THE
SOURCEBOOK
To Public Record Information

*The Comprehensive Guide to County, State, & Federal
Public Records Sources*

Seventh Edition

BRB Publications, Inc.
www.brbpub.com

Dedicated to the Searching & Understanding of Public Records

BRB Publications

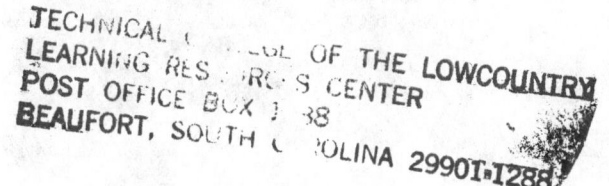
THE
SOURCEBOOK
TO PUBLIC RECORD INFORMATION - *Seventh Edition*

Edited by: Peter J. Weber and Michael Sankey

©2006 By BRB Publications, Inc.
206 West Julie Dr, Suite 2
Tempe, AZ 85283
800-929-3811   Fax 800-929-4981

www.brbpub.com

ISBN 1-879792-81-1

The sourcebook to public record information : the
comprehensive guide to county, state, & federal public
records sources / [edited by Peter J. Weber and Michael
Sankey]. -- 7th ed.
    p. cm.
    ISBN 1-879792-81-8

    1. Public records--United States--States--Information
services--Directories. 2. Courts--United States--States
--Directories. 3. Public records--United States--States
--Computer network resources.   I. Weber, Peter J.
(Peter Julius), 1952- II. Sankey, Michael L., 1949-

JK468.P76S693 2005   352.3'87'02573
                QBI05-1196

Replaces *The Guide to Background Investigations*

Contents

Section II: State Chapters

Introduction

Over 20,000 Government Agencies at Your Fingertips

This *Sourcebook* reveals where government records are kept, outlines the access requirements, gives searching hints and tells which agencies are online. Over 20,000 government agencies are profiled so you can explore the depths of government maintained records.

The public has a broad right of access to government information. Public records are meant to be used for the benefit of society. As a member of the public, you or someone in authority is entitled to review the public records held by government agencies. Whether you are a business owner, a reporter, an investigator, or even a father trying to check on your daughter's first date, you can access public records to meet your needs.

Herein, we examine these paper trails that begin or are maintained at the federal, state, county, and in certain instances, the city and town level. This *Sourcebook* is especially useful for these applications:

> Legal Research
>
> Pre-Employment Screening
>
> Background Investigation
>
> Tenant Screening
>
> Locating People
>
> Locating Assets
>
> Skiptracing
>
> Genealogy

Equipped with the information contained in these pages, you can find the facts, gain access to the information you need, and even track your own "information trail."

What Is New in the Seventh Edition

The Seventh Edition contains 16 additional pages compared to last year's book. Not only has the research for this year's edition led to an enormous amount of updated material, but we have also added many new phone numbers and online access sites. In fact, over 400 online accessible sources for record searching have been added since last year.

Specifically, within the County Courts section, additional information includes—

- Throughput date of public use terminals and differences in copy fees when self serve or if copied by court personnel.

Within the County Recorder section, additional information includes—

- Search fees and copy fees differentiated between different indices (real estate, UCC, judgments, etc.).

The Guide to Background Investigations

In 2003, BRB Publications purchased the rights to a very successful publication known as *The Guide to Background Investigations*.

Since 1996, BRB provided the majority of the content found in *The Guide*. Thus, rather than publish two very similar books, BRB Publications chose to print one book – *The Sourcebook* – and incorporate the best of both products into one.

Updated Content is Available on the Internet

The Seventh Edition of *The Sourcebook to Public Record Information* represents thousands of hours of research right up to the day of printing. We have compiled what we feel is the most up-to-date and unique compendium of its kind. However, users should also remember that the information reported in *The Sourcebook* can, and does change.

For those of you who need to know more or need to have this information constantly updated, we recommend an expanded version of this product. **The Public Records Research System** (PRRS) is available as a subscription service on the Internet.

Updated weekly, PRRS contains all the information found in *The Sourcebook*, *The National Directory to College and University Student Records*, and *The County Locator*.

For additional information, visit www.brbpub.com.

Thank You from the Research and Editorial Staff at BRB Publications—

BRB Publications is 100% devoted to the understanding of public records. We hope you find the Seventh Edition of *The Sourcebook* to be a valuable asset.

Kiala Flanagan

Jill Von Rotz

Annette Talley

William Roberts

Michael Young

Peter J. Weber

Michael Sankey

How This Book Is Organized

General Layout

The Sourcebook is organized into two Sections—

1. Public Record Primer

2. 51 Individual State Chapters (with an Appendix of Canadian Provinces and U.S. Territories)

The Public Record Primer

The purpose of *The Public Record Primer* is to assist the reader in knowing *where categories of records can be found* and *how to search*. The Primer contains many searching hints and is an excellent overall resource, especially helpful to those not familiar with searching government records.

An important discussion starting on page 9 examines privacy issues including public information vs. personal information and how records enter the public domain.

The **Searching Other Federal Records Online** chapter contains an excellent article (see page 36) contributed by Alan Schlein, author of *Find it Online! The Complete Guide to Online Research* (Facts on Demand Press). Mr. Schlein presents a unique dissertation about the best federal government Internet sites for finding usual information quickly and efficiently.

Another important chapter **Using a Public Record Vendor** (see page 60) contains a wealth of information about using commercial public record vendors.

The State Chapters

The individual state chapters in *The Sourcebook* have been compiled into an easy to use format. Six sub-chapters or sections are presented in this order:

1. State Public Record Agencies

2. State Licensing and Regulatory Boards

3. Federal Courts (U.S. District and Bankruptcy), shown by state

4. County Courts

5. County Recorder Offices

6. County Locator

After the State Chapters there is short section for Canadian Provinces and U.S. Territories.

Information Found in the Agency Profiles

The depth of knowledge presented about each government agency is what separates this *Sourcebook* from a typical address and telephone listing reference book. The beginning of each state and/or county sub-chapter has an overall discussion of the public records policies, with important characteristics and searching hints.

The following details have been researched and presented (when applicable) within each profile:

- **Agency Facts**: office hours; time zone; websites.

- **Searching Facts**: methods of access; indexing; search requirements; if records are available online; when free public access terminals are at the counter; turnaround times for mail requests; how far back (years) records or indices are kept.

- **Privacy Facts**: restrictions the agencies impose on searchers or on the use of the record; when signed releases or notarized statements are required.

- **Fees**: access fees, copy fees; certification fees; expedited fees, if credit cards accepted; what types of checks accepted; to whom to make the check payable.

- **Other Access:** how to purchase databases or customized lists; if more than one agency must be visited in the county to get all records; when subscription or registration is required; if results or specific documents will be returned by fax, etc.

Using The County Locator

The County Locator portion of each state chapter is extremely useful when it is unclear in which county to perform a localized record search. This section contains two cross-reference indices. The City/County Cross Reference will indicate in what county(s) a "place" (city or town) is located. There are over 40,000 places referenced. The ZIP Code/City Cross Reference assists those people who have an address with ZIP Code, but are unsure in which county the ZIP in located.

Keep in mind that over 8,000 ZIP Codes cross county lines.

The Sourcebook includes maps showing each state's county borders, county seats, and major cities.

Note: The Internet version of the book content has an additional 45,000 place names and show when ZIP Codes cross county lines.

Guidelines for Searching Public Records

Definition of Public Records

The strict **definition** of **public records** is—

> *"Those records maintained by government agencies*
> *that are open without restriction to public inspection,*
> *either by statute or by tradition."*

If access to a record that is held by a government agency is restricted in some way, then it is not a public record.

Accessibility Paradox

Adding to the mystique of government records is the accessibility paradox. For example, in some states a specific category of records is severely restricted, and therefore those records are not "public," while the very same category of records may be 100% open in other states. Among these categories are criminal histories, vehicle ownership records and workers' compensation records.

The text in the box printed below is significant. We are not trying to fill up space. As your public record searching takes you from state-to-state, this is the one important adage to keep in mind.

> "Just because records are maintained in a certain way in
> your state or county, do not assume that any other county or
> state does things the same way you are used to."

Public vs. Private vs. Personal

Before reading further, let us define types of records held by government or by private industry. Of course, not all information about a company or individual is public. The boundaries between public and private information are not well understood, and continually undergo intense scrutiny. The following is an introduction to the subject from a viewpoint of a professional record searcher.

Public Record

Public records are records of **incidents** or **actions** filed or recorded with a government agency for the purpose of notifying others— the "public" — about the matter. The **deed** to your house recorded at the county recorder's office is a public record — it is a legal requirement that you record with the county recorder. Anyone requiring details about your property may review or copy the documents.

Public Information

Your **telephone listing** in the phone book is public information; that is, you freely furnished the information to ease the flow of commercial and private communications.

Personal Information

Any information about a person or business that the person or business might consider private and confidential in nature, such as your **Social Security Number, DOB or address**, is personal information. Such information will remain private to a limited extent unless it is disclosed to some outside entity that could make it public. **Personal information may be found in either public records or in public information.**

How Personal Information Enters the Public Domain

Many people confuse the three categories above, lump them into one and wonder how "big brother" accumulated so much information about them. Therefore, these distinctions are important. The reality is that **much of this information is given willingly**.

Actually, there are two ways that personal information can enter the public domain — statutory and voluntary. In a **voluntary** transaction, you **share** personal information of your own free will. In a **statutory** transaction, you **disclose** personal information because the law requires you to.

The confusion of terms used today feeds the increasing conflict between privacy advocates and commercial interests. This, in turn, is driving legislation towards more and more **restrictions** on the **dissemination of personal information** — the same personal information that, in fact, is willingly shared by most people and companies in order to participate in our market economy.

Of course, the increased number of identity theft incidents has precipitated well deserved scrutiny on the manner in which personal information is maintained by the government and the private sector.

Where Public Records are Held

There are two places you can find public records—

1. at a government agency

2. within the database of a private company

Government agencies maintain records in a variety of ways. While many state agencies and highly populated county agencies are computerized, many others use microfiche, microfilm, and paper to store files and indexes. Agencies that have converted to computer will not necessarily place complete file records on their system; they are more apt to include only an index, pointer or summary data to the files.

Private enterprises develop their databases in one of two ways: they buy the records in bulk from government agencies; or they send personnel to the agencies and compile this information by using a copy machine or keying information into a laptop computer. The database is then available for internal use or for resale purposes. An example of such a company is *Superior Information* (800 848-0489). Superior maintains a very comprehensive database of civil judgments, tax liens, Uniform Commercial Code filings, and bankruptcy data gathered from the Mid-Atlantic States. For more information about vendors, see page 60.

The Common Methods Used to Access Public Records

The following is a look at the various methods available to access public records.

Visit in Person

This is easy if you live close by. Many courthouses and recorders offices have free access terminals open to the public. Certain records, such as corporate or UCC records generally found at the Secretary of State, can be viewed or pulled for free, but will incur a fee for copies. A signed release is a common requirement for accessing motor vehicle and criminal records.

Mail, Fax, or Telephone

Although some agencies permit phone or fax requests, the majority of agencies prefer mail requests. Some agencies consider fax requesting to be an expedited service that incurs higher fees. Agencies that permit telephone requests may merely answer "Yes" or "No" to questions such as "Does John Doe have a civil court case in his name?" We have indicated when telephone and fax requesting is available, as well as the extent of the service. Some courts that will not fax search requests will fax specific documents, if the case file or docket number is given.

Online

The Internet may serve as a free means to certain agency records or may be the conduit to a subscription or commercial site. Also, a few private dial systems (non-Internet) still exist for some subscription services. There is a significant difference between viewing an image of a record vs. looking at an index of available records. Keep in mind that most Internet access sites permit the latter, not the former. Usually the searchable and viewable information is limited to name indexes and summary data, rather than document images.

Also, keep in mind many agencies, such as DMVs, only provide access to pre-approved, high volume, ongoing accounts. Typically, this access involves fees and a specified, minimum amount of usage.

The Internet is a good place to find *general* information about a government agency. Many web sites contain detailed descriptions of policies and regulations. If records or indices are not searchable on the web, many sites enable one to download or print record request forms,

Hire Someone Else

As mentioned previously, one method to access public records is from a vendor. These vendors must comply with state and federal laws. Thus if the government agency will not release a record, chances are a vendor company will not either. There are a variety of companies that can be hired to perform record searches. An excellent, quick source to find the right vendor for a particular need is the Resource Center at www.brbpub.com or *Public Records Online* by Facts on Demand Press.

Bulk or Database Purchases

Many agencies offer programs to purchase all or parts of their database for statistical or commercial purposes. The restrictions vary widely from state to state, even within the same record type or category. Typically, records are available (to those who qualify) in the following media types; FTP, cartridges, paper printouts, labels, disks, CDs, microfiche and/or microfilm. Throughout the individual state chapters, we have indicated where these bulk purchases are available, to whom, and for what purposes as well as the costs involved.

Using the Freedom of Information Act and Other Acts

The Federal Freedom of Information Act has no bearing on state, county or local government agencies because these agencies are subject to that state's individual act. Further, the government agencies profiled in this book generally already have systems in place to release information and the act is not needed. However, if you are trying to obtain records from agencies beyond the scope of this book, there are many useful Internet sites that will give you the information you need to complete such a request. We can recommend these sites:

> www.usdoj.gov/04foia/
>
> www.spj.org/foia.asp

Fees, Charges, and Usage

Public records are not necessarily free of charge, certainly not if they are maintained by private industry. Remember that **public records are records of incidents or transactions**. These incidents can be civil or criminal court actions, recordings, filings or occurrences such as speeding tickets or accidents. **It costs money** (time, salaries, supplies, etc.) **to record and track these events**. Common charges found at the government level include copy fees (to make copies of the document), search fees (for clerical personnel to search for the record), and certification fees (to certify a document as being accurate and coming from the particular agency). Fees can vary from $.10 per page for copies to a $52.00 search fee for government personnel to do the actual look-up. Also, higher fees are usually involved if records must be pulled from off-site storage. Some government agencies will allow you to walk in and view records at no charge. Fewer will release information over the phone for no fee.

If a private enterprise is in the business of maintaining a public records database, it generally does so to offer these records for resale. Typical clients include financial institutions, the legal industry, the insurance industry, and pre-employment screening firms among others. Usually, records are sold via online access or on a CD-ROM.

Also, there are a number of public record vendors (we call them search firms) companies that will do a name search — for a fee. These companies do not warehouse the records, but search on demand for a specific name.

Private companies usually offer different price levels based on volume of usage, while government agencies have one price per category, regardless of the amount of requests.

Using Identifiers

Every source will require certain identifiers to process a search request. For example, an agency may ask for the full name, Social Security Number, date of birth and even the last known address of the person to be checked. These "Identifiers" serve two different, though related purposes. First, these identifiers ensure that the repository will be able to properly conduct a search of existing records. For example, perhaps records are indexed by only a correct full name or the Social Security Number. Thus, the office simply may not be able to process a record request if it does not have one or the other of these identifiers.

Second, the identifiers act as an important safeguard for both the requesting party and the subject of the search. There is always the chance that the "Harold Johnson" on whom a given repository has a record is not the same "Harold Johnson" on whom a check has been requested. However, the possibility of a misidentification can be decreased substantially if other identifiers can be matched on the individual.

In general, each record source listed in *The Sourcebook* will include the identifiers required to process a search (as well as some other information that the record-holder said would be "helpful"). This is the minimum data required for the office to proceed with your search. Sometimes a signed release is needed and is so indicated throughout the book.

As a general rule, information beyond the minimum should be provided whenever possible. Every available piece of information can aid their search. For example, maiden, alias or other previous names should always be included. Although no repository can be expected to give a 100% positive identification (without a fingerprint card), the more pointers matched, the smaller the chance of a mistake.

A Few Myths About Searching Public Records Online

The availability of online public records is not as widespread as one might think. According to our research:

- only 35% of public records can be found online;
- nearly every free government public record website contains no personal identifiers.

The federal, state, and local agencies that maintain public record systems make substantial efforts to limit the disclosure of Social Security Numbers, phone numbers, addresses, and dates of birth. The Social Security Number is no longer the key search tool identifier it was in the 1980's and early 1990's. The websites with open record searching available to the public generally require only a name, unless a specific case file or docket number or registration number, etc. is given.

The government agencies that offer online access on a fee or subscription basis generally disclose at least partial personal identifiers. But very few give Social Security Numbers anymore, and those that do may cloak or mask the first 5 digits. Some even cloak the month and day of the birth and only release the year of birth. For example, most U.S. District Court and Bankruptcy Court online systems give no personal identifiers on search results, thus making a "name search" nearly impossible.

The lack of identifiers is a real problem for employers or financial institutions who require a certain amount of due diligence. The existence of any possible adverse information may have to be checked by a hands-on search to insure the proper identify of the subject.

Also, many government websites offering online record access include a warning or disclosure stating that the data can have errors and/or should be used for informational purposes only. Such sites should be considered as supplemental or secondary sources only. For example, a criminal record search from such as source usually does not in and by itself comply with the Fair Credit Reporting Act regulations involving pre-employment screening.

Public Record & Public Information Categories

The following descriptions of the record categories fall into our definitions of either "public records" or "public information."

In considering these definitions, keep the following point in mind:

♦ Just because your state or county has certain rules, regulations and practices regarding the accessibility and content of public records does not mean that any other state or county follows the same rules.

Business Records

Corporation Records (found at the state level)

Checking to see if a company is incorporated is considered a **"status check."** The information that results from a status check typically includes the date of incorporation, status, type, registered agent and, sometimes, officers or directors. This is a good way to find the start of a paper trail and/or to find affiliates of the subject of your search. Some states permit status checks over the telephone.

If available, articles of incorporation (or amendments to them) as well as copies of annual reports may also provide useful information about a business or business owner. However, corporate records may *not* be a good source for a business address because most states allow corporations to use a registered agent as their address for service of process.

Many state agencies provide a business name check so that a new entity can make sure the name is not already used by an existing business entity.

Partnership Records (found at the state level)

Some state statutes require registration of certain kinds of partnerships at the state level. Sometimes, these partner names and addresses may be available from the same office that handles corporation records. Some states have a department created specifically to administer limited partnerships and the records associated with them. These filings provide a wealth of information about other partners. Such information can be used to uncover other businesses that may be registered as well.

Limited Liability Companies (found at state level)

A newer form of business entity, similar to a corporation but with the favorable tax characteristics of a partnership, is known as the Limited Liability Company (LLC). An LLC is legal in most every state. An offspring of this, which many states now permit, is the Limited Liability Partnership (LLP).

Trademark and Trade Name (found at state or county levels)

"Trade names" and "trademarks" are relative terms. A trademark may be known as a "service mark." Trade names may be referred to as "fictitious names," "assumed names," or "DBAs." States (or counties) will not let two entities register and use the same or close to the same name or trademark

Typically, the agency that oversees corporation records usually maintains the files for trademarks and/or trade names. Most states will allow verbal status checks of names or worded marks. Some states will administer "fictitious names" at the state level while county agencies administer "trade names," or vice versa.

Sales Tax Registrations (found at state level)

Any individual or firm that sells applicable goods or services to an end-user, is required to register with the appropriate state agency. Such registration is necessary to collect applicable sales tax on the goods and services, and to ensure remittance of those taxes to the state.

45 states collect some sort of sales tax on a variety of goods and services. Of these, 38 will at the very least confirm that a tax permit exists. Each sales tax registrant is given a special state tax permit number, which may be called by various names, including tax ID number or seller's permit number. These numbers are not to be confused with the federal employer identification number.

SEC and Other Financial Data

The Federal Securities and Exchange Commission (SEC) is the public repository for information about publicly held companies. These companies are required to share their material facts with existing and prospective stockholders. See page 36 for information about the SEC database EDGAR.

Private companies, on the other hand, are not subject to public scrutiny. Their financial information is public information only to the extent that the company itself decides to disclose information.

Lien and Security Interest Records

Uniform Commercial Code (found at state and sometimes at county or city levels)

All 50 states and the District of Columbia have passed a version of the model Uniform Commercial Code (UCC). UCC filings are used to record liens in financing transactions such as equipment loans, leases, inventory loans, and accounts receivable financing. The Code allows potential lenders to be notified that certain assets of a debtor are already used to secure a loan or lease. *Therefore, examining UCC filings is an excellent way to find bank accounts, security interests, financiers, and assets.*

Revised Article 9 (see page 52) of the Code made significant changes to the location of filings and records. Prior to July 2001, of the 7.5 million new UCC financing statements filed annually, 2.5 million were filed at the state level; 5 million were filed at the local level. Now, less than 3% of filings are done so at the local level. Although there are significant variations among state statutes, the state level is now the best starting place to uncover liens filed against an individual or business.

Tax Liens (found at state and sometimes at county or city levels)

The federal government and every state have some sort of taxes, such as those associated with sales, income, withholding, unemployment, and/or personal property. When these taxes go unpaid, the appropriate state agency can file a lien on the real or personal property of the subject. *Normally, the state agency that maintains UCC records also maintains tax liens.*

Individuals vs. Businesses

Tax liens filed against individuals are frequently maintained at separate locations from those liens filed against businesses. For example, a large number of states require liens filed against businesses to be filed at a central state location (i.e., Secretary of State's office) and liens against individuals to be filed at the county level (i.e., Recorder, Register of Deeds, Clerk of Court, etc.).

State vs. Federal Liens

Liens on a company may not all be filed in the same location. A federal tax lien will not necessarily be filed (recorded) at the same location/jurisdiction as a lien filed by the state. This holds true for both individual liens and as well as business liens filed against personal property. Typically, state tax liens on personal property will be found where UCCs are filed. *Tax liens on real property will be found where real property deeds are recorded*, with few exceptions. Unsatisfied state and federal tax liens may be renewed if prescribed by individual state statutes. However, once satisfied, the time the record will remain in the repository before removal varies by jurisdiction.

Real Estate and Tax Assessor (found at county and local levels)

Traditionally, real estate records are public so that everyone can know who owns what property. Liens on real estate must be public so a buyer knows all the facts. The county (or parish) recorder's office is the record source. However, many private companies purchase entire county record databases and create their own database for commercial purposes.

This category of public record is perhaps the fastest growing in regards to being freely accessible over the Internet. We have indicated all the recorder offices that offer web **name queries;** many more offer location searches (using maps and parcel numbers to locate an address).

Bankruptcies (found at federal court level)

This entails case information about people and businesses that have filed for protection under the bankruptcy laws of the United States. Only federal courts handle bankruptcy cases. Many types of financial records maintained by government agencies are considered public records; bankruptcy records, unlike some other court records, are in this class of fully open court records. There are several private companies that compile databases with names and dates of these records.

Important Individual Records

Criminal Records (found at state level, county courts, and federal courts)

Every state has a central repository of major misdemeanor, felony arrest records and convictions. States submit criminal record activity to the National Crime Information Center (which is not open to the public). *Not all states open their criminal records to the public*. Of those states that *will* release records to the public, many require fingerprints or signed release forms. The information that *could be* disclosed on the report includes the arrest record, criminal charges, fines, sentencing and incarceration information.

In states where records are not released, the best places to search for criminal record activity is at the city or county level with the county or district court clerk. Many of these searches can be done with a phone call. Further information regarding the access and use of criminal records is found in the Searching State Agency Records chapter on page 23.

Litigation and Civil Judgments (found at county, local, and federal courts)

Actions under federal laws are found at U.S. District Courts. Actions under state laws are found within the state court system at the county level. Municipalities also have courts. Records of civil litigation case and records about judgments are often collected by commercial database vendors. For more information, please refer to the **County Court Records** chapter.

Motor Vehicle Records (found at state level, but, on occasion, accessible at county level)

The retrieval industry often refers to driving records as "MVRs." Typical information on an MVR might include full name, address, Social Security Number, physical description and date of birth along with the conviction and accident history. Also, the license type, restrictions and/or endorsements can provide background data on an individual.

The release of motor vehicle data to the public is governed by the federal Driver's Privacy Protection Act (DPPA). States must differentiate between *permissible uses* (14 are designated in DPPA) and *casual requesters* to determine who may receive a record and/or how much personal information is reported on the record. For example, if a state DMV chooses to sell a record to a "casual requester," the record can contain personal information (address, etc.), but **only** with the **consent** of the subject.

Pay particular attention to the restriction requirements mentioned in this category throughout this publication. Refer to Searching State Agency Records chapter on page 24 for more about this subject. Also, for those interested in extensive, detailed information about either driver or vehicle records, refer to BRB Publications' *The MVR Book*.

Vehicle and Vessel Ownership, Registration, VINs, Titles, and Liens (found at state and, on occasion, at county level)

State repositories of vehicle/vessel registration and ownership records hold a wide range of information. Generally, record requesters submit a name to uncover vehicle(s) owned or submit vehicle information to obtain an owner name and address. However, this category of record information is also subject to the DPPA as described above.

The original language of DPPA required the states to offer an "opt out" option to drivers and vehicle owners, if they (the states) sold marketing lists or individual records to casual requesters (those requesters not specifically mentioned in DPPA). Public Law 106-69 reversed this. Effective June 1, 2000, states automatically opted out all individuals, unless the individual specifically asked to be included. Since nearly all states have this "opt-in" procedure in place, very few individuals request to be placed on marketing lists.

Therefore, passage of Public Law 106-69 was dramatic since it essentially did away with sales of:

- marketing lists;
- records (with addresses and other personal information) to "casual" requesters;
- record databases to information vendors and database compilers (except for vehicle recall purposes, etc.).

Accident or Crash Reports (found at state level or local level)

The State Police or Department of Public Safety usually maintains accident reports. For the purposes of this publication, "accident records" are designated as those prepared by the investigating officer. Copies of a *citizen's* accident report are not usually available to the public and are not reviewed herein. Typical information found on a state accident report includes drivers' addresses and license numbers as well as a description of the incident. Accidents investigated by local officials or minor accidents where the damage does not exceed a reporting limit (such as $1,000), are not available from state agencies. When the accident reports are maintained by state DMVs, the DPPA guidelines are followed with regards to honoring record requests.

Occupational Licensing and Business Registration (found at state boards)

Occupational licenses and business registrations contain a plethora of information readily available from various state agencies. A common reason to call these agencies is to corroborate professional or industry credentials. Often, a telephone call to the agency may secure an address and phone number. Refer to the chapter Searching State Occupational Licensing Boards for further information.

GED Records (found at state level)

By contacting the state offices that oversee GED Records, one can verify whether someone truly received a GED certificate for the high school education equivalency. These records are useful for pre-employment screening or background checking purposes. Most state agencies will verify over the phone the existence of a GED certificate or give a "yes-no" answer by fax. Copies of transcripts or diplomas usually are not free-of-charge. When doing a record search, you must know the name of the student at the time of the test and a general idea of the year and test location. GED Records are *not* useful when trying to locate an individual.

Hunting and Fishing Licenses (found at state, county and local levels)

We have singled out one type of state license that merits a closer look. When trying to locate an individual, state hunting and fishing license information can be very informative. Currently 44 states maintain a central repository of fishing and/or hunting license records and 31 states permit access in some capacity by the public.

The trend is that many of these record repositories are becoming more computerized and are progressing from the days of storing in boxes in the basement. This movement began in 1992 when the U.S. Fish and Wildlife Service implemented a Migratory Bird Harvest Information Program that changed state hunting licensing procedures. Under this cooperative program, many states began to computerize their collection of licensees' names and addresses. The release of these records for investigative or search purposes may depend upon individual state "sunshine laws."

Workers' Compensation Records (found at state level)

Research at state workers' compensation boards is generally limited to determining if an employee has filed a claim and/or obtaining copies of the claim records themselves. With the passage of the Americans with Disabilities Act (ADA) in the early 1990s, using information from workers' compensation boards for pre-employment screening was virtually eliminated. Per the ADA, *a review of workers' compensation histories may only be conducted after a conditional job offer has been made* and when medical information is reviewed. However, the ability of conducting this review is still subject to individual state statutes, which vary widely and be stricter than the ADA..

Voter Registration (found at state and county levels)

Voting Registration Records are a good place to find addresses and voting history, and can generally be viewed at the local level.

Every state has a central election agency or commission, and all have a central repository of voter information collected from the county level agencies per the federal mandate HAVA. The degree or level of accessibility to these records varies widely from state to state. Over half of the states will sell portions of the registered voter database, but only a handful of states permit individual searching by name through the state office. Name searches are best performed at the county level. States will allow access for political purposes such as "Get Out the Vote" campaigns or compilation of campaign contribution lists. Nearly every state and local agency blocks the release of Social Security Numbers and telephone numbers found on these records.

Vital Records: Birth, Death, Marriage, and Divorce Records (found at state and county levels)

Copies of vital record certificates are needed for a variety of reasons — social security, jobs, passports, family history, litigation, lost heir searching, proof of identity, etc. Most states understand the urgency of these requests, and many offer an expedited service. *A number of states will take requests over the phone or by fax if you use a credit card.* Searchers must also be aware that in many instances certain vital records are *not* kept at the state level. The searcher must then turn to city and county record repositories to find the information needed.

Most states offer expedited fax and online ordering through the services from an outside vendor, either VitalChek or USCerts. These state-endorsed vendors maintain individual fax order telephone lines for each state they service. They require the use of a credit card and with that an extra fee in the range of $5.50 to $10.05. Their websites at www.vitalchek.com and www.uscerts.com are good places to order vital records online from many states; keep in mind that results are still mailed.

Older vital records are usually found in the state archives. There is an excellent website of extensive historical genealogy-related databases at http://ancestry.com/default.aspx. Another source of historical vital record information is the Family History Library of the Church of Jesus Christ of Latter Day Saints (located at 35 North West Temple, Salt Lake City 84150). They have millions of microfilmed records from church and civil registers from all over the world.

Credit Information and Social Security Numbers

Social Security Numbers

The Social Security Number (SSN) is the subject of a persistent struggle between privacy rights groups and legitimate business interests that wish to confirm the identity of an individual. The truth is that many individuals gave up the privacy of their number by writing it on a voter registration form, product registration form, or any of a myriad of other voluntary disclosures made over the years. With the justifiable increased concerns over identity theft, the release of SSNs in records, without consent of the subject, is very uncommon. In the past, a major source of finding a SSN was in the "header" of a credit report. But not any more, see below.

Credit Information

Credit data is derived from financial transactions of people or businesses. **Private companies maintain this information; government only regulates access.** Certain credit information about individuals is restricted by law, such as the Fair Credit Reporting Act, at the federal level and by even more restrictive laws in many states. Credit information about businesses is not restricted by law and is fully open to anyone who requests (pays for) it.

A credit report essentially has two parts — the credit header and the credit history. A credit header is essentially the upper portion of a credit report containing the Social Security Number, age, phone number, last several addresses, and any AKAs. Recently, access to credit header information (see below) was closed to most business entities.

Credit Header Ban Went Into Effect July 1st, 2001

July 1st, 2001 was an important date for skiptracers, fraud investigators, and other businesses that rely on "credit headers." This information has always been available without the consent of the individual subject. Per a federal court ruling, beginning July 1st 2001, access to credit header information was treated in the same manner as access to credit reports—there has to be permission granted by the individual.

The basis of this ban is traced to the Gramm-Leach-Bliley Act (GLB). Section 502 of this act prohibits a financial institution from disclosing nonpublic personal information about a consumer to non-affiliated third parties unless a consumer has elected not to opt out from disclosure. Trans Union and other members of the Individual References Services Group (IRSG), among others, filed suit in an effort to keep this information open for "appropriate commercial purposes." The ruling, dated April 30th, denied this argument. The sale of credit headers seemed to be on borrowed time anyway—originally, the ban was to begin November 2000. However, due to the lawsuits and action involving the FTC, a provision changed the start of the ban until July 1st, 2001.

Impact of Changes

The impact of the ruling (and an FTC opinion) was far ranging. The ruling restricted credit bureaus from selling the above-mentioned data to information vendors who compile their own proprietary databases. But there are some alternatives to those business entities that rely on this type of public record information. The data is grandfathered. Provider companies that purchased files from the credit bureaus can continue to sell the data to their customers. Although data will never be updated from the credit bureaus, the existing data can still be used without the restrictions imposed by the ruling.

The Gramm-Leach-Bliley Act did not deny access to public record sources or databases that may contain age, SSN, phone, prior addresses, and AKAs. The Act only forbade financial institutions from disclosing this data. Therefore, those businesses shut-off from using credit headers had to investigate alternative sources of public records.

Additional Record Sources Worth Reviewing

Education and Employment

Information about an employee's or prospective employee's schooling, training, education, and jobs is important to any employer. Learning institutions maintain their own records of attendance, completion and degree/certification granted. Also, employers will confirm certain information about former employees. This is an example of private information that becomes public by voluntary disclosure. As part of your credit record, this information would be considered restricted. If, however, you disclose this information to Who's Who, or to a credit card company, it becomes public information.

Environment

Information about hazards to the environment is critical. There is little tradition and less law regarding how open or restricted information is at the state and local (recorder's office) levels. Most information on hazardous materials, soil composition, even OSHA inspection reports is public record. But many federal websites have removed information since 9-11-2001.

OSHA stands for Occupational Safety and Health Administration, which is part of the U.S. Department of Labor. Their website is www.osha.gov.

Another federal government source is the U.S. Environmental Protection Agency found at www.epa.gov/records. According to *Find it Online* author Alan Schlein, the EPA "…no longer allows direct access to the Envirofacts databases, which explain what toxic chemicals are found in water, hazardous waste, toxic waste, and Superfund sites, and is broken down by community. The EPA had originally created the database to provide the public with direct access to the wealth of information contained in its databases. The public is no longer able to access the information."

The same can be said for the U.S. Geological Survey (www.usgs.gov); this agency has removed a number of its reports on water resources.

Medical

Medical record Information about an individual's medical status and history are summarized in various repositories that are accessible only to authorized insurance and other private company employees. Medical information is neither public information nor a closed record. Like credit information, it is not meant to be shared with anyone unless you give authorization.

Military

Each branch maintains its own records. Much of this, such as years of service and rank, is open public record. However, some details in the file of an individual may be subject to restrictions on access — approval by the subject may be required.

For more information about military records, turn to page 37.

Searching State Agency Records

The previous chapter includes a wealth of knowledge about the various types of public records found at the state level. This chapter explains how to use the State Agencies Sections found in each state chapter in this *Sourcebook* and gives a more detailed look at criminal and motor vehicle records.

The State Summary Page

Each state chapter begins with a list of four important state offices and other logistics that may be helpful to your record searching needs.

The office of the Governor is a good place to start if you are looking for an obscure agency, phone number or address. We have found that typically the person who answers the phone will point you in the right direction if he or she cannot answer your question.

The Attorney General's Office is another excellent starting point. For example, if you are looking for a non-profit organization, this may be able to help you out.

Most State Legislative bodies offer free Internet access to bill text and status; some even offer subject queries. Notwithstanding federal guidelines, the state legislatures and legislators control the policies and provisions for the release of state held information. Every year there is a multitude of bills introduced in state legislatures that would, if passed, create major changes in the access and retrieval of records and personal information.

The State Archives contain an abundance of historical documents and records, especially useful to those interested in genealogy.

"Just because records are maintained in a certain way in your state, do not assume that any other state does things the same way you are used to."

The State Record Repository Agency Profiles

After the preceding page, the state record repository agency profiles are presented, starting with the state criminal records agency. Each of these state agency profiles is broken into distinct segments that create a total picture of record searching, including access methods and privacy restrictions.

Indexing and Storage

This segment examines the following—

- How many years of records are accessible
- How long before new records are available
- How records are indexed and in what format are they maintained.

Searching

This segment looks in depth at the searching requirements and when privacy restrictions are in place. For example, here you learn what the agencies requirements are for doing a search, such as if a signed release is needed from the subject, or if a certain state form must be used.

Access Methods

The following access methods are both listed and described in a detailed paragraph—

- Mail
- Phone
- In person
- Fax
- Online

Here you will learn the turnaround time for mail requests, if there is free Internet access, if the agency will release any information over the phone, fax, email, etc. In addition, there is a section describing expedited services or bulk database purchases, when applicable.

Fee and Payments

Fee coverage includes search fees, copy fees, certification fees, and expedite fees. Also covered: if credit cards are accepted, if personal checks (many agencies only accept business checks) are accepted, and whom to make the check payable.

Special Situations in State Records

We won't waste your time reading about agencies if the record data is truly unavailable. The following special situations are noted—

- When the state agency does not release any information period, except to government personnel.
- When the records are not maintained by a state level agency...and where to find these records if they are held at the local level.

More About Criminal Records

All states have a central repository of criminal records of those individuals who have been subject to that state's criminal justice system. The information at the state repository is obtained from local county, parish, and municipal courts as well as from law enforcement. Records include fingerprint files and files containing identification segments, and notations of arrests and dispositions. Although usually housed in the Department of Public Safety, often it is the State Police or other state agency that maintains the central repository.

Most states make this repository available to the public, but there is a high degree of non-uniformity regarding what information is released and to whom. Consider the following—

- 21 states release criminal records to the general public without consent of the subject
- 20 states release criminal records to the general public with signed release from the subject
- 16 states require statutory authority to access their records

For those readers who are quick at math (57 states?), please note that some states have two types of records they release and fall into several categories above.

By far, the vast majority of criminal records used outside of law enforcement are used for employment purposes, generally referred to as pre-employment screening as background checks.

Criminal Records and Pre-Employment Screening

A background screen is not meant to stop individual who has a criminal record in the past from being hired. The purpose of a background screen is to enable the employers to verify the information presented by the applicants in order to determine if the applicants are really truthful about the past and really are whom they are (and not someone with a false ID or even a terrorist). Employers encourage and expect applicants to be truthful about past activity and employment.

State and federal laws are very strict about what employers can and cannot ask or use when making hiring decisions. The following statistics pertain to state restrictions on criminal record use by employers—

- 19 states prohibit the use of arrest records (i.e., non-conviction records)
- 5 states prohibit the use of misdemeanor convictions
- 13 states prohibit the use of expunged or sealed records
- 4 states restrict the use of records based on time periods
- 2 states limit the use of first offense records

The federal regulations concerning the use of criminal records by employers comes from the Fair Credit Reporting Act (FCRA). If you are an employer ordering criminal records on potential employees, or a pre-employment screening company, it is imperative to become familiar with this law.

Per Derek Hinton, author of the *Criminal Records Manual*, "…there are three main areas in which the FCRA can affect an employer ordering criminal records—

- Releases—What notifications must be made and permissions granted from the subject of the search.
- Arrest vs. convictions, seven-year rule—What information can appear on the report, and what must be suppressed.

- Aged public record for employment purposes—When the vendor databases records, what additional notifications to the subject must be performed."

For detailed specifics regarding FCRA and criminal records, it is suggested to obtain Derek's book or to obtain *The Safe Hiring Manual* by Les Rosen (both available from Facts on Demand Press and BRB Publications).

More About Motor Vehicle Records

The Driver's Privacy Protection Act Title XXXI — Protection of Privacy of Information in State Motor Vehicle Records — was attached as an amendment to the Violent Crime Control Act of 1994 and was signed by President Clinton late in that summer. The intent of the DPPA is to protect the personal privacy of persons licensed to drive by prohibiting certain disclosures of information maintained by the states.

This federal mandate declared that the federal government had the right to restrict or prohibit the release of personal information of persons licensed to drive or own motor vehicles. DPPA prohibits disclosure of personal information from the driver history, vehicle registration, title files held by state DMVs, except for 14 specific "permissible uses." The Act's definition of Personal Information is…

"..information that identifies an individual, including an individual's photograph, social security number, driver identification number, name, address (but not the 5-digit zip code), telephone number, and medical or disability information, but does not include information on vehicular accidents, driving violations, and driver's status."

The permissible uses do, in general, permit ongoing, legitimate businesses and individuals to obtain full record data, but with added compliance procedures.

The Effect of Public Law 106-69

As explained earlier, the original language of DPPA required the states offer an "opt out" option to drivers and vehicle owners, if they (the states) sell marketing lists or individual records to casual requesters (those requesters not specifically mentioned in DPPA). Public Law 106-69, and amendment to DPPA, reverses this. Effective June 1, 2000, it instructed the states to automatically opt out all individuals, unless the individual specifically asks to be included. Now, nearly all states have an "opt in" procedure in place. Thus, the states' compliance with Public Law 106-69 essentially did away with the sale of marketing lists and sales of bulk or database formats to information vendors and database compilers.

Also, 106-69 created a new category of personal information called sensitive personal information. This category includes the driver's license photograph, Social Security Number, medical and disability information. Subsection 350(b) restricts the dissemination of sensitive personal information without the express consent of the person to whom the information pertains. However, expressed consent is not required for the dissemination of sensitive personal information if released under the following permissible uses in DPPA 2721(b) —

- (1) For use by any government agency, including any court or law enforcement agency;

- (4) For use in connection with any civil, criminal, administrative, or arbitral proceeding;

- (6) For use by any insurer or insurance support organization;

- (9) For use by an employer or its agent or insurer to obtain or verify information relating to a holder of a commercial driver's license.

Therefore, Public Law 106-69 blocks any of the other 10 permissible users mentioned in DPPA from obtaining the four categories of sensitive personal information. Clear as mud, isn't it? Unless you have a very good and legitimate reason, do not expect a state motor vehicle departments to release photos, addresses, SSNs or disability information.

Searching State Occupational Licensing Boards

The Privacy Question

While some agencies consider this information private and confidential, most agencies freely release at least some basic data over the phone or by mail.

Our research indicates that many agencies appear to make their own judgments regarding what specifically is private and confidential in their files. For example, approximately 45% of the agencies indicate that they will disclose adverse information about a registrant, and many others will only disclose selected portions of the information or merely verify a credential.

In any event, the basic rule to follow when you contact a licensing agency is to **ask for the specific kinds of information available.**

What Information May Be Available

An agency may be willing to release part or all of the following—

- Field of Certification
- Status of License/Certificate
- Date License/Certificate Issued
- Date License/Certificate Expires
- Current or Most Recent Employer
- Social Security Number
- Address of Subject
- Complaints, Violations or Disciplinary Actions

How to Use the State Licenses Section

Each *State Licenses* section is separated into three parts—

1. Licenses Searchable Online
2. Licensing Quick Finder
3. Licensing Agency Information

A "Key Number" ties the sections together.

The License Searchable Online List

This is a list of boards and their corresponding URLs that offer **free Internet access** to their records. This means that you can do a name search or query from this website.

Using the Quick Finder

The place to start a verification search is in the **Licensing Quick Finder.** Here you will find, licenses, registrations or occupations listed in alphabetical order.

Although we reflect the official name used in a state for most items, names of some of the major license types have been standardized to make them easier to locate. For example, some states use the word "Physician" rather than "Medical Doctor." We have chosen to use the latter.

Agency Information

This section gives the address and telephone number of the agency or board where the records are maintained.

Use the "Key Number"

The **Key Number** is the *identifying number* for the agency that maintains information about this license. By matching the Key Number found in the Quick Finder to the profile in the Agency Information, you will have the address and other details about how this agency operates. The key number follows the "#" sign in the Quick Finder Section.

An Example of How to Use the Sections

Let us say the following appears in the *Quick Finder Section*:

Beautician #3   216-123-4536

As stated above, the Key Number, which follows the # sign, leads you to the Agency Information Section, where you will find the Agency or Board's address and phone number. For example, "#3" refers to the following:

3 Department of Health & Social Services, Division of Public Health,
123 Sesame Street, Mapletown, OH 44414, 216-123-4536

Search Fees

Several trends are observed when verifying search fees of the various licensing agencies. They are—

1. There is no charge to verify if a particular person is licensed; this can usually be done by phone.

2. The fee for copies or faxes ranges from $.25 to $2.00.

3. A fee of $5 to $20 usually applies to written requests. This is due to the fact that written certifications give more information than verbal inquiries, i.e. disciplinary action, exam scores, specific dates.

4. A fee that is $25 or more is typically for a list of licensed professionals. For example, a hospital might need a roster of registered nurses in a certain geographic area.

Searching Tip – Distinguish the Type of Agency

Within the agency category listings, it is important to note that there are five general types of agencies. When you are verifying credentials, you should be aware of what distinguishes each type, which in turn could alter the questions you ask.

Private Certification

Private Licensing and Certification — requires a proven level of minimum competence before a license is granted. These professional licenses separate the true "professions" from the third category below. In many of these professions, the certification body, such as the American Institute of Certified Public Accountants, is a private association whereas the licensing body, such as the New York State Education Department, is the licensing agency. Also, many professions may provide additional certifications in specialty areas.

State Certification

State Licensing and Certification — requires certification through an *examination* and/or other *requirements supervised* directly *by the state* rather than by a private association.

By Individual

Individual Registration — required if an individual intends to offer specified products or services in the designated area, but does not require certification that the person has met minimum requirements. An everyday example would be registering a handgun in a state that does not require passing a gun safety course.

By Business

Business Registration — required if a business intends to do business or offer specified products or services in a designated area, such as registering a liquor license. Some business license agencies require testing or a background check. Others merely charge a fee after a cursory review of the application.

Special Permits

Permits — give the grantee specific permission to do something, whether it is to sell hotdogs on the corner or to erect a three story high sign. Permits are usually granted at the local level rather than the state level of government.

Other Forms of Licensing and Registration

Although the state level is where much of the licensing and registration occurs, you should be aware of other places you may want to search.

Local Government Agencies

Local government agencies at both the **county** and **municipal levels** require a myriad of business registrations and permits in order to do business (construction, signage, etc.) within their borders. Even where you think a business or person, such as a remodeling contractor, should have local registrations you want to check out, it is still best to start at the state level.

County Recording Office and City Hall

If you decide to check on local registrations and permits, call the offices at both the county — try the **county recording office** — and municipal level — try **city hall** — to find out what type of registrations may be required for the person or business you are checking out.

Like the state level, you should expect that receiving basic information will only involve a phone call and that you will not be charged for obtaining a status summary.

Professional Associations

As mentioned above, many professional licenses are based on completion of the requirements of professional associations. In addition, there are *many professional designations* from such associations that *are not recognized as official licenses by government*. Other designations are basic certifications in fields that are so specialized that they are not of interest to the states, but rather only to the professionals within an industry. For example, if your company needs to hire an investigator to check out a potential fraud against you, you might want to hire a CFE — Certified Fraud Examiner — who has met the minimum requirements for that title from the Association of Certified Fraud Examiners.

Other Media Sources

Mail Lists and Databases

Many agencies make their lists available in reprinted or computer form, and a few maintain online access to their files. If you are interested in the availability of licensing agency information in bulk (e.g. mailing lists, magnetic tapes, disks) or online, call the agency and ask about formats that are available.

Vendor Databases

A number of private vendors also compile lists from these agencies and make them available online or on CD-ROM. We do not necessarily suggest these databases for credential searching because they may not be complete, may not be up-to-date and may not contain all the information you can obtain directly from the licensing agency. However, these databases are extremely valuable as a general source of background information on an individual or company that you wish to do business with.

Searching Federal Court Records

In addition to detailing how to obtain Federal Court information, another objective of this publication is to show searchers how the Federal Court system has evolved during the past few years. One problem searchers encounter is that older records may be in a different form or in a different location from newer records. For example, a searcher can go astray trying to find bankruptcy cases in Ohio unless he or she knows about changes in Dayton.

Many courts no longer provide the date of birth or the Social Security Number on search results. However, many do provide the last four digits of the SSN, or they may provide the month and year of birth, but not the day. This edition of *The Sourcebook* indicates what a court will or will not provide.

One development that continues to change the fundamental nature of Federal Courts case record access is, of course, computerization. Now, every Federal Court in the United States has converted to a computerized index. Courts are increasing computerized and rely less on paper.

Federal Court Structure

The Federal Court system includes three levels of courts, plus some special courts —

Supreme Court of the United States

The Supreme Court of the United States is the court of last resort in the United States. It is located in Washington, DC, where it hears appeals from the United States Courts of Appeals and from the highest courts of each state.

United States Court of Appeals

The United States Court of Appeals consists of thirteen appellate courts that hear appeals of verdicts from the courts of general jurisdiction. They are designated as follows:

The Federal Circuit Court of Appeals hears appeals from the U.S. Claims Court and the U.S. Court of International Trade. It is located in Washington, DC.

The District of Columbia Circuit Court of Appeals hears appeals from the district courts in Washington, DC as well as from the Tax Court.

Eleven geographic **Courts of Appeals** — each of these appeal courts covers a designated number of states and territories. The chart on the pages 34-35 lists the circuit numbers (1 through 11) and location of the Court of Appeals for each state.

United States District Courts

The United States District Courts are the courts of general jurisdiction, or trial courts, and are subdivided into two categories—

The District Courts are courts of general jurisdiction, or trial courts, for federal matters, excluding bankruptcy. Essentially, this means they hear cases involving federal law and cases where there is diversity of citizenship. Both **civil** and **criminal** cases come before these courts.

The **Bankruptcy Courts** generally follow the same geographic boundaries as the U.S. District Courts. There is at least one bankruptcy court for each state; within a state there may be one or more judicial districts and within a judicial district there may be more than one location (division) where the courts hear cases. While civil lawsuits may be filed in either state or federal courts depending upon the applicable law, all bankruptcy actions are filed with the U.S. Bankruptcy Courts.

Special Courts/Separate Courts

The Special Courts/Separate Courts have been created to hear cases or appeals for certain areas of litigation demanding special expertise. Examples include the U.S. Tax Court, the Court of International Trade and the U.S. Claims Court.

How Federal Trial Courts are Organized

At the federal level, all cases involve federal or U.S. constitutional law or interstate commerce. The task of locating the right court is seemingly simplified by the nature of the federal system—

- All court locations are based upon the plaintiff's county of domicile.
- All civil and criminal cases go to the U.S. District Courts.
- All bankruptcy cases go to the U.S. Bankruptcy Courts.

However, a plaintiff or defendant may have cases in any of the 500 court locations, so it is really not all that simple to find them.

There is at least one District Court and one Bankruptcy Court in each state. In many states there is more than one court, often divided further into judicial districts — e.g., the State of New York consists of four judicial districts: the Northern, Southern, Eastern, and Western. Further, many judicial districts contain more than one court location (usually called a division).

The Bankruptcy Courts generally use the same hearing locations as the District Courts. If court locations differ, the usual variance is to have fewer Bankruptcy Court locations.

Case Numbering

When a case is filed with a federal court, a case number is assigned. This is the primary indexing method. Therefore, in searching for case records, you will need to know or find the applicable case number. If you have the number in good form already, your search should be fast and inexpensive.

You should be aware that case numbering procedures are not consistent throughout the Federal Court system: one judicial district may assign numbers by district while another may assign numbers by location (division) within the judicial district or by judge. Remember that case numbers appearing in legal text citations may not be adequate for searching unless they appear in the proper form for the particular court.

All the basic civil case information that is entered onto docket sheets, and into computerized systems like PACER (see below), starts with standard form JS-44, the Civil Cover Sheet, or the equivalent.

Docket Sheet

As in the state court system, information from cover sheets, and from documents filed as a case goes forward, is recorded on the **docket sheet**, which then contains the case history from initial filing to its current status. While docket sheets differ somewhat in format, the basic information contained on a docket sheet is consistent from court to court. As noted earlier in the state court section, all docket sheets contain:

- Name of court, including location (division) and the judge assigned;

- Case number and case name;

- Names of all plaintiffs and defendants/debtors;

- Names and addresses of attorneys for the plaintiff or debtor;

- Nature and cause (e.g., U.S. civil statute) of action;

- Listing of documents filed in the case, including docket entry number, the date and a short description (e.g., 12-2-92, #1, Complaint).

Assignment of Cases and Computerization

Traditionally, cases were assigned within a district by county. Although this is still true in most states, the introduction of computer systems to track dockets has led to a more flexible approach to case assignment, as is the case in Minnesota and Connecticut. Rather than blindly assigning all cases from a county to one judge, their districts are using random numbers and other logical methods to balance caseloads among their judges.

This trend may appear to confuse the case search process. Actually, the only problem the searcher may face is to figure out where the case records themselves are located. Finding cases has become significantly easier with the wide availability of PACER and Case Management/Electronic Case Filings at remote access, Internet, and onsite terminals in each court location with the same district-wide information base.

Computerized Indexes are Available

Computerized courts generally index each case record by the names of some or all the parties to the case — the plaintiffs and defendants (debtors and creditors in Bankruptcy Court) as well as by case number. Therefore, when you search by name you will first receive a listing of all cases in which the name appears, both as plaintiff and defendant.

Electronic Access to Federal Courts

Numerous programs have been developed for electronic access to Federal Court records. Over the years the Administrative Office of the United States Courts in Washington, DC has developed three innovative public access programs: VCIS, PACER, and most recently the Case Management/ Electronic Case Files (CM/ECF) project. The most useful program for online searching is now CM/ECF. VCIS access is via telephone; PACER via Internet or remote dial-up.

Case Management/Electronic Case Files (CM/ECF)

CM/ECF is the new case management system for the Federal Judiciary for all bankruptcy, district and appellate courts. CM/ECF allows courts to accept filings and provide access to filed documents over the Internet. CM/CDF replaced aging electronic docketing and case management systems in all federal courts in 2005. Nearly every federal court is currently CM/ECF operational as we go to press, and the remaining courts are in the process of implementing CM/ECF. Courts currently using CM/ECF are noted in this directory. It is important to note that when you search ECF, you may be ONLY searching cases that have been filed electronically. A case may not have been filed electronically through CM/ECF, so you must still conduct a search using PACER (where PACER is still operational) if you want to know if a case exists.

One important feature of this system is their *National Locator*, known as the *United States Party Index*. This is a name search, used to locate the specific court where records are available.

To sign-up for CM/ECF access, do so through the court. For further information about CM/ECF visit http://pacer.psc.uscourts.gov/cmecf/index.html. Most courts offer tutorials on how to use CM/ECF.

PACER

PACER, the acronym for **P**ublic **A**ccess to **E**lectronic **C**ourt **R**ecords, provides docket information online for open cases at **all U.S. Bankruptcy courts** and **most U.S. District courts**. Currently most courts are available on the Internet. A few systems can be dialed directly using communication software (such as ProComm Plus, pcAnywhere, or Hyperterminal) and a modem. Cases for the U.S. Court of Federal Claims are also available.

Each court maintains its own databases with case information. Because PACER and CM/ECF database systems are maintained within each court, each jurisdiction will have a different URL or modem number. Accessing and querying information from each service is comparable; however, the format and content of information provided may differ slightly.

Sign-up and technical support is handled at the PACER Service Center in San Antonio, Texas; phone 800-676-6856. You can sign up for all or multiple districts at once. In many judicial districts, when you sign up for PACER access, you will receive a PACER Primer that has been customized for each district. The primer contains a summary of how to access PACER, how to select cases, how to read case numbers and docket sheets, some searching tips, who to call for problem resolution, and district specific program variations.

A problem with PACER is that each court determines when records will be purged and how records will be indexed, leaving you to guess how a name is spelled or abbreviated and how much information about closed cases your search will uncover. A PACER search for anything but open cases **cannot** take the place of a full seven-year search of the federal court records available by written request from the court itself or through a local document retrieval company. Many districts report that they have closed records back a number of years, but at the same time indicate they purge docket items every six months.

Another problem is the lack of identifiers. Most federal courts do not show the DOB on records available to the public. Thus, if a record searcher has a common name and gets one or more hits, each individual case file may need to be reviewed to determine if the case belongs to the subject in mind.

An excellent FAQ on PACER is found at http://pacer.psc.uscourts.gov/faq.html.

Before Accessing PACER of CM/ECF, Search the "National" U.S. Party/Case Index

The U.S. Party/Case Index is a national index for U.S. District, Bankruptcy, and Appellate courts. A small subset of information from each case will be transferred to the U.S. Party/Case Index each night. The system serves as a locator index for PACER. You may conduct nationwide searches to determine whether or not a party is involved in federal litigation. For detailed information on cases found while searching the U.S. Party/Case Index, you will need to visit the PACER or CM/ECF site for the particular jurisdiction where the case is located. The Case Number field in the output will be a direct link to the full case information on the court's computers, whether the court is running the Internet version of PACER or CM/ECF.

You may access the U.S. Party/Case Index by via the Internet at http://pacer.uspci.uscourts.gov.

Miscellaneous Online Systems

Some courts have developed their own online systems. In addition to RACER, Idaho's Bankruptcy and District Courts have other searching options available on their website. Likewise, the Southern District Court of New York offers CourtWeb, which provides information to the public on selected recent rulings of those judges who have elected to make information available in electronic form.

VCIS

Another access system is **VCIS** (Voice Case Information System). At one time, nearly all of the U.S. Bankruptcy Court judicial districts provide **VCIS**, a means of accessing information regarding open bankruptcy cases by merely using a touch-tone telephone. The advantage? There is no charge. Individual names are entered last name first with as much of the first name as you wish to include.

For example, Carl R. Ernst could be entered as ERNSTC or ERNSTCARL. Do not enter the middle initial. Business names are entered as they are written, without blanks.

VCIS, like the RACER System, is being replaced by newer technology. **Each Bankruptcy Court that now offers VCIS access includes that court's VCIS phone number(s) in its profile.**

RACER

RACER stands for Remote Access to Court Electronic Records. Accessed through the Internet, RACER offers access to the same records as PACER. At present, searching RACER is free in a few courts and has been changed to PACER or CM/ECF in almost all others, using fee structures there.

Federal Courts Searching Hints

- VCIS should *only* be used to locate information about open cases. Do not attempt to use VCIS as a substitute for a PACER search.

- This publication includes the counties of jurisdiction for each court. The county list in each Court profile is a good starting point for determining where case records may be found.

- Before performing a general PACER or CM/ECF search to determine whether cases exist under a particular plaintiff, debtor, or defendant name, first be certain to review that Court's profile, which may indicate the earliest dates of case records available on PACER. Also, searchers need to be sure that the Court's case index includes all cases, open and closed, for that particular period, especially important if using CM/ECF. Be aware that some courts purge older, closed cases after a period of time, making a PACER search incomplete. Wherever known, this publication indicates within the court profiles the purge timeframe for PACER records. Purge times vary from court to court and state to state.

- Experience shows that court personnel are typically not aware of — nor concerned about — the types of searches performed by readers of this publication. Court personnel often focus on only open cases, whereas a searcher may want to know as much about closed cases as open ones. Thus, court personnel are sometimes fuzzy in answering questions about how far back case records go on PACER, and whether closed cases have been purged. If you are looking for cases older than a year or two, there is no substitute for a real, onsite search performed by the court itself or by a local search expert (if that court allows full access to its indexes).

- Some courts may be more willing than others to give out information by telephone. This is because most courts have converted from the old card index system to fully computerized indexes that are easily accessible while on the phone.

Federal Records Centers and the National Archives

After a federal case is closed, the documents are held by Federal Courts themselves for a number of years, then stored at a designated Federal Records Center (FRC). After 20 to 30 years, the records are then transferred from the FRC to the regional archives offices of the National Archives and Records Administration (NARA). The length of time between a case being closed and its being moved to an FRC varies widely by district. Each court has its own transfer cycle and determines access procedures to its case records even after they have been sent to the FRC.

When case records are sent to an FRC, the boxes of records are assigned accession, location, and box numbers. These numbers, which are called **case locator information, must be obtained from the originating court and are necessary to retrieve documents from the FRC.** Some courts will provide case locator information over the telephone, but other courts may require a written request. This information is now available on PACER in certain judicial districts. The Federal Records Center for each state is as follows:

State	Circuit	Appeals Court	Federal Records Center
AK	9	San Francisco, CA	Anchorage (Some records are in temporary storage in Seattle)
AL	11	Atlanta, GA	Atlanta
AR	8	St. Louis, MO	Fort Worth
AZ	9	San Francisco, CA	Los Angeles
CA	9	San Francisco, CA	Los Angeles (Central & Southern CA) San Francisco (Eastern & Northern CA)
CO	10	Denver, CO	Denver
CT	2	New York, NY	Boston
DC		Washington, DC	Washington, DC
DE	3	Philadelphia, PA	Philadelphia
FL	11	Atlanta, GA	Atlanta
GA	11	Atlanta, GA	Atlanta
GU	9	San Francisco, CA	San Francisco
HI	9	San Francisco, CA	San Francisco
IA	8	St. Louis, MO	Kansas City, MO
ID	9	San Francisco, CA	Seattle
IL	7	Chicago, IL	Chicago
IN	7	Chicago, IL	Chicago
KS	10	Denver, CO	Kansas City, MO
KY	6	Cincinnati, OH	Atlanta
LA	5	New Orleans, LA	Fort Worth
MA	1	Boston, MA	Boston
MD	4	Richmond, VA	Philadelphia
ME	1	Boston, MA	Boston
MI	6	Cincinnati, OH	Chicago
MN	8	St. Louis, MO	Chicago
MO	8	St. Louis, MO	Kansas City, MO
MS	5	New Orleans, LA	Atlanta
MT	9	San Francisco, CA	Denver
NC	4	Richmond, VA	Atlanta
ND	8	St. Louis, MO	Denver
NE	8	St. Louis, MO	Kansas City, MO
NH	1	Boston, MA	Boston
NJ	3	Philadelphia, PA	New York
NM	10	Denver, CO	Denver
NV	9	San Francisco, CA	Los Angeles (Clark County, NV) San Francisco (Other NV counties)
NY	2	New York, NY	New York
OH	6	Cincinnati, OH	Chicago; Dayton has some bankruptcy
OK	10	Denver, CO	Fort Worth

State	Circuit	Appeals Court	Federal Records Center
OR	9	San Francisco, CA	Seattle
PA	3	Philadelphia, PA	Philadelphia
PR	1	Boston, MA	New York
RI	1	Boston, MA	Boston
SC	4	Richmond, VA	Atlanta
SD	8	St. Louis, MO	Denver
TN	6	Cincinnati, OH	Atlanta
TX	5	New Orleans, LA	Fort Worth
UT	10	Denver, CO	Denver
VA	4	Richmond, VA	Philadelphia
VI	3	Philadelphia, PA	New York
VT	2	New York, NY	Boston
WA	9	San Francisco, CA	Seattle
WI	7	Chicago, IL	Chicago
WV	4	Richmond, VA	Philadelphia
WY	10	Denver, CO	Denver

Notes to the Chart:

GU is Guam, PR is Puerto Rico, and VI is the Virgin Islands.

According to some odd logic, the following Federal Records Centers are not located in the city named above, but are actually somewhere else. Below are the exceptions:

Atlanta—in East Point, GA; Boston—in Waltham, MA; Los Angeles—in Laguna Niguel, CA; New York—in Bayonne, NJ; San Francisco—in San Bruno, CA

Note: The Los Angeles Records Center now houses its records in Perris, CA (Riverside, for all practical purposes). Telephone number for Perris is 951- 956-2011.

The administrative offices remain in Laguna Niguel.

Searching Other Federal Records Online

EDGAR

EDGAR – the **E**lectronic **D**ata **G**athering **A**nalysis and **R**etrieval system – was established by the U.S. Securities and Exchange Commission (SEC) to allow companies to make required filing to the SEC by direct transmission. As of May 6, 1996, all public domestic companies are required to make their filings on EDGAR, except for filings made to the Commission's regional offices and those filings made on paper due to a hardship exemption.

EDGAR is an extensive repository of U.S. corporation information and it is available online.

What Information is Available on EDGAR?

Companies must file the following reports with the SEC:

- 10-K – an annual financial report that includes audited year-end financial statements.

- 10-Q – a quarterly, un-audited report.

- 8K – a report detailing significant or unscheduled corporate changes or events.

- Securities offering, trading registrations, and the final prospectus.

The list above is not conclusive. There are other miscellaneous reports filed, including those dealing with security holdings by institutions and insiders. Access to these documents provides a wealth of information.

How to Access EDGAR Online

EDGAR is searchable online at http://www.sec.gov/info/edgar.shtml. Also, a number of private vendors offer access to EDGAR records. LexisNexis acts as the data wholesaler or distributor on behalf of the government. LexisNexis sells data to information retailers, including its own Nexis service.

Aviation Records

The Federal Aviation Association (FAA) is the U.S. government agency with the responsibility for all matters related to the safety of civil aviation. Among its functions the FAA provides the system that registers aircraft and the documents showing title or interest in aircraft. Their website, at www.faa.gov, is the ultimate source of aviation records, airports and facilities, safety regulations, and civil research and engineering.

The Aircraft Owners and Pilots Association is the largest organization of its kind with 340,000+ members. Their website is www.aopa.org and is an excellent source of information regarding the aviation industry.

Another excellent source of aircraft information is *Jane's World Airlines* at www.janes.com.

Military Records

This topic is so broad that there can be a book written about it, and in fact there is! *The Armed Forces Locator Directory* from MIE Publishing (864- 595-0891) is an excellent source. The book, now in its 8th edition, covers every conceivable topic regarding military records. Their website www.militaryusa.com offers free access to some useful databases.

The Privacy Act of 1974 (5 U.S.C. 552a) and Department of Defense directives require a written request, signed and dated, to access military personnel records. For further details, visit the NPRC site listed below.

Military Internet Sources

There are a number of great internet sites that provide valuable information on obtaining military and military personnel records. The National Personnel Records Center (NPRC), maintained by the National Archives & Records Administration, is on the Internet at www.nara.gov/regional/mpr.html. The NPRC site is full of useful information and links. Other excellent sites include:

www.army.mil	The official site of the U.S. Army
www.af.mil	The official site of the U.S. Air Force
www.navy.mil	The official site of the U.S. Navy
www.usmc.mil	The official site of the U.S. Marine Corps
www.arng.army.mil	The official site of the Army National Guard
www.ang.af.mil	The official site of the Air National Guard
www.uscg.mil/USCG.shtm	The official site of the U.S. Coast Guard

Best U.S. Government Gateways

The remainder of this Chapter is written and contributed by online pioneer and award winning journalist Alan M. Schlein, author of Find It Online.

We sincerely thank Alan for permitting the use of his material in The Sourcebook. *Alan can be reached at* www.deadlineonline.com. *Check out his website— it is a great source with lots of useful links!*

In the U.S., almost every federal government agency is online. There is a nationwide network of depository libraries, including the enormous resources of the National Archives (www.nara.gov), the twelve presidential libraries, and four national libraries – the Library of Congress, the National Agricultural Library, the National Library of Education, and the National Library of Medicine. There are almost 5000 government websites from more than forty-two U.S. departments and agencies.

Because there are so many government websites, in order to find the starting point for your research, you may need to turn to specialized, purpose-built websites called *government gateways*, that organize and link government sites. Some gateways are simply collections of links. Others provide access to bulletin boards of specific government agencies so that you find and contact employees with specific knowledge. This "human guidance" is becoming increasingly important in light of the growing number of reports and publications that are no longer printed but simply posted online.

Best Government Gateways (listed alphabetically)

Documents Center
www.lib.umich.edu/govdocs/index.html

Documents Center is a clearinghouse for local, state, federal, foreign, and international government information. It is one of the more comprehensive online searching aids for all kinds of government information on the Internet. It is especially useful as a meta-site of meta-sites.

Federal Web Locators
www.infoctr.edu/fwl/

This web locator is really two sites in one: a federal government website (www.infoctr.edu/fwl) and a separate site that tracks federal courts (www.infoctr.edu/fwl/fedweb.juris.htm), both of which are browsable by category or by keyword. Together they provide links to thousands of government agencies and departments.

FedLaw
www.thecre.com/fedlaw/default.htm

Containing 1,600+ links to law-related information, FedLaw is an extremely broad resource for federal legal and regulatory research. It has very good topical and title indices that group web links into hundreds of subjects. It is operated by the General Services Administration (GSA).

Fedstats

www.fedstats.gov

A terrific collection of statistical sites from the federal government and a good central clearinghouse for other federal statistics sites.

FedWorld Information Network

www.fedworld.gov

FedWorld helps you search over thirty million U.S. government pages. It is a massive collection of 15,000 files and databases of government sites, including bulletin boards that can help you identify government employees with expertise in a broad range of subjects. A surprising number of these experts will take the time to discuss questions from the general public.

FirstGov

www.firstgov.gov

Responding to the need for a central clearinghouse of U.S. federal government sites, the U.S. government developed FirstGov and linked every federal agency to its site as well as every state government. It has an easy-to-use search tool, allowing you to specify if you want federal or state agencies and to easily locate business regulations and vital records. It also lets you look for federal government phone numbers and email addresses. This is an easy-to-use starting point, powered by the AlltheWeb search engine. Also, check out the FAQs of the U.S. government for questions and answers about the U.S. government (www.faq.gov).

Google's Uncle Sam

www.google.com/unclesam

Google's Uncle Sam site is a search engine geared to looking at U.S. government sites. It is an easy-to-use tool if you know what you are looking for.

Healthfinder

www.healthfinder.gov

This is a great starting point for health-related government information. See the Health and Medicine Information Tools sidebar in Chapter 5, Specialized Tools, for more health sites.

InfoMine: Scholarly Internet Resource Collections

http://infomine.ucr.edu

InfoMine provides collections of scholarly internet resources, best for academics. It is one of the best academic resources anywhere, from the librarians at the University of California Riverside. InfoMine's Government Information section is easily searchable by subject. It has detailed headings and its resource listings are very specific. Since it is run by a university, some of its references are limited to student use only.

SearchGov.com

www.searchgov.com

A private company that has an effective search for U.S. government sites.

Speech & Transcript Center

www.freepint.com/gary/speech.htm

This site links directly to websites containing transcripts of speeches. Pulled together by former George Washington University reference librarian and *Invisible Web* author Gary Price, it encompasses government resources, business leaders, and real audio. A large section is devoted to U.S. and international government speech transcripts including Congressional hearings, experts' testimony, and transcripts.

U.S. Federal Government Agencies Directory
`www.lib.lsu.edu/gov/fedgov.html`

This directory of federal agencies is maintained by Louisiana State Univ. It links to hundreds of federal government internet sites. It is divided by branch and agency and is very thorough, but focus on your target because it is easy to lose your way or become overwhelmed en route.

Best U.S. Federal Government Websites

U.S. tax dollars are put to good and visible use here. A few of the government's web pages are rated as excellent. Some can be used in lieu of commercial tools but only if you have the time to invest.

A few of the top government sites – the Census and the Securities and Exchange Commission – are models of content and presentation. They are very deep, very thorough, and easy to use. If only the rest of the federal government would follow suit. Unfortunately, the best of the federal government is just that: the best. Not all agencies maintain such detailed and relevant resources.

Following are the crown jewels of the government's collection, in ranked order:

U.S. Census Bureau
`www.census.gov`

Without question, this is the U.S. government's top site. It is saturated with information and census publications – at times overwhelmingly so – but worth every minute of your time. A few hours spent here is a worthwhile investment for almost anyone seeking to background a community, learn about business, or find any kind of demographic information. You can search several ways: alphabetically by subject, by word, by location, and by geographic map. The only problem is the sheer volume of data.

One feature, the Thematic Mapping System, allows users to extract data from Census CD-ROMs and display them in maps by state or county. You can create maps on all kinds of subjects – for examples, tracking violent crime or comparing farm income. The site also features the Statistical Abstract of the U.S. with a searchable index at `www.census.gov/statab/www/stateabs.html`

The potential uses of census data are infinite. Marketers use it to find community information. Reporters search out trends by block, neighborhood or region. Educators conduct research. Businesses evaluate new business prospects. Genealogists trace family trees – though full census data is not available for seventy-two years from the date the census is taken. You can even use it to identify ideal communities in which to raise a family. Jennifer LaFleur, now at *The Dallas Morning News* did a story while at *The San Jose Mercury News* using the census site to find eligible bachelors in specific areas of San Jose.

Additional census resources include:

U.S. Census Data Access Tools
`http://www.census.gov/main/www/access.html`

This site provides a myriad of detailed census data and software that may be downloaded.

State and County QuickFacts
`http://quickfacts.census.gov/qfd/`

At all its levels, this site has very easy-to-use census information.

Census FactFinder
`http://factfinder.census.gov`

An easy way to find quickie facts from within the Census' huge website. This is an excellent and easy to use site. Start here when looking for Census documents, since it has a search capability.

Census Industry Statistics

www.census.gov/main/www/industries.html

Industry-by-industry statistics.

And one other census-related site that is superb is the University of Virginia's Fisher Library's historical census data browser, going all the way back to 1790. It can be found at http://fisher.lib.virginia.edu/collections/stats/histcensus/

U.S. Securities and Exchange Commission (SEC)

www.sec.gov

Only the Census site is better than the SEC site, which is a first-rate, must-stop place for information shopping on U.S. companies. Its EDGAR database search site (www.sec.gov/edaux/searches.htm) is easy to use and provides access to documents that companies and corporations are required to file under regulatory laws.

The SEC site is a great starting point for information about specific companies and industry trends. The SEC requires all publicly-held corporations and some large privately-held corporations to disclose detailed financial information about their activities, plans, holdings, executives' salaries and stakes, legal problems and so forth. For more details, see Chapter 9, Business Tools.

Library of Congress (LOC)

www.loc.gov

This site is an extraordinary collection of documents. Thomas, the Library's Congressional online center site (http://thomas.loc.gov/home) provides an exhaustive collection of congressional documents, including bill summaries, voting records, and the full Congressional Record, which is the official record of Congressional action. This LOC site also links to many international, federal, state, and local government sites. You can also access the library's more than five million records online, some versions in full-text and some in abstract form. Though the library's entire 121 million item collection is not yet available online, the amount online increases daily. In addition to books and papers, it includes an extensive images collection ranging from Frank Lloyd Wright's designs to the Dead Sea Scrolls to the world's largest online collection of baseball cards. The Library of Congress also has a terrific collection of international data on its website at www.loc.gov/rr/international/portals.html

U.S. Government Printing Office Home Page (GPO)

www.access.gpo.gov/

The GPO is the federal government's primary information printer and distributor. All federally funded information from every agency is sent here, which makes the GPO's holdings priceless. Luckily, the GPO site is well-constructed and easy to use. For example, it has the full text of the *Federal Register*, which lists all federal regulations and proposals, and full-text access to the *Congressional Record*. The GPO also produces an online version of the *Congressional Directory*, providing details on every congressional district, profiles of members, staff profiles, maps of every district and historical documents about Congress. This site will expand exponentially over the next few years, as an increased number of materials go out of print and online. GPO Access also allows you to electronically retrieve much of the bureaucratic paper in Washington, electronically, from the Government Printing Office including searching more than seventy databases and indices. If you need some help finding things, use the topic-specific finder at this site.

National Technical Information Service (NTIS)

www.ntis.gov

The best place to find federal government reports related to technology and science, NTIS is the nation's clearinghouse for unclassified technical reports of government-sponsored research. NTIS collects, indexes, abstracts, and sells U.S. and foreign research – mostly in science, technology, behavioral, and social science data.

IGnet

www.ignet.gov

This is a truly marvelous collection of reports and information from the Inspector Generals of about sixty federal agency departments. They find waste and abuse within government agencies. It is well worth checking when starting research on government-related matters.

General Accounting Office GAO Reports

www.gao.gov/decisions/decision.htm

The Comptroller General Opinions from the last sixty days are posted on this GAO website. These reports and opinions are excellent references. For historical opinions back to 1995, go online to www.gpoaccess.gov/gaodecisions/index.html

DefenseLINK – U.S. Department of Defense (DOD)

www.defenselink.mil

This is the brand-name site for Pentagon-related information. There is a tremendous amount of data here – categorized by branch of service – including U.S. troop deployments worldwide. To the Pentagon's credit, they have made this a very easy site to use.

Defense Technical Information Center (DTIC)

www.dtic.mil

The DTIC site is loaded with links and defense information – everything from contractors to weapon systems. It even includes de-classified information about the Gulf War. It is the best place to start for defense information. You can even find a list of all military-related contracts, including beneficiary communities and the kinds of contracts awarded. The only problem with the site is there is no search engine to make it easy to find information.

Bureau of Transportation Statistics

www.bts.gov

The U.S. Department of Transportation's enormous collection of information about every facet of transportation. There is a lot of valuable material here including the Transportation Statistics Annual Report. It also holds financial data for airlines and searchable databases containing information about fatal accidents and on-time statistics for airlines, which can be narrowed to your local airport.

National Archives and Records Administration

www.archives.gov/index.html

A breathtaking collection of research online, for example the National Archives has descriptions of more than 170,000 documents related to the Kennedy assassination. It also contains a world-class database holding descriptions of more than 95,000 records held by the Still Picture and Motion Picture, Sound and Video Branches. This site also links to the twelve Presidential Archives with their records of every person ever mentioned in Executive Branch correspondence. You can view an image of the original document. The Archives Research Center Online has great collections of family history/genealogy research and veterans' service records.

FedWorld.gov

www.fedworld.gov

This thorough government clearinghouse site, run by the Commerce Department's National Technical Information Service, offers access to FirstGov, the U.S. Government's comprehensive site, but also allows you to search government publications, U.S. Supreme Court decisions, and helps you find government jobs.

Federal Consumer Information Center National Contact Center
www.info.gov

While this is largely a telephone service that gets more than a million calls a year, this website tries to provide a way through the maze of federal agencies. It includes a clearinghouse of phone numbers for all federal agencies, state, and local government sites.

SciTechResources.gov
www.scitechresources.gov

This is a tremendous directory of about 700 science and technology resources on U.S. government sites from the U.S. Department of Commerce, National Technical Information Service.

Department of Homeland Security
http://www.whitehouse.gov/infocus/homeland/index.html

While the U.S. Government has made the Department of Homeland Security a separate agency, it maintains the website under the White House's auspices. As a result, it has good information, but is, like the White House site, more about public relations for the current president and his staff than it is about information. Nonetheless, you can find useful information about the current threat level and information about what U.S. state and local governments are doing on homeland security.

Bureau of National Affairs, The
www.bna.com

An expensive but useful group of topic-focused newsletters providing details on U.S. government action at different federal agencies. Titles include *The Daily Labor Report, Bankruptcy Law Daily*, and *The Biotech Watch*. This private company has hundreds of newsletters you will not find elsewhere.

Searching County Court Records

The purpose of the County Court Records Section is to provide detailed access information on the more than 6,400 major courts that have jurisdiction over significant criminal and civil cases under state law.

Some Court Basics

Before trudging into a courthouse and demanding to view a document, you should first be aware of some basic court procedures. Whether the case is filed in a state, municipal, or federal court, each case follows a similar process.

A **civil case** usually commences when a plaintiff files a complaint with a court against defendants. The defendants respond to the complaint with an answer. After this initial round, there may be literally hundreds of activities before the court issues a judgment. These activities can include revised complaints and their answers, motions of various kinds, discovery proceedings (including depositions) to establish the documentation and facts involved in the case. All of these activities are listed on a **docket sheet**, which may be a piece of paper or a computerized index.

Once the court issues a judgment, either party may appeal the ruling to an appellate division or court. In the case of a money judgment, the winning side can usually file it as a judgment lien with the county recorder. Appellate divisions usually deal only with legal issues and not the facts of the case.

In a **criminal case**, the plaintiff is a government jurisdiction. The Government brings the action against the defendant for violation of one or more of its statutes.

In a **bankruptcy case,** which can be heard only in federal courts, there is neither defendant nor plaintiff. Instead, the debtor files voluntarily for bankruptcy protection against creditors, or the creditors file against the debtor in order to force the debtor into involuntary bankruptcy.

State Court Structure

The first step to determining where a particular state court case is located is to understand how the court system is structured in that particular state. The general structure of all state court systems has four parts:

Appellate courts   **Limited jurisdiction trial courts**

Intermediate appellate courts   **General jurisdiction trial courts**

The two highest levels, appellate and intermediate appellate courts, only hear cases on appeal from the trial courts. Opinions of these appellate courts are of interest primarily to attorneys seeking legal precedents for new cases.

General jurisdiction trial courts usually handle a full range of civil and criminal litigation. These courts usually handle felonies and larger civil cases.

Limited jurisdiction trial courts come in two varieties. First, many limited jurisdiction courts handle smaller civil claims (usually $10,000 or less), misdemeanors, and pretrial hearing for felonies. Second, some of these courts — sometimes called special jurisdiction courts — are limited to one type of litigation, for example the Court of Claims in New York which only handles liability cases against the state. Some limited jurisdiction courts operate as state courts and some are local courts, usually known such as City, Municipal, or Justice Courts.

The Sourcebook lists and profiles all the general jurisdiction courts and most of the limited jurisdiction courts.

Some states, for instance Iowa, have consolidated their general and limited jurisdiction court structure into one combined court system. In other states there may be a further distinction between state-supported courts and municipal courts. Notable is the state of New York where nearly 1,300 Justice Courts handle misdemeanors, local ordinance violations, and traffic violations including DWI.

Generalizations should not be made about where specific types of cases are handled in the various states. Misdemeanors, probate, landlord/tenant (eviction), domestic relations, and juvenile cases may be handled in either or both the general and limited jurisdiction courts. To help you locate the correct court to perform your search in, this *Sourcebook* specifically lists the types of cases handled by each court.

Types of Litigation in Trial Courts

Criminal

Criminal cases are categorized as *felonies* or *misdemeanors*. A general rule, a felony involves a jail term of one year or more, whereas a misdemeanor may only involve a monetary *fine*.

Civil

Civil cases are categorized as *tort*, *contract*, and *real property* rights. Torts can include *automobile accidents*, *medical malpractice*, and *product liability* cases. Actions for small money damages, typically under $3,000, are known as *small claims*.

Other

Other types of cases that frequently are handled by separate courts or specialized divisions of courts include *juvenile*, *probate* (wills and estates), and *domestic relations*.

How Courts Maintain Records

Case Numbering

When a case is filed, it is assigned a case number. This is the primary indexing method in every court. Therefore, in searching for case records, you will need to know — or find — the applicable case number. If you have the case number in good form already, your search should be fast and reasonably inexpensive.

You should be aware that case numbering procedures are not consistent throughout a state court system. One district may assign numbers by district while another may assign numbers by location (division) within the district, or by judge. Remember: case numbers appearing in legal text citations may not be adequate for searching unless they appear in the proper form for the particular court in which you are searching.

All basic civil case information is entered onto docket sheets.

Docket Sheet

Information from cover sheets and from documents filed as a case goes forward is recorded on the docket sheet. The docket sheet then contains an outline of the case history from initial filing to its current status. While docket sheets differ somewhat in format, the basic information contained on a docket sheet is consistent from court to court. All docket sheets contain:

- Name of court, including location (division) and the judge assigned;

- Case number and case name;

- Names of all plaintiffs and defendants/debtors;

- Names and addresses of attorneys for the plaintiff or debtor;

- Nature and cause (e.g., statute) of action.

Computerization

Most courts are computerized, which means the docket sheet data is entered into a computer system. Within a state or judicial district, the courts *may* be linked together via a single computer system.

Docket sheets from cases closed before the advent of computerization may not be in the computer system. For pre-computer cases, most courts keep summary case information on microfilm, microfiche, or index cards.

Case documents are not generally available on computer because courts are still experimenting with and developing electronic filing and imaging of court documents. Generally, documents are only available to be copied by contacting the court where the case records are located.

Using the County Court Records Section

Included in *The Sourcebook* are all state felony courts, larger claim civil courts, and probate courts in the United States. Since most courts have jurisdiction over a number of categories of cases, we also include many of the courts that hear misdemeanor, eviction, and small claims court cases. In addition, each County Court Records Section begins with an introduction that summarizes where other major categories of court cases — DUI, preliminary hearings, and juvenile cases — can be found.

The term "County Courts" — as used in this publication — refers to those courts of original jurisdiction (trial courts) within each state's court system that handle…

- **Felonies** -- Generally defined as crimes punishable by one year or more of jail time

- **Misdemeanors** -- Generally defined as minor infractions with a fine or minimal jail time

- **Civil Actions** -- For money damages (usually greater than $3,000)

- **Probate** -- Estate matters

- **Evictions** -- Landlord/tenant actions

- **Small Claims** -- Actions for minor money damages (generally under $3,000)

Useful Applications

The County Court Record sections are especially useful for four kinds of applications—

General litigation searching/background searching... Combined with the *Federal Court section*, you have complete coverage of all the important courts in the United States.

Employment background screening... Included is full coverage of local criminal courts at the felony level, and many misdemeanor courts as well.

Tenant background checking... Courts where landlord/tenant cases are filed are indicated in the state introduction charts, and most of the courts handling such cases are profiled.

Asset searching... The probate courts have records of wills and estate matters that can be used to determine assets, related parties, and useful addresses.

The State Court Chart Pages

At the beginning of each state's County Court Records Section is an excellent summary of that state's court structure.

The First Chart

The chart at the top of the page summarizes the structure of the court system, listing the court of general jurisdiction, followed underneath by the courts of limited, municipal, and special jurisdiction. Court types with an asterisk (*) after their names are profiled in *The Sourcebook*.

The number of case record locations is indicated for each court. Where two classifications of courts are combined into one location and only one entry appears in the profiles, the number of combined courts is noted. The number of locations for the courts not profiled in *The Sourcebook* are estimates.

Where useful, the number and type of organization of each of the classifications of court are indicated under the "How Organized" column. When searching for case records, keep in mind that many of the higher level courts also handle appeals from lower courts.

The Civil and Criminal Charts

The other two charts consolidate information about what types of cases each court hears, i.e. the "jurisdiction" of the type of court.

Where more than one court has jurisdiction for a particular kind of civil case, the minimum and maximum claim fields clarify whether there is overlapping jurisdiction in the state. In most states, the lower and upper court civil claim limits dovetail nicely between the court levels, so you can readily tell which court has the type of civil case you are concerned about.

Although these charts oversimplify complex sets of state statutes, their purpose is to provide you with a practical starting point to help you decide where to search for case records.

Beyond the Charts

The address, telephone number, and Internet address of the administrative office in each state are listed under the heading "Administration." This is a good contact point for technical or complex questions about a particular state's court system. After the charts are summaries of significant statewide online access systems and overviews of statewide policies and procedures. This text is especially help.

The Court Profile Pages and Court Record Searching Tips

Basic Information

All the U.S. counties (and where applicable, parishes, boroughs, independent cities, etc.) are listed in alphabetical order within each state. When a county has more than one court profiled, the courts appear in order beginning with the court of general jurisdiction then proceed down to more limited jurisdictions. Each profile specifically lists the types of cases handled by that court. If a level of court has divisions, civil courts are listed before criminal courts. Where more than one court of the same type is located in a county, they are listed in alphabetical order by the name of the city where they are located.

All city/ZIP Code combinations have been verified against our latest version of *The County Locator* database for accuracy. In addition to the address and telephone number, the time zone is indicated (see below for an explanation of the abbreviations used). Fax numbers are given for most courts.

Watch for Name Variations From State to State

Do not assume that the structure of the court system in another state is anything like your own. In one state, the Circuit Court may be the highest trial court whereas in another it is a limited jurisdiction court. Examples are: New York, where the Supreme Court is not very "supreme" and the downstate court structure varies from upstate; and Tennessee, where circuit courts are in districts.

Access and Searching Tips

Each court profile indicates acceptable searching methods including phone, fax mail, in person, and online. The profiles also indicate all fees (including search, copy and certification) and acceptable payment methods. For example, some courts accept credit cards, some do not accept personal checks, and some may bill for copies.

Here are some searching hints to keep in mind:

- When a county has multiple courts of the same level, general information is provided to help determine which office to search in, depending upon the subject's address.

- In many instances two types of courts within a county (e.g., circuit and district) are combined. When phoning or writing these courts, we recommend that your request specifically state that you want both courts included in the search.

- If you are conducting a name search – that is, you do not supply a specific case number, just a name – then you may find that many courts that previously conducted searches of court records on behalf of the public are no longer making that service available. Typically, these courts do one of two things. In some states, such as Kentucky, the courts only refer the searcher to a state agency that maintains a database combining individual court records, which may not be current. In other states, Nebraska for instance, the court has public access terminals or microfilm/fiche readers available for public use.

- If you need copies of a specific case record and you know the case number, court personnel generally will honor mail, fax, and sometimes phone requests to make copies for you. Also, court personnel may certify the document for you for a fee.

- If you cannot come to the courthouse yourself, and the court personnel will not perform the search for you, then you must hire a local retrieval firm or other individual to conduct the search. An excellent source of local court record searchers is the Public Record Retriever Network found at www.brbpub.com/prrn.

Index and Record Systems

Most profiles of the civil courts indicate whether the plaintiffs as well as the defendants are indexed. A plaintiff search is useful, for example, to determine if someone is especially litigious.

During the past decade, thousands of courts have installed computerized indexing systems. The year when computer indexing started in each of these courts is indicated in the profile of most of the automated courts. Computerized systems are considerably faster and easier to search, allowing for more indexing capability than the microfilm and card indexes that preceded them.

Search Requirements

There is a strong tendency for courts to overstate their search requirements. For civil cases, the usual reasonable requirement is a defendant (or plaintiff) name — full name if it is a common name — and the time frame to search —e.g., 1993-2002. For criminal cases, the court may require more identification, such as date of birth (DOB), to ascertain the correct individual. Other information "required" by courts — such as Social Security Number (SSN) — is often just "helpful" to narrow the search on a common name. Further, we have indicated when certain pieces of information may be helpful but are not required.

Restricted Records

Most courts have a number of types of case records, such as juvenile and adoptions, which are not released without a court order. These restricted record types are indicated in each profile.

Fees and Other Requirements

As mentioned above, search, copy, and certification fees are given for most courts, as well as fax fees if known.

Sometimes there is a difference in the copy fee depending if the court makes the copy or if a self-serve machine is used. These differences are indicated within the profile.

Where specified, we indicate whether the court requires a self-addressed stamped envelope (SASE) to accompany a written search request. Even where it is not indicated, we recommend including a SASE to make sure the results are returned to you.

Searching State Courts Online

Online searching is generally limited to a copy of the courts' docket sheets, as explained above. Most courts are computerized in-house, which means that the docket sheet data is entered into a computer system of the courthouse itself. Checking a courthouse's computer index is the quickest way to find if case records exist online. Some states offer statewide access to docket information, as described below.

The State Court Administrator's Office

The court administrator oversees the state court system, which is also known as the county court system. The state judicial website is a good place to find opinions from the state supreme court and for appeals court opinions. In some states, the state court administration office oversees a statewide online access system to court records. Some of these systems are commercial fee-based. Other systems offer free access, but are usually very limited in comparison. *The Sourcebook* contains profiles of each statewide system that offers access to a centralized database of trial court records.

A growing number of state courts provide electronic access to their records. For example, in Alabama, Maryland, Minnesota, New Mexico, Oregon, Washington, and Wisconsin where "statewide" online systems are available, you still need to understand (1) the court structure in that state, (2) which particular courts are included in their online system, and (3) what types of cases are included.

Recommended State Court Resources

The National Center for State Courts

www.ncsconline.org

NASCIO

https://www.nascio.org/aboutNascio/profiles/ - (click on a State then the Judicial Link)

Searching Recording Office Records

Combined, the Recording Offices section for each state section contains 4,266 local recording offices where Uniform Commercial Code and real estate records are maintained.

The Lowdown on Recorded Documents

Documents filed and recorded at local county, parish, city or town offices represent some of the best opportunities to gain access to open public records, more so if they are available for searching online by name. In fact, recorded documents are one of the most available types of public records that can be viewed online and obtained over the Internet, either for free or at a reasonable fee. Even better, if you are lucky enough to live in close proximity, you can visit your local office and view complete records for free and acquire copies.

Real Estate

Real estate records are public so that everyone can know who owns what property. Liens on real estate must be public so a buyer knows all the facts. The county (or parish or city) recording office is the source. Also, access is also available from many private companies that purchase entire county record databases and create their own database for commercial purposes.

Uniform Commercial Code (UCC)

UCC filings are to personal property what mortgages are to real estate property. UCCs are in the category of financial records that must be fully open to public scrutiny so that other potential lenders are on notice about which assets of the borrower have been pledged as collateral.

As with tax liens, UCC recordings are filed, according to state law, either at the state or local (county, town, parish) level. Until June 30, 2001, liens on certain types of companies required dual filing (must file at BOTH locations, thus records can be searched at BOTH locations). As of July 1, 2001, UCC filings other than those that go into real estate records are no longer filed at the local filing offices in most states, but older filings can still be located there until 2008. As with real estate records, there are a number of private companies who have created their own databases for commercial resale.

A Great Source of Information

Although recorded documents are a necessity to making an informed business-related decision, they are also a virtual treasure trove of data. UCC filing documents give you the names and addresses of creditors and debtors, describe the asset offered for collateral, the date of the filing, and whether or not the loan has been satisfied. This information contained on the statements can lead an experienced investigator to other avenues along the information trail. For example, if the collateral is a plane or a vessel, this will lead to registration records; if the debtor is a business, other names on the filing may lead to other traceable business partners or ventures.

How the Recording Offices Section is Organized

General Organization

The mailing address, telephone, time zone and fax number are listed for each office. If online access is available from the agencies, a detailed profile is provided. Included are other categories of information offered online from this or a related agency, such as tax assessor information and vital records, licenses, etc. Searching fees are listed. Other important phone numbers in the county are listed to the extent that we have researched and verified these numbers. Examples are telephone numbers for the assessor, treasurer, vital records, and elections offices.

An introduction to each state Recording Offices section contains a summary of the facts about where and how real estate records are maintained, as well as indicating information about Uniform Commercial Code and tax lien filings. It mentions any unusual conditions pertaining to real estate, tax lien and UCC searching in that state. A list of some of the other liens that are filed at the local level is also included.

Recording Office Searching Rules

The general rules for background searching of UCC records are as follows:

- *Except in local filing states, a search at the state level is adequate to locate all UCC records on a subject.*

- *Mortgage record searches will include any real estate related UCC filings.*

See the sections below for discussions of special collateral rules.

Due diligence searching, however, usually demands searching the local records in dual filing states, especially for older UCC records.

Special Categories of Collateral

Real Estate Related UCC Collateral

A specific purpose of lien statutes under both the UCC and real estate laws is to put a buyer or potential secured creditor on notice that someone has a prior security interest in real or personal property. UCC financing statements are to personal property what mortgages or deeds of trust are to real property.

One problem addressed by the UCC is that certain types of property have the characteristics of both real and personal property. In those instances, it is necessary to have a way to provide lien notice to two different categories of interested parties: those who deal with the real estate aspect of the property and those who deal with the "personal" aspect of the property.

In general, our definition of real estate related UCC collateral is any property that in one form is attached to land, but that in another form is not attached. For the sake of simplicity, we can define the characteristics of two broad types of property that meet this definition:

Property that is initially attached to real property, but then is separated.
Three specific types of collateral have this characteristic: *minerals* (including oil and gas), *timber*, and *crops*. These things are grown on or extracted from land. While they are on or in the ground they are thought of as real property, but once they are harvested or extracted they become personal property. Some states have a separate central filing system for crops.

*Property that is initially personal property, but then is attached to land, is generally called **fixtures**.*
Equipment such as telephone systems or heavy industrial equipment permanently affixed to a building are examples of fixtures. It is important to realize that what is a fixture, like beauty, is in the eye of the beholder, since it is a somewhat vague definition.

UCC financing statements applicable to real estate related collateral must be filed where the real estate and mortgage records are kept, which is generally at the county level — except in Connecticut, Rhode Island and Vermont where the Town/City Clerk maintains these records. The chart gives the titles of the local official who maintains these records.

Consumer Goods

Among the state-to-state variations, some states required filing where real estate is filed for certain consumer goods. However, as of July 1, 2001 all non-realty related UCC filings in most states, including consumer goods, now go only to the central filing office in the state.

Equipment Used in Farming Operations

33 states required only local filing for equipment used in farming operations. However as of July 1, 2001, all non-realty-related UCC filing has been centralized.

Searching Note

If you are looking for information on subjects that might have these types of filings against them, a search of county records may still be revealing even if you would normally search only at the state level.

The Importance of Revised Article 9

Revised Article 9

On July 1, 2001, Revised Article 9 became law in 46 states and the District of Columbia, with 4 states adopting the law later; Alabama (January 1, 2002), Connecticut (October 1, 2001), Florida (January 1, 2002) and Mississippi (January 1, 2002). Under this new law, most UCC filings will go to the state where a business is organized, not where the collateral or chief executive offices are located. Thus, you will find new filings against IBM only in Delaware (IBM and many other public companies are Delaware corporations), and not in New York or in any other states where it has branch offices. Therefore, you will need to know where a company is organized in order to know where to find new UCC filings against it.

The place to file against individuals is the state where the person resides.

However, the new law does not apply to federal tax liens, which are still generally filed where the chief executive office is located. IBM's chief executive offices, for example, may still be in New York state.

As stated above, realty-related UCC filings continue to go to land recording offices where the property is located.

How to Search for Filings Under Old Article 9

Under old Article 9, Uniform Commercial Code financing statements and changes to them might be filed at two or three government agencies in each state, depending upon the type of collateral involved in the transaction. Each state's UCC statute contained variations on a nationally recommended Model Act. Each variation is explained below. The charts appear at the end of this chapter.

You will still need to know about where UCC filings are located under old Article 9 because the transition period to Revised Article 9 is five years long. UCC filings on record before July 1, 2001 remain effective until they lapse, which is generally five years from initial filing date.

A lot of UCC filings against IBM, for example, made before July 1, 2001 will still be on record in New York's central filing office, and may also be found in county filing offices since New York was a dual filing state, as explained below.

Under old Article 9, 33 states were central filing states. Central filing states are those where most types of personal property collateral require filing of a UCC financing statement only at a central filing location within that state.

Under old Article 9, five states had statewide UCC database systems. Some of these systems are still in effect under Revised Article 9. Minnesota and **Wisconsin** were central filing states with a difference: UCC financing statements filed at the county level are also entered into a statewide database. In **North Dakota** UCC financing statements may be filed at either the state or county level, and all filings are entered into a statewide database. In **Louisiana**, **Nebraska**, and **Georgia**, UCC financing statements may be filed with **any** county (parish). Under Revised Article 9, Minnesota has established a county/state system like North Dakota in all but six county offices, and Nebraska is now a central filing state. In each of these six states the records are entered into a central, statewide database that is available for searching in each county, as well as at the state agency (no state agency in Louisiana or Georgia).

Under old Article 9, eight states required dual filing of certain types of UCC financing statements. The usual definition of a dual filing state is one in which financing statements containing collateral such as inventory, equipment or receivables *must* be filed in *both* a central filing office, usually with the Secretary of State, and in a local (county) office where the collateral or business is located. The three states below were also dual filing states, with a difference. Under Revised Article 9, no dual filing is required within a state

Under old Article 9, the filing systems in three states, MA, NH, and PA, can be described as triple filing because the real estate portion of the filings goes to an office separate from the UCC filing offices. In Massachusetts and New Hampshire, UCC filings were submitted to the town/city while real estate filings go to the county. In Pennsylvania, county government was separated into the *Prothonotary* for UCC filings and the *Recorder* for real estate filings. The local filing offices for non-realty-related UCC filings no longer take filings under Revised Article 9, but they will continue to perform searches of the old records.

Some counties in other states do have separate addresses for real estate recording, but this is usually just a matter of local departmentalization.

Under old Article 9, Kentucky and Wyoming were the only *local filing only* states. In both of these states a few filings were also found at the state level because filings for out of state debtors went to the Secretary of State. And in Wyoming, filings for Wyoming debtor accounts receivable and farm products require dual filing. However, under Revised Article 9, all filings have been centralized.

The Old Article 9 UCC Locator Chart

This handy chart will tell you at a glance where UCC and real estate records are filed under old Article 9 on a state-by-state basis. Under Revised Article 9, effective July 1, 2001 except as noted later for Alabama, Connecticut, Florida and Mississippi, all new personal property filings go to the central filing office.

State	Most Personal Property		All Real Property Filing Office
	Central Filing Office	Local Filing Office	
AK	Department of Natural Resources		District Recorder
AL	Secretary of State		Judge of Probate
AR	Secretary of State	and Circuit Clerk	Circuit Clerk
AZ	Secretary of State		County Recorder
CA	Secretary of State		County Recorder
CO	Secretary of State	or any County Recorder (as of July 1, 1996)	County Clerk & Recorder
CT	Secretary of State		Town/City Clerk
DC	County Recorder		County Recorder
DE	Secretary of State		County Recorder
FL	Secretary of State		Clerk of Circuit Court
GA	None	Clerk Superior Court	Clerk of Superior Court
HI	Bureau of Conveyances		Bureau of Conveyances
IA	Secretary of State		County Recorder
ID	Secretary of State		County Recorder
IL	Secretary of State		County Recorder
IN	Secretary of State		County Recorder
KS	Secretary of State		Register
KY	Secretary of State (Out of state only)	County Clerk	County Clerk
LA	None	Clerk of Court	Clerk of Court
MA	Secretary of the Commonwealth	and Town/City Clerk	Register of Deeds
MD	Department of Assessments & Taxation	and Clerk of Circuit Court (until 7/1/95)	Clerk of Circuit Court
ME	Secretary of State		County Register
MI	Secretary of State		County Register
MN	Secretary of State or Recorder		County Recorder
MO	Secretary of State	and County Recorder	County Recorder
MS	Secretary of State	and Chancery Clerk	Chancery Clerk

| State | Most Personal Property | | All Real Property |
	Central Filing Office	Local Filing Office	Filing Office
MT	Secretary of State		Clerk & Recorder
NC	Secretary of State	and Register of Deeds	Register of Deeds
ND	Secretary of State or County Register		County Register
NE	Secretary of State (Out of state only)	County Clerk	County Register
NH	Secretary of State	and Town/City Clerk	County Register
NJ	Secretary of State		County Clerk/Register
NM	Secretary of State		County Clerk
NV	Secretary of State		County Recorder
NY	Secretary of State	and County Clerk (Register)	County Clerk (Register)
OH	Secretary of State	and County Recorder	County Recorder
OK	Oklahoma County Clerk		County Clerk
OR	Secretary of State		County Clerk
PA	Department of State	and Prothonotary	County Recorder
RI	Secretary of State		County Clerk & Recorder
SC	Secretary of State		County Register/Clerk
SD	Secretary of State		County Register
TN	Secretary of State		County Register
TX	Secretary of State		County Clerk
UT	Division of Corporations & Commercial Code		County Recorder
VA	Corporation Commission	and Clerk of Circuit Court	Clerk of Circuit Court
VT	Secretary of State	and Town/City Clerk (until 7/1/95)	Town/City Clerk
WA	Department of Licensing		County Auditor
WI	Dept. of Financial Institutions		County Register
WV	Secretary of State		County Clerk
WY	Secretary of State (Out of state and A/R only)	County Clerk	County Clerk

Using the County Locator Section

A list at the end of each state section cross references place names to counties. Comprised of every official U.S. Postal Service place name, the city/county cross references contain more that 40,000 entries. This information is summarized from the BRB publication The County Locator.

The cross references contain a special feature that identifies ZIP Codes that cross county lines.

Using ZIP Codes When Searching For Public Records

A place name (capitalized type) may be listed more than once in the city/county cross-references. For example,

> LOS GATOS (95030) Santa Clara (88), Santa Cruz (12)
> LOS GATOS Santa Clara

This duplicate listing indicates that the bulk of LOS GATOS addresses is in Santa Clara county, but those addresses with the ZIP Code 95030 may be in Santa Cruz county. Specifically, ZIP Code 95030 is approximately 88% in Santa Clara and 12% in Santa Cruz.

Note: county names are listed in upper and lower case type, and place names are always capitalized.

10,000 Problems Pointed Out

Multiple county ZIP Codes always appear, as in the above example, before the main entry for a place name. The percentages may not always add up to 100% because of rounding off. Counties that represent less than 1% of the addresses in a ZIP Code have also been eliminated. In all, there are almost 10,000 ZIP Codes shown in this *Sourcebook* that cross county lines.

Using Multiple County Information

The special multiple county entries put you on notice that addresses within a ZIP Code may not be in the county usually associated with that place name. This information can be crucial to finding public records, including court cases that are filed based on the location of property or residence. Remember, if you search in the wrong county, then you may get a false "no hit" response.

Non-Geographic Zip Codes

When trying to locate public records based upon place names and ZIP Codes, be aware that 10,000 ZIP Codes are useless in determining county of residence because they are assigned exclusively to post office boxes or rural routes. Anyone can have a post office box in any county. Never use an address containing one of these non-geographic ZIP Codes to determine where to search.

Maps

The Sourcebook contains 116 pages of useful state maps and tables. County outlines and major cities are shown.

For More Extensive Information

BRB Publications has several products that take a deeper look at counties, place names and ZIP Codes. The Public Record Research System on CD and on the Web each contain an additional 40,000 place names, as well as information about the characteristics of each ZIP Code. For example, these products indicate whether the ZIP Code only contains post office boxes, high rise building, or general delivery.

A resource recently added to the above products is the Adjoining County Lookup. This gives the user the ability to choose a subject county and find all adjoining counties with most recent Census population numbers.

For more information, visit www.brbpub.com

Using a Public Record Vendor

Hiring Someone to Obtain the Record

There are five main categories of public record professionals: distributors; gateway; search firms and local document retrievers; investigative firms; and verification-screening firms.

Distributors (Proprietary Database Vendors)

These vendors (also known as Primary Distributors) are automated public record firms who combine public sources of bulk data and/or online access to develop their own database product(s). They collect or buy public record information from government repositories and reformat the information in some useful way. They may also purchase or license records from other information vendors, like the phone companies. In the past they purchased the "credit header" information from the credit bureaus, but this is no longer a standard practice. There are approximately 250 public record vendors in this category that collect and warehouse information (not counting marketing companies). Most of these entities are either vertical (multiple types of info collected on a local or regional basis) or horizontal (one type of info collected on a national basis) in nature. Less than 10% are large entities that are both vertical and horizontal with massive amount of data (like ChoicePoint). When a database vendor sells the data, the **vendor is bound by the same disclosure laws attached to the government repository data.** This can range from zero (recorded documents, level three sexual predators, etc.) to severe (voter registration, criminal court case records, etc.).

Gateways

Gateways are companies that provide automated electronic gateway to Proprietary Database Vendors or to government agencies online systems. Gateways do not warehouse records. Gateways thus provide "one-stop shopping" for multiple geographic areas and/or categories of information. Gateways are the companies that are most evident on the Internet as they advertise access to records for many different purposes.

Companies can be *both* Primary Distributors and Gateways. For example, a number of online database companies are both primary distributors of corporate information and also gateways to real estate information from other Primary Distributors

Search Firms

Search firms are companies that furnish public record search and document retrieval services using online services and/or through a network of specialists, including their own employees or correspondents (see Retrievers below). Search firms rely on, primary distributors and/or networks of retrievers, or they may go direct to the government agency. They combine online proficiency with document retrieval expertise. Search firms may focus either on one geographic region — like New England — or on one specific type of public record information — like criminal records.

A very common sub-category of search firms is known as **Local Document Retrievers**. Retrievers search specific requested categories of public records usually in order to obtain documentation for legal compliance (e.g., incorporations), for lending, and for litigation. They do not usually review or interpret the results or issue reports in the sense that investigators do, but rather return documents with the results of searches. They tend to be localized, but there are companies that offer a national network of retrievers and/or correspondents. The retriever or his/her personnel goes directly to the agency to look up the information. A retriever may be relied upon for strong knowledge in a local area, whereas a search generalist has a breadth of knowledge and experience in a wider geographic range. There are thousands of entities that can be classified as search firms in the U.S., including approximately 3,000 local document retrievers.

The 775+ members of the **Public Record Retriever Network (PRRN)** can be found, by state and counties served, at www.brbpub.com/PRRN. This organization has set industry standards for the retrieval of public record documents and operates under a Code of Professional Conduct. Using one of these record retrievers is an excellent way to access records in those jurisdictions that do not offer online access.

Verification Firms (Pre-employment Screeners, Tenant Screeners, MVR Vendors)

Verification firms provide services to employers and businesses when the subject has given consent. In this category are pre-employment screening firms and tenant screening firms (both governed by the Fair Credit Reporting Act - FCRA) and motor vehicle record vendors (governed by the Drivers Privacy Protection Act – DPPA). Since these entities usually only perform their services for clients who have specifically received consent from the subjects, they do not warehouse or collect data to be resold. Many times the service provided by a pre-employment screening company is called a background screen or a background report. Their service should not be confused with an investigation as provided by private investigators (see below) or with search firms with an Internet presences that advertise their services for background checks. There are at least 500 pre-employment screening firms in the U.S., not counting many private investigators that may also offer that service, when asked. After the FCRA was passed, many, many PIs ceased doing employment screening.

Private Investigation Firms

Investigators use public records as tools rather than as ends in themselves, in order to create an overall, comprehensive "picture" of an individual or company for a particular purpose. They interpret the information they have gathered in order to identify further investigation tracks. They summarize their results in a report compiled from all the sources used. In addition, an investigator may be licensed and may perform the types of services traditionally thought of as detective work, such as surveillance. In many instances, a private investigator doing an investigation and does not have the consent of the subject.

Many investigators also act as search firms or record retrievers and provide search results to other investigators. Some investigators offer pre-employment screening per the FCRA.

Other Vendors of Note

There are two other types of firm worthy of mention that occasionally utilize public records. The Association of Independent Information Professionals (AIIP), at www.aiip.org, has over 700 experienced professional information specialist members from 21 countries. They refer to themselves as Information Brokers (IBS). They gather information that will help their clients make informed business decisions. Their work is usually done on a custom basis with each project being unique. IBs are extremely knowledgeable in online research of full text databases and most specialize in a particular subject area, such as patent searching or competitive intelligence.

A similar organization is the Society of Competitive Intelligence Professionals (SCIP) whose home page is www.scip.org. Per their web "...SCIP provides education and networking opportunities for business professionals working in the rapidly growing field of competitive intelligence (the legal and ethical collection and analysis of information regarding the capabilities, vulnerabilities, and intentions of business competitors)."

Which Type of Vendor is Right for You?

With all the variations of vendors and the categories of information, the obvious question is; "How do I find the right vendor to go to for the public record information I need?" Before you start calling every interesting online vendor that catches your eye, you need to narrow your search to the **type** of vendor for your needs. To do this, ask yourself the following questions—

What is the Frequency of Usage?

If you have on-going, recurring requests for a particular type of information, it is probably best to choose a different vendor then if you have infrequent requests. Setting up an account with a primary distributor, such as LEXIS or Westlaw will give you an inexpensive per search fee, but the monthly minimum requirements will be prohibitive to the casual requester, who would be better off finding a vendor who accesses or is a gateway to one of these vendors.

What is the Complexity of the Search?

The importance of hiring a vendor who understands and can interpret the information in the final format increases with the complexity of the search. Pulling a corporation record in Maryland is not difficult, but doing an online criminal record search in Maryland, when only a portion of the felony records are online, is not so easy.

Thus, part of the answer to determining which vendor or type of vendor to use is to become conversant with what is (and is not) available from government agencies. Without knowing what is available (and what restrictions apply), you cannot guide the search process effectively. Once you are comfortable knowing the kinds of information available in the public record, you are in a position to find the best method to access needed information.

What are the Geographic Boundaries of the Search?

A search of local records close to you may require little assistance, but a search of records nationally or in a state 2,000 miles away will require seeking a vendor who covers the area you need to search. Many national primary distributors and gateways combine various local and state databases into one large comprehensive system available for searching. However, if your record searching is narrowed by a region or locality, then an online source that specializes in a specific geographic region (like Superior Information Services in NJ) may be an alternative to a national vendor. Keep in mind that many national firms allow you to order a search online, even though results cannot be delivered immediately and some hands-on local searching is required.

Of course, you may want to use the government agency online system, if available, for the kind of information you need.

10 Questions to Ask a Public Records Vendor

(Or a Vendor Who Uses Online Sources)

The following discussion focuses specifically on automated sources of information because many valuable types of public records have been entered into a computer and, therefore, require a computer search to obtain reliable results. The original version of the text to follow was written by **Mr. Leroy Cook.** Mr. Cook is the founder and Director of ION and The Investigators Anywhere Resource Line (800-338-3463, http://ioninc.com). Mr. Cook has graciously allowed us to edit the article and reprint it for our readers.

1. Where does he or she get the information?

You may feel awkward asking a vendor where he or she obtained the information you are purchasing. The fake Rolex watch is a reminder that even buying physical things based on looks alone — without knowing where they come from — is dangerous.

Reliable information vendors *will* provide verification material such as the name of the database or service accessed, when it was last updated, and how complete it is.

It is important that you know the gathering process in order to better judge the reliability of the information being purchased. There *are* certain investigative sources that a vendor will not be willing to disclose to you. However, that type of source should not be confused with the information that is being sold item by item. Information technology has changed so rapidly that some information vendors may still confuse "items of information" with "investigative reports." Items of information sold as units are *not* investigative reports. The professional reputation of an information vendor is a guarantee of sorts. Still, because information as a commodity is so new, there is little in the way of an implied warranty of fitness.

2. How long does it take for the new information or changes to get into the system?

Any answer *except* a clear, concise date and time or the vendor's personal knowledge of an ongoing system's methods of maintaining information currency is a reason to keep probing. In view of the preceding question, this one might seem repetitive, but it *really* is a different issue. Microfiche or a database of records may have been updated last week at a courthouse or a DMV, but the department's computer section may also be working with a three-month backlog. In this case, a critical incident occurring one month ago would *not* show up in the information updated last week. The importance of timeliness is a variable to be determined by you, but to be truly informed you need to know how "fresh" the information is. Ideally, the mechanism by which you purchase items of information *should* include an update or statement of accuracy — as a part of the reply — *without* having to ask.

3. What are the searchable fields? Which fields are mandatory?

If your knowledge of "fields" and "records" is limited to the places where cattle graze and those flat, round things that play music, you *could* have a problem telling a good database from a bad one. An MVR vendor, for example, should be able to tell you that a subject's middle initial is critical when pulling an Arizona driving record. You don't have to become a programmer to use a computer and you needn't know a database management language to benefit from databases, *but* it is very helpful to understand how databases are constructed and (*at the least*) what fields, records, and indexing procedures are used.

As a general rule, the computerized, public-record information world is not standardized from county to county or from state to state; in the same way, there is little standardization within or between information vendors. Look at the system documentation from the vendor. The manual should include this sort of information.

4. How much latitude is there for error (misspellings or inappropriate punctuation) in a data request?

If the vendor's requirements for search data appear to be concise and meticulous, then you're probably on the right track. Some computer systems will tell (or "flag") an operator when they make a mistake such as omitting important punctuation or using an unnecessary comma. Other systems allow you to make inquiries by whatever means or in whatever format you like — and then tell you the requested information has *not* been found. In this instance, the desired information may *actually* be there, but the computer didn't understand the question because of the way in which it was asked. It is easy to misinterpret "no record found" as "there is no record." Please take note that the meanings of these two phrases are quite different.

5. What method is used to place the information in the repository and what error control or edit process is used?

In some databases, information may be scanned in or may be entered by a single operator as it is received and, in others, information may be entered *twice* to allow the computer to catch input errors by searching for non-duplicate entries. You don't have to know *everything* about all the options, but the vendor selling information in quantity *should*.

6. How many different databases or sources does the vendor access *and* how often?

The chance of obtaining an accurate search of a database increases with the frequency of access and the vendor's/searcher's level of knowledge. If he or she only makes inquiries once a month — and the results are important — you may need to find someone who sells data at higher volume. The point here is that it is better to find someone who specializes in the type of information you are seeking than it is to utilize a vendor who *can* get the information, but actually specializes in another type of data.

7. Does the price include assistance in interpreting the data received?

A report that includes coding and ambiguous abbreviations may look impressive in your file, but may not be too meaningful. For all reports, except those you deal with regularly, interpretation assistance can be *very* important. Some information vendors offer searches for information they really don't know much about through sources that they only use occasionally. Professional pride sometimes prohibits them from disclosing their limitations — until *you* ask the right questions.

8. Do vendors "keep track" of requesters and the information they seek (usage records)?

This may not seem like a serious concern when you are requesting information you're legally entitled to; however, there *is* a possibility that your usage records could be made available to a competitor. Most probably, the information itself is *already* being (or will be) sold to someone else, but you may not necessarily want *everyone* to know what you are requesting and how often. If the vendor keeps records of who-asks-what, the confidentiality of that information should be addressed in your agreement with the vendor.

9. Will the subject of the inquiry be notified of the request?

If your inquiry is sub rosa or if the subject's discovery of the search could lead to embarrassment, double check! There are laws that mandate the notification of subjects when certain types of inquiries are made into their files. If notification is required, the way it is accomplished could be critical.

10. Is the turnaround time and cost of the search made clear at the outset?

You should be crystal clear about what you expect and/or need; the vendor should be succinct when conveying exactly what will be provided and how much it will cost. Failure to address these issues can lead to disputes and hard feelings.

These are excellent questions and concepts to keep in mind when searching for the right public record vendor to meet your needs.

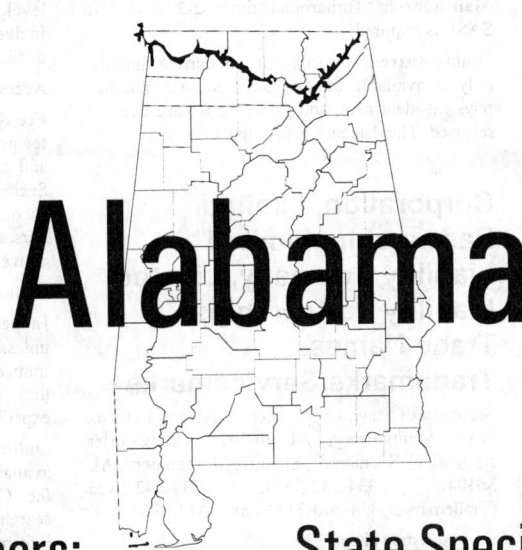

Alabama

General Help Numbers:

Governor's Office
600 Dexter Ave, #N-104   334-242-7100
Montgomery, AL 36130   Fax 334-353-0004
www.governor.state.al.us   8AM-5PM

Attorney General's Office
State House   334-242-7300
11 S. Union Street, 3rd Fl   Fax 334-242-4891
Montgomery, AL 36130   8AM-5PM
www.ago.state.al.us

Legislative Records
State House   334-242-7800 (Senate)
11 S Union St   334-242-7600 (House)
Montgomery, AL 36130-4600   Fax 334-242-8819
www.legislature.state.al.us   8:30AM-4:30PM

State Archives
Archives & History Department   334-242-4435
Reference Room, PO Box 300100   Fax 334-240-3433
Montgomery, AL 36130-0100   8AM-5PM T-F,
www.archives.state.al.us   9AM-5PM SA

State Specifics:

Capital:	Montgomery
	Montgomery County
Time Zone:	CST
Number of Counties:	67
Population:	4,530,182
Website:	www.alabama.gov

State Agencies

Criminal Records

Alabama Bureau of Investigation, Identification Unit Record Checks, PO Box 1511, Montgomery, AL 36102-1511 (Courier address: 301 S Ripley St, Montgomery, AL 36104); 334-353-4340, 8AM-5PM.

www.dps.state.al.us/public/abi

Records are available from 1942 on. It takes about 7 days before new records are available for inquiry. 40% of arrests in database have final dispositions recorded, 65% for those arrests in last 5 years.

Searching: The request must be on state form ABI-46. The form can be obtained from the webpage at www.dps.state.al.us/public/abi/forms/ABI-46.pdf, or call to have copy sent. Include the following in your request-notarized release from subject, date of birth, Social Security Number, full name, race, sex. Fingerprints optional. 100% of the record files have fingerprints. The following data is not released: juvenile records. All records or arrests are released, including those without dispositions.

Access by: mail, in person.

Fee & Payment: The fee is $25.00 per name. For those entities entitled by statute to an FBI fingerprint check, the fee is $49.00 per name. The FBI check is not available to the public or employers not entitled per statute. Fee payee: Alabama Bureau of Investigation. Cashier checks and money orders accepted. No credit cards or personal checks accepted.

Mail search: Turnaround time: 4 to 6 weeks. No SASE is required.

In person search: You may bring in the required release and request form.

Statewide Court Records

Administrative Office of Courts, 300 Dexter Ave, Montgomery, AL 36104-3741; 334-954-5000, 334-242-2099-Fax; 8AM-5PM.

www.alacourt.gov

Except for certain online research capabilities, all trial court record access must be done at the local level.

Access by: online.

Online search: In the past, commercial remote access to the State Judicial Information System (SJIS) was offered, but this is no longer available. This agency reccommends that searchers contact a commercial vendor at www.alacourt.com. State Supreme Court and Appellate decisions are available at www.alalinc.net and at www.judicial.state.al.us/.

Sexual Offender Registry

Department of Public Safety, Sexual Offender Registry, PO Box 1511, Montgomery, AL 36102-1511 (Courier address: 301 S Ripley, Montgomery, AL 36109); 334-353-1172, 334-353-2563-Fax; 8AM-5PM.

www.dps.state.al.us

Sections 15-20-21 to 37, Code of Alabama 1975, makes it a class C felony for any criminal sex offender to violate most provisions of the Alabama Community Notification Act.

Records are available from 08/01/98. It takes about 7 days before new records are available for inquiry. Records are normally destroyed after the death of the offender.

Searching: Include the following in your request-name, DOB, and SSN. The following data is not released: information on the victim.

Access by: mail, phone, fax, online.

Fee & Payment: None

Mail search: Turnaround time: 7 days. A SASE is required.

Phone search: Limited searching available.

Fax search: Requests may be faxed.

Online search: Sex offender data and a felony fugitives list are available online at www.dps.state.al.us/public/abi/system. Search by name, ZIP Code or geographic area.

Incarceration Records

Alabama Department of Corrections, Central Records Office, PO Box 301501, Montgomery, AL 36130 (Courier address: 301 S. Ripley Street, Montgomery, AL 36130); 334-353-9500, 8AM-5PM.

http://doc.state.al.us

Questions regarding specific inmates can be sent to pio@doc.state.al.us.

Records are available on current and former inmates by mail; current inmates only online. No information is available on youthful offenders. It takes about 2-3 weeks before new records are available for inquiry. Records are normally destroyed after (kept indefinitely).

Searching: Include the following in your request-full name; AIS number helpful, as is DOB & SSN.

Access by: mail, online.

Fee & Payment: There is no fee.

Mail search: Turnaround time: 2-3 days. No SASE is required.

Online search: Information on current inmates only is available online. Location, AIS number, physical identifiers, and projected release date are released. The database is updated weekly.

Corporation, Limited Partnership, Limited Liability Company, Limited Liability Partnerships, Trade Names, Trademarks/Servicemarks

Secretary of State, Corporations Division, PO Box 5616, Montgomery, AL 36103-5616 (Courier address: 11 S Union St, Ste 207, Montgomery, AL 36104); 334-242-5324, 334-242-5325 (Trademarks), 334-240-3138-Fax; 8AM-5PM.

www.sos.state.al.us

The office for Trademarks, Trade Names, and Servicemarks is located in Room 200.

Records are available for corporations, active or inactive. All information here on file is considered public information. It takes 1 month before new records are available for inquiry. Records are indexed on images and on inhouse computer.

Searching: Include the following in your request-full name of business. In addition to the articles of incorporation, corporation records include the following information: Officers, Prior (Merged) names, Inactive and Reserved names.

Access by: mail, phone, fax, in person, online.

Fee & Payment: There is no search fee, but copies are $1.00 per page. Fee payee: Secretary of State. Prepayment required. Personal checks & credit cards accepted.

Mail search: Turnaround time: 7 to 10 days. A SASE is requested.

Fax search: Search requests accepted by fax.

In person search: Call first for page amount before going to their office. Expedite fees may apply.

Online search: The website has free searches of corporate and UCC records. Search individual files for Active Names at http://arc-sos.state.al.us/CGI/SOSCRP01.MBR/INPUT.

Expedited service: Expedited service is available for mail and phone searches, call for fees. Turnaround time: 72 hours. Expedited service ends at Noon each day.

Uniform Commercial Code, Federal and State Tax Liens

UCC Division - SOS, UCC Records, PO Box 5616, Montgomery, AL 36103-5616 (Courier address: 11 South Union St, Suite 200, Montgomery, AL 36104); 334-242-5231, 334-353-8269-Fax; 8AM-5PM.

www.sos.state.al.us

It takes 72 hours before new records are available for inquiry. Records are indexed on inhouse computer. Records are normally destroyed after 1 year after lapse date.

Searching: Use search request form UCC-11. The search includes tax liens. Federal and state tax liens on individuals may also be filed at the county

level. All tax liens on businesses are filed here. Include the following in your request-debtor name or file number.

Access by: mail, in person, online.

Fee & Payment: In addition to the $20.00 search fee per debtor name, the copy fee is $1.00 per page and certification is $5.00 per filing. Fee payee: Secretary of State. Prepayment required. Prepaid accounts available, minimum $500 deposit. Personal checks accepted. Credit cards accepted, convenience fee added.

Mail search: Turnaround time: 72 hours.

In person search: Turnaround time is 72 hours unless an expedited fee of $100 is paid for immediate service. However, if workload is light, they may do the search that day without the expedited fee.

Online search: The agency has UCC information available to search at the web address, there is no fee. Corporation data is also available. You can search by debtor's name or file number. Collateral information and /or image is not available to view online.

Other access: Bulk sale by CD for $1,500 plus $300 a week for updates.

Expedited service: This service is available for an additional $100.00, usually same day service.

Sales Tax Registrations
Access to Records is Restricted.

Alabama Department of Revenue, Sales, Use and Business Tax Division, 4303 Gordon Persons Bldg, 50 N Ripley St, Montgomery, AL 36104; 334-353-7867, 334-242-8916-Fax; 8AM-5PM.

www.revenue.alabama.gov

According to state law 40-2A-10, Code of Alabama 1975, this agency is unable to release any information about tax registrations. Note, their website has motor vehicle dealer regulatory license information.

Birth Certificates

Center for Health Statistics, Record Services Division, PO Box 5625, Montgomery, AL 36103-5625 (Courier address: RSA Tower Suite 1150, 201 Monroe St, Montgomery, AL 36104); 334-206-5418, 334-262-9563-Fax; 8AM-5PM.

http://ph.state.al.us/chs/VitalRecords/VRECORDS.HTMl

Certificates can, also, be delivered in any County Health Department for any vital record event occurring in AL. Delivery time is usually 15-30 minutes.

Records are available from 1908 to present. New records are available for inquiry immediately. Records are indexed on inhouse computer.

Searching: Birth certificates under 125 years old may be requested by an immediate family member or person with legal right to certificate. Include the following in your request-full name, names of father, full maiden name of mother, date of birth, county, reason for information request. Include a daytime phone number and a signature.

Access by: mail, phone, fax, in person, online.

Fee & Payment: Fee is $12.00, add $4.00 per copy for additional copies, add $5.50 for use of a credit card. Fee payee: State Board of Health. Prepayment required. Credit cards accepted for phone, fax and expedited requests only. Personal checks accepted. Major credit cards accepted.

Mail search: Turnaround time: 5 to 10 days. No SASE is required.

Phone search: Telephone requests allowed using a credit card, see expedited service.

Fax search: Same criteria as phone searching.

In person search: Also, go to the nearest County Health Department.

Online search: Online ordering is available from the webpage through a service provider.

Expedited service: Expedited service is available for phone, fax and online orders. Turnaround time: 1 day. Additional expedite fee is $10.00, use of credit card is $5.50, add overnight shipping fee if needed.

Death Records

Center for Health Statistics, Record Services Division, PO Box 5625, Montgomery, AL 36103-5625 (Courier address: RSA Tower Suite 1150, 201 Monroe St, Montgomery, AL 36104); 334-206-5418, 334-262-9563-Fax; 8AM-5PM.

http://ph.state.al.us/chs/VitalRecords/VRECORDS.HTMl

Certificates can, also, be delivered in any County Health Department for any vital record event occurring in AL. Delivery time is usually 15-30 minutes.

Records are available from 1908 on. New records are available for inquiry immediately. Records are indexed on inhouse computer.

Searching: Must be immediate family for ordering death records less than 25 years old. Include the following in your request-full name, DOB, names of parents with mother's maiden name, county or city, reason for request, relationship to subject, signature and daytime phone of requester.

Access by: mail, phone, fax, in person, online.

Fee & Payment: Fee is $12.00, add $4.00 per copy for additional copies, add $5.50 for use of a credit card. Fee payee: Vital Records Prepayment required. Personal checks accepted. Major credit cards accepted.

Mail search: Turnaround time: 5 to 10 days. No SASE is required.

Phone search: Telephone requests allowed using a credit card, see expedited service.

Fax search: Same criteria as phone searching.

In person search: Also, you can go to the nearest County Health Department.

Online search: Online ordering is available from the webpage through a service provider.

Other access: Index to records are available on microfilm for $40.00 per roll. There are 6 rolls of records for 1908 through 1959.

Expedited service: Expedited service is available for phone, fax and online orders. Additional expedite fee is $10.00, use of credit card is $5.50, add overnight shipping fee if needed.

Marriage Certificates

Center for Health Statistics, Record Services Division, PO Box 5625, Montgomery, AL 36103-5625 (Courier address: RSA Tower Suite 1150, 201 Monroe St, Montgomery, AL 36104); 334-206-5418, 334-262-9563-Fax; 8AM-5PM.

http://ph.state.al.us/chs/VitalRecords/VRECORDS.HTMl

Certificates can, also, be delivered in any County Health Department for any vital record event occurring in AL. Delivery time is usually 15-30 minutes.

Records are available from 1936 to present. New records are available for inquiry immediately. Records are indexed on inhouse computer.

Searching: Include the following in your request-names of husband and wife, date of marriage, county of license issue. Include a daytime phone number and signature of requester.

Access by: mail, phone, fax, in person, online.

Fee & Payment: Fee is $12.00, add $4.00 per copy for additional copies, add $5.50 for use of a credit card. Fee payee: State Board of Health Prepayment required. Personal checks accepted. Major credit cards accepted.

Mail search: Turnaround time: 5 to 10 days. No SASE is required.

Phone search: Telephone requests allowed using a credit card, see expedited service.

Fax search: Same criteria as phone searches.

In person search: Also, you can go to the nearest County Health Department.

Online search: Online ordering is available from the webpage through a service provider.

Other access: Microfilm rolls are available for purchase at $40.00 each. There are 11 rolls available which includes index to records for 1936 to 1969.

Expedited service: Expedited service is available for phone, fax and online orders. Turnaround time: 1 to 2 days. Additional expedite fee is $10.00, use of credit card is $5.50, add overnight shipping fee if needed.

Divorce Records

Center for Health Statistics, Record Services Division, PO Box 5625, Montgomery, AL 36103-5625 (Courier address address: RSA Tower Suite 1150, 201 Monroe St, Montgomery, AL 36104); 334-206-5418, 334-206-2659-Fax; 8AM-5PM.

http://ph.state.al.us/chs/VitalRecords/VRECORDS.HTMl

Certificates can, also, be delivered in any County Health Department for any vital record event occurring in AL. Delivery time is usually 15-30 minutes.

Records are available from 1950 to present. New records are available for inquiry immediately. Records are indexed on inhouse computer.

Searching: Include the following in your request-names of husband and wife, date of divorce, county. Include a daytime phone number, all requests must have signature of the requester.

Access by: mail, phone, fax, in person, online.

Fee & Payment: Fee is $12.00, add $4.00 per copy for additional copies, add $5.50 for use of a credit card. Fee payee: State Board of Health Prepayment required. Personal checks accepted. Major credit cards accepted.

Mail search: Turnaround time: 5 to 10 days. No SASE is required.

Phone search: Telephone requests allowed using a credit card, see expedited service.

Fax search: Same criteria as phone searches.

In person search: Also, you can go to the nearest County Health Department.

Online search: Online ordering is available from the webpage through a service provider.

Other access: There is one microfilm roll of index for records for 1950-59 available for $40.00.

Expedited service: Expedited service is available for phone, fax and online orders. Turnaround time: 1 to 2 days. Additional expedite fee is $10.00, use of credit card is $5.50, add overnight shipping fee if needed.

Workers' Compensation Records

Department of Industrial Relations, Central Cashier-Disclosure Unit, 649 Monroe Street, Rm. 2684, Montgomery, AL 36131; 334-242-8981, 334-242-2304-Fax; 7AM-5PM.

http://dir.alabama.gov/wc

Records are available on computer (summarized) in index form. Retention period is based on type of record. Actual file copies are placed on microfilm after 6 months. It takes 3 days before new records are available for inquiry. Records are normally destroyed after 12 years.

Searching: Must have a written, notarized release from claimant. Include the following in your request-claimant name, Social Security Number.

Access by: mail, fax, in person.

Fee & Payment: The fee is $10.00 per record. Fee payee: Department of Industrial Relations Prepayment required. No personal checks or credit cards accepted.

Mail search: Turnaround time: 1 week. No SASE is required.

Fax search: Records can be returned (not ordered) by fax if desired.

In person search: A notarized release form is required.

Driver Records

Department of Public Safety, Driver Records-License Division, PO Box 1471, Montgomery, AL 36102-1471 (Courier address address: 301 S Ripley Street, Montgomery, AL 36104); 334-242-4400, 334-242-9926-Fax; 8AM-5PM.

www.dps.state.al.us

Ticket information must be secured at the local level.

Records are available for convictions in last three years for moving violations, and accidents. New records are available for inquiry immediately.

Searching: Some juvenile records are considered confidential and are not released. The driver's address and personal information is not included, even if the requester is a DPPA permissible user, for mail or in person requesters. The address is released online. Need full name, DOB and license number to obtain a record. Use Form MV-DPPA1 if you are a permissible user.

Access by: mail, in person, online.

Fee & Payment: The fee is $5.75 per record, online is higher. Fee payee: Alabama DPS, Drivers License Division. Prepayment required. Personal checks not accepted. Credit cards accepted.

Mail search: Turnaround time: 3 to 5 days. Providing a self-addressed return envelope usually means quicker service.

In person search: Locations offering driving records and crash reports include Birmingham, Dothan, Foley, Huntsville, Jacksonville, Mobile, Montgomery, Opelika, Sheffield, and Tuscaloosa.

Online search: Alabama Interactive has been designated the state's agent for online access of state driving records. A Subscriber Registration Agreement must be submitted and both Alabama Interactive and the Alabama DPS must approve all customers. There is a $75.00 annual administrative fee for new accounts and the search fee is $7.00 per record. The driver license number is needed to search. The system, open 24 hours daily, is Internet-based. Alabama Interactive can be reached at 2 N. Jackson St, #301, Montgomery AL, 36104, telephone 866-353-3468, www.alabamainteractive.org.

Vehicle Ownership, Vehicle Identification

Motor Vehicle Division, Records & Registration Unit, PO Box 327630, Montgomery, AL 36132-7630 (Courier address: 50 North Ripley St, #1229, 1202 Gordon Persons Bldg, Montgomery, AL 36140); 334-242-9056 (Registration), 334-242-9102 (Title Inquiry), 334-353-8038-Fax; 8AM-5PM.

www.ador.state.al.us/motorvehicle/index.html

Tile history requests should be mailed to PO Box 327640, Montgomery 36132-7640.

Records are available 24 years for title records and 10 years for registration records. It takes 4-6 weeks before new records are available for inquiry. Records are normally destroyed after 24 years.

Searching: The restrictions specified under the DPPA (Driver's Privacy Protection Act) apply. Access is restricted to permissible users who must use Form MV-DPPA1 (found on web). Non-permissible users must have notarized release of subject. Include the following in your request-name, specific year to search, address of the title or registration holder. The following data is not released: bulk information or lists for commercial purposes.

Access by: mail.

Fee & Payment: Fees are $3.00 per record per year for registration records and $15.00 per year for title searches (includes lien data). Fee payee: Alabama Department of Revenue. Prepayment required. Only certified funds are accepted. No credit cards accepted.

Mail search: Turnaround time: 1 to 2 weeks. No SASE is required.

Accident Reports

Alabama Department of Public Safety, Accident Records, PO Box 1471, Montgomery, AL 36102-1471; 334-242-4241, 8AM-5PM.

Records are available for a minimum of 10 years. After 2 years, they put reports on microfiche. It takes 2 weeks before new records are available for inquiry.

Searching: Include the following in your request-date of accident, location of accident, county. Also, submit names of drivers.

Access by: mail, in person.

Fee & Payment: The fee is $15.00 and prepayment is required. Fee payee: Alabama DPS, Accident Reports. Only certified funds or cash is accepted. No credit cards accepted.

Mail search: Turnaround time: within 2 weeks. A SASE is requested.

In person search: Locations offering driving records and crash reports include Birmingham, Dothan, Foley, Huntsville, Jacksonville, Mobile, Montgomery, Opelika, Sheffield, and Tuscaloosa. Turnaround time is while you wait.

Vessel Ownership, Vessel Registration

Dept of Conservation & Natural Resources, Marine Police Div. Boat Reg. Records, PO Box 301451, Montgomery, AL 36130 (Courier address: 64 N Union St, Montgomery, AL 36104); 334-242-3673, 334-242-3647-Fax; 8AM-5PM.

www.dcnr.state.al.us

Records are not freely open to the public. Must give reason why record is requested.

Records are available from 1985 to the present. Records are indexed on computer. All mechanically propelled, sail or rental boats must be registered. It takes 2 months before new records are available for inquiry. Records are normally destroyed after 7 years.

Searching: Vessels that have been commercially documented by the Coast Guard are not required to register with Alabama. Liens are not recorded here, but at the central state locations for UCC filings. Include the following in your request-one of the following is required; owner's name, hull id number, current decal number, or registration number For purged records, the registration number is required to search.

Access by: mail, phone, fax, in person.

Fee & Payment: There is no search fee, except for bulk searches (see below) or lengthy lists ($1.00 per record). Fee payee: Department of Conservation. Prepayment required. Personal checks accepted. No credit cards accepted.

Mail search: Turnaround time: 1 to 2 days. No SASE is required.

Phone search: Records are available by phone.

Fax search: Turnaround time is within 1 day.

In person search: Immediate records available, if list not lengthy. Request must be in writing.

Other access: This agency accepts e-mail requests for records at rthornell@dcnr.state.al.us. This agency will sell all or parts of its database. Fees start at $100.00 for the first 2,500 records.

Voter Registration

Access to Records is Restricted.

Secretary of State-Elections Division, PO Box 5616, State Capitol E-210, Montgomery, AL 36103 (Courier address: 600 Dexter Avenue, Room E-210, Montgomery Alabama 36130); 334-242-4337, 334-242-2444-Fax; 8AM-5PM.

www.sos.state.al.us/election/index.cfm

Individual name requests must be done at the county level, there are no restrictions. The web site does provide searches to Contributions & Disbursements and PAC information. Bulk requests can be ordered from this office for data from all 67 counties. Call for fees and breakdowns of customized requests.

GED Certificates

State Dept of Education, GED Testing Office, 401 Adams Ave #280, Montgomery, AL 36104; 334-353-4886, 334-353-4884-Fax; 8AM-5PM.

www.acs.cc.al.us/ged/ged.aspx

Release of your GED information is prohibited without written authorization

Searching: Requests should be writing. Include the following in your request-a signed release, name, year of test, date of birth, Social Security Number, and city of testing. All required for a verification or for copy of transcript.

Access by: mail, fax, in person.

Fee & Payment: There is no verification or search fee, but there is a $10.00 fee for either a copy of grades, transcript or diploma. Fee payee: GED Testing. Only cashier's checks and money orders are accepted. No credit cards or personal checks accepted.

Mail search: Turnaround time: 1-2 days. No SASE is required.

Fax search: Turnaround time is same day. Results will be called or faxed.

In person search: Turnaround time is a few minutes.

Hunting and Fishing License Information

Records not maintained by a state level agency.

They do not have a central computerized database. Records must be hand searched and are grouped by issuing agent. This makes searching very time consuming and thus it is discouraged.

However, the agency will sell a list of lifetime license purchasers. Also, the state is assembling a database of electronically sold records, but it is not available for sale.

Alabama State Licensing Agencies

For details about the agency responsible for licensing/certifying/registering an item below or in the Agency Quick Finder section, match an item's number with the number of the agency in the *Licensing Agency Information* section.

Licenses Searchable Online

Abortion/Reproductive Health Ctr #31 .. www.adph.org/providers/
Ambulatory Surgery Center #31 .... www.adph.org/providers/
Anesthesiologist Assistant #19 .... www.docboard.org/al/
Architect #8 .... www.boa.state.al.us/rostersearch/rostersearch.asp
Assisted Living Facility/Unit #31 .... www.adph.org/providers/
Auctioneer #9 .... www.auctioneer.state.al.us/roster/roster-search-form.asp
Bank #5 .... www.bank.state.al.us/bank_search.aspx
Birthing Center #31 .... www.adph.org/providers/
Cerebral Palsy Center #31 .... www.adph.org/providers/
Check Casher #5 .... www.bank.state.al.us/Search_All_Licences2.asp
Chiropractor #10   https://www.alabamainteractive.org/asbce/VerificationEntryPoint.do;jsessionid=ap_JoQrUmjsg
Consumer Finance Company #5 .... www.bank.state.al.us/Search_All_Licences2.asp
Contractor, General #7 .... www.genconbd.state.al.us/DATABASE-LIVE/roster.asp
Electrical Contractor #14 .... www.aecb.state.al.us/Search/new_search.asp
Electrician, Journeyman #14 .... www.aecb.state.al.us/Search/new_search.asp
Engineer/Engineer in Training #27 .... www.bels.alabama.gov
Forester #26 .... www.alsbrf.org
Gas Fitter #46 .... www.pgfb.state.al.us/inquiries.aspx
Geologist #37 .... www.algeobd.state.al.us/roster_search.asp
Heating/Air Conditioning Cont'r #38 ..... www.hvacboard.state.al.us/Lic_Search/searchform.asp
Home Builder #53 .... www.hblb.state.al.us/Lic_Search/all-ind.asp
Home Health Agency #31 .... www.adph.org/providers/
Home Inspector #42 .... www.sos.state.al.us/sosinfo/inquiry.cfm
Hospice #31 .... www.adph.org/providers/
Hospital #31 .... www.adph.org/providers/
Insurance Adjuster #39 .... www.aldoi.org/LicenseeSearch/
Insurance Agent/Broker/Producer #39 . www.aldoi.org/LicenseeSearch/
Insurance Corp/Co./Partnership #39 .... www.aldoi.org/CompanySearch/
Interior Designer #54 .... www.idboard.alabama.gov/search/start.aspx
Landscape Architect #18 .... www.abela.state.al.us/architects.html
Lender/Loan Source #5 .... www.bank.state.al.us/Search_All_Licences2.asp
Marriage/Family Therapist #9 .... www.mft.state.al.us/Search/search.asp
Massage Therapist #56 .... www.almtbd.state.al.us/roster_search.asp
Medical Doctor #19 .... www.docboard.org/al/
Medical Gas Piper #46 .... www.pgfb.state.al.us/inquiries.aspx
Mental Health Center #31 .... www.adph.org/providers/
Mortgage Broker #5 .... www.bank.state.al.us/Search_All_Licences2.asp
Notary Public #42 .... www.sos.state.al.us/sosinfo/inquiry.cfm?area=notaries%20public
Nursing Home #31 .... www.adph.org/providers/
Nursing Home Administrator #22 .... www.alboenha.state.al.us/logon.html
Optometrist #20 .... www.al-optometry.org
Osteopathic Physician #19 .... www.docboard.org/al/
Pawn Shop #5 .... www.bank.state.al.us/Search_All_Licences2.asp
Petroleum Product Seller #30 .... www.agi.state.al.us/Bonded.asp
Physical Therapist/Therapist Asst #24 . www.pt.state.al.us/License/searchform.asp
Physician Assistant #19 .... www.docboard.org/al/
Physiological Lab, Clinical #31 .... www.adph.org/providers/
Plumber #46 .... www.pgfb.state.al.us/inquiries.aspx
Podiatrist #4 .... www.alabamapodiatryboard.org/pages/licensee.html
Pre-Need Sales Agent #39 .... www.aldoi.org/LicenseeSearch/
Public Account.-CPA- non-licensee #25. www.asbpa.state.al.us/register/register.asp
Real Estate Agent/Sales #2 .... www.arec.state.al.us/search.asp
Real Estate Appraiser #43 .... http://reab.state.al.us/appraisers/searchform.asp

Real Estate Broker #2 .... www.arec.state.al.us/search.asp
Rehabilitation Center #31 .... www.adph.org/providers/
Reinsurance Intermediary #39 .... www.aldoi.org/LicenseeSearch/
Renal Disease Ter'l Treatment Ctr #31 . www.adph.org/providers/
Rural Primary Care Hospital #31 .... www.adph.org/providers/
School Superintendent #49 .... www.alsde.edu/html/super_listing.asp?menu=none&footer=general
Sleep Disorder Center #31 .... www.adph.org/providers/
Social Worker #6 .... www.abswe.state.al.us/Lic_Search/search.asp
Social Worker, Independ't Practice #6 .. www.abswe.state.al.us/Lic_Search/searchpip.asp
Sports Agent #42 .... www.sos.state.al.us/cf/sportsagents/sasrch1.cfm
Surplus Line Broker #39 .... www.aldoi.org/LicenseeSearch/
Surveyor, Land #27 .... www.bels.alabama.gov
Therapist, Marriage and Family #9 .... www.mft.state.al.us/Search/search.asp
U-Pick Location #30 .... www.agi.state.al.us/PDFs/UPick.PDF
X-ray (Portable) Supplier #31 .... www.adph.org/providers/

Alabama Licensing Quick Finder

Abortion/Reproductive Health Ctr #31...334-206-5175
Aircraft/Pilot-related Personnel #51......205-731-1557
Ambulatory Surgery Center #31............334-206-5175
Anesthesiologist Assistant #19.............334-242-4116
Architect #8 334-242-4179
Assisted Living Facility/Unit #31 334-206-5175
Attorney #3 334-269-1515
Auctioneer #9.............................334-269-9990 x14
Audiologist #28 334-269-1434
Bank #5..334-242-3452
Beauty Shop/Booth Rental #11 334-242-1918
Beauty Shop/Salon #11.......................334-242-1918
Bee, Queen & Package Shipper #30 ... 334-240-7239
Birthing Center #31................................334-206-5175
Boxer/Wrestler - not regulated #52 334-242-1380
Broker/Dealer Agent #48 334-242-2984
Cerebral Palsy Center #31 334-206-5175
Charitable Filing #48.............................334-242-2984
Check Casher #5...................................334-242-3452
Check Seller #48 334-242-2984
Chiropractor #10 205-755-8000
Clinical Nurse Specialist #21 334-242-0767
Consumer Finance Company #5.........334-242-3452
Contractor, General #7 334-272-5030
Cosmetic Studio #11 334-242-1918
Cosmetologist & Cosmetology Instruc./Mgr #11
....334-242-1918
Cosmetologist/Esthetician/Manicurist #11
....334-242-1918
Cosmetology Mgr Pending Exam #11...334-242-1918
Cosmetology School/Instruc/Exam #11 334-242-1918
Cosmetology Student/Apprentice #11..334-242-1918
Cosmetology, Restricted Managing#11 334-242-1918
Counselor, Professional #15 205-458-8716
Dental Hygienist #12 205-985-7267
Dentist #12..205-985-7267
Dietitian/Nutritionist #33.......................334-242-4505
Education Administrator #49 334-242-9977
Electrical Contractor #14 334-269-9990
Electrician, Journeyman #14................334-269-9990
Embalmer #17 334-242-4049
Emergency Medical Technician #50 334-206-5383
Engineer/Engineer in Training #27.......334-242-5568
Esthetician School/Salon #11...............334-242-1918
Esthetician Student/Instruct/School/Exam #11
....334-242-1918
Esthetician/Esthetician Apprentice #11.334-242-1918
Firefighter #36..205-391-3743
Forester #26 334-353-3640
Funeral Director #17..............................334-242-4049
Gas Fitter #46 205-945-4857
Geologist #37.............................334-269-9990 x10
Ginseng Dealer #30...............................334-240-7239

Hearing Instrument Dealer #35 334-242-1925
Heating/Air Condition Contracort #38 . 334-242-5550
Home Builder #53...................................334-242-2230
Home Health Agency #31 334-206-5175
Home Inspector #42..............................334-242-7205
Hospice #31...334-206-5175
Hospital #31...334-206-5175
Industrial Revenue Bond #48...............334-242-2984
Insurance Adjuster #39 334-241-4126
Insurance Agent #39.............................334-241-4126
Insurance Broker/Producer #39 334-241-4126
Insurance Corp/Co./Partnership #39....334-241-4126
Interior Designer #54.............................205-879-4232
Investment Advisor #48.........................334-242-2984
Investment Advisor Rep. #48 334-242-2984
Landscape Architect #18.......................334-262-1351
Landscape Designer #55 334-240-7241
Landscape Planter #55 334-240-7241
Law Enforcement Personnel #44 334-242-4047
Lead Abatement Contractor #13 334-206-5373
Lead Abatement Professional #13........334-206-5373
Legal/Dental Svc Representative #39..334-241-4126
Lender/Loan Source #5..........................334-242-3452
Livestock Market Operator #30 334-240-7263
LPG-Liquefied Petrol. Gas Broker #40.334-242-5649
Manicurist Salon/School/Student/Instruc #11
....334-242-1918
Manicurist/Manicurist Apprentice/Exam #11
....334-242-1918
Marriage/Family Therapist #9........ 334-269-9990 x14
Massage Therapist #56.........................334-269-9990
Medical Doctor #19................................334-242-4116
Medical Gas Piper #46 205-945-4857
Mental Health Center #31 334-206-5175
Midwife Nurse #21.................................334-242-0767
Mine Land Reclamation #32.................205-945-8671
Mine Personnel #34 205-254-1275
Mine Safety and Inspection #32...........205-254-1275
Mobile Home Manufacturer #41............334-242-4036
Mobile Home Set-up/Install'r/Sales #41 334-242-4036
Mortgage Broker #5...............................334-242-3452
Motor Club Representative #39 334-241-4126
Notary Public #42..................................334-242-7205
Nurse Anesthetist #21 334-242-0767
Nurse-LPN/RN #21................................334-242-0767
Nursing Disciplinary Action #21 334-242-0767
Nursing Home #31.................................334-206-5175
Nursing Home Administrator #22..........334-271-6214
Occup. Therapist Assistant #57 334-353-4466
Occupational Therapist #57..................334-353-4466
Optometrist #20 205-481-9993
Osteopathic Physician #19....................334-242-4116
Pawn Shop #5..334-242-3452

Pest Control #30.....................................334-240-7239
Pesticide Applicator/Dealer #30 334-240-7239
Petroleum Product Seller #30 334-240-7127
Pharmacist #23 205-967-0130
Physical Therapist/Therapist Asst #24. 334-242-4064
Physician Assistant #19.........................334-242-4116
Physiological Lab, Clinical #31 334-206-5175
Pilot/Bar Pilot #45..................................251-432-2639
Plant & Quarantine Inspector #30........334-240-7239
Plumber #46...205-945-4857
Podiatrist #4 205-995-8537
Polygraph Examiner #47.......................334-353-1881
Pre-Need Sales Agent #39 334-241-4126
Psychological Technician #16...............334-242-4127
Psychologist #16 334-242-4127
Public Account.-CPA-non licensee #25 334-242-5700
Real Estate Agent/Sales #2 334-242-5544
Real Estate Appraiser #43 334-242-8747
Real Estate Broker #2............................334-242-5544
Registered Nurse Practitioner #21.......334-242-0767
Rehabilitation Center #31......................334-206-5175
Reinsurance Intermediary #39 334-241-4126
Renal Disease Terminal Treatment Ctr #31
....334-206-5175
Rural Primary Care Hospital #31 334-206-5175
School Bus Driver #49 334-242-9730
School Counselor #49............................334-242-9977
School Superintendent #49...................334-242-9977
Securities Broker/Dealer/Seller #48.....334-242-2984
Shampoo Assistant #11 334-242-1918
Sleep Disorder Center #31....................334-206-5175
Social Worker #6 334-242-5860
Social Worker, Pvt. Independent Practice #6
....334-242-5860
Soil Classifier #1....................................334-242-2620
Speech Pathologist/Audiologist #28 . 334-269-1434
Sports Agent #42...................................334-242-7591
Subcontractor #7...................................334-272-5030
Surface Mining (non-fuel) #32..............334-242-8265
Surplus Line Broker #39 334-241-4126
Surveyor, Land #27 334-242-5568
Teacher #49 334-242-9977
Teacher, Elementary School #49..........334-242-9977
Therapist, Marriage & Family #9... 334-269-9990 x14
Timeshare Real Estate Seller #43 334-242-8747
Timeshare Seller #2..............................334-242-5544
Tree Surgeon #55 334-240-7241
U-Pick Location #30 334-240-7100
Veterinarian #29 256-353-3544
Veterinary Premise Permit #29 256-353-3544
Veterinary Technician #29 256-353-3544
Weights & Measures #30.......................334-240-7133
X-ray (Portable) Supplier #31 334-206-5175

Alabama Licensing Agency Information

1 Soil and Water Conservation Committee, 100 N Union St #334 (PO Box 304800 - 36130), Montgomery, AL 36104-3702; 334-242-2620, Fax: 334-242-0551. www.swcc.state.al.us/ Email: vpayne@swcc.state.al.us

2 Real Estate Commission, 1201 Carmichael Way, Montgomery, AL 36106; 334-242-5544, Fax: 334-270-9118. www.arec.state.al.us/ Email: arec@arec.state.al.us Search Database at www.arec.state.al.us/search.asp

3 Alabama State Bar Association, 415 Dexter Ave (PO Box 671), Montgomery, AL 36104; 334-269-1515, Fax: 334-261-6310. www.alabar.org Email: info@alabar.org

4 Board of Podiatry, 610 S McDonough St, Montgomery, AL 36104; 334-269-9990, Fax: 334-263-6115. www.alabamapodiatryboard.org Email: alpodboard@aol.com Search Database at www.alabamapodiatryboard.org/pages/licensee.html

5 State Banking Department, Licensing and Registration, 401 Adams St, #680, Montgomery, AL 36130; 334-242-3452, Fax: 334-242-3500. www.bank.state.al.us Search Database at www.bank.state.al.us/search_all_licenses2.asp Note: Bureau of Loans fax number is 334-353-5961.

6 Board of Social Work Examiners, 100 N Union St. #736, Montgomery, AL 36130; 888-879-3672, 334-242-5860, Fax: 334-242-0280. www.abswe.state.al.us Search Database at www.abswe.state.al.us/Lic_Search/searchpip.asp

7 License Board for General Contractors, 2525 Fairlane Drive, Montgomery, AL 36116; 334-272-5030, Fax: 334-395-5336. www.genconbd.state.al.us Search Database at www.genconbd.state.al.us/DATABASE-LIVE/roster.asp

8 Board for Registration of Architects, 770 Washington Ave, #150, Montgomery, AL 36130-4450; 334-242-4179, Fax: 334-242-4531. www.boa.state.al.us/ Email: cgainey@boa.state.al.us Search Database at www.boa.state.al.us/rostersearch/rostersearch.asp

9 Board of Auctioneers, and, Board of Examiners in Marriage & Family Therapy, 7245 Halcyon Summit Dr, Montgomery, AL 36104; 334-215-7233, Fax: 334-215-7231. www.mft.state.al.us/ Email: paula.scout@mft.alabama.gov Search Database at www.auctioneer.state.al.us/roster/roster-search-form.asp

10 Board of Chiropractic Examiners, 737 Logan Road, Clanton, AL 35045; 205-755-8000, Fax: 205-755-0081. http://chiro.state.al.us

Email: sbolton@chiro.state.al.us Search Database at https://www.alabamainteractive.org/asbce/VerificationEntryPoint.do;jsessionid=ap_JoQrUmjsg Note: Verification is on-line.

11 Board of Cosmetology, RSA Union Bldg, 100 N Union St #320 (PO Box 301750), Montgomery, AL 36130; 334-242-1918, Fax: 334-242-1926. www.aboc.state.al.us Email: cosmetology@aboc.state.al.us

12 Board of Dental Examiners, 5346 Stadium Trace Pkwy #112, Hoover, AL 35244; 205-985-7267, Fax: 205-985-0674. www.dentalboard.org Email: BDEAAL@bellsouth.net Note: They will not verify over the phone; they recommend you send a fax.

13 Department of Public Health, Indoor Air Quality/Lead Branch, Div. of Comm. Environmental Protection - Lead Contractors, P.O. Box 303017, (201 Monroe St, The RSA Tower, Suite 1250), Montgomery, AL 36130-3017; 800-819-7644, 334-206-5373. www.adph.org/lead/

14 Board of Electrical Contractors, 610 S McDonough St, Montgomery, AL 36104; 334-269-9990, Fax: 334-263-6115. www.aecb.state.al.us Email: alelectricalbd@aol.com Search Database at www.aecb.state.al.us/Search/new_search.asp

15 Board of Examiners in Counseling, 950 22nd St N. #670, Birmingham, AL 35203; 205-458-8716, Fax: 205-458-8718. www.abec.state.al.us Email: fhemphill@abec.state.al.us

16 Board of Examiners in Psychology, 660 Adams Ave, #360, Mongomery, AL 36104; 334-242-4127. www.psychology.state.al.us Email: albdpsychology@mindspring.com

17 Board of Funeral Service, Box 309522, Montgomery, AL 36130; 334-242-4049, Fax: 334-353-7988.

18 Board of Landscape Architects, 908 S Hull St, Montgomery, AL 36104; 334-262-1351, Fax: 334-262-1351. www.abela.state.al.us/ Email: abela@bellsouth.net Search Database at www.abela.state.al.us/architects.html

19 Board of Medical Examiners, PO Box 887 (848 Washington Ave), Montgomery, AL 36101; 334-242-4116, Fax: 334-242-4155. www.albme.org Email: webmaster@albme.org Search Database at www.docboard.org/al/ Note: Will sell lists at $.05 per record.

20 Board of Optometry, 1431 2nd Ave, N, Bessemer, AL 35020; 205-481-9993, Fax: 205-481-9959. www.al-optometry.org Email: fwallace@al-optometry.org Search Database at www.al-optometry.org

21 Board of Nursing, 770 Washington Ave #250, Montgomery, AL 36104; 334-242-4060, Fax: 334-242-4360. www.abn.state.al.us Email: abn@abn.state.al.us Note: Individial verifications are $30.00 each. A group online license verification is available by subscription.

22 Board of Nursing Home Administrators, 4156 Carmichael Road, Montgomery, AL 36106; 334-271-6214, Fax: 334-244-6509. www.alboenha.state.al.us Search Database at www.alboenha.state.al.us/logon.html

23 Board of Pharmacy, 1 Perimeter Park S, #425 South, Birmingham, AL 35243; 205-967-0130, Fax: 205-967-1009. www.albop.com

24 Board of Physical Therapy, 100 N Union St, #724, Montgomery, AL 36130-5040; 334-242-4064, Fax: 334-240-3288. www.pt.state.al.us Email: kbrown@pt.state.al.us Search Database at www.pt.state.al.us/License/searchform.asp Note: Will sell directories of licensees for $50.00 each.

25 Board of Public Accountancy, PO Box 300375 (770 Washington Ave, #226), Montgomery, AL 36130-0375; 334-242-5700, Fax: 334-240-2711. www.asbpa.state.al.us Search Database at www.asbpa.state.al.us/register/register.asp

26 Board of Registration for Foresters, 513 Madison Ave, Montgomery, AL 36130; 334-353-3640, Fax: 334-353-3641. www.alsbrf.org Email: psears@almore.rr.com Search Database at www.alsbrf.org

27 Board of Licensure for Professional Engineers & Land Surveyors, PO Box 304451 (100 North Union St #382), Montgomery, AL 36130-4451; 334-242-5568, Fax: 334-242-5105. www.bels.alabama.gov Email: bonnie.kelly@bels.alabama.gov Search Database at www.bels.alabama.gov

28 Board of Examiners for Speech-Language Pathology & Audiology, PO Box 304760 (400 S Union St #225), Montgomery, AL 36130-4760; 334-269-1434, Fax: 334-834-9618. www.abespa.org/ Email: abespa@mindspring.com

29 Board of Veterinary Medical Examiners, 2128 6th Avenue SE, Bldg 5 Ste 501, Decatur, AL 35601; 256-353-3544, Fax: 256-350-5629. http://asbvme.us Email: asbvme@mindspring.com

30 Department of Agriculture & Industries, Executive Division - Licensing, PO Box 3336 (1445 Federal Dr), Montgomery, AL 36109-0336; 334-240-7282, 800-642-7761, Fax: 334-240-7190. www.agi.state.al.us Note: Fax number for the Pesticide Management Section is 334-240-7168. Weights & Measures fax is 334-240-7175. Admin Dept. fax is 334-240-7194.

31 Department of Health, Provider Services Division - Licensing, 201 Monroe St, Montgomery, AL 36130-3017; 334-206-5175, Fax: 334-206-5219. www.adph.org Search Database at www.adph.org/providers/ Note: Enter search area by clicking on "Facility Directory."

32 Department of Industrial Relations, Mining & Reclamation, 649 Monroe St, Montgomery, AL 36131-5200; 334-242-8265, Fax: 334-242-8403. http://dir.alabama.gov/

33 Dietetic/Nutrition Examiners Board, 400 S Union St #445, Montgomery, AL 36104-0500; 334-242-4505, Fax: 334-834-6398. Note: Will sell mail list for $50.00. Verification by phone, mail no charge.

34 Examiners of Mine Personnel, Division of Safety and Inspection, 11 W Oxmoor, Birmingham, AL 35202; 205-254-1275, Fax: 205-945-8685.

35 Hearing Aid Dealers, Executive Secretary, 400 S Union St, #445, Montgomery, AL 36130-3010; 334-242-1925, Fax: 334-834-6398. Note: Mail lists are available for $25.00. Verifications made by phone and mail.

36 Fire College & Personnel Standards Commission, 2501 Phoenix Dr, Tuscaloosa, AL 35405; 205-391-3779, Fax: 205-391-3747. www.alabamafirecollege.org

37 Board of Licensure of Professional Geologists, 610 S McDonough St, Montgomery, AL 36104; 334-269-9990 x10, Fax: 334-263-6115. www.algeobd.state.al.us/ Email: ALGEOBD@aol.com

38 Heating & Air Conditioning Contractors Board, 100 N Union St, #630, Montgomery, AL 36130; 866-855-1912, 334-242-5550, Fax: 334-353-7050. www.hvacboard.state.al.us Search Database at www.hvacboard.state.al.us/ Lic_Search/searchform.asp

39 Department of Insurance, Agent Licensing Division, 201 Monroe St #1700, Mongomery, AL 36104; 334-269-3550, Fax: 334-240-3282. www.aldoi.gov Search Database at www.aldoi.org/LicenseeSearch/

40 Liquefied Petroleum Gas Board, 818 S Perry St, Montgomery, AL 36104; 334-242-5649, Fax: 334-240-3255. www.lpgb.state.al.us

41 Manufactured Housing Commission, 350 S Decatur St, Montgomery, AL 36104; 334-242-4036, Fax: 334-240-3178. www.amhc.state.al.us

42 Registrations for Sports Agents and Notaries, Office of the Secretary of State, PO Box 5616, Montgomery, AL 36103-5616; 334-242-7205, Fax: 334-353-8993. www.sos.state.al.us Email: wsullivan@sos.al.gov Search Database at www.sos.state.al.us/sosinfo/inquiry.cfm

43 Office of the Secretary of State, Real Estate Appraisers Licensing, PO Box 304355 (100 North Union St #370), Montgomery, AL 36104; 334-242-8747, Fax: 334-242-8749. http://reab.state.al.us/ Email: lbrooks@reab.state.al.us

44 Peace Officers Standards & Training Commission, PO Box 300075 (100 Union St, RSA Union Bldg, #600), Montgomery, AL 36130-0075; 334-242-4045, Fax: 334-242-4633. www.apostc.state.al.us

45 Pilotage Commission, PO Box 273, Mobile, AL 36601; 251-432-2639, Fax: 251-432-9964.

46 Plumbers & Gas Fitters Examining Board, 11 W Oxmoor, #104, Birmingham, AL 35209; 205-945-4857, Fax: 205-945-9915. www.pgfb.state.al.us Email: staff@pgfb.state.al.us Search Database at www.pgfb.state.al.us/inquiries.aspx

47 Polygraph Examiners Board, PO Box 1511, Montgomery, AL 36102-1511; 334-353-1881, Fax: www.polygraph.alabama.gov/.

48 Securities Commission, 770 Washington Ave, #570, Montgomery, AL 36130; 334-242-2984, Fax: 334-242-0240. www.asc.state.al.us Email: asc@asc.state.al.us

49 Department of Education, Teacher Education & Certification, PO Box 302101 (50 N Ripley St), Montgomery, AL 36104; 334-242-9977, Fax: 334-242-0498. www.alsde.edu Email: tcert@alsde.edu

50 Department of Health, Emergency Medical Services Division, PO Box 303017 [RSA Tower - 201 Monroe St, #750 (36104)], Birmingham, AL 36130-3017; 334-206-5383, Fax: 334-206-5260. www.adph.org/ems/

51 Department of Transportation, Flight Standards District Office, 1500 Urban Center Dr #250, Vestavia Hills, AL 35242; 205-731-1557, Fax: 205-731-0939. www.faa.gov/fsdo/bhm/

52 Department of Revenue, Athletic Commission - Inactive, 50 N Ripley St Rm 4131, Montgomery, AL 36132; 334-242-1380.

53 Home Builders Licensure Board, 400 S Union St #195, Montgomery, AL 36130; 334-242-2230, Fax: 334-263-1397. www.hblb.state.al.us/ Search Database at www.hblb.state.al.us/Lic_Search/search.asp

54 Board of Registration for Interior Designers, PO Box 11026 (65 Bagby Dr #3B), Birmingham, AL 35202; 205-879-4232, Fax: 205-942-8285*51. www.idboard.alabama.gov/contact.htm

55 Department of Agriculture & Industries, Plant Protection & Pesticide Management Division, PO Box 3336 - Beard Building, Montgomery, AL 36109-0336; 334-240-7243, Fax: 334-240-7168. www.agi.state.al.us/ Email: commone@agi.state.al.us

56 Board of Massage Therapy, 610 S McDonough St, Montgomery, AL 36104; 334-269-9990, Fax: 334-263-6115. www.almtbd.state.al.us/ Email: almtbd@aol.com Search Database at www.almtbd.state.al.us/roster_search.asp

57 Board of Occupational Therapy, 64 N Union St #734 (PO Box 304510), Montgomery, AL 36130-4510; 334-353-4466, Fax: 334-353-4465. www.asbot.state.al.us/ Email: acosby@asbot.state.al.us

Alabama Federal Courts

The following list indicates the district and division name for each county in the state. If the bankruptcy court location is different from the district court, then the location of the bankruptcy court appears in parentheses.

County/Court Cross Reference

County	District	Division
Autauga	Middle	Montgomery
Baldwin	Southern	Mobile
Barbour	Middle	Montgomery
Bibb	Northern	Birmingham (Tuscaloosa)
Blount	Northern	Birmingham
Bullock	Middle	Montgomery
Butler	Middle	Montgomery
Calhoun	Northern	Birmingham (Anniston)
Chambers	Middle	Opelika (Montgomery)
Cherokee	Northern	Gadsden (Anniston)
Chilton	Middle	Montgomery
Choctaw	Southern	Mobile
Clarke	Southern	Mobile
Clay	Northern	Birmingham (Anniston)
Cleburne	Northern	Birmingham (Anniston)
Coffee	Middle	Dothan (Montgomery)
Colbert	Northern	Florence (Decatur)
Conecuh	Southern	Mobile
Coosa	Middle	Montgomery
Covington	Middle	Montgomery
Crenshaw	Middle	Montgomery
Cullman	Northern	Huntsville (Decatur)
Dale	Middle	Dothan (Montgomery)
Dallas	Southern	Selma (Mobile)
De Kalb	Northern	Gadsden (Anniston)
Elmore	Middle	Montgomery
Escambia	Southern	Mobile
Etowah	Northern	Gadsden (Anniston)
Fayette	Northern	Jasper (Tuscaloosa)
Franklin	Northern	Florence (Decatur)
Geneva	Middle	Dothan (Montgomery)
Greene	Northern	Birmingham (Tuscaloosa)
Hale	Southern	Selma (Mobile)
Henry	Middle	Dothan (Montgomery)
Houston	Middle	Dothan (Montgomery)
Jackson	Northern	Huntsville (Decatur)
Jefferson	Northern	Birmingham
Lamar	Northern	Jasper (Tuscaloosa)
Lauderdale	Northern	Florence (Decatur)
Lawrence	Northern	Huntsville (Decatur)
Lee	Middle	Opelika (Montgomery)
Limestone	Northern	Huntsville (Decatur)
Lowndes	Middle	Montgomery
Macon	Middle	Opelika (Montgomery)
Madison	Northern	Huntsville (Decatur)
Marengo	Southern	Selma (Mobile)
Marion	Northern	Jasper (Tuscaloosa)
Marshall	Northern	Gadsden (Anniston)
Mobile	Southern	Mobile
Monroe	Southern	Mobile
Montgomery	Middle	Montgomery
Morgan	Northern	Huntsville (Decatur)
Perry	Southern	Selma (Mobile)
Pickens	Northern	Birmingham (Tuscaloosa)
Pike	Middle	Montgomery
Randolph	Middle	Opelika (Montgomery)
Russell	Middle	Opelika (Montgomery)
Shelby	Northern	Birmingham
St. Clair	Northern	Gadsden (Anniston)
Sumter	Northern	Birmingham (Tuscaloosa)
Talladega	Northern	Birmingham (Anniston)
Tallapoosa	Middle	Opelika (Montgomery)
Tuscaloosa	Northern	Birmingham (Tuscaloosa)
Walker	Northern	Jasper (Tuscaloosa)
Washington	Southern	Mobile
Wilcox	Southern	Selma (Mobile)
Winston	Northern	Jasper (Tuscaloosa)

Standards for Federal Courts: Search fee is $26.00 per item (one party name or case number). Copy fee is $.50 per page. Certification fee is $9.00 per document, double for exemplification, if available. All fees standard unless noted in profile. Mail Search: always enclose a stamped self addressed envelope unless otherwise noted. Most courts accept fax requests or will suggest a copying/search vendor. Before releasing records, all courts require prepayment, unless noted.

Open records are located at the court unless otherwise noted. District courts index by defendant and plaintiff as well as by case number. Bankruptcy courts usually index by debtor and case number. While most courts now have their indexes on computer, many may still maintain index card files as well.

Courts offering internet access via CM-ECF or older RACER, PACER, or Web-PACER systems charge $.08 per page fee unless noted as free. Where PACER is available, the universal sign-up number is 800-676-6856. Find PACER and the US Party/Case Index at http://pacer.psc.uscourts.gov.

US District Court

Middle District of Alabama

Dothan Division c/o Montgomery Division, PO Box 711, Montgomery, AL 36101 (courier address: 1 Church St, Montgomery, AL 36104), 334-954-3600, records rm- 334-954-3600, Fax-334-954-3615.   Hours-   8AM-5PM. www.almd.uscourts.gov

Counties: Coffee, Dale, Geneva, Henry, Houston.

Searches & Indexing: Results do not include SSN or DOB. Computer index maintained. New cases in the index immediately after filing date. Open records located at Montgomery Division.

Fee & Payment: Pay by no business or personal checks accepted. Payee: U S District Court.

Phone Search: No searching by telephone.

Mail Search: search usually completed- within 2 days.

In Person Search: permitted. No self-serve copier available.

E-Services: ECF replaces PACER whose records did go back to 1994. New records online after 1 day. ECF at https://ecf.almd.uscourts.gov

Montgomery Division Records Search Dept, PO Box 711, Montgomery, AL 36101-0711 (courier address: 1 Church St, Montgomery, AL 36104), 334-223-7308, records rm- 334-954-3600, Fax-334-954-3614.   Hours-   8AM-5PM. www.almd.uscourts.gov

Counties: Autauga, Barbour, Bullock, Butler, Chilton, Coosa, Covington, Crenshaw, Elmore, Lowndes, Montgomery, Pike.

Searches & Indexing: Results do not include SSN or DOB. Computer, microfiche and card indexes maintained. New cases in the index immediately after filing date.

Fee & Payment: Pay by money order, cashier check, business check. No personal checks. Payee: Clerk, US District Court. Prepayment required.

Phone Search: No searching by telephone.

Mail Search: search usually completed- 48 hours.

In Person Search: Fee charged if court performs your search. Public allowed to search the microfiche index. No self-serve copier available.

E-Services: ECF replaces PACER whose records did go back to 1994. New records online after 1 day. ECF at https://ecf.alsd.uscourts.gov

Opelika Division c/o Montgomery Division, PO Box 711, Montgomery, AL 36101 (courier address: 1 Church St, Montgomery, AL 36104), 334-954-3600, Fax-334-954-3615. Hours- 8AM-5PM. www.almd.uscourts.gov

Counties: Chambers, Lee, Macon, Randolph, Russell, Tallapoosa.

Searches & Indexing: Results do not include SSN or DOB. Computer index maintained. New cases in the index immediately after filing date. Open records located at Montgomery Division.

Fee & Payment: Pay by no business or personal checks accepted. Payee: U S District Court.

Phone Search: No searching by telephone.

Mail Search: search usually completed- within 2 days. SASE not required.

In Person Search: permitted. No self-serve copier available.

E-Services: ECF replaces PACER whose records did go back to 1994. New records online after 1 day. ECF at https://ecf.almd.uscourts.gov

US Bankruptcy Court

Middle District of Alabama

Montgomery Division Court Clerk, PO Box 1248, Montgomery, AL 36102-1248 (courier address: 1 Church St, Montgomery, AL 36104), 334-954-3800, Fax-334-954-3819. Hours-8:30AM-4PM. www.almb.uscourts.gov

Counties: Autauga, Barbour, Bullock, Butler, Chambers, Chilton, Coffee, Coosa, Covington, Crenshaw, Dale, Elmore, Geneva, Henry, Houston, Lee, Lowndes, Macon, Montgomery, Pike, Randolph, Russell, Tallapoosa.

Searches & Indexing: Results include last 4 SSN digits. Computer index maintained. New cases in the index immediately after filing date. Records purged every 6 months.

Fee & Payment: Pay by money order, cashier check, business check. No personal checks. Payee: Clerk of Court. Court may bill upon request. Will fax back $1.50 per page.

Phone Search: Docket information available by phone. Voice Case Information Service available at 334-954-3868.

Mail Search: search usually completed- 2-3 days.

In Person Search: Fee charged if court performs your search. No self-serve copier available.

E-Services: WebPACER is at https://ecf.almb.uscourts.gov. Document images available. NIBS court. PACER records go back to 8/2000. New records online after 2-3 days. ECF at https://ecf.almb.uscourts.gov **Opinions Online:** https://ecf.almb.uscourts.gov/cgi-bin/PublicOpinion.pl. **Other Online:** Calendars free at www.almb.uscourts.gov/calendar.htm.

US District Court

Northern District of Alabama

Birmingham Division Court Clerk, Rm 104, Hugo Black US Courthouse, 1729 5th Ave N, Birmingham, AL 35203 (also use mail address for courier delivery), 205-278-1700. Hours- 8:30AM-4:30PM. www.alnd.uscourts.gov

Counties: Bibb, Blount, Calhoun, Clay, Cleburne, Greene, Jefferson, Pickens, Shelby, Sumter, Talladega, Tuscaloosa.

Searches & Indexing: Results do not include SSN or DOB. Computer and microfiche indexes maintained. New cases in the index immediately after filing date.

Fee & Payment: Pay by money order, cashier's or personal check. No credit cards. Payee: Clerk of Court. Prepayment required.

Phone Search: No searching by telephone.

Mail Search: search usually completed- 24 hours.

In Person Search: Fee charged if court performs your search. Self-serve copier available.

E-Services: PACER records go back to 1994. ECF at https://ecf.alnd.uscourts.gov **Opinions Online:** www.alnd.uscourts.gov/judge_pages.htm.

Florence Division Court Clerk, PO Box 776, Florence, AL 35630 (courier address: 210 Court St, Florence, AL 35631), 205-760-8415, Fax-205-760-5727. Hours- 8:30AM-4:30PM. www.alnd.uscourts.gov

Counties: Colbert, Franklin, Lauderdale. No public access at this court.

Searches & Indexing: Results do not include SSN or DOB. Computer and microfiche indexes maintained. New cases in the index 2-3 days after filing date. Records purged every 18 months. Open records located in Birmingham.

Fee & Payment: Pay by money order, cashier's or personal check. Payee: US District Court. Prepayment required.

Phone Search: Only docket information is available by phone.

Mail Search: search usually completed- 24 hours. SASE not required.

In Person Search: Fee charged if court performs your search. No self-serve copier available.

E-Services: PACER records go back to 1994. New records online after 1 day. ECF at https://ecf.alnd.uscourts.gov **Opinions Online:** www.alnd.uscourts.gov/judge_pages.htm.

Gadsden Division c/o Birmingham Division, Rm 140, US Courthouse, 1729 5th Ave N, Birmingham, AL 35203 (also use mail address for courier delivery), 205-278-1700 x2, Fax-n/a. Hours- 8:30AM-4:30PM. www.alnd.uscourts.gov

Counties: Cherokee, De Kalb, Etowah, Marshall, St. Clair.

Searches & Indexing: Results do not include SSN or DOB. Computer index back to 1987 maintained. New cases in the index 2-3 days after filing date. Records purged every 18 months. Open records located at Birmingham Division.

Fee & Payment: Pay by money order, cashier's or personal check. No business checks or credit cards accepted.

Phone Search: No searching by telephone.

Mail Search: search usually completed- 2 days.

In Person Search: permitted. No self-serve copier available.

E-Services: PACER records go back to 1994. New records online after 1 day. ECF at https://ecf.alnd.uscourts.gov **Opinions Online:** www.alnd.uscourts.gov/judge_pages.htm.

Huntsville Division Clerk's Office, US Post Office & Courthouse #302, 101 Holmes Ave NE, Huntsville, AL 35801 (also use mail address for courier delivery), 256-534-6495, Fax-256-551-0741. Hrs- 8AM-4:30PM. www.alnd.uscourts.gov

Counties: Cullman, Jackson, Lawrence, Limestone, Madison, Morgan.

Searches & Indexing: Results do not include SSN or DOB. Computer index back to 1996 maintained; index also on microfiche. New cases in the index 2 days after filing date. Records purged every 18 months.

Fee & Payment: Pay by money order, cashier's or personal check. No credit cards. Payee: US District Court Clerk. Prepayment required.

Phone Search: All public information is released via phone.

Mail Search: search usually completed- 24 hours. All requests for criminal searches sent to Birmingham.

In Person Search: Fee charged if court performs your search. No self-serve copier available.

E-Services: PACER records go back to 1994. New records online after 1 day. ECF at https://ecf.alnd.uscourts.gov **Opinions Online:** www.alnd.uscourts.gov/judge_pages.htm.

Jasper Division c/o Birmingham Division, Rm 140, US Courthouse, 1729 5th Ave N, Birmingham, AL 35203 (also use mail address for courier delivery), 205-278-1700 x2. Hours-8:30AM-4:30PM. www.alnd.uscourts.gov

Counties: Fayette, Lamar, Marion, Walker, Winston.

Searches & Indexing: Some case records may be held in Florence, depending upon the judge assigned. Results do not include SSN or DOB. Computer index maintained. New cases in the index 2-3 days after filing date. Records purged every 18 months. Open records located at Birmingham Division.

Fee & Payment: Pay by money order, cashier's or personal check. No business checks or credit cards accepted.

Phone Search: No searching by telephone.

Mail Search: search usually completed- 2 days.

In Person Search: No self-serve copier available.

E-Services: PACER records go back to 1994. New records online after 1 day. ECF at https://ecf.alnd.uscourts.gov **Opinions Online:** www.alnd.uscourts.gov/judge_pages.htm.

US Bankruptcy Court

Northern District of Alabama

Anniston Division Court Clerk, PO Box 2008, Anniston, AL 36202-2008 (courier address: 914 Noble St, Anniston, AL 36202), 256-741-1500, Fax-256-741-1503. Hours- 8AM-4:30PM. www.alnb.uscourts.gov

Counties: Calhoun, Cherokee, Clay, Cleburne, De Kalb, Etowah, Marshall, St. Clair, Talladega.

Searches & Indexing: Results include last 4 SSN digits. Computer index maintained. New cases in the index immediately after filing date.

Fee & Payment: Pay by money order, cashier's or personal check. Payee: Clerk, US Bankruptcy Court, Northern District. Prepayment required.

Phone Search: Voice Case Information Service available at 877-466-0795 or 205-254-7337.

Mail Search: search usually completed- 1 day.

In Person Search: Fee charged if court performs your search. No self-serve copier available.

E-Services: ECF replaces PACER whose records did go back to 11/1976. ECF at https://ecf.alnb.uscourts.gov **Opinions Online:** www.alnb.uscourts.gov/opinions.htm. **Other Online Access:** Calendars free at http://207.41.17.39/index.cfm?prg=publiccalsearch

Birmingham Division Court Clerk, Rm 120, 1800 5th Ave N, Birmingham, AL 35203 (also use mail address for courier delivery), 205-714-4000, Fax-205-714-3913. Hours- 8AM-4:30PM. www.alnb.uscourts.gov

Counties: Blount, Jefferson, Shelby.

Searches & Indexing: Along with debtor name and the case number, provide the year the case closed and location where case was filed. Results include last 4 SSN digits. Computer index maintained. New cases in the index immediately after filing date. Records purged every 6 months.

Fee & Payment: Pay by money order, cashier's or personal check. No debtor's checks accepted. Payee: Clerk, US Bankruptcy Court. Prepayment required.

Phone Search: Only docket information is available by phone. Voice Case Information Service available at 877-466-0795 or 205-254-7337.

Mail Search: search usually completed- 1-2 days.

In Person Search: Fee charged if court performs your search. No self-serve copier available.

E-Services: ECF replaces PACER whose records did go back to 1992. ECF at https://ecf.alnb.uscourts.gov **Opinions Online:** www.alnb.uscourts.gov/opinions.htm. **Other Online Access:** Calendars free at http://207.41.17.39/index.cfm?prg=publiccalsearch

Decatur Division Court Clerk, PO Box 2748, Decatur, AL 35602 (courier address: Rm 220, 400 Well St, Decatur, AL 35601), 256-584-7900, Fax-256-584-7977. Hours- 8AM-4:30PM. www.alnb.uscourts.gov

Counties: Colbert, Cullman, Franklin, Jackson, Lauderdale, Lawrence, Limestone, Madison, Morgan. The part of Winston County north of Double Springs is handled by this division.

Searches & Indexing: Along with debtor name and the case number, provide the year the case closed and location where case was filed. Results include last 4 SSN digits. Computer index maintained. New cases in the index immediately after filing date. Records purged every 6 months.

Fee & Payment: Pay by money order, cashier's or personal check. Payee: Clerk, US Bankruptcy Court. Prepayment required.

Phone Search: Via phone, this court will indicate charges but not release information. Voice Case Information Service available at 877-466-0795 or 205-254-7337.

Mail Search: search usually completed- 24 hours.

In Person: Fee charged if court performs your search. No self-serve copier available.

E-Services: ECF replaces PACER whose records did go back to 1992. ECF at https://ecf.alnb.uscourts.gov **Opinions Online:** www.alnb.uscourts.gov/opinions.htm. **Other Online Access:** Calendars free at http://207.41.17.39/index.cfm?prg=publiccalsearch

Tuscaloosa Division Court Clerk, PO Box 3226, Tuscaloosa, AL 35403 (courier address: 1118 Greensboro Ave, Tuscaloosa, AL 35401), 205-561-1600, Fax-205-561-1641. Hours- 8AM-4:30PM. www.alnb.uscourts.gov

Counties: Bibb, Fayette, Greene, Lamar, Marion, Pickens, Sumter, Tuscaloosa, Walker, Winston. The part of Winston County North of Double Springs is handled by Decatur Division.

Searches & Indexing: Results include last 4 SSN digits. Both computer and card indexes maintained; on computer back to 10/1979. New cases in the index immediately after filing date. Records purged never.

Fee & Payment: Pay by money order, cashier check, business check. No personal checks. Payee: Clerk, Bankruptcy Court. Prepayment required.

Phone Search: Voice Case Information Service available, call 877-466-0795 or 205-254-7337.

Mail Search: search usually completed- 2 days.

In Person: Fee charged if court performs your search. No self-serve copier available.

E-Services: ECF replaces PACER whose records did go back to 1990. ECF at https://ecf.alnb.uscourts.gov **Opinions Online:** www.alnb.uscourts.gov/opinions.htm. **Other Online Access:** Calendars free at http://207.41.17.39/index.cfm?prg=publiccalsearch

US District Court
Southern District of Alabama

Mobile Division Clerk of Court, 113 St Joseph St, Mobile, AL 36602 (also use mail address for courier delivery), 251-690-2371, Fax-251-694-4297. Hours- 8AM-5PM. www.als.uscourts.gov

Counties: Baldwin, Choctaw, Clarke, Conecuh, Escambia, Mobile, Monroe, Washington.

Searches & Indexing: Results do not include SSN or DOB. Computer index maintained back to 1992 for criminal cases, 1991 for civil. New cases in the index immediately after filing date.

Fee & Payment: Pay by Visa/MC, money order, cashier's or personal check. Payee: Clerk, US District Court. Prepayment required.

Phone Search: Via phone, court will only check docket information for a case.

Mail Search: search usually completed- 1-2 days.

In Person Search: Fee charged if court performs your search. Self-serve copier available - $.25 per page.

E-Services: ECF replaces PACER whose records did go back to 1993. ECF at https://ecf.almd.uscourts.gov **Opinions Online:** www.als.uscourts.gov/page.cfm?page=120.

Selma Division c/o Mobile Division, 113 St Joseph St, Mobile, AL 36602 (also use mail address for courier delivery), 251-690-2371, Fax-251-694-4297. 8AM-5PM. www.als.uscourts.gov

Counties: Dallas, Hale, Marengo, Perry, Wilcox.

Searches & Indexing: Results do not include SSN or DOB. Computer index back to 1990 maintained. New cases in the index immediately after filing date. Open records located at Mobile Division.

Fee & Payment: Pay by Visa/MC, money order, cashier's or personal check.

Phone Search: No searching by telephone.

In Person Search: permitted. No self-serve copier available.

E-Services: ECF replaces PACER whose records did go back to 1993. ECF at https://ecf.almd.uscourts.gov **Opinions Online:** www.als.uscourts.gov/page.cfm?page=120.

US Bankruptcy Court
Southern District of Alabama

Mobile Division Clerk of Court, 201 St. Louis St, Mobile, AL 36602 (also use mail address for courier delivery), 251-441-5391, Fax-251-441-6286. Hours- 8:30AM-5PM. www.alsb.uscourts.gov

Counties: Baldwin, Choctaw, Clarke, Conecuh, Dallas, Escambia, Hale, Marengo, Mobile, Monroe, Perry, Washington, Wilcox.

Searches & Indexing: Results include last 4 SSN digits. Both computer and card indexes maintained. New cases in the index immediately after filing date. District wide computer searches available here back to 1985.

Fee & Payment: Pay by money order, cashier check, business check. No personal checks. Payee: Clerk, US Bankruptcy Court. Prepayment required.

Phone Search: Only name and case number is released via phone. Voice Case Information Service available at 251-441-5637.

Mail Search: search usually completed- 2-3 days. SASE not required.

In Person Search: Fee charged if court performs your search. Self-serve copier available - $.25 per page.

E-Services: ECF replaces PACER whose records did go back to 1993. New records online after 1 day. ECF at https://ecf.alsb.uscourts.gov **Opinions Online:** www.alsb.uscourts.gov/opinions.htm. **Other Online Access:** Dockets free at www.alsb.uscourts.gov/crtcal.htm.

Alabama County Courts

Court	Jurisdiction	No. of Courts	How Organized
Circuit Courts*	General	17	40 Circuits
District Courts*	Limited	15	67 Districts
Combined Courts*		61	
Municipal Courts	Municipal	253	
Probate Courts*	Probate	68	

* Profiled in this Sourcebook.

Court	CIVIL								
	Tort	Contract	Real Estate	Min. Claim	Max. Claim	Small Claims	Estate	Eviction	Domestic Relations
Circuit Courts*	X	X	X	$3000	No Max				X
District Courts*	X	X	X	$3000	$10,000	$3000		X	
Municipal Courts									
Probate Courts*							X		

Court	CRIMINAL				
	Felony	Misdemeanor	DWI/DUI	Preliminary Hearing	Juvenile
Circuit Courts*	X				
District Courts*		X	X	X	X
Municipal Courts		X	X		
Probate Courts*					

ADMINISTRATION Director of Courts, 300 Dexter Ave, Montgomery, AL, 36104; 334-954-5000, Fax: 334-242-2099. www.alacourt.gov

COURT STRUCTURE Circuit Courts are the courts of general jurisdiction; District Courts have limited jurisdiction in civil matters. These courts are combined in all but eight larger counties. Barbour, Coffee, Jefferson, St. Clair, Talladega, and Tallapoosa Counties have two court locations within the county.

Jefferson County (Birmingham), Madison (Huntsville), Marshall, and Tuscaloosa Counties have separate criminal divisions for Circuit and/or District Courts. Misdemeanors committed with felonies are tried with the felony. The Circuit Courts are appeals courts for misdemeanors.

District Courts can receive guilty pleas in felony cases.

ONLINE ACCESS The state has a remote access program called (SJIS), but it is only open to government agencies. They recommend new users to contact a designated private vendor. For more information, visit their web site at www.alacourt.com. Note that fees are involved.

State Supreme Court and Appellette decisions are available online at www.judicial.state.al.us/.

ADDITIONAL INFORMATION Although in most counties Circuit and District courts are combined, each index may be separate. Therefore, when you request a search of both courts, be sure to state that the search is to cover "both the Circuit and District Court records." Several offices do not perform searches. Some offices do not have public access computer terminals.

Autauga County

Circuit & District Court 134 N Court St, #114, Prattville, AL 36067-3049; criminal phone: 334-361-3737; civil phone: 334-361-3736; hours 8AM-5PM (CST). *Felony, Misdemeanor, Civil, Eviction, Small Claims.*
Civil Records: Access: Mail, online, in person. Both court and visitors may perform in person searches. No search fee. Court makes copy: $.25 per page. Required to search: name, years to search. Civil cases indexed by defendant, plaintiff. Civil records on computer since 1977 and in books from 1950. Online access at www.alacourt.com. Mail turnaround time 1-2 weeks.
Criminal Records: Access: Mail, online, in person. Both court and visitors may perform in person searches. No search fee. Court makes copy: $.25 per page. Required to search: name, years to search; also helpful: DOB, SSN. Criminal records on computer since 1977 and in books from 1950. Online access via www.alacourt.com. Mail turnaround time 1-2 weeks.
General Information: No public access terminal. No sealed, adoptions, youthful offenders or juvenile records released. Certification fee: $2.00. Payee: Circuit Court. Only cashiers checks and money orders accepted. Prepayment required.

Probate Court 176 W 5th, Prattville, AL 36067; phone: 334-361-3728/4842; fax: 334-361-3740; hours 8:30AM-5PM (CST). *Probate.*

Baldwin County

Circuit & District Court 312 Courthouse Sq #10, Bay Minette, AL 36507; phone: 251-937-0370; criminal phone: 251-937-0280; civil phone: 251-937-0299; hours 8AM-4:30PM (CST). *Felony, Misdemeanor, Civil, Eviction, Small Claims, Traffic.* Note: Court will not do name searches.
Civil Records: Access: Online, in person. Visitors must perform in person searches themselves. Court makes copy: $.25 per page; same fee for self serve.

Required to search: name, years to search. Civil cases indexed by defendant, plaintiff. Civil records indexed on computer from 1977, index books by case # to early 1900s. Online access at www.alacourt.com.

Criminal Records: Access: Online, in person. Visitors must perform in person searches themselves. Court makes copy: $.25 per page; same fee for self search. Required to search: name, years to search, DOB. Criminal records indexed on computer from 1977, index books by case # to early 1900s. Online access via www.alacourt.com.

General Information: Public access terminal goes back to 1990 for records; 1977 for indices. No sealed, youthful offenders or juvenile records released. Will not fax documents. Certification fee: $1.25 per page. Payee: Circuit Court Clerk. Only cashiers checks and money orders accepted. Prepayment required.

Probate Court PO Box 459, 220 Courthouse Sq, Bay Minette, AL 36507; phone: 251-937-9561; fax: 251-937-0252; hours 8AM-4:30PM (CST). *Probate.*
Note: Online access to probate property records is free at www.deltacomputersystems.com/al/al05/probatea.html.

Barbour County

Circuit & District Court - Clayton Division PO Box 219, Clayton, AL 36016; phone: 334-775-8366; probate phone: 334-775-8371; fax: 334-775-1125; hours 8AM-4:30PM (CST). *Felony, Misdemeanor, Civil, Eviction, Small Claims, Probate.*
Note: Probate court is separate from this court; probate phone number above.

Civil Records: Access: Phone, mail, online, in person. Both court and visitors may perform in person searches. Search fee: $5.00 per name. Fee is per division. Court makes copy: $.50 per page; same fee for self serve. Required to search: name, years to search; a release of liability is requested. Civil cases indexed by defendant. Civil records on computer back to 1993; books from 1977; archives back to 1920. Online access at www.alacourt.com. Mail turnaround time 2-3 days.

Criminal Records: Access: Mail, online, in person. Both court and visitors may perform in person searches. Search fee: $5.00 per name. $5.00 per division. Court makes copy: $.50 per page; same fee for self serve. Required to search: name, years to search, DOB; also helpful: SSN. Criminal records on computer back to 1993, books from 1977; archives back to 1920. Online access via www.alacourt.com. Mail turnaround time 2-3 days.

General Information: No public access terminal. No sealed, adoptions, youthful offenders records released. Fee to fax documents is $.50 per page. Certification fee: $1.50 per cert. Payee: David S Nix. Business checks accepted. SASE required.

Circuit & District Court - Eufaula Division 303 E Broad St, Rm 201, Eufaula, AL 36027; phone: 334-687-1515/16; probate phone: 334-687-1530; fax: 334-687-1599; hours 8AM-4:30PM (CST). *Misdemeanor, Civil, Eviction, Small Claims, Probate.*
Note: Probate court is separate from this court at Rm 101, and can be contacted at the telephone number above.

Civil Records: Access: Online, in person. Visitors must perform in person searches themselves. Court makes copy: $.25 per page. Required to search: name, years to search. Civil cases indexed by defendant, plaintiff. Civil records on computer from 1993. Index from 1977 to present; prior to 1977 difficult to search. Online access through SJIS. See state introduction or visit www.alacourt.com. If case number is known, will provide copies within 2 days.

Criminal Records: Access: Online, in person. Visitors must perform in person searches themselves. Court makes copy: $.25 per page. Required to search: name, years to search; also

helpful: DOB, SSN. Civil records on computer from 1993. Index from 1977 to present; prior to 1977 difficult to search. Online access through SJIS. See state introduction or visit www.alacourt.com. If case number is known, will provide copies within 2 days.

General Information: Public access terminal goes back to 1977. No sealed, adoptions, youthful offenders or juvenile records released. Certification fee: $3.00. Payee: Clerk of Courts. Personal checks accepted. No credit cards. Prepayment required.

Bibb County

Circuit & District Court Bibb County Courthouse, PO Box 185, Centreville, AL 35042; phone: 205-926-3103 Civil (Circuit); criminal phone: 205-926-3107; civil phone: 205-926-3100 (Dist); probate phone: 205-926-3108; fax: 205-926-3132; hours 8AM-4:30PM (CST). *Felony, Misdemeanor, Civil, Eviction, Small Claims, Probate.*
Note: Probate court is separate from this court; probate phone number above.

Civil Records: Access: Mail, online, in person. Both court and visitors may perform in person searches. No search fee. Court makes copy: $.25 per page; same fee for self serve. Required to search: name, years to search. Civil cases indexed by defendant. Civil records on index book back to 1940s. Online access at www.alacourt.com. Mail turnaround time 3-4 days.

Criminal Records: Access: Mail, online, in person. Both court and visitors may perform in person searches. No search fee. Court makes copy: $.25 per page; same fee for self serve. Required to search: name, years to search, DOB; also helpful: SSN. Criminal records on computer from 1995, on index books back to 1940s. Online access via www.alacourt.com. Mail turnaround time 1-2 days.

General Information: Public access terminal goes back to 1995. No sealed, adoptions, youthful offenders or juvenile records released. Certification fee: $1.00. Payee: John H Stacy, Clerk. Business checks accepted; no personal checks. Prepayment and SASE required.

Blount County

Circuit & District Court 220 2nd Ave East Rm 208, Oneonta, AL 35121; phone: 205-625-4153; hours 8AM-5PM (CST). *Felony, Misdemeanor, Civil, Eviction, Small Claims.*
Civil Records: Access: Mail, online, in person. Both court and visitors may perform in person searches. Court makes copy: $.25 per page. Required to search: name, years to search. Civil cases indexed by defendant, plaintiff. Civil records on computer from 3/1994, on index books from 1977. Online access at www.alacourt.com. Mail turnaround time up to 1 month.

Criminal Records: Access: Mail, online, in person. Both court and visitors may perform in person searches. Court makes copy: $.25 per page. Required to search: name, years to search, DOB; also helpful: SSN. Criminal records on computer from 3/1994, on index books from 1977. Online access via www.alacourt.com. Mail turnaround time up to 1 month.

General Information: Public access terminal goes back to 1994. No sealed, adoptions, youthful offenders or juvenile records released. Certification fee: $1.00 per cert. Payee: Mike Chriswell. No personal checks accepted. Prepayment and SASE required.

Probate Court 220 2nd Ave E, Oneonta, AL 35121; phone: 205-625-4191/4180; fax: 205-625-4206; hours 8AM-5PM (CST). *Probate.*

Bullock County

Circuit & District Court PO Box 230, Union Springs, AL 36089; phone: 334-738-2280; probate phone: 334-738-2250; fax: 334-738-2282; hours 8AM-4:30PM (CST). *Felony, Misdemeanor, Civil, Eviction, Small Claims, Probate.*
Note: Probate court is separate from this court; probate phone number above.

Civil Records: Access: Phone, fax, mail, online, in person. Both court and visitors may perform in person searches. No search fee. Required to search: name, years to search. Civil cases indexed by defendant, plaintiff. Civil records on index books back to 1930s; on computer back to 1995. Online access at www.alacourt.com. Mail turnaround time depends on clerk availability.

Criminal Records: Access: Phone, fax, mail, online, in person. Only the court performs in person searches; visitors may not. No search fee. Required to search: name, years to search, DOB; also helpful: SSN, signed release. Criminal records on index books back to 1930s; on computer back to 1995. Online access via www.alacourt.com. Mail turnaround time depends on clerk availability.

General Information: No public access terminal. No sealed, adoptions, youthful offenders or juvenile records released. No fee to fax documents. Prepayment and SASE required.

Butler County

Circuit & District Court PO Box 236, Greenville, AL 36037; phone: 334-382-3521; probate phone: 334-382-3512; fax: 334-382-7488; hours 7:30AM-4:30PM (CST). *Felony, Misdemeanor, Civil, Eviction, Small Claims, Probate.*
Note: Probate court is separate from this court; probate phone number above.

Civil Records: Access: Mail, online, in person. Both court and visitors may perform in person searches. Search fee: $5.00 per name. Fee is for first 2-3 years. Court makes copy: $1.00 per page; same fee for self serve. Required to search: name, years to search. Civil cases indexed by defendant, plaintiff. Civil records on computer from 1992, books to 1979. Online access at www.alacourt.com. Mail turnaround time 1-2 weeks.

Criminal Records: Access: Mail, online, in person. Both court and visitors may perform in person searches. Search fee: $5.00 per name. Fee for first 2-3 years. Court makes copy: $1.00 per page; same fee for self serve. Required to search: name, years to search; also helpful: SSN, DOB. Criminal records on computer from 1992, books to 1979. Online access via www.alacourt.com. Mail turnaround time 1-2 weeks.

General Information: Public access terminal has criminal back to 1992 and civil back to 1994. No sealed, adoptions, youthful offenders or juvenile records released. Fee to fax documents is $1.00 per page. Certification fee: $1.50 per page. Payee: Butler County District Court. Business checks accepted. Prepayment required. SASE requested.

Calhoun County

Circuit Court 25 W 11th St, #300, Anniston, AL 36201; phone: 256-231-1750; fax: 256-231-1826; hours 8AM-4:30PM (CST). *Felony, Civil Actions Over $10,000.*
Civil Records: Access: Online, in person. Visitors must perform in person searches themselves. Court makes copy: $.25 per page. Required to search: name, years to search. Civil cases indexed by defendant, plaintiff. Civil records indexed on computer from 1970s, prior in books. Online access at www.alacourt.com.
Criminal Records: Access: Online, mail, in person. Visitors must perform in person searches themselves. Court makes copy: $.25 per page. Required to search: name, years to search, DOB; also helpful: SSN. Criminal records indexed on computer

from 1970s, prior on books. Online access via www.alacourt.com. The County sex offender registry is online at www.calhouncountysheriff.org/html/Framsex.html . From Sept. 1999 forward only. Mail turnaround time 2-4 days.

General Information: Public access terminal goes back to 1970. No sealed, adoptions, youthful offenders or juvenile records released. Certification fee: $1.00. Personal checks accepted. Prepayment required.

District Court 25 W 11th St, Box 9, Anniston, AL 36201; phone: 256-231-1850; fax: 256-231-1863; hours 8AM-4:30PM (CST). *Misdemeanor, Civil Actions Under $10,000, Eviction, Small Claims.*

Civil Records: Access: Online, in person. Visitors must perform in person searches themselves. Court makes copy: $.25 per page; same fee for self serve. Required to search: name, years to search. Civil cases indexed by defendant, plaintiff. Civil records on computer from 1989, books from 1977 to 1989. Online access at www.alacourt.com.

Criminal Records: Access: Online, in person. Visitors must perform in person searches themselves. Court makes copy: $.25 per page; same fee for self serve. Required to search: name, years to search; also helpful: SSN. Criminal records on computer from 1989, books from 1977 to 1989. Online access via www.alacourt.com.

General Information: Public access terminal goes back to 1977. (Terminal located in law Library.) No sealed, adoptions, youthful offenders or juvenile records released. Certification fee: $1.00 per cert. Payee: District Court. No personal checks or credit cards. Prepayment required.

Probate Court 1702 Noble St, #102, Anniston, AL 36201; phone: 256-241-2825; fax: 256-231-1728; hours 8AM-4:30PM (CST). *Probate.* www.calhouncounty.org/probate.html

Chambers County

Circuit & District Court Chambers County Courthouse - Clerks Office, Lafayette, AL 36862; phone: 334-864-4348; probate phone: 334-864-4372; hours 8AM-N, 1-4:30PM (CST). *Felony, Misdemeanor, Civil, Eviction, Small Claims, Probate.*

Note: Probate court is separate from this court; probate phone number above.

Civil Records: Access: Mail, online, in person. Both court and visitors may perform in person searches. Search fee: No fee for mail. Court makes copy: $.25 per page; same fee for self serve. Required to search: name, years to search. Civil cases indexed by defendant, plaintiff. Civil records on computer from 4/93, on index books to early 1900s. Online access at www.alacourt.com. Mail turnaround time 1 week.

Criminal Records: Access: Mail, online, in person. Only the court performs in person searches; visitors may not. Search fee: No fee for mail. Court makes copy: $.25 per page; same fee for self serve. Required to search: name, years to search; also helpful: DOB, SSN. Criminal records are computerized since 1993. Online access via www.alacourt.com. Mail turnaround time 1 week.

General Information: Public access terminal goes back to 1993. No sealed, adoptions, youthful offenders or juvenile records released. Certification fee: $1.00 per cert. Business checks accepted. No personal checks or credit cards. SASE required.

Cherokee County

Circuit & District Court 100 Main St, Rm 203, Centre, AL 35960-1532; phone: 256-927-3340; hours 8AM-4:30PM (CST). *Felony, Misdemeanor, Civil, Eviction, Small Claims.*

Civil Records: Access: In person, online. Visitors must perform in person searches themselves. No search fee. Court makes copy: $.25 per page; same fee for self serve. Required to search: name, years to search. Civil cases indexed by defendant, plaintiff.

Civil records on books from 1977. Online access at www.alacourt.com.

Criminal Records: Access: Online, in person. Visitors must perform in person searches themselves. No search fee. Court makes copy: $.25 per page; same fee for self serve. Required to search: name, years to search; also helpful: DOB, SSN. Criminal records on books from 1977. Online access via www.alacourt.com.

General Information: Public access terminal goes back to 8/1995. No sealed, adoptions, youthful offenders or juvenile records released. Certification fee: $1.00 per cert. Payee: Circuit Clerk. Business checks accepted. Prepayment required.

Probate Court 260 Cedar Bluff Rd, Rm 101, Centre, AL 35960; phone: 256-927-3363; fax: 256-927-9218; hours 8AM-4PM (CST). *Probate.*

Chilton County

Circuit & District Court PO Box 1946, Clanton, AL 35046; phone: 205-755-4275 Dist; 280-1844 Dist.; probate phone: 205-755-1555; hours 8AM-5PM (CST). *Felony, Misdemeanor, Civil, Eviction, Small Claims, Probate.*

Note: Probate court is separate from this court; probate phone number above.

Civil Records: Access: Online, in person. Visitors must perform in person searches themselves. Court makes copy: $.25 per page; same fee for self serve. Required to search: name, years to search. Civil cases indexed by defendant, plaintiff. Civil records on computer from 9/93, on books from 1950s. Online access at www.alacourt.com.

Criminal Records: Access: Online, in person. Visitors must perform in person searches themselves. Court makes copy: $.25 per page; same fee for self serve. Required to search: name, years to search; also helpful: DOB, SSN. Criminal records on computer since 1977. Online access via www.alacourt.com.

General Information: Public access terminal goes back to 1994. No sealed, adoptions, youthful offenders or juvenile records released. Certification fee: $1.00 per cert. Payee: Clerk. Business checks accepted. No personal checks or credit cards. Prepayment required.

Choctaw County

Circuit & District Court Choctaw County Courthouse, #10, PO Box 428, Butler, AL 36904; phone: 205-459-2155; probate phone: 205-459-2417; hours 8AM-4:30PM (CST). *Felony, Misdemeanor, Civil, Eviction, Small Claims, Probate.*

Note: Probate court is separate from this court; probate phone number above.

Civil Records: Access: Online, in person. Both court and visitors may perform in person searches. No search fee. Court makes copy: $.50 per page. Required to search: name, years to search. Civil cases indexed by defendant, plaintiff. Civil records on index books from 1940. Putting records on computer from 9/1994. Online access at www.alacourt.com.

Criminal Records: Access: Online, in person. Visitors must perform in person searches themselves. Court makes copy: $.50 per page. Required to search: name, years to search; also helpful: DOB, SSN. Criminal records on index books from 1940. Putting records on computer from 9/1994. Online access via www.alacourt.com.

General Information: Public access terminal available. No sealed, adoptions, youthful offenders or juvenile records released. Certification fee: $1.00. Payee: Circuit Clerk. Business checks accepted. Prepayment required.

Clarke County

Circuit & District Court PO Box 921, Grove Hill, AL 36451; phone: 251-275-3363; probate phone: 251-275-3251; fax: 251-275-2080; hours 8AM-5PM (CST). *Felony, Misdemeanor, Civil,*

Eviction, Small Claims, Probate.

Note: Probate court is separate from this court; probate phone number above.

Civil Records: Access: Mail, online, in person. Both court and visitors may perform in person searches. Search fee: $5.00 per name. Court makes copy: $.40 per page. Required to search: name, years to search. Civil cases indexed by defendant, plaintiff. Civil records on index cards from 1977. Online access at www.alacourt.com. Mail turnaround time 1 week.

Criminal Records: Access: Mail, online, in person. Both court and visitors may perform in person searches. Search fee: $5.00 per name. Court makes copy: $.40 per page. Required to search: name, years to search; also helpful: DOB, SSN. Criminal records on index cards from 1977. Online access via www.alacourt.com. Mail turnaround time 1 week.

General Information: Public access terminal available. No sealed, adoptions, youthful offenders or juvenile records released. Will not fax documents. Certification fee: $2.50. Payee: Circuit Clerk. Business checks accepted. Prepayment required.

Clay County

Circuit & District Court PO Box 816, Ashland, AL 36251; phone: 256-354-7926; probate phone: 256-354-2198; fax: 256-354-2249; hours 8AM-4:30PM (CST). *Felony, Misdemeanor, Civil, Eviction, Small Claims, Probate.*

Note: Probate court is separate from this court, and can be reached at the telephone number given above.

Civil Records: Access: Mail, online, in person. Visitors must perform in person searches themselves. Court makes copy: $.50 per page. Required to search: name, years to search. Civil cases indexed by defendant, plaintiff. Overall records go back to 1977; computerized records go back to 1994. Online access at www.alacourt.com. Mail turnaround time 10-14 days.

Criminal Records: Access: Mail, online, in person. Visitors must perform in person searches themselves. Court makes copy: $.50 per page. Required to search: name, years to search; also helpful: SSN, DOB, signed release. Overall records go back to 1977; computerized records go back to 1994. Online access via www.alacourt.com. Mail turnaround time 10-14 days.

General Information: Public access terminal goes back to 1994. No sealed, adoptions, youthful offenders or juvenile records released. Fee to fax documents is $1.00 per page. Certification fee: $1.25. Payee: Circuit Clerk. Business checks accepted. Prepayment required.

Cleburne County

Circuit & District Court 120 Vickery St Rm 202, Heflin, AL 36264; phone: 256-463-2651; probate phone: 256-463-5655; fax: 256-463-2257; probate fax: 256-463-1044; hours 8AM-4:30PM (CST). *Felony, Misdemeanor, Civil, Eviction, Small Claims, Probate.*

Note: Probate is a separate index located in Rm 101.

Civil Records: Access: Phone, mail, online, in person. Both court and visitors may perform in person searches. No search fee. Court makes copy: $.25 per page; same fee for self serve. Required to search: name, years to search. Civil cases indexed by defendant, plaintiff. Civil records on computer from 1993, on books and cards from 1900. Online access at www.alacourt.com. Mail turnaround time 1-2 days.

Criminal Records: Access: Mail, online, in person. Only the court performs in person searches; visitors may not. No search fee. Court makes copy: $.25 per page; same fee for self serve. Required to search: name, years to search, DOB; also helpful: SSN. Criminal records on computer from 1993, on books and cards from 1900. Online access via www.alacourt.com. Mail turnaround time 1-2 days.

General Information: No public access terminal. No sealed, adoptions, youthful offenders or juvenile records released. Will fax documents for no fee. Certification fee: $1.00. Payee: Clerk. Only cashiers checks and money orders accepted. Prepayment and SASE required.

Coffee County

Circuit & District Court - Elba Division
230 M Court Ave, Elba, AL 36323; phone: 334-897-2954; Hours: 8:30AM-N, 1-4;30PM (CST). *Felony, Misdemeanor, Civil, Eviction, Small Claims, Probate.*
Civil Records: Access: Mail, online, in person. Both court and visitors may perform in person searches. No search fee. Court makes copy: $.25 per page; same fee for self serve. Required to search: name, years to search. Civil cases indexed by defendant. Civil records on computer back to 8/1993. Online access at www.alacourt.com. Mail turnaround time 3-4 days.
Criminal Records: Access: Mail, online, in person. Only the court performs in person searches; visitors may not. No search fee. Court makes copy: $.25 per page; same fee for self serve. Required to search: name, years to search; also helpful: DOB. Criminal records on computer back to 8/1993. Online access via www.alacourt.com. Mail turnaround time varies.
General Information: No public access terminal. No sealed, adoptions, youthful offenders or juvenile records released. Certification fee: $1.25 per cert includes copy. Payee: Circuit Clerk. Business checks accepted. SASE required.

Circuit & District Court - Enterprise Division
PO Box 311284, Enterprise, AL 36331; phone: 334-347-2519; hours 8AM-5PM (CST). *Felony, Misdemeanor, Civil, Eviction, Small Claims.*
Civil Records: Access: Mail, fax, online, in person. Both court and visitors may perform in person searches. No search fee. Court makes copy: $.25 per page. Required to search: name, years to search. Civil cases indexed by defendant, plaintiff. Civil records on computer since 8/1993. Online access at www.alacourt.com. Mail turnaround time up to 1 week.
Criminal Records: Access: Mail, online, in person. Both court and visitors may perform in person searches. No search fee. Court makes copy: $.25 per page. Required to search: name, years to search, DOB; also helpful: SSN. Criminal records on computer since 8/1993. Online access via www.alacourt.com. Mail turnaround time up to 1 week.
General Information: Public access terminal goes back to 1980. No sealed, adoptions, youthful offenders or juvenile records released. Certification fee: $1.25 per cert includes copy. Payee: Clerk of Courts. Only cashiers checks and money orders accepted. Prepayment and SASE required.

Probate Court - Enterprise Division
PO Box 311247, Enterprise, AL 36331; phone: 334-347-2688; fax: 334-347-2095; hours 8AM-4:30PM (CST). *Probate.*

Colbert County

Circuit Court
Colbert County Courthouse, 201 N Main St, Tuscumbia, AL 35674; phone: 256-386-8512; probate phone: 256-386-8542; hours 8AM-N, 1-4:30PM; no phones 11AM-2PM (CST). *Felony, Civil Actions Over $10,000, Probate.*
Note: Probate court is separate from this court; probate phone number above.
Civil Records: Access: Online, in person. Visitors must perform in person searches themselves. Court makes copy: $.25 per page; same fee for self serve. Required to search: name, years to search. Civil cases indexed by defendant. Civil records on computer from 1993, books from 1959. Online access at www.alacourt.com.
Criminal Records: Access: Online, in person. Visitors must perform in person searches themselves. Court makes copy: $.25 per page; same

fee for self serve. Required to search: name, years to search; also helpful: DOB, SSN. Criminal records on computer from 1993, books prior. Online access via www.alacourt.com.
General Information: Public access terminal has criminal back to 1977 and civil back to 1993. No sealed, youthful offenders or juvenile records released. Certification fee: $1.00 per page. Payee: Circuit Court Clerk. Business checks accepted. Prepayment required.

District Court
Colbert County Courthouse, 201 N Main St, Tuscumbia, AL 35674; phone: 256-386-8518; hours 8AM-N; 1PM-4:30PM (CST). *Misdemeanor, Civil Actions Under $10,000, Eviction, Small Claims.*
Civil Records: Access: Online, in person. Visitors must perform in person searches themselves. Court makes copy: $.25 per page. Required to search: name, years to search. Civil cases indexed by defendant, plaintiff. Civil records on computer from 1993, prior on books. Online access at www.alacourt.com.
Criminal Records: Access: Online, in person. Visitors must perform in person searches themselves. Court makes copy: $.25 per page. Required to search: name, years to search; also helpful: SSN. Criminal records on computer from 1993, prior on books. Online access via www.alacourt.com.
General Information: Public access terminal goes back to 4/1997. No sealed, adoptions, youthful offenders or juvenile records released. Certification fee: $1.00. Payee: District Clerk. Only cashiers checks and money orders accepted. Prepayment required.

Conecuh County

Circuit & District Court
PO Box 107, Evergreen, AL 36401; phone: 251-578-2066; probate phone: 251-578-1221; hours 8AM-4:30PM (CST). *Felony, Misdemeanor, Civil, Eviction, Small Claims, Probate.*
Note: Probate court is separate from this court; probate phone number above.
Civil Records: Access: In person, online. Both court and visitors may perform in person searches. Court makes copy: $1.00 per page. Self serve copy fee: $.50 per page. Required to search: name, years to search. Civil cases indexed by defendant, plaintiff. Civil records on index cards from 1977, on computer back to 12/1994. Online access at www.alacourt.com.
Criminal Records: Access: In person, online. Both court and visitors may perform in person searches. No search fee. Court makes copy: $1.00 per page. Self serve copy fee: $.50 per page. Required to search: name, years to search, DOB; also helpful: SSN. Criminal records on index cards from 1977, on computer back to 1994. Online access via www.alacourt.com.
General Information: Public access terminal goes back to 12/94. No sealed, adoptions, youthful offenders or juvenile records released. Will fax specific case file requests for $1.00 per page. Certification fee: $2.50. Payee: Circuit Clerk, George Hendrix. Business checks accepted. Prepayment required.

Coosa County

Circuit & District Court
PO Box 98, Rockford, AL 35136; phone: 256-377-4988; probate phone: 256-377-4919; fax: 256-377-1599; hours 8AM-4:30PM (CST). *Felony, Misdemeanor, Civil, Eviction, Small Claims, Probate.*
Note: Probate court is separate from this court; probate phone number above.
Civil Records: Access: Online, in person. Visitors must perform in person searches themselves. Court makes copy: $.25 per page. Required to search: name, years to search. Civil cases indexed by plaintiff. Civil records on books from the late 1800s, computerized records go back to 7/1994. Online access at www.alacourt.com.
Criminal Records: Access: Online, in person, fax, mail. Visitors must perform in person searches

themselves. Court makes copy: $.25 per page. Required to search: name, years to search; also helpful: DOB, SSN. Criminal records from the late 1800s, computerized records go back to 7/1994. Online access via www.alacourt.com. Mail turnaround time 2-3 days.
General Information: No public access terminal. No sealed, adoptions, youthful offenders or juvenile records released. Certification fee: $1.00. Payee: Clerk of Court. Business checks accepted. Prepayment and SASE required.

Covington County

Circuit & District Court
Covington County Courthouse, Andalusia, AL 36420; phone: 334-428-2520; probate phone: 334-428-2510; hours 8AM-5PM (CST). *Felony, Misdemeanor, Civil, Eviction, Small Claims, Probate.*
Note: Probate court is separate from this court; probate telephone number above.
Civil Records: Access: Online, in person. Both court and visitors may perform in person searches. Search fee: Copy fee only. Court makes copy: $.25 per page; same fee for self serve. Required to search: name, years to search. Civil cases indexed by defendant, plaintiff. Civil records on computer from 3/94; prior on books to 1920. Online access at www.alacourt.gov. Also, online access to probate records is by subscription at www.recordsusa.com/Alabama/CovingtonCnAl.htm. Credit card-username-password required; choose monthly or per-use plan. Visit the website or call Lisa at 601-264-7701 for information.
Criminal Records: Access: Online, in person. Visitors must perform in person searches themselves. Court makes copy: $.25 per page; same fee for self serve. Required to search: name, years to search, DOB; also helpful: SSN. Criminal records on computer from 3/94; prior on books to 1920. Online access via www.alacourt.gov.
General Information: Public access terminal available. No sealed, adoptions, youthful offenders or juvenile records released. Will not fax documents. Certification fee: $1.00 per cert. Payee: Circuit Clerk. Business checks accepted. Prepayment required.

Crenshaw County

Circuit & District Court
PO Box 167, Luverne, AL 36049; phone: 334-335-6575; probate phone: 334-335-6568; fax: 334-335-2076; hours 8AM-4:30PM (CST). *Felony, Misdemeanor, Civil, Eviction, Small Claims, Probate.*
Note: Probate court is separate from this court, and can be contacted at the telephone number above. Probate address is PO Box 328, Luverne, 36049.
Civil Records: Access: Mail, online, in person. Both court and visitors may perform in person searches. No search fee. Court makes copy: $.50 per page; same fee for self serve. Required to search: name, years to search. Civil cases indexed by defendant, plaintiff. Civil records on computer from 1993, on book from 1977. Online access at www.alacourt.com. Mail turnaround time 2-3 days.
Criminal Records: Access: Mail, online, in person. Both court and visitors may perform in person searches. No search fee. Court makes copy: $.50 per page; same fee for self serve. Required to search: name, years to search, DOB; also helpful: SSN. Criminal records on computer from 1993, on book from 1977. Online access via www.alacourt.com. Mail turnaround time 2-3 days.
General Information: Public access terminal goes back to 1993. No sealed, adoptions, youthful offenders or juvenile records released. Will fax documents. Certification fee: $1.00. Payee: Circuit Clerk. Only cashiers checks and money orders accepted. SASE requested.

Cullman County

Circuit Court Cullman County Courthouse, Rm 303, 500 2nd Ave SW, Cullman, AL 35055; phone: 256-775-4654; criminal phone: 256-775-4799; civil phone: 256-775-4800; probate phone: 256-775-4652; hours 8AM-4:30PM (CST). *Felony, Civil Actions Over $10,000, Probate.*

Civil Records: Access: Phone, mail, online, in person. Both court and visitors may perform in person searches. No search fee. Court makes copy: $.25 per page. Add postage costs if by mail; same fee for self serve. Required to search: name, years to search. Civil cases indexed by defendant, plaintiff. Civil records on computer back to 1993, index back to 1977; books from 1900s. Online access at www.alacourt.com. Mail turnaround time 10 days.

Criminal Records: Access: Mail, online, in person. Both court and visitors may perform in person searches. No search fee. Court makes copy: $.25 per page. Add postage costs if by mail; same fee for self serve. Required to search: name, years to search, DOB; also helpful: SSN. Criminal records on computer back to 1993; index back to 1977; prior in books. Online access via www.alacourt.com. Mail turnaround time 10 days.

General Information: Public access terminal goes back to 1977. (Indices only.) No sealed, adoptions, youthful offenders or juvenile records released. Will not fax documents. Certification fee: $1.00 per doc. Payee: Robert Bates, Circuit Clerk. Business checks accepted. Prepayment required. SASE not required.

District Court 500 2nd Ave SW, Courthouse Rm 211, Cullman, AL 35055-4197; phone: 256-775-4660; hours 8AM-4:30PM (CST). *Misdemeanor, Civil Actions Under $10,000, Eviction, Small Claims.*

Civil Records: Access: Mail, online, in person. Visitors must perform in person searches themselves. Court makes copy: $.25 per page. Required to search: name, years to search. Civil cases indexed by defendant. Civil records on computer from 11/92, on books 10 yrs back. Online access at www.alacourt.com. Mail turnaround time 1 week.

Criminal Records: Access: Mail, online, in person. Visitors must perform in person searches themselves. Court makes copy: $.25 per page. Required to search: name, years to search, DOB; also helpful: SSN. Criminal records on computer from 11/92, on books 10 yrs back. Online access via www.alacourt.com. Mail turnaround time 1 week.

General Information: Public access terminal available. No sealed, adoptions, youthful offenders or juvenile records released. Will not fax documents. Certification fee: $1.25. Payee: District Clerk. Only cashiers checks and money orders accepted. Prepayment and SASE required.

Dale County

Circuit & District Court PO Box 1350, Ozark, AL 36361; phone: 334-774-5003; probate phone: 334-774-2754; hours 8AM-1:30PM, 3:30-5PM (CST). *Felony, Misdemeanor, Civil, Eviction, Small Claims, Probate.*

Note: Probate court is separate from this court; probate phone number above.

Civil Records: Access: Online, in person. Visitors must perform in person searches themselves. Court makes copy: $.25 per page. Required to search: name, years to search. Civil cases indexed by defendant, plaintiff. Civil records on computer from 8/92, on books and index cards from the 1920s. Online access at www.alacourt.com.

Criminal Records: Access: Online, in person. Visitors must perform in person searches themselves. Court makes copy: $.25 per page. Required to search: name, years to search, DOB; also helpful: SSN. Criminal records on computer from 8/92, on books and index cards from the 1920s. Online access via www.alacourt.com.

General Information: Public access terminal goes back to 1994. No sealed, adoptions, youthful

offenders or juvenile records released. Certification fee: $1.00 per page. Payee: Dale County Circuit Clerk. Only cashiers checks and money orders accepted. Prepayment required.

Dallas County

Circuit Court PO Box 1148, Selma, AL 36702; phone: 334-874-2523; hours 9AM-4PM (CST). *Felony, Civil Actions Over $10,000, Probate.*

Note: Probate court is separate from this court, and can be contacted 334-874-2500

Civil Records: Access: Mail, online, in person. Both court and visitors may perform in person searches. No search fee. Court makes copy: $.25 per page. Self serve copy fee: $.10 per page. Required to search: name, years to search. Civil cases indexed by defendant, plaintiff. Civil records on computer from 1980, on microfiche from the late 1800s, index books prior. Online access at www.alacourt.com. Mail turnaround time less than 1 week for civil cases.

Criminal Records: Access: Phone, mail, online, in person. Both court and visitors may perform in person searches. No search fee. Court makes copy: $.25 per page. Self serve copy fee: $.10 per page. Required to search: name, years to search, DOB; also helpful: SSN. Criminal records on computer from 1980, on microfiche from the late 1800s, index books prior. Online access via www.alacourt.com. Mail turnaround time less than 1 week for civil cases.

General Information: Public access terminal goes back to 1992. (Terminal may not include recent activity.) No sealed, adoptions, youthful offenders or juvenile records released. Certification fee: $1.00 per file. Payee: Dallas County Circuit Court. Personal checks accepted. Prepayment and SASE required.

District Court PO Box 1148, Selma, AL 36702; phone: 334-874-2523; fax: 334-877-0637; hours 9AM-4PM (CST). *Misdemeanor, Civil Actions Under $10,000, Eviction, Small Claims.*

Note: Probate court is separate from this court and can be reached at 334-874-2500. Traffic division phone- 877-252-7294.

Civil Records: Access: Phone, mail, online, in person. Visitors must perform in person searches themselves. Court makes copy: $.25 per page; same fee for self serve. Required to search: name, years to search. Civil cases indexed by defendant. Civil records on books from 1967, on computer since 1993. Online access at www.alacourt.com. Mail turnaround time varies.

Criminal Records: Access: Mail, online, in person. Visitors must perform in person searches themselves. Court makes copy: $.25 per page; same fee for self serve. Required to search: name, years to search; also helpful: DOB, SSN. Criminal records on books from 1967, on computer since 1992. Online access via www.alacourt.com. Mail turnaround time varies.

General Information: Public access terminal goes back to 1993. No sealed, adoptions, youthful offenders or juvenile records released. Certification fee: $1.00 per cert. Payee: District Clerk. Cashiers checks and money orders only. Prepayment required.

De Kalb County

Circuit & District Court PO Box 681149, Fort Payne, AL 35968; phone: 256-845-8525; probate phone: 256-845-8510; hours 8AM-4PM (CST). *Felony, Misdemeanor, Civil, Eviction, Small Claims, Probate.*

Note: Probate court is separate from this court; probate phone number above.

Civil Records: Access: Mail, online, in person. Both court and visitors may perform in person searches. No search fee. Court makes copy: $.25 per page. Required to search: name, years to search. Civil cases indexed by defendant. Civil records on computer from 8/1991, on books from 1959. Online access at www.alacourt.com. Mail turnaround time 1 week.

Criminal Records: Access: Mail, online, in person. Both court and visitors may perform in person

searches. No search fee. Court makes copy: $.25 per page. Required to search: name, years to search; also helpful: DOB, SSN. Criminal records on computer from 8/1991, on books from 1959. Online access via www.alacourt.com. Mail turnaround time 1 week.

General Information: Public access terminal goes back to 1993. No sealed, adoptions, youthful offenders or juvenile records released. Certification fee: $1.00. Business checks accepted.

Elmore County

Circuit & District Court - Civil Division PO Box 310, Wetumpka, AL 36092; phone: 334-567-1123; probate phone: 334-567-1139; fax: 334-567-5957; hours 8AM-4:30PM (CST). *Civil, Probate.*

Note: Probate court is separate from this court, but can be contacted at the telephone number above.

Civil Records: Access: Online, in person. Visitors must perform in person searches themselves. Court makes copy: $.25 per page; same fee for self serve. Required to search: name, years to search. Civil cases indexed by defendant, plaintiff. Civil records on computer from 1997, books from 1930. Online access at www.alacourt.com.

General Information: Public access terminal has only civil records back to 1990. No sealed, adoptions, youthful offenders or juvenile records released. Certification fee: $1.00 per cert. Payee: Circuit Court Clerk. Business checks accepted. Prepayment required.

Circuit Court - Criminal Division PO Box 310, 8935 US Hwy 23, Wetumpka, AL 36092; phone: 334-567-1123; fax: 334-567-5957; hours 8AM-4:30PM (CST). *Felony, Misdemeanor.*

Criminal Records: Access: Online, in person. Visitors must perform in person searches themselves. Court makes copy: $.25 per page; same fee for self serve. Required to search: name, years to search, DOB, SSN. Criminal records on computer from mid-1991, books from 1960-1992. Online access through SJIS. See state introduction

General Information: Public access terminal has criminal back to 1991 and civil back to 1990. No sealed, adoptions, youthful offenders or juvenile records released. Certification fee: $1.00 per cert. Payee: Circuit Court Clerk. Only cashiers checks and money orders accepted. Prepayment required.

Escambia, County

Circuit & District Court PO Box 856, Brewton, AL 36427; phone: 251-867-0305; criminal phone: 251-867-0220; civil phone: 251-867-0285; probate phone: 251-867-0201; fax: 251-867-0365; probate fax: 251-867-0284; hours 8AM-4:30PM (CST). *Felony, Misdemeanor, Civil, Eviction, Small Claims, Probate.*

Note: Probate court has separate mailing address: PO Box 557.

Civil Records: Access: Mail, fax, online, in person. Both court and visitors may perform in person searches. No search fee. Court makes copy: $.25 per page; same fee for self serve. Required to search: name, years to search. Civil cases indexed by defendant, plaintiff. Civil records on computer from 10/93, books and cards back to 1990. Online access at www.alacourt.com. Mail turnaround time 2-3 days.

Criminal Records: Access: Mail, fax, online, in person. Both court and visitors may perform in person searches. No search fee. Court makes copy: $.25 per page; same fee for self serve. Required to search: name, years to search, DOB. Criminal records on computer from 10/93, books and cards back to 1950. Online access via www.alacourt.com. Mail turnaround time 2-3 days.

General Information: Public access terminal goes back to 10/1993. No sealed, adoptions, youthful offenders or juvenile records released. Fee to fax documents is $1.00 per document and $.25 per page. Certification fee: $1.00 per page. Payee: Escambia

County Circuit Court. Business checks accepted. Prepayment and SASE required.

Etowah County

Circuit & District Court 801 Forrest Ave #202, Gadsden, AL 35901; phone: 256-549-2150; criminal phone: 256-549-5437; civil phone: 256-549-5350; probate phone: 256-549-5333; hours 8:30AM-4:30PM (CST). *Felony, Misdemeanor, Civil, Eviction, Small Claims.*
Note: Probate court is separate from this court.

Civil Records: Access: Mail, online, in person. Both court and visitors may perform in person searches. No search fee. Court makes copy: $.25 per page. Self serve copy fee: $.10 per page. Required to search: name, years to search. Civil cases indexed by defendant, plaintiff. Civil records on computer from 1984, index on computer since 1977, books prior to 1977. Online access at www.alacourt.com. Mail turnaround time 4-6 weeks.
Criminal Records: Access: Mail, online, in person. Both court and visitors may perform in person searches. No search fee. Court makes copy: $.25 per page. Self serve copy fee: $.10 per page. Required to search: name, years to search; also helpful: DOB, SSN. Criminal records on computer from 1984, index on computer since 1977, books prior to 1977. Online access via www.alacourt.com. Mail turnaround time 4-6 weeks.
General Information: Public access terminal goes back to 1984. No sealed, adoptions, youthful offenders or juvenile records released. Will not fax documents. Certification fee: $1.00 per page. Payee: Clerk of Court. Only cashiers checks and money orders accepted. Prepayment required. SASE requested.

Probate Court 801 Forest Ave, #202, PO Box 187, Gadsden, AL 35901; phone: 256-549-2150, 256-549-5333; fax: 256-546-1149; hours 8AM-5PM. *Probate.*

Fayette County

Circuit & District Court PO Box 906, 113 N Temple Ave, Fayette, AL 35555; phone: 205-932-4617; probate phone: 205-932-4519; fax: 205-932-2697; probate fax: 205-932-7600; hours 8AM-4:30PM (CST). *Felony, Misdemeanor, Civil, Eviction, Small Claims, Probate.*
Note: Probate court is separate from this court; mail to Probate at PO Box 670.

Civil Records: Access: Online, mail, fax, in person. Visitors must perform in person searches themselves. Court makes copy: $.25 per page; same fee for self serve. Required to search: name, years to search. Civil cases indexed by defendant. Civil records on computer from 3/94, on books and cards from 1977. Online access at www.alacourt.com.
Criminal Records: Access: Online, mail, fax, in person. Visitors must perform in person searches themselves. Court makes copy: $.25 per page; same fee for self serve. Required to search: name, years to search, DOB; also helpful: SSN. Criminal records on computer from 3/94, on books and cards from 1977. Online access via www.alacourt.com.
General Information: Public access terminal goes back to 1994. No sealed, adoptions, youthful offenders or juvenile records released. Will fax documents for $.25 per page. Certification fee: $1.00 per page. Payee: Circuit Clerk. Business checks accepted. Prepayment required.

Franklin County

Circuit & District Court PO Box 160, Russellville, AL 35653; phone: 256-332-8861; probate phone: 256-332-8802; hours 8AM-4:30PM (CST). *Felony, Misdemeanor, Civil, Eviction, Small Claims, Probate.*
Note: Probate court is separate and can be contacted at the telephone number above or PO Box 70.

Civil Records: Access: Mail, online, in person. Both court and visitors may perform in person searches.

Court makes copy: $.25 per page; same fee for self serve. Required to search: name, years to search; also helpful: address. Civil cases indexed by defendant, plaintiff. Civil records on computer from 1993, on index books prior. SSN and DOB helpful, but records are not indexed by SSN. Online access at www.alacourt.com. Mail turnaround time 3-4 days.
Criminal Records: Access: Mail, online, in person. Both court and visitors may perform in person searches. Court makes copy: $.25 per page; same fee for self serve. Required to search: name, years to search, DOB; also helpful: SSN. Criminal records on computer from 1993, on index books prior. SSN and DOB helpful, but records are not indexed by SSN. Online access via www.alacourt.com. Mail turnaround time 3-4 days.
General Information: Public access terminal goes back to 1993. No sealed, youthful offenders or juvenile released. Certification fee: $2.00. Payee: Circuit Court Clerk. Business checks accepted. Prepayment and SASE required.

Geneva County

Circuit & District Court PO Box 86, Geneva, AL 36340; phone: 334-684-5620; probate phone: 334-684-5640; fax: 334-684-5605; hours 8AM-5PM (CST). *Felony, Misdemeanor, Civil, Eviction, Small Claims, Probate.*
Note: Probate court is separate index at this same address.

Civil Records: Access: Mail, online, in person. Visitors must perform in person searches themselves. Search fee: $5.00 per name. Court makes copy: $.25 per page; same fee for self serve. Required to search: name, years to search; also helpful: address. Civil cases indexed by defendant, plaintiff. Civil records on computer from 1992. Online access at www.alacourt.com. Mail turnaround time varies.
Criminal Records: Access: Mail, online, in person. Visitors must perform in person searches themselves. Search fee: $5.00 per name. Court makes copy: $.25 per page; same fee for self serve. Required to search: name, years to search, DOB; also helpful: SSN. Criminal records on computer from 1992. Online access via www.alacourt.com. Mail turnaround time varies.
General Information: Public access terminal goes back to 1992. No sealed, adoptions, youthful offenders or juvenile records released. Will not fax documents. Certification fee: $2.00 per case. Payee: Circuit Clerk. Business checks accepted. Out of state personal checks not accepted. Prepayment and SASE required.

Greene County

Circuit & District Court PO Box 307, Eutaw, AL 35462; phone: 205-372-3598; probate phone: 205-372-3340; criminal records fax: 205-372-1510; civil records fax: same; hours 8AM-12;00-1-4:30PM (CST). *Felony, Misdemeanor, Civil, Eviction, Small Claims, Probate.*
Note: Probate is a separate court.

Civil Records: Access: Mail, online, in person. Both court and visitors may perform in person searches. No search fee. Court makes copy: $.25 per page; same fee for self serve. Required to search: name, years to search; also helpful: DOB, SSN and signed release. Civil cases indexed by defendant, plaintiff. Civil records on books from 1984. Online access at www.alacourt.com. Mail turnaround time 1 week.
Criminal Records: Access: Mail, online, in person. Visitors must perform in person searches themselves. No search fee. Court makes copy: $.25 per page; same fee for self serve. Required to search: name, years to search; also helpful: DOB, SSN and signed release. Criminal records on books from 1984. Online access via www.alacourt.com. Mail turnaround time 1 week.
General Information: Public access terminal goes back to 1993. No sealed, adoptions, youthful offenders or juvenile records released. Certification

fee: $1.00 per page. Payee: Circuit Clerk. Business checks accepted. Prepayment and SASE required.

Hale County

Circuit & District Court Hale County Courthouse, Rm 8, PO Drawer 99, Greensboro, AL 36744; phone: 334-624-4334; probate phone: 334-624-8740; hours 8AM-5PM (CST). *Felony, Misdemeanor, Civil, Eviction, Small Claims, Probate.*
Note: Probate court is separate from this court; probate phone number above.

Civil Records: Access: Mail, online, in person. Both court and visitors may perform in person searches. No search fee. Court makes copy: $.25 per page. Required to search: name, years to search. Civil cases indexed by defendant, plaintiff. Civil records on books from 1985. Online access at www.alacourt.com. Mail turnaround time 1 week.
Criminal Records: Access: Mail, online, in person. Both court and visitors may perform in person searches. No search fee. Court makes copy: $.25 per page. Required to search: name, years to search; also helpful: DOB, SSN. Criminal records on books from 1985. Online access via www.alacourt.com. Mail turnaround time 1 week.
General Information: Public access terminal has criminal back to 1997 and civil back to 1994. No sealed, adoptions, youthful offenders or juvenile records released. Will fax documents to local and toll free lines. Certification fee: $1.00 per page. Payee: Clerk of the Court. Business checks accepted. No personal checks accepted. Prepayment and SASE required.

Henry County

Circuit & District Court 101 W Court St, #J, Abbeville, AL 36310-2135; phone: 334-585-2753; probate phone: 334-585-3257; fax: 334-585-5006; hours 8AM-4:30PM (CST). *Felony, Misdemeanor, Civil, Eviction, Small Claims, Probate.*
Note: Probate court is separate from this court; probate phone number above.

Civil Records: Access: Mail, online, in person. Both court and visitors may perform in person searches. Search fee: $3.00 per name. Court makes copy: $.25 per page; same fee for self serve. Required to search: name, years to search. Civil cases indexed by defendant. Civil records on computer from 1994, index cards 10 yrs back. Online access at www.alacourt.com. Mail turnaround time 2-3 days.
Criminal Records: Access: Mail, online, in person. Both court and visitors may perform in person searches. Search fee: $3.00 per name. Court makes copy: $.25 per page; same fee for self serve. Required to search: name, years to search, DOB; also helpful: SSN. Criminal records on computer from 5/93, index cards 10 yrs back. Online access via www.alacourt.com. Mail turnaround time 2-3 days.
General Information: Public access terminal has criminal back to 1993 and civil back to 1994. No sealed, adoptions, youthful offenders or juvenile records released. Certification fee: $1.00 per cert. Payee: Circuit Clerk. No personal checks accepted. Prepayment and SASE required.

Houston County

Circuit & District Court PO Drawer 6406, Dothan, AL 36302; phone: 334-677-4800/4872; criminal phone: Circ-334-677-4863; Dist-334-677-4872; civil phone: Circ-334-677-4858; Dist-334-677-4868; probate phone: 334-677-4734; probate fax: 334-702-0032; hours 7:30AM-4:30PM (CST). *Felony, Misdemeanor, Civil, Eviction, Small Claims, Probate.*
Note: Probate court is separate from this court; probate phone number above.

Civil Records: Access: Mail, online, in person. Both court and visitors may perform in person searches. No search fee. Court makes copy: $.25 per page.

Required to search: name, years to search. Civil cases indexed by defendant. Civil records on computer from 1977, index books from 1950s. Online access at www.alacourt.com. Mail turnaround time 1 week.

Criminal Records: Access: Mail, online, in person. Both court and visitors may perform in person searches. No search fee. Court makes copy: $.25 per page; same fee for self serve. Required to search: name, years to search; also helpful: DOB, SSN. Criminal records on computer from 1977, index books from 1950s. Online access via www.alacourt.com. Mail turnaround time 1 week.

General Information: Public access terminal available. No sealed, adoptions, youthful offenders or juvenile records released. Certification fee: $1.00. Payee: Judy Byrd. Business checks accepted. Prepayment required.

Jackson County

Circuit & District Court PO Box 397, Scottsboro, AL 35768; phone: 256-574-9320; criminal phone: 256-574-9320; civil phone: 256-574-9320; probate phone: 256-574-9290; fax: 256-259-9981; probate fax: 256-574-9318; hours 8AM-4:30PM (CST). *Felony, Misdemeanor, Civil, Eviction, Small Claims, Probate.*

Note: Probate office is at a separate office at the courthouse (PO Box 128) and can be contacted at the telephone number above or 256-574-9295.

Civil Records: Access: Mail, fax, online, in person. Both court and visitors may perform in person searches. No search fee. Court makes copy: $.25 per page; same fee for self serve. Required to search: name, years to search. Civil cases indexed by defendant. Civil records on computer from 5/1993, on cards from 1977. Online access at www.alacourt.com. Mail turnaround time 1-2 weeks.

Criminal Records: Access: Mail, fax, online, in person. Both court and visitors may perform in person searches. No search fee. Court makes copy: $.25 per page; same fee for self serve. Required to search: name, years to search, DOB; also helpful: SSN. Criminal records on computer from 5/1993, on cards from 1977. Online access via www.alacourt.com. Mail turnaround time 1-2 weeks.

General Information: Public access terminal available. No sealed, adoptions, youthful offenders or juvenile records released. Will fax documents only if situation urgent enough to require quick return. Certification fee: $2.00. Payee: Circuit Court Clerk. Only cashiers checks and money orders accepted. Prepayment and SASE required.

Jefferson County

Circuit Court - Bessemer Division Rm 606, Courthouse Annex, Bessemer, AL 35020; phone: 205-481-4165; hours 8AM-5PM (CST). *Felony, Civil Actions Over $10,000.*

Civil Records: Access: Mail, online, in person. Visitors must perform in person searches themselves. No search fee. Court makes copy: $.25 per page. Required to search: name, years to search. Civil cases indexed by defendant, plaintiff. Civil records on computer from 1988, on index books from 1930s to 1977. Online access at www.alacourt.com.

Criminal Records: Access: Online, in person. Visitors must perform in person searches themselves. Court makes copy: $.25 per page. Required to search: name, years to search, DOB; also helpful: SSN. Criminal records on computer from 1988, on index books from 1930s to 1977. Online access via www.alacourt.com.

General Information: Public access terminal available. No sealed, adoptions, youthful offenders or juvenile records released. Certification fee: $1.25. Payee: Clerk of Circuit Court. Only cashiers checks and money orders accepted. Prepayment required.

District Court - Bessemer Division Rm 506, Courthouse Annex, 1801 Third Ave N, Bessemer, AL 35020; phone: 205-481-4187; probate phone: 205-481-4100; hours 8AM-5PM (CST). *Misdemeanor, Civil Actions Under $10,000, Eviction, Small Claims.*

Civil Records: Access: Online, in person. Visitors must perform in person searches themselves. Court makes copy: $.25 per page; same fee for self serve. Required to search: name, years to search. Civil cases indexed by defendant, plaintiff. Civil records on computer from 1986, on index cards from 1977, prior on docket books. Online access at www.alacourt.com.

Criminal Records: Access: Online, in person, mail. Visitors must perform in person searches themselves. No search fee. Court makes copy: $.25 per page; same fee for self serve. Required to search: name, years to search, DOB; also helpful: SSN. Criminal records on computer from 1986, on index cards from 1977, prior on docket books. Online access via www.alacourt.com. Mail turnaround time varies.

General Information: Public access terminal goes back to 1995. No sealed, adoptions, youthful offenders or juvenile records released. Certification fee: $1.00 per cert. Payee: Bessemer District Court. Business checks accepted; no personal checks. Prepayment required. SASE not required.

Circuit Court - Birmingham Civil Division 716 N 21st St, Rm 400, Birmingham, AL 35263; phone: 205-325-5355; hours 8AM-5PM (CST). *Civil Actions Over $10,000 (Over $5,000 if jury trial).*

Civil Records: Access: Phone, mail, online, in person. Both court and visitors may perform in person searches. Court makes copy: $.25 per page. Required to search: name, years to search. Civil cases indexed by defendant, plaintiff. Civil records on computer from 1976, on index books from 1976 to 1986, prior to 1976 archived. Online access at www.alacourt.com. Mail turnaround time 1-2 weeks.

General Information: Public access terminal available. No sealed, adoptions, youthful offenders or juvenile records released. Will not fax documents. Certification fee: $1.25. Payee: Clerk of Circuit Court. Business checks accepted. Prepayment required.

Circuit Court - Birmingham Criminal Division 801 Richard Arrington Blvd, Rm 901, Birmingham, AL 35263; phone: 205-325-5285; criminal phone: 205-325-5285; civil phone: 205-325-5355; hours 8AM-4:55PM (CST). *Felony.*

Criminal Records: Access: Online, in person. Visitors must perform in person searches themselves. Court makes copy: $.25 per page. Required to search: name, years to search, DOB, signed release; also helpful: address, SSN. Criminal records on computer from 1960s, index books prior. Online access through SJIS. See state introduction.

General Information: Public access terminal has only criminal records. No sealed, adoptions, youthful offenders, sex offender cases or juvenile records released. Will not fax documents. Certification fee: $1.00 per page. Payee: Clerk of Court. Only cashiers checks and money orders accepted. Prepayment required.

District Court - Birmingham Civil Division 716 Richard Arrington BLVD N, Birmingham, AL 35203; phone: 205-325-5331; probate phone: 205-325-5420; hours 8AM-5PM (CST). *Civil Actions Under $10,000, Eviction, Small Claims.*

Civil Records: Access: Online, in person. Both court and visitors may perform in person searches. No search fee. Court makes copy: $.25 per page; same fee for self serve. Required to search: name, years to search. Civil cases indexed by defendant, plaintiff. Civil records on computer from 1977, index books stored in warehouse. Online access at www.alacourt.com. Mail turnaround time 1-7 days.

General Information: Public access terminal has only civil records back to 1977; also some criminal records. No sealed, adoptions, youthful offenders or juvenile records released. Will not fax documents. Certification fee: $1.00. Payee: District Court. Only cashiers checks and money orders accepted. Prepayment required.

District Court - Birmingham Criminal Division 801 Richard Arrington Blvd N, Rm 207, Birmingham, AL 35203; phone: 205-325-5309; hours 8AM-5PM (CST). *Misdemeanor.*

Criminal Records: Access: Mail, online, in person. Both court and visitors may perform in person searches. Search fee: $1.25. Court makes copy: $.25 per page. Required to search: name, DOB; also helpful: years to search, SSN, sex, date of arrest. Criminal records on computer from 1986. To search for records prior to 1987, require arrest date. Online access through SJIS. See state introduction Mail turnaround time 5-10 days.

General Information: Public access terminal has only criminal records back to 1986. No sealed, sexual abuse, adoptions, youthful offenders or juvenile records released. Certification fee: $1.25. Payee: District Court. Only cashiers checks and money orders accepted. Prepayment and SASE required.

Probate Court 716 Richard Arrington Jr Blvd N., Birmingham, AL 35203; phone: 205-325-5411; fax: 205-325-4885; hours 8AM-4:45PM (CST). *Probate.*

Lamar County

Circuit & District Court PO Box 434, Vernon, AL 35592; phone: 205-695-7193; probate phone: 205-695-9119; fax: 205-695-0046; hours 8AM-4:30PM (CST). *Felony, Misdemeanor, Civil, Eviction, Small Claims, Probate.*

Note: Probate court is separate from this court; probate phone number above.

Civil Records: Access: Mail, online, in person. Visitors must perform in person searches themselves. No search fee. Court makes copy: $.25 per page; same fee for self serve. Required to search: name, years to search; also helpful: address. Civil cases indexed by defendant, plaintiff. Civil records on books from 1900; computerized records go back to 1995. Online access at www.alacourt.com. Mail turnaround time 1-2 days.

Criminal Records: Access: Mail, fax, online, in person. Visitors must perform in person searches themselves. No search fee. Court makes copy: $.25 per page; same fee for self serve. Required to search: name, years to search, DOB, signed release; also helpful: SSN. Criminal records on books from 1900; computerized records go back to 1995. Online access via www.alacourt.com. Mail turnaround time 1-2 days.

General Information: Public access terminal has criminal back to 1995 and civil back to 1992. No sealed, adoptions, youthful offenders or juvenile records released. Certification fee: $2.25. Payee: Circuit Clerk. Only cashiers checks and money orders accepted. Prepayment required. Will bill copy fees. SASE required.

Lauderdale County

Circuit Court PO Box 795, Florence, AL 35631; phone: 256-760-5710; criminal phone: 256-760-5713; probate phone: 256-760-5800; fax: 256-760-5727; hours 8AM-N, 1-5PM (CST). *Felony, Civil Actions Over $10,000, Probate.*

Note: Probate court is separate from this court; probate phone number above.

Civil Records: Access: Online, in person. Visitors must perform in person searches themselves. Court makes copy: $.25 per page. Self serve copy fee: $.25 per page. Required to search: name, years to search. Civil cases indexed by defendant, plaintiff. Civil records on computer from 1977, index books from the 1930s. Online access at www.alacourt.com.

Criminal Records: Access: Online, in person. Visitors must perform in person searches themselves. Court makes copy: $.25 per page. Self serve copy fee: $.25 per page. Required to search: name, years to search, DOB; also helpful: SSN. Criminal records on computer from 1977, index books from the 1930s. Online access via www.alacourt.com.

General Information: Public access terminal available. No sealed, adoptions, youthful offenders or juvenile records released. Certification fee: $1.00. Payee: Circuit Court Clerk. Personal checks accepted. Prepayment required.

District Court PO Box 776, Florence, AL 35631; phone: 256-760-5726; criminal phone: 256-760-5724; civil phone: 256-760-5722; fax: 256-760-5727; hours 8AM-N, 1-5PM (CST). *Misdemeanor, Civil Actions Under $10,000, Eviction, Small Claims.*

Civil Records: Access: Mail, fax, online, in person. Visitors must perform in person searches themselves. No search fee. Court makes copy: $.25 per page. Required to search: name, years to search. Civil cases indexed by defendant, plaintiff. Civil records on computer from 1986, books from 1930s. Online access at www.alacourt.com. Mail turnaround time 1 week.

Criminal Records: Access: Mail, fax, online, in person. Visitors must perform in person searches themselves. No search fee. Court makes copy: $.25 per page. Required to search: name, years to search, DOB; also helpful: SSN. Criminal records on computer from 1986, books from the 1930s. Online access via www.alacourt.com. Mail turnaround time 1 week.

General Information: Public access terminal available. No sealed, adoptions, youthful offenders or juvenile records released. No fee to fax documents. Certification fee: $1.00. Payee: District Clerk. Personal checks accepted. Prepayment required.

Lawrence County

Circuit & District Court PO Box 249, Moulton, AL 35650; phone: 256-974-2432; criminal phone: 256-974-2436; civil phone: 256-974-2435; probate phone: 256-974-2439; hours 8AM-N, 1-4PM (CST). *Felony, Misdemeanor, Civil, Eviction, Small Claims, Probate.*

Note: Probate court is separate from this court; probate phone number above.

Civil Records: Access: Online, in person. Visitors must perform in person searches themselves. Court makes copy: $.25 per page. Required to search: name, years to search. Civil cases indexed by defendant. Civil records on computer from mid-1994, on books and index cards from 1920s. Online access at www.alacourt.com.

Criminal Records: Access: Online, in person. Visitors must perform in person searches themselves. Court makes copy: $.25 per page. Required to search: name, years to search; also helpful: DOB, SSN. Criminal records on computer from mid-1994, on books and index cards from 1920s. Online access via www.alacourt.com.

General Information: Public access terminal goes back to 1994. No sealed, adoption, youthful offender, juvenile records released. Certification fee: $1.00 per cert. Payee: Court clerk. Prepayment required.

Lee County

Circuit & District Court 2311 Gateway Dr, Rm 104, Opelika, AL 36801; phone: 334-749-7141; fax: 334-737-3520; hours 8:30AM-4:30PM; no phone svc 12-2PM (CST). *Felony, Misdemeanor, Civil, Eviction, Small Claims.*

Note: Probate court is separate from this court, and can be contacted at 334-745-9761 or at Lee County Courthouse, 215 S 9 St, Opelika, AL 36801.

Civil Records: Access: Phone, mail, online, in person. Only the court performs in person searches; visitors may not. No search fee. Court makes copy: $.50 per page. Required to search: name, years to

search. Civil cases indexed by defendant, plaintiff. Civil records on computer from 1980s, on index cards from 1988. Online access at www.alacourt.com. Mail turnaround time 1 week.

Criminal Records: Access: Phone, mail, online, in person. Only the court performs in person searches; visitors may not. No search fee. Court makes copy: $.50 per page. Required to search: name, years to search; also helpful: DOB, SSN. Criminal records on computer from 1980s, on index cards from 1988. Online access via www.alacourt.com. Mail turnaround time 1 week/varies

General Information: No public access terminal. No sealed, adoptions, youthful offenders or juvenile records released. Certification fee: $1.00 per page. Payee: Clerk's Office. Only cashiers checks and money orders accepted. SASE required.

Limestone County

Circuit & District Court 200 Washington St West, Athens, AL 35611; phone: 256-233-6406; probate phone: 256-233-6427; hours 8AM-4:30PM (CST). *Felony, Misdemeanor, Civil, Eviction, Small Claims, Probate.*

Note: Probate court is separate from this court; probate phone number above.

Civil Records: Access: Mail, in person. Both court and visitors may perform in person searches. No search fee. Court makes copy: $.25 per page. Required to search: name, years to search. Civil cases indexed by defendant, plaintiff. Civil records on computer since 1992; prior in docket books. Mail turnaround time 2 weeks.

Criminal Records: Access: Mail, in person. Both court and visitors may perform in person searches. No search fee. Court makes copy: $.25 per page. Required to search: name, years to search, DOB; also helpful: SSN, sex. Criminal records on computer since 1992, prior in docket books. Mail turnaround time 2 weeks.

General Information: Public access terminal goes back to 1900. No juvenile, youthful offender records released. Certification fee: $1.00. Payee: Clerk of Court. Personal checks accepted. Prepayment and SASE required.

Lowndes County

Circuit & District Court PO Box 876, Hayneville, AL 36040; phone: 334-548-2252; probate phone: 334-548-2365; criminal records fax: 334-548-2548; civil records fax: same; hours 8AM-4:30PM (CST). *Felony, Misdemeanor, Civil, Eviction, Small Claims, Probate.*

Note: Probate court is separate from this court; probate phone number above.

Civil Records: Access: Mail, online, in person. Both court and visitors may perform in person searches. Search fee: $10.00 per name. Court makes copy: $.25 per page; same fee for self serve. Required to search: name, years to search. Civil cases indexed by defendant, plaintiff. Civil records on index cards from 1977; computerized since 1996. Online access at www.alacourt.com. Mail turnaround time up to 1 week.

Criminal Records: Access: Mail, online, in person. Both court and visitors may perform in person searches. Search fee: $10.00 per name. Court makes copy: $.25 per page; same fee for self serve. Required to search: name, years to search; also helpful: DOB, SSN. Criminal records on index cards from 1977; computerized since 1996. Online access via www.alacourt.com. Mail turnaround time up to 1 week.

General Information: Public access terminal goes back to 1995. No sealed, adoptions, youthful offenders or juvenile records released. Will fax documents to local or toll free line. Certification fee: $1.00 per cert. Payee: District Court Clerk. Business checks accepted. SASE required.

Macon County

Circuit & District Court PO Box 830723, Tuskegee, AL 36083; phone: 334-724-2614; probate phone: 334-724-2611; hours 8AM-12;00-1-4:30PM (CST). *Felony, Misdemeanor, Civil, Eviction, Small Claims, Probate.*

Note: Probate court is separate from this court; probate phone number above.

Civil Records: Access: Mail, online, in person. Both court and visitors may perform in person searches. Search fee: $10.00 per name. Court makes copy: $.25 per page. Required to search: name, years to search. Civil cases indexed by defendant, plaintiff. Civil records on index books from 1977; on computer back to 1993. Online access at www.alacourt.com. Mail turnaround time 30 days.

Criminal Records: Access: Mail, online, in person. Only the court performs in person searches; visitors may not. Search fee: $10.00 per name. Court makes copy: $.25 per page. Required to search: name, years to search; also helpful: DOB, SSN. Criminal records go back to 1977; on computer back to 1993. Online access via www.alacourt.com. Mail turnaround time 30 days.

General Information: No public access terminal. No sealed, adoption, youthful offender, juvenile records released. Will fax documents to local or toll free line. Certification fee: $2.50 per page includes copy fee. Payee: Office of Circuit Clerk. Business checks accepted. Prepayment required. SASE not required.

Madison County

Circuit Court - Civil 100 N Side Square, Courthouse, Huntsville, AL 35801; phone: 256-532-3381; probate phone: 256-532-3330; fax: 256-532-3768; hours 8AM-5PM (CST). *Civil Actions Over $10,000, Probate.*

Note: Probate court is separate from this court, and can be contacted at the telephone number above

Civil Records: Access: Online, in person. Visitors must perform in person searches themselves. Court makes copy: $.25 per page; same fee for self serve. Required to search: name, years to search; also helpful: address. Civil cases indexed by defendant, plaintiff. Civil records on computer from 1977, index books from 1937. Online access through SJIS. See state introduction

General Information: Public access terminal has only civil records back to 1977. No sealed, adoptions, youthful offenders or juvenile records released. Certification fee: $1.00. Personal checks accepted. Prepayment required.

Circuit Court - Criminal 100 N Side Square, Courthouse, Huntsville, AL 35801-4820; phone: 256-532-3386; Hours: 8:30AM-5PM (CST). *Felony.*

Criminal Records: Access: Online, in person. Visitors must perform in person searches themselves. Court makes copy: $.25 per page. Required to search: name, years to search; also helpful: DOB, SSN. Criminal records on computer from 1977, books from 1937. Online access through SJIS. See state introduction

General Information: Public access terminal has only criminal records back to 1977. No sealed, adoptions, youthful offenders or juvenile records released. Certification fee: $1.00 per cert. Payee: Circuit Court Clerk. No personal checks accepted. Prepayment required.

District Court 100 N Side Square, Rm 822 Courthouse, Huntsville, AL 35801; criminal phone: 256-532-3373; civil phone: 256-532-3622; fax: 256-532-6972; hours 8:30AM-5PM (CST). *Misdemeanor, Civil Actions Under $10,000, Eviction, Small Claims.*

Civil Records: Access: Online, in person. Visitors must perform in person searches themselves. Court makes copy: $.25 per page. Required to search: name, years to search. Civil cases indexed by defendant, plaintiff. Civil records on computer from 1982, index books prior. Online access at www.alacourt.com.

Criminal Records: Access: Online, in person. Visitors must perform in person searches themselves. Court makes copy: $.25 per page. Required to search: name, years to search; also helpful: DOB, SSN. Criminal records on computer from 1982, index books prior since 1979. Online access via www.alacourt.com.

General Information: Public access terminal has criminal back to 1977 and civil back to 1980. No sealed, adoptions, youthful offenders or juvenile records released. Certification fee: $1.00 per cert. Payee: District Court. Only cashiers checks and money orders accepted. Prepayment required.

Marengo County

Circuit & District Court PO Box 480566, Linden, AL 36748; phone: 334-295-2220; hours 8-11AM, 1-4:30PM (CST). *Felony, Misdemeanor, Civil, Eviction, Small Claims, Probate.*

Civil Records: Access: Mail, online, in person. Both court and visitors may perform in person searches. No search fee. Court makes copy: $.25 per page. Self serve copy fee: none. Required to search: name, years to search. Civil cases indexed by defendant, plaintiff. Civil records on computer from 6/94, on books and index cards from 1965. Online access at www.alacourt.com. Mail turnaround time 1 week.

Criminal Records: Access: Mail, online, in person. Both court and visitors may perform in person searches. No search fee. Court makes copy: $.25 per page. Self serve copy fee: none. Required to search: name, years to search; also helpful: DOB, SSN. Criminal records on computer from 6/94, on books and index cards from 1965. Online access via www.alacourt.com. Mail turnaround time 1 week.

General Information: Public access terminal goes back to 1994. No sealed, adoptions, youthful offenders or juvenile records released. Certification fee: $1.00 per page. Payee: Circuit Clerk. Business checks accepted. No personal checks or credit cards. Prepayment required.

Marion County

Circuit & District Court PO Box 1595, Hamilton, AL 35570; phone: 205-921-7451; probate phone: 205-921-2471; hours 8AM-5PM (CST). *Felony, Misdemeanor, Civil, Eviction, Small Claims, Probate.*

Note: Probate court is separate from this court; probate phone number above.

Civil Records: Access: Mail, online, in person. Both court and visitors may perform in person searches. No search fee. Court makes copy: $.50 per page. Required to search: name, years to search. Civil cases indexed by defendant, plaintiff. Civil records on computer from 5/94, on books from 1950s. Online access at www.alacourt.com. Mail turnaround time 7-10 days.

Criminal Records: Access: Mail, online, in person. Both court and visitors may perform in person searches. No search fee. Court makes copy: $.50 per page. Required to search: name, years to search; also helpful: DOB, SSN. Criminal records on computer from 5/94, on books from 1950s. Online access via www.alacourt.com. Mail turnaround time 7-10 days.

General Information: Public access terminal available. No sealed, adoptions, youthful offenders or juvenile records released. Certification fee: $1.50. Payee: Circuit Clerk. Only cashiers checks and money orders accepted. SASE required.

Marshall County

Circuit & District Court - Albertville Division 133 S.Emmet St., Albertville, AL 35950; phone: 256-878-4522/4521/4515; criminal phone: 256-878-4522; civil phone: 256-878-4521; probate phone: 256-571-7764; hours 8AM-4:30PM (CST). *Felony, Misdemeanor, Civil, Eviction, Small Claims.*

Civil Records: Access: Mail, online, in person. Both court and visitors may perform in person searches. No search fee. Court makes copy: $.25 per page. Self

serve copy fee: $.12 per page. Required to search: name, years to search. Civil cases indexed by defendant. Civil records on computer from 1974. Online access at www.alacourt.com.

Criminal Records: Access: In person, online. Both court and visitors may perform in person searches. No search fee. Court makes copy: $.25 per page. Self serve copy fee: $.12 per page. Required to search: name, years to search, DOB; also helpful: SSN. Criminal records on computer from 8/92, on index books from 1974. Online access via www.alacourt.com.

General Information: Public access terminal has only civil records back to 8/1992. No sealed, adoptions, youthful offenders or juvenile records released. Will not fax documents. Certification fee: $1.00 per page plus court copy fee. Payee: Clerk of Courts. Business checks accepted. Prepayment required.

Circuit Court - Guntersville Civil Division 424 Blount Ave #201, Guntersville, AL 35976; phone: 256-571-7788; probate phone: 256-571-7764; hours 8AM-Noon; 1-4:30PM (CST). *Civil Actions Over $10,000, Small Claims, Probate.*

Note: Probate court is separate from this court, and can be contacted at the telephone number above

Civil Records: Access: Online, in person. Visitors must perform in person searches themselves. Court makes copy: $.25 per page. Required to search: name, years to search. Civil cases indexed by defendant, plaintiff. Civil records on computer for past 10 years, on index books early 1900s. Online access through SJIS. See state introduction

General Information: Public access terminal has only civil records back to 1992. No sealed, adoptions, youthful offenders or juvenile records released. Certification fee: $1.00. Payee: Circuit Clerk. Business checks accepted. Prepayment required.

Circuit Court - Guntersville Criminal Division 424 Blount Ave #201, Guntersville, AL 35976; phone: 256-571-7791; hours 7-11AM; 2-4:30PM (CST). *Felony, Misdemeanor.*

Criminal Records: Access: Online, in person. Visitors must perform in person searches themselves. Court makes copy: $.25 per page. Required to search: name, years to search; also helpful: DOB, SSN. Criminal records on computer from 1992, on index books from 1984, prior back to 1930s. Online access through SJIS. See state introduction

General Information: Public access terminal has only criminal records. No sealed, adoptions, youthful offenders or juvenile records released. Certification fee: $1.00. Payee: Circuit Clerk. Business checks accepted. Prepayment required.

Mobile County

Circuit Court 205 Government St #C-913, Mobile, AL 36644-2913; phone: 251-574-8786; criminal phone: 251-574-8430; civil phone: 251-574-8525; hours 8AM-1:30PM (CST). *Felony, Civil Actions Over $10,000.*

Note: Courthouse information line is 251-574-4636.

Civil Records: Access: Online, in person. Visitors must perform in person searches themselves. Court makes copy: $.25 per page. Required to search: name, years to search. Civil cases indexed by defendant. Civil records on computer from 1977, microfiche from early 1900s. Online access at www.alacourt.com.

Criminal Records: Access: Online, in person. Visitors must perform in person searches themselves. Court makes copy: $.25 per page. Required to search: name, years to search; also helpful: DOB, SSN. Criminal records on computer from 1977, microfiche from early 1900s. Online access via www.alacourt.com.

General Information: Public access terminal available. No sealed, adoptions, youthful offenders or

juvenile records released. Certification fee: $1.25. Payee: Circuit Clerk. Cashiers checks and money orders accepted. Exact change for payment is required. Prepayment required. Exact change for payments is required.

District Court 205 Government St, Mobile, AL 36644; phone: 251-574-8520, 251-690-8525 (small claims); criminal phone: 251-574-8511; civil phone: 251-574-8526; probate phone: 251-574-8502; fax: 251-574-4840; hours 8AM-5PM (CST). *Misdemeanor, Civil Actions Under $10,000, Eviction, Small Claims, Probate.*

Note: Probate court is a separate court and can be reached at the telephone number given above.

Civil Records: Access: Phone, fax, mail, online, in person. Both court and visitors may perform in person searches. No search fee. Court makes copy: $.25 per page. Required to search: name, years to search. Civil cases indexed by defendant, plaintiff. Civil records on computer from 1977, index books from 1950s. Online access at www.alacourt.com. Access to the Probate court's recordings database is free at www.mobilecounty.org/probatecourt/recordssearch.htm. A second search is at www.mobilecounty.org/probatecourt/judicial.asp. Mail turnaround time 7 days.

Criminal Records: Access: Phone, mail, online, in person. Both court and visitors may perform in person searches. No search fee. Court makes copy: $.25 per page. Required to search: name, years to search, DOB; also helpful: SSN. Criminal records on computer from 1977, index books from 1950s. Online access via www.alacourt.com. Mail turnaround time 7 days.

General Information: Public access terminal available. No sealed, youthful offenders, protected files or juvenile records released. Will not fax documents. Certification fee: $1.25. Payee: Clerk, District Court. Business checks accepted if pre-approved. Prepayment and SASE required.

Monroe County

Circuit & District Court County Courthouse, 65 N Alabama Ave, Monroeville, AL 36460; phone: 251-743-2283; probate phone: 251-743-4107; hours 8AM-5PM (CST). *Felony, Misdemeanor, Civil, Eviction, Small Claims, Probate.*

Note: Probate court is separate from this court; probate phone number above.

Civil Records: Access: Mail, online, in person. Both court and visitors may perform in person searches. No search fee. Court makes copy: $.25 per page; same fee for self serve. Required to search: name, years to search. Civil cases indexed by defendant. Civil records on index cards from 1977 and on computer since 7/1994. Online access at www.alacourt.com. Mail turnaround time 1 week.

Criminal Records: Access: Mail, online, in person. Both court and visitors may perform in person searches. No search fee. Court makes copy: $.25 per page; same fee for self serve. Required to search: name, years to search; also helpful: DOB, SSN. Criminal records on index cards from 1977 and on computer since 7/1994. Online access via www.alacourt.com. Mail turnaround time 1 week.

General Information: Public access terminal goes back to 1977. No sealed, adoptions, youthful offenders or juvenile records released. Certification fee: $1.25 per page. Cert fee includes copies. Payee: John Sawyer, Circuit Clerk. Business checks accepted. Prepayment and SASE required.

Montgomery County

Circuit Court PO Box 1667, Montgomery, AL 36102-1667; phone: 334-832-1260; probate phone: 334-832-1237; hours 8AM-11:00-11:30- 4PM (CST). *Felony, Civil Actions Over $10,000, Probate.*

Note: Probate court is separate from this court; probate phone number above.

Civil Records: Access: Mail, online, in person. Both court and visitors may perform in person searches. No search fee. Court makes copy: $.25 per page. Required to search: name, years to search. Civil cases indexed by defendant, plaintiff. Civil records on computer from 1982, microfiche from 1976. Online access at www.alacourt.com. Mail turnaround time 3-4 days.

Criminal Records: Access: Mail, online, in person. Both court and visitors may perform in person searches. No search fee. Court makes copy: $.25 per page. Required to search: name, years to search; also helpful: DOB, SSN. Criminal records on computer from 1982, microfiche from 1976. Online access via www.alacourt.com. Mail turnaround time 3-4 days.

General Information: Public access terminal available. No sealed, youthful offenders or juvenile records released. Certification fee: $1.00 per copy. Cert fee includes copies. Payee: Circuit Clerk. Business checks accepted. Prepayment and SASE required.

District Court PO Box 1667, Montgomery, AL 36102; phone: 334-832-4950; Hours: 8AM-11:30AM, 12:30PM-4PM (CST). *Misdemeanor, Civil Actions Under $10,000, Eviction, Small Claims.*

Civil Records: Access: Mail, online, in person. Both court and visitors may perform in person searches. No search fee. Court makes copy: $.25 per page. Required to search: name, years to search. Civil cases indexed by defendant. Civil records on computer from the 1980s, index books from 1977. Online access at www.alacourt.com. Mail turnaround time 2 weeks.

Criminal Records: Access: Mail, online, in person. Both court and visitors may perform in person searches. No search fee. Court makes copy: $.25 per page. Required to search: name, years to search; also helpful: DOB, SSN. Criminal records on computer from the 1980s, index books from 1977. Online access via www.alacourt.com. Mail turnaround time 2 weeks.

General Information: Public access terminal goes back to 1995. No sealed, youthful offender, juvenile records released. Certification fee: $1.00 per cert. Payee: District Court. Only cashiers checks and money orders accepted. SASE not required.

Morgan County

Circuit Court PO Box 668, Decatur, AL 35602; phone: 256-351-4790; probate phone: 256-351-4675; hours 8AM-4:30PM (CST). *Felony, Civil Actions Over $10,000, Probate.*

Note: Probate court is separate from this court; probate phone number above.

Civil Records: Access: Online, in person. Visitors must perform in person searches themselves. Court makes copy: $.25 per page. Required to search: name, years to search. Civil cases indexed by defendant, plaintiff. Civil records on computer from 1994, on microfiche from 1950s, books from 1965. Online access at www.alacourt.com.

Criminal Records: Access: Online, in person. Visitors must perform in person searches themselves. Court makes copy: $.25 per page. Required to search: name, years to search; also helpful: DOB, SSN. Criminal records on computer from 1992. Online access via www.alacourt.com.

General Information: Public access terminal available. No sealed, adoption, youthful offender, juvenile records released. Certification fee: $1.00 per page. Payee: John Pat Orr, Circuit Clerk. Only cashiers checks and money orders accepted. Prepayment required.

District Court PO Box 668, Decatur, AL 35602; phone: 256-351-4649; hours 8:30AM-4:30PM (CST). *Misdemeanor, Civil Actions Under $10,000, Eviction, Small Claims.*

Civil Records: Access: Online, in person. Visitors must perform in person searches themselves. Court makes copy: $.25 per page. Required to search: name, years to search. Civil cases indexed by defendant.

Civil records on computer from 1992, books from 1960. Online access at www.alacourt.com.

Criminal Records: Access: Online, in person, mail. Visitors must perform in person searches themselves. Court makes copy: $.25 per page. Required to search: name, years to search; also helpful: DOB, SSN. Criminal records on computer from 1992, books from 1960. Online access via www.alacourt.com. Mail turnaround time varies.

General Information: Public access terminal available. No sealed, adoption, youthful offender, juvenile records released. Certification fee: $1.00. Payee: District Court. Only cashiers checks and money orders accepted. Prepayment and SASE required.

Perry County

Circuit & District Court PO Box 505, Marion, AL 36756; phone: 334-683-6106; probate phone: 334-683-2210; hours 8AM-4:30PM (CST). *Felony, Misdemeanor, Civil, Eviction, Small Claims, Probate.*

Note: Probate court is separate from this court; probate phone number above.

Civil Records: Access: Mail, online, in person. Both court and visitors may perform in person searches. No search fee. Court makes copy: $.25 per page. Required to search: name, years to search. Civil cases indexed by defendant, plaintiff. Civil records on books from 1900's, on computer back to 1990. Online access at www.alacourt.com. Mail turnaround time 2-3 days.

Criminal Records: Access: Mail, online, in person. Both court and visitors may perform in person searches. No search fee. Court makes copy: $.25 per page. Required to search: name, years to search; also helpful: DOB, SSN. Criminal records on index cards back to 1900, computerized back to 1990. Online access via www.alacourt.com. Mail turnaround time 2-3 days.

General Information: Public access terminal goes back to 1990. No sealed, adoption, youthful offender, juvenile records released. Certification fee: $1.00 per page. Payee: District Court Clerk. Business checks accepted. Prepayment and SASE required.

Pickens County

Circuit & District Court PO Box 418, Carrollton, AL 35447; phone: 205-367-2050; probate phone: 205-367-2010; hours 8AM-4:30PM (CST). *Felony, Misdemeanor, Civil, Eviction, Small Claims, Probate.*

Civil Records: Access: Mail, online, in person. Only the court performs in person searches; visitors may not. No search fee. Court makes copy: $.25 per page; same fee for self serve. Required to search: name, years to search. Civil cases indexed by defendant, plaintiff. Civil records on computer from 10/93, on books and index cards from 1840s. Online access at www.alacourt.com. Mail turnaround time 1-2 weeks.

Criminal Records: Access: Mail, online, in person. Only the court performs in person searches; visitors may not. No search fee. Court makes copy: $.25 per page; same fee for self serve. Required to search: name, years to search; also helpful: DOB, SSN. Criminal records on computer, on books and index cards from 1840s. Online access via www.alacourt.com. Mail turnaround time 1-2 weeks.

General Information: No public access terminal. No sealed, adoption, youthful offender, juvenile records released. Will not fax documents. Certification fee: $1.00 includes copy fee. Payee: District Court. Business checks accepted. Prepayment and SASE required.

Pike County

Circuit & District Court 120 W Church St, Troy, AL 36081; phone: 334-566-4622; criminal phone: 334-566-5113; civil phone: 334-566-5113; probate phone: 334-566-1246; hours 8AM-5PM

(CST). *Felony, Misdemeanor, Civil, Eviction, Small Claims, Probate.*

Note: Probate court is separate from this court, probate phone number above.

Civil Records: Access: Mail, online, in person. Both court and visitors may perform in person searches. Search fee: $5.00 per name. Court makes copy: $.25 per page. Required to search: name, years to search. Civil cases indexed by defendant, plaintiff. Civil records on computer from 1977, on books from 1938. Online access at www.alacourt.com. Mail turnaround time same day.

Criminal Records: Access: Mail, online, in person. Both court and visitors may perform in person searches. Search fee: $5.00 per name. Court makes copy: $.25 per page. Required to search: name, years to search, DOB, SSN. Criminal records on computer from 1977, on books from 1938. Online access via www.alacourt.com. Mail turnaround time same day.

General Information: Public access terminal goes back to 1993. (The index goes back further but there is very little case info.) No sealed, adoption, youthful offender, juvenile records released. Will not fax documents. Certification fee: $1.00 per page. Payee: Pike County Circuit/District Court. Only cashiers checks and money orders accepted. Prepayment and SASE required.

Randolph County

Circuit & District Court PO Box 328, Wedowee, AL 36278; phone: 256-357-4551; probate phone: 256-357-4933; hours 8AM-N, 1-5PM (CST). *Felony, Misdemeanor, Civil, Eviction, Small Claims, Probate.*

Note: Probate court is separate from this court; probate phone number above.

Civil Records: Access: Online, in person. Visitors must perform in person searches themselves. Court makes copy: $.25 per page; same fee for self serve. Required to search: name, years to search. Civil cases indexed by defendant, plaintiff. Civil records on computer from 1994. Online access at www.alacourt.gov.

Criminal Records: Access: Online, in person. Visitors must perform in person searches themselves. Court makes copy: $.25 per page; same fee for self serve. Required to search: name, years to search; also helpful: DOB, SSN. Criminal records index on computer from 1977. Online access via www.alacourt.gov.

General Information: Public access terminal available. No sealed, adoption, youthful offender, juvenile records released. Certification fee: $1.50 per page. Visitors may not make certifiable copies. Payee: Kim S Benefield. Business checks accepted. Prepayment required.

Russell County

Circuit & District Court PO Box 518, Phenix City, AL 36868; phone: 334-298-0516; probate phone: 334-298-7979; criminal records fax: 334-297-6250; civil records fax: same; hours 8:30AM-4:PM (EST). *Felony, Misdemeanor, Civil, Eviction, Small Claims, Probate.*

Note: Probate is separate office and separate index at this same address.

Civil Records: Access: Mail, in person, online. Visitors must perform in person searches themselves. No search fee. Court makes copy: $.25 per page. Required to search: name, years to search. Civil cases indexed by defendant, plaintiff. Civil records on computer from 1988, books from 1800s (prior to 1940 extremely difficult to find). Online access at www.alacourt.com from 1988 to present. Mail turnaround time 2 weeks.

Criminal Records: Access: Mail, in person, online. Visitors must perform in person searches themselves. No search fee. Court makes copy: $.25 per page. Required to search: name, years to search; also helpful: DOB, SSN. Criminal records on computer from 1988, books from 1800s (prior to 1940

extremely difficult to find). Online access via www.alacourt.com, from 1988 to present. Mail turnaround time 2 weeks.

General Information: Public access terminal has criminal back to 1977 and civil back to 1937 for divorce. No sealed, adoption, youthful offender, juvenile records released. Will not fax documents. Certification fee: $1.00 per cert. Payee: Clerk of Circuit Court. Business checks accepted. Prepayment required.

Shelby County

Circuit & District Court PO Box 1810, Columbiana, AL 35051; phone: 205-669-3760; probate phone: 205-669-3711; hours 8AM-4:30PM (CST). *Felony, Misdemeanor, Civil, Eviction, Small Claims, Probate.*
http://18jc.alacourt.gov
Note: Probate court is separate office at this same address.

Civil Records: Access: Mail, fax, online, in person. Visitors must perform in person searches themselves. No search fee. Court makes copy: $.25 per page. Self serve copy fee: $.25 per page. Required to search: name, years to search. Civil cases indexed by defendant, plaintiff. Civil records on computer from 1993, on index books from 1820s. Online access at www.alacourt.com.
Criminal Records: Access: Mail, fax, online, in person. Visitors must perform in person searches themselves. No search fee. Court makes copy: $.25 per page. Self serve copy fee: $.25 per page. Required to search: name, years to search, DOB; also helpful: SSN. Criminal records on computer from 1993, on index books from 1820s. Online access via www.alacourt.com.
General Information: Public access terminal goes back to 1993. No sealed, adoption, youthful offender, juvenile records released. Will not fax documents. Certification fee: $1.00 per page. Payee: Mary Harris, Circuit Clerk. Only cashiers checks and money orders accepted. Prepayment required.

St. Clair County

Circuit & District Court - Ashville Division PO Box 1569, Ashville, AL 35953; phone: 205-594-2184; probate phone: 205-594-2120; hours 8AM-5PM (CST). *Felony, Misdemeanor, Civil, Eviction, Small Claims, Probate.*
www.stclairco.com/
Note: Probate court is separate from this court; probate phone number above.

Civil Records: Access: Mail, online, in person. Both court and visitors may perform in person searches. No search fee. Court makes copy: $.25 per page; same fee for self serve. Required to search: name, years to search. Civil cases indexed by defendant, plaintiff. Civil records on computer from 1/94, in books from 1800s, no index before 1940. Online access at www.alacourt.com. Also, online access to probate records is by subscription at www.recordsusa.com/Alabama/CovingtonCnAl.htm. Credit card-username-password required; choose monthly or per-use plan. Visit the website or call Lisa at 601-264-7701 for information. Mail turnaround time 10 days.
Criminal Records: Access: Mail, online, in person. Both court and visitors may perform in person searches. No search fee. Court makes copy: $.25 per page; same fee for self serve. Required to search: name, years to search, DOB; also helpful: SSN. Criminal records on computer from 1/94, in books from 1800s, no index before 1940. The office will only do record searches by written request. Online access via www.alacourt.com. Mail turnaround time 10 days.
General Information: Public access terminal goes back to 1993. No sealed, adoption, youthful offender, juvenile records released. Certification fee: $1.25. Payee: Jeff Wyatt Circuit Clerk. Business checks accepted. Prepayment and SASE required.

Circuit & District Court - Pell City Division 1815 Cogswell Ave, #217, Pell City, AL 35125; phone: 205-338-2511; Circuit: 205-338-7224 District; probate phone: 205-338-9449; hours 8AM-5PM (CST). *Felony, Misdemeanor, Civil, Eviction, Small Claims, Probate.*
Note: Probate court is separate from this court; probate phone number above.

Civil Records: Access: Mail, online, in person. Both court and visitors may perform in person searches. No search fee. Court makes copy: $.25 per page; same fee for self serve. Required to search: name, years to search. Civil cases indexed by defendant, plaintiff. Civil records on computer from 11/93, on books from 1970s. Online access at www.alacourt.com. Also, online access to probate records is by subscription at www.recordsusa.com/Alabama/CovingtonCnAl.htm. Credit card-username-password required; choose monthly or per-use plan. Visit the website or call Lisa at 601-264-7701 for information. Mail turnaround time 7-14 days.
Criminal Records: Access: Mail, online, in person. Both court and visitors may perform in person searches. No search fee. Court makes copy: $.25 per page; same fee for self serve. Required to search: name, years to search, DOB; also helpful: SSN, signed release. Criminal records on computer from 11/93, on books from 1950s. Online access via www.alacourt.com. Mail turnaround time 7-14 days.
General Information: Public access terminal goes back to 1993. No sealed, adoption, youthful offender, juvenile records released. Certification fee: $1.25. Payee: Clerk of Courts. Business checks accepted. Prepayment and SASE required.

Sumter County

Circuit & District Court PO Box 936, 115 Franklin St, Livingston, AL 35470; phone: 205-652-2291; probate phone: 205-652-7281; hours 8AM-4:30PM (CST). *Felony, Misdemeanor, Civil, Eviction, Small Claims.*
Civil Records: Access: Mail, online, in person. Both court and visitors may perform in person searches. No search fee. Court makes copy: $.50 per page. Required to search: name, years to search. Civil cases indexed by defendant, plaintiff. Civil records on computer from early 1995, on index books from 1962. Online access at www.alacourt.com. Mail turnaround time 2 weeks.
Criminal Records: Access: Mail, online, in person. Both court and visitors may perform in person searches. No search fee. Court makes copy: $.50 per page. Required to search: name, years to search; also helpful: DOB, SSN. Criminal records on computer from early 1995, on index books from 1962. Online access via www.alacourt.com. Mail turnaround time 2 weeks.
General Information: Public access terminal available. No sealed, adoption, youthful offender, juvenile records released. Will not fax documents. Certification fee: $1.50. Payee: Circuit Court Clerk. Business checks accepted. Prepayment and SASE required.

Probate Court PO Box 1040, 115 Marshall St, Livingston, AL 35470; phone: 205-652-7281; fax: 205-652-6206; hours 8AM-4PM (CST). *Probate.*

Talladega County

Circuit & District Court - Northern Division PO 6137, 148 E. St N, Talladega, AL 35161; phone: 256-761-2102; hours 8AM-5PM (CST). *Felony, Misdemeanor, Civil, Eviction, Small Claims Probate.*
Civil Records: Access: Online, in person. Visitors must perform in person searches themselves. Court makes copy: $.25 per page; same fee for self serve. Required to search: name, years to search. Civil cases indexed by defendant, plaintiff. Civil records on computer from 1989, index books from 1970s. Online access at www.alacourt.com.

Criminal Records: Access: Online, in person. Visitors must perform in person searches themselves. Court makes copy: $.25 per page; same fee for self serve. Required to search: name, years to search; also helpful: DOB, SSN. Criminal records on computer from 1989, index books from 1970s. Online access via www.alacourt.com.
General Information: Public access terminal has criminal back to 1985 and civil back to 1989. No sealed, adoption, youthful offender, juvenile records released. Certification fee: $1.00 per cert. Payee: Circuit Court Clerk. Business checks accepted, no personal checks. Prepayment required.

District Court - Southern Division PO Box 183, Sylacauga, AL 35150; phone: 256-245-4352; fax: 256-249-1013; hours 7:30AM-4:30AM (CST). *Misdemeanor, Civil Actions Under $10,000, Eviction, Small Claims.*
Civil Records: Access: Mail, online, in person. Visitors must perform in person searches themselves. No search fee. Court makes copy: $.25 per page; same fee for self serve. Required to search: name, years to search. Civil cases indexed by defendant. Civil records on computer from 1977, on index books and cards prior to 1982 at the Northern Division District Court. Online access at www.alacourt.com. Mail turnaround time up to 7-10 days.
Criminal Records: Access: Mail, online, in person. Visitors must perform in person searches themselves. No search fee. Court makes copy: $.25 per page; same fee for self serve. Required to search: name, years to search; also helpful: DOB, SSN. Criminal records on computer from 1977, on index books and cards prior to 1982 at the Northern Division District Court. Online access via www.alacourt.com. Mail turnaround time up to 7-10 days.
General Information: Public access terminal available. No juvenile, youthful offender records released. Will fax documents to local or toll free line. Certification fee: $1.25 per page includes copy fee. Payee: Clerk of District Court. Business checks accepted. Prepayment and SASE required.

Probate Court PO Box 737, Talladega, AL 35161; phone: 256-362-4175; fax: 256-761-2128; hours 8AM-5PM (CST). *Probate.*

Tallapoosa County

Circuit & District Court - Eastern Division Tallapoosa County Courthouse, Dadeville, AL 36853; phone: 256-825-1098; probate phone: 256-825-4266; hours 8AM-5PM (CST). *Felony, Misdemeanor, Civil, Eviction, Small Claims, Probate.*
Note: Probate court is separate from this court; probate phone number above.

Civil Records: Access: Mail, online, in person. Only the court performs in person searches; visitors may not. Search fee: $3.00 per name. Court makes copy: $.50 per page. Required to search: name, years to search. Civil cases indexed by defendant, plaintiff. Civil records on computer from 1993, on index books from 1977. Online access at www.alacourt.com. Mail turnaround time 1-2 weeks.
Criminal Records: Access: Mail, online, in person. Only the court performs in person searches; visitors may not. Search fee: $3.00 per name. Court makes copy: $.50 per page. Required to search: name, years to search, DOB; also helpful: SSN. Criminal records on computer from 1993, on index books from 1977. Online access via www.alacourt.com. Mail turnaround time 1-2 weeks.
General Information: No public access terminal. No sealed, adoption, youthful offender, juvenile records released. Certification fee: $1.00. Payee: Circuit Clerk. Business checks accepted. Prepayment and SASE required.

Circuit & District Court - Western Division PO Box 189, Alexander City, AL 35011; phone: 256-329-8123/234-4361; criminal phone: 205-234-4361; civil phone: same; criminal records fax: 205-234-4389; civil records fax: same; hours 8AM-5PM (CST). *Felony, Misdemeanor, Civil, Eviction, Small Claims.*

Civil Records: Access: Mail, online, in person. Both court and visitors may perform in person searches. Search fee: $3.00 per name. Court makes copy: $.50 per page; same fee for self serve. Required to search: name, years to search. Civil cases indexed by defendant, plaintiff. Civil records on index books from 1977, prior in docket books; on computer back to 1994. Online access at www.alacourt.com. Mail turnaround time up to 2 weeks.

Criminal Records: Access: Mail, online, in person. Both court and visitors may perform in person searches. Search fee: $3.00 per name. Court makes copy: $.50 per page; same fee for self serve. Required to search: name, years to search, DOB; also helpful: SSN, signed release. Criminal records on index books from 1977, prior in docket books; on computer back to 1994. Online access via www.alacourt.com. Mail turnaround time up to 2 weeks.

General Information: No public access terminal. No sealed, adoption, youthful offender, juvenile records released. Will fax documents to local or toll free line. Certification fee: $1.00 per cert. Payee: Clerk of Courts. Business checks accepted. Prepayment required. SASE requested.

Tuscaloosa County

Circuit Court - Civil 714 Greensboro Ave, 2nd Fl, Tuscaloosa, AL 35401; phone: 205-349-3870; civil phone: Circ-205-349-3870 X260; Dist: X357; probate phone: 205-349-3870 X203; hours 8:30AM-5PM (CST). *Civil Actions over $10,000.*
Note: Probate is on 1st Fl and is separate from this court; probate phone number above.

Civil Records: Access: Online, in person. Visitors must perform in person searches themselves. Court makes copy: $.25 per page; same fee for self serve. Required to search: name, years to search. Civil cases indexed by defendant, plaintiff. Civil records on computer from 1977, index books early 1900s. Online access at www.alacourt.com.

General Information: Public access terminal goes back to 1977. (Terminal search requires name, other names used, and DOB.) No sealed, adoption, youthful offender, juvenile records released. Will not fax documents. Certification fee: $1.00. Payee: Circuit Clerk. Business checks accepted. Prepayment required.

District Courts - Civil PO Box 2883, 714 Greensboro Ave, 6th Fl, Tuscaloosa, AL 35403; phone: 205-349-3870; civil phone: 205-349-3870 x355; probate phone: 205-349-3870 x203; hours 8:30AM-4:30PM (CST). *Civil Actions Under $10,000, Probate.*
Note: Probate court is separate from this court and can be contacted at the telephone number above.

Civil Records: Access: Online, in person. Visitors must perform in person searches themselves. Court makes copy: $.25 per page. Required to search: name, years to search. Civil cases indexed by defendant, plaintiff. Civil records on computer from 1977, index books early 1900s. Online access at www.alacourt.com.

General Information: Public access terminal has only civil records back to 1977. No sealed, adoption, youthful offender, juvenile records released. Certification fee: $1.00 per page. Payee: District Clerk. Business checks accepted. No credit cards. Prepayment required.

Circuit Court - Criminal 714 Greensboro Ave, 3rd Fl, Tuscaloosa, AL 35401; phone: 205-349-3870 X326; hours 8AM-5PM (CST). *Felony.*
Criminal Records: Access: Mail, online, in person. Both court and visitors may perform in person searches. No search fee. Court makes copy: $.25 per page; same fee for self serve. Required to search:

name, years to search, DOB; also helpful: SSN. Criminal records on computer and index books back to 1977. Online access through SJIS. See state introduction Mail turnaround time 1-2 days.

General Information: Public access terminal goes back to 1977. No sealed, adoption, youthful offender, juvenile records released. Certification fee: $1.00 per cert. Payee: Circuit Clerk. Business checks accepted. Prepayment and SASE required.

District Court - Criminal Division PO Box 1687, 714 Greensboro Ave, 6th Fl, Tuscaloosa, AL 35403; phone: 205-349-3870 x357; hours 8:30AM-4:30PM (CST). *Misdemeanor.*

Criminal Records: Access: Phone, mail, online, in person. Both court and visitors may perform in person searches. No search fee. Court makes copy: $.25 per page. Required to search: name, years to search, signed release; also helpful: DOB, SSN. Criminal records on computer from 1985, books in storage from early 1965. Online access through SJIS. See state introduction Mail turnaround time 5 days.

General Information: Public access terminal has only criminal records back to 1997. No sealed, youthful offender records released. Will fax documents to local or toll free line. Certification fee: $1.00 per page. Payee: District Court Clerk. Business checks accepted. No credit cards. Prepayment required. SASE preferred.

Walker County

Circuit & District Court PO Box 749, Jasper, AL 35502; phone: 205-384-7268; probate phone: 205-384-7281; fax: 205-384-7271; hours 8AM-2:30PM (CST). *Felony, Misdemeanor, Civil, Eviction, Small Claims, Probate.*
Note: Probate court is separate from this court at PO Box 502.

Civil Records: Access: Online, in person. Visitors must perform in person searches themselves. Court makes copy: $.25 per page. Required to search: name, years to search. Civil cases indexed by defendant, plaintiff. Civil records on computer from 3/93, on index books from 1920s. Online access at www.alacourt.com.

Criminal Records: Access: Online, in person. Visitors must perform in person searches themselves. Court makes copy: $.25 per page. Required to search: name, years to search. Criminal records on computer from 3/93, on index books from 1920s. Online access via www.alacourt.com.

General Information: Public access terminal goes back to 1993. No sealed, adoption, youthful offender, juvenile records released. Certification fee: $1.00 per page. Payee: Vinita Thomspon, Circuit Clerk. Business checks accepted. Prepayment required.

Washington County

Circuit & District Court PO Box 548, Chatom, AL 36518; phone: 251-847-2239; hours 8AM-4:30PM (CST). *Felony, Misdemeanor, Civil, Eviction, Small Claims, Probate.*
www.millry.net/~spgrimes
Note: Probate is a separate court and separate index.

Civil Records: Access: Online, in person. Visitors must perform in person searches themselves. Court makes copy: $.25 per page. Required to search: name, years to search. Civil cases indexed by defendant. Civil records on computer since 9/1994; prior 7 years on index cards. Online access at www.alacourt.com. Also, online access to probate records is by subscription at www.recordsusa.com/Alabama/CovingtonCnAl.htm. Credit card-username-password required; choose monthly or per-use plan. Visit the website or call Lisa at 601-264-7701 for information.

Criminal Records: Access: Online, in person. Visitors must perform in person searches themselves. Court makes copy: $.25 per page. Required to search: name, years to search, DOB; also helpful: SSN. Criminal records on computer since

9/1994; prior 7 years on index cards. Online access via www.alacourt.com.

General Information: Public access terminal available. No sealed, adoption, youthful offender, juvenile records released. Certification fee: $1.00. Payee: Circuit Clerk. Only cashiers checks and money orders accepted. Prepayment required.

Wilcox County

Circuit & District Court PO Box 608, Camden, AL 36726; phone: 334-682-4126; probate phone: 334-682-4883; hours 8AM-N, 1-5PM (CST). *Felony, Misdemeanor, Civil, Eviction, Small Claims, Probate.*
Note: Probate court is separate from this court; probate phone number above.

Civil Records: Access: Mail, online, in person. Visitors must perform in person searches themselves. Court makes copy: $.25 per page; same fee for self serve. Required to search: name, years to search, address. Civil cases indexed by defendant, plaintiff. Civil records on computer since 1995; prior records on index books from 1970s, prior to 1970s in vault. Online access at www.alacourt.com.

Criminal Records: Access: Mail, online, in person. Visitors must perform in person searches themselves. Court makes copy: $.25 per page; same fee for self serve. Required to search: name, years to search; also helpful: DOB. Criminal records on computer since 1995; prior records on index books from 1970s, prior to 1970s in vault. Online access via www.alacourt.com.

General Information: No public access terminal. No sealed, adoption, youthful offender, juvenile records released. Certification fee: $1.50. Payee: Circuit Clerk. Business checks accepted. Prepayment required.

Winston County

Circuit & District Court PO Box 309, Double Springs, AL 35553; phone: 205-489-5533; probate phone: 205-489-5219; hours 8AM-4:30PM (CST). *Felony, Misdemeanor, Civil, Eviction, Small Claims, Probate.*
Note: Probate court is separate from this court; probate phone number above.

Civil Records: Access: Mail, online, in person. Visitors must perform in person searches themselves. No search fee. Court makes copy: $.25 per page. Required to search: name, years to search. Civil cases indexed by defendant, plaintiff. Civil records on index books from 1977, on computer since 6/1994 including pending cases. Online access at www.alacourt.com.

Criminal Records: Access: Mail, online, in person. Visitors must perform in person searches themselves. No search fee. Court makes copy: $.25 per page. Required to search: name, years to search, DOB; also helpful: SSN. Criminal records on index books from 1977, on computer since 6/1994 including pending cases. Online access via www.alacourt.com.

General Information: Public access terminal goes back to 1994. No sealed, adoption, youthful offender, juvenile records released. Certification fee: $2.00 per cert. Payee: Circuit Clerk. Business checks accepted, no personal checks. Prepayment required.

Alabama Recording Offices

ORGANIZATION: 67 counties, 71 recording offices. The recording officer is Judge of Probate. Four counties have two recording offices-Barbour, Coffee, Jefferson, and St. Clair. See the notes under each county regarding how to determine which office is appropriate to search. The state is in the Central Time Zone (CST).

REAL ESTATE RECORDS: Most counties do not perform real estate searches. Copy fees vary. Certification fees vary. Tax records are located at the Assessor's Office.

UCC RECORDS: Alabama adopted Revised Article 9 effective 01/01/2002. Financing statements are filed at the state level; real estate related collateral with the County Judge of Probate. Prior to 01/01/2002, consumer goods and farm collateral were filed with the county Judge of Probate. Only one-third of counties will perform UCC searches. Use search request form UCC-11. Search fees vary from $2.00 to $12.00 per debtor. Copies usually cost $1.00 per page.

TAX LIEN RECORDS: Federal and state tax liens on personal property of businesses are filed with the Secretary of State. Other federal and state tax liens are filed with the County Judge of Probate. Counties do not perform separate tax lien searches although the liens are usually filed in the same index with UCC financing statements.

OTHER LIENS: Mechanics, judgment, lis pendens, hospital, vendor.

ONLINE ACCESS: There is no statewide system, but a limited number of counties offer free online access to recorded documents and tax assessor data.

Autauga County

County Judge of Probate, 176 W 5th St, Prattville, AL 36067-3041. 334-361-3731, R/E recording phone-334-361-3732, UCC recording phone-334-361-3732; fax-334-361-3740; hours: 8:30AM-5PM
All records in one index. Records indexed on a public use terminal back to 10/1/1996. Only the public may search. Copy fee $1.00 per page. Cert fee- $3.00 per doc plus copy fee. Payee- County Judge of Probate. **Online access to Property, Assessor, Map records:** Access to the GIS-property information database and Tax Office is free at www.emapsplus.com/ALAutauga/maps/. Click on search by name. **Other phones:** Treasurer- 334-361-3701; Appraiser/Auditor- 334-361-3712; Elections-334-361-3728. **Property tax/Assessor-** 334-361-3709.

Baldwin County

County Judge of Probate, PO Box 459, Bay Minette, AL 36507. RE & UCC recording phone-251-937-0230; fax-251-580-2563; hours: 8AM-4:30PM www.co.baldwin.al.us
Separate indices to search include books and computer. Records indexed on a public use terminal back to 1987. Only the public may search. Copy fee $1.00 per page. Cert fee- $3.00 per doc plus copy fee. Payee- Baldwin County Judge of Probate. **Online access to Property, Deed, Recording, UCC records:** Access to recordings, deeds, and UCCs is at the website, see the "Recording" box. Also, search property appraiser records at www.deltacomputersystems.com/AL/AL05/pappraisal a.html. Access to probate's property information att www.deltacomputersystems.com/al/al05/probatea.html. Property tax information is at www.deltacomputersystems.com/AL/AL05/plinkquery a.html. **Other phones:** Treasurer- 251-937-0282; Appraiser/Auditor- 251-937-0245; Elections- 251-937-0399. **Property tax/Assessor-** 251-937-0245.

Barbour County Clayton Division

County Judge of Probate, PO Box 158, Clayton, AL 36016. 334-775-8371; fax-334-775-1126; 8AM-5PM
File and search here for addresses in Clayton. File and search for Eufaula addresses there. For other county addresses, call for where to search. Records indexed on a public use terminal back to 1/1999. Only the public may search. Copy fee $.50 per page. Cert fee- $2.50 per doc after 5 pages $.50 per sheet. Payee- Barbour County Judge of Probate. **Other phones:** Treasurer- 334-775-3203. **Property tax/Assessor-** PO Box 267, Clayton, AL 36016; 334-775-1110.

Barbour County Eufaula Division

County Judge of Probate, PO Box 758, Eufaula, AL 36072. 334-687-1530; fax-334-687-0921; 8AM-5PM
File and search for Eufaula addresses here. File and search for Clayton addresses there. For other county addresses, call for where to search. Only the public may search. Copy fee $1.00 per page. RE or tax lien copy- $.50 per page. Cert fee- $3.00 per doc plus copy fee. Payee- Barbour County Judge of Probate. **Other phones:** Treasurer- 334-775-3203. **Property tax/Assessor-** 334-687-1575.

Bibb County

County Judge of Probate, 8 Court Sq W, #A, Centerville, AL 35042. 205-926-3104, R/E recording phone-205-926-3108; fax-205-926-3131; 8AM-5PM
All records in one index. Office will perform a UCC search but public must search other records themselves. Search fee $6.00 per name. Copy fee $1.00 per page. Cert fee- $1.00 per doc plus copy fee. Payee- Bibb County Judge of Probate. **Other phones:** Treasurer- 205-926-3114. **Property tax/Assessor-** 8 Court Sq W, #B, Centerville, AL 35042; 205-926-3105.

Blount County

County Judge of Probate, 220 2nd Ave East, Oneonta, AL 35121. 205-625-4180; fax-205-625-4206; hours: 8AM-4PM
Only the public may search. Copy fee $1.00 per page. Cert fee- $4.00 per doc plus copy fee. Payee- Blount County Judge of Probate. **Other phones:** Treasurer- 205-625-4117. **Property tax/Assessor-** 205-625-4117.

Bullock County

County Judge of Probate, PO Box 71, Union Springs, AL 36089. RE & UCC recording phone-334-738-2250; fax-334-738-3839; hours: 8AM-4:30PM

Separate indices to search. Record index not computerized. Only the public may search. Copy fee $1.00 per page. Real estate deed copy- $3.10. Cert fee- $5.00 per doc plus copy fee. Payee-Bullock County Judge of Probate. **Other phones:** Elections- 334-738-2250; Vital Records- 334-738-2250. **Property tax/Assessor-** 217 N. Prairie St, Union Springs, AL 36089; 334-738-2888.

Butler County

County Judge of Probate, PO Box 756, Greenville, AL 36037. RE & UCC recording phone-334-382-3512; fax-334-382-5489; hours: 8AM-4PM M,T,Th,F; 8AM-N W
Record index not computerized. Only the public may search. Copy fee $1.00 per page. Cert fee- $3.00 per doc plus copy fee. Payee- Butler County Judge of Probate. **Other phones:** Treasurer- 334-382-3612; Elections- 334-382-3512; Vital Records- 334-382-3512. **Property tax/Assessor-** same address as above. 334-382-3221.

Calhoun County

County Judge of Probate, 1702 Noble St; #102, Anniston, AL 36201. 256-241-2825; fax-256-231-1728; hours: 8AM-4:30PM
Office will help visitors perform a real estate search but public must search other records themselves. Copy fee $1.00 per page. Cert fee- $3.00 per doc plus copy fee. Payee- Calhoun County Judge of Probate. **Other phones:** ; Tax Collector- 256-241-2840. **Property tax/Assessor-** 256-241-2855.

Chambers County

County Judge of Probate, Courthouse, Lafayette, AL 36862. 334-864-4384, R/E recording phone-334-864-4397, UCC recording phone-334-864-4393; fax-334-864-4394; hours: 8AM-4:30PM
Separate indices to search. Records indexed on a public use terminal back to 10/1997. Only the public may search. Copy fee $1.00 per page. Cert fee- $3.00 per doc plus copy fee. Payee- Chambers County Judge of Probate. **Online access to Real Estate, UCC records:** Access real estate and UCC information for a $49.95 monthly fee. For information, call 706-643-1010. Records are live and go back 5 years. **Other phones:** Appraiser/Auditor- 334-864-

4379; Elections- 334-864-4380; Vital Records- 334-864-4393; Tax Collector- 334-864-4386. **Property tax/Assessor-** 334-864-4389.

Cherokee County

County Judge of Probate, 260 Cedar Bluff Rd #10; Cherokee County Admin Center, Centre, AL 35960. 256-927-3363; fax-256-927-6949; hours: 8AM-4PM
All records in one index since February, 1990. Records indexed on a public use terminal. Only the public may search. Copy fee $1.00 per page. Cert fee- $3.00 per doc plus copy fee. Payee- Cherokee County Judge of Probate. **Property tax/Assessor-** 256-927-5527.

Chilton County

County Judge of Probate, PO Box 270, Clanton, AL 35046. RE & UCC recording phone-205-755-1555; fax-205-280-7204; hours: 8AM-4PM
Only the public may search. Copy fee $1.00 per page. RE record copy- $.50 per page. Cert fee- $2.00 per doc, does not include copy fee. Payee- Chilton County Judge of Probate. **Other phones:** Appraiser/Auditor- 205-755-0160. **Property tax/Assessor-** 205-755-0155.

Choctaw County

County Judge of Probate, 117 S. Mulberry; Courthouse, Butler, AL 36904. 205-459-2417; fax-205-459-4248; hours: 8AM-4:30PM
Record index not computerized. Only the public may search. Copy fee $.50 per page. Cert fee- $3.00 per doc plus copy fee. Payee- Choctaw County Judge of Probate. **Other phones:** Treasurer- 205-459-2411. **Property tax/Assessor-** 205-459-2412.

Clarke County

County Judge of Probate, PO Box 10, Grove Hill, AL 36451. RE & UCC recording phone-251-275-3251; fax-251-275-8427; hours: 8AM-5PM
All records in one index. Records indexed on a public use terminal back to 1999. Office will perform a UCC search (must be made by UCC-11 request forms only), but public must search other records themselves. UCC search per debtor name- $20.00. Copy fee $1.00 per page. Cert fee- $3.00; UCCs are $5.00 per file plus copy fee. Payee- Clarke County Judge of Probate. **Other phones:** Treasurer- 251-275-3507; Appraiser/Auditor- 251-275-3010; Elections- 251-275-3251; Vital Records- 251-275-3251 (marriages); Circuit Clerk (divorce records)- 251-275-3163. **Property tax/Assessor-** PO Box 9, Grove Hill, AL 36451; 251-275-3376.

Clay County

County Judge of Probate, PO Box 1120, Ashland, AL 36251. 256-354-3006; fax-256-354-4778; hours: 8AM-4:30PM
All records in one index. Records indexed on a public use terminal back to 1986. Only the public may search. Copy fee $1.00 per page. Cert fee- $5.00 per doc plus copy fee. Payee- Clay County Judge of Probate. **Property tax/Assessor-** 256-354-2454.

Cleburne County

County Judge of Probate, 120 Vickery St, Rm 101, Heflin, AL 36264. RE & UCC recording phone-256-463-5655; fax-256-463-1044; hours: 8AM-5PM
Separate indices to search include real estate, UCC. Only the public may search. Copy fee $1.00 per page; $.50 self serve. Cert fee- $6.00 per doc includes 1 copy page. Payee- Cleburne County Judge of Probate. **Other phones:** Treasurer- 256-463-2873; Appraiser/Auditor- 256-463-2873; Elections- 256-463-5299; Vital Records- 256-463-2296. **Property tax/Assessor-** 120 Vickery St, #102, Heflin, AL 36264; 256-463-5419.

Coffee County Elba Division

County Judge of Probate, 230-P N. Court Ave, Elba, AL 36323. 334-897-2211, R/E recording phone-334-897-2211/12, UCC recording phone-334-897-2211/12; fax-334-897-2028; hours: 8AM-4:30PM
All records in one index. Records indexed on a public use terminal back to 1999. Only the public may search. Copy fee $1.00 per page. Cert fee- $3.00 per page plus copy fee. Payee- Coffee County Judge of Probate. **Other phones:** Elections- 334-897-2211/12. **Property tax/Assessor-** same address as above. not known.

Coffee County Enterprise Div.

County Judge of Probate, PO Box 311247, Enterprise, AL 36331. 334-347-2688; fax-334-347-2095; hours: 8AM-4:30PM www.probateoffice.info
All records in one index. Records indexed Prior to 1990, separately. Only the public may search. Copy fee $1.00 per page. Cert fee- $3.00 per doc, plus copy fee. Payee- Coffee County Judge of Probate. **Property tax/Assessor-** 334-347-8734.

Colbert County

County Judge of Probate, PO Box 47, Tuscumbia, AL 35674. 256-386-8546; fax-256-386-8547; hours: 8AM-4:30PM
Only the public may search. Copy fee $1.00 per page. Cert fee- $3.00 per doc plus copy fee. Payee- Colbert County Judge of Probate. **Online access to Property Tax records:** Access property tax records free at www.deltacomputersystems.com/search.html. **Property tax/Assessor-** 256-386-8530.

Conecuh County

County Judge of Probate, PO Box 149, Evergreen, AL 36401. 251-578-1221; fax-251-578-7034; hours: 8AM-4:30PM
All records in one index. Records indexed on a public use terminal back to 6/2001. Only the public may search. Copy fee $1.00 per page. Cert fee- $3.00 plus copy fee. Payee- Conecuh County Judge of Probate. **Property tax/Assessor-** 251-578-7019.

Coosa County

County Judge of Probate, PO Box 218, Rockford, AL 35136. RE & UCC recording phone-256-377-4919; fax-256-377-1549; hours: 8AM-4PM
All records in one index. Only the public may search. Copy fee $1.00 per page. Cert fee- $3.00 for 1st page; $1.00 each add'l. Payee- Coosa County Judge of Probate. **Other phones:** Appraiser/Auditor- 256-377-4916. **Property tax/Assessor-** 256-377-4916.

Covington County

County Judge of Probate, PO Box 789, Andalusia, AL 36420-0789. 334-428-2518/2519, R/E recording phone-334-428-2518, UCC recording phone-334-428-2519; fax-334-428-2563; hours: 8AM-5PM
All records in one index. Records indexed on a public use terminal back to 1987 R/P. Only the public may search. Copy fee $1.00 per page. Cert fee- $3.00 per doc, plus copy fee. Payee- Probate Judge. **Online access to Real Estate records:** Access real estate recording records via a private company subscription service at www.recordsusa.com/Alabama/CovingtonCnAl.htm. **Property tax/Assessor-** 334-428-2540.

Crenshaw County

County Judge of Probate, PO Box 328, Luverne, AL 36049-0328. 334-335-6568, R/E recording phone-x227, UCC recording phone-x227; fax-334-335-4749; hours: 8AM-4:30PM
Separate indices to search include mortgage/deed, miscellaneous, Probate, UCC, direct and reverse. Record index not computerized. Only the public may search. Copy fee $1.00 per page. Cert fee- $3.00 per doc plus copy fee. Payee- Crenshaw County Judge of Probate. **Other phones:** Treasurer-

334-335-6568 x222; Appraiser/Auditor- 334-335-6568 x236; Elections- 334-335-6568 x254; Vital Records- 334-335-2471. **Property tax/Assessor-** 334-335-6568 x231.

Cullman County

County Judge of Probate, PO Box 970, Cullman, AL 35055. RE & UCC recording phone-256-775-4807; fax-256-775-4813; hours: 8AM-4:30PM
All records in one index. Records indexed on a public use terminal back to April, 1997. Only the public may search. Copy fee $.30 per page. Cert fee- $2.00 per doc plus copy fee. Payee- Cullman County Judge of Probate. **Other phones:** Appraiser/Auditor- 256-775-4825; Elections- 256-775-4815. **Property tax/Assessor-** 256-775-4844.

Dale County

County Judge of Probate, PO Box 580, Ozark, AL 36361-0580. RE & UCC recording phone-334-774-2754; fax-334-774-0468; hours: 8AM-5PM
Separate indices to search include books back to 1884, mtgs, deeds, misc, judgments. Records indexed on a public use terminal back to 1986. Only the public may search. Copy fee $1.00 per page, $.25 self serve. Cert fee- $4.00 per doc plus copy fee. Payee- Dale County Judge of Probate. **Other phones:** Appraiser/Auditor- 334-774-7208; Elections- 334-774-9038; Vital Records- 334-774-5146. **Property tax/Assessor-** 334-774-2226.

Dallas County

County Judge of Probate, PO Box 987, Selma, AL 36702-0987. 334-874-2516; hours: 8:30AM-4:30PM www.dallascounty-al.org
Separate indices to search include corporation, judgment & real property. Office will perform a UCC search, which includes tax liens, but public must search other records themselves. UCC search per debtor name- $25.00. Separate state/federal tax lien search fee- $5.00 per debtor. Copy fee $1.50 per page. Cert fee- $3.00 per cert. Payee- Dallas County Judge of Probate. **Other phones:** ; Tax Collector- 334-874-2519. **Property tax/Assessor-** same address as above. 334-874-2520.

De Kalb County

County Judge of Probate, 300 Grand SW #100; Courthouse, Fort Payne, AL 35967. 256-845-8510; fax-256-845-8514; hours: 7:45AM-4:15PM
All records in one index. Records indexed on a public use terminal back to 5/2005. Only the public may search. Copy fee $.25 per page. Cert fee- $3.00 per doc plus copy fee. Payee- De Kalb County Judge of Probate. **Online access to Property, Assessor, Mapping records:** Access to property information on the GIS site is free at www.emapsplus.com/aldekalb/maps/. Click on Owner to search by name. **Other phones:** Treasurer- 256-845-8520. **Property tax/Assessor-** 301 Grand SW, Fort Payne, AL 35967; 256-845-8515.

Elmore County

County Judge of Probate, PO Box 280, Wetumpka, AL 36092. Main phone & R/E recording-334-567-1143, UCC recording phone-334-567-1143 or 1145; fax-334-567-1144; hours: 8AM-4:30PM
All records in one index. Records indexed on a public use terminal back to 1995. Only the public may search. Copy fee $1.00 per page. Cert fee- $3.00 per doc plus copy fee. Payee- Elmore County Judge of Probate. **Other phones:** Treasurer- 334-567-1156; Appraiser/Auditor- 334-567-1117; Elections- 334-567-1140; Vital Records- 334-567-1145. **Property tax/Assessor-** 334-567-1118.

Escambia County

County Judge of Probate, PO Box 557, Brewton, AL 36427. 251-867-0206, R/E recording phone-251-867-0291, UCC recording phone-251-867-0291; fax-251-867-0284; 8-4 www.co.escambia.al.us/probate.htm
All records in one index. Records indexed on a public use terminal back to 10/1991. Only the

public may search. Copy fee $1.00 per page. Cert fee- $1.00 per doc plus copy fee. Payee- Escambia County Judge of Probate. **Online access to Property Appraiser records:** Access county property appraisal data free at http://property.co.escambia.al.us/search.php?type=appraisal. **Other phones:** Appraiser/Auditor- 251-867-9168; Elections- 251-867-0201. **Property tax/Assessor-** PO Box 556, Brewton, AL 36427; 251-867-0214.

Etowah County

County Judge of Probate, PO Box 187, Gadsden, AL 35902. 256-549-5341; fax-256-546-1149; hours: 8AM-5PM

Only the public may search. Copy fee $1.00 per page. Cert fee- $1.50 per doc plus copy fee. Payee- Etowah County Judge of Probate. **Online access to Property Appraisal, Property Tax records:** Access to property data through a private company is free at www.deltacomputersystems.com/AL/AL31/pappraisala.html. Also, tax records are free at www.deltacomputersystems.com/AL/AL31/plinkquerya.html. **Property tax/Assessor-** 256-549-5341 x121.

Fayette County

County Judge of Probate, PO Box 670, Fayette, AL 35555. 205-932-4519; fax-205-932-7600; hours: 8AM-4PM

Separate indices to search include deed, mortgages, judgments, UCC, notaries. Records indexed on a public use terminal back to 2000. Only the public may search. Copy fee $1.00 per page. RE or tax lien copy- $.50 per page. Cert fee- $1.00 per doc plus copy fee. Payee- Fayette County Judge of Probate. **Other phones:** Treasurer- 205-932-4510; Appraiser/Auditor- 205-932-6081; Elections- 205-932-5432. **Property tax/Assessor-** 205-932-6081.

Franklin County

County Judge of Probate, PO Box 70, Russellville, AL 35653. 256-332-8801, R/E recording phone-256-332-8804, UCC recording phone-256-332-8804; fax-256-332-8423; hours: 8AM-5PM; 8AM-N Sat

All records in one index. Records indexed on computer. Only the public may search. Copy fee $1.00 per page. Cert fee- $4.00 per doc plus copy fee. Payee- Franklin County Judge of Probate. **Other phones:** Treasurer- 256-332-8850; Elections- 256-332-8805. **Property tax/Assessor-** 256-332-8831.

Geneva County

County Judge of Probate, PO Box 430, Geneva, AL 36340-0430. RE & UCC recording phone-334-684-5647; fax-334-684-5602; hours: 8AM-5PM

Records indexed on a public use terminal back to 10/1985. Only the public may search. Copy fee $1.00 per page. Cert fee- $2.00 per doc plus copy fee. Payee- Geneva County Judge of Probate. **Other phones:** Appraiser/Auditor- 334-684-5713; Elections- 334-684-5655; Main Number- 334-684-5600. **Property tax/Assessor-** 334-684-3119.

Greene County

County Judge of Probate, PO Box 790, Eutaw, AL 35462-0790. 205-372-3340, R/E recording phone-205-372-3340 or 6945, UCC recording phone-205-372-3340 or 6945; fax-205-372-0499; hours: 8AM-4PM

Index: Records prior to 1994 are in real estate books; 1994 to present on computer. Office will perform a UCC search but public must search other records themselves. UCC search per debtor name- $9.00. Copy fee $1.00 per page. Cert fee- $3.00 per page plus copy fee. Payee- Greene County Judge of Probate. **Other phones:** Appraiser/Auditor- 205-372-3202; Elections- 205-372-3340 or 6943; Vital Records- 205-372-3340 or 6945. **Property tax/Assessor-** 205-372-3202.

Hale County

County Judge of Probate, 1001 Main St; Courthouse, Greensboro, AL 36744. RE & UCC recording phone-334-624-8740; fax-334-624-8725; hours: 8AM-4PM

All records in one index. Record index not computerized. Only the public may search. UCC copy fee $2.00 per page. RE record copy- $1.00 per page. Tax lien copy- $1.50 per page. Cert fee- $3.00 per doc plus copy fee. Payee- Hale County Judge of Probate. **Other phones:** Treasurer- 334-624-4257; Appraiser/Auditor- 334-624-0705. **Property tax/Assessor-** same as above. 334-624-3854.

Henry County

County Judge of Probate, 101 Court Sq, #A, Abbeville, AL 36310. RE & UCC recording phone-334-585-3257; fax-334-585-3610; hours: 8AM-4:30PM

All records in one index. Records indexed on a public use terminal back to 11/1/1995. Only the public may search. Copy fee $1.00 per page. Cert fee- $2.00 per doc plus copy fee. Payee- Henry County Judge of Probate. **Property tax/Assessor-** 334-585-3043.

Houston County

County Judge of Probate, PO Drawer 6406, Dothan, AL 36302. RE & UCC recording phone-334-677-4723; fax-334-677-4733; hours: 8AM-4:30PM

All records in one index. Records indexed on a public use terminal back to 1985. Only the public may search. Copy fee $1.00 per page. Cert fee- $2.00 per document plus copy fee. Payee- Houston County Judge of Probate. **Property tax/Assessor-** 334-677-4714.

Jackson County

County Judge of Probate, PO Box 128, Scottsboro, AL 35768. 256-574-9292; fax-256-574-9318; hours: 8AM-4:30PM

Separate indices to search include Deeds, Mortgages, Marriages, Probate, UCC. The office personnel will assist if you have book and page #. They will make copies. Will not search real estate records. Will search UCC records, but not tax liens. Copy fee $1.00 per page. Cert fee- $3.00 per doc + $1.00 per page plus copy fee. Payee- Gloyd Hambrick Jr, Judge of Probate. **Property tax/Assessor-** 256-574-9270.

Jefferson County Bessemer Div.

County Judge of Probate, 1801 3rd Ave., Bessemer, AL 35020. 205-481-4100; hours: 8AM-4:45PM

Separate indices to search include Real, Personal, and UCCs. Records indexed on a public use terminal back to 1987. Office will perform a UCC search but public must search other records themselves. Search fee $20.00. Copy fee $1.00 per page. Cert fee- $2.00 per doc plus copy fee. Payee- Jefferson County Judge of Probate. **Property tax/Assessor-** 205-481-4125.

Jefferson County Birmingham Div.

County Judge of Probate, 716 Richard Arrington Jr Blvd; Courthouse, Birmingham, AL 35203. 205-325-5512- records, R/E recording phone-205-325-5411, UCC recording phone-205-325-5411; fax-205-325-1437; 8AM-4:45PM www.jeffcointouch.com

Index: Indices by instrument type. Records indexed on computer back to 1985. Only the public may search. Copy fee $1.00 per page. Cert fee- $2.00 per doc plus copy fee. Payee- Jefferson County Judge of Probate. **Online access to Property Tax, Unclaimed Property, Inmate records:** Access to the property tax due inquiry is free at http://tc.jeffcointouch.com/taxcollection/HTML/index.asp. No name searching. Also, access the unclaimed property list free at www.jeffcointouch.com/jeffcointouch/ieindex.asp. Click on treasurer. Site may be under re-construction. Also, access the sheriff's most wanted list at www.jeffcosheriff.org/most_wanted.php. Search inmate lists at http://sheriff.jccal.org. **Other phones:** Treasurer- 205-325-5372; Vital Records- 205-325-

5182. **Property tax/Assessor-** 716 Richard Arrington, Jr. Blvd N, Rm 710, Birmingham, AL 35203; 205-325-5505.

Lamar County

County Judge of Probate, PO Box 338, Vernon, AL 35592. 205-695-9119; fax-205-695-9253; hours: 8AM-5PM M,T,Th,F; 8AM-Noon W,Sat

Only the public may search. Copy fee $1.00 per page. RE or tax lien copy- $9.00 1st page, $3.00 each add'l page. Payee- Lamar County Judge of Probate. **Other phones:** Treasurer- 205-695-7151. **Property tax/Assessor-** 205-695-9139.

Lauderdale County

County Judge of Probate, PO Box 1059, Florence, AL 35631-1059. 256-760-5800; fax-256-760-5807; hours: 8AM-5PM

Only the public may search. Copy fee $1.00 per page. Cert fee- $1.00. Payee- Lauderdale County Judge of Probate. **Online access to Real Estate, Appraisal, Property Tax records:** Access property appraisal data free at http://deltacomputersystems.com/AL/AL41/pappraisala.html. Also, property tax records are free at http://deltacomputersystems.com/AL/AL41/plinkquerya.html. **Property tax/Assessor-** 256-760-5785.

Lawrence County

County Judge of Probate, PO Box 310, Moulton, AL 35650. RE & UCC recording phone-256-974-2440; fax-256-974-3188; hours: 8AM-4PM

All records in one index. Only the public may search. Copy fee $.25 per page. Cert fee- $3.00 per doc plus copy fee. Payee- Lawrence County Judge of Probate. **Other phones:** Treasurer- 256-974-2401; Appraiser/Auditor- 256-974-2546; Elections- 256-974-2440; Vital Records- 256-974-2440. **Property tax/Assessor-** 750 Main St, Moulton, AL 35650; 256-974-2476.

Lee County

County Judge of Probate, PO Drawer 2266, Opelika, AL 36803. 334-745-9761; fax-334-745-5082; hours: 8:30AM-4:30PM

Separate indices to search include books, computer. Records indexed on a public use terminal back to 6/1997. Only the public may search. Copy fee $1.00 per page. Cert fee- $3.00 per page plus copy fee. Payee- Lee County Judge of Probate. **Online access to Real Estate, Appraisal, Property Tax, Sex Offender records:** Assess to property appraisal records is free at http://deltacomputersystems.com/AL/AL43/pappraisala.html. Also, search property tax records free at http://deltacomputersystems.com/AL/AL41/plinkquerya.html. Also search the sheriff's sex offender list at www.leecountysheriff.org/offenders.html. **Property tax/Assessor-** 334-745-9786.

Limestone County

County Judge of Probate, 100 S Clinton St, #D, Athens, AL 35612. RE & UCC recording phone-256-233-6427; fax-256-233-6474; hours: 8AM-4:30PM

All records in one index. Records indexed on a public use terminal back to 3/1984. Only the public may search. Copy fee $1.00 per page. Cert fee- $3.00 per doc plus copy fee. Payee- Limestone County Judge of Probate. **Other phones:** Appraiser/Auditor- 256-233-6437; Elections- 256-233-6427. **Property tax/Assessor-** 256-233-6435.

Lowndes County

County Judge of Probate, PO Box 5, Hayneville, AL 36040-0005. 334-548-2365; fax-334-548-5399; hours: 8AM-4:30PM

Records indexed on a public use terminal back to 2002. Only the public may search. Copy fee $1.00 per page. Cert fee- $4.00 per doc plus copy fee. Payee- Lowndes County Judge of Probate. **Other phones:** Appraiser/Auditor- 334-548-5619. **Property tax/Assessor-** PO Box 186, Hayneville, AL 36040; 334-548-2271.

Macon County

County Judge of Probate, 101 E. Northside St.; #101, Tuskegee, AL 36083-1731. 334-724-2611, R/E recording phone-334-724-2508, UCC recording phone-334-724-2508; fax-334-724-2512; hours: 8:30AM-4:30PM

All records in one index. Records indexed on a public use terminal back to 6/97. Only the public may search. Copy fee $1.00 per page. Cert fee-$5.00 per doc plus copy fee. Payee- Macon County Judge of Probate. **Other phones:** Treasurer- 334-724-5120; Appraiser/Auditor- 334-724-2607; Elections-334-724-2617; Vital Records- 334-724-2611. **Property tax/Assessor-** 210 N Elm St, Tuskegee, AL 36083; 334-724-2603.

Madison County

County Judge of Probate, 100 Northside Sq, Rm 101, Huntsville, AL 35801-4820. 256-532-3339, R/E recording phone-256-532-3784; fax-256-532-3338; hours: 8:30AM-5PM www.co.madison.al.us

All records in one index. Records indexed on a public use terminal back to 1971. Only the public may search. Copy fee $1.00 per page. Cert fee-$2.00 per doc plus copy fee. Payee- Madison County Judge of Probate. **Other phones:** Treasurer-256-532-3370; Appraiser/Auditor- 256-532-3350; Elections- 256-532-3332; Vital Records- 256-532-3342. **Property tax/Assessor-** 100 Northside Sq, Rm 121, Huntsville, AL 35801; 256-532-3350.

Marengo County

County Judge of Probate, PO Box 480668, Linden, AL 36748. 334-295-2210, R/E recording phone-334-295-2212, UCC recording phone-334-295-2212; fax-334-295-2254; hours: 8AM-4:30PM

All records in one index. Records indexed on a public use terminal. Search fee $5.00; will perform a limited RE search; provide date, name, etc. General copy fee $3.00. RE record copy- $2.00 per page includes certification. Cert fee- $2.00 per page plus copy fee. Payee- Marengo County Judge of Probate. **Other phones:** Appraiser/Auditor- 334-295-2250; Elections- 334-295-2210. **Property tax/Assessor-** same address as above. 334-295-2215.

Marion County

County Judge of Probate, PO Box 1687, Hamilton, AL 35570. RE & UCC recording phone-205-921-2471; fax-205-921-5109; hours: 8AM-N, 1-5PM

Only the public may search. Copy fee $1.00 per page. Cert fee- $1.00 per copy. Payee- Marion County Judge of Probate. **Online access to Property Tax, Land, Mapping records:** Access the county GIS-mapping and property information data for free at www.marioncountymaps.com/FrameSet.htm. **Other phones:** Treasurer- 205-921-3561; Appraiser/Auditor- 205-921-2606; Elections- 205-921-2471; Vital Records- 205-921-2471. **Property tax/Assessor-** 205-921-2606.

Marshall County

County Judge of Probate, 425 Gunter Ave, Guntersville, AL 35976. 256-571-7767, R/E recording phone-256-571-7764 x208, UCC recording phone-256-571-7764 x208; fax-256-571-7732; hours: 8AM-4:30PM

Separate indices to search include real estate reveres and direct, misc, UCCs. Records indexed on a public use terminal back to October, 1990. Only the public may search. Copy fee $1.00 per page. Cert fee- $.50 per doc plus copy fee. Payee-Marshall County Judge of Probate. **Online access to Property, GIS Mapping records:** Access to property data requires free registration and password at www.marshallgis.com. **Other phones:** Treasurer- 256-571-7758; Elections- 256-571-7764 x202. **Property tax/Assessor-** 424 Blount Ave, Guntersville, AL 35976; 256-571-5733.

Mobile County

County Judge of Probate, PO Box 7, Mobile, AL 36601. 251-574-8497, R/E recording phone-251-690-8497, UCC recording phone-251-690-8497; fax-251-690-4939; hours: 8AM-5PM www.mobile-county.net/probate/

Separate indices to search include film/book-1958-1983, film-1813-1958. Records indexed on a public use terminal back to 1984. Only the public may search. Copy fee $1.00 1st 10 pgs, $.50 add'l per page. Cert fee- $2.00 per doc plus copy fee. Payee- Mobile County Judge of Probate. **Online access to Deed, UCC, Property, Incs, Marriage, Estate Claim, Mortgage, Real/Personal Property, Voter Registration records:** Access to the Probate court's recordings database is free at www.mobilecounty.org/probatecourt/recordssearch.htm Marriages and estate claims are in a separate index here. Also, search real and personal property at http://apps.siteonestudio.com/siteone/towns/mobilecoproptax/. Search registered voters at www.mobilecounty.org/probatecourt/voters/index.asp. Also, City of Mobile property ownership data is free at http://maps.cityofmobile.org/webmapping.htm. Click on Property ownership information and choose to search by name. **Other phones:** Treasurer- 251-690-8585; Appraiser/Auditor- 251-690-8531; Elections-251-574-8480; Vital Records- 251-574-8490. **Property tax/Assessor-** 251-574-8530.

Monroe County

County Judge of Probate, PO Box 665, Monroeville, AL 36461-0665. 251-743-4107, R/E recording phone-251-743-4107 x121, UCC recording phone-251-743-4107 x121; fax-251-575-4756; hours: 8AM-5PM M,T,W,F; 8AM-N Th

Index: Indices; Deeds, Mtgs, Corporation records, marriage records, probate records, adoption records, and election. Only the public may search. Copy fee $1.00 per page. Cert fee- $2.00 per page plus copy fee. Payee- Monroe County Judge of Probate. **Other phones:** Appraiser/Auditor- 251-743-4107 x124; Elections- 251-743-4107 x120; Vital Records- 251-743-4107 x121. **Property tax/Assessor-** same address as above. 251-743-4107 x124.

Montgomery County

County Judge of Probate, PO Box 223, Montgomery, AL 36195. 334-832-1237, R/E recording phone-334-832-1236/1237; hours: 8AM-5PM

All records in one index. Records indexed on a public use terminal back to 1974. Only the public may search. Copy fee $1.00 per page. Cert fee-$2.00 per doc plus copy fee. Payee- Montgomery County Judge of Probate. **Online access to Unclaimed Property records:** Access to Probate Court's unclaimed property list is free at www.mc-ala.org/probate/unclprop/default.asp. **Property tax/Assessor-** 334-832-4950.

Morgan County

County Judge of Probate, PO Box 848, Decatur, AL 35602-0848. RE & UCC recording phone-256-351-4680; hours: 8AM-4:30PM

Only the public may search. Copy fee $1.00 per page. Cert fee- $3.00 per doc plus copy fee. Payee-Morgan County Judge of Probate. **Online access to Property, Appraisal, Assessor, Tax Payment records:** Access is free at www.deltacomputersystems.com/AL/AL52/INDEX.html. Also, search property assessor data free at www.deltacomputersystems.com/AL/AL52/plinkquerya.html. There is also a property tax payment search at https://secure.termnetinc.com/morgan/paymentType.jsp but no name searching. **Property tax/Assessor-** 256-351-4690.

Perry County

County Judge of Probate, PO Box 478, Marion, AL 36756. RE & UCC recording phone-334-683-2210; fax-334-683-2211; hours: 8AM-4:30PM

Will not search real estate records. Will not search UCC records or tax liens. Copy fee $1.00 per page. Cert fee- $3.00 per cert plus copy fee. Payee- Perry County Judge of Probate. **Other phones:** Appraiser/Auditor- 334-683-2221; Elections- 334-683-2210; Collector- 334-683-2220. **Property tax/Assessor-** PO Box 117, Marion, AL 36756; 334-683-2219.

Pickens County

County Judge of Probate, PO Box 370, Carrollton, AL 35447. RE & UCC recording phone-205-367-2010; fax-205-367-2011; hours: 8AM-4PM

All records in one index. Only the public may search. Copy fee $1.00 per page. Cert fee- $3.00 per instrument plus copy fee. Payee- Pickens County Judge of Probate. **Other phones:** Elections-205-367-2010. **Property tax/Assessor-** 205-367-2040.

Pike County

County Judge of Probate, 120 W Church St, Troy, AL 36081. RE & UCC recording phone-334-566-1246; fax-334-566-8585; hours: 8AM-5PM

Separate indices to search include deeds, mortgages, Liens, Incorp, judgment, marriage, Misc., plat, UCC, Lis pendens, advers possession, probate, and elections. Records indexed on a public use terminal back to 10/1/2003. Only the public may search. Copy fee $.50 per page. Cert fee- $2.00, plus copy fee. Payee- Pike County Judge of Probate. **Other phones:** Treasurer- 334-566-6374; Appraiser/Auditor- 334-566-0706; Elections-334-566-1246. **Property tax/Assessor-** same address as above. 334-566-0706.

Randolph County

County Judge of Probate, PO Box 249, Wedowee, AL 36278. 256-357-4933; fax-256-357-9053; hours: 8AM-5PM

Only the public may search. Copy fee $1.00 per page. Cert fee- $2.00. Payee- Randolph County Judge of Probate. **Property tax/Assessor-** 256-357-4343.

Russell County

County Judge of Probate, PO Box 700, Phenix City, AL 36868-0700. RE & UCC recording phone-334-298-7979; fax-334-298-7979; hours: 8:30AM-5PM

Separate indices to search include books, computer. Records indexed on a public use terminal back to 6/21/2002. Only the public may search. Copy fee $1.00 per page. Cert fee- $3.00 per doc plus copy fee. Payee- Russell County Judge of Probate. **Other phones:** Treasurer- 334-298-6426; Appraiser/Auditor- 334-297-8996. **Property tax/Assessor-** same address as above. 334-298-4441.

Shelby County

County Judge of Probate, PO Box 825, Columbiana, AL 35051. 205-669-3720; fax-205-669-3714; hours: 8AM-4:30PM www.shelbycountyalabama.com

Index: Books, computer. Records indexed on a public use terminal back to 1971. Only the public may search. Copy fee $1.00 per page. Cert fee-$3.00 per page plus copy fee. Payee- Shelby County Judge of Probate. **Online access to Recording, Land, Judgment, Deed, UCC, Notary, Fictitious Name, Marriage, Probate, Property Tax records:** Access to the probate court recording data is free at www.shelbycountyalabama.com/probate/. Also, search property tax records free at www.shelbycountyalabama.com/taxc_search.asp. **Other phones:** Appraiser/Auditor- 205-669-3902. **Property tax/Assessor-** 205-669-3902.

St. Clair County
Northern Congressional District

County Judge of Probate, PO Box 220, Ashville, AL 35953. RE & UCC recording phone-205-594-2124; fax-205-594-2125; hours: 8AM-5PM www.stclairco.com/index.php

All records in one index. Records indexed on a public use terminal back to 1986. Only the public may search. Copy fee $1.00 per page. Cert fee-$3.00 per doc plus copy fee. Payee- Judge of Probate. **Online access to Property, Appraisal, Assessor records:** Access to property appraiser data is free at www.deltacomputersystems.com/AL/AL59/pappraisala.html. Also, access county assessor data free at www.deltacomputersystems.com/AL/AL59/plinkquerya.html. Access to real estate recording records via a private company subscription service is at www.recordsusa.com/Alabama/StClairCnAl.htm. **Other phones:** Appraiser/Auditor- 205-594-2168; Vital Records- 334-206-5418. **Property tax/Assessor-** 205-594-2160.

St. Clair County
Southern Congressional District

County Judge of Probate, 1815 Cogswell Ave, #212, Pell City, AL 35125. RE & UCC recording phone-205-338-9449; fax-205-884-1182; hours: 8AM-5PM
Only the public may search. Copy fee $1.00 per page. Cert fee- $3.00 per doc plus copy fee. Payee- St. Clair Judge of Probate. **Online access to Property, Appraisal, Assessor records:** Access to property appraiser data is free at www.deltacomputersystems.com/AL/AL59/pappraisala.html. Also, access to county assessor data is free at www.deltacomputersystems.com/AL/AL59/plinkquerya.html. Access to real estate recording records via a private company subscription service is at www.recordsusa.com/Alabama/StClairCnAl.htm. **Other phones:** Appraiser/Auditor- 205-884-2395. **Property tax/Assessor-** 205-884-2395.

Sumter County

County Judge of Probate, PO Box 1040, Livingston, AL 35470-1040. RE & UCC recording phone-205-652-7281; fax-205-652-6206; hours: 8AM-4PM
All records in one index. Only the public may search. Copy fee $1.00 per page. Cert fee- $3.00 per doc, copies extra. Payee- Sumter County Judge of Probate. **Other phones:** Treasurer- 205-652-2731; Appraiser/Auditor- 205-652-2424; Elections- 205-652-7281; Vital Records- 205-652-7281. **Property tax/Assessor-** 205-652-2424.

Talladega County

County Judge of Probate, PO Box 737, Talladega, AL 35161. RE & UCC recording phone-256-362-4175; fax-256-761-2128; hours: 8AM-5PM
Index: Books. Records indexed on a public use terminal back to 11/1997. Office will perform a UCC and Tax lien search but public must search

other records themselves. No search fee. Copy fee $1.00 per page. Cert fee- $4.00 per page includes copy fee. Payee- Talladega County Judge of Probate. **Property tax/Assessor-** 256-761-2123.

Tallapoosa County

County Judge of Probate, 125 N. Broadnax St.; Courthouse, Rm 126, Dadeville, AL 36853. RE & UCC recording phone-256-825-1090; fax-256-825-1604; hours: 8AM-5PM
Only the public may search. Copy fee $1.00 per page. Cert fee- $3.00 per instrument. Payee- Tallapoosa County Judge of Probate. **Other phones:** Appraiser/Auditor- 256-825-7831. **Property tax/Assessor-** 256-825-7831.

Tuscaloosa County

County Judge of Probate, PO Box 20067, Tuscaloosa, AL 35402-0067. 205-349-3870 x205/6; hours: 8:30AM-5PM www.tuscco.com
Office will perform a real estate search as time permits, but public must search other records themselves. Copy fee $1.00 per page. Cert fee-$3.00 per doc plus copy fee. Payee- Judge of Probate. **Online access to Real Estate, Lien, UCC, Grantor/Grantee, Probate, Marriage, Mortgage, Incorporation, Property, Jail, Sex Offender, Most Wanted records:** Access to the records database is free at www.tuscco.com/OnlineServices.cfm. Also included are searches for mortgages, incorporations, bonds, discharges, exemptions. Also, access property assessor data free at www.emapsplus.com/ALTuscaloosa/maps/. Click on owner search. Also, a search is proposed for probate and judgment records at www.tuscco.com/RecordsRoom_Probate.cfm. Also, search for inmates, most wanted, sex offenders, and missing persons at www.tcsoal.org. **Property tax/Assessor-** 205-349-3870 x370.

Walker County

County Judge of Probate, PO Box 502, Jasper, AL 35502-0502. 205-384-7282, R/E recording phone-205-384-7281; fax-205-384-7005; hours: 8;30AM-4PM
Separate indices to search include books, computer. Records indexed on a public use terminal back to 1992. Only the public may search. Copy fee $1.00 per page. Cert fee- $3.00 per doc plus copy fee. Payee- Walker County Judge of Probate. **Other phones:** Treasurer- 205-384-7276; Elections- 205-384-7284. **Property tax/Assessor-** 205-384-7265.

Washington County

County Judge of Probate, PO Box 549, Chatom, AL 36518. RE & UCC recording phone-251-847-2201; fax-251-847-6450; hours: 8AM-4:30PM
Separate indices to search include corp, judgment, will, bond, partnership, prior to 12/1995. Only the public may search. Copy fee $1.00 per page 1st 10, then $.50 per page. Cert fee- $3.00 per doc plus copy fee. Payee- Washington County Judge of Probate. **Online access to Real Estate records:** Access to real estate recording records via a private company subscription service is at www.recordsusa.com/Alabama/WashingtonCnAl.htm. **Other phones:** Treasurer- 251-847-2208; Elections- 251-847-2201. **Property tax/Assessor-** 251-847-2780.

Wilcox County

County Judge of Probate, PO Box 668, Camden, AL 36726. RE & UCC recording phone-334-682-4883; fax-334-682-9484; hours: 8-11:30AM,Noon-4:30PM
All records in one index. Records indexed on a public use terminal back to 7/2001. Only the public may search. Copy fee $1.00 per page. Cert fee- $3.00 per cert; $1.00 per page. Payee- Wilcox County Judge of Probate. **Other phones:** Treasurer- 334-682-9112. **Property tax/Assessor-** 334-682-4625.

Winston County

County Judge of Probate, PO Box 27, Double Springs, AL 35553. RE & UCC recording phone-205-489-5219; fax-205-489-5135; hours: 8AM-4:30PM (8AM-N 1st Sat of every month)
All records in one index. Records indexed on a public use terminal back to 3/1999. Only the public may search. Copy fee $1.00 per page. Cert fee- $3.00 per doc plus copy fee. Payee- Winston County Judge of Probate. **Other phones:** Appraiser/Auditor- 205-489-5166; Vital Records- 205-489-5219 (marriages). **Property tax/Assessor-** PO Box 160, Double Springs, AL 35553; 205-489-5166.

Alabama County Locator

You will usually be able to find the city name in the City/County Cross Reference below. In that case, it is a simple matter to determine the county from the cross reference. However, only the official US Postal Service city names are included in this index. There are an additional 40,000 place names that people use in their addresses. Therefore, we have also included a ZIP/City Cross Reference immediately following the City/County Cross Reference.

If you know the ZIP Code but the city name does not appear in the City/County Cross Reference index, look up the ZIP Code in the ZIP/City Cross Reference, find the city name, then look up the city name in the City/County Cross Reference. For example, you want to know the county for an address of Menands, NY 12204. There is no "Menands" in the City/County Cross Reference. The ZIP/City Cross Reference shows that ZIP Codes 12201-12288 are for the city of Albany. Looking back in the City/County Cross Reference, Albany is in Albany County.

Alabama City/County Cross Reference

ABBEVILLE Henry
ABERNANT Tuscaloosa
ADAMSVILLE Jefferson
ADDISON (35540) Winston(95), Cullman(4)
ADGER (35006) Jefferson(91), Walker(6), Tuscaloosa(2)
AKRON Hale
ALABASTER Shelby
ALBERTA Wilcox
ALBERTVILLE (35951) Marshall(73), De Kalb(26)
ALBERTVILLE Marshall
ALEXANDER CITY (35010) Tallapoosa(95), Elmore(2), Coosa(1)
ALEXANDER CITY Tallapoosa
ALEXANDRIA Calhoun
ALICEVILLE (35442) Pickens(87), Sumter(11)
ALLEN Clarke
ALLGOOD Blount
ALMA Clarke
ALPINE Talladega
ALTON Jefferson
ALTOONA (35952) Etowah(57), Blount(41)
ANDALUSIA (36420) Covington(97), Escambia(2)
ANDALUSIA (36421) Covington(98), Conecuh(1)
ANDERSON (35610) Lauderdale(74), Limestone(25)
ANNEMANIE Wilcox
ANNISTON (36203) Calhoun(79), Talladega(20)
ANNISTON Calhoun
ARAB (35016) Marshall(82), Cullman(14), Blount(2)
ARDMORE (35739) Limestone(77), Madison(22)
ARITON (36311) Dale(66), Barbour(23), Coffee(10)
ARLEY Winston
ARLINGTON (36722) Wilcox(97), Marengo(2)
ASHFORD Houston
ASHLAND Clay
ASHVILLE St. Clair
ATHENS Limestone
ATMORE (36502) Escambia(93), Monroe(4), Baldwin(2)
ATMORE Escambia
ATTALLA Etowah
AUBURN (36830) Lee(90), Macon(9)
AUBURN Lee
AUBURN UNIVERSITY Lee
AUTAUGAVILLE Autauga
AXIS Mobile

BAILEYTON (35019) Cullman(73), Morgan(26)
BANKS (36005) Pike(67), Bullock(32)
BANKSTON Fayette
BAY MINETTE Baldwin
BAYOU LA BATRE Mobile
BEAR CREEK Marion
BEATRICE Monroe
BEAVERTON Lamar
BELK Fayette
BELLAMY Sumter
BELLE MINA Limestone
BELLWOOD Geneva
BERRY (35546) Fayette(65), Tuscaloosa(31), Walker(3)
BESSEMER (35022) Jefferson(95), Shelby(4)
BESSEMER Jefferson
BIGBEE Washington
BILLINGSLEY (36006) Autauga(59), Chilton(41)
BIRMINGHAM (35244) Jefferson(53), Shelby(46)
BIRMINGHAM (35242) Shelby(90), Jefferson(9)
BIRMINGHAM Jefferson
BLACK Geneva
BLOUNTSVILLE Blount
BOAZ (35957) Marshall(78), De Kalb(18), Blount(3)
BOAZ Etowah
BOLIGEE Greene
BOLINGER Choctaw
BON AIR Talladega
BON SECOUR Baldwin
BOOTH Autauga
BOYKIN Wilcox
BRANTLEY (36009) Crenshaw(94), Coffee(5)
BREMEN (35033) Cullman(90), Walker(9)
BRENT (35034) Bibb(98), Perry(1)
BREWTON (36426) Escambia(98), Conecuh(1)
BREWTON Escambia
BRIDGEPORT Jackson
BRIERFIELD (35035) Bibb(97), Shelby(2)
BRILLIANT Marion
BROOKLYN Conecuh
BROOKSIDE Jefferson
BROOKWOOD (35444) Tuscaloosa(97), Jefferson(2)
BROWNSBORO Madison
BRUNDIDGE (36010) Pike(77), Coffee(21)
BRYANT Jackson
BUCKS Mobile

BUHL Tuscaloosa
BURNT CORN Monroe
BURNWELL Walker
BUTLER Choctaw
BYNUM Calhoun
CALERA (35040) Shelby(86), Chilton(13)
CALVERT Washington
CAMDEN Wilcox
CAMP HILL (36850) Tallapoosa(76), Chambers(19), Lee(3)
CAMPBELL Clarke
CAPSHAW Limestone
CARBON HILL (35549) Walker(83), Fayette(16)
CARDIFF Jefferson
CARLTON Clarke
CARROLLTON Pickens
CASTLEBERRY (36432) Conecuh(67), Escambia(32)
CATHERINE Wilcox
CECIL (36013) Montgomery(94), Macon(5)
CEDAR BLUFF Cherokee
CENTRE Cherokee
CENTREVILLE Bibb
CHANCELLOR (36316) Geneva(53), Coffee(46)
CHAPMAN Butler
CHATOM Washington
CHELSEA Shelby
CHEROKEE Colbert
CHILDERSBURG Talladega
CHOCCOLOCCO Calhoun
CHUNCHULA Mobile
CITRONELLE (36522) Mobile(95), Washington(4)
CLANTON (35046) Chilton(97), Coosa(2)
CLANTON Chilton
CLAY Jefferson
CLAYTON Barbour
CLEVELAND Blount
CLINTON Greene
CLIO Barbour
CLOPTON (36317) Henry(88), Barbour(6), Dale(5)
CLOVERDALE Lauderdale
COALING Tuscaloosa
CODEN Mobile
COFFEE SPRINGS (36318) Geneva(70), Coffee(29)
COFFEEVILLE Clarke
COKER Tuscaloosa
COLLINSVILLE (35961) De Kalb(79), Etowah(10), Cherokee(10)
COLUMBIA (36319) Henry(51), Houston(48)

COLUMBIANA Shelby
COOK SPRINGS St. Clair
COOSADA Elmore
CORDOVA Walker
COTTONDALE Tuscaloosa
COTTONTON Russell
COTTONWOOD Houston
COURTLAND Lawrence
COWARTS Houston
COY Wilcox
CRAGFORD (36255) Clay(97), Tallapoosa(2)
CRANE HILL Cullman
CREOLA Mobile
CROMWELL Choctaw
CROPWELL St. Clair
CROSSVILLE (35962) De Kalb(93), Marshall(6)
CUBA Sumter
CULLMAN Cullman
CUSSETA (36852) Lee(74), Chambers(25)
DADEVILLE Tallapoosa
DALEVILLE (36322) Dale(95), Coffee(2), Geneva(2)
DANVILLE (35619) Lawrence(49), Morgan(49)
DAPHNE Baldwin
DAUPHIN ISLAND Mobile
DAVISTON (36256) Tallapoosa(96), Clay(3)
DAWSON De Kalb
DAYTON Marengo
DE ARMANVILLE Calhoun
DEATSVILLE (36022) Elmore(82), Autauga(17)
DECATUR (35603) Morgan(98), Lawrence(1)
DECATUR Morgan
DEER PARK Washington
DELMAR Winston
DELTA (36258) Clay(55), Cleburne(29), Randolph(15)
DEMOPOLIS Marengo
DETROIT (35552) Marion(56), Lamar(43)
DICKINSON Clarke
DIXONS MILLS Marengo
DOCENA Jefferson
DOLOMITE Jefferson
DORA (35062) Jefferson(52), Walker(47)
DOTHAN (36303) Houston(92), Dale(7)
DOTHAN Houston
DOUBLE SPRINGS Winston
DOUGLAS Marshall
DOZIER (36028) Covington(56), Crenshaw(43)

DUNCANVILLE (35456) Tuscaloosa(98), Bibb(1)
DUTTON Jackson
EAST TALLASSEE Tallapoosa
EASTABOGA (36260) Calhoun(64), Talladega(35)
ECHOLA Tuscaloosa
ECLECTIC Elmore
EDWARDSVILLE Cleburne
EIGHT MILE Mobile
ELBA Coffee
ELBERTA Baldwin
ELDRIDGE (35554) Fayette(64), Walker(29), Marion(5)
ELKMONT Limestone
ELMORE Elmore
ELROD Tuscaloosa
EMELLE Sumter
EMPIRE (35063) Walker(72), Blount(19), Jefferson(8)
ENTERPRISE (36330) Coffee(90), Dale(9)
ENTERPRISE Coffee
EPES Sumter
EQUALITY (36026) Elmore(61), Coosa(38)
ESTILLFORK Jackson
ETHELSVILLE Pickens
EUFAULA Autauga
EUFAULA Barbour
EUTAW Greene
EVA (35621) Morgan(91), Cullman(8)
EVERGREEN Conecuh
EXCEL Monroe
FACKLER Jackson
FAIRFIELD Jefferson
FAIRHOPE Baldwin
FALKVILLE (35622) Morgan(78), Cullman(21)
FAUNSDALE Marengo
FAYETTE (35555) Fayette(92), Tuscaloosa(5), Lamar(1)
FITZPATRICK (36029) Macon(49), Bullock(32), Montgomery(18)
FIVE POINTS Chambers
FLAT ROCK (35966) Jackson(64), De Kalb(35)
FLOMATON Escambia
FLORALA Covington
FLORENCE Lauderdale
FOLEY Baldwin
FOREST HOME (36030) Butler(96), Wilcox(3)
FORKLAND Greene
FORT DAVIS Macon
FORT DEPOSIT (36032) Lowndes(75), Butler(24)
FORT MITCHELL Russell
FORT PAYNE (35967) De Kalb(96), Cherokee(3)
FORT PAYNE De Kalb
FORT RUCKER Dale
FOSTERS Tuscaloosa
FRANKLIN Monroe
FRANKVILLE Washington
FRISCO CITY Monroe
FRUITDALE Washington
FRUITHURST Cleburne
FULTON Clarke
FULTONDALE Jefferson
FURMAN Wilcox
FYFFE De Kalb
GADSDEN (35907) Etowah(98), Calhoun(1)
GADSDEN Etowah
GAINESTOWN Clarke

GAINESVILLE (35464) Sumter(86), Greene(13)
GALLANT (35972) Etowah(75), St. Clair(24)
GALLION (36742) Marengo(95), Hale(4)
GANTT Covington
GARDEN CITY Cullman
GARDENDALE Jefferson
GAYLESVILLE Cherokee
GENEVA Geneva
GEORGIANA (36033) Butler(98), Conecuh(1)
GERALDINE De Kalb
GILBERTOWN Choctaw
GLEN ALLEN Fayette
GLENWOOD (36034) Crenshaw(70), Pike(29)
GOODSPRINGS Walker
GOODWATER (35072) Clay(47), Coosa(32), Tallapoosa(18)
GOODWAY Monroe
GORDO (35466) Pickens(93), Tuscaloosa(6)
GORDON Houston
GOSHEN (36035) Pike(76), Crenshaw(23)
GRADY (36036) Montgomery(75), Crenshaw(24)
GRAHAM Randolph
GRAND BAY Mobile
GRANT Marshall
GRAYSVILLE Jefferson
GREEN POND Bibb
GREENSBORO Hale
GREENVILLE Butler
GROVE HILL Clarke
GROVEOAK (35975) De Kalb(92), Marshall(7)
GUIN (35563) Marion(91), Fayette(4), Lamar(4)
GULF SHORES Baldwin
GUNTERSVILLE (35976) Marshall(97), Blount(2)
GURLEY (35748) Madison(94), Jackson(5)
HACKLEBURG Marion
HALEYVILLE (35565) Winston(66), Marion(28), Franklin(4)
HAMILTON Marion
HANCEVILLE Cullman
HARDAWAY Macon
HARPERSVILLE Shelby
HARTFORD Geneva
HARTSELLE Morgan
HARVEST (35749) Madison(74), Limestone(25)
HATCHECHUBBEE Russell
HAYDEN Blount
HAYNEVILLE Lowndes
HAZEL GREEN Madison
HEADLAND (36345) Henry(83), Houston(10), Dale(6)
HEFLIN (36264) Cleburne(92), Randolph(7)
HELENA Shelby
HENAGAR (35978) De Kalb(79), Jackson(20)
HIGDON (35979) De Kalb(66), Jackson(33)
HIGHLAND HOME (36041) Crenshaw(97), Montgomery(2)
HILLSBORO Lawrence
HODGES (35571) Franklin(69), Marion(30)
HOLLINS Clay
HOLLY POND Cullman
HOLLYTREE Jackson

HOLLYWOOD Jackson
HOLY TRINITY Russell
HONORAVILLE (36042) Crenshaw(54), Butler(45)
HOPE HULL (36043) Montgomery(65), Lowndes(34)
HORTON (35980) Marshall(66), Blount(33)
HOUSTON Winston
HUNTSVILLE Madison
HURTSBORO (36860) Russell(86), Bullock(8), Macon(4)
HUXFORD Escambia
IDER De Kalb
IRVINGTON Mobile
JACHIN Choctaw
JACK Coffee
JACKSON Clarke
JACKSONS GAP Tallapoosa
JACKSONVILLE Calhoun
JASPER (35503) Walker(92), Winston(7)
JASPER Walker
JEFFERSON Marengo
JEMISON Chilton
JONES (36749) Dallas(53), Autauga(46)
JOPPA (35087) Cullman(50), Morgan(37), Marshall(11)
KANSAS Walker
KELLERMAN Tuscaloosa
KELLYTON (35089) Tallapoosa(60), Coosa(39)
KENNEDY (35574) Lamar(55), Pickens(33), Fayette(11)
KENT Elmore
KILLEN Lauderdale
KIMBERLY Jefferson
KINSTON (36453) Coffee(53), Geneva(42), Covington(3)
KNOXVILLE (35469) Greene(52), Tuscaloosa(47)
LACEYS SPRING (35754) Morgan(98), Marshall(1)
LAFAYETTE Chambers
LAMISON Wilcox
LANETT Chambers
LANGSTON (35755) Marshall(58), Jackson(41)
LAPINE (36046) Crenshaw(51), Montgomery(48)
LAVACA Choctaw
LAWLEY (36793) Bibb(68), Chilton(24), Perry(7)
LEEDS (35094) Jefferson(76), Shelby(13), St. Clair(10)
LEESBURG (35983) Cherokee(98), De Kalb(1)
LEIGHTON Colbert
LENOX Conecuh
LEROY Washington
LESTER Limestone
LETOHATCHEE (36047) Lowndes(68), Montgomery(31)
LEXINGTON Lauderdale
LILLIAN Baldwin
LINCOLN (35096) Talladega(89), Calhoun(10)
LINDEN Marengo
LINEVILLE (36266) Clay(82), Randolph(17)
LISMAN Choctaw
LITTLE RIVER Baldwin
LIVINGSTON Sumter
LOACHAPOKA Lee
LOCKHART Covington
LOCUST FORK Blount
LOGAN (35098) Cullman(89), Winston(10)

LOUISVILLE Barbour
LOWER PEACH TREE (36751) Monroe(47), Wilcox(28), Clarke(23)
LOWNDESBORO Lowndes
LOXLEY Baldwin
LUVERNE Crenshaw
LYNN Winston
MADISON (35756) Limestone(81), Madison(18)
MADISON Madison
MAGNOLIA Marengo
MAGNOLIA SPRINGS Baldwin
MALCOLM Washington
MALVERN Geneva
MAPLESVILLE (36750) Chilton(94), Bibb(5)
MARBURY (36051) Autauga(43), Elmore(30), Chilton(26)
MARGARET St. Clair
MARION Perry
MARION JUNCTION (36759) Dallas(94), Perry(5)
MATHEWS (36052) Montgomery(93), Bullock(6)
MAYLENE Shelby
MC CALLA (35111) Tuscaloosa(62), Jefferson(35), Bibb(1)
MC INTOSH Washington
MC KENZIE (36456) Butler(74), Covington(12), Conecuh(12)
MC SHAN Pickens
MC WILLIAMS Wilcox
MEGARGEL Monroe
MELVIN Choctaw
MENTONE (35984) De Kalb(81), Cherokee(18)
MERIDIANVILLE Madison
MEXIA Monroe
MIDLAND CITY (36350) Dale(91), Houston(8)
MIDWAY (36053) Barbour(79), Bullock(20)
MILLBROOK Elmore
MILLERS FERRY Wilcox
MILLERVILLE Clay
MILLPORT (35576) Lamar(89), Pickens(10)
MILLRY (36558) Washington(84), Choctaw(15)
MINTER (36761) Dallas(59), Lowndes(39), Wilcox(1)
MOBILE Mobile
MONROEVILLE Monroe
MONTEVALLO (35115) Shelby(83), Chilton(15), Bibb(1)
MONTGOMERY Montgomery
MONTROSE Baldwin
MOODY St. Clair
MOORESVILLE Limestone
MORRIS Jefferson
MORVIN Clarke
MOULTON Lawrence
MOUNDVILLE (35474) Hale(87), Tuscaloosa(12)
MOUNT HOPE (35651) Lawrence(98), Franklin(1)
MOUNT MEIGS Montgomery
MOUNT OLIVE Jefferson
MOUNT VERNON Mobile
MULGA Jefferson
MUNFORD Talladega
MUSCADINE Cleburne
MUSCLE SHOALS Colbert
MYRTLEWOOD Marengo
NANAFALIA Marengo
NATURAL BRIDGE Winston

NAUVOO (35578) Walker(79), Winston(20)
NEEDHAM Choctaw
NEW BROCKTON Coffee
NEW CASTLE Jefferson
NEW HOPE (35760) Madison(88), Marshall(11)
NEW MARKET Madison
NEWBERN (36765) Hale(85), Perry(14)
NEWELL Randolph
NEWTON (36352) Houston(55), Dale(42), Geneva(1)
NEWVILLE (36353) Henry(72), Dale(27)
NORMAL Madison
NORTHPORT Tuscaloosa
NOTASULGA (36866) Macon(73), Tallapoosa(20), Lee(5)
OAK HILL Wilcox
OAKMAN (35579) Walker(98), Tuscaloosa(1)
ODENVILLE St. Clair
OHATCHEE Calhoun
ONEONTA Blount
OPELIKA (36801) Lee(98), Chambers(1)
OPELIKA (36804) Lee(97), Macon(1), Russell(1)
OPELIKA Lee
OPP (36467) Covington(95), Coffee(4)
ORANGE BEACH Baldwin
ORRVILLE Dallas
OWENS CROSS ROADS Madison
OZARK Dale
PAINT ROCK Jackson
PALMERDALE Jefferson
PANOLA Sumter
PANSEY Houston
PARRISH Walker
PAUL Conecuh
PELHAM Shelby
PELL CITY St. Clair
PENNINGTON Choctaw
PERDIDO (36562) Baldwin(90), Escambia(9)
PERDUE HILL Monroe
PEROTE Bullock
PETERMAN (36471) Monroe(96), Conecuh(3)
PETERSON Tuscaloosa
PETREY Crenshaw
PHENIX CITY (36870) Lee(72), Russell(27)
PHENIX CITY (36867) Russell(90), Lee(9)
PHENIX CITY Russell
PHIL CAMPBELL (35581) Franklin(87), Marion(12)
PIEDMONT (36272) Calhoun(61), Cherokee(26), Etowah(8), Cleburne(3)
PIKE ROAD Montgomery
PINCKARD Dale
PINE APPLE Wilcox
PINE HILL Wilcox
PINE LEVEL Montgomery
PINSON (35126) Jefferson(96), Blount(3)
PISGAH (35765) Jackson(92), De Kalb(7)

PITTSVIEW Russell
PLANTERSVILLE (36758) Dallas(90), Autauga(7), Chilton(1)
PLEASANT GROVE Jefferson
POINT CLEAR Baldwin
PRAIRIE Wilcox
PRATTVILLE Autauga
PRINCETON Jackson
QUINTON (35130) Walker(65), Jefferson(34)
RAGLAND St. Clair
RAINBOW CITY Etowah
RAINSVILLE De Kalb
RALPH (35480) Tuscaloosa(97), Greene(2)
RAMER Montgomery
RANBURNE Cleburne
RANDOLPH (36792) Bibb(72), Chilton(27)
RANGE Conecuh
RED BAY Franklin
RED LEVEL (36474) Covington(97), Conecuh(2)
REFORM Pickens
REMLAP (35133) Blount(93), St. Clair(6)
REPTON (36475) Conecuh(64), Monroe(35)
RIVER FALLS Covington
RIVERSIDE St. Clair
ROANOKE (36274) Randolph(93), Chambers(6)
ROBERTSDALE Baldwin
ROCKFORD Coosa
ROGERSVILLE (35652) Lauderdale(98), Limestone(1)
RUSSELLVILLE (35654) Franklin(80), Colbert(14), Lawrence(5)
RUTLEDGE (36071) Crenshaw(97), Butler(2)
RYLAND Madison
SAFFORD (36773) Dallas(89), Marengo(10)
SAGINAW Shelby
SAINT ELMO Mobile
SAINT STEPHENS Washington
SALEM (36874) Lee(95), Russell(4)
SALITPA Clarke
SAMANTHA Tuscaloosa
SAMSON (36477) Geneva(91), Coffee(8)
SARALAND Mobile
SARDIS (36775) Dallas(81), Lowndes(18)
SATSUMA Mobile
SAWYERVILLE Hale
SAYRE Jefferson
SCOTTSBORO (35769) Jackson(70), Marshall(29)
SCOTTSBORO Jackson
SEALE Russell
SECTION (35771) Jackson(96), De Kalb(3)
SELMA (36701) Dallas(98), Perry(1)
SELMA (36703) Dallas(97), Autauga(2)
SELMA Dallas
SEMINOLE Baldwin
SEMMES Mobile

SHANNON Jefferson
SHEFFIELD Colbert
SHELBY Shelby
SHORTER Macon
SHORTERVILLE Henry
SILAS Choctaw
SILURIA Shelby
SILVERHILL Baldwin
SIPSEY Walker
SKIPPERVILLE (36374) Dale(60), Barbour(39)
SLOCOMB (36375) Geneva(84), Houston(15)
SMITHS Lee
SMITHS STATION Lee
SNOW HILL Wilcox
SOMERVILLE Morgan
SPANISH FORT Baldwin
SPRING GARDEN Cherokee
SPRINGVILLE (35146) St. Clair(81), Blount(17), Jefferson(1)
SPROTT Perry
SPRUCE PINE Franklin
STANTON Chilton
STAPLETON Baldwin
STEELE St. Clair
STERRETT Shelby
STEVENSON Jackson
STOCKTON Baldwin
SULLIGENT Lamar
SUMITON Walker
SUMMERDALE Baldwin
SUNFLOWER Washington
SWEET WATER Marengo
SYCAMORE Talladega
SYLACAUGA Talladega
SYLVANIA De Kalb
TALLADEGA (35160) Talladega(96), Clay(3)
TALLADEGA Talladega
TALLASSEE (36078) Elmore(81), Tallapoosa(18)
TANNER Limestone
THEODORE Mobile
THOMASTON Marengo
THOMASVILLE (36784) Clarke(79), Marengo(16), Wilcox(3)
THORSBY Chilton
TIBBIE Washington
TITUS (36080) Elmore(98), Coosa(1)
TONEY (35773) Madison(72), Limestone(27)
TOWN CREEK (35672) Lawrence(97), Colbert(2)
TOWNLEY Walker
TOXEY Choctaw
TRAFFORD (35172) Blount(83), Jefferson(16)
TRENTON Jackson
TRINITY (35673) Lawrence(78), Morgan(21)
TROY (36079) Pike(93), Coffee(6)
TROY (36081) Pike(98), Bullock(1)
TROY Pike
TRUSSVILLE (35173) Jefferson(81), St. Clair(18)
TUSCALOOSA Tuscaloosa

TUSCUMBIA Colbert
TUSKEGEE Macon
TUSKEGEE INSTITUTE Macon
TYLER (36785) Lowndes(75), Dallas(25)
UNION GROVE (35175) Marshall(89), Morgan(10)
UNION SPRINGS Bullock
UNIONTOWN (36786) Perry(88), Hale(5), Marengo(5)
URIAH Monroe
VALHERMOSO SPRINGS Morgan
VALLEY (36854) Chambers(74), Lee(25)
VALLEY Lee
VALLEY HEAD De Kalb
VANCE Tuscaloosa
VANDIVER Shelby
VERBENA (36091) Chilton(95), Autauga(3)
VERNON Lamar
VINA (35593) Franklin(85), Marion(14)
VINCENT (35178) Shelby(70), St. Clair(29)
VINEGAR BEND Washington
VINEMONT Cullman
VREDENBURGH Monroe
WADLEY (36276) Randolph(68), Chambers(15), Clay(11), Tallapoosa(4)
WAGARVILLE Washington
WALKER SPRINGS Clarke
WALNUT GROVE Etowah
WARD (36922) Choctaw(91), Sumter(8)
WARRIOR (35180) Jefferson(55), Blount(44)
WATERLOO Lauderdale
WATSON Jefferson
WATTSVILLE St. Clair
WAVERLY (36879) Chambers(50), Lee(49)
WEAVER Calhoun
WEBB Houston
WEDOWEE Randolph
WELLINGTON Calhoun
WEOGUFKA Coosa
WEST BLOCTON (35184) Bibb(98), Tuscaloosa(1)
WEST GREENE Greene
WESTOVER Shelby
WETUMPKA Elmore
WHATLEY (36482) Clarke(97), Monroe(2)
WILMER Mobile
WILSONVILLE Shelby
WILTON Shelby
WINFIELD (35594) Fayette(56), Marion(43)
WING (36483) Covington(63), Escambia(36)
WOODLAND Randolph
WOODSTOCK (35188) Bibb(88), Tuscaloosa(11)
WOODVILLE (35776) Jackson(82), Marshall(15), Madison(1)
YORK Sumter

Alabama ZIP/City Cross Reference

ZIP Range	City	ZIP Range	City	ZIP Range	City	ZIP Range	City
35004-35004	MOODY	35143-35143	SHELBY	35563-35563	GUIN	35768-35769	SCOTTSBORO
35005-35005	ADAMSVILLE	35144-35144	SILURIA	35564-35564	HACKLEBURG	35771-35771	SECTION
35006-35006	ADGER	35146-35146	SPRINGVILLE	35565-35565	HALEYVILLE	35772-35772	STEVENSON
35007-35007	ALABASTER	35147-35147	STERRETT	35570-35570	HAMILTON	35773-35773	TONEY
35010-35011	ALEXANDER CITY	35148-35148	SUMITON	35571-35571	HODGES	35774-35774	TRENTON
35013-35013	ALLGOOD	35149-35149	SYCAMORE	35572-35572	HOUSTON	35775-35775	VALHERMOSO SPRINGS
35014-35014	ALPINE	35150-35151	SYLACAUGA	35573-35573	KANSAS	35776-35776	WOODVILLE
35015-35015	ALTON	35160-35161	TALLADEGA	35574-35574	KENNEDY	35800-35899	HUNTSVILLE
35016-35016	ARAB	35171-35171	THORSBY	35575-35575	LYNN	35901-35905	GADSDEN
35019-35019	BAILEYTON	35172-35172	TRAFFORD	35576-35576	MILLPORT	35906-35906	RAINBOW CITY
35020-35023	BESSEMER	35173-35173	TRUSSVILLE	35577-35577	NATURAL BRIDGE	35907-35907	GADSDEN
35031-35031	BLOUNTSVILLE	35175-35175	UNION GROVE	35578-35578	NAUVOO	35950-35951	ALBERTVILLE
35032-35032	BON AIR	35176-35176	VANDIVER	35579-35579	OAKMAN	35952-35952	ALTOONA
35033-35033	BREMEN	35178-35178	VINCENT	35580-35580	PARRISH	35953-35953	ASHVILLE
35034-35034	BRENT	35179-35179	VINEMONT	35581-35581	PHIL CAMPBELL	35954-35954	ATTALLA
35035-35035	BRIERFIELD	35180-35180	WARRIOR	35582-35582	RED BAY	35956-35957	BOAZ
35036-35036	BROOKSIDE	35181-35181	WATSON	35584-35584	SIPSEY	35958-35958	BRYANT
35038-35038	BURNWELL	35182-35182	WATTSVILLE	35585-35585	SPRUCE PINE	35959-35959	CEDAR BLUFF
35040-35040	CALERA	35183-35183	WEOGUFKA	35586-35586	SULLIGENT	35960-35960	CENTRE
35041-35041	CARDIFF	35184-35184	WEST BLOCTON	35587-35587	TOWNLEY	35961-35961	COLLINSVILLE
35042-35042	CENTREVILLE	35185-35185	WESTOVER	35592-35592	VERNON	35962-35962	CROSSVILLE
35043-35043	CHELSEA	35186-35186	WILSONVILLE	35593-35593	VINA	35963-35963	DAWSON
35044-35044	CHILDERSBURG	35187-35187	WILTON	35594-35594	WINFIELD	35964-35964	DOUGLAS
35045-35046	CLANTON	35188-35188	WOODSTOCK	35601-35609	DECATUR	35966-35966	FLAT ROCK
35048-35048	CLAY	35200-35299	BIRMINGHAM	35610-35610	ANDERSON	35967-35968	FORT PAYNE
35049-35049	CLEVELAND	35401-35407	TUSCALOOSA	35611-35614	ATHENS	35971-35971	FYFFE
35051-35051	COLUMBIANA	35440-35440	ABERNANT	35615-35615	BELLE MINA	35972-35972	GALLANT
35052-35052	COOK SPRINGS	35441-35441	AKRON	35616-35616	CHEROKEE	35973-35973	GAYLESVILLE
35053-35053	CRANE HILL	35442-35442	ALICEVILLE	35617-35617	CLOVERDALE	35974-35974	GERALDINE
35054-35054	CROPWELL	35443-35443	BOLIGEE	35618-35618	COURTLAND	35975-35975	GROVEOAK
35055-35058	CULLMAN	35444-35444	BROOKWOOD	35619-35619	DANVILLE	35976-35976	GUNTERSVILLE
35060-35060	DOCENA	35446-35446	BUHL	35620-35620	ELKMONT	35978-35978	HENAGAR
35061-35061	DOLOMITE	35447-35447	CARROLLTON	35621-35621	EVA	35979-35979	HIGDON
35062-35062	DORA	35448-35448	CLINTON	35622-35622	FALKVILLE	35980-35980	HORTON
35063-35063	EMPIRE	35449-35449	COALING	35630-35634	FLORENCE	35981-35981	IDER
35064-35064	FAIRFIELD	35452-35452	COKER	35640-35640	HARTSELLE	35983-35983	LEESBURG
35068-35068	FULTONDALE	35453-35453	COTTONDALE	35643-35643	HILLSBORO	35984-35984	MENTONE
35070-35070	GARDEN CITY	35456-35456	DUNCANVILLE	35645-35645	KILLEN	35986-35986	RAINSVILLE
35071-35071	GARDENDALE	35457-35457	ECHOLA	35646-35646	LEIGHTON	35987-35987	STEELE
35072-35072	GOODWATER	35458-35458	ELROD	35647-35647	LESTER	35988-35988	SYLVANIA
35073-35073	GRAYSVILLE	35459-35459	EMELLE	35648-35648	LEXINGTON	35989-35989	VALLEY HEAD
35074-35074	GREEN POND	35460-35460	EPES	35649-35649	MOORESVILLE	35990-35990	WALNUT GROVE
35077-35077	HANCEVILLE	35461-35461	ETHELSVILLE	35650-35650	MOULTON	35999-35999	GADSDEN
35078-35078	HARPERSVILLE	35462-35462	EUTAW	35651-35651	MOUNT HOPE	36003-36003	AUTAUGAVILLE
35079-35079	HAYDEN	35463-35463	FOSTERS	35652-35652	ROGERSVILLE	36004-36004	EUFAULA
35080-35080	HELENA	35464-35464	GAINESVILLE	35653-35653	RUSSELLVILLE	36005-36005	BANKS
35082-35082	HOLLINS	35466-35466	GORDO	35660-35660	SHEFFIELD	36006-36006	BILLINGSLEY
35083-35083	HOLLY POND	35468-35468	KELLERMAN	35661-35662	MUSCLE SHOALS	36008-36008	BOOTH
35085-35085	JEMISON	35469-35469	KNOXVILLE	35670-35670	SOMERVILLE	36009-36009	BRANTLEY
35087-35087	JOPPA	35470-35470	LIVINGSTON	35671-35671	TANNER	36010-36010	BRUNDIDGE
35089-35089	KELLYTON	35471-35471	MC SHAN	35672-35672	TOWN CREEK	36013-36013	CECIL
35091-35091	KIMBERLY	35473-35473	NORTHPORT	35673-35673	TRINITY	36015-36015	CHAPMAN
35094-35094	LEEDS	35474-35474	MOUNDVILLE	35674-35674	TUSCUMBIA	36016-36016	CLAYTON
35096-35096	LINCOLN	35475-35476	NORTHPORT	35677-35677	WATERLOO	36017-36017	CLIO
35097-35098	LOCUST FORK	35477-35477	PANOLA	35699-35699	DECATUR	36020-36020	COOSADA
35098-35098	LOGAN	35478-35478	PETERSON	35739-35739	ARDMORE	36022-36022	DEATSVILLE
35111-35111	MC CALLA	35480-35480	RALPH	35740-35740	BRIDGEPORT	36023-36023	EAST TALLASSEE
35112-35112	MARGARET	35481-35481	REFORM	35741-35741	BROWNSBORO	36024-36024	ECLECTIC
35114-35114	MAYLENE	35482-35482	SAMANTHA	35742-35742	CAPSHAW	36025-36025	ELMORE
35115-35115	MONTEVALLO	35485-35487	TUSCALOOSA	35744-35744	DUTTON	36026-36026	EQUALITY
35116-35116	MORRIS	35490-35490	VANCE	35745-35745	ESTILLFORK	36027-36027	EUFAULA
35117-35117	MOUNT OLIVE	35491-35491	WEST GREENE	35746-35746	FACKLER	36028-36028	DOZIER
35118-35118	MULGA	35501-35504	JASPER	35747-35747	GRANT	36029-36029	FITZPATRICK
35119-35119	NEW CASTLE	35540-35540	ADDISON	35748-35748	GURLEY	36030-36030	FOREST HOME
35120-35120	ODENVILLE	35541-35541	ARLEY	35749-35749	HARVEST	36031-36031	FORT DAVIS
35121-35121	ONEONTA	35542-35542	BANKSTON	35750-35750	HAZEL GREEN	36032-36032	FORT DEPOSIT
35123-35123	PALMERDALE	35543-35543	BEAR CREEK	35751-35751	HOLLYTREE	36033-36033	GEORGIANA
35124-35124	PELHAM	35544-35544	BEAVERTON	35752-35752	HOLLYWOOD	36034-36034	GLENWOOD
35125-35125	PELL CITY	35545-35545	BELK	35754-35754	LACEYS SPRING	36035-36035	GOSHEN
35126-35126	PINSON	35546-35546	BERRY	35755-35755	LANGSTON	36036-36036	GRADY
35127-35127	PLEASANT GROVE	35548-35548	BRILLIANT	35756-35758	MADISON	36037-36037	GREENVILLE
35128-35128	PELL CITY	35549-35549	CARBON HILL	35759-35759	MERIDIANVILLE	36038-36038	GANTT
35130-35130	QUINTON	35550-35550	CORDOVA	35760-35760	NEW HOPE	36039-36039	HARDAWAY
35131-35131	RAGLAND	35551-35551	DELMAR	35761-35761	NEW MARKET	36040-36040	HAYNEVILLE
35133-35133	REMLAP	35552-35552	DETROIT	35762-35762	NORMAL	36041-36041	HIGHLAND HOME
35135-35135	RIVERSIDE	35553-35553	DOUBLE SPRINGS	35763-35763	OWENS CROSS ROADS	36042-36042	HONORAVILLE
35136-35136	ROCKFORD	35554-35554	ELDRIDGE	35764-35764	PAINT ROCK	36043-36043	HOPE HULL
35137-35137	SAGINAW	35555-35555	FAYETTE	35765-35765	PISGAH	36045-36045	KENT
35139-35139	SAYRE	35559-35559	GLEN ALLEN	35766-35766	PRINCETON	36046-36046	LAPINE
35142-35142	SHANNON	35560-35560	GOODSPRINGS	35767-35767	RYLAND	36047-36047	LETOHATCHEE

ZIP Range	Location
36048-36048	LOUISVILLE
36049-36049	LUVERNE
36051-36051	MARBURY
36052-36052	MATHEWS
36053-36053	MIDWAY
36054-36054	MILLBROOK
36057-36057	MOUNT MEIGS
36061-36061	PEROTE
36062-36062	PETREY
36064-36064	PIKE ROAD
36065-36065	PINE LEVEL
36066-36068	PRATTVILLE
36069-36069	RAMER
36071-36071	RUTLEDGE
36072-36072	EUFAULA
36075-36075	SHORTER
36078-36078	TALLASSEE
36079-36079	TROY
36080-36080	TITUS
36081-36082	TROY
36083-36083	TUSKEGEE
36087-36088	TUSKEGEE INSTITUTE
36089-36089	UNION SPRINGS
36091-36091	VERBENA
36092-36093	WETUMPKA
36100-36199	MONTGOMERY
36201-36207	ANNISTON
36250-36250	ALEXANDRIA
36251-36251	ASHLAND
36253-36253	BYNUM
36254-36254	CHOCCOLOCCO
36255-36255	CRAGFORD
36256-36256	DAVISTON
36257-36257	DE ARMANVILLE
36258-36258	DELTA
36260-36260	EASTABOGA
36261-36261	EDWARDSVILLE
36262-36262	FRUITHURST
36263-36263	GRAHAM
36264-36264	HEFLIN
36265-36265	JACKSONVILLE
36266-36266	LINEVILLE
36267-36267	MILLERVILLE
36268-36268	MUNFORD
36269-36269	MUSCADINE
36270-36270	NEWELL
36271-36271	OHATCHEE
36272-36272	PIEDMONT
36273-36273	RANBURNE
36274-36274	ROANOKE
36275-36275	SPRING GARDEN
36276-36276	WADLEY
36277-36277	WEAVER
36278-36278	WEDOWEE
36279-36279	WELLINGTON
36280-36280	WOODLAND
36301-36305	DOTHAN
36310-36310	ABBEVILLE
36311-36311	ARITON
36312-36312	ASHFORD
36313-36313	BELLWOOD
36314-36314	BLACK
36316-36316	CHANCELLOR
36317-36317	CLOPTON
36318-36318	COFFEE SPRINGS
36319-36319	COLUMBIA
36320-36320	COTTONWOOD
36321-36321	COWARTS
36322-36322	DALEVILLE
36323-36323	ELBA
36330-36331	ENTERPRISE
36340-36340	GENEVA
36343-36343	GORDON
36344-36344	HARTFORD
36345-36345	HEADLAND
36346-36346	JACK
36349-36349	MALVERN
36350-36350	MIDLAND CITY
36351-36351	NEW BROCKTON
36352-36352	NEWTON
36353-36353	NEWVILLE
36360-36361	OZARK
36362-36362	FORT RUCKER
36370-36370	PANSEY
36371-36371	PINCKARD
36373-36373	SHORTERVILLE
36374-36374	SKIPPERVILLE
36375-36375	SLOCOMB
36376-36376	WEBB
36401-36401	EVERGREEN
36419-36419	ALLEN
36420-36421	ANDALUSIA
36425-36425	BEATRICE
36426-36427	BREWTON
36429-36429	BROOKLYN
36431-36431	BURNT CORN
36432-36432	CASTLEBERRY
36435-36435	COY
36436-36436	DICKINSON
36439-36439	EXCEL
36441-36441	FLOMATON
36442-36442	FLORALA
36444-36444	FRANKLIN
36445-36445	FRISCO CITY
36446-36446	FULTON
36449-36449	GOODWAY
36451-36451	GROVE HILL
36453-36453	KINSTON
36454-36454	LENOX
36455-36455	LOCKHART
36456-36456	MC KENZIE
36457-36457	MEGARGEL
36458-36458	MEXIA
36460-36462	MONROEVILLE
36467-36467	OPP
36469-36469	EVERGREEN
36469-36469	PAUL
36470-36470	PERDUE HILL
36471-36471	PETERMAN
36473-36473	RANGE
36474-36474	RED LEVEL
36475-36475	REPTON
36476-36476	RIVER FALLS
36477-36477	SAMSON
36480-36480	URIAH
36481-36481	VREDENBURGH
36482-36482	WHATLEY
36483-36483	WING
36501-36501	ALMA
36502-36504	ATMORE
36505-36505	AXIS
36507-36507	BAY MINETTE
36509-36509	BAYOU LA BATRE
36510-36510	BIGBEE
36511-36511	BON SECOUR
36512-36512	BUCKS
36513-36513	CALVERT
36515-36515	CARLTON
36518-36518	CHATOM
36521-36521	CHUNCHULA
36522-36522	CITRONELLE
36523-36523	CODEN
36524-36524	COFFEEVILLE
36525-36525	CREOLA
36526-36526	DAPHNE
36527-36527	SPANISH FORT
36528-36528	DAUPHIN ISLAND
36529-36529	DEER PARK
36530-36530	ELBERTA
36532-36533	FAIRHOPE
36535-36536	FOLEY
36538-36538	FRANKVILLE
36539-36539	FRUITDALE
36540-36540	GAINESTOWN
36541-36541	GRAND BAY
36542-36542	GULF SHORES
36543-36543	HUXFORD
36544-36544	IRVINGTON
36545-36545	JACKSON
36547-36547	GULF SHORES
36548-36548	LEROY
36549-36549	LILLIAN
36550-36550	LITTLE RIVER
36551-36551	LOXLEY
36553-36553	MC INTOSH
36555-36555	MAGNOLIA SPRINGS
36556-36556	MALCOLM
36558-36558	MILLRY
36559-36559	MONTROSE
36560-36560	MOUNT VERNON
36561-36561	ORANGE BEACH
36562-36562	PERDIDO
36564-36564	POINT CLEAR
36567-36567	ROBERTSDALE
36568-36568	SAINT ELMO
36569-36569	SAINT STEPHENS
36570-36570	SALITPA
36571-36571	SARALAND
36572-36572	SATSUMA
36574-36574	SEMINOLE
36575-36575	SEMMES
36576-36576	SILVERHILL
36577-36577	SPANISH FORT
36578-36578	STAPLETON
36579-36579	STOCKTON
36580-36580	SUMMERDALE
36581-36581	SUNFLOWER
36582-36582	THEODORE
36583-36583	TIBBIE
36584-36584	VINEGAR BEND
36585-36585	WAGARVILLE
36586-36586	WALKER SPRINGS
36587-36587	WILMER
36590-36590	THEODORE
36600-36612	MOBILE
36613-36613	EIGHT MILE
36614-36695	MOBILE
36701-36703	SELMA
36720-36720	ALBERTA
36721-36721	ANNEMANIE
36722-36722	ARLINGTON
36723-36723	BOYKIN
36726-36726	CAMDEN
36727-36727	CAMPBELL
36728-36728	CATHERINE
36731-36731	DAYTON
36732-36732	DEMOPOLIS
36736-36736	DIXONS MILLS
36738-36738	FAUNSDALE
36740-36740	FORKLAND
36741-36741	FURMAN
36742-36742	GALLION
36744-36744	GREENSBORO
36745-36745	JEFFERSON
36747-36747	LAMISON
36748-36748	LINDEN
36749-36749	JONES
36750-36750	MAPLESVILLE
36751-36751	LOWER PEACH TREE
36752-36752	LOWNDESBORO
36753-36753	MC WILLIAMS
36754-36754	MAGNOLIA
36756-36756	MARION
36758-36758	PLANTERSVILLE
36759-36759	MARION JUNCTION
36760-36760	MILLERS FERRY
36761-36761	MINTER
36762-36762	MORVIN
36763-36763	MYRTLEWOOD
36764-36764	NANAFALIA
36765-36765	NEWBERN
36766-36766	OAK HILL
36767-36767	ORRVILLE
36768-36768	PINE APPLE
36769-36769	PINE HILL
36771-36771	PRAIRIE
36773-36773	SAFFORD
36775-36775	SARDIS
36776-36776	SAWYERVILLE
36778-36778	SNOW HILL
36779-36779	SPROTT
36782-36782	SWEET WATER
36783-36783	THOMASTON
36784-36784	THOMASVILLE
36785-36785	TYLER
36786-36786	UNIONTOWN
36790-36790	STANTON
36792-36792	RANDOLPH
36793-36793	LAWLEY
36801-36804	OPELIKA
36830-36832	AUBURN
36849-36849	AUBURN UNIVERSITY
36850-36850	CAMP HILL
36851-36851	COTTONTON
36852-36852	CUSSETA
36853-36853	DADEVILLE
36854-36854	VALLEY
36855-36855	FIVE POINTS
36856-36856	FORT MITCHELL
36858-36858	HATCHECHUBBEE
36859-36859	HOLY TRINITY
36860-36860	HURTSBORO
36861-36861	JACKSONS GAP
36862-36862	LAFAYETTE
36863-36863	LANETT
36865-36865	LOACHAPOKA
36866-36866	NOTASULGA
36867-36870	PHENIX CITY
36871-36871	PITTSVIEW
36872-36872	VALLEY
36874-36874	SALEM
36875-36875	SEALE
36877-36877	SMITHS
36877-36877	SMITHS STATION
36879-36879	WAVERLY
36901-36901	BELLAMY
36903-36903	BOLINGER
36904-36904	BUTLER
36906-36906	CROMWELL
36907-36907	CUBA
36908-36908	GILBERTOWN
36910-36910	JACHIN
36911-36911	LAVACA
36912-36912	LISMAN
36913-36913	MELVIN
36915-36915	NEEDHAM
36916-36916	PENNINGTON
36919-36919	SILAS
36921-36921	TOXEY
36922-36922	WARD
36925-36925	YORK

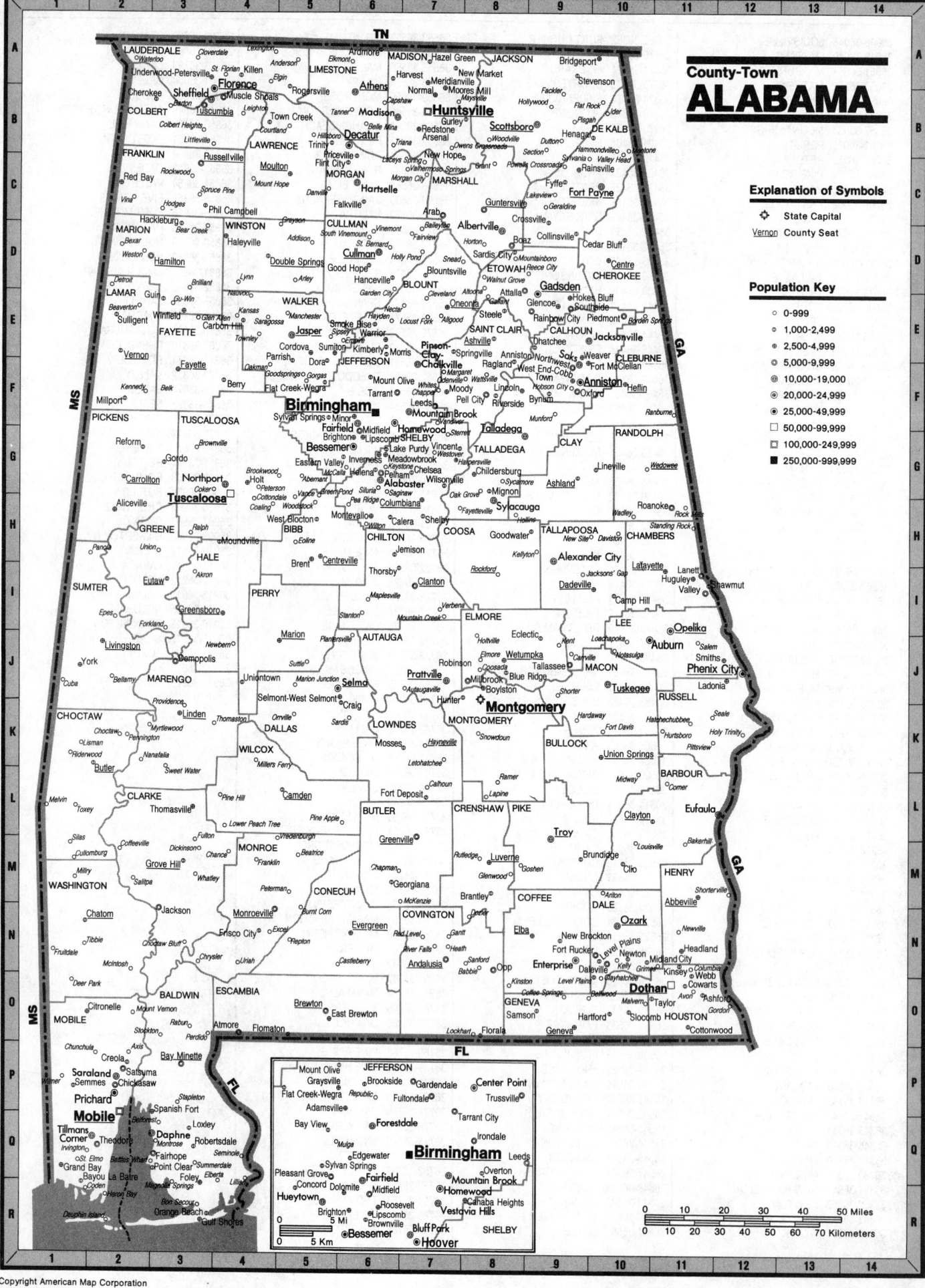

County-Town
ALABAMA

Explanation of Symbols

✧ State Capital
Vernon County Seat

Population Key

○ 0-999
◔ 1,000-2,499
◉ 2,500-4,999
◉ 5,000-9,999
◉ 10,000-19,000
◉ 20,000-24,999
◉ 25,000-49,999
□ 50,000-99,999
□ 100,000-249,999
■ 250,000-999,999

COUNTIES

(67 Counties)

Name of County	Population	Location on Map
AUTAUGA	34,222	J-6
BALDWIN	98,280	O-3
BARBOUR	25,417	L-11
BIBB	16,576	H-5
BLOUNT	39,248	D-7
BULLOCK	11,042	K-9
BUTLER	21,892	L-6
CALHOUN	116,034	E-9
CHAMBERS	36,876	H-10
CHEROKEE	19,543	D-10
CHILTON	32,458	H-6
CHOCTAW	16,018	K-1
CLARKE	27,240	L-2
CLAY	13,252	G-9
CLEBURNE	12,730	E-10
COFFEE	40,240	M-8
COLBERT	51,666	B-2
CONECUH	14,054	M-5
COOSA	11,063	H-7
COVINGTON	36,478	N-7
CRENSHAW	13,635	L-7
CULLMAN	67,613	D-5
DALE	49,633	M-10
DALLAS	48,130	K-4
DEKALB	54,651	B-10
ELMORE	49,210	I-8
ESCAMBIA	35,518	O-4
ETOWAH	99,840	D-8
FAYETTE	17,962	E-3
FRANKLIN	27,814	C-2
GENEVA	23,647	O-8
GREENE	10,153	H-2
HALE	15,498	H-3
HENRY	15,374	M-11
HOUSTON	81,331	O-11
JACKSON	47,796	A-8
JEFFERSON	651,525	F-6
LAMAR	15,715	E-2
LAUDERDALE	79,661	A-2
LAWRENCE	31,513	B-4
LEE	87,146	I-10
LIMESTONE	54,135	A-5
LOWNDES	12,658	K-6
MACON	24,928	J-9
MADISON	238,912	A-7
MARENGO	23,084	J-3
MARION	29,830	D-2
MARSHALL	70,832	C-7
MOBILE	378,643	O-1
MONROE	23,968	M-4
MONTGOMERY	209,085	K-7
MORGAN	100,043	C-5
PERRY	12,759	I-4
PICKENS	20,699	F-2
PIKE	27,595	L-8
RANDOLPH	19,881	G-10
RUSSELL	46,860	J-11
SAINT CLAIR	50,009	E-8
SHELBY	99,358	G-7
SUMTER	16,174	I-1
TALLADEGA	74,107	G-8
TALLAPOOSA	38,826	H-9
TUSCALOOSA	150,522	F-3
WALKER	67,670	E-5
WASHINGTON	16,694	M-1
WILCOX	13,568	K-4
WINSTON	22,053	D-4
Total	4,040,587	

CITIES AND TOWNS

Note: The first name is that of the city or town, second, that of the county in which it is located, then the population and location on the map.

- Abbeville, Henry, 3,173 ... M-11
- Adamsville, Jefferson, 4,161 ... P-6
- Alabaster, Shelby, 14,732 ... G-6
- Albertville, Marshall, 14,507 ... D-8
- Alexander City, Tallapoosa, 14,917 ... H-9
- Aliceville, Pickens, 3,009 ... H-2
- Andalusia, Covington, 9,269 ... N-7
- Anniston, Calhoun, 26,623 ... F-9
- Anniston Northwest, Calhoun ... F-9
- Arab, Cullman/Marshall, 6,321 ... C-7
- Ardmore, Limestone, 1,090 ... A-6
- Ashford, Houston, 1,926 ... O-11
- Ashland, Clay, 2,034 ... G-9
- Ashville, St. Clair, 1,494 ... E-8
- Athens, Limestone, 16,901 ... B-6
- Atmore, Escambia, 8,046 ... O-4
- Attalla, Etowah, 6,859 ... E-8
- Auburn, Lee, 33,830 ... J-10
- Bay Minette, Baldwin, 7,168 ... P-3
- Bay View, Jefferson ... Q-5
- Bayou La Batre, Mobile, 2,456 ... R-1
- Berry, Fayette, 1,218 ... F-4
- Bessemer, Jefferson, 33,497 ... G-6
- Birmingham, Jefferson/Shelby, 265,968 ... F-6
- Blountsville, Blount, 1,527 ... D-7
- • Blue Ridge, Elmore, 1,151 ... J-8
- Bluff Park, Jefferson ... R-7
- Boaz, Etowah/Marshall, 6,928 ... D-8
- Boylston, Montgomery ... J-8
- Brantley, Crenshaw, 1,015 ... M-8
- Brent, Bibb, 2,776 ... H-5
- Brewton, Escambia, 5,885 ... O-5
- Bridgeport, Jackson, 2,936 ... A-10
- Brighton, Jefferson, 4,518 ... G-6
- Brookside, Jefferson, 1,365 ... P-6
- Brownville, Jefferson ... R-6
- Brundidge, Pike, 2,472 ... M-9
- Butler, Choctaw, 1,872 ... K-2
- • Bynum, Calhoun, 1,917 ... F-9
- • Cahaba Heights, Jefferson, 4,778 ... R-8
- Calera, Shelby, 2,136 ... H-6
- Camden, Wilcox, 2,414 ... L-5
- Camp Hill, Tallapoosa, 1,415 ... I-10
- Carbon Hill, Walker, 2,115 ... E-4
- Carrollton, Pickens, 1,170 ... G-2
- Cedar Bluff, Cherokee, 1,174 ... D-10
- • Center Point, Jefferson, 22,658 ... P-8
- Centre, Cherokee, 2,893 ... D-10
- Centreville, Bibb, 2,508 ... H-5
- Chatom, Washington, 1,094 ... N-2
- • Chelsea, Shelby, 1,329 ... G-7
- Cherokee, Colbert, 1,479 ... B-3
- Chickasaw, Mobile, 6,649 ... P-2
- Childersburg, Talladega, 4,579 ... G-8
- Citronelle, Mobile, 3,671 ... O-2
- Clanton, Chilton, 7,669 ... I-7
- Clayton, Barbour, 1,564 ... L-11
- Clio, Barbour, 1,365 ... M-10
- Collinsville, Cherokee/DeKalb, 1,429 ... D-9
- Columbiana, Shelby, 2,968 ... H-7
- Concord, Jefferson ... R-5
- Cordova, Walker, 2,623 ... E-5
- Cottonwood, Houston, 1,385 ... O-11
- Cowarts, Houston, 1,400 ... O-11
- Craig, Dallas ... K-6
- Creola, Mobile, 1,896 ... P-2
- Crossville, DeKalb, 1,350 ... C-9
- Cullman, Cullman, 13,367 ... D-6
- Dadeville, Tallapoosa, 3,276 ... I-10
- Daleville, Dale, 5,117 ... N-10
- Daphne, Baldwin, 11,290 ... Q-3
- Decatur, Limestone/Morgan, 48,761 ... B-6
- Demopolis, Marengo, 7,512 ... J-3
- Dolomite, Jefferson ... R-6
- Dora, Walker, 2,214 ... F-5
- Dothan, Dale/Houston, 53,589 ... O-11
- Double Springs, Winston, 1,138 ... D-4
- East Brewton, Escambia, 2,579 ... O-5
- Eastern Valley, Jefferson ... G-6
- Eclectic, Elmore, 1,087 ... J-9
- Edgewater, Jefferson ... Q-6
- Elba, Coffee, 4,011 ... N-9
- Enterprise, Coffee/Dale, 20,123 ... N-9
- Eufaula, Barbour, 13,220 ... L-12
- Eutaw, Greene, 2,281 ... I-3
- Evergreen, Conecuh, 3,911 ... N-6
- Fairfield, Jefferson, 12,200 ... F-6
- Fairhope, Baldwin, 8,485 ... Q-3
- Falkville, Morgan, 1,337 ... C-6
- Fayette, Fayette, 4,909 ... F-3
- Flat Creek-Wegra, Jefferson/Walker ... F-5
- Flint City, Morgan, 1,033 ... C-6
- Flomaton, Escambia, 1,811 ... O-5
- Florala, Covington, 2,075 ... O-8
- Florence, Lauderdale, 36,426 ... B-3
- Foley, Baldwin, 4,937 ... R-3
- • Forestdale, Jefferson, 10,395 ... Q-6
- Fort Deposit, Lowndes, 1,240 ... L-7
- • Fort McClellan, Calhoun, 4,128 ... F-9
- Fort Payne, DeKalb, 11,838 ... C-10
- • Fort Rucker, Dale, 7,593 ... N-10
- Frisco City, Monroe, 1,581 ... N-4
- Fultondale, Jefferson, 6,400 ... P-7
- Fyffe, DeKalb, 1,094 ... C-9
- Gadsden, Etowah, 42,523 ... E-9
- Gardendale, Jefferson, 9,251 ... P-7
- Geneva, Geneva, 4,681 ... O-9
- Georgiana, Butler, 1,933 ... M-6
- Glencoe, Calhoun/Etowah, 4,670 ... E-9
- Good Hope, Cullman, 1,700 ... D-6
- Goodwater, Coosa, 1,840 ... H-9
- Gordo, Pickens, 1,918 ... G-3
- • Grand Bay, Mobile, 3,383 ... Q-1
- Graysville, Jefferson, 2,241 ... P-6
- Greensboro, Hale, 3,047 ... I-4
- Greenville, Butler, 7,492 ... M-7
- Grove Hill, Clarke, 1,551 ... M-3
- Guin, Marion, 2,464 ... E-3
- Gulf Shores, Baldwin, 3,261 ... R-3
- Guntersville, Marshall, 7,038 ... C-8
- Gurley, Madison, 1,007 ... B-8
- Hackleburg, Marion, 1,161 ... C-3
- Haleyville, Marion/Winston, 4,452 ... D-4
- Hamilton, Marion, 5,787 ... D-3
- Hanceville, Cullman, 2,246 ... D-6
- Hartford, Geneva, 2,448 ... O-10
- Hartselle, Morgan, 10,795 ... C-6
- • Harvest, Madison, 1,922 ... A-6
- Hayneville, Lowndes, 969 ... K-7
- • Hazel Green, Madison, 2,208 ... A-7
- Headland, Henry, 3,266 ... N-11
- Heflin, Cleburne, 2,906 ... F-10
- Helena, Shelby, 3,918 ... G-6
- Henagar, DeKalb, 1,934 ... B-9
- Hokes Bluff, Etowah, 3,739 ... E-9
- • Holt, Tuscaloosa, 4,125 ... G-4
- Homewood, Jefferson, 22,922 ... F-6
- Hoover, Jefferson/Shelby, 39,788 ... R-7
- Hueytown, Jefferson, 15,280 ... R-5
- • Huguley, Chambers, 3,161 ... I-11
- Hunter, Montgomery ... J-7
- Huntsville, Limestone/Madison, 159,789 ... B-7
- • Inverness, Shelby, 2,528 ... G-6
- Irondale, Jefferson, 9,454 ... Q-8
- Jackson, Clarke, 5,819 ... N-3
- Jacksonville, Calhoun, 10,283 ... E-10
- Jasper, Walker, 13,553 ... E-5
- Jemison, Chilton, 1,898 ... H-6
- Killen, Lauderdale, 1,047 ... A-4
- Kimberly, Jefferson, 1,096 ... E-6
- Kinsey, Houston, 1,679 ... N-11
- • Ladonia, Russell, 2,905 ... J-12
- Lafayette, Chambers, 3,151 ... I-11
- • Lake Purdy, Shelby, 1,840 ... G-6
- Lanett, Chambers, 8,985 ... I-11
- Leeds, Jefferson/St. Clair/Shelby, 9,946 ... F-7
- Level Plains, Dale, 1,473 ... N-10
- Lincoln, Talladega, 2,941 ... F-8
- Linden, Marengo, 2,548 ... K-3
- Lineville, Clay, 2,394 ... G-10
- Lipscomb, Jefferson, 2,892 ... G-6
- Livingston, Sumter, 3,530 ... J-2
- Loxley, Baldwin, 1,161 ... Q-3
- Luverne, Crenshaw, 2,555 ... M-8
- Madison, Limestone/Madison, 14,904 ... B-6
- Marion, Perry, 4,211 ... J-5
- • Meadowbrook, Shelby, 4,621 ... G-6
- • Meridianville, Madison, 2,852 ... A-7
- Midfield, Jefferson, 5,559 ... G-6
- Midland City, Dale, 1,819 ... N-11
- • Mignon, Talladega, 1,548 ... G-8
- Millbrook, Elmore, 6,050 ... J-8
- Millport, Lamar, 1,203 ... F-2
- • Minor, Jefferson, 3,313 ... F-6
- Mobile, Mobile, 196,278 ... Q-2
- Monroeville, Monroe, 6,993 ... N-4
- Montevallo, Shelby, 4,239 ... H-6
- Montgomery, Montgomery, 187,106 ... K-8
- • Moody, St. Clair, 4,921 ... F-7
- • Moores Mill, Madison, 3,362 ... B-7
- Morris, Jefferson, 1,136 ... F-6
- Mosses, Lowndes, 1,072 ... K-6
- Moulton, Lawrence, 3,248 ... C-5
- Moundville, Hale/Tuscaloosa, 1,348 ... H-4
- Mount Olive, Jefferson ... F-6
- Mountain Brook, Jefferson, 19,810 ... F-7
- Muscle Shoals, Colbert, 9,611 ... B-4
- New Brockton, Coffee, 1,184 ... N-9
- New Hope, Madison, 2,248 ... C-7
- • New Market, Madison, 1,094 ... A-7
- Newton, Dale, 1,580 ... N-10
- Normal, Madison ... B-7
- Northport, Tuscaloosa, 17,366 ... G-4
- Ohatchee, Calhoun, 1,042 ... E-8
- Oneonta, Blount, 4,844 ... E-7
- Opelika, Lee, 22,122 ... I-11
- Opp, Covington, 6,985 ... N-8
- Orange Beach, Baldwin, 2,253 ... R-3
- Overton, Jefferson ... Q-8
- Oxford, Calhoun/Talladega, 9,362 ... F-9
- Ozark, Dale, 12,922 ... N-10
- Parrish, Walker, 1,433 ... F-5
- Pelham, Shelby, 9,765 ... G-6
- Pell City, St. Clair, 8,118 ... F-8
- Phenix City, Lee/Russell, 25,312 ... J-12
- Phil Campbell, Franklin, 1,317 ... C-3
- Piedmont, Calhoun/Cherokee, 5,288 ... E-10
- • Pinson-Clay-Chalkville, Jefferson, 10,987 ... F-7
- Pleasant Grove, Jefferson, 8,458 ... Q-5
- • Point Clear, Baldwin, 2,125 ... Q-3
- Prattville, Autauga/Elmore, 19,587 ... J-7
- Priceville, Morgan, 1,323 ... B-6
- Prichard, Mobile, 34,311 ... P-2
- Ragland, St. Clair, 1,807 ... F-8
- Rainbow City, Etowah, 7,673 ... E-9
- Rainsville, DeKalb, 3,875 ... C-9
- Red Bay, Franklin, 3,451 ... C-2
- • Redstone Arsenal, Madison, 4,909 ... B-7
- Reform, Pickens, 2,105 ... G-2
- Riverside, St. Clair, 1,004 ... F-8
- Roanoke, Randolph, 6,362 ... H-11
- Robertsdale, Baldwin, 2,401 ... Q-3
- Rockford, Coosa, 461 ... I-8
- Rogersville, Lauderdale, 1,125 ... B-5
- Roosevelt, Jefferson ... R-6
- Russellville, Franklin, 7,812 ... C-3
- • Saks, Calhoun, 11,138 ... F-9
- Samson, Geneva, 2,190 ... O-9
- Saraland, Mobile, 11,751 ... P-2
- Sardis City, DeKalb/Etowah/Marshall, 1,301 ... D-8
- Satsuma, Mobile, 5,194 ... P-2
- Scottsboro, Jackson, 13,786 ... B-9
- Selma, Dallas, 23,755 ... J-6
- • Selmont-West Selmont, Dallas, 3,823 ... J-6
- Semmes, Mobile ... P-1
- Sheffield, Colbert, 10,380 ... B-3
- Shelby, Shelby ... H-7
- Slocomb, Geneva, 1,906 ... O-10
- • Smiths, Lee, 3,456 ... J-12
- • Smoke Rise, Blount, 1,367 ... E-6
- Southside, Calhoun/Etowah, 5,580 ... E-9
- • Spanish Fort, Baldwin, 3,732 ... P-3
- Springville, St. Clair, 1,910 ... E-7
- Steele, St. Clair, 1,046 ... E-8
- Stevenson, Jackson, 2,046 ... A-9
- Sulligent, Lamar, 1,886 ... E-2
- Sumiton, Jefferson/Walker, 2,604 ... E-5
- Sylacauga, Talladega, 12,520 ... H-8
- Sylvan Springs, Jefferson, 1,470 ... F-5
- Talladega, Talladega, 18,175 ... G-9
- Tallassee, Elmore/Tallapoosa, 5,112 ... J-9
- Tarrant, Jefferson, 8,046 ... F-6
- Taylor, Houston, 1,352 ... O-11
- • Theodore, Mobile, 6,509 ... Q-2
- Thomasville, Clarke, 4,301 ... L-3
- Thorsby, Chilton, 1,465 ... I-6
- • Tillmans Corner, Mobile, 17,988 ... Q-2
- Town Creek, Lawrence, 1,379 ... B-4
- Trinity, Morgan, 1,380 ... B-5
- Troy, Pike, 13,051 ... L-9
- Trussville, Jefferson, 8,266 ... P-8
- Tuscaloosa, Tuscaloosa, 77,759 ... H-4
- Tuscumbia, Colbert, 8,413 ... B-3
- Tuskegee, Macon, 12,257 ... J-10
- • Underwood-Petersville, Lauderdale, 3,092 ... A-3
- Union Springs, Bullock, 3,975 ... K-10
- Uniontown, Perry, 1,730 ... J-4
- Valley, Chambers, 8,173 ... I-10
- Vernon, Lamar, 2,247 ... E-2
- Vestavia Hills, Jefferson, 19,749 ... R-7
- Vincent, St. Clair/Shelby/Talladega, 1,767 ... G-7
- Warrior, Jefferson, 3,280 ... E-6
- Weaver, Calhoun, 2,715 ... E-9
- Webb, Houston, 1,039 ... N-11
- Wedowee, Randolph, 796 ... G-10
- West Blocton, Bibb, 1,468 ... H-5
- • West End-Cobb Town, Calhoun, 4,034 ... F-9
- Wetumpka, Elmore, 4,670 ... J-8
- Wilsonville, Shelby, 1,185 ... G-7
- Winfield, Fayette/Marion, 3,689 ... E-3
- York, Sumter, 3,160 ... J-1

Explanation of symbols: • – Census Designated Place (CDP)

Alaska

General Help Numbers:

Governor's Office
PO Box 110001   907-465-3500
Juneau, AK 99811-0001   Fax 907-465-3532
www.gov.state.ak.us   8AM-5PM

Attorney General's Office
Law Department   907-465-3600, 465-2122
PO Box 110300   Fax 907-465-2075
Juneau, AK 99811-0300   8AM-4:30PM
www.law.state.ak.us

Legislative Records
Alaska State Legislative Affairs Agency   907-465-4648
Legislative Information Office   Fax 907-465-2864
120 4th St #111-State Capitol   8AM-5PM
Juneau, AK 99801-1182   www.legis.state.ak.us

State Archives
Alaska State Archives   907-465-2270
141 Willoughby Ave   Fax 907-465-2465
Juneau, AK 99801-1720   9AM-5PM
www.archives.state.ak.us

State Specifics:

Capital: Juneau
Juneau Borough

Time Zone: AK (Alaska Standard Time)*
* Alaska's Aleutian Islands are HT (Hawaii Standard Time)

Number of Boroughs/Political Divisions: 23

Population: 655,435

Website: www.state.ak.us

State Agencies

Criminal Records

Department of Public Safety, Records and Identification, 5700 E Tudor Rd, Anchorage, AK 99507; 907-269-5767, 907-269-5091-Fax; 8AM-4:30PM.

www.dps.state.ak.us

The state has a "Request for Criminal Justice Information Form" (one for the subject and one for third parties) for "Any Person" reports, which can be requested by email at tracey_brown@dps.state.ak.us.

Records are available for 10 years from the unconditional discharge date of the incident. 86% of arrests in database have final dispositions recorded; 85% for those arrests in last 5 years.

Searching: To receive full record, requester must provide verification of status as "Interested Party" defined as person who employs, appoints or permits the subject to have supervisory power over others, primarily in the child care industry. Include the following in your request-set of fingerprints, full name. "Any Person" reports are processed for those who are not "Interested Person" qualified

and who have a release, proper letter of explanation, and fingerprints. Approximately 62% of records are fingerprint-supported. The following data is not released: sealed records. All records are released, including those without dispositions to "Interested Person" requesters. "Any Person" requesters receive criminal records only with dispositions.

Access by: mail, in person.

Fee & Payment: The fee is $35.00 per search. The subject may - in person - request a search for $20.00, without fingerprints. This also applies to government agencies. If authorized, a requester may also request a national check by the FBI for an additional $24.00. Fee payee: State of Alaska. Prepayment required. No credit cards and no personal checks accepted.

Mail search: Turnaround time: 5 days. The fee is $5.00 for a 2nd copy.

In person search Results usually returned by mail

Other access: Name searching of limited trial court records and calendars are available free online at www.state.ak.us/courts/names.htm. See the Statewide Court Records profile.

Statewide Court Records

Office of the Administrative Director, Alaska Court System, 820 W 4th Ave, Anchorage, AK 99501; 907-264-8269, 907-264-8291-Fax; 8AM-4:30PM.

www.state.ak.us/courts

The state is in the process of migrating to a new case management system. Records form courts on the new ssytem are updated daily; on the old system the records are updated every 90 days.

Records are available online only. It takes 1-90 days before new records are available for inquiry.

Searching: Records are not destroyed.

Access by: online.

Online search: The home web page gives access to Appellate opinions. You may do a name search of a partial statewide Alaska Trial Courts database index at www.state.ak.us/courts/names.htm. Search results give case number, file date, disposition date, charge, and sentence. The index gives the name used on the first pleading only. The index is for only those courts on the new case managmentsystem. Until all courts are on, this search is not FCRA-compliant for employment screening purposes.

Other access: The civil/criminal name index is available to anyone who sends a blank CD-ROM each quarter to the Administrative Director.

Sexual Offender Registry

Department of Public Safety, Statewide Services Div-SOCR Unit, 5700 E Tudor Rd, Anchorage, AK 99507; 907-269-0396, 907-269-0394-Fax; 8AM-4:30PM.

www.dps.state.ak.us/nSorcr/asp

AS 18.65.087 authorizes the Department of Public Safety to maintain a central registry of sex offenders required to register under AS 12.63.010 and to make information about the offender available to the public.

Records are available since August 10, 1994. There are no levels or classes of sexual offenders in this state. All registration forms of offenders who register locally are forwarded to this address.

Searching: Only offenders convicted of the sex offenses specified under AS 12.63.100 are required to register. Persons who have been arrested or charged with a sex offense are not required to register unless the arrest or charge results in a conviction. The following information about those offenders available to the public: name, address, photograph, place of employment, date of birth, crime for which convicted, date of conviction and place and court of conviction. The following data is not released: sealed records.

Access by: mail, in person, online.

Mail search: Turnaround time: 2-4 days.

In person search Results usually returned by mail

Online search: Name searching and geographic searching is available at the website.

Incarceration Records

Alaska Department of Corrections, DOC Classification Office, 4500 Diplomacy Drive, Suite 340, Anchorage, AK 99508-5918; 907-269-7426, 907-269-7439-Fax; 8AM-4:30PM.

www.correct.state.ak.us

Records are available on current and former inmates. It takes 1 to 2 days before new records are available for inquiry.

Searching: Location, physical identifiers, charges, bail data, conviction and sentencing data are released. Include the following in your request-full name; DOB and SSN helpful.

Access by: mail, phone, fax.

Fee & Payment: No fee for search.

Mail search: Turnaround time: 1-3 days.

Phone search: Limited data given over the phone.

Fax search: Requests accepted by fax, if not extensive in nature.

Corporation, Trademarks, Servicemarks, Fictitious Name, Assumed Name, Limited Partnership, Limited Liability Company, Limited Liability Partnership Records

Corporation Section, Department of Commerce, Community & Econ Dev, PO Box 110808, Juneau, AK 99811-0808 (Courier address: 150 Third Street Rm 217, Juneau, AK 99801); 907-465-2530, 907-465-3257-Fax; 8AM-5PM.

www.dced.state.ak.us/bsc/corps.htm

Records are available from early 1900's on. Prior to 1960, the records are kept at the State Archives. You must go through this office in order to get records. New records are available for inquiry immediately. Records are indexed on microfiche, inhouse computer.

Searching: All information contained is considered public record. Include the following in your request-full name of business. In addition to the articles of incorporation, corporation records include the following information: Annual Reports, Officers, Directors, DBAs, Prior (Merged) names, Inactive and Reserved names.

Access by: mail, phone, fax, in person, online.

Fee & Payment: A copy of a document that is more than one page is $10.00. A copy of all documents pertaining to one file is $30.00 up to 50 pages and an additional $1.00 per page after 50 pages. A copy of a biennial report is $1.00. Fee payee: State of Alaska. Prepayment required. Personal checks accepted. Credit cards accepted: MasterCard, Visa.

Mail search: Turnaround time: 1 to 2 weeks.

Phone search: You can make a search request only if you are local and you plan to pick-up.

Fax search: Typical fax searches involve use of a credit card.

In person search: All results are mailed unless request is being processed using expedited service. The agency will call the requester when his/her request has been processed and is ready for pick-up, if it is a local call.

Online search: At the website, one can access status information on corps, LLCs, LLP, LP (all both foreign and domestic), registered and reserved names. Search by entity name, registered agent name, or by officer name. There is no fee.

Other access: Bulk purchase is available to approved entities. Call 907-465-2530 for more information.

Expedited service: Expedited service is available for mail, phone and in person searches. Turnaround time: 48 hours. Add $50.00 per business name.

Uniform Commercial Code

UCC Central File Systems Office, State Recorder's Office, 550 West 7th Ave #1200A, Anchorage, AK 99501-3564; 907-269-8873, 907-269-8899, 907-269-8945-Fax; 8AM-3:30PM.

www.dnr.state.ak.us/ssd/ucc/index.cfm

The statewide recording system consists of 34 separate recording districts serviced by a total of 14 separate offices.

Records are available from 1961 when the UCC system was established. Records are computerized since October 20, 1986 or earlier if with continuations. Records are kept on microfiche since 1-14-63 or prior if continuations filed. It takes 24 hours before new records are available for inquiry.

Searching: Use search request form UCC-11. Search results include all filings up to one year after lapse. All tax liens are filed at the local District Recorder offices. Include the following in your request-debtor name. All requests must be in writing.

Access by: mail, fax, in person, online.

Fee & Payment: Fee to search by name is $15.00 per debtor name. For information and copies, fee is $25.00 per debtor name. Certification costs an additional $5.00. Document page copies are $2.00 per file. Fee payee: Alaska Department of Revenue. Prepayment required. Personal checks accepted. Credit cards accepted: MasterCard, Visa.

Mail search: Turnaround time: 1 to 2 days. No SASE is required.

Fax search: Credit cards accepted.

In person search: A public access terminal is available, there is no fee to use the terminal.

Online search: One can search by granter-grantee name, date, document number or dcoument type at www.dnr.state.ak.us/ssd/ucc/search.cfm. There is no fee.

Other access: Bulk media of the entire UCC database can be purchased from the State Recorder's Office (907-269-8881).

Federal and State Tax Liens

Records not maintained by a state level agency.

All tax liens are filed at local District Recorder Offices.

Sales Tax Registrations

State does not impose sales tax.

Birth Certificates

Department of Health & Social Services, Bureau of Vital Statistics, 5441 Commercial Blvd, Juneau, AK 99801; 907-465-3391, 907-465-3618-Fax; 8AM-4:30PM.

www.hss.state.ak.us/dph/bvs

Birth records are strictly confidential until they become public records which is 100 years after the event.

Records are available from 1913 to present. New records are available for inquiry immediately. Records are indexed on microfiche, inhouse computer.

Searching: Person requesting must be a parent or guardian or give a justifying reason for request. No adoption information will be given except according to statute. Include the following in your request-full name, names of parents, mother's maiden name, date of birth, place of birth, reason for information request, relationship to person of record, and copy of requester's ID. Also, include a day time phone number.

Access by: mail, phone, fax, in person, online.

Fee & Payment: The $20.00 search fee includes a 3 year search. Add $1.00 per year searched for each year over 3 years. Fee payee: Bureau of Vital Statistics. Prepayment required. Personal checks accepted. Major credit cards accepted.

Mail search: Turnaround time: 2 weeks. No SASE is required.

Phone search: See expedited services.

Fax search: See expedited services.

In person search: Turnaround time 10 minutes.

Online search: Records may be ordered online via a state-designated vendor at www.vitalchek.com. There is a $5.50 service fee. Use of credit card required.

Expedited service: Expedited service is available for mail, phone, online and fax searches. Turnaround time: 2 days. Add $11.00 for using a credit card and $15.50 for Fed Ex or $11.75 for Express Mail.

Death Records

Department of Health & Social Services, Bureau of Vital Statistics, 5441 Commercial Blvd, Juneau, AK 99801; 907-465-3391, 907-465-3618-Fax; 8AM-4:30PM.

www.hss.state.ak.us/dph/bvs

Records are available from 1913 to present. New records are available for inquiry immediately. Records are indexed on microfiche, inhouse computer.

Searching: You must be next of kin or have a notarized release statement from immediate family. Records are public after 50 years. Include the following in your request-full name, date of death, place of death, names of parents, reason for information request, relationship to person of record. Also, include a daytime phone number.

Access by: mail, phone, fax, in person, online.

Fee & Payment: The $20.00 search fee includes a 3 year search. Add $1.00 per year searched for each year over 3 years. Fee payee: Bureau of Vital

Statistics. Prepayment required. Personal checks accepted. Major credit cards accepted.

Mail search: Turnaround time: 2 weeks.

Phone search: See expedited service.

Fax search: See expedited service.

In person search: Turnaround time 10 minutes.

Online search: Records may be ordered online via a state-designated vendor at www.vitalchek.com. There is a $5.50 service fee. Use of credit card required.

Expedited service: Expedited service is available for mail, phone, online and fax searches. Turnaround time: 2 days. Add $11.00 for using a credit card and add $15.50 for Fed Ex or $11.75 for Express Mail.

Marriage Certificates

Department of Health & Social Services, Bureau of Vital Statistics, 5441 Commercial Blvd, Juneau, AK 99801; 907-465-3391, 907-465-3618-Fax; 8AM-4:30PM.

www.hss.state.ak.us/dph/bvs

Records are available from 1913 to present. New records are available for inquiry immediately. Records are indexed on microfiche, inhouse computer.

Searching: Person requesting must be one of the registrants or an attorney representing a registrant. Records are public after 50 years. Include the following in your request-names of husband and wife, date of marriage, place or county of marriage. Include wife's maiden name and a daytime phone number.

Access by: mail, phone, fax, in person, online.

Fee & Payment: The $20.00 search fee includes a 3 year search. Add $1.00 per year searched for each year over 3 years. Fee payee: Bureau of Vital Statistics. Prepayment required. Personal checks accepted. Credit cards accepted: MasterCard, Visa.

Mail search: Turnaround time: 2 weeks.

Phone search: See expedited service.

Fax search: See expedited service.

In person search: Turnaround time 10 minutes.

Online search: Records may be ordered online via a state-designated vendor at www.vitalchek.com. There is a $5.50 service fee. Use of credit card required.

Expedited service: Expedited service is available for mail, phone, online and fax searches. Turnaround time: 2 days. Add $11.00 for using a credit card and add $15.50 for Fed Ex or $11.75 for Express Mail.

Divorce Records

Department of Health & Social Services, Bureau of Vital Statistics, 5441 Commercial Blvd, Juneau, AK 99801; 907-465-3391, 907-465-3618-Fax; 8AM-4:30PM.

www.hss.state.ak.us/dph/bvs

Records are available from 1950 to present. New records are available for inquiry immediately. Records are indexed on microfiche, inhouse computer.

Searching: Person requesting must be one of the registrants or an attorney representing a registrant. Records are public after 50 years. Include the following in your request-names of husband and

wife, date of divorce, place of divorce. Also, include a daytime phone number.

Access by: mail, phone, fax, in person, online.

Fee & Payment: The $20.00 search fee includes a 3 year search. Add $1.00 per year searched for each year over 3 years. Fee payee: Bureau of Vital Statistics. Prepayment required. Personal checks accepted. Major credit cards accepted.

Mail search: Turnaround time: 2 weeks. No SASE is required.

Phone search: See expedited service.

Fax search: See expedited service.

In person search: Turnaround time 10 minutes.

Online search: Records may be ordered online via a state-designated vendor at www.vitalchek.com. There is a $5.50 service fee. Use of credit card required.

Expedited service: Expedited service is available for mail, phone, online and fax searches. Turnaround time: 2 days. Add $11.00 for using a credit card and add $15.50 for Fed Ex or $11.75 for Express Mail.

Workers' Compensation Records

Workers' Compensation, PO Box 25512, Juneau, AK 99802 (Courier address: 1111 W Eighth St, Room 307, Juneau, AK 99802); 907-465-2790, 907-465-2797-Fax; 8AM-4:30PM.

www.labor.state.ak.us/wc/wc.htm

Records are available from 1982 on the computer if active, and prior to 1982 the records are on microfilm and/or microfiche to the 1960s. It takes one week before new records are available for inquiry.

Searching: All requests must be in writing. To receive a copy of a file, a signed medical release from claimant is required. Include the following in your request-claimant name, Social Security Number, date of accident. All requests handled on a first come first serve basis.

Access by: mail, phone, fax, in person.

Fee & Payment: Copies cost $.35 per page for active files and $.75 per page for microfilmed files. A computer printout costs $.50 per screen. There is no search fee. Fee payee: State of Alaska. Large orders require prepayment. Personal checks accepted. No credit cards accepted.

Mail search: Turnaround time: 10 to 14 days. No SASE is required.

Phone search: The agency will let you know if a file exists.

Fax search: Fax searching available.

In person search: Records are returned by mail.

Other access: Microfiche is available at $50.00 per fiche, prepaid.

Driver Records

Division of Motor Vehicles, Driver's Records, 2760 Sherwood Lane #B, Juneau, AK 99801; 907-465-4361 (Motor Vehicle Reports Desk), 907-465-4363 (Licensing), 907-465-5509-Fax; 8AM-5PM.

www.state.ak.us/dmv

Copies of tickets are only released, in writing, to the participant, legal representative, or insurance representative.

Records are available for minor moving violations and suspensions for three years, major moving violations for five years. Convictions are automatically purged from public record by conviction date. Accidents are reported only if action is taken.

Searching: Records are considered confidential. Any private company or individual requester must have a signed release from the licensee or a subpoena. High volume requesters may maintain these forms rather than send in with requests. Include the following in your request-name, driver's license number, date of birth. Driver's residence and mailing address are included as part of the search report.

Access by: mail, in person, online.

Fee & Payment: Search costs $5.00 per record. Prepayment is required. Fee payee: State of Alaska. Personal checks accepted. Credit cards are accepted.

Mail search: Turnaround time: 3 to 4 working days. No SASE is required.

In person search turnaround time- while you wait

Online search: Online access costs $5.00 per record. This is for pre-approved, ongoing requesters only. Inquiries may be made at any time, 24 hours a day. Batch inquiries may call back within thirty minutes for responses. Search by the first four letters of driver's name, license number and date of birth. At present, there is only one phone line available for users; you may experience a busy signal.

Vehicle Ownership, Vehicle Identification, Vessel Registration

Division of Motor Vehicles, Research, 1300 W Benson Blvd #200, Anchorage, AK 99503-3600; 907-269-5551, 8:30AM-4:30PM.

www.state.ak.us/dmv

All powered boats, and all non-powered boats over 10 ft or with auxiliary power units used on any water of the state must be registered. Records are available for 7 years to present. However, until Jan. 1, 2001, all boat registrations were done through the US Coast Guard.

Searching: Record requests are honored for employment, insurance, court or impound purposes. Otherwise, a signed release is required, signed by requester, attesting to purpose of request. Use of Form 851-Request for Vehicle Record is required if not a pre-approved, ongoing requester; form may be downloaded form the web.

Access by: mail, in person.

Fee & Payment: The fee is $5.00 per record. There is no fee to do a vessel search. Fee payee: State of Alaska. Prepayment required. No credit cards accepted.

Mail search: Turnaround time: 2 to 3 weeks. No SASE is required.

In person search: Typically a search request is limited to three items and is a computer printout. Other research requests are mailed and can take up to 2-3 weeks to complete.

Other access: The entire master tape file of registration information is available at a cost of approximately $50 per 1,000 records. Call the Director's Office (907-269-5551) for more info.

Accident Reports

Department of Public Safety, Driver Services, 2760 Sherwood Lane #B, Juneau, AK 99801; 907-465-4361, 8AM-5PM.

www.state.ak.us/dmv

Accidents involving property damage in excess of $500, injury or death must be reported to the local police or state troopers. Records are available from seven years. Records are normally destroyed after seven years.

Searching: Only legal representatives and insurance agents of the participants, or the participant him/herself may obtain copies. The lawyer or legal representative must have a notarized request, an insurance agent a signed request with reason. Include the following in your request-names, date of incident, city, physical location of the accident.

Access by: mail, phone, in person.

Fee & Payment: The fee is $5.00 per record. Fee payee: State of Alaska, Department of Public Safety. Prepayment required. Personal checks accepted. No credit cards accepted.

Mail search: Turnaround time: 1 to 2 weeks. No SASE is required.

Phone search: Phone requests are available for pre-approved accounts.

In person search Turnaround time while you wait

Vessel Ownership

Records not maintained by a state level agency.

Alaska is not a title state. Liens are filed with the Department of Natural Resources, Recorder's Section at 907-269-8882. Also, until Jan. 1, 2001, all boat registrations were done through the US Coast Guard (970-463-2294).

Voter Registration

Division of Elections, PO Box 110017, Juneau, AK 99811-0017 (Courier: Court Plaza Building, 4th Floor, 240 Main Street, Juneau, AK 99801); 907-465-4611, 907-465-3203-Fax; 8AM-5PM.

www.elections.state.ak.us

There are four regional Elections Offices, besides this office. Each has access to the election records database.

Records are available from 1968. It takes 1 day before new records are available for inquiry. Records are normally destroyed after placed on microfilm and become permanent.

Searching: Searching by name is permitted. The following data is not released: Social Security Number, place or date of birth, phone number, and voter ID #.

Access by: mail, phone, fax, in person.

Fee & Payment: There is no fee. There is a copy fee of $.20 per copy if request exceeds 20 copies. Prepayment required. Personal checks accepted.

Mail search: Turnaround time: 1 day.

Phone search: Will search if research time not lengthy.

Fax search: Fax searching available.

In person search: Turnaround time is immediate unless extensive lists or requests for older records are presented.

Other access: The agency offers the complete record database on CD-ROM for $178. Individual districts (there are 40) can be purchased on disk for $20.00 per district.

GED Certificates

Department of Labor, Employment Security Division, PO Box 25509, Juneau, AK 99802-5509 (Courier address: 1111 8th Street #210, Juneau, AK 99801); 907-465-4685, 907-465-4186-Fax; 8AM-4:30PM.

www.ajcn.state.ak.us/abe

The documents are referred to as GED Diplomas by this agency. It takes 1 day before new records are available for inquiry.

Searching: Include the following in your request-full name, DOB, SSN, year of test and city of test. All requesters must include a signed release. E-mail requests accepted at ged@labor.state.ak.us.

Access by: mail, fax, in person.

Fee & Payment: There is no fee for a verification or a transcript copy. There is a $10.00 fee for a copy of a diploma.

Mail search: Turnaround time: 1 to 2 weeks. No SASE is required.

Fax search: A written release form is required.

In person search: Simple requests may be processed while you wait.

Hunting and Fishing License Information

Department of Fish & Game, Licensing Section, PO Box 25525, Juneau, AK 99802-5525 (Courier address: 1255 W 8th St, Juneau, AK 99802); 907-465-2376, 907-465-2440-Fax; 8AM-5PM.

www.adfg.state.ak.us

Records are available from 10 years to present. It takes 4 weeks before new records are available for inquiry.

Searching: Information used to search includes name, SSN, DOB, address, driver's license number, or year license issued. The following data is not released: Social Security Numbers or telephone numbers.

Access by: mail, phone, fax, in person.

Fee & Payment: No fee unless you request a large list. For certified copies the turnaround time is 6 weeks. Fee payee: State of Alaska. Prepayment required. Personal checks accepted. Credit cards accepted.

Mail search: Turnaround time: within 2 weeks. No SASE is required.

Phone search: Limited number of requests given over the phone.

Fax search: Same criteria as phone searches.

In person search: Large lists will not be processed immediately.

Other access: The vendor file is available for $25 on paper or disk. The entire license file is available for $350 on CD.

Alaska State Licensing Agencies

For details about the agency responsible for licensing/certifying/registering an item below or in the Agency Quick Finder section, match an item's number with the number of the agency in the *Licensing Agency Information* section.

Alaska Licenses Searchable Online

Acupuncturist #20	www.dced.state.ak.us/occ/search3.htm
Anesthetist, Dental, General/Permit #20	www.dced.state.ak.us/occ/search3.htm
Architect #20	www.dced.state.ak.us/occ/search3.htm
Athletic Event Promoter #20	www.dced.state.ak.us/occ/search3.htm
Athletic Trainer #20	www.dced.state.ak.us/occ/search3.htm
Attorney #11	www.alaskabar.org/index.cfm?id=4954
Audiologist/Hearing Aid Dealer #20	www.dced.state.ak.us/occ/search3.htm
Bail Bondsman #13	www.dced.state.ak.us/ins/apps/InsLicStart.cfm
Bank #15	www.dced.state.ak.us/bsc/pub/2003_directory.pdf
Barber #20	www.dced.state.ak.us/occ/search3.htm
Barber Shop Owner/School/Instr. #20	www.dced.state.ak.us/occ/search3.htm
BIDCOS/CFAB #15	www.dced.state.ak.us/bsc/pub/2003_directory.pdf
Big Game Guide/Assist./Transporter #20	www.dced.state.ak.us/occ/search3.htm
Boxer #20	www.dced.state.ak.us/occ/search3.htm
Boxing Physician #20	www.dced.state.ak.us/occ/search3.htm
Boxing/Wrestling Personnel #20	www.dced.state.ak.us/occ/search3.htm
Chiropractor #20	www.dced.state.ak.us/occ/search3.htm
Collection Agency/Operator #20	www.dced.state.ak.us/occ/search3.htm
Concert Promoter #20	www.dced.state.ak.us/occ/search3.htm
Construction Contractor #20	www.dced.state.ak.us/occ/search3.htm
Contractor, Civil/Elect./Mech./Petrol. #20	www.dced.state.ak.us/occ/search3.htm
Contractor, Residential #20	www.dced.state.ak.us/occ/search3.htm
Cosmetologist/Hairdresser #20	www.dced.state.ak.us/occ/search3.htm
Cosmetology Shop Owner/School/Instr #20	www.dced.state.ak.us/occ/search3.htm
Counselor, Professional #20	www.dced.state.ak.us/occ/OccSearch/main.cfm
Credit Union #15	www.dced.state.ak.us/bsc/pub/2003_directory.pdf
Defibrillator Technician #17	http://chems.alaska.gov/emsdata/
Dental Hygienist #20	www.dced.state.ak.us/occ/search3.htm
Dentist/Dental Examiner #20	www.dced.state.ak.us/occ/search3.htm
Dietitian/Nutritionist #20	www.dced.state.ak.us/occ/OccSearch/main.cfm
Drug Distributor/Drug Room #20	www.dced.state.ak.us/occ/search3.htm
Electrical Administrator #20	www.dced.state.ak.us/occ/search3.htm
Emergency Medical Technician #17	http://chems.alaska.gov/emsdata/
Employment Agency Operator #5	www.dced.state.ak.us/occ/search3.htm
Engineer #20	www.dced.state.ak.us/occ/search3.htm
Esthetician #20	www.dced.state.ak.us/occ/search3.htm
Funeral Director/Establishment #20	www.dced.state.ak.us/occ/search3.htm
Geologist #20	www.dced.state.ak.us/occ/search3.htm
Guide/Outfitter, Hunting #20	www.dced.state.ak.us/occ/search3.htm
Hairdresser/Esthetician #20	www.dced.state.ak.us/occ/search3.htm
Hearing Aid Dealer #20	www.dced.state.ak.us/occ/search3.htm
Independent Adjuster #13	www.dced.state.ak.us/ins/apps/InsLicStart.cfm
Insurance Agent, Managing General #13	www.dced.state.ak.us/ins/apps/InsLicStart.cfm
Insurance Occupation #13	www.dced.state.ak.us/ins/apps/InsLicStart.cfm
Insurance Producer #13	www.dced.state.ak.us/ins/apps/InsLicStart.cfm
Landscape Architect #20	www.dced.state.ak.us/occ/search3.htm
Lobbyist/Lobbyist Employer #9	www.state.ak.us/local/akpages/ADMIN/apoc/lobcov.htm
Marriage & Family Therapist #20	www.dced.state.ak.us/occ/OccSearch/main.cfm
Mechanical Administrator #20	www.dced.state.ak.us/occ/search3.htm
Medical Doctor/Surgeon #20	www.dced.state.ak.us/occ/search3.htm
Midwife #20	www.dced.state.ak.us/occ/OccSearch/main.cfm
Mortician/Embalmer #20	www.dced.state.ak.us/occ/search3.htm
Naturopathic Physician #20	www.dced.state.ak.us/occ/search3.htm
Nurse Anesthetist #20	www.dced.state.ak.us/occ/search3.htm
Nurse-RN/LPN #20	www.dced.state.ak.us/occ/search3.htm
Nurses' Aide #20	www.dced.state.ak.us/occ/search3.htm
Nursing Home Administrator #20	www.dced.state.ak.us/occ/search3.htm

Occupational Therapist/Assist #20	www.dced.state.ak.us/occ/search3.htm
Optician, Dispensing #20	www.dced.state.ak.us/occ/search3.htm
Optometrist #20	www.dced.state.ak.us/occ/search3.htm
Osteopathic Physician #20	www.dced.state.ak.us/occ/search3.htm
Paramedic #20	www.dced.state.ak.us/occ/search3.htm
Parenteral Sedation (Dental) #20	www.dced.state.ak.us/occ/search3.htm
Pharmacist/Pharmacist Intern #20	www.dced.state.ak.us/occ/search3.htm
Pharmacy/Pharmacy Technician #20	www.dced.state.ak.us/occ/search3.htm
Physical Therapist/Assistant #20	www.dced.state.ak.us/occ/search3.htm
Physician Assistant #20	www.dced.state.ak.us/occ/search3.htm
Pilot, Marine #20	www.dced.state.ak.us/occ/search3.htm
Podiatrist #20	www.dced.state.ak.us/occ/search3.htm
Premium Finance Company #15	www.dced.state.ak.us/bsc/pub/2003_directory.pdf
Process Server #10	www.dps.state.ak.us/PermitsLicensing/images/CPSlist.pdf
Psychologist/Psychological Assistant #20	www.dced.state.ak.us/occ/search3.htm
Public Accountant-CPA #20	www.dced.state.ak.us/occ/OccSearch/main.cfm
Real Estate Agent/Broker/Assoc. #20	www.dced.state.ak.us/occ/search3.htm
Real Estate Appraiser #20	www.dced.state.ak.us/occ/search3.htm
Referee #20	www.dced.state.ak.us/occ/OccSearch/main.cfm
Reinsurance Intermediary Broker/Mgr #13	www.dced.state.ak.us/ins/apps/InsLicStart.cfm
School Administrator #1	www.eed.state.ak.us/TeacherCertification/CertSearchForm.cfm
School Special Service #1	www.eed.state.ak.us/TeacherCertification/CertSearchForm.cfm
Small Loan Company #15	www.dced.state.ak.us/bsc/pub/2003_directory.pdf
Social Worker #20	www.dced.state.ak.us/occ/OccSearch/main.cfm
Social Worker, Clinical #20	www.dced.state.ak.us/occ/OccSearch/main.cfm
Speech/Language Pathologist #20	www.dced.state.ak.us/occ/search3.htm
Surplus Line Broker #13	www.dced.state.ak.us/ins/apps/InsLicStart.cfm
Surveyor, Land #20	www.dced.state.ak.us/occ/search3.htm
Tattoo Artist/Body Piercer #20	www.dced.state.ak.us/occ/search3.htm
Teacher #1	www.eed.state.ak.us/TeacherCertification/CertSearchForm.cfm
Thrift #15	www.dced.state.ak.us/bsc/pub/2003_directory.pdf
Transporter, Game #20	www.dced.state.ak.us/occ/search3.htm
Trust Company #15	www.dced.state.ak.us/bsc/pub/2003_directory.pdf
Undergr'nd Storage Tank Worker/Contr. #20	www.dced.state.ak.us/occ/search3.htm
Vessel Agent #20	www.dced.state.ak.us/occ/search3.htm
Veterinarian/Veterinary Technician #20	www.dced.state.ak.us/occ/search3.htm
Viatical Settlement Broker #13	www.dced.state.ak.us/ins/apps/InsLicStart.cfm
Waste Water System Operator #3	http://info.dec.state.ak.us/SPS/Permitall2.asp
Wrestler #20	www.dced.state.ak.us/occ/OccSearch/main.cfm

Alaska Licensing Quick Finder

Acupuncturist #20	907-465-2695
Aircraft-related Occupation #18	907-271-2158
Alcohol Establishment #21	907-269-0350
Alcohol Server #21	907-269-0350
Amusement Ride #7	907-269-4963
Anesthetist, Dental, Gen/Permit #20	907-465-2542
Architect #20	907-465-2540
Art Exhibit, Cabaret #21	907-269-0350
Asbestos Removal Worker #14	907-269-4963
Asbestos Worker #227	907-269-4960
Athletic Event Promoter #20	907-465-2695
Athletic Trainer #20	907-465-2695
Attorney #11	907-272-7469
Audiologist/Hearing Aid Dealer #20	907-465-2695
Bail Bondsman #13	907-465-2515
Bank #15	907-465-2521
Barber #20	907-465-2547
Barber Shop Owner/School/Instr. #20	907-465-2547
BIDCOS/CFAB #15	907-465-2521
Big Game Guide/Assistant/Transporter #20	907-465-2543
Boiler Operator #7	907-269-4963
Boxer #20	907-465-2695
Boxing Physician #20	907-465-2695
Boxing/Wrestling Personnel #20	907-465-2695
Broker/Dealer #12	907-465-2521
Charter Boat, Sport Fishing #6	907-267-2369
Child Care Provider/Home/Center/Group Home #16	907-465-4756
Chiropractor #20	907-465-2589
Collection Agency/Operator #20	907-465-2695
Concealed Handgun Registrant #10	907-269-0392
Concert Promoter #20	907-465-2534
Construction Contractor #20	907-465-2546
Contractor, Civil/Elect./Mech./Mining/Petrol. #20	907-465-2546
Contractor, Residential #20	907-465-2546
Cosmetologist/Hairdresser #20	907-465-2547
Cosmetology Shop Owner/School/Instr #20	907-465-2547
Counselor, Professional #20	907-465-2551
Credit Union #15	907-465-2521
Crewmember, Fishing Boat #4	907-465-2376
Defibrillator Technician #17	907-465-3029
Dental Hygienist #20	907-465-2542
Dentist/Dental Examiner #20	907-465-2542
Dietitian/Nutritionist #20	907-465-2534
Drug Distributor/Drug Room #20	907-465-2589
Electrical Administrator #20	907-465-2589
Electrician #7	907-269-4963
Elevator #7	907-269-4963
Emergency Medical Technician #17	907-465-3029
Employment Agency Operator #5	907-269-8160
Engineer #20	907-465-2540
Esthetician #20	907-465-2547
Explosives Handler #14	907-269-4963
Fisher #4	907-465-2376
Fishing Operation, Kenai #8	907-260-4882
Funeral Director/Establishment #20	607-465-2695
Fur Dealer #4	907-465-2376
Game Farm #4	907-465-2376
Geologist #20	907-465-2695
Guide, Sport Fishing #6	907-267-2369
Guide, Sport Fishing, Kenai Only #8	907-260-4882
Guide/Outfitter, Hunting #20	907-465-2543
Hairdresser/Esthetician #20	907-465-2547
Hearing Aid Dealer #20	907-465-2695
Hunting Guide #20	907-465-2543
Independent Adjuster #13	907-465-2515
Insurance Agent, Mng General #13	907-465-2515
Insurance Occupation #13	907-465-2515
Insurance Producer #13	907-465-2515
Investment Advisor #12	907-465-2521
Investment Broker/Dealer/Occupation #12	907-465-2521
Landscape Architect #20	907-465-2540
Lobbyist/Lobbyist Employer #9	907-465-4864
Marriage & Family Therapist #20	907-465-2551
Mechanical Administrator #20	907-465-2589
Medical Doctor/Surgeon #20	907-465-2541
Midwife #20	907-465-2580

Mobile Home Dealer #20 907-465-2547	Physician Assistant #20 907-269-8163	Social Worker #20 907-465-2551
Mortician/Embalmer #20 607-465-2695	Pilot, Aircraft #18 907-271-2158	Social Worker, Clinical #20 907-465-2551
Naturopathic Physician #20 907-465-2695	Pilot, Marine #20 907-465-2548	Speech/Language Pathologist #20 907-465-2534
Notary Public #19 907-465-3509	Plumber #7 907-269-4963	Surplus Line Broker #13 907-465-2515
Nurse #20 907-465-2544	Podiatrist #20 907-465-2541	Surveyor, Land #20 907-465-2540
Nurse Anesthetist #20 907-465-2544	Premium Finance Company #15 907-465-2521	Tattoo Artist/Body Piercer #20 907-465-2547
Nurse-RN/LPN #20 907-465-2544	Process Server #10 907-269-0393	Taxidermist #4 907-465-2376
Nurses' Aide #20 907-269-8169	Psychologist/Psychological Assistant #20	Teacher #1 907-465-2831
Nursing Home Administrator #20 907-465-2695	 907-465-3811	Thrift #15 907-465-2521
Occupational Therapist/Assist #20 907-465-2580	Public Accountant-CPA #20 907-465-3817	Transporter, Game #20 907-465-2543
Optician, Dispensing #20 907-465-5470	Real Estate Agent/Broker/Assoc. #20.. 907-269-8162	Trapper #4 907-465-2376
Optometrist #20 907-465-2580	Real Estate Appraiser #20 907-465-2542	Trust Company #15 907-465-2521
Osteopathic Physician #20 907-465-2541	Referee #20 907-465-2695	Undergr'nd Storage Tank Worker/Contractor #20
Painter #14 907-269-4963	Reinsurance Intermediary Broker/Mgr #13	 907-465-5470
Paramedic #20 907-465-2541	 907-465-2515	Vessel Agent #20 907-465-2548
Parenteral Sedation (Dental) #20 907-465-2542	School Administrator #1 907-465-2831	Veterinarian/Veterinary Technician #20 907-465-5470
Pesticide Applicator #2 907-376-1858	School Special Service #1 907-465-2831	Viatical Settlement Broker #13 907-465-2515
Pharmacist/Pharmacist Intern #20 907-465-2589	Securities Agent #12 907-465-2521	Waste Water System Operator #3 907-465-5140
Pharmacy #20 907-465-2589	Security Guard #10 907-269-0393	Wrestler #20 907-465-2695
Pharmacy Technician #20 907-465-2589	Ski Lift #7 907-269-4963	
Physical Therapist/Assistant #20 907-465-2580	Small Loan Company #15 907-465-2521	

Alaska Licensing Agency Information

1 Department of Education & Early Development, Teacher Education & Certification, 801 W 10th St, #200, Juneau, AK 99801-1894; 907-465-2831, Fax: 907-465-2441.
www.eed.state.ak.us/TeacherCertification/
Email: tcwebmail@eed.state.ak.us
Search Database at www.eed.state.ak.us/Teach erCertification/CertSearchForm.cfm

2 Department of Environmental Conservation, Division of Environmental Health, 1700 E Bogard Rd, Bldg B #202, Wasilla, AK 99654; 907-376-1858, Fax: 907-745-8125.
Email: dick_barrett@dec.state.ak.us

3 Department of Environmental Conservation, Facility Construction & Operation, 410 Willoughby Ave, #303, Juneau, AK 99801-1795; 907-465-5140, Fax: 907-465-5177.
www.state.ak.us/local/akpages/ENV.CONSERV/
Search Database at
http://info.dec.state.ak.us/SPS/Permitall2.asp

4 Department of Fish & Game, Licensing Section, PO Box 25525, Juneau, AK 99802-5525; 907-465-2376, Fax: 907-465-2440. www.adfg.state.ak.us/
Email: Kris_Wright@fishgame.state.ak.us

5 Department of Labor, Department of Commerce, Div of Occupational Licensing, 550 W 7th Ave #1500, Anchorage, AK 99501-3567; 907-269-8160, Fax: 907-261-8156.
www.gov.state.ak.us/ltgov Search Database at
www.dced.state.ak.us/occ/search3.htm

6 Department of Fish and Game, Division of Sport Fish - RTS, 333 Raspberry Rd, Anchorage, AK 99518-1599; 907-267-2369, Fax: 907-267-2422.
www.sf.adfg.state.ak.us/statewide/Guides/guide.cfm

7 Department of Labor, Labor & Safety Standards, Mechanical Inspection Section, 3301 Eagle St #302, Anchorage, AK 99503-4149; 907-269-4963, Fax: 907-269-4932.
www.labor.state.ak.us/lss/mihome.htm
Email: Anchorage_LSS-MI@labor.state.ak.us

8 Department of Natural Resources, Division of Parks & Outdoor Recreation - Kenai, 514 Funny River Rd, Soldotna, AK 99669; 907-260-4882, Fax: 907-260-5992.
www.dnr.state.ak.us/parks/

9 Public Offices Commission, PO Box 110222 (240 Main. St, Rm 201), Juneau, AK 99811-0222; 907-465-4864, Fax: 907-465-4832.
www.state.ak.us/local/akpages/ADMIN/apoc/lobc ov.htm Email: tammy_kempton@admin.stae.ak.us
Search Database at www.state.ak.us/local/akpage s/ADMIN/apoc/lobcov.htm Note: Download directories of licensed lobbyists at the website. The Anchorage phone is 907-276-4176.

10 Alaska State Troopers, Dept. of Public Safety/ Permits & Licensing Unit, 5700 E Tudor Rd, Anchorage, AK 99507-1225; 907-269-0391, Fax: 907-269-5609.
www.dps.state.ak.us/PermitsLicensing/index.asp
Email: maryellen_thomas@dps.state.ak.us

11 Alaska Bar Association, Board of Governors, PO Box 100279 (550 W 7th Ave #1900), Anchorage, AK 99510-0279; 907-272-7469, Fax: 907-272-2932. www.alaskabar.org
Email: info@alaskabar.org Search Database at
www.alaskabar.org/index.cfm?id=4954 Note: Recent yearly bar exam name results are available at www.alaskabar.org/ada.cfm?id=5239.

12 Department of Community & Economic Development, Division of Banking; Securities Section, PO Box 110807, Juneau, AK 99811-0807; 907-465-2521, Fax: 907-465-1230.
www.dced.state.ak.us/bsc/secur.htm
Email: dbsc@dced.state.ak.us

13 Department of Community & Economic Development, Division of Insurance, PO Box 110805 (9th Floor State Office Bldg), Juneau, AK 99811-0805; 907-465-2515, Fax: 907-465-3422.
www.dced.state.ak.us/insurance/
Email: insurance@dced.state.ak.us
Search Database at
www.dced.state.ak.us/ins/apps/InsLicStart.cfm

14 Dept. of Labor, Labor & Safety Standards, Occupational Safety & Health, 3301 Eagle St #302, Anchorage, AK 99503; 907-269-4963.
www.labor.state.ak.us/lss/mihome.htm
Email: Anchorage_LSS-MI@labor.state.ak.us

15 Department of Community & Economic Development, Division of Banking; Banking Section, PO Box 110807, Juneau, AK 99811; 907-465-2521, Fax: 907-465-1231.
www.dced.state.ak.us/bsc/banking.htm

Search Database at
www.dced.state.ak.us/bsc/pub/2003_directory.pdf

16 Department of Health & Social Services, Division of Public Asst - Child Care Licensing, SE, PO Box 110640 (SE Division Only), Juneau, AK 99811; 907-465-4756, Fax: 907-465-6982.
www.hss.state.ak.us/dpa Search Database at
www.hss.state.ak.us/dpa/programs/ccare/ Note: There are 3 other divisions that handle facility licensing: Anchorage Area.: 907-343-4748; South Central Alaska (except Anchorage): 907-269-4600; Fairbanks: 907-451-3198.

17 Department of Health & Social Services, Division of Public Health/Section of Community Health and EMS, 410 Willoughby Rm 109 Box 110616, Juneau, AK 99811-0616; 907-465-3027, Fax: 907-465-4101. www.chems.alaska.gov
Email: matt_anderson@health.state.ak.us Search Database at http://chems.alaska.gov/emsdata/

18 Federal Aviation Administration, FSDO, 4510 W International Airport Rd, Anchorage, AK 99502; 907-271-2158, Fax: 907-271-3877.

19 Notary Public Section, Office of Lieutenant Governor, PO Box 110015, State Capitol, Juneau, AK 99811-0015; 907-465-3509, Fax: 907-465-5400. www.gov.state.ak.us/ltgov
Email: notary@gov.state.ak.us

20 Department of Community & Economic Development, Div of Occupational Licensing, PO Box 110806, Juneau, AK 99811-0806; 907-465-2534, Fax: 907-465-2974.
www.dced.state.ak.us/occ
Email: license@dced.state.ak.us Search Database at
www.dced.state.ak.us/occ/search3.htm Note: You may download business license lists at
www.dced.state.ak.us/occ/buslic4.cfm.

21 Department of Revenue, Alcoholic Beverage Control Board, 5848 E. Tudor Rd, Anchorage, AK 99507-1286; 907-269-0350, Fax: 907-272-9412.
www.dps.state.ak.us/abc/

Alaska Federal Courts

The following list indicates the district and division name for each jurisdiction in the state. If the bankruptcy court location is different from the district court, then the location of the bankruptcy court appears in parentheses.

Alaska County/Court Cross Reference

Aleutian Islands, East..Anchorage

Aleutian Islands, West..Anchorage

Anchorage Borough Borough ....Anchorage

Bethel...Fairbanks (Anchorage)

Bristol Bay Borough Borough...............................Anchorage

Fairbanks North Star Borough Borough ....Fairbanks (Anchorage)

Haines. Borough Borough.....................................Juneau (Anchorage)

Juneau Borough Borough ....Juneau (Anchorage)

Kenai Peninsula Borough Borough ....Anchorage

Ketchikan Gateway Borough Borough ....Ketchikan (Anchorage)

Kodiak Island Borough Borough ....Anchorage

Matanuska-Susitna Borough Borough ....Anchorage

Nome ....Nome (Anchorage)

North Slope Borough Borough...........................Fairbanks (Anchorage)

Northwest Arctic Borough.................................Fairbanks (Anchorage)

Prince of Wales-Outer Ketchikan ....Juneau (Anchorage)

Sitka Borough Borough ....Juneau (Anchorage)

Southeast Fairbanks..Fairbanks (Anchorage)

Valdez-Cordova...Anchorage

Wade Hampton ....Fairbanks (Anchorage)

Wrangell-Petersburg..Juneau (Anchorage)

Yakutat ....Juneau (Anchorage)

Yukon-Koyukuk ....Fairbanks (Anchorage)

Standards for Federal Courts: Search fee is $26.00 per item (one party name or case number). Copy fee is $.50 per page. Certification fee is $9.00 per document, double for exemplification, if available. All fees standard unless noted in profile. Mail Search: always enclose a stamped self addressed envelope unless otherwise noted. Most courts accept fax requests or will suggest a copying/search vendor. Before releasing records, all courts require prepayment, unless noted.

Open records are located at the court unless otherwise noted. District courts index by defendant and plaintiff as well as by case number. Bankruptcy courts usually index by debtor and case number. While most courts now have their indexes on computer, many may still maintain index card files as well.

Courts offering internet access via CM-ECF or older RACER, PACER, or Web-PACER systems charge $.08 per page fee unless noted as free. Where PACER is available, the universal sign-up number is 800-676-6856. Find PACER and the US Party/Case Index at http://pacer.psc.uscourts.gov.

US District Court

Anchorage Division Court Clerk, 222 W 7th Ave, #4, Anchorage, AK 99513-7564 (courier address: 222 W 7th Ave, Rm 229, Anchorage), 907-677-6100, 866-243-3814. Hours- 9:00AM-12:30PM, 1:30-4:30PM. www.akd.uscourts.gov

Jurisdiction: Aleutian Islands-East, Aleutian Islands-West, Anchorage Borough, Bristol Bay Borough, Dillingham, Kenai Peninsula Borough, Kodiak Island Borough, Lake and Peninsula, Matanuska-Susitna Borough, Valdez-Cordova.

Searches & Indexing: Results do not include SSN or DOB. Both computer and card indexes maintained. Names and docket sheets after 5/1987 on computer. New cases in the index ASAP after filing date. If a case was tried, file sent to Anchorage Records Center. If the case did not go to trial, file sent to Seattle Records Center.

Fee & Payment: Pay by money order, cashier's or personal check. Payee: Clerk, US District Court. Prepayment required.

Phone Search: Only docket information available by phone. Voice Case Information Service available, call VCIS at 907-222-6940.

Mail Search: search usually completed- 1-2 weeks. Include SASE for return.

In Person: Fee charged if court performs your search. Self-serve copier available - $.50 per page.

E-Services: PACER toll-free: 888-271-6212. PACER local phone: 907-677-6178, . PACER records go back to 1987. New records online after 1 day. Currently in the process of implementing CM/ECF. **Other Online Access:** Court does not participate in the US party case index. Current and next day calendars at www.akd.uscourts.gov.

Fairbanks Division Court Clerk, Rm 332, 101 12th Ave, Fairbanks, AK 99701 (also use mail address for courier delivery), 907-451-5791, 866-243-3813. Hours- 8AM-4:30PM. www.akd.uscourts.gov

Jurisdiction: Bethel, Denali, Fairbanks North Star Borough, North Slope Borough, Northwest Arctic Borough, Southeast Fairbanks, Wade Hampton, Yukon-Koyukuk.

Searches & Indexing: Results do not include SSN or DOB. Computer index maintained. New cases in the index 1-2 days after filing date. Records purged every 6 months.

Fee & Payment: Pay by money order, cashier's or personal check. Payee: US District Court. Prepayment required unless payment arrangement is made.

Phone Search: Only docket information available by phone. Voice Case Information Service available, call VCIS at 907-222-6940.

Mail Search: search usually completed- week-10 days. Include SASE for return.

In Person: Fee charged if court performs your search. No self-serve copier available.

E-Services: PACER toll-free: 888-271-6212. PACER local phone: 907-677-6178, . PACER records go back to 1987. New records online after 1 day. Currently in the process of implementing CM/ECF. **Other Online Access:** Court does not participate in the US party case index. Current and next day calendars at www.akd.uscourts.gov.

Juneau Division Court Clerk, PO Box 020349, Juneau, AK 99802-0349 (courier address: Rm 979, Federal Bldg-US Courthouse, 709 W 9th Ave, Juneau, AK 99802), 907-586-7458, 866-243-3812. Hours- 9AM-4PM. www.akd.uscourts.gov

Jurisdiction: Haines Borough, Juneau Borough, Prince of Wales-Outer Ketchikan, Sitka Borough, Skagway-Hoonah-Angoon, Wrangell-Petersburg.

Searches & Indexing: Results do not include SSN or DOB. Computer index maintained. Case files indexed on computer, then stored in file cabinets. New cases in the index immediately after filing date. Records purged every 6 months. If case was tried, file sent to division where it was filed. If the case did not go to trial, file sent to the Seattle Records Center some time after case closed.

Fee & Payment: Pay by money order, cashier's or personal check. Payee: Clerk, US District Court.

Phone Search: Only docket information is available by phone. Voice Case Information Service available, call VCIS at 907-222-6940.

Mail Search: search usually completed- 2 days. Include SASE for return.

In Person: Fee charged if court performs your search. Public may view original case files. No self-serve copier available.

E-Services: PACER toll-free: 888-271-6212. PACER local phone: 907-677-6178, . PACER records go back to 1987. New records online after 1 day. Currently in the process of implementing CM/ECF. **Other Online Access:** Court does not participate in the US party case index. Current and next day calendars at www.akd.uscourts.gov.

Ketchikan Division Court Clerk, 648 Mission St, Rm 507, Ketchikan, AK 99901 (also use mail address for courier delivery), 907-247-7576. Hours- 9-11AM. www.akd.uscourts.gov

Jurisdiction: Ketchikan Gateway Borough.

Searches & Indexing: Results do not include SSN or DOB. Computer index maintained. Case files indexed on computer, then stored in file cabinets. New cases in the index immediately after filing date. Records purged every 6 months. If case was tried, file sent to Anchorage Division. If the case did not go to trial, it will be sent to the Seattle Records Center. Case records sent to a Center after case closed.

Fee & Payment: Pay by money order, cashier check, business check. No personal checks. Payee: Clerk, US District Court. Prepayment required.

Phone Search: Only docket information available by phone. Voice Case Information Service available, call VCIS at 907-222-6940.

Mail Search: search usually completed- 2 days. Include SASE for return.

In Person Search: Fee charged if court performs your search. No self-serve copier available.

E-Services: PACER toll-free: 888-271-6212. PACER local phone: 907-677-6178, . PACER records go back to 1987. New records online after 1 day. Currently in the process of implementing CM/ECF. **Other Online Access:** Court does not participate in the US party case index. Current and next day calendars at www.akd.uscourts.gov.

Nome Division Court Clerk, PO Box 130, Nome, AK 99762 (courier address: 2nd Fl, Federal Bldg, 113 Front St, Nome, AK 99762), 907-443-5216, Fax-907-443-2192. Hours- 8AM-4:30PM. www.akd.uscourts.gov

Jurisdiction: Nome.

Searches & Indexing: Records have been retained at this court since 1960. Results do not include SSN or DOB. A card index is maintained. New cases in the index immediately after filing date. Records purged every 6 months. No records have been sent to the repository.

Fee & Payment: Pay by money order, cashier's or personal check. Prepayment is not required, but preferred. For copies, make checks payable to Alaska Court System. For searches and certified copies, make checks payable to US District Court. Prefers not to fax results, but will in expedited cases at cost of fax, search, and copies.

Phone Search: Only docket information available by phone. Court prefers that requests be submitted in writing. Voice Case Information Service available, call VCIS at 907-222-6940.

Mail Search: search usually completed- 5 day maximum. SASE not required.

In Person Search: Fee charged if court performs your search. No self-serve copier available.

E-Services: PACER toll-free: 888-271-6212. PACER local phone: 907-677-6178, . PACER records go back to 1987. New records online after 1 day. Currently in the process of implementing CM/ECF. **Other Online Access:** Court does not participate in the US party case index. Current and next day calendars at www.akd.uscourts.gov.

US Bankruptcy Court

Anchorage Division Court Clerk, Historic Courthouse, 605 W 4th Ave, #138, Anchorage, AK 99501-2296 (also use mail address for courier delivery), 907-271-2655. Hours- 9AM-12:30PM, 1:30-4:30PM. www.akb.uscourts.gov

Jurisdiction: All boroughs and districts in Alaska.

Searches & Indexing: Results do not include DOB; SSN only before 12/04. Computer index maintained. New cases in the index 1-2 days after filing date. Records purged 6 months. If a case was tried, file sent to Anchorage Records Center. If the case did not go to trial, file sent to Seattle Records Center. Case records sent to a Center 60 days after case closed.

Fee & Payment: Pay by money order, cashier's or personal check. Payee: Clerk, US Bankruptcy Court. Prepayment required.

Phone Search: Accession number released via phone if case number is provided. If case number is unknown, information must be requested in writing along with search fee. Voice Case Information Service available, call VCIS at 888-878-3110 or 907-271-2658.

Mail Search: search usually completed- 24 hours. Include SASE for return.

In Person Search: Fee charged if court performs your search. Self-serve copier available - $.20 per page.

E-Services: ECF replaces PACER. Document images available. PACER records go back to 7/1991. ECF at https://ecf.akb.uscourts.gov opinions online www.akb.uscourts.gov/index.htm. **Other Online Access:** The old RACER system has been replaced. Court calendars free at www.akb.uscourts.gov/calendars.htm.

Alaska Local Courts

Court	Jurisdiction	No. of Courts	How Organized
Superior Courts*	General		4 Districts
District Courts*	Limited	6	4 Districts
Combined Courts*		16	
Magistrate Courts*	Limited	40	4 Districts

* Profiled in this Sourcebook

Court	CIVIL								
	Tort	Contract	Real Estate	Min. Claim	Max. Claim	Small Claims	Estate	Eviction	Domestic Relations
Superior Courts*	X	X	X	$0	No Max		X	X	X
District Courts*	X	X		$0	$50,000	$7500		X	X
Magistrate Courts*	X	X		$0	$7500	$7500			

Court	CRIMINAL				
	Felony	Misdemeanor	DWI/DUI	Preliminary Hearing	Juvenile
Superior Courts*	X				X
District Courts*		X	X	X	X
Magistrate Courts*		X	X	X	

ADMINISTRATION

Office of the Administrative Director, 820 W 4th Ave, Anchorage, AK, 99501; 907-264-8269, Fax: 907-264-8291. www.state.ak.us/courts

COURT STRUCTURE

Alaska is not organized into counties, but rather into 15 boroughs (3 unified home rule municipalities that are combination borough and city, and 12 boroughs) and 12 home rule cities, which do not directly coincide with the 4 Judicial Districts into which the judicial system is divided. In other words, judicial boundaries cross borough boundaries. Alaska has a unified, centrally administered, and totally state-funded judicial system. Municipal governments do not maintain separate court systems.

The four levels of courts in the Alaska Court System are the supreme court, the court of appeals, the superior court and the district court. The supreme court and the court of appeals are appellate courts, while the superior and district courts are trial courts. Probate is handled by the superior courts.

The superior court is the trial court of general jurisdiction. There are 34 superior court judgeships located throughout the state. The district court is a trial court of limited jurisdiction. The district court currently has 17 judges in the state. The superior court serves as an appellate court for appeals from civil and criminal cases which have been tried in the district court.

We have listed the courts by their borough or home rule city in keeping with a convenient alphabetical format. You should search through the city court location names to determine the correct court for your search.

The First District encompasses all of S.E. Alaska. Magistrates act as judicial officers. This 1st District has five trial/Superior courts: Ketchikan, Wrangell, Petersburg, Sitka and Juneau. District Magistrate Courts are Haines, Skagway, Yakutat, Angoon, Kake, Hoona, Craig.

ONLINE ACCESS

You may do a name search of a partial statewide Alaska Trial Courts database index at www.state.ak.us/courts/names.htm. Search results give case number, file date, disposition date, charge, and sentence. The index gives the name used on the first pleading only. The index is for only those courts on the new case management system. Until all courts are on, this search is not FCRA-compliant for employment screening purposes. The civil/criminal name index is available to anyone who sends a blank CD-ROM each quarter to the Administrative Director. The home web page gives access to Appellate opinions.

ADDITIONAL INFORMATION

Documents may not be filed by fax in any Alaska court without prior authorization of a judge.

The fees established by court rules for Alaska courts are: search fee - $15.00 per hour or fraction thereof; certification fee - $5.00 per document and $2.00 per additional copy of the document. Copy fee is $.25 per page. Magistrate Courts vary widely in how records are maintained and in the hours of operation (some are open only a few hours per week)

📖 📖 📖 📖 📖 📖 📖

Aleutian Islands

Unalaska District Court (3rd District) PO Box 245, Unalaska, AK 99685-0245; phone: 907-581-1266; fax: 907-581-2809; hours 8AM-4:30PM (AK). *Felony, Misdemeanor, Civil.*
Civil Records: Access: In person, mail, online. Both court and visitors may perform in person searches. Search fee: $15.00 per name. Court makes copy: $.25 per page. Required to search: name, DOB. Civil records on computer back to 1992. Search names on the Alaska Trial Courts database at www.state.ak.us/courts/names.htm. Web gives basic info. Mail turnaround time 1-2 weeks.
Criminal Records: Access: In person, mail, online. Both court and visitors may perform in person searches. Search fee: $15.00 per name. Court makes copy: $.25 per page. Required to search: name, years to search, DOB. Criminal records on computer back to 1992. Online access to criminal records is the same as civil. Mail turnaround time 1-2 weeks.
General Information: Public access terminal available. Will fax documents to local or toll free line. Certification fee: $5.00 per copy. Payee: State of Alaska. Prepayment required.

Sand Point Magistrate Court (3rd District), AK. *Felony, Misdemeanor, Civil Actions Under $7,500, Small Claims.* Note: Court closed; records at Cordova Court in Valdez-Cordova District.

St Paul Island Magistrate Court (3rd District), AK. *Misdemeanor, Civil Actions Under $7,500, Small Claims.* Note: court closed, see Seward Magistrate Court in Kenai Peninsula Borough.

Anchorage Borough

Superior & District Court (3rd District) 825 W 4th, Anchorage, AK 99501-2004; phone: 907-264-0491; probate phone: 907-264-0436; fax: 907-264-0873; probate fax: 907-264-0598; hours 8AM-4:30PM (AK). *Felony, Misdemeanor, Civil, Eviction, Small Claims, Probate.*
Civil Records: Access: Fax, mail, in person, online. Both court and visitors may perform in person searches. Search fee: $15.00 per hour. Court makes copy: $.25 per page; same fee for self serve. Required to search: name, years to search; also helpful: address. Civil cases indexed by defendant, plaintiff. Civil records on computer from 1990, on microfiche and archived from 1977 to 1989, on roll index from 1940s. Search court records free at new CourtView system at www.courtrecords.alaska.gov/. Mail turnaround time 2-3 weeks.
Criminal Records: Access: Fax, mail, in person, online. Both court and visitors may perform in person searches. Search fee: $15.00 per hour. Court makes copy: $.25 per page; same fee for self serve. Required to search: name, years to search; also helpful: address, DOB, SSN. Criminal records on computer from 1990, on microfiche and archived from 1977 to 1989, on roll index from 1940s. Online access to criminal records is the same as civil. Mail turnaround time 2-3 weeks.
General Information: Public access terminal goes back to 1990. No adoption, juvenile, sealed or mental records released. Will fax documents to local or toll-free number. Certification fee: $5.00. Cert fee includes copies. Payee: AK Court System. Personal checks accepted. Prepayment and SASE required.

Bethel District

Superior & District Court (4th District) PO Box 130, Bethel, AK 99559-0130; phone: 907-543-2298; fax: 907-543-4419; hours 8AM-4:30PM; 9-4:30 W (AK). *Felony, Misdemeanor, Civil, Eviction, Small Claims, Probate.*
Civil Records: Access: Fax, mail, in person, online. Visitors must perform in person searches themselves. Search fee: $15.00 per name. Court makes copy: $.25 per page. Required to search: name, years to search. Civil cases indexed by defendant, plaintiff. Civil records on computer back to 1983, on microfiche, archived and on index from 1977. Search names on the Alaska Trial Courts database at www.state.ak.us/courts/names.htm. Web gives case number only. Mail turnaround time 2 weeks.
Criminal Records: Access: Fax, mail, in person, online. Visitors must perform in person searches themselves. Search fee: $15.00 per name. Court makes copy: $.25 per page. Required to search: name, years to search, DOB; also helpful- case number. Criminal records on computer back to 1983, on microfiche, archived and on index from 1977. Online access to criminal records is the same as civil. Mail turnaround time 2 weeks.
General Information: Public access terminal available. No adoption, juvenile, guardianship or mental records released. Fee to fax documents is $.25 per page. Certification fee: $5.00 plus $2.00 per page after first. Payee: Clerk of Court. Personal checks accepted. Prepayment and SASE required.

Aniak District Court (4th District) PO Box 147, Aniak, AK 99557-0147; phone: 907-675-4325; fax: 907-675-4278; 8AM-4:30PM *Misdemeanor, Civil Actions Under $7,500, Small Claims.*
Civil Records: Access: Phone, mail, fax, in person. Both court and visitors may perform in person searches. Search fee: $15.00 per search. Court makes copy: $.25 per page. Required to search: name plus DOB, SSN, years to search. Civil records go back to 1960; on computer back to 1998. Mail turnaround time 1-2 weeks.
Criminal Records: Access: Phone, mail, fax, in person. Both court and visitors may perform in person searches. Search fee: $15.00 per search. Court makes copy: $.25 per page. Required to search: name, years to search, DOB. Civil records go back to 1960; on computer to 1998. Mail turnaround 1-2 weeks.
General Information: No public access terminal. Will fax documents. Cert fee: $5.00 per document. Payee: Aniak District Court. Prepayment required.

Quinhagak Magistrate Court (Bethel Area) c/o Bethel Clerk, PO Box 130, Bethel, AK 99559-0130; phone: 907-543-1105. *Misdemeanor, Civil Actions Under $7,500, Small Claims.* Note: Court closed; records at Bethel Clerk of Courts at address and phone here.

Bristol Bay Borough

Naknek District Court (3rd District) PO Box 229, Naknek, AK 99633-0229; phone: 907-246-6151; fax: 907-246-7418; hours 8:30AM-4PM (AK). *Felony, Misdemeanor, Civil Actions Under $7,500, Small Claims.*
Note: Naknek is 3NA on the state court record numbers. Some Lake and Peninsula cases heard here.
Civil Records: Access: Mail, in person, online. Only the court performs in person searches; visitors may not. Search fee: $15.00 per hour. Court makes copy: $.25 per page. Required to search: name. Records go back to 1970's; computerized from 1993. Search names on the Alaska Trial Courts database at www.state.ak.us/courts/names.htm. Web gives case number only. Mail turnaround time same day.
Criminal Records: Access: Mail, in person, online. Only the court performs in person searches; visitors may not. Search fee: $15.00 per hour. Court makes copy: $.25 per page. Required to search: name, years to search. Records go back to 1970's; computerized from 1993. Online access to criminal records is the same as civil. Mail turnaround time same day.
General Information: No public access terminal. Certification fee: $10.00 per cert. Payee: Alaska Court System. Prepayment required. SASE requested.

Denali Borough

Healy Magistrate Court (4th District) PO Box 298, Healy, AK 99743-0298; phone: 907-683-2213; fax: 907-683-1383; hours 8AM-4:30PM (AK). *Misdemeanor, Civil Actions Under $7,500, Small Claims.* Note: Felony cases are at Fairbanks Superior & District Court.

Civil Records: Access: Phone, mail, fax, in person, online. Both court and visitors may perform in person searches. Search fee: $15.00 per hour. Court makes copy: $.25 per page. Required to search: name, years to search, DOB. Records on computer back to 1972. Search names on the Alaska Trial Courts database at www.state.ak.us/courts/names.htm. Web gives case number only. Mail turnaround time 2 weeks.
Criminal Records: Access: Phone, mail, fax, in person, online. Both court and visitors may perform in person searches. Search fee: $15.00 per name. Court makes copy: $.25 per page. Required to search: name, years to search, DOB. Records on computer back to 1972. Online access to criminal records is the same as civil. Mail turnaround time 2 weeks.
General Information: Public access terminal goes back to 1997. Certification fee: $5.00. Payee: State of Alaska. Personal check accepted. No credit cards accepted. Prepayment and SASE required.

Dillingham

Dillingham Superior Court (3rd District) PO Box 909, Dillingham, AK 99576-0909; phone: 907-842-5215; fax: 907-842-5746; 8AM-4:30PM (AK). *Felony, Misdemeanor, Civil, Small Claims.*
Civil Records: Access: In person, mail, online. Only the court performs in person searches; visitors may not. Search fee: $15.00. Court makes copy: $.25 per page. Search names on the Alaska Trial Courts database at www.state.ak.us/courts/names.htm. Web gives case number only. Mail turnaround time 1-2 weeks.
Criminal Records: Access: In person, mail, online. Only the court performs in person searches; visitors may not. Search fee: $15.00 per name. Court makes copy: $.25 per page. Required to search: name, years to search, DOB. Online access to criminal records is the same as civil. Mail turnaround time 1-2 weeks.
General Information: No public access terminal. Certification fee: $3.00 per doc. Payee: State of Alaska. Cashiers checks, money orders, personal checks accepted. Prepayment and SASE required.

Fairbanks North Star Borough

Superior & District Court (4th District) 101 Lacey St, Fairbanks, AK 99701-4761; phone: 907-452-9277; criminal phone: 907-452-9289; civil phone: 907-452-9267; probate phone: 907-452-9256; fax: 907-452-9330; 8AM-4:30PM (AK). *Felony, Misdemeanor, Civil, Eviction, Small claims, Probate*
Civil Records: Access: In person, online. Visitors must perform in person searches themselves. Court makes copy: $.25 per page. Required to search: name, years to search. Civil cases indexed by defendant, plaintiff. Civil records on computer from 1988, on microfiche, archived and on index from 1900s. Search court records free at new CourtView system at www.courtrecords.alaska.gov/. Note: Access to closed civil cases goes back 6 months.
Criminal Records: Access: In person, online. Visitors must perform in person searches themselves. Court makes copy: $.25 per page. Required to search: name, years to search, DOB. Criminal records on computer from 1988, on microfiche, archived and on index from 1900s. Online access to criminal records is same as civil.
General Information: Public access terminal goes back to 1988. No adoption, juvenile, guardianship or mental records released. Certification fee: $5.00 plus $2.00 per copy after first. Payee: Clerk of Court. Personal checks accepted. In person only. Prepayment required.

Haines Borough

District Court (1st District) PO Box 169, Haines, AK 99827-0169; phone: 907-766-2801; fax: 907-766-3148; hours 8AM-N, 1-4:30PM (AK). *Misdemeanor, Civil Actions Under $50,000, Small Claims.* Note: Felony cases are at Juneau Superior & District Court.

Civil Records: Access: Phone, fax, mail, in person, online. Only the court performs in person searches; visitors may not. Search fee: $15.00 per hour if time consuming. Court makes copy: $.25 per page. Required to search: name, years to search; also helpful: address. Civil cases indexed by defendant, plaintiff. Civil records on computer since 1993, index from 1960s. Search names on the Alaska Trial Courts database at www.state.ak.us/courts/names.htm. Web gives case number only. Note: Limited information is available by phone. Mail turnaround time 1-2 days.

Criminal Records: Access: Phone, fax, mail, in person, online. Only the court performs in person searches; visitors may not. Search fee: $15.00 per hour if time consuming. Court makes copy: $.25 per page. Required to search: name, years to search; also helpful: address, DOB, SSN. Criminal records on computer since 1993, index from 1960s. Online access to criminal records is the same as civil. Mail turnaround time 1-2 days.

General Information: No public access terminal. No juvenile records released. Certification fee: $5.00 plus $2.00 per each add'l document requested at same time. Payee: Alaska Court System. Personal checks accepted. Prepayment and SASE required.

Juneau Borough

Superior & District Court (1st District)
Dimond Courthouse, PO Box 114100, Juneau, AK 99811-4100; phone: 907-463-4700; probate phone: same; fax: 907-463-3788; hours 8AM-4:30PM M-Th, 9AM-4:30 F (AK). *Felony, Misdemeanor, Civil, Eviction, Small Claims, Probate.*

Civil Records: Access: Fax, mail, in person, online. Both court and visitors may perform in person searches. Search fee: $15.00 per hour. Court makes copy: $.25 per page. Required to search: name, years to search. Civil cases indexed by defendant. Civil records on computer back to 1987, on microfiche from 1960 to 1986, on index from 1959 to 1987. Search names on the Alaska Trial Courts database at www.state.ak.us/courts/names.htm. Web gives case number only. Mail turnaround time 2-5 days.

Criminal Records: Access: Fax, mail, in person, online. Both court and visitors may perform in person searches. Search fee: $15.00 per hour. Court makes copy: $.25 per page. Required to search: name, years to search. Criminal records on computer back to 1987, on microfiche from 1960 to 1986, on index 1959 to 1987. Online access to criminal records is the same as civil. Mail turnaround time 2-5 days.

General Information: Public access terminal goes back to 1980s. No adoption, juvenile, guardianship or mental records released. Certification fee: $5.00 plus $2.00 per page after first. Payee: Juneau Trial Court. Personal checks accepted. Prepayment and SASE required.

Kenai Peninsula Borough

Superior & District Court (3rd District)
125 Trading Bay Dr, #100, Kenai, AK 99611; phone: 907-283-3110; probate phone: same; fax: 907-283-8535; 8AM-4:30PM (AK). *Felony, Misdemeanor, Civil, Eviction, Small Claims, Probate.*

Civil Records: Access: Mail, in person, online. Both court and visitors may perform in person searches. Search fee: $15.00 per hour. Court makes copy: $.25 per page. Required to search: name, years to search. Civil cases indexed by defendant, plaintiff. Civil records on computer from 1982, on microfiche, archived and on index from 1959. Search names on the Alaska Trial Courts database at www.state.ak.us/courts/names.htm. Web gives case number only. Mail turnaround time 1 week.

Criminal Records: Access: Mail, in person, online. Both court and visitors may perform in person searches. Search fee: $15.00 per hour. Court makes copy: $.25 per page. Required to search: name, years to search, DOB. Criminal records on computer from 1982, on microfiche, archived and on index from

1959. Online access to criminal records is the same as civil. Mail turnaround time 1 week.

General Information: Public access terminal goes back to 1982. No adoption, guardianship, children's, conservatorship or coroner records released. Certification fee: $5.00 plus $2.00 per page after first. Payee: Clerk of Court. Personal checks accepted. Prepayment required. SASE not required.

Homer District Court (3rd District)
3670 Lake St, #400, Homer, AK 99603-9647; phone: 907-235-8171; fax: 907-235-4257; hours 8AM-4:30PM (AK). *Felony, Misdemeanor, Civil Actions Under $100,000, Small Claims.* Note: Felony cases heard only once a week, if needed. Records for these felony cases could be here or at the Kenai District Court.

Civil Records: Access: Phone, fax, mail, in person, online. Visitors must perform in person searches themselves. Search fee: $15.00 per hour. Court makes copy: $.25 per page. Required to search: name, years to search. Civil cases indexed by defendant, plaintiff. Civil records on computer back to 1984. Search names on the Alaska Trial Courts database at www.state.ak.us/courts/names.htm. Web gives case number only. Mail turnaround time 5 days.

Criminal Records: Access: Phone, fax, mail, in person, online. Visitors must perform in person searches themselves. Search fee: $15.00 per hour. Court makes copy: $.25 per page. Required to search: name, years to search. Criminal records on computer back to 1984. Online access to criminal records is the same as civil. Mail turnaround time 5 days.

General Information: Public access terminal available. No confidential or sealed records released. Certification fee: $5.00. Cert fee includes copies. Payee: Alaska Court System. Personal checks accepted. Prepayment and SASE required.

Seward Magistrate Court (3rd District)
PO Box 1929, 5th and Adams Strs, Seward, AK 99664-1929; phone: 907-224-3075; fax: 907-224-7192; hours 8AM-4:30PM (AK). *Misdemeanor, Civil Actions Under $7,500, Small Claims.*
Note: Handles cases for St. Paul Island.

Civil Records: Access: In person, mail, online. Both court and visitors may perform in person searches. Search fee: $15.00 per name; may do for free as time permits. Court makes copy: $.25 per page. Civil records on computer since 1983. Search names on Alaska Trial Courts database at www.state.ak.us/courts/names.htm. Web gives case number only. Mail turnaround time 1-2 weeks.

Criminal Records: Access: In person, mail, online. Both court and visitors may perform in person searches. Search fee: $15.00 per name. Court makes copy: $.25 per page. Required to search: name, years to search, DOB. Criminal records on computer since 1983. Online access to criminal records is the same as civil. Mail turnaround time 1-2 weeks.

General Information: Public access terminal goes back to 1983. Recommends against faxing back documents. Certification fee: $5.00. Payee: State of Alaska. Prepayment required. SASE helpful.

Ketchikan Gateway Borough

Superior & District Court (1st District)
415 Main, Rm 400, Ketchikan, AK 99901-6399; phone: 907-225-3195; fax: 907-225-7849; hours 8AM-4:30PM M-Th, 9AM-4:30PM F (AK). *Felony, Misdemeanor, Civil, Eviction, small claims, Probate.*

Civil Records: Access: Mail, in person, online. Both court and visitors may perform in person searches. Search fee: $15.00 per hour. Court makes copy: $.25 per page. Required to search: name, years to search. Civil cases indexed by defendant, plaintiff. Civil records on computer from 1983, on microfiche from 1972 to 1989, index from 1972. Search names on the Alaska Trial Courts database at www.state.ak.us/courts/names.htm. Web gives case number only. Mail turnaround time 2 weeks.

Criminal Records: Access: Mail, in person, online. Both court and visitors may perform in person searches. Search fee: $15.00 per hour. Court makes copy: $.25 per page. Required to search: name, years

to search, DOB. Criminal records on computer from 1983, on microfiche from 1972 to 1989, index from 1972. Online access to criminal records is the same as civil. Mail turnaround time 2 weeks.

General Information: Public access terminal available. No confidential probate or children's records released. No fee to fax documents if toll-free. Cert fee: $5.00. Payee: Alaska Court System. Personal checks accepted. Prepayment and SASE required.

Kodiak Island Borough

Superior & District Court (3rd District)
204 Mission Road, Rm 10, Kodiak, AK 99615-7312; phone: 907-486-1600; fax: 907-486-1660; hours 8AM-4:30PM M,T,Th,F; 9AM-4:30PM W (AK). *Felony, Misdemeanor, Civil, Eviction, Small Claims, Probate.*

Civil Records: Access: Mail, fax, in person, online. Both court and visitors may perform in person searches. Search fee: $15.00 per hour. Court makes copy: $.25 per page. Required to search: name, years to search; also helpful: address. Civil cases indexed by defendant, plaintiff. Civil records on computer from 1982, on microfiche, index and archived from 1959. Search names on the Alaska Trial Courts database at www.state.ak.us/courts/names.htm. Web gives case number only. Mail turnaround time 10 days.

Criminal Records: Access: Mail, fax, in person, online. Both court and visitors may perform in person searches. Search fee: $15.00 per hour. Court makes copy: $.25 per page. Required to search: name, years to search; also helpful: address, DOB, SSN. Criminal records on computer from 1982, on microfiche, index and archived from 1959. Online access to criminal records is the same as civil. Mail turnaround time 10 business days.

General Information: Public access terminal goes back to 1983. No adoption, juvenile, guardianship or mental records released. Certification fee: $5.00 plus $2.00 per add'l copy. Payee: Clerk of Court. Personal checks accepted. Prepayment and SASE required.

Matanuska-Susitna Borough

Superior & District Court (3rd District)
435 S Denali, Palmer, AK 99645-6437; criminal phone: 907-746-8104; civil phone: 907-746-8108; fax: 907-746-4151; 8AM-4:30PM (AK). *Felony, Misdemeanor, Civil, Eviction, small claims, Probate.*

Civil Records: Access: Mail, in person, online. Both court and visitors may perform in person searches. Search fee: $15.00 per hour. Court makes copy: $.25 per page. Required to search: name, years to search; also helpful: address. Civil cases indexed by defendant, plaintiff. Civil records on computer from 1988, on microfiche, archived and index from 1974. Search court records free at new CourtView system at www.courtrecords.alaska.gov/. Mail turnaround time 1-3 weeks.

Criminal Records: Access: Mail, in person, online. Both court and visitors may perform in person searches. Search fee: $15.00 per hour. Court makes copy: $.25 per page. Required to search: name, years to search; also helpful: address, DOB, SSN. Criminal records on computer from 1988, on microfiche, archived and index from 1974. Online access to criminal records is the same as civil. Mail turnaround time 1-3 weeks.

General Information: Public access terminal goes back to 1988. No adoption, juvenile, guardianship or mental records released. Certification fee: $5.00 per document. A second copy is $2.00 per document. Payee: State of Alaska. Personal checks accepted. Prepayment and SASE required.

Nome

Superior & District Court (2nd District)
PO Box 1110, Nome, AK 99762-1110; phone: 907-443-5216; fax: 907-443-2192; hours 8AM-4:30PM (AK). *Felony, Misdemeanor, Civil, Eviction, Small Claims, Probate.*

Civil Records: Access: Fax, mail, in person, online. Both court and visitors may perform in person searches. Search fee: $15.00 per hour or fraction of. Court makes copy: $.25 per page; same fee for self serve. Required to search: name, years to search; also helpful: DOB. Civil cases indexed by defendant, plaintiff. Civil records on computer from 1983, on microfiche from 1960 to 1983, on index and archived from 1960. Search names on Alaska Trial Courts database at www.state.ak.us/courts/names.htm. Web gives case number only. Mail turnaround time 5 days.

Criminal Records: Access: Fax, mail, in person, online. Both court and visitors may perform in person searches. Search fee: $15.00 per hour or fraction of. Court makes copy: $.25 per page; same fee for self serve. Required to search: name, years to search; also helpful: DOB, SSN. Criminal records on computer from 1983, on microfiche from 1960 to 1983, on index and archived from 1960. Online access to criminal records is the same as civil. Mail turnaround time 5 days.

General Information: Public access terminal goes back to 1983. No adoption, juvenile, guardianship or mental records released. Will fax documents to toll-free number only. Certification fee: $5.00 plus $2.00 per copy after first. Payee: Nome Trial Courts. Personal checks accepted. Prepayment and SASE required.

Gambell Magistrate Court (2nd District)
PO Box 110, Nome, AK 99762-1110; phone: 907-443-5216; fax: 907-443-2192; hours 8AM-4:30PM (AK). *Misdemeanor, Civil Actions Under $7,500, Small Claims.* Note: Court is vacant; records at Superior Court in Nome at address and phone here.

Unalakleet Magistrate Court (2nd District)
PO Box 250, Unalakleet, AK 99684-0250; phone: 907-624-3015; fax: 907-624-3118; hours 8AM-4PM (AK). *Misdemeanor, Civil Actions Under $7,500, Small Claims.*
Note: This is a one-person court and very quiet.

Civil Records: Access: In person, mail, fax. Only the court performs in person searches; visitors may not. Search fee: $15.00 per hour. Court makes copy: $.25 per page. Required to search: name, years to search. Mail turnaround time 1-2 weeks.

Criminal Records: Access: In person, mail, fax. Only the court performs in person searches; visitors may not. Search fee: $15.00 per hour. Court makes copy: $.25 per page. Required to search: name, years to search. Mail turnaround time 1-2 weeks.

General Information: No public access terminal. Will fax documents for free. Certification fee: $5.00 per doc. Payee: Magistrate Court. Prepayment required. SASE not required.

North Slope Borough
Superior & District Court (2nd District)
PO Box 270, Barrow, AK 99723-0270; phone: 907-852-4800 X80; fax: 907-852-4804; hours 8AM-4:30PM (AK). *Felony, Misdemeanor, Civil, Eviction, Small Claims, Probate.*
Civil Records: Access: Fax, mail, in person, online. Both court and visitors may perform in person searches. Search fee: $15.00 per hour. Court makes copy: $.25 per page. Required to search: name, years to search; also helpful: address. Civil cases indexed by defendant, plaintiff. Civil records on computer from 1983, prior on microfiche. Search names on the Alaska Trial Courts database at www.state.ak.us/courts/names.htm. Web gives case number only. Mail turnaround time 3 weeks.
Criminal Records: Access: Fax, mail, in person, online. Both court and visitors may perform in person searches. Search fee: $15.00 per hour. Court makes copy: $.25 per page. Required to search: name, years to search; also helpful: address, DOB, SSN. Criminal records on computer from 1983, prior on microfiche. Online access to criminal records is the same as civil. Mail turnaround time 3 weeks.
General Information: Public access terminal available. No confidential records released. No fee to fax documents. Certification fee: $5.00 plus $2.00 per

page after first. Payee: Alaska Court System. Personal checks accepted. Prepayment and SASE required.

Northwest Arctic Borough
Superior & District Court (2nd District)
PO Box 317, 605 3rd Ave, Kotzebue, AK 99752-0317; phone: 907-442-3208; probate phone: same; fax: 907-442-3974; hours 8AM-4:30PM (AK). *Felony, Misdemeanor, Civil, Eviction, Small Claims, Probate.*
Note: This court holds records for the closed Magistrate Court formerly in Ambler, Kiana, Selawick and Noowik.

Civil Records: Access: Phone, fax, mail, in person, online. Both court and visitors may perform in person searches. Search fee: $15.00. Court makes copy: $.25 per page; same fee for self serve. Required to search: name, years to search. Civil cases indexed by defendant and plaintiff. Civil records on computer from 1983, prior records on microfilm, archived and index from 1966. Search names on the Alaska Trial Courts database at www.state.ak.us/courts/names.htm. Web gives case number only. Note: Copy of check required for fax access. Mail turnaround time 2 day to 3 weeks.

Criminal Records: Access: Mail, fax, in person, online. Both court and visitors may perform in person searches. Search fee: $15.00. Court makes copy: $.25 per page; same fee for self serve. Required to search: name, years to search, DOB; also helpful: SSN. Criminal records on computer from 1983, prior records on microfilm, archived and index from 1966. Online access to criminal records is the same as civil. Mail turnaround time 2 days to 3 weeks.

General Information: Public access terminal available. No adoption, juvenile, guardianship or mental records released. Certification fee: $5.00 plus $2.00 per page after first. Notary fee is $3.00. Payee: Alaska Court System. Personal checks accepted. Prepayment required.

Kiana Magistrate Court (2nd District)
PO Box 317, Kotzebue, AK 99752-0317; phone: 907-442-3208; hours 8AM-4;30PM (AK). *Misdemeanor, Civil Actions Under $7,500, Small Claims.*
Note: Court is temporarily vacant; for records, contact Kotzebue Court at address and phone here.

Selawik Magistrate Court (2nd District)
PO Box 317, Kotzebue, AK 99752; phone: 907-442-3208; fax: 907-442-3974; hours variable (AK). *Misdemeanor, Civil Actions Under $7,500, Small Claims.*
Note: Contact the Kotzebue Court for record information; Kotzebue court address and phones given here.

Prince of Wales - Outer Ketchikan
Craig Magistrate Court (1st District)
PO Box 646, Craig, AK 99921-0646; phone: 907-826-3316/3306; fax: 907-826-3904; hours 8AM-4:30PM (AK). *Misdemeanor, Civil Actions Under $10,000, Small Claims.* Note: Felony cases are at Ketchican Superior & District Court.
Civil Records: Access: In person, phone, fax, mail, online. Only the court performs in person searches; visitors may not. Search fee: $15.00 per name. Court makes copy: $.25. Required to search: name, years to search; also helpful: DOB. Search names on the Alaska Trial Courts database at www.state.ak.us/courts/names.htm. Web gives case number only. Mail turnaround time 2 weeks.
Criminal Records: Access: In person, phone, fax, mail, online. Only the court performs in person searches; visitors may not. Search fee: $15.00 per name. Court makes copy: $.25. Required to search: name, years to search; also helpful: DOB. Online access to criminal records is the same as civil. Mail turnaround time 2 weeks.
General Information: Will fax documents for free. Certification fee: $5.00. Payee: Alaska Court System. Prepayment required. SASE requested.

Sitka Borough
Superior & District Court (1st District)
304 Lake St, Rm 203, Sitka, AK 99835-7759; phone: 907-747-3291; fax: 907-747-6690; hours 8AM-4:30PM (AK). *Felony, Misdemeanor, Civil, Eviction, Small Claims, Probate.*
Note: Probate is in a separate index at this address.

Civil Records: Access: Phone, fax, mail, in person, online. Both court and visitors may perform in person searches. Search fee: $15.00 per hour. Court makes copy: $.25 per page. Self serve copy fee: $.10 per page. Required to search: name. Civil cases indexed by defendant, plaintiff. Civil records on computer from 1983, on microfilm and archived from 1970 to 1987, on index from 1960. Search names on the Alaska Trial Courts database at www.state.ak.us/courts/names.htm. Web gives case number only. Mail turnaround time 1 week.

Criminal Records: Access: Phone, fax, mail, in person, online. Both court and visitors may perform in person searches. Search fee: $15.00 per hour. Court makes copy: $.25 per page. Self serve copy fee: $.10 per page. Required to search: name. Criminal records on computer from 1983, on microfilm and archived from 1970 to 1987, on index from 1960. Online access to criminal records is the same as civil. Mail turnaround time 1 week.

General Information: Public access terminal goes back to 1980s. No adoption, juvenile, guardianship or mental records released. No fee to fax documents. Will fax to toll free number. Certification fee: $5.00 per document. Payee: Alaska Court System. Personal checks accepted. Prepayment and SASE required.

Skagway-Yakutat-Angoon
Hoonah District Court (1st District)
PO Box 430, Hoonah, AK 99829-0430; phone: 907-945-3668; fax: 907-945-3637; hours 8AM-N, 1-4:30PM (AK). *Misdemeanor, Civil Actions Under $50,000, Small Claims.* Note: Felony cases are at Juneau Superior & District Court.
Civil Records: Access: Mail, in person. Only the court performs in person searches; visitors may not. No search fee. Court makes copy: $.25 per page. Required to search: name, years to search. Civil cases indexed by defendant, plaintiff. Civil records on index from 1971 to present. Mail turnaround- 2-3 days.
Criminal Records: Access: Mail, in person. Only the court performs in person searches; visitors may not. No search fee. Court makes copy: $.25 per page. Required to search: name, years to search; also helpful: DOB. Criminal records on index from 1971 to present. Mail turnaround time 2-3 days.
General Information: No public access terminal. No confidential, juvenile or sex related records released. Will fax documents to toll-free number only. Certification fee: $5.00 plus $2.00 per page after first. Payee: Alaska Court System. Personal checks accepted. Prepayment required. SASE not required.

Angoon Magistrate Court (1st District)
PO Box 250, Angoon, AK 99820-0123; phone: 907-788-3229; fax: 907-788-3108; hours 1PM-4:30PM (AK). *Misdemeanor, Civil Actions Under $7,500, Small Claims.* Note: Felony cases are at Sitka Superior & District Court.
Civil Records: Access: Phone, mail, fax, in person. Only the court performs in person searches; visitors may not. Search fee: $15.00 per hour. Court makes copy: $.25 per page. Required to search: name, years to search. Records go back to 1994. Mail turnaround time 1 week.
Criminal Records: Access: Phone, mail, fax, in person. Only the court performs in person searches; visitors may not. Search fee: $15.00 per hour. Court makes copy: $.25 per page. Required to search: name, years to search, date of birth. Records go back to 1994. Mail turnaround time 1 week.
General Information: No public access terminal. Fee to fax documents is $5.00 per page or $15.00 per document. Certification fee: $5.00 per doc. Payee:

Alaska Court System. Personal checks and money orders accepted. Prepayment required. SASE helpful.

Pelican Magistrate Court (1st District)
304 Lake St #203, Sitka, AK 99835; phone: 907-747-3291; fax: 907-747-6690. *Misdemeanor, Civil Actions Under $7,500, Small Claims.*

Note: This Pelican court closed permanently on 12/31/99. All records are at the Sitka court, address and phone given here.

Skagway District Magistrate Court PO
Box 495, Skagway, AK 99840-0495; phone: 907-983-2368; fax: 907-983-3801; hours Closed Mondays and closed for lunch (AK). *Misdemeanor, Civil Actions Under $10,500, Small Claims.*

Note: Hours will vary from Summer to Winter. Summer hours-M-Tu 8:30-4; W-8:45-4; Th-9-4; F-8:15-10AM, closed 12-1PM for lunch. Felony cases are at Juneau Superior & District Court.

Civil Records: Access: Mail, fax, in person. Only the court performs in person searches; visitors may not. Search fee: $15.00 per hour. Court makes copy: $.25 per page. Civil records go back to 1970; on computer back to 1998. Mail turnaround: 1-2 weeks
Criminal Records: Access: In person, fax, mail. Only the court performs in person searches; visitors may not. Search fee: $15.00 per hour. Court makes copy: $.25 per page. Required to search: name, years to search, DOB. Criminal records go back to 1970; on computer back to 1998. No charge for a simple name search. Mail turnaround time 1-2 weeks.
General Information: No public access terminal. Will fax to toll-free numbers no charge. Certification fee: $5.00 per doc. Payee: State of Alaska. Prepayment required.

Yakutat Magistrate Court (1st District)
PO Box 426, Yakutat, AK 99689-0426; phone: 907-784-3274; fax: 907-784-3257; hours 9AM-4:30PM M-Th (AK). *Misdemeanor, Civil Actions Under $7,500, Small Claims.*

Note: Felony cases are at Juneau Superior & District Court. Telephone number subject to change.

Civil Records: Access: Phone, mail, fax, in person, email. Only the court performs in person searches; visitors may not. Search fee: $15.00 per hour. Court makes copy: $.25 per page. Required to search: name. Civil records go back to 1998; on computer back to 1976. Mail turnaround time 7-12 days.
Criminal Records: Access: Mail, fax, in person, email. Only the court performs in person searches; visitors may not. Search fee: $15.00 per hour. Court makes copy: $.25 per page. Required to search: name and DOB or SSN. Criminal records go back to 1959; on computer back to 1998. Mail turnaround time 7-12 days.
General Information: No public access terminal. Certification fee: $5.00. Payee: Alaska Court System. Prepayment required.

Southeast Fairbanks

Delta Junction Magistrate Court (4th District)
PO Box 401, Delta Junction, AK 99737-0401; phone: 907-895-4211; fax: 907-895-4204; hours 8AM-N, 1-4:30PM (AK). *Misdemeanor, Civil Actions Under $7,500, Small Claims.* Note: Felony cases are at Fairbanks Superior & District Court.
Civil Records: Access: In person, mail, online. Only the court performs in person searches; visitors may not. Court makes copy: $.25 per page. Search names on the Alaska Trial Courts database at www.state.ak.us/courts/names.htm. Web gives case number only. Mail turnaround time 1 week.
Criminal Records: Access: phone, mail, fax, in person, online. Only the court performs in person searches; visitors may not. Search fee: $15.00 per hour. Court makes copy: $.25 per page. Required to search: name, years to search. Criminal records computerized go back to 1980; prior records go back to mid-70's. Online access to criminal records is the same as civil. Mail turnaround time 1 week.

General Information: No public access terminal. Certification fee: $5.00 per doc. Payee: District Court. Prepayment required.

Tok Magistrate Court (4th District) PO
Box 187, Tok, AK 99780-0187; phone: 907-883-5171; fax: 907-883-4367; hours 8AM-N; 1PM-4:30PM (AK). *Misdemeanor, Civil Actions Under $7,500, Small Claims.*

Note: Felony cases are at Fairbanks Superior & District Court.

Civil Records: Access: In person, phone, mail, online. Visitors must perform in person searches themselves. Court makes copy: $.25 per page. Required to search: Name, DOB, SSN. Civil records computerized since 1994. Search names on the Alaska Trial Courts database at www.state.ak.us/courts/names.htm. Web gives case number only. Mail turnaround time 5 days.
Criminal Records: Access: In person, phone, mail, online. Visitors must perform in person searches themselves. No search fee. Court makes copy: $.25 per page. Required to search: name, years to search, DOB. Criminal records computerized since 1994. Online access to criminal records is the same as civil. Mail turnaround time 5 days.
General Information: Public access terminal goes back to 1994. Will fax documents. Certification fee: $5.00 per doc. Prepayment required.

Valdez-Cordova

Superior & District Court (3rd District)
PO Box 127, 213 Meals, Valdez, AK 99686-0127; phone: 907-835-2266; fax: 907-835-3764; hours 8AM-4:30PM (AK). *Felony, Misdemeanor, Civil, Eviction, Small Claims, Probate.*

Note: In rare instances, some of the older Valdez felony records may be found at Cordova.

Civil Records: Access: Fax, mail, in person, online. Only the court performs in person searches; visitors may not. No search fee. Court makes copy: $.25 per page. Required to search: name, years to search; also helpful: address. Civil cases indexed by defendant, plaintiff. Civil records on computer from 1984, on microfiche, archived and index from 1960. Search names on the Alaska Trial Courts database at www.state.ak.us/courts/names.htm. Web gives case number only. Mail turnaround time 1-3 weeks.
Criminal Records: Access: Fax, mail, in person, online. Only the court performs in person searches; visitors may not. No search fee. Court makes copy: $.25 per page. Required to search: name, years to search; also helpful: address, DOB, SSN. Criminal records on computer from 1984, on microfiche, archived and index from 1960. Online access to criminal records is the same as civil. Mail turnaround time 1-3 weeks.
General Information: No public access terminal. No adoption, juvenile, guardianship or mental records released. Will fax documents for $15.00 fee. Certification fee: $5.00 per doc. Payee: Valdez Trial Court of Alaska. Personal checks accepted. Prepayment and SASE required.

Cordova District Court (3rd District) PO
Box 898, 500 Water St, Cordova, AK 99574-0898; phone: 907-424-3378; fax: 907-424-7581; hours 8AM-4:30PM (AK). *Felony, Misdemeanor, Civil, Small Claims, Probate.*

Note: Some very old Valdez court records may also reside here. Although some felony cases may be assigned to a Valdez judge or a Anchorage judge, the actual case records will be found here in Cordova. Sand Point cases handled here.

Civil Records: Access: Phone, mail, fax, in person, online. Both court and visitors may perform in person searches. Search fee: $15.00 per hour. Court makes copy: $.25. Required to search: DOB, years to search. Civil records on computer back to 1993; other records back to 1975. Search names on the Alaska Trial Courts database at www.state.ak.us/courts/names.htm. Web gives case number only.

Note: Access by phone if time allows. Mail turnaround time 1 week.
Criminal Records: Access: Phone, mail, fax, in person, online. Both court and visitors may perform in person searches. Search fee: $15.00 per hour. Court makes copy: $.25. Required to search: name, years to search, DOB. Criminal records on computer back to 1993; other records back to 1975. Online access to criminal records is the same as civil. Note: Will take phone requests if time allows. Mail turnaround time 1 week.
General Information: Public access terminal goes back to 7-10 years. Will not fax documents. Certification fee: $5.00 per doc. Payee: State of Alaska. Prepayment required.

Glennallen District Court (3rd District)
PO Box 86, Glennallen, AK 99588-0086; phone: 907-822-3405; hours 8AM-4:30PM (AK). *Misdemeanor, Civil, Small Claims.*
Civil Records: Access: Mail, in person, online. Only the court performs in person searches; visitors may not. Search fee: $15.00 per hour. Court makes copy: $.25 per page. Records go back to 1960; on computer back to 1992. Search names on the Alaska Trial Courts database at www.state.ak.us/courts/names.htm. Web gives case number only. Mail turnaround time 1-2 weeks.
Criminal Records: Access: Mail, in person, online. Only the court performs in person searches; visitors may not. Search fee: $15.00 per hour. Court makes copy: $.25 per page. Required to search: name, years to search, DOB. Records go back to 1960; on computer back to 1992. Online access to criminal records is the same as civil. Mail turnaround time 1-2 weeks.
General Information: No public access terminal. Certification fee: $5.00 per document. Payee: Alaska Court System. Prepayment required.

Whittier Magistrate Court (3rd District)
825 W 4th Ave, Anchorage, AK 99501-2004; phone: 907-264-0479. *Misdemeanor, Civil Actions Under $7,500, Small Claims.* Note: Court closed; records available at the address and phone above.

Wade Hampton

Chevak Magistrate Court (Bethel Area)
PO Box 238, Chevak, AK 99563-0238; phone: 907-858-7231; fax: 907-858-7230; hours 8AM-4:30PM (AK). *Misdemeanor, Civil Actions Under $7,500, Small Claims.* Note: Felony cases at Bethel Superior & District Court.
Civil Records: Access: Mail, fax, in person. Only the court performs in person searches; visitors may not. Search fee: $15.00. Court makes copy: $.25 per page; same fee for self serve. Required to search: name, years to search. Civil records go back to 1993; on computer back to 1997. Mail turnaround time 1-2 weeks.
Criminal Records: Access: Mail, fax, in person. Both court and visitors may perform in person searches. Search fee: $15.00 per hour. Court makes copy: $.25 per page; same fee for self serve. Required to search: name, years to search, address, DOB, SSN, signed release. Criminal records go back to 1993; on computer back to 1997. Mail turnaround time 1-2 weeks.
General Information: No public access terminal. Will fax documents. Certification fee: $3.00 per document includes copy fee. Payee: Magistrate Court. Prepayment required.

Emmonak Magistrate Court (Bethel Area)
PO Box 176, Emmonak, AK 99581-0176; phone: 907-949-1748; fax: 907-949-1535; hours 8AM-4:30PM (AK). *Misdemeanor, Civil Actions Under $15,000, Small Claims.* Note: Felony cases are at Bethel Superior & District Court.
Civil Records: Access: Mail, in person. Only the court performs in person searches; visitors may not. Search fee: $15.00 per hour. Court makes copy: $.25 per page. Required to search: years to search, DOB, SSN, signed release. Overall records go back to

1995. Computerized records go back to 2000. Mail turnaround time 1-2 weeks.

Criminal Records: Access: Mail, in person. Only the court performs in person searches; visitors may not. Search fee: $15.00 per hour. Court makes copy: $.25 per page. Required to search: name, years to search, address, DOB, signed release; also helpful: SSN. Overall records go back to 1995. Computerized records go back to 2000. Mail turnaround time 1-2 weeks.

General Information: No public access terminal. Will fax documents. Certification fee: $5.00 includes copy fee. Payee: Magistrate Court. Prepayment required.

St Mary's Magistrate Court (Bethel Area)

PO Box 269, St Mary's, AK 99658-0183; phone: 907-438-2912; fax: 907-438-2819; hours 8AM-N, 1-4:30PM (AK). *Misdemeanor, Civil Actions Under $10,000, Small Claims.* Note: Felony cases are at Bethel Superior & District Court.

Civil Records: Access: Mail, in person. Only the court performs in person searches; visitors may not. Search fee: $15.00 per hour. Court makes copy: $.25 per page; same fee for self serve. Civil records computerized go back to 1996. Mail turnaround time 3 weeks.

Criminal Records: Access: Mail, in person. Only the court performs in person searches; visitors may not. Search fee: $15.00 per hour. Court makes copy: $.25 per page; same fee for self serve. Required to search: name, years to search; also helpful: DOB. Criminal records computerized go back to 1996. Mail turnaround time 3 weeks.

General Information: No public access terminal. Will fax documents. Prepayment required.

Wrangell-Petersburg

Petersburg Superior & District Court (1st District)

PO Box 1009, Petersburg, AK 99833-1009; phone: 907-772-3824; fax: 907-772-3018; hours 8AM-4:30PM (AK). *Felony, Misdemeanor, Civil, Eviction, Small Claims, Probate.*

Civil Records: Access: Phone, fax, mail, in person, online. Only the court performs in person searches; visitors may not. Search fee: None unless on microfilm-$15.00 hr. Court makes copy: $.25 per page. Required to search: name, years to search; also helpful: address. Civil cases indexed by defendant, plaintiff. Civil records on computer from 1988, on microfiche and index from 1960s, archived from 1920s. Search names on the Alaska Trial Courts database at www.state.ak.us/courts/names.htm. Web gives case number only. Mail turnaround time 1 week.

Criminal Records: Access: Phone, fax, mail, in person, online. Only the court performs in person searches; visitors may not. Search fee: There is a $15.00 per hour fee on archive cases. Court makes copy: $.25 per page. Required to search: name, years to search; also helpful: address, DOB. Criminal records on computer from 1988, on microfiche and index from 1960s, archived from 1920s. Online access to criminal records is the same as civil. Mail turnaround time 1 week.

General Information: No public access terminal. No adoption, juvenile, guardianship or mental records released. Outgoing fax limited to 10 pages; call for fee. Certification fee: $5.00 per doc. Payee: Alaska Court System. Personal checks accepted. Prepayment and SASE required.

Wrangell Superior & District Court (1st District)

PO Box 869, Wrangell, AK 99929-0869; phone: 907-874-2311; fax: 907-874-3509; hours 8AM-4:30PM (AK). *Felony, Misdemeanor, Civil, Eviction, Small Claims, Probate.* Note: The TDD office can be reached at 907-874-2313.

Civil Records: Access: Phone, fax, mail, in person, online. Only the court performs in person searches; visitors may not. Search fee: $15.00 per hour. Search fee is charged for all written responses. Court makes copy: $.25 per page. Required to search: name, years

to search. Civil cases indexed by defendant, plaintiff. Civil records on computer from 1988, on microfiche and card files from 1959, archived from 1900s. Search names on the Alaska Trial Courts database at www.state.ak.us/courts/names.htm. Web gives case number and court location only. Mail turnaround time 3 days.

Criminal Records: Access: Phone, fax, mail, in person, online. Only the court performs in person searches; visitors may not. Search fee: $15.00 per hour. Court makes copy: $.25 per page. Required to search: name, years to search, DOB. Criminal records on computer from 1988, on microfiche and card files from 1959, archived from 1900s. Online access to criminal records is the same as civil. Mail turnaround time 3 days.

General Information: No public access terminal. No adoption, juvenile, guardianship or mental records released. Fee to fax documents is $15.00 per document. Certification fee: $5.00 plus $2.00 per copy after first. Payee: Alaska Court System or State of Alaska. Personal checks accepted. Prepayment and SASE required.

Kake Magistrate Court (1st District)

PO Box 100, Kake, AK 99830-0100; phone: 907-785-3651; fax: 907-785-3152; hours 8AM-N (AK). *Misdemeanor, Civil Actions Under $7,500, Small Claims.*

Civil Records: Access: Fax, mail, in person. Only the court performs in person searches; visitors may not. Search fee: $15.00 per name. Court makes copy: $.25 per page. Required to search: name. Mail turnaround time 1-2 weeks.

Criminal Records: Access: Fax, mail, in person. Only the court performs in person searches; visitors may not. Search fee: $15.00 per name. Court makes copy: $.25 per page. Required to search: name, years to search, DOB, SSN, signed release. Mail turnaround 1-2 weeks.

General Information: No public access terminal. Certification fee: $5.00 per doc. Payee: Alaska Court System. Prepayment required.

Yukon-Koyukuk

Fort Yukon Magistrate Court (4th District)

PO Box 211, Fort Yukon, AK 99740-0211; phone: 907-662-2336; fax: 907-662-2824; hours 9:30AM-3PM (AK). *Misdemeanor, Civil Actions Under $7,500, Small Claims.* Note: Felony cases are at Fairbanks Superior & District Court.

Civil Records: Access: Fax, mail, in person. Only the court performs in person searches; visitors may not. Search fee: $15.00 per name. Court makes copy: $.25 per page. Required to search: name, DOB. Records go back to 1960s. Mail turnaround time 1-2 weeks.

Criminal Records: Access: Fax, mail, in person. Only the court performs in person searches; visitors may not. Search fee: $15.00 per hour. Court makes copy: $.25 per page. Required to search: name, years to search, DOB. Records go back to 1960s. Mail turnaround time 1-2 weeks.

General Information: No public access terminal. Will fax documents to local or toll free line. Certification fee: $5.00 per doc. Payee: District Court. Prepayment required.

Galena Magistrate Court (4th District)

PO Box 167, Galena, AK 99741-0167; phone: 907-656-1322; fax: 907-656-1546; hours 8AM-4:30PM (AK). *Misdemeanor, Civil Actions Under $7,500, Small Claims.* Note: Felony cases are at Fairbanks Superior & District Court.

Civil Records: Access: Mail, in person. Only the court performs in person searches; visitors may not. Search fee: $15.00 per name. Court makes copy: $.25 per page. Required to search: name. Civil record computerized since 1995. Mail turnaround time 1-2 weeks.

Criminal Records: Access: Mail, in person. Only the court performs in person searches; visitors may not. Search fee: $15.00 per hour. Required to search:

name, years to search. Criminal records computerized since 1995. Mail turnaround time 1-2 weeks.

General Information: No public access terminal. Certification fee: $5.00 per doc. Payee: Magistrate Court. Prepayment required.

McGrath Magistrate Court (4th District)

PO Box 167, Galena, AK 99741-0167; phone: 907-656-1322; fax: 907-656-1546; hours 8:30AM-4:30PM (AK). *Misdemeanor, Civil Actions Under $7,500, Small Claims.*

Note: McGrath Court is vacant. Court records at Galena Magistrate Court, address and phone here.

Nenana Magistrate Court (4th District)

PO Box 449, Nenana, AK 99760-0449; phone: 907-832-5430; fax: 907-832-5841; hours 8:30AM-4PM (AK). *Misdemeanor, Civil Actions Under $7,500, Small Claims.* Note: Felony cases are at Fairbanks Superior & District Court.

Civil Records: Access: In person, phone, online. Both court and visitors may perform in person searches. Search fee: $15.00 per name. Court makes copy: $.25 per page. Required to search: name, years to search, DOB. Search names on the Alaska Trial Courts database at www.state.ak.us/courts/names.htm. Web gives case number only.

Criminal Records: Access: In person, phone, online. Both court and visitors may perform in person searches. No search fee. Court makes copy: $.25 per page. Required to search: name, years to search, DOB. Criminal records on computer back to 1995. Online access to criminal records is the same as civil.

General Information: Public access terminal goes back to 1995. Certification fee: $5.00 per doc.

Tanana Magistrate Court (4th District)

PO Box 449, Nenana, AK 99777; phone: 907-832-5430; fax: 907-832-5841; hours Th-F 2nd full week each month (AK). *Misdemeanor, Civil Actions Under $7,500, Small Claims.*

Note: Magistrate may also be contacted by phone at 907-832-5430. Felony cases are at Fairbanks Superior & District Court. All case record files moved to Galena Court 6/2005.

Civil Records: Access: In person, phone, mail. Both court and visitors may perform in person searches. Search fee: $15.00 per name. Court makes copy: $.25 per page. Mail turnaround time 1-2 weeks.

Criminal Records: Access: In person, phone, mail. Both court and visitors may perform in person searches. Search fee: $15.00 per name. Court makes copy: $.25 per page. Required to search: name, years to search, DOB, signed release. Mail turnaround time 1-2 weeks.

General Information: Public access terminal goes back to 1995. Will not fax documents. Certification fee: $5.00 per doc. Payee: Magistrate Court. Prepayment required.

Alaska Recording Offices

ORGANIZATION: The 23 Alaskan counties are called boroughs. However, real estate recording is done under a system that was established at the time of the Gold Rush (whenever that was) of 34 Recording Districts. Some of the Districts are identical in geography to boroughs, such as the Aleutian Islands, but other boroughs and districts overlap. Therefore, you need to know which recording district any given town or city is located in. A helpful web site www.dnr.state.ak.us/recorders/findYourDistrict.htm

The entire state except the Aleutian Islands is in the Alaska Time Zone (AK).

REAL ESTATE RECORDS: Districts do not perform real estate searches. Certification fees are usually $5.00 per document. Copies usually cost $1.25 for the first page, $.25 per additional page.

UCC RECORDS: Financing statements are filed at the state level, except for real estate related collateral, which are filed with the District Recorder. However, prior to 07/2001, consumer goods and farm collateral were filed at the District Recorder and can be searched there. All districts will perform UCC searches now at $15.00 per debtor name for information and $25.00 with copies. Use search request form UCC-11. Copies ordered separately usually cost $2.00 per financing statement.

TAX LIEN RECORDS: All state and federal tax liens are filed with the District Recorder. Districts do not perform separate tax lien searches.

ONLINE ACCESS: Online access to the state recorder's office database from the Dept. of Natural Resources is available free at http://www.dnr.state.ak.us/ssd/recoff/search.cfm. This includes property information, liens, deeds, bankruptcies and more. Images go back to 6/2001; index to 2000. Also, a DNR "land records" database is searchable at www.dnr.state.ak.us/cgi-bin/lris/landrecords.

Aleutian Islands District

District Recorder, 550 W 7th Ave, #1200; #1140, Anchorage, AK 99501. 907-269-8899, R/E recording phone-907-762-2444; hours: 8AM-3:30PM
Separate indices to search. Records indexed on a public use terminal back to 2001. Only the public may search. Copy fee $2.00 per financing statement; tax lien or real estate copy fee $1.25 1st page, $.25 each add'l. Cert fee- $5.00 per doc plus copy fee. Payee- Department of Revenue. **Online access to Real Estate, UCC records:** Access is free on the statewide DNR system at www.dnr.state.ak.us/ssd/recoff/search.cfm. **Property tax/Assessor**- 907-343-6770.

Anchorage District

District Recorder, 550 W 7th Ave, #1200; #1140, Anchorage, AK 99501. 907-269-8879, R/E recording phone-907-762-2443;   fax-907-269-8912;   hours: 8AM-3:30PM www.akrecorder.info
All records in one index. Records indexed on a public use terminal back to 1971. Only the public may search. Copy fee $1.25 1st page plus $.25 each add'l. Cert fee- $5.00 per doc plus copy fee. Payee- Department of Revenue. **Online access to Real Estate, UCC, Property Tax, Most Wanted, Stolen Vehicle records:** Access is on the statewide DNR system at www.dnr.state.ak.us/ssd/recoff/search.cfm. UCC records can be accessed by phone at 907-269-8899. Also, access to Anchorage real estate property taxes is free at www.muni.org/services/departments/treasury/property/viewer.cfm Also, the sheriff's most wanted and stolen vehicle lists are at www.muni.org/apd1/apd911.cfm. Also, court list of divorces from 6/25/2003 to 10/22/2003 is at www.state.ak.us/courts/WEBDIV.3AN.   **Property tax/Assessor**- 907-343-6770.

Barrow District

District Recorder, 1648 S Cushman St. #201, Fairbanks, AK 99701-6206. 907-452-3521; fax-907-452-2951; hours: 8AM-4PM
Office will perform a UCC search but public must search other records themselves. UCC info request only per debtor name- $15.00. UCC search & copy request per debtor name- $25.00. UCC copy fee $2.00 per financing statement. RE record copy- $1.25 1st page, $.25 each add'l page. Cert fee- $5.00 per doc plus copy fee. Payee- Department of Revenue. **Online access to Real Estate, UCC records:** Access is on the statewide DNR system at www.dnr.state.ak.us/ssd/recoff/search.cfm.   **Property tax/Assessor**- 907-459-1000.

Bethel District

District Recorder, PO Box 426, Bethel, AK 99559. 907-543-3391; fax-907-543-7053; hours: 9:15AM-N, 1-3:15PM
Records indexed on computer back to 2001. Only the public may search. UCC copy fee $1.25 1st page, $.25 each add'l. Cert fee- $5.00 per doc plus copy fee. Payee- Department of Revenue. **Online access to Real Estate, UCC records:** Access is on the statewide DNR system at www.dnr.state.ak.us/ssd/recoff/search.cfm Or at akrecorder.info . **Other phones:** Treasurer- 907-543-2298. **Property tax/Assessor**- 907-543-2296.

Bristol Bay District

District Recorder, 550 W 7th Ave, #1200; #1140, Anchorage, AK 99501. 907-269-8899, R/E recording phone-907-762-2443; hours: 8AM-3:30PM
Office will perform a UCC search but public must search other records themselves. UCC info request only per debtor name- $15.00. UCC search & copy request per debtor name- $25.00 + $1.00. per page. UCC copy fee $2.00 per financing statement. RE record copy- $1.25 1st page, $.25 each add'l page. Cert fee- $5.00 per doc plus copy fee. Payee-

Department of Revenue. **Online access to Real Estate, UCC records:** Access is on the statewide DNR system at www.dnr.state.ak.us/ssd/recoff/search.cfm. **Property tax/Assessor**- 907-343-6770.

Cape Nome District

District Recorder, Box 431, Nome, AK 99762. 907-443-5178; fax-907-452-2951; hours: 8AM-12:30PM
Temporarily closed until further notice; Fairbanks office now processes recordings. Office will perform a UCC search but public must search other records themselves. UCC info request only per debtor name- $15.00. UCC search & copy request per debtor name- $25.00. Copy fee $2.00 per financing statement. Tax lien or real estate copy- $1.25 1st page, $.25 each add'l page. Cert fee- $5.00 per doc plus copy fee. Payee- Department of Revenue. **Online access to Real Estate, UCC records:** Access is on the statewide DNR system at www.dnr.state.ak.us/ssd/recoff/search.cfm.

Chitina District

District Recorder, Box 2023, Valdez, AK 99686. 907-835-2266, R/E recording phone-907-745-9683, UCC recording phone-907-269-8899; hours: 8:30AM-4PM
Chitna office records are now in Valdez; address and telephone given here. Only the public may search. Copy fee $2.00 per financing statement. Tax lien or real estate copy- $1.25 1st page, $.25 each add'l page. Cert fee- $5.00 per doc plus copy fee. Payee- Department of Revenue. **Online access to Real Estate, UCC, Deed records:** Access is on the statewide DNR system at www.dnr.state.ak.us/ssd/recoff/search.cfm. **Other phones:** Elections- 907-451-2835; Vital Records- 907-465-8606.

Cordova District

District Recorder, 550 W 7th Ave, #1200; #1140, Anchorage, AK 99501. 907-269-8899, R/E recording phone-907-762-2443; hours: 8AM-3:30PM
Office will perform a UCC search but public must search other records themselves. UCC info request

only per debtor name- $15.00. UCC search & copy request per debtor name- $25.00. UCC copy fee $2.00 per financing statement. RE record copy- $1.25 1st page, $.25 each add'l page. Cert fee- $5.00 per doc plus copy fee. Payee- Department of Revenue. **Online access to Real Estate, UCC records:** Access is on the statewide DNR system at www.dnr.state.ak.us/ssd/recoff/search.cfm. **Property tax/Assessor-** 907-343-6770.

Fairbanks District

District Recorder, 1648 S Cushman St. #201, Fairbanks, AK 99701-6206. 907-452-3521; fax-907-269-8912; hours: 8AM-3:30PM www.co.fairbanks.ak.us
Office will perform a UCC search but public must search other records themselves. UCC info request only per debtor name- $15.00. UCC search & copy request per debtor name- $25.00. Copy fee $2.00 per financing statement. Tax lien or real estate copy- $1.25 1st page, $.25 each add'l page. Cert fee- $5.00 per doc plus copy fee. Payee- Department of Revenue. **Online access to Real Estate, UCC, Cemetery records:** Access to the Fairbanks North Star Borough property database is free at www.co.fairbanks.ak.us/PropertyDB/default.asp. Also, access is on the statewide DNR system at www.dnr.state.ak.us/ssd/recoff/search.cfm. Also, access cemetery records for a fee through a private company at www.ancestry.com/search/db.aspx?dbid=4044. **Property tax/Assessor-** 907-459-1000.

Fort Gibbon District

District Recorder, 1648 S Cushman St. #201, Fairbanks, AK 99701-6206. 907-452-3521; fax-907-452-2951; hours: 8:30AM-4PM
Office will perform a UCC search but public must search other records themselves. UCC info request only per debtor name- $15.00. UCC search & copy request per debtor name- $25.00. Copy fee $2.00 per financing statement. Tax lien or real estate copy- $1.25 1st page, $.25 each add'l page. Cert fee- $5.00 per doc plus copy fee. Payee- Department of Revenue. **Online access to Real Estate, UCC records:** Access the statewide DNR system at www.dnr.state.ak.us/ssd/recoff/search.cfm. **Property tax/Assessor-** 907-459-1000.

Haines District

District Recorder, 400 Willoughby; 3rd Fl, Juneau, AK 99801. 907-465-3449; hours: 8:30AM-4PM
Office will perform a UCC search but public must search other records themselves. UCC info request only per debtor name- $15.00. UCC search & copy request per debtor name- $25.00. Copy fee $2.00 per financing statement. Tax lien or real estate copy- $1.25 1st page, $.25 each add'l page. Cert fee- $5.00 per doc plus copy fee. Payee- Department of Revenue. **Online access to Real Estate, UCC records:** Access the statewide DNR system at www.dnr.state.ak.us/ssd/recoff/search.cfm. **Property tax/Assessor-** 907-586-5220.

Homer District

District Recorder, 195 E Bunnell Ave.; #A, Homer, AK 99603. 907-235-8136; hours: 8:30AM-N, 1-4PM
Office will perform a UCC search but public must search other records themselves. UCC info request only per debtor name- $15.00. UCC search & copy request per debtor name- $25.00. Copy fee $2.00 per financing statement. Tax lien or real estate copy- $1.25 1st page, $.25 each add'l page. Cert fee- $5.00 per doc plus copy fee. Payee- Department of Revenue. **Online access to Real Estate, UCC, Assessor records:** Access is the statewide DNR system at www.dnr.state.ak.us/ssd/recoff/search.cfm. Also, access the borough tax assessor rolls free at www.borough.kenai.ak.us/assessingdept/Parcel_QUERY/SEARCH.HTM.

Iliamna District

District Recorder, 550 W 7th Ave, #1200; #1140, Anchorage, AK 99501. 907-269-8899, R/E recording phone-907-762-2443; hours: 8AM-3:30PM
Office will perform a UCC search but public must search other records themselves. UCC info request only per debtor name- $15.00. UCC search & copy request per debtor name- $25.00 + $1.00. per page. Copy fee $2.00 per financing statement. Tax lien or real estate copy- $1.25 1st page, $.25 each add'l page. Cert fee- $5.00 per doc plus copy fee. Payee-Department of Revenue. **Online access to Real Estate, UCC records:** Access the statewide DNR system at www.dnr.state.ak.us/ssd/recoff/search.cfm. **Property tax/Assessor-** 907-343-6770.

Juneau District

District Recorder, 400 Willoughby; 3rd Fl, Juneau, AK 99801. 907-465-3449; hours: 8:30AM-4PM www.juneau.org/cbj/index.php
Office will perform a UCC search but public must search other records themselves. UCC info request only per debtor name- $15.00. UCC search & copy request per debtor name- $25.00. Copy fee $2.00 per financing statement. Tax lien or real estate copy- $1.25 1st page, $.25 each add'l page. Cert fee- $5.00 per doc plus copy fee. Payee-Department of Revenue. **Online access to Real Estate, UCC, Assessor records:** Access to City of Juneau Property Records database is free online at www.juneau.org/assessordata/sqlassessor.php. Also includes link access to Juneau rentals data and the Records home page. Access is via the statewide DNR system at www.dnr.state.ak.us/ssd/recoff/search.cfm. **Property tax/Assessor-** 907-586-5220.

Kenai District

District Recorder, 120 Trading Bay Rd #190, Kenai, AK 99611. 907-283-3118, R/E recording phone-907-225-3142; hours: 8:30AM-4PM
Office will perform a UCC search but public must search other records themselves. UCC info request only per debtor name- $15.00. UCC search & copy request per debtor name- $25.00. Copy fee $2.00 per financing statement. Tax lien or real estate copy- $1.25 1st page, $.25 each add'l page. Cert fee- $5.00 per doc plus copy fee. Payee-Department of Revenue. **Online access to Assessor, Real Estate, UCC records:** Access Kenai Peninsula Borough Assessing Dept. Search Page is free at www.borough.kenai.ak.us/assessingdept/Parcel_QUERY/SEARCH.HTM. Also, access data on the statewide DNR system at www.dnr.state.ak.us/ssd/recoff/search.cfm. **Property tax/Assessor-** 907-343-6770.

Ketchikan District

District Recorder, 415 Main St; Rm 310, Ketchikan, AK 99901. 907-225-3142; fax-907-247-3142; hours: 8:30AM-4PM; closed for lunch hour.
Office will perform a UCC search but public must search other records themselves. UCC info request only per debtor name- $15.00. UCC search & copy request per debtor name- $25.00. Copy fee $2.00 per financing statement. Tax lien or real estate copy- $1.25 1st page, $.25 each add'l page. Cert fee- $5.00 per doc plus copy fee. Payee-Department of Revenue. **Online access to Real Estate, UCC records:** Access the statewide DNR system at www.dnr.state.ak.us/ssd/recoff/search.cfm. **Property tax/Assessor-** 907-225-0277.

Kodiak District

District Recorder, 204 Mission Rd; Rm 110, Kodiak, AK 99615. 907-486-9432; fax-907-486-9432; hours: 8AM-N, 1-4PM
Only the public may search. Copy fee $2.00 per financing statement. Tax lien or real estate copy- $1.25 1st page, $.25 each add'l page. Cert fee- $5.00 per doc plus copy fee. Payee- Department of Revenue. **Online access to Real Estate, UCC, Assessor, Property records:** Access the statewide DNR system at www.dnr.state.ak.us/ssd/recoff/search.cfm. Also, search property assessor real

property records free at www.kib.co.kodiak.ak.us. Click on "Real Property Records.". **Property tax/Assessor-** 907-486-9310.

Kotzebue District

District Recorder, 1648 S. Cushman St. #201, Fairbanks, AK 99701-6206. 907-452-3521; fax-907-452-2951; hours: 8AM-4PM
Office will perform a UCC search but public must search other records themselves. UCC info request only per debtor name- $15.00. UCC search & copy request per debtor name- $25.00. Copy fee $2.00 per financing statement. Tax lien or real estate copy- $1.25 1st page, $.25 each add'l page. Cert fee- $5.00 per doc plus copy fee. Payee-Department of Revenue. **Online access to Real Estate, UCC records:** Access the statewide DNR system at www.dnr.state.ak.us/ssd/recoff/search.cfm. **Property tax/Assessor-** 907-459-1000.

Kuskokwim District

District Recorder, PO Box 426, Bethel, AK 99559. 907-543-3391; fax-907-543-7053; hours: 9:15AM-N, 1-3:15PM
Office will perform a UCC search but public must search other records themselves. UCC info request only per debtor name- $15.00. UCC search & copy request per debtor name- $25.00. Copy fee $2.00 per financing statement. Tax lien or real estate copy- $1.25 1st page, $.25 each add'l page. Cert fee- $5.00 per doc plus copy fee. Payee-Department of Revenue. **Online access to Real Estate, UCC records:** Access the statewide DNR system at www.dnr.state.ak.us/ssd/recoff/search.cfm.

Kvichak District

District Recorder, 550 W 7th Ave, #1200; #1140, Anchorage, AK 99501. 907-269-8899, R/E recording phone-907-762-2443; hours: 8AM-3:30PM
Office will perform a UCC search but public must search other records themselves. UCC info request only per debtor name- $15.00. UCC search & copy request per debtor name- $25.00. Copy fee $2.00 per financing statement. Tax lien or real estate copy- $1.25 1st page, $.25 each add'l page. Cert fee- $5.00 per doc plus copy fee. Payee-Department of Revenue. **Online access to Real Estate, UCC records:** Access the statewide DNR system at www.dnr.state.ak.us/ssd/recoff/search.cfm. **Property tax/Assessor-** 907-343-6770.

Manley Hot Springs District

District Recorder, 1648 S Cushman St. #201, Fairbanks, AK 99701-6206. 907-452-3521; fax-907-452-2951; hours: 8:30AM-4PM
Office will perform a UCC search but public must search other records themselves. UCC info request only per debtor name- $15.00. UCC search & copy request per debtor name- $25.00. Copy fee $2.00 per financing statement. Tax lien or real estate copy- $1.25 1st page, $.25 each add'l page. Cert fee- $5.00 per doc plus copy fee. Payee-Department of Revenue. **Online access to Real Estate, UCC records:** Access the statewide DNR system at www.dnr.state.ak.us/ssd/recoff/search.cfm. **Property tax/Assessor-** 907-459-1000.

Mount McKinley District

District Recorder, 1648 S Cushman St. #201, Fairbanks, AK 99701-6206. 907-452-3521; fax-907-452-2951; hours: 8:30AM-4PM
Office will perform a UCC search but public must search other records themselves. UCC info request only per debtor name- $15.00. UCC search & copy request per debtor name- $25.00. Copy fee $2.00 per financing statement. Tax lien or real estate copy- $1.25 1st page, $.25 each add'l page. Cert fee- $5.00 per doc plus copy fee. Payee-Department of Revenue. **Online access to Real Estate, UCC records:** Access the statewide DNR system at www.dnr.state.ak.us/ssd/recoff/search.cfm. **Property tax/Assessor-** 907459-1000.

Nenana District

District Recorder, 1648 S Cushman St. #201, Fairbanks, AK 99701-6206. 907-452-3521; fax-907-452-2951; hours: 8:30AM-4PM

Office will perform a UCC search but public must search other records themselves. UCC info request only per debtor name- $15.00. UCC search & copy request per debtor name- $25.00. Copy fee $2.00 per financing statement. Tax lien or real estate copy- $1.25 1st page, $.25 each add'l page. Cert fee- $5.00 per doc plus copy fee. Payee-Department of Revenue. **Online access to Real Estate, UCC records:** Access the statewide DNR system at www.dnr.state.ak.us/ssd/recoff/search.cfm. **Property tax/Assessor-** 907-459-1000.

Nulato District

District Recorder, 1648 S Cushman St. #201, Fairbanks, AK 99701-6206. 907-452-3521; fax-907-452-2951; hours: 8:30AM-4PM

Office will perform a UCC search but public must search other records themselves. UCC info request only per debtor name- $15.00. UCC search & copy request per debtor name- $25.00. Copy fee $2.00 per financing statement. Tax lien or real estate copy- $1.25 1st page, $.25 each add'l page. Cert fee- $5.00 per doc plus copy fee. Payee-Department of Revenue. **Online access to Real Estate, UCC records:** Access the statewide DNR system at www.dnr.state.ak.us/ssd/recoff/search.cfm. **Property tax/Assessor-** 907-459-1000.

Palmer District

District Recorder, 1800 Glenn Hwy #7, Palmer, AK 99645. 907-745-3080; fax-907-745-0958; hours: 8:30AM-4PM

Office will perform a UCC search but public must search other records themselves. UCC info request only per debtor name- $15.00. UCC search & copy request per debtor name- $25.00. Copy fee $2.00 per financing statement. Tax lien or real estate copy- $1.25 1st page, $.25 each add'l page. Cert fee- $5.00 per doc plus copy fee. Payee-Department of Revenue. **Online access to Real Estate, UCC records:** Access the statewide DNR system at www.dnr.state.ak.us/ssd/recoff/search.cfm.

Petersburg District

District Recorder, 415 Main St; Rm 310, Ketchikan, AK 99901. 907-225-3142; fax-907-247-3142; hours: 8:30AM-4PM; closed for lunch hour.

Office will perform a UCC search but public must search other records themselves. UCC info request only per debtor name- $15.00. UCC search & copy request per debtor name- $25.00. Copy fee $2.00 per financing statement. Tax lien or real estate copy- $1.25 1st page, $.25 each add'l page. Cert fee- $5.00 per doc plus copy fee. Payee-Department of Revenue. **Online access to Real Estate, UCC records:** Access the statewide DNR system at www.dnr.state.ak.us/ssd/recoff/search.cfm. **Property tax/Assessor-** 907-225-0277.

Rampart District

District Recorder, 1648 S. Cushman St. #201, Fairbanks, AK 99701-6206. 907-452-3521; fax-907-452-2951; hours: 8AM-4PM

Office will perform a UCC search but public must search other records themselves. UCC info request only per debtor name- $15.00. UCC search & copy request per debtor name- $25.00. Copy fee $2.00 per financing statement. Tax lien or real estate copy- $1.25 1st page, $.25 each add'l page. Cert fee- $5.00 per doc plus copy fee. Payee-Department of Revenue. **Online access to Real Estate, UCC records:** Access the statewide DNR system at www.dnr.state.ak.us/ssd/recoff/search.cfm. **Property tax/Assessor-** 907-459-1000.

Seldovia District

District Recorder, 195 E Bunnell Ave.; #A, Homer, AK 99603. 907-235-8136; hours: 8:30AM-N, 1-4PM

Office personnel or visitors may perform searches. UCC info request only per debtor name- $15.00. UCC search & copy request per debtor name- $25.00. Copy fee $2.00 per financing statement. Tax lien or real estate copy- $1.25 1st page, $.25 each add'l page. Cert fee- $5.00 per doc plus copy fee. Payee- Department of Revenue. **Online access to Real Estate, UCC, Assessor records:** Access the statewide DNR system at www.dnr.state.ak.us/ssd/recoff/search.cfm. Also, access the borough tax assessor rolls free at www.borough.kenai.ak.us/assessingdept/Parcel_QUERY/SEARCH.HTM.

Seward District

District Recorder, Box 246, Seward, AK 99664. 907-224-7032; fax-907-224-7192; hours: 8:30AM-4PM

Office will perform a UCC search but public must search other records themselves. UCC info request only per debtor name- $15.00. UCC search & copy request per debtor name- $25.00. Copy fee $2.00 per financing statement. Tax lien or real estate copy- $1.25 1st page, $.25 each add'l page. Cert fee- $5.00 per doc plus copy fee. Payee-Department of Revenue. **Online access to Real Estate, UCC, Assessor records:** Access the statewide DNR system at www.dnr.state.ak.us/ssd/recoff/search.cfm. Also, access borough tax assessor rolls free at www.borough.kenai.ak.us/assessingdept/Parcel_QUERY/SEARCH.HTM.

Sitka District

District Recorder, 210C Lake St, Sitka, AK 99835. 907-747-3275; hours: 8:30AM-N, 1-4PM M-Th

Office will perform a UCC search but public must search other records themselves. UCC info request only per debtor name- $15.00. UCC search & copy request per debtor name- $25.00. Copy fee $2.00 per financing statement. Tax lien or real estate copy- $1.25 1st page, $.25 each add'l page. Cert fee- $5.00 per doc plus copy fee. Payee-Department of Revenue. **Online access to Real Estate, UCC records:** Access the statewide DNR system at www.dnr.state.ak.us/ssd/recoff/search.cfm. **Property tax/Assessor-** 907-343-6770.

Skagway District

District Recorder, 400 Willoughby; 3rd Fl, Juneau, AK 99801. 907-465-3449; hours: 8:30AM-4PM

Only the public may search. Copy fee $2.00 per financing statement. Tax lien or real estate copy- $1.25 1st page, $.25 each add'l page. Cert fee- $5.00 per doc plus copy fee. Payee- Department of Revenue. **Online access to Real Estate, UCC records:** Access is on the statewide DNR system at www.dnr.state.ak.us/ssd/recoff/search.cfm.

Talkeetna District

District Recorder, 1800 Glenn Hwy #7, Palmer, AK 99645. 907-745-3080; fax-907-745-0958; hours: 8:30AM-4PM

Office will perform a UCC search but public must search other records themselves. UCC info request only per debtor name- $15.00. UCC search & copy request per debtor name- $25.00. Copy fee $2.00 per financing statement. Tax lien or real estate copy- $1.25 1st page, $.25 each add'l page. Cert fee- $5.00 per doc plus copy fee. Payee-Department of Revenue. **Online access to Real Estate, UCC records:** Access the statewide DNR system at www.dnr.state.ak.us/ssd/recoff/search.cfm.

Valdez District

District Recorder, Box 2023, Valdez, AK 99686. 907-835-3153, R/E recording phone-907-835-2266; hours: 8:30AM-N, 1-4PM

Office will perform a UCC search but public must search other records themselves. UCC info request only per debtor name- $15.00. UCC search & copy request per debtor name- $25.00. Copy fee $2.00 per financing statement. Tax lien or real estate copy- $1.25 1st page, $.25 each add'l page. Cert fee- $5.00 per doc plus copy fee. Payee-Department of Revenue. **Online access to Real Estate, UCC records:** Access the statewide DNR system at www.dnr.state.ak.us/ssd/recoff/search.cfm.

Wrangell District

District Recorder, 415 Main St; Rm 310, Ketchikan, AK 99901. 907-225-3142; fax-907-247-3142; hours: 8:30AM-4PM; closed for lunch hour.

Office will perform a UCC search but public must search other records themselves. UCC info request only per debtor name- $15.00. UCC search & copy request per debtor name- $25.00. Copy fee $2.00 per financing statement. Tax lien or real estate copy- $1.25 1st page, $.25 each add'l page. Cert fee- $5.00 per doc plus copy fee. Payee-Department of Revenue. **Online access to Real Estate, UCC records:** Access the statewide DNR system at www.dnr.state.ak.us/ssd/recoff/search.cfm. **Property tax/Assessor-** 907-225-0277.

Alaska County Locator

You will usually be able to find the city name in the City/County Cross Reference below. In that case, it is a simple matter to determine the county from the cross reference. However, only the official US Postal Service city names are included in this index. There are an additional 40,000 place names that people use in their addresses. Therefore, we have also included a ZIP/City Cross Reference immediately following the City/County Cross Reference.

If you know the ZIP Code but the city name does not appear in the City/County Cross Reference index, look up the ZIP Code in the ZIP/City Cross Reference, find the city name, then look up the city name in the City/County Cross Reference. For example, you want to know the county for an address of Menands, NY 12204. There is no "Menands" in the City/County Cross Reference. The ZIP/City Cross Reference shows that ZIP Codes 12201-12288 are for the city of Albany. Looking back in the City/County Cross Reference, Albany is in Albany County.

Alaska City/County Cross Reference

ADAK Aleutian Islands, West
AKIACHAK Bethel
AKIAK Bethel
AKUTAN Aleutian Islands, East
ALAKANUK Wade Hampton
ALEKNAGIK Dillingham
ALLAKAKET Yukon-Koyukuk
AMBLER Northwest Arctic
ANAKTUVUK PASS North Slope Borough
ANCHOR POINT Kenai Peninsula Borough
ANCHORAGE Anchorage Borough
ANDERSON Denali
ANGOON Yakutat
ANIAK Bethel
ANVIK Yukon-Koyukuk
ARCTIC VILLAGE Yukon-Koyukuk
ATKA Aleutian Islands, West
ATQASUK North Slope Borough
AUKE BAY Juneau Borough
BARROW North Slope Borough
BEAVER Yukon-Koyukuk
BETHEL Bethel
BETTLES FIELD Yukon-Koyukuk
BIG LAKE Matanuska-Susitna Borough
BREVIG MISSION Nome
BUCKLAND Northwest Arctic
CANTWELL Denali
CENTRAL Yukon-Koyukuk
CHALKYITSIK Yukon-Koyukuk
CHEFORNAK Bethel
CHEVAK Wade Hampton
CHICKEN Southeast Fairbanks
CHIGNIK Lake & Peninsula
CHIGNIK LAGOON Lake & Peninsula
CHIGNIK LAKE Lake & Peninsula
CHITINA Valdez-Cordova
CHUGIAK Anchorage Borough
CIRCLE Yukon-Koyukuk
CLAM GULCH Kenai Peninsula Borough
CLARKS POINT Dillingham
CLEAR Denali
COFFMAN COVE Prince of Wales-Outer
  Ketchikan
COLD BAY Aleutian Islands, East
COOPER LANDING Kenai Peninsula
  Borough
COPPER CENTER Valdez-Cordova
CORDOVA Valdez-Cordova
CRAIG Prince of Wales-Outer Ketchikan
CROOKED CREEK Bethel
DEERING Northwest Arctic
DELTA JUNCTION Southeast Fairbanks
DENALI NATIONAL PARK Denali
DILLINGHAM Dillingham
DOUGLAS Juneau Borough
DUTCH HARBOR Aleutian Islands, West
EAGLE Southeast Fairbanks
EAGLE RIVER Anchorage Borough
EEK Bethel
EGEGIK Lake & Peninsula
EIELSON AFB Fairbanks North Star
  Borough

EKWOK Dillingham
ELFIN COVE Yakutat
ELIM Nome
ELMENDORF AFB Anchorage Borough
EMMONAK Wade Hampton
ESTER Fairbanks North Star Borough
FAIRBANKS Fairbanks North Star Borough
FALSE PASS Aleutian Islands, East
FLAT Yukon-Koyukuk
FORT GREELY Southeast Fairbanks
FORT RICHARDSON Anchorage Borough
FORT WAINWRIGHT Fairbanks North Star
  Borough
FORT YUKON Yukon-Koyukuk
GAKONA Valdez-Cordova
GALENA Yukon-Koyukuk
GAMBELL Nome
GIRDWOOD Anchorage Borough
GLENNALLEN Valdez-Cordova
GOODNEWS BAY Bethel
GRAYLING Yukon-Koyukuk
GUSTAVUS Yakutat
HAINES Haines Borough
HEALY Denali
HOLY CROSS Yukon-Koyukuk
HOMER Kenai Peninsula Borough
HOONAH Yakutat
HOOPER BAY Wade Hampton
HOPE Kenai Peninsula Borough
HOUSTON Matanuska-Susitna Borough
HUGHES Yukon-Koyukuk
HUSLIA Yukon-Koyukuk
HYDABURG Prince of Wales-Outer
  Ketchikan
HYDER Prince of Wales-Outer Ketchikan
ILIAMNA Lake & Peninsula
INDIAN Anchorage Borough
JUNEAU Juneau Borough
KAKE Wrangell-Petersburg
KAKTOVIK North Slope Borough
KALSKAG Bethel
KALTAG Yukon-Koyukuk
KARLUK Kodiak Island Borough
KASIGLUK Bethel
KASILOF Kenai Peninsula Borough
KENAI Kenai Peninsula Borough
KETCHIKAN Ketchikan Gateway Borough
KIANA Northwest Arctic
KING COVE Aleutian Islands, East
KING SALMON (99613) Bristol Bay
  Borough(84), Lake & Peninsula(15)
KIPNUK Bethel
KIVALINA Northwest Arctic
KLAWOCK Prince of Wales-Outer
  Ketchikan
KOBUK Northwest Arctic
KODIAK Kodiak Island Borough
KOTLIK Wade Hampton
KOTZEBUE Northwest Arctic
KOYUK Nome
KOYUKUK Yukon-Koyukuk
KWETHLUK Bethel

KWIGILLINGOK Bethel
LAKE MINCHUMINA Yukon-Koyukuk
LARSEN BAY Kodiak Island Borough
LEVELOCK Lake & Peninsula
LOWER KALSKAG Bethel
MANLEY HOT SPRINGS Yukon-Koyukuk
MANOKOTAK Dillingham
MARSHALL Wade Hampton
MC GRATH Yukon-Koyukuk
MEKORYUK Bethel
METLAKATLA Prince of Wales-Outer
  Ketchikan
MEYERS CHUCK Prince of Wales-Outer
  Ketchikan
MINTO Yukon-Koyukuk
MOOSE PASS Kenai Peninsula Borough
MOUNTAIN VILLAGE Wade Hampton
NAKNEK Bristol Bay Borough
NAPAKIAK Bethel
NENANA Yukon-Koyukuk
NEW STUYAHOK Dillingham
NIGHTMUTE Bethel
NIKISKI Kenai Peninsula Borough
NIKOLAI Yukon-Koyukuk
NIKOLSKI Aleutian Islands, West
NINILCHIK Kenai Peninsula Borough
NOATAK Northwest Arctic
NOME Nome
NONDALTON Lake & Peninsula
NOORVIK Northwest Arctic
NORTH POLE Fairbanks North Star
  Borough
NORTHWAY Southeast Fairbanks
NUIQSUT North Slope Borough
NULATO Yukon-Koyukuk
NUNAM IQUA Wade Hampton
NUNAPITCHUK Bethel
OLD HARBOR Kodiak Island Borough
OUZINKIE Kodiak Island Borough
PALMER Matanuska-Susitna Borough
PEDRO BAY Lake & Peninsula
PELICAN Yakutat
PERRYVILLE Lake & Peninsula
PETERSBURG Wrangell-Petersburg
PILOT POINT Lake & Peninsula
PILOT STATION Wade Hampton
PLATINUM Bethel
POINT BAKER Prince of Wales-Outer
  Ketchikan
POINT HOPE North Slope Borough
POINT LAY North Slope Borough
PORT ALEXANDER Wrangell-Petersburg
PORT ALSWORTH Lake & Peninsula
PORT HEIDEN Lake & Peninsula
PORT LIONS Kodiak Island Borough
PRUDHOE BAY North Slope Borough
QUINHAGAK Bethel
RAMPART Yukon-Koyukuk
RED DEVIL Bethel
RUBY Yukon-Koyukuk
RUSSIAN MISSION Wade Hampton

SAINT GEORGE ISLAND Aleutian Islands,
  West
SAINT MARYS Wade Hampton
SAINT MICHAEL Nome
SAINT PAUL ISLAND Aleutian Islands,
  West
SALCHA Fairbanks North Star Borough
SAND POINT Aleutian Islands, East
SAVOONGA Nome
SCAMMON BAY Wade Hampton
SELAWIK Northwest Arctic
SELDOVIA Kenai Peninsula Borough
SEWARD Kenai Peninsula Borough
SHAGELUK Yukon-Koyukuk
SHAKTOOLIK Nome
SHELDON POINT Wade Hampton
SHISHMAREF Nome
SHUNGNAK Northwest Arctic
SITKA Sitka Borough
SKAGWAY Yakutat
SKWENTNA Matanuska-Susitna Borough
SLEETMUTE Bethel
SOLDOTNA Kenai Peninsula Borough
SOUTH NAKNEK Bristol Bay Borough
STEBBINS Nome
STERLING Kenai Peninsula Borough
STEVENS VILLAGE Yukon-Koyukuk
SUTTON Matanuska-Susitna Borough
TAKOTNA Yukon-Koyukuk
TALKEETNA Matanuska-Susitna Borough
TANACROSS Southeast Fairbanks
TANANA Yukon-Koyukuk
TATITLEK Valdez-Cordova
TELLER Nome
TENAKEE SPRINGS Yakutat
TETLIN Southeast Fairbanks
THORNE BAY Prince of Wales-Outer
  Ketchikan
TOGIAK Dillingham
TOK Southeast Fairbanks
TOKSOOK BAY Bethel
TRAPPER CREEK Matanuska-Susitna
  Borough
TULUKSAK Bethel
TUNTUTULIAK Bethel
TUNUNAK Bethel
TWO RIVERS Fairbanks North Star
  Borough
TYONEK Kenai Peninsula Borough
UNALAKLEET Nome
UNALASKA Aleutian Islands, West
VALDEZ Valdez-Cordova
VENETIE Yukon-Koyukuk
WAINWRIGHT North Slope Borough
WALES Nome
WARD COVE Ketchikan Gateway Borough
WASILLA Matanuska-Susitna Borough
WHITE MOUNTAIN Nome
WHITTIER Valdez-Cordova
WILLOW Matanuska-Susitna Borough
WRANGELL Wrangell-Petersburg
YAKUTAT Yakutat-Not Used

Alaska ZIP/City Cross Reference

99500-99504 ANCHORAGE	99638-99638 NIKOLSKI	99736-99736 DEERING	99926-99926 METLAKATLA
99505-99505 FORT RICHARDSON	99639-99639 NINILCHIK	99737-99737 DELTA JUNCTION	99927-99927 POINT BAKER
99506-99506 ELMENDORF AFB	99640-99640 NONDALTON	99738-99738 EAGLE	99928-99928 WARD COVE
99507-99530 ANCHORAGE	99641-99641 NUNAPITCHUK	99739-99739 ELIM	99929-99929 WRANGELL
99540-99540 INDIAN	99643-99643 OLD HARBOR	99740-99740 FORT YUKON	99950-99950 KETCHIKAN
99546-99546 ADAK	99644-99644 OUZINKIE	99741-99741 GALENA	
99547-99547 ATKA	99645-99645 PALMER	99742-99742 GAMBELL	
99548-99548 CHIGNIK LAKE	99647-99647 PEDRO BAY	99743-99743 HEALY	
99549-99549 PORT HEIDEN	99648-99648 PERRYVILLE	99744-99744 ANDERSON	
99550-99550 PORT LIONS	99649-99649 PILOT POINT	99745-99745 HUGHES	
99551-99551 AKIACHAK	99650-99650 PILOT STATION	99746-99746 HUSLIA	
99552-99552 AKIAK	99651-99651 PLATINUM	99747-99747 KAKTOVIK	
99553-99553 AKUTAN	99652-99652 BIG LAKE	99748-99748 KALTAG	
99554-99554 ALAKANUK	99653-99653 PORT ALSWORTH	99749-99749 KIANA	
99555-99555 ALEKNAGIK	99654-99654 WASILLA	99750-99750 KIVALINA	
99556-99556 ANCHOR POINT	99655-99655 QUINHAGAK	99751-99751 KOBUK	
99557-99557 ANIAK	99656-99656 RED DEVIL	99752-99752 KOTZEBUE	
99558-99558 ANVIK	99657-99657 RUSSIAN MISSION	99753-99753 KOYUK	
99559-99559 BETHEL	99658-99658 SAINT MARYS	99754-99754 KOYUKUK	
99561-99561 CHEFORNAK	99659-99659 SAINT MICHAEL	99755-99755 DENALI NATIONAL PARK	
99563-99563 CHEVAK	99660-99660 SAINT PAUL ISLAND	99756-99756 MANLEY HOT SPRINGS	
99564-99564 CHIGNIK	99661-99661 SAND POINT	99757-99757 LAKE MINCHUMINA	
99565-99565 CHIGNIK LAGOON	99662-99662 SCAMMON BAY	99758-99758 MINTO	
99566-99566 CHITINA	99663-99663 SELDOVIA	99759-99759 POINT LAY	
99567-99567 CHUGIAK	99664-99664 SEWARD	99760-99760 NENANA	
99568-99568 CLAM GULCH	99665-99665 SHAGELUK	99761-99761 NOATAK	
99569-99569 CLARKS POINT	99666-99666 SHELDON POINT	99762-99762 NOME	
99571-99571 COLD BAY	99666-99666 NUNAM IQUA	99763-99763 NOORVIK	
99572-99572 COOPER LANDING	99667-99667 SKWENTNA	99764-99764 NORTHWAY	
99573-99573 COPPER CENTER	99668-99668 SLEETMUTE	99765-99765 NULATO	
99574-99574 CORDOVA	99669-99669 SOLDOTNA	99766-99766 POINT HOPE	
99575-99575 CROOKED CREEK	99670-99670 SOUTH NAKNEK	99767-99767 RAMPART	
99576-99576 DILLINGHAM	99671-99671 STEBBINS	99768-99768 RUBY	
99577-99577 EAGLE RIVER	99672-99672 STERLING	99769-99769 SAVOONGA	
99578-99578 EEK	99674-99674 SUTTON	99770-99770 SELAWIK	
99579-99579 EGEGIK	99675-99675 TAKOTNA	99771-99771 SHAKTOOLIK	
99580-99580 EKWOK	99676-99676 TALKEETNA	99772-99772 SHISHMAREF	
99581-99581 EMMONAK	99677-99677 TATITLEK	99773-99773 SHUNGNAK	
99583-99583 FALSE PASS	99678-99678 TOGIAK	99774-99774 STEVENS VILLAGE	
99584-99584 FLAT	99679-99679 TULUKSAK	99775-99775 FAIRBANKS	
99585-99585 MARSHALL	99680-99680 TUNTUTULIAK	99776-99776 TANACROSS	
99586-99586 GAKONA	99681-99681 TUNUNAK	99777-99777 TANANA	
99587-99587 GIRDWOOD	99682-99682 TYONEK	99778-99778 TELLER	
99588-99588 GLENNALLEN	99683-99683 TRAPPER CREEK	99779-99779 TETLIN	
99589-99589 GOODNEWS BAY	99684-99684 UNALAKLEET	99780-99780 TOK	
99590-99590 GRAYLING	99685-99685 UNALASKA	99781-99781 VENETIE	
99591-99591 SAINT GEORGE ISLAND	99686-99686 VALDEZ	99782-99782 WAINWRIGHT	
99599-99599 ANCHORAGE	99687-99687 WASILLA	99783-99783 WALES	
99602-99602 HOLY CROSS	99688-99688 WILLOW	99784-99784 WHITE MOUNTAIN	
99603-99603 HOMER	99689-99689 YAKUTAT	99785-99785 BREVIG MISSION	
99604-99604 HOOPER BAY	99690-99690 NIGHTMUTE	99786-99786 AMBLER	
99605-99605 HOPE	99691-99691 NIKOLAI	99788-99788 CHALKYITSIK	
99606-99606 ILIAMNA	99692-99692 DUTCH HARBOR	99789-99789 NUIQSUT	
99607-99607 KALSKAG	99693-99693 WHITTIER	99790-99790 FAIRBANKS	
99608-99608 KARLUK	99694-99694 HOUSTON	99791-99791 ATQASUK	
99609-99609 KASIGLUK	99695-99695 ANCHORAGE	99801-99811 JUNEAU	
99610-99610 KASILOF	99697-99697 KODIAK	99820-99820 ANGOON	
99611-99611 KENAI	99701-99701 FAIRBANKS	99821-99821 AUKE BAY	
99612-99612 KING COVE	99702-99702 EIELSON AFB	99824-99824 DOUGLAS	
99613-99613 KING SALMON	99703-99703 FORT WAINWRIGHT	99825-99825 ELFIN COVE	
99614-99614 KIPNUK	99704-99704 CLEAR	99826-99826 GUSTAVUS	
99615-99619 KODIAK	99705-99705 NORTH POLE	99827-99827 HAINES	
99620-99620 KOTLIK	99706-99712 FAIRBANKS	99829-99829 HOONAH	
99621-99621 KWETHLUK	99714-99714 SALCHA	99830-99830 KAKE	
99622-99622 KWIGILLINGOK	99716-99716 TWO RIVERS	99832-99832 PELICAN	
99624-99624 LARSEN BAY	99720-99720 ALLAKAKET	99833-99833 PETERSBURG	
99625-99625 LEVELOCK	99721-99721 ANAKTUVUK PASS	99835-99835 SITKA	
99626-99626 LOWER KALSKAG	99722-99722 ARCTIC VILLAGE	99836-99836 PORT ALEXANDER	
99627-99627 MC GRATH	99723-99723 BARROW	99840-99840 SKAGWAY	
99628-99628 MANOKOTAK	99724-99724 BEAVER	99841-99841 TENAKEE SPRINGS	
99629-99629 WASILLA	99725-99725 ESTER	99850-99850 JUNEAU	
99630-99630 MEKORYUK	99726-99726 BETTLES FIELD	99901-99901 KETCHIKAN	
99631-99631 MOOSE PASS	99727-99727 BUCKLAND	99903-99903 MEYERS CHUCK	
99632-99632 MOUNTAIN VILLAGE	99729-99729 CANTWELL	99918-99918 COFFMAN COVE	
99633-99633 NAKNEK	99730-99730 CENTRAL	99919-99919 THORNE BAY	
99634-99634 NAPAKIAK	99731-99731 FORT GREELY	99921-99921 CRAIG	
99635-99635 NIKISKI	99732-99732 CHICKEN	99922-99922 HYDABURG	
99636-99636 NEW STUYAHOK	99733-99733 CIRCLE	99923-99923 HYDER	
99637-99637 TOKSOOK BAY	99734-99734 PRUDHOE BAY	99925-99925 KLAWOCK	

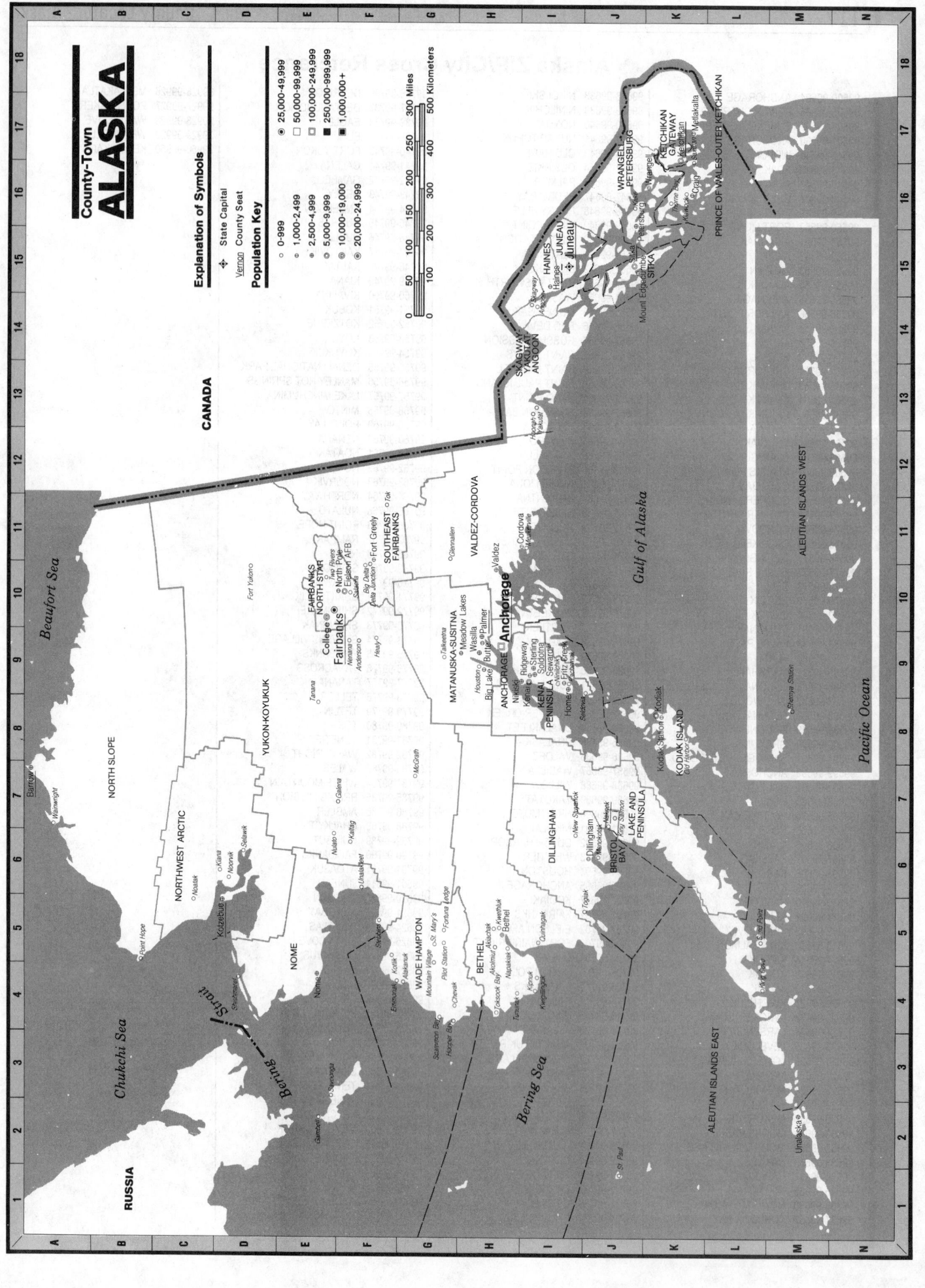

County-Town
ALASKA

Explanation of Symbols

◈ State Capital

Vernon County Seat

Population Key

Symbol	Population
○	0-999
◉	1,000-2,499
⊕	2,500-4,999
◉	5,000-9,999
◉	10,000-19,000
◉	20,000-24,999
◉	25,000-49,999
□	50,000-99,999
▣	100,000-249,999
■	250,000-999,999
■	1,000,000+

Scale: 300 Miles / 500 Kilometers

CANADA

RUSSIA

Chukchi Sea

Beaufort Sea

Bering Strait

Bering Sea

Gulf of Alaska

Pacific Ocean

NORTH SLOPE

NORTHWEST ARCTIC

YUKON-KOYUKUK

NOME

WADE HAMPTON

BETHEL

DILLINGHAM

LAKE AND PENINSULA

BRISTOL BAY

ALEUTIAN ISLANDS EAST

ALEUTIAN ISLANDS WEST

KODIAK ISLAND

KENAI PENINSULA

MATANUSKA-SUSITNA

ANCHORAGE

FAIRBANKS NORTH STAR

SOUTHEAST FAIRBANKS

VALDEZ-CORDOVA

SKAGWAY YAKUTAT ANGOON

HAINES

JUNEAU

SITKA

WRANGELL PETERSBURG

KETCHIKAN GATEWAY

PRINCE OF WALES-OUTER KETCHIKAN

Barrow
Wainwright
Point Hope
Kivalina
Noatak
Kiana
Noorvik
Selawik
Kotzebue
Shishmaref
Teller
Nome
Savoonga
Gambell
Unalakleet
Kaltag
Nulato
Galena
Tanana
Nenana
Anderson
Healy
McGrath
Fort Yukon
Two Rivers
College
Fairbanks
North Pole
Salcha
Eielson AFB
Big Delta
Delta Junction
Fort Greely
Fort Yukon
Tok
Talkeetna
Houston
Wasilla
Meadow Lakes
Palmer
Big Lake
Butte
Glennallen
Valdez
Cordova
Whittier
Anchorage
Ridgeway
Kenai
Soldotna
Sterling
Seward
Nikiski
Kalifornsky
Fritz Creek
Homer
Kasilof
Ninilchik
Seldovia
Kodiak
Port Lions
Old Harbor
Sand Point
King Cove
Unalaska
St. Paul
Nikolski
Kokhanok
New Stuyahok
Dillingham
Aleknagik
Manokotak
Togiak
Quinhagak
Kwigillingok
Napakiak
Kasigluk
Napaskiak
Kipnuk
Tuntutuliak
Toksook Bay
Bethel
Akiachak
Kwethluk
Akiak
Alakanuk
Emmonak
Kotlik
Mountain Village
Pilot Station
St. Mary's
Chevak
Hooper Bay
Scammon Bay
Fortuna Ledge
Shageluk
Hoonah
Yakutat
Gustavus
Skagway
Haines
Klukwan
Juneau
Sitka
Mount Edgecumbe
Angoon
Kake
Petersburg
Wrangell
Craig
Klawock
Hydaburg
Thorne Bay
Ketchikan
Saxman
Hyder
Metlakatla
Shemya Station
Adak Station

18 17 16 15 14 13 12 11 10 9 8 7 6 5 4 3 2 1

A B C D E F G H I J K L M N

BOROUGHS AND CENSUS AREAS

(25 Boroughs and Census Areas)

Name of Borough or Census Area	Population	Location on Map
ALEUTIANS EAST Borough	2,464	L-3
ALEUTIANS WEST Census Area	9,478	M-11
ANCHORAGE Borough	226,338	H-8
BETHEL Census Area	13,656	H-4
BRISTOL BAY Borough	1,410	J-6
DILLINGHAM Census Area	4,012	I-6
FAIRBANKS NORTH STAR Borough	77,720	E-10
HAINES Borough	2,117	I-15
JUNEAU Borough	26,751	I-15
KENAI PENINSULA Borough	40,802	I-8
KETCHIKAN GATEWAY Borough	13,828	K-17
KODIAK ISLAND Borough	13,309	K-7
LAKE AND PENINSULA Borough	1,668	J-7
MATANUSKA-SUSITNA Borough	39,683	G-8
NOME Census Area	8,288	E-4
NORTH SLOPE Borough	5,979	B-7
NORTHWEST ARCTIC Borough	6,113	C-6
PRINCE OF WALES-OUTER KETCHIKAN Census Area	6,278	L-15
SITKA Borough	8,588	K-15
SKAGWAY-YAKUTAT-ANGOON Census Area	4,385	H-13
SOUTHEAST FAIRBANKS Census Area	5,913	F-11
VALDEZ-CORDOVA Census Area	9,952	H-11
WADE HAMPTON Census Area	5,791	G-4
WRANGELL-PETERSBURG Census Area	7,042	J-16
YUKON-KOYUKUK Census Area	8,478	D-8
TOTAL	550,043	

CITIES AND TOWNS

Note: The first name is that of the city or town, second, that of the county in which it is located, then the population and location on the map.

• Adak Station, Aleutians West Census Area, 4,633 — N-12
Anchorage, Anchorage Borough, 226,338 — H-9
Barrow, North Slope Borough, 3,469 — A-7
Bethel, Bethel Census Area, 4,674 — H-5
• Big Lake, Matanuska-Susitna Borough, 1,477 — H-9
• Butte, Matanuska-Susitna Borough, 2,039 — H-9
• College, Fairbanks North Star Borough, 11,249 — E-10
Cordova, Valdez-Cordova Census Area, 2,110 — I-11
Craig, Prince of Wales-Outer Ketchikan Census Area, 1,260 — K-16
Dillingham, Dillingham Census Area, 2,017 — J-6
• Eielson AFB, Fairbanks North Star Borough, 5,251 — F-10
Fairbanks, Fairbanks North Star Borough, 30,843 — E-10

• Fort Greely, Southeast Fairbanks Census Area, 1,147 — F-11
• Fritz Creek, Kenai Peninsula Borough, 1,426 — I-9
Haines, Haines Borough, 1,238 — I-14
Homer, Kenai Peninsula Borough, 3,660 — I-9
Juneau, Juneau Borough, 26,751 — I-15
Kenai, Kenai Peninsula Borough, 6,327 — I-9
Ketchikan, Ketchikan Gateway Borough, 8,263 — K-17
Kodiak, Kodiak Island Borough, 6,365 — K-8
• Kodiak Station, Kodiak Island Borough, 2,025 — K-8
Kotzebue, Northwest Arctic Borough, 2,751 — D-5
• Meadow Lakes, Matanuska-Susitna Borough, 2,374 — G-9
• Metlakatla, Prince of Wales-Outer Ketchikan Census Area, 1,407 — K-17
Mount Edgecumbe, Sitka — J-15
• Nikiski, Kenai Peninsula Borough, 2,743 — I-8
Nome, Nome Census Area, 3,500 — E-4
North Pole, Fairbanks North Star Borough, 1,456 — E-10
Palmer, Matanuska-Susitna Borough, 2,866 — H-9
Petersburg, Wrangell-Petersburg Census Area, 3,207 — J-16
• Ridgeway, Kenai Peninsula Borough, 2,018 — I-9
Seward, Kenai Peninsula Borough, 2,699 — I-9
Sitka, Sitka Borough, 8,588 — J-16
Soldotna, Kenai Peninsula Borough, 3,482 — I-9
Sterling, Kenai Peninsula Borough, 3,802 — I-9
Unalaska, Aleutians West Census Area, 3,089 — M-3
Valdez, Valdez-Cordova Census Area, 4,068 — H-10
Wasilla, Matanuska-Susitna Borough, 4,028 — H-9
Wrangell, Wrangell-Petersburg Census Area, 2,479 — K-16

Explanation of symbols: • – Census Designated Place (CDP)

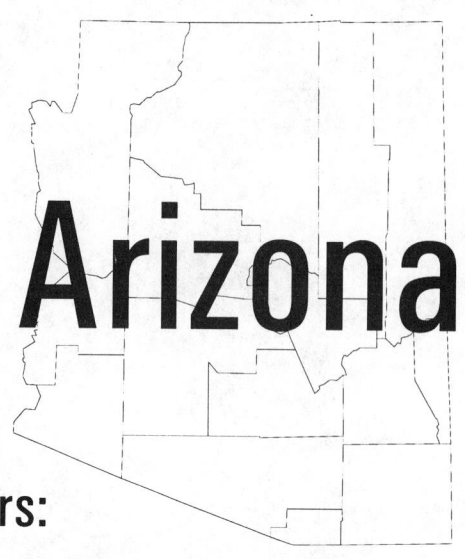

Arizona

General Help Numbers:

Governor's Office
1700 W Washington   602-542-4331
Phoenix, AZ 85007   Fax 602-542-1381
www.governor.state.az.us   8AM-5PM

Attorney General's Office
1275 W Washington   602-542-5025
Phoenix, AZ 85007   Fax 602-542-4085
www.attorneygeneral.state.az.us   8AM-5PM

Legislative Records
Arizona Legislature   602-542-3559 Senate
1700 W Washington   602-542-4221 House
Phoenix, AZ 85007   Fax 602-542-4099
www.azleg.state.az.us   8AM-5PM

State Archives
1700 W Washington, Room 342   602-542-4159
Phoenix, AZ 85007   Fax 602-542-4402
www.dlapr.lib.az.us/archives   8AM-5PM

State Specifics:

Capital:

Phoenix
Maricopa County

Time Zone:

MST
Note that Arizona does not go on daylight Savings Time

Number of Counties: 15

Population: 5,743,834

Website: www.az.gov/webapp/portal/

State Agencies

Criminal Records

Department of Public Safety, Applicant Team One, PO Box 18430//Mail Code 2250, Phoenix, AZ 85005-8430 (Courier address: 2320 N 20th Ave, Phoenix, AZ 85005); 602-223-2223, 602-223-2972-Fax; 8AM-5PM. www.dps.state.az.us

Records are available from 1988. It takes about 14 days before new records are available for inquiry. Records are indexed on computer back to 1983; non-automated records may go back as far as 1960's, depending on charge. Records are normally destroyed after age 99 or 2 years after subject's death. 50% of arrests in database have final dispositions recorded.

Searching: Record access is limited to agencies that have specific authorization by law including employers or pre-employment search firms located

in AZ. Fingerprints are required for a search. 100% of arrest records are fingerprint supported. Include the following in your request-full set of fingerprints plus demographic information on the applicant. Be sure to address requests to Applicant Team One. All records are released, including those without dispositions.

Access by: mail.

Fee & Payment: The fee is $5.00 per name. Fee payee: Department of Public Safety. Only cashier's checks and money orders accepted

Mail search: Turnaround time: 2 to 3 days. Arizona employers may call 602-223-2223 to request fingerprint cards and forms. No SASE is required.

Statewide Court Records

Administrative Offices of the Courts, Arizona Supreme Court Bldg, 1501 W Washington, Phoenix, AZ 85007; 602-542-9310, 602-542-9484-Fax; 8AM-5PM. www.supreme.state.az.us

Except for their excellent online research capabilities, all trial court record access must be done at the local level.

Access by: online.

Online search: The Public Access to Court Case Information is a valuable web service providing a resource for information about court cases from 141 out of 180 courts in Arizona. Courts not covered include certain parts of Pima, Yavapai, Mohave, and Maricopa counties. Access information includes: detailed case information, i.e., case type, charges, filing and disposition dates; the parties in the case, not including victims and witnesses; and the court mailing address & location. Go to www.supreme.state.az.us/publicaccess/default.htm. Opinions from the AZ Supreme Court & Court of Appeals available from website.

Other access: The Maricopa and Pima county courts maintain their own online access systems, but will also, under current planning, be part of the above system.

Sexual Offender Registry

Department of Public Safety, Sex Offender Compliance, PO Box 6638//Mail Code 9999, Phoenix, AZ 85005-6638 (Courier address: 2102 W Encanto, Phoenix, AZ 85009); 602-255-0611, 602-223-2949-Fax; 8AM-5PM.

http://az.gov/webapp/offender/main.do

The county sheriff is responsible for registering sex offenders living within their county. Arizona has approximately 12,000 registered sex offenders.

Records are available on or after June 1,1996 with risk assessment scores of Level 2 (Intermediate) or Level 3 (High). It takes 45 days before new records are available for inquiry.

Searching: The agency has a policy to assist those individuals that do not have access to the webpage and wish to do a record search.

Access by: mail, phone, fax, online.

Mail search: Turnaround time: 2 to 3 days. No SASE is required.

Phone search: Phone search requests accepted.

Fax search: Fax requests accepted.

Online search: Searching of Level 2 and Level 3 offenders is available online at the website above. Search for an individual by name, or search by ZIP Code or address for known offenders. The site also lists, with pictures, absconders who are individuals whose whereabouts are unknown.

Other access: A download is available from the webpage for $25.00.

Incarceration Records

Arizona Department of Corrections, Records Department, 1601 W. Jefferson St., Phoenix, AZ 85007; 602-542-5586, 602-542-1638-Fax; 8AM-5PM. www.adc.state.az.us

Records are available on current and former inmates. It takes about 7 days before new records are available for inquiry. Records are indexed on computer. Records are normally destroyed after 25 years.

Searching: Include the following in your request-Full name, ADC number, and what you want. DOB, and SSN helpful.

Access by: mail, fax, in person, online.

Fee & Payment: Fee is $.25 for every copy. Fee payee: Arizona Department of Corrections. Business checks accepted, but not personal checks or credit cards.

Mail search: An SASE is not required.

Fax search: Fax requires full name, the DOB and SSN are helpful.

In person search: Visitors can fill out record request form; turnaround time is up to 7 days and office can return by mail.

Online search: For online search, you must provide last name, first initial or ADC number. Any add'l identifiers are welcomed. Location,

ADC number, physical Identifiers and sentencing information are released. Inmates admitted and released from 1972 to 1985 may not be searchable on the web. Also available is ADC Fugitives - an alphabetical Inmate Datasearch listing of Absconders and Escapees from ADC.

Other access: A private company offers free web access at www.vinelink.com/index.jsp.

Expedited service: Will expedite for attorneys, public defenders, etc. Fed-Ex must be prepaid.

Corporation, Limited Liability Company Records

Corporation Commission, Corporation Records, 1300 W Washington, Room 101, Phoenix, AZ 85007; 602-542-3026 (Status), 602-542-3285 (Annual Reports), 602-542-3414-Fax; 8AM-5PM.

www.cc.state.az.us/corp/index.htm

Fictitious Name & Assumed Name records are found at the county level.

Records are available from 1809 on. You must go through this office for records. If copies are needed for historical records, it can take as long as 4 to 6 weeks due to the filming process. It takes after 2-3 months before new records are available for inquiry. Records are indexed on microfiche, inhouse computer, microfilm.

Searching: Include the following in your request-full name of business, specific records that you need copies of. In addition to the articles of incorporation, corporation records include the following information: Annual Reports, Officers, Directors, Prior (Merged) Names, Inactive and Reserved Names.

Access by: mail, in person, online.

Fee & Payment: There is no charge for a search. Uncertified LLC copies cost $5.00 plus .50 per page; a certified copy is $10.00. A certified corporation document is $5.00 plus $.50 per page. The cost for the Good Standing is $10.00. Fee payee: Arizona Corporation Commission. Prepayment required. Personal checks accepted. No credit cards accepted.

Mail search: Turnaround time: 3 to 5 days. Enclose a check marked "Not to exceed $10.00." A SASE is requested.

In person search: Turnaround time is while you wait for up to 5 corporate names.

Online search: The website provides free access to all corporation information. Also, an online system called STARPAS functions 24 hours a day, 7 days a week. Go to http://starpas.cc.state.az.us/instruct.html. Also, to purchase the entire database, call 602-364-4433.

Expedited service: Expedited service is available for mail and in person searches. Turnaround time: 24 hours. Add $35.00 per request. The fee applies to large orders that must be completed within 24 hours. Generally, smaller orders or single document orders do not require this fee.

Fictitious Name, Assumed Name

Records not maintained by a state level agency.

Records are found at the county level.

Trademarks/Servicemarks, Trade Names, Limited Partnerships, Limited Liability Partnerships, Foreign Limited Partnerships

Secretary of State, Trademarks/Tradenames/Limited Partnership Division, 1700 W Washington, 7th Floor, Phoenix, AZ 85007 (Courier: Customer Service, 14 N 18th Ave, Phoenix, AZ); 602-542-6187, 602-542-7386-Fax; 8AM-5PM.

www.azsos.gov/business_services/trademarksandtradenames.htm

Note that corporations are filed with the Arizona Corporation Commission.

Records are available from 1984 to present on computer. It takes 1 to 3 days before new records are available for inquiry.

Searching: Provide the entity name, owner name or file number to search. A record request form may be downloaded from the web.

Access by: mail, phone, in person, online.

Fee & Payment: Copies fee $.10 per page . Certified copies of Trade Name and Trademark filings $3.00. Certificate of Existence or Non-Existence for Trade Name or Trademark $3.00. Certification of Existence for LP, FLP, LLP, LLLP $5.00. Fee payee: Secretary of State. Prepayment required. Personal checks accepted. No credit cards accepted.

Mail search: Turnaround time: 1 to 3 days. Trademarks may take longer. SASE is requested.

Phone search: They will give general information at no charge over the phone for up to 3 searches, such as owner's name, date of application, mailing address & expiration date.

In person search: If there are more than 5 pages of copies, service is overnight. You may view microfiche at no charge.

Online search: The website links to three searchable databases. One searches for Registered Names, Trade Names, and Trademarks. Also available is the full Trade Name and Trademark index in data format. Anther lists the registered names in alpha order and states the type of records available. **Other access:** Bulk purchase is available on microfiche.

Expedited service: Expedited service is available for mail, phone and in person searches. Add $25.00 per filing.

Uniform Commercial Code, Federal and State Tax Liens

UCC Division, Secretary of State, 1700 W Washington, 7th Floor, Phoenix, AZ 85007 (Courier address: Customer Service Center, 14 North 18th Ave, Phoenix, AZ 85007); 602-542-6187, 602-542-7386-Fax; 8AM - 5PM.

www.azsos.gov/business_services/ucc.htm

Records are available from 3/80 to present on microfiche; from 6/95 to present on the Internet.

Searching: Use search request form UCC-11. The search includes tax liens recorded here. Please note that tax liens recorded on individuals may be filed at the county level and not here. Include the following in your request-debtor name.

Access by: mail, phone, fax, in person, online.

Fee & Payment: The search fee is $6.00 per debtor name, except via the web which is no charge. Copies are $.10 each. Certification is an additional $3.00. Fee payee: Secretary of State. Prepayment required. Personal checks accepted. No credit cards accepted.

Mail search: Turnaround time: 5 days.

Phone search: Records are available by phone.

Fax search: Records are available by fax.

In person search: They usually do not charge expedited fees for same day service, if the counter is not busy. Be sure to visit the 18th Ave address.

Online search: UCC records can be searched for free over the website. Searching can be done by debtor, secured party name, or file number. From this site you can also download the full UCC index in data format. Note there are 2 searches - a pre 07/01/01 search of the old database, and a strict Revised Article 9 which is current up within 4 days of present.

Other access: E-mail requests are accepted. Microfilm of filings is available for purchase.

Expedited service: Expedited service is available for mail and phone searches. Turnaround time: same day if possible. Add $25.00 per package.

Sales Tax Registrations

Revenue Department, Transaction (Sales) Tax Licenses and Registration, 1600 W Monroe, Phoenix, AZ 85007; 602-542-4565, 602 255-2060, 602-542-4772-Fax; 8AM-5PM.

www.revenue.state.az.us

Records are available from 1980.

Searching: This agency will only confirm that a business is registered and whether it is active. It will provide no other information without a power of attorney. Include the following in your request-business name. Tax permit number is very helpful.

Access by: mail, phone, in person.

Mail search: A SASE is requested. No fee for mail request.

Phone search: They will confirm license on phone, if given permit number.

In person search: No fee for request.

Birth Certificates

Department of Health Services, Vital Records Section, PO Box 3887, Phoenix, AZ 85030 (Courier address: 1818 West Adams, Phoenix, AZ 85007); 602-255-3260, 602-364-1300 (Recording), 888-816-5907 (In-state), 602-249-3040-Fax; 8AM-5PM.

www.azdhs.gov/vitalrcd/index.htm

Arizona is a "closed record" state meaning that vital records are not public record. A certificate of birth resulting in stillbirth is available as of 08/09/2001. All records are available from late 1800's to present. Records are computerized from 1950 to present. Records are indexed on file folders.

Searching: Must by 18 years of age or older to request a record and be the person named or that person's parent or legal guardian. Records 75 years or older available to the public for a $2.00 fee. Include the following in your request-full name, names of parents, mother's maiden name, date of birth, place of birth, relationship to person of

record, reason for information request. A copy of a valid government issued ID is required or the requestor signature must be notarized.

Access by: mail, fax, in person, online.

Fee & Payment: Certified copies of birth certificates for births occurring 1990 to present are $10.00 each. Prior certified records are $15.00 each. Fee payee: Vital Records Section. Prepayment required. Personal checks are not accepted. Major credit cards accepted.

Mail search: Turnaround time: 2 weeks. No SASE is required.

Fax search: Include the following additional information on the request: copy of government ID with your signature, return address, phone #, credit card #, and expiration date. Fee is $5.50 plus copy cost. Turnaround time is 2 days.

In person search: Turnaround time is usually less than 1 hour.

Online search: Records may be ordered online via www.vitalchek.com, a state-endorsed vendor. Images of birth certificates from 1887 to 1929 are available free online at http://genealogy.az.gov. Death certificates 1878-1953 are also available.

Expedited service: Expedited service is available for fax and online ordering. Turnaround time: 1 day. There is an additional $27.00 fee to use a credit card have the results returned by Courier address.

Death Records

Department of Health Services, Vital Records Section, PO Box 3887, Phoenix, AZ 85030 (Courier: 1818 West Adams, Phoenix, AZ 85007); 602-255-3260, 602-364-1300 (Recording), 888-816-5907 (in-state), 602-249-3040-Fax; 8-5PM.

www.azdhs.gov/vitalrcd/index.htm

Arizona is a "closed record" state meaning that vital records are not public record.

Records are available from late 1800's to present. New records are available for inquiry immediately. Records are indexed on file folders.

Searching: Must have notarized release from immediate family. Only immediate family, attorney or funeral director acting for immediate family can get records. Records 50 years or older are available to the public for a $2.00 fee. Include the following in your request-full name, date of death, place of death, relationship to person of record, reason for information request. A copy of a valid government issued ID is required or the requestor signature must be notarized.

Access by: mail, fax, in person, online.

Fee & Payment: The search fee is $4.00 for the first 10 years and $3.00 each add'l. A certified photocopy is $10.00. The fee for use of a credit card is $5.50. Fee payee: Vital Records Section. Prepayment required. Personal checks are not accepted. Major credit cards accepted.

Mail search: Turnaround time: 2 weeks. A SASE is requested.

Fax search: Include the following additional information on the request: copy of government ID with signature, return address, phone #, credit card number, and expiration date. Fee is $5.00 for processing/handling. Certification fee is $6.00.

In person search: Turnaround time is usually 30-50 minutes.

Online search: Death certificate images 1878-1953 are available free online at

http://genealogy.az.gov. Also available are images of birth certificates from 1887 to 1928. Records may be ordered online via www.vitalchek.com, a state-endorsed vendor.

Expedited service: Expedited service is available for fax and online orders. There is an additional $27.00 fee to use a credit card have the results returned by Courier address.

Marriage Certificates, Divorce Records

Records not maintained by a state level agency.

These records are not available from this agency; records must be requested from the county or court of issue.

Workers' Compensation Records

State Compensation Fund, Claims Information, 3030 N 3rd Street, Phoenix, AZ 85012; 602-631-2883, 602-631-2884-Fax; 8AM-5PM.

www.scfaz.com

Records are available from 1926 on. New records available for inquiry immediately. Records indexed on microfilm, hard copy, imaging system.

Searching: Records that are closed or inactive are stored on microfilm. All active records are on the imaging system. Claim and policy records are confidential, but you can get claim records with release from claimant. Most other records are public. Include the following in your request-claimant name, Social Security Number, claim number. Requester must have signed release from claimant or policyholder prior to obtaining confidential records. Copies of legal, claims, and policy working files are not released otherwise.

Access by: mail, in person.

Fee & Payment: Copies are $.25 per page. There is no search fee. Copy of file on CD available for $10.00. Fee payee: SCF of Arizona Requesters will be billed. Personal checks and MasterCard/VISA accepted.

Mail search: Turnaround time: 1 to 2 weeks. No SASE is required.

In person search: Simple requests will receive immediate service.

Driver Records

Motor Vehicle Division, Correspondence Unit, PO Box 2100, Mail Drop 539M, Phoenix, AZ 85001-2100 (Courier address: Customer Records Services, 1801 W Jefferson, Lobby, Phoenix, AZ 85007); 602-712-8420, 8AM-5PM.

www.dot.state.az.us/MVD/mvd.htm

Arizona will suspend the license for unpaid out-of-state tickets.

Records are available for either a thirty-nine month record or for a five-year record. Records may be available for ten years under special circumstances and approval. It takes seconds before new records are available for inquiry.

Searching: Requesters must state the reason for the request and present ID may be required. Casual requesters (per DPPA) must submit notarized consent from the subject. Form 46-4416 is suggested. Include the following in your request-full name, date of birth or license expiration date, driver's license number, notarized consent if necessary. Certain "exempt requesters" as identified by law need only supply 2 out of the 3 items required to search. The driver's mailing address is provided as part of the record to exempt requesters.

Access by: mail, in person, online.

Fee & Payment: The fees are $3.00 for 39 month records ($2.00 if picked up overnight at counter) and $5.00 for certified 5 year records. Electronic access fees differ. Insurers may only receive the 39 month record. All non-exempt requests must be signed and notarized. Fee payee: Motor Vehicle Division, Record Services. Prepayment required. Personal checks accepted.; no credit cards.

Mail search: Turnaround time: 1 week to 10 days. If express mail is requested, then envelope must be pre-paid. If mail requester is not DPPA permissible, the requester's signature must be notarized. No SASE is required.

In person search: Records are available at any of the MVD field offices. There is a limit of 4 requests for immediate service. There is a $1.00 discount if requests are picked up next day.

Online search: Arizona's online system is interactive and open 24 hours daily. Fee is $3.25 per record. This system is primarily for those requesters who qualify per DPPA. For more information call 602-712-7235.

Other access: Overnight cartridge ordering is available. Fee is $2.00 for 39 month record, $3.00 for 5 year record. Call 602-712-7235 for details.

Vehicle Ownership, Vehicle Identification

Motor Vehicle Division - Director's Office, Record Services Section, PO Box 2100, Mail Drop 504M, Phoenix, AZ 85001-2100 (Courier address: Customer Records Services, 1801 W Jefferson, Rm 111, Phoenix, AZ 85007); 602-712-8420, 8AM-5PM.

www.dot.state.az.us/MVD/mvd.htm

The record Services Section also handles search requests for mobile homes, both attached and unattached. Records are available for 5 years to present. It takes 2 weeks before new records are available for inquiry.

Searching: The record searcher must state the reason for the request and have his/her signature notarized. Records are not given by merely giving a plate license number or a name for ownership searches. The vehicle's owner, VIN, and plate number must be submitted to receive a vehicle history. If not a permissible use, need notarized release from subject.

Access by: mail, in person, online.

Fee & Payment: The fee is $3.00, $2.00 if walk-in is willing to pick up the next day, and $5.00 if the record is certified. Fee payee: Motor Vehicle Division. Prepayment required. Money orders and checks are accepted through the mail. Walk-ins may pay with cash. Personal checks accepted. No credit cards accepted.

Mail search: Turnaround time: 1 week to 10 days. A SASE is requested.

In person search: You may request information in person.

Online search: Online access is offered but only to permissible users. Fee is $3.00 per record. The

system is open 24 hours a day, seven days a week. For more information, call 602-712-7235.

Accident Reports

Department of Public Safety, Accident Reports, PO Box 6638, Mail Drop 1110, Phoenix, AZ 85005 (Courier address: 2102 W Encanto, 1st Floor, Phoenix, AZ 85005-6638); 602-223-2230, 623-223-2945-Fax; 8AM-5PM.

www.azdps.gov/reports/collision/default.asp

It takes 2 weeks before new records are available for inquiry. Records indexed on inhouse computer. Records are normally destroyed after 25 years.

Searching: A written request is required and the requester must state his/her connection to the incident. Include the following in your request-relationship to person of record, date of accident, location of accident, full name, report number.

Access by: mail, in person.

Fee & Payment: The fee is $9.00 per record for up to first 9 pages, then $1.00 for each additional page. Fee payee: Department of Public Safety. Prepayment required; Business check or money order. Personal checks accepted in person with ID. No credit cards accepted.

Mail search: Turnaround time: 1 week to 14 days. A SASE is requested.

In person search: Turnaround time is while you wait, provided record is on file.

Vessel Ownership, Vessel Registration

Game & Fish Dept, Watercraft Department, 2221 W Greenway Rd, Phoenix, AZ 85023-4399; 602-942-3000, 602-789-3729-Fax; 8AM-5PM M-F.

www.azgfd.gov/outdoor_recreation/boating.shtml

Lien information is recorded at the county level. Maricopa County has some liens from other counties. Records are available from 1977 to present. Records are indexed on computer for the last 5 years. No titles are issued. All watercraft must be registered unless they are non-motorized. Records are normally destroyed after microfilmed.

Searching: To search, the following information is required: Arizona #, hull ID, owner's name, and a picture ID.

Access by: mail, phone, fax, in person.

Fee & Payment: There is no search fee.

Mail search: Turnaround time: 1 day. No SASE is required. **Phone search:** Only lawyers, private investigators, and government representatives can search by phone or fax. **Fax search:** Same criteria as phone searching. **In person search:** Turnaround time is normally immediate.

Other access: Commercial records are given as bulk lists, CDs or labels.

Voter Registration
Access to Records is Restricted.

Secretary of State, Election Division, 1700 W Washington, 7th Floor, Phoenix, AZ 85007; 602-542-8683, 8AN-5PM.

www.azsos.gov/election

The state is "HAVA compliant" with a central, computerized, statewide voter registration system. However, by state statute, the record database is

not available to the public. Presently, record information can only be purchased at the county recorder offices. Their records are permitted to be sold in bulk only for political related purposes. Go to the county level to confirm names on a single inquiry basis.

GED Certificates

Department of Education, GED Testing, 1535 W Jefferson #30, Phoenix, AZ 85007 (Courier address: 333 East Virginia Avenue, Suite 205, Phoenix, AZ 85004); 602-254-0265, 602-258-2410, 602-258-4977-Fax; 8AM-5PM.

www.ade.az.gov/adult-ed

This agency will not do a verification only; a transcript must be purchased.

Records are available from 1945 to present. It takes 3 to 4 weeks before new records are available for inquiry. Records are indexed on microfilm prior to 1985.

Searching: Request forms are available from the website. Include the following in your request-name at date of test, date of birth, Social Security Number, signed release, year of test and test site. All requests must be in writing, all require student signature.

Access by: mail, in person.

Fee & Payment: There is a $10.00 fee for a copy of transcript. This agency will not do a verification only; a transcript must be purchased. Fee payee: AZ Department of Education

Mail search: Turnaround time: 5 to 7 days. No SASE is required.

In person search: Counter service is available at the East Virginia Ave address. Records are available in minutes if the test was taken after 1985, otherwise research can take 1-2 hours.

Hunting and Fishing License Information

Game & Fish Department, Information & Licensing Division, 2222 W Greenway Rd, Phoenix, AZ 85023-4399; 602-942-3000, 602-789-3924-Fax; 8AM-5PM.

www.azgfd.com/h_f/hunting_fishing.shtml

Records are available for past 3 years. It takes 30 days before new records are available for inquiry. Records are normally destroyed after placed on microfilm.

Searching: Records are not available to the public except as a mailing list. A Public record Request form must be used, call to obtain. They will release certain data to attorneys or private investigators for pending litigation, use of form required.

Access by: mail.

Fee & Payment: Prepayment required. Fee payee: Arizona Game & Fish. Personal checks accepted. Credit cards accepted: MasterCard, Visa.

Mail search: Turnaround time: variable. Must complete a request form. No SASE is required.

Other access: There is a program to purchase the database or portions of. You can get 3 years of approximately 160,000 to 190,000 names for $.10 per name, which includes addresses. This is available for commercial purposes. Lists are completed within 30 days days.

Arizona State Licensing Agencies

For details about the agency responsible for licensing/certifying/registering an item below or in the Agency Quick Finder section, match an item's number with the number of the agency in the *Licensing Agency Information* section.

Arizona Licenses Searchable Online

Acupuncturist Chiropractor #11 .... www.azchiroboard.com/ASPSearch.htm
Advance Fee Loan Broker #5 .... www.azbanking.com/Lists/Lists.htm
Aerial Applicator, Pesticide #33 .... www.kellysolutions.com/az/Pilots/index.asp
Agricultural Grower Permit / Grower/Seller #33 .... www.kellysolutions.com/az/RUPBuyers/index.asp
Agricultural Pest Control Advisor #33 .... www.kellysolutions.com/az/PCA/index.asp
Ambulatory Surgical Center #43 .... www.azdhs.gov/als/medical/index.htm
Applicator (Pesticide), Private/Com'c'l #33 .... www.kellysolutions.com/AZ/Applicators/index.asp
Architect #29 .... www.btr.state.az.us/RegistrantSearch.asp
Assayer #29 .... www.btr.state.az.us/RegistrantSearch.asp
Assisted Living Facility #49 .... www.hs.state.az.us/als/hcb/index.htm
Attorney #30 .... www.azbar.org/content.cfm?text=/LegalResources/findlawyer
Audiologist #49 .... www.hs.state.az.us/als/hcb/index.htm
Bank #5 .... www.azbanking.com/Lists/Lists.htm
Behavioral Health Emerg./Resi. Svcs #47 .... www.hs.state.az.us/als/databases/
Behavioral Outpatient Clinic/Rehab Ctr #47 .... www.hs.state.az.us/als/databases/
Charity #62 .... www.azsos.gov/scripts/Charity_Search.dll
Charter School #38 .... www.ade.state.az.us/CharterSchools/search/
Child Residential Home #37 .... www.hs.state.az.us/als/databases/providers_cc.pdf
Chiropractor #11 .... www.azchiroboard.com/ASPSearch.htm
Citrus Broker/Dealer/Packer/Shipper #35 .... www.kellysolutions.com/az
Clinic, Recovery Core #43 .... www.azdhs.gov/als/medical/index.htm
Clinic, Rural Health #43 .... www.azdhs.gov/als/medical/index.htm
Collection Agency #5 .... www.azbanking.com/Lists/Lists.htm
Consumer Lender #5 .... www.azbanking.com/Lists/Lists.htm
Contractor #70 .... www.rc.state.az.us/clsc/AZROCLicenseQuery
Court Reporter #63 .... www.supreme.state.az.us/cr/pdf/merged%20directory2wpd.pdf
Credit Union #5 .... www.azbanking.com/Lists/Lists.htm
Day Care Establishment #45 .... www.hs.state.az.us/als/childcare/index.htm
Debt Management #5 .... www.azbanking.com/Lists/Lists.htm
Deferred Presentment Company #5 .... www.azbanking.com/Lists/DPC_List.HTML
Degree Program, Vocational #6 .... http://azppse.state.az.us/directory.html
Detoxification Service #47 .... www.hs.state.az.us/als/databases/
Development Disabled Group Home #49 .... www.hs.state.az.us/als/hcb/index.htm
Dispensing Naturopath #19 .... www.npbomex.az.gov/directories.html
Dry Well Registration #41 .... www.adeq.state.az.us/environ/water/permits/drywell.html
Embalmer #15 .... www.funeralbd.state.az.us/dir.htm
Engineer #29 .... www.btr.state.az.us/RegistrantSearch.asp
Escrow Agent #5 .... www.azbanking.com/Lists/Lists.htm
Family Day Care Home #37 .... www.hs.state.az.us/als/databases/providers_cc.pdf
Feed Dealer #33 .... www.kellysolutions.com/az/feeddealers/index.asp
Feed Distribution, Commercial #34 .... www.kellysolutions.com/az/FeedDealers/index.asp
Fertilizer Dealer/Distributor #33 .... www.kellysolutions.com/az/fertdealers/index.asp
Fertilizer Product #33 .... www.kellysolutions.com/AZ/Fertilizer/fertilizerindex.asp
Food Packer/Grower/Shipper, Contract #35 .... www.kellysolutions.com/az
Foster Care Home #49 .... www.hs.state.az.us/als/hcb/index.htm
Fruit/Vegetable Broker/Dealer #35 .... www.kellysolutions.com/az
Funeral Director #15 .... www.funeralbd.state.az.us/dir.htm
Funeral Pre-Need Trust Company #5 .... www.azbanking.com/Lists/Lists.htm
Geologist #29 .... www.btr.state.az.us/RegistrantSearch.asp
Headstart Facility #45 .... www.hs.state.az.us/als/childcare/index.htm
Hearing Aid Dispenser #49 .... www.hs.state.az.us/als/hcb/index.htm
Home Health Agency #43 .... www.azdhs.gov/als/medical/index.htm
Home Inspector #29 .... www.btr.state.az.us/RegistrantSearch.asp
Homeopathic Physician #16 .... http://home.mindspring.com/~bhme/
Hospice #43 .... www.azdhs.gov/als/medical/index.htm
Hospital/ Infirmary #43 .... www.azdhs.gov/als/medical/index.htm

Insurance Agent #51 .... www.id.state.az.us/
Insurance Broker P&C only #51 .... www.id.state.az.us/
Landscape Architect #29 .... www.btr.state.az.us/RegistrantSearch.asp
Liquor Producer/Whsle #52 .... www.azll.com/query.htm
Liquor Retail Co-Operative/Agent/Mgr. #52 .... www.azll.com/query.htm
Lobbyist #62 .... www.azsos.gov/scripts/Lobbyist_Search.dll
Long Term Care Facility #49 .... www.hs.state.az.us/als/hcb/index.htm
Massage Therapy School #19 .... http://massagetherapy.az.gov/approvedschools.htm
Medical Doctor, Intern/Resident #17 .... www.bomex.org/getlicense.asp
Medical Facility #49 .... www.hs.state.az.us/als/hcb/index.htm
Midwife, Lay #50 .... www.hs.state.az.us/als/midwife/
Money Transmitter #5 .... www.azbanking.com/Lists/Lists.htm
Mortgage Banker/Broker #5 .... www.azbanking.com/Lists/Lists.htm
Motor Vehicle Dealer/Sales Finance #5 .... www.azbanking.com/Lists/Lists.htm
Naturopathic Physician/Medical Asst. #19 .... www.npbomex.az.gov/directories.html
Naturopathic School #19 .... www.npbomex.az.gov/School%20Directory.html
Notary Public #62 .... www.azsos.gov/scripts/Notary_Search.dll
Nurse-LPN / RN #20 .... www.azbn.org/onlineverificationbatch.asp
Nurses' Aide #20 .... www.azbn.org/onlineverificationbatch.asp
Optometrist #22 .... www.asbo.state.az.us
Osteopathic Physician #23 .... http://docfinder.state.az.us
Outpatient Physical Therapy #43 .... www.azdhs.gov/als/medical/index.htm
Out-Patient Surgical Center #43 .... www.azdhs.gov/als/medical/index.htm
Out-Patient Treatment Clinic #43 .... www.azdhs.gov/als/medical/index.htm
P&C Broker #51 .... www.id.state.az.us/
P&C Managing Agent, Life/Disability #51 .... www.id.state.az.us/
Pesticide Company #18 .... www.sb.state.az.us/spccsearch.htm
Pesticide Custom Applicator #33 .... www.kellysolutions.com/az/CustomAppl/index.asp
Pesticide Distribution #34 .... www.kellysolutions.com/az/Dealers/index.asp
Pesticide Registration #33 .... www.kellysolutions.com/az/pesticideindex.htm
Pesticide Seller #33 .... www.kellysolutions.com/az/Dealers/index.asp
Physical Therapist/Therapist Assist. #25 .... www.ptboard.state.az.us
Physician Assistant #17 .... www.bomex.org/getlicense.asp
Physiotherapist #11 .... www.azchiroboard.com/ASPSearch.htm
Podiatrist #26 .... www.podiatry.state.az.us/directory.htm
Political Action Committee #62 .... www.azsos.gov/scripts/superpac.cgi
Post-Secondary Educ. Institution #6 .... http://azppse.state.az.us/directory.html
Post-Secondary Voc. Program, Private #6 .... http://azppse.state.az.us/directory.html
Premium Finance Company #5 .... www.azbanking.com/Lists/Lists.htm
Preschool #45 .... www.hs.state.az.us/als/childcare/index.htm
Property Tax Agent #8 .... www.appraisal.state.az.us/Directory/TAXAOUT.TXT
Psychologist #27 .... www.psychboard.az.gov/directory.htm
Public Accountant-CPA #7 .... www.accountancy.state.az.us/scripts/BOAsearch.exe
Public Accounting Firm-CPA/PA #7 .... www.accountancy.state.az.us/scripts/BOAsearch.exe
Real Estate Agent/Broker/Sales/Firm #55 .... www.re.state.az.us/db.html
Real Estate Appraiser #8 .... www.appraisal.state.az.us/Directory/directory.html
Rehabilitation Agency #43 .... www.azdhs.gov/als/medical/index.htm
Renal Disease Facility #43 .... www.azdhs.gov/als/medical/index.htm
Sales Finance Company #5 .... www.azbanking.com/Lists/Lists.htm
School Bus Transportation Provider #1 .... www.dps.state.az.us/license/schoolbusdriver/default.asp
Seed Dealer/Labeler #33 .... www.kellysolutions.com/az/SeedDealers/index.asp
Speech Pathology #43 .... www.azdhs.gov/als/medical/index.htm
Speech-Language Pathologist #49 .... www.hs.state.az.us/als/hcb/index.htm
Surveyor, Land #29 .... www.btr.state.az.us/RegistrantSearch.asp
Telemarketing Firm #62 .... www.azsos.gov/scripts/TS_Search_engine.cgi
Trust Company #5 .... www.azbanking.com/Lists/Lists.htm
Trust Div. of Chartered Fin. Inst. #5 .... www.azbanking.com/Lists/Lists.htm
Well Drilling Firm #58 .... http://water.az.gov/adwr/content/drillers/default.asp
X-ray, Portable #43 .... www.azdhs.gov/als/medical/index.htm

Arizona Licensing Quick Finder

Acupuncturist #25 ... 602-542-3095
Acupuncturist Chiropractor #11 ... 602-864-5088
Adult Care Home Manager #68 ... 602-364-2273
Advance Fee Loan Broker #5 ... 602-255-4421
Aerial Applicator, Pesticide #33 ... 602-542-0904
Aesthetician #12 ... 480-784-4539
Aesthetics Instructor #12 ... 480-784-4539
Agricultural Aircraft Pilot #33 ... 602-542-0904
Agricultural Grower Permit #33 ... 602-542-0904
Agricultural Grower/Seller #33 ... 602-542-0904
Agricultural Pest Control Advisor #33 ... 602-542-0904
Agricultural Seller Permit #33 ... 602-542-0904
Air Pollution Source #39 ... 602-771-2338
Air Quality Permit #65 ... 602-506-6970
Aircraft Dealer for Wreckers or Salvage #57 ... 602-294-9144
Aircraft Dealer/Retail #57 ... 602-294-9144
Aircraft Mfg/Importer/Dist./Transporter #57 ... 602-294-9144
Aircraft Owner #57 ... 602-294-9144
Aircraft Pilot Trainer School/Instr #57 ... 602-294-9144
Aircraft Use Fuel Dealer/Mfg #56 ... 602-542-4565
Ambulance Service #48 ... 602-364-3184
Ambulatory Surgical Center #43 ... 602-364-3030
Amusement Park #56 ... 602-542-4565
Amusement Printing & Advertising #56 ... 602-542-4565
Applicator (Pesticide), Pvt/Comm #33 ... 602-542-0904
Appraiser, Real/Personal Property #56 ... 602-542-4565
Aquifer Protection Permit #41 ... 602-771-4644
Architect #29 ... 602-364-4930
Assayer #29 ... 602-364-4930
Assisted Living Facility #49 ... 602-364-2536
Attorney #30 ... 602-252-4804
Audiologist #49 ... 602-364-2536
Bank #5 ... 602-255-4421
Barber School/Instruction #9 ... 602-542-4498
Barber/Barber Shop #9 ... 602-542-4498
Bathing Place #65 ... 602-506-6970
Bedding/Furniture Manufacturer #65 ... 602-506-6970
Behavioral Health Emergency/Resi. Svcs #47 ... 602-364-2536
Behavioral Outpatient Clinic #47 ... 602-364-2536
Behavioral Outpatient Rehab Ctr #47 ... 602-364-2536
Bingo Operation #56 ... 602-542-4565
Bondsman (Insurance) #51 ... 602-912-8470
Bone Densitometer Operator #66 602-255-4845 x242
Bottled Water Processor #65 ... 602-506-6970
Boxer #3 ... 602-364-1721
Boxing Physician #3 ... 602-364-1721
Boxing Professional #3 ... 602-364-1721
Campground Membership Broker/Salesman #55 ... 602-468-1414
Cannabis & Controlled Substance Dealer #56 ... 602-542-4565
Cemetery Broker/Salesman #55 ... 602-468-1414
Charity #62 ... 602-542-6670
Charter School #38 ... 602-542-5968
Child Adoption Agency #37 ... 602-364-2539
Child Foster Home #37 ... 602-364-2539
Child Placing Agency #37 ... 602-364-2539
Child Residential Home #37 ... 602-364-2539
Chiropractor #11 ... 602-864-5088
Citrus Fruit Broker/Dealer/Packer/Shipper #35 ... 602-542-0944
Clinic, Recovery Core #43 ... 602-364-3030
Clinic, Rural Health #43 ... 602-364-3030
Clinical Laboratory #44 ... 602-364-0741
Collection Agency #5 ... 602-255-4421
Commercial Leasing #56 ... 602-542-4565
Concealed Weapon Permit #53 ... 602-256-6280
Consumer Lender #5 ... 602-255-4421
Contractor #70 ... 602-542-1525
Cosmetologist #12 ... 480-784-4539
Cosmetology Instructor #12 ... 480-784-4539
Cosmetology or Nail Technology Salon or School #12 ... 480-784-4539
Counselor, Professional #10 ... 602-542-1864
Court Reporter #63 ... 602-364-0878
Credit Union #5 ... 602-255-4421
Cremationist #15 ... 602-542-3095
Crematory #15 ... 602-542-3095
Day Care Establishment #45 ... 602-364-2536
Debt Management #5 ... 602-255-4421
Deferred Presentment Company #5 ... 602-255-4421
Degree Program, Vocational #6 ... 602-542-5709
Dental Assistant #13 ... 602-242-1492
Dental Hygienist #13 ... 602-242-1492
Dentist #13 ... 602-242-1492
Denturist #13 ... 602-242-1492
Detoxification Service #47 ... 602-364-2536
Developmentally Disabled Group Home #49 ... 602-364-2536
Dispensing Naturopath #19 ... 602-542-8242
Dog Racing Kennel #54 ... 602-364-1700
Drug Mfg/Wholesaler #24 ... 623-463-2727
Dry Well Registration #41 ... 602-771-4385
DUI Education Agency #47 ... 602-364-2536
DUI Screening/Treatment Agency #47 602-364-2536
Embalmer #15 ... 602-542-3095
Embalmer Assistant #15 ... 602-542-3095
Emergency Medl Tech. Instructor #48 ... 602-364-3150
Emergency Medical Technician #48 ... 602-364-3186
Emergency Response Div. #66 ... 602-255-4845 x239
Engineer #29 ... 602-364-4930
Environmental Laboratory #44 ... 602-364-0741
Escrow Agent #5 ... 602-255-4421
Falconer #59 ... 602-942-3000
Family Day Care Home #37 ... 602-364-2539
Feed Dealer #33 ... 602-542-0904
Feed Distribution, Commercial #34 ... 602-542-0814
Feed, Wholesale #56 ... 602-542-4565
Fertilizer Dealer #33 ... 602-542-0904
Fertilizer Distribution, Commercial #34 ... 602-542-0814
Fertilizer Product #33 ... 602-542-0904
Field Trial License #59 ... 602-942-3000
Food Establishment #65 ... 602-506-6970
Food Packer/Grower/Shipper, Contract #35 ... 602-542-0944
Foster Care Home #49 ... 602-364-2536
Fruit/Vegetable Broker/Dealer #35 ... 602-542-0944
Funeral Director #15 ... 602-542-3095
Funeral Establishment #15 ... 602-542-3095
Funeral Pre-Need Trust Company #5 ... 602-255-4421
Fur Dealer #59 ... 602-942-3000
Game Farm, Private #59 ... 602-942-3000
Game Resident Guide #59 ... 602-942-3000
Geologist #29 ... 602-364-4930
Groom #54 ... 602-364-1700
Guidance Counselor #38 ... 602-542-4367
Hazardous Waste Facility #40 ... 602-771-4153
Headstart Facility #45 ... 602-364-2536
Hearing Aid Dispenser #49 ... 602-364-2536
Home Health Agency #43 ... 602-364-3030
Home Inspector #29 ... 602-364-4930
Homeopathic Physician #16 ... 602-542-3095
Horse or Greyhound Racing #54 ... 602-364-1700
Horse Owner/Trainer #54 ... 602-364-1700
Hospice #43 ... 602-364-3030
Hospital #43 ... 602-364-3030
Hotel/Motel/Tourist Court #65 ... 602-506-6970
Hunting & Fishing License Dealer #59 ... 602-942-3000
Industrial Laser #66 ... 602-255-4845 x237
Infirmary #43 ... 602-364-3030
Insurance Agent #51 ... 602-912-8470
Insurance Broker P&C only #51 ... 602-912-8470
Intern #15 ... 602-542-3095
Investment Advisor #32 ... 602-542-0678
Investment Advisor Rep. #32 ... 602-542-0678
Jockey #54 ... 602-364-1700
Landscape Architect #29 ... 602-364-4930
Laser Light Show #56 ... 602-255-4845
Laser, Medical #66 ... 602-255-4845 x237
Liquor Producer/Whsle #52 ... 602-542-5141
Liquor Retail Co-Operative/Agent/Mgr. #52 .. 602-542-5141
Lobbyist #62 ... 602-542-8683
Long Term Care Facility #49 ... 602-364-2536
Lottery Retailer #4 ... 480-921-4400
LPG Service Agency/Rep #2 ... 602-255-5211
Marriage & Family Therapist #10 ... 602-542-1864
Massage Therapy School #19 ... 602-542-8242
Medical Doctor, Intern/Resident #17 ... 480-551-2700
Medical Facility #49 ... 602-364-2536
Mental Health Screening/Evaluation/Treatment #47 ... 602-364-2536
Midwife, Lay #50 ... 602-364-2536
Mine Reclamation Plan #67 ... 602-542-5971
Mining #56 ... 602-542-4565
Mining Elevator/Diesel #67 ... 602-542-5971
Mining Operator/Start-up #67 ... 602-542-5971
Minnow Dealer #59 ... 602-942-3000
Mobile Home Dealer/Broker/Salesperson #36 ... 602-364-1094
Mobile Home Installer/Mfg. #36 ... 602-364-1094
Money Transmitter #5 ... 602-255-4421
Mortgage Banker, Commercial #5 ... 602-255-4421
Mortgage Banker/Broker #5 ... 602-255-4421
Motor Vehicle Dealer/Sales Finance #5602-255-4421
MRI License #66 ... 602-255-4845 x237
Nail Technician #12 ... 480-784-4539
Nail Technology Instructor #12 ... 480-784-4539
Naturopathic Medical Asst. #19 ... 602-542-8242
Naturopathic Physician #19 ... 602-542-8242
Naturopathic School #19 ... 602-542-8242
Notary Public #62 ... 602-542-4086
Nuclear Medicine Tech #66 ... 602-255-4845 x242
Nurse-LPN #20 ... 602-889-5150
Nurse-RN #20 ... 602-889-5150
Nurses' Aide #20 ... 602-889-5150
Nursing Care Inst. Administrator #68 ... 602-364-2273
Occupational Therapist/Assistant #21 ... 602-589-8352
Oil & Gas Production #56 ... 602-542-4565
Optical Establishment #14 ... 602-542-3095
Optician #14 ... 602-542-3095
Optometrist #22 ... 602-542-3095
Osteopathic Physician #23 ... 480-657-7703
Outpatient Physical Therapy #43 ... 602-364-3030
Out-Patient Surgical Ctr./Treatment Clinic #43 ... 602-364-3030
P&C Broker #51 ... 602-912-8470
P&C Managing Agent, also Life/Disability #51 ... 602-912-8470
Pesticide Appl./Supv./Advisor #18 ... 602-255-3664
Pesticide Company #18 ... 602-255-3664
Pesticide Custom Applicator #33 ... 602-542-0904
Pesticide Distribution #34 ... 602-542-0949
Pesticide Qualifying Party #18 ... 602-255-3664
Pesticide Registration #33 ... 602-542-0904
Pesticide Seller #33 ... 602-542-0904
Pharmacist #24 ... 623-463-2727
Pharmacy Intern #24 ... 623-463-2727
Physical Therapist/Therapist Assistant #25 ... 602-542-3095
Physician Assistant #17 ... 480-551-2700
Physiotherapist #11 ... 602-864-5088
Pipeline #56 ... 602-542-4565
Plant Operator #41 ... 602-771-4644
Podiatrist #26 ... 602-542-3095
Political Action Committee #62 ... 602-542-8683
Pollutant Discharge Permit #41 ... 602-771-4644
Post-Secondary Educ. Institution #6 ... 602-542-5709
Post-Secondary Voc. Pgm, Private #6. 602-542-5709

Premium Finance Company #5 602-255-4421
Pre-Need Endorsement, Establishment #15
.... 602-542-3095
Pre-Need Salesperson #15 602-542-3095
Preschool #45 602-364-2536
Private Car, Rail & Aircraft #56 602-542-4565
Private Investigator #53 602-223-2361
Property Broker #51 602-912-8470
Property Tax Agent #8 602-542-1539
Psychiatric Unit #47 602-364-2536
Psychologist #27 602-542-8162
Public Accountant-CPA #7 602-364-0804
Public Accounting Firm-CPA/PA #7 .. 602-364-0804
Publishing #56 602-542-4565
Radiation Machine Possession Facility #66
.... 602-255-4845 x231
Radiation Therapy Tech #66 .... 602-255-4845 x242
Radioactive Material Possessor #66
.... 602-255-4845 x227
Radioactive Materials Lab #66 .... 602-255-4845 x246
Radiologic Technologist #66 ...... 602-255-4845 x242
Radiology Practical Techt #66 ..... 602-255-4845 x242
Radon Mitigation Specialist #66 .. 602-255-4845 x244
Real Estate Agent/Broker/Sales #55 .. 602-468-1414
Real Estate Appraiser #8 602-542-1539
Real Estate Division #62 602-542-1704
Real Estate Firm #55 602-468-1414
Real Estate School/Instructor/Course #55
.... 602-468-1414
Rehabilitation Agency #43 602-364-3030
Rehabilitation Unit #47 602-364-2536
Renal Disease Facility #43 602-364-3030
Rental of Personal Property #56 602-542-4565
Respiratory Therapist #28 602-542-5995
Restaurant/Bar #56 602-542-4565
Retail Sales Outlet #56 602-542-4565
Risk Management Company #51 602-912-8470

Sales Finance Company #5 602-255-4421
Sanitarian #46 602-364-3118
School Bus Driver #1 602-223-2646
School Bus Driver Instructor #1 602-223-2646
School Bus transportation provider #1 .. 602-223-2646
School Librarian #38 602-542-4367
School Psycholog't/Psychometrist #38 602-542-4367
School Superintendent #38 602-542-4367
School Supervisor #38 602-542-4367
Scientific Collector #59 602-942-3000
Securities Salesperson/Dealer #32 602-542-0678
Security Guard #53 602-223-2361
Seed Dealer #33 602-542-0904
Seed Labeler #33 602-542-0904
Self Insured Employer #60 602-542-1836
Sewage/Sludge/Septic Pumping Vehicle #40
.... 602-771-4153
Shooting Preserve #59 602-942-3000
Social Worker #10 602-542-1864
Solid Waste Facility #40 602-771-4153
Speech Pathology #43 602-364-3030
Speech-Language Pathologist #49 602-364-2536
Spray Process Appli./Sterilizer/Renovator #65
.... 602-506-6970
Subdivision Public Report #55 602-468-1414
Substance Abuse Counselor #10 602-542-1864
Substance Abuse Treatment Service #47
.... 602-364-2536
Surety #51 602-912-8470
Surplus Line Broker #51 602-912-8470
Surveyor, Land #29 602-364-4930
Tanning Facility #66 .... 602-255-4845 x237
Taxidermist #59 602-942-3000
Teacher, Elementary/Special Education. #38
.... 602-542-4367
Telemarketing Firm #62 602-542-6670
Timbering #56 602-542-4565

Timeshare Public Report #55 602-468-1414
Tobacco Product Distributor #56 602-542-4565
Trailer Coach Park #65 602-506-6970
Transporting/Towing Company #56 602-542-4565
Travel Agent, Limited #51 602-912-8470
Trust Company #5 602-255-4421
Trust Div. of Chartered Fin. Inst. #5 .. 602-255-4421
Vehicle Emission Fleet Insp station#42 602-207-7007
Vehicle Emission Fleet Inspector #42.. 602-207-7007
Vendor/Concession on State Park Land #69
.... 602-542-2155
Veterinary Medicine/Surgery #64 602-364-1738
Veterinary Premise (Hospital) #64 602-364-1738
Veterinary Technician #64 602-364-1738
Vocational Rehabilitation #61 602-542-3294
Waste Water Collection/Treatment/Construction #41
.... 602-771-4644
Waste Water Facility Operator #41 602-771-4644
Waste Water Reuse #41 602-771-4644
Water Distrib'n System Operator #41 .. 602-771-4644
Water Quality Certification #41 602-771-4644
Water Rights Assignment #58 602-417-2405
Water Transporter, out of state #58 602-417-2405
Watercraft Registration Agent #59 602-942-3000
Weighmaster, Public #2 602-255-5211
Weights & Measures Rep./Svc. Agency #2
.... 602-255-5211
Well Drilling Firm #58 .... 602-417-2470 x 7141
Well Registration/Construction #58...... 602-417-2405
White Amor Stocker #59 602-942-3000
Wildlife Hobby License #59 602-942-3000
Wildlife Holding Permit #59 602-942-3000
Wildlife Rehab/Service #59 602-942-3000
X-ray Supplier #66 .... 602-255-4845 x231
X-ray, Portable0. #43 602-364-3030
Zoo #59 602-942-3000

Arizona Licensing Agency Information

1 Department of Public Safety, Student Transportation, PO Box 6638 - Mail Drop 1250, Phoenix, AZ 85005-6638; 602-223-2646, Fax: 602-223-2923. www.dps.state.az.us   Search Database at www.dps.state.az.us/license/schoolbusdriver/default.asp

2 Department of Weights & Measures, 4425 W Olive Av #134, Glendale, AZ 85302-3844; 602-255-5211, Fax: 602-255-1950. www.weights.az.gov

3 Boxing Commission, 1110 W Washington, #260, Phoenix, AZ 85007; 602-364-1721, Fax: 602-364-1703.

4 Arizona State Lottery, PO Box2913, AZ 85063-2913., 4740 E University Dr, Phoenix, AZ 85034; 800-921-4400, Fax: 480-921-4512. www.arizonalottery.com Email: feedback@arizonalottery.com

5 Banking Department, 2910 N 44th St, #310, Phoenix, AZ 85018; 602-255-4421, Fax: 602-381-1225. www.azbanking.com Email: mailbox@azbanking.com Search Database at www.azbanking.com/Lists/Lists.htm   Note: On-line or phone verifications ONLY.

6 Board for Private Postsecondary Education, 1400 W Washington, Rm 260, Phoenix, AZ 85007; 602-542-5709, Fax: 602-542-1253. http://azppse.state.az.us

Search Database at http://azppse.state.az.us/directory.html

7 Board of Accountancy, 100 N,.15th Ave #165, Phoenix, AZ 85007; 602-364-0804, Fax: 602-364-0903.   www.accountancy.state.az.us Email: info@mail.accountancy.state.az.us Search Database at www.accountancy.state.az.us/scripts/BOAsearch.exe   Note: Lists of names and addresses are available for $1.00 per name.

8 Board of Appraisal, 1400 W Washington, #360, Phoenix, AZ 85007; 602-542-1539, Fax: 602-542-1598.   www.appraisal.state.az.us Email: appraisal@appraisal.state.az.us Search Database at www.appraisal.state.az.us/Directory/directory.html

9 Board of Barbers, 1400 W Washington, Rm 220, Phoenix, AZ 85007; 602-542-4498.

10 Board of Behavioral Health Examiners, 1400 W Washington St #350, Phoenix, AZ 85007; 602-542-1882, Fax: 602-364-0890. www.bbhe.state.az.us Email: azbbhe@bbhe.state.az.us   Note: A public record request form is available at www.bbhe.state.az.us/Forms/pubinfo.pdf. Fee for verifications is $15.00; copies are $.25 each.

11 Board of Chiropractic Examiners, 5060 N 19th Ave #416, Phoenix, AZ 85015; 602-864-5088, Fax: 602-864-5099. www.azchiroboard.com Email: merriejoh@earthlink.net

Search Database at www.azchiroboard.com Note: Accupuncture and physiotherapy are certifications under a Chiropractic license.

12 Information Services, Board of Cosmetology, 1721 E Broadway Rd, Tempe, AZ 85282; 480-784-4539, Fax: 480-255-3680. www.cosmetology.state.az.us/

13 Board of Dental Examiners, 5060 N 19th Ave, #406, Phoenix, AZ 85015; 602-242-1492, Fax: 602-242-1445. www.azdentalboard.org

14 Board of Dispensing Opticians, 1400 W Washington, Rm 230, Phoenix, AZ 85007; 602-542-3095, Fax: 602-542-3093. Email: director@asbdo.state.az.us

15 Board of Funeral Directors & Embalmers, 1400 W Washington, Room 230, Phoenix, AZ 85007; 602-542-3095, Fax: 602-542-3093. www.funeralbd.state.az.us

16 Board of Homeopathic Medical Examiners, 1400 W Washington, Rm 230, Phoenix, AZ 85007; 602-542-3095, Fax: 602-542-3093. http://home.mindspring.com/~bhme/ Email: bhme@mindspring.com   Note: A public records request must be completed.

17 Board of Medical Examiners, 9545 E Doubletree Ranch Dr, Scottsdale, AZ 85258-5539; 480-551-2700, Fax: 480-551-2704. www.bomex.org   Email: questions@bomex.org Search Database at www.bomex.org/getlicense.asp

18 Structural Pest Control Commission, 9535 E Doubletree Ranch Rd, Scottsdale, AZ 85258-5514; 602-255-3664, Fax: 602-255-1281. www.sb.state.az.us

19 Board of Naturopathic Physicians Examiners, 1400 W Washington, Rm 230, Phoenix, AZ 85007; 602-542-8242, Fax: 602-542-3093. www.npbomex.az.gov Email: gail.anthony@npbomex.az.gov Search Database at www.npbomex.az.gov/directories.html   Note: Licensing lookup may be under construction.

20 Board of Nursing, 1651 E Morton, #210, Phoenix, AZ 85020-7605; 602-889-5150, Fax: 602-889-5155. www.azbn.org Email: arizona@azbn.org Search Database at www.azbn.org/onlineverificationbatch.asp   Note: You may request verification via email only at www.azboardofnursing.org/verification.htm.

21 Board of Occupational Therapy Examiners, 5060 N 19th Av #209, Phoenix, AZ 85015; 602-589-8352, Fax: 602-589-8354. www.mindspring.com/~abote/ Email: azot@mindspring.com

22 Board of Optometry, 1400 W Washington, Rm 230, Phoenix, AZ 85007; 602-542-3095, Fax: 602-542-3093. www.asbo.state.az.us Email: margaret.whelan@webmail.state.az.us Search Database at www.asbo.state.az.us

23 Board of Osteopathic Medicine & Surgery Examiners, 9535 E Doubletree Ranch Rd, Scottsdale, AZ 85258-5539; 480-657-7703, Fax: 480-657-7715. www.azosteoboard.org Email: information@azostedboard.org Search Database at http://docfinder.state.az.us

24 Board of Pharmacy, 4425 W Olive #140, Glendale, AZ 85302-3844; 623-463-2727, Fax: 623-934-0583. www.pharmacy.state.az.us Email: info@azsbp.com

25 Board of Physical Therapy & Acupuncture, 1400 W Washington, Rm 230, Phoenix, AZ 85007; 602-542-3095, Fax: 602-542-3093. www.ptboard.state.az.us Email: info@ptboard.state.az.us Search Database at www.ptboard.state.az.us Note: Online searching will be available 1/1/2003.

26 Board of Podiatry Examiners, 1400 W Washington, Rm 230, Phoenix, AZ 85007; 602-542-3095, Fax: 602-542-3093. www.podiatry.state.az.us/ Search Database at www.podiatry.state.az.us/directory.htm

27 Board of Psychologist Examiners, 1400 W Washington St, #235, Phoenix, AZ 85007; 602-542-8162, Fax: 602-542-8279. www.psychboard.az.gov/ Email: info@psychboard.az.gov Search Database at www.psychboard.az.gov/directory.htm   Note: Will sell lists of licensees.

28 Board of Respiratory Care Examiners, 1400 W Washington, #200, Phoenix, AZ 85007; 602-542-5995, Fax: 602-542-5900. www.rb.state.az.us Email: recept@rb.state.az.us

29 Board of Technical Registration, 1110 W Washington #240, Phoenix, AZ 85007; 602-364-4930, Fax: 602-364-4931. www.btr.state.az.us Email: azbtrweb@yahoo.com Search Database at www.btr.state.az.us/RegistrantSearch.asp

30 State Bar of Arizona, 4201 N 24th St #200, Phoenix, AZ 85016-6288; 602-252-4804, Fax: 602-271-4930.   www.azbar.org Email: azbar@azbar.org Search Database at www.azbar.org/content.cfm?text=/LegalResources/findlawyer

31 Maricopa County Community College District, 2411 W. 14th Street, Tempe, AZ 85281; 480-731-8000, Fax: 480-731-8506.

32 Registration Department, Securities Division, Corporation Commission, 1300 W Washington, 3rd Fl, Phoenix, AZ 85007; 602-542-4242, Fax: 602-594-7470. www.ccsd.cc.state.az.us/licensing_and_registration/index.asp Email: accsec@ccsd.cc.state.az.us

33 Department of Agriculture, Environmental Services Division, 1688 W Adams St, Phoenix, AZ 85007; 602-542-0904, Fax: 602-542-0466. Email: adaweb@getnet.com Search Database at www.kellysolutions.com/az/

34 Department of Agriculture, Environmental Services Division, 1688 W Adams St, 1st Fl, Phoenix, AZ 85007; 602-542-5578, Fax: 602-542-0466. www.kellysolutions.com/az/ Email: adaweb@getnet.com

35 Department of Agriculture, Plant Services, Citrus, Fruit & Vegetable Standardization, 1688 W Adams, Phoenix, AZ 85007; 602-542-0947, Fax: 602-542-0898. www.kellysolutions.com/az Email: cfv@agriculture.state.az.us Search Database at www.kellysolutions.com/az

36 Department of Building & Fire Safety, 1110 W. Washington #100, Phoenix, AZ 85007; 602-364-1094.

37 Dept of Health Services, Child Care Facility Licensing, 150 N 18th Ave, Phoenix, AZ 85007; 602-364-2539, Fax: 602-364-4768. www.hs.state.az.us/als/childcare/index.htm

38 Department of Education, Teacher Certification Unit, PO Box 6490 (1535 W Jefferson St, Bin 34), Phoenix, AZ 85005-6490; 602-542-4367, Fax: 602-542-1141. www.ade.state.az.us Email: ade@ade.az.gov

39 Department of Environmental Quality, Office of Air Quality, 1110 W. Washington, Phoenix, AZ 85007; 602-771-2338, Fax: 602-771-2299. www.adeq.state.az.us

40 Department of Environmental Quality, Office of Waste Programs, 1110 W. Washington, Phoenix, AZ 85007; 602-771-4208, Fax: 602-771-2302.

41 Department of Environmental Quality, Office of Water Quality, 1110 W. Washington, Phoenix, AZ 85007; 602-771-4644, Fax: 602-771-4634. www.azdeq.state.gov

42 Department of Environmental Quality, Vehicle Emissions Section, 600 N 40th St, Phoenix, AZ 85008; 602-207-7007, Fax: 602-207-7020. www.adeq.state.az.us/environ/air/vei/index.html Email: gibbons.john@ev.state.az.us

43 Department of Health Services, Facilities Licensing, 150 N 18th Ave #450, Phoenix, AZ 85007-3245; 602-364-3030, Fax: 602-364-4765. www.hs.state.az.us/als/index.htm Search Database at www.azdhs.gov/als/medical/index.htm

44 Department of Health Services, Bureau of State Lab Services/Licensure/Cert, 250 N 17th Ave, Phoenix, AZ 85007; 602-364-0741, Fax: 602-364-0759. www.hs.state.az.us

45 Child Care Licensing, Division of Child Care, 150 N 18th Ave, 4th Fl, Phoenix, AZ 85007; 602-364-2536, Fax: 602-364-4806. www.hs.state.az.us/als/childcare/index.htm   Note: No license searches, only provider lists.

46 Department of Health Services, Office of Environmental Health, 150 N 18th Ave St.340, Phoenix, AZ 85007; 602-364-3118, Fax: 602-364-3146. www.azdhs.gov/phs/oeh/rs/

47 Department of Health Services, Office of Behavioral Health Licensure, 150 N.18th Ave, Phoenix, AZ 85007; 602-364-2536, Fax: 602-542-0883.   www.hs.state.az.us Search Database at www.hs.state.az.us/als/databases/

48 Arizona Department of Health Services, Bureau of EMS, 150 N. 18th Ave #540, Phoenix, AZ 85007; 602-364-3150, Fax: 602-364-3568. www.hs.state.az.us/bems/

49 Department of Health Services, The Division of Licensing Services, 150 N 18th Ave, Phoenix, AZ 85007; 602-364-2536, Fax: 602-364-4808. www.hs.state.az.us Search Database at www.hs.state.az.us

50 Department of Health Services, Office of Women & Children, 150 N 18th Ave, Phoenix, AZ 85017-5253; 602-364-2536, Fax: 602-364-4808. www.hs.state.az.us Search Database at www.hs.state.az.us/als/midwife/

51 Department of Insurance, Licensing Section, 2910 N 44th St, #210, Phoenix, AZ 85018-7256; 602-912-8470, Fax: 602-912-8453. www.id.state.az.us/ Email: licensing@id.state.az.us Search Database at www.id.state.az.us/

52 Department of Liquor License & Control, 800 W Washington, 5th Fl, Phoenix, AZ 85007; 602-542-5141, Fax: 602-542-5707. www.azll.com Search Database at www.azll.com/query.htm Note: Search recently issued, expired, closed, suspended and inactive licenses at the website.

53 Department of Public Safety, Security Guard & Private Investigator Licensing, PO Box 6328 (2102 W Encanto Blvd, 85009), Phoenix, AZ 85005-6328; 602-223-2361, Fax: 602-223-2938. www.dps.state.az.us/

54 Department of Racing, Licensing Division, 1110 W Washington #260, Phoenix, AZ 85007; 602-364-1700, Fax: 602-364-1703.
www.racing.state.az.us/
Email: ador@racing.state.az.us

55 Department of Real Estate, 2910 N 44th St #100, Phoenix, AZ 85018; 602-468-1414, Fax: 602-468-0562.
www.re.state.az.us
Email: cdowns@adre.org
Search Database at www.re.state.az.us/db.html

56 Department of Revenue, License & Registration, 1600 W Monroe, Phoenix, AZ 85007-2650; 602-542-4565.
www.revenue.state.az.us

57 Department of Transportation, Aeronautics Division, 255 E Osborn #101, Phoenix, AZ 85012; 602-294-9144, Fax: 602-294-9141.
www.azdot.gov/Aviation/index.asp
Email: aeroinfo@dot.state.az.us

58 Department of Water Resources, 500 N 3rd St (PO Box 458), Phoenix, AZ 85004; 602-417-2400, Fax: 602-417-2401.
http://water.az.gov/adwr/

59 Game & Fish Department, 2222 W Greenway Rd, Phoenix, AZ 85023; 602-942-3000, Fax: 602-789-3921.
http://azgfd.com/

60 Division of Administration, Industrial Commission of Arizona, 800 W Washington, 3rd Fl, Phoenix, AZ 85007; 602-542-4653, Fax: 602-542-3070.
www.ica.state.az.us

61 Special Fund Division, Industrial Commission of Arizona, 800 W Washington, 4th Fl, Rm 401, Phoenix, AZ 85007; 602-542-3294, Fax: 602-542-3696.
www.ica.state.az.us

62 Secretary of State, 1700 W Washington St, 7th Fl, Phoenix, AZ 85007-2888; 602-542-4285, Fax: 602-542-6172.
www.azsos.gov/
Email: lobbyist@azsos.gov   Note: Search lobbyists using the public body's name, the lobbyist's name or the lobbyist's employee's name.

63 Arizona Supreme Court, Court Reporter Program, 1501 W. Washington St, #104, Phoenix, AZ 85007-3231; 602-364-0878, Fax: 602-307-1210.
www.supreme.state.az.us/cr/
Email: courtrep@supreme.sp.state.az.us

64 Veterinary Medical Examining Board, 1400 W Washington, #240, Phoenix, AZ 85007; 602-364-1738, Fax: 602-542-3093.
www.vetbd.state.az.us

65 Maricopa Environmental Services, 1001 N Central, #550, Phoenix, AZ 85004; 602-506-6970, Fax: 602-506-6862.
www.maricopa.gov/envsvc/default.asp
Email: webmail@mail.maricopa.co

66 Medical Radiologic Technology Board of Examiners, 4814 S 40th St, Phoenix, AZ 85040-2940; 602-255-4845, Fax: 602-437-0705.
www.arra.state.az.us
Email: agodwin@arra.state.az.us

67 Mine Inspector, 1700 W Washington, #400, Phoenix, AZ 85007-2805; 602-542-5971, Fax: 602-542-5335.
www.asmi.state.az.us
Email: admin@mi.state.az.us

68 Nursing Care Board, 1400 W Washington, #230, Phoenix, AZ 85007; 602-364-2273.
www.nciabd.state.az.us
Email: information@nciabd.state.az.us

69 Parks Board, 1300 W Washington, #221, Phoenix, AZ 85007; 602-542-2155, Fax: 602-542-4180.
www.pr.state.az.us/
Email: info@pr.state.az.us

70 Registrar of Contractors, 800 W Washington, 6th Fl, Phoenix, AZ 85007; 602-542-1525, Fax: 602-542-1599.
www.rc.state.az.us
Email: webmaster@roc1.rc.state.az.us
Search Database at www.rc.state.az.us/clsc/AZROCLicenseQuery

Arizona Federal Courts

The following list indicates the district and division name for each county in the state. If the bankruptcy court location is different from the district court, then the location of the bankruptcy court appears in parentheses.

County/Court Cross Reference

Apache	Prescott (Phoenix)	Mohave	Prescott (Yuma)
Cochise	Tucson	Navajo	Prescott (Phoenix)
Coconino	Prescott (Phoenix)	Pima	Tucson
Gila	Phoenix	Pinal	Phoenix (Tucson)
Graham	Tucson	Santa Cruz	Tucson
Greenlee	Tucson	Yavapai	Prescott (Phoenix)
La Paz	Phoenix (Yuma)	Yuma	Phoenix (Yuma)
Maricopa	Phoenix		

Standards for Federal Courts: Search fee is $26.00 per item (one party name or case number). Copy fee is $.50 per page. Certification fee is $9.00 per document, double for exemplification, if available. All fees standard unless noted in profile. Mail Search: always enclose a stamped self addressed envelope unless otherwise noted. Most courts accept fax requests or will suggest a copying/search vendor. Before releasing records, all courts require prepayment, unless noted.

Open records are located at the court unless otherwise noted. District courts index by defendant and plaintiff as well as by case number. Bankruptcy courts usually index by debtor and case number. While most courts now have their indexes on computer, many may still maintain index card files as well.

Courts offering internet access via CM-ECF or older RACER, PACER, or Web-PACER systems charge $.08 per page fee unless noted as free. Where PACER is available, the universal sign-up number is 800-676-6856. Find PACER and the US Party/Case Index at http://pacer.psc.uscourts.gov.

US District Court

District of Arizona

Phoenix Division Court Clerk, Sandra Day O'Connor US Courthouse, #130, 401 W Washington St, SPC 1, Phoenix, AZ 85025-2118 (also use mail address for courier delivery), 602-322-7200, records rm- 602-322-7205. Hours- 8:30AM-5PM. www.azd.uscourts.gov

Counties: Gila, La Paz, Maricopa, Pinal, Yuma. This office manages the Prescott Division records. Some Yuma cases handled by San Diego Division of the Southern District of California.

Searches & Indexing: Results do not include SSN or DOB. Computer index maintained; public access terminal in lobby provides docket access. New cases in the index 2-3 days after filing date. Records purged every 12 months.

Fee & Payment: Pay by Visa/MC, money order, cashier check, business check. In state personal checks also accepted. Payee: Clerk, US District Court. Prepayment required.

Phone Search: If case number is provided via phone, basic information will be released.

Mail Search: search usually completed- 3-5 days. Include SASE for return.

In Person Search: Fee charged if court performs your search. No self-serve copier available.

E-Services: ECF replaces PACER whose records did go back to 1992. New records online after 1 day. ECF at https://ecf.azd.uscourts.gov **Opinions Online:** www.azd.uscourts.gov. Click on "cases of interest." **Other Online Access:** Access to court calendars can be found at www.azd.uscourts.gov.

Prescott Division Court Clerk, 101 W Goodwin St, US Post Office Bldg, Prescott, AZ 86303 (also use mail address for courier delivery), 928-445-6598; 602-322-7200- Phoenix, records rm- 602-322-7205- Phoenix. www.azd.uscourts.gov

Counties: Apache, Coconino, Mohave, Navajo, Yavapai. Currently, this is an unmanned office; direct record requests to the Phoenix Division.

Searches & Indexing: Cases indexed by and case number. Results do not include SSN or DOB. Open records located at Phoenix Division.

Fee & Payment: Pay by money order, cashier check, in state personal check accepted. Payee: Clerk, US District Court. Prepayment required.

Phone Search: No searching by telephone.

In Person Search: permitted. No self-serve copier available.

E-Services: ECF replaces PACER. ECF at https://ecf.azd.uscourts.gov **Opinions Online:** www.azd.uscourts.gov. Click on "cases of interest." **Other Online Access:** Access to court calendars can be found at www.azd.uscourts.gov.

Tucson Division Court Clerk, US Court House, 405 W Congress Ste 1500, Tucson, AZ 85701-5010 (also use mail address for courier delivery), 520-205-4200, Fax-520-205-4209. Hours- 8:30AM-5PM. www.azd.uscourts.gov

Counties: Cochise, Graham, Greenlee, Pima, Santa Cruz. The Globe Division was closed effective 1/1994, and all case records for that division are now found here.

Searches & Indexing: Results do not include SSN or DOB. Computer index maintained; criminal back to 1990. New cases in the index immediately after filing date. Records purged every 12 months.

Fee & Payment: Pay by Visa/MC, money order, cashier check, business check. In state personal checks also accepted. Payee: Clerk, US District Court. Prepayment required.

Phone Search: Only docket information is available by phone.

Mail Search: search usually completed- 1 day. SASE not required.

In Person Search: Fee charged if court performs your search. A copy service may be used in lieu of court staff; copy service has a 1 day turnaround. No self-serve copier available.

E-Services: ECF replaces PACER whose records did go back to 1992. New records online after 1 day. ECF at https://ecf.azd.uscourts.gov **Opinions Online:** www.azd.uscourts.gov. Click on "cases of interest." **Other Online Access:** Access to court calendars can be found at www.azd.uscourts.gov.

US Bankruptcy Court

District of Arizona

Phoenix Division Court Clerk, 230 N First Ave, # 101, Phoenix, AZ 85003 (also use mail address for courier delivery), 602-682-4000. Hours- 9AM-4PM. www.azb.uscourts.gov

Counties: Apache, Coconino, Gila, Maricopa, Navajo, Yavapai.

Searches & Indexing: Results include last 4 SSN digits only. Computer index maintained. New cases in the index immediately after filing date. Records purged every 6 months.

Fee & Payment: Pay by money order, cashier check, business check. No personal checks. Payee: Clerk, US Bankruptcy Court. Prepayment required.

Phone Search: Only docket information is available by phone. Voice Case Information Service available, call VCIS at 602-682-4001.

Mail Search: search usually completed- 1 week. Include SASE for return.

In Person Search: Fee charged if court performs your search. No self-serve copier available.

E-Services: ECF replaces PACER whose records did go back to 1986. ECF at https://ecf.azb.uscourts.gov **Opinions Online:** www.azb.uscourts.gov/opinions. **Other Online Access:** Judge's court calendars free at www.azb.uscourts.gov.

Tucson Division Court Clerk, 38 S Scott Ave #100, Tucson, AZ 85701-1608 (also use mail address for courier delivery), 520-202-7500. Hours- 9AM-4PM. www.azb.uscourts.gov

Counties: Cochise, Graham, Greenlee, Pima, Pinal, Santa Cruz.

Searches & Indexing: Records also indexed by adversary case number, if applicable. A master list of creditors available for each case back to 1995. Results include last 4 SSN digits only. Computer index maintained. New cases in the index immediately after filing date. Records purged every 6 months.

Fee & Payment: Pay by money order, cashier check, business check. No personal checks. Payee: Clerk, US Bankruptcy Court. Prepayment required.

Phone Search: Only docket and cover sheet information is released via phone. Voice Case Information Service available, call VCIS at 888-299-6032.

Mail Search: search usually completed- 24 hours. Include SASE for return.

In Person Search: Fee charged if court performs your search. Copies obtained at the Office of the Bankruptcy Clerk or through an off-site copy service. No self-serve copier available.

E-Services: ECF replaces PACER whose records did go back to 1914. ECF at https://ecf.azb.uscourts.gov **Opinions Online:** www.azb.uscourts.gov/opinions. **Other Online Access:** Judge's court calendars free at www.azb.uscourts.gov.

Yuma Division Court Clerk, PO Box 13011, Yuma, AZ 85366 (courier address: 325 W 19th St, Yuma, AZ 85364), 928-783-2288. Hours- 9AM-4PM. www.azb.uscourts.gov

Counties: La Paz, Mohave, Yuma.

Searches & Indexing: Results do not include SSN or DOB. Computer index maintained. New cases in the index immediately after filing date. Records purged every 6 months.

Fee & Payment: Pay by money order, cashier check, business check. No personal checks. Payee: Clerk, US Bankruptcy Court. Prepayment required.

Phone Search: Docket information available by phone. Voice Case Information Service available, call VCIS at 888-299-6032.

Mail Search: search usually completed- 1-2 days. Include SASE for return.

In Person Search: Fee charged if court performs your search. No self-serve copier available.

E-Services: ECF replaces PACER whose records did go back to the mid 1980's. ECF at https://ecf.azb.uscourts.gov **Opinions Online:** www.azb.uscourts.gov/opinions. **Other Online Access:** Judge's court calendars free at www.azb.uscourts.gov.

Arizona County Courts

Court	Jurisdiction	No. of Courts	How Organized
Superior Courts*	General	15	15 Counties
Justice of the Peace Courts*	Limited	79	79 Precincts
Municipal Courts	Municipal	85	

* Profiled in this Sourcebook.

CIVIL									
Court	Tort	Contract	Real Estate	Min. Claim	Max. Claim	Small Claims	Estate	Eviction	Domestic Relations
Superior Court*	X	X	X	$5000	No Max			X	
Justice of the Peace Courts*	X	X	X	$0	$10,000	$2500		X	X
Municipal Courts									X

CRIMINAL					
Court	Felony	Misdemeanor	DWI/DUI	Preliminary Hearing	Juvenile
Superior Court*	X	X			X
Justice of the Peace Courts*		X	X	X	
Municipal Courts		X	X		

ADMINISTRATION

Administrative Office of the Courts, Arizona Supreme Court Bldg, 1501 W Washington, Phoenix, AZ, 85007; 602-542-9310, Fax: 602-542-9484.

www.supreme.state.az.us

COURT STRUCTURE

The Superior is the court of general jurisdiction. Justice, and Municipal courts generally have separate jurisdiction over case types as indicated in the text. Most courts will search their records by plaintiff or defendant. Estate cases are handled by Superior Court. Fees are the same as for civil and criminal case searching.

ONLINE ACCESS

The Public Access to Court Case Information is a valuable web service providing a resource for information about court cases from 141 out of 180 courts in Arizona. Courts not covered include certain parts of Pima, Yavapai, Mohave, and Maricopa counties. Access information includes: detailed case information, i.e., case type, charges, filing and disposition dates; the parties in the case, not including victims and witnesses; and the court mailing address & location. Go to www.supreme.state.az.us/publicaccess/default.htm.

Opinions from the AZ Supreme Court and Court of Appeals are available from the website.

ADDITIONAL INFORMATION

Public access to all Maricopa County court case indexes is available at a central location - 1 W Madison Ave in downtown Phoenix. Copies, however, must be obtained from the court where the case is heard.

Justice Courts accept civil actions up to $10,000 due to higher value claims in landlord/tenant cases. Civil cases between $5,000 and $10,000 may be filed at either Justice or Superior Courts.

Many offices do not perform searches due to personnel and/or budget constraints. As computerization of record offices increases across the state, more record offices are providing public access computer terminals.

Fees across all jurisdictions, as established by the Arizona Supreme Court and State Legislature, are as follows as of August 9, 2001: search - Superior Court: $18.00 per name; lower courts: $17.00 per name; certification - Superior Court: $18.00 per document; lower courts: $17.00 per document; copies - $.50 per page. Courts may choose to charge no fees.

Apache County

Superior Court PO Box 365, St Johns, AZ 85936; phone: 928-337-7550; probate phone: same; fax: 928-337-2771; hours 8AM-5PM (MST). *Felony, Civil Actions Over $10,000, Probate.* www.co.apache.az.us/clerk

Civil Records: Access: Mail, in person, online. Both court and visitors may perform in person searches. Search fee: $18.00 per name. Court makes copy: $.50 per page; same fee for self serve. Required to search: name, years to search; also helpful: address. Civil cases indexed by defendant, plaintiff. Civil records on computer and docket books. Access to records from 1995 forward is free at www.supreme.state .az.us/publicaccess/. Mail turnaround time 2 days.

Criminal Records: Access: Mail, in person, online. Both court and visitors may perform in person searches. Search fee: $18.00 per name. Add $5.00 if no SASE or not a toll free serve. Court makes copy: $.50 per page; same fee for self serve. Required to search: name, years to search, DOB; also helpful: address, SSN. Criminal records on computer and docket books. Access to records from 1995 forward is free at www.supreme.state.az.us/publicaccess/. Mail turnaround time 2 days.

General Information: Public access terminal goes back to 1995. No juvenile dependencies, mental health, victims, sealed or adoption records released. Will fax documents to local or toll-free line; $5.00 if not. Certification fee: $18.00 per document. Payee: Clerk of the Court. Business checks accepted. Credit cards accepted. Prepayment and SASE required.

Chinle Justice Court PO Box 888, Chinle, AZ 86503; phone: 928-674-5922; fax: 928-674-5926; hours 8AM-5PM (MST). *Misdemeanor, Civil Actions Under $10,000, Eviction, Small Claims.*

Civil Records: Access: Fax, mail, in person, online. Both court and visitors may perform in person searches. Search fee: $17.00 per name. Court makes copy: $.50 per page; same fee for self serve. Required to search: name, years to search; also helpful: address. Civil cases indexed by defendant. Civil records on docket books from 1977, computerized back to 2000. Access to records is free at www.supreme.stat e.az.us/publicaccess/. Mail turnaround 1-2 days.

Criminal Records: Access: Fax, mail, in person, online. Both court and visitors may perform in person searches. Search fee: $17.00 per name. Court makes copy: $.50 per page; same fee for self serve. Required to search: name, years to search; also helpful: address, DOB, SSN. Criminal records on docket books from 1977, computerized back to 2000. Access to records is free at www.supreme.state.az.us/publicaccess/. Phone access is discouraged. Mail turnaround 1-2 days.

General Information: Public access terminal goes back to 2000. No juvenile, mental health, victims, sealed or adoption records released. Fee to fax documents is $1.25 per page. Certification fee: $17.00. Payee: Chinle Justice Court. Business checks accepted. Prepayment and SASE required.

Puerco Justice Court PO Box 610, Sanders, AZ 86512; phone: 928-688-2954; fax: 928-688-2244; hours 8AM-N, 1-5PM (MST). *Misdemeanor, Civil Actions Under $10,000, Eviction, Small Claims.*

Civil Records: Access: Mail, in person, online. Only the court performs in person searches; visitors may not. Search fee: $17.00 per name. Court makes copy: $.50 per page. Required to search: name, years to search; also helpful: address. Civil cases indexed by defendant. Civil records on docket books. Access to records is free at www.supreme.state.az.us/publ icaccess/. Mail turnaround time ASAP.

Criminal Records: Access: Mail, in person, online. Only the court performs in person searches; visitors may not. Search fee: $17.00 per name. Court makes copy: $.50 per page. Required to search: name, years to search, DOB; also helpful: address, SSN. Criminal records on docket books. Access to records

is free at www.supreme.state.az.us/publicaccess/. Mail turnaround time ASAP.

General Information: No public access terminal. No juvenile, mental health, victims, sealed or adoption records released. Certification fee: $17.00 per doc. Payee: Sanders Justice Court. Only cashiers checks and money orders accepted. Prepayment and SASE required.

Round Valley Justice Court PO Box 1356, Springerville, AZ 85938; phone: 928-333-4613; fax: 928-333-4205; hours 8AM-N, 1-5PM (MST). *Misdemeanor, Civil Actions Under $10,000, Eviction, Small Claims.*

Civil Records: Access: Phone, fax, mail, in person, online. Both court and visitors may perform in person searches. Search fee: $17.00 per name. Court makes copy: $.50 per page. Required to search: name, years to search; also helpful: address. Civil cases indexed by defendant, plaintiff. Civil records on docket books from 1990, computerized since 2/96. Access to records is free at www.supreme.st ate.az.us/publicaccess/. Mail turnaround time 5 working days.

Criminal Records: Access: Phone, fax, mail, in person, online. Both court and visitors may perform in person searches. Search fee: $17.00 per name. Court makes copy: $.50 per page. Required to search: name, years to search; also helpful: address, DOB, SSN. Criminal records from docket books from 1990, computerized since 2/96. Access to records is free at www.supreme.state.az.us/publicaccess/. Mail turnaround time 5 working days.

General Information: No public access terminal. No juvenile, mental health, victims, sealed or adoption records released. Will not fax documents. Certification fee: $17.00. Payee: Round Valley Justice Court. Only cashiers checks and money orders accepted. Prepayment and SASE required.

St Johns Justice Court PO Box 308, St Johns, AZ 85936; phone: 928-337-7558; fax: 928-337-2683; hours 8AM-5PM (MST). *Misdemeanor, Civil Actions Under $10,000, Eviction, Small Claims.*

Civil Records: Access: Mail, in person, online. Both court and visitors may perform in person searches. Search fee: $17.00 per name. Court makes copy: $.50 per page; same fee for self serve. Required to search: name, years to search; also helpful: address. Civil cases indexed by defendant. Civil records on docket books since 1972; on computer since 1996. Access to records is free at www.supreme.state.az.us/pu blicaccess/. Mail turnaround time 48 hours.

Criminal Records: Access: Mail, in person, online. Both court and visitors may perform in person searches. Search fee: $17.00 per name. Court makes copy: $.50 per page; same fee for self serve. Required to search: name, years to search, DOB; also helpful: address, SSN. Criminal records on docket books since 1972; on computer since 1996. Access to records is free at www.supreme.state.az.us/publicaccess/. Mail turnaround time 48 hours.

General Information: No public access terminal. No juvenile, mental health, victims, sealed or adoption records released. Will fax documents. Certification fee: $17.00. Payee: St John's Justice Court. Only cashiers checks and money orders accepted. Prepayment and SASE required.

Cochise County

Superior Court PO Box CK, Bisbee, AZ 85603; phone: 520-432-8604; criminal phone: 520-432-8581; fax: 520-432-4850; hours 8AM-5PM (MST). *Felony, Civil Actions Over $5,000, Probate.* www.co.cochise.az.us/Court

Civil Records: Access: Fax, mail, in person, email, online. Both court and visitors may perform in person searches. Search fee: $18.00 per name per year. Court makes copy: $.50 per page; same fee for self serve. Required to search: name, years to search. Civil cases indexed by defendant, plaintiff. Civil records on computer since 1996 and on index books from 1881 to present. Access to records is free at

www.supreme.state.az.us/publicaccess/.   Mail turnaround time 7-14 days.

Criminal Records: Access: Fax, mail, in person, email, online. Both court and visitors may perform in person searches. Search fee: $18.00 per name. Per every 5 years. Court makes copy: $.50 per page; same fee for self serve. Required to search: name, years to search; also helpful: DOB, SSN. Criminal records on computer since 1996; prior records on index books. Access to records is free at www.supreme.st ate.az.us/publicaccess/. Mail turnaround 7-14 days.

General Information: Public access terminal goes back to 1996. No juvenile, mental health, victims, sealed or adoption records released. Fee to fax documents is $.50 per page. Certification fee: $18.00. Payee: Clerk of Superior Court. Cashiers checks and money orders accepted; prepayment/SASE required

Benson Justice Court 126 W 5th St, #1, Benson, AZ 85602; phone: 520-586-8100; criminal phone: 520-586-8106; civil phone: 520-586-8103; fax: 520-586-9647; hours 8AM-5PM (MST). *Misdemeanor, Civil Actions Under $10,000, Eviction, Small Claims.*

Civil Records: Access: Fax, mail, in person, online. Only the court performs in person searches; visitors may not. Search fee: $17.00 per name. Court makes copy: $.50 per page. Required to search: name, years to search; also helpful: address. Civil cases indexed by defendant and plaintiff. Civil records go back to 1997. Access to records is free at www.supreme.state.az.us/publicaccess/.   Mail turnaround time 1-3 days.

Criminal Records: Access: Fax, mail, in person, online. Only the court performs in person searches; visitors may not. Search fee: $17.00 per name. Court makes copy: $.50 per page. Required to search: name, years to search; also helpful: address, DOB, SSN. Criminal records go back to 1997. Access to records is free at www.supreme.state.az.us/publicaccess/. Mail turnaround time 1-3 days.

General Information: No public access terminal. No juvenile, mental health, victims, sealed records released. No fee to fax documents. Certification fee: $17.00 per doc. Payee: Benson Justice Court. Only cashiers checks and money orders accepted. Prepayment and SASE required.

Bisbee Justice Court 207 N Judd Dr, Bisbee, AZ 85603; phone: 520-432-9542; fax: 520-432-5271; hours 8AM-5PM (MST). *Misdemeanor, Civil Actions Under $10,000, Eviction, Small Claims.*

Civil Records: Access: Fax, mail, in person, online. Only the court performs in person searches; visitors may not. Search fee: $17.00 per name. Court makes copy: $.50 per page. Required to search: name, years to search; also helpful: address. Civil cases indexed by defendant, plaintiff. Civil records on computer from 1992. Some records on dockets. Access to records is free at www.supreme.state.az.us/publicaccess/.   Mail turnaround time 1-7 days.

Criminal Records: Access: Fax, mail, in person, online. Only the court performs in person searches; visitors may not. Search fee: $17.00 per name. Court makes copy: $.50 per page. Required to search: name, years to search; also helpful: address, DOB, SSN. Criminal records on computer from 7/92. Some records on dockets; computerized records since 1992. Access to records is free at www.supreme.state.az.us/publicaccess/.   Mail turnaround time 1-7 days.

General Information: No public access terminal. No juvenile, mental health, victims, sealed or adoption records released. No fee to fax documents. Certification fee: $17.00. Payee: Bisbee Justice Court #1. Personal checks accepted. Prepayment and SASE required.

Bowie Justice Court PO Box 317, Bowie, AZ 85605; phone: 520-847-2303; fax: 520-847-2242; hours 8AM-5PM (MST). *Misdemeanor, Civil Actions Under $10,000, Eviction, Small Claims.*

Civil Records: Access: Phone, fax, mail, in person, online. Only the court performs in person searches;

visitors may not. Search fee: $17.00 per name. Court makes copy: $.50 per page. Required to search: name, years to search; also helpful: address. Civil cases indexed by defendant. Civil records on computer from 7/85, some from 1994. Files maintained for 5 years after closure. Access to records is free at www.supreme.state.az.us/publicaccess/. Mail turnaround time 1-3 days.

Criminal Records: Access: Phone, fax, mail, in person, online. Only the court performs in person searches; visitors may not. Search fee: $17.00 per name. Court makes copy: $.50 per page. Required to search: name, years to search, DOB; also helpful: address, SSN. Criminal records on computer from 1989. Files maintained for 5 years after closure. Access to records is free at www.supreme.state.az.us/publicaccess/. Mail turnaround time 1-3 days.

General Information: No public access terminal. No juvenile, mental health, victims, sealed or adoption records released. Will fax documents $2.00 per page. Certification fee: $17.00 per doc includes copy fee. Payee: Bowie Justice Court. Only cashiers checks and money orders accepted. Visa, MC accepted. Prepayment and SASE required.

Douglas Justice Court 661 G Ave, Douglas, AZ 85607; phone: 520-805-5640; fax: 520-364-3684; hours 8AM-5PM (MST). *Misdemeanor, Civil Actions Under $10,000, Eviction, Small Claims.*

Civil Records: Access: Fax, mail, in person, online. Both court and visitors may perform in person searches. Search fee: $17.00 per name. Court makes copy: $.50 per page; same fee for self serve. Required to search: name, years to search; also helpful: address. Civil cases indexed by defendant, plaintiff. Civil records on computer from 1991. Some records on dockets. Access to records is free at www.supreme.state.az.us/publicaccess/. Mail turnaround time 1-7 days.

Criminal Records: Access: Fax, mail, in person, online. Both court and visitors may perform in person searches. Search fee: $17.00 per name. Court makes copy: $.50 per page; same fee for self serve. Required to search: name, years to search, DOB; also helpful: address, SSN. Criminal records on computer from 1990. Some records on dockets. Access to records is free at www.supreme.state.az.us/publicaccess/. Mail turnaround time 1-7 days.

General Information: Public access terminal has criminal back to 5 years, then file destroyed and civil back to - traffic records 1 year, then file destroyed. No juvenile, mental health, victims, sealed or adoption records released. Fee to fax certified search documents is $.50 per page. Certification fee: $17.00 per doc. Payee: Douglas Justice Court. Personal checks accepted. Prepayment and SASE required.

Sierra Vista Justice Court 4001 E Foothills Dr, Sierra Vista, AZ 85635; phone: 520-803-3801; fax: 520-803-3800; hours 8AM-5PM (MST). *Misdemeanor, Civil Actions Under $10,000, Eviction, Small Claims.*

Civil Records: Access: Fax, mail, in person, online. Only the court performs in person searches; visitors may not. Search fee: $17.00 per name. Court makes copy: $.50 per page. Required to search: name, years to search; also helpful: address. Civil cases indexed by plaintiff and defendant. Civil records on computer since 8/96. Access to records is free at www.supreme.state.az.us/publicaccess/. Note: In person access requires a written request. Mail turnaround time 3-7 days.

Criminal Records: Access: Fax, mail, in person, online. Only the court performs in person searches; visitors may not. Search fee: $17.00 per name. Court makes copy: $.50 per page. Required to search: name, years to search; also helpful: address, DOB, SSN. Criminal records by case number, on computer back to 8/1996. Access to records is free at www.supreme.state.az.us/publicaccess/. Note: In person access requires a written request. Mail turnaround time 3-7 days.

General Information: No public access terminal. No juvenile, mental health, victims, sealed, financial, or adoption records released. Will fax documents to local or toll free line. Certification fee: $17.00. Payee: Cochise County Treasurer. Personal checks or Visa, MC accepted. Prepayment and SASE required.

Willcox Justice Court 450 S Haskell, Willcox, AZ 85643; phone: 520-384-7000; fax: 520-384-4305; hours 8AM-5PM (MST). *Misdemeanor, Civil Actions Under $10,000, Eviction, Small Claims.*

Civil Records: Access: Phone, fax, mail, in person, online. Both court and visitors may perform in person searches. Search fee: $17.00. Court makes copy: $.50 per page. Required to search: name; also helpful: years to search, address. Civil cases indexed by defendant, plaintiff. Civil records on computer from 1996. Some records on dockets. Access to records is free at www.supreme.state.az.us/publicaccess/. Mail turnaround time usually 1-3 days.

Criminal Records: Access: Phone, fax, mail, in person, online. Both court and visitors may perform in person searches. Search fee: $17.00. Court makes copy: $.50 per page. Required to search: name, DOB; also helpful: years to search, address, SSN. Criminal records on computer from 1996. Some records on dockets. Access to records is free at www.supreme.state.az.us/publicaccess/. Mail turnaround time usually 1-3 days.

General Information: Public access terminal goes back to 1996. No juvenile, mental health, victims, sealed or adoption records released. No fee to fax documents. Certification fee: $17.00. Payee: Willcox Justice Court. Only cashiers checks and money orders accepted. Prepayment and SASE required.

Coconino County

Superior Court 200 N San Francisco St, Flagstaff, AZ 86001; phone: 928-779-6535; hours 8AM-5PM (MST). *Felony, Civil Actions Over $5,000, Probate.*

Civil Records: Access: Mail, in person, online. Both court and visitors may perform in person searches. Search fee: $22.00 per name per year. Court makes copy: $.50 per page. Required to search: name, years to search; also helpful: address. Civil cases indexed by defendant. Civil records on handwritten ledger books from 1890. Some records on microfiche and dockets; computer from 1994. Access to records is free at www.supreme.state.az.us/publicaccess/. Mail turnaround time 2 weeks.

Criminal Records: Access: Mail, in person, online. Both court and visitors may perform in person searches. Search fee: $22.00 per name per year. Court makes copy: $.50 per page. Required to search: name, years to search, DOB; also helpful: address, SSN. Criminal records on handwritten ledger books from 1890. Some records on microfiche and dockets; computer from 1994. Access to records is free at www.supreme.state.az.us/publicaccess/. Mail turnaround time 2 weeks.

General Information: No public access terminal. No mental health, victims, sealed or adoption records released. Certification fee: $18.00. Payee: Clerk of Superior Court. Business checks accepted. Prepayment and SASE required.

Flagstaff Justice Court 200 N San Franciso St., Flagstaff, AZ 86001; phone: 928-779-6806; Hours: 8AM-5PM (MST). *Misdemeanor, Civil Actions Under $10,000, Eviction, Small Claims.*

Civil Records: Access: Mail, in person, online. Only the court performs in person searches; visitors may not. Search fee: $17.00 per name. Court makes copy: $.50 per page. Required to search: name, years to search; also helpful: address. Civil records on docket books. Will only maintain records for 5 years. Access to records is free at www.supreme.state.az.us/publicaccess/. Mail turnaround time 14-20 days.

Criminal Records: Access: Mail, in person, online. Only the court performs in person searches; visitors may not. Search fee: $17.00 per name per year. Court makes copy: $.50 per page. Required to

search: name, years to search, DOB; also helpful: address, SSN. Criminal records on computer since 1987. Will only maintain records for 5 years. Access to records is free at www.supreme.state.az.us/publicaccess/. Mail turnaround time 14-20 days.

General Information: No public access terminal. No juvenile, mental health, victims, sealed or adoption records released. Certification fee: $17.00 per doc. Payee: Flagstaff Justice Court. Only cashiers checks and money orders accepted. Prepayment and SASE required.

Fredonia Justice Court PO Box 559, 112 N Main, Fredonia, AZ 86022-0559; phone: 928-643-7472; fax: 928-643-7491; hours 8AM-5PM (closed 1 hr at noon) (MST). *Misdemeanor, Civil Actions Under $10,000, Eviction, Small Claims.*

Civil Records: Access: Mail, in person, online. Only the court performs in person searches; visitors may not. Search fee: $17.00 per name. Court makes copy: $.50 per page. Required to search: name, years to search; also helpful: address. Civil cases indexed by number. Civil records on docket books. Will only maintain records for 5 years. Access to records is free at www.supreme.state.az.us/publicaccess/. Mail turnaround time 5 business days.

Criminal Records: Access: Mail, in person, online. Only the court performs in person searches; visitors may not. Search fee: $17.00 per name. Court makes copy: $.50 per page. Required to search: name, years to search, DOB; also helpful: address, SSN. Criminal records for misdemeanors on computer from 1992, all others on docket books. Access to records is free at www.supreme.state.az.us/publicaccess/. Mail turnaround time 5 days.

General Information: No public access terminal. No juvenile, mental health, victims, sealed or adoption records released. Will fax documents for $1.00 per page. Certification fee: $17.00. Payee: Justice Court. Only cashiers checks and money orders accepted. Prepayment and SASE required.

Page Justice Court PO Box 1565, Page, AZ 86040; phone: 928-645-8871; fax: 928-645-1869; hours 8AM-5PM (MST). *Misdemeanor, Civil Actions Under $10,000, Eviction, Small Claims.*

Civil Records: Access: Mail, in person, online. Only the court performs in person searches; visitors may not. Search fee: $17.00 per name. Court makes copy: $.50 per page. Required to search: name, years to search; also helpful: address. Civil cases indexed by defendant. Civil records on computer since 9/96; prior on docket books. Will only maintain records for 5 years. Access to records is free at www.supreme.state.az.us/publicaccess/. Mail turnaround time 5 days.

Criminal Records: Access: Mail, in person, online. Only the court performs in person searches; visitors may not. Search fee: $17.00 per name. Court makes copy: $.50 per page. Required to search: name, years to search, DOB; also helpful: address, SSN. Criminal records for misdemeanors on computer from 1987, felony since 1991, all others on docket books. Access to records is free at www.supreme.state.az.us/publicaccess/. Mail turnaround time 5 days.

General Information: No public access terminal. No juvenile, mental health, victims, sealed or adoption records released. Will fax documents. Certification fee: $17.00 per doc. Payee: Page Justice Court. Only cashiers checks and money orders accepted. Visa, MC accepted. Prepayment and SASE required.

Williams Justice Court 700 W Rail Road Ave, Williams, AZ 86046; phone: 928-635-2691; hours 8AM-N; 1-5PM (MST). *Misdemeanor, Civil Actions Under $10,000, Eviction, Small Claims.*

Civil Records: Access: Mail, in person, online. Both court and visitors may perform in person searches. Search fee: $17.00 per name. Court makes copy: $1.25 per page. Required to search: name, years to search; also helpful: address. Civil cases indexed by defendant, plaintiff. Civil records on docket books. Will only maintain records for 5 years. Access to

records is free at www.supreme.state.az.us/p ublicaccess/. Mail turnaround time 2-3 weeks.
Criminal Records: Access: Mail, in person, online. Both court and visitors may perform in person searches. Search fee: $22.00 per name. Court makes copy: $1.25 per page. Required to search: name, years to search, DOB; also helpful: address, SSN. Criminal records on docket books. Access to records is free at www.supreme.state.az.us/publicaccess/. Mail turnaround time 2-3 weeks.
General Information: Public access terminal has criminal back to 5 years and civil back to 3 years. No juvenile, mental health, victims, sealed or adoption records released. Will not fax documents. Certification fee: $17.00. Payee: Williams Justice Court. Only cashiers checks and money orders accepted. Prepayment and SASE required.

Gila County

Superior Court 1400 E Ash, Globe, AZ 85501; phone: 928-425-3231 X8553; hours 8AM-5PM (MST). *Felony, Civil Actions Over $5,000, Probate.*
Civil Records: Access: Mail, in person, online. Both court and visitors may perform in person searches. Search fee: $18.00 per name per year. Court makes copy: $.50 per page. Required to search: name, years to search; also helpful: address. Civil cases indexed by defendant, plaintiff. Civil records indexed on computer from 1982. On microfiche from 1913 to 1982. Some records on docket books and index cards. Access to records is free at www.supreme.state.az.us/publicaccess/. Mail turnaround time 10 days to 2 weeks.
Criminal Records: Access: Mail, in person, online. Both court and visitors may perform in person searches. Search fee: $18.00 per name. Court makes copy: $.50 per page. Required to search: name, years to search, DOB; also helpful: address, SSN. Criminal records on computer from 1913. Access to records is free at www.supreme.state.az.us/publicaccess/. Mail turnaround time 10 days to 2 weeks.
General Information: Public access terminal available. No juvenile prior to June 1996, mental health, victims, sealed or adoption records released. Will not fax documents. Certification fee: $18.00. Payee: Clerk of Superior Court. Personal checks accepted. Prepayment and SASE required.

Northern Regional Justice Court 714 S Beeline Hwy, #103, Payson, AZ 85541; phone: 928-474-5267; fax: 928-474-6214; hours 8AM-5PM (MST). *Misdemeanor, Civil Actions Under $10,000, Eviction, Small Claims.*
Note: This court holds the records for the Pine Justice Court which is closed.
Civil Records: Access: Fax, mail, in person, online. Only the court performs in person searches; visitors may not. Search fee: $17.00 per name. Court makes copy: $.50 per page. Required to search: name, years to search; also helpful: address. Civil cases indexed by party names; defendant and plaintiff. Civil records on computer since 1992. Records on dockets. Will retain criminal and civil for 5 years. Access to records is free at www.supreme.state.az.us/publicaccess/. Mail turnaround time 10 days.
Criminal Records: Access: Phone, fax, mail, in person, online. Only the court performs in person searches; visitors may not. Search fee: $17.00 per name. Court makes copy: $.50 per page. Required to search: name, years to search, DOB; also helpful: address, SSN. Criminal records on computer since 1992. Records on dockets. Will retain criminal and civil for 5 years. Access to records is free at www.supreme.state.az.us/publicaccess/. Mail turnaround time 10 days.
General Information: No public access terminal. No juvenile, mental health, victims, sealed or adoption records released. Will not fax documents. Certification fee: $17.00 per doc includes copy fee. Payee: Payson Justice Court. No personal checks accepted. Prepayment and SASE required.

Southern Regional Justice Court

Globe/Miami Magistrate Court, 1400 E Ash, Globe, AZ 85501; phone: 928-425-3231 x8545; fax: 928-425-4773; hours 8AM-5PM (MST). *Misdemeanor, Civil Actions Under $10,000, Eviction, Small Claims.*
Note: This courts holds the records for the justice courts formerly located in Miami and Hayden/Winkelman.
Civil Records: Access: Mail, fax, in person, online. Both court and visitors may perform in person searches. Search fee: $17.00 per name. Court makes copy: $.50 per page. Required to search: name, years to search. Civil cases indexed by defendant, plaintiff. Civil records on computer from 1997. Some records on dockets. Will retain criminal and civil for 5 years. Access to records is free at www.supreme.state.az.us/publicaccess/. Mail turnaround time 2-4 days.
Criminal Records: Access: Mail, fax, in person, online. Both court and visitors may perform in person searches. Search fee: $17.00 per name. Court makes copy: $.50 per page. Required to search: name, years to search; also helpful: SSN, DOB, signed release. Criminal records on computer from 1997. Some records on dockets. Will retain criminal and civil for 5 years. Access to records is free at www.supreme.state.az.us/publicaccess/. Mail turnaround time 2-4 days.
General Information: Public access terminal goes back to 1997. (The public access terminal is in the Law Library on the 1st floor.) No juvenile, mental health, victims, sealed or adoption records released. Will fax documents to local or toll free line. Certification fee: $17.00. Payee: Globe Justice Court. Business checks accepted. Prepayment and SASE required.

Winkleman Justice Court 1400 E Ash St, c/o Globe Regional Justice Court, Globe, AZ 85501-1414. *Misdemeanor, Civil Actions Under $10,000, Eviction, Small Claims.*
Note: Now part of the Globe Regional Justice Court.

Graham County

Superior Court 800 Main St, Safford, AZ 85546-3803; phone: 928-428-3100; criminal records fax: 928-428-0061; same fax for civil and probate; hours 8AM-5PM (MST). *Felony, Civil Actions Over $5,000, Probate.*
Civil Records: Access: Fax, mail, in person, online. Both court and visitors may perform in person searches. Search fee: $18.00 per name. Court makes copy: $.50 per page; same fee for self serve. Required to search: name, years to search. Civil cases indexed by defendant, plaintiff. Civil records on dockets. Access to records is free at www.supreme.state.az.us/publicaccess/. Mail turnaround time 3 days minimum.
Criminal Records: Access: Phone, fax, mail, in person, online. Both court and visitors may perform in person searches. Search fee: $18.00 per name per year. Court makes copy: $.50 per page; same fee for self serve. Required to search: name, years to search. Criminal records on dockets. Access to records is free at www.supreme.state.az.us/publicaccess/. Mail turnaround time 3 days minimum.
General Information: Public access terminal goes back to 9/1995. No mental health, victims, sealed or adoption records released. Will fax documents for $5.00. Certification fee: $18.00 per document includes copy fee. Payee: Clerk of Superior Court. Personal checks accepted. Prepayment and SASE required.

Justice Court Precinct #1 800 W Main St, Safford, AZ 85546; phone: 928-428-1210; fax: 928-428-3523; hours 8AM-5PM (MST). *Misdemeanor, Civil Actions Under $10,000, Eviction.*
Civil Records: Access: Mail, in person, online. Both court and visitors may perform in person searches. Search fee: $17.00 per name. Court makes copy: $.50 per page. Required to search: name, years to search; also helpful: address. Civil cases indexed by case number. Civil records on computer from 1995, on

dockets prior. Access to records is free at www.supreme.state.az.us/publicaccess/. Mail turnaround time 3-4 days.
Criminal Records: Access: Mail, in person, online. Both court and visitors may perform in person searches. Search fee: $17.00 per name. Court makes copy: $.50 per page. Required to search: name, years to search, DOB; also helpful: address, SSN. Criminal records on computer from 1995, on dockets prior. Access to records is free at www.supreme.state.az.us/publicaccess/. Mail turnaround time 2-3 days.
General Information: No public access terminal. No juvenile, mental health, victims, sealed or adoption records released. Will fax documents to local or toll free line. Certification fee: $17.00 per doc includes copy fee. Payee: Safford Justice Court. Only cashiers checks and money orders accepted. VISA/MC/Discover accepted. Prepayment and SASE required.

Pima Justice Court Precinct #2 PO Box 1159, 136 W Center St, Pima, AZ 85543; phone: 928-485-2771; fax: 928-485-9961; hours 8AM-5PM (MST). *Misdemeanor, Civil Actions Under $10,000, Eviction, Small Claims.*
www.supreme.state.az.us
Note: They also handle criminal traffic.
Civil Records: Access: Fax, mail, in person, online. Both court and visitors may perform in person searches. Search fee: $17.00 per name. Court makes copy: $.50; same fee for self serve. Required to search: name, years to search; also helpful: address, docket number. Civil cases indexed by defendant. Civil records on dockets back to 1985; on computer back to 1995. Retained for 5 years. Access to records is free at www.supreme.state.az.us/publicaccess/. Mail turnaround time 2 weeks.
Criminal Records: Access: Fax, mail, in person, online. Both court and visitors may perform in person searches. Search fee: $17.00 per name. Court makes copy: $.50; same fee for self serve. Required to search: name, years to search, DOB; also helpful: address, SSN, docket number. Criminal records on dockets back to 1985; on computer back to 1995. Retained for 5 years. Access to records is free at www.supreme.state.az.us/publicaccess/. Mail turnaround time 2 weeks.
General Information: No public access terminal. No juvenile, mental health, victims, sealed or adoption records released. Will fax documents $17.00 per doc. Certification fee: $17.00. Payee: Graham Justice Court. Credit cards, cashiers checks and money orders accepted. Prepayment and SASE required.

Greenlee County

Superior Court PO Box 1027, Clifton, AZ 85533; phone: 928-865-4242; fax: 928-865-5358; hours 8AM-5PM (MST). *Felony, Civil Actions Over $5,000, Probate.*
Civil Records: Access: Mail, in person, online. Both court and visitors may perform in person searches. Search fee: $18.00 per name per year. Court makes copy: $.50 per page. Required to search: name, years to search. Civil cases indexed by defendant, plaintiff. Civil records in docket books from 1911; on computer from 12/97. Access to records is free at www.supreme.state.az.us/publicaccess/. Mail turnaround time 3 days.
Criminal Records: Access: Mail, in person, online. Both court and visitors may perform in person searches. Search fee: $18.00 per name per year. Court makes copy: $.50 per page. Required to search: name, years to search. Criminal records on computer since 12/97; on books from 1911. Access to records is free at www.supreme.state.az.us/publicaccess/. Mail turnaround time 7 days.
General Information: No public access terminal. No adoptions released. Will fax documents to local or toll free line. Certification fee: $18.00. Payee: Clerk of Superior Court. Personal checks accepted. Prepayment and SASE required.

Justice Court Precinct #1 PO Box 517, Clifton, AZ 85533; phone: 928-865-4312; fax: 928-865-5644; hours 9AM-5PM (MST). *Misdemeanor, Civil Actions Under $10,000, Eviction, Small Claims.*
Civil Records: Access: Mail, in person, online. Only the court performs in person searches; visitors may not. Search fee: $17.00 per name. No copy fee.Required to search: name, years to search. Civil cases indexed by defendant, plaintiff. Civil records in docket books. Access to records is free at www.supreme.state.az.us/publicaccess/. Mail turnaround time 1 week.
Criminal Records: Access: Mail, in person, online. Only the court performs in person searches; visitors may not. Search fee: $17.00 per name. No copy fee.Required to search: name, years to search; also helpful: DOB, SSN. Criminal records in docket books. Access to records is free at www.supreme.state.az.us/publicaccess/. Mail turnaround time 1 week.
General Information: No public access terminal. No juvenile, sealed, victims, mental health or adoption records released. Certification fee: $17.00 per doc includes copies. Payee: Justice of the Peace. Only cashiers checks and money orders accepted. Prepayment required. SASE not required.

Justice Court Precinct #2 PO Box 208, Duncan, AZ 85534; phone: 928-359-2536; fax: 928-359-1936; hours 9AM-5PM (MST). *Misdemeanor, Civil Actions Under $10,000, Eviction, Small Claims.*
Civil Records: Access: Mail, in person, online. Both court and visitors may perform in person searches. Search fee: $17.00 per name. Court makes copy: $.50 per page; same fee for self serve. Required to search: name, years to search. Civil cases indexed by defendant, plaintiff. Civil records on computer since 1996. Documents retained for 5 years. Access to records is free at www.supreme.state.az.us/publicaccess/. Mail turnaround time 2 days.
Criminal Records: Access: Mail, in person, online. Both court and visitors may perform in person searches. Search fee: $17.00 per name. Court makes copy: $.50 per page; same fee for self serve. Required to search: name, years to search. Criminal Records computerized since 1996. Access to records is free at www.supreme.state.az.us/publicaccess/. Mail turnaround time 2 days.
General Information: Public access terminal goes back to 1996-97. No juvenile, victims, sealed, mental health or adoption records released. Will fax documents for no fee. Certification fee: $17.00 per doc. Payee: Justice Court. Personal checks not accepted. Prepayment required.

La Paz County

Superior Court 1316 Kofa Ave, #607, Parker, AZ 85344; phone: 928-669-6131; hours 8AM-5PM (MST). *Felony, Civil Actions Over $5,000, Probate.* www.co.la-paz.az.us/courts.htm
Civil Records: Access: Mail, in person, online. Both court and visitors may perform in person searches. Search fee: $18.00 per name per year. Court makes copy: $.50 per page. Required to search: name, years to search; also helpful: address. Civil cases indexed by defendant, plaintiff. Civil records computerized since 1996, to 1983 on docket books. For records prior to 1983, check with Yuma County Superior Court. Access to records is free at www.supreme.state.az.us/publicaccess/. Mail turnaround time 2-3 days.
Criminal Records: Access: Mail, in person, online. Both court and visitors may perform in person searches. Search fee: $18.00 per name per year. Court makes copy: $.50 per page. Required to search: name, years to search; also helpful: address, DOB, SSN. Criminal records computerized since 1996, to 1983 on docket books. For records prior to 1983, check with Yuma County Superior Court. Access to records is free at www.supreme.state.az.us/publicaccess/. Mail turnaround time 2-3 days.

General Information: No public access terminal. No dependency or adoption records released. Will fax documents for certification fee. Certification fee: $18.00 per document. Payee: Clerk of Superior Court. Business checks accepted. Prepayment and SASE required.

Parker Justice Court 1105 Arizona Ave, Parker, AZ 85344; phone: 928-669-2504; fax: 928-669-2915; hours 8AM-5PM (MST). *Misdemeanor, Civil Actions Under $10,000, Eviction, Small Claims.*
Civil Records: Access: Mail, in person, online. Only the court performs in person searches; visitors may not. Search fee: $17.00. Court makes copy: $.50 per page. Required to search: name, years to search; also helpful: address. Civil cases indexed by defendant. Civil records on dockets back to 1800s, computerized since 1996. Access to records is free at www.supreme.state.az.us/publicaccess/. Mail turnaround time 2-3 weeks.
Criminal Records: Access: Mail, in person, online. Only the court performs in person searches; visitors may not. Search fee: $17.00. Court makes copy: $.50 per page. Required to search: name, years to search, DOB; also helpful: address, SSN. Criminal records on dockets back to 1800s, computerized since 1996. Access to records is free at www.supreme.state.az.us/publicaccess/. Mail turnaround time 2-3 weeks.
General Information: No public access terminal. No juvenile, mental health, victims or sealed records released. Certification fee: $17.00 per doc. Payee: Clerk of Justice Court. Only cashiers checks and money orders accepted. Prepayment and SASE required.

Quartzsite Justice Court PO Box 580, Quartzsite, AZ 85346; phone: 928-927-6313; fax: 928-927-4842; 8AM-5PM (MST). *Misdemeanor, Civil Actions Under $10,000, Eviction, Small Claims.*
Civil Records: Access: Fax, mail, in person, online. Both court and visitors may perform in person searches. Search fee: $17.00 per name/year. Court makes copy: $.50 per page. Required to search: name, years to search. Civil cases indexed by defendant, plaintiff. Civil records computerized since 7/96. Files retained for 5 yrs after final disposition. Access to records is free at www.supreme.state.az.us/publicaccess/. Mail turnaround time within 3 weeks.
Criminal Records: Access: Fax, mail, in person, online. Both court and visitors may perform in person searches. Search fee: $17.00 per name. Court makes copy: $.50 per page. Required to search: name, years to search, date of offense; also helpful: DOB, SSN, offense. Criminal records computerized since 7/96. Files retained for 5 yrs after final disposition. Access to records is free at www.supreme.state.az.us/publicaccess/. Mail turnaround time within 3 weeks.
General Information: No public access terminal. No juvenile, mental health, victims, sealed or adoption records released. Will fax documents to local or toll-free number. Certification fee: $17.00 per doc includes copies. Payee: Quartsite Justice Court. Only cashiers checks and money orders accepted. Prepayment and SASE required.

Salome Justice Court PO Box 661, Salome, AZ 85348; phone: 928-859-3871; fax: 928-859-3709; hours 8AM-5PM (MST). *Misdemeanor, Civil Actions Under $10,000, Eviction, Small Claims.*
Civil Records: Access: Mail, in person, online. Only the court performs in person searches; visitors may not. Search fee: $17.00. Court makes copy: $.50 per page. Required to search: name, years to search; also helpful: address. Civil cases indexed by defendant. Civil records on dockets from mid-1960s. Records destroyed after 5 years. Computerized back to 1996. Access to records is free at www.supreme.state.az.us/publicaccess/. Mail turnaround time 2-3 days.
Criminal Records: Access: Mail, in person, online. Only the court performs in person searches;

visitors may not. Search fee: $17.00. Court makes copy: $.50 per page. Required to search: name, years to search, DOB; also helpful: address, SSN. Criminal records on dockets from mid-1960s. Records destroyed after 5 years. Computerized back to 1996. Access to records is free at www.supreme.state.az.us/publicaccess/. Mail turnaround time 2-3 days.
General Information: No public access terminal. No juvenile, mental health, victims, sealed or adoption records released. Certification fee: $17.00 per doc. Payee: Salome Justice Court. Only cashiers checks and money orders accepted. Prepayment required. SASE not required.

Maricopa County

Superior Court Correspondence, 201 W Jefferson, Phoenix, AZ 85003; phone: 602-506-3360; fax: 602-506-7619; hours 8AM-5PM (MST). *Felony, Civil Actions Over $5,000, Probate.* www.superiorcourt.maricopa.gov
Note: Physical address is 601 W Jackson St.

Civil Records: Access: Fax, mail, online, in person. Both court and visitors may perform in person searches. Search fee: $18.00 per name. Court makes copy: $.50 per page. Required to search: name, years to search. Civil cases indexed by defendant, plaintiff. Civil records on computer from 7/87, on microfiche from 1969 to present. Some records on docket books. Access to civil case dockets free at www.superiorcourt.maricopa.gov/docket/index.asp Case file can be printed. Also, access to probate court dockets is at www.superiorcourt.maricopa.gov/docket/probate/index.asp. Family court filings at www.superiorcourt.maricopa.gov/docket/family/index.asp Mail turnaround time 2 weeks.
Criminal Records: Access: Fax, mail, online, in person. Both court and visitors may perform in person searches. Search fee: $18.00 per name. Court makes copy: $.50 per page. Required to search: name, years to search; also helpful: DOB. Criminal records on computer from 7/87, on microfiche from 1969 to present. Some records on docket books. Access to criminal case dockets is free at www.superiorcourt.maricopa.gov/docket/criminal/index.asp. Mail turnaround time 2 weeks.
General Information: Public access terminal goes back to 7/1987. No mental health, victims, sealed or adoption records released. Will fax documents $5.00 plus $.50 per page. Certification fee: $18.00 per doc. Payee: Clerk of Superior Court. Personal checks, Visa/MC accepted. Prepayment required. SASE not required.

Buckeye Justice Court 100 N Apache Rd, Buckeye, AZ 85326; phone: 623-386-4222; fax: 623-386-5796; hours 8AM-5PM (MST). *Misdemeanor, Civil Actions Under $10,000, Eviction, Small Claims.*
Civil Records: Access: Mail, in person. Only the court performs in person searches; visitors may not. Search fee: $17.00 per name. Court makes copy: $.50 per page. Required to search: name, years to search. Civil cases indexed by defendant, plaintiff. Civil records on dockets by number, computerized since 1990. Mail turnaround time 1-2 weeks.
Criminal Records: Access: Mail, in person. Only the court performs in person searches; visitors may not. Search fee: $17.00 per name. Court makes copy: $.50 per page. Required to search: name, years to search, DOB. Criminal records on dockets by number, computerized since 1990. Mail turnaround time 1-2 weeks.
General Information: No public access terminal. No juvenile, mental health, victims, sealed or adoption records released. Will fax documents to local or toll free line. Certification fee: $17.00. Payee: Buckeye Justice Court. Personal checks or Visa, MC accepted. Prepayment and SASE required.

Central Phoenix Justice Court 1 W Madison St, Phoenix, AZ 85003; phone: 602-254-1488; fax: 602-254-1496; hours 8AM-5PM (MST). *Misdemeanor, Civil Actions Under $10,000, Eviction, Small Claims.*

Civil Records: Access: Phone, fax, mail, in person. Visitors must perform in person searches themselves. Search fee: $17.00 per name. Court makes copy: $.50 per page. Required to search: name, years to search. Civil cases indexed by defendant, plaintiff. Civil records on computer since 1985. Mail turnaround time 1-2 weeks.

Criminal Records: Access: Mail, fax, in person. Visitors must perform in person searches themselves. Search fee: $17.00 per name. Court makes copy: $.50 per page. Required to search: name, years to search, DOB, SSN. Criminal records on computer back to 1985. Mail turnaround time 1-2 weeks.

General Information: Public access terminal available. (Allows public access to electronic Justice Courts countywide.) No sealed records released. Certification fee: $17.00. Payee: Central Phoenix Justice Court. Personal checks accepted with DL. Visa, MC accepted. Prepayment and SASE required.

Chandler Justice Court 2051 W Warner Rd, #20, Chandler, AZ 85224; phone: 480-963-6691; fax: 480-786-6210; hours 8AM-5PM (MST). *Misdemeanor, Civil Actions Under $10,000, Eviction, Small Claims.*

Civil Records: Access: Mail, in person. Only the court performs in person searches; visitors may not. Search fee: $17.00 per name. Court makes copy: $.50 per page; same fee for self serve. Required to search: name, years to search; also helpful: address. Civil records on dockets by number; records go back 5 years; on computer back to 1991. Mail turnaround time 1-2 weeks.

Criminal Records: Access: Mail, in person. Only the court performs in person searches; visitors may not. Search fee: $17.00 per name. Court makes copy: $.50 per page; same fee for self serve. Required to search: name, years to search, DOB; also helpful: address, SSN. Criminal records on dockets by number; records on computer go back to 1991. Mail turnaround time 1-2 weeks.

General Information: No public access terminal. No juvenile, mental health, victims, sealed or adoption records released. Certification fee: $17.00. Payee: Clerk of Justice Court. Personal checks or Visa, MC accepted. Prepayment and SASE required.

East Mesa Justice Court 4811 E Julep, #128, Mesa, AZ 85205; phone: 480-985-0188; fax: 480-396-6327; 8AM-5PM (MST). *Misdemeanor, Civil Actions Under $10,000, Eviction, Small Claims.*

Civil Records: Access: Mail, in person. Only the court performs in person searches; visitors may not. Search fee: $17.00 per name. Court makes copy: $.50 per page. Required to search: name, years to search; also helpful: address. Civil cases indexed by defendant, plaintiff. Civil records on computer since 1990. Prior records in docket books by number. Mail turnaround time 1-2 weeks.

Criminal Records: Access: Mail, in person. Only the court performs in person searches; visitors may not. Search fee: $17.00 per name. Court makes copy: $.50 per page. Required to search: name, years to search, DOB; also helpful: address, SSN. Criminal records on computer since 1990. Prior records in docket books by number. Mail turnaround time 1-2 weeks.

General Information: No public access terminal. No juvenile, mental health, victims, sealed or adoption records released. Certification fee: $17.00 per doc. Payee: East Mesa Justice Court. Personal checks or Visa, MC accepted. Prepayment and SASE required.

East Phoenix Justice Court #1 1 W Madison St, #1, Phoenix, AZ 85003; phone: 602-254-1599; fax: 602-254-1603; hours 8AM-5PM (MST). *Misdemeanor, Civil Actions Under $10,000, Eviction, Small Claims.*

Civil Records: Access: Phone, mail, in person. Visitors must perform in person searches themselves. Court makes copy: $.50 per page. Required to search: name, years to search. Civil cases indexed by defendant, plaintiff. Civil records on dockets by number; computerized records since 1990's. Mail turnaround time 1-2 weeks.

Criminal Records: Access: Phone, mail, in person. Visitors must perform in person searches themselves. Court makes copy: $.50 per page. Required to search: name, years to search, DOB. Criminal records on dockets by number; computerized records since 1990's. Mail turnaround time 1-2 weeks.

General Information: Public access terminal available. (Terminal allows access to Justice Courts countywide.) No mental health, victims or sealed records released. Certification fee: $17.00 per doc. Payee: East Phoenix #1 Justice Court. Personal checks or Visa, MC accepted. Credit cards only if paid in person. Prepayment and SASE required.

East Phoenix Justice Court #2 4109 N 12th St, Phoenix, AZ 85014; phone: 602-266-3741; fax: 602-277-9442; hours 8AM-5PM (MST). *Misdemeanor, Civil Actions Under $10,000, Eviction, Small Claims.*

Civil Records: Access: Mail, in person. Both court and visitors may perform in person searches. Search fee: $17.00 per name. Court makes copy: $.50 per page. Required to search: name, years to search. Civil cases indexed by defendant, plaintiff. Civil records on computer since 1981. Mail turnaround time same day.

Criminal Records: Access: Mail, in person. Both court and visitors may perform in person searches. Search fee: $17.00 per name. Court makes copy: $.50 per page. Required to search: name, years to search, DOB. Criminal records computerized since 1991. Mail turnaround time same day.

General Information: Public access terminal goes back to 1991. No juvenile, mental health, victims, sealed or adoption records released. Certification fee: $17.00. Payee: East Phoenix #2 Justice Court. Personal checks or Visa, MC accepted. Prepayment and SASE required.

East Tempe Justice Court 1845 E Broadway, #8, Tempe, AZ 85282; phone: 480-967-8856; fax: 480-921-7413; hours 8AM-5PM (MST). *Misdemeanor, Civil Actions Under $10,000, Eviction, Small Claims.*

Civil Records: Access: Mail, in person. Only the court performs in person searches; visitors may not. Search fee: $17.00 per name. Court makes copy: $.50 per page. Required to search: name, years to search. Civil cases indexed by defendant, plaintiff. Civil records on computer by case number.

Criminal Records: Access: Mail, in person. Only the court performs in person searches; visitors may not. Search fee: $17.00 per name. Court makes copy: $.50 per page. Required to search: name, years to search, DOB. Criminal records on computer by case number.

General Information: No public access terminal. No juvenile, mental health, victims, sealed records released. Certification fee: $17.00 per doc. Payee: Tempe Justice Court. Personal checks or Visa, MC accepted. Prepayment and SASE required.

Gila Bend Justice Court PO Box 648 (209 E Pima St), Gila Bend, AZ 85337; phone: 928-683-2651; fax: 928-683-6412; hours 8AM-5PM (MST). *Misdemeanor, Civil Actions Under $10,000, Eviction, Small Claims.*

Civil Records: Access: Mail, in person. Only the court performs in person searches; visitors may not. Search fee: $17.00 per name. Court makes copy: $.50 per page. Required to search: name, years to search. Civil cases indexed by defendant, plaintiff. Civil records on computer since 1987. Public access terminal only in main Phoenix court. Mail turnaround time 1-2 weeks.

Criminal Records: Access: Mail, in person. Only the court performs in person searches; visitors may not. Search fee: $17.00 per name. Court makes copy: $.50 per page. Required to search: name, years to search; also helpful: DOB. Criminal records on computer since 1987. Public access terminal only in main Phoenix court. Mail turnaround 1-2 weeks.

General Information: No public access terminal. No juvenile, mental health, victims, sealed or adoption records released. Certification fee: included in search fee. Payee: Gila Bend Justice Court. Personal checks or Visa, MC accepted. Prepayment & SASE required.

Glendale Justice Court 5222 W Glendale, Glendale, AZ 85301; phone: 623-939-9477; fax: 623-842-2260; hours 8AM-5PM (MST). *Misdemeanor, Civil Actions Under $10,000, Eviction, Small Claims.*

Civil Records: Access: Mail, in person. Only the court performs in person searches; visitors may not. Search fee: $17.00 per name. Court makes copy: $.50 per page. Required to search: name, years to search. Civil records on dockets by case number, computerized since 1993. Public access for all searches at Justice Court Administration, 1 W Madison St, Phoenix, in person only. Mail turnaround time 1-2 weeks.

Criminal Records: Access: Mail, in person. Only the court performs in person searches; visitors may not. Search fee: $17.00 per name. Court makes copy: $.50 per page. Required to search: name, years to search, DOB; also helpful: SSN. Criminal records on dockets by case number, computerized since 1992. Public access for all searches at Justice Court Administration, 1 W Madison, Phoenix in person only. Mail turnaround time 1-2 weeks.

General Information: No public access terminal. No juvenile, mental health, victims, sealed or adoption records released. Certification fee: $17.00 per doc. Payee: Glendale Justice Court. Personal checks or Visa, MC accepted. Prepayment and SASE required.

Maryvale Justice Court 4622 W Indian School Rd, Bldg D, Phoenix, AZ 85031; phone: 623-245-0432; fax: 623-245-1216; hours 8AM-5PM (MST). *Misdemeanor, Civil Actions Under $10,000, Eviction, Small Claims.*

Civil Records: Access: Mail, in person. Only the court performs in person searches; visitors may not. Search fee: $17.00 per name. Court makes copy: $.50 per page. Required to search: name, years to search, address. Civil records on dockets by number. Mail turnaround time 2-4 weeks.

Criminal Records: Access: Mail, in person. Only the court performs in person searches; visitors may not. Search fee: $17.00 per name. Court makes copy: $.50 per page. Required to search: name, years to search, address, DOB; also helpful: SSN, aliases. Criminal records on dockets by number. Mail turnaround time 2-4 weeks.

General Information: No public access terminal. No juvenile, mental health, victims, sealed or adoption records released. Certification fee: $17.00. Payee: Maryvale Justice Court. Personal checks or Visa, MC accepted. Prepayment and SASE required.

North Mesa Justice Court 1837 S Mesa Dr, #B-103, Mesa, AZ 85210; phone: 480-926-9731; fax: 480-926-7763; hours 8AM-5PM (MST). *Misdemeanor, Civil Actions Under $10,000, Eviction, Small Claims.*

Civil Records: Access: Fax, mail, in person. Only the court performs in person searches; visitors may not. Search fee: $17.00 per name, limit 3 names. Court makes copy: $.50 per page. Required to search: name, years to search. Civil cases indexed by defendant, plaintiff. Civil records on computer by case number. Public access terminal only in main Phoenix court. Mail turnaround time 1-2 weeks.

Criminal Records: Access: Fax, mail, in person. Only the court performs in person searches; visitors may not. Search fee: $17.00 per name, limit 3 names. Court makes copy: $.50 per page. Required to search: name, years to search, offense; also helpful: DOB. Criminal records on computer by case number. Public access terminal only in main Phoenix court. Mail turnaround time 1-2 weeks.

General Information: No public access terminal. No juvenile, mental health, victims or sealed records released. No fee to fax documents. Certification fee: $17.00 per doc. Payee: North Mesa Justice Court. Personal checks or Visa, MC accepted. Prepayment and SASE required.

North Valley Justice Court 5222 W Glendale, Glendale, AZ 85301; phone: 623-915-2877; fax: 623-463-0670; hours 8AM-5PM (MST). *Misdemeanor, Civil Actions Under $10,000, Eviction, Small Claims.*

Civil Records: Access: Mail, in person. Only the court performs in person searches; visitors may not. Search fee: $17.00 per name. Court makes copy: $.50 per page. Required to search: name, years to search. Civil records on dockets by case number; on computer back to 1999. Public access for all searches at Justice Court Administration, 1 W Madison St, Phoenix in person only. Mail turnaround time 1-2 weeks.

Criminal Records: Access: Mail, in person. Only the court performs in person searches; visitors may not. Search fee: $17.00 per name. Court makes copy: $.50 per page. Required to search: name, years to search, DOB; also helpful: SSN. Criminal records on dockets by case number; on computer back to 1999. Public access for all searches at Justice Court Administration, 1 W Madison, Phoenix in person only. Mail turnaround time 1-2 weeks.

General Information: No public access terminal. No juvenile, mental health, victims, sealed or adoption records released. Certification fee: $17.00 per doc. Payee: North Valley Justice Court. Personal checks or Visa, MC accepted. Prepayment and SASE required.

Northeast Phoenix Justice Court 10255 N 32nd St, Phoenix, AZ 85028; phone: 602-494-0620; fax: 602-953-2315; hours 8AM-5PM (MST). *Misdemeanor, Civil Actions Under $10,000, Eviction, Small Claims.*

Civil Records: Access: Mail, in person. Only the court performs in person searches; visitors may not. Search fee: $17.00 per name; no fee if records are onsite. Court makes copy: $.50 per page. Required to search: name, years to search; also helpful: address. Civil cases indexed by defendant, plaintiff. Civil records on computer since 1993. Records on dockets by name and case number. Mail turnaround time 1-2 weeks.

Criminal Records: Access: Phone, mail, in person. Only the court performs in person searches; visitors may not. Search fee: $17.00 per name; no fee if records are onsite. Court makes copy: $.50 per page. Required to search: name, years to search, DOB; also helpful: address, SSN. Criminal records on dockets by name & case number. Mail turnaround 1-2 weeks.

General Information: No public access terminal. No juvenile, mental health, victims, sealed or adoption records released. Certification fee: $17.00 per doc. Payee: Clerk of Justice Court-Northeast. Visa/MC accepted. Personal checks accepted for civil filings; for traffic: cashier's check or MO only. Prepayment and SASE required.

Northwest Phoenix Justice Court 8230 E Butherus Dr, Scottsdale, AZ 85260; phone: 602-395-0293; fax: 602-678-4508; hours 8AM-5PM (MST). *Misdemeanor, Civil Actions Under $10,000, Eviction, Small Claims.*

Note: This court is co-located with the Scottsdale Justice Court.

Civil Records: Access: Mail, in person. Only the court performs in person searches; visitors may not. Search fee: $17.00 per name. Court makes copy: $.50 per page. Required to search: name, years to search. Civil cases indexed by defendant, plaintiff. Civil records on dockets. Will retain criminal and civil for 5 years; computerized records since 1987. Mail turnaround time 1 week.

Criminal Records: Access: Mail, in person. Only the court performs in person searches; visitors may not. Search fee: $17.00 per name. Court makes copy: $.50 per page. Required to search: name, years to search. Criminal records on dockets. Will retain

criminal and civil for 5 years; computerized records since 1987. Mail turnaround time 1 week.

General Information: No public access terminal. Certification fee: $17.00 per doc. Payee: Northwest Phoenix Justice Court. Personal checks or Visa, MC accepted. Prepayment and SASE required.

Peoria Justice Court 11601 N 19th Ave, Phoenix, AZ 85029; phone: 602-395-0294; fax: 602-997-1677; hours 8AM-5PM (MST). *Misdemeanor, Civil Actions Under $10,000, Eviction, Small Claims.*
www.superiorcourt.maricopa.gov/justiceCourts

Civil Records: Access: Phone, mail, in person. Only the court performs in person searches; visitors may not. Search fee: $17.00 per name. Court makes copy: $.50 per page. Required to search: name, years to search. Civil cases indexed by defendant, plaintiff. Civil records on computer by case number. Mail turnaround time 1-2 weeks.

Criminal Records: Access: Phone, mail, in person. Only the court performs in person searches; visitors may not. Search fee: $17.00 per name. Court makes copy: $.50 per page. Required to search: name, years to search; also helpful: DOB. Criminal records on computer by case number. Mail turnaround time 1-2 weeks.

General Information: No public access terminal. No juvenile, mental health, victims, sealed or adoption records released. Will fax documents to 602, 480, 623 area codes only- $1.25 per page. Certification fee: $17.00 per doc. Payee: Peoria Justice Court. Personal checks or Visa, MC accepted. Prepayment and SASE required.

Scottsdale Justice Court 8230 E Butherus Dr, Scottsdale, AZ 85260; phone: 480-443-6600; fax: 480-443-5981; hours 8AM-5PM (MST). *Misdemeanor, Civil Actions Under $10,000, Eviction, Small Claims.*

Civil Records: Access: Phone, mail, in person. Only the court performs in person searches; visitors may not. Search fee: $17.00 per name. Court makes copy: $.50 per page. Required to search: name, years to search. Civil cases indexed by defendant, plaintiff. Civil records on computer since 1985. Records kept for 5 years on closed cases. Mail turnaround time 2-3 weeks.

Criminal Records: Access: Phone, mail, in person. Only the court performs in person searches; visitors may not. Search fee: $17.00 per name. Court makes copy: $.50 per page. Required to search: name, years to search. Criminal records on computer since 1985. Records kept for 5 years on closed cases. Mail turnaround time 2-3 weeks.

General Information: No public access terminal. No juvenile, mental health, victims, sealed or adoption records released. Certification fee: $17.00 per doc. Payee: Scottsdale Justice Court. Personal checks or Visa, MC accepted. Prepayment and SASE required.

South Mesa/Gilbert Justice Court 55 E Civic Center Dr, #102, Gilbert, AZ 85296-3468; phone: 480-926-3051; fax: 480-545-1638; hours 8AM-5PM (MST). *Misdemeanor, Civil Actions Under $10,000, Eviction, Small Claims.*

Civil Records: Access: Mail, in person. Only the court performs in person searches; visitors may not. Search fee: $17.00 per name. Court makes copy: $.50 per page. Required to search: name, years to search, DOB, SSN, signed release. Civil cases indexed by defendant, plaintiff. Civil records on computer by case number back to 1994. Public access terminal at Justice Court Administration 1 W Madison St, Phoenix, AZ. Mail turnaround time 1-2 weeks.

Criminal Records: Access: Mail, in person. Only the court performs in person searches; visitors may not. Search fee: $17.00 per name. Court makes copy: $.50 per page. Required to search: name, years to search, DOB, SSN, signed release. Criminal records on computer by case number; computerized back to 1994. Public access terminal at Justice Court Administration 1 West Madison, Phoenix, AZ. Mail turnaround time 1-2 weeks.

General Information: No public access terminal. No juvenile, mental health, victims, sealed or adoption records released. Certification fee: $17.00 per doc. Payee: South Mesa/Gilbert Justice Court. Only cashiers checks and money orders accepted. Prepayment and SASE required.

South Phoenix Justice Court 217 E Olympic Dr, Phoenix, AZ 85040; phone: 602-243-0318; fax: 602-243-6389; hours 8AM-5PM (MST). *Misdemeanor, Civil Actions Under $10,000, Eviction, Small Claims.*

Civil Records: Access: In person only. Visitors must perform in person searches themselves. Court makes copy: $.50 per page. Required to search: name, years to search; also helpful: address. Civil cases indexed by defendant, plaintiff. Civil records on computer since 1990, on dockets by number.

Criminal Records: Access: In person only. Visitors must perform in person searches themselves. Court makes copy: $.50 per page. Required to search: name, years to search; also helpful: DOB. Criminal records on dockets by number.

General Information: Public access terminal available. No juvenile, mental health, victims, sealed or adoption records released. Certification fee: $17.00. Payee: South Phoenix Justice Court. Personal checks or Visa, MC accepted. Prepayment required.

Tolleson Justice Court 9550 W Van Buren, #6, Tolleson, AZ 85353; phone: 623-936-1449; fax: 623-936-4859; hours 8AM-5PM (MST). *Misdemeanor, Civil Actions Under $10,000, Eviction, Small Claims.*

Civil Records: Access: Mail, in person. Only the court performs in person searches; visitors may not. Search fee: $17.00 per name. Court makes copy: $.50 per page. Required to search: name, years to search; also helpful: address. Civil cases indexed by defendant, plaintiff. Civil records on computer since 1993. Mail turnaround time 1-2 weeks.

Criminal Records: Access: Mail, in person. Only the court performs in person searches; visitors may not. Search fee: $17.00 per name. Court makes copy: $.50 per page. Required to search: name, years to search, DOB; also helpful: address, SSN. Criminal records on computer since 1993. Mail turnaround time 1-2 weeks.

General Information: No public access terminal. No juvenile, mental health, victims, sealed or adoption records released. Certification fee: $17.00 per doc. Payee: Tolleson Justice Court. Personal checks or Visa, MC accepted. Prepayment and SASE required.

West Mesa Justice Court 2050 W University Dr, Mesa, AZ 85201; phone: 480-964-2958; fax: 480-969-1098; hours 8AM-5PM (MST). *Misdemeanor, Civil Actions Under $10,000, Eviction, Small Claims.*

Civil Records: Access: Mail, in person. Only the court performs in person searches; visitors may not. Search fee: $17.00 per name. Court makes copy: $.50 per page. Required to search: name, years to search. Civil cases indexed by defendant, plaintiff. Civil records on computer since 1990 by case number.

Criminal Records: Access: Mail, in person. Only the court performs in person searches; visitors may not. Search fee: $17.00 per name. Court makes copy: $.50 per page. Required to search: name, years to search, DOB; also helpful: SSN. Criminal records on computer since 1990 by case number.

General Information: No public access terminal. No juvenile, mental health, victims, sealed or adoption records released. Certification fee: $17.00 per doc. Payee: West Mesa Justice Court. Personal checks or Visa, MC accepted. Prepayment required.

West Phoenix Justice Court 1 W Madison St, Phoenix, AZ 85003; phone: 602-256-0292; fax: 602-256-7959; hours 8AM-5PM (MST). *Misdemeanor, Civil Actions Under $10,000, Eviction, Small Claims.*

Civil Records: Access: Mail, in person. Both court and visitors may perform in person searches. Search fee: $17.00 per name. Court makes copy: $.50

per page. Required to search: name, years to search. Civil cases indexed by defendant, plaintiff. Civil records on computer since 1993.

Criminal Records: Access: In person. Both court and visitors may perform in person searches. Search fee: $17.00 per name. Court makes copy: $.50 per page. Required to search: name, years to search, DOB. Criminal records on computer by case number. Mail turnaround time 1-2 days

General Information: Public access terminal available. No juvenile, mental health, victims, sealed or adoption records released. Certification fee: $17.00. Payee: West Phoenix Justice Court. Personal checks or Visa, MC accepted. Prepayment and SASE required.

West Tempe Justice Court 8240 S Kyrene Rd, #113, Bldg A, Tempe, AZ 85284; phone: 480-705-7349; fax: 480-785-4577; hours 8AM-5PM (MST). *Misdemeanor, Civil Actions Under $10,000, Eviction, Small Claims.*

Civil Records: Access: Mail, in person. Only the court performs in person searches; visitors may not. No search fee. Court makes copy: $.50 per page. Required to search: name, years to search. Civil cases indexed by defendant, plaintiff. Civil records on computer by case number.

Criminal Records: Access: Mail, in person. Only the court performs in person searches; visitors may not. No search fee. Court makes copy: $.50 per page. Required to search: name, years to search, DOB. Criminal records on computer by case number.

General Information: No public access terminal. No juvenile, mental health, victims, sealed records released. Certification fee: $17.00. Payee: Tempe West Justice Court. Personal checks or Visa, MC accepted. Prepayment and SASE required.

Wickenburg Justice Court 155 N Tegner, #D, Wickenburg, AZ 85390; phone: 602-506-1554; fax: 928-684-9639; hours 8AM-5PM (MST). *Misdemeanor, Civil Actions Under $10,000, Eviction, Small Claims.*

Note: Town Court telephone number is 928-684-5451.

Civil Records: Access: Mail, in person. Only the court performs in person searches; visitors may not. Search fee: $17.00 per name. Court makes copy: $.50 per page. Required to search: name, years to search; also helpful: address. Civil cases indexed by defendant, plaintiff. Civil records on computer since 1994. Mail turnaround time 1-2 weeks.

Criminal Records: Access: Mail, in person. Only the court performs in person searches; visitors may not. Search fee: $17.00 per name. Court makes copy: $.50 per page. Required to search: name, years to search, DOB; also helpful: SSN. Criminal records on computer by name and case number. Mail turnaround time 1-2 weeks.

General Information: No public access terminal. No juvenile, mental health, victims, sealed records released. Certification fee: $17.00 per doc. Payee: Wickenburg Justice Court. Personal checks or Visa, MC accepted. Prepayment and SASE required.

Mohave County

Superior Court PO Box 7000, Kingman, AZ 86402-7000; phone: 928-753-0713; fax: 928-753-0781; hours 8AM-5PM (MST). *Felony, Civil Actions Over $5,000, Probate.*

www.mohavecourts.com

Civil Records: Access: Phone, fax, mail, in person. Both court and visitors may perform in person searches. Search fee: $18.00 per name. Fee is per source. Court makes copy: $.50 per page; same fee for self serve. Required to search: name, years to search. Civil cases indexed by defendant, plaintiff. Civil records on computer since 11/95; prior records on microfiche and index books. Mail turnaround time 3 days.

Criminal Records: Access: Phone, fax, mail, in person. Both court and visitors may perform in person searches. Search fee: $18.00 per name per yr. Court makes copy: $.50 per page; same fee for self

serve. Required to search: name, years to search; also helpful: DOB, SSN. Criminal records on computer since 11/95; prior records on microfiche and index books. Mail turnaround time 3 days.

General Information: Public access terminal goes back to 1995. No juvenile, mental health, victims, sealed or adoption records released. Will fax documents for $18.00. Certification fee: $18.00 per cert. Payee: Clerk of Superior Court. Business checks accepted. Prepayment and SASE required.

Bullhead City Justice Court 2225 Trane Rd, Bullhead City, AZ 86442; phone: 928-758-0709 x2015; fax: 928-758-2644; hours 8AM-5PM (MST). *Misdemeanor, Civil Actions Under $10,000, Eviction, Small Claims.*

www.mohavecourts.com

Civil Records: Access: Phone, fax, mail, in person. Search fee: $17.00 per name. Court makes copy: $.50 per page. Required to search: name, years to search. Civil cases indexed by defendant, plaintiff. Civil records on computer from 1988. Some records on docket books. Records retained for 5 years. Will only search back to 1988 unless w/docket number. Mail turnaround time 2-3 days.

Criminal Records: Access: Mail, in person. Both court and visitors may perform in person searches. Search fee: $17.00 per name. Court makes copy: $.50 per page. Required to search: name, years to search; also helpful: DOB, SSN. Criminal records on computer from 1988. Some records on docket books. Records retained for 5 years. Will only search back to 1988 unless w/docket number. Mail turnaround time 2-3 days.

General Information: Public access terminal goes back to 1997. No juvenile, mental health, victims, sealed or adoption records released. Certification fee: $17.00 per doc. Payee: Bullhead City Justice Court. Personal checks accepted. Prepayment required. SASE requested.

Kingman/Cerbat Justice Court 524 W Beale St, PO Box 29, Kingman, AZ 86401-0029; phone: 928-753-0710; fax: 928-753-7840; hours 8AM-5PM (MST). *Misdemeanor, Civil Actions Under $10,000, Eviction, Small Claims.*

www.mohavecourts.com

Civil Records: Access: Phone, fax, mail, in person. Only the court performs in person searches; visitors may not. Search fee: $17.00 per name. Court makes copy: $.50 per page. Required to search: name, years to search. Civil cases indexed by defendant, plaintiff. Civil records on computer from 1988. Some records on docket books. Records retained for 5 years. Mail turnaround time 2-3 days.

Criminal Records: Access: Phone, fax, mail, in person. Only the court performs in person searches; visitors may not. Search fee: $17.00 per name. Court makes copy: $.50 per page. Required to search: name, years to search; also helpful: DOB, SSN. Criminal records on computer from 1988. Some records on docket books. Records retained for 5 years. Mail turnaround time 2-3 days.

General Information: No public access terminal. No juvenile, mental health, victims, sealed or adoption records released. Will fax documents $.50 per page. Certification fee: $17.00. Payee: Kingman/Cerbat Justice Court. Personal checks or Visa, MC accepted. Prepayment and SASE required.

Lake Havasu Consolidated Court 2001 College Dr, #148, Lake Havasu City, AZ 86403; phone: 928-453-0705; fax: 928-680-0193; hours 8AM-5PM (MST). *Misdemeanor, Civil Actions Under $10,000, Eviction, Small Claims.*

www.mohavecourts.com

Civil Records: Access: Mail, fax, in person. Only the court performs in person searches; visitors may not. Search fee: $17.00 per name. Court makes copy: $.50 per page. Required to search: name, years to search. Civil cases indexed by defendant, plaintiff. Civil records on computer from 1983. Some records on docket books. Records retained for 5 years after closed/satisfied. Mail turnaround time 3 days.

Criminal Records: Access: Fax, mail, in person. Only the court performs in person searches; visitors may not. Search fee: $17.00 per name. Court makes copy: $.50 per page. Required to search: name, years to search; also helpful: DOB. Criminal records on computer from 1983. Some records on docket books. Records retained for 5 years after closed/satisfied. Mail turnaround time 3 days.

General Information: No public access terminal. No juvenile or victims records released. Will fax non-certified documents. Certification fee: $17.00 per doc. Payee: Lake Havasu Consolidated Court. Personal checks accepted. Prepayment and SASE required.

Moccasin Justice Court HC-65, PO Box 90, Moccasin, AZ 86022; phone: 928-643-7104; fax: 928-643-6206; hours 8AM-5PM (MST). *Misdemeanor, Civil Actions Under $10,000, Eviction, Small Claims.*

www.mohavecourts.com

Note: This court is also the Magistrate Court for Colorado City.

Civil Records: Access: Mail, in person. Both court and visitors may perform in person searches. Search fee: $17.00 per name. Court makes copy: $.50 per page. Required to search: name, years to search. Civil cases indexed by defendant, plaintiff. Civil records on docket books. Records retained for 5 years. Mail turnaround time 7-14 days.

Criminal Records: Access: Mail, in person. Both court and visitors may perform in person searches. Search fee: $17.00 per name. Court makes copy: $.50 per page. Required to search: name, years to search. Criminal records on docket books. Records retained for 5 years. Mail turnaround time 14 to 30 days.

General Information: Public access terminal has criminal back to 5 years and civil back to 1 year. No juvenile, mental health, victims, sealed or adoption records released. Certification fee: $17.00. Payee: Moccasin Justice Court. Personal checks accepted. Prepayment and SASE required.

Navajo County

Superior Court PO Box 668, Holbrook, AZ 86025; phone: 928-524-4188; fax: 928-524-4261; hours 8AM-5PM (MST). *Felony, Civil Actions Over $5,000, Probate.*

Civil Records: Access: Phone, fax, mail, in person, online. Both court and visitors may perform in person searches. Search fee: $18.00 per document. Court makes copy: $.50 per page; same fee for self serve. Required to search: name, years to search. Civil cases indexed by defendant, plaintiff. Civil records on docket books, index cards and microfiche back to 1890; computerized back to 1994. Access to records is free at www.supreme.state.az.us/publicaccess/. Mail turnaround time ASAP

Criminal Records: Access: Phone, fax, mail, in person, online. Both court and visitors may perform in person searches. Search fee: $18.00 per document. Court makes copy: $.50 per page; same fee for self serve. Required to search: name, years to search; also helpful: DOB, SSN. Criminal records on docket books, index cards and microfiche back to 1890; computerized back to 1994. Access to records is free at www.supreme.state.az.us/publicaccess/. Mail turnaround time ASAP.

General Information: Public access terminal goes back to 1994. No mental health, victims, sealed or adoption records released. Fee to fax documents is $18.00. Certification fee: $18.00 per document. Payee: Clerk of Superior Court. Only cashiers checks and money orders accepted. Prepayment and SASE required.

Holbrook Justice Court PO Box 668, Holbrook, AZ 86025; phone: 928-524-4720; fax: 928-524-4725; hours 8AM-5PM (MST). *Misdemeanor, Civil Actions Under $10,000, Eviction, Small Claims.*

www.supreme.state.az.us

Civil Records: Access: Mail, in person, online. Both court and visitors may perform in person searches. Search fee: $17.00 per name. Court makes copy: $.50

per page. Required to search: name, years to search. Civil cases indexed by defendant, plaintiff. Civil records on computer since 1994. Records on dockets and index cards back for 5 years. Access to records is free at www.supreme.state.az.us/publicaccess/. Mail turnaround time 1 week.

Criminal Records: Access: Mail, in person, online. Both court and visitors may perform in person searches. Search fee: $17.00 per name. Court makes copy: $.50 per page. Required to search: name, years to search. Criminal records on computer since 1992. Records on dockets and stat books back for 5 years. Access to records is free at www.supreme.state.az.us/publicaccess/. Mail turnaround time 1 week.

General Information: Public access terminal has criminal back to 1992 and civil back to 1994. No victim names or sealed records released. Certification fee: $17.00 per doc. Payee: Holbrook Justice Court. Business checks accepted. Prepayment and SASE required.

Kayenta Justice Court PO Box 38, Kayenta, AZ 86033; phone: 928-697-3522; fax: 928-697-3528; hours 8AM-N,1-5PM (MST). *Misdemeanor, Civil Actions Under $10,000, Eviction, Small Claims.*
Note: If planning to make an in-person search, call to make an appointment.

Civil Records: Access: Mail, in person, online. Only the court performs in person searches; visitors may not. Search fee: $17.00 per name. Court makes copy: $.50 per page. Required to search: name, years to search, address. Civil cases indexed by defendant, plaintiff. Civil records on docket books and index cards; on computer back to 1994. Access to records is free at www.supreme.state.az.us/publicaccess/. Mail turnaround time 1 week.

Criminal Records: Access: Mail, in person, online. Only the court performs in person searches; visitors may not. Search fee: $17.00 per name. Court makes copy: $.50 per page. Required to search: name, years to search, address, DOB, SSN, signed release. Criminal records on docket books and index cards; on computer back to 1994. Access to records is free at www.supreme.state.az.us/publicaccess/. Mail turnaround time 1 week.

General Information: No public access terminal. No victim's names released. Certification fee: $17.00. Payee: Kayenta Justice Court. Only cashiers checks and money orders accepted. Prepayment and SASE required.

Pinetop-Lakeside Justice Court PO Box 2020, 1360 Neils Hansen Dr, Lakeside, AZ 85929; phone: 928-368-6200; fax: 928-368-8674; hours 8AM-5PM (MST). *Misdemeanor, Civil Actions Under $10,000, Eviction, Small Claims.*

Civil Records: Access: Fax, mail, in person, online. Only the court performs in person searches; visitors may not. Search fee: $17.00 per name. Court makes copy: $.50 per page. Required to search: name, years to search. Civil cases indexed by case number. Civil records on electronic dockets by case number and case files by numeric. Access to records is free at www.supreme.state.az.us/publicaccess/. Mail turnaround time 7-10 days.

Criminal Records: Access: Fax, mail, in person, online. Only the court performs in person searches; visitors may not. Search fee: $17.00 per name. Court makes copy: $.50 per page. Required to search: name, years to search. Criminal records on electronic dockets by case number and case files by alpha back to 1970. Computerized back to 1996. Access to records is free at www.supreme.state.az.us/publicaccess/. Mail turnaround time 7-10 days.

General Information: No public access terminal. No victim's names released. No fee to fax documents. Certification fee: $17.00 per doc. Payee: Pinetop-Lakeside Justice Court. Personal checks accepted. Prepayment required. SASE requested.

Show Low Justice Court PO Box 3085, 561 E Duece of Clubs, Show Low, AZ 85902-3085; phone: 928-532-6030; fax: 928-532-6035; hours 8AM-5PM (MST). *Misdemeanor, Civil Actions Under $10,000, Eviction, Small Claims.*

Civil Records: Access: Mail, in person, online. Only the court performs in person searches; visitors may not. Search fee: $17.00 per name. Court makes copy: $.50 per page. Required to search: name, years to search. Civil cases indexed by defendant, plaintiff. Civil records on computer. Access to records is free at www.supreme.state.az.us/publicaccess/. Note: In person access requires a written request. Mail turnaround time 1 week.

Criminal Records: Access: Mail, in person, online. Only the court performs in person searches; visitors may not. Search fee: $17.00 per name per year. Court makes copy: $.50 per page. Required to search: name, years to search; also helpful: DOB, SSN. Criminal records on computer for five years. Access to records is free at www.supreme.state.az.us/publicaccess/. Note: In person access requires a written request. Mail turnaround time 1 week.

General Information: No public access terminal. No victim's names released. Will fax documents if fees prepaid. Certification fee: $17.00. Payee: Show Low Justice Court. Personal checks accepted. Prepayment and SASE required.

Snowflake Justice Court 73 W 1st S, Snowflake, AZ 85937; phone: 928-536-4141; fax: 928-536-3511; hours 8AM-5PM (MST). *Misdemeanor, Civil Actions Under $10,000, Eviction, Small Claims.*

Civil Records: Access: Phone, fax, mail, in person, online. Only the court performs in person searches; visitors may not. Search fee: $17.00 per name. Court makes copy: $1.25 per page. Required to search: name, years to search. Civil cases indexed by defendant, plaintiff. Civil records on computer back to 6/96, prior on docket books and index cards. Misdemeanors, DUI's and traffic records kept for 3 years, others held for 5 years. Access to records is free at www.supreme.state.az.us/publicaccess/. Mail turnaround time 2 weeks.

Criminal Records: Access: Fax, mail, in person, online. Only the court performs in person searches; visitors may not. Search fee: $17.00 per name. Court makes copy: $1.25 per page. Required to search: name, years to search; also helpful: DOB, SSN. Criminal records on computer back to 6/96, prior on docket books and index cards. Misdemeanors, DUI's and traffic records kept for 3 years, others held for 5 years. Access to records is free at www.supreme.state.az.us/publicaccess/. Mail turnaround time 2 weeks.

General Information: No public access terminal. No victim's names or search warrants released, no juvenile records released. Certification fee: $17.00 per doc. Payee: Snowflake Justice Court. Only cashiers checks and money orders accepted. Prepayment and SASE required.

Winslow Justice Court Box 808, Winslow, AZ 86047; phone: 928-289-6840; fax: 928-289-6847; hours 8AM-5PM (MST). *Misdemeanor, Civil Actions Under $10,000, Eviction, Small Claims.*

Civil Records: Access: Fax, mail, in person, online. Only the court performs in person searches; visitors may not. Search fee: $20.00. Court makes copy: $.50 per page. Required to search: name, years to search. Civil cases indexed by defendant, plaintiff. Civil records on docket books; on computer since 1994. Access to records is free at www.supreme.state.az.us/publicaccess/. Mail turnaround time 1 week.

Criminal Records: Access: Fax, mail, in person, online. Only the court performs in person searches; visitors may not. Search fee: $20.00. Court makes copy: $.50 per page. Required to search: name, years to search; also helpful: DOB, SSN. Criminal records on docket books; on computer since 1995. Access to records is free at

www.supreme.state.az.us/publicaccess/. Mail turnaround time 1 week.

General Information: No public access terminal. No victim's names released. Will fax documents to local or toll free line. Certification fee: $20.00. Payee: Winslow Justice Court. Personal checks accepted. Prepayment and SASE required.

Pima County

Superior Court 110 W Congress, Tucson, AZ 85701; phone: 520-740-3240; fax: 520-798-3531; hours 8AM-5PM (MST). *Felony, Civil Actions Over $5,000, Probate.*
www.cosc.co.pima.az.us
Note: Address correspondence to attention of civil or criminal section.

Civil Records: Access: Phone, mail, in person, online. Both court and visitors may perform in person searches. Search fee: $18.00 per name. Court makes copy: $.50 per page. Required to search: name, years to search, DOB. Civil cases indexed by defendant, plaintiff. Civil records on computer since 1980s, on microfilm since late 1800s. Online access to superior court records is free at www.cosc.co.pima.az.us/record_search/. Mail turnaround time 14 days; include $5.00 mailing fee.

Criminal Records: Access: Mail, in person, online. Both court and visitors may perform in person searches. Search fee: $18.00 per name. Add $5.00 for postage and handling. Court makes copy: $.50 per page. Required to search: name, years to search, DOB. Criminal records on computer since 1980s, on microfilm since late 1800s. Online access to superior court records is free at www.cosc.co.pima.az.us/record_search/. Cases without dispositions are not included online. Mail turnaround time 14 days; include $5.00 mailing fee.

General Information: Public access terminal has criminal back to 1983 and civil back to 1970s. No juvenile, mental health, adoption, victims or sealed records released. Fee to fax documents is $5.00 plus $.50 per page. Certification fee: $18.00 per doc. Payee: Clerk of Superior Court. Only cashiers checks and money orders accepted. Visa, MC accepted. In person only. Prepayment required. SASE not required.

Ajo Justice Court 111 La Mina, Ajo, AZ 85321; phone: 520-387-7684; Hours: 8AM-5PM (MST). *Misdemeanor, Civil Actions Under $10,000, Eviction, Small Claims.*

Civil Records: Access: Mail, in person, online. Only the court performs in person searches; visitors may not. No search fee. Court makes copy: $.50 per page. Required to search: name, years to search. Civil cases indexed by defendant, plaintiff. Civil records on computer since 1987, prior in docket books. Access to records is free at www.supreme.state.az.us/publicaccess/. Mail turnaround time 2 weeks.

Criminal Records: Access: Mail, in person, online, fax. Only the court performs in person searches; visitors may not. Search fee: $17.00 per name. Court makes copy: $.50 per page. Required to search: name, years to search. Criminal records on computer since 1987, prior in docket books. Access to records is free at www.supreme.state.az.us/publicaccess/. Mail turnaround time 2 weeks.

General Information: No public access terminal. No juvenile, sealed, victim records released. Certification fee: $17.00 per doc. Payee: Ajo Justice Court. Personal checks accepted. Prepayment required. SASE not required.

Green Valley Justice Court 601 N LaCanada, Green Valley, AZ 85614; phone: 520-648-0658; fax: 520-648-2235; hours 8AM-5PM (MST). *Misdemeanor, Civil Actions Under $10,000, Eviction, Small Claims.*

Civil Records: Access: Mail, in person, online. Only the court performs in person searches; visitors may not. Search fee: $17.00 per name. Court makes copy:

$.50 per page. Required to search: name, years to search. Civil cases indexed by defendant, plaintiff. Civil records on computer back to 1996; card files prior. Access to records is free at www.supreme.state.az.us/publicaccess/. Note: Clerk will only search computerized records. Mail turnaround time 2 weeks.

Criminal Records: Access: Mail, in person, online. Only the court performs in person searches; visitors may not. Search fee: $17.00 per name. Court makes copy: $.50 per page. Required to search: name, years to search, DOB. Criminal records on computer back to 1996; card files prior. Access to records is free at www.supreme.state.az.us/publicaccess/. Note: Clerk will only search computerized records. Mail turnaround time 14 days.

General Information: No public access terminal. No juvenile, mental health, victims, sealed or adoption records released. Certification fee: $17.00. Payee: Green Valley Justice Court. Personal checks and credit cards accepted. Prepayment and SASE required.

Pima County Consolidated Justice Court
115 N Church Ave, Tucson, AZ 85701; phone: 520-740-3171; fax: 520-884-0346; hours 8AM-4:30PM (MST). *Misdemeanor, Civil Actions Under $10,000, Eviction, Small Claims.*
www.jp.pima.gov
Civil Records: Access: Fax, mail, online, in person. Both court and visitors may perform in person searches. Search fee: $10.00 per name. Court makes copy: $1.25 per page. Required to search: name, years to search. Civil cases indexed by defendant, plaintiff. Civil records on computer since 1988, on docket books prior. Online access is free http://jp.co.pima.az.us/casesearch/index.php. You can search docket information for civil, criminal or traffic cases by name, docket or citation number. Mail turnaround time 10 days.
Criminal Records: Access: Fax, mail, online, in person. Both court and visitors may perform in person searches. Search fee: $17.00 per name. Court makes copy: $1.25 per page. Required to search: name, years to search, DOB, SSN. Criminal records on computer since 1988, on docket books prior. Online access to criminal records is the same as civil. Mail turnaround time 10 days.
General Information: Public access terminal available. No information about set-aside judgments, unserved search warrants or felony warrants released. Certification fee: $17.00 per page. Payee: Pima County Justice Court. Personal checks or Visa, MC accepted. Visa, MC. Prepayment and SASE required.

Pinal County

Superior Court
PO Box 2730, Florence, AZ 85232-2730; phone: 520-866-5300; probate phone: same; fax: 520-866-5320; probate fax: same; hours 8AM-5PM (MST). *Felony, Civil Actions Over $5,000, Probate.*
www.co.pinal.az.us/clerksc
Civil Records: Access: Phone, mail, in person, online. Both court and visitors may perform in person searches. Search fee: $18.00 per name. Court makes copy: $.50 per page. Required to search: name, years to search. Civil cases indexed by defendant, plaintiff. Civil records on computer from 1993. Some records on docket books back to 1775. Access to records is free at www.supreme.state.az.us/publicaccess/. Mail turnaround time 7 days.
Criminal Records: Access: Phone, mail, in person, online. Both court and visitors may perform in person searches. Search fee: $18.00 per name. Court makes copy: $.50 per page. Required to search: name, years to search. Criminal records on computer from 1987. Some records on docket books back to 1875. Access to records is free at www.supreme.state.az.us/publicaccess/. Mail turnaround time 7 days.
General Information: Public access terminal has criminal back to 1987 and civil back to 1993. No

victim names, adoption records released. Fee to fax documents is $.50 per page. Certification fee: $18.00. Payee: Clerk of Superior Court. Business checks accepted. Prepayment and SASE required.

Apache Junction Justice Court
575 N Idaho, #200, Apache Junction, AZ 85219; phone: 480-982-2921; fax: 520-866-6153; hours 8AM-5PM (MST). *Misdemeanor, Civil Actions Under $10,000, Eviction, Small Claims.*
http://co.pinal.az.us/JusticeCourts/
Note: Yes, the area code for the fax number is different than the voice number.
Civil Records: Access: Fax, mail, in person, online. Both court and visitors may perform in person searches. Search fee: $17.00. Court makes copy: $.50 per page. Required to search: name, years to search. Civil cases indexed by defendant, plaintiff. Civil records on computer since 1999. Records retained for 5 years. Access to records is free at www.supreme.state.az.us/publicaccess/. Mail turnaround time varies.
Criminal Records: Access: Fax, mail, in person, online. Only the court performs in person searches; visitors may not. Search fee: $17.00. Court makes copy: $.50 per page. Required to search: name, years to search. Criminal records on computer since 1993. Records retained for 5 years. Access to records is free at www.supreme.state.az.us/publicaccess/. Mail turnaround time varies.
General Information: No public access terminal. Will fax documents $1.25 per page. Certification fee: $17.00 per doc. Payee: Apache Junction Justice Court. Personal checks accepted. Prepayment required.

Casa Grande Justice Court
820 E Cottonwood Ln, Bldg B, Casa Grande, AZ 85222; phone: 520-836-5471; fax: 520-866-7404; hours 8AM-5PM (MST). *Misdemeanor, Civil Actions Under $10,000, Eviction, Small Claims.*
http://co.pinal.az.us/JusticeCourts
Civil Records: Access: Mail, in person, online. Only the court performs in person searches; visitors may not. Search fee: $17.00 per name. Court makes copy: $.50; same fee for self serve. Required to search: name, years to search. Civil cases indexed by defendant, plaintiff. Civil records on computer since 1999, index back to 1995. Access to records is free at www.supreme.state.az.us/publicaccess/. Mail turnaround time 1 day.
Criminal Records: Access: Mail, in person, online. Only the court performs in person searches; visitors may not. Search fee: $17.00 per name. Court makes copy: $.50; same fee for self serve. Required to search: name, years to search, DOB; also helpful: SSN. Criminal records on computer since 1999, index back to 1995. Access to records is free at www.supreme.state.az.us/publicaccess/. Mail turnaround time 1 day.
General Information: No public access terminal. No juvenile, mental health, victims, sealed or adoption records released. Will fax documents. Certification fee: $17.00 includes copy fee. Payee: Casa Grande Justice Court. Business checks must be pre-approved. Visa, MC accepted. Prepayment and SASE required.

Eloy Justice Court
PO Box 586, Eloy, AZ 85231; phone: 520-466-9221; fax: 520-466-4473; hours 8AM-N, 1-5PM (MST). *Misdemeanor, Civil Actions Under $10,000, Eviction, Small Claims.*
http://co.pinal.az.us/JusticeCourts
Civil Records: Access: Mail, in person, online. Only the court performs in person searches; visitors may not. Search fee: $17.00 per name. Court makes copy: $.50 per page. Required to search: name, years to search. Civil cases indexed by defendant, plaintiff. Civil records on computer since 8/92. On docket books and index cards from 1981. Access to records is free at www.supreme.state.az.us/publicaccess/. Mail turnaround time 1-2 weeks.
Criminal Records: Access: Mail, in person, online. Only the court performs in person searches; visitors may not. Search fee: $17.00 per name. Court makes copy: $.50 per page. Required to search: name, years to search, DOB. Criminal records on computer

since 8/92. On docket books and index cards from 1981. Access to records is free at www.supreme.state.az.us/publicaccess/. Mail turnaround time 1-2 weeks.
General Information: No public access terminal. No juvenile, mental health, victims, sealed or adoption records released. Certification fee: $17.00. Payee: Eloy Justice Court. No personal checks accepted. Prepayment and SASE required.

Florence Justice Court
PO Box 1818, Florence, AZ 85232; phone: 520-866-7194; fax: 520-866-7190; hours 8AM-5PM (MST). *Misdemeanor, Civil Actions Under $10,000, Eviction, Small Claims.*
http://co.pinal.az.us/JusticeCourts
Civil Records: Access: Mail, in person, online. Only the court performs in person searches; visitors may not. Search fee: $17.00 per name. Court makes copy: $.50 per page. Required to search: name, years to search. Civil cases indexed by defendant, plaintiff. Civil records are on computer since 1/1999. Access to records is free at www.supreme.state.az.us/publicaccess/. Mail turnaround time 1 week.
Criminal Records: Access: Mail, in person, online. Only the court performs in person searches; visitors may not. Search fee: $17.00 per name. Court makes copy: $.50 per page. Required to search: name, years to search. Criminal records are on computer since 1/1999. Access to records is free at www.supreme.state.az.us/publicaccess/. Mail turnaround time 1 week.
General Information: No juvenile, mental health, victims, sealed or adoption records released. Certification fee: $17.00. Payee: Florence Justice Court. Only cashiers checks and money orders accepted. Prepayment and SASE required.

Mammoth Justice Court
PO Box 777, Mammoth, AZ 85618; phone: 520-487-2262; fax: 520-866-7839; hours 8AM-5PM (MST). *Misdemeanor, Civil Actions Under $10,000, Eviction, Small Claims.*
http://co.pinal.az.us/JusticeCourts
Civil Records: Access: Mail, fax, in person, online. Both court and visitors may perform in person searches. Search fee: $17.00 per name. Court makes copy: $.50 per page. Required to search: name, years to search. Civil cases indexed by defendant, plaintiff. Civil records on docket books. Misdemeanor and civil records retained for 7 years; on computer back 5 years. Access records free at www.supreme.state.az.us/publicaccess/. Mail turnaround time 2 days.
Criminal Records: Access: Mail, in person, online. Both court and visitors may perform in person searches. Search fee: $17.00 per name. Court makes copy: $.50 per page. Required to search: name, years to search, DOB. Criminal records on docket books. Misdemeanor and civil records retained for 7 years; on computer back 5 years. Access to records is free at www.supreme.state.az.us/publicaccess/. Mail turnaround time 2 days.
General Information: Public access terminal goes back to 5 years. No juvenile, mental health, victims, sealed or adoption records released. Will fax documents to local or toll free line. Certification fee: $17.00. Cert fee includes copies. Payee: Mammoth Justice Court. Personal checks accepted. Prepayment and SASE required.

Maricopa Justice Court
PO Box 201, 44625 W Garvey Rd, Maricopa, AZ 85239; phone: 520-568-2451; fax: 520-568-2924; hours 8AM-5PM (MST). *Misdemeanor, Civil Actions Under $10,000, Eviction, Small Claims.*
http://co.pinal.az.us/JusticeCourts
Civil Records: Access: Fax, mail, in person, online. Only the court performs in person searches; visitors may not. Search fee: $17.00 per name. Court makes copy: $.50 per page. Required to search: name, years to search. Civil cases indexed by defendant. Civil records on computer since 1999; on dockets to 1993. Access to records is free at www.supreme.state.az.us/publicaccess/. Mail turnaround time 7 days.

Criminal Records: Access: Fax, mail, in person, online. Only the court performs in person searches; visitors may not. Search fee: $17.00 per name. Court makes copy: $.50 per page. Required to search: name, years to search. Criminal records on computer since 1999; on dockets to 1993. Access to records is free at www.supreme.state.az.us/publicaccess/. Mail turnaround time 7 days.

General Information: No public access terminal. No juvenile, mental health, victims, sealed or adoption records released. Certification fee: $17.00 per doc. Payee: Maricopa Justice Court. Personal checks accepted. Prepayment and SASE required.

Oracle Justice Court PO Box 3924, Oracle, AZ 85623; phone: 520-896-9250; fax: 520-866-7812; hours 8AM-5PM (MST). *Misdemeanor, Civil Actions Under $10,000, Eviction, Small Claims, Traffic.* http://co.pinal.az.us/JusticeCourts

Civil Records: Access: Mail, in person, online. Both court and visitors may perform in person searches. Search fee: $17.00 per name. Court makes copy: $1.50 per page; same fee for self serve. Required to search: name, years to search; also helpful: address. Civil cases indexed by defendant. Civil records on docket books and computer back to 1991. Access to records is free at www.supreme.state.az.us/publicaccess/. Mail turnaround time 5 days

Criminal Records: Access: Mail, in person, online. Both court and visitors may perform in person searches. Search fee: $17.00 per name. Court makes copy: $1.50 per page; same fee for self serve. Required to search: name, years to search, DOB; also helpful: address, SSN. Criminal records on docket books and computer back to 1991. Access to records is free at www.supreme.state.az.us/publicaccess/. Mail turnaround time 5 days

General Information: Public access terminal goes back to 1991. No juvenile, mental health, victims, sealed, adoption records released. Fee to fax documents is $1.00 per page. Certification fee: $17.00. Payee: Oracle Justice Court. Personal checks not accepted; money orders, cashier's checks or cash only. Prepayment and SASE required.

Superior/Kearny Justice Court 60 E Main St, Superior, AZ 85273; phone: 520-689-5871; fax: 520-689-2369; hours 8AM-N, 1-5PM (MST). *Misdemeanor, Civil Actions Under $10,000, Eviction, Small Claims.* http://co.pinal.az.us/JusticeCourts

Civil Records: Access: Fax, mail, in person, online. Only the court performs in person searches; visitors may not. Search fee: $17.00 per name. Court makes copy: $.50 per page. Required to search: name, years to search. Civil cases indexed by defendant, plaintiff. Civil records go back 5 years; computerized records go back 5 years. Access to records is free at www.supreme.state.az.us/publicaccess/. Mail turnaround time 3 days.

Criminal Records: Access: Fax, mail, in person, online. Only the court performs in person searches; visitors may not. Search fee: $17.00 per name. Court makes copy: $.50 per page. Required to search: name, years to search, DOB; also helpful: SSN. Criminal records go back 5 years; computerized records go back 5 years. Access to records is free at www.supreme.state.az.us/publicaccess/. Mail turnaround time 3 days.

General Information: No public access terminal. No juvenile, mental health, victims, sealed or adoption records released. No fee to fax documents. Certification fee: $17.00 includes copies. Payee: Superior/Kearny Justice Court. Personal checks accepted. Prepayment and SASE required.

Santa Cruz County

Superior Court PO Box 1265, Nogales, AZ 85628; phone: 520-375-7700; criminal phone: 520-375-7703; hours 8AM-5PM (MST). *Felony, Civil Actions Over $5,000, Probate.* http://sccazcourts.org

Civil Records: Access: Mail, fax, in person, online. Both court and visitors may perform in person

searches. Search fee: $18.00 per year/source. Court makes copy: $.50 per page; same fee for self serve. Required to search: name, years to search. Civil cases indexed by defendant, plaintiff. Civil records on microfiche from 1898 to 1950. Records on docket books from 1950 to 1996; on computer after 1996. Access civil records free at www.supreme.state.az.us/publicaccess/. Mail turnaround time 10 days.

Criminal Records: Access: Mail, fax, in person, online. Both court and visitors may perform in person searches. Search fee: $18.00 per year/source. Court makes copy: $.50 per page; same fee for self serve. Required to search: name, years to search, DOB; also helpful: SSN. Criminal records archived on microfiche from 1898 to 1989. Records on docket books from 1977 to 1996; on computer after 1996. Access criminal records free at www.supreme.state.az.us/publicaccess/. Mail turnaround time 1 1/2 weeks.

General Information: Public access terminal has criminal back to 1896 and civil back to 1920. No mental health, victims, sealed or adoption records released. Fee to fax documents is $.50 per page. Certification fee: $18.00. Payee: Clerk of Superior Court. Personal checks accepted. Prepayment and SASE required.

East Santa Cruz County Justice Court - Precinct #2 PO Box 100, Patagonia, AZ 85624; phone: 520-455-5796; fax: 520-455-5133; hours 8:30AM-5PM (MST). *Misdemeanor, Civil Actions Under $10,000, Eviction, Small Claims.*

Note: Send fax requests to Attention: Justice Court.

Civil Records: Access: Mail, in person, online. Only the court performs in person searches; visitors may not. Search fee: $17.00 per name. Court makes copy: $.50 per page. Required to search: name, years to search; also helpful: address. Civil cases indexed by plaintiff. Civil records on docket books. Access civil records free at www.supreme.state.az.us/publicaccess/. Mail turnaround time 3-5 days.

Criminal Records: Access: Mail, in person, online. Only the court performs in person searches; visitors may not. Search fee: $17.00 per name. Court makes copy: $.50 per page. Required to search: name, years to search, DOB, SSN, signed release; also helpful: address. Criminal records on docket books. Access to records is free at www.supreme.state.az.us/publicaccess/. Mail turnaround time 3-5 days.

General Information: No public access terminal. No juvenile, mental health, victims, sealed or adoption records released. Will fax documents to local or toll free line. Certification fee: $17.00 per doc. Payee: East Santa Cruz County Justice Court. Personal checks accepted. Prepayment required. SASE not required.

Santa Cruz Justice Court PO Box 1150, Nogales, AZ 85628; phone: 520-375-7762; fax: 520-375-7759; hours 8AM-5PM (MST). *Misdemeanor, Civil Actions Under $10,000, Eviction, Small Claims.* www.sccazcourts.org

Civil Records: Access: Fax, mail, in person, online. Both court and visitors may perform in person searches. Search fee: $17.00 per name. Court makes copy: $.50 per page; same fee for self serve. Required to search: name, years to search; also helpful: address. Civil cases indexed by defendant, plaintiff. Civil records go back to 1975; on computer back to 2/96. Access civil records free at www.supreme.state.az.us/publicaccess/. Also, weekly court calendars are at www.sccazcourts.org/court_calendars.htm. Mail turnaround time 1-3 weeks.

Criminal Records: Access: Fax, mail, in person, online. Both court and visitors may perform in person searches. Search fee: $17.00 per name. Court makes copy: $.50 per page; same fee for self serve. Required to search: name, years to search, DOB; also helpful: address, SSN. Criminal records go back to 1975; on computer back to 2/96. Access to records is free at www.supreme.state.az.us/publicaccess/.

Also, weekly court calendars are at www.sccazcourts.org/court_calendars.htm. Mail turnaround time 1-3 weeks.

General Information: Public access terminal available. No juvenile, mental health, victims, sealed or adoption records released. Certification fee: $17.00. Payee: Santa Cruz Justice Court. Personal checks accepted. Prepayment and SASE required.

Yavapai County

Superior Court Yavapai County Courthouse, 120 S Cortez, Prescott, AZ 86303; phone: 928-771-3312; fax: 928-771-3111; hours 8AM-5PM (MST). *Felony, Civil Actions Over $1,000, Probate.*

Civil Records: Access: Fax, mail, in person, online. Both court and visitors may perform in person searches. Search fee: $18.00 per name. Court makes copy: $.50 per page. Required to search: name, years to search. Civil cases indexed by defendant, plaintiff. Civil records archived from 1900s. Some records on handwritten index book. Access to Superior Court records is free at www.supreme.state.az.us/publicaccess/. Mail turnaround time 10 days.

Criminal Records: Access: Fax, mail, in person, online. Both court and visitors may perform in person searches. Search fee: $18.00 per name per year. Court makes copy: $.50 per page. Required to search: name, years to search, offense. Criminal records archived from 1900s. Some records on handwritten index book. Free access to Superior Court records at www.supreme.state.az.us/publicaccess/. Mail turnaround time 10 days.

General Information: Public access terminal goes back to 1992. No juvenile, mental health, victims, sealed or adoption records released. Will fax documents $5.00 per doc. Certification fee: $18.00. Payee: Clerk of Superior Court. Personal checks accepted. Prepayment and SASE required.

Bagdad Justice Court PO Box 243, Bagdad, AZ 86321; phone: 928-633-2141; fax: 928-633-4451; hours 8AM-5PM M; 8:00AM-4:00PM T-Th (MST). *Misdemeanor, Civil Actions Under $10,000, Eviction, Small Claims.*

Civil Records: Access: Mail, in person, online. Only the court performs in person searches; visitors may not. Search fee: $17.00 per name. Court makes copy: $.50 per page. Required to search: name, years to search; also helpful: address. Civil records on computer since 3/94. Records on docket books and index cards. Records purged after 10 years. Access to records is free at www.supreme.state.az.us/publicaccess/. Mail turnaround time 2 days.

Criminal Records: Access: Mail, in person, online. Only the court performs in person searches; visitors may not. Search fee: $17.00 per name. Court makes copy: $.50 per page. Required to search: name, years to search, DOB; also helpful: address, SSN. Criminal records on computer since 3/94. Records on docket books and index cards. Records purged after 5 years. Access to records is free at www.supreme.state.az.us/publicaccess/. Mail turnaround time 2 days.

General Information: No public access terminal. No juvenile, mental health, victims, sealed or adoption records released. Will not fax documents. Certification fee: $17.00 per cert. Payee: Bagdad Justice Court. Only cashiers checks and money orders accepted. Prepayment and SASE required.

Mayer Justice Court PO Box 245, Mayer, AZ 86333; phone: 928-771-3355; hours 8AM-5PM (MST). *Misdemeanor, Civil Actions Under $10,000, Eviction, Small Claims.*

Civil Records: Access: Mail, in person, online. Only the court performs in person searches; visitors may not. Search fee: $17.00 per name. Court makes copy: $.50 per page. Required to search: name, years to search. Civil cases indexed by defendant, plaintiff. Civil records on computer back to 1989. Records purged after 5 years. Access to records is free at www.supreme.state.az.us/publicaccess/. Mail turnaround time 4 days.

Criminal Records: Access: Mail, in person, online. Only the court performs in person searches; visitors may not. Search fee: $17.00 per name. Court makes copy: $.50 per page. Required to search: name, years to search; also helpful: DOB. Criminal records on computer back to 1989. Records purged after 5 years. Access to records is free at www.supreme.state.az.us/publicaccess/. Mail turnaround time 4 days.

General Information: No public access terminal. No juvenile, mental health, victims, sealed or adoption records released. Will not fax documents. Certification fee: $17.00 per doc includes copies. Payee: Mayer Justice Court. Only cashiers checks and money orders accepted. Prepayment/SASE required.

Prescott Justice Court Yavapai County Courthouse, 120 S Cortez, Rm 103, Prescott, AZ 86301; phone: 928-771-3300; fax: 928-771-3302; hours 8AM-5PM (MST). *Misdemeanor, Civil Actions Under $10,000, Eviction, Small Claims.* www.co.yavapai.az.us

Civil Records: Access: Fax, mail, in person. Both court and visitors may perform in person searches. Search fee: $17.00. Court makes copy: $.50 per page. Required to search: name, years to search; also helpful: address. Civil cases indexed by defendant, plaintiff. Civil records are indexed on computer then purged after 5 years. Searches only for past 5 years. Mail turnaround time 2 days.

Criminal Records: Access: Fax, mail, in person. Both court and visitors may perform in person searches. Search fee: $17.00. Court makes copy: $.50 per page. Required to search: name, years to search, DOB; also helpful: address, SSN. Criminal records are indexed on computer then purged after 5 years. Searches only available for past 5 years. Mail turnaround time 2 days.

General Information: Public access terminal goes back to 5 years. No juvenile, victims or sealed records released. Will fax documents $17.00 per doc. Certification fee: $17.00 per doc. Payee: City of Prescott. No two party checks accepted. Visa, MC, AmEX accepted. Prepayment and SASE required.

Seligman Justice Court PO Box 56, Seligman, AZ 86337-0056; phone: 928-422-3281; fax: 928-422-3282; hours 8AM-5PM (MST). *Misdemeanor, Civil Actions Under $10,000, Eviction, Small Claims.*

Civil Records: Access: Phone, fax, mail, in person, online. Both court and visitors may perform in person searches. No search fee. Court makes copy: $1.25 per page. Required to search: name, years to search; also helpful: address. Civil cases indexed by defendant, plaintiff. Civil records on computer. Records purged after 5 years. Access to records is free at www.supreme.state.az.us/publicaccess/. Mail turnaround time 2 days.

Criminal Records: Access: Phone, fax, mail, in person, online. Both court and visitors may perform in person searches. No search fee. Court makes copy: $1.25 per page. Required to search: name, years to search, DOB; also helpful: address, SSN. Criminal records on computer. Records purged after 5 years. Access records free at www.supreme.state.az.us/publicaccess/. Mail turnaround time 2 days.

General Information: No public access terminal. No juvenile or victims records released. No fee to fax documents. Certification fee: $17.00. Payee: Seligman Justice Court. Business checks accepted. Prepayment and SASE required.

Verde Valley Justice Court 10 S 6th St, Cottonwood, AZ 86326; phone: 928-639-5820; fax: 928-639-5828; hours 8AM-5PM (MST). *Misdemeanor, Civil Actions Under $10,000, Eviction, Small Claims.*

Civil Records: Access: Mail, in person, online. Both court and visitors may perform in person searches. Search fee: $17.00. Court makes copy: $.50 per page. Required to search: name, years to search; also helpful: address. Civil cases indexed by defendant, plaintiff. Civil records on computer from 6/99. Records purged after 5 years. Access to records is

free at www.supreme.state.az.us/publicaccess/. Mail turnaround time 2 days.

Criminal Records: Access: Mail, in person, online. Both court and visitors may perform in person searches. Search fee: $17.00. Court makes copy: $.50 per page. Required to search: name, years to search, DOB; also helpful: address, SSN. Criminal records computerized since 6/99. Records purged after 5 years. Access to records is free at www.supreme.state.az.us/publicaccess/. Mail turnaround time 2 days.

General Information: No public access terminal. No juvenile, mental health, victims, sealed records released. Will not fax documents. Certification fee: $17.00 per doc includes copy fee. Payee: Verde Valley Justice Court. Prepayment and SASE required.

Yarnell Justice Court PO Box 65, Justice Court Bldg, Yarnell, AZ 85362; phone: 928-427-3318; fax: 928-771-3362; hours 8AM-5PM (MST). *Misdemeanor, Civil Actions Under $10,000, Eviction, Small Claims.*

Civil Records: Access: Mail, in person, online. Only the court performs in person searches; visitors may not. Search fee: $17.00 per name. Court makes copy: $.50 per page. Required to search: name, years to search. Civil cases indexed by defendant, plaintiff. Civil records on computer from 1989. Prior records on docket books. Records purged after 10 years. Access records free at www.supreme.state.az.us/publicaccess/. Mail turnaround time 5 days.

Criminal Records: Access: Mail, in person, online. Only the court performs in person searches; visitors may not. Search fee: $17.00 per name. Court makes copy: $.50 per page. Required to search: name, years to search. Criminal records on computer from 1989, prior on docket books. Records purged after 5 years. Access to records is free at www.supreme.state.az.us/publicaccess/. Mail turnaround time 5 days.

General Information: No juvenile, mental health, victims, sealed or adoption records released. Certification fee: $17.00 per doc. Payee: Yarnell Justice Court. Only cashiers checks and money orders accepted. Prepayment and SASE required.

Yuma County

Superior Court 168 S 2nd Ave, Yuma, AZ 85364; phone: 928-329-2164; criminal phone: 928-329-2167; civil phone: 928-329-2164; probate phone: 928-329-2163; fax: 928-329-2007; hours 8AM-5PM (MST). *Felony, Civil Actions Over $5,000, Probate.*

Civil Records: Access: Fax, mail, in person, online. Both court and visitors may perform in person searches. Search fee: $18.00 per name. Court makes copy: $.50 per page. Required to search: name, years to search. Civil cases indexed by defendant or plaintiff. Civil records on docket books from 1900s, new and pending cases from 11/1994 on computer. Access to records is free at www.supreme.state.az.us/publicaccess/. Mail turnaround time 1 week.

Criminal Records: Access: Fax, mail, in person, online. Both court and visitors may perform in person searches. Search fee: $18.00 per name. Court makes copy: $.50 per page. Required to search: name, years to search. Criminal records on docket books from 1900s, new and pending cases from 11/1994 on computer. Access to records is free at www.supreme.state.az.us/publicaccess/. Mail turnaround time 1 week.

General Information: Public access terminal goes back to 1995. No adoption, mental health records released. Will fax documents $18.00 per doc. Certification fee: $18.00 per cert. Payee: Clerk of Superior Court. Business checks or Visa, MC accepted. Prepayment and SASE required.

Somerton Justice Court PO Box 458, 350 W Main St, Somerton, AZ 85350; phone: 928-627-2722; fax: 928-627-1076; hours 8AM-5PM (MST). *Misdemeanor, Civil Actions Under $10,000, Eviction, Small Claims.* www.somertoncourts.com

Civil Records: Access: Phone, fax, mail, in person, online. Both court and visitors may perform in person searches. Search fee: $17.00 per name. Court makes copy: $.50 per page. Required to search: name, years to search. Civil cases indexed by defendant. Civil records on computer. Access to records is free the website above and at www.supreme.state.az.us/publicaccess/. Mail turnaround time 2-4 days.

Criminal Records: Access: Phone, fax, mail, in person, online. Only the court performs in person searches; visitors may not. Search fee: $17.00 per name. Court makes copy: $.50 per page. Required to search: name, years to search, DOB, SSN, offense, date of offense. Criminal records on computer. Access to records is free at the website above as well at www.supreme.state.az.us/publicaccess/. Mail turnaround time 2-4 days.

General Information: No public access terminal. No set aside judgment records released. Will fax documents for $.50 per page. Certification fee: $17.00 per doc. Payee: Somerton Justice Court. Business checks accepted. Prepayment and SASE required.

Wellton Justice Court PO Box 384, Wellton, AZ 85356; phone: 928-785-3321; fax: 928-785-4933; hours 8AM-5PM (MST). *Misdemeanor, Civil Actions Under $10,000, Eviction, Small Claims.*

Civil Records: Access: Phone, fax, mail, in person, online. Only the court performs in person searches; visitors may not. No search fee. Court makes copy: $.50 per page. Required to search: name, years to search. Civil cases indexed by defendant, plaintiff. Civil records on computer to 1992. Access to records is free at www.supreme.state.az.us/publicaccess/. Mail turnaround time same day.

Criminal Records: Access: Phone, fax, mail, in person, online. Only the court performs in person searches; visitors may not. No search fee. Court makes copy: $.50 per page. Required to search: name, years to search, offense, date of offense. Criminal records on computer to 1992. Access to records is free at www.supreme.state.az.us/publicaccess/. Mail turnaround time same day.

General Information: No public access terminal. No set aside judgment records released. Will fax documents to local or toll free line. No certification fee . Payee: Wellton Justice Court. Personal checks accepted. Credit cards accepted: Visa, MC, Discover, AmEx. Prepayment required. SASE not required.

Yuma Justice Court 168 S 2nd Ave, Yuma, AZ 85364; phone: 928-329-2180; fax: 928-329-2005; hours 8AM-5PM (MST). *Misdemeanor, Civil Actions Under $10,000, Eviction, Small Claims.* Note: The office hopes to have a public access terminal available for the public in early 2006.

Civil Records: Access: Mail, in person, online. Both court and visitors may perform in person searches. Search fee: $17.00 per name. Court makes copy: $.50 per page. Required to search: name, years to search. Civil cases indexed by defendant. Civil records on computer. Purged after 5 years. Info available only for cases after 9/01/97; computerized since 1997. Access to records is free at www.supreme.state.az.us/publicaccess/. Mail turnaround time 2-4 days.

Criminal Records: Access: Mail, in person, online. Only the court performs in person searches; visitors may not. Search fee: $17.00 per name. Court makes copy: $.50 per page. Required to search: name, years to search. Criminal records on computer. Purged after 5 years. Info available only for cases after 9/01/97; computerized records since 1997. Access to records is free at www.supreme.state.az.us/publicaccess/. Mail turnaround time 2-4 days.

General Information: Public access terminal has only civil records. Will not release victim's names. Certification fee: $17.00. Payee: Justice Court #1. Personal checks or Visa, MC accepted. Prepayment and SASE required.

Arizona Recording Offices

ORGANIZATION: 15 counties, 16 recording offices. The Navajo Nation is profiled here. The recording officer is County Recorder. Recordings are usually placed in a Grantor/Grantee index. The entire state is in the Mountain Time Zone (MST), and does not change to daylight savings time. Note that no less than four new telephone area codes have added in recent years: 480 and 623 for east and west Phoenix Metro area respectively, 520 for south and southeastern state, 924 for west and north of state.

REAL ESTATE RECORDS: Counties do not perform real estate searches. Copy fees are usually $1.00 per page. Certification fees are usually $3.00 per document.

UCC RECORDS: Financing statements are filed at the state level, except for real estate related collateral, which are filed with the County Recorder. However, prior to 07/2001, consumer goods and farm collateral were filed at the County Recorder and these older records can be searched there. All counties will perform UCC searches. Use search request form UCC-3. Search fees are generally $10.00 per debtor name. Copies usually cost $1.00 per page.

TAX LIEN RECORDS: Federal and state tax liens on personal property of businesses are filed with the Secretary of State. Other federal and state tax liens are filed with the County Recorder. Several counties will do a separate tax lien search.

OTHER LIENS: Executions, judgments, labor.

ONLINE ACCESS: A number of county assessor offices offer online access:. The Secretary of State offers online access to UCC records at http://www.azsos.gov/business_services/ucc.htm

Apache County

County Recorder, PO Box 425, St. Johns, AZ 85936. RE & UCC recording phone-928-337-7515; fax-928-337-7676; hours: 8AM-5PM www.co.apache.az.us/Recorder/
Separate indices to search. Records indexed on a public use terminal back to 1986. Office will perform a UCC search but public must search other records themselves. Search fee $10.00 per name. Will not search real estate records. Copy fee $1.00 per page. Cert fee- $3.00 per doc plus copy fee. Payee- Apache County Recorder. **Online access to Real Estate, Recording, Deed, Judgment, Lien records:** Access to the recorder is free at www.thecountyrecorder.com/Search.aspx?CountyKey =5. Index goes back to 1985. Also, search the assessor property tax records free at www.co.mohave.az.us/apache/assessor/assessdatalink.a sp. **Other phones:** Treasurer- 928-337-7513; Elections- 928-337-7537. **Property tax/Assessor-** PO Box 770, St. Johns, AZ 85936; 928-337-7521.

Cochise County

County Recorder, PO Box 184, Bisbee, AZ 85603. RE & UCC recording phone-520-432-8350; fax-520-432-8368; hours: 8AM-5PM www.co.cochise.az.us/recorders/Default.htm
All records in one index. Records indexed on computer back to 7/1/1985. Office will perform a UCC search but public must search other records themselves. Search fee $10.00. Copy fee $1.00 per page. Cert fee- $3.00 per cert plus copy fee. Payee- Cochise County Recorder. **Online access to Treasurer Back Tax, Restaurant Inspection records:** Access the treasurer's back tax list free at http://209.180.126.252/treasurer/backtax.htm. Also, search restaurant inspections results at www.co.cochise.az.us/ccwebsite/SelectDistrict.asp. **Other phones:** Treasurer- 520-432-8400; Elections- 520-432-8970; Voter Registration- 520-432-8354. **Property tax/Assessor-** PO Box 168, Bisbee, AZ 85603; 520-432-8650.

Coconino County

County Recorder, 110 E. Cherry Ave, Flagstaff, AZ 86001. RE & UCC recording phone-928-779-6585; fax-928-779-6739; hours: 8AM-5PM http://co.coconino.az.us/recorder/
All records in one index. Records indexed on a public use terminal back to 1983. Office will perform a UCC and Tax liens search but public must search other records themselves. Search fee $10.00. Copy fee $1.00 per page. Cert fee- $3.00 per doc plus copy fee. Payee- Coconino County Recorder. **Online access to Recording, Grantor/Grantee, Real Estate records:** Access to county iCRIS system is free at http://coco-criswf.infomagic.net/icris/splash.jsp. Registration required. Documents: $1.00 to print; signup and request documents at 800-793-6181. Online records go back to 1983; images back to 3/1999. Also for property owner site for free go to http://gis-map.coconino.az.gov/website/coconino/getgisdata.asp. **Other phones:** Treasurer- 928-779-6615; Appraiser/Auditor- 928-779-6502; Elections- 928-779-6589; Vital Records- 602-364-1300. **Property tax/Assessor-** 928-779-6502.

Gila County

County Recorder, 1400 E. Ash St, Globe, AZ 85501. 928-425-3231, R/E recording phone-928-425-3231 x8738, UCC recording phone-928-425-3231 x8738; fax-928-425-9270; hours: 8AM-5PM www.co.gila.az.us
All records in one index. Office personnel or visitors may perform searches. General index search fee $10.00 per hour for searches 1985 to present; $15 per hour if prior to 1985. UCC search per debtor name- $18.00. Copy fee $1.00 per page. Cert fee- $3.00 per doc plus copy fee. Payee- Gila County Recorder. **Online access to Recording, Deed, Lien, Grantor/Grantee records:** Access to the recorder's index are free at http://63.241.138.77/icris/splash.jsp. Search for free, but official copies are $1.00 per page. Records go back to 1985, images back to 1998. **Other phones:** Treasurer- 928-425-3231 x8701; Elections- 928-425-3231 x8740.

Property tax/Assessor- same address as above. 928-425-3231 x8720.

Graham County

County Recorder, 921 Thatcher Blvd., Safford, AZ 85546. RE & UCC recording phone-928-428-3560; fax-928-348-8625; hours: 8AM-5PM www.graham.az.gov
All records in one index. Office will perform a UCC search but public must search other records themselves. UCC search per debtor name- $10.00. Copy fee $1.00 per finding. Cert fee- $3.00 per instrument plus copy fee. Payee- Graham County Recorder. **Online access to Assessor, Property, Most Wanted, Recording, Deed, Divorce, Judgment, Lien records:** Access the assessor database of property and assessments is free at www.co.mohave.az.us/graham/assessor/assessdatalink.asp. Search the most wanted list at www.eaznet.com/~gcso/wanted.htm. Also access to recorder records is at www.thecountyrecorder.com/Search.aspx?CountyKey =1.Index goes back to 1984. **Other phones:** Treasurer- 928-428-3440; Elections- 928-428-3930; Vital Records- 928-428-0110. **Property tax/Assessor-** same address as above. 928-428-2828.

Greenlee County

County Recorder, PO Box 1625, Clifton, AZ 85533-1625. 928-865-2632, UCC recording phone-928-865-2632 or 928-865-1717; fax-928-865-4417; hours: 8AM-5PM www.co.greenlee.az.us/Recorder/RecorderHomeP age.aspx
All records in one index. Will not search real estate records. Will search UCC records, but not tax liens. UCC search per debtor name- $10.00. Copy fee $1.00 per page. Cert fee- $3.00 per doc plus copy fee. Payee- Greenlee County Recorder. **Online access to Real Estate, Deed, Lien, Judgment, Vital Statistic, Recording records:** Access to recorder records is free at www.thecountyrecorder.com/Search.aspx?CountyKey=2. Index back to 1979. **Other phones:** Treasurer- 928-865-3422; Elections- 928-865-1717. **Property tax/Assessor-** PO Box 777, Clifton, AZ 85533; 928-865-5302.

La Paz County

County Recorder, 1112 Joshua Ave, #201, Parker, AZ 85344. RE & UCC recording phone-928-669-6136; fax-928-669-5638; hours: 8AM-5PM www.co.la-paz.az.us/recorder.htm
Only the public may search. Copy fee $1.00 per page. Cert fee- $3.00 per doc plus copy fee. Payee- La Paz County Recorder. **Online access to Recorder, Deed, Judgment, Lien records:** Access to the recorder document index only is free at www.thecountyrecorder.com. **Other phones:** Treasurer- 928-669-6145; Elections- 928-669-6115; Vital Records- 928-669-6131 (marriages only). **Property tax/Assessor-** 1112 Joshua Ave #204, Parker, AZ 85344; 928-669-6165.

Maricopa County

County Recorder, 111 S. 3rd Ave #103, Phoenix, AZ 85003. 602-506-3535; fax-602-506-3273; hours: 8AM-5PM http://recorder.maricopa.gov
All records in one index. Records indexed on a public use terminal back to 1991. Office personnel or visitors may perform searches. Search fee $10.00 per name. Will not search real estate records. Copy fee $1.00 per page. Cert fee- $3.00 per doc plus copy fee. Payee- Maricopa County Recorder. **Online access to Real Estate, Lien, Property, Assessor records:** Access by direct dial-up or the Internet. Dial-up access requires one-time set-up fee of $300 plus $.06 per minute. Dial-up hours are 8am-10pm M-F, 8-5 S-S. Records date back to 1983. For add'l info, contact Linda Kinchloe, 602-506-3637. Also, access to Recorder's database is at http://recorder.maricopa.gov/recdocdata. Records go back to 1968. Also search data back to 2002 for free at the clerk's office. Also search most wanted list at www.mcso.org/submenu.asp?file=mostwanted.
Assessor database is at www.maricopa.gov/assessor. Residential data available. Also, perform tax appeal lookups at SBOE site at www.sboe.state.az.us/cgi-bin/name_lookup.pl. Search inmates at www.mcso.org/submenu.asp?file=MugIndex.
Property tax/Assessor- 301 W Jefferson, Phoenix, AZ 85003; 602-506-3406.

Mohave County

County Recorder, PO Box 70, Kingman, AZ 86402-0070. RE & UCC recording phone-928-753-0701; fax-928-753-0727; hours: 8AM-5PM www.co.mohave.az.us
All records in one index. Will not search real estate records. Will search UCC records, but not tax liens. UCC search per debtor name- $10.00. Copy fee $1.00 per page. Cert fee- $3.00 per doc plus copy fee. Payee- Mohave County Recorder. **Online access to Real Estate, Grantor/Grantee, Lien, Assessor, Most Wanted, Sex Offender records:** Access to the Recorder's System is free at http://icris.co.mohave.az.us/splash.jsp. Registration and password is required. Sheriff's most wanted list is at www.co.mohave.az.us/mcso/wanted.htm. Also, online access to the Assessor's property database is free (no registration) at www.co.mohave.az.us/1moweb/depts_files/assessor.htm. A sales history database is also here. Sex offender list is at www.ctaz.com/~mcso/page19.html. Also, the treasurer's tax sale parcel search is at www.co.mohave.az.us/depts/treas/tax_sale.asp. Also, search health inspection rating for food establishments at www.co.mohave.az.us/webapts/aptsnew.htm. **Other phones:** Treasurer- 928-753-0737; Appraiser/Auditor- 928-753-0703; Elections- 928-753-0733; Vital Records- 602-364-1300 (Phoenix). **Property tax/Assessor-** 315 Oak St, Kingman, AZ 86401; 928-753-0703.

Navajo County

County Recorder, PO Box 668, Holbrook, AZ 86025-0668. 928-524-4194; fax-928-524-4308; hours: 8AM-5PM www.co.navajo.az.us
All records in one index. Records indexed on a public use terminal back to 1989. Office will perform a UCC search but public must search other records themselves. Search fee $10.00 per name. Copy fee $1.00 per page. Cert fee- $3.00 per seal plus copy fee. Payee- Navajo County Recorder. **Online access to Property, Assessor, Grantor/Grantee, Recording, UCC, Tax Lien, Death, Tax Sale records:** Access to the recorder's database of land information, UCCs, Liens, and Grantor/Grantee indices is free at www.thecountyrecorder.com/Introduction.aspx?CountyKey=4. Documents go back to 1989; images to 1995. Also, access property assessor database free at www.thecountyrecorder.com/(s14kqeqdyurl2o55f3hripih)/Search.aspx. Also, search a list of tax sales property at the county website. **Other phones:** Treasurer- 928-524-4172. **Property tax/Assessor-** same address as above. 928-524-4086.

Navajo Nation

County Recorder, PO Box 663, Divison of Economic Development, Window Rock, AZ 86515. 928-871-7365; fax-928-871-7381; hours: 8AM-N, 1-5PM www.co.navajo.az.us
Navajo Nation UCCs are here. Land recording is handled by Navajo County. While assessing is performed by Navajo Nation, the Assessor is county assessor located at Navajo County. Will not search real estate records. UCC search per debtor name- $.50 per page found. Copy fee $.50 per page. Cert fee- $5.00 per page plus copy fee. Payee- Navajo Nation Business Regulatory Dept. **Online access to Property, Assessor, Grantor/Grantee, Recording, UCC, Tax Lien, Death, Tax Sale records:** Access to the recorder's database of land information, UCCs, Liens, and Grantor/Grantee indices is free at www.thecountyrecorder.com/Introduction.aspx?CountyKey=4. Documents go back to 1989; images to 1995. Also, access property assessor database free at http://co.navajo.az.us/theCountyRecorder/DataSearch/WebForm1.aspx. Site may be temp down. Also, a list of tax sales property is via the Navajo County website. **Other phones:** Treasurer- 928-524-4172. **Property tax/Assessor-** 928-524-4086.

Pima County

County Recorder, 115 N. Church Ave, Tucson, AZ 85701. 520-740-4350; fax-520-623-1785; hours: 8AM-5PM www.recorder.co.pima.az.us
All records in one index. Records indexed on a public use terminal back to 4/1987. Office personnel or visitors may perform searches. Search fee $10.00 per name. Copy fee $1.00 per page. Cert fee- $3.00 per doc plus copy fee. Payee- Pima County Recorder. **Online access to Assessor, Real Estate, Lien, Recording, Deed, Property Tax records:** Access recorder records free at www.recorder.co.pima.az.us/search/search.html. Also, records on the Pima County Tax Assessor database are free at www.asr.co.pima.az.us/apiq/index.html. Also, a name/parcel/property tax lookup may be performed free on the SBOE site at www.sboe.state.az.us/cgi-bin/name_lookup.pl. Also, search the property tax inquiry database at www.to.co.pima.az.us/inquiry.html. **Property tax/Assessor-** same address as above. 520-740-8630.

Pinal County

County Recorder, PO Box 848, Florence, AZ 85232-0848. Main phone & R/E recording-520-866-7100, UCC recording phone-520-866-6179; fax-520-866-7170; hours: 8AM-5PM http://co.pinal.az.us
Will be re-locating to the County Courthouse after renovation. Also has branch offices in Casa Grande (520-866-7488) and Apache Junction (480-983-7038). Public access terminals available. Will not search real estate records. Will not search UCC records or tax liens. Copy fee $1.00 per page. Cert fee- $3.00 per doc

plus copy fee. Payee- Pinal County Recorder. **Online access to Grantor/Grantee, Tax Bill, Tax Lien, Tax Sale, Assessor records:** Access to the recorder's index is free at http://apps.co.pinal.az.us/Recorder/Search/. Also, access to the county treasurer's database of tax liens, tax bills, and tax sales is free at http://co.pinal.az.us/treasurer. Click on appropriate "Tax Searches" button. Also, search the assessor's property tax database free at http://apps.co.pinal.az.us/Assessor/Search/?T=Pinfo. **Other phones:** Treasurer- 520-866-6425; Appraiser/Auditor- 520-866-6361; Elections- 520-866-7101. **Property tax/Assessor-** 520-866-6361.

Santa Cruz County

County Recorder, 2150 N. Congress; County Complex, Nogales, AZ 85621. RE & UCC recording phone-520-375-7990; fax-520-761-7938; hours: 8AM-5PM www.co.santa-cruz.az.us
Records indexed on a public use terminal back to 4/1987. Only the public may search. Copy fee $1.00 per page. Cert fee- $3.00 per doc plus $1.00 per page copy. Payee- Santa Cruz County Recorder. **Online access to Assessor, Property records:** Access to the County Assessor data is free at www.co.mohave.az.us./santacruz/assessor/assessdatalink.asp. **Other phones:** Treasurer- 520-375-7980; Appraiser/Auditor- 520-375-8030; Elections- 520-375-7990; Courthouse Main- 520-375-7800. **Property tax/Assessor-** PO Box 1150, Nogales, AZ 85621; 520-375-8030.

Yavapai County

County Recorder, 1015 Fair St, Rm 228, Prescott, AZ 86305. 928-771-3244; fax-928-771-3258; hours: 8AM-5PM www.co.yavapai.az.us
A second office is located at 10 S 6th St, Cottonwood AZ 86326, phone 928-639-5807, fax: 928-639-5812. Separate indices to search. Records indexed on a public use terminal back to 1973. Will not perform open-ended real estate records searches. Copy fee $1.00 per page. Cert fee- $3.00 per seal plus copy fee. Payee- Yavapai County Recorder. **Online access to Assessor, Real Estate, Recording, Inmate/Offender records:** Access to the recording office iCRIS database is free at http://icris.co.yavapai.az.us/icris/splash.jsp. Records from 1976 to present; images from 1986 to present. Also, assessor and land records on the County Geographic Information Systems (GIS) database are free at http://mapserver.co.yavapai.az.us/interactive/map.asp. Information also at http://mapserver.co.yavapai.az.us/parcelinfo/map.asp. Also, the board of supervisors tax sale list is at www.co.yavapai.az.us/events/TaxSales/BOS/taxsalelist.htm. Search the county offender/inmate list for free at www.vinelink.com/offender/searchNew.jsp?siteID=3007. **Other phones:** Treasurer- 928-771-3233; Elections- 928-771-3250; Voter Registration- 928-771-3248. **Property tax/Assessor-** same address as above. 520-771-3220.

Yuma County

County Recorder, 410 S Maiden Lane, Yuma, AZ 85364-2311. 928-373-6020, R/E recording phone-928-373-6029, UCC recording phone-928-373-6028; fax-928-373-6024; 8AM-5PM www.co.yuma.az.us
All records in one index. Records indexed on a public use terminal back to 9/1993. Only the public may search. Copy fee $1.00 per page. Cert fee- $3.00 per doc plus copy fee. Payee- Yuma County Recorder. **Online access to Property, Assessor records:** Access to county property data is free at http://itax.co.yuma.az.us:8080/itax/taxSplash.jsp; registration is required. **Other phones:** Treasurer- 928-539-7781; Elections- 928-373-1014; Vital Records- 928-317-4530. **Property tax/Assessor-** 928-373-6040.

Arizona County Locator

You will usually be able to find the city name in the City/County Cross Reference below. In that case, it is a simple matter to determine the county from the cross reference. However, only the official US Postal Service city names are included in this index. There are an additional 40,000 place names people use in their addresses. We have included a ZIP/City Cross Reference following the City/County Cross Reference.

If you know the ZIP Code but the city name does not appear in the City/County Cross Reference index, look up the ZIP Code in the ZIP/City Cross Reference, find the city name, then look up the city name in the City/County Cross Reference.

Arizona City/County Cross Reference

AGUILA Maricopa
AJO Pima
ALPINE Apache
AMADO (85645) Pima(90), Santa Cruz(9)
ANTHEM Maricopa
APACHE JUNCTION (85220) Pinal(85), Maricopa(14)
APACHE JUNCTION Pinal
ARIVACA Pima
ARIZONA CITY Pinal
ARLINGTON Maricopa
ASH FORK Yavapai
AVONDALE Maricopa
BAGDAD Yavapai
BAPCHULE Pinal
BELLEMONT Coconino
BENSON (85602) Cochise(93), Pima(6)
BISBEE Cochise
BLACK CANYON CITY Yavapai
BLUE Greenlee
BLUE GAP Navajo
BOUSE La Paz
BOWIE Cochise
BUCKEYE Maricopa
BULLHEAD CITY Mohave
BYLAS Graham
CAMERON Coconino
CAMP VERDE Yavapai
CAREFREE Maricopa
CASA GRANDE Pinal
CASHION Maricopa
CATALINA Pima
CAVE CREEK Maricopa
CENTRAL Graham
CHAMBERS Apache
CHANDLER Maricopa
CHANDLER HEIGHTS Maricopa
CHINLE Apache
CHINO VALLEY Yavapai
CHLORIDE Mohave
CIBICUE Navajo
CIBOLA La Paz
CLARKDALE Yavapai
CLAY SPRINGS Navajo
CLAYPOOL Gila
CLIFTON Greenlee
COCHISE Cochise
COLORADO CITY Mohave
CONCHO Apache
CONGRESS Yavapai
COOLIDGE Pinal
CORNVILLE Yavapai
CORTARO Pima
COTTONWOOD Yavapai
CROWN KING Yavapai
DATELAND Yuma
DENNEHOTSO Apache
DEWEY Yavapai
DOLAN SPRINGS Mohave
DOUGLAS Cochise
DRAGOON Cochise
DUNCAN Greenlee
EAGAR Apache
EDEN Graham
EHRENBERG La Paz
EL MIRAGE Maricopa
ELFRIDA Cochise
ELGIN Santa Cruz
ELOY Pinal

FLAGSTAFF Coconino
FLORENCE Pinal
FOREST LAKES Coconino
FORT APACHE Navajo
FORT DEFIANCE Apache
FORT HUACHUCA Cochise
FORT MCDOWELL Maricopa
FORT MOHAVE Mohave
FORT THOMAS Graham
FOUNTAIN HILLS Maricopa
FREDONIA Coconino
GADSDEN Yuma
GANADO Apache
GILA BEND Maricopa
GILBERT Maricopa
GLENDALE Maricopa
GLOBE Gila
GOLDEN VALLEY Mohave
GOODYEAR Maricopa
GRAND CANYON Coconino
GRAY MOUNTAIN Coconino
GREEN VALLEY Pima
GREER Apache
HACKBERRY Mohave
HAPPY JACK Coconino
HAYDEN Gila
HEBER Navajo
HEREFORD Cochise
HIGLEY Maricopa
HOLBROOK Navajo
HOTEVILLA Navajo
HOUCK Apache
HUACHUCA CITY Cochise
HUALAPAI Mohave
HUMBOLDT Yavapai
INDIAN WELLS Navajo
IRON SPRINGS Yavapai
JEROME Yavapai
JOSEPH CITY Navajo
KAIBITO Coconino
KAYENTA Navajo
KEAMS CANYON Navajo
KEARNY Pinal
KINGMAN Mohave
KIRKLAND Yavapai
KYKOTSMOVI VILLAGE Navajo
LAKE HAVASU CITY Mohave
LAKE MONTEZUMA Yavapai
LAKESIDE Navajo
LAVEEN Maricopa
LEUPP Coconino
LITCHFIELD PARK Maricopa
LITTLEFIELD Mohave
LUKACHUKAI Apache
LUKE AFB Maricopa
LUKEVILLE Pima
LUPTON Apache
MAMMOTH Pinal
MANY FARMS Apache
MARANA (85653) Pima(84), Pinal(15)
MARBLE CANYON Coconino
MARICOPA Pinal
MAYER Yavapai
MC NARY Apache
MC NEAL Cochise
MEADVIEW Mohave
MESA (85212) Maricopa(92), Pinal(7)
MESA Maricopa
MIAMI Gila

MOHAVE VALLEY Mohave
MORENCI Greenlee
MORMON LAKE Coconino
MORRISTOWN Maricopa
MOUNT LEMMON Pima
MUNDS PARK Coconino
NACO Cochise
NAZLINI Apache
NEW RIVER Maricopa
NOGALES Santa Cruz
NORTH RIM Coconino
NUTRIOSO Apache
OATMAN Mohave
ORACLE Pinal
OVERGAARD Navajo
PAGE Coconino
PALO VERDE Maricopa
PARADISE VALLEY Maricopa
PARKER La Paz
PARKS Coconino
PATAGONIA Santa Cruz
PAULDEN Yavapai
PAYSON Gila
PEACH SPRINGS Mohave
PEARCE Cochise
PEORIA Maricopa
PERIDOT Gila
PETRIFIED FOREST NATL PK Apache
PHOENIX Maricopa
PICACHO Pinal
PIMA Graham
PINE Gila
PINEDALE Navajo
PINETOP Navajo
PINON Navajo
PIRTLEVILLE Cochise
POLACCA Navajo
POMERENE Cochise
POSTON La Paz
PRESCOTT Yavapai
PRESCOTT VALLEY Yavapai
QUARTZSITE La Paz
QUEEN CREEK (85242) Maricopa(61), Pinal(38)
RED ROCK Pinal
RED VALLEY Apache
RILLITO Pima
RIMROCK Yavapai
RIO RICO Santa Cruz
RIO VERDE Maricopa
ROCK POINT Apache
ROLL Yuma
ROOSEVELT Gila
ROUND ROCK Apache
SACATON Pinal
SAFFORD Graham
SAHUARITA Pima
SAINT DAVID Cochise
SAINT JOHNS Apache
SAINT MICHAELS Apache
SALOME La Paz
SAN CARLOS Gila
SAN LUIS Yuma
SAN MANUEL Pinal
SAN SIMON Cochise
SANDERS Apache
SASABE Pima
SAWMILL Apache
SCOTTSDALE Maricopa

SECOND MESA Navajo
SEDONA (86336) Yavapai(67), Coconino(32)
SEDONA Coconino
SEDONA Yavapai
SELIGMAN Yavapai
SELLS Pima
SHONTO Navajo
SHOW LOW Navajo
SIERRA VISTA Cochise
SKULL VALLEY Yavapai
SNOWFLAKE Navajo
SOLOMON Graham
SOMERTON Yuma
SONOITA (85637) Santa Cruz(82), Pima(17)
SPRINGERVILLE Apache
STANFIELD Pinal
SUN CITY Maricopa
SUN CITY WEST Maricopa
SUN VALLEY Navajo
SUPAI Coconino
SUPERIOR Pinal
SURPRISE Maricopa
TACNA Yuma
TAYLOR Navajo
TEEC NOS POS Apache
TEMPE Maricopa
TEMPLE BAR MARINA Mohave
THATCHER Graham
TOLLESON Maricopa
TOMBSTONE Cochise
TONALEA Coconino
TONOPAH Maricopa
TONTO BASIN Gila
TOPAWA Pima
TOPOCK Mohave
TORTILLA FLAT Maricopa
TSAILE Apache
TUBA CITY Coconino
TUBAC Santa Cruz
TUCSON (85739) Pima(57), Pinal(42)
TUCSON Pima
TUMACACORI Santa Cruz
VAIL Pima
VALENTINE Mohave
VALLEY FARMS Pinal
VERNON Apache
WADDELL Maricopa
WELLTON Yuma
WENDEN La Paz
WHITE MOUNTAIN LAKE Navajo
WHITERIVER Navajo
WICKENBURG Maricopa
WIKIEUP Mohave
WILLCOX (85643) Cochise(98), Graham(1)
WILLCOX Cochise
WILLIAMS Coconino
WILLOW BEACH Mohave
WINDOW ROCK Apache
WINKELMAN (85292) Pinal(54), Gila(45)
WINSLOW Navajo
WITTMANN Maricopa
WOODRUFF Navajo
YARNELL Yavapai
YOUNG Gila
YOUNGTOWN Maricopa
YUCCA Mohave
YUMA Yuma

Arizona ZIP/City Cross Reference

85000-85086	PHOENIX
85086-85086	ANTHEM
85087-85087	NEW RIVER
85098-85099	PHOENIX
85201-85216	MESA
85217-85220	APACHE JUNCTION
85221-85221	BAPCHULE
85222-85222	CASA GRANDE
85223-85223	ARIZONA CITY
85224-85226	CHANDLER
85227-85227	CHANDLER HEIGHTS
85228-85228	COOLIDGE
85230-85230	CASA GRANDE
85231-85231	ELOY
85232-85232	FLORENCE
85233-85234	GILBERT
85235-85235	HAYDEN
85236-85236	HIGLEY
85237-85237	KEARNY
85239-85239	MARICOPA
85240-85240	MESA
85241-85241	PICACHO
85242-85243	QUEEN CREEK
85244-85244	CHANDLER
85245-85245	RED ROCK
85246-85246	CHANDLER
85247-85247	SACATON
85248-85249	CHANDLER
85250-85252	SCOTTSDALE
85253-85253	PARADISE VALLEY
85254-85262	SCOTTSDALE
85263-85263	RIO VERDE
85264-85264	FORT MCDOWELL
85266-85267	SCOTTSDALE
85268-85269	FOUNTAIN HILLS
85271-85271	SCOTTSDALE
85272-85272	STANFIELD
85273-85273	SUPERIOR
85274-85277	MESA
85278-85278	APACHE JUNCTION
85279-85279	FLORENCE
85280-85289	TEMPE
85290-85290	TORTILLA FLAT
85291-85291	VALLEY FARMS
85292-85292	WINKELMAN
85296-85299	GILBERT
85301-85308	GLENDALE
85309-85309	LUKE AFB
85310-85318	GLENDALE
85320-85320	AGUILA
85321-85321	AJO
85322-85322	ARLINGTON
85323-85323	AVONDALE
85324-85324	BLACK CANYON CITY
85325-85325	BOUSE
85326-85326	BUCKEYE
85327-85327	CAVE CREEK
85328-85328	CIBOLA
85329-85329	CASHION
85331-85331	CAVE CREEK
85332-85332	CONGRESS
85333-85333	DATELAND
85334-85334	EHRENBERG
85335-85335	EL MIRAGE
85336-85336	GADSDEN
85337-85337	GILA BEND
85338-85338	GOODYEAR
85339-85339	LAVEEN
85340-85340	LITCHFIELD PARK
85341-85341	LUKEVILLE
85342-85342	MORRISTOWN
85343-85343	PALO VERDE
85344-85344	PARKER
85345-85345	PEORIA
85346-85346	QUARTZSITE
85347-85347	ROLL
85348-85348	SALOME
85349-85349	SAN LUIS
85350-85350	SOMERTON
85351-85351	SUN CITY
85352-85352	TACNA
85353-85353	TOLLESON
85354-85354	TONOPAH
85355-85355	WADDELL
85356-85356	WELLTON
85357-85357	WENDEN
85358-85358	WICKENBURG
85359-85359	QUARTZSITE
85360-85360	WIKIEUP
85361-85361	WITTMANN
85362-85362	YARNELL
85363-85363	YOUNGTOWN
85364-85369	YUMA
85371-85371	POSTON
85372-85373	SUN CITY
85374-85374	SURPRISE
85375-85376	SUN CITY WEST
85377-85377	CAREFREE
85378-85379	SURPRISE
85380-85385	PEORIA
85387-85388	SURPRISE
85388-85388	SUN CITY
85390-85390	WICKENBURG
85396-85396	BUCKEYE
85501-85502	GLOBE
85530-85530	BYLAS
85531-85531	CENTRAL
85532-85532	CLAYPOOL
85533-85533	CLIFTON
85534-85534	DUNCAN
85535-85535	EDEN
85536-85536	FORT THOMAS
85539-85539	MIAMI
85540-85540	MORENCI
85541-85541	PAYSON
85542-85542	PERIDOT
85543-85543	PIMA
85544-85544	PINE
85545-85545	ROOSEVELT
85546-85546	SAFFORD
85547-85547	PAYSON
85548-85548	SAFFORD
85550-85550	SAN CARLOS
85551-85551	SOLOMON
85552-85552	THATCHER
85553-85553	TONTO BASIN
85554-85554	YOUNG
85601-85601	ARIVACA
85602-85602	BENSON
85603-85603	BISBEE
85605-85605	BOWIE
85606-85606	COCHISE
85607-85608	DOUGLAS
85609-85609	DRAGOON
85610-85610	ELFRIDA
85611-85611	ELGIN
85613-85613	FORT HUACHUCA
85614-85614	GREEN VALLEY
85615-85615	HEREFORD
85616-85616	HUACHUCA CITY
85617-85617	MC NEAL
85618-85618	MAMMOTH
85619-85619	MOUNT LEMMON
85620-85620	NACO
85621-85621	NOGALES
85622-85622	GREEN VALLEY
85623-85623	ORACLE
85624-85624	PATAGONIA
85625-85625	PEARCE
85626-85626	PIRTLEVILLE
85627-85627	POMERENE
85628-85628	NOGALES
85629-85629	SAHUARITA
85630-85630	SAINT DAVID
85631-85631	SAN MANUEL
85632-85632	SAN SIMON
85633-85633	SASABE
85634-85634	SELLS
85635-85636	SIERRA VISTA
85637-85637	SONOITA
85638-85638	TOMBSTONE
85639-85639	TOPAWA
85640-85640	TUMACACORI
85641-85641	VAIL
85643-85644	WILLCOX
85645-85645	AMADO
85646-85646	TUBAC
85648-85648	RIO RICO
85650-85650	SIERRA VISTA
85652-85652	CORTARO
85653-85653	MARANA
85654-85654	RILLITO
85655-85655	DOUGLAS
85662-85662	NOGALES
85670-85670	FORT HUACHUCA
85671-85671	SIERRA VISTA
85700-85737	TUCSON
85738-85738	CATALINA
85739-85777	TUCSON
85901-85902	SHOW LOW
85911-85911	CIBICUE
85912-85912	WHITE MOUNTAIN LAKE
85920-85920	ALPINE
85922-85922	BLUE
85923-85923	CLAY SPRINGS
85924-85924	CONCHO
85925-85925	EAGAR
85926-85926	FORT APACHE
85927-85927	GREER
85928-85928	HEBER
85929-85929	LAKESIDE
85930-85930	MC NARY
85931-85931	FOREST LAKES
85932-85932	NUTRIOSO
85933-85933	OVERGAARD
85934-85934	PINEDALE
85935-85935	PINETOP
85936-85936	SAINT JOHNS
85937-85937	SNOWFLAKE
85938-85938	SPRINGERVILLE
85939-85939	TAYLOR
85940-85940	VERNON
85941-85941	WHITERIVER
85942-85942	WOODRUFF
86001-86011	FLAGSTAFF
86015-86015	BELLEMONT
86016-86016	GRAY MOUNTAIN
86017-86017	MUNDS PARK
86018-86018	PARKS
86020-86020	CAMERON
86021-86021	COLORADO CITY
86022-86022	FREDONIA
86023-86023	GRAND CANYON
86024-86024	HAPPY JACK
86025-86025	HOLBROOK
86028-86028	PETRIFIED FOREST NATL PARK
86029-86029	SUN VALLEY
86030-86030	HOTEVILLA
86031-86031	INDIAN WELLS
86032-86032	JOSEPH CITY
86033-86033	KAYENTA
86034-86034	KEAMS CANYON
86035-86035	LEUPP
86036-86036	MARBLE CANYON
86038-86038	MORMON LAKE
86039-86039	KYKOTSMOVI VILLAGE
86040-86040	PAGE
86042-86042	POLACCA
86043-86043	SECOND MESA
86044-86044	TONALEA
86045-86045	TUBA CITY
86046-86046	WILLIAMS
86047-86047	WINSLOW
86052-86052	NORTH RIM
86053-86053	KAIBITO
86054-86054	SHONTO
86301-86305	PRESCOTT
86312-86312	PRESCOTT VALLEY
86313-86313	PRESCOTT
86314-86314	PRESCOTT VALLEY
86320-86320	ASH FORK
86321-86321	BAGDAD
86322-86322	CAMP VERDE
86323-86323	CHINO VALLEY
86324-86324	CLARKDALE
86325-86325	CORNVILLE
86326-86326	COTTONWOOD
86327-86327	DEWEY
86329-86329	HUMBOLDT
86330-86330	IRON SPRINGS
86331-86331	JEROME
86332-86332	KIRKLAND
86333-86333	MAYER
86334-86334	PAULDEN
86335-86335	RIMROCK
86336-86336	SEDONA
86337-86337	SELIGMAN
86338-86338	SKULL VALLEY
86339-86341	SEDONA
86342-86342	LAKE MONTEZUMA
86343-86343	CROWN KING
86351-86351	SEDONA
86401-86402	KINGMAN
86403-86406	LAKE HAVASU CITY
86409-86409	KINGMAN
86411-86411	HACKBERRY
86412-86412	HUALAPAI
86413-86413	GOLDEN VALLEY
86426-86427	FORT MOHAVE
86429-86430	BULLHEAD CITY
86431-86431	CHLORIDE
86432-86432	LITTLEFIELD
86433-86433	OATMAN
86434-86434	PEACH SPRINGS
86435-86435	SUPAI
86436-86436	TOPOCK
86437-86437	VALENTINE
86438-86438	YUCCA
86439-86439	BULLHEAD CITY
86440-86440	MOHAVE VALLEY
86441-86441	DOLAN SPRINGS
86442-86442	BULLHEAD CITY
86443-86443	TEMPLE BAR MARINA
86444-86444	MEADVIEW
86445-86445	WILLOW BEACH
86446-86446	MOHAVE VALLEY
86502-86502	CHAMBERS
86503-86503	CHINLE
86504-86504	FORT DEFIANCE
86505-86505	GANADO
86506-86506	HOUCK
86507-86507	LUKACHUKAI
86508-86508	LUPTON
86509-86509	CHAMBERS
86510-86510	PINON
86511-86511	SAINT MICHAELS
86512-86512	SANDERS
86514-86514	TEEC NOS POS
86515-86515	WINDOW ROCK
86520-86520	BLUE GAP
86535-86535	DENNEHOTSO
86538-86538	MANY FARMS
86540-86540	NAZLINI
86544-86544	RED VALLEY
86545-86545	ROCK POINT
86547-86547	ROUND ROCK
86549-86549	SAWMILL
86556-86556	TSAILE

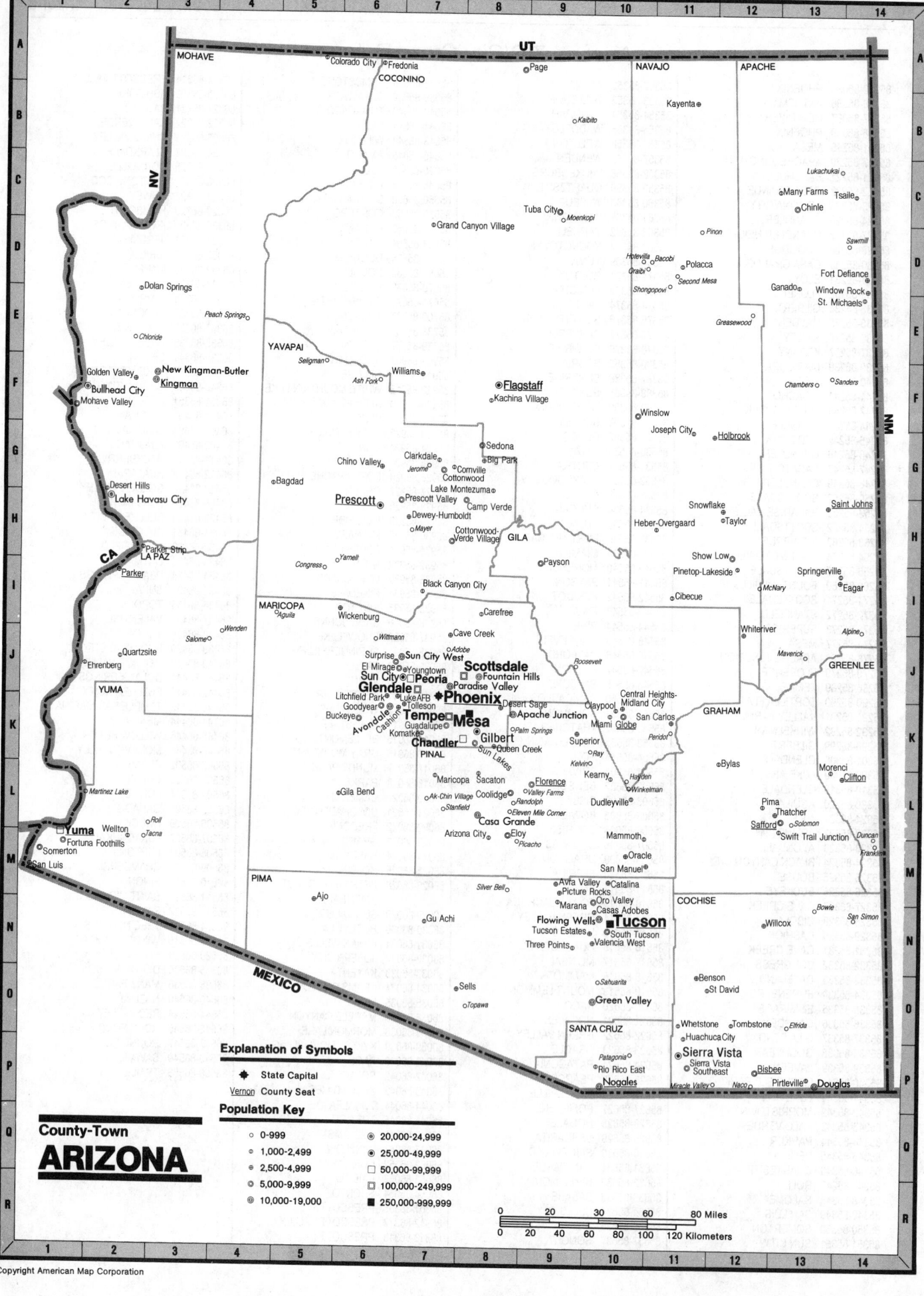

County-Town
ARIZONA

Explanation of Symbols

✦ State Capital

<u>Vernon</u> County Seat

Population Key

○ 0-999	⊕ 20,000-24,999	
⊕ 1,000-2,499	⊛ 25,000-49,999	
⊕ 2,500-4,999	▫ 50,000-99,999	
⊕ 5,000-9,999	◻ 100,000-249,999	
⊛ 10,000-19,000	■ 250,000-999,999	

0   20   30   60   80 Miles

0 20 40 60 80 100 120 Kilometers

COUNTIES

(15 Counties)

Name of County	Population	Location on Map
APACHE	61,591	A-12
COCHISE	97,624	M-11
COCONINO	96,591	A-6
GILA	40,216	H-8
GRAHAM	26,554	K-11
GREENLEE	8,008	J-13
LA PAZ	13,844	H-2
MARICOPA	2,122,101	I-4
MOHAVE	93,497	A-3
NAVAJO	77,658	A-10
PIMA	666,880	M-4
PINAL	116,379	K-7
SANTA CRUZ	29,676	O-9
YAVAPAI	107,714	E-4
YUMA	106,895	J-2
TOTAL	**3,665,228**	

CITIES AND TOWNS

Note: The first name is that of the city or town, second, that of the county in which it is located, then the population and location on the map.

- Ajo, Pima, 2,919 ... N-5
- Apache Junction, Maricopa/Pinal, 18,100 ... K-8
- Arizona City, Pinal, 1,940 ... L-8
- Avondale, Maricopa, 16,169 ... K-6
- Avra Valley, Pima, 3,403 ... M-9
- Bagdad, Yavapai, 1,858 ... G-4
- Benson, Cochise, 3,824 ... O-11
- Big Park, Yavapai, 3,024 ... G-8
- Bisbee, Cochise, 6,288 ... P-12
- Black Canyon City, Yavapai, 1,811 ... I-7
- Buckeye, Maricopa, 5,038 ... K-6
- Bullhead City, Mohave, 21,951 ... F-1
- Bylas, Graham, 1,219 ... K-12
- Camp Verde, Yavapai, 6,243 ... H-8
- Carefree, Maricopa, 1,666 ... I-8
- Casa Grande, Pinal, 19,082 ... L-8
- Casas Adobes, Pima ... N-10
- Catalina, Pima, 4,864 ... M-10
- Cave Creek, Maricopa, 2,925 ... J-7
- Central Heights-Midland City, Gila, 2,969 ... J-10
- Chandler, Maricopa, 90,533 ... K-8
- Chinle, Apache, 5,059 ... C-13
- Chino Valley, Yavapai, 4,837 ... G-6
- Cibecue, Navajo, 1,254 ... I-11
- Clarkdale, Yavapai, 2,144 ... G-7
- Claypool, Gila, 1,942 ... K-10
- Clifton, Greenlee, 2,840 ... L-14
- Colorado City, Mohave, 2,426 ... A-5
- Coolidge, Pinal, 6,927 ... L-8
- Cornville, Yavapai, 2,089 ... G-7
- Cottonwood, Yavapai, 5,918 ... G-7
- Cottonwood-Verde Village, Yavapai, 7,037 ... H-7
- Desert Hills, Mohave, 1,700 ... G-2
- Desert Sage, Maricopa ... K-8
- Dewey-Humboldt, Yavapai, 3,640 ... H-7
- Dolan Springs, Mohave, 1,090 ... D-2
- Douglas, Cochise, 12,822 ... P-13
- Dudleyville, Pinal, 1,356 ... L-10
- Eagar, Apache, 4,025 ... I-14
- Ehrenberg, La Paz, 1,226 ... J-2
- El Mirage, Maricopa, 5,001 ... J-7
- Eloy, Pinal, 7,211 ... M-8
- Flagstaff, Coconino, 45,857 ... F-8
- Florence, Pinal, 7,510 ... L-9
- Flowing Wells, Pima, 14,013 ... N-10
- Fort Defiance, Apache, 4,489 ... D-14
- Fortuna Foothills, Yuma, 7,737 ... M-1
- Fountain Hills, Maricopa, 10,030 ... J-8
- Fredonia, Coconino, 1,207 ... A-6
- Ganado, Apache, 1,257 ... D-13
- Gila Bend, Maricopa, 1,747 ... L-6
- Gilbert, Maricopa, 29,188 ... K-8
- Glendale, Maricopa, 148,134 ... J-7
- Globe, Gila, 6,062 ... K-10
- Golden Valley, Mohave, 2,619 ... F-2
- Goodyear, Maricopa, 6,258 ... K-6
- Grand Canyon Village, Coconino, 1,499 ... D-7
- Green Valley, Pima, 13,231 ... O-10
- Gu Achi, Pima ... N-7
- Guadalupe, Maricopa, 5,458 ... K-7
- Heber-Overgaard, Navajo, 1,581 ... H-11
- Holbrook, Navajo, 4,686 ... G-12
- Huachuca City, Cochise, 1,782 ... O-11
- Joseph City, Navajo ... G-11
- Kachina Village, Coconino, 1,711 ... F-8
- Kayenta, Navajo, 4,372 ... B-11
- Kearny, Pinal, 2,262 ... L-10
- Kingman, Mohave, 12,722 ... F-3
- Komatke, Maricopa, 1,116 ... K-7
- Lake Havasu City, Mohave, 24,363 ... H-2
- Lake Montezuma, Yavapai, 1,841 ... G-8
- Litchfield Park, Maricopa, 3,303 ... J-6
- Luke AFB, Maricopa, 4,371 ... J-6
- Mammoth, Pinal, 1,845 ... M-10
- Many Farms, Apache, 1,294 ... C-13
- Marana, Pima, 2,187 ... M-9
- Mesa, Maricopa, 288,091 ... K-8
- Miami, Gila, 2,018 ... K-10
- Mohave Valley, Mohave, 6,962 ... F-1
- Morenci, Greenlee, 1,799 ... L-13
- New Kingman-Butler, Mohave, 11,627 ... F-3
- Nogales, Santa Cruz, 19,489 ... P-10
- Oracle, Pinal, 3,043 ... M-10
- Oro Valley, Pima, 6,670 ... N-10
- Page, Coconino, 6,598 ... A-8
- Paradise Valley, Maricopa, 11,671 ... J-7
- Parker, La Paz, 2,897 ... I-2
- Parker Strip, La Paz, 1,646 ... H-3
- Payson, Gila, 8,377 ... I-9
- Peoria, Maricopa, 50,618 ... J-7
- Phoenix, Maricopa, 983,403 ... J-7
- Picture Rocks, Pima, 4,026 ... M-9
- Pima, Graham, 1,725 ... K-12
- Pinetop-Lakeside, Navajo, 2,422 ... I-12
- Pirtleville, Cochise, 1,364 ... P-13
- Polacca, Navajo, 1,108 ... D-11
- Prescott, Yavapai, 26,455 ... H-6
- Prescott Valley, Yavapai, 8,858 ... H-6
- Quartzsite, La Paz, 1,876 ... J-2
- Queen Creek, Maricopa, 2,667 ... K-8
- Rio Rico East, Santa Cruz, 1,407 ... P-10
- Sacaton, Pinal, 1,452 ... L-8
- Safford, Graham, 7,359 ... L-13
- Saint David, Cochise, 1,468 ... O-11
- Saint Johns, Apache, 3,294 ... H-13
- Saint Michaels, Apache, 1,119 ... E-14
- San Carlos, Gila, 2,918 ... K-11
- San Luis, Yuma, 4,212 ... M-1
- San Manuel, Pinal, 4,009 ... M-10
- Scottsdale, Maricopa, 130,069 ... J-8
- Sedona, Coconino/Yavapai, 7,720 ... G-8
- Sells, Pima, 2,750 ... O-7
- Show Low, Navajo, 5,019 ... H-12
- Sierra Vista, Cochise, 32,983 ... P-11
- Sierra Vista Southeast, Cochise, 9,237 ... P-11
- Snowflake, Navajo, 3,679 ... H-12
- Somerton, Yuma, 5,282 ... M-1
- South Tucson, Pima, 5,093 ... N-10
- Springerville, Apache, 1,802 ... I-14
- Sun City, Maricopa, 38,126 ... J-7
- Sun City West, Maricopa, 15,997 ... J-7
- Sun Lakes, Maricopa, 6,578 ... K-8
- Superior, Pinal, 3,468 ... K-9
- Surprise, Maricopa, 7,122 ... J-6
- Swift Trail Junction, Graham, 1,203 ... L-13
- Taylor, Navajo, 2,418 ... H-12
- Tempe, Maricopa, 141,865 ... K-7
- Thatcher, Graham, 3,763 ... L-13
- Three Points, Pima, 2,175 ... N-9
- Tolleson, Maricopa, 4,434 ... K-7
- Tombstone, Cochise, 1,220 ... O-12
- Tsaile, Apache, 1,043 ... C-14
- Tuba City, Coconino, 7,323 ... C-9
- Tucson, Pima, 405,390 ... N-10
- Tucson Estates, Pima, 2,662 ... N-10
- Valencia West, Pima, 3,277 ... N-10
- Wellton, Yuma, 1,066 ... M-2
- Whetstone, Cochise, 1,289 ... O-11
- Whiteriver, Navajo, 3,775 ... J-12
- Wickenburg, Maricopa, 4,515 ... I-6
- Willcox, Cochise, 3,122 ... N-12
- Williams, Coconino, 2,532 ... F-7
- Window Rock, Apache, 3,306 ... D-14
- Winslow, Navajo, 8,190 ... F-10
- Youngtown, Maricopa, 2,542 ... J-7
- Yuma, Yuma, 54,923 ... M-1

Explanation of symbols: ●– Census Designated Place (CDP)

Arkansas

General Help Numbers:

Governor's Office

State Capitol, #250
Little Rock, AR 72201
www.arkansas.gov/governor

501-682-2345
Fax 501-682-3597
8AM-5PM

Attorney General's Office

323 Center St #200
Little Rock, AR 72201
www.ag.state.ar.us

501-682-2007
Fax 501-682-8084
8AM-5PM

Legislative Records

Elections Department
State Capitol, Room 026
Little Rock, AR 72201
www.arkleg.state.ar.us

501-682-5070
Fax 501-682-3408
8AM-5PM

State Archives

State Archives
One Capitol Mall
Little Rock, AR 72201
www.ark-ives.com/

501-682-6900

8AM-4:30PM M-SAT.

State Specifics:

Capital:

Little Rock
Pulaski County

Time Zone:

CST

Number of Counties:

75

Population:

2,752,629

Website:

www.state.ar.us

State Agencies

Criminal Records

Arkansas State Police, Identification Bureau, #1 State Police Plaza Dr, Little Rock, AR 72209; 501-618-8500, 501-618-8404-Fax; 7:30AM-4:30PM.

www.asp.state.ar.us

Under Act 63 of the 1st Ext Sess of 2003, employers and professional licensing boards are permitted access to felony arrests not yet resulting in disposition. Generally if such arrest is more than three years old, state personnel will research record.

Records are available for the past 25 years. Older records are located in the off-site State Archives. It takes 2-3 weeks before new records are available

for inquiry. Records are indexed on computer by name, and on fingerprint cards. Records are normally destroyed after it is determined the subject will probably not commit a crime again (i.e. death). 58% of arrests in database have final dispositions recorded, 77% for those arrests in last 5 years.

Searching: You must use the Bureau's request form. Include the following in your request- notarized release from subject, name, date of birth, sex, Social Security Number, driver's license number. Fingerprints are not required, but may be included. 100% of the arrest records are fingerprint supported. The following data is not released: pardons and juvenile records. Felony records

without dispositions are released only to employers and licensing boards, otherwise all records without disposition are not released.

Access by: mail, in person, online.

Fee & Payment: The fee is $20.00 per record. Fee payee: Arkansas State Police. Prepayment required. Personal checks accepted, credit or debit cards are not.

Mail search: Turnaround time: 5 to 7 days. A SASE is required.

In person search: Bring in signed, notarized release. Results of less than 10 request can usually be done as you wait.

Online search: Online access available but only to employers and professional licensing boards. Registration is required. Agents or 3rd party vendors representing employers are blocked from access, per the state legislators. There is an additional $2.00 to the standard $20.00 search fee. Searches are conducted by name. Search results includes registered sex offenders. For more info on this online service, see https://www.ark.org/criminal/index.php. Accounts must maintain the signed release documents in-house for three years.

Statewide Court Records

Administrative Office of Courts, 625 Marshall Street, 1100 Justice Bldg, Little Rock, AR 72201-1078; 501-682-9400, 501-682-9410-Fax; 8AM-5PM.

www.courts.state.ar.us

There is no statewide access to county court records. Except for certain online research capabilities, all court record access must be done at the local level.

Access by: online.

Online search: The home web page gives online access to Supreme Court Opinions and Appellate Court dockets, or access via http://courts.state.ar.us/online/or.html where you will also find Court of Appeals dockets, corrected opinions, and parallel citations. An Attorney search and court rules and administrative orders are also available.

Sexual Offender Registry

Access to Records is Restricted.

Arkansas Crime Information Center, Sexual Offender Registry, One Capitol Mall, 4D200, Little Rock, AR 72201; 501-682-2222, 501-682-2269 (Fax). www.acic.org/Registration/index.htm

Based on information obtained from the risk assessment process, offenders are assigned the following levels: Level 1: Low Risk; Level 2: Moderate Risk; Level 3: High Risk; Level 4: Sexually Violent Predator. ACIC provides information on registered sex offenders to all law enforcement agencies in the county where the offender resides. Local law enforcement agencies release names of those determined most likely to re-offend.

Incarceration Records

Arkansas Department of Corrections, Records Supervisor, PO Box 8707, Pine Bluff, AR 71611-8707; 870-267-6424, 870-267-6999, 8AM-4:30PM.

www.accessarkansas.org/doc/index.html

Questions may be directed to info@adc.state.ar.us or adc.inmate.info@arkansas.gov.

Records are available on current and former inmates; however, the online access is limited to current inmates. It takes 2-3 weeks before new records are available for inquiry.

Searching: Include the following in your request-first and last name or ADC number. Location, ADC number, physical Identifiers and sentencing information, release dates are released.

Access by: mail, online.

Fee & Payment: There is no fee.

Mail search: Turnaround time: 5 to 7 days. A mail search can also be directed through the Attorney General's office (phone 510-682-2007).

Online search: The online access at www.accessarkansas.org/doc/inmate_info/ has many search criteria capabilites. Also, a private company offers free web access at www.vinelink.com/index.jsp, including state, DOC, and many county jail systems.

Other access: The inmate access web page offers a download of the inmate database. Fee includes an annual INA subscription of $50.00 plus $0.10 per record enhanced access fee.

Corporation, Fictitious Name, Limited Liability Company, Limited Partnerships

Secretary of State, Business & Commercial Service Division, State Capitol Bldg, Little Rock, AR 72201 (Courier address: Business & Commercial Service Division, 1401 W Capitol Ave Ste 250, Little Rock, AR 72201); 501-682-3409, 888-233-0325, 501-682-3437-Fax; 8AM-5PM (4:30 on F).

www.sos.arkansas.gov/corps

Records are available from late 1800's on. Corporation records are on computer from 1987 on. Prior records, such as dissolved corporations, may be in paper files. New records are available for inquiry immediately. Records are indexed on inhouse computer, file folders.

Searching: Franchise tax information is not released except for names and addressees of parties involved and certain information about the shares of stock. Include the following in your request-full name of business. In addition to the articles of incorporation, corporation records include the following information: Prior (Merged) names, Reserved names, Good standing. Officers listed on franchise tax form is now public information.

Access by: mail, phone, in person, online.

Fee & Payment: There are no search fees. Copies are $.50 a page. Certification of records is an additional $5.00. Fee payee: Secretary of State. Prepayment required. Personal checks accepted. No credit cards accepted.

Mail search: Turnaround time: same day if possible. Call first for copy fees. Records prior to 1988 will take longer to search. No SASE is required. Copies cost $.50 per page, minimum $2.50 by mail.

Phone search: They will give incorporation dates, history, agent name, and status over the phone.

In person search: Copies cost $.50 per page.

Online search: The Internet site permits free searching of corporation records. You can search by name, registered agent, or filing number.

Other access: Bulk release of records is available for $.50 per page. Contact Records Dept. 501-682-3409 or visit website for details.

Trademarks/Servicemarks

Secretary of State, Trademarks Section, State Capitol Bldg, Little Rock, AR 72201 (Courier address: Business & Commercial Services Div, 1401 W Capitol Ave #250, Little Rock, AR 72201); 501-682-3409, 888-233-0325, 501-682-3437-Fax; 8AM-5PM (4:30PM on F).

www.sos.arkansas.gov/corps/trademk

Records are available from the 1950s. It takes minutes before new records are available for inquiry. Records are indexed on inhouse computer.

Searching: Include the following in your request-name.

Access by: mail, phone, in person, online.

Fee & Payment: There is no search fee, copy fees are $.50 per copy. Fee payee: Secretary of State. Prepayment required. Personal checks accepted. No credit cards accepted.

Mail search: Turnaround time: 24-48 hours. Minimum fee for copies by mail is $2.50. No SASE is required.

Phone search: They will give information over the phone.

In person search: Turnaround time is within a few minutes.

Online search: Searching is available at no fee over the Internet site. Search by name, owner, city, or filing number. You can also search via email at corprequest@sosmail.state.ar.us.

Other access: Records can be provided in bulk for $.50 per page. Call 501-682-3409 or visit website for details.

Uniform Commercial Code, Federal Tax Liens

UCC Division - Commercial Srvs, Secretary of State, State Capitol Bldg, Little Rock, AR 72201 (Courier address: Commercial Business & Service Division, 1401 W Capitol Ave Rm 250, Little Rock, AR 72201); 501-682-5078, 501-682-3500-Fax; 8AM-5PM.

www.sos.arkansas.gov

Records are available from 1962. You can make requests by fax, but they will be returned by mail. Records are not searched by phone, but they will inform if there is anything on file. It takes minutes before new records are available for inquiry.

Searching: Use search request form UCC-11. A search includes federal tax liens on businesses, via a lien search certificate. Federal tax liens on individuals and all state tax liens (AKA municipal judgments before 1978) are filed at the county. Include the following in your request-debtor name.

Access by: mail, fax, in person, online.

Fee & Payment: A lien search certificate is $6.00. Photostat copies of financing statements are $6.00 for the first page, $.50 each additional, maximum $100.00. The fee for certification of a copy of a filed financing statement is $.50 Fee payee: Secretary of State. Personal checks accepted. No credit cards accepted.

Mail search: Turnaround time: 1 to 2 days. No SASE is required.

Fax search: There is an additional fee of $5.00 to return by fax.

In person search: Requesters can leave request and pick up the next day.

Online search: Subscribers of INA (Information Netwrok of Arkansas) can search by file number or charter number; subscription fees and search fees involved. Check website for details. UCC Download is available via the Internet, but only to subscribers. Fee is $2,000.00 per month for weekly, bi-weekly or monthly downloads. Watch notifications are available for a $35.00 monthly fee.

State Tax Liens

Records not maintained by a state level agency.

Records are at the county level.

Sales Tax Registrations

Finance & Administration Department, Sales & Use Tax Office - Reg. Dept, PO Box 1272, Little Rock, AR 72203; 501-682-1895, 501-682-7900-Fax; 8AM-4:30PM.

www.state.ar.us/dfa/taxes/salestax

Records are available from the 1940s.

Searching: This agency will only confirm that a business is registered. They will provide no other information. All searches are based upon tax permit number

Access by: mail, phone, fax, in person.

Mail search: Turnaround time: 3 to 5 days. A SASE is requested. No fee for mail request.

Phone search: No fee for telephone request. This is the recommended search request method.

Fax search: Fax searching available.

In person search: No fee for request.

Birth Certificates

Arkansas Department of Health, Division of Vital Records, 4815 W Markham St, Slot 44, Little Rock, AR 72205; 501-661-2174, 501-661-2336 (Message Number), 501-661-2726 (Credit Card Line), 800-637-9314 (Toll Free), 501-663-2832-Fax; 8AM-4:30PM.

www.healthyarkansas.com

Three types of records are available; certification copy, actual copy, and wallet size copy.

Records are available from 02/01/1914 to present. New records are available for inquiry immediately. Records are indexed on microfiche, inhouse computer.

Searching: Must have a signed release from person of record if requester is not a member of parents, grandparents or spouse. Include your name, address and signature on the request. Include the following in your request-full name, names of parents, mother's maiden name, date of birth, place of birth, relationship to person of record, reason for information request. Also include your phone number.

Access by: mail, phone, fax, in person, online.

Fee & Payment: The fee is $12.00 for the first copy and $10.00 for each add'l of same record. Fee payee: Division of Vital Records. Prepayment required. Personal checks accepted. Major credit cards accepted.

Mail search: Turnaround time: 4 weeks. No SASE is required.

Phone search: See expedited service. You must use a credit card. Turnaround time is 1 week.

Fax search: See expedited service.

In person search: Turnaround time: While you wait.

Online search: Records may requested from www.vitalchek.com, or www.uscerts.com, both are state-endorsed vendors. Expedited service fees apply.

Other access: Research projects require the approval of the director.

Expedited service: Expedited service is available for phone, online, and fax requests. Turnaround time: 1-5 days. Add $10.95 for use of credit card and additional funds for the delivery method desired.

Death Records

Arkansas Department of Health, Division of Vital Records, 4815 W Markham St, Slot 44, Little Rock, AR 72205; 501-661-2174, 501-661-2336 (Message number), 501-661-2726 (Credit Card Line), 501-663-2832-Fax; 8AM-4:30PM.

www.healthyarkansas.com

This agency does not hold the actual records, but does have an index of all deaths since 1914 and some death index records for Fort Smith and Little Rock prior to 1914.

Records are available from 02/01/1914 to present. New records are available for inquiry immediately. Records are indexed on microfiche, inhouse computer.

Searching: Must have a signed release from immediate family member if requester is not a member of family, unless record is over 50 years old. Include the following in your request-full name, date of death, place of death, relationship to person of record, reason for information request, wife's maiden name. Include requester's signature and phone number.

Access by: mail, phone, fax, in person, online.

Fee & Payment: The fee is $10.00 for the first copy and $8.00 for each add'l of same record. Add $6.00 if you use a credit card. Fee payee: Division of Vital Records. Prepayment required. Personal checks accepted. Major credit cards accepted.

Mail search: Turnaround time: 4 weeks. Turnaround time with a credit card is 1 week. No SASE is required.

Phone search: You must use a credit card.

Fax search: You must use a credit card or prepay before record is sent.

In person search: Turnaround time is usually 1 to 2 hours.

Online search: Records may requested from www.vitalchek.com, or www.uscerts.com, both are state-endorsed vendors. Expedited service fees apply.

Expedited service: Expedited service is available for online, phone and fax searches. Turnaround time: 1-5 days. Add $10.95 for use of credit card and additional funds for the delivery method desired.

Marriage Certificates

Arkansas Department of Health, Division of Vital Records, 4815 W Markham St, Slot 44, Little Rock, AR 72205; 501-661-2174, 501-661-2336 (Message Number), 501-661-2726 (Credit Card Line), 501-663-2832-Fax; 8AM-4:30PM.

www.healthyarkansas.com

The Division of Vital Records does not have either the actual marriage license or divorce decree. Customers who want a copy of the actual license or decree must contact the County Clerk or Circuit Clerk office where the record was recorded.

Records are available from 1917 on. The Division of Vital Records issues a certified copy of the coupon of marriage or divorce in paper form. New records are available for inquiry immediately. Records are indexed on microfiche, inhouse computer.

Searching: Must have a signed release from person of record if requester is not a member of immediate family. Include the following in your request-full names of husband and wife, registration number, date of marriage, place or county of marriage, wife's maiden name. Requester must sign request and provide phone number.

Access by: mail, phone, fax, in person, online.

Fee & Payment: The fee is $10.00, add $6.00 if you use a credit card. Fee payee: Division of Vital Records. Prepayment required. Personal checks accepted. Major credit cards accepted.

Mail search: Turnaround time: 4 weeks. Turnaround time with a credit card is 1 week. No SASE is required.

Phone search: You may call in your request, but you must use a credit card. Turnaround time is 1 week.

Fax search: A credit card is required or must prepay before records sent.

In person search: Turnaround time is 30 minutes to an hour.

Online search: Records may requested from www.vitalchek.com, a state-endorsed vendor. Expedited service fees apply.

Expedited service: Expedited service is available for online, phone and fax searches. Turnaround time: 1-5 days. Add $10.95 for use of credit card and additional funds for the delivery method desired.

Divorce Records

Arkansas Department of Health, Division of Vital Records, 4815 W Markham St, Slot 44, Little Rock, AR 72205; 501-661-2174, 501-661-2336 (Message Number), 866-209-9482 (Credit Card Line), 800-637-9314, 501-663-2832-Fax; 8AM-4:30PM.

www.healthyarkansas.com

The Division of Vital Records does not have either the actual marriage license or divorce decree. Customers who want a copy of the actual license or decree must contact the County Clerk or Circuit Clerk office where the record was recorded.

Records are available from 1923 to present. The Division of Vital Records issues a certified copy of the coupon of marriage or divorce in paper form. It takes 30 days before new records are available for inquiry. Records are indexed on mainframe computer and microfiche.

Searching: Must have a signed release from person of record if requester is not a member of the immediate family. Include the following in your request-names of husband and wife, date of divorce, place of divorce. Signature of requester required.

Access by: mail, phone, fax, in person, online.

Fee & Payment: The fee is $10.00. Fee payee: Division of Public Records. Prepayment required. Personal checks and major credit cards accepted.

Mail search: Turnaround time: 4 weeks. Turnaround time with a credit card is 1 week. No SASE is required.

Phone search: See expedited service. You must use a credit card. Turnaround time is 1 week.

Fax search: See expedited service.

In person search: Turnaround time is within 1 hour.

Online search: Records may requested from www.vitalchek.com, a state-endorsed vendor. See expedited service.

Expedited service: Expedited service is available for online, phone and fax searches. Turnaround time: 1-5 days. Add $10.95 for use of credit card and additional funds for the delivery method desired.

Workers' Compensation Records

Workers Compensation Commission, Operations/Compliance, 324 Spring Street, PO Box 950, Little Rock, AR 72203-0950; 501-682-3930, 800-622-4472, 501-682-6761-Fax; 8AM-4:30PM M-F.

www.awcc.state.ar.us

Records are available from 1940s on. New records are available for inquiry immediately. Records are indexed on microfilm, inhouse computer.

Searching: Only written requests are accepted. You may fax a request, but it is returned by mail. Include the following in your request-claimant name, Social Security Number, place of employment at time of accident, file number (if known). The following data is not released: Social Security Numbers or medical information.

Access by: mail, phone, fax, in person, online.

Fee & Payment: The fee is $5.00 per name searched and $.50 per page for copies. Fee payee: Workers' Compensation Commission. An invoice is mailed with the results of the request. Personal checks accepted. No credit cards accepted.

Mail search: Turnaround time: 10 days. No SASE is required.

Phone search: Records are available by phone.

Fax search: Same criteria as mail searching.

In person search: You may make copies at $.50 per page. You are allowed to look through the files without charge.

Online search: To perform an online claim search, one must be a subscriber to the Information Network of Arkansas (INA). Records are from May 1, 1997 forward. There is an annual $50 subscriber fee to INA. Each record request is $3.50; if more than 20 are ordered in one month, the fee is $2.50 each request over 20. For more information, visit www.awcc.state.ar.us/electron.html.

Driver Records

Department of Driver Services, Driving Records Division, PO Box 1272, Room 1130, Little Rock, AR 72203-1272 (Courier address: 1900 W 7th, #1130, Little Rock, AR 72201); 501-682-7207, 501-682-7908, 501-682-2075-Fax; 8AM-4:30PM.

www.accessarkansas.org/dfa/driverservices

Copies of tickets must be requested from the local jurisdiction where the ticket was issued.

Records are available for 3 years for moving violations, 3 years for employment or insurance purposes and are retained indefinitely for departmental purposes. DWI and suspensions show until all requirements are met. It takes less than 1 day before new records are available for inquiry. Records are indexed on inhouse computer.

Searching: Arkansas requires signed authorization by the driver to obtain a driving record. Volume requesters must have these authorizations on file. Violations on an interstate highway not exceeding 75 mph won't show on records requested for insurance purposes. Include the following in your request-full name, driver's license number, date of birth. Driver's address is included as part of the search report for permissible requesters.

Access by: mail, in person, online.

Fee & Payment: Fees are $7.00 for insurance record and $10.00 for records on commercial drivers. There is a full charge for a "no record found." Fee payee: State of Arkansas, Driver Services. Prepayment required. Personal checks accepted. No credit cards accepted.

Mail search: Turnaround time: 24 hours. Requester must enclose written release, full name, DOB, driver's license number, and proper fees. No SASE is required.

In person search: The state will process up to 5 requests while you wait.

Online search: Access is available through the Information Network of Arkansas (INA). The system offers both batch and interactive service. The system is only available to INA subscribers who have statutory rights to the data. The record fee is $8.00, or $11.00 for commercial drivers. Visit www.arkansas.gov/sub_services.php.

Other access: High volume requesters use magnetic tape-to-tape for overnight access.

Vehicle Ownership, Vehicle Identification

Office of Motor Vehicles, MV Title Records, PO Box 1272, Room 1100, Little Rock, AR 72203 (Courier address: 7th & Battery Sts, Ragland Bldg, Room 1100, Little Rock, AR 72201); 501-682-4692, 800-662-8247, 501-682-4756-Fax; 8AM-4:30PM.

www.accessarkansas.org/dfa

Records are available from 1950 for titles; license plate records from 1968 on microfilm; plate number and name from 1981 on microfiche. It takes 4 to 6 weeks before new records are available for inquiry.

Searching: Vehicle registration information cannot be sold or used for solicitation purposes. Requesters that do not have DPPA approved purpose, cannot receive records with personal information, unless consent of subject is given. Include the following in your request-vehicle make and VIN. Approved account holders may request

via e-mail. The following data is not released: Social Security Numbers or date of birth.

Access by: mail, phone, fax, in person, online.

Fee & Payment: The fee for vehicle and/or ownership searches is $1.00 per copy and $1.00 per search. Fee payee: Department of Finance and Administration. Prepayment required. If mailing a check to open a new account, place "Attn: Search Account" on the request. If mailing an information request, place "Attn: Correspondence Desk" on the request. Personal checks accepted. No credit cards accepted.

Mail search: Turnaround time: 24 hours. No SASE is required.

Phone search: Searching by phone is available for established accounts. A $25.00 deposit is required.

Fax search: For approved account holders only.

In person search: Turnaround time: while you wait.

Online search: Approved, DPPA compliant accounts may access records online by VIN, plate, or title number. The fee is $1.50. Name searches and certificated documents may be ordered. For further info, go to www.arkansas.gov/itrl/.

Other access: The bulk purchase of records, except for recall or statistical purposes, is prohibited.

Accident Reports

Arkansas State Police, Crash Records Section, 1 State Police Plaza Drive, Little Rock, AR 72209; 501-618-8130, 501-618-8131-Fax; 8AM-5PM.

www.asp.state.ar.us/cr/cr.html

Records are available from 1995 to present. It takes 30-40 days before new records are available for inquiry.

Searching: Include the following in your request-date of accident, location, name of at least on driver.

Access by: mail, phone, in person, online.

Fee & Payment: The fee is $10.00 per record. There is no charge for a "no record found." Payment will be refunded. Fee payee: Arkansas State Police, Accident Records. Prepayment required. Personal checks accepted. No credit cards accepted.

Mail search: Turnaround time: 4 to 6 weeks. A SASE is requested.

Phone search: Limited information is available.

In person search: Turnaround time is while you wait, if staffing available.

Online search: Limited information is available from the webpage for no charge (names involved), date, county. A record copy s may be purchased for $10.00 plus an additional $2.00 fee. Search by name, license number and/or date range. Once purchased, reports will be available for 30 days and may be repeatedly accessed with an Order ID. For further information regarding the contents of the report, please contact the Arkansas State Police at 501-618-8130. Credit card is required, unless requester is member of INA. Available records date back to 01/02/00.

Vessel Ownership, Vessel Registration

Office of Motor Vehicles, Boat Registration, PO Box 1272, Little Rock, AR 72203; 501-682-4692, 501-682-1116-Fax; 8AM-4:30PM.

www.arkansas.gov/dfa/motorvehicle/index.html

Lien information may be filed at the Secretary of State.

Records are available from 1980. All boats propelled by sail or machinery must be registered. Vessels are not titled in this state. New records are available for inquiry immediately.

Searching: Motor vehicle title, registration and lien information is available for users that qualify under DPPA. Ongoing requesters should become account holders. Include the following in your request-name and address of requester and account number if applicable. Search by name or registration number or hull number.

Access by: mail, phone, fax, in person.

Fee & Payment: The search fee is $1.00 per search and $1.00 per copy of a record. Fee payee: Office of Motor Vehicles. Prepayment required. Personal checks accepted. No credit cards accepted.

Mail search: Turnaround time: 2 weeks. No SASE is required.

Phone search: Requests only accepted for account holders.

Fax search: Requests only accepted for account holders.

In person search: Records are usually obtained at once, unless they require extensive research.

Other access: Bulk access to approved users is available via FTP.

Voter Registration

Access to Records is Restricted.

Secretary of State, Voter Services, State Capitol, Room 026, Little Rock, AR 72201; 501-682-3204, 501-682-3548-Fax; 8AM-5PM.

www.sosweb.state.ar.us/elections.html

The state will sell the voter database for voting or election purposes. All individual search requests must be at the local County Clerk's office. The SSN will not be released. The state will comply with the HAVA mandate by 01/06. Requests for bulk release of records must be in writing and state "pursuant to the Freedom of Information Act." Information released on a CD includes name, address, and DOB, as well as district data.

GED Certificates

GED Testing, Dept of Workforce Education, #3 Capitol Mall, Room 305D, Little Rock, AR 72201; 501-682-1978 (Main Number), 501-682-1982-Fax; 8AM-4:30PM.

http://dwe.arkansas.gov/ged.htm

Records are available from 1980 forward. It takes one month before new records are available for inquiry.

Searching: For verification or for a copy of a transcript, all of the following is required: a signed release, name, year of test, date of birth, and SSN.

Access by: mail, fax, in person.

Fee & Payment: There is no fee.

Mail search: Turnaround time: 2 to 31 days. No SASE is required.

Fax search: Turnaround time is next day, but results returned by mail.

In person search: Records can be accessed immediately.

Expedited service: Will provide expedited service if needed for immediate hiring or enrollment in college, and documented by signature of company/school official. Turnaround time: 1 day or less.

Hunting and Fishing License Information

Access to Records is Restricted.

Game & Fish Commission, Attn: Licensing, Two Natural Resources Dr, Little Rock, AR 72205; 501-223-6300, 800-364-4263, 501-223-6425-Fax; 8AM-4:30PM.

www.agfc.com

Requests for records are only processed in accordance with the Arkansas Freedom of Information Act. This agency refuses to make any further statements regarding the procedure. Must mention request is under the Freedom of Information Act.

Arkansas State Licensing Agencies

For details about the agency responsible for licensing/certifying/registering an item below or in the Agency Quick Finder section, match an item's number with the number of the agency in the *Licensing Agency Information* section.

Arkansas Licenses Searchable Online

Aesthetician #49	www.arkansas.gov/cos/
Agriculture Education #32	www.as-is.org/directory/search_lic.html
Architect #6	www.state.ar.us/arch/search.html
Asbestos Abatem't Inspector/Planner #28	www.adeq.state.ar.us/compsvs/webmaster/databases.htm
Asbestos Abatem't Training Provider #28	www.adeq.state.ar.us/compsvs/webmaster/databases.htm
Asbestos Removal Worker #28	www.adeq.state.ar.us/compsvs/webmaster/databases.htm
Athletic Trainer #24	www.aratb.org/search.php
Attorney #43	http://courts.state.ar.us/attylist/new/
Bank #38	www.sos.arkansas.gov/corps/search_all.php
Business Education Teacher #32	www.as-is.org/directory/search_lic.html
Career Education Coordinator #32	www.as-is.org/directory/search_lic.html
Career Orientation Teacher #32	www.as-is.org/directory/search_lic.html
Cemetery, Perpetual Care #39	www.ark.org/arsec/database/dbsearch.cgi?dbname=7&LIMIT=20&LISTALL=ON
Child Care Provider #26	www.state.ar.us/childcare/search.html
Chiropractor #9	www.accessarkansas.org/asbce/search.html
Contractor #23	www.state.ar.us/clb/search.html
Cosmetologist/Cosmetology Instr. #49	www.arkansas.gov/cos/
Counselor, Professional #51	www.state.ar.us/abec/search.php
Dental Hygienist #11	www.asbde.org
Dentist #11	www.asbde.org
Electrologist/Electrolysis Instructor #49	www.arkansas.gov/cos/
Embalmer/Embalmer Apprentice #12	www.arkansas.gov/fdemb/
Engineer/Engineer in Training #19	www.accessarkansas.org/pels/search.php
Fire Equipment Inspector/Repairer #47	www.arfireprotection.org/roster/index.html
Fire Extinguisher Sprinkler Inspector #47	www.arfireprotection.org/roster/index.html
Funeral Director/Apprentice #12	www.arkansas.gov/fdemb/
Funeral Home/Crematory #12	www.arkansas.gov/fdemb/
Insurance Agency #2	http://insurance.arkansas.gov/is/Agency/agency.asp
Insurance Agency #38	www.sos.arkansas.gov/corps/search_all.php
Insurance Company #2	http://insurance.arkansas.gov/is/companysearch/cosearch.asp
Insurance Sales Agent #2	http://insurance.arkansas.gov/is/agentsearch/agent.asp
Investment Advisor #39	www.ark.org/arsec/database/search.html
Landscape Architect #6	www.state.ar.us/arch/search.html
Lobbyist #38	www.sosweb.state.ar.us/elections/elections_pdfs/lobby_lists/2005/2005list.pdf
Manicurist #49	www.arkansas.gov/cos/
Marriage & Family Therapist #51	www.state.ar.us/abec/search.php
Medical Corporation #31	https://www.armedicalboard.org/licenseverf/
Medical Doctor/Surgeon #31	https://www.armedicalboard.org/licenseverf/
Midwife Nurse #15	www.arsbn.org/registry/index.html
Mortgage Loan Broker/Company #39	www.ark.org/arsec/database/search.html
Motor Vehicle Dealer/Distributor #35	www.armvc.com/licensee_search/index.html
Motor Vehicle Mfg/Rep, New #35	www.armvc.com/licensee_search/index.html
Notary Public #38	www.sos.arkansas.gov/corps/notary/
Nurse #15	www.arsbn.org/registry/index.html
Nurse Anesthetist #15	www.arsbn.org/registry/index.html
Nurse-LPN #15	www.arsbn.org/registry/index.html
Occupational Therapist/Assistant #31	https://www.armedicalboard.org/licenseverf/
Optician #50	www.ark.org/directory/detail2.cgi?ID-1050
Optometrist #16	www.arbo.org/index.php?action=findanoptometrist
Osteopathic Physician #31	https://www.armedicalboard.org/licenseverf/
P & C Company #2	http://insurance.arkansas.gov/pclh/pcweb.asp
Physical Therapist #3	www.arptb.org/ptroster/search.php
Physician Assistant #31	https://www.armedicalboard.org/licenseverf/
Political Action Committee #38	www.sosweb.state.ar.us/elections/elections_pdfs/pac_lists/pac_list_02-03-05.pdf
Public Accountant-CPA #18	www.arkansas.gov/asbpa/
Real Estate Agent/Broker/Sales #37	www.accessarkansas.org/arec/db/
Real Estate Appraiser #37	www.arkansas.gov/alcb/search.php

Respiratory Care Practitioner #31 ....https://www.armedicalboard.org/licenseverf/
School Counselor #32 ....www.as-is.org/directory/search_lic.html
School Principal/Admin/Super #32 ....www.as-is.org/directory/search_lic.html
Securities Agent #39...www.ark.org/arsec/database/search.html
Securities Broker/Dealer #39.................................www.ark.org/arsec/database/search.html
Social Worker #40 ....www.state.ar.us/swlb/search/index.html
Solid Waste Facility Operator #28 ....www.adeq.state.ar.us/compsvs/webmaster/databases.htm
Surveyor, Land #19 ....www.accessarkansas.org/pels/search.php
Surveyor-in-Training #19 ....www.accessarkansas.org/pels/search.php
Teacher #32 ....www.as-is.org/directory/search_lic.html
Waste Water Plant Operator #28............................www.adeq.state.ar.us/compsvs/webmaster/databases.htm

Arkansas Licensing Quick Finder

Abstractor #48 870-942-8064	Emergency Medical Technician #25 501-661-2284	Nurse-LPN #15.................................... 501-682-2200
Acupuncturist #46 501-683-3583	Emergency Medical Tech-Paramedic #25	Nurseryman #33............................... 501-225-1598
Aesthetician #49 501-682-2168	 501-661-2284	Nursing Home Administrator #52 501-682-1873
Agricultural Consultant #33 501-225-1598	Employment Agency Manager #27 501-682-4505	Occupational Therapist/Assistant #31 . 501-296-1802
Agriculture Education #32 501-682-4695	Employment Agent/Counselor #27 501-682-4505	Optician #50 870-572-2847
Alcohol/Drug Treatment Prgm #25....... 501-661-2000	Engineer/Engineer in Training #19...... 501-682-2824	Optometrist #16................................. 501-268-4351
Anesthetician #15 501-682-2200	Exterminator #33 501-225-1598	Osteopathic Physician #31................. 501-296-1802
Announcer, Athletic Event (Ring) #4 501-666-5544	Fire Equipment Inspector/Repairer #47 501-661-7903	Permanent Cosmetic/Tattoo Artist #25 501-661-2171
Architect #6...................................... 501-682-3171	Fire Extinguisher Sprinkler Inspt. #47 .. 501-661-7903	Pesticide Applicator #33.................... 501-225-1598
Armored Car Guard #42 501-618-8600	Forester #20 501-296-1998	Petroleum Dealer #30 501-683-4100
Asbestos Abatem't Inspr/Planner #28 ... 501-682-0718	Funeral Director/Apprentice #12 501-682-0574	Pharmacist #17 501-682-0190
Asbestos Abatement Training Provider #28	Funeral Home/Crematory #12.............. 501-682-0574	Pharmacist Intern #17 501-682-0190
.... 501-682-0718	Gas Fitter/Trainee #25 501-661-2242	Pharmacy Technician #17................... 501-682-0190
Asbestos Removal Worker #28............. 501-682-0718	Geologist #21 501-683-0150	Pharmacy, Hospital #17..................... 501-682-0190
Athletic Manager #4.......................... 501-666-5544	Grain Warehouseman #33 501-225-1598	Pharmacy, Institutional #17................ 501-682-0190
Athletic Promoter/Matchmaker #4 501-666-5544	Greyhound Racing #36 501-682-1467	Pharmacy, Specialty #17 501-682-0190
Athletic Trainer #24........................... 501-683-4076	Handgun, Concealed #42 501-618-8600	Pharmacy-In-State, Retail #17 501-682-0190
Attorney #43 501-682-6849	Health Facility #25 501-661-2201	Pharmacy-Out-of-State, Retail #17 501-682-0190
Auctioneer #5................................... 501-682-1156	Hearing Instrument Dispenser #14 501-663-5869	Physical Therapist #3......................... 501-228-7100
Audiologist #41 501-320-4319	HMO #25 501-661-2518	Physician Assistant #31 501-296-1802
Bail Bondsman #2............................. 501-682-9050	Home Health Agency #25 501-661-2518	Podiatrist #34 501-664-3668
Bank #38.. 501-682-3409	Home Inspector #38........................... 501-682-3409	Political Action Committee #38 501-682-1010
Barber Instructor #7 501-682-4035	Homebuilders #23 501-372-4661	Polygraph Examiner #42..................... 501-618-8600
Barber/Barber Technician #7............... 501-682-4035	Horse Racing #36.............................. 501-682-1467	Precious Metals Dealer #42 501-618-8600
Birthing Center #25........................... 501-661-2518	Hospice Facility #25 501-661-2518	Private Investigator #42 501-618-8600
Boiler Inspector/Installer/Repairer #27 . 501-682-4513	Hospital Maintenance Plumber #25 501-661-2698	Psychological Examiner #13................ 501-682-6167
Boiler Operator #27 501-682-4513	Industrial Maintenance Electrician #27 501-682-4549	Psychologist #13............................... 501-682-6167
Boxer #4.. 501-666-5544	Insurance Agency #38........................ 501-682-3409	Public Accountant-CPA #18................ 501-682-1520
Boxing/Wrestling Referee #4............... 501-666-5544	Insurance Sales Agent #2 501-371-2750	Pump Installer #45 501-682-1025
Burglar Alarm Systems Agent/Mgr #42. 501-618-8600	Investment Advisor #39...................... 501-324-9260	Radiologic Technician #25.................. 501-661-2306
Business Education Teacher #32.......... 501-682-4695	Laboratory #25 501-661-2191	Real Estate Agent/Broker/Sales #37 ... 501-683-8010
Career Education Coordinator #32........ 501-682-4695	Landscape Architect #6...................... 501-682-3393	Real Estate Appraiser #37 501-683-8010
Career Orientation Teacher #32............ 501-682-4695	Liquor Distributor #1 501-682-1105	Residential Journeyman #27............... 501-682-4549
Cemetery, Perpetual Care #39............. 501-324-9260	Livestock Brand #53 501-907-2400	Respiratory Care Practitioner #31........ 501-296-1802
Check Casher #10.............................. 501-376-1438	Livestock Dealer #53.......................... 501-907-2400	School Counselor #32......................... 501-682-4344
Chemicals, List 1, Whoelsale Dist. #17. 501-682-0190	Lobbyist #38 501-682-1010	School Principal/Admin/Super #32 501-682-4344
Child Care Provider #26 501-682-9699	LPG Safety Supervisor #30 501-683-4100	Securities Agent #39 501-324-9260
Chiropractor #9................................. 501-682-9015	Manicurist #49 501-682-2168	Securities Broker/Dealer #39 501-324-9260
Claims Adjuster #2............................ 501-371-2750	Manufactured Home Dealer/Mfg #54 ... 501-324-9032	Security Guard #42 501-618-8600
Clinics, Health #25............................ 501-661-2518	Manufactured Home Installer #54 501-324-9032	Seed Dealer #33 501-225-1598
Collection Agency #10........................ 501-376-1438	Manufactured Home Salesperson #54. 501-324-9032	Septic Tank Cleaner #25.................... 501-661-2171
Collection Agency Collector/Mgr. #10 .. 501-376-1438	Marriage & Family Therapist #51 870-901-7055	Social Worker #40 501-372-5071
Contractor #23.................................. 501-372-4661	Martial Arts #4 501-666-5544	Solid Waste Facility Operator #28 501-682-0585
Cosmetologist/Cosmetology Instr. #49.. 501-682-2168	Massage Therapy Technician (Masseur/Masseuse)	Speech Pathologist #41 501-320-4319
Counselor, Professional #51 870-901-7055	#22.. 501-623-0444	State Trooper #42 501-618-8282
Court Reporter #8.............................. 501-682-6850	Medical Corporation #31 501-296-1802	Supplier of Med Equipment, Legend Device,
Dental Assistant #11.......................... 501-682-2085	Medical Doctor/Surgeon #31................ 501-296-1802	Medical Gas #17 501-682-0190
Dental Hygienist #11 501-682-2085	Medicare Certified Facility #25............. 501-661-2201	Surveyor, Land #19............................ 501-682-2824
Dentist #11....................................... 501-682-2085	Midwife Nurse #15............................. 501-682-2200	Surveyor-in-Training #19..................... 501-682-2824
Dietitian #29.............501-221-0566, 580-9294	Mortgage Loan Broker/Company #39 .. 501-324-9260	Teacher #32 501-682-4695
Drugs, Legend, Wholesale Dist. #17.... 501-682-0190	Motor Vehicle Dealer/Distributor #35 ... 501-682-1428	Veterinarian #44 501-224-2836
Egg Grader #53................................. 501-907-2400	Motor Vehicle Dealer/Salesperson, Used #42	Veterinary Technician #44 501-224-2836
Electrical Contractor #27 501-682-4549	 501-618-8600	Waste Water Treatment Plant Op.#28.. 501-682-0998
Electrician Journeyman/ Master #27 501-682-4549	Motor Vehicle Mfg/Rep, New #35 501-682-1428	Water Supply Operator #25................. 501-661-2623
Electrologist/Electrolysis Instructor #49 501-682-2168	Notary Public #38 501-682-3409	Water Well Driller #45 501-682-1025
Elevator/Lifting Device Inspector #27... 501-682-4531	Nurse #15 501-682-2200	Wrestler #4 501-666-5544
Embalmer/Embalmer Apprentice #12 .. 501-682-0574	Nurse Anesthetist #15 501-682-2200	

Arkansas Licensing Agency Information

1 Alcoholic Beverage Control Division, 1515 W 7th St #503, Little Rock, AR 72201; 501-682-1105, Fax: 501-682-2221.

2 Department of Insurance, Licensing Division, 1200 W 3rd St, Little Rock, AR 72201; 800-282-9134, Fax: 501-371-2618.
http://insurance.arkansas.gov
Email: Insurance.License@mail.state.ar.us
Search Database at http://insurance.arkan sas.gov/is/a1searchhome.html

3 Board of Physical Therapy, 9 Shackelford Plaza, #3, Little Rock, AR 72211; 501-228-7100, Fax: 501-228-0294.
www.arptb.org
Email: axptb@sbcglobal.net
Search Database at
www.arptb.org/ptroster/search.php

4 Athletic Commission, 809 N Palm St, Little Rock, AR 72205-1946; 501-666-5544, Fax: 501-666-5546.

5 Auctioneers Licensing Board, 101 E Capitol, #112B, Little Rock, AR 72201; 501-682-1156, Fax: 501-682-1158.
www.state.ar.us/directory/detail2.cgi?ID=962
Email: betty.king@mail.state.ar.us

6 Board of Architecture, 101 E Capitol, #101, Little Rock, AR 72201; 501-682-3171, Fax: 501-682-3172.
www.accessarkansas.org/arch
Email: arch@mac.state.ar.us
Search Database at
www.state.ar.us/arch/search.html

7 Board of Barber Examiners, 103 E 7th St Rm 212, Little Rock, AR 72201-4512; 501-682-4035, Fax: 501-682-5073.
www.state.ar.us/directory/detail2.cgi?ID=1044
Email: charles.kirkpatrick@mail.state.ar.us

8 Board of Certified Court Reporter Examiners, 625 Marshall St, Justice Bldg, Little Rock, AR 72201; 501-682-6850.
Email: renee.herndon@mail.state.ar.us

9 Board of Chiropractic Examiners, 101 E Capital, #209, Little Rock, AR 72201; 501-682-9015, Fax: 501-682-9016.
www.accessarkansas.org/asbce/
Email: ann.gates@mail.state.ar.us
Search Database at
www.accessarkansas.org/asbce/search.html

10 Board of Collection Agencies, 523 S Louisiana St, #460, Little Rock, AR 72201; 501-376-1438, Fax: 501-372-5383.
www.asbca.org/

11 Board of Dental Examiners, 101 E Capitol Ave, #111, Little Rock, AR 72201; 501-682-2085, Fax: 501-682-3543.
www.asbde.org
Email: asbde@arkansas.gov
Search Database at www.asbde.org

12 Board of Embalmers & Funeral Directors, 101 E Capitol Ave, #113, Little Rock, AR 72201; 501-682-0574, Fax: 501-682-0575.
www.arkansas.gov/fdemb/
Search Database at www.arkansas.gov/fdemb/

13 Board of Examiners in Psychology, 101 E Capitol Ave, #415, Little Rock, AR 72201; 501-682-6167, Fax: 501-682-6165.
www.accessarkansas.org/abep/
Email: rebecca.wright@arkansas.gov Note: They do accept verifications by phone or fax. They require a written request only plus a $10.00 per per verification. A form may be downloaded from their website to fill out and return. They do not have web access for verifications.

14 Board of Hearing Instrument Dispensers, 305 N Monroe, Little Rock, AR 72205; 501-663-5869, Fax: 501-663-6359.

15 Board of Nursing, 1123 S University, University Tower Bldg, #800, Little Rock, AR 72204-1619; 501-686-2700, Fax: 501-686-2714.
www.arsbn.org/ Search Database at
www.arsbn.org/registry/index.html

16 Board of Optometry, 407 N. Elm St., Searcy, AR 72143; 501-268-4351, Fax: 501-268-5631.
www.aroptometry.org/
Email: hflippin@cswnet.com
Search Database at www.arbo.org/index.php?acti on=findanoptometrist

17 Board of Pharmacy, 101 E Capitol, #218, Little Rock, AR 72201; 501-682-0190, Fax: 501-682-0195. www.arkansas.gov/asbp
Email: margaret.lincourt@arkansas.gov

18 Board of Public Accountancy, 101 E Capitol, #450, Little Rock, AR 72201; 501-682-1520, Fax: 501-682-5538.
www.arkansas.gov/asbpa/
Search Database at www.arkansas.gov/asbpa/

19 Board of Registration for Engineers/Land Surveyors, PO Box 3750, Little Rock, AR 72203; 501-682-2824, Fax: 501-682-2827.
www.state.ar.us/pels/
Email: joseph.clement@mail.state.ar.us
Search Database at
www.accessarkansas.org/pels/search.php

20 Board of Registration for Foresters, PO Box 7424, Little Rock, AR 72207; 501-296-1998, Fax: 501-296-1949.
http://members.aol.com/JOSTNIX/rf.htm
Email: robert.mcfarland@arkansas.org

21 Board of Registration for Professional Geologists, 3815 W Roosevelt Rd, Little Rock, AR 72204; 501-683-0150, Fax: 501-663-7360.
Email: connie.raper@arkansas.gov

22 Board of Massage Therapy, PO Box 20739, Hot Springs, AR 71903-0739; 501-623-0444, Fax: 501-623-4130.
www.arkansasmassagetherapy.com/
Email: info@arkansasmassagetherapy.com

23 Contractors Licensing Board, 4100 Richards Road, North Little Rock, AR 72117; 501-372-4661, Fax: 501-372-2247.
www.accessarkansas.org/clb/
Search Database at
www.state.ar.us/clb/search.html

24 State Board of Athletic Training, 9 Shackleford Plaza #3, Litttle Rock, AR 72211; 501-683-4076, Fax: 501-228-0294.
www.aratb.org
Email: aratb@sbcglobal.net
Search Database at www.aratb.org/search.php

25 Department of Health, Bureau of Health Resources; Administration/Licencing, 4815 West Markham, Little Rock, AR 72205-3867; 501-661-2000, Fax: 501-280-4901.
www.healthyarkansas.com/index.html

26 Department of Human Services, Division of Child Care & Early Childhood Education, PO Box 1437 Slot S140, Little Rock, AR 72203; 501-682-4891, Fax: 501-682-2317.
www.accessarkansas.org/childcare/
Email: Jennifer.Spriggs@mail.state.ar.us
Search Database at
www.state.ar.us/childcare/search.html

27 Department of Labor, 10421 W Markham, Little Rock, AR 72205; 501-682-4500, Fax: 501-682-4535.
www.arkansas.gov/labor/
Email: sharon.adams@arkansas.gov Note: Online rosters available.

28 Department of Environmental Quality, 8001 National Dr, Little Rock, AR 72209; 501-682-0680, Fax: 501-682-0707.
www.adeq.state.ar.us
Email: rogersk@adeq.state.ar.us
Search Database at
www.adeq.state.ar.us/compsvs/webmaster/databas es.htm

29 Dietetics Licensing Board, PO Box 1016, Little Rock, AR 72115; 501-221-0566, Fax: 501-843-0878.

30 Liquefied Petroleum Gas Board, 3800 Richards Rd, North Little Rock, AR 72117; 501-683-4100, Fax: 501-683-4110.

31 Medical Board, 2100 Riverside Dr., Little Rock, AR 72202-1435; 501-296-1802, Fax: 501-296-1805.
www.armedicalboard.org
Email: asmb@mail.state.ar.us
Search Database at
https://www.armedicalboard.org/licenseverf/
Note: They also offer online verification system that includes additional professional information.

32 Department of Education, Office of Teacher Education & Licensure, State Education Bldg, Rm 106, Capitol Mall #4, Little Rock, AR 72201; 501-682-4695, Fax: 501-682-4898.
Email: qmorris@arkedu.k12.ar.us
Search Database at www.as-is.org/directory/search_lic.html

33 Plant Board, PO Box 1069 (One Natural Resources Dr), Little Rock, AR 72203; 501-225-1598, Fax: 501-225-3590.
www.plantboard.org
Email: info@aspb.state.ar.us

34 Arkansas Board of Podiatric Medicine, 2001 Georgia Ave, Little Rock, AR 72207-5014; 501-664-3668, Fax: 501-666-3338. Note: Verifications in writing are free if a toll free fax number is provided, and/or a self addressed stamped envelope is provided with request.

35 Motor Vehicle Commission, 101 E Capitol #212, Little Rock, AR 72201; 501-682-1428, Fax: 501-682-5573.
www.armvc.com
Email: amvc@mail.state.ar.us
Search Database at
www.armvc.com/licensee_search/index.html

36 Racing Commission, 1515 W. 7th St #505, Little Rock, AR 72203; 501-682-1467, Fax: 501-682-5273.
www.arkansas.gov/dfa/racing/
Email: bob.cohen@dfa.state.ar.us

37 Real Estate Commission, 612 Summit St, Little Rock, AR 72201; 501-683-8010, Fax: 501-682-8020.
www.arkansas.gov/arec/
Search Database at www.arkansas.gov/arec/

38 Secretary of State, 256 State Capitol, Little Rock, AR 72201; 501-682-3409, Fax: 501-682-3437.
www.sosweb.state.ar.us/corps/
Search Database at www.sosweb.state.ar.us/corps/

39 Securities Department, 201 W Markham, Heritage West Bldg, 3rd Fl, Little Rock, AR 72201; 501-324-9260, Fax: 501-324-9268.
www.accessarkansas.org/arsec/
Search Database at
www.accessarkansas.org/asbce/search.html

40 Social Work Licensing Board, PO Box 250381, Little Rock, AR 72225; 501-372-5071, Fax: 501-372-6301.
www.accessarkansas.org/swlb/
Email: swlb@mail.state.ar.us
Search Database at
www.state.ar.us/swlb/search/index.html

41 Speech Pathology & Audiology, Arkansas Children's Hospital, 800 Marshall St., Little Rock, AR 72202; 501-364-4319, Fax: 501-364-6881.
www.archildrens.org

42 Regulartory Service Section, State Police Admin. Svcs. Section, #1 State Police Plaza Drive, Little Rock, AR 72209; 501-618-8600, Fax: 501-618-8621.
www.asp.state.ar.us
Email: info@asp.state.ar.us

43 Supreme Court, 625 Marshall, Justice Bldg, Little Rock, AR 72201; 501-682-6849.
http://courts.state.ar.us
Email: denise.parks@arkansas.gov
Search Database at
http://courts.state.ar.us/attylist/new/

44 Veterinary Medical Examining Board, PO Box 8505, Little Rock, AR 72215; 501-224-2836, Fax: 501-224-1100.
Email: sherry.glover@aspb.ar.gov   Note: Veterinary/Tech Roster (hard copy printed) each year- $25.00.

45 Water Well Construction Commission, 101 E Capitol #350, Little Rock, AR 72201; 501-682-1025, Fax: 501-682-3991.
www.accessarkansas.org/awwcc

46 Board of Acupuncture & Related Techniques, 813 West 3rd St, Little Rock, AR 72207; 501-683-3583, Fax: 501-244-2333.
www.state.ar.us/directory/detail2.cgi?ID=1254

47 Fire Protection Licensing Board, 7509 Cantrell Rd #103-A, Little Rock, AR 72207; 501-661-7903, Fax: 501-603-3540.
www.arfireprotection.org
Email: afplb@aristotle.net
Search Database at
www.arfireprotection.org/roster/index.html

48 Abstractor's Board of Examiners, #5 Pinecrest Circle, Sheridan, AR 72150; 870-942-8064, Fax: 870-942-3101.
www.ark.org

49 Board of Cosmetology, 101 E Capitol #108, Little Rock, AR 72201; 501-682-2168, Fax: 501-682-5640.
www.arkansas.gov/cos/
Search Database at www.arkansas.gov/cos/

50 Board of Dispensing Opticians, Box 627, Helena, AR 72342; 870-572-2847, Fax: 870-572-2847.
www.ark.org

51 Board of Examiners for Counselors & Marriage/Family Therapists, 124 South Jackson #312 (PO Box 70, AR 71754), Magnolia, AR 71754-0070; 870-901-7055, Fax: 870-234-1842.
www.accessarkansas.org/abec/
Email: arboec@global.net
Search Database at
www.state.ar.us/abec/search.php   Note: They provide lists in email, fax, land line and written requests.

52 Department of Human Services, Office of Long Term Care, 7th & Main Streets, Little Rock, AR 72203; 501-682-8430, Fax: 501682-8551.

53 Livestock & Poultry Commission, 1 Natural Resources Dr, PO Box 8505, Little Rock, AR 72215; 501-907-2400, Fax: 501-907-2425.
www.arlpc.org
Email: info@arlpc.org

54 Manufactured Home Commission, 101 E Capitol Ave #210, Little Rock, AR 72201; 501-324-9032, Fax: 501-324-9032.

Arkansas Federal Courts

The following list indicates the district and division name for each county in the state. If the bankruptcy court location is different from the district court, then the location of the bankruptcy court appears in parentheses.

County/Court Cross Reference

County	District	Location
Arkansas	Eastern	Pine Bluff (Little Rock)
Ashley	Western (Eastern)	El Dorado (Little Rock)
Baxter	Western	Harrison (Fayetteville)
Benton	Western	Fayetteville
Boone	Western	Harrison (Fayetteville)
Bradley	Western (Eastern)	El Dorado (Little Rock)
Calhoun	Western (Eastern)	El Dorado (Little Rock)
Carroll	Western	Harrison (Fayetteville)
Chicot	Eastern	Pine Bluff (Little Rock)
Clark	Western (Eastern)	Hot Springs (Little Rock)
Clay	Eastern	Jonesboro (Little Rock)
Cleburne	Eastern	Batesville (Little Rock)
Cleveland	Eastern	Pine Bluff (Little Rock)
Columbia	Western (Eastern)	El Dorado (Little Rock)
Conway	Eastern	Little Rock
Craighead	Eastern	Jonesboro (Little Rock)
Crawford	Western	Fort Smith (Fayetteville)
Crittenden	Eastern	Jonesboro (Little Rock)
Cross	Eastern	Helena (Little Rock)
Dallas	Eastern	Pine Bluff (Little Rock)
Desha	Eastern	Pine Bluff (Little Rock)
Drew	Eastern	Pine Bluff (Little Rock)
Faulkner	Eastern	Little Rock
Franklin	Western	Fort Smith (Fayetteville)
Fulton	Eastern	Batesville (Little Rock)
Garland	Western (Eastern)	Hot Springs (Little Rock)
Grant	Eastern	Pine Bluff (Little Rock)
Greene	Eastern	Jonesboro (Little Rock)
Hempstead	Western (Eastern)	Texarkana (Little Rock)
Hot Spring	Western (Eastern)	Hot Springs (Little Rock)
Howard	Western (Eastern)	Texarkana (Little Rock)
Independence	Eastern	Batesville (Little Rock)
Izard	Eastern	Batesville (Little Rock)
Jackson	Eastern	Batesville (Little Rock)
Jefferson	Eastern	Pine Bluff (Little Rock)
Johnson	Western	Fort Smith (Fayetteville)
Lafayette	Western (Eastern)	Texarkana (Little Rock)
Lawrence	Eastern	Jonesboro (Little Rock)
Lee	Eastern	Helena (Little Rock)
Lincoln	Eastern	Pine Bluff (Little Rock)
Little River	Western (Eastern)	Texarkana (Little Rock)
Logan	Western	Fort Smith (Fayetteville)
Lonoke	Eastern	Little Rock
Madison	Western	Fayetteville
Marion	Western	Harrison (Fayetteville)
Miller	Western (Eastern)	Texarkana (Little Rock)
Mississippi	Eastern	Jonesboro (Little Rock)
Monroe	Eastern	Helena (Little Rock)
Montgomery	Western (Eastern)	Hot Springs (Little Rock)
Nevada	Western (Eastern)	Texarkana (Little Rock)
Newton	Western	Harrison (Fayetteville)
Ouachita	Western (Eastern)	El Dorado (Little Rock)
Perry	Eastern	Little Rock
Phillips	Eastern	Helena (Little Rock)
Pike	Western (Eastern)	Hot Springs (Little Rock)
Poinsett	Eastern	Jonesboro (Little Rock)
Polk	Western	Fort Smith (Fayetteville)
Pope	Eastern	Little Rock
Prairie	Eastern	Little Rock
Pulaski	Eastern	Little Rock
Randolph	Eastern	Jonesboro (Little Rock)
Saline	Eastern	Little Rock
Scott	Western	Fort Smith (Fayetteville)
Searcy	Western	Harrison (Fayetteville)
Sebastian	Western	Fort Smith (Fayetteville)
Sevier	Western (Eastern)	Texarkana (Little Rock)
Sharp	Eastern	Batesville (Little Rock)
St. Francis	Eastern	Helena (Little Rock)
Stone	Eastern	Batesville (Little Rock)
Union	Western (Eastern)	El Dorado (Little Rock)
Van Buren	Eastern	Little Rock
Washington	Western	Fayetteville
White	Eastern	Little Rock
Woodruff	Eastern	Helena (Little Rock)
Yell	Eastern	Little Rock

Standards for Federal Courts: Search fee is $26.00 per item (one party name or case number). Copy fee is $.50 per page. Certification fee is $9.00 per document, double for exemplification, if available. All fees standard unless noted in profile. Mail Search: always enclose a stamped self addressed envelope unless otherwise noted. Most courts accept fax requests or will suggest a copying/search vendor. Before releasing records, all courts require prepayment, unless noted.

Open records are located at the court unless otherwise noted. District courts index by defendant and plaintiff as well as by case number. Bankruptcy courts usually index by debtor and case number. While most courts now have their indexes on computer, many may still maintain index card files as well.

Courts offering internet access via CM-ECF or older RACER, PACER, or Web-PACER systems charge $.08 per page fee unless noted as free. Where PACER is available, the universal sign-up number is 800-676-6856. Find PACER and the US Party/Case Index at http://pacer.psc.uscourts.gov.

US District Court

Eastern District of Arkansas

Batesville Division c/o Little Rock Division, 600 W Capitol, Rm 402, Little Rock, AR 72201 (also use mail address for courier delivery), 501-604-5351. www.are.uscourts.gov

Counties: Cleburne, Fulton, Independence, Izard, Jackson, Sharp, Stone.

Searches & Indexing: Cases indexed by and case number. Results do not include SSN or DOB. Open records located at Little Rock Division.

Fee & Payment: Pay by money order or cashier's check.

Phone Search: No searching by telephone.

In Person Search: Fee charged if court performs your search.

E-Services: Search records on the Internet using RACER at https://pacer.login.uscourts.gov/cgi-bin/login.pl?court_id=r_aredc. Fees now apply. Document images available. No PACER access to this court. ECF at https://ecf.ared.uscourts.gov **Other Online Access:** Search records on the Internet using RACER at www.are.uscourts.gov/perl/bkplog.html. Access fee is $.08 per page.

Helena Division c/o Little Rock Division, 600 W Capital, Rm 402, Little Rock, AR 72201-3325 (also use mail address for courier delivery), 501-604-5351. Hours- 8AM-5PM. www.are.uscourts.gov

Counties: Cross, Lee, Monroe, Phillips, St. Francis, Woodruff.

Searches & Indexing: Cases indexed by debtor name and case number. Results do not include SSN or DOB. Computer index back to 1993 maintained. Records purged every 5 years. Open records located at Little Rock Division.

Fee & Payment: Pay by money order, cashier's, business or personal check.

Phone Search: Will search name via phone.

Mail Search: Include SASE for return.

In Person Search: permitted. Self-serve copier available - $.10 per page.

E-Services: Search records on the Internet using RACER at https://pacer.login.uscourts.gov/cgi-bin/login.pl?court_id=r_aredc. Fees now apply. Document images available. PACER records go back to 1987-89. New records online after 1 day. ECF at https://ecf.ared.uscourts.gov

Jonesboro Division Court Clerk, PO Box 7080, Jonesboro, AR 72403 (courier address: Federal Office Bldg, Rm 312, 615 S Main St, Jonesboro, AR 72401), phone- 870-972-4610, Fax-870-972-4612. Hours- 8AM-5PM. www.are.uscourts.gov

Counties: Clay, Craighead, Crittenden, Greene, Lawrence, Mississippi, Poinsett, Randolph.

Searches & Indexing: Results do not include SSN or DOB. Computer index maintained back to 1989. New cases in the index immediately after filing date. Records purged every 5 years.

Fee & Payment: Pay by money order, cashier's or personal check. Payee: Clerk, US District Court. Prepayment required.

Phone Search: Docket information available via phone.

Mail Search: search usually completed- 1-2 weeks. SASE not required.

In Person Search: Fee charged if court performs your search. No self-serve copier available.

E-Services: Search records on the Internet using RACER at https://pacer.login.uscourts.gov/cgi-bin/login.pl?court_id=r_aredc. Fees now apply. Document images available. No PACER access to this court. ECF at https://ecf.ared.uscourts.gov

Little Rock Division Court Clerk, Rm 402, 600 W Capitol, Little Rock, AR 72201 (also use mail address for courier delivery), 501-604-5351. Hours- 8AM-5PM. www.are.uscourts.gov

Counties: Conway, Faulkner, Lonoke, Perry, Pope, Prairie, Pulaski, Saline, Van Buren, White, Yell.

Searches & Indexing: Results do not include SSN or DOB. Computer, microfiche and card indexes maintained, computer back to 3/92. New cases in the index immediately after filing date. Records purged every 5 years.

Fee & Payment: Pay by Visa/MC, money order, cashier's or personal check. Payee: Clerk, US District Court. Prepayment required.

Phone Search: Docket information available via phone.

Mail Search: search usually completed- 1-2 weeks. Include SASE for return.

In Person Search: Fee charged if court performs your search. No self-serve copier available.

E-Services: Search records on the Internet using RACER at https://pacer.login.uscourts.gov/cgi-bin/login.pl?court_id=r_aredc. Fees now apply. Document images available. No PACER access to this court. ECF at https://ecf.ared.uscourts.gov

Pine Bluff Division Court Clerk, PO Box 8307, Pine Bluff, AR 71611-8307 (courier address: US Post Office & Courthouse, 100 E 8th St, Rm 3103, Pine Bluff, AR 71601), 870-536-1190, Fax-870-536-6330. Hours- 8AM-4:30PM. www.are.uscourts.gov

Counties: Arkansas, Chicot, Cleveland, Dallas, Desha, Drew, Grant, Jefferson, Lincoln.

Searches & Indexing: Results do not include SSN or DOB. Computer index back to 1989 maintained; also on microfiche. New cases in the index immediately after filing date. Records purged every 5 years.

Fee & Payment: Pay by money order, cashier's or personal check. Payee: US District Clerk. Prepayment required for copies and certification.

Phone Search: Searching is not available by phone.

Mail Search: search usually completed- soon as work load permits. Include SASE for return.

In Person Search: Fee charged if court performs your search. No self-serve copier available.

E-Services: Search records on the Internet using RACER at https://pacer.login.uscourts.gov/cgi-bin/login.pl?court_id=r_aredc. Fees now apply. Document images available. Search records on the Internet using RACER at www.are.uscourts.gov/perl/bkplog.html. Document images available. PACER records go back to 1987-89. New records online after 1 day. ECF at https://ecf.ared.uscourts.gov

US Bankruptcy Court

Eastern District of Arkansas

Little Rock Division Court Clerk, 300 W 2nd St, Little Rock, AR 72203 (also use mail address for courier delivery), 501-918-5500, Fax-501-918-5520. Hours- 8AM-5PM. www.areb.uscourts.gov

Counties: Same counties as included in Eastern District of Arkansas, plus the counties included in the Western District divisions of El Dorado, Hot Springs and Texarkana. All bankruptcy cases in Arkansas prior to mid-1993 were heard here.

Searches & Indexing: Cases indexed by debtor, creditors, and case number. Results include last 4 SSN digits. Computer, microfiche and card indexes maintained. New cases in the index immediately after filing date. Records purged every 6 months.

Fee & Payment: Pay by Visa/MC, money order, cashier's or personal check. No debtor's checks accepted. Payee: Clerk, US Bankruptcy Court. Prepayment required. Will fax documents if copy fee paid.

Phone Search: Only basic info not provided on VCIS is released via phone; includes case number, chapter, judge, attorney, trustee, date case closed, etc. Voice Case Information Service available, call VCIS at 800-891-6741 or 501-918-5555.

Mail Search: search usually completed- 1-2 weeks. Include SASE for return.

In Person Search: permitted. No self-serve copier available.

E-Services: ECF replaces PACER whose records did go back to 5/1989. New records online after 1 day. ECF at https://ecf.areb.uscourts.gov **Opinions Online:** www.arb.uscourts.gov/Orders-Rules-Opinions/opinions/opinions.htm. **Other Online Access:** Search court calendars free at www.arb.uscourts.gov/calendars/calendars.htm.

US District Court

Western District of Arkansas

El Dorado Division Court Clerk, PO Box 1566, El Dorado, AR 71731 (courier address: Rm 205, 101 S Jackson, El Dorado, AR 71730), 870-862-1202, Fax-870-863-488. Hours- 8AM-4:30PM. www.arwd.uscourts.gov

Counties: Ashley, Bradley, Calhoun, Columbia, Ouachita, Union.

Searches & Indexing: Results do not include SSN or DOB. Computer index maintained. Files maintained numerically by year. New cases in the index immediately after filing date. Records purged every 5 years.

Fee & Payment: Pay by Visa/MC, money order, cashier's or personal check. Payee: Clerk, US District Court. Prepayment required for out of state searchers.

Phone Search: Only docket information is available by phone.

Mail Search: search usually completed- 1 week. Include SASE for return.

In Person Search: Fee charged if court performs your search. No self-serve copier available.

E-Services: PACER online at http://pacer.arwd.uscourts.gov. PACER records go back to 9/1990. New records online after 1 day.

ECF at https://ecf.arwd.uscourts.gov **Opinions Online:** www.arwd.uscourts.gov/pleadings.cfm. Selected pleadings only; opinions to be online later in 2005. **Other Online Access:** "Pending Cases" at www.arwd.uscourts.gov/docs/pendcases.txt. Court now participate in the US party case index.

Fayetteville Division Court Clerk, PO Box 6420, Fayetteville, AR 72702 (courier address: Rm 510, 35 E Mountain, Fayetteville, AR 72702), 479-521-6980, Fax-479-575-0774. Hours- 8AM-5PM. www.arwd.uscourts.gov

Counties: Benton, Madison, Washington.

Searches & Indexing: Results include full SSN, DOB. Computer index back to 1992 maintained. Files maintained numerically by year. New cases in the index immediately after filing date. Records purged every 5 years.

Fee & Payment: Pay by Visa/MC, money order, cashier's or personal check. Payee: Clerk, Western District of Arkansas. Prepayment required for out of state searchers.

Phone Search: Only docket information is available by phone.

Mail Search: search usually completed- 24 hours. SASE not required.

In Person Search: Fee charged if court performs your search. Searches can be done in person for free if no written record is furnished. Self-serve copier available - $.50 per page.

E-Services: PACER online at http://pacer.arwd.uscourts.gov. PACER records go back to 9/1990. New records online after 1 day. ECF at https://ecf.arwd.uscourts.gov **Opinions Online:** www.arwd.uscourts.gov/pleadings.cfm. Selected pleadings only; opinions to be online later in 2005. **Other Online Access:** "Pending Cases" at www.arwd.uscourts.gov/docs/pendcases.txt. Court now participate in the US party case index.

Fort Smith Division Court Clerk, PO Box 1547, Fort Smith, AR 72902 (courier address: Judge Isaac C. Parker Federal Bldg #1038, 6th & Rogers Ave, Fort Smith, AR 72901), 479-783-6833, Fax-479-783-6308. Hours- 8AM-5PM. www.arwd.uscourts.gov

Counties: Crawford, Franklin, Johnson, Logan, Polk, Scott, Sebastian.

Searches & Indexing: Results do not include SSN or DOB. Computer index maintained. Files maintained numerically by year. New cases in the index immediately after filing date. Records purged every 5 years.

Fee & Payment: Pay by Visa/MC, money order, cashier's or personal check. Payee: Clerk of Court. Prepayment required for out of state searchers.

Phone Search: Only docket information is available by phone.

Mail Search: search usually completed- week-10 days. SASE not required.

In Person Search: Fee charged if court performs your search. Self-serve copier available - $.50 per page.

E-Services: PACER online at http://pacer.arwd.uscourts.gov. PACER records go back to 9/1990. New records online after 1 day. ECF at https://ecf.arwd.uscourts.gov **Opinions Online:** www.arwd.uscourts.gov/pleadings.cfm. Selected pleadings only; opinions to be online later in 2005. **Other Online Access:** "Pending Cases" at www.arwd.uscourts.gov/docs/pendcases.txt. Court now participate in the US party case index.

Hot Springs Division Court Clerk, PO Drawer 6486, Hot Springs, AR 71902 (courier address: Federal Bldg, Rm 347, 100 Reserve, Hot Springs, AR 71901), 501-623-6411. Hours- 8AM-4:30PM. www.arwd.uscourts.gov

Counties: Clark, Garland, Hot Springs, Montgomery, Pike.

Searches & Indexing: Results do not include SSN or DOB. Computer index maintained. Files maintained numerically by year. New cases in the index immediately after filing date. Records purged every 5 years.

Fee & Payment: Pay by money order, cashier's or personal check. Payee: Clerk, Western District of Arkansas. Prepayment required for out of state searchers.

Phone Search: Searching is not available by phone.

Mail Search: search usually completed- 2 days. Include SASE for return.

In Person Search: Fee charged if court performs your search. No self-serve copier available.

E-Services: PACER online at http://pacer.arwd.uscourts.gov. PACER records go back to 9/1990. New records online after 1 day. ECF at https://ecf.arwd.uscourts.gov **Opinions Online:** www.arwd.uscourts.gov/pleadings.cfm. Selected pleadings only; opinions to be online later in 2005. **Other Online Access:** "Pending Cases" at www.arwd.uscourts.gov/docs/pendcases.txt. Court now participate in the US party case index.

Texarkana Division Court Clerk, PO Box 2746, Texarkana, AR 75504-2746 (courier address: 500 State Line Ave, Rm 302, Texarkana, AR 71854), 870-773-3381. Hours- 8AM-4:30PM. www.arwd.uscourts.gov

Counties: Hempstead, Howard, Lafayette, Little River, Miller, Nevada, Sevier.

Searches & Indexing: Results do not include SSN or DOB. Computer index back to 1990 maintained; also on microfiche. Files maintained numerically by year. New cases in the index immediately after filing date. Records purged every 5 years.

Fee & Payment: Pay by money order, cashier's or personal check. Payee: Clerk of the Court. Prepayment required for out of state searchers.

Phone Search: Case numbers are released via phone; anything else depends on workload of deputy clerk.

Mail Search: search usually completed- 24 hours. SASE not required.

In Person Search: Fee charged if court performs your search. Self-serve copier available - $.50 per page.

E-Services: PACER online at http://pacer.arwd.uscourts.gov. PACER records go back to 9/1990. New records online after 1 day. ECF at https://ecf.arwd.uscourts.gov **Opinions Online:** www.arwd.uscourts.gov/pleadings.cfm. Selected pleadings only; opinions to be online later in 2005. **Other Online Access:** "Pending Cases" at www.arwd.uscourts.gov/docs/pendcases.txt. Court now participate in the US party case index.

US Bankruptcy Court

Western District of Arkansas

Fayetteville Division Court Clerk, PO Box 3097, Fayetteville, AR 72702-3097 (courier address: 35 E Mountain, Rm 316, Fayetteville, AR 72701), 479-582-9800, Fax-479-582-9825. Hours- 8AM-5PM. www.arb.uscourts.gov

Counties: Same counties as included in US District Court - Western District of Arkansas except that counties included in El Dorado and Texarkana Divisions are heard in Little Rock.

Searches & Indexing: Cases indexed by debtor, creditors, and case number. Results include last 4 SSN digits only. Computer index maintained. New cases in the index immediately after filing date. Records purged every 6 months.

Fee & Payment: Pay by Visa, money order, cashier's or personal check. No debtor's checks accepted. Payee: Clerk, US Bankruptcy Court. Prepayment required. Licensed attorneys may be invoiced for copy work.

Phone Search: Only basic info not provided on VCIS is released via phone; includes case number, chapter, judge, attorney, trustee. Voice Case Information Service available, call VCIS at 800-891-6741 or 501-918-5555.

Mail Search: search usually completed- 1 day. Include SASE for return.

In Person Search: Fee charged if court performs your search. No self-serve copier available.

E-Services: ECF replaces PACER whose records did go back to 5/1989. New records online after 1 day. ECF at https://ecf.arwb.uscourts.gov **Opinions Online:** www.arb.uscourts.gov/Orders-Rules-Opinions/opinions/opinions.htm. **Other Online Access:** Search court calendars free at www.arb.uscourts.gov/calendars/calendars.htm.

Arkansas County Courts

Court	Jurisdiction	No. of Courts	How Organized
Circuit Courts*	General	38	28 Circuits
District Courts*	Limited	126	
City Courts	Limited	1084	
Court of Common Pleas	Limited	4	
Justice of the Peace Courts	Limited	55	
Police Courts	Limited	5	

* Profiled in this Sourcebook.

Court	CIVIL								
	Tort	Contract	Real Estate	Min. Claim	Max. Claim	Small Claims	Estate	Eviction	Domestic Relations
Circuit Courts*	X	X	X	$5000	No Max		X		X
District Courts*		X	X	$0	$5000	$5000		X	
City Courts		X	X	$0	$300				
Court of Common Pleas		X		$500	$1000				
Justice of the Peace Courts						$300			
Police Courts		X	X	$0	$300				

Court	CRIMINAL				
	Felony	Misdemeanor	DWI/DUI	Preliminary Hearing	Juvenile
Circuit Courts*	X				
District Courts*		X	X	X	
City Courts		X	X	X	
Court of Common Pleas					
Justice of the Peace Courts		X			
Police Courts		X	X		

ADMINISTRATION   Administrative Office of Courts, 625 Marshall St, 1100 Justice Bldg, Little Rock, AR, 72201; 501-682-9400, Fax: 501-682-9410. www.courts.state.ar.us/

COURT STRUCTURE   Circuit Courts are the courts of general jurisdiction and are arranged in 28 circuits. Circuit courts consist of five subject matter divisions: criminal, civil, probate, domestic relations, and juvenile. The Circuit Clerk handles the records and recordings; however, some counties have a County Clerk that handles probate. District courts, formerly known as municipal courts before passage of Amendment 80 to the Arkansas Constitution, exercise county-wide jurisdiction over misdemeanor cases, preliminary felony cases, and civil cases in matters of less than $5,000, including small claims. The City Courts operate in smaller communities where District Courts do not exist and exercise city-wide jurisdiction.

ONLINE ACCESS   A limited but newly improved online computer system at http://courts.state.ar.us/online/or.html from the Administrative Office of Courts offers access to Supreme Court and Court of Appeals opinions and parallel citations, also Appellate Court and Court of Appeals dockets. There is also an AR licensed attorney search and court rules and administrative orders. However, online access to courts at the county level remains almost non-existant.

ADDITIONAL INFORMATION   Many courts that allow written search requests require an SASE. Fees vary widely across jurisdictions as do prepayment requirements.

Arkansas County

Circuit Court - Northern District 302 S College St, Stuttgart, AR 72160; phone: 870-673-2056; probate phone: 870-673-7311; fax: 870-673-3869; hours 8AM-4:30PM (CST). *Felony, Civil Actions, Probate.*
Note: The court is not bonded to search Civil or Chancery records. Probate has a different Clerk.

Civil Records: Access: In person only. Visitors must perform in person searches themselves. Court makes copy: $.50 per page; same fee for self serve. Required to search: name, years to search. Civil cases indexed by defendant, plaintiff, in files from 1913.
Criminal Records: Access: In person only. Visitors must perform in person searches themselves. Court makes copy: $.50 per page; same fee for self serve. Required to search: name, years to search, DOB. Criminal records in files from 1913, earlier records located in DeWitt.
General Information: Public access terminal goes back to 2004. No juvenile records released. Certification fee: $4.00 per doc includes copy fee. Payee: Arkansas Circuit Court. Personal checks accepted. Prepayment required.

Circuit Court - Southern District 101 Courthouse Sq, De Witt, AR 72042; phone: 870-946-4219; fax: 870-946-1394; hours 8AM-4:30PM (CST). *Felony, Civil Actions Over $5,000.*
Civil Records: Access: In person only. Both court and visitors may perform in person searches. Search fee: $6.00 per name. Court makes copy: $.50 per page; same fee for self serve. Required to search: name, years to search. Civil cases indexed by defendant, plaintiff. Civil records in files from 1923, computerized since 1995, prior records (the two other courts in this county also) located at this court.
Criminal Records: Access: In person only. Both court and visitors may perform in person searches. Search fee: $6.00 per name. Court makes copy: $.50 per page; same fee for self serve. Required to search: name, DOB; also helpful: SSN. Criminal records in files from 1923, computerized since 1995, prior records (the two other courts in this county also) located at this court. Note: Search request must be in writing.
General Information: Public access terminal goes back to 2004. No juvenile, expunged records released. Will not fax back documents. Certification fee: $4.00 per doc includes copies. Payee: Arkansas County Circuit Clerk. Personal checks accepted. Prepayment required.

Stuttgart District Court PO Box 848, 514 S. Main, Stuttgart, AR 72160; phone: 870-673-7951; fax: 870-673-6522; hours 8AM-4:30PM (CST). *Misdemeanor, Civil Actions Under $5,000, Eviction, Small Claims.*
Civil Records: Access: Phone, mail, fax, in person. Both court and visitors may perform in person searches. No search fee. Court makes copy: $.25 per page. Required to search: name plus SSN. Records go back to 1990; on computer back to 1991. Mail turnaround time 3 days.
Criminal Records: Access: Phone, mail, fax, in person. Both court and visitors may perform in person searches. No search fee. Court makes copy: $.25. Required to search: name, years to search, SSN; also helpful: DOB. Records go back to 1990; on computer back to 1991. Mail turnaround time 3 days.
General Information: No public access terminal. Will fax documents. No certification fee . SASE required.

Ashley County

Circuit Court Ashley County Courthouse, 205 E Jefferson, Hamburg, AR 71646; phone: 870-853-2030; fax: 870-853-2034; hours 8AM-4:30PM (CST). *Felony, Civil Actions Over $5,000, Probate.*
Civil Records: Access: Mail, in person. Visitors must perform in person searches themselves. No

search fee. Court makes copy: $.50 per page; same fee for self serve. Required to search: name, years to search. Civil cases indexed by defendant, plaintiff; on files and index cards from 1950s. Mail turnaround time 2 days.
Criminal Records: Access: Mail, in person. Visitors must perform in person searches themselves. Court makes copy: $.50 per page; same fee for self serve. Required to search: name, years to search; also helpful: DOB, SSN. Criminal records on files and index cards from 1950s. Note: No name searches by mail; mail requests must have case numbers. Mail turnaround time 2 days.
General Information: No public access terminal. No juvenile records released. Fee to fax documents is $1.00 per page. Certification fee: $2.00 per doc. Payee: Circuit Clerk's Office. Personal checks accepted. Prepayment and SASE required.

Hamburg District Court PO Box 72, Hamburg, AR 71646; phone: 870-853-8326; fax: 870-853-5433; hours 8AM-4:30PM (CST). *Misdemeanor, Civil Actions Under $5,000, Eviction, Small Claims.*
Civil Records: Access: Mail, in person. Both court and visitors may perform in person searches. No search fee. Court makes copy: $.25 per page; same fee for self serve. Required to search: name. Civil records go back 10 years; on computer back to 1989. Mail turnaround time 1-2 days.
Criminal Records: Access: Mail, in person. Both court and visitors may perform in person searches. Search fee: $5.00. Court makes copy: $.25 per page; same fee for self serve. Required to search: name, years to search, DOB. Criminal records go back to 1976; on computer back to 1989. Mail turnaround time 1-2 days.
General Information: Public access terminal goes back to 1989. Will not fax documents. Certification fee: $10.00 per document. Payee: District Court. Prepayment required.

Baxter County

Circuit Court 1 E 7th St, Rm 103, Courthouse Square, Mountain Home, AR 72653; phone: 870-425-3475; probate phone: same; fax: 870-424-5105; hours 8AM-4:30PM (CST). *Felony, Civil Actions Over $5,000, Probate.*
Civil Records: Access: Fax, mail, in person. Both court and visitors may perform in person searches. Search fee: $6.00 per name. Court makes copy: $.25 per page. Required to search: name, years to search. Civil cases indexed by defendant, plaintiff; on computer from 1982, on criminal fee book from early 1900s. Mail turnaround time 1-2 days.
Criminal Records: Access: Mail, in person. Both court and visitors may perform in person searches. Search fee: $6.00 per name. Court makes copy: $.25 per page. Required to search: name, years to search, SSN. Criminal records on computer from 1982, on criminal fee book from early 1900s. Mail turnaround time 1-2 days.
General Information: Public access terminal goes back to 1995. No adoption or juvenile records released. Will fax documents $5.00 per page. Certification fee: $5.00 per doc. Payee: Baxter County Clerk. Personal checks accepted. Prepayment and SASE required.

District Court 301 E 6th St #130, Mountain Home, AR 72653; phone: 870-425-3140; criminal phone: 870-425-3140; civil phone: 870-425-8910; criminal records fax: 870-425-8470; civil records fax: same; hours 8AM-4:30PM (CST). *Misdemeanor, Civil Actions Under $5,000, Eviction, Small Claims.*
Civil Records: Access: Mail, in person. Only the court performs in person searches. Court makes copy: $.25 per page. Required to search: name, years to search; also helpful-DOB, SSN, signed release. Civil records go back to 1980's; computerized records since 1995. Mail turnaround time 3 days.
Criminal Records: Access: Mail, in person. Only the court performs in person searches. No search

fee. Court makes copy: $.25 per page. Required to search: name, years to search, DOB, SSN. Criminal records go back to 1980's; computerized since 1995. Mail turnaround time 3 days.
General Information: No public access terminal. Will not fax documents. Certification fee: $5.00.

Benton County

Circuit Court 102 NE "A" St, Bentonville, AR 72712; phone: 479-271-1015; probate phone: 479-271-5727; criminal records fax: 479-271-5719; civil records fax: same; hours 8AM-4:30PM (CST). *Felony, Civil Actions Over $5,000, Probate.*
www.co.benton.ar.us
Note: Probate records managed by the County Clerk.

Civil Records: Access: Phone, mail, online, in person. Visitors must perform in person searches themselves. No search fee. Court makes copy: $.10 per page; same fee for self serve. Required to search: name, years to search. Civil cases indexed by defendant, plaintiff; on computer from 1991, on dockets from 1880s. Civil court docket information is free at http://209.183.170.177:5061/. Use "option" 21. Mail turnaround time in 24 hours.
Criminal Records: Access: Phone, mail, online, in person. Visitors must perform in person searches themselves. No search fee. Court makes copy: $.10 per page; same fee for self serve. Required to search: name, years to search. Criminal records on computer from 1991, on dockets from 1880s. Online access to criminal records is the same as civil. Mail turnaround time in 24 hours.
General Information: Public access terminal goes back to 1987. No juvenile records released. Will fax documents to local or toll free line. Certification fee: $2.00. Payee: Benton County Circuit Clerk. Personal checks accepted. Prepayment required.

District Court 117 W Central, Bentonville, AR 72712; criminal phone: 479-271-3120; civil phone: 479-271-3121; fax: 479-271-3134; hours 8AM-4:30PM (CST). *Misdemeanor, Civil Actions Under $5,000, Small Claims.*
Civil Records: Access: Mail, in person. Only the court performs in person searches. No search fee. Court makes copy: $5.00 - only certified copies released. Civil records computerized to 1996; other records go back to 1985. Mail turnaround time 5 days.
Criminal Records: Access: Mail, in person. Only the court performs in person searches. No search fee. Court makes copy: only certified copies released. Required to search: name, years to search, DOB. Criminal records computerized to 1992; other records go back to 1982. Mail turnaround time 5 days.
General Information: Will fax documents to local or toll free line. Certification fee: $5.00 per doc includes copies. Payee: Bentonville District Court. Prepayment required.

Boone County

Circuit Court 100 N Main St #200, Harrison, AR 72601; phone: 870-741-5560; fax: 870-741-4335; hours 8AM-4:30PM (CST). *Felony, Civil Actions Over $5,000.*
Note: Probate records are in the County Clerk's office, 870-741-8428.

Civil Records: Access: Mail, in person, online. Both court and visitors may perform in person searches. Search fee: $5.00. Court makes copy: $.25 per page; same fee for self serve. Required to search: name, years to search. Civil cases indexed by defendant, plaintiff. Civil records archived from 1940, index from 1977, computerized from 1990. Access court orders online at www.etitlesearch.com; registration and fees apply. Mail turnaround time 1 day.
Criminal Records: Access: Mail, in person, online. Both court and visitors may perform in person searches. Search fee: $5.00. Court makes copy: $.25 per page; same fee for self serve. Required to search: name, years to search. Criminal records archived from 1940, index from 1977, computerized from 1990. Access court orders online at

www.etitlesearch.com; registration and fees apply. Mail turnaround time 1 day.

General Information: Public access terminal goes back to 1997. No indictments or juvenile records released. Fee to fax documents is $5.00 per document. Certification fee: $5.00. Payee: Circuit Clerk. Personal checks accepted. Prepayment and SASE required.

District Court PO Box 968, Harrison, AR 72602; phone: 870-741-2788; fax: 870-741-4329; hours 8AM-4:30PM (CST). *Misdemeanor, Civil Actions Under $5,000, Eviction, Small Claims.*

Civil Records: Access: Mail, in person. Both court and visitors may perform in person searches. No search fee. Self serve copy fee: $.25 per copy. Required to search: name, years to search. Records indexed since 1996. Mail turnaround 2 weeks.

Criminal Records: Access: Mail, in person. Both court and visitors may perform in person searches. No search fee. Self serve copy fee: $.25 per copy. Required to search: name, years to search; also helpful: DOB. Records indexed since 1990 on computer. Mail turnaround time 2 weeks.

General Information: No public access terminal. Will fax documents for $1.00 per page. Certification fee: $5.00 per doc. Payee: Boone County District Court. Prepayment required.

Bradley County

Circuit Court Bradley County Courthouse - Records, 101 E Cedar, Warren, AR 71671; phone: 870-226-2272; probate phone: 870-226-3464; fax: 870-226-8404; hours 8AM-4:30PM (CST). *Felony, Civil Actions Over $5,000, Probate.*

Civil Records: Access: In person only. Visitors must perform in person searches themselves. Court makes copy: $.50 per page; same fee for self serve. Required to search: name, years to search. Civil cases indexed by defendant, plaintiff. Civil records (active cases) on dockets, retired cases on indexes from 1880, no computerization.

Criminal Records: Access: Mail, in person. Both court and visitors may perform in person searches. Search fee: $6.00. Court makes copy: $.50 per page; same fee for self serve. Required to search: name, years to search; also helpful: DOB, SSN. Criminal records (active cases) on dockets, retired cases on indexes from 1880, no computerization. Mail turnaround time 1 week.

General Information: No public access terminal. No juvenile released. Certification fee: $3.00. Payee: Circuit Court. Personal checks accepted. Prepayment and SASE required.

District Court PO Box 352, Warren, AR 71671; phone: 870-226-2567; criminal records fax: 870-226-2567; civil records fax: same; hours 8AM-4:30PM (CST). *Misdemeanor, Civil Actions Under $5,000, Eviction, Small Claims.*

Civil Records: Access: Mail, in person. Both court and visitors may perform in person searches. Search fee: $6.00 per name. No copy fee. Required to search: name; also helpful address, other names used, case number. Computerized records since 1993. Note: Only the court may search on computer; visitors may hand-search indexed records indexed by case number only. Mail turnaround 2-3 days.

Criminal Records: Access: Mail, in person. Only the court performs in person searches. Search fee: $6.00 per name. No copy fee. Required to search: name, years to search, DOB; searcher may be required to provide DR number. Computerized records since 1993. Mail turnaround time 3-5 days.

General Information: No public access terminal. Will fax documents to local or toll free line. Certification fee: $6.00 search fee includes certification. Payee: District Court. Prepayment and SASE required.

Calhoun County

Circuit Court PO Box 1175, Hampton, AR 71744; phone: 870-798-2517; hours 8AM-4:30PM (CST). *Felony, Civil Actions Over $5,000, Probate.*

Civil Records: Access: Mail, in person. Both court and visitors may perform in person searches. Search fee: $6.00. Court makes copy: $.25 per page. Required to search: name, years to search. Civil cases indexed by defendant, plaintiff; on dockets from 1851. Mail turnaround time 1-3 days.

Criminal Records: Access: Mail, in person. Visitors must perform in person searches themselves. Search fee: $6.00. Court makes copy: $.25 per page. Required to search: name, years to search, DOB; also helpful: SSN. Criminal records on dockets from 1851. Mail turnaround time 1-3 days.

General Information: Public access terminal available. No juvenile or adoption released. Certification fee: $5.00. Payee: Calhoun County Clerk. Personal checks accepted. Prepayment and SASE required.

District Court PO Box 783, Courthouse, Hampton, AR 71744; phone: 870-798-2753; civil phone: 870-798-2165; hours 8AM-4:30PM (CST). *Misdemeanor, Civil Actions Under $5,000, Eviction, Small Claims.*

Note: Separate PO Box for civil court - PO Box 864. Archives located across street. Phone city's Municipal Clerk at 870-798-3201.

Civil Records: Access: Mail, in person. Both court and visitors may perform in person searches. No search fee. Court makes copy: $5.00 per document. Records on computer back to 1997. Mail turnaround time 2 days.

Criminal Records: Access: Mail, in person. Both court and visitors may perform in person searches. No search fee. Court makes copy: $5.00 per document. Required to search: name, years to search, SSN. Records on computer back to 1997. Mail turnaround time 2 days.

General Information: No public access terminal. Will fax documents. Certification fee: $5.00 per doc. SASE requested.

Carroll County

Berryville Circuit Court - Eastern District Carroll County Circuit Court, PO Box 71, Berryville, AR 72616; phone: 870-423-2422; probate phone: 870-423-2022; fax: 870-423-4796; probate fax: 870-423-7400; hours 8:30AM-4:30PM (CST). *Felony, Civil Actions Over $5,000, Eviction, Probate.*

Note: Probate located at 210 W Church Ave.

Civil Records: Access: Mail, in person. Both court and visitors may perform in person searches. Search fee: $6.00 per name. Court makes copy: $.25 per page; $.50 per page if to be mailed. Self serve copy fee: $.25 per page. Required to search: name, years to search. Civil cases indexed by defendant, plaintiff; on computer from 1997, on index books since 1869. Mail turnaround time same or next day.

Criminal Records: Access: Fax, mail, in person. Both court and visitors may perform in person searches. Search fee: $6.00 per name. Court makes copy: $.25 per page; $.50 per page if to be mailed. Self serve copy fee: $.25 per page. Required to search: name, years to search, DOB, SSN. Criminal records computerized to 1997, on index books since 1869. Mail turnaround time 1-2 days.

General Information: Public access terminal goes back to 1997. No juvenile records released. Fee to fax documents is $1.00 per page. Certification fee: $2.00 per document. Payee: Circuit Clerk of Carroll County. Personal checks accepted. Prepayment and SASE required.

Eureka Springs Circuit Court - Western District 44 S Main, PO Box 109, Eureka Springs, AR 72632; phone: 479-253-8646; hours 8:30AM-4:30PM (CST). *Felony, Civil Actions Over $5,000, Eviction, Probate.*

Civil Records: Access: In person only. Visitors must perform in person searches themselves. Court makes copy: $.50 per page. Required to search: name, years to search. Civil cases indexed by defendant, plaintiff; on indexes from 1883.

Criminal Records: Access: Phone, mail, in person. Both court and visitors may perform in person searches. Search fee: $6.00 per name. Court makes copy: $.50 per page. Self serve copy fee: $.25 per page. Required to search: name, years to search; also helpful: DOB. Criminal records on indexes from 1883, computerized since 2/21/02. Mail turnaround time varies.

General Information: Public access terminal has only criminal records. (Only for recent criminal cases.) No expunged criminal records released. Fee to fax documents is $1.00 per page. Certification fee: $2.00; $5.00 for Probate records. Payee: Circuit Clerk of Carroll County or County Clerk. Personal checks accepted. Prepayment and SASE required.

Berryville District Court 103 S Springs, Berryville, AR 72616; phone: 870-423-6247; fax: 870-423-7069; hours 8AM-4:30PM (CST). *Misdemeanor, Civil Actions Under $5,000, Small Claims.*

Civil Records: Access: Mail, fax, in person. Both court and visitors may perform in person searches. Court makes copy: $.25 per page. Required to search: name, DOB. Records computerized since 1987. Mail turnaround time 1-2 days.

Criminal Records: Access: Mail, in person. Both court and visitors may perform in person searches. No search fee. Court makes copy: $.25 per page. Required to search: name, years to search; also helpful: DOB. Records computerized since 1987. Mail turnaround time 1-2 days.

General Information: No public access terminal. Prepayment required.

Eureka Springs District Court Courthouse, 44 S Main, Eureka Springs, AR 72632; phone: 479-253-8574; hours 8AM-5PM (CST). *Misdemeanor, Civil Actions Under $5,000, Small Claims.*
www.cityofeurekasprings.org/muncourt.html

Civil Records: Access: Phone, mail, in person. Both court and visitors may perform in person searches. No search fee. No copy fee. Required to search: name. Records on computer back to 1990. Mail turnaround time 1 week.

Criminal Records: Access: Phone, mail, in person. Both court and visitors may perform in person searches. No search fee. Required to search: name, years to search. Criminal records computerized to 1990. Mail turnaround time 1 week.

General Information: No public access terminal. No certification fee . SASE required.

Chicot County

Circuit Court 108 Main St, County Courthouse, Lake Village, AR 71653; phone: 870-265-8010; probate phone: 870-265-8000; fax: 870-265-8012; hours 8AM-4:30PM (CST). *Felony, Civil Actions Over $5,000, Probate.*

Note: Probate is located here in a separate office.

Civil Records: Access: Mail, in person. Both court and visitors may perform in person searches. Search fee: $6.00 per name. Court makes copy: $.50 per page; same fee for self serve. Required to search: name, years to search. Civil cases indexed by defendant, plaintiff; on dockets and files from 1900s; computerized since 1999. Mail turnaround time 1-2 days.

Criminal Records: Access: Mail, in person. Both court and visitors may perform in person searches. Search fee: $6.00 per name. Court makes copy: $.50 per page; same fee for self serve. Required to search: name, years to search. Criminal records on dockets and files from 1900s; computerized since 1999. Mail turnaround time 1-2 days.

General Information: No public access terminal. No juvenile records released. Certification fee: $2.00 per doc. Payee: Circuit Clerk. Personal checks accepted. Prepayment and SASE required.

Lake Village District Court PO Box 832, Lake Village, AR 71653; phone: 870-265-3283; criminal records fax: 870-265-3283; civil records fax: same; hours 9AM-4:30PM (CST). *Misdemeanor, Civil Actions Under $5,000, Eviction, Small Claims.*
Civil Records: Access: Mail, fax, in person. Both court and visitors may perform in person searches. Search fee: $5.00 per name. No copy fee.Required to search: name, years to search, other names used; also helpful-DOB, SSN, address, signed release. Civil records on computer go back to 10/02; other records go back to 1977. Mail turnaround time ASAP.
Criminal Records: Access: Mail, in person. Both court and visitors may perform in person searches. Search fee: $5.00 per name. No copy fee.Required to search: name, years to search; also helpful: DOB, SSN. Criminal records on computer go back to 8/2000; other records go back to 1977. Mail turnaround time ASAP.
General Information: No public access terminal. Will fax documents. Certification fee: $5.00 per document. Payee: Lake Village District Court. Prepayment and SASE required.

Clark County

Circuit Court PO Box 576, Arkadelphia, AR 71923; phone: 870-246-4281; probate phone: 870-246-4491; criminal records fax: 870-246-1419; civil records fax: same; hours 8:30AM-4:30PM (CST). *Felony, Civil Actions Over $5,000, Probate.*
Note: Probate is a separate index, separate address
Civil Records: Access: Mail, in person. Both court and visitors may perform in person searches. Search fee: $5.00 per name. Court makes copy: $.50 per page; same fee for self serve. Required to search: name, years to search. Civil cases indexed by defendant, plaintiff; on computer since 1985. Mail turnaround time 1-2 days.
Criminal Records: Access: Mail, in person. Both court and visitors may perform in person searches. Search fee: $5.00 per name. Court makes copy: $.50 per page; same fee for self serve. Required to search: name, years to search. Criminal records on computer since 1985. Mail turnaround time 1-2 days.
General Information: Public access terminal goes back to 1985. No juvenile records released. Will fax documents for $1.00 per page. Certification fee: $5.00 per document includes copies. Payee: Penny R Ross Circuit Clerk. Personal checks accepted. Prepayment and SASE required.

District Court PO Box 449, Arkadelphia, AR 71923; phone: 870-246-9552; fax: 870-246-1415; hours 8:30AM-4:30PM (CST). *Misdemeanor, Civil Actions Under $5,000, Eviction, Small Claims.*
Civil Records: Access: Phone, mail, fax, in person. Both court and visitors may perform in person searches. No search fee. No copy fee.Required to search: name, DOB, SSN, signed release, other names used; also helpful-DL number. Records go back to 1980; on computer since 1990. Mail turnaround time 3 days.
Criminal Records: Access: Phone, mail, fax, in person. Both court and visitors may perform in person searches. No search fee. No copy fee.Required to search: name, years to search; also helpful: DOB. Records go back to 1980; on computer since 1990. Mail turnaround time 3 days.
General Information: No public access terminal. No certification fee. SASE required.

Clay County

Corning Circuit Court 800 SW 2nd St, Corning, AR 72422-2715; phone: 870-857-3271; probate phone: 870-857-3480; fax: 870-857-9201; probate fax: 870-857-3480; hours 8AM-4:30PM (CST). *Felony, Civil Actions Over $5,000, Probate.*
Note: Probate is a separate office and separate index at this same address.
Civil Records: Access: In person only. Both court and visitors may perform in person searches. No search fee. Court makes copy: $1.00 per page if

mailed, $.25 if in person. Self serve copy fee: $.25 per page. Required to search: name, years to search. Civil cases indexed by defendant, plaintiff; on books from 1893.
Criminal Records: Access: In person only. Both court and visitors may perform in person searches. Court makes copy: $1.00 per page if mailed, $.25 if in person. Self serve copy fee: $.25 per page. Required to search: name, years to search; also helpful: DOB, SSN. Criminal records on books from 1893. Court personnel will not do a name search, but will pull specific case data if docket number given.
General Information: No public access terminal. No juvenile records released. Will not fax specific case file. Certification fee: $5.00 per document. Payee: Circuit Clerk. Personal checks accepted. Prepayment required.

Piggott Circuit Court 151 S 2nd, Piggott, AR 72454; phone: 870-598-2524; probate phone: 870-598-2813; hours 8AM-4:30PM (CST). *Felony, Civil Actions Over $5,000.*
Civil Records: Access: In person only. Visitors must perform in person searches themselves. Court makes copy: $.25 per page; same fee for self serve. Required to search: name, years to search. Civil cases indexed by defendant, plaintiff; on books from 1893.
Criminal Records: Access: In person only. Visitors must perform in person searches themselves. Court makes copy: $.25 per page; same fee for self serve. Required to search: name, years to search, DOB, SSN. Criminal records on books from 1893.
General Information: No public access terminal. No expunged criminal records released. Will fax documents $5.00 per doc. Certification fee: $5.00 per doc. Payee: Circuit Clerk. Personal checks accepted. Prepayment required.

District Court 151 S 2nd Ave, Piggott, AR 72454; phone: 870-598-2265; fax: 870-598-2229; hours 8AM-4:30PM (CST). *Misdemeanor, Civil Actions Under $5,000, Eviction, Small Claims.*
Note: Office is open 20 hours per week only. For eviction information the court says to contact Clay County Sheriff, 151 S 2nd St, Piggott, AR 72454, 870-598-2266.
Civil Records: Access: Mail, in person. Only the court performs in person searches. Search fee: $8.00. Court makes copy: $.25 per page. Required to search: name, DOB, years. Records on computer back to 1998. Mail turnaround time 3-4 days.
Criminal Records: Access: Mail, in person. Only the court performs in person searches. Search fee: $8.00. Court makes copy: $.25 per page. Required to search: name, years to search, SSN; also helpful: DOB. Records on computer back to 1998. Mail turnaround time 3-4 days.
General Information: No public access terminal. Will fax documents to local or toll free line. Payee: District Court. Prepayment and SASE required.

Cleburne County

Circuit Court PO Box 543, Heber Springs, AR 72543; phone: 501-362-8149; criminal records fax: 501-362-4650; same fax for civil and probate; hours 8:30AM-4:30PM (CST). *Felony, Civil Actions Over $5,000, Probate.*
Note: Probate is on a separate index at this address.
Civil Records: Access: Fax, mail, in person. Both court and visitors may perform in person searches. Search fee: $6.00 per name. Court makes copy: $.25 per page; same fee for self serve. Required to search: name, years to search. Civil cases indexed by defendant, plaintiff; on dockets from 1883. Mail turnaround time 1-2 days.
Criminal Records: Access: Phone, mail, in person. Both court and visitors may perform in person searches. Search fee: $6.00 per name. Court makes copy: $.25 per page; same fee for self serve. Required to search: name, years to search. Criminal records on dockets from 1883. Mail turnaround time 1-2 days.
General Information: No public access terminal. No juvenile records released. Will fax documents for

$4.00 1st page; $1.00 each add'l page. Certification fee: $1.00 per document. Payee: Circuit Clerk. Personal checks accepted. Prepayment and SASE required.

District Court 102 E Main, Heber Springs, AR 72543; phone: 501-362-6585; hours 8:30AM-4:30PM (CST). *Misdemeanor, Civil Actions Under $5,000, Small Claims, Eviction.*
Civil Records: Access: Phone, mail, fax, in person. Both court and visitors may perform in person searches. No search fee. Civil records computerized to 1989. Mail turnaround time 10 working days.
Criminal Records: Access: Phone, mail, fax, in person. Both court and visitors may perform in person searches. No search fee. Required to search: name, years to search, offense, DOB. Criminal records computerized to 1989. Mail turnaround time 10 working days.
General Information: No public access terminal.

Cleveland County

Circuit Court PO Box 368, Rison, AR 71665; phone: 870-325-6521; criminal records fax: 870-325-6144; same fax for civil and probate; hours 8AM-4:30PM (CST). *Felony, Civil Actions Over $5,000, Probate.*
Note: Probate is a separate office and separate index at this same address.
Civil Records: Access: Mail, in person. Visitors must perform in person searches themselves. No search fee. Court makes copy: $.25 per page; same fee for self serve. Required to search: name, years to search. Civil cases indexed by defendant, plaintiff. Civil records from 1980. Mail turnaround time same day, if possible.
Criminal Records: Access: Mail, in person. Both court and visitors may perform in person searches. No search fee. Court makes copy: $.25 per page; same fee for self serve. Required to search: name, years to search, DOB. Criminal records from 1980. Mail turnaround time same day, if possible.
General Information: No public access terminal. No juvenile or adoption records released. Fee to fax documents is $1.00 per page. Certification fee: $5.00 per document. Payee: Clerk of Circuit Court. Personal checks accepted. Prepayment required.

District Court PO Box 405, City Hall, 405 Main St, Rison, AR 71665; phone: 870-325-7382; fax: 870-325-6152; hours 8AM-4PM (CST). *Misdemeanor, Civil Actions Under $5,000, Eviction, Small Claims.*
Civil Records: Access: In person only. Both court and visitors may perform in person searches. Search fee: None; court will charge for multiple records. No copy fee. Computerized records go back 1 and one-half years.
Criminal Records: Access: In person only. Both court and visitors may perform in person searches. Search fee: none; court will charge for multiple records. No copy fee. Required to search: name, years to search, SSN. Computerized records go back 1 and one-half years.
General Information: No public access terminal. No certification fee .

Columbia County

Circuit Court 1 Court Sq #3, Magnolia, AR 71753-3595; phone: 870-235-3700; probate phone: 870-325-3774; criminal records fax: 870-235-3786; civil records fax: same; hours 8AM-4:30PM (CST). *Felony, Civil Actions Over $5,000, Probate.*
Note: Probate is a separate office and separate index at this same address.
Civil Records: Access: Mail, in person. Both court and visitors may perform in person searches. Search fee: $10.00 per name. Court makes copy: $1.00 per page. Self serve copy fee: $.50 per page. Required to search: name, years to search. Civil cases indexed by defendant, plaintiff; on dockets and index cards; computerized records since 8/97. Mail turnaround time 2-4 days.

Criminal Records: Access: Mail, in person. Both court and visitors may perform in person searches. Search fee: $10.00 per name. Court makes copy: $1.00 per page. Self serve copy fee: $.50 per page. Required to search: name, years to search, DOB, SSN. Criminal records on dockets and index cards; computerized records since 8/97. Mail turnaround time 2-4 days.

General Information: No public access terminal. No juvenile or adoption. Will fax documents. Certification fee: $3.00 per document. Payee: Circuit Clerk. Personal checks accepted. Prepayment and SASE required.

Magnolia District Court 121 S Jefferson, Magnolia, AR 71753; phone: 870-234-7312; hours 8AM-5PM (CST). *Misdemeanor, Civil Actions Under $5,000, Eviction, Small Claims.*

Civil Records: Access: Mail, in person. Both court and visitors may perform in person searches. No search fee. Court makes copy: $1.00 per page. Required to search: DOB and SSN. Civil records available since 1993. Mail turnaround time 3 days.

Criminal Records: Access: Mail, in person. Only the court performs in person searches. Search fee: $1.00 per name. Court makes copy: $1.00 per page. Required to search: name, DOB and SSN, years to search; also helpful: address. Criminal records available sine 1987. Mail turnaround time 3 days.

General Information: No public access terminal. Will fax documents to local or toll-free number. Certification fee: $5.00 includes copy fee. Payee: District Court Clerk. Prepayment and SASE required.

Conway County

Circuit Court Conway County Courthouse, Rm 206, 115 S Moose, Morrilton, AR 72110; phone: 501-354-9617; probate phone: 501-354-9621; fax: 501-354-9612; hours 8AM-5PM (CST). *Felony, Civil Actions Over $5,000, Probate.*

Civil Records: Access: Phone, fax, mail, in person. Both court and visitors may perform in person searches. Search fee: $8.00 per name. Court makes copy: $1.00 per page; same fee for self serve. Required to search: name, years to search. Civil cases indexed by defendant, plaintiff. Civil records (child support) on computer. All others on dockets from 1900s. Mail turnaround time 1-2 days.

Criminal Records: Access: Phone, mail, in person. Both court and visitors may perform in person searches. Search fee: $8.00 per name. Court makes copy: $1.00 per page; same fee for self serve. Required to search: name, years to search, DOB; also helpful: sex, SSN. Criminal records indexed in books back to 1900's. Mail turnaround time 1-2 days.

General Information: No public access terminal. No juvenile records released. Fee to fax documents is $1.00 per page. Certification fee: $5.00 per doc. Payee: Circuit Clerk. Personal checks accepted. Prepayment and SASE required.

District Court Conway County Courthouse, PO Box 127, Morrilton, AR 72110; phone: 501-354-9615; fax: 501-354-9633; hours 8AM-4:30PM (CST). *Misdemeanor, Civil Actions Under $5,000, Eviction, Small Claims.*

Civil Records: Access: Mail, in person. Both court and visitors may perform in person searches. No search fee. Court makes copy: $.50 per page; same fee for self serve. Computerized records since 1994. Mail turnaround time 1-2 days.

Criminal Records: Access: Mail, in person. Only the court performs in person searches. No search fee. Court makes copy: $.50 per page; same fee for self serve. Required to search: name, years to search; also helpful: DOB. Computerized records since 1994. Mail turnaround time 1-2 days.

General Information: Public access terminal available. Certification fee: $5.00. Payee: District Court Clerk. Prepayment required.

Craighead County

Jonesboro Circuit Court PO Box 120, Jonesboro, AR 72403; phone: 870-933-4530; probate phone: 870-933-4520; fax: 870-933-4534; probate fax: 870-933-4514; hours 8AM-5PM (CST). *Felony, Civil Actions Over $5,000, Probate.*

Civil Records: Access: Fax, mail, in person. Both court and visitors may perform in person searches. Search fee: $6.00 per name. Court makes copy: $.50 per page; same fee for self serve. Required to search: name, years to search. Civil cases indexed by defendant, plaintiff; on computer from 1972, on microfiche from 1800s. Mail turnaround time 1-2 days.

Criminal Records: Access: Fax, mail, in person. Both court and visitors may perform in person searches. Search fee: $6.00 per name. Court makes copy: $.50 per page; same fee for self serve. Required to search: name, years to search, DOB; also helpful: address, SSN. Criminal records on computer from 1972, on microfiche from 1800s. Mail turnaround time 1-2 days.

General Information: Public access terminal goes back to 1997. No juvenile records released. Will fax documents $1.00 per page. Certification fee: $3.00 per document. Payee: Circuit Clerk. Personal checks accepted. Prepayment and SASE required.

Lake City Circuit Court - Eastern District PO Box 537, Lake City, AR 72437; phone: 870-237-4342; fax: 870-237-8174; hours 8AM-5PM (CST). *Felony, Civil Actions Over $5,000, Probate.*

Civil Records: Access: In person only. Both court and visitors may perform in person searches. Court makes copy: $.25 per page; same fee for self serve. Required to search: name, years to search, address. Civil cases indexed by defendant, plaintiff; on computer from 1976. Mail turnaround time 1-2 days.

Criminal Records: Access: In person only. Both court and visitors may perform in person searches. Court makes copy: $.25 per page; same fee for self serve. Required to search: name, years to search, address, DOB; also helpful: SSN. Criminal records on computer from 1976.

General Information: Public access terminal goes back to 1976. No adoption records released. Will fax documents to local or toll free line. Certification fee: $3.00 per doc. Payee: Circuit Clerk. Business checks accepted. Prepayment required.

District Court 410 W Washington, Jonesboro, AR 72401; phone: 870-933-4508; criminal records fax: 870-933-4582; civil records fax: same; hours 8AM-5PM (CST). *Misdemeanor, Civil Actions Under $5,000, Eviction, Small Claims.*

Civil Records: Access: Mail, in person. Only the court performs in person searches. Search fee: $4.00 per name. Court makes copy: $.20 per page. Required to search: name, DOB. Computerized records go back 10 years. Mail turnaround time 1-2 days.

Criminal Records: Access: Mail, in person. Only the court performs in person searches. Search fee: $4.00 per name. Court makes copy: $.20 per page. Required to search: name, years to search, SSN. Computerized records go back 10 years. Mail turnaround time 1-2 days.

General Information: No public access terminal. Will fax documents. Certification fee: $2.00 each include copy fee. Payee: District Court. Prepayment required.

Crawford County

Circuit Court County Courthouse, 300 Main St, Rm 22, Van Buren, AR 72956; phone: 479-474-1821; probate phone: 479-474-1312; fax: 479-471-0622; hours 8AM-5PM (CST). *Felony, Civil Actions Over $5,000, Probate.*

www.crawford-county.org/circuit_court.htm

Note: Probate is a separate office, separate index.

Civil Records: Access: Mail, in person, online. Both court and visitors may perform in person searches.

Search fee: $6.00 per name, if written response needed. Court makes copy: $1.00 per page if mailed, otherwise $.50. Self serve copy fee: $.50 per page. Required to search: name, years to search. Civil cases indexed by defendant, plaintiff; on computer from 1992, on dockets from 1877. Access court orders online at www.etitlesearch.com; registration and fees apply. Mail turnaround time same day.

Criminal Records: Access: Mail, in person, online. Both court and visitors may perform in person searches. Search fee: $6.00 per name, if written response needed. Court makes copy: $1.00 per page if mailed, otherwise $.50. Self serve copy fee: $.50 per page. Required to search: name, years to search. Criminal records on computer from 1992, on dockets from 1877. Access court orders online at www.etitlesearch.com; registration and fees apply. Mail turnaround time 1-2 days.

General Information: Public access terminal goes back to 1992. No juvenile records released. Will fax documents to toll-free line. Certification fee: $2.00. Payee: Circuit Clerk. Personal checks accepted. Prepayment and SASE required.

District Court 1003 Broadway, Van Buren, AR 72956; phone: 479-474-1671; fax: 479-471-5005; hours 8AM-5PM, (CST). *Misdemeanor, Civil Actions Under $5,000, Eviction, Small Claims.*

Civil Records: Access: Mail, in person. Both court and visitors may perform in person searches. No search fee. Court makes copy: $.50. Records available from 1975, computerized from 2000. Mail turnaround time 2-3 days.

Criminal Records: Access: Mail, in person. Both court and visitors may perform in person searches. No search fee. Court makes copy: $.50. Required to search: name, years to search; also helpful: DOB, SSN. Specific court cases prior to 2000 need the conviction date. Records available from 1975, computerized from 2000. Mail turnaround time 2-3 days.

General Information: Public access terminal goes back to 2000. (Terminal only available Fridays.) Certification fee: $10.00 per document. Payee: Van Buren District Court. Prepayment and SASE required.

Crittenden County

Circuit Court 100 Court St, Marion, AR 72364; phone: 870-739-3248; probate phone: 870-739-4434; criminal records fax: 870-739-3287; civil records fax: same; hours 8AM-4:30PM (CST). *Felony, Civil Actions Over $5,000, Probate.*

Note: Probate is managed by the County Clerk office.

Civil Records: Access: Mail, in person. Both court and visitors may perform in person searches. Search fee: $6.00 per name. Court makes copy: $.25 per page; same fee for self serve. Required to search: name, years to search. Civil cases indexed by plaintiff only. Civil records on dockets from 1930s; manual lookups.

Criminal Records: Access: In person only. Visitors must perform in person searches themselves. Court makes copy: $.25 per page; same fee for self serve. Required to search: name, case number. Criminal records on dockets from 1930s; manual lookups. The court suggests to send for criminal record inquiries to Ark. State Police, 501-681-8100.

General Information: No public access terminal. No juvenile records released. Fee to fax documents is $4.50 per document. Certification fee: $3.00. Payee: Circuit Court. Personal checks accepted. Prepayment and SASE required.

District Court PO Box 766, West Memphis, AR 72303; phone: 870-732-7560; civil phone: 870-732-7563; fax: 870-732-7538; hours 8AM-5PM (CST). *Misdemeanor, Civil Actions Under $5,000, Eviction, Small Claims.*

Civil Records: Access: Phone, fax, mail, in person. Both court and visitors may perform in person searches. No search fee. Court makes copy: $.25 per page. Required to search: name, years to search, DOB or SSN. Civil records computerized to 1989; other records go back to 1945. Mail turnaround time 2-3 days.

Criminal Records: Access: Phone, mail, in person. Both court and visitors may perform in person searches. No search fee. Court makes copy: $.25 per page. Required to search: name, years to search; also helpful: SSN, race, sex, DOB. Criminal records computerized to 1989; other records go back to 1945. Mail turnaround time 2-3 days.

General Information: Public access terminal available. No fee to fax documents. No certification fee. Payee: District Court. Prepayment required.

Cross County

Circuit Court County Courthouse, 705 E Union, Rm 9, Wynne, AR 72396; phone: 870-238-5720; probate phone: 870-238-5735; fax: 870-238-5722; hours 8AM-4PM (CST). *Felony, Civil Actions Over $5,000, Probate.*

Civil Records: Access: In person only. No search fee. Court makes copy: $.25 per page. Required to search: name, years to search. Civil cases indexed by defendant. Civil records (child support) on computer. All on dockets from 1800s.

Criminal Records: Access: In person only. Visitors must perform in person searches themselves. Court makes copy: $.25 per page. Required to search: name, years to search; SSN helpful. Criminal records (child support) on computer. All on dockets from 1800s.

General Information: Public access terminal goes back to 2001. No juvenile records released. Certification fee: $3.00 per doc. Payee: Cross County Circuit Court. Personal checks accepted. Prepayment required.

District Court 205 Mississippi St, Wynne, AR 72396; phone: 870-238-9171; hours 8AM-4PM (CST). *Misdemeanor, Civil Actions Under $5,000, Eviction, Small Claims.*

Civil Records: Access: Mail, in person. Both court and visitors may perform in person searches. Search fee: $5.00. Court makes copy: $.50 per page. Required to search: name, years to search. Records on computer back to 1986. Mail turnaround time 5-7 days.

Criminal Records: Access: Mail, in person. Both court and visitors may perform in person searches. Search fee: $5.00. Court makes copy: $.50 per page. Required to search: name, years to search, signed release; also helpful: SSN. Records on computer back to 1986. Mail turnaround time 5-7 days.

General Information: No public access terminal. Fee to fax documents is $2.00 per document. Certification fee: $5.00. Payee: Cross County Court. Prepayment required.

Dallas County

Circuit Court Dallas County Courthouse, Fordyce, AR 71742; phone: 870-352-2307; fax: 870-352-7179; hours 8:30AM-4:30PM (CST). *Felony, Civil Actions Over $5,000, Probate.*

Civil Records: Access: Phone, fax, mail, in person. Both court and visitors may perform in person searches. Search fee: $6.00. Court makes copy: $.50 per page; same fee for self serve. Required to search: name, years to search. Civil cases indexed by defendant, plaintiff. Civil records go back to 1863; on computer back to 8/1997.

Criminal Records: Access: In person only. Visitors must perform in person searches themselves. Court makes copy: $.50 per page; same fee for self serve. Required to search: name, years to search, DOB; SSN helpful. Criminal records go back to 1863; on computer back to 8/1997.

General Information: Public access terminal goes back to 8/1997. No juvenile records released. Will fax documents $2.00 plus $.25 per page. Certification fee: $5.00. Payee: Circuit Clerk. Business checks accepted. Law firm accounts, money orders and cashier checks allowed. Prepayment and SASE required.

District Court 202 W 3rd St, Fordyce, AR 71742; phone: 870-352-2332; fax: 870-352-3414; hours 8AM-4:30PM (CST). *Misdemeanor, Civil Actions Under $5,000, Eviction, Small Claims.*

Civil Records: Access: In person, mail. Only the court performs in person searches. No search fee. Court makes copy: $.25 per page. Required to search: name. Computerized records since 1997. Mail turnaround time 1-2 days.

Criminal Records: Access: In person only. Only the court performs in person searches. No search fee. Court makes copy: $.25 per page. Required to search: name, years to search, SSN; also helpful: DOB. Computerized records since 1997. Mail turnaround time 1-2 days.

General Information: No public access terminal. No certification fee . Payee: Dallas County District Court. Checks or cash accepted.

Desha County

Circuit Court PO Box 309, Arkansas City, AR 71630; phone: 870-877-2411; probate phone: 870-877-2323; fax: 870-877-3407; hours 8AM-4PM (CST). *Felony, Civil Actions Over $5,000, Probate.*

Civil Records: Access: Fax, mail, in person. Both court and visitors may perform in person searches. Search fee: $5.00 per name. Court makes copy: $.50 per page. Required to search: name, years to search. Civil cases indexed by defendant, plaintiff; on dockets from 1920s; on computer back to 1997. Mail turnaround time 1-2 days.

Criminal Records: Access: Fax, mail, in person. Both court and visitors may perform in person searches. Search fee: $5.00 per name. Court makes copy: $.50 per page. Required to search: name, years to search, SSN. Criminal records on dockets from 1920s, on computer back to 1997. Mail turnaround time 1-2 days.

General Information: Public access terminal available. (Terminal may only have deeds, mortgages, judgments.) No juvenile records released. No fee to fax documents. Certification fee: $3.00 per doc. Payee: Skippy Leek, Circuit Court Clerk. Personal checks accepted. Prepayment and SASE required.

District Court PO Box 157, Dumas, AR 71639-2226; phone: 870-382-6972; criminal phone: 870-382-6852; civil phone: 870-382-6972; criminal records fax: 870-382-1106; civil records fax: same; hours 8AM-4:30PM (CST). *Misdemeanor, Civil Actions Under $5,000, Eviction, Small Claims.*

Civil Records: Access: Mail, in person. Only the court performs in person searches. Search fee: $5.00 per name. Court makes copy: included in search fee. Required to search: name, years to search, signed release; also helpful: address. Civil records go back to 1988. Note: search fee includes copy fee if record found Mail turnaround time 1-2 days.

Criminal Records: Access: Mail, in person. Only the court performs in person searches. Search fee: $5.00 per name. Court makes copy: search fee includes copy fee if record found. Required to search: name, years to search, signed release; also helpful: address. Criminal records go back to 1988. Mail turnaround time 1-2 days.

General Information: No public access terminal. Will fax documents for no fee. Certification fee: $5.00 per record includes copy fee. Payee: Dumas District Court. Prepayment required.

Drew County

Circuit Court 210 S Main, Monticello, AR 71655; phone: 870-460-6250; probate phone: 870-460-6260; fax: 870-460-6246; hours 8AM-4:30PM (CST). *Felony, Civil Actions Over $5,000, Probate.*

Civil Records: Access: Phone, fax, mail, in person. Both court and visitors may perform in person searches. No search fee. Court makes copy: $.50 per page. Self serve copy fee: $.25 per page. Required to search: name, years to search. Civil cases indexed by defendant, plaintiff; on dockets from 1846; on computer back to 1996 approx. Mail turnaround time 1 day.

Criminal Records: Access: In person only. Visitors must perform in person searches themselves. Court makes copy: $.50 per page. Self serve copy fee: $.25 per page. Required to search: name, years to search. Criminal records on dockets from 1846; on computer back to 1997 approx.

General Information: Public access terminal has criminal back to 1997 and civil back to 1996. No juvenile or expunged records released. Will fax documents $1.25 1st page, $1.00 each add'l. Certification fee: $2.50 per doc. Payee: Drew County Circuit Clerk. Personal checks accepted. Prepayment and SASE required.

District Court PO Box 505, Monticello, AR 71655; phone: 870-367-4420; criminal records fax: 870-460-9056; civil records fax: same; hours 8AM-4:30PM (CST). *Misdemeanor, Civil Actions Under $5,000, Eviction, Small Claims.*

Civil Records: Access: Mail, fax, in person. Only the court performs in person searches. No search fee. No copy fee. Required to search: name, years to search, DOB, SSN, signed release. Records overall since 1980, on computer since 1987. Mail turnaround time 1-2 days.

Criminal Records: Access: Mail, fax, in person. Only the court performs in person searches. No search fee. No copy fee. Required to search: name, years to search, DOB; also helpful: sex, signed release. Records overall since 1980, on computer since 1987. Mail turnaround time 1-2 days.

General Information: No public access terminal. Will fax documents to local or toll free line. Certification fee: No fee to certify.

Faulkner County

Circuit Court Circuit Clerk, PO Box 9, Conway, AR 72033; phone: 501-450-4911; probate phone: 501-450-4909; fax: 501-450-4948; hours 8AM-4:30PM (CST). *Felony, Civil Actions Over $5,000, Probate.*

Note: Probate handled at different office, number above.

Civil Records: Access: Fax, mail, in person. Both court and visitors may perform in person searches. Search fee: $6.00 per name. Court makes copy: $.25 per page. Required to search: name, years to search. Civil cases indexed by defendant, plaintiff. Civil records computerized to 1987; on docket from 1800s. Mail turnaround time 1-2 days.

Criminal Records: Access: Fax, mail, in person. Both court and visitors may perform in person searches. Search fee: $6.00 per name. Court makes copy: $.25 per page. Required to search: name, years to search. Criminal records computerized to 1987; on docket from 1800s. Mail turnaround time 1-2 days.

General Information: Public access terminal goes back to 1987. No juvenile records released. Will fax documents $1.00 if local, $3.50 plus $.25 per page if long distance. Certification fee: $3.00 per doc. Payee: Faulkner County Circuit Clerk. Personal checks accepted. Prepayment and SASE required.

District Court 810 Parkway, Conway, AR 72034; phone: 501-450-6112; fax: 501-450-6184; hours 8AM-4:30PM (CST). *Misdemeanor, Civil Actions Under $5,000, Small Claims.*

Civil Records: Access: Mail, fax, in person. Both court and visitors may perform in person searches. No search fee. Court makes copy: if over 25 copies, then $.02 per page. Required to search: name, years to search, DOB, signed release; also helpful: address, SSN. Computerized records go back to 1993. Mail turnaround time 2 days.

Criminal Records: Access: Mail, fax, in person. Both court and visitors may perform in person searches. No search fee. Court makes copy: if over 25 copies, then $.02 per page. Required to search: name, years to search, DOB, signed release; also helpful: address, SSN. Computerized records go back to 1993. Mail turnaround time 2 days.

General Information: Public access terminal has only criminal records back to 1993. Will fax documents to local or toll free number. Certification fee: $5.00. Payee: Conway District Court. Prepayment required.

Franklin County

Charleston Circuit Court 607 E main, Charleston, AR 72933; phone: 479-965-7332; probate phone: 479-965-2129; fax: 479-965-9322; hours 8AM-4:30PM (CST). *Felony, Civil Actions Over $5,000, Probate.*

Civil Records: Access: Mail, in person. Both court and visitors may perform in person searches. Search fee: $6.00 per name. Court makes copy: $.25 per page; same fee for self serve. Required to search: name, years to search, DOB. Civil cases indexed by defendant, plaintiff; on dockets from 1900s. Mail turnaround time 1-2 days.

Criminal Records: Access: Mail, in person. Both court and visitors may perform in person searches. Search fee: $6.00 per name. Court makes copy: $.25 per page; same fee for self serve. Required to search: name, years to search, DOB. Criminal records on dockets from 1900s. Mail turnaround time 1-2 days.

General Information: No public access terminal. No juvenile records released. Will fax documents $1.00 per page. Certification fee: $5.00. Payee: Franklin County. Personal checks accepted. Prepayment and SASE required.

Ozark Circuit Court PO Box 1112, 211 W Commercial, Ozark, AR 72949; phone: 479-667-3818; probate phone: 479-667-3607; fax: 479-667-5174; hours 8AM-4:30PM (CST). *Felony, Civil Actions Over $5,000, Probate.*
Note: Probate is maintained at the County Clerk's Office.

Civil Records: Access: Fax, mail, in person. Both court and visitors may perform in person searches. Search fee: $6.00 per name. Court makes copy: $.25 per page; same fee for self serve. Required to search: name, years to search. Civil cases indexed by plaintiff. Civil records on dockets from 1900s. Mail turnaround time 1-2 days.

Criminal Records: Access: Fax, mail, in person. Both court and visitors may perform in person searches. Search fee: $6.00 per name. Court makes copy: $.25 per page; same fee for self serve. Required to search: name, years to search. Criminal records on dockets from 1900s. Mail turnaround time 1-2 days.

General Information: No public access terminal. No juvenile records released. Will fax documents $1.00 per page. Certification fee: $2.00. Payee: Circuit Clerk. Personal checks accepted. Prepayment and SASE required.

District Court PO Box 426, Charleston, AR 72933; phone: 479-965-7455; fax: 479-965-9980; hours 8AM-5PM (CST). *Misdemeanor, Civil Actions Under $5,000, Small Claims.*

Civil Records: Access: Mail, fax, in person. Both court and visitors may perform in person searches. No search fee. No copy fee. Civil records are not computerized, records index in docket books. Mail turnaround time 3-4 days.

Criminal Records: Access: Mail, fax, in person. Both court and visitors may perform in person searches. No search fee. No copy fee. Required to search: name, years to search, DOB; also helpful SSN, signed release. Criminal records computerized to 1/2000. Mail turnaround time 3-4 days.

General Information: No public access terminal. Will fax documents. No certification fee .

Fulton County

Circuit Court PO Box 219, Salem, AR 72576; phone: 870-895-3310; criminal records fax: 870-895-3383; same fax for civil and probate; hours 8AM-4:30PM (CST). *Felony, Civil Actions Over $5,000, Probate.*

Civil Records: Access: Mail, in person. Both court and visitors may perform in person searches. Search fee: $6.00 per name. Court makes copy: $.20 per page; same fee for self serve. Required to search: name, years to search. Civil cases indexed by

defendant, plaintiff; on dockets from 1900s; on computer back to 2000. Mail turnaround time 1-2 days.

Criminal Records: Access: Mail, in person. Both court and visitors may perform in person searches. Search fee: $6.00 per name. Court makes copy: $.20 per page; same fee for self serve. Required to search: name, years to search. Criminal records on dockets from 1900s; on computer back to 2000. Mail turnaround time 1-2 days.

General Information: Public access terminal goes back to 2000. No juvenile records released. Will fax documents. No certification fee . Payee: Fulton County Clerks. Personal checks accepted. Prepayment and SASE required.

District Court PO Box 928, Salem, AR 72576; phone: 870-895-4136; fax: 870-895-4114; hours 8AM-4:30PM (CST). *Misdemeanor, Civil Actions Under $5,000, Eviction, Small Claims.*

Civil Records: Access: Mail, in person. Only the court performs in person searches. No search fee. No copy fee. Required to search: name. Computerized records since 1995. Mail turnaround time 1 week.

Criminal Records: Access: Phone, mail, in person. Both court and visitors may perform in person searches. No search fee. No copy fee. Required to search: name, years to search, DOB. Computerized records since 1995. Mail turnaround time 1 week.

General Information: No public access terminal. No certification fee . SASE required.

Garland County

Circuit Court Garland County Courthouse, 501 Ouachita Ave, Rm 207, Hot Springs, AR 71901; criminal phone: 501-622-3640; civil phone: 501-622-3630; probate phone: 501-622-3610; criminal records fax: 501-609-9043; civil records fax: same; hours 8AM-5PM (CST). *Felony, Civil Actions Over $5,000, Probate.*
Note: Probate records are handled by the County Clerk, phone number above.

Civil Records: Access: In person only. Visitors must perform in person searches themselves. Court makes copy: $.25 per page; same fee for self serve. Required to search: name; also helpful: years to search. Civil cases indexed by defendant, plaintiff; on microfiche and docket from 1900s; on computer back to 1989.

Criminal Records: Access: Fax, mail, in person. Both court and visitors may perform in person searches. No search fee. Court makes copy: $.25 per page; same fee for self serve. Required to search: name, years to search; also helpful: DOB, SSN, maiden name, race, aliases, sex. Criminal records on microfiche and docket from 1900s; on computer back to 1989. Mail turnaround time 1-2 days.

General Information: No public access terminal. No expunged, sealed records released. Fee to fax documents is $2.00 plus $.25 per page. Certification fee: $.50 per page. Payee: Garland County Circuit Clerk. Personal checks accepted. Prepayment and SASE required.

District Court 607 Ouachita, Hot Springs, AR 71901; phone: 501-321-6765; fax: 501-321-6764; hours 8AM-4:30PM (CST). *Misdemeanor, Civil Actions Under $5,000, Eviction, Small Claims.*

Civil Records: Access: In person only. Only the court performs in person searches. No search fee. Court makes copy: $.25 per page. Required to search: name, DOB, SSN, years to search. Civil record on computer back to 2000.

Criminal Records: Access: In person only. Only the court performs in person searches. No search fee. Court makes copy: $.25 per page. Required to search: name, years to search, offense. Criminal records computerized to 1990.

General Information: No public access terminal. Certification fee: $5.00 per document. Payee: HSDC. Prepayment required.

Grant County

Circuit Court Grant County Courthouse, 101 W Center, Rm 106, Sheridan, AR 72150; phone: 870-942-2631; criminal records fax: 870-942-3564; same fax for civil and probate; hours 8AM-4:30PM (CST). *Felony, Civil Actions Over $5,000, Probate.*

Civil Records: Access: In person only. Visitors must perform in person searches themselves. Court makes copy: $.25 per page; same fee for self serve. Required to search: name, years to search. Civil cases indexed by defendant, plaintiff; on dockets and index from 1877.

Criminal Records: Access: In person only. Visitors must perform in person searches themselves. Court makes copy: $.25 per page; same fee for self serve. Required to search: name, years to search. Criminal records on dockets and index from 1982.

General Information: No public access terminal. No juvenile, probate or adoption records released. Will fax specific case file for $3.00 fax fee. Certification fee: $5.00 per certification includes copies. Payee: Circuit Clerk. Personal checks accepted. Prepayment required.

District Court PO Box 603, Sheridan, AR 72150; phone: 870-942-3464; criminal phone: 870-942-2631; criminal records fax: 870-942-8885; same fax for civil and probate; hours 8AM-4:15PM (CST). *Misdemeanor, Civil Actions Under $5,000, Eviction, Small Claims.*
Note: Probate is a separate index at this same address.

Civil Records: Access: Mail, in person. Both court and visitors may perform in person searches. No search fee. Court makes copy: $.25; same fee for self serve. Computerized records since 1992. Mail turnaround time 3 days.

Criminal Records: Access: Mail, in person. Both court and visitors may perform in person searches. No search fee. Court makes copy: $.25; same fee for self serve. Required to search: name, years to search. Computerized records since 1992. Mail turnaround time 3 days.

General Information: No public access terminal. Will fax documents for $3.00 per fax. Certification fee: $5.00. Payee: Grant County District Court. Personal checks accepted. SASE required.

Greene County

Circuit Court 320 W Court #124, Paragould, AR 72450; phone: 870-239-6330; fax: 870-239-3550; hours 8AM-4:30PM (CST). *Felony, Civil Actions Over $5,000, Probate.*

Civil Records: Access: Fax, mail, in person. Both court and visitors may perform in person searches. Search fee: $6.00 per name. Court makes copy: $.20 per page; same fee for self serve. Required to search: name, years to search. Civil cases indexed by plaintiff. Civil records on computer from 1980, on index from 1830. Mail turnaround time 1-2 days.

Criminal Records: Access: Fax, mail, in person. Both court and visitors may perform in person searches. Search fee: $6.00 per name. Court makes copy: $.20 per page; same fee for self serve. Required to search: name, years to search; also helpful: DOB, SSN. Criminal records computerized since 1986, archived to 1876. Mail turnaround time 1-2 days.

General Information: Public access terminal has criminal back to 1970 and civil back to 1980. No juvenile records released. For fax return, $1.00 for first 3 pages then $.25 per page. Certification fee: $3.00 per doc. Payee: Greene County Circuit Clerk. Personal checks accepted. Prepayment and SASE required.

District Court 320 W Court, Rm 227, Paragould, AR 72450; phone: 870-239-7507; fax: 870-239-7506; hours 8AM-4:30PM (CST). *Misdemeanor, Civil Actions Under $5,000, Eviction, Small Claims.*
www.gccourt.com

Civil Records: Access: Mail, in person. Only the court performs in person searches. No search fee. Court makes copy: $.50 per page. Required to search: name, years to search, DOB or SSN. Records on computer back to 1989. Mail turnaround time 2 days.

Criminal Records: Access: Mail, in person. Only the court performs in person searches. Search fee: $5.00 per name. Court makes copy: $.50 per page. Required to search: name, years to search, DOB or SSN. Records on computer back to 1989. Mail turnaround time 2 days.

General Information: No public access terminal. Certification fee: $5.00 per doc. Payee: District Clerk. Only cashiers checks and money orders accepted. Prepayment and SASE required.

Hempstead County

Circuit Court PO Box 1420, Hope, AR 71802; phone: 870-777-2384; probate phone: 870-777-2241; fax: 870-777-7827; hours 8AM-4PM (CST). *Felony, Civil Actions Over $5,000, Probate.*

Note: Probate is handled by the County Clerk at same address.

Civil Records: Access: Phone, fax, mail, in person. Both court and visitors may perform in person searches. Search fee: $6.00 per name. Court makes copy: $.50 per page. Self serve copy fee: $.25 per page. Required to search: name, years to search. Civil cases indexed by defendant, plaintiff; on dockets from 1910. Mail turnaround time 1-2 days.

Criminal Records: Access: Phone, fax, mail, in person. Both court and visitors may perform in person searches. Search fee: $6.00 per name. Court makes copy: $.50 per page. Self serve copy fee: $.25 per page. Required to search: name, years to search, DOB, SSN. Criminal records on dockets from 1910; computerized since 198. Mail turnaround time 1-2 days.

General Information: No public access terminal. No juvenile records released. Certification fee: $5.00. Payee: Circuit Clerk. Personal checks accepted. Prepayment and SASE required.

District Court PO Box 1420, Hope, AR 71802-1420; phone: 870-777-2525; fax: 870-777-7830; hours 8AM-4PM (CST). *Misdemeanor, Civil Actions Under $5,000, Eviction, Small Claims.*

Civil Records: Access: Mail, in person. Both court and visitors may perform in person searches. Search fee: $5.00 per name includes copies. Required to search: name, years to search. Civil records not computerized. Mail turnaround time less than 1 week.

Criminal Records: Access: Mail, in person. Both court and visitors may perform in person searches. Search fee: $5.00 per name includes copies. Required to search: name, years to search, SSN, DOB. Criminal records computerized to 1987. Mail turnaround time less than 1 week.

General Information: No public access terminal. Will not fax documents. Certification fee: $5.00 per doc includes copies. Payee: District Court. Prepayment required.

Hot Spring County

Circuit Court PO Box 1220, 210 Locust St, Malvern, AR 72104; phone: 501-332-2281; probate phone: 501-332-2291; Hours: 8:00AM-4:30PM (CST). *Felony, Civil Actions Over $5,000.*

Civil Records: Access: Mail, in person. Both court and visitors may perform in person searches. No search fee. Court makes copy: $.50 per page. Self serve copy fee: $.25 per page. Required to search: name, years to search. Civil cases indexed by plaintiff. Civil records on dockets from 1800s. Mail turnaround time 1-2 days.

Criminal Records: Access: Mail, in person. Both court and visitors may perform in person searches. No search fee. Court makes copy: $.50 per page. Self serve copy fee: $.25 per page. Required to search: name, years to search, DOB or SSN. Criminal records on dockets from 1800s. Mail turnaround time 1-2 days.

General Information: Public access terminal goes back to 1994. No juvenile records released. Certification fee: $5.00 per doc. Payee: Circuit Clerk.

Personal checks accepted. Prepayment and SASE required.

Malvern District Court 305 Locust St, Rm 201, Malvern, AR 72104; phone: 501-332-7604; fax: 501-332-3144; hours 8AM-4:30PM (CST). *Misdemeanor, Civil Actions Under $5,000, Eviction, Small Claims.*

Note: Formerly known as Malvern Municipal Court before 7/1/01.

Civil Records: Access: Mail, fax, in person. Visitors must perform in person searches themselves. No search fee. Court makes copy: $.25. Required to search: name, years to search and DOB or SSN. Records computerized back to 1994. Mail turnaround time 3 days.

Criminal Records: Access: Mail, fax, in person. Visitors must perform in person searches themselves. No search fee. Court makes copy: $.25. Required to search: name, years to search, DOB; also helpful: address, SSN. Records computerized back to 1994. Mail turnaround time 3 days.

General Information: No public access terminal. Will fax documents for f$.25 per record. Prepayment and SASE required.

Howard County

Circuit Court 421 N Main, Rm 7, Nashville, AR 71852; phone: 870-845-7506; probate phone: 870-845-7503; hours 8AM-4:30PM (CST). *Felony, Civil Actions Over $5,000, Probate.*

Note: Probate is handled by the County Clerk at this address in Room 10.

Civil Records: Access: Phone, mail, in person. Both court and visitors may perform in person searches. Search fee: $6.00. Court makes copy: $.25 per page; same fee for self serve. Required to search: name, years to search. Civil cases indexed by defendant, plaintiff; on dockets from 1873.

Criminal Records: Access: In person only. Visitors must perform in person searches themselves. Court makes copy: $.25 per page; same fee for self serve. Required to search: name, years to search, DOB. Criminal records on dockets from 1873.

General Information: Public access terminal goes back to 7/2003. No juvenile or sealed records released. Will fax documents for $.50 per page. Certification fee: $2.00. Payee: Circuit Clerk. Personal checks accepted. Prepayment and SASE required.

District Court 426 N Main, ##7, Nashville, AR 71852-2009; phone: 870-845-7522; criminal records fax: 870-845-3705; civil records fax: same; hours 8AM-4:30PM (CST). *Misdemeanor, Civil Actions Under $5,000, Eviction, Small Claims.*

Civil Records: Access: Mail, in person. Visitors must perform in person searches themselves. No copy fee. Required to search: name, years to search. Civil records viewable back to 1989. Mail turnaround time 1-3 days.

Criminal Records: Access: Mail, in person. Both court and visitors may perform in person searches. No search fee. No copy fee.Required to search: name, years to search, DOB; also helpful: address, SSN. Criminal records viewable past 7 years. Mail turnaround time 1-3 days.

General Information: No public access terminal. Will fax documents to local or toll free line. Certification fee: $5.00 per doc. Prepayment required.

Independence County

Circuit Court PO Box 2155, 192 E Main at Broad St, Batesville, AR 72503; phone: 870-793-8833; fax: 870-793-8888; hours 8AM-4:30PM (CST). *Felony, Civil Actions Over $5,000.*

Civil Records: Access: In person only. Visitors must perform in person searches themselves. Court makes copy: $.25 per page. Required to search: name, years to search; also helpful: address. Civil cases indexed by defendant, plaintiff. Civil judgments on computer from 1980, all others on index books from 1970s.

Criminal Records: Access: Mail, in person. Both court and visitors may perform in person searches. Search fee: $6.00 per name. Court makes copy: $.25 per page. Required to search: name, years to search, DOB; also helpful: address. Criminal records on index books from 1970s. Mail turnaround time varies, but usually same day.

General Information: No public access terminal. No juvenile records released. No certification fee . Payee: Circuit Clerk. Personal checks accepted. Prepayment and SASE required.

District Court 549 W Main, Batesville, AR 72501; phone: 870-793-8817; fax: 870-793-8875; hours 8AM-4:30PM (CST). *Misdemeanor, Civil Actions Under $5,000, Eviction, Small Claims.*

Civil Records: Access: Mail, in person. Both court and visitors may perform in person searches. No search fee. No copy fee.Civil records go back to 1975. Mail turnaround time 1-2 days.

Criminal Records: Access: Mail, in person. Both court and visitors may perform in person searches. No search fee. No copy fee.Required to search: name, years to search. Criminal records go back to 1975. Mail turnaround time 1-2 days.

General Information: No public access terminal. Will fax documents. No certification fee . Payee: District Court. Only cashiers checks and money orders accepted. Prepayment and SASE required.

Izard County

Circuit Court PO Box 95, Melbourne, AR 72556; phone: 870-368-4316; fax: 870-368-4748; hours 8:30AM-4:30PM (CST). *Felony, Civil Actions Over $5,000, Probate.*

Civil Records: Access: Fax, mail, in person. Visitors must perform in person searches themselves. Search fee: $6.00 per name. Court makes copy: $.20 per page; same fee for self serve. Required to search: name, years to search. Civil cases indexed by plaintiff. Civil records on judgment books from 1889. Mail turnaround time 2 weeks.

Criminal Records: Access: Fax, mail, in person. Both court and visitors may perform in person searches. Search fee: $6.00 per name. Court makes copy: $.20 per page; same fee for self serve. Required to search: name, years to search, DOB; also helpful: address. Criminal records on judgment books from 1889. Mail turnaround time 2 weeks.

General Information: No public access terminal. No juvenile records released. No fee to fax documents locally; is $1.00 per page if long distance. Certification fee: $5.00 per document. Payee: Izard County and Circuit Clerk. Personal checks accepted. Prepayment and SASE required.

District Court PO Box 337, Melbourne, AR 72556; phone: 870-368-4390; fax: 870-368-2267; hours 8:30AM-4:30PM (CST). *Misdemeanor, Civil Actions Under $5,000, Small Claims.*

Civil Records: Access: Mail, fax, in person. Both court and visitors may perform in person searches. Search fee: $6.00. Court makes copy: $.20 per page; same fee for self serve. Required to search: name, years to search, DOB. Civil records go back to 1977; on computer back to 1993. Mail turnaround time varies.

Criminal Records: Access: Mail, fax, in person. Both court and visitors may perform in person searches. Search fee: $6.00. Court makes copy: $.20 per page; same fee for self serve. Required to search: name, years to search, DOB. Criminal records go back to 1977; on computer back to 1993. Mail turnaround time varies.

General Information: No public access terminal. Will fax documents for $1.00 per page. Certification fee: $5.00. Payee: District Court. Prepayment required.

Jackson County

Circuit Court Jackson County Courthouse, 208 Main St, Newport, AR 72112; phone: 870-523-7423; fax: 870-523-3682; hours 8AM-4:30PM (CST). *Felony, Civil Actions Over $5,000, Probate.*
Civil Records: Access: Mail, in person. Visitors must perform in person searches themselves. Court makes copy: $.25 per page; same fee for self serve. Required to search: name, years to search. Civil cases indexed by defendant, plaintiff; on dockets from 1800s.
Criminal Records: Access: Mail, in person. Visitors must perform in person searches themselves. No search fee. Court makes copy: $.25 per page; same fee for self serve. Required to search: name, years to search. Criminal records on dockets from 1800s, computerized back to 1997. Mail turnaround time 1-2 days.
General Information: Public access terminal has criminal back to 1997 and civil back to 1997. (Terminal has name index.) No juvenile records released. Certification fee: $3.00 per doc. Payee: Circuit Clerk. Personal checks accepted. Prepayment and SASE required.

District Court 615 3rd St, Newport, AR 72112; phone: 870-523-9555; criminal phone: x118; civil phone: Ext 120; fax: 870-523-4365; hours 8AM-4:30PM (CST). *Misdemeanor, Civil Actions Under $5,000, Eviction, Small Claims.*
Civil Records: Access: Phone, mail, fax, in person. Both court and visitors may perform in person searches. No search fee. Court makes copy: $5.00 for 10+ pages. Civil records go back to 1987. Mail turnaround time 5-7 days.
Criminal Records: Access: Mail, fax, in person. Both court and visitors may perform in person searches. No search fee. Court makes copy: $5.00 for 10+ pages. Required to search: name, years to search, DOB. Criminal records go back to 1993 on computer, searchable to 1950. Mail turnaround time 5-7 days.
General Information: No public access terminal. Will fax documents to local or toll free line. No certification fee . Payee: Newport District Court. Prepayment and SASE required.

Jefferson County

Circuit Court PO Box 7433, Pine Bluff, AR 71611; criminal phone: 870-541-5306; civil phone: 870-541-5307; hours 8:30PM-5PM (CST). *Felony, Civil Actions Over $5,000, Probate.*
Civil Records: Access: In person only. Visitors must perform in person searches themselves. Court makes copy: $.50 per page; same fee for self serve. Required to search: name, years to search. Civil cases indexed by defendant, plaintiff; on dockets from 1950.
Criminal Records: Access: In person only. Visitors must perform in person searches themselves. Court makes copy: $.50 per page; same fee for self serve. Required to search: name, years to search, DOB. Criminal records on dockets from 1950.
General Information: Public access terminal goes back to 1991. No juvenile records released. Certification fee: $.50 per page. Payee: Circuit Clerk. Only cashiers checks and money orders accepted. Prepayment required.

District Court 200 E 8th Ave, Pine Bluff, AR 71601; phone: 870-543-1860 Div.I; 850-7584 Div. II; fax: 870-543-1889; hours 8AM-5PM (CST). *Misdemeanor, Civil Actions Under $5,000, Eviction, Small Claims.*
Civil Records: Access: Mail, in person. Both court and visitors may perform in person searches. Search fee: $5.00. Court makes copy: $.25 per page. Required to search: name. Mail turnaround time 3 days.
Criminal Records: Access: Mail, in person. Both court and visitors may perform in person searches. Search fee: $5.00. Court makes copy: $.25 per page. Required to search: name, years to search; also helpful: DOB, SSN. Criminal records go back to

1989; computerized records since 1997. Mail turnaround time 3 days.
General Information: No public access terminal. No certification fee . Payee: District Court. Only cashiers checks and money orders accepted. SASE required.

Johnson County

Circuit Court PO Box 189, Clarksville, AR 72830-0189; phone: 479-754-2977; probate phone: 479-754-3967; fax: 479-754-4235; hours 8AM-4:30PM (CST). *Felony, Civil Actions Over $5,000, Probate.*
Note: Probate is handled by County Clerk, PO Box 57.
Civil Records: Access: Fax, mail, in person. Both court and visitors may perform in person searches. No search fee. Court makes copy: $.50 per page. Required to search: name, years to search. Civil cases indexed by defendant, plaintiff; on index from 1900s. Fax access limited to 800#'s. Mail turnaround time 1-2 days.
Criminal Records: Access: Mail, in person. Both court and visitors may perform in person searches. No search fee. Court makes copy: $.50 per page. Required to search: name, years to search, DOB; also helpful: SSN. Criminal records on index from 1900s. Fax access limited to 800#'s. Mail turnaround time 1-2 days.
General Information: No public access terminal. No juvenile records released. Will fax to 800 numbers only. Certification fee: $1.00 per cert. Personal checks accepted. SASE required.

District Court PO Box 581, 301 Porter Industrial Rd, Clarksville, AR 72830; phone: 479-754-8533; fax: 479-754-6014; hours 8AM-4PM (CST). *Misdemeanor, Civil Actions Under $5,000, Eviction, Small Claims.*
Civil Records: Access: Mail, in person. Both court and visitors may perform in person searches. No search fee. Court makes copy: no charge for 1st 10 pages; same fee for self serve. Required to search: name. Turnaround time 1-2 days. Civil records go back 10 years. Mail turnaround time 1-2 days.
Criminal Records: Access: Mail, in person. Both court and visitors may perform in person searches. No search fee. Court makes copy: no charge for 1st 10 pages; same fee for self serve. Required to search: name, years to search; also helpful: DOB, SSN. Records not computerized. Mail turnaround time 1-2 days.
General Information: No public access terminal. Will fax documents if only a page or two. No certification fee . Will accept checks, but prefer not to. Prepayment and SASE required.

Lafayette County

Circuit Court #3 Courthouse Square, Lewisville, AR 71845; phone: 870-921-4878; probate phone: 870-921-4633; hours 8AM-4:30PM (CST). *Felony, Civil Actions Over $5,000, Probate.*
Note: Civil fax is 870-921-4879. Probate is located at #2 Courthouse Square.
Civil Records: Access: Phone, mail, in person. Both court and visitors may perform in person searches. Search fee: $6.00 per name. Court makes copy: $.50 per page; same fee for self serve. Required to search: name, years to search. Civil cases indexed by defendant, plaintiff; on dockets from 1950s. Mail turnaround time 2 days.
Criminal Records: Access: Mail, in person. Visitors must perform in person searches themselves. Court makes copy: $.50 per page; same fee for self serve. Required to search: name, years to search. Criminal records on dockets from 1950s. Mail turnaround time 2 days.
General Information: No public access terminal. No juvenile records released without written order form the judge. Will fax documents to local or toll-free number. Certification fee: $3.00. Payee: Circuit Clerk. Personal checks accepted. Prepayment and SASE required.

District Court 110 E Fourth, #1, Lewisville, AR 71845; phone: 870-921-5555; fax: 870-921-4256; hours 8AM-4:30PM (CST). *Misdemeanor, Civil Actions Under $5,000, Eviction, Small Claims.*
Civil Records: Access: In person only. Both court and visitors may perform in person searches. Court makes copy: $.25 per page. Self serve copy fee: $.25 per page. Required to search: name.
Criminal Records: Access: In person, mail. Both court and visitors may perform in person searches. Court makes copy: $.25 per page. Self serve copy fee: $.25 per page. Required to search: name, years to search; helpful- DOB, SSN. Records on computer back to 1994. Court will only search misdemeanor records.
General Information: Public access terminal has only criminal records back to 1996. Certification fee: $5.00 per doc. Payee: District Court.

Lawrence County

Circuit Court PO Box 581, 315 W. Main St., Rm 7, Walnut Ridge, AR 72476; phone: 870-886-1112; probate phone: 870-886-1111; criminal records fax: 870-886-1128; civil records fax: same; hours 8AM-4:30PM (CST). *Felony, Civil Actions Over $5,000, Probate, Family.*
Note: Probate is a separate index, separate mailing address.
Civil Records: Access: Mail, in person. Visitors must perform in person searches themselves. Search fee: $6.00. Court makes copy: $.50 per page; same fee for self serve. Required to search: name, years to search. Civil cases indexed by defendant, plaintiff; on index from 1981, on docket sheets from 1960s. Mail turnaround time 2-5 days.
Criminal Records: Access: Mail, in person. Visitors must perform in person searches themselves. Search fee: $6.00. Court makes copy: $.50 per page; same fee for self serve. Required to search: name, years to search. Criminal records on index from 1981, on docket sheets from 1960s. Mail turnaround time 2-5 days.
General Information: No public access terminal. No juvenile records released. Will fax documents for $1.00 per page. Certification fee: $3.00 per document. Payee: Circuit Clerk. Personal checks accepted. Prepayment and SASE required.

Walnut Ridge District Court 201 SW 2nd St, Walnut Ridge, AR 72476; phone: 870-886-3905; hours 8AM-4:30PM (CST). *Misdemeanor, Civil Actions Under $5,000, Eviction, Small Claims.*
Civil Records: Access: Mail, in person. Both court and visitors may perform in person searches. No search fee. Computerized records since 1992. Mail turnaround time 2-3 days.
Criminal Records: Access: Mail, in person. Both court and visitors may perform in person searches. No search fee. Required to search: name, years to search, offense. Computerized records since 1992. Mail turnaround time 2-3 days.
General Information: No public access terminal. Will fax documents to local or toll free line.

Lee County

Circuit Court 15 E Chestnut, Marianna, AR 72360; phone: 870-295-7710; probate phone: 870-295-7715; fax: 870-295-7712; probate fax: 870-295-7766; hours 8:30AM-4:30PM (CST). *Felony, Civil Actions Over $5,000, Probate.*
Civil Records: Access: In person only. Visitors must perform in person searches themselves. Court makes copy: $.25 per page; same fee for self serve. Required to search: name, years to search. Civil cases indexed by defendant, plaintiff; on index books from 1873; computerized records since 1/2002.
Criminal Records: Access: In person only. Visitors must perform in person searches themselves. Court makes copy: $.25 per page; same fee for self serve. Required to search: name, years to search, DOB. Criminal records on index books from 1873; computerized records since 1/2002.

General Information: No public access terminal. No juvenile records released. Certification fee: $2.50. Payee: Circuit Court. Personal checks accepted. Prepayment required.

District Court 45 W Mississippi, Marianna, AR 72360; phone: 870-295-3813; fax: 870-295-5726; hours 8AM-N; 1-5PM (CST). *Misdemeanor, Civil Actions Under $5,000, Eviction, Small Claims.*
Civil Records: Access: Mail, in person. Only the court performs in person searches. Court makes copy: $.25 per page. Computerized records since 1994. Mail turnaround time 5 days.
Criminal Records: Access: Mail, in person. Only the court performs in person searches. No search fee. Court makes copy: $.25 per page. Required to search: name, years to search. Computerized records since 1994. Mail turnaround time 5 days.
General Information: No public access terminal. Certification fee: $5.00 per document. Payee: City of Marianna. Personal checks accepted. SASE requested.

Lincoln County

Circuit Court Courthouse, 300 S Drew, Star City, AR 71667; phone: 870-628-3154; probate phone: 870-628-5114; criminal records fax: 870-628-5546; civil records fax: same; hours 8AM-4:30PM (CST). *Felony, Civil Actions Over $5,000, Probate.*
Note: Probate is a separate index and separate office at this address.
Civil Records: Access: In person only. Both court and visitors may perform in person searches. No search fee. Court makes copy: $.50 per page; same fee for self serve. Required to search: name, years to search. Civil cases indexed by defendant, plaintiff; on index from 1920, archived from 1920.
Criminal Records: Access: In person only. Visitors must perform in person searches themselves. Court makes copy: $.50 per page; same fee for self serve. Required to search: name, years to search. Criminal records on index from 1920, archived from 1920.
General Information: No public access terminal. No sealed records released. Certification fee: $3.00 per document. Payee: Lincoln County Circuit Court. Personal checks accepted. Prepayment required.

Lincoln County District Court 300 S Drew St, Star City, AR 71667; phone: 870-628-4904; civil phone: 870-628-4166; fax: 870-628-6442; hours 8AM-4:30PM (CST). *Misdemeanor, Civil Actions Under $5,000, Eviction, Small Claims.*
Civil Records: Access: Mail, in person. Both court and visitors may perform in person searches. Search fee: $6.00 per name. Court makes copy: $.50 per page; same fee for self serve. Required to search: name, years to search, DOB. Civil records go back to 1980. Mail turnaround time 3-5 days.
Criminal Records: Access: Mail, in person. Both court and visitors may perform in person searches. Search fee: $6.00 per name. Court makes copy: $.50 per page; same fee for self serve. Required to search: name, years to search, DOB, signed release; also helpful: address, SSN, DL#. Criminal records go back to 1980; on computer back to 1991. Mail turnaround time 3-5 days.
General Information: No public access terminal. No fee to fax 5 pages or less; if more, $.50 per page. Certification fee: $25.00 includes copies. Payee: District Court of Star City. Prepayment required.

Little River County

Circuit Court PO Box 575, Ashdown, AR 71822; phone: 870-898-7211; probate phone: 870-898-7210; criminal records fax: 870-898-5783; same fax for civil and probate; hours 8AM-4:30PM (CST). *Felony, Civil Actions Over $5,000, Probate.*
Civil Records: Access: Phone, mail, in person. Both court and visitors may perform in person searches. Search fee: $6.00 per name. Court makes copy: $.50 per page; same fee for self serve. Required to search: name, years to search. Civil cases indexed by plaintiff. Civil records docket books from early 1900s.

Criminal Records: Access: In person only. Visitors must perform in person searches themselves. Court makes copy: $.50 per page; same fee for self serve. Required to search: name. Criminal records on docket books back to 1868. Note: Direct criminal records searches to AR state police; 870-777-4641
General Information: No public access terminal. No juvenile records released. Will not fax documents. Certification fee: $5.00 per document. Payee: Circuit Clerk. Personal checks accepted. Prepayment required.

District Court 351 N 2nd St, #8, Ashdown, AR 71822; phone: 870-898-7230; fax: 870-898-7262; hours 8:30AM-4:30PM (CST). *Misdemeanor, Civil Actions Under $5,000, Eviction, Small Claims.*
Civil Records: Access: Mail, in person. Both court and visitors may perform in person searches. Court makes copy: $.50 per page. Civil records on computer since 1987. Mail turnaround time 1 week.
Criminal Records: Access: Mail, in person. Both court and visitors may perform in person searches. No search fee. Court makes copy: $.50 per page. Required to search: name, years to search; also helpful: DOB, SSN. Criminal records on computer since 1987. Mail turnaround time 1 week.
General Information: Public access terminal has only criminal records back to 10 years. Certification fee: $5.00 per document. Payee: District Court. Only cashiers checks and money orders accepted. SASE required.

Logan County

Circuit Court Courthouse, 25 W Walnut, Paris, AR 72855; phone: 479-963-2164; probate phone: 479-963-2618; fax: 479-963-3304; probate fax: 479-963-9017; hours 8AM-4:30PM (CST). *Felony, Civil Actions Over $5,000, Probate.*
Note: Probate is handled by the county clerk in Rm #25.
Civil Records: Access: Fax, mail, in person. Visitors must perform in person searches themselves. Search fee: $6.00 per name. Court makes copy: $.50 per page. Required to search: name, years to search. Civil cases indexed by defendant, plaintiff; on criminal index from 1901.
Criminal Records: Access: Fax, mail, in person. Visitors must perform in person searches themselves. Search fee: $6.00 per name. Court makes copy: $.50 per page. Required to search: name, years to search. Criminal records on criminal index from 1901.
General Information: No public access terminal. Will not fax documents. Certification fee: $5.00. Payee: Circuit Clerk. Personal checks accepted. Prepayment required.

Paris District Court Paris Courthouse, 25 W Walnut, Paris, AR 72855; phone: 479-963-3792; fax: 479-963-2762; hours 8:30AM-4:30PM (CST). *Misdemeanor, Civil Actions Under $5,000, Eviction, Small Claims.*
Civil Records: Access: Mail, in person. Both court and visitors may perform in person searches. No search fee. No copy fee.Civil records go back to the 1970's; computerized records since 1994. Mail turnaround time 1-2 days.
Criminal Records: Access: Mail, in person. Both court and visitors may perform in person searches. No search fee. No copy fee.Required to search: name, years to search; also helpful: DOB. Criminal records go back to 1970's; computerized records since 1994. Mail turnaround time 1-2 days.
General Information: No public access terminal. Will fax documents to local or toll free line. No certification fee . SASE required.

Lonoke County

Circuit Court PO Box 219, Attn: Circuit Clerk, Lonoke, AR 72086; phone: 501-676-2316; probate phone: 501-676-2368; hours 8AM-4:30PM (CST). *Felony, Civil Actions Over $5,000, Probate.*

Civil Records: Access: in person only. Visitors must perform in person searches themselves. Court makes copy: $.25 per page; same fee for self serve. Required to search: name, years to search. Civil cases indexed by defendant. Civil records on computer from 1989, on dockets from 1918's.
Criminal Records: Access: Mail, in person. Both court and visitors may perform in person searches. Search fee: $6.00 per name. Court makes copy: $.25 per page; same fee for self serve. Required to search: name, years to search, SSN. Criminal records on computer from 1989, on dockets from 1918's (not for public use). Mail turnaround time 1-2 days.
General Information: Public access terminal available. No juvenile records released. Certification fee: $6.00. Payee: Circuit Clerk. Personal checks accepted. Prepayment and SASE required.

Lonoke District Court 107 W 2nd St, Lonoke, AR 72086-2701; phone: 501-676-3585; fax: 501-676-2500; hours 8AM-4:30PM (CST). *Misdemeanor, Civil Actions Under $5,000, Eviction, Small Claims.*
Civil Records: Access: Mail, in person. Both court and visitors may perform in person searches. Search fee: $5.00. No copy fee.Computerized records since 1999. Mail turnaround time 1-2 days.
Criminal Records: Access: Mail, in person. Both court and visitors may perform in person searches. No search fee. No copy fee.Required to search: name, years to search. Computerized records since 1999. Mail turnaround time 1-2 days.
General Information: No public access terminal. No certification fee . Payee: District Court. Prepayment and SASE required.

Madison County

Circuit Court PO Box 626, Courthouse, Huntsville, AR 72740; phone: 479-738-2215; probate phone: 479-738-2747; fax: 479-738-1544; probate fax: 479-738-2735; hours 8AM-4:30PM (CST). *Felony, Civil Actions Over $5,000, Probate.*
Note: Probate is in the County Clerk's office, PO Box 37.
Civil Records: Access: In person only. Both court and visitors may perform in person searches. Search fee: $10.00 per name. Court makes copy: $.25 per page; same fee for self serve. Required to search: name, years to search; also helpful: address. Civil cases indexed by defendant, plaintiff; on dockets back to 1892.
Criminal Records: Access: In person only. Both court and visitors may perform in person searches. Search fee: $10.00 per name. Court makes copy: $.25 per page; same fee for self serve. Required to search: name, years to search; also helpful: DOB, SSN. Criminal records on dockets back to 1906.
General Information: No public access terminal. No juvenile records released. Will fax specific document for $5.00 per fax; if over 20 pages, add $.25 each add'l page. Certification fee: $2.00. Payee: Circuit Clerk. Personal checks accepted. Prepayment required.

District Court PO Box 549, 208 E Regal, Huntsville, AR 72740; phone: 479-738-2911; fax: 479-738-6846; hours 8AM-4:30PM (CST). *Misdemeanor, Civil Actions Under $5,000, Eviction, Small Claims.*
Civil Records: Access: Mail, fax, in person. Both court and visitors may perform in person searches. No search fee. Self serve copy fee: $.25 per page. Records go back to 1991; computerized records since 1999. Note: Court will search only if time permits. Mail turnaround time 1 week.
Criminal Records: Access: In person, mail, fax. Both court and visitors may perform in person searches. No search fee. Self serve copy fee: $.25 per page. Required to search: name, years to search, DOB, SSN. Criminal records go back to 1991; on computer back to 1999. Note: Court will in person criminal search only if time permits. Mail turnaround time 1 week.

General Information: Public access terminal goes back to 1999. Certification fee: $5.00 per doc. Payee: City of Huntsville. Personal checks accepted. SASE required.

Marion County

Circuit Court PO Box 385, Yellville, AR 72687; phone: 870-449-6226; fax: 870-449-4979; hours 8AM-4:30PM (CST). *Felony, Civil Actions Over $5,000, Probate.*

Note: Probate is separate index as this same address.

Civil Records: Access: In person only. Visitors must perform in person searches themselves. Court makes copy: $.25 per page; same fee for self serve. Required to search: name, years to search. Civil cases indexed by plaintiff. Civil records on dockets from 1956, records are not computerized.

Criminal Records: Access: In person only. Visitors must perform in person searches themselves. Court makes copy: $.25 per page; same fee for self serve. Required to search: name, years to search. Criminal records on dockets from 1956, records are not computerized.

General Information: No public access terminal. No juvenile or adoption records released. Will fax specific case file for $1.00 per page (for specific case information). Certification fee: $5.00 per document includes copies. Payee: Marion County Circuit Clerk. Personal checks accepted. Prepayment required.

District Court PO Box 301, Yellville, AR 72687; phone: 870-449-6030; Hours: 8AM-4:30PM (CST). *Misdemeanor, Civil Actions Under $5,000, Small Claims.*

Civil Records: Access: Mail, in person. Both court and visitors may perform in person searches. Search fee: $6.00 per name. Court makes copy: $.25 per page; same fee for self serve. Required to search: name. Civil records go back to 1985. Mail turnaround time 1-2 days.

Criminal Records: Access: Mail, in person. Both court and visitors may perform in person searches. Search fee: $6.00 per name. Court makes copy: $.25 per page; same fee for self serve. Required to search: name, years to search, DOB. Criminal records go back to 1985; on computer back to 1996. Mail turnaround time 1-2 days.

General Information: No public access terminal. Will fax documents to local or toll free line. Certification fee: $5.00 per doc. Prepayment required.

Miller County

Circuit Court 412 Laurel St Rm 109, Texarkana, AR 71854; phone: 870-774-4501; probate phone: 870-774-1501; criminal records fax: 870-772-5293; civil records fax: same; hours 8AM-4:30PM (CST). *Felony, Civil Actions Over $5,000, Probate.*

Note: Probate is at the County Clerk's office.

Civil Records: Access: Phone, mail, in person, online. Both court and visitors may perform in person searches. Search fee: $6.00 per name. Court makes copy: $1.00 per page; same fee for self serve. Required to search: name, years to search. Civil cases indexed by defendant, plaintiff; on index from 1850s. Access to court dockets is by subscription service at www.recordsusa.com/Arkansas/MillerCnAr.htm. Base fee is $49.95 per month and also includes land imaging and unlimited instrument access. Mail turnaround time 1-2 days.

Criminal Records: Access: Mail, in person, online. Both court and visitors may perform in person searches. Search fee: $6.00 per name. Court makes copy: $1.00 per page; same fee for self serve. Required to search: name, years to search. Criminal records on index from 1850s; computerized back since 2000. Online access to criminal records is the same as civil. Mail turnaround time 1-2 days.

General Information: Public access terminal goes back to 2003. No expunged records released. Will fax documents to local or toll free line. Certification fee: $3.50 per document. Payee: Miller County

Circuit Clerk. Personal checks accepted. Prepayment and SASE required.

District Court 2300 East St, Texarkana, AR 71854; phone: 870-772-2780; fax: 870-773-3595; hours 8AM-4:30PM (CST). *Misdemeanor, Eviction.*

Criminal Records: Access: Mail, in person. Only the court performs in person searches. No search fee. No copy fee. Required to search: name, years to search, DOB. Criminal records computerized to 1997. Mail turnaround time 2 days.

General Information: No public access terminal. Will fax documents to local or toll free line. SASE required.

District Court 100 N Stateline, Texarkana, AR 75501; phone: 903-798-3016; fax: 903-798-3588; hours 8AM-5PM (CST). *Misdemeanor, Civil Actions Under $5,000, Small Claims, Evictions.*
www.txkusa.org/ar/departments/arcourt/arcourt.html

Civil Records: Access: Mail, in person. Both court and visitors may perform in person searches. Search fee: None, unless extensive searching involved. Court makes copy: $1.00 (computer screen). Civil records computerized to 1997. Mail turnaround time 2 days.

General Information: No public access terminal. Will fax documents to local or toll free line. Certification fee: $10.00 per transcript. Payee: Miller District Court. Only cashiers checks and money orders accepted. Prepayment and SASE required.

Mississippi County

Blytheville Circuit Court PO Box 1498, Blytheville, AR 72316; phone: 870-762-2332; fax: 870-762-8148; hours 9AM-4:30PM (CST). *Felony, Civil Actions Over $5,000, Probate.*

Civil Records: Access: In person only. Visitors must perform in person searches themselves. Court makes copy: $.25 per page; same fee for self serve. Required to search: name, years to search. Civil cases indexed by plaintiff. Civil records prior on index from 1940.

Criminal Records: Access: In person only. Both court and visitors may perform in person searches. Court makes copy: $.25 per page; same fee for self serve. Required to search: name, years to search, DOB, SSN. Criminal records prior on index from 1940. Note: Court will search 7 years only.

General Information: No public access terminal. No juvenile records released. Will fax specific case file $5.00 per doc. Certification fee: $3.00 includes copy fee. Court may add add'l copy fee is document is lengthy. Payee: Circuit Clerk. Personal checks accepted. Prepayment required.

Osceola Circuit Court PO Box 466, 200 W Hale, County Courthouse, Osceola, AR 72370; phone: 870-563-6471; fax: 870-563-5063; hours 9AM-4:30PM (CST). *Felony, Civil Actions Over $5,000, Probate.*

Civil Records: Access: Mail, in person. Visitors must perform in person searches themselves. Court makes copy: $.25 per page; same fee for self serve. Required to search: name, years to search. Civil cases indexed by defendant, plaintiff. Civil records computerized since 1992, on index from 1940.

Criminal Records: Access: In person only. Visitors must perform in person searches themselves. Court makes copy: $.25 per page; same fee for self serve. Required to search: name, years to search, DOB, SSN. Criminal records on computer (not for public use) since 1992.

General Information: Public access terminal available. No juvenile records released. Certification fee: $3.00 per document. Payee: Circuit Clerk. Personal checks accepted. Prepayment required.

Blytheville District Court 121 N 2nd St, #104, Blytheville, AR 72315; phone: 870-763-7513; fax: 870-762-0433; hours 8AM-5PM (CST). *Misdemeanor, Civil Actions Under $5,000, Small Claims.*

Civil Records: Access: Mail, fax, in person. Both court and visitors may perform in person searches.

Search fee: $4.00 per name. Court makes copy: $.50 per page. Self serve copy fee: $.25 per page. Civil records go back to 1960; on computer back to 1987. Mail turnaround time 1 day, sometimes 2.

Criminal Records: Access: Mail, fax, in person. Both court and visitors may perform in person searches. Search fee: $4.00 per name. Court makes copy: $.50 per page. Self serve copy fee: $.25 per page. Required to search: name, years to search; also helpful: DOB, SSN. Criminal records go back to 1960; on computer back to 1987. Mail turnaround time 1-2 days.

General Information: No public access terminal. Will fax documents to local or toll free line. Certification fee: $5.00. Payee: City of Blytheville. Prepayment required.

Osceola District Court 397 W Keiser, Osceola, AR 72370; phone: 870-563-1303; criminal records fax: 870-563-8439; civil records fax: same; hours 8AM-4PM (CST). *Misdemeanor, Civil Actions Under $5,000, Small Claims.*

Civil Records: Access: Mail, in person, fax. Only the court performs in person searches. Search fee: $5.00. Court makes copy: $1.00 per page; same fee for self serve. Required to search: name, DOB and SSN. Records computerized for at least 7 years. Mail turnaround time 1-2 days.

Criminal Records: Access: Mail, in person. Only the court performs in person searches. Search fee: $5.00. Court makes copy: $1.00 per page; same fee for self serve. Required to search: name, years to search; also helpful: address, DOB, SSN. Records computerized for at least 7 years. Mail turnaround time 1-2 days.

General Information: No public access terminal. Will fax documents to local or toll free line. Certification fee: $1.00 per page. Payee: Osceola District Court. Prepayment required.

Monroe County

Circuit Court 123 Madison St, Courthouse, Clarendon, AR 72029; phone: 870-747-3615; probate phone: 870-747-3632; fax: 870-747-3710; hours 8AM-4:30PM (CST). *Felony, Civil Actions Over $5,000, Probate.*

Civil Records: Access: Fax, mail, in person. Both court and visitors may perform in person searches. No search fee. Court makes copy: $.50 per page; same fee for self serve. Required to search: name, years to search. Civil cases indexed by defendant, plaintiff; on index books from 1931.

Criminal Records: Access: In person only. Visitors must perform in person searches themselves. Court makes copy: $.50 per page; same fee for self serve. Required to search: name, years to search. Criminal records on index books from 1933.

General Information: No public access terminal. No juvenile records released. Will fax documents $2.50 per page and $2.50 per doc. Add $.50 per page if more than 10. Certification fee: $2.50. Payee: Monroe County Circuit Clerk. Personal checks accepted. Prepayment and SASE required.

District Court City Hall, 270 Madison St, Clarendon, AR 72029; phone: 870-747-5200; criminal records fax: 870-747-9969; civil records fax: same; hours 8AM-5PM (CST). *Misdemeanor, Civil Actions Under $5,000, Small Claims.*

Civil Records: Access: Mail, in person. Both court and visitors may perform in person searches. No search fee. Court makes copy: $.25 per page; same fee for self serve. Required to search: name, years to search, DOB. Records go back to 1988, on computer since 1994. Mail turnaround time 1-2 days.

Criminal Records: Access: Mail, in person. Both court and visitors may perform in person searches. No search fee. Court makes copy: $.25 per page; same fee for self serve. Required to search: name, years to search, DOB, SSN. Records go back to 1988, on computer since 1994. Mail turnaround time 1-2 days.

General Information: No public access terminal. Will fax documents to local or toll free line.

Certification fee: $5.00 per document includes copy fee. Payee: Clarendon District Court. Prepayment required.

Montgomery County

Circuit Court PO Box 369, Courthouse, Mount Ida, AR 71957; phone: 870-867-3521; criminal records fax: 870-867-2177; same fax for civil and probate; hours 8AM-4:30PM (CST). *Felony, Civil Actions Over $5,000, Probate.*
Note: Probate is a separate index at the courthouse.
Civil Records: Access: Phone, fax, mail, in person. Both court and visitors may perform in person searches. Court makes copy: $.50 per page. Required to search: name, years to search; also helpful: address. Civil cases indexed by defendant, plaintiff; on card files from 1960s.
Criminal Records: Access: In person only. Visitors must perform in person searches themselves. Court makes copy: $.50 per page. Required to search: name, years to search; also helpful: DOB, SSN. Criminal records on card files from 1960s.
General Information: No public access terminal. No juvenile or adoption records released. Certification fee: $5.00. Payee: Circuit Clerk. Personal checks accepted. Prepayment and SASE required.

District Court PO Box 548, Mount Ida, AR 71957; phone: 870-867-2221; fax: 870-867-3695; hours 8AM-4:30PM M-Th, other days hours may vary (CST). *Misdemeanor, Civil Actions Under $5,000, Eviction, Small Claims.*
Civil Records: Access: Mail, in person. Both court and visitors may perform in person searches. No search fee. No copy fee.Self serve copy fee: none. Required to search: name, years to search, DOB, SSN. Records go back to 1973; computerized records go back to 1993. Mail turnaround time 1-2 days.
Criminal Records: Access: Mail, in person. Both court and visitors may perform in person searches. No search fee. No copy fee.Self serve copy fee: none. Required to search: name, years to search, DOB, SSN. Records go back to 1973; computerized records go back to 1993. Mail turnaround time 1-2 days.
General Information: No public access terminal. No fee to fax documents. No certification fee .

Nevada County

Circuit Court PO Box 204, Prescott, AR 71857; phone: 870-887-2511; fax: 870-887-1911; hours 8AM-5PM (CST). *Felony, Civil Actions Over $5,000, Probate.*
Civil Records: Access: Phone, fax, mail, in person. Both court and visitors may perform in person searches. Search fee: $6.00 per name. Court makes copy: $.25 per page; same fee for self serve. Required to search: name, years to search. Civil cases indexed by defendant, plaintiff; on index since 1850. Mail turnaround time 1-2 days.
Criminal Records: Access: Mail, in person. Both court and visitors may perform in person searches. Search fee: $6.00 per name. Court makes copy: $.25 per page; same fee for self serve. Required to search: name, years to search, DOB. Criminal records on index since 1850. Mail turnaround time 1-2 days.
General Information: No public access terminal. No juvenile records released. Will fax documents $.25 per page. Certification fee: $2.00 plus $.25 per page. Payee: Nevada County Circuit Clerk. Personal checks accepted. Prepayment and SASE required.

District Court PO Box 22, Prescott, AR 71857; phone: 870-887-6016; fax: 870-887-3244; hours 8AM-5PM (CST). *Misdemeanor, Civil Actions Under $5,000, Small Claims.*
Civil Records: Access: Phone, mail, fax, in person. Both court and visitors may perform in person searches. Search fee: $6.00. Court makes copy: $.25 per page; same fee for self serve. Records on computer go back to 1994. Mail turnaround time 2-5 days.
Criminal Records: Access: Phone, mail, fax, in person. Visitors must perform in person searches

themselves. Search fee: $6.00. Self serve copy fee: $.25 per page. Required to search: name, years to search, DOB, SSN. Records on computer go back to 1994. Mail turnaround time 2-5 days.
General Information: No public access terminal. Will fax documents to local or toll free line. Certification fee: $2.00. Will only certify civil records, not criminal. Prepayment required. SASE requested.

Newton County

Circuit Court PO Box 410, Jasper, AR 72641; phone: 870-446-5125; probate phone: same; fax: 870-446-5755; hours 8AM-4:30PM (CST). *Felony, Civil Actions Over $5,000, Probate.*
Civil Records: Access: Fax, mail, in person. Both court and visitors may perform in person searches. Search fee: $6.00 per name. Court makes copy: $.25 per page; same fee for self serve. Required to search: name, years to search. Civil cases indexed by defendant, plaintiff; on dockets from 1800s. Mail turnaround time varies.
Criminal Records: Access: Fax, mail, in person. Both court and visitors may perform in person searches. Search fee: $6.00 per name. Court makes copy: $.25 per page; same fee for self serve. Required to search: name, years to search, DOB. Criminal records on dockets from 1800s. Mail turnaround time varies.
General Information: No public access terminal. No juvenile records released. Will fax documents $2.50 1st page, $.50 each add'l. Certification fee: $5.00. Payee: Circuit Clerk. Personal checks accepted. Prepayment and SASE required.

District Court PO Box 550, Jasper, AR 72641; phone: 870-446-5335; fax: 870-446-2234; hours 8AM-4:30PM (CST). *Misdemeanor, Civil Actions Under $5,000, Eviction, Small Claims.*
Civil Records: Access: Phone, mail, fax, in person. Only the court performs in person searches. Court makes copy: $.25 per page; same fee for self serve. Required to search: name plus years to search, and DOB or SSN. Records go back to 1984, civil records not computerized. Mail turnaround time 24 hours.
Criminal Records: Access: Phone, mail, fax, in person. Only the court performs in person searches. No search fee. Court makes copy: $.25 per page; same fee for self serve. Required to search: name plus years to search, and DOB or SSN. Records go back to 1972, on computer back to 1993. Mail turnaround time 24 hours.
General Information: No public access terminal. Will fax documents to local or toll free line. Certification fee: $10.00. Payee: District Court. Prepayment required.

Ouachita County

Circuit Court PO Box 667, Camden, AR 71701; phone: 870-837-2230 (Circuit); probate phone: 870-837-2220; fax: 870-837-2252; probate fax: 870-837-2251; hours 8AM-4:30PM (CST). *Felony, Civil Actions Over $5,000, Probate.*
Note: Probate is a separate index at this same address.
Civil Records: Access: In person only. Visitors must perform in person searches themselves. Court makes copy: $.50 per page; same fee for self serve. Required to search: name, years to search. Civil cases indexed by defendant, plaintiff. Civil records archived from 1950s; on computer back to 3/1999.
Criminal Records: Access: In person only. Visitors must perform in person searches themselves. Court makes copy: $.50 per page; same fee for self serve. Required to search: name, years to search; also helpful: DOB, SSN. Criminal records archived from 1950s; on computer back to 3/1999.
General Information: Public access terminal goes back to 1999. No juvenile records released. Will fax specific case file for $3.00 per fax. Certification fee: $2.50 per cert. Payee: Circuit Clerk of Ouachita County. Personal checks accepted. Prepayment required.

District Court 213 Madison St, Camden, AR 71701; phone: 870-836-0331; criminal records fax: 870-837-5530; civil records fax: same; hours 8AM-4:30PM (CST). *Misdemeanor, Civil Actions Under $5,000, Eviction, Small Claims.*
Civil Records: Access: Mail, fax, in person. Both court and visitors may perform in person searches. Search fee: $5.00 per name. Court makes copy: $.25 per page; same fee for self serve. Required to search: name, years to search. Records go back to 1950; computerized since 1987. Mail turnaround time 1-2 days.
Criminal Records: Access: Mail, fax, in person. Both court and visitors may perform in person searches. Search fee: $5.00 per name. Court makes copy: $.25 per page; same fee for self serve. Required to search: name, years to search, DOB; also helpful: SSN. Records go back to 1950; computerized since 1987. Mail turnaround time 1-2 days.
General Information: No public access terminal. Will fax documents to local or toll free line. Certification fee: $5.00 per document. Payee: District Court. Prepayment required.

Perry County

Circuit Court PO Box 358, Perryville, AR 72126; phone: 501-889-5126; criminal records fax: 501-889-5759; civil records fax: same; hours 8AM-4:30PM (CST). *Felony, Civil Actions Over $5,000, Probate.*
Civil Records: Access: In person only. Visitors must perform in person searches themselves. Court makes copy: $.50 for 1st page, $.25 each add'l; same fee for self serve. Required to search: name, years to search. Civil cases indexed by defendant, plaintiff; on computer from 1997, on dockets from 1974.
Criminal Records: Access: In person only. Visitors must perform in person searches themselves. Court makes copy: $.50 for first page, $.25 each add'l; same fee for self serve. Required to search: name, years to search, DOB. Criminal records on computer from 1997, on dockets from 1974.
General Information: Public access terminal goes back to 1997. No juvenile or adoption records released. Will fax specific case file for $2.00 per page. Certification fee: $5.00 per document. Payee: Circuit Clerk. Personal checks accepted. Prepayment required.

District Court PO Box 186, Perryville, AR 72126; phone: 501-889-5296; fax: 501-889-5835; hours 8AM-4:30PM (CST). *Misdemeanor, Civil Actions Under $5,000, Eviction, Small Claims, Traffic.*
Civil Records: Access: Mail, fax, in person. Only the court performs in person searches. Search fee: $2.00 per name. No copy fee.Required to search: name. Records back to 1993. Mail turnaround time 3-5 days.
Criminal Records: Access: Mail, in person. Only the court performs in person searches. Search fee: $2.00. No copy fee.Required to search: name, years to search, DOB, SSN. Computerized records back to 1997, prior on hard copy back to 1993. Mail turnaround time 3-5 days.
General Information: No public access terminal. Will fax documents. Certification fee: $2.00 per doc. Payee: District Court. Prepayment required.

Phillips County

Circuit Court 620 Cherry St #206, Courthouse, Helena, AR 72342; phone: 870-338-5515; probate phone: 870-338-5505; criminal records fax: 870-338-5513; civil records fax: same; hours 8AM-4:30PM (CST). *Felony, Civil Actions Over $5,000, Probate.*
Note: Probate records located in the County Clerk office.
Civil Records: Access: Mail, in person, online. Visitors must perform in person searches themselves. Search fee: $6.00 per name. Court makes copy: $.25 per page; same fee for self serve. Required to search: name, years to search, DOB. Civil cases

indexed by plaintiff. Civil records on fee books from 1970; on computer back to 1998. Access court orders online at www.etitlesearch.com; registration and fees apply. Mail turnaround time 1-3 days.

Criminal Records: Access: Mail, in person. Visitors must perform in person searches themselves. Search fee: $6.00 per name. Court makes copy: $.25 per page; same fee for self serve. Required to search: name, years to search; also helpful-DOB, SSN. Criminal records on fee books from 1970; on computer back to 2000. Mail turnaround time 1-3 days.

General Information: Public access terminal has criminal back to 2000 and civil back to 2000 (orders only). No juvenile records released. Fee to fax documents is $1.00 per document. Certification fee: $3.00 per cert. Payee: Circuit Clerk Wanda McIntosh. Personal checks accepted. Prepayment and SASE required.

District Court 226 Perry ST, City Hall, Helena, AR 72342; phone: 870-338-8825; fax: 870-338-9832; hours 8AM-4:30PM (CST). *Misdemeanor, Civil Actions Under $5,000, Eviction, Small Claims.*
Civil Records: Access: Mail, in person. Both court and visitors may perform in person searches. Search fee: $9.00. Court makes copy: $.25 per page. Computerized from 1993-2000. Mail turnaround time 3 days.
Criminal Records: Access: Mail, in person. Both court and visitors may perform in person searches. Search fee: $5.00 per name. Court makes copy: $.25 per page. Required to search: name, years to search, address, DOB, SSN. Computerized back to 1993. Mail turnaround time 3 days.
General Information: No public access terminal. Certification fee: $5.00 per page. Payee: City of Helena District Court. Prepayment required.

Pike County

Circuit Court PO Box 219, Murfreesboro, AR 71958; phone: 870-285-2231; fax: 870-285-3281; hours 8AM-4:30PM (CST). *Felony, Civil Actions Over $5,000, Probate.*
Civil Records: Access: Fax, mail, in person. Both court and visitors may perform in person searches. Search fee: $6.00 per name. Court makes copy: $.50 per page. Required to search: name, years to search. Civil cases indexed by defendant. Civil records archived from 1895. Some records on dockets books, computerized since 1989. Mail turnaround time 1 week.
Criminal Records: Access: Fax, mail, in person. Both court and visitors may perform in person searches. Search fee: $6.00 per name. Court makes copy: $.50 per page. Required to search: name, years to search, DOB. Criminal records archived from 1895. Some records on dockets, fee books. Computerized records from 1992. Mail turnaround time 1 week.
General Information: No public access terminal. No juvenile or adoption records released. Will fax documents for $1.50 1st 3 pages, $.50 each add'l. Certification fee: $5.00 per doc. Payee: Pike County Clerk. Prepayment required.

District Court PO Box 197, Murfreesboro, AR 71958; phone: 870-285-3865; fax: 870-285-3865; hours 8:30AM-4:30PM (CST). *Misdemeanor, Civil Actions Under $5,000, Eviction, Small Claims.*
Civil Records: Access: Mail, in person. Both court and visitors may perform in person searches. Court makes copy: $.50 per page; same fee for self serve. Mail turnaround time 2-3 days.
Criminal Records: Access: Mail, in person. Both court and visitors may perform in person searches. Search fee: $6.00 per name. Court makes copy: $.50 per page; same fee for self serve. Required to search: name, years to search, offense. Mail turnaround time 2-3 days.
General Information: No public access terminal. Will fax documents. Certification fee: $5.00 per case. Payee: Pike County District Court. Prepayment required.

Poinsett County

Circuit Court PO Box 46, Harrisburg, AR 72432; phone: 870-578-4420; fax: 870-578-4427; hours 8:30AM-4:30PM (CST). *Felony, Civil Actions Over $5,000, Probate.*
Civil Records: Access: Mail, in person. Both court and visitors may perform in person searches. Search fee: $6.00 per name. Court makes copy: $.25 per page. Required to search: name, years to search. Civil cases indexed by defendant, plaintiff; on computer from 1985. Some records on dockets. All requests must be in writing. Mail turnaround time 1-2 days.
Criminal Records: Access: Mail, in person. Both court and visitors may perform in person searches. Search fee: $6.00 per name. Court makes copy: $.25 per page. Required to search: name, years to search, DOB. Criminal records on computer from 1985. Some records on dockets. All requests must be in writing. Mail turnaround time 1-2 days.
General Information: No public access terminal. No juvenile records released. Certification fee: $2.00 per doc. Payee: Circuit Clerk. Personal checks accepted. Prepayment and SASE required.

Harrisburg District Court 202 N East St, Harrisburg, AR 72432; phone: 870-578-4110; fax: 870-578-4123; hours 8AM-4:30PM (CST). *Misdemeanor, Civil Actions Under $5,000, Eviction, Small Claims.*
Civil Records: Access: Mail, in person. Both court and visitors may perform in person searches. Search fee: $2.00. Court makes copy: $.25 per page. Required to search: name, DOB, SSN, signed release. Civil records go back to 1978. Mail requests must include SASE. Mail turnaround time 1 day.
Criminal Records: Access: Mail, in person. Both court and visitors may perform in person searches. Search fee: $2.00. Court makes copy: $.25 per page. Required to search: name, years to search; also helpful: DOB, SSN, signed release. Criminal records computerized to 1987. Mail requests must include SASE. Mail turnaround time 1 day.
General Information: No public access terminal. Certification fee: $5.00. Payee: Harrisburg District Court. Prepayment required.

Lepanto District Court PO Box 610, Lepanto, AR 72354; phone: 870-475-2415; fax: 870-475-3161; hours 8AM-4:30PM (CST). *Misdemeanor, Civil Actions Under $5,000, Eviction, Small Claims.*
Civil Records: Access: Mail, in person. Both court and visitors may perform in person searches. Search fee: $2.00. Court makes copy: $.25 per page. Required to search: name, DOB, SSN, signed release. Civil records go back to 1978. Mail turnaround time 1-2 days.
Criminal Records: Access: Mail, in person. Both court and visitors may perform in person searches. Search fee: $2.00. Court makes copy: $.25 per page. Required to search: name, years to search; also helpful: DOB, SSN, signed release. Criminal records computerized to 1987. All requests must be in writing. Mail turnaround time 1-2 days.
General Information: No public access terminal. Certification fee: $5.00 per doc. Payee: District Court. Prepayment required.

Marked Tree District Court #1 Elm St, Marked Tree, AR 72365; phone: 870-358-2024; fax: 870-358-7867; hours 8AM-4:30PM (CST). *Misdemeanor, Civil Actions Under $5,000, Eviction, Small Claims.*
Civil Records: Access: Mail, in person. Both court and visitors may perform in person searches. Search fee: $2.00. Court makes copy: $.25 per page. Required to search: name, DOB, SSN, signed release. Civil records go back to 1978. Mail turnaround time 1-2 days.
Criminal Records: Access: Mail, in person. Both court and visitors may perform in person searches. Search fee: $2.00. Court makes copy: $.25 per page. Required to search: name, years to search; also helpful: DOB, SSN, signed release. Criminal records

computerized to 1987. Mail turnaround time 1-2 days.
General Information: No public access terminal. Certification fee: $5.00. Payee: District Court. Prepayment required.

Trumann District Court PO Box 120, Trumann, AR 72472; phone: 870-483-7771; criminal records fax: 870-483-2620; civil records fax: same; hours 8AM-4:30PM (CST). *Misdemeanor, Civil Actions Under $5,000, Eviction, Small Claims.*
Civil Records: Access: Mail, in person. Both court and visitors may perform in person searches. Court makes copy: $.25 per page; same fee for self serve. Required to search: name, DOB, SSN, signed release. Civil records go back to 1978. Mail turnaround time 1-2 days.
Criminal Records: Access: Mail, in person. Both court and visitors may perform in person searches. Court makes copy: $.25 per page; same fee for self serve. Required to search: name, years to search; also helpful: DOB, SSN, signed release. Criminal records computerized to 1987. Mail turnaround time 1-2 days.
General Information: No public access terminal. Will fax documents. Certification fee: $5.00 per document includes copies. Payee: District Court. Prepayment required.

Tyronza District Court PO Box 275, Tyronza, AR 72386; phone: 870-487-2168; criminal records fax: 870-487-2729; civil records fax: same; hours 8AM-4:30PM (CST). *Misdemeanor, Civil Actions Under $5,000, Eviction, Small Claims.*
Civil Records: Access: Mail, in person. Both court and visitors may perform in person searches. Search fee: $2.00. Court makes copy: $.25 per page. Required to search: name, DOB, SSN, signed release. Civil records go back to 1994.
Criminal Records: Access: Mail, in person. Both court and visitors may perform in person searches. Search fee: $2.00. Court makes copy: $.25 per page. Required to search: name, years to search; also helpful: DOB, SSN, signed release. Criminal records computerized to 1994. All requests must be in writing.
General Information: No public access terminal. Will fax documents. Certification fee: $5.00 per document includes copy fee. Payee: District Court. Prepayment required.

Polk County

Circuit Court 507 Church St, Mena, AR 71953; phone: 479-394-8100; probate phone: 479-394-8123; fax: 479-394-8170; hours 8AM-4:30PM (CST). *Felony, Civil Actions Over $5,000, Probate.* Note: Probate is handled separately from the court.

Civil Records: Access: Mail, in person. Both court and visitors may perform in person searches. Search fee: $6.00 per name. Court makes copy: $.25 per page. $.50 for legal size; same fee for self serve. Required to search: name, years to search. Civil cases indexed by defendant, plaintiff; on dockets and index from late 1800s. Mail turnaround time 1-2 days.
Criminal Records: Access: Mail, in person. Both court and visitors may perform in person searches. Search fee: $6.00 per name. Court makes copy: $.25 per page. $.50 legal size page; same fee for self serve. Required to search: name, years to search, DOB. Criminal records on dockets and index from late 1800s. Mail turnaround time 1-2 days.
General Information: Public access terminal goes back to 7/03. No juvenile records released. Will fax documents to local or toll free line. Certification fee: $2.00. Payee: Circuit Clerk. Personal checks accepted. Prepayment and SASE required.

District Court 507 Church St, Courthouse, Mena, AR 71953; phone: 479-394-8140; criminal records fax: 479-394-6199; civil records fax: same; hours 8AM-4:30PM (CST). *Misdemeanor, Civil Actions Under $5,000, Eviction, Small Claims.*

Civil Records: Access: In person only. Visitors must perform in person searches themselves. No copy fee. Civil records go back 10 years; computerized records go back 10 years. Note: Court will assist visitors with search.

Criminal Records: Access: In person only. Visitors must perform in person searches themselves. No search fee. No copy fee.Required to search: name, years to search, DOB; SSN helpful. Criminal records go back 10 years; computerized records go back 10 years. Note: Court will assist visitors with search.

General Information: No public access terminal. Will not fax specific case file. No certification fee.

Pope County

Circuit Court 100 W Main, Russellville, AR 72801; phone: 479-968-7499; probate phone: 479-968-6064; fax: 479-880-8463; hours 8AM-4PM (CST). *Felony, Civil Actions Over $5,000.*
Note: Probate is a separate index at this same address.

Civil Records: Access: In person, online. Visitors must perform in person searches themselves. Court makes copy: $1.00 per page. Required to search: name, years to search. Civil cases indexed by defendant, plaintiff; on dockets from early 1900s; on computer back to 1998. Access court orders online at www.etitlesearch.com; registration and fees apply.

Criminal Records: Access: In person, online. Visitors must perform in person searches themselves. Court makes copy: $1.00 per page. Self serve copy fee: $.25 per page. Required to search: name, years to search, DOB; also helpful: SSN. Criminal records on dockets from early 1900s; on computer back to 1998. Access court orders online at www.etitlesearch.com; registration and fees apply.

General Information: Public access terminal goes back to 1998. No juvenile records released. Will not fax specific case file. Certification fee: $3.00. Payee: Pope County. Personal checks accepted. Prepayment required.

District Court 205 W Second, Russellville, AR 72801; phone: 479-968-1393; fax: 479-968-4166; hours 8AM-5PM (CST). *Misdemeanor, Civil Actions Under $5,000, Small Claims.*
Civil Records: Access: Phone, fax, mail, in person. Both court and visitors may perform in person searches. No search fee. Court makes copy: $.25 per page. Required to search: name, DOB, years to search. Civil records go back to 1970s; on computer back to 1991. Mail turnaround time 2-3 days.
Criminal Records: Access: Phone, fax, mail, in person. Both court and visitors may perform in person searches. No search fee. Court makes copy: $.25 per page. Required to search: name, years to search; also helpful: DOB. Criminal records go back to 1970s; on computer back to 1991. Mail turnaround time 2-3 days.
General Information: No public access terminal. Will fax documents to local or toll free line. Certification fee: $5.00. Cert fee includes copies. Payee: District Court. Prepayment required.

Prairie County

Circuit Court - Southern District PO Box 283, De Valls Bluff, AR 72041; phone: 870-998-2314; fax: 870-998-2314; hours 8AM-4:30PM (CST). *Felony, Civil Actions Over $5,000, Probate.*
Civil Records: Access: Phone, fax, mail, in person. Both court and visitors may perform in person searches. Search fee: $6.00. Court makes copy: $.25 per page; same fee for self serve. Required to search: name, years to search. Civil cases indexed by defendant, plaintiff; on dockets from 1800s. Mail turnaround time 1 day.
Criminal Records: Access: Phone, fax, mail, in person. Both court and visitors may perform in person searches. Search fee: $6.00. Court makes copy: $.25 per page; same fee for self serve. Required to search: name, years to search, DOB, SSN. Criminal

records on dockets from 1800s. Mail turnaround time 1 day.
General Information: No public access terminal. No juvenile or adoption records released. Will fax documents $1.00 per page. Certification fee: $5.00. Payee: Circuit Clerk. Personal checks accepted. Prepayment and SASE required.

Circuit Court - Northern District PO Box 1011, Des Arc, AR 72040; phone: 870-256-4434; criminal records fax: 870-256-4434; same fax for civil and probate; hours 8AM-4:30PM (CST). *Felony, Civil Actions Over $5,000, Probate.*
Note: Probate is a separate index at this same address.
Civil Records: Access: Mail, in person. Both court and visitors may perform in person searches. Search fee: $6.00 per name. Court makes copy: $1.00 per page. Self serve copy fee: $.25 per page. Required to search: name, years to search. Civil cases indexed by defendant, plaintiff; on dockets from 1800s; limited records on computer. Mail turnaround time 1 day.
Criminal Records: Access: Mail, in person. Both court and visitors may perform in person searches. Search fee: $6.00 per name. Court makes copy: $1.00 per page. Self serve copy fee: $.25 per page. Required to search: name, years to search. Criminal records on dockets from 1800s; limited records on computer. Mail turnaround time 1 day.
General Information: No public access terminal. No juvenile, adoption records released. Fee to fax documents is $1.00 per page. Certification fee: $5.00 per cert. Payee: Circuit Clerk. Personal checks accepted. Prepayment and SASE required.

Des Arc District Court PO Box 389, Des Arc, AR 72040; phone: 870-256-3011; fax: 870-256-4612; hours 8AM-4:30PM (CST). *Misdemeanor, Civil Actions Under $5,000, Small Claims.*
Civil Records: Access: Mail, in person. Both court and visitors may perform in person searches. No search fee. Court makes copy: $.50 per page. Self serve copy fee: $.25 per page. Civil records available since 1988. Mail turnaround time 1-2 days.
Criminal Records: Access: Mail, in person. Both court and visitors may perform in person searches. No search fee. Court makes copy: $.50 per page. Self serve copy fee: $.25 per page. Required to search: name, years to search. Criminal records available since 1988. Mail turnaround time 1-2 days.
General Information: No public access terminal.

Pulaski County

District Court 3001 W Roosevelt, Little Rock, AR 72204; phone: 501-340-6824; fax: 501-340-6899; hours 8AM-4:30PM (CST). *Misdemeanor, Civil Actions Under $5,000, Eviction, Small Claims.*
Civil Records: Access: Phone, mail, in person. Both court and visitors may perform in person searches. No search fee. Court makes copy: $.50 per page. Required to search: DOB, SNS, case number. Overall records and computerized records go to 1988. Mail turnaround time 2-3 days.
Criminal Records: Access: Phone, mail, in person. Both court and visitors may perform in person searches. No search fee. Court makes copy: $.50 per page. Required to search: name, years to search; also helpful: SSN. Mail turnaround time 2-3 days.
General Information: No public access terminal. Certification fee: $1.00 per page.

Circuit Court Courthouse, Rm 102, 401 W Markham St, #102, Little Rock, AR 72201; phone: 501-340-8431; probate phone: 501-340-5605; fax: 510-340-8420; hours 8:30AM-4:30PM (CST). *Felony, Civil Actions Over $5,000, Probate.*
Note: Probate was handled by the Chancery Court #12 until July 1, 2001.
Civil Records: Access: In person only. Visitors must perform in person searches themselves. Court makes copy: $.50 first page; $.25 per each add'l page. Self serve copy fee: $.15 per page. Required to search: name, years to search. Civil cases indexed by

defendant, plaintiff; on computer from 1982, on microfiche from 1974 to 1982, archived from 1900.
Criminal Records: Access: In person only. Visitors must perform in person searches themselves. Court makes copy: $.50 first page; $.25 per each add'l page. Self serve copy fee: $.15 per page. Required to search: name, years to search, DOB, SSN. Criminal records on computer from 1982, on microfiche from 1974 to 1982, archived from 1900.
General Information: Public access terminal has criminal back to mid-1980s and civil back to early 1990s. No expunged records released. Certification fee: $5.00 per cert. Payee: Circuit Clerk. Personal checks accepted. Prepayment required.

Randolph County

Circuit Court 107 W Broadway, Pocahontas, AR 72455; phone: 870-892-5522; probate phone: same; fax: 870-892-8794; hours 8AM-4:30PM (CST). *Felony, Civil Actions Over $5,000, Probate.*
Note: Probate records are located at the same address, right down the hall.

Civil Records: Access: Mail, in person. Both court and visitors may perform in person searches. Search fee: $6.00 per name. Court makes copy: $.25 per page. Required to search: name, years to search. Civil cases indexed by defendant, plaintiff; on criminal index from 1836. Mail turnaround time same day.
Criminal Records: Access: Mail, in person. Both court and visitors may perform in person searches. Search fee: $6.00 per name. Court makes copy: $.25 per page. Required to search: name, years to search, DOB. Criminal records on criminal index from 1836. Mail turnaround time same day.
General Information: No public access terminal. No juvenile records released. Will fax documents for $1.00 per page prepaid. Certification fee: $2.00. Payee: Circuit Clerk. Personal checks accepted. Prepayment and SASE required.

District Court 1510 Pace Rd, Pocahontas, AR 72455; phone: 870-892-4033; criminal records fax: 870-892-4392; civil records fax: same; hours 8:00AM-4:30PM (CST). *Misdemeanor, Civil Actions Under $5,000, Eviction, Small Claims.*
Civil Records: Access: Mail, in person. Both court and visitors may perform in person searches. Search fee: $6.00. No copy fee. Required to search: name, years to search, DOB, SSN. Records maintained since 1980s. Mail turnaround time 1 day.
Criminal Records: Access: Mail, in person. Both court and visitors may perform in person searches. Search fee: $6.00. No copy fee.Required to search: name, years to search, DOB, SSN. Records maintained since 1980. Mail turnaround time 1 day.
General Information: No public access terminal. Will fax documents to local or toll free line. Certification fee: $5.00 per cert includes copies. Payee: District Court. Prepayment required.

Saline County

Circuit Court 200 N Main St, Benton, AR 72015; phone: 501-303-5615; probate phone: 501-303-5630; fax: 501-303-5675; probate fax: 501-303-5684; hours 8AM-4:30PM (CST). *Felony, Civil Actions Over $5,000, Probate.*
www.salinecounty.org
Note: Probate records located at 215 N Main St.

Civil Records: Access: In person only. Visitors must perform in person searches themselves. Court makes copy: $.25 per page; same fee for self serve. Required to search: name, years to search. Civil cases indexed by defendant, plaintiff; on computer since 1991, prior on docket books.
Criminal Records: Access: In person only. Visitors must perform in person searches themselves. Court makes copy: $.25 per page; same fee for self serve. Required to search: name, years to search. Criminal records on computer since 1991, prior on docket books.

General Information: Public access terminal goes back to 1991. No juvenile records released. Will fax specific case file for $1.00 per page. Certification fee: $3.00. Payee: Circuit Court. Personal checks accepted. Prepayment required.

Benton District Court 1605 Edison Ave #19, Benton, AR 72015; phone: 501-303-5670/1 & 5975; fax: 501-303-5656; hours 8AM-4:30PM (CST). *Misdemeanor, Civil Actions Under $5,000, Eviction, Small Claims.*

Civil Records: Access: Mail, in person. Only the court performs in person searches. Search fee: $5.00 per name. Court makes copy: $5.00 per document. Required to search: name. Civil records go back to 1982. Mail turnaround time 72 hours.

Criminal Records: Access: Mail, in person. Only the court performs in person searches. Search fee: $5.00 per name. Court makes copy: $5.00. Required to search: name, years to search, DOB; also helpful: DOB, SSN, DL. Criminal records go back to 1994 on computer. Mail turnaround time 72 hours.

General Information: No public access terminal. Will fax documents. Certification fee: $5.00.

Scott County

Circuit Court PO Box 2165, 190 W First St Box 10, Waldron, AR 72958; phone: 479-637-2642; criminal records fax: 479-637-0124; same fax for civil and probate; hours 8AM-4:30PM (CST). *Felony, Civil Actions Over $5,000, Probate.*

Civil Records: Access: Phone, mail, fax, in person. Both court and visitors may perform in person searches. No search fee. No copy fee.Self serve copy fee: $.25 per page. Required to search: name, years to search. Civil cases indexed by defendant, plaintiff; on index books from 1882. Mail turnaround time 1 week.

Criminal Records: Access: Phone, mail, fax, in person. Both court and visitors may perform in person searches. No search fee. No copy fee.Self serve copy fee: $.25 per page. Required to search: name, years to search, DOB, SSN. Criminal records on index books from 1882. Mail turnaround time 1 week.

General Information: No public access terminal. No juvenile or adoption records released. Will fax documents for no fee. Certification fee: $5.00 per cert includes copies. Payee: Scott County. Personal checks accepted. Prepayment and SASE required.

District Court 190 W 1st St, Box 15, Waldron, AR 72958; phone: 479-637-4694; criminal records fax: 479-637-4712; civil records fax: same; hours 8AM-4:30PM (CST). *Misdemeanor, Civil Actions Under $5,000, Eviction, Small Claims.*

Civil Records: Access: Mail, in person. Both court and visitors may perform in person searches. No copy fee. Required to search: name, years to search, DOB; also helpful-other names used, SSN. Records on computer go back to 1998. Mail turnaround time 1-2 days.

Criminal Records: Access: Mail, in person. Both court and visitors may perform in person searches. No search fee. No copy fee. Required to search: name, years to search. Records go back to 1998; on computer back to 10/1998. Mail turnaround time 1-2 days.

General Information: No public access terminal. No certification fee .

Searcy County

Circuit Court PO Box 998, Marshall, AR 72650; phone: 870-448-3807; fax: 870-448-5005; hours 8AM-4:30PM (CST). *Felony, Civil Actions Over $5,000, Probate.*

Civil Records: Access: Mail, in person. Visitors must perform in person searches themselves. Search fee: $6.00 per name. Court makes copy: $.25 per page. Required to search: name, years to search. Civil cases indexed by defendant, plaintiff. Civil records archived from 1881. Some records on dockets.

Criminal Records: Access: Mail, in person. Visitors must perform in person searches themselves. Search fee: $6.00 per name. Required to search: name, years to search, offense; also helpful: DOB, SSN. Criminal records archived from 1881. Some records on dockets.

General Information: No public access terminal. No juvenile or adoption records released. Certification fee: $5.00 per document. Payee: Searcy County Clerk. Personal checks accepted. Prepayment and SASE required.

District Court PO Box 885, Marshall, AR 72650; phone: 870-448-5411; fax: 870-448-5927; hours 9AM-5PM (CST). *Misdemeanor, Civil Actions Under $5,000, Eviction, Small Claims.*

Civil Records: Access: Mail, in person. Both court and visitors may perform in person searches. Search fee: $6.00 per name. Court makes copy: $.25 per page. Required to search: name. Mail turnaround time 1 week.

Criminal Records: Access: Mail, in person. Both court and visitors may perform in person searches. No search fee. Court makes copy: $.25 per page. Required to search: name, years to search, DOB, SSN. Mail turnaround time 1 week.

General Information: No public access terminal. Certification fee: $5.00 per document. Prepayment required. SASE helpful.

Sebastian County

Circuit Court - Greenwood Division PO Box 310, County Courthouse, Greenwood, AR 72936; phone: 479-996-4175; fax: 479-996-6885; hours 8AM-5PM (CST). *Felony, Civil Actions Over $5,000, Probate.*

www.sebastiancountyonline.com

Note: Records from both Circuit Courts - Fort Smith and Greenwood Division - are on the same computer system, but copies of case files must be pulled from individual courts.

Civil Records: Access: Mail, in person. Both court and visitors may perform in person searches. Search fee: $6.00 per name. Court makes copy: $1.00 per page. Required to search: name, years to search. Civil cases indexed by defendant, plaintiff; on computer from 10/87, on dockets from 1900. Mail turnaround time 1-2 weeks.

Criminal Records: Access: Mail, in person. Both court and visitors may perform in person searches. Search fee: $6.00 per name. Court makes copy: $1.00 per page. Required to search: name, years to search; also helpful: SSN. Criminal records on computer from 10/87, on dockets from 1900. Mail turnaround time 1-2 weeks.

General Information: Public access terminal goes back to 1988. No juvenile records released. Will fax documents $1.00 per page. Certification fee: $2.50 per cert. Payee: Circuit Clerk. Personal checks accepted. Prepayment and SASE required.

Circuit Court - Fort Smith 35 S 6th St,Rm 203, PO Box 1179, Fort Smith, AR 72902; phone: 479-782-1046; fax: 479-784-1580; hours 8AM-5PM (CST). *Felony, Civil Actions Over $5,000, Probate.*

www.sebastiancountyonline.com

Note: Records from both Circuit Courts-Fort Smith and Greenwood Division-are on the same computer system, but copies of case files must be pulled from the individual courts. Closed files in this Circuit are maintained at 40 S 4th St in Fort Smith.

Civil Records: Access: Fax, mail, in person. Both court and visitors may perform in person searches. Search fee: $6.00 per name. Court makes copy: $1.00 per page. Self serve copy fee: $.50 per page. Required to search: name, years to search; also helpful: address. Civil cases indexed by defendant, plaintiff. Civil records computerized from 1988, on dockets from 1900. Mail turnaround time 1-2 days.

Criminal Records: Access: Fax, mail, in person. Both court and visitors may perform in person searches. Search fee: $6.00 per name. Court makes

copy: $1.00 per page. Self serve copy fee: $.50 per page. Required to search: name, years to search; also helpful: address, DOB, SSN. Criminal records computerized from 1988, on dockets from 1900. Note: Court will only perform searches for criminal justice purposes. Mail turnaround time 1-2 days.

General Information: Public access terminal goes back to 1988. No juvenile records released. Will fax documents $1.00 per page. Certification fee: $2.50. Payee: Circuit Clerk. Personal checks accepted. Prepayment and SASE required.

Fort Smith District Court Courthouse, 35 S 6th St, Fort Smith, AR 72901; phone: 479-784-2420; fax: 479-784-2438; hours 8:30AM-5PM (CST). *Misdemeanor, Civil Actions Under $5,000, Traffic, Small Claims.*

www.districtcourtfortsmith.org

Civil Records: Access: Phone, fax, mail, in person. Both court and visitors may perform in person searches. No search fee. Court makes copy: $.50 per page. Record stored from 1984. Note: If copies are required, then your request must be in writing. Mail turnaround time 1-2 days.

Criminal Records: Access: Phone, fax, mail, in person. Both court and visitors may perform in person searches. No search fee. Court makes copy: $.50 per page. Required to search: name, years to search, DOB; also helpful: SSN. Records are computerized since 1993. Note: If copies are required, then your request must be in writing. Mail turnaround time 1-2 days.

General Information: Public access terminal goes back to 1993. Fee to fax documents is $.50 per page. Certification fee: $5.00. Payee: Fort Smith District Court. Prepayment required.

Sevier County

Circuit Court 115 N 3rd, Courthouse, De Queen, AR 71832; phone: 870-584-3055; probate phone: 870-642-2852; criminal records fax: 870-642-3119; civil records fax: same; hours 8AM-4:30PM (CST). *Felony, Civil Actions Over $5,000, Probate.*

Note: Probate index in the same building at County Clerk.

Civil Records: Access: Phone, mail, fax, in person. Visitors must perform in person searches themselves. No search fee. Court makes copy: $.25 per page; same fee for self serve. Required to search: name, years to search. Civil cases indexed by defendant, plaintiff. Civil records archived from 1900.

Criminal Records: Access: In person only. Visitors must perform in person searches themselves. Court makes copy: $.25 per page; same fee for self serve. Required to search: name, years to search. Criminal records index goes back to 1961, prior back to 1912.

General Information: Public access terminal goes back to 2003. No juvenile records released. Fee to fax documents is $5.00 per document; free if to a toll-free number. Certification fee: $5.00 per document. Payee: Circuit Clerk. Personal checks accepted. Prepayment and SASE required.

District Court 115 N 3rd St, Rm 215, De Queen, AR 71832; phone: 870-584-7311; criminal records fax: 870-642-6651; civil records fax: same; hours 8AM-4:30PM (CST). *Misdemeanor, Civil Actions Under $5,000, Eviction, Small Claims.*

Civil Records: Access: Mail, in person. Both court and visitors may perform in person searches. No search fee. No copy fee.Required to search: name, DOB, SSN, address. Records available since 1991. Mail turnaround time 1-2 weeks.

Criminal Records: Access: Mail, in person. Both court and visitors may perform in person searches. No search fee. No copy fee. Required to search: name, years to search, DOB. Records available since 1991. Mail turnaround time 1-2 weeks.

General Information: No public access terminal. Will fax documents. No certification fee.

Sharp County

Circuit Court PO Box 307, Ash Flat, AR 72513; phone: 870-994-7361; fax: 870-994-7712; hours 8AM-4PM (CST). *Felony, Civil Actions Over $5,000, Probate.*

Civil Records: Access: Fax, mail, in person, online. Both court and visitors may perform in person searches. Search fee: $6.00 per name. Court makes copy: $.25 per page. Required to search: name, years to search. Civil cases indexed by defendant, plaintiff; on card files from 1970s. Some records on dockets, computerized since 1986. Court has outsourced online access to civil, probate, criminal, and all recordings to www.ecourtstor.com; fees are involved.

Criminal Records: Access: In person, online. Visitors must perform in person searches themselves. Court makes copy: $.25 per page. Required to search: name, years to search; also helpful: DOB, SSN. Criminal records on card files from 1970s. Some records on dockets, computerized since 1986. Court has outsourced online access to civil, probate, criminal, and all recordings to www.ecourtstor.com; fees are involved. Mail turnaround time 1 day.

General Information: Public access terminal goes back to 1986. No juvenile or expunged records released. No fee to fax documents to toll free numbers only. Certification fee: $5.00 per doc. Payee: Sharp County Clerk. Personal checks accepted. Prepayment and SASE required.

District Court PO Box 2, Ash Flat, AR 72513; phone: 870-994-2745; fax: 870-994-7901; hours 8AM-4PM (CST). *Misdemeanor, Civil Actions Under $5,000, Eviction, Small Claims.*

Civil Records: Access: Mail, in person. Both court and visitors may perform in person searches. Court makes copy: $.50 per page; same fee for self serve. Mail turnaround time 1 day.

Criminal Records: Access: Mail, in person. Both court and visitors may perform in person searches. No search fee. Court makes copy: $.50 per page; same fee for self serve. Required to search: name, years to search; also helpful: DOB, SSN. Mail turnaround time 1 day.

General Information: Public access terminal has criminal back to 1999 and civil back to 1991.

St. Francis County

Circuit Court PO Box 1775, Forrest City, AR 72336; phone: 870-261-1715; fax: 870-261-1723; probate fax: 870-630-1210; hours 8AM-4:30PM (CST). *Felony, Civil Actions Over $5,000, Probate.* Note: Probate is a separate index at this same address.

Civil Records: Access: Fax, mail, in person. Both court and visitors may perform in person searches. Search fee: $5.00 per name. Court makes copy: $.25 per page; same fee for self serve. Required to search: name, years to search. Civil cases indexed by defendant, plaintiff; on index from 1982, archived from 1920s.

Criminal Records: Access: In person only. Visitors must perform in person searches themselves. Court makes copy: $.25 per page; same fee for self serve. Required to search: name, years to search, DOB, SSN. Criminal records on index from 1982, archived from 1920s. Court directs criminal searches to AR State Police, phone 501-618-8500.

General Information: No public access terminal. No juvenile records released. Will fax documents for $5.00 fee. Certification fee: $3.00 per cert includes copy fee. Payee: Circuit Clerk. Personal checks accepted. Prepayment and SASE required.

District Court 615 E Cross, Forrest City, AR 72335; phone: 870-261-1410; fax: 870-261-1411; hours 8AM-4:30PM (CST). *Misdemeanor, Civil Actions Under $5,000, Eviction, Small Claims.*

Civil Records: Access: Mail, in person. Only the court performs in person searches. Search fee: $5.00 per name. Court makes copy: $.25 per page.

Civil records on computer since 1994. Mail turnaround time 5 days.

Criminal Records: Access: Mail, in person. Only the court performs in person searches. Search fee: $5.00 per name. Court makes copy: $.25 per page. Required to search: name, years to search. Criminal records on computer since 1990. Mail turnaround time 5 days.

General Information: No public access terminal. Will fax documents. Certification fee: $5.00 per page. Payee: District Court. Prepayment required.

Stone County

Circuit Court 107 W Mail #D, Mountain View, AR 72560; phone: 870-269-3271; fax: 870-269-2303; hours 8AM-4:30PM (CST). *Felony, Civil Actions Over $5,000, Probate.* www.16thdistrictark.org

Civil Records: Access: In person only. Visitors must perform in person searches themselves. Court makes copy: $.25 per page; same fee for self serve. Required to search: name, years to search. Civil cases indexed by defendant, plaintiff; on dockets from 1960s; computerized records since 1992. Mountain View Abstract Corp does searches by mail. Call 870-269-3470.

Criminal Records: Access: In person only. Visitors must perform in person searches themselves. Court makes copy: $.25 per page; same fee for self serve. Required to search: name, years to search, DOB; SSN helpful. Criminal records on dockets from 1960s; computerized records since 1992.

General Information: Public access terminal goes back to 1992. No juvenile or adoption records released. Certification fee: $5.00 per document. Payee: Stone County Clerk. Personal checks accepted. Prepayment required.

District Court 107 W Main, #H, Mountain View, AR 72560; phone: 870-269-3465; fax: 870-269-3465; hours 8AM-4:30PM (CST). *Misdemeanor, Civil Actions Under $5,000, Eviction, Small Claims.*

Civil Records: Access: Phone, fax, mail, in person. Both court and visitors may perform in person searches. Court makes copy: $.25 per page. Self serve copy fee: $.25 per page. Required to search: names, years to search. Records available since 1984, not computerized. Mail turnaround time varies.

Criminal Records: Access: Phone, fax, mail, in person. Both court and visitors may perform in person searches. No search fee. Court makes copy: $.25 per page. Self serve copy fee: $.25 per page. Required to search: name, years to search; also helpful: DOB, SSN. Records on computer since 1990. Mail turnaround time varies.

General Information: No public access terminal. Certification fee: $3.00. Payee: District Court. Prepayment required.

Union County

Circuit Court PO Box 1626, El Dorado, AR 71730; phone: 870-864-1940; probate phone: 870-864-1910; fax: 870-864-1994; hours 8:30AM-5PM (CST). *Felony, Civil Actions Over $5,000, Probate.*

Civil Records: Access: In person, online. Visitors must perform in person searches themselves. Court makes copy: $.50 per page; same fee for self serve. Required to search: name, years to search. Civil cases indexed by defendant, plaintiff. Civil records computerized to 1996 on dockets from 1800s. Online access to circuit court dockets by subscription through RecordsUSA.com. Credit card, username and password is required; choose either monthly or per-use plan. Visit the website for sign-up or call Lisa at 601-264-7701 for information.

Criminal Records: Access: In person, online. Visitors must perform in person searches themselves. No search fee. Court makes copy: $.50 per page for self serve. Required to search: name, years to search, DOB; also helpful: SSN. Criminal records computerized to 1996 on dockets from 1800s. Online access to criminal dockets is the same as civil.

General Information: Public access terminal goes back to 1999. No juvenile records released. Will fax specific case file requests for $1.00 per page. Certification fee: $3.00. Payee: Circuit Clerk. Personal checks accepted. Prepayment required.

District Court 250 American #A, El Dorado, AR 71730; phone: 870-864-1950; fax: 870-864-1955; hours 8:30AM-5PM (CST). *Misdemeanor, Civil Actions Under $5,000, Eviction, Small Claims.*

Civil Records: Access: In person, fax, mail. Both court and visitors may perform in person searches. No search fee. No copy fee. Required to search: name. Computerized records since 1987. Mail turnaround time 1-2 days.

Criminal Records: Access: In person, fax, mail. Both court and visitors may perform in person searches. No search fee. No copy fee. Required to search: name, years to search, DOB; also helpful: SSN. Computerized records since 1987. Mail turnaround time 1-2 days.

General Information: No public access terminal. No certification fee .

Van Buren County

Circuit Court 451 Main St, Clinton, AR 72031; phone: 501-745-4140; fax: 501-745-7400; hours 8AM-5PM (CST). *Felony, Civil Actions Over $5,000, Probate.*

Civil Records: Access: Mail, in person. Visitors must perform in person searches themselves. Search fee: $1.00. Court makes copy: $.50 per page; same fee for self serve. Required to search: name, years to search; also helpful: address. Civil cases indexed by defendant, plaintiff; on computer from 1987, archived from 1900s. Mail turnaround time 7-10 days.

Criminal Records: Access: Mail, in person. Both court and visitors may perform in person searches. Search fee: $1.00 per name. Court makes copy: $.50 per page; same fee for self serve. Required to search: name, years to search; also helpful: address, DOB, SSN. Criminal records on computer from 1987, archived from 1900s. Mail turnaround time 7-10 days.

General Information: Public access terminal available. No juvenile or adoption records released. Will fax documents to local or toll free line. Certification fee: $5.00. Payee: Van Buren County Clerk's Office. Personal checks accepted. Prepayment and SASE required.

District Court 339 Boykin St, Clinton, AR 72031; phone: 501-745-8894; criminal records fax: 501-745-5810; civil records fax: same; hours 8AM-5PM (CST). *Misdemeanor, Civil Actions Under $5,000, Small Claims.*

Civil Records: Access: Phone, mail, fax, in person. Visitors must perform in person searches themselves. Required to search: name, years to search, DOB. Civil records computerized to 1992; in books back to 1992.

Criminal Records: Access: Phone, mail, fax, in person. Both court and visitors may perform in person searches. Search fee: $5.00 per name. Required to search: name, years to search, DOB, SSN; also helpful-docket or ticket number. Criminal records computerized to 1992; in books back to 1992; computerized since 1992.

General Information: No public access terminal. Will fax documents. Certification fee: $5.00 per document. Payee: Clinton District Court. Prepayment required.

Washington County

Circuit Court 280 N College, #302, Fayetteville, AR 72701; phone: 479-444-1538; probate phone: 479-444-1711; fax: 479-444-1537; hours 8AM-4:30PM (CST). *Felony, Civil Actions Over $5,000, Probate.* www.co.washington.ar.us Note: Probate is a separate index in the County Clerk's office.

Civil Records: Access: Fax, mail, in person, online. Both court and visitors may perform in person searches. No search fee. Court makes copy: $.15 per page; same fee for self serve. Required to search: name, years to search. Civil cases indexed by defendant, plaintiff; on computer from 1992, on index from 1950. Online case index at www.co.washington.ar.us/resolution/. Civil cases indexed from 1992 forward. This is a commercial system, $50.00 per month prepaid. Pre-1973 court indices free at www.co.washington.ar.us/ArchiveSearch/CourtRecordSearch.asp. Mail turnaround time 1-2 days.

Criminal Records: Access: Fax, mail, in person, online. Both court and visitors may perform in person searches. No search fee. Court makes copy: $.15 per page; same fee for self serve. Required to search: name, years to search. Criminal records on computer from 1992, on index from 1950. Online case index at www.co.washington.ar.us/resolution/. Criminal cases indexed from 1992 forward. This is a commercial system, $50.00 per month prepaid. Pre-1973 court indices free at www.co.washington.ar.us/ArchiveSearch/CourtRecordSearch.asp. Mail turnaround time 1-2 days.

General Information: Public access terminal has criminal back to 1992 and civil back to 1992. No juvenile records released. Will fax documents $5.00 per doc. Certification fee: $2.00 per document includes copy fee. Payee: Circuit Clerk. Personal checks accepted. Prepayment required.

Fayetteville District Court 100 B W Rock, Fayetteville, AR 72701; phone: 479-587-3596; fax: 479-444-3480; hours 8AM-5PM (CST). *Misdemeanor, Civil Actions Under $5,000, Small Claims.*
www.co.washington.ar.us
Civil Records: Access: Phone, mail, fax, in person. Both court and visitors may perform in person searches. Search fee: $5.00 per name. Court makes copy: $5.00 per document. Required to search: name, years to search. Civil records on computer go back to 1984. Mail turnaround time 1 week.

Criminal Records: Access: Mail, in person. Only the court performs in person searches. Search fee: $5.00 per name. Court makes copy: $5.00 per document. Required to search: name, years to search, DOB, SSN, signed release; also helpful: address. Criminal records on computer go back to 1984. Mail turnaround time 1 week.

General Information: No public access terminal. Will fax documents no charge. No certification fee . Payee: City of Fayetteville. Prepayment required. SASE not required.

White County

Circuit Court 301 W Arch, Searcy, AR 72143; phone: 501-279-6223; probate phone: 501-279-6204; criminal records fax: 501-279-6218; civil records fax: same; hours 8AM-4:30PM (CST). *Felony, Civil Actions Over $5,000, Probate.*
Note: Probate is a separate office and separate index at this same address.

Civil Records: Access: Mail, in person. Both court and visitors may perform in person searches. Search fee: $6.00 per name. Court makes copy: $.50 per page; same fee for self serve. Required to search: name, years to search; also helpful: address. Civil cases indexed by plaintiff. Records indexed back to 2000. Mail turnaround time 1 day.

Criminal Records: Access: Mail, in person. Both court and visitors may perform in person searches. Search fee: $6.00 per name. Court makes copy: $.50 per page; same fee for self serve. Required to search: name, years to search, DOB, SSN; also helpful:

address. Criminal records on dockets from 1982. Mail turnaround time 1 day.
General Information: No public access terminal. No juvenile records released. Will fax documents $1.00 per page. Certification fee: $2.50 per certification. Payee: Circuit Clerk. Personal checks accepted. Prepayment and SASE required.

Searcy District Court PO Box 958, 406 E Booth St, Searcy, AR 72145; phone: 501-279-1040, 268-7622; fax: 501-279-1043; hours 8:00AM-4:30PM (CST). *Misdemeanor, Civil Actions Under $5,000, Small Claims.*
www.cityofsearcy.org
Note: On 1/27/05 the courthouse burned down and a significant amount of records were lost. Until 10/2006, temporarily located at city hall, enter via side door.

Civil Records: Access: Mail, fax, phone, in person. Only the court performs in person searches. Search fee: $6.00 per name. Court makes copy: $.50 per page. Required to search: name plus SSN, years to search. Records go back to 1998; on computer since 6/1995. Mail turnaround time 5 days.

Criminal Records: Access: In person, phone, fax, mail. Only the court performs in person searches. Search fee: $6.00 per name. Court makes copy: $.50 per page. Required to search: name, years to search, DOB, SSN. Records go back since 1993; on computer since 6/1995. Mail turnaround time 5 days.

General Information: No public access terminal. Will fax documents. No certification fee . Payee: Searcy District Court. Prepayment required. SASE requested.

Woodruff County

Circuit Court PO Box 492, Augusta, AR 72006; phone: 870-347-2391; probate phone: 870-347-2871; fax: 870-347-8703; hours 8AM-4PM (CST). *Felony, Civil Actions Over $5,000.*
Note: Probate is handled by the County Clerk.

Civil Records: Access: Phone, mail, in person, fax. Both court and visitors may perform in person searches. No search fee. Court makes copy: $1.00 per page. Self serve copy fee: $.50 per page. Required to search: name, years to search. Civil cases indexed by defendant, plaintiff; on dockets from 1982. Mail turnaround time 1-2 days.

Criminal Records: Access: Phone, mail, in person. Both court and visitors may perform in person searches. No search fee. Court makes copy: $1.00 per page. Self serve copy fee: $.50 per page. Required to search: name, years to search, DOB. Criminal records on dockets from 1980. Mail turnaround time 1-2 days.

General Information: No public access terminal. No juvenile records released. Certification fee: $5.00. Payee: Circuit Clerk. Personal checks accepted. Prepayment and SASE required.

District Court PO Box 381, Augusta, AR 72006; phone: 870-347-2790; fax: 870-347-2436; hours 8:30AM-4PM (CST). *Misdemeanor, Civil Actions Under $5,000, Eviction, Small Claims.*
Civil Records: Access: Mail, in person. Only the court performs in person searches. Search fee: $5.00 per name. No copy fee.Required to search: name. Computerized records go back to 1995. Mail turnaround time 10 days.

Criminal Records: Access: Mail, in person. Only the court performs in person searches. Search fee: $5.00 per name. No copy fee.Required to search: name, years to search, DOB, signed release. Computerized records go back to 1995. Mail turnaround time 10 days.

General Information: No public access terminal. No fee to fax documents. Certification fee: $.25 per

page. Payee: Augusta District Court. Prepayment required.

Yell County

Danville Circuit Court PO Box 219, Danville, AR 72833; phone: 479-495-4850; criminal records fax: 479-495-4875; same fax for civil and probate; hours 8AM-4PM (CST). *Felony, Civil Actions Over $5,000, Probate.*
Note: Probate is a separate index at this same address.

Civil Records: Access: Mail, fax, in person. Both court and visitors may perform in person searches. Search fee: $6.00 per name. Court makes copy: $.25 per page. Self serve copy fee: $.25 per page. Required to search: name, years to search; also helpful: address. Civil cases indexed by defendant. Civil records on dockets from 1900s. Mail turnaround time 1 day.

Criminal Records: Access: Mail, fax, in person. Both court and visitors may perform in person searches. Search fee: $6.00 per name. Court makes copy: $.25 per page. Self serve copy fee: $.25 per page. Required to search: name, years to search, DOB; also helpful: address. Criminal records on dockets from 1900s. Mail turnaround time 1 day.

General Information: No public access terminal. No juvenile or adoption records released. Will fax documents for $3.00 if lengthy. Certification fee: $5.00 per document. Payee: Circuit Clerk of Yell County. Personal checks accepted. Prepayment and SASE required.

Dardanelle Circuit Court County Courthouse, PO Box 457, Dardanelle, AR 72834; phone: 479-229-4404; fax: 479-229-4PM (CST). *Felony, Civil Actions Over $5,000, Probate.*
Civil Records: Access: Mail, in person. Both court and visitors may perform in person searches. Search fee: $6.00 per name. Court makes copy: $.25 per page; same fee for self serve. Required to search: name, years to search. Civil cases indexed by defendant. Civil records on dockets from 1800s. Mail turnaround time 1 day.

Criminal Records: Access: Mail, in person. Both court and visitors may perform in person searches. Search fee: $6.00 per name. Court makes copy: $.25 per page; same fee for self serve. Required to search: name, years to search; also helpful: DOB. Criminal records on dockets from 1800s. Mail turnaround time 1 day.

General Information: No public access terminal. No adoption or juvenile records released. Will fax documents for a fee of $3.00 per document. Certification fee: $5.00 per doc. Payee: Circuit Clerk of Yell County. Personal checks accepted. Prepayment and SASE required.

District Court County Courthouse, Dardanelle, AR 72834; phone: 479-229-1389; fax: 479-229-5740; hours 8AM-4PM (CST). *Misdemeanor, Civil Actions Under $5,000, Eviction, Small Claims.*
Civil Records: Access: Mail, in person. Both court and visitors may perform in person searches. Search fee: $3.00 per name. Court makes copy: $.25 per page. Civil records go back to 1982. Mail turnaround time 2-4 days.

Criminal Records: Access: Mail, in person. Both court and visitors may perform in person searches. Search fee: $3.00 per name. Court makes copy: $.25 per page. Required to search: name, years to search, signed release; also helpful: address, DOB, SSN. Criminal records go back to 1982, on computer back to 1994. Mail turnaround time 2-4 days.

General Information: No public access terminal. Will fax documents to local or toll free line. No certification fee . Payee: District Court. Prepayment required.

Arkansas Recording Offices

ORGANIZATION: 75 counties, 85 recording offices. The recording officer is the Clerk of Circuit Court, who is Ex Officio Recorder. Ten counties have two recording offices - Arkansas, Carroll, Clay, Craighead, Franklin, Logan, Mississippi, Prairie, Sebastian, and Yell. See the notes under each county for how to determine which office is appropriate to search. The entire state is in the Central Time Zone (CST).

REAL ESTATE RECORDS: Most counties do not perform real estate searches. Copy fees and certification fees vary.

UCC RECORDS: Prior to 07/01 this was a dual filing state. Financing statements were filed at the state level and with the Circuit Clerk, except for consumer goods, farm and real estate related collateral, which were filed only with the Circuit Clerk. Now all financing statements are filed at the state level, except for real estate related collateral, which is still filed with the Circuit Clerk. Most counties will perform UCC searches. Use search request form UCC-11. Search fees are usually $10.00 per debtor name. Copy fees vary.

TAX LIEN RECORDS: Federal tax liens on personal property of businesses are filed with the Secretary of State. Other federal and all state tax liens are filed with the Circuit Clerk. Many counties will perform separate tax lien searches. Search fees are usually $6.00 per name.

OTHER LIENS: Mechanics, lis pendens, judgments, hospital, child support, materialman.

ONLINE ACCESS: There is no statewide access. Benton county offers records via their website. Also, there is a commercial system available for a limited number of participating counties. Registration and logon is required, the signup fee is $200 minimum plus $.10 per minute usage. For signup or information call 479-631-8054 or visit www.arcountydata.com

Arkansas County
Northern District

County Circuit Clerk, 302 S. College St., Stuttgart, AR 72160. RE & UCC recording phone-870-673-2056; fax-870-673-3869; hours: 8AM-4:30PM
Will not search real estate records. Will search UCC records, but not tax liens. UCC search per debtor name- $6.00. Copy fee $1.00 per page. Cert fee- $4.00 per doc plus copy fee. Payee- Arkansas County Circuit Clerk. **Online access to Assessor, Property records:** Registration and logon is required to search assessor records at www.arcountydata.com. Signup fee is $200 plus $.10 per minute usage. For signup or information call 479-631-8054 or visit the website. **Property tax/Assessor-** 870-673-6586.

Arkansas County
Southern District

County Circuit Clerk, 101 Court Sq, De Witt, AR 72042. RE & UCC recording phone-870-946-4219; fax-870-946-1394; hours: 8AM-N,12:30-4:30PM
Index: Books, computer. Records indexed on a public use terminal back to 1996. Office will perform a UCC search but public must search other records themselves. Search fee $6.00. Copy fee $.50 per copy. $1.00 for fax copy. Cert fee- $4.00 per page includes copy fee. Payee- Arkansas County Circuit Clerk. **Online access to Assessor, Property records:** Registration and logon is required to search assessor records at www.arcountydata.com. Signup fee is $200 plus $.10 per minute usage. For signup or information call 479-631-8054 or visit the website. **Other phones:** Treasurer- 870-946-4210; Elections- 870-846-4347; Tax Collector- 870-946-2911. **Property tax/Assessor-** 870-946-1795.

Ashley County

County Circuit Clerk, 205 E. Jefferson St; Courthouse, Hamburg, AR 71646. RE & UCC recording phone-870-853-2030; fax-870-853-2034; 8AM-4:30PM
All records in one index. Record index not computerized. Office will perform a UCC search but public must search other records themselves. Search fee $6.00. Copy fee $.50 per page. Cert fee- $2.50 per doc plus copy fee. Payee- Ashley County Circuit Clerk. **Other phones:** Treasurer- 870-853-2010; Elections- 870-853-2020; Tax Collector- 870-853-2050. **Property tax/assessor-** 870-853-2060.

Baxter County

County Circuit Clerk, 1 E. 7th St #103; Courthouse Sq, Mountain Home, AR 72653. 870-425-3475; fax-870-424-5105; hours: 8AM-4:30PM
UCC records are now filed at the office of the Secretary of State. All records in one index. Records indexed on a public use terminal back to 9/1995. Office will perform a UCC and Tax lien search but public must search other records themselves. Search fee $6.00. Copy fee $6.00 1st page; $1.00 each add'l. Cert fee- $5.00 per doc plus copy fee. Payee- Baxter County Circuit Clerk. **Online access to Assessor, Property, Real Estate Recording, Deed records:** Registration and logon is required to search assessor records at www.arcountydata.com. Signup fee is $200 plus $.10 per minute usage. For signup or information call 479-631-8054 or visit the website. Also, access recording office land data at www.etitlesearch.com; registration required, fee based on usage. **Other phones:** ; Tax Collector- 870-425-3444. **Property tax/Assessor-** 870-425-3453.

Benton County

County Circuit Clerk, 215 E. Central St, #6, Bentonville, AR 72712. RE & UCC recording phone-479-271-1017; fax-479-271-5719; hours: 8AM-4:30PM www.co.benton.ar.us
Separate indices to search include deed, mortgage books. Records indexed on a public use terminal back to 1990. Only the public may search. Copy fee $.10 per page. Cert fee- $2.00 per page. Payee- Benton County Circuit Clerk. **Online access to Real Estate, Deed, Circuit Court, Lien, Plat, Property Tax, Judgment, Medical Lien, Inmate, Personal Property records:** County Assessor, tax collector, medical liens, plats and circuit court information is free online at http://209.183.170.177:5061/. Land records are at http://etitlesearch.com; call 870-856-3055 for subscription info. Also, registration and logon required to search assessor records at www.arcountydata.com. Signup fee is $200 min. plus $.10 per minute usage. For info, call 479-631-8054. Also, search inmate records free at www.co.benton.ar.us/Sheriff/Inmate.htm. Also, search property and personal property data free at www.countyservice.net/bentax.html. Also access land court records by subscription at www.recordsusa.com/Arkansas/bentonCnAr.htm or phone 800-932-5029 or 888-85-IMAGE. $49.95/$79.90 or monthly. **Other phones:** Treasurer-

479-271-1018; Elections- 479-271-1013; Tax Collector- 479-271-1040. **Property tax/Assessor-** 215 E Central, Bentonville, AR 72712; 479-271-1037.

Boone County

County Circuit Clerk, 100 N Main; Courthouse, #200, Harrison, AR 72601. RE & UCC recording phone-870-741-5560; fax-870-741-4335; hours: 8AM-4:30PM
Separate indices to search include land & court records are indexed on the computer as of mid 1990. UCC's are in a card index file. Older records for land & court are indexed in books. Records indexed on a public use terminal back to 1990. Only the public may search. Copy fee $.25 per page. Cert fee- $5.00 per doc includes copy fee. Payee- Boone County Circuit Clerk. **Online access to Real Estate Recording, Deed, Assessor, Property records:** Land records are at http://etitlesearch.com. You can do a name search; choose from $45.00 monthly subscription or per click account. Also, registration and logon is required to search all participating counties' assessor records at www.arcountydata.com. Signup fee is $200 minimum plus $.10 per minute usage. For signup or information call 479-631-8054 or visit www.arcountydata.com. **Other phones:** Treasurer- 870-741-3068; Elections- 870-741-8428; Tax Collector- 870-741-6646; Marriages -870-741-8428. **Property tax/Assessor-** PO Box 2425, Harrison, AR 72602; 870-741-3783.

Bradley County

County Circuit Clerk, 101 E. Cedar St; Courthouse, Warren, AR 71671. RE & UCC recording phone-870-226-2272; fax-870-226-8401; hours: 8AM-4:30PM
Only the public may search. Copy fee $1.00 per page. RE or tax lien copy- $.50 per page. Cert fee- $3.00 per doc plus copy fee. Payee- Bradley County Circuit Clerk. **Online access to Assessor, Property records:** Registration and logon is required to search assessor records at www.arcountydata.com. Signup fee is $200 plus $.10 per minute usage. For signup or information call 479-631-8054 or visit the website. **Other phones:** Treasurer- 870-226-8402; Elections- 870-226-3464. **Property tax/Assessor-** 870-226-2211.

Calhoun County

County Circuit Clerk, PO Box 1175, Hampton, AR 71744. RE & UCC recording phone-870-798-2517; fax-870-798-2428; hours: 8AM-4:30

Separate indices to search. Office will perform a UCC search but public must search other records themselves. UCC search per debtor name- $6.00. Copy fee $.25 per page. Cert fee- $5.00 per doc plus copy fee. Payee- Calhoun County Circuit Clerk. **Other phones:** Treasurer- 870-798-2827; Tax Collector- 870-798-2357. **Property tax/Assessor**- PO Box 276, Hampton, AR 71744; 870-798-2740.

Carroll County Eastern District

County Circuit Clerk, PO Box 71, Berryville, AR 72616. RE & UCC recording phone-870-423-2422; fax-870-423-4796; hours: 8:30AM-4:30PM

Separate indices to search include deeds, mortgages, UCCs, judgments, liens. Records indexed on a public use terminal back to 1997. Office personnel or visitors may perform searches. Will not search real estate records. UCC search per debtor name- $6.00. Separate federal/state combined tax lien search- $6.00 per debtor. Copy fee $.25 per page. Cert fee- $2.00 per doc plus copy fee. Payee- Carroll County Circuit Clerk. **Online access to Assessor, Property, Jail records:** Registration and logon is required to search assessor records at www.arcountydata.com. Signup fee is $200 plus $.10 per minute usage. For signup or information call 479-631-8054 or visit the website. Also, access to the weekly county jail roster is free at www.carrollcounty.org/sheriff/jail.phtm. **Other phones:** Treasurer- 870-423-3189; Appraiser/Auditor- 870-423-2388; Elections- 870-423-2022; Vital Records- 870-423-2022; Tax Collector- 870-423-2867. **Property tax/Assessor**- 870-423-2388.

Carroll County Western District

County Circuit Clerk, PO Box 109, Eureka Springs, AR 72632. R/E recording phone-870-423-8646, R/E recording phone-870-423-2422, UCC recording phone-870-423-2422; fax-479-253-6013; hours: 8:30AM-4:30PM

Office will perform a UCC or Tax liens search but public must search other records themselves. Search fee $6.00. Copy fee $.25 per page. Cert fee- $2.00. Payee- Carroll County Circuit Clerk. **Online access to Assessor, Property, Jail records:** Registration and logon is required to search assessor records at www.arcountydata.com. Signup fee is $200 plus $.10 per minute usage. For signup or information call 479-631-8054 or visit the website. Also, access to the weekly county jail roster is free at www.carrollcounty.org/sheriff/jail.phtm. **Other phones:** Treasurer- 870-423-3189; Appraiser/Auditor- 870-423-2388; Elections- 870-423-2022; Vital Records- 870-423-2022 (marriage); Tax Collector- 870-423-2867. **Property tax/Assessor**- 870-423-2388.

Chicot County

County Circuit Clerk, 108 Main St; Courthouse, Lake Village, AR 71653. 870-265-8010, R/E recording phone-870-265-236; fax-870-265-8012; hours: 8AM-4:30PM

Record index not computerized. Office will perform a UCC and Tax lien search but public must search other records themselves. Search fee $6.00. Copy fee $.50 per page. Cert fee- $2.00 per cert plus copy fee. Payee- Chicot County Circuit Clerk. **Online access to Assessor, Property records:** Registration and logon is required to search assessor records at www.arcountydata.com. Signup fee is $200 plus $.10 per minute usage. For signup or information call 479-631-8054 or visit the website. **Other phones:** ; Tax Collector- 870-265-8040. **Property tax/Assessor**- same address as above. 870-265-8025.

Clark County

County Circuit Clerk, PO Box 576, Arkadelphia, AR 71923. RE & UCC recording phone-870-246-4281; fax-870-246-1419; hours: 8:30AM-4:30PM www.clarkcountyarkansas.org

All records in one index. Records indexed on a public use terminal back to 1985. Only the public may search. Copy fee $1.00 per page, $.25 self serve. Cert fee- $5.00 per doc includes copy fee. Payee- Clark County Circuit Clerk. **Online access**

to **Real Estate Recording, Deed records:** Access land records at http://etitlesearch.com. You can do a name search, fees involved. **Other phones:** Treasurer- 870-246-4361; Tax Collector- 870-246-2211. **Property tax/Assessor**- 870-246-4431.

Clay County Eastern District

County Circuit Clerk, 151 S Second St, Piggott, AR 72454. RE & UCC recording phone-870-598-2524; fax-870-598-1107; hours: 8AM-N, 1-4:30PM

Separate indices to search include real estate, judgments. Office will perform a UCC search but public must search other records themselves. UCC search per debtor name- $10.00. Copy fee $.25 per page. Cert fee- $5.00 per cert includes copies. Payee- Clay County Circuit Clerk. **Online access to Assessor, Property records:** Registration and logon is required to search assessor records at www.arcountydata.com. Signup fee is $200 plus $.10 per minute usage. For signup or information call 479-631-8054 or visit the website. **Other phones:** Treasurer- 870-598-3879; Elections- 870-598-2813; Vital Records- 870-598-2813. **Property tax/Assessor**- same address as above. 870-598-3870.

Clay County Western District

County Circuit Clerk, 800 W. Second St., Corning, AR 72422. 870-857-3271; fax-870-857-9201; hours: 8AM-N, 1PM-4:30PM

Separate indices to search include books, computer. Records indexed on a public use terminal back to 1/2005. Office will perform a UCC and Tax lien search but public must search other records themselves. Search fee $6.00. Copy fee $1.00 per page. Cert fee- $5.00 per cert plus copy fee. Payee- Clay County Circuit Clerk. **Other phones:** ; Tax Collector- 870-855-3011. **Property tax/Assessor**- same address as above. 870-857-3133.

Cleburne County

County Circuit Clerk, PO Box 543, Heber Springs, AR 72543. RE & UCC recording phone-501-362-8149; fax-501-362-4650; hours: 8:30AM-4:30PM

All records in one index. Office will perform a UCC search but public must search other records themselves. Search fee $6.00. Copy fee $.25 per page; fax fee $6.00 1st page, $2.00 each add'l. Cert fee- $1.00 per cert plus copy fee. Payee- Cleburne County Circuit Clerk. **Other phones:** ; Tax Collector- 501-362-8124. **Property tax/Assessor**- 501-362-8147.

Cleveland County

County Circuit Clerk, PO Box 368, Rison, AR 71665. RE & UCC recording phone-870-325-6521; fax-870-325-6144; hours: 8AM-4:30PM

Separate indices to search include deeds and mortgages. Records indexed on a public use terminal back to 1993. Office personnel or visitors may perform searches. Will not search tax liens. Copy fee $.25 per page. Cert fee- $8.00 1st pg, $3.00 each add'l plus copy fee. Payee- Cleveland County Circuit Clerk. **Other phones:** Treasurer- 870-325-6681; Elections- 870-325-6521; Tax Collector- 870-325-6681. **Property tax/Assessor**- 870-325-6695.

Columbia County

County Circuit Clerk, PO Box 327, Magnolia, AR 71753. RE & UCC recording phone-870-235-3700; fax-870-235-3786; hours: 8AM-4:30PM

All records in one index except for juvenile. Records indexed on a public use terminal back to 1997. Only the public may search. Copy fee $1.00 per page. Cert fee- $3.00 per page plus copy fee. Payee- Columbia County Circuit Clerk. **Other phones:** Treasurer- 870-235-3704; Appraiser/Auditor- 870-234-4380; Elections- 870-235-3774; Vital Records- Little Rock; Tax Collector- 870-235-4171. **Property tax/Assessor**- County Annex, South Court Sq, Magnolia, AR 71753; 870-234-4380.

Conway County

County Circuit Clerk, 115 S. Moose St; County Courthouse, Rm 206, Morrilton, AR 72110. RE & UCC recording phone-501-354-9617; fax-501-354-9612; hours: 8AM-5PM

Separate indices to search include deeds, Mtgs, misc, oil and gas, UCCs. Records indexed on a public use terminal back to 1994. Only the public may search. Copy fee $1.00 per page. Cert fee- $5.00 per doc plus copy fee. Payee- Conway County Circuit Clerk. **Other phones:** Treasurer- 501-354-9623; Elections- 501-354-9621; Tax Collector- 501-354-9600. **Property tax/Assessor**- 501-354-9622.

Craighead County Eastern District

County Circuit Clerk, PO Box 537, Lake City, AR 72437. RE & UCC recording phone-870-237-4342; fax-870-237-8174; hours: 8AM-5PM

Separate indices to search include deeds, mtgs. Records indexed on a public use terminal back to 1979. Office will perform a UCC and Tax lien search but public must search other records themselves. Search fee $6.00. Copy fee $.25 per page. Cert fee- $3.00 per doc plus copy fee. Payee- Craighead County Circuit Clerk. **Online access to Real Estate Recording, Deed, Property, Personal Property records:** Access recording office land data at www.etitlesearch.com; registration required, fee based on usage. Also, search property and personal property data free at www.countyservice.net.

Craighead County Western District

County Circuit Clerk, PO Box 120, Jonesboro, AR 72401. 870-933-4530; fax-870-933-4534; hours: 8AM-5PM www.craigheadcounty.org

All records in one index. General index search fee $6.00 per page. Will search real estate records. Will not search tax liens. Copy fee $.25 per page. Cert fee- $3.00 per doc includes copy fee. Payee- Craighead County Circuit Clerk. **Online access to Assessor, Property, Personal Property, Assessor, Real Estate records:** Registration and logon is required to search assessor records at www.arcountydata.com. Signup fee is $200 plus $.10 per minute usage. For signup or information call 479-631-8054 or visit the website. Also, access land records at http://etitlesearch.com. You can do a name search; choose from $100.00 monthly subscription or per click account. Also, search personal property, real estate, and assessor records free at www.cratax.countyservice.net. **Other phones:** Treasurer- 870-933-4549; Tax Collector- 870-933-4540. **Property tax/Assessor**- 511 Union St, Jonesboro, AR 72401; 870-933-4570.

Crawford County

County Circuit Clerk, 300 Main; Courthouse - Rm 22, Van Buren, AR 72956-5799. RE & UCC recording phone-479-474-1821; fax-479-471-0622; hours: 8AM-5PM www.ecourtstor.com

Separate indices to search include computer index and non-computer index. Records indexed on a public use terminal back to 1992. Office personnel or visitors may perform searches. Search fee $6.00 if search finds record. Copy fee $1.00 per page by fax, $.50 per page if picked up in person. Cert fee- $2.00 per doc plus copy fee. Payee- Crawford County Circuit Clerk. **Online access to Real Estate Recording, Deed records:** Land records are at http://etitlesearch.com. You can do a name search; choose from $30.00 monthly subscription or per click account. **Other phones:** Treasurer- 479-474-6641; Vital Records- 501-661-2000; Tax Collector- 479-474-1111. **Property tax/Assessor**- 479-471-1751.

Crittenden County

County Circuit Clerk, 100 Court St., Marion, AR 72364. RE & UCC recording phone-870-739-3248; fax-870-739-3072; hours: 8AM-4:30PM

All records in one index. Records indexed on computer back to 1998. Office will perform a

UCC search but public must search other records themselves. UCC search per debtor name- $6.00. Separate tax lien search- $6.00 per debtor. Copy fee $.25 per page. Cert fee- $3.00 per doc plus copy fee. Payee- Crittenden County Circuit Clerk. **Online access to Assessor, Property records:** Registration and logon is required to search assessor records at www.arcountydata.com. Signup fee is $200 plus $.10 per minute usage. For signup or information call 479-631-8054 or visit the website. **Other phones:** Treasurer- 870-739-4112; Appraiser/Auditor- 870-739-3606; Elections- 870-739-4434. **Property tax/Assessor-** 870-739-3606.

Cross County

County Circuit Clerk, 705 E Union; Rm 9, Wynne, AR 72396. RE & UCC recording phone-870-238-5720; fax-870-238-5739; hours: 8AM-4PM
Index: Books, computer. Records indexed on a public use terminal back to 1992. Office will perform a UCC search but public must search other records themselves. Search fee $6.00. Copy fee $.25 per page. RE or tax lien copy- $.25 per page. Cert fee- $3.00 per page includes copy fee. Payee- Cross County Circuit Clerk. **Other phones:** Treasurer- 870-238-5725; Appraiser/Auditor- 870-238-5715; Elections- 870-238-5735; Vital Records- 870-238-5735; Tax Collector- 870-238-5710. **Property tax/Assessor-** 705 E. Union #5715, Wynne, AR 72396; 870-238-5715.

Dallas County

County Circuit Clerk, 206 W 3rd St; Courthouse, Fordyce, AR 71742-3299. RE & UCC recording phone-870-352-2307; fax-870-352-7179; hours: 8:30AM-4:30PM
All records in one index. Records indexed on computer back to 8/26/1997. Office will perform a UCC search but public must search other records themselves. Search fee $6.00 per name. Copy fee $.50 per page. Cert fee- $5.00 per doc plus copy fee. Payee- Dallas County Circuit Clerk. **Online access to Assessor, Property records:** Registration and logon is required to search assessor records at www.arcountydata.com. Signup fee is $200 plus $.10 per minute usage. For signup or information call 479-631-8054 or visit the website. **Other phones:** Treasurer- 870-352-2333; Appraiser/Auditor- 870-352-3342; Elections- 870-352-3965; Vital Records- 870-352-7688; Tax Collector- 870-352-5181. **Property tax/Assessor-** same address as above. 870-352-7983.

Desha County

County Circuit Clerk, PO Box 309, Arkansas City, AR 71630. 870-877-2411; fax-870-877-3407; 8AM-4PM
Record index not computerized. Only the office personnel may search. Search fee $6.00 per name. Copy fee $.50 per page. Cert fee- $3.00 per doc plus copy fee. Payee- Circuit Clerk of Desha County. **Online access to Real Estate, Recording, Assessor, Property records:** Access to recorder records is by subscription at www.recordsusa.com. Credit card, username and password is required; Visit the website or call Lisa at 601-264-7701 for information. Also, registration and logon is required to search assessor records at www.arcountydata.com. Signup fee is $200 plus $.10 per minute usage. For signup or information call 479-631-8054 or visit the website. **Other phones:** ; Tax Collector- 870-877-2353. **Property tax/Assessor-** 870-877-2431.

Drew County

County Circuit Clerk, 210 S. Main, Monticello, AR 71655. RE & UCC recording phone-870-460-6250; fax-870-460-6246; hours: 8AM-4:30PM
All records in one index. Records indexed on a public use terminal back to 2001. Only the public may search. Copy fee $.50 per page, $.25 self serve. Cert fee- $2.50 per doc plus copy fee. Payee- Drew County Circuit Clerk. **Online access to Real Estate, Deed, Circuit Court, Lien, Judgment records:** Access county land and court records by

subscription at www.recordsusa.com/Arkansas/drewCnAr.htm or phone 800-932-5029 or 888-85-IMAGE. Monthly packages are $49.95 or $79.90. **Other phones:** Treasurer- 870-460-6225; Elections- 870-460-6220; Tax Collector- 870-460-6225. **Property tax/Assessor-** same address as above. 870-460-6225.

Faulkner County

Faulkner County Circuit Clerk, PO Box 9, Conway, AR 72033. RE & UCC recording phone-501-450-4911; fax- 501-450-4948; hours: 8AM-4:30PM www.faulknercc.org
Records indexed on a public use terminal back to 6/1989. Office will perform a UCC search but public must search other records themselves. Search fee $6.00. Copy fee $6.00 per name plus $2.00 each add'l page to maximum of $100.00. RE or tax lien copy- $.25 per copy. Cert fee- $3.00 per doc, plus copy fee. Payee- Faulkner County Circuit Clerk. **Online access to Assessor, Property, Personal Property records:** Registration and logon is required to search assessor records at www.arcountydata.com. Signup fee is $200 plus $.10 per minute usage. For signup or information call 479-631-8054 or visit the website. Also, search property and personal property data free at www.countyservice.net. **Other phones:** Treasurer- 501-450-4902; Elections- 501-450-4909; Tax Collector- 501-450-4921. **Property tax/Assessor-** 501-450-4905.

Franklin County
Charleston District

County Circuit Clerk, 607 E Main St, Charleston, AR 72933. RE & UCC recording phone-479-965-7332; fax-479-965-9322; hours: 8AM-N, 12:30-4:30PM
Will not search real estate records. Will not search UCC records or tax liens. Copy fee $.25 per page. Cert fee- $2.00 per doc plus copy fee. Payee- Franklin County Circuit Clerk. **Property tax/Assessor-** 479-965-7797.

Franklin County Ozark District

County Circuit Clerk, PO Box 1112, Ozark, AR 72949. 479-667-3818; fax-479-667-5174; 8AM-4:30PM
All records in one index. Only the public may search. Copy fee $.25 per page. Cert fee- $5.00 per instrument plus copy fee. Payee- Franklin County Circuit Clerk. **Other phones:** Vital Records- 479-965-2129. **Property tax/Assessor-** PO Box152, Ozark, AR 72949; 479-667-2415.

Fulton County

County Circuit Clerk, PO Box 219, Salem, AR 72576. 870-895-3310; fax-870-895-3383; hours: 8AM-4:30PM
Records indexed on computer name search since 2000. Office will perform a UCC search but public must search other records themselves. Search fee $6.00 per name. Copy fee $.20 per page. Cert fee- No fee for certification but must pay for copies. Payee- Fulton County Circuit Clerk. **Online access to Assessor, Property records:** Registration and logon is required to search assessor records at www.arcountydata.com. Signup fee is $200 plus $.10 per minute usage. For signup or information call 479-631-8054 or visit the website. **Other phones:** Treasurer- 870-895-3522; Vital Records- 501-661-2336; Tax Collector- 870-895-2547. **Property tax/Assessor-** 870-895-3592.

Garland County

County Circuit Clerk, Courthouse - Rm207; Quachita & Hawthorn Sts, Hot Springs, AR 71901. RE & UCC recording phone-501-622-3630; fax-501-609-9043; hours: 8AM-5PM
Only the public may search. Copy fee $.25 per page. Cert fee- $.50 per cert plus copy fee. Payee- Garland County Circuit Clerk. **Online access to Sex Offender records:** Access to the sheriff's sex offender list is free at www.hsnp.com/megan/garland_index.cgi. No recording records available through Garland County; reportedly available via a private provider County Professional Solicitations, PO Box 55, Brenton,

AR 72015. **Other phones:** Treasurer- 501-622-3650; Elections- 501-622-3610; Tax Collector- 501-622-3710. **Property tax/Assessor-** 501-622-3730.

Grant County

County Circuit Clerk, 101 W. Center, Rm 106; Courthouse, Sheridan, AR 72150. RE & UCC recording phone-870-942-2631; fax-870-942-3564; hours: 8AM-4:30PM
Records indexed on a public use terminal back to 2001. Only the public may search. Copy fee $.25 per page. Cert fee- $5.00 per page includes copy fee. Payee- Grant County Circuit Clerk. **Online access to Assessor, Property records:** Registration and logon is required to search assessor records at www.arcountydata.com. Signup fee is $200 plus $.10 per minute usage. For signup or information call 479-631-8054 or visit the website. **Other phones:** Treasurer- 870-942-2031; Elections- 870-942-4363; Tax Collector- 870-942-4315. **Property tax/Assessor-** same address as above. 870-942-3711.

Greene County

County Circuit Clerk, 320 W. Court St, Rm 124, Paragould, AR 72450. RE & UCC recording phone-870-239-6330; fax-870-239-3550; 8AM-4:30PM
All records in one index. Records indexed on a public use terminal back to 1982, Deeds,1987, Mtg. Office personnel or visitors may perform searches. Search fee $6.00. Will not search real estate records. Copy fee $.50 per page. Tax lien copy- $.20 per page. Cert fee- $3.00 per doc plus copy fee. Payee- Greene County Circuit Clerk. **Online access to Assessor, Property records:** Registration and logon is required to search assessor records at www.arcountydata.com. Signup fee is $200 plus $.10 per minute usage. For signup or information call 479-631-8054 or visit the website. **Other phones:** Treasurer- 870-239-6304; Elections- 870-239-6311. **Property tax/Assessor-** same address as above. 870-239-6303.

Hempstead County

County Circuit Clerk, PO Box 1420, Hope, AR 71802. RE & UCC recording phone-870-777-2384; fax-870-777-7827; hours: 8AM-4PM
Index: Books, computer. Records indexed on a public use terminal back to 1993. Office will perform a UCC search but public must search other records themselves. Search fee $6.00. Copy fee $1.00 per page, self serve $.25 per page. Cert fee- $5.00 per page includes copy fee. Payee- Hempstead County Circuit Clerk. **Other phones:** Treasurer- 870-777-3141; Appraiser/Auditor- 870-777-6190; Elections- 870-777-2241; Vital Records- 501-661-2000; Tax Collector- 870-777-4103. **Property tax/Assessor-** same address as above. 870-777-6190.

Hot Spring County

Circuit Clerk, PO Box 1220, Malvern, AR 72104. 501-332-2281; hours: 8AM-4:30PM
Records indexed on computer back to 1994. Office will perform a UCC search but public must search other records themselves. Search fee $5.00. Copy fee $.50 per page. Cert fee- $5.00 per doc plus copy fee. Payee- Hot Spring County Circuit Clerk. **Other phones:** Treasurer- 501-337-7411; Elections- 501-332-2291; Tax Collector- 501-332-7211. **Property tax/Assessor-** same address as above. 501-332-2461.

Howard County

County Circuit Clerk, 421 N. Main St; Rm 7, Nashville, AR 71852. RE & UCC recording phone-870-845-7506; hours: 8AM-4:30PM
All records in one index. Office will perform a UCC or tax lien search but public must search other records themselves. UCC search per debtor name- $6.00. Copy fee $.50 per page; UCC copy $1.00. Cert fee- $2.00 plus $.50 per page. Payee- Howard County Circuit Clerk. **Online access to Assessor, Property records:** Registration and logon is

required to search assessor records at www.arcountydata.com. Signup fee is $200 plus $.10 per minute usage. For signup or information call 479-631-8054 or visit the website. **Other phones:** Treasurer- 870-845-7504; Elections- 870-845-7503. **Property tax/Assessor-** 421 N. Main St #4, Nashville, AR 71852; 870-845-7511.

Independence County

County Circuit Clerk, PO Box 2155, Batesville, AR 72503. RE & UCC recording phone-870-793-8865; fax-870-793-8888; hours: 8AM-4:30PM
All records in one index. Records indexed on computer, liens and UCC's back to 1980; deeds back to 1967; deed of trust back to March, 1992. Office will perform a UCC search but public must search other records themselves. UCC search per debtor name- $6.00. Copy fee $.25 per page. Cert fee- $3.00 per instrument plus copy fee. Payee-Independence County Circuit Clerk. **Online access to Real Estate Recording, Deed records:** Land records are at http://etitlesearch.com. You can do a name search; choose from $200.00 monthly subscription or per click account. **Other phones:** Treasurer- 870-793-8899. **Property tax/Assessor-** 870-793-8842.

Izard County

County Circuit Clerk, PO Box 95, Melbourne, AR 72556. RE & UCC recording phone-870-368-4316; fax-870-368-4748; hours: 8:30AM-4:30PM
All records in one index. Records indexed on computer back to 2000. Office personnel or visitors may perform searches. Search fee $6.00 per name. Copy fee $.20 per page. Cert fee- $5.00 per cert includes copy fee. Payee- Izard County Circuit Clerk. **Online access to Assessor, Property records:** Registration and logon is required to search assessor records at www.arcountydata.com. Signup fee is $200 plus $.10 per minute usage. For signup or information call 479-631-8054 or visit the website. **Other phones:** Treasurer- 870-368-7247; Elections-870-368-4316; Vital Records- 501-661-2726; Tax Collector- 870-368-4394. **Property tax/Assessor-** 870-368-7810.

Jackson County

County Circuit Clerk, 208 Main St; Courthouse, Newport, AR 72112. 870-523-7423, R/E recording phone-870-523-3826; fax-870-523-3682; hours: 8AM-4:30PM
Only the public may search. Copy fee $.25 per page. Cert fee- $3.00 per doc plus copy fee. Payee-Jackson County Circuit Clerk. **Other phones:** ; Tax Collector- 870-523-7401. **Property tax/Assessor-** 870-523-7410.

Jefferson County

County Circuit Clerk, PO Box 7433, Pine Bluff, AR 71611. 870-541-5309, R/E recording phone-870-541-5360, UCC recording phone-870-541-5304; fax-none; hours: 8:30AM-5PM
Only the public may search. Copy fee $.50; if real estate record- $2.00 1st 2 pages, $3.00 next 3, then $.25 per page. Cert fee- $.50 per doc plus copy fee. Payee- Jefferson County Circuit Clerk. **Online access to Property, Personal Property records:** Search property and personal property data free at www.countyservice.net. **Other phones:** ; Tax Collector- 870-541-5302. **Property tax/Assessor-** 870-541-5338.

Johnson County

County Circuit Clerk, PO Box 189, Clarksville, AR 72830-0189. RE & UCC recording phone-479-754-2977; fax-479-754-4235; hours: 8AM-4:30PM
Only the public may search. Copy fee $.50 per page. Cert fee- $1.00 per page. Payee- Johnson County Circuit Clerk. **Online access to Assessor, Property records:** Registration and logon is required to search all participating counties at www.arcountydata.com. Signup fee is $200 minimum plus $.10 per minute usage. For signup or information

call 479-631-8054 or visit www.arcountydata.com. **Other phones:** Appraiser/Auditor- 479-754-8839; Tax Collector- 479-754-3056. **Property tax/Assessor-** 479-754-8839.

Lafayette County

County Circuit Clerk, 3 Courthouse Sq; Third & Spruce, Lewisville, AR 71845. RE & UCC recording phone-870-921-4878; fax-870-421-4879; hours: 8AM-4:30PM
Index: Books, computer. Records indexed on a public use terminal back to 2001. Office will perform a UCC search but public must search other records themselves. Search fee $6.00. Copy fee $.50 per page. Cert fee- $3.00 + $.50 per page. Payee- Lafayette County Circuit Clerk. **Other phones:** Treasurer- 870-921-4755; Tax Collector- 870-921-4755. **Property tax/Assessor-** #7 Courthouse Sq, Lewisville, AR 71845; 870-921-4808.

Lawrence County

County Circuit Clerk, PO Box 581, Walnut Ridge, AR 72476. RE & UCC recording phone-870-886-1112; fax-870-886-1128; hours: 8AM-4:30PM
Separate indices to search include books, misc, deeds, mtgs, Lis Pendens. Records indexed on a public use terminal back to 1990. Office will perform a UCC search but public must search other records themselves. Search fee $6.00. Copy fee $.50 per page. Cert fee- $3.00 per doc plus copy fee. Payee- Lawrence County Circuit Clerk. **Other phones:** Treasurer- 870-886-1116; Elections-870-866-1111; Tax Collector- 870-886-1114. **Property tax/Assessor-** 870-886-1135.

Lee County

County Circuit Clerk, 15 E. Chestnut St; Courthouse, Marianna, AR 72360. RE & UCC recording phone-870-295-7710; fax-870-295-7712; 8:30AM-4:30PM
Separate indices to search include deeds, judgments, mortgages. Records indexed on a public use terminal back to 2002. Office will perform a UCC search (5 years) but public must search other records themselves. UCC search per debtor name- $6.00. Copy fee $.25 per page. Cert fee- $2.50 per doc plus copy fee. Payee- Lee County Circuit Clerk. **Online access to Assessor, Property records:** Registration and logon is required to search assessor records at www.arcountydata.com. Signup fee is $200 plus $.10 per minute usage. For signup or information call 479-631-8054 or visit the website. **Other phones:** Treasurer- 870-295-5296; Tax Collector- 870-295-7752. **Property tax/Assessor-** same address as above. 870-295-7750.

Lincoln County

County Circuit Clerk, 300 S. Drew St, Star City, AR 71667. RE & UCC recording phone-870-628-3154; fax-870-628-5546; hours: 8AM-5PM
Separate indices to search include deeds, mortgages together; all others in separate books. Record index not computerized. Office will perform a UCC search but public must search other records themselves. UCC search per debtor name- $6.00. Copy fee $.50 per page. Cert fee- $3.00 per doc plus copy fee. Payee- Lincoln County Circuit Clerk. **Other phones:** Treasurer- 870-628-4816; Elections- 870-628-5114; Tax Collector- 870-628-5320. **Property tax/Assessor-** same address as above. 870-628-4401.

Little River County

County Circuit Clerk, PO Box 575, Ashdown, AR 71822-0575. RE & UCC recording phone-870-898-7211; fax-870-898-4783; hours: 8AM-4:30PM
Separate indices to search include prior to 2003, direct and indirect indexes for real estate, UCC records are in cards and in a separate index book. Records indexed on a public use terminal back to 2003. Office will perform a tax search (5 year only) but public must search other records themselves. Search fee $6.00 per name. Copy fee $.50 per page. Cert fee- $5.00 per doc plus copy

fee. Payee- Little River County Circuit Clerk. **Other phones:** Treasurer- 870-898-7215; Elections-870-898-7210. **Property tax/Assessor-** 351 N 2nd #3, Ashdown, AR 71822; 870-898-7204.

Logan County Northern District

County Circuit Clerk, 25 W. Walnut, Courthouse, Paris, AR 72855. 479-963-2164, R/E recording phone-479-963-2618; fax-479-963-3304; hours: 8AM-4:30PM
All records in one index. Records indexed on a public use terminal back to 1991. Only the public may search. Copy fee $.25 per page. Cert fee-$5.00 per doc plus copy fee. Payee- Logan County Circuit Clerk. **Online access to Assessor, Property records:** Registration and logon is required to search assessor records at www.arcountydata.com. Signup fee is $200 plus $.10 per minute usage. For signup or information call 479-631-8054 or visit the website. **Other phones:** ; Tax Collector- 479-963-2038. **Property tax/Assessor-** same address as above. 479-963-2716.

Logan County Southern District

County Circuit Clerk, 366 N Broadway #2; Courthouse, Booneville, AR 72927. 479-675-2894; fax-479-675-0577; hours: 8AM-N, 1-4:30PM
All records in one index. Records indexed on a public use terminal back to 1998. Office personnel or visitors may perform searches. Search fee $6.00 per name. Copy fee $.25 per page. Cert fee- $5.00 per doc plus copy fee. Payee- Logan County Circuit Clerk. **Online access to Assessor, Property records:** Registration and logon is required to search assessor records at www.arcountydata.com. Signup fee is $200 plus $.10 per minute usage. For signup or information call 479-631-8054 or visit the website. **Other phones:** ; Tax Collector- 479-675-5131. **Property tax/Assessor-** 479-675-3942.

Lonoke County

County Circuit Clerk, PO Box 219, Lonoke, AR 72086-0219. RE & UCC recording phone-501-676-2316; hours: 8AM-4:30PM
Office will perform a UCC search but public must search other records themselves. UCC search per debtor name- $6.00. Copy fee $.25 per page. Cert fee- $6.00 per doc plus copy fee. Payee- Lonoke County Circuit Clerk. **Online access to Assessor, Property records:** Registration and logon is required to search assessor records at www.arcountydata.com. Signup fee is $200 plus $.10 per minute usage. For signup or information call 479-631-8054 or visit the website. **Property tax/Assessor-** 501-676-6938.

Madison County

County Circuit Clerk, PO Box 626, Huntsville, AR 72740. RE & UCC recording phone-479-738-2215; fax-479-738-1544; hours: 8AM-4:30PM
Index: All recorded documents have a separate index. Will search UCC real estate records. Will search UCC records, but not tax liens. UCC search per debtor name- $10.00. Copy fee $.25 per page. Cert fee- $2.00 per doc includes free copies. Payee-Madison County Circuit Clerk. **Other phones:** Treasurer- 479-738-6514; Elections- 479-738-2747; Tax Collector- 479-738-6673. **Property tax/Assessor-** 479-738-2325.

Marion County

County Circuit Clerk, PO Box 385, Yellville, AR 72687. RE & UCC recording phone-870-449-6226; fax-870-449-4979; hours: 8AM-4:30PM
Separate indices to search include real estate in computer since 1998, everything else in individual books. Records indexed on a public use terminal back to 1998 (real estate only). Office will perform a UCC search but public must search other records themselves. UCC search per debtor name- $6.00. Copy fee $.25 per page. Cert fee- $5.00 plus $.25 per page. Payee- Marion County Circuit Clerk. **Other phones:** Treasurer- 870-449-6331; Tax Collector- 870-449-6253. **Property tax/Assessor-** 870-449-4113.

Miller County

County Circuit Clerk, 412 Laurel St.; County Courthouse, #109, Texarkana, AR 71854. 870-774-4501; fax-870-772-5293; hours: 8AM-4:30PM
Separate indices to search. Office personnel or visitors may perform searches. UCC search per debtor name- $8.00. Do not do lien search or mortgage searches. Copy fee $1.00 per page. Cert fee- $3.50 per doc plus copy fee. Payee- Miller County Circuit Clerk. **Online access to Land, Deed records:** Access to recorder land records and images are via a private company at www.recordsusa.com/Arkansas/MillerCnAr.htm. Subscription required; basic monthly package including court dockets is $49.95. Call 888-85-IMAGE or visit the website. **Other phones:** ; Tax Collector- 870-772-0003. **Property tax/Assessor-** 870-772-1502.

Mississippi County Chickasawba District

County Circuit Clerk, PO Box 1498, Blytheville, AR 72316-1498. 870-762-2332; fax-870-762-8148; hours: 9AM-4:30PM
Separate indices to search include COT Indexes and Computer. Records indexed on a public use terminal back to 1991. Office will perform a UCC search but public must search other records themselves. Search fee $6.00. Copy fee $.25 per page. Cert fee- $3.00 per doc plus copy fee. Payee- Mississippi County Circuit Clerk. **Other phones:** ; Tax Collector- 870-762-2152. **Property tax/Assessor-** 870-763-6860.

Mississippi County Osceola District

County Circuit Clerk, PO Box 466, Osceola, AR 72370. 870-563-6471; fax-870-563-5063; hours: 9AM-4:30PM
All records in one index. Record index not computerized. Only the public may search. Copy fee $.25 per page. Cert fee- $3.00 per doc plus copy fee. Payee- Mississippi County Circuit Clerk. **Other phones:** ; Tax Collector- 870-762-2152. **Property tax/Assessor-** 870-563-2682.

Monroe County

County Circuit Clerk, 123 Madison St, Clarendon, AR 72029. RE & UCC recording phone-870-747-3615; fax-870-747-3710; hours: 8AM-4:30PM
Separate indices to search include books, computer. Real estate records indexed on computer back to 3/1/2005. Office will perform a UCC search but public must search other records themselves. UCC search per debtor name- $6.00. Copy fee $.25 per page. Cert fee- $2.50 per doc includes copies. Payee- Monroe County Circuit Clerk. **Other phones:** Treasurer- 870-747-3722; Elections- 870-747-3632; Tax Collector- 870-747-3819. **Property tax/Assessor-** same address as above. 870-747-3847.

Montgomery County

County Circuit Clerk, PO Box 369, Mount Ida, AR 71957-0369. 870-867-3521; fax-870-867-2177; hours: 8AM-4:30PM
All records in one index. Record index not computerized. Only the public may search. Copy fee $.50 per page. RE record copy- $1.00 if from vault. Cert fee- $5.00 per doc includes copy fee. Payee- Montgomery County Circuit Clerk. **Other phones:** Treasurer- 870-867-3411; Tax Collector- 870-867-3155. **Property tax/Assessor-** 870-867-3271.

Nevada County

County Circuit Clerk, PO Box 204, Prescott, AR 71857. RE & UCC recording phone-870-887-2511; fax-870-887-1911; hours: 8AM-5PM
Record index not computerized. Office personnel or visitors may perform searches. Search fee $6.00 per name. Copy fee $.25 per page. Cert fee- $2.00 per doc plus copy fee. Payee- Nevada County Circuit Clerk. **Other phones:** Treasurer- 870-887-

2811; Tax Collector- 870-887-2811. **Property tax/Assessor-** same address as above. 870-887-3410.

Newton County

County Circuit Clerk, PO Box 410, Jasper, AR 72641. 870-446-5125; fax-870-446-5755; hours: 8AM-4:30PM
All records in one index. Only the public may search. Search fee $6.00 per hour. Copy fee $.25 per page. Cert fee- $5.00 per doc plus copy fee. Payee- Newton County Circuit Clerk. **Online access to Assessor, Property records:** Registration and logon is required to search assessor records at www.arcountydata.com. Signup fee is $200 plus $.10 per minute usage. For signup or information call 479-631-8054 or visit the website. **Other phones:** Treasurer- 870-446-2936; Tax Collector- 870-446-2936. **Property tax/Assessor-** PO Box 45, Jasper, AR 72641; 870-446-2937.

Ouachita County

County Circuit Clerk, PO Box 667, Camden, AR 71701. RE & UCC recording phone-870-837-2230; fax-870-837-2252; hours: 8AM-4:30PM
All records in one index since 1999. Office will perform a UCC search but public must search other records themselves. UCC search per debtor name- $10.00. Copy fee $.50 per page. Cert fee- $2.50 per doc plus copy fee. Payee- Ouachita County Circuit Clerk. **Other phones:** Treasurer- 870-837-2250; Appraiser/Auditor- 870-837-2240; Elections- 870-837-2220; Vital Records- 501-661-2336. **Property tax/Assessor-** 145 Jefferson St, Camden, AR 71701; 870-837-2240.

Perry County

County Circuit Clerk, PO Box 358, Perryville, AR 72126. 501-889-5126; fax-501-889-5759; hours: 8AM-4:30PM
All records in one index. Records indexed on computer back to 7/1997. Only the public may search. Copy fee $1.00 per page. Cert fee- $5.00 per doc plus copy fee. Payee- Perry County Circuit Clerk. **Other phones:** Treasurer- 501-889-5285; Tax Collector- 501-889-2710. **Property tax/Assessor-** 501-889-2865.

Phillips County

County Circuit Clerk, 620 Cherry St.; Courthouse, #206, Helena, AR 72342. RE & UCC recording phone-870-338-5515; fax-870-338-5513; hours: 8AM-4:30PM
Records indexed on computer. Only the public may search. Copy fee $.25 per page. Cert fee- $3.00 per page plus copy fee. Payee- Phillips County Circuit Clerk. **Online access to Real Estate Recording records:** Access land records at http://etitlesearch.com. You can do a name search; choose from $25.00 monthly subscription or per-click account. **Other phones:** Treasurer- 870-338-5510; Tax Collector- 870-338-5580. **Property tax/Assessor-** 870-338-5535.

Pike County

County Circuit Clerk, PO Box 219, Murfreesboro, AR 71958. RE & UCC recording phone-870-285-2231; fax-870-285-3281; hours: 8AM-4:30PM
All records in one index. Only the public may search. Copy fee $.50 per page. Cert fee- $5.00 per doc plus copy fee. Payee- Pike County Circuit Clerk. **Online access to Assessor, Property records:** Registration and logon is required to search assessor records at www.arcountydata.com. Signup fee is $200 plus $.10 per minute usage. For signup or information call 479-631-8054 or visit the website. **Other phones:** Treasurer- 870-285-2422; Tax Collector- 870-285-3121; County Clerk -870-285-2743. **Property tax/Assessor-** PO Box 356, Murfreesboro, AR 71958; 870-285-3121.

Poinsett County

County Circuit Clerk, PO Box 46, Harrisburg, AR 72432-0046. 870-578-4420; fax-870-578-4427; hours: 8:30AM-4:30PM
Index: Books, computer. Records indexed on a public use terminal back to 1998. Office will perform a UCC and Tax lien search but public must search other records themselves. Search fee $6.00. Copy fee $.25 per page. Cert fee- $2.00 per doc plus copy fee. Payee- Poinsett County Circuit Clerk. **Online access to Assessor, Property records:** Registration and logon is required to search assessor records at www.arcountydata.com. Signup fee is $200 plus $.10 per minute usage. For signup or information call 479-631-8054 or visit the website. **Other phones:** Treasurer- 870-578-4405; Tax Collector- 870-578-4405. **Property tax/Assessor-** same address as above. 870-578-4430.

Polk County

Circuit Clerk, 507 Church St; Courthouse, Mena, AR 71953. RE & UCC recording phone-479-394-8100; fax-479-394-8170; hours: 8AM-4:30PM
Separate indices to search include deed, mortgages, liens, judgments, UCCs. Records indexed on a public use terminal back to 7/2002. Office will perfom a UCC or separate fed tax lien search but public must search other records themselves. Search fee $6.00 per name. Copy fee $5.00 per UCC. RE record copy- $.50 per page. Tax lien copy- $.25 per page. Cert fee- $2.00 per doc includes copy fee. Payee- Polk County Circuit Clerk. **Online access to Real Estate, Deed, Circuit Court, Lien, Judgment records:** Access to county land and court records is by subscription; visit www.recordsusa.com/Arkansas/PolkCnAr.htm or phone 800-932-5029 or 888-85-IMAGE. Monthly packages are $49.95 or $79.90 per month. **Other phones:** Treasurer- 479-394-8150; Appraiser/Auditor- 479-394-8121; Elections- 479-394-8123; Tax Collector- 479-394-8150. **Property tax/Assessor-** same address as above. 479-394-8121.

Pope County

Circuit Clerk, 100 W. Main, 3rd Fl; County Courthouse, Russellville, AR 72801. Main phone & R/E recording-479-968-7499, UCC recording phone-479-968-6989; fax-none; hours: 8AM-5PM
Will not search real estate records. Will search UCC and criminal records, but not tax liens. UCC search per debtor name- $6.00. Copy fee $.25 per page. Cert fee- $3.00 per doc plus copy fee. Payee- Pope County Circuit Clerk. **Online access to Assessor, Property, Real Estate, Deed, Personal Property records:** Registration and logon is required to search assessor records at www.arcountydata.com. Signup fee is $200 plus $.10 per minute usage. For signup or information call 479-631-8054 or visit the website. Also, free access to assessor data is at www.countyservice.net/poptax.html. Last name and zip code are required. Also, search property and personal property data free at www.countyservice.net. Also, access recording office land data at www.etitlesearch.com; registration required, fee based on usage. **Other phones:** Treasurer- 479-968-7016; Tax Collector- 479-968-7016. **Property tax/Assessor-** 100 W Main, Russellville, AR 72801; 479-968-7418.

Prairie County Northern District

County Circuit Clerk, PO Box 1011, Des Arc, AR 72040. 870-256-4434; fax-870-256-4434; hours: 8AM-4:30PM
Separate indices to search include Deed and mortgage indexes. Will not search real estate records. Will search UCC records, but not tax liens. UCC search per debtor name- $6.00. Copy fee $1.00 per page. Cert fee- $5.00 per doc plus copy fee. Payee- Prairie County Circuit Clerk. **Online access to Real Estate Recording, Deed records:** Access recording office land data at www.etitlesearch.com; registration required, fee based on usage. **Other phones:** Treasurer-

870-256-4786; Tax Collector- 870-256-4764. **Property tax/Assessor-** 870-256-4692.

Prairie County Southern District

County Circuit Clerk, PO Box 283, De Valls Bluff, AR 72041-0283. RE & UCC recording phone-870-998-2314; fax-870-998-2314; hours: 8AM-N, 1-4:30PM Separate indices to search. Only the public may search. Copy fee $.25 per page. Cert fee- $5.00 per doc plus copy fee. Payee- Prairie County Circuit Clerk. **Online access to Real Estate Recording records:** Access recording office land data at www.etitlesearch.com; registration required, fee based on usage. **Other phones:** Treasurer- 870-256-4786; Tax Collector- 870-256-4764. **Property tax/Assessor-** 870-256-4692.

Pulaski County

County Circuit Clerk, 401 W. Markham St, Rm S216, Little Rock, AR 72201. 501-340-8433; fax-501-340-8889; hours: 8:30AM-4:30PM
Only the public may search. Copy fee $1.00 per page. Cert fee- $2.50 per doc plus copy fee. Payee-Pulaski County Circuit Clerk. **Online access to Assessor, Property, Personal Property, Real Estate Recording, Deed records:** Registration and logon is required to search assessor records at www.arcountydata.com. Signup fee is $200 plus $.10 per minute usage. For signup or information call 479-631-8054 or visit the website. Also, search the personal property and real estate database for free at www.pultax.countyservice.net. For personal property, click on "Access Vehicles." Name and zip code required. Also, access recording office land data at www.etitlesearch.com; registration required, fee based on usage. **Other phones:** Treasurer- 501-340-8345; Elections- 501-340-8683 (Vote); Tax Collector- 501-340-8345. **Property tax/Assessor-** 501-340-6170.

Randolph County

County Circuit Clerk, 107 W. Broadway, Pocahontas, AR 72455. RE & UCC recording phone-870-892-5522; fax-870-892-8794; hours: 8AM-4:30PM
Records indexed on a public use terminal back to 1836. Office will perform a UCC search but public must search other records themselves. Search fee $6.00. Copy fee $.25; real estate $.50 per page. Cert fee- $2.00 per cert plus copy fee. Payee-Randolph County Circuit Clerk. **Online access to Property, Personal Property records:** Also, search property and personal property data free at www.countyservice.net. **Other phones:** Treasurer- 870-892-5238; Elections- 870-892-5822; Tax Collector- 870-892-5491. **Property tax/Assessor-** same address as above. 870-892-3200.

Saline County

County Circuit Clerk, 200 N. Main St. #113, Benton, AR 72018. 501-303-5615; fax-501-303-5675; hours: 8AM-4:30PM www.salinecounty.org
Separate indices to search include 1991 to present on computer; prior separate books for deeds, mortgages, etc. Records indexed on a public use terminal back to 1991. Office will perform a UCC search but public must search other records themselves. UCC search per debtor name- $6.00. Copy fee $.25 per page. Cert fee- $3.00 per doc plus copy fee. Payee- Saline County Circuit Clerk. **Online access to Assessor, Property, Real Estate Recording, Personal Property records:** Registration and logon is required to search assessor records at www.arcountydata.com. Signup fee is $200 plus $.10 per minute usage. For signup or information call 479-631-8054 or visit the website. Also, access land records at http://etitlesearch.com. You can do a name search; choose from $25.00 monthly subscription or per-click account. Also, search assessor real estate and personal property records free at www.countyservice.net/saltax.html. **Other phones:** Treasurer- 501-776-5633; Tax Collector- 501-776-5633. **Property tax/Assessor-** 501-776-5622.

Scott County

County Circuit Clerk, PO Box 2165, Waldron, AR 72958. RE & UCC recording phone-479-637-2642; fax-479-637-0124; hours: 8AM-4:30PM
Separate indices to search arranged by years. Records indexed on a public use terminal back to 11/2002. Office will perform a UCC search but public must search other records themselves. UCC search (no tax liens) per debtor name- $6.00. Copy fee $.25 per page. Cert fee- $5.00 per doc plus copy fee. Payee- Scott County Circuit Clerk. **Other phones:** Treasurer- 479-637-2780; Tax Collector- 479-637-4156. **Property tax/Assessor-** PO Box 12, 190 W. First, Waldron, AR 72958; 479-637-2666.

Searcy County

County Circuit Clerk, PO Box 998, Marshall, AR 72650. 870-448-3807; fax-870-448-5005; hours: 8AM-4:30PM
Will not search real estate records. Will search UCC records and tax liens. UCC search per debtor name- $8.00. Tax lien search fee- $6.00 per search. Copy fee $.50 per copy. Cert fee- $5.00 per doc plus copy fee. Payee- Searcy County Circuit Clerk. **Other phones:** Treasurer- 870-448-3828; Appraiser/Auditor- 870-448-2464; Tax Collector- 870-448-5050. **Property tax/Assessor-** 870-448-2464.

Sebastian County Fort Smith District

County Clerk and Recorder, PO Box 1089, Fort Smith, AR 72902-1089. RE & UCC recording phone-479-782-5065; fax-479-784-1567; hours: 8AM-5PM www.sebastiancountyonline.com
All records in one index. Records indexed on a public use terminal back to 1988. Office will perform a UCC and Tax lien search but public must search other records themselves. Search fee $6.00. Copy fee $.50 1st 10 pages, $.25 add'l per page. Tax lien copy- $1.00 per page. Cert fee- $2.50 per doc plus copy fee. Payee- Sebastian County Clerk and Recorder. **Online access to Assessor, Property, Personal Property records:** Registration and logon is required to search assessor records at www.arcountydata.com. Signup fee is $200 plus $.10 per minute usage. For signup or information call 479-631-8054 or visit the website. Also, search property and personal property data free at www.countyservice.net. **Other phones:** Elections- 479-782-5065. **Property tax/Assessor-** 35 S 6th St, Rm 108, Fort Smith, AR 72901; 479-783-8948.

Sebastian County Southern District

County Clerk, PO Box 428, Greenwood, AR 72936. RE & UCC recording phone-479-996-4195; fax-479-996-4165; hours: 8AM-5PM
Sebastian County has (2) courthouses. Separate indices to search. Records indexed on computer back to 1984, on index books from 1983 to 1882. Office personnel or visitors may perform searches (real estate only). Will not search real estate records. Will search UCC records, but not tax liens. UCC search per debtor name- $6.00. Copy fee $.50 per page for 1st 10 copies. $.25 each above 10 copies. If attained by mail $1.00 each. Cert fee- $3.00 per doc plus copy fee. Payee- Sebastian County Clerk-Doris Tate. **Online access to Assessor, Property, Personal Property records:** Registration and logon is required to search assessor records at www.arcountydata.com. Signup fee is $200 plus $.10 per minute usage. For signup or information call 479-631-8054 or visit the website. Also, search property and personal property data free at www.countyservice.net. **Other phones:** Elections- 479-996-4195; Vital Records- 479-996-4195 (marriages). **Property tax/Assessor-** 479-996-6591.

Sevier County

County Circuit Clerk, 115 N. 3rd St, De Queen, AR 71832. RE & UCC recording phone-870-584-3055; fax-870-642-3119; hours: 8AM-4:30PM
Will not search real estate records. Will not search UCC records or tax liens. Copy fee $.25 per page. Cert fee- $5.00 per doc plus copy fee. Payee- Sevier County Circuit Clerk. **Other phones:** Treasurer- 870-642-2358; Tax Collector- 870-642-2358. **Property tax/Assessor-** 870-584-3182.

Sharp County

County Circuit Clerk, PO Box 307, Ash Flat, AR 72513. RE & UCC recording phone-870-994-7361; fax-870-994-7712; hours: 8AM-4PM
Records indexed on a public use terminal back to 1997. Office will perform a UCC search but public must search other records themselves. Search fee $6.00. Copy fee $.25 per page. Cert fee- $5.00 per page includes copy fee. Payee- Sharp County Circuit Clerk. **Online access to Assessor, Property, Real Estate Recording, Deed records:** Registration and logon is required to search assessor records at www.arcountydata.com. Signup fee is $200 plus $.10 per minute usage. For signup or information call 479-631-8054 or visit the website. Also, access land records at http://etitlesearch.com. You can do a name search; choose from $25.00 monthly subscription or per-click account. **Other phones:** Treasurer- 870-994-7347; Elections- 870-994-7361; Tax Collector- 870-994-7347. **Property tax/Assessor-** same address as above. 870-994-7328.

St. Francis County

County Circuit Clerk, PO Box 1775, Forrest City, AR 72336-1775. Main phone & R/E recording-870-261-1715, UCC recording phone-870-261-1721; fax-870-261-1723; hours: 8AM-4:30PM
Records indexed on a public use terminal back to 2003. Office will perform a UCC search but public must search other records themselves. Search fee $6.00. Copy fee $.25 per page. Cert fee- $3.00 per page includes copy fee. Payee- St. Francis County Circuit Clerk. **Online access to Assessor, Property records:** Registration and logon is required to search assessor records at www.arcountydata.com. Signup fee is $200 plus $.10 per minute usage. For signup or information call 479-631-8054 or visit the website. **Other phones:** Treasurer- 870-261-1705; Tax Collector- 870-261-1792. **Property tax/Assessor-** same address as above. 870-261-1710.

Stone County

County Circuit Clerk, 107 W Main #D, Mountain View, AR 72560. RE & UCC recording phone-870-269-3271; fax-870-269-2303; hours: 8AM-4:30PM
Separate indices to search include Land, Court, UCC, and Marriage. Records indexed on a public use terminal back to 1990. Office will perform a UCC search but public must search other records themselves. Search fee $6.00. Copy fee $5.00 for 1st 3 pages, $1.00 each add'l. RE or tax lien copy- $.25 per page. Cert fee- $5.00 per doc plus copy fee up to 10 pages. Payee- Stone County Circuit Clerk. **Online access to Assessor, Property records:** Registration and logon is required to search assessor records at www.arcountydata.com. Signup fee is $200 plus $.10 per minute usage. For signup or information call 479-631-8054 or visit the website. **Other phones:** Treasurer- 870-269-8426; Elections- 870-269-5550; Tax Collector- 870-269-8426. **Property tax/Assessor-** 108 W Washington, Mountain View, AR 72560; 870-269-3524.

Union County

County Circuit Clerk, PO Box 1626, El Dorado, AR 71731-1626. 870-864-1940; fax-870-864-1994; hours: 8:30AM-5PM
Will not search real estate records. Will search UCC records; search includes tax liens if requested. UCC search per debtor name- $6.00. Separate federal tax lien search- $6.00 per debtor. Separate state tax lien search- $6.00 per debtor. Separate

federal/state combined tax lien search- $12.00 per debtor. General copy fee $5.00 1st 3 pages; $1.00 each add'l. RE or tax lien copy- $.50 per page. Cert fee- $1.00 per page. Payee- Union County Circuit Clerk. **Online access to Real Estate, Deed, Circuit Court, Lien, Judgment records:** Access to county land and court records is by subscription; visit www.recordsusa.com/Arkansas/UnionCnAr.htm or phone 800-932-5029 or 888-85-IMAGE. Monthly packages are $49.95 or $79.90 per month. **Other phones:** Treasurer- 870-864-1928; Tax Collector- 870-864-1928. **Property tax/Assessor-** same address as above. 870-864-1920.

Van Buren County

County Circuit Clerk, 451 Main St. #2, Clinton, AR 72031-9806. RE & UCC recording phone-501-745-4140; fax-501-745-7400; hours: 8AM-5PM
All records in one index. Records indexed on a public use terminal back to 1996. Office personnel or visitors may perform searches. Search fee-none. Real estate owner, mortgage, and property transfer searches available. Will not search UCC records or tax liens. Copy fee $.50 per page. Cert fee- $5.00 per doc plus copy fee. Payee- Van Buren County Circuit Clerk. **Online access to Real Estate Recording, Deed, Property, Personal Property records:** Access land records at http://etitlesearch.com. You can do a name search; call 870-856-3055 for subscription information. Also, search property and personal property data free at www.countyservice.net. **Other phones:** Treasurer- 501-745-2400; Appraiser/Auditor- 501-745-2474; Elections- 501-745-4140. **Property tax/Assessor-** 501-745-2464.

Washington County

County Circuit Clerk, 280 N. College, #302; Courthouse, Fayetteville, AR 72701. 479-444-1538; fax-479-444-1537; hours: 8AM-4:30PM www.co.washington.ar.us
All records in one index. Only the public may search. Copy fee $.15 per page. Cert fee- $2.00 per doc plus copy fee. Payee- Washington County Circuit Clerk. **Online access to Real Estate, Deed, Lien, UCC, Recording, Court, Vital Statistic records:** Search Clerk's index of real estate, liens, and UCCs (to '92) at www.co.washington.ar.us/resolution/. Username, password and $50.00 subscription required. Also, search property records for free at www.co.washington.ar.us/PropertySearch/MapSearch.asp. Also, search court record archives at www.co.washington.ar.us/ArchiveSearch/CourtRecordSearch.asp. Also, access land records at http://etitlesearch.com. You can do a name search, fees involved, call 870-856-3055 for info. **Other phones:** Treasurer- 479-444-1526; Tax Collector- 479-444-1526. **Property tax/Assessor-** 479-444-1520.

White County

County Circuit Clerk, White County Courthouse; 300 N. Spruce, Searcy, AR 72143. 501-279-6203; fax-501-279-6233; hours: 8AM-4:30PM
Separate indices to search. Records indexed on a public use terminal back to 1998. Office will perform a tax liens search but public must search other records themselves. Search fee $9.00 per name. Copy fee $.50 per page. Cert fee- $2.50 per doc plus copy fee. Payee- White County Circuit Clerk. **Online access to Assessor, Property records:** Registration and logon is required to search assessor records at www.arcountydata.com. Signup fee is $200 plus $.10 per minute usage. For signup or information call 479-631-8054 or visit the website. **Other phones:** Treasurer- 501-279-6206; Tax Collector- 501-279-6206. **Property tax/Assessor-** 501-279-6205.

Woodruff County

County Circuit Clerk, PO Box 492, Augusta, AR 72006. RE & UCC recording phone-870-347-2391; fax-870-347-8703; hours: 8AM-4PM
Separate indices to search. Records indexed on a public use terminal back to 1998. Office will perform a tax lien search but public must search other records themselves. Search fee $9.00. Copy fee $.50 per page. Cert fee- $5.00 per doc plus copy fee. Payee- Woodruff County Circuit Clerk. **Online access to Real Estate Recording records:** Access land records at http://etitlesearch.com. You can do a name search; choose from $25.00 monthly subscription or per-click account. **Other phones:** Treasurer- 870-347-5416; Tax Collector- 870-347-5151. **Property tax/Assessor-** 870-347-5151.

Yell County Danville District

County Circuit Clerk, PO Box 219, Danville, AR 72833. RE & UCC recording phone-479-495-4850; fax-479-495-4875; hours: 8AM-4PM
All records in one index. Record index not computerized. Only the office personnel may search. Search fee $6.00 per name. Will not search real estate records. Copy fee $.25 per page. Cert fee- $5.00 per doc plus copy fee. Payee- Yell County Circuit Clerk. **Other phones:** Treasurer- 479-495-2933; Elections- 479-495-4850; Vital Records- 479-495-4850. **Property tax/Assessor-** 479-495-2940.

Yell County Dardanelle District

County Circuit Clerk, PO Box 457, Dardanelle, AR 72834. 479-229-4404; fax-479-229-5634; hours: 8AM-4PM
Separate indices to search include computer, books, UCCs, judgments. Search fee $6.00 per name. Will not search real estate records. A federal and state tax lien search is combined. Copy fee $.25 per page. Cert fee- $5.00 per doc includes copy fee. Payee- Yell County Circuit Clerk. **Property tax/Assessor-** 479-229-2693.

Arkansas County Locator

You will usually be able to find the city name in the City/County Cross Reference below. In that case, it is a simple matter to determine the county from the cross reference. However, only the official US Postal Service city names are included in this index. There are an additional 40,000 place names that people use in their addresses. Therefore, we have also included a ZIP/City Cross Reference immediately following the City/County Cross Reference.

If you know the ZIP Code but the city name does not appear in the City/County Cross Reference index, look up the ZIP Code in the ZIP/City Cross Reference, find the city name, then look up the city name in the City/County Cross Reference. For example, you want to know the county for an address of Menands, NY 12204. There is no "Menands" in the City/County Cross Reference. The ZIP/City Cross Reference shows that ZIP Codes 12201-12288 are for the city of Albany. Looking back in the City/County Cross Reference, Albany is in Albany County.

Arkansas City/County Cross Reference

ADONA (72001) Perry(53), Conway(46)
ALCO (72610) Stone(95), Searcy(4)
ALEXANDER (72002) Saline(93), Pulaski(6)
ALICIA Lawrence
ALIX Franklin
ALLEENE Little River
ALMA Crawford
ALMYRA Arkansas
ALPENA (72611) Boone(50), Carroll(49)
ALPINE Clark
ALTHEIMER Jefferson
ALTUS (72821) Franklin(75), Johnson(24)
AMAGON Jackson
AMITY (71921) Clark(54), Pike(29), Hot Spring(16)
ANTOINE Pike
ARKADELPHIA (71923) Clark(96), Hot Spring(3)
ARKADELPHIA Clark
ARKANSAS CITY Desha
ARMOREL Mississippi
ASH FLAT (72513) Fulton(48), Sharp(45), Izard(6)
ASHDOWN Little River
ATKINS (72823) Pope(97), Conway(2)
ATKINS Pope
AUBREY Lee
AUGUSTA Woodruff
AUSTIN Lonoke
AVOCA Benton
BALCH Jackson
BALD KNOB White
BANKS Bradley
BARLING Sebastian
BARTON Phillips
BASS Newton
BASSETT Mississippi
BATES Scott
BATESVILLE Independence
BAUXITE Saline
BAY Craighead
BEARDEN (71720) Ouachita(85), Dallas(11), Calhoun(3)
BEAVER Carroll
BEE BRANCH (72013) Van Buren(96), Conway(3)
BEEBE White
BEECH GROVE Greene
BEEDEVILLE Jackson
BEIRNE Clark
BELLA VISTA Benton
BELLEVILLE Yell
BEN LOMOND Sevier
BENTON (72015) Saline(98), Grant(1)
BENTON Saline
BENTONVILLE Benton
BERGMAN Boone
BERRYVILLE Carroll
BEXAR Fulton
BIG FLAT (72617) Baxter(75), Searcy(18), Stone(6)

BIGELOW (72016) Perry(52), Pulaski(47)
BIGGERS (72413) Randolph(92), Clay(7)
BIRDEYE Cross
BISCOE Prairie
BISMARCK Hot Spring
BLACK OAK Craighead
BLACK ROCK Lawrence
BLAKELY Garland
BLEVINS Hempstead
BLUE MOUNTAIN Logan
BLUFF CITY Nevada
BLUFFTON (72827) Yell(89), Scott(10)
BLYTHEVILLE Mississippi
BOARD CAMP Polk
BOLES Scott
BONNERDALE (71933) Hot Spring(46), Garland(35), Montgomery(17)
BONO (72416) Craighead(77), Greene(22)
BOONEVILLE (72927) Logan(85), Scott(8), Sebastian(5)
BOSWELL Izard
BRADFORD (72020) Jackson(48), White(37), Independence(13)
BRADLEY Lafayette
BRANCH Franklin
BRICKEYS Lee
BRIGGSVILLE Yell
BRINKLEY (72021) Monroe(98), Woodruff(1)
BROCKWELL Izard
BROOKLAND Craighead
BRUNO Marion
BRYANT (72022) Saline(96), Pulaski(3)
BRYANT Saline
BUCKNER (71827) Lafayette(78), Nevada(21)
BULL SHOALS Marion
BURDETTE Mississippi
CABOT (72023) Lonoke(75), Pulaski(23)
CADDO GAP Montgomery
CALDWELL St. Francis
CALE Nevada
CALICO ROCK (72519) Baxter(66), Stone(18), Izard(14)
CALION Union
CAMDEN (71701) Ouachita(97), Calhoun(2)
CAMDEN Ouachita
CAMP Fulton
CANEHILL Washington
CARAWAY (72419) Craighead(94), Poinsett(5)
CARLISLE (72024) Lonoke(96), Prairie(3)
CARTHAGE (71725) Dallas(92), Cleveland(7)
CASA (72025) Perry(80), Conway(18), Yell(2)
CASH (72421) Craighead(77), Poinsett(19), Jackson(2)
CASSCOE Arkansas
CAVE CITY (72521) Sharp(69), Independence(30)

CAVE SPRINGS Benton
CECIL (72930) Franklin(80), Sebastian(19)
CEDARVILLE Crawford
CENTER RIDGE (72027) Conway(97), Faulkner(1)
CENTERTON Benton
CENTERVILLE Yell
CHARLESTON (72933) Franklin(83), Sebastian(16)
CHARLOTTE Independence
CHATFIELD Crittenden
CHEROKEE VILLAGE (72529) Sharp(77), Fulton(22)
CHEROKEE VILLAGE Sharp
CHERRY VALLEY (72324) Cross(90), Poinsett(9)
CHESTER Crawford
CHIDESTER Ouachita
CHOCTAW Van Buren
CLARENDON Monroe
CLARKEDALE Crittenden
CLARKRIDGE Baxter
CLARKSVILLE Johnson
CLEVELAND (72030) Conway(52), Van Buren(47)
CLINTON (72031) Van Buren(95), Stone(2), Conway(1)
COAL HILL Johnson
COLLEGE STATION Pulaski
COLLINS Drew
COLT (72326) St. Francis(87), Cross(12)
COLUMBUS (71831) Hempstead(60), Howard(40)
COMBS Madison
COMPTON (72624) Newton(83), Carroll(16)
CONCORD (72523) Cleburne(87), Independence(12)
CONWAY Faulkner
CORD Independence
CORNING Clay
COTTER Baxter
COTTON PLANT (72036) Woodruff(88), Monroe(11)
COVE Polk
COY Lonoke
CRAWFORDSVILLE Crittenden
CROCKETTS BLUFF Arkansas
CROSSETT Ashley
CRUMROD Phillips
CURTIS Clark
CUSHMAN Independence
DAMASCUS (72039) Van Buren(71), Faulkner(28)
DANVILLE Yell
DARDANELLE (72834) Yell(98), Logan(1)
DATTO Clay
DE QUEEN Sevier
DE VALLS BLUFF Prairie
DE WITT Arkansas
DECATUR Benton
DEER Newton

DELAPLAINE Greene
DELAWARE Logan
DELIGHT Pike
DELL Mississippi
DENNARD Van Buren
DERMOTT (71638) Chicot(84), Drew(12), Desha(3)
DES ARC Prairie
DESHA Independence
DIAMOND CITY Boone
DIAZ Jackson
DIERKS (71833) Howard(94), Sevier(5)
DODDRIDGE Miller
DOLPH Izard
DONALDSON Hot Spring
DOVER Pope
DRASCO (72530) Cleburne(94), Stone(5)
DRIVER Mississippi
DUMAS (71639) Desha(97), Lincoln(2)
DYER Crawford
DYESS Mississippi
EARLE (72331) Crittenden(95), Cross(4)
EDGEMONT (72044) Cleburne(80), Stone(19)
EDMONDSON Crittenden
EGYPT Craighead
EL DORADO Union
EL PASO (72045) White(98), Faulkner(1)
ELAINE Phillips
ELIZABETH (72531) Baxter(53), Fulton(46)
ELKINS (72727) Madison(50), Washington(49)
ELM SPRINGS Washington
EMERSON Columbia
EMMET (71835) Nevada(78), Hempstead(21)
ENGLAND (72046) Lonoke(81), Pulaski(10), Jefferson(7)
ENOLA Faulkner
ETHEL Arkansas
ETOWAH Mississippi
EUDORA Chicot
EUREKA SPRINGS Carroll
EVANSVILLE Washington
EVENING SHADE Sharp
EVERTON (72633) Boone(59), Marion(37), Searcy(3)
FAIRFIELD BAY (72088) Van Buren(91), Cleburne(8)
FARMINGTON Washington
FAYETTEVILLE Washington
FERNDALE Pulaski
FIFTY SIX Stone
FISHER (72429) Poinsett(97), Cross(3)
FLIPPIN Marion
FLORAL (72534) Independence(86), Cleburne(13)
FORDYCE (71742) Dallas(96), Calhoun(3)
FOREMAN Little River
FORREST CITY St. Francis
FORT SMITH Sebastian
FOUKE Miller

FOUNTAIN HILL (71642) Ashley(82),
  Drew(17)
FOX Stone
FRANKLIN Izard
FRENCHMANS BAYOU Mississippi
FRIENDSHIP Hot Spring
FULTON Hempstead
GAMALIEL Baxter
GARFIELD Benton
GARLAND CITY (71839) Miller(96),
  Lafayette(4)
GARNER White
GASSVILLE Baxter
GATEWAY Benton
GENOA Miller
GENTRY Benton
GEPP (72538) Fulton(94), Baxter(5)
GILBERT Searcy
GILLETT (72055) Arkansas(89),
  Jefferson(10)
GILLHAM (71841) Sevier(89), Polk(10)
GILMORE Crittenden
GLENCOE Fulton
GLENWOOD (71943) Pike(56),
  Montgomery(39), Hot Spring(4)
GOODWIN St. Francis
GOSHEN Washington
GOSNELL Mississippi
GOULD (71643) Lincoln(88), Desha(11)
GRADY (71644) Jefferson(64), Lincoln(35)
GRANNIS Polk
GRAPEVINE Grant
GRAVELLY (72838) Yell(93), Scott(6)
GRAVETTE Benton
GREEN FOREST Carroll
GREENBRIER Faulkner
GREENLAND Washington
GREENWAY Clay
GREENWOOD Sebastian
GREGORY Woodruff
GRIFFITHVILLE (72060) White(70),
  Prairie(29)
GRUBBS Jackson
GUION Izard
GURDON Clark
GUY Faulkner
HACKETT Sebastian
HAGARVILLE (72839) Johnson(97),
  Pope(2)
HAMBURG Ashley
HAMPTON Calhoun
HARDY (72542) Sharp(86), Fulton(13)
HARRELL Calhoun
HARRIET (72639) Searcy(95), Marion(4)
HARRISBURG Poinsett
HARRISON Boone
HARTFORD Sebastian
HARTMAN Johnson
HARVEY (72841) Scott(81), Yell(18)
HASTY Newton
HATFIELD Polk
HATTIEVILLE (72063) Conway(94),
  Pope(5)
HATTON Polk
HAVANA (72842) Yell(98), Logan(1)
HAYNES Lee
HAZEN Prairie
HEBER SPRINGS Cleburne
HECTOR Pope
HELENA Phillips
HENDERSON Baxter
HENSLEY (72065) Saline(84), Pulaski(11),
  Grant(4)
HERMITAGE Bradley
HETH (72346) St. Francis(94), Cross(4),
  Crittenden(1)
HICKORY PLAINS Prairie
HICKORY RIDGE (72347) Cross(80),
  Jackson(18)
HIGDEN (72067) Cleburne(89), Van
  Buren(10)
HIGGINSON White

HINDSVILLE (72738) Madison(80),
  Washington(12), Benton(6)
HIWASSE Benton
HOLLY GROVE (72069) Monroe(91),
  Phillips(8)
HOPE Hempstead
HORATIO Sevier
HORSESHOE BEND Izard
HOT SPRINGS NATIONAL PARK Garland
HOT SPRINGS VILLAGE (71909)
  Garland(74), Saline(25)
HOT SPRINGS VILLAGE Garland
HOUSTON Perry
HOWELL Woodruff
HOXIE Lawrence
HUGHES (72348) St. Francis(48),
  Crittenden(45), Lee(5)
HUMNOKE (72072) Lonoke(90),
  Jefferson(9)
HUMPHREY (72073) Arkansas(77),
  Jefferson(22)
HUNT Johnson
HUNTER Woodruff
HUNTINGTON Sebastian
HUTTIG Union
IDA Cleburne
IMBODEN (72434) Randolph(71),
  Lawrence(28)
IVAN Dallas
JACKSONPORT Jackson
JACKSONVILLE (72076) Pulaski(95),
  Lonoke(4)
JACKSONVILLE Pulaski
JASPER Newton
JEFFERSON (72079) Jefferson(85),
  Grant(14)
JENNIE Chicot
JEROME Drew
JERSEY Bradley
JERUSALEM (72080) Van Buren(48),
  Conway(41), Pope(10)
JESSIEVILLE Garland
JOHNSON Washington
JOINER Mississippi
JONES MILLS Hot Spring
JONESBORO (72401) Craighead(98),
  Greene(1)
JONESBORO Craighead
JUDSONIA White
JUNCTION CITY Union
KEISER Mississippi
KENSETT White
KEO Lonoke
KINGSLAND Cleveland
KINGSTON (72742) Madison(91),
  Newton(8)
KIRBY Pike
KNOBEL (72435) Clay(93), Greene(6)
KNOXVILLE Johnson
LA GRANGE Lee
LAFE (72436) Greene(84), Clay(15)
LAKE CITY Craighead
LAKE VILLAGE Chicot
LAKEVIEW Baxter
LAMAR (72846) Johnson(97), Pope(2)
LAMBROOK Phillips
LANEBURG Nevada
LANGLEY Pike
LAVACA Sebastian
LAWSON Union
LEACHVILLE (72438) Mississippi(87),
  Craighead(12)
LEAD HILL (72644) Boone(89), Marion(10)
LEOLA (72084) Grant(54), Hot Spring(27),
  Dallas(18)
LEPANTO (72354) Poinsett(78),
  Mississippi(21)
LESLIE (72645) Van Buren(42),
  Searcy(34), Stone(22)
LETONA White
LEWISVILLE Lafayette
LEXA (72355) Phillips(88), Lee(11)

LIGHT Greene
LINCOLN Washington
LITTLE ROCK (72210) Pulaski(92),
  Saline(7)
LITTLE ROCK Pulaski
LITTLE ROCK AIR FORCE BASE Pulaski
LOCKESBURG Sevier
LOCUST GROVE (72550)
  Independence(56), Cleburne(28),
  Stone(14)
LONDON (72847) Pope(62), Johnson(37)
LONOKE Lonoke
LONSDALE (72087) Saline(57),
  Garland(42)
LOUANN Ouachita
LOWELL Benton
LUXORA Mississippi
LYNN Lawrence
MABELVALE (72103) Saline(79),
  Pulaski(20)
MADISON St. Francis
MAGAZINE Logan
MAGNESS Independence
MAGNOLIA (71753) Columbia(98),
  Union(1)
MAGNOLIA Columbia
MALVERN (72104) Hot Spring(98),
  Saline(1)
MAMMOTH SPRING (72554) Fulton(68),
  Sharp(31)
MANILA Mississippi
MANSFIELD (72944) Sebastian(59),
  Scott(40)
MARBLE FALLS Newton
MARCELLA Stone
MARIANNA Lee
MARION Crittenden
MARKED TREE Poinsett
MARMADUKE Greene
MARSHALL (72650) Searcy(90), Stone(9)
MARVELL (72366) Phillips(96), Monroe(1),
  Lee(1)
MAUMELLE Pulaski
MAYFLOWER Faulkner
MAYNARD Randolph
MAYSVILLE Benton
MC CASKILL Hempstead
MC CRORY (72101) Woodruff(89),
  Jackson(8), Cross(2)
MC CRORY Cross
MC CRORY Woodruff
MC DOUGAL Clay
MC GEHEE Desha
MC NEIL Columbia
MC RAE White
MELBOURNE Izard
MELLWOOD Phillips
MENA Polk
MENIFEE Conway
MIDLAND Sebastian
MIDWAY Baxter
MINERAL SPRINGS Howard
MINTURN Lawrence
MOKO Fulton
MONETTE Craighead
MONROE Monroe
MONTICELLO Drew
MONTROSE Ashley
MORO (72368) Lee(90), Monroe(9)
MORRILTON Conway
MORROW Washington
MOSCOW Jefferson
MOUNT HOLLY Union
MOUNT IDA Montgomery
MOUNT JUDEA Newton
MOUNT PLEASANT Izard
MOUNT VERNON (72111) Faulkner(64),
  White(35)
MOUNTAIN HOME (72653) Baxter(98),
  Marion(1)
MOUNTAIN HOME Baxter
MOUNTAIN PINE Garland

MOUNTAIN VIEW (72560) Stone(98),
  Izard(1)
MOUNTAINBURG Crawford
MULBERRY (72947) Crawford(61),
  Franklin(38)
MURFREESBORO Pike
NASHVILLE (71852) Howard(87),
  Hempstead(6), Pike(6)
NATURAL DAM (72948) Crawford(95),
  Washington(4)
NEW BLAINE Logan
NEW EDINBURG (71660) Cleveland(96),
  Bradley(3)
NEWARK Independence
NEWHOPE (71959) Pike(60), Howard(39)
NEWPORT Jackson
NORFORK Baxter
NORMAN Montgomery
NORPHLET Union
NORTH LITTLE ROCK Pulaski
O KEAN Randolph
OAK GROVE Carroll
OAKLAND Marion
OARK (72852) Johnson(90), Newton(5),
  Madison(4)
ODEN Montgomery
OGDEN Little River
OIL TROUGH Independence
OKOLONA Clark
OLA (72853) Perry(64), Yell(35)
OMAHA (72662) Boone(98), Carroll(1)
ONEIDA Phillips
ONIA Stone
OSCEOLA Mississippi
OXFORD Izard
OZAN Hempstead
OZARK (72949) Franklin(97), Johnson(1),
  Logan(1)
OZONE (72854) Johnson(94), Newton(5)
PALESTINE (72372) St. Francis(85),
  Lee(14)
PANGBURN (72121) White(69),
  Cleburne(30)
PARAGOULD Greene
PARIS Logan
PARKDALE (71661) Ashley(88), Chicot(11)
PARKIN Cross
PARKS Scott
PARON (72122) Saline(69), Pulaski(30)
PARTHENON Newton
PATTERSON Woodruff
PEA RIDGE Benton
PEACH ORCHARD (72453) Greene(89),
  Clay(10)
PEARCY (71964) Garland(90), Hot
  Spring(9)
PEEL Marion
PELSOR (72856) Pope(52), Newton(47)
PENCIL BLUFF Montgomery
PERRY (72125) Perry(71), Conway(28)
PERRYVILLE (72126) Perry(96), Pulaski(3)
PETTIGREW (72752) Madison(84),
  Johnson(14)
PICKENS (71662) Lincoln(53), Desha(46)
PIGGOTT Clay
PINDALL Searcy
PINE BLUFF (71602) Jefferson(98),
  Grant(1)
PINE BLUFF Jefferson
PINEVILLE Izard
PLAINVIEW (72857) Yell(70), Perry(29)
PLEASANT GROVE Stone
PLEASANT PLAINS (72568)
  Independence(92), White(7)
PLUMERVILLE Conway
POCAHONTAS Randolph
POLLARD Clay
PONCA Newton
POPLAR GROVE (72374) Phillips(98),
  Lee(1)
PORTIA Lawrence
PORTLAND (71663) Ashley(65), Chicot(34)

POTTSVILLE Pope
POUGHKEEPSIE Sharp
POWHATAN Lawrence
POYEN (72128) Grant(98), Hot Spring(1)
PRAIRIE GROVE Washington
PRATTSVILLE Grant
PRESCOTT (71857) Nevada(96), Hempstead(3)
PRIM Cleburne
PROCTOR (72376) Crittenden(98), St. Francis(1)
PYATT Marion
QUITMAN (72131) Cleburne(82), Faulkner(9), Van Buren(7)
RATCLIFF (72951) Logan(58), Franklin(41)
RAVENDEN (72459) Lawrence(50), Randolph(35), Sharp(13)
RAVENDEN SPRINGS Randolph
RECTOR (72461) Clay(91), Greene(8)
REDFIELD (72132) Jefferson(84), Grant(15)
REYDELL Jefferson
REYNO Randolph
RISON (71665) Cleveland(98), Jefferson(1)
RIVERVALE Poinsett
ROE (72134) Monroe(82), Arkansas(13), Prairie(3)
ROGERS Benton
ROLAND Pulaski
ROMANCE White
ROSE BUD (72137) White(58), Cleburne(41)
ROSIE Independence
ROSSTON Nevada
ROUND POND St. Francis
ROVER Yell
ROYAL Garland
RUDY Crawford
RUSSELL White
RUSSELLVILLE Pope
SAFFELL (72572) Lawrence(66), Independence(33)
SAGE Izard
SAINT CHARLES Arkansas
SAINT FRANCIS Clay
SAINT JOE (72675) Marion(60), Searcy(39)
SAINT PAUL Madison
SALADO Independence
SALEM Fulton

SARATOGA (71859) Hempstead(60), Howard(40)
SCOTLAND Van Buren
SCOTT (72142) Pulaski(62), Lonoke(37)
SCRANTON Logan
SEARCY White
SEDGWICK Lawrence
SHERIDAN (72150) Grant(98), Jefferson(1)
SHERRILL Jefferson
SHERWOOD (72120) Pulaski(96), Faulkner(3)
SHIRLEY (72153) Van Buren(93), Stone(6)
SIDNEY (72577) Sharp(73), Izard(26)
SILOAM SPRINGS Benton
SIMS Montgomery
SMACKOVER (71762) Union(96), Ouachita(3)
SMITHVILLE (72466) Lawrence(63), Sharp(36)
SNOW LAKE Desha
SOLGOHACHIA Conway
SPARKMAN (71763) Dallas(92), Ouachita(4), Clark(2)
SPRINGDALE (72764) Washington(97), Benton(2)
SPRINGDALE Washington
SPRINGFIELD Conway
SPRINGTOWN Benton
STAMPS (71860) Lafayette(94), Columbia(5)
STAR CITY (71667) Lincoln(97), Cleveland(1)
STATE UNIVERSITY Craighead
STEPHENS (71764) Ouachita(57), Columbia(35), Nevada(5), Union(1)
STEPROCK White
STORY Montgomery
STRAWBERRY (72469) Lawrence(80), Sharp(19)
STRONG Union
STURKIE Fulton
STUTTGART (72160) Arkansas(96), Prairie(1), Jefferson(1)
SUBIACO Logan
SUCCESS Clay
SULPHUR ROCK (72579) Independence(94), Sharp(5)
SULPHUR SPRINGS Benton
SUMMERS Washington
SUMMIT Marion

SWEET HOME Pulaski
SWIFTON Jackson
TAYLOR (71861) Columbia(63), Lafayette(36)
TEXARKANA Miller
THIDA Independence
THORNTON (71766) Calhoun(97), Ouachita(2)
TICHNOR Arkansas
TILLAR (71670) Desha(81), Drew(18)
TILLY (72679) Pope(61), Van Buren(25), Searcy(12)
TIMBO Stone
TOMATO Mississippi
TONTITOWN Washington
TRASKWOOD (72167) Saline(80), Hot Spring(14), Grant(4)
TRUMANN Poinsett
TUCKER Jefferson
TUCKERMAN Jackson
TUMBLING SHOALS Cleburne
TUPELO Jackson
TURNER Phillips
TURRELL Crittenden
TWIST Cross
TYRONZA (72386) Poinsett(63), Mississippi(18), Crittenden(17)
ULM Prairie
UMPIRE (71971) Howard(78), Pike(21)
UNIONTOWN Crawford
URBANA Union
VALLEY SPRINGS (72682) Marion(83), Boone(16)
VAN BUREN Crawford
VANDERVOORT Polk
VANNDALE Cross
VENDOR Newton
VILLAGE Columbia
VILONIA Faulkner
VIOLA Fulton
VIOLET HILL Izard
WABASH Phillips
WABBASEKA (72175) Jefferson(98), Arkansas(1)
WALCOTT Greene
WALDENBURG Poinsett
WALDO (71770) Columbia(88), Nevada(11)
WALDRON Scott

WALNUT RIDGE (72476) Lawrence(91), Randolph(3), Craighead(2), Greene(2)
WARD (72176) Lonoke(98), Prairie(1)
WARM SPRINGS Randolph
WARREN (71671) Bradley(97), Cleveland(2)
WASHINGTON Hempstead
WATSON Desha
WAVELAND Yell
WEINER (72479) Poinsett(85), Jackson(9), Craighead(4)
WESLEY (72773) Madison(98), Washington(1)
WEST FORK Washington
WEST HELENA Phillips
WEST MEMPHIS Crittenden
WEST POINT White
WEST RIDGE Mississippi
WESTERN GROVE (72685) Newton(92), Searcy(4), Boone(2)
WHEATLEY (72392) St. Francis(78), Monroe(14), Woodruff(5), Lee(1)
WHEELER Washington
WHELEN SPRINGS Clark
WHITE HALL Jefferson
WICKES (71973) Polk(93), Howard(6)
WIDEMAN Izard
WIDENER St. Francis
WILBURN Cleburne
WILLIFORD Sharp
WILLISVILLE Nevada
WILMAR (71675) Drew(92), Bradley(7)
WILMOT (71676) Ashley(94), Chicot(5)
WILSON Mississippi
WILTON Little River
WINCHESTER Drew
WINSLOW (72959) Washington(87), Crawford(12)
WINTHROP Little River
WISEMAN (72587) Izard(94), Fulton(5)
WITTER Madison
WITTS SPRINGS (72686) Searcy(90), Pope(9)
WOODSON Pulaski
WOOSTER Faulkner
WRIGHT Jefferson
WRIGHTSVILLE Pulaski
WYNNE Cross
YELLVILLE Marion
YORKTOWN Lincoln

Arkansas ZIP/City Cross Reference

71601-71612 PINE BLUFF	71663-71663 PORTLAND	71749-71749 JUNCTION CITY	71833-71833 DIERKS
71612-71612 WHITE HALL	71665-71665 RISON	71750-71750 LAWSON	71834-71834 DODDRIDGE
71613-71613 PINE BLUFF	71666-71666 MC GEHEE	71751-71751 LOUANN	71835-71835 EMMET
71630-71630 ARKANSAS CITY	71667-71667 STAR CITY	71752-71752 MC NEIL	71836-71836 FOREMAN
71631-71631 BANKS	71670-71670 TILLAR	71753-71754 MAGNOLIA	71837-71837 FOUKE
71634-71634 COLLINS	71671-71671 WARREN	71758-71758 MOUNT HOLLY	71838-71838 FULTON
71635-71635 CROSSETT	71674-71674 WATSON	71759-71759 NORPHLET	71839-71839 GARLAND CITY
71638-71638 DERMOTT	71675-71675 WILMAR	71762-71762 SMACKOVER	71840-71840 GENOA
71639-71639 DUMAS	71676-71676 WILMOT	71763-71763 SPARKMAN	71841-71841 GILLHAM
71640-71640 EUDORA	71677-71677 WINCHESTER	71764-71764 STEPHENS	71842-71842 HORATIO
71642-71642 FOUNTAIN HILL	71678-71678 YORKTOWN	71765-71765 STRONG	71844-71844 LANEBURG
71643-71643 GOULD	71701-71711 CAMDEN	71766-71766 THORNTON	71845-71845 LEWISVILLE
71644-71644 GRADY	71720-71720 BEARDEN	71767-71767 HAMPTON	71846-71846 LOCKESBURG
71646-71646 HAMBURG	71721-71721 BEIRNE	71768-71768 URBANA	71847-71847 MC CASKILL
71647-71647 HERMITAGE	71722-71722 BLUFF CITY	71769-71769 VILLAGE	71851-71851 MINERAL SPRINGS
71649-71649 JENNIE	71724-71724 CALION	71770-71770 WALDO	71852-71852 NASHVILLE
71650-71650 JEROME	71725-71725 CARTHAGE	71772-71772 WHELEN SPRINGS	71853-71853 OGDEN
71651-71651 JERSEY	71726-71726 CHIDESTER	71801-71802 HOPE	71854-71854 TEXARKANA
71652-71652 KINGSLAND	71728-71728 CURTIS	71820-71820 ALLEENE	71855-71855 OZAN
71653-71653 LAKE VILLAGE	71730-71731 EL DORADO	71822-71822 ASHDOWN	71857-71857 PRESCOTT
71654-71654 MC GEHEE	71740-71740 EMERSON	71823-71823 BEN LOMOND	71858-71858 ROSSTON
71655-71657 MONTICELLO	71742-71742 FORDYCE	71825-71825 BLEVINS	71859-71859 SARATOGA
71658-71658 MONTROSE	71743-71743 GURDON	71826-71826 BRADLEY	71860-71860 STAMPS
71659-71659 MOSCOW	71744-71744 HAMPTON	71827-71827 BUCKNER	71861-71861 TAYLOR
71660-71660 NEW EDINBURG	71745-71745 HARRELL	71828-71828 CALE	71862-71862 WASHINGTON
71661-71661 PARKDALE	71747-71747 HUTTIG	71831-71831 COLUMBUS	71864-71864 WILLISVILLE
71662-71662 PICKENS	71748-71748 IVAN	71832-71832 DE QUEEN	71865-71865 WILTON

ZIP Range	City	ZIP Range	City	ZIP Range	City	ZIP Range	City
71866-71866	WINTHROP	72042-72042	DE WITT	72153-72153	SHIRLEY	72383-72383	TURNER
71901-71903	HOT SPRINGS NATIONAL PARK	72043-72043	DIAZ	72156-72156	SOLGOHACHIA	72384-72384	TURRELL
71909-71910	HOT SPRINGS VILLAGE	72044-72044	EDGEMONT	72157-72157	SPRINGFIELD	72385-72385	TWIST
71913-71914	HOT SPRINGS NATIONAL PARK	72045-72045	EL PASO	72158-72158	BENTON	72386-72386	TYRONZA
71920-71920	ALPINE	72046-72046	ENGLAND	72159-72159	STEPROCK	72387-72387	VANNDALE
71921-71921	AMITY	72047-72047	ENOLA	72160-72160	STUTTGART	72389-72389	WABASH
71922-71922	ANTOINE	72048-72048	ETHEL	72164-72164	SWEET HOME	72390-72390	WEST HELENA
71923-71923	ARKADELPHIA	72051-72051	FOX	72165-72165	THIDA	72391-72391	WEST RIDGE
71929-71929	BISMARCK	72052-72052	GARNER	72166-72166	TICHNOR	72392-72392	WHEATLEY
71931-71931	BLAKELY	72053-72053	COLLEGE STATION	72167-72167	TRASKWOOD	72394-72394	WIDENER
71932-71932	BOARD CAMP	72055-72055	GILLETT	72168-72168	TUCKER	72395-72395	WILSON
71933-71933	BONNERDALE	72057-72057	GRAPEVINE	72169-72169	TUPELO	72396-72397	WYNNE
71935-71935	CADDO GAP	72058-72058	GREENBRIER	72170-72170	ULM	72397-72397	MC CRORY
71937-71937	COVE	72059-72059	GREGORY	72173-72173	VILONIA	72401-72404	JONESBORO
71940-71940	DELIGHT	72060-72060	GRIFFITHVILLE	72175-72175	WABBASEKA	72410-72410	ALICIA
71941-71941	DONALDSON	72061-72061	GUY	72176-72176	WARD	72411-72411	BAY
71942-71942	FRIENDSHIP	72063-72063	HATTIEVILLE	72178-72178	WEST POINT	72412-72412	BEECH GROVE
71943-71943	GLENWOOD	72064-72064	HAZEN	72179-72179	WILBURN	72413-72413	BIGGERS
71944-71944	GRANNIS	72065-72065	HENSLEY	72180-72180	WOODSON	72414-72414	BLACK OAK
71945-71945	HATFIELD	72066-72066	HICKORY PLAINS	72181-72181	WOOSTER	72415-72415	BLACK ROCK
71946-71946	HATTON	72067-72067	HIGDEN	72182-72182	WRIGHT	72416-72416	BONO
71949-71949	JESSIEVILLE	72068-72068	HIGGINSON	72183-72183	WRIGHTSVILLE	72417-72417	BROOKLAND
71950-71950	KIRBY	72069-72069	HOLLY GROVE	72189-72189	MC CRORY	72419-72419	CARAWAY
71951-71951	HOT SPRINGS NATIONAL PARK	72070-72070	HOUSTON	72190-72199	NORTH LITTLE ROCK	72421-72421	CASH
71952-71952	LANGLEY	72071-72071	HOWELL	72200-72207	LITTLE ROCK	72422-72422	CORNING
71953-71953	MENA	72072-72072	HUMNOKE	72208-72208	FERNDALE	72424-72424	DATTO
71956-71956	MOUNTAIN PINE	72073-72073	HUMPHREY	72209-72297	LITTLE ROCK	72425-72425	DELAPLAINE
71957-71957	MOUNT IDA	72074-72074	HUNTER	72301-72303	WEST MEMPHIS	72426-72426	DELL
71958-71958	MURFREESBORO	72075-72075	JACKSONPORT	72310-72310	ARMOREL	72427-72427	EGYPT
71959-71959	NEWHOPE	72076-72078	JACKSONVILLE	72311-72311	AUBREY	72428-72428	ETOWAH
71960-71960	NORMAN	72079-72079	JEFFERSON	72312-72312	BARTON	72429-72429	FISHER
71961-71961	ODEN	72080-72080	JERUSALEM	72313-72313	BASSETT	72430-72430	GREENWAY
71962-71962	OKOLONA	72081-72081	JUDSONIA	72314-72314	BIRDEYE	72431-72431	GRUBBS
71964-71964	PEARCY	72082-72082	KENSETT	72315-72317	BLYTHEVILLE	72432-72432	HARRISBURG
71965-71965	PENCIL BLUFF	72083-72083	KEO	72319-72319	GOSNELL	72433-72433	HOXIE
71966-71966	ODEN	72084-72084	LEOLA	72320-72320	BRICKEYS	72434-72434	IMBODEN
71968-71968	ROYAL	72085-72085	LETONA	72321-72321	BURDETTE	72435-72435	KNOBEL
71969-71969	SIMS	72086-72086	LONOKE	72322-72322	CALDWELL	72436-72436	LAFE
71970-71970	STORY	72087-72087	LONSDALE	72323-72323	CHATFIELD	72437-72437	LAKE CITY
71971-71971	UMPIRE	72088-72088	FAIRFIELD BAY	72324-72324	CHERRY VALLEY	72438-72438	LEACHVILLE
71972-71972	VANDERVOORT	72089-72089	BRYANT	72325-72325	CLARKEDALE	72439-72439	LIGHT
71973-71973	WICKES	72099-72099	LITTLE ROCK AIR FORCE BASE	72326-72326	COLT	72440-72440	LYNN
71998-71999	ARKADELPHIA	72100-72100	NORTH LITTLE ROCK	72327-72327	CRAWFORDSVILLE	72441-72441	MC DOUGAL
72001-72001	ADONA	72101-72101	MC CRORY	72328-72328	CRUMROD	72442-72442	MANILA
72002-72002	ALEXANDER	72102-72102	MC RAE	72329-72329	DRIVER	72443-72443	MARMADUKE
72003-72003	ALMYRA	72103-72103	MABELVALE	72330-72330	DYESS	72444-72444	MAYNARD
72004-72004	ALTHEIMER	72104-72104	MALVERN	72331-72331	EARLE	72445-72445	MINTURN
72005-72005	AMAGON	72105-72105	JONES MILLS	72332-72332	EDMONDSON	72447-72447	MONETTE
72006-72006	AUGUSTA	72106-72106	MAYFLOWER	72333-72333	ELAINE	72449-72449	O KEAN
72007-72007	AUSTIN	72107-72107	MENIFEE	72335-72336	FORREST CITY	72450-72451	PARAGOULD
72009-72009	BALCH	72108-72108	MONROE	72338-72338	FRENCHMANS BAYOU	72453-72453	PEACH ORCHARD
72010-72010	BALD KNOB	72110-72110	MORRILTON	72339-72339	GILMORE	72454-72454	PIGGOTT
72011-72011	BAUXITE	72111-72111	MOUNT VERNON	72340-72340	GOODWIN	72455-72455	POCAHONTAS
72012-72012	BEEBE	72112-72112	NEWPORT	72341-72341	HAYNES	72456-72456	POLLARD
72013-72013	BEE BRANCH	72113-72113	MAUMELLE	72342-72342	HELENA	72457-72457	PORTIA
72014-72014	BEEDEVILLE	72114-72119	NORTH LITTLE ROCK	72346-72346	HETH	72458-72458	POWHATAN
72015-72015	BENTON	72120-72120	SHERWOOD	72347-72347	HICKORY RIDGE	72459-72459	RAVENDEN
72016-72016	BIGELOW	72121-72121	PANGBURN	72348-72348	HUGHES	72460-72460	RAVENDEN SPRINGS
72017-72017	BISCOE	72122-72122	PARON	72350-72350	JOINER	72461-72461	RECTOR
72018-72018	BENTON	72123-72123	PATTERSON	72351-72351	KEISER	72462-72462	REYNO
72020-72020	BRADFORD	72124-72124	NORTH LITTLE ROCK	72352-72352	LA GRANGE	72464-72464	SAINT FRANCIS
72021-72021	BRINKLEY	72125-72125	PERRY	72353-72353	LAMBROOK	72465-72465	SEDGWICK
72022-72022	BRYANT	72126-72126	PERRYVILLE	72354-72354	LEPANTO	72466-72466	SMITHVILLE
72023-72023	CABOT	72127-72127	PLUMERVILLE	72355-72355	LEXA	72467-72467	STATE UNIVERSITY
72024-72024	CARLISLE	72128-72128	POYEN	72358-72358	LUXORA	72469-72469	STRAWBERRY
72025-72025	CASA	72129-72129	PRATTSVILLE	72359-72359	MADISON	72470-72470	SUCCESS
72026-72026	CASSCOE	72130-72130	PRIM	72360-72360	MARIANNA	72471-72471	SWIFTON
72027-72027	CENTER RIDGE	72131-72131	QUITMAN	72364-72364	MARION	72472-72472	TRUMANN
72028-72028	CHOCTAW	72132-72132	REDFIELD	72365-72365	MARKED TREE	72473-72473	TUCKERMAN
72029-72029	CLARENDON	72133-72133	REYDELL	72366-72366	MARVELL	72474-72474	WALCOTT
72030-72030	CLEVELAND	72134-72134	ROE	72367-72367	MELLWOOD	72475-72475	WALDENBURG
72031-72031	CLINTON	72135-72135	ROLAND	72368-72368	MORO	72476-72476	WALNUT RIDGE
72032-72035	CONWAY	72136-72136	ROMANCE	72369-72369	ONEIDA	72478-72478	WARM SPRINGS
72036-72036	COTTON PLANT	72137-72137	ROSE BUD	72370-72370	OSCEOLA	72479-72479	WEINER
72037-72037	COY	72139-72139	RUSSELL	72372-72372	PALESTINE	72482-72482	WILLIFORD
72038-72038	CROCKETTS BLUFF	72140-72140	SAINT CHARLES	72373-72373	PARKIN	72501-72503	BATESVILLE
72039-72039	DAMASCUS	72141-72141	SCOTLAND	72374-72374	POPLAR GROVE	72512-72512	HORSESHOE BEND
72040-72040	DES ARC	72142-72142	SCOTT	72376-72376	PROCTOR	72513-72513	ASH FLAT
72041-72041	DE VALLS BLUFF	72143-72149	SEARCY	72377-72377	RIVERVALE	72515-72515	BEXAR
		72150-72150	SHERIDAN	72378-72378	ROUND POND	72516-72516	BOSWELL
		72152-72152	SHERRILL	72379-72379	SNOW LAKE	72517-72517	BROCKWELL
				72381-72381	TOMATO	72519-72519	CALICO ROCK

72520-72520 CAMP	72650-72650 MARSHALL	72837-72837 DOVER
72521-72521 CAVE CITY	72651-72651 MIDWAY	72838-72838 GRAVELLY
72522-72522 CHARLOTTE	72653-72654 MOUNTAIN HOME	72839-72839 HAGARVILLE
72523-72523 CONCORD	72655-72655 MOUNT JUDEA	72840-72840 HARTMAN
72524-72524 CORD	72657-72657 TIMBO	72841-72841 HARVEY
72525-72525 CHEROKEE VILLAGE	72658-72659 NORFORK	72842-72842 HAVANA
72526-72526 CUSHMAN	72660-72660 OAK GROVE	72843-72843 HECTOR
72527-72527 DESHA	72661-72661 OAKLAND	72844-72844 HUNT
72528-72528 DOLPH	72662-72662 OMAHA	72845-72845 KNOXVILLE
72529-72529 CHEROKEE VILLAGE	72663-72663 ONIA	72846-72846 LAMAR
72530-72530 DRASCO	72666-72666 PARTHENON	72847-72847 LONDON
72531-72531 ELIZABETH	72668-72668 PEEL	72851-72851 NEW BLAINE
72532-72532 EVENING SHADE	72669-72669 PINDALL	72852-72852 OARK
72533-72533 FIFTY SIX	72670-72670 PONCA	72853-72853 OLA
72534-72534 FLORAL	72672-72672 PYATT	72854-72854 OZONE
72536-72536 FRANKLIN	72675-72675 SAINT JOE	72855-72855 PARIS
72537-72537 GAMALIEL	72677-72677 SUMMIT	72856-72856 PELSOR
72538-72538 GEPP	72679-72679 TILLY	72857-72857 PLAINVIEW
72539-72539 GLENCOE	72680-72680 TIMBO	72858-72858 POTTSVILLE
72540-72540 GUION	72682-72682 VALLEY SPRINGS	72860-72860 ROVER
72542-72542 HARDY	72683-72683 VENDOR	72863-72863 SCRANTON
72543-72543 HEBER SPRINGS	72685-72685 WESTERN GROVE	72865-72865 SUBIACO
72544-72544 HENDERSON	72686-72686 WITTS SPRINGS	72867-72867 WAVELAND
72545-72545 HEBER SPRINGS	72687-72687 YELLVILLE	72901-72919 FORT SMITH
72546-72546 IDA	72701-72704 FAYETTEVILLE	72921-72921 ALMA
72550-72550 LOCUST GROVE	72711-72711 AVOCA	72923-72923 BARLING
72553-72553 MAGNESS	72712-72712 BENTONVILLE	72924-72924 BATES
72554-72554 MAMMOTH SPRING	72714-72715 BELLA VISTA	72926-72926 BOLES
72555-72555 MARCELLA	72716-72716 BENTONVILLE	72927-72927 BOONEVILLE
72556-72556 MELBOURNE	72717-72717 CANEHILL	72928-72928 BRANCH
72557-72557 MOKO	72718-72718 CAVE SPRINGS	72930-72930 CECIL
72560-72560 MOUNTAIN VIEW	72719-72719 CENTERTON	72932-72932 CEDARVILLE
72561-72561 MOUNT PLEASANT	72721-72721 COMBS	72933-72933 CHARLESTON
72562-72562 NEWARK	72722-72722 DECATUR	72934-72934 CHESTER
72564-72564 OIL TROUGH	72727-72727 ELKINS	72935-72935 DYER
72565-72565 OXFORD	72728-72728 ELM SPRINGS	72936-72936 GREENWOOD
72566-72566 PINEVILLE	72729-72729 EVANSVILLE	72937-72937 HACKETT
72567-72567 PLEASANT GROVE	72730-72730 FARMINGTON	72938-72938 HARTFORD
72568-72568 PLEASANT PLAINS	72732-72732 GARFIELD	72940-72940 HUNTINGTON
72569-72569 POUGHKEEPSIE	72733-72733 GATEWAY	72941-72941 LAVACA
72571-72571 ROSIE	72734-72734 GENTRY	72943-72943 MAGAZINE
72572-72572 SAFFELL	72735-72735 GOSHEN	72944-72944 MANSFIELD
72573-72573 SAGE	72736-72736 GRAVETTE	72945-72945 MIDLAND
72575-72575 SALADO	72737-72737 GREENLAND	72946-72946 MOUNTAINBURG
72576-72576 SALEM	72738-72738 HINDSVILLE	72947-72947 MULBERRY
72577-72577 SIDNEY	72739-72739 HIWASSE	72948-72948 NATURAL DAM
72578-72578 STURKIE	72740-72740 HUNTSVILLE	72949-72949 OZARK
72579-72579 SULPHUR ROCK	72741-72741 JOHNSON	72950-72950 PARKS
72581-72581 TUMBLING SHOALS	72742-72742 KINGSTON	72951-72951 RATCLIFF
72583-72583 VIOLA	72744-72744 LINCOLN	72952-72952 RUDY
72584-72584 VIOLET HILL	72745-72745 LOWELL	72955-72955 UNIONTOWN
72585-72585 WIDEMAN	72747-72747 MAYSVILLE	72956-72957 VAN BUREN
72587-72587 WISEMAN	72749-72749 MORROW	72958-72958 WALDRON
72601-72602 HARRISON	72751-72751 PEA RIDGE	72959-72959 WINSLOW
72610-72610 ALCO	72752-72752 PETTIGREW	
72611-72611 ALPENA	72753-72753 PRAIRIE GROVE	
72612-72612 BASS	72756-72758 ROGERS	
72613-72613 BEAVER	72760-72760 SAINT PAUL	
72615-72615 BERGMAN	72761-72761 SILOAM SPRINGS	
72616-72616 BERRYVILLE	72762-72766 SPRINGDALE	
72617-72617 BIG FLAT	72767-72767 SPRINGTOWN	
72618-72618 BRUNO	72768-72768 SULPHUR SPRINGS	
72619-72619 BULL SHOALS	72769-72769 SUMMERS	
72623-72623 CLARKRIDGE	72770-72770 TONTITOWN	
72624-72624 COMPTON	72773-72773 WESLEY	
72626-72626 COTTER	72774-72774 WEST FORK	
72628-72628 DEER	72775-72775 WHEELER	
72629-72629 DENNARD	72776-72776 WITTER	
72630-72630 DIAMOND CITY	72801-72812 RUSSELLVILLE	
72631-72632 EUREKA SPRINGS	72820-72820 ALIX	
72633-72633 EVERTON	72821-72821 ALTUS	
72634-72634 FLIPPIN	72822-72823 ATKINS	
72635-72635 GASSVILLE	72824-72824 BELLEVILLE	
72636-72636 GILBERT	72826-72826 BLUE MOUNTAIN	
72638-72638 GREEN FOREST	72827-72827 BLUFFTON	
72639-72639 HARRIET	72828-72828 BRIGGSVILLE	
72640-72640 HASTY	72829-72829 CENTERVILLE	
72641-72641 JASPER	72830-72830 CLARKSVILLE	
72642-72642 LAKEVIEW	72832-72832 COAL HILL	
72644-72644 LEAD HILL	72833-72833 DANVILLE	
72645-72645 LESLIE	72834-72834 DARDANELLE	
72648-72648 MARBLE FALLS	72835-72835 DELAWARE	

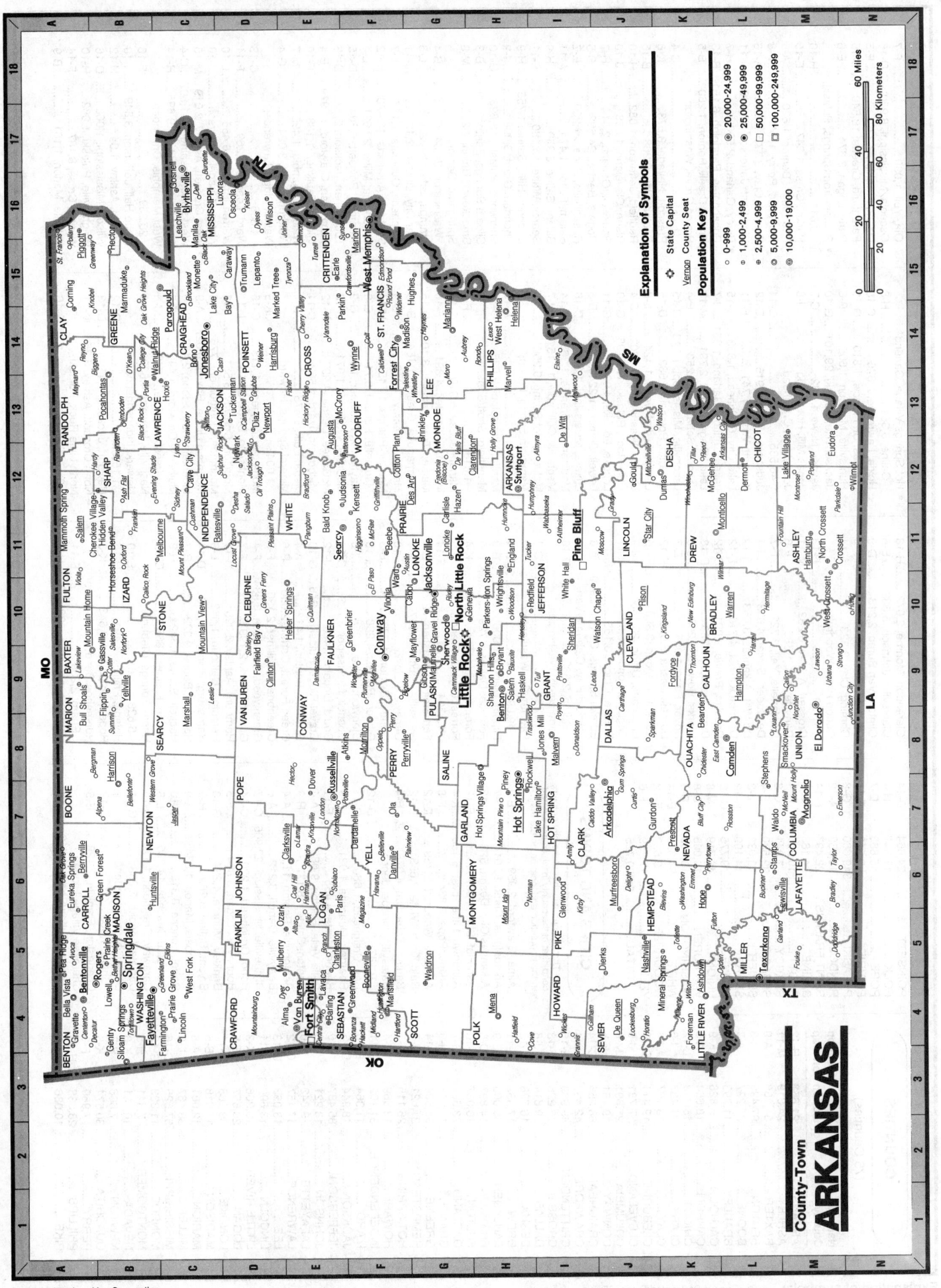

County-Town
ARKANSAS

Explanation of Symbols

✧ State Capital
Vernon ● County Seat

Population Key

○ 0-999	◉ 20,000-24,999
● 1,000-2,499	◉ 25,000-49,999
● 2,500-4,999	☐ 50,000-99,999
◉ 5,000-9,999	☐ 100,000-249,999
◉ 10,000-19,000	

60 Miles
80 Kilometers

CITIES AND TOWNS

Note: The first name is that of the city or town, second, that of the county in which it is located, then the population and location on the map.

Explanation of symbols: • — Census Designated Place (CDP)

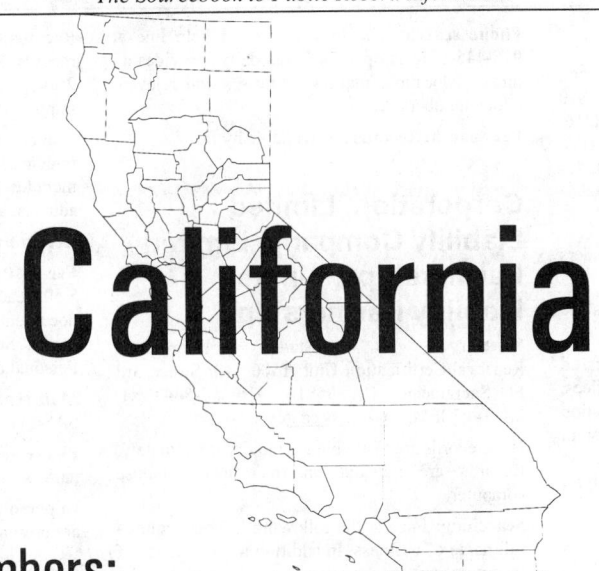

California

General Help Numbers:

Governor's Office
State Capitol, 1st Floor
Sacramento, CA 95814
www.governor.ca.gov/state
/govsite/gov_homepage.jsp

916-445-2841
Fax 916-445-4633
8:30AM-5PM

Attorney General's Office
Justice Department
PO Box 944255
Sacramento, CA 94244-2550
http://caag.state.ca.us

916-445-9555,445-3360
Fax 916-323-5341
8AM-5PM

Legislative Records
State Capitol, Room B-32
Sacramento, CA 95814
www.leginfo.ca.gov

916-445-2323
Fax 916-322-1257
8AM-5PM

State Archives
1020 "O" St
Sacramento, CA 95814
www.ss.ca.gov/archives/archives.htm

916-653-7715/2246
Fax 916-653-7363
9:30AM-4PM

State Specifics:

Capital:
Sacramento
Sacramento County

Time Zone:
PST

Number of Counties:
58

Population:
35,893,799

Website:
www.state.ca.us/state/portal/myca_homepage.jsp

State Agencies

Criminal Records

Access to Records is Restricted.

Department of Justice, Records Security Section, PO Box 903417, Sacramento, CA 94203-4170 (Courier address: 4949 Broadway, Sacramento, CA 95820); 916-227-3460 (Dept of Justice), 916-227-3849 (General Information), 916-227-3812 (Sealing & Dismissal), 916-227-4815-Fax; 8AM-5PM.

www.caag.state.ca.us

SEVERE LIMITATIONS! Penal Code Sec. 11105.3 limits access to searches involving child care, education, the handicapped and mentally impaired. The subject can obtain their own copy. Entities must be pre-approved before records can be ordered. 99% of arrest records are fingerprint supported, entered from final disposition.

Statewide Court Records

Administration Office of Courts, Office of Communications, 455 Golden Gate Ave, San Francisco, CA 94102-3660; 415-865-4200, 415-865-4205-Fax; 8AM-5PM.

www.courtinfo.ca.gov

All trial court record access must be done at the local level.

Access by: online.

Online search: There is no statewide online computer access available for county court records. The website offers access to all opinions from the Supreme and Appeals courts from 1850 to present. Opinions not certified for publications are available for last 60 days. The site is an excellent source of information about court procedures.

Sexual Offender Registry

Department of Justice, Sexual Offender Program, PO Box 903387, Sacramento, CA 94203-3870 (Courier address: 4949 Broadway, Rm H216, Sacramento, CA 95820); 900-448-3000 (Fee Search), 916-227-4199 (Tracking), 916-227-4345-Fax; 8AM-5PM.

www.caag.state.ca.us

There are over 99,715 registered sexual offenders in CA.

It takes 48 hours or less before new records are available for inquiry.

Searching: Offender information can be accessed 3 ways: 1) in person at DOJ offices, sheriff offices, and police departments in cities with population exceeding 200,000; 2) fee-based phone system from DOJ; 3) mail requests to DOJ. Include the following in your request-full name; also helpful DOB and SSN.

Access by: mail, phone, online.

Fee & Payment: name search by mail is $4.00, there is no fee to search using the online system. Fee payee: CA Department of Justice

Mail search: Turnaround time: 3 to 5 business days. Names searches are $4.00 per name and the request must contain 6 names or more. Mail requests are available to businesses and organizations.

Phone search: The public may call the CA Sexual Offender 900 service at 900-448-3000. There is a fee of $10.00 per call for checks on up to two names.

Online search: Search free at http://meganslaw.ca.gov/index.htm. This site will provide access to information on more than 63,000 persons required to register in California as sex offenders. One may search by a sex offender's specific name or by geographic location including ZIP Code. Specific home addresses are displayed on more than 33,500 offenders.

Incarceration Records

California Department of Corrections & Reh, ID & Warrants, PO Box 942883, Sacramento, CA 94283-0001; 916-557-5933 (Inmate Check Line (Media Only)), 916-445-6713 (ID & Warrants (Public Inquiry)), 916-445-7682 (Dept. of Corrections Main #), 916-327-1988-Fax; 8AM-5PM.

www.cdcr.ca.gov

The state provides no online searching, however a private company offers free web access to state/DOC records at www.vinelink.com/index.jsp.

Records are available on current and former inmates. It takes about 70 days before new records are available for inquiry.

Searching: Please note that for new or transferring inmates it can take up to seven business days to update location information. Include the following in your request-full name, DOB, your fax and phone numbers; also helpful: inmate number. Location, conviction and sentencing information, and county of conviction are released. Agency prefers to return results via fax. The following data is not released: case specifics, which should be acquired from the courts.

Access by: mail, phone, fax.

Fee & Payment: There is no fee.

Mail search: Turnaround time: 4-6 days.

Phone search: The Inmate Locator help line at 916-445-6713 is open 24 hours daily. Provides an inmate's location, mailing addresses and relevant phone numbers.

Fax search: Records are available by fax.

Corporation, Limited Liability Company, Limited Partnerships, Limited Liability Partnerships

Secretary of State, Information Retrieval/Certification Unit, 1500 11th Street, 3rd Fl, Sacramento, CA 95814; 916-657-5448 x1, 8AM-4:30PM. www.ss.ca.gov

New records are available for inquiry immediately. Records are indexed on microfiche, inhouse computer.

Searching: Include the following in your request-full name of business. In addition to the articles of incorporation, corporation records include the following information: Statement of Officers (up to 2), Prior (merged) or amended names, Inactive and Reserved names. Reserved names are not available on the online search.

Access by: mail, phone, fax, in person, online.

Fee & Payment: Statement of Officers or articles of incorporation and amendments is $1.00 first page, $.50 each add'l. A status report with officers is $4.00. Add $5.00 for certification for any document. Fee payee: Secretary of State. Prepayment required. Personal checks accepted. No credit cards accepted.

Mail search: Turnaround time: 3 to 5 weeks. A SASE is requested.

Phone search: Only pre-paid accounts have telephone access to corporate status and name availability/reservation. Fee is $4.00 per name searched.

Fax search: Return of documents and/or status information is an additional $5.00 per document, $10.00 if international.

In person search: Turnaround time is while you wait for computer printouts of status reports, but a $10.00 expedite fee is charged.

Online search: The website at http://kepler.ss.ca.gov/list.html offers access to more than 2 million records including corporation, LLC, LP and LLP. Information available includes status, file number, date of filing and agent for service of process. The file is updated weekly.

Expedited service: Over-the counter requests for immediate service, other than for computer printouts of status reports, entails an additional $10.00 fee.

Assumed Name, Fictitious Name

Records not maintained by a state level agency.

Records are found at the county level.

Trademarks/Servicemarks

Secretary of State, Trademark Unit, PO Box 942877, Sacramento, CA 94277-0001 (Courier address: 1500 11th Street, 2nd Fl, Sacramento, CA 95814); 916-653-3984 (Trademark/Servicemarks), 8AM-5PM. www.ss.ca.gov/business/ts/ts.htm

Records are available for active and expired records. Records are microfilmed monthly. It takes 2 to 3 weeks before new records are available for inquiry. Records are indexed on index cards.

Searching: Include the following in your request-trademark/servicemark name. Information returned includes name of trademark, name of owner and address, and date of filing.

Access by: mail, phone, in person.

Fee & Payment: Copies are $1.00 per page and $.50 each add'l. Certification is $5.00 per document. A Certificate of Status is $5.00. Fee payee: Secretary of State. Prepayment required. Personal checks accepted but no credit cards.

Mail search: Turnaround time: 2 to 3 weeks. A SASE is requested. No fee for mail request.

Phone search: No fee for telephone request of a name search. There is a limit of 2 searches per call.

In person search: You can wait for results. If lists are presented, then the results are returned by mail.

Uniform Commercial Code, Federal & State Tax Liens

UCC Division, Secretary of State, PO Box 942835, Sacramento, CA 94235 (Courier address: 1500 11th St, Room 255, Sacramento, CA 95814); 916-653-3516 x2, 8AM-5PM.

www.ss.ca.gov/business/ucc/ucc.htm

This office does not currently offer fax service, but may make it available in the near future.

Records are available for current records and expired records up to 1 year after lapse. There is an index on computer dating back to 1965. New records are available for inquiry immediately. Records are indexed on inhouse computer.

Searching: Use search request form UCC-11; one form per debtor name. The search includes federal and some state tax liens on businesses. Federal tax liens on individuals are filed at the county level, state tax liens are filed at either location. Include the following in your request-debtor name. Item 3b-3d on the UCC11 provide fields for narrowing the search by a specific address, by a date range or by a Social Security or federal tax number

Access by: mail, in person, online.

Fee & Payment: The search fee is $10.00 per debtor name. The copy fee is $1.00 for the first page of the document and $.50 each additional page. There is a certification fee of $5.00 if the state seal is needed. Note that fees are different for the online system, Fee payee: Secretary of State. Prepayment required. Credit cards are only for over-the-counter services. Those conducting business frequently with this office may utilize a prepaid account option. Personal checks accepted. Major credit cards accepted.

Mail search: Turnaround time: 2-3 days.

In person search: There is an additional $6.00 special handling fee for each document received over the counter.

Online search: UCC Connect provides an online service at https://uccconnect.ss.ca.gov/acct/acct-login.asp to conduct a variety of inquiries and place orders for copies and debtor search certificates on records and submit UCC filings. Ongoing requesters can become subscribers. Fees are based on name inquires ($5.00) and images viewed ($1.00). The web page has a complete list of fees and excellent FAQ section. Click on the Help tab.

Sales Tax Registrations

Board of Equalization, Sales and Use Tax Department, PO Box 942879, Sacramento, CA 94279-0001; 916-445-6362, 800-400-7115 (In California Only), 800-735-2922, 916-324-4433-Fax; 8AM-5PM.

www.boe.ca.gov

A list of the field offices is available at www.boe.ca.gov/info/phone.htm.

Searching: This Board will provide owners' name, firm name, business address, account number, starting date, whether account is active or closed and, if closed, the closing date. The responsibility of assisting taxpayers in verifying the validity of resale certificates is primarily at the District level, but this office will provide search services. Requesters must provide the name of the business, its location, and the permit #.

Access by: mail, phone, fax, online.

Fee & Payment: No charge is required for verification of resale certificates and permits. However, a fee for other requests, such as those received from attorneys and collection agencies, is $3.00 per name searched. Fee payee: Board of Equalization. Prepayment required. Monthly billing is available for ongoing requesters. Personal checks accepted. No credit cards accepted.

Mail search: Turnaround time: 2 weeks. A SASE is requested.

Phone search: No fee for telephone request. The 24 hour phone service is offered to verify a seller's permit is valid. Calls are not limited to number of requests.

Fax search: Generally, turnaround time is 2 weeks.

Online search: The Internet site provides a permit verification service. Permit number is needed. System is open 5AM to midnight.

Other access: Lists, available for a fee, are sorted in a number of ways including CA Industry Code. For further information and fees, call the Technical Services Division at 916-445-5848

Birth Certificates

State Department of Health Svcs, Office of Vital Records - MS 5103, PO Box 997410, Sacramento, CA 95899-7410 (Courier address: 1501 Capitol Ave, Rm 71-1110, Sacramento, CA 95814); 916-445-2684 (Recording), 8AM-4:30PM.

www.dhs.ca.gov/chs/OVR/default.htm

If requesting an Authorized Certified Birth or Death certificate online or by fax, applicants must complete a Sworn Statement and a notarized Certificate of Acknowledgment in the presence of a Notary Public.

Records are available from July 1905 on. It takes 1 to 3 months before new records are available for inquiry. Records are indexed on microfiche, inhouse computer. Records are normally destroyed after (records kept indefinitely).

Searching: Certified records are not open to the public. Requester must be related to the subject or attorney representing subject or subject's family. However, persons who are not eligible to receive a Certified Copy can receive a Certified Informational Copy. Include the following in your request-full name, mother's full maiden name, date of birth, place of birth, father's full name is optional. Certified copy must included notarized

signature of requester. If you do not use their form, the search may be delayed 2-3 weeks.

Access by: mail, fax, online.

Fee & Payment: The fee for a certified copy is $15.00, if the birth date is not known, a fee of $15.00 is charged for each decade searched. Fee payee: Office of Vital Records. Prepayment required. Personal checks and money orders accepted. Credit cards accepted only by the vendor Vitalchek.

Mail search: Turnaround time: may exceed 1 month. Always include your daytime phone number. No SASE is required. Download and use the request form at the website.

Fax search: Applicant must complete a Sworn Statement and a notarized Certificate of Acknowledgment in the presence of a Notary Public.

Online search: Applicant must complete a Sworn Statement and a notarized Certificate of Acknowledgment in the presence of a Notary Public. Records may be ordered from a state-designated vendor - www.vitalchek.com.

Expedited service: This is only available online or fax via the www.vitalchek.com (not through the state). Turnaround time: 22-25 days. Add $60.00 per event for express delivery service and use of credit card.

Death Records

State Department of Health Svcs, Office of Vital Records - MS 5103, PO Box 997410, Sacramento, CA 95899-7410 (Courier address: 1501 Capitol Ave, Rm 71-1110, Sacramento, CA 95814); 916-445-2684, 8AM-4:30PM.

www.dhs.ca.gov/chs/default.htm

Records are available from July 1905 to present. It takes 1 to 3 months before new records are available for inquiry. Records are indexed on microfiche, inhouse computer. Records are kept indefinitely.

Searching: Certified records are not open to the public. Requester must be related to the subject or attorney representing subject or subject's family. However, persons who are not eligible to receive a Certified Copy can receive a Certified Informational Copy. Include the following in your request-full name, date of death, date of birth, place of death, Social Security Number. Certified copy must included notarized signature of requester. There will be a 2-3 week delay if you do not use their form.

Access by: mail, online.

Fee & Payment: Search fee is $13.00 per name for each decade searched, the fee is $9.00 for a fetal death certificate. Fee payee: Office of Vital Records. Prepayment required. Personal checks accepted. Credit cards accepted only by the vendor Vitalchek.

Mail search: Turnaround time: 1 month or more. Download and use the request form at the website.

Online search: Access death records from 1940 thru 1997 at http://vitals.rootsweb.com/ca/death/search.cgi. Also, records are available from a state-designated vendor - www.vitalchek.com.

Expedited service: This is only available online or fax via the www.vitalchek.com (not through the state). Turnaround time: 22-25 days. Add $60.00 per event for express delivery service and use of credit card.

Marriage Certificates, Death Certificates

Access to Records is Restricted.

State Department of Health Svcs, Office of Vital Records - MS 5103, PO Box 997410, Sacramento, CA 95899-7410 (Courier address: 1501 Capitol Ave, Rm 71-1110, Sacramento, CA 95814); 916-445-2684, 8AM-4:30PM.

www.dhs.ca.gov/chs/default.htm

It can take 2 to 3 years for this agency to process requests. Therefore it is strongly urged to search at the county level. This office holds records from July 1905 to March 1986 and 1998 to 2000. ($13.00 fee, 2-3 year turnaround time.) Records between 1986 to 1997 and 2000 to present must be searched at the county level; state does not have access to these records.

Workers' Compensation Records

Division of Workers' Compensation, Headquarters, 455 Golden Gate Ave, 9th Fl, San Francisco, CA 94102; 415-703-4600, 415-703-4717-Fax; 8AM-5PM.

www.dir.ca.gov/dwc/dwc_home_page.htm

Per law, no addresses of any injured workers are given out. There are 3 claims offices as follows - Oakland (415-703-4955); Los Angeles (213-576-7300; and Sacramento (916-263-2774).

Records are available for varying periods depending on injury.

Searching: Using the proper forms, one can either view a file or ask if records exist. This authorization process does not require the signature or approval of the claimant. Forms may be faxed. All forms must be obtained from this agency and require approval before a searcher can present a request at the district office.

Access by: mail, fax, in person.

Fee & Payment: There is no search fee.

Mail search: Turnaround time: variable. You must use "Request for WCAB Case # Search Form" and the agency will let you know if there is a record. The state suggests that out-of-state requesters use a local CA retriever who already has the necessary authorization to search. No SASE is required.

Fax search: Turnaround is usually 1 week.

In person search: Requester must be authorized first (by this office) with either the "Request to View a WCAB Case File" or "Request for DWC Authorization # for Access to Index Cards." Then, with a case number, requester can visit any of the 25 district offices.

Driver Records

Department of Motor Vehicles, Information Services Branch, PO Box 944247, Mail Station G199, Sacramento, CA 94244-2470 (Courier address: 2415 First Ave, Sacramento, CA 95818); 916-657-8098, 916-657-5564 (Requester Accounts), 8AM-5PM.

www.dmv.ca.gov

The public counter is closed for record access by walk-in requesters. Copies of tickets are not available at the state level.

Records are available for 3 years from accidents and minor moving violations dates and 7 years for major violations. A Failure to Appear is reported for 5 years, and 10 years if for a DUI offense. It takes 10 days or more (as received from the courts) before new records are available for inquiry. Records are normally destroyed after the Director determines they are no longer necessary to retain.

Searching: Commercial requesters/users who meet certain criteria must maintain a Commercial Requester Account, which may require a $50,000 bond if confidential address information is released. For more details call 916-657-5564 or visit www.dmv.ca.gov/forms. Include the following in your request-driver's license number, full name, date of birth. Non-commercial requesters are known as "casual requesters." These requests may be held for 10 days and the state notifies the licensee of each release. If released, address is shielded unless a permissible use shown. The following data is not released: mental health records, medical records, pending records, and Social Security Numbers.

Access by: mail, phone, in person, online.

Fee & Payment: Manual searches are $5.00; electronic MVRs are $2.00; guarantor's signature-$20.00; license status only $1.00 via an approved vendor. Fee payee: California Department of Motor Vehicles. Prepayment required. Personal checks accepted. No credit cards accepted.

Mail search: Turnaround time: 1 to 2 weeks.

Phone search: Available, however, records are only released to the subject. Call 916-657-6525.

In person search: The counter is closed to the general public, unless it is your own record. A licensee may purchase a copy of own record at any DMV Field Office.

Online search: The department offers online access, but a $10,000 one-time setup fee is required. The fee is $2.00 per record. The system is available 24 hours, 7 days a week. For more information call 916-657-5582.

Other access: Employers may monitor their drivers in the Pull Notice Program. The DMV informs the organization when there is activity on enrolled drivers. Call 916-657-6346 for details.

Vehicle Ownership, Vehicle Identification, Vessel Ownership, Vessel Registration

Department of Motor Vehicle, Office of Information Services, PO Box 944247, MS-G199, Sacramento, CA 94244-2470 (Courier address: 2415 First Ave, Sacramento, CA 95818); 916-657-8098, 916-657-5564 (Commercial Accounts), 916-657-6893 (Vessel Registration), 8AM-5PM.

www.dmv.ca.gov

All watercraft must be registered if over 8 ft (except rowboats).

Records are available for thirteen years when microfilmed. It takes up to 10 days before new records are available for inquiry.

Searching: It is suggested to use departmental forms, which can be obtained the webpage or fax request to 916-657-7243. Include the following in your request-license plate, CF number, VIN or vessel hull number. There are two types of requesters: "casual requesters" and "requester account holders." For those businesses and entities who need to access on a regular basis, call 916-657-5564. A bond may be required.

Access by: mail, in person, online.

Fee & Payment: Current record by license, VIN or CF#, by registration owner name and address-$5.00; magnetic tape inquiry-$2.00; owner as of data by license, VIN or CF#-$5.00; current automated history data-$5.00; photocopies-$20.00 per year. Fee payee: California Department of Motor Vehicles. Prepayment required. Personal checks accepted. No credit cards accepted.

Mail search: Turnaround time: 1 to 2 weeks. A SASE is requested.

In person search: Only the registered, owner, spouse, or minor child (with same address) can purchase a copy of their vehicle/vessel record at any DMV field office.

Online search: 24 hour online access is limited to certain Authorized Vendors. Requesters may not use the data for direct marketing, solicitation, nor resell for those purposes. A bond is required and very high fees are involved. For more information, call the Electronic Access Administration Section at 916-657-5582.

Other access: California offers delivery of registration information on FTP VPN, magnetic tape, disk or paper within special parameters. Release of information is denied for commercial marketing purposes.

Accident Reports

Department of Motor Vehicles, Accident Reports, PO Box 942884, Sacramento, CA 94284; 800-777-0133, 8AM-5PM (open at 9AM of F).

www.dmv.ca.gov

Most accident reports are held by the California Highway Patrol or local law enforcement agency that filed the report. There are 115 area offices of the California Highway Patrol. Fees vary. Limited reports are held by this office.

It takes 30 to 60 days before new records are available for inquiry. Records are normally destroyed after 4 years.

Searching: Reports are made if there was property damage of more than $750 ($500 for accidents prior to January 1, 2003), bodily injury or death. Include the following in your request-name and DOB of driver, location, date, and name of requester. Copies of SR-1 accident reports are provided to limited requesters by the Department of Motor Vehicles. Note the CA Highway Patrol has a centralized database of older records (at least 3 years old or more).

Access by: mail.

Fee & Payment: The fee is $20.00.

Mail search: SR-1 accident reports are available by mail from this office.

Voter Registration

Access to Records is Restricted.

Secretary of State, Elections Division, 1500 11th Street, 5th Fl, Sacramento, CA 95814; 916-657-2166, 916-653-3214-Fax; 8AM-5PM.

www.ss.ca.gov/elections/elections.htm

Records are not open and cannot be viewed at this agency. Individual verification must be done at the local level. The state will sell CDs with all or portions of the statewide database for political or pre-approved purposes. Call for details.

GED Certificates

GED Records Center, PO Box 4005, Concord, CA 94524-4005; 866-370-4740, 800-331-6316, 8AM-5PM.

www.cde.ca.gov/ta/tg/gd

Records are available from July 1990, prior are archived. It takes 2 months before new records are available for inquiry.

Searching: To verify or to obtain a copy of a transcript, all of the following is required: a signed release, name, date of birth, date/year of test, SSN, and city of test.

Access by: mail.

Fee & Payment: There is no fee for verifications. Score reports are provided for $5.00; there is a $12.00 fee (money order only) for duplicate certificates. Fee payee: Ca Dept of Ed Prepayment required. Personal checks not accepted. Credit cards not accepted.

Mail search: Turnaround time is 7-10 working days or 2-3 weeks if the information is older than 1990. SASE is suggested.

Hunting and Fishing License Information

Access to Records is Restricted.

Department of Fish & Game, License & Revenue Branch, 3211 "S" St, Sacramento, CA 95816; 916-227-2245, 916-227-2261-Fax; 9AM-5PM.

www.dfg.ca.gov

Records are not available to the public.

California State Licensing Agencies

For details about the agency responsible for licensing/certifying/registering an item below or in the Agency Quick Finder section, match an item's number with the number of the agency in the *Licensing Agency Information* section.

California Licenses Searchable Online

Acupuncturist #1 .... www.acupuncture.ca.gov
Administrative Services #26 .... www.ctc.ca.gov/credentials/default.html
Adoption Agency #50.................................... www.ccld.ca.gov/docs/ccld_search/ccld_search.aspx
Air Conditioning Contractor #28................... http://www2.cslb.ca.gov/CSLB_LIBRARY/Name+Request.asp
Alarm Company/Employee/Mgr. #22.............. www.dca.ca.gov/bsis/lookup.htm
Apprentice Program #48................................ www.dir.ca.gov/databases/das/aigstart.asp
Architect #7 .... www.cab.ca.gov/querylic.htm
Asbestos Consultant/Surveillance #52 .... www.dir.ca.gov/databases/doshcaccsst/caccsst_query_1.html
Asbestos Contractor #52 .... www.dir.ca.gov/databases/doshacru/acrusearch.html
Asbestos Trainer #52..................................... www.dir.ca.gov/databases/doshcaccsst/aheratp.asp
Asbestos Worker/Trainee #52 .... www.dir.ca.gov/DOSH/ACRU/TP_AsbestosTrainingCertificates.html
Attorney #23 .... http://members.calbar.ca.gov/search/member.aspx
Audiologist #42 .... www.slpab.ca.gov/
Automobile Dealer/Repair #19....................... www.smogcheck.ca.gov/stdPage.asp?Body=/Consumer/verify_a_license.htm
Bank #11.. www.dfi.ca.gov/directry/tl.asp
Bar Association #23.. http://members.calbar.ca.gov/search/ba_search.aspx
Barber Instructor/School #4 .... www.barbercosmo.ca.gov/license.htm
Barber Shop/Barber/Barber Apprentice #4...... www.barbercosmo.ca.gov/license.htm
Baton Training Facility/Instructor #22 .... www.dca.ca.gov/bsis/lookup.htm
Brake & Lamp Adjuster #19............................ www.smogcheck.ca.gov/stdPage.asp?Body=/Consumer/verify_a_license.htm
Brake Station #19 .... www.smogcheck.ca.gov/stdPage.asp?Body=/Consumer/verify_a_license.htm
Building Contr., General-Class B #28.............. http://www2.cslb.ca.gov/CSLB_LIBRARY/Name+Request.asp
Business/Industrial Dev. Company #11............ www.dfi.ca.gov/directry/bidco.asp
Cabinet/Millwork Contractor #28.................... http://www2.cslb.ca.gov/CSLB_LIBRARY/Name+Request.asp
Care Facility for Children, Transitional #50...... www.ccld.ca.gov/docs/ccld_search/ccld_search.aspx
Care Facility for Chronically Ill #50 .... www.ccld.ca.gov/docs/ccld_search/ccld_search.aspx
Cemetery, Cemetery Broker/Seller #25........... www.dca.ca.gov/cemetery/lookup.htm
Child Care Center #50 .... www.ccld.ca.gov/docs/ccld_search/ccld_search.aspx
Chiropractic Business #46.............................. www.chiro.ca.gov/licsearch/
Chiropractor #46.. www.chiro.ca.gov/licsearch/
Clinic Pharmaceutical Permit #13................... www.pharmacy.ca.gov/verify_lic.htm
Community Treatment Facility #50.................. www.ccld.ca.gov/docs/ccld_search/ccld_search.aspx
Concrete Contractor/Company #28.................. http://www2.cslb.ca.gov/CSLB_LIBRARY/Name+Request.asp
Conscious Sedation Permit #9 .... www.dbc.ca.gov/license_verification.html
Continuing Education Provider #8 .... www.bbs.ca.gov/weblokup.htm
Contractor, Business/Individual #28 .... www.cslb.ca.gov
Cosmetician/Cosmetologist #4....................... www.barbercosmo.ca.gov/license.htm
Cosmetology School #4.................................. https://app.dca.ca.gov/bppve/school-search/default.htm
Cosmetology/Electrology Busin's/Instr. #4 ...... www.barbercosmo.ca.gov/license.htm
Court Reporter (Shorthand Reporter) #29....... www.courtreportersboard.ca.gov
CPA/CPA Firm #6... www.dca.ca.gov/cba/lookup.htm
Crane Operator #52 .... www.dir.ca.gov/databases/crane/cranesearch.html
Credit Union #11.. www.dfi.ca.gov/directry/cu.asp
Cremated Remains Disposer #25.................... www.dca.ca.gov/cemetery/lookup.htm
Crematory #25 .... www.dca.ca.gov/cemetery/lookup.htm
Day Care, Adult/Child #50 .... www.ccld.ca.gov/docs/ccld_search/ccld_search.aspx
Dental Anesthesia Permit #9 .... www.dbc.ca.gov/license_verification.html
Dental Assistant #27...................................... www.comda.ca.gov/licensestatus.html
Dental Hygienist #27...................................... www.comda.ca.gov/licensestatus.html
Dental Registered Provider #9........................ www.dbc.ca.gov/license_verification.html
Dentist #9.. www.dbc.ca.gov/license_verification.html
Dentist Fictitious Name #9.............................. www.dbc.ca.gov/license_verification.html
Development Corporation #11......................... www.dfi.ca.gov/directry/directry.asp
Driving School #49... https://eg.dmv.ca.gov/olinq/SvOIDs
Drug Wholesaler/Drug Room #13................... www.pharmacy.ca.gov/verify_lic.htm
Drywall Contractor #28 .... http://www2.cslb.ca.gov/CSLB_LIBRARY/Name+Request.asp

Earthwork/Paving Contractor #28.....................http://www2.cslb.ca.gov/CSLB_LIBRARY/Name+Request.asp
Electrical Contr. & Electric Sign Contr. #28.....http://www2.cslb.ca.gov/CSLB_LIBRARY/Name+Request.asp
Electrologist #4.....................www.barbercosmo.ca.gov/license.htm
Electrology School #4.....................https://app.dca.ca.gov/bppve/school-search/default.htm
Electronics & Appliance Repair #20.....................www.bear.ca.gov/look-up.htm
Elevator Installation Contr. #28.....................http://www2.cslb.ca.gov/CSLB_LIBRARY/Name+Request.asp
Embalmer/Embalmer Apprentice #25.....................www.dca.ca.gov/cemetery/lookup.htm
Engineer (various disciplines) #10.....................www.dca.ca.gov/pels/l_lookup.htm
Esthetician #4.....................www.barbercosmo.ca.gov/license.htm
Family Child Care Home #50.....................www.ccld.ca.gov/docs/ccld_search/ccld_search.aspx
Farm Labor Contractor #48.....................www.dir.ca.gov/databases/dlselr/Farmlic.html
Fencing Contractor #28.....................http://www2.cslb.ca.gov/CSLB_LIBRARY/Name+Request.asp
Firearm Permit #22.....................www.dca.ca.gov/bsis/lookup.htm
Firearm Training Facility/Instr. #22.....................www.dca.ca.gov/bsis/lookup.htm
Flooring/Floor Covering Contr. #28.....................http://www2.cslb.ca.gov/CSLB_LIBRARY/Name+Request.asp
Foster Family Agency #50.....................www.ccld.ca.gov/docs/ccld_search/ccld_search.aspx
Fumigation #44.....................www.cdpr.ca.gov/docs/license/currlic.htm
Funeral Director/Establishment #25.....................www.dca.ca.gov/cemetery/lookup.htm
Funerary Training Establ./Apprentice #25.......www.dca.ca.gov/cemetery/lookup.htm
Garment Mfg #48.....................www.dir.ca.gov/databases/dlselr/Garmreg.html
Geologist / Geophysicist #18.....................www.geology.ca.gov/
Geologist, Engineering #18.....................www.geology.ca.gov/
Glazier #28.....................http://www2.cslb.ca.gov/CSLB_LIBRARY/Name+Request.asp
Group Home #50.....................www.ccld.ca.gov/docs/ccld_search/ccld_search.aspx
Healing Art Supervisor #31.....................www.applications.dhs.ca.gov/rhbxray/
Hearing Aid Dispenser #34.....................www.dca.ca.gov/hearingaid/
Heating & Warm-Air Vent. Contr. #28.....................http://www2.cslb.ca.gov/CSLB_LIBRARY/Name+Request.asp
Home Furnishings #21.....................www2.dca.ca.gov/pls/wllpub/wllqryna$lcev2.startup?p_qte_code=LIC&p_qte_pgm_code=5710
Horse Racing Entity/Occupation #24.....................www.chrb.ca.gov/license_search.htm
Hospital Pharmaceutical Exemptee #13.....................www.pharmacy.ca.gov/verify_lic.htm
Hydrogeologist #18.....................www.geology.ca.gov/
Hypodermic Needle & Syringe Dist. #13.....................www.pharmacy.ca.gov/verify_lic.htm
Industrial Loan Company, Premium #11.....................www.dfi.ca.gov/directry/tl.asp
Infant Center #50.....................www.ccld.ca.gov/docs/ccld_search/ccld_search.aspx
Insulation/Acoustical Contr. #28.....................http://www2.cslb.ca.gov/CSLB_LIBRARY/Name+Request.asp
Insurance Adjuster #32.....................www.insurance.ca.gov/docs/FS-Licensestatus.htm
Insurance Agent/Broker #32.....................www.insurance.ca.gov/docs/FS-Licensestatus.htm
Lamp Station #19.....................www.smogcheck.ca.gov/stdPage.asp?Body=/Consumer/verify_a_license.htm
Landscape Architect #35.....................www.latc.dca.ca.gov/licenseeinfo/search.htm
Landscaping Contractor #28.....................http://www2.cslb.ca.gov/CSLB_LIBRARY/Name+Request.asp
Legal Specialist #23.....................http://members.calbar.ca.gov/search/ls_search.aspx
Legal Specialization Provider #23.....................http://members.calbar.ca.gov/search/cert.aspx
Lobbyist #47.....................http://cal-access.ss.ca.gov/Lobbying/
Locksmith/Locksmith Company #22.....................www.dca.ca.gov/bsis/lookup.htm
Mammographic Facility #31.....................www.applications.dhs.ca.gov/rhbxray/
Manicurist #4.....................www.barbercosmo.ca.gov/license.htm
Marriage & Family Therapist #8.....................www.bbs.ca.gov/weblokup.htm
Masonry Contractor #28.....................http://www2.cslb.ca.gov/CSLB_LIBRARY/Name+Request.asp
Medical Doctor/Surgeon #36.....................www2.dca.ca.gov/pls/wllpub/wllqryna$lcev2.startup?p_qte_code=MDX&p_qte_pgm_code=6301
Medical Evaluator #52.....................www.dir.ca.gov/databases/imc/imcstartnew.asp
Midwife #36.....................http://www2.dca.ca.gov/pls/wllpub/wllqryna$lcev2.startup?p_qte_code=LM&p_qte_pgm_code=6200
Money Orders Issuer #11.....................www.dfi.ca.gov/directry/pi.asp
Nuclear Medicine Technologist #31.....................www.applications.dhs.ca.gov/rhbxray/
Nurse #16.....................www.rn.ca.gov/online/online.htm
Nursing Continuing Edu. Provider #16.....................www.rn.ca.gov/online/online.htm
Occupational Therapist or Assistant #51.......http://www2.dca.ca.gov/pls/wllpub/wllqryna$lcev2.startup?p_qte_code=OT&p_qte_pgm_code=1475
Optometrist #12.....................www.optometry.ca.gov/search.htm
Optometry Practice/Branch Office #12.....................www.optometry.ca.gov/search.htm
Ornamental Metal Contractor #28.....................http://www2.cslb.ca.gov/CSLB_LIBRARY/Name+Request.asp
Osteopath #36.....................www.opsc.org/displaycommon.cfm?an=1&subarticlenbr=9
Painting/Decorating Contractor #28.....................http://www2.cslb.ca.gov/CSLB_LIBRARY/Name+Request.asp
Parking/Highway Improvement Contr. #28.....................http://www2.cslb.ca.gov/CSLB_LIBRARY/Name+Request.asp
Patrol Operator, Private #22.....................www.dca.ca.gov/bsis/lookup.htm
Payment Instrument Issuer #11.....................www.dfi.ca.gov/directry/directry.asp
Pest Control Field Rep./Operator #44.....................www.cdpr.ca.gov/docs/license/currlic.htm

Pesticide Applicator #44 .... www.cdpr.ca.gov/docs/license/currlic.htm
Pharmaceutical Dist., Out-of-State #13 .... www.pharmacy.ca.gov/verify_lic.htm
Pharmaceutical Whlse./Exemptee #13............ www.pharmacy.ca.gov/verify_lic.htm
Pharmacist/Pharmacist Intern #13.................... www.pharmacy.ca.gov/verify_lic.htm
Pharmacy #13.. www.pharmacy.ca.gov/verify_lic.htm
Pharmacy Technician #13.................................. www.pharmacy.ca.gov/verify_lic.htm
Physical Therapist/Assistant #38.................... http://www2.dca.ca.gov/pls/wllpub/wllqryna$lcev2.startup?p_qte_code=PT&p_qte_pgm_code=6800
Physician Assistant #39.................................. http://www2.dca.ca.gov/pls/wllpub/wllqryna$lcev2.startup?p_qte_code=PA&p_qte_pgm_code=7000
Plastering Contractor #28 .... http://www2.cslb.ca.gov/CSLB_LIBRARY/Name+Request.asp
Plumber #28 .... http://www2.cslb.ca.gov/CSLB_LIBRARY/Name+Request.asp
Podiatrist #14.. www.bpm.ca.gov
Premium Finance Company #11 .... www.dfi.ca.gov/directry/pf.asp
Private Investigator #22 .... www.dca.ca.gov/bsis/lookup.htm
Psychiatric Technician #17 .... www.bvnpt.ca.gov/licverif.htm
Psychological Assistant #15 .... www.psychboard.ca.gov
Psychologist #15.. www.psychboard.ca.gov
Psychologist, Educational #8 .... www.bbs.ca.gov/weblokup.htm
Psychologist, Registered #15 .... www.psychboard.ca.gov/
Public Accountant-CPA #6 .... www.dca.ca.gov/cba/lookup.htm
Public Works Trainer #48 .... www.dir.ca.gov/databases/das/pwaddrstart.asp
Radioactive Material Licensee #31................. www.applications.dhs.ca.gov/rhbxray/
Radiologic Technologist #31 .... www.applications.dhs.ca.gov/rhbxray/
Real Estate Agent/Sales #33 .... www.dre.ca.gov/licstats.htm
Real Estate Broker/Corporation #33............... www.dre.ca.gov/licstats.htm
Refrigeration Contractor #28 .... http://www2.cslb.ca.gov/CSLB_LIBRARY/Name+Request.asp
Registered Veterinary Technician #40 .... www.vmb.ca.gov/lic1list.htm
Repossessor Agency/Mgr./Employee #22 ...... www.dca.ca.gov/bsis/lookup.htm
Residential Care for Elderly #50 .... www.ccld.ca.gov/docs/ccld_search/ccld_search.aspx
Residential Facility, Adult #50 .... www.ccld.ca.gov/docs/ccld_search/ccld_search.aspx
Respiratory Care Practitioner #41 .... www.rcb.ca.gov/license_verification_forms_instructions.htm
Roofing Contractor #28................................... http://www2.cslb.ca.gov/CSLB_LIBRARY/Name+Request.asp
Sanitation System Contractor #28................... http://www2.cslb.ca.gov/CSLB_LIBRARY/Name+Request.asp
Security Guard #22.. www.dca.ca.gov/bsis/lookup.htm
Service Contract Seller (Appliance) #20.......... www.bear.ca.gov/look-up.htm
Sheet Metal Contractor #28............................. http://www2.cslb.ca.gov/CSLB_LIBRARY/Name+Request.asp
Shelter, Temporary #50 .... www.ccld.ca.gov/docs/ccld_search/ccld_search.aspx
Smog Check Station/Technician #19............... www.smogcheck.ca.gov/stdPage.asp?Body=/Consumer/verify_a_license.htm
Social Rehabilitation Facility #50 .... www.ccld.ca.gov/docs/ccld_search/ccld_search.aspx
Social Worker, Clinical #8 .... www.bbs.ca.gov/weblokup.htm
Social Worker, Clinical Assoc #8 .... www.bbs.ca.gov/weblokup.htm
Solar Energy Contractor #28 .... http://www2.cslb.ca.gov/CSLB_LIBRARY/Name+Request.asp
Specialty Contractor-Class C #28................... http://www2.cslb.ca.gov/CSLB_LIBRARY/Name+Request.asp
Speech Pathologist/Audiologist Aide #42........ www.slpab.ca.gov/
Speech-Language Pathologist #42.................. www.slpab.ca.gov/
Steel Contractor #28....................................... http://www2.cslb.ca.gov/CSLB_LIBRARY/Name+Request.asp
Studio Teacher #48 .... www.dir.ca.gov/databases/dlselr/StudTch.html
Support Center, Adult #50 .... www.ccld.ca.gov/docs/ccld_search/ccld_search.aspx
Surgical Clinic Pharm., Nonprofit #13............. www.pharmacy.ca.gov/verify_lic.htm
Surveyor, Land #10 .... www.dca.ca.gov/pels/l_lookup.htm
Swimming Pool Contractor #28 .... http://www2.cslb.ca.gov/CSLB_LIBRARY/Name+Request.asp
Talent Agency #48... www.dir.ca.gov/databases/dlselr/Talag.html
Tax Education Provider #45 .... www.ctec.org/index.asp?pid=10
Tax Preparer #45... www.ctec.org/verify.asp
Termite Control #44... www.cdpr.ca.gov/docs/license/currlic.htm
Thrift & Loan Company #11 .... www.dfi.ca.gov/directry/directry.asp
Tile Contractor, Ceramic/Mosaic #28 .... http://www2.cslb.ca.gov/CSLB_LIBRARY/Name+Request.asp
Trainer, Public Works #48 .... www.dir.ca.gov/databases/das/pwaddrstart.asp
Travelers Checks Issuer #11 .... www.dfi.ca.gov/directry/tc.asp
Trust Company #11 .... www.dfi.ca.gov/directry/trust.asp
Veterinarian / Veterinary Premises #40........... www.vmb.ca.gov/lic1list.htm
Veterinary Food/Animal Drug Retailer #13...... www.pharmacy.ca.gov/verify_lic.htm
Vocational Nurse #17 .... www.bvnpt.ca.gov/licverif.htm
Water Well Driller #28...................................... http://www2.cslb.ca.gov/CSLB_LIBRARY/Name+Request.asp
X-ray Machine Registration #31 .... www.applications.dhs.ca.gov/rhbxray/
X-ray Technician #31 .... www.applications.dhs.ca.gov/rhbxray/

California Licensing Quick Finder

Acupuncturist #1 916-445-3021
Administrative Services #26 916-445-7254
Adoption Agency #50 916-274-6200
Agricultural Engineer #10 916-263-2222
Air Conditioning Contractor #28 800-321-2752
Alarm Company/Employee/Mgr. #22 ... 800-952-5210
Announcer, Athletic Event (Ring) #3 916-263-2195
Apprentice Program #48 415-703-5100
Arbitrator, Consumer (Lemon Law)
Auto Mfg. Arbitration Program #2 ... 916-323-3406
Architect #7 916-445-3394
Asbestos Consultant/Surveillance #52 . 415-703-5100
Asbestos Contractor #52 415-703-5100
Asbestos Trainer #52 415-703-5100
Asbestos Worker/Trainee #52 415-703-5100
Athletic Event Box Office Employee/Ticket Seller #3
.... 916-263-2195
Athletic Event Mgr/Promoter/Matchmaker #3
.... 916-263-2195
Athletic Event-related Occupation #3 ... 916-263-2195
Athletic Gym #3 916-263-2195
Athletic Trainer/Second #3 916-263-2195
Attorney #23 415-538-2577
Audiologist #42 916-263-2666
Automobile Dealer/Repair #19 916-322-4000
Bank #11 800-622-0620
Bar Association #23 415-538-2577
Barber Instructor/School #4 916-445-7061
Barber Shop/Barber/Barber Apprentice #4
.... 916-445-7061
Baton Training Facility/Instructor #22 .. 800-952-5210
Bedding Mfg./Renovator/Retailer/Whlse. #21
.... 800-952-5210
Boiler, Hot Water & Steam Fitting #28 . 800-321-2752
Boxer #3 916-263-2195
Boxing Second #3 916-263-2195
Brake & Lamp Adjuster #19 916-322-4000
Brake Station #19 916-322-4000
Building Contr., General-Class B #28 .. 800-321-2752
Building Moving/Demolition #28 800-321-2752
Business/Industrial Dev. Company #11
.... 800-622-0620, 916-323-0189
Cabinet/Millwork Contractor #28 800-321-2752
Care Facility for Children, Transitional #50
.... 916-274-6200
Care Facility for Chronically Ill #50 916-274-6200
Cemetery, Cemetery Broker/Sales Agent #25
.... 916-322-7737
Child Care Center #50 916-274-6200
Chiropractic Business #46 916-263-5355
Chiropractor #46 916-263-5355
Clinic Pharmaceutical Permit #13 916-445-5014
Clinical Nurse Specialist #16
.... 800-838-6828 L, 916-322-3350
Community Treatment Facility #50 916-274-6200
Concrete Contractor/Company #28 800-321-2752
Conscious Sedation Permit #9 916-263-2300
Continuing Education Provider #8 916-445-4933
Contractor, Business/Individual #28 800-321-2752
Cosmetician/Cosmetologist #4 916-445-7061
Cosmetology School #4 916-445-7061
Cosmetology/Electrology Business/Instr. #4
.... 916-445-7061
Court Reporter (Shorthand Rptr) #29 ... 916-263-3660
CPA/CPA Firm #6 916-263-3680
Crane Operator #52 415-703-5100
Credit Union #11 800-622-0620
Cremated Remains Disposer #25 916-322-7737
Crematory #25 916-322-7737
Day Care, Adult/Child #50 916-274-6200
Dental Anesthesia Permit #9 916-263-2300
Dental Assistant #27 916-263-2595
Dental Assist, Extended Function #27 . 916-263-2595
Dental Hygienist #27 916-263-2595
Dental Registered Provider #9 916-263-2300

Dentist #9 916-263-2300
Dentist Fictitious Name #9 916-263-2300
Development Corporation #11
.... 800-622-0620, 916-323-0189
Driving School #49 916-229-3127
Drug Wholesaler/Drug Room #13 916-445-5014
Dry Cleaning Plant #21 916-574-0280
Drywall Contractor #28 800-321-2752
Earthwork/Paving Contractor #28 800-321-2752
Electrical Contr. & Electric Sign Contr. #28
.... 800-321-2752
Electrologist #4 916-445-7061
Electrology School #4 916-445-7061
Electroneuromyographer #38 916-561-8200
Electronics & Appliance Repair #20 916-574-2069
Elementary School Teacher #26 916-445-7254
Elevator Installation Contr. #28 800-321-2752
Embalmer/Embalmer Apprentice #25 .. 916-322-7737
Engineer (various disciplines) #10 916-263-2222
Esthetician #4 916-445-7061
Family Child Care Home #50 916-274-6200
Farm Labor Contractor #48 415-703-4854
Fencing Contractor #28 800-321-2752
Fire Protection #28 800-321-2752
Firearm Permit #22 800-952-5210
Firearm Training Facility/Instr. #22 800-952-5210
Flooring/Floor Covering Contr. #28 800-321-2752
Foster Family Agency #50 916-274-6200
Fumigation #44 916-561-8704
Fundraiser to Establish Training School #43
.... 916-324-9328
Funeral Director/Establishment #25 916-322-7737
Funerary Training Establishment/Apprentice #25
.... 916-322-7737
Furniture & Bedding Retailer #21 916-574-0280
Furniture Mfg./Retailer/Whlse. #21 916-574-0280
Garment Mfg #48 415-703-4848
Geologist #18 916-263-2113
Geologist, Engineering #18 916-263-2113
Geophysicist #18 916-263-2113
Glazier #28 800-321-2752
Group Home #50 916-274-6200
Hearing Aid Dispenser #34 916-263-2288
Heating & Warm-Air Vent. Contr. #28 .. 800-321-2752
Home Furnishings #21 916-574-0280
Home Improvement Salesperson #28 .. 800-321-2752
Horse Racing Entity #24 916-263-6000
Horse Racing Occupation #24 916-263-6000
Hospital Pharmaceutical Exemptee #13 916-445-5014
Hydrogeologist #18 916-263-2113
Hypodermic Needle&Syringe Dist. #13. 916-445-5014
Industrial Loan Company, Premium #11
.... 800-622-0620, 916-323-0189
Infant Center #50 916-274-6200
Insulation/Acoustical Contr. #28 800-321-2752
Insurance Adjuster #32 916-322-3555
Insurance Agent/Broker #32 916-322-3555
Insurance Company #32 916-322-3555
Investment Advisors #30 916-445-3062
Kickboxer, Amateur #3 916-263-2195
Kickboxer/Full Contact Karate #3 916-263-2195
Kinesiological Electromyographer #38 .. 916-561-8200
Lamp Station #19 916-322-4000
Landscape Architect #35 916-445-4954
Landscaping Contractor #28 800-321-2752
Lathing Contractor #28 800-321-2752
Legal Specialist #23 415-538-2577
Legal Specialization Provider #23 415-538-2577
Lobbyist #47 916-653-6224
Locksmith/Locksmith Company #22 800-952-5210
Mammographic Facility #31 916-323-2772
Manicurist #4 916-445-7061
Manufactured Housing Contractor #28 800-321-2752
Marriage & Family Therapist #8 916-445-4933
Masonry Contractor #28 800-321-2752

Medical Doctor/Surgeon #36 916-263-2382
Medical Evaluator #52 415-703-5100
Midwife #36 916-263-2393
Midwife Nurse #16 .... 800-838-6828 L, 916-322-3350
Money Order Issuer#11 800-622-0620 916-323-0189
Notary Public #37 916-653-3595
Nurse #16 .... 800-838-6828 L, 916-322-3350
Nurse Anesthetist #16 800-838-6828 L, 916-322-3350
Nursing Continuing Edu. Provider #16
.... 800-838-6828 L, 916-322-3350
Nursing Home Administrator #5 916-916-552-8780
Occupational Therapist #51 916-322-3394
Occupational Therapist Assistant #51 . 916-322-3394
Optician, Dispensing #36 916-263-2634
Optometric Corporation #12 916-323-8720
Optometrist #12 916-323-8720
Optometrist Diagnostic/Pharmaceutical #12
.... 916-323-8720
Optometry Practice/Branch Office #12 916-323-8720
Ornamental Metal Contractor #28 800-321-2752
Osteopath #36 916-263-3100
Painting/Decorating Contractor #28 800-321-2752
Parking/Highway Improvement Contr. #28
.... 800-321-2752
Patrol Operator, Private #22 800-952-5210
Payment Instrument Issuer #11
.... 800-622-0620, 916-323-0189
Pest Control Field Rep./Operator #44 .. 916-561-8704
Pesticide Applicator #44 916-561-8704
Pharmaceutical Dist., Out-of-state #13 916-445-5014
Pharmaceutical Whlse./Exemptee #13 916-445-5014
Pharmacist/Pharmacist Intern #13 916-445-5014
Pharmacy #13 916-445-5014
Pharmacy Technician #13 916-445-5014
Pharmacy, Non-resident #13 916-445-5014
Photogrammetrist #10 916-263-2222
Physical Therapist/Assistant #38 916-561-8200
Physician Assistant #39 916-263-2670
Pipeline Contractor #28 800-321-2752
Plastering Contractor #28 800-321-2752
Plumber #28 800-321-2752
Podiatrist #14 916-263-2382
Premium Finance Company #11
.... 800-622-0620, 916-323-0189
Private Investigator #22 800-952-5210
Psychiatric Mental Health Nurse #16
.... 800-838-6828 L, 916-322-3350
Psychiatric Technician #17 916-263-7800
Psychoanalyst, Research #36 916-263-2370
Psychological Assistant #15 916-263-2699
Psychologist #15 916-263-2699
Psychologist, Educational #8 916-445-4933
Psychologist, Registered #15 916-263-2699
Public Accountant-CPA #6 916-263-3680
Public Health Nurse #16
.... 800-838-6828 L, 916-322-3350
Public Works Trainer #48 415-703-5100
Real Estate Agent/Sales #33 916-227-0931
Real Estate Broker/Corporation #33 916-227-0931
Refrigeration Contractor #28 800-321-2752
Registered Veterinary Technician #40. 916-263-2610
Repossessor Agency/Mgr./Employee #22
.... 800-952-5210
Residential Care for Elderly #50 916-274-6200
Residential Facility, Adult #50 916-274-6200
Respiratory Care Practitioner #41 916-323-9983
Roofing Contractor #28 800-321-2752
Sanitation System Contractor #28 800-321-2752
Sanitizer of Home Furnishings #21 916-574-0280
Savings & Loan Association #11
.... 800-622-0620, 916-323-0189
Secondary School Teacher #26 916-445-7254
Securities Broker/Dealer #30 916-445-3062
Security Guard #22 800-952-5210
Service Contract Seller (appliance) #20 916-574-2069

Sheet Metal Contractor #28..................800-321-2752
Shelter, Temporary #50......................916-274-6200
Smog Check Station/Technician #19 ...916-322-4000
Social Rehabilitation Facility #50..........916-274-6200
Social Worker, Clinical #8...................916-445-4933
Social Worker, Clinical Assoc #8..........916-445-4933
Solar Energy Contractor #28...............800-321-2752
Sparring Permit #3............................916-263-2195
Specialty Contractor-Class C #28........800-321-2752
Specialty Sublicenses, Limited #28.......800-321-2752
Speech Pathologist/Audiolog't aide #42 916-263-2666
Speech Pathology Assistant #42..........916-263-2666
Speech-Language Pathologist #42 916-263-2666
Steel Contractor #28.........................800-321-2752

Studio Teacher #48 415-703-4854
Support Center, Adult #50...................916-274-6200
Surgical Clinic Pharm., Nonprofit #13 ..916-445-5014
Surveyor, Land #10...........................916-263-2222
Surveyor-in-Training #10.....................916-263-2222
Swimming Pool Contractor #28............800-321-2752
Talent Agency #48............................415-703-4846
Tax Education Provider #45 916-492-0457
Tax Interviewer #45...........................916-492-0457
Tax Preparer #45..............................916-492-0457
Termite Control #44...........................916-561-8704
Thermal Insulation Manufacturer #21 ..916-574-0280
Thrift & Loan Company #11
.... 800-622-0620, 916-323-0189

Tile Contractor, Ceramic/Mosaic #28... 800-321-2752
Trainer, Public Works #48....................415-703-5100
Travelers Checks Issuer #11
.................................800-622-0620, 916-323-0189
Trust Company #11......800-622-0620, 916-323-0189
Upholsterer, Custom #21 800-952-5210
Veterinarian #40...............................916-263-2610
Veterinary Food/Animal Drug Retailer #13
....916-445-5014
Veterinary Premise #40......................916-263-2610
Vocational Nurse #17.........................916-263-7800
Water Well Driller #28 800-321-2752
X-ray Technician #31 916-323-2775

California Licensing Agency Information

1 Acupuncture Board, 444 N. 3rd Street, #260, Sacramento, CA 95825-3233; 916-445-3021, Fax: 916-263-3015.
www.acupuncture.ca.gov
Email: acupuncture@dca.ca.gov
Search Database at www.acupuncture.ca.gov

2 Arbitration Certification Program, 401 S St #201, Sacramento, CA 95814; 916-323-3406, Fax: 916-323-3968.
www.dca.ca.gov/acp/arbprocess.htm
Email: acp@dca.ca.gov

3 Athletic Commission, 1424 Howe Ave, #33, Sacramento, CA 95825; 916-263-2195, Fax: 916-263-2197.
www.dca.ca.gov/csac/
Search Database at
www.dca.ca.gov/csac/directories.htm

4 Board of Barbering & Cosmetology, 400 R St, #5100 (PO Box 944226), Sacramento, CA 95814-6200; 916-445-1254, Fax: 916-323-5037.
www.barbercosmo.ca.gov
Email: barbercosmo@dca.ca.gov
Search Database at
www.barbercosmo.ca.gov/license.htm Note: 800-952-5210 is number when calling in-state.

5 Nursing Home Administrator Program, PO Box 997416, MS 3302 (1800 3rd St #162), Sacramento, CA 95899-7416; 916-552-8780, Fax: 916-552-8777.
www.dhs.ca.gov
Email: nhap@dhs.ca.gov

6 Board of Accountancy, 2000 Evergreen St, #250, Sacramento, CA 95815-3832; 916-263-3680, Fax: 916-263-3675.
www.dca.ca.gov/cba/
Email: enforcementinfo@cba.ca.gov
Search Database at
www.dca.ca.gov/cba/lookup.htm Note: Search either individual or company names.

7 Architects Board, 400 R St, #4000, Sacramento, CA 95814-6238; 916-445-3394, Fax: 916-445-8524. www.cab.ca.gov
Email: cab@dca.ca.gov
Search Database at www.cab.ca.gov/querylic.htm

8 Board of Behavioral Sciences, 400 R St, #3150, Sacramento, CA 95814-6200; 916-445-4933, Fax: 916-323-0707.
www.bbs.ca.gov
Email: BBSWebMaster@bbs.ca.gov
Search Database at
www.bbs.ca.gov/weblokup.htm

9 Dental Board, 1432 Howe Ave, #85-B, Sacramento, CA 95825-3241; 916-263-2300, Fax: 916-263-2140.
www.dca.ca.gov
Email: DentalBoard@dca.ca.gov
Search Database at
www.dbc.ca.gov/license_verification.html

10 Board of Professional Engineers & Land Surveyors, 2535 Capitol Oaks Dr #300, Sacramento, CA 95833-2944; 916-263-2222, Fax: 916-263-2246.
www.dca.ca.gov/pels
Email: bpels-license-verifications@dca.ca.gov
Search Database at
www.dca.ca.gov/pels/l_lookup.htm Note: Member lists may be downloaded. Engineers include: civil, fire protection, electrical, mechanical, geotechnical, structural, traffic, oil, nuclear, control system, chemical, industrial, manufacturing, metallurgical, petroleum, corrosion, quality, safety.

11 Department of Financial Institutions, Consumer Affairs, 1801 13th Street #2124, Sacramento, CA 95814; 916-322-5966, Fax: 916-445-2123.
www.dfi.ca.gov/consumer/
Search Database at
www.dfi.ca.gov/directry/directry.asp

12 Board of Optometry, 400 R St, #4090, Sacramento, CA 95814-6200; 916-323-8720, 800-547-4576, Fax: 916-445-8711.
www.optometry.ca.gov
Email: boardemail@dea.ca.gov
Search Database at
http://www.optometry.ca.gov/search

13 Board of Pharmacy, 400 R St, #4070, Sacramento, CA 95814-6200; 916-445-5014, Fax: 916-327-6308.
www.pharmacy.ca.gov
Search Database at
www.pharmacy.ca.gov/verify_lic.htm

14 Board of Podiatric Medicine, 1420 Howe Ave, #8, Sacramento, CA 95825-3229; 916-263-2647, Fax: 916-263-2651.
www.bpm.ca.gov
Email: bpm@dca.ca.gov
Search Database at www.bpm.ca.gov

15 Board of Psychology, 1422 Howe Ave, #22, Sacramento, CA 95825-3200; 916-263-2699, Fax: 916-263-2697.
www.psychboard.ca.gov
Email: bopmail@dca.ca.gov
Search Database at www.psychboard.ca.gov

16 Board of Registered Nursing, 400 R St, #4030, Sacramento, CA 95814-6200; 916-322-3350, Fax: 916-327-4402.   www.rn.ca.gov
Email: brnappdesk@dca.ca.gov
Search Database at
www.rn.ca.gov/online/online.htm Note: The toll-free number is available 24 hours a day. Also, a license verification request form is available online at www.ncsbn.org/public/regulation/res/verific ation.pdf.

17 Board of Vocational Nursing & Psychiatric Technicians, 2535 Capitol Oaks Dr, #205, Sacramento, CA 95833; 916-263-7800, Fax: 916-263-7855.
www.bvnpt.ca.gov
Email: webmaster@bvnpt.ca.gov
Search Database at www.bvnpt.ca.gov/licverif.htm

18 Board for Geologists & Geophysicists, 2535 Capitol Oaks Dr, #300A, Sacramento, CA 95833; 916-263-2113, Fax: 916-263-2099.
www.geology.ca.gov/
Email: geology@dca.ca.gov
Search Database at www.geology.ca.gov/ Note: To search directories, click on "Directory of Licenses."

19 Bureau of Automotive Repair, PO Box 989001, West Sacramento, CA 95798-9001; 916-322-4000, Fax: 916-322-4274.
www.smogcheck.ca.gov/stdhome.asp
Search Database at
www.smogcheck.ca.gov/stdPage.asp?Body=/Cons umer/verify_a_license.htm

20 Department of Consumer Affairs, Bureau of Electronic & Appliance Repair, 3485 Orange Grove Ave., North Highlands, CA 95660; 916-574-2069, Fax: 916-574-2120.
www.bear.ca.gov
Email: beartalk@dca.ca.gov
Search Database at www.bear.ca.gov/look-up.htm

21 Department of Consumer Affairs, Bureau of Home Furnishings & Thermal Insulation, 3485 Orange Grove Ave, North Highlands, CA 95660; 916-574-0280, Fax: 916-574-2043.
www.dca.ca.gov/bhfti/

22 Bureau of Security & Investigative Services, 401 S St #101, Sacramento, CA 95814; 916-322-4000, Fax: 916-445-1694.
www.dca.ca.gov/bsis
Email: bsis@dca.ca.gov
Search Database at
www.dca.ca.gov/bsis/lookup.htm

23 State Bar of California, California Committee of Bar Examiners, 180 Howard St, San Francisco, CA 94105; 415-538-2577, Fax: 415-538-2361.
www.calbar.ca.gov/state/calbar/calbar_home.jsp
Email: memrec@calbar.ca.gov
Search Database at
www.calbar.ca.gov/state/calbar/calbar_home.jsp
Note: The member records online database does not include judges or deceased former members.

24 Horse Racing Board, 1010 Hurley Way, #300, Sacramento, CA 95825;
916-263-6000, Fax: 916-263-6042.
www.chrb.ca.gov
Search Database at
www.chrb.ca.gov/license_search.htm

25 Cemetery and Funeral Bureau, 400 R St, #3080, Sacramento, CA 95814; 916-327-3219.
www.cfb.ca.gov
Search Database at
www.dca.ca.gov/cemetery/lookup.htm

26 Commission on Teacher Credentialing, 1900 Capitol Ave (95814-4213), Sacramento, CA 95814-7000; 916-445-7254, Fax: 916-445-7255.
www.ctc.ca.gov
Email: credentials@ctc.ca.gov
Search Database at
www.ctc.ca.gov/credentials/default.html

27 Committee on Dental Auxiliaries, 1428 Howe Ave, #58, Sacramento, CA 95825; 916-263-2595, Fax: 916-263-2709.
www.comda.ca.gov
Search Database at
www.comda.ca.gov/licensestatus.html

28 Contractors License Board, PO Box 26000 (9821 Business Park Dr), Sacramento, CA 95826; 916-255-3900, 800-321-2752, Fax: 916-361-7497.
www.cslb.ca.gov
Email: licensing@dca.cslb.ca.gov
Search Database at
http://www2.cslb.ca.gov/CSLB_LIBRARY/Name+Request.asp

29 Court Reporters Board of California, 2535 Capitol Oaks Dr, #230, Sacramento, CA 95833; 916-263-3660, Fax: 916-263-3664.
www.courtreportersboard.ca.gov
Search Database at
www.courtreportersboard.ca.gov   Note: To search, click on "License Verification."

30 Department of Corporations, 1515 K St #200, Sacramento, CA 95814; 916-445-7205.
www.corp.ca.gov
Email: Webmaster@corp.ca.gov

31 Department of Health Services, Radiological Health Branch, PO Box 997414, Sacramento, CA 95899-7414; 916-327-5106.
www.dhs.ca.gov/rhb/
Search Database at
www.applications.dhs.ca.gov/rhbxray/

32 Department of Insurance, Producer Licensing Bureau, 320 Capitol Mall [PO Box 1437 (95812-1437)], Sacramento, CA 95814; 916-322-3555, Fax: 916-327-6907.
www.insurance.ca.gov
Email: license.bureau@insurance.ca.gov
Search Database at
www.insurance.ca.gov/docs/FS-Licensestatus.htm

33 Department of Real Estate, 2201 Broadway, Sacramento, CA 95818-2500; 916-227-0931, Fax: 916-227-0925.
www.dre.ca.gov
Search Database at www.dre.ca.gov/licstats.htm

34 Hearing Aid Dispensers Examining Committee; PO Box 980490, West Sacramento, CA 95798-0490; 916-327-3433, Fax: 916-445-1696.
www.dca.ca.gov/hearingaid/
Email: hearingaid@dca.ca.gov
Search Database at www.dca.ca.gov/hearingaid/

35 Landscape Architects Technical Committee, 400 R St, #4000, Sacramento, CA 95814-6200; 916-445-4954, Fax: 916-324-2333.
www.latc.dca.ca.gov
Email: latc@dca.ca.gov
Search Database at
www.latc.dca.ca.gov/licenseeinfo/search.htm

36 Medical Board of California, 1426 Howe Ave, #54, Sacramento, CA 95825-3236; 916-263-2382, Fax: 916-263-2944.
www.medbd.ca.gov   Note: Facilities and professionals may search at
www.docboard.org/ca/df/casearch.htm; logon and password required.

37 Office of the Secretary of State, 1500 11th St, 2nd Fl, Sacramento, CA 95814; 916-653-3595, Fax: 916-653-9580.
www.ss.ca.gov/business/notary/notary.htm
Email: notaries@ss.ca.gov

38 Physical Therapy Examining Committee, 1418 Howe Ave #16, Sacramento, CA 95825-3204; 916-561-8200, Fax: 916-263-2560.
www.ptb.ca.gov

39 Department of Consumer Affairs, Physician Assistant Committee, 1424 Howe Ave, #35, Sacramento, CA 95825-3237; 916-263-2670, Fax: 916-263-2671.
www.physicianassistant.ca.gov/index.html

40 Veterinary Medical Board, 1420 Howe Ave, #6, Sacramento, CA 95825-3228; 916-263-2610, Fax: 916-263-2621.
www.vmb.ca.gov
Email: vmb@dca.ca.gov
Search Database at www.vmb.ca.gov/lic1list.htm

41 Respiratory Care Board of California, 444 N 3rd St #270, Sacramento, CA 95814; 916-323-9983, Fax: 916-323-9999.
www.rcb.ca.gov
Email: rcbinfo@dca.ca.gov
Search Database at
www.rcb.ca.gov/license_verification_forms_instructions.htm   Note: Click on "License Verification On-Line".

42 Speech Language Pathology & Audiology Board, 1422 Howe Ave, #3, Sacramento, CA 95825; 916-263-2666, Fax: 916-263-2668.
www.slpab.ca.gov/
Email: slpab@dca.ca.gov

43 Board of Guide Dogs for the Blind, 400 R St #5100-A, Sacramento, CA 95814; 916-324-9328, Fax: 916-324-9340.
www.dca.ca.gov/guidedogboard
Email: guidedogboard@dca.ca.gov

44 Structural Pest Control Board, 1418 Howe Ave #18, Sacramento, CA 95825-3280; 800-737-8188, Fax: 916-263-2469.
www.cdpr.ca.gov
Search Database at
www.cdpr.ca.gov/docs/license/currlic.htm

45 Tax Preparer Program, CA Tax Education Council, PO Box 2890, Sacramento, CA 95812-2840; 877-850-2832.
Email: info@ctec.org
Search Database at www.ctec.org/verify.asp

46 California Board of Chiropractic Examiners, 2525 Natromas Park Dr #260, Sacramento, CA 95833-2931; 916-263-5355, Fax: 916-263-5369.
www.chiro.ca.gov/default.asp
Search Database at www.chiro.ca.gov/licsearch/

47 Secretary of State, Political Reform Division, 1500 11th Street, Room 495, Sacramento, CA 95814; 916-653-6224, Fax: 916-653-5045.
http://cal-access.ss.ca.gov
Email: PoliticalReform@ss.ca.gov
Search Database at http://cal-access.ss.ca.gov/Lobbying/

48 Division of Labor Standards Enforcement, Licensing and Registration Unit, PO Box 420603, San Francisco, CA 94142; 415-703-5100, Fax: 415-703-4808.
www.dir.ca.gov
Email: DLSE.licensing@dir.ca.gov
Search Database at
www.dir.ca.gov/dirdatabases.html

49 Driving School Complaint Unit, Occupational Licensing, PO Box 932342 L228, Sacramento, CA 94232-3420; 916-229-3127.
www.dmv.ca.gov/vehindustry/ol/drschool_faq.htm
Search Database at
https://eg.dmv.ca.gov/olinq/SvOlDs

50 Department of Social Services, Community Care Licensing Division, 744 P St, Sacramento, CA 95814; 916-274-6200, Fax: 916-274-6205.
http://ccld.ca.gov
Email: cclwebmaster@dss.ca.gov
Search Database at www.ccld.ca.gov/docs/ccld_search/ccld_search.aspx

51 Board of Occupational Therapy, 444 N 3rd St, #410, Sacramento, CA 95814; 916-322-3394, Fax: 916-445-6167.
www.bot.ca.gov
Email: cbot@dca.ca.gov
Search Database at
http://www2.dca.ca.gov/pls/wllpub/wllqryna$lcev2.startup?p_qte_code=OT&p_qte_pgm_code=1475   Note: Will provide certification/ letter of good standing.

52 Department of Industrial Relations, Division of Occupational Health, 455 Golden Gate Ave, 10th Fl, San Francisco, CA 94102; 415-703-5100, Fax: 415-703-5135.
www.dir.ca.gov
Search Database at
www.dir.ca.gov/dirdatabases.html

California Federal Courts

The following list indicates the district and division name for each county in the state. If the district or division name of the bankruptcy court is different from the civil/criminal court, it appears in parentheses.

For California counties of Alameda, Contra Costa, Del Norte, Humboldt, Lake, Marin, Mendocino, Napa, San Francisco, San Mateo, and Sonoma in the Northern District of California District Court, cases may be filed at either the San Francisco Division or Oakland Division. From there a case may be assigned to either division. Records are available electronically or on public access terminals at either Division, and at the San Jose Division. To find the actual locations of records, first search by name to find case numbers; the first number of the case number indicates the file location: 3~=San Francisco, 4~=Oakland., 5~=San Jose.

County/Court Cross Reference

County	District	Division
Alameda	Northern	Oakland/SF (Oakland)
Alpine	Eastern	Sacramento
Amador	Eastern	Sacramento
Butte	Eastern	Sacramento
Calaveras	Eastern	Sacramento (Modesto)
Colusa	Eastern	Sacramento
Contra Costa	Northern	Oakland/SF (Oakland)
Del Norte	Northern	San Francisco/Oakland (Santa Rosa)
El Dorado	Eastern	Sacramento
Fresno	Eastern	Fresno
Glenn	Eastern	Sacramento
Humboldt	Northern	San Francisco/Oakland (Santa Rosa)
Imperial	Southern	San Diego
Inyo	Eastern	Fresno
Kern	Eastern	Fresno
Kings	Eastern	Fresno
Lake	Northern	San Francisco/Oakland (Santa Rosa)
Lassen	Eastern	Sacramento
Los Angeles	Central	Los Angeles (Western)
Madera	Eastern	Fresno
Marin	Northern	San Francisco/Oakland (Santa Rosa)
Mariposa	Eastern	Fresno
Mendocino	Northern	San Francisco/Oakland (Santa Rosa)
Merced	Eastern	Fresno
Modoc	Eastern	Sacramento
Mono	Eastern	Sacramento
Monterey	Northern	San Jose
Napa	Northern	San Francisco/Oakland (Santa Rosa)
Nevada	Eastern	Sacramento
Orange	Central	Santa Ana (Southern)
Placer	Eastern	Sacramento
Plumas	Eastern	Sacramento
Riverside	Central	Riverside (Eastern)
Sacramento	Eastern	Sacramento
San Benito	Northern	San Jose
San Bernardino	Central	Riverside (Eastern)
San Diego	Southern	San Diego
San Francisco	Northern	San Francisco/Oakland (San Francisco)
San Joaquin	Eastern	Sacramento (Sacramento- Modesto to 11/04)
San Luis Obispo	Central	Los Angeles (Western)
San Mateo	Northern	San Francisco/Oakland (San Francisco)
Santa Barbara	Central	Los Angeles (Western)
Santa Clara	Northern	San Jose
Santa Cruz	Northern	San Jose
Shasta	Eastern	Sacramento
Sierra	Eastern	Sacramento
Siskiyou	Eastern	Sacramento
Solano	Eastern	Sacramento
Sonoma	Northern	San Francisco/Oakland (Santa Rosa)
Stanislaus	Eastern	Fresno (Modesto)
Sutter	Eastern	Sacramento
Tehama	Eastern	Sacramento
Trinity	Eastern	Sacramento
Tulare	Eastern	Fresno
Tuolumne	Eastern	Fresno (Modesto)
Ventura	Central	Los Angeles (Western)
Yolo	Eastern	Sacramento
Yuba	Eastern	Sacramento

Standards for Federal Courts: Search fee is $26.00 per item (one party name or case number). Copy fee is $.50 per page. Certification fee is $9.00 per document, double for exemplification, if available. All fees standard unless noted in profile. Mail Search: always enclose a stamped self addressed envelope unless otherwise noted. Most courts accept fax requests or will suggest a copying/search vendor. Before releasing records, all courts require prepayment, unless noted.

Open records are located at the court unless otherwise noted. District courts index by defendant and plaintiff as well as by case number. Bankruptcy courts usually index by debtor and case number. While most courts now have their indexes on computer, many may still maintain index card files as well.

Courts offering internet access via CM-ECF or older RACER, PACER, or Web-PACER systems charge $.08 per page fee unless noted as free. Where PACER is available, the universal sign-up number is 800-676-6856. Find PACER and the US Party/Case Index at http://pacer.psc.uscourts.gov.

U.S. District Court

Central District of California

Los Angeles (Western) Division Attn: Correspondence, US Courthouse, 312 N Spring St, Rm G-8, Los Angeles, CA 90012 (also use mail address for courier delivery), 213-894-2215. www.cacd.uscourts.gov
Counties: Los Angeles, San Luis Obispo, Santa Barbara, Ventura.
Searches & Indexing: Results do not include SSN or DOB. Both computer and card indexes maintained. Persons with a valid ID may search microfiche. New cases in the index 3 days after filing date. In general, criminal case records from 1989 back and civil cases from 1992 back sent to archives.
Fee & Payment: Pay by money order, cashier check, business check. No personal checks. Payee: Clerk, US District Court. Prepayment required.
Phone Search: No searching by telephone.
Mail Search: search usually completed- 2-4 days. Include SASE for return.
In Person Search: Fee charged if court performs your search. Copy service available, call 213-253-9413 No self-serve copier available.
E-Services: PACER online at http://pacer.cacd.uscourts.gov. Document images available. PACER records go back to 1993. New records online after 1 day. ECF at

https://ecf.cacd.uscourts.gov **Opinions Online:** www.cacd.uscourts.gov. Click on Recent Opinions. **Other Online Access:** Limited calendars at website.

Riverside (Eastern) Division US District Court Clerk, 3470 12th St, Riverside, CA 92501 (also use mail address for courier delivery), 951-328-4450, records rm- 213-894-3863. Hours- 10AM-4PM. www.cacd.uscourts.gov
Counties: Riverside, San Bernardino.
Searches & Indexing: Results do not include SSN or DOB. Both computer and card indexes maintained. New cases in the index 3 days after filing date.
Fee & Payment: Pay by money order, cashier check, business check. No personal checks. Payee: Clerk, US District Court. Prepayment required.
Phone Search: No searching by telephone.
Mail Search: search usually completed- 4-7 days. Include SASE for return.
In Person Search: Fee charged if court performs your search. Copy service available, call 951-328-9995. No self-serve copier available.
E-Services: PACER online at http://pacer.cacd.uscourts.gov. Document images available. PACER records go back to 1993. New records online after 1 day. ECF at https://ecf.cacd.uscourts.gov **Opinions Online:** www.cacd.uscourts.gov. Click on Recent

Opinions. **Other Online Access:** Limited calendars at website.

Santa Ana (Southern) Division Court Clerk, 411 W 4th St Rm 1053, Santa Ana, CA 92701-4516 (also use mail address for courier delivery), 714-338-4750. Hours- 10AM-4PM. www.cacd.uscourts.gov

Counties: Orange.

Searches & Indexing: Results do not include SSN or DOB. Both computer and card indexes maintained. New cases in the index 3 days after filing date.

Fee & Payment: Pay by money order, cashier check, business check. No personal checks. Payee: Clerk, US District Court. Prepayment required unless a deposit account has been set up.

Phone Search: Only docket information is available by phone.

Mail Search: search usually completed- 4-7 days. Include SASE for return.

In Person Search: Fee charged if court performs your search. Copy service available, call 741-543-8123. No self-serve copier available.

E-Services: PACER online at http://pacer.cacd.uscourts.gov. Document images available. PACER records go back to 1993. New records online after 1 day. ECF at https://ecf.cacd.uscourts.gov **Opinions Online:** www.cacd.uscourts.gov. Click on Recent Opinions. **Other Online Access:** Limited calendars at website.

US Bankruptcy Court

Central District of California

Los Angeles Division Court Clerk, 255 E Temple St, Roybal Bldg, #945, Los Angeles, CA 90012 (use mail address for courier delivery), 213-894-3118, records rm- 213-894-7205, Fax-213-894-1261. 9AM-4PM. www.cacb.uscourts.gov

Counties: Los Angeles (cases filed in certain northern Los Angeles County ZIP Codes may be shared with the San Fernando Valley Division.)

Searches & Indexing: Results include SSN. Records indexed on microfiche, computer, cards. New cases in the index immediately after filing date. Records purged once a year.

Fee & Payment: Pay by no business or personal checks accepted. Payee: Clerk, US Bankruptcy Court. Prepayment required.

Phone Search: Voice Case Information Service available, call VCIS at 213-894-4111.

Mail Search: search usually completed- 2 days. Include SASE for return.

In Person Search: Fee charged if court performs your search. No self-serve copier available.

E-Services: PACER online https://pacer.login.uscourts.gov/cgi-bin/login.pl?court_id=CACBLA. Document images available. PACER records go back to 1992. New records online after 1 day. ECF at https://ecf.cacb.uscourts.gov. Cases of Interest-www.cacb.uscourts.gov/cacb/notices.nsf/Cases+of+Interest?OpenView

Riverside (East) Division Court Clerk, 3420 12th St #125, Riverside, CA 92501-3819 (also use mail address for courier delivery), 951-774-1000. 9AM-4PM. www.cacb.uscourts.gov

Counties: Riverside, San Bernardino.

Searches & Indexing: Results do not include SSN or DOB. Computer index maintained. Files stored in numerically. New cases in the index

immediately after filing date. Records purged as deemed necessary.

Fee & Payment: Pay by Visa/MC (in person only), money order, cashier check only. No personal or business checks accepted. Payee: US Bankruptcy Court. Prepayment required.

Phone Search: Only docket information is available by phone. Voice Case Information Service available, call VCIS at 951-774-1150.

Mail Search: search usually completed- 24 hours. Include case number, document title, document number (if available), your phone number and any applicable fees. Include SASE for return.

In Person Search: Fee charged if court performs your search. Coping available from West Coast Copy Svc, 909-788-4371. No self-serve copier.

E-Services: PACER online at https://pacer.login.uscourts.gov/cgi-bin/login.pl?court_id=CACBRS. Document images available. PACER records go back to 1992. New records online after 1 day. ECF at https://ecf.cacb.uscourts.gov. Cases of Interest at www.cacb.uscourts.gov/cacb/notices.nsf/Cases+of+Interest?OpenView

San Fernando Valley Division Court Clerk, 21041 Burbank Blvd, Woodland Hills, CA 91367 (also use mail address for courier delivery), 818-587-2900. Hours- 9AM-4PM. www.cacb.uscourts.gov

Counties: Los Angeles, Ventura (cases filed in certain northern Los Angeles County ZIP Codes are shared with the Los Angeles Division, and cases filed in certain eastern Ventura County ZIP Codes are shared with the Ventura Division.)

Searches & Indexing: Results do not include SSN or DOB. New cases in the index immediately after filing date. Records purged once a year.

Fee & Payment: Pay by money order, cashier check only. Payee: Clerk, US Bankruptcy Court. Prepayment required.

Phone Search: Voice Case Information Service available, call VCIS at 818-587-2936.

Mail Search: search usually completed- 2 days. Include SASE for return.

In Person Search: Fee charged if court performs your search. No self-serve copier available.

E-Services: PACER at https://pacer.login.uscourts.gov/cgi-bin/login.pl?court_id=CACBSV. Document images available. PACER records go back to 1992. New records online after 1 day. ECF at https://ecf.cacb.uscourts.gov. Cases of Interest-www.cacb.uscourts.gov/cacb/notices.nsf/Cases+of+Interest?OpenView

Santa Ana Division Court Clerk, 411 W 4th St, #2030, Ronald Reagan Federal Bldg & US Courthouse, Santa Ana, CA 92701-4593 (also use mail address for courier delivery), 714-338-5300. Hours- 9AM-4PM. www.cacb.uscourts.gov

Counties: Orange.

Searches & Indexing: Cases indexed by debtor, creditors, and case number. Results include last 4 SSN digits. Computer index maintained back to 1990. New cases in the index 24-48 hours after filing date.

Fee & Payment: Pay by Visa/MC (in person only), money order, cashier check, business check. No personal checks. Payee: US Bankruptcy Court. Prepayment required unless prior arrangements made.

Phone Search: Docket information available via phone. Voice Case Information Service available, call VCIS at 714-338-5401.

Mail Search: search usually completed- 1 week. Include SASE for return.

In Person Search: Fee charged if court performs your search. No self-serve copier available.

E-Services: PACER online at https://pacer.login.uscourts.gov/cgi-bin/login.pl?court_id=CACBSA. Document images available. PACER records go back to 6/3/1991. New records online after 1 day. ECF at https://ecf.cacb.uscourts.gov. Cases of Interest at www.cacb.uscourts.gov/cacb/notices.nsf/Cases+of+Interest?OpenView

Santa Barbara (Northern) Division Court Clerk, 1415 State St, Santa Barbara, CA 93101 (also use mail address for courier delivery), 805-884-4800. Hours- 9AM-4PM. www.cacb.uscourts.gov

Counties: San Luis Obispo, Santa Barbara, Ventura. Certain Ventura County ZIP Codes are assigned to the new office in San Fernando Valley.

Searches & Indexing: Computer index back to 1995 maintained. New cases in the index immediately after filing date. No set time for sending records to repository.

Fee & Payment: Pay by Visa/MC, no business or personal checks accepted. Payee: US Bankruptcy Court. Prepayment required.

Phone Search: Voice Case Information Service available, call VCIS at 805-884-4805.

Mail Search: search usually completed- 24 hours. Include case number, document title, document number (if available), your phone number and any applicable fees. Include SASE for return.

In Person Search: Fee charged if court performs your search. No self-serve copier available.

E-Services: PACER online at https://pacer.login.uscourts.gov/cgi-bin/login.pl?court_id=CACBND. Document images available. PACER records go back to 6/1992. New records online after 1 day. ECF at https://ecf.cacb.uscourts.gov. Cases of Interest at www.cacb.uscourts.gov/cacb/notices.nsf/Cases+of+Interest?OpenView

US District Court

Eastern District of California

Fresno Division Court Clerk, US Courthouse, Rm 5000, 1130 "O" St, Fresno, CA 93721-2201 (also use mail address for courier delivery), 559-498-7483, records rm- 559-498-7372, crim dockets- 559-498-7235, civil dockets- 559-498-7235. 8:30AM-4:30PM. www.caed.uscourts.gov

Counties: Fresno, Inyo, Kern, Kings, Madera, Mariposa, Merced, Stanislaus, Tulare, Tuolumne.

Searches & Indexing: Results do not include SSN or DOB. Computer index back to 1991 maintained. Records stored by case type and case number. New cases in the index 24 hours after filing date. Records purged at varying intervals.

Fee & Payment: Pay by money order, cashier's or personal check. Credit cards accepted. Payee: Clerk, US District Court. Prepayment required.

Phone Search: Only docket information is available by phone.

Mail Search: search usually completed- 2 days. SASE not required.

In Person Search: Fee charged if court performs your search. Court will copy a maximum of 20 pages, otherwise searchers must contact an outside copy service. In person search between 8:30AM and 4:30PM. No self-serve copier available.

E-Services: ECF replaces PACER whose records did go back to 1990, some earlier. New records online after 1 day. ECF at https://ecf.caed.uscourts.gov **Opinions Online:** www.caed.uscourts.gov. **Other Online Access:** Judges calendars free at http://207.41.18.73/caed/staticOther/page_460.htm

Sacramento Division Court Clerk, 501 I St, Sacramento, CA 95814 (also use mail address for courier delivery), 916-930-4000, records rm- 916-498-5415, Fax-916-930-4015. Hours- 8:30AM-4:30PM. www.caed.uscourts.gov
Counties: Alpine, Amador, Butte, Calaveras, Colusa, El Dorado, Glenn, Lassen, Modoc, Mono, Nevada, Placer, Plumas, Sacramento, San Joaquin, Shasta, Sierra, Siskiyou, Solano, Sutter, Tehama, Trinity, Yolo, Yuba.
Searches & Indexing: Archived records stored by case number; research case number by plaintiff or defendant name. Results do not include SSN or DOB. Computer index maintained back to 1990. Archived case records indexed on microfiche. New cases in the index immediately after filing date. Records purged at varying intervals.
Fee & Payment: Pay by money order, cashier check, business check. No personal checks. Payee: Clerk, US District Court. Prepayment required.
Phone Search: Only docket information is available by phone.
Mail Search: search usually completed- 1-2 days. Include SASE for return.
In Person Search: Fee charged if court performs your search. For copy service, call 916-448-8875. A 24-hour drop box is located on the premises. Self-serve copier available - $.15 per page.
E-Services: ECF replaces PACER whose records did go back to 1990, some earlier. New records online after 1 day. ECF at https://ecf.caed.uscourts.gov. **Opinions Online:** www.caed.uscourts.gov. **Other Online Access:** Judges calendars free at http://207.41.18.73/caed/staticOther/page_460.htm

US Bankruptcy Court

Eastern District of California

Fresno Division Court Clerk, Rm 2656, 1130 O Street, Fresno, CA 93721 (also use mail address for courier delivery), 559-498-7217. Hours- 9AM-4PM. www.caeb.uscourts.gov
Counties: Fresno, Inyo, Kern, Kings, Madera, Mariposa, Merced, Tulare. Three Kern ZIP Codes - 93243, 93523, 93524 -handled by San Fernando Valley in the Central District.
Searches & Indexing: Results include last 4 SSN digits. Computer index back to 1979 maintained. New cases in the index immediately after filing date. Records purged every 6 months.
Fee & Payment: Pay by money order, cashier check, business check. No personal checks or credit cards accepted. Payee: Clerk, US Bankruptcy Court. Prepayment required.
Phone Search: Only docket information is available by phone. Voice Case Information Service available, call VCIS at 916-498-5583 or 916-498-5584.
Mail Search: search usually completed- 2 weeks. Include SASE for return.
In Person Search: Fee charged if court performs your search. Self-serve copier - $.15 per page.
E-Services: PACER online at http://pacer.caeb.uscourts.gov/pacerhome.html. Document images available. PACER records go

back to 8/1990. New records online after 1 day. Currently implementing CM/ECF. **Opinions:** www.caeb.uscourts.gov/cortinfo/opinions.asp. Opinions after 2/16/2005 at www.caeb.uscourts.gov/search/search.asp. **Other Online Access:** Calendars free at www.caeb.uscourts.gov/calendar/calendar.asp.

Modesto Division Court Clerk, Suite C, 1130 12th St, Modesto, CA 95354 (also use mail address for courier delivery), 209-521-5160. Hours- 9AM-4PM. www.caeb.uscourts.gov
Counties: Calaveras, Stanislaus, Tuolumne. Pre-11/2004 San Joaquin records for these ZIP Codes are here: 95220, 95227, 95234, 95237, 95240-95242, 95253, 95258, 95286. Mariposa and Merced counties were transferred to the Fresno Division as of 1/1995.
Searches & Indexing: Research case numbers using debtor name. Results do not include SSN or DOB. Computer index maintained. New cases in the index 1 day after filing date.
Fee & Payment: Pay by money order, cashier's or personal check. Payee: Clerk, US Bankruptcy Court. Prepayment required.
Phone Search: Only docket information is available by phone. Voice Case Information Service available, call VCIS at 916-498-5583 or 916-498-5584.
Mail Search: search usually completed- within 1 week. SASE required.
In Person Search: Fee charged if court performs your search. Copies printed from the lobby computer are $.10 each. Self-serve copier available - $.25 per page.
E-Services: PACER online at http://pacer.caeb.uscourts.gov/pacerhome.html. Document images available. PACER records go back to 8/1990. New records online after 1 day. Currently implementing CM/ECF. **Opinions:** www.caeb.uscourts.gov/cortinfo/opinions.asp. Opinions after 2/16/2005 at www.caeb.uscourts.gov/search/search.asp. **Other Online Access:** Calendars free at www.caeb.uscourts.gov/calendar/calendar.asp.

Sacramento Division Court Clerk, US Courthouse Rm 3-200, 501 I St, Sacramento, CA 95814 (also use mail address for courier delivery), 916-930-4400. Hours- 9AM-4PM. www.caeb.uscourts.gov
Counties: Alpine, Amador, Butte, Colusa, El Dorado, Glenn, Lassen, Modoc, Mono, Nevada, Placer, Plumas, Sacramento, San Joaquin, Shasta, Sierra, Siskiyou, Solano, Sutter, Tehama, Trinity, Yolo, Yuba. Pre-11/2004 San Joaquin records are at Modesto Division for these ZIP Codes: 95220, 95227, 95234, 95237, 95240-95242, 95253, 95258, 95286. There is a hearing location in Bakersfield at 1300 18th St, but no cases or case records there.
Searches & Indexing: Office will confirm, by phone, if a SSN matches a SSN in the case file. Computer index maintained. New cases in the index within 48 hours after filing date.
Fee & Payment: Pay by money order, cashier check, business check. No personal checks or credit cards accepted. Payee: Clerk, US Bankruptcy Court. Prepayment required.
Phone Search: Only docket information is available by phone. Voice Case Information Service available, call VCIS at 916-498-5583 or 916-498-5584.
Mail Search: search usually completed- 24-48 hours. Include SASE for return.

In Person Search: Fee charged if court performs your search. You must make an appointment in order to conduct a search yourself. Self-serve copier available - $.15 per page.
E-Services: PACER online at http://pacer.caeb.uscourts.gov/pacerhome.html. Document images available. PACER records go back to 8/1990. New records online after 1 day. Currently implementing CM/ECF. **Opinions:** www.caeb.uscourts.gov/cortinfo/opinions.asp. Opinions after 2/16/2005 at www.caeb.uscourts.gov/search/search.asp. **Other Online Access:** Calendars free at www.caeb.uscourts.gov/calendar/calendar.asp.

US District Court

Northern District of California

Oakland Division Court Clerk, 1301 Clay St, Ste 400S, Oakland, CA 94612-5212 (also use mail address for courier delivery), 510-637-3530. Hours- 9AM-4PM. www.cand.uscourts.gov
Counties: Alameda, Contra Costa. (Note: Cases may be filed here or at San Francisco Div.; records available electronically at either; the 1st number of the case number indicates the file location: 3=SF, 4=Oak., 5=SJ.
Searches & Indexing: Records stored by case number; case number can be found by using plaintiff or defendant name. Results do not include SSN or DOB. Computer and microfiche indexes maintained; on computer back to 1990. New cases in the index immediately after filing date. Records purged every 6 months.
Fee & Payment: Pay by money order, cashier's or personal check. Payee: Clerk, US District Court. Prepayment required.
Phone Search: Only docket information available by phone.
Mail Search: search usually completed- 7 days. Include SASE for return.
In Person Search: Fee charged if court performs your search. Self-serve copier $.20 per page.
E-Services: ECF replaces PACER whose records did go back to 1984. New records online after 1 day. ECF at https://ecf.cand.uscourts.gov. ECF cases data back to 4/2001. **Other Online Access:** Access to court calendars can be found at www.cand.uscourts.gov.

San Francisco Division Court Clerk, 450 Golden Gate Ave, 16th Fl, San Francisco, CA 94102 (also use mail address for courier delivery), 415-522-2000. Hours- 9AM-4PM. www.cand.uscourts.gov
Counties: Del Norte, Humboldt, Lake, Marin, Mendocino, Napa, San Francisco, San Mateo, Sonoma. (Note: Cases may be filed here or at Oakland Div; records available electronically at either; the 1st number of the case number indicates the file location: 3=SF, 4=Oak., 5=SJ.
Searches & Indexing: Records stored by case number; use plaintiff or defendant name to find case number. Results do not include SSN or DOB. Computer and microfiche indexes maintained; comptuer back to 1994. New cases in the index immediately after filing date. Records purged every 6 months.
Fee & Payment: Pay by money order, cashier's or personal check. Payee: Clerk, US District Court. Prepayment required.
Phone Search: Only docket information is available by phone.

Mail Search: search usually completed- 7 days. Include SASE for return.

In Person Search: Fee charged if court performs your search. Self-serve copier $.20 per page.

E-Services: ECF replaces PACER whose records did go back to 1984. New records online after 1 day. ECF at https://ecf.cand.uscourts.gov. ECF cases data back to 4/2001. **Other Online Access:** Access to court calendars can be found at www.cand.uscourts.gov.

San Jose Division Court Clerk, 280 S 1st St, Rm 2112, San Jose, CA 95113 (also use mail address for courier delivery), 408-535-5364. Hours- 9AM-4PM. www.cand.uscourts.gov

Counties: Monterey, San Benito, Santa Clara, Santa Cruz.

Searches & Indexing: Records stored by case number; case number can be found by using plaintiff or defendant name. Results do not include SSN or DOB. Computer and microfiche indexes maintained. New cases in the index immediately after filing date. Records purged every 6 months.

Fee & Payment: Pay by money order, cashier check. No personal checks. Payee: Clerk, US District Court. Prepayment required.

Phone Search: Only docket information is available by phone.

Mail Search: search usually completed- 7 days. Include SASE for return.

In Person Search: Fee charged if court performs your search. Self-serve copier $.20 per page.

E-Services: ECF replaces PACER whose records did go back to 1984. New records online after 1 day. ECF at https://ecf.cand.uscourts.gov. ECF includes civil cases filed after 4/1/2001 and criminal and miscellaneous cases after 1/1/2004. **Other Online Access:** Access to court calendars can be found at www.cand.uscourts.gov.

US Bankruptcy Court

Northern District of California

Oakland Division Court Clerk, PO Box 2070, Oakland, CA 94604 (courier address: 1300 Clay St, Rm 300, Oakland, CA 94612), 510-879-3600. Hours- 9AM-4:30PM. www.canb.uscourts.gov

Counties: Alameda, Contra Costa.

Searches & Indexing: Results include last 4 SSN digits. Both computer and card indexes maintained. New cases in the index immediately after filing date. Records purged every 6 months to 1 year.

Fee & Payment: Pay by money order, cashier check, business check. No personal checks. Payee: Clerk, Bankruptcy Court. Prepayment required.

Phone Search: Voice Case Information Service available, call 888-457-0604 or 415-705-3160.

Mail Search: search usually completed- 2-4 days. Include SASE for return.

In Person Search: Fee charged if court performs your search. Self-serve copier - $.25 per page.

E-Services: ECF replaces PACER whose records did go back to 1993. New records online after 1 day. ECF at https://ecf.canb.uscourts.gov. **Opinions Online:** www.canb.uscourts.gov. Click on Judges Decisions. **Other Online Access:** For calendars, click on Calendars at main website.

San Francisco Division Court Clerk, PO Box 7341, San Francisco, CA 94120-7341 (courier address: 235 Pine St, 19th Fl, San Francisco, CA

94104), 415-268-2300. Hours- 9AM-4:30PM. www.canb.uscourts.gov

Counties: San Francisco, San Mateo.

Searches & Indexing: All searches conducted by a copy service; call 415-781-4910. Results include last 4 SSN digits. Computer index back to 1984 maintained; also on microfiche. New cases in the index immediately after filing date. Records purged every 6 months to 1 year.

Fee & Payment: Pay by money order, cashier check, business check. No personal checks or credit cards accepted. Payee: Clerk of the Court. Prepayment required.

Phone Search: Only information from dockets of open cases is released via phone. Voice Case Information Service available, call VCIS at 888-457-0604 or 415-705-3160.

Mail Search: search usually completed- 1-2 weeks. SASE not required.

In Person Search: Fee charged if court performs your search. Self-serve copier- $.25 per page.

E-Services: ECF replaces PACER whose records did go back to 1993. New records online after 1 day. ECF at https://ecf.canb.uscourts.gov. **Opinions Online:** www.canb.uscourts.gov. Click on Judges Decisions. **Other Online Access:** For calendars, click on Calendars at main website.

San Jose Division Court Clerk, Rm 3035, 3rd Fl, 280 S 1st St, San Jose, CA 95113-3099 (use mail address for courier delivery), 408-535-5118. Hours- 9AM-4PM. www.canb.uscourts.gov

Counties: Monterey, San Benito, Santa Clara, Santa Cruz.

Searches & Indexing: Results include last 4 SSN digits. Computer index back to 1980 maintained. New cases in the index immediately after filing date. Records purged every 6 months to 1 year.

Fee & Payment: Pay by money order, cashier check, business check. No personal checks. Payee: Clerk, Bankruptcy Court. Prepayment required.

Phone Search: Only basic information, such as date of filing is released via phone. Voice Case Information Service available, call VCIS at 888-457-0604 or 415-705-3160.

Mail Search: search usually completed- 2-3 days. Include SASE for return.

In Person Search: Fee charged if court performs your search. Copying available from BK Copy Ctr. No self-serve copier available.

E-Services: ECF replaces PACER whose records did go back to 1993. New records online after 1 day. ECF at https://ecf.canb.uscourts.gov. **Opinions Online:** www.canb.uscourts.gov. Click on Judges Decisions. **Other Online Access:** For calendars, click on Calendars at main website.

Santa Rosa Division Court Clerk, 99 South E St, Santa Rosa, CA 95404 (use mail address for courier delivery), 707-525-8539, Fax-707-579-0374. 9AM-4:30PM. www.canb.uscourts.gov

Counties: Del Norte, Humboldt, Lake, Marin, Mendocino, Napa, Sonoma.

Searches & Indexing: Results include last 4 SSN digits. Computer index maintained. New cases in the index immediately after filing date. Records purged every 6 months to 1 year.

Fee & Payment: Pay by money order, cashier check, business check. No personal checks. Payee: Clerk - Bankruptcy Court. Prepayment required.

Phone Search: Names and accession numbers is released via phone. Voice Case Information Service available, call VCIS at 888-457-0604 or 415-705-3160.

Mail Search: search usually completed- 5 days. Include SASE for return.

In Person Search: Fee charged if court performs your search. This court urges use of their contracted copy service, Attorney's Diversified, 707-545-5455. Self-serve copier- $.20 per page.

E-Services: ECF replaces PACER whose records did go back to 1993. New records online after 1 day. ECF at https://ecf.canb.uscourts.gov **Opinions Online:** www.canb.uscourts.gov. Click on Judges Decisions. **Other Online Access:** For calendars, click on Calendars at main website.

US District Court

Southern District of California

San Diego Division Clerk of Court, Rm 4290, 880 Front St, San Diego, CA 92101-8900 (use mail address for courier delivery), 619-557-5600, records rm- 619-702-9941, Fax-619-557-6684. 8:30AM-4:30PM. www.casd.uscourts.gov

Counties: Imperial, San Diego. Court also handles some cases from Yuma County, AZ.

Searches & Indexing: Results do not include SSN or DOB. Computer index maintained. New cases in the index 24 hours after filing date.

Fee & Payment: Pay by Visa/MC, money order, cashier's or personal check. Payee: US District Court. Prepayment required.

Phone Search: No searching by telephone.

Mail Search: search usually completed- 7-10 days. SASE not required.

In Person Search: Fee charged if court performs your search. A copy service is available. No self-serve copier available.

E-Services: PACER online at http://pacer.casd.uscourts.gov. Document images available. PACER records go back to 1990. New records online after 1 day. Currently in the process of implementing CM/ECF. **Other Online Access:** Access computer bulletin board at 619-557-6779.

US Bankruptcy Court

Southern District of California

San Diego Division Office of the Clerk, US Courthouse, 325 West "F" St, San Diego, CA 92101 (also use mail address for courier delivery), 619-557-5620. Hours- 9AM-4PM. www.casb.uscourts.gov

Counties: Imperial, San Diego.

Searches & Indexing: Cases indexed by debtor name and case number. Results include last 4 SSN digits. Computer index maintained back to 1998. New cases in the index 3 days after filing date. Records purged every 6 months.

Fee & Payment: Pay by money order, cashier check. Payee: Clerk, US Bankruptcy Court. Prepayment required.

Phone Search: Only docket information is available by phone. Voice Case Information Service available, call VCIS at 619-557-6521.

Mail Search: search usually completed- 7 days. SASE not required.

In Person Search: Fee charged if court performs your search. No self-serve copier available.

E-Services: PACER online at http://pacer.casb.uscourts.gov. Document images available. PACER records go back to 1989. New records online after 1 day. ECF at http://ecf.casb.uscourts.gov

California County Courts

Court	Jurisdiction	No. of Courts	How Organized
Superior Courts*	General	29	
Limited Superior Courts*	Limited	122	
Combined Superior Courts*	Limited & General	58	

* Profiled in this Sourcebook.

CIVIL									
Court	Tort	Contract	Real Estate	Min. Claim	Max. Claim	Small Claims	Estate	Eviction	Domestic Relations
General Jurisdiction*	X	X	X	$25,000	No Max		X		X
Limited Jurisdiction*	X	X	X	$0	$25,000	$5000		X	

CRIMINAL					
Court	Felony	Misdemeanor	DWI/DUI	Preliminary Hearing	Juvenile
General Jurisdiction*	X	X	X		X
Limited Jurisdiction*		X	X	X	

ADMINISTRATION

Administrative Office of Courts, 455 Golden Gate Ave, San Francisco, CA, 94102; 415-865-4200, Fax: 415-865-4205. www.courtinfo.ca.gov

COURT STRUCTURE

In July, 1998, the judges in individual counties were given the opportunity to vote on unification of superior and municipal courts within their respective counties. By late 2000, all counties had voted to unify these courts. Courts that were formally Municipal Courts are now known as Limited Jurisdiction Superior Courts. In some counties, superior and municipal courts were combined into one superior court. Civil under $25,000 is a Limited Civil Court, over $25,000 is an Unlimited Civil Court, and if both are over and under, then the court is a Combined Civil Court.

It is important to note that Limited Courts may try minor felonies not included under our felony definition.

Due to its large number of courts, the Los Angeles County section is arranged uniquely in this book. Each Branch or Division of the Los Angeles Superior Court is given by name, which usually indicates a court's general jurisdictional and geographic boundary (the actual jurisdiction area is noted in the text). The court name is followed by the District it is located in - South Central, West, Northeast, Central, etc. Also, a court name may mention whether its jurisdiction is "Civil" only or "Criminal" only.

ONLINE ACCESS

The site at www.courtinfo.ca.gov offers access to all opinions from the Supreme and Appeals courts from 1850 to present. Opinions not certified for publications are available for last 60 days. This site also contains very useful information about the state court system, inlcuding opinions from the Supreme and Appeals courts.

There is no statewide online computer access available. However, a number of counties have developed their own online access sytems and provide Internet access at no fee. Los Angeles County has a fee-based online system to obtain criminal records county wide or civil case records for limits exceeding $25,000. There is a free lookup by case number only for probate and civil case summaries when under $25,000. Go to www.lasuperiorcourt.org/.

ADDITIONAL INFORMATION

If there is more than one court of a type within a county, where the case is tried and where the record is held depends on how a citation is written, where the infraction occurred, or where the filer chose to file the case.

Some courts now require signed releases from the subject in order to perform criminal searches and will no longer allow the public to conduct such searches.

Personal checks are acceptable by state law.

Although fees are set by statute, courts interpret them differently. For example, the search fee is supposed to be $6.00 per name per year searched, but many courts charge only $5.00 per name. Generally, certification is $6.60 per document and copies are usually $.75 per page, but can range from $.50 to $1.10, and in Los Angeles County copies are $.57 each.

A convenient Los Angeles County Court Locator web page is available free at www.lasuperiorcourt.org/locations/

Alameda County

Superior Court - Criminal 1225 Fallon St, Rm 107, Oakland, CA 94612; phone: 510-272-6777; fax: 510-835-4850; hours 8:30AM-4PM (PST). *Felony.* www.alameda.courts.ca.gov/courts/
Note: Located at the Rene C Davidson Alameda County Courthouse.

Criminal Records: Access: Mail, in person. Both court and visitors may perform in person searches. Search fee: $5.00 per name. There is no fee if you do the search. Court makes copy: $.75 per page. Required to search: name, years to search, signed release; also helpful: DOB, SSN. Criminal records on computer back 10 years; on microfiche from 1940, archived and indexed from 1880. At the website, search "Find Your Court Date" to determine if a name has an upcoming court date. Mail turnaround time 1 week.

General Information: Public access terminal has only criminal records back to 1998. No probation, medical, adoption, juvenile or sealed records released. Will fax documents. Certification fee: $6.60 per doc. Payee: Clerk of Superior Court. Personal checks accepted. Prepayment and SASE required.

Superior Court - Civil 1225 Fallon St, Rm 109, Oakland, CA 94612; 510-272-6503; 8:30AM-4:30PM (PST). *Civil Actions Over $25,000, Probate.* www.alameda.courts.ca.gov/courts/
Note: Located at the Rene C Davidson Courthouse.

Civil Records: Access: Mail, in person, online. Both court and visitors may perform in person searches. Search fee: $5.00 per name per year. Additional $5.00 fee for years prior to 1974. Court makes copy: $.75 per page. Required to search: name, years to search. Civil cases indexed by defendant, plaintiff. Civil records on computer from 1974, on microfiche and archived from 1900s. Online access to calendars, limited civil case summaries and complex litigations are free from Domain Web at the website. Search limited cases by number; litigations by case name or number. At the website, search "Find Your Court Date" to determine if a name has an upcoming court date. Note: Court prefers you use their "consent form." Mail turnaround time 2 weeks.

General Information: Public access terminal has only civil records back to 1998. No sealed records nor adoption records released unless court ordered. Certification fee: $6.60 per doc. Payee: Superior Court. Personal checks accepted. Prepayment and SASE required.

Superior Court South Branch/Hayward - Civil 24405 Amador St, Rm 108, Hayward, CA 94544; phone: 510-670-5060; hours 8:30AM-5PM (PST). *Civil, Probate.*
www.alameda.courts.ca.gov/courts/
Note: Located at the Hayward Hall of Justice.

Civil Records: Access: Mail, in person, online. Visitors must perform in person searches themselves. Search fee: $5.00 per name. Court makes copy: $.75 per page. Required to search: name, years to search. Civil cases indexed by defendant, plaintiff. Civil records on computer from 1974, on microfiche and archived from 1900s. Online access to calendars, limited civil case summaries and complex litigations are free from Register of Actions/Domain Web at the website. Search limited cases by number; litigations by case number. At the website, search "Find Your Court

Date" to determine if a name has an upcoming court date. Mail turnaround time 2-3 weeks.
General Information: Public access terminal has only civil records. No sealed files, paternity or adoption records released. Certification fee: $6.60 per doc. Payee: Clerk of Superior Court. Personal checks accepted. Prepayment and SASE required.

Alameda Branch Superior Court 2233 Shoreline Dr, Alameda, CA 94501; phone: 510-268-4209; criminal phone: 510-268-7484; civil phone: 510-268-4219; fax: 510-268-4273; hours 8:30AM-4:00PM (PST). *Felony, Misdemeanor, Civil Actions Under $25,000, Eviction, Small Claims.*
www.alameda.courts.ca.gov/courts/
Note: Co-extensive with the city limits of Alameda only. Located at George E McDonald Hall of Justice.

Civil Records: Access: Mail, in person, online. Both court and visitors may perform in person searches. Search fee: $5.00 per name. Court makes copy: $.75 per page. Required to search: name, years to search. Civil cases indexed by defendant, plaintiff. Civil records on computer since 1987. Online access to calendars, limited civil case summaries and complex litigations are free from Domain Web at the website. Search limited cases by number; litigations by case number. Mail turnaround time 1 week.

Criminal Records: Access: Mail, in person. Both court and visitors may perform in person searches. Search fee: $5.00 per name. Court makes copy: $.75 per page. Required to search: name, years to search, DOB, signed release; also helpful: SSN. Criminal records on computer 7 years back. At the website, search "Find Your Court Date" to determine if a name has an upcoming court date. Mail turnaround time 1 week.

General Information: Public access terminal available. No confidential records released. Will fax documents to local or toll free line. Certification fee: $6.60 per doc. Payee: Alameda Superior Court. Personal checks accepted. Credit cards accepted. Accepted in person only. Prepayment and SASE required.

Berkeley/Albany Superior Court - Civil 2120 Martin Luther King Jr Way, Berkeley Courthouse, Berkeley, CA 94704; phone: 510-647-4423, 510-647-4424; fax: 510-883-9359; hours 8:30AM-4:00PM (PST). *Civil Actions Under $25,000, Eviction, Small Claims.*
www.alameda.courts.ca.gov/courts/
Note: Co-extensive with the city limits of Berkeley and Albany.

Civil Records: Access: Mail, in person, online. Both court and visitors may perform in person searches. Search fee: $5.00 per name. Court makes copy: $.75 per page. Required to search: name, years to search. Civil cases indexed by defendant, plaintiff. Civil records on computer from 1986. Online access to calendars, limited civil case summaries and complex litigations are free from Domain Web at the website. Search limited cases by number; litigations by case name or number. At the website, search "Find Your Court Date" to determine if a name has an upcoming court date. Mail turnaround time 1 week.
General Information: Public access terminal has only civil records back to 1987. No sealed, judge's notes or confidential records released. Will not fax documents. Certification fee: $6.60 per doc. Payee: Berkeley Superior Court. Personal checks accepted. Prepayment and SASE required.

Fremont Superior Court 39439 Paseo Padre Pky, Fremont, CA 94538; criminal phone: 510-795-2300; civil phone: 510-795-2360; fax: 510-795-2418; hours 8:30AM-4PM (PST). *Misdemeanor, Civil Actions Under $25,000, Eviction, Small Claims.* www.alameda.courts.ca.gov/courts/
Note: Jurisdiction includes Fremont, Newark and Union City. Located at the Fremont Hall of Justice.

Civil Records: Access: Fax, mail, in person, online. Both court and visitors may perform in person searches. Search fee: $5.00 per name. Court makes copy: $.75 per page. Required to search: name, years to search. Civil cases indexed by defendant, plaintiff. Civil records on computer from 1990. Online access to calendars, limited civil case summaries and complex litigations are free at the DomainWeb section at the website. Search limited cases by number; litigations by case name or number. Mail turnaround time 1 week.

Criminal Records: Access: Mail, in person. Both court and visitors may perform in person searches. Search fee: $5.00 per name. Court makes copy: $.75 per page. Required to search: name, years to search, DOB, signed release. Criminal records on computer only go back 7 years. At the website, search "Find Your Court Date" to determine if a name has an upcoming court date. Mail turnaround - 1 week.

General Information: Public access terminal has criminal back to 7 years and civil back to 15 years. No sealed or confidential records released. Will fax civil documents only, $1.00 per page. Certification fee: $6.75 per doc. Payee: Fremont Superior Court. Personal checks accepted. Prepayment and SASE required.

Hayward Superior Court 24405 Amador St, Hayward, CA 94544; criminal phone: 510-670-6434; civil phone: 510-670-5059; fax: 510-670-5953; hours 8:30AM-4PM (PST). *Misdemeanor, Civil Actions Under $25,000, Eviction, Small Claims.* www.alameda.courts.ca.gov/courts/
Note: Formerly San Leandro/Hayward Superior Ct. Includes the cities of San Leandro, Hayward and adjoining unincorporated areas of Castro Valley and San Lorenzo. Located at the Hayward Hall of Justice.

Civil Records: Access: Mail, in person, online. Both court and visitors may perform in person searches. Search fee: $5.00 per name. Court makes copy: $.75 per page. Required to search: name, years to search. Civil cases indexed by defendant, plaintiff. Civil records on computer back 20 years; also on paper index. Online access to calendars, limited civil case summaries and complex litigations are free from Domain Web at the website. Search limited cases by number; litigations by case name or number. Mail turnaround time 2-3 days.

Criminal Records: Access: Mail, in person. Both court and visitors may perform in person searches. Search fee: $5.00 per name. Fee is per case. Will only search back 7 years. Court makes copy: $.75 per page. Required to search: name, years to search, DOB, signed release; also helpful: SSN. Criminal records on computer back 20 years; also on paper index. At the website, search "Find Your Court Date" to determine if a name has an upcoming court date. Mail turnaround time 2-3 days.

General Information: Public access terminal goes back to 1998. No sealed or confidential records released. No fee to fax documents. Certification fee: $6.60 per doc. Payee: Clerk of the Court. Local personal checks accepted. Visa, MC accepted in person only. ATM card accepted. Prepayment and SASE required.

Oakland/Piedmont/Emeryville Superior Court - Civil

661 Washington St, 2nd Fl, Oakland, CA 94607; phone: 510-268-4222; fax: 510-268-7807; hours: 8:30AM-4PM (PST). *Civil Actions Under $25,000, Eviction, Small Claims.* www.alameda.courts.ca.gov/courts/

Note: Comprises the cities of Oakland, Piedmont and Emeryville. Located at the Allen E Broussard Justice Center.

Civil Records: Access: Mail, in person, online. Both court and visitors may perform in person searches. Search fee: $5.00 per name. Court makes copy: $.75 per page. Required to search: name, years to search. Civil cases indexed by defendant, plaintiff. Civil records on computer from 1990. Online access to calendars, limited civil case summaries and complex litigations are free from Domain Web at the website. Search limited cases by number; litigations by case name or number. At the website, search "Find Your Court Date" to determine if a name has an upcoming court date. Mail turnaround time 2-3 weeks.

General Information: Public access terminal has only civil records back to 10 years. No sealed or confidential records released. Certification fee: $6.60 per doc. Payee: Oakland Superior Court. Personal checks accepted. Prepayment and SASE required.

Oakland/Piedmont/Emeryville Superior Court - Criminal

661 Washington St, 2nd Fl, Oakland, CA 94607; phone: 510-268-7700; fax: 510-268-7705; hours 8:30AM-4PM (PST). *Misdemeanor, Felony.* www.alameda.courts.ca.gov/courts/

Note: Comprises the cities of Oakland, Piedmont and Emeryville, Albany and Berkeley. Located at the Wiley W Manuel Courthouse.

Criminal Records: Access: Mail, in person. Both court and visitors may perform in person searches. Search fee: $5.00 per name. Court makes copy: $.75 per page. Required to search: name, years to search. Criminal records on computer from 1994, maintained since 1972. At the website, search "Find Your Court Date" to determine if a name has an upcoming court date. Mail turnaround - 1 week.

General Information: Public access terminal has only criminal records back to 1998. No sealed or confidential records released. Certification fee: $6.60 per doc. Payee: Oakland Superior Court. Personal checks accepted. Will accept Mc/Visa in person only. Prepayment and SASE required.

Pleasanton Superior Court

5672 Stoneridge Dr, Hall of Justice, Pleasanton, CA 94588; phone: 925-803-7123; criminal phone: 925-803-7995; civil phone: 925-551-6886; probate phone: 925-551-6886; criminal records fax: 925-551-6862; civil records fax: 925-803-7979; hours 8:30AM-4PM (PST). *Misdemeanor, Civil Actions over $25,000, Eviction, Small Claims, Probate.* www.alameda.courts.ca.gov/courts/

Note: Includes the cities of Livermore, Dublin, Sunol and Pleasanton and all areas east to San Joaquin County line, north of Highway 580 to Contra Costa line. Located at the Gale/Schenone Hall of Justice.

Civil Records: Access: Mail, in person, online. Both court and visitors may perform in person searches. Search fee: $5.00 per name. Court makes copy: $.75 per page. Required to search: name, years to search. Civil cases indexed by defendant, plaintiff. Civil records on computer from 1990. Online access to calendars, civil case summaries, probate, family law, and complex litigations are free from Domain Web at the website. Search all cases by case number. Mail turnaround time 4-6 weeks.

Criminal Records: Access: Mail, in person. Both court and visitors may perform in person searches. Search fee: $5.00 per name. Court makes copy: $.75 per page. Required to search: name, years to search; also helpful: address, DOB. Criminal records on computer from 1990. At the website, search "Find

Your Court Date" to determine if a name has an upcoming court date within five days. Note: Court prefers that you use their "consent form." Mail turnaround time 4-6 weeks.

General Information: Public access terminal goes back to 1998. No records older than 10 years are released. Certification fee: $6.60 per doc. Payee: Alameda County Superior Court. Personal checks accepted. Visa, MC accepted in person only. Prepayment and SASE required.

Berkeley/Albany Superior Court - Traffic

2120 Martin Luther King Jr Way, Berkeley, CA 94704; phone: 510-647-4405; hours 8:30AM-4:PM (PST). *Traffic.* www.alameda.courts.ca.gov/courts/

Note: This court no longer handles Misdemeanor cases; records are at the Oakland/Piedmont/ Emeryville Superior Ct Criminal Div. at 661 Washington St, Oakland. Co-extensive with the city limits of Berkeley and Albany. Located at the Berkeley Courthouse.

Alpine County

Superior Court

PO Box 518, Markleeville, CA 96120; phone: 530-694-2113; probate phone: same; fax: 530-694-2119; hours 8AM-N, 1-5PM (PST). *Felony, Misdemeanor, Civil, Eviction, Small Claims, Probate.* www.alpine.courts.ca.gov

Civil Records: Access: Mail, in person. Both court and visitors may perform in person searches. Search fee: $5.00 per name per year. Court makes copy: $.50 per page; same fee for self serve. Required to search: name, years to search. Civil cases indexed by defendant, plaintiff. Civil records on index file from 1981, archived from 1800s. Computer records go back 10 years. Mail turnaround time 2 days.

Criminal Records: Access: Mail, in person. Both court and visitors may perform in person searches. Search fee: $5.00 per name per year. Court makes copy: $.50 per page; same fee for self serve. Required to search: name, years to search; also helpful-SSN. Criminal records on index file from 1981, archived from 1800s. Computer records go back 10 years. Mail turnaround time 2 to 5 days.

General Information: No public access terminal. No juvenile, paternity, adoption or sealed released. Fee to fax documents is $1.00 per page. Certification fee: $7.00 per page. Payee: Alpine County Superior Court. Personal checks accepted. Prepayment and SASE required.

Amador County

Superior Court

108 Court St, Jackson, CA 95642; criminal phone: 209-223-6320; civil phone: 209-223-6463; Hours: 9:3AM-4PM (PST). *Felony, Misdemeanor, Civil, Eviction, Small Claims, Probate.* www.amadorcourt.org

Civil Records: Access: Mail, in person, online. Both court and visitors may perform in person searches. Search fee: $5.00 per name; clerk will search for specific information only. Court makes copy: $1.00 for first page, $.20 each add'l. Required to search: name, years to search. Civil cases indexed by defendant, plaintiff. Civil records on computer from 1989, archived and indexed from 1800s. Court calendars are by date up to 10 days ahead at www.amadorcourt.org/courtcal/courtcal.html. Tentative rulings including previous year are free at www.amadorcourt.org/rulings/rulings.html. Mail turnaround time 7-14 days.

Criminal Records: Access: Mail, in person, online. Only the court performs in person searches; visitors may not. Search fee: $5.00 per name. $5.00 for search by case number. Court makes copy: $1.00 for first page, $.20 each add'l. Required to search: name, years to search. Criminal records on computer from 1989, archived and indexed from 1800s. Court calendars are by date up to 10 days ahead at www.amadorcourt.org/courtcal/courtcal.html. Tentative rulings including previous year are free at www.amadorcourt.org/rulings/rulings.html. Note: Phone and fax access limited to agency searches. Mail turnaround time 4-6 weeks.

General Information: No public access terminal. No adoption, juvenile or paternity records released. Will fax documents to 800 numbers only. Certification fee: $6.60 per doc. Payee: Superior Court Clerk. No personal checks accepted. Prepayment and SASE required.

Butte County

Superior Court

One Court St, Oroville, CA 95965; phone: 530-532-7002; criminal phone: 530-532-7012; civil phone: 530-532-7009; probate phone: 530-532-7017; fax: 530-892-8516; 8:30AM-4PM *Felony, Misdemeanor, Small Claims, Eviction.* www.courtinfo.ca.gov/courts/trial/butte

Note: This courthouse physically holds most criminal court files for the county, including Gridley and Paradise Branches; however, one can search the countywide computer index at any court. Civil cases were transferred to the Chico court in 2003.

Civil Records: Access: Mail, in person, online. Both court and visitors may perform in person searches. Search fee: $5.00 per name. Court makes copy: $.50 per page. $1.00 minimum. Required to search: name, years to search; also helpful: address. Civil cases indexed by defendant, plaintiff. Civil records on computer from 1988, on microfiche from 1983 thru 1988. Limited case index searching by name is free online at www.buttecourt.ca.gov/online_index/cms search.cfm. There is also a calendar lookup at www.buttecourt.ca.gov/calendarlookup/cmscalend arlookup.cfm. Mail turnaround time 2-5 days.

Criminal Records: Access: Mail, in person, online. Both court and visitors may perform in person searches. Search fee: $5.00 per name. Court makes copy: $.50 per page. $1.00 minimum. Required to search: name, years to search; also helpful: DOB. Criminal records on computer from 1988, on microfiche from 1983 thru 1988. Limited case index searching by name is free online at www.buttecourt.ca.gov/online_index/cmssearch.cf m. There is also a calendar lookup, see above. Mail turnaround time 1-2 weeks.

General Information: Public access terminal goes back to 1990. No juvenile, paternity or adoption records released. Will fax documents $5.00 1st page, $1.00 each add'l. Certification fee: $6.60 per doc. Payee: Butte County Superior Court. Personal checks or Visa, MC accepted. Prepayment required. SASE helpful.

Chico Branch - Superior Court

655 Oleander Ave, Chico, CA 95926; phone: 530-892-9407 (Traffic); criminal phone: 530-532-7011; civil phone: 530-892-0849; Hours: 8:30AM-4PM (PST). *Misdemeanor, Civil Actions, Eviction, Small Claims, Probate.*

Note: Active county Probate case records are located here; closed cases are archived in the basement at the main Superior Court in Oroville. This court handles civil cases previously handled by Oroville court.

Civil Records: Access: Mail, in person, online. Both court and visitors may perform in person searches. Search fee: $5.00 per name. Court makes copy: $1.00 for first page, $.50 each add'l. Required to search: name, years to search. Civil cases indexed by defendant, plaintiff. Civil records in index files. Records destroyed after 10 years. Limited case index searching by name is free at www.buttecourt.ca.gov/online_index/cmssearch.cf m. There is also a calendar lookup at www.buttecourt.ca.gov/calendarlookup/cmscalend arlookup.cfm. Mail turnaround time 4 weeks.

Criminal Records: Access: Mail, in person, online. Both court and visitors may perform in person searches. Search fee: $5.00 per name. Court makes copy: $1.00 for first page, $.50 each add'l. Required to search: name, years to search; also helpful: DOB. Criminal records in index files. Records destroyed after 10 years. Limited case index searching by name is free at www.buttecourt.ca.gov/on line_index/cmssearch.cfm. There is also a calendar lookup, see civil. Mail turnaround time 4 weeks.

General Information: Public access terminal goes back to 1986. No sealed records released. Court says to get copies made at Oroville. Certification fee: $6.60 per doc. Payee: Superior Court. Personal checks accepted. Prepayment and SASE required.

Gridley Branch - Superior Court 1 Court St, Oroville, CA 95965; phone: 530-846-5701 or 538-7551; hours 8AM-1PM 1st & 3rd Tuesday of month (PST). *Misdemeanor-Traffic, Eviction, Small Claims.*

Note: Closed cases must be searched at either Chico or Oroville. When court is closed (all but 2 days a month) calls are routed to the Oroville court, address given here.

Paradise Branch - Superior Court 747 Elliott Rd, Paradise, CA 95969; phone: 530-532-7018; criminal phone: 530-532-7011; civil phone: 530-532-7009; probate phone: 530-532-7017; criminal records fax: 530-538-9017; civil records fax: 530-538-8516; probate fax: 530-538-8516; hours 8:30AM-4PM (PST). *Misdemeanor-Traffic, Eviction, Small Claims.*

Civil Records: Access: Mail, in person, online. Only the court performs in person searches; visitors may not. Search fee: $5.00 per name. Court makes copy: $1.00 for first page, $.50 each add'l. Required to search: name; also helpful: years to search. Civil cases indexed by defendant, plaintiff. Civil records are located in The Chico Superior Court. Records go back to 1980; on computer back to 1997. Limited case index searching by name is free at www.buttecourt.ca.gov/online_index/cmssearch.cfm. There is also a calendar lookup at www.buttecourt.ca.gov/calendarlookup/cmscalendarlookup.cfm.

Criminal Records: Access: Online. Both court and visitors may perform in person searches. Search fee: $5.00 per name. Court makes copy: $1.00 for first page, $.50 each add'l. Required to search: Name, DOB, years to search, other names used; helpful-case/docket number. Criminal records indexed back to 1980. Criminal records are located in Oroville Superior Court. Records go back to 1980; on computer back to 1997.

General Information: No public access terminal. No sealed records released. Will fax documents if civil record. Certification fee: $6.60 per doc. Payee: Superior Court. Personal checks accepted. Prepayment and SASE required.

Calaveras County

Superior Court 891 Mt Ranch Rd, San Andreas, CA 95249; phone: 209-754-6311 info; criminal phone: 209-754-6338; civil phone: 209-754-6310; probate phone: 209-754-6310; criminal records fax: 209-754-6689; same fax for civil and probate; hours 8AM-4PM (PST). *Misdemeanor, Civil, Small Claims, Probate.*
www.calaveras.courts.ca.gov

Civil Records: Access: Mail, in person. Both court and visitors may perform in person searches. Search fee: $5.00 per name. Fee is for each 15 year period. Court makes copy: $.50 per page. Required to search: name, years to search. Civil cases indexed by defendant, plaintiff. Civil records on computer since 6/96; in index books and microfiche from 1975. Mail turnaround time 2-3 weeks.

Criminal Records: Access: Mail, in person. Both court and visitors may perform in person searches. Search fee: $5.00 per name. Fee is for each 15 year period. Court makes copy: $.50 per page. Required to search: name, years to search, DOB; also helpful: aliases. Criminal records on computer since 6/96; in index books and microfiche from 1975. Mail turnaround time 2-3 weeks.

General Information: No public access terminal. No juvenile or confidential records released. Will not fax documents. Certification fee: $6.60 per doc. Payee: Calaveras Superior Court. Personal checks accepted. No credit cards. Prepayment and SASE required.

Colusa County

Superior Court 532 Oak St, Colusa, CA 95932; phone: 530-458-5149; fax: 530-458-2230; hours 8:30AM-5PM (PST). *Felony, Civil Actions Over $25,000, Probate.*

Note: Since 1995, the records have been combined for both courts in this county; prior records must be searched at the individual courts. Dept. 1's courtroom is at 547 Market St.

Civil Records: Access: Mail, in person. Both court and visitors may perform in person searches. Search fee: $5.00 per name. Court makes copy: $.50 per page. Required to search: name, years to search. Civil cases indexed by defendant, plaintiff. Civil records on computer from 1986, in index files from 1800s. Mail turnaround time 7 days.

Criminal Records: Access: Mail, in person. Both court and visitors may perform in person searches. Search fee: $5.00 per name. Court makes copy: $.50 per page. Required to search: name, years to search. Criminal records on computer from 1986, in index files from 1800s. Mail turnaround time 7 days.

General Information: Public access terminal goes back to 1995. No juvenile, paternity (except Judgment) or adoption records released. Certification fee: $6.60 per doc. Payee: Colusa County Superior Court. Personal checks accepted. Prepayment and SASE required.

Colusa Superior Court 532 Oak St, Colusa, CA 95932; phone: 530-458-5149; fax: 530-458-2230; hours 8:30AM-5PM (PST). *Felony, Misdemeanor, Civil, Eviction, Small Claims.*
www.colusa.courts.ca.gov

Note: Since 1995, records from both courts in this county have been combined; prior records must be searched at the individual courts.

Civil Records: Access: Mail, in person. Both court and visitors may perform in person searches. Search fee: $5.00 per name per year. Court makes copy: $.50 per page; same fee for self serve. Required to search: name, years to search. Civil cases indexed by defendant, plaintiff. Civil records on computer from 1994, index books prior. Mail turnaround time up to 2 weeks.

Criminal Records: Access: Mail, in person. Both court and visitors may perform in person searches. Search fee: $5.00 per name per year. Court makes copy: $.50 per page; same fee for self serve. Required to search: name, years to search, DOB. Criminal records on computer from 1994, index books prior. Mail turnaround time up to 2 weeks.

General Information: Public access terminal goes back to 1995. No sealed records released. Certification fee: $6.60 per doc. Payee: Colusa Superior Court. Personal checks accepted. Prepayment and SASE required.

Contra Costa County

Superior Court 725 Court St, Martinez, CA 94553; phone: 925-646-2950; criminal phone: 925-646-2440; civil phone: 925-646-2951; hours 8AM-3PM (PST). *Felony, Civil Actions Over $25,000, Probate.* www.cc-courts.org
Family Law Center can be reached at 925-957-7866.

Civil Records: Access: Mail, online, in person. Both court and visitors may perform in person searches. Search fee: $5.00 per name. Court makes copy: $1.00 per page. Required to search: name, years to search. Civil cases indexed by defendant, plaintiff. Civil records on computer from 1987, on microfiche from 1900s. Civil case, Probate, Family and Small Claims information is free at www.cc-courts.org/civilcms.htm. Visitors can view microfiche. Mail turnaround time 1 week.

Criminal Records: Access: Mail, in person. Both court and visitors may perform in person searches. Search fee: $5.00 per name. Court makes copy: $1.00 per page. Required to search: name, DOB. Criminal records on computer from 1987, on microfiche from 1900s. Send written requests to Room 127. Visitors can view microfiche. Mail turnaround time 1 week.

General Information: No public access terminal. No adoption, juvenile or sealed records released. Certification fee: $6.60 per doc. Payee: Clerk of the Superior Court. Business checks accepted. Prepayment and SASE required.

Walnut Creek Branch - Superior Court 640 Ygnacio Valley Rd, Walnut Creek, CA 94596-3820; criminal phone: 925-646-6763; civil phone: 925-646-6579; Hours: 8AM-3PM (PST). *Felony, Misdemeanor, Civil Actions Under $25,000, Eviction, Small Claims.*
www.co.contra-costa.ca.us

Note: Includes Alamo, Canyon, Danville, Lafayette, Moraga, Orinda, Rheem, San Ramon, St Mary's College, Walnut Creek and Ygnacio Valley. Effective 01/01/99, this court has all civil records formerly at the municipal court in Concord.

Civil Records: Access: Phone, mail, online, in person. Both court and visitors may perform in person searches. Search fee: $5.00 per name. Add $5.00 archive retrieval fee for older cases. In person searching of microfiche is free. Court makes copy: $1.00 per page. Required to search: name; also helpful: years to search. Civil cases indexed by defendant, plaintiff. Civil records on computer from 1991. Records are destroyed after 10 years. Civil case, Probate, Family and Small Claims information is free at www.cc-courts.org/civilcms.htm. Mail turnaround time 1 week.

Criminal Records: Access: Mail, in person. Both court and visitors may perform in person searches. Search fee: $5.00 per name. Add $5.00 archive retrieval fee for older cases. In person searching of microfiche is free. Court makes copy: $1.00 per page. Required to search: name, years to search, DOB. Criminal records go back 10 years. Mail turnaround time 1 week.

General Information: No public access terminal. No probation reports or sealed case records released. Certification fee: $6.60 per doc. Payee: Walnut Creek Superior Court. Personal checks accepted. Prepayment and SASE required.

Pittsburg Branch - Superior Court 45 Civic Ave, Pittsburg, CA 94565-0431; criminal phone: 925-427-8173; civil phone: 925-427-8159; Hours: 8AM-3PM (PST). *Felony, Misdemeanor, Civil Actions $25,000 and under, Eviction, Small Claims.* www.co.contra-costa.ca.us

Note: Includes Antioch, Bay Pt., Bradford Island, Brentwood, Byron, Discovery Bay, Knightsen, Oakley, Pittsburg.

Civil Records: Access: Mail, online, in person. Both court and visitors may perform in person searches. Search fee: $5.00 per name. Court makes copy: $1.00 per page. Required to search: name, years to search. Civil cases indexed by defendant, plaintiff. Civil records on computer from 1991. Records are destroyed after 10 years. Civil case, Probate, Family and Small Claims information is free at www.cc-courts.org/index.htm Mail turnaround time 1 week.

Criminal Records: Access: Mail, in person. Both court and visitors may perform in person searches. Search fee: $5.00 per name. Court makes copy: $1.00 per page. Required to search: name, years to search, DOB. Criminal records on computer from 1991, index files for 10 years. Records are destroyed after 10 years. Note: Visitor may search microfiche only. Mail turnaround time 1 week.

General Information: No public access terminal. No probation reports released. Certification fee: $6.60 per doc. Payee: Superior Court. Personal checks accepted. Prepayment and SASE required.

Richmond Superior Court 100 37th St, Rm 185, Richmond, CA 94805; criminal phone: 510-374-3156; civil phone: 510-374-3137; fax: 510-374-3812; hours 8AM-3PM (PST). *Misdemeanor, Civil Actions Under $25,000, Eviction, Small Claims.*
www.co.contra-costa.ca.us

Note: Includes Crockett, El Cerrito, El Sobrante, Hercules, Kensington, North Richmond, Pinole, Point Richmond, Port Costa, Richmond, Rodeo, Rollingwood and San Pablo.

Civil Records: Access: Mail, in person, online. Both court and visitors may perform in person searches. Search fee: $5.00 per name. Court makes copy: $1.00 per page. Required to search: name. Civil cases indexed by defendant, plaintiff. Civil records on computer from 1991. Records are destroyed after 10 years unless renewal of judgment filed. Civil case, Probate, Family and Small Claims information is free at www.cc-courts.org/civilcms.htm. Mail turnaround time 5 days.

Criminal Records: Access: Mail, in person. Only the court performs in person searches; visitors may not. Search fee: $5.00 per name. There is an additional fee for retrieval of archive files. Court makes copy: $1.00 per page. Required to search: name, years to search; also helpful: address, DOB, SSN. Criminal records maintained for 10 years, but can be destroyed after 2 years depending on violation code. Mail turnaround time 5 days.

General Information: No public access terminal. No probation reports released. Certification fee: $6.60 per doc. Payee: Richmond Superior Court. Personal checks accepted. Prepayment and SASE required.

Del Norte County

Superior Court 450 "H" St, Rm 209, Crescent City, CA 95531; phone: 707-464-8115; fax: 707-465-4005; 8AM-5PM (PST). *Felony, Misdemeanor, Civil, Eviction, Small Claims, Probate.*
www.delnorte.courts.ca.gov
Civil Records: Access: Fax, mail, in person. Only the court performs in person searches; visitors may not. Search fee: $5.00 per name per year. Court makes copy: $.50 per page. Required to search: name, years to search. Civil cases indexed by defendant, plaintiff. Civil records archived and in index files. Mail turnaround time 3 days.

Criminal Records: Access: Mail, fax, in person. Only the court performs in person searches; visitors may not. Search fee: $5.00 per name per year. Court makes copy: $.50 per page. Required to search: name, years to search, DOB, middle name; also helpful-SSN. Criminal records archived and in index files. Mail turnaround time 1-2 days.

General Information: No public access terminal. No adoption, juvenile, probate, LPS conservatorship released. Certification fee: $7.00 per doc. Add'l fee for copies. Payee: Superior Court. Personal checks accepted. Prepayment and SASE required.

El Dorado County

Placerville Branch - Superior Court 495 Main St, Placerville, CA 95667; phone: 530-621-6426; criminal phone: 530-621-6427; fax: 530-622-9774; hours 8AM-2PM (PST). *Felony.*
http://eldocourtweb.eldoradocourt.org
Criminal Records: Access: Mail, in person. Both court and visitors may perform in person searches. Search fee: $5.00 per name. Court makes copy: $.50 per page. Self serve copy fee: $.15 per page. Required to search: name, years to search. Criminal records on computer from 2000, in hardbound books from 1979 to 1999, prior archived in Placerville. Mail turnaround time 2 weeks.

General Information: No public access terminal. No adoption, juvenile, mental or confidential released. Will not fax documents. Certification fee: $6.60 per doc. Payee: Superior Court. Personal checks accepted. Prepayment and SASE required.

South Lake Tahoe Branch - Superior Court - Civil 1354 Johnson Blvd, #2, South Lake Tahoe, CA 96150; phone: 530-573-3075; fax: 530-544-6532; hours 8AM-2PM (PST). *Civil, Eviction, Probate.* http://eldocourtweb.eldoradocourt.org
Civil Records: Access: Mail, in person. Both court and visitors may perform in person searches. Search fee: $5.00 per name. Court makes copy: $.50 per page. Required to search: name, years to search;

also helpful-case number. Civil cases indexed by defendant, plaintiff. Civil records on computer from 1989, in hardbound books from 1979 to 1989, prior archived in Placerville. Judge's weekly tentative rulings may be free online at the website. Mail turnaround time 2 weeks.

General Information: No public access terminal. No adoption, juvenile, mental or confidential released. Certification fee: $6.60 per doc. Payee: Superior Court. Personal checks accepted. Prepayment and SASE required.

South Lake Tahoe Branch - Superior Court - Criminal 1354 Johnson Blvd, #1, South Lake Tahoe, CA 96150; phone: 530-573-3044; fax: 530-542-9102; hours 8AM-2PM (PST). *Felony, Misdemeanor.*
http://eldocourtweb.eldoradocourt.org
Criminal Records: Access: Mail, in person. Both court and visitors may perform in person searches. Search fee: $5.00 per name. Court makes copy: $.50 per page. Required to search: name, years to search; also helpful: DOB, SSN. Criminal records on computer from 1991, index files from 1983. Records are destroyed after 10 years. Judge's weekly tentative rulings may be free online at the website. Mail turnaround time 2 weeks.

General Information: No public access terminal. No probation reports released. Faxed record request must be prepaid. Certification fee: $6.60 per doc. Payee: El Dorado Superior Court. Personal checks accepted. Credit cards not accepted. Prepayment and SASE required.

Cameron Park Branch - Superior Court 3321 Cameron Park Dr, Cameron Park, CA 95682; phone: 530-621-5867; probate phone: same; fax: 530-672-2413; hours 8AM-3PM (PST). *Civil, Probate.*
http://eldocourtweb.eldoradocourt.org/
Note: This is a Trial and Law & Motion court. Only records after 2000 are housed here. Records from 1999 and prior are available at the Placerville Branch Superior Court or at record storage location in Sacramento.
Civil Records: Access: Mail, in person. Both court and visitors may perform in person searches. Search fee: $5.00 per name. Court makes copy: $.50 per page. Required to search: name, years to search. Civil records on computer from 2000, index cards prior. Records are destroyed after 10 years. Mail turnaround time 1 week.

General Information: No public access terminal. Will not fax documents. Certification fee: $6.60 per doc. Payee: Superior Court. Personal checks accepted. Prepayment and SASE required.

Westen Slope Branch Superior Court 2850 Fairlane Ct, Bldg C, Placerville, CA 95667; criminal phone: 530-621-7464; civil phone: 530-621-7470; hours 8AM-3PM M-F (PST). *Misdemeanor, Small Claims, Evictions, Traffic.*
http://eldocourtweb.eldoradocourt.org/
Note: Also known as the Fairlane Branch. Also hears felony arraignments.
Civil Records: Access: Mail, in person. Both court and visitors may perform in person searches. Search fee: $5.00 per name per year. Court makes copy: $.50 per page. Required to search: name, years to search. Civil cases indexed by defendant, plaintiff. Civil records on computer from 2000. Judge's weekly tentative rulings may be free online at the website. Note: Address search requests to Dept. 8. Mail turnaround time 2 weeks.

Criminal Records: Access: Mail, in person. Both court and visitors may perform in person searches. Search fee: $5.00 per name. Court makes copy: $.50 per page. Required to search: name, years to search; also helpful: DOB. Criminal records on computer from 2000, prior on index books, index files from 1983. Records are destroyed after 10 years. Note: Address search requests to Dept 7. Mail turnaround time 2 weeks.

General Information: No public access terminal. No probation reports released. Will not fax documents. Certification fee: $6.60 per doc. Payee: El Dorado County Superior Courts. Personal checks accepted. Prepayment and SASE required.

Fresno County

Superior Court 1100 Van Ness Ave, #401, Fresno, CA 93724; criminal phone: 559-488-3142 misd.; 559-488-3388 felony; civil phone: 559-488-3452; probate phone: 559-488-3618; criminal records fax: 559-488-6799; civil records fax: 559-488-1976; probate fax: 559-488-3334; hours 8AM-3PM; clerk open to researcher 9AM-3PM (PST). *Felony, Misdemeanor, Civil, Small Claims, Probate.*
www.fresnosuperiorcourt.org/
Note: Felony address is B-102; Misdemeanor address is Rm 402; Civil unlimited is RM 401. Fax number for misdemeanors is 599-488-1654.

Civil Records: Access: Phone, fax, mail, in person, online. Both court and visitors may perform in person searches. Search fee: $5.00 per name. Court makes copy: $.50 per page. Required to search: name, years to search. Civil cases indexed by defendant, plaintiff. Civil records on computer back to 1976, on microfiche, index files and archived from 1800s. Online access to civil, probate, family, small claims cases is free at www.fresnosuperiorcourt.org/case_info/. Mail turnaround time 3-5 days.

Criminal Records: Access: Phone, fax, mail, in person. Both court and visitors may perform in person searches. Search fee: $5.00 per name per year. Court makes copy: $.50 per page. Required to search: name, years to search. Criminal records on computer back to 1976, microfiche, index files and archived from 1800s. Mail turnaround time 3-5 days.

General Information: Public access terminal available. No confidential, adoption or juvenile records released. Certification fee: $6.60 per doc. Payee: Superior Court Clerk's Office. Personal checks accepted. Prepayment and SASE required.

Clovis Division - Superior Court 1011 5th St, Clovis, CA 93612; phone: 559-299-4964; fax: 559-299-2595; hours 8AM-3PM (PST). *Traffic, Misdemeanor, Civil Actions Under $25,000, Eviction, Small Claims.*
www.fresnosuperiorcourt.org
Note: Includes Alder Springs, Auberry, Big Creek, Burroughs Valley, Clovis, Friant, Huntington Lake, Millerton Lake, Pine Ridge, Prather, Shaver, Tollhouse, and Watts. Does felony welfare fraud cases only.

Civil Records: Access: Mail, in person, online. Only the court performs in person searches; visitors may not. Search fee: $5.00. Court makes copy: $.50 per page. Required to search: name, years to search. Civil cases indexed by defendant, plaintiff. Civil records on computer and index files from 1983. Records destroyed after 10 years. Online access to civil, probate, family, small claims cases is free at www.fresnosuperiorcourt.org/case_info/. Mail turnaround time 1 week.

Criminal Records: Access: Mail, in person. Only the court performs in person searches; visitors may not. Search fee: $5.00. Court makes copy: $.50 per page. Required to search: name, years to search, DOB. Criminal records on computer and index files from 1983. Records destroyed after 10 years. Mail turnaround time 1 week.

General Information: No public access terminal. No probation reports released. Will not fax documents. Certification fee: $6.60 per doc. Payee: Clovis Superior Court. Personal checks accepted. Prepayment and SASE required.

Coalinga Division - Superior Court 160 W Elm St, Coalinga, CA 93210; phone: 559-935-2017/2018; fax: 559-935-5324; hours 8AM-3PM (PST). *Misdemeanor, Civil Actions Under $25,000, Eviction, Small Claims.*
www.fresnosuperiorcourt.org
Note: Includes Coalinga and Huron.

Civil Records: Access: Mail, in person, online. Only the court performs in person searches; visitors may not. Search fee: $5.00 per name. Court makes copy: $.50 per page. Required to search: name, years to search; also helpful: address. Civil cases indexed by defendant, plaintiff. Civil records on index cards and are computerized since 1990. Will only search back 10 years. Online access to civil, probate, family and small claims cases are free at www.fresnosuperiorcourt.org/case_info/. Mail turnaround time 1 week.

Criminal Records: Access: Mail, in person. Only the court performs in person searches; visitors may not. Search fee: $5.00 per name. Court makes copy: $.50 per page. Required to search: name, years to search, DOB; also helpful: address. Criminal records on computer from 1990, on index cards prior. Will only search back 10 years, Traffic 10 years. Mail turnaround time 1 week.

General Information: No public access terminal. No confidential records or cases not finished released. Certification fee: $6.60 per doc. Payee: Superior Court. Personal checks accepted. Prepayment and SASE required.

Firebaugh Division - Superior Court
1325 "O" St, Firebaugh, CA 93622; phone: 559-659-2011/2012; fax: 559-659-6228; hours 8AM-3PM (PST). *Misdemeanor, Civil Actions Under $25,000, Eviction, Small Claims.*
www.fresnosuperiorcourt.org/
Note: Includes Firebaugh and Mendota.

Civil Records: Access: Phone, fax, mail, in person, online. Only the court performs in person searches; visitors may not. Search fee: $5.00 per name. Court makes copy: $.50 per page. Required to search: name, years to search. Civil cases indexed by defendant, plaintiff. Civil records on computer from 1990, index cards prior. Will only search back 7 years. Online access to civil, probate, family, small claims cases is free at www.fresnosuperiorcourt.org/case_info/. Mail turnaround time 1 week.

Criminal Records: Access: Phone, fax, mail, in person. Only the court performs in person searches; visitors may not. Search fee: $5.00 per name. Court makes copy: $.50 per page. Required to search: name, years to search, DOB. Criminal records on computer from 1990. Will only search back 7 years. Mail turnaround time 1 week.

General Information: No public access terminal. No confidential records released. Will not fax documents. Certification fee: $6.60 Per doc. Payee: Firebaugh Superior Court. Personal checks accepted. Prepayment and SASE required.

Fowler Division - Superior Court
PO Box 400, Fowler, CA 93625; phone: 559-834-3215; fax: 559-834-1645; hours 8AM-3PM (PST). *Misdemeanor, Civil Actions Under $25,000, Eviction, Small Claims.*
www.fresnosuperiorcourt.org
Note: This court holds the records for the closed courts in Caruthers, Parlier, and Selma (no criminal) as well as cases from the cities of Bowles, Del Rey, Fowler, Kinopburg, Monmouth, and Raisin City (no criminal).

Civil Records: Access: Mail, in person, online. Only the court performs in person searches; visitors may not. Search fee: $5.00 per name. Court makes copy: $.50 per page; same fee for self serve. Required to search: name, years to search. Civil cases indexed by defendant, plaintiff. Civil records on index cards. Will only search back 7 years. Online access to civil, probate, family, small claims cases is free at www.fresnosuperiorcourt.org/case_info/. Mail turnaround time 1 week.

Criminal Records: Access: Mail, in person. Only the court performs in person searches; visitors may not. Search fee: $5.00 per name. Court makes copy: $.50 per page; same fee for self serve. Required to search: name, years to search; also helpful: DOB, SSN. Criminal records on computer from 1990, index cards prior. Will only search back 7 years. Mail turnaround time 1 week.

General Information: No public access terminal. No confidential records released. Certification fee: $6.60 per doc. Payee: Fowler Superior Court. Personal checks accepted. Prepayment and SASE required.

Kerman Division - Superior Court
719 S Madera Ave, Kerman, CA 93630; phone: 559-846-7371/7372; fax: 559-846-5751; hours 8AM-3PM M-F (PST). *Misdemeanor, Civil Actions Under $25,000, Eviction, Small Claims.*
www.fresnosuperiorcourt.org/
Note: The court holds preliminary hearings for felonies. Includes Biola, Biola Junction, Cantua, Five Points, Helm, Kerman, Rolinda, San Joaquin, and Tranquility.

Civil Records: Access: Phone, mail, in person, online. Only the court performs in person searches; visitors may not. No search fee. Court makes copy: $.50 per page. Required to search: name, years to search. Civil cases indexed by defendant, plaintiff. Civil records on index cards, computerized since 1994. Court will only search back 7 years. Online access to civil, probate, family, and small claims cases are free at www.fresnosuperiorcourt.org/case_info/. Mail turnaround time 1 week.

Criminal Records: Access: Phone, mail, in person. Only the court performs in person searches; visitors may not. No search fee. Court makes copy: $.50 per page. Required to search: name, years to search. Criminal records on computer from 1994 index cards prior. Court will only search back 7 years. Note: May have terminals available at archives location; 1963 E St, Kerman, CA, Ph-559-233-2800. Mail turnaround time 1 week.

General Information: No public access terminal. No confidential records released. Certification fee: $7.00 per doc. Payee: Superior Court. Personal checks accepted. Prepayment and SASE required.

Kingsburg Division - Superior Court
1600 California St, Kingsburg, CA 93631; phone: 559-897-2241; fax: 559-897-1419; hours 8AM-3PM *Felony, Misdemeanor, Civil (Limited), Traffic.*
www.fresnosuperiorcourt.org/
Note: This court includes records from the branch court closed in Riverdale, Selma/Parlick/Fowler (criminal only), and cases from the cities of Burrel, Camden, Kingsburg, Lanare, Laton, and Riverdale.

Civil Records: Access: Mail, in person, online. Only the court performs in person searches; visitors may not. Search fee: $5.00 per name. Court makes copy: $.50 per page. Required to search: name, years to search. Online access to civil, probate, family, small claims cases is free at www.fresnosuperiorcourt.org/case_info/. Mail turnaround time 1 week.

Criminal Records: Access: Mail, in person. Only the court performs in person searches; visitors may not. Search fee: $5.00 per name. Court makes copy: $.50 per page. Required to search: name, years to search, DOB. Criminal records on computer from 4/1994, index cards prior. Mail turnaround time 1 week.

General Information: No public access terminal. No confidential records released. Will not fax documents. Certification fee: $7.00 per doc. Payee: Superior Court. Personal checks accepted. Prepayment and SASE required.

Reedley Division - Superior Court
815 "G" St, Reedley, CA 93654; phone: 559-638-3114; fax: 559-637-1534; hours 8AM-3PM (PST). *Misdemeanor, Civil Actions Under $25,000, Eviction, Small Claims.*
www.fresnosuperiorcourt.org/
Note: Includes Badger, Cedarbrook, Cedar Pines, Centerville, Dunlap, Hume, Kings River Canyon, Navalencia, Minkler, Miramonte, Orange Cove, Piedra, Reedley, Sanger, Squaw Valley, Trimmer Springs and Wahtoke.

Civil Records: Access: Mail, in person, online. Both court and visitors may perform in person searches. No search fee. Court makes copy: $.50 per page.

Required to search: name, years to search. Civil cases indexed by defendant, plaintiff. Civil records on computer back 10 years, index cards prior. Will only search back 7 years. Online access to civil, probate, family, small claims cases is free at www.fresnosuperiorcourt.org/case_info/. Mail turnaround time 1 week.

Criminal Records: Access: Mail, in person. Both court and visitors may perform in person searches. No search fee. Court makes copy: $.50 per page. Required to search: name, years to search, DOB. Criminal records on computer back 10 years, index cards prior. Will only search back 7 years. Mail turnaround time 1 week.

General Information: No public access terminal. No confidential records released. Certification fee: $6.60 per doc. Payee: Reedley Superior Court. Personal checks accepted. Prepayment and SASE required.

Sanger Division - Superior Court
c/o Reedley Division Superior Court, 815 "G" St, Reedley, CA 93654; phone: 559-638-3114; fax: 559-637-1534; hours 8AM-N, 1-4PM (1-4 for phone calls) (PST). *Misdemeanor, Civil Actions Under $25,000, Eviction, Small Claims.*
www.fresnosuperiorcourt.org/
Note: This court closed as of 07/03. Case files went to the Court in Reedley. The Sanger court had jurisdiction over Centerville, Minkler, Piedra, Sanger, and Trimmer Springs.

Selma Division - Superior Court
Fowler, CA 93626. *Misdemeanor, Civil Actions Under $25,000, Eviction, Small Claims.*
www.fresnosuperiorcourt.org/
Note: This court, formerly on Mercer St in Flowler, closed as of 06/03. Criminal case files went to the Court in Kingsburg. Civil and small claims to court in Fowler.

Glenn County

Superior Court 526 W Sycamore, Willows, CA 95988; phone: 530-934-6446; fax: 530-934-6728; hours 8AM-5PM (PST). *Felony, Misdemeanor, Civil, Small Claims, Probate.*
Note: Records from the municipal court were combined with this court when the courts were consolidated. Records-530-934-6461

Civil Records: Access: Mail, in person. Both court and visitors may perform in person searches. Search fee: $5.00 per search. Court makes copy: $.50 per page; same fee for self serve. Required to search: name, years to search. Civil cases indexed by defendant, plaintiff. Civil records on computer back to 1996, on microfiche, archived and in index file from 1894. Mail turnaround time 1 day.

Criminal Records: Access: Mail, in person. Both court and visitors may perform in person searches. Search fee: $5.00 per search. Court makes copy: $.50 per page; same fee for self serve. Required to search: name, years to search; also helpful: DOB. Criminal records on computer back to 1996, on microfiche, archived and in index file from 1894. Mail turnaround time 1 day.

General Information: Public access terminal goes back to 1996. No adoption, juvenile or paternity released. Certification fee: $7.00 per doc. Payee: Superior Court. Personal checks accepted. Prepayment and SASE required.

Humboldt County

Superior Court 825 5th St, Eureka, CA 95501; phone: 707-445-7256; hours 10AM-4PM (PST). *Felony, Civil, Small Claims, Eviction, Probate.*
Note: Address for the civil window is 421 I St. Countywide searching can be done from this court, records computerized for 10 years. The former Eureka, Eel River, and North Humboldt Muni. Court Divisions now part of this court.

Civil Records: Access: Mail, in person. Both court and visitors may perform in person searches. Search fee: $5.00 per name. Court makes copy: $.50

per page. Required to search: name, years to search. Civil cases indexed by defendant, plaintiff. Civil records on computer back to 1993; on microfiche and archived from 1964. Mail turnaround time 3 weeks.

Criminal Records: Access: Mail, in person. Both court and visitors may perform in person searches. Search fee: $5.00 per name. Court makes copy: $.50 per page. Required to search: name, years to search; also helpful: DOB. Criminal records on computer back to 1985; on microfiche and archived from 1964. Mail turnaround time 3 weeks.

General Information: No public access terminal. No probation, medical, adoption, juvenile or sealed records released. Certification fee: $6.60 per doc. Payee: Humboldt Superior Court. Personal checks accepted. Prepayment and SASE required.

Garberville Branch - Superior Court C/O Eureka Superior Court, 825 5th St, Eureka, CA 95501; phone: 707-445-7256; hours 9AM-3PM Fri only (PST). *Misdemeanor, Eviction, Small Claims.*
Note: Court is open one day a week no longer opens new civil cases. All mail inquires or research are directed to the Superior Court in Eureka.

Klamath/Trinity Branch - Superior Court, Eureka, CA 95501. *Misdemeanor, Civil Actions Under $25,000, Eviction, Small Claims.*
Note: Records for this branch are housed at the main court in Eureka.

Imperial County

Imperial Branch - Superior Court 939 W Main St, El Centro, CA 92243; criminal phone: 760-482-4256; civil phone: 760-482-4217; criminal records fax: 760-482-4918; civil records fax: 760-482-4219; 8AM-4PM (PST). *Felony, Misdemeanor, Civil, Eviction, Small Claims, Probate.*
Note: All record searching for Imperial county must be done at each location.

Civil Records: Access: Mail, in person. Both court and visitors may perform in person searches. Search fee: $5.00 per name. Court makes copy: $1.00 for first page, $.50 each add'l. Required to search: name, years to search. Civil cases indexed by defendant, plaintiff. Civil records on microfiche from 1972, in index file from 1917. Mail turnaround time 7 days.

Criminal Records: Access: Mail, in person. Both court and visitors may perform in person searches. Search fee: $5.00 per name. Court makes copy: $1.00 for first page, $.50 each add'l. Required to search: name, years to search, year action filed. Criminal records on microfiche from 1972, index file from 1917. Mail turnaround time 2 weeks.

General Information: No public access terminal. No adoptions, juvenile, medical, probation or sealed records released. Will fax documents for $1.00. Certification fee: $7.00 per doc. Payee: Imperial County Superior Court. Personal checks accepted. Prepayment and SASE required.

Brawley Branch - Superior Court 220 Main St., Brawley, CA 92227; phone: 760-351-2840; fax: 760-351-7703; hours 8AM-4PM (PST). *Misdemeanor, Civil Actions Under $25,000, Eviction, Small Claims.*
Note: There is no countywide database in this county.

Civil Records: Access: Phone, fax, mail, in person. Both court and visitors may perform in person searches. Search fee: $5.00 per name. Court makes copy: $1.00 for first page, $.50 each add'l. Required to search: name, years to search. Civil cases indexed by defendant, plaintiff. Civil records on computer from 09/93 (traffic from 1991), in index files from 1983. Records destroyed after 10 years. Mail turnaround time 1 week.

Criminal Records: Access: Phone, fax, mail, in person. Only the court performs in person searches; visitors may not. Search fee: $5.00 per name. Court makes copy: $1.00 for first page, $.50 each add'l. Required to search: name, years to search, DOB. Criminal records on computer back 2 years (traffic

only from 1991), in index files from 1983. Records destroyed after 10 years. Mail turnaround - 1 week.

General Information: No public access terminal. No probation reports released. Certification fee: $7.00 per doc. Payee: Brawley Superior Court. Personal checks accepted. Prepayment and SASE required.

Calexico Branch - Superior Court 415 4th St, Calexico, CA 92231; phone: 760-357-3726; fax: 760-357-6571; hours 8AM-4PM (PST). *Misdemeanor, Civil Actions Under $25,000, Eviction, Small Claims, Traffic.*
Note: There is no countywide database in this county.

Civil Records: Access: Fax, mail, in person. Both court and visitors may perform in person searches. Search fee: $5.00 per name. Court makes copy: $1.00 per page, $.50 add'l. Required to search: name, years to search. Civil cases indexed by defendant, plaintiff. Civil records on computer from 1991, index files from 1983. Records destroyed after 10 years. Mail turnaround time 1-2 weeks.

Criminal Records: Access: Fax, mail, in person. Only the court performs in person searches; visitors may not. Search fee: $5.00 per name. Court makes copy: $1.00 per page, $.50 each add'l. Required to search: name, years to search. Criminal records on computer from 1991, index files from 1983. Records destroyed after 10 years. Mail turnaround time 1-2 weeks.

General Information: No public access terminal. No probation reports released. Certification fee: $7.00 per doc. Payee: Superior Court. Personal checks accepted. Write case number on check. Prepayment and SASE required.

Winterhaven Branch - Superior Court PO Box 1087 (2124 Winterhaven Dr), Winterhaven, CA 92283-1087; phone: 760-572-0354; fax: 760-572-2683; 8AM-N, 1-4PM (PST). *Small Claims, Traffic.*
Note: Misdemeanor and civil records have been moved to the Calexico Branch. Only small claims and traffic records remain here.

Inyo County

Superior Court PO Drawer U, 168 N Edwards St, Independence, CA 93526; phone: 760-878-0218; fax: 760)-878-0334; hours 8AM- 4PM (PST). *Felony, Civil Actions Over $25,000, Probate.*
www.inyocourt.ca.gov
Note: There is no countywide database; branch court must be searched separately.

Civil Records: Access: Mail, in person. Both court and visitors may perform in person searches. Search fee: $6.00 per name. Court makes copy: $1.00 per page. Required to search: name, years to search. Civil cases indexed by defendant, plaintiff. Civil records on computer to mid-1999, on microfiche and in index files from 1800s. Mail turnaround time 2-3 business days.

Criminal Records: Access: Mail, in person. Both court and visitors may perform in person searches. Search fee: $6.00 per name. Court makes copy: $1.00 per page. Required to search: name, years to search. Criminal records on computer back to 1993, on microfiche and in index files from 1800s. Mail turnaround time 2-3 business days.

General Information: No public access terminal. No adoptions, juvenile, medical, probation or sealed records released. Will fax to 800 number no fee; otherwise $1.00 per page. Certification fee: $7.00 per doc. Payee: Inyo Superior Court. Personal checks or credit cards accepted. Prepayment and SASE required.

Bishop Branch - Superior Court 301 W Line St, Bishop, CA 93514; phone: 760-872-4971; fax: 760-872-1067; hours 8AM-4PM (PST). *Misdemeanor, Civil Actions Under $25,000, Eviction, Small Claims, Traffic.*
www.inyocourt.ca.gov
Note: There is no countywide database; each branch court must be searched.

Civil Records: Access: Mail, in person. Only the court performs in person searches; visitors may

not. Search fee: $6.00 per name. Court makes copy: $1.00 per page. Required to search: name, years to search. Civil cases indexed by defendant, plaintiff. Civil records on index cards. Will only search back 7 years. Mail turnaround time 1 week.

Criminal Records: Access: Mail, in person. Only the court performs in person searches; visitors may not. Search fee: $6.00 per name. Court makes copy: $1.00 per page. Required to search: name, years to search. Criminal records on computer from 1993, index cards prior. Will only search back 7 years. Mail turnaround time 1 week.

General Information: No confidential records released. Will fax to 800 number no fee; otherwise $1.00 per page. Certification fee: $7.00 per doc. Payee: Superior Court. Personal checks or credit cards accepted. Prepayment and SASE required.

Independence Limited Branch - Superior Court PO Drawer 518, 168 N Edwards St, Independence, CA 93526; phone: 760-878-0319; fax: 760-878-0334; hours 8AM-4PM (PST). *Misdemeanor, Civil Actions Under $25,000, Eviction, Small Claims.*
www.inyocourt.ca.gov Note: there is no countywide database, each branch court must be searched.

Civil Records: Access: Mail, in person. Both court and visitors may perform in person searches. Search fee: $6.00 per name. Court makes copy: $1.00 per page; same fee for self serve. Required to search: name, years to search. Civil cases indexed by defendant, plaintiff. Civil records on computer back to 1999, in index books and index cards. Will only search back 7 years. Mail turnaround time 1 week.

Criminal Records: Access: Mail, in person. Both court and visitors may perform in person searches. Search fee: $6.00 per name. Court makes copy: $1.00 per page; same fee for self serve. Required to search: name, years to search, DOB. Criminal records on computer from 2/1993, index books and index cards prior. Will only search back 7 years. Mail turnaround time 1 week.

General Information: No public access terminal. No confidential records released. Will fax to 800 number no fee; otherwise $1.00 per page. Certification fee: $7.00 per doc. Payee: Inyo County Court. Personal checks accepted. Prepayment and SASE required.

Kern County

Superior Court 1415 Truxtun Ave, Bakersfield, CA 93301; phone: 661-868-5393; criminal phone: 661-868-5393; civil phone: 661-868-7205; criminal records fax: 661-868-4883; civil records fax: 661-868-4883; hours 8AM-5PM (PST). *Felony, Civil Actions, Eviction, Small Claims.*
www.co.kern.ca.us/courts/
Note: Has electronic access to all divisions. Felonies in Rm 111. Note that misdemeanors at a separate address - see separate listing. No faxing to criminal record section. Small claims phone: 661-868-2456

Civil Records: Access: Mail, fax, in person. Both court and visitors may perform in person searches. Search fee: $5.00 per name per year. Court makes copy: $.75 per page. Required to search: name, years to search. Civil cases indexed by defendant, plaintiff. Civil records on microfiche from 1964, archived and in index file from 1800s. Civil case info and calendars available on special kiosk computers located at every court location; calendars soon to be online at website. Mail turnaround time 1 day to 1 week.

Criminal Records: Access: Mail, in person, online. Both court and visitors may perform in person searches. Search fee: $5.00 per name per year. Court makes copy: $.75 per page. Required to search: name, years to search, DOB. Criminal records on computer from 1989, on microfiche, archived, and in index files. Access defendant search database free at www.co.kern.ca.us/courts/crimcal/crim_index_def.asp; new system with old records being added. Current court calendars are free online at www.co.kern.ca.us/courts/crim_index_case_info_c

al.asp. Also, access court defendant hearings schedule by name at www.co.kern.ca.us/courts/crimcal/crim_hearing_srch.asp. Also, search county sheriff inmate list at www.co.kern.ca.us/courts/caseinfo_menu.asp. Click on "inmate search." Note: Visitors may search court counter index which excludes identifiers; court searches electronically with identifiers. Mail turnaround time 1 day to 1 week.

General Information: Public access terminal has criminal back to 1989; new system goes back to 2003 and civil (dates not known). (Older records on the old terminal system which is now located in 3rd Fl Law Library.) No adoptions, juvenile, medical, probation or sealed records released. Certification fee: $6.60 per doc. Payee: Kern County Superior Court. Personal checks accepted. Prepayment and SASE required.

Delano/McFarland Branch Superior Court - North Division
1122 Jefferson St, Delano, CA 93215; phone: 661-720-5800; criminal phone: x3; civil phone: x4; fax: 661-721-1237; hours 8AM-5PM (PST). *Misdemeanor, Civil Actions Under $25,000, Eviction, Small Claims.*
www.co.kern.ca.us/courts/

Note: You should be able to access all recent court division criminal defendant records from this division computer.

Civil Records: Access: Fax, mail, in person. Both court and visitors may perform in person searches. Search fee: $5.00 per name per year. Court makes copy: $.75 per page. Required to search: name, years to search. Civil cases indexed by defendant, plaintiff. Civil records in index files from 1983. Records destroyed after 10 years. Civil case info and calendars available on special kiosk computers located at every court location; calendars soon to be online at website. Mail turnaround time 2 days.

Criminal Records: Access: Mail, in person, online. Both court and visitors may perform in person searches. Search fee: $5.00 per name per year. Court makes copy: $.75 per page. Required to search: name, years to search; also helpful: DOB. Criminal records on computer from 1988, in index files from 1983. Records destroyed after 10 years. Access defendant search database free at www.co.kern.ca.us/courts/crimcal/crim_index_def.asp; new system with old records being added. Current court calendars are free at www.co.kern.ca.us/courts/crim_index_case_info_cal.asp. Also, access court defendant hearings schedule by name at www.co.kern.ca.us/courts/crimcal/crim_hearing_srch.asp. Also, search county sheriff inmate list at www.co.kern.ca.us/courts/caseinfo_menu.asp. Click on "inmate search." Note: Visitors may search counter index which excludes identifiers; court searches electronically with identifiers. Mail turnaround time 2 days.

General Information: Public access terminal has only criminal records back to 1988. No probation reports released. Will not fax documents. Certification fee: $6.60 per doc. Payee: Superior Court Kern County-Delano/McFarland Branch. Personal checks accepted. Prepayment and SASE required.

Kern River Branch Superior Court - East Division
7046 Lake Isabella Blvd, Lake Isabella, CA 93240; phone: 760-549-2000; fax: 760-549-2120; hours 8AM-4PM M-Th 8AM-5PM F (PST). *Misdemeanor, Civil Actions Under $25,000, Eviction, Small Claims.*
www.co.kern.ca.us/courts/

Note: Includes the communities of Lake Isabella, Kern River, Weldon, Onxy, and Mt Mesa. You should be able to access all recent court division criminal defendant records from this division computer.

Civil Records: Access: Phone, fax, mail, in person. Only the court performs in person searches; visitors may not. Search fee: $5.00. Court makes copy: $.75 per page, $1.10 if certified. Required to search: name, DOB, years to search. Civil cases

indexed by defendant, plaintiff. Civil records on computer from 1991, in index files from 1983. Records destroyed after 10 years. Civil case info and calendars available on special kiosk computers located at every court location; calendars soon to be online at website. Mail turnaround time 2 days.

Criminal Records: Access: Phone, mail, in person, online. Both court and visitors may perform in person searches. Search fee: $5.00 per name. Court makes copy: $.75 per page, $1.10 if certified. Required to search: name, years to search. Criminal records on computer from 1991, in index files from 1983. Records destroyed after 10 years. Access defendant search database free at www.co.kern.ca.us/courts/crimcal/crim_index_def.asp; new system with old records being added. Current court calendars are free online at www.co.kern.ca.us/courts/crim_index_case_info_cal.asp. Also, access court defendant hearings schedule by name at www.co.kern.ca.us/courts/crimcal/crim_hearing_srch.asp. Mail turnaround time 2 days.

General Information: Public access terminal has only criminal records back to 1987. No probation reports released. Certification fee: $6.60 per doc. Payee: East Kern Superior Court. Personal checks accepted. Visa, AmEx accepted. Prepayment and SASE required.

Lamont/Arvin Branch Superior Court - South Division
12022 Main St, Lamont, CA 93241; phone: 661-868-5800; fax: 661-845-9142; hours 8AM-5PM (PST). *Misdemeanor, Civil Actions Under $25,000, Eviction, Small Claims.*
www.co.kern.ca.us/courts/

Note: You should be able to access all recent court division criminal defendant records from this division computer.

Civil Records: Access: Mail, in person. Both court and visitors may perform in person searches. Search fee: $5.00 per name. Court makes copy: $.75 per page. Required to search: name, years to search. Civil cases indexed by defendant, plaintiff. Civil records on computer from 1989. Records destroyed after 10 years. Civil case info and calendars available on special kiosk computers located at every court location; calendars soon to be online at website. Mail turnaround time 2 days.

Criminal Records: Access: Fax, mail, in person, online. Both court and visitors may perform in person searches. Search fee: $5.00 per name. Court makes copy: $.75 per page. Required to search: name, years to search, DOB; also helpful CA DL#, SSN, signed release. Criminal records on computer from 1989. Records destroyed after 10 years. Access defendant search database free at www.co.kern.ca.us/courts/crimcal/crim_index_def.asp; new system with old records being added. Current court calendars are free online at www.co.kern.ca.us/courts/crim_index_case_info_cal.asp. Also, access court defendant hearings schedule by name at www.co.kern.ca.us/courts/crimcal/crim_hearing_srch.asp. Also, search county sheriff inmate list at www.co.kern.ca.us/courts/caseinfo_menu.asp. Click on "inmate search." Note: Visitors may search court counter index which excludes identifiers; court searches electronically with identifiers. Mail turnaround time 2 days.

General Information: Public access terminal goes back to 1989. No probation reports released. No fee to fax documents. Certification fee: $6.60 per doc. Payee: Superior Court Lamont Branch. Personal checks accepted. Visa, AmEx accepted. Prepayment and SASE required.

Mojave Branch Superior Court - East Division
1773 Hwy 58, Mojave, CA 93501; phone: 661-824-7100; fax: 661-824-7089; hours 8AM-5PM (PST). *Misdemeanor, Civil Actions Under $25,000, Eviction, Small Claims.*
www.co.kern.ca.us/courts/

Note: Includes California City, Edwards AFB, Mojave, Boron, Rosemond, Cantil, and Tehachapi.

You should be able to access all recent court division criminal defendant records from this division computer.

Civil Records: Access: Mail, fax, in person. Both court and visitors may perform in person searches. Search fee: $5.00 per name. Court makes copy: $.75 per page. Required to search: name, years to search. Civil cases indexed by defendant, plaintiff. Civil records on computer from 1991, in index files from 1983. Records destroyed after 10 years. Civil case info and calendars available on special kiosk computers located at every court location; calendars soon to be online at website. Mail turnaround time up to 1 week.

Criminal Records: Access: Mail, fax, in person, online. Both court and visitors may perform in person searches. Search fee: $5.00. Court makes copy: $.75 per page. Required to search: name, years to search, DOB. Criminal records on computer from 1991, in index files from 1983. Access defendant search database free at www.co.kern.ca.us/courts/crimcal/crim_index_def.asp; new system with old records being added. Current court calendars are free online at www.co.kern.ca.us/courts/crim_index_case_info_cal.asp. Also, access court defendant hearings schedule by name at www.co.kern.ca.us/courts/crimcal/crim_hearing_srch.asp. Mail turnaround time up to 1 week.

General Information: Public access terminal goes back to 1991. No probation reports released. Will not fax documents. Certification fee: $6.60 per doc. Payee: East Kern Superior Court. Personal checks accepted. Visa, AmEx accepted; there is a $7.50 credit card charge. Additional fee charged for use of credit card. Prepayment and SASE required.

Ridgecrest Branch Superior Court - East Division
132 E Coso St, Ridgecrest, CA 93555; phone: 760-384-5900; civil phone: 760-384-5986; fax: 760-384-5899; hours 8AM-5PM (PST). *Misdemeanor, Civil Actions Under $25,000, Eviction, Small Claims.*
www.co.kern.ca.us/courts/

Note: Includes the communities of Ridgecrest, Inyokern, China Lake, Johanesburg, and Randsburg. Possible to access all recent court division criminal defendant records from this division computer.

Civil Records: Access: Mail, in person. Both court and visitors may perform in person searches. Search fee: $5.00 per name. Court makes copy: $.75 per page. Required to search: name, years to search. Civil cases indexed by defendant, plaintiff. Civil records on computer from 1990, in index files from 1983. Records destroyed after 10 years. Civil case info and calendars available on special kiosk computers located at every court location; calendars soon to be online at website. Mail turnaround time 2 days.

Criminal Records: Access: Phone, fax, mail, in person, online. Both court and visitors may perform in person searches. Search fee: $5.00 per name. Court makes copy: $.75 per page. Required to search: name, years to search; also helpful: DOB, SSN. Criminal records on computer from 1990, in index files from 1983. Records destroyed after 5 years. Access defendant search database free at www.co.kern.ca.us/courts/crimcal/crim_index_def.asp; new system with old records being added. Current court calendars are free online at www.co.kern.ca.us/courts/crim_index_case_info_cal.asp. Also, access court defendant hearings schedule by name at www.co.kern.ca.us/courts/crimcal/crim_hearing_srch.asp. Also, search county sheriff inmate list at www.co.kern.ca.us/courts/caseinfo_menu.asp. Click on "inmate search." Mail turnaround time 2 days.

General Information: Public access terminal goes back to 1990. No probation reports released. Will not fax documents. Certification fee: $6.60 per doc. Payee: Kern County Superior Court. Personal checks accepted. Visa, AmEx accepted. Prepayment and SASE required.

Shafter/Wasco Branch Superior Court - North Division
325 Central Valley Hwy, Shafter, CA 93263; phone: 661-746-7500; fax: 661-746-0545; hours 8AM-5PM (PST). *Misdemeanor, Civil Actions Under $25,000, Eviction, Small Claims.* www.co.kern.ca.us/courts/

Note: You should be able to access all recent court division criminal defendant records from this division computer.

Civil Records: Access: Phone, fax, mail, in person. Both court and visitors may perform in person searches. Search fee: $5.00 per name per year. Court makes copy: $.75 per page. Required to search: name, years to search; also helpful: address. Civil cases indexed by defendant, plaintiff. Civil records go back to 1994. Civil case info and calendars available on special kiosk computers located at every court location; calendars soon to be online at website. Note: Visitors may search counter index that excludes identifiers; court searches electronically with identifiers. Mail turnaround time 2 days.

Criminal Records: Access: Mail, in person, online. Both court and visitors may perform in person searches. Search fee: $5.00 per name per year. Court makes copy: $.75 per page. Required to search: name, years to search, DOB; also helpful: address, SSN. Criminal records on computer since 1988, traffic since 1991. Access defendant search database free at www.co.kern.ca.us/courts/crimcal/crim_index_def.asp; new system with old records being added. Current court calendars are free online at www.co.kern.ca.us/courts/crim_index_case_info_cal.asp. Also, access court defendant hearings schedule by name at www.co.kern.ca.us/courts/crimcal/crim_hearing_srch.asp. Also, search county sheriff inmate list at www.co.kern.ca.us/courts/caseinfo_menu.asp. Click on "inmate search." Note: Visitors may search court counter index which excludes identifiers; court searches electronically with identifiers. Phone searches limited to a few names only. Mail turnaround time 2 days.

General Information: Public access terminal has only criminal records back to 1988. No probation reports released. No fee to fax documents. Certification fee: $6.60 per doc; $10.00 if a dissolution. Payee: Superior Court North Division. Personal checks accepted. Prepayment and SASE required.

Superior Court Metropolitan Division
1215 Truxtun Ave, Bakersfield, CA 93301; phone: 661-868-2482; 868-2534 search requests; fax: 661-868-2695; hours 8AM-5PM (PST). *Misdemeanor, Traffic.* www.co.kern.ca.us/courts

Note: Formerly Bakersfield Municipal Court. Includes Bakersfield, Oildale, Edison, Glenville, Woody. You should be able to access all recent court division criminal defendant records from this division computer.

Criminal Records: Access: Mail, in person, online. Both court and visitors may perform in person searches. Search fee: $5.00 per name per year. Court makes copy: $.75 per page. Required to search: name, years to search. Criminal records on computer since 1988, microfilm since 1952. Access defendant search database free at www.co.kern.ca.us/crimcal/crim_index_def.asp; new system with old records being added. Current court calendars are free at www.co.kern.ca.us/courts/crim_index_case_info_cal.asp. Also, access court defendant hearings schedule by name at www.co.kern.ca.us/courts/crimcal/crim_hearing_srch.asp. Also, search county sheriff inmate list at www.co.kern.ca.us/courts/caseinfo_menu.asp. Click on "inmate search." Note: Visitors may search court counter index which excludes identifiers; court searches electronically with identifiers. Mail turnaround time 1 weeks.

General Information: Public access terminal goes back to 1988. No probation reports, rap sheets, medical or financial released. No fee to fax

documents. Will only fax one or two pages due to time constraints. Certification fee: $6.60 per doc. Payee: Superior Court of California. Personal checks accepted. Prepayment required. SASE helpful.

Taft Branch Superior Court - South Division
311 N Lincoln St, Taft, CA 93268; phone: 661-763-8531; fax: 661-763-2439; hours 8AM-N,1-5PM (PST). *Misdemeanor, Civil Actions Under $25,000, Eviction, Small Claims.* www.co.kern.ca.us/courts/

Access all recent court division criminal defendant records from this division computer.

Civil Records: Access: Phone, mail, in person. Both court and visitors may perform in person searches. Search fee: $5.00 per name. Court makes copy: $.75 per page. Required to search: name, years to search; also helpful: address. Civil cases indexed by defendant, plaintiff. Civil records on computer from 1988, in index files from 1983. Records destroyed after 10 years. Civil case info and calendars available on special kiosk computers located at every court location; calendars soon to be online at website. Mail turnaround time 2 days.

Criminal Records: Access: Phone, mail, in person, online. Both court and visitors may perform in person searches. Search fee: $5.00 per name. Purchase of complaint and docket required. Court makes copy: $.75 per page. Required to search: name, years to search, DOB; also helpful: address, SSN. Criminal records on computer from 1988, in index files from 1983. Records destroyed after 10 years. Access defendant search database free at www.co.kern.ca.us/courts/crimcal/crim_index_def.asp; new system with old records being added. Current court calendars are free online at www.co.kern.ca.us/courts/crim_index_case_info_cal.asp. Also, access court defendant hearings schedule by name at www.co.kern.ca.us/courts/crimcal/crim_hearing_srch.asp. Also, search county sheriff inmate list at www.co.kern.ca.us/courts/caseinfo_menu.asp. Click on "inmate search." Mail turnaround time 2 days.

General Information: Public access terminal goes back to 1988. No probation reports released. Certification fee: $6.60 per doc. Payee: South Taft Court. Personal checks or Visa, MC, AmEx accepted. Prepayment and SASE required.

Kings County

Superior Court - Criminal
1426 South Dr, Hanford, CA 93230; phone: 559-582-1010 x3042; fax: 559-585-3267; hours 8AM-5PM (PST). *Felony, Misdemeanor.* www.kings.courts.ca.gov

Criminal Records: Access: Mail, in person. Both court and visitors may perform in person searches. Search fee: $5.00 per name. Court makes copy: $.50 per page. Required to search: name, years to search, DOB. Criminal records on computer from 1991, in index files from 1983. Records destroyed after 10 years. Mail turnaround time 1 week.

General Information: Public access terminal has only criminal records. No probation or police reports released. Will not fax documents. Certification fee: $6.60 per doc. Payee: Kings County Superior Court. Personal checks accepted. Credit cards not accepted. Prepayment and SASE required.

Superior Court - Civil
1426 South Dr, Hanford, CA 93230; phone: 559-582-1010; probate phone: x3083; fax: 559-584-0319; hours 8AM-5PM (PST). *Civil Actions, Eviction, Small Claims, Probate.* www.kings.courts.ca.gov

Civil Records: Access: Mail, in person. Both court and visitors may perform in person searches. Search fee: $5.00 per name. Court makes copy: $.50 per page. Required to search: name, years to search. Civil cases indexed by defendant, plaintiff. Civil records on computer from 1989, on microfiche and archived from 1970s, in index file from 1914. Mail turnaround time 4 weeks.

General Information: Public access terminal has only civil records back to 1989. No adoptions,

juvenile, medical, probation or sealed records released. Certification fee: $6.60 per doc. Payee: Superior Court of the State of California. Business checks accepted. Checks accepted with proper identification. Prepayment and SASE required.

Avenal Division Superior Court
501 E Kings St, Avenal, CA 93204; phone: 559-582-1010 x4094; fax: 559-585-3269; hours 8AM-5PM (PST). *Misdemeanor, Civil Actions Under $25,000, Eviction, Small Claims.* www.kings.courts.ca.gov

Civil Records: Access: Phone, fax, mail, in person. Both court and visitors may perform in person searches. Search fee: $5.00 per name. Court makes copy: $.50 per page. Required to search: name, years to search. Civil records on index cards, computerized. Mail turnaround time 1 week.

Criminal Records: Access: Fax, mail, in person. Both court and visitors may perform in person searches. Search fee: $5.00 per name. Court makes copy: $.50 per page. Required to search: name, years to search, DOB. Criminal records on computer from 1991, index cards prior. Mail turnaround - 1 week.

General Information: Public access terminal has only civil records. No juvenile or adoption records released. Certification fee: $6.60 per doc. Payee: Avenal Superior Court. Personal checks accepted. Prepayment and SASE required.

Corcoran Division Superior Court
1000 Chittenden Ave, Corcoran, CA 93212; phone: 559-9582-1010 x3004; fax: 559-585-3270; hours 8AM-5PM (PST). *Misdemeanor, Civil Actions Under $25,000, Eviction, Small Claims.* www.kings.courts.ca.gov

Civil Records: Access: Mail, in person
Mail, in person. Only the court performs in person searches; visitors may not. Search fee: $5.00 per name. Court makes copy: $.50 per page. Required to search: name, years to search; also helpful: address. Civil cases indexed by defendant, plaintiff. Civil records on computer from 1990, index cards to 1974. Will only search back 7 years. Mail turnaround time 1 week.

Criminal Records: Access: Mail, in person. Only the court performs in person searches; visitors may not. Search fee: $5.00 per name. Court makes copy: $.50 per page. Required to search: name, years to search, DOB; also helpful: address, aka's. Criminal records on computer from 1990, index cards to 1974. Will only search back 7 years. Mail turnaround time 1 week.

General Information: No juvenile or adoption records released. Will not fax documents. Certification fee: $6.60 per doc. Payee: Superior Court of California. Personal checks accepted. Prepayment and SASE required.

Lemoore Division Superior Court
449 "C" St, Lemoore, CA 93245; phone: 559-924-7757; hours 8AM-5PM (PST). *Misdemeanor, Civil Actions Under $25,000, Eviction, Small Claims.* www.kings.courts.ca.gov/

Note: Court says to search records at Hanford court; 1426 South Dr, Hanford, CA 93230, Ph-559-582-1010 x3034 Criminal; x2075 Civil.

Civil Records: Access: Fax, mail, in person. Both court and visitors may perform in person searches. Search fee: $5.00 per name. Court makes copy: $.50 per page. Required to search: name, years to search. Civil cases indexed by defendant, plaintiff. Civil records computerized since 1990, on index cards back to 1977. In person access limited. Fax requests are accepted, though the court will recommend a fax processing service; add'l charge for fax requests. Mail turnaround time 10 days.

Criminal Records: Access: None. No criminal searching at this court. Criminal records on computer since 1990, index cards back to 1977. No criminal records located in Lemoore Division.

General Information: No public access terminal. Certification fee: $6.60 per doc. Payee: Clerk of Courts. Personal checks accepted. Prepayment and SASE required.

Lake County

Superior Court 255 N Forbes St, Lakeport, CA 95453; phone: 707-263-2374; fax: 707-262-1327; hours 8AM-1PM (PST). *Felony, Misdemeanor, Civil, Eviction, Small Claims, Probate.*
www.courtinfo.ca.gov/courts/trial/lake/lakeport.htm
Note: This court holds the records for the former Northlake Municipal Court. Please note that there are also felony records at the South Lake Division, and both courts should be checked when doing a criminal record search.
Civil Records: Access: Mail, in person. Only the court performs in person searches; visitors may not. Search fee: $5.00 per name. Court makes copy: $.25 per page. Required to search: name, years to search. Civil cases indexed by defendant, plaintiff. Civil records on computer from 1991, on microfiche, archived, and in index files from 1800s. Mail turnaround time 1-3 weeks.
Criminal Records: Access: Mail, in person. Only the court performs in person searches; visitors may not. Search fee: $5.00 per name. Court makes copy: $.25 per page. Required to search: name, years to search, DOB. Criminal records on computer from 1991, on microfiche, archived, and in index files from 1800s. Mail turnaround time 1-3 weeks.
General Information: No public access terminal. No adoptions, juvenile, medical, probation or sealed records released. Certification fee: $6.60 per doc. Payee: Lake County Superior Court. Personal checks accepted. Prepayment and SASE required.

South Lake Division - Superior Court 7000 S Center Dr, Clearlake, CA 95422; phone: 707-994-4859; criminal phone: 707-994-6598; civil phone: 707-994-8262; fax: 707-994-1625; hours 8AM-1PM; Phone hours 8:30AM-12:30PM (PST). *Felony, Misdemeanor, Civil Actions Under $25,000, Eviction, Small Claims.*
Note: Some felony cases here will not be on the computer index at the Superior Court in Lakeport. The court recommends searching both courts when doing criminal record searches.
Civil Records: Access: Mail, in person. Visitors must perform in person searches themselves. Search fee: $5.00 per name. Court makes copy: $.25 per page. Required to search: name, years to search. Civil cases indexed by defendant, plaintiff. Civil records on index books. Mail turnaround time 1 week for civil or 30 days for criminal.
Criminal Records: Access: Mail, in person. Only the court performs in person searches; visitors may not. Search fee: $5.00 per name. Court makes copy: $.25 per page. Required to search: name, years to search, DOB. Criminal records on computer from 1990, index books prior. Mail turnaround time 1 week for civil or 30 days for criminal.
General Information: No public access terminal. No police reports or sealed records released. Certification fee: $6.60 per doc. Payee: Lake County Superior Court. Personal checks accepted. Prepayment and SASE required.

Lassen County

Superior Court 220 S Lassen St, #2, Susanville, CA 96130; phone: 530-251-8205; criminal records fax: 530-257-9061; same fax for civil and probate; 7:30AM-5:30PM (PST). *Felony, Misdemeanor, Civil, Eviction, Small Claims, Probate.*
Civil Records: Access: Phone, mail, in person. Both court and visitors may perform in person searches. Search fee: $5.00 per name. Court makes copy: $1.50 for first page, $.50 each add'l; same fee for self serve. Required to search: name, years to search. Civil cases indexed by defendant, plaintiff. Civil records on computer from 11/89, archived and in index files from 1900s. Mail turnaround time 1-5 days.
Criminal Records: Access: Phone, mail, in person. Both court and visitors may perform in person searches. Search fee: $5.00 per name. Court makes copy: $1.50 for first page, $.50 each add'l; same fee for self serve. Required to search: name, years to

search. Criminal records on computer from 11/89, archived and in index files from 1900s. Mail turnaround time 1-5 days.
General Information: No public access terminal. No adoptions, juvenile, medical, probation or sealed records released. Will fax documents if all fees paid. Certification fee: $6.60 per doc. Payee: Lassen County Superior Court. Business checks accepted. Prepayment and SASE required.

Los Angeles County

Los Angeles Superior Court - Central District - Civil Stanley Mosk Courthouse, 110 N Grand Ave, Rm 426, Los Angeles, CA 90012; phone: 213-974-6135 (974-5171 if over $25,000); fax: 213-621-2701; hours 8:30AM-4:30PM (PST). *Civil Actions, Eviction, Small Claims, Probate.*
www.lasuperiorcourt.org
Note: Any civil cases here under $25,000 are co-extensive with the city limits of Los Angeles and includes the City of San Fernando and sections designated as San Pedro, West Los Angeles, Van Nuys, Venice and the unincorporated county area known as Florence.
Civil Records: Access: Phone, mail, online, in person. Both court and visitors may perform in person searches. Search fee: $5.00 per name. Court makes copy: $.57 per page. Required to search: name, years to search. Civil cases indexed by defendant, plaintiff. Civil records on computer from 1991, index files from 1983. Records destroyed after 10 years. For cases over $25,000 there is a fee-based lookup for case images at https://www.lasuperiorcourt.org/OnlineServices/CivilImages/index.asp. Search fee is $4.75, case document file is $7.50. Free case summary lookup for cases under $25,000 at https://www.lasuperiorcourt.org/OnlineServices/CivilImages/index.asp, but the lookup is by case number, not by name. Includes probate from 01/97. Mail turnaround time 24 hours, more if busy.
General Information: Public access terminal available. No probation reports released. Certification fee: $6.60 per doc. Payee: Los Angeles Superior Court. Personal checks or Visa, MC accepted. Prepayment and SASE required.

Los Angeles Superior Court - Central District - Felony Criminal Justice Center, 210 W Temple St, Rm M-6, Los Angeles, CA 90012; phone: 213-974-5259; criminal phone: 213-974-6535 Felony; 974-6141 Misd.; fax: 213-617-1224; hours 8:30AM-4:30PM (PST). *Felony, Misdemeanor.*
www.lasuperiorcourt.org
Note: court now handles felonies and misdemeanors; they can do misdemeanor searches for the Central District area of downtown LA, East LA, and Hollywood. Fax number above is for agency use only.
Criminal Records: Access: Mail, in person, online. Only the court performs in person searches; visitors may not. Search fee: $5.00 per name. Court makes copy: $.57 per page. Required to search: name, years to search, DOB, sex. Criminal records on microfiche and index files since 1956, computerized misdemeanors since 1988; felonies since 1996. Felony and misdemeanor defendant records are online for a fee at www.lasuperiorcourt.org/OnlineServices/criminalindex/. Search fee is $4 to $4.75. Note: In requests, court suggests to include full spelling of middle name. Mail turnaround time 24 hours; up to 3 weeks if busy.
General Information: No public access terminal. No adoptions, juvenile, medical, probation or sealed records released. Certification fee: $6.60 per doc. Payee: Los Angeles Superior Court. Personal checks accepted. Prepayment and SASE required.

Los Angeles Superior Court - Probate Department 111 N Hill St, Rm 258, Los Angeles, CA 90012; phone: 213-974-5471; hours 8AM-4PM (PST). *Probate.* www.lasuperiorcourt.org/probate
Note: Case summaries (notes) available free at website; search by case number. Also, probate for current cases in Central Dist., Burbank, Compton, Glendale, Lancaster, Long Beach, Pasadena, Pomona, San Fernando, Santa Monica, Torrance District Courts.

Airport Superior Court - West District 11701 S La Cienega Blvd, Los Angeles, CA 90045; phone: 310-727-6020; criminal phone: 310-727-6100; hours 8:30AM-4:30PM (PST). *Felony, Misdemeanor.*
www.lasuperiorcourt.org/Locations/LAX.htm
Note: New Court in 2000, includes the areas of Palms, Mar Vista, Rancho Park, Marina del Rey, Venice, Playa del Rey and Sawtelle. Holds records for the former West LA Court covering Culver, El Segundo, Hawthorne.
Criminal Records: Access: In person, online. Only the court performs in person searches; visitors may not. Search fee: $5.00 per name. Court makes copy: $.57 per page. Required to search: name, years to search; also helpful: DOB, address. Criminal records index goes back to. Felony and misdemeanor defendant records are online for a fee at www.lasuperiorcourt.org/OnlineServices/criminalindex/. Search fee is $4 to $4.75. Note: Will do search if you have a case number.
General Information: No public access terminal. No probation reports released. Will not fax documents. Certification fee: $6.60 per doc. Payee: Los Angeles Superior Court. Personal checks accepted. Prepayment required.

Alhambra Superior Court - Northeast District 150 W Commonwealth Ave, Alhambra, CA 91801; criminal phone: 626-308-5525; civil phone: 626-308-5521; hours 8AM-4:30PM (PST). *Misdemeanor, Civil Actions Under $25,000, Eviction, Small Claims.*
www.lasuperiorcourt.org
Note: Includes cities of Alhambra, Monterey Park, San Gabriel, Temple City and the unincorporated County area known as South San Gabriel. Address the specific division (criminal, civil, small claims) in correspondence.
Civil Records: Access: Mail, online, in person. Only the court performs in person searches; visitors may not. Search fee: $5.00 per name. Court makes copy: $.57 per page. Required to search: name, years to search. Civil cases indexed by defendant, plaintiff. Civil records on computer back to 1991, index files from 1983. Records destroyed after 10 years. There is a free case summary lookup at https://www.lasuperiorcourt.org/OnlineServices/CivilImages/index.asp, but the lookup is by case number, not by name. There is a fee-based name search for records back to 1991 (if Small Claims 1992) at https://www.lasuperiorcourt.org/OnlineServices/CivilImages/index.asp. Fee is $4.75 per search. Mail turnaround time 2 days.
Criminal Records: Access: Mail, in person, online. Only the court performs in person searches; visitors may not. Search fee: $5.00 per name. Court makes copy: $.57 per page. Required to search: name, years to search, DOB; also helpful: CDL. Criminal records on computer from 1996, index files from 1991. Records destroyed after 10 years. Felony and misdemeanor defendant records are online for a fee at www.lasuperiorcourt.org/OnlineServices/criminalindex/. Search fee is $4 to $4.75. Mail turnaround time 2 days.
General Information: No public access terminal. No probation records released. Certification fee: $6.60 per doc. Payee: Los Angeles Superior Court. Personal checks accepted. Prepayment and SASE required.

Bellflower Superior Court - Southeast District
10025 E Flower St, Bellflower, CA 90706; phone: 562-804-8025; criminal phone: 562-804-8019; civil phone: 562-804-8011; hours 8AM-4:30PM (PST). *Misdemeanor, Civil Actions Under $25,000, Eviction, Small Claims.*
www.lasuperiorcourt.org/Locations/LosCerritos.htm
Note: Includes Artesia, Bellflower, Hawaiian Gardens, Lakewood and Cerritos. Also includes Norwalk for criminal cases only. Specify civil or criminal search request.
Civil Records: Access: Mail, online, in person. Both court and visitors may perform in person searches. Search fee: $5.00 per name. Court makes copy: $.57 per page. Required to search: name, years to search. Civil cases indexed by defendant, plaintiff. Civil records on computer from 1991, index files from 1983. Records destroyed after 10 years. There is a free case summary lookup at https://www.lasuperiorcourt.org/OnlineServices/CivilImages/index.asp, but the lookup is by case number, not by name. There is a fee-based name search for records back to 1991 (if Small Claims 1992) at https://www.lasuperiorcourt.org/OnlineServices/CivilImages/index.asp. Fee is $4.75 per search. Note: Always specify that it is a "civil records" search request. Mail turnaround time 2-3 days.
Criminal Records: Access: Mail, in person, online. Only the court performs in person searches; visitors may not. Search fee: $5.00 per name. Court makes copy: $.57 per page. Required to search: name, years to search, DOB; also helpful: SSN, sex. Criminal records on computer from 1991, index files from 1983. Records destroyed after 10 years. Criminal defendant records are online for a fee at www.lasuperiorcourt.org/OnlineServices/criminalindex/index.asp/. Search fee is $4 to $4.75. Note: Always specify that it is a "criminal records" search request. Mail turnaround time 2-3 days.
General Information: Public access terminal has only civil records back to 10 years. No probation reports released. Certification fee: $6.60 per doc. Payee: Los Angeles Superior Court. Personal checks or Visa, MC, Discover accepted. Prepayment and SASE required.

Beverly Hills Superior Court - West District
9355 Burton Way, Beverly Hills, CA 90210; phone: 310-860-0070; hours 8:30AM-4:30PM (PST). *Misdemeanor, Civil Actions Under $25,000, Eviction, Small Claims.*
www.lasuperiorcourt.org
Note: Includes cities of Beverly Hills and West Hollywood.
Civil Records: Access: Phone, mail, online, in person. Both court and visitors may perform in person searches. Search fee: $5.00 per name. Fee is per data bank per year. Court makes copy: $.57 per page. Required to search: name, years to search; also helpful: address. Civil cases indexed by defendant, plaintiff. Civil records on computer from 1991, index files from 1983. Records destroyed after 10 years. There is a free case summary lookup at https://www.lasuperiorcourt.org/OnlineServices/CivilImages/index.asp, but the lookup is by case number, not by name. There is a fee-based name search for records back to 1991 (if Small Claims 1992) at https://www.lasuperiorcourt.org/OnlineServices/CivilImages/index.asp. Fee is $4.75 per search. Mail turnaround time 3 days.
Criminal Records: Access: Phone, mail, in person, online. Only the court performs in person searches; visitors may not. Search fee: $5.00 per name. Fee is per data bank per year. Court makes copy: $.57 per page. Required to search: name, years to search, DOB; also helpful: address, SSN, sex, signed release. Criminal records on computer from 1991, index files from 1983. Records destroyed after 10 years. Felony and misdemeanor defendant records for a fee at www.lasuperiorcourt.org/OnlineServices/criminalindex/. Search fee is $4 to $4.75. Mail turnaround time 3 days.

General Information: No public access terminal. No probation, arrest records released. Certification fee: $6.60 per doc. Payee: Los Angeles Superior Court. Personal checks or Visa, MC, Discover accepted. Use Visa or Discover; plus user fees. Prepayment and SASE required.

Burbank Superior Court - North Central District
300 E Olive Ave, Burbank, CA 91502-1215; criminal phone: 818-557-3466; civil phone: 818-557-3482 Civ; 818-557-3461 Sm Claims; criminal records fax: 818-569-7413; civil records fax: 818-953-9455; hours 8:15AM-4:30PM (PST). *Felony, Misdemeanor, Civil Actions, Eviction, Small Claims, Probate.*
www.lasuperiorcourt.org
Civil Records: Access: Mail, online, in person. Both court and visitors may perform in person searches. Search fee: $5.00 per name. Court makes copy: $.57 per page. Required to search: name, years to search. Civil cases indexed by defendant, plaintiff. Civil records on computer from 1991. Limited hard copy civil records, destroyed ten years after judgment. There is a free case summary lookup at https://www.lasuperiorcourt.org/OnlineServices/CivilImages/index.asp, but the lookup is by case number, not by name. Includes probate from 03/98. There is a fee-based name search for records back to 1991 (if Small Claims 1992) at https://www.lasuperiorcourt.org/OnlineServices/CivilImages/index.asp. Fee is $4.75 per search. Mail turnaround time 3-5 days.
Criminal Records: Access: Mail, in person, online. Only the court performs in person searches; visitors may not. Search fee: $5.00 per name. Court makes copy: $.57 per page. Required to search: name, years to search, DOB. Criminal records on computer from 1991, index files from 1983. Records destroyed after ten years. Felony and misdemeanor defendant records are online for a fee at www.lasuperiorcourt.org/OnlineServices/criminalindex/. Search fee is $4 to $4.75. Mail turnaround time 3-5 days.
General Information: Public access terminal has only civil records back to 1977. (From Courtnet, includes probate also.) No probation reports released. They may charge a $3.37 fee for faxing back documents. Certification fee: $6.60 per doc; domestic judgments cert-$11.00. Payee: Los Angeles Superior Court. Personal checks accepted. Prepayment and SASE required.

Chatsworth Courthouse
9425 Penfield Avenue, Chatsworth, CA 91311; phone: 818-576-8575; hours 8:30AM-4:30PM (PST). *Limited Civil, Small Claims, Traffic.*
www.lasuperiorcourt.org
Civil Records: Access: Mail, online, in person. Both court and visitors may perform in person searches. Search fee: $5.00 per name. Court makes copy: $.57. Civil cases indexed by defendant, plaintiff. A fee-based name search for records back to 1991 (if Small Claims 1992) is available at https://www.lasuperiorcourt.org/OnlineServices/CivilImages/index.asp is $4.75 per search. Mail turnaround time 1-3 days.
General Information: No probation reports released. Certification fee: $6.60 per doc. Payee: Los Angeles Superior Court. SASE requested.

Compton Superior Court - South Central District
200 W Compton Blvd, Compton, CA 90220; criminal phone: 310-603-7112; civil phone: 310-603-7842; fax: 310-223-5941; hours 8:30AM-4:30PM (PST). *Felony, Misdemeanor, Civil Actions, Eviction, Small Claims, Probate.* www.lasuperiorcourt.org
Note: Includes cities of Carson, Compton, Lynwood and Paramount and the unincorporated portions of county that surround them.
Civil Records: Access: Mail, online, in person. Both court and visitors may perform in person searches. Search fee: $5.00 per name. Fee is per year prior to 1991. Court makes copy: $.57 per page. Required to search: name, years to search. Civil cases indexed by

defendant, plaintiff. Civil records on computer from 1991, index files from 1983. Records destroyed after 10 years. There is a free case summary lookup at https://www.lasuperiorcourt.org/OnlineServices/CivilImages/index.asp, but the lookup is by case number, not by name. Includes probate from 09/99. There is a fee-based name search for records back to 1991 (if Small Claims 1992) at https://www.lasuperiorcourt.org/OnlineServices/CivilImages/index.asp. Fee is $4.75 per search. Mail turnaround time 7 days.
Criminal Records: Access: Mail, in person, online. Both court and visitors may perform in person searches. Search fee: $5.00 per name. Court makes copy: $.57 per page. Required to search: name, years to search, DOB. Criminal records maintained per G.C. 68152(E). Felony and misdemeanor defendant records are online for a fee at www.lasuperiorcourt.org/OnlineServices/criminalindex/. Search fee is $4 to $4.75. Mail turnaround time 7 days.
General Information: Public access terminal available. No complaint records released. Certification fee: $6.60 per doc. Payee: Los Angeles Superior Court-Compton. Personal checks or Visa, MC, Discover accepted. Prepayment and SASE required.

Culver City Superior Court - West District
1725 Main St, Rm224, Santa Monica, CA 90401; phone: 310-260-3522 Admin; civil phone: 310-206-1876; probate phone: 310-260-1876; fax: 310-576-1399; hours 8AM-4:30PM (PST). *Civil Actions Under $25,000, Eviction, Small Claims, Probate.*
www.lasuperiorcourt.org
Note: Now combined with Santa Monica; new phone and address given here. Small Claims- 310-260-1887. Culver City did include Angelus Vista, portions of Marina del Rey, View Park and Windsor Hills, all surrounded by City of LA, on south bounded by Inglewood.

Downey Superior Court - Southeast District
7500 E Imperial Hwy, Downey, CA 90242; criminal phone: 562-803-7049; civil phone: 562-803-7052; hours 8:30AM-4:30PM T-F; 8:30AM-6PM M (PST). *Misdemeanor, Civil Actions Under $25,000, Eviction, Small Claims.*
www.lasuperiorcourt.org
Note: Comprises the cities of Downey, Norwalk and La Mirada.
Civil Records: Access: Mail, online, in person. Both court and visitors may perform in person searches. Search fee: $5.00 per name. Court makes copy: $.57 per page. Required to search: name, years to search. Civil cases indexed by defendant, plaintiff. Civil records on microfiche from 1964, archived and index file from 1800s. There is a free case summary lookup at https://www.lasuperiorcourt.org/OnlineServices/CivilImages/index.asp, but the lookup is by case number, not by name. There is a fee-based name search for records back to 1991 (if Small Claims 1992) at https://www.lasuperiorcourt.org/OnlineServices/CivilImages/index.asp. Fee is $4.75 per search. Mail turnaround time 5 days.
Criminal Records: Access: Mail, in person, online. Only the court performs in person searches; visitors may not. Search fee: $5.00 per name. Court makes copy: $.57 per page. Required to search: name, years to search; also helpful: DOB. Criminal records on computer from 1989, on microfiche, archived, and index files. Felony and misdemeanor defendant records are online for a fee at www.lasuperiorcourt.org/OnlineServices/criminalindex/. Search fee is $4 to $4.75. Note: Mail or in person - court may choose not to run lists of names. Mail turnaround time 5 days.
General Information: No adoptions, juvenile, medical, probation or sealed records released. Certification fee: $6.60 per doc. Payee: Los Angeles Superior Court. Personal checks accepted. Credit cards accepted. Prepayment and SASE required.

East Los Angeles Superior Court - Central District
214 S Fetterly Ave, Los Angeles, CA 90022; criminal phone: 323-780-2025; civil phone: 323-780-2017; fax: 323-415-0139; hours 8AM-4:30PM (PST). *Misdemeanor.*
www.lasuperiorcourt.org
Note: Includes cities of Montebello and Commerce and adjacent unincorporated territory bordering Monterey Park on the north and Los Angeles on the west. Civil actions discontinued as of 5/2003.

Criminal Records: Access: Mail, in person, online. Only the court performs in person searches; visitors may not. Search fee: $5.00 per name. Court makes copy: $.57 per page. Required to search: name, years to search, DOB; also helpful: SSN. Criminal records on computer from 1991, index files from 1983. Records destroyed after 10 years. Felony and misdemeanor defendant records are online for a fee at www.lasuperiorcourt.org/OnlineServices/criminalindex/. Search fee is $4 to $4.75. Mail turnaround time 2 days.

General Information: No probation reports released. Certification fee: $6.60 per doc. Payee: Superior Court of East Los Angeles. Personal checks accepted. Credit cards accepted: Discover. Prepayment and SASE required.

El Monte Superior Court - East District
11234 E Valley Blvd, El Monte, CA 91731; criminal phone: 626-575-4121; civil phone: 626-575-4117; fax: 626-444-9029; hours 8AM-4:30PM (PST). *Misdemeanor, Civil Actions Under $25,000, Eviction, Small Claims.*
www.lasuperiorcourt.org   Note: Includes cities of El Monte, South El Monte, La Puente, Rosemead and adjacent unincorporated county area.

Civil Records: Access: Mail, online, in person. Only the court performs in person searches; visitors may not. Court makes copy: $.57 per page. Required to search: name, years to search. Civil cases indexed by defendant, plaintiff. Civil records on computer since 1989, microfiche since 1980. Records destroyed after 10 years. There is a free case summary lookup at https://www.lasuperiorcourt.org/OnlineServices/CivilImages/index.asp, but the lookup is by case number, not by name. There is a fee-based name search for records back to 1991 (if Small Claims 1992) at https://www.lasuperiorcourt.org/OnlineServices/CivilImages/index.asp. Fee is $4.75 per search. Mail turnaround time 5 days.

Criminal Records: Access: Phone, mail, in person, online. Only the court performs in person searches; visitors may not. Search fee: $5.00 per name. Court makes copy: $.57 per page. Required to search: name, years to search; also helpful: DOB. Criminal records on computer since 1985, microfiche since 1980. Felony and misdemeanor defendant records are online for a fee at www.lasuperiorcourt.org/OnlineServices/criminalindex/. Search fee is $5. Mail turnaround time 5 days.

General Information: Will not release unlawful detainer for 60 days. No probation reports, medical records, search warrants, rap sheet, and any sealed cases per CCP Sec 1161.2(e), CLETS report, transcripts or sealed records released. Certification fee: $6.60 per doc. Payee: Los Angeles Superior Court. Two-party checks not accepted. Write "not to exceed $x.xx" on check. Prepayment and SASE required.

Glendale Superior Court - NorthCentral District
Los Angeles Superior Court, 600 E Broadway, Glendale, CA 91206; criminal phone: 818-500-3530; civil phone: 818-500-3551; criminal records fax:; civil records fax: 818-548-0486; hours 8:15AM-4:30PM (PST). *Misdemeanor, Civil Actions Under $25,000, Eviction, Small Claims, Probate.*   www.lasuperiorcourt.org
Note: Includes cities of Glendale, LaCanada-Flintridge and unincorporated county are known as Montrose, La Crescenta, Verdugo City, Highway Highlands, and Kogel Canyon.

Civil Records: Access: Mail, online, in person. Only the court performs in person searches; visitors may

not. Search fee: $5.00 per name. Court makes copy: $.57 per page. Required to search: name, years to search. Civil cases indexed by defendant, plaintiff. Civil records on computer from 1990, small claims from 7/92, index files from 1983. Records destroyed after 10 years. Free case summary lookup at https://www.lasuperiorcourt.org/OnlineServices/CivilImages/index.asp, but the lookup is by case number, not by name. Also includes probate cases from 01/06/98. There is a fee-based name search for records back to 1991 (if Small Claims 1992) at https://www.lasuperiorcourt.org/OnlineServices/CivilImages/index.asp. Fee is $4.75 per search. Mail turnaround time 2 weeks.

Criminal Records: Access: Mail, in person, online. Only the court performs in person searches; visitors may not. Search fee: $5.00 per name. Court makes copy: $.57 per page. Required to search: name, years to search. Criminal records on computer from 1990, microfilm past 10 years. Felony and misdemeanor defendant records are online for a fee at www.lasuperiorcourt.org/OnlineServices/criminalindex/. Search fee is $4 to $4.75. Mail turnaround time 2 weeks.

General Information: No probation reports, police reports, CII records released. Certification fee: $6.60 per doc. Payee: Los Angeles Superior Court. Personal checks or Visa, MC accepted. Prepayment and SASE required.

Hollywood Superior Court - Central District
5925 Hollywood Blvd, Los Angeles, CA 90028; phone: 323-856-5747; hours 8:30AM-4:30PM (PST). *Misdemeanor.*
www.lasuperiorcourt.org
Note: High-grade and low-grade Misdemeanors for the Hollywood area.

Criminal Records: Access: Mail, in person, online. Only the court performs in person searches; visitors may not. Search fee: $5.00 per name. Court makes copy: $.57 per page; same fee for self serve. Required to search: name, years to search, DOB. Criminal records on computer go back 10 years, prior on microfiche. Felony and misdemeanor defendant records are online for a fee at www.lasuperiorcourt.org/OnlineServices/criminalindex/. Search fee is $4 to $4.75. Note: Mail or in person request will be expedited if a SASE provided. Mail turnaround time 2-3 days.

General Information: No probation, driver's license, medical, arrest report or confidential reports released. Will not fax documents. Certification fee: $6.60 per doc. Payee: Los Angeles Superior Court. Personal checks accepted. Credit cards accepted (except AMEX). Prepayment and SASE required.

Huntington Park Superior Court - Southeast District
6548 Miles Ave, Huntington Park, CA 90255; criminal phone: 323-586-6362; civil phone: 323-586-6365; fax: 323-589-6769; hours 8AM-4:30PM (PST). *Misdemeanor, Civil Actions Under $25,000, Eviction, Small Claims.*
www.lasuperiorcourt.org
Note: Includes cities of Bell, Bell Gardens, Cudahy, Huntington Park, Maywood and Vernon. Also includes South Gate, Hollydale and unincorporated area of Walnut Park from closed court at South Gate.

Civil Records: Access: Mail, online, in person. Only the court performs in person searches; visitors may not. Search fee: $5.00 per name. Court makes copy: $.57 per page. Required to search: name, years to search. Civil cases indexed by defendant, plaintiff. Civil records on computer from 1991, index files from 1983. Records destroyed after 10 years. There is a free case summary lookup at https://www.lasuperiorcourt.org/OnlineServices/CivilImages/index.asp, but the lookup is by case number, not by name. There is a fee-based name search for records back to 1991 (if Small Claims 1992) at https://www.lasuperiorcourt.org/OnlineServices/CivilImages/index.asp. Fee is $4.75 per search. Mail turnaround time 2 days.

Criminal Records: Access: Phone, mail, in person, online. Only the court performs in person searches;

visitors may not. Search fee: $5.00 per name. Court makes copy: $.57 per page. Required to search: name, years to search; also helpful: DOB. Criminal records on computer from 1991, index files from 1983. Records destroyed after 10 years. Felony and misdemeanor defendant records are online for a fee at www.lasuperiorcourt.org/OnlineServices/criminalindex/. Search fee is $4 to $4.75. Mail turnaround time 2 days.

General Information: No probation reports released. Certification fee: $6.60 per doc. Payee: Los Angeles Superior Court. Personal checks or Visa, MC, Discover accepted. Prepayment and SASE required.

Inglewood Superior Court - Southwest District
One Regent St, Inglewood, CA 90301; phone: 310-419-5132; criminal records fax: 310-680-7053; civil records fax: 310-680-7055; hours 8AM-4:30PM (PST). *Felony, Misdemeanor, Civil Actions Under $25,000, Eviction, Small Claims.*
www.lasuperiorcourt.org
Note: Includes cities of Inglewood, Hawthorne, El Segundo, Lennox and adjoining unincorporated area. Felony cases are only from these areas. Administration "clarification" fax-310-674-4862.

Civil Records: Access: Mail, online, in person. Only the court performs in person searches; visitors may not. Search fee: $5.00 per name. Court makes copy: $.57 per page; same fee for self serve. Required to search: name, years to search. Civil cases indexed by defendant, plaintiff. Civil records on computer from 1991, index files from 1983. Records destroyed after 10 years. There is a free case summary lookup at https://www.lasuperiorcourt.org/OnlineServices/CivilImages/index.asp, but the lookup is by case number, not by name. There is a fee-based name search for records back to 1991 (if Small Claims 1992) at https://www.lasuperiorcourt.org/OnlineServices/CivilImages/index.asp. Fee is $4.75 per search. Mail turnaround time 2 days.

Criminal Records: Access: Mail, in person, online. Only the court performs in person searches; visitors may not. Search fee: $5.00 per name. Court makes copy: $.57 per page; same fee for self serve. Required to search: name, years to search; also helpful: DOB. Criminal records on computer from 1991, index files from 1983. Records destroyed after 10 years. Felony and misdemeanor defendant records are online for a fee at www.lasuperiorcourt.org/OnlineServices/criminalindex/. Search fee is $4 to $4.75. Mail turnaround time 2 days.

General Information: No probation reports released. Will not fax documents. Certification fee: $6.60 per doc. Payee: Los Angeles Superior Court. Personal checks accepted. Major credit cards accepted. Prepayment and SASE required.

Lancaster Superior Court - North District
Antelope Valley Courthouse, 42011 4th St West, Lancaster, CA 93534; phone: 661-974-7200; hours 8AM-4:30PM (PST). *Felony, Misdemeanor, Civil, Small Claims, Probate.*
www.lasuperiorcourt.org
Note: Formerly Antelope; includes Lancaster, City of Palmdale, and unincorporated County territory including Acton, Agua Dulce, Fairmont, Lake Hughes, Llano, Leona Valley, Littlerock, Pearblossom, Quartz Hill, Roosevelt, Green Valley Big Pines, Lake Elizabeth

Civil Records: Access: Phone, mail, online, in person. Only the court performs in person searches; visitors may not. Search fee: $5.00 per name. Court makes copy: $.57 per page. Required to search: name, years to search. Civil cases indexed by defendant, plaintiff. Civil records on computer since 1989, index books since 1983. Records destroyed after 10 years. There is a free case summary lookup at https://www.lasuperiorcourt.org/OnlineServices/CivilImages/index.asp, but the lookup is by case number, not by name. Also includes probate cases from 06/05. There is a fee-based name search for records back to 1991 (if Small Claims 1992) at https://www.lasuperiorcourt.org/OnlineServices/Ci

vilImages/index.asp. Fee is $4.75 per search. Mail turnaround time 2 days.

Criminal Records: Access: Mail, in person, online. Only the court performs in person searches; visitors may not. Search fee: $5.00 per name. Court makes copy: $.57 per page. Required to search: name, years to search; also helpful: case number. Criminal records on computer since 1989, index books since 1983. Records destroyed after 10 years. Felony and misdemeanor defendant records for a fee at www.lasuperiorcourt.org/OnlineServices/criminalindex/. Search fee is $4 to $4.75. Mail turnaround time 2 days.

General Information: No probation reports released. Certification fee: $6.60 per doc. Payee: Los Angeles Superior Court. Personal checks accepted; must be pre-imprinted. Prepayment and SASE required.

Long Beach Superior Court - South District
415 W Ocean Blvd, Long Beach, CA 90802; phone: 562-491-6201; criminal phone: 562-491-6226/6227; civil phone: 562-491-6234 Civ; 562-491-6235 Sm Claims; probate phone: 562-491-5926; hours 8:30AM-4:30PM (PST). *Misdemeanor, Civil Actions Under $25,000, Eviction, Small Claims, Probate.* www.lasuperiorcourt.org
Note: Includes cities of Long Beach and Signal Hill and adjoining unincorporated area. Address requests to civil or criminal division.

Civil Records: Access: Mail, online, in person. Both court and visitors may perform in person searches. Search fee: $5.00 per name. Court makes copy: $.57 per page. Required to search: name, years to search. Civil cases indexed by defendant, plaintiff. Civil records on computer from 1991, index files from 1983. Records destroyed after 10 years. There is a free case summary lookup at https://www.lasuperiorcourt.org/OnlineServices/CivilImages/index.asp, but the lookup is by case number, not by name. Includes probate from 01/97. There is a fee-based name search for records back to 1991 (if Small Claims 1992) at https://www.lasuperiorcourt.org/OnlineServices/CivilImages/index.asp. Fee is $4.75 per search. Mail turnaround time 2 days.

Criminal Records: Access: Mail, in person, online. Both court and visitors may perform in person searches. Search fee: $5.00 per name. Court makes copy: $.57 per page. Required to search: name, years to search, DOB. Criminal records on computer from 1991, index files from 1983. Records destroyed after 10 years. Felony and misdemeanor defendant records are online for a fee at www.lasuperiorcourt.org/OnlineServices/criminalindex/, search fee on line depends on volume. Mail turnaround time 2 days.

General Information: Public access terminal goes back to 1991. (Terminals are on first floor as well as room 207 and room 401.) No probation reports released. Certification fee: $6.60 per doc. Payee: Los Angeles Superior Court. Personal checks accepted. Credit cards accepted: Discover. Accepted in person only. Prepayment and SASE required.

Malibu Superior Court - West District
23525 W Civic Center Way, Malibu, CA 90265; phone: 310-317-1335; fax: 310-456-0194; hours 8AM-4:30PM (PST). *Misdemeanor, Civil Actions Under $25,000, Eviction, Small Claims.* www.lasuperiorcourt.org
Note: Includes Malibu, Agoura Hills, Calabasas, Westlake Village, Hidden Hills and unincorporated areas known as Topanga and Chatsworth Lake, bounded by Ventura County on the west and north, Pacific Ocean on the south and City of Los Angeles on the east.

Civil Records: Access: Mail, online, in person. Only the court performs in person searches; visitors may not. Search fee: $5.00 per name. Court makes copy: $.57 per page. Required to search: name, years to search. Civil cases indexed by defendant, plaintiff. Civil records on computer from 1991, index files from 1983. Records destroyed after 10 years. There is a free case summary lookup at https://www.lasup

eriorcourt.org/OnlineServices/CivilImages/index.asp, but the lookup is by case number, not by name. There is a fee-based name search for records back to 1991 (if Small Claims 1992) at https://www.lasuperiorcourt.org/OnlineServices/CivilImages/index.asp. Fee is $4.75 per search. Mail turnaround time 1-5 days.

Criminal Records: Access: Mail, in person, online. Only the court performs in person searches; visitors may not. Search fee: $5.00 per name. Court makes copy: $.57 per page. Required to search: name, years to search; also helpful: DOB. Criminal records on computer from 1991, index files from 1983. Records destroyed after 10 years. Felony and misdemeanor defendant records for a fee at www.lasuperiorcourt.org/OnlineServices/criminalindex/. Search fee is $4 to $4.75. Mail turnaround time 1-5 days.

General Information: No probation reports released. Certification fee: $6.60 per doc. Payee: Los Angeles Superior Court. Personal checks accepted. Prepayment and SASE required.

Metropolitan Branch Superior Court - Central District
1945 S Hill St, Rm 200, Los Angeles, CA 90007; phone: 213-744-4023; fax: 213-744-1879; 8AM-4:30PM (PST). *Misdemeanor.* www.lasuperiorcourt.org
Note: Vehicle Code misdemeanor and traffic citations for the incorporated City of Los Angeles excluding the areas known as San Pedro, W. Los Angeles and communities of San Fernando Valley and the unincorporated County area more commonly known as Florence.

Criminal Records: Access: Mail, in person, online. Only the court performs in person searches; visitors may not. Search fee: $5.00 per name. Court makes copy: $.57 per page. Required to search: name, years to search, DOB. Criminal records on computer from 1991, index files from 1983. Records destroyed after 10 years. Felony and misdemeanor defendant records are online for a fee at www.lasuperiorcourt.org/OnlineServices/criminalindex/. Search fee is $4 to $4.75. Mail turnaround time 2-3 days.

General Information: No probation, driver's license, medical, arrest report or confidential reports released. Certification fee: $6.60 per doc. Payee: Los Angeles Superior Court. Personal checks accepted. Credit cards accepted. Prepayment required. SASE requested.

Norwalk Superior Court - Southeast District
12720 Norwalk Blvd, Norwalk, CA 90650; phone: 562-807-7266; fax: 560-863-8757; hours 8:30AM-4:30PM (PST). *Felony, Civil Actions Over $25,000, Probate.*
www.lasuperiorcourt.org
Civil Records: Access: Mail, online, in person. Both court and visitors may perform in person searches. Search fee: $5.00 per name. Court makes copy: $.57 per page. Required to search: name, years to search. Civil cases indexed by defendant, plaintiff. Civil records on computer from 1991, index files from 1983. There is a free case summary lookup at https://www.lasuperiorcourt.org/OnlineServices/CivilImages/index.asp, but the lookup is by case number, not by name. Also includes probate cases from 02/11/03. There is a fee-based name search for records back to 1991 (if Small Claims 1992) at https://www.lasuperiorcourt.org/OnlineServices/CivilImages/index.asp. Fee is $4.75 per search. Mail turnaround time 2-10 days.

Criminal Records: Access: Mail, in person, online. Both court and visitors may perform in person searches. Search fee: $5.00 per name. Court makes copy: $.57 per page. Required to search: name, years to search, DOB; also helpful: SSN, sex. Criminal records on computer from 1991, index files from 1983. Felony and misdemeanor defendant records are online for a fee at www.lasuperiorcourt.org/OnlineServices/criminalindex/. Search fee is $4 to $4.75. Mail turnaround time 2-10 days.

General Information: Public access terminal available. (Public terminal to find case number only.)

No probation reports released. Certification fee: $6.60 per doc. Payee: Los Angeles Superior Court. Personal checks accepted. Credit cards accepted. Prepayment and SASE required.

Pasadena Superior Court - Northeast District
300 E Walnut, Pasadena, CA 91101; criminal phone: 626-356-5254; civil phone: 626-356-5695; fax: 626-568-3903; hours 8:30AM-4:30PM (PST). *Misdemeanor, Civil Actions Under $25,000, Eviction, Small Claims, Probate.*
www.lasuperiorcourt.org
Note: Includes cities of Pasadena, South Pasadena, San Marino, Sierra Madre and the area of Altadena and East Pasadena.

Civil Records: Access: Mail, online, in person. Both court and visitors may perform in person searches. Search fee: $5.00 per name. Court makes copy: $.57 per page. Required to search: name, years to search. Civil cases indexed by defendant, plaintiff. Civil records on computer from 1991, index files from 1983. Records destroyed after 10 years. Free case summary lookup at https://www.lasuperiorcourt.org/OnlineServices/CivilImages/index.asp, but the lookup is by case number, not by name. Also includes probate cases from 06/97. There is a fee-based name search for records back to 1991 (if Small Claims 1992) at https://www.lasuperiorcourt.org/OnlineServices/CivilImages/index.asp. Fee is $4.75 per search. Mail turnaround time 2 days.

Criminal Records: Access: Mail, in person, online. Only the court performs in person searches; visitors may not. Search fee: $5.00 per name. Court makes copy: $.57 per page. Required to search: name, years to search. Criminal records on computer from 1991, index files from 1983. Records destroyed after 10 years. Felony and misdemeanor defendant records are online for a fee at www.lasuperiorcourt.org/OnlineServices/criminalindex/. Search fee is $4 to $4.75. Mail turnaround time 2 days.

General Information: No public access terminal. No probation reports released. Certification fee: $6.60 per doc. Payee: Los Angeles Superior Court. Personal checks accepted. Prepayment and SASE required.

Pomona Superior Court - North
350 W Mission Blvd, Pomona, CA 91766; phone: 909-802-9944; fax: 909-865-6767; hours 8AM-4:30PM (PST). *Misdemeanor, Civil Actions Under $25,000, Eviction, Small Claims, Probate.*
www.lasuperiorcourt.org
Note: Includes cities of Pomona, Claremont, La Verne, Walnut, San Dimas and unincorporated area including Diamond Bar. There is another court in Pomona on 400 Civic Center that deals with family and juvenile matters.

Civil Records: Access: Fax, mail, online, in person. Only the court performs in person searches; visitors may not. Search fee: $5.00 per name. Court makes copy: $.57 per page. Required to search: name, years to search. Civil cases indexed by defendant, plaintiff. Civil records on computer from 1990, index files from 1983. Records destroyed after 10 years. There is a free case summary lookup at https://www.lasuperiorcourt.org/OnlineServices/CivilImages/index.asp, but the lookup is by case number, not by name. Also includes probate cases from 01/95. There is a fee-based name search for records back to 1991 (if Small Claims 1992) at https://www.lasuperiorcourt.org/OnlineServices/CivilImages/index.asp. Fee is $4.75 per search. Mail turnaround time 1-2 days.

Criminal Records: Access: Mail, in person, online. Only the court performs in person searches; visitors may not. Search fee: $5.00 per name. Court makes copy: $.57 per page. Required to search: name, years to search, DOB. Criminal records on computer from 1990, index files from 1983. Records destroyed after 10 years. Felony and misdemeanor defendant records are online for a fee at www.lasuperiorcourt.org/OnlineServices/criminalindex/. Search fee is $4 to $4.75. Note: Drop box available. Mail turnaround time 2-4 days.

General Information: No probation, mental health or police reports released. Certification fee: $6.60 per doc. Payee: Los Angeles Superior Court. Personal checks accepted. Prepayment and SASE required.

Redondo Beach Superior Court - Southwest District
117 W Torrance Blvd, Redondo Beach, CA 90277-3638; phone: 310-798-6875; fax: 310-376-4051; hours 8:15AM-4:30PM (PST). *Civil Actions under $25,000.*
www.lasuperiorcourt.org
Note: Also known as the Southwest District South Bay Court - Beach Cities Branch.

Civil Records: Access: Mail, online, in person. Only the court performs in person searches; visitors may not. Search fee: $5.00 per name. Court makes copy: $.57 for first page, $.20 each add'l. Required to search: name, years to search. Civil cases indexed by defendant, plaintiff. Civil records on computer from 1991, index files from 1983. Records destroyed after 10 years. There is a free case summary lookup at https://www.lasuperiorcourt.org/OnlineServices/CivilImages/index.asp, but the lookup is by case number, not by name. There is a fee-based name search for records back to 1991 at https://www.lasuperiorcourt.org/OnlineServices/CivilImages/index.asp. Fee is $4.75 per search. Mail turnaround time 3-4 days.

General Information: No public access terminal. Unlawful detainers held for 60 days. Certification fee: $6.60 per doc. Payee: Los Angeles Superior Court. Personal checks accepted. Prepayment and SASE required.

San Fernando Superior Court - North Valley District
900 3rd St, #1137, San Fernando, CA 91340; phone: 818-898-2401; criminal phone: 818-898-2655 Felony, 818-898-2407 Misc; hours 8:30AM-4:30PM (PST). *Felony, Misdemeanor, Small Claims.* www.lasuperiorcourt.org
Includes Granada Hills, Northridge, Chatsworth, Sunland, Tujunga, Pacoima, Mission Hills, Sylmar, Arleta, Lake View Terrace, Sun Valley and City of San Fernando. They merged with the Newhall Court to become North Valley District Court.

Criminal Records: Access: Mail, online, in person. Only the court performs in person searches; visitors may not. Search fee: $5.00 per name. Court makes copy: $.57 per page. Required to search: name, years to search; also helpful: DOB. Criminal records on computer from 1988. Records destroyed after 10 years. Felony and misdemeanor defendant records are online for a fee at www.lasuperiorcourt.org/OnlineServices/criminalindex/. Search fee is $4 to $4.75. Note: The Misdemeanor clerk's office is Rm 1137. Mail turnaround time 2 days.

General Information: No probation reports or arrest reports released. Certification fee: $6.60 per doc. Payee: Los Angeles Superior Court. Personal checks accepted. No 3rd party checks. Credit cards accepted. Prepayment and SASE required.

San Pedro Superior Court - South District
505 S Centre St, Rm 202, San Pedro, CA 90731; phone: 310-519-6014; 519-6016 Traffic; civil phone: 310-519-6015; hours 8:30AM-4:30PM (civ, sm claims & criminal); 8AM-4:30PM (traffic) (PST). *Civil Actions, Eviction, Small Claims, Traffic.* www.lasuperiorcourt.org
Note: Includes San Pedro, Wilmington and a county strip in Torrance extending up to Western Ave.

Civil Records: Access: Mail, online, in person. Only the court performs in person searches; visitors may not. Search fee: $5.00 per name. Court makes copy: $.57 per page. Required to search: name, years to search. Civil cases indexed by defendant, plaintiff. Civil records on computer go back 10 years; on index files from 1984. Records destroyed after 10 years. There is a free case summary lookup at https://www.lasuperiorcourt.org/OnlineServices/CivilImages/index.asp, but the lookup is by case number, not by name. There is a fee-based name search for records back to 1991 at https://www.lasuperiorcourt.org/OnlineServices/Ci

villImages/index.asp. Fee is $4.75 per search. Mail turnaround time 2 days.
General Information: No public access terminal. No probation, arrest, records released. Will fax documents for $3.37 per page. Certification fee: $6.60 per doc. Payee: Los Angeles Superior Court. Personal checks accepted. Credit cards accepted: Visa (add'l 6% fee charged). Prepayment and SASE required.

Santa Clarita Superior Court - North Valley District
23747 W Valencia Blvd, Santa Clarita, CA 91355; phone: 661-253-7316; criminal phone: 661-253-7384; civil phone: 661-253-7313; criminal records fax: 661-254-4107; civil records fax: 661-286-1546; hours 8:30AM-4:30PM (PST). *Misdemeanor, Civil Actions Under $25,000, Eviction, Small Claims.*
www.lasuperiorcourt.org
Note: Formerly known as Newhall Sup. Court. Includes Saugus, Canyon Country, Valencia, Santa Clarita and unincorporated area bound by Ventura County (west), Kern County line (north), Agua Dulce (east), and Glendale and Los Angeles city limits (south).

Civil Records: Access: Mail, online, in person. Only the court performs in person searches; visitors may not. Search fee: $5.00 per name, no fee to on microfiche. Court makes copy: $.57 per page. Required to search: name, years to search. Civil cases indexed by defendant, plaintiff. Civil records on computer from 1991, on files from 1983. Records destroyed after 10 years, many records on microfiche. There is a free case summary lookup at web, but the lookup is by case number, not by name. A fee-based name search for records back to 1991 (if Small Claims 1992) at https://www.lasuperiorcourt.org/OnlineServices/CivilImages/index.asp is $4.75 per search. Mail turnaround time 7-10 days.

Criminal Records: Access: Mail, in person, online. Only the court performs in person searches; visitors may not. Search fee: $5.00 per name, 5 name limit. Court makes copy: $.57 per page. Required to search: name, years to search; also helpful: DOB, SSN. Records on computer from 1991, indices from 1983. Records destroyed after 10 years, many records on microfiche. Criminal defendant records online for a fee at www.lasuperiorcourt.org/OnlineServices/criminalindex/. Search fee is $4 to $4.75. Note: Visitors may view microfiche records only. Mail turnaround time 7-10 days.

General Information: No probation, or police reports w/out court approval released. Will fax civil documents for $3.37 per doc. Certification fee: $6.60 per doc. Payee: Los Angeles Superior Court. Personal checks accepted. Prepayment and SASE required.

Santa Monica Superior Court - West District
1725 Main St, Rm 224, Santa Monica, CA 90401; phone: 310-260-3522; civil phone: 310-260-1876; probate phone: 310-260-1876; fax: 310-576-1399; hours 8:30AM-4:30PM (PST). *Civil Actions Under $25,000, Eviction, Small Claims, Probate.*
www.lasuperiorcourt.org
Note: Includes City of Santa Monica and the unincorporated territory of the Veteran's Administration facilities located at West Los Angeles. Criminal section moved to LAX Courthouse, 2004, 310-727-6020. Now has Culver City records. Small claims-310-260-1887.

Civil Records: Access: Mail, online, in person. Both court and visitors may perform in person searches. Search fee: $5.00 per name. Court makes copy: $.57 per page. Required to search: name, years to search. Civil cases indexed by defendant, plaintiff. Civil records on computer from 1991, files from 1983. There is a free case summary lookup at web, but the lookup is by case number, not by name. Also includes probate cases from 07/02/04. A fee-based name search for records back to 1991 (if Small Claims 1992) at https://www.lasuperiorcourt.org/OnlineServices/CivilImages/index.asp is $4.75 per search. Mail turnaround time 1-2 days.

Criminal Records: Access: Mail, in person, online. Only the court performs in person searches; visitors may not. Search fee: $5.00 per name. Court makes copy: $.57 per page. Required to search: name, years to search. Criminal records on computer from 1991, index files from 1983. Records destroyed after 10 years. Felony and misdemeanor defendant records are online for a fee at www.lasuperiorcourt.org/OnlineServices/criminalindex/. Search fee is $4 to $4.75. Mail turnaround time 1-2 days.

General Information: No public access terminal. No probation reports or unlawful detainer records released. Certification fee: $6.60 per doc. Payee: Los Angeles Superior Court. Personal checks accepted. Prepayment and SASE required.

Torrance Superior Court - Southwest District
825 Maple Ave, Torrance, CA 90503-5058; phone: 310-222-6505, 222-6501 Admin.; criminal phone: 310-222-6506; civil phone: 310-222-8809 Civ, 222-6400 Sm Claims; probate phone: 310-222-8803; criminal records fax: 310-783-5108; civil records fax: 310-782-7326; hours 8:30AM-4:30PM (PST). *Misdemeanor, Civil, Traffic, Eviction, Small Claims, Probate.* www.lasuperiorcourt.org
Note: Includes cities of Torrance, Gardena, Rolling Hills, Rolling Hills Estates, Manhattan Beach, Lomita, Redondo Beach, Hermosa Beach, Palos Verdes Estates, Rancho Palos Verdes, and Lawndale.

Civil Records: Access: Mail, online, in person. Only the court performs in person searches; visitors may not. Search fee: $5.00 per name. Court makes copy: $.57 per page. Required to search: name, years to search. Civil cases indexed by defendant, plaintiff. Civil records on computer from 1991, index files from 1983. Records destroyed after 10 years. Free case summary lookup at https://www.lasuperiorcourt.org/OnlineServices/CivilImages/index.asp, but the lookup is by case number, not by name. Also includes probate cases from 02/97. A fee-based name search for records back to 1991 (if Small Claims 1992) at https://www.lasuperiorcourt.org/OnlineServices/CivilImages/index.asp is $4.75 per search. Mail turnaround time 5 days.

Criminal Records: Access: Mail, in person, online. Only the court performs in person searches; visitors may not. Search fee: $5.00 per name. Court makes copy: $.57 per page. Required to search: name, years to search, DOB. Criminal records on computer from 1991, index files from 1983. Records destroyed after 10 years. Criminal defendant records are online for a fee at www.lasuperiorcourt.org/OnlineServices/criminalindex/. Search fee is $4 to $4.75. Mail turnaround time 5 days.

General Information: No probation reports, medical or psychiatric reports, criminal history rap sheets released. Certification fee: $6.60 per doc. Payee: LA Superior Court. Personal checks accepted. Prepayment and SASE required.

Van Nuys Superior Court - East - Civil
6230 Sylmar St, Van Nuys, CA 91401; phone: 818-374-2208; criminal phone: 818-374-2903; civil phone: 818-374-2904; probate phone: 818-374-2199; fax: 818-779-7713; hours 8:30AM-4:30PM (PST). *Civil Actions, Eviction, Small Claims, Family Law, Probate.* www.lasuperiorcourt.org
Note: Small Claims for Sherman Oaks, Van Nuys, Reseda, North Hollywood, Woodland Hills, Canoga Park, Tarzana, Porter Ranch, Winnetka and Panorama City. Civil jurisdiction depends on whether limited or general.

Civil Records: Access: Mail, online, in person. Both court and visitors may perform in person searches. Search fee: $5.00 per name. Court makes copy: $.57 per page. Required to search: name, years to search. Civil cases indexed by defendant, plaintiff. Civil records on computer from 1991, index files from 1983. Records destroyed after 10 years. There is a free case summary lookup at https://www.lasuperiorcourt.org/OnlineServices/CivilImages/index.asp, but the lookup is by case number, not by name. Also includes probate cases from 02/01. A fee-based name search for records back to 1991 (if Small Claims 1992) at https://www.lasuperiorcourt.org/OnlineServices/CivilImages/index.asp is $4.75 per search. Mail turnaround time 2-3 days.

General Information: Public access terminal has only civil records back to 1991. No probation reports or arrest reports released. Will not fax documents. Certification fee: $6.60 per doc. Payee: Los Angeles Superior Court or LASC. Personal checks and credit cards accepted. Prepayment and SASE required.

Van Nuys Superior Court - West - Criminal
14400 Erwin St, Mall, 2nd Fl, Van Nuys, CA 91401; phone: 818-374-2903; hours 8:30AM-4:30PM (PST). *Felony, Misdemeanor.*

www.lasuperiorcourt.org

Note: Misdemeanors for that part of city known as Sherman Oaks, Van Nuys, Reseda, North Hollywood, Woodland Hills, Canoga Park, Tarzana, Proter Ranch, Winnetka and Panorama City

Criminal Records: Access: Phone, mail, in person, online. Only the court performs in person searches; visitors may not. Search fee: $5.00 per name. Court makes copy: $.57 per page. Required to search: name, years to search, sex; also helpful: DOB. Criminal records on computer from 1991, index files from 1983. Felony and misdemeanor defendant records are online for a fee at www.lasuperiorcourt.org/OnlineServices/criminalindex/. Search fee is $4 to $4.75. Mail turnaround time 2-3 days.

General Information: No probation reports or arrest reports released. Will not fax documents. Certification fee: $6.60 per doc. Payee: Los Angeles Superior Court. Personal checks accepted. Prepayment and SASE required.

West Covina Superior Court - East District
1427 W Covina Pky, West Covina, CA 91790; criminal phone: 626-813-3239; civil phone: 626-813-3236 Civ, 626-813-3226 Sm Claims; fax: 626-338-7364; hours 8AM-4:30PM (PST). *Misdemeanor, Civil Actions Under $25,000, Eviction, Small Claims.*

www.lasuperiorcourt.org

Note: Formerly known as Citrus Court, this includes cities of Azusa, Baldwin Park, Covina, Glendora, Industry, Irwindale, Valinda, West Covina and surrounding unincorporated County area.

Civil Records: Access: Mail, online, in person. Both court and visitors may perform in person searches. Search fee: $5.00 per name. Court makes copy: $.57 per page. Required to search: name, years to search. Civil cases indexed by defendant, plaintiff. Civil records on computer from 1991, index files from 1983. Records destroyed after 10 years. There is a free case summary lookup at https://www.lasuperiorcourt.org/OnlineServices/CivilImages/index.asp, but the lookup is by case number, not by name. A fee-based name search for records back to 1991 (if Small Claims 1992) at https://www.lasuperiorcourt.org/OnlineServices/CivilImages/index.asp is $4.75 per search.

Criminal Records: Access: In person, online. Both court and visitors may perform in person searches. Search fee: $5.00 per name. Court makes copy: $.57 per page. Required to search: name, years to search. Criminal records on computer from 1991, index files from 1983. Records destroyed after 10 years. Felony and misdemeanor defendant records are online for a fee at www.lasuperiorcourt.org/OnlineServices/criminalindex/. Search fee is $4 to $4.75. Note: Direct criminal records searches to; LA County Court, Felony; phone-213-974-6145, address-210 W Temple St, LA, CA 90012. Mail turnaround time 1 week.

General Information: Public access terminal available. No probation reports released. Certification fee: $6.60 per doc. Payee: Los Angeles Superior Court. Personal checks accepted. Prepayment and SASE required.

West Los Angeles Superior Court - West District
1633 Purdue Ave, Los Angeles, CA 90025; phone: 310-312-6545; fax: 310-312-2902; hours 8:30AM-4:30PM (PST). *Civil Actions Under $25,000, Eviction, Small Claims.*

www.lasuperiorcourt.org

Note: Includes the areas of Palms, Mar Vista, Rancho Park, Marina del Rey, Venice, Playa del Rey and Sawtelle. Holds records for the former Robertson branch. Criminal felony and misdemeanors are at the new Airport Court.

Civil Records: Access: Phone, mail, online, in person. Both court and visitors may perform in person searches. Search fee: $5.00 per name. Court makes copy: $.57 per page. Required to search: name, years to search. Civil cases indexed by defendant, plaintiff. There is a free case summary lookup at https://www.lasuperiorcourt.org/OnlineServices/CivilImages/index.asp, but the lookup is by case number, not by name. A fee-based name search for records back to 1991 (if Small Claims 1992) at https://www.lasuperiorcourt.org/OnlineServices/CivilImages/index.asp is $4.75 per search.

Criminal Records: Access: Mail, in person, online. Both court and visitors may perform in person searches. Search fee: $5.00 per name. Court makes copy: $.57 per page. Required to search: name, years to search; also helpful: DOB. Felony and misdemeanor defendant records for a fee at www.lasuperiorcourt.org/OnlineServices/criminalindex/. Search fee is $4 to $4.75. Note: Felony and misdemeanor records have been moved to the Airport Court. Mail turnaround time 1-5 days.

General Information: Public access terminal available. Certification fee: $6.60 per doc. Payee: Los Angeles Superior Court. Personal checks accepted. Prepayment and SASE required.

Whittier Superior Court - Southeast District
7339 S Painter Ave, Whittier, CA 90602; criminal phone: 562-907-3113; civil phone: 562-907-3127; hours 8AM-4:30PM (PST). *Misdemeanor, Civil Actions Under $25,000, Eviction, Small Claims.* www.lasuperiorcourt.org

Note: Includes cities of Whittier, Santa Fe Springs, Pico Rivera, La Habra Heights plus unincorporated territory in the Whittier area including areas designated as Los Nietos and South Whittier.

Civil Records: Access: Mail, online, in person. Both court and visitors may perform in person searches. No search fee. Court makes copy: $.57 per page. Required to search: name, years to search. Civil cases indexed by defendant, plaintiff. Civil records on computer from 1991, index files from 1983. Records destroyed after 10 years. There is a free case summary lookup at https://www.lasuperiorcourt.org/OnlineServices/CivilImages/index.asp, but the lookup is by case number, not by name. A fee-based name search for records back to 1991 (if Small Claims 1992) at https://www.lasuperiorcourt.org/OnlineServices/CivilImages/index.asp is $4.75 per search. Mail turnaround time 2 days.

Criminal Records: Access: Mail, in person, online. Only the court performs in person searches; visitors may not. Search fee: $5.00 per name. Court makes copy: $.57 per page. Required to search: name, years to search; also helpful: DOB. Criminal records computerized since 1987. Felony and misdemeanor defendant records are online for a fee at www.lasuperiorcourt.org/OnlineServices/criminalindex/. Search fee is $4 to $4.75. Mail turnaround time 2 days.

General Information: No public access terminal. No probation reports released. Certification fee: $6.60 per doc. Payee: Los Angeles Superior Court. Personal checks or Visa, MC, Discover accepted. Prepayment and SASE required.

Santa Anita Superior Court - Northeast District
150 W Commonwealth Ave, Alhambra, CA 91801; criminal phone: 626-308-5525; civil phone: 626-308-5521; *Civil Actions Under $25,000, Eviction, Small Claims.* Note: Court closed - merged with Alhambra Court; phone and address given above. Formerly included cities of Monrovia, Arcadia, Duarte, Bradbury and unincorporated county territory in surrounding area.

Madera County

Superior Court
209 W Yosemite Ave, Madera, CA 93637; phone: 559-675-7944; criminal phone: 559-675-7734; civil phone: 559-675-7995; probate phone: 559-675-7795; criminal records fax: 559-675-7618; civil records fax: 559-675-6565; hours 8AM-4PM (PST). *Felony, Civil, Probate, Eviction, Small Claims.*

www.madera.courts.ca.gov

Note: The Superior and Municipal courts located in the City of Madera have combined into a consolidated court. There is a countywide index of criminal records.

Civil Records: Access: Mail, fax, in person. Both court and visitors may perform in person searches. Search fee: $5.00 per name. There is no fee if searcher comes to court and does search. Court makes copy: $.50 per page. Required to search: name, years to search. Civil cases indexed by defendant, plaintiff. Civil records on microfiche, archived and index file from 1893. Mail turnaround time 2-3 weeks.

Criminal Records: Access: Mail, fax, in person. Both court and visitors may perform in person searches. Search fee: $5.00 per name. There is no fee if searcher comes to court and does search. Court makes copy: $.50 per page. Required to search: name, years to search; also helpful: DOB, signed release. Criminal records on microfiche, archived and index file from 1893. Mail turnaround time 2-3 weeks.

General Information: Public access terminal available. No adoptions, juvenile, medical, probation or sealed records released. Certification fee: $6.60 per doc. Payee: Madera Superior Court. Personal checks accepted. Prepayment and SASE required.

Sierra Division - Superior Court
40601 Road 274, Bass Lake, CA 93604; phone: 559-642-3235; probate phone: same; fax: 559-642-3445; hours 8:30AM-12:30, 1:30-4:00PM (PST). *Felony, Misdemeanor, Civil Actions, Eviction, Small Claims, Probate.*

www.madera.courts.ca.gov/

Note: There is a countywide index database of court records.

Civil Records: Access: Mail, in person. Only the court performs in person searches; visitors may not. Search fee: $5.00 per name. Court makes copy: $.50 per page. Required to search: name, years to search. Civil cases indexed by defendant, plaintiff. Civil records on computer back to 3/30/03 prior on index cards. Will only search back 7 years. Mail turnaround time 1-2 weeks.

Criminal Records: Access: Mail, in person. Only the court performs in person searches; visitors may not. Search fee: $5.00 per name. Court makes copy: $.50 per page. Required to search: name, years to search; also helpful: DOB. Criminal records on computer back to 3/30/03 prior on index cards for criminal. Mail turnaround time 1-2 weeks.

General Information: No adoptions, juvenile, medical, probation or sealed records released. Will not fax documents. Certification fee: $6.60 per doc. Payee: Madera Superior Court. Personal checks accepted. Prepayment and SASE required.

Chowchilla Division - Superior Court
141 S 2nd St, Chowchilla, CA 93610; phone: 559-665-4861/4862; fax: 559-665-3185; hours 8AM-5PM (PST). *Traffic.*

www.madera.courts.ca.gov

Marin County

Superior Court PO Box 4988, San Rafael, CA 94913-4988; criminal phone: 415-473-6225; civil phone: 415-473-6407; hours 8:30AM-4PM (PST). *Felony, Misdemeanor, Civil, Eviction, Small Claims, Probate.* www.co.marin.ca.us/courts

Civil Records: Access: Phone, mail, in person, online. Both court and visitors may perform in person searches. Search fee: $5.00 per name per year. Court makes copy: $1.00 per page. Required to search: name, years to search. Civil cases indexed by defendant, plaintiff. Civil records on computer from 1986, on microfiche from 1973 to 1985, archived from 1900 to 1972, on reel from 1900. Online access to the current court calendar is free at www.co.marin.ca.us/depts/MC/main/courtcal/name.cfm. Note: Phone requests are limited to one name. Mail turnaround time 3 weeks.

Criminal Records: Access: Mail, in person, online. Both court and visitors may perform in person searches. Search fee: $5.00 per name per year. Court makes copy: $1.00 per page. Required to search: name, years to search. Criminal records on computer from 1986, on microfiche from 1973 to 1985, archived from 1900 to 1972, on reel from 1900. Online Access to the active criminal calendar is the same as civil. Note: Phone requests are limited to one name. Mail turnaround time 3 weeks.

General Information: Public access terminal available. No adoptions, paternity, sole custody, juvenile, medical, probation or sealed records released. Will not fax documents. Certification fee: $7.00 per abstract. Payee: Marin County Superior Court. Personal checks accepted. Out-of-state checks not accepted. Write "not to exceed $x.xx" on check. Call first. Prepayment and SASE required.

Mariposa County

Superior Court PO Box 28, 5088 Bullion St, Mariposa, CA 95338; phone: 209-966-2005; criminal phone: 209-966-2005; civil phone: 209-966-6599; probate phone: 209-966-6599; fax: 209-742-6860; 8:30AM-4PM (PST). *Felony, Misdemeanor, Civil, Small Claims, Eviction, Probate.* www.mariposacourts.org

Civil Records: Access: Mail, in person. Both court and visitors may perform in person searches. Search fee: $5.00 per name, if prior to 1990, add $1.75 per search. Court makes copy: $.50 per page. Required to search: name, years to search. Civil records on computer from 1989, on microfiche and index files from 1800s. Mail turnaround: 1-2 weeks.

Criminal Records: Access: Mail, in person. Both court and visitors may perform in person searches. Search fee: $5.00 per name, if prior to 1990, add $1.75 per search. Court makes copy: $.50 per page. Required to search: name, years to search. Criminal records on computer from 1989, on microfiche and index files from 1800s. Mail turnaround: 1-2 weeks.

General Information: Public access terminal goes back to 1989. No adoptions, juvenile, medical, probation or sealed records released. Certification fee: $6.60 per doc. Payee: Mariposa Superior Court. Personal checks accepted. Prepayment and SASE required.

Mendocino County

Superior Court PO Box 337, Criminal Division, 100 N State & Perkins Sts, Ukiah, CA 95482; criminal phone: 707-463-4466; civil phone: 707-463-4481; fax: 707-463-4655; hours 8AM-2:30 PM; to noon on Friday (PST). *Felony, Civil Actions Over $25,000, Probate.* www.mendocino.courts.ca.gov/ Mailing address for Civil Division is PO Box 996.

Civil Records: Access: Mail, in person, online. Both court and visitors may perform in person searches. Search fee: $5.00 per name. Fee for mail search only. Court makes copy: $1.00 for first page, $.50 each add'l. Civil cases indexed by defendant, plaintiff. Civil records on computer from 1990s, on microfilm from 1800 to 1940. Search index at www.mendocino.courts.ca.gov/caseindex.html. Mail turnaround time 2 weeks.

Criminal Records: Access: Mail, in person, online. Both court and visitors may perform in person searches. Search fee: $5.00 per case. Court makes copy: $1.00 for first page, $.50 each add'l. Criminal records on computer from 1990s, on microfilm from 1800 to 1940. Search index at www.mendocino.courts.ca.gov/caseindex.html. Mail turnaround time 2 weeks.

General Information: Public access terminal available. No adoptions, juvenile, medical, probation or sealed records released. Certification fee: $6.60 per doc. Payee: Mendocino Superior Court. Personal checks accepted. Prepayment and SASE required.

Ten Mile Branch - Superior Court
700 S Franklin St, Fort Bragg, CA 95437; phone: 707-964-3192; fax: 707-961-2611; hours 8AM-2:30PM (Noon on Fri) (PST). *Felony, Misdemeanor, Civil Actions, Eviction, Small Claims.* www.mendocino.courts.ca.gov/fortbragg.html

Civil Records: Access: Mail, in person, online. Only the court performs in person searches; visitors may not. Search fee: $5.00 per name. Court makes copy: $1.00 for first page, $.50 each add'l. Required to search: name, years to search. Civil cases indexed by defendant, plaintiff. Will only search back 7 years. Search index at www.mendocino.courts.ca.gov/caseindex.html. Mail turnaround time 2 weeks.

Criminal Records: Access: Mail, in person, online. Only the court performs in person searches; visitors may not. Search fee: $5.00 per name. Court makes copy: $1.00 for first page, $.50 each add'l. Required to search: name, years to search, DOB. Criminal records go back to 1990; on computer back 1995; will only search back 7 years. Search index at www.mendocino.courts.ca.gov/caseindex.html. Mail turnaround time 2 weeks.

General Information: No juvenile or probation records released. Will not fax documents. Certification fee: $6.60 per doc. Payee: Superior Court. Personal checks accepted. Prepayment and SASE required.

Willits Branch - Superior Court
125 E Commercial St, Rm 100, Willits, CA 95490; phone: 707-459-5554; fax: 707-459-7818; hours 8AM-2:30PM (Noon on Fri) (PST). *Felony, Misdemeanor, Civil Actions Under $25,000, Eviction, Small Claims.* www.mendocino.courts.ca.gov

Civil Records: Access: Mail, in person, online. Only the court performs in person searches; visitors may not. Search fee: $5.00 per name. Court makes copy: $1.00 for 1st page, $.50 each add'l. Required to search: name, years to search. Civil cases indexed by defendant, plaintiff. Civil records on computer since 1992, index files prior. Search index at www.mendocino.courts.ca.gov/caseindex.html. Mail turnaround time 1 week.

Criminal Records: Access: Mail, in person, online. Both court and visitors may perform in person searches. Search fee: $5.00 per name. Court makes copy: $1.00 for 1st page, $.50 per add'l page. Required to search: name, years to search, DOB. Criminal records on computer since 1992, index files prior. Search index at www.mendocino.courts.ca.gov/caseindex.html. Mail turnaround time 1 week.

General Information: No public access terminal. No probation reports released. Certification fee: $6.60 per doc. Payee: MCSC. Personal checks accepted. Prepayment and SASE required.

Anderson Branch in Boonville - Superior Court
CA; fax: 707-895-2349. *Misdemeanor, Civil Actions Under $25,000, Eviction, Small Claims.* Note: This court was closed. Records were transferred to Ukiah. Everything east of Mile post marker 13.6 on Highway 128 is now in Ukiah; everything west is in Ft Bragg.

Round Valley Branch - Superior Court
CA. *Misdemeanor, Civil Actions Under $25,000, Eviction, Small Claims.* Note: This court has been merged with the Willits Division.

Arena Branch - Superior Court, CA.
www.mendocino.courts.ca.gov/ptarena.html Note: Effective June 30, 2003, operations for the Arena Branch of the Superior Court merged with the Ten Mile Court in Fort Bragg.

Merced County

Superior Court 627 W 21st St, Merced, CA 95340; criminal phone: 209-725-4113; civil phone: 209-725-4111; criminal records fax: 209-725-4114; civil records fax: 209-725-4112; hours 8AM-4PM (PST). *Felony, Civil Actions Over $25,000, Probate.*

Civil Records: Access: Mail, in person. Both court and visitors may perform in person searches. Search fee: $5.00 per name. Court makes copy: $.50 per page. Required to search: name, years to search. Civil cases indexed by defendant, plaintiff. Civil records in index files from 1900s, computer from 1979, on microfiche from 1900s. Mail turnaround time 1 week.

Criminal Records: Access: Mail, in person. Both court and visitors may perform in person searches. Search fee: $5.00 per name. Court makes copy: $.50 per page. Required to search: name, years to search. Criminal records in index files from 1900s, computer from 1979, on microfiche from 1900s. Mail turnaround time 1 week.

General Information: Public access terminal available. No juvenile nor adoption records released. Certification fee: $6.60 per doc. Payee: Merced County Superior Court. Business checks accepted. Prepayment and SASE required.

4, 5, 7 & 8 Divisions - Merced Limited Superior Court
670 W 22nd St, Merced, CA 95340; phone: 209-725-4113; civil phone: 209-385-7335; civil phone: 209-385-7337; fax: 209-725-4114; hours 8AM-4PM (PST). *Misdemeanor, Civil Actions Under $25,000, Eviction, Small Claims.*

Civil Records: Access: Mail, in person. Search fee: $5.00 per name. Court makes copy: $.50 per page. Required to search: name, years to search. Civil cases indexed by defendant, plaintiff. Civil records on computer from 1992, index cards prior. Will only search back 7 years. Mail turnaround time 2-5 days.

Criminal Records: Access: Mail, in person. Both court and visitors may perform in person searches. Search fee: $5.00 per name. Court makes copy: $.50 per page. Required to search: name, years to search. Criminal records on computer from 1992; prior on microfiche. Will only search back 7 years. Mail turnaround time 2-5 days.

General Information: Public access terminal goes back to 1992. No juvenile or probation records released. Certification fee: $6.60 per doc. Payee: County Superior Court. Only cashiers checks/money orders accepted. Prepayment & SASE required.

Los Banos Branch - Superior Court
445 "I" St, Los Banos, CA 93635; phone: 209-725-4124; fax: 209-725-4125; hours 8AM-4PM (PST). *Misdemeanor, Civil Actions Under $25,000, Eviction, Small Claims.* Note: This court was combined with the old Dos Palos and Gustine Municipal Courts.

Civil Records: Access: Mail, in person. Only the court performs in person searches; visitors may not. Search fee: $5.00 per name. Court makes copy: $.50 per page. Required to search: name, years to search. Civil cases indexed by defendant, plaintiff. Civil records on microfiche. Mail turnaround time 2-3 days.

Criminal Records: Access: Mail, in person. Only the court performs in person searches; visitors may not. Search fee: $5.00 per name. Court makes copy: $.50 per page. Required to search: name, years to search; also helpful: DOB. Criminal records on microfiche. Mail turnaround time 2-3 days.

General Information: No juvenile or probation records released. Will fax documents to local or toll free line. Certification fee: $6.60 per doc. Payee: Merced Superior Court. Personal checks accepted. Prepayment and SASE required.

Modoc County

Superior Court 205 S East St, Alturas, CA 96101; phone: 530-233-6515/6; fax: 530-233-6500; 8:30AM-5PM (PST). *Felony, Misdemeanor, Civil, Small Claims, Eviction, Probate.*

Civil Records: Access: Mail, in person. Only the court performs in person searches; visitors may not. Search fee: $5.00 per name. Court makes copy: $.50 per page. Required to search: name, years to search. Civil cases indexed by plaintiff. Civil records in index file from 1874, computerized since 7/25/95. Mail turnaround time 1-2 weeks.

Criminal Records: Access: Fax, mail, in person. Only the court performs in person searches; visitors may not. Search fee: $5.00 per name. Court makes copy: $.50 per page. Required to search: name, years to search; also helpful: DOB. Criminal records computerized since 1991. Mail turnaround time 1-2 weeks.

General Information: No adoptions, juvenile, medical, probation or sealed records released. Certification fee: $6.60 per doc. Payee: Modoc County Superior Courts. Personal checks accepted. Prepayment and SASE required.

Mono County

Mammoth Lakes Division - Superior Court PO Box 1037, Mammoth Lakes, CA 93546; phone: 760-924-5444; fax: 760-924-5419; hours 9AM-5PM (PST). *Felony, Misdemeanor, Civil, Eviction, Small Claims.*
www.monosuperiorcourt.ca.gov/
Note: This court performs all record searches for the Bridgeport Branch.

Civil Records: Access: Mail, in person. Only the court performs in person searches; visitors may not. Search fee: $5.00 per name. Court makes copy: $.50 per page. Required to search: name, years to search. Civil cases indexed by defendant, plaintiff. Civil records on index cards. Will only search back 10 years. Mail turnaround time 1 week.

Criminal Records: Access: Mail, in person. Only the court performs in person searches; visitors may not. Search fee: $5.00 per name. Court makes copy: $.50 per page. Required to search: name, years to search. Criminal records on computer from 1989, index cards prior. Will only search back 7 years. Mail turnaround time 1 week.

General Information: No juvenile or probation records released. Will fax documents for $3.00. Certification fee: $6.60 per doc $1.10 per page copy fee. Payee: Mono Superior Court. Personal checks accepted. Prepayment and SASE required.

Superior Court - Bridgeport Branch PO Box 537, Bridgeport, CA 93517; phone: 760-932-5239; probate phone: same; hours 8:30AM-5PM (PST). *Felony, Civil, Probate.*
Note: All record searches are directed to the court in Mammoth Lakes. There are only 2 staff people at this court.

Monterey County

Superior Court - Monterey Branch 1200 Aguajito Rd, 1st Fl, Monterey, CA 93940; phone: 831-647-5800; hours 9:30AM-4PM (PST). *Civil, Probate.*
www.monterey.courts.ca.gov/
Note: This court holds the civil records from the city of Salinas. Criminal records for Monterey are held in Salinas.

Civil Records: Access: Mail, in person. Both court and visitors may perform in person searches. Search fee: $5.00 per name per year. Court makes copy: $.75 per page. Required to search: name, years to search. Civil cases indexed by defendant, plaintiff. Some civil records computerized since 7/03, on microfiche from 1973, index books prior. Online access to calendars is free at webpage. Mail turnaround time 1 week.

General Information: No public access terminal. No juvenile or probation records released.

Certification fee: $7.00 general; $10.00 if for final dissolution. Payee: Superior Court. Personal checks accepted. Prepayment and SASE required.

Superior Court - Salinas Division 240 Church St, Rm 318, Salinas, CA 93901; phone: 831-755-5400; hours 9:30AM-4PM (PST). *Felony, Misdemeanor.*
www.monterey.courts.ca.gov/
Note: All criminal records are filed at the Salinas courthouse. All civil, probate, and family law cases are files at the Monterey courthouse.

Criminal Records: Access: Mail, in person. Both court and visitors may perform in person searches. Search fee: $5.00 per name. Court makes copy: $.75 per page. Required to search: name, years to search; also helpful: DOB. Felony records computerized since 1998, on microfiche to 1940s. Misdemeanor records computerized since 1992, on microfiche since 1986. Online access to calendars is free at webpage. Mail turnaround time 2 weeks.

General Information: Public access terminal available. No adoptions, juvenile, medical, probation or sealed records released. Certification fee: $6.60 per doc. Payee: Clerk of Court. Personal checks accepted. Prepayment and SASE required.

King City Division - Consolidated Trial Court PO Box 647, 250 Franciscan Way, King City, CA 93930; phone: 831-386-5200; fax: n/s; hours 8AM-5PM; Public hrs: 9:30AM-4PM (PST). *Felony, Misdemeanor, Civil Actions Under $25,000, Eviction, Small Claims.*
www.monterey.courts.ca.gov/
Note: Encompasses the cities of King City, Greenfield, Soledad, areas south of King City to the San Luis Obispo County line.

Civil Records: Access: Mail, in person. Both court and visitors may perform in person searches. Search fee: $5.00 per name. Court makes copy: $.75 per page. Required to search: name, years to search. Civil cases indexed by defendant, plaintiff. Civil records on computer from 1992, index files from 1983. Records destroyed after 10 years. Online access to calendars is free at webpage. Mail turnaround time 2-4 weeks.

Criminal Records: Access: Mail, in person. Both court and visitors may perform in person searches. Search fee: $5.00 per name. Court makes copy: $.75 per page. Required to search: name, years to search; also helpful: DOB. Criminal records on computer from 1992, index files from 1983. Records destroyed after 10 years. Online access to calendars is free at webpage. Mail turnaround time 2-4 week.

General Information: No public access terminal. No probation reports released. Certification fee: $7.00 per doc. Payee: Monterey County Courts. Personal checks accepted. Visa, AmEx accepted. Additional fee charged. Prepayment required. SASE requested.

Superior Court - Marina Division 3180 Del Monte Blvd, Marina, CA 93933; phone: 831-883-5300; fax: 831-884-0106; hours 8AM-4PM M-W, 8AM-2PM Fri; Closed Thursdays (PST). *Small Claims, Traffic.* www.monterey.courts.ca.gov

Napa County

Superior Court - Civil Division 825 Brown St, Napa, CA 94559; phone: 707-299-1130; criminal phone: 702-299-1180; fax: 707-253-4229; hours 8AM-5PM (PST). *Civil, Eviction, Small Claims, Probate.*
www.napa.courts.ca.gov
Civil Records: Access: Mail, in person. Both court and visitors may perform in person searches. Search fee: $5.00 per name per year. Court makes copy: $1.00 per page. Required to search: name, years to search. Civil cases indexed by defendant, plaintiff. Civil records on computer since 1989; prior records on index books or microfilm back to 1800s. Access to Tentative Rulings is online free at www.napa.courts.ca.gov/Civil/civil_tentative.asp. These only go back about 1 week. Mail turnaround time 2 weeks.

General Information: Public access terminal has only civil records back to 1989. No adoptions, juvenile, medical, probation or sealed records released. Certification fee: $6.60 per doc. Payee: Napa Superior Court. Personal checks accepted. Prepayment and SASE required.

Superior Court - Criminal Division 1111 3rd St, Napa, CA 94559; phone: 707-299-1180; fax: 707-253-4673; hours 8AM-5PM (PST). *Felony, Misdemeanor.* www.napa.courts.ca.gov
Criminal Records: Access: Mail, in person, fax, online. Both court and visitors may perform in person searches. Search fee: $5.00 per name. Court makes copy: $1.00 per page; same fee for self serve. Required to search: name, years to search, DOB; also helpful: address. Records on computer back to 1990. Online access is at www.napa.courts.ca.gov/. There is no fee to search by case number. Mail turnaround time 2 weeks.

General Information: Public access terminal has only criminal records back to 1990. No adoptions, juvenile, medical, probation or sealed records released. Certification fee: $6.60 per doc. Payee: Napa Superior Court. Personal checks accepted. Prepayment and SASE required.

Nevada County

Superior Court - Civil Division 201 Church St, #5, Nevada City, CA 95959; criminal phone: 530-265-1311; civil phone: 530-265-1293; probate phone: 530-265-1293; hours 8AM-5PM (PST). *Civil, Eviction, Small Claims.*
www.court.co.nevada.ca.us
Note: Phone number for Evictions and Small Claims is 530-265-1294 or 530-265-1318.

Civil Records: Access: Phone, mail, in person, online. Both court and visitors may perform in person searches. Search fee: $5.00 per name. Court makes copy: $.50 per page. Required to search: name or case number. Civil cases indexed by defendant, plaintiff. Civil records on computer back to 1983. Cases with previous disposition are available on microfilm in most cases. Some of the Limited Civil, Small Claims and Unlawful Detainer cases have been destroyed. Access to case calendar is free at www.court.co.nevada.ca.us/cgi/dba/casecal/db.cgi. Mail turnaround time 2 days.

General Information: Public access terminal has civil records back to 10-15 years. No probation reports released. Will not fax documents. Certification fee: $6.60 per doc. Payee: Nevada County Superior Court. Personal checks accepted. Prepayment and SASE required.

Superior Court - Criminal 201 Church St, #7, Nevada City, CA 95959; phone: 530-265-1311; fax: 530-478-1938; hours 8AM-5PM (PST). *Felony, Misdemeanor.*
www.courts.co.nevada.ca.us
Criminal Records: Access: Phone, mail, in person, online. Only the court performs in person searches; visitors may not. Search fee: No fee unless extensive research required. Court makes copy: $.50 per page. Required to search: name, years to search; also helpful: DOB. Criminal records on computer from 1987, prior in books back to 1800s. Access to case calendar is free at www.court.co.nevada.ca.us/cgi/dba/casecal/db.cgi. Mail turnaround time 2 weeks.

General Information: No adoptions, paternity, juvenile, medical, probation or sealed records released. Will fax documents to local or toll free line. Certification fee: $6.60 per doc. Payee: Nevada County Superior Courts. Personal checks accepted. Prepayment and SASE required.

Truckee Branch - Superior Court 10075 Levon Ave, #301, Truckee, CA 96161; criminal phone: 530-582-7835; civil phone: 530-582-7835; fax: 530-582-7875; hours 8AM-5PM (PST). *Misdemeanor, Civil, Eviction, Small Claims.*
http://nevadacountycourts.com

Civil Records: Access: Mail, in person, online. Both court and visitors may perform in person searches. Search fee: $5.00 per name. Court makes copy: $.50 per page. Required to search: name, years to search. Civil cases indexed by defendant, plaintiff. Civil records on computer from 1991, index files from 1983. Records destroyed after 10 years. Access to case calendar is free at www.court.co.nevada.ca.us/cgi/dba/casecal/db.cgi. Mail turnaround time 1 week.

Criminal Records: Access: Mail, in person, online. Both court and visitors may perform in person searches. Search fee: $5.00 per name. Court makes copy: $.50 per page. Required to search: name, years to search. Criminal records on computer from 1991, index files from 1983. Records destroyed after 10 years. Access to case calendar is free at www.court.co.nevada.ca.us/cgi/dba/casecal/db.cgi. Mail turnaround time 1 week.

General Information: Public access terminal has criminal back to 1992 and civil back to 1989. No probation reports released. Will not fax documents. Certification fee: $6.60 per doc. Payee: Superior Court. Personal checks accepted. Prepayment and SASE required.

Orange County

Superior Court - Civil 700 Civic Center Dr W, Santa Ana, CA 92701; phone: 714-834-2200; fax: 714-834-5589; hours 8AM-4PM (PST). *Civil Actions, Small Claims.*

www.occourts.org   Note: This court handles civil actions over $25,000 countywide, but holds only limited civil and small claims cases for this central jurisdiction venue (Santa Ana area).

Civil Records: Access: Mail, in person. Both court and visitors may perform in person searches. Search fee: $5.00 per name per index. Court makes copy: $.80 per page. Required to search: name, years to search. Civil cases indexed by defendant, plaintiff. Records on computer from mid 1980s, partial prior to 1986, microfiche and index file from 1900s. Civil, small claims, probate cases index for the county can be purchased on CD; index goes back to 12/31/01; can be purchased on monthly basis. See www.occourts.org/caseinfo/ or email tthompson@occourts.org. Unlimited civil and family court calendars are online at www.occourts.org/calendars/. Fax fee to this court is $1.00 per page. Mail turnaround time 1-2 weeks.

General Information: Public access terminal has civil records back to 9/2003. No adoptions, juvenile, medical, probation or sealed records released. Will not fax documents. Certification fee: $6.60 per doc. Payee: Clerk of the Court. Personal checks accepted. Prepayment and SASE required.

Superior Court - Criminal Operations 700 Civic Center Dr W, Santa Ana, CA 92701; phone: 714-834-2200; criminal phone: 714-834-2266; hours 8AM-4PM (PST). *Felony, Misdemeanor.*

www.occourts.org

Criminal Records: Access: Mail, in person. Both court and visitors may perform in person searches. Search fee: $5.00 per name per year. Court makes copy: $.80 per page. Required to search: name, years to search, DOB. Criminal records on computer from 1988, on microfiche and archived from 1966. Felony record index for the county can be purchased on CD; index goes back to 12/31/01 or can be purchased on monthly basis. See www.occourts.org/caseinfo/ or email tthompson@occourts.org. Mail turnaround time 1-2 weeks.

General Information: No public access terminal. No adoptions, juvenile, medical, probation or sealed records released. Certification fee: $6.60 per doc. Payee: Clerk of the Court. Personal checks accepted. Prepayment and SASE required.

Central Orange County Superior Court - Limited Jurisdiction PO Box 1138, 700 Civic Ctr Dr W, Santa Ana, CA 92702; criminal phone: 714-834-3575; civil phone: 714-834-3580; fax: 714-834-5589; 8AM-4PM (PST). *Misdemeanor, Civil*

Actions Under $25,000, Eviction, Small Claims.

www.occourts.org

Note: Includes cities of Santa Ana, Orange, Tustin and surrounding unincorporated territories including Cowan Heights, El Modena, Tustin Marine Air Base, Lemon Heights, Modjeska, Orange Park Acres, Silverado Canyon and Villa Park.

Civil Records: Access: Mail, in person. Both court and visitors may perform in person searches. Search fee: $5.00 per name per year. Court makes copy: $1.00 per page. Required to search: name, years to search. Civil cases indexed by defendant, plaintiff. Civil records on index files and microfiche from 1985. Records destroyed after 10 years. Civil and family court calendars at www.occourts.org/calendars/. Civil, small claims, probate cases index for the county can be purchased on CD; index goes back to 12/31/01 or can be purchased on monthly basis. See www.occourts.org/caseinfo/ or email tthompson@occourts.org. Mail turnaround time 2-4 days.

Criminal Records: Access: Mail, in person. Both court and visitors may perform in person searches. Search fee: $5.00 per name per year. Court makes copy: $1.00 per page. Required to search: name, years to search, DOB. Criminal records on index files and microfiche from 1986; on computer since 1995. Records destroyed after 7 years, no physical file available then. Mail turnaround time 2-4 days.

General Information: Public access terminal goes back to 1995. (Terminal is in Rm K107.) No probation reports released. Certification fee: $7.00 per doc. Payee: Clerk of Court. Personal checks or Visa, MC accepted. Prepayment and SASE required.

Harbor - Laguna Hills Superior Court - Civil Division 23141 Moulton Pky, Laguna Hills, CA 92653; phone: 949-472-6964; fax: 714-647-6937; hours 8AM-4PM (PST). *Civil Actions Under $25,000, Eviction, Small Claims.*

www.occourts.org

Note: Formerly known as South Orange, this includes Aliso Viejo, Capistrano Bch, Coto De Caza, Dana Pt, Laguna (various), Lake Forest, Mission Viejo, Rancho St. Margarita, San Clemente, San Juan Capistrano, Trabuco Canyon.

Civil Records: Access: Mail, in person. Both court and visitors may perform in person searches. Search fee: $5.00 per name per year. Fee only applies if court does search and case number is required. Court makes copy: $.80 per page. Required to search: name, years to search. Civil cases indexed by defendant, plaintiff. Civil records in index files and on microfiche back to 1987; on computer back to 2000. Civil and family court calendars are online at www.occourts.org/calendars/. Civil, small claims, probate cases index for the county can be purchased on CD; index goes back to 12/31/01 or can be purchased on monthly basis. See www.occourts.org/caseinfo/ or email tthompson@occourts.org. Mail turnaround time 2-3 days. Mail turnaround time 2-3 days.

General Information: Public access terminal has only civil records back to 12/89. No unlawful detainer records released for 60 days. Certification fee: $6.60 per doc. Payee: Clerk of Courtnex. Personal checks or Visa, MC, Discover accepted. Prepayment and SASE required.

Harbor - Laguna Niguel Superior Court - Criminal Division 30143 Crown Valley Pky, Justice Center, Laguna Niguel, CA 92677; phone: 949-249-5000; hours 8AM-4PM (PST). *Misdemeanor.* www.occourts.org

Note: Also known as South Orange County Superior Court. Includes Capistrano Bch, Coto De Caza, Dana Pt, Laguna Hills, Laguna Niguel, Mission Viejo, Rancho St. Margarita, San Clemente, San Juan Capistrano, Trabuco Canyon.

Criminal Records: Access: Mail, in person. Both court and visitors may perform in person searches. Search fee: $5.00 per name per year. Court makes copy: $.80 per page. Required to search: name, years to search, DOB; also helpful: SSN. Criminal records

on computer since 1987; prior records on books. Mail turnaround time 2-3 days.

General Information: No public access terminal. No probation report, unlawful detainer records released. Certification fee: $6.60 per doc. Payee: Clerk of Court. Personal checks and Visa/MC/Discover accepted. Prepayment and SASE required.

Harbor - Newport Beach Superior Court Justice Center, 4601 Jamboree Rd, Newport Beach, CA 92660-2595; phone: 949-476-4699; hours 8AM-4PM (PST). *Misdemeanor, Civil Actions Under $25,000, Eviction, Small Claims.*

www.occourts.org

Note: Includes Balboa Island, Corona Del Mar, Costa Mesa, Newport Beach, Irvine, Santa Ana Heights, John Wayne/Orange Co Airport, Lido Isle and surrounding unincorporated areas.

Civil Records: Access: Mail, in person. Both court and visitors may perform in person searches. Search fee: $5.00 per name. Court makes copy: $.80 per page. Required to search: name, years to search. Civil cases indexed by defendant, plaintiff. Civil records go back 10 years. Civil and family court calendars are at www.occourts.org/calendars/. Civil, small claims, probate cases index for the county can be purchased on CD; index goes back to 12/31/01 or can be purchased on monthly basis. See www.occourts.org/caseinfo/ or email tthompson@occourts.org. Mail turnaround time 5-10 days.

Criminal Records: Access: Mail, in person. Only the court performs in person searches; visitors may not. Search fee: $5.00 per name. Court makes copy: $.80 per page. Required to search: name, years to search; also helpful: DOB. Criminal records on computer go back 10 years; on microfiche -- felonies kept 75 years, misdemeanors 5 years. Mail turnaround time 5-10 days.

General Information: No public access terminal. No probation reports nor police reports released. Certification fee: $6.60 per doc. Payee: Clerk of Court. Personal checks accepted. Checks must be in-state and be imprinted with name and address. Visa, MC, Discover accepted. Prepayment and SASE required.

North Orange County Superior Court 1275 N Berkeley Ave, PO Box 5000, Fullerton, CA 92838-0500; phone: 714-773-4555; 773-4667 (Small Claims); criminal phone: 714-773-4668; civil phone: 714-773-4664; hours 8AM-4PM (PST). *Felony, Misdemeanor, Civil Actions Under $25,000, Eviction, Small Claims.*

www.occourts.org

Note: Traffic phone: 714-773-4615. Includes the cities of Anaheim, Brea, Buena Park, Fullerton, La Habra, La Palma, Placentia, Yorba Linda and surrounding unincorporated area including Anaheim Hills.

Civil Records: Access: Mail, in person. Both court and visitors may perform in person searches. Search fee: $5.00 per name, per year, per index. Fee also applies to requests by case number. Court makes copy: $.80 per page. Required to search: name, years to search. Civil cases indexed by defendant, plaintiff. Civil records on computer from 1991, index files from 1983. Records destroyed after 10 years. Family court calendars are at www.occourts.org/calendars/. Civil, small claims, probate cases index for the county can be purchased on CD; index goes back to 12/31/01 or can be purchased on monthly basis. See www.occourts.org/caseinfo/ or email tthompson@occourts.org. Mail turnaround time 5 days.

Criminal Records: Access: Mail, in person. Only the court performs in person searches; visitors may not. Search fee: $5.00 per name per index. Court makes copy: $.80 per page. Required to search: name, years to search. All Criminal records are on computer. Records destroyed after 5-7 years from date of conviction. Criminal cases index for the county can be purchased on CD; index goes back to 12/31/01 or can be purchased on monthly basis. See www.occourts.org/caseinfo/ or email tthompson@occourts.org. Mail turnaround time 5 days.

General Information: No public access terminal. No probation reports or UD's for 60 days released. Certification fee: $6.60 per doc. Payee: Clerk of Court. Personal checks accepted with proper ID. Visa, MC, Discover accepted. Prepayment and SASE required.

West Orange County Superior Court

8141 13th St, Westminster, CA 92683; phone: 714-896-7181; criminal phone: 714-896-7351; civil phone: 714-896-7191; criminal records fax: 714-896-7404; civil records fax: 714-896-7404; hours 8AM-4PM (PST). *Misdemeanor, Civil Actions Under $25,000, Eviction, Small Claims.*
www.occourts.org
Note: Includes the cities of Cypress, Fountain Valley, Garden Grove, Huntington Beach, Los Alamitos, Rossmore, Seal Beach, Stanton, Sunset Beach, Surfside, Westminster and adjoining and unincorporated territory.

Civil Records: Access: Mail, in person. Both court and visitors may perform in person searches. Search fee: $5.00 per name per year per index. Court makes copy: $.80 per page. Required to search: name, years to search. Civil cases indexed by defendant, plaintiff. Civil records on computer back to 1992, microfiche from 1983. Records destroyed after 10 years. Civil and family court calendars are online at www.occourts.org/calendars/. Civil, small claims, probate cases index for the county can be purchased on CD; index goes back to 12/31/01 or can be purchased on monthly basis. See www.occourts.org/caseinfo/ or email tthompson@occourts.org. Mail turnaround time 2 days.

Criminal Records: Access: Mail, in person. Both court and visitors may perform in person searches. Search fee: $5.00 per name per year per index. Court makes copy: $.80 per page. Required to search: name, years to search, DOB. Criminal records on computer back to 1996, microfiche from 1983. Misdemeanor records destroyed after 10 years. Mail turnaround time 2 days.

General Information: No public access terminal. No probation reports, unlawful detainer (under 60 days old) records released. Will not fax documents. Certification fee: $6.60 per doc. Payee: Clerk of Court. Personal checks or Visa, MC, Discover accepted. Prepayment and SASE required.

Orange County Probate Court

341 The City Dr, Orange, CA 92868; phone: 714-935-8043; hours 8AM-4PM (PST). *Probate.*
www.occourts.org/probate/
Note: Jurisdiction includes juvenile, family law, and mental health filings. Search court calendars free at www.occourts.org/calendars/calendarsprob.asp; indices at www.occourts.org/caseinfo/.

Placer County

Superior Court

101 Maple St, Auburn, CA 95603; criminal phone: 530-886-1200; civil phone: 530-889-6550; Hours: 8AM-3PM (PST). *Felony, Civil, Eviction, Probate.*
www.placercourts.org
Civil Records: Access: Phone, mail, in person. Both court and visitors may perform in person searches. Search fee: $5.00 per year for records prior to 1974; 1975 and forward are $5.00 per name. Court makes copy: $1.00 for first page, $.50 each add'l. Required to search: name, years to search. Civil cases indexed by defendant, plaintiff. Civil records on computer from 1992, on microfiche from 1974, archived and index file from 1800s. Mail turnaround time 2 weeks.
Criminal Records: Access: Phone, mail, in person. Both court and visitors may perform in person searches. Search fee: Same fees as civil. Court makes copy: $1.00 per page. Required to search: name, years to search. Criminal records on computer from 1992, on microfiche from 1974, archived and index file from 1800s. Mail turnaround time 2 weeks.

General Information: Public access terminal goes back to 1992. No adoptions, juvenile, medical, paternity, probation or sealed records released. Certification fee: $6.60 per doc. Payee: Clerk of the Court. Personal checks accepted. Prepayment and SASE required.

Auburn Branch - Superior Court

11532 "B" Ave, Auburn, CA 95603; phone: 530-886-1200; fax: 530-886-1209; hours 8AM-3PM Office (8AM-3PM phone hours) (PST). *Felony, Misdemeanor.*
www.placercourts.org
Note: Includes Auburn, Penryn, Newcastle, Bowman, Colfax, Weimar, Alta, Dutch Flat, Loomis. Also includes criminal for Roseville, Rocklin, Lincoln.

Criminal Records: Access: Mail, in person. Both court and visitors may perform in person searches. Search fee: $5.00 per name per year. Court makes copy: $1.00 per page; same fee for self serve. Required to search: name, years to search, DOB. Criminal Records indexed on computer back to 1992; felonies back to 1999; records go back 10 years. Mail turnaround time 2 weeks.
General Information: Public access terminal has only criminal records back to 1999. No probation reports or copies of warrants released. Will not fax documents. Certification fee: $6.60 per doc. Payee: Clerk of the Court. Personal checks accepted. Prepayment and SASE required.

Tahoe Division - Superior Court

PO Box 5669, Tahoe City, CA 96145; phone: 530-581-6336; criminal phone: 530-581-6339; civil phone: 530-581-6340; fax: 530-581-6344; hours 8AM-3PM (PST). *Misdemeanor, Civil, Eviction, Small Claims.*
www.placercourts.org
Note: This court does all areas of law with the exception of Adoptions and Probate.

Civil Records: Access: Mail, in person. Only the court performs in person searches; visitors may not. Search fee: $5.00 per name. Court makes copy: $1.00 per page. Required to search: name, years to search. Civil cases indexed by defendant, plaintiff. Civil records computerized since 1999, previous on index cards. Mail turnaround time 1 week.
Criminal Records: Access: Mail, in person. Only the court performs in person searches; visitors may not. Search fee: $5.00 per name. Court makes copy: $1.00 per page. Required to search: name, years to search. Criminal records on index cards. Will only search back 7 years; computerized records since 1999. Mail turnaround time 1 week.
General Information: No probation reports released. Certification fee: $6.60 per doc. Payee: Clerk of Court. Personal checks accepted. Write "not to exceed $x.xx" on check. Prepayment and SASE required.

Lincoln Division - Superior Court, CA.

www.placercourts.org
Note: This Lincoln Division is now fully consolidated with the Roseville Court. All traffic cases have been transferred to Roseville custody; all small claims cases have been transferred to Historic Courthouse at 101 Maple St, Auburn, CA 95603, 530-889-6550.

Roseville Division - Superior Court

300 Taylor St, Roseville, CA 95678; phone: 916-783-1600; fax: 916-783-1690; hours 8AM-3PM (PST). *Traffic.* www.placercourts.org
This court holds the records for the closed Foresthill Division Court, also Lincoln Court Traffic only.

Plumas County

Superior Court - Civil Division

520 Main St, Rm 104, Quincy, CA 95971; phone: 530-283-6305; criminal phone: 530-283-6232; probate phone: same; fax: 530-283-6415; hours 8AM-5PM (PST). *Civil, Small Claims, Probate.*
www.plumascourt.ca.gov
Civil Records: Access: Phone, fax, mail, in person. Both court and visitors may perform in person searches. Search fee: $5.00 per name per year. Court makes copy: $1.00 per page. Required to search: name, years to search. Civil cases indexed by

defendant, plaintiff. Civil records on computer from 1993, archived from 1980, index file from 1850. Mail turnaround time 1 week.
General Information: No public access terminal. No adoptions, juvenile, confidential, medical, probation or sealed records released. Will fax documents $5.00 per doc. Certification fee: $7.00 per doc. Payee: Plumas County Courts. Personal checks accepted. Prepayment and SASE required.

Superior Court - Criminal Division

520 Main St, Rm 104, Quincy, CA 95971; phone: 530-283-6232; fax: 530-283-6415; hours 8AM-5PM (PST). *Felony, Misdemeanor.*
www.plumascourt.ca.gov
Criminal Records: Access: Mail, in person. Only the court performs in person searches; visitors may not. Search fee: $5.00 per name. Court makes copy: $1.00 per page. Required to search: name, years to search, DOB; also, signed release if juvenile. Criminal records indexed on computer back to 1989. Mail turnaround time 1-2 days.
General Information: No probation reports, financial statements or juvenile released. Will fax documents. Certification fee: $7.00 per doc. Payee: Superior Court. Personal checks accepted. Prepayment and SASE required.

Chester Branch - Superior Court

PO Box 722, 1st & Willow Way, Chester, CA 96020; phone: 530-258-2646; fax: 530-258-2652; hours 8AM-4PM (PST). *Civil Actions Under $25,000, Eviction, Small Claims.*
www.psln.com/pccourt
Civil Records: Access: Phone, mail, in person. Only the court performs in person searches; visitors may not. Search fee: $5.00 per name per year. Court makes copy: $1.00 per page. Required to search: name, years to search. Civil cases indexed by defendant, plaintiff. Traffic on computer, index cards for civil records. Will only search back 7 years. Records on computer go back 13 years. Mail turnaround time 1-2 days.
General Information: No probation reports released. Fee to fax documents is $5.00 per document. Certification fee: $6.60 per doc; dissolution- $10.00. Payee: Superior Court. Personal checks accepted. Prepayment and SASE required.

Portola Branch - Superior Court

PO Box 1054, 161 Nevada St, Portola, CA 96122; phone: 530-832-6232; fax: 530-832-5838; hours 8AM-3:30PM (PST). *Civil Actions Under $25,000, Eviction, Small Claims, Traffic.*
Note: 530-832-4286 is Traffic Division.

Civil Records: Access: Phone, fax, mail, in person. Only the court performs in person searches; visitors may not. Search fee: $5.00 per name. Court makes copy: $1.00 per page. Required to search: name, years to search. Civil cases indexed by defendant, plaintiff. Traffic on computer, computer for civil records. Court will only search back 10 years. Mail turnaround time ASAP.
Criminal Records: Access: Phone, mail, in person. Only the court performs in person searches; visitors may not. Search fee: $5.00 per name. Court makes copy: $1.00 per page. Required to search: name, years to search. Traffic on computer, computer for criminal records. Court will only search back 10 years. Mail turnaround time ASAP.
General Information: No public access terminal. No probation reports released. Will not fax documents. Certification fee: $6.60 per doc. Payee: Superior Court. Personal checks accepted. Prepayment and SASE required.

Greenville Branch - Superior Court

PO Box 706 (115 Hwy 89), Greenville, CA 95947; phone: 530-284-7213; fax: 530-284-0857; hours 8AM-4PM (PST). *Small Claims.*

Riverside County

Superior Court - Civil Division 4050 Main St, Riverside, CA 92501; phone: 951-955-1960; probate phone: 951-955-1970; fax: 909-955-1751; hours 8AM-4PM (PST). *Civil Actions, Small Claims, Probate.*
www.courts.co.riverside.ca.us/
Note: All Superior Court Files and Limited Jurisdiction files except for those cases filed within the Mt. San Jacinto Judicial District and Three Lakes Judicial District. Includes case from closed branch in Lake Elsinore.

Civil Records: Access: Phone, fax, mail, online, in person. Both court and visitors may perform in person searches. No search fee. Court makes copy: $.50 per page. Required to search: name, years to search. Civil cases indexed by defendant, plaintiff. Civil records on computer and microfiche from 1970, index file from 1956, archived from 1900s. Access to civil records is free at the web page. Online records date back to 1991 for Riverside, 1994 for Corona, and 1996 forward for most of the remaining limited court cases. Note: Also, civil indexes are on CD-Rom including DOBs. CD-Rom fee is $25.00 per month per department. Overall index goes back to 10/91 and complete name index history is $300 per department. Mail turnaround time 3 days.

General Information: Public access terminal has civil records back to 1991. No adoptions, juvenile, medical, probation, unlawful detainers for 60 days or sealed records released. Will fax documents $1.00 per page. Certification fee: $7.00 per doc. Payee: Riverside County Superior Court. Personal checks or Visa, MC, Discover accepted. Prepayment and SASE required.

Superior Court - Criminal Division 4100 Main St, Riverside, CA 92501; phone: 951-955-2300; fax: 951-955-4007; hours 7:30AM-4PM (PST). *Felony, Misdemeanor.*
www.courts.co.riverside.ca.us
Criminal Records: Access: Phone, fax, mail, online, in person. Both court and visitors may perform in person searches. No search fee. Court makes copy: $.50 per page. Required to search: name, years to search, DOB; also helpful: SSN. Criminal Records on microfiche and computer since 1970, index file from 1956. For free Internet access to records visit the web page. Includes Desert and Riverside felony, misdemeanor, & traffic; and misdemeanor from Corona, Palm Springs, Indio and Blythe. Note: Also, criminal indexes are on CD-Rom, but no DOBs. CD-Rom fee is $25.00 per month per department. Overall index goes back to 6/90 and complete name index history is $300.00 per department. For info, contact S Griffin at 951-955-1431. Mail turnaround time 2 to 4 weeks.

General Information: Public access terminal has only criminal records. No adoptions, juvenile, medical, probation, unlawful detainers for 60 days or sealed records released. Will fax documents $1.00 for 1st page, $.50 each add'l. Must pay fax fee by credit card. Certification fee: $7.00 per doc. Payee: Clerk of the Court. Personal checks or Visa, MC, Discover accepted. Prepayment and SASE required.

Blythe Division - Superior Court 265 N Broadway, Blythe, CA 92225; criminal phone: 760-921-7828 (incl: traffic); civil phone: 760-921-7981; criminal records fax: 760-921-7942; civil records fax: 760-921-7941; hours 7:30AM-4PM (PST). *Felony, Misdemeanor, Civil Actions, Eviction, Small Claims.*
www.courts.co.riverside.ca.us/
Note: Includes Blythe, Ripley. Phone for Family Law is 760-921-7982.

Civil Records: Access: Phone, fax, mail, online, in person. Both court and visitors may perform in person searches. No search fee. Court makes copy: $.50 per page. Required to search: name, years to search. Civil cases indexed by defendant, plaintiff. Civil records on computer from 1991, index files from 1983. Records destroyed after 10 years. See Riverside Division for online information. Also, see Riverside Civil Division for information on name indexes back to 3/89 on CD-rom. Mail turnaround time 2 days.

Criminal Records: Access: Phone, fax, mail, online, in person. Both court and visitors may perform in person searches. No search fee. Court makes copy: $.50 per page. Required to search: name, years to search; also helpful: DOB, sex. Criminal records on computer from 1991, index files from 1983. Records destroyed after 10 years. See Riverside Division for online information. Also, see Riverside Criminal Division for information on name indexes back to 11/89 on CD-rom. Note: See Riverside Division for information on name indexes on CD-rom. Mail turnaround time 2 days.

General Information: Public access terminal has criminal back to 11/1992 and civil back to 1994. No probation reports released. Will charge $1.00 per page to fax in or fax documents out. Certification fee: $7.00. Payee: Clerk of the Court. Personal checks or Visa, MC, Discover accepted. Prepayment and SASE required.

Banning Division - Superior Court 155 E Hays St, Banning, CA 92220; criminal phone: 951-922-7145; civil phone: 951-922-7155; criminal records fax: 951-922-7150; civil records fax: 951-922-7160; hours 7:30AM-4PM (PST). *Felony, Misdemeanor, Civil Actions Under $25,000, Eviction, Small Claims.*
www.courts.co.riverside.ca.us
Note: Includes Banning, Cabazon, Highland Springs, Poppet Flatt, Silent Valley, Beaumont, Calimesa, Cherry Valley and Whitewater.

Civil Records: Access: Phone, mail, online, in person. Both court and visitors may perform in person searches. No search fee. Court makes copy: $.50 per page. Required to search: name, years to search; also helpful-case number. Civil cases indexed by defendant, plaintiff. Civil records on computer from 1991, index files from 1983. Records destroyed after 10 years. See Riverside Division location for online information. Also, see Riverside Civil Division for information on name indexes back to 3/89 on CD-rom. Note: Phone access limited to short searches. Mail turnaround time 2 days.

Criminal Records: Access: Phone, mail, online, in person. Only the court performs in person searches; visitors may not. No search fee. Court makes copy: $.50 per page. Required to search: name, years to search; also helpful-case number. Criminal records on computer back to 1992, index files from 1983. Records destroyed after 10 years. See Riverside Division for online information. Also, see Riverside Criminal Division for information on name indexes back to 11/89 on CD-rom. Note: Will perform phone searches for one or two names only. Mail turnaround time 2 days.

General Information: Public access terminal has only civil records back to 1997. No probation reports released. Certification fee: $7.00. Payee: Clerk of the Court. Personal checks or Visa, MC, Discover accepted. Prepayment and SASE required.

Hemet Division - Superior Court 880 N State St, Hemet, CA 92543; phone: 951-766-2322; fax: 951-766-2317; hours 7:30AM-4PM (PST). *Civil Actions Under $25,000, Eviction, Small Claims.*
www.courts.co.riverside.ca.us/
Note: Includes Aguanga, Anza, Gilman Hot Springs, Hemet, Idylwild, Mountain Center, Pine Cove, Redec, Sage, San Jacinto, Sobba Hot Spring, Valle Vista and Winchester.

Civil Records: Access: Mail, online, in person. Both court and visitors may perform in person searches. No search fee. Court makes copy: $1.00 per page. Required to search: name, years to search. Civil cases indexed by defendant, plaintiff. Civil records on computer from 1996, index files from 1983. Records destroyed after 10 years. See Riverside Division location for online information. Also, see

Riverside Civil Division for information on name indexes back to 3/89 on CD-rom.
General Information: No public access terminal. Certification fee: $6.60 per doc. Payee: Clerk of the Court. Personal checks or Visa, MC, Discover accepted. Prepayment and SASE required.

Indio Division - Superior Court 46-200 Oasis St, Indio, CA 92201; phone: 760-863-8426; 863-7585-post court svcs; criminal phone: 760-863-8206; civil phone: 760-863-8208; probate phone: 760-863-8207; fax: 760-863-8707; hours 7:30AM-4PM (PST). *Misdemeanor, Civil Actions Under $25,000, Eviction, Small Claims, Probate.*
www.courts.co.riverside.ca.us/
Note: Includes Desert Center, Eagle Mountain, Indio, La Quinta, Coachella, Bermuda Dunes, Mecca, North Shore, Pinyon Pines, Palm Springs, Salton Sea, Oasis, Thermal. Most Palm Springs records here.

Civil Records: Access: Phone, fax, mail, online, in person. Visitors must perform in person searches themselves. No search fee. Court makes copy: $.50 per page. Required to search: name, years to search. Civil cases indexed by defendant, plaintiff. Civil records on computer from 1993, index files from 1983. Records destroyed after 10 years. See Riverside Division for online information. Also, see Riverside Civil Division for information on name indexes back to 3/89 on CD-rom. Note: Phone and fax access limited to short searches. Mail turnaround time 2 days.

Criminal Records: Access: Phone, fax, mail, online, in person. Visitors must perform in person searches themselves. No search fee. Court makes copy: $.50 per page. Required to search: name, years to search, signed release. Criminal records on computer from 1993, index files from 1983. Records destroyed after 10 years. See Riverside Division for online information. Also, see Riverside Criminal Division for information on name indexes back to 11/89 on CD-rom. Mail turnaround time 2 days.

General Information: Public access terminal goes back to 1993. No probation reports released. Will fax documents $1.00 per page. Certification fee: $7.00. Payee: Clerk of the Court. Personal checks or Visa, MC, Discover accepted. Prepayment and SASE required.

Southwest Justice Center - Superior Court 30755 "D" Auld Rd, #1226, Murrieta, CA 92563; phone: 951-304-5000; fax: 951-304-5250; hours 7:30AM-4PM (PST). *Felony, Misdemeanor, Family Law.*
www.courts.co.riverside.ca.us/
Note: This is a new court (01/21/03) that took in the criminal court cases from the closed Superior Courts in Hemet and Perris.

Criminal Records: Access: Fax, mail, online, in person. Both court and visitors may perform in person searches. No search fee. Court makes copy: $.50 per page. Required to search: name, years to search. Criminal records on computer since 1992; prior records on fiche. See Riverside Division for online information. See Riverside Criminal Division for information on name indexes back to 11/89 on CD-Rom. Note: Phone & fax access limited to short searches. Mail turnaround time 1 week.

General Information: Public access terminal has only criminal records. No adoptions, juvenile, medical, probation or sealed records released. Will fax documents for $1.00 per page. Certification fee: $7.00 per doc. Payee: Clerk of the Court. Personal checks or Visa, MC, Discover accepted. Prepayment and SASE required.

Temecula Branch - Superior Court 41002 County Center Dr, Temecula, CA 92591; phone: 951-600-6435; fax: 951-600-6423; hours 7:30AM-4PM (PST). *Civil Actions Under $25,000, Eviction, Small Claims.* www.courts.co.riverside.ca.us/
Note: Includes Perris, Sun City, Romoland, Homeland, Lakeview, Glenn Valley, Mead Valley, Quail Valley, Nuevo.

Civil Records: Access: Phone, mail, online, in person. Both court and visitors may perform in person searches. No search fee. Court makes copy: $.50 per page. Required to search: name, years to search, DOB. Civil cases indexed by defendant, plaintiff. Civil records on computer go back 10-12 years; records held for 10 years. See Riverside Division location for online information. Also, see Riverside Civil Division for information on name indexes back to 3/89 on CD-rom. Note: Visitors may search on computer only. Mail turnaround time 7 days.

General Information: Public access terminal has only civil records. No confidential, adoption or sealed records released. Unlawful detainers not released for 60 days. Will not fax documents. Certification fee: $7.00 per doc. Payee: Clerk of the Court. Personal checks or Visa, MC, Discover accepted. Prepayment and SASE required.

Corona Branch - Superior Court, CA; phone: 909-272-5620. *Felony, Misdemeanor, Civil Actions Under $25,000, Eviction, Small Claims.*
www.courts.co.riverside.ca.us/
Note: This court closed as of 7/03.

Lake Elsinore Division - Superior Court
Note: This court closed 01/01/03. Refer to the Riverside Superior Court for case files.

Palm Springs Division - Superior Court, CA. *Misdemeanor, Evictions, Traffic.*
Note: This Court closed as of 07/03. Records sent to court in Indio.

Perris Branch - Superior Court, CA.
Note: This court closed 01/01/03. Refer to the Riverside Superior Court for case files.

Sacramento County

Superior Court 720 9th St, Rm 102, Sacramento, CA 95814; phone: 916-874-5664; criminal phone: 916-874-5744; civil phone: 916-874-6868; fax: 916-874-5620; hours 8:30AM-4:30PM (PST). *Felony, Misdemeanor, Civil.*
www.saccourt.com
Note: Galt, Elk Grove, and Walnut Grove branches are closed. This court now holds their records. Probate is located at 3341 Power Inn Rd, Sacramento 95826 (916-875-3400).

Civil Records: Access: Phone, fax, mail, online, in person. Both court and visitors may perform in person searches. Search fee: $5.00 per name per year. Also charge $9.00 per hour for court. Court makes copy: $.50 per page. Required to search: name, years to search; also helpful: address. Civil cases indexed by defendant, plaintiff. Civil records on microfiche and archived from 1937, index books from 1800s. Access to court records back to 1993 is free at www.saccourt.com/indexes/. Search using the DOB, but results are not shown with the DOB. Includes civil, probate, small claims, unlawful detainer, family as well as criminal. Mail turnaround time 1-3 weeks.

Criminal Records: Access: Phone, mail, online, in person. Both court and visitors may perform in person searches. Search fee: $5.00 per name. Court makes copy: $.50 per page. Required to search: name, years to search; also helpful: address, DOB, SSN. Criminal records on computer since 1993 (Superior), on microfiche and archived from 1962. Access to criminal records back to 1993 is free at https://services.saccourt.com/indexsearch/. Search using the DOB, but results are not shown with the DOB. Mail turnaround time 1-3 weeks.

General Information: No public access terminal. No adoptions, juvenile, medical, probation or sealed records released. Certification fee: $6.60 per doc. Payee: Superior Court. Personal checks accepted. Prepayment and SASE required.

Carol Miller Justice Center 301 Bicentennial Cir, Sacramento, CA 95826; phone: 916-875-7800/7354; hours 8:30AM-4:30PM (PST). *Small Claims, Evictions, Traffic, Juvenile.*
www.saccourt.com/geninfo/location/cmjc.asp

Galt Division - Superior Court, *Misdemeanor, Small Claims.*
Note: This court is closed as of 03/03. Misdemeanor records and files are now housed at the Sacramento Superior Court. Traffic records were sent to the Carol Miller Justice Center (916-875-7354/7800).

South Sacramento Superior Court - Elk Grove Branch, CA. *Misdemeanor, Civil Actions Under $25,000, Eviction, Small Claims.*
www.saccourt.com
Note: This court has been closed. All records are located at the Superior Court in Sacramento.

Walnut Grove Branch - Superior Court,
Note: This court was closed, records are now at the Superior Court in Sacramento.

San Benito County

Superior Court Courthouse, 440 5th St, Rm 205, Hollister, CA 95023; phone: 831-636-4057; fax: 831-636-2046; hours 8AM-4PM (PST). *Felony, Misdemeanor, Civil, Small Claims, Eviction, Probate.* www.sanbenito.courts.ca.gov/
Note: As of 11/2000, Family Law records are located at the Limited Jurisdiction Court, 390 5th St, Hollister. Phone: 831-636-4425. fax: 831-636-4117. Same search requirements as stated below.

Civil Records: Access: Mail, in person. Both court and visitors may perform in person searches. Search fee: $5.00 per name. Court makes copy: $.50 per page. Required to search: name, years to search. Civil cases indexed by defendant, plaintiff. Civil records on computer since 1990, index books and archived from 1873. Mail turnaround time 1-2 weeks.

Criminal Records: Access: Mail, in person. Both court and visitors may perform in person searches. Search fee: $5.00 per name. Court makes copy: $.50 per page. Required to search: name, years to search. Criminal records on computer since 1989, index books and archived from 1900. Mail turnaround time 1-2 weeks.

General Information: Public access terminal goes back to 1990. No adoptions, juvenile, medical, probation or sealed records released. Will not fax documents. Certification fee: $7.00 per doc. Payee: Superior Court. Personal checks accepted. Prepayment and SASE required.

San Bernardino County

Barstow District - Superior Court 235 E Mountain View, Barstow, CA 92311; phone: 760-256-4814; criminal phone: 760-256-4785; civil phone: 760-256-4907; fax: 760-256-4884; hours 8AM-4PM (PST). *Felony, Misdemeanor, Civil, Eviction, Small Claims.*
www.sbcounty.gov/courts/
Note: Includes the City of Barstow and the unincorporated areas of Yermo, Lenwood, Daggett, Hinkley and Baker.

Civil Records: Access: Mail, in person, online. Both court and visitors may perform in person searches. Search fee: $5.00 per name per year. Court makes copy: $.50 per page. Required to search: name, years to search. Civil cases indexed by defendant, plaintiff. Civil records on computer from 1991, index books and microfilm. Microfilm is 3 to 4 weeks current. Records destroyed after 10 years. Access to civil cases is free at www.sbcounty.gov/courts/genInfo/openaccess.htm Includes calendars. Daily calendars also at main website. Mail turnaround time 2-5 days.

Criminal Records: Access: Mail, in person, online. Both court and visitors may perform in person searches. Search fee: $5.00 per name per year. Court makes copy: $.50 per page. Required to search: name,

years to search. Criminal records on computer from 1999, index books and microfilm. Microfilm is 3 to 4 weeks current. Records destroyed after 10 years. Access to criminal cases and traffic is free at www.sbcounty.gov/courts/genInfo/openaccess.htm. Includes calendars. Also, the daily criminal docket is free at the court main website. Mail turnaround time 2-5 days.

General Information: Public access terminal goes back to 1999. No probation or confidential reports released. Will not fax documents. Certification fee: $6.60 per doc. Payee: Clerk of the Court. Only cashiers checks and money orders. Credit cards accepted for filings only. Prepayment and SASE required.

Central District - Superior Court 351 N Arrowhead Ave, San Bernardino, CA 92415; phone: 909-885-0139; criminal phone: 909-384-1888; civil phone: 909-387-3922; probate phone: 909-387-3952; criminal records fax: 909-387-4993; civil records fax: 909-387-4428; hours 8AM-4PM (PST). *Felony, Misdemeanor, Civil Actions, Small Claims, Probate.*
www.sbcounty.gov/courts/
Note: Small claims phone: 909-885-0139. Evictions now handled by Redlands Division.

Civil Records: Access: Mail, fax, in person, online. Both court and visitors may perform in person searches. Search fee: $5.00 per name per year. Court makes copy: $.50 per page. Required to search: name, years to search. Civil cases indexed by defendant, plaintiff. Civil records on computer from 1992, microfiche from 1972, archived and index file from 1856. Online access to civil cases is free at www.sbcounty.gov/courts/genInfo/openaccess.htm. Includes calendars. Online access to "Probate Notes" is free at www.co.san-bernardino.ca.us/courts/ Click on Probate. Daily calendars also at main website. Note: Address mail search access requests to Research Dept. Mail turnaround time 7-10 days.

Criminal Records: Access: Mail, in person, online. Both court and visitors may perform in person searches. Search fee: $5.00 per name per year. Court makes copy: $.50 per page. Required to search: name, years to search, DOB, SSN. Criminal records on computer from 1996, microfiche from 1972, index files from 1983, archived back to 1856. Online access to criminal cases and traffic is free at www.sbcounty.gov/courts/genInfo/openaccess.htm. Includes calendars. Also, the daily criminal docket is free at the court main website. Mail turnaround time 7-10 days.

General Information: Public access terminal goes back to 1998. No adoptions, juvenile, medical, probation or sealed records released. Certification fee: $6.60 per doc. Payee: Superior Court. Business and personal checks accepted. Prepayment and SASE required.

Joshua Tree District - Superior Court PO Box 6602, 6527 White Feather Rd, Joshua Tree, CA 92252; phone: 760-366-5770; criminal phone: 760-366-5775; civil phone: 760-366-5770; fax: 760-366-4156; hours 8AM-4PM (PST). *Felony, Misdemeanor, Civil, Eviction, Small Claims.*
www.sbcounty.gov/courts/
Note: Includes the incorporated area of City of Twenty-Nine Palms, Town of Yucca Valley and unincorporated areas of Morongo Valley, Pioneertown, Landers, Johnson Valley and Wonder Valley.

Civil Records: Access: Mail, in person, online. Both court and visitors may perform in person searches. Search fee: $5.00 per name per year. Court makes copy: $.50 per page. Required to search: name, years to search. Civil cases indexed by defendant, plaintiff. Civil records on computer from 1991, index books from 1983. Records destroyed after 10 years. Online access to civil cases is free at www.sbcounty.gov/courts/genInfo/openaccess.htm. Includes calendars. Daily calendars also at main website. Mail turnaround time 1 week.

Criminal Records: Access: Mail, in person, online. Both court and visitors may perform in person searches. Search fee: $5.00 per name per year. Court makes copy: $.50 per page. Required to search: name, years to search, DOB. Criminal records on computer from 1991, index books from 1983. Records destroyed after 10 years. Online access to criminal cases and traffic is free at www.sbcounty.gov/courts/genInfo/openaccess.htm . Includes calendars. Also, the daily criminal docket is free at the court main website. Mail turnaround time 1 week.

General Information: Public access terminal goes back to 1998. No probation reports, confidential records released. Will not fax documents. Certification fee: $6.60 per doc. Payee: Joshua Tree Superior Court. Personal checks accepted. Prepayment and SASE required.

Rancho Cucamonga District - Superior Court
8303 N Haven Ave, Rancho Cucamonga, CA 91730; phone: 909-945-4131 info.; criminal phone: 909-350-9764; civil phone: 909-945-4131; fax: 909-945-4154; hours 8AM-4PM (PST). *Felony, Misdemeanor, Civil, Eviction, Small Claims, Probate.*

www.co.san-bernardino.ca.us/courts/

Note: Formerly West District Superior Ct. Includes cities of Montclair, Ontario, Upland, Rancho Cucamonga, Alta Loma, Etiwanda, Guasti and surrounding unincorporated area of Mt Baldy.

Civil Records: Access: Phone, fax, mail, in person, online. Both court and visitors may perform in person searches. Search fee: $5.00 per name. Court makes copy: $.50 per page. Required to search: name, years to search. Civil cases indexed by defendant, plaintiff. Civil records on computer since 4/1994, index cards prior. Records destroyed after 10 years. Online access to civil cases is free at www.sbcounty.gov/courts/genInfo/openaccess.htm . Includes calendars. Online access to "Probate Notes" is free at www.co.san-bernardino.ca.us/courts/ Click on Probate. Daily calendars also at main website. Mail turnaround time 2-4 days.

Criminal Records: Access: Phone, fax, mail, in person, online. Both court and visitors may perform in person searches. Search fee: $5.00 per name. Court makes copy: $.50 per page. Required to search: name, years to search; also helpful: DOB. Criminal records computerized since 1994, also on index cards, microfiche. Access to criminal and traffic is free at www.sbcounty.gov/courts/genInfo/openaccess.htm . Includes calendars. Also, the daily criminal docket is free at the court main website. Mail turnaround time 2-4 days.

General Information: Public access terminal goes back to 1998. No probation reports released. Will not fax documents. Certification fee: $6.60 per doc. Payee: Superior Court. Personal checks accepted. Only checks over $10.00 accepted. Visa, AmEx accepted for civil records. Prepayment and SASE required.

Victorville District - Superior Court
14455 Civic Dr, Victorville, CA 92392; phone: 760-245-6215; criminal records fax: 760-243-8794; civil records fax: 760-243-8790; hours 8AM-4PM (PST). *Felony, Misdemeanor, Civil, Eviction, Small Claims, Probate.*

www.sbcounty.gov/courts/

Note: Includes the Cities of Victorville, Adelanto Hesperia and the areas of Apple Valley, El Mirage, Helendale, Lucerne Valley, Oro Grande, Phelan, Pinon Hill, Oakhills and Wrightwood.

Civil Records: Access: Mail, in person, online. Both court and visitors may perform in person searches. Search fee: $5.00 per name. Court makes copy: $.50 per page. Self serve copy fee: $.15 per page. Required to search: name, years to search. Civil cases indexed by defendant, plaintiff. Civil records on microfiche from 1982 to 7/1999, on computer from 1989 to present, index books prior. Records destroyed after 10 years. Online access to civil cases is free at

www.sbcounty.gov/courts/genInfo/openaccess.htm . Includes calendars. Daily calendars also at main website. Mail turnaround time within 2 weeks.

Criminal Records: Access: Mail, in person, online. Both court and visitors may perform in person searches. Search fee: $5.00 per name. Court makes copy: $.50 per page. Self serve copy fee: $.15 per page. Required to search: name, years to search; also helpful: DOB, date of offense. Criminal index books by defendant 1986 - present. Online access to criminal cases and traffic is free at www.sbcounty.gov/courts/genInfo/openaccess.htm . Includes calendars. Also, the daily criminal docket is free at the court main website. Note: Only court allowed to search computer index. Mail turnaround time within 2 weeks.

General Information: Public access terminal has criminal back to 1998 and civil back to 1984. No probation reports released. Will not fax documents. Certification fee: $6.60 per doc. Payee: Superior Court. Personal checks accepted. $5.00 minimum. Prepayment and SASE required.

Big Bear Lake District - Superior Court
PO Box 2806 (477 Summit Blvd), Big Bear Lake, CA 92315; phone: 909-866-0150; fax: 909-866-0160; hours 8AM-4PM (PST). *Misdemeanor, Civil Actions Under $25,000, Eviction, Small Claims.*

www.sbcounty.gov/courts

Civil Records: Access: Mail, in person, online. Both court and visitors may perform in person searches. Search fee: $5.00 per name. Court makes copy: $.50 per page. Required to search: name, years to search. Civil cases indexed by defendant, plaintiff. Civil records on computer since 9/1/96; prior on index books. Will only search back 7 years. Access to civil cases is free at www.sbcounty.gov/courts/genInfo/openaccess.htm. Includes calendars. Daily calendars also at main website. Mail turnaround time 1 week.

Criminal Records: Access: Mail, in person, online. Both court and visitors may perform in person searches. Search fee: $5.00 per name per year. Court makes copy: $.50 per page. Required to search: name, years to search, DOB; also helpful: SSN. Criminal records on index books. Will only search back 7 years. Online access to criminal cases and traffic is free at www.sbcounty.gov/courts/genInfo/openaccess.htm. Includes calendars. Also, the daily criminal docket is free at the court main website. Mail turnaround time 1 week.

General Information: No public access terminal. No probation reports released. Certification fee: $6.60 per doc. Payee: Superior Court. Personal checks accepted. Prepayment and SASE required.

Chino Division - Superior Court
13260 Central Ave, Chino, CA 91710; phone: 909-356-5337; criminal phone: 909-465-5260; fax: 909-465-5221; hours 8AM-4PM (PST). *Felonies, Misdemeanor, Eviction, Small Claims.*

www.sbcounty.gov/courts/

Note: Includes City of Chino and surrounding unincorporated area. Rancho Cucamonga Courts handles all civil cases since 01/01/99.

Civil Records: Access: Fax, mail, in person. Only the court performs in person searches; visitors may not. Search fee: $5.00 per name. Court makes copy: $.50 per page. Required to search: name, years to search; also helpful: address. Civil cases indexed by defendant, plaintiff. Civil records on computer from 1991, index books from 1983. Records destroyed after 10 years. Daily calendars at main website. Mail turnaround time 2 days.

Criminal Records: Access: Mail, in person, online. Only the court performs in person searches; visitors may not. Search fee: $5.00 per name. Court makes copy: $.50 per page. Required to search: name, years to search, DOB; also helpful: address. Criminal records on computer from 1991, index books from 1983. Records destroyed after 10 years. Online access to criminal cases and traffic is free at www.sbcounty.gov/courts/genInfo/openaccess.htm . Includes calendars. Also, the daily criminal

docket is free at the court main website. Mail turnaround time 2 days.

General Information: No probation reports released. Will fax documents. Certification fee: $6.60 per doc. Payee: Chino Superior Court. Personal checks accepted. Prepayment and SASE required.

Fontana District - Superior Court
17780 Arrow Blvd, Fontana, CA 92335; phone: 909-350-9322; hours 8AM-4PM (PST). *Felony, Misdemeanor, Civil Actions Under $25,000, Eviction, Small Claims, Traffic.*

www.sbcounty.gov/courts/

Note: Includes the Cities of Fontana, Rialto, Crestmore and the unincorporated areas of Lytle Creek Canyon and Bloomington.

Civil Records: Access: Mail, in person, online. Only the court performs in person searches; visitors may not. Search fee: $5.00 per name. Court makes copy: $.50 per page. Required to search: name, years to search; also helpful: address. Civil cases indexed by defendant, plaintiff. Civil records on computer from 1987, microfilm prior. Access to civil cases free at www.sbcounty.gov/courts/genInfo/openaccess.htm . Includes calendars. Daily calendars also at main website. Mail turnaround time 2-5 days.

Criminal Records: Access: Mail, in person, online. Both court and visitors may perform in person searches. Search fee: $5.00 per name. Court makes copy: $.50 per page. Required to search: name, years to search; also helpful: DOB. Criminal records on computer from 1987, microfilm prior. Online access to criminal cases and traffic is free at www.sbcounty.gov/courts/genInfo/openaccess.htm . Includes calendars. Also, the daily criminal docket is free at the court main website. Mail turnaround time 2-5 days.

General Information: No public access terminal. No probation reports or police records released. Certification fee: $6.60 per doc. Payee: Fontana Courts. Personal checks accepted. Prepayment and SASE required.

Needles District - Superior Court
1111 Bailey Ave, Needles, CA 92363; phone: 760-326-9245; fax: 760-326-9254; hours 8AM-4PM (PST). *Felony, Misdemeanor, Civil Actions Under $25,000, Eviction, Small Claims.*

www.sbcounty.gov/courts

Civil Records: Access: Mail, in person, online. Only the court performs in person searches; visitors may not. Search fee: $5.00 per name. Court makes copy: $.50 per page. Required to search: name, years to search. Civil cases indexed by plaintiff. Civil records in index books. Will only search back 7 years. Online access to civil cases is free at www.sbcounty.gov/courts/genInfo/openaccess.htm . Includes calendars. Daily calendars also at main website. Mail turnaround time 1-2 weeks.

Criminal Records: Access: Mail, in person, online. Only the court performs in person searches; visitors may not. Search fee: $5.00 per name. Court makes copy: $.50 per page. Required to search: name, years to search. Criminal records on computer from 1990, index books prior. Will only search back 7 years. Access to criminal cases and traffic is free at www.sbcounty.gov/courts/genInfo/openaccess.htm . Includes calendars. Also, the daily criminal docket is free at the court main website. Mail turnaround time 1-2 weeks.

General Information: No probation reports released. Will not fax documents. Certification fee: $6.60 per doc. Payee: Superior Court. Personal checks accepted. Prepayment and SASE required.

Redlands District - Superior Court
216 Brookside Ave, Redlands, CA 92373; criminal phone: 909-885-1269; civil phone: 909-888-4260; fax: 909-798-8588; hours 8AM-4PM (PST). *Traffic Misdemeanor, Eviction, Small Claims.*

www.sbcounty.gov/courts/

Note: All felonies and non-traffic misdemeanors filed at Central Dist. Court. This Court's district includes Redlands, Yucaipa and unincorporated areas of

Angeles Oaks, Barton Flats, Colton, Forest Home, Grand Terrace, Highland, Loma Linda and Mentone.

Civil Records: Access: Mail, in person. Visitors must perform in person searches themselves. Search fee: $5.00 per name. Court makes copy: $.50 per page. Required to search: name, years to search. Civil cases indexed by defendant, plaintiff. Civil records on computer from 1991, index books prior. Records destroyed after 10 years. Daily calendars at main website. Note: All evictions records for Riverside and Redlands are managed here. Mail turnaround time 2 days.

Criminal Records: Access: Mail, in person, online. Visitors must perform in person searches themselves. Search fee: $5.00 per name. Court makes copy: $.50 per page. Required to search: name, years to search, DOB. Criminal records on computer from 1998, index books prior. Records destroyed after 10 years. Access to criminal cases and traffic is free at www.sbcounty.gov/courts/genInfo/openaccess.htm Includes calendars. Also, the daily criminal docket is free at the court main website. Mail turnaround time 2 days.

General Information: Public access terminal goes back to 1998. No probation reports released. Will not fax documents. Exemplified copy $20.00. Certification fee: $6.60 per doc. Payee: Superior Court. Prepayment and SASE required.

Twin Peaks District - Superior Court PO Box 394, 26010 State Hwy 189, Twin Peaks, CA 92391; phone: 909-336-0620; fax: 909-336-0683; hours 8AM-4:30PM Monday only (PST). *Traffic Misdemeanor, Civil under $25,000, Eviction, Small Claims.*

www.sbcounty.gov/courts/
Note: Felony and misdemeanors are now heard at the San Bernardino District Courthouse. For information on Twin Peaks cases Tuesdays to Fridays, call the San Bernardino District Courthouse.

Civil Records: Access: Mail, in person, online. Both court and visitors may perform in person searches. Search fee: $5.00 per name per year. Court makes copy: $.50 per page. Required to search: name, years to search. Civil cases indexed by defendant, plaintiff. Civil records on index cards. Will only search back 7 years. Online access to civil cases is free at www.sbcounty.gov/courts/genInfo/openaccess.htm . Includes calendars. Daily calendars also at main website. Mail turnaround time 1 week.

Criminal Records: Access: Mail, in person, online. Both court and visitors may perform in person searches. Search fee: $5.00 per name per year. Court makes copy: $.50 per page. Required to search: name, years to search, DOB. Criminal records on computer from 1990, index cards prior. Will only search back 7 years. Online access to criminal traffic is free at www.sbcounty.gov/courts/genInfo/openaccess.htm . Includes calendars. Also, the daily criminal docket is free at the court main website. Mail turnaround time 1 week.

General Information: Public access terminal goes back to 1998. No probation or arrest reports released. Will not fax documents. Certification fee: $6.60 per doc. Payee: Superior Court. No personal checks accepted. SASE required.

San Diego County

Superior Court - Civil PO Box 120128, 330 W Broadway, Hall of Justice, San Diego, CA 92112-0128; civil phone: 619-531-3141; probate phone: 619-236-3781; hours 8:30AM-4:30PM (PST). *Civil, Probate, Eviction, Small Claims, Probate.*

www.sdcourt.ca.gov
Note: Now has Central Division Limited Jurisdiction civil cases. For any San Diego County requests, always specify which division - Central, East, North or South. Probate is located at the Madge Bradley Bldg, 1409 4th Ave, 92101.

Civil Records: Access: Mail, in person, online. Both court and visitors may perform in person searches. Search fee: $5.00 per name. Court makes copy: $.50 per page. Required to search: name, years to search.

Civil cases indexed by defendant, plaintiff. Civil records index on computer from 6/74. The court sells a county-wide CD-ROM of civil, domestic, mental health, and probate indices, generally from 1974 to 1999. Online searching for case information and calendars is free at www.sdcourt.ca.gov/. Mail turnaround time 1 day.

General Information: Public access terminal has civil records. No probation reports released. Will not fax documents. Certification fee: $6.60 per doc. Payee: Clerk of Superior Court. Personal checks accepted. Prepayment and SASE required.

Superior Court - Criminal PO Box 120128 (220 W Broadway), San Diego, CA 92112-0128; phone: 619-531-3040 Misdemeanor; hours 8:30AM-4:30PM (PST). *Felony, Misdemeanor.*

www.sdcourt.ca.gov/
Note: Both General and Limited Criminal records are located here.

Criminal Records: Access: Mail, in person, online. Both court and visitors may perform in person searches. Search fee: $5.00 per name. Fee is per index. Court makes copy: $.50 per page. Required to search: name, years to search, DOB. Criminal records on computer from 1974 to present, paper ledgers from 1860s. The county sells a CD-ROM of criminal records; felonies from 6/1974 to 1999; misdemeanors back 10 years. Online searching for case information and calendars is free at www.sdcourt.ca.gov/. Mail turnaround time 1 week.

General Information: Public access terminal has criminal records back to 25 yrs for felony, 10 yrs for misd. No adoptions, juvenile, medical, probation or sealed records released. Will not fax documents. Certification fee: $6.60 per doc. Payee: San Diego Superior Court. No out of state personal checks. Prepayment and SASE required.

East County Division - Superior Court 250 E Main St, El Cajon, CA 92020; phone: 619-441-4100; criminal phone: 619-441-4342; civil phone: 619-441-4461; hours 8AM-4:30PM (PST). *Felony, Misdemeanor, Civil, Small Claims, Eviction.*

www.sdcourt.ca.gov/
Note: Court now houses the former municipal court records. Includes El Cajon, La Mesa, Lemon Grove, Santee and unincorporated towns of Alpine, Boulevard, Campo, Dulzura, Grossmont, Jacumba, Jamul, Julian, Lakeside, Mesa Grande, Ramona, Spring Valley, Tecate.

Civil Records: Access: Mail, in person, online. Both court and visitors may perform in person searches. Search fee: $5.00 per name. Court makes copy: $.50 per page. Required to search: name, years to search. Civil cases indexed by defendant, plaintiff. Civil records on computer since 1974; microfilm prior. Online searching for case information and calendars is free at www.sdcourt.ca.gov/. Also, there is a free party name case search at www.sandiego.courts.ca.gov:8080/CISPublic/enter . Mail turnaround time 3-5 days.

Criminal Records: Access: Mail, in person, online. Both court and visitors may perform in person searches. Search fee: $5.00 per name. Court makes copy: $.50 per page. Required to search: name, years to search; also helpful: DOB. Criminal records on computer since 1974; microfilm prior. The county system sells a CD-ROM of criminal records; felonies from 6/1974 to 1999; misdemeanors back 10 years. Online searching for case information and calendars is free at www.sdcourt.ca.gov/. Mail turnaround time 3-5 days.

General Information: Public access terminal available. Certification fee: $6.60 per doc. Payee: Clerk of Superior Court. Personal checks accepted. Law firm and Calif. checks with preprinted name and address only. Prepayment and SASE required.

North County Branch - Superior Court 325 S Melrose Dr, Vista, CA 92081; phone: 760-726-9595; probate phone: 760-806-6150; hours 8:30AM-4:30PM (PST). *Felony, Misdemeanor, Civil Actions, Eviction, Small Claims, Probate.*

www.sdcourt.ca.gov/
Note: Includes Cities of Oceanside, Del Mar, Carlsbad, Solana Beach, Encinitas, Escondido, San Marcos, Vista and unincorporated towns of Del Dios, Olivehain, San Luis Rey, San Pasqual, Rancho Santa Fe, Valley Ctr., Bonsall, Palomar Mt., Borrego Spr., Pala, etc.

Civil Records: Access: Mail, in person, online. Both court and visitors may perform in person searches. Search fee: $5.00 per name. Court makes copy: $.50 per page. Required to search: name, years to search. Civil cases indexed by defendant, plaintiff. Civil records on computer back to 1993; prior on microfiche and index books. Online searching for case information and calendars is free at www.sdcourt.ca.gov/. Mail turnaround time 2-3 days.

Criminal Records: Access: Mail, in person, online. Both court and visitors may perform in person searches. Search fee: $5.00 per name. Court makes copy: $.50 per page. Required to search: name, years to search. Criminal records on computer back to 1993; prior on microfiche and index books. The county system sells a CD-ROM of criminal records; felonies from 6/1974 to 1999; misdemeanors back 10 years. Online searching for case information and calendars is free at www.sdcourt.ca.gov/. Mail turnaround time 2-3 days.

General Information: Public access terminal goes back to 10 years. No sealed or confidential documents released. Certification fee: $6.60 per doc. Payee: Clerk of the Superior Court. Personal checks accepted. Out of state checks not accepted. Prepayment and SASE required.

South County Branch - Superior Court 500-C 3rd Ave, Chula Vista, CA 91910; criminal phone: 619-691-4726; civil phone: 619-691-4439; criminal records fax: 619-691-4864; civil records fax: 619-691-4969; hours 8:30AM-4:30PM (PST). *Felony, Misdemeanor, Civil Actions, Probate, Eviction, Small Claims.*

www.sdcourt.ca.gov/
Note: Includes National City, Chula Vista, Coronado, Imperial Beach and that portion of the City of San Diego lying south of the City of Chula Vista and contiguous unincorporated areas. Family phone is 619-691-4875

Civil Records: Access: Fax, mail, in person, online. Both court and visitors may perform in person searches. Search fee: $5.00 per name per year. Court makes copy: $.50 per page. Required to search: name, years to search. Civil cases indexed by defendant, plaintiff. Civil records on computer; for case files prior to 1991, contact Superior Court's Main Records Division, Downtown. Online searching for case information and calendars is free at www.sdcourt.ca.gov/. Mail turnaround time up to 1 week (civil) or depends on availability of clerk (criminal).

Criminal Records: Access: Phone, fax, mail, in person, online. Both court and visitors may perform in person searches. Search fee: $5.00 per name. Court makes copy: $.50 per page. Required to search: name, years to search, DOB. Criminal records on computer, cases files in or before 1986 on microfiche. The county system sells a CD-ROM of criminal records; felonies from 6/1974 to 1999; misdemeanors back 10 years. Online searching for case information and calendars is free at www.sdcourt.ca.gov/. Mail turnaround time up to 1 week (civil) or depends on availability of clerk (criminal).

General Information: Public access terminal goes back to 10 years. Certification fee: $6.60 per doc. Payee: Superior Court (Civil)-Clerk of the Court (Criminal). Personal checks accepted. Prepayment and SASE required.

Kearny Mesa Branch - Central Division
8950 Clairemont Mesa Blvd, San Diego, CA 92123; phone: 858-694-2066 Small Claims; fax: 858-694-2252; hours 8AM-4PM (PST). *Small Claims, Traffic, Infractions.*
www.sdcourt.ca.gov/
Note: Traffic phone is 858-565-1006. Some minor infractions are heard at this court.

Ramona Branch - East Division 1428
Montecito Rd, Ramona, CA 92065; phone: 760-738-2435; hours 8AM-4:30PM (PST). *Misdemeanor, Civil Actions Under $25,000, Eviction, Small Claims.*
www.sdcourt.ca.gov/
Note: Jurisdiction over the northeast area of the county. Closed noon to 1PM T, W, TH.

Civil Records: Access: Mail, in person, online. Only the court performs in person searches; visitors may not. Search fee: $5.00 per name. Court makes copy: $.50 per page. Required to search: name, years to search. Civil cases indexed by defendant, plaintiff. Civil records on computer from 1991, index files since 1983. Files destroyed after 10 years. Online searching for case information and calendars is free at www.sdcourt.ca.gov/. Mail turnaround time 2-3 days.
Criminal Records: Access: Mail, in person, online. Only the court performs in person searches; visitors may not. Search fee: $5.00 per name. Court makes copy: $.50 per page. Required to search: name, years to search, SSN; also helpful: DOB. Criminal records on computer from 1991, index files since 1983. Files destroyed after 10 years. The county system sells a CD-ROM of criminal records; felonies from 6/1974 to 1999; misdemeanors back 10 years. Online searching for case information and calendars is free at www.sdcourt.ca.gov/. Mail turnaround time 2-3 days.
General Information: No probation reports or DMV records released. Will not fax documents. Certification fee: $6.60. Payee: Clerk of the Court. Personal checks or Visa, MC accepted. Prepayment and SASE required.

San Marcos Branch - North Divison, CA.
Misdemeanor, Traffic.
Note: On July 14th 2003, they moved into the Superior Court at 325 S Melrose Dr, #350, Annex Bldg, Vista CA 92081.

San Francisco County

Superior Court - Criminal Division 850
Bryant St, Rm 201, Hall of Justice, San Francisco, CA 94107/94103; phone: 415-553-9394; hours 8AM-4:30PM (PST). *Felony.*
www.sftc.org
Note: Misdemeanor records dept.-415-553-1665. Court Mgr-415-553-1897.
Criminal Records: Access: Mail, in person. Both court and visitors may perform in person searches. Search fee: $5.00 per name per year. Add warehouse retrieval fee of $5.00 for archived records. Court makes copy: $1.00 per page. Required to search: name, years to search, DOB. Note: If searching by mail, direct your request to "Prior Convictions" Mail turnaround time 1 week.
General Information: No public access terminal. No medical, probation or sealed records released. No fee to fax documents if prepaid. Certification fee: $6.60 per doc. Payee: Clerk of the Superior Court. Personal checks accepted with ID. Cashier checks and money orders accepted. Prepayment and SASE required.

Superior Court - Civil Division 400
McAllister St, #103, San Francisco, CA 94102; phone: 415-551-4000 (general info); civil phone: 415-551-3888; probate phone: 415-551-3892; hours 8AM-3PM M-F (PST). *Civil, Small Claims, Eviction, Probate.*
http://sfgov.org/site/courts_index.asp

Civil Records: Access: Mail, in person, online. Both court and visitors may perform in person searches. Search fee: $5.00 per name per year. Court makes copy: $1.00 per page. Required to search: name, years to search. Civil records indexed by defendant, plaintiff. Civil records on computer since 1987 for unlimited jurisdiction; 1992 for Limited jurisdiction; prior records on microfilm and microfiche. For pre-1987 records, contact: Research at 415-551-3813. Online access to the case management system is free at www.sftc.org but does not include family law or small claims. Also, access probate case data free at www.sftc.org/browser_pages/Probate/probate_frame.htm. Click on "Probate Case View." Mail turnaround time 2-3 weeks; in person turnaround is 5 days.
General Information: Public access terminal has civil records back to 1987. No medical, probation or sealed records released without court order. Will not fax documents. Certification fee: $6.60 per doc. Payee: San Francisco Superior Court. Personal checks or Visa, MC accepted. Prepayment and SASE required.

Limited Superior - Civil Division 400
McAllister St, #103, San Francisco, CA 94102; phone: 415-551-3802 records section; civil phone: 415-551-4000; fax: 415-551-3801; hours 8AM-4:30PM; 8AM-3PM Wed (PST). *Civil Actions Under $25,000, Eviction, Small Claims.* www.sftc.org
Note: Includes all of San Francisco County, including former municipal court on Folsom St.
Civil Records: Access: Mail, in person, online. Both court and visitors may perform in person searches. Search fee: $5.00 per name per year. No charge if easily pulled from computer - after 1987. Court makes copy: $1.00 per page. Required to search: name, years to search. Civil cases indexed by defendant, plaintiff. Civil records on computer from 1991, index files from 1983. Records destroyed after 10 years. Online access to the case management system is free at www.sftc.org but does not include family law or small claims. Mail turnaround time 2 days.
General Information: Public access terminal has civil records back to 1991. No sealed records released. Will not fax documents. Certification fee: $6.60 per document. Payee: Superior Court. Personal checks accepted. Prepayment and SASE required.

Superior Court - Misdemeanor Division
850 Bryant St, Rm 101, Records Section, San Francisco, CA 94103; phone: 415-553-1665 (Records Dept); criminal phone: 415-553-9395; hours 8AM-4:30PM (PST). *Misdemeanor.*
www.ci.sf.ca.us/courts
Note: Includes all San Francisco County.
Criminal Records: Access: Mail, in person, online. Both court and visitors may perform in person searches. Search fee: $5.00 per name per year. Court makes copy: $1.00 per page. Microfilm copies $1.50 per page. Required to search: name, years to search; also helpful: DOB. Criminal records (pending) on computer from 1991, index files from 1983. Records are destroyed after 10 years. Online access to the case management system is free at www.sftc.org. Mail turnaround time 3-4 weeks.
General Information: No public access terminal. No probation reports released. Certification fee: $1.75. Payee: Superior Court. Personal checks accepted. Prepayment and SASE required.

San Joaquin County

Superior Court - Civil 222 E Weber Ave, Rm 303, Stockton, CA 95202-2709; phone: 209-468-2355; civil phone: 209-468-2933; probate phone: 209-468-2843; fax: 209-468-0539; hours 7:30AM-4PM-office; 8AM-5PM -phones (PST). *Civil Actions, Eviction, Small Claims, Probate.*
www.stocktoncourt.org/courts/
Note: Includes City of Stockton and suburban areas Farmington and Linden, Delta area and surrounding unincorporated areas

Civil Records: Access: Mail, in person, online. Both court and visitors may perform in person searches. Search fee: $5.00 per name. No fee if search is done by customer. Court makes copy: $.50 per page. Required to search: name, years to search. Civil cases indexed by defendant, plaintiff. Civil records on computer from 1996; indices/books from 1850-1977; Microfiche 1977-1996. Records destroyed after 10 years. Free access to civil case summaries, with name searching, at www.stocktoncourt.org/courts/caseinfo.htm. Also, access court calendars free at www.stocktoncourt.org/stkcrtwwwV5web/SCCalDayIndex.html. Mail turnaround time 5-7 days.
General Information: Public access terminal has civil records back to 1996. No probation, confidential records released. Will not fax documents. Certification fee: $6.60 per doc. Payee: Superior Court. Personal checks accepted. Prepayment and SASE required.

Superior Court - Criminal Division 222 E Weber Ave, Rm 101, Stockton, CA 95202; phone: 209-468-2935; fax: 209-468-8577; hours 7:30AM-4PM (PST). *Felony, Misdemeanor.*
www.stocktoncourt.org/courts
Criminal Records: Access: Mail, fax, in person, online. Both court and visitors may perform in person searches. Search fee: $5.00 per name. Court makes copy: $.50 per page. Required to search: name, years to search; also helpful: DOB, SSN. Criminal Records on computer since 1991, on microfiche since 1972, older records archived to 1800s. Access criminal case summaries free at www.stocktoncourt.org/courts/caseinfo.htm. Also, access court calendars free at www.stocktoncourt.org/stkcrtwwwV5web/SCCalDayIndex.html. Mail turnaround time 1-2 weeks.
General Information: Public access terminal has criminal records back to 1991. No juvenile, medical, probation, sealed records released. Certification fee: $6.60 per doc. Payee: San Joaquin Superior Court. Personal checks accepted. Prepayment and SASE required.

Lodi Division - Superior Court - Civil 315
W Elm St, Lodi, CA 95240; phone: 209-331-2101; fax: 209-331-2133; hours 8AM-4PM (PST). *Misdemeanor Traffic, Civil Actions Under $25,000, Eviction, Small Claims.*
www.stocktoncourt.org/courts/
Note: Includes City of Lodi, eight mile road to Sacramento County line, towns of Acampo, Clements, Lockeford, Terminous, Thornton, Woodbridge.
Civil Records: Access: Phone, mail, fax, in person, online. Both court and visitors may perform in person searches. Search fee: $5.00 per name. Court makes copy: $.50 per page. Required to search: name, years to search. Civil cases indexed by defendant, plaintiff. Civil records on computer from 1994, index files from 1989. Records destroyed after 10 years. Free access to civil case summaries, with name searching, at www.stocktoncourt.org/courts/caseinfo.htm. Also, access court calendars free at www.stocktoncourt.org/stkcrtwwwV5web/SCCalDayIndex.html. Mail turnaround time 5 days.
General Information: No public access terminal. No probation reports released. Will not fax documents. Certification fee: $6.60 per doc. Payee: Superior Court. Personal checks accepted. Prepayment and SASE required.

Lodi Division - Superior Court - Criminal
230 W Elm St, Lodi, CA; phone: 209-331-2121; fax: 209-331-2135; hours 8AM-4PM (PST). *Felony, Misdemeanor.*
www.stocktoncourt.org/courts/
Note: Includes City of Lodi, eight mile road to Sacramento County line, towns of Acampo, Clements, Lockeford, Terminous, Thornton, Woodbridge.
Criminal Records: Access: Phone, mail, fax, in person, online. Both court and visitors may perform in person searches. Search fee: $5.00 per name.

Court makes copy: $.50 per page. Required to search: name, years to search, DOB; also helpful: address, SSN, sex. Criminal records on computer from 1991, index files from 1983. Records destroyed after 10 years. Access criminal case summaries free at www.stocktoncourt.org/courts/caseinfo.htm. Also, access court calendars free at www.stocktoncourt.org/stkcrtwwwV5web/SCCal DayIndex.html. Mail turnaround time 5 days.

General Information: Public access terminal has criminal records back to 1991. No probation reports released. Will not fax documents. Certification fee: $6.60 per doc. Payee: Superior Court. Personal checks accepted. Prepayment and SASE required.

Manteca Branch - Superior Court
315 E Center St, Manteca, CA 95336; criminal phone: 209-239-1316; civil phone: 209-239-9188; hours 8AM-4PM (PST). *Felony, Misdemeanor, Civil Actions Under $25,000, Eviction, Small Claims.* www.stocktoncourt.org/courts/

Note: Includes Cities of Manteca, Ripon, Escalon, French Camp, Lathrop and surrounding unincorporated areas.

Civil Records: Access: Mail, in person, online. Only the court performs in person searches; visitors may not. Search fee: $5.00 per name. Court makes copy: $.50 per page. Required to search: name, years to search. Civil cases indexed by defendant, plaintiff. Records on microfiche since 1986, index files from 1983. Records destroyed after 10 years. Free access to civil case summaries, with name searching, at www.stocktoncourt.org/courts/caseinfo.htm. Also, access court calendars free at www.stocktoncourt.org/stkcrtwwwV5web/SCCal DayIndex.html. Mail turnaround time 1-2 days.

Criminal Records: Access: Mail, in person, online. Only the court performs in person searches; visitors may not. Search fee: $5.00 per name. Court makes copy: $.50 per page. Required to search: name, years to search; also helpful: DOB. Criminal records on computer since 1990, microfiche since 1986, index files from 1983. Records destroyed after 10 years. Access criminal case summaries free at www.stocktoncourt.org/courts/caseinfo.htm. Also, access court calendars at www.stocktoncourt.or g/stkcrtwwwV5web/SCCalDayIndex.html. Note: Use of special request form required to view files in person. Mail turnaround time 1-2 days.

General Information: No judge's notes, probation or police reports released. Certification fee: $6.60 per doc. Payee: Superior Court. Personal checks accepted. Prepayment and SASE required.

Tracy Branch - Superior Court
475 E 10th St, Tracy, CA 95376; criminal phone: 209-831-5900; civil phone: 209-831-5902; fax: 209-831-5919; hours 8AM-4PM (PST). *Felony, Misdemeanor, Civil Actions Under $25,000, Eviction, Small Claims.* www.stocktoncourt.org/courts/

Note: Includes Cities of Tracy, Banta, portion of Vernalis and surrounding unincorporated area.

Civil Records: Access: Phone, mail, in person, online. Only the court performs in person searches; visitors may not. Search fee: $5.00 per name. If on computer, no charge. Court makes copy: $.50 per page. Required to search: name, years to search. Civil cases indexed by defendant, plaintiff. Civil records on computer since 3/95; on index files from 1983. Records destroyed after 10 years. Free access to civil case summaries, with name searching, at www.stocktoncourt.org/courts/caseinfo.htm. Also, access court calendars free at www.stocktoncourt.org/stkcrtwwwV5web/SCCal DayIndex.html. Mail turnaround time 5-10 days.

Criminal Records: Access: Mail, in person, online. Only the court performs in person searches; visitors may not. Search fee: $5.00 per name. Court makes copy: $.50 per page. Required to search: name, years to search, DOB. Criminal records on computer from 1991; on index files from 1983. Records destroyed after 10 years. Access criminal case summaries free at www.stocktoncourt.org/co urts/caseinfo.htm. Also, access court calendars at

www.stocktoncourt.org/stkcrtwwwV5web/SCCal DayIndex.html. Mail turnaround time 5-10 days.

General Information: No probation reports, DMV history and criminal history records released. Will not fax documents. Certification fee: $6.60 per doc. Payee: Tracy Superior Court. Personal checks accepted. Prepayment and SASE required.

San Luis Obispo County

Superior Court - Civil Division
1035 Palm St, Rm 385, Government Ctr, San Luis Obispo, CA 93408; phone: 805-781-5677; probate phone: 805-781-5242; hours 8:30AM-4PM (PST). *Civil Actions, Small Claims, Eviction, Probate, Family Law.* www.slocourts.net

Note: This Court has jurisdiction over all of San Luis Obispo County for Civil actions over $25,000, and also the current and former "limited jurisdiction" (under $25,000) civil cases and small claims in the immediate area.

Civil Records: Access: Mail, in person. Both court and visitors may perform in person searches. Search fee: $5.00 per name. Court makes copy: $1.00 per page. Required to search: name, years to search. Civil cases indexed by defendant, plaintiff. Civil records on computer from 1975, index files from 1865. Records destroyed after 10 years. Access daily calendars from their website. Mail turnaround time 2-5 days.

General Information: Public access terminal has civil records. No probation reports released. Will not fax documents. Certification fee: $6.60 per doc. Payee: Superior Court. Personal checks accepted. Prepayment and SASE required.

Superior Court - Criminal Division
Government Center, Rm 220, 1050 Monterey St., San Luis Obispo, CA 93408; phone: 805-781-5670; hours 8:30AM-4PM (PST). *Felony, Misdemeanor.* www.slocourts.net

Criminal Records: Access: Mail, in person. Both court and visitors may perform in person searches. Search fee: $5.00 per name. Court makes copy: $1.00 per page. Required to search: name, years to search. Criminal records on computer and microfiche from 1975, archived and index felony files from late 1800s. Access daily calendars from their website. Note: A "11 search" is for 1985 to present for Misd, felonies, and non-traffic infractions; a name search of 1975-1985 misd. Records is a "10 search,' or a electronic felony index 1975-1995. Mail turnaround time 7-10 days.

General Information: Public access terminal has criminal records back to 1975-felony; 1985-misdemeanors. No adoptions, juvenile, medical, probation or sealed records released. Will not fax documents. Certification fee: $6.60 per doc. Payee: Superior Court Criminal Court Operations. Personal checks accepted. Prepayment and SASE required.

Grover Beach Branch - Superior Court
214 S 16th St, Grover Beach, CA 93433-2299; criminal phone: 805-473-7072; civil phone: 805-473-7077; hours 8:30AM-4PM (PST). *Misdemeanor, Civil Actions Under $25,000, Eviction, Small Claims.* www.slocourts.net

Note: Includes Nipomo, Grover Beach, Arroyo Grande, Pismo Beach, Oceano, South Coast unincorporated areas.

Civil Records: Access: Phone, mail, in person. Both court and visitors may perform in person searches. Search fee: First name is free, then $5.00 per name. Court makes copy: $1.00 per page. Required to search: name, years to search. Civil cases indexed by defendant, plaintiff. Civil records on index cards to 1976; on computer back to 1986. Records destroyed after 10 years. Access daily calendar from their website. Mail turnaround time 2-3 weeks if civil; 1 week if criminal.

Criminal Records: Access: Phone, mail, in person. Both court and visitors may perform in person searches. Search fee: First name is free, then $5.00 per name. Court makes copy: $1.00 per page.

Required to search: name, years to search. Criminal records on index cards to 1976; on computer back to 1986. Records destroyed after 10 years. Access daily calendar from their website. Mail turnaround time 2-3 weeks if civil; 1 week if criminal.

General Information: Public access terminal goes back to 10 years. No probation reports released. Will not fax documents. Certification fee: $6.60 per doc. Payee: Superior Court. Personal checks accepted. Prepayment and SASE required.

Paso Robles Branch - Superior Court
549 10th St, Paso Robles, CA 93446-2593; criminal phone: 805-237-3080; civil phone: 805-237-3079; hours 8:30AM-4PM (PST). *Misdemeanor, Civil Actions Under $25,000, Eviction, Small Claims.* www.slocourts.net/

Note: Includes Atascadero, Templeton, Paso Robles, San Miguel, Shandon, Cholame, areas north and east of the Cuesta Grade.

Civil Records: Access: Phone, mail, in person. Both court and visitors may perform in person searches. Search fee: $5.00 per name. Search is free if only one name. Court makes copy: $1.00 per page. Required to search: name, years to search. Civil cases indexed by defendant, plaintiff. Civil records on computer from 1975, index files from 1983. Records destroyed after 10 years. Access daily calendar from their website. Note: Mail requests limited to 5 at a time. Mail turnaround time 1-2 days.

Criminal Records: Access: Phone, mail, in person. Both court and visitors may perform in person searches. Search fee: $5.00. Search is free for only one name. Court makes copy: $1.00 per page. Required to search: name, years to search; also helpful: DOB. Criminal records on computer from 1975, index files from 1983. Records destroyed after 10 years. Access daily calendar from their website. Note: Mail requests limited to 5 at a time. Mail turnaround time 1-2 days.

General Information: Public access terminal goes back to 10 years. No driving histories, rap sheets, sealed or probation reports released. Certification fee: $6.60 per doc. Payee: Superior Court. Personal checks accepted. Prepayment and SASE required.

San Mateo County

Superior Court
400 County Center, Redwood City, CA 94063; criminal phone: 650-363-4302; civil phone: 650-363-4711; probate phone: 650-363-4711; fax: 650-363-4914; hours 8AM-4PM (PST). *Felony, Civil Actions Over $25,000, Probate.* www.sanmateocourt.org

Note: Southern Area Limited Criminal, lower-value civil actions, evictions and small claims are also located here.

Civil Records: Access: Mail, in person, online. Both court and visitors may perform in person searches. Search fee: $5.00 per name. Court makes copy: $.75 per page per side. Required to search: name, years to search. Civil cases indexed by defendant, plaintiff. Civil records and Family Law on computer from 1978; index books prior. Online access to civil, probate, family and small claims records is free at www.sanmateocourt.org. Click on "Access Public Court Records Online." Mail turnaround time 1 week.

Criminal Records: Access: Mail, in person, online. Both court and visitors may perform in person searches. Search fee: $5.00 per name. Court makes copy: $.75 per page per side. Required to search: name, years to search; also helpful: address, DOB, SSN. Criminal records on computer since 1964; prior on books. Criminal matters only filed by Belmont, Foster City, Half Moon Bay, San Carlos, Menlo Pk, East Palo Alto and unincorporated areas are heard at the Southern Branch. Search all types of county case records including criminal for free at www.sanmateocourt.org/midx/searchform4_tim.p hp. Mail turnaround time 1 week.

General Information: Public access terminal has criminal back to 1964 and civil back to 1978. (Probate records to 1972.) No confidential jackets on conservatorships & guardianships, adoptions, juvenile, medical, probation or sealed records released. Certification fee: $6.60 per doc. Payee: Superior Court. Personal checks accepted. Prepayment and SASE required.

Northern Branch - Superior Court 1050

Mission Rd, South San Francisco, CA 94080; phone: 650-877-5773; criminal phone: 650-877-5771; civil phone: 650-877-5705; criminal records fax: 650-877-5703; civil records fax: 650-615--0875; hours 8AM-4PM *Misdemeanor, Small Claims, Traffic.* www.sanmateocourt.org

Note: Includes Brisbane, Daly City (including Westlake), Pacifica, San Bruno, South San Francisco, the northern coastal towns and all unincorporated areas in the north end of the county including Colma, Bart and Broadmoor. Small Claims phone is 650-877-5778.

Civil Records: Access: Mail, in person, online. Both court and visitors may perform in person searches. Search fee: $5.00 per name. Court makes copy: $.75 per page. Required to search: name, years to search. Civil cases indexed by defendant, plaintiff. Civil records go back to 1978 by name index. Online access to civil, probate, family and small claims records is free at www.sanmateocourt.org. Click on Open Access. Note: Probate filings are accepted here, but there are no records to search here. Mail turnaround time 2 days to 2 weeks.

Criminal Records: Access: Mail, in person, online. Both court and visitors may perform in person searches. Search fee: $5.00 per name. Court makes copy: $.75 per page. Required to search: name, years to search; also helpful: DOB. Criminal records on computer back to 1991, index files from 1983. Records destroyed after 10 years. Search all types of county case records including criminal for free at www.sanmateocourt.org/midx/searchform4_tim.php. Also, search traffic citations at https://www.sanmateocourt.org/traffic/. Mail turnaround time 2 days to 2 weeks.

General Information: Public access terminal has criminal back to 1964 and civil back to 1978. No probation reports or confidential information records released. Will fax documents to local or toll free line. Certification fee: $6.60 per doc. Payee: Superior Court. Personal checks accepted. Prepayment and SASE required.

San Mateo Central Branch 800 N Humboldt

St, San Mateo, CA 94401; phone: 650-573-2628; 650-573-2616 Traf.; fax: 650-342-5438; hours 8AM-4PM (PST). *Small Claims, Traffic, Infractions.*

www.sanmateocourt.org offers online access to court records; click on "Access Public Court Records Online." Also, search traffic citations at https://www.sanmateocourt.org/traffic/. Note: Small claims phone is 650-573-2628. Includes small claims for Belmont, Burlingame, El Granada, Foster City, Half Moon Bay, Hillsborough, Millbrae, Miramar, Montara, Moss Beach, San Mateo and adjoining unincorporated areas.

Superior Court - Southern Branch 400

County Center, Redwood City, CA 94063; criminal phone: 650-363-4302; civil phone: 650-363-4576; hours 8AM-4PM (PST). *Misdemeanor, Civil, Eviction, Small Claims.*
www.sanmateocourt.org

Note: Limited Criminal - Includes Atherton, Belmont, Foster City, Half Moon Bay, Menlo Park, Portola Valley, Redwood City, San Carlos, Woodside, East Palo Alto and unincorporated areas including La Honda, Pescadera, and San Gregorio.

Civil Records: Access: Mail, in person, online. Both court and visitors may perform in person searches. Search fee: $5.00 per name. Court makes copy: $.75 per page. Required to search: name, years to search. Civil cases indexed by defendant, plaintiff. Civil Records on computer since 1978. Online access to civil and small claims records is free at www.sanmateocourt.org. Click on "Access Public

Court Records Online." Mail turnaround time 2 weeks.

Criminal Records: Access: Mail, in person, online. Both court and visitors may perform in person searches. Search fee: $5.00 per name. Court makes copy: $.75 per page. Required to search: name, years to search. Limited Criminal records on computer from 1991, index files from 1983. Records destroyed after 10 years. Search all types of county case records including criminal for free at www.sanmateocourt.org/midx/searchform4_tim.php. Also, search traffic citations at https://www.sanmateocourt.org/traffic/. Note: Only limited criminal cases for the Southern District can be found at this location. Mail turnaround time 2 weeks.

General Information: Public access terminal has criminal back to 1991 and civil back to 1978. No probation reports or confidential information records released. Certification fee: $6.60 per doc. Payee: Superior Court. Personal checks accepted. Write "not to exceed $x.xx" on check. Visa/MC accepted. Credit card accepted in person only. Prepayment and SASE required.

Santa Barbara County

Superior Court - Civil - Anacapa

Division Box 21107, 1100 Anacapa St, Santa Barbara, CA 93121; phone: 805-568-2220; criminal phone: 805-568-2753; civil phone: 805-568-2238; fax: 805-568-2219; hours 8AM-4PM; closed on mandatory furlough days; call for dates (PST). *Civil Actions, Eviction, Small Claims, Probate.*
www.sbcourts.org/index.asp

Note: Also known as the Anacapa Division. Includes the City of Santa Barbara, Goleta, and adjacent unincorporated areas, Carpenteria and Montecito. Daily calendars free at www.sbcourts.org/pubcal/.

Civil Records: Access: Phone, fax, mail, in person. Both court and visitors may perform in person searches. Search fee: $5.00 per name. Court makes copy: $.75 per page. Required to search: name, years to search. Civil cases indexed by defendant, plaintiff. Civil records on computer and microfiche from 1975, archived and index file from 1920. Mail turnaround time 1 week.

General Information: Public access terminal has civil records. No adoptions, juvenile, medical, probation or sealed records released. A CD-Rom of monthly court indices from all divisions is for $40.00. Certification fee: $6.60 per doc; marriage dissolution $10.00. Payee: Superior Court. Personal checks or Visa, MC accepted. Prepayment and SASE required.

Superior Court - Criminal - Figueroa

Division 118 E Figueroa St, Santa Barbara, CA 93101; phone: 805-568-2735; criminal phone: 805-568-2778; fax: 805-568-3208; hours 7:45AM-4PM; closed on mandatory furlough days; call for dates (PST). *Felony, Misdemeanor.*
www.sbcourts.org/index.asp

Note: Includes the City of Santa Barbara, Goleta and adjacent unincorporated areas, Carpentaria, Montecito. For civil cases call Anacapa Division at 805-568-2220. Daily calendars free at www.sbcourts.org/pubcal/.

Criminal Records: Access: Mail, in person. Both court and visitors may perform in person searches. Search fee: $5.00 per name. Court makes copy: $.75 per page. Required to search: name, years to search; also helpful: DOB. Criminal records on computer from 1991, index files from 1983, microfiche from 1975. Records destroyed after 10 years. Note: Will accept fax requests from gov't agencies only. Mail turnaround time 3-5 days.

General Information: Public access terminal has criminal records back to 1991. No probation reports released. A CD-Rom of monthly court indices from all divisions is for $40.00. Certification fee: $6.60 per doc. Payee: Clerk of the Court. Personal checks accepted. Prepayment and SASE required.

Santa Maria Cook Division - Superior

Court PO Box 5369, 312-C E Cook St, Santa Maria, CA 93454-5369; phone: 805-346-7414; civil phone: 805-346-7405; fax: 805-346-7616; hours 8AM-3PM (PST). *Civil Actions, Probate, Eviction, Small Claims.*
www.sbcourts.org/index.asp

The Cook Division handles Civil; its sister court (Miller Division) handles Criminal. Includes Betteravia, Casmalia, Cuyama, Guadalupe, Gary, Los Alamos, New Cuyama, Orcutt, Santa Maria, Sisquoc, Tepusquet and sections of the Vandenburg Air Force Base

Civil Records: Access: Mail, in person. Both court and visitors may perform in person searches. Search fee: $5.00 per name. Court makes copy: $.75 per page. Required to search: name, years to search. Civil cases indexed by defendant, plaintiff. Civil records in index files from 1964. Records destroyed after 10 years. Daily calendars free at www.sbcourts.org/pubcal/. Mail turnaround time 5 days. Mail turnaround time 5 days.

General Information: Public access terminal has civil records. No probation reports, financial, judges notes, confidential or sealed records released. Will fax documents for $1.00 per page fax fee. A CD-Rom of monthly court indices from all divisions is for $40.00. Certification fee: $6.60 per doc. Payee: Clerk of Court. Personal checks or Visa, MC accepted. Prepayment and SASE required.

Santa Maria Miller Division - Superior

Court 312-M E Cook St, Bldg E, Santa Maria, CA 93454-5165; phone: 805-346-7590; criminal phone: 805-346-7650; fax: 805-346-7591; hours 8AM-3PM (PST). *Felony, Misdemeanor, Traffic.*
www.sbcourts.org/index.asp

Note: Miller Division is in the same building complex as the Cook Division, which handles civil, small claims, family cases. Miller includes the same jurisdictional area as Cook Division. A CD-Rom of monthly court indices from all divisions is for $40.00.

Criminal Records: Access: Mail, fax, in person. Both court and visitors may perform in person searches. Search fee: $5.00 per name. Court makes copy: $.75 per page. Required to search: complete name and alias, years to search, DOB. Criminal records in index files from 7/1964. Mail turnaround time 5 days.

General Information: No public access terminal. No probation reports, financial, judges notes, confidential or sealed records released. Will fax documents for $1.00 per page. Certification fee: $6.60 per doc. Payee: Clerk of Court. Personal checks or Visa, MC accepted. Prepayment and SASE required.

Lompoc Division - Superior Court 115

Civic Center Plz, Lompoc, CA 93436; criminal phone: 805-737-7790; civil phone: 805-737-7909; fax: 805-737-7786; hours 8AM-3PM (PST). *Felony, Misdemeanor, Civil Actions Under $25,000, Eviction, Small Claims.*
www.sbcourts.org/index.asp

Note: Includes Lompoc and adjacent unincorporated areas including sections of Vandenburg Air Force Base. Daily calendars free at www.sbcourts.org/pubcal/. A CD-Rom of monthly court indices from all divisions is for $40.00.

Civil Records: Access: Mail, in person. Both court and visitors may perform in person searches. Search fee: $5.00. Court makes copy: $.75 per side. Required to search: name, years to search. Civil cases indexed by defendant, plaintiff. Civil records on computer from 1991, index files from 1983. Records destroyed after 10 years. Mail turnaround time 1 week.

Criminal Records: Access: Mail, in person. Both court and visitors may perform in person searches. Search fee: $5.00. Court makes copy: $.75 per side. Required to search: name, years to search, DOB; also helpful: address. Criminal records on computer from 1991, index files from 1983. Records destroyed after 10 years. Includes Solvang jurisdiction filings from 1997 to present. Mail turnaround time 1 week.

General Information: Public access terminal available. No probation reports released. Will fax documents for $1.00 per page. Certification fee: $6.60 per doc. Payee: Clerk of the Superior Court. Personal checks accepted. Prepayment and SASE required.

Solvang Division - Superior Court

1745 Mission Dr, #C, Solvang, CA 93463; phone: 805-686-5040; fax: 805-686-5079; hours 8AM-3PM (PST). *Misdemeanor, Small Claims, Traffic.*

www.sbcourts.org/index.asp

Note: Includes the City of Solvang, Buelton, and adjacent unincorporated areas, Los Olivos and Santa Ynez. Daily calendars free at www.sbcourts.org/pubcal/. A CD-Rom of monthly court indices from all divisions is for $40.00.

Civil Records: Access: Phone, mail, in person. Both court and visitors may perform in person searches. Search fee: $5.00. Court makes copy: $.75 per page. Required to search: name, years to search. Civil cases indexed by defendant, plaintiff. Civil records on computer from 1997 to present, index lists prior. Mail turnaround time 1 week.

Criminal Records: Access: Mail, in person. Both court and visitors may perform in person searches. No search fee. Court makes copy: $.75 per page. Required to search: name, years to search, DOB. Criminal records on computer from 1988 to 1997. There are no criminal filings at this court since 1/1997. Mail turnaround time 1 week.

General Information: Public access terminal has criminal back to 1987 and civil back to 1976. No sealed or confidential records released. Will not fax documents. Certification fee: $6.75. Payee: Superior Court. Personal checks accepted. Visa, MC only accepted at the counter and by phone. Prepayment and SASE required.

Santa Clara County

Superior Court - Civil

191 N 1st St, San Jose, CA 95113; phone: 408-882-2100; hours 8:30AM-4PM (PST). *Civil, Eviction, Probate.*

www.sccsuperiorcourt.org

Note: Handles cases for San Jose, Milpitas, Santa Clara, Los Gatos and Campbell areas.

Civil Records: Access: Mail, in person, online. Both court and visitors may perform in person searches. Search fee: $5.00 per name per year. Court makes copy: $1.00 per page. Required to search: name, years to search. Civil records on computer 1993 to present; prior on books to 1800s. Civil, Family, Probate, and Small Claims case records and court calendars are free online at www.sccaseinfo.org. CD-rom is also available, fee-$150.00. Mail turnaround time 2 weeks.

General Information: Public access terminal has civil records back to 1993. No probation reports or confidential records released. Certification fee: $6.00 per doc. Payee: Clerk of Superior Court. Personal checks accepted. Prepayment and SASE required.

Superior Court - Criminal

191 N 1st St, San Jose, CA 95113-1001; phone: 408-808-6600; criminal phone: 408-808-6600; hours 8:30AM-4PM (PST). *Felony, Misdemeanor.*

www.sccsuperiorcourt.org

Note: Includes the Cities of Alviso, Campbell, Los Gatos, Milpitas, Monte Sereno, San Jose, Santa Clara, and Saratoga.

Criminal Records: Access: Mail, in person. Both court and visitors may perform in person searches. Search fee: $5.00 per name per year. Court makes copy: $1.00 per page. Postage also charged based on number of pages copied. Required to search: name, years to search, DOB. Criminal indexes on microfiche from 1975-present. Old files are kept in archives or on microfilm. Mail turnaround time 3-7 days.

General Information: No public access terminal. No probation, confidential or sealed records released. Will not fax documents. Certification fee: $6.60 per doc. Payee: Santa Clara Superior Court. Personal checks accepted. Prepayment and SASE required.

South County Facility - Superior Court

12425 Monterey Rd, San Martin, CA 95046-9590; phone: 408-695-5000; criminal phone: 408-695-5014; civil phone: 408-695-5012; hours 8:30AM-4PM (PST). *Felony, Misdemeanor, Civil Actions Under $25,000, Eviction, Small Claims.*

http://sccsuperiorcourt.org

Note: Jurisdiction includes the Cities of Gilroy, Morgan Hill, San Martin and surrounding unincorporated areas. Traffic case phone number is 408-695-5011.

Civil Records: Access: Mail, in person, onliine. Both court and visitors may perform in person searches. Search fee: $5.00 per name per year. Court makes copy: $1.00 per page. Required to search: name, years to search. Civil records on microfiche. Civil, Family, Probate, and Small Claims case records and court calendars are free online at www.sccaseinfo.org. CD-rom is also available, fee-$150.00. Mail turnaround time 1 week.

Criminal Records: Access: Mail, in person. Both court and visitors may perform in person searches. Search fee: $5.00 per name per year. Court makes copy: $1.00 per page. Required to search: name, years to search; also helpful: DOB. Same record keeping as civil. Mail turnaround time 1 week.

General Information: No public access terminal. No adoptions, juvenile, medical, probation or sealed records released. Certification fee: $6.60 per doc. Payee: Superior Court. Personal checks accepted. Prepayment and SASE required.

Palo Alto Facility - Superior Court

270 Grant Ave, Palo Alto, CA 94306; phone: 650-462-3800; hours 8:30AM-4PM (PST). *Felony, Misdemeanor, Small Claims, Traffic.*

www.sccsuperiorcourt.org

Note: Includes Palo Alto, Mountain View, Los Altos, Los Altos Hills, Stanford University, Sunnyvale and the surrounding unincorporated areas.

Civil Records: Access: Mail, in person, online. Both court and visitors may perform in person searches. Search fee: $5.00 per name per year. Court makes copy: $1.00 per page. Required to search: name, years to search. Civil, Family, Probate, and Small Claims case records and court calendars are free online at www.sccaseinfo.org. CD-rom is also available, fee-$150.00. Mail turnaround time 1 week.

Criminal Records: Access: Mail, in person. Both court and visitors may perform in person searches. Search fee: $5.00 per name per year. Court makes copy: $1.00 per page. Required to search: name, years to search; also helpful: DOB. Criminal Records on microfiche. Mail turnaround time 1 week.

General Information: No public access terminal. No probation, doctor report, pretrial report records released. Certification fee: $6.60 per doc. Payee: Superior Court. Personal checks accepted. Prepayment and SASE required.

Sunnyvale Facility - Superior Court

270 Grant Ave, #204, Palo Alto, CA 94306; phone: 408-462-3800; hours 8:30AM-3PM (PST). *Felony, Misdemeanor.*

www.sccsuperiorcourt.org

Note: Court closed; records now at Palo Alto Court facility; address and phone given here. Also, traffic and small claims are filed at the Palo Alto Facility.

Los Gatos Facility - Superior Court

191 N 1st St, San Jose, CA 95113; phone: 408-370-4440; hours 8:30AM-4PM (PST). *Small Claims.*

http://sccsuperiorcourt.org

Note: Includes the towns of Los Gatos and Monte Sereno and the cities of Campbell, Saratoga, and surrounding unincorporated areas as well as San Jose, Milpitas and Santa Clara. Physical address is 14205 Capri Dr, Los Gatos, 95032

Civil Records: Access: Phone, mail, in person, online. Both court and visitors may perform in person searches. Search fee: $5.00 per name per year. Court makes copy: $1.10 per page. Required to search: name, years to search. Civil cases indexed by defendant, plaintiff. Civil record index on microfiche.

Civil, Family, Probate, and Small Claims case records and court calendars are free online at www.sccaseinfo.org. CD-rom is also available, fee-$150.00.

General Information: No public access terminal. Certification fee: $6.60 per doc. Payee: Superior Court. Personal checks accepted. Prepayment required.

Santa Cruz County

Superior Court - Civil

701 Ocean St, Rm 110, Santa Cruz, CA 95060; phone: 831-454-2020; hours 8AM-4PM (PST). *Civil, Probate.*

www.santacruzcourt.org/

Note: This court also handles Family Law.

Civil Records: Access: Phone, mail, in person, online. Both court and visitors may perform in person searches. Search fee: $5.00 per name. Court makes copy: $.50 per page. Required to search: name, years to search. Civil cases indexed by defendant, plaintiff. Civil records on computer back to 6/1985; microfiche, archived and index books from 1880. Access civil records free at www.santacruzcourt.org/CaseInquiry.htm Access using case number or party name. Mail turnaround time 10-15 days.

General Information: Public access terminal has civil records back to 1985. No adoptions, juvenile, medical, probation or sealed records released. Certification fee: $6.60 plus $1.10 per page. Payee: Superior Court. Personal checks accepted. Prepayment and SASE required.

Superior Court - Criminal

701 Ocean St, Rm 120, Santa Cruz, CA 95060; phone: 831-454-2230; fax: 831-454-2215; hours 8AM-4PM (PST). *Felony, Misdemeanor.*

www.santacruzcourt.org

Criminal Records: Access: Fax, mail, in person, online. Both court and visitors may perform in person searches. Search fee: $5.00 per name. Court makes copy: $.50 per page. Required to search: name; also helpful: years to search, DOB. Records on computer since 1984; older records on microfiche index by party name to 1880's. Free index search at www.santacruzcourt.org/CaseInquiry.htm. Access case information using case number or party name. Mail turnaround time 2-4 weeks.

General Information: Public access terminal available. No juvenile, probation or sealed records released. Will fax documents to local or toll free line. Certification fee: $6.60 per doc. Payee: Clerk of Court. Personal checks accepted. Prepayment and SASE required.

Watsonville Division - Superior Court

1430 Freedom Blvd, Watsonville, CA 95076; phone: 831-763-8060; fax: 831-763-8069; hours 8AM-4PM (PST). *Misdemeanor, Civil Actions Under $25,000, Eviction, Small Claims.*

www.santacruzcourt.org/

Note: Includes all of Santa Cruz County.

Civil Records: Access: Mail, in person, online. Both court and visitors may perform in person searches. Search fee: $5.00 per name. Court makes copy: $.50 per page. Required to search: name, years to search. Civil cases indexed by defendant, plaintiff. Civil records on computer from 1992, index books prior. Records destroyed after 10 years. Search the index at www.santacruzcourt.org/CaseInquiry.htm. Includes small claims. Mail turnaround time 2-5 days.

Criminal Records: Access: Mail, in person, online. Both court and visitors may perform in person searches. Search fee: $5.00 per name. Court makes copy: $.50 per page. Required to search: name, years to search; also helpful: DOB. Criminal records on computer from 1992, microfilm to 1993, index books prior. Records destroyed after 10 years. Search the index at www.santacruzcourt.org/CaseInquiry.htm. Access case information using case number or party name. In person searchers may use microfilm - records back to 1993. Mail turnaround time 2-5 days.

General Information: No public access terminal. No probation or juvenile records released. Certification fee: $6.60 plus $1.10 per page. Payee: Superior Court. Personal checks accepted. Prepayment and SASE required.

Shasta County

Superior Court 1500 Court St, Redding, CA 96001; phone: 530-245-6789; criminal records fax: 530-245-6483; civil records fax: 530-225-5564; 8:30AM-4:30PM (PST). *Felony, Misdemeanor, Civil, Small Claims, Eviction, Probate.* www.shastacourts.com
Note: Address #319 for civil division and #219 for criminal division.

Civil Records: Access: Phone, mail, in person, online. Both court and visitors may perform in person searches. Search fee: $5.00 per name per year. Court makes copy: $.50 per page. Required to search: name, years to search. Civil cases indexed by defendant, plaintiff. Civil records on computer from 1992, index books prior. Access to civil division index free at www.shastacourts.com/indexes.php. Mail turnaround time 2-7 days.
Criminal Records: Access: Mail, in person, online. Both court and visitors may perform in person searches. Search fee: $5.00 per name per year. Court makes copy: $.50 per page. Required to search: name, years to search. Criminal records on computer from 1992, index books prior. Access the criminal division index free at www.shastacourts.com/indexes/index_menu.php Also, access using Integrated Justice Mail turnaround time 2-7 days.
General Information: Public access terminal goes back to 1992. No probation or confidential records released. Will fax documents to local or toll free line. Certification fee: $6.60 per doc. Payee: Superior Court. Personal checks accepted. Prepayment and SASE required.

Burney Branch - Superior Court 20509 Shasta St, Burney, CA 96013; phone: 530-335-3571; fax: 530-225-5684; hours 8AM-N, 1-4:30PM (PST). *Misdemeanor, Civil, Eviction, Small Claims.* www.shastacourts.com
Note: Civil actions handled by Redding Branch since 1992. Prior civil limited jurisdiction records maintained here.

Civil Records: Access: Mail, in person. Only the court performs in person searches; visitors may not. Search fee: $5.00 per name per year. Court makes copy: $.50 per page. Required to search: name, years to search. Civil cases indexed by defendant, plaintiff. Civil records on computer from 1993, index books prior. Mail turnaround time 2-14 days.
Criminal Records: Access: Mail, in person, online. Only the court performs in person searches; visitors may not. Search fee: $5.00 per name per year. Court makes copy: $.50 per page. Required to search: name, years to search, DOB. Criminal records on computer from 1993, index books prior. Online access to the criminal division index is free at www.shastacourts.com/indexes/index_menu.php. Also, the Integrated Justice Mail turnaround time 2-14 days.
General Information: No probation, juvenile, or DMV reports released. Certification fee: $6.60 per doc. Payee: Superior Court. Personal checks accepted. Prepayment and SASE required.

Sierra County

Superior Court PO Box 476, Courthouse Sq, Downieville, CA 95936; phone: 530-289-3698; criminal phone: 530-289-2903; civil phone: 530-289-2926; probate phone: 530-289-2926; fax: 530-289-0205; hours 8AM-N, 1-5PM *Felony, Misdemeanor, Civil, Eviction, Small Claims, Probate.* www.sierracourt.org
Note: Probate is a separate index at this same address.

Civil Records: Access: Phone, fax, mail, in person. Only the court performs in person searches;

visitors may not. Search fee: $5.00 per name per year. Court makes copy: $1.00 per page. Required to search: name, plaintiff. Civil records on computer from 1985, index books from 1852. Mail turnaround time 2-4 days.
Criminal Records: Access: Phone, fax, mail, in person. Both court and visitors may perform in person searches. Search fee: $5.00 per name per year. Court makes copy: $1.00 per page. Required to search: name, years to search. Criminal records on computer from 1985, index books from 1852. Mail turnaround time 2-4 days.
General Information: No public access terminal. No adoptions, juvenile, medical, probation or sealed records released. Will fax documents $1.00 per page. Certification fee: $7.00 per doc. Payee: Superior Court. Personal checks accepted. Prepayment and SASE required.

Siskiyou County

Superior Court 311 4th St, PO Box 1026, Yreka, CA 96097; criminal phone: 530-842-8195; civil phone: 530-842-8196; criminal records fax: 530-842-8178; civil records fax: 530-842-0164; hours 8AM-5PM; 8AM-3PM (phone hours) (PST). *Felony, Misdemeanor, Civil, Probate.* www.siskiyou.courts.ca.gov
Civil Records: Access: Phone, mail, in person, online. Both court and visitors may perform in person searches. Search fee: $5.00 per name. Fee is per 10 years searched. Court makes copy: $.50 per page. Required to search: name, years to search. Civil cases indexed by defendant, plaintiff. Civil records on computer since 1991, archived and index book from 1900. Access county superior court records free at www.siskiyou.courts.ca.gov/CaseHistory.asp. Includes traffic but not juvenile. Mail turnaround time 1 week.
Criminal Records: Access: Mail, in person, online. Both court and visitors may perform in person searches. Search fee: $5.00 per name. Fee is per 10 years searched. Court makes copy: $.50 per page. Required to search: name, years to search. Criminal records on computer since 1991, archived and index book from 1900. Online access to criminal records is available; see civil. Mail turnaround time 1 week.
General Information: Public access terminal goes back to 1991. No adoptions, juvenile, medical, probation or sealed records released. Will fax documents to local or toll free line. Certification fee: $6.60 per doc. Payee: Siskiyou Superior Court. Personal checks accepted. Prepayment and SASE required.

Weed Branch - Superior Court 550 Main St, Weed, CA 96094; phone: 530-938-2483; civil phone: 530-842-0107; fax: 530-842-0109; hours 8AM-4PM (PST). *Misdemeanor, Small Claims.* www.siskiyou.courts.ca.gov
Civil Records: Access: Mail, fax, in person, online. Both court and visitors may perform in person searches. Search fee: $5.00 per name per 10 years. Court makes copy: $.50 per page. Required to search: full name, years to search. Civil cases indexed by defendant, plaintiff. Civil records go back to 1980; on computer since 1995. Access to county superior court records is free at www.siskiyou.courts.ca.gov/CaseHistory.asp. Includes traffic but not juvenile. Mail turnaround time 10 days.
Criminal Records: Access: Mail, fax, in person, online. Both court and visitors may perform in person searches. Search fee: $5.00 per name per 10 years. Court makes copy: $.50 per page. Required to search: full name, years to search, DOB, SSN. Criminal records go back to 1994; computerized records back 7 years. Online access to criminal records is available; see civil. Mail turnaround time 10 days.
General Information: Public access terminal has criminal back to 7 years and civil back to 1995.

Fee to fax documents is $1.00 per page. Certification fee: $6.60 per doc. Payee: Siskiyou Superior Court. Personal checks accepted only from party to the case. Prepayment and SASE required.

Dorris Branch - Superior Court PO Box 828, 324 N Pine St, Dorris, CA 96023; phone: 530-397-3161; fax: 530-397-3169; hours 8AM-N, 1-4PM (PST). *Civil Actions Under $25,000, Eviction, Small Claims.* www.siskiyou.courts.ca.gov
Note: All new misdemeanor cases are referred to Weed, CA Branch. This court only maintains a few criminal records for a year

Civil Records: Access: Mail, in person, online. Only the court performs in person searches; visitors may not. Search fee: $5.00 per name. Court makes copy: $.50 per page. Required to search: name, years to search. Civil records on computer back to 1998; prior on books back to 1992. Access to county superior court records is free at www.siskiyou.courts.ca.gov/CaseHistory.asp. Includes traffic but not juvenile. Mail turnaround time 10 days.
General Information: No probation reports released. Certification fee: $6.60 per doc. Payee: Siskiyou Superior Court. Personal checks accepted. Prepayment and SASE required.

Solano County

Superior Court - Civil 600 Union Ave, Fairfield, CA 94533; phone: 707-421-6053; probate phone: 707-421-6471; hours 8AM-3PM (PST). *Civil, Eviction, Probate.* www.solanocourts.com/
Note: Northern Solano Muni. Ct. has been combined with this Court. Probate is a separate office at this same address. Small claims phone-707-421-7435. Includes Fairfield, Suisun, Vacaville, Dixon, Rio Vista, and surrounding area.

Civil Records: Access: Phone, mail, online, in person. Both court and visitors may perform in person searches. Search fee: $5.00 per name. Court makes copy: $1.00 per page. Required to search: name, years to search. Civil cases indexed by defendant, plaintiff. Civil records on computer since 1992, microfiche since 1971, archived and index files since 1800s. Online access to civil records is free at http://courtconnect.solanocourts.com/pls/bprod_cc/ck_public_qry_main.cp_main_idx. Also, civil tentative rulings and probate notes are free at www.solanocourts.com/civil_tent.htm. Note: Phone access limited to short searches. Mail turnaround time 2-3 days.
General Information: Public access terminal has civil records back to 1992. No sealed records released. Certification fee: $6.60 per doc. Payee: Solano County Courts. Personal checks accepted. Prepayment and SASE required.

Superior Court - Criminal 530 Union Ave, #200, Fairfield, CA 94533; phone: 707-421-7440; 421-7834 Sup Court Records; fax: 707-421-7439; hours 8AM-3PM (PST). *Felony, Misdemeanor.* www.solanocourts.com
Note: The Northern Solano Municipal Court has been combined with the Superior Court. This court includes Fairfield, Suisun, Vacaville, Dixon, Rio Vista and the adjacent unincorporated areas.

Criminal Records: Access: Mail, in person, online. Visitors must perform in person searches themselves. Search fee: $5.00 per name. Court makes copy: $1.00 for first page. Required to search: name, years to search; also helpful: DOB, SSN. Superior Court records on computer since 1992, microfiche since 1971; Municipal Court records on computer for past 10 years. Access criminal records free at http://courtconnect.solanocourts.com/pls/bprod_cc/ck_public_qry_main.cp_main_idx. Note: Phone questions can only be answered between 10AM and 3PM. Records from this court found here only, not at other divisions. Mail turnaround time 1-3 weeks.

General Information: No public access terminal. No probation reports released. Certification fee: $6.60 per doc. Payee: Solano Superior Court. Personal checks accepted. Prepayment and SASE required.

Vallejo Branch - Superior Court 321 Tuolumne St, Vallejo, CA 94590; criminal phone: 707-553-5341; civil phone: 707-553-5346; fax: 707-553-5661; hours 8AM-3PM (PST). *Misdemeanor, Civil, Eviction, Small Claims, Felony, Probate.*
www.solanocourts.com
Note: Includes Cities of Vallejo and Benicia and the adjacent unincorporated areas.

Civil Records: Access: Mail, in person, online. Both court and visitors may perform in person searches. Search fee: $5.00 per name. Court makes copy: $1.00 per page. Required to search: name, years to search. Civil cases indexed by defendant, plaintiff. Civil records on computer from 1991, index files from 1983. Records destroyed after 10 years. Online access to civil records is free at the website; click on "Court Connect." Also, civil tentative rulings and probate notes are free at www.solanocourts.com/civil_tent.htm. Mail turnaround time 2 days.

Criminal Records: Access: Mail, in person, online. Only the court performs in person searches; visitors may not. Search fee: $5.00 per name. Court makes copy: $1.00 per page. Required to search: name, years to search. Criminal records on computer from 1991, index files from 1983. Records destroyed after 10 years. Access to criminal records is free at http://courtconnect.solanocourts.com/pls/bprod_cc/ck_public_qry_main.cp_main_idx. Mail turn around time 2 days.

General Information: Public access terminal has only civil records back to 1991. No probation reports released. Will not fax documents. Certification fee: $6.60 per doc. Payee: Superior Court. Personal checks accepted. Visa, AmEx accepted. Prepayment and SASE required.

Sonoma County

Superior Court - Criminal 600 Administration Dr, Rm 105J, Santa Rosa, CA 95403-0281; phone: 707-565-1100; hours 8AM-3PM, M,W,F; 8-6PM Th (PST). *Felony, Misdemeanor, Probate.*
www.sonomasuperiorcourt.com

Civil Records: Access: Phone, mail, in person. Both court and visitors may perform in person searches. Search fee: $15.00 per hour. Court makes copy: $1.00 per page. 10 page limit. If more than 10 pages must wait 3-5 days. Required to search: name, years to search. Civil cases indexed by defendant, plaintiff. Civil records on computer from 1985, microfiche and index books from 1850 to 1984. Phone access limited to 2 names or cases per call. The phone is only answered from 8AM to noon. Mail turnaround time 2-3 weeks.

Criminal Records: Access: Phone, mail, in person. Both court and visitors may perform in person searches. Search fee: $15.00 per hour. Court makes copy: $1.00 per page. 10 page limit. If more than 10 pages must wait 3-5 days. Required to search: name, years to search, DOB. Criminal Records on computer back to 1985, microfiche and index books 1850 to 1984. Misdemeanor records can be destroyed after 10 years. Mail turnaround time 2-3 weeks.

General Information: Public access terminal available. No adoptions, juvenile, medical, probation or sealed records released. Certification fee: $6.60 per doc. Payee: Superior Court. No out of state personal checks accepted. Prepayment and SASE required.

Superior Court - Civil Division 600 Administration Dr, Rm 107J, Santa Rosa, CA 95403; phone: 707-565-1100; hours 8AM-3PM M,T,W,F; till 6PM Th (PST). *Civil, Eviction, Small Claims.*
www.sonomasuperiorcourt.com

Civil Records: Access: Mail, in person. Both court and visitors may perform in person searches. Search fee: $15.00 per hour; minimum is $5.00. Court makes copy: $1.00 per page. Required to search: name, years to search. Civil cases indexed by

defendant, plaintiff. Civil records on computer to 10/84, index files prior. Judgment records destroyed after 10 years, dismissals after 1. Computer index include criminal from 10/1984. Mail turnaround time 3 days to 2 weeks

General Information: Public access terminal has civil records back to 1984. (Access terminal includes probate records.) No probation reports or sealed records released. Will not fax documents. Certification fee: $6.60 per doc. Payee: Superior Court. Personal checks accepted. Prepayment and SASE required.

Stanislaus County

Superior Court - Criminal PO Box 1098, 800 11 St, Rm 140, 95354, Modesto, CA 95353; phone: 209-558-6000; Hours: 8AM-3PM (PST). *Felony, Misdemeanor.*
www.stanct.org/courts/index.html

Criminal Records: Access: Phone, mail, in person, online. Both court and visitors may perform in person searches. Search fee: $5.00 per name per year if in archives, but will search on computer for free. Court makes copy: $.75 per page. Required to search: name, years to search, DOB; also helpful- charges, felony of misd. Criminal Records on microfiche since 1974, archived back to 1800s. Access the case indices free at www.stanct.org/case_index/. Mail turnaround time 1-2 weeks.

General Information: Public access terminal has criminal records back to 1995. (Index and case numbers only on terminal. Some records go back further than 1995.) No adoptions, juvenile, medical, probation or sealed records released. Certification fee: $6.60 per doc. Payee: Superior Court Clerk. Personal checks accepted. No credit cards accepted. Prepayment and SASE required.

Superior Court - Civil 1100 "I" St, PO Box 828, Modesto, CA 95353; phone: 209-558-6000; criminal records fax: 209-525-4348; civil records fax: 209-525-4348; hours 8AM-3PM (PST). *Civil, Eviction, Small Claims, Probate.*
www.stanct.org/courts/index.html
Ceres Branch is operation, but all filings are here.

Civil Records: Access: Mail, fax, in person, online. Both court and visitors may perform in person searches. Search fee: $5.00 per name. Court makes copy: $.75 per page. Required to search: name, years to search. Civil cases indexed by defendant, plaintiff. Civil records on computer from 1991, in index files from 1983. Records destroyed after 10 years. The case index is searchable by name and year at www.stanct.org/case_index/. Mail turnaround time 2-5 days.

General Information: Public access terminal has civil records. No probation or juvenile records released. Certification fee: $6.60 per doc. Payee: Superior Court. Personal checks accepted. Prepayment and SASE required.

Turlock Division - Superior Court 300 Starr Ave, Turlock, CA 95380; phone: 209-558-6000; fax: 209-664-8009; hours 8AM-N, 12:30-3PM T-F (PST). *Small Claims, Traffic.*
www.stanct.org/courts/index.html

Sutter County

Superior Court - Civil Division 463 2nd St, Rm 211, Courthouse East, 2nd Fl, Yuba City, CA 95991; phone: 530-822-7352; probate phone: same; fax: 530-822-7192; hours 8AM-5PM (PST). *Civil, Eviction, Small Claims, Probate.*
www.suttercourts.com

Civil Records: Access: Mail, in person. Both court and visitors may perform in person searches. Search fee: $5.00 per name. Court makes copy: $.50 per page. Required to search: name, years to search. Civil cases indexed by defendant, plaintiff. Civil records in index books and archived from 1800s, on computer back to 1/95. Mail turnaround time 2 days if records on site.

General Information: Public access terminal goes back to 1995. No adoptions, juvenile, medical, probation or sealed records released. Certification fee: $6.60 per doc. Payee: Superior Court. Personal checks accepted. Prepayment and SASE required.

Superior Court - Criminal Division 446 2nd St, Yuba City, CA 95991; phone: 530-822-7360; fax: 530-822-7159; hours 8AM-5PM (PST). *Felony, Misdemeanor.*
www.suttercourts.com

Criminal Records: Access: Fax, mail, in person. Both court and visitors may perform in person searches. Search fee: $5.00 per name. Court makes copy: $.50 per page. Required to search: name, years to search. Criminal records in index books and archived from 1800s, computerized since 1995. Mail turnaround time 1 week.

General Information: Public access terminal has criminal records back to 1995. No police reports or probation records released. Will fax documents to local or toll free line. Certification fee: $6.60 per doc. Payee: Sutter County Superior Court. Personal checks accepted. Prepayment required.

Tehama County

Superior Court - Civil Division PO Box 310, Red Bluff, CA 96080; phone: 530-527-6441; hours 8AM-5PM (PST). *Civil, Small Claims, Eviction, Probate, Family Law.*

Civil Records: Access: Mail, in person. Only the court performs in person searches; visitors may not. Search fee: $2.50 per name. Fee is $5.00 if years before 1992 are requested. Court makes copy: $.50 per page. Required to search: name, years to search. Civil cases indexed by defendant, plaintiff. Civil records on computer back to 1992, archived and index books from 1900s. Mail turnaround time same day.

General Information: No adoptions, juvenile, mental, probation or sealed records released. Will not fax documents. Certification fee: $6.60 per doc. Payee: Tehama County Superior Court Clerk. Personal checks accepted. Prepayment and SASE required.

Superior Court - Criminal Division 445 Pine St, PO Box 1170, Red Bluff, CA 96080; phone: 530-527-3563; criminal phone: 530-527-7314; fax: 530-527-0956; hours 8AM-5PM (PST). *Felony, Misdemeanor.*

Criminal Records: Access: Mail, in person. Both court and visitors may perform in person searches. Search fee: $5.00 per name if not computerized; $2.50 if name in computer. Court makes copy: $.50 per page. Required to search: name, years to search; also helpful: DOB. Criminal records on computer from 1991, index cards prior. Will only search back 7 years. Mail turnaround time within 1 week.

General Information: No public access terminal. No probation reports released. Certification fee: $6.60 per doc. Payee: Superior Court. Personal checks accepted. Prepayment and SASE required.

Corning Branch - Superior Court 720 Hoag St, Corning, CA 96021; phone: 530-824-4601; fax: 530-824-6457; hours 8AM-5PM (PST). *Misdemeanor, Civil Actions Under $25,000, Eviction, Small Claims.*

Civil Records: Access: Mail, in person. Both court and visitors may perform in person searches. Search fee: $2.50 per name. Court makes copy: $.50 per page. Required to search: name, years to search. Civil cases indexed by defendant, plaintiff. Civil records in index cards. Will only search back 7 years; records on computer since 1990. Requests must be in writing. Mail turnaround time 1 week.

Criminal Records: Access: Mail, in person. Only the court performs in person searches; visitors may not. Search fee: $2.50. Court makes copy: $.50 per page. Required to search: name, years to search; also helpful: DOB. Criminal records on computer from 1990, index cards prior. Will only search back 7 years. Requests must be in writing. Mail turnaround time 1 week.

General Information: No probation reports released. Will fax documents to local or toll free line, if paid in advance. Certification fee: $7.00 per doc. Payee: Tehama Superior Court. Personal checks accepted. Prepayment and SASE required.

Trinity County

Superior Court 101 Court St, PO Box 1258, Weaverville, CA 96093; phone: 530-623-1208; criminal records fax: 530-623-3762; same fax for civil and probate; hours 9AM-4PM (PST). *Felony, Misdemeanor, Civil, Eviction, Small Claims, Probate.*

Civil Records: Access: Mail, in person. Both court and visitors may perform in person searches. Search fee: $5.00 per name per year. Court makes copy: $.50 per page. Required to search: name, years to search. Civil cases indexed by defendant, plaintiff. Civil records on microfiche, archived and index files from 1900s. Mail turnaround time 2-3 weeks.

Criminal Records: Access: Mail, in person. Both court and visitors may perform in person searches. Search fee: $5.00 per name per year. Court makes copy: $.50 per page. Required to search: name, years to search. Criminal records on microfiche, archived and index files from 1900s. Mail turnaround time 2-3 weeks.

General Information: No public access terminal. No adoptions, juvenile, medical, probation or sealed records released. Will not fax documents. Certification fee: $6.60 per doc. Payee: Superior Court. Personal checks accepted. Prepayment and SASE required.

Tulare County

Superior Court Courthouse, 221 S Mooney, Visalia, CA 93291; criminal phone: 559-733-6830; civil phone: 559-733-6374; fax: 559-737-4547; hours 8AM-4PM (PST). *Felony, Civil, Eviction, Small Claims, Probate.*
www.tularesuperiorcourt.ca.gov
Note: This court has records from Exeter, Woodlake, Farmersville, Goshen and Three Rivers. Address criminal record requests to Rm. 124; civil to Rm. 201.

Civil Records: Access: Mail, in person. Both court and visitors may perform in person searches. Search fee: $5.00 per name. Court makes copy: $.50 per page. Required to search: name, years to search. Civil cases indexed by defendant, plaintiff. Civil records on computer back to 2/1986; microfiche and index books from 1800s. Daily calendar and civil and probate recommendations at www.tularesuperiorcourt.ca.gov. Mail turnaround time 1 week.

Criminal Records: Access: Mail, in person. Both court and visitors may perform in person searches. Search fee: $5.00 per name. Court makes copy: $.50 per page. Required to search: name, years to search, DOB or SSN. Criminal records on computer back to 2/1986; microfiche and index books from 1800s. Daily calendar and civil and probate recommendations are at www.tularesuperior court.ca.gov. Mail turnaround time 1 week.

General Information: Public access terminal goes back to 1986. No adoptions, juvenile, mental, probation reports or sealed records released. Certification fee: $6.60 per doc. Payee: Tulare County Superior Court. Personal checks accepted. Prepayment and SASE required.

Dinuba Division - Superior Court 640 S
Alta Dinuba, Dinuba, CA 93618; phone: 559-591-5815; fax: 559-591-5871; hours 8AM-4PM (PST). *Felony, Misdemeanor, Civil Actions Under $25,000, Eviction, Small Claims.*
http:www.tularesuperiorcourt.ca.gov
Note: Includes Dinuba, Cutler, Orosi, Seville, Traver, London, Delf, Orange Cove.

Civil Records: Access: Mail, in person. Both court and visitors may perform in person searches. Search fee: $5.00 per name. Court makes copy: $.50 per page. Required to search: name, years to search;

helpful- case number. Civil cases indexed by defendant, plaintiff. Civil records on computer from 1993, index files from 1983. Records destroyed after 10 years. Mail turnaround time 2-3 days.

Criminal Records: Access: Mail, in person. Both court and visitors may perform in person searches. Search fee: $5.00 per name. Court makes copy: $.50 per page. Required to search: name, years to search, DOB. Criminal records on computer from 1993, index files from 1983. Records destroyed after 10 years. Mail turnaround time 2-3 days.

General Information: Public access terminal goes back to 1993. No probation reports released. Will not fax documents. Certification fee: $6.60 per doc. Payee: Dinuba Superior Court. In state checks accepted. Prepayment and SASE required.

Porterville Division - Superior Court 87 E
Morton Ave, Porterville, CA 93257; phone: 559-782-4710; fax: 559-782-4805; hours 8AM-4PM (PST). *Misdemeanor, Civil Actions Under $25,000, Eviction, Small Claims.*
Note: Includes Porterville, Springville, Camp Nelson, Johnsondale, Terra Bella, Ducor, Richgrove, Poplar, Strathmore and surrounding areas.

Civil Records: Access: Mail, in person. Both court and visitors may perform in person searches. Search fee: $5.00 per name. also is per case. Court makes copy: $.50 per page. Required to search: name, years to search, DOB, SSN, case #. Civil cases indexed by defendant, plaintiff. Civil records on computer from 2/1992, index book prior. Records destroyed after 10 years. Mail turnaround - 3-5 days.

Criminal Records: Access: Mail, in person. Both court and visitors may perform in person searches. Search fee: $5.00 per name. Also is per case. Court makes copy: $.50 per page. Required to search: name, years to search; also helpful: DOB, SSN, case #. Criminal records on computer from 2/1992, index book prior. Records destroyed after 10 years. Mail turnaround time 3-5 days.

General Information: Public access terminal goes back to 2/1992. No probation reports released. Certification fee: $6.60 per doc. Payee: Porterville Superior Court. Personal checks accepted. Prepayment and SASE required.

Tulare/Pixley Division - Superior Court
PO Box 1136, 425 E Kern St, Tulare, CA 93275; phone: 559-685-2556; fax: 559-685-2663; hours 8AM-4PM (PST). *Misdemeanor, Civil Actions Under $25,000, Eviction, Small Claims.*
Note: Includes Tulare, Pixley, Tipton, Earlimart, Alpaugh, Allensworth, Woodville, Waukena and surrounding areas.

Civil Records: Access: Mail, fax, in person. Both court and visitors may perform in person searches. Search fee: $5.00 per name. Court makes copy: $.50 per page. Required to search: name, years to search. Civil cases indexed by defendant, plaintiff. Civil records in index books. Records destroyed after 10 years; on computer back to 1992. Mail turnaround time 2 days.

Criminal Records: Access: Mail, fax, in person. Both court and visitors may perform in person searches. Search fee: $5.00 per name. Court makes copy: $.50 per page. Required to search: name, years to search, DOB; also helpful: address, SSN. Criminal records in index books. Records destroyed after 10 years; on computer back to 1992. Mail turnaround time 2 days.

General Information: Public access terminal goes back to 1992. No probation reports released. Certification fee: $6.60 per doc. Payee: Superior Court. Personal checks accepted. Prepayment and SASE required.

Tuolumne County

Superior Court - Civil 41 W Yaney, Sonora, CA 95370; phone: 209-533-5555; fax: 209-533-6944; hours 8AM-5PM (PST). *Civil, Eviction, Small Claims, Probate.*
www.tuolumne.courts.ca.gov

Note: Departments 1, 2, and 5. The small claims court can be reach at 209-533-6509.

Civil Records: Access: Mail, in person, online. Both court and visitors may perform in person searches. Search fee: $5.00 per name. Fee is per record. Court makes copy: $.50 per page. Required to search: name, years to search. Civil cases indexed by defendant, plaintiff. Civil records on computer back to 1994, microfiche and archived from 1900s, index files from 1800s. May have civil cases online late in 2005; click on "Civil Division" at website. Mail turnaround time 1 week.

General Information: Public access terminal has civil records back to 1994. No adoptions, juvenile, medical, probation or sealed records released. Certification fee: $6.60 per doc. Payee: Superior Court. Personal checks accepted. Out of state checks not accepted. Prepayment and SASE required.

Superior Court - Criminal 60 N Washington St, Sonora, CA 95370; phone: 209-533-5563; fax: 209-533-5581; hours 8AM-4PM (PST). *Felony, Misdemeanor, Traffic.*
www.tuolumne.courts.ca.gov
Note: Departments 3 and 4. Traffic court can be reach at 209-533-5671.

Criminal Records: Access: Mail, in person, online. Both court and visitors may perform in person searches. Search fee: $5.00 per name. Court makes copy: $.50 per page. Required to search: name, years to search, DOB. Felony records on computer from 1993; misdemeanors from 1999; index files prior. Will only search back 7 years. Access criminal records by case number of DR# at www.tuolumne.courts.ca.gov; click on "Criminal Division." Mail turnaround time 1 week to 10 days.

General Information: Public access terminal has criminal records back to 1993. No sealed records released. Most records are public. Will only fax to public agencies. Certification fee: $6.60 per doc. Payee: Tuolumne County Superior Court. Personal checks accepted. Prepayment and SASE required.

Ventura County

Ventura Superior Court 800 S Victoria Ave, PO Box 6489, Ventura, CA 93006-6489; criminal phone: 805-654-2611; civil phone: 805-654-2609; probate phone: 805-654-2264; fax: 805-650-4032; hours 8AM-5PM (PST). *Felony, Misdemeanor, Civil, Eviction, Small Claims, Probate.*
www.ventura.courts.ca.gov

Civil Records: Access: Phone, mail, online, in person. Both court and visitors may perform in person searches. Search fee: $5.00 per name. Court makes copy: $.50 per page. Required to search: name, years to search. Civil cases indexed by defendant, plaintiff. Civil records prior to 10/93 are on microfiche, after are on computer. Access to case information, calendars and dockets is free at www.ventura.courts.ca.gov/vent_frameset_puba.htm. Search by defendant or plaintiff name, case number, or date. Note: Search probate at www.cagenweb.com/ventura/Probate.html. Mail turnaround time 5-10 days.

Criminal Records: Access: Phone, mail, online, in person. Both court and visitors may perform in person searches. Search fee: $5.00 per name. Court makes copy: $.50 per page. Required to search: name, years to search, DOB. Criminal records go back to 1893; criminal records on computer back to 1989. Free access to case calendars and dockets at www.ventura.courts.ca.gov/vent_frameset_puba.htm. Mail turnaround time 5-10 days.

General Information: Public access terminal available. No adoptions, mental health, paternity actions, juvenile, medical, probation or sealed records released. Certification fee: $7.00 per doc. Payee: Superior Court. Personal checks or Visa, MC, AmEx, Discover accepted. Additional fee charged. Prepayment and SASE required.

East County Superior Court PO Box 1200 (3855F Alamo St), Simi Valley, CA 93062-1200; criminal phone: 805-582-8080; civil phone: 805-582-8086; hours 8AM-11:30AM; 1:30PM-5PM (PST). *Misdemeanor, Civil, Eviction, Small Claims, Family Law.*
www.ventura.courts.ca.gov/
Note: Other phones are: Eviction 582-8086; Small Claims 582-8078; Family Law 582-8086.
Civil Records: Access: Phone, mail, online, in person. Both court and visitors may perform in person searches. Search fee: $5.00 per name. Fee is per court. Court makes copy: $.50 per page. Required to search: name, years to search. Civil records back to 4/92. Access to civil records 10/93-present free at www.ventura.courts.ca.gov/vent_frameset_puba.htm. Search by defendant or plaintiff name, case number, or date. Mail turnaround time 5 days.
Criminal Records: Access: Phone, mail, in person, online. Both court and visitors may perform in person searches. Search fee: $5.00 per name. Fee is per court. Court makes copy: $.50 per page. Required to search: name, years to search, DOB. Same record keeping as civil. Access to case information, calendars and dockets is free at webpage. Mail turnaround time 5 days.
General Information: Public access terminal has only civil records back to 10/93. No adoptions, mental health, paternity actions, juvenile, medical, probation or sealed records released. Will not fax documents. Certification fee: $7.00 per doc. Payee: Ventura County Superior Courts. Personal checks accepted. Credit cards accepted: Visa, MC, Discover, AmEx. Additional fee charged to fax back. Prepayment and SASE required.

Yolo County

Superior Court 725 Court St, Rm 308, Woodland, CA 95695; phone: 530-406-6700; criminal phone: 530-406-6705; civil phone: 530-406-6704; criminal fax: 530-406-6763; civil records fax: 530-406-6734; probate Hours: 8AM-3PM (PST). *Felony, Misdemeanor, Civil, Eviction, Small Claims, Probate.*
www.yolocourts.com
Note: Address civil requests to Rm 103 and criminal to Rm 111. Small claims phone is 530-406-6706
Civil Records: Access: Phone, mail, in person. Both court and visitors may perform in person searches. Search fee: $5.00 per name. Court makes copy: $1.10 per copy. Self serve copy fee: $.25 per page. Required to search: name, years to search. Civil cases indexed by defendant, plaintiff. Civil records on computer from 1995, microfiche, archived and index files from 1800s. Calendars are online free at www.yolocourts.com/calendar_daily.html. Search Probate Notes at www.yolocourts.com/probate_notes.html. Mail turnaround time 2 weeks.
Criminal Records: Access: Phone, mail, in person. Both court and visitors may perform in person searches. Search fee: $5.00 per name. Court makes copy: $1.10 per copy. Self serve copy fee: $.25 per page. Required to search: name, years to search; also helpful: DOB. Criminal records on computer from 1995, microfiche, archived and index files from 1800s. Calendars are free at www.yolocourts.com/calendar_daily.html. Mail turnaround time 2 weeks.
General Information: No public access terminal. No adoptions, juvenile, medical, probation or sealed records released. Will not fax documents. Certification fee: $6.60 per doc. Payee: Yolo Superior Court. Personal checks accepted. Prepayment and SASE required.

Yuba County

Superior Court 215 5th St, #200, Marysville, CA 95901; phone: 530-749-7600; fax: 530-749-7351; hours 8:30AM-4:30PM (PST). *Felony, Misdemeanor, Civil, Small Claims, Probate.*
www.yubacourts.org
Civil Records: Access: Mail, in person. Both court and visitors may perform in person searches. Search fee: $5.00 per name. Court makes copy: $1.00 per page. Required to search: name, years to search. Civil cases indexed by defendant, plaintiff. Civil records on computer from 1992, index books through 1962, archives and index files from 1854. Mail turnaround time 1-2 weeks.
Criminal Records: Access: Mail, in person. Both court and visitors may perform in person searches. Search fee: $5.00 per name. Court makes copy: $1.00 per page. Required to search: name, years to search. Criminal records on computer from 1992, index books through 1962, archives and index files from 1854. Mail turnaround time 1-2 weeks.
General Information: Public access terminal available. No adoptions, paternity, juvenile, medical, probation or sealed records released. Certification fee: $6.60 per doc. Payee: Yuba County Superior Court. Personal checks accepted. Prepayment and SASE required.

Marysville Civil Limited Superior Court 215 5th St, #200, Marysville, CA 95901; phone: 530-749-7600; fax: 530-749-7351; hours 8:30AM-4:30PM (PST). *Civil Actions Under $25,000, Eviction, Small Claims.*
www.yubacourts.org
Civil Records: Access: Mail, in person. Both court and visitors may perform in person searches. Search fee: $5.00 per name. Court makes copy: $1.00 per page. Required to search: name, years to search, DOB. Civil cases indexed by defendant, plaintiff. Civil records on computer through 1993, index books prior back to 1850's. Mail turnaround 1-2 weeks.
General Information: Public access terminal has only civil records. No labor commissioner judgment, juvenile, or judge's records released. Will fax documents $20.00 per doc and $1.00 per page. Certification fee: $6.60 per doc. Payee: Yuba County Superior Court. Personal checks accepted. Prepayment and SASE required.

California Recording Offices

ORGANIZATION: 58 counties, 58 recording offices. The recording officer is County Recorder. Recordings are usually located in a Grantor/Grantee or General index. The entire state is in the Pacific Time Zone (PST).

REAL ESTATE RECORDS: Most counties do not perform real estate name searches. Copy fees and certification fees vary.

UCC RECORDS: Financing statements are filed at the state level, except for real estate related collateral, which are filed with the County Recorder. However, prior to 07/2001, consumer goods and farm collateral were also filed at the County Recorder and these older records can be searched there. All counties will perform UCC searches. Use search request form UCC-11. Search fees are usually $15.00 per debtor name. Copy costs vary.

TAX LIEN RECORDS: Federal and state tax liens on personal property of businesses are filed with the Secretary of State. Other federal and state tax liens are filed with the County Recorder. Some counties will perform separate tax lien searches. Fees vary for this type of search.

OTHER LIENS: Judgment (note - many judgments are also filed at the Sec. of State), child support, mechanic.

ONLINE ACCESS: A number of counties offer online access to assessor and real estate information. The system in Los Angeles is a commercial subscription system.

Alameda County

County Recorder, 1106 Madison St, 1st Fl, Oakland, CA 94607. 510-272-6362; fax-510-208-9957; hours: 8:30AM-4:30PM www.co.alameda.ca.us
Separate indices to search. Records indexed on a public use terminal back to 1969. Office personnel or visitors may perform searches. Search fee $25.00 per name. UCC copy fee $2.00 per page. RE record copy- $1.50 per page. Cert fee- $12.00 per doc plus copy fee. Payee- Alameda County Recorder. **Online access to Assessor, Recording, Deed, Mortgage, Lien, Fictitious Business Name, Property Tax, Inmates, Offender records:** The clerk-recorder's official public records and fictitious name databases are free at http://rechart1.co.alameda.ca.us/localization/menu.asp. Also, Property Assessment database is free online at www.co.alameda.ca.us/jsp_app/assessor/property_info/index.jsp. No name searching. Also, to search offender site go to www.vinelink.com. **Other phones:** Treasurer- 510-272-6800. **Property tax/Assessor-** 1225 Fallen, Oakland, CA 94607; 510-272-3755.

Alpine County

County Recorder, PO Box 217, Markleeville, CA 96120. RE & UCC recording phone-530-694-2286; fax-530-694-2491; hours: 9AM-N,1-4PM
All records in one index. Record index not computerized. Only the public may search. Copy fee $1.00 1st page, $.50 each add'l page plus 7.25% tax. Cert fee- $1.75 per cert plus copy fee. Payee- Alpine County Recorder. **Online access to Birth records:** Search births 1905-1995 free at www.mariposaresearch.net/php/. **Other phones:** Treasurer- 530-694-2286; Elections- 530-694-2281; Vital Records- 530-694-2286. **Property tax/Assessor-** PO Box 171, Markleeville, CA 96120; 530-694-2283.

Amador County

County Recorder, 500 Argonaut Lane, Jackson, CA 95642. RE & UCC recording phone-209-223-6468; fax-209-223-6204; hours: 8AM-5PM www.co.amador.ca.us/depts/recorder/index.htm
Separate indices to search include computer-1991 to current; Cott Indexes-1935 to1990; General Index-1887 to 1935. Records indexed on a public use terminal back to 1991. Only the public may search. Copy fee $2.00 for 1st page, $1 each add'l. Cert fee- $4.00 per cert plus copy fee. Payee- Amador County Recorder. **Online access to Recording, Deed, Lien, Judgment, Fictitious name, Tax Sale records:** Access to the county clerk database is free at www.co.amador.ca.us/depts/recorder/criis.htm or www.criis.com/amador/recorded.htm Also, tax sale info at www.co.amador.ca.us/depts/treasurer/index.htm; search by year. **Other phones:** Treasurer- 209-223-6364; Appraiser/Auditor- 209-223-6351; Elections- 209-223-6465; Vital Records- 209-223-6468. **Property tax/Assessor-** same address as above. 209-223-6351.

Butte County

County Recorder, 25 County Ctr Dr, Oroville, CA 95965-3375. RE & UCC recording phone-530-538-7691; fax-530-538-7975; hours: 9AM-5PM; Recording hours: 9AM-4PM http://clerk-recorder.buttecounty.net
All records in one index. Records indexed on a public use terminal back to 1/1/1988. Only the public may search. Copy fee $2.00 per page. Cert fee- $2.00 per cert plus copy fee. Payee- Butte County Recorder. **Online access to Real Estate, Recording, Fictitious Business Name, Inmate records:** Access to the recorder's database of official documents is free at http://clerk-recorder.buttecounty.net/Riimsweb/Asp/ORInquiry.asp. Records go back to 1988. Marriages, births and deaths are no longer available. Also, search fictitious business names free online at http://clerk-recorder.buttecounty.net/RiimsWeb/ASP/FBNInquiry.asp. Also, search the inmate list free at www.vinelink.com/offender/searchNew.jsp?siteID=5099. **Other phones:** Treasurer- 530-538-7576; Appraiser/Auditor- 530-538-7721; Elections- 530-538-7761; Vital Records- 530-538-7690. **Property tax/Assessor-** address above. 530-538-7721.

Calaveras County

County Recorder, 891 Mountain Ranch Rd; Government Ctr, San Andreas, CA 95249. 209-754-6372; fax-209-754-6733; hours: 8AM-4PM
All records in one index. Records indexed on computer back to 9/1995. Only the public may search. Copy fee $1.00 1st page; $.50 each add'l. Cert fee- $1.00 per cert plus copy fee. Payee- Calaveras County Recorder. **Online access to Property, Assessor records:** Access property data free at www.co.calaveras.ca.us/parcelsearch.asp. No name searching. Also, access the GIS Project of property data free at www.co.calaveras.ca.us/departments/gisproj.asp. Click on "The Parcel Information System." No name search at this site. **Other phones:** Treasurer- 209-754-6350; Appraiser/Auditor- 209-754-6356; Elections- 209-754-6376; Vital Records- 209-754-6372. **Property tax/Assessor-** same address as above. 209-754-6356.

Colusa County

County Recorder, 546 Jay St #200, Colusa, CA 95932. RE & UCC recording phone-530-458-0500; fax-530-458-0512; hours: 8:30AM-5PM www.colusacountyclerk.com
All records in one index. Search fee $5.00 per name plus $1.00 per page. Will search real estate records. Will not search UCC records or tax liens. Copy fee $1.00 per page. Cert fee- $1.00 per doc plus copy fee. Payee- Colusa County Recorder. **Other phones:** Treasurer- 530-458-0440; Appraiser/Auditor- 530-458-0450; Elections- 530-458-0500; Vital Records- 530-458-0500. **Property tax/Assessor-** 547 Market St, Colusa, CA 95932; 530-458-0450.

Contra Costa County

County Recorder, PO Box 350, Martinez, CA 94553. 925-646-2360; fax-925-646-2135; hours: 8AM-4PM www.co.contra-costa.ca.us/depart/elect/Rindex.html
The County Clerk is located at 822 Main St, Martinez, CA 94553, 925-646-2955. All records in one index. Records indexed on a public use terminal back to 1992. Only the public may search. Copy fee $1.00 per page. Cert fee- $2.50 per cert plus copy fee. Payee- Contra Costa County Recorder. **Online access to Recording, Fictitious Business Name, Deed, Lien, Judgment, Real Estate, Most Wanted, Marriage records:** Recorder office records back to 1992 and marriages free at www.criis.com/contracosta/official.shtml. By order of governor, vital statistic records have been removed from the internet. Fictitious Business names at www.criis.com/contracosta/sfictitious.shtml. Also, search the sheriff's most wanted list at www.cocosheriff.org/wanted/wanted.htm. **Phones:** Elections- 925-646-4166; Vital Records- 925-646-2360. **Property tax/Assessor-** 925-313-7400 (resi); 313-7500 (busi).

Del Norte County

County Recorder, 981 H St #160, Crescent City, CA 95531. RE & UCC recording phone-707-464-7216; fax-707-464-0321; hours: 8AM-N,1-5PM
All records in one index. Records indexed on a public use terminal back to 1973. Only the public may search. Copy fee $2.00 1st page, $1.00 each add'l. Cert fee- $2.00 per seal plus copy fee. Payee- Del Norte County Recorder. **Other phones:** Treasurer- 707-464-7283; Elections- 707-465-0383; Vital Records- 707-464-7216. **Property tax/Assessor-** 981 H St #120, Crescent City, CA 95531; 707-464-7200.

El Dorado County

County Recorder, 360 Fair Lane, Placerville, CA 95667-4197. RE & UCC recording phone-530-621-5490; fax-530-621-2147; hours: 8AM-5PM (No recordings after 4PM) www.co.el-dorado.ca.us/countyclerk/
All records in one index. Records indexed on computer back to 1850 (excluding 1911-1948). Only the public may search. Copy fee $1.00 1st page, $.50 each add'l. Cert fee- $1.00 per cert plus copy fee. Payee- El Dorado County Recorder. **Online access to Real Estate, Personal Property, Vital Statistic, Fictitious Name, Restaurant Insp records:** Access to the Recorder's index is free at http://main.co.el-dorado.ca.us/CGI/WWB012/WWM 501/R. Records go back to 1949. Search business licenses free at http://main.co.el-dorado.ca.us/CG I/WWB012/WWM200/T?S=A Official records on the recorder database are free at http://main.co.el-dorado.ca.us/CGI/WWB012/WWM501/C. Search by date range, name or document number. Search inmates at www.vinelink.com/offender/searchNew.jsp?siteI D=5099 County non-confidential marriages and fictitious names are free at http://main.co.el-dorado.ca.us/CGI/WWB012/WWM500/C. Births and deaths removed. **Other phones:** Treasurer- 530-621-5800; Elections- 530-621-7480; Vital Records- 530-621-5490. **Property tax/Assessor-** same address as above. 530-621-5719.

Fresno County

County Recorder, PO Box 766, Fresno, CA 93712. RE & UCC recording phone-559-488-3471; fax-559-488-6774; hours: 9AM-4PM www.co.fresno.ca.us/04 20/recorders_web/index.htm
Husband and wife count as one search, if so indicated. Only the public may search. Copy fee $1.50 1st page; $.50 each add'l. Cert fee- $1.00 per cert plus copy fee. Payee- Fresno County Recorder. **Online access to Recorder, Property, Birth, Death, Marriage, Lien, Deed, Mortgage, Inmate records:** Access to the recorder database is free at www.criis.com/fresno/srecord.shtml. Marriage records are at www.criis.com/fresno/smarriage.shtml. County Birth Records and death records have been removed from the internet. Also, search inmate info on private company website at www.vinelink.com/index.jsp. **Other phones:** Treasurer- 559-488-3486; Vital Records- 559-488-3476. **Property tax/Assessor-** 559-488-3514.

Glenn County

County Recorder, 526 W. Sycamore St, Willows, CA 95988. RE & UCC recording phone-530-934-6412; fax-530-934-6305; hours: 8AM-5PM
All records in one index. Records indexed on a public use terminal back to 7/1989. Only the public may search. Copy fee $1.50 per page. Cert fee- $2.00 per cert plus copy fee. Payee- Glenn County Recorder. **Other phones:** Treasurer- 530-934-6410; Appraiser/Auditor- 530-934-6402; Elections- 530-934-6414; Vital Records- 530-934-6412. **Property tax/Assessor-** 516 W. Sycamore St, Willows, CA 95988; 530-934-6402.

Humboldt County

County Recorder, 825 Fifth St, 5th Fl, Eureka, CA 95501. RE & UCC recording phone-707-445-7593; fax-707-445-7324; hours: 8:30AM-5PM www.co.humboldt.ca.us/recorder/
Only the public may search. Copy fee $2.00 1st page; $1.00 each add'l. Cert fee- $2.00 per cert plus copy fee. Payee- Humboldt County Recorder. **Online access to Inmate, Offender records:** Access to the county correction facility inmate lists is free at www.vinelink.com/offender/searchNew.jsp?siteID=50 99. **Other phones:** Treasurer- 707-445-7331; Elections- 707-445-7481; Vital Records- 707-445-7382. **Property tax/Assessor-** 707-445-7663.

Imperial County

County Recorder, 940 Main St, Rm 202, El Centro, CA 92243-2865. 760-482-4272, R/E recording phone-760-482-4275, UCC recording phone-760-482-4275; hours: 9AM-4:30PM www.co.imperial.ca.us/
All records in one index. Records indexed on a public use terminal back to 4/1986. Only the public may search. Copy fee $1.00 per page; $.50 each add'l. Cert fee- $1.00 per cert plus copy fee. Payee- Imperial County Clerk/Recorder. **Online access to Inmate, Offender, Most Wanted records:** Search the county inmate list for free at www.vinelink.com/offender/searchNew.jsp?siteID=50 11. View the sheriff office most wanted list at www.icso.org/most_wanted.htm . **Other phones:** Treasurer- 760-482-6281; Elections- 760-482-4226; Vital Records- 760-482-4272. **Assessor** - 940 Main #115, El Centro, CA 92243; 760-482-4244.

Inyo County

County Recorder, PO Box F, Independence, CA 93526. RE & UCC recording phone-760-878-0222; fax-760-878-1805; 9AM-N,1-5PM www.countyofinyo.org
All records in one index. Records indexed on a public use terminal back to 1982. Search fee $.50 per name per year, unless otherwise indicated. Will not search real estate records. UCC search per debtor name- $15.00. Copy fee $1.00 per page. Cert fee- $3.00 for 1st page; $1.00 each add'l, plus copy fee. Payee- Inyo County Recorder. **Online access to Recording, Fictitious Business Name records:** Access to the county clerk recording database may be available free at www.criis.com/inyo/official.shtml. May include Fictitious names. **Other phones:** Treasurer- 760-878-0333; Appraiser/Auditor- 760-878-0302; Elections- 760-878-0223; Vital Records- 760-878-0410. **Property tax/Assessor-** PO Drawer J, Independence, CA 93526; 760-878-0302.

Kern County

County Recorder, 1655 Chester Ave; Hall of Records, Bakersfield, CA 93301. 661-868-6400, R/E recording phone-661-868-6448, UCC recording phone-661-868-6448; fax-661-868-6401; hours: 8AM-5PM; Recording 8AM-2PM; Copy Svc 8AM-4:30PM http://recorder.co.kern.ca.us
All records in one index. Records indexed on a public use terminal back to 1974. Only the public may search. Copy fee $3.00 1st page, $.50 each add'l. Cert fee- $.50 per doc plus copy fee. Payee- Kern County Recorder. **Online access to Assessor, Property Tax, Fictitious Business Name, Vital Statistic, Recording, Real Estate, Tax Collector, Unclaimed Property records:** Assessor database records are free at http://assessor.co.kern.ca.us/kips/pr operty_search.asp. Purchase Birth, Death records from Vitalchek at www.vitalchek.com. Also, search county clerk's fictitious business name database free at www.co.kern.ca.us/ctyclerk/dba/default.asp. Recorders database of deeds is free at http://recorder.co.kern.ca.u s/kips/property_search.asp. Search fictitious business names and property tax assessment data at http://kerndata.com. Search tax collector data at www.kcttc.co.kern.ca.us/payment/mainsearch.aspx. Search unclaimed property at www.kcttc.co.kern.ca.us/searches/unclaimed_monies.cf m. **Other phones:** Treasurer- 661-868-3490; Appraiser/Auditor- 661-868-3485; Elections- 661-868-3590; Vital Records- 661-868-6449. **Property tax/Assessor-** 1115 Truxtun Ave, Bakersfield, CA 93301; 661-868-3485.

Kings County

County Recorder, 1400 W. Lacey Blvd., Hanford, CA 93230. RE & UCC recording phone-559-582-3211 x2470; fax-559-582-6639; hours: 8AM-3PM www.countyofkings.com
Search records in person with office assistance. Copy fee $1.00 per page. Cert fee- $2.00 per cert plus copy fee. Payee- Kings County Clerk Recorder. **Online access to Inmate records:** Search inmate info on private company website at www.vinelink.com/index.jsp. **Other phones:**

Treasurer- 559-582-3211 x2477; Elections- 559-582-3211 x2439; Vital Records- 559-582-3211 x2470. **Property tax/Assessor-** 559-582-3211 x2486.

Lake County

County Recorder, 255 N. Forbes, Rm 223, Lakeport, CA 95453. RE & UCC recording phone-707-263-2293; fax-707-263-3703; hours: 9AM-5PM
All records in one index. Office will perform a UCC search but public must search other records themselves. Search fee $15.00 per debtor. Copy fee $1.00 for 1st page; $.50 each add'l. Cert fee- $1.00 per cert plus copy fee. Payee- Lake County Recorder. **Other phones:** Treasurer- 707-263-2236; Elections- 707-263-2372; Vital Records- 707-263-2293. **Property tax/Assessor-** same address as above. 707-263-2302.

Lassen County

County Recorder, 220 S. Lassen St, #5, Susanville, CA 96130. RE & UCC recording phone-530-251-8234; fax-530-257-3480; hours: Public Hours: 10AM-N, 1-3PM; Phone Hours: 8AM-N http://clerk.lassencounty.org
All records in one index. Only the public may search. Copy fee $1.50 per page; $.50 each add'l. Cert fee- $1.75 1st page plus copy fee. Payee- Lassen County Recorder. **Online access to Real Estate, Recording, Deed, Tax Sale records:** Access to the recorder database is free at http://icris.lassencounty.org/icris/splash.jsp. Registration is required. Recorded documents go back to 7/1985. Also, access to tax sales lists is free through a private company at www.bid4assets.com. **Other phones:** Treasurer- 530-251-8220; Elections- 530-251-8217; Vital Records- 530-251-8234. **Property tax/Assessor-** 220 S. Lassen St, #4, Susanville, CA 96130; 530-251-8241; 251-8242.

Los Angeles County

County Recorder, PO Box 53195; Real Estate Records Section, Los Angeles, CA 90053-0115. 562-462-2125, 800-815-2666; fax-562-929-5086; hours: 8AM-5PM http://regrec.co.la.ca.us
County sells a variety of data; view the list and details at http://assessor.co.la.ca.us/extranet/Outsidesales/catalog. aspx. An application for real estate record form is at http://regrec.co.la.ca.us/recorder/appraealstaterec.htm. Separate indices to search. Will not name search real estate records. Search fee with document number is $.50 per name per year. To request a credit card order by telephone, contact the Real Estate Records Section at 562-462-2133. Will search UCC records, but not tax liens. UCC search per debtor name- $.50 per year with $1.00 minimum. Copy fee see certification fee. Cert fee- $6.00 for 1st page; $3.00 each add'l page. Payee- Los Angeles County Recorder; no out of state checks. Credit card orders-add $6.00. All major cards accepted. **Online access to Assessor, Fictitious Business Name, Inmate, Property Tax, Sex Offender, Most Wanted records:** For assessments use the PDB Inquiry System dial-up svc. for $100 monthly plus $1.00 per inquiry, also $75 sign-up fee for 3-year dial-up with usage fee of $6.50 per hr or $.11 per minute. PDB registration data is at: http://assessor.co.la.ca.us/extranet/outsidesales/online.as px. Tax info line: 213-974-3838. County most wanted list- www.lapdonline.org/get_involved/most_wanted/m ost_wanted_main.htm. Search county inmates at http://app1.lasd.org/iic/ajis_search.cfm. Also search property/assessor data (no name searching) free at http://assessormap.co.la.ca.us/mapping/viewer.asp. Search Fictitious Names at http://regrec.co.la.ca.us/fbn/ FBN.cfm. Sex offenders- http://gismap.co.la.ca.us/so ls/viewer.asp. **Other phones:** Treasurer- 562-974-2101. **Property tax/Assessor-** 562-974-3211.

Madera County

County Recorder, 209 W. Yosemite, Madera, CA 93637. RE & UCC recording phone-559-675-7724; fax-559-675-7870; hours: 8AM-3:30PM www.madera-county.com

Separate indices to search include computer, roll film. Records indexed on a public use terminal back to 9/1990. Only the public may search. Copy fee $1.00 1st page; $.50 each add'l. Cert fee- $1.75 per cert plus copy fee. Payee- Madera County Recorder. **Other phones:** Treasurer- 559-675-7713; Elections- 559-675-7720; Vital Records- 559-675-7724. **Property tax/Assessor-** same address as above. 559-675-7710.

Marin County

County Recorder, PO Box C, San Rafael, CA 94913. RE & UCC recording phone-415-499-6092; fax-415-499-7893; hours: 9AM-4PM research & copies; 9AM-3PM recording www.co.marin.ca.us/depts/AR/main/index.cfm

All records in one index. Records indexed on a public use terminal back to 1974. Only the public may search. Copy fee $4.00 1st page, $1.00 each add'l page. Cert fee- $4.00 per cert plus copy fee. Payee- Marin County Recorder. **Online access to Real Estate, Property Tax, Grantor/Grantee, Recording, Vital Statistic, Business Name, Booking Log records:** Search county Grantor/Grantee index free at www.co.marin.ca.us/depts/AR/RiiMs/index.asp. Also, search the property tax database at www.co.marin.ca.us/depts/AR/COMPASS/index.asp but there is no name searching. Also, search the real estate sales lists by month and year by selecting the year. Also, search vital records for document index # at www.co.marin.ca.us/depts/AR/VitalStatistics/index.asp. Birth records go back to 1967; deaths to 1979. Marriage records go back to 1948. Search business names at http://marinfo.marin/Bizmo/index.cfm. Search the sheriff's booking log at www.co.marin.ca.us/depts/SO/bklog/XMLProj/index.asp. **Other phones:** Treasurer- 415-499-6145; Vital Records- 415-499-6094. **Property tax/Assessor-** PO Box C, Civic Center Branch, Rm 208, San Rafael, CA 94913; 415-499-7215.

Mariposa County

County Recorder, PO Box 35, Mariposa, CA 95338. 209-966-5719; hours: 8AM-5PM (Recording hours 8AM-3:30PM)

All records in one index. Only the public may search. Copy fee $1.00 per page. Cert fee- $1.00 per doc plus copy fee. Payee- Mariposa County Recorder. **Online access to Birth records:** Search birth records 1905-1995 free at www.mariposaresearch.net/php/. **Other phones:** Treasurer- 209-966-2621. **Property tax/Assessor-** 209-966-2332.

Mendocino County

County Recorder, 501 Low Gap Rd, Rm 1020, Ukiah, CA 95482. RE & UCC recording phone-707-463-4376; fax-707-463-4257; hours: 8AM-5PM www.co.mendocino.ca.us

All records in one index. Records indexed on a public use terminal back to 1966. Will honor mailed in requests for real estate records searches, otherwise the public must search for themselves. Search fee $5.00 per name. Copy fee $2.50 1st page, $.50 each add'l. Cert fee- $1.00 per cert plus copy fee. Payee- Mendocino County Recorder. **Online access to Inmate, Offender records:** Access to the county inmate list is free at www.vinelink.com/offender/searchNew.jsp?siteID=5009. **Other phones:** Treasurer- 707-463-4388; Appraiser/Auditor- 707-463-4311; Elections- 707-463-4374; Vital Records- 707-463-4371. **Property tax/Assessor-** 707-463-4311.

Merced County

County Recorder, 2222 M St, Merced, CA 95340. 209-385-7627; fax-209-385-7626; hours: 8AM-4:30PM http://web.co.merced.ca.us/recorder/

Only the public may search. Copy fee $3.00 for 1st page; $1 each add'l. Cert fee- $2.00 per cert plus copy fee. Payee- Merced County Recorder. **Online access to Recorder, Grantor/Grantee, Deed, Real Estate, Most Wanted, Missing Person, Sex Offender records:** Access to the recorder official records index

PARIS system is free at http://139.151.191.2/cgi-bin/odsmnu1.html/input. Search the county most wanted and missing person sites for free at www.co.merced.ca.us/sheriff/. A short list of high risk sex offenders at www.co.merced.ca.us/da/so_high_risk.htm. **Other phones:** Treasurer- 209-385-7307. **Property tax/Assessor-** 209-385-7631.

Modoc County

County Recorder, 204 Court St, Alturas, CA 96101. RE & UCC recording phone-530-233-6205; fax-530-233-6666; hours: 8:30AM-N, 1-5PM

Separate indices to search. Records indexed on a public use terminal back to 1987. Office will perform a UCC search but public must search other records themselves. UCC search per debtor name- $1.00 for 1st page; $.50 each add'l. Cert fee- $1.00 per cert plus copy fee. Payee- Modoc County Recorder. **Online access to Recording, Fictitious Business Name, Tax Sale records:** Access to the county clerk recording database soon to be free at www.criis.com/modoc/official.shtml. Fictitious business names may also be found. Also, access to tax sales lists is free through a private company at www.bid4assets.com. **Other phones:** Treasurer- 530-233-6223; Appraiser/Auditor- 530-233-6221; Elections- 530-233-6201; Vital Records- 530-233-6205. **Property tax/Assessor-** same address as above. 530-233-6217; 233-6218.

Mono County

County Recorder, PO Box 237, Bridgeport, CA 93517. RE & UCC recording phone-760-932-5530; fax-760-932-5531; hours: 9AM-5PM www.monocounty.ca.gov/departments.html

Office personnel or visitors may perform searches. General index search fee $2.00 per year per name. Real estate record owner searches available. Will search UCC records, UCC search does not include tax liens. UCC search per debtor name- $15.00 per name per 5 years. Tax lien search fee- $2.00 per year per debtor. Copy fee $.05 per page. Cert fee- $1.75 per cert plus copy fee. Payee- Mono County Recorder. **Other phones:** Treasurer- 760-932-5480; Elections- 760-932-5537; Vital Records- 760-932-5535. **Property tax/Assessor-** 760-932-5510.

Monterey County

County Recorder, 168 Alisal St, 1st Fl, Salinas, CA 93901. RE & UCC recording phone-831-755-5041; fax-831-755-5064; hours: 8AM-5PM www.co.monterey.ca.us/recorder/

All records in one index. Records indexed on computer back to 1978. Only the public may search. Copy fee $2.00 per page. Cert fee- $2.00 per cert plus copy fee. Payee- Monterey County Recorder. **Online access to Inmate, Offender, Most Wanted, Tax Sale records:** Access to the county jail inmates list is available free at www.vinelink.com/offender/searchNew.jsp?siteID=5099. The county tax defaulted property list is at www.co.monterey.ca.us/taxcollector/Auction.htm. Search assessor data free at www.co.monterey.ca.us/assessor/intro2asmt-query.htm; no name searching. **Other phones:** Treasurer- 831-755-5015; Elections- 831-796-1499; Vital Records- 813-755-5041. **Property tax/Assessor-** 831-755-5035.

Napa County

County Recorder, PO Box 298, Napa, CA 94559-0298. 707-253-4246, R/E recording phone-707-253-4105, UCC recording phone-707-253-4105; fax-707-259-8149; hours: 8AM-5PM www.mynapa.info/Gov/Departments/DeptDefault.asp?DID=28000

All records in one index. Records indexed on a public use terminal back to 1986. Office personnel or visitors may perform searches. Search fee $5.00 per name, per year. Real estate record owner searches available at www.co.napa.ca.us/orpublic/ORInquiry.asp Federal tax lien search- $15.00 per debtor. Copy fee $2.00 per page. Cert fee- $3.00 per doc, plus copy fee. Fee to fax results is $3 for 1st page, $1 each add'l. Payee- Napa County Recorder. **Online**

access to Grantor/Grantee, Property, Recording, Deed, Judgment, Lien records: Access "Official Records" by subscription; tentative fee- $3600 per year. Index goes back to May, 1986; images back to March, 1999. Search Grantor/Grantee index back to 5/86 free at www.co.napa.ca.us/orpublic/ORInquiry.asp. **Other phones:** Treasurer- 707-253-4311; Elections- 707-253-4321; Vital Records- 707-253-4247. **Property tax/Assessor-** 1127 1st St #128, Napa, CA 94559; 707-253-4466.

Nevada County

County Recorder, 950 Maidu Ave, Nevada City, CA 95959. 530-265-1221; fax-530-265-9842; hours: 9AM-4PM www.mynevadacounty.com/recorder

All records in one index. Records indexed on a public use terminal back to 1987. Only the public may search. Copy fee $3.00 for 1st page; $.50 each add'l. Will fax results for $2.00 per page fee. Cert fee- $1.00 per cert plus copy fee. Payee- Nevada County Recorder. **Online access to Real Estate, Recorder, Deed, Judgment, Fictitious Name, Property Tax, GIS records:** Access to the county clerk database of recordings and assumed names is free at www.criis.com/nevada/official.shtml. Also, search property tax payment records at http://treas-tax.co.nevada.ca.us/searchtax.php; no name searching. Also, subscription access to Recorders full database is $200 per month fee. Also, daily/weekly/monthly CD-roms are available. Also, search the GIS mapping site by address for property info for free at http://63.205.214.10:1711. **Other phones:** Treasurer- 530-265-1285; Elections- 530-265-1298. **Property tax/Assessor-** same address as above. 530-265-1232.

Orange County

County Clerk Recorder, PO Box 238, Santa Ana, CA 92702-0238. 714-834-2500 (questions), R/E recording phone-714-834-2500 (recorded info only); fax-714-834-2575; hours: 8AM-4:30PM www.ocrecorder.com

For questions about requesting documents, call Tom Daly, 714-834-2500. Fax requests not accepted. Only the public may search. Copy fee $1.00 per page. Cert fee- $1.00 per complete doc plus copy fee. Payee- Orange County Clerk-Recorder. **Online access to Grantor/Grantee, Deed, Lien, Judgment, Fictitious Business Name, Property Tax, Wanted, Missing Person, Inmate, Arrest records:** Orange County Grantor/Grantee index is free online at http://cr.ocgov.com/grantorgrantee/index.asp. Also, search fictitious business names at http://cr.ocgov.com/fbn/index.asp. Also, search property tax records at http://tax.ocgov.com/tcweb/search_page.asp; no name searching. Search sheriff's wanted, missing persons and blotter lists at www.ocsd.org; click on "Crime Bulletins." For inmates, arrests (search by date only), arrest warrants, click on "e-services." Also, search inmate/offender lists www.vinelink.com/offender/searchNew.jsp?siteID=5004. **Other phones:** Treasurer- 714-834-2682; Vital Records- 714-834-2568. **Property tax/Assessor-** 714-834-2727.

Placer County

County Recorder, 2954 Richardson Dr., Auburn, CA 95603. RE & UCC recording phone-530-886-5600; fax-530-886-5687; hours: 8AM-5PM (Recording 9AM-4PM) www.placer.ca.gov/clerk/clerk.htm

All records in one index. Records indexed on a public use terminal back to 1972. Office will perform a UCC search but public must search other records themselves. Search fee $10.00. Copy fee $2.00 per page. Cert fee- $2.00 per doc plus copy fee. Payee- Placer County Recorder. **Online access to Recording, Fictitious Name, Marriage, Most Wanted, Missing Person, Jail, Assessor, Property Tax records:** Recorder office records are free at the website. County Birth and death records have been removed from the internet. Marriage records are at www.criis.com/placer/smarriage.shtml. Search county Fictitious Business Names at www.criis.com/placer/sfictitious.shtml. Search sheriff's most wanted, missing person, and sex offender map at www.placer.ca.gov/sheriff/aware/. The county in-custody roster is at www.placer.ca.gov/sheriff/jail/icr.htm. The assessor's property assessment data is free at www.placer.ca.gov/assessor/assessment-inquiry.htm, no name searching. **Other phones:** Elections- 530-886-5650; Vital Records- 530-886-5600. **Property tax/Assessor-** 530-889-4300.

Plumas County

County Recorder, 520 Main St, Rm 102, Quincy, CA 95971. 530-283-6218; fax-530-283-6155; hours: 8AM-5PM www.countyofplumas.com
Office will perform a UCC search but public must search other records themselves. UCC search per debtor name- $10.00. Separate federal/state combined tax lien search- $10.00 per debtor. Copy fee $1.00 1st page, $.50 each add'l. Large books $1.50 1st page, $.80 each add'l. Cert fee- $1.00 per cert plus copy fee. Payee- Plumas County Recorder. **Other phones:** Treasurer- 530-283-6260; Elections- 530-283-6256. **Property tax/Assessor-** 530-283-6380.

Riverside County

County Recorder, PO Box 751; Attn: County Recorder/Clerk, Riverside, CA 92502-0751. RE & UCC recording phone-951-486-7000; fax-951-486-7047; hours: 8AM-4:30PM (recording hours 8AM-2PM) http://riverside.asrclkrec.com
Separate indices to search. Records indexed on a public use terminal back to 1998. Office personnel or visitors may perform searches. Search fee $2.00 1st page found, $1.00 each add'l page. Will not search real estate records. Copy fee $2.00 1st page, $1.00 each add'l. Cert fee- $1.00 per cert plus copy fee. Payee- Riverside County Recorder. **Online access to Assessor, Property Tax, Fictitious Name, Grantor/Grantee, Wanted, Missing Person records:** Property tax information from the County Treasurer database is free from EZproperty.com at https://riverside.ca.ezgov.com/ezproperty/review_search.jsp. Also, access to county fictitious name database is at http://riverside.asrclkrec.com/OS.asp. The FBN search is free; a fee is charged for documents from Grantor/Grantee index and assessor data at www.enetwizard.com/shop/affiliates/11467_01/. Also, access sheriff's most wanted, missing person, sex offender map at www.co.riverside.ca.us/sheriff/crime/. **Other phones:** Treasurer- 951-955-3900; Vital Records- 951-486-7000. **Property tax/Assessor-** PO Box 12004, Riverside, CA 92500-2204 951-955-6250.

Sacramento County

County Recorder, PO Box 839, Sacramento, CA 95812-0839. 916-874-6334; 800-313-7133, R/E recording phone-916-874-6334, UCC recording phone-916-874-6334; fax-916-874-8012; hours: 8AM-5PM (recording 8AM-3PM) www.saccounty.net
Separate indices to search include grantor and grantee. Records indexed on computer back to 1965. Only the public may search. Copy fee $1.50 for 1st page; $1.00 each add'l. Cert fee- $.50 per cert plus copy fee. Payee- Sacramento County Clerk and Recorder. **Online access to Assessor, Grantor/Grantee, Deed, Business License, Wanted Suspect, Inmate records:** Access Clerk-recorder Grantor/Grantee index back to 1965 for free at www.erosi.saccounty.net/Inputs.asp. Search restaurant inspections at www.emd.saccounty.net/eh/emdfoodprotect.htm. Sex offenders at www.sacpd.org/sexoffender/. Fictitious names at www.efbn.saccounty.net. Also search property tax & parcels at www.eproptax.saccounty.net; no name searching. Also, find proptax data at http://assessorparcelviewer.saccounty.net/website/assessor/pv_blank.aspx?g=; no name searching. Also, search City of West Sacramento business licenses at www.ci.west-sacramento.ca.us/cityhall/departments/finance/buslic/blfind.cfm. Search the county wanted suspect list at www.crimealert.org/wanted.cfm. Inmates at

www.vinelink.com/index.jsp. **Other phones:** Treasurer- 916-874-6725; Appraiser/Auditor- 916-875-0700; Elections- 916-874-6451; Vital Records- 916-874-7850. **Property tax/Assessor-** 3701 Power Inn Rd., Sacramento, CA 95814; 916-875-0700.

San Benito County

County Recorder, 440 Fifth St; Rm 206, Hollister, CA 95023. RE & UCC recording phone-831-636-4046; fax-831-636-2939; hours: 8AM-5PM (Recording hours 9AM-4PM) www.san-benito.ca.us
All records in one index. Only the public may search. Copy fee $2.00 1st page; $1.00 each add'l. Cert fee- $3.00 per doc plus copy fee. Payee- San Benito County Clerk. **Online access to Most Wanted records:** Access the sheriff's most wanted list at www.sbcsheriff.org/wanted.html. **Other phones:** Treasurer- 831-636-4043; Elections- 831-636-4016; Vital Records- 831-636-4029. **Property tax/Assessor-** 440 Fifth St, 1st Fl, Rm 107, Hollister, CA 95023; 831-636-4043, assessor fax- 831-636-4033.

San Bernardino County

County Recorder, 222 W. Hospitality Ln.; 1st Fl, San Bernardino, CA 92415-0022. RE & UCC recording phone-909-387-8306; fax-909-386-9050; hours: 8AM-4:30PM www.co.san-bernardino.ca.us
All records in one index. Records indexed on a public use terminal back to 1980. Only the public may search. Copy fee $2.00 1st page, $1.25 each add'l. Cert fee- $3.25 per doc plus copy fee. Payee- San Bernardino County Recorder. **Online access to Recorder, Assessor, Fictitious Name, Grantor/Grantee, Inmate, Property Tax records:** Records on the County Assessor database are free at www.co.san-bernardino.ca.us/tax/trsearch.asp. No name searching. Also, for automated call distribution, call 909-387-8306; for fictitious names information, call 909-386-8970. Search fictitious business names at http://170.164.50.51/fbn/index.html. Also, Auditor/Controller Grantor/Grantee recording index back to 1980 is free at http://acrparis.co.san-bernardino.ca.us/cgi-bin/odsmnu1.html/input. Property can also be searched on PIMS system, registration required, https://nppublic.co.san-bernardino.ca.us/newpims/. Also, search the inmates/offender list at www.vinelink.com/offender/searchNew.jsp?siteID=5006. **Other phones:** Treasurer- 909-387-8308; Appraiser/Auditor- 909-387-6730; Elections- 909-387-8300; Vital Records- 909-387-8314; Admin.- 909-387-8924. **Property tax/Assessor-** 172 W 3rd St, San Bernardino, CA 92413; 909-387-6730.

San Diego County

County Recorder, PO Box 121750, San Diego, CA 92112. RE & UCC recording phone-619-238-8158; fax-619-557-4155; hours: 8AM-5PM www.co.san-diego.ca.us
Separate indices to search. Records indexed on a public use terminal back to 1982. Office will perform a UCC search but public must search other records themselves. UCC search per debtor name- $10.00. Copy fee $2.00 per page. Cert fee- $1.00 per cert plus copy fee. Payee- San Diego Recorder/Clerk. **Online access to Assessor, Fictitious Name, Real Estate, Grantor/Grantee, Inmates, Most Wanted, Warrant, Sex Offender, Pet, Missing Children, Tax Sale records:** Records on the County Assessor/Recorder/County Clerk Online Services site are free at www.sdcounty.ca.gov/arcc/arcc_home.html including fictitious business names, indexes, maps, property information. Grantee/grantor index search by name for individual record data at http://arcc.co.san-diego.ca.us/services/grantorgrantee. Search inmates at www.sdsheriff.net/wij/wij.aspx. Property characteristics at- http://arcc.co.san-diego.ca.us/services/propchar/. Search for property data at www.sdcounty.ca.gov/arcc/services/propsales_search.html; no name searching. **Other phones:** Treasurer- 619-236-3121; Vital Records- 619-237-0502. **Property tax/Assessor-** 1600 Pacific Hwy, #103, San Diego, CA 92101; 619-236-3771.

San Francisco County

County Recorder, 1 Dr. Carlton E. Goodlet Pl.; City Hall, Rm 190, San Francisco, CA 94102. 415-554-4176; fax-415-554-4179; hours: 8AM-4PM www.sf.org
Only the public may search. Copy fee $3.00 for 1st 3 pages; $.50 after 3rd page. Cert fee- $1.00 per doc plus copy fee. Payee- San Francisco County Assessor-Recorder. **Online access to Assessor, Property, Fictitious Business Name, Birth, Death records:** Access to the City Property Tax database is free at https://services.sfgov.org/ptx/intro.asp. Click on begin. No name searching; address or block/lot number is required. Also search parcel addresses on the GIS site at http://gispub.sfgov.org/website/sfparcel/index.htm. Sex offenders are at www.sfgov.org/site/police_index.asp?id=24681 Fictitious business names are also searchable at http://services.sfgov.org/bns/start.asp. Limited vital statistic information is searchable at www.sfgenealogy.com/sf/, a privately operated site. **Property tax/Assessor-** 415-554-5516.

San Joaquin County

County Recorder, PO Box 1968, Stockton, CA 95201. 209-468-3939; fax-209-468-8040; www.co.san-joaquin.ca.us
All records in one index. Only the public may search. Copy fee $2.00 per page staff assisted, $1.00 per page self assisted. Cert fee- $1.00 per page. Payee- San Joaquin County Recorder. **Online access to Most Wanted, Missing Person records:** Access the sheriff most wanted and missing person pages at http://207.104.50.55/wanted/information.jsp. **Other phones:** Treasurer- 209-468-2133; Vital Records- 803-245-8075. **Property tax/Assessor-** 24 S Hunke, Rm 303, Stockton, CA 95202; 209-468-2630.

San Luis Obispo County

County Recorder, 1055 Monterey St, Rm D120, San Luis Obispo, CA 93408. RE & UCC recording phone-805-781-5080; fax-805-781-1111; hours: 8AM-5PM www.sloclerkrecorder.org
There is also a North County office at 5955 Capistrano, #B, Atascadero CA 93422, 805-461-6041. All records in one index. Records indexed on a public use terminal back to 1924. Office will perform a UCC search if by mail, but public must search other records themselves. UCC search per debtor name- $10.00. Copy fee $1.00 per page. Cert fee- $1.00 per doc, plus copy fee. Payee- San Luis Obispo County Recorder. **Online access to Grantor/Grantee, Deed, Judgment, Lien, Real Estate, Mortgage, Divorce, Fictitious Business Name, Missing Person, Most Wanted records:** Search the recorder database for free at www.sloclerkrecorder.org/recorder/searchform.cfm. Search fictitious names at www.sloclerkrecorder.org/countyclerk/fbnstartpage.htm. Also, search the assessor property tax rolls for free at www.slocoassr.net/#; no name searching. There is also an "unsecured roll" search. Also, search the sheriff's alerts page for missing persons and most wanted at http://slosheriff.org/alerts.php. **Other phones:** Treasurer- 805-781-5842; Elections- 805-781-5228; Vital Records- 805-781-5080. **Property tax/Assessor-** 805-781-5643.

San Mateo County

County Recorder, 555 County Ctr, 1st Fl, Redwood City, CA 94063. RE & UCC recording phone-650-363-4713; fax-650-363-4843; hours: 8AM-5PM www.smcare.org
All records in one index. Records indexed on a public use terminal back to 1985. Only the public may search. Copy fee $2.00 1st page, $1.00 each add'l. Cert fee- $1.00 per cert plus copy fee. Payee- San Mateo County Recorder. **Online access to Property Tax, Fictitious Name records:** Records on county property tax data site is free at http://smctweb1.co.sanmateo.ca.us/index.html. Search by address or parcel ID#. There is also a secured property search, but no name searching, at

http://smctweb1.co.sanmateo.ca.us/SMCWPS/pages/secureSearch.jsp. Also, search fictitious business names at www.care.co.sanmateo.ca.us/business/fictitious/default.asp. **Other phones:** Treasurer- 650-363-4840; Appraiser/Auditor- 650-363-4500; Elections- 650-312-5222; Vital Records- 650-363-4500. **Property tax/Assessor-** address above. 650-363-4500.

Santa Barbara County

County Recorder, PO Box 159, Santa Barbara, CA 93102-0159. RE & UCC recording phone-805-568-2250; fax-805-568-2266; hours: 8AM-4:30PM www.sbcrecorder.com
County also has a branch office in Santa Maria at 511 E Lakeside Pkwy, #115, 93455, 805-346-8370; but that office does not handle recordings. All records in one index. Records indexed on a public use terminal back to 1989. Office will perform a UCC search but public must search other records themselves. Search fee $15.00. Copy fee $1.00 per page. Cert fee- $3.00 per cert plus copy fee. Payee- Santa Barbara County Recorder. **Online access to Assessor, Recorder, Real Estate, Lien, Deed, Vital Statistic, Judgment, Property Tax, Most Wanted records:** Access to assessor online property info system (OPIS) in free at the website with parcel number. Records go back 10 years. Database is free to view but only subscribers will be able to download. Full access requires registration. Contact Larry Herrera for an account. herrera@co.santa-barbara.ca.us. Also, search the records database for free at www.sb-democracy.com/opis/logon.htf. Logon as "public" password "access." Also, search property tax bills at http://taxes.co.santa-barbara.ca.us/propertytax.asp; click on View/Search Secured Property Tax Bills. No name searching. Search the Sheriff's most wanted list at www.sbsheriff.org/mw/index.html. **Other phones:** Treasurer- 805-568-2490; Appraiser/Auditor- 805-568-2550; Elections- 805-568-2200; Vital Records- 805-568-2257. **Property tax/Assessor-** same address as above. 805-568-2550.

Santa Clara County

County Clerk-Recorder, 70 W. Hedding St, 1st Fl, East Wing; County Gov't Ctr, San Jose, CA 95110. 408-299-2481, R/E recording phone-408-299-5667; fax-408-280-1768; hours: 8AM-4:30PM www.clerkrecordersearch.org
Separate indices to search include computer; microfiche/film for pre-1981. Records indexed on a public use terminal back to 1981. Office will perform a tax lien search but public must search other records themselves. Tax lien search fee- $15.00 per debtor. Separate federal/state combined tax lien search- $.50 per debtor per year. RE or tax lien copy- $9.00 for the 1st page, $2.00 each add'l page. Cert fee- $2.00 per cert plus copy fee. Payee- Santa Clara County Recorder. **Online access to Recording, Grantor/Grantee, Fictitious Business Name, Assessor, Tax Collector, Birth records:** Access to the County Clerk-Recorder database is free at www.clerkrecordersearch.org/cgi-bin/odsmnu1.html/input. Search births 1905-1995 free at www.mariposaresearch.net/php/. Also, search fictitious business names free at www.clerkrecordersearch.org/cgi-bin/FBNSearch.html/input. Also search the assessment roll free at www.scc-assessor.org/ari/home. No name searching. Also, search tax collector database at http://payments.scctax.org/payment/jsp/startup.jsp. No name searching. Also, search for county sex offenders at www.sjpd.org/SexOffenders.cfm. **Other phones:** Vital Records- 408-299-5669; Official Record Copies- 408-299-5670. **Property tax/Assessor-** 408-299-5500.

Santa Cruz County

County Recorder, 701 Ocean St, Rm 230, Santa Cruz, CA 95060. 831-454-2800; fax-831-454-3169; hours: 8AM-4PM www.co.santa-cruz.ca.us/rcd/
All records in one index. Records indexed on computer. Only the public may search. Copy fee $1.75 per page. Cert fee- $2.50 per cert plus copy fee. Payee- Santa Cruz County Recorder. **Online**

access to Assessor, Property Tax, Fictitious Business Name, Recording, Deed, Judgment, Vital Statistic, Inmate records: Access to the assessor's parcel information data is free at http://sccounty01.co.santa-cruz.ca.us/ASR/. No name searching. Also, search for property information using the GIS map at http://gis.co.santa-cruz.ca.us. Search fictitious business names at http://sccounty01.co.santa-cruz.ca.us/clerkrecorder/Asp/FBNInquiry.asp. Search city business licenses at www.ci.santa-cruz.ca.us/bldb/index.html. Search inmates at- www.vinelink.com/offender/searchNew.jsp?siteID=5099. Also, access to the recorder's official records is free at http://sccounty01.co.santa-cruz.ca.us/clerkrecorder/Asp/ORInquiry.asp. Online indexes go back to 1978. Births, Deaths, and Marriages are also searchable back to 1984. **Other phones:** Treasurer- 831-454-2510; Elections- 831-454-2060; Vital Records- 831-454-2429. **Property tax/Assessor-** same address as above. 831-454-2002.

Shasta County

County Recorder, 1500 Court St, Rm 102, Redding, CA 96001. 530-225-5671; fax-530-225-5152; hours: 8AM-5PM www.co.shasta.ca.us
Only the public may search. General copy fee $1.00 1st page, $.50 each add'l. RE or tax lien copy- $1.00 1st page; $.50 each add'l page. Cert fee- $1.00 per doc plus copy fee. Payee- Shasta County Recorder. **Online access to Assessor, Recorder, Real Estate, Vital Statistic records:** Search assessor and recorded documents at www.co.shasta.ca.us/Departments/AssessorRecorder/PubInqDisclaimer.shtml Also, a private site lists various birth, death, and marriage records of the county and more at http://myclouds.tripod.com/shasta/shastaco.html. Records on the City of Redding Parcel Search By Parcel Number Server are free at http://cor400.ci.redding.ca.us/nd/gow3lkap.ndm/input. CA state law has removed owner names. **Property tax/Assessor-** 530-225-3600.

Sierra County

County Recorder, PO Drawer D, Downieville, CA 95936. RE & UCC recording phone-530-289-3295; fax-530-289-3300; hours: 9AM-N,1-4PM www.sierracounty.ws
Records indexed on computer back to 1985. Only the public may search. Copy fee $1.00 per page. Cert fee- $1.75 per cert plus copy fee. Payee-Sierra County Recorder. **Online access to Tax Sale records:** Access to tax sales lists is free through a private company at www.bid4assets.com . **Other phones:** Treasurer- 530-289-3286; Appraiser/Auditor- 530-289-3283; Elections- 530-289-3295; Vital Records- 530-289-3295. **Property tax/Assessor-** PO Box 8, Downieville, CA 95936; 530-289-3283.

Siskiyou County

County Recorder, PO Box 8, Yreka, CA 96097. 530-842-8065; fax-530-842-8077; hours: 8AM-4PM
All records in one index. Records indexed on a public use terminal back to 1975. Only the public may search. Copy fee $1.00 1st page, $.50 each add'l. Cert fee- $1.00 per doc plus copy fee. Payee- Siskiyou County Recorder. **Online access to Recording, Deed, Lien, Land, Fictitious Business Name, Tax Sale records:** Access to the Recorder records database is free at www.criis.com/siskiyou/srecord_current.shtml. Also, access to the fictitious names database is at www.criis.com/siskiyou/sfictitious.shtml. Also, access to tax sales lists is free through a private company at www.bid4assets.com. **Other phones:** Vital Records- 530-842-8065. **Property tax/Assessor-** 530-842-8036.

Solano County

County Recorder, 675 Texas St #2700, Fairfield, CA 94533. 707-784-6290, R/E recording phone-707-421-6290, UCC recording phone-707-421-6290; fax-707-421-6911; hours: 8AM-4PM; 8AM-3:30PM recording hours; copies 8AM-3P www.solanocounty.com

Separate indices to search. Records indexed on a public use terminal back to 1990. Office will perform a UCC search but public must search other records themselves. UCC search per debtor name- $4.00 plus $2.00 add'l copy. Copy fee $4.00 for 1st page; $2.00 each add'l. Cert fee- $4.00 per cert plus copy fee. Payee- Solano County Recorders Office. **Online access to Property Tax, Recording, Grantor/Grantee, Deed, Judgment, Lien, Death, Inmate records:** The recorder's and assessor's indexes are free at www.solanocounty.com/assessrecord/. Also, search the treasurer/tax collector/county clerk property tax database free at www.solanocounty.com/resources/scips/tax/situssearch.asp?navid=531. No name searching. Also, search the county jail inmate list at www.vinelink.com/offender/searchNew.jsp?siteID=5099. **Other phones:** Treasurer- 707-421-7485; Appraiser/Auditor- 707-421-6210; Elections- 707-421-7485; Vital Records- 707-421-6294. **Property tax/Assessor-** same address as above. 707-421-6200.

Sonoma County

County Recorder, PO Box 1709, Santa Rosa, CA 95402-1709. 707-565-2651; fax-707-565-3905; hours: 8AM-4:30PM www.sonoma-county.org/recorder
All records in one index. Records indexed on computer back to 1/1/1964. Only the public may search. Copy fee $1.75 per page. Cert fee- $2.00 per doc plus copy fee. Payee- Sonoma County Recorder. **Online access to Real Estate, Recorder, Deed, Lien, Death, Birth, UCC records:** Access recorder records free at www.sonoma-county.org/recorder. **Other phones:** Treasurer- 707-565-2281; Elections- 707-565-6800; Vital Records- 707-565-2645. **Property tax/Assessor-** 585 Fiscal Drive, Rm 104F, Santa Rosa, CA 95403; 707-565-1888.

Stanislaus County

County Recorder, PO Box 1008, Modesto, CA 95353. RE & UCC recording phone-209-525-5260; fax-209-525-5207; hours: 8AM-N,1-4PM www.co.stanislaus.ca.us
Assessor is located at 1010 10th St. #2400. Records indexed on a public use terminal back to 4/1993. Only the public may search. Copy fee $3.00 1st page, $2.00 each add'l. Cert fee- $2.00 per doc, plus copy fee. Payee- Stanislaus County Recorder. **Online access to Recording, Fictitious Name, Deed, Lien, Land, Most Wanted, Missing Person records:** Recorder office records index of recent records are free at www.criis.com/stanislaus/srecord_current.shtml. Birth, death and marriage records have been removed from the internet. County Fictitious Business Name records are free at www.criis.com/stanislaus/sfictitious.shtml. Also, search sheriff's missing persons and most wanted lists at www.stanislaussheriff.com/crimebulletin/. **Other phones:** Elections- 209-525-5200; Vital Records- 209-525-5291. **Property tax/Assessor-** 1010 Tenth St, Modesto, CA 95354; 209-525-6461.

Sutter County

County Recorder, PO Box 1555, Yuba City, CA 95992-1555. RE & UCC recording phone-530-822-7134; fax-530-822-7214; hours: 8AM-5PM www.suttercounty.org
All records in one index. Records indexed on a public use terminal back to 1995. Only the public may search. Copy fee $1.25 per page. Cert fee- $2.25 per doc plus copy fee. Payee- Sutter County Recorder. **Online access to Recorder, Grantor/Grantee, Real Estate, Fictitious Name, Inmate, Offender records:** Access recorder database free at www.suttercounty.org/apps/recordsquery/clerk/. Records go back to 12/29/1994. Also, access assessment and property tax records free at www.suttercounty.org/doc/apps/recordsquery/recordsquery. Also, to search offender site go to www.vinelink.com. **Other phones:** Treasurer- 530-822-7117; Appraiser/Auditor- 530-822-7160;

Elections- 530-822-7122; Vital Records- 530-822-7134. **Property tax/Assessor-** 4160 Civic Center Blvd., Yuba City, CA 95992; 530-822-7160.

Tehama County

County Recorder, PO Box 250, Red Bluff, CA 96080. RE & UCC recording phone-530-527-3350; fax-530-527-1745; hours: 8AM-5PM www.co.tehama.ca.us Separate indices to search include births, deaths, marriages. Records indexed on a public use terminal back to 1975. Only the public may search. Copy fee $1.50 per page. Cert fee- $2.00 per cert plus copy fee. Payee- Tehama County Recorder. **Online access to Inmate records:** Access to the county sheriff inmate list is at www.tehamaso.org/inmates/ICURRENT.HTM. **Other phones:** Treasurer- 530-527-4535; Appraiser/Auditor- 530-527-5931; Elections- 530-527-8190; Vital Records- 530-527-3350. **Property tax/Assessor-** PO Box 428, Red Bluff, CA 96080; 530-527-5931.

Trinity County

County Recorder, PO Box 1215, Weaverville, CA 96093-1258. 530-623-1215; fax-530-623-8398; hours: 8AM-5PM www.trinitycounty.org/Departments/assessor-clerk-elect/clerkrecorder.htm Index: Books, Microfiche, and Computer. Records indexed on a public use terminal back to 10/1994. Only the public may search. Copy fee $1.25 per page. Cert fee- $2.00 per cert plus copy fee. Payee- Trinity County Recorder. **Online access to Fictitious Business Name records:** Access to the Recorder's fictitious business names database is free at http://halfile.trinitycounty.org. For user name, enter "fbn"; leave password field empty. **Other phones:** Treasurer- 530-623-1251; Elections- 530-623-1220; Vital Records- 530-623-1215. **Property tax/Assessor-** same address as above. 530-623-1257.

Tulare County

County Recorder, 221 S. Mooney Blvd.; County Civic Ctr, Rm 103, Visalia, CA 93291-4593. 559-733-6377; fax-559-740-4329; hours: 8AM-5PM (recording hours 8AM-3PM) www.co.tulare.ca.us Records indexed on a public use terminal back to 1987. Only the public may search. Copy fee $3.00 per page. Cert fee- $6.60 per page. Payee- Tulare County Recorder. **Online access to Recording, Deed, Judgment, Lien, Vital Statistic, Fictitious Name records:** Search the recorders database including births, marriages, deaths free at http://209.78.90.65/riimsweb/orinquiry.asp. **Other phones:** Elections- 559-733-6377. **Property tax/Assessor-** 559-733-6361.

Tuolumne County

County Recorder, 2 S. Green St; County Admin. Ctr, Sonora, CA 95370. 209-533-5531; fax-209-533-6543; hours: 8AM-5PM www.tuolumnecounty.ca.gov All records in one index. Records indexed on a public use terminal back to 1972. Only the public may search. General copy fee $3.00 per page. RE or tax lien copy- $2.00 1st page, $1.00 per add'l page. Cert fee- $1.00 per doc plus copy fee. Payee- Tuolumne County Recorder. **Other phones:** Treasurer- 209-533-5544; Appraiser/Auditor- 209-533-5535; Elections- 209-533-5570; Vital Records- 209-533-5531. **Property tax/Assessor-** same address as above. 209-533-5535.

Ventura County

County Recorder, 800 S. Victoria Ave; Government Ctr, Ventura, CA 93009. 805-654-2292, R/E recording phone-805-654-3665; fax-805-654-2392; hours: 8AM-4PM http://recorder.countyofventura.org/venclrk.htm Will not search real estate records. Will not search UCC records or tax liens. Copy fee $2.00 1st page, $1.00 each add'l. Cert fee- $3.00 for 1st page; $1.00 each add'l, plus copy fee. Payee- Ventura County Recorder. **Online access to Recording, Deed, Grantor/Grantee, Fictitious Name, Most Wanted, Property Tax records:** Access the county clerks database free at http://recorder.countyofventura.org/venclrk.htm. Also, search property tax data for free at http://prop-tax.countyofventura.org/pisearch.asp; no name searching. Also, the county most wanted list is www.vcsd.org/wanted_and_offenders/most_wanted.htm. **Other phones:** Treasurer- 805-654-3735; Elections- 805-654-2664; Vital Records- 805-654-3666. **Property tax/Assessor-** same address as above. 805-654-2181.

Yolo County

County Recorder, PO Box 1130, Woodland, CA 95776-1130. 530-666-8130; fax-530-666-8109; hours: 8AM-4PM www.yolocounty.org/org/Recorder All records in one index. Records indexed on a public use terminal back to 1970. Office will perform a UCC and Tax lien(10yrs) search but public must search other records themselves. Copy fee $3.50 for 1st page; $.50 each add'l. Cert fee- $2.00 per cert plus copy fee. Payee- Yolo County Recorder. **Online access to Assessor, Birth, Death, Marriage, Fictitious Business Name, Davis Cemetery, Restaurant Insp records:** Access to recordings on the county clerk database are free at www.criis.com/yolo/srecord_current.shtml. Marriage records are at www.criis.com/yolo/smarriage.shtml. County Fictitious Business Name records are at www.criis.com/yolo/sfictitious.shtml. County Birth records Death records have been removed from the Internet. Also, City of Davis business licenses are free at www.city.davis.ca.us/ed/business/. Davis Cemetery District search is free at http://www2.dcn.org/orgs/cemetery. Also verify or find addresses free at www.ci.davis.ca.us/gis/choosemap.cfm. **Other phones:** Treasurer- 530-666-8625. **Property tax/Assessor-** 530-666-8135.

Yuba County

County Recorder, 915 8th St #107, Marysville, CA 95901. 530-749-7850; fax-530-749-7854; hours: 8AM-5PM www.co.yuba.ca.us/content/departments/clerk/ Index: All indexes are searchable except vital records. Records indexed on a public use terminal back to 1989. Only the public may search. Copy fee $2.00 1st page, $.50 each add'l. Cert fee- $1.50 per document plus copy fee. Payee- Yuba County Recorder. **Online access to Recording, Deed, Judgment, Lien, Property, GIS-mapping, Property Tax, Assessor records:** Access the Recorded Document Index free at http://www2.co.yuba.ca.us/records/CriteriaPage.aspx. Online record go back to 1989. Search property data on the GIS-mapping site, or assessor data free, no name search: www.co.yuba.ca.us/content/departments/assessor/parcelinfo.asp. **Other phones:** Treasurer- 530-749-7840; Elections- 530-749-7855; Vital Records- 530-749-7850; Clerk- 530-749-7851. **Property tax/Assessor-** 915 8th St. #101, Marysville, CA 95901; 530-749-7820, assessor fax- 530-749-7824.

California County Locator

You will usually be able to find the city name in the City/County Cross Reference below. In that case, it is a simple matter to determine the county from the cross reference. However, only the official US Postal Service city names are included in this index. There are an additional 40,000 place names that people use in their addresses. Therefore, we have also included a ZIP/City Cross Reference immediately following the City/County Cross Reference.

If you know the ZIP Code but the city name does not appear in the City/County Cross Reference index, look up the ZIP Code in the ZIP/City Cross Reference, find the city name, then look up the city name in the City/County Cross Reference. For example, you want to know the county for an address of Menands, NY 12204. There is no "Menands" in the City/County Cross Reference. The ZIP/City Cross Reference shows that ZIP Codes 12201-12288 are for the city of Albany. Looking back in the City/County Cross Reference, Albany is in Albany County.

California City/County Cross Reference

ACAMPO San Joaquin
ACTON Los Angeles
ADELANTO San Bernardino
ADIN (96006) Modoc(66), Lassen(33)
AGOURA HILLS Los Angeles
AGUANGA Riverside
AHWAHNEE (93601) Madera(96), Mariposa(3)
ALAMEDA Alameda
ALAMO Contra Costa
ALBANY Alameda
ALBION Mendocino
ALDERPOINT Humboldt
ALHAMBRA Los Angeles
ALISO VIEJO Orange
ALLEGHANY Sierra
ALPAUGH Tulare
ALPINE San Diego
ALTA Placer
ALTA LOMA San Bernardino
ALTADENA Los Angeles
ALTAVILLE Calaveras
ALTURAS Modoc
ALVISO Santa Clara
AMADOR CITY Amador
AMBOY San Bernardino
AMERICAN CANYON Napa
ANAHEIM Orange
ANDERSON Shasta
ANGELS CAMP Calaveras
ANGELUS OAKS San Bernardino
ANGWIN Napa
ANNAPOLIS Sonoma
ANTELOPE Sacramento
ANTIOCH Contra Costa
ANZA Riverside
APPLE VALLEY San Bernardino
APPLEGATE Placer
APTOS Santa Cruz
ARBUCKLE (95912) Colusa(98), Yolo(1)
ARCADIA Los Angeles
ARCATA Humboldt
ARMONA Kings
ARNOLD Calaveras
AROMAS (95004) Monterey(53), San Benito(46)
ARROYO GRANDE San Luis Obispo
ARTESIA Los Angeles
ARTOIS Glenn
ARVIN Kern
ATASCADERO San Luis Obispo
ATHERTON San Mateo
ATWATER Merced
ATWOOD Orange
AUBERRY Fresno
AUBURN (95602) Placer(73), Nevada(26)
AUBURN Placer
AVALON Los Angeles
AVENAL Kings
AVERY Calaveras
AVILA BEACH San Luis Obispo
AZUSA Los Angeles
BADGER Tulare
BAKER San Bernardino

BAKERSFIELD Kern
BALDWIN PARK Los Angeles
BALLICO Merced
BANGOR (95914) Butte(90), Yuba(10)
BANNING Riverside
BANTA San Joaquin
BARD Imperial
BARSTOW San Bernardino
BASS LAKE Madera
BAYSIDE Humboldt
BEALE AFB Yuba
BEAUMONT Riverside
BECKWOURTH Plumas
BELDEN Plumas
BELL Los Angeles
BELL GARDENS Los Angeles
BELLA VISTA Shasta
BELLFLOWER Los Angeles
BELMONT San Mateo
BELVEDERE TIBURON Marin
BEN LOMOND Santa Cruz
BENICIA Solano
BENTON Mono
BERKELEY (94708) Alameda(83), Contra Costa(16)
BERKELEY Alameda
BERRY CREEK Butte
BETHEL ISLAND Contra Costa
BEVERLY HILLS Los Angeles
BIEBER Lassen
BIG BAR Trinity
BIG BEAR CITY San Bernardino
BIG BEAR LAKE San Bernardino
BIG BEND Shasta
BIG CREEK Fresno
BIG OAK FLAT Tuolumne
BIG PINE Inyo
BIG SUR Monterey
BIGGS Butte
BIOLA Fresno
BIRDS LANDING Solano
BISHOP (93514) Inyo(93), Mono(6)
BISHOP Inyo
BLAIRSDEN-GRAEAGLE Plumas
BLOCKSBURG Humboldt
BLOOMINGTON San Bernardino
BLUE JAY San Bernardino
BLUE LAKE Humboldt
BLYTHE Riverside
BODEGA Sonoma
BODEGA BAY Sonoma
BODFISH Kern
BOLINAS Marin
BONITA San Diego
BONSALL San Diego
BOONVILLE Mendocino
BORON (93516) Kern(93), San Bernardino(6)
BORON Kern
BORREGO SPRINGS (92004) San Diego(94), Imperial(5)
BOULDER CREEK Santa Cruz
BOULEVARD San Diego
BOYES HOT SPRINGS Sonoma

BRADLEY (93426) Monterey(69), San Luis Obispo(30)
BRANDEIS Ventura
BRANSCOMB Mendocino
BRAWLEY Imperial
BREA Orange
BRENTWOOD Contra Costa
BRIDGEPORT Mono
BRIDGEVILLE (95526) Humboldt(90), Trinity(10)
BRISBANE San Mateo
BROOKDALE Santa Cruz
BROOKS Yolo
BROWNS VALLEY Yuba
BROWNSVILLE Yuba
BRYN MAWR San Bernardino
BUELLTON Santa Barbara
BUENA PARK Orange
BURBANK Los Angeles
BURLINGAME San Mateo
BURNEY Shasta
BURNT RANCH Trinity
BURREL Fresno
BURSON Calaveras
BUTTE CITY Glenn
BUTTONWILLOW Kern
BYRON (94514) Contra Costa(89), Alameda(9), San Joaquin(1)
CABAZON Riverside
CADIZ San Bernardino
CALABASAS Los Angeles
CALEXICO Imperial
CALIENTE Kern
CALIFORNIA CITY Kern
CALIFORNIA HOT SPRINGS Tulare
CALIMESA Riverside
CALIPATRIA Imperial
CALISTOGA (94515) Napa(88), Sonoma(11)
CALLAHAN Siskiyou
CALPELLA Mendocino
CALPINE Sierra
CAMARILLO Ventura
CAMBRIA San Luis Obispo
CAMINO El Dorado
CAMP MEEKER Sonoma
CAMP NELSON Tulare
CAMP PENDLETON San Diego
CAMPBELL Santa Clara
CAMPO San Diego
CAMPO SECO Calaveras
CAMPTONVILLE (95922) Yuba(85), Sierra(14)
CANBY Modoc
CANOGA PARK Los Angeles
CANTIL Kern
CANTUA CREEK Fresno
CANYON Contra Costa
CANYON COUNTRY Los Angeles
CANYONDAM Plumas
CAPAY Yolo
CAPISTRANO BEACH Orange
CAPITOLA Santa Cruz
CARDIFF BY THE SEA San Diego

CARLOTTA Humboldt
CARLSBAD San Diego
CARMEL Monterey
CARMEL VALLEY Monterey
CARMICHAEL Sacramento
CARNELIAN BAY Placer
CARPINTERIA Santa Barbara
CARSON Los Angeles
CARUTHERS Fresno
CASMALIA Santa Barbara
CASPAR Mendocino
CASSEL Shasta
CASTAIC Los Angeles
CASTELLA Shasta
CASTRO VALLEY Alameda
CASTROVILLE Monterey
CATHEDRAL CITY Riverside
CATHEYS VALLEY Mariposa
CAYUCOS San Luis Obispo
CAZADERO Sonoma
CEDAR GLEN San Bernardino
CEDAR RIDGE Nevada
CEDARPINES PARK San Bernardino
CEDARVILLE Modoc
CERES Stanislaus
CERRITOS Los Angeles
CHALLENGE (95925) Butte(56), Yuba(43)
CHATSWORTH (91311) Los Angeles(98), Ventura(1)
CHATSWORTH Los Angeles
CHESTER Plumas
CHICAGO PARK Nevada
CHICO Butte
CHILCOOT Plumas
CHINESE CAMP Tuolumne
CHINO San Bernardino
CHINO HILLS San Bernardino
CHOLAME San Luis Obispo
CHOWCHILLA (93610) Madera(97), Merced(2)
CHUALAR Monterey
CHULA VISTA San Diego
CIMA San Bernardino
CITRUS HEIGHTS Sacramento
CITY OF INDUSTRY Los Angeles
CLAREMONT Los Angeles
CLARKSBURG Yolo
CLAYTON Contra Costa
CLEARLAKE Lake
CLEARLAKE OAKS Lake
CLEARLAKE PARK Lake
CLEMENTS San Joaquin
CLIO Plumas
CLIPPER MILLS Butte
CLOVERDALE (95425) Sonoma(98), Mendocino(1)
CLOVIS Fresno
COACHELLA Riverside
COALINGA Fresno
COARSEGOLD Madera
COBB Lake
COLEVILLE Mono
COLFAX Placer
COLLEGE CITY Colusa

COLOMA El Dorado
COLTON (92324) San Bernardino(96),
    Riverside(3)
COLUMBIA Tuolumne
COLUSA Colusa
COMPTCHE Mendocino
COMPTON Los Angeles
CONCORD Contra Costa
COOL El Dorado
COPPEROPOLIS Calaveras
CORCORAN (93212) Kings(97), Tulare(2)
CORNING Tehama
CORONA (92880) Riverside(98), San
    Bernardino(1)
CORONA Riverside
CORONA DEL MAR Orange
CORONADO San Diego
CORTE MADERA Marin
COSTA MESA Orange
COTATI Sonoma
COTTONWOOD (96022) Tehama(51),
    Shasta(48)
COULTERVILLE (95311) Mariposa(92),
    Tuolumne(7)
COURTLAND Sacramento
COVELO Mendocino
COVINA Los Angeles
COYOTE Santa Clara
CRESCENT CITY Del Norte
CRESCENT MILLS Plumas
CRESSEY Merced
CREST PARK San Bernardino
CRESTLINE San Bernardino
CRESTON San Luis Obispo
CROCKER NAT BANK San Francisco
CROCKETT Contra Costa
CROWS LANDING Stanislaus
CULVER CITY Los Angeles
CUPERTINO Santa Clara
CUTLER Tulare
CUTTEN Humboldt
CUYAMA Santa Barbara
CYPRESS Orange
DAGGETT San Bernardino
DALY CITY San Mateo
DANA POINT Orange
DANVILLE Contra Costa
DARDANELLE Tuolumne
DARWIN Inyo
DAVENPORT Santa Cruz
DAVIS Yolo
DAVIS CREEK Modoc
DEATH VALLEY Inyo
DEER PARK Napa
DEL MAR San Diego
DEL REY Fresno
DELANO (93215) Kern(92), Tulare(7)
DELANO Kern
DELHI Merced
DENAIR Stanislaus
DESCANSO San Diego
DESERT CENTER Riverside
DESERT HOT SPRINGS Riverside
DI GIORGIO Kern
DIABLO Contra Costa
DIAMOND BAR Los Angeles
DIAMOND SPRINGS El Dorado
DILLON BEACH Marin
DINUBA (93618) Tulare(98), Fresno(1)
DIXON Solano
DOBBINS Yuba
DORRIS Siskiyou
DOS PALOS (93620) Merced(85),
    Fresno(14)
DOS RIOS Mendocino
DOUGLAS CITY Trinity
DOUGLAS FLAT Calaveras
DOWNEY Los Angeles
DOWNIEVILLE Sierra
DOYLE Lassen
DRYTOWN Amador
DUARTE Los Angeles

DUBLIN Alameda
DUCOR Tulare
DULZURA San Diego
DUNCANS MILLS Sonoma
DUNLAP Fresno
DUNNIGAN Yolo
DUNSMUIR (96025) Siskiyou(93),
    Shasta(6)
DURHAM Butte
DUTCH FLAT Placer
EAGLEVILLE Modoc
EARLIMART Tulare
EARP San Bernardino
EAST IRVINE Orange
ECHO LAKE El Dorado
EDISON Kern
EDWARDS Kern
EL CAJON San Diego
EL CENTRO Imperial
EL CERRITO Contra Costa
EL DORADO El Dorado
EL DORADO HILLS El Dorado
EL GRANADA San Mateo
EL MACERO Yolo
EL MONTE Los Angeles
EL NIDO Merced
EL PORTAL Mariposa
EL SEGUNDO Los Angeles
EL SOBRANTE Contra Costa
EL TORO Orange
EL VERANO Sonoma
ELDRIDGE Sonoma
ELK Mendocino
ELK CREEK (95939) Glenn(94), Colusa(5)
ELK GROVE Sacramento
ELMIRA Solano
ELVERTA (95626) Sacramento(84),
    Placer(12), Sutter(2)
EMERYVILLE Alameda
EMIGRANT GAP Placer
EMPIRE Stanislaus
ENCINITAS San Diego
ENCINO Los Angeles
ESCALON San Joaquin
ESCONDIDO San Diego
ESPARTO Yolo
ESSEX San Bernardino
ETNA Siskiyou
EUREKA Humboldt
EXETER Tulare
FAIR OAKS Sacramento
FAIRFAX Marin
FAIRFIELD Solano
FALL RIVER MILLS Shasta
FALLBROOK San Diego
FARMERSVILLE Tulare
FARMINGTON (95230) Stanislaus(34),
    San Joaquin(33), Calaveras(28),
    Tuolumne(2)
FAWNSKIN San Bernardino
FEATHER FALLS Butte
FELLOWS Kern
FELTON Santa Cruz
FERNDALE Humboldt
FIDDLETOWN (95629) El Dorado(75),
    Amador(24)
FIELDS LANDING Humboldt
FILLMORE Ventura
FINLEY Lake
FIREBAUGH (93622) Fresno(89),
    Madera(8), Merced(2)
FISH CAMP (93623) Mariposa(81),
    Madera(18)
FIVE POINTS Fresno
FLORISTON Nevada
FLOURNOY Tehama
FOLSOM Sacramento
FONTANA San Bernardino
FOOTHILL RANCH Orange
FORBESTOWN (95941) Butte(84),
    Yuba(15)
FOREST FALLS San Bernardino

FOREST KNOLLS Marin
FOREST RANCH Butte
FORESTHILL Placer
FORESTVILLE Sonoma
FORKS OF SALMON Siskiyou
FORT BIDWELL Modoc
FORT BRAGG Mendocino
FORT DICK Del Norte
FORT IRWIN San Bernardino
FORT JONES Siskiyou
FORT ORD Monterey
FORTUNA Humboldt
FOUNTAIN VALLEY Orange
FOWLER Fresno
FRAZIER PARK Kern
FREEDOM Santa Cruz
FREMONT Alameda
FRENCH CAMP San Joaquin
FRENCH GULCH Shasta
FRESNO Fresno
FRIANT (93626) Fresno(58), Madera(41)
FT ORD Monterey
FULLERTON Orange
FULTON Sonoma
GALT (95632) Sacramento(95), San
    Joaquin(4)
GARBERVILLE Humboldt
GARDEN GROVE Orange
GARDEN VALLEY El Dorado
GARDENA Los Angeles
GASQUET (95543) Del Norte(98), Trinity(2)
GAZELLE Siskiyou
GEORGETOWN El Dorado
GERBER Tehama
GEYSERVILLE Sonoma
GILROY Santa Clara
GLEN ELLEN Sonoma
GLENCOE Calaveras
GLENDALE Los Angeles
GLENDORA Los Angeles
GLENHAVEN Lake
GLENN Glenn
GLENNVILLE Kern
GOLD RUN Placer
GOLETA Santa Barbara
GONZALES Monterey
GOODYEARS BAR Sierra
GOSHEN Tulare
GRANADA HILLS Los Angeles
GRAND TERRACE San Bernardino
GRANITE BAY Placer
GRASS VALLEY Nevada
GRATON Sonoma
GREEN VALLEY LAKE San Bernardino
GREENBRAE Marin
GREENFIELD Monterey
GREENVIEW Siskiyou
GREENVILLE Plumas
GREENWOOD El Dorado
GRENADA Siskiyou
GRIDLEY Butte
GRIMES Colusa
GRIZZLY FLATS El Dorado
GROVELAND (95321) Tuolumne(97),
    Mariposa(2)
GROVER BEACH San Luis Obispo
GUADALUPE Santa Barbara
GUALALA Mendocino
GUASTI San Bernardino
GUATAY San Diego
GUERNEVILLE Sonoma
GUINDA Yolo
GUSTINE Merced
HACIENDA HEIGHTS Los Angeles
HALF MOON BAY San Mateo
HAMILTON CITY Glenn
HANFORD Kings
HAPPY CAMP Siskiyou
HARBOR CITY Los Angeles
HARMONY San Luis Obispo
HAT CREEK Shasta
HATHAWAY PINES Calaveras

HAWAIIAN GARDENS Los Angeles
HAWTHORNE Los Angeles
HAYFORK Trinity
HAYWARD Alameda
HEALDSBURG Sonoma
HEBER Imperial
HELENDALE San Bernardino
HELM Fresno
HEMET Riverside
HERALD Sacramento
HERCULES Contra Costa
HERLONG Lassen
HERMOSA BEACH Los Angeles
HESPERIA San Bernardino
HICKMAN Stanislaus
HIDDEN VALLEY LAKE Lake
HIGHLAND San Bernardino
HILMAR Merced
HINKLEY San Bernardino
HOLLISTER San Benito
HOLT San Joaquin
HOLTVILLE Imperial
HOLY CITY Santa Clara
HOMELAND Riverside
HOMEWOOD Placer
HONEYDEW Humboldt
HOOD Sacramento
HOOPA Humboldt
HOPLAND Mendocino
HORNBROOK Siskiyou
HORNITOS Mariposa
HORSE CREEK Siskiyou
HUGHSON Stanislaus
HUME Fresno
HUNTINGTON BEACH Orange
HUNTINGTON LAKE Fresno
HUNTINGTON PARK Los Angeles
HURON Fresno
HYAMPOM Trinity
HYDESVILLE Humboldt
IDYLLWILD Riverside
IGO Shasta
IMPERIAL Imperial
IMPERIAL BEACH San Diego
INDEPENDENCE Inyo
INDIAN WELLS Riverside
INDIO Riverside
INGLEWOOD Los Angeles
INVERNESS Marin
INYOKERN (93527) Kern(93), Inyo(3),
    Tulare(2)
IONE Amador
IRVINE Orange
ISLETON Sacramento
IVANHOE Tulare
JACKSON Amador
JACUMBA San Diego
JAMESTOWN Tuolumne
JAMUL San Diego
JANESVILLE Lassen
JENNER Sonoma
JOHANNESBURG Kern
JOLON Monterey
JOSHUA TREE San Bernardino
JULIAN San Diego
JUNCTION CITY Trinity
JUNE LAKE Mono
KAWEAH Tulare
KEELER Inyo
KEENE Kern
KELSEYVILLE Lake
KENTFIELD Marin
KENWOOD Sonoma
KERMAN Fresno
KERNVILLE (93238) Kern(89), Tulare(10)
KETTLEMAN CITY Kings
KEYES Stanislaus
KING CITY Monterey
KINGS BEACH Placer
KINGS CANYON NATIONAL PK Tulare
KINGSBURG (93631) Fresno(83),
    Tulare(11), Kings(4)

KIRKWOOD Alpine
KIT CARSON Amador
KLAMATH Del Norte
KLAMATH RIVER Siskiyou
KNEELAND Humboldt
KNIGHTS LANDING (95645) Sutter(84), Yolo(15)
KNIGHTSEN Contra Costa
KORBEL Humboldt
KYBURZ El Dorado
LA CANADA FLINTRIDGE Los Angeles
LA COUNTY TAX COLLECTOR Los Angeles
LA CRESCENTA Los Angeles
LA GRANGE (95329) Tuolumne(57), Mariposa(34), Stanislaus(8)
LA HABRA (90631) Orange(87), Los Angeles(12)
LA HABRA Orange
LA HONDA San Mateo
LA JOLLA San Diego
LA MESA San Diego
LA MIRADA (90638) Los Angeles(98), Orange(1)
LA MIRADA Los Angeles
LA PALMA Orange
LA PUENTE Los Angeles
LA QUINTA Riverside
LA VERNE Los Angeles
LADERA RANCH Orange
LAFAYETTE Contra Costa
LAGUNA BEACH Orange
LAGUNA HILLS Orange
LAGUNA NIGUEL Orange
LAGUNITAS Marin
LAKE ARROWHEAD San Bernardino
LAKE CITY Modoc
LAKE ELSINORE Riverside
LAKE FOREST Orange
LAKE HUGHES Los Angeles
LAKE ISABELLA Kern
LAKEHEAD Shasta
LAKEPORT Lake
LAKESHORE Fresno
LAKESIDE San Diego
LAKEVIEW Riverside
LAKEWOOD Los Angeles
LAMONT Kern
LANCASTER Los Angeles
LANDERS San Bernardino
LARKSPUR Marin
LATHROP San Joaquin
LATON (93242) Fresno(84), Kings(15)
LAWNDALE Los Angeles
LAYTONVILLE Mendocino
LE GRAND Merced
LEBEC (93243) Kern(73), Los Angeles(26)
LEE VINING Mono
LEGGETT Mendocino
LEMON COVE Tulare
LEMON GROVE San Diego
LEMOORE Kings
LEWISTON Trinity
LIKELY Modoc
LINCOLN Placer
LINCOLN ACRES San Diego
LINDEN (95236) San Joaquin(95), Calaveras(4)
LINDSAY Tulare
LITCHFIELD Lassen
LITTLE LAKE Inyo
LITTLERIVER Mendocino
LITTLEROCK Los Angeles
LIVE OAK Sutter
LIVERMORE (94551) Alameda(97), Contra Costa(2)
LIVERMORE Alameda
LIVINGSTON Merced
LLANO Los Angeles
LOCKEFORD San Joaquin
LOCKWOOD Monterey
LODI San Joaquin

LOLETA Humboldt
LOMA LINDA San Bernardino
LOMA MAR San Mateo
LOMITA Los Angeles
LOMPOC Santa Barbara
LONE PINE Inyo
LONG BARN Tuolumne
LONG BEACH Los Angeles
LOOKOUT Modoc
LOOMIS Placer
LOS ALAMITOS Orange
LOS ALAMOS Santa Barbara
LOS ALTOS Santa Clara
LOS ANGELES Los Angeles
LOS BANOS Merced
LOS GATOS (95033) Santa Cruz(66), Santa Clara(33)
LOS GATOS Santa Clara
LOS MOLINOS Tehama
LOS OLIVOS Santa Barbara
LOS OSOS San Luis Obispo
LOST HILLS Kern
LOTUS El Dorado
LOWER LAKE Lake
LOYALTON Sierra
LUCERNE Lake
LUCERNE VALLEY San Bernardino
LUDLOW San Bernardino
LYNWOOD Los Angeles
LYOTH San Joaquin
LYTLE CREEK San Bernardino
MACDOEL Siskiyou
MAD RIVER Trinity
MADELINE Lassen
MADERA Madera
MADISON Yolo
MAGALIA Butte
MALIBU (90265) Los Angeles(94), Ventura(5)
MALIBU Los Angeles
MAMMOTH LAKES Mono
MANCHESTER Mendocino
MANHATTAN BEACH Los Angeles
MANTECA San Joaquin
MANTON (96059) Tehama(67), Shasta(32)
MARCH AIR FORCE BASE Riverside
MARICOPA (93252) Kern(60), Santa Barbara(24), Ventura(12), San Luis Obispo(2)
MARINA Monterey
MARINA DEL REY Los Angeles
MARIPOSA Mariposa
MARKLEEVILLE Alpine
MARSHALL Marin
MARTELL Amador
MARTINEZ Contra Costa
MARYSVILLE Yuba
MATHER Sacramento
MAXWELL Colusa
MAYWOOD Los Angeles
MC FARLAND Kern
MC KITTRICK Kern
MCARTHUR (96056) Lassen(54), Shasta(31), Modoc(14)
MCARTHUR Lassen
MCCLELLAN Sacramento
MCCLELLAN AFB Sacramento
MCCLOUD Siskiyou
MCKINLEYVILLE Humboldt
MEADOW VALLEY Plumas
MEADOW VISTA Placer
MECCA Riverside
MENDOCINO Mendocino
MENDOTA Fresno
MENIFEE Riverside
MENLO PARK San Mateo
MENTONE San Bernardino
MERCED Merced
MERIDIAN (95957) Sutter(97), Colusa(2)
MI WUK VILLAGE Tuolumne
MIDDLETOWN Lake
MIDPINES Mariposa

MIDWAY CITY Orange
MILFORD Lassen
MILL CREEK Tehama
MILL VALLEY Marin
MILLBRAE San Mateo
MILLVILLE Shasta
MILPITAS Santa Clara
MINERAL Tehama
MIRA LOMA Riverside
MIRAMONTE (93641) Fresno(90), Tulare(10)
MIRANDA Humboldt
MISSION HILLS Los Angeles
MISSION VIEJO Orange
MOBIL OIL CREDIT CORPORATION Contra Costa
MOCCASIN Tuolumne
MODESTO Stanislaus
MOJAVE Kern
MOKELUMNE HILL Calaveras
MONO HOT SPRINGS Fresno
MONROVIA Los Angeles
MONTAGUE Siskiyou
MONTARA San Mateo
MONTCLAIR San Bernardino
MONTE RIO Sonoma
MONTEBELLO Los Angeles
MONTEREY Monterey
MONTEREY PARK Los Angeles
MONTGOMERY CREEK Shasta
MONTGOMERY WARD Contra Costa
MONTROSE Los Angeles
MOORPARK Ventura
MORAGA Contra Costa
MORENO VALLEY Riverside
MORGAN HILL Santa Clara
MORONGO VALLEY San Bernardino
MORRO BAY San Luis Obispo
MOSS BEACH San Mateo
MOSS LANDING Monterey
MOUNT AUKUM El Dorado
MOUNT HAMILTON Santa Clara
MOUNT HERMON Santa Cruz
MOUNT LAGUNA San Diego
MOUNT SHASTA Siskiyou
MOUNT WILSON Los Angeles
MOUNTAIN CENTER Riverside
MOUNTAIN PASS San Bernardino
MOUNTAIN RANCH Calaveras
MOUNTAIN VIEW Santa Clara
MT BALDY Los Angeles
MURPHYS Calaveras
MURRIETA Riverside
MYERS FLAT Humboldt
NAPA Napa
NATIONAL CITY San Diego
NAVARRO Mendocino
NEEDLES San Bernardino
NELSON Butte
NESTOR San Diego
NEVADA CITY Nevada
NEW ALMADEN Santa Clara
NEW CUYAMA Santa Barbara
NEWARK Alameda
NEWBERRY SPRINGS San Bernardino
NEWBURY PARK Ventura
NEWCASTLE Placer
NEWHALL Los Angeles
NEWMAN Stanislaus
NEWPORT BEACH Orange
NEWPORT COAST Orange
NICASIO Marin
NICE Lake
NICOLAUS Sutter
NILAND Imperial
NIPOMO San Luis Obispo
NIPTON San Bernardino
NORCO Riverside
NORDEN Nevada
NORTH FORK Madera
NORTH HIGHLANDS Sacramento
NORTH HILLS Los Angeles

NORTH HOLLYWOOD Los Angeles
NORTH PALM SPRINGS Riverside
NORTH SAN JUAN (95960) Nevada(61), Sierra(31), Yuba(6)
NORTHRIDGE Los Angeles
NORWALK Los Angeles
NOVATO Marin
NUBIEBER Lassen
NUEVO Riverside
O NEALS Madera
OAK PARK Ventura
OAK RUN Shasta
OAK VIEW Ventura
OAKDALE Stanislaus
OAKHILLS San Bernardino
OAKHURST Madera
OAKLAND Alameda
OAKLEY Contra Costa
OAKVILLE Napa
OBRIEN Shasta
OCCIDENTAL Sonoma
OCEANO San Luis Obispo
OCEANSIDE San Diego
OCOTILLO Imperial
OJAI Ventura
OLANCHA Inyo
OLD STATION Shasta
OLEMA Marin
OLIVEHURST Yuba
OLYMPIC VALLEY Placer
ONTARIO San Bernardino
ONYX Kern
ORANGE Orange
ORANGE COVE (93646) Fresno(90), Tulare(10)
ORANGEVALE Sacramento
OREGON HOUSE Yuba
ORICK Humboldt
ORINDA Contra Costa
ORLAND Glenn
ORLEANS Humboldt
ORO GRANDE San Bernardino
OROSI Tulare
OROVILLE Butte
OXNARD Ventura
PACIFIC GROVE Monterey
PACIFIC PALISADES Los Angeles
PACIFICA San Mateo
PACOIMA Los Angeles
PAICINES San Benito
PALA San Diego
PALERMO Butte
PALM DESERT Riverside
PALM SPRINGS Riverside
PALMDALE Los Angeles
PALO ALTO (94303) Santa Clara(51), San Mateo(48)
PALO ALTO San Mateo
PALO ALTO Santa Clara
PALO CEDRO Shasta
PALO VERDE Imperial
PALOMAR MOUNTAIN San Diego
PALOS VERDES PENINSULA Los Angeles
PANORAMA CITY Los Angeles
PARADISE Butte
PARAMOUNT Los Angeles
PARKER DAM San Bernardino
PARLIER Fresno
PASADENA Los Angeles
PASKENTA Tehama
PASO ROBLES San Luis Obispo
PATTERSON Stanislaus
PATTON San Bernardino
PAUMA VALLEY San Diego
PAYNES CREEK Tehama
PEARBLOSSOM Los Angeles
PEBBLE BEACH Monterey
PENN VALLEY Nevada
PENNGROVE Sonoma
PENRYN Placer
PERRIS Riverside

PESCADERO San Mateo
PETALUMA Sonoma
PETROLIA Humboldt
PHELAN San Bernardino
PHILLIPSVILLE Humboldt
PHILO Mendocino
PICO RIVERA Los Angeles
PIEDMONT Alameda
PIEDRA Fresno
PIERCY Mendocino
PILOT HILL El Dorado
PINE GROVE Amador
PINE VALLEY San Diego
PINECREST Tuolumne
PINOLE Contra Costa
PINON HILLS San Bernardino
PIONEER Amador
PIONEERTOWN San Bernardino
PIRU Ventura
PISMO BEACH San Luis Obispo
PITTSBURG Contra Costa
PIXLEY Tulare
PLACENTIA Orange
PLACERVILLE El Dorado
PLANADA Merced
PLATINA (96076) Tehama(46), Trinity(27),
    Shasta(25)
PLAYA DEL REY Los Angeles
PLEASANT GROVE (95668) Sutter(72),
    Placer(27)
PLEASANT HILL Contra Costa
PLEASANTON Alameda
PLEASANTON Contra Costa
PLYMOUTH Amador
POINT ARENA Mendocino
POINT MUGU NAWC Ventura
POINT REYES STATION Marin
POLLOCK PINES El Dorado
POMONA (91766) Los Angeles(95), San
    Bernardino(4)
POMONA Los Angeles
POPE VALLEY Napa
PORT COSTA Contra Costa
PORT HUENEME Ventura
PORT HUENEME CBC BASE Ventura
PORTERVILLE Tulare
PORTOLA Plumas
PORTOLA VALLEY San Mateo
POSEY Tulare
POTRERO San Diego
POTTER VALLEY Mendocino
POWAY San Diego
PRATHER Fresno
PRINCETON (95970) Glenn(79),
    Colusa(20)
PROBERTA Tehama
QUINCY Plumas
RACKERBY Yuba
RAIL ROAD FLAT Calaveras
RAISIN Fresno
RAMONA San Diego
RANCHITA San Diego
RANCHO CORDOVA Sacramento
RANCHO CUCAMONGA San Bernardino
RANCHO MIRAGE Riverside
RANCHO PALOS VERDES Los Angeles
RANCHO SANTA FE San Diego
RANCHO SANTA MARGARITA Orange
RANDSBURG Kern
RAVENDALE Lassen
RAYMOND (93653) Madera(79),
    Mariposa(20)
RED BLUFF Tehama
RED MOUNTAIN Kern
REDCREST Humboldt
REDDING Shasta
REDLANDS (92373) San Bernardino(96),
    Riverside(3)
REDLANDS San Bernardino
REDONDO BEACH Los Angeles
REDWAY Humboldt
REDWOOD CITY San Mateo

REDWOOD ESTATES Santa Clara
REDWOOD VALLEY Mendocino
REEDLEY (93654) Fresno(97), Tulare(2)
REPRESA Sacramento
RESCUE El Dorado
RESEDA Los Angeles
RIALTO San Bernardino
RICHGROVE Tulare
RICHMOND Contra Costa
RICHVALE Butte
RIDGECREST (93555) Kern(98), San
    Bernardino(1)
RIDGECREST Kern
RIMFOREST San Bernardino
RIO DELL Humboldt
RIO LINDA Sacramento
RIO NIDO Sonoma
RIO OSO Sutter
RIO VISTA (94571) Solano(94),
    Sacramento(5)
RIPLEY (92272) Riverside(98), San
    Diego(1)
RIPON San Joaquin
RIVER PINES Amador
RIVERBANK Stanislaus
RIVERDALE (93656) Fresno(88), Kings(11)
RIVERSIDE Riverside
ROBBINS Sutter
ROCKLIN Placer
RODEO Contra Costa
ROHNERT PARK Sonoma
ROSAMOND (93560) Kern(98), Los
    Angeles(1)
ROSEMEAD Los Angeles
ROSEVILLE Placer
ROSS Marin
ROUGH AND READY Nevada
ROUND MOUNTAIN Shasta
ROWLAND HEIGHTS Los Angeles
RUMSEY Yolo
RUNNING SPRINGS San Bernardino
RUTHERFORD Napa
RYDE Sacramento
SACRAMENTO (95837) Sacramento(70),
    Sutter(29)
SACRAMENTO Sacramento
SAINT HELENA Napa
SALIDA Stanislaus
SALINAS Monterey
SALTON CITY Imperial
SALYER Trinity
SAMOA Humboldt
SAN ANDREAS Calaveras
SAN ANSELMO Marin
SAN ARDO Monterey
SAN BERNARDINO San Bernardino
SAN BRUNO San Mateo
SAN CARLOS San Mateo
SAN CLEMENTE Orange
SAN DIEGO San Diego
SAN DIMAS Los Angeles
SAN FERNANDO Los Angeles
SAN FRANCISCO San Francisco
SAN FRANCISCO San Mateo
SAN GABRIEL Los Angeles
SAN GERONIMO Marin
SAN GREGORIO San Mateo
SAN JACINTO Riverside
SAN JOAQUIN Fresno
SAN JOSE Santa Clara
SAN JUAN BAUTISTA San Benito
SAN JUAN CAPISTRANO Orange
SAN LEANDRO Alameda
SAN LORENZO Alameda
SAN LUCAS Monterey
SAN LUIS OBISPO San Luis Obispo
SAN LUIS REY San Diego
SAN MARCOS San Diego
SAN MARINO Los Angeles
SAN MARTIN Santa Clara
SAN MATEO San Mateo

SAN MIGUEL (93451) San Luis
    Obispo(58), Monterey(41)
SAN PABLO Contra Costa
SAN PEDRO Los Angeles
SAN QUENTIN Marin
SAN RAFAEL Marin
SAN RAMON Contra Costa
SAN SIMEON San Luis Obispo
SAN YSIDRO San Diego
SANGER Fresno
SANTA ANA Orange
SANTA BARBARA Santa Barbara
SANTA CLARA Santa Clara
SANTA CLARITA Los Angeles
SANTA CRUZ Santa Cruz
SANTA FE SPRINGS Los Angeles
SANTA MARGARITA San Luis Obispo
SANTA MARIA (93454) Santa Barbara(98),
    San Luis Obispo(1)
SANTA MARIA Santa Barbara
SANTA MONICA Los Angeles
SANTA PAULA Ventura
SANTA RITA PARK Merced
SANTA ROSA Sonoma
SANTA YNEZ Santa Barbara
SANTA YSABEL San Diego
SANTEE San Diego
SARATOGA Santa Clara
SAUSALITO Marin
SCOTIA Humboldt
SCOTT BAR Siskiyou
SCOTTS VALLEY Santa Cruz
SEAL BEACH Orange
SEASIDE Monterey
SEBASTOPOL Sonoma
SEELEY Imperial
SEIAD VALLEY Siskiyou
SELMA Fresno
SEQUOIA NATIONAL PARK Tulare
SHAFTER Kern
SHANDON San Luis Obispo
SHASTA Shasta
SHASTA LAKE Shasta
SHAVER LAKE Fresno
SHEEP RANCH Calaveras
SHERIDAN Placer
SHERMAN OAKS Los Angeles
SHINGLE SPRINGS El Dorado
SHINGLETOWN Shasta
SHOSHONE Inyo
SIERRA CITY Sierra
SIERRA MADRE Los Angeles
SIERRAVILLE Sierra
SIGNAL HILL Los Angeles
SILVERADO Orange
SIMI VALLEY Ventura
SKYFOREST San Bernardino
SLOUGHHOUSE Sacramento
SMARTVILLE (95977) Nevada(62),
    Yuba(37)
SMITH RIVER Del Norte
SNELLING Merced
SODA SPRINGS Nevada
SOLANA BEACH San Diego
SOLEDAD Monterey
SOLVANG Santa Barbara
SOMERSET El Dorado
SOMES BAR Siskiyou
SOMIS Ventura
SONOMA Sonoma
SONORA Tuolumne
SOQUEL Santa Cruz
SOULSBYVILLE Tuolumne
SOUTH DOS PALOS Merced
SOUTH EL MONTE Los Angeles
SOUTH GATE Los Angeles
SOUTH LAKE TAHOE El Dorado
SOUTH PASADENA Los Angeles
SOUTH SAN FRANCISCO San Mateo
SPRECKELS Monterey
SPRING VALLEY San Diego
SPRINGVILLE Tulare

SQUAW VALLEY Fresno
STANDARD Tuolumne
STANDISH Lassen
STANTON Orange
STEVENSON RANCH Los Angeles
STEVINSON Merced
STEWARTS POINT Sonoma
STINSON BEACH Marin
STIRLING CITY Butte
STOCKTON San Joaquin
STONYFORD Colusa
STORRIE Plumas
STRATFORD Kings
STRATHMORE Tulare
STRAWBERRY Tuolumne
STRAWBERRY VALLEY (95981)
    Yuba(66), Plumas(33)
STUDIO CITY Los Angeles
SUGARLOAF San Bernardino
SUISUN CITY Solano
SULTANA Tulare
SUMMERLAND Santa Barbara
SUN CITY Riverside
SUN VALLEY Los Angeles
SUNLAND Los Angeles
SUNNYVALE Santa Clara
SUNOL Alameda
SUNSET BEACH Orange
SURFSIDE Orange
SUSANVILLE Lassen
SUTTER Sutter
SUTTER CREEK Amador
SYLMAR Los Angeles
TAFT Kern
TAHOE CITY Placer
TAHOE VISTA Placer
TAHOMA El Dorado
TALMAGE Mendocino
TARZANA Los Angeles
TAYLORSVILLE Plumas
TECATE San Diego
TECOPA Inyo
TEHACHAPI Kern
TEHAMA Tehama
TEMECULA Riverside
TEMPLE CITY Los Angeles
TEMPLETON San Luis Obispo
TERMO Lassen
TERRA BELLA Tulare
THE SEA RANCH Sonoma
THERMAL (92274) Riverside(65),
    Imperial(34)
THORNTON San Joaquin
THOUSAND OAKS (91362) Ventura(83),
    Los Angeles(16)
THOUSAND OAKS Ventura
THOUSAND PALMS Riverside
THREE RIVERS Tulare
TIPTON Tulare
TOLLHOUSE Fresno
TOLUCA LAKE Los Angeles
TOMALES Marin
TOPANGA Los Angeles
TOPAZ Mono
TORRANCE Los Angeles
TRABUCO CANYON Orange
TRACY (95391) San Joaquin(88),
    Alameda(11)
TRACY San Joaquin
TRANQUILLITY Fresno
TRAVER Tulare
TRAVIS AFB Solano
TRES PINOS San Benito
TRINIDAD Humboldt
TRINITY CENTER (96091) Trinity(56),
    Siskiyou(43)
TRONA San Bernardino
TRUCKEE (96161) Nevada(89), Placer(10)
TRUCKEE Nevada
TUJUNGA Los Angeles
TULARE Tulare

TULELAKE (96134) Modoc(71), Siskiyou(28)
TUOLUMNE Tuolumne
TUPMAN Kern
TURLOCK Stanislaus
TUSTIN Orange
TWAIN Plumas
TWAIN HARTE Tuolumne
TWENTYNINE PALMS San Bernardino
TWIN BRIDGES El Dorado
TWIN PEAKS San Bernardino
UKIAH Mendocino
UNION CITY Alameda
UNIVERSAL CITY Los Angeles
UPLAND San Bernardino
UPPER LAKE Lake
VACAVILLE Solano
VALENCIA Los Angeles
VALLECITO Calaveras
VALLEJO Solano
VALLEY CENTER San Diego
VALLEY FORD Sonoma
VALLEY HOME Stanislaus
VALLEY SPRINGS Calaveras
VALLEY VILLAGE Los Angeles
VALYERMO Los Angeles
VAN NUYS Los Angeles
VENICE Los Angeles
VENTURA Ventura
VERDUGO CITY Los Angeles
VERNALIS (95385) Stanislaus(76), San Joaquin(23)

VICTOR San Joaquin
VICTORVILLE San Bernardino
VIDAL San Bernardino
VILLA GRANDE Sonoma
VILLA PARK Orange
VINA Tehama
VINEBURG Sonoma
VINTON Plumas
VISALIA Tulare
VISTA San Diego
VOLCANO Amador
WALLACE Calaveras
WALNUT Los Angeles
WALNUT CREEK Contra Costa
WALNUT GROVE (95690) Sacramento(73), Solano(17), San Joaquin(8)
WARNER SPRINGS San Diego
WASCO Kern
WASHINGTON Nevada
WATERFORD Stanislaus
WATSONVILLE (95076) Santa Cruz(86), Monterey(13)
WATSONVILLE Santa Cruz
WAUKENA Tulare
WEAVERVILLE Trinity
WEED Siskiyou
WEIMAR Placer
WELDON Kern
WENDEL Lassen
WEOTT Humboldt
WEST COVINA Los Angeles

WEST HILLS (91307) Los Angeles(94), Ventura(5)
WEST HILLS Los Angeles
WEST HOLLYWOOD Los Angeles
WEST POINT Calaveras
WEST SACRAMENTO Yolo
WESTLAKE VILLAGE (91361) Ventura(74), Los Angeles(25)
WESTLAKE VILLAGE Los Angeles
WESTLAKE VILLAGE Ventura
WESTLEY Stanislaus
WESTMINSTER Orange
WESTMORLAND Imperial
WESTPORT Mendocino
WESTWOOD (96137) Plumas(70), Lassen(29)
WHEATLAND Yuba
WHISKEYTOWN Shasta
WHITE WATER Riverside
WHITETHORN (95589) Humboldt(95), Mendocino(4)
WHITMORE Shasta
WHITTIER Los Angeles
WILDOMAR Riverside
WILLIAMS Colusa
WILLITS Mendocino
WILLOW CREEK Humboldt
WILLOWS Glenn
WILMINGTON Los Angeles
WILSEYVILLE Calaveras
WILTON Sacramento
WINCHESTER Riverside

WINDSOR Sonoma
WINNETKA Los Angeles
WINTERHAVEN Imperial
WINTERS (95694) Yolo(85), Solano(14)
WINTON Merced
WISHON Madera
WITTER SPRINGS Lake
WOFFORD HEIGHTS Kern
WOODACRE Marin
WOODBRIDGE San Joaquin
WOODLAKE Tulare
WOODLAND Yolo
WOODLAND HILLS Los Angeles
WOODY Kern
WRIGHTWOOD San Bernardino
YERMO San Bernardino
YETTEM Tulare
YOLO Yolo
YORBA LINDA Orange
YORKVILLE Mendocino
YOSEMITE NATIONAL PARK Mariposa
YOUNTVILLE Napa
YREKA Siskiyou
YUBA CITY Sutter
YUCAIPA (92399) San Bernardino(98), Riverside(1)
YUCCA VALLEY San Bernardino
ZAMORA Yolo
ZENIA Trinity

California ZIP/City Cross Reference

90000-90068 LOS ANGELES	90680-90680 STANTON	91225-91226 GLENDALE	91395-91395 MISSION HILLS
90069-90069 WEST HOLLYWOOD	90701-90702 ARTESIA	91301-91301 AGOURA HILLS	91396-91396 WINNETKA
90070-90189 LOS ANGELES	90703-90703 CERRITOS	91302-91302 CALABASAS	91399-91399 WOODLAND HILLS
90201-90201 BELL	90704-90704 AVALON	91303-91305 CANOGA PARK	91400-91401 VAN NUYS
90202-90202 BELL GARDENS	90706-90707 BELLFLOWER	91306-91306 WINNETKA	91402-91402 PANORAMA CITY
90209-90213 BEVERLY HILLS	90710-90710 HARBOR CITY	91307-91308 WEST HILLS	91403-91403 SHERMAN OAKS
90220-90224 COMPTON	90711-90715 LAKEWOOD	91309-91309 CANOGA PARK	91404-91411 VAN NUYS
90230-90233 CULVER CITY	90716-90716 HAWAIIAN GARDENS	91310-91310 CASTAIC	91412-91412 PANORAMA CITY
90239-90242 DOWNEY	90717-90717 LOMITA	91311-91313 CHATSWORTH	91413-91413 SHERMAN OAKS
90245-90245 EL SEGUNDO	90720-90721 LOS ALAMITOS	91316-91316 ENCINO	91416-91416 ENCINO
90247-90249 GARDENA	90723-90723 PARAMOUNT	91319-91320 NEWBURY PARK	91423-91423 SHERMAN OAKS
90250-90251 HAWTHORNE	90731-90734 SAN PEDRO	91321-91322 NEWHALL	91426-91436 ENCINO
90254-90254 HERMOSA BEACH	90740-90740 SEAL BEACH	91324-91330 NORTHRIDGE	91461-91494 VAN NUYS
90255-90255 HUNTINGTON PARK	90742-90742 SUNSET BEACH	91331-91334 PACOIMA	91495-91495 SHERMAN OAKS
90260-90261 LAWNDALE	90743-90743 SURFSIDE	91335-91337 RESEDA	91496-91499 VAN NUYS
90262-90262 LYNWOOD	90744-90744 WILMINGTON	91340-91341 SAN FERNANDO	91500-91526 BURBANK
90263-90265 MALIBU	90745-90747 CARSON	91342-91342 SYLMAR	91600-91603 NORTH HOLLYWOOD
90266-90267 MANHATTAN BEACH	90748-90748 WILMINGTON	91343-91343 NORTH HILLS	91604-91604 STUDIO CITY
90270-90270 MAYWOOD	90749-90749 CARSON	91344-91344 GRANADA HILLS	91605-91606 NORTH HOLLYWOOD
90272-90272 PACIFIC PALISADES	90755-90755 SIGNAL HILL	91345-91346 MISSION HILLS	91607-91607 VALLEY VILLAGE
90274-90274 PALOS VERDES PENINSULA	90800-90899 LONG BEACH	91350-91350 SANTA CLARITA	91608-91608 UNIVERSAL CITY
90275-90275 RANCHO PALOS VERDES	90895-90895 CARSON	91351-91351 CANYON COUNTRY	91609-91609 NORTH HOLLYWOOD
90277-90278 REDONDO BEACH	91001-91003 ALTADENA	91352-91353 SUN VALLEY	91610-91610 TOLUCA LAKE
90280-90280 SOUTH GATE	91006-91007 ARCADIA	91354-91355 VALENCIA	91611-91612 NORTH HOLLYWOOD
90290-90290 TOPANGA	91009-91010 DUARTE	91356-91357 TARZANA	91614-91614 STUDIO CITY
90291-90291 VENICE	91011-91012 LA CANADA FLINTRIDGE	91358-91358 THOUSAND OAKS	91615-91616 NORTH HOLLYWOOD
90292-90292 MARINA DEL REY	91016-91017 MONROVIA	91359-91359 WESTLAKE VILLAGE	91617-91617 VALLEY VILLAGE
90293-90293 PLAYA DEL REY	91020-91021 MONTROSE	91360-91360 THOUSAND OAKS	91618-91618 UNIVERSAL CITY
90294-90294 VENICE	91023-91023 MOUNT WILSON	91361-91361 WESTLAKE VILLAGE	91618-91618 NORTH HOLLYWOOD
90295-90295 MARINA DEL REY	91024-91025 SIERRA MADRE	91362-91362 THOUSAND OAKS	91701-91701 ALTA LOMA
90296-90296 PLAYA DEL REY	91030-91031 SOUTH PASADENA	91363-91363 WESTLAKE VILLAGE	91702-91702 AZUSA
90300-90398 INGLEWOOD	91040-91041 SUNLAND	91364-91371 WOODLAND HILLS	91706-91706 BALDWIN PARK
90400-90411 SANTA MONICA	91042-91043 TUJUNGA	91372-91372 CALABASAS	91708-91708 CHINO
90500-90510 TORRANCE	91046-91046 VERDUGO CITY	91375-91376 AGOURA HILLS	91709-91709 CHINO HILLS
90601-90612 WHITTIER	91050-91051 PASADENA	91377-91377 OAK PARK	91710-91710 CHINO
90620-90622 BUENA PARK	91052-91052 LA COUNTY TAX COL'R	91380-91380 SANTA CLARITA	91711-91711 CLAREMONT
90623-90623 LA PALMA	91066-91077 ARCADIA	91381-91381 STEVENSON RANCH	91714-91716 CITY OF INDUSTRY
90624-90624 BUENA PARK	91100-91107 PASADENA	91382-91383 SANTA CLARITA	91718-91720 CORONA
90630-90630 CYPRESS	91108-91108 SAN MARINO	91384-91384 CASTAIC	91722-91724 COVINA
90631-90633 LA HABRA	91109-91117 PASADENA	91385-91385 VALENCIA	91729-91730 RANCHO CUCAMONGA
90637-90639 LA MIRADA	91118-91118 SAN MARINO	91386-91387 CANYON COUNTRY	91731-91732 EL MONTE
90640-90640 MONTEBELLO	91121-91191 PASADENA	91388-91388 VAN NUYS	91733-91733 SOUTH EL MONTE
90650-90659 NORWALK	91200-91210 GLENDALE	91390-91390 SANTA CLARITA	91734-91735 EL MONTE
90660-90665 PICO RIVERA	91214-91214 LA CRESCENTA	91392-91392 SYLMAR	91737-91737 ALTA LOMA
90670-90671 SANTA FE SPRINGS	91221-91222 GLENDALE	91393-91393 NORTH HILLS	91739-91739 RANCHO CUCAMONGA
	91224-91224 LA CRESCENTA	91394-91394 GRANADA HILLS	91740-91741 GLENDORA

Zip Range	City	Zip Range	City	Zip Range	City	Zip Range	City
91743-91743	GUASTI	92069-92069	SAN MARCOS	92314-92314	BIG BEAR CITY	92606-92606	IRVINE
91744-91744	LA PUENTE	92070-92070	SANTA YSABEL	92315-92315	BIG BEAR LAKE	92607-92607	LAGUNA NIGUEL
91745-91745	HACIENDA HEIGHTS	92071-92072	SANTEE	92316-92316	BLOOMINGTON	92609-92609	EL TORO
91746-91747	LA PUENTE	92073-92073	SAN DIEGO	92317-92317	BLUE JAY	92610-92610	FOOTHILL RANCH
91748-91748	ROWLAND HEIGHTS	92074-92074	POWAY	92318-92318	BRYN MAWR	92612-92612	IRVINE
91749-91749	LA PUENTE	92075-92075	SOLANA BEACH	92319-92319	CADIZ	92613-92613	ORANGE
91750-91750	LA VERNE	92078-92079	SAN MARCOS	92320-92320	CALIMESA	92614-92614	IRVINE
91752-91752	MIRA LOMA	92081-92081	VISTA	92321-92321	CEDAR GLEN	92615-92615	HUNTINGTON BEACH
91754-91756	MONTEREY PARK	92082-92082	VALLEY CENTER	92322-92322	CEDARPINES PARK	92616-92620	IRVINE
91758-91758	ONTARIO	92083-92085	VISTA	92323-92323	CIMA	92621-92622	BREA
91759-91759	MT BALDY	92086-92086	WARNER SPRINGS	92324-92324	COLTON	92623-92623	IRVINE
91760-91760	NORCO	92088-92088	FALLBROOK	92325-92325	CRESTLINE	92624-92624	CAPISTRANO BEACH
91761-91762	ONTARIO	92090-92090	EL CAJON	92326-92326	CREST PARK	92625-92625	CORONA DEL MAR
91763-91763	MONTCLAIR	92091-92091	RANCHO SANTA FE	92327-92327	DAGGETT	92626-92628	COSTA MESA
91764-91764	ONTARIO	92092-92093	LA JOLLA	92328-92328	DEATH VALLEY	92629-92629	DANA POINT
91765-91765	DIAMOND BAR	92096-92096	SAN MARCOS	92329-92329	PHELAN	92630-92630	LAKE FOREST
91766-91769	POMONA	92100-92117	SAN DIEGO	92332-92332	ESSEX	92631-92631	BREA
91770-91772	ROSEMEAD	92118-92118	CORONADO	92333-92333	FAWNSKIN	92632-92635	FULLERTON
91773-91773	SAN DIMAS	92119-92142	SAN DIEGO	92334-92337	FONTANA	92637-92637	LAGUNA HILLS
91775-91778	SAN GABRIEL	92143-92143	SAN YSIDRO	92338-92338	LUDLOW	92640-92640	FULLERTON
91780-91780	TEMPLE CITY	92145-92172	SAN DIEGO	92339-92339	FOREST FALLS	92641-92645	GARDEN GROVE
91784-91786	UPLAND	92173-92173	SAN YSIDRO	92340-92340	HESPERIA	92646-92649	HUNTINGTON BEACH
91788-91789	WALNUT	92174-92177	SAN DIEGO	92341-92341	GREEN VALLEY LAKE	92650-92650	EAST IRVINE
91790-91793	WEST COVINA	92178-92178	CORONADO	92342-92342	HELENDALE	92651-92652	LAGUNA BEACH
91795-91795	WALNUT	92179-92199	SAN DIEGO	92344-92345	HESPERIA	92653-92654	LAGUNA HILLS
91797-91797	BALDWIN PARK	92201-92203	INDIO	92346-92346	HIGHLAND	92655-92655	MIDWAY CITY
91797-91797	POMONA	92210-92210	INDIAN WELLS	92347-92347	HINKLEY	92656-92656	ALISO VIEJO
91798-91798	ONTARIO	92211-92211	PALM DESERT	92350-92350	LOMA LINDA	92657-92657	NEWPORT COAST
91799-91799	POMONA	92220-92220	BANNING	92351-92351	BAKER	92658-92663	NEWPORT BEACH
91800-91899	ALHAMBRA	92222-92222	BARD	92352-92352	LAKE ARROWHEAD	92664-92669	ORANGE
91901-91901	ALPINE	92223-92223	BEAUMONT	92353-92353	LAKEVIEW	92670-92670	PLACENTIA
91902-91902	BONITA	92225-92226	BLYTHE	92354-92354	LOMA LINDA	92672-92674	SAN CLEMENTE
91903-91903	ALPINE	92227-92227	BRAWLEY	92356-92356	LUCERNE VALLEY	92675-92675	SAN JUAN CAPISTRANO
91905-91905	BOULEVARD	92230-92230	CABAZON	92357-92357	LOMA LINDA	92676-92676	SILVERADO
91906-91906	CAMPO	92231-92232	CALEXICO	92358-92358	LYTLE CREEK	92677-92677	LAGUNA NIGUEL
91908-91908	BONITA	92233-92233	CALIPATRIA	92359-92359	MENTONE	92678-92679	TRABUCO CANYON
91909-91915	CHULA VISTA	92234-92235	CATHEDRAL CITY	92363-92363	NEEDLES	92680-92681	TUSTIN
91916-91916	DESCANSO	92236-92236	COACHELLA	92364-92364	NIPTON	92683-92685	WESTMINSTER
91917-91917	DULZURA	92239-92239	DESERT CENTER	92365-92365	NEWBERRY SPRINGS	92686-92687	YORBA LINDA
91921-91921	CHULA VISTA	92240-92241	DESERT HOT SPRINGS	92366-92366	MOUNTAIN PASS	92688-92688	RANCHO SANTA MARGARITA
91931-91931	GUATAY	92242-92242	EARP	92368-92368	ORO GRANDE	92690-92692	MISSION VIEJO
91932-91933	IMPERIAL BEACH	92243-92244	EL CENTRO	92369-92369	PATTON	92693-92693	SAN JUAN CAPISTRANO
91934-91934	JACUMBA	92247-92248	LA QUINTA	92371-92371	PHELAN	92694-92694	MISSION VIEJO
91935-91935	JAMUL	92249-92249	HEBER	92372-92372	PINON HILLS	92694-92694	LADERA RANCH
91941-91944	LA MESA	92250-92250	HOLTVILLE	92373-92375	REDLANDS	92697-92698	IRVINE
91945-91946	LEMON GROVE	92251-92251	IMPERIAL	92376-92377	RIALTO	92698-92698	ALISO VIEJO
91947-91947	LINCOLN ACRES	92252-92252	JOSHUA TREE	92378-92378	RIMFOREST	92701-92707	SANTA ANA
91948-91948	MOUNT LAGUNA	92253-92253	LA QUINTA	92382-92382	RUNNING SPRINGS	92708-92708	FOUNTAIN VALLEY
91950-91951	NATIONAL CITY	92254-92254	MECCA	92384-92384	SHOSHONE	92709-92710	IRVINE
91962-91962	PINE VALLEY	92255-92255	PALM DESERT	92385-92385	SKYFOREST	92711-92712	SANTA ANA
91963-91963	POTRERO	92256-92256	MORONGO VALLEY	92386-92386	SUGARLOAF	92713-92720	IRVINE
91976-91979	SPRING VALLEY	92257-92257	NILAND	92389-92389	TECOPA	92725-92725	SANTA ANA
91980-91987	TECATE	92258-92258	NORTH PALM SPRINGS	92391-92391	TWIN PEAKS	92728-92728	FOUNTAIN VALLEY
91990-91995	POTRERO	92259-92259	OCOTILLO	92392-92395	VICTORVILLE	92730-92730	IRVINE
92003-92003	BONSALL	92260-92261	PALM DESERT	92397-92397	WRIGHTWOOD	92735-92735	SANTA ANA
92004-92004	BORREGO SPRINGS	92262-92264	PALM SPRINGS	92398-92398	YERMO	92780-92782	TUSTIN
92007-92007	CARDIFF BY THE SEA	92266-92266	PALO VERDE	92399-92399	YUCAIPA	92799-92799	SANTA ANA
92008-92013	CARLSBAD	92267-92267	PARKER DAM	92400-92427	SAN BERNARDINO	92800-92809	ANAHEIM
92014-92014	DEL MAR	92268-92268	PIONEERTOWN	92500-92517	RIVERSIDE	92811-92811	ATWOOD
92018-92018	CARLSBAD	92270-92270	RANCHO MIRAGE	92518-92518	MARCH AIR FORCE BASE	92812-92817	ANAHEIM
92019-92022	EL CAJON	92272-92272	RIPLEY	92519-92522	RIVERSIDE	92821-92823	BREA
92023-92024	ENCINITAS	92273-92273	SEELEY	92530-92532	LAKE ELSINORE	92825-92825	ANAHEIM
92025-92027	ESCONDIDO	92274-92274	THERMAL	92536-92536	AGUANGA	92831-92838	FULLERTON
92028-92028	FALLBROOK	92275-92275	SALTON CITY	92539-92539	ANZA	92840-92846	GARDEN GROVE
92029-92033	ESCONDIDO	92276-92276	THOUSAND PALMS	92543-92546	HEMET	92850-92850	ANAHEIM
92036-92036	JULIAN	92277-92278	TWENTYNINE PALMS	92548-92548	HOMELAND	92856-92859	ORANGE
92037-92039	LA JOLLA	92280-92280	VIDAL	92549-92549	IDYLLWILD	92860-92860	NORCO
92040-92040	LAKESIDE	92281-92281	WESTMORLAND	92551-92557	MORENO VALLEY	92861-92861	VILLA PARK
92046-92046	ESCONDIDO	92282-92282	WHITE WATER	92561-92561	MOUNTAIN CENTER	92862-92869	ORANGE
92049-92052	OCEANSIDE	92283-92283	WINTERHAVEN	92562-92564	MURRIETA	92870-92871	PLACENTIA
92053-92053	NESTOR	92284-92284	YUCCA VALLEY	92567-92567	NUEVO	92877-92883	CORONA
92054-92054	OCEANSIDE	92285-92285	LANDERS	92570-92572	PERRIS	92885-92887	YORBA LINDA
92055-92055	CAMP PENDLETON	92286-92286	YUCCA VALLEY	92581-92583	SAN JACINTO	92899-92899	ANAHEIM
92056-92058	OCEANSIDE	92292-92292	PALM SPRINGS	92584-92584	MENIFEE	93001-93009	VENTURA
92059-92059	PALA	92301-92301	ADELANTO	92585-92587	SUN CITY	93010-93012	CAMARILLO
92060-92060	PALOMAR MOUNTAIN	92304-92304	AMBOY	92589-92593	TEMECULA	93013-93014	CARPINTERIA
92061-92061	PAUMA VALLEY	92305-92305	ANGELUS OAKS	92595-92595	WILDOMAR	93015-93016	FILLMORE
92064-92064	POWAY	92307-92308	APPLE VALLEY	92596-92596	WINCHESTER	93020-93021	MOORPARK
92065-92065	RAMONA	92309-92309	BAKER	92599-92599	PERRIS	93022-93022	OAK VIEW
92066-92066	RANCHITA	92310-92310	FORT IRWIN	92601-92601	ATWOOD	93023-93024	OJAI
92067-92067	RANCHO SANTA FE	92311-92312	BARSTOW	92602-92604	IRVINE	93030-93036	OXNARD
92068-92068	SAN LUIS REY	92313-92313	GRAND TERRACE	92605-92605	HUNTINGTON BEACH	93040-93040	PIRU

93041-93041 PORT HUENEME	93402-93402 LOS OSOS	93605-93605 BIG CREEK	94013-94017 DALY CITY
93042-93042 POINT MUGU NAWC	93403-93410 SAN LUIS OBISPO	93606-93606 BIOLA	94018-94018 EL GRANADA
93043-93043 PORT HUENEME CBC BASE	93412-93412 LOS OSOS	93607-93607 BURREL	94019-94019 HALF MOON BAY
93044-93044 PORT HUENEME	93420-93421 ARROYO GRANDE	93608-93608 CANTUA CREEK	94020-94020 LA HONDA
93060-93061 SANTA PAULA	93422-93423 ATASCADERO	93609-93609 CARUTHERS	94021-94021 LOMA MAR
93062-93063 SIMI VALLEY	93424-93424 AVILA BEACH	93610-93610 CHOWCHILLA	94022-94024 LOS ALTOS
93064-93064 BRANDEIS	93426-93426 BRADLEY	93611-93613 CLOVIS	94025-94026 MENLO PARK
93065-93065 SIMI VALLEY	93427-93427 BUELLTON	93614-93614 COARSEGOLD	94027-94027 ATHERTON
93066-93066 SOMIS	93428-93428 CAMBRIA	93615-93615 CUTLER	94028-94028 PORTOLA VALLEY
93067-93067 SUMMERLAND	93429-93429 CASMALIA	93616-93616 DEL REY	94029-94029 MENLO PARK
93093-93099 SIMI VALLEY	93430-93430 CAYUCOS	93618-93618 DINUBA	94030-94031 MILLBRAE
93101-93111 SANTA BARBARA	93431-93431 CHOLAME	93619-93619 CLOVIS	94035-94035 MOUNTAIN VIEW
93116-93118 GOLETA	93432-93432 CRESTON	93620-93620 DOS PALOS	94037-94037 MONTARA
93120-93190 SANTA BARBARA	93433-93433 GROVER BEACH	93621-93621 DUNLAP	94038-94038 MOSS BEACH
93199-93199 GOLETA	93434-93434 GUADALUPE	93622-93622 FIREBAUGH	94039-94043 MOUNTAIN VIEW
93201-93201 ALPAUGH	93435-93435 HARMONY	93623-93623 FISH CAMP	94044-94045 PACIFICA
93202-93202 ARMONA	93436-93438 LOMPOC	93624-93624 FIVE POINTS	94059-94059 REDWOOD CITY
93203-93203 ARVIN	93440-93440 LOS ALAMOS	93625-93625 FOWLER	94060-94060 PESCADERO
93204-93204 AVENAL	93441-93441 LOS OLIVOS	93626-93626 FRIANT	94061-94065 REDWOOD CITY
93205-93205 BODFISH	93442-93443 MORRO BAY	93627-93627 HELM	94066-94067 SAN BRUNO
93206-93206 BUTTONWILLOW	93444-93444 NIPOMO	93628-93628 HUME	94070-94071 SAN CARLOS
93207-93207 CALIFORNIA HOT SPRINGS	93445-93445 OCEANO	93629-93629 HUNTINGTON LAKE	94074-94074 SAN GREGORIO
93208-93208 CAMP NELSON	93446-93447 PASO ROBLES	93630-93630 KERMAN	94080-94083 SOUTH SAN FRANCISCO
93210-93210 COALINGA	93448-93449 PISMO BEACH	93631-93631 KINGSBURG	94085-94091 SUNNYVALE
93212-93212 CORCORAN	93450-93450 SAN ARDO	93633-93633 KINGS CANYON NAT PK	94096-94098 SAN BRUNO
93214-93214 CUYAMA	93451-93451 SAN MIGUEL	93634-93634 LAKESHORE	94099-94099 SOUTH SAN FRANCISCO
93215-93216 DELANO	93452-93452 SAN SIMEON	93635-93635 LOS BANOS	94100-94199 SAN FRANCISCO
93217-93217 DI GIORGIO	93453-93453 SANTA MARGARITA	93637-93639 MADERA	94203-94299 SACRAMENTO
93218-93218 DUCOR	93454-93458 SANTA MARIA	93640-93640 MENDOTA	94300-94310 PALO ALTO
93219-93219 EARLIMART	93460-93460 SANTA YNEZ	93641-93641 MIRAMONTE	94400-94497 SAN MATEO
93220-93220 EDISON	93461-93461 SHANDON	93642-93642 MONO HOT SPRINGS	94501-94502 ALAMEDA
93221-93221 EXETER	93463-93464 SOLVANG	93643-93643 NORTH FORK	94503-94503 AMERICAN CANYON
93222-93222 FRAZIER PARK	93465-93465 TEMPLETON	93644-93644 OAKHURST	94504-94504 MOBIL OIL CREDIT CORP
93223-93223 FARMERSVILLE	93475-93475 OCEANO	93645-93645 O NEALS	94506-94506 DANVILLE
93224-93224 FELLOWS	93483-93483 GROVER BEACH	93646-93646 ORANGE COVE	94507-94507 ALAMO
93225-93225 FRAZIER PARK	93501-93502 MOJAVE	93647-93647 OROSI	94508-94508 ANGWIN
93226-93226 GLENNVILLE	93504-93505 CALIFORNIA CITY	93648-93648 PARLIER	94509-94509 ANTIOCH
93227-93227 GOSHEN	93510-93510 ACTON	93649-93649 PIEDRA	94510-94510 BENICIA
93230-93232 HANFORD	93512-93512 BENTON	93650-93650 FRESNO	94511-94511 BETHEL ISLAND
93234-93234 HURON	93513-93513 BIG PINE	93651-93651 PRATHER	94512-94512 BIRDS LANDING
93235-93235 IVANHOE	93514-93515 BISHOP	93652-93652 RAISIN	94513-94513 BRENTWOOD
93237-93237 KAWEAH	93516-93516 BORON	93653-93653 RAYMOND	94514-94514 BYRON
93238-93238 KERNVILLE	93517-93517 BRIDGEPORT	93654-93654 REEDLEY	94515-94515 CALISTOGA
93239-93239 KETTLEMAN CITY	93518-93518 CALIENTE	93656-93656 RIVERDALE	94516-94516 CANYON
93240-93240 LAKE ISABELLA	93519-93519 CANTIL	93657-93657 SANGER	94517-94517 CLAYTON
93241-93241 LAMONT	93522-93522 DARWIN	93660-93660 SAN JOAQUIN	94518-94522 CONCORD
93242-93242 LATON	93523-93524 EDWARDS	93661-93661 SANTA RITA PARK	94523-94523 PLEASANT HILL
93243-93243 LEBEC	93526-93526 INDEPENDENCE	93662-93662 SELMA	94524-94524 CONCORD
93244-93244 LEMON COVE	93527-93527 INYOKERN	93664-93664 SHAVER LAKE	94525-94525 CROCKETT
93245-93246 LEMOORE	93528-93528 JOHANNESBURG	93665-93665 SOUTH DOS PALOS	94526-94526 DANVILLE
93247-93247 LINDSAY	93529-93529 JUNE LAKE	93666-93666 SULTANA	94527-94527 CONCORD
93249-93249 LOST HILLS	93530-93530 KEELER	93667-93667 TOLLHOUSE	94528-94528 DIABLO
93250-93250 MC FARLAND	93531-93531 KEENE	93668-93668 TRANQUILLITY	94529-94529 CONCORD
93251-93251 MC KITTRICK	93532-93532 LAKE HUGHES	93669-93669 WISHON	94530-94530 EL CERRITO
93252-93252 MARICOPA	93534-93539 LANCASTER	93670-93670 YETTEM	94531-94531 ANTIOCH
93254-93254 NEW CUYAMA	93541-93541 LEE VINING	93673-93673 TRAVER	94533-94534 FAIRFIELD
93255-93255 ONYX	93542-93542 LITTLE LAKE	93675-93675 SQUAW VALLEY	94535-94535 TRAVIS AFB
93256-93256 PIXLEY	93543-93543 LITTLEROCK	93700-93888 FRESNO	94536-94539 FREMONT
93257-93258 PORTERVILLE	93544-93544 LLANO	93901-93915 SALINAS	94540-94545 HAYWARD
93260-93260 POSEY	93545-93545 LONE PINE	93920-93920 BIG SUR	94546-94546 CASTRO VALLEY
93261-93261 RICHGROVE	93546-93546 MAMMOTH LAKES	93921-93923 CARMEL	94547-94547 HERCULES
93262-93262 SEQUOIA NATIONAL PARK	93549-93549 OLANCHA	93924-93924 CARMEL VALLEY	94548-94548 KNIGHTSEN
93263-93263 SHAFTER	93550-93552 PALMDALE	93925-93925 CHUALAR	94549-94549 LAFAYETTE
93265-93265 SPRINGVILLE	93553-93553 PEARBLOSSOM	93926-93926 GONZALES	94550-94551 LIVERMORE
93266-93266 STRATFORD	93554-93554 RANDSBURG	93927-93927 GREENFIELD	94552-94552 CASTRO VALLEY
93267-93267 STRATHMORE	93555-93556 RIDGECREST	93928-93928 JOLON	94553-94553 MARTINEZ
93268-93268 TAFT	93558-93558 RED MOUNTAIN	93930-93930 KING CITY	94555-94555 FREMONT
93270-93270 TERRA BELLA	93560-93560 ROSAMOND	93932-93932 LOCKWOOD	94556-94556 MORAGA
93271-93271 THREE RIVERS	93561-93561 TEHACHAPI	93933-93933 MARINA	94557-94557 HAYWARD
93272-93272 TIPTON	93562-93562 TRONA	93940-93940 MONTEREY	94558-94559 NAPA
93274-93275 TULARE	93563-93563 VALYERMO	93941-93941 FT ORD	94560-94560 NEWARK
93276-93276 TUPMAN	93570-93570 KEENE	93941-93941 FORT ORD	94561-94561 OAKLEY
93277-93279 VISALIA	93581-93582 TEHACHAPI	93941-93944 MONTEREY	94562-94562 OAKVILLE
93280-93280 WASCO	93584-93586 LANCASTER	93950-93950 PACIFIC GROVE	94563-94563 ORINDA
93282-93282 WAUKENA	93590-93591 PALMDALE	93953-93953 PEBBLE BEACH	94564-94564 PINOLE
93283-93283 WELDON	93592-93592 TRONA	93954-93954 SAN LUCAS	94565-94565 PITTSBURG
93285-93285 WOFFORD HEIGHTS	93596-93596 BORON	93955-93955 SEASIDE	94566-94566 PLEASANTON
93286-93286 WOODLAKE	93599-93599 PALMDALE	93960-93960 SOLEDAD	94567-94567 POPE VALLEY
93287-93287 WOODY	93601-93601 AHWAHNEE	93962-93962 SPRECKELS	94568-94568 DUBLIN
93290-93292 VISALIA	93602-93602 AUBERRY	94002-94003 BELMONT	94569-94569 PORT COSTA
93300-93399 BAKERSFIELD	93603-93603 BADGER	94005-94005 BRISBANE	94570-94570 MORAGA
93401-93401 SAN LUIS OBISPO	93604-93604 BASS LAKE	94010-94012 BURLINGAME	94571-94571 RIO VISTA

Zip Range	Place
94572-94572	RODEO
94573-94573	RUTHERFORD
94574-94574	SAINT HELENA
94575-94575	MORAGA
94576-94576	DEER PARK
94577-94579	SAN LEANDRO
94580-94580	SAN LORENZO
94581-94581	NAPA
94582-94582	PLEASANTON
94582-94583	SAN RAMON
94585-94585	SUISUN CITY
94586-94586	SUNOL
94587-94587	UNION CITY
94588-94588	PLEASANTON
94589-94592	VALLEJO
94593-94593	CROCKER NAT BANK
94594-94594	MONTGOMERY WARD
94595-94598	WALNUT CREEK
94599-94599	YOUNTVILLE
94601-94607	OAKLAND
94608-94608	EMERYVILLE
94609-94619	OAKLAND
94620-94620	PIEDMONT
94621-94661	OAKLAND
94662-94662	EMERYVILLE
94666-94666	OAKLAND
94701-94705	BERKELEY
94706-94706	ALBANY
94707-94720	BERKELEY
94801-94802	RICHMOND
94803-94803	EL SOBRANTE
94804-94805	RICHMOND
94806-94806	SAN PABLO
94807-94808	RICHMOND
94820-94820	EL SOBRANTE
94850-94875	RICHMOND
94901-94903	SAN RAFAEL
94904-94904	GREENBRAE
94911-94913	SAN RAFAEL
94914-94914	KENTFIELD
94915-94915	SAN RAFAEL
94920-94920	BELVEDERE TIBURON
94922-94922	BODEGA
94923-94923	BODEGA BAY
94924-94924	BOLINAS
94925-94925	CORTE MADERA
94926-94926	COTATI
94927-94928	ROHNERT PARK
94929-94929	DILLON BEACH
94930-94930	FAIRFAX
94931-94931	COTATI
94933-94933	FOREST KNOLLS
94937-94937	INVERNESS
94938-94938	LAGUNITAS
94939-94939	LARKSPUR
94940-94940	MARSHALL
94941-94942	MILL VALLEY
94945-94945	NOVATO
94946-94946	NICASIO
94947-94949	NOVATO
94950-94950	OLEMA
94951-94951	PENNGROVE
94952-94955	PETALUMA
94956-94956	POINT REYES STATION
94957-94957	ROSS
94960-94960	SAN ANSELMO
94963-94963	SAN GERONIMO
94964-94964	SAN QUENTIN
94965-94966	SAUSALITO
94970-94970	STINSON BEACH
94971-94971	TOMALES
94972-94972	VALLEY FORD
94973-94973	WOODACRE
94974-94974	SAN QUENTIN
94975-94975	PETALUMA
94976-94976	CORTE MADERA
94977-94977	LARKSPUR
94978-94978	FAIRFAX
94979-94979	SAN ANSELMO
94998-94998	NOVATO
94999-94999	PETALUMA
95001-95001	APTOS
95002-95002	ALVISO
95003-95003	APTOS
95004-95004	AROMAS
95005-95005	BEN LOMOND
95006-95006	BOULDER CREEK
95007-95007	BROOKDALE
95008-95009	CAMPBELL
95010-95010	CAPITOLA
95011-95011	CAMPBELL
95012-95012	CASTROVILLE
95013-95013	COYOTE
95014-95016	CUPERTINO
95017-95017	DAVENPORT
95018-95018	FELTON
95019-95019	FREEDOM
95020-95021	GILROY
95023-95024	HOLLISTER
95026-95026	HOLY CITY
95030-95033	LOS GATOS
95035-95036	MILPITAS
95037-95038	MORGAN HILL
95039-95039	MOSS LANDING
95041-95041	MOUNT HERMON
95042-95042	NEW ALMADEN
95043-95043	PAICINES
95044-95044	REDWOOD ESTATES
95045-95045	SAN JUAN BAUTISTA
95046-95046	SAN MARTIN
95050-95056	SANTA CLARA
95060-95065	SANTA CRUZ
95066-95067	SCOTTS VALLEY
95070-95071	SARATOGA
95073-95073	SOQUEL
95075-95075	TRES PINOS
95076-95077	WATSONVILLE
95100-95139	SAN JOSE
95140-95140	MOUNT HAMILTON
95141-95196	SAN JOSE
95201-95219	STOCKTON
95220-95220	ACAMPO
95221-95221	ALTAVILLE
95222-95222	ANGELS CAMP
95223-95223	ARNOLD
95224-95224	AVERY
95225-95225	BURSON
95226-95226	CAMPO SECO
95227-95227	CLEMENTS
95228-95228	COPPEROPOLIS
95229-95229	DOUGLAS FLAT
95230-95230	FARMINGTON
95231-95231	FRENCH CAMP
95232-95232	GLENCOE
95233-95233	HATHAWAY PINES
95234-95234	HOLT
95236-95236	LINDEN
95237-95237	LOCKEFORD
95240-95242	LODI
95245-95245	MOKELUMNE HILL
95246-95246	MOUNTAIN RANCH
95247-95247	MURPHYS
95248-95248	RAIL ROAD FLAT
95249-95249	SAN ANDREAS
95250-95250	SHEEP RANCH
95251-95251	VALLECITO
95252-95252	VALLEY SPRINGS
95253-95253	VICTOR
95254-95254	WALLACE
95255-95255	WEST POINT
95257-95257	WILSEYVILLE
95258-95258	WOODBRIDGE
95267-95296	STOCKTON
95296-95296	LYOTH
95297-95298	STOCKTON
95301-95301	ATWATER
95303-95303	BALLICO
95304-95304	BANTA
95305-95305	BIG OAK FLAT
95306-95306	CATHEYS VALLEY
95307-95307	CERES
95309-95309	CHINESE CAMP
95310-95310	COLUMBIA
95311-95311	COULTERVILLE
95312-95312	CRESSEY
95313-95313	CROWS LANDING
95314-95314	DARDANELLE
95315-95315	DELHI
95316-95316	DENAIR
95317-95317	EL NIDO
95318-95318	EL PORTAL
95319-95319	EMPIRE
95320-95320	ESCALON
95321-95321	GROVELAND
95322-95322	GUSTINE
95323-95323	HICKMAN
95324-95324	HILMAR
95325-95325	HORNITOS
95326-95326	HUGHSON
95327-95327	JAMESTOWN
95328-95328	KEYES
95329-95329	LA GRANGE
95330-95330	LATHROP
95333-95333	LE GRAND
95334-95334	LIVINGSTON
95335-95335	LONG BARN
95336-95337	MANTECA
95338-95338	MARIPOSA
95340-95341	MERCED
95342-95342	ATWATER
95343-95344	MERCED
95345-95345	MIDPINES
95346-95346	MI WUK VILLAGE
95347-95347	MOCCASIN
95348-95348	MERCED
95350-95358	MODESTO
95360-95360	NEWMAN
95361-95361	OAKDALE
95363-95363	PATTERSON
95364-95364	PINECREST
95365-95365	PLANADA
95366-95366	RIPON
95367-95367	RIVERBANK
95368-95368	SALIDA
95369-95369	SNELLING
95370-95370	SONORA
95372-95372	SOULSBYVILLE
95373-95373	STANDARD
95374-95374	STEVINSON
95375-95375	STRAWBERRY
95376-95378	TRACY
95379-95379	TUOLUMNE
95380-95382	TURLOCK
95383-95383	TWAIN HARTE
95384-95384	VALLEY HOME
95385-95385	VERNALIS
95386-95386	WATERFORD
95387-95387	WESTLEY
95388-95388	WINTON
95389-95389	YOSEMITE NATIONAL PARK
95390-95390	RIVERBANK
95391-95391	TRACY
95397-95397	MODESTO
95401-95409	SANTA ROSA
95410-95410	ALBION
95412-95412	ANNAPOLIS
95415-95415	BOONVILLE
95416-95416	BOYES HOT SPRINGS
95417-95417	BRANSCOMB
95418-95418	CALPELLA
95419-95419	CAMP MEEKER
95420-95420	CASPAR
95421-95421	CAZADERO
95422-95422	CLEARLAKE
95423-95423	CLEARLAKE OAKS
95424-95424	CLEARLAKE PARK
95425-95425	CLOVERDALE
95426-95426	COBB
95427-95427	COMPTCHE
95428-95428	COVELO
95429-95429	DOS RIOS
95430-95430	DUNCANS MILLS
95431-95431	ELDRIDGE
95432-95432	ELK
95433-95433	EL VERANO
95435-95435	FINLEY
95436-95436	FORESTVILLE
95437-95437	FORT BRAGG
95439-95439	FULTON
95441-95441	GEYSERVILLE
95442-95442	GLEN ELLEN
95443-95443	GLENHAVEN
95444-95444	GRATON
95445-95445	GUALALA
95446-95446	GUERNEVILLE
95448-95448	HEALDSBURG
95449-95449	HOPLAND
95450-95450	JENNER
95451-95451	KELSEYVILLE
95452-95452	KENWOOD
95453-95453	LAKEPORT
95454-95454	LAYTONVILLE
95456-95456	LITTLERIVER
95457-95457	LOWER LAKE
95458-95458	LUCERNE
95459-95459	MANCHESTER
95460-95460	MENDOCINO
95461-95461	MIDDLETOWN
95462-95462	MONTE RIO
95463-95463	NAVARRO
95464-95464	NICE
95465-95465	OCCIDENTAL
95466-95466	PHILO
95467-95467	HIDDEN VALLEY LAKE
95468-95468	POINT ARENA
95469-95469	POTTER VALLEY
95470-95470	REDWOOD VALLEY
95471-95471	RIO NIDO
95472-95473	SEBASTOPOL
95476-95476	SONOMA
95480-95480	STEWARTS POINT
95481-95481	TALMAGE
95482-95482	UKIAH
95485-95485	UPPER LAKE
95486-95486	VILLA GRANDE
95487-95487	VINEBURG
95488-95488	WESTPORT
95490-95490	WILLITS
95492-95492	WINDSOR
95493-95493	WITTER SPRINGS
95494-95494	YORKVILLE
95497-95497	THE SEA RANCH
95501-95503	EUREKA
95511-95511	ALDERPOINT
95514-95514	BLOCKSBURG
95518-95518	ARCATA
95519-95519	MCKINLEYVILLE
95521-95521	ARCATA
95524-95524	BAYSIDE
95525-95525	BLUE LAKE
95526-95526	BRIDGEVILLE
95527-95527	BURNT RANCH
95528-95528	CARLOTTA
95531-95532	CRESCENT CITY
95534-95534	CUTTEN
95536-95536	FERNDALE
95537-95537	FIELDS LANDING
95538-95538	FORT DICK
95540-95540	FORTUNA
95542-95542	GARBERVILLE
95543-95543	GASQUET
95545-95545	HONEYDEW
95546-95546	HOOPA
95547-95547	HYDESVILLE
95548-95548	KLAMATH
95549-95549	KNEELAND
95550-95550	KORBEL
95551-95551	LOLETA
95552-95552	MAD RIVER
95553-95553	MIRANDA
95554-95554	MYERS FLAT
95555-95555	ORICK
95556-95556	ORLEANS
95558-95558	PETROLIA
95559-95559	PHILLIPSVILLE
95560-95560	REDWAY
95562-95562	RIO DELL
95563-95563	SALYER

ZIP Range	City	ZIP Range	City	ZIP Range	City	ZIP Range	City
95564-95564	SAMOA	95678-95678	ROSEVILLE	95947-95947	GREENVILLE	96055-96055	LOS MOLINOS
95565-95565	SCOTIA	95679-95679	RUMSEY	95948-95948	GRIDLEY	96056-96056	MCARTHUR
95567-95567	SMITH RIVER	95680-95680	RYDE	95949-95949	GRASS VALLEY	96057-96057	MCCLOUD
95568-95568	SOMES BAR	95681-95681	SHERIDAN	95950-95950	GRIMES	96058-96058	MACDOEL
95569-95569	REDCREST	95682-95682	SHINGLE SPRINGS	95951-95951	HAMILTON CITY	96059-96059	MANTON
95570-95570	TRINIDAD	95683-95683	SLOUGHHOUSE	95953-95953	LIVE OAK	96061-96061	MILL CREEK
95571-95571	WEOTT	95684-95684	SOMERSET	95954-95954	MAGALIA	96062-96062	MILLVILLE
95573-95573	WILLOW CREEK	95685-95685	SUTTER CREEK	95955-95955	MAXWELL	96063-96063	MINERAL
95585-95585	LEGGETT	95686-95686	THORNTON	95956-95956	MEADOW VALLEY	96064-96064	MONTAGUE
95587-95587	PIERCY	95687-95688	VACAVILLE	95957-95957	MERIDIAN	96065-96065	MONTGOMERY CREEK
95589-95589	WHITETHORN	95689-95689	VOLCANO	95958-95958	NELSON	96067-96067	MOUNT SHASTA
95595-95595	ZENIA	95690-95690	WALNUT GROVE	95959-95959	NEVADA CITY	96068-96068	NUBIEBER
95601-95601	AMADOR CITY	95691-95691	WEST SACRAMENTO	95960-95960	NORTH SAN JUAN	96069-96069	OAK RUN
95602-95604	AUBURN	95692-95692	WHEATLAND	95961-95961	OLIVEHURST	96070-96070	OBRIEN
95605-95605	WEST SACRAMENTO	95693-95693	WILTON	95962-95962	OREGON HOUSE	96071-96071	OLD STATION
95606-95606	BROOKS	95694-95694	WINTERS	95963-95963	ORLAND	96073-96073	PALO CEDRO
95607-95607	CAPAY	95695-95695	WOODLAND	95965-95966	OROVILLE	96074-96074	PASKENTA
95608-95609	CARMICHAEL	95696-95696	VACAVILLE	95967-95967	PARADISE	96075-96075	PAYNES CREEK
95610-95611	CITRUS HEIGHTS	95697-95697	YOLO	95968-95968	PALERMO	96076-96076	PLATINA
95612-95612	CLARKSBURG	95698-95698	ZAMORA	95969-95969	PARADISE	96078-96078	PROBERTA
95613-95613	COLOMA	95699-95699	DRYTOWN	95970-95970	PRINCETON	96079-96079	SHASTA LAKE
95614-95614	COOL	95701-95701	ALTA	95971-95971	QUINCY	96080-96080	RED BLUFF
95615-95615	COURTLAND	95703-95703	APPLEGATE	95972-95972	RACKERBY	96084-96084	ROUND MOUNTAIN
95616-95617	DAVIS	95709-95709	CAMINO	95973-95973	CHICO	96085-96085	SCOTT BAR
95618-95618	EL MACERO	95712-95712	CHICAGO PARK	95974-95974	RICHVALE	96086-96086	SEIAD VALLEY
95619-95619	DIAMOND SPRINGS	95713-95713	COLFAX	95975-95975	ROUGH AND READY	96087-96087	SHASTA
95620-95620	DIXON	95714-95714	DUTCH FLAT	95976-95976	CHICO	96088-96088	SHINGLETOWN
95621-95621	CITRUS HEIGHTS	95715-95715	EMIGRANT GAP	95977-95977	SMARTVILLE	96089-96089	SHASTA LAKE
95622-95622	NICOLAUS	95717-95717	GOLD RUN	95978-95978	STIRLING CITY	96090-96090	TEHAMA
95623-95623	EL DORADO	95720-95720	KYBURZ	95979-95979	STONYFORD	96091-96091	TRINITY CENTER
95624-95624	ELK GROVE	95721-95721	ECHO LAKE	95980-95980	STORRIE	96092-96092	VINA
95625-95625	ELMIRA	95722-95722	MEADOW VISTA	95981-95981	STRAWBERRY VALLEY	96093-96093	WEAVERVILLE
95626-95626	ELVERTA	95724-95724	NORDEN	95982-95982	SUTTER	96094-96094	WEED
95627-95627	ESPARTO	95726-95726	POLLOCK PINES	95983-95983	TAYLORSVILLE	96095-96095	WHISKEYTOWN
95628-95628	FAIR OAKS	95728-95728	SODA SPRINGS	95984-95984	TWAIN	96096-96096	WHITMORE
95629-95629	FIDDLETOWN	95735-95735	TWIN BRIDGES	95986-95986	WASHINGTON	96097-96097	YREKA
95630-95630	FOLSOM	95736-95736	WEIMAR	95987-95987	WILLIAMS	96099-96099	REDDING
95631-95631	FORESTHILL	95741-95743	RANCHO CORDOVA	95988-95988	WILLOWS	96101-96101	ALTURAS
95632-95632	GALT	95746-95746	GRANITE BAY	95991-95993	YUBA CITY	96103-96103	BLAIRSDEN-GRAEAGLE
95633-95633	GARDEN VALLEY	95747-95747	ROSEVILLE	96001-96003	REDDING	96104-96104	CEDARVILLE
95634-95634	GEORGETOWN	95757-95759	ELK GROVE	96006-96006	ADIN	96105-96105	CHILCOOT
95635-95635	GREENWOOD	95762-95762	EL DORADO HILLS	96007-96007	ANDERSON	96106-96106	CLIO
95636-95636	GRIZZLY FLATS	95763-95763	FOLSOM	96008-96008	BELLA VISTA	96107-96107	COLEVILLE
95637-95637	GUINDA	95765-95765	ROCKLIN	96009-96009	BIEBER	96108-96108	DAVIS CREEK
95638-95638	HERALD	95776-95776	WOODLAND	96010-96010	BIG BAR	96109-96109	DOYLE
95639-95639	HOOD	95798-95799	WEST SACRAMENTO	96011-96011	BIG BEND	96110-96110	EAGLEVILLE
95640-95640	IONE	95800-95842	SACRAMENTO	96013-96013	BURNEY	96111-96111	FLORISTON
95641-95641	ISLETON	95843-95843	ANTELOPE	96014-96014	CALLAHAN	96112-96112	FORT BIDWELL
95642-95642	JACKSON	95851-95899	SACRAMENTO	96015-96015	CANBY	96113-96113	HERLONG
95643-95643	PLACERVILLE	95901-95901	MARYSVILLE	96016-96016	CASSEL	96114-96114	JANESVILLE
95644-95644	KIT CARSON	95903-95903	BEALE AFB	96017-96017	CASTELLA	96115-96115	LAKE CITY
95645-95645	KNIGHTS LANDING	95910-95910	ALLEGHANY	96019-96019	SHASTA LAKE	96116-96116	LIKELY
95646-95646	KIRKWOOD	95912-95912	ARBUCKLE	96020-96020	CHESTER	96117-96117	LITCHFIELD
95648-95648	LINCOLN	95913-95913	ARTOIS	96021-96021	CORNING	96118-96118	LOYALTON
95650-95650	LOOMIS	95914-95914	BANGOR	96022-96022	COTTONWOOD	96119-96119	MADELINE
95651-95651	LOTUS	95915-95915	BELDEN	96023-96023	DORRIS	96120-96120	MARKLEEVILLE
95652-95652	MCCLELLAN AFB	95916-95916	BERRY CREEK	96024-96024	DOUGLAS CITY	96121-96121	MILFORD
95652-95652	MCCLELLAN	95917-95917	BIGGS	96025-96025	DUNSMUIR	96122-96122	PORTOLA
95653-95653	MADISON	95918-95918	BROWNS VALLEY	96027-96027	ETNA	96123-96123	RAVENDALE
95654-95654	MARTELL	95919-95919	BROWNSVILLE	96028-96028	FALL RIVER MILLS	96124-96124	CALPINE
95655-95655	MATHER	95920-95920	BUTTE CITY	96029-96029	FLOURNOY	96125-96125	SIERRA CITY
95656-95656	MOUNT AUKUM	95922-95922	CAMPTONVILLE	96031-96031	FORKS OF SALMON	96126-96126	SIERRAVILLE
95658-95658	NEWCASTLE	95923-95923	CANYONDAM	96032-96032	FORT JONES	96127-96127	SUSANVILLE
95659-95659	NICOLAUS	95924-95924	CEDAR RIDGE	96033-96033	FRENCH GULCH	96128-96128	STANDISH
95660-95660	NORTH HIGHLANDS	95925-95925	CHALLENGE	96034-96034	GAZELLE	96129-96129	BECKWOURTH
95661-95661	ROSEVILLE	95926-95926	CHICO	96035-96035	GERBER	96130-96130	SUSANVILLE
95662-95662	ORANGEVALE	95930-95930	CLIPPER MILLS	96037-96037	GREENVIEW	96132-96132	TERMO
95663-95663	PENRYN	95931-95931	COLLEGE CITY	96038-96038	GRENADA	96133-96133	TOPAZ
95664-95664	PILOT HILL	95932-95932	COLUSA	96039-96039	HAPPY CAMP	96134-96134	TULELAKE
95665-95665	PINE GROVE	95934-95934	CRESCENT MILLS	96040-96040	HAT CREEK	96135-96135	VINTON
95666-95666	PIONEER	95935-95935	DOBBINS	96041-96041	HAYFORK	96136-96136	WENDEL
95667-95667	PLACERVILLE	95936-95936	DOWNIEVILLE	96044-96044	HORNBROOK	96137-96137	WESTWOOD
95668-95668	PLEASANT GROVE	95937-95937	DUNNIGAN	96045-96045	HORSE CREEK	96140-96140	CARNELIAN BAY
95669-95669	PLYMOUTH	95938-95938	DURHAM	96046-96046	HYAMPOM	96141-96141	HOMEWOOD
95670-95670	RANCHO CORDOVA	95939-95939	ELK CREEK	96047-96047	IGO	96142-96142	TAHOMA
95671-95671	REPRESA	95940-95940	FEATHER FALLS	96048-96048	JUNCTION CITY	96143-96143	KINGS BEACH
95672-95672	RESCUE	95941-95941	FORBESTOWN	96049-96049	REDDING	96145-96145	TAHOE CITY
95673-95673	RIO LINDA	95942-95942	FOREST RANCH	96050-96050	KLAMATH RIVER	96146-96146	OLYMPIC VALLEY
95674-95674	RIO OSO	95943-95943	GLENN	96051-96051	LAKEHEAD	96148-96148	TAHOE VISTA
95675-95675	RIVER PINES	95944-95944	GOODYEARS BAR	96052-96052	LEWISTON	96150-96158	SOUTH LAKE TAHOE
95676-95676	ROBBINS	95945-95945	GRASS VALLEY	96053-96053	MCARTHUR	96160-96162	TRUCKEE
95677-95677	ROCKLIN	95946-95946	PENN VALLEY	96054-96054	LOOKOUT	96635-96688	FPO

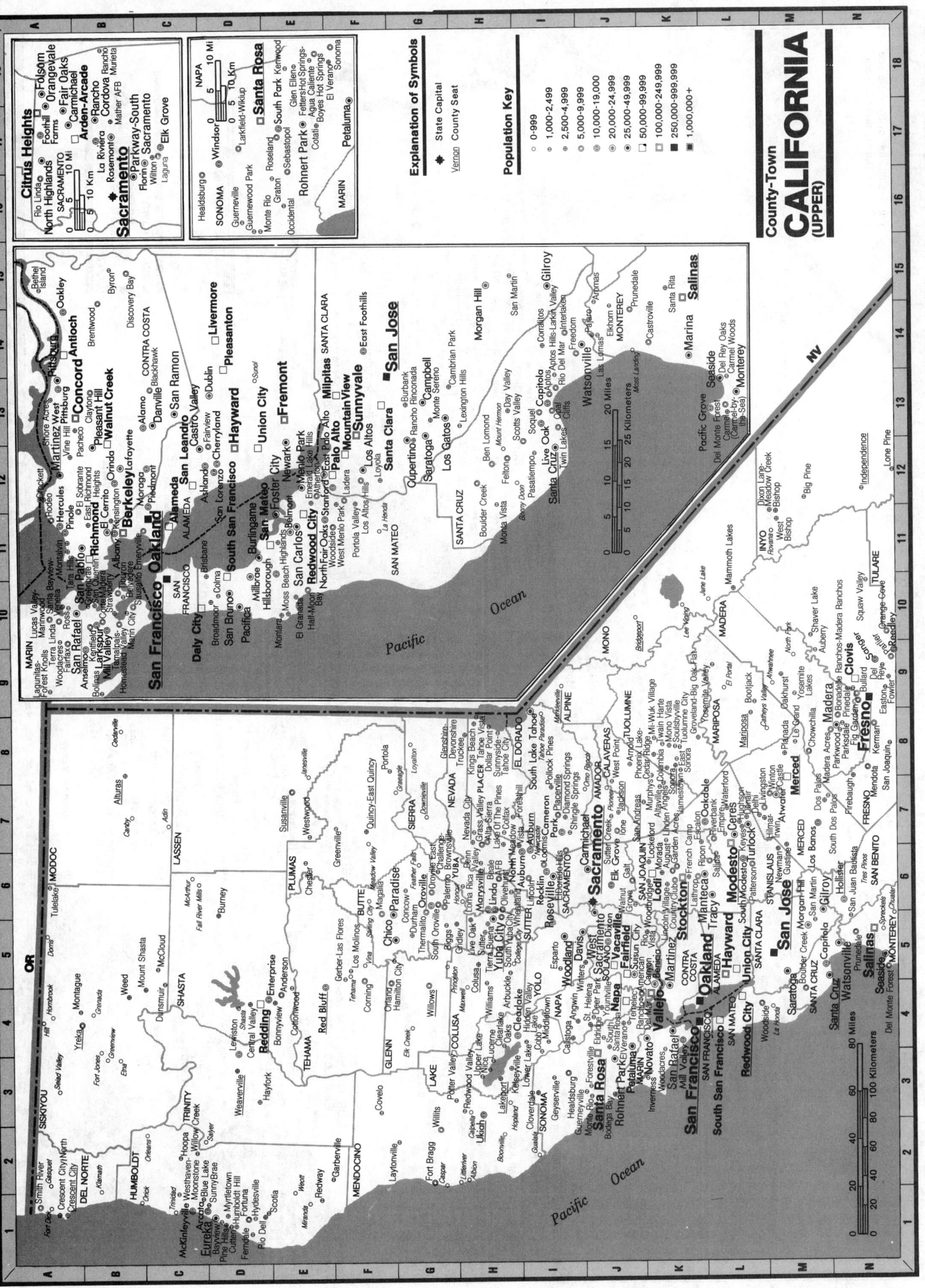

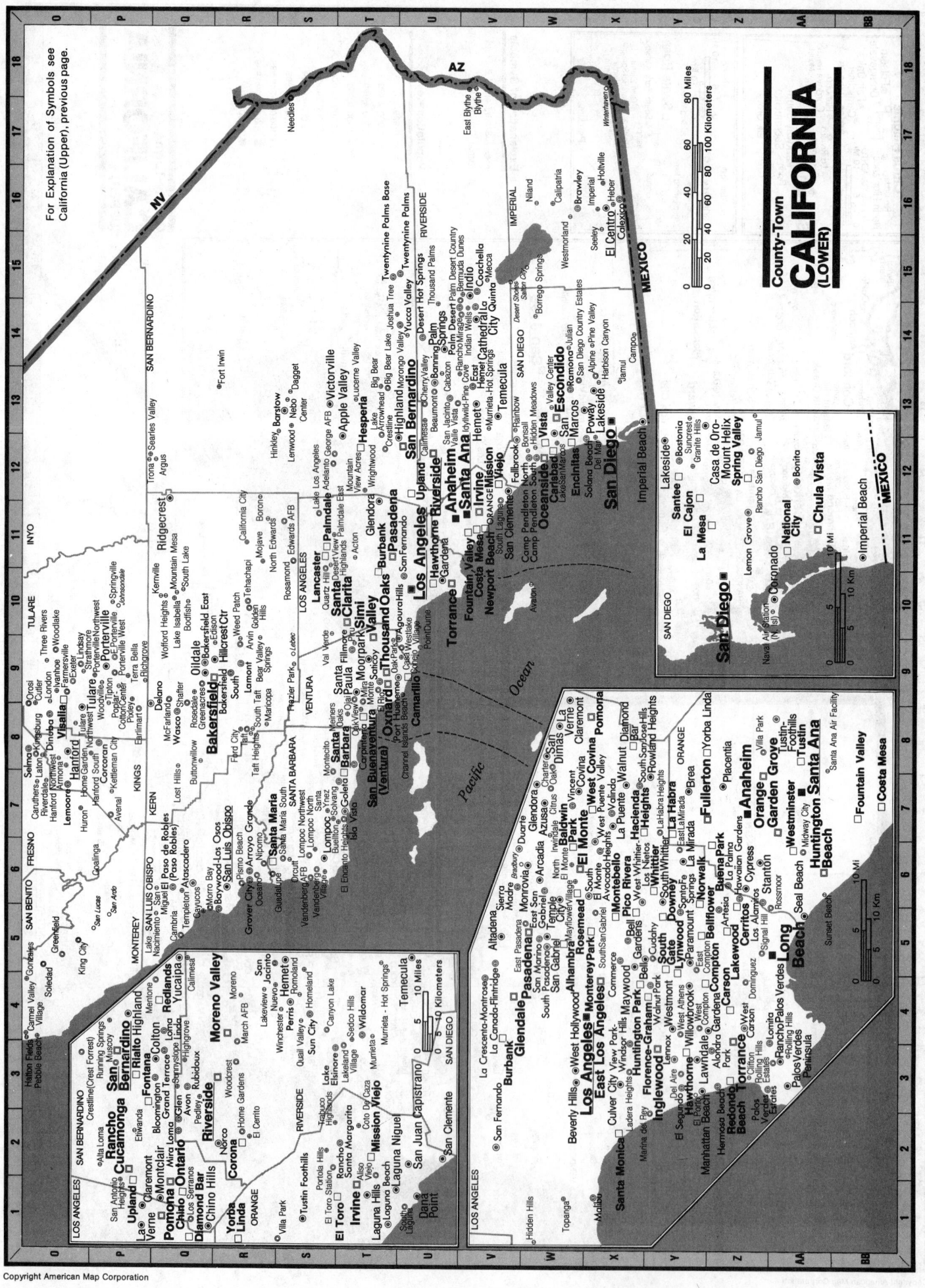

County-Town
CALIFORNIA
(LOWER)

For Explanation of Symbols see California (Upper), previous page.

80 Miles
100 Kilometers

COUNTIES

CITIES AND TOWNS

Note: The first name is that of the city or town; second, that of the county in which it is located; then the population and location on the map.

Explanation of symbols: • — Census Designated Place (CDP)

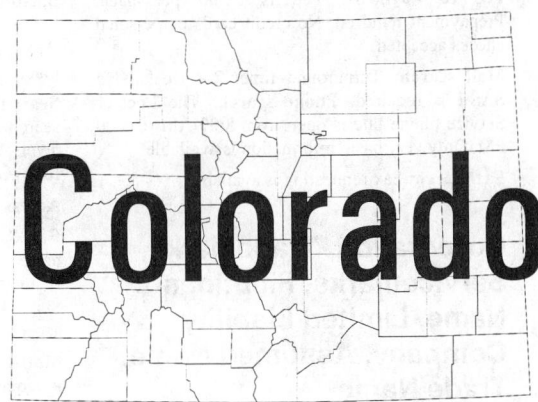

General Help Numbers:

Governor's Office

136 State Capitol Bldg
Denver, CO 80203-1792
www.colorado.gov/governor

303-866-2471
Fax 303-866-2003
8AM-5PM

Attorney General's Office

Department of Law
1525 Sherman St, 5th Floor
Denver, CO 80203
www.ago.state.co.us

303-866-4500
Fax 303-866-5691
8AM-5PM

Legislative Records

State Capitol, 200 E Colfax Ave
Devcer, CO 80203-1776
www.leg.state.co.us/

303-866-3055
303-866-2316
8AM-5PM

State Archives

Archives & Public Records
1313 Sherman St, Room 1B-20
Denver, CO 80203
http://statearchives.us/colorado.htm

303-866-2555
Fax 303-866-2257
8AM-4:30PM

State Specifics:

Capital:	Denver Denver County
Time Zone:	MST
Number of Counties:	64
Population:	4,601,403
Website:	www.state.co.us

State Agencies

Criminal Records

Bureau of Investigation, State Repository, Identification Unit, 690 Kipling St, Suite 3000, Denver, CO 80215; 303-239-4208, 303-239-5858-Fax; 8AM-4:30PM. http://cbi.state.co.us

Records are available from 1967 on. Records prior to 1967 are in on-site computer archives. It takes less than 72 hours before new records are available for inquiry. Records are indexed on inhouse computer, fingerprint cards. Records are not destroyed or removed. 12% of all arrests in database have final dispositions recorded, over 12% for those arrests within last 5 years.

Searching: The requester must sign a disclaimer stating "This record shall not be used for the direct solicitation of business for pecuniary gain." Include the following in your request-full name, date of birth, and disclaimer. The SSN, race, and gender are optional. Fingerprints are optional unless statutorily-required. Records are 100% fingerprint supported. If charged after fingerprinted, the practice of notifying the state is becoming more common, though this not yet statewide. The following data is not released: sealed records, juvenile records and pending mental comps. All records or arrests are released, including those without dispositions.

Access by: mail, in person, online.

Fee & Payment: Name check-$13.00 per name; fingerprint search-$16.50 per fingerprint. A state mandated fingerprint search plus notification of subsequent arrest in CO-$17.50; or nationwide fingerprint search-$22.00. Internet searches are $6.85 each. Fee payee: Colorado Bureau of Investigations (CBI). Prepayment required. No personal checks accepted. Credit cards accepted: MasterCard, Visa.

Mail search: Turnaround time: 3 days. No SASE is required. **In person search:** You may request information in person, but responses are normally returned by mail.

Online search: There is an Internet access at www.cbirecordscheck.com. Requesters must use a credit card, an account does not need to be established. However, account holders may set up a batch system. The fee is $6.85 per record.

Statewide Court Records

State Court Administrator, 1301 Pennsylvania St, Suite 300, Denver, CO 80203; 303-861-1111, 800-888-0001, 303-837-2340-Fax; 8AM-5PM.

www.courts.state.co.us

Except for certain online research capabilities, all trial court record access must be done at the local level.

Access by: online.

Online search: Search opinions at the website. As a result of an initiative of the Colorado Judicial Branch, all district court and all county court records are available through www.cocourts.com, e-screening.com, cojustice.com and Sol Communications. An index (Register of Actions) is available from the vendors for civil, civil water, small claims, domestic, felony, misdemeanor, and traffic cases. Images or copies of documents are not available from any of the commercial sites and may only be obtained by contacting the individual court where the documents were filed.

Sexual Offender Registry

Colorado Bureau of Investigation, SOR Unit, 690 Kipling St, Suite 3000, Denver, CO 80215; 303-239-4222, 303-239-4661-Fax; 8AM-4:30PM.

http://sor.state.co.us

Each police or sheriff's agency is required to maintain a list of convicted sex offenders in their jurisdiction and may release that information to the public.

Searching: Requesters are screened for purpose, they must be at least 18 years of age. Include the following in your request-name, address. Requester should include DL# and phone number.

Access by: mail, in person, online.

Fee & Payment: The CBI may assess reasonable fees for the search, retrieval, and copying of information requested. Fee payee: CBI Personal checks are not accepted. Credit cards are accepted.

Mail search: Turnaround time: 10 days. Lists of names can be ordered by city or by ZIP Code.

In person search: Lists of names can be ordered by city or by ZIP Code.

Online search: The website gives access to only certain high-risk registered sex offenders in the following categories: Sexually Violent Predator (SVP), Multiple Offenses, and Failed to Register.

Incarceration Records

Colorado Department of Corrections, Offender Records Customer Support, 2862 South Circle Dr. #418, Colorado Springs, CO 80906-4195; 719-226-4884, 719-226-4880 (Locator Service), 719-226-4899-Fax; 8AM-5PM. www.doc.state.co.us

Email locator requests to pio@doc.state.co.us.

Records are available on current and former inmates to 1976. This office can release: sentence information (crime/sentencing court/docket #); location of incarceration; parole eligibility date/approved parole date; and mandatory release date. It takes 4 weeks before new records are available for inquiry. Records are normally destroyed after 10 years.

Searching: Include the following in your request-full name, date of birth, DOC # if available.

Access by: mail, phone, fax.

Fee & Payment: Fee is $1.00 per page. Prepayment required. No credit cards or personal checks accepted.

Mail search: Turnaround time: 2-4 weeks. No SASE is required. **Phone search:** The Locator Service phone line is open from 8:00 AM to 5:00 PM. Only very basic information is available.

Fax search: Fax requesting is available.

Corporation, Trademarks, Servicemarks, Fictitious Name, Limited Liability Company, Assumed Name, Trade Name

Secretary of State, Business Division, 1700 Broadway, Suite 200, Denver, CO 80290; 303-894-2200 x2 (Business Entities), 303-869-4864-Fax; 7:30AM-5PM. www.sos.state.co.us

Records are available for all active companies. Inactive company records are archived. New records are available for inquiry immediately. Records are indexed on microfilm, inhouse computer. Records are normally destroyed after once scanned & available on web.

Searching: Include the following in your request-full name of business.

Access by: mail, phone, fax, in person, online.

Fee & Payment: There is no fee for searching active companies online. There is a $25.00 per business name searched via paper request, $25.00 fee for archived records. The copy fee is $.50 per page. Certification is $2.00. Fee payee: Secretary of State. Personal checks accepted; no credit cards.

Mail search: Turnaround time: 2 to 3 days. **Phone search:** Limit of 3 names. **Fax search:** Orders requested by fax are processed the same as other searches. **In person search:** A public access terminal offers free searching.

Online search: The Sec. of State's Business Record Search page offers free searching of corporate names and associate information at www.sos.state.co.us/pubs/business/main.htm. Effective 07/04, some e-filing documents are available. Click on Business Center. Also, search for charitable nonprofit members of CANPO - Colorado Assoc. of Nonprofit Organizations - at www.canpo.org/directory_members_search.cfm. Search trade names at www.businesstax.state.co.us/tradenames/.

Other access: Various information is available as a one time order or via subscription. Transmittal can be through CDs, tapes or FTP.

Expedited service: Expedited service is available for mail, in person and fax searches. Turnaround time: 1 day. Add $150.00 per business name.

Uniform Commercial Code, Federal and State Tax Liens

Secretary of State, UCC Division, 1560 Broadway, Suite 200, Denver, CO 80202; 303-894-2200 x2, 303-869-4864-Fax; 7:30AM-5PM.

www.sos.state.co.us

State tax liens are handled by the Department of Revenue. These liens can be filed at any one of the state's county recording offices, and so should be searched as such.

Records are available from 1966. Records are indexed on computer from 1979, and on microfiche from 1987 to 1997. It takes 5 days before new records are available for inquiry. Records are normally destroyed after scanning and placed online.

Searching: Use search request form UCC-11. The search includes all tax liens recorded at the state level. This includes all IRS liens. Include the following in your request-debtor name.

Access by: mail, phone, fax, in person, online.

Fee & Payment: The search fee is $13.00 per name searched. Copies are $1.25 per page. There is no fee to view online. Fee payee: Secretary of State. Personal checks accepted. No credit cards accepted.

Mail search: Turnaround time: 10 days. A SASE is requested. **Phone search:** The latest 4 liens are available by telephone, press 2 when connected using number listed above. **Fax search:** Fax searching available. **In person search:** Simple requests may be processed while you wait.

Online search: There is free record searching at this agency's website. More extensive data is also available via subscription for ongoing business requesters.

Other access: Various information is available as a one time order or via subscription. Transmittal can be through CDs, tapes or FTP.

Expedited service: Expedited service is available for mail, phone and in person searches. Turnaround time: 1 day. There is a $150.00 fee per debtor name to expedite search.

Sales Tax Registrations

Revenue Department, Taxpayers Services Office, 1375 Sherman St, Denver, CO 80261; 303-238-7378, 303-866-3211-Fax; 8AM-4:30PM.

www.revenue.state.co.us/main/home.asp

Records are available from 1988 and are computerized. It takes 2 weeks before new records are available for inquiry. Records are indexed on computer. Records are normally destroyed after 10 years.

Searching: This agency will confirm that a business is registered. Include the following in your request-business name. They will also search by tax permit number.

Access by: phone, in person, online.

Fee & Payment: There is no search fee.

Phone search: No fee for telephone request. They will only search by trade name.

In person search: They will release the owner's name if petitioned in writing.

Online search: You can verfiy a sales tax license or exemption number at www.taxview.state.co.us.

Birth Certificates

Department of Public Health & Environment, Vital Records Section HSVR-A1, 4300 Cherry Creek Dr S, Denver, CO 80246-1530; 303-756-4464 (Recorded Message), 303-692-2224 (Credit Card Ordering), 303-692-2234 (General Info), 800-423-1108-Fax; 8:30AM-4:30PM.

www.cdphe.state.co.us/hs/certs.asp

Certified copies for birth years 1910 to present can also be ordered at most county health departments.

Records are available from 1910 to present. New records are available for inquiry immediately. Records are indexed on microfiche, inhouse computer.

Searching: The person named on the record, members of the immediate family, legal representatives of those named above, and others demonstrating a direct and tangible interest in the record may request a copy. Include the following in your request-full name, names of parents, mother's maiden name, date of birth, place of birth, relationship to person of record, reason for information request. Birth Certificates are filed under person of record's last name.

Access by: mail, phone, fax, in person, online.

Fee & Payment: Search fee is $15.00 per name. Add $6.00 if you use a credit card. Add $6.00 per name requested for additional copies. You can order by fax using a credit card. Also include copy of requester's ID (government issued). Fee payee: Vital Records. Prepayment required. Personal checks accepted. Major credit cards accepted.

Mail search: Turnaround time: 2 weeks. Include a daytime telephone number. No SASE is required.

Phone search: You must use a credit card for an additional $6.00 fee. Turnaround time is 5 working days. **Fax search:** Turnaround time 5 days, credit card required. **In person search:** Turnaround time is 30-45 minutes. **Online search:** Records can be ordered online from state designated vendors. Go to www.vitalchek.com/default.asp or www.uscerts.com.

Expedited service: available for online searches. Turnaround time: next day. Add credit card fee ($6.00) and express delivery fee.

Death Records

Department of Public Health & Environment, Vital Records Section HSVR-A1, 4300 Cherry Creek Dr S, Denver, CO 80246-1530; 303-756-4464 (Recorded Message), 303-692-2224 (Credit Card Ordering), 303-692-2234, 800-423-1108-Fax; 8:30AM-4:30PM.

www.cdphe.state.co.us/hs/certs.asp

Records are available from 1900 to present. It takes within 4 weeks before new records are available for inquiry. Records are indexed on microfiche, inhouse computer.

Searching: Certified copies may be issued to: parents; grandparents; stepparents; siblings; spouse; adult children, stepchildren or grandchildren of the deceased; legal representatives of above; genealogists, probate researchers or those with a tangible interest. Include the following in your request-full name, date of death, place of death, names of parents, relationship to person of record, reason for information request. Death certificates are indexed by decedent's last name and the year of death. Include date of birth or age at death.

Access by: mail, phone, fax, in person, online.

Fee & Payment: Search fee is $15.00 per name. Add $6.00 if you use a credit card. Add $6.00 per name requested for an additional copy. Also include copy of requester's ID (government issued). Fee payee: Vital Records. Prepayment required. Personal checks accepted. Major credit cards accepted.

Mail search: Turnaround time: 2 weeks. Also include a day time phone number.

Phone search: You must use a credit card. Turnaround time is 5 working days. **Fax search:** Same criteria as phone searching. **In person search:** You may request records in person for same day service. Turnaround time 30-45 minutes.

Online search: Records can be ordered online from state designated vendors at www.vitalchek.com/default.asp or www.uscerts.com

Expedited service: available for fax searches. Turnaround time: next day. Add use of credit card fee ($6.00) and express delivery fee.

Marriage Certificates

Department of Public Health & Environment, Vital Records Section, 4300 Cherry Creek Dr S, Denver, CO 80246-1530; 303-756-4464 (Recorded Message), 303-692-2224 (Credit Card Ordering), 303-692-2234, 800-423-1108-Fax; 8:30AM-4:30PM.

www.cdphe.state.co.us/hs/certs.asp

Records available include 1900 to 1939, and 1975 to present. Verifications for the years 1940 to 1974 are not available from this office and must be obtained from the county where the license was obtained.

It takes 3 months before new records are available for inquiry.

Searching: Records are open to the public. This agency refers to the records as "verifications." Include the following in your request-date of marriage, county of license issue. Also include copy of requester's ID (government issued).

Access by: mail, phone, fax, in person, online.

Fee & Payment: The state fee for a marriage verification is $15.00. If the year is not known and the entire index is searched, there is an additional $5.00. Fee payee: Vital Records. Prepayment required. Credit card use is only for fax, phone, and Internet searches. Personal checks accepted. Major credit cards accepted.

Mail search: Turnaround time: 2 weeks.

Phone search: Turnaround time is 5 days. There is an additional $6.00 fee for use of a credit card.

Fax search: Use of credit card (extra $6.00) required, turnaround time 1 day.

In person search: Turnaround time is 30 to 45 minutes. These indexes can also be searched, for no fee, at many public libraries throughout the state and at State Archives.

Online search: Search marriages from 1975 to present in the state of Colorado at www.sctc.state.co.us/marriages/default.aspx. There is no fee. Records can be ordered online from state designated vendors. Go to www.vitalchek.com/default.asp or www.uscerts.com/.

Expedited service: Expedited service is available. Use of credit card is required (extra $6.00 fee). Total fee depends on delivery service requested.

Divorce Records

Department of Public Health & Environment, Vital Records Section, 4300 Cherry Creek Dr S, Denver, CO 80246-1530; 303-756-4464 (Recorded Message), 303-692-2224 (Credit Card Ordering), 303-692-2234, 800-423-1108-Fax; 8:30AM-4:30PM.

www.cdphe.state.co.us/hs/certs.asp

This office holds record index from 1851 to 1939, and 1968 to present. Searches must be performed at the county level for all other years. Records include annulments and separations.

Records are available 1900 to 1939 and 1968 to current at this office. It takes 6 months before new records are available for inquiry.

Searching: Records are open to the public. Include the following in your request-names of parties, date of action, county. Also include copy of requester's ID (government issued). The agency only has an INDEX of the records and will provide a certified verification. Actual copies of the dissolution must be obtained from the county where the event was finalized.

Access by: mail, phone, fax, in person, online.

Fee & Payment: The state fee for a divorce verification is $15.00. If the year is not known and the entire index is searched, there is an additional $5.00. Fee payee: Vital Records. Prepayment required. Personal checks accepted. Major credit cards accepted.

Mail search: Turnaround time: 2 weeks. **Phone search:** A credit card is required with an additional fee of $6.00. Turnaround time is 5 business days. **Fax search:** Same criteria as phone searching, but turnaround time is 5 business days. **In person search:** Records can be obtained across the counter within 30 to 45 minutes.

Online search: Search all divorces/dissolutions from 1851 to 1939 and 1968 to present at www.sctc.state.co.us/marriages/divorces.aspx. There is no fee.

Expedited service: Expedited service is available for online searches. Turnaround time: 1 day. Use of credit card is required (extra $6.00 fee). Total fee depends on delivery service requested.

Workers' Compensation Records

Division of Workers' Compensation, Customer Service, 633 17th Street 400, Denver, CO 80202-3660; 303-318-8700, 303-318-8710-Fax; 8AM-5PM. www.coworkforce.com/DWC

Records are available as far back 1979, many records have been scanned and are stored electronically. If the physical records have been destroyed, the wage information is still on computer. New records are available for inquiry immediately. Records are indexed on inhouse computer.

Searching: If you are not a party to the claim, you must have a notarized release from claimant not older than 90 days. Judges notes, transcripts and depositions are not released. Older purged files will get a screen print only. Include the following in your request-claimant name, Social Security Number, DOB. There is a search form that is suggested; form not yet onthe web page.

Access by: mail, phone, fax, in person.

Fee & Payment: There is no search fee, copies are $.25 per page, rush copies are $.50 per page, the fee to return via fax is $1.00 per page. Certification is $2.00. Fee payee: Division of Workers' Compensation. Prepayment required. Approved accounts are billed monthly. Personal checks not accepted. No credit cards accepted.

Mail search: Turnaround time: 1 to 2 days. A SASE is requested. **Phone search:** Limited information is given over the phone only if caller is a party to the case. **Fax search:** Turnaround time is 1-2 days, unless otherwise requested. **In person search:** You should call first so that they can locate records. Bring ID and notarized statement.

Other access: Lists and/or labels of carriers, adjusting companies, and attorneys are available upon request. Fees range from $3.00 to $7.00 (for list, not per name) plus postage.

Driver Records

Motor Vehicle Business Group, Driver Control, Denver, CO 80261-0016 (Courier address: 1881 Pierce Street, Lakewood, CO 80214); 303-205-5613, 303-205-5990-Fax; 8AM-5PM.

www.mv.state.co.us

Copies of tickets may be obtained this address for a fee of $2.20 per record. All requests must be submitted in writing and include the driver's name, DOB, and the specific ticket number.

Records are available for up to 7 years. It takes 3 to 12 days before new records are available for inquiry.

Searching: Address and personal data is given to certain pre-approved, permissible requesters. Otherwise the "Requester Release and Information Request/Notice of Intended Use" form must be signed by requester. Include the following in your request-name, date of birth, driver's license number. The middle initial and DL are optional, but suggested.

Access by: mail, in person, online.

Fee & Payment: The fee for manually processed records is $2.20 per record, $2.70 if certified. Online access has been privatized, there is no state fee. Fee payee: Department of Revenue. Prepayment required. Personal checks accepted. No credit cards accepted.

Mail search: Turnaround time: 24 hours. No SASE is required. **In person search:** Turnaround time is immediate. Up to 50 records will be processed while you wait.

Online search: Online access is available via a state-designated vendor. The vendors receive nightly updates from the state of the entire DMV record history file, then charge a processing fee per record to users and customers. These vendors provide access online to end users. Call Mary Tuttle at 303-205-5762 for a list of the vendors.

Other access: Colorado offers FTP retrieval for high volume users, call 303-205-5762.

Vehicle Ownership, Vehicle Identification

Division of Motor Vehicle, Title and Registration Section, Denver, CO 80261-0016 (Courier address: 1881 Pierce Street, Lakewood, CO 80214); 303-205-5608 (Titles), 303-205-5607 (Registration), 303-205-5765-Fax; 8AM-5PM.

www.mv.state.co.us/mv.html

Records are available 10 years back plus the current year. It takes (varies - depend on when county submits record) before new records are available for inquiry. Records are normally destroyed after being microfilmed.

Searching: Handicap and disabled vet plate data are not released. Include the following in your request-Vehicle Identification Number. To obtain vehicle or ownership information, or for title and lien records, the requester's driver license number, and the Requestor Release and Information Request Form (DR 2539) and Affidavit of Intended Use (DR2489) are required.

Access by: mail, in person.

Fee & Payment: The fee for searches is $2.20 per record. Fee payee: Department of Revenue. Prepayment required. Personal checks accepted. No credit cards accepted.

Mail search: Turnaround time: 24 hours. **In person search:** Turnaround time is while you wait.

Other access: Bulk requests of vehicle information on magnetic tape, computer paper, and on microfiche are available. Direct inquires to the Data Services Section, Motor Vehicle Extractions, DMV, Driver Control, Denver, CO 80261-0016.

Expedited service: Will expedite if a prepaid FedEx envelope is provided with request.

Accident Reports

Motor Vehicle Business Group, Driver Control, Denver, CO 80261-0016 (Courier address: 1881 Pierce Street, Lakewood, CO 80261); 303-205-5613, 8AM-5PM.

www.mv.state.co.us

Records are available for 6 years plus current year from date of the accident. It takes 30 to 60 days before new records are available for inquiry.

Searching: Use of "Requestor Release and Information Request" Form DR 2559 is required. If requester is not involved in accident, permission must be given by one of involved drivers. Include the following in your request-full name, date of accident, location of accident, and requester's mailing address.

Access by: mail, in person.

Fee & Payment: The fee is $2.20 per record for walk-in or mail-in searches. Fee payee: Department of Revenue. Prepayment required. Personal checks accepted. No credit cards accepted.

Mail search: Turnaround time: variable. No SASE is required. **In person search:** Turnaround time depends on availability of report.

Vessel Ownership, Vessel Registration

Colorado State Parks, Registration, 13787 S Highway 85, Littleton, CO 80125; 303-791-1920, 303-470-0782-Fax; 8AM-5PM.

http://parks.state.co.us/boating

Liens must be searched at the Secretary of State.

Records are available since 1994. Older records are available on microfiche. All sail and motorized vessels must be registered. It takes 24 hours or less before new records are available for inquiry.

Searching: To search, a Release of Registration Records Form must be completed and signed. The following data is not released: owner DOB.

Access by: mail, fax, in person.

Fee & Payment: There is a $2.00 search fee plus a $1.00 charge per page for copies. Fee payee: Colorado State Parks. Prepayment required. Personal checks accepted, no credit cards.

Mail search: Turnaround time: 1-3 weeks. No SASE is required. **Fax search:** Turnaround time varies. Results are faxed or mailed back. **In person search:** Availability depends on how extensive search is.

Voter Registration

Department of State, Elections Department, 1700 Broadway #270, Denver, CO 80290; 303-894-2200 x6307, 303-869-4861-Fax; 8:30AM-5PM.

www.sos.state.co.us/pubs/elections/main.htm

Records available for the current year only. Takes 1-2 days before new records available for inquiry.

Searching: Voters may request not to have their information released. Include the following in your request-a signed statement requesting confidentiality. Provide name and address or DOB to search. The following data is not released: Social Security Numbers.

Access by: mail, fax, in person, online.

Fee & Payment: The fee is $.50 per name. Fee payee: Department of State. Prepayment required. No credit cards accepted.

Mail search: Turnaround time: 2 to 3 days. A SASE is requested. **Fax search:** Same criteria as mail searching. **In person search:** Availability depends on how extensive search is.

Online search: Search campaign finance data at www.sos.state.co.us/cpf/FcpaHome.do.

Other access: The entire database is available on tape or CD-ROM. The cost is $500. No customization is available.

GED Certificates

Colorado Dept of Education, GED Testing, 201 E Colfax Ave Rm 100, Denver, CO 80203; 303-866-6613, 303-866-6947-Fax; 8AM-4:55PM.

www.cde.state.co.us/cdeadult/GEDindex.htm

Searching: All written requests must have a yes or no answer to the following question in the upper right hand corner of the request: Did the person who received the GED ever attend a Colorado public school (as in elementary or high school)? All of the following are required to search: a signed release, name, date/year of test, date of birth, SSN, and location of testing.

Access by: mail, fax, in person.

Fee & Payment: There is no fee for a "yes or no" verification. The search fee $15.00 per transcript. Fee payee: GED Testing. Prepayment required. Money orders & personal checks accepted. No credit cards accepted.

Mail search: Turnaround time: 14 working days. The agency requests use of their request form, which can be downloaded from the web site. No SASE is required. **Fax search:** One may do a verification by fax. Signed release is still needed.

In person search: Turnaround time is 24 hours, you must come back next day.

Hunting and Fishing License Information

Access to Records is Restricted.

Department of Natural Resources, Division of Wildlife, 6060 Broadway, Denver, CO 80216; 303-297-1192, 303-291-7106-Fax; 8AM-5PM.

www.wildlife.state.co.us

The state attorney general has decided that no information on holders of individual hunting and fishing licenses can be given to the public. It is only available to law enforcement officials or to the licensed individual.

Colorado State Licensing Agencies

For details about the agency responsible for licensing/certifying/registering an item below or in the Agency Quick Finder section, match an item's number with the number of the agency in the *Licensing Agency Information* section.

Colorado Licenses Searchable Online

Accident & Health Insurer #10 .... www.dora.state.co.us/pls/real/INS_Search.Disclaimer_Page

Acupuncturist #14 .... www.dora.state.co.us/pls/real/ARMS_Search.Set_Up

Addiction Counselor #20 .... www.dora.state.co.us/pls/real/ARMS_Search.Disclaimer_Page

Architect/Architectural Firm #15 .... www.dora.state.co.us/pls/real/ARMS_Search.Set_Up

Attorney #4 .... www.coloradosupremecourt.com/Search/AttSearch.asp

Audiologist #14 .... www.dora.state.co.us/pls/real/ARMS_Search.Set_Up

Barber #16 .... www.dora.state.co.us/pls/real/ARMS_Search.Disclaimer_Page

Bus, Charter/Scenic/Children's #30 .... www.dora.state.co.us/pls/real/puc_permit.search_form

Casualty Company #10 .... www.dora.state.co.us/pls/real/INS_Search.Disclaimer_Page

Charitable Organization #37 .... www.sos.state.co.us/cgi-
       forte/fortecgi?serviceName=ccsaprodaccess&templateName=/sessauto/mainMenu_outer_form.forte&hasr=T&hast=T

Chiropractor #17 .... www.dora.state.co.us/pls/real/ARMS_Search.Disclaimer_Page

Common Carrier/Contract Carrier #30 ...... www.dora.state.co.us/pls/real/puc_permit.search_form

Contractor Registration #41 .... www.dora.state.co.us/pls/real/ARMS_Search.Disclaimer_Page

Cosmetologist #16 .... www.dora.state.co.us/pls/real/ARMS_Search.Disclaimer_Page

Counselor, Professional #20 .... www.dora.state.co.us/pls/real/ARMS_Search.Disclaimer_Page

Credit Union #9 .... www.dora.state.co.us/financial-services/homeregu.html

Dental Hygienist #18 .... www.dora.state.co.us/pls/real/ARMS_Search.Disclaimer_Page

Dentist #18 .... www.dora.state.co.us/pls/real/ARMS_Search.Disclaimer_Page

Electrician/ Electrical Contractor #41 .... www.dora.state.co.us/pls/real/ARMS_Search.Disclaimer_Page

Engineer/Engineer in Training #19 .... www.dora.state.co.us/pls/real/ARMS_Search.Disclaimer_Page

Family Therapist #20 .... www.dora.state.co.us/pls/real/ARMS_Search.Disclaimer_Page

Fundraising Consultant #37 .... www.sos.state.co.us/cgi-
       forte/fortecgi?serviceName=ccsaprodaccess&templateName=/sessauto/mainMenu_outer_form.forte&hasr=T&hast=T

HazMat Carrier #30 .... www.dora.state.co.us/pls/real/puc_permit.search_form

Hearing Aid Dealer #14 .... www.dora.state.co.us/pls/real/ARMS_Search.Set_Up

Household Goods/Property Carrier #30 .... www.dora.state.co.us/pls/real/puc_permit.search_form

Insurance Agency/Company #10 .... www.dora.state.co.us/pls/real/INS_Agent.Search_Form

Insurance Producer #10 .... www.dora.state.co.us/pls/real/INS_Agent.Search_Form

Land Surveyor/Land Surveyor Intern #19 . www.dora.state.co.us/pls/real/ARMS_Search.Disclaimer_Page

Life Care Institution #9 .... www.dora.state.co.us/financial-services/homeregu.html

Life Insurance Company #10 .... www.dora.state.co.us/pls/real/INS_Search.Disclaimer_Page

Limousine #30 .... www.dora.state.co.us/pls/real/puc_permit.search_form

Lobbyist #37 .... www.sos.state.co.us/cgi-
       forte/fortecgi?serviceName=lobbyprodaccess&templateName=/sessauto/inquiryHome_outer_form.forte&hasr=T&hast=T

Lobbyist Employer #37 .... www.sos.state.co.us/pubs/elections/employer_clientdir.pdf

Lobbyist Volunteer #37 .... www.state.co.us/gov_dir/leg_dir/vollob03.pdf

Manicurist #16 .... www.dora.state.co.us/pls/real/ARMS_Search.Disclaimer_Page

Manufactured Housing Mfg. #22 .... www.dola.state.co.us/doh/Documents/parkt.htm

Marriage Therapist #20 .... www.dora.state.co.us/pls/real/ARMS_Search.Disclaimer_Page

Medical Doctor #21 .... www.dora.state.co.us/pls/real/ARMS_Search.Disclaimer_Page

Midwife #28 .... www.dora.state.co.us/pls/real/ARMS_Search.Disclaimer_Page

Nurse / Nurses' Aide #1 .... www.dora.state.co.us/pls/real/ARMS_Search.Disclaimer_Page

Nursing Care Facility #23 .... www.dora.state.co.us/pls/real/ARMS_Search.Set_Up

Nursing Home Administrator #23 .... www.dora.state.co.us/pls/real/ARMS_Search.Set_Up

Off-Road Charter #30 .... www.dora.state.co.us/pls/real/puc_permit.search_form

Optometrist #33 .... www.dora.state.co.us/pls/real/ARMS_Search.Disclaimer_Page

Outfitter #24 .... www.dora.state.co.us/pls/real/ARMS_Search.Disclaimer_Page

Pharmacist/Pharmacy #26 .... www.dora.state.co.us/pls/real/ARMS_Search.Disclaimer_Page

Physical Therapist #32 .... www.dora.state.co.us/pls/real/ARMS_Search.Disclaimer_Page

Physician Assistant #21 .... www.dora.state.co.us/pls/real/ARMS_Search.Disclaimer_Page

Plumber Journeym'n/Master/Resid'l #35 .. www.dora.state.co.us/pls/real/ARMS_Search.Disclaimer_Page

Podiatrist #27 .... www.dora.state.co.us/pls/real/ARMS_Search.Disclaimer_Page

Psychologist #20 .... www.dora.state.co.us/pls/real/ARMS_Search.Disclaimer_Page

Public Accountant-CPA #13 .... www.dora.state.co.us/pls/real/ARMS_Search.Disclaimer_Page

Real Estate Agent/Broker/Sales #12 .... www.dora.state.co.us/pls/real/re_estate_home

Real Estate Appraiser #12 .... www.dora.state.co.us/pls/real/re_estate_home

Reinsurance Intermediary Manager #10 ... www.dora.state.co.us/pls/real/INS_Search.Disclaimer_Page

Respiratory Therapist #16 .... www.dora.state.co.us/pls/real/ARMS_Search.Disclaimer_Page

River Outfitter #38 .... www.dora.state.co.us/pls/real/ARMS_Search.Disclaimer_Page

Savings & Loan Association #9 .... www.dora.state.co.us/financial-services/homeregu.html
Securities Broker/Dealer #34 .... http://pdpi.nasdr.com/pdpi/disclaimer_frame.htm
Social Worker #20 .... www.dora.state.co.us/pls/real/ARMS_Search.Disclaimer_Page
Solicitor, Paid #37 .... www.sos.state.co.us/cgi-
              forte/fortecgi?serviceName=ccsaprodaccess&templateName=/sessauto/mainMenu_outer_form.forte&hasr=T&hast=T
Stock Broker #34 .... http://pdpi.nasdr.com/pdpi/disclaimer_frame.htm
Towing Carrier #30 .... www.dora.state.co.us/pls/real/puc_permit.search_form
Veterinarian / Veterinary Student #31 .... www.dora.state.co.us/pls/real/ARMS_Search.Disclaimer_Page
Wireman, Residential #41 .... www.dora.state.co.us/pls/real/ARMS_Search.Disclaimer_Page

Colorado Licensing Quick Finder

Accident & Health Insurer #10 303-894-2419
Acupuncturist #14 303-894-2464
Addiction Counselor #20 303-894-7766
Architect/Architectural Firm #15 303-894-7441
Artificial Inseminator #31 303-894-7755
Asbestos Building Inspector #5 303-692-3158
Asbestos Inspector/Management Planner or related
    occupation #5 303-692-3158
Attorney #4 303-893-8096
Audiologist #14 303-894-2464
Bail Bond/ Cash Bail Bond Agent #10 .. 303-894-7583
Bank, Commercial/Industrial #8 303-894-7575
Barber #16 303-894-7772
Bulk Milk Hauler #6 303-692-3643
Bus, Charter/Scenic/Children's #30 303-894-2867
Casualty Company #10 303-894-2419
Charitable Organization #37 303-894-2200
Child Care Facility #29 800-799-5876
Chiropractor #17 303-894-7762
Collection Agency #3 303-866-5706
Commercial Driving School #7 303-934-9211
Common Carrier/Contract Carrier #30 .. 303-894-2870
Contractor Registration #41 303-894-2300
Cosmetologist #16 303-894-7772
Counselor, Professional #20 303-894-7766
Court Reporter #36 303-837-3695
Credit Union #9 303-894-2336
Dairy Farm / Dairy Plant #6 303-692-3643
Debt Management Company #8 303-894-7575
Dental Hygienist #18 303-894-7758
Dentist #18 303-894-7758
Egg Seller #2 303-239-4140
Electrical Contractor #41 303-894-2300
Electrician Journeyman/Master #41 303-894-2300
Engineer/Engineer in Training #19 303-894-7788
Family Care Home #29 303-866-5958
Family Therapist #20 303-894-7766
Food Plant Operator #2 303-239-4140
Fundraising Consultant #37 303-894-2200

Greyhound Racing #11 303-205-2990
HazMat Carrier #30 303-894-2868
Hearing Aid Dealer #14 303-894-2464
Horse Racing #11 303-205-2990
Household Goods/Property Carrier #30 303-894-2868
Insurance Agency/Company #10 303-894-2419
Insurance Producer #10 303-894-2419
Investment Advisor #34 303-894-2320
Kennel #2 303-239-4166
Land Surveyor/Land Surv. Intern #19 .. 303-894-7788
Lead Abatement Inspector/Risk Assessor or related
    occupation #5 303-692-3158
Life Care Institution #9 303-894-2336
Life Insurance Company #10 303-894-2419
Limousine #30 303-894-2867
Liquor Control #39 303-205-2300
Lobbyist / Lobbyist Employer #37 303-894-2200
Lobbyist Volunteer #37 303-894-2200
Manicurist #16 303-894-7772
Manufact'd Housing Dealer/Mfg #22 303-866-4616
Manufacturer Housing Installer #22 303-866-4616
Marriage Therapist #20 303-894-7766
Medical Doctor #21 303-894-7690
Midwife #28 303-894-2464
Milk/Cream Sampler/Tester #6 303-692-3643
Money Order Company #8 303-894-7575
Motor Vehicle Buyer/Wholesaler #42 .. 303-205-5604
Motor Vehicle Dealer #42 303-205-5604
Motor Vehicle Manufacturer Rep. #42 . 303-205-5604
Motor Vehicle Salesperson #42 303-205-5604
Notary Public #37 303-894-2680
Nurse #1 303-894-2430
Nursery #2 303-239-4140
Nurses' Aide #1 303-894-2816
Nursing Care Facility #23 303-894-7800
Nursing Home Administrator #23 303-894-7760
Off-Road Charter #30 303-894-2867
Optometrist #33 303-894-7750
Outfitter #24 303-894-7778

Pesticide Applicator #2......................... 303-239-4140
Pet Animal/Bird Dealer #2 303-239-4166
Pharmacist/Pharmacy #26 303-894-7750
Physical Therapist #32.......................... 303-894-2440
Physician Assistant #21 303-894-7690
Physiotherapist #32............................... 303-894-2440
Plumber Journeyman/Master/Residential #35
    .... 303-894-2300 x110
Podiatrist #27 303-894-2464
Psychiatric Technician #1 303-894-2430
Psychologist #20 303-894-7766
Public Accountant-CPA #13................... 303-894-7441
Public Adjuster #10 303-894-7499
Real Estate Agent/Broker/Sales #12 .. 303-894-2166
Real Estate Appraiser #12 303-894-2166
Reinsurance Intermediary Mngr #10.... 303-894-2419
Respiratory Therapist #16
    ....303-894-7851, 303-894-2440
River Outfitter #38 303-894-7772
Savings & Loan Association #9 303-894-2336
School Administrator/Principal #40 303-866-6628
School Special Service Associate #40.. 303-866-6628
Securities Broker/Dealer #34 303-894-2320
Securities Sales Promoter #34 303-894-2320
Ski Lift #25.. 303-894-7785
Small Business Development Credit Corp. #9
    303-894-2336
Social Worker #20 303-894-7766
Solicitor, Paid #37 303-894-2200
Solicitor/Telemarketer #3 303-866-5079
Stock Broker #34 303-894-2320
Substitute Teacher #40 303-866-6968
Teacher #40 303-866-6628
Towing Carrier #30 303-894-2846
Tramway #25... 303-894-7785
Trust Company #8 303-894-7575
Veterinarian / Veterinary Student #31 .. 303-894-7755
Vocational Education Teacher #40 303-866-6628
Wireman, Residential #41 303-894-2300

Colorado Licensing Agency Information

1 Board of Nursing, 1560 Broadway, #880, Denver, CO 80202; 303-894-2430, Fax: 303-894-2821. www.dora.state.co.us/nursing Search Database at www.dora.state.co.us/pls/real/ARMS_Search.Disclaimer_Page

2 Agriculture Department, 700 Kipling St, #4000, Lakewood, CO 80215-8000; 303-239-4100, Fax: 303-239-4125. www.ag.state.co.us

3 Attorney General's Office, 1525 Sherman St, 5th Fl, Denver, CO 80203; 303-866-4500, Fax: 303-866-5691. www.ago.state.co.us Email: attorney.general@state.co.us

4 Colorado Supreme Court, Board of Law Examiners, 600 17th St, #520 S, Denver, CO 80202; 303-893-8096, Fax: 303-534-3643. www.coloradosupremecourt.com/Regulation/Contacts.htm   Email: kuenhold@amigo.net Search Database at www.coloradosupremecourt.com/Search/AttSearch.asp

5 Department of Public Health & Environment, Air Pollution Control Division, 4300 Cherry Creek Dr S, Denver, CO 80246; 303-692-3150, Fax: 303-782-0278. www.cdphe.state.co.us/a p/asbeshom.asp

6 Consumer Protection Division, Department of Public Health and Environment, 4300 Cherry Creek, Denver, CO 80246-1530; 303-692-3620, Fax: 303-753-6809. www.cdphe.state.co.us/cp/Dairy/dairy.asp

7 Department of Revenue, 1375 Sherman St, Denver, CO 80261; 303-866-3091, Fax: 303-205-5634. www.revenue.state.co.us/main/home.asp

8 Division of Banking, 1560 Broadway, #1175, Denver, CO 80202; 303-894-7575, Fax: 303-894-7570. www.dora.state.co.us/Banking Email: Banking@dora.state.co.us

9 Division of Financial Services, 1560 Broadway, #1520, Denver, CO 80202; 303-894-2336, Fax: 303-894-7886. www.dora.state.co.us/financial-services Search Database at www.dora.state.co.us/financial-services/homeregu.html

10 Division of Insurance, 1560 Broadway, #850, Denver, CO 80202; 303-894-7499, Fax: 303-894-7455. www.dora.state.co.us/Insurance Email: nancy.ryan@dora.state.co.us Search Database at www.dora.state.co.us/pls/real/INS_Search.Disclaimer_Page

11 Division of Racing Events, 1881 Pierce St, #108, Lakewood, CO 80214; 303-205-2990, Fax: 303-205-2950. www.revenue.state.co.us/racing_dir/home.asp Email: Racing@spike.dor.state.co.us

12 Division of Real Estate, 1900 Grant St, #600, Denver, CO 80203; 303-894-2166, Fax: 303-894-

2683. Search Database at www.dora.state.co.us/pls/real/re_estate_home

13 Division of Registrations, Board of Accountancy, 1560 Broadway, #1340, Denver, CO 80202; 303-894-7800, Fax: 303-894-7802. www.dora.state.co.us/Accountants Email: robert.longway@state.co.us   Search Database at www.dora.state.co.us/pls/real/ARMS_Search.Disclaimer_Page

14 Division of Registrations, Audiology Registration Ofc / Acupuncture Licensing, 1560 Broadway, #1550, Denver, CO 80202; 303-894-2464, Fax: 303-894-7802. www.dora.state.co.us Email: acupuncture@dora.state.co.us Search Database at www.dora.state.co.us/pls/real/ARMS_Search.Set_Up

15 Division of Registrations, Board of Examiners of Architects, 1560 Broadway, #1300, Denver, CO 80202; 303-894-7801, Fax: 303-894-7790. www.dora.state.co.us/Architects/ Search Database at www.dora.state.co.us/pls/real/ARMS_Search.Disclaimer_Page

16 Division of Registrations, Office of Barber & Cosmetologists, 1560 Broadway, #1340, Denver, CO 80202; 303-894-7772, Fax: 303-894-7764. www.dora.state.co.us/Barbers_Cosmetologists Email: barber-cosmetology@dora.state.co.us Search Database at www.dora.state.co.us/pls/real/ARMS_Search.Disclaimer_Page

17 Division of Registrations, Board of Chiropractors, 1560 Broadway, #1310, Denver, CO 80202; 303-894-7762, Fax: 303-894-7764. Search Database at www.dora.state.co.us/real/ARMS_Search.Disclaimer_Page

18 Division of Registrations, Board of Dental Examiners, 1560 Broadway, #1310, Denver, CO 80202; 303-894-7758, Fax: 303-894-7764. www.dora.state.co.us/dental Email: Dental@dora.state.co.us Search Database at www.dora.state.co.us/real/ARMS_Search.Disclaimer_Page

19 Division of Registrations, Board of Reg for Prof Engineers and Land Surveyors, 1560 Broadway, #1300, Denver, CO 80202; 303-894-7788, Fax: 303-894-7790. www.dora.state.co.us/Engineers_Surveyors/ Search Database at www.dora.state.co.us/pls/real/ARMS_Search.Disclaimer_Page

20 Division of Registrations, Mental Health Licening Section, 1560 Broadway, #880, Denver, CO 80202; 303-894-7766, Fax: 303-894-7747. www.dora.state.co.us/Mental-Health Email: MentalHealth@dora.state.co.us Search Database at www.dora.state.co.us/real/ARMS_Search.Disclaimer_Page

21 Div of Registrations, Dept of Regulatory Agencies, Board of Medical Examiners, 1560 Broadway, #1300, Denver, CO 80202-5140; 303-894-7690, Fax: 303-894-7692. www.dora.state.co.us/medical/ Email: medical@dora.state.co.us Search Database at www.dora.state.co.us/real/ARMS_Search.Disclaimer_Page

22 Division of Housing, 1313 Sherman St Rm 518, Denver, CO 80203; 303-866-2033, Fax: 303-866-4077. www.dola.state.co.us/doh/Index.htm Email: dola.helpdesk@state.co.us

23 Division of Registrations, Board of Examiners of Nursing Home Adminstrators, 1560 Broadway, #1310, Denver, CO 80202; 303-894-7760, Fax: 303-894-7764. www.dora.state.co.us/nursing-home-administrators/   Search Database at www.dora.state.co.us/pls/real/ARMS_Search.Set_Up

24 Division of Registrations, Office of Outfitters Registration, 1560 Broadway, #1340, Denver, CO 80202; 303-894-7778, Fax: 303-894-7692. www.dora.state.co.us/Outfitters Email: Outfitters@dora.state.co.us   Search Database at www.dora.state.co.us/pls/real/ARMS_Search.Disclaimer_Page

25 Division of Registrations, Colorado Tramway Passenger Safety Board, 1560 Broadway, #1300, Denver, CO 80202; 303-894-7785, Fax: 303-894-7790.   www.dora.state.co.us/Tramway Email: webmaster@dora.state.co.us

26 Division of Registrations, Board of Pharmacy, 1560 Broadway, #1310, Denver, CO 80202-5146; 303-894-7750, Fax: 303-894-7764. www.dora.state.co.us/Pharmacy Email: pharmacy@dora.state.co.us   Search Database at www.dora.state.co.us/pls/real/ARMS_Search.Disclaimer_Page

27 Division of Registrations, Podiatry Board, 1560 Broadway, #1300, Denver, CO 80202; 303-894-7690, Fax: 303-894-7692. www.dora.state.co.us/Podiatrists Email: podiatrists@dora.state.co.us Search Database at www.dora.state.co.us/pls/real/ARMS_Search.Disclaimer_Page

28 Division of Registrations, Midwives Registration, 1560 Broadway, #1340, Denver, CO 80202; 303-894-2440, Fax: 303-894-7764. www.dora.state.co.us/Midwives Email: midwives@dora.state.co.us Search Database at www.dora.state.co.us/pls/real/ARMS_Search.Disclaimer_Page

29 Department of Human Services, Division of Child Care, 1575 Sherman St, Denver, CO 80202; 800-799-5876, Fax: 303-866-4453. www.cdhs.state.co.us/childcare/home.html Search Database at www.cdhs.state.co.us/childcare/word%20files/FIRST%20AID%20&%20CPR%20VENDORS%202-05.doc

30 Public Utilities Commission, Department of Regulatory Agencies, 1580 Logan St, OL 2, Denver, CO 80203; 800-456-0858, 303-894-2070. www.dora.state.co.us/puc/index.htm Email: terry.willert@dora.state.co.us Search Database at www.dora.state.co.us/pls/real/puc_permit.search_form

31 Division of Registrations, Board of Veterinary Medicine, 1560 Broadway, #1310, Denver, CO 80202-5146; 303-894-7755, Fax: 303-894-7764. www.dora.state.co.us/Veterinarians Search Database at www.dora.state.co.us/pls/real/ARMS_Search.Disclaimer_Page

32 Division of Registrations, Physical Therapy Registration, 1560 Broadway, #1340, Denver, CO 80202; 303-894-2440, Fax: 303-894-7764. www.dora.state.co.us/Physical-Therapy Email: pt@dora.state.co.us Search Database at www.dora.state.co.us/pls/real/ARMS_Search.Disclaimer_Page

33 Division of Registrations, Board of Optometry Examiners, 1560 Broadway, #1310, Denver, CO 80202-5146; 303-894-7751, Fax: 303-894-7764. www.dora.state.co.us/Optometry Email: optometry@dora.state.co.us Search Database at www.dora.state.co.us/pls/real/ARMS_Search.Disclaimer_Page

34 Department of Regulatory Agencies, Division of Securities, 1580 Lincoln, #420, Denver, CO 80203-1506; 303-894-2320, Fax: 303-861-2126. www.dora.state.co.us/Securities/brokers.htm Email: Securities@DORA.state.co.us Search Database at http://pdpi.nasdr.com/pdpi/disclaimer_frame.htm

35 Examining Board of Plumbers, 1580 Logan St, #550, Denver, CO 80203-1941; 303-894-2300, Fax: 303-894-2310. www.dora.state.co.us/Plumbing Email: Plumbing@dora.state.co.us Search Database at www.dora.state.co.us/pls/real/ARMS_Search.Disclaimer_Page

36 Judicial Department, Human Resources Office, 1301 Pennsylvania St, #300, Denver, CO 80203; 303-837-3695, Fax: 303-837-2340. www.courts.state.co.us

37 Licensing Division, Office of Secretary of State, 1560 Broadway, #200, Denver, CO 80202; 303-894-2200, Fax: 303-869-4864. www.sos.state.co.us/pubs/business/main.htm Email: licensing@sos.state.co.us Search Database at www.sos.state.co.us/pubs/bingo_raffles/main.htm Note: The Colorado Assoc. of NonProfit Organizations member list is avaialble free at www.canpo.org/directory_members_search.cfm.

38 Division of Registrations, Outfitters Registration, 1560 Broadway, #1340, Denver, CO 80202; 303-894-7778, Fax: 303-894-7692. www.dora.state.co.us/Outfitters Email: outfitters@dora.state.co.us Search Database at www.dora.state.co.us/pls/real/ARMS_Search.Disclaimer_Page Note: For a list of all registered outfitters, please send a check or money order in the amount of $11.00 to: Office of Outfitters Reg. 1560 Broadway #1340, Denver, CO 80202.

39 Revenue Department, Alcohol Control Division, 1881 Pierce, #108A, Lakewood, CO 80214; 303-205-2300, Fax: 303-205-2341. www.revenue.state.co.us/liquor_dir/licenses.htm Email: nhamby@spike.dor.state.co.us

40 Department of Education, 201 E Colifax Ave, Denver, CO 80203; 303-866-6600, Fax: 303-830-0793. www.cde.state.co.us/index_license.htm Email: webmaster@cde.state.co.us

41 Electrical Board, 1580 Logan St, #550, Denver, CO 80203-1939; 303-894-2300, Fax: 303-894-2310. www.dora.state.co.us/Electrical Email: roberta.aceves@dora.state.co.us Search Database at www.dora.state.co.us/pls/real/ARMS_Search.Disclaimer_Page

42 Motor Vehicle Dealer Board, 1881 Pierce St Rm 142, Lakewood, CO 80215; 303-205-5604, Fax: 303-205-5977. www.revenue.state.co.us/mv_dir/home.asp Email: dealers@spike.dor.state.co.us

Colorado Federal Courts

The following list indicates the district and division name for each county in the state.

County/Court Cross Reference

Adams	Denver	Fremont	Denver	Montrose	Denver
Alamosa	Denver	Garfield	Denver	Morgan	Denver
Arapahoe	Denver	Gilpin	Denver	Otero	Denver
Archuleta	Denver	Grand	Denver	Ouray	Denver
Baca	Denver	Gunnison	Denver	Park	Denver
Bent	Denver	Hinsdale	Denver	Phillips	Denver
Boulder	Denver	Huerfano	Denver	Pitkin	Denver
Chaffee	Denver	Jackson	Denver	Prowers	Denver
Cheyenne	Denver	Jefferson	Denver	Pueblo	Denver
Clear Creek	Denver	Kiowa	Denver	Rio Blanco	Denver
Conejos	Denver	Kit Carson	Denver	Rio Grande	Denver
Costilla	Denver	La Plata	Denver	Routt	Denver
Crowley	Denver	Lake	Denver	Saguache	Denver
Custer	Denver	Larimer	Denver	San Juan	Denver
Delta	Denver	Las Animas	Denver	San Miguel	Denver
Denver	Denver	Lincoln	Denver	Sedgwick	Denver
Dolores	Denver	Logan	Denver	Summit	Denver
Douglas	Denver	Mesa	Denver	Teller	Denver
Eagle	Denver	Mineral	Denver	Washington	Denver
El Paso	Denver	Moffat	Denver	Weld	Denver
Elbert	Denver	Montezuma	Denver	Yuma	Denver

US District Court

District of Colorado

Denver Division Court Clerk, 901 19th St, US Courthouse, Denver, CO 80294-3589 (also use mail address for courier delivery), 303-335-2075, crim dockets- 303-844-2115, civil dockets- 303-844-3434, Fax-303-335-2714. Hours- 8AM-5PM. www.co.uscourts.gov

Counties: All counties in Colorado.

Searches & Indexing: Results do not include SSN or DOB. Computer index maintained. New cases in the index immediately after filing date. Records purged schedule varies.

Fee & Payment: Pay by Visa/MC, money order, cashier's or personal check. Payee: Clerk, US District Court. No prepayment required unless bill over $100.00.

Phone Search: This court releases anything of public record via phone but will not read long excerpts via phone.

Mail Search: search usually completed- 1 day. Include SASE for return.

In Person Search: Fee charged if court performs your search. No self-serve copier available.

E-Services: ECF replaces PACER whose records go back to 1990. New records online after 1 day. ECF at www.co.uscourts.gov/cmecf_frame.htm **Opinions Online:** www.co.uscourts.gov/opinions_frame2.htm. **Other Online Access:** Current and next week calendars- www.co.uscourts.gov/calendars_frame.htm.

US Bankruptcy Court

District of Colorado

Denver Division Court Clerk, US Custom House, Rm 114, 721 19th St, Denver, CO 80202-2508 (also use mail address for courier delivery), 303-844-4045, records rm- 303-844-0235. Hours- 8AM-4:30PM. www.cob.uscourts.gov

Counties: All counties in Colorado.

Searches & Indexing: Results do not include SSN or DOB. Computer index maintained. Pre-6/1996 case records on microfilm. New cases in the index 24-48 hours after filing date.

Fee & Payment: Pay by money order, cashier check only. No debtor's personal checks accepted. Payee: Clerk, US Bankruptcy Court. Prepayment required.

Phone Search: Voice Case Information Service available, call VCIS at 303-844-0267.

Mail Search: search usually completed- within 7 days. SASE not required.

In Person Search: Fee charged if court performs your search. View records from 8:00AM-4:45PM in Room 114. Self-serve copier available - $.10 per page.

E-Services: ECF replaces PACER whose records did go back to 7/ 1981. ECF at https://ecf.cob.uscourts.gov **Opinions Online:** www.cob.uscourts.gov/opinions.asp. **Other Online Access:** Calendars free at www.cob.uscourts.gov/calendar.asp.

Standards for Federal Courts: Search fee is $26.00 per item (one party name or case number). Copy fee is $.50 per page. Certification fee is $9.00 per document, double for exemplification, if available. All fees standard unless noted in profile. Mail Search: always enclose a stamped self addressed envelope unless otherwise noted. Most courts accept fax requests or will suggest a copying/search vendor. Before releasing records, all courts require prepayment, unless noted.

Open records are located at the court unless otherwise noted. District courts index by defendant and plaintiff as well as by case number. Bankruptcy courts usually index by debtor and case number. While most courts now have their indexes on computer, many may still maintain index card files as well.

Courts offering internet access via CM-ECF or older RACER, PACER, or Web-PACER systems charge $.08 per page fee unless noted as free. Where PACER is available, the universal sign-up number is 800-676-6856. Find PACER and the US Party/Case Index at http://pacer.psc.uscourts.gov.

Colorado County Courts

Court	Jurisdiction	No. of Courts	How Organized
District Courts*	General	14	22 Districts
County Courts*	Limited	17	63 Counties
Combined Courts*		49	
Denver Probate Courts*	Probate	1	
Municipal Courts	Municipal	206	
Denver Juvenile Courts	Special	1	
Water Courts	Special	7	7 Districts

* Profiled in this Sourcebook.

Court	CIVIL								
	Tort	Contract	Real Estate	Min. Claim	Max. Claim	Small Claims	Estate	Eviction	Domestic Relations
District Courts*	X	X	X	$0	No Max		X		X
County Courts*	X	X	X	$0	$15,000	$7500		X	
Denver Probate*							X		
Denver Juvenile Courts									
Water Courts			X	$0	No Max				

Court	CRIMINAL				
	Felony	Misdemeanor	DWI/DUI	Preliminary Hearing	Juvenile
District Courts*	X				X
County Courts*		X	X	X	
Denver Probate*					
Denver Juvenile Courts					X
Water Courts					

ADMINISTRATION   State Court Administrator, 1301 Pennsylvania St, Suite 300, Denver, CO, 80203; 303-861-1111, Fax: 303-837-2340. www.courts.state.co.us

COURT STRUCTURE   As of 9/1/2001, the maximum civil claim in County Courts was increased to $15,000. The District and County Courts have overlapping jurisdiction over civil cases involving less than $15,000 ($10,000 prior to 9/1/2001). Fortunately, District and County Courts are combined in most counties. Combined courts usually search both civil or criminal indexes for a single fee, except as indicated in the profiles.

Municipal courts only have jurisdiction over traffic, parking, and ordinance violations.

ONLINE ACCESS   As a result of an initiative of the Colorado Judicial Branch, all district court and all county court records are available through www.cocourts.com, e-screening.com, cojustice.com and Sol Communications. An index (Register of Actions) is available from the vendors for civil, civil water, small claims, domestic, felony, misdemeanor, and traffic cases. Images or copies of documents are not available from any of the commercial sites and may only be obtained by contacting the individual court where the documents were filed.

Opinions from the Court of Appeals are available from the web site.

ADDITIONAL INFORMATION

November 15, 2001, Broomfield City & County came into existence, derived from the counties of Adams, Boulder, Jefferson and Weld. A District and County Court (in 17th Judicial District) was established.

All state agencies require a self-addressed, stamped envelope (SASE) for return of information.

Co-located with seven district courts are divisions known as Water Courts. The Water Courts are located in Weld, Pueblo, Alamosa, Montrose, Garfield, Routt, and La Platta counties; see the District Court discussion for those counties to determine the jurisdictional area for the Water Court. Water Court records are maintained by the Water Clerk and fees are similar to those for other court records. To retrieve a Water Court record, one must furnish the Case Number or the Legal Description (section, township, and range) or the Full Name of the respondent (note that the case number or legal description are preferred).

PROBATE COURTS

Denver is the only county where Probate Court is separate from the District Court.

Adams County

17th District Court 1100 Judicial Center Dr, Brighton, CO 80601; phone: 303-659-1161; criminal phone: 303-654-3314; civil phone: 303-654-3237; probate phone: 303-654-3237; criminal fax: 303-654-3216; same fax for civil and probate; hours 8AM-N, 1-5PM (MST). *Felony, Civil Actions Over $10,000, Probate.*
www.17thjudicialdistrict.com
Note: The District and County courts have combined, but records are searched separately unless requester asks to search both courts (at no extra fee). Probate is in a separate index.

Civil Records: Access: Mail, in person, online. Both court and visitors may perform in person searches. Search fee: $5.00 per name. Fee is $10.00 for cases before 1976. There is no fee if search done by party of case. Court makes copy: $.75 per page. Self serve copy fee: $.25 per page. Required to search: name, years to search. Civil cases indexed by defendant, plaintiff. Civil records on computer from 1/1976, index books back to early 1900s. Civil records online access at www.cocourts.com. Mail turnaround time 2 days.

Criminal Records: Access: Mail, in person, online. Both court and visitors may perform in person searches. Search fee: $5.00 per name. Fee is $10.00 for cases before 1976. Court makes copy: $.75 per page. Self serve copy fee: $.25 per page. Required to search: name, years to search, DOB. Criminal records on computer from 1/1976, index books back to early 1900s. Access criminal records at www.cocourts.com. Mail turnaround time 2 days.

General Information: No public access terminal. No adoptions, sealed, juvenile, mental health or expunged cases released. Will not fax documents. Certification fee: $10.00. Payee: Clerk of the District Court. Personal checks accepted. Credit cards accepted. Accepted in person only. Prepayment and SASE required.

County Court 1100 Judicial Center Dr, Brighton, CO 80601; phone: 303-659-1161; criminal phone: 303-654-3314; civil phone: 303-654-3335; hours 8AM-5PM; closed Noon-1PM (MST). *Misdemeanor, Civil Actions Under $15,000, Eviction, Small Claims.*
www.17thjudicialdistrict.com/
Note: The District and County courts have combined, but records are searched separately unless specifically asked to search both courts for no add'l fee.

Civil Records: Access: Mail, in person, online. Both court and visitors may perform in person searches. Search fee: $5.00 per name. $10.00 per name for pre-computer records. Court makes copy: $.75 per page. Self serve copy fee: $.25 per page. Required to search: name, years to search. Civil cases indexed by defendant, plaintiff. Civil records on computer from 1/1990, index books back to 1965. Civil records online access at www.cocourts.com. Mail turnaround time 3 working days.

Criminal Records: Access: Mail, in person, online. Both court and visitors may perform in person searches. Search fee: $5.00 per name. $10.00 per name for pre-computer records. Court makes copy: $.75 per page. Self serve copy fee: $.25 per page. Required to search: name, years to search, DOB. Criminal records on computer from 1/1990, index books back to 1965. Access criminal records at www.cocourts.com. Mail turnaround time 3 working days.

General Information: No public access terminal. No adoptions, sealed, juvenile, mental health or expunged cases released. Will not fax documents. Certification fee: $10.00 per document. Payee: Adams County Combined Court. Personal checks or Visa, MC accepted. Prepayment and SASE required.

Alamosa County

Alamosa Combined Court 702 4th St, Alamosa, CO 81101; phone: 719-589-4996; fax: 719-589-4998; hours 8AM-N, 1-4PM (MST). *Felony, Misdemeanor, Civil, Eviction, Small Claims, Probate, Traffic.*
Civil Records: Access: Mail, in person, online. Only the court performs in person searches. Search fee: $5.00 per name. Court makes copy: $.75 per page. Required to search: name, years to search. Civil cases indexed by defendant, plaintiff. Civil records on computer from 5/1978, index books back to 1913. Civil records online access at www.cocourts.com. Mail turnaround time 10 days.

Criminal Records: Access: Mail, in person, online. Only the court performs in person searches. Search fee: $5.00 per name. Court makes copy: $.75 per page. Required to search: name, years to search, DOB. Criminal records on computer from 5/1978, index books back to 1913. Access criminal records at www.cocourts.com. Mail turnaround time 10 days.

General Information: No adoptions, juvenile, mental health, sealed or expunged cases released. Fee to fax documents is $10.00 minimum plus $1.00 per page after 1st 10. Certification fee: $5.00. Payee: Clerk, Combined Court. Personal checks accepted. Prepayment and SASE required.

Arapahoe County

18th District Court 7325 S Potomac St, Centennial, CO 80112; phone: 303-649-6355; hours 8AM-N, 1:15-4PM (MST). *Felony, Civil Actions Over $15,000, Probate.*
www.courts.state.co.us/district/18th/18dist.htm
Civil Records: Access: Phone, mail, in person, online. Both court and visitors may perform in person searches. Search fee: $5.00 per name. Court makes copy: $.75 per page. Required to search: name, years to search. Civil cases indexed by defendant, plaintiff. Civil records on computer from 1985, microfiche back to 1903. Civil records online access at www.cocourts.com. Mail turnaround time 10 working days.

Criminal Records: Access: Phone, mail, in person, online. Both court and visitors may perform in person searches. Search fee: $5.00 per name. Court makes copy: $.75 per page. Required to search: name, years to search, DOB. Criminal records on computer from 1985, microfiche back to 1903. Access criminal records at www.cocourts.com. Mail turnaround time 7-10 days.

General Information: No public access terminal. No adoptions, sealed, juvenile, mental health or expunged cases released. Will not fax documents. Certification fee: $10.00. Payee: Clerk of District Court. Personal checks accepted. Prepayment and SASE required.

Arapahoe County Court Division A 1790 W Littleton Blvd, Littleton, CO 80120-2060; phone: 303-798-4591; fax: 303-798-0524; hours 8AM-N-1;30-4PM (MST). *Misdemeanor, Civil Actions Under $15,000, Eviction, Small Claims.*
www.courts.state.co.us/district/18th/18dist.htm
Civil Records: Access: Mail, in person, online. Both court and visitors may perform in person searches. Search fee: $5.00 per name. Court makes copy: $.75 per page. Required to search: name, years to search. Civil cases indexed by defendant, plaintiff. Civil records on computer from 1986, index cards from 1965, microfiche from 1861 in District Court. Civil records online access at www.cocourts.com. Registration required; transaction fee. Note: Only court performs searches prior to March 1986. Mail turnaround time 5-10 business days.

Criminal Records: Access: Mail, in person, online. Both court and visitors may perform in person searches. Search fee: $5.00 per name. Court makes copy: $.75 per page. Required to search: name, years to search, DOB. Criminal records on computer from 1986, index cards from 1965, microfiche from 1861 in District Court. Access criminal records at www.cocourts.com. Note: Only court performs searches prior to March 1986. Mail turnaround time 5-10 business days.

General Information: No public access terminal. No adoptions, sealed, juvenile, mental health or expunged cases released. Will fax documents for $1.00 per page fax fee. Certification fee: $10.00 per document. Payee: Clerk of County Court. Personal checks or Visa, MC, Discover accepted. Prepayment and SASE required.

Arapahoe County Court Division B 15400 E 14th Pl, Aurora, CO 80011; phone: 303-363-8004; fax: 303-363-7155; hours 8AM-N, 1:30-4PM (MST). *Misdemeanor, Civil Actions Under $15,000, Eviction, Small Claims.*
www.courts.state.co.us/district/18th/18dist.htm
Civil Records: Access: Phone, mail, in person, online. Only the court performs in person searches. Search fee: $5.00 per name or $25.00 per hour. Court makes copy: $.75 per page. Required to search: name, years to search. Civil cases indexed by defendant, plaintiff. Civil records on computer from 4/1986, microfiche from 1980-1983, index cards from 1980.

Civil records online access at www.cocourts.com. Mail turnaround time 5-10 days.

Criminal Records: Access: Phone, mail, in person, online. Only the court performs in person searches. Search fee: $5.00 per name $25.00 per hour. Court makes copy: $.75 per page. Required to search: name, years to search, DOB. Criminal records on computer from 4/1986, microfiche from 1980-1983, index cards from 1980. Access criminal records at www.cocourts.com. Mail turnaround time 5-10 days.

General Information: No adoptions, sealed, juvenile, mental health or expunged records released. Will fax documents. Certification fee: $10.00. Payee: Clerk of County Court. Personal checks or Visa, MC accepted. Prepayment and SASE required.

Archuleta County

Archuleta Combined Courts PO Box 148, Pagosa Springs, CO 81147; phone: 970-264-5932; fax: 970-264-2407; hours 8AM-4PM (MST). *Felony, Misdemeanor, Civil, Eviction, Small Claims, Probate.*

Civil Records: Access: Mail, in person, online. Only the court performs in person searches. Search fee: $5.00 per name. Specific case information is $2.00 per file. Court makes copy: $.75 per page. Required to search: name, years to search. Civil cases indexed by defendant, plaintiff. Civil records on index cards from 1976, index books back to 1885, on computer since 8/95. Civil records online access at www.cocourts.com. Mail turnaround time 5 days.

Criminal Records: Access: Mail, in person, online. Only the court performs in person searches. Search fee: $5.00 per name. Specific case information $2.00 per file. Court makes copy: $.75 per page. Required to search: name, years to search, DOB. Criminal records on index cards from 1976, index books back to 1885, on computer since 8/95. Access criminal records at www.cocourts.com. Mail turnaround time 5 days.

General Information: No adoptions, sealed, juvenile, mental health or expunged cases released. Will fax documents to local or toll free line, otherwise $1.00 per page. Certification fee: $10.00 per doc. Payee: Archuleta Combined Court. Personal checks accepted. Prepayment and SASE required.

Baca County

Baca County District & County Courts 741 Main St, Springfield, CO 81073; phone: 719-523-4555; fax: 719-523-4552; hours 8AM-5PM (MST). *Felony, Misdemeanor, Civil, Eviction, Small Claims, Probate.*

www.courts.state.co.us/district/15th/15dist.htm

Civil Records: Access: Mail, in person, online. Only the court performs in person searches. Search fee: $5.00 per name. Court makes copy: $.75 per page. Required to search: name, years to search. Civil cases indexed by defendant, plaintiff. Civil records on index cards from 1945, index books back to 1910, computerized since 1995. Records accessed at www.cocourts.com. Mail turnaround 1-2 days.

Criminal Records: Access: Mail, in person, online. Only the court performs in person searches. Search fee: $5.00 per name. Court makes copy: $.75 per page. Required to search: name, years to search, DOB. Criminal records on index cards from 1945, index books back to 1910, computerized since 1995. Access criminal records at www.cocourts.com. Mail turnaround time 1-2 days.

General Information: No adoptions, sealed, juvenile, mental health or expunged cases released. Will fax documents for $1.00 per page. If only two pages-nothing lengthy. Certification fee: $10.00 per document. Payee: Baca County Courts. Personal checks accepted. Prepayment and SASE required.

Bent County

16th District Court Bent County Courthouse, 725 Bent, Las Animas, CO 81054; phone: 719-456-1353; probate phone: same; fax: 719-456-0040; hours 8AM-12, 1-5PM (MST). *Felony,*

Misdemeanor, Civil, Eviction, Small Claims, Probate.

www.courts.state.co.us/district/16th/16dist.htm

Civil Records: Access: Mail, in person, online. Only the court performs in person searches. Search fee: $5.00 per name. Court makes copy: $.75 per page; same fee for self serve. Required to search: name, years to search. Civil cases indexed by defendant, plaintiff. Civil records on index cards from 1975, prior to 1975 some on microfilm, on computer from 11/95 forward- all indexes available at this office. Civil records online access at www.cocourts.com. Mail turnaround time 4-5 days.

Criminal Records: Access: Mail, in person, online. Only the court performs in person searches. Search fee: $5.00 per name. Court makes copy: $.75 per page; same fee for self serve. Required to search: name, years to search, DOB. Criminal records on index cards from 1975, prior to 1975 some on microfilm, on computer from 11/95 forward- all indexes available at this office. Access criminal records at www.cocourts.com. Mail turnaround time 4-5 days.

General Information: No adoptions, sealed, juvenile, mental health or expunged cases released. Will fax documents to local or toll free line. Certification fee: $10.00. Payee: Clerk of Combined Court. Personal checks accepted. Prepayment and SASE required.

Boulder County

20th District & County Courts 6th & Canyon, 1777 6th St, Boulder, CO 80306; phone: 303-441-3750; civil phone: 303-441-4860; probate phone: 303-441-4760; fax: 303-441-3737; probate fax: 303-441-4750; hours 8AM-4PM (MST). *Felony, Misdemeanor, Civil, Eviction, Small Claims, Probate.*

Civil Records: Access: Mail, in person, online. Only the court performs in person searches. Search fee: $5.00 per name. Court makes copy: $.75 per page. Self serve copy fee: $.25 per page. Required to search: name, years to search. Civil cases indexed by defendant, plaintiff. Civil records on computer from 1983, microfiche prior from 1977, all prior records in books. Civil records online access at www.cocourts.com. Mail turnaround time 5 days.

Criminal Records: Access: Mail, in person, online. Only the court performs in person searches. Search fee: $5.00 per name. Court makes copy: $.75 per page. Self serve copy fee: $.25 per page. Required to search: name, years to search, DOB, signed release. Criminal records on computer from 1983, microfiche prior from 1977, all prior records in books. Access criminal records at www.cocourts.com. Mail turnaround time 5 days.

General Information: No adoptions, sealed, juvenile, mental health or expunged cases released. Currently will not fax documents. Certification fee: $10.00. Payee: 20th Judicial District. Business checks, attorney checks or Visa, MC accepted. Prepayment and SASE required.

Broomfield County

Broomfield Combined Court (District, County & Municipal, 17 DesCombes Dr, Broomfield, CO 80020; phone: 720-887-2100; fax: 720-887-2122; hours 8AM-5PM (MST). *Felony, Misdemeanor, Civil, Eviction, Small Claims, Probate.*

www.co.broomfield.co.us

Note: This is a new county created in late 2001, record keeping is limited. Older records should be searched in Adams, Boulder, Jefferson or Weld counties. This court holds Municipal court records prior to county organization.

Civil Records: Access: Mail, in person, online. Only the court performs in person searches. Court makes copy: $.75. Self serve copy fee: $.25 per page. Civil cases indexed by defendant, plaintiff. Civil records on computer since 11/01. Online access is at www.cocourts.com. Mail turnaround 2-3 days.

Criminal Records: Access: Mail, in person, online. Only the court performs in person searches. Search fee: $5.00 per name. Court makes copy: $.75 per page. Self serve copy fee: $.25 per page. Required to search: name, also helpful: address, DOB. Online access is at www.cocourts.com. Mail turnaround time 2-3 days.

General Information: No Juvenile or protective custody records released. Certification fee: $10.00. Payee: Broomfield County Courts. Will accept credit cards and checks. Prepayment and SASE required.

Chaffee County

11th District & County Courts PO Box 279, Salida, CO 81201; phone: 719-539-2561/6031; criminal fax: 719-539-6281; same fax for civil and probate; hours 8AM-5PM (MST). *Felony, Misdemeanor, Civil, Eviction, Small Claims, Probate.*

www.courts.state.co.us/district/11th/dist11.htm

Civil Records: Access: Phone, mail, in person, online. Only the court performs in person searches. Search fee: $5.00 per name. Fee applies if 3 or more files involved. Court makes copy: $.75 per page. Required to search: name, years to search. Civil cases indexed by defendant, plaintiff. Civil records on computer back to 1995; index cards from 4/1976, index books back to late 1800s. Civil records online access at www.cocourts.com. Mail turnaround time ASAP

Criminal Records: Access: Phone, mail, in person, online. Only the court performs in person searches. Search fee: $5.00 per name. Fee applies if 3 or more files involved. Court makes copy: $.75 per page. Required to search: name, years to search, DOB. Criminal records on computer back to 1995; index cards back to 4/1976, index books back to late 1800s. Access criminal records at www.cocourts.com. Mail turnaround time 2-3 days.

General Information: No adoptions, sealed, juvenile, mental health or expunged cases released. Fee to fax documents is $.50 per page. Certification fee: $10.00 per certification. Payee: Clerk of District Court. Personal checks accepted. Prepayment and SASE required.

Cheyenne County

District & County Courts PO Box 696, Cheyenne Wells, CO 80810; phone: 719-767-5649; fax: 719-767-5671; hours 8AM-4PM, till noon on Fri (MST). *Felony, Misdemeanor, Civil, Eviction, Small Claims, Probate.*

www.courts.state.co.us/district/15th/15dist.htm

Civil Records: Access: Mail, in person, online. Only the court performs in person searches. Search fee: $5.00 per name. Court makes copy: $.75 per page. Required to search: name, years to search. Civil cases indexed by defendant, plaintiff. Civil records on computer since 11/1/95, index cards from 1960, index books back to early 1900s. Civil records online access at www.cocourts.com. Mail turnaround time 5-7 days.

Criminal Records: Access: Mail, in person, online. Only the court performs in person searches. Search fee: $5.00 per name. Court makes copy: $.75 per page. Required to search: name, years to search, DOB, notarized signed release. Criminal records on computer since 11/1/95, index cards from 1960, index books back to early 1900s. Access criminal records at www.cocourts.com. Mail turnaround time 5-7 days.

General Information: No public access terminal. No adoptions, sealed, juvenile, mental health or expunged cases released. Will fax documents for $1.00 per page. Certification fee: $10.00 per document. Payee: Cheyenne County Combined Court. Business checks accepted. Prepayment required. Will bill attorneys only. SASE required.

Clear Creek County

Clear Creek Combined Courts PO Box 367, Georgetown, CO 80444; phone: 303-569-3273; fax: 303-569-3274; hours 8AM-4PM (MST). *Felony, Misdemeanor, Civil, Eviction, Small Claims, Probate.*

Civil Records: Access: Mail, in person, online. Both court and visitors may perform in person searches. Search fee: $5.00 per name. Court makes copy: $.75 per page. Required to search: name, years to search. Civil cases indexed by defendant, plaintiff. Civil records on index cards from 1976, ledger books back to late 1800. Civil records online access at www.cocourts.com. Note: No searches done on records prior to 1976. Mail turnaround time 1 week.

Criminal Records: Access: Mail, in person, online. Both court and visitors may perform in person searches. Search fee: $5.00 per name. Court makes copy: $.75 per page. Required to search: name, years to search, DOB. Criminal records on index cards from 1976, ledger books back to late 1800, computerized since 9/95. Access criminal records at www.cocourts.com. Mail turnaround time 1 week.

General Information: No public access terminal. No adoptions, sealed, juvenile, mental health or expunged cases released. Certification fee: $10.00 per doc. Payee: Clerk of Combined Court. Personal checks accepted. Prepayment and SASE required.

Conejos County

12th District & County Courts 6683 County Road 13, Conejos, CO 81129; phone: 719-376-5466; probate phone: 719-376-5465; fax: 719-376-5939; hours 8AM-4PM (MST). *Felony, Misdemeanor, Civil, Eviction, Small Claims, Probate.*

Civil Records: Access: Mail, in person, online. Only the court performs in person searches. Search fee: $5.00 per name. Court makes copy: $.75 per page. Required to search: name, years to search. Civil cases indexed by defendant, plaintiff. Civil records on computer since 6/94, on index cards from 1980. Civil records online access at www.cocourts.com. Mail turnaround time 2 weeks.

Criminal Records: Access: Mail, in person, online. Only the court performs in person searches. Search fee: $5.00 per name. Court makes copy: $.75 per page. Required to search: name, years to search, DOB. Criminal records on computer since 6/94, on index cards from 1980. Access criminal records at www.cocourts.com. Mail turnaround time 2 weeks.

General Information: No public access terminal. No adoptions, sealed, juvenile, mental health or expunged cases released. Will not fax documents. Certification fee: $10.00. Payee: Conejos Combined Court. Personal checks accepted. Prepayment and SASE required.

Costilla County

12th District & County Courts PO Box 301, San Luis, CO 81152; phone: 719-672-3681; criminal fax: 719-672-4493; same fax for civil and probate; hours 8AM-N, 1-4PM (MST). *Felony, Misdemeanor, Civil, Eviction, Small Claims, Probate.*
www.courts.state.co.us/district/12th/12dist.htm
Civil Records: Access: Mail, in person, online. Both court and visitors may perform in person searches. Search fee: $5.00 per name. Records prior to 1994 are $25.00 per hour. Court makes copy: $.75 per page. Self serve copy fee: $.25 per page. Required to search: name, years to search; also helpful: address. Civil cases indexed by defendant, plaintiff. Civil records on index cards from 1970, index books back to 1865, indexed on computer since 1994. In CO state archives prior to 1970. Civil records online access at www.cocourts.com. Mail turnaround time 1-2 weeks.

Criminal Records: Access: Fax, mail, in person, online. Only the court performs in person searches.

Search fee: $5.00 per name, records prior to 1994 are $25.00 per hour. Court makes copy: $.75 per page. Self serve copy fee: $.25 per page. Required to search: name, years to search, DOB; also helpful: address, SSN. Criminal records on index cards from 1970, index books back to 1865, indexed on computer since 1994. In CO state archived prior to 1970. Access criminal records at www.cocourts.com. Mail turnaround time 1-2 weeks.

General Information: No public access terminal. No adoptions, sealed, juvenile, mental health, certain criminal cases or expunged cases released. Fee to fax documents is $10.00 per document. Certification fee: $10.00 per document. Payee: Costilla Combined Courts. Personal checks accepted. Prepayment and SASE required.

Crowley County

16th District & County Courts 110 E 6th St, #303, Ordway, CO 81063; phone: 719-267-4468; fax: 719-267-3753; hours 8AM-5PM (MST). *Felony, Misdemeanor, Civil, Eviction, Small Claims, Probate.*
www.courts.state.co.us/district/16th/16dist.htm
Civil Records: Access: Phone, mail, fax, in person, online. Only the court performs in person searches. Search fee: $5.00 per name. Court makes copy: $.75 per page. Required to search: name, years to search. Civil cases indexed by defendant, plaintiff. Civil records on computer back to 1993, fiche since 1980s, index books back to 1925. Civil records online access at www.cocourts.com. Mail turnaround time 3-5 days.

Criminal Records: Access: Mail, fax, in person, online. Only the court performs in person searches. Search fee: $5.00 per name. Court makes copy: $.75 per page. Required to search: name, years to search, DOB, SSN. Criminal records on computer back to 1993, fiche since 1980's, index books back to 1925. Access criminal records at www.cocourts.com. Mail turnaround time 3-5 days.

General Information: No public access terminal. No adoptions, sealed, juvenile, mental health or expunged cases released. Fee to fax documents is $1.00 per page. Certification fee: $10.00 per doc. Payee: Crowley Combined Court. Personal checks accepted. Prepayment and SASE required.

Custer County

11th District & County Courts PO Box 60, Westcliffe, CO 81252; phone: 719-783-2274; fax: 719-783-2995; hours 9AM-2PM (MST). *Felony, Misdemeanor, Civil, Eviction, Small Claims, Probate.*
www.courts.state.co.us/district/11th/dist11.htm
Civil Records: Access: Mail, in person, online. Only the court performs in person searches. Search fee: $5.00 per name. Court makes copy: $.75 per page. Required to search: name, years to search. Civil cases indexed by defendant, plaintiff. Civil records on index cards from 1973, ledger books back to 1965, on computer since 1993, archived from 1879-1972. Civil records online access at www.cocourts.com. Mail turnaround time 3-4 days.

Criminal Records: Access: Mail, in person, online. Only the court performs in person searches. Search fee: $5.00 per name. Court makes copy: $.75 per page. Required to search: name, years to search, DOB. Criminal records on index cards from 1973, ledger books back to 1965, on computer since 1993, archived from 1879-1972. Access criminal records at www.cocourts.com. Mail turnaround time 3-4 days.

General Information: No public access terminal. No adoptions, sealed, juvenile, mental health or expunged cases released. Will fax documents for $1.00 per page. Certification fee: $10.00. Payee: Custer Combined Court. Personal checks accepted. Prepayment and SASE required.

Delta County

District & County Courts 501 Palmer St, Rm 338, Delta, CO 81416; phone: 970-874-6280; fax: 970-874-4306; hours 9AM-4PM (MST). *Felony, Misdemeanor, Civil, Eviction, Small Claims, Probate.*
www.7thjudicialdistrictco.org/delta.html
Civil Records: Access: Mail, in person, online. Only the court performs in person searches. Search fee: $5.00 per name. Court makes copy: $.75 per page. Required to search: name, years to search. Civil cases indexed by defendant, plaintiff. Civil records on computer back to 10/1994, index cards from 1972, index books back to 1900. Civil records online access at www.cocourts.com. Also, weekly dockets for the 7th district courts are at www.7thjudicialdistrictco.org/docket.html. Mail turnaround time 10 days.

Criminal Records: Access: Mail, in person, online. Only the court performs in person searches. Search fee: $5.00 per name. Court makes copy: $.75 per page. Required to search: name, years to search, DOB, signed release. Criminal records on computer back to 10/1994, index cards from 1972, index books back to 1900. Access criminal records at www.cocourts.com. Also, weekly dockets are available, see civil, above. Mail turnaround time 10 days.

General Information: No public access terminal. No adoptions, sealed, juvenile, mental health or expunged cases released. Will fax documents for $1.00 per page prepaid. Certification fee: $10.00 per cert. Payee: Clerk of Court. Only cashiers checks and money orders accepted. Prepayment and SASE required.

Denver County

2nd District Court 1437 Bannock, Office of the Court Clerk, Denver, CO 80202; phone: 720-865-8301; hours 8:30AM-4PM (MST). *Felony, Civil Actions Over $10,000.*
www.courts.state.co.us/district/02nd/02dist.htm
Note: This court will not process written requests for name searches. You must use the Internet or hire a retriever, or visit in person.

Civil Records: Access: In person, online. Both court and visitors may perform in person searches. No search fee. Court makes copy: $.75 per page. Self copy fee: $.25 per page. Required to search: name, years to search. Civil cases indexed by defendant, plaintiff. Civil records on computer from 1974, index books back to the late 1800s if convicted of criminal charges. Online access to civil records is at www.cocourts.com.

Criminal Records: Access: In person, online. Both court and visitors may perform in person searches. No search fee. Court makes copy: $.75 per page. Self serve copy fee: $.25 per page. Required to search: name, years to search, DOB. Criminal records on computer from 1974, index books back to the late 1800s if convicted of criminal charges. Access criminal records at www.cocourts.com and at www.denvergov.org/court/courtselect.asp.

General Information: Public access terminal goes back to 1974. No adoptions, sealed, juvenile, mental health or expunged cases released. Certification fee: $10.00. Payee: Denver District Court. Personal checks accepted. Prepayment required.

County Court - Civil Division 1515 Cleveland Pl, 4th Fl, Denver, CO 80202; phone: 303-640-5161; fax: 303-640-4730; hours 8AM-5PM (MST). *Civil Actions Under $15,000, Eviction, Small Claims.*
www.courts.state.co.us/district/counties.htm
Civil Records: Access: Mail, in person, online. Only the court performs in person searches. No search fee. Court makes copy: $1.00 per page. Self serve copy fee: $.25 per page. Required to search: name, years to search. Civil cases indexed by defendant, plaintiff. Civil records on computer from 1987, microfiche since 1965. Online searching of Denver

County Civil Division court cases is at www.denvergov.org/court/civilcourts.asp. Search by name, business name, or case number. You can also search at www.cocourts.com. Mail turnaround time 1 week.

Mail turnaround time 1 week.

General Information: No public access terminal. No adoptions, sealed, juvenile, mental health or expunged cases released. Will not fax documents. Certification fee: $10.00. Payee: Denver County Court. Personal checks accepted. Prepayment and SASE required.

County Court - Criminal Division 1437 Bannock St, Rm 111A, Denver, CO 80202; phone: 720-865-7820; hours 8AM-5PM (MST). *Misdemeanor.*

www.courts.state.co.us/district/02nd/02dist.htm

Criminal Records: Access: Mail, in person, online. Only the court performs in person searches. Search fee: None, until after 2nd request then $5.00. Court makes copy: $.75 per page. Required to search: name, years to search, DOB; also helpful: address. Criminal records computerized since 1978. Access criminal records at www.denvergov.org/court/courtselect.asp. Mail turnaround time 1 week.

General Information: No public access terminal. No adoptions, sealed, juvenile, mental health or expunged cases released. Will fax documents for $5.00 per name plus $.75 per page. Certification fee: $10.00. Payee: Denver County Court. Personal checks accepted. Prepayment and SASE required.

Probate Court 1437 Bannock, Rm 230, Denver, CO 80202; phone: 720-865-8310; fax: 720-865-8576; hours 8:30AM-4PM (MST). *Probate.*

www.courts.state.co.us/district/02nd/02dist.htm

Dolores County

22nd District & County Courts PO Box 511, Dove Creek, CO 81324; phone: 970-677-2258; hours 8AM-5PM M, T, Th; 8AM-N Fri (MST). *Felony, Misdemeanor, Civil, Eviction, Small Claims, Probate.*

Note: Office is closed on Wednesday & Thursday.

Civil Records: Access: Phone, mail, in person, online. Only the court performs in person searches. No search fee. Court makes copy: $.75 per page. Required to search: name, years to search. Civil cases indexed by defendant, plaintiff. Civil records on index cards from 1972, index books back to 1895, on computer from 6/95 to present. Civil records online access at www.cocourts.com. Mail turnaround time 1 week.

Criminal Records: Access: Phone, mail, in person, online. Only the court performs in person searches. No search fee. Court makes copy: $.75 per page. Required to search: name, years to search, DOB. Criminal records on index cards from 1972, index books back to 1895, on computer from 6/95 to present. Access criminal records at www.cocourts.com. Mail turnaround time 1 week.

General Information: No public access terminal. No adoptions, sealed, juvenile, mental health or expunged cases released. Will not fax documents. Certification fee: $10.00. Payee: Dolores County Combined. Only cashiers checks and money orders accepted. Prepayment and SASE required.

Douglas County

Douglas County Combined Court 4000 Justice Way, #2009, Castle Rock, CO 80104; phone: 303-663-7200; criminal fax: 303-688-1962; same fax for civil and probate; hours 8:00AM-N; 1:15PM-4PM (MST). *Felony, Misdemeanor, Civil, Eviction, Small Claims, Probate.*

www.courts.state.co.us/district/18th/18dist.htm

Civil Records: Access: Mail, in person, online. Both court and visitors may perform in person searches. Search fee: $5.00 per name. $20.00 per hour for extensive search. Court makes copy: $.75 per page. Self serve copy fee: $.25 per page. Required to search:

name, years to search. Civil cases indexed by defendant, plaintiff. Civil records on computer back to 1/1988, index cards from 1975, index books to 1880s. Civil records online access at www.cocourts.com. Mail turnaround time 1-2 weeks.

Criminal Records: Access: Mail, in person, online. Both court and visitors may perform in person searches. Search fee: $5.00 per name. $20.00 per hour for extensive search. Court makes copy: $.75 per page. Self serve copy fee: $.25 per page. Required to search: name, years to search. Criminal records on computer back to 1/1988, index cards from 1975, index books to 1880s. Access criminal records at www.cocourts.com. Mail turnaround time 1-2 weeks.

General Information: No public access terminal. No adoptions, sealed, juvenile, mental health or expunged cases released. Will not fax documents. Certification fee: $10.00 per cert. Payee: Clerk of Court. No out of state checks accepted. Prepayment and SASE required.

Eagle County

Eagle Combined Court PO Box 597, Eagle, CO 81631; phone: 970-328-6373; fax: 970-328-6328; hours 8AM-Noon; 1-4PM (MST). *Felony, Misdemeanor, Civil, Eviction, Small Claims, Probate.*

Civil Records: Access: Fax, mail, in person, online. Visitors must perform in person searches themselves. Search fee: $5.00 per name. Court makes copy: $.75 per page. Required to search: name, years to search. Civil cases indexed by defendant, plaintiff. Civil records on computer since 9/95; prior on fiche to 1970, books to 1930. Civil records online access at www.cocourts.com. Mail turnaround time 5-7 days.

Criminal Records: Access: Fax, mail, in person, online. Visitors must perform in person searches themselves. Search fee: $5.00 per name. Court makes copy: $.75 per page. Required to search: name, years to search, DOB. Criminal records on computer since 9/95; prior on fiche to 1970, books to 1930. Access criminal records at www.cocourts.com. Mail turnaround time 5-7 days.

General Information: No public access terminal. No adoptions, sealed, juvenile, mental health or expunged cases released. Will fax documents $1.00 per page. Fax fee must be paid with credit card. Certification fee: $10.00 per doc. Payee: Eagle Combined Courts. Personal checks or Visa, MC accepted. Prepayment and SASE required.

El Paso County

El Paso Combined Court PO Box 2980, Colorado Springs, CO 80901-2980; phone: 719-448-7599; fax: 719-448-7685; hours 8AM-5PM (closed at noon 1 hr) (MST). *Felony, Misdemeanor, Civil Actions, Probate.*

www.gofourth.org

Note: Records for the County and District Courts are combined.

Civil Records: Access: Fax, mail, in person, online. Both court and visitors may perform in person searches. Search fee: $5.00 per name, if records prior to 1988 then $5.00 each 15 minutes. Add $1.00 to fax or mail. Court makes copy: $.75 per page. Required to search: name, years to search. Civil cases indexed by defendant, plaintiff. Civil records on computer from 1/1975, index cards to 1975, index books to 1861. Civil records online access at www.cocourts.com. Mail turnaround time 5-7 days.

Criminal Records: Access: Fax, mail, in person, online. Both court and visitors may perform in person searches. Search fee: $5.00 per name; if pre-1988, fee is $20.00 per hour. Add $1.00 to fax or mail. Court makes copy: $.75 per page. Required to search: name, years to search, DOB; also helpful: SSN. Criminal records on computer from 1/1975, index cards to 1975, index books to 1861. Access criminal records at www.cocourts.com. Mail turnaround time 5-7 days.

General Information: No public access terminal. No adoptions, sealed, juvenile, mental health, expunged cases or other access restricted cases released. Fee is fax documents is $.75 per page plus $1.50 if long distance. Certification fee: $10.00. Payee: Clerk of District Court. Personal checks or Visa, MC, Discover accepted. Prepayment and SASE required.

Elbert County

Elbert District & County Courts PO Box 232, Kiowa, CO 80117; phone: 303-621-2131; probate phone: same; hours 8AM-4PM (MST). *Felony, Misdemeanor, Civil, Eviction, Small Claims, Probate.*

www.courts.state.co.us/district/18th/18dist.htm

Civil Records: Access: Mail, in person, online. Only the court performs in person searches. Search fee: $5.00 per name. Court makes copy: $.75 per page. Required to search: full name, years to search. Civil cases indexed by defendant, plaintiff. Civil records on computer back to 1995, index cards from 1978-1994, index books from 1920s, archived prior to 1920. Civil records online access at www.cocourts.com. Mail turnaround time 1-2 weeks.

Criminal Records: Access: Mail, in person, online. Only the court performs in person searches. Search fee: $5.00 per name. Court makes copy: $.75 per page. Required to search: full name, years to search, DOB, signed release. Criminal records on computer back to 1995, index cards from 1978, index books from 1920s. Access criminal records at www.cocourts.com. Mail turnaround time 1-2 weeks.

General Information: No public access terminal. No adoptions, sealed, juvenile, mental health or expunged cases released. Certification fee: $10.00. Payee: Elbert Combined Courts. Business checks accepted. Prepayment and SASE required.

Fremont County

District & County Courts 136 Justice Center Rd, Rm 103, Canon City, CO 81212; phone: 719-269-0100; fax: 719-269-0134; hours 8AM-5PM (MST). *Felony, Misdemeanor, Civil, Eviction, Small Claims, Probate, Traffic.*

www.courts.state.co.us/district/11th/dist11.htm

Civil Records: Access: Mail, fax, in person, online. Only the court performs in person searches. Search fee: $5.00 per name. Court makes copy: $.75 per page. Required to search: name, years to search; also helpful: address. Civil cases indexed by defendant, plaintiff. Civil records computerized since 1995, on index cards from 1978, index books in Denver back to 1861. Civil records online access at www.cocourts.com. Mail turnaround time up to 14 working days.

Criminal Records: Access: Mail, in person, online. Only the court performs in person searches. Search fee: $5.00 per name. Court makes copy: $.75 per page. Required to search: name, years to search; also helpful: address, DOB. Criminal records computerized since 1995, on index cards from 1978. Access criminal records at www.cocourts.com. Mail turnaround time up to 14 working days.

General Information: No public access terminal. No adoptions, sealed, juvenile, mental health or expunged cases released. Certification fee: $10.00. Payee: Clerk of the Combined Courts. Personal checks accepted. Prepayment and SASE required.

Garfield County

9th District & County Courts 109 8th St, #104, Glenwood Springs, CO 81601; phone: 970-945-5075; fax: 970-945-8756; hours 8AM-5PM (MST). *Felony, Misdemeanor, Civil, Eviction, Small Claims, Probate.*

www.courts.state.co.us/district/09th/dist09.htm

Note: This court handles cases in the county for the area east of New Castle.

Civil Records: Access: Mail, in person, online. Only the court performs in person searches. Search fee:

$5.00 per name. Court makes copy: $.75 per page. Self serve copy fee: $.25 per page. Required to search: name, years to search. Civil cases indexed by defendant, plaintiff. Civil records on computer from 1992, on fiche from 1970, index books back to late 1800s. Civil records online access at www.cocourts.com. Mail turnaround time 1-2 weeks.

Criminal Records: Access: Mail, in person, online. Only the court performs in person searches. Search fee: $5.00 per name. Court makes copy: $.75 per page. Self serve copy fee: $.25 per page. Required to search: name, years to search. Criminal records on computer from 1992, on fiche from 1970, index books back to late 1800s. Access criminal records at www.cocourts.com. Mail turnaround time 1-2 weeks.

General Information: No public access terminal. No adoptions, sealed, juvenile, mental health or expunged cases released. Will fax documents for $1.00 per page. Certification fee: $10.00 per document. Payee: Garfield Combined Courts. Personal checks or Visa, MC accepted. Prepayment and SASE required.

County Court - Rifle 110 E 18th St, Rifle, CO 81650; phone: 970-625-5100; fax: 970-625-1125; hours 8AM-5PM (MST). *Misdemeanor, Civil Actions Under $15,000, Eviction, Small Claims.*
www.courts.state.co.us/district/09th/dist09.html
Note: This court handles cases in the county for the area from New Castle to the west.

Civil Records: Access: Phone, fax, mail, in person, online. Only the court performs in person searches. No search fee. Court makes copy: $.75 per page. Required to search: name, years to search. Civil cases indexed by defendant, plaintiff. Civil records on index cards from 1965, computerized since 1994. Civil records online access at www.cocourts.com. Mail turnaround time 1 week.

Criminal Records: Access: Phone, fax, mail, in person, online. Only the court performs in person searches. No search fee. Court makes copy: $.75 per page. Required to search: name, years to search, DOB. Criminal records on index cards from 1965, computerized since 1994. Access criminal records at www.cocourts.com. Mail turnaround time 1 week.

General Information: No public access terminal. No adoptions, sealed, juvenile, mental health or expunged cases released. Will fax documents $1.00 per page to send or receive. Certification fee: $10.00 per page. Payee: Associate County Court. Personal checks or Visa, MC accepted. Prepayment and SASE required.

Gilpin County

1st District & County Courts 2960 Dory Hill Rd, #200, Golden, CO 80403-8768; phone: 303-582-5522; fax: 303-582-3112; hours 8AM-5PM (MST). *Felony, Misdemeanor, Civil, Eviction, Small Claims, Probate.*

Civil Records: Access: Mail, in person, online. Only the court performs in person searches. Search fee: $5.00 per name. Fee is for past 7 years. Court makes copy: $.75 per page. Required to search: name, years to search. Civil cases indexed by defendant, plaintiff. Civil records on computer (County-1993, District-1994), on index cards from 1970s, index books from 1950s. Civil records online access at www.cocourts.com. Mail turnaround time 5 days.

Criminal Records: Access: Mail, in person, online. Only the court performs in person searches. Search fee: $10.00 per name. Fee is for past 7 years. Court makes copy: $.75 per page. Required to search: name, years to search, DOB. Criminal records on computer (County-1993, District-1994), on index cards from 1970s, index books from 1950s. Access criminal records at www.cocourts.com. Mail turnaround time 5 days.

General Information: No public access terminal. No adoptions, sealed, juvenile, mental health or expunged cases released. Will fax documents to local or toll free line. Certification fee: $10.00 per doc.

Payee: Clerk of the Combined Courts. Personal checks accepted. Prepayment and SASE required.

Grand County

14th District & County Courts PO Box 192, Hot Sulphur Springs, CO 80451; phone: 970-725-3357; hours 8AM-4PM (MST). *Felony, Misdemeanor, Civil, Eviction, Small Claims, Probate.*

Civil Records: Access: Phone, mail, in person, online. Only the court performs in person searches. Search fee: $5.00 per name if 1976-1991; $20.00 if pre-1976; No fee 1992-present. Court makes copy: $.75 per page. Required to search: name, years to search. Civil cases indexed by defendant, plaintiff. Civil records on computer from 7/1991, fiche from 1970, index books from 1900. Civil records online access at www.cocourts.com. Note: Phone requests accepted only if no fees involved. Mail turnaround time 1 week.

Criminal Records: Access: Phone, mail, in person, online. Only the court performs in person searches. Search fee: $5.00 per name if 1976-1991; $20.00 if pre-1976; No fee 1992-present. Court makes copy: $.75 per page. Required to search: name, years to search, DOB. Criminal records on computer from 7/1991, fiche from 1970, index books from 1900. Access criminal records at www.cocourts.com. Note: Phone requests accepted only if no fees involved. Mail turnaround time 1 week.

General Information: No public access terminal. No adoptions, sealed, juvenile, mental health or expunged cases released. Certification fee: $10.00. Payee: Grand County Combined Court. Personal checks accepted. Prepayment and SASE required.

Gunnison County

7th District & County Courts 200 E Virginia Ave, Gunnison, CO 81230; phone: 970-641-3500; fax: 970-641-6876; hours 8:30AM-4:30PM M-Th; 8:30AM-3PM F (MST). *Felony, Misdemeanor, Civil, Eviction, Small Claims, Probate.*
www.courts.state.co.us/district/07th/dist07.htm

Civil Records: Access: Mail, in person, online. Only the court performs in person searches. Search fee: $5.00 per name. Court makes copy: $.75 per page. Required to search: name, years to search. Civil cases indexed by defendant. Civil records on computer from 1994, index cards from 1977, index books back to 1877. Civil records online access at www.cocourts.com. Mail turnaround 1-2 days.

Criminal Records: Access: Mail, in person, online. Only the court performs in person searches. Search fee: $5.00 per name. Court makes copy: $.75 per page. Required to search: name, years to search, DOB. Criminal records on computer from 1994, index cards from 1977, index books back to 1877. Access criminal records at www.cocourts.com. Mail turnaround time 1-2 days.

General Information: No public access terminal. No adoptions, sealed, juvenile, mental health or expunged cases released. Will fax documents. Certification fee: $10.00. Payee: Gunnison Combined Courts. Personal checks accepted. Prepayment and SASE required.

Hinsdale County

7th District & County Courts PO Box 245, Lake City, CO 81235; phone: 970-944-2227; criminal fax: 970-944-2289; same fax for civil and probate; hours 8:30-N M,W,F (Jun-Aug); 8:30AM-N M&F (Sept-May) (MST). *Felony, Misdemeanor, Civil, Eviction, Small Claims, Probate.*
www.courts.state.co.us/district/07th/dist07.htm

Civil Records: Access: Phone, fax, mail, in person, online. Only the court performs in person searches. No search fee. Court makes copy: $.75 per page. Required to search: name, years to search. Civil cases indexed by defendant, plaintiff. Civil records on index cards from 1975, index books back to 1900. Civil records online access at www.cocourts.com. Mail turnaround time 2-4 weeks.

Criminal Records: Access: Phone, fax, mail, in person, online. Only the court performs in person searches. Search fee: Fee depends on time required for search. Court makes copy: $.75 per page. Required to search: name, years to search. Criminal records on index cards from 1975, index books back to 1900. Access criminal records at www.cocourts.com. Mail turnaround time 2-4 weeks.

General Information: No public access terminal. No adoptions, sealed, juvenile, mental health or expunged cases released. Will fax documents $.75 per page. 1-10 pgs $2.00, 11-20 pgs $5.00, 21-30 pgs $10.00. Certification fee: $10.00 per cert. Payee: Clerk of the Combined Courts. Personal checks accepted. Prepayment and SASE required.

Huerfano County

3rd District & County Courts 401 Main St, #304, Walsenburg, CO 81089; phone: 719-738-1040; fax: 719-738-1267; hours 8AM-4PM (MST). *Felony, Misdemeanor, Civil, Eviction, Small Claims, Probate.*
www.courts.state.co.us/district/03rd/03dist.htm

Civil Records: Access: Mail, in person, online. Only the court performs in person searches. Search fee: $5.00 per name. Court makes copy: $.75 per page. Required to search: name, years to search. Civil cases indexed by defendant, plaintiff. Civil records on computer from 1995 (county court only), index cards from 1978, index books from 1861. Civil records online access at www.cocourts.com. Mail turnaround time 2 weeks.

Criminal Records: Access: Mail, in person, online. Only the court performs in person searches. Search fee: $5.00 per name. Court makes copy: $.75 per page. Required to search: name, years to search, DOB. Criminal records on computer from 1995 (county court only), index cards from 1978, index books from 1861. Access criminal records at www.cocourts.com. Mail turnaround 2 weeks.

General Information: No public access terminal. No adoptions, sealed, juvenile, mental health or expunged cases released. Fee to fax documents is $2.00 per page. Certification fee: $10.00. Payee: Huerfano County Combined Courts. Personal checks accepted. Prepayment and SASE required.

Jackson County

8th District & County Courts PO Box 308, Walden, CO 80480; phone: 970-723-4363; hours 9AM-1PM (MST). *Felony, Misdemeanor, Civil, Eviction, Small Claims, Probate.*
www.courts.state.co.us/district/08th/08dist.htm

Civil Records: Access: Mail, in person, online. Both court and visitors may perform in person searches. No search fee. Court makes copy: $.75 per page. Will bill in excess of 10 pages; same fee for self serve. Required to search: name, years to search. Civil cases indexed by defendant, plaintiff. Civil records on computer since 1994; prior on index cards from 1974, index books from the 1900s. Civil records online access at www.cocourts.com. Mail turnaround time 2 weeks.

Criminal Records: Access: Mail, in person, online. Both court and visitors may perform in person searches. No search fee. Court makes copy: $.75 per page. Will bill in excess of 10 pages; same fee for self serve. Required to search: name, years to search, DOB. Criminal records on computer since 1994; prior on index cards from 1974, index books from the 1900s. Access criminal records at www.cocourts.com. Mail turnaround time 2 weeks.

General Information: No public access terminal. No adoptions, sealed, juvenile, mental health or expunged cases released. Will fax documents to a local or toll free line. Certification fee: $10.00. Payee: Clerk of the Combined Courts. Personal checks accepted. Prepayment required. If a file has been pulled and exceeds 10 pages, will bill the requesting party. SASE required.

Jefferson County

1st District & County Courts 100 Jefferson County Pky, Golden, CO 80401-6002; phone: 303-271-6267; criminal phone: 303-271-6237; civil phone: 303-271-6228; probate phone: 303-271-6135; criminal fax: 303-271-6188; same fax for civil and probate; hours 8AM-4PM (MST). *Felony, Misdemeanor, Civil, Eviction, Small Claims, Probate, Traffic.*

Civil Records: Access: Mail, in person, online. Both court and visitors may perform in person searches. Search fee: $5.00 per name. Fee is per case. Add $5.00 if search includes microfilm records. Court makes copy: $.75 per page. Self serve copy fee: $.25 per page. Required to search: name, years to search; also helpful: DOB. Civil cases indexed by defendant, plaintiff. Civil records on computer from 1985, microfiche from 1975, index books from 1963-1974, archived prior to 1963. Civil records online access at www.cocourts.com. Mail turnaround time 1 week.

Criminal Records: Access: Mail, in person, online. Both court and visitors may perform in person searches. Search fee: $5.00 per name. Fee varies depending on number of years searched. Add $5.00 if search includes microfilm records. Court makes copy: $.75 per page. Self serve copy fee: $.25 per page. Required to search: name, years to search, DOB; also helpful: address. Criminal records on computer from 1985, microfiche from 1975, index books from 1963-1974, archived prior to 1963. Access criminal records at www.cocourts.com. Mail turnaround time 1 week.

General Information: No public access terminal. No adoptions, sealed, juvenile, mental health or expunged cases released. Will not fax documents. Certification fee: $10.00 per document. Payee: Clerk of Combined Courts. Personal checks accepted. Prepayment and SASE required.

Kiowa County

15th District & County Courts PO Box 353, Eads, CO 81036; phone: 719-438-5558; fax: 719-438-5300; hours 9AM-4PM (MST). *Felony, Misdemeanor, Civil, Eviction, Small Claims, Probate.*

www.courts.state.co.us/district/15th/15dist.html
Civil Records: Access: Phone, fax, mail, in person, online. Only the court performs in person searches. Search fee: $5.00 per name. Court makes copy: $.75 per page. Required to search: name, years to search. Civil cases indexed by defendant, plaintiff. Civil records on index cards from the 1960s, index books from 1889. Recent records are computerized. Civil records online access at www.cocourts.com. Mail turnaround time 1 week.

Criminal Records: Access: Phone, fax, mail, in person, online. Only the court performs in person searches. Search fee: $5.00 per name. Court makes copy: $.75 per page. Required to search: name, years to search, DOB. Criminal records on index cards from the 1960s, index books from 1889. Recent records are computerized. Access criminal records at www.cocourts.com. Mail turnaround time 1 week.

General Information: No public access terminal. No adoptions, sealed, juvenile, mental health or expunged cases released. Will fax documents $1.00 per doc. Certification fee: $10.00 per doc. Payee: Kiowa County Court. Business checks accepted. Prepayment and SASE required.

Kit Carson County

Kit Carson Combined Court 251 16th St, #301, Burlington, CO 80807; phone: 719-346-5524; fax: 719-346-7805; hours 8AM-4PM (MST). *Felony, Misdemeanor, Civil, Eviction, Small Claims, Probate.*

www.courts.state.co.us/district/13th/13dist.htm
Civil Records: Access: Mail, in person, online. Only the court performs in person searches. Search fee: $5.00 per name. Court makes copy: $.75 per page. Required to search: name, years to search. Civil cases

indexed by defendant, plaintiff. Civil records on index cards from 1910, index books from 1889. Civil records online access at www.cocourts.com. Mail turnaround time 1 week.

Criminal Records: Access: Mail, in person, online. Only the court performs in person searches. Search fee: $5.00 per name. Court makes copy: $.75 per page. Required to search: name, years to search, DOB. Criminal records on index cards from 1910, index books from 1889. Access criminal records at www.cocourts.com. Mail turnaround time 1 week.

General Information: No adoptions, sealed, juvenile, mental health or expunged cases released. Will fax documents $5.00 per doc. Certification fee: $10.00. Payee: Combined Courts. No personal checks accepted. Prepayment and SASE required.

La Plata County

La Plata Combined Courts 1060 E 2nd Ave, Durango, CO 81301; phone: 970-247-2304; criminal fax: 970-247-4348; civil records fax: 970-259-0258; hours 8AM-4PM (MST). *Felony, Misdemeanor, Civil, Small Claims, Probate.*
Note: Fax for civil section is 970-259-0258.

Civil Records: Access: Mail, in person, online. Only the court performs in person searches. Search fee: $5.00 per name. Fee is per case and can be as much as $20.00. Court makes copy: $.75 per page. Required to search: name, years to search. Civil cases indexed by defendant, plaintiff. Civil records on computer from 1990, index cards from 1976, index books from 1874. Civil records online access at www.cocourts.com. Mail turnaround time 3-7 days.

Criminal Records: Access: Mail, in person, online. Only the court performs in person searches. Search fee: $5.00 per name. Fee is per case and can be as much as $20.00. Court makes copy: $.75 per page. Required to search: name, years to search, DOB. Criminal records on computer from 1990, index cards from 1976, index books from 1874. Access criminal records at www.cocourts.com. Mail turnaround time 3-7 days.

General Information: No public access terminal. No adoptions, sealed, juvenile, mental health or expunged cases released. Fee to fax documents is $3.00 per document. Certification fee: $15.00. Payee: Clerk of the Combined Courts. Personal checks accepted. Prepayment and SASE required.

Lake County

Lake County Combined Courts PO Box 55, Leadville, CO 80461; phone: 719-486-0535; hours 8AM-N, 1-4PM (MST). *Felony, Misdemeanor, Civil, Eviction, Small Claims, Probate.*

Civil Records: Access: Mail, in person, online. Only the court performs in person searches. Search fee: $20.00 per name. Court makes copy: $.75 per page. Required to search: name, years to search. Civil cases indexed by defendant, plaintiff. Civil records on index cards from 1988 (District), 1970 (County), index books from 1865. Civil records online access at www.cocourts.com. Mail turnaround time 7 days.

Criminal Records: Access: Mail, in person, online. Only the court performs in person searches. Search fee: $20.00 per name. Court makes copy: $.75 per page. Required to search: name, years to search, DOB. Criminal records on index cards from 1988 (District), 1970 (County), index books from 1865. Access criminal records at www.cocourts.com. Mail turnaround time 7 days.

General Information: No public access terminal. No adoptions, sealed, juvenile, mental health or expunged cases released. Certification fee: $10.00 per cert. Payee: Lake County Court. Business checks accepted. Prepayment and SASE required.

Larimer County

8th District Court 201 La Porte Ave, #100, Ft Collins, CO 80521; phone: 970-498-6100; probate phone: 970-498-6111; fax: 970-498-6110; hours 8AM-4PM (MST). *Felony, Civil Actions Over $10,000, Probate.*

www.courts.state.co.us/district/08th/08dist.htm
Civil Records: Access: Phone, mail, in person, online. Both court and visitors may perform in person searches. Search fee: $5.00 per name. Court makes copy: $.75 per page. Self serve copy fee: $.25 per page. Required to search: name; also helpful: years to search. Civil cases indexed by defendant, plaintiff. Civil records on computer from 1976, index books back to 1861. Civil records online access at www.cocourts.com. Mail turnaround time 1-2 weeks.

Criminal Records: Access: Mail, in person, online. Only the court performs in person searches. Search fee: $5.00 per name. Court makes copy: $.75 per page. Self serve copy fee: $.25 per page. Required to search: name; also helpful: years to search, DOB, SSN. Criminal records on computer from 1976, index books back to 1861. Access criminal records at www.cocourts.com. Mail turnaround time 7-10 days.

General Information: No public access terminal. No adoptions, sealed, juvenile, mental health or expunged cases released. Certification fee: $10.00. Payee: Clerk of District Court. Personal checks accepted. Prepayment and SASE required.

County Court 201 La Porte Ave, #100, Ft Collins, CO 80521; phone: 970-498-6100; fax: 970-498-6110; hours 8AM-4PM (MST). *Misdemeanor, Civil Actions Under $15,000, Eviction, Small Claims.*

www.courts.state.co.us/district/08th/08dist.htm
Civil Records: Access: Mail, in person, online. Both court and visitors may perform in person searches. Search fee: $5.00 per name. Court makes copy: $.75 per page. Self serve copy fee: $.25 per page. Required to search: name, years to search; also helpful: address. Civil cases indexed by defendant, plaintiff. Some records on computer from 1986, index cards from 1965. Civil records online access at www.cocourts.com. Mail turnaround time 1-2 weeks.

Criminal Records: Access: Mail, in person, online. Both court and visitors may perform in person searches. Search fee: $5.00 per name. Court makes copy: $.75 per page. Self serve copy fee: $.25 per page. Required to search: name, years to search, DOB, signed release, offense; also helpful: address. Some records on computer from 1986, index cards from 1965. Access criminal records at www.cocourts.com. Mail turnaround time 1-2 weeks.

General Information: No public access terminal. No sealed cases released. Certification fee: $10.00. Payee: Larimer County Combined Court. Personal checks accepted. Prepayment and SASE required.

Las Animas County

3rd District Court 200 E 1st St, Rm 304, Trinidad, CO 81082; phone: 719-846-3316/2221; probate phone: 719-846-3316; fax: 719-846-9367; hours 8AM-4PM (MST). *Felony, Misdemeanor, Civil, Eviction, Small Claims, Probate.*

www.courts.state.co.us/district/03rd/03dist.htm
Civil Records: Access: Mail, in person, online. Both court and visitors may perform in person searches. Search fee: $5.00 per name. Court makes copy: $.75 per page. Required to search: name, years to search. Civil cases indexed by defendant, plaintiff. Civil records on index cards from 1976, index books to 1950. Civil records online access at www.cocourts.com. Mail turnaround time 1 week.

Criminal Records: Access: Mail, in person, online. Both court and visitors may perform in person searches. Search fee: $5.00 per name. Court makes copy: $.75 per page. Required to search: name, years to search, DOB; also helpful: SSN. Criminal records on index cards from 1976, index books to 1950. Access criminal records at www.cocourts.com. Mail turnaround time 1 week.

General Information: No public access terminal. No adoptions, sealed, juvenile, mental health or expunged cases released. Fee to fax documents is $2.00 per page. Certification fee: $10.00. Payee:

Combined Courts. Only cashiers checks and money orders accepted. Prepayment and SASE required.

Lincoln County

18th District & County Courts PO Box 128, Hugo, CO 80821; phone: 719-743-2455; hours 8AM-5PM (MST). *Felony, Misdemeanor, Civil, Eviction, Small Claims, Probate.*
www.courts.state.co.us/district/18th/18dist.htm
Civil Records: Access: Phone, mail, in person, online. Only the court performs in person searches. Search fee: $5.00. Court makes copy: $.75 per page. Required to search: name, years to search. Civil cases indexed by defendant, plaintiff. Civil records on computer since 12/94, index cards from 1977, index books back to 1889, archived 10 years back. Civil records online access at www.cocourts.com. Mail turnaround time within 10 days.
Criminal Records: Access: Phone, mail, in person, online. Only the court performs in person searches. Search fee: $5.00. Court makes copy: $.75 per page. Required to search: name, years to search, DOB. Criminal records on computer since 12/94, index cards from 1977, index books to 1889, archived 10 years. Access records at www.cocourts.com. Mail turnaround within 10 days.
General Information: No public access terminal. No adoptions, sealed, juvenile, mental health or expunged cases released. Will not fax documents. Certification fee: $10.00 per document. Payee: Lincoln County Combined Courts. Personal checks accepted. Prepayment and SASE required.

Logan County

13th District Court 110 N Riverview Rd, Rm 205, Sterling, CO 80751; phone: 970-522-6565; fax: 970-522-6566; hours 8AM-4PM (MST). *Felony, Civil Actions Over $10,000, Probate.*
www.courts.state.co.us/district/13th/13dist.htm
Civil Records: Access: Mail, in person, online. Only the court performs in person searches. Search fee: $5.00 per name. Court makes copy: $.75 per page. Required to search: name, years to search. Civil cases indexed by defendant, plaintiff. Civil records computerized since 8/95, on index cards from 1973, index books back to 1887. Civil records online access at www.cocourts.com. Mail turnaround time 1 week.
Criminal Records: Access: Mail, in person, online. Only the court performs in person searches. Search fee: $5.00 per name. Court makes copy: $.75 per page. Required to search: name, years to search, DOB. Criminal records computerized since 8/95, on index cards from 1973, index books back to 1887. Access criminal records at www.cocourts.com. Mail turnaround time 1 week.
General Information: No adoptions, sealed, juvenile, mental health or expunged cases released. Fee to fax documents is $1.00 per page local; $2.00 per page long distance. Certification fee: $10.00 per doc. Payee: Logan District Court. Personal checks accepted. Prepayment and SASE required.

County Court 110 N Riverview Rd, Rm 210, Sterling, CO 80751; phone: 970-522-1572; fax: 970-526-5359; hours 8AM-4PM (MST). *Misdemeanor, Civil Actions Under $15,000, Eviction, Small Claims.*
www.courts.state.co.us/district/counties.htm
Civil Records: Access: Phone, mail, in person, online. Both court and visitors may perform in person searches. Search fee: $5.00 per name. Court makes copy: $.75 per page. Required to search: name, years to search. Civil cases indexed by defendant, plaintiff. Civil records on computer since 8/95; prior on index cards from 1972 and index books from 1965. Civil records online access at www.cocourts.com.
Criminal Records: Access: In person, online. Both court and visitors may perform in person searches. Search fee: $5.00 per name. Court makes copy: $.75 per page. Required to search: name, years to search, DOB. Criminal records on computer since 8/95; prior

on index cards from 1972 and index books from 1965. Access criminal records at www.cocourts.com.
General Information: No public access terminal. No adoptions, sealed, juvenile, mental health or expunged cases released. Will fax documents for $2.00 per document. Certification fee: $10.00 per document. Payee: Logan County Court. Business checks accepted. Prepayment required.

Mesa County

Mesa County Combined Court Mesa County District Court, PO Box 20000-5030, Grand Junction, CO 81502; phone: 970-257-3625; criminal phone: 970-257-3640; civil phone: 970-257-3640; probate phone: 970-257-3640; hours 8AM-4PM (MST). *Felony, Civil Actions Over $10,000, Probate.*
Civil Records: Access: Phone, mail, in person, online. Only the court performs in person searches. Search fee: $5.00 per name. Court makes copy: $.75 per page. Required to search: name, years to search. Civil cases indexed by defendant, plaintiff. Civil records on computer since 1989, on microfiche to 1970s. Civil records online access at www.cocourts.com. Mail turnaround time 7-10 days up to 2 weeks.
Criminal Records: Access: Mail, in person, online. Only the court performs in person searches. Search fee: $5.00 per name. Court makes copy: $.75 per page. Required to search: name, years to search, DOB. Criminal records on computer since 1989, on microfiche to 1970s. Access criminal records at www.cocourts.com. Mail turnaround time 7-10 days up to 2 weeks.
General Information: No public access terminal. No adoptions, sealed, juvenile, mental health or expunged cases released. Will not fax documents. Certification fee: $10.00 per document. Payee: Mesa County Combined Court. Business checks or Visa, MC accepted. Prepayment and SASE required.

Mineral County

12th District & County Courts PO Box 337, Creede, CO 81130; phone: 719-658-2575; fax: 719-658-2575; hours 8AM-12;00-1-3PM (MST). *Felony, Misdemeanor, Civil, Eviction, Small Claims, Probate.*
Civil Records: Access: Mail, in person, online. Only the court performs in person searches. Search fee: $5.00 per name. Court makes copy: $.75 per page. Required to search: name, years to search. Civil cases indexed by defendant, plaintiff. Civil records on computer since 7/1993, on index cards from 1977, index books back to 1893. Civil records online access at www.cocourts.com. Mail turnaround time 2-3 days.
Criminal Records: Access: Mail, in person, online. Only the court performs in person searches. Search fee: $5.00 per name. Court makes copy: $.75 per page. Required to search: name, years to search, DOB. Criminal records on computer since 7/1993, on index cards from 1977, index books back to 1893. Access criminal records at www.cocourts.com. Mail turnaround time 2-3 days.
General Information: No public access terminal. No adoptions, sealed, juvenile, mental health or expunged cases released. Certification fee: $10.00 per doc. Payee: Mineral Combined Courts. Personal checks accepted. Prepayment and SASE required.

Moffat County

Moffat County Combined Court 221 W Victory Wy, #300, Craig, CO 81625; phone: 970-824-8254; hours 8AM-4PM (MST). *Felony, Misdemeanor, Civil, Eviction, Small Claims, Probate.*
Civil Records: Access: Phone, mail, in person, online. Only the court performs in person searches. Search fee: $5.00 for records 1976-91; $20.00 prior to 1976. Court makes copy: $.75 per page. Required to search: name, years to search. Civil cases indexed by defendant, plaintiff. Civil records on computer from 1992, index cards from 1976, either microfilmed or

archived back to 1911. Access records at www.cocourts.com. Mail turnaround time 1-2 weeks.
Criminal Records: Access: Mail, in person, online. Only the court performs in person searches. Search fee: $5.00 1976-1991; $20.00 prior to 1976. Court makes copy: $.75 per page. Required to search: name, years to search, DOB. Criminal records on computer from 1992, index cards from 1976, either microfilmed or archived back to 1911. Access to criminal records at www.cocourts.com. Mail turnaround 1-2 weeks.
General Information: No adoptions, sealed, juvenile, mental health or expunged cases released. Certification fee: $10.00 per document. Payee: Moffat County Combined Courts. Personal checks accepted. Prepayment and SASE required.

Montezuma County

22nd District Court 109 W Main St, #210, Cortez, CO 81321; phone: 970-565-1111; hours 8AM-4PM (MST). *Felony, Civil Actions Over $15,000, Probate.*
www.courts.state.co.us/district/22nd/22distindex.htm
Note: Fax requests must be pre-approved.
Civil Records: Access: Phone, mail, in person, online. Only the court performs in person searches. Search fee: $5.00 per name or case number, or $20.00 per hour to search. Court makes copy: $.75 per page. Required to search: name, years to search. Civil cases indexed by defendant, plaintiff. Civil records on computer back to 6/95, microfiche up to 1988, index cards from 1975, index books back to late 1890s. Civil records online access at www.cocourts.com. Mail turnaround time 1-2 weeks.
Criminal Records: Access: Mail, in person, online. Only the court performs in person searches. Search fee: $5.00 per name or case number, or $20.00 per hour to search. Court makes copy: $.75 per page. Required to search: name, years to search, DOB. Criminal records on computer back to 6/95, microfiche up to 1988, index cards from 1975, index books back to late 1890s. Access criminal records at www.cocourts.com. Mail turnaround 1-2 weeks.
General Information: No public access terminal. No adoptions, sealed, juvenile, mental health or expunged cases released. Will not fax documents. Certification fee: $10.00. Payee: Montezuma District Court. Personal checks accepted. Prepayment required. Will bill mailing and copy costs. SASE required.

County Court 601 N Mildred Rd, Cortez, CO 81321; phone: 970-565-7580; fax: 970-565-8798; hours 8AM-4PM (MST). *Misdemeanor, Civil Actions Under $15,000, Eviction, Small Claims.*
www.courts.state.co.us/district/22nd/22distindex.htm
Civil Records: Access: Mail, in person, online. Only the court performs in person searches. Search fee: $5.00. Court makes copy: $.75 per page. Required to search: name, years to search. Civil cases indexed by defendant, plaintiff. Civil records on computer since 1993. Civil records online access at www.cocourts.com. Mail turnaround 20-30 days.
Criminal Records: Access: Mail, in person, online. Only the court performs in person searches. Search fee: $5.00. Court makes copy: $.75 per page. Required to search: name, years to search, DOB. Criminal records on index cards from 1975, index books prior. Access criminal records at www.cocourts.com. Mail turnaround time 5-7 days.
General Information: No adoptions, sealed, juvenile, mental health or expunged cases released. Will not fax documents. Certification fee: $10.00. Payee: Montezuma County Court. Personal checks accepted. Prepayment and SASE required.

Montrose County

7th District & County Courts 1200 N Grand Ave, Bin B, Montrose, CO 81401-3164; phone: 970-252-4305; fax: 970-252-4345; hours 9AM-4PM (MST). *Felony, Misdemeanor, Civil, Eviction, Small Claims, Probate.*

www.courts.state.co.us/district/07th/dist07.htm

Civil Records: Access: Mail, in person, online. Search fee: $5.00 per name. Court makes copy: $.75 per page. Required to search: name, years to search. Civil cases indexed by defendant, plaintiff. Civil records on index cards from 1975, index books back to 1890. Civil records online access at www.cocourts.com. Also, weekly dockets for the 7th district county courts only are at www.7thjudicialdistrictco.org/docket.html. Mail turnaround time 10 days.

Criminal Records: Access: Mail, in person, online, fax. Only the court performs in person searches. Search fee: $5.00 per name. Court makes copy: $.75 per page. Required to search: name, years to search, DOB. Criminal records on index cards from 1975, index books back to 1890. Access criminal records at www.cocourts.com. Also, County Court weekly dockets are available, see civil, above. Mail turnaround time 10 days.

General Information: No public access terminal. No adoptions, sealed, juvenile, mental health or expunged cases released. Certification fee: $10.00 per doc. Payee: Montrose Combined Courts. Personal checks accepted. Prepayment and SASE required.

Morgan County

13th District Court PO Box 130, Ft Morgan, CO 80701; phone: 970-542-3435; fax: 970-542-3436; hours 8AM-4PM (MST). *Felony, Civil Actions Over $10,000, Probate.*
www.courts.state.co.us/district/13th/13dist.htm

Civil Records: Access: Fax, mail, in person, online. Only the court performs in person searches. Search fee: $5.00. Court makes copy: $.75 per page. Required to search: name, years to search. Civil cases indexed by defendant, plaintiff. Civil records on index cards from 1967, index books back to 1906; computerized since 8/95. Civil records online access at www.cocourts.com. Mail turnaround time 1 week.

Criminal Records: Access: Fax, mail, in person, online. Only the court performs in person searches. Search fee: $5.00. Court makes copy: $.75 per page. Required to search: name, years to search, DOB, SSN; also helpful: signed release. Criminal records on index cards from 1967, index books back to 1906, computerized since 8/95. Access criminal records at www.cocourts.com. Mail turnaround time 1 week.

General Information: No public access terminal. No adoptions, sealed, juvenile, mental health or expunged cases released. Will fax documents if less than 5 pages for $1.00 per page if local or toll-free call. Certification fee: $10.00. Payee: Morgan District Court. Personal checks accepted. Prepayment required. Will bill copy fees to attorneys. Mail requests: Written request and SASE required.

County Court PO Box 695, Ft Morgan, CO 80701; phone: 970-542-3414; fax: 970-542-3416; hours 8AM-4PM (MST). *Misdemeanor, Civil Actions Under $15,000, Eviction, Small Claims, Traffic.*
www.courts.state.co.us/district/13th/13dist.htm

Civil Records: Access: Mail, in person, online. Only the court performs in person searches. Search fee: $5.00 per name. Court makes copy: $.75 per page. Required to search: name, years to search. Civil cases indexed by defendant, plaintiff. Civil records on computer since 8/95; prior on index cards from 1980. Civil records online access at www.cocourts.com. Mail turnaround time 7 days.

Criminal Records: Access: Mail, in person, online. Only the court performs in person searches. Search fee: $5.00 per name. Court makes copy: $.75 per page. Required to search: name, years to search, DOB. Criminal records on computer since 8/95; prior on index cards from 1980. Access criminal records at www.cocourts.com. Mail turnaround time 7 days.

General Information: No public access terminal. Certification fee: $10.00 per document includes

copies. Payee: Morgan County Court. Personal checks accepted. Prepayment required.

Otero County

Otero County Combined Courts Courthouse, Rm 207, 13 W 3rd St, La Junta, CO 81050; phone: 719-384-4951; criminal fax: 719-384-4991; same fax for civil and probate; hours 8AM-5PM (MST). *Felony, Civil, Probate.*
www.courts.state.co.us/district/16th/16dist.htm

Note: While this court has been "combined" with the County Court, there are separate offices and record databases. Probate is also a separate index.

Civil Records: Access: Mail, in person, online. Only the court performs in person searches. Search fee: $5.00 per name. Court makes copy: $.75 per page. Self serve copy fee: $.75 per page. Required to search: name, years to search. Civil cases indexed by defendant, plaintiff. Civil records on index cards from 1978, index books back to 1889, microfiche from 1889-1992. Civil records online access at www.cocourts.com. Mail turnaround time 10 days.

Criminal Records: Access: Mail, in person, online. Only the court performs in person searches. Search fee: $5.00 per name. Court makes copy: $.75 per page. Self serve copy fee: $.75 per page. Required to search: name, years to search, DOB. Criminal records on index cards from 1978, index books back to 1889, microfiche from 1889-1992. Access criminal records at www.cocourts.com. Mail turnaround time 10 days.

General Information: No adoptions, sealed, juvenile, mental health or expunged cases released. Will fax documents for $1.00 per page. Certification fee: $10.00 per document. Payee: Otero County Combined Courts. Personal checks accepted. Prepayment and SASE required.

Ouray County

7th District & County Courts PO Box 643, Ouray, CO 81427; phone: 970-325-4405; criminal fax: 970-325-7364; same fax for civil and probate; hours 8:30AM-N, 1-4PM M-Th; Closed Fri (MST). *Felony, Misdemeanor, Civil, Eviction, Small Claims, Probate.*
www.courts.state.co.us/district/07th/dist07.htm

Civil Records: Access: Mail, in person, online. Only the court performs in person searches. Search fee: $5.00 per name. Court makes copy: $.75 per page. Self serve copy fee: $.25 per page. Required to search: name, years to search. Civil cases indexed by defendant, plaintiff. Civil records on computer since 1994, index cards from 1976, index books back to 1876, archived prior to 1925. Civil records online access at www.cocourts.com. Mail turnaround time 1 week.

Criminal Records: Access: Mail, in person, online. Only the court performs in person searches. Search fee: $5.00 per name. Court makes copy: $.75 per page. Self serve copy fee: $.25 per page. Required to search: name, years to search, DOB. Criminal records on computer since 1994, index cards from 1976, index books back to 1876, archived prior to 1925. Access criminal records at www.cocourts.com. Mail turnaround time 1 week.

General Information: No adoptions, sealed, juvenile, financial, drug-alcohol evaluations, or mental health cases released. Fee to fax documents is $1.00 per page. Certification fee: $10.00. Payee: Ouray Combined Courts. Personal checks accepted. Prepayment required. SASE requested.

Park County

Park County Combined Courts PO Box 190, Fairplay, CO 80440; phone: 719-836-2940; fax: 719-836-2892; hours 8AM-5PM (MST). *Felony, Misdemeanor, Civil, Eviction, Small Claims, Probate.*
www.courts.state.co.us/district/11th/dist11.htm

Civil Records: Access: Mail, in person, online. Only the court performs in person searches. Search fee: $5.00 per name. Court makes copy: $.75 per page.

Required to search: name, years to search. Civil cases indexed by defendant, plaintiff. Civil records computerized since 1995, on index cards from 1978, index books back to 1950, archived prior to 1950. Civil records online access at www.cocourts.com. Mail turnaround time within 1 week.

Criminal Records: Access: Mail, in person, online. Only the court performs in person searches. Search fee: $5.00 per name. Court makes copy: $.75 per page. Required to search: name, years to search, DOB, signed release. Criminal records computerized since 1995, on index cards from 1978, index books back to 1950, archived prior to 1950. Access criminal records at www.cocourts.com. Mail turnaround time within 1 week.

General Information: No public access terminal. No adoptions, sealed, juvenile, mental health or expunged cases released. Fee to fax documents is $1.00 per page. Certification fee: $10.00. Payee: Park County Combined Court. Personal checks accepted. Prepayment and SASE required.

Phillips County

13th District & County Courts 221 S Interocean, Holyoke, CO 80734; phone: 970-854-3279; fax: 970-854-3179; hours 8AM-1PM (MST). *Felony, Misdemeanor, Civil, Eviction, Small Claims, Probate.*
www.courts.state.co.us/district/13th/13dist.htm

Civil Records: Access: Phone, fax, mail, in person, online. Only the court performs in person searches. No search fee. Court makes copy: $.75 per page. Required to search: name, years to search. Civil cases indexed by defendant, plaintiff. Civil records on computer since 1995; records go back to 1880. Civil records online access at www.cocourts.com. Mail turnaround time 1-3 days.

Criminal Records: Access: Phone, fax, mail, in person, online. Only the court performs in person searches. No search fee. Court makes copy: $.75 per page. Required to search: name, years to search, DOB. Criminal records on computer since 1995; records go back to 1880. Access criminal records at www.cocourts.com. Mail turnaround time 1-3 days.

General Information: No public access terminal. No adoptions, sealed, juvenile, mental health or expunged cases released. Certification fee: $10.00 per document. Payee: Phillips County Combined Court. Personal checks accepted. Prepayment and SASE required.

Pitkin County

9th District & County Courts 506 E Main St, #300, Aspen, CO 81611; phone: 970-925-7635; fax: 970-925-6349; hours 8AM-N, 1-5PM (MST). *Felony, Misdemeanor, Civil, Eviction, Small Claims, Probate.*
www.courts.state.co.us/district/09th/dist09.htm

Civil Records: Access: Phone, mail, fax, in person, online, email. Both court and visitors may perform in person searches. Search fee: No fee for computer search. Court makes copy: $.75 per page. Required to search: name, years to search. Civil cases indexed by defendant. Civil records on computer back to 1990, microfiche from 1940-1970, index cards from 1975. Civil records online access at www.cocourts.com. Search probate 1881-1953 at www.colorado.gov/dpa/doit/archives/probate/pitkin_probate.htm Mail turnaround time 1 week.

Criminal Records: Access: Mail, fax, in person, online. Both court and visitors may perform in person searches. Search fee: There is no fee for searching computer, otherwise rate determined by time and volume. Court makes copy: $.75 per page. Required to search: name, years to search, DOB, SSN. Criminal records on computer back to 1990, microfiche from 1940-1970, index cards from 1975. Access criminal records at www.cocourts.com. Mail turnaround time 1 week.

General Information: No public access terminal. No adoptions, sealed, juvenile, mental health or expunged cases released. Fee to fax documents is

$1.00 per page. Certification fee: $10.00 per doc. Payee: Pitkin County Combined Court. Only cashiers checks and money orders accepted. Visa, MC accepted. Prepayment required.

Prowers County

15th District Court 301 S Main St, #300, Lamar, CO 81052-2834; phone: 719-336-7424; fax: 719-336-9757; hours 8AM-5PM (MST). *Felony, Civil Actions Over $10,000, Probate.*
www.courts.state.co.us/district/15th/15dist.htm
Civil Records: Access: Fax, mail, in person, online. Only the court performs in person searches. Search fee: $5.00. Court makes copy: $.75 per page. Required to search: name, years to search. Civil cases indexed by defendant, plaintiff. Civil records computerized since 1995, on microfiche from 1920, index books from the late 1800s. Civil records online access at www.cocourts.com. Mail turnaround time 1 week.
Criminal Records: Access: Fax, mail, in person, online. Only the court performs in person searches. Search fee: $5.00. Court makes copy: $.75 per page. Required to search: name, years to search, DOB. Criminal records computerized since 1995, on microfiche from 1920, index books from the late 1800s. Access criminal records at www.cocourts.com. Mail turnaround time 1 week.
General Information: No adoptions, sealed, juvenile, mental health or expunged cases released. Will fax documents $1.00 per page. Certification fee: $10.00 per doc. Payee: Clerk of District Court. Only cashiers checks and money orders accepted. Prepayment and SASE required.

County Court 301 S Main St, #100, Lamar, CO 81052-2634; phone: 719-336-7416; fax: 719-336-4145; hours 8AM-Noon; 1-5PM (MST). *Misdemeanor, Civil Actions Under $15,000, Eviction, Small Claims.*
www.courts.state.co.us/district/15th/15dist.htm
Civil Records: Access: Mail, phone, in person, online. Only the court performs in person searches. No search fee. Court makes copy: $.75 per page. Required to search: name, years to search. Civil cases indexed by defendant, plaintiff. Civil records on computer since 10/95, prior on books to 1965. Civil records online access at www.cocourts.com. Mail turnaround time 7-14 days.
Criminal Records: Access: Mail, in person, online, fax. Only the court performs in person searches. Search fee: $5.00 per name-1st. 5 names. Court makes copy: $.75 per page. Required to search: name, years to search; also helpful: DOB. Criminal records on computer since 10/95, prior on books to 1965. Access criminal records at www.cocourts.com. Mail turnaround time 7-14 days.
General Information: No public access terminal. No adoptions, sealed, juvenile, mental health or expunged cases released. Certification fee: $10.00 per doc. Payee: Prowers County Court. Only cashiers checks and money orders accepted. Prepayment and SASE required.

Pueblo County

Combined Courts 320 W 10th St, Pueblo, CO 81003; phone: 719-583-7000; civil phone: 719-583-7026; probate phone: 719-583-7030; fax: 719-583-7184; hours 8AM-4PM (MST). *Felony, Misdemeanor, Civil, Eviction, Small Claims, Probate.*
www.courts.state.co.us/district/10th/10dist.htm
Civil Records: Access: Mail, in person, online. Only the court performs in person searches. Search fee: $5.00 per name. Court makes copy: $.75 per page. Required to search: name, years to search; also helpful: address. Civil cases indexed by defendant, plaintiff. Civil records on computer from 1976, index books back to the 1890s. Civil records online access at www.cocourts.com. Mail turnaround time 3-5 days.
Criminal Records: Access: Mail, in person, online. Only the court performs in person searches. Search

fee: $5.00 per name. Court makes copy: $.75 per page. Required to search: name, years to search, DOB; also helpful: address. Criminal records on computer from 1976, index books back to the 1890s. Access criminal records at www.cocourts.com. Mail turnaround time 3-5 days.
General Information: No public access terminal. No adoptions, sealed, juvenile, mental health or expunged cases released. Will fax documents for $1.00 per page. Certification fee: $10.00 per doc. Payee: Clerk of Court. Personal checks accepted. Prepayment and SASE required.

Rio Blanco County

9th District & County Courts PO Box 1150, 555 Main St, Rm 303, Meeker, CO 81641; phone: 970-878-5622; fax: 970-878-4295; hours 8AM-N, 1-5PM (MST). *Felony, Misdemeanor, Civil, Eviction, Small Claims, Probate.*
www.courts.state.co.us/district/09th/dist09.htm
Note: You may fax in after agreeing to $1.00 per page fax fee.
Civil Records: Access: Phone, fax, mail, in person, online. Only the court performs in person searches. Search fee: $5.00 per name. May charge for lengthy in-person search request. Court makes copy: $.75 per page. Required to search: name; also helpful: years to search. Civil cases indexed by defendant, plaintiff. Civil records on computer since 8/1994, on index cards from 4/1976, index books back to 1889. Civil records online access at www.cocourts.com. Mail turnaround time 2 days.
Criminal Records: Access: Phone, fax, mail, in person, online. Only the court performs in person searches. Search fee: $5.00 per name. May charge for lengthy in-person search request. Court makes copy: $.75 per page. Required to search: name, years to search; also helpful: DOB. Criminal records on computer since 8/1994, on index cards from 4/1976, index books back to 1889. Access criminal records at www.cocourts.com. Mail turnaround time 2 days.
General Information: No public access terminal. No adoptions, sealed, juvenile, mental health or expunged cases released. Fee to fax documents is $1.00 per page. Certification fee: $10.00 per doc. Payee: Clerk of the Combined Courts. Business checks accepted. Prepayment and SASE required.

Rio Grande County

12th District & County Courts 6th & Cherry, PO Box 427, Del Norte, CO 81132; phone: 719-657-3394; hours 8AM-N, 1-4PM (MST). *Felony, Misdemeanor, Civil, Eviction, Small Claims, Probate.*
Civil Records: Access: Mail, in person, online. Only the court performs in person searches. Search fee: $5.00 per name, additional $25.00 to search archived records. Court makes copy: $.75 per page. Required to search: name, years to search. Civil cases indexed by defendant, plaintiff. Civil records on computer from 5/95, County on index cards from 1950s, District from 1977. All on index books from the 1800s. Online access to civil records 1995 to present is at www.cocourts.com. Mail turnaround time 2-4 days.
Criminal Records: Access: Mail, in person, online. Only the court performs in person searches. Search fee: $5.00 per name, additional $25.00 to search archived records. Court makes copy: $.75 per page. Required to search: name, DOB; also helpful: years to search. Criminal records on computer from 5/95, County on index cards from 1950s, District from 1977. All on index books from the 1800s. Access criminal records at www.cocourts.com. Mail turnaround time 2-4 days.
General Information: No public access terminal. No adoptions, sealed, juvenile, mental health or expunged cases released. Will fax documents for $1.00 per page. Certification fee: $10.00. Payee: Rio Grande Combined Court. Personal and business checks accepted. Prepayment and SASE required.

Routt County

Routt Combined Courts PO Box 773117, Steamboat Springs, CO 80477; phone: 970-879-5020; fax: 970-879-3531; hours 8AM12;00-1-4PM (MST). *Felony, Misdemeanor, Civil, Eviction, Small Claims, Probate.*
Civil Records: Access: Mail, in person, online. Both court and visitors may perform in person searches. Search fee: $5.00 for 1976-1991; prior to 1976 $20.00. There is no fee to search computer records. Court makes copy: $.75 per page. Required to search: name, years to search. Civil cases indexed by defendant. Civil records on computer back to 1994, on index cards from 1977, microfiche from 1/1977 to 12/1990, archived from 1877. Civil records online access at www.cocourts.com. Mail turnaround time 7-10 days.
Criminal Records: Access: Mail, in person, online. Both court and visitors may perform in person searches. Same fees as civil. Court makes copy: $.75 per page. Required to search: name, years to search, DOB, maiden name, aliases. Criminal records on computer back to 1994, on index cards from 1977, microfiche from 1/1977 to 12/1990, archived from 1877. Criminal records at www.cocourts.com. Mail turnaround time 7-10 days.
General Information: No public access terminal. No adoptions, sealed, juvenile, mental health or expunged cases released. Certification fee: $10.00 per doc. Payee: Routt Combined Court. Personal checks accepted. Visa/MC accepted. Prepayment and SASE required.

Saguache County

12th District & County Courts PO Box 197, 4th and Christy Sts, Saguache, CO 81149; phone: 719-655-2522; fax: 719-655-0109; hours 8AM-N, 1-4PM (MST). *Felony, Misdemeanor, Civil, Eviction, Small Claims, Probate.*
Civil Records: Access: Mail, in person, online. Only the court performs in person searches. Search fee: $5.00 per name. Court makes copy: $.75 per page. Required to search: name, years to search. Civil cases indexed by defendant, plaintiff. Civil records on computer since 6/94, on index cards from 1980s, index books back to 1866. Civil records online access at www.cocourts.com. Note: Civil records containing financial information are not available by mail. Mail turnaround time 7-10 days.
Criminal Records: Access: Mail, in person, online. Only the court performs in person searches. Search fee: $5.00 per name. Court makes copy: $.75 per page. Required to search: name, years to search, DOB. Criminal records on computer since 6/94, on index cards from 1980s, index books back to 1866. Access criminal records at www.cocourts.com. Note: Criminal record search at this office will reveal dispositions only, generally. Mail turnaround time 10-12 days.
General Information: No public access terminal. No adoptions, sealed, juvenile, mental health or expunged cases released. Certification fee: $10.00 per doc. Payee: Saguache Combined Courts. Personal checks accepted. Prepayment and SASE required.

San Juan County

6th District & County Courts PO Box 441, Silverton, CO 81433; phone: 970-387-5790; fax: 970-387-0295; hours 8AM-4PM T & Th, 8AM-N Wed (MST). *Felony, Misdemeanor, Civil, Eviction, Small Claims, Probate.*
Civil Records: Access: Phone, mail, in person, online. Only the court performs in person searches. Search fee: $20.00 per hour. Fee is for lengthy search. Court makes copy: $.75 per page. Required to search: name, years to search. Civil cases indexed by defendant, plaintiff. Civil records on computer since 1995; prior on index cards from 1975, index books back to 1876. Civil records online access at www.cocourts.com. Mail turnaround time 1 week.

Criminal Records: Access: Mail, in person, online. Only the court performs in person searches. Search fee: $8.00 per name. Court makes copy: $.75 per page. Required to search: name, years to search, DOB, signed release. Criminal records on computer since 1995; prior on index cards from 1975, index books back to 1876. Access criminal records at www.cocourts.com. Mail turnaround time 1 week.

General Information: No adoptions, sealed, juvenile, mental health, open domestic, probate or expunged cases released. Will fax documents to local or toll free line. Certification fee: $10.00 per doc. Payee: San Juan County Court. Business checks accepted. Prepayment and SASE required.

San Miguel County

7th District & County Courts PO Box 919, 305 W Colorado St, Telluride, CO 81435; phone: 970-728-3891; fax: 970-728-6216; hours 9AM-N, 1-4PM (MST). *Felony, Misdemeanor, Civil, Eviction, Small Claims, Probate.*
www.7thjudicialdistrictco.org
Civil Records: Access: Phone, mail, in person, online. Only the court performs in person searches. Search fee: $5.00 per name if after 1994. Court makes copy: $.75 per page. Required to search: name, years to search. Civil cases indexed by defendant, plaintiff. Civil records on index cards from 1970, index books back to 1861, archived back to 1880; on computer back to 1994. Civil records online access at www.cocourts.com. Note: Will do very limited phone searches back to 1994. Mail turnaround time 30 days.
Criminal Records: Access: Phone, mail, in person, online. Only the court performs in person searches. Search fee: $5.00 per name if after 1994. Court makes copy: $.75 per page. Required to search: name, years to search, DOB. Criminal records on index cards from 1970, index books back to 1861, archived back to 1880; on computer back to 1994. Access criminal records at www.cocourts.com. Note: Will do very limited phone searches back to 1994. Mail turnaround time 30 days.
General Information: No adoptions, sealed, juvenile, mental health or expunged cases released. Will fax documents if prepaid. Certification fee: $10.00 per doc. Payee: Combined Courts. Personal checks accepted. Prepayment and SASE required.

Sedgwick County

13th District & County Courts 3rd & Pine, Julesburg, CO 80737; phone: 970-474-3627; criminal fax: 970-474-2026; same fax for civil and probate; hours 8AM-1PM (MST). *Felony, Misdemeanor, Civil, Eviction, Small Claims, Probate.*
www.courts.state.co.us/district/13th/13dist.htm
Civil Records: Access: Fax, mail, in person, online. Both court and visitors may perform in person searches. Search fee: The court reserves the right to charge if an extensive search is required. Court makes copy: $.75 per page. Required to search: name; also helpful: years to search. Civil cases indexed by defendant, plaintiff, records on index cards from early 1970s, index books to 1889; on computer back to 8/1995. Civil records online access at www.cocourts.com. Mail turnaround 1-2 days.
Criminal Records: Access: Fax, mail, in person, online. Both court and visitors may perform in person searches. Search fee: The court reserves the right to charge if an extensive search is required. Court makes copy: $.75 per page. Required to search: name, DOB; also helpful: years to search. Criminal records on index cards from early 1970s, index books back to 1889; on computer back to 8/1995. Access criminal records at www.cocourts.com. Mail turnaround time 1-2 days.
General Information: No public access terminal. No adoptions, sealed, juvenile, mental health or expunged cases released. Fee to fax documents is $2.00 per document. Certification fee: $10.00 per doc.

Payee: Sedgwick County Combined Court. Personal checks accepted. Prepayment and SASE required.

Summit County

Summit Combined Courts PO Box 185, Breckenridge, CO 80424; phone: 970-453-2241 District; 970-453-2272 County; hours 8AM-N, 1-4PM (MST). *Felony, Misdemeanor, Civil, Eviction, Small Claims, Probate.*
www.courts.state.co.us
Note: District Court uses PO Box 269.
Civil Records: Access: In person, online. Visitors must perform in person searches themselves. Court makes copy: $.75 per page. Required to search: name. Civil cases indexed by defendant, plaintiff. Civil records on computer back to 1995, index cards from the early 1970s, index books back to 1861, archived from 1980 and prior. Civil records online access at www.cocourts.com. Records prior to 2003 in storage. Must request in writing and pay fee prior to court providing record.
Criminal Records: Access: In person, online. Visitors must perform in person searches themselves. Court makes copy: $.75 per page. Required to search: name, DOB, signed release. Criminal records name index on computer as of 9/95. Access criminal records at www.cocourts.com. Records prior to 2003 in storage. Must request in writing and pay fee prior to court providing record.
General Information: No public access terminal. No adoptions, sealed, juvenile, mental health or expunged cases released. Certification fee: $10.00. Only cashiers checks and money orders accepted. Cash accepted in person. Prepayment required.

Teller County

Teller Combined Courts PO Box 997, Cripple Creek, CO 80813; phone: 719-689-2574; hours 9AM-N; 1PM-4PM (MST). *Felony, Misdemeanor, Civil, Eviction, Small Claims, Probate.*
www.tellercountycourts.com
Civil Records: Access: Mail, in person, online. Only the court performs in person searches. Search fee: $5.00 per name. If not on computer, fee is $20.00 per hour. Court makes copy: $.75 per page. Required to search: name, years to search. Civil cases indexed by defendant, plaintiff. Civil records computerized back to 1988, on index cards from 1960, index books to 1899. Civil records access at www.cocourts.com. Also, a record request form is to download at https://33.securedata.net/gofourth/pub_data_req_form.htm. Mail turnaround time 5-7 days; 4-6 weeks if not computerized.
Criminal Records: Access: Mail, in person, online. Only the court performs in person searches. Search fee: $5.00 per name. If records not on computer, fee is $20.00 per hour. Court makes copy: $.75 per page. Required to search: name, years to search, DOB; also helpful: address, SSN. Criminal records computerized back to 1988, on index cards from 1960, index books back to 1899. Access criminal records at www.cocourts.com. Mail turnaround time 5-7 days; 4-6 weeks if not computerized.
General Information: No public access terminal. No adoptions, sealed, juvenile, mental health or expunged cases released. Will fax documents for $1.00 per page. Certification fee: $10.00. Payee: Teller County Combined Courts. Any form of payment is acceptable, including Visa/MC. Prepayment and SASE required.

Washington County

Washington County Combined Court PO Box 455 (26861 Hwy 34), Akron, CO 80720; phone: 970-345-2756; fax: 970-345-2829; hours 8AM-N, 1-5PM (MST). *Felony, Misdemeanor, Civil, Eviction, Small Claims, Probate.*
www.courts.state.co.us/district/13th/13dist.htm
Civil Records: Access: Phone, mail, in person, online. Only the court performs in person searches. No search fee. Court makes copy: $.75 per page; same fee for self serve. Required to search: name, years to

search. Civil cases indexed by defendant. Civil records on index cards from 1970, index books back to 1887; computerized since 1995. Civil records online access at www.cocourts.com. Mail turnaround time 2-3 days.
Criminal Records: Access: Phone, mail, in person, online. Only the court performs in person searches. No search fee. Court makes copy: $.75 per page; same fee for self serve. Required to search: name, years to search, DOB. Criminal records on index cards from 1970, index books to 1887; computerized since 1995. Access criminal records at www.cocourts.com. Mail turnaround time 2-3 days.
General Information: No public access terminal. No adoptions, sealed, juvenile, mental health or expunged cases released. Will fax documents. Certification fee: $10.00. Payee: Washington County Combined Court. Personal checks accepted. Prepayment and SASE required.

Weld County

19th District & County Courts PO Box 2038, Greeley, CO 80632; phone: 970-351-7300; probate phone: x5400; fax: 970-336-7245; hours 8AM-4PM closed at noon for 1 hour (MST). *Felony, Misdemeanor, Civil, Eviction, Small Claims, Probate.*
Note: Probate/water offices fax is 970-346-9136.
Civil Records: Access: Mail, in person, online. Only the court performs in person searches. Search fee: $10.00 per name. Court makes copy: $.75 per page. Required to search: name, years to search. Civil cases indexed by defendant, plaintiff. Civil records on computer from 1975 (District), 1990 (County), index cards from 1958, index books back to 1876. Civil records online access at www.cocourts.com. Fees involved. Mail turnaround time asap.
Criminal Records: Access: Mail, in person, online. Only the court performs in person searches. Search fee: $10.00 per name. Court makes copy: $.75 per page. Required to search: name, years to search; also helpful: DOB. Criminal records on computer from 1975 (District), 1990 (County), index cards from 1958, index books back to 1876. Access criminal records at www.cocourts.com. Fees involved. Mail turnaround time ASAP.
General Information: No adoptions, sealed, juvenile, mental health or expunged cases released. Certification fee: $20.00 per doc. Payee: Clerk of Combined Court. Personal checks accepted. Prepayment and SASE required.

Yuma County

13th District & County Courts PO Box 347, Wray, CO 80758; phone: 970-332-4118; fax: 970-332-4119; hours 8AM-4PM (MST). *Felony, Misdemeanor, Civil, Eviction, Small Claims, Probate.*
www.courts.state.co.us/district/13th/13dist.htm
Civil Records: Access: Mail, in person, online. Only the court performs in person searches. Search fee: $5.00 per name. Court makes copy: $.75 per page. Required to search: name, years to search. Civil cases indexed by defendant. Civil records on computer back to 3/1996; on index cards from 1982, index books back to 1889. Civil records online access at www.cocourts.com. Mail turnaround 2-5 days.
Criminal Records: Access: Mail, in person, online. Only the court performs in person searches. Search fee: $5.00 per name. Court makes copy: $.75 per page. Required to search: name. Criminal records on computer back to 3/1996; on index cards from 1982, index books back to 1889. Access criminal records at www.cocourts.com. Mail turnaround 2-5 days.
General Information: No adoptions, sealed, juvenile, mental health or expunged cases released. Will fax documents to local or toll free line. Certification fee: $10.00. Payee: Yuma County Combined Court. Personal checks accepted. Prepayment and SASE required.

Colorado Recording Offices

ORGANIZATION: 63 counties, 63 recording offices. The recording officer is County Clerk and Recorder. The entire state is in the Mountain Time Zone (MST).

November 15, 2001, Broomfield City and County comes into existence, derived from portions of Adams, Boulder, Jefferson and Weld counties. County offices are located at 1 Descombes Dr, Broomfield, CO 80020; 303-469-3301; hours 8AM-5PM. To determine if an address is in Broomfield, parcel search by address at www.co.broomfield.co.us/centralrecords/assessor.shtml

REAL ESTATE RECORDS: Counties do not perform real estate searches. Copy fees are usually $1.25 per page and certification fees are usually $1.00 per document. Tax records are located in Assessor's Office.

UCC RECORDS: Financing statements are filed at the state level, except for real estate related collateral, which are filed with the County Clerk & Recorder. However, prior to 07/2001, consumer goods and farm collateral were also filed at the County Clerk & Recorder and these older records can be searched there. Nearly all counties perform UCC searches. Use search request form UCC-11. Search fees are usually $5.00 per debtor name for the first year and $2.00 for each additional year searched (or $13.00 for a five year search). Copies usually cost $1.25 per page.

TAX LIEN RECORDS: Federal and some state tax liens on personal property are filed with the Secretary of State. Other federal and state tax liens are filed with the County Clerk and Recorder. Many counties will perform a tax lien search, usually the same fee as UCC search. Usually copies $1.25 per page.

OTHER LIENS: Judgments, motor vehicle, mechanics.

ONLINE ACCESS: Over 20 Colorado Counties offer free access to property assessor records. Also, the state archives provides limited inheritance tax records for 14 Colorado counties at www.colorado.gov/dpa/doit/archives/inh_tax/index.html; generally records extend forward only to the 1940s.

At the state level, the Secretary of State offers web access to UCCs, and the Department of Revenue offers trade name searches. See the State Agencies section for details.

Adams County

County Clerk & Recorder, 450 S. 4th Ave; Admin. Bldg., Brighton, CO 80601-3197. RE & UCC recording phone-303-654-6020; fax-303-654-6009; hours: 8AM-4:30PM www.co.adams.co.us
All records in one index. Office will perform a UCC search, which includes tax liens, but public must search other records themselves. Search fee $5.00 per name. Copy fee $1.25 per page. Cert fee- $1.00 per cert plus copy fee. Payee- Adams County Clerk and Recorder. **Online access to Assessor, Property records:** Records from the Adams County Assessor database are free at www.co.adams.co.us/gis/html/QuickSearchFSIE.htm. Also, search property information on the GIS mapping page for free at www.co.adams.co.us/gis/. **Other phones:** Treasurer- 303-654-6160; Elections- 303-920-7800; Vital Records- 303-654-6020. **Property tax/Assessor-** same address as above. 303-654-6038, assessor fax- 303-654-6037.

Alamosa County

County Clerk & Recorder, PO Box 630, Alamosa, CO 81101. 719-589-6681; fax-719-589-6118; hours: 8AM-4:30PM
All records in one index. Records indexed on a public use terminal back to 1984. Only the public may search. Copy fee $1.25 per page. Cert fee- $1.00 per page plus copy fee. Payee- Alamosa County Clerk and Recorder. **Other phones:** Treasurer- 719-589-3626; Elections- 719-589-6681; Vital Records- 719-589-6681. **Property tax/Assessor-** 719-589-6365, assessor fax- 719-589-6118.

Arapahoe County

County Clerk & Recorder, 5334 S. Prince St; Adminstration Bldg., Littleton, CO 80166-0060. 303-795-4520; R/E recording phone-303-795-4200; fax-303-794-4625; 7-4:30 www.co.arapahoe.co.us
Records indexed on a public use terminal back to 1979. Office personnel or visitors may perform searches. Will not search UCC records. Copy fee $1.25 per page. Cert fee- $1.00 per doc plus copy fee. Payee- Arapahoe County Clerk and Recorder.

Online access to Assessor, Property Tax, Real Estate, Deed, Judgment, Lien, Recording, Personal Property records: Access to the recorders database is free at www.co.arapahoe.co.us/OnlineTools/index.asp. **Other phones:** Treasurer- 303-795-4550; Appraiser/Auditor- 303-795-4611; Elections- 303-795-4511; Vital Records- 303-756-4464. **Property tax/Assessor-** 303-738-7949, assessor fax- 303-797-1295.

Archuleta County

County Clerk & Recorder, PO Box 2589, Pagosa Springs, CO 81147-2589. RE & UCC recording phone-970-264-8350; fax-970-264-8357; hours: 8AM-4PM http://archuletacounty.org/
All records in one index. Records indexed on computer 1985 to current; prior is a book search. Will not search real estate records. Will not search UCC records. Will do a federal tax lien search, but not state tax liens. Copy fee $1.25 per page. Cert fee- $1.00 per cert plus copy fee. Payee- Archuleta County Clerk and Recorder. **Online access to Sex Offender, Property records:** Search for property records at www.qpublic.net/co/archuleta/index.html for a fee. Also, search the sex offender site is free at www.archuletacounty.org/so/offenders/offenders/offender.htm. **Other phones:** Treasurer- 970-264-8325; Elections- 970-264-8350. **Property tax/Assessor-** PO Box 1089, Pagosa Springs, CO 81147; 970-264-8310, assessor fax- 970-264-8319.

Baca County

County Clerk & Recorder, 741 Main St; Courthouse, Springfield, CO 81073. RE & UCC recording phone-719-523-4372; fax-719-523-4881; hours: 8:30AM-4:30PM www.bacacounty.net
All records in one index. Only the public may search. Copy fee $1.25 per page. Cert fee- $.50 per cert plus copy fee. Payee- Baca County Clerk and Recorder. **Other phones:** Treasurer- 719-523-4262; Appraiser/Auditor- 719-523-4332; Elections- 719-523-4372; Vital Records- 719-523-6665. **Property tax/Assessor-** same address as above. 719-523-4332, assessor fax- 719-523-4735.

Bent County

County Clerk & Recorder, PO Box 350, Las Animas, CO 81054. RE & UCC recording phone-719-456-2009; fax-719-456-0375; hours: 8:30AM-4:30PM
Will not search real estate records. Will search UCC records, but not tax liens. UCC search per debtor name- $5.00. Copy fee $1.25 per page. Cert fee- $1.00 per cert plus copy fee. Payee- Bent County Clerk and Recorder. **Other phones:** Treasurer- 719-456-2211; Elections- 719-456-2009; Vital Records- 719-456-6042. **Property tax/Assessor-** 719-456-2010, assessor fax- 719-456-3108.

Boulder County

County Clerk & Recorder, 1750 33rd St #201, Boulder, CO 80301. 303-413-7770; hours: 8AM-5PM www.co.boulder.co.us/clerk
Index: Military records are the only index that are confidential. Records indexed on a public use terminal back to 1862. Only the public may search. Copy fee $1.25 per page. Cert fee- $1.00 per cert plus copy fee. Payee- Boulder County Clerk and Recorder. **Online access to Assessor, Property Tax, Voter Registration, Recording, Grantor/Grantee, Deed, Judgment, Lien, Most Wanted records:** Search the assessor's property database for free at www.co.boulder.co.us/assessor/disclaimer.htm. No name searching. Also, recorder data is on the iCris system at http://icris.co.boulder.co.us/splash.jsp. To search free, login as public, password public. Also, search free property tax records at www.co.boulder.co.us/treas/disclaim.htm. No name searching. Also, the county treasurer offers data electronically and on microfiche. Alpha index by owner name is $25.00 per set. Also, search voter registration at www.co.boulder.co.us/clerk/elections/promptforname.html. Name and DOB required. Search sheriff's most wanted at www.co.boulder.co.us/Sheriff/most_wanted/wanted.htm. **Other phones:** Treasurer- 303-441-3520; Elections- 303-413-7740. **Property tax/Assessor-** 303-441-3530, assessor fax- 303-441-4996.

Broomfield County

County/City Clerk & Recorder, One DesCombes Dr, Broomfield, CO 80020. 303-469-3301; fax-303-438-6252; hours: 8AM-5PM www.co.broomfield.co.us Became a county in 2001; further information is at website. Includes Zip Codes 80005, 80020, 80021, 80038, 80234. Only the public may search. Copy fee $1.25, if real estate $.50 per page. Cert fee- $1.00 per doc plus copy fee. Payee- City and County of Broomfield. **Online access to Real Estate, Assessor, Voter Registration records:** Access to the assessor property database is free at http://ims.ci.broomfield.co.us/website/htmlviewer/Parcelsearch/. Search by address or parcel ID only. Also, search property and tax assessment data for free at http://info.ci.broomfield.co.us/Tax/. No name searching. Also search voter registration records at www.ci.broomfield.co.us/election/voter_inquiry/. **Other phones:** ; Central Records, all departments- 303-464-5819. **Property tax/Assessor-** 303-464-5819, assessor fax- 303-438-6252.

Chaffee County

County Clerk & Recorder, PO Box 699, Salida, CO 81201. 719-539-6913, R/E recording phone-719-539-4004; fax-719-539-8588; hours: 8AM-4PM Recording; 8AM-5PM Researching All records in one index. Only the public may search. Copy fee $1.25 per page. Cert fee- $1.00 per cert plus copy fee. Payee- Chaffee County Clerk and Recorder. **Other phones:** Treasurer- 719-539-6808; Elections- 719-539-6913. **Property tax/Assessor-** 104 Crestone Ave., Salida, CO 81201; 719-539-4016, assessor fax- 719-539-8513.

Cheyenne County

County Clerk & Recorder, PO Box 567, Cheyenne Wells, CO 80810. RE & UCC recording phone-719-767-5685; fax-719-767-5540; hours: 8AM-4PM All records in one index. Only the public may search. Copy fee $1.25 per page. Cert fee- $1.00 per cert plus copy fee. Payee- Cheyenne County Clerk and Recorder. **Other phones:** Treasurer- 719-767-5657; Elections- 719-767-5685; Vital Records- 719-767-5661. **Property tax/Assessor-** PO Box 36, Cheyenne Wells, CO 80810; 719-767-5664, assessor fax- 719-767-5540.

Clear Creek County

County Clerk & Recorder, PO Box 2000, Georgetown, CO 80444-2000. RE & UCC recording phone-303-679-2339; fax-303-679-2416; hours: 8:30AM-4:30PM www.co.clear-creek.co.us/depts/clerk.htm All records in one index. Records indexed on a public use terminal back to 1995. Only the public may search. Will do a federal tax lien search if requested. Copy fee $1.25 per page. Cert fee- $1.00 per cert plus copy fee. Payee- Clear Creek County Clerk and Recorder. **Other phones:** Treasurer- 303-679-2353; Appraiser/Auditor- 303-679-2322; Elections- 303-679-2339; Vital Records- 303-679-2357. **Property tax/Assessor-** same address as above. 303-679-2322, assessor fax- 303-679-2441.

Conejos County

County Clerk & Recorder, PO Box 127, Conejos, CO 81129-0127. RE & UCC recording phone-719-376-5422; fax-719-376-5997; hours: 8AM-4:30PM Records indexed on a public use terminal back to 1994. Office personnel or visitors may perform searches. Search fee $5.00. Copy fee $1.25 per page. Cert fee- $1.00 per cert plus copy fee. Payee- Conejos County Clerk and Recorder. **Other phones:** Treasurer- 719-376-5919; Elections- 719-376-5422; Vital Records- 719-376-5787. **Property tax/Assessor-** PO Box 67, Conejos, CO 81129; 719-376-5585, assessor fax- 719-376-2442.

Costilla County

County Clerk & Recorder, PO Box 308, San Luis, CO 81152. RE & UCC recording phone-719-672-3301; fax-719-672-3962; hours: 8AM-N, 1-5PM

Records indexed on a public use terminal back to 1997. Office will perform a UCC search but public must search other records themselves. Copy fee $1.25 per page. Cert fee- $1.00 per page. Payee- Costilla County Clerk and Recorder. **Other phones:** Treasurer- 719-672-3542; Elections- 719-672-3301; Vital Records- 719-672-3301. **Property tax/Assessor-** 719-672-3642, assessor fax- 719-672-3206.

Crowley County

County Clerk & Recorder, 631 Main #104, Ordway, CO 81063-1092. 719-267-4643 x3, R/E recording phone-719-267-5555 x3, UCC recording phone-719-267-5555 x3; fax-719-267-4608; hours: 8AM-4PM Only the public may search. Copy fee $1.25 per page. Cert fee- $1.00 per cert plus copy fee. Payee- Crowley County Clerk and Recorder. **Other phones:** Treasurer- 719-267-4624 x4; Elections- 719-267-5555 x3. **Property tax/Assessor-** 631 Main #105, Ordway, CO 81063; 719-267-4421 x5, assessor fax- 719-267-4608.

Custer County

County Clerk & Recorder, PO Box 150, Westcliffe, CO 81252. RE & UCC recording phone-719-783-2441; fax-719-783-2885; hours: 8AM-4PM All records in one index. Records indexed on a public use terminal back to 1986. Office will perform a UCC search but public must search other records themselves. UCC search per debtor name- $15.00 for 1st yr; $5.00 each add'l yr. Copy fee $1.25 per page. $1.50 per page faxed back. Cert fee- $1.00 per cert plus copy fee. Payee- Custer County Clerk and Recorder. **Other phones:** Treasurer- 719-783-2341; Appraiser/Auditor- 719-783-2218; Elections- 719-783-2441; Vital Records- 719-783-2441. **Property tax/Assessor-** PO Box 518, Westcliffe, CO 81252; 719-783-2218, assessor fax- 719-783-2885.

Delta County

County Clerk & Recorder, 501 Palmer St, #211, Delta, CO 81416. Main phone & R/E recording-970-874-2150, UCC recording phone-970-874-2200; fax-970-874-2161; hours: 8:30AM-4:30PM All records in one index. Only the public may search. Copy fee $1.25 per page. Cert fee- $1.00 per cert plus copy fee. Payee- Delta County Clerk and Recorder. **Other phones:** Treasurer- 970-874-2135; Appraiser/Auditor- 970-874-2120; Elections- 970-874-2150; Vital Records- 970-874-2150. **Property tax/Assessor-** same address as above. 970-874-2120, assessor fax- 970-874-2482.

Denver County

County Clerk & Recorder, 201 W Colfax Ave Dept 101, Denver, CO 80202. 720-865-8400; fax-720-865-8580; hours: 9AM-4PM www.denvergov.org Will not search real estate records. Will search UCC records. Tax liens not included in UCC search. UCC search per debtor name-$5.00 per name, 1st year, $2.00 add'l 1 year. Separate tax lien searches performed at same cost as UCC searches. Copy fee $1.00 per page. RE or tax lien copy- $1.25 per page. Cert fee- $1.00 per cert plus copy fee. Payee- Denver County Clerk and Recorder. **Online access to Assessor, Real Estate, Property Tax, Personal Property, Contract, Inmate, Solicitation Arrest, Restaurant records:** Records on the Denver City and Denver County Assessor database are free at www.denvergov.org/realproperty.asp. Search business personal property at www.denvergov.org/PersProperty.asp. Also, search real estate property tax data for free at www.denvergov.org/treasurypt/PropertyTax.asp. Address or parcel number required to search. Search restaurant inspections at www.denvergov.org/eh/search.asp. Also, search county contracts at www.denvergov.org/contracts/contrak.asp. Search county inmates list at www.vinelink.com/offender/searchNew.jsp?siteID=6001; Prostitution solicitation arrests are at www.denvergov.org/johnstv/. **Other phones:** Treasurer- 720-865-7070; Appraiser/Auditor- 720-913-4032; Elections- 720-913-

8683; Vital Records- 303-436-7350. **Property tax/Assessor-** 720-913-4162.

Dolores County

County Clerk & Recorder, PO Box 58, Dove Creek, CO 81324-0058. RE & UCC recording phone-970-677-2381; fax-970-677-2815; 8:30AM-4:30PM Office personnel or visitors may perform searches. Search fee $5.00 for 1st year; $2.00 each add'l year. Copy fee $1.25 per page. Cert fee- $1.00 per cert plus copy fee. Payee- Dolores County Clerk and Recorder. **Other phones:** Treasurer- 970-677-2386; Appraiser/Auditor- 970-677-2385; Elections- 970-677-2381; Vital Records- 970-677-2381. **Property tax/Assessor-** PO Box 478, Dove Creek, CO 81324; 970-677-2385, assessor fax- 970-677-3068.

Douglas County

County Clerk & Recorder, PO Box 1360, Castle Rock, CO 80104. RE & UCC recording phone-303-660-7446; fax-303-814-2776; 8-4:30 www.douglas.co.us All records in one index. Records indexed on a public use terminal back to 1983. Office will perform a UCC search but public must search other records themselves. Search fee $5.00. Copy fee $1.25 per page. Cert fee- $1.00 per cert plus copy fee. Payee- Douglas County Clerk and Recorder. **Online access to Deed, Grantor/Grantee, Judgment, Lien, Mortgage, UCC, Vital Statistic, Assessor, Property records:** Access to recorders data is free at www.douglas.co.us/Orgchart_top.htm; click on "Advance Doc Search" to search by name. Records on the county assessor database are free at www.douglas.co.us/Assessor_Search/default.htm. **Other phones:** Treasurer- 303-660-7455; Appraiser/Auditor- 303-660-7450; Elections- 303-660-7444. **Property tax/Assessor-** 303-660-7450, assessor fax- 303-663-7356.

Eagle County

County Clerk & Recorder, PO Box 537, Eagle, CO 81631. 970-328-8710, R/E recording phone-970-328-8723, UCC recording phone-970-328-8723; fax-970-328-8716; hours: 8AM-5PM www.eaglecounty.us Will not search real estate records. Will search UCC records, search includes tax liens. UCC search per debtor name- $5.00 first year; $2.00 per name ea add'l year. Copy fee $1.00 per page. Cert fee- $1.00 per cert plus copy fee. Payee- Eagle County Clerk and Recorder. **Online access to Assessor, Property, Grantor/Grantee, Deed, Judgment, Lien, Vital Statistic, Will, UCC, Property Sale, Most Wanted, Pet records:** Search clerk and recorder data free at www.eaglecounty.us/cloe/search.cfm. Also, access the County Assessor-Treasurer databases free at www.eaglecounty.us/patie/index_content.cfm. Search comps sales at www.eaglecounty.us/assessor/saleslist.cfm. Also, view the sheriff's most wanted list at www.eaglecounty.us/sheriff/mostWanted.cfm. Pet lost and found database at www.eaglecounty.us/doggie/lfpetsform.cfm. **Other phones:** Treasurer- 970-328-8860; Election- 970-328-8715. **Property tax/Assessor-** 970-328-8640, assessor fax- 970-328-8679.

El Paso County

County Clerk & Recorder, PO Box 2007, Colorado Springs, CO 80901-2007. 719-520-6200; fax-719-520-6230; hours: 8AM-5PM www.car.elpasoco.com/ Only the public may search. Copy fee $1.25 per page. Cert fee- $1.00 per cert plus copy fee. Payee- El Paso County Clerk and Recorder. **Online access to Assessor, Public Trustee Sale, Inmate, Contractor, Granter-Grantee records:** Records on the county Assessor database are free at http://land.elpasoco.com/default.htm. Also, public trust weekly sale list at http://put.elpasoco.com/ptweeklysaledetail.asp?rm=47119. Search the county contractor list at www.pprbd.org/contrnames.html. Search the Grantor/Grantee index at www.car.elpasoco.com/rcdquery.asp. **Other phones:** Treasurer- 719-520-6666; Elections- 719-520-8683; Vital Records- 719-520-7475. **Property tax/Assessor-** 719-520-6600, assessor fax- 719-520-6635.

Elbert County

County Clerk & Recorder, PO Box 37, Kiowa, CO 80117. 303-621-3129, 303-621-3116, R/E recording phone-303-621-3128, UCC recording phone-303-621-3128; fax-303-621-3168; hours: 8AM-4:30PM
All records in one index. Records indexed on computer back to 1984. Only the public may search. Copy fee $1.00 per page. RE or tax lien copy- $1.25 per page. Cert fee- $1.00 per cert plus copy fee. Payee- Elbert County Clerk and Recorder. **Other phones:** Treasurer- 303-621-3117; Elections- 303-621-3127. **Property tax/Assessor-** 303-621-3101, assessor fax- 303-621-3173.

Fremont County

County Clerk & Recorder, 615 Macon Ave; Rm 102, Canon City, CO 81212-3311. 719-276-7336; fax-719-275-7338; hours: 8:30AM-4:30PM
All records in one index. Records indexed on a public use terminal back to 1/1987. Only the public may search. Copy fee $1.25 per page. Cert fee- $1.00 per cert plus copy fee. Payee- Fremont County Clerk and Recorder. **Online access to Assessor, Property, Property Sale records:** Access to the assessors database is free at www.qpublic.net/fremont/search1.html. **Other phones:** Treasurer- 719-276-7380; Elections- 719-276-7332; Vital Records- 719-276-1556. **Property tax/Assessor-** same address as above. 719-276-7310.

Garfield County

County Clerk & Recorder, 109 8th St; #200, Glenwood Springs, CO 81601. 970-945-2377x1840, R/E recording phone-970-945-2377 x1845, UCC recording phone-970-945-2377 x1845; fax-970-947-1078; hours: 8:30AM-5PM
All records in one index. Only the public may search. Copy fee $1.25 per page. Cert fee- $1.00 per cert plus copy fee. Payee- Garfield County Clerk and Recorder. **Online access to Assessor, Treasurer records:** Search the assessor and treasurer at www.mitchandco.com/realEstate/garfield/index.cfm. **Other phones:** Treasurer- 970-945-6382; Elections- 970-945-2377 x1770; Vital Records- 970-945-2377 x1950. **Property tax/Assessor-** same address as above. 970-945-9134, assessor fax- 970-945-3953.

Gilpin County

County Clerk & Recorder, PO Box 429, Central City, CO 80427. 303-582-5321; fax-303-582-3086; hours: 7:30AM-5:30PM
All records in one index. Records indexed on a public use terminal back to 1988. Only the public may search. Copy fee $1.25 per page. Cert fee- $1.00 per cert plus copy fee. Payee- Gilpin County Clerk and Recorder. **Online access to Marriage records:** Access county marriage records from 1864 to 1944 free at www.colorado.gov/dpa/doit/archives/marriage/gilpin_index.htm. **Other phones:** Treasurer- 303-582-5222; Appraiser/Auditor- 303-582-5451; Elections- 303-582-5321. **Property tax/Assessor-** 303-582-5451, assessor fax- 303-582-3086.

Grand County

County Clerk & Recorder, PO Box 120, Hot Sulphur Springs, CO 80451. 970-725-3347 x273, R/E recording phone-970-725-3347 x115; fax-970-725-0100; hours: 8:30AM-5PM
http://co.grand.co.us/Clerk/clerkand.htm
All records in one index. Only the public may search. Copy fee $1.25 per page. Cert fee- $1.00 per cert plus copy fee. Payee- Grand County Clerk and Recorder. **Online access to Property, Assessor, Grantor/Grantee, Recording records:** Access Clerk&Recorder database free at http://co.grand.co.us/Clerk/lookup/. Also, assessor database is free at http://co.grand.co.us/Assessor/PropertySearch2/. Also, property ownership information is free at www.co.grand.co.us/Assessor/Download_Page.html. **Other phones:** Treasurer- 970-725-3347 x131; Elections- 970-725-3347 x114; Vital Records- 970-725-3347 x113. **Property tax/Assessor-** 970-725-3347 x119, assessor fax- 970-725-3505.

Gunnison County

County Clerk & Recorder, 221 N Wisconsin #C; Courthouse, Gunnison, CO 81230. 970-641-1516, R/E recording phone-970-641-2038; fax-970-641-7690; hours: 8AM-5PM www.co.gunnison.co.us
Records indexed on a public use terminal back to 1992. Only the public may search. Copy fee $1.25 per page. Cert fee- $1.00 per cert plus copy fee. Payee- Gunnison County Clerk and Recorder. Treasurer- 970-641-2231; Elections- 970-641-7927. **Property tax/Assessor-** same address as above. 970-641-1085, assessor fax- 970-641-7920.

Hinsdale County

County Clerk & Recorder, PO Box 9, Lake City, CO 81235. 970-944-2228; fax-970-944-2202; 7-5:30
All records in one index. Only the public may search. General copy fee $.25 per page. RE record copy- $1.25 per page. Tax lien copy- $5.00 per 1st year. Cert fee- $1.00 per cert plus copy fee. Payee- Hinsdale County Clerk and Recorder. **Other phones:** Treasurer- 970-944-2223; Elections- 970-944-2228. **Property tax/Assessor-** PO Box 28, Lake City, CO 81235; 970-944-2224.

Huerfano County

County Clerk & Recorder, 410 Main St.; Courthouse, #204, Walsenburg, CO 81089. 719-738-2380; fax-719-738-2364; hours: 8AM-4PM
Treasurer performs tax lien searches. Only the public may search. Copy fee $1.25 per page. Cert fee- $1.00 per cert plus copy fee. Payee- Huerfano County Clerk and Recorder. **Other phones:** Treasurer- 719-738-1280. **Property tax/Assessor-** 719-782-1191, assessor fax- 719-782-1191.

Jackson County

County Clerk & Recorder, PO Box 337, Walden, CO 80480-0337. 970-723-4334; fax-970-723-3214; 8 to 5. Records indexed on a public use terminal back to 1996. Only the public may search. Copy fee $1.25 per page. Cert fee- $1.00 per cert plus copy fee. Payee- Jackson County Clerk and Recorder. **Other phones:** Treasurer- 970-723-4220; Elections- 970-723-4334; Vital Records- 970-723-4334. **Property tax/Assessor-** 970-723-4751.

Jefferson County

County Clerk & Recorder, 100 Jefferson County Parkway, #2530, Golden, CO 80419-2530. 303-271-8121; fax-303-271-8180; 8:30AM-4:30PM http://co.jefferson.co.us/ext/dpt/officials/clkrec/index.htm
All records in one index. Records indexed on a public use terminal back to 1963. Office will perform a UCC search but public must search other records themselves. UCC search per debtor name- $5.00 per 1st year. Copy fee $1.25 per page. Cert fee- $1.00 per cert plus copy fee. Payee-Jefferson County Clerk and Recorder. **Online access to Assessor, Property, Grantor/Grantee, Deed, Judgment, Recording records:** Records on the county Assessor database are free at http://ww14.co.jefferson.co.us/ats/splash.do. No name searching. Also, recorder's Grantor/Grantee index free at http://ww14.co.jefferson.co.us/crint/disclaimer.htm. **Other phones:** Treasurer- 303-271-8330; Elections- 303-271-8111; Vital Records- 303-271-6450. **Property tax/Assessor-** 100 Jefferson Cty Pky, #2500, Golden, CO 80419; 303-271-8666.

Kiowa County

County Clerk & Recorder, PO Box 37, Eads, CO 81036-0037. RE & UCC recording phone-719-438-5421; fax-719-438-5327; hours: 8AM-4:30PM
All records in one index. Record index not computerized. Only the public may search. Copy fee $1.25 per page. Cert fee- $1.00 per cert plus copy fee. Payee- Kiowa County Clerk and Recorder. **Other phones:** Treasurer- 719-438-5831; Elections- 719-438-5421; Vital Records- 719-438-5590. **Property tax/Assessor-** PO Box 295, Eads, CO 81036; 719-438-5521.

Kit Carson County

County Clerk & Recorder, PO Box 249, Burlington, CO 80807-0249. 719-346-8638; fax-719-346-7242; hours: 8AM-4PM
All records in one index. Only the public may search. Copy fee $1.25 per page. Cert fee- $1.00 per cert plus copy fee. Payee- Kit Carson County Clerk & Recorder. **Other phones:** Treasurer- 719-346-8434; Elections- 719-346-8638; Vital Records- 719-346-8133. **Property tax/Assessor-** 251 16th St, Burlington, CO 80807; 719-346-8946.

La Plata County

County Clerk & Recorder, PO Box 519, Durango, CO 81302-0519. 970-382-6294, R/E recording phone-970-382-6280/6281; fax-970-382-6299; hours: 8AM-5PM http://co.laplata.co.us
All records in one index. Only the public may search. Copy fee $1.25 per page. Cert fee- $1.00 per cert plus copy fee. Payee- La Plata County Clerk and Recorder. **Online access to Real Estate, Sale, Property records:** Records on the county Real Estate Search Page are free at www.laplatainfo.com/search2.html. This is basic property data; for sales and tax data, there is a subscription service for $20.00 per month, credit cards accepted. **Other phones:** Treasurer- 970-382-6245. **Property tax/Assessor-** 970-382-6221.

Lake County

County Clerk & Recorder, PO Box 917, Leadville, CO 80461. Main phone & R/E recording-719-486-4131, UCC recording phone-719-894-2200; fax-719-486-3972; hours: 9AM-5PM
Records indexed on computer 1981 forward, prior in vault. Only the public may search, terminal available. Copy fee $1.25 per page. Cert fee- $1.00 per cert plus copy fee. Payee- Lake County Clerk and Recorder. **Other phones:** Treasurer- 719-486-0530; Elections- 719-486-1410; Vital Records- 719-486-0708. **Property tax/Assessor-** PO Box 28, Leadville, CO 80461; 719-486-0413.

Larimer County

County Clerk & Recorder, PO Box 1280, Fort Collins, CO 80522-1280. RE & UCC recording phone-970-498-7860; fax-970-498-7830; hours: 8AM-5PM www.larimer.org
All records in one index. Will not search real estate records. Will search UCC records, search includes tax liens. UCC search per debtor name- $5.00 per name. Separate tax lien search costs the same as UCC search. Copy fee $1.25 per page. Cert fee- $1.00 per cert plus copy fee. Payee- Larimer County Clerk and Recorder. **Online access to Property Tax, Assessor, Treasurer, UCC, Lien, Deed, Judgment, Recording, Voter Registration, Most Wanted records:** Search county Public Record Databases free at www.larimer.org/databases/index.htm. Also, search the sheriff most wanted list at www.co.larimer.co.us/Sheriff/MostWanted/Wanted0.htm. **Other phones:** Treasurer- 970-498-7020; Elections- 970-498-7820; Vital Records- 970-498-5710. **Property tax/Assessor-** 200 W Oak, #2000, Ft Collins, CO 80521; 970-498-7050, assessor fax- 970-498-7070.

Las Animas County

County Clerk & Recorder, PO Box 115, Trinidad, CO 81082. 719-846-3314; fax-719-845-2573; 8AM-4PM
Only the public may search. Copy fee $1.25 per page. Cert fee- $2.25 per cert plus copy fee. Payee- Las Animas County Clerk and Recorder. **Other phones:** Treasurer- 719-846-2295. **Property tax/Assessor-** 719-846-2295,.

Lincoln County

County Clerk & Recorder, PO Box 67, Hugo, CO 80821-0067. 719-743-2444; fax-719-743-2524; hours: 8AM-4:30PM
All records in one index. Will not search real estate records. Will not search UCC records. Copy fee $1.25 per page; fax back- $1.00 per page. Cert fee- $1.00

per doc, plus copy fee. Payee- Lincoln County Clerk and Recorder. **Other phones:** Treasurer- 719-743-2633; Elections- 719-743-2444; Vital Records-719-743-2444. **Property tax/Assessor-** PO Box 277, Hugo, CO 80821; 719-743-2358.

Logan County

County Clerk & Recorder, 315 Main St #3; Logan County Courthouse, Sterling, CO 80751. RE & UCC recording phone-970-522-1544; fax-970-522-2063; 8AM-5PM www.loganco.gov/departments.htm
Separate indices to search include grantor/grantee, marriage licenses. Records indexed on a public use terminal back to 1/21/1997. Office will perform a UCC search but public must search other records themselves. UCC search per debtor name- $5.00 per name per year; $2.00 each add'l year. Copy fee $1.25 per page. Plat copy $5.00, marriage copy-$2.00. Cert fee- $1.00 per cert plus copy fee. Payee- Logan County Clerk and Recorder. **Other phones:** Treasurer- 970-522-2462; Elections- 970-522-1544; Vital Records- 970-522-1544 (marriage); Birth & Death Certificates- 970-522-3741. **Property tax/Assessor-** 315 Main St #1, Sterling, CO 80751; 970-522-2797, assessor fax- 970-522-1987.

Mesa County

County Clerk & Recorder, PO Box 20000-5007, Grand Junction, CO 81502-5007. RE & UCC recording phone-970-244-1679; fax-970-256-1588; hours: 8:30AM-5PM www.mesacounty.us
an interactive Voice Response System lets callers access real property data at 970-256-1563. Fax back service available. All records in one index. Records indexed on a public use terminal back to 1979. Only the public may search. Copy fee $1.25 per page. Cert fee- $1.00 per cert plus copy fee. Payee- Mesa County Clerk and Recorder. **Online access to Grantor/Grantee, Judgment, Lien, Real Estate, Assessor, Real Estate, Property Tax, Voter Registration records:** Records on the county Assessor database are free at www.mesacounty.us. Click on Assessor lookup and search by address or parcel number. Search on the GIS-mapping/property page at www.gjcity.org/CityDeptWebPages/AdministrativeServices/InformationSystems/GIS/GIS.htm. Also, search the Grantor/Grantee index, liens, judgments, mortgages, etc. at www.co.mesa.co.us/sireweb/sireweb.asp. **Other phones:** Treasurer- 970-244-1824; Elections- 970-244-1662; Vital Records- 970-248-6900 (birth/death); Marriage Records- 970-244-1679. **Property tax/Assessor-** same address as above. 970-244-1610, assessor fax- 970-244-1790.

Mineral County

County Clerk & Recorder, PO Box 70, Creede, CO 81130. RE & UCC recording phone-719-658-2440; fax-719-658-2931; hours: 8AM-4PM
All records in one index. Records indexed on a public use terminal back to 12/1996. Only the public may search. Copy fee $1.25 per page. Cert fee- $1.00 per page plus copy fee. Payee- Mineral County Clerk and Recorder. **Online access to Property, records:** Access property records free at www.qpublic.net/co/mineral/. **Other phones:** Treasurer- 719-658-2325; Elections- 719-658-2440; Vital Records- 719-658-2497. **Property tax/Assessor-** PO Box 574, Creede, CO 81130; 719-658-2669.

Moffat County

County Clerk & Recorder, 221 W. Victory Way #200, Craig, CO 81625-2716. RE & UCC recording phone-970-824-9104; fax-970-824-4975; hours: 8AM-4PM
Separate indices to search include in books by Marriage, Real Estate, UCCs, and liens. Records indexed on a public use terminal back to 1990. Only the public may search. Copy fee $1.25 per page. Cert fee- $1.00 per page plus copy fee. Payee- Moffat County Clerk and Recorder. **Online access to Most Wanted records:** Access to the sheriff's most wanted list is at www.moffatcountysheriff.com/mostwanted.htm. **Other phones:** Treasurer- 970-824-9111; Elections- 970-824-

9104; Vital Records- 970-824-8233. **Property tax/Assessor-** 970-824-9102,.

Montezuma County

County Clerk & Recorder, 109 W. Main St, Rm #108, Cortez, CO 81321. 970-565-3728, R/E recording phone-970-565-3728 x3, UCC recording phone-303-894-2200; fax-970-564-0215; hours: 8:30AM-4:30PM www.co.montezuma.co.us/
Records indexed from 6/3/96 are on Crist Plus system before that are in Grantor/Grantee book indexes. Only the public may search books, time permitting they try to help on computer. Will not search real estate records. Will not search UCC records or tax liens. Copy fee $1.25 per page. Cert fee-$1.00 per cert plus copy fee. Payee- Montezuma County Clerk and Recorder. **Online access to Property Tax, Property Sale records:** Access to county property information is free at http://itax.co.montezuma.co.us/itax/taxSplash.jsp and registration is required. **Other phones:** Treasurer- 970-565-7550; Elections- 970-565-3728 x4; Vital Records- 970-565-3728 x3. **Property tax/Assessor-** 970-565-3428, assessor fax- 970-565-1247.

Montrose County

County Clerk & Recorder, PO Box 1289, Montrose, CO 81402. 970-249-3362, R/E recording phone-970-249-3362 x2; fax-970-249-0757; 8:30AM-4:30PM
All records in one index. Records indexed on a public use terminal back to 1996. Only the public may search. General copy fee $1.00 per page. RE or tax lien copy- $1.25 per page. Cert fee- $1.00 per cert plus copy fee. Payee- Montrose County Clerk and Recorder. **Online access to Property, Assessor records:** Access Property Information Search System free at http://itax.co.montrose.co.us/itax/taxSplash.jsp. Free registration is required. **Other phones:** Treasurer- 970-249-3565; Elections-970-249-3362 x3; Vital Records- 970-249-3362 x0. **Property tax/Assessor-** 970-249-3753.

Morgan County

County Clerk & Recorder, PO Box 1399, Fort Morgan, CO 80701. RE & UCC recording phone-970-542-3521; fax-970-542-3520; hours: 8AM-4PM
All records in one index. Only the public may search. Copy fee $1.25 per page. Cert fee- $1.00 per page plus copy fee. Payee- Morgan County Clerk and Recorder. **Online access to Assessor, Property records:** Search the assessor database free at http://morgancounty.coloproperty.com/search/search.cfm. **Other phones:** Treasurer- 970-542-3518; Appraiser/Auditor- 970-542-3512; Elections- 970-542-3521; Vital Records- 970-867-4918. **Property tax/Assessor-** 970-542-3512.

Otero County

County Clerk & Recorder, PO Box 511, La Junta, CO 81050-0511. 719-383-3020, R/E recording phone-719-383-3023; fax-719-383-3026; hours: 8AM-5PM
All records in one index. Records indexed on a public use terminal back to 1993. Only the public may search. Copy fee $1.25 per page. Cert fee-$1.00 per cert plus copy fee. Payee- Otero County Clerk and Recorder. **Online access to Assessor, Property records:** Access property data free at www.oterocountyassessor.net. **Other phones:** Treasurer- 719-383-3030; Elections- 719-383-3024; Vital Records- 719-383-3040. **Property tax/Assessor-** 13 W 3rd St. Rm 211, La Junta, CO 81050; 719-383-3010, assessor fax- 719-383-3019.

Ouray County

County Clerk & Recorder, PO Bin C, Ouray, CO 81427. Main phone & R/E recording-970-325-4961, UCC recording phone-970-894-2200; fax-970-325-0452; hours: 9AM-5PM http://co.ouray.co.us
All records in one index. Records indexed on a public use terminal back to 1995. Office will perform a UCC search but public must search other records themselves. Copy fee $1.25 per page. Payee- Ouray County Clerk and Recorder. **Other**

phones: Treasurer- 970-325-4487; Elections- 970-325-4961; Vital Records- 970-325-4487. **Property tax/Assessor-** 970-325-4371.

Park County

County Clerk & Recorder, PO Box 220, Fairplay, CO 80440. 719-836-4222, R/E recording phone-719-836-4226 or 4224, UCC recording phone-719-836-4226 or 4224; fax-719-836-4348; hours: 7AM-5PM www.parkco.org
All records in one index. Only the public may search. Copy fee $1.25 per page. Cert fee- $1.00 per cert plus copy fee. Payee- Park County Clerk and Recorder. **Online access to Assessor, Property Tax, Divorce records:** Records on the county Assessor database are free at www.parkco.org/Search2.asp? including tax information, owner, address, building characteristics, legal and deed information. Also, county divorce records from 1957 to 1974 are free at www.colorado.gov/dpa/doit/archives/divorce/1park.htm. **Other phones:** Treasurer- 719-836-2771 x242; Elections- 719-836-4223; Vital Records- 719-836-4227; 719-836-4333. **Property tax/Assessor-** same address as above. 719-836-4189.

Phillips County

County Clerk & Recorder, 221 S. Interocean, Holyoke, CO 80734. RE & UCC recording phone-970-854-3131; fax-970-854-4745; hours: 8AM-4:30PM
Separate indices to search include books and computer. Records indexed on a public use terminal back to 1997. Only the public may search. Copy fee $1.25 per page. Cert fee- $1.00 per cert plus copy fee. Payee- Phillips County Clerk and Recorder. **Other phones:** Treasurer- 970-852-2822; Appraiser/Auditor- 970-854-3151; Elections- 970-854-3131; Vital Records- 970-854-3350. **Property tax/Assessor-** 970-854-3151.

Pitkin County

County Clerk & Recorder, 530 E. Main St.; #101, Aspen, CO 81611. RE & UCC recording phone-970-920-5180; fax-970-920-5196; hours: 8:30AM-4:30PM www.aspenpitkin.com
All records in one index. Records indexed on a public use terminal. Office will perform a UCC search but public must search other records themselves. UCC search per debtor name-$13.00 per 5 year search. Copy fee $1.25 per page. Cert fee- $1.00 per cert plus copy fee. Payee- Pitkin County Clerk and Recorder. **Online access to Assessor, Inmates, Divorce, Probate, Grantor/Grantee records:** Assessor database free at www.mitchandco.com/realestate/pitkin/index.cfm.
Search recorded documents at www.pitkinassessor.org/Clerk/search.asp. Also, sheriff's current inmate list is free at www.aspenpitkin.com/depts/28/inmates.cfm. Divorce records 1931 to 1964 are at www.colorado.gov/dpa/doit/archives/divorce/1pitkin.htm. Also, probate records from 1881 to 1953 are at www.colorado.gov/dpa/doit/archives/probate/pitkin_probate.htm. Grantor/Grantee index at www.pitkinassessor.org/clerk. **Other phones:** Treasurer- 970-920-5170; Elections- 970-920-5180. **Property tax/Assessor-** 970-920-5160.

Prowers County

County Clerk & Recorder, 301 S. Main St #210, Lamar, CO 81052. RE & UCC recording phone-719-336-8011; fax-719-336-5306; 8:30AM-4:30PM
Separate indices to search include grantor/grantee & general reception book (numeric order). Records indexed on a public use terminal back to 7/1/1994. Only the public may search. Copy fee $1.25 per page. Cert fee- $1.00 per cert plus copy fee. Payee- Prowers County Clerk and Recorder. **Other phones:** Treasurer- 719-336-8081; Appraiser/Auditor- 719-336-8000; Elections- 719-336-8011; Vital Records- 719-336-2606. **Property tax/Assessor-** 301 S. Main St #205, Lamar, CO 81052; 719-336-8000, assessor fax- 719-336-7232.

Pueblo County

County Clerk & Recorder, PO Box 878, Pueblo, CO 81002-0878. 719-583-6625, R/E recording phone-719-583-6629; fax-719-583-4625; hours: 8AM-4:30PM www.co.pueblo.co.us/clerk/

All records in one index. Records indexed on a public use terminal back to 5/1/1991. Office will perform a tax lien search but public must search other records themselves. Search fee, tax lien-$5.00 per debtor for 1st year; $2.00 each add'l year. Copy fee $1.25 per page. Cert fee- $1.00 per doc plus copy fee. Payee- Pueblo County Clerk and Recorder. **Online access to Assessor, Real Estate, Property Sale, Registered Voter, Grantor/Grantee, Marriage Certificates records:** Access to the county assessor database is free at http://assessor.co.pueblo.co.us. Also, access to voter registration data is free at www.co.pueblo.co.us; click on "Registered Voters" Also, for online index of recorded documents go to iCRIS http://icris.co.pueblo.co.us/icris/Login.jsp. Includes grantor/grantee, marriage certificates, etc. **Other phones:** Treasurer- 719-583-6015; Appraiser/Auditor-719-583-6596; Elections- 719-583-6620; Vital Records- 719-583-4555; Main switchboard- 719-583-6000. **Property tax/Assessor-** 215 W 10th St, Pueblo, CO 81003; 719-583-6564, assessor fax-719-583-6600.

Rio Blanco County

County Clerk & Recorder, PO Box 1067, Meeker, CO 81641. 970-878-9460; fax-970-878-3587; 8AM-5PM

All records in one index. Records indexed on a public use terminal back to 6/1/1983. Only the public may search. Copy fee $1.25 per page. Cert fee- $1.00 per cert plus copy fee. Payee- Rio Blanco County Clerk and Recorder. **Other phones:** Treasurer- 970-878-9660; Elections- 970-878-5068; Vital Records- 970-878-9460. **Property tax/Assessor-** 970-878-9410, assessor fax- 970-878-5701.

Rio Grande County

County Clerk & Recorder, PO Box 160, Del Norte, CO 81132. Main phone & R/E recording-719-657-3334, UCC recording phone-719-657-3334 real estate only; fax-719-657-2621; hours: 8AM-4PM www.qpublic.net/riogrande/

Only the public may search. Copy fee $1.25 per page. Cert fee- $1.00 per doc plus copy fee. Payee- Rio Grande County Clerk and Recorder. **Online access to Property Tax, Assessor, Sale records:** Access to the property assessor's data is free at www.qpublic.net/riogrande/search1.html. A property sale search is also at the assessor website. **Other phones:** Treasurer- 719-657-2747; Appraiser/Auditor-719-657-3326; Elections- 719-657-3334; Vital Records- 719-657-3334. **Property tax/Assessor-** 719-657-3326, assessor fax- 719-657-2514.

Routt County

County Clerk & Recorder, PO Box 773598, Steamboat Springs, CO 80477. RE & UCC recording phone-970-870-5556; fax-970-870-1329; hours: 8AM-4:30PM www.co.routt.co.us

All records in one index. Records indexed on computer back to 1983. Only the public may search. Copy fee $1.25 per page. Cert fee- $1.00 per doc plus copy fee. Payee- Routt County Clerk and Recorder. **Online access to Real Estate, Assessor, Property Tax, Treasurer, Deed, Judgment, Property Sale records:** Records on the county Assessor/Treasurer Property Search database are free at www.co.routt.co.us/assessor.html. Also, search records free on the County Clerk & Recorder Reception Search database at www.co.routt.co.us/clerk.html. Also, a gis-mapping site has property data for free at http://maps.co.routt.co.us/website/parcels/index.asp. Search by name. **Other phones:** Treasurer- 970-870-5555; Appraiser/Auditor- 970-870-5554; Elections-970-870-5556; Vital Records- 970-879-1632. **Property tax/Assessor-** PO Box 773210, 522 Lincoln Ave, Steamboat Springs, CO 80477; 970-870-5544, assessor fax- 970-870-5461.

Saguache County

County Clerk & Recorder, PO Box 176, Saguache, CO 81149-0176. RE & UCC recording phone-719-655-2512; fax-719-655-2730; hours: 8AM-4PM

All records in one index. Records indexed on a public use terminal. Only the public may search. Copy fee $1.25 per page. Cert fee- $1.00 per cert plus copy fee. Payee- Saguache County Clerk and Recorder. **Online access to Recording, Real Estate, Deed, Lien, Death, Marriage records:** Access to the Recorder data base is free at www.thecountyrecorder.com/Search.aspx?CountyKey=6. Index goes back to 1984; images back to 1994. Search Assessor database at www.qpublic.net/co/saguache/. **Other phones:** Treasurer- 719-655-2656; Elections-719-655-2512; Vital Records- 719-655-2559. **Property tax/Assessor-** PO Box 38, Saguache, CO 81149; 719-655-2521, assessor fax- 719-655-0152.

San Juan County

County Clerk & Recorder, PO Box 466, Silverton, CO 81433-0466. RE & UCC recording phone-970-387-5671; fax-970-387-5671; hours: 9AM-5PM

All records in one index. Only the public may search. Copy fee $1.25 per page. Cert fee- $1.00 per page. Payee- San Juan County Clerk and Recorder. **Other phones:** Treasurer- 970-389-5488; Elections- 970-387-5671; Vital Records- 970-387-5488; Admin- 970-387-5766. **Property tax/Assessor-** same address as above. 970-387-5632.

San Miguel County

County Clerk & Recorder, PO Box 548, Telluride, CO 81435-0548. RE & UCC recording phone-970-728-3954; fax-970-728-4808; hours: 9AM-5PM www.sanmiguelcounty.org/

Separate indices to search include computer, microfiche, older grantor/grantee books. Only the public may search. Copy fee $1.25 per page. Cert fee- $1.00 per cert plus copy fee. Payee- San Miguel County Clerk and Recorder. **Online access to Inmate records:** Access the sheriff's county inmates list free at www.sanmiguelsheriff.com/index.cfm?fuseaction=standard&categoryId=5&subcategoryId=4 . **Other phones:** Treasurer- 970-728-4451; Appraiser/Auditor- 970-728-3174; Elections- 970-728-3954; Vital Records- 970-728-4451. **Property tax/Assessor-** PO Box 506, 333 W Colorado Ave, Telluride, CO 81435-0506; 970-728-3174, assessor fax- 970-369-1007.

Sedgwick County

County Clerk & Recorder, 315 Cedar St., Julesburg, CO 80737. RE & UCC recording phone-970-474-3346; fax-970-474-0954; hours: 8AM-4PM

Separate indices to search include from 1997 forward index in computer, prior to 1997 in books in vault. Records indexed on a public use terminal back to November, 1997. Only the public may search. Copy fee $1.25 per page. Cert fee- $1.00 per cert plus copy fee. Payee- Sedgwick County Clerk and Recorder. **Other phones:** Treasurer- 970-474-3473; Elections- 970-474-3346; Vital Records-970-474-3473. **Property tax/Assessor-** 970-474-2531, assessor fax- 970-474-0954.

Summit County

County Clerk & Recorder, PO Box 1538, Breckenridge, CO 80424. RE & UCC recording phone-970-453-3475; fax-970-453-3540; hours: 8AM-5PM www.co.summit.co.us

All records in one index. Records indexed on a public use terminal back to 1990. Office personnel or visitors may perform searches. Copy fee $1.25 per page. Cert fee- $1.00 per cert plus copy fee. Payee- Summit County Clerk and Recorder. **Online access to Property, GIS-mapping records:** Access to the GIS-mapping site property data is free at www.co.summit.co.us/scripts/esrimap.dll. **Other phones:** Treasurer- 970-453-3440; Appraiser/Auditor-970-453-3480; Elections- 970-453-3479; Vital Records- 970-453-3472. **Property tax/Assessor-** 970-453-3480, assessor fax- 970-453-3481.

Teller County

County Clerk & Recorder, PO Box 1010, Cripple Creek, CO 80813-1010. 719-689-2951, R/E recording phone-719-686-8035; fax-719-686-8030; hours: 8AM-4:30PM www.co.teller.co.us

All records in one index. Records indexed on a public use terminal. Only the public may search. Copy fee $1.25 per page. Cert fee- $1.00 per cert plus copy fee. Payee- Teller County Clerk and Recorder. **Online access to Real Estate, Grantor/Grantee, Assessor, Property Tax records:** Access the county clerk real estate database free at http://data.co.teller.co.us/AsrData/wc.dll?Doc~GrantSearch. Records go back to 1978; fee for documents-$1.25 per page. Also, search assessor database free at http://data.co.teller.co.us/AsrData/wc.dll?AsrDataProc~OwnerNameSearch. **Other phones:** Treasurer- 719-689-2985; Elections- 719-686-8031; Vital Records-719-686-8035. **Property tax/Assessor-** PO Box 1008, Cripple Creek, CO 80813; 719-689-2941, assessor fax- 719-689-0988.

Washington County

County Clerk & Recorder, PO Box L, Akron, CO 80720-0380. Main phone & R/E recording-970-345-6565, UCC recording phone-303-894-2200; fax-970-345-6607; hours: 8AM-4:30PM

All records in one index. Records indexed on a public use terminal back to 9/1996. Office will perform a Tax lien search but public must search other records themselves. Copy fee $1.00 per page. RE or tax lien copy- $1.25 per page. Cert fee-$1.00 per cert plus copy fee. Payee- Washington County Clerk. **Other phones:** Treasurer- 970-345-6601; Appraiser/Auditor- 970-345-6662; Elections-970-345-6565; Vital Records- 970-345-6562. **Property tax/Assessor-** same address as above. 970-345-6662, assessor fax- 970-345-2329.

Weld County

County Clerk & Recorder, PO Box 459, Greeley, CO 80632-0459. 970-304-6530, R/E recording phone-970-304-6530 x3065, UCC recording phone-970-304-6530 x3065; fax-970-353-1964; hours: 8AM-5PM www.co.weld.co.us

All records in one index. Records indexed on computer back to 1982. Office will perform a tax lien search but public must search other records themselves. Federal/state combined tax lien search- $25.00 per debtor. Copy fee $1.25 per page. Cert fee- $1.00 per cert plus copy fee. Payee- Weld County Clerk and Recorder. **Online access to Real Estate, Assessor, Treasurer, Property Tax, Most Wanted, Sex Offender records:** Search property information on the map server database at http://maps.merrick.com/website/weld/ or click on the "Property Information" button then search assessor data by name. Also, search treasurer's property database free at www.co.weld.co.us/departments/treasurer/tax/index1.cfm. Also, access the sheriff's most wanted and sex offender pages at www.co.weld.co.us/Sheriff/. **Other phones:** Treasurer- 970-304-3845 x3260; Elections-970-304-6525 x3070. **Property tax/Assessor-** 1400 N 17th Ave, Greeley, CO 80631; 970-304-3845 x3650, assessor fax- 970-304-6433.

Yuma County

County Clerk & Recorder, 310 Ash St, #F, Wray, CO 80758. RE & UCC recording phone-970-332-5809; fax-970-332-5919; hours: 8:30AM-4:30PM

All records in one index. Records indexed on computer. Office will perform a UCC search but public must search other records themselves. Search fee $2.00 per name per year. Copy fee $1.25 per page. Cert fee- $1.00 per cert plus copy fee. Payee- Yuma County Clerk and Recorder. Treasurer- 970-332-4965; Appraiser/Auditor- 970-332-5032; Elections- 970-332-5809; Vital Records- 970-332-5809; Birth/Death Records- 970-332-4431/970-848-3878. **Property tax/Assessor-** same address as above. 970-332-5032, assessor fax- 970-332-3373.

Colorado County Locator

You will usually be able to find the city name in the City/County Cross Reference below. In that case, it is a simple matter to determine the county from the cross reference. However, only the official US Postal Service city names are included in this index. There are an additional 40,000 place names that people use in their addresses. Therefore, we have also included a ZIP/City Cross Reference immediately following the City/County Cross Reference.

If you know the ZIP Code but the city name does not appear in the City/County Cross Reference index, look up the ZIP Code in the ZIP/City Cross Reference, find the city name, then look up the city name in the City/County Cross Reference. For example, you want to know the county for an address of Menands, NY 12204. There is no "Menands" in the City/County Cross Reference. The ZIP/City Cross Reference shows that ZIP Codes 12201-12288 are for the city of Albany. Looking back in the City/County Cross Reference, Albany is in Albany County.

Colorado City/County Cross Reference

AGATE Elbert
AGUILAR Las Animas
AKRON Washington
ALAMOSA (81101) Alamosa(98), Conejos(1)
ALAMOSA Alamosa
ALLENSPARK (80510) Boulder(95), Larimer(4)
ALMA Park
ALMONT Gunnison
AMHERST Phillips
ANTON Washington
ANTONITO Conejos
ARAPAHOE Cheyenne
ARBOLES Archuleta
ARLINGTON (81021) Kiowa(80), Lincoln(19)
ARRIBA Lincoln
ARVADA (80003) Jefferson(86), Adams(13)
ARVADA Jefferson
ASPEN Pitkin
ATWOOD Logan
AULT Weld
AURORA (80010) Adams(52), Arapahoe(47)
AURORA (80011) Arapahoe(61), Adams(38)
AURORA (80014) Arapahoe(91), Denver(8)
AURORA Adams
AURORA Arapahoe
AUSTIN Delta
AVON Eagle
AVONDALE Pueblo
BAILEY Park
BASALT (81621) Eagle(68), Pitkin(31)
BATTLEMENT MESA Garfield
BAYFIELD La Plata
BEDROCK Montrose
BELLVUE Larimer
BENNETT (80102) Adams(51), Arapahoe(44), Elbert(3)
BERTHOUD (80513) Larimer(90), Weld(9)
BETHUNE Kit Carson
BEULAH Pueblo
BLACK HAWK Gilpin
BLANCA Costilla
BONCARBO Las Animas
BOND Eagle
BOONE Pueblo
BOULDER Boulder
BOYERO Lincoln
BRANSON Las Animas
BRECKENRIDGE Summit
BRIGGSDALE Weld
BRIGHTON (80603) Weld(54), Adams(45)
BRIGHTON Adams
BRISTOL Prowers
BROOMFIELD (80020) Broomfield(77), Jefferson(11), Adams(8), Boulder(2)
BROOMFIELD (80021) Jefferson(84), Broomfield(15)
BROOMFIELD Boulder

BRUSH (80723) Morgan(98), Washington(1)
BUENA VISTA Chaffee
BUFFALO CREEK Jefferson
BURLINGTON Kit Carson
BURNS Eagle
BYERS (80103) Arapahoe(87), Adams(12)
CAHONE Dolores
CALHAN (80808) El Paso(97), Elbert(2)
CAMPO Baca
CANON CITY Fremont
CAPULIN Conejos
CARBONDALE (81623) Garfield(62), Eagle(15), Pitkin(11), Gunnison(9)
CARR (80612) Weld(95), Larimer(4)
CASCADE El Paso
CASTLE ROCK Douglas
CEDAREDGE Delta
CENTER (81125) Saguache(67), Rio Grande(31), Alamosa(1)
CENTRAL CITY Gilpin
CHAMA Costilla
CHERAW Otero
CHEYENNE WELLS Cheyenne
CHIMNEY ROCK Archuleta
CHROMO Archuleta
CIMARRON (81220) Gunnison(81), Montrose(18)
CLARK Routt
CLIFTON Mesa
CLIMAX Lake
COAL CREEK Fremont
COALDALE Fremont
COALMONT Jackson
COKEDALE Las Animas
COLLBRAN Mesa
COLORADO CITY Pueblo
COLORADO SPRINGS (80926) El Paso(98), Fremont(1)
COLORADO SPRINGS El Paso
COMMERCE CITY Adams
COMO Park
CONEJOS Conejos
CONIFER Jefferson
COPE Washington
CORTEZ Montezuma
CORY Delta
COTOPAXI Fremont
COWDREY Jackson
CRAIG Moffat
CRAWFORD (81415) Delta(80), Montrose(19)
CREEDE Mineral
CRESTED BUTTE Gunnison
CRESTONE Saguache
CRIPPLE CREEK Teller
CROOK Logan
CROWLEY Crowley
DACONO Weld
DE BEQUE (81630) Mesa(63), Garfield(36)
DEER TRAIL (80105) Arapahoe(63), Elbert(26), Adams(9)

DEL NORTE (81132) Rio Grande(88), Saguache(11)
DELTA (81416) Delta(96), Montrose(3)
DENVER (80221) Adams(87), Denver(12)
DENVER (80234) Adams(97), Broomfield(2)
DENVER (80212) Denver(77), Jefferson(18), Adams(3)
DENVER (80216) Denver(60), Adams(39)
DENVER (80222) Denver(94), Arapahoe(5)
DENVER (80230) Denver(98), Adams(1)
DENVER (80247) Denver(69), Arapahoe(27), Adams(3)
DENVER (80249) Denver(96), Adams(3)
DENVER (80235) Jefferson(61), Denver(38)
DENVER Adams
DENVER Denver
DENVER Jefferson
DILLON Summit
DINOSAUR Moffat
DIVIDE Teller
DOLORES Montezuma
DOVE CREEK (81324) Dolores(98), San Miguel(1)
DRAKE Larimer
DUMONT Clear Creek
DUPONT Adams
DURANGO La Plata
EADS Kiowa
EAGLE Eagle
EASTLAKE Adams
EATON Weld
ECKERT Delta
ECKLEY Yuma
EDWARDS Eagle
EGNAR (81325) Dolores(85), San Miguel(14)
EL JEBEL Eagle
ELBERT (80106) El Paso(60), Elbert(37), Douglas(2)
ELDORADO SPRINGS Boulder
ELIZABETH Elbert
EMPIRE Clear Creek
ENGLEWOOD (80110) Arapahoe(98), Denver(1)
ENGLEWOOD (80112) Arapahoe(90), Douglas(5), Denver(4)
ENGLEWOOD Arapahoe
ERIE (80516) Weld(59), Boulder(40)
ESTES PARK Larimer
EVANS Weld
EVERGREEN (80439) Jefferson(88), Clear Creek(11)
EVERGREEN Jefferson
FAIRPLAY Park
FIRESTONE Weld
FLAGLER (80815) Kit Carson(86), Washington(13)
FLEMING Logan
FLORENCE Fremont
FLORISSANT (80816) Teller(78), Park(21)
FORT COLLINS Larimer

FORT GARLAND Costilla
FORT LUPTON Weld
FORT LYON Bent
FORT MORGAN Morgan
FOUNTAIN El Paso
FOWLER (81039) Otero(91), Pueblo(6), Crowley(1)
FOXTON Jefferson
FRANKTOWN Douglas
FRASER Grand
FREDERICK Weld
FRISCO Summit
FRUITA Mesa
GALETON Weld
GARCIA Costilla
GARDNER Huerfano
GATEWAY Mesa
GENOA (81818) Lincoln(83), Washington(16)
GEORGETOWN Clear Creek
GILCREST Weld
GILL Weld
GLADE PARK Mesa
GLEN HAVEN Larimer
GLENWOOD SPRINGS Garfield
GOLDEN (80403) Jefferson(74), Gilpin(21), Boulder(4)
GOLDEN Jefferson
GRANADA (81041) Prowers(92), Baca(7)
GRANBY Grand
GRAND JUNCTION Mesa
GRAND LAKE Grand
GRANITE (81228) Lake(62), Chaffee(37)
GRANT Park
GREELEY Weld
GREEN MOUNTAIN FALLS El Paso
GROVER Weld
GUFFEY Park
GULNARE Las Animas
GUNNISON Gunnison
GYPSUM (81637) Eagle(91), Garfield(8)
HAMILTON (81638) Moffat(59), Routt(30), Rio Blanco(9)
HARTMAN Prowers
HARTSEL Park
HASTY Bent
HASWELL (81045) Kiowa(63), Lincoln(20), Cheyenne(16)
HAXTUN (80731) Phillips(55), Logan(23), Yuma(21)
HAYDEN Routt
HENDERSON Adams
HEREFORD Weld
HESPERUS La Plata
HILLROSE Morgan
HILLSIDE Fremont
HOEHNE Las Animas
HOLLY (81047) Prowers(92), Kiowa(4), Baca(2)
HOLYOKE (80734) Phillips(95), Yuma(4)
HOMELAKE Rio Grande
HOOPER (81136) Alamosa(94), Saguache(5)

HOT SULPHUR SPRINGS Grand
HOTCHKISS Delta
HOWARD Fremont
HUDSON (80642) Weld(67), Adams(32)
HUGO Lincoln
HYGIENE Boulder
IDAHO SPRINGS Clear Creek
IDALIA Yuma
IDLEDALE Jefferson
IGNACIO La Plata
ILIFF Logan
INDIAN HILLS Jefferson
JAMESTOWN Boulder
JAROSO Costilla
JEFFERSON Park
JOES Yuma
JOHNSTOWN Weld
JULESBURG Sedgwick
KARVAL Lincoln
KEENESBURG (80643) Weld(88),
    Adams(11)
KERSEY Weld
KIM Las Animas
KIOWA Elbert
KIRK Yuma
KIT CARSON Cheyenne
KITTREDGE Jefferson
KREMMLING (80459) Grand(98),
    Summit(1)
LA JARA Conejos
LA JUNTA Otero
LA SALLE Weld
LA VETA Huerfano
LAFAYETTE Boulder
LAKE CITY Hinsdale
LAKE GEORGE (80827) Teller(71),
    Park(28)
LAKEWOOD (80226) Jefferson(98),
    Denver(1)
LAKEWOOD Jefferson
LAMAR (81052) Prowers(98), Bent(1)
LAPORTE Larimer
LARKSPUR Douglas
LAS ANIMAS Bent
LAZEAR Delta
LEADVILLE Lake
LEWIS Montezuma
LIMON (80828) Lincoln(70), Elbert(29)
LIMON Lincoln
LINDON Washington
LITTLETON (80128) Jefferson(94),
    Arapahoe(5)
LITTLETON Arapahoe
LITTLETON Douglas
LITTLETON Jefferson
LIVERMORE Larimer
LOG LANE VILLAGE Morgan
LOMA Mesa
LONGMONT (80504) Weld(75),
    Boulder(22), Larimer(1)
LONGMONT Boulder
LOUISVILLE Boulder
LOUVIERS Douglas
LOVELAND (80537) Larimer(98), Weld(1)
LOVELAND Larimer
LUCERNE Weld
LYONS (80540) Larimer(53), Boulder(46)

MACK Mesa
MAHER Delta
MANASSA Conejos
MANCOS (81328) Montezuma(96), La
    Plata(3)
MANITOU SPRINGS El Paso
MANZANOLA (81058) Otero(78),
    Crowley(21)
MARVEL La Plata
MASONVILLE Larimer
MATHESON Elbert
MAYBELL Moffat
MC CLAVE Bent
MC COY (80463) Eagle(80), Routt(20)
MEAD Weld
MEEKER (81641) Rio Blanco(93),
    Moffat(4), Garfield(1)
MEREDITH Pitkin
MERINO (80741) Logan(90),
    Washington(7), Morgan(1)
MESA Mesa
MESA VERDE NATIONAL PARK
    Montezuma
MILLIKEN Weld
MINTURN Eagle
MODEL (81059) Las Animas(77), Otero(22)
MOFFAT Saguache
MOLINA Mesa
MONARCH Chaffee
MONTE VISTA (81144) Rio Grande(96),
    Alamosa(3)
MONTROSE (81401) Montrose(96),
    Ouray(3)
MONTROSE Montrose
MONUMENT El Paso
MORRISON Jefferson
MOSCA Alamosa
NATHROP Chaffee
NATURITA Montrose
NEDERLAND Boulder
NEW CASTLE Garfield
NEW RAYMER (80742) Weld(66),
    Morgan(33)
NIWOT Boulder
NORWOOD San Miguel
NUCLA Montrose
NUNN Weld
OAK CREEK Routt
OHIO CITY Gunnison
OLATHE Montrose
OLNEY SPRINGS (81062) Crowley(94),
    Pueblo(5)
OPHIR San Miguel
ORCHARD (80649) Morgan(55), Weld(44)
ORDWAY (81063) Crowley(95), Lincoln(4)
OTIS (80743) Washington(97), Logan(2)
OURAY Ouray
OVID Sedgwick
PADRONI Logan
PAGOSA SPRINGS Archuleta
PALISADE Mesa
PALMER LAKE El Paso
PAOLI Phillips
PAONIA Delta
PARACHUTE Garfield
PARADOX Montrose
PARKER Douglas

PARLIN Gunnison
PARSHALL Grand
PEETZ Logan
PENROSE Fremont
PEYTON El Paso
PHIPPSBURG Routt
PIERCE Weld
PINE (80470) Jefferson(69), Park(30)
PINECLIFFE Boulder
PITKIN Gunnison
PLACERVILLE San Miguel
PLATTEVILLE Weld
PLEASANT VIEW Montezuma
PONCHA SPRINGS Chaffee
POWDERHORN Gunnison
PRITCHETT (81064) Baca(77), Las
    Animas(22)
PRYOR Huerfano
PUEBLO (81008) Pueblo(84), El Paso(15)
PUEBLO Pueblo
RAMAH (80832) Elbert(48), El Paso(46),
    Lincoln(5)
RAND Jackson
RANGELY Rio Blanco
RED CLIFF Eagle
RED FEATHER LAKES Larimer
RED WING Huerfano
REDVALE Montrose
RICO Dolores
RIDGWAY Ouray
RIFLE (81650) Garfield(96), Rio Blanco(3)
ROCKVALE Fremont
ROCKY FORD Otero
ROGGEN Weld
ROLLINSVILLE Gilpin
ROMEO Conejos
RUSH (80833) El Paso(49), Lincoln(40),
    Elbert(10)
RYE Pueblo
SAGUACHE Saguache
SALIDA Chaffee
SAN ACACIO Costilla
SAN LUIS Costilla
SAN PABLO Costilla
SANFORD (81151) Conejos(77),
    Costilla(21), Rio Grande(1)
SARGENTS Saguache
SEDALIA Douglas
SEDGWICK Sedgwick
SEGUNDO Las Animas
SEIBERT (80834) Kit Carson(90),
    Washington(9)
SEVERANCE Weld
SHAWNEE Park
SHERIDAN LAKE Kiowa
SILT Garfield
SILVER CLIFF Custer
SILVER PLUME Clear Creek
SILVERTHORNE Summit
SILVERTON San Juan
SIMLA (80835) Elbert(89), El Paso(10)
SLATER Moffat
SLICK ROCK San Miguel
SNOWMASS Pitkin
SNOWMASS VILLAGE Pitkin
SNYDER Morgan

SOMERSET (81434) Gunnison(90),
    Delta(9)
SOUTH FORK Rio Grande
SPRINGFIELD Baca
STARKVILLE Las Animas
STEAMBOAT SPRINGS Routt
STERLING Logan
STONEHAM Weld
STONINGTON Baca
STRASBURG (80136) Adams(66),
    Arapahoe(33)
STRATTON Kit Carson
SUGAR CITY (81076) Crowley(94),
    Lincoln(3), Kiowa(1)
SWINK Otero
TABERNASH Grand
TELLURIDE San Miguel
TIMNATH Larimer
TOPONAS Routt
TOWAOC Montezuma
TRINCHERA Las Animas
TRINIDAD Las Animas
TWIN LAKES Lake
TWIN LAKES CPO Lake
TWO BUTTES (81084) Baca(89),
    Prowers(10)
U S A F ACADEMY El Paso
VAIL Eagle
VERNON Yuma
VICTOR Teller
VILAS Baca
VILLA GROVE Saguache
VIRGINIA DALE Larimer
VONA Kit Carson
WALDEN Jackson
WALSENBURG Huerfano
WALSH Baca
WARD Boulder
WATKINS (80137) Arapahoe(59),
    Adams(40)
WELDONA Morgan
WELLINGTON (80549) Larimer(95),
    Weld(4)
WESTCLIFFE Custer
WESTMINSTER (80031) Adams(93),
    Jefferson(6)
WESTMINSTER Adams
WESTON Las Animas
WETMORE (81253) Custer(69),
    Fremont(26), Pueblo(4)
WHEAT RIDGE Jefferson
WHITEWATER Mesa
WIGGINS (80654) Morgan(92), Weld(4),
    Adams(2)
WILD HORSE Cheyenne
WILEY (81092) Prowers(60), Bent(36),
    Kiowa(3)
WINDSOR (80550) Weld(94), Larimer(5)
WINDSOR Weld
WINTER PARK Grand
WOLCOTT Eagle
WOODLAND PARK Teller
WOODROW Washington
WOODY CREEK Pitkin
WRAY Yuma
YAMPA Routt
YELLOW JACKET Montezuma
YODER El Paso

Colorado ZIP/City Cross Reference

ZIP	City	ZIP	City	ZIP	City	ZIP	City
80001-80007	ARVADA	80454-80454	INDIAN HILLS	80651-80651	PLATTEVILLE	81001-81015	PUEBLO
80010-80019	AURORA	80455-80455	JAMESTOWN	80652-80652	ROGGEN	81019-81019	COLORADO CITY
80020-80021	BROOMFIELD	80456-80456	JEFFERSON	80653-80653	WELDONA	81020-81020	AGUILAR
80022-80022	COMMERCE CITY	80457-80457	KITTREDGE	80654-80654	WIGGINS	81021-81021	ARLINGTON
80024-80024	DUPONT	80459-80459	KREMMLING	80701-80701	FORT MORGAN	81022-81022	AVONDALE
80025-80025	ELDORADO SPRINGS	80461-80461	LEADVILLE	80705-80705	LOG LANE VILLAGE	81023-81023	BEULAH
80026-80026	LAFAYETTE	80463-80463	MC COY	80720-80720	AKRON	81024-81024	BONCARBO
80027-80028	LOUISVILLE	80465-80465	MORRISON	80721-80721	AMHERST	81025-81025	BOONE
80030-80031	WESTMINSTER	80466-80466	NEDERLAND	80722-80722	ATWOOD	81026-81026	EADS
80033-80034	WHEAT RIDGE	80467-80467	OAK CREEK	80723-80723	BRUSH	81027-81027	BRANSON
80035-80036	WESTMINSTER	80468-80468	PARSHALL	80726-80726	CROOK	81028-81028	BRISTOL
80037-80037	COMMERCE CITY	80469-80469	PHIPPSBURG	80727-80727	ECKLEY	81029-81029	CAMPO
80038-80038	BROOMFIELD	80470-80470	PINE	80728-80728	FLEMING	81030-81030	CHERAW
80040-80047	AURORA	80471-80471	PINECLIFFE	80729-80729	GROVER	81032-81032	COKEDALE
80101-80101	AGATE	80473-80473	RAND	80731-80731	HAXTUN	81033-81034	CROWLEY
80102-80102	BENNETT	80474-80474	ROLLINSVILLE	80732-80732	HEREFORD	81036-81036	EADS
80103-80103	BYERS	80475-80475	SHAWNEE	80733-80733	HILLROSE	81038-81038	FORT LYON
80104-80104	CASTLE ROCK	80476-80476	SILVER PLUME	80734-80734	HOLYOKE	81039-81039	FOWLER
80105-80105	DEER TRAIL	80477-80477	STEAMBOAT SPRINGS	80735-80735	IDALIA	81040-81040	GARDNER
80106-80106	ELBERT	80478-80478	TABERNASH	80736-80736	ILIFF	81041-81041	GRANADA
80107-80107	ELIZABETH	80479-80479	TOPONAS	80737-80737	JULESBURG	81042-81042	GULNARE
80108-80109	CASTLE ROCK	80480-80480	WALDEN	80740-80740	LINDON	81043-81043	HARTMAN
80110-80113	ENGLEWOOD	80481-80481	WARD	80741-80741	MERINO	81044-81044	HASTY
80116-80116	FRANKTOWN	80482-80482	WINTER PARK	80742-80742	NEW RAYMER	81045-81045	HASWELL
80117-80117	KIOWA	80483-80483	YAMPA	80743-80743	OTIS	81046-81046	HOEHNE
80118-80118	LARKSPUR	80487-80488	STEAMBOAT SPRINGS	80744-80744	OVID	81047-81047	HOLLY
80120-80130	LITTLETON	80497-80498	SILVERTHORNE	80745-80745	PADRONI	81049-81049	KIM
80131-80131	LOUVIERS	80501-80504	LONGMONT	80746-80746	PAOLI	81050-81050	LA JUNTA
80132-80132	MONUMENT	80510-80510	ALLENSPARK	80747-80747	PEETZ	81052-81052	LAMAR
80133-80133	PALMER LAKE	80511-80511	ESTES PARK	80749-80749	SEDGWICK	81054-81054	LAS ANIMAS
80134-80134	PARKER	80512-80512	BELLVUE	80750-80750	SNYDER	81055-81055	LA VETA
80135-80135	SEDALIA	80513-80513	BERTHOUD	80751-80751	STERLING	81057-81057	MC CLAVE
80136-80136	STRASBURG	80514-80514	DACONO	80754-80754	STONEHAM	81058-81058	MANZANOLA
80137-80137	WATKINS	80515-80515	DRAKE	80755-80755	VERNON	81059-81059	MODEL
80138-80138	PARKER	80516-80516	ERIE	80757-80757	WOODROW	81062-81062	OLNEY SPRINGS
80150-80155	ENGLEWOOD	80517-80517	ESTES PARK	80758-80758	WRAY	81063-81063	ORDWAY
80160-80166	LITTLETON	80520-80520	FIRESTONE	80759-80759	YUMA	81064-81064	PRITCHETT
80201-80214	DENVER	80521-80528	FORT COLLINS	80801-80801	ANTON	81065-81065	PRYOR
80215-80215	LAKEWOOD	80530-80530	FREDERICK	80802-80802	ARAPAHOE	81066-81066	RED WING
80216-80225	DENVER	80532-80532	GLEN HAVEN	80804-80804	ARRIBA	81067-81067	ROCKY FORD
80226-80226	LAKEWOOD	80533-80533	HYGIENE	80805-80805	BETHUNE	81069-81069	RYE
80227-80227	DENVER	80534-80534	JOHNSTOWN	80806-80806	BOYERO	81070-81070	SEGUNDO
80228-80228	LAKEWOOD	80535-80535	LAPORTE	80807-80807	BURLINGTON	81071-81071	SHERIDAN LAKE
80229-80231	DENVER	80536-80536	LIVERMORE	80808-80808	CALHAN	81073-81073	SPRINGFIELD
80232-80232	LAKEWOOD	80537-80539	LOVELAND	80809-80809	CASCADE	81074-81074	STARKVILLE
80233-80299	DENVER	80540-80540	LYONS	80810-80810	CHEYENNE WELLS	81075-81075	STONINGTON
80301-80329	BOULDER	80541-80541	MASONVILLE	80812-80812	COPE	81076-81076	SUGAR CITY
80401-80419	GOLDEN	80542-80542	MEAD	80813-80813	CRIPPLE CREEK	81077-81077	SWINK
80420-80420	ALMA	80543-80543	MILLIKEN	80814-80814	DIVIDE	81081-81081	TRINCHERA
80421-80421	BAILEY	80544-80544	NIWOT	80815-80815	FLAGLER	81082-81082	TRINIDAD
80422-80422	BLACK HAWK	80545-80545	RED FEATHER LAKES	80816-80816	FLORISSANT	81084-81084	TWO BUTTES
80423-80423	BOND	80546-80546	SEVERANCE	80817-80817	FOUNTAIN	81087-81087	VILAS
80424-80424	BRECKENRIDGE	80547-80547	TIMNATH	80818-80818	GENOA	81089-81089	WALSENBURG
80425-80425	BUFFALO CREEK	80548-80548	LAPORTE	80819-80819	GREEN MOUNTAIN FALLS	81090-81090	WALSH
80426-80426	BURNS	80548-80548	VIRGINIA DALE	80820-80820	GUFFEY	81091-81091	WESTON
80427-80427	CENTRAL CITY	80549-80549	WELLINGTON	80821-80821	HUGO	81092-81092	WILEY
80428-80428	CLARK	80550-80551	WINDSOR	80822-80822	JOES	81101-81102	ALAMOSA
80429-80429	CLIMAX	80553-80553	FORT COLLINS	80823-80823	KARVAL	81120-81120	ANTONITO
80430-80430	COALMONT	80601-80603	BRIGHTON	80824-80824	KIRK	81121-81121	ARBOLES
80432-80432	COMO	80610-80610	AULT	80825-80825	KIT CARSON	81122-81122	BAYFIELD
80433-80433	CONIFER	80611-80611	BRIGGSDALE	80826-80826	LIMON	81123-81123	BLANCA
80434-80434	COWDREY	80612-80612	CARR	80827-80827	LAKE GEORGE	81124-81124	CAPULIN
80435-80435	DILLON	80614-80614	EASTLAKE	80828-80828	LIMON	81125-81125	CENTER
80436-80436	DUMONT	80615-80615	EATON	80829-80829	MANITOU SPRINGS	81126-81126	CHAMA
80437-80437	EVERGREEN	80620-80620	EVANS	80830-80830	MATHESON	81127-81127	CHIMNEY ROCK
80438-80438	EMPIRE	80621-80621	FORT LUPTON	80831-80831	PEYTON	81128-81128	CHROMO
80439-80439	EVERGREEN	80622-80622	GALETON	80832-80832	RAMAH	81129-81129	CONEJOS
80440-80440	FAIRPLAY	80623-80623	GILCREST	80833-80833	RUSH	81130-81130	CREEDE
80441-80441	FOXTON	80624-80624	GILL	80834-80834	SEIBERT	81131-81131	CRESTONE
80442-80442	FRASER	80631-80639	GREELEY	80835-80835	SIMLA	81132-81132	DEL NORTE
80443-80443	FRISCO	80640-80640	HENDERSON	80836-80836	STRATTON	81133-81133	FORT GARLAND
80444-80444	GEORGETOWN	80642-80642	HUDSON	80840-80841	U S A F ACADEMY	81134-81134	GARCIA
80446-80446	GRANBY	80643-80643	KEENESBURG	80860-80860	VICTOR	81135-81135	HOMELAKE
80447-80447	GRAND LAKE	80644-80644	KERSEY	80861-80861	VONA	81136-81136	HOOPER
80448-80448	GRANT	80645-80645	LA SALLE	80862-80862	WILD HORSE	81137-81137	IGNACIO
80449-80449	HARTSEL	80646-80646	LUCERNE	80863-80863	WOODLAND PARK	81138-81138	JAROSO
80451-80451	HOT SULPHUR SPRINGS	80648-80648	NUNN	80864-80864	YODER	81140-81140	LA JARA
80452-80452	IDAHO SPRINGS	80649-80649	ORCHARD	80866-80866	WOODLAND PARK	81141-81141	MANASSA
80453-80453	IDLEDALE	80650-80650	PIERCE	80900-80997	COLORADO SPRINGS	81143-81143	MOFFAT

81144-81144 MONTE VISTA	81221-81221 COAL CREEK	81243-81243 POWDERHORN	81325-81325 EGNAR
81146-81146 MOSCA	81222-81222 COALDALE	81244-81244 ROCKVALE	81326-81326 HESPERUS
81147-81147 PAGOSA SPRINGS	81223-81223 COTOPAXI	81246-81246 CANON CITY	81327-81327 LEWIS
81148-81148 ROMEO	81224-81225 CRESTED BUTTE	81247-81247 GUNNISON	81328-81328 MANCOS
81149-81149 SAGUACHE	81226-81226 FLORENCE	81248-81248 SARGENTS	81329-81329 MARVEL
81150-81150 SAN ACACIO	81227-81227 MONARCH	81249-81249 SILVER CLIFF	81330-81330 MESA VERDE NATIONAL
81151-81151 SANFORD	81228-81228 GRANITE	81250-81250 COTOPAXI	PARK
81152-81152 SAN LUIS	81230-81231 GUNNISON	81251-81251 TWIN LAKES	81331-81331 PLEASANT VIEW
81153-81153 SAN PABLO	81232-81232 HILLSIDE	81251-81251 TWIN LAKES CPO	81332-81332 RICO
81154-81154 SOUTH FORK	81233-81233 HOWARD	81252-81252 WESTCLIFFE	81333-81333 SLICK ROCK
81155-81155 VILLA GROVE	81235-81235 LAKE CITY	81253-81253 WETMORE	81334-81334 TOWAOC
81157-81157 PAGOSA SPRINGS	81236-81236 NATHROP	81290-81290 FLORENCE	81335-81335 YELLOW JACKET
81201-81201 SALIDA	81237-81237 OHIO CITY	81301-81303 DURANGO	81401-81402 MONTROSE
81210-81210 ALMONT	81239-81239 PARLIN	81320-81320 CAHONE	81410-81410 AUSTIN
81211-81211 BUENA VISTA	81240-81240 PENROSE	81321-81321 CORTEZ	81411-81411 BEDROCK
81212-81215 CANON CITY	81241-81241 PITKIN	81323-81323 DOLORES	81413-81413 CEDAREDGE
81220-81220 CIMARRON	81242-81242 PONCHA SPRINGS	81324-81324 DOVE CREEK	81414-81414 CORY
81415-81415 CRAWFORD	81432-81432 RIDGWAY	81615-81615 SNOWMASS VILLAGE	81640-81640 MAYBELL
81416-81416 DELTA	81433-81433 SILVERTON	81620-81620 AVON	81641-81641 MEEKER
81418-81418 ECKERT	81434-81434 SOMERSET	81621-81621 BASALT	81642-81642 MEREDITH
81419-81419 HOTCHKISS	81435-81435 TELLURIDE	81623-81623 CARBONDALE	81643-81643 MESA
81420-81420 LAZEAR	81501-81506 GRAND JUNCTION	81624-81624 COLLBRAN	81645-81645 MINTURN
81421-81421 MAHER	81520-81520 CLIFTON	81625-81626 CRAIG	81646-81646 MOLINA
81422-81422 NATURITA	81521-81521 FRUITA	81628-81628 EL JEBEL	81647-81647 NEW CASTLE
81423-81423 NORWOOD	81522-81522 GATEWAY	81630-81630 DE BEQUE	81648-81648 RANGELY
81424-81424 NUCLA	81523-81523 GLADE PARK	81631-81631 EAGLE	81649-81649 RED CLIFF
81425-81425 OLATHE	81524-81524 LOMA	81632-81632 EDWARDS	81650-81650 RIFLE
81426-81426 OPHIR	81525-81525 MACK	81633-81633 DINOSAUR	81652-81652 SILT
81427-81427 OURAY	81526-81526 PALISADE	81635-81635 PARACHUTE	81653-81653 SLATER
81428-81428 PAONIA	81527-81527 WHITEWATER	81636-81636 BATTLEMENT MESA	81654-81654 SNOWMASS
81429-81429 PARADOX	81601-81602 GLENWOOD SPRINGS	81637-81637 GYPSUM	81655-81655 WOLCOTT
81430-81430 PLACERVILLE	81610-81610 DINOSAUR	81638-81638 HAMILTON	81656-81656 WOODY CREEK
81431-81431 REDVALE	81611-81612 ASPEN	81639-81639 HAYDEN	81657-81658 VAIL

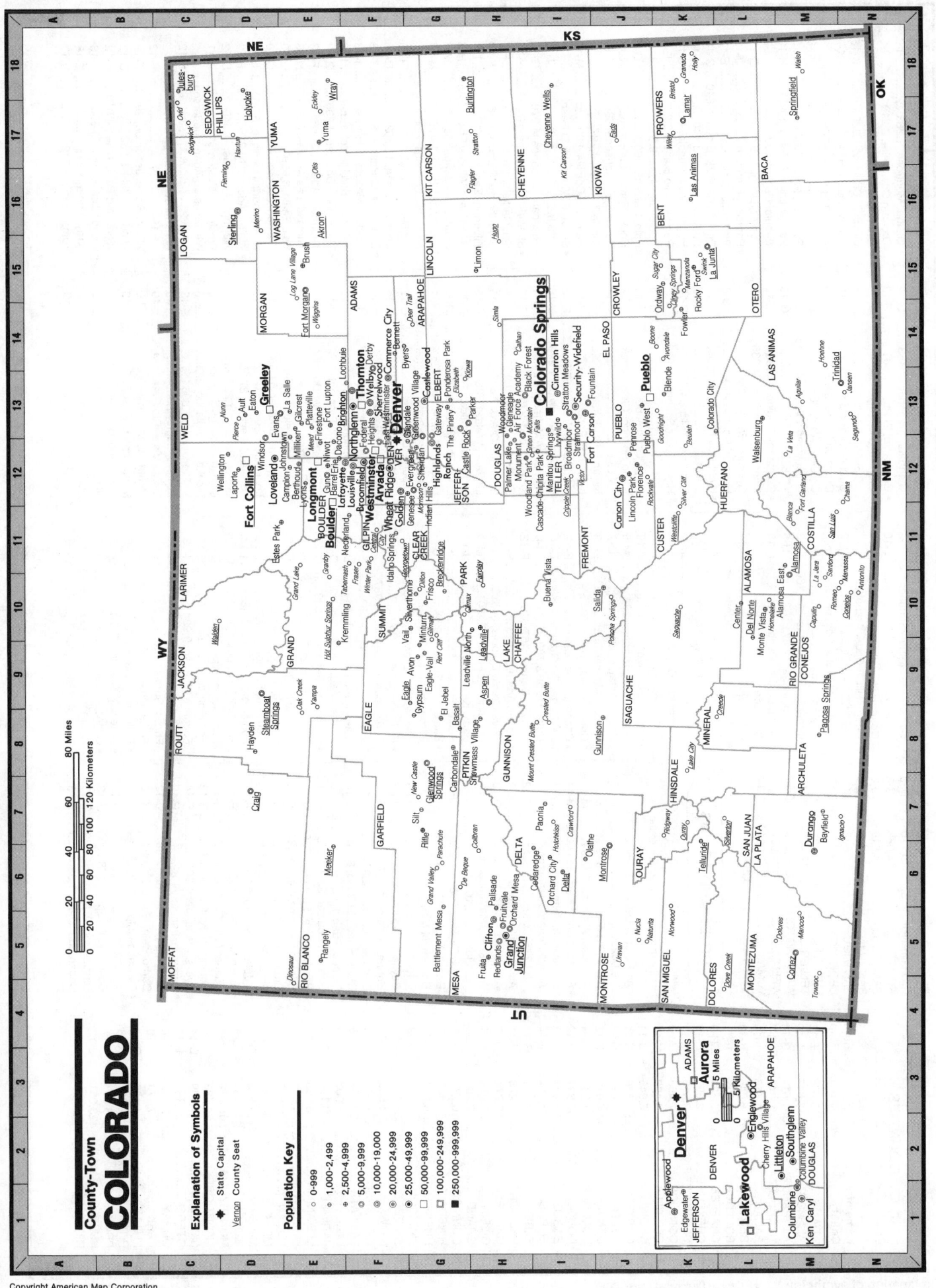

County-Town
COLORADO

Explanation of Symbols

✦ State Capital

<u>Vernon</u> ⊙ County Seat

Population Key

- ○ 0-999
- ⊙ 1,000-2,499
- ⊕ 2,500-4,999
- ⊕ 5,000-9,999
- ◉ 10,000-19,000
- ◉ 20,000-24,999
- ◉ 25,000-49,999
- □ 50,000-99,999
- ☐ 100,000-249,999
- ■ 250,000-999,999

COUNTIES

(63 Counties)

Name of County	Population	Location on Map
ADAMS	265,038	F-14
ALAMOSA	13,617	L-10
ARAPAHOE	391,511	G-14
ARCHULETA	5,345	M-7
BACA	4,556	L-16
BENT	5,048	K-16
BOULDER	225,339	E-11
CHAFFEE	12,684	H-9
CHEYENNE	2,397	H-16
CLEAR CREEK	7,619	G-11
CONEJOS	7,453	M-9
COSTILLA	3,190	M-11
CROWLEY	3,946	J-14
CUSTER	1,926	K-11
DELTA	20,980	H-6
DENVER	467,610	F-12
DOLORES	1,504	K-4
DOUGLAS	60,391	H-12
EAGLE	21,928	F-8
EL PASO	397,014	J-14
ELBERT	9,646	G-13
FREMONT	32,273	I-11
GARFIELD	29,974	F-7
GILPIN	3,070	F-11
GRAND	7,966	E-9
GUNNISON	10,273	H-7
HINSDALE	467	K-7
HUERFANO	6,009	L-11
JACKSON	1,605	C-9
JEFFERSON	438,430	G-12
KIOWA	1,688	J-16
KIT CARSON	7,140	G-16
LA PLATA	32,284	L-6
LAKE	6,007	H-9
LARIMER	186,136	C-10
LAS ANIMAS	13,765	L-13
LINCOLN	4,529	G-15
LOGAN	17,567	C-15
MESA	93,145	G-4
MINERAL	558	K-8
MOFFAT	11,357	C-5
MONTEZUMA	18,672	L-4
MONTROSE	24,423	J-4
MORGAN	21,939	D-14
OTERO	20,185	L-14
OURAY	2,295	J-6
PARK	7,174	G-10
PHILLIPS	4,189	D-17
PITKIN	12,661	G-8
PROWERS	13,347	K-17
PUEBLO	123,051	J-13
RIO BLANCO	5,972	E-4
RIO GRANDE	10,770	M-9
ROUTT	14,088	C-8
SAGUACHE	4,619	J-8
SAN JUAN	745	L-6
SAN MIGUEL	3,653	K-4
SEDGWICK	2,690	C-17
SUMMIT	12,881	F-10
TELLER	12,468	H-12
WASHINGTON	4,812	D-15
WELD	131,821	C-13
YUMA	8,954	D-17
TOTAL	**3,294,394**	

CITIES AND TOWNS

Note: The first name is that of the city or town, second, that of the county in which it is located, then the population and location on the map.

- Air Force Academy, El Paso, 9,062 — H-13
Akron, Washington, 1,599 — E-16
- Alamosa, Alamosa, 7,579 — M-10
- Alamosa East, Alamosa, 1,389 — M-11
- Applewood, Jefferson, 11,069 — K-1
Arvada, Adams/Jefferson, 89,235 — F-12
Aspen, Pitkin, 5,049 — H-9
Ault, Weld, 1,107 — D-13
Aurora, Adams/Arapahoe/Douglas, 222,103 — K-3
Avon, Eagle, 1,798 — F-9
Basalt, Eagle/Pitkin, 1,128 — G-8
- Battlement Mesa, Garfield, 1,477 — G-6
Bayfield, La Plata, 1,090 — M-7
Bennett, Adams, 1,757 — F-14
Berthoud, Larimer, 2,990 — E-12
- Black Forest, El Paso, 8,143 — H-13
Blende, Pueblo — K-13
Boulder, Boulder, 83,312 — E-11
Breckenridge, Summit, 1,285 — G-10
Brighton, Adams/Weld, 14,203 — F-13
Broadmoor, El Paso — I-13
Broomfield, Adams/Boulder/Jefferson/Weld, 24,638 — F-12
Brush, Morgan, 4,165 — E-15
Buena Vista, Chaffee, 1,752 — I-10
Burlington, Kit Carson, 2,941 — G-18
Byers, Arapahoe, 1,065 — F-14
- Campion, Larimer, 1,692 — E-12
Canon City, Fremont, 12,687 — J-12
- Carbondale, Garfield, 3,004 — G-8
- Cascade-Chipita Park, El Paso, 1,479 — H-13
Castle Rock, Douglas, 8,708 — G-13
- Castlewood, Arapahoe, 24,392 — G-13
Cedaredge, Delta, 1,380 — I-6
Center, Rio Grande/Saguache, 1,963 — L-10
Central City, Gilpin, 335 — F-11
Cherry Hills Village, Arapahoe, 5,245 — L-2
Cheyenne Wells, Cheyenne, 1,128 — I-18
- Cimarron Hills, El Paso, 11,160 — I-13
- Clifton, Mesa, 12,671 — H-5
- Colorado City, Pueblo, 1,149 — K-13
Colorado Springs, El Paso, 281,140 — I-13
- Columbine, Arapahoe/Jefferson, 23,969 — M-1
Columbine Valley, Arapahoe, 1,071 — M-2
Commerce City, Adams, 16,466 — F-13
Conejos, Conejos — N-10
Cortez, Montezuma, 7,284 — M-5
Craig, Moffat, 8,091 — D-7
Creede, Mineral, 362 — L-8
Cripple Creek, Teller, 584 — I-12
Dacono, Weld, 2,228 — E-12
Del Norte, Rio Grande, 1,674 — L-10
Delta, Delta, 3,789 — I-6
Denver, Denver, 467,610 — F-12
- Derby, Adams, 6,043 — F-14
Dove Creek, Dolores, 643 — L-4
Durango, La Plata, 12,430 — M-6
Eads, Kiowa, 780 — J-17
Eagle, Eagle, 1,580 — F-9
- Eagle-Vail, Eagle, 1,922 — G-9
Eaton, Weld, 1,959 — D-13
Edgewater, Jefferson, 4,613 — K-1
- El Jebel, Eagle, 2,605 — G-8
Englewood, Arapahoe, 29,387 — L-2
Erie, Boulder/Weld, 1,258 — E-12
Estes Park, Larimer, 3,184 — D-11
Evans, Weld, 5,877 — D-13
Evergreen, Jefferson, 7,582 — G-12
Fairplay, Park, 387 — H-10
Federal Heights, Adams, 9,342 — F-12
Firestone, Weld, 1,358 — E-12
Florence, Fremont, 2,990 — J-12
Fort Carson, El Paso, 11,309 — I-13
Fort Collins, Larimer, 87,758 — D-12
Fort Lupton, Weld, 5,159 — E-13
Fort Morgan, Morgan, 9,068 — E-15
Fountain, El Paso, 9,984 — I-13
Fowler, Otero, 1,154 — K-14
Frisco, Summit, 1,601 — G-10
Fruita, Mesa, 4,045 — H-5
Fruitvale, Mesa, 5,222 — H-5
- Gateway, Mesa, 7,510 — G-12
Genesee, Jefferson, 2,737 — F-12
Georgetown, Clear Creek, 891 — F-11
Gilcrest, Weld, 1,084 — E-13
Glendale, Arapahoe, 2,453 — G-12
- Gleneagle, El Paso, 1,661 — H-13
Glenwood Springs, Garfield, 6,561 — G-8
Golden, Jefferson, 13,116 — F-12
Grand Junction, Mesa, 29,034 — H-5
Greeley, Weld, 60,536 — D-13
Greenwood Village, Arapahoe, 7,589 — L-2
- Gunbarrel, Boulder, 9,388 — E-12
Gunnison, Gunnison, 4,636 — J-8
Gypsum, Eagle, 1,750 — F-8
Hayden, Routt, 1,444 — D-8
- Highlands Ranch, Douglas, 10,181 — G-12
Holyoke, Phillips, 1,931 — D-18
Hot Sulphur Springs, Grand, 347 — E-10
Hugo, Lincoln, 660 — H-15
Idaho Springs, Clear Creek, 1,834 — F-11
Indian Hills, Jefferson — G-12
Ivywild, El Paso — I-13
Johnstown, Weld, 1,579 — E-12
Julesburg, Sedgwick, 1,295 — C-18
- Ken Caryl, Jefferson, 24,391 — M-1
Kiowa, Elbert, 275 — G-13
Kremmling, Grand, 1,166 — E-9
La Junta, Otero, 7,637 — K-15
La Salle, Weld, 1,783 — E-13
Lafayette, Boulder, 14,548 — F-12
Lake City, Hinsdale, 223 — K-8
Lakewood, Jefferson, 126,481 — L-1
Lamar, Prowers, 8,343 — K-17
Laporte, Larimer — D-12
Las Animas, Bent, 2,481 — K-16
Leadville, Lake, 2,629 — H-10
- Leadville North, Lake, 1,757 — H-10
Limon, Lincoln, 1,831 — H-15
Lincoln Park, Fremont, 3,728 — J-12
Littleton, Arapahoe/Douglas, 33,685 — M-2
Lochbuie, Weld, 1,168 — E-13
Longmont, Boulder, 51,555 — E-12
Louisville, Boulder, 12,361 — F-12
Loveland, Larimer, 37,352 — D-12
Lyons, Boulder, 1,227 — E-12
Manitou Springs, El Paso, 4,535 — I-13
Meeker, Rio Blanco, 2,098 — E-6
Milliken, Weld, 1,605 — E-13
Minturn, Eagle, 1,066 — G-9
Monte Vista, Rio Grande, 4,324 — L-10
Montrose, Montrose, 8,854 — J-6
Monument, El Paso, 1,020 — H-13
Nederland, Boulder, 1,099 — F-11
Niwot, Boulder, 2,666 — E-12
Northglenn, Adams/Weld, 27,195 — F-13
Olathe, Montrose, 1,263 — I-6
Orchard City, Delta, 2,218 — I-6
- Orchard Mesa, Mesa, 5,977 — H-5
Ordway, Crowley, 1,025 — K-15
Ouray, Ouray, 644 — K-7
Pagosa Springs, Archuleta, 1,207 — M-8
Palisade, Mesa, 1,871 — H-6
Palmer Lake, El Paso, 1,480 — H-12
Paonia, Delta, 1,403 — I-7
Parker, Douglas, 5,450 — G-13
Penrose, Fremont, 2,235 — J-12
Platteville, Weld, 1,515 — E-13
- Ponderosa Park, Elbert, 1,640 — G-13
Pueblo, Pueblo, 98,640 — J-13
Pueblo West, Pueblo, 4,386 — J-13
Rangely, Rio Blanco, 2,278 — E-5
- Redlands, Mesa, 9,355 — H-5
Rifle, Garfield, 4,636 — G-7
Rocky Ford, Otero, 4,162 — K-15
Saguache, Saguache, 584 — K-10
Salida, Chaffee, 4,737 — J-10
San Luis, Costilla, 800 — M-11
- Security-Widefield, El Paso, 23,822 — I-13
Sheridan, Arapahoe, 4,976 — G-12
Sherrelwood, Adams, 16,636 — F-13
Silt, Garfield, 1,095 — F-7
Silverthorne, Summit, 1,768 — F-10
Silverton, San Juan, 716 — L-7
Snowmass Village, Pitkin, 1,449 — H-8
- Southglenn, Arapahoe, 43,087 — M-2
Springfield, Baca, 1,475 — M-17
Steamboat Springs, Routt, 6,695 — D-9
Sterling, Logan, 10,362 — D-16
Stratmoor, El Paso, 5,854 — I-13
Stratton Meadows, El Paso, 1,309 — K-6
- The Pinery, Douglas, 4,885 — G-13
Thornton, Adams, 55,031 — F-13
Trinidad, Las Animas, 8,580 — N-13
Vail, Eagle, 3,659 — G-10
Walden, Jackson, 890 — C-10
Walsenburg, Huerfano, 3,300 — L-13
- Welby, Adams, 10,218 — F-13
Wellington, Larimer, 1,340 — D-12
Westcliffe, Custer, 312 — K-11
Westminster, Adams/Jefferson, 74,625 — F-12
- Westminster East, Adams, 5,197 — F-12
Wheat Ridge, Jefferson, 29,419 — F-12
Windsor, Weld, 5,062 — D-12
Woodland Park, Teller, 4,610 — H-12
- Woodmoor, El Paso, 3,858 — H-13
Wray, Yuma, 1,998 — E-18
Yuma, Yuma, 2,719 — E-17

Explanation of symbols: ● – Census Designated Place (CDP)

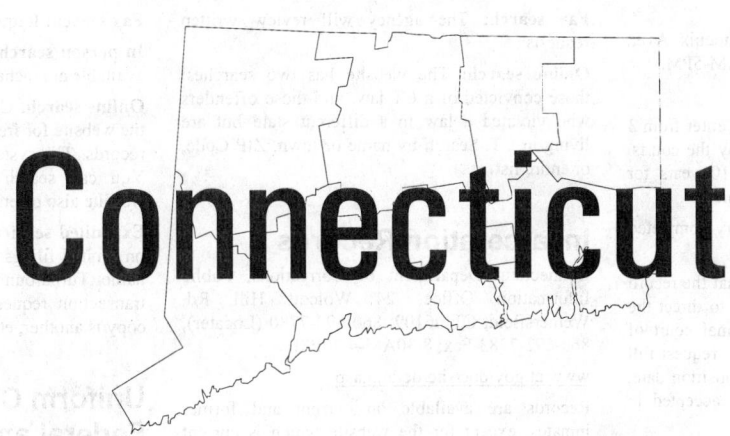

Connecticut

General Help Numbers:

Governor's Office

State Capitol, 210 Capitol Ave
Hartford, CT 06106
www.ct.gov/governor

860-566-4840
Fax 860-566-4677
8AM-5PM

Attorney General's Office

PO Box 120
Hartford, CT 06141-0120
www.cslib.org/attygenl

860-808-5318
Fax 860-808-5387
8:30AM-4:30PM

Legislative Records

State Library, Bill Room 231
Hartford, CT 06106
www.cga.ct.gov

860-757-6550
Fax 860-757-6594
9AM-5PM

State Archives

History & Genealogy Unit
231 Capitol Ave
Hartford, CT 06106
www.cslib.org/archives.htm

860-757-6580
Fax 860-757-6677
9AM-5PM M-F

State Specifics:

Capital:

Hartford
Hartford County

Time Zone:

EST

Number of Counties:

8

Population:

3,503,604

Website:

www.ct.gov

State Agencies

Criminal Records

Department of Public Safety, Bureau of Identification, 1111 Country Club Rd, Middletown, CT 06457; 860-685-8480, 860-685-8361-Fax; 8:30AM-4:30PM.

www.state.ct.us/dps/spbi.htm

DPS-846-C Form "State Police Bureau of Identification Request" can be downloaded from the website.

Records are available from the 1950's on. Records were first computerized in 1983. It takes about 30 days before new records are available for inquiry.

Records are normally destroyed after subject reaches 100th birthdate. 90% of all arrests in database have final dispositions recorded, 90% for those arrests within last 5 years.

Searching: Records are open to the public using a name search. Fingerprint searches are not available to the public. Pending case information is available. Include the following in your request-date of birth. Request forms may be downloaded from the website. Approximately 90% of the records on file are fingerprint supported. The following data is not released: dismissals or juvenile records. The records released to the public

only contain convictions. Nolles are usually released if in conjunction with a conviction.

Access by: mail, in person.

Fee & Payment: The fee is $25.00 per request. Fee payee: Commissioner of Public Safety. Prepayment required. Personal checks accepted. No credit cards accepted.

Mail search: Turnaround time: 7 to 10 days. Records must be in writing. SASE helpful.

In person search: Request must be on agency form; results are mailed only. If you come in-person, the results are still mailed.

Statewide Court Records - Records Center

Connecticut Record Center, 111 Phoenix Ave,, Enfield, CT 06082; 860-741-3714, 9AM-5PM.

www.jud.state.ct.us

Case records are sent to the Record Center from 3 months to 5 years after disposition by the courts. These records are then maintained 10 years for misdemeanors and 20+ years for felonies.

Records are available for all data entry completed by close of business the previous day.

Searching: If a requester is certain that the record is at the Record Center, it is quicker to direct the request here rather than to the original court of record. Include the following in your request-full defendant name, docket number, disposition date, and court action. Requests are only accepted in writing.

Access by: mail.

Fee & Payment: Fee is $3.00 for each docket, $5.00 if certifed. Fee payee: Treasurer-State of Connecticut Personal checks must have name and address printed on the check; if requesting in person, check must have same address as drivers' license.

Mail search: No searching by mail.

Statewide Court Records

Chief Court Administrator, 231 Capitol Ave, Hartford, CT 06106; 860-757-2100, 860-757-2270 (External Affairs), 860-757-2215-Fax; 8AM-5PM.

www.jud.state.ct.us

Specific requests for case information should be obtained from the court itself.

Records are available for all data entry completed by close of business the previous day.

Searching: Records are retained per Sec 7-13 of the Superior Court General provision.

Access by: online.

Online search: Online access allows for civil, housing and family cases only at the party name inquiry page at www.jud2.state.ct.us/Civil_Inquiry/GetParty.asp. Assignment lists and calendars are also available free at www.jud2.state.ct.us. Opinions from the Supreme and Appellate courts are available from the general website.

Sexual Offender Registry

Department of Public Safety, Sex Offender Registry Unit, PO Box 2794, Middletown, CT 06757-9294 (Courier address: 1111 Country Club Rd, Middleton, CT 06457); 860-685-8060, 860-685-8349-Fax; 8:30AM-4:30PM.

www.state.ct.us/dps/Sex_Offender_Registry.htm

It is suggested to visit local law enforcement if you cannot search online.

Records are available from October 1, 1988. It takes 1 day before new records are available for inquiry. Records are normally destroyed after registry term expires.

Searching: Include the following in your request-date of birth. The following data is not released: names of victims and treatment information.

Access by: mail, fax, online.

Fee & Payment: There is no fee.

Mail search: The agency will review written requests.

Fax search: The agency will review written requests.

Online search: The website has two searches: those convicted of a CT law, and those offenders who violated a law in a different state but are living in CT. Search by name or town, ZIP Code, or entire list.

Incarceration Records

Connecticut Department of Corrections, Public Information Office, 24 Wolcott Hill Rd, Wethersfield, CT 06109; 860-692-7780 (Locater), 860-692-7783-Fax; 8:30AM-4:30PM.

www.ct.gov/doc/site/default.asp

Records are available on current and former inmates, except for the website which is current only. Computerized records go back to 1970. It takes about 30 days before new records are available for inquiry.

Searching: Records are open to the public using a name search. Location, conviction and sentencing information, bond, and release dates are released. An FOI request must be submitted to access records for inmates not currently incarcerated. Include the following in your request-name; DOB and SSN are helpful.

Access by: mail, phone, online.

Fee & Payment: There is no fee.

Mail search: Turnaround time: 7 to 10 days.

Phone search: For phone search, use the "Locater" number listed above.

Online search: Current inmates may be searched at www.ctinmateinfo.state.ct.us/searchop.asp.

Corporation, Limited Partnership, Trademarks/Servicemarks, Limited Liability Company and Limited Liability Partnership, Statutory Trust Records

Secretary of State, Commercial Recording Division, 30 Trinity St, Hartford, CT 06106; 860-509-6003, 860-509-6069-Fax; 8:30AM-4PM.

www.sots.state.ct.us

Assumed names are found at the town level.

New records are available for inquiry immediately. Records are indexed on microfilm, inhouse computer.

Searching: Include the following in your request-full name of business, specific records that you need copies of. In addition to the articles of incorporation, corporation records include the following information: Annual Reports, Officers, Directors, Prior (merged) names, Inactive and Reserved names.

Access by: mail, phone, fax, in person, online.

Fee & Payment: The search fee is $20.00 per business name for copies of documents on record. Add $5.00 for certification. Fee payee: Secretary of State. Prepayment required. Personal checks accepted. Credit cards accepted: MasterCard, Visa.

Mail search: Turnaround time: 2 to 3 days. No SASE is required.

Phone search: Only limited, basic information is available by phone.

Fax search: Requests accepted by fax.

In person search: Certain, limited information is available at no charge.

Online search: Click on the CONCORD option at the website for free access to corporation and UCC records. The system is open from 7AM to 11PM. You can search by business name only. The website also offers online filing.

Expedited service: Expedited service is available on limited filings for an add'l $25.00 per business name. Turnaround time: 24 hours. The fee is per transaction requested; review is one transaction, copy is another, etc.

Uniform Commercial Code, Federal and State Tax Liens

UCC Division, Secretary of State, PO Box 150470, Hartford, CT 06115-0470 (Courier address: 30 Trinity St, Hartford, CT 06106); 860-509-6002, 860-509-6069-Fax; 8:30AM-4PM.

www.sots.state.ct.us

Records are available from 8/94 on computer, earlier records are on microfilm from 10/80. It takes one month or less before new records are available for inquiry.

Searching: Use search request form UCC-11. The search includes tax liens. Include the following in your request-debtor name or original .

Access by: mail, fax, in person, online.

Fee & Payment: UCC searches include tax liens and are free if requested in person, $25.00 per name by mail. Copies are $20.00 for a plain copy or $25.00 for a certified copy. Fee payee: Secretary of State. Prepayment required. Credit cards are accepted for in-person searching only. Personal checks accepted. Credit cards accepted: MasterCard, Visa.

Mail search: Turnaround time: 3 to 5 days.

Fax search: Use of credit card required.

In person search: Walk-in service available, excepted for prepared documents.

Online search: Records may be accessed at no charge on the Internet. Click on the CONCORD ON-LINE option (lower right corner). The system is open 7AM to 11PM.

Other access: Bulk lists and CDs are available for purchase. Call the Financial Area at 860-509-6165.

Sales Tax Registrations

Dept of Revenue - Taxpayer Services Division, Sales Tax Registrations, 25 Sigourney St, Hartford, CT 06106; 860-297-4885, 860-297-5714-Fax; 8AM-5PM.

www.ct.gov/drs/site/default.asp

It takes up to 3 weeks before new records are available for inquiry. Records are normally destroyed after 5 years after date of abatement for abated taxpayer files and 5 years after "out-of-business notice" for out-of-business taxpayer files.

Searching: This agency will only confirm that the business is registered and active. They will provide no other information. Include the following in your request-business name. They will also search by tax permit number. Authorized business representatives may request copies of their records only by mail, fax, or in person.

Access by: mail, phone, fax, in person.

Fee & Payment: There is no search fee

Mail search: Turnaround time: 1 day.

Phone search: Records available by phone only to verify a permit was issued.

Fax search: Same criteria as mail searches.

In person search: If the question is more than "has a permit been issued," the requester must have documents completed and have legal authority to make request.

Birth Certificates, Death Records, Marriage Certificates
Access to Records is Restricted.

Department of Public Health, Vital Records Section MS# 11VRS, PO Box 340308, Hartford, CT 06134-0308 (Courier address: 410 Capitol Ave, Hartford, CT 06134); 860-509-7897, 860-509-7964-Fax; 8:30AM-4:30PM M-F.

www.dph.state.ct.us/OPPE/hpvital.htm

The state is in the process of microfilming birth, death and marriage records. You must contact the town/city clerk of occurrence to obtain copies of records. The website has a list of towns and phone numbers. Records are $5.00 each at the town level.

Divorce Records
Records not maintained by a state level agency.

The state does not maintain divorce records; records are available from the Chief Clerks of the 15 Judicial District Courts; See the County Courts Section. The State Vital Records Section (860-509-7897) will also provide contact info for the 15 courts.

Workers' Compensation Records

Workers Compensation Commission, 21 Oak Street, Hartford, CT 06106; 860-493-1500, 860-247-1361-Fax; 7:45AM-4:30PM.

http://wcc.state.ct.us

All files are kept at one of the eight district offices. This agency will forward the request to the proper district office, or you can order direct from the D. Office. Requesters with authorization may email requests to peter.miecznikowski@postate.ct.us.

Records are available on microfilm from 1914 thru 1985 and computerized from 1985 forward, for insurance coverage files. The case files since 1995 are indexed on computer. Records are not destroyed. It takes 1 month before new records are available for inquiry.

Searching: Claims information is not released without a signed release from the employee, for employment checks. Include the following in your request-claimant name, Social Security Number (if available), date of injury, name and address of employer. Include as much information as possible. The following data is not released: medical records, commissioner's notes.

Access by: mail, phone, fax, in person.

Fee & Payment: Fees vary depending upon the nature of the request and are determined at that time. Fee payee: Workers Compensation Commission. Personal checks accepted. No credit cards accepted.

Mail search: Turnaround time: variable. A SASE is requested.

Phone search: You may call for information.

Fax search: A mail request must follow.

In person search: You may request information in person.

Other access: The agency will sell self-insured lists for $5.00.

Driver Records

Department of Motor Vehicles, Copy Records Unit, 60 State St., Wethersfield, CT 06161-0503; 860-263-5154, 8:30AM-4:30PM T-F.

www.ct.gov/dmv/site/default.asp

Copies of tickets may be obtained from the Superior Court Records Center, 860-741-3714 for a fee of $3.00, or $5.00 for certified copy.

Records are available for 3/5/10 years to present, dependent upon the type of violation. It takes 5 to 7 days before new records are available for inquiry. Records are normally destroyed after 5 years at the discretion of the commissioner. The state does not report accidents on the driving record.

Searching: Mail and in person requesters must complete Form J-23 and state permissible use. Casual requests must include evidence of the individual's consent and form. The form can be ordered from the web at http://dmvct.org/formsrec.htm or by calling 860-263-5700. Include the following in your request-two forms of ID (one with photo), signed Form J-23. The driver's license number, name and address are needed when searching, the DOB is optional. A DWI first offense violation will not appear if the offender attends an "Accelerated Alcohol Class."

Access by: mail, in person, online.

Fee & Payment: The fee for walk-in or mail-in driving records is $20.00 per record (the highest fee in the US for a driving record). The fee for ordering online is $15.00. The fee for a license status check is $20.00. Fee payee: Department of Motor Vehicles. Prepayment required. Personal checks accepted. No credit cards accepted.

Mail search: Turnaround time: 2 weeks.

In person search: The state will process up to 3 requests (at one time) for walk-in requesters who have a permissible use as stipulated in C.G.S.#14-10. Please note the office is closed on Mondays.

Online search: Online access is provided to approved businesses that enter into written contract. The contract requires a $37,500 prepayment deposit for the first 2,500 records. Fee is $15.00 per record. The address is part of the record. For more information, call 203-805-6093.

Other access: Batch requests are available for approved users, call 203-805-6093 for details.

Vehicle Ownership, Vehicle Identification

Department of Motor Vehicles, Copy Record Unit, 60 State St,, Wethersfield, CT 06161-1896; 860-263-5154, 8:AM-4:30PM T- F.

www.ct.gov/dmv/site/default.asp

Section 14-10 of the Connecticut General Statutes regulates the release of record information in accordance with federal DPPA guidelines.

Records are available for 3 years to present. Any records prior to this period may be destroyed at the discretion of the commissioner. It takes six weeks before new records are available for inquiry.

Searching: Permissible users of the information are listed on back of Form J-23. Otherwise, requester must include evidence of subject's written consent. Form J-23 can be ordered from the website or obtained by calling 860-263-5700. Include the following in your request-two forms of ID and one must contain a photo of the person signing the Form. Name searches and license plate searches are available to J-23 approved requesters. Businesses requesting for permissible purposes may only confirm the accuracy of personal information submitted by an individual to them.

Access by: mail, in person, online.

Fee & Payment: Record searches are $20.00 each, including title, lien, and current owner searches. Certification is an additional $20.00. A full charge is for a "no record found." Fee payee: Department of Motor Vehicles. Prepayment required. Personal checks accepted. No credit cards accepted.

Mail search: Turnaround time: 3 to 4 working days. The agency requests that you use their Form J-23. A SASE is requested.

In person search: The state will process up to 3 requests (file information only) for walk-in customers. Drop off requests accepted. Please note the office is closed on Mondays.

Online search: Vehicle record information is available on a volume basis to approved businesses that enter into a written agreement. The contract requires an annual fee and a surety bond. For more information, call 860-805-6093.

Accident Reports

Department of Public Safety, Reports and Records Unit, 1111 Country Club Rd, Middletown, CT 06457; 860-685-8250, 8:30AM-4:30PM.

Records are available from 10 years to present. Searching by name only goes back 5 years.

Searching: The request should include data and location of incident, names of operators, and the 8 digit case number (if known). The following data is not released: pending cases or sealed records.

Access by: mail.

Fee & Payment: Prepayment of the $8.00 search fee per record is required. Fee payee: Commissioner of Public Safety. Personal checks accepted. No credit cards accepted.

Mail search: Turnaround time: 2 to 4 weeks. A SASE is requested.

Vessel Ownership, Vessel Registration

Department of Motor Vehicles, Marine Vessel Section, 60 State Street, Wethersfield, CT 06161-3032; 860-263-5151, 860-263-5555-Fax; 8AM-5PM T-F; til 12:30 PM Sat.

www.ct.gov/dmv/cwp/view.asp?A=818&Q=245044

Lien information is found at the Secretary of State.

Records are available from 1982, records are maintained on computer for 4 years then placed on microfiche. All motorized boats any length, and all vessels over 19.5 ft without motor must be registered. It takes within minutes before new records are available for inquiry. Records are normally destroyed after 5 years.

Searching: All requests must be in writing. Requests follow requirements of DPPA. Use Form J-23B. Include the following in your request-photo ID and money. Either the name, CT registration number or hull number is needed to do a search.

Access by: mail, in person.

Fee & Payment: The fee is $20.00 for a current owner search or for a copy of the registration and $17.50 for a complete boat history. Certification is an additional $20.00. Fee payee: Department of Motor Vehicles. Prepayment required. Personal checks accepted. No credit cards accepted.

Mail search: Turnaround time: 1 to 2 weeks. No SASE is required.

In person search: In some instances, results are returned by mail. The agency is closed to the public on Mondays.

Other access: Bulk list information is available by contract. The fee depends on data requested. Call 860-263-5241 for ordering procedures.

Voter Registration
Access to Records is Restricted.

Secretary of State, Election Services Division, 30 Trinity Street, 2nd Fl, Hartford, CT 06106; 860-509-6100.

www.sots.state.ct.us/#

Presently, records are open at the town level. There are 169 towns. However, the Federal Help America Vote Act of 2002 (HAVA) law requires implementation of a central, computerized, statewide voter registration system by 01/01/2006. The state will comply.

GED Certificates

Department of Education, GED Records, 25 Industrial Park Rd, Middletown, CT 06457; 860-807-2110, 860-807-2112-Fax; 8AM-5PM.

www.state.ct.us/sde

It takes 6 weeks before new records are available for inquiry.

Searching: Include the following in your request-signed release, Social Security Number, date of birth. The year of the test is helpful. For records prior to 1982, the location of the test is needed.

Access by: mail, fax, in person.

Fee & Payment: There is no search fee.

Mail search: Turnaround time: 2 to 3 days. No SASE is required.

Fax search: There is no fee to fax back to a local phone number.

In person search: Photo ID is required.

Hunting and Fishing License Information

Department of Environmental Protection, License Division, 79 Elm St, Hartford, CT 06106; 860-424-3105, 860-424-4072-Fax; 9AM-4PM.

www.dep.state.ct.us

Records are available from 1999 to present. It takes 1 day before new records are available for inquiry. Records are indexed on inhouse computer. Records are normally destroyed after 5 years.

Searching: Only deer tag information is released. Include the following in your request-full name, address. All requests must be in writing.

Access by: mail, in person.

Fee & Payment: There is no search fee. Copies are $.25 per page. Fee payee: Department of Environmental Protection. Prepayment required. Personal checks accepted. No credit cards accepted.

Mail search: Turnaround time: 1 to 3 days. No SASE is required.

In person search: Must have the request in writing.

Other access: CDs are available, usually $50.00 per disk.

Connecticut State Licensing Agencies

For details about the agency responsible for licensing/certifying/registering an item below or in the Agency Quick Finder section, match an item's number with the number of the agency in the *Licensing Agency Information* section.

Connecticut Licenses Searchable Online

Acupuncturist #11	www.dph.state.ct.us/scripts/hlthprof.asp
Alcohol/Drug Counselor #11	www.dph.state.ct.us/scripts/hlthprof.asp
Antenna Svcs Dealer/Technician #5	www.dcpaccess.state.ct.us/DCPPublic/LicenseLookup.asp
Appraiser, MVPD/MVR #2	www.ct-clic.com
Architect #3	www.dcpaccess.state.ct.us/DCPPublic/LicenseLookup.asp
Architectural Firm #3	www.dcpaccess.state.ct.us/DCPPublic/LicenseLookup.asp
Asbestos Abatement Worker/Supr. #31	www.dph.state.ct.us/scripts/hlthprof.asp
Asbestos Consultant/Contractor #31	www.dph.state.ct.us/scripts/hlthprof.asp
Athletic Promoter #7	www.dcpaccess.state.ct.us/DCPPublic/LicenseLookup.asp
Attorney/Attorney Firm #1	www.jud2.state.ct.us/Civil_Inquiry/GetAtty.asp
Audiologist #11	www.dph.state.ct.us/scripts/hlthprof.asp
Auto Insurance Adjuster #2	www.ct-clic.com
Bail Bond Agent #2	www.ct-clic.com
Bail Enforcement Agent #13	www.state.ct.us/dps/SLFU/BailEnforcementLicensed.htm
Bail Enforcement Firearm Instructor #13	www.state.ct.us/dps/SLFU/BailEnforcementFirearmsPermit.htm
Bailbondsman #13	www.state.ct.us/dps/SLFU/BailBondsmanLicensed.htm
Bakery #8	www.dcpaccess.state.ct.us/DCPPublic/LicenseLookup.asp
Bank / Bank & Trust Company #6	www.state.ct.us/dob/pages/bcharter.htm
Bank Branch #6	www.state.ct.us/dob/pages/branch1.htm
Barber #11	www.dph.state.ct.us/scripts/hlthprof.asp
Bazaar/Raffle Permit #12	www.ct-clic.com/
Bedding Mfg/Renovation / Bedding Supply/Sterilizer #4	www.dcpaccess.state.ct.us/DCPPublic/LicenseLookup.asp
Beekeeper #14	www.caes.state.ct.us/InspectandRegandGeneral/inspecti.htm
Beverage/Water Bottler #4	www.dcpaccess.state.ct.us/DCPPublic/LicenseLookup.asp
Bingo Registration #12	www.ct-clic.com/
Boxer/Boxing Professional #7	www.dcpaccess.state.ct.us/DCPPublic/LicenseLookup.asp
Building Contractor #7	www.dcpaccess.state.ct.us/DCPPublic/LicenseLookup.asp
Casino #12	www.ct-clic.com/
Casino Occupation #12	www.ct-clic.com/
Casualty Adjuster #2	www.ct-clic.com
Check Cashing Service #6	www.state.ct.us/dob/pages/chckcash.htm
Child Caring Agency/Facility #37	www.state.ct.us/dcf/Licensed_Facilities/listing_CCF.asp
Child Placing Agency #37	www.state.ct.us/dcf/Licensed_Facilities/listing_CPA.asp
Child Psychiatric Clinic #37	www.state.ct.us/dcf/Licensed_Facilities/listing_OPCC.asp
Chiropractor #11	www.dph.state.ct.us/scripts/hlthprof.asp
Coach, High/Grade School #9	www.state.ct.us/sde/
Collection Agency #6	www.state.ct.us/dob/pages/collect.htm
Collection Agency, Consumer #6	www.state.ct.us/dob/pages/collect.htm
College/University #29	www.ctdhe.org/database/default.htm
Contractor, Mechanical #4	www.dcpaccess.state.ct.us/DCPPublic/LicenseLookup.asp
Cosmetologist #11	www.dph.state.ct.us/scripts/hlthprof.asp
Counselor, Professional #11	www.dph.state.ct.us/scripts/hlthprof.asp
Credit Union #6	www.state.ct.us/dob/pages/culist.htm
Day Treatment Facility, Extended #37	www.state.ct.us/dcf/Licensed_Facilities/listing_EDT.asp
Debt Adjuster #6	www.state.ct.us/dob/pages/debtadj.htm
Dental Anes/Conscious Sedater #11	www.dph.state.ct.us/scripts/hlthprof.asp
Dentist/Dental Hygienist #11	www.dph.state.ct.us/scripts/hlthprof.asp
Dessert Mfg, Frozen #8	www.dcpaccess.state.ct.us/DCPPublic/LicenseLookup.asp
Dietician/Nutritionist #11	www.dph.state.ct.us/scripts/hlthprof.asp
Dog Racing Owner/Trainer #12	www.ct-clic.com/
Druggist Liquor Permittee #15	www.dcpaccess.state.ct.us/DCPPublic/LicenseLookup.asp
Electrical Contr./Inspector #7	www.dcpaccess.state.ct.us/DCPPublic/LicenseLookup.asp
Electrical Journeyman/Apprentice #4	www.dcpaccess.state.ct.us/DCPPublic/LicenseLookup.asp

Electrical Sign Installer #7 .... www.dcpaccess.state.ct.us/DCPPublic/LicenseLookup.asp
Electrician #7 .... www.dcpaccess.state.ct.us/DCPPublic/LicenseLookup.asp
Electrologist/Hypertricologist #11 .... www.dph.state.ct.us/scripts/hlthprof.asp
Electronics Service Dealer/Tech. #5........................ www.dcpaccess.state.ct.us/DCPPublic/LicenseLookup.asp
Elevator Inspector/Mechanic #4 .... www.dcpaccess.state.ct.us/DCPPublic/LicenseLookup.asp
Embalmer #11 .... www.dph.state.ct.us/scripts/hlthprof.asp
Emergency Medical Svc Professional #11 .... www.dph.state.ct.us/scripts/hlthprof.asp
Engineer #4 .... www.dcpaccess.state.ct.us/DCPPublic/LicenseLookup.asp
Family Residence, Permanent #37........................... www.state.ct.us/dcf/Licensed_Facilities/listing_PFR.asp
Farm Winery #15 .... www.dcpaccess.state.ct.us/DCPPublic/LicenseLookup.asp
Fire Investigator, PI #13.. www.state.ct.us/dps/SLFU/PrivateDetectivesLicensed.htm
Fire Protection Inspector/Contr. #4.......................... www.dcpaccess.state.ct.us/DCPPublic/LicenseLookup.asp
Funeral Director/Home #11 .... www.dph.state.ct.us/scripts/hlthprof.asp
Glazier #4 .... www.dcpaccess.state.ct.us/DCPPublic/LicenseLookup.asp
Hairdresser #11 .... www.dph.state.ct.us/scripts/hlthprof.asp
Health Care Ctr. Insurer #2....................................... www.ct-clic.com
Health Club #4 .... www.dcpaccess.state.ct.us/DCPPublic/LicenseLookup.asp
Hearing Instrument Specialist #11 .... www.dph.state.ct.us/scripts/hlthprof.asp
Heating, Piping, Cooling Cont./Journey. #4............ www.dcpaccess.state.ct.us/DCPPublic/LicenseLookup.asp
Homeopathic Physician #11 .... www.dph.state.ct.us/scripts/hlthprof.asp
Honey Bee Registration #14...................................... www.caes.state.ct.us/InspectandRegandGeneral/inspecti.htm
Hypertrichologist #11 .... www.dph.state.ct.us/scripts/hlthprof.asp
Insurance Adjuster/Public Adjuster #2..................... www.ct-clic.com
Insurance Agent, Fraternal #2 .... www.ct-clic.com
Insurance Appraiser #2 .... www.ct-clic.com
Insurance Company/Producer/Consultant #2............ www.ct-clic.com
Interior Designer #4 .... www.dcpaccess.state.ct.us/DCPPublic/LicenseLookup.asp
Juice Producer #8.. www.dcpaccess.state.ct.us/DCPPublic/LicenseLookup.asp
Land Surveyor Firm #3 .... www.dcpaccess.state.ct.us/DCPPublic/LicenseLookup.asp
Landscape Architect #3 .... www.dcpaccess.state.ct.us/DCPPublic/LicenseLookup.asp
Lead Abatement Professional #11............................ www.dph.state.ct.us/scripts/hlthprof.asp
Lead Abatement Worker/Supervisor #31................... www.dph.state.ct.us/scripts/hlthprof.asp
Lead Abatement/Consul't Contractor #31................. www.dph.state.ct.us/scripts/hlthprof.asp
Lead Planner/Project Designer #11........................... www.dph.state.ct.us/scripts/hlthprof.asp
Legalized Gaming Occupation #12............................ www.ct-clic.com/
Liquor License #15 .... www.dcpaccess.state.ct.us/DCPPublic/LicenseLookup.asp
Liquor Mfg/Dist/Whlse/Store/Broker/Shipper #15 ..... www.dcpaccess.state.ct.us/DCPPublic/LicenseLookup.asp
Loan Company, Small #6 .... www.state.ct.us/dob/pages/smalloan.htm
Lobbyist #18 .... www.ethics.state.ct.us/publicinfo.htm
Lottery #12.. www.ct-clic.com/
Lottery Sales Agent #12 .... www.ct-clic.com/
Marriage & Family Therapist #11.............................. www.dph.state.ct.us/scripts/hlthprof.asp
Marshall, State #34.. www.jud.state.ct.us/faq/marshals.htm
Martial Arts Facility #4 .... www.dcpaccess.state.ct.us/DCPPublic/LicenseLookup.asp
Massage Therapist #11 .... www.dph.state.ct.us/scripts/hlthprof.asp
Mausoleum #11.. www.dph.state.ct.us/scripts/hlthprof.asp
Medical Doctor #11.. www.dph.state.ct.us/scripts/hlthprof.asp
Medical Response Technician #11 .... www.dph.state.ct.us/scripts/hlthprof.asp
Midwife #11.. www.dph.state.ct.us/scripts/hlthprof.asp
Mobile Home Park/Seller #17 .... www.dcpaccess.state.ct.us/DCPPublic/LicenseLookup.asp
Money Forwarder #6... www.state.ct.us/dob/pages/$forward.htm
Mortgage (1st) Broker/Lender #6.............................. www.state.ct.us/dob/pages/1stmtg.htm
Mortgage (2nd) Broker/Lender #6 .... www.state.ct.us/dob/pages/2ndmtg.htm
Naturopathic Physician #11 .... www.dph.state.ct.us/scripts/hlthprof.asp
New Home Construction Contr. #4 .... www.dcpaccess.state.ct.us/DCPPublic/LicenseLookup.asp
Nurse #11... www.dph.state.ct.us/scripts/hlthprof.asp
Nurse, Advance Registered Practice #11 .... www.dph.state.ct.us/scripts/hlthprof.asp
Nurse-LPN #11... www.dph.state.ct.us/scripts/hlthprof.asp
Nursery Plant Dealer #14 .... www.caes.state.ct.us/InspectandRegandGeneral/inspecti.htm
Nursery, Plant #14 .... www.caes.state.ct.us/InspectandRegandGeneral/inspecti.htm
Nursing Home Administrator #11............................... www.dph.state.ct.us/scripts/hlthprof.asp
Occupational Therapist/Assistant #11 .... www.dph.state.ct.us/scripts/hlthprof.asp

Off-Track Betting #12	www.ct-clic.com/
Optical Shop #11	www.dph.state.ct.us/scripts/hlthprof.asp
Optician #11	www.dph.state.ct.us/scripts/hlthprof.asp
Optometrist #11	www.dph.state.ct.us/scripts/hlthprof.asp
Osteopathic Physician #11	www.dph.state.ct.us/scripts/hlthprof.asp
Paramedic #11	www.dph.state.ct.us/scripts/hlthprof.asp
Pesticide Applicator #26	www.kellysolutions.com/CT/Applicators/index.htm
Pesticide-related Business #26	www.kellysolutions.com/CT/Business/index.htm
Pharmacist/Pharmacist Intern #4	www.dcpaccess.state.ct.us/DCPPublic/LicenseLookup.asp
Pharmacy #4	www.dcpaccess.state.ct.us/DCPPublic/LicenseLookup.asp
Pharmacy Technician #4	www.dcpaccess.state.ct.us/DCPPublic/LicenseLookup.asp
Physical Therapist/Assistant #11	www.dph.state.ct.us/scripts/hlthprof.asp
Physician #11	www.dph.state.ct.us/scripts/hlthprof.asp
Physician Assistant #11	www.dph.state.ct.us/scripts/hlthprof.asp
Pipefitter #7	www.dcpaccess.state.ct.us/DCPPublic/LicenseLookup.asp
Plumber #4	www.dcpaccess.state.ct.us/DCPPublic/LicenseLookup.asp
Podiatrist #11	www.dph.state.ct.us/scripts/hlthprof.asp
Premium Finance Company #2	www.ct-clic.com
Private Detective Company #13	www.state.ct.us/dps/SLFU/PrivateDetectivesLicensed.htm
Private Investigator #13	www.state.ct.us/dps/SLFU/PrivateDetectivesLicensed.htm
Private Occupational School #29	www.ctdhe.org/database/default.htm
Psychologist #11	www.dph.state.ct.us/scripts/hlthprof.asp
Public Service Technician #4	www.dcpaccess.state.ct.us/DCPPublic/LicenseLookup.asp
Radiographer #11	www.dph.state.ct.us/scripts/hlthprof.asp
Real Estate Agent/Broker/Sales #17	www.dcpaccess.state.ct.us/DCPPublic/LicenseLookup.asp
Real Estate Appraiser #17	www.dcpaccess.state.ct.us/DCPPublic/LicenseLookup.asp
Reinsurance Intermediary #2	www.ct-clic.com
Rental Car Company #2	www.ct-clic.com
Respiratory Care Practitioner #11	www.dph.state.ct.us/scripts/hlthprof.asp
Risk Purchasing/Retention Group #2	www.ct-clic.com
Sales Finance Company #6	www.state.ct.us/dob/pages/salefinc.htm
Sanitarian #11	www.dph.state.ct.us/scripts/hlthprof.asp
Sanitarian, Registered #31	www.dph.state.ct.us/scripts/hlthprof.asp
Savings & Loan Association Bank #6	www.state.ct.us/dob/pages/bcharter.htm
Savings Bank #6	www.state.ct.us/dob/pages/bcharter.htm
School Administrator/Supervisor/Guidance Counselor #9	www.state.ct.us/sde/
School Library Media Associate #9	www.state.ct.us/sde/
School Principal/Superintendent #9	www.state.ct.us/sde/
School Psychologist/Social Worker #9	www.state.ct.us/sde/
Security Company, Private #13	www.state.ct.us/dps/SLFU/PrivateSecurityLicensed.htm
Security Service #13	www.state.ct.us/dps/SLFU/PrivateDetectivesLicensed.htm
Sheet Metal Cont./Journeyman #4	www.dcpaccess.state.ct.us/DCPPublic/LicenseLookup.asp
Shorthand Court Reporter #4	www.dcpaccess.state.ct.us/DCPPublic/LicenseLookup.asp
Social Worker #11	www.dph.state.ct.us/scripts/hlthprof.asp
Solar Energy Contr./Journeyman #4	www.dcpaccess.state.ct.us/DCPPublic/LicenseLookup.asp
Speech Pathologist #11	www.dph.state.ct.us/scripts/hlthprof.asp
Speech/Language Pathologist #9	www.state.ct.us/sde/
Sprinkler Layout Technician #4	www.dcpaccess.state.ct.us/DCPPublic/LicenseLookup.asp
Student Athlete Agent #4	www.dcpaccess.state.ct.us/DCPPublic/LicenseLookup.asp
Subsurface Sewage Cleaner/Installer #11	www.dph.state.ct.us/scripts/hlthprof.asp
Surplus Line Broker #2	www.ct-clic.com
Surveyor, Land #3	www.dcpaccess.state.ct.us/DCPPublic/LicenseLookup.asp
Teacher #9	www.state.ct.us/sde/
Utilization Review Company #2	www.ct-clic.com
Vending Machine Operator #8	www.dcpaccess.state.ct.us/DCPPublic/LicenseLookup.asp
Vendor, Itinerant #4	www.dcpaccess.state.ct.us/DCPPublic/LicenseLookup.asp
Veterinarian #11	www.dph.state.ct.us/scripts/hlthprof.asp
Viatical Settlement Broker/Provider #2	www.ct-clic.com
Weights/MeasureDealer/Repair/Regular #8	www.dcpaccess.state.ct.us/DCPPublic/LicenseLookup.asp
Well Driller #7	www.dcpaccess.state.ct.us/DCPPublic/LicenseLookup.asp
Wrestler/Wrestling Manager #7	www.dcpaccess.state.ct.us/DCPPublic/LicenseLookup.asp
Youth Camp #11	www.dph.state.ct.us/BRS/Youth_camps/youthcamps.htm

Connecticut Licensing Quick Finder

Acupuncturist #11	860-509-7603
Air Emission Permittee #30	860-424-4152
Airport/Heliport #43	860-594-2544
Alcohol/Drug Counselor #11	860-509-7603
Ambulance #11	860-509-7552
Amusement Park #25	860-685-8470
Antenna Svcs Dealer/Technician #5	860-566-3275
Appraiser, MVPD/MVR #2	860-297-3954
Aquaculture Operation #20	203-874-0696
Arborist #26	860-424-3369
Architect #3	860-713-6145
Architectural Firm #3	860-713-6145
Asbestos Abatement Worker/Supr. #31	860-509-7559
Asbestos Consultant/Contractor #31	860-509-7559
Assisted Living Service #11	860-509-7400
Athletic Promoter #7	860-566-6980
Attorney/Attorney Firm #1	860-568-5157
Audiologist #11	860-509-7603
Auto Auction #44	203-805-6307
Auto Insurance Adjuster #2	860-297-3954
Auto Parts Manufacturer #27	860-263-5057
Auto Racing Permit #27	860-263-5057
Auto Renter/Leasor #27	860-263-5057
Backflow Tester #11	860-509-7333
Bail Bond Agent #2	860-297-3954
Bail Enforcement Agent #13	860-685-8046
Bail Enforcement Firearm Instr. #13	860-685-8160
Bailbondsman #13	860-685-8046
Bait Seller (Live Bait) #10	860-424-3474
Bakery #8	860-713-6160
Bank #6	860-240-8299
Bank & Trust Company #6	860-240-8299
Bank Branch #6	860-240-8299
Banking Office, Non-depository #6	860-240-8299
Barber #11	860-509-7603
Bazaar/Raffle Permit #12	860-594-5480
Bedding Mfg/Renovation #4	860-713-6000
Bedding Supply/Sterilizer #4	860-713-6000
Beekeeper #14	203-974-8479
Beverage/Water Bottler #4	860-713-6000
Bingo Registration #12	860-594-5480
Bird/Poultry Permit/Buyer #22	860-713-2512
Boxer/Boxing Professional #7	860-713-6155
Broker/Dealer Agent #6	860-240-8299
Building Contractor #7	860-566-2825
Building Inspector #33	860-685-8330
Building Official #25	860-685-8330
Bus Driver #23	860-263-5720
Business Opportunity Offering #6	860-240-8299
Car Dealer #27	860-263-5056
Carnival/Circus Operator #25	860-685-8470
Casino #12	860-594-0643
Casino Occupation #12	860-594-0643
Casualty Adjuster #2	860-297-3954
Cattle/Swine Dealer #22	860-713-2512
Charitable Solicitor #36	860-808-5030
Charter Fishing Vessel #42	860-434-6043
Chauffeur/Livery Company #24	860-594-2865
Check Cashing Service #6	860-240-8299
Cheese Dealer #22	860-713-2512
Child Caring Agency/Facility #37	860-550-6445
Child Clinic (Well Child) #11	860-509-7444
Child Placing Agency #37	860-550-6445
Child Psychiatric Clinic #37	860-550-6445
Chiropractor #11	860-509-7603
Cigarette Seller/Dist. #21	860-297-5962
Coach, High/Grade School #9	860-713-6969
Coastal/Tidal/Navigatable Waters Permit #32	860-424-3034
Collection Agency #6	860-240-8299
Collection Agency, Consumer #6	860-240-8299
College/University #29	860-947-1822
Community Assoc. Manager #7	860-713-6150
Community Living arrangement for Mentally Retarded #38	860-418-6081
Conch/Depuration/Oyster License #20	203-874-0696
Construction Inspector #25	860-685-8310
Contractor, Mechanical #4	860-713-6135
Controlled Substance License #7	860-713-6065
Convalescent Hursing Home #11	860-509-7400
Cosmetologist #11	860-509-7603
Counselor, Professional #11	860-509-7603
Crane Operator #25	860-685-8470
Cranes/Hoisting Equipment #25	860-685-8470
Credit Union #6	860-240-8299
Crematorium #11	860-509-7296
Cross-Connection Survey Insp. #11	860-509-7333
Dairy Laboratory Analyst #22	860-713-2512
Dairy Sample Collector #22	860-713-2512
Dairy Transporter #22	860-713-2512
Day Care Provider #11	860-509-8000
Day Treatment Facility, Extended #37	860-550-6445
Debt Adjuster #6	860-240-8299
Demolition Operator #25	860-685-8470
Dental Anes/Conscious Sedation Permittee #11	860-509-7603
Dentist/Dental Hygienist #11	860-509-7603
Dessert Mfg, Frozen #8	860-713-6160
Diesel Fuel Distributor #21	860-297-5962
Dietician/Nutritionist #11	860-509-7603
Digger of Shellfish #20	203-874-0696
Dog Racing Owner/Trainer #12	860-594-0643
Dog Training Facility #22	860-713-2512
Driver Education Instr/School #27	860-263-5057
Driving Instructor #23	860-263-5720/5442
Driving School #23	860-263-5442
Druggist Liquor Permittee #15	860-713-6200
Egg Grader #22	860-713-2513
Electrical Contr./Inspector #7	860-566-2825
Electrical Journeyman/Apprentice #4	860-713-6000
Electrical Sign Installer #7	860-566-2825
Electrician #7	860-566-2825
Electrologist/Hypertricologist #11	860-509-7603
Electronics Service Dealer/Tech. #5	860-566-3275
Elevator Inspector/Mechanic #4	860-713-6000
Embalmer #11	860-509-7603
Emergency Medical Svc Prof'l #11	860-509-7603
Emissions Technician #35	203-805-6244
Employment Agency #39	860-263-6790
EMS First Responder #11	860-509-7552
EMS Instructor #11	860-509-7975
Engineer #4	860-713-6000
Enviromental Professional #40	860-424-3705
Environmental Lab Director #11	860-509-7389
Explosive Handler #25	860-685-8470
Explosive Hauler #25	860-685-8470
Family Planning Clinic #11	860-509-8000
Family Residence, Permanent #37	860-550-6445
Farm Winery #15	860-713-6200
Fire Investigator, PI #13	860-685-8046
Fire Officer/Driver/Instructor #41	860-627-6363 x225
Fire Protection Inspector/Contr. #4	860-713-6000
Fire/Life Safety Educator #41	860-627-6363 x225
Firearms Dealer #13	860-685-8046
Firearms Registration #19	860-685-8290
Firefighter #41	860-627-6363 x225
Fireworks Display Operator #25	860-685-8470
Fireworks Occupation/Permit #25	860-685-8470
Fisher #10	860-424-3105
Fishery #10	860-424-3474
Food Service Inspector #11	860-509-7297
Food Tester #11	860-509-7297
Forest Products Harvestor/Practitioner #10	860-424-3630
Fruit Storage #22	860-713-2548
Fund Raiser, Paid #36	860-808-5030
Funeral Director/Home #11	860-509-7603
Fur Breeder #22	860-713-2512
Fur Buyer #10	860-424-3011
Game Breeder #10	860-424-3011
Gasoline Dealer #8	860-713-6160
Glazier #4	860-713-6000
Gun Dealer #19	860-685-8290
Hairdresser #11	860-509-7603
Hatchery #20	203-874-0696
Hazardous Material Tech. #41	860-627-6363 x225
Hazardous Waste Disposer #40	860-424-3372
Hazardous Waste Transporter #40	860-424-3372
Health Care Ctr. Insurer #2	860-297-3814
Health Club #4	860-713-6000
Hearing Instrument Specialist #11	860-509-7603
Heating, Piping, Cooling Contractor/Journeyman #4	860-713-6000
Home Health Aide Agency #11	860-509-7400
Home Health Aide Homemaker #11	860-509-7400
Home Heating Oil Seller #8	860-713-6160
Home Improvement Contr./Seller #4	860-713-6110
Home Inspector #4	860-713-6145
Homeopathic Physician #11	860-509-7603
Honey Bee Registration #14	203-974-8479
Hospice #11	860-509-7400
Hospital #11	860-509-7400
Hypertrichologist #11	860-509-7603
Industrial Truck #24	860-594-2874
Insurance Adjuster/Public Adjuster #2	860-297-3954
Insurance Agent, Fraternal #2	860-297-3954
Insurance Appraiser #2	860-297-3954
Insurance Company/Producer #2	860-297-3845
Insurance Consultant #2	860-297-3954
Interior Designer #4	860-566-2825
Investment Advisor/Agent #6	860-240-8299
Issuer Agent (Financial) #6	860-240-8299
Juice Producer #8	860-713-6160
Junkyard Operator #27	860-263-5057
Kennel #22	860-713-2512
Laboratory, Animal #11	860-509-7400
Laboratory, Clinical #11	860-509-7400
Land Surveyor Firm #3	860-713-6145
Landscape Architect #3	860-713-6145
Lead Abatement Professional #11	860-509-7603
Lead Abatement Worker/Supv'r #31	860-509-7559
Lead Abatement/Consultant Contractor #31	860-509-7559
Lead Consultant #31	860-509-7559
Lead Planner/Project Designer #11	860-509-7603
Legalized Gaming Occupation #12	860-594-0643
Lender #6	860-240-8200
Lender, Correspondent #6	860-240-8299
Liquor License #15	860-713-6200
Liquor Mfg/Dist/Whlse #15	860-713-6200
Liquor Permittee #15	860-713-6200
Liquor Store/Broker/Shipper #15	860-713-6200
Livestock Dealer #22	860-713-2512
Loan Broker/Originator #6	860-240-8299
Loan Company, Small #6	860-240-8299
Lobbyist #18	860-566-4472
Lobster Seller #10	860-424-6043
Lottery #12	860-594-0643
Lottery Sales Agent #12	860-594-0643
Marine Fishing License #42	860-434-6043
Marriage & Family Therapist #11	860-609-7603
Marshall, State #34	860-566-7109
Martial Arts Facility #4	860-713-6000
Massage Therapist #11	860-509-7603
Materialman #21	860-297-5962
Maternity Home #11	860-509-7400
Mausoleum #11	860-509-7603
Medical Doctor #11	860-509-7603
Medical Gas/Vacuum System #4	860-713-6135
Medical Response Technician #11	860-509-7603
Medication Administration for Mentally Retarded #38	860-418-6081
Mental Health Facility/Clinic #11	860-509-7400
Midwife #11	860-509-7603
Mikdwife Nurse #11	860-509-7603/7570

Milk Dealer/Producer #22 860-713-2512
Milk/Cream Weigher #22 860-713-2512
Mobile Home Park/Seller #17 860-713-6150
Money Forwarder #6 860-240-8299
Money Order/Traveler Check Issuer #6 860-240-8299
Mooring Space #43 860-594-2544
Mooring/Swim Float #32 860-424-3034
Mortgage (1st) Broker/Lender #6 860-240-8299
Mortgage (2nd) Broker/Lender #6 860-240-8299
Motion Picture Theater #25 860-685-8470
Motion Picture Theater Mgr #25 860-685-8470
Motor Bus Company #24 860-594-2865
Motor Vehicle Recycler #27 860-263-5056
Mover, Household Goods #24 860-594-2863
Naturopathic Physician #11 860-509-7603
New Home Construction Contr. #4 860-713-6000
Notary Public #16 860-509-6200
Nurse #11 .... 860-509-7603/7570
Nurse, Advance Registered Practice #11
.... 860-509-7603/7570
Nurse-LPN #11 860-509-7603
Nursery Plant Dealer #14 203-974-8481
Nursery, Plant #14 203-974-8481
Nurses' Aide #11 860-509-7603
Nursing Home #11 860-509-7400
Nursing Home Administrator #11 860-509-7603
Occupational Therapist/Assistant #11 .. 860-509-7603
Off-Track Betting #12 860-594-0643
Optical Shop #11 860-509-7603
Optician #11 860-509-7603
Optometrist #11 860-509-7603
Osteopathic Physician #11 860-509-7603
Outpatient Clinic #11 860-509-7400
Parachute Jump Area #43 860-594-2544
Paramedic #11 860-509-7603
Pawnbroker #21 860-297-4874
Pesticide Applicator #26 860-424-3369
Pesticide-related Business #26 860-424-3369
Pet Groomer #22 860-713-2512
Pet Store Operator #22 860-713-2512
Pharmacist/Pharmacist Intern #4 860-713-6000
Pharmacy #4 860-713-6000
Pharmacy Technician #4 860-713-6000
Physical Therapist/Assistant #11 860-509-7603
Physician / Physician Assistant #11 860-509-7603
Pilot, Marine #43 860-443-3856
Pipefitter #7 860-566-2825

Plan Review Technician #25 860-685-8310
Plumber #4 860-713-6000
Plumbing Inspector #25 860-685-8310
Podiatrist #11 860-509-7603
Police Officer #45 203-238-6694
Poultry Buyer #22 860-713-2512
Premium Finance Company #2 860-297-3916
Private Detective Company #13 860-685-8046
Private Investigator #13 860-685-8046
Private Occupational School #29 860-947-1822
Psychologist #11 860-509-7603
Public Accountant-CPA #16 860-509-6179
Public Service Technician #4 860-713-6000
Radiation Permittee #30 860-424-3029
Radiographer #11 860-509-7603
Real Estate Agent/Broker/Sales #17 860-713-6150
Real Estate Appraiser #17 860-713-6150
Recycler #40 860-424-3365
Reinsurance Intermediary #2 860-297-3954
Rental Car Company #2 860-297-3953
Residence for Mentally Retarded #38 .. 860-418-6081
Residential Care Home #11 860-509-7400
Respiratory Care Practitioner #11 860-509-7603
Rest Home #11 860-509-7400
Risk Purchasing/Retention Group #2 ... 860-297-3880
Safety Officer #41 .... 860-627-6363 x225
Sales Finance Company #6 860-240-8299
Sanitarian #11 860-509-7603
Sanitarian, Registered #31 860-509-7559
Savings & Loan Association Bank #6 .. 860-240-8299
Savings Bank #6 860-240-8299
School Administrator/Supervisor #9 860-713-6969
School Bus Driver #23 860-263-5720
School Guidance Counselor #9 860-713-6969
School Library Media Associate #9 860-713-6969
School Principal/Superintendent #9 860-713-6969
School Psychologist #9 860-713-6969
School Social Worker #9 860-713-6969
Scientific Collector #10 860-424-3589
SCOR #6 860-240-8299
Seafood Dealer #42 860-434-6043
Securities Agent #6 860-240-8299
Securities Broker/Dealer #6 860-240-8299
Security Company, Private #13 860-685-8046
Security Guard / Security Service #13 .. 860-685-8046
Septic Tank Cleaner #11 860-509-8000
Sewage Disposal System Instal'r #11 .. 860-509-8000

Sheet Metal Cont./Journeyman #4 860-713-6000
Shellfish Professional #20 203-874-0696
Shorthand Court Reporter #4 860-713-6000
Social Worker #11 860-509-7603
Solar Energy Contr./Journeyman #4 860-713-6000
Solid Waste Facility Operator #40 860-424-4051
Special Effects Permit #25 860-685-8470
Speech Pathologist #11 860-509-7603
Speech/Language Pathologist #9 860-713-6969
Sprinkler Layout Technician #4 860-713-6000
Student Athlete Agent #4 860-713-6000
Substance Abuse Clinic #11 860-509-7400
Subsurface Sewage Cleaner/Instal. #11 860-509-7603
Surplus Line Broker #2 860-297-3868
Surveyor, Land #3 860-713-6145
Tattoo Artist #11 860-509-8000
Taxable Entity #21 860-297-4874
Taxi Company #24 860-594-2865
Taxidermist #10 860-424-3105
Teacher #9 860-713-6969
Theatre Manager #25 860-685-8470
Tobacco Products Permit #21 860-297-5962
Towing Operator #27 860-263-5056
Training Home for Mentally Retarded #38
.... 860-418-6081
Trapper #10 860-424-3105
Tree Surgeon #7 860-566-2825
Truck Driver #23 860-263-5720
Underground Storage Tank #40 860-424-3374
Utilization Review Company #2 860-297-3862
Vehicle Dealer #27 860-263-5056
Vehicle Repairer #27 860-263-5057
Vending Machine Operator #8 860-713-6160
Vendor, Itinerent #4 860-713-6000
Veterinarian #11 860-509-7603
Viatical Settlement Broker/Provider #2 . 860-297-3882
Waste Disposal Permittee #40 860-424-3360
Water Distribnt'n System Operator #11 860-509-8000
Water Treatment Plant Operator #11 860-509-8000
Weigher #8 860-713-6000
Weights/Measures Dealer/Repairer/Regulator #8
.... 860-713-6000
Well Driller #7 860-566-2825
Wildlife Control Operator/Rehabil. #10 . 860-424-3011
Winery, Small #21 860-297-5962
Wrestler/Wrestling Manager #7 860-566-2825
Youth Camp #11 .... 860-509-8045, 800-282-6063

Connecticut Licensing Agency Information

1 Attorney Registration, Statewide Grievance Committee, 287 Main St, East Hartford, CT 06118; 860-568-5157, Fax: 860-568-4953. www.jud.state.ct.us/   Search Database at www.jud2.state.ct.us/Civil_Inquiry/GetAtty.asp

2 Department of Insurance, Licensing Division, PO Box 816 (153 Market St), Hartford, CT 06142-0816; 860-297-3845, Fax: 860-297-3978. www.ct.gov/cid
Email: ctinsdept.licensing@po.state.ct.us
Search Database at www.ct-clic.com Note: Fees for pre-programed lists: printed report-$7.88 + $.25 per page, labels-$7.88 + $.25 per 100 labels, Diskette-$7.88 + $.17 per diskette, CD-ROM-$7.88 + $.57 per CD, Email-$7.88.

3 Department of Consumer Protection, Board of Architects, 165 Capitol Ave, #110, Hartford, CT 06106; 860-713-6135, Fax: 860-713-7239. www.dcpaccess.state.ct.us/default.asp
Search Database at www.dcpaccess.state.ct.us/DCPPublic/LicenseLookup.asp Note: Lists can be downloaded at www.dcpaccess.state.ct.us/DCPRosterDownload/pRosterDownload.asp.

4 Department of Consumer Protection, Board of Trades Division, 165 Capitol Ave, Hartford, CT 06106; 860-713-6000, Fax: 860-713-7239. www.dcp.state.ct.us
Email: License.services@po.state.ct.us
Search Database at www.dcpaccess.state.ct.us/verify.htm Note: Lists can be downloaded at www.dcpaccess.state.ct.us/DCPRosterDownload/pRosterDownload.asp.

5 Department of Consumer Protection/Occupational Licensing, Board of Television & Radio Service Examiners, 165 Capitol Ave, Hartford, CT 06106; 860-713-6135, Fax: 860-713-7239. www.state.ct.us/dcp/
Search Database at www.dcpaccess.state.ct.us/verify.htm

6 Department of Banking, 260 Constitution Plaza, Hartford, CT 06103-1800; 860-240-8299, Fax: 860-240-8178. www.state.ct.us/dob/
Email: john.burke@po.state.ct.us
Search Database at www.state.ct.us/dob/

7 Department of Consumer Protection, Occupational Licensing Division, 165 Capitol Ave, Hartford, CT 06106; 860-713-6300, Fax: 860-713-7239. www.dcpaccess.state.ct.us
Email: license.services@po.state.ct.us
Search Database at www.dcpaccess.state.ct.us/verify.htm Note: Lists can be downloaded at www.dcpaccess.state.ct.us/DCPRosterDownload/pRosterDownload.asp.

8 Department of Consumer Protection, Food Standards Division, 165 Capitol Ave, State Office Bldg, Hartford, CT 06106-1630; 860-713-6160, Fax: 860-713-7229. www.dcp.state.ct.us/licensing/food.htm
Email: license.services@po.state.ct.us
Search Database at www.dcpaccess.state.ct.us/DCPPublic/LicenseLookup.asp Note: Lists can be downloaded at www.dcpaccess.state.ct.us/DCPRosterDownload/pRosterDownload.asp.

9 Department of Education, Bureau of Certification & Professional Development, PO Box 150471, Rm 243, Hartford, CT 06115-0471; 860-713-6969, Fax: 860-713-7017. www.state.ct.us/sde/   *more*

Email: teacher.cert@po.state.ct.us Note: License verification available through "Freedom of Information" (FOI). Request must be submitted in writing.

10 Department of Environmental Protection, Bureau of Natural Resources, 79 Elm St, Hartford, CT 06106; 860-424-3010, Fax: 860-424-4078.
www.dep.state.ct.us/burnatr/index.htm

11 Department of Public Health, Health Care or Environmental Health Licensing, PO Box 340308 (410 Capital Ave, MS 12MQA), Hartford, CT 06134-0308; 860-509-7603, Fax: 860-509-7607.
www.dph.state.ct.us
Search Database at
www.dph.state.ct.us/scripts/hlthprof.asp

12 Division of Special Revenue, Licensing Section, PO Box 11424 (555 Russell Rd), Newington, CT 06111; 860-594-0643, Fax: 860-594-0696.
www.dosr.state.ct.us/
Email: dosr@po.state.ct.us
Search Database at www.ct-clic.com/

13 Division of State Police, Special Licensing & Firearms Division, 1111 Country Club Rd, Middletown, CT 06457; 860-685-8046, Fax: 860-685-8496.
www.state.ct.us/dps/SLFU/
Email: DPS.Spec.Licensing@po.state.ct.us
Search Database at www.state.ct.us/dps/SLFU/

14 Office of the State Entomologist, Connecticut Agricultural Experiment Station, PO Box 1106 (125 Huntington St), New Haven, CT 06504; 203-974-8466, Fax: 203-974-8502.
www.caes.state.ct.us/InspectandRegandGeneral/inspecti.htm

15 Department of Consumer Protection, Liquor Control Divison, 165 Capitol Ave, Hartford, CT 06106; 860-713-6200, Fax: 860-713-7235.
Email: dosr@po.state.ct.us
Search Database at
www.dcpaccess.state.ct.us/DCPPublic/LicenseLookup.asp Note: Lists can be downloaded at
www.dcpaccess.state.ct.us/DCPRosterDownload/pRosterDownload.asp.

16 Office of the Secretary of the State, Records Division, 30 Trinity St, (PO Box 150470, 06115), Hartford, CT 06106; 860-509-6200, Fax: 860-509-6230.
www.sots.state.ct.us
Email: rls@po.state.ct.us

17 Department of Consumer Protection, Real Estate Division, 165 Capitol Ave, Rm 110, Hartford, CT 06106; 860-713-6150, Fax: 860-713-7230.
www.ct.gov/dcp/cwp/view.asp?a=1622&Q=287752&PM=1
Email: license.services@po.state.ct.us
Search Database at www.dcpaccess.state.ct.us/verify.htm Note: Lists can be downloaded at
www.dcpaccess.state.ct.us/DCPRosterDownload/pRosterDownload.asp.

18 Ethics Commission, 20 Trinity St #2, Hartford, CT 06106; 860-566-4472, Fax: 860-566-3806.
www.ethics.state.ct.us
Search Database at
www.ethics.state.ct.us/publicinfo.htm Note: May not have full lobbyist rosters. Also search reports and enforcement actions.

19 Department of Public Safety, Division of State Police, Licensing/Registration, 1111 Country Club Rd, Middletown, CT 06457-9294; 860-685-8290, Fax: 860-685-8496.
www.state.ct.us/dps/

20 Department of Agriculture, Bureau of Aquaculture, PO Box 97 (190 Rogers Ave), Milford, CT 06460; 203-874-0696, Fax: 203-783-9976.
www.state.ct.us/doag/

21 Department of Revenue Svcs, Audit Unit (Licensing), 25 Sigourney St, Hartford, CT 06106; 860-297-5962, Fax: 860-297-4797.
http://ct.gov/drs/site/default.asp

22 Department of Agriculture, Bureau of Regulation & Inspection, 165 Capitol Avenue, Hartford, CT 06106; 860-713-2504, Fax: 860-713-2514.
www.state.ct.us/doag
Email: ctdeptag@po.state.ct.us

23 Department of Motor Vehicles, Specialized Licenses & Permits, 60 State St, Wethersfield, CT 06109; 860-263-5720.
www.ct.gov/dmv/site/default.asp

24 Department of Transportation, Motor Transport Svcs, PO Box 317546 (2800 Berlin Turnpike,), Newington, CT 06131-7546; 860-594-2865, Fax: 860-594-2859.
www.ct.gov

25 Department of Public Safety, Division of Fire, Emergency & Building Svcs, 1111 Country Club Rd, Middletown, CT 06457-9294; 860-685-8470.
www.state.ct.us/dps/DFEBS/index.html

26 Department of Environmental Protection, Pesticide Division, Bureau of Waste Management, 79 Elm St, Hartford, CT 06106; 860-424-3369, Fax: 860-424-4060.
www.dep.state.ct.us/wst/pesticides/index.htm
Search Database at www.kellysolutions.com/CT/

27 Department of Motor Vehicles, Dealer and Repairer Division, 60 State St, Wethersfield, CT 06109; 860-263-5057, Fax: 860-263-5554.
www.ct.gov/dmv/site/default.asp Note: Licenses cannot be verified by phone; must use form J23 available at all DMV offices.

28 Police Officers Standards & Training Council, Certification, Assessment & Audit Unit, 285 Preston Ave, Meriden, CT 06450; 203-238-6694, Fax: 203-238-6643.
www.post.state.ct.us
Email: gary.pfeifer@po.state.ct.us

29 CT Department of Higher Education, Academic Affairs, 61 Woodland St, Hartford, CT 06105-2326; 860-947-1801, Fax: 860-947-1310.
www.ctdhe.org
Email: info@ctdhe.org

30 Department of Environmental Protection, Bureau of Air Mgmt; Compliance & Filed Ops Div., 79 Elm St, Hartford, CT 06106; 860-424-4152, Fax: 860-424-4064.

31 Department of Public Health, Asbestos Licensure, 410 Capitol Ave, MS 51 AIR, PO Box 340308, Hartford, CT 06134; 860-509-7559, Fax: 860-509-7378.
www.dph.state.ct.us Search Database at www.dph.state.ct.us/scripts/hlthprof.asp

32 Department of Environmental Protection, Office of Long Island Sound Programs, 79 Elm St, Hartford, CT 06106; 860-424-3034, Fax: 860-424-4045.
www.dep.state.ct.us/

33 Department of Public Safety, Office of Education & Data Management, PO Box 2794 (1111 County Club Rd), Middletown, CT 06457-9294; 860-685-8330, Fax: 860-685-8611.
www.state.ct.us/dps/dfebs/oedm/oedmbcol.htm

34 State Marshall Commission, State of Connecticut Judicial Branch, 765 Asylum Ave, Hartford, CT 06105; 860-566-7109, Fax: 860-566-3743.
www.jud.state.ct.us
Email: rob.rudewicz@po.state.ct.us
Search Database at
www.jud.state.ct.us/faq/marshals.htm

35 Department of Motor Vehicles, Emissions Divison, 55 West Main St, Rowland State Gov. Ctr, Waterbury, CT 06072; 800-842-8222, 203-805-6244.
www.ct.gov/dmv/cwp/view.asp?a=800&Q=244982

36 Department of Consumer Protection, Public Charities Unit - Ofc. of the Attorney General, 55 Elm St, Hartford, CT 06106; 860-808-5030, Fax: 860-808-5347.

37 DCF Licensing, Department of Children & Families, 505 Hudson St, Hartford, CT 06106; 860-550-6445.
www.state.ct.us/dcf/

38 Department of Mental Retardation, 460 Capitol Ave, Hartford, CT 06106; 860-418-6000, Fax: 860-418-6079.
www.dmr.state.ct.us/

39 Department of Labor, Wage and Workplace Standards, 200 Folly Brook Blvd, Wethersfield, CT 06109-1114; 860-263-6790, Fax: 860-263-6541.
www.ctdol.state.ct.us/wgwkstnd/wgemenu.htm

40 Department of Environmental Protection, Bureau of Waste Management, 79 Elm St, 2nd Fl, Hartford, CT 06106; 860-424-3705.
www.dep.state.ct.us/wst/prgactiv.htm

41 Commission on Fire Prevention & Control, Director of Certification, 34 Perimeter Rd, Windsor Locks, CT 06096; 860-623-6363 x225, Fax: 860-654-1889.
www.ct.gov/cfpc/taxonomy/ct_taxonomy.asp
Email: denice.fortin@po.state.ct.us

42 Department of Environmental Protection, Marine Fisheries Division, PO Box 719 (333 Ferry Rd), Old Lyme, CT 06371; 860-434-6043, Fax: 860-434-6150.
www.dep.state.ct.us/burnatr/fishing/fdhome.htm

43 Department of Transportation, Bureau of Aviation and Ports, State Pier, New London, CT 06320; 860-443-3856, Fax: 860-437-7251.
www.ct.gov/dot/site/default.asp
Email: Kevin.Lynch@po.state.ct.us

44 Department of Motor Vehicles, Fiscal Services Divison, 55 W Main St, Waterbury, CT 06702; 203-805-6307, Fax: 203-805-6161.

Connecticut Federal Courts

The following list indicates the district and division name for each county in the state. If the bankruptcy court location is different from the district court, then the location of the bankruptcy court appears in parentheses.

County/Court Cross Reference

Fairfield	Bridgeport	New Haven	New Haven
Hartford	Hartford	New London	New Haven
Litchfield	New Haven (Hartford)	Tolland	Hartford
Middlesex	New Haven (Hartford)	Windham	Hartford

Standards for Federal Courts: See Colorado Federal Courts section for information on Federal Courts standards and fees.

US District Court

Bridgeport Division Office of the Clerk, Rm 400, 915 Lafayette Blvd, Bridgeport, CT 06604 (also use mail address for courier delivery), 203-579-5861. 9AM-4PM. www.ctd.uscourts.gov
Counties: Litchfield (after 2004), Fairfield (prior to 1993). Since 1/1993, cases from any county may be assigned to any division in the district.
Searches & Indexing: Results do not include SSN or DOB. Computer index maintained. New cases in the index immediately after filing date.
Fee & Payment: Pay by exact amount cash, money order, cashier check. Business and personal checks accepted with address and phone number on check. Payee: Clerk, US District Court. Prepayment required.
Phone Search: Only docket information is available by phone. **Mail Search:** search usually completed- 7 days. SASE not required. **In Person Search:** Fee charged if court performs your search. Copy fee from CM/ECF public terminal $.10 per page. Self-serve copier available - $.25 per page.
E-Services: ECF replaces PACER whose records did go back to 11/1991. New records online after 1 day. ECF at https://ecf.ctd.uscourts.gov. Copies off the ECF terminal are $.10 per page. **Selected opinions:** www.ctd.uscourts.gov/Opinions.htm..

Hartford Division Court Clerk, 450 Main St, Hartford, CT 06103 (use mail address for courier delivery), 860-240-3200. www.ctd.uscourts.gov
Counties: Hartford, Tolland, Windham (prior to 1993). Since 1993, cases from any county may be assigned to any of the divisions in the district.
Searches & Indexing: Results do not include SSN or DOB. Computer index back to 2003 maintained. Records kept where the assigned judge sits, then stored by the federal record number system. New cases in the index immediately after filing date.
Fee & Payment: Pay by money order, cashier's or personal check. Payee: Clerk, US District Court. Prepayment required.
Phone Search: Only docket information is available by phone. **Mail Search:** search usually completed- 2 weeks. Include SASE for return. **In Person Search:** Fee charged if court performs your search. Self-serve copier - $.25 per page.
E-Services: ECF replaces PACER whose records did go back to 11/1991. New records online after 1 day. ECF at https://ecf.ctd.uscourts.gov **Opinions Online:** www.ctd.uscourts.gov/Opinions.htm. Selected opinions only.

New Haven Division Court Clerk, 141 Church St, New Haven, CT 06510 (also use mail address for courier delivery), 203-773-2140. Hours- 9AM-4PM. www.ctd.uscourts.gov
Counties: Middlesex, New Haven, New London (prior to 1993), Litchfield (prior to 2004). Since 1993, cases from any county may be assigned to any of the divisions in the district.
Searches & Indexing: Results do not include SSN or DOB. Computer index maintained. Older records indexed on microfiche. New cases in the index immediately after filing date. District-wide searches available here back to 1982.
Fee & Payment: Pay by money order, cashier check, business check. No personal checks. Payee: District Court Clerk.
Phone Search: Only docket information is available by phone.
Mail Search: search usually completed- 3-4 days. Include SASE for return.
In Person Search: Fee charged if court performs your search. Self-serve copier- $.25 per page.
E-Services: ECF replaces PACER whose records did go back to 11/1991. New records online after 1 day. ECF at https://ecf.ctd.uscourts.gov **Opinions Online:** www.ctd.uscourts.gov/Opinions.htm. Selected opinions only.

US Bankruptcy Court

Bridgeport Division Court Clerk, 915 Lafayette Blvd, Bridgeport, CT 06604 (also use mail address for courier delivery), 203-579-5808, records rm- 203-579-5808, Fax-203-579-5827. Hours- 9AM-4PM. www.ctb.uscourts.gov
Counties: Fairfield.
Searches & Indexing: Results include SSN. Computer index maintained. New cases in the index immediately after filing date. Records purged every 6 months. District-wide searches available here.
Fee & Payment: Pay by money order, cashier check, business check. No personal checks. Payee: Clerk, Bankruptcy Court. Prepayment required.
Phone Search: Voice Case Information Service available, call at 800-800-5113 or 860-240-3345.
Mail Search: search usually completed- up to 2 weeks. Include SASE for return.
In Person Search: Fee charged if court performs your search. Self-serve copier - $.25 per page.
E-Services: ECF replaces PACER. Document images available. PACER records go back to 1979. New records online after 1 day. ECF at https://ecf.ctb.uscourts.gov **Opinions Online:** www.ctb.uscourts.gov. Click on Opinions. **Other Online Access:** calendars at https://ecf.ctb.uscourts.gov/cgi-bin/PublicCalendar.pl.

Hartford Division Court Clerk, 450 Main St, Hartford, CT 06103 (also use mail address for courier delivery), 860-240-3675. Hours- 9AM-4PM. www.ctb.uscourts.gov
Counties: Hartford, Tolland, Windham.
Searches & Indexing: Results include SSN. Computer index maintained. New cases in the index 1 day after filing date. Records purged every 6 months.
Fee & Payment: Pay by money order, cashier's or personal check. Payee: Clerk, US Bankruptcy Court. Prepayment required.
Phone Search: Only docket information is available by phone. Voice Case Information Service available, call VCIS at 800-800-5113 or 860-240-3345.
Mail Search: search usually completed- week-10 days. Include SASE for return.
In Person Search: Fee charged if court performs your search. Self-serve copier- $.25 per page.
E-Services: ECF replaces PACER. Document images available. PACER records go back to 1979. New records online after 1 day. ECF at https://ecf.ctb.uscourts.gov **Opinions Online:** www.ctb.uscourts.gov. Click on Opinions. **Other Online Access:** calendars at https://ecf.ctb.uscourts.gov/cgi-bin/PublicCalendar.pl.

New Haven Division Court Clerk, 157 Church St, 18th Fl, Connecticut Financial Center, New Haven, CT 06510 (also use mail address for courier delivery), 203-773-2009. Hours- 9AM-4PM. www.ctb.uscourts.gov
Counties: Litchfield, Middlesex, New Haven, New London.
Searches & Indexing: Results include SSN. Computer index maintained. New cases in the index 1 week after filing date. Records purged every 6 months.
Fee & Payment: Pay by money order, cashier's or personal check. Payee: Clerk, US Bankruptcy Court. Prepayment required.
Phone Search: Only docket information is available by phone. Voice Case Information Service available, call VCIS at 800-800-5113 or 860-240-3345.
Mail Search: search usually completed- week-10 days. Include SASE for return.
In Person Search: Fee charged if court performs your search. Self-serve copier - $.25 per page.
E-Services: ECF replaces PACER. Document images available. PACER records go back to 1979. New records online after 1 day. ECF at https://ecf.ctb.uscourts.gov **Opinions Online:** www.ctb.uscourts.gov. Click on Opinions. **Other Online Access:** calendars at https://ecf.ctb.uscourts.gov/cgi-bin/PublicCalendar.pl.

Connecticut County Courts

Court	Jurisdiction	No. of Courts	How Organized
Judicial District Courts*	General	15	15 Geographic Areas
Geographic Area Courts*	Limited	20	20 Geographic Areas
Probate Courts*	Probate	129	

* Profiled in this Sourcebook.

Court	CIVIL								
	Tort	Contract	Real Estate	Min. Claim	Max. Claim	Small Claims	Estate	Eviction	Domestic Relations
Judicial District Courts*	X	X	X	No Min	No Max				X
Geographic Area Courts*						$3500		X	
Probate Courts*							X		

Court	CRIMINAL				
	Felony	Misdemeanor	DWI/DUI	Preliminary Hearing	Juvenile
Judicial District Courts*	X				X
Geographic Area Courts*		X	X	X	
Probate Courts*					

ADMINISTRATION

Chief Court Administrator, 231 Capitol Av, Hartford, CT, 06106; 860-757-2100, Fax: 860-757-2130. www.jud.state.ct.us

COURT STRUCTURE

The Superior Court is the sole court of original jurisdiction for all causes of action, except for matters over which the probate courts have jurisdiction as provided by statute. The state is divided into 15 Judicial Districts, 20 Geographic Area Courts, and 14 Juvenile Districts. The Superior Court - comprised primarily of the Judicial District Courts and the Geographical Area Courts - has five divisions: Criminal, Civil, Family, Juvenile, and Administrative Appeals. When not combined, the Judicial District Courts handle felony and civil cases while the Geographic Area Courts handle misdemeanors, and most handle small claims.

Divorce records are maintained by the Chief Clerk of the Judicial District Courts.

ONLINE ACCESS

The Judicial Branch provides access to civil, small claims and/or family court records via the Internet, located online at www.jud2.state.ct.us. Click on "Party Name Inquiry." The site contains party name search, assignment lists and calendars. Also, questions about the fuller commercial system available through Judicial Information Systems should be directed to the CT JIS Office at 860-282-6500. There is currently no online access to criminal records; however, criminal and motor vehicle data is available for purchase in database format. Opinions from the Supreme and Appellete courts are available from the general web site.

ADDITIONAL INFORMATION

The Superior Court Record Center in Enfield, CT is the repository for criminal and some civil records; open 9AM-5PM M-F. Case records are sent to the Record Center from 3 months to 5 years after disposition by the courts. These records are then maintained 10 years for misdemeanors and 20+ years for felonies. If a requester is certain that the record is at the Record Center, it is quicker to direct the request there rather than to the original court of record. Only written requests are accepted. Search requirements: full defendant name, docket number, disposition date, and court action. Fee is $3.00 for each docket, $5.00 if certifed. Fee payee is Treasurer-State of Connecticut. Direct Requests to: Connecticut Record Center, 111 Phoenix Avenue, Enfield CT 06082, 860-741-3714.

Personal checks must have name and address printed on the check; if requesting in person, check must have same address as drivers' license.

PROBATE

Probate is handled by city Probate Courts, which we have listed, and are not part of the state court system. Information request requirements are consistent across the state; requesters must provide full name of decedent, year and place of death, and SASE. There is no search fee; the certification fee is $5.00 for 1st 2 pages and $2.00 for each additional page; and, the copy fee is $1.00 per page.

Fairfield County

Bridgeport Judicial District Court 1061 Main St, Attn: criminal or civil, Bridgeport, CT 06604; phone: 203-579-6527; fax: 203-382-8406; hours 9AM-5PM (EST). *Felony, Civil Actions, Divorce.*

Civil Records: Access: Mail, online, in person. Only the court performs in person searches; visitors may not. No search fee. Court makes copy: $1.00 per page. Required to search: name, years to search. Civil cases indexed by defendant, plaintiff. Civil records on computer from 1990, on microfiche from 1975 to 1990, prior on index cards. After 5 years sent to Records Center at Enfield, CT. Access to civil, family, and small claims case records is free at www.jud.state.ct.us. Mail turnaround time 2-3 weeks.

Criminal Records: Access: Mail, in person. Only the court performs in person searches; visitors may not. No search fee. Court makes copy: $1.00 per page. Required to search: name, years to search, DOB. Criminal records on computer since 1997, on microfiche from 1975 to 1996. Mail turnaround time 4 week.

General Information: No public access terminal. No sealed, adoption records released. Certification fee: $2.00 per cert. Payee: Chief Clerk Superior Court. Personal checks accepted. Prepayment and SASE required.

Danbury Judicial District Court 146 White St, Danbury, CT 06810; phone: 203-207-8600; criminal phone: same; civil phone: same; hours 9AM-5PM (EST). *Felony, Civil Actions, Divorce, Eviction, Small Claims.*

Civil Records: Access: Mail, online, in person. Only the court performs in person searches; visitors may not. No search fee. Court makes copy: $1.00 per page. Required to search: name, years to search. Civil cases indexed by plaintiff and defendant. Civil records on microfilm from 11-87, prior on index cards. Access to civil and family case records is free at www.jud.state.ct.us. Mail turnaround time 2-4 days for civil and family.

Criminal Records: Access: Mail, in person. Only the court performs in person searches; visitors may not. No search fee. Court makes copy: $1.00 per page. Required to search: name, years to search, DOB. Criminal records on microfilm from 11-87, prior on index cards but only list docket number and disposal date. Mail turnaround time 3-4 days.

General Information: No public access terminal. No sealed records released. Will not fax documents. Certification fee: $2.00 per cert. Will not certify unless copies are made by the court personnel. Payee: Clerk of Superior Court. ID required with personal check. Prepayment required.

Stamford-Norwalk Judicial District Court 123 Hoyt St, Stamford, CT 06905; criminal phone: 203-965-5208; civil phone: 203-965-5307; criminal records fax: 203-965-5355; civil records fax: 203-965-5370; hours 9AM-5PM (EST). *Felony, Misdemeanors, Civil Actions, Divorce.*

Civil Records: Access: Mail, online, in person. Both court and visitors may perform in person searches. No search fee. Court makes copy: $1.00 per page. Required to search: name, years to search. Civil cases indexed by defendant, plaintiff. Only pending civil cases on computer, on microfiche from 1970s, on index cards from 1958. Access to current civil case records is free at www.jud.state.ct.us.

Criminal Records: Access: Mail, in person. Both court and visitors may perform in person searches. No search fee. Court makes copy: $1.00 per page. Required to search: name, years to search. Only pending cases on computer, on microfiche from 1970s, on index cards from 1962.

General Information: Public access terminal available. (Terminal has pending cases only.) No sealed records released. Will not fax documents. Certification fee: $2.00. Payee: Clerk of Superior

Court. Personal checks accepted. Prepayment required.

Geographical Area Court #2 172 Golden Hill St, Bridgeport, CT 06604; criminal phone: 203-579-6560; civil phone: 203-579-6527; hours 9AM-4PM (EST). *Misdemeanor, Eviction, Small Claims.*

Note: Serving the towns of Bridgeport, Easton, Fairfield, Monroe, Stratford and Trumbull.

Civil Records: Access: Phone, mail, online, in person. Both court and visitors may perform in person searches. Court makes copy: $1.00 per page. Required to search: name, years to search. Civil cases indexed by defendant. Civil records pending and from 1990 on computer, on microfiche from 1982 to 1990, prior on index cards. After microfilmed and entered on index cards, sent to Records Center at Enfield, CT. Access to civil, family, and small claims case records is free at www.jud.state.ct.us.

Criminal Records: Access: In person only. Visitors must perform in person searches themselves. Court makes copy: $1.00 per page. Required to search: name, years to search. Criminal records pending and from 1990 on computer, on microfiche from 1982. Note: Refer mail requests to the state criminal records agency, PO Box 2794, Middletown CT 06457, www.state.ct.us/dps/SPBI.htm

General Information: No sealed records released. Certification fee: $3.00. Payee: Clerk of Superior Court. Personal checks accepted. Prepayment required.

Geographical Area Court #20 17 Belden Ave, Norwalk, CT 06850; phone: 203-846-3237; criminal phone: 203-846-3237; civil phone: 203-846-4206; fax: 203-847-8710; hours 9AM-5PM (EST). *Misdemeanor, Eviction, Small Claims.*

Note: Serving the towns of New Canaan, Norwalk, Weston, Westport and Wilton.

Civil Records: Access: Online, in person. Visitors must perform in person searches themselves. Court makes copy: $1.00 per page. Required to search: name, years to search. Civil cases indexed by defendant, plaintiff. Civil records on computer from 1986. Access to small claims case records is free at www.jud.state.ct.us.

Criminal Records: Access: In person only. Visitors must perform in person searches themselves. Court makes copy: $1.00 per page. Required to search: name, years to search; also helpful: DOB. Criminal records on computer from 1986, prior records on index cards.

General Information: No public access terminal. Certification fee: $2.00 per cert. Payee: Superior Court GA #20. Only cashiers checks and money orders accepted. Prepayment required.

Geographical Area Court #3 146 White St, Danbury, CT 06810; phone: 203-207-8600; fax: 203-207-8642; hours 9AM-5PM (EST). *Misdemeanor, Eviction, Small Claims.*

Note: Serving the towns of Bethel, Brookfield, Danbury, New Fairfield, Newtown, Redding, Ridgefield and Sherman.

Civil Records: Access: Mail, online, in person. Only the court performs in person searches; visitors may not. No search fee. Court makes copy: $1.00 per page. Required to search: name, years to search. Civil cases indexed by defendant. Civil records on microfilm from 11-87, prior on index cards, but only list docket number and disposal date, then referred to Records Center at Enfield, CT. Access to civil, family, and small claims case records is free at www.jud.state.ct.us. Note: In person searches are returned by mail.

Criminal Records: Access: In person only. Visitors must perform in person searches themselves. Court makes copy: $1.00 per page. Required to search: name, years to search; also helpful: DOB. Criminal records on computer from 11/9/87. Note: The court refers all requests to one of the 2 statewide agencies.

General Information: No public access terminal. No youthful offender or dispositions by dismissal after 20 days from date of judgment records released. Certification fee: $2.00 per cert. Payee: Clerk of Superior Court. Personal checks accepted. Prepayment and SASE required.

Bethel Probate Court 1 School St, PO Box 144, Bethel, CT 06801; phone: 203-794-8508; fax: 203-794-8587; hours 9AM-1:00PM (EST). *Probate.*

Bridgeport Probate District 202 State St, McLevy Hall, 3rd Fl, Bridgeport, CT 06604; phone: 203-576-3945; fax: 203-576-7898; hours 8:30AM-5PM M-Th; 8:30AM-4PM F (EST). *Probate.*

Brookfield Probate Court PO Box 5192, 100 Pocono Rd, Brookfield, CT 06804; phone: 203-775-3700; fax: 203-775-5246; hours 9AM-3:30PM (EST). *Probate.*

Danbury Probate Court 155 Deer Hill Ave, Danbury, CT 06810; phone: 203-797-4521; fax: 203-796-1563; hours 8:30AM-4:30PM (EST). *Probate.*

Darien Probate Court Town Hall, 2 Renshaw Rd, Darien, CT 06820; phone: 203-656-7342; fax: 203-656-0774; hours 8:30AM-12:30PM, 1:30-4:30PM; M-Th; 9AM-12:30PM F - July-Labor Day (EST). *Probate.*

Fairfield Probate Court Independence Hall, 725 Old Post Rd, Fairfield, CT 06824; phone: 203-256-3041; fax: 203-256-3044; hours 8:30AM-4:30PM (EST). *Probate.*

Greenwich Probate Court 101 Field Point Rd, PO Box 2540, Greenwich, CT 06836; phone: 203-622-7879; fax: 203-622-6451; hours 8AM-4PM, 8AM-N Fri July-Aug (EST). *Probate.*

New Canaan Probate Court 77 Main St, New Canaan, CT 06840; phone: 203-594-3050; fax: 203-594-3128; hours 8:30AM-4:30PM; 8:30AM-1PM Fri July-Aug (EST). *Probate.*

New Fairfield Probate Court 4 Brush Hill Rd, Town Hall, New Fairfield, CT 06812; phone: 203-312-5627; hours 8AM-5PM T-W-Th; closed 12:30-3:30PM Th; also by app't (EST). *Probate.*

Newtown Probate Court Edmond Town Hall, 45 Main St, Newtown, CT 06470; phone: 203-270-4280; fax: 203-270-4283; hours 8:30AM-N,1-4:30PM (EST). *Probate.*

Norwalk Probate Court 125 East Ave, PO Box 2009, Norwalk, CT 06852-2009; phone: 203-854-7737; fax: 203-854-7825; hours 9AM-4:30PM (EST). *Probate.*

Note: District includes Town of Wilton.

Redding Probate Court Town Hall, Lonetown Rd, PO Box 1125, Redding, CT 06875-1125; phone: 203-938-2326; fax: 203-938-8816; hours 9AM-1PM (EST). *Probate.*

Ridgefield Probate Court Town Hall, 400 Main St, Ridgefield, CT 06877; phone: 203-431-2776; fax: 203-431-2722; hours 8:30AM-4:30PM (EST). *Probate.*

Shelton Probate Court 60 Perry Hill Rd, PO Box 127, Shelton, CT 06484; phone: 203-924-8462; fax: 203-924-8943; hours 9AM-5PM; 9AM-6:30PM 1st & 3rd Tues of month (EST). *Probate.*

Sherman Probate Court 4 Brush Hill Rd, NewFairfield, CT 06812; phone: 203-312-5627; hours 9AM-N T-Th (EST). *Probate.*

Note: Records now located at New Fairfield.

Stamford Probate Court 888 Washington Blvd, 8th Fl, PO Box 10152, Stamford, CT 06904-2152; phone: 203-323-2149; fax: 203-964-1830; hours 9AM-4PM (EST). *Probate.*

Stratford Probate Court 468 Birdseye St, 2nd Fl, Stratford, CT 06615; phone: 203-385-4023; fax: 203-375-6253; hours 9:30AM-4:30PM (EST). *Probate.*

Trumbull Probate Court Town Hall, 5866 Main St, Trumbull, CT 06611-5416; phone: 203-452-5068; fax: 203-452-5092; hours 9AM-4:30PM (EST). *Probate.*
Note: District includes Town of Easton, and Monroe.

Westport Probate Court Town Hall, 110 Myrtle Ave, Westport, CT 06880; phone: 203-341-1100; fax: 203-341-1102; hours 9AM-4:30PM (EST). *Probate.*
Note: District includes Town of Weston.

Hartford County

Hartford Judicial District Court - Civil 95 Washington St, Hartford, CT 06106; phone: 860-548-2700; fax: 860-548-2711; hours 9AM-5PM (EST). *Civil Actions, Divorce.*
Civil Records: Access: Mail, online, in person. Both court and visitors may perform in person searches. No search fee. Court makes copy: $1.00 per page. Required to search: name, years to search. Civil cases indexed by defendant, plaintiff. Civil records on computer if active, otherwise on microfiche, older records at Enfield Records Center. Access to civil case records is free at www.jud.state.ct.us. Mail turnaround time 7-10 days.
General Information: Public access terminal has only civil records. Certification fee: $2.00 per cert. Payee: Clerk of Superior Court. Personal checks or Visa, MC accepted. Accepted in person only. $10.00 minimum. Prepayment and SASE required.

Hartford Judicial District Court - Criminal 101 LaFayette St, Hartford, CT 06106; phone: 860-566-1630; fax: 860-566-1983; hours 9AM-5PM (EST). *Felony.*
Note: This court shares phone line and address with Geo. Court #14.
Criminal Records: Access: Mail, in person. Only the court performs in person searches; visitors may not. No search fee. Court makes copy: $1.00 per page. Required to search: name, years to search; also helpful: DOB. Criminal records on computer from 1989. Mail turnaround time 7-10 days.
General Information: No public access terminal. No youthful offender records or dismissals released. Will fax documents. Certification fee: $3.00. Payee: Clerk of Superior Court. Personal checks accepted. Prepayment and SASE required.

New Britain Judicial District Court 20 Franklin Square, New Britain, CT 06051; criminal phone: 860-515-5080; civil phone: 860-515-5180; criminal fax: 860-515-5103; civil records fax: 860-515-5185; hours 9AM-5PM (EST). *Felony, Civil Actions, Small Claims, Divorce.*
Civil Records: Access: Phone, mail, online, in person. Both court and visitors may perform in person searches. No search fee. Court makes copy: $1.00 per page. Required to search: name, years to search. Civil cases indexed by plaintiff. Civil records on computer up to one year after closing, index cards back to 1989, prior in Hartford. Access to civil, family, and small claims case records is free at www.jud.state.ct.us. Mail turnaround time 3 days.
Criminal Records: Access: Phone, mail, in person. Both court and visitors may perform in person searches. No search fee. Court makes copy: $1.00 per page. Required to search: name, years to search. Criminal records on computer for 2 years, then purged when cases sent to State Record Center. Mail turnaround time 3 days.
General Information: Public access terminal available. Certain paternity, family case studies and sealed records not released. Certification fee: $2.00. Payee: Clerk of Superior Court. Prepayment and SASE required.

Geographic Area Court #15 20 Franklin Square, New Britain, CT 06051; criminal phone: 860-515-5080; civil phone: 860-515-5180; fax: 860-515-5185; hours 9AM-5PM (EST). *Misdemeanor, Eviction, Small Claims.*
Note: Serving the towns of Berlin, New Britain, Newington, Rocky Hill and Wethersfield.
Civil Records: Access: Mail, online, in person. Only the court performs in person searches; visitors may not. No search fee. Court makes copy: $1.00 per page. Required to search: name, years to search. Civil cases indexed by defendant, plaintiff. Civil records on computer for 3 years, then on microfiche. All info in archives at Record Center at Enfield, CT. Access to civil, family, and small claims case records is free at www.jud.state.ct.us. Mail turnaround time 1 month.
Criminal Records: Access: Mail, in person. Only the court performs in person searches; visitors may not. No search fee. Court makes copy: $1.00 per page. Required to search: name, years to search; DOB. Criminal records on computer from 1985, then on microfiche. All info in archives at Record Center @ Enfield, CT. Data is purged every two years. Mail turnaround time 1 month.
General Information: No public access terminal. No sealed records released. Certification fee: $2.00 per cert, criminal division. Civil fee varies. Payee: Clerk of Superior Court. No out-of-state checks accepted. Prepayment and SASE required.

Geographical Area Court #12 410 Center St, Manchester, CT 06040; phone: 860-647-1091; fax: 860-645-7540; hours 9AM-5PM; Phone Hours: 9AM-4PM (EST). *Misdemeanor, Eviction, Small Claims.*
Note: Evictions are handled by a special Housing Court, 80 Washington St, Hartford, CT, 860-756-7920. Serving the towns of East Hartford, Glastonbury, Manchester, Marlborough and South Windsor.
Civil Records: Access: Mail, online, in person. Both court and visitors may perform in person searches. No search fee. Court makes copy: $1.00 per page. Required to search: name, years to search. Civil cases indexed by defendant. Civil records on computer for 3 years. Access to family and small claims case records is free at www.jud.state.ct.us. Mail turnaround time 1-2 weeks.
Criminal Records: Access: Mail, in person. Only the court performs in person searches; visitors may not. No search fee. Court makes copy: $1.00 per page. Required to search: name, years to search, DOB. Criminal records on computer since 2002, available since 1979. In person search results returned by mail only. The court urges requesters to go to the State Police for criminal record searches. Mail turnaround time 1-2 weeks.
General Information: No non disclosable records released. Certification fee: $3.00 first page, $1.00 ea add'l. Payee: Clerk of Superior Court. Prepayment and SASE required.

Geographical Area Court #13 111 Phoenix, Enfield, CT 06082; phone: 860-741-3727; fax: 860-741-3474; hours 9AM-5PM (EST). *Misdemeanor.*
Note: Eviction cases are handled by Hartford Housing, 860-756-7920. Serving the towns of East Granby, East Windsor, Enfield, Granby, Simsbury, Suffield, Windsor and Windsor Locks.
Civil Records: Access: Mail, in person. Visitors must perform in person searches themselves. Court makes copy: $1.00 per page. Required to search: name, years to search. Civil cases indexed by defendant. Civil records on computer for 1 year, microfiche by year, archived at Record Center at Enfield, CT.
Criminal Records: Access: Mail, in person. Visitors must perform in person searches themselves. Court makes copy: $1.00 per page. Required to search: name, years to search, DOB. Criminal records on computer for 3 years, microfiche by year, archived at Record Center at Enfield, CT.

General Information: No public access terminal. Certification fee: $2.00 per doc. Payee: Clerk of Superior Court. Will take personal check with ID. Prepayment required.

Geographical Area Court #17 131 N Main St, Bristol, CT 06010; phone: 860-582-8111; hours 9AM-5PM (EST). *Misdemeanor, Eviction, Small Claims.*
Note: Serving the towns of Bristol, Burlington, Plainville, Plymouth and Southington.
Civil Records: Access: Phone, mail, in person. No search fee. Court makes copy: $1.00 per page. Required to search: name, years to search, docket #. Civil cases indexed by defendant. Mail turnaround time 1-2 days.
Criminal Records: Access: Mail, in person. Only the court performs in person searches; visitors may not. No search fee. Court makes copy: $3.00 per disposition. Required to search: name, years to search, DOB. Criminal records on computer from 1986, on microfiche from 1982, prior on index cards from 1979-1992, microfiche 1988-1996 and docket books; records on computer for 5 years, then put on microfiche. Mail turnaround time 1-2 days.
General Information: No public access terminal. No dismissals, not guilty, youthful offender or NOLLE records released. Certification fee: $2.00. Payee: Clerk of Superior Court. Personal checks accepted. Prepayment and SASE required.

Geographical Area Court #14 101 LaFayette St, Hartford, CT 06106; phone: 860-566-1630; fax: 860-566-1983; hours 9AM-5PM (EST). *Misdemeanor.*
Note: Serving the towns of Avon, Bloomfield, Canton, Farmington, Hartford and West Hartford.
Criminal Records: Access: Mail, in person. Only the court performs in person searches; visitors may not. No search fee. Court makes copy: $1.00 per page. Required to search: name, years to search, DOB. Computerized records for past 3 years. Mail turnaround time 1 week.
General Information: No public access terminal. Will fax documents. Certification fee: $2.00. Payee: Clerk of Superior Court. Only cashiers checks and money orders accepted. Prepayment and SASE required.

Avon Probate Court 60 W Main St, Avon, CT 06001-0578; phone: 860-409-4348; fax: 860-409-4368; hours 9am-2:30M,T,Th; 9-12;00-W,Fri (EST). *Probate.*

Berlin Probate Court 1 Liberty Square, PO Box 400, New Britain, CT 06050-0400; phone: 860-826-2696; fax: 860-826-2695; hours 9AM-4PM (EST). *Probate.*
Note: District includes towns of New Britain, Kennsington, East Berlin.

Bloomfield Probate Court Town Hall, 800 Bloomfield Ave, Bloomfield, CT 06002; phone: 860-769-3548; fax: 860-242-1167; hours 9AM-1PM, 2PM-4:30PM (EST). *Probate.*
www.bloomfieldct.org/Pages/BloomfieldCT_Probate/index

Bristol Probate Court 111 N Main St, City Hall, 3rd Fl, Bristol, CT 06010; phone: 860-584-6230; fax: 860-584-3818; hours 9AM-5PM (EST). *Probate.*

Burlington Probate Court 200 Spielman Hwy, Burlington, CT 06013; phone: 860-673-2108 x213; fax: 860-673-8607; hours 1PM-6PM M-Th and by app't (EST). *Probate.*

Canton Probate Court 4 Market St, Canton Town Hall, 3rd Fl, PO Box 175, Collinsville, CT 06022-0175; phone: 860-693-7851; fax: 860-693-7889; hours 8:30AM-2PM M,Tu,Th; 8:30AM-N, 1-4PM W; and by app't (EST). *Probate.*

East Granby Probate Court PO Box 542, 9 Center St, East Granby, CT 06026-0542; phone: 860-653-3434; fax: 860-653-7085; hours 9AM-N T, W-Th (and by app't) (EST). *Probate.*

East Hartford Probate Court Town Hall, 740 Main St, East Hartford, CT 06108; phone: 860-291-7278; fax: 860-291-7211; hours 9AM-4PM (EST). *Probate.*

East Windsor Probate Court Town Hall, 1540 Sullivan Ave, South Windsor, CT 06074; phone: 860-644-2511 X271; fax: 860-648-5047; hours 8:00AM-3:00PM (EST). *Probate.*
Note: District also includes Town of South Windsor.

Enfield Probate Court 820 Enfield St, Enfield, CT 06082; phone: 860-253-6305; fax: 860-253-6388; hours 9AM-4:30PM (EST). *Probate.*

Farmington Probate Court One Monteith Dr, Farmington, CT 06032; phone: 860-675-2360; fax: 860-673-8262; hours 9AM-4PM (EST). *Probate.*

Glastonbury Probate Court PO Box 6523, 2155 Main St, Glastonbury, CT 06033-6523; phone: 860-652-7629; fax: 860-368-2520; hours 9:30AM-4:30PM (7PM on T) (EST). *Probate.*

Granby Probate Court PO Box 240, 15 N Granby Rd, Town Hall, Granby, CT 06035-0240; phone: 860-844-5314; fax: 860-653-4769; hours 9AM-12:30 M, T,W (EST). *Probate.*

Hartford Probate Court 250 Constitution Plaza, 3rd Fl, Hartford, CT 06103; phone: 860-757-9150; fax: 860-724-1503; hours 9AM-4PM M-F; (4-6:30PM Mon by app't) (EST). *Probate.*

Manchester Probate Court 66 Center St, Manchester, CT 06040; phone: 860-647-3227; fax: 860-647-3236; hours 8:30AM-N, 1-4:30PM (EST). *Probate.*

Marlborough Probate Court 26 N Main St, PO Box 29, Marlborough, CT 06447; phone: 860-295-6239; fax: 860-295-0317; hours 10:30-12;00 M; 10:30-N,1-4PM T,W; 9am-12pm Th-and by app't) (EST). *Probate.*

New Hartford Probate Court 530 Main, New Hartford, CT 06057; phone: 860-379-3254; fax: 860-379-0940; hours 8:30-3PM-M,Tu,Th; 8:30AM-N Wed; 8AM-N Fri (EST). *Probate.*
Note: Also serving Barkhamsted and Hartland.

Newington Probate Court 66 Cedar St, Rear, Newington, CT 06111; phone: 860-665-1285; fax: 860-665-1331; hours 9AM-4PM M-W, F; 9AM-6PM Th (EST). *Probate.*
Note: District includes towns of Rocky Hill, Wethersfield, Newington.

Plainville Probate Court 1 Central Square, Plainville, CT 06062; phone: 860-793-0221 x250; fax: 860-793-2424; hours 8:30AM-N, 1-3:30PM M-Th; Closed Fri (EST). *Probate.*

Simsbury Probate Court 933 Hopmeadow St, PO Box 495, Simsbury, CT 06070; phone: 860-658-3277; fax: 860-658-3204; hours 8:30-1, 2-4:30 M-F (EST). *Probate.*

Southington Probate Court Town Hall, 75 Main St, PO Box 165, Southington, CT 06489; phone: 860-276-6253; fax: 860-276-6255; hours 8:30AM-4:30PM; 8:30AM-7PM Th (EST). *Probate.*

Suffield Probate Court 83 Mountain Rd, Town Hall, Suffield, CT 06078; phone: 860-668-3835; fax: 860-668-3029; hours 9AM-1PM (EST). *Probate.*
Note: Passport applications by appointment.

West Hartford Probate Court 50 S Main St, West Hartford, CT 06107; phone: 860-523-3174; fax: 860-561-7591; hours 8:30AM-4:30PM (EST). *Probate.*

Windsor Locks Probate Court Town Office Bldg, 50 Church St, Windsor Locks, CT 06096; phone: 860-627-1450; fax: 860-654-8919; hours 9AM-2PM M-Th (EST). *Probate.*

Windsor Probate Court 275 Broad St, PO Box 342, Windsor, CT 06095; phone: 860-285-1976; fax: 860-285-1909; hours 8:30AM-4:30PM M-Th; 8:30AM-N Fri (EST). *Probate.*

Litchfield County

Litchfield Judicial District Court PO Box 247, Litchfield, CT 06759; phone: 860-567-0885; fax: 860-567-4779; hours 9AM-5PM (EST). *Felony, Civil Actions, Divorce.*
Civil Records: Access: Fax, mail, online, in person. Only the court performs in person searches; visitors may not. No search fee. Court makes copy: $1.00 per page. Required to search: name, years to search. Civil cases indexed by defendant, plaintiff. Pending cases only on computer, on index cards from 1972. Access to civil case records is free at www.jud.state.ct.us. Mail turnaround time 3-4 weeks.
Criminal Records: Access: Fax, mail, in person. Only the court performs in person searches; visitors may not. No search fee. Court makes copy: $1.00 per page. Required to search: name, years to search; also helpful: DOB. Pending cases only on computer, on index cards from 1972. Mail turnaround time 3-4 weeks.
General Information: No public access terminal. No sealed files released. No fee to fax documents. Certification fee: $2.00 per cert. Payee: Clerk of Superior Court. Personal checks accepted. Prepayment and SASE required.

Geographical Area Court #18 PO Box 667, 80 Doyle Rd, Bantam, CT 06750; phone: 860-567-3942; fax: 860-567-3934; hours 9AM-5PM (EST). *Misdemeanor, Eviction, Small Claims.*
Note: Serving Barkhamsted, Bethlehem, Bridgewater, Canaan, Colebrook, Cornwall, Goshen, Hartland, Harwinton, Kent, Litchfield, Morris, New Hartford, New Milford, Norfolk, North Canaan, Roxbury, Salisbury, Sharon, Thomaston, Torrington, Warren, Wash & Winchester
Civil Records: Access: Mail, online, in person. Both court and visitors may perform in person searches. No search fee. Court makes copy: $1.00 per page. Required to search: name, years to search. Civil cases indexed by defendant. Civil records on computer for 2 years, on microfiche from 1986. Access to small claims case records is free at www.jud.state.ct.us. Mail turnaround time 1 week.
Criminal Records: Access: Mail, in person. Only the court performs in person searches; visitors may not. No search fee. Court makes copy: $1.00 per page. Required to search: name, years to search, DOB; also helpful: address. Criminal records on computer for 1 year, microfiche from 1986, on index cards for 40 years. Archived at Records Center at Enfield, CT. Mail turnaround time 1 week.
General Information: No public access terminal. No youthful offender or non-discloseable records released. Certification fee: $2.00 per doc. Payee: Clerk of Superior Court. Personal checks accepted. Prepayment and SASE required.

Barkhamsted Probate Court, CT 06063. *Probate.*
Note: Merged w/ New Hartford-860-379-3254.

Canaan Probate Court Town Hall, 100 Pease St, PO Box 905, Canaan, CT 06018-0905; phone: 860-824-7114; fax: 860-824-3139; hours 9AM-1PM (and by app't) (EST). *Probate.*

Cornwall Probate Court PO Box 157, Town Office Bldg, Cornwall, CT 06753-0157; phone: 860-672-2677; hours 9AM-12, 1-4PM, T & Th (EST). *Probate.*

Harwinton Probate Court Town Hall, 100 Bentley Dr, Harwinton, CT 06791; phone: 860-485-1403; fax: 860-485-0051; hours 1-6PM Tu-W (and by app't) (EST). *Probate.*
Note: Fax is in First Selectman's office, so put "Attention Probate Court" on fax cover.

Kent Probate Court Town Hall, 41 Kent Green Blvd, PO Box 185, Kent, CT 06757-0185; phone: 860-927-3729; fax: 860-927-1313; hours 9AM-N Tu & Th (and by app't) (EST). *Probate.*

Litchfield Probate Court PO Box 505, 74 West St, Litchfield, CT 06759; phone: 860-567-8065; fax: 860-567-2538; hours 9AM-1PM (and by app't) (EST). *Probate.*
Note: District includes towns of Morris, Warren, and Litchfield.

New Hartford Probate Court Town Hall, 530 Main St, PO Box 308, New Hartford, CT 06057; phone: 860-379-3254; fax: 860-379-0940; hours 8:30AM-3PM M,T,Th; 8AM-N W,F (EST). *Probate.*
Note: Includes towns of New Hartford, Barkhamsted, and Hartland

New Milford Probate Court 10 Main St, Town Hall, New Milford, CT 06776; phone: 860-355-6029; fax: 860-355-6024; hours 9AM-N 1-5PM T-Th; 9AM-N 1-4PM Mon; closed Friday (EST). *Probate.*
Note: District includes Town of Bridgewater.

Norfolk Probate Court 19 Maple Ave, PO Box 648, Norfolk, CT 06058; phone: 860-542-5134; fax: 860-542-5876; hours 9AM-N T & Th (and by app't) (EST). *Probate.*

Plymouth Probate Court 80 Main St, Terryville, CT 06786; phone: 860-585-4014; fax: 860-585-4098; hours 9AM-2PM Tu & Th (and by app't) (EST). *Probate.*

Roxbury Probate Court Town Hall, 29 North St, PO Box 203, Roxbury, CT 06783; phone: 860-354-1184; fax: 860-355-3091; hours 9AM-3PM Tu-Th (and by app't) (EST). *Probate.*

Salisbury Probate Court Town Hall, 27 Main St, PO Box 525, Salisbury, CT 06068; phone: 860-435-5183; fax: 860-435-5172; hours 9AM-N (and by app't) (EST). *Probate.*

Sharon Probate Court 63 Main St, PO Box 1177, Sharon, CT 06069; phone: 860-364-5514; fax: 860-364-5789; hours 2-4PM M-W & F (and by app't) (EST). *Probate.*

Thomaston Probate Court 158 Main St, Town Hall Bldg, PO Box 136, Thomaston, CT 06787; phone: 860-283-4874; fax: 860-283-1013; hours 3-6PM T-Th (and by app't) (EST). *Probate.*

Torrington Probate Court Municipal Bldg, 140 Main St, Torrington, CT 06790; phone: 860-489-2215; fax: 860-496-5910; hours 8:30AM-4:00PM, M-W; 8:30AM-6:30PM, Tu; 8:30AM-12:30PM F (EST). *Probate.*
Note: District includes Town of Goshen.

Washington Probate Court Town Hall, 2 Bryan Mem. Plaza, PO Box 295, Washington Depot, CT 06794; phone: 860-868-7974; fax: 860-868-0512; hours 9AM-N, 1-5PM M,W,F and by app't (EST). *Probate.*
www.washingtonct.org/probate.html

Watertown Probate Court PO Box 843, Woodbury, CT 06798; phone: 203-263-2417; fax: 203-263-2748; hours 9AM-N, 1-3PM (EST). *Probate.*

Note: Waterbury probate Court merged with Woodbury Probate Court on 01/08/03.

Winchester Probate Court 338 Main St, PO Box 625, Winsted, CT 06098; phone: 860-379-5576; fax: 860-738-7053; hours 9AM-12,1-4PM M-W, 9Am-2PM, 3-7PM Th, til noon Fri (EST). *Probate.*

Note: District includes towns of Colebrook, Winsted.

Woodbury Probate Court 281 Main St S, PO Box 843, Woodbury, CT 06798; phone: 203-263-2417; fax: 203-263-2748; hours 9AM-N, 1PM-4PM M-Th (EST). *Probate.*

Note: District includes Town of Bethlehem, Watertown and Oakville.

Middlesex County

Middlesex District Court - Criminal & GA Court #9 1 Court St, 1st Fl, Middletown, CT 06457-3348; phone: 860-343-6445; fax: 860-343-6566; hours 9AM-5PM (EST). *Felony, Misdemeanor.*

Note: Serving the towns of Chester, Clinton, Cromwell, Deep River, Durham, East Haddam, East Hampton, Essex, Haddam, Killingworth, Middlefield, Middletown, Old Saybrook, Portland and Westbrook.

Criminal Records: Access: Mail, in person. Only the court performs in person searches; visitors may not. No search fee. Court makes copy: $1.00 per page. Required to search: name, years to search, DOB, signed release; also helpful: address, SSN. Criminal records on computer for 1 year from disposition or sentence, on microfiche prior to 1984, prior on index cards to 1961. Mail turnaround time 3-4 days.

General Information: No public access terminal. No youthful offender records or dismissals released. Certification fee: $2.50. Payee: Clerk, Superior Court. Personal checks accepted. Prepayment and SASE required.

Middlesex Judicial District Court - Civil 1 Court St, 2nd Fl, Middletown, CT 06457-3374; phone: 860-343-6400; fax: 860-343-6423; hours 9AM-5PM (EST). *Civil Actions, Divorce, Eviction, Small Claims.*

Civil Records: Access: Mail, online, in person. Only the court performs in person searches; visitors may not. No search fee. Court makes copy: $1.00 per page. Required to search: name, years to search; also helpful: type of case, docket number. Civil cases indexed by defendant, plaintiff. Civil records on computer 1 year post-judgment; on index card back 15 years, prior on docket books, microfiche. Access to civil and family case records is free at www.jud.state.ct.us. Mail turnaround time 1 week.

General Information: Public access terminal has only civil records back to 1980. No sealed records released. Will not fax documents. Certification fee: $2.00; judgment file copy-$15.00 ($25 if certified); judgment in foreclosure action-$20.00. Exemplification copies-$20.00. Payee: Clerk, Superior Court. Personal checks accepted. Name and address must be on pre-printed check. Prepayment and SASE required.

Clinton Probate Court 50 E Main St, PO Box 130, Clinton, CT 06413-0130; phone: 860-669-6447; hours 10AM-3PM M-Th; Fri by app't (EST). *Probate.*

Note: Call before faxing.

Deep River Probate Court Town Hall, 174 Main St, PO Box 391, Deep River, CT 06417; phone: 860-526-6026; fax: 860-526-6094; hours 9AM-N M,F; 9AM-5PM T,Th; 9-12;00 and 2:30-5PM Wed (EST). *Probate.*

Note: Call before faxing.

East Haddam Probate Court PO Box 217, 7 Main St, East Haddam, CT 06423; phone: 860-873-5028; fax: 860-873-5025; hours 10AM-2PM (and by app't) (EST). *Probate.*

East Hampton Probate Court 20 E High St, Annex, East Hampton, CT 06424; phone: 860-267-9262; fax: 860-267-6453; hours 9AM-2PM M-Th (EST). *Probate.*

Essex Probate Court Town Hall, 29 West Ave, Essex, CT 06426; phone: 860-767-4340 X125; fax: 860-767-2538; hours 9AM-3PM (and by app't) (EST). *Probate.*
www.essexprobate.com

Haddam Probate Court 30 Field Park Dr, Haddam, CT 06438; phone: 860-345-8531; probate phone: 860-345-8531 x210; fax: 860-345-3730; hours 10AM-2PM T-Th (and by app't) (EST). *Probate.*

Killingworth Probate Court 323 Rte 81, Killingworth, CT 06419; phone: 860-663-2304; fax: 860-663-3305; hours 9AM-N M,W,F (and by app't) (EST). *Probate.*

Middletown Probate Court 94 Court St, Middletown, CT 06457; phone: 860-347-7424; fax: 860-346-1520; hours 8:30AM-4:30PM (EST). *Probate.*

Note: District includes towns of Cromwell, Durham, Middlefield, Middletown.

Old Saybrook Probate Court 251 Main St, Old Saybrook, CT 06475; phone: 860-395-3128; fax: 860-395-3128; hours 9AM-1PM M,T,Th,F (Wed eves by app't) (EST). *Probate.*

Note: Court is open on Wed. evenings, also

Portland Probate Court 33 E Main St, PO Box 71, Portland, CT 06480; phone: 860-342-6739; hours 9AM-2PM and by app't (EST). *Probate.*

Saybrook Probate Court PO Box 628, 203 Middlesex Ave, Chester, CT 06412; phone: 860-526-0013 X221; fax: 860-526-0004; hours 9:30AM-12:30PM Tue, Wed, Thur (and by app't) (EST). *Probate.*

Note: District includes Town of Chester

Westbrook Probate Court 866 Boston Post Rd, Westbrook, CT 06498; phone: 860-399-5661; fax: 860-399-3092; hours 1-4:30PM (EST). *Probate.*

New Haven County

Ansonia-Milford Judicial District Court PO Box 210, 14 W River St, Milford, CT 06460; phone: 203-877-4293; fax: 203-876-8640; hours 9AM-4PM (EST). *Felony, Civil Actions, Divorce.*

Civil Records: Access: Mail, fax, online, in person. Only the court performs in person searches; visitors may not. No search fee. Court makes copy: $1.00 per page. Required to search: name, years to search. Civil cases indexed by defendant, plaintiff. Civil records on computer back to 1993, on index cards from 1978. Purged computer records are on microfilm. Maintain 75 years at Records Center at Enfield, CT. Access to civil, family, and small claims case records is free at www.jud.state.ct.us. Mail turnaround time 1-2 weeks.

Criminal Records: Access: Mail, in person. Only the court performs in person searches; visitors may not. No search fee. Court makes copy: $1.00 per page. Required to search: name, years to search, DOB; also helpful-SSN. Criminal records on computer back to 1993, on index cards from 1978. Purged computer records are on microfilm. Maintain 75 years at Records Center at Enfield, CT. Mail turnaround time 1-2 weeks.

General Information: No public access terminal. Will fax documents only to toll-free or local numbers. Certification fee: $2.00 per cert. Payee: Clerk of Superior Court. Personal checks accepted. Prepayment and SASE required.

Meriden Judicial District Court 54 W Main St, Rm 128, Meriden, CT 06451; phone: 203-238-6666; fax: 203-238-6322; hours 9AM-4PM (EST). *Civil Actions, Divorce, Eviction, Housing Small Claims.*

Civil Records: Access: Mail, online, in person. Only the court performs in person searches; visitors may not. No search fee. Court makes copy: $1.00 per page. Required to search: name, years to search. Civil cases indexed by defendant, plaintiff. Pending and 1 yr after disposed cases on computer, on microfiche from 1984, prior on index cards. Access to civil, family, and small claims case records is free at www.jud.state.ct.us. Mail turnaround time 1-2 days.

General Information: No public access terminal. No acknowledgments of paternity, agreements to support prior to 10/01/95 records released. Certification fee: $2.00 per doc. Payee: Clerk of Superior Court. In state personal checks accepted. Prepayment and SASE required.

New Haven Judicial District Court 235 Church St, New Haven, CT 06510; phone: 203-503-6800; fax: 203-789-6424; hours 9AM-5PM (EST). *Felony, Civil Actions, Family, Divorce, Small Claims.*
www.jud.state.ct.us/directory/directory/location/newhaven.htm

Civil Records: Access: Phone, mail, online, in person. Only the court performs in person searches; visitors may not. No search fee. Court makes copy: $1.00 per page. Required to search: name, years to search. Civil cases indexed by defendant, plaintiff. Pending cases on computer, disposed cases deleted after 1 year, on microfiche from 1972, prior on index cards. Access to civil and family case records is free at www.jud.state.ct.us. Note: Visits may search live cases only in person. Mail turnaround time 2-5 weeks.

Criminal Records: Access: Mail, in person. Only the court performs in person searches; visitors may not. No search fee. Court makes copy: $1.00 per page. Required to search: name, years to search, DOB. Pending criminal cases on computer, disposed deleted after 1 year, prior on index cards. Mail turnaround time 2-5 weeks.

General Information: Public access terminal has only civil records back to - has llive cases only. No sealed records released. Certification fee: $2.00. Payee: Clerk of Superior Court. CT personal checks accepted if address on check matches address on drivers license. Prepayment and SASE required.

Waterbury Judicial District Court 300 Grand St, Waterbury, CT 06702; phone: 203-591-3300; criminal phone: 203-236-8100; civil phone: small claims: 203-591-3320; fax: 203-591-3325; hours 9AM-5PM (EST). *Civil Actions, Small Claims, Divorce.*

Note: Address mail requests for Misdemeanor criminal searches to 400 Grand St. (Geographical Area Court #4)

Civil Records: Access: Fax, mail, online, in person. Only the court performs in person searches; visitors may not. No search fee. Court makes copy: $1.00 per page. Required to search: name, years to search. Civil cases indexed by defendant. Civil records on computer back to 1990; none-computer records go back to 1900. Access to civil, family, and small claims case records is free at www.jud.state.ct.us. Note: Phone access limited to one search. Mail turnaround time 1-2 weeks.

General Information: No public access terminal. Certification fee: $2.00 per page. Payee: Clerk of Superior Court. Personal checks accepted. Prepayment and SASE required.

Geographical Area Court #22 14 W River St, Milford, CT 06460; phone: 203-874-0674-Small Claims; criminal phone: 203-874-1116; civil phone: 203-877-4293; fax: 203-874-5233; hours 1-2:30PM, 4-5PM (EST). *Misdemeanor, Eviction, Housing Small Claims.*
Note: Serving the towns of Milford and West Haven.

Civil Records: Access: Mail, online, in person. Only the court performs in person searches; visitors may not. No search fee. Court makes copy: $1.00 per page. Required to search: name, years to search. Civil cases indexed by defendant, plaintiff. Civil records on computer for 6 months, after disposal, on microfiche from 1986, prior on index cards and docket books. Access to civil, family, and small claims case records is free at www.jud.state.ct.us. Mail turnaround time 1 week.

Criminal Records: Access: Mail, in person. Only the court performs in person searches; visitors may not. No search fee. Court makes copy: $1.00 per page. Required to search: name, years to search; also helpful: DOB. Criminal records on computer for 6 months, after disposal, on microfiche from 1986, prior on index cards and docket books. Mail turnaround time 1 week.

General Information: No public access terminal. Certification fee: $2.00 per cert. Payee: Clerk of Superior Court. Personal checks accepted. Prepayment and SASE required.

Geographical Area Court #23 121 Elm St, New Haven, CT 06510; phone: 203-789-7461; civil phone: 203-503-6800; fax: 203-789-7492; hours 9AM-5PM (EST). *Misdemeanor, Eviction.*
Note: Small claims is located at 235 Church St, Clerk's Office, New Haven, CT 06510, 203-503-6800. Serving the towns of Bethany, Branford, East Haven, Guilford, Madison, New Haven, North Branford and Woodbridge.

Civil Records: Access: Mail, online, in person. Only the court performs in person searches; visitors may not. No search fee. Court makes copy: $1.00 per page. Required to search: name, years to search. Civil records on log book for small claims. Records go back to 1800s. Access to civil, family, and small claims case records is free at www.jud.state.ct.us. Mail turnaround time 2-3 weeks.

Criminal Records: Access: Mail, in person. Only the court performs in person searches; visitors may not. No search fee. Court makes copy: $1.00 per page. Required to search: name, years to search, DOB. Criminal records on computer back 13 months, microfiche from 1986, prior archived for criminal and motor vehicle. Note: In person search results mailed back. Mail turnaround time 2-3 weeks.

General Information: No public access terminal. No dismissals, juvenile records released. Certification fee: $2.00 per cert. Payee: Superior Court. Personal checks accepted. Prepayment and SASE required.

Geographical Area Court #4 400 Grand St, Waterbury, CT 06702; phone: 203-236-8100; fax: 203-236-8099; hours 9AM-5PM (EST). *Felony, Misdemeanor, Traffic.*
Note: Serving the towns of Middlebury, Naugatuck, Prospect, Southbury, Waterbury, Watertown, Wolcott and Woodbury.

Criminal Records: Access: Phone, mail, in person. Only the court performs in person searches; visitors may not. No search fee. Court makes copy: $1.00 per page. Required to search: name, years to search; also helpful: DOB. Criminal records on computer since 1985. Note: No certification of records available. Mail turnaround time 1-2 weeks.

General Information: No public access terminal. No youthful offenders records or dismissals released. Certification fee: $2.00 per doc. Payee: Clerk of Superior Court. Personal checks accepted. Prepayment and SASE required.

Geographical Area Court #5 106 Elizabeth St, Derby, CT 06418; phone: 203-735-7438; criminal phone: 203-735-7438; civil phone: 203-735-9654; fax: 203-735-2047; hours 9AM-5PM (EST). *Misdemeanor, Eviction, Small Claims.*
Note: Serving the towns of Ansonia, Beacon Falls, Derby, Orange, Oxford, Seymour and Shelton.

Civil Records: Access: Mail, in person. Only the court performs in person searches; visitors may not. No search fee. Court makes copy: $1.00 per page. Required to search: name, years to search. Civil cases indexed by defendant, plaintiff. Pending and records for 1 yr after disposal on computer, prior on index cards. They only hold small claims civil records in this office. Access to small claims case records is free at www.jud.state.ct.us. Note: In person search results are mailed back. Mail turnaround time 1-2 weeks.

Criminal Records: Access: Mail, in person. Only the court performs in person searches; visitors may not. No search fee. Court makes copy: $1.00 per page. Required to search: name, years to search, DOB. Pending and records for 1 yr after disposal on computer, on microfiche from 1986, prior on index cards. Note: In person search results returned by mail only. Mail turnaround time 1-2 weeks.

General Information: No public access terminal. No sealed records released. Certification fee: $2.00 per cert. Payee: Clerk of Superior Court. Personal checks accepted. Prepayment required. SASE not required.

Geographical Area Court #7 54 W Main St, Meriden, CT 06451; criminal phone: 203-238-6130; civil phone: 203-238-6128; fax: 203-238-6016; hours 9AM-5PM (EST). *Misdemeanor, Small Claims.*
Note: Serving the towns of Cheshire, Hamden, Meriden, North Haven and Wallingford.

Civil Records: Access: Mail, online, in person. Only the court performs in person searches; visitors may not. No search fee. Court makes copy: $1.00 per page. Required to search: name, years to search. Civil cases indexed by defendant, plaintiff. Pending and 1 yr after disposed cases on computer, on microfiche from 1985, prior on index cards. All manual records by docket number. Access to civil, family, and small claims case records is free at www.jud.state.ct.us. Mail turnaround time 1-2 days.

Criminal Records: Access: Phone, mail, in person. Only the court performs in person searches; visitors may not. No search fee. Court makes copy: $1.00 per page. Required to search: name, years to search, DOB. Criminal records on computer since 1986, purged every 6 months and maintained in Enfield, CT. Mail turnaround time 1-2 days.

General Information: No public access terminal. No sealed records released. Certification fee: $10.00. Payee: Clerk of Superior Court. Personal checks accepted. Prepayment and SASE required.

Bethany Probate Court Town Hall, 40 Peck Rd, Bethany, CT 06524; phone: 203-393-3744; fax: 203-393-0821; hours 9AM-1PM, by appt (EST). *Probate.*

Branford Probate Court PO Box 638, 1019 Main St, Branford, CT 06405-0638; phone: 203-488-0318; fax: 203-315-4715; hours 9AM-N, 1-4:30PM (till Noon, Fridays in Summer) (EST). *Probate.*

Cheshire Probate Court 84 S Main St, Cheshire, CT 06410; phone: 203-271-6608; fax: 203-271-6628; hours 8:30AM-1PM, 1:30PM-4PM M-Th (EST). *Probate.*
Note: District includes town of Prospect. Courts closed on Fridays.

Derby Probate Court 253 Main St, 2nd Fl, Ansonia, CT 06401; phone: 203-734-1277; fax: 203-736-1434; hours 8:30AM-5PM M-Th; 8;30-4 F (EST). *Probate.*
Note: District includes towns of Ansonia, Seymour.

East Haven Probate Court 250 Main St, Town Hall, East Haven, CT 06512; phone: 203-468-3895; fax: 203-468-5155; hours 9:30AM-4:30PM, M; 9:30AM-3:30PM, Tu; 8:30AM-3:30PM, W; 8:30AM-4:30PM, Th; 9AM-1PM, F; (EST). *Probate.*

Guilford Probate Court Town Hall, 31 Park St, Guilford, CT 06437; phone: 203-453-8006; fax: 203-453-8132; hours 9AM-N,1-4PM M,T,Th,F; 9AM-N W (EST). *Probate.*

Hamden Probate Court Govt Center, 2750 Dixwell Ave, Hamden, CT 06518; phone: 203-287-7082; fax: 203-287-7087; hours 9AM-4:30PM (EST). *Probate.*

Madison Probate Court PO Box 205, 8 Campus Dr, Madison, CT 06443; phone: 203-245-5661; fax: 203-245-5653; hours 9AM-3PM and by app't (EST). *Probate.*

Meriden Probate Court City Hall, 142 E Main St, Rm 113, Meriden, CT 06450; phone: 203-630-4150; fax: 203-630-4043; hours 8:30AM-7PM M; 8:30-4:30 T-F (EST). *Probate.*

Milford Probate Court Parsons Government Office Complex, 70 W River St, PO Box 414, Milford, CT 06460; phone: 203-783-3205; fax: 203-783-3364; hours 9AM-5PM (EST). *Probate.*

Naugatuck Probate Court Town Hall, 229 Church St, Naugatuck, CT 06770; phone: 203-720-7046; fax: 203-720-5476; hours 8:45AM-4PM M-Th; 8:45AM-2PM F (EST). *Probate.*
Note: District includes Town of Beacon Falls.

New Haven Probate Court 200 Orange St, 1st Fl, PO Box 905, New Haven, CT 06504; phone: 203-946-4880; fax: 203-946-5962; hours 9AM-4PM (EST). *Probate.*

North Branford Probate Court 909 Foxon Rd, PO Box 214, North Branford, CT 06471; phone: 203-484-6007; fax: 203-484-6017; hours 8:45AM-12:45PM (EST). *Probate.*

North Haven Probate Court PO Box 175, 18 Church St, North Haven, CT 06473-0175; phone: 203-239-5321 x775; fax: 203-239-1874; hours 8:30AM-4:30PM M-Th (and by app't) (EST). *Probate.*

Orange Probate Court 525 Orange Center Rd, Orange, CT 06477; phone: 203-891-2160; fax: 203-891-2161; hours 8:30AM-N (EST). *Probate.*

Oxford Probate Court Town Hall, Rte 67, Oxford, CT 06478; phone: 203-888-2543 x3014; fax: 203-888-2136; hours 7-9PM M,Tu,W, 1-5PM, 9AM-5PM, 7-9PM Th (EST). *Probate.*

Southbury Probate Court Townhall Annex, 421 Main St S, PO Box 674, Southbury, CT 06488; phone: 203-262-0641; fax: 203-264-9310; hours 9AM-4:30PM (and by app't) (EST). *Probate.*

Wallingford Probate Court Town Hall, 45 S Main St, Rm 114, Wallingford, CT 06492; phone: 203-294-2100; fax: 203-294-2109; hours 9AM-5PM (EST). *Probate.*

Waterbury Probate Court 236 Grand St, Waterbury, CT 06702; phone: 203-755-1127; fax: 203-597-0824; hours 9AM-4:45PM (EST). *Probate.*
Note: District includes towns of Middlebury, Wolcott.

West Haven Probate Court 355 Main St, PO Box 127, West Haven, CT 06516; phone: 203-937-3552/3/4/5; fax: 203-937-3556; hours 9AM-4PM (EST). *Probate.*

Woodbridge Probate Court Town Hall, 11 Meetinghouse Ln, Woodbridge, CT 06525; phone: 203-389-3410; fax: 203-387-5878; hours 9AM-1PM M, 9AM-2PM W (EST). *Probate.*

New London County

New London Judicial District Court 70 Huntington St, New London, CT 06320; phone: 860-443-5363; fax: 860-442-7703; hours 9AM-5PM (EST). *Felony, Civil Actions, Divorce.*

Civil Records: Access: Mail, online, in person. No search fee. Court makes copy: $1.00 per page; same fee for self serve. Required to search: exact name, years to search. Civil cases indexed by defendant, plaintiff. Civil records pending and 1 yr after disposed on computer, on microfiche from mid-70s. Access to civil and family case records is free at www.jud.state.ct.us. Note: In person access limited to five names. Mail turnaround time 2 weeks.

Criminal Records: Access: Mail, in person. Only the court performs in person searches; visitors may not. No search fee. Court makes copy: $1.00 per page; same fee for self serve. Required to search: name, years to search; also helpful: DOB. Criminal records on computer from 1991, prior on index cards. Mail turnaround time 2 weeks.

General Information: Public access terminal has only civil records. No sealed or youthful offender records released. Certification fee: $2.00. Payee: Clerk of Superior Court. Personal checks accepted. Prepayment and SASE required.

Norwich Judicial District Court 1 Courthouse Sq, Norwich, CT 06360; phone: 860-887-3515; fax: 860-887-8643; hours 9AM-5PM (EST). *Civil Actions, Divorce.*

Civil Records: Access: Phone, mail, fax, online, in person. Both court and visitors may perform in person searches. No search fee. Court makes copy: $1.00 per page. Judgment copies $15.00. Required to search: name, years to search. Civil cases indexed by defendant, plaintiff. Pending and disposed cases on computer from 1992, on microfiche from 1975, prior on index cards. Access to civil case records is free at www.jud.state.ct.us. Mail turnaround time up to 2 months.

General Information: Public access terminal has only civil records back to 1992. No criminal search warrant, acknowledgement of paternity prior to 1995, sealed records released. Certification fee: $2.00 per doc. Certified copy of Judgment $25.00. Payee: Clerk of Superior Court. Personal checks accepted. Checks must have imprinted name and address and match valid CT driver license. Prepayment and SASE required.

Geographical Area Court #10 112 Broad St, New London, CT 06320; phone: 860-443-8343; civil phone: 860-443-8346; fax: 860-447-1168; hours 9AM-5PM (EST). *Misdemeanor, Eviction, Small Claims.*

Note: Serving the towns of East Lyme, Groton, Ledyard, Lyme, New London, North Stonington, Old Lyme, Stonington and Waterford.

Civil Records: Access: Mail, online, in person. Both court and visitors may perform in person searches. No search fee. Court makes copy: $1.00 per page. Required to search: name, years to search. Civil cases indexed by defendant. Civil records on index cards and docket books. Access to civil, family, and small claims case records is free at www.jud.state.ct.us. Mail turnaround time up to 2 months.

Criminal Records: Access: Mail, in person. Only the court performs in person searches; visitors may not. No search fee. Court makes copy: $1.00 per page. Required to search: name, years to search, DOB. Criminal records on computer for 2 years; on microfiche back to 1962. Mail turnaround time up to 2 months.

General Information: No public access terminal. No sealed, dismissed, youth or program records released. Certification fee: $2.00 per page. Payee: Clerk, Superior Court. Personal checks accepted. Prepayment and SASE required.

Geographical Area Court #21 1 Courthouse Sq, Norwich, CT 06360; criminal phone: 860-889-7338; civil phone: 860-887-3515; fax: 860-885-0509; hours 1-2:30PM, 4-5PM (EST). *Misdemeanor, Eviction, Small Claims.*

Note: Serving the towns of Bozrah, Colchester, Franklin, Griswold, Lebanon, Montville, Norwich, Preston, Salem, Sprague and Voluntown.

Civil Records: Access: Mail, online, in person. No search fee. Court makes copy: $1.00 per page. Required to search: name, years to search. Civil cases indexed by defendant. Pending and 2-4 years history of disposed on computer, on microfiche from 1986, prior on index cards and docket books. Small claims, evictions not on computer. Access to civil case records is free at www.jud.state.ct.us.

Criminal Records: Access: In person only. Visitors must perform in person searches themselves. Court makes copy: $1.00 per page. Required to search: name, years to search, DOB. Pending and 2-4 years history of disposed on computer, on microfiche from 1986, prior on index cards and docket books. Small claims, evictions not on computer. Note: Mail requests are referred to the Judicial Records Center in Enfield.

General Information: Public access terminal available. No youthful offender or dismissed/erased records released. Certification fee: $2.00 per cert. Certified copy of Judgment $15.00. Payee: Superior Court GA #21. Personal checks accepted. Prepayment and SASE required.

Bozrah Probate Court Town Hall, 2nd Fl, One River Rd, Bozrah, CT 06334; phone: 860-889-2958; fax: 860-887-7571; hours 10AM-1PM M,W (and by app't) (EST). *Probate.*

Colchester Probate Court Town Hall, 127 Norwich Ave, Colchester, CT 06415; phone: 860-537-7290; fax: 860-537-7298; hours 12:30PM-4:30PM M,F; 9AM-4:30PM T,W,Th (EST). *Probate.* Note: The court also holds records for former probate court in Lebanon fro Jan '03 to date.

East Lyme Probate Court PO Box 519, 108 Pennsylvania Ave, Niantic, CT 06357; phone: 860-739-6931; fax: 860-739-6930; hours 8:30AM-12:30PM (EST). *Probate.*

Griswold Probate Court Town Hall, 28 Main St, PO Box 369, Jewett City, CT 06351; phone: 860-376-7060 x213; fax: 860-376-6628; hours 10AM-2PM, M,T,Th; 1PM-5;30PM W; 10AM-1;30 F (EST). *Probate.*

Lebanon Probate Court, CT. *Probate.* Note: Court records now located at Colchester Probate Court at 860-537-7290.

Ledyard Probate Court 741 Colonel Ledyard Hwy, Rte 17, Ledyard, CT 06339; phone: 860-464-3219; probate phone: 860-464-3218; fax: 860-464-8531; hours 8:30AM-12:30PM M, T, Th; 8:30AM-4:30PM Wed; closed Fri (app't only) (EST). *Probate.*

Lyme Probate Court Town Hall, 480 Hamburg Rd, Lyme, CT 06371; phone: 860-434-7733; fax: 860-434-2989; hours 2-4PM T-Th (and by app't) (EST). *Probate.*

Montville Probate Court 310 Norwich-New London Turnpike, Uncasville, CT 06382; phone: 860-848-3030 x319; fax: 860-848-2116; hours 9AM-1PM M,T,Th,F; 9AM-4PM W (EST). *Probate.*

New London Probate Court PO Box 148, 181 State St, Municipal Bldg, New London, CT 06320; phone: 860-443-7121; fax: 860-437-8155; hours 9AM-4PM (EST). *Probate.* Note: District includes Town of Waterford.

North Stonington Probate Court 391 Norwich Westerly Rd, Rte #2, PO Box 204, North Stonington, CT 06359; phone: 860-535-8441; fax: 860-535-8441; hours 9AM-N M & W; 1-4PM T; 1-5:30PM Th (EST). *Probate.* Note: Call before faxing.

Norwich Probate Court PO Box 38, 100 Broadway, Rm 122, Norwich, CT 06360; phone: 860-887-2160; fax: 860-887-2401; hours 9AM-4:30PM (EST). *Probate.* Note: District includes Towns of Franklin, Lisbon, Norwich, Preston, Sprague, Voluntown

Old Lyme Probate Court 52 Lyme St, Memorial Town Hall, Old Lyme, CT 06371; phone: 860-434-1605 X222; fax: 860-434-9283; hours 9AM-N, 1-4PM (EST). *Probate.*

Salem Probate Court 270 Hartford Rd, Salem, CT 06420; phone: 860-859-3873, 203-859-3036 (After hours); fax: 860-537-0547; hours 10:00-N Fridays and app't (EST). *Probate.*

Stonington Probate Court 152 Elm St, PO Box 312, Stonington, CT 06378; phone: 860-535-5090; fax: 860-535-0520; hours 9AM-N, 1-4PM (EST). *Probate.* Note: District includes Town of Mystic.

Tolland County

Tolland Judicial District Court - Civil 69 Brooklyn St, Rockville, CT 06066; phone: 860-896-4920; fax: 860-875-0777; hours 9AM-5PM (EST). *Civil Actions, Family.*

Civil Records: Access: Mail, online, in person. Only the court performs in person searches; visitors may not. No search fee. Court makes copy: $1.00 per page; Copy of judgment is $15.00. Required to search: name, years to search. Civil cases indexed by defendant, plaintiff. Civil records on computer from 2001, on microfiche from 1980, all prior on index cards. Access to civil and family case records is free at www.jud.state.ct.us. Mail turnaround time 1-2 weeks.

General Information: No public access terminal. No youthful offender, dismissed or not guilty verdict records released. Will not fax documents. Certification fee: $2.00. A full Certified Copy of Judgment is $25.00 including copy fee. Payee: Clerk of Superior Court. Personal checks accepted. Prepayment and SASE required.

Tolland Judicial District Court - Criminal 20 Park St, Vernon, CT 06066; phone: 860-870-3200; fax: 860-870-3290; hours 9AM-5PM (EST). *Felony.* Note: The address can use either Rockville or Vernon, but the US Postal Service will sometimes return mail addressed to Rockville.

Criminal Records: Access: In person only. Only the court performs in person searches; visitors may not. No search fee. Court makes copy: $1.00 per page. Required to search: name, years to search; also helpful: DOB. Criminal records are for active cases only. Completed cases must be searched State Police. Mail requests should be sent to the State Police Bureau in Middletown, CT. Mail turnaround time 1 week.

General Information: No public access terminal. No youthful offender, dismissed or not guilty verdict records released. Certification fee: $2.00. Payee: Clerk of Superior Court. Personal checks accepted. Prepayment required.

Geographical Area Court #19 PO Box 980, 20 Park St, Rockville, CT 06066-0980; phone: 860-870-3200; fax: 860-870-3290; hours 9AM-5PM (EST). *Misdemeanor.*

Note: Serving the towns of Andover, Bolton, Columbia, Coventry, Ellington, Hebron, Mansfield, Somers, Stafford, Tolland, Union, Vernon and Willington.

Criminal Records: Access: Mail, in person. Only the court performs in person searches; visitors may not. No search fee. Court makes copy: $1.00 per page. Required to search: name, years to search, DOB. Criminal records on computer approx. 2 yrs from disposition, on microfiche from 1985, prior on index cards. Mail turnaround time 7-14 days.

General Information: No public access terminal. No youthful offender records released. Will not fax documents. Certification fee: $2.00. Payee: Clerk of Superior Court. Personal checks accepted. Prepayment and SASE required.

Hebron Probate Court 15 Gilead St, Hebron, CT 06248; phone: 860-228-5971 x127; fax: 860-228-4859; hours 8AM-N Tu-W; 8-10AM Fri; and by app't (EST). *Probate.*

Andover Probate Court 222 Bolton Center Rd, Bolton, CT 06043; phone: 860-647-7979; fax: 860-649-8674; hours 8:30-4:30PM M,T-Th; 8:30-1PM Fri (EST). *Probate.*
Note: District includes towns of Andover, Bolton and Columbia

Ellington Probate Court PO Box 268, 14 Park Pl, Rockville, CT 06066; phone: 860-872-0519; fax: 860-870-5140; hours M-closed,T,W-9am-4pm,Th-9am-7pm,Fri-9am-1pm (EST). *Probate.*
Note: District includes Towns of Vernon, Ellington.

Mansfield Probate Court 4 S Eagleville Rd, Storrs, CT 06268; phone: 860-429-3313; fax: 860-429-4088; hours 9AM-12PM, 2PM-5PM, Tu; 2-5PM W; 2-6:0PM, Th; 9AM-12pm, F (EST). *Probate.*

Stafford Probate Court Town Hall, 1 Main St, PO Box 63, Stafford Springs, CT 06076; phone: 860-684-1783; fax: 860-684-1797; hours 9AM-N, 1-4:30PM M; 9AM-N Tu-F (and by app't) (EST). *Probate.*
Note: District includes towns of Union, Stafford and Somers. Somers Probate Court merged with this court in Jan. 1999.

Tolland Probate Court 21 Tolland Green, Tolland, CT 06084; phone: 860-871-3640; fax: 860-871-3641; hours 9AM-1:30 M-W; 4:30-7:30PM Th (and by app't) (EST). *Probate.*
Note: District includes Town of Willington.

Windham County

Windham Judicial District Court 155 Church St, Putnam, CT 06260; phone: 860-928-7749; civil phone: 860-779-8480-small claims; fax: 860-928-7076; hours 9AM-5PM (EST). *Civil Actions, Divorce.*
Civil Records: Access: Phone, mail, online, in person. Only the court performs in person searches; visitors may not. No search fee. Court makes copy: $1.00 per page. Required to search: name, years to search. Civil cases indexed by defendant, plaintiff. Civil records on computer for 1 year, prior on index cards, prior to 70s archived. Access to civil and family case records is free at www.jud.state.ct.us. Mail turnaround time 1-2 days.

General Information: No public access terminal. No sealed, dismissed criminal, not guilty verdict records released. Will not fax documents. Certification fee: $2.00 per cert. Payee: Clerk of Superior Court. Personal checks accepted. Prepayment and SASE required.

Geographical Area Court #11 120 School St, #110, Danielson, CT 06239-3024; phone: 860-779-8480; fax: 860-779-8488; hours 9AM-5PM (EST). *Felony, Misdemeanor, Eviction, Small Claims.*
Note: Serving the towns of Ashford, Brooklyn, Canterbury, Chaplin, Eastford, Hampton, Killingly, Plainfield, Pomfret, Putnam, Scotland, Sterling, Thompson, Windham and Woodstock.
Civil Records: Access: Phone, mail, online, in person. Both court and visitors may perform in person searches. No search fee. Court makes copy: $1.00 per page. Required to search: name, years to search. Civil cases indexed by defendant. Small claims records on computer since 8/96; all other records on index cards. Access to small claims case records is free at www.jud.state.ct.us. Mail turnaround time 1-2 weeks.
Criminal Records: Access: Phone, mail, in person. Only the court performs in person searches; visitors may not. No search fee. Court makes copy: $1.00 per page. Required to search: name, years to search, DOB. Pending criminal and 1 year after disposed on computer, on microfiche from 1986, prior on index cards. Mail turnaround time 1-2 weeks.
General Information: Public access terminal has only civil records back to 8/1996. No sealed records released. Will not fax documents. Certification fee: $2.00 per page. Payee: Clerk of Superior Court. Personal checks accepted. Prepayment and SASE required.

Ashford Probate Court 20 Pompey Hollow Rd, PO Box 61, Ashford, CT 06278; phone: 860-429-4986; fax: 860-429-1114; hours 1PM-3:30PM Th (and by app't) (EST). *Probate.*

Brooklyn Probate Court Town Hall, 4 Wolf Den Rd, PO Box 356, Brooklyn, CT 06234-0356; phone: 860-774-5973; fax: 860-779-3744; hours 11AM-4:30PM T (and by app't) (EST). *Probate.*

Canterbury Probate Court, CT. *Probate.*
Note: Closed. See Plainfield Probate District.

Chaplin Probate Court c/o Eastford Probate District, PO Box 61, Ashford, CT 06278-0061; phone: 860-974-1885; fax: 860-974-0624. *Probate.*
Note: See Eastford probate Court; Champlin Court merged with Eastford in late 1990's.

Eastford Probate Court PO Box 98, 16 Westford Rd, Eastford, CT 06242-0207; phone: 860-974-3024; fax: 860-974-0624; hours 2-5PM and by app't (EST). *Probate.*

Hampton Probate Court Town Hall, 164 Main St, PO Box 143, Hampton, CT 06247; phone: 860-455-9132 x8; fax: 860-455-0517; hours 1-4PM T, Th (EST). *Probate.*
http://hamptonct.org/probate.htm

Killingly Probate Court 172 Main St, Danielson, CT 06239; phone: 860-779-5319; fax: 860-779-5394; hours 1-4:30PM (EST). *Probate.*
Note: Also handles passports, marriages, guardianships, adoptions, name changes.

Plainfield Probate Court Town Hall, 8 Community Ave, Plainfield, CT 06374; phone: 860-230-3031; fax: 860-230-3033; hours 8:30-3:30PM M-Th; 8:30AM-N Fri (EST). *Probate.*
Note: The Probate Court merged into this court Jan. 2003.

Pomfret Probate Court 5 Haven Rd, Rt. 44, Pomfret Center, CT 06259; phone: 860-974-0186; fax: 860-974-3950; hours 10AM-4PM T-Th (and by app't) (EST). *Probate.*

Putnam Probate Court PO Box 548, 126 Church St, Putnam, CT 06260; phone: 860-963-6868; fax: 860-963-6817; hours 9AM-3PM M-F (EST). *Probate.*

Sterling Probate Court, CT. *Probate.*
Note: This court merged into the Plainfield Probate Court.

Thompson Probate Court 815 Riverside Dr, Town Hall, PO Box 74, North Grosvenordale, CT 06255; phone: 860-923-2203; fax: 860-923-3836; hours 8:30-11:30 M T W F; 3-6PM Th; 9-N 1st Sat of month (and by app't) (EST). *Probate.*
www.thompsonct.org/Government/gov_1.html

Windham Probate Court 979 Main St, PO Box 34, Willimantic, CT 06226; phone: 860-465-3049; fax: 860-465-2162; hours 9AM-1PM M-Th; 9AM-N F (EST). *Probate.*
Note: District includes Willimanitc, Scotland and Windham.

Woodstock Probate Court 415 Rte 169, Woodstock, CT 06281; phone: 860-928-2223; fax: 860-963-7557; hours 3PM-6PM W, 1:30PM-4:30PM Th (and by app't) (EST). *Probate.*

Connecticut Recording Offices

ORGANIZATION:	8 counties and 170 towns/cities. There is no county recording in this state. The recording officer is Town/City Clerk. Be careful not to confuse searching in the following towns/cities as equivalent to a county-wide search: Fairfield, Hartford, Litchfield, New Haven, New London, Tolland, and Windham. The entire state is in the Eastern Time Zone (EST).
REAL ESTATE RECORDS:	Many towns do not perform real estate searches. Copy fees are usually $1.00 per page. Certification fees are usually $1.00 per document or per page.
UCC RECORDS:	Connecticut adopted Revised Article 9 on October 1, 2001. Financing statements are filed at the state level, except for real estate related collateral, which are filed only with the Town/City Clerk. Some towns will perform UCC searches. Copies usually cost $1.00 per page.
TAX LIEN RECORDS:	All federal and state tax liens on personal property are filed with the Secretary of State. Federal and state tax liens on real property are filed with the Town/City Clerk. Towns will not perform tax lien searches.
OTHER LIENS:	Mechanics, judgments, lis pendens, municipal, welfare, carpenter, sewer & water, city/town.
ONLINE ACCESS:	A number of towns offer free access to assessor information. The State's Municipal Public Access Initiative has produced a website of Town and Municipality general information at http://www.munic.state.ct.us/. Also, a private vendor has placed assessor records from a number of towns on the Internet. Visit http://data.visionappraisal.com

Andover Town

Town Clerk, 17 School Rd, Andover, CT 06232-0328. RE & UCC recording phone-860-742-0188; fax-860-742-7535; hours: M 8:3AM-7PM; Tues-Th 8:30AM-3PM; F 8:30AM-12PM www.andoverct.org
Separate indices to search include day book, grantor/grantee. Only the public may search. Copy fee $1.00 per page. Cert fee- $1.00 per doc plus copy fee. Payee- Andover Town Clerk. **Online access to Assessor records:** Search town assessor database at http://data.visionappraisal.com/AndoverCT/. Free registration for full data. **Other phones:** Treasurer- 860-742-4035; Elections- 860-742-7305; Vital Records- 860-742-0188; Tax Collector- 860-742-4035. **Property tax/Assessor-** same address as above. 860-742-7305.

Ansonia City

City Clerk, 253 Main St; City Hall, Ansonia, CT 06401. 203-736-5980; hours: 8AM-5:30PM, M, T, W, F; 8AM-6:30PM, TH
All records in one index. Records indexed on computer back to 1968. Only the public may search. Copy fee $1.00 per page. Cert fee- $1.00 per cert plus copy fee. Payee- Ansonia City Clerk. **Other phones:** Treasurer- 203-734-5920; Elections- 203-736-5970; Vital Records- 203-736-5980. **Property tax/Assessor-** 253 Main St, Ansonia, CT 06401; 203-734-5950.

Ashford Town

Town Clerk, 5 Town Hall, Ashford, CT 06278. 860-429-7044; fax-860-487-2025; hours: 8:30AM-3PM M-W & F; 7-9PM Wed
All records in one index. Record index not computerized. Only the public may search. Copy fee $1.00 per page. Cert fee- $2.00 per page plus copy fee. Payee- Town of Ashford. **Property tax/Assessor-** same address as above. 860-429-8583.

Avon Town

Town Clerk, 60 W. Main St, Avon, CT 06001. 860-409-4310; fax-860-677-8428; hours: 8:30AM-4:30PM (Summer hours: 8AM-4:45PM M-Th)
Only the public may search. Copy fee $1.00 per page. Cert fee- $1.00 per cert plus copy fee. Payee- Avon Town Clerk. **Online access to Property**

Assessor records: Access to property data is free at www.avonassessor.com/index.shtml. **Other phones:** Elections- 860-409-4350; Vital Records- 860-409-4310. **Property tax/Assessor-** 860-409-4335.

Barkhamsted Town

Town Clerk, 67 Ripley Hill Rd., Pleasant Valley, CT 06063. RE & UCC recording phone-860-379-8665; fax-860-379-9284; hours: 9AM-4PM (1PM on Fri)
All records in one index. Records indexed on computer back to December, 1986. Only the public may search. Copy fee $1.00 per page. Cert fee- $1.00 per doc plus copy fee. Payee- Town of Barkhamsted. **Other phones:** Treasurer- 860-379-8285; Elections- 860-738-4695; Vital Records- 860-379-8665. **Property tax/Assessor-** PO Box 555, Pleasant Valley, CT 06063; 860-379-3600.

Beacon Falls Town

Town Clerk, 10 Maple Ave, Beacon Falls, CT 06403. RE & UCC recording phone-203-729-8254; fax-203-720-1078; hours: 9AM-N, 1-4PM www.beaconfalls.us
Record index not computerized. Only the public may search. Copy fee $1.00 per page. Cert fee- $1.00 per cert plus copy fee. Payee- Beacon Falls Town Clerk. **Other phones:** Treasurer- 203-729-4340; Elections- 203-729-4216; Vital Records- 203-729-8254. **Property tax/Assessor-** same address as above. 203-723-5253.

Berlin Town

Town Clerk, 240 Kensington Rd, Kensington, CT 06037. RE & UCC recording phone-860-828-7035; fax-860-828-8628; hours: M-W, 8:30AM-4:30PM; Th 8:30AM-7PM; F 8:30AM-1PM www.town.berlin.ct.us
Separate indices to search include grantor, grantee. Only the public may search. Copy fee $1.00 per page. Cert fee- $1.00 per cert plus copy fee. Payee- Berlin Town Clerk. **Online Real Estate, Marriage, Recorder, Assessor records:** Access the recorders index free at www.town.berlin.ct.us/resolution/. Also, search town assessor database at http://data.visionappraisal.com/BerlinCT/. Free regristration for full data. **Other phones:** Treasurer- 860-828-7023; Elections- 860-828-7035; Vital Records- 860-828-7035. **Property tax/Assessor-** same address as above. 860-828-7039.

Bethany Town

Town Clerk, 40 Peck Rd, Bethany, CT 06524-3338. 203-393-2100 x104, x105, R/E recording phone-203-393-2100 x104,x105,x106; fax-203-393-0821; hours: 9AM-4:30PM (No copying after 4PM)
All records in one index. Records indexed on computer back to 1981. Only the public may search. Copy fee $1.00 per page. Cert fee- $1.00 per cert plus copy fee. Payee- Bethany Town Clerk. **Other phones:** Treasurer- 203-393-2100 x104, x105, x106; Vital Records- 203-393-2100 x104, x105, x106. **Property tax/Assessor-** same address as above. 203-393-2100 x112.

Bethel Town

Town Clerk, 1 School St., Bethel, CT 06801. RE & UCC recording phone-203-794-8505; fax-203-794-8588; hours: 9AM-5PM
Separate indices to search include computer, paper. Records indexed on computer back to 1989. Only the public may search. Copy fee $1.00 per page. Cert fee- $1.00 per cert plus copy fee. Payee- Bethel Town Clerk. **Other phones:** Vital Records- 203-794-8505. **Property tax/Assessor-** 203-794-8507.

Bethlehem Town

Town Clerk, PO Box 160, Bethlehem, CT 06751. RE & UCC recording phone-203-266-7510; fax-203-266-7670; hours: 9AM-Noon T,W,Th,F,Sat www.ci.bethlehem.ct.us
Record index not computerized. Only the public may search. Copy fee $1.00 per page. Cert fee- $1.00 per page plus copy fee. Payee- Bethlehem Town Clerk. **Other phones:** Treasurer- 203-266-7677; Elections- 203-266-7961; Vital Records- 203-266-7510. **Property tax/Assessor-** 203-266-5479.

Bloomfield Town

Town Clerk, PO Box 337, Bloomfield, CT 06002. 860-769-3507; fax-860-769-3597; hours: 9AM-5PM
All records in one index. Only the public may search. Copy fee $1.00 per page. Cert fee- $1.00 per cert plus copy fee. Payee- Town of Bloomfield. **Online access to Property, Assessor records:** Access property data free at www.prophecyone.us. No name searching. **Other phones:** Elections- 860-769-3507; Vital Records- 860-

769-3507. **Property tax/Assessor**- same address as above. 860-769-3530.

Bolton Town

Town Clerk, 222 Bolton Ctr Rd, Bolton, CT 06043-7698. 860-649-8066, R/E recording phone-860-649-8066 x106, UCC recording phone-860-649-8066 x107; fax-860-643-0021; hours: 8:30AM-4PM M,W,Th; 8:30A-6:30PM, T; 8:30AM-PM F
All records in one index. Only the public may search. Copy fee $1.00 per page. Cert fee- $1.00 per cert plus copy fee. Payee- Bolton Town Clerk. **Online access to Assessor, Property records:** Access property data free at www.prophecyone.us. No name searching. **Other phones:** Treasurer- 860-649-7780; Elections- 860-649-8066 x116; Vital Records- 860-649-8066 x106. **Property tax/Assessor**- same address as above. 860-649-8066 x100.

Bozrah Town

Town Clerk, I River Rd, Bozrah, CT 06334. 860-889-2689; fax-860-887-5449; hours: 9AM-4PM T,W; 9AM-4PM Th; 9AM-N Fri
Separate land indices to search are 3 years each. Records indexed on computer back to 1/2002; computer is not for public use. Only the public may search. Copy fee $1.00 per page. Cert fee- $1.00 per page plus copy fee. Payee- Bozrah Town Clerk. **Property tax/Assessor**- 860-889-2689.

Branford Town

Town Clerk, PO Box 150, Branford, CT 06405. 203-488-6305; fax-203-481-5561; hours: 8:30AM-4:30PM (9AM-4PM recording hours)
All records in one index. Records indexed on a public use terminal back to July, 1994. Images start 11/22/04. Only the public may search. Copy fee $1.00 per page. Cert fee- $1.00 per cert plus copy fee. Payee- Branford Town Clerk. **Online access to Assessor records:** Search the town assessor data at http://data.visionappraisal.com/BranfordCT/. Free registration for full data. **Other phones:** Treasurer- 203-488-8394; Elections- 203-483-3998; Vital Records- 203-488-4305. **Property tax/Assessor**- same address as above. 203-488-2039 x144.

Bridgeport Town

Town Clerk, 45 Lyon Terrace; City Hall, Rm 124, Bridgeport, CT 06604. 203-576-7207; hours: 9AM-4:30PM; Recording until 4PM
Separate indices to search include tax liens, tradenames, military discharges, maps of land records, political filings. Only the public may search. Copy fee $1.00 per page. Cert fee- $1.00 per page plus copy fee. Payee- Bridgeport Town Clerk. **Other phones:** Treasurer- 203-576-7286; Appraiser/Auditor- 203-576-7241; Elections- 203-576-7281; Vital Records- 203-576-7445; City Hall Information- 203-576-7200. **Property tax/Assessor**- 45 Lyon Terrace, Rm 105, Bridgeport, CT 06604; 203-576-7241.

Bridgewater Town

Town Clerk, PO Box 216, Bridgewater, CT 06752-0216. RE & UCC recording phone-860-354-5102; fax-860-350-5944; hours: 8AM-Noon M,W,F; 8AM-5PM T www.bridgewatertownhall.org
Separate indices to search include indexes from 1856-1958, 1959-1984, 6/1/84-6/30/97, 7/1/97-12/31/02, 1/1/03-12/31/04, 1/1/05 to present. Record index not computerized. Only the public may search. Copy fee $1.00 per page. Cert fee- $1.00 per cert plus copy fee. Payee- Bridgewater Town Clerk. **Other phones:** Treasurer- 860-354-2683; Elections- 860-354-5102; Vital Records- 860-354-5102. **Property tax/Assessor**- PO Box 171, Bridgewater, CT 06752; 860-355-9379.

Bristol City

Town Clerk, PO Box 114, Bristol, CT 06011-0114. 860-584-7600, R/E recording phone-860-584-6200, UCC recording phone-860-584-6200; hours: 8:30AM-5PM

Separate indices to search include trade names, land records, maps. Records indexed on computer back to 1975. Only the public may search. Copy fee $1.00 per page. Cert fee- $1.00 per cert plus copy fee. Payee- Bristol Town Clerk. **Other phones:** Elections- 860-584-6285; Elections- 860-584-6200; Vital Records- 860-584-6200. **Property tax/Assessor**- same address as above. 860-584-6240.

Brookfield Town

Town Clerk, PO Box 5106, Brookfield, CT 06804-5106. 203-775-7314, R/E recording phone-203-775-7313; fax-203-775-5231; hours: 8:30AM-4:30PM; Most Th to 7PM-Call. www.brookfield.org
All records in one index. Only the public may search. Copy fee $1.00 per page. Cert fee- $1.00 per cert plus copy fee. Payee- Brookfield Town Clerk. **Online access to Assessor records:** Search the town assessor field cards at http://data.visionappraisal.com/BrookfieldCT/. Free registration for full data. **Other phones:** Treasurer- 203-775-7308; Elections- 203-775-7343; Vital Records- 203-775-7313. **Property tax/Assessor**- same address as above. 203-775-7302.

Brooklyn Town

Town Clerk, PO Box 356, Brooklyn, CT 06234. RE & UCC recording phone-860-774-9543; fax-860-779-3744; hours: M-W 9AM-4:30PM; Th 9AM-6PM; F 9AM-1PM www.brooklynct.org
All records in one index. Records indexed on a public use terminal back to 1920. Only the public may search. Copy fee $1.00 per page. Cert fee- $1.00 per page plus copy fee. Payee- Town of Brooklyn. **Other phones:** Treasurer- 860-779-3411; Elections- 860-779-3411; Vital Records- 860-774-9543. **Property tax/Assessor**- same address as above. 860-774-5611.

Burlington Town

Town Clerk, 200 Spielman Highway, Burlington, CT 06013. RE & UCC recording phone-860-673-2108; fax-860-675-9312; hours: 8:30AM-4PM
Separate indices to search include Grantor/Grantee. Records indexed on a public use terminal back to 1990. Only the public may search. Copy fee $1.00 per page. Cert fee- $1.00 per cert plus copy fee. Payee- Burlington Town Clerk. **Other phones:** Treasurer- 860-673-6789; Elections- 860-673-2108; Vital Records- 860-673-2108. **Property tax/Assessor**- same address as above. 860-673-3901.

Canaan Town

Town Clerk, PO Box 47, Falls Village, CT 06031. 860-824-0707; fax-860-824-4506; hours: 9AM-3PM M-Th
All records in one index. Only the public may search. Copy fee $1.00 per page. Cert fee- $1.00 per page plus copy fee. Payee- Town of Canaan. **Other phones:** Treasurer- 860-824-0707; Appraiser/Auditor- 860-824-0707; Elections- 860-824-0707; Vital Records- 860-824-0707. **Property tax/Assessor**- same address as above. 860-824-0707.

Canterbury Town

Town Clerk, PO Box 27, Canterbury, CT 06331-0027. RE & UCC recording phone-860-546-9377; fax-860-546-9295; hours: 9AM-4PM M-W; 9AM-6:30PM TH; 9AM-1:30PM F
All records in one index. Records indexed on a public use terminal back to 7/1986. Only the public may search. Copy fee $1.00 per page. Cert fee- $1.00 per cert plus copy fee. Payee- Canterbury Town Clerk. **Other phones:** Treasurer- 860-546-2089; Elections- 860-546-9377; Vital Records- 860-546-9377. **Property tax/Assessor**- same address as above. 860-546-6035.

Canton Town

Town Clerk, PO Box 168, Collinsville, CT 06022. RE & UCC recording phone-860-693-7870; fax-860-693-7840; hours: 8:30AM-4:30PM www.townofcantonct.org
All records in one index. Only the public may search. Copy fee $1.00 per page. Cert fee- $1.00 per cert plus copy fee. Payee- Town of Canton. **Online access to Property records:** For search of property address, search by owner name or search sales go to www.cantonassessor.com. **Other phones:** Treasurer- 860-693-7852; Elections- 860-693-7870; Vital Records- 860-693-7870. **Property tax/Assessor**- 860-693-7842.

Chaplin Town

Town Clerk, PO Box 286, Chaplin, CT 06235. RE & UCC recording phone-860-455-9455; fax-860-455-0027; hours: 9AM-3PM M, W, Th; 1-7PM Tues
Only the public may search. Copy fee $1.00 per page. Cert fee- $1.00 per cert plus copy fee. Payee- Town of Chaplin. **Other phones:** Treasurer- 860-455-2170; Appraiser/Auditor- 860-455-9333; Elections- 860-455-9455; Vital Records- 860-455-9455. **Property tax/Assessor**- 860-455-9333.

Cheshire Town

Town Clerk, 84 S. Main St; Town Hall, Cheshire, CT 06410. RE & UCC recording phone-203-271-6601; hours: 8:30AM-4PM (Recording until 3:30PM) www.cheshirect.org
All records in one index. Only the public may search. Copy fee $1.00 per page. Cert fee- $1.00 per cert plus copy fee. Payee- Cheshire Town Clerk. **Online access to Assessor, Property records:** Access property data free at www.prophecyone.us. No name searching. **Other phones:** Elections- 203-271-6680; Vital Records- 203-271-6601. **Property tax/Assessor**- same address as above. 203-271-6620.

Chester Town

Town Clerk, PO Box 218, Chester, CT 06412-0218. RE & UCC recording phone-860-526-0013 x511; fax-860-526-0004; hours: 9AM-N, 1-4PM M,W,Th; 9AM-N, 1-7PM T; 9AM-N Fri. www.chesterct.com
All records in one index. Only the public may search. Copy fee $1.00 per page. Cert fee- $1.00 per cert plus copy fee. Payee- Chester Town Clerk. **Other phones:** Treasurer- 860-526-0013 x214; Elections- 860-526-0013 x211; Vital Records- 860-526-0013 x511. **Property tax/Assessor**- same address as above. 860-526-0013 x512.

City of New London

City Clerk, 181 State St, New London, CT 06320. RE & UCC recording phone-860-447-5205; fax-860-447-1644; hours: 8:30AM-3:50PM www.ci.new-london.ct.us
File here only for the city of New London, not for the county. There is no county filing in Connecticut. All records in one index. Records indexed on a public use terminal back to 1/1/1969. Only the public may search. Copy fee $1.00 per page. Cert fee- $1.00 per cert plus copy fee. Payee- New London City Clerk. **Online access to Assessor records:** Search the city assessor's database at http://data.visionappraisal.com//NewLondonCT. Free registration required for full access. **Other phones:** Treasurer- 860-447-5209; Appraiser/Auditor- 860-447-5216; Elections- 860-447-5206; Vital Records- 860-447-5205; Tax Collector- 860-447-5208. **Property tax/Assessor**- P O Box 92, New London, CT 06320; 860-447-5216.

Clinton Town

Town Clerk, 54 E. Main St, Clinton, CT 06413. RE & UCC recording phone-860-669-9101; hours: 9AM-4PM
All records in one index. Only the public may search. Copy fee $1.00 per page. Cert fee- $1.00

per cert plus copy fee. Payee- Clinton Town Clerk. **Online to Assessor, Property records:** Assessor records at http://data.visionappraisal.com/ClintonCT/. **Other phones:** Treasurer- 860-669-9465; Elections- 860-669-6436; Vital Records- 860-669-9101. **Property tax/Assessor-** same address as above. 860-669-9269.

Colchester Town

Town Clerk, 127 Norwich Ave, Colchester, CT 06415. RE & UCC recording phone-860-537-7215; fax-860-537-0547; hours: 8:30AM-4:30PM M-W & F; 8:30-7PM Th www.colchesterct.net
All records in one index. Records indexed on computer back to 1933. Only the public may search. Copy fee $1.00 per page. Cert fee- $1.00 per doc plus copy fee. Payee- Town of Colchester. **Online to Assessor records:** Search the town assessor data at http://data.visionappraisal.com/ColchesterCT/. Free registration for full data. **Other phones:** Treasurer- 860-537-7225; Elections- 860-537-7204; Vital Records- 860-537-7215. **Property tax/Assessor-** same address as above. 860-537-7205.

Colebrook Town

Town Clerk, PO Box 5, Colebrook, CT 06021. 860-379-3359 ext 213, R/E recording phone-203-379-3359 x213; fax-860-379-2342; hours: 9AM-N, 1-4:30PM
All records in one index. Office personnel will perform small searches or visitors may perform searches. Will not search real estate records. Will not search UCC records or tax liens. Copy fee $1.00 per page. Cert fee- $1.00 per cert plus copy fee. Payee- Colebrook Town Clerk. **Online access to Assessor records:** Assessor records online at http://data.visionappraisal.com/ColebrookCT/.
Property tax/Assessor- PO Box 5, Colebrook, CT 06021; 203-379-3359 x206.

Columbia Town

Town Clerk, 323 Jonathan Trumbull Hwy, Columbia, CT 06237. 860-228-3284; fax-860-228-2335; hours: 8AM-4PM M-W; 8AM-6PM Th; 8AM-N Fri www.columbiact.org
All records in one index. Record index not computerized. Only the public may search. Copy fee $1.00 per page. Cert fee- $1.00 per cert plus copy fee. Payee- Columbia Town Clerk. **Property tax/Assessor-** same address as above. 860-228-9555.

Cornwall Town

Town Clerk, PO Box 97, Cornwall, CT 06753-0097. RE & UCC recording phone-860-672-2709; hours: 9AM-4PM M-Th
All records in one index. Only the public may search. Copy fee $1.00 per page. Cert fee- $1.00 per cert, plus copy fee. Payee- Town of Cornwall. **Other phones:** Treasurer- 860-672-2707; Vital Records- 860-672-2709; Tax Collector- 860-672-2705. **Property tax/Assessor-** PO Box 178, Cornwall, CT 06754; 860-672-2703.

Coventry Town

Town Clerk, 1712 Main St, Coventry, CT 06238. RE & UCC recording phone-860-742-7966; fax-860-742-8911; hours: 8:30AM-4:30PM M-W; 8:30AM-6:30PM Th; 8:30AM-1:30PM
All records in one index. Only the public may search. Copy fee $1.00 per page for land record books, $.50 per copy for maps. Cert fee- $1.00 per cert plus copy fee. ($7.00 for full map). Payee- Town of Coventry. **Other phones:** Treasurer- 860-742-3528; Elections- 860-742-4061; Vital Records- 860-742-7966. **Property tax/Assessor-** 1712 Main St, Coventry, CT 06238; 860-742-4067.

Cromwell Town

Town Clerk, 41 West St, Cromwell, CT 06416-2100. RE & UCC recording phone-860-632-3440; fax-860-632-3425; hours: 8:30AM-4PM www.cromwellct.com

All records in one index. Only the public may search. Copy fee $1.00 per page. Cert fee- $1.00 per cert plus copy fee. Payee- Town of Cromwell. **Other phones:** Treasurer- 860-632-3440; Elections- 860-632-3418; Vital Records- 860-632-3440. **Property tax/Assessor-** same address as above. 860-632-3442.

Danbury City

Town Clerk, 155 Deer Hill Ave; City Hall, Danbury, CT 06810. 203-797-4531; hours: 8:30AM-4:30PM www.ci.danbury.ct.us
Only the public may search. Copy fee $1.00 per page. Cert fee- $1.00 per cert plus copy fee. Payee- City of Danbury. **Online to Assessor, Land, Permit, Water Information records:** Search the city assessor database at http://data.visionappraisal.com/DanburyCT/. Free registration for full data. Also, search land, permits, and other records on the city public access at www.ci.danbury.ct.us/Public_Documents/DanburyCT_WebDocs/publicaccess. Follow prompts and use "public" for username and password. Site may be temporarily down. **Other phones:** Treasurer- 203-797-4650. **Property tax/Assessor-** 203-797-4556.

Darien Town

Town Clerk, 2 Renshaw Rd, Darien, CT 06820-5397. 203-656-7307; hours: 8:30AM-4:30PM www.darien.org
All records in one index. Records indexed on computer back to 06/83. Only the public may search. Copy fee $1.00 per page. Cert fee- $1.00 per cert plus copy fee. Payee- Town of Darien. **Other phones:** Treasurer- 203-656-7334. **Property tax/Assessor-** same address. 203-656-7310.

Deep River Town

Town Clerk, 174 Main St; Town Hall, Deep River, CT 06417. RE & UCC recording phone-860-526-6024; fax-860-526-6023; hours: 9AM-4PM
All records in one index. Record index not computerized. Only the public may search. Copy fee $1.00 per page. Cert fee- $1.00 per cert plus copy fee. Payee- Deep River Town Clerk. **Other phones:** Elections- 860-526-6024; Vital Records- 860-526-6024. **Property tax/Assessor-** same address as above. 860-526-6029.

Derby City

Town Clerk, 1 Elizabeth St, Derby, CT 06418. RE & UCC recording phone-203-736-1462; fax-203-736-1458; hours: 9AM-5PM
Only the public may search. Copy fee $1.00 per page. Cert fee- $1.00 per cert plus copy fee. Payee- Derby Town Clerk. **Other phones:** Treasurer- 203-736-1452; Appraiser/Auditor- 203-736-1452; Elections- 203-736-1462; Vital Records- 203-736-1462. **Property tax/Assessor-** 203-736-1455.

Durham Town

Town Clerk, PO Box 428, Durham, CT 06422. RE & UCC recording phone-860-349-3453; fax-860-349-0547; hours: 9AM-4:30PM M-F, 10AM-N Sat except holiday weekends http://townofdurhamct.org
Separate indices to search include land, maps. Records indexed on a public use terminal back to 1979. Only the public may search. Copy fee $1.00 per page. Cert fee- $1.00 per cert plus copy fee. Payee- Durham Town Clerk. **Online access to Assessor, Property, Map records:** Access the assessor's database at http://durham.univers-clt.com. Also, Assessor Maps access at www.townofdurhamct.org/content/18701/18791/default.aspx. **Other phones:** Treasurer- 860-349-3625; Elections- 860-349-3452; Vital Records- 860-349-3453. **Property tax/Assessor-** same address as above. 860-349-3452.

East Granby Town

Town Clerk, PO Box TC, East Granby, CT 06026-0459. RE & UCC recording phone-860-653-6528; fax-860-653-4017; hours: 8:30AM-N, 1-4PM M-Th; 8:30AM-1PM F
All records in one index. Record index not computerized. Only the public may search. Copy fee $1.00 per page. Cert fee- $1.00 per doc plus copy fee. Payee- Town of East Granby. **Other phones:** Treasurer- 860-653-0096; Elections- 860-653-0097; Vital Records- 860-653-6528; Selectmen- 860-653-2576. **Property tax/Assessor-** PO Box 1858, East Granby, CT 06026; 860-653-2852.

East Haddam Town

Town Clerk, PO Box K; Town Office Bldg, East Haddam, CT 06423. 860-873-5027; hours: 9AM-4PM M,W,Th; 9AM-N F (Tues until 7PM) http://easthaddam.org
Only the public may search. Copy fee $1.00 per page. Cert fee- $1.00 per page. Payee- East Haddam Town Clerk. **Online access to Assessor, Property records:** Access property data free at http://easthaddam.org/property_value.htm. **Other phones:** Treasurer- 860-873-5022; Elections- 860-873-5027; Vital Records- 860-873-5027. **Property tax/Assessor-** same address as above. 860-873-5026.

East Hampton Town

Town Clerk, 20 E. High St; Town Hall, East Hampton, CT 06424. 860-267-2519, R/E recording phone-203-267-2519; fax-860-267-1027; hours: 8AM-4PM M,W,Th; 8AM-7:30PM T; 8AM-12:30PM F www.easthamptonct.org/
All records in one index. Records indexed on a public use terminal. Only the public may search. Copy fee $1.00 per page. Cert fee- $2.00 per page. Payee- East Hampton Town Clerk. **Property tax/Assessor-** 203-267-2510.

East Hartford Town

Town Clerk, 740 Main St, East Hartford, CT 06108-3126. 860-291-7230; fax-860-289-0831; hours: 8:30AM-4:30PM www.ci.east-hartford.ct.us
All records in one index. Office will perform UCC search but public must search other records themselves. Copy fee $1.00 per page. Cert fee- $1.00 per cert. Payee- Town Clerk, East Hartford. **Other phones:** Vital Records- 860-291-7230. **Property tax/Assessor-** 860-291-7260 x268.

East Haven Town

Town Clerk, 250 Main St, East Haven, CT 06512-3034. 203-468-3201; hours: 8:30AM-4:15PM
All records in one index except for municipal liens. Only the public may search. Copy fee $1.00 per page. Cert fee- $1.00 per cert plus copy fee. Payee- East Haven Town Clerk. **Online access to Assessor, Property records:** Access property data free at www.prophecyone.us. No name searching. **Other phones:** Elections- 203-468-3320; Vital Records- 203-468-3201. **Property tax/Assessor-** same address as above. 203-468-3233.

East Lyme Town

Town Clerk, PO Box 519, Niantic, CT 06357. RE & UCC recording phone-860-739-6931; fax-860-739-6930; hours: 8AM-4PM www.eltownhall.com
All records in one index. Only the public may search. Copy fee $1.00 per page. Cert fee- $1.00 per cert plus copy fee. Payee- East Lyme Town Clerk. **Online access to Assessor, Property records:** Search the town assessor database at http://data.visionappraisal.com/EastLymeCT/. Free registration for full data. **Other phones:** Treasurer- 860-739-6931; Vital Records- 860-739-6931. **Property tax/Assessor-** 860-739-6931.

East Windsor Town

Town Clerk, PO Box 213, Broad Brook, CT 06016-0213. 860-623-9467, R/E recording phone-860-292-8255, UCC recording phone-860-292-8255; fax-860-623-4798; hours: 8:30-4:30PM M,T,W; 8:30AM-7PM Th; 8:30AM-1PM www.eastwindsorct.com/Home/

Only the public may search. Copy fee $1.00 per page. Cert fee- $1.00 per cert plus copy fee. Payee- Town of East Windsor. **Online access to Assessor, Property records:** Access property data free at www.prophecyone.us. No name searching. **Other phones:** Treasurer- 860-292-5909; Elections- 860-292-5915; Vital Records- 860-292-8255; Selectmen- 860-623-8122. **Property tax/Assessor-** 11 Rye St, Broad Brook, CT 06016-0213; 860-623-8878.

Eastford

Town Clerk, PO Box 98, Eastford, CT 06242-0098. 860-974-1885; fax-860-974-0624; hours: 2nd & 4th Tue, 5;30-7;30PM
Record index not computerized. Only the public may search. Copy fee $1.00 per page. Cert fee-$1.00 per page plus copy fee. Payee- Eastford Town Clerk. **Other phones:** Treasurer- 860-974-0133; Elections- 860-974-1885; Vital Records- 860-974-1885. **Property tax/Assessor-** same address as above. 860-974-1291.

Easton Town

Town Clerk, PO Box 61, Easton, CT 06612. 203-268-6291; fax-203-261-6080; hours: 9AM-2PM www.eastonct.org
Only the public may search. Copy fee $1.00 per page. Cert fee- $1.00 per cert plus copy fee. Payee- Town of Easton. **Other phones:** Treasurer- 203-268-6291; Appraiser/Auditor- 203-268-6291; Elections- 203-268-6291; Vital Records- 203-268-6291. **Property tax/Assessor-** 203-268-6291.

Ellington Town

Town Clerk, PO Box 187, Ellington, CT 06029-0187. RE & UCC recording phone-860-870-3105; hours: 8:30AM-6PM M; 8:30-4 T,W; 8:30AM-1:30PM Fri www.ellington-ct.gov
All records in one index. Records indexed on a public use terminal back to 1984. Only the public may search. Copy fee $1.00 per page. Cert fee-$1.00 per cert plus copy fee. Payee- Ellington Town Clerk. **Other phones:** Treasurer- 860-870-3115; Elections- 860-870-3107; Vital Records- 860-870-3105; Tax Collector- 860-870-3113. **Property tax/Assessor-** same address as above. 860-870-3109.

Enfield Town

Town Clerk, 820 Enfield St, Enfield, CT 06082-2997. 860-253-6440, R/E recording phone-860-253-6435, UCC recording phone-860-253-6435; hours: 9AM-5PM www.enfield.org
All records in one index. Only the public may search. Copy fee $1.00 per page. Cert fee- $1.00 per doc plus copy fee. Payee- Town of Enfield. **Online access to Tax Sale records:** Search the town's tax sale list free at www.enfield.org/Link_Tax.HTM. Use Control+F and search for name. **Other phones:** Treasurer- 860-253-6330; Elections- 860-253-6320; Vital Records- 860-253-6440. **Property tax/Assessor-** same address as above. 860-253-6339.

Essex Town

Town Clerk, PO Box 98, Essex, CT 06426. RE & UCC recording phone-860-767-4344 x129; fax-860-767-4560; hours: 9AM-4PM www.essexct.gov/departments/townclerk.html
All records in one index. Only the public may search. Copy fee $1.00 per page. Cert fee- $1.00 per page plus copy fee. Payee- Essex Town Clerk. **Online access to Property, Assessor records:** Access to property data is at http://data.visionappraisal.com/EssexCT/. **Other phones:** Treasurer- 860-767-4340 x127; Elections- 860-767-4344 x129; Vital Records- 860-767-4344 x129. **Property tax/Assessor-** same address as above. 860-767-4340 x124.

Fairfield Town

Town Clerk, 611 Old Post Rd, Fairfield, CT 06430-6690. RE & UCC recording phone-203-256-3090; hours: 8:30AM-4:30PM

Only the public may search. Copy fee $1.00 per page. Cert fee- $1.00 per page. Payee- Fairfield Town Clerk. **Online access to Assessor records:** Search the town assessor database at http://data.visionappraisal.com/FairfieldCT/. Free registration for full data. **Other phones:** Elections- 203-256-3090; Vital Records- 203-256-3090. **Property tax/Assessor-** same address as above. 203-256-3110.

Farmington Town

Town Clerk, 1 Monteith Drive, Farmington, CT 06032-1053. 860-675-2380, R/E recording phone-860-673-2380; fax-860-675-2389; hours: 8:30AM-4:30PM www.farmington-ct.org/TownServices/TownClerk/
All records in one index. Only the public may search. Copy fee $1.00 per page. Cert fee- $1.00 per cert plus copy fee. Payee- Farmington Town Clerk. **Online access to Assessor, Property records:** Access to the property assessor data is free at www.farmington-ct.org; click on Assessor Property search . **Property tax/Assessor-** One Monteith Dr, Farminton, CT 06032; 860-673-2370.

Franklin Town

Town Clerk, 7 Meeting House Hill Rd; Town Hall, Franklin, CT 06254. 860-642-7352; fax-860-642-6606; hours: 8:30AM-3PM M-Th; 6PM-8PM T
All records in one index. Records indexed on computer back to 2/05. Only the public may search. Copy fee $1.00 per page. Cert fee- $1.00 per cert plus copy fee. Payee- Franklin Town Clerk. **Other phones:** Treasurer- 860-642-6055. **Property tax/Assessor-** same address as above. 860-642-6475.

Glastonbury Town

Town Clerk, 2155 Main St, Glastonbury, CT 06033. RE & UCC recording phone-860-652-7616; fax-860-652-7639; hours: 8AM-4:30PM www.glasct.org
All records in one index. Records indexed on computer back to 1/1/1973. Only the public may search. Copy fee $1.00 per page. Cert fee- $1.00 per page plus copy fee. Payee- Glastonbury Town Clerk. **Online access to Property, Assessor records:** Search town property information free on the GIS Interactive Mapping site at http://gis.glasct.org/. Click on the binoculars for "Parcels" page where you can name search. **Other phones:** Treasurer- 860-652-7586; Elections- 860-652-7616; Vital Records- 860-652-7616. **Property tax/Assessor-** same address as above. 860-652-7600.

Goshen Town

Town Clerk, PO Box 54, Goshen, CT 06756-0054. RE & UCC recording phone-860-491-3647; hours: 9AM-N,1-4PM M-Th; 9AM-1PM F
Separate indices to search include maps, tradenames, grantor/grantee. Only the public may search. Copy fee $1.00 per page. Cert fee- $1.00 per doc, plus copy fee. Payee- Town Clerk. **Online access to Assessor records:** Search the town assessor database at http://data.visionappraisal.com/goshenCT/. Free registration for full data. **Other phones:** Treasurer- 860-491-2308; Elections- 860-491-2308 x236; Vital Records- 860-491-3647; Tax Office- 860-491-3275 X226. **Property tax/Assessor-** PO Box 187, Goshen, CT 06756; 860-491-2115.

Granby Town

Town Clerk, 15 N. Granby Rd, Granby, CT 06035. 860-844-5308; hours: 9AM-N,1-4PM
Only the public may search. Copy fee $1.00 per page. Cert fee- $1.00 per cert plus copy fee. Payee- Town of Granby. **Online access to Assessor records:** Search the town assessor's database at http://data.visionappraisal.com/GranbyCT. Free registration for full data. **Property tax/Assessor-** 203-844-5311.

Greenwich Town

Town Clerk, PO Box 2540, Greenwich, CT 06836. 203-622-7897; hours: 8AM-4PM

All records in one index. Only the public may search. Copy fee $1.00 per page. Cert fee- $1.00 per cert plus copy fee. Payee- Town of Greenwich. **Other phones:** ; Main Switchboard- 203-622-7700. **Property tax/Assessor-** same address as above. 203-622-7885.

Griswold Town

Town Clerk, PO Box 369, Jewett City, CT 06351. 860-376-7060 x100, R/E recording phone-860-376-7060 x101, UCC recording phone-860-376-7060 x101; fax-860-376-7070; hours: 8:30AM-4PM M,T, 8;30AM-6;30PM Th, 8;30AM-1;30PM Fr www.griswold-ct.org
All records in one index. Only the public may search. Copy fee $1.00 per page. Cert fee- $1.00 per page plus copy fee. Payee- Town of Griswold. **Other phones:** Treasurer- 860-376-7060 x205; Appraiser/Auditor- 860-376-7060 x101; Elections- 860-376-7060 x208; Vital Records- 860-376-7060 x101. **Property tax/Assessor-** same address as above. 860-376-7060 x105.

Groton Town

Town Clerk, 45 Fort Hill Rd, Groton, CT 06340. RE & UCC recording phone-860-441-6642; hours: 8:30AM-4:30PM M-W & F; 9AM-4:30PM Th
All records in one index. Only the public may search. Copy fee $1.00 per page. Cert fee- $1.00 per cert plus copy fee. Payee- Groton Town Clerk. **Online access to Property, GIS records:** Access property data free at http://grotongis.town.groton.ct.us. Click on Interactive Mapping, then Property Viewer, then owner name. Records back to 1990. **Other phones:** Treasurer- 860-441-6609; Elections- 860-441-6640; Vital Records- 860-441-6640. **Property tax/Assessor-** same address as above. 860-441-6660.

Guilford Town

Town Clerk, 31 Park St; Town Hall, Guilford, CT 06437. 203-453-8001; hours: 8:30AM-4:30PM www.ci.guilford.ct.us
All records in one index. Record index not computerized. Only the public may search. Copy fee $1.00 per page. Cert fee- $1.00 per cert plus copy fee. Payee- Guilford Town Clerk. **Other phones:** Treasurer- 203-453-8022; Elections- 203-453-8028; Vital Records- 203-453-8001. **Property tax/Assessor-** same address as above. 203-453-8010.

Haddam Town

Town Clerk, PO Box 87, Haddam, CT 06438. 860-345-8531; fax-860-345-3730; hours: 9AM-4PM M,T,W,; 9AM-7PM Th; 9AM-N F
Records indexed on computer. Only the public may search. Copy fee $1.00 per page. Cert fee- $1.00 per cert plus copy fee. Payee- Town of Haddam. **Property tax/Assessor-** 860-345-8531 x213.

Hamden Town

Town Clerk, 2372 Whitney Ave; Memorial Town Hall, Hamden, CT 06518. 203-287-2510, R/E recording phone-203-287-7112; fax-203-287-2518; hours: 9AM-4PM www.hamden.com
Records indexed on a public use terminal back to 1968. Only the public may search. Copy fee $1.00 per page. Cert fee- $1.00 per cert plus copy fee. Payee- Hamden Town Clerk. **Online access to Assessor records:** Search the town assessor's database at http://data.visionappraisal.com/hamdenct. Free registration required for full access. **Other phones:** Treasurer- 203-387-7007; Appraiser/Auditor- 203-287-7128; Elections- 203-287-7081; Vital Records- 203-287-7112. **Property tax/Assessor-** 2750 Dixwell Ave, Hamden, CT 06518; 203-287-7128, assessor fax- 203-287-7125.

Hampton Town

Town Clerk, PO Box 143, Hampton, CT 06247-0143. 860-455-9132, R/E recording phone-860-455-9132 x1,

UCC recording phone-860-455-9132 x1; fax-860-455-0517; hours: 9AM-4PM T,Th; 6-8PM Th
Only the public may search. Copy fee $1.00 per page. Cert fee- $1.00 per cert plus copy fee. Payee-Hampton Town Clerk. **Other phones:** Treasurer- 860-455-9132 x7; Elections- 860-455-9132 x1; Vital Records- 860-455-9132 x1. **Property tax/Assessor-** 860-455-9132 x5.

Hartford City

City Clerk, 550 Main St, Hartford, CT 06103-2992. 860-543-8580, R/E recording phone-860-722-8040; fax-860-772-8041; hours: 8:30AM-4:30 PM
Only the public may search. Copy fee $1.00 per page. Cert fee- $1.00 per cert plus copy fee. Payee-Hartford City Clerk. **Other phones:** Treasurer- 860-543-8530. **Property tax/Assessor-** 860-543-8540.

Hartland Town

Town Clerk, PO Box 297, East Hartland, CT 06027. 860-653-0285; fax-860-653-0452; 10AM-N, 1-4PM M,T,W www.munic.state.ct.us/hartland/hartland.htm
Separate indices to search. Office personnel or visitors may perform searches. Office will do short search as time allows only. Copy fee $1.00 per page. Cert fee- $1.00 per cert plus copy fee. Payee-Hartland Town Clerk. **Other phones:** Vital Records- 860-653-0285; Selectmen- 860-653-6800; Tax Collector -860-653-0609 x105. **Property tax/Assessor-** 22 South Rd, East Hartland, CT 06027; 860-653-0609 X106.

Harwinton Town

Town Clerk, 100 Bentley Drive; Town Hall, Harwinton, CT 06791. RE & UCC recording phone-860-485-9613; fax-860-485-0051; hours: 8:30AM-4PM
All records in one index. Only the public may search. Copy fee $1.00 per page. Cert fee- $1.00 per cert plus copy fee. Payee- Harwinton Town Clerk. **Other phones:** Treasurer- 860-485-9051; Elections- 860-485-9613; Vital Records- 860-485-9613; Tax Collector- 860-485-0446. **Property tax/Assessor-** 100 Bentley Dr, Harwinton, Ct 06791; 860-485-0898.

Hebron Town

Town Clerk, PO Box 156, Hebron, CT 06248. 860-228-5971 x124, R/E recording phone-860-228-5971, UCC recording phone-860-228-5971; fax-860-228-4859; hours: 8AM-4PM M-W; 8AM-6PM Th; 8AM-1PM F www.hebronct.com
All records in one index. Only the public may search. Copy fee $1.00 per page. Cert fee- $1.00 per cert plus copy fee. Payee- Town of Hebron. **Other phones:** Treasurer- 860-228-5971; Appraiser/Auditor- 860-228-5971; Elections- 860-228-5971; Vital Records- 860-228-5971. **Property tax/Assessor-** 860-228-5971.

Kent Town

Town Clerk, PO Box 678, Kent, CT 06757-0678. 860-927-3433; fax-860-927-4541; hours: 9AM-4PM www.kentct.org
Separate indices to search include grantor, grantee. Record index not computerized. Only the public may search. Copy fee $1.00 per page. Cert fee- $1.00 per page. Payee- Kent Town Clerk. **Online access to Assessor, Property records:** Access to property assessor data is at http://data.visionappraisal.com/KentCT/. Free registration required. **Other phones:** Treasurer- 860-927-1313; Vital Records- 860-927-3433. **Property tax/Assessor-** same address as above. 860-927-3160.

Killingly Town

Town Clerk, PO Box 6000, Danielson, CT 06239. RE & UCC recording phone-860-779-5307; fax-860-779-5394; hours: 8:30AM-4:30PM www.killinglyct.gov
Records indexed on a public use terminal back to 1939. Only the public may search. Copy fee $1.00

per page. Cert fee- $1.00 per page plus copy fee. Payee- Killingly Town Clerk. **Other phones:** Treasurer- 860-779-5337; Elections- 203-779-5302; Vital Records- 860-779-5307. **Property tax/Assessor-** same address as above. 860-779-5323.

Killingworth Town

Town Clerk, 323 Route 81, Killingworth, CT 06419-1298. 860-663-1616, R/E recording phone-860-663-1765; fax-860-663-3305; hours: 9AM-N,1-4PM
Index: Recorded by years or groups of years. Only the public may search. Copy fee $1.00 per page. Cert fee- $1.00 per cert plus copy fee. Payee-Town of Killingworth. **Other phones:** Vital Records- 860-663-1616. **Property tax/Assessor-** same address as above. 203-663-2002.

Lebanon Town

Town Clerk, 579 Exeter Rd; Town Hall, Lebanon, CT 06249. 860-642-7319; fax-860-642-7716; hours: 8AM-4PM M,Th,F; 8AM-6PM T www.lebanontownhall.org
Only the public may search. Copy fee $1.00 per page. Cert fee- $1.00 per cert plus copy fee. Payee-Town of Lebanon. **Other phones:** Vital Records- 860-642-7319. **Property tax/Assessor-** same address as above. 860-642-6141.

Ledyard Town

Town Clerk, 741 Col. Ledyard Highway, Ledyard, CT 06339. 860-464-3259; fax-860-464-1126; hours: 8:30AM-4:30PM Mon-Fri www.town.ledyard.ct.us
Only the public may search. Copy fee $1.00 per page. Cert fee- $1.00 per cert plus copy fee. Payee-Town of Ledyard. **Other phones:** Treasurer- 860-464-3228; Vital Records- 860-464-3259. **Property tax/Assessor-** 860-464-3237.

Lisbon Town

Town Clerk, 1 Newent Rd; RD 2 Town Hall, Lisbon, CT 06351-9802. 860-376-2708; fax-860-376-6545; hours: 9AM-3PM M-Th; 6PM-8PM W; 9AM-1PM F; 9AM-N Sat
All records in one index. Only the public may search. Copy fee $1.00 per page. Cert fee- $1.00 per cert plus copy fee. Payee- Lisbon Town Clerk. **Other phones:** Treasurer- 860-376-3400. **Property tax/Assessor-** 1 Newent Rd, Lisbon, CT 06351; 860-376-5115.

Litchfield Town

Town Clerk, PO Box 488, Litchfield, CT 06759-0488. RE & UCC recording phone-860-567-7561; hours: 9AM-4:30PM
Separate indices to search. Only the public may search. Copy fee $1.00 per page. Cert fee- $1.00 per cert plus copy fee. Payee- Litchfield Town Clerk. **Other phones:** Treasurer- 860-567-7554; Vital Records- 860-567-7561; Registrar- 860-567-7558. **Property tax/Assessor-** 860-567-7559.

Lyme Town

Town Clerk, 480 Hamburg Rd.; Town Hall, Lyme, CT 06371. RE & UCC recording phone-860-434-7733; fax-860-434-2989; hours: 9AM-4PM
All records in one index. Record index not computerized. Only the public may search. Copy fee $1.00 per page. Cert fee- $1.00 per page plus copy fee. Payee- Lyme Town Clerk. **Online access to Assessor, Property records:** Access to property data is at http://data.visionappraisal.com/LymeCT/. Free registration required. **Other phones:** Treasurer- 860-434-7733; Appraiser/Auditor- 860-434-8094; Elections- 860-434-7733; Vital Records- 860-434-7733. **Property tax/Assessor-** same address as above. 860-434-8094.

Madison Town

Town Clerk, 8 Campus Dr., Madison, CT 06443-2538. RE & UCC recording phone-203-245-5672; fax-203-245-5613; hours: 8:30AM-4PM www.madisonct.org

All records in one index. Only the public may search. Copy fee $1.00 per page. Cert fee- $1.00 per cert plus copy fee. Payee- Madison Town Clerk. **Online access to Assessor, Property records:** Search the town assessor database at http://data.visionappraisal.com/MadisonCT/. Free registration required for full access. **Other phones:** Elections- 203-245-5671; Vital Records- 203-245-5672. **Property tax/Assessor-** same address as above. 203-245-5652.

Manchester Town

Town Clerk, PO Box 191, Manchester, CT 06045-0191. RE & UCC recording phone-860-647-3037; fax-860-647-3029; hours: 8:30AM-5PM www.ci.manchester.ct.us/Town_Clerk/index.htm
All records in one index. Only the public may search. Copy fee $1.00 per page. Cert fee- $1.00 per cert plus copy fee. Payee- Manchester Town Clerk. **Online access to Assessor records:** Search the town assessor database at http://data.visionappraisal.com/ManchesterCT/. Free registration required for full access. **Other phones:** Treasurer- 860-647-3023; Appraiser/Auditor- 860-647-3017; Elections- 860-647-3037; Vital Records- 860-647-3037. **Property tax/Assessor-** 860-647-3016.

Mansfield Town

Town Clerk, 4 S. Eagleville Rd, Mansfield, CT 06268. 860-429-3302; hours: 8:15AM-4:30PM M-W; 8:15AM-6:30PM Th; 8AM-N Fri www.mansfieldct.org
All records in one index. Only the public may search. Copy fee $1.00 per page. Cert fee- $1.00 per page plus copy fee. Payee- Town of Mansfield. **Other phones:** Elections- 860-429-3369. **Property tax/Assessor-** same address as above. 860-429-3327.

Marlborough Town

Town Clerk, PO Box 29, Marlborough, CT 06447. RE & UCC recording phone-860-295-6206; fax-860-295-0317; hours: 8AM-4:30PM M-Th; 8AM-7PM T; 8AM-N Fri www.marlboroughct.com
All records in one index. Records indexed on a public use terminal back to 9/10/04. Only the public may search. Copy fee $1.00 per page. Cert fee- $1.00 per doc plus copy fee. Payee-Marlborough Town Clerk. **Other phones:** Treasurer- 860-295-6165; Elections- 860-295-6166; Vital Records- 860-295-6206. **Property tax/Assessor-** same address as above. 860-295-6201.

Meriden City

City Clerk, 142 E. Main St, Meriden, CT 06450-8022. RE & UCC recording phone-203-630-4030; fax-203-630-4059; hours: 9AM-7PM M; 9AM-5PM T-F www.cityofmeriden.org
All records in one index. Records indexed on a public use terminal back to 1983. Only the public may search. Copy fee $1.00 per page. Cert fee- $1.00 per page plus copy fee. Payee- Meriden City Clerk. **Online to Property, Assessor records:** Search by parcel ID or address for property assessor data at www.meridenrealestate.org/meriden208/LandRover.asp. **Other phones:** Treasurer- 203-630-4134; Elections- 203-630-4075; Vital Records- 203-630-4030. **Property tax/Assessor-** same address. 203-630-4071.

Middlebury Town

Town Clerk, PO Box 392, Middlebury, CT 06762-0392. RE & UCC recording phone-203-758-2557; fax-203-758-2915; hours: 9AM-N,1-5PM www.middlebury-ct.org
All records in one index. Records indexed on a public use terminal back to 1934. Only the public may search. Copy fee $1.00 per page. Cert fee- $1.00 per cert plus copy fee. Payee- Middlebury Town Clerk. **Other phones:** Treasurer- 203-758-1770; Elections- 203-758-2557; Vital Records- 203-758-2557. **Property tax/Assessor-** same address as above. 203-758-1447.

Middlefield Town

Town Clerk, PO Box 179, Middlefield, CT 06455. RE & UCC recording phone-860-349-7116; fax-860-349-7115; 9AM-5PM M; -4PM T-Th; -3PM F www.munic.state.ct.us/MIDDLEFIELD/contents.htm Only the public may search. Copy fee $1.00 per page. Cert fee- $1.00 per cert plus copy fee. Payee-Middlefield Town Clerk. **Online access to Assessor records:** Search the town assessor database at http://data.visionappraisal.com/MiddlefieldCT/. Free registration required for full data. **Other phones:** Treasurer- 860-349-7114; Elections- 860-349-7119; Vital Records- 860-349-7116. **Property tax/Assessor-** 860-349-7111.

Middletown City

City Clerk, PO Box 1300, Middletown, CT 06457. RE & UCC recording phone-860-344-3459; fax-860-344-3591; hours: 8:30AM-4:30PM www.cityofmiddletown.com/Departments.htm Only the public may search. Copy fee $1.00 per page. Cert fee- $1.00 per cert plus copy fee. Payee-Middletown Town Clerk. **Other phones:** Treasurer- 860-344-3438; Elections- 860-344-3459; Vital Records- 860-344-3474. **Property tax/Assessor-** 860-344-3454.

Milford City

City Clerk, 70 W River St, Milford, CT 06460-3364. RE & UCC recording phone-203-783-3210; fax-203-783-3362; hours: 8:30AM-5PM www.ci.milford.ct.us All records in one index. Only the public may search. Copy fee $1.00 per page. Cert fee- $1.00 per cert plus copy fee. Payee- Milford City Clerk. **Online to Assessor records:** Search the city assessor's database at http://data.visionappraisal.com/milfordct/. Free registration required for full data. **Other phones:** Treasurer- 203-783-3257; Appraiser/Auditor- 203-783-3215; Elections- 203-783-3339 (DEM); 203-783-3242 (REP); Vital Records- 203-783-3210. **Property tax/Assessor-** 70 W River St, Milford, CT 06460; 203-783-3215.

Monroe Town

Town Clerk, 7 Fan Hill Rd, Monroe, CT 06468-1800. 203-452-5417, R/E recording phone-203-452-5427, UCC recording phone-203-452-5427; fax-203-261-6197; hours: 9AM-5PM Records indexed on computer back to 1968. Only the public may search. Copy fee $1.00 per page. Cert fee- $1.00 per cert plus copy fee. Payee-Town of Monroe. **Other phones:** Treasurer- 203-452-5433; Appraiser/Auditor- 203-452-5469; Elections- 203-452-5414; Vital Records- 203-452-5427. **Property tax/Assessor-** same address as above. 203-452-5469.

Montville Town

Town Clerk, 310 Norwich-New London Tpke.; Town Hall, Uncasville, CT 06382. 860-848-1349; fax-860-848-1521; hours: 9AM-5PM www.townofmontville.org All records in one index. Records indexed on computer back to 1950. Only the public may search. Copy fee $1.00 per page. Cert fee- $1.00 per cert plus copy fee. Payee- Montville Town Clerk. **Other phones:** Treasurer- 860-848-0139. **Property tax/Assessor-** 860-848-8221 #5.

Morris Town

Town Clerk, PO Box 66, Morris, CT 06763-0066. RE & UCC recording phone-860-567-7433; fax-860-567-7432; hours: 9AM-N, 1-4PM M T F; 9AM-N, 1PM-5PM W TH All records in one index. Only the public may search. Copy fee $1.00 per page. Cert fee- $1.00 per cert plus copy fee. Payee- Morris Town Clerk. **Other phones:** Treasurer- 860-567-6094; Elections-860-567-7433; Vital Records- 860-567-7433; Tax Collector- 860-567-7435. **Property tax/Assessor-** same address as above. 860-567-6096.

Naugatuck Town

Town Clerk, 229 Church St; Town Hall, Naugatuck, CT 06770. 203-720-7000, R/E recording phone-203-720-7055; fax-203-720-7099; hours: 8:30AM-4PM Only the public may search. Copy fee $1.00 per page. Cert fee- $1.00 per cert plus copy fee. Payee-Naugatuck Town Clerk. **Online access to Assessor records:** Search the town assessor database at http://data.visionappraisal.com/NaugatuckCT/. Free registration required for full data. **Other phones:** Treasurer- 203-720-7021; Elections- 203-720-7047; Vital Records- 203-720-7055. **Property tax/Assessor-** 203-720-7016.

New Britain Town

Town Clerk, 27 W. Main St, New Britain, CT 06051. 860-826-3344; fax-860-826-3348; hours: 8:15AM-3:45PM M-W & F; 8:15AM-6:45PM Th Only the public may search. Copy fee $1.00 per page. Cert fee- $1.00 per cert plus copy fee. Payee-New Britain Town Clerk. **Online access to Assessor records:** Search the city assessor database at http://data.visionappraisal.com/NewbritainCT/. Free registration for full data. **Property tax/Assessor-** 860-826-3323.

New Canaan Town

Town Clerk, 77 Main St; Town Hall, New Canaan, CT 06840. 203-594-3070; fax-203-594-3130; hours: 8:30AM-4:30PM www.newcanaan.info All records in one index. Records indexed on computer back to 1981. Only the public may search. Copy fee $.25 per page. Cert fee- $1.00 per cert plus copy fee. Payee- New Canaan Town Clerk. **Online access to Assessor, Property records:** Access to property data is at http://data.visionappraisal.com/NewCanaanCT/. Free registration required. **Other phones:** Treasurer- 203-594-3024; Elections- 203-594-3060; Vital Records- 203-594-3070. **Property tax/Assessor-** 203-594-3005.

New Fairfield Town

Town Clerk, 4 Brushhill Rd, New Fairfield, CT 06812. 203-312-5616; hours: 8:30AM-5PM T-F; 8:30AM-N Sat Separate indices to search. Records indexed on a public use terminal. Only the public may search. Copy fee $1.00 per page. Cert fee- $2.00 per cert plus copy fee. Payee- New Fairfield Town Clerk. **Online access to Assessor records:** To access accessor database go to http://data.visionappraisal.com/NewfairfieldCT/. Does not require a username & password to enter database. Just click on link. **Property tax/Assessor-** 203-312-5625.

New Hartford Town

Town Clerk, PO Box 426, New Hartford, CT 06057. RE & UCC recording phone-860-379-5037; fax-860-379-1367; hours: 9AM-N, 12:40-4PM M,T,Th; 9AM-N, 1PM-6PM W; www.town.new-hartford.ct.us All records in one index. Only the public may search. Copy fee $1.00 per page. Cert fee- $1.00 per cert plus copy fee. Payee- New Hartford. **Online access to Assessor, Property records:** Access to property data is at http://data.visionappraisal.com/NewhartfordCT/. Free registration required. **Other phones:** Treasurer- 860-379-3389; Elections- 860-738-9721; Vital Records-860-379-5037. **Property tax/Assessor-** PO Box 316, New Hartford, CT 06057; 860-379-5235.

New Haven City

City Clerk, 200 Orange St, Rm 202, New Haven, CT 06510. 203-946-8339, R/E recording phone-203-946-8344, UCC recording phone-203-946-8344; fax-203-946-6974; hours: 9AM-5PM Records indexed on a public use terminal back to 1960. Only the public may search. Copy fee $.50 per page. Cert fee- $1.00 per page plus copy fee. Payee- New Haven City Clerk. **Online access to Assessor records:** Search the city assessor database at http://data.visionappraisal.com/NewhavenCT/. Free registration required for full data. **Other phones:** Treasurer- 203-946-8300; Elections- 203-946-8346; Vital Records- 203-946-8084. **Property tax/Assessor-** 203-787-8066.

New Milford Town

Town Clerk, 10 Main St, New Milford, CT 06776. 860-355-6020; fax-860-210-2096; hours: 8;30AM-4;30PM www.newmilford.org/ All records in one index. Records indexed on a public use terminal back to 1971. Only the public may search. Copy fee $1.00 per page. Cert fee-$1.00 per cert plus copy fee. Payee- New Milford Town Clerk. **Online access to Assessor records:** Search the town assessor database at http://data.visionappraisal.com/NewMilfordCT/. Free registration required for full access. **Other phones:** Vital Records- 860-355-6020. **Property tax/Assessor-** same address as above. 860-355-6070.

Newington Town

Town Clerk, 131 Cedar St, Newington, CT 06111-2696. RE & UCC recording phone-860-665-8545; hours: 8:30AM-4:30PM www.ci.newington.ct.us Only the public may search. Copy fee $1.00 per page. Cert fee- $1.00 per page. Payee- Newington Town Clerk. **Other phones:** Elections- 860-665-8516; Vital Records- 860-665-8545. **Property tax/Assessor-** 860-665-8530.

Newtown Town

Town Clerk, 45 Main St, Newtown, CT 06470. 203-270-4210; hours: 8AM-4:30PM All records in one index. Records indexed on a public use terminal back to 1900. Only the public may search. Copy fee $1.00 per page. Cert fee-$1.00 per cert plus copy fee. Payee- Town of Newtown. **Online access to Property, Assessor records:** Access property data free at www.prophecyone.us. No name searching. **Other phones:** Treasurer- 203-270-4221; Elections- 203-270-4250; Vital Records- 203-270-4210. **Property tax/Assessor-** 203-270-4240.

Norfolk Town

Town Clerk, PO Box 552, Norfolk, CT 06058-0552. 860-542-5679; hours: 8:30AM-N, 1-4PM M-Th, 8:30AM-N F All records in one index. Only the public may search. All land records copy fee $1.00 per page. Cert fee- $1.00 per doc plus copy fee. Payee- Town of Norfolk. **Other phones:** Elections- 860-542-5679; Vital Records- 860-542-5679. **Property tax/Assessor-** PO Box 552, Norfolk, CT 06058; 860-542-5287.

North Branford Town

Town Clerk, PO Box 287, North Branford, CT 06471-0287. 203-484-6015; hours: 8:30AM-4:30PM Only the public may search. Copy fee $1.00 per page. Cert fee- $1.00 per cert plus copy fee. Payee-North Branford Town Clerk. **Other phones:** Treasurer- 203-484-6002; Elections- 203-484-1033; Vital Records- 203-484-6015. **Property tax/Assessor-** 909 Foxon Rd, North Branford, CT 06471; 203-484-6013.

North Canaan Town

Town Clerk, PO Box 338, North Canaan, CT 06018. 860-824-3138; fax-860-824-3139; hours: 9:30AM-N, 1-4PM; Fri till 1PM All records in one index. Only the public may search. Copy fee $1.00 per page. Cert fee- $1.00 per cert plus copy fee. Payee- North Canaan Town Clerk. **Property tax/Assessor-** same address as above. 860-824-3137.

North Haven Town

Town Clerk, 18 Church St; Town Hall, North Haven, CT 06473. 203-239-5321 x541; fax-203-234-2130; hours: 8:30AM-4:30PM

Separate indices to search include liens, etc. Record index not computerized. Only the public may search. Copy fee $1.00 per page. Cert fee- $1.00 per cert plus copy fee. Payee- North Haven Town Clerk. **Other phones:** Elections- 203-239-5321 x755; Vital Records- 203-239-5321 x541. **Property tax/Assessor-** same address as above. 203-239-5321 x700.

North Stonington Town

Town Clerk, 40 Main St, North Stonington, CT 06359. RE & UCC recording phone-860-535-2877 x21; fax-860-535-4554;   hours: 9AM-4PM www.munic.state.ct.us/N_Stonington/

All records in one index. Only the public may search. Copy fee $1.00 per page. Cert fee- $1.00 per cert plus copy fee. Payee- North Stonington Town Clerk. **Other phones:** Treasurer- 860-535-2877 x10; Elections- 860-535-2877 x28; Vital Records- 860-535-2877 x21. **Property tax/Assessor-** PO Box 263, North Stonington, CT 06359; 860-535-2877 x23.

Norwalk City

Town Clerk, PO Box 5125, Norwalk, CT 06856-5125. 203-854-7746; fax-203-854-7817; hours: 8:30AM-4:30PM M T W F; 8:30 AM-7PM Th www.norwalkct.org

Separate indices to search include computer, books. Records indexed on computer back to 1974. Only the public may search. Copy fee $1.00 per page. Cert fee- $1.00 per cert plus copy fee. Payee- Town Clerk of Norwalk. **Online access to Property, Assessor records:** Access to Norwalk property records is free at www.norwalkct.org/norwalk/pckls.asp. **Other phones:** Elections- 203-854-7746; Vital Records- 203-854-7746. **Property tax/Assessor-** 125 East Ave, Rm 102, Norwalk, CT 06851; 203-854-7887.

Norwich City

City Clerk, 100 Broadway; City Hall, Rm 215, Norwich, CT 06360. 860-823-3732; fax-860-823-3790; hours: 8:30AM-4:30PM www.norwichct.org

Records indexed on index books. Only the public may search. Copy fee $1.00 per page. Cert fee- $1.00 per cert plus copy fee. Payee- Norwich City Clerk. **Online access to Assessor, Real Estate records:** Search the city assessor's database at http://data.visionappraisal.com/NorwichCT. Free registration required for full data. Also, access to the clerk's town land records is online by subscription. Index goes back to 1929 and images to 1997. Fee is $350.00 per year; sign-up online at www.norwichct.org/clerk.htm or call 860-823-3734. **Other phones:** Vital Records- 860-823-3734. **Property tax/Assessor-** 100 Broadway, Norwich, CT 06360; 860-823-3723.

Old Lyme Town

Town Clerk, 52 Lyme St, Old Lyme, CT 06371. RE & UCC recording phone-860-434-1605 x221; fax-860-434-9283; hours: 9AM-N,1-4PM

All records in one index. Records indexed on computer back to 2/14/2005. Only the public may search. Copy fee $1.00 per page. Cert fee- $1.00 per cert plus copy fee. Payee- Old Lyme Town Clerk. **Online access to Assessor records:** Search the town Assessor's database at http://data.visionappraisal.com/OLDLYMECT. Free registration required for full access. **Other phones:** Treasurer- 860-434-1605 x232; Appraiser/Auditor- 860-434-1605 x218; Elections- 860-434-1605 x230; Vital Records- 860-434-1605 x221. **Property tax/Assessor-** same address as above. 860-434-1605 x218.

Old Saybrook Town

Town Clerk, 302 Main St, Old Saybrook, CT 06475. RE & UCC recording phone-860-395-3135; fax-860-395-5014;   hours: 8:30AM-4:30PM www.oldsaybrookct.com

All records in one index. Records indexed on a public use terminal back to 9/24/04. Only the public may search. Copy fee $1.00 per page. Cert fee- $1.00 per cert plus copy fee. Payee- Old Saybrook Town Clerk. **Online access to Real Estate records:** Real Estate Sales records on the Assessor's database are free at http://oldsaybrookct.com/assessor/. No name searching. **Other phones:** Treasurer- 860-395-3073; Elections- 860-395-3135; Vital Records- 860-395-3135. **Property tax/Assessor-** same address as above. 860-395-3137.

Orange Town

Town Clerk, 617 Orange Center Rd.; Town Hall, Orange, CT 06477. 203-891-2122, R/E recording phone-203-891-2122 x730; fax-203-891-2185; hours: 8:30AM-4:30PM www.orange-ct.gov

All records in one index. Only the public may search. Copy fee $1.00 per page. Cert fee- $1.00 per cert plus copy fee. Payee- Orange Town Clerk. **Other phones:** ; First Selectman- 203-891-2122 x737. **Property tax/Assessor-** same address as above. 203-891-2122 x722.

Oxford Town

Town Clerk, 486 Oxford Rd, Oxford, CT 06478. 203-888-2543; fax-203-888-2136; hours: 9AM-5PM M-Th; 7-9PM Mon & Th

All records in one index. Records indexed on a public use terminal back to 1978. Only the public may search. Copy fee $1.00 per page. Cert fee- $1.00 per cert plus copy fee. Payee- Oxford Town Clerk. **Other phones:** Treasurer- 203-888-2543; Elections- 203-888-2543; Vital Records- 203-888-2543. **Property tax/Assessor-** 203-888-2543.

Plainfield Town

Town Clerk, 8 Community Ave; Town Hall, Plainfield, CT 06374. 860-564-4075, R/E recording phone-860-230-3009, UCC recording phone-860-230-3009; hours: 8:30AM-4:30PM M,T,W; 8:30AM-6:30PM Th; 8:30AM-1PM

Separate indices to search. Only the public may search. Copy fee $1.00 per page. Cert fee- $1.00 per cert plus copy fee. Payee- Town of Plainfield. **Other phones:** Treasurer- 860-230-3003; Elections- 860-230-3009; Vital Records- 860-230-3009. **Property tax/Assessor-** 8 Community Ave, Plainfield, CT 06374; 860-230-3006.

Plainville Town

Town Clerk, 1 Central Sq; Municipal Ctr, Plainville, CT 06062. 860-793-0221; hours: 8:30AM-4:30PM

All records in one index. Only the public may search. Copy fee $1.00 per page. Cert fee- $1.00 per page, plus copy fee. Payee- Town of Plainville. **Property tax/Assessor-** 860-793-0221 x242.

Plymouth Town

Town Clerk, 80 Main St; Town Hall, Terryville, CT 06786. RE & UCC recording phone-860-585-4039; fax-860-585-4015;   hours: 8:30-4:30PM www.plymouthct.us

All records in one index. Records indexed on a public use terminal back to the 1960's. Only the public may search. Copy fee $1.00 per page. Cert fee- $1.00 per page plus copy fee. Payee- Plymouth Town Clerk. **Other phones:** Treasurer- 860-585-4009; Elections- 860-585-4033; Vital Records- 860-585-4039. **Property tax/Assessor-** same address as above. 860-585-4006.

Pomfret Town

Town Clerk, 5 Haven Rd, Pomfret Center, CT 06259. RE & UCC recording phone-860-974-0343; fax-860-974-3950; hours: 9AM-4PM http://pomfretct.org

Separate indices to search include trade names, vitals, armed forces discharges, land maps. Only the public may search. Copy fee $1.00 per page. Cert fee- $1.00 per doc, plus copy fee. Payee- Town of Pomfret. **Online access to Assessor records:** Search town assessor database at http://data.visionappraisal.com/PomfretCT/. Free registration for full data. Also, can find subdivisions, wetlands and zoning regulations at http://pomfretct.org. **Other phones:** Treasurer- 860-974-0343; Vital Records- 860-974-0343. **Property tax/Assessor-** same address as above. 860-974-1674.

Portland Town

Town Clerk, PO Box 71, Portland, CT 06480. RE & UCC recording phone-860-342-6743; fax-860-342-0001; hours: 9AM-4:30PM

All records in one index. Records indexed on a public use terminal back to 1929. Only the public may search. Copy fee $1.00 per page. Cert fee- $1.00 per doc, plus copy fee. Payee- Portland Town Clerk. **Other phones:** Treasurer- 860-342-6726; Elections- 860-342-6743; Vital Records- 860-342-6743. **Property tax/Assessor-** 33 E Main St, PO box 71, Portland, CT 06480; 860-342-6744.

Preston Town

Town Clerk, 389 Route 2; Town Hall, Preston, CT 06365-8830. 860-887-9821; fax-860-885-1905; hours: 9AM-4:30PM   T-F;   Th   until   6:30 http://prestonlibrary.org/town_of_preston.htm

Only the public may search. Copy fee $1.00 per page. Cert fee- $1.00 per cert plus copy fee. Payee- Preston Town Clerk. **Property tax/Assessor-** 860-889-2529.

Prospect Town

Town Clerk, 36 Center St, Prospect, CT 06712-1699. 203-758-4461; fax-203-758-4466; hours: 8:30AM-4PM

All records in one index. Only the public may search. Copy fee $1.00 per page. Cert fee- $1.00 per page plus copy fee. Payee- Prospect Town Clerk. **Other phones:** Vital Records- 203-758-4461. **Property tax/Assessor-** same address as above. 203-758-4461.

Putnam Town

Town Clerk, 126 Church St, Putnam, CT 06260. RE & UCC recording phone-860-963-6807; fax-860-963-2001;   hours: 8:30AM-N,1-4:15PM www.putnamct.us

All records in one index. Only the public may search. Copy fee $1.00 per page. Cert fee- $1.00 per cert plus copy fee. Payee- Town of Putnam. **Online access to Assessor, Property records:** Access to   property   data   is   at http://data.visionappraisal.com/PutnamCT/. Free registration required. **Other phones:** Treasurer- 860-963-6809. **Property tax/Assessor-** 860-963-6802.

Redding Town

Town Clerk, PO Box 1028, Redding, CT 06875-1028. RE & UCC recording phone-203-938-2377; fax-203-938-8816; hours: 9AM-4:30PM

Only the public may search. Copy fee $1.00 per page. Cert fee- $1.00 per cert plus copy fee. Payee- Redding Town Clerk. **Other phones:** Treasurer- 203-938-3616; Appraiser/Auditor- 203-938-2626; Elections- 203-938-5012; Vital Records- 203-938-2377. **Property tax/Assessor-** 203-938-2626.

Ridgefield Town

Town Clerk, 400 Main St, Ridgefield, CT 06877. 203-431-2783; fax-203-431-2722; hours: 8:30AM-4:30PM www.ridgefieldct.org/government/townclerk/town clerk.htm

All records in one index. Only the public may search. Copy fee $1.00 per page. Cert fee- $1.00 per instrument plus copy fee. Payee- Ridgefield Town Clerk. **Other phones:** Treasurer- 203-431-

2763; Elections- 203-431-2771/2772; Vital Records- 203-431-2783. **Property tax/Assessor**- same address as above. 203-431-2706.

Rocky Hill Town

Town Clerk, 761 Old Main St., Rocky Hill, CT 06067. 860-258-2705; hours: 8:30AM-4:30PM M-W; 8:30-7PM Th; 8:30AM-12:30PM F www.ci.rocky-hill.ct.us
Only the public may search. Copy fee $1.00 per page. Cert fee- $1.00 per cert plus copy fee. Payee- Rocky Hill Town Clerk. **Online access to Land, Marriage, Death, Trade Name, Recording records:** Access to the Town Clerk's Index Search is free at www.ci.rocky-hill.ct.us/resolution/. Land records go back to 1973; Marriages/Deaths to 1990; trade names to 1987; maps to 1982. **Other phones:** Elections- 860-258-2715. **Property tax/Assessor**- 860-258-2772.

Roxbury Town

Town Clerk, 29 North St., Roxbury, CT 06783-1405. RE & UCC recording phone-860-354-3328; fax-860-354-0560; hours: 9AM-N, 1-4PM T Th; 9AM-N W; 9AM-N F www.roxburyct.com
Separate indices to search include grantor/grantee. Records indexed on a public use terminal back to 1999. Only the public may search. Copy fee $1.00 per page. Cert fee- $1.00 per page plus copy fee. Payee- Roxbury Town Clerk. **Online access to Assessor, Property records:** Access to property data is at www.visionappraisal.com/databases/ct/index.htm. Free registration required. Also, the search town assessor database go to http://data.visionappraisal.com/RoxburyCT/. Free registratoin for full data. **Other phones:** Treasurer- 860-354-9938; Vital Records- 860-354-3328. **Property tax/Assessor**- 860-354-2634.

Salem Town

Town Clerk, 270 Hartford Rd; Town Office Bldg., Salem, CT 06420. RE & UCC recording phone-860-859-3873 x170; fax-860-859-1184; hours: 8AM-4PM M-W; 8AM-5PM Th; 8AM-N Fri. www.salemct.gov
Separate indices by years. Records indexed on a public use terminal from 1986-7; more records being added. Only the public may search. Copy fee $1.00 per page. Cert fee- $1.00 per page plus copy fee. Payee- Town of Salem. **Other phones:** Treasurer- 860-859-3873 x125; Elections- 860-859-3873 x230; Vital Records- 860-859-3873 x170; Tax Collector- 860-859-3873 x150. **Property tax/Assessor**- same address as above. 860-859-3873 x130.

Salisbury Town

Town Clerk, PO Box 548, Salisbury, CT 06068. 860-435-5182; fax-860-435-5172; hours: 9AM-4PM www.salisburyct.us
Only the public may search. Copy fee $1.00 per page. Cert fee- $1.00 per cert plus copy fee. Payee- Salisbury Town Clerk. **Other phones:** Treasurer- 860-435-5174; Vital Records- 860-435-5182. **Property tax/Assessor**- PO Box 548, Salisbury, CT 06068; 860-435-5176.

Scotland Town

Town Clerk, PO Box 122, Scotland, CT 06264. RE & UCC recording phone-860-423-9634; fax-860-423-3666; hours: 9AM-3PM M,T,Th; Noon-8PM W; closed Friday
Separate indices to search. Record index not computerized. Only the public may search. Copy fee $1.00 per page. Cert fee- $1.00 per cert plus copy fee. Payee- Scotland Town Clerk. **Other phones:** Treasurer- 860-423-9634; Elections- 860-423-9634; Vital Records- 860-423-9634. **Property tax/Assessor**- 9 Devotion Rd, Scotland, CT 06264; 860-423-9634.

Seymour Town

Town Clerk, 1 First St; Town Hall, Seymour, CT 06483-2817. 203-888-0519; fax-203-881-5005; hours: 9AM-5PM (No recording after 4:15PM)

Index: Indices arranged by years. Records indexed on computer back to 8/2005, hopefully. Only the public may search. Copy fee $1.00 per page. Cert fee- $1.00 per cert plus copy fee. Payee- Seymour Town Clerk. **Other phones:** Treasurer- 203-888-0581; Elections- 203-881-5039; Vital Records- 203-888-0519. **Property tax/Assessor**- same address as above. 203-881-5013.

Sharon Town

Town Clerk, PO Box 224, Sharon, CT 06069. 860-364-5224; fax-860-364-5224; hours: M- Th 8:30AM-N, 1-4PM ; Fri 8:30AM-N
All records in one index. Only the public may search. Copy fee $1.00 per page. Cert fee- $1.00 per cert plus copy fee. Payee- Sharon Town Clerk. **Online access to Assessor records:** Access assessor data at http://data.visionappraisal.com/SharonCT/. **Other phones:** Treasurer- 860-364-5789; Vital Records- 860-364-5224. **Property tax/Assessor**- same address as above. 860-364-0205.

Shelton City

City Clerk, PO Box 364, Shelton, CT 06484-0364. 203-924-1555, R/E recording phone-203-924-1555 x377; fax-203-924-1721; hours: 8AM-5:30PM www.cityofshelton.org
All records in one index. Records indexed on a public use terminal back to 1954. Only the public may search. Copy fee $1.00 per page. Cert fee- $1.00 per cert plus copy fee. Payee- Shelton City Clerk. **Other phones:** Treasurer- 203-924-1555 x318; Elections- 203-924-1555 x337; Vital Records- 203-924-1555 x321. **Property tax/Assessor**- 203-924-1555 x335.

Sherman Town

Town Clerk, PO Box 39, Sherman, CT 06784-0039. RE & UCC recording phone-860-354-5281; fax-860-350-5041; hours: 9AM-N, 1-4PM T,W,Th,F; 9AM-N Sat
All records in one index. Only the public may search. Copy fee $1.00 per page. Cert fee- $1.00 per cert plus copy fee. Payee- Town of Sherman. **Other phones:** Treasurer- 860-355-1139; Elections- 860-350-4694; Vital Records- 860-354-5281. **Property tax/Assessor**- same address as above. 860-355-0376.

Simsbury Town

Town Clerk, PO Box 495, Simsbury, CT 06070. 860-658-3243; fax-860-658-3206; hours: 8:30AM-4:30PM
Only the public may search. Copy fee $1.00 per page. Cert fee- $1.00 per cert plus copy fee. Payee- Town of Simsbury. **Property tax/Assessor**- 860-658-3251.

Somers Town

Town Clerk, PO Box 308, Somers, CT 06071. 860-763-8206; fax-860-763-8228; hours: 8:30AM-4:30PM M-W,F; 8:30AM-7PM Th www.somersnow.com
Separate indices to search. Record index not computerized. Only the public may search. Copy fee $1.00 per page. Cert fee- $1.00 per doc, plus copy fee. Payee- Somers Town Clerk. **Online access to Property, Assessor records:** Access property data free at www.prophecyone.us. No name searching. **Other phones:** Treasurer- 860-763-8204; Elections- 860-763-8211; Vital Records- 860-763-8206. **Property tax/Assessor**- same address as above. 860-763-8203.

South Windsor Town

Town Clerk, 1540 Sullivan Ave, South Windsor, CT 06074. 860-644-2511 x225, R/E recording phone-860-644-2511 x225/226/227; fax-860-644-3781; hours: 8AM-4:30PM www.southwindsor.org
All records in one index. Only the public may search. Copy fee $1.00 per page. Cert fee- $1.00 per cert plus copy fee. Payee- Town of South Windsor. **Online access to Property Transfer**

records: Access to town clerk's lists of property transfers by year are free at www.southwindsor.org/TownHall/Property%20Transfer/property.htm. Search back to 1999. **Other phones:** Treasurer- 860-644-2511 x261; Elections- 860-644-2511 x275; Vital Records- 860-644-2511 x225/226/227; Tax Collector- 860-644-2511 X220. **Property tax/Assessor**- same address as above. 860-644-2511 x213.

Southbury Town

Town Clerk, 501 Main St South, Southbury, CT 06488-2295. RE & UCC recording phone-203-262-0657; fax-203-264-9762; hours: 8:30AM-4:30PM
All records in one index. Records indexed on a public use terminal back to 1787. Only the public may search. Copy fee $1.00 per page. Cert fee- $1.00 per cert plus copy fee. Payee- Southbury Town Clerk. **Other phones:** Treasurer- 203-262-0663; Elections- 203-262-0657; Vital Records- 203-262-0657. **Property tax/Assessor**- 203-262-0674.

Southington Town

Town Clerk, PO Box 152, Southington, CT 06489. 860-276-6211; fax-860-276-6229; hours: 8:30AM-4PM M, T, W, F; 8:30AM-7PM TH www.southington.org
All records in one index. Records indexed on a public use terminal back to 1968. Only the public may search. Copy fee $1.00 per page. Cert fee- $1.00 per cert plus copy fee. Payee- Southington Town Clerk. **Online access to Most Wanted records:** Access to the Town's most wanted list is at www.southingtonpolice.org/warrant.htm. **Other phones:** Treasurer- 860-276-6228; Elections- 860-276-6268; Vital Records- 860-276-6211. **Property tax/Assessor**- same address as above. 860-276-6205.

Sprague Town

Town Clerk, PO Box 162, Baltic, CT 06330. 860-822-3000 x220; fax-860-822-3013; hours: 8AM-4:30PM M-T (W Open Until 5:30PM)
Recording done on Town level not County. Only the public may search. Copy fee $1.00 per page. Cert fee- $1.00 per cert plus copy fee. Payee- Town of Sprague. **Other phones:** Treasurer- 860-822-3000 x209. **Property tax/Assessor**- same address as above. 860-822-3000 x222.

Stafford Town

Town Clerk, PO Box 11, Stafford Springs, CT 06076. RE & UCC recording phone-860-684-1765; fax-860-684-1765; hours: 8:15AM-4PM M-W; 8:15AM-6:30PM Th; 8AM-N Fri
Records indexed on a public use terminal back to 1977. Only the public may search. Copy fee $1.00 per page. Cert fee- $1.00 per page plus copy fee. Payee- Stafford Town Clerk. **Other phones:** Treasurer- 860-684-1772; Elections- 860-684-1765; Vital Records- 860-684-1765. **Property tax/Assessor**- 860-684-1788.

Stamford City

City Clerk, PO Box 10152, Stamford, CT 06904. Main phone & R/E recording-203-977-4054, UCC recording phone-203-977-4707; fax-203-977-4943; hours: 8AM-3:45PM www.cityofstamford.org/Welcome.htm
Records indexed on a public use terminal back to 1967. Office personnel or visitors may perform searches. Will not search UCC records. Copy fee $1.00 per page. RE or tax lien copy- $.50 per page. Cert fee- $1.00 per cert plus copy fee. Payee- City of Stamford. **Online access to Assessor, Real Estate, Personal Property, City Businesses records:** Access to the city tax assessor database is free online at www.cityofstamford.org/Tax/default.htm. Also, search the city registry of trade names for free at www.cityofstamford.org/TradeNames/default.htm. Also, access assessor at www.cityofstamford.org/TaxCollectionAssessment/default.htm. **Other phones:** Treasurer- 203-977-4185;

Elections- 203-977-4011; Vital Records- 203-977-4054. **Property tax/Assessor-** 203-977-4019.

Sterling Town

Town Clerk, PO Box 157, Oneco, CT 06373-0157. RE & UCC recording phone-860-564-2657; fax-860-564-1660; hours: 8:30AM-3:30PM-M,T,TH; 8AM-6PM-W; 8AM-N Fri. www.sterlingct.us

All records in one index. Records indexed on a public use terminal. Only the public may search. Copy fee $1.00 per page. Cert fee- $1.00 per cert plus copy fee. Payee- Sterling Town Clerk. **Other phones:** Treasurer- 860-564-8488; Elections- 860-564-2657; Vital Records- 860-564-2657. **Property tax/Assessor-** 1114 Plainfield Pike, Oneco, CT 06373; 860-564-3030.

Stonington Town

Town Clerk, PO Box 352, Stonington, CT 06378. RE & UCC recording phone-860-535-5060; fax-860-535-5062; hours: 8:30AM-4PM www.townofstonington.com

All records in one index. Only the public may search. Copy fee $1.00 per page. Cert fee- $1.00 per cert plus copy fee. Payee- Stonington Town Clerk. **Other phones:** Elections- 860-535-5047; Vital Records- 860-535-5060; Finance Phone:- 860-535-5070. **Property tax/Assessor-** same address as above. 860-535-5098.

Stratford Town

Town Clerk, 2725 Main St; Rm 101, Stratford, CT 06615. 203-385-4020; fax-203-385-4005; hours: 8AM-4:30PM www.townofstratford.com

All records in one index. Records indexed on computer back to 1984. Only the public may search. Copy fee $1.00 per page. Cert fee- $1.00 per page; $2.00 per certification. Payee- Town of Stratford. **Online access to Assessor records:** Search town assessor database at http://data.visionappraisal.com/StratfordCT/. Free registration for full data. **Other phones:** Elections- 203-385-4048; Vital Records- 203-385-4020. **Property tax/Assessor-** same address as above. 203-385-4025.

Suffield Town

Town Clerk, 83 Mountain Rd; Town Hall, Suffield, CT 06078. 860-668-3880; fax-860-668-3898; hours: 8:30AM-4:30PM; Summer: 8AM-4:30PM M-Th; 8AM-1PM F www.suffieldtownhall.com

All records in one index. Record index not computerized. Only the public may search. Copy fee $1.00 per page. Cert fee- $1.00 per page. Payee- Town of Suffield. **Online access to Assessor records:** Search the town assessor's database at http://data.visionappraisal.com/SuffieldCT. Free registration required for full access. **Other phones:** Treasurer- 860-668-3851; Appraiser/Auditor- 860-668-3850; Elections- 860-668-3880; Vital Records- 860-668-3880. **Property tax/Assessor-** 860-668-3866.

Thomaston Town

Town Clerk, 158 Main St, Thomaston, CT 06787. RE & UCC recording phone-860-283-4141; fax-860-283-1013; hours: 9AM-4:30PM

Only the public may search. Copy fee $1.00 per page. Cert fee- $1.00 per cert plus copy fee. Payee- Thomaston Town Clerk. **Other phones:** Treasurer- 860-283-9678. **Property tax/Assessor-** 860-283-0305.

Thompson Town

Town Clerk, PO Box 899, No. Grosvenor Dale, CT 06255. 860-923-9900; fax-860-923-3836; hours: 9AM-5PM www.thompsonct.org

All records in one index. Records indexed on computer. Only the public may search. Copy fee $1.00 per page. Cert fee- $1.00 per cert plus copy fee. Payee- Town of Thompson. **Online access to Assessor records:** Search the town assessor database at http://data.visionappraisal.com/ThompsonCT/. Free registration for full data. **Other phones:** Treasurer-

860-923-3593; Elections- 860-923-9900; Vital Records- 860-923-9900. **Property tax/Assessor-** same address as above. 860-923-2259.

Tolland Town

Town Clerk, 21 Tolland Green; Hicks Memorial Muni. Ctr, Tolland, CT 06084. RE & UCC recording phone-860-871-3630; fax-860-871-3663; hours: 8:30AM-4PM MTW; 8:30AM-7:30PM TH; 8:30AM-N Fri. www.toland.org

Do not confuse this town with the County of Tolland. Only Town of Tolland filings go here. All records in one index. Only the public may search. Copy fee $1.00 per page. Cert fee- $1.00 per doc plus copy fee. Payee- Tolland Town Clerk. **Online access to Assessor records:** Search town assessor database at http://data.visionappraisal.com/TollandCT/. Does not require a username & password. Simply click on link. **Other phones:** Treasurer- 860-871-3658; Elections- 860-871-3634; Vital Records- 860-871-3630. **Property tax/Assessor-** 21 Tolland Green, Tolland, CT 06084; 860-871-3650.

Torrington City

Town Clerk, 140 Main St; City Hall, Torrington, CT 06790. 860-489-2236, R/E recording phone-860-489-2238, UCC recording phone-860-489-2237; fax-860-489-2548; hours: 8:30AM-4:PM M-W; 8:30AM-6:30PM Th; 8:30-12:30 Fri www.torrington-ct.org

All records in one index. Records indexed on a public use terminal back to 1955. Only the public may search. Copy fee $1.00 per page. Cert fee- $1.00 per cert plus copy fee. Payee- Town of Torrington. **Online access to Assessor, Property records:** Access to property data is at http://data.visionappraisal.com/TorringtonCT/. Free registration required. **Other phones:** Treasurer- 860-489-2334; Elections- 860-489-2239; Vital Records- 860-489-2236. **Property tax/Assessor-** same address as above. 860-489-2222.

Trumbull Town

Town Clerk, 5866 Main St, Trumbull, CT 06611. 203-452-5035; fax-203-452-5094; hours: 9AM-5PM

All records in one index. Only the public may search. Copy fee $1.00 per page. Cert fee- $1.00 per cert plus copy fee. Payee- Trumbull Town Clerk. **Other phones:** Treasurer- 203-452-5014; Elections- 203-452-5058; Vital Records- 203-452-5035. **Property tax/Assessor-** same address as above. 203-452-5016.

Union Town

Town Clerk, 1043 Buckley Highway; Route 171, Union, CT 06076-9520. RE & UCC recording phone-860-684-3770; fax-860-684-8830; hours: 9AM-N T,Th; 9AM-N, 1-3PM W

All records in one index. Records index not computerized. Only the public may search. Copy fee $1.00 per page. Cert fee- $1.00 per cert plus copy fee. Payee- Union Town Clerk. **Other phones:** Treasurer- 860-684-8831; Elections- 860-684-3770; Vital Records- 860-684-3770; Tax Collector- 860-684-8834. **Property tax/Assessor-** same address as above. 860-684-5705.

Vernon Town

Town Clerk, 14 Park Pl, Vernon, CT 06066. RE & UCC recording phone-860-870-3662; fax-860-870-3683; hours: 8:30AM-4:30PM M-W; 8:30AM-7PM Th; 8:30AM-1PM F www.munic.state.ct.us/VERNON/

Separate indices to search include Grantor/Grantee. Only the public may search. Copy fee $1.00 per page. Cert fee- $1.00 per cert plus copy fee. Payee- Town of Vernon. **Other phones:** Treasurer- 860-870-3660 (Tax Collector); Elections- 860-870-3685 (Reg of Voters); Vital Records- 860-870-3662. **Property tax/Assessor-** 8 Park Pl, Vernon, CT 06066; 860-870-3625.

Voluntown Town

Town Clerk, PO Box 96, Voluntown, CT 06384-0096. RE & UCC recording phone-860-376-4089; fax-860-376-3295; hours: 9AM-2PM; 6-8PM T Evening www.voluntown.gov

All records in one index. Only the public may search. Copy fee $1.00 per page. Cert fee- $1.00 per cert plus copy fee. Payee- Town of Voluntown. **Other phones:** Treasurer- 860-376-3927. **Property tax/Assessor-** PO Box 96, Voluntown, CT 06384; 860-376-3927.

Wallingford Town

Town Clerk, Omit PO Box, Wallingford, CT 06492. RE & UCC recording phone-203-294-2145; fax-203-294-2150; hours: 9AM-5PM

Only the public may search. Copy fee $1.00 per page. Cert fee- $1.00 per cert plus copy fee. Payee- Wallingford Town Clerk. **Other phones:** Treasurer- 203-294-2042; Appraiser/Auditor- 203-294-2001; Elections- 203-294-2125; Vital Records- 203-294-2145. **Property tax/Assessor-** 203-294-2001.

Warren Town

Town Clerk, 7 Sackett Hill Rd; Town Hall, Warren, CT 06754. 860-868-0090; fax-860-868-7746; hours: 10AM-4PM W,Th; 10AM-Noon M,F

Records indexed on computer back to 1996. Only the public may search. Copy fee $1.00 per page. Cert fee- $1.00 per cert plus copy fee. Payee- Warren Town Clerk. **Property tax/Assessor-** same address as above. 860-868-7881.

Washington Town

Town Clerk, PO Box 383, Washington Depot, CT 06794. 860-868-2786; fax-860-868-3103; hours: 9AM-N, 1-4:45PM www.washingtonct.org

All records in one index. Record index not computerized. Only the public may search. Copy fee $1.00 per page. Cert fee- $1.00 per page plus copy fee. Payee- Town of Washington. **Other phones:** Vital Records- 860-868-2786. **Property tax/Assessor-** Bryan Memorial Town Hall, Main level, Washington Depot, CT 06794; 860-868-0398, assessor fax- 860-868-3103.

Waterbury City

Town Clerk, 235 Grand St; City Hall, Waterbury, CT 06702. RE & UCC recording phone-203-574-6806; fax-203-574-6887; hours: 8:30AM-4:30PM

Only the public may search. Copy fee $1.00 per page. Cert fee- $1.00 per page. Payee- Waterbury Town Clerk. **Online access to Assessor, Property, Real Estate Sale records:** Access to the assessor property data is free at www.waterburyrealestate.org/Waterbury208/LandRover.asp and at http://data.visionappraisal.com/watertownct/. **Other phones:** Elections- 203-574-6751; Vital Records- 203-574-6801. **Property tax/Assessor-** 203-574-6821.

Waterford Town

Town Clerk, 15 Rope Ferry Rd, Waterford, CT 06385. RE & UCC recording phone-860-444-5831; fax-860-437-0352; hours: 8AM-4PM

All records in one index. Records indexed on computer back to 1959. Only the public may search. Copy fee $1.00 per page. Cert fee- $1.00 per cert plus copy fee. Payee- Waterford Town Clerk. **Online access to Assessor, Property records:** Access property data free at www.prophecyone.us. No name searching. **Other phones:** Vital Records- 860-444-5831. **Property tax/Assessor-** 860-444-5820.

Watertown Town

Town Clerk, 37 DeForest St, Watertown, CT 06795. RE & UCC recording phone-860-945-5230; fax-860-945-2706; hours: 9AM-5PM www.watertownct.org

All records in one index. Only the public may search. Copy fee $1.00 per page. Cert fee- $1.00 per page plus copy fee. Payee- Watertown Town Clerk. **Online access to Property, Assessor records:**

Access property data free at http://data.visionappraisal.com/watertownct/. Free registration for full data. **Other phones:** Treasurer- 860-945-5261; Elections- 860-945-5230; Vital Records- 860-945-5230; Town Manager- 860-945-5255. **Property tax/Assessor**- same address as above. 860-945-5235.

West Hartford Town

Town Clerk, 50 S. Main St; Rm 313 Town Hall Common, West Hartford, CT 06107-2431. 860-561-7430; fax-860-561-7438; hours: 8:30AM-4:30PM www.west-hartford.com
All records in one index. Records indexed on a public use terminal back to 1963. Only the public may search. Copy fee $1.00 per page. Cert fee- $1.00 per cert plus copy fee. Payee- Town of West Hartford. **Online access to Assessor, Property records:** Access to the assessor property records requires a $50 annual subscription for one user; $200 for 5 users. Details and sign-up at www.westhartford.org/whprs/. **Other phones:** Treasurer- 860-561-7474; Appraiser/Auditor- 860-561-7410; Elections- 860-561-7450; Vital Records- 860-561-7431. **Property tax/Assessor**- 860-561-7410.

West Haven City

City Clerk, PO Box 526, West Haven, CT 06516. 203-937-3534, R/E recording phone-203-937-3535; fax-203-937-3706; hours: 9AM-5PM
Only the public may search. Copy fee $1.00 per page. Cert fee- $1.00 per cert plus copy fee. Payee- West Haven City Clerk. **Online access to Assessor records:** Search the town assessor's database at http://data.visionappraisal.com/Westhavenct/. Free registration required for full access. **Property tax/Assessor**- 203-937-3517.

Westbrook Town

Town Clerk, 866 Boston Post Rd, Westbrook, CT 06498-1881. 860-399-3044; fax-860-399-3092; hours: 9AM-4PM M-W & F; 9AM-7PM Th; 9AM-N F
Records indexed on a public use terminal back to 2/2005. Only the public may search. Copy fee $1.00 per page. Cert fee- $1.00 per cert plus copy fee. Payee- Westbrook Town Clerk. **Property tax/Assessor**- 860-399-3045.

Weston Town

Town Clerk, PO Box 1007, Weston, CT 06883. 203-222-2616, R/E recording phone-203-222-2617; fax-203-222-8871; hours: 9AM-4:30PM www.weston-ct.com
All records in one index. Records indexed on a public use terminal back to 1950. Only the public may search. General copy fee $1.00 per page. RE record copy- $.50 per page. Cert fee- $1.00 per cert plus copy fee. Payee- Weston Town Clerk. **Online access to Land, Marriage, Death, Trade Name, Grantor/Grantee records:** Access the Town Clerk's index records free online at www.weston-ct.com/resolution/. For username and password use cott, cott. Maps and surveys are also available. Search page access at www.weston-ct.com/resolution. **Other phones:** Elections- 203-222-2616; Vital Records- 203-222-2616; General Information- 203-222-2500. **Property tax/Assessor**- same address as above. 203-222-2606.

Westport Town

Town Clerk, PO Box 549, Westport, CT 06881. RE & UCC recording phone-203-341-1110; fax-203-341-1112; hours: 8:30AM-4:30PM www.ci.westport.ct.us/govt/services
All records in one index. Only the public may search. Copy fee $1.00 per page. Cert fee- $1.00 per cert plus copy fee. Payee- Westport Town Clerk. **Online access to Assessor records:** Access to the assessments database is free at www.westport.ct.us/govt/services/finance/assessor/default.asp. **Other phones:** Elections- 203-341-1115; Vital Records- 203-341-1110; Main number- 203-341-

1000. **Property tax/Assessor**- same address as above. 203-341-1070.

Wethersfield Town

Town Clerk, 505 Silas Deane Highway, Wethersfield, CT 06109. RE & UCC recording phone-860-721-2880; fax-860-721-2994; hours: 8AM-4:30PM http://wethersfieldct.com/govt.htm
All records in one index. Records indexed on computer. Only the public may search. Copy fee $1.00 per page. Cert fee- $1.00 per cert plus $1.00 per copy page. Payee- Wethersfield Town. **Online access to Assessor, Property records:** Access to property data is at http://data.visionappraisal.com/WethersfieldCT/. Free registration for full data. **Other phones:** Treasurer- 860-721-2861; Elections- 860-721-2819; Vital Records- 860-721-2880. **Property tax/Assessor**- same address as above. 860-721-2810.

Willington Town

Town Clerk, 40 Old Farms Rd, Willington, CT 06279. RE & UCC recording phone-860-487-3121; fax-860-487-3103; hours: 9AM-2PM T-F www.willingtonct.org
All records in one index. Only the public may search. Copy fee $1.00 per page. Cert fee- $1.00 per cert plus copy fee. Payee- Willington Town Clerk. **Other phones:** Treasurer- 860-487-3133; Elections- 860-487-3120; Vital Records- 860-487-3121. **Property tax/Assessor**- same address as above. 860-487-3122.

Wilton Town

Town Clerk, 238 Danbury Rd, Wilton, CT 06897. RE & UCC recording phone-203-563-0106; fax-203-563-0130; hours: 8:30AM-4:30PM www.wiltonct.org/info.htm
All records in one index. Only the public may search. Copy fee $1.00 per page. Cert fee- $1.00 per page + $1.00. Payee- Town of Wilton. **Online access to Assessor records:** Search the town assessor database at http://data.visionappraisal.com/WiltonCT/. Free registration for full data. **Other phones:** Treasurer- 203-563-0114; Elections- 203-563-0112; Vital Records- 203-563-0106. **Property tax/Assessor**- same address as above. 203-563-0121.

Winchester Town

Town Clerk, 338 Main St; Town Hall, Winsted, CT 06098-1697. RE & UCC recording phone-860-738-6963; fax-860-738-6595; 8AM-4PM M-W, 8AM-7PM Th, 8AM-noon F www.townofwinchester.org
All records in one index, arranged by year. Only the public may search. Copy fee $1.00 per page. Cert fee- $1.00 per cert plus copy fee. Payee- Town of Winchester. **Online to Property, Assessor records:** Access property tax data after free registration at http://data.visionappraisal.com/WinchesterCT/. **Other phones:** Treasurer- 860-738-6961; Appraiser/Auditor- 860-379-5461; Elections- 860-379-2713 x355; Vital Records- 860-738-6963. **Property tax/Assessor**- same address. 860-379-5461.

Windham Town

Town Clerk, PO Box 94, Willimantic, CT 06226. 860-465-3013; fax-860-465-3012; hours: 8AM-5PM M-W; 8AM-7:30PM Th; 8AM-N Fri www.windhamct.com
All records in one index. Only the public may search. Copy fee $1.00 per page. Cert fee- $1.00 per cert plus copy fee. Payee- Windham Town Clerk. **Other phones:** Treasurer- 860-465-3013. **Property tax/Assessor**- same address as above. 860-465-3025.

Windsor Locks Town

Town Clerk, 50 Church St; Town Office Bldg., Windsor Locks, CT 06096. RE & UCC recording phone-860-627-1441; hours: 8AM-4PM M-W; 8AM-6PM Th; 8AM-1PM F
All records in one index. Only the public may search. Copy fee $1.00 per page. Cert fee- $1.00

per cert plus copy fee. Payee- Town of Windsor Locks. **Online access to Assessor records:** Search the town assessor database at http://data.visionappraisal.com/WINDSORLOCKSCT/. Free registration for full data. **Other phones:** Treasurer- 860-627-1449; Elections- 860-654-1619; Vital Records- 860-627-1441; Tax Collector- 860-627-1415. **Property tax/Assessor**- same address as above. 860-627-1448.

Windsor Town

Town Clerk, PO Box 472, Windsor, CT 06095-0472. RE & UCC recording phone-860-285-1902; fax-860-285-1909; 8AM-5PM www.townofwindsorct.com
All records in one index. Only the public may search. Copy fee $1.00 per page. Cert fee- $1.00 per cert plus copy fee. Payee- Town of Windsor. **Online access to Assessor, Real Estate records:** Search the town clerk's land records index for free at www.townofwindsorct.com/records.htm. Index goes back to 1970. Also, search the town assessor's Taxpayer Information System database at http://data.visionappraisal.com/WINDSORCT/. Free registration required for full access. Town services search page at www.townofwindsorct.com. **Other phones:** Treasurer- 860-285-1890; Elections- 860-285-1902; Vital Records- 860-285-1902. **Property tax/Assessor**- 275 Broad St, Windsor, CT 06095; 860-285-1817.

Wolcott Town

Town Clerk, 10 Kenea Ave; Town Hall, Wolcott, CT 06716. RE & UCC recording phone-203-879-8100; fax-203-879-8105; hours: 8:30AM-4:30PM (Recording until 4PM)
Records indexed on computer back to 2001. Only the public may search. Copy fee $1.00 per page. Cert fee- $1.00 per cert plus copy fee. Payee- Wolcott Town Clerk. **Other phones:** Treasurer- 203-879-8100; Elections- 203-879-8100; Vital Records- 203-879-8100. **Property tax/Assessor**- same address as above. 203-879-8100.

Woodbridge Town

Town Clerk, 11 Meetinghouse Lane, Woodbridge, CT 06525. RE & UCC recording phone-203-389-3422; fax-203-389-3473; hours: 8;30AM-4PM www.munic.state.ct.us/WOODBRIDGE/woodbridge.htm
Records indexed on a public use terminal back to 1987. Only the public may search. Copy fee $1.00 per page. Cert fee- $1.00 per cert plus copy fee. Payee- Woodbridge Town Clerk. **Online access to Assessor records:** Search the town assessor's database at http://data.visionappraisal.com/woodbridgeCT. Free registration required for full data. **Other phones:** Treasurer- 203-389-3414; Appraiser/Auditor- 203-389-3414; Elections- 203-389-3408; Vital Records- 203-389-3424. **Property tax/Assessor**- same address as above. 203-389-3416.

Woodbury Town

Town Clerk, PO Box 369, Woodbury, CT 06798-3407. 203-263-2144; fax-203-263-4755; hours: 8:30AM-4:30PM (Summer Hours 8AM-4PM)
All records in one index. Only the public may search. Copy fee $1.00 per page. Cert fee- $1.00 per cert plus copy fee. Payee- Woodbury Town Clerk. **Other phones:** Treasurer- 203-263-2449; Elections- 203-263-4750; Vital Records- 203-263-2144. **Property tax/Assessor**- same address as above. 203-263-2435.

Woodstock Town

Town Clerk, 415 Route 169; Town Hall, Woodstock, CT 06281. 860-928-6595; fax-860-963-7557; hours: 8:30AM-4:30PM M,T,Th; 8:30AM-6PM W; 8:30AM-3PM F
Only the public may search. Copy fee $1.00 per page. Cert fee- $1.00 per cert plus copy fee. Payee- Town of Woodstock. **Property tax/Assessor**- 860-928-6929.

Connecticut County Locator

You will usually be able to find the city name in the City/County Cross Reference below. In that case, it is a simple matter to determine the county from the cross-reference. However, only the official US Postal Service city names are included in this index. Included is a ZIP/City Cross Reference following the City/County Cross Reference. If you know the ZIP Code but the city name does not appear in the City/County Cross list, look up the ZIP Code in the ZIP/City Cross Reference, find the city name, then look up the city in the City/County Cross Reference.

Connecticut City/County Cross Reference

ABINGTON Windham
AMSTON Tolland
ANDOVER Tolland
ANSONIA New Haven
ASHFORD Windham
AVON Hartford
BALLOUVILLE Windham
BALTIC (06330) New London(92), Windham(7)
BANTAM Litchfield
BARKHAMSTED Litchfield
BEACON FALLS New Haven
BETHANY New Haven
BETHEL Fairfield
BETHLEHEM Litchfield
BLOOMFIELD Hartford
BOLTON Tolland
BOTSFORD Fairfield
BOZRAH New London
BRANFORD New Haven
BRIDGEPORT Fairfield
BRIDGEWATER Litchfield
BRISTOL Hartford
BROAD BROOK Hartford
BROOKFIELD Fairfield
BROOKLYN Windham
BURLINGTON Hartford
CANAAN Litchfield
CANTERBURY Windham
CANTON Hartford
CANTON CENTER Hartford
CENTERBROOK Middlesex
CENTRAL VILLAGE Windham
CHAPLIN Windham
CHESHIRE New Haven
CHESTER Middlesex
CLINTON Middlesex
COBALT Middlesex
COLCHESTER (06415) New London(90), Middlesex(9)
COLEBROOK Litchfield
COLLINSVILLE Hartford
COLUMBIA Tolland
CORNWALL Litchfield
CORNWALL BRIDGE Litchfield
COS COB Fairfield
COVENTRY Tolland
CROMWELL Middlesex
DANBURY Fairfield
DANIELSON Windham
DARIEN Fairfield
DAYVILLE Windham
DEEP RIVER Middlesex
DERBY New Haven
DURHAM Middlesex
EAST BERLIN Hartford
EAST CANAAN Litchfield
EAST GLASTONBURY Hartford
EAST GRANBY Hartford
EAST HADDAM Middlesex
EAST HAMPTON Middlesex
EAST HARTFORD Hartford
EAST HARTLAND Hartford
EAST HAVEN New Haven
EAST KILLINGLY Windham
EAST LYME New London
EAST WINDSOR Hartford
EAST WINDSOR HILL Hartford
EAST WOODSTOCK Windham
EASTFORD (06242) Windham(96), Tolland(3)

EASTON Fairfield
ELLINGTON Tolland
ENFIELD Hartford
ESSEX Middlesex
FABYAN Windham
FAIRFIELD Fairfield
FALLS VILLAGE Litchfield
FARMINGTON Hartford
GALES FERRY New London
GAYLORDSVILLE Litchfield
GEORGETOWN Fairfield
GILMAN New London
GLASGO New London
GLASTONBURY Hartford
GOSHEN Litchfield
GRANBY Hartford
GREENS FARMS Fairfield
GREENWICH Fairfield
GROSVENOR DALE Windham
GROTON New London
GUILFORD New Haven
HADDAM Middlesex
HADLYME New London
HAMDEN New Haven
HAMPTON Windham
HANOVER New London
HARTFORD Hartford
HARWINTON Litchfield
HAWLEYVILLE Fairfield
HEBRON Tolland
HIGGANUM Middlesex
IVORYTON Middlesex
JEWETT CITY New London
KENSINGTON Hartford
KENT Litchfield
KILLINGWORTH Middlesex
LAKESIDE Litchfield
LAKEVILLE Litchfield
LEBANON New London
LEDYARD New London
LITCHFIELD Litchfield
MADISON New Haven
MANCHESTER (06040) Hartford(98), Tolland(1)
MANCHESTER Hartford
MANSFIELD CENTER (06250) Tolland(97), Windham(2)
MANSFIELD DEPOT Tolland
MARION Hartford
MARLBOROUGH Hartford
MASHANTUCKET New London
MELROSE Hartford
MERIDEN New Haven
MIDDLE HADDAM Middlesex
MIDDLEBURY New Haven
MIDDLEFIELD Middlesex
MIDDLETOWN Middlesex
MILFORD New Haven
MILLDALE Hartford
MONROE Fairfield
MONTVILLE New London
MOODUS Middlesex
MOOSUP Windham
MORRIS Litchfield
MYSTIC New London
NAUGATUCK New Haven
NEW BRITAIN Hartford
NEW CANAAN Fairfield
NEW FAIRFIELD Fairfield
NEW HARTFORD Litchfield
NEW HAVEN New Haven

NEW LONDON New London
NEW MILFORD Litchfield
NEW PRESTON MARBLE DALE Litchfield
NEWINGTON Hartford
NEWTOWN Fairfield
NIANTIC New London
NORFOLK Litchfield
NORTH BRANFORD New Haven
NORTH CANTON Hartford
NORTH FRANKLIN New London
NORTH GRANBY Hartford
NORTH GROSVENORDALE Windham
NORTH HAVEN New Haven
NORTH STONINGTON New London
NORTH WESTCHESTER New London
NORTH WINDHAM Windham
NORTHFIELD Litchfield
NORTHFORD New Haven
NORWALK Fairfield
NORWICH New London
OAKDALE New London
OAKVILLE Litchfield
OLD GREENWICH Fairfield
OLD LYME New London
OLD MYSTIC New London
OLD SAYBROOK Middlesex
ONECO Windham
ORANGE New Haven
OXFORD New Haven
PAWCATUCK New London
PEQUABUCK Litchfield
PINE MEADOW Litchfield
PLAINFIELD Windham
PLAINVILLE Hartford
PLANTSVILLE Hartford
PLEASANT VALLEY Litchfield
PLYMOUTH Litchfield
POMFRET Windham
POMFRET CENTER Windham
POQUONOCK Hartford
PORTLAND Middlesex
PRESTON New London
PROSPECT New Haven
PUTNAM Windham
QUAKER HILL New London
QUINEBAUG Windham
REDDING Fairfield
REDDING CENTER Fairfield
REDDING RIDGE Fairfield
RIDGEFIELD Fairfield
RIVERSIDE Fairfield
RIVERTON Litchfield
ROCKFALL Middlesex
ROCKY HILL Hartford
ROGERS Windham
ROXBURY Litchfield
SALEM New London
SALISBURY Litchfield
SANDY HOOK Fairfield
SCOTLAND Windham
SEYMOUR New Haven
SHARON Litchfield
SHELTON Fairfield
SHERMAN (06784) Fairfield(98), Litchfield(1)
SIMSBURY Hartford
SOMERS Tolland
SOMERSVILLE Tolland
SOUTH BRITAIN New Haven
SOUTH GLASTONBURY Hartford
SOUTH KENT Litchfield

SOUTH LYME New London
SOUTH WILLINGTON Tolland
SOUTH WINDHAM Windham
SOUTH WINDSOR Hartford
SOUTH WOODSTOCK Windham
SOUTHBURY New Haven
SOUTHINGTON Hartford
SOUTHPORT Fairfield
STAFFORD Tolland
STAFFORD SPRINGS (06076) Tolland(93), Windham(6)
STAFFORDVILLE Tolland
STAMFORD Fairfield
STERLING Windham
STEVENSON Fairfield
STONINGTON New London
STORRS MANSFIELD Tolland
STRATFORD Fairfield
SUFFIELD Hartford
TACONIC Litchfield
TAFTVILLE New London
TARIFFVILLE Hartford
TERRYVILLE Litchfield
THOMASTON Litchfield
THOMPSON Windham
TOLLAND Tolland
TORRINGTON Litchfield
TRUMBULL Fairfield
UNCASVILLE New London
UNIONVILLE Hartford
VERNON ROCKVILLE Tolland
VERSAILLES New London
VOLUNTOWN (06384) New London(97), Windham(2)
W HARTFORD Hartford
WALLINGFORD New Haven
WASHINGTON DEPOT Litchfield
WATERBURY New Haven
WATERFORD New London
WATERTOWN Litchfield
WAUREGAN Windham
WEATOGUE Hartford
WEST CORNWALL Litchfield
WEST GRANBY Hartford
WEST HARTFORD Hartford
WEST HARTLAND Hartford
WEST HAVEN New Haven
WEST MYSTIC New London
WEST SIMSBURY Hartford
WEST SUFFIELD Hartford
WESTBROOK Middlesex
WESTON Fairfield
WESTPORT Fairfield
WETHERSFIELD Hartford
WILLIMANTIC Windham
WILLINGTON Tolland
WILTON Fairfield
WINCHESTER CENTER Litchfield
WINDHAM Windham
WINDSOR Hartford
WINDSOR LOCKS Hartford
WINSTED Litchfield
WOLCOTT New Haven
WOODBRIDGE New Haven
WOODBURY Litchfield
WOODSTOCK Windham
WOODSTOCK VALLEY Windham
YANTIC New London

Connecticut ZIP/City Cross Reference

ZIP	City
06001-06001	AVON
06002-06002	BLOOMFIELD
06006-06006	WINDSOR
06010-06011	BRISTOL
06013-06013	BURLINGTON
06016-06016	BROAD BROOK
06018-06018	CANAAN
06019-06019	CANTON
06020-06020	CANTON CENTER
06021-06021	COLEBROOK
06022-06022	COLLINSVILLE
06023-06023	EAST BERLIN
06024-06024	EAST CANAAN
06025-06025	EAST GLASTONBURY
06026-06026	EAST GRANBY
06027-06027	EAST HARTLAND
06028-06028	EAST WINDSOR HILL
06029-06029	ELLINGTON
06030-06030	FARMINGTON
06031-06031	FALLS VILLAGE
06032-06032	FARMINGTON
06033-06033	GLASTONBURY
06034-06034	FARMINGTON
06035-06035	GRANBY
06037-06037	KENSINGTON
06039-06039	LAKEVILLE
06040-06042	MANCHESTER
06043-06043	BOLTON
06045-06045	MANCHESTER
06049-06049	MELROSE
06050-06053	NEW BRITAIN
06057-06057	NEW HARTFORD
06058-06058	NORFOLK
06059-06059	NORTH CANTON
06060-06060	NORTH GRANBY
06061-06061	PINE MEADOW
06062-06062	PLAINVILLE
06063-06063	PLEASANT VALLEY
06063-06063	BARKHAMSTED
06064-06064	POQUONOCK
06065-06065	RIVERTON
06066-06066	VERNON ROCKVILLE
06067-06067	ROCKY HILL
06068-06068	SALISBURY
06069-06069	SHARON
06070-06070	SIMSBURY
06071-06071	SOMERS
06072-06072	SOMERSVILLE
06073-06073	SOUTH GLASTONBURY
06074-06074	SOUTH WINDSOR
06075-06075	STAFFORD
06076-06076	STAFFORD SPRINGS
06077-06077	STAFFORDVILLE
06078-06078	SUFFIELD
06079-06079	TACONIC
06080-06080	SUFFIELD
06081-06081	TARIFFVILLE
06082-06083	ENFIELD
06084-06084	TOLLAND
06085-06087	UNIONVILLE
06088-06088	EAST WINDSOR
06089-06089	WEATOGUE
06090-06090	WEST GRANBY
06091-06091	WEST HARTLAND
06092-06092	WEST SIMSBURY
06093-06093	WEST SUFFIELD
06094-06094	WINCHESTER CENTER
06095-06095	WINDSOR
06096-06096	WINDSOR LOCKS
06098-06098	WINSTED
06100-06106	HARTFORD
06107-06107	W HARTFORD
06107-06107	WEST HARTFORD
06108-06108	EAST HARTFORD
06109-06109	WETHERSFIELD
06110-06110	W HARTFORD
06110-06110	WEST HARTFORD
06111-06111	NEWINGTON
06112-06115	HARTFORD
06117-06117	W HARTFORD
06117-06117	WEST HARTFORD
06118-06118	EAST HARTFORD
06119-06119	W HARTFORD
06119-06119	WEST HARTFORD
06120-06126	HARTFORD
06127-06127	W HARTFORD
06127-06127	WEST HARTFORD
06128-06128	EAST HARTFORD
06129-06129	WETHERSFIELD
06131-06131	NEWINGTON
06132-06132	HARTFORD
06133-06133	W HARTFORD
06133-06133	WEST HARTFORD
06134-06134	HARTFORD
06137-06137	W HARTFORD
06137-06137	WEST HARTFORD
06138-06138	EAST HARTFORD
06140-06199	HARTFORD
06226-06226	WILLIMANTIC
06230-06230	ABINGTON
06231-06231	AMSTON
06232-06232	ANDOVER
06233-06233	BALLOUVILLE
06234-06234	BROOKLYN
06235-06235	CHAPLIN
06237-06237	COLUMBIA
06238-06238	COVENTRY
06239-06239	DANIELSON
06241-06241	DAYVILLE
06242-06242	EASTFORD
06243-06243	EAST KILLINGLY
06244-06244	EAST WOODSTOCK
06245-06245	FABYAN
06246-06246	GROSVENOR DALE
06247-06247	HAMPTON
06248-06248	HEBRON
06249-06249	LEBANON
06250-06250	MANSFIELD CENTER
06251-06251	MANSFIELD DEPOT
06254-06254	NORTH FRANKLIN
06255-06255	NORTH GROSVENORDALE
06256-06256	NORTH WINDHAM
06258-06258	POMFRET
06259-06259	POMFRET CENTER
06260-06260	PUTNAM
06262-06262	QUINEBAUG
06263-06263	ROGERS
06264-06264	SCOTLAND
06265-06265	SOUTH WILLINGTON
06266-06266	SOUTH WINDHAM
06267-06267	SOUTH WOODSTOCK
06268-06269	STORRS MANSFIELD
06277-06277	THOMPSON
06278-06278	ASHFORD
06279-06279	WILLINGTON
06280-06280	WINDHAM
06281-06281	WOODSTOCK
06282-06282	WOODSTOCK VALLEY
06320-06320	NEW LONDON
06330-06330	BALTIC
06331-06331	CANTERBURY
06332-06332	CENTRAL VILLAGE
06333-06333	EAST LYME
06334-06334	BOZRAH
06335-06335	GALES FERRY
06336-06336	GILMAN
06337-06337	GLASGO
06338-06338	MASHANTUCKET
06339-06339	LEDYARD
06340-06349	GROTON
06350-06350	HANOVER
06351-06351	JEWETT CITY
06353-06353	MONTVILLE
06354-06354	MOOSUP
06355-06355	MYSTIC
06357-06357	NIANTIC
06359-06359	NORTH STONINGTON
06360-06360	NORWICH
06365-06365	PRESTON
06370-06370	OAKDALE
06371-06371	OLD LYME
06372-06372	OLD MYSTIC
06373-06373	ONECO
06374-06374	PLAINFIELD
06375-06375	QUAKER HILL
06376-06376	SOUTH LYME
06377-06377	STERLING
06378-06378	STONINGTON
06379-06379	PAWCATUCK
06380-06380	TAFTVILLE
06382-06382	UNCASVILLE
06383-06383	VERSAILLES
06384-06384	VOLUNTOWN
06385-06386	WATERFORD
06387-06387	WAUREGAN
06388-06388	WEST MYSTIC
06389-06389	YANTIC
06401-06401	ANSONIA
06403-06403	BEACON FALLS
06404-06404	BOTSFORD
06405-06405	BRANFORD
06408-06408	CHESHIRE
06409-06409	CENTERBROOK
06410-06411	CHESHIRE
06412-06412	CHESTER
06413-06413	CLINTON
06414-06414	COBALT
06415-06415	COLCHESTER
06416-06416	CROMWELL
06417-06417	DEEP RIVER
06418-06418	DERBY
06419-06419	KILLINGWORTH
06420-06420	SALEM
06422-06422	DURHAM
06423-06423	EAST HADDAM
06424-06424	EAST HAMPTON
06426-06426	ESSEX
06430-06432	FAIRFIELD
06436-06436	GREENS FARMS
06437-06437	GUILFORD
06438-06438	HADDAM
06439-06439	HADLYME
06440-06440	HAWLEYVILLE
06441-06441	HIGGANUM
06442-06442	IVORYTON
06443-06443	MADISON
06444-06444	MARION
06447-06447	MARLBOROUGH
06450-06454	MERIDEN
06455-06455	MIDDLEFIELD
06456-06456	MIDDLE HADDAM
06457-06459	MIDDLETOWN
06460-06460	MILFORD
06461-06461	BRIDGEPORT
06466-06466	MILFORD
06467-06467	MILLDALE
06468-06468	MONROE
06469-06469	MOODUS
06470-06470	NEWTOWN
06471-06471	NORTH BRANFORD
06472-06472	NORTHFORD
06473-06473	NORTH HAVEN
06474-06474	NORTH WESTCHESTER
06475-06475	OLD SAYBROOK
06477-06477	ORANGE
06478-06478	OXFORD
06479-06479	PLANTSVILLE
06480-06480	PORTLAND
06481-06481	ROCKFALL
06482-06482	SANDY HOOK
06483-06483	SEYMOUR
06484-06484	SHELTON
06487-06487	SOUTH BRITAIN
06488-06488	SOUTHBURY
06489-06489	SOUTHINGTON
06490-06490	SOUTHPORT
06491-06491	STEVENSON
06492-06495	WALLINGFORD
06497-06497	STRATFORD
06498-06498	WESTBROOK
06500-06511	NEW HAVEN
06512-06512	EAST HAVEN
06513-06513	NEW HAVEN
06514-06514	HAMDEN
06515-06515	NEW HAVEN
06516-06516	WEST HAVEN
06517-06517	HAMDEN
06519-06521	NEW HAVEN
06524-06524	BETHANY
06525-06525	WOODBRIDGE
06530-06540	NEW HAVEN
06600-06610	BRIDGEPORT
06611-06611	TRUMBULL
06612-06612	EASTON
06614-06615	STRATFORD
06650-06699	BRIDGEPORT
06701-06710	WATERBURY
06712-06712	PROSPECT
06716-06716	WOLCOTT
06720-06749	WATERBURY
06750-06750	BANTAM
06751-06751	BETHLEHEM
06752-06752	BRIDGEWATER
06753-06753	CORNWALL
06754-06754	CORNWALL BRIDGE
06755-06755	GAYLORDSVILLE
06756-06756	GOSHEN
06757-06757	KENT
06758-06758	LAKESIDE
06759-06759	LITCHFIELD
06762-06762	MIDDLEBURY
06763-06763	MORRIS
06770-06770	NAUGATUCK
06776-06776	NEW MILFORD
06777-06777	NEW PRESTON MARBLE DALE
06778-06778	NORTHFIELD
06779-06779	OAKVILLE
06781-06781	PEQUABUCK
06782-06782	PLYMOUTH
06783-06783	ROXBURY
06784-06784	SHERMAN
06785-06785	SOUTH KENT
06786-06786	TERRYVILLE
06787-06787	THOMASTON
06790-06790	TORRINGTON
06791-06792	HARWINTON
06792-06792	TORRINGTON
06793-06794	WASHINGTON DEPOT
06795-06795	WATERTOWN
06796-06796	WEST CORNWALL
06798-06798	WOODBURY
06801-06801	BETHEL
06804-06804	BROOKFIELD
06807-06807	COS COB
06810-06811	DANBURY
06812-06812	NEW FAIRFIELD
06813-06817	DANBURY
06820-06820	DARIEN
06824-06828	FAIRFIELD
06829-06829	GEORGETOWN
06830-06836	GREENWICH
06838-06838	GREENS FARMS
06840-06842	NEW CANAAN
06850-06860	NORWALK
06870-06870	OLD GREENWICH
06875-06875	REDDING CENTER
06876-06876	REDDING RIDGE
06877-06877	RIDGEFIELD
06878-06878	RIVERSIDE
06879-06879	RIDGEFIELD
06880-06881	WESTPORT
06883-06883	WESTON
06888-06889	WESTPORT
06890-06890	SOUTHPORT
06896-06896	REDDING
06897-06897	WILTON
06900-06928	STAMFORD

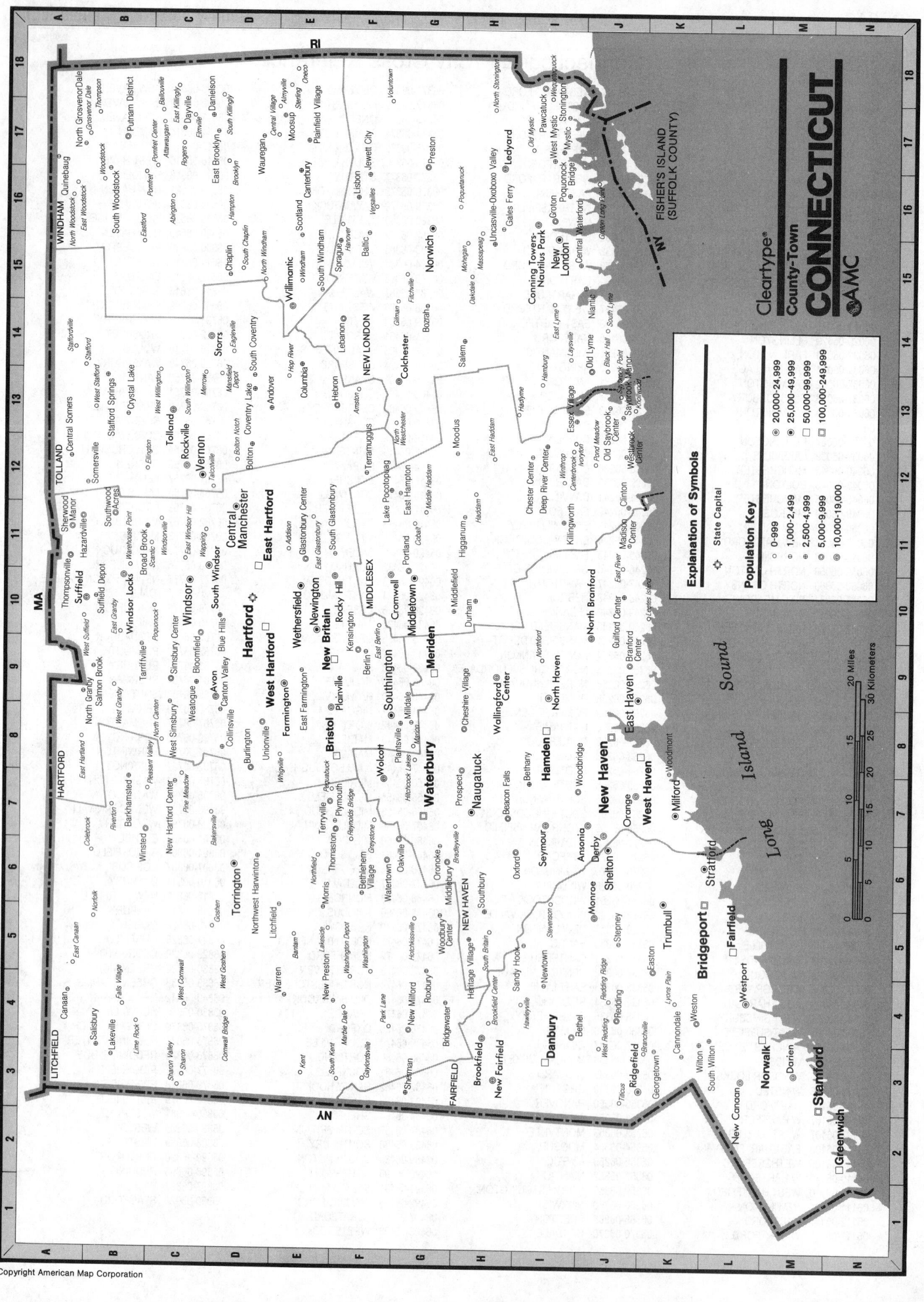

Explanation of symbols:

● – Census Designated Place (CDP)

▲ *italics* – Township (shown on the map)

● *italics* – Township shown which is also a CDP

italics – Township (not shown on the map)

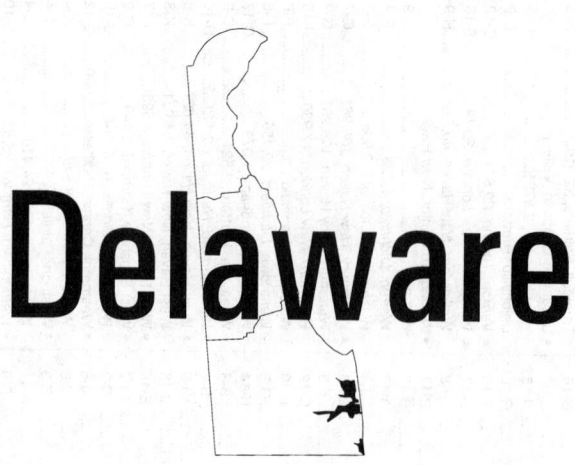

Delaware

General Help Numbers:

Governor's Office

820 N. French St
Wilmington, DE 19801
www.state.de.us/governor/index.shtml

302-577-3210
Fax 302-577-3118
8AM-5:30PM

Attorney General's Office

Carvel State Office Bldg
820 N French St
Wilmington, DE 19801
www.state.de.us/attgen

302-577-8400
Fax 302-577-6630
8:30AM-5PM

Legislative Records

Division of Research
PO Box 1401
Wilmington, DE 19903
www.legis.state.de.us/Legislature.nsf?Open

302-744-4114
302-739-5318
8AM-4:30PM

State Archives

121 Duke of York St
Dover, DE 19901
www.state.de.us/sos/dpa/

302-744-5000
Fax 302-739-6710
8:30AM-4:15PM M-F
(till 8PM on E & TH)

State Specifics:

Capital:	Dover
	Kent County
Time Zone:	EST
Number of Counties:	3
Population:	830,364
Website:	http://delaware.gov

State Agencies

Criminal Records

Delaware State Police, State Bureau of Identification, PO Box 430, Dover, DE 19903-0430 (Courier address: 1407 N Dupont Highway, Dover, DE 19930); 302-739-2134, 302-739-5888-Fax; 8AM-4PM.

www.state.de.us/dsp

Records are available from 1935. It takes up to 3 days before new records are available for inquiry. Records are normally destroyed after expunged, otherwise kept indefinitely. 81% of all arrests in database have final dispositions recorded, 92% for those arrests within last 5 years.

Searching: Must have a signed release from the subject for the fingerprint search and release of information. You do not need to use the state's forms. Include the following in your request- fingerprints, full name, signed release. Will not expedite requests; their policy is first come first served. The following data is not released: traffic ticket information. If the disposition is not known by this agency, the record will say "disposition not known." Will only release records with dispositions to pre-employment screeners.

Access by: mail, in person.

Fee & Payment: The search fee is $30.00 per request. Fee payee: Delaware State Police. Prepayment required. Funds must be certified or money order. Credit cards accepted for in person searches only

Mail search: Turnaround time: 14 days. Must have a signed release and full set of fingerprints. A SASE is requested.

In person search: Records can be requested, but results are mailed.

Statewide Court Records

Administrative Office of the Courts, Supreme Court of Delaware, 500 N King St, #11600, Wilmington, DE 19801; 302-255-0090, 302-255-2217-Fax; 8:30AM-5PM.

http://courts.state.de.us

All trial court record access must be done at the local level.

Access by: online.

Online search: Supreme Court Final Orders and Opinions (also lower state court opinions) are available at the webpage. There is no statewide access to trial court data.

Sexual Offender Registry

Delaware State Police, Sex Offender Central Registry, PO Box 430, Dover, DE 19903-0430 (Courier address: 1407 N Dupont Highway, Dover, DE 19901); 302-739-5882, 302-739-5888-Fax; 8AM-4PM.

www.state.de.us/dsp/sexoff

There are three Tiers or Levels of offenders in the state. The public is only made aware of Tiers 2 and 3 via the Internet through public notification programs by local law enforcement. Door-to-door is used for Tier 3 notification.

Records are available from 06/24/94. It takes up to 3 days before new records are available for inquiry.

Searching: Name searching is not available in the state except through the web page. Email questions to soffender@state.de.us.

Access by: online.

Online search: Statewide registry can be searched at the web site. The site gives the ability to search by Last Name, Development, and city or Zip Code. Any combination of these fields may be used; however, a search cannot be performed if both a city and Zip Code are entered.

Incarceration Records

Delaware Department of Corrections, Central Records, 511 Maple Parkway, Dover, DE 19901; 302-739-5387 (Locator), 302-739-7486-Fax; 8AM-4PM.

www.state.de.us/correct/index.htm

The Department of Correction does not offer the public access to an automated database of offender information.

Records are available and maintained on current and former inmates. Records are normally destroyed after three years (retired).

Searching: However, the public may receive basic information about an offender, including whether the individual is incarcerated in Delaware, where the individual is incarcerated and, how to contact an offender, by calling the number above. Include the following in your request-name and DOB.

Access by: phone.

Phone search: Call the Department's Office of Community Relations at 302-739-5601 Ext. 246.

Other access: An escapees list is available online at www.state.de.us/correct/Data/Escapees.htm.

Corporation Records General Partnerships, Limited Partnership, Trademarks/Servicemarks, Limited Liability Company, Limited Liability Partnerships

Secretary of State, Corporation Records, PO Box 898, Dover, DE 19903 (Courier address: 401 Federal Street #4, Dover, DE 19901); 302-739-3073, 302-739-3812-Fax; 8AM-4:30PM.

www.state.de.us/corp

There is no online access to the public; however, there is a system available to only registered agents.

Records are available from the formation of the Division. Indexes are maintained on imaging system and in-house computer. Delaware Registered Agents have online access. New records are available for inquiry immediately.

Searching: Include the following in your request-full name of business. In addition to the articles of incorporation, corporation records include the following information: Annual Reports, Officers, Directors, Prior (merged) names, Inactive and Reserved names.

Access by: mail, phone, fax, in person, online.

Fee & Payment: Record search is $30.00. Certification is $30.00 (plus $2.00 per page if annual report). Plain copies are $10.00 first page and $2.00 each additional. Fee payee: Delaware Secretary of State. Prepayment required. Personal checks and MasterCard, Visa, Discover accepted.

Mail search: Turnaround time: 3 - 5 days. No SASE is required.

Phone search: There is no fee for general information given over the phone.

Fax search: Fax requests can be received by fax, but are not returned by fax.

In person search: Requests are returned by regular mail unless expedite fee is paid.

Online search: Information is available at https://sos-res.state.de.us/tin/GINameSearch.jsp. The entity information provided on this website, free of charge, consists of the entity name, file number, incorporation/formation date, registered agent name, address, phone number and residency. Additional, detailed information can be obtained for a fee of $20.00.

Expedited service: Expedited services available for mail, fax, phone, and in person. Add $2.00 for 24 hour service for plain copies. Add $10.00 for a same day search. Otherwise, fees will basically double if 24 hours. If same day, then 133% higher. $1,000 for one hour service. $500 for 2 hour service. Ouch.

Uniform Commercial Code, Federal Tax Liens

UCC Division, Secretary of State, PO Box 793, Dover, DE 19903 (Courier address: Townsend Bldg, 401 Federal Street #4, Dover, DE 19901); 302-739-3077, 302-739-3813-Fax; 8:30AM-4:30PM.

www.state.de.us/corp/ucc.shtml

All non "Search to Reflect" UCC Searches are outsourced to a Delaware Authorized Searcher, who performs the search. The website maintains a list of these private vendors. All UCC searches performed by these agents are Certified UCC Searches.

Records are available from 1967. Records are computerized since 1992. Records are indexed on inhouse computer.

Searching: Use search request form UCC-11, downloadable from web. The search includes federal tax liens on businesses since 1976. Federal tax liens on individuals may show here, also. All state tax liens are filed at the county level. Include the following in your request-debtor name.

Access by: mail, in person.

Fee & Payment: Copies are $10.00 first page, $2.00 each additional. Add $25.00 for certification. Fee payee: Secretary of State. Prepayment required. Volume users may establish an account. Personal checks and MasterCard, Visa, Discover accepted.

Other access: Bulk purchase of paper copies is $2.00 per page.

Expedited service: Expedited service is available for mail and phone searches. Three levels of expedited service are available at extra fees as follows: 24 hrs-$25.00; same day-$50.00; 2 hrs-$75.00.

State Tax Liens

Records not maintained by a state level agency.

Records are at the county level.

Sales Tax Registrations

Finance Department - Div. Rev., Gross Receipt Tax Registration, PO Box 8750, Wilmington, DE 19899-8750 (Courier address: Carvel State Office Bldg, 820 N French St, 9th Fl, Wilmington, DE 19801); 302-577-8230, 302-577-8203-Fax; 8AM-4:30PM.

www.state.de.us/revenue/divisions.shtml

This state has a gross receipts tax, not a sales tax per se. They will release the information found on the face of the business licensee issued to the business.

Records are available for the past 3 years.

Searching: This agency will do an alpha search for a business name and will provide the business name, address and business license number, type of business, and amount of license fee paid. They will not release business owner or officer names. Include the following in your request-business name. The federal tax ID can also be used.

Access by: mail, phone, fax, in person.

Mail search: Turnaround time: 1 week. A SASE is requested. No fee for mail request.

Phone search: No fee for telephone request. There is a limit of 3 searches per phone call.

Fax search: There is no fee for fax searches. Turnaround time is 2 days.

In person search: No fee for request.

Birth Certificates

Department of Health, Office of Vital Statistics, PO Box 637, Dover, DE 19903 (Courier address: William Penn & Federal Sts, Jesse Cooper Bldg, Dover, DE 19901); 302-744-4549, 8AM-4:30PM (Counter closes at 4:15 PM).

www.state.de.us/dhss/dph/ss/vitalstats.html

Records are available from 1932 to present. Prior records are at the State Archives. It takes 1 month before new records are available for inquiry. Records are indexed on microfilm, microfiche, and index cards.

Searching: Must have a signed release from person of record or immediate family member. Others may only obtain records if they demonstrate the record is needed for the determination or protection of their personal property rights or for genealogical uses. Include the following in your request-full name, names of parents, mother's maiden name, date of birth, place of birth, reason for information request, relationship to person of record, photo ID.

Access by: mail, in person, online.

Fee & Payment: Search fee is $10.00 per name for every 5 years searched. Add $6.00 if you use a credit card via vitalchek.com. Fee payee: Office of Vital Statistics. Prepayment required. Personal checks accepted. Major credit cards accepted by VitalChek (not state).

Mail search: Turnaround time: 1 day to 1 week. No SASE is required.

In person search: Records may be ordered in person at this agency or at the local county agency. Turnaround time is generally 10 minutes or less.

Online search: Access available at vitalchek.com, a state designated vendor.

Expedited service: VitalChek offers expedited services when ordered online or by fax. Turnaround time: 3 to 5 days. Include $23.50 for use of credit card and delivery, as well as the $10.00 record fee.

Death Records

Department of Health, Office of Vital Statistics, PO Box 637, Dover, DE 19903 (Courier address: William Penn & Federal Sts, Jesse Cooper Bldg, Dover, DE 19901); 302-744-4549, 8AM-4:30PM.

www.state.de.us/dhss/dph/ss/vitalstats.html

Records are available from 1964 to present. Prior records are at the State Archives. It takes 3 days before new records are available for inquiry. Records are indexed on microfilm, microfiche, and index cards.

Searching: Must have a signed release from immediate family member. Include the following in your request-full name, date of death, place of death, names of parents, reason for information request, relationship to person of record, photo ID.

Access by: mail, in person, online.

Fee & Payment: The search fee is $10.00 per name for every 5 years searched. Add $6.00 if you use a credit card via vitalchek.com. Fee payee: Office of Vital Statistics. Prepayment required.

Personal checks accepted. Major credit cards accepted by VitalChek (not state).

Mail search: Turnaround time: 1 day. No SASE is required.

In person search: Records may be ordered in person at this agency or at the local county agency. Turnaround time is 10 to 15 minutes.

Online search: Access available at vitalchek.com, a state designated vendor.

Expedited service: VitalChek offers expedited services when ordered online or by fax. Turnaround time: 3 to 5 days. Include $23.50 for use of credit card and delivery, as well as the $10.00 record fee.

Marriage Certificates

Department of Health, Office of Vital Statistics, PO Box 637, Dover, DE 19903 (Courier address: William Penn & Federal Sts, Jesse Cooper Bldg, Dover, DE 19901); 302-744-4549, 8AM-4:30PM.

www.state.de.us/dhss/dph/ss/vitalstats.html

Records are available from 1964 to present. Prior records are in the State Public Archives. It takes 1 month before new records are available for inquiry. Records are indexed on microfilm, microfiche, and index cards.

Searching: Must have a signed release from person or persons of record or immediate family member. Include the following in your request-names of husband and wife, date of marriage, place or county of marriage, relationship to person of record, reason for information request, wife's maiden name, photo ID.

Access by: mail, in person, online.

Fee & Payment: The search fee is $10.00 per name for every 5 years searched. Add $6.00 if you use a credit card via vitalchek.com. Fee payee: Office of Vital Statistics. Prepayment required. Personal checks accepted. Major credit cards accepted by VitalChek (not state).

Mail search: Turnaround time: 1 day. No SASE is required.

In person search: Records may be ordered in person at this agency or at the local county agency. Turnaround time is 10 to 15 minutes.

Online search: Access is available via VitalChek.com, a state designated vendor.

Expedited service: VitalChek offers expedited services when ordered online or by fax. Turnaround time: 3 to 5 days. Include $23.50 for use of credit card and delivery, as well as the $10.00 record fee.

Divorce Records

Records not maintained by a state level agency.

This agency will verify whether a divorce occurred after 1935, but will issue no copies of the record. For records 1976 to present, go to the Family Court at the county; prior to 1976, go to the Prothonotary at the county level.

Workers' Compensation Records

Labor Department, Industrial Accident Board, 4425 N Market Street, 3rd Fl, Wilmington, DE 19802; 302-761-8200 x2, 302-761-6601-Fax; 8AM-4:30PM.
www.delawareworks.com/industrialaffairs/services/workerscomp.shtml

Case records must have been adjudicated to be considered public. First reports of injury only (non-adjudicated) are not covered under FOIA.

Records are available from 1985. New records are available for inquiry immediately.

Searching: Must have signed authorization from injured party in letter form or a court subpoena. They will not honor out-of-state requests. Information required includes claimant name, SSN, and date of accident.

Access by: mail.

Fee & Payment: There is no fee. Copies are $.25 each. Fee payee: DOL/IA. Prepayment required. Payment is for copies only. Personal checks accepted. No credit cards accepted.

Mail search: Turnaround time: 2 to 5 days. A SASE is requested.

Driver Records

Division of Motor Vehicles, Driver's License Unit, PO Box 698, Dover, DE 19903 (Courier address: 303 Transportation Circle, Dover, DE 19901); 302-744-2506, 302-739-2602-Fax; 8AM-4:30PM (12-8PM W). www.dmv.de.gov

Records are available for 3 years to present for public record purposes. It takes 2 to 3 weeks before new records are available for inquiry.

Searching: Records cannot be sold from one vendor to another unless approved. Casual requesters can obtain records only with MV703 Form requiring notarized signature of requester. Include the following in your request-full name, driver's license number, date of birth, Form MV703. Authorized account holders must complete an Application and a Contract for Direct Access. The following data is not released: Social Security Numbers or medical information.

Access by: mail, in person, online.

Fee & Payment: The fee for all search modes is $15.00 per request. Fee payee: Division of Motor Vehicles. Prepayment required. Personal checks accepted. No credit cards accepted.

Mail search: Turnaround time: 3 to 5 days. A SASE is requested.

In person search: Three requests will be processed while you wait, additional requests are processed overnight. Walk-in requesters may obtain records from centers in Wilmington, New Castle, Dover, and Georgetown.

Online search: Online searching is single inquiry only, no batch request mode is offered. Searching is done by driver's license number or name and DOB. A signed contract application and valid "business license" is required. Access is provided 24 hours daily through a 900 number at a fee of $1.50 per minute, plus the $15.00 per screen/record fee. For info, call 302-744-2606.

Other access: Tape-to-tape is offered for high volume, batch requesters. The $1.50 per minute line charge also applies. Also, this agency will release data from the driver license file on tapes or cartridges, but this cannot be resold.

Vehicle Ownership, Vehicle Identification

Division of Motor Vehicles, Correspondence Section, PO Box 698, Dover, DE 19903 (Courier address: 303 Transportation Circle, Dover, DE 19901); 302-744-2511, 302-744-2538, 302-739-2042-Fax; 8AM-4:30PM M-T-TH-F; 12-8PM W.

www.dmv.de.gov/services/vehicle_svcs.shtml

Records are available for 3 years to present. It takes 2 to 3 weeks before new records are available for inquiry.

Searching: Those routinely seeking information must complete an Application and Contract for Direct Access to become an account holder. Casual requesters must use Form MV703 which requires notarized signature of subject.

Access by: mail, in person, online.

Fee & Payment: The fee for ownership, plate, and registration searches is $15.00 per record, $20.00 if certified. Fee payee: Division of Motor Vehicles. Prepayment required. Personal checks accepted. No credit cards accepted.

Mail search: Turnaround time: 3 to 5 days. A SASE is requested.

In person search: Turnaround time is while you wait.

Online search: There is an additional $1.50 per minute fee for using the online "900 number" system. Records are $5.00 each. The system is single inquiry mode and open 24/7. Call 302-744-2606. This program is strictly monitored and not available for non-permissible uses.

Other access: Bulk information can be obtained on a customized basis in tape, cartridge or paper format. However, the purpose of the request is carefully screened and information cannot be resold.

Accident Reports

Delaware State Police, Traffic Control Section, PO Box 430, Dover, DE 19903 (Courier address: 1441 N Dupont Hwy, Dover, DE 19901); 302-739-5931, 302-739-5982-Fax; 8AM-4PM.

It takes 2 to 3 weeks before new records are available for inquiry.

Searching: Include the following in your request-full names, date of accident, location of accident.

Access by: mail, phone.

Fee & Payment: The fee is $25.00 per report, $60.00 if fatal accident report. Fee payee: Delaware State Police. Prepayment required. Personal checks accepted. No credit cards accepted.

Mail search: Turnaround time: 5 to 10 days. A SASE is requested.

Phone search: You can only verify if a report exists.

Vessel Ownership, Vessel Registration

Dept of Natural Resources & Environmental Control, Delaware Boat Registration Office, 89 Kings Highway, Dover, DE 19901; 302-739-3498, 302-739-6157-Fax; 8AM-4:30PM.

www.dnrec.state.de.us/dnrec2000/Boating.asp

Liens are filed with UCC filings, not at this location. Records are confidential and not released to general public per DPPA.

Records are available from 1978 to present. Records are registration only, no titles, and are indexed on microfiche from 1978 to 1989. Records are computer indexed from 1990 to the present. All motorized craft are registered. It takes one month or less before new records are available for inquiry. Records are normally destroyed after original paperwork scanned.

Searching: No searching of records is allowed. However, they will verify information over the phone using "yes" and "no" only. Liens are not filed here, they are filed with UCCs. Either the owner's name, hull ID# or registration number must be submitted for a verification.

Access by: mail, phone, fax, in person.

Fee & Payment: There is no fee.

Mail search: Turnaround time: 3 days. Records are available by mail.

Phone search: They will verify information over the phone using "yes" and "no" only.

Fax search: If DPPA approved.

In person search: Verification only.

Voter Registration

Commissioner of Elections, Voter Registration Records, 111 S West St #10, Dover, DE 19904; 302-739-4277, 302-739-6794-Fax; 8AM-4:30PM.

www.state.de.us/election

Records are available for both active and inactive records.

Searching: There is no individual record searching permitted, except in person. The following data is not released: Social Security Numbers or telephone numbers.

Access by: mail, in person.

Fee & Payment: There is no search fee, the copy fee is $.25 per copy. Fee payee: State of Delaware. Prepayment required. Personal checks accepted No credit cards accepted.

Mail search: Turnaround time: 7 to 10 days. Records are available by mail.

In person search: available.

Other access: The entire state database is available on CD for $250. Individual districts (432) are available on disk for $2.00 per district or $.025 per name on labels. Also, there are several different types of printed lists available.

GED Certificates

Department of Education, Adult Education - GED Testing, 401 Federal St #2, Dover, DE 19901; 302-857-3348, 302-739-1770-Fax; 8AM-4:30PM.

www.doe.state.de.us

It takes 8-12 weeks before new records are available for inquiry.

Searching: Consent of subject is needed for all third-party searches. Include the following in your request-signed release, name, date of birth, Social Security Number, location of test center. Requests must be in writing. The year of the test is very helpful.

Access by: mail, fax, in person.

Fee & Payment: There is no fee for a verification. A duplicate certificate is available for $5.00. Fee payee: Department of Education Strongly suggest using a money order. Personal checks not accepted.

Mail search: Turnaround time: 2 to 3 weeks. No SASE is required.

Fax search: Same criteria as mail searching.

In person search: Requester must present a photo ID.

Hunting and Fishing License Information

Access to Records is Restricted.

Division of Fish & Wildlife, License Records, 89 Kings Hwy, Dover, DE 19901; 302-739-5296, 302-739-6157-Fax; 8AM-4:30PM.

www.dnrec.state.de.us/fw/index.htm

Records are not on a computerized database, but kept on paper and filed alphabetically. Per Delaware Code, license holder information is restricted and not available for public access.

Delaware State Licensing Agencies

For details about the agency responsible for licensing/certifying/registering an item below or in the Agency Quick Finder section, match an item's number with the number of the agency in the *Licensing Agency Information* section.

Delaware Licenses Searchable Online

Counselors(Elementary/ Secondary) #4 .... https://deeds.doe.k12.de.us/public/deeds_pc_findeducator.aspx

Engineer #12 .... www.dape.org/App/peRoster.asp

Engineering Firm #12 .... www.dape.org/App/peRoster.asp

Insurance Broker/Dealer #8.............................. www.state.de.us/inscom/berg/authorizedcompanies.htm

Library/Media Specialist #4............................... https://deeds.doe.k12.de.us/public/deeds_pc_findeducator.aspx

Optometrist #11 .... www.arbo.org/index.php?action=findanoptometrist

Real Estate Appraiser #11................................. www.asc.gov/content/category1/appr_by_state.asp

School Admin. Supervisor/Asst. #4 .... https://deeds.doe.k12.de.us/public/deeds_pc_findeducator.aspx

School Counselor/Principal/Superintendent #4 ... https://deeds.doe.k12.de.us/public/deeds_pc_findeducator.aspx

Teacher #4... https://deeds.doe.k12.de.us/public/deeds_pc_findeducator.aspx

Delaware Licensing Quick Finder

Adult Entertainment #11 302-744-4506	EmergencyMedicalTechParamedic #11 302-739-6637	Pharmacy/Pharmacy-related Business #11
Aesthetician #11 302-744-4518	EMT-B #13 302-739-4773	 320-744-4547
Alarm Company/Employee #3.............. 302-739-5991	Engineer #12 302-577-6500	Physical Therapist/Assistant #11 302-744-4506
Alcoholic Bev. Establishment #1 302-577-5222	Engineering Firm #12 302-577-6500	Physician Assistant #11 302-744-4507
Amateur Boxing #11 320-744-4533	Fire Company #13 302-739-4773	Pilot, River #11 302-744-4504
Ambulance Attendant #13 302-739-4773	Funeral Director #11............ 302-744-4505	Plumber #11 302-744-4504
Architect #11 302-744-4505	Gaming Control #11 302-744-4530	Podiatrist #11 302-744-4530
Armored Car Agency/Employee #3....302-739-5991	Geologist #11 302-744-4533	Private Investigative Agency/Employee #3
Asbestos Abatement Worker #15........302-739-4611	Harness Racing #6 302-698-4500	 302-739-5991
Athletic Agent #11................ 302-744-4511	Hearing Aid Dealer/Fitter #11.............. 302-744-4533	Private Security Agency/Employee #3. 302-739-5991
Athletic Trainer #11.............. 302-744-4506	Horse Racing (Thorobred) #6 302-698-4500	Professional Svc. Firm #15 302-739-4611
Attorney #2 302-739-4155	Insurance Adjuster/Advisor #8 302-739-4254	Project Monitor (Const.) #15 302-739-4611
Audiologist #11 302-744-4533	Insurance Agent/Consultant #8............ 302-739-4254	Psychological Assistant #11........... 302-744-4534
Bail Enforcement Agent #3.................. 302-739-5991	Insurance Broker/Dealer #8.............. 302-739-4254	Psychologist #11 302-744-4534
Barber #11 302-744-4518	Landscape Architect #11 302-744-4504	Public Accountant-CPA #11.............. 302-744-4505
Bodyworker #11.................. 302-744-4506	Library/Media Specialist #4 888-759-9133	Radiation Therapist #16............. 302-744-4546
Boiler Inspector #14............. 302-744-2735	Lobbyist #9 302-739-2397	Real Estate Agent/Broker #11 302-744-4519
Boxer/Boxing Professional #11 302-787-5720	Massage #11 302-744-4506	Real Estate Appraiser #11 302-744-4505
Charitable Gaming Permittee #11 302-744-4530	Medical Doctor/Surgeon #11................ 302-744-4530	Rental Car Insurer #8.............. 302-739-4254
Chiropractor #11................. 302-744-4509	Medical Practice #11 302-744-4530	Respiratory Care Practitioner #11........ 302-744-4507
Constable #3........................ 302-739-5991	Mental Health Counselor #11.............. 302-744-4507	School Admin. Supervisor/Asst. #4..... 888-759-9133
Contractor Class A #15 302-739-4611	Midwife Nurse #11............... 302-744-4517	School Counselor #4 888-759-9133
Contractor, General #5 302-577-8778	Nail Technician #11.............. 302-744-4518	School Principal/Superintendent #4..... 888-759-9133
Cosmetologist #11............... 302-744-4518	Notary Public #9 302-739-3073	Securities Agent #8 302-739-4254
Counselor, Professional #11 302-744-4534	Nuclear Medicine Technologist #16..... 302-744-4546	Social Worker #11 302-744-4534
Counselor, School #4 888-759-9133	Nurse #11 302-744-4517	Speech Pathologist/Audiologist #11 302-744-4533
Deadly Weapons Dealer #11 302-744-4506	Nursing Home Administrator #11 302-744-4505	Surplus Lines Broker #8............. 302-739-4254
Dental Hygienist #11 302-744-4518	Nutritionist #11.................... 302-744-4512	Surveyor, Land #11 302-744-4518
Dental Radiographer #16 302-744-4546	Occupational Therapist/Assistant #11.. 302-744-4511	Teacher #4 888-759-9133
Dentist #11.......................... 302-744-4518	Optometrist #11 302-744-4512	Veterinarian #11................... 302-744-4506
Dietician/Nutritionist #11 302-744-4512	Osteopathic Physician #11.................. 302-744-4529	Waste Water Operator #17 302-739-5731
Electrical Inspector #11 302-744-4505	Pesticide Applicator #10...................... 302-698-4570	Water Supply Operator #7 302-739-5410
Electrician #11 302-744-4504	Pharmacist #11.................... 302-744-4547	X-ray Technician #7 302-744-4546
Electrologist #11 302-744-4518		

Delaware Licensing Agency Information

1 Alcoholic Beverage Control Division, 820 N French St, Carvel State Office Bldg, Wilmington, DE 19801; 302-577-5222, Fax: 302-577-3204.

2 Board of Bar Examiners, 820 N French St 11th Fl., Wilmington, DE 19801-3545; 302-577-7038, Fax: 302-577-7037.
http://courts.state.de.us/bbe

3 State Police, State Bureau of Identification, Detective Licensing, PO Box 430, Dover, DE 19903; 302-739-5991, Fax: 302-739-5888.
www.state.de.us/dsp/sbi.htm
Email: panderson@state.de.us

4 Department of Education, Certification Division, 401 Federal St, Dover, DE 19903; 888-759-9133, 302-739-4601, Fax: 302-739-3092.
www.doe.state.de.us
Search Database at
https://deeds.doe.k12.de.us/public/deeds_pc_finde ducator.aspx

5 Division of Revenue, 820 N French St, Carvel State Office Bldg, Wilmington, DE 19801; 302-577-8200, Fax: 302-577-8202.
www.state.de.us/revenue/default.shtml
Email: wremington@state.de.us

6 Harness Racing Commission, 2320 S DuPont Hwy, Dover, DE 19901;
302-698-4500, Fax: 302-697-4748.
www.state.de.us/deptagri/harness/index.shtml
Email: johnwayne@dda.state.de.us

7 Health & Social Services Department, Division of Public Health, PO Box 637 (Federal & Water Sts), Dover, DE 19903; 302-744-4701.
www.state.de.us/dhss/dph/index.htm
Email: dhssinfo@state.de.us

8 Insurance Department, Producer Licencing, 841 Silver Lake Blvd, Dover, DE 19904; 302-739-4254, Fax: 302-739-5280.
www.state.de.us/inscom/departments/licensing/lic ensing.shtml
Email: licensing@deins.state.de.us

9 Notary Division, Office of Secretary of State, 401 Federal St #3, Dover, DE 19903;
302-739-4111, Fax: 302-739-3812.
www.state.de.us/sos/nphome.shtml

10 Department of Agriculture, Pesticide Section, 2320 S DuPont Hwy, Dover, DE 19901;
302-698-4570, Fax: 302-697-4483.
www.state.de.us/deptagri/pesticides/index.shtml
Email: grier.stayton@state.de.us

11 Division of Professional Regulations, Department of Admin. Svcs., 861 Silver Lake Blvd, Cannon Bldg #203, Dover, DE 19904; 302-739-4522, Fax: 302-739-2711.
www.professionallicensing.state.de.us

12 Assoc. of Professional Engineers, Engineering Licensing Board, 56 W Main St #208, Plaza 273, Christiana, DE 19702-1500;
302-368-6708, Fax: 302-368-6710.

www.dape.org   Email: office@dape.org
Search Database at www.dape.org/Ap p/peRoster.asp   Note: Searchable rosters link is on left hand margin of web page.

13 Fire Prevention Commission, 1463 Chestnut Grove Rd, Dover, DE 19904;
302-739-3169, Fax: 302-739-4436.
www.delawarestatefirecommission.com/default.sh tml
Email: firecommission@state.de.us

14 Department of Public Safety, Division of Boiler Safety, PO Box 674, Dover, DE 19903-0674; 302-744-2735, Fax: 302-739-2526.
www.delawareboilersafety.com

15 Division of Facilities Mgmt, 540 S. DuPont Hwy, Thomas Collins Building #1, Dover, DE 19901; 302-739-3930, Fax: 302-739-3127.

16 Division of Public Health, Office of Radiation Control, PO Box 637 (417 Federal St), Dover, DE 19903; 302-744-4546, Fax: 302-739-3839.

17 Department of Natural Resources & Environmental Control, Division of Water Resources, 89 Kings Hwy, Dover, DE 19901; 302-739-4860, Fax: 302-739-8369.

Delaware Federal Courts

The following list indicates the district and division name for each county in the state.

County/Court Cross Reference

Kent...Wilmington
New Castle...Wilmington
Sussex...Wilmington

US District Court

Wilmington Division Court Clerk, Lock Box 18, 844 N King St, US Courthouse, Wilmington, DE 19801 (courier address: US Courthouse, 844 N King St, Clerk's Office, 4th Fl, Rm 4209, Wilmington, DE 19801), 302-573-6170, records rm- 302-573-6158. Hours- 8:30AM-4:30PM. www.ded.uscourts.gov

Counties: All counties in Delaware.

Searches & Indexing: Results do not include SSN or DOB. Computer index maintained. New cases in the index 1 day after filing date. Records purged every few years.

Fee & Payment: Pay by money order, cashier's or personal check. Payee: Clerk, US District Court. Prepayment required.

Phone Search: Via phone, this court will search civil and criminal cases back to 1982; will only say if a case was found and a case number.

Mail Search: search usually completed- 2-3 days. Search can include all computer, microfiche and judgment indexes. SASE not required.

In Person Search: Fee charged if court performs your search. For civil court document copies you may place orders directly with Parcels Inc, 800-343-1742. No self-serve copier available.

E-Services: ECF replaces PACER whose records did go back to 1/1991. New records online after 1 day. ECF at https://ecf.ded.uscourts.gov

Opinions Online:
www.lawlib.widener.edu/pages/deopind.htm.

US Bankruptcy Court

Wilmington Division Court Clerk, 824 N Market St, 3rd Fl, Marine Midland Plaza, Wilmington, DE 19801 (also use mail address for courier delivery), 888-667-5530, records rm- x 5136. Hours- 8AM-4PM. www.deb.uscourts.gov

Counties: All counties in Delaware.

Searches & Indexing: Results do not include SSN or DOB. Computer index maintained. New cases in the index 1 day after filing date. Records purged every 4 years.

Fee & Payment: Pay by money order, cashier's or personal check. Payee: Clerk, US Bankruptcy Court. Prepayment required.

Phone Search: Via telephone, this court will only say whether the search is positive or negative. If positive they will release case number. Voice Case Information Service available, call VCIS at 302-252-2560.

Mail Search: search usually completed- 1-2 days. Include SASE for return.

In Person Search: Fee charged if court performs your search. An in-house private copy service is available for your use. Self-serve copier available - $.50 per page.

E-Services: ECF replaces PACER whose records did go back to 1991. New records online after 1 day. ECF at https://ecf.deb.uscourts.gov

Opinions Online:
www.deb.uscourts.gov/Opinions/opinions_cover.htm. **Other Online Access:** Online access to WebPacer is available is available at www.deb.uscourts.gov and click on "Case Information." Chapter 11 filing monthly lists are free at www.deb.uscourts.gov/Chapter11/chapter11_filings.htm.

Standards for Federal Courts: Search fee is $26.00 per item (one party name or case number). Copy fee is $.50 per page. Certification fee is $9.00 per document, double for exemplification, if available. All fees standard unless noted in profile. Mail Search: always enclose a stamped self addressed envelope unless otherwise noted. Most courts accept fax requests or will suggest a copying/search vendor. Before releasing records, all courts require prepayment, unless noted.

Open records are located at the court unless otherwise noted. District courts index by defendant and plaintiff as well as by case number. Bankruptcy courts usually index by debtor and case number. While most courts now have their indexes on computer, many may still maintain index card files as well.

Courts offering internet access via CM-ECF or older RACER, PACER, or Web-PACER systems charge $.08 per page fee unless noted as free. Where PACER is available, the universal sign-up number is 800-676-6856. Find PACER and the US Party/Case Index at http://pacer.psc.uscourts.gov.

Delaware County Courts

Court	Jurisdiction	No. of Courts	How Organized
Superior Courts*	General	3	
Chancery Courts*	General	3	
Court of Common Pleas*	Limited	3	
Justice of the Peace Courts*	Municipal	19	
Alderman's Courts	Municipal	9	
Family Courts	Special	3	

* Profiled in this Sourcebook.

Court	CIVIL								
	Tort	Contract	Real Estate	Min. Claim	Max. Claim	Small Claims	Estate	Eviction	Domestic Relations
Superior Courts*	X	X	X	$50000	No Max				
Chancery Courts*	X	X	X	$0	No Max		X		
Court of Common Pleas*	X	X	X	$0	$50000				
Justice of the Peace Courts*			X	$0	$15000	$5000		X	
Alderman's Courts						$2500			
Family Courts									X

Court	CRIMINAL				
	Felony	Misdemeanor	DWI/DUI	Preliminary Hearing	Juvenile
Superior Courts*	X	X			
Chancery Courts*					
Court of Common Pleas*		X		X	
Justice of the Peace Courts*		X	X		
Alderman's Courts		X	X		
Family Courts		X			X

ADMINISTRATION Administrative Office of the Courts, Supreme Court of Delaware, 500 N King St, #11600, Wilmington, DE, 19801; 302-255-0090, Fax: 302-255-2217. 8:30AM-5PM. courts.state.de.us/

COURT STRUCTURE The Superior Court, the State's court of general jurisdiction, has original jurisdiction over criminal and civil cases except equity cases. The Court has exclusive jurisdiction over felonies and almost all drug offenses. The Court of Common Pleas has jurisdiction in civil cases where the amount in controversy, exclusive of interest, does not exceed $50,000. In criminal cases, the Court of Common Pleas handles all misdemeanors occurring in the State except certain drug-related offenses and traffic offenses. The Court of Chancery has jurisdiction to hear all matters relating to equity. The litigation in this tribunal deals largely with corporate issues, trusts, estates, other fiduciary matters, disputes involving the purchase of land and questions of title to real estate as well as commercial and contractual matters. The Justice of the Peace Court, the initial entry level into the court system for most citizens, has jurisdiction over civil cases in which the disputed amount is less than $15,000. In criminal cases, the Justice of the Peace Court hears certain misdemeanors and most motor vehicle cases (excluding felonies) and the Justices of the Peace may act as committing magistrates for all crimes.

ONLINE ACCESS Chancery, Superior, Common Pleas and Supreme Court opinions and orders are available free online at http://courts.state.de.us/opinions. Supreme, Superior and Common Pleas Court calendars are available free at http://courts.state.de.us/calendars. Chancery and Supreme Court filings are available at www.virtualdocket.com. Registration and fees required.

Kent County

Superior Court Office of Prothonotary, 38 The Green, Dover, DE 19901; phone: 302-739-3184; fax: 302-739-6717; hours 8AM-4:30PM (EST). *Felony, Misdemeanor, Civil Actions Over $50,000.*
http://courts.state.de.us/superior
Note: Court refers records request to State Agency-302-739-5961.

Civil Records: Access: In person only. Visitors must perform in person searches themselves. Court makes copy: $1.50 per page; copies off the computer are free; same fee for self serve. Required to search: name, years to search. Civil cases indexed by defendant, plaintiff. Judgments on computer from 1996, on books from 1918.

Criminal Records: Access: In person only. Both court and visitors may perform in person searches. Search fee: None, but $25.00 search fee for pre-1996 records. Court makes copy: $1.50 per page; copies off the computer are free; same fee for self serve. Required to search: name, years to search, DOB. Judgments on computer from 1996, on microfiche from 1918.

General Information: Public access terminal goes back to 7/1996. No sealed or psychological evaluation records released. Certification fee: $6.00 fee for 3 pages; add copy fee for add'l pages. Payee: Prothonotary. Personal checks accepted. Prepayment required.

Chancery Court 38 The Green, Dover, DE 19901; phone: 302-736-2242; probate phone: 302-744-2330; fax: 302-736-2240; hours 8:30AM-4:30PM (EST). *Civil, Probate.*
http://courts.state.de.us/chancery
Civil Records: Access: In person only. Visitors must perform in person searches themselves. Court makes copy: $1.50 per page. Required to search: name, years to search. Civil cases indexed by defendant, plaintiff. Civil records on index books. The Court of Chancery oversees corporate and equity matters and guardianship. The Register of Wills oversees estate, and probate matters.
Mail turnaround time 24 hrs.

General Information: Public access terminal has only civil records. No juvenile, sealed or mental health records released. Fee to fax documents is $10.00 1st page, $2.00 each add'l. Certification fee: $25.00 per document. Payee: Register in Chancery (Register of Wills for Probate). Personal checks accepted. Prepayment required. May bill law firms and businesses.

Court of Common Pleas 38 The Green, Dover, DE 19901; phone: 302-739-4618; fax: 302-739-4501; hours 8AM-4:30PM (EST). *Misdemeanor, Civil Actions Under $50,000.*
http://courts.state.de.us/commonpleas
Civil Records: Access: Mail, in person. Both court and visitors may perform in person searches. Court makes copy: $1.00 per page. Required to search: name, years to search. Civil cases indexed by defendant, plaintiff. Civil records on computer from 1992, on microfiche from 10/85, archived prior. Mail turnaround time 1-3 days.

Criminal Records: Access: Mail, in person. Visitors must perform in person searches themselves. Court makes copy: $1.00 per page. Required to search: name, years to search, DOB, offense, date of offense. Criminal records on computer from 1/94, on microfiche from 10/85, archived prior. Mail turnaround time 1-3 days.

General Information: Public access terminal available. No sealed records released. Will fax documents to local or toll free line. Certification fee: $10.00. Payee: Court of Common Pleas. Personal checks accepted. Prepayment and SASE required.

Dover Justice of the Peace #16 480 Bank Ln, Dover, DE 19904; phone: 302-739-4316; fax: 302-739-6797; hours 8AM-4PM (EST). *Civil Actions Under $15,000, Eviction, Small Claims.*
http://courts.state.de.us/jpcourt

Civil Records: Access: Mail, in person. Both court and visitors may perform in person searches. No search fee. Court makes copy: $.25 per page. Required to search: name, years to search. Civil cases indexed by defendant, plaintiff. Civil records computerized since 10/98. Mail turnaround varies.

General Information: No public access terminal. Certification fee: $10.00 per doc. Payee: JCP Court 16. Personal checks accepted. Prepayment required. SASE requested.

Dover Justice of the Peace #7 480 Bank Ln, Dover, DE 19903; phone: 302-739-4554; fax: 302-739-6797; hours Open 24 hours (EST). *Misdemeanor.*
http://courts.state.de.us/jpcourt
Criminal Records: Only the court performs in person searches. Search fee: $7.00 per name. Fee includes copy certification. Court makes copy: $.25 per page. Required to search: name, years to search, DOB, signed release; also helpful: address, offense, date of offense. Record computerized since 1992, manually searched from 1992 to 1967.

General Information: Certification fee: $7.00 per case/file. Payee: State of Delaware. Prepayment required.

Harrington Justice of the Peace #6 35 Cams Fortune Way, Harrington, DE 19952; phone: 302-422-5922; fax: 302-422-1527; hours 8AM-4PM (EST). *Misdemeanor.*
http://courts.state.de.us/jpcourt
Criminal Records: Access: Mail, in person. Only the court performs in person searches. No search fee. Court makes copy: $.25 per page. Required to search: name, years to search, DOB. Note: Court form required for all searches. Mail turnaround time 2-3 days.

General Information: Certification fee: $7.00 per doc includes copies.

Smyrna Justice of the Peace #8 100 Monrovia Ave, Smyrna, DE 19977; phone: 302-653-7083; fax: 302-653-2888; hours 8AM-4PM (EST). *Misdemeanor.*
http://courts.state.de.us/jpcourt
Criminal Records: Access: Mail, in person. Only the court performs in person searches. No search fee. Court makes copy: $.30 per page. Required to search: name, years to search; also helpful: DOB. Note: Search requests must be on court's form.

General Information: Certification fee: $7.00 per doc includes copies.

New Castle County

Superior Court Office of the Prothonotary, 500 N King St, #500, Wilmington, DE 19801; phone: 302-255-0800; fax: 302-255-2264; hours 8:30AM-5PM (EST). *Felony, Misdemeanor, Civil Actions Over $50,000.*
http://courts.state.de.us/superior
Civil Records: Access: In person only. Visitors must perform in person searches themselves. Court makes copy: $1.50 per page. Required to search: name, years to search. Civil cases indexed by defendant, plaintiff. Civil records on computer from 4/80, prior on microfiche.

Criminal Records: Access: In person only. Visitors must perform in person searches themselves. Court makes copy: $1.50 per page. Required to search: name, DOB, years to search. Criminal records on computer from 4/80, prior on microfiche.

General Information: Public access terminal has criminal back to 1980 and civil back to 1985. No psychological evaluation, sealed records released. Certification fee: $6.00. Payee: Prothonotary's Office. Personal checks accepted. Prepayment required.

Chancery Court 500 N King St, #1551, Wilmington, DE 19801; phone: 302-255-0544; probate phone: 302-395-7800; fax: 302-255-2213; probate fax: 302-395-7801; hours 8:30AM-5PM (EST). *Civil, Probate.*
http://courts.state.de.us/chancery
Civil Records: Access: Phone, fax, mail, in person. Both court and visitors may perform in person searches. No search fee. Court makes copy: $.50 per page. $2.00 per pg if from microfilm. Required to search: name; also helpful: years to search. Civil cases indexed by defendant, plaintiff. Civil records indexed on computer since 1963, in books prior to 1963. The civil records for the Court of Chancery deal with corporate and equity matters, there is no money jurisdiction. The Register of Wills oversees estates, guardianships and probate. Mail turnaround 2 days.

General Information: Public access terminal has only civil records back to 1963. No guardianship records released. Will fax documents $10.00 1st page, $2.00 each add'l. Certification fee: $25.00. Payee: Register in Chancery (Register of Wills for Probate). Personal checks accepted. Prepayment required. Will bill fax requests. SASE requested.

Court of Common Pleas 500 N King St, Wilmington, DE 19801-3704; phone: 302-255-0900; fax: 302-255-2244; hours 8:30AM-4:30PM (EST). *Misdemeanor, Civil Actions Under $50,000.*
http://courts.state.de.us/commonpleas
Note: Fax for civil is 302-255-2245.

Civil Records: Access: Phone, fax, mail, in person. Both court and visitors may perform in person searches. No search fee. Court makes copy: $1.00 per page. Required to search: name, years to search. Civil cases indexed by defendant, plaintiff. Civil records on computer from 1989; prior records on docket books. Mail turnaround time up to 3 weeks.

Criminal Records: Access: Phone, fax, mail, in person. Both court and visitors may perform in person searches. No search fee. Court makes copy: $1.00 per page. Required to search: name, years to search; also helpful: DOB. Criminal records on computer from 1993; prior records on docket books. Mail turnaround time up to 3 weeks.

General Information: Public access terminal goes back to 1974. No closed records released. Will fax documents $1.00 per page. Certification fee: $10.00. Payee: Court of Common Pleas. No personal checks accepted. Prepayment and SASE required.

Middletown Justice of the Peace #9 757 N Broad St, Middletown, DE 19709; phone: 302-378-5221; fax: 302-378-5220; hours 8AM-4PM M,T,Th,F, Noon-8PM W (EST). *Civil Actions Under $15,000, Misdemeanor, Eviction, Small Claims.*
http://courts.state.de.us/jpcourt
Note: Due to a court fire, criminal cases 7/24/2000 to 5/1/2001 are heard at New Castle JP Court 11, 323-4450. Civil cases were heard at Prices Corner JP Court 12, 995-8646. Now, all new cases are back at here at Middletown.

Civil Records: Access: In person only. Both court and visitors may perform in person searches. Search fee: none. Court makes copy: $.25 per page. Required to search: name, years to search. Civil cases indexed by defendant. Due to fire, records on computer only back to mid-1990s. Discrepancy within this office as whether or not they will search. In the past, the Court said they will not do name searches, but will search if a civil action # is presented.

Criminal Records: Access: In person only. Both court and visitors may perform in person searches. Court makes copy: $.25 per page. Required to search: name, years to search, DOB. Due to fire, records on computer only back to mid-1990s. This office prefers that you search through the state agency, though this office did not say they would refuse all search requests.

General Information: No public access terminal. Certification fee: $10.00 per Civil doc includes copies; $7.00 per criminal doc. Only cashiers checks and money orders accepted.

New Castle Justice of the Peace #11 61

Christiana Rd, New Castle, DE 19720; phone: 302-323-4450; fax: 302-323-4452; hours Open 24 hours (EST). *Misdemeanor.*
http://courts.state.de.us/jpcourt
Criminal Records: Access: Mail, in person. Visitors must perform in person searches themselves. Search fee: $7.00 per search. Court makes copy: $7.00 per case. Required to search: name, years to search. Records indexed on computer to 1966, older records hand written in log book. Mail turnaround time 2-3 weeks.
General Information: No public access terminal. Certification fee: $7.00. Cert fee includes copies. Payee: State of Delaware. Only cashiers checks and money orders accepted. SASE required.

Prices Corner Justice of the Peace #10

210 Greenbank Rd, Wilmington, DE 19808; phone: 302-995-8640; fax: 302-995-8642; hours 8AM-10PM (EST). *Misdemeanor Traffic.*
http://courts.state.de.us/jpcourt
Criminal Records: Access: Mail, in person. Only the court performs in person searches. Search fee: $7.00 per name. Court makes copy: $.25 per page. Required to search: name, years to search, DOB. Mail turnaround time 2 weeks.
General Information: No public access terminal. Certification fee: $10.00 per doc. Payee: Justice of the Peace Court 10. Only cashiers checks and money orders accepted. Prepayment and SASE required.

Prices Corner Justice of the Peace #12

212 Greenbank Rd, Wilmington, DE 19808; phone: 302-995-8646; fax: 302-995-8642; hours 8AM-4PM (EST). *Civil Actions Under $15,000, Eviction, Small Claims.*
http://courts.state.de.us/jpcourt
Civil Records: Access: Mail, in person. Visitors must perform in person searches themselves. Court makes copy: $.25 per page; same fee for self serve. Required to search: name, years to search. Records are computerized since 8/99, prior records must be searched manually.
General Information: Public access terminal has only civil records back to 8/1999. No sealed, juvenile, adoption or mental health records released. Will fax documents to local or toll free line. Certification fee: $10.00. Payee: Justice of the Peace Court 12. Personal checks accepted. Prepayment required.

Wilmington Justice of the Peace #13

1010 Concord Ave, Concord Professional Ctr, Wilmington, DE 19802; phone: 302-577-2550; fax: 302-577-2526; hours 8AM-4PM (EST). *Civil Actions Under $15,000, Eviction, Small Claims.*
http://courts.state.de.us/jpcourt
Civil Records: Access: In person only. Visitors must perform in person searches themselves. Court makes copy: $.25 per page. Required to search: name, years to search. Civil cases indexed by defendant, plaintiff. Civil records are computerized since 9/01/99. The court will pull specific case data if CA# given, if and when time permitting.
General Information: No public access terminal. No sealed, juvenile, adoption or mental health records released. Certification fee: $10.00 per doc. Payee: Justice of the Peace Court #13. Personal checks accepted. Prepayment required.

Wilmington Justice of the Peace #15 130

Hickman Rd, #13, Claymont, DE 19703; phone: 302-798-5327; fax: 302-798-4508; hours 8AM-4PM (EST). *Misdemeanor.*
http://courts.state.de.us/jpcourt
Criminal Records: Access: Mail, in person. Only the court performs in person searches. Search fee: $7.00 per name. Fee is per case & includes certification & copy fees. Court makes copy: $.25 per page. Required to search: name, years to search, DOB; also helpful: offense. Mail turnaround time 2-4 weeks.
General Information: No public access terminal. Payee: State of Delaware. Prepayment required.

Wilmington Justice of the Peace #20

Public Safety Bldg, 300 N Walnut St, Wilmington, DE 19801; phone: 302-577-7234; fax: 302-577-7237; hours 8AM-midnight (EST). *Misdemeanor.*
http://courts.state.de.us/jpcourt
Note: This court also maintains the case records from the former JP Court #18.
Criminal Records: Access: In person only. Visitors must perform in person searches themselves. Court makes copy: $7.00 per disposition (1 copy only). Required to search: name, years to search.
General Information: No public access terminal. Certification fee: $7.00. Payee: Justice of the Peace Court #13. Only cashiers checks and money orders accepted.

Sussex County

Superior Court 1The Circle #2, Georgetown, DE

19947; criminal phone: 302-856-5741; civil phone: 302-856-5742; fax: 302-856-5739; hours 8:30AM-4:30PM (EST). *Felony, Misdemeanor, Civil Actions.*
http://courts.state.de.us/superior
Civil Records: Access: In person only. Visitors must perform in person searches themselves. Court makes copy: $.25 per page; same fee for self serve. Required to search: name, years to search. Civil cases indexed by defendant, plaintiff. Civil records on computer from 6/91 or as far back as 1980 if case was pending in 1991; microfiche prior.
Criminal Records: Access: In person only. Visitors must perform in person searches themselves. Court makes copy: $.25 per page; same fee for self serve. Required to search: name, years to search, DOB. Criminal records on manual index; computerized records since 1983.
General Information: Public access terminal has criminal back to 1983 and civil back to 1980s. No divorce, victim info, sealed records, expungments, or CCDW permit records released. Certification fee: $6.00 plus $1.00 per page after 1st three. Payee: Prothonotary. Personal checks accepted. Prepayment required.

Chancery Court 34 The Circle, PO Box 424,

Georgetown, DE 19947; phone: 302-856-5775; probate phone: 302-855-7875; hours 8:30AM-4:30PM (EST). *Civil, Probate.*
http://courts.state.de.us/chancery
Note: For probate, sent to Attention: Register in Chancery. Fees charged by Register of Wills for Probate are separate.
Civil Records: Access: Phone, mail, in person. Both court and visitors may perform in person searches. Court makes copy: $1.50 per page; same fee for self serve. Required to search: name, years to search. Civil cases indexed by defendant, plaintiff. Civil records on index books; on computer back to 1999. Mail turnaround time 1-3 days.
Mail turnaround time 1-3 days.
General Information: Public access terminal has only civil records back to 1999. All records public. Will fax documents for $10.00 plus $2.00 per each add'l page. Certification fee: $25.00 per cert. Payee: Register in Chancery (or Register of Wills for Probate). Personal checks accepted. Prepayment required.

Court of Common Pleas 1 The Circle #1,

Georgetown, DE 19947; phone: 302-856-5333; fax: 302-856-5056; hours 8:30AM-4:30PM (EST). *Misdemeanor, Civil Actions Under $50,000.*
http://courts.state.de.us/commonpleas
Civil Records: Access: Phone, fax, mail, in person. Both court and visitors may perform in person searches. Search fee: $10.00 per name. Court makes copy: $1.00 per page. Required to search: name, years to search. Civil cases indexed by defendant. Civil records on computer from 1993, on microfiche from 9/53, archived prior. Mail turnaround 1-2 weeks.
Criminal Records: Access: Phone, fax, mail, in person. Both court and visitors may perform in person searches. Search fee: $10.00 per name. Court

makes copy: $1.00 per page. Required to search: name, years to search, DOB, offense, date of offense. Criminal records on computer from 1994, on microfiche from 10/65, archived prior. Mail turnaround time 1-2 weeks.
General Information: Public access terminal has criminal back to 1994 and civil back to 1993. No closed case records released. No fee to fax documents. Certification fee: $5.00. Payee: Court of Common Pleas. Personal checks accepted. Prepayment and SASE required.

Georgetown Justice of the Peace #17

23730 Shortly Rd, Georgetown, DE 19947; phone: 302-856-1447; fax: 302-856-4654; hours 8AM-4PM (EST). *Civil Actions Under $15,000, Eviction, Small Claims.*
http://courts.state.de.us/jpcourt
Civil Records: Access: Mail, in person. Only the court performs in person searches. No search fee. Court makes copy: $.25 per page. Required to search: name, years to search. Civil cases indexed by defendant, plaintiff. Civil records on index books from 1966 to present. Mail turnaround time 1-2 days.
General Information: No public access terminal. Will fax documents to local or toll-free number. Certification fee: $10.00. Payee: State of Delaware. Personal checks accepted. Prepayment required. SASE requested.

Georgetown Justice of the Peace #3

23730 Shortly Rd, Georgetown, DE 19947; phone: 302-856-1445; fax: 302-856-5844; hours 24 hours daily (EST). *Misdemeanor.*
http://courts.state.de.us/jpcourt
Criminal Records: Access: Mail, in person. Only the court performs in person searches. Search fee: $7.00 per case. Search fee includes certification. Also must be recent case. Court makes copy: $.25 per page. Required to search: name, years to search, DOB; also helpful: SSN. Records are here from 1999 to present. On microfilm 1966-1983. From 1984-1999, records archived.
General Information: Will fax documents to local or toll-free number. Payee: State of Delaware. Prepayment required.

Millsboro Justice of the Peace #1 9 Main

St, Frankford, DE 19945; phone: 302-732-9580; fax: 302-732-9586; hours 8AM-4PM (EST). *Misdemeanor.*
http://courts.state.de.us/jpcourt
Criminal Records: Access: Mail, in person. Only the court performs in person searches. No search fee. Court makes copy: $.25 per page. Required to search: name, years to search, DOB. Records available from 1983, computerized since 1990. Mail turnaround time same day.
General Information: Prepayment required.

Rehoboth Beach Justice of the Peace #2 35252 Hudson Way, #1, Rehoboth Beach, DE

19971-9738; phone: 302-645-6163; fax: 302-645-8842; hours 8AM-Midnight (EST). *Misdemeanor.*
http://courts.state.de.us/jpcourt
Criminal Records: Access: Mail, in person. Both court and visitors may perform in person searches. No search fee. Court makes copy: $1.00 per page. Required to search: name, years to search, DOB. Records available since 1990, computerized since 1992.
General Information: No public access terminal. Certification fee: $7.00. Payee: State of Delaware. Prepayment required.

Seaford Justice of the Peace #19 408 Stein

Hwy, Seaford, DE 19973; phone: 302-629-5433; fax: 302-628-6517; hours 8AM-4PM (EST). *Civil Actions Under $15,000, Eviction, Small Claims.*
http://courts.state.de.us/jpcourt
Civil Records: Access: In person, mail. Visitors must perform in person searches themselves. Court makes copy: $.25 per page. Required to search: name, years to search. Civil cases indexed by defendant, plaintiff. Civil records in docket books since 1985;

computerized records since 9/98. In person access requires identification. Mail turnaround time 5 days.

General Information: No public access terminal. Will fax documents to local or toll-free number. Certification fee: $10.00. Payee: State of Delaware. Personal checks accepted. Prepayment required.

Seaford Justice of the Peace #4
408 Stein Hwy, Seaford, DE 19973; phone: 302-628-2036; fax: 302-528-2049; hours 8:00 am - Midnight (EST). *Misdemeanor.*
http://courts.state.de.us/jpcourt

Criminal Records: Access: Mail, in person. Visitors must perform in person searches themselves. Search fee: $7.00 per name. Court makes copy: $.25 per page. Required to search: name, years to search. Mail turnaround time varies.

General Information: No public access terminal. Certification fee: $7.00 per cert. Payee: JP Court 4. SASE required.

Justice of the Peace #6
35 Cams Fortune Way, Harrington, DE 19952-1790; phone: 302-422-5922; fax: 302-422-1527; hours 8AM-4PM (EST). *Misdemeanor.*
http://courts.state.de.us/jpcourt

Note: Some old civil cases also located here.

Criminal Records: Access: In person only. Visitors must perform in person searches themselves. Court makes copy: $1.00 per page. Required to search: name, years to search, DOB. Court refers written requests to State Bureau of Investigation in Dover at 302-739-5882.

General Information: Public access terminal has only criminal records back to 1990. No juvenile records released. Certification fee: $7.00. Payee: State of Delaware. Personal checks or Visa, MC, Discover accepted. Prepayment required.

Delaware Recording Offices

ORGANIZATION: Delaware has 3 counties and 3 recording offices. The recording officer is County Recorder in both jurisdictions. Delaware is in the Eastern Time Zone (EST).

REAL ESTATE RECORDS: Counties do not perform real estate searches, but will provide copies.

UCC RECORDS: Financing statements are filed at the state level, except for real estate related collateral, which are filed only with the County Recorder. All counties perform UCC searches. Copy and certification fees vary.

TAX LIEN RECORDS: Federal tax liens on personal property of businesses are filed with the Secretary of State. Other federal and all state tax liens on personal property are filed with the County Recorder. Copy and certification fees vary.

ONLINE ACCESS: There is no statewide online system for county recorded documents.

Kent County

County Recorder of Deeds, 414 Federal St.; County Admin. Bldg, Rm 218, Dover, DE 19901. 302-744-2314; fax-302-736-2035; hours: 8:30AM-4:30PM www.co.kent.de.us
Separate indices to search include Real property, financial statements. Records indexed on a public use terminal back to 1973. Only the public may search. Copy fee $1.00 per page. Cert fee- $5.00 per page. Payee- Kent County Recorder of Deeds. **Online access to Most Wanted records:** City of Dover most wanted list is at www.doverpolice.org/wanted.htm. **Other phones:** Treasurer- 302-744-2341; Prothonotary- 302-739-5328. **Property tax/Assessor-** 555 Bay Rd, Dover, DE 19901; 302-744-2401.

New Castle County

County Recorder of Deeds, 800 French St, 4th Fl, Wilmington, DE 19801. RE & UCC recording phone-302-395-7700; fax-302-395-7732; hours: 9AM-5PM www.ncc-deeds.com
Separate indices to search include deed, mortgage, assignments, fed liens, UCCs, satisfactions. Office will perform a UCC search but public must search other records themselves. UCC search per debtor name- $16.00. Copy fee $1.00 per page if mailed; $.25 in person. Cert fee- $1.00 per page; $5.00 if pages supplied by office, plus copy fee. Payee- New Castle County Recorder of Deeds. **Online access to Real Estate, Property Assessor, Recorder, Deed, Marriage, Incs, Sex Offender, Most Wanted records:** Records on the City of New Castle Geographic Information System database are free at www.2isystems.com/newcastle/Search2.CFM.
Property information can also be found at www.co.new-castle.de.us/ParcelView/parcelsearch.asp. No name searching. Also, access to the Recorder of Deeds database is free at www.ncc-deeds.com. Also, the sheriff's Most Wanted, sex offender and missing persons lists are at www.nccpd.com Also, City of New Castle provides an acreage search for free at www.2isystems.com/newcastle/Search2.CFM. **Other phones:** Treasurer- 302-395-5177; Appraiser/Auditor-302-395-5400; Elections- 302-577-3464; Prothonotary-302-255-0800. **Property tax/Assessor-** 302-395-5400.

Sussex County

County Recorder of Deeds, PO Box 827, Georgetown, DE 19947-0827. 302-855-7785; fax-302-855-7787; hours: 8:30AM-4:30PM
All records in one index. Records indexed on a public use terminal back to 1952. Office will perform a UCC search but public must search other records themselves. UCC search per debtor name- $10.00. General copy fee $2.00. RE record copy $5.00 1st page; $.50 each add'l pg. Cert fee-$5.00 per cert plus copy fee. Payee- Sussex County Recorder of Deeds. **Online access to Real Estate, Property Tax, Sheriff Sale records:** Access to the tax information website is free at www.sussexcounty.net/e-gov/propertytaxes/index.cfm. Also, search the GIS-mapping page for free at www.smartmap.com/sussex/. At the map page, click on "search by" and choose "tax parcel (Name)". Also access to sheriff sales data is at www.sussexsheriff.com/SheriffsSales.htm. **Other phones:** Treasurer- 302-855-7763; Prothonotary- 302-856-5740. **Property tax/Assessor-** 302-855-7824.

Delaware County Locator

You will usually be able to find the city name in the City/County Cross Reference below. In that case, it is a simple matter to determine the county from the cross reference. However, only the official US Postal Service city names are included in this index. There are an additional 40,000 place names that people use in their addresses. Therefore, we have also included a ZIP/City Cross Reference immediately following the City/County Cross Reference.

If you know the ZIP Code but the city name does not appear in the City/County Cross Reference index, look up the ZIP Code in the ZIP/City Cross Reference, find the city name, then look up the city name in the City/County Cross Reference. For example, you want to know the county for an address of Menands, NY 12204. There is no "Menands" in the City/County Cross Reference. The ZIP/City Cross Reference shows that ZIP Codes 12201-12288 are for the city of Albany. Looking back in the City/County Cross Reference, Albany is in Albany County.

Delaware City/County Cross Reference

BEAR New Castle	FELTON Kent	LINCOLN Sussex	REHOBOTH BEACH Sussex
BETHANY BEACH Sussex	FENWICK ISLAND Sussex	LITTLE CREEK Kent	ROCKLAND New Castle
BETHEL Sussex	FRANKFORD Sussex	MAGNOLIA Kent	SAINT GEORGES New Castle
BRIDGEVILLE Sussex	FREDERICA Kent	MARYDEL Kent	SEAFORD Sussex
CAMDEN WYOMING Kent	GEORGETOWN Sussex	MIDDLETOWN New Castle	SELBYVILLE Sussex
CHESWOLD Kent	GREENWOOD (19950) Sussex(65), Kent(34)	MILFORD (19963) Sussex(61), Kent(38)	SMYRNA (19977) Kent(89), New Castle(10)
CLAYMONT New Castle		MILLSBORO Sussex	
CLAYTON (19938) Kent(89), New Castle(10)	HARBESON Sussex	MILLVILLE Sussex	TOWNSEND New Castle
	HARRINGTON Kent	MILTON Sussex	VIOLA Kent
DAGSBORO Sussex	HARTLY Kent	MONTCHANIN New Castle	WILMINGTON New Castle
DELAWARE CITY New Castle	HOCKESSIN New Castle	NASSAU Sussex	WINTERTHUR New Castle
DELMAR Sussex	HOUSTON Kent	NEW CASTLE New Castle	WOODSIDE Kent
DOVER Kent	KENTON Kent	NEWARK New Castle	YORKLYN New Castle
DOVER AFB Kent	KIRKWOOD New Castle	OCEAN VIEW Sussex	
ELLENDALE Sussex	LAUREL Sussex	ODESSA New Castle	
FARMINGTON Kent	LEWES Sussex	PORT PENN New Castle	

Delaware ZIP/City Cross Reference

BEAR New Castle	FELTON Kent	LINCOLN Sussex	REHOBOTH BEACH Sussex
BETHANY BEACH Sussex	FENWICK ISLAND Sussex	LITTLE CREEK Kent	ROCKLAND New Castle
BETHEL Sussex	FRANKFORD Sussex	MAGNOLIA Kent	SAINT GEORGES New Castle
BRIDGEVILLE Sussex	FREDERICA Kent	MARYDEL Kent	SEAFORD Sussex
CAMDEN WYOMING Kent	GEORGETOWN Sussex	MIDDLETOWN New Castle	SELBYVILLE Sussex
CHESWOLD Kent	GREENWOOD (19950) Sussex(65), Kent(34)	MILFORD (19963) Sussex(61), Kent(38)	SMYRNA (19977) Kent(89), New Castle(10)
CLAYMONT New Castle		MILLSBORO Sussex	
CLAYTON (19938) Kent(89), New Castle(10)	HARBESON Sussex	MILLVILLE Sussex	TOWNSEND New Castle
	HARRINGTON Kent	MILTON Sussex	VIOLA Kent
DAGSBORO Sussex	HARTLY Kent	MONTCHANIN New Castle	WILMINGTON New Castle
DELAWARE CITY New Castle	HOCKESSIN New Castle	NASSAU Sussex	WINTERTHUR New Castle
DELMAR Sussex	HOUSTON Kent	NEW CASTLE New Castle	WOODSIDE Kent
DOVER Kent	KENTON Kent	NEWARK New Castle	YORKLYN New Castle
DOVER AFB Kent	KIRKWOOD New Castle	OCEAN VIEW Sussex	
ELLENDALE Sussex	LAUREL Sussex	ODESSA New Castle	
FARMINGTON Kent	LEWES Sussex	PORT PENN New Castle	

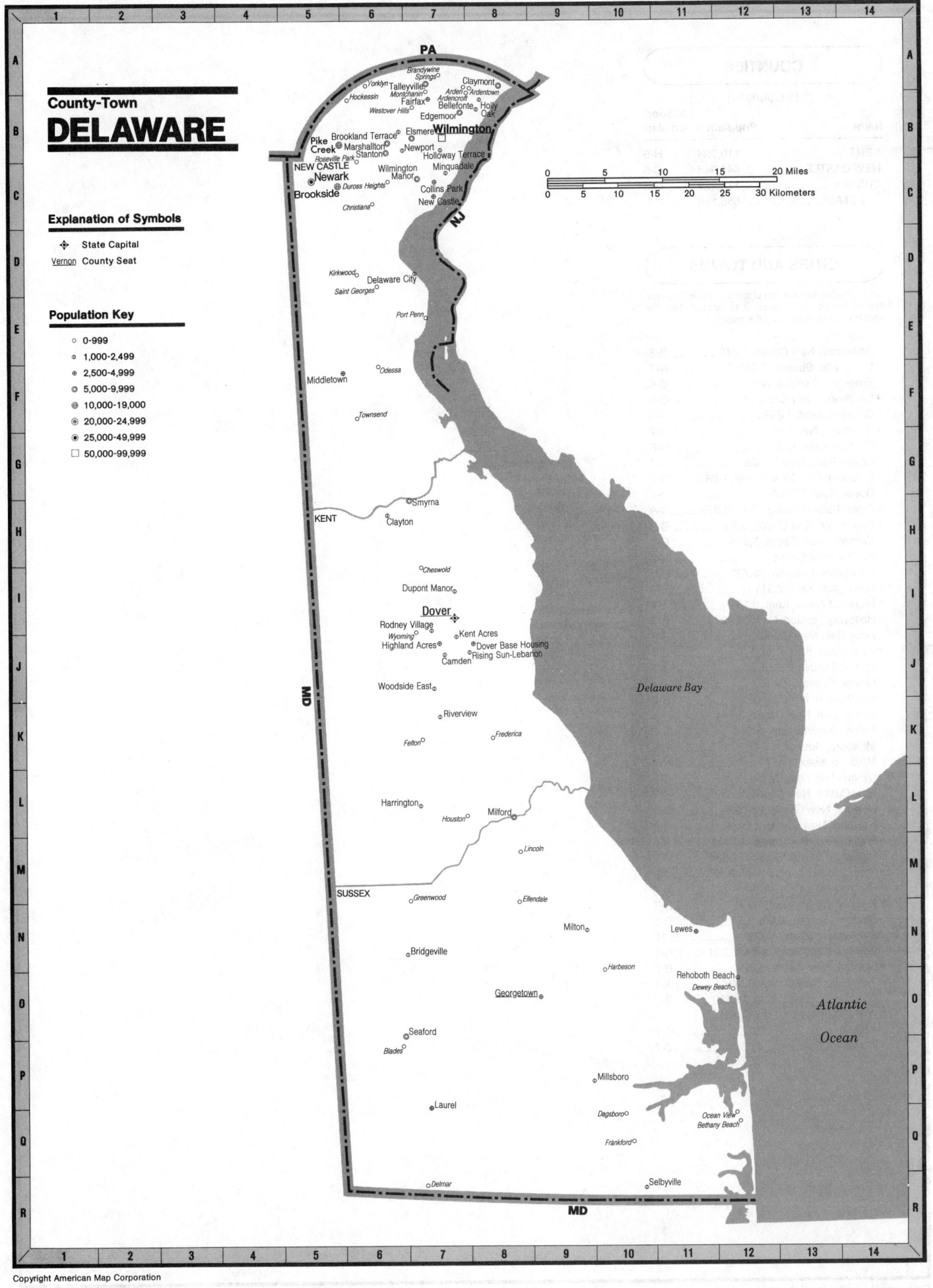

County-Town
DELAWARE

Explanation of Symbols

✛ State Capital

Vernon County Seat

Population Key

○ 0-999
◎ 1,000-2,499
◉ 2,500-4,999
◍ 5,000-9,999
◉ 10,000-19,000
◉ 20,000-24,999
◉ 25,000-49,999
☐ 50,000-99,999

COUNTIES

(3 Counties)

Name	Population	Location on Map
KENT	110,993	H-5
NEW CASTLE	441,946	C-5
SUSSEX	113,229	M-5
TOTAL	666,168	

CITIES AND TOWNS

Note: The first name is that of the city or town, second, that of the county in which it is located, then the population and location on the map.

Bellefonte, New Castle, 1,243 .... B-8
Bridgeville, Sussex, 1,210 .... N-7
Brookland Terrace, New Castle B-6
• Brookside, New Castle, 15,307 .... C-5
Camden, Kent, 1,899 .... J-7
• Claymont, New Castle, 9,800 .... A-7
Clayton, Kent, 1,163 .... H-6
Collins Park, New Castle C-7
Delaware City, New Castle, 1,682 ...... D-7
Dover, Kent, 27,630 .... I-7
• Dover Base Housing, Kent, 4,376 .... J-8
• Edgemoor, New Castle, 5,853 .... B-7
Elsmere, New Castle, 5,935 .... B-7
Fairfax, New Castle B-7
Georgetown, Sussex, 3,732 .... O-9
Harrington, Kent, 2,311 .... L-7
• Highland Acres, Kent, 3,151 .... J-7
Holloway Terrace, New Castle B-7
Holly Oak, New Castle B-8
• Kent Acres, Kent, 1,807 .... J-7
Laurel, Sussex, 3,226 .... Q-7
Lewes, Sussex, 2,295 .... N-11
Marshallton, New Castle B-6
Middletown, New Castle, 3,834 .... F-5
Milford, Kent/Sussex, 6,040 .... L-8
Millsboro, Sussex, 1,643 .... P-9
Milton, Sussex, 1,417 .... N-9
Minquadale, New Castle C-7
New Castle, New Castle, 4,837 .... C-7
Newark, New Castle, 25,098 .... C-5
Newport, New Castle, 1,240 .... B-6
• Pike Creek, New Castle, 10,163 .... B-5
Rehoboth Beach, Sussex, 1,234 ...... O-12
• Rising Sun-Lebanon, Kent, 2,177 .... J-8
• Riverview, Kent, 1,138 .... K-7
• Rodney Village, Kent, 1,745 .... I-7
Seaford, Sussex, 5,689 .... O-6
Selbyville, Sussex, 1,335 .... R-10
Smyrna, Kent/New Castle, 5,231 .... H-7
• Stanton, New Castle, 5,028 .... B-6
• Talleyville, New Castle, 6,346 .... A-7
Wilmington, New Castle, 71,529 .... B-7
• Wilmington Manor, New Castle,
  8,568 .... C-7
• Woodside East, Kent, 1,655 .... J-7

District of Columbia

General Help Numbers:

Mayor's Office

1350 Pennsylvania Ave NW
Washington, DC 20004
http://dc.gov/mayor/index.shtm

202-727-2980
Fax 202-727-0505
8:30AM-6:00PM

Legislative Records

Council of the District of Columbia
441 4th Street, Rm 714
Washington, DC 20004
www.dccouncil.washington.dc.us

202-724-8050
Fax 202-347-3070
9AM-5:30PM

District Archives

Office of Archives/Public Records
1300 Naylor Ct NW
Washington, DC 20001-4225 9AM4:00PM research hours

202-671-1105
Fax 202-727-6076

District Specifics:

Time Zone: EST

Population: 553,523

Website: www.washingtondc.gov

District Agencies

Criminal Records

Metropolitan Police Department, Identification and Records Section, 300 Indiana Ave NW, Rm 3055, Washington, DC 20001; 202-727-4245 (Police), 202-442-4247-Fax; 8AM-5PM.

www.mpdc.dc.gov/main.shtm

Records are also available with less restrictions from the Superior Court, Criminal Div. at 500 Indiana NW, Rm 4001, phone 202-879-1373. The court record mail/fax search fee is $10.00; a signed release not required there.

Records are available for 10 years. It takes 1 day before new records are available for inquiry. 46% of all arrests in database have final dispositions recorded, 84% for those arrests within last 5 years.

Searching: Records are referred to as Police Clearances. Include the following in your request-

signed, notarized release from subject, full name (middle initial), date and place of birth, year. The SSN, race, current address and case number, if known, are helpful. Although 80% of the records are fingerprint supported, fingerprints searches are not available. The following data is not released: pending cases. Neither records location will supply records without dispositions.

Access by: mail, in person.

Fee & Payment: The fee is $7.00 per name from the Police Dept. Fee payee: Superior Court, Criminal Division Out of state personal checks accepted. No credit cards accepted.

Mail search: Turnaround time: 2 to 4 weeks. A SASE is required.

In person search: Counter service is available at this address.

Sexual Offender Registry

Metropolitan Police Department, Sex Offender Registry Unit, 300 Indiana Ave NW, Rm 3009, Washington, DC 20001; 202-727-4407, 202-727-9292-Fax; 8AM-5PM.

http://mpdc.dc.gov/mpdc/site/default.asp

In general, an offense requiring registration is a felony sexual assault (regardless of the age of the victim); an offense involving sexual abuse or exploitation of minors; or sexual abuse of wards, patients, or clients.

It takes 1 day before new records are available for inquiry.

Searching: Searchers can visit any police station and inspect a public registry that will contain current information on all registered sex offenders in the District of Columbia. The following data is not released: pending cases.

Access by: fax, in person, online.

Fax search: Records may be requested by fax.

In person search: Records for all classes may be searched at this office and all local police stations in DC.

Online search: A list of Class A & B registered sex offenders is provided on the website. Under "Services" click on Sex Offender Registry.

Incarceration Records

District of Columbia Department of Corrections, DC Detention Facility, Office of Records, 1901 D. Street, SE, Washington, DC 20003; 202-673-8136, 202-673-8136 option 2 (VINE Inmate Information Line), 202-673-8257 (Administration), 8AM-5PM.

http://mpdc.dc.gov/mpdc/site/default.asp

Records are available on current and former inmates. It takes 1 day before new records are available for inquiry. Records are normally destroyed after never; records are archived.

Searching: For full information, a subpoena or signed release is required. The reason for the search must be stated in your request. For general "public" information, this agency prefers that you access the VINE telephone locator system. Include the following in your request-first and last name, DOB. SSN and PVID number helpful and requested. Type of data released varies depending on request.

Access by: mail.

Mail search: Turnaround time: 2 to 4 weeks minimum. For a search, you must provide first and last name, DOB; SSN and/or PVID number helpful.

Corporation, Limited Partnership, Limited Liability Company Records

Department of Consumer & Regulatory Affairs, Corporations Division, 941 N Capitol St NE, Washington, DC 20002; 202-442-4432, 202-442-4523-Fax; 8:30AM-4PM.

http://dcra.dc.gov/dcra/site/default.asp

Records are available from the 1850s. There is no trademark or servicemark statute. Records are indexed on inhouse computer.

Searching: Include the following in your request-full name of business. The website provides download capability of forms.

Access by: mail, phone, in person.

Fee & Payment: The fee is $35.00 per certified legal document, plain copies are not available. A Good Standing is $15.00, $18.00 for partnerships, and $30.00 if a not-for-profit. Fee payee: DC Treasury. Prepayment required. Personal checks accepted. Credit cards accepted for in person searches only.

Mail search: Turnaround time: 5 to 10 days.

Phone search: They will release agent's name and address, date of incorporation, and status over the phone at no fee. Names and addresses of Officers and Directors will not be released over the phone, unless time permits.

In person search: You may request information in person. There is no fee unless copies of documents are needed. You may use a credit card.

Other access: For information concerning lists and bulk file purchases, contact the Office of Information Services.

Uniform Commercial Code, Federal and State Tax Liens

UCC Recorder, District of Columbia Recorder of Deeds, 941 North Capitol Street, NE, Washington, DC 20002;, 202-727-5374, 8:30AM-4:30PM.

http://cfo.dc.gov/otr/site/default.asp

Records from 1983 forward are located in Room 101, prior records are in Room 304. This agency will not perform name searches (you must do yourself or hire someone).

Records are available from the 1900's; 1979 from the online system. Records are indexed on microfiche.

Searching: Local tax liens are called district tax liens. Include the following in your request-debtor name. Searches from 1973 forward are not performed by state personnel. Use the inhouse terminal or the website. Searches prior to 1973 need a book and page number.

Access by: mail, in person, online.

Fee & Payment: Copies cost $2.25 per page. Fee payee: DC Treasurer. Prepayment required. Personal checks accepted. Credit cards accepted for online service only.

Mail search: Turnaround time: 2 weeks. No name searches.

In person search: There is a public access terminal available to look up names to find instrument numbers.

Online search: Search the index by name or document number at www.washington.dc.us.landata.com/. Registration is required. There are two commercial plans to purchase images. Note this for all recorded documents, not just UCC. A Subscriber pays $175 per month for unlimited views of images and $2.00 per document image downloaded. Accounts are also available for larger firms with multiple users. A registered "non-subscriber" pays no fee to view documents and $4.00 per document mage downloaded.

Sales Tax Registrations

Office of Tax and Revenue, Sales Tax Certificates, 941 N. Capitol Street NE, Washington, DC 20002; 202-727-4829, 8:15AM-4:30PM.

http://brc.dc.gov/tax/tax.asp

Records are available from the 1980's. Records are computerized since 1990, otherwise are hard copies.

Searching: This agency will only confirm that a tax certificate number is registered. If a request is made to search by company name, requester should talk to the agency's legal department. They will provide no other information. Include the following in your request-business name, tax certification number, federal employer identification number, address.

Access by: mail, phone, fax, in person.

Mail search: Turnaround time: 3 to 5 days. A SASE is requested. No fee for mail request.

Phone search: No fee for telephone request.

Fax search: Same criteria as mail searches.

In person search: Immediate turnaround time. The Customer Service Center is on the 1st Fl.

Birth Certificates

Department of Health, Vital Records Division, 825 North Capitol St NE, 1st Fl, Washington, DC 20002; 202-442-9009, 877-572-6332 (Order), 202-442-4848-Fax; 8:30AM-3:30PM.

http://dchealth.dc.gov/services/vital_records/index.shtm

Records are available from 1874 to present. New records are available for inquiry immediately. Records are indexed on microfiche, inhouse computer. Records are normally destroyed after (records not destroyed).

Searching: Records less than 100 years old are only released to person of record or immediate family members or to legal representative of family. Requester should include a copy of photo ID and daytime phone number. Include the following in your request-full name, date of birth, place of birth, names of parents, name of the hospital.

Access by: mail, phone, fax, in person, online.

Fee & Payment: The $18.00 fee is for the short form of birth certificate for every consecutive 3 years searched. The archival long form costs $23.00. All copies are certified. Fee payee: DC Treasurer. Prepayment required. Credit cards are only accepted for expedited services. Personal checks accepted. Major credit cards accepted.

Mail search: Turnaround time: 2 weeks. All genealogical searches must be done by mail and cannot be expedited. No SASE is required.

Phone search: Phone requests are through VitalChek, are considered expedited and extra fees are involved.

Fax search: Order by fax from VitalChek at 202-783-0136.

In person search: Simple requests may be processed while you wait.

Online search: Orders may be placed online via a state designated vendor at www.vitalchek.com.

Expedited service: Expedited service is available for phone, fax and online orders. Expedited service is available from VitalChek 800-255-2414 and requires a credit card and additional $12.95 for 7-10 day delivery or $29.95 for 3-5 day service.

Death Records

Department of Health, Vital Records Division, 825 North Capitol St NE, 1st Fl, Washington, DC 20002; 202-442-9009, 877-572-6332 (Order), 8:30AM-3:30PM.

http://dchealth.dc.gov/index.asp

Request forms are available from the website.

Records are available from August 1874 on. New records are available for inquiry immediately. Records are indexed on microfiche, inhouse computer.

Searching: Records up to 50 years old are only released to immediate family members of person of record or to legal representative of family. Requester should include copy of a photo ID and daytime phone number. Include the following in your request-full name, date of death, Social Security Number.

Access by: mail, phone, fax, in person, online.

Fee & Payment: The fee is $18.00 per record. All copies are certified. Fee payee: DC Treasurer. Prepayment required. Credit cards are only accepted for expedited services. Personal checks accepted. Major credit cards accepted.

Mail search: Turnaround time: 2 weeks. Genealogical searches must be in writing and cannot be expedited. No SASE is required.

Phone search: Phone requests are through VitalChek, are considered expedited and extra fees are involved.

Fax search: Order from VitalChek at 202-783-0136.

In person search: Turnaround time is 1/2 hour unless extensive search required.

Online search: Orders may be placed online via a state designated vendor at www.vitalchek.com.

Expedited service: Expedited service is available for phone, fax and online orders. Expedited service is available from VitalChek 800-255-2414 and requires a credit card and additional $12.95 for 7-10 day delivery or $29.95 for 3-5 day service.

Marriage Certificates

Superior Court House, Marriage Bureau, 500 Indiana Ave, NW, Room 4485, Washington, DC 20001; 202-879-4840, 202-879-1280-Fax; 9AM-4PM.

Records are available from 1811 on. New records are available for inquiry immediately. Records are indexed on microfilm, books (volumes).

Searching: Include the following in your request-both names, wife's maiden name, date of marriage.

Access by: mail, in person.

Fee & Payment: Search fee is $10.00. Extra copies are $.50 per page. To search prior to 1921 there is an additional $10.00 per year charge to search. Fee payee: Clerk of the Superior Court. Prepayment required. Only money orders are accepted unless requester is an attorney or a minister/priest/rabbi. No credit cards or personal checks accepted.

Mail search: Turnaround time: 2 weeks. A SASE is requested.

In person search: Unless the request is a simple search, the results are mailed within 15 days. Turnaround time is within the same day.

Divorce Records

Superior Court House, Divorce Records, 500 Indiana Ave, NW, Room 4230, Washington, DC 20001; 202-879-1261, 202-879-1572-Fax; 8:30AM-5PM.

Records are available from 1956 on. Records prior to 1956 are located at the US District Court at 202-273-0520. New records are available for inquiry immediately. Records are indexed on microfilm, books (volumes).

Searching: Include the following in your request-names of husband and wife, date of divorce, year divorce case began, case number (if known). The following data is not released: sealed records.

Access by: mail, in person.

Fee & Payment: Search fee is $10.00. Certification is $6.50. Copy fee is $.50 per page. Fee payee: Clerk of the Superior Court. Prepayment required. Use either a money order or a cashier's check if ordering by mail. Personal checks not accepted. No credit cards accepted.

Mail search: Turnaround time: 3-6 weeks. Written requests must include requester's phone number so the court can call back with the charge. A SASE is requested.

In person search: Turnaround time is same day for record after 1993. Prior records are kept off site and will take longer to retrieve.

Workers' Compensation Records

Office of Workers' Compensation, PO Box 56098 2nd Floor, Washington, DC 20011 (Courier address: 77 P St, NE 2nd Fl, Washington, DC 20011); 202-671-1000, 202-671-1929-Fax; 8:30AM-5PM.

www.does.dc.gov/main.shtm

Records are available from June 1982 on. Records are archived after a year and will take longer to locate. Records are only from private employers. New records are available for inquiry immediately. Records are indexed on inhouse computer.

Searching: Only claimant or parties to claim can access records. All others must have signed release from claimant. Include the following in your request-claimant name, Social Security Number, date of accident, employer.

Access by: mail, fax, in person.

Fee & Payment: There is no search fee, copies are $.25 per page. Fee payee: DC Treasurer. Prepayment required. Personal checks accepted. No credit cards accepted.

Mail search: Turnaround time: 2 to 3 days. A SASE is requested.

Fax search: Limit 2 pages, turnaround time is 2-3 days.

In person search: Limited to interested parties or with signed release from claimant.

Driver Records

Department of Motor Vehicles, Driver Records Division, 65 K Street NE, Rm 200A, Washington, DC 20002; 202-727-1530, 202-727-5000 (General), 8:15AM-4PM.

www.dmv.dc.gov

Copies of tickets are available from the Bureau of Traffic Adjudication, same address. The fee is $1.00 per ticket.

Records are available for 3 years for moving violations, suspensions/revocations for 5 years, and DWIs for an indefinite period. Accidents are listed on the record if there is a conviction, but fault is not indicated.

Searching: The agency's policy is stricter than DPPA. Personal information is suppressed unless authority is granted by subject. Mail requesters must submit name and DL number; DOB is optional. Online requesters must submit DL, name and DOB; the sex and middle initial is optional. The following data is not released: SSN, height, and weight

Access by: mail, in person, online.

Fee & Payment: The cost for a driving record is $7.00 for a three or five year record and $13.00 for a ten year record. Fee payee: DC Treasurer. Prepayment required. Personal checks accepted. Credit cards accepted for in person requests.

Mail search: Turnaround time: 5 to 10 days. No SASE is required.

In person search: Walk-in requesters may obtain up to 5 records at once. Additional records are available the next day.

Online search: Online requests are taken throughout the day and are available in batch the next morning after 8:15 am. There is no minimum order requirement. Fee is $7.00 per record. Billing is a "bank" system which draws from pre-paid account. Requesters are restricted to high volume, ongoing users. Each requester must be approved and sign a contract. For more information, call 202-727-5692.

Vehicle Ownership, Vehicle Identification

Department of Motor Vehicles, Service Center, 301 "C" St, NW, Room 1157, Washington, DC 20001; 202-727-5000, 8:15AM-4PM M-T-TH-F.

www.dmv.dc.gov

Searching: Records are classified as either "Authorized" or "General." Authorized is for law enforcement. General records (DPPA permissible use purposes) suppress the SSN but show personal information. Casual requesters must have permission of the subject. The following data is not released: Social Security Numbers or financial information.

Access by: mail, in person.

Fee & Payment: The current fee is $7.00 per request for VIN, registration or lien information. Fee payee: DC Treasurer. Prepayment required. Cash is accepted for in person transactions. Personal checks accepted. No credit cards accepted.

Mail search: Turnaround time: 10 days. No SASE is required.

In person search: You may request information in person.

Other access: Bulk requests can be obtained for commercial purposes upon approval by the Director, Department of Motor Vehicles if it is determined that the requested use "is for the public interest." Commercial purposes are not permitted.

Accident Reports

Metro. Police Dept., Accident Report Section, 300 Indiana Ave NW, Room 3075, Washington, DC 20001; 202-727-4357, 9AM-4PM.

http://mpdc.dc.gov/mpdc/site/default.asp

This office holds the officer investigated accident reports known as PD-10s. "Citizen reports" are no longer required (effective 12/12/03), but older reports may be secured for $2.00 each at the Insurance Operations Branch at 202-727-4601.

Searching: Include the following in your request-full name and either date of accident and location of accident or the six-digit report number. The agency will not perform a "name only" search.

Access by: mail, in person.

Fee & Payment: The fee is $3.00 per report for walk-in or mail-in requests. There is no charge for complainants, their spouses, and parents/guardians. Fee payee: DC Treasurer. Prepayment required. Personal checks accepted. No credit cards accepted.

Mail search: Turnaround time: 3 days. A SASE is requested.

In person search: You may request information in person.

Vessel Ownership, Vessel Registration

Access to Records is Restricted.

Metropolitan Police Dept, Harbor Patrol, 550 Water St SW, Washington, DC 20024; 202-727-4582, 202-727-4383, 202-727-3663-Fax; 7AM-3PM.

http://mpdc.dc.gov/main.shtm

All vessels regardless of size must be titled and registered. Information is not open to the public. Record verifications are handled on a case-by-case basis. The agency uses discretion in release of data for lawful purposes, but does not follow DPPA.

Voter Registration

DC Board of Elections and Ethics, Voter Registration Records, 441 4th St NW, #250 North, Washington, DC 20001; 202-727-2525, 202-347-2648-Fax; 8:30AM-4:45PM.

www.dcboee.org

Records are available for active records. The database is updated every four months.

Searching: Records are open to the public. The following data is not released: Social Security Numbers or date of birth.

Access by: mail, phone, fax, in person, online.

Fee & Payment: There is no fee for a search, but there is a $.25 copy fee. Fee payee: DC Treasurer. Prepayment required. If purchasing the database,

certified funds are required. No credit cards accepted.

Mail search: Turnaround time: 7 to 10 days.

Phone search: For verification purposes only.

Fax search: Fax searching available.

In person search: Information is available immediately.

Online search: One may check voter regiatration status at www.dcboee.org/voterreg/vic_step1.asp. Name, DOB and ZIP are required.

Other access: Records can be purchased on CD, tape, and printed lists. A variety of data is available from party registration to voter history. Minimum fee is $50 plus $10 for a CD. Call at 202-727-2525 for details.

GED Certificates

GED Testing Center, State Education Agency, 4200 Connecticut Ave NW, Washington, DC 20008; 202-274-7173, 9AM-1PM.

www.dcadultliteracy.org/services/ged.html

There is a request form available from the web page.

Records are available from 1940 to present.

Searching: An examinee must request in writing that an official score report or verification be sent to a specific institution, employer, or other organization. Include the following in your request-a signed release, name at time of test, DOB, date/year test, SSN, and city of test. The requester can submit a "Fax Waiver" form so that

the transcript copy can be sent to a designated third party.

Access by: mail, in person.

Fee & Payment: There is no "verification" service. All record requests or verification requests are considered to be requests of copies of transcripts. This is $5.00 per copy. Fee payee: UDC - GED Testing Center Money orders are accepted. No credit cards accepted.

Mail search: Turnaround time is 7-10 days if record is after 1994, 2-3 weeks if prior to 1994.

In person search: Results are mailed or can be picked up.

Fishing & Hunting License Information

Access to Records is Restricted.

Environmental Health Regulation, Fisheries & Wildlife Division, 51 N Street NE - 5th Fl, Washington, DC 20002-3323; 202-535-2266, 202-535-1359-Fax; 8AM-5PM.

http://doh.dc.gov/doh/cwp/view,a,1374,Q,584468, dohNav_GID,1810,.asp

Hunting of any kind is prohibited within the District of Columbia. Fishing records are not available to the public, they are only released as a Freedom of Information Act request. Certain data may be released to attorneys for pending litigation or statistical use with a written request.

District of Columbia Licensing Agencies

For details about the agency responsible for licensing/certifying/registering an item below or in the Agency Quick Finder section, match an item's number with the number of the agency in the *Licensing Agency Information* section.

Licenses Searchable Online

Acupuncturist #2	http://dchealth.dc.gov/prof_license/services/search_licensing.asp
Addiction Counselor #2	http://dchealth.dc.gov/prof_license/services/search_licensing.asp
Alcohol Mfg./Vendor/Dist. #1	http://app.abra.dc.gov/services/license_holders.asp
Alcohol Servers/Sellers #1	http://app.abra.dc.gov/services/license_holders.asp
Alcohol Susp'd/Revoked License #1	http://app.abra.dc.gov/services/suspended_licenses.asp
Appraiser, Real Estate #5	www.asc.gov/content/category1/appr_by_state.asp
Attorney #3	www.dcbar.org/find_a_member/index.cfm
Bank #10	http://dbfi.dc.gov/dbfi/cwp/view,a,3,q,585840,dbfiNav,|31299|.asp
Check Casher #10	http://app.dbfi.dc.gov/ifs/default.asp
Chiropractor #2	http://dchealth.dc.gov/prof_license/services/search_licensing.asp
Counselor, Professional #2	http://dchealth.dc.gov/prof_license/services/search_licensing.asp
Dance Therapist #2	http://dchealth.dc.gov/prof_license/services/search_licensing.asp
Dental Hygienist #2	http://dchealth.dc.gov/prof_license/services/search_licensing.asp
Dentist #2	http://dchealth.dc.gov/prof_license/services/search_licensing.asp
Dietitian/Nutritionist #2	http://dchealth.dc.gov/prof_license/services/search_licensing.asp
Educational Institution, Higher #8	http://dcra.dc.gov/dcra/cwp/view,a,1342,q,600631,dcraNav_GID,1697,dcraNav,|33466|.asp
Insurance Company #12	http://disb.dc.gov/disr/cwp/view,a,1300,q,581346,disrnav_gid,1644.asp
Investment Advisor #7	www.nasdbrokercheck.com
Investment Advisor Rep. #7	www.nasdbrokercheck.com
Lobbyist #9	http://ocf.dc.gov/rep/repocf4.shtm
Massage Therapist #2	http://dchealth.dc.gov/prof_license/services/search_licensing.asp
Medical Doctor #2	http://dchealth.dc.gov/prof_license/services/search_licensing.asp
Midwife Nurse #2	http://dchealth.dc.gov/prof_license/services/search_licensing.asp
Money Lender #10	http://app.dbfi.dc.gov/ifs/default.asp
Money Transmitter #10	http://app.dbfi.dc.gov/ifs/default.asp
Mortgage Broker/Lender #10	http://app.dbfi.dc.gov/ifs/default.asp
Naturopath #2	http://dchealth.dc.gov/prof_license/services/search_licensing.asp
Nurse Anesthetist #2	http://dchealth.dc.gov/prof_license/services/search_licensing.asp
Nurse, Clinical #2	http://dchealth.dc.gov/prof_license/services/search_licensing.asp
Nurse-LPN #2	http://dchealth.dc.gov/prof_license/services/search_licensing.asp
Nurse-RN #2	http://dchealth.dc.gov/prof_license/services/search_licensing.asp
Nursing Home Administrator #2	http://dchealth.dc.gov/prof_license/services/search_licensing.asp
Occupational Therapist #2	http://dchealth.dc.gov/prof_license/services/search_licensing.asp
Optometrist #2	www.arbo.org/index.php?action=findanoptometrist
Osteopath #2	http://dchealth.dc.gov/prof_license/services/search_licensing.asp
Pharmacist/Pharmacy #2	http://dchealth.dc.gov/prof_license/services/search_licensing.asp
Physical Therapist #2	http://dchealth.dc.gov/prof_license/services/search_licensing.asp
Physician Assistant #2	http://dchealth.dc.gov/prof_license/services/search_licensing.asp
Podiatrist #2	http://dchealth.dc.gov/prof_license/services/search_licensing.asp
Political Campaign Contributor #9	http://ocf.dc.gov/dsearch/dsearch.asp
Psychologist #2	http://dchealth.dc.gov/prof_license/services/search_licensing.asp
Real Estate Appraiser #5	www.asc.gov/content/category1/appr_by_state.asp
Real Estate School #5	http://dcra.dc.gov/dcra/cwp/view,a,1342,q,600757,dcraNav_GID,1697,dcraNav,|33466|.asp
Recreational Therapist #2	http://dchealth.dc.gov/prof_license/services/search_licensing.asp
Respiratory Care #2	http://dchealth.dc.gov/prof_license/services/search_licensing.asp
Sales Finance Company #10	http://app.dbfi.dc.gov/ifs/default.asp
Securities Agent #7	www.nasdbrokercheck.com
Securities Broker/Dealer #7	www.nasdbrokercheck.com
Social Worker #2	http://dchealth.dc.gov/prof_license/services/search_licensing.asp
Taxi Dispatch #6	www.dctaxi.dc.gov/dctaxi/cwp/view.asp?a=1187&q=487917
Taxi Fleet/Company #6	www.dctaxi.dc.gov/dctaxi/cwp/view.asp?a=1187&q=487910
Taxi Insurer #6	www.dctaxi.dc.gov/dctaxi/cwp/view.asp?a=1187&q=487938

District of Columbia Licensing Quick Finder

Acupuncturist #2	202-724-4900
Addiction Counselor #2	202-724-4900
Air Conditioning/Refrigeration #5	202-442-4459
Alcohol Mfg./Vendor/Dist. #1	202-442-4423
Alcohol Permit #1	202-442-4423
Alcohol Servers/Sellers #1	202-442-4423
Alcohol Susp'd/Revoked License #1	202-442-4423
Appraiser, Real Estate #5	202-442-4472
Architect #5	202-442-4461
Asbestos Abatement Worker/Contr. #5	202-442-4459
Attorney #3	202-626-3475
Attorney Discipline Case #3	202-638-1501
Auctioneer #5	202-442-9200
Automobile Repossessor #5	202-442-9200
Bank #10	202-727-1563
Barber #5	202-442-4459
Bingo Operation #13	202-645-8041
Boxing Event/Professional #5	202-442-4472
Check Casher #10	202-727-1563
Chiropractor #2	202-724-4900
Contractor, Mechanical/Residential #5	202-442-4459
Cosmetologist #5	202-442-4459
Counselor, Professional #2	202-724-4900
Credit Union #10	202-727-1563
Dance Therapist #2	202-724-4900
Dental Hygienist #2	202-724-4900
Dentist #2	202-724-4900
Dietitian/Nutritionist #2	202-724-4900
Educational Institution, Higher #8	202-442-5377
Electrician #5	202-442-4459
Emergency Medical Technician #11	202-442-9111
Engineer #5	202-442-4459
Engineer, Steam #5	202-442-4459
Fair Housing Provider #5	202-442-4400
Firearms Instructor #14	410-799-0191
Firearms Permit #14	410-799-0191
Funeral Director #5	202-442-4461

Gas Fitter #5	202-442-4459
Hearing Aid Dispenser #2	202-724-4900
Insurance Broker/Agent #12	202-727-7425
Insurance Company #12	202-727-7425
Interior Designer #5	202-442-4461
Investment Advisor #7	202-442-4934
Investment Advisor Rep. #7	202-442-4934
K-9 Units #14	410-799-0191
Lobbyist #9	202-671-0550
Lottery Retailer #13	202-645-8042
Massage Therapist #2	202-724-4900
Mechanic, Master #5	202-442-9200
Medical Doctor #2	202-724-4900
Midwife Nurse #2	202-724-4900
Money Lender #10	202-727-1563
Money Transmitter #10	202-727-1563
Mortgage Broker/Lender #10	202-727-1563
Motor Vehicle Dealer/Salesperson #5	202-442-9200
Naturopath #2	202-724-4900
Notary Public #15	202-727-3117
Nurse Anesthetist #2	202-724-4900
Nurse, Clinical #2	202-724-4900
Nurse-LPN / RN #2	202-724-4900
Nursing Home Administrator #2	202-724-4900
Occupational Therapist #2	202-724-4900
Optometrist #2	202-724-4900
Osteopath #2	202-724-4900
Parking Lot Attendant #5	202-442-9200
Pesticide Applicator #4	202-535-2299
Pesticide Dealer #4	202-535-2299
Pesticide Employee/Operator #4	202-535-2299
Pharmacist/Pharmacy #2	202-724-4900
Physical Therapist #2	202-724-4900
Physician Assistant #2	202-724-4900
Plumber #5	202-727-1000
Podiatrist #2	202-724-4900
Political Campaign Contributor #9	202-671-0550

Private Investigator #14	410-799-0191
Property Manager #5	202-442-9200
Psychologist #2	202-724-4900
Psychometrist/School Psychologist #8	202-442-5377
Public Accountant #5	202-442-4461
Real Estate Agent/Broker/Sales #5	202-442-4400
Real Estate Appraiser #5	202-442-4472
Real Estate School #5	202-442-4400
Recreational Therapist #2	202-724-4900
Respiratory Care #2	202-724-4900
Sales Finance Company #10	202-727-1563
Savings & Loan Company #10	202-727-1563
School Athletic Trainer/Coach #8	202-442-5377
School Attendance Officer/Worker #8	202-442-5377
School Counselor #8	202-442-5377
School Librarian/Media Specialist #8	202-442-5377
School Social Worker #8	202-442-5377
School, Degree/Non-Degree Granting #5	202-442-4314 or 4465
Securities Agent/Broker/Dealer #7	202-442-4934
Security Agency / Guard #14	410-799-0191
Security Alarm Dealer/Agent #5	202-442-9200
Social Worker #2	202-724-4900
Solicitor #5	202-442-9200
Solid Waste Collector #5	202-442-9200
Speech Language Pathologist/Audiologist #8	202-442-5377
Steam Fitter #5	202-442-4459
Surveyor, Land #5	202-442-4459
Taxi Dispatch #6	202-645-6018
Taxi Fleet/Company #6	202-645-6018
Taxi Insurer #6	202-645-6018
Teacher/Teacher Trainer #8	202-442-5377
Tour Guide #5	202-442-9200
Trust Company #10	202-727-1563
Veterinarian #5	202-442-9200
Wrestling Event/Professional #5	202-442-4472

Licensing Agency Information

1 Department of Consumer Regulatory Affairs, Alcohol & Beverage Control Division, 941 N Capitol St NE #7200, Washington, DC 20002-4259; 202-442-4423, Fax: 202-727-9685. www.abra.dc.gov Search Database at http://app.abra.dc.gov/services/license_holders.asp

2 Department of Consumer & Regulatory Affairs, Health Professional Licensing, 717 14th Street NW #600, Washington, DC 20005; 202-724-4900, Fax: 202-727-8471. http://dchealth.dc.gov/prof_license/services/main.asp Search Database at http://dchealth.dc.gov/prof_license/services/search_licensing.asp

3 District of Columbia Bar Association, 1250 H St NW, 6th Fl, Washington, DC 20005; 202-737-4700, Fax: 202-626-3471. www.dcbar.org Search Database at www.dcbar.org/find_a_member/index.cfm

4 Department of Health, Bureau of Hazardous & Toxic Substances, 51 N St NE, 3rd Fl, #3032, Washington, DC 20002; 202-535-2299, Fax: 202-535-2483. http://doh.dc.gov/services/administration_offices/environmental/services2/tsd/index.shtm Email: gholmes@dchealth.com Note: Also, check licensees through the Dept. of Consumer Affairs at 202-442-4400.

5 Department of Consumer & Regulatory Affairs, License & Certification Division - Central

Verifications, 941 N Capitol St NE, Washington, DC 20002-4259; 202-442-4400. http://dcra.dc.gov/dcra/site/default.asp

6 DC Taxicab Commission, 2041 Martin Luther King Junior Ave, SE, #204, Washaington, DC 20020-7024; 202-645-6018, Fax: 202-889-3604. www.dctaxi.dc.gov/dctaxi/site/default.asp Email: dctc@dc.gov Search Database at www.dctaxi.dc.gov/dctaxi/site/default.asp

7 Department of Insurance & Securities Regulation, Securities Bureau, 810 1st St NE #602, Washington, DC 20002-4227; 202-727-8000, Fax: 202-442-0661. www.disr.dc.gov Email: Maurice.goff@dc.gov

8 District of Columbia Public Schools, Licensure & Credentials, 825 N Capitol St NE, 7th Floor, Washington, DC 20002; 202-442-5377, Fax: 202-442-5311. www.k12.dc.us/dcps/home.html

9 Director of Campaign Finance, Office of Campaign Finance, 2000 14th St NW, #420, Washington, DC 20009; 202-671-0550, Fax: 202-671-0658. http://ocf.dc.gov/index.shtm

10 Economic Development, Banking & Financial Institutions Office, 810 1st St NE #701, Washington, DC 20002; 202-727-1563, Fax: 202-727-1290.

http://dbfi.dc.gov/dbfi Search Database at http://app.dbfi.dc.gov/ifs/default.asp

11 Emergency, Health & Medical Svcs. Office, 64 New York Ave NE #5000, Washington, DC 20002; 202-671-4222, Fax: 202-671-0707. http://doh.dc.gov/services/administration_offices/ehms/services.shtm Email: sadams@dchealth.com

12 Department of Insurance & Securities Regulation, Insurance Licensing Division, 810 1st St NE #701, Washington, DC 20002; 202-727-8000. www.disr.washingtondc.gov Email: disr@dcgov.org

13 Lottery & Charitable Games Control Board, 2101 Martin Luther King Jr Ave SE, Washington, DC 20020; 202-645-8041, Fax: 202-645-0006. www.dclottery.com/

14 Metropolitian Police Department, Licensing Division, 7751 Washington Blvd, Jessup, MD 20794; 410-799-0191, Fax: 410-799-5934.

15 Notary Commissions & Authentications Section, Office of the Secretary, 441 4th St NW #810A South, Washington, DC 20001; 202-727-3117, Fax: 202-727-8457. http://os.dc.gov/os/cwp/view%2Ca%2C1206%2Cq%2C522329.asp

District of Columbia Federal Courts

US District Court

District of Columbia

Washington DC Division Clerk's Office, US Courthouse, Rm 1225, 333 Constitution Ave NW, Washington, DC 20001 (also use mail address for courier delivery), 202-727-3000, records rm- 202-354-3080, crim dockets- 202-354-3060, civil dockets- 202-354-3120, Fax-202-354-3524. Hours- 8:30AM-4:30PM. www.dcd.uscourts.gov

Counties: District of Columbia.

Searches & Indexing: Results include DOB. Both computer and card indexes maintained. Civil records indexed on computer back to 1987; includes an archive program of some older cases. Microfiche from 1932 to mid-1991. Criminal records indexed on computer since mid-1991; microfiche 1932 to mid-1991. New cases in the index 48 hours after filing date. District-wide searches available here. Copies available through a copy service; turnaround time 3-5 days.

Fee & Payment: Pay by money order or cashier's check. Payee: Clerk, US District Court. Prepayment required.

Phone Search: Searchers calling locally are not given information via phone. Out of state calls are given the 3 most current docket entries only. Archived records not available via phone; court must be contacted in writing.

Mail Search: search usually completed- 7 days. Include SASE for return.

In Person Search: Fee charged if court performs your search. Copying available from I.T.S. copy service, 202-857-3800.

E-Services: ECF replaces PACER. ECF at https://ecf.dcd.uscourts.gov **Opinions Online:** www.dcd.uscourts.gov/court-opinions.html. **Other Online Access:** Weekly court schedules at www.dcd.uscourts.gov/court-schedules.html.

US Bankruptcy Court

District of Columbia

Washington DC Division Court Clerk, E Barrett Prettyman Courthouse, Rm 4400, 333 Constitution Ave NW, Washington, DC 20001 (also use mail address for courier delivery), 202-565-2500. Hours- 9AM-4PM. www.dcb.uscourts.gov

Counties: District of Columbia.

Searches & Indexing: Cases indexed by debtor, creditors, and case number. Results include last 4 SSN digits. Both computer and card indexes maintained, after 10/6/03 records on computer only. Records indexed on computer back to 1990. New cases in the index 24 hours after filing date. Records purged every 6 months.

Fee & Payment: Pay by money order, cashier check, business check. No personal checks. Payee: Clerk, US Bankruptcy Court. Prepayment required. Cash accepted in person.

Phone Search: Voice Case Information Service available, call VCIS at 202-208-1365.

Mail Search: search usually completed- within 7 days. Include SASE for return.

In Person Search: permitted. Outside copy service available for more than 10 copies; call I.T.S., 202-857-3837. No self-serve copier available.

E-Services: ECF replaces PACER whose records did go back to 1991. ECF at https://ecf.dcb.uscourts.gov **Opinions Online:** www.dcb.uscourts.gov/decisions.htm.

Standards for Federal Courts: Search fee is $26.00 per item (one party name or case number). Copy fee is $.50 per page. Certification fee is $9.00 per document, double for exemplification, if available. All fees standard unless noted in profile. Mail Search: always enclose a stamped self addressed envelope unless otherwise noted. Most courts accept fax requests or will suggest a copying/search vendor. Before releasing records, all courts require prepayment, unless noted.

Open records are located at the court unless otherwise noted. District courts index by defendant and plaintiff as well as by case number. Bankruptcy courts usually index by debtor and case number. While most courts now have their indexes on computer, many may still maintain index card files as well.

Courts offering internet access via CM-ECF or older RACER, PACER, or Web-PACER systems charge $.08 per page fee unless noted as free. Where PACER is available, the universal sign-up number is 800-676-6856. Find PACER and the US Party/Case Index at http://pacer.psc.uscourts.gov.

District of Columbia Courts

Court	Jurisdiction	No. of Courts	How Organized
Superior Courts*	General	3	
Probate/Tax Court*	Special	1	

* Profiled in this Sourcebook.

Court	CIVIL								
	Tort	Contract	Real Estate	Min. Claim	Max. Claim	Small Claims	Estate	Eviction	Domestic Relations
Superior Courts*	X	X	X	$5000	No Max	$5000		X	X
Probate/Tax Courts*							X		

Court	CRIMINAL				
	Felony	Misdemeanor	DWI/DUI	Preliminary Hearing	Juvenile
Superior Courts*	X	X	X	X	X
Probate/Tax Courts*					

ADMINISTRATION   Executive Office, 500 Indiana Av NW, Room 1500, Washington, DC, 20001; 202-879-1700, Fax: 202-879-4829. www.dcsc.gov

COURT STRUCTURE   The Superior Court in DC is divided into 17 divisions, 4 of which are shown in this book: Criminal, Civil, Landlord & Tenant, and Tax-Probate. The Tax-Probate Div. of the Superior Court handles probate. Eviction is part of the Landlord & Tenant Branch (202-879-4879).

ONLINE ACCESS   The Superior Court and Court of Appeals offer access to opinions at www.dcbar.org

Superior Court - Criminal Division 500 Indiana Ave NW, Rm 4001, Washington, DC 20001; phone: 202-879-1373; fax: 202-879-0146; hours 8:30AM-5PM (EST). *Felony, Misdemeanor.* www.dcsc.gov

Criminal Records: Access: Mail, fax, in person. Visitors must perform in person searches themselves. Search fee: $10.00 (if name search required). No copy fee.Self serve copy fee: $.25 per page. Required to search: name, years to search, DOB. Criminal records on computer from 1978, on microfiche from 1974, on index from 1970, archived from 1962. This court recommends that you contact the Metro DC Police to perform a "police clearance" record check for $7.00. ID and signed release is required. Metro Police is at 202-727-4245, ID & Records Sec., Mail Correspondence Sec., 300 Indiana Av NW, DC 20001 See the State section under District of Columbia "Criminal Records" Mail turnaround time depends on case involved.

General Information: Public access terminal has criminal records back to 1978. (Three public access terminals available, includes Traffic cases index.) No sealed records released. Will not fax documents. No certification fee .

Superior Court - Civil Division 500 Indiana Ave NW, JM 170, Washington, DC 20001; phone: 202-879-1133; criminal phone: 202-879-1373; fax: 202-879-8335; hours 8:30AM-5PM (EST). *Civil Actions, Small Claims.* www.dcbar.org/dcsc/

Note: Small Claims is a separate branch that handles claims of $5,000 or less.

Civil Records: Access: Phone, mail, in person, online. Both court and visitors may perform in person searches. Search fee: $10.00 per name. Court makes copy: $.25 per page. Required to search: name. Civil cases indexed by defendant, plaintiff. Civil records on computer from 1983, on microfiche, archived and on index from 1976. Attorneys and legal professionals participating in the e-Filing Project must register for the CourtLink eFile service either by logging onto www.courtlink.com or calling 1-888-529-7587. Note: Only out-of-District inquires are taken by phone. Mail turnaround time depends on case involved.

General Information: Public access terminal has civil records back to 1983. No sealed records released. Certification fee: $5.00. Payee: Clerk-Superior Court of DC. Only cashiers checks and money orders accepted. Prepayment and SASE required.

Superior Court - Landlord & Tenant Branch 409 E Street NW Rm110, Washington, DC 20001; phone: 202-879-4879; hours 8:30AM-5PM M-F; 9AM-N Sat; 6:30-8PM Wed evenings (EST). *Eviction.* www.dcsc.gov

Note: This information applies to the Landlord & Tenant Branch only.

Civil Records: Access: In person, mail. Both court and visitors may perform in person searches. Search fee: $10.00. Court makes copy: $.50 each. Required to search: name, years to search; also helpful-case number. Civil records go back to 1994; computerized records go back 5 years. Note: Only out-of-District inquires are taken by phone. Mail turnaround time depends on case involved.

General Information: Public access terminal has civil records. Certification fee: $5.00. Payee: Clerk-Superior Court of DC. Prepayment required.

Superior Court - Probate Division 500 Indiana Ave NW, #5000, Washington, DC 20001; phone: 202-879-1499; fax: 202-393-5849; hours 8:30AM-5PM (EST). *Probate.*

District of Columbia Recording Offices

ORGANIZATION: District of Columbia is in the Eastern Time Zone (EST).

REAL ESTATE RECORDS: The District does not perform real estate searches.

UCC RECORDS: Financing statements are filed with the Recorder, including real estate related collateral. UCC searches performed for $30.00 per debtor name. Copies cost $2.25 per page.

TAX LIEN RECORDS: Federal tax liens on personal property of businesses are filed with the Secretary of State. Other federal and all state tax liens on personal property are filed with the Recorder.

ONLINE ACCESS: Search the recorders database at http://www.washington.dc.us.landata.com/. Registration is required; images are available for free, temporarily. Also, search the real property tax database for free at http://cfo.dc.gov/otr/cwp/view,a,1330,q,594345.asp

District of Columbia

Recorder of Deeds, 515 D St NW; Rm 203, Washington, DC 20001. 202-727-5374; fax-202-727-9629; hours: 8:30AM-4:30PM www.dc.gov

All records in one index. Only the public may search. Copy fee $2.25. A $6.50 surcharge is added to each Land Document or General Document processed. Cert fee- $2.25 per page includes copy fee. Payee- D.C. Treasurer.

Online access to Real Estate, Assessor, Recording, Deed, Judgment, Lien, UCC records: Search the recorders database at www.washington.dc.us.landata.com. Registration is required; search index for free; $4.00 fee to view and copy. Subscribe for $175.00 per month or per use, and get docs for $2.00 per page. Records go back to 1973.

Also, you may search the real property tax database online free at http://cfo.dc.gov/otr/cwp/view,a,1330,q,594345.asp Search the DC legislation record at www.dccouncil.washington.dc.us/lims/SearchForm.asp

Other phones: Treasurer- 202-727-6055.

Property tax/Assessor- 941 N Cap St NE, Washingtin, DC 20002; 202-442-7024.

District of Columbia County Locator

You will usually be able to find the city name in the City/County Cross Reference below. In that case, it is a simple matter to determine the county from the cross reference. However, only the official US Postal Service city names are included in this index. There are an additional 40,000 place names that people use in their addresses. Therefore, we have also included a ZIP/City Cross Reference immediately following the City/County Cross Reference.

If you know the ZIP Code but the city name does not appear in the City/County Cross Reference index, look up the ZIP Code in the ZIP/City Cross Reference, find the city name, then look up the city name in the City/County Cross Reference. For example, you want to know the county for an address of Menands, NY 12204. There is no "Menands" in the City/County Cross Reference. The ZIP/City Cross Reference shows that ZIP Codes 12201-12288 are for the city of Albany. Looking back in the City/County Cross Reference, Albany is in Albany County.

District of Columbia
City/County Cross Reference

ANACOSTIA ANNEX District of Columbia

NAVAL ANACOST ANNEX District of Columbia

WASHINGTON District of Columbia

WASHINGTON NAVY YARD District of Columbia

District of Columbia
ZIP/City Cross Reference

20000-20099	WASHINGTON
20201-20330	WASHINGTON
20332-20373	WASHINGTON
20373-20373	ANACOSTIA ANNEX
20373-20373	NAVAL ANACOST ANNEX
20374-20374	WASHINGTON
20374-20374	WASHINGTON NAVY YARD
20375-20376	WASHINGTON
20376-20376	WASHINGTON NAVY YARD
20380-20388	WASHINGTON
20388-20388	WASHINGTON NAVY YARD
20389-20391	WASHINGTON
20391-20391	WASHINGTON NAVY YARD
20392-20398	WASHINGTON
20398-20398	WASHINGTON NAVY YARD
20401-20599	WASHINGTON
20511-20511	WASHNGTON, DIR NATIONAL INTELLIGENCE
56901-56920	WASHINGTON

General Help Numbers:

Governor's Office

The Capitol,PL05 400 S Monroe St   850-488-4441
Tallahassee, FL 32399-0001   Fax 850-487-0801
www.myflorida.com/b_eog/owa/b_eog_www.html.main_page
    8AM-5PM

Attorney General's Office

Legal Affairs Department   850-414-3300
The Capitol, PL-01   Fax 850-410-1630
Tallahassee, FL 32399-1050   8AM-5PM
http://myfloridalegal.com/

Legislative Records

Legislative Information Services Division   850-488-4371
111 W Madison St, Rm 704   Fax 850-921-5334
Tallahassee, FL 32399-1400   8AM-5PM
www.flsenate.gov/Welcome/index.cfm

State Archives

Archives & Records   850-245-6700
R A Gray Bldg, 500 S Bronough   Fax 850-488-4894
Tallahassee, FL 32399-1400   8AM-5PM
http://dlis.dos.state.fl.us/barm/

State Specifics:

Capital: Tallahassee
Leon County

Time Zone: EST*

* Florida's ten western-most counties are CST:
They are: Bay, Calhoun, Escambia, Gulf, Holmes,
Jackson, Okaloosa, Santa Rosa, Walton, Washington.

Number of Counties: 67

Population: 17,397,161

Website: www.myflorida.com/

State Agencies

Criminal Records

Florida Department of Law Enforcement, User Services Bureau, PO Box 1489, Tallahassee, FL 32302 (Courier address: 2331 Phillip Rd, Tallahassee, FL 32308); 850-410-8109, 850-410-8107, 850-410-8201-Fax; 8AM-5PM.

www.fdle.state.fl.us

Records are available from the early 1930's. It takes 1 day before new records are available for inquiry. Records are indexed on microfilm, NIST

Archive inhouse computer. 70% of all felony arrests in database have final dispositions recorded; 63% of misdemeanors. 68% of all records within last 5 years include dispositions.

Searching: The SSN is suppressed except for the last 4 digits. Include the following in your request-date of birth, race, sex, name. You can submit fingerprints, for the same fee, but it is not required. 100% of the arrest records are fingerprint-supported. The following data is not released: sealed or expunged records, juvenile records prior

to 10/94. All records are released, including those without dispositions.

Access by: mail, in person, online.

Fee & Payment: The fee is $23.00 per individual. Pre-paid accounts receive turnaround time of two to five working days. Fee payee: Department of Law Enforcement. Prepayment required. Personal checks accepted. Credit cards accepted only for online requests.

Mail search: Turnaround time: 5 working days. No SASE is required.

In person search: In person requests are treated the same as mail requests; processing takes 5 working days.

Online search: Criminal history information from 1967 forward may be ordered over the Department Program Internet site at http://www2.fdle.state.fl.us. The $23.00 fee applies. Juvenile records from 10/1994 forward are also available. Credit card ordering will return records to your screen or via email. Search state's most wanted list at http://www3.fdle.state.fl.us/fdle/wpersons_search.asp.

Statewide Court Records

State Courts Administrator, 500 S Duval, Supreme Court Bldg, Tallahassee, FL 32399-1900; 850-922-5081, 850-488-0156-Fax; 8AM-5PM.

www.flcourts.org

Except for certain online research capabilities, all trial court record access must be done at the local level.

Searching: The Clerk of the Circuit Court cannot place an image or copy of the following documents on a publicly available Internet website for general public display.

Access by: online.

Online search: Many Clerk of Courts/Recorders give access to index data at www.myflorida.com, a government sponsored web site. Supreme Court dockets are available online at http://jweb.flcourts.org/pls/docket/ds_docket_search.

Sexual Offender Registry

Florida Department of Law Enforcement, Sexual Offender/Predator Unit, PO Box 1489, Tallahassee, FL 32302 (Courier: 2331 Phillips Rd, Tallahassee, FL 32308); 888-357-7332, 850-410-8572, 850-410-8599-Fax; 8AM-6:30PM.

http://www3.fdle.state.fl.us/sopu/index.asp?PSessionId=824514917&

Chapter 97-299, Laws of Florida, requires certain sex offenders to directly register with law enforcement or to have information compiled by the Department of Corrections, with the information to be provided to FDLE.

Records are available from 10/01/97. It takes 1 day before new records are available for inquiry.

Searching: Under Chapter 119, Florida Statutes, the Public Records Law, any of the public records of the Department of Law Enforcement are available for review upon request, subject to statutorily-authorized editing of exempt or confidential information. Include the following in your request-name and address.

Access by: mail, phone, fax, online.

Fee & Payment: If documents need printing or are substandard forms, then fees may be involved. Fee payee: FDLE Prepayment required. Personal checks accepted. Credit cards not accepted.

Mail search: Turnaround time: 5 working days. No SASE required.

Phone search: The toll free number is manned from 8AM until 6:30PM.

Fax search: Search criteria is the same phone search.

Online search: Search the registry from the web page. Searching can be done by name or by geographic area.

Incarceration Records

Florida Department of Corrections, Central Records Office, 2601 Blair Stone Rd, Tallahassee, FL 32399-2500; 850-2533, 850-488-1503 (Records), 850-922-0000 (Parole Commission), 850-413-8302-Fax; 8AM-5PM.

www.dc.state.fl.us

Full records are housed at the individual institutions, though inmate information available through this agency and the website should sufficiently fulfill most searches.

Records are available on current and former inmates. It takes 1 day before new records are available for inquiry. Records are indexed on paper, then scanned and stored in database. Image database goes back to 1997. Records are normally destroyed after imaging the paper records.

Searching: Location, DOC number, physical identifiers, conviction information, and release dates are released. Include the following in your request-first and last name and DOB. The SSN and DOC number are helpful.

Access by: mail, phone, fax, in person, online.

Fee & Payment: Fee is $.15 per copy. There is $12.00 per hour search fee (minimum is $12.00). Fee payee: Florida Department of Corrections

Mail search: Turnaround time: 14-30 working days. No SASE is required.

Phone search: Searching limited to general "public" information is available by phone.

Fax search: Fax requesting available.

In person search: In person requesters must call for appointment for a Public File Review; please call two weeks in advance.

Online search: Extensive search capabilities are offered from the website. Click on Inmate Population Information Search. Also, a private company offers free web access at www.vinelink.com/index.jsp. Includes state, DOC, and 44 county jail systems.

Other access: The monthly-updated inmate database is available for $83.00.

Corporation Records
Limited Partnership,
Limited Liability Company,
Trademarks/Servicemarks,
Fictitious Names,
Federal Tax Liens

Division of Corporations, Department of State, PO Box 6327, Tallahassee, FL 32314 (Courier address: 409 E Gaines St, Tallahassee, FL 32399); 800-755-5111 (Telephone Inquiries), 850-245-6053 (Copy Requests), 850-245-6056 (Annual Reports), 8AM-5PM.

www.sunbiz.org

This agency recommends accessing the Internet site. Send requests for Judgment Lien Filings to PO Box 6250, Tallahassee 32314.

Records are available from the late 1800's. New records are available for inquiry immediately. Records are indexed on inhouse computer, on-line.

Searching: Other fees note - LLC status is $5.00, LLC certified copy of record is $30.00. Include the following in your request-full name of business. In addition to the articles of incorporation, corporation records include the following information: Annual Reports (date of filing and updates), Officers, Directors, Prior (merged) names, Inactive names, and US Tax ID number. The following data is not released: addresses of judges and police.

Access by: mail, phone, fax, in person, online.

Fee & Payment: In person copies are $1.00 per page, certified copies are $8.75 for the first 8 pages and $1.00 for each additional page, not to exceed $52.50. By mail, a flat fee of $8.75 for certification and $10.00 for copies of complete record. Fee payee: Secretary of State. Prepayment required. Personal checks accepted. Accepts credit cards for online filing of annuals, only.

Mail search: Turnaround time: 3 to 5 days.

Phone search: The agency will release officer/director/registered agent name and address information for $4.00 per entity via the 800 number. Add $1.00 to have the information returned by fax.

Fax search: Results returned by fax for $1.00 per page.

In person search: Limted searches available at the counter.

Online search: The state's excellent Internet site gives detailed information on all corporate, trademark, limited liability company and limited partnerships; fictitious names; and lien records. Images of filed documents are available from 1996/7 to present.

Other access: This agency offers record purchases on microfiche sets and on CD disks.

Uniform Commercial Code

UCC Filings, FLORIDAUCC, Inc, 2670 Executive Center Circle West, #100, Tallahassee, FL 32301; 850-222-8526, 8AM-5PM.

www.floridaucc.com

The Secretary of State privatized the filing and searching of UCC. The vendor, FLORIDAUCC, is responsible for all filings, photocopy and certification requests, forms, and database availability for searches.

Records are available from 1966, if active, 1997 forward on the web. Records are on computer and microfiche. Records filed by electronic process are available in image format. New records are available for inquiry immediately. Records are normally destroyed after 1997, if lapsed.

Searching: Information on Tax Liens is maintained at the Department of State, Division of Corporations. Tax liens are not filed here, unless filed as a UCC. It is suggested to search tax liens at the county level. Include the following in your request-debtor name. The agency will not do a search. You must hire an outside firm, the web page, or use the state designated vendor.

Access by: mail, in person, online.

Fee & Payment: Fees are $1.00 per page for mail searching. Fee payee: Secretary of State. Prepayment required. Personal checks accepted. No credit cards accepted.

Mail search: Turnaround time: 3 to 5 days.

In person search: Simple requests may be processed while you wait.

Online search: The Internet site allows access for no charge. Search by name or document number, for records 1997 to present. Images of documents are available from 1997 to present at this site. Tax Liens are not included with UCC filing information.

Other access: Microfilm reels and CD's of images are available for bulk purchase requesters. Call for more information.

State Tax Liens

Records not maintained by a state level agency.

These records are filed and found at the county level.

Sales Tax Registrations

Florida Department of Revenue, Sales Tax Registration Records, 168 Blountstown Highway #C, Tallahassee, FL 32304-3702; 850-488-9925, 850-922-5936-Fax; 8AM-5PM.

www.state.fl.us/dor

Records are available for 5 years, then they are purged.

Searching: This agency will confirm that a business is registered and has filed returns with the department. The following are required to search; business name, tax ID number, and business location. Federal ID is helpful. They can also search by the owner's name.

Access by: mail, fax, in person.

Fee & Payment: There is no fee.

Mail search: The turnaround time is 7-10 days.

Fax search: Same criteria as mail searching.

In person search: Records still returned by mail.

Birth Certificates

Department of Health, State Office of Vital Statistics, PO Box 210, Jacksonville, FL 32231-0042 (Courier address: 1217 Pearl St, Jacksonville, FL 32202); 904-359-6900 x9000, 877-550-7330 (Order Line), 877-550-7428 (Fax Order Line), 904-359-6633-Fax; 8AM-5PM.

www.doh.state.fl.us

The website includes general information and ordering instructions. The vendor www.vitalchek.com also can process orders via online or by fax.

Records are available from 1865 to present, however few records were filed prior to 1917. Birth registration was not required until 1917. It takes 4 weeks after birth before new records are available for inquiry. Records are indexed on microfiche, inhouse computer.

Searching: Certified copies released only to individual named, if of legal age, or to parents or legal guardians. All letters or applications must include a copy of a valid picture ID of the applicant and the signature and relationship must be notarized. Include the following in your request-full name, names of parents including mother's maiden name, date of birth, county. Include relationship of requester to subject and ID. Legal guardian or representative must submit an affidavit along with current government issued photo ID.

Access by: mail, phone, fax, in person.

Fee & Payment: Fee is $9.00 for a certified computer copy or $14.00 for a certified photocopy. Extra fees involved for expedited services. $4.00 per copy when ordering additional same name at the same time. Fee payee: Office of Vital Statistics. Prepayment required. Personal checks accepted. Major credit cards accepted.

Mail search: Turnaround time: 10 to 15 days. No SASE is required.

Phone search: See expedited services. This is an automated phone service open 24 hours daily.

Fax search: See expedited services.

In person search: Turnaround time is normally the same day.

Other access: Commemorative birth certificates in large size, signed by the governor, and suitable for framing are available. The fee is $34.00 or $25.00 when ordered in conjunction with other certified copies of the same record. Allow 4 to 6 weeks for delivery.

Expedited service: Expedited service is available for mail, phone and fax searches. Fax phone is 877-550-7428. Add $10.00 for "2 to 3 day rush service" or $24.95 for overnight service. Add $5.00 for use of credit card (required for phone or fax service).

Death Records

Department of Health, State Office of Vital Statistics, PO Box 210, Jacksonville, FL 32231-0042 (Courier address: 1217 Pearl St, Jacksonville, FL 32202); 904-359-6900 x9000, 877-550-7330 (Order Line), 877-550-7428 (Fax Order Line), 904-359-6633-Fax; 8AM-5PM.

www.doh.state.fl.us

The website contains general information, ordering instructions, and forms. The vendor www.vitalchek.com also can process orders via online or by fax.

Records are available from 1877 to present. Note that death registration was not required by state law until 1917. It takes 4 weeks after death before new records are available for inquiry. Records are indexed on microfiche, inhouse computer.

Searching: The death certificate minus cause of death is public information. Certification with cause of death is released after 50 years to public. Otherwise, requester must be family member or demonstrate legal interest in the estate. Include the following in your request-full name, sex, date of death, county. Valid photo ID required if cause of death information released.

Access by: mail, phone, fax, in person.

Fee & Payment: Fee is $5.00 for the first year searched. If the specific year is not known, additional years may be searched for $2.00 per year with a maximum fee of $55.00. Add $4.00 per copy when ordering additional copies at the same time. Fee payee: Office of Vital Statistics. Prepayment required. Personal checks accepted. Major credit cards accepted.

Mail search: Turnaround time: 10 to 15 days. No SASE is required.

Phone search: See expedited service. Order line is open 24 hours daily.

Fax search: See expedited service.

In person search: Turnaround time is normally the same day.

Expedited service: Expedited service is available for mail, phone and fax searches. Fax phone is 877-550-7428. Add $10.00 for "2 to 3 day rush service" or $24.95 for overnight service. Add $5.00 for use of credit card (required for phone or fax service).

Marriage Certificates

Department of Health, State Office of Vital Statistics, PO Box 210, Jacksonville, FL 32231-0042 (Courier address: 1217 Pearl St, Jacksonville, FL 32202); 904-359-6900 x9000, 877-550-7330, 904-359-6633-Fax; 8AM-5PM.

www.doh.state.fl.us

The website contains general information, ordering instructions and order forms to download. The vendor www.vitalchek.com also can process orders via online or by fax.

Records are available from June 1927 to present on microfiche, from 1970 to present on computer. It takes 6 weeks before new records are available for inquiry.

Searching: Records are indexed by husband's name and/or by wife's maiden name. Include date of marriage and county of marriage in request. The following data is not released: Social Security Numbers.

Access by: mail, phone, fax, in person.

Fee & Payment: The fee is $5.00 per name for the first year searched. Additional years may be searched for $2.00 per year with a maximum fee of $55.00. Add $4.00 per copy when ordering additional copies at the same time. Credit card fee is $5.00 Fee payee: Office of Vital Statistics. Prepayment required. Personal checks accepted. Major credit cards accepted.

Mail search: Turnaround time: 15 to 20 days. No SASE is required.

Phone search: See expedited service.

Fax search: See expedited service.

In person search: Turnaround time is same day.

Other access: A large size, commemorative marriage certificate signed by the governor is available for $30.00 or $25.00 when ordered in conjunction with other certified copies of the same record. Allow 4 to 6 weeks for delivery.

Expedited service: Expedited service is available for mail, phone and fax searches. Use 904-359-6633 for the fax number. Add $10.00 for "2 to 3 day rush service" or $24.95 for overnight service. Add $5.00 for use of credit card (required for phone or fax service).

Divorce Records

Department of Health, State Office of Vital Statistics, PO Box 210, Jacksonville, FL 32231-0042 (Courier address: 1217 Pearl St, Jacksonville, FL 32202); 904-359-6900 x9000, 877-550-7330, 904-359-6633-Fax; 8AM-5PM.

www.doh.state.fl.us

The website provides general information and ordering instructions. The vendor www.vitalchek.com also can process orders via online or by fax.

Records are available from June 1927 to present. It takes 6-8 weeks after divorce before new records are available for inquiry.

Searching: Records are indexed by husband's name and wife's first name only. Include county of divorce in request. In each of the last 5 years in Florida, there have been 140,000 marriages and

80,000 divorces per year. (This is over 1025 per court day.)

Access by: mail, phone, fax, in person.

Fee & Payment: Fees are $5.00 per request for the first year and $2.00 per year for each additional search year, with a maximum search fee of $55.00. Add $4.00 per copy per name when ordering additional copies at the same time. Fee payee: Office of Vital Statistics. Prepayment required. Personal checks accepted. Major credit cards accepted.

Mail search: Turnaround time: 15 to 20 days. No SASE is required.

Phone search: See expedited service.

Fax search: See expedited service.

In person search: The fee is nonrefundable. Turnaround time is same day.

Expedited service: Expedited service is available for mail, phone and fax searches. Use 904-359-6633 for the fax number. Turnaround time: 2 days. Add $10.00 for "2 to 3 day rush service" or $24.95 for overnight service. Add $5.00 for use of credit card (required for phone or fax service).

Workers' Compensation Records

Workers Compensation Division, Data Quality and Collector, 200 E Gaines St, Tallahassee, FL 32399-4226; 850-413-1712, 850-414-7341-Fax; 8AM-5PM.

www.fldfs.com/wc

All information that would identify an ill or injured worker contained on the first notice of injury (DWC-1) is confidential and may not be disclosed to the public.

It takes 3 days (imaged) before new records are available for inquiry. Records are indexed on microfilm, microfiche, and electronic image.

Searching: To get medical records you must have a signed release of subject, except for legal representatives or an involved insurance company. Include the following in your request-claimant name, Social Security Number, date of accident.

Access by: mail, in person, online.

Fee & Payment: There is no search fee, but copies are $.50 per page plus an additional $.55 per page for "special service" if more than 9 pages. Fee payee: Workers Compensation Trust Fund. Prepayment required. Personal checks accepted. No credit cards accepted.

Mail search: Turnaround time: 1 week. They will send an invoice, and will send you the copies after they receive the check. No SASE is required.

In person search: Requests are still returned by mail, unless you have a subpoena.

Online search: A myriad of information is available at www.fldfs.com/wc/databases.html.

Driver Records

Division of Drivers Licenses, Bureau of Records, PO Box 5775, Tallahassee, FL 32314-5775 (Courier address: 2900 Apalachee Pky, MS90, Neil Kirkman Bldg, Tallahassee, FL 32399); 850-488-0250, 850-922-9000, 8AM-5PM.

www.hsmv.state.fl.us

Copies of tickets may be obtained from the same address listed above. The search fee is $2.00 plus $.50 copy fee or $1.00 for certified copies.

Records are available for a 3 year record or for a 7 year record. Accidents will appear only if convicted of a violation.

Searching: Florida adopted the amendment to DPPA. Casual requesters can obtain personal information only with consent of the subject. Either the driver license number or the name, DOB and sex are required for ordering.

Access by: mail, in person, online.

Fee & Payment: The fee is $3.10 for a certified three or seven year record. Uncertified or online is $2.10. There is a full charge for a "no record found." Fee payee: Division of Drivers Licenses. Prepayment required. Personal checks accepted. No credit cards accepted.

Mail search: Turnaround time: 10 days. No SASE is required.

In person search: Normally, up to 50 requests can be processed for walk-in requests, while you wait. Some Clerks of Courts will also process driving records.

Online search: Online requests an sold on an interactive basis. The state differentiates between high and low volume users. Requesters with 5,000 or more records per month are considered Network Providers. Call 850-488-6264 to become a Provider. Requesters with less than 5,000 requests per month (called Individual Users) are directed to a Provider. A list of providers is found at the website. Check the status of any Florida Driver License free at https://www6.hsmv.state.fl.us/dlcheck/dlchecking. Simply enter the driver license number.

Other access: This agency will process magnetic tape requests on a batch basis, for approved users. Call 850-487-4467 for more details.

Vehicle Ownership, Vehicle Identification

Division of Motor Vehicles, Information Research Unit, Neil Kirkman Bldg, A-126, Tallahassee, FL 32399; 850-922-9000, 850-488-8983-Fax; 8AM-4:30PM.

www.hsmv.state.fl.us

The state' policy is in compliance with the DPPA.

Records are available for 10 years.

Searching: Non DPPA compliant requesters cannot obtain personal information without the specific consent of subject. Please submit the city (residence) and DOB if doing a name search.

Access by: mail, in person, online.

Fee & Payment: The fee for a computer printout of information is $.50, $1.00 per page copy fee, add $3.00 if certification is needed. The current license plate registration or copy of title is $2.00. A complete 10 year history is available for $15.00. Fee payee: Division of Motor Vehicles. Prepayment required. Personal checks accepted. No credit cards accepted.

Mail search: Turnaround time: 2 to 3 weeks. No SASE is required.

In person search: In cases when the information is not readily available the wait is 2 to 3 days.

Online search: Florida has contracted to release vehicle information through approved Network Providers. Accounts must first be approved by the state. For each record accessed, the charge is $.50 plus a transactional fee, and the subscriber fee. Users must work from an estimated 2 1/2 month pre-paid bank. New subscribers must complete an application with the Department 850-488-6710.

Accident Reports

DHSMV- MS-28, Crash Records-Room A-325, 2900 Apalachee Prky, Tallahassee, FL 32399-0537; 850-488-5017, 850-488-1009 (Older Homicide Records (5 yrs)), 850-922-0488-Fax; 8AM-4:45PM.

www.hsmv.state.fl.us

They will not provide homicide reports, which must come from the investigating agency.

Records are available from 1942 to the present. Records are stored on microfilm from 1983 forward. It takes 12 weeks before new records are available for inquiry. Records are indexed on microfilm and computer.

Searching: Records sealed by court order and juvenile information cannot be accessed. Homicide reports less than 5 years old should be requested from the local law enforcement agency that wrote the report, if over 5 years call 850-188-1009. Include the following in your request-the full name of driver, exact date of crash (after 1983), county and city, local agency that investigated. For reports prior to 1983 the exact date, county, location and if crash involved a fatality must be supplied with request.

Access by: mail, in person.

Fee & Payment: The cost is $2.00 per report, $25.00 if homicide. You cannot search by phone; however, you can call to determine if report is available. Fee payee: Department of Highway Safety and Motor Vehicles. Prepayment required. Personal checks accepted. No credit cards accepted.

Mail search: Turnaround time: 2 to 4 weeks. A SASE is requested.

In person search: You may request information in person at the customer service counter on 1st floor (Room B-133).

Other access: List or bulk purchase is available by special request.

Vessel Ownership, Vessel Registration

Dept of Highway Safety and Motor Vehicles, Bureau of Titles & Registrations, 2900 Apalachee Parkway, MS 68, Tallahassee, FL 32399; 850-922-9000, 850-921-1935-Fax; 8AM-5PM.

www.hsmv.state.fl.us

The state does not offer online access, but has outsourced some online access to vendors. Check the web page for details.

Records are available for 10 yrs to present. Records indexed on computer. Motorized vessels must be titled and registered. Registration of non-powered vessels is not required, but non-powered vessels 16 ft and over must be titled. Liens show on records. It takes 6 weeks before new records are available for inquiry. Records are normally destroyed after 10 years.

Searching: A written request is required for all searches. To search one of the following is required: Florida registration #, title #, hull id #, or the exact name. If doing name search, submit DOB and city.

Access by: mail, in person.

Fee & Payment: $.50 per page for computer print-out. $1.00 per photocopy of record. Additional $3.00 for each item to be certified. Fee payee: Dept of Highway Safety. Personal checks accepted. No credit cards accepted.

Mail search: Turnaround time: 1-2 weeks. No SASE is required.

In person search: Simple requests may be processed while you wait.

Other access: A bulk purchase program is available for magnetic tape, labels or printed list. There is a $50.00 deposit required and a fee of $.01 per record.

Voter Registration

Access to Records is Restricted.

Dept of State - Division of Elections, 500 South Bronough St, RA Gray Building, Room 316, Tallahassee, FL 32399-0250; 850-245-6200, 850-245-6217-Fax; 8AM-5PM.

http://election.dos.state.fl.us

All individual searching must be done at the county level. The state maintains a central voter file for data and statistical purposes.

GED Certificates

GED Transcripts/Certificates, 325 W Gaines St Rm 634, Tallahassee, FL 32399; 850-245-0449, 850-245-0990-Fax; 8AM-5PM.

www.firn.edu/doe/workforce/ged_dipl.htm

It takes 24 hours or less before new records are available for inquiry. Records are normally destroyed after never.

Searching: To verify, the following is required: name, date of birth, year of test, SSN, and county/city of test. If known, the GED Diploma number is helpful. A signed release is needed to get a copy of a transcript or diploma.

Access by: mail, phone, fax, in person.

Fee & Payment: The fee is $4.00 per copy of transcript or diploma. There is no fee for verification. Fee payee: FDOE Prepayment required. Money orders and cashiers' checks are required. Personal checks and credit cards are not accepted.

Mail search: Turnaround time 7-10 working days. A SASE is required

Phone search: Depending on workload, personnel may be able to verify over the telephone.

Fax search: Requests are accepted via fax.

In person search: Suggest to call first.

Hunting and Fishing License Information

Fish & Wildlife Cons. Comm, Licensing & Permit Board, 2590 Executive Center Circle, #200, Tallahassee, FL 32301; 850-488-3641, 850-414-8212-Fax; 8AM-5PM.

www.floridaconservation.org

Records are available from 2/97 forward.

Searching: Requests must be in writing. The agency will release address, telephone number, and type of license. Include the following in your request-name, date of birth. The following data is not released: SSN, DOB

Access by: mail, in person.

Fee & Payment: There is no search fee.

Mail search: Turnaround time: 2 to 4 days.

In person search: Turnaround time while you wait.

Other access: Will sell entire database of records. Request must be in writing. Ask for Susan Weaver.

Florida State Licensing Agencies

For details about the agency responsible for licensing/certifying/registering an item below or in the Agency Quick Finder section, match an item's number with the number of the agency in the *Licensing Agency Information* section.

Florida Licenses Searchable Online

Acupuncturist #1	http://ww2.doh.state.fl.us/irm00praes/praslist.asp
Air Ambulance #20	www.doh.state.fl.us/demo/ems/Providers/Providers.html
Air Conditioning Contractor #16	https://www.myfloridalicense.com/licensing/wl11.jsp?SID=
Alcoholic Beverage Permit #6	https://www.myfloridalicense.com/licensing/wl11.jsp?SID=
Ambulance Service #20	www.doh.state.fl.us/demo/ems/Providers/Providers.html
Architectural Business/Individual #11	https://www.myfloridalicense.com/licensing/wl11.jsp?SID=
Asbestos Remover/Contractor/Consultant #16	https://www.myfloridalicense.com/licensing/wl11.jsp?SID=
Assisted Living Facility #26	www.fdhc.state.fl.us/licensing_cert.shtml
Athletic Agent #6	https://www.myfloridalicense.com/licensing/wl11.jsp?SID=
Athletic Trainer #1	http://ww2.doh.state.fl.us/irm00praes/praslist.asp
Attorney #23	www.flabar.org/newflabar/findlawyer.html
Auctioneer/Auction Company #22	https://www.myfloridalicense.com/licensing/wl11.jsp?SID=
Audiologist #1	http://ww2.doh.state.fl.us/irm00praes/praslist.asp
Automobile Repossessor #18	http://licgweb.doacs.state.fl.us/access/individual.html
Bank #5	www.dbf.state.fl.us/cf/dogi/Inst_search.cfm
Barber/Barber Assist./Barber Shop #6	https://www.myfloridalicense.com/licensing/wl11.jsp?SID=
Boxer #6	https://www.myfloridalicense.com/licensing/wl11.jsp?SID=
Building Code Administrator #6	https://www.myfloridalicense.com/licensing/wl11.jsp?SID=
Building Contractor #16	https://www.myfloridalicense.com/licensing/wl11.jsp?SID=
Building Inspector #6	https://www.myfloridalicense.com/licensing/wl11.jsp?SID=
Chiropractic-related Occupation #1	http://ww2.doh.state.fl.us/irm00praes/praslist.asp
Chiropractor #1	http://ww2.doh.state.fl.us/irm00praes/praslist.asp
Clinical Lab Personnel #1	http://ww2.doh.state.fl.us/irm00praes/praslist.asp
Collection Agency #5	https://ssl.dbf.state.fl.us/cf/lic/pubinqry/pub2/index.cfm
Community Association Manager #6	https://www.myfloridalicense.com/licensing/wl11.jsp?SID=
Company in Receivership #14	www.fldfs.com/Receiver/receivership_list.asp
Construction Business #16	https://www.myfloridalicense.com/licensing/wl11.jsp?SID=
Continuing Edu. Provider, Medical #1	http://ww2.doh.state.fl.us/irm00praes/praslist.asp
Contractor, General #16	https://www.myfloridalicense.com/licensing/wl11.jsp?SID=
Cosmetologist, Nails/Salon #6	https://www.myfloridalicense.com/licensing/wl11.jsp?SID=
Credit Union #5	www.dbf.state.fl.us/cf/dogi/Inst_search.cfm
Crematory #6	https://www.myfloridalicense.com/licensing/wl11.jsp?SID=
Dentist/Dental Assistant #1	http://ww2.doh.state.fl.us/irm00praes/praslist.asp
Dietician/Nutritionist #1	http://ww2.doh.state.fl.us/irm00praes/praslist.asp
Doctor, Limited #1	http://ww2.doh.state.fl.us/irm00praes/praslist.asp
Electrical Contractor #16	https://www.myfloridalicense.com/licensing/wl11.jsp?SID=
Electrologist/Electrologist Facility #1	http://ww2.doh.state.fl.us/irm00praes/praslist.asp
Elevator Certificates of Operation #6	https://www.myfloridalicense.com/licensing/wl11.jsp?SID=
Embalmer #6	https://www.myfloridalicense.com/licensing/wl11.jsp?SID=
Emergency Medical Technician #20	www.doh.state.fl.us/demo/ems/Providers/Providers.html
Employee Leasing Company #16	https://www.myfloridalicense.com/licensing/wl11.jsp?SID=
Engineer #17	www.fbpe.org/search/
Engineering Firm #17	www.fbpe.org/search/
Finance Company, Consumer #5	https://ssl.dbf.state.fl.us/cf/lic/pubinqry/pub3/index.cfm
Financial Institution #5	www.dbf.state.fl.us/cf/dogi/Inst_search.cfm
Firearms Instructor #18	http://licgweb.doacs.state.fl.us/access/individual.html
Firearms License, Statewide #18	http://licgweb.doacs.state.fl.us/access/individual.html
Food Services Establishment #6	https://www.myfloridalicense.com/licensing/wl11.jsp?SID=
Funeral Director/Funeral Home #6	https://www.myfloridalicense.com/licensing/wl11.jsp?SID=
Geologist/Geology Firm #6	https://www.myfloridalicense.com/licensing/wl11.jsp?SID=
Hair Braider #6	https://www.myfloridalicense.com/licensing/wl11.jsp?SID=
Health Facility #26	www.fdhc.state.fl.us/licensing_cert.shtml
Hearing Aid Specialist #1	http://ww2.doh.state.fl.us/irm00praes/praslist.asp
Home Health Care Agency #26	www.fdhc.state.fl.us/licensing_cert.shtml
Hospital #26	www.fdhc.state.fl.us/licensing_cert.shtml
Hotel/Restaurant #6	https://www.myfloridalicense.com/licensing/wl11.jsp?SID=
Insect Sting Treatment Specialist #20	www.doh.state.fl.us/demo/ems/Providers/Providers.html
Installment Seller, Retail #5	www.dbf.state.fl.us/licensing/
Insurance Adjuster/Agent/Title Agent #14	www.fldfs.com/data/aar_alis1/
Insurance-related Company #14	www.fldfs.com/Data/CompanySearch/index.asp

Interior Design Business/Individual #11 ....https://www.myfloridalicense.com/licensing/wl11.jsp?SID=
International Bank Office #5 ....www.dbf.state.fl.us/cf/dogi/Inst_search.cfm
Kickboxer #6 ....https://www.myfloridalicense.com/licensing/wl11.jsp?SID=
Lab License #26 ....www.fdhc.state.fl.us/licensing_cert.shtml
Landscape Architect #11 ....https://www.myfloridalicense.com/licensing/wl11.jsp?SID=
Liquor Store #6 ....https://www.myfloridalicense.com/licensing/wl11.jsp?SID=
Lobbyist/Principal #28   www.flsenate.gov/lobbyist/index.cfm?requesttimeout=500&mode=list&submenu=2&tab=lobbyist
Lodging Establishment #6 ....https://www.myfloridalicense.com/licensing/wl11.jsp?SID=
Marriage & Family Therapist #1 ....http://ww2.doh.state.fl.us/irm00praes/praslist.asp
Massage Therapist/School/Facility #1 ....http://ww2.doh.state.fl.us/irm00praes/praslist.asp
Mechanical Contractor #16 ....https://www.myfloridalicense.com/licensing/wl11.jsp?SID=
Medical Doctor #1 ....http://ww2.doh.state.fl.us/irm00praes/praslist.asp
Medical Faculty Member #1 ....http://ww2.doh.state.fl.us/irm00praes/praslist.asp
Mental Health Counselor #1 ....http://ww2.doh.state.fl.us/irm00praes/praslist.asp
Midwife #1 ....http://ww2.doh.state.fl.us/irm00praes/praslist.asp
Mortgage Broker School #5 ....https://ssl.dbf.state.fl.us/cf/lic/mbschools/index.cfm
Mortgage Broker/Firm #5 ....https://ssl.dbf.state.fl.us/cf/lic/pubinqry/pub1/index.cfm
Motel/Restaurant #6 ....https://www.myfloridalicense.com/licensing/wl11.jsp?SID=
Nail Specialist #6 ....https://www.myfloridalicense.com/licensing/wl11.jsp?SID=
Naturopath #1 ....http://ww2.doh.state.fl.us/irm00praes/praslist.asp
Naturopathic Physician #1 ....http://ww2.doh.state.fl.us/irm00praes/praslist.asp
Notary Public #19 ....http://notaries.dos.state.fl.us/not001.html
Nuclear Radiology Physicist #1 ....http://ww2.doh.state.fl.us/irm00praes/praslist.asp
Nurse #1 ....http://ww2.doh.state.fl.us/irm00praes/praslist.asp
Nursing Assistant #1 ....http://ww2.doh.state.fl.us/irm00praes/praslist.asp
Nursing Home Administrator #1 ....http://ww2.doh.state.fl.us/irm00praes/praslist.asp
Nutrition Counselor #1 ....http://ww2.doh.state.fl.us/irm00praes/praslist.asp
Occupational Therapist #1 ....http://ww2.doh.state.fl.us/irm00praes/praslist.asp
Optician/Optician Apprentice #1 ....http://ww2.doh.state.fl.us/irm00praes/praslist.asp
Optometrist #1 ....http://ww2.doh.state.fl.us/irm00praes/praslist.asp
Orthotist/Prosthetist #1 ....http://ww2.doh.state.fl.us/irm00praes/praslist.asp
Osteopathic Physician #1 ....http://ww2.doh.state.fl.us/irm00praes/praslist.asp
Paramedic #20 ....www.doh.state.fl.us/demo/ems/Providers/Providers.html
Pari-Mutuel Wagering #6 ....https://www.myfloridalicense.com/licensing/wl11.jsp?SID=
Pedorthist #1 ....http://ww2.doh.state.fl.us/irm00praes/praslist.asp
Pest Control Operator #4 ....www.safepesticideuse.com/search/PersonSearch.asp
Pesticide Applicator #4 ....www.safepesticideuse.com/search/PersonSearch.asp
Pesticide Appl., Com./Private/Public #15 ....http://licgweb.doacs.state.fl.us/index.html
Pesticide Dealer #15 ....http://licgweb.doacs.state.fl.us/index.html
Pharmacist, Consulting #1 ....http://ww2.doh.state.fl.us/irm00praes/praslist.asp
Pharmacist/Pharmacist Intern #1 ....http://ww2.doh.state.fl.us/irm00praes/praslist.asp
Physical Therapist/Assistant #1 ....http://ww2.doh.state.fl.us/irm00praes/praslist.asp
Physician Assistant #1 ....http://ww2.doh.state.fl.us/irm00praes/praslist.asp
Physicist, Medical #1 ....http://ww2.doh.state.fl.us/irm00praes/praslist.asp
Pilot, State/Deputy #6 ....https://www.myfloridalicense.com/licensing/wl11.jsp?SID=
Plumbing Contractor #16 ....https://www.myfloridalicense.com/licensing/wl11.jsp?SID=
Polygraph Examiner / Assn. Member #27 ....www.floridapolygraph.org/directory/
Private Investigator/Agency #18 ....http://licgweb.doacs.state.fl.us/access/individual.html
Psychologist/Ltd Lic. Psychologist #1 ....http://ww2.doh.state.fl.us/irm00praes/praslist.asp
Public Accountant-CPA #21 ....https://www.myfloridalicense.com/licensing/wl11.jsp?SID=
Racing, Dog/Horse #6 ....https://www.myfloridalicense.com/licensing/wl11.jsp?SID=
Radiologic Physician #1 ....http://ww2.doh.state.fl.us/irm00praes/praslist.asp
Radiologist #1 ....http://ww2.doh.state.fl.us/irm00praes/praslist.asp
Real Estate Agent/Broker/Sales #24 ....https://www.myfloridalicense.com/licensing/wl11.jsp?sid=
Real Estate Appraiser #24 ....https://www.myfloridalicense.com/licensing/wl11.jsp?sid=
Recovery Agent School/Instrct./Mgr. #18 ....http://licgweb.doacs.state.fl.us/access/agency.html
Recovery Agent/Agency/Intern #18 ....http://licgweb.doacs.state.fl.us/access/agency.html
Respiratory Care Therapist/Provider #1 ....http://ww2.doh.state.fl.us/irm00praes/praslist.asp
Roofing Contractor #16 ....https://www.myfloridalicense.com/licensing/wl11.jsp?SID=
Sales Finance Company #5 ....www.dbf.state.fl.us/licensing/
Savings & Loan Assoc., Charter #5 ....www.dbf.state.fl.us/cf/dogi/Inst_search.cfm
School Psychologist #1 ....http://ww2.doh.state.fl.us/irm00praes/praslist.asp
Security Officer School #18 ....http://licgweb.doacs.state.fl.us/access/agency.html
Security Officer/Instructor #18 ....http://licgweb.doacs.state.fl.us/access/individual.html
Social Worker, Clinical/Master #1 ....http://ww2.doh.state.fl.us/irm00praes/praslist.asp
Solar Energy Contractor #16 ....https://www.myfloridalicense.com/licensing/wl11.jsp?SID=
Speech-Language Pathol./Audiolog't #1 ....http://ww2.doh.state.fl.us/irm00praes/praslist.asp
Surveyor, Mapping #6 ....https://www.myfloridalicense.com/licensing/wl11.jsp?SID=
Swimming Pool/Spa Contr. #16 ....https://www.myfloridalicense.com/licensing/wl11.jsp?SID=

Talent Agency #6 ... https://www.myfloridalicense.com/licensing/wl11.jsp?SID=
Therapeutic Radiologic Physician #1 ... http://ww2.doh.state.fl.us/irm00praes/praslist.asp
Tobacco Wholesale #6 ... https://www.myfloridalicense.com/licensing/wl11.jsp?SID=
Trust Company #5 ... www.dbf.state.fl.us/cf/dogi/Inst_search.cfm
Underground Utility Contractor #16 ... https://www.myfloridalicense.com/licensing/wl11.jsp?SID=
Veterinarian/Veterinary Business #6 ... https://www.myfloridalicense.com/licensing/wl11.jsp?SID=
Visiting Mental Health Faculty #1 ... http://ww2.doh.state.fl.us/irm00praes/praslist.asp
X-ray, Pod, Assistant #1 ... http://ww2.doh.state.fl.us/irm00praes/praslist.asp
Yacht & Ship Broker/Salesman #6 ... https://www.myfloridalicense.com/licensing/wl11.jsp?SID=

Florida Licensing Quick Finder

Acupuncturist #1 ... 850-488-0595
Adoption Service #9 ... 850-922-6656
Adult & Foster Care #9 ... 850-487-2383
Air Ambulance #20 ... 850-245-4440
Air Conditioning Contractor #16 ... 850-487-1395
Alcoholic Beverage Permit #6 ... 850-487-1395
Ambulance Service #20 ... 850-245-4440
Animal Registration (Livestock Marks/Brands) #3 ... 850-922-0187
Architectural Business/Individual #11 ... 850-487-1395
Asbestos Remover/Contractor #16 ... 850-487-1395
Asbestos Surveyor Consultant #16 ... 850-487-1395
Assisted Living Facility #26 ... 850-487-2515
Athletic Agent #6 ... 850-488-8500
Athletic Trainer #1 ... 850-488-0595
Attorney #23 ... 850-561-5832
Auctioneer/Auction Company #22 ... 850-487-1395
Audiologist #1 ... 850-488-0595
Automobile Dealer/Sales #13 ... 850-488-4958
Automobile Repossessor #18 ... 850-488-5381
Bail Bondsman #14 ... 850-413-3137
Bank #5 ... 850-410-9111
Barber/Barber Asst./Barber Shop #6 ... 850-487-1395
Boxer #6 ... 850-488-8500
Broker Dealer/Branch Office #5 ... 850-410-9805
Broker/Dealer/Associated Person #5 ... 850-410-9805
Building Code Administrator #6 ... 850-487-1395
Building Contractor #16 ... 850-487-1395
Building Inspector #6 ... 850-487-1395
Cemetery Lot Salesperson #5 ... 850-410-9898
Child Care Center #10 ... 850-922-6454
Child Care/Child Placing Facility #9 ... 850-922-6656
Chiropractic-related Occupation #1 ... 850-488-0595
Chiropractor #1 ... 850-488-0595
Clinical Lab Personnel #1 ... 850-488-0595
Clinical Laboratory #26 ... 850-487-3109
Collection Agency #5 ... 850-410-9805
Community Association Manager #6 ... 850-487-1395
Company in Receivership #14 ... 800-882-3054
Concealed Weapon License #18 ... 850-488-5381
Construction Business #16 ... 850-487-1395
Continuing Edu. Provider, Medical #1 ... 850-488-0595
Contractor, General #16 ... 850-487-1395
Cosmetologist, Hair Braider, Nails/Salon #6 ... 850-487-1395
Credit Union #5 ... 850-410-9111
Crematory #6 ... 850-487-1395
Day Care Center/Child Care Center/Nursery School #10 ... 850-922-6454
Dentist/Dental Assistant #1 ... 850-488-0595
Dietician/Nutritionist #1 ... 850-488-0595
Doctor, Limited #1 ... 850-488-0595
Electrical Contractor #16 ... 850-488-3109
Electrologist/Electrologist Facility #1 ... 850-488-0595
Elevator Certificates of Operation #6 ... 850-487-1395
Embalmer #6 ... 850-487-1395
Emergency Medical Technician #20 ... 850-245-4440
Employee Leasing Company #16 ... 850-487-1395
Engineer / Engineering Firm #17 ... 850-521-0500
Feed Distributor #15 ... 850-245-5691
Fertilizer Distributor #15 ... 850-245-5691
Finance Company, Consumer #5 ... 850-410-9805
Financial Institution #5 ... 850-410-9111
Firearms Instructor #18 ... 850-488-5381
Firearms License, Statewide #18 ... 850-488-5381
Fishing, Commercial Fresh Water #25 ... 850-488-3641
Food Services Establishment #6 ... 850-487-1395
Foster Family Home #9 ... 850-922-6656
Fumigation Performance Special ID #4 850-921-4177
Funeral Director/Funeral Home #6 ... 850-487-1395
Geologist/Geology Firm #6 ... 850-488-1105
Guidance Counselor #2 ... 800-445-6739
Health Facility #26 ... 850-922-5455
Hearing Aid Specialist #1 ... 850-488-0595
Home Health Care Agency #26 ... 850-414-6010
Hospital #26 ... 850-487-2717
Hotel/Restaurant #6 ... 850-488-7891
In Home Family Day Care Center #10 ... 850-922-6454
Insect Sting Treatment Specialist #20 ... 850-245-4440
Installment Seller, Retail #5 ... 850-410-9805
Insurance Adjuster/Agent/Title Agent #14 ... 850-413-3137
Insurance-related Company #14 ... 850-413-3137
Interior Design Business/Individual #11 850-487-1395
International Bank Office #5 ... 850-410-9111
Investment Advisor #5 ... 850-410-9805
Investment Advisor (Credit Unions) #5 850-410-9805
Kickboxer #6 ... 850-488-8500
Lab License #26 ... 850-487-3109
Labor Org Business Agent #7 ... 850-488-3131
Labor Organization #7 ... 850-488-3131
Landscape Architecture Business/Individual #11 ... 850-487-1395
Landscape Maint. & Pest Control Mgmt Co #4 ... 850-921-4177
Liquor Store #6 ... 850-488-8288
Livestock Hauler #3 ... 850-922-0187
Lobbyist/Principal #28 ... 850-922-4990
Lodging Establishment #6 ... 850-487-1395
LPG-Liquefied Petroleum Gas Apr'vd #15 ... 850-245-5691
Marriage & Family Therapist #1 ... 850-488-0595
Massage Therapist/School/Facility #1 ... 850-488-0595
Mechanical Contractor #16 ... 850-487-1395
Medical Doctor #1 ... 850-488-0595
Medical Faculty Member #1 ... 850-488-0595
Mental Health Counselor #1 ... 850-488-0595
Midwife #1 ... 850-488-0595
Milk Hauler/Tester #12 ... 850-487-1450
Mobile Home Dealer/Broker/Mfg #13 ... 850-488-4958
Money Transmitter #5 ... 850-410-9805
Mortgage Broker School #5 ... 850-410-9805
Mortgage Broker/Firm #5 ... 850-410-9805
Motel/Restaurant #6 ... 904-488-1133
Nail Specialist #6 ... 850-487-1395
Naturopath #1 ... 850-488-0595
Naturopathic Physician #1 ... 850-488-0595
Notary Public #19 ... 850-245-6975
Nuclear Radiology Physicist #1 ... 850-488-0595
Nurse / Nursing Assistant #1 ... 850-488-0595
Nursing Home Administrator #1 ... 850-488-0595
Nutrition Counselor #1 ... 850-488-0595
Occupational Therapist #1 ... 850-488-0595
Optician/Optician Apprentice #1 ... 850-488-0595
Optometrist #1 ... 850-488-0595
Orphanage #9 ... 850-922-6656
Orthotist/Prosthetist #1 ... 850-488-0595
Osteopathic Physician #1 ... 850-488-0595
Paramedic #20 ... 850-245-4440
Pari-Mutuel Wagering #6 ... 850-488-9161
Pedorthist #1 ... 850-488-0595
Pest Control, Structural #4 ... 850-921-4177
Pesticide Applicator/Operator #4 ... 850-921-4177
Pesticide Applicator, Comm./Private/Public, Dealer #15 ... 850-245-5691
Pet Shop #25 ... 850-488-3641
Pharmacist, Consulting #1 ... 850-488-0595
Pharmacist/Pharmacist Intern #1 ... 850-488-0595
PHPC Public Health Pest Control #4 ... 850-921-4177
Physical Therapist/Assistant #1 ... 850-488-0595
Physician Assistant #1 ... 850-488-0595
Physicist, Medical #1 ... 850-488-0595
Pilot, State/Deputy #6 ... 850-488-0698
Plumbing Contractor #16 ... 850-487-1395
Polygraph Assn Member #27 ... 954-321-4264
Polygraph Examiner #27 ... 954-321-4264
Private Investigator/Agency #18 ... 850-488-5381
Psychologist/Limited License Psychologist #1 ... 850-488-0595
Public Accountant-CPA #21 ... 850-487-1395
Racing, Dog/Horse #6 ... 850-488-9130
Radiologic Physician, Diagnostic/Therapeutic #1 ... 850-488-0595
Radiologist #1 ... 850-488-0595
Real Estate Agent/Broker/Sales #24 ... 407-245-0800
Real Estate Appraiser #24 ... 407-245-0800
Recovery Agent School/Instrc./Mgr.#18 850-488-5381
Recovery Agent/Agency/Intern #18 ... 850-488-5381
Recreational Vehicle Dealer #13 ... 850-488-4958
Respiratory Care Therapist/Provid'r #1 ... 850-488-0595
Roofing Contractor #16 ... 850-487-1395
Sales Finance Company #5 ... 850-410-9805
Savings & Loan Assoc., Charter #5 ... 850-410-9111
School Admin./Supervisor #2 ... 800-445-6739
School Educ. Media Specialist #2 ... 800-445-6739
School Principal #2 ... 800-445-6739
School Psychologist #1 ... 850-488-0595
Securities Agent/Dealer #5 ... 850-410-9805
Securities Registration #5 ... 850-410-9805
Security Officer School #18 ... 850-488-5381
Security Officer/Instructor #18 ... 850-488-5381
Seed Dealer #15 ... 850-245-5691
Social Worker, Clinical/Master #1 ... 850-488-0595
Solar Energy Contractor #16 ... 850-487-1395
Solid Waste Facility Operator #8 ... 850-245-8705
Speech-Language Pathologist/Audiologist #1 ... 850-488-0595
Surveyor, Mapping #6 ... 850-487-1395
Sweepstakes Operator #18 ... 850-488-5381
Swimming Pool/Spa Contr. #16 ... 850-487-1395
Talent Agency #6 ... 850-487-1395
Teacher #2 ... 800-445-6739
Therapeutic Radiologic Physician #1 ... 850-488-0595
Timeshare Agent #5 ... 850-410-9805
Tobacco Wholesale #6 ... 850-487-6793
Trust Company #5 ... 850-410-9111
Underground Utility Contractor #16 ... 850-487-1395
Veterinarian/Veterinary Estblshmnt#6 ... 850-487-1395
Visiting Mental Health Faculty #1 ... 850-488-0595
X-ray, Pod, Assistant #1 ... 850-488-0595
Yacht & Ship Broker/Salesman #6 ... 850-488-1636
Zoo #25 ... 850-488-3641

Florida Licensing Agency Information

1 Department of Health, Division of Medical Quality Assurance, 4052 Bald Cypress Way, Tallahassee, FL 32399; 850-245-4111, Fax: 850-414-8209. www.doh.state.fl.us/mqa   Search Database at http://ww2.doh.state.fl.us/irm00praes/praslist.asp

2 Education Center, Bureau of Teacher Certification, 325 W Gaines, #1514, Tallahassee, FL 32399; 800-445-6739, Fax: 850-245-9667. www.fldoe.org

3 Department of Agriculture & Consumer Services, Division of Animal Industry, 407 S Calhoun, Mayo Bldg, Rm 335, Tallahassee, FL 32399-0800; 850-410-0900, Fax: 850-487-3641. Email: brown@doacs.state.fl.us

4 Department of Agriculture & Consumer Services, Bureau of Entomology & Pest Control, 1203 Governors Square Blvd #300, Tallahassee, FL 32301; 850-921-4177, Fax: 850-410-0724. www.floridatermitehelp.org/ Email: galet@doacs.state.fl.us Search Database at www.safepesticideuse.com/search/PersonSearch.asp

5 Department of Financial Services, Banking & Finance Division, 200 E Gaines St, Larsen Bldg, Tallahassee, FL 32399; 850-410-9805, Fax: 850-410-9914. www.dbf.state.fl.us Search Database at www.dbf.state.fl.us/cf/dogi/Inst_search.cfm Note: Formerly the Dept of Banking and Finance.

6 Department of Business & Professional Regulation, DBPR Licensing, 1940 N Monroe St #300, Tallahassee, FL 32399; 850-487-1395, Fax: 850-488-1514. www.state.fl.us/dbpr Search Database at https://www.myfloridalicense.com/licensing/wl11.jsp?SID=

7 Department of Business and Professional Regulation, Farm and Child Labor Program, Post Office Box 1698, Tallahassee, FL 32302-1698; 850-488-3131, Fax: 850-488-0512. Email: Rebecca.Gregory@dbpr.state.fl.us

8 Department of Environmental Regulation, Division of Waste Management, 2600 Blair Stone Rd, Tallahassee, FL 32399-2400; 850-245-8705, Fax: 850-245-8703.   www.dep.state.fl.us

9 Department of Children & Families, Interstate Corporate Office, 1317 Winewood Blvd, Bldg 7, #202, Tallahassee, FL 32399-0700; 850-487-2383, Fax: 850-488-0751. www.state.fl.us/cf_web/ Email: dcf-osc@dcf.state.state.us Note: This agency provides an informative searchable online list of children available for adoption through them.

10 Department of Children & Families, Day Care Facilities Licensing, 1317 Winewood Blvd., Tallahassee, FL 32399-0700; 850-487-1111. www.state.fl.us/cf_web/

11 Department of Professional Regulation, Bureau of Architects, Interior Desigers & Landscape Architects, 1940 N Monroe St, Tallahassee, FL 32399-1027; 850-487-1395, Fax: 850-922-4191. www.state.fl.us/dbpr/pro/arch/arc_index.shtml Search Database at https://www.myfloridalicense.com/licensing/wl11.jsp?SID=

12 Department of Agriculture & Consumer Services, Division of Dairy Industry, 3125 Conner Blvd, Mail Stop C-27, Tallahassee, FL 32399-1650; 850-487-1450, Fax: 850-922-9444. http://doacs.state.fl.us/~dairy/index.html

13 Department of Highway Safety & Motor Vehicles, Bureau of Field Operations, 2900 Apalachee Pkwy MS65, Tallahassee, FL 32399-0500; 850-488-4958, Fax: 850-922-9840. www.hsmv.state.fl.us Email: Reynolds.Ron@hsmv.state.fl.us Note: List are available $25.00 each. Request must be in writing.

14 Department of Financial Services, Office of Insurance Regulation; Agents & Agency Licensing, 200 E Gaines St, Larsen Bldg, Tallahassee, FL 32399; 850-413-3137. www.fldfs.com Search Database at www.fldfs.com/data/aar_alis1/ Note: Formerly the Department of Insurance.

15 Agriculture and Consumer Services, Division of Licensing, Post Office Box 6687, Tallahassee, FL 32314-6687; 850-245-5691. http://licgweb.doacs.state.fl.us/index.html

16 Department of Professional Regulation, Construction Industry Licensing Board, 1940 N Monroe St, Tallahassee, FL 32399; 850-487-1395, Fax: 850-487-9529. www.state.fl.us/dbpr Email: cathleen.o'dowd@mail.dbpr.state.fl.us Search Database at https://www.myfloridalicense.com/licensing/wl11.jsp?SID=

17 Board of Professional Engineers, 2507 Calloway Rd. #200, Tallahassee, FL 32303-5267; 850-521-0500, Fax: 850-521-0521. www.fbpe.org Search Database at www.fbpe.org/search/

18 Division of Licensing, Bureau of License Issuance, Post Office Box 6687, Tallahassee, FL 32314-6687; 850-488-5381, Fax: 850-487-7950. http://licgweb.doacs.state.fl.us/ Email: eshores@mail.dos.state.fl.us Search Database at http://licgweb.doacs.state.fl.us

19 Department of State, Division of Corporations, Division of Corporation, Notary Section, PO Box 6327, Tallahassee, FL 32314; 850-245-6975, Fax: 850-245-6966. http://notaries.dos.state.fl.us Email: gkoonce@mail.state.fl.us Search Database at http://notaries.dos.state.fl.us/not001.html

20 Emergency Medical Services, 4025 Esplanade Way Bin C-18, Tallahassee, FL 32399; 850-245-4440, Fax: 850-488-9408. www.doh.state.fl.us/ems Email: lisa_vanderwerf-hourigan@doh.state.fl.us Search Database at www.doh.state.fl.us/demo/ems/Providers/Providers.html

21 Board of Accountancy, Dept. of Business & Professional Regulation, 240 NW 76th Dr, Ste. A, Gainesville, FL 32607; 850-487-1395, Fax: 352-333-2508. www.state.fl.us/dbpr/cpa/index.shtml Email: CallCenter@dbpr.state.fl.us Search Database at https://www.myfloridalicense.com/licensing/wl11.jsp?SID=

22 Department of Business & Professional Regulation, Board of Auctioneers, 1940 N Monroe St, Tallahassee, FL 32399; 850-487-1395. www.state.fl.us/dbpr/pro/auct/auc_index.shtml Email: Julie.Baker@dbpr.state.fl.us Search Database at https://www.myfloridalicense.com/licensing/wl11.jsp?SID=

23 Florida Bar Membership Records Dept, Board of Bar Examiners, 651 E. Jefferson St, Tallahassee, FL 32399-2300; 850-561-5832, Fax: 850-561-1141. www.barexam.org/florida Email: memberaddress@flabar.org Search Database at www.flabar.org/newflabar/findlawyer.html

24 Department of Business & Professional Regulation, Real Estate Commission, 1940 N Monroe St, Talahassee, FL 32399; 407-245-0800. www.state.fl.us/dbpr/re/frec_welcome.shtml Search Database at https://www.myfloridalicense.com/licensing/wl11.jsp?sid=

25 Florida Fish & Wildlife Conservation Commision, 2590 Executive Center Cir, Tallahassee, FL 32301; 850-488-3641, Fax: 850-488-1961. www.marinefisheries.org

26 Facilities Licensing, Agency for Health Care Administration (AHCA), 2727 Mahan Dr, Tallahassee, FL 32308-5401; 850-414-9796, Fax: 850-487-6240. www.fdhc.state.fl.us/index.shtml Search Database at www.fdhc.state.fl.us/licensing_cert.shtml

27 Florida Polygraph Association, Lt. Scott A. Gooding, BCSO, 2601 West Broward Boulevard, Ft. Lauderdale, FL 33311; 954-321-4264, Fax: 954-321-4566. www.floridapolygraph.org/ Search Database at www.floridapolygraph.org/

28 Lobbyist Registration, 111 W Madison St Rm G-68, Tallahassee, FL 32399-1425; 850-922-4990. www.leg.state.fl.us/lobbyist/index.cfm Search Database at www.flsenate.gov/lobbyist/index.cfm?requesttimeout=500&mode=list&submenu=2&tab=lobbyist

Florida Federal Courts

The following list indicates the district and division name for each county in the state. If the bankruptcy court location is different from the district court, then the location of the bankruptcy court appears in parentheses.

County/Court Cross Reference

County	District	Location
Alachua	Northern	Gainesville (Tallahassee)
Baker	Middle	Jacksonville
Bay	Northern	Panama City (Tallahassee)
Bradford	Middle	Jacksonville
Brevard	Middle	Orlando
Broward	Southern	Fort Lauderdale (Miami)
Calhoun	Northern	Panama City (Tallahassee)
Charlotte	Middle	Fort Myers (Tampa)
Citrus	Middle	Ocala (Jacksonville)
Clay	Middle	Jacksonville
Collier	Middle	Fort Myers (Tampa)
Columbia	Middle	Jacksonville
Dade	Southern	Miami
De Soto	Middle	Fort Myers (Tampa)
Dixie	Northern	Gainesville (Tallahassee)
Duval	Middle	Jacksonville
Escambia	Northern	Pensacola
Flagler	Middle	Jacksonville
Franklin	Northern	Tallahassee
Gadsden	Northern	Tallahassee
Gilchrist	Northern	Gainesville (Tallahassee)
Glades	Middle	Fort Myers (Tampa)
Gulf	Northern	Panama City (Tallahassee)
Hamilton	Middle	Jacksonville
Hardee	Middle	Tampa
Hendry	Middle	Fort Myers (Tampa)
Hernando	Middle	Tampa
Highlands	Southern	Fort Pierce (Miami)
Hillsborough	Middle	Tampa
Holmes	Northern	Panama City (Tallahassee)
Indian River	Southern	Fort Pierce (Miami)
Jackson	Northern	Panama City (Tallahassee)
Jefferson	Northern	Tallahassee
Lafayette	Northern	Gainesville (Tallahassee)
Lake	Middle	Ocala (Orlando)
Lee	Middle	Fort Myers (Tampa)
Leon	Northern	Tallahassee
Levy	Northern	Gainesville (Tallahassee)
Liberty	Northern	Tallahassee
Madison	Northern	Tallahassee
Manatee	Middle	Tampa
Marion	Middle	Ocala (Jacksonville)
Martin	Southern	Fort Pierce (Miami)
Monroe	Southern	Key West (Miami)
Nassau	Middle	Jacksonville
Okaloosa	Northern	Pensacola
Okeechobee	Southern	Fort Pierce (Miami)
Orange	Middle	Orlando
Osceola	Middle	Orlando
Palm Beach	Southern	W. Palm Beach (Miami)
Pasco	Middle	Tampa
Pinellas	Middle	Tampa
Polk	Middle	Tampa
Putnam	Middle	Jacksonville
Santa Rosa	Northern	Pensacola
Sarasota	Middle	Tampa
Seminole	Middle	Orlando
St. Johns	Middle	Jacksonville
St. Lucie	Southern	Fort Pierce (Miami)
Sumter	Middle	Ocala (Jacksonville)
Suwannee	Middle	Jacksonville
Taylor	Northern	Tallahassee
Union	Middle	Jacksonville
Volusia	Middle	Orlando (Jacksonville)
Wakulla	Northern	Tallahassee
Walton	Northern	Pensacola
Washington	Northern	Panama City (Tallahassee)

Standards for Federal Courts: Search fee is $26.00 per item (one party name or case number). Copy fee is $.50 per page. Certification fee is $9.00 per document, double for exemplification, if available. All fees standard unless noted in profile. Mail Search: always enclose a stamped self addressed envelope unless otherwise noted. Most courts accept fax requests or will suggest a copying/search vendor. Before releasing records, all courts require prepayment, unless noted.

Open records are located at the court unless otherwise noted. District courts index by defendant and plaintiff as well as by case number. Bankruptcy courts usually index by debtor and case number. While most courts now have their indexes on computer, many may still maintain index card files as well.

Courts offering internet access via CM-ECF or older RACER, PACER, or Web-PACER systems charge $.08 per page fee unless noted as free. Where PACER is available, the universal sign-up number is 800-676-6856. Find PACER and the US Party/Case Index at http://pacer.psc.uscourts.gov.

US District Court

Middle District of Florida

Fort Myers Division Court Clerk, 2110 First St, Rm 2-194, Fort Myers, FL 33901 (also use mail address for courier delivery), 239-461-2000. Hours- 8:30AM-4PM. www.flmd.uscourts.gov

Counties: Charlotte, Collier, De Soto, Glades, Hendry, Lee.

Searches & Indexing: Civil case index is computerized; criminal index is not. Results do not include SSN or DOB. Microfiche and card indexes maintained. New cases in index immediately after filing date. Records purged 3 years after closed.

Fee & Payment: Pay by money order, cashier's or personal check. Payee: Clerk, US District Court. Prepayment required.

Phone Search: Docket information available.

Mail Search: search usually completed- 3 days. Include SASE for return.

In Person Search: Fee charged if court performs your search. Self-serve copier - - current fee is not known - per page.

E-Services: ECF replaces PACER. Document images available. PACER records go back to 1989-90. ECF at https://ecf.flmd.uscourts.gov **Opinions Online:** www.flmd.uscourts.gov. Selected notable opinions only. **Other Online Access:** Calendars free at www.flmd.uscourts.gov.

Jacksonville Division Court Clerk, PO Box 53558, Jacksonville, FL 32201 (courier address: Suite 9-150, 300 N Hogan St, Jacksonville, FL 32202), 904-549-1900. Hours- 8:30AM-4PM. www.flmd.uscourts.gov

Counties: Baker, Bradford, Clay, Columbia, Duval, Flagler, Hamilton, Nassau, Putnam, St. Johns, Suwannee, Union.

Searches & Indexing: Results do not include SSN or DOB. Computer index maintained. New cases in the index 1 day after filing date. Records purged 3 years after case closed.

Fee & Payment: Pay by money order, cashier's or personal check. Payee: Clerk, US District Court. Prepayment required.

Phone Search: No searching by telephone.

Mail Search: search usually completed- 3-5 days. Include SASE for return.

In Person Search: Fee charged if court performs your search. Self-serve copier - $.50 per page.

E-Services: ECF replaces PACER. Document images available. PACER records go back to 1989-90. ECF at https://ecf.flmd.uscourts.gov **Opinions Online:** www.flmd.uscourts.gov. Selected notable opinions only. **Other Online Access:** Calendars free at www.flmd.uscourts.gov.

Ocala Division Court Clerk, 207 NW Second St, US Court House, Ocala, FL 34475 (also use mail address for courier delivery), 352-369-4860. Hours- 9AM-4:30PM. www.flmd.uscourts.gov

Counties: Citrus, Lake, Marion, Sumter.

Searches & Indexing: Cases indexed by defendant and case number. Index on computer back to 1995 Results do not include SSN or DOB. Records purged 3 years after case closed. Open records located at Jacksonville Division.

Fee & Payment: Pay by money order, cashier's or personal check. No business checks accepted.

Phone Search: No searching by telephone.

Mail Search: Include SASE for return.

In Person Search: permitted. No self-serve copier available.

E-Services: ECF replaces PACER. Document images available. PACER records go back to 1989-90. ECF at https://ecf.flmd.uscourts.gov **Opinions Online:** www.flmd.uscourts.gov. Selected notable opinions only. **Other Online Access:** Calendars free at www.flmd.uscourts.gov.

Orlando Division Court Clerk, 80 N Hughey Ave, Rm 218, Orlando, FL 32801 (also use mail address for courier delivery), 407-835-4200. Hours- 8:30AM-4PM. www.flmd.uscourts.gov

Counties: Brevard, Orange, Osceola, Seminole, Volusia.

Searches & Indexing: Results do not include SSN or DOB. Computer index back to 1995 maintained. Records stored by case number according to year closed. New cases in the index immediately after filing date. Records purged 3 years after case closed.

Fee & Payment: Pay by Personal or business check accepted. No foreign checks accepted. Payee: Clerk, US District Court.

Phone Search: Docket information available.

Mail Search: search usually completed- 3 days. Include SASE for return.

In Person Search: Fee charged if court performs your search. Self-serve copier - $.50 per page.

E-Services: ECF replaces PACER. Document images available. PACER records go back to 1989-90. ECF at https://ecf.flmd.uscourts.gov **Opinions Online:** www.flmd.uscourts.gov. Selected notable opinions only. **Other Online Access:** Calendars free at www.flmd.uscourts.gov.

Tampa Division Office of the Clerk, 801 N Florida Ave #223, Tampa, FL 33602-4500 (also use mail address for courier delivery), 813-301-5400, Fax-n/a. Hours- 9AM-4:30PM. www.flmd.uscourts.gov

Counties: Hardee, Hernando, Hillsborough, Manatee, Pasco, Pinellas, Polk, Sarasota.

Searches & Indexing: Results do not include SSN or DOB. Computer index back to 1996 maintained. New cases in index 1 day after filing date. Records purged 3 years after case closed.

Fee & Payment: Pay by money order, cashier's or personal check. Payee: Clerk, US District Court. Prepayment required.

Phone Search: Only docket information is available by phone.

Mail Search: search usually completed- 3-5 days. Include SASE for return.

In Person Search: Fee charged if court performs your search. Self-serve copier - $.25 per page.

E-Services: ECF replaces PACER. Document images available. PACER records go back to 1989-90. ECF at https://ecf.flmd.uscourts.gov **Opinions Online:** www.flmd.uscourts.gov. Selected notable opinions only. **Other Online Access:** Calendars free at www.flmd.uscourts.gov.

US Bankruptcy Court

Middle District of Florida

Jacksonville Division Court Clerk, 300 North Hogan St #3-350, Jacksonville, FL 32202 (also use mail address for courier delivery), 904-301-6490. Hours- 8:30AM-4PM. www.flmb.uscourts.gov

Counties: Baker, Bradford, Citrus, Clay, Columbia, Duval, Flagler, Hamilton, Marion, Nassau, Putnam, St. Johns, Sumter, Suwannee, Union, Volusia.

Searches & Indexing: Computer index maintained. New cases in the index immediately after filing date. Records purged yearly. No specific time when closed records sent to Atlanta Records Center.

Fee & Payment: Pay by money order, cashier check, business check. No personal checks. Payee: Clerk, Bankruptcy Court. Prepayment required.

Phone Search: Voice Case Information Service available, call 866-879-1286 or 904-301-6490.

Mail Search: search usually completed- 1-2 days. SASE not required.

In Person Search: permitted. Judicial Research will search and copy for this district- 904-356-9110. No self-serve copier available.

E-Services: PACER online at http://pacer.flmb.uscourts.gov. PACER records go back to 1981. New records online after 1 day. ECF at https://ecf.flmb.uscourts.gov **Opinions Online:** http://207.41.16.66/cgi/foxweb.exe/dcs-new/dcs. **Other Online Access:** Court now participates in the US party case index.

Orlando Division Court Clerk, Suite 950, 135 W Central Blvd, Orlando, FL 32801 (also use mail address for courier delivery), 407-648-6365. Hours- 8:30AM-4PM. www.flmb.uscourts.gov

Counties: Brevard, Lake, Orange, Osceola, Seminole.

Searches & Indexing: Results include last 4 SSN digits. Computer index maintained. New cases in the index 1-2 days after filing date. Records purged never. No specific time when closed records sent to Atlanta Records Center.

Fee & Payment: Pay by money order, cashier check, business check. No personal checks. Payee: Clerk, Bankruptcy Court. Prepayment required.

Phone Search: Voice Case Information Service available, call VCIS at 866-879-1286.

Mail Search: search usually completed- 1-2 days. Include SASE for return.

In Person Search: permitted. There may be a 5 page photocopy limit at court. Judicial Research will search and copy for this district- 407-999-7717. No self-serve copier available.

E-Services: PACER online at http://pacer.flmb.uscourts.gov. PACER records go back to 1986. New records online after 1 day. ECF at https://ecf.flmb.uscourts.gov **Opinions Online:** http://207.41.16.66/cgi/foxweb.exe/dcs-new/dcs. **Other Online Access:** Court now participates in the US party case index.

Tampa Division Court Clerk, 801 N Florida Ave #727, Tampa, FL 33602 (also use mail address for courier delivery), 813-301-5065, records rm- 813-228-7200, Fax-813-228-7200. Hours- 8:30AM-4PM. www.flmb.uscourts.gov

Counties: Charlotte, Collier, De Soto, Glades, Hardee, Hendry, Hernando, Hillsborough, Lee, Manatee, Pasco, Pinellas, Polk, Sarasota.

Searches & Indexing: Results do not include SSN or DOB. Computer index maintained. New cases in the index immediately after filing date. Records purged every 6 months. No specific time when closed records sent to Atlanta Records Center.

Fee & Payment: Pay by money order, cashier check, business check. No personal checks. Payee: Clerk, Bankruptcy Court. Prepayment required.

Phone Search: Voice Case Information Service available, call VCIS at 813-301-5210.

Mail Search: search usually completed- 1-2 days. Include SASE for return.

In Person Search: permitted. Judicial Research will search and copy for this district- 904-356-9110. No self-serve copier available.

E-Services: PACER online at http://pacer.flmb.uscourts.gov. PACER records go back to 1992. New records online after 1 day. ECF at https://ecf.flmb.uscourts.gov **Opinions Online:** http://207.41.16.66/cgi/foxweb.exe/dcs-new/dcs. **Other Online Access:** Court now participates in the US party case index.

US District Court

Northern District of Florida

Gainesville Division Court Clerk, 401 SE First Ave, Rm 243, Gainesville, FL 32601 (also use mail address for courier delivery), 352-380-2400, Fax-352-380-2424. Hours- 8:30AM-5:00PM. www.flnd.uscourts.gov

Counties: Alachua, Dixie, Gilchrist, Lafayette, Levy. Records for cases prior to 7/1996 are maintained at the Tallahassee Division.

Searches & Indexing: Results do not include SSN or DOB. Both computer and card indexes maintained. New cases in index 3 days after filing date. Records purged 3 years after case closed.

Fee & Payment: Pay by money order, cashier's or personal check. Payee: Clerk, US District Court. Prepayment required.

Phone Search: Only 1-3 names may be searched via phone, and only docket information is released.

Mail Search: search usually completed- 3 days. Include SASE for return.

In Person Search: Fee charged if court performs your search. No self-serve copier available.

E-Services: ECF replaces PACER whose records did go back to 1992. New records online after 1 day. ECF at https://ecf.flnd.uscourts.gov

Panama City Division Court Clerk, 30 W Government St, Panama City, FL 32401 (also use mail address for courier delivery), 850-769-4556, Fax-850-769-7528. Hours- 8:30AM-4:30PM. www.flnd.uscourts.gov

Counties: Bay, Calhoun, Gulf, Holmes, Jackson, Washington.

Searches & Indexing: Cases indexed by and case number. Records on computer back to 1995 and cards. Results do not include SSN or DOB. Records purged 3 years after case closed.

Fee & Payment: Pay by Visa/MC, money order, cashier's or personal check. No business checks accepted. Payee: Clerk, US District Court. Prepayment required.

Mail Search: search usually completed- 24-48 hours. Include SASE for return.

In Person Search: permitted. No self-serve copier available.

E-Services: ECF replaces PACER whose records did go back to 1992. New records online after 1 day. ECF at https://ecf.flnd.uscourts.gov

Pensacola Division Court Clerk, US Courthouse, #226, 1 N Palafox St, Pensacola, FL 32502 (also use mail address for courier delivery), 850-435-8440, Fax-850-433-5972. Hours- 8AM-4:30AM. www.flnd.uscourts.gov

Counties: Escambia, Okaloosa, Santa Rosa, Walton.

Searches & Indexing: Pensacola also maintains records for Panama City office. Results do not include SSN or DOB. Both computer and card indexes maintained; on computer back to 8/1992. New cases in the index 2-3 days after filing date. Records purged 3 years after case closed. District-wide searches available back to 8/1992.

Fee & Payment: Pay by money order, cashier's or personal check. Payee: Clerk, US District Court. Prepayment required.

Phone Search: Only basic information is released via phone. Court will not release all docket data via phone.

Mail Search: search usually completed- 2-3 days. Include SASE for return.

In Person Search: Fee charged if court performs your search. No self-serve copier available.

E-Services: ECF replaces PACER whose records did go back to 1992. New records online after 1 day. ECF at https://ecf.flnd.uscourts.gov

Tallahassee Division Court Clerk, 111 N Adams St, Suite 322, Tallahassee, FL 32301 (also use mail address for courier delivery), 850-521-3501, Fax-850-521-3656. www.flnd.uscourts.gov

Counties: Franklin, Gadsden, Jefferson, Leon, Liberty, Madison, Taylor, Wakulla.

Searches & Indexing: Results do not include SSN or DOB. Computer index maintained. Records also indexed by year closed. New cases in the index

immediately after filing date. Records purged 3 years after case closed.

Fee & Payment: Pay by money order, cashier's or personal check. Payee: Clerk, US District Court. Prepayment required.

Phone Search: Basic case information requested by name (reveals case number) or by case number (reveals names of parties or their attorneys, date of complaint, general status) is available free by phone.

Mail Search: search usually completed- 3 days. SASE not required.

In Person Search: Fee charged if court performs your search. No self-serve copier available.

E-Services: ECF replaces PACER whose records did go back to 1992. New records online after 1 day. ECF at https://ecf.flnd.uscourts.gov

US Bankruptcy Court

Northern District of Florida

Pensacola Division Court Clerk, Suite 700, 220 W Garden St, Pensacola, FL 32502 (also use mail address for courier delivery), 850-435-8475. Hours- 9AM-4PM. www.flnb.uscourts.gov

Counties: Escambia, Okaloosa, Santa Rosa, Walton.

Searches & Indexing: Results include last 4 SSN digits. Both computer and card indexes maintained. New cases in the index 1-2 days after filing date. Records purged when case closed.

Fee & Payment: Pay by money order, cashier check, business check. No personal checks. Payee: Clerk, Bankruptcy Court. Prepayment required.

Phone Search: Voice Case Information Service available., call VCIS at 850-435-8477.

Mail Search: search usually completed- 1-2 days. SASE not required.

In Person Search: Fee charged if court performs your search. No self-serve copier available.

E-Services: ECF replaces PACER whose records did go back to 9/1985. ECF at https://ecf.flnb.uscourts.gov **Opinions Online:** www.flnb.uscourts.gov/webapps/opinion_search/default.aspx. **Other Access:** Calendars at www.flnb.uscourts.gov/Calendar/calendar_ack.htm.

Tallahassee Division Court Clerk, 110 E Park Ave #100, Tallahassee, FL 32301-7726 (also use mail address for courier delivery), 850-521-5001, Fax-850-521-5004. Hours- 9AM-4PM. www.flnb.uscourts.gov

Counties: Alachua, Bay, Calhoun, Dixie, Franklin, Gadsden, Gilchrist, Gulf, Holmes, Jackson, Jefferson, Lafayette, Leon, Levy, Liberty, Madison, Taylor, Wakulla, Washington.

Searches & Indexing: Results do not include SSN or DOB. Computer index maintained. New cases in the index 2-3 days after filing date. Records purged every 6 months.

Fee & Payment: Pay by money order, cashier check, business check. No personal checks. Payee: Clerk, Bankruptcy Court. Prepayment required.

Phone Search: Only docket information is available by phone. Voice Case Information Service available, call VCIS at 850-521-5040.

Mail Search: search usually completed- 1-2 days. Include SASE for return.

In Person Search: Fee charged if court performs your search. No self-serve copier available.

E-Services: ECF replaces PACER whose records did go back to 9/23/1985. ECF at https://ecf.flnb.uscourts.gov **Opinions Online:** www.flnb.uscourts.gov/webapps/opinion_search/default.aspx. **Other Online Access:** Calendars at www.flnb.uscourts.gov/Calendar/calendar_ack.htm.

US District Court

Southern District of Florida

Fort Lauderdale Division Court Clerk, 299 E Broward Blvd, Fort Lauderdale, FL 33301 (use mail address for courier delivery), 954-769-5400. Hours- 9AM-4:30PM. www.flsd.uscourts.gov

Counties: Broward.

Searches & Indexing: Full name of any party, case number or case type required to search. Results do not include SSN or DOB. Both computer and card indexes maintained. Civil cases on computer back to 8/1990; criminal to 1/1992. Cases from 1983 on microfiche; prior on microfilm. New cases in the index immediately after filing date. Records purged 3 years after case closed. Records over 5 years old are, at clerk's discretion, sent to Atlanta Records Center. Call records department to get records location.

Fee & Payment: Pay by Visa/MC, money order, cashier check, business check, local personal check. No out of state personal checks accepted. Payee: U.S. Courts. Prepayment required.

Phone Search: Only docket information is available by phone.

Mail Search: search usually completed- 10 working days. Include SASE for return.

In Person Search: Fee charged if court performs your search. A copy service at 954-832-0111 will pull records and make copies. Self-serve copier available in lobby - $.25 per page.

E-Services: PACER online at http://pacer.flsd.uscourts.gov. Document images available. PACER records go back to 8/1990. New records online after 1 day. ECF at https://ecf.flsd.uscourts.gov. To be available soon. **Opinions Online:** www.flsd.uscourts.gov/default.asp?file=cases/index.html. Filings/verdicts free at www.flsd.uscourts.gov/default.asp?file=fileverdicts.html.

Fort Pierce Division Court Clerk, U S Court House, 300 S Sixth St, Miami, FL 33128 (also use mail address for courier delivery), 772-595-9691, Hours- 9AM-4:30PM. www.flsd.uscourts.gov

Counties: Highlands, Indian River, Martin, Okeechobee, St. Lucie.

Searches & Indexing: Results do not include SSN or DOB. Computer index maintained; civil back to 1985, criminal to 1990. New cases in the index immediately after filing date. Records purged 3 years after case closed. Open records located at Miami Division. Records over 5 years old are, at clerk's discretion, sent to Federal Records Ctr.

Fee & Payment: Pay by money order, cashier's or personal check. Payee: US Court. Prepayment required.

Phone Search: Docket information available.

Mail Search: search usually completed- 10 working days. Include SASE for return.

In Person Search: Fee charged if court performs your search. No Self-serve copier - $.50 per page.

E-Services: PACER online at http://pacer.flsd.uscourts.gov. Document images available. PACER records go back to 8/1990. New records online after 1 day. ECF at https://ecf.flsd.uscourts.gov. To be available soon. **Opinions Online:** www.flsd.uscourts.gov/default .asp?file=cases/index.html. Filings/verdicts free at www.flsd.uscourts.gov/default.asp?file=fileverdict s.html.

Key West Division Court Clerk, 301 Simonton St, Key West, FL 33040 (also use mail address for courier delivery), 305-295-8100, records rm- 305-523-5210. Hours- 10AM-N, 1-3PM. www.flsd.uscourts.gov

Counties: Monroe.

Searches & Indexing: Full name of any party, case number or case type required to search. Recent cases do not include SSN or DOB. Computer index back to 1991 maintained. New cases in the index immediately after filing date. Records purged 3 years after case closed. Open records located at Miami Division. Records over 5 years old are, at clerk's discretion, sent to Atlanta Records Center. Call records department to get records location.

Fee & Payment: Pay by money order, cashier's or personal check. Credit cards accepted. Payee: U.S. Courts. Prepayment required.

Phone Search: No searching by telephone. **Mail Search:** search usually completed- 10 working days. Include SASE for return. **In Person:** Fee charged if court performs your search. A copy service will pull records and make copies for a fee. Self-serve copier - $.50 per page.

E-Services: PACER online at http://pacer.flsd.uscourts.gov. Document images available. PACER records go back to 8/1992. New records online after 1 day. ECF at https://ecf.flsd.uscourts.gov. To be available soon. **Opinions Online:** www.flsd.uscourts.gov/default .asp?file=cases/index.html. Filings/verdicts free at www.flsd.uscourts.gov/default.asp?file=fileverdict s.html.

Miami Division Court Clerk, Rm 150, 301 N Miami Ave, Miami, FL 33128-7788 (also use mail address for courier delivery), 305-523-5100. Hours- 10AM-N, 1-3PM. www.flsd.uscourts.gov

Counties: Dade, Miami-Dade.

Searches & Indexing: Full name of any party, case number or case type required to search. SSN is on criminal, DOB on judgments. Computer index back to 1990 maintained. New cases in the index 1 day after filing date. Records purged 3 years after case closed. Records over 5 years old are, at clerk's discretion, sent to Atlanta Records Center. Call records dept. to get records location.

Fee & Payment: Pay by Visa/MC, money order, cashier's or personal check. Payee: U.S. Courts. Prepayment required.

Phone Search: Only docket information is available by phone.

Mail Search: search usually completed- 10 working days. Include SASE for return.

In Person Search: Fee charged if court performs your search. Copy machines in the lobby area of Records and Docketing Section. An onsite copy service can also pull records and make copies; call for info. Self-serve copier - $.25 per page.

E-Services: PACER online at http://pacer.flsd.uscourts.gov. Document images available. PACER records go back to 8/1990. New records online after 1 day. ECF at https://ecf.flsd.uscourts.gov. To be available soon. **Opinions Online:** www.flsd.uscourts.gov/default .asp?file=cases/index.html. Filings/verdicts free at www.flsd.uscourts.gov/default.asp?file=fileverdict s.html.

West Palm Beach Division Court Clerk, Rm 402, 701 Clematis St, West Palm Beach, FL 33401 (also use mail address for courier delivery), 561-803-3400. Hours- No public access. www.flsd.uscourts.gov

Counties: Palm Beach. Not open to public - records at Ft Lauderdale Division.

Searches & Indexing: Results do not include SSN or DOB. Computer index maintained. New cases in the index immediately after filing date.

Fee & Payment: Pay by Visa/MC, money order, cashier check, business check. No personal checks. Payee: U.S. Courts. Prepayment required.

Phone Search: Docket information available.**Mail Search:** search usually completed- 1-2 days. Include SASE for return. **In Person Search:** Fee charged if court performs your search. A copy service is available to pull records and copy. Self-serve copy - $.50 per page.

E-Services: PACER online at http://pacer.flsd.uscourts.gov. Document images available. PACER records go back to 8/1990. New records online after 1 day. ECF at https://ecf.flsd.uscourts.gov. To be available soon. **Opinions Online:** www.flsd.uscourts.gov/default .asp?file=cases/index.html. Filings/verdicts free at www.flsd.uscourts.gov/default.asp?file=fileverdict s.html.

US Bankruptcy Court
Southern District of Florida

Fort Lauderdale Division Court Clerk, 299 E Broward Blvd, Courthouse, Rm 112, Fort Lauderdale, FL 33301 (also use mail address for courier delivery), 954-769-5700. www.flsb.uscourts.gov   **Counties:** Broward

Searches & Indexing: Cases indexed by debtor, creditors, and case number. Records may also include some older records from Miami-Dade County, particularly Chapter 13s. Results include last 4 SSN digits only. Computer index includes dockets from the 3 division courts. Older records also on books and microfiche. New cases in the index immediately after filing date. Records purged every 6 months.

Fee & Payment: Pay by money order, cashier check only. Law firm checks accepted. Payee: US Courts. Prepayment required.

Phone Search: Voice Case Information Service available, call 800-473-0226 or 305-536-5979. **Mail Search:** search usually completed- 3-5 days. Include SASE for return. **In Person Search:** Fee charged if court performs your search.

E-Services: PACER online at http://pacer.flsb.uscourts.gov. PACER records go back to 1986. New records online after 1 day. ECF at https://ecf.flsb.uscourts.gov **Opinions Online:** www.flsb.uscourts.gov/FRAMES/court_opi.pl. **Other Online Access:** Judges calendars at www.flsb.uscourts.gov/FRAMES/judge_cal.pl.

Miami Division Court Clerk, Rm 1517, 51 SW 1st Ave, Miami, FL 33130 (also use mail address for courier delivery), 305-714-1800. www.flsb.uscourts.gov

Counties: Dade, Miami-Dade, Monroe. Select Chapter 13 cases may be assigned to Fort Lauderdale judges.

Searches & Indexing: Cases indexed by debtor, creditors, and case number. Results include last 4 SSN digits only. Computer index includes dockets from the 3 division courts. Older records also on books and microfiche. New cases in the index immediately after filing date. Records purged every 6 months. Older case records may be held in Fort Lauderdale or West Palm Beach offices, depending on the judge assigned.

Fee & Payment: Pay by money order, cashier check only. Law firm checks accepted. Payee: US Courts. Prepayment required.

Phone Search: Voice Case Information Service available, call 800-473-0226 or 305-536-5979.

Mail Search: search usually completed- 3-5 days. Include SASE for return.

In Person Search: Fee charged if court performs your search. No self-serve copier available.

E-Services: PACER online at http://pacer.flsb.uscourts.gov. PACER records go back to 1986. New records online after 1 day. ECF at https://ecf.flsb.uscourts.gov **Opinions Online:** www.flsb.uscourts.gov/FRAMES/court_opi.pl. **Other Online Access:** Judges calendars at www.flsb.uscourts.gov/FRAMES/judge_cal.pl.

West Palm Beach Division Court Clerk, 1675 Palm Beach Lakes Blvd, 8th Fl, Forum Building Complex, West Palm Beach, FL 33401 (also use mail address for courier delivery), 561-514-4100. www.flsb.uscourts.gov

Counties: Highlands, Indian River, Martin, Okeechobee, Palm Beach, St. Lucie.

Searches & Indexing: Cases indexed by debtor, creditors, and case number. Records may also include some older records from Miami-Dade County, particularly Chapter 13s. Results include last 4 SSN digits only. Computer index includes dockets from the 3 division courts. New cases in the index immediately after filing date. Records purged every 6 months.

Fee & Payment: Pay by money order, cashier check only. Law firm checks accepted. Payee: US Courts. Prepayment required.

Phone Search: Voice Case Information Service available, call VCIS at 800-473-0226 or 305-536-5979.

Mail Search: search usually completed- 3-5 days. Include SASE for return.

In Person Search: Fee charged if court performs your search.

E-Services: PACER online at http://pacer.flsb.uscourts.gov. PACER records go back to 1986. New records online after 1 day. ECF at https://ecf.flsb.uscourts.gov **Opinions Online:** www.flsb.uscourts.gov/FRAMES/court_opi.pl. **Other Online Access:** Judges calendars at www.flsb.uscourts.gov/FRAMES/judge_cal.pl.

Florida County Courts

Court	Jurisdiction	No. of Courts	How Organized
Circuit Courts*	General	10	20 Circuits
County Courts*	Limited	13	
Combined Courts*		81	

* Profiled in this Sourcebook.

Court	CIVIL								
	Tort	Contract	Real Estate	Min. Claim	Max. Claim	Small Claims	Estate	Eviction	Domestic Relations
Circuit Courts*	X	X	X	$15,000	No Max		X		X
County Courts*	X	X	X	$0	$15,000	$2500		X	

Court	CRIMINAL				
	Felony	Misdemeanor	DWI/DUI	Preliminary Hearing	Juvenile
Circuit Courts*	X				X
County Courts*		X	X	X	

ADMINISTRATION   Office of State Courts Administrator, Supreme Court Bldg, 500 S Duval, Tallahassee, FL, 32399-1900; 850-922-5081, Fax: 850-488-0156. www.flcourts.org

COURT STRUCTURE   All counties have combined Circuit and County Courts. The Circuit Court is the court of general jurisdiction.

ONLINE ACCESS   Many Clerk of Courts/Recorders give access to index data at www.myflorida.com, a government sponsored web site. Supreme Court dockets are available online at http://jweb.flcourts.org/pls/docket/ds_docket_search. A large number of the courts do offer online access to the public, usually, through the Clerk of the Circuit Court. The Florida Legislature mandated that court documents must be imaged and available for inspection over a publicly available web site. In response to concerns of identity theft and fraud, the Florida Legislature recently passed new laws concerning privacy of public documents on public web sites. These laws now make it possible for certain of these documents viewed on the Clerk web sites to be either redacted of sensitive information or in some cases removed completely. The Clerk of the Circuit Court cannot place an image or copy of the following documents on a publicly available Internet web site for general public display: Military discharges; Death certificates; Court files, records or papers relating to Family Law, Juvenile Law or Probate Law cases.

ADDITIONAL INFORMATION   All courts have one address and switchboard; however, the divisions within a court are completely separate. Requesters should specify which court and which division, e.g., Circuit Civil, County Civil, etc., the request is directed to, even though some counties will automatically check both with one request.

Fees are set by statute and are as follows as of July 1, 2004: Search Fee - $1.50 per name per year; Certification Fee - $1.50 per document plus copy fee; Copy Fee - $1.00 per page; some county copy fees may vary.

Most courts have very lengthy phone recording systems.

📖 📖 📖 📖 📖 📖 📖

Alachua County

Circuit & County Courts PO Box 600, 201 E University Ave, Gainesville, FL 32602; phone: 352-374-3636; criminal phone: 352-374-3681 (felony); civil phone: 352-374-3636; criminal fax: 352-381-0144; civil records fax: 352-338-3207; hours 8:15AM-5PM (EST). *Felony, Misdemeanor, Civil, Eviction, Small Claims, Probate.* www.alachuaclerk.org

Note: Misdemeanor records phone number-352-337-6250. Fax number for older records is 352-337-6158.

Civil Records: Access: Phone, fax, mail, in person, online. Both court and visitors may perform in person searches. Search fee: $1.50 per name per year. Court makes copy: $1.00 per page. Required to search: name, years to search; also helpful: address. Civil cases indexed by defendant, plaintiff. Civil records on computer from 1979, some records on docket books. Civil records can be searched www.clerk-alachua-fl.org/clerk/pubrec.html. Also, access an index of judgments & recorded documents at www.myfloridacounty.com. Fees involved to order copies; save $1.50 per record by becoming a subscriber. Note: Also, search probate and other ancient records free at www.clerk-alachua-fl.org/archive/default.cfm.

Criminal Records: Access: Fax, mail, in person. Both court and visitors may perform in person searches. Search fee: $1.50 per name per year. Court makes copy: $1.00 per page. Required to search: name, years to search, DOB; also helpful-address, SSN, race, sex. Criminal records on computer since 1974.

General Information: Public access terminal has criminal back to 1974 and civil back to 1979. No juvenile, child abuse or sexual battery records released. Will fax documents for $1.50 per page. Certification fee: $1.50. Payee: Clerk of Circuit Court. No personal checks or Visa, MC, Discover accepted. Prepayment required. SASE not required.

Baker County

Circuit & County Courts - Civil 339 E Macclenny Ave, Macclenny, FL 32063; phone: 904-259-0202, 904-259-0209; civil phone: 904-259-0208; probate phone: 904-259-8449; fax: 904-259-4176; hours 8:30AM-5PM (EST). *Civil, Eviction, Small Claims, Probate.*
http://bakercountyfl.org/clerk
Civil Records: Access: Mail, in person, online. Both court and visitors may perform in person searches. Search fee: $1.50 per name per year. Court makes copy: $1.00 per page. Required to search: name, years to search; also helpful: address. Civil cases indexed by defendant, plaintiff. Civil records on computer back to 1996; prior on index cards and docket books. Access an index of judgments, liens, recorded documents at www.myfloridacounty.com. Fees involved to order copies; save $1.50 per record by becoming a subscriber. Mail turnaround time 2 days.
General Information: Public access terminal has only civil records. No juvenile, child abuse or sexual battery records released. Certification fee: $1.50. Payee: Clerk of Circuit Court. Business checks accepted. Prepayment required. SASE preferred.

Circuit & County Courts - Criminal 339 E Macclenny Ave, Macclenny, FL 32063; phone: 904-259-0206; fax: 904-259-4176; hours 8:30AM-5PM (EST). *Felony, Misdemeanor.*
http://bakercountyfl.org/clerk/
Note: County Court Misdemeanor phone number is 904-259-0204.
Criminal Records: Access: Mail, in person, online. Only the court performs in person searches; visitors may not. Search fee: $1.00 per name per year. Court makes copy: $1.00 per page; same fee for self serve. Required to search: name, years to search, DOB. Criminal records on computer since 1989. Some records on docket books. Access the circuit-wide criminal quick lookup at http://circuit8.org/golem/gencrim.html. Account and password is required; restricted usage. Call the court for details. Mail turnaround time 1-2 days.
General Information: No public access terminal. No juvenile or guardianship records released. Certification fee: $1.50. Payee: Clerk of Circuit Court. Business checks accepted. Prepayment and SASE required.

Bay County

Circuit Court - Civil PO Box 2269, Panama City, FL 32402; criminal phone: 850-747-5123; civil phone: 850-747-5715; probate phone: 850-747-5118; fax: 850-747-5188; hours 8AM-4:30PM (CST). *Civil Actions Over $15,000, Probate.*
www.baycoclerk.com
Civil Records: Access: Phone, fax, mail, in person, online. Both court and visitors may perform in person searches. Search fee: $1.50 per name per year. Court makes copy: $1.00 per page. Required to search: name, years to search. Civil cases indexed by defendant, plaintiff. Civil records on computer from 1984, on microfiche from 1950 to 1980, archived from 1913 to 1979. Some records on dockets. Access the clerk's case search database free at www.clerk.co.bay.fl.us/ovationweb/search.aspx. Access an index of judgments, liens, recorded documents at www.myfloridacounty.com. Fees involved to order copies; save $1.50 per record by becoming a subscriber. Mail turnaround time varies.
General Information: No public access terminal. No juvenile, adoption, child abuse or sexual battery records released. Will not fax back documents. Certification fee: $1.50. Payee: Clerk of Circuit Court. Personal checks not accepted. Prepayment and SASE required.

Circuit Court - Criminal PO Box 2269, Panama City, FL 32402; phone: 850-747-5125; fax: 850-747-5188; hours 8AM-4:30PM (CST). *Felony.*
www.baycoclerk.com
Criminal Records: Access: Fax, mail, in person, online. Both court and visitors may perform in person searches. Search fee: $1.50 per name per year. Court makes copy: $1.00 per page. Required to search: name, years to search, DOB; also helpful: SSN, signed release. Criminal records on computer back to 1986, on microfilm from 1938 to 1982, prior archived. Search the clerk's case search database for free at www.clerk.co.bay.fl.us/ovationweb/search.aspx. Mail turnaround time 3-5 days.
General Information: No public access terminal. No sealed, juvenile or expunged records released. Will fax documents $2.00 per doc. Certification fee: $1.50 per page. Payee: Clerk of Circuit Court. Personal checks accepted. Prepayment required. SASE requested.

County Court - Civil PO Box 2269, Panama City, FL 32402; phone: 850-747-5114; fax: 850-747-5188; hours 8AM-4:30PM (CST). *Civil Actions Under $15,000, Eviction, Small Claims.*
www.baycoclerk.com
Civil Records: Access: Phone, fax, mail, in person, online. Both court and visitors may perform in person searches. Search fee: $1.50 per name per year. Court makes copy: $1.00 per page. Required to search: name, years to search. Civil cases indexed by defendant, plaintiff. Civil records on computer from 1986, on microfiche from 1950 to 1980, archived from 1913 to 1979. Some records on docket books. Access an index of judgments, liens, recorded documents at www.myfloridacounty.com. Fees involved to order copies; save $1.50 per record by becoming a subscriber. Also, search the clerk's case search database for free at www.clerk.co.bay.fl.us/ovationweb/search.aspx. Mail turnaround time 2 days.
General Information: No public access terminal. No juvenile, child abuse or sexual battery records released. Will fax documents $2.00 per page. Certification fee: $1.50 per page. Payee: Clerk of Circuit Court. Personal checks accepted. Prepayment required. SASE requested.

County Court - Misdemeanor PO Box 2269, Panama City, FL 32402; phone: 850-747-5146; fax: 850-747-5188; hours 8AM-4:30PM (CST). *Misdemeanor.*
www.baycoclerk.com
Criminal Records: Access: Phone, fax, mail, in person, online. Both court and visitors may perform in person searches. Search fee: $1.50 per name per year. Court makes copy: $1.00 per page. Required to search: name, years to search; also helpful: DOB, SSN. Criminal records on computer from 1984, felonies on microfilm from 1950 to 1987, archived from 1913. Misdemeanors from 1996-present; pending cases back to 1980. Search the clerk's case search database for free at www.clerk.co.bay.fl.us/ovationweb/search.aspx. Mail turnaround time 7-10 days.
General Information: No public access terminal. No sealed or expunged records released. Will fax documents $2.00 per doc. Certification fee: $1.50. Payee: Clerk of Circuit Court. Personal checks accepted. Prepayment required. SASE requested.

Bradford County

Circuit Court PO Drawer B, Starke, FL 32091; phone: 904-964-6280; fax: 904-964-4454; hours 8AM-5PM (EST). *Felony, Civil Actions Over $15,000, Probate.*
http://circuit8.org
Civil Records: Access: Phone, mail, in person, online. Both court and visitors may perform in person searches. Search fee: $1.50 per name per year. Court makes copy: $1.00 per page. Required to search: name, years to search. Civil cases indexed by defendant, plaintiff. Civil records on computer since late 1987, others on index books. Access an index of judgments, liens, recorded documents at www.myfloridacounty.com. Fees involved to order copies; save $1.50 per record by becoming a subscriber. Mail turnaround time 1 week.

Criminal Records: Access: Phone, mail, in person, online. Both court and visitors may perform in person searches. Search fee: $1.50 per name per year. Court makes copy: $1.00 per page. Required to search: name, years to search, DOB, SSN. Criminal records on computer since 1989, others on index books. Access to the circuit-wide criminal quick lookup is at http://circuit8.org/golem/gencrim.html. Account and password is required; restricted usage. Mail turnaround time 1 week.
General Information: No public access terminal. No juvenile, child abuse or sexual battery records released. Certification fee: $1.50 per document. Payee: Clerk at Circuit Court. Credit cards, business and personal checks accepted. Prepayment and SASE required.

County Court PO Drawer B, Starke, FL 32091; phone: 904-964-6280; fax: 904-964-4454; hours 8AM-5PM (EST). *Misdemeanor, Civil Actions Under $15,000, Eviction, Small Claims.*
www.bradford-co-fla.org/
Note: Send mail requests to "Attention Records."
Civil Records: Access: Mail, in person, online. Only the court performs in person searches; visitors may not. Search fee: $1.50 per name per year. Court makes copy: $1.50 per page. Required to search: name, years to search. Civil cases indexed by defendant, plaintiff. Civil records on computer back to 1989. Some records on docket books, some microfilm. Access index of judgments, liens, recorded documents at www.myfloridacounty.com. Fees involved to order copies; save $1.50 per record by becoming a subscriber. Mail turnaround time up to 1 week.
Criminal Records: Access: Mail, in person. Only the court performs in person searches; visitors may not. Search fee: $1.50 per name per year. Court makes copy: $1.50 per page. Required to search: name, years to search, DOB, SSN. Criminal records on computer back to 1988. Records back to 1970's on docket books. Mail turnaround time up to 1 week.
General Information: No public access terminal. No juvenile records released. Certification fee: $1.50 per document. Payee: Clerk of Court. Business checks accepted. Prepayment and SASE required.

Brevard County

Circuit Court - Civil PO Box 2767, Offical Records Copy Desk, Titusville, FL 32781-2767; phone: 321-264-5245; fax: 321-264-5246; hours 8AM-5PM (EST). *Civil, Eviction, Small Claims, Probate.*
www.brevardclerk.us
Civil Records: Access: Phone, fax, mail, online, in person. Both court and visitors may perform in person searches. Search fee: $1.50 per name per year. Court makes copy: $1.00 per page; same fee for self serve. Required to search: name, years to search. Civil cases indexed by defendant, plaintiff. Civil records on computer since 1987, on microfiche since early 1900s. Some records on docket books. Access County Court records free at www.brevardclerk.us/pages/pubrec9.htm. Online records back to 1988 can be searched by name, case number or citation number. Mail turnaround time 1 week.
General Information: Public access terminal has civil records back to 1981. No juvenile, child abuse or sexual battery victim records released. If local, no add'l charges. Fax fee for long distance $3.00 1st page, $1.00 each add'l page. Certification fee: $1.50. Payee: Circuit Clerk. Personal checks accepted. Check by fax or phone accepted. Visa, MC, Discover accepted. Prepayment required. SASE not required.

Circuit Court - Felony PO Box H, 700 S Park Ave, Titusville, FL 32781-0239; phone: 321-264-5245; fax: 321-264-5345; hours 8AM-5PM (EST). *Felony.*
www.brevardclerk.us
Criminal Records: Access: Phone, fax, mail, online, in person. Both court and visitors may perform in person searches. Search fee: $1.50 per name per

year. Court makes copy: $1.00 per page; same fee for self serve. Required to search: name, DOB, SSN. Criminal records on computer since 1988, on microfiche from early 1900s. Some records on docket books. Online access to county criminal court records is free at www.brevard clerk.us/pages/pubrec9.htm. Search by name, case number or citation number. Mail turnaround time 1 week; phone turnaround is same day.

General Information: Public access terminal has criminal records back to 1987. No juvenile, child abuse, sexual battery or adoption records released. Will fax documents $1.00 per page. Fax fee for long distance $2.00. Certification fee: $1.50. Payee: Circuit Clerk. Personal checks or Visa, MC accepted. Prepayment required. SASE not required.

County Court - Misdemeanor PO Box 2767, 700 S Park Ave, Bldg B, Titusville, FL 32781; phone: 321-637-5445; fax: 321-264-5246; hours 8AM-4:30PM (EST). *Misdemeanor.* www.brevardclerk.us
Criminal Records: Access: Phone, fax, mail, online, in person. Both court and visitors may perform in person searches. Search fee: $1.50 per name per year. Court makes copy: $1.00 per page; same fee for self serve. Required to search: name, years to search, DOB; also helpful: SSN, race, sex, signed release. Criminal records on computer since 1990, on microfiche from early 1900s. Some records on docket books and index cards. Online access to county criminal court records is free at free at www.brevardclerk.us/pages/pubrec9.htm. Online records back to 1988 can be searched by name, case number or citation number. Mail turnaround time 1 week; phone turnaround is 2 days.

General Information: Public access terminal has criminal records back to 1987. No juvenile, child abuse, sexual battery or adoption records released. Will fax documents $1.00 per page. Fax fee for long distance $2.00 for 1st page. Certification fee: $1.50. Payee: Circuit Clerk. Personal checks or Visa, MC, AmEx, Discover accepted. Prepayment required. SASE not required.

Broward County

Circuit & County Courts 201 SE 6th St, Ft Lauderdale, FL 33301; phone: 954-712-7899; criminal phone: 954-831-5680; civil phone: 954-831-5740; probate phone: 954-831-7154; fax: 954-831-7166; hours 9AM-4PM (EST). *Felony, Misdemeanor, Civil, Eviction, Small Claims, Probate.* www.browardclerk.org
Civil Records: Access: Phone, fax, mail, online, in person, email. Both court and visitors may perform in person searches. Search fee: $1.50 per name per year. Add $4.00 for written response (affidavit). Court makes copy: $1.00 per page. Required to search: name, years to search. Civil cases indexed by defendant, plaintiff. Civil records on computer from 1986. Some records on dockets. Will search back 10 years. The county clerk online fee system is being replaced by a web system. Basic information is free at www.browardclerk.org/bccoc2/default.asp. Search by name or case number or case type. Mail turnaround time 1-14 days.
Criminal Records: Access: Mail, online, in person, email. Both court and visitors may perform in person searches. Search fee: $1.50 per name per year. Add $4.00 for written response (affidavit). Court makes copy: $1.00 per page. Required to search: name, years to search, DOB; also helpful: SSN. Criminal records on computer since 1980. The county clerk online fee system is being replaced by a web system. The web allows basic information free at www.browardclerk.org/bccoc2/default.asp. Search by name or case number or case type. The "Premium Access" for detailed case information requires a fee, registration and password. Call 954-831-5654 for information or visit the website. Mail turnaround time 1-14 days.

General Information: Public access terminal goes back to 2003. Certification fee: $1.50. Payee: Clerk of the Court. Only cashiers checks and money orders accepted. Prepayment required.

Calhoun County

Circuit & County Court 20859 E Central Ave #130, 425 E Central, Blountstown, FL 32424; phone: 850-674-4545; fax: 850-674-5553; hours 8AM-4PM (CST). *Felony, Misdemeanor, Civil, Eviction, Small Claims, Probate.*
www.calhounclerk.com
Civil Records: Access: Phone, mail, in person, online. Both court and visitors may perform in person searches. Search fee: $7.00 per name. Court makes copy: $.15 per page. Required to search: name, years to search. Civil cases indexed by defendant, plaintiff. Civil records on computer back to 1986, books from 1970s. Access an index of judgments, liens, recorded documents at www.myfloridacounty.com. Fees involved to order copies; save $1.50 per record by becoming a subscriber. Mail turnaround time 2 days.
Criminal Records: Access: Phone, mail, in person. Both court and visitors may perform in person searches. Search fee: $7.00 per name. Court makes copy: $.15 per page. Required to search: name, years to search. Criminal records on computer back to 1986, on docket books from 1970s. Mail turnaround time 2 days.

General Information: Public access terminal available. No juvenile, child abuse or sexual battery records released. Certification fee: $1.00 per page. Cert fee includes copy fee. Payee: Clerk of Court. Personal checks accepted. Prepayment and SASE required.

Charlotte County

Circuit & County Courts - Civil Division PO Box 511687, Punta Gorda, FL 33951-1687; phone: 941-637-2279; fax: 941-637-2116; hours 8AM-5PM (EST). *Civil, Eviction, Small Claims, Probate.*
http://co.charlotte.fl.us/clrkinfo/clerk_default.htm
Civil Records: Access: Mail, in person, online. Both court and visitors may perform in person searches. Search fee: $1.50 per name per year. Court makes copy: $1.00 per page. Required to search: name, years to search. Civil cases indexed by defendant, plaintiff. Civil records on computer back to 1982, on microfiche since 1987. Online access to civil and probate records is by subscription, see the website. Original payment is $186.00 ($150 refundable) plus a usage fee based on number of transactions. Allows printing of copies. For more information, call 941-637-4848. Access an index of judgments, liens, recorded documents at www.myfloridacounty.com. Fees involved to order copies; save $1.50 per record by becoming a subscriber. Mail turnaround time 1-2 days.
General Information: Public access terminal has civil records back to 1980. No juvenile, child abuse, sexual battery, adoption records released. Will not fax back documents. Certification fee: $1.50 per doc. Payee: Clerk of Circuit Court. Personal checks accepted. Prepayment required. SASE requested.

Circuit & County Courts - Criminal Division PO Box 511687, Punta Gorda, FL 33951-1687; phone: 941-637-2269; fax: 941-637-2159; hours 8AM-5PM (EST). *Felony, Misdemeanor.*
http://co.charlotte.fl.us/clrkinfo/clerk_default.htm
Criminal Records: Access: Phone, mail, in person, online. Both court and visitors may perform in person searches. Search fee: $1.50 per name per year. Court makes copy: $1.00 per page; same fee for self serve. Required to search: name, years to search, DOB; also helpful: address, SSN, race, sex. Criminal records on computer since 1985, misdemeanors on index cards, felonies on judgment books, imaging on disc from 1993. Online access free at https://www.co.charlotte.fl.us/scripts/mgrqispi.dll?appname=MPI%20Criminal&prgname=PUBSEARCHF requires that you provide a name and birthdate. Also, full records back to 1990 available by subscription at http://co.charlotte.fl.us/clrk info/services/criminalInformation.htm; initial setup cost is $250.00, plus $50.00 monthly payment in advance. Mail turnaround time 1 week.

General Information: Public access terminal goes back to 1985. No juvenile, child abuse or sexual battery records released. Fee to fax documents is $2.00 per page. Certification fee: $1.50 per page. Payee: Clerk of Circuit Court. Personal checks or Visa/MC accepted. Prepayment required. SASE requested.

Citrus County

Circuit Court 110 N Apopka, Rm 101, Inverness, FL 34450-4299; phone: 352-341-6400; fax: 352-341-6413; hours 8AM-5PM (EST). *Felony, Civil Actions Over $15,000, Probate.*
www.clerk.citrus.fl.us
Note: Marriage license data is found online at the website.

Civil Records: Access: Phone, fax, mail, in person, online. Both court and visitors may perform in person searches. Search fee: $1.50 per name per year. Court makes copy: $1.00 per page. Required to search: name, years to search; also helpful: address. Indicate on search request the type(s) of cases to search. Civil cases indexed by defendant, plaintiff. Civil records on computer from 1989, archived from 1940 to 1991. Some records on docket books. By phone only back to 1989. The web page has a subscription service to view court record index, fees are involved. Images are not on this system. Also there is an index of judgments, liens, recorded documents at www.myfloridacounty.com. Fees involved to order copies; save $1.50 per record by becoming a subscriber. Mail turnaround time 1-2 days.
Criminal Records: Access: Phone, fax, mail, in person, online. Both court and visitors may perform in person searches. Search fee: $1.50 per name per year. Court makes copy: $1.00 per page. Required to search: name, years to search, DOB; also helpful: address, SSN, race, sex. Criminal records on computer from 1989, on microfiche from 1948 to 1987, archived from 1940-1991. The web page has a subscription service to view court record index, fees are involved. Images are not on this system. Note: By phone only back to 1989. Mail turnaround time 1 week.

General Information: Public access terminal goes back to 1982. No juvenile, adoption, child abuse or sexual battery records released. Will fax documents $1.00 per page if local; $2.00 per page long distance. Certification fee: $1.50. Payee: Clerk of Circuit Court. Personal checks accepted. Prepayment and SASE required.

County Court 110 N Apopka, Rm 101, Inverness, FL 34450; phone: 352-341-6400; fax: 352-341-6413; hours 8AM-5PM (EST). *Misdemeanor, Civil Actions Under $15,000, Eviction, Small Claims.*
www.clerk.citrus.fl.us
Civil Records: Access: Phone, fax, mail, in person, online. Both court and visitors may perform in person searches. Search fee: $1.50 per name per year. Court makes copy: $1.00 per page. Required to search: name, years to search; also helpful: address. Civil cases indexed by defendant, plaintiff. Civil records on computer from 1990, prior records on docket books. The web page has a subscription service to view court record index, fees are involved. Images are not on this system. Also, access an index of judgments, liens, recorded documents at www.myfloridacounty.com. Fees involved to order copies; save $1.50 per record by becoming a subscriber. Mail turnaround 1-3 days.
Criminal Records: Access: Phone, fax, mail, in person, online. Both court and visitors may perform in person searches. Search fee: $1.50 per name per year. Court makes copy: $1.00 per page. Required to search: name, years to search, DOB; also helpful: address, SSN, race, sex. Criminal records on computer from 1990, prior records on docket books. The web page has a subscription service to view court record index, fees are involved. Images are not on this system. Mail turnaround time 1-3 days.

General Information: Public access terminal goes back to 2003. No juvenile, child abuse or sexual battery records released. Will fax documents $1.00 per page. Fax fee for long distance $2.00 per page. Certification fee: $1.50 per cert. Payee: Clerk of Circuit Court. Personal checks accepted. Prepayment and SASE required.

Clay County

Circuit Court PO Box 698, Green Cove Springs, FL 32043; phone: 904-284-6302; probate phone: ext 6516; fax: 904-284-6390; hours 8:15AM-4:30PM (EST). *Felony, Civil Actions Over $15,000, Probate.* http://clerk.co.clay.fl.us
Civil Records: Access: Mail, online, in person. Both court and visitors may perform in person searches. Search fee: $1.50 per name per year. Court makes copy: $1.00 per page; same fee for self serve. Required to search: name, years to search; also helpful: address. Civil cases indexed by defendant, plaintiff. Civil records on computer from 1985, prior records on docket books. Clerk of the circuit court provides free access to records at http://clerk.co.clay.fl.us/asp/pub_pi_queryname.asp. Access an index of judgments, liens, recorded documents at www.myfloridacounty.com. Fees involved to order copies; save $1.50 per record by becoming a subscriber. Mail turnaround time 1-3 days.
Criminal Records: Access: Mail, in person. Both court and visitors may perform in person searches. Search fee: $1.50 per name per year. Court makes copy: $1.00 per page; same fee for self serve. Required to search: name, years to search, DOB; also helpful: address, SSN, race, sex. Criminal records (Felony) on computer from 1967, prior records on docket books. Access to criminal records is free at http://clerk.co.clay.fl.us/asp/cr_pi_queryname.asp. Mail turnaround time 1-3 days.
General Information: Public access terminal available. No juvenile, child abuse or sexual battery records released. Certification fee: $1.50. Payee: Clerk of Circuit Court. Only cashiers checks and money orders accepted. Prepayment required.

County Court PO Box 698, Green Cove Springs, FL 32043; phone: 904-284-6316; fax: 904-284-6390; hours 8:30AM-4:30PM (EST). *Misdemeanor, Civil Actions Under $15,000, Eviction, Small Claims.* http://clerk.co.clay.fl.us
Civil Records: Access: Mail, online, in person. Both court and visitors may perform in person searches. Search fee: $1.50 per name per year. Court makes copy: $1.00 per page. Required to search: name, years to search; also helpful: address. Civil cases indexed by defendant, plaintiff. Civil records on computer back to 1992, prior records on docket books. Access civil records free at http://clerk.co.clay.fl.us/asp/pub_pi_queryname.asp. Online records go back to 1992. Mail turnaround time 1-2 days.
Criminal Records: Access: Mail, in person, online. Both court and visitors may perform in person searches. Search fee: $1.50 per name per year. Court makes copy: $1.00 per page. Required to search: name, years to search, DOB, SSN; also helpful: address, race, sex. Criminal records on computer back to 1992, prior records on docket books. Access criminal records free at http://clerk.co.clay.fl.us/asp/cr_pi_queryname.asp. Mail turnaround time 1 week.
General Information: Public access terminal goes back to 1991. No juvenile, child abuse or sexual battery records released. Fee to fax documents is $2.00 1st page; $1.00 each add'l. Certification fee: $1.50 per cert. Payee: Clerk of Circuit Court. Credit cards accepted; no personal checks. Prepayment required.

Collier County

Circuit Court PO Box 413044, Naples, FL 34101-3044; phone: 239-732-2646; criminal phone: 239-732-2648; hours 8AM-5PM (EST). *Felony, Civil Actions Over $15,000, Probate.* www.clerk.collier.fl.us
Civil Records: Access: Mail, online, in person. Both court and visitors may perform in person searches. Search fee: $1.50 per name per year. Court makes copy: $1.00 per page. Required to search: name, years to search. Civil cases indexed by defendant, plaintiff. Civil records on computer from 1990, on microfiche from 1922 to 1997, archived from 1922. Online access is free at www.clerk.collier.fl.us/clerkspublicac/Default.htm. Records include probate, traffic and domestic. Access an index of judgments, liens, recorded documents at www.myfloridacounty.com. Fees involved to order copies; save $1.50 per record by becoming a subscriber. Mail turnaround time within 1 week.
Criminal Records: Access: Mail, online, in person. Both court and visitors may perform in person searches. Search fee: $1.50 per name per year. Court makes copy: $1.00 per page. Required to search: name, years to search, DOB; also helpful: SSN, add your phone number. Criminal records on computer from 1990, on microfiche from 1922 to 1994, archived from 1922. Criminal records access free at www.clerk.collier.fl.us/clerkspublicac/Default.htm. Mail turnaround time within 1 week.
General Information: Public access terminal goes back to 1988. (The terminal is on the 6th Fl.) No sealed by court or statute records released. Certification fee: $1.50. Payee: Clerk of Circuit Court. Personal checks accepted. Prepayment and SASE required.

County Court PO Box 413044, 3301 Tamiami Trail East, Naples, FL 34101-3044; criminal phone: 239-732-2648; civil phone: 239-732-2646; criminal fax: 239-732-2717; civil records fax: 239-774-8020; hours 8AM-5PM (EST). *Misdemeanor, Civil Actions Under $15,000, Eviction, Small Claims.* www.clerk.collier.fl.us
Civil Records: Access: Mail, online, in person. Both court and visitors may perform in person searches. Search fee: $1.50 per name per year. Court makes copy: $1.00 per page. Required to search: name, years to search; also helpful: address. Civil cases indexed by defendant, plaintiff. Civil records on computer from 1990, on microfiche from 1922 to 1995. Online access is free at www.clerk.collier.fl.us/clerkspublicac/Default.htm. Records include probate, traffic and domestic. Mail turnaround time 1 week.
Criminal Records: Access: Mail, online, in person. Both court and visitors may perform in person searches. Search fee: $1.50 per name per year. Court makes copy: $1.00 per page. Required to search: name, years to search, DOB; also helpful: address, SSN, race, sex. Criminal records on computer from 1988; felony on microfiche from 1922 to 1999 - misdemeanors to 2000. Criminal records access is free at www.clerk.collier.fl.us/clerkspublicac/Default.htm. Mail turnaround time 1 week.
General Information: Public access terminal has criminal back to 1988 and civil back to 1990. No juvenile, child abuse or sexual battery records released. Will fax documents; $2.00 if local, $3.00 if long distance. Certification fee: $1.50. Payee: Clerk of County Court. Personal checks accepted. Prepayment and SASE required.

Columbia County

Circuit & County Courts PO Drawer 2069, Lake City, FL 32056; phone: 386-758-1342; criminal phone: 386-758-1164; civil phone: 386-758-1036; probate phone: 386-758-1054; fax: 386-758-1337; hours 8AM-5PM (EST). *Felony, Misdemeanor, Circuit/County, Civil, Eviction, Small Claims, Probate.* http://www2.myfloridacounty.com/wps/wcm/connect/columbiaclerk
Civil Records: Access: Mail, in person, online. Both court and visitors may perform in person searches. Search fee: $1.50 per name per year. Fee is per department. Court makes copy: $1.00 per page; same fee for self serve. Required to search: name, years to search. Civil cases indexed by defendant, plaintiff. Civil records on computer from 1990, archived from 1800s. DOB and SSN also helpful for searching. Access an index of judgments, liens, recorded documents at www.myfloridacounty.com. Fees involved to order copies; save $1.50 per record by becoming a subscriber.
Criminal Records: Access: In person only. Both court and visitors may perform in person searches. Court makes copy: $1.00 per page; same fee for self serve. Required to search: name, years to search, DOB; SSN helpful. Criminal records on computer from 1989, archived from 1800s.
General Information: Public access terminal has criminal back to 1989 and civil back to 1990. No names of victims of sex related offenses, juveniles, incompetence or mental health records released. Fee to fax documents is $3.00 per page. Certification fee: $1.50 per cert. Payee: Clerk of Circuit Court. Cashiers check or money order only. Prepayment and SASE required.

Dade County

Circuit & County Courts - Civil 73 W Flagler St, #242, Miami, FL 33130; phone: 305-275-1155; fax: 305-349-7410; hours 9AM-4PM (EST). *Civil under $15,000, Eviction, Small Claims, Probate.* www.miami-dadeclerk.com/dadecoc
Note: Better known as Miami-Dade County.

Civil Records: Access: Mail, online, in person. Both court and visitors may perform in person searches. Search fee: $1.50 per name per year. Court makes copy: $1.00 per page. Required to search: name, years to search. Civil and domestic relations cases indexed by plaintiff/petitioner, defendant/respondent. Civil and domestic relations records on computer back to 1973; archives from 1836; microfilm in county recorder office. Access a wealth of information through the Clerk of Court's online services website. Choose between Standard (free of charge) and Premier (fee-based) online services. By subscribing to the Premier service, you may access 3 advanced options: Civil/Family/Probate, Public Records, and Traffic. Fees are based on number of units purchased; minimum $5.00, paid in advance. Also, though limited, you may search felony, misdemeanor, civil and county ordinance violations free at Note: www.miami-dadeclerk.com/cjis/search1.asp. Also, search Civil/Family/Probate free at www.miami-dadeclerk.com/default.asp and choose Standard Case Search. Also, now search traffic cases free at www.miami-dadeclerk.com/spirit/publicsearch/defnamesearch.asp. Mail turnaround time 10 days.

General Information: Public access terminal has only civil records. No juvenile, adoption, mental health records releases. Will not fax documents. Certification fee: $1.50. Payee: Clerk of Circuit & County Courts. Personal checks and money orders accepted; will accept Visa/MC. Prepayment required. SASE requested.

Circuit & County Courts - Criminal 1351 NW 12th St, #9000, Miami, FL 33125; phone: 305-275-1155; criminal phone: 305-548-5527; fax: 305-548-5526; hours 9AM-4PM (EST). *Felony, Misdemeanor.*

www.miami-dadeclerk.com/dadecoc/

Note: Better known as Miami-Dade County. Although located in the same building, the records of the felony and the misdemeanor courts are not co-mingled. Search the Circuit Court for felony and the County Court for misdemeanor records.

Criminal Records: Access: Mail, online, in person. Both court and visitors may perform in person searches. Search fee: $1.50 per year. Court makes copy: $1.00 per page. Required to search: name, years to search, DOB; also helpful: address, SSN, race, sex. Criminal records on computer back to 1971, on microfiche from 1975, archived from 1836. The website offers free and Premier (Fee Based) Online Services. Though limited, you may search felony, misdemeanor, civil and county ordinance violations free at www.miami-dadeclerk.com/cjis/search1.asp. By subscribing to the Clerk's Premier Services, you will be able to access advanced options in three of the Clerk's internet-based systems: Civil/Family/Probate, Public Records, and Traffic. Fees are $.25 per search, paid in advance. Note: Search traffic cases free at www.miami-dadeclerk.com/spirit/publicsearch/defnamesearch.asp. Mail turnaround time 10-15 days.

General Information: Public access terminal has criminal records back to 1970. No juvenile, child abuse or sexual battery records released. Certification fee: $1.50. Payee: Clerk of Circuit and County Court. Personal checks or Visa, MC accepted. Credit cards accepted in person only. Prepayment and SASE required.

De Soto County

Circuit & County Courts 115 E Oak St, Arcadia, FL 34266; phone: 863-993-4876; criminal phone: 863-993-4876; civil phone: 863-993-4880; probate phone: 863-993-4880; criminal fax: 863-993-4669; same fax for civil and probate; hours 8AM-4:45PM (EST). *Felony, Misdemeanor, Civil, Eviction, Small Claims, Probate.*

www.desotoclerk.com

Note: Misdemeanors 863-993-4880. County Court & Evictions 863-993-4880.

Civil Records: Access: Phone, fax, mail, in person, online. Both court and visitors may perform in person searches. Search fee: $1.50 per name per year. Court makes copy: $1.00 per page; same fee for self serve. Required to search: name, years to search. Civil cases indexed by defendant, plaintiff. Civil records on computer from 1986, on microfiche from 1974, archived from 1887. Free access to civil, marriage/divorce, small claims, probate, Uresa, traffic/parking, Muni ordinances, domestic relations, name changes, foreclosures at www.desotoclerk.com/dpa/cvweb.htm. Also, access an index of judgments, liens, recorded documents at www.myfloridacounty.com. Fees involved to order copies; save $1.50 per record by becoming a subscriber. Mail turnaround time 2 days.

Criminal Records: Access: Phone, fax, mail, in person. Both court and visitors may perform in person searches. Search fee: $1.50 per name per year. Court makes copy: $1.00 per page; same fee for self serve. Required to search: name, years to search, DOB; also helpful: SSN, aliases. Criminal records on computer since 1986, archived since 1887. Criminal records are soon to be available at the 12th Judicial Circuit website. Mail turnaround time 2 days.

General Information: Public access terminal available. No juvenile or sex related records released. Will fax documents $1.00 per page. Certification fee: $1.50. Payee: Clerk of the Court. Personal checks accepted. Prepayment required. SASE requested.

Dixie County

Circuit & County Courts PO Drawer 1206, Cross City, FL 32628-1206; phone: 352-498-1200; fax: 352-498-1201; hours 9AM-5PM (EST). *Felony, Misdemeanor, Civil, Eviction, Small Claims, Probate.*

Civil Records: Access: Mail, in person, online. Both court and visitors may perform in person searches. Search fee: $1.50 per name per year. Court makes copy: $1.00 per page. Required to search: name, years to search; also helpful: address. Civil cases indexed by defendant, plaintiff. Civil records on computer since 1987, archived to 1920's. Access an index of judgments, liens, recorded documents at www.myfloridacounty.com. Fees involved to order copies; save $1.50 per record by becoming a subscriber. Mail turnaround time 1 week.

Criminal Records: Access: Mail, in person. Both court and visitors may perform in person searches. Search fee: $1.50 per name per year. Court makes copy: $1.00 per page. Required to search: name, years to search, DOB; also helpful: address, SSN, race, sex. Criminal records on computer since 1989, archived to 1920's. Mail turnaround time 1 week.

General Information: No public access terminal. No juvenile, child abuse or sexual battery records released. Fee to fax documents is $1.00 per page. Certification fee: $1.50 per document. Payee: Clerk of Circuit Court. Personal checks accepted. Prepayment and SASE required.

Duval County

Circuit & County Courts - Civil Division 330 E Bay St, Jacksonville, FL 32202; phone: 904-630-2031; fax: 904-630-7506; hours 8:30AM-4:30PM *Civil, Eviction, Small Claims, Probate.*

www.coj.net/Departments/Fourth+Judicial+Circuit+Court/default.htm

Civil Records: Access: Fax, mail, online, in person. Both court and visitors may perform in person searches. Search fee: $1.50 per name per year. Court makes copy: $1.00 per page. Required to search: name, years to search; also helpful: address. Civil cases indexed by defendant, plaintiff. Civil records (Circuit) on computer from 1968, county from 1984. County civil on index books from 1975 to 1986, prior on docket books. Circuit civil on index books from 1950s to 1968. Two sources are available. First, online access requires $100.00 setup fee, but no access charges. For more information, call 904-630-1212 x5115. Access an index of judgments, liens, recorded documents at www.myfloridacounty.com. Fees involved to order copies; save $1.50 per record by becoming a subscriber. Mail turnaround time for county records 5-7 days, circuit 2-4 days.

General Information: Public access terminal has civil records back to 1968. No juvenile, child abuse or sexual battery records released. Fee to fax documents is $1.00 per page. Certification fee: $1.50 per doc. Payee: Clerk of Circuit Court. Business checks accepted. Prepayment required.

Circuit & County Courts - Criminal Division Attn; Records, 501 E Bay St, Jacksonville, FL 32202; phone: 904-630-2065; fax: 904-630-1115; hours 8:30AM-4:30PM (EST). *Felony, Misdemeanor.*

Criminal Records: Access: Mail, fax, online, in person. Visitors must perform in person searches themselves. Search fee: $5.00. Court makes copy: $1.00 per page. Required to search: name, years to search, DOB; also helpful: address, SSN, race, sex. Criminal records (Circuit) on computer from 1968, county from 1986. County civil on index books from 1975 to 1986, prior on docket books. Circuit civil on index books from 1900s to 1968. Online access to criminal records requires $100.00 setup fee, but no access charges. Records go back to 1992. For more information, call Leslie Peterson at 904-630-1212 x5115. Note: For search without case number, search fee involved. Contact JSO Records, must be in writing. Mail turnaround time 2-3 days.

General Information: Public access terminal goes back to 1981. No juvenile, child abuse or sexual battery records released. Certification fee: $1.50. Payee: Clerk of the Court. Business checks accepted. Prepayment required. SASE helpful.

Escambia County

Circuit & County Courts - Civil Division PO Box 333, 190 Governmental Ctr, Pensacola, FL 32591-0333.; phone: 850-595-4170; civil phone: 850-595-4130 (Circ Ct. Civil); probate phone: 850-595-4300; hours 8AM-5PM (CST). *Civil, Eviction, Small Claims, Probate.*

www.clerk.co.escambia.fl.us

Note: Archive Dept. performs searches.

Civil Records: Access: Phone, fax, mail, in person, online. Both court and visitors may perform in person searches. Search fee: $1.00 per year per name. $6.00 for cover letter response (no record found, etc). Court makes copy: $1.00 per page. Required to search: name, years to search; also helpful: address. Civil cases indexed by defendant, plaintiff. County civil records on computer from mid 1986, Circuit Court civil on computer from mid 1987. Prior on index books. Judgments and small claims on microfiche from 1952, evictions from 1973. Online access to county clerk records is free at www.clerk.co.escambia.fl.us/public_records.html. Search by name, citation, or case number. Small claims, traffic, and marriage data also available. Access an index of judgments, liens, recorded documents at www.myfloridacounty.com. Fees involved to order copies; save $1.50 per record by becoming a subscriber. Mail turnaround 1-5 days.

General Information: Public access terminal has civil records back to 1999. No juvenile, child abuse, adoption, mental health or sexual battery records released. Will fax documents; $1.00 per call. Certification fee: $1.50 per page. Payee: Clerk of Circuit Court. Personal checks accepted. Credit cards accepted. Prepayment required. SASE requested.

Circuit & County Courts - Criminal Division 190 Governmental Ctr, Pensacola, FL 32501; phone: 850-595-4150; criminal phone: 850-595-4185; criminal fax: 850-595-4198; hours 8AM-5PM (CST). *Felony, Misdemeanor.*

www.clerk.co.escambia.fl.us

Note: Misdemeanor records phone is 850-595-4185.

Criminal Records: Access: Fax, mail, in person, online. Both court and visitors may perform in person searches. Search fee: $1.50 per name per year. Court makes copy: $1.00 per page. Required to search: name, years to search, DOB; also helpful: address, SSN, race, sex. Criminal records on computer and microfiche from 1973, archived from 1940-1972. Online access criminal records free at www.clerk.co.escambia.fl.us/public_records.html. Search by name, citation, or case number. Mail turnaround time within 1 week.

General Information: Public access terminal has criminal back to 1984 and civil back to 3/1986. No juvenile, child abuse, mental health, adoption or sexual battery records released. Will fax documents $1.00 per page. Over 5 pages $2.00, each add'l group of 5 pages charge increases by $1.00, plus phone charge. Certification fee: $1.50. Payee: Clerk of Circuit Court. Personal checks accepted. Prepayment required. SASE requested.

Flagler County

Circuit & County Courts PO Box 787, Bunnell, FL 32110; criminal phone: 386-437-7419; civil phone: 386-437-7430; probate phone: 386-437-7458; criminal fax: 386-437-7454; civil fax: 386-586-2116; hours 8:30AM-4:30PM (EST). *Felony, Misdemeanor, Civil, Eviction, Small Claims, Probate.* www.flaglerclerk.com

Civil Records: Access: Phone, fax, mail, in person, email, online. Both court and visitors may perform in person searches. Search fee: $1.50 per name per year. Court makes copy: $1.00 per page. Required to search: name, years to search; also helpful: address.

Civil cases indexed by defendant, plaintiff. Civil records on computer from 1990. All archived from 1917, some on index books. Access an index of judgments, liens, recorded documents at www.myfloridacounty.com. Fees involved to order copies. Mail turnaround time 2-7 days.

Criminal Records: Access: Phone, fax, mail, in person, email. Both court and visitors may perform in person searches. Search fee: $1.50 per name per year. Court makes copy: $1.00 per page. Required to search: name, years to search, DOB; also helpful: address, SSN, race, sex. Felony records on computer back to 1999; misdemeanors back to 1988. All archived from 1917, some on index books. Mail turnaround time 2-7 days.

General Information: Public access terminal has criminal back to 1999 felony; 1988 misdemeanor and civil back to 1990. No juvenile, adoption, child abuse or sexual battery records released. Will fax documents $1.00 per page. Certification fee: $1.50. Payee: Clerk of Circuit Court. Local business checks, money orders, or cashiers checks accepted. Prepayment required.

Franklin County

Circuit & County Courts 33 Market St, #203, Apalachicola, FL 32320; phone: 850-653-8861; criminal phone: x166 or x107; civil phone: x106 or x149; probate phone: sx193; criminal fax: 850-653-2261; same fax for civil and probate; hours 8:30AM-4:30PM (EST). *Felony, Misdemeanor, Civil, Eviction, Small Claims, Probate.*
www.franklinclerk.com/
Note: Probate is a separate index at this courthouse.

Civil Records: Access: Mail, in person, online. Both court and visitors may perform in person searches. Search fee: $1.50 per name per year. Court makes copy: $1.00 per page; same fee for self serve. Required to search: name, years to search; also helpful: address. Civil cases indexed by defendant, plaintiff. Civil records on computer from 3/92. Access an index of judgments, liens, recorded documents at www.myfloridacounty.com. Fees involved to order copies; save $1.50 per record by becoming a subscriber. Mail turnaround 2-5 days.

Criminal Records: Access: Mail, in person, online. Both court and visitors may perform in person searches. Search fee: $1.50 per name per year. Court makes copy: $1.00 per page; same fee for self serve. Required to search: name, years to search, DOB; also helpful: address, SSN, race, sex. Criminal records on computer since 1989. Public records may be obtained online at https://www.myfloridacounty.com/subscription/. Fees are involved. Mail turnaround time 2-5 days.

General Information: Public access terminal has criminal back to 1989 and civil back to 1992. No juvenile, child abuse or sexual battery records released. Will fax documents if prepaid. Certification fee: $1.50. Payee: Clerk of Circuit Court. In county personal checks accepted. Prepayment required. SASE requested.

Gadsden County

Circuit & County Courts - Criminal Division 24 N Adams, Quincy, FL 32351; phone: 850-875-8610; fax: 850-875-7265; hours 8:30AM-5PM (EST). *Felony, Misdemeanor.*
www.co.leon.fl.us/court/court.htm
Note: Requests may be sent to PO Box 1649, ZIP is 32353.

Criminal Records: Access: Fax, mail, in person. Only the court performs in person searches; visitors may not. Search fee: $1.50 per name per year. Court makes copy: $.25 per page. Required to search: name, years to search, DOB; also helpful: SSN. Criminal records on computer from 1984, some on index books and cards. Mail turnaround time 3-5 days.

General Information: No public access terminal. No juvenile or sex offender records released. Will fax documents for $1.00 per page. Certification fee: $1.50

per page. Payee: Clerk of Circuit Court. Personal checks accepted. Prepayment required. SASE not required.

Circuit & County Courts - Civil Division PO Box 1649, Quincy, FL 32353; phone: 850-875-8601; probate phone: 850-875-8601 ext 232; fax: 850-875-8612; hours 8:30AM-5PM (EST). *Civil, Eviction, Small Claims, Probate.*
www.clerk.co.gadsden.fl.us
Note: Extension 231 is Circuit; Ext. 246 is County Clerk.

Civil Records: Access: Phone, fax, mail, online, email, in person. Both court and visitors may perform in person searches. Search fee: $1.50 per name, per yr. Court makes copy: $.25 per page; $1.00 per page of recorded; same fee for self serve. Required to search: name, years to search. Civil cases indexed by defendant, plaintiff. Civil records on computer since 1984. Access to the index of civil court judgments, etc. are free from the County Clerk at www.clerk.co.gadsden.fl.us. Also, access an index of judgments, liens, recorded documents at www.myfloridacounty.com. Fees involved to order copies; save $1.50 per record by becoming a subscriber. Mail turnaround time 1 week.

General Information: Public access terminal has only civil records. No juvenile, child abuse or sexual battery records released. Will fax documents $1.00 per page. Certification fee: $1.75. Payee: Clerk of Circuit Court. Only cashiers checks and money orders accepted. Prepayment and SASE required.

Gilchrist County

Circuit & County Courts PO Box 37, Trenton, FL 32693; phone: 352-463-3170; probate phone: same; fax: 352-463-3166; hours 8:30AM-5PM (EST). *Felony, Misdemeanor, Civil, Eviction, Small Claims, Probate.* www.co.gilchrist.fl.us/cophone

Civil Records: Access: Mail, in person, online. Only the court performs in person searches; visitors may not. Search fee: $1.50 per name per year. Add $4.00 for written response (affidavit). Court makes copy: $1.00 per page; same fee for self serve. Required to search: name, years to search; also helpful: address. Civil cases indexed by defendant, plaintiff. Civil records on computer from 1987, prior on index books. Search judgments and liens online at the website. Mail turnaround time 2-3 days.

Criminal Records: Access: Mail, in person. Only the court performs in person searches; visitors may not. Search fee: $1.50 per name per year. Add $4.00 for written response (affidavit). Court makes copy: $1.00 per page; same fee for self serve. Required to search: name, years to search, DOB; also helpful: address, SSN, race, sex. Criminal records on computer since 1989, prior on index books. Mail turnaround time 2-3 days.

General Information: No public access terminal. No juvenile, child abuse or sexual battery records released. Will fax documents $1.00 per page; available for civil only. Certification fee: $1.50. Payee: Clerk of Circuit Court. Personal checks accepted. Prepayment and SASE required.

Glades County

Circuit & County Courts PO Box 10, Moore Haven, FL 33471; phone: 863-946-6011; criminal fax: 863-946-0560; same fax for civil and probate; hours 8AM-5PM (EST). *Felony, Misdemeanor, Civil, Eviction, Small Claims, Probate.*
Note: Probate is separate index at this same address.

Civil Records: Access: Mail, in person, online. Only the court performs in person searches; visitors may not. Search fee: $1.50 per name per year. Court makes copy: $1.00 per page; same fee for self serve. Required to search: name, years to search; also helpful: address. Civil cases indexed by defendant, plaintiff. Civil records on computer from 1991. Access an index of judgments only available at www.myfloridacounty.com. Fees involved to order copies; save $1.50 per record by becoming a subscriber. Mail turnaround time 2-3 days.

Criminal Records: Access: Mail, in person. Only the court performs in person searches; visitors may not. Search fee: $1.50 per name per year. Court makes copy: $1.00 per page; same fee for self serve. Required to search: name, years to search. Criminal records on computer from 1991. Mail turnaround time 2-3 days.

General Information: No public access terminal. No juvenile, child abuse or sexual battery records released. Will fax documents for $3.00 per page. Certification fee: $1.50 per document. Payee: Clerk of Circuit Court. Personal checks accepted. Prepayment and SASE required.

Gulf County

Circuit & County Courts 1000 Cecil Costin Blvd, Port St Joe, FL 32456; phone: 850-229-6112; fax: 850-229-6174; hours 9AM-5PM (EST). *Felony, Misdemeanor, Civil, Eviction, Small Claims, Probate.* www.gulfclerk.com

Civil Records: Access: Fax, mail, in person, online. Only the court performs in person searches; visitors may not. Search fee: $1.50 per name per year. Court makes copy: $.15 per page. Required to search: name, years to search. Civil cases indexed by defendant, plaintiff. Civil records on computer from 1990; archived to 1925. Access an index of judgments, liens, recorded documents at www.myfloridacounty.com. Fees involved to order copies; save $1.50 per record by becoming a subscriber. Mail turnaround time 1-3 days.

Criminal Records: Access: Fax, mail, in person. Only the court performs in person searches; visitors may not. Search fee: $1.50 per name per year. Court makes copy: $.15 per page. Required to search: name, years to search, DOB; also helpful: SSN. Criminal records on computer from 1990; archived to 1925. Mail turnaround time 1-3 days.

General Information: No juvenile, adoption, child abuse or sexual battery records released. Will fax documents $1.50 per page. Certification fee: $1.50. Payee: Clerk of Circuit Court. Personal checks accepted. Prepayment and SASE required.

Hamilton County

Circuit & County Courts 207 NE 1st St, #106, Jasper, FL 32052; phone: 386-792-1288; fax: 386-792-3524; hours 8:30AM-4:30PM (EST). *Felony, Misdemeanor, Civil, Eviction, Small Claims, Probate.*

Civil Records: Access: Mail, in person, online. Both court and visitors may perform in person searches. Search fee: $1.50 per name per year. Court makes copy: $1.00 per page; same fee for self serve. Required to search: name, years to search; also helpful: address. Civil records on computer from 1/91, county civil from 3/91. Access an index of judgments, liens, recorded documents at www.myfloridacounty.com. Fees involved to order copies; save $1.50 per record by becoming a subscriber. Mail turnaround time 2-3 days.

Criminal Records: Access: Mail, in person. Both court and visitors may perform in person searches. Search fee: $1.50 per name per year. Court makes copy: $1.00 per page; same fee for self serve. Required to search: name, years to search, DOB; also helpful: address, SSN, race, sex. Criminal records on computer since 1/89. Mail turnaround 2-3 days.

General Information: No public access terminal. No juvenile, child abuse or sexual battery records released. Will fax documents for $2.00 per page. Certification fee: $1.00. Payee: Clerk of Circuit Court. Personal checks not accepted. Prepayment required. SASE requested.

Hardee County

Circuit & County Courts PO Drawer 1749, Wauchula, FL 33873-1749; criminal phone: 863-773-2096; civil phone: 863-773-4174; probate phone: 863-773-4174; criminal fax: 863-773-9637; civil records fax: 863-773-9636; hours 8AM-5PM (EST). *Felony, Misdemeanor, Civil, Eviction, Small Claims, Probate.* www.hardeeclerk.com
Civil Records: Access: Mail, in person, online. Both court and visitors may perform in person searches. Search fee: $1.50 per name per year. Court makes copy: $1.00 per page. Required to search: name, years to search; also helpful: address. Civil records on computer from 1984. Access an index of judgments, liens, recorded documents at www.myfloridacounty.com. Fees involved to order copies; save $1.50 per record by becoming a subscriber. Mail turnaround time 2 days.
Criminal Records: Access: Mail, in person. Both court and visitors may perform in person searches. Search fee: $1.50 per name per year. Court makes copy: $1.00 per page. Required to search: name, years to search, DOB; also helpful: address, race, sex. Criminal records on computer from 1984. Mail turnaround time 3 days.
General Information: Public access terminal goes back to 1984. No juvenile, child abuse or sexual battery records released. Fee to fax documents is $1.00 per page. Certification fee: $3.00 per document. Payee: Clerk of Circuit Court. Business checks accepted. Prepayment required. SASE requested.

Hendry County

Circuit & County Courts PO Box 1760, LaBelle, FL 33975-1760; phone: 863-675-5369; criminal phone: 863-675-5214; civil phone: 863-675-5206; criminal fax: 863-612-4748; civil fax: 863-612-5299; 8:30AM-5PM *Felony, Misdemeanor, Civil, Eviction, Small Claims, Probate.*
Civil Records: Access: Mail, in person, online. Both court and visitors may perform in person searches. Search fee: $1.50 per name per year plus cert fee. Court makes copy: $1.00 per page. Required to search: name, years to search, DOB, SSN or DL, specify index to search; also helpful: address. Civil cases indexed by defendant, plaintiff. Civil records on computer since 5/92; on microfiche prior to 1989 if filed. Access www.myfloridacounty.com for an index of judgments, liens, recorded documents at. Fees involved to order copies; save $1.50 per record by becoming a subscriber. Mail turnaround time varies.
Criminal Records: Access: Mail, in person. Both court and visitors may perform in person searches. Search fee: $1.50 per name per year plus cert fee. Court makes copy: $1.00 per page. Required to search: name, years to search, DOB, SSN or DL, specify index to search; also helpful: address, race, sex. Misdemeanor records on computer since 1989, felony back to 1986; prior on microfiche. Mail turnaround time varies.
General Information: No public access terminal. No juvenile, child abuse or sexual battery records released. Will fax documents to local or toll-free number. Certification fee: $6.00 per document if they do search; $1.50 for simple cert seal per page. Payee: Clerk of Circuit Court. Only cashiers checks and money orders accepted. Prepayment required. Pay as you go plan. SASE requested.

Hernando County

Circuit & County Courts 20 N Main St, Brooksville, FL 34601; phone: 352-540-6377; criminal phone: 352-540-6444; civil phone: 352-540-6377; probate phone: 352-540-6366; fax: 352-754-4247; hours 8AM-5PM (EST). *Felony, Misdemeanor, Civil, Eviction, Small Claims, Probate.* www.clerk.co.hernando.fl.us
Civil Records: Access: Mail, online, in person. Both court and visitors may perform in person searches. Search fee: $1.50 per name per year. Court makes copy: $1.00 per page; same fee for self serve.

Required to search: name, years to search. Civil cases indexed by defendant, plaintiff. Civil records on computer from 1982, archived from late 1800s. Online access to court records is now free at www.clerk.co.hernando.fl.us/SearchType.asp. Online records may go as far back as 1/1983. Your browser must be JavaScript enables (MS Explorer 4.0 or above). Access an index of judgments, liens, recorded documents at www.myfloridacounty.com. Fees involved to order copies; save $1.50 per record by becoming a subscriber. Mail turnaround time approx. 5 days.
Criminal Records: Access: Mail, online, in person. Both court and visitors may perform in person searches. Search fee: $1.50 per name per year. Court makes copy: $1.00 per page; same fee for self serve. Required to search: name, years to search, DOB; also helpful: SSN. Criminal records on computer from 1982, archived from late 1800s. Index and docket information is available for felony and misdemeanor records. Online access to criminal records is the same as civil. Mail turnaround- approx. 5 days.
General Information: Public access terminal goes back to 1983. No juvenile, child abuse or sexual battery records released. Certification fee: $1.50. Payee: Clerk of Circuit Court. Personal checks accepted. Prepayment required.

Highlands County

Circuit & County Courts 590 S Commerce Ave, Sebring, FL 33870-3867; criminal phone: 863-402-6597; civil phone: 863-402-6591; probate phone: 863-402-6595; fax: 863-402-6575; probate fax: 863-402-6903; hours 8AM-5PM (EST). *Felony, Misdemeanor, Civil, Eviction, Small Claims, Probate.* www.clerk.co.highlands.fl.us
Civil Records: Access: Mail, in person, online. Both court and visitors may perform in person searches. Search fee: $1.50 per name per year. Court makes copy: $1.00 per page. Required to search: name, years to search. Civil cases indexed by defendant, plaintiff. Civil records on computer since 1992, prior on microfiche and film. Access to county clerk civil and probate records is free at www.clerk.co.highlands.fl.us/civil/search.masn, from 1991. Also includes small claims, probate, and tax deeds. Access an index of judgments, liens, recorded documents at www.myfloridacounty.com. Fees involved to order copies; save $1.50 per record by becoming a subscriber. Mail turnaround time 1 week.
Criminal Records: Access: Mail, in person. Both court and visitors may perform in person searches. Search fee: $1.50 per name per year. Court makes copy: $1.00 per page. Required to search: name, years to search; also helpful: SSN. Criminal records on computer since 1991, prior on microfiche and film. Mail turnaround time 1 week.
General Information: Public access terminal goes back to 1991. No juvenile, child abuse or sexual battery records released. Certification fee: $2.00. Payee: Clerk of Courts. Personal checks accepted. Prepayment required.

Hillsborough County

Circuit & County Courts 419 Pierce St, Tampa, FL 33602; phone: 813-276-8100; criminal phone: x7802; civil phone: x7803; hours 8AM-5PM (EST). *Felony, Misdemeanor, Civil, Eviction, Small Claims, Probate.* www.hillsclerk.com
Civil Records: Access: Fax, mail, online, in person. Both court and visitors may perform in person searches. Search fee: $1.50 per name per year. Court makes copy: $1.00 per page. Required to search: name, years to search; also helpful: address. Civil cases indexed by defendant, plaintiff. Civil records on computer since 5/85, prior on microfiche. Online access to records at http://207.156.115.73/or_wb1/or_sch_1.asp. Search the Court Progress Dockets free at http://publicrecord.hillsclerk.com/courtdisclaimer. html. A subscription service is also available for records, visit the home page for details and fees.

Note: Also, access an index of judgments, liens, recorded documents at www.myfloridacounty.com. Fees involved to order copies; save $1.50 per record by becoming a subscriber. Mail turnaround time 1-2 days.
Criminal Records: Access: Fax, mail, online, in person. Both court and visitors may perform in person searches. Search fee: $1.50 per name per year. Court makes copy: $1.00 per page. Required to search: name, years to search, DOB; also helpful: address, SSN, race, sex. Criminal records on computer since 1989, prior on microfiche to 1975, archived 1953 to 1974. Online access to the Court Progress Dockets Search is same as civil. Mail turnaround time 1-2 days.
General Information: Public access terminal available. No juvenile, child abuse or sexual battery records released. No fee to fax documents. Fax account required. Certification fee: $1.50. Payee: Clerk of Circuit Court. Local personal checks accepted. Prepayment required.

Holmes County

Circuit & County Courts PO Box 397, Bonifay, FL 32425; phone: 850-547-1100; fax: 850-547-6630; 8AM-4PM (CST). *Felony, Misdemeanor, Civil, Eviction, Small Claims, Probate.*
Civil Records: Access: Mail, in person, online. Both court and visitors may perform in person searches. Search fee: $1.50 per name per year. Court makes copy: $1.00 per page. Required to search: name, years to search; also helpful: address. Civil cases indexed by defendant, plaintiff. Civil records on computer from 10/91, archived from early 1900s. Access an index of judgments, liens, recorded documents at www.myfloridacounty.com. Fees involved to order copies; save $1.50 per record by becoming a subscriber. Mail turnaround time 1 week.
Criminal Records: Access: Mail, in person. Both court and visitors may perform in person searches. Search fee: $1.50 per name per year. Court makes copy: $1.00 per page. Required to search: name, years to search, DOB; also helpful: address, SSN, race, sex. Criminal records on computer since 1989, prior archived since early 1900s. Mail turnaround 1 week.
General Information: Public access terminal goes back to 1983. No juvenile, child abuse or sexual battery records released. Certification fee: $1.50 per page. Payee: Holmes County Clerk of Court. Personal checks accepted. Prepayment and SASE required.

Indian River County

Circuit & County Courts PO Box 1028, Vero Beach, FL 32961; phone: 772-770-5185; fax: 772-770-5008; hours 8:30AM-5PM (EST). *Felony, Misdemeanor, Civil, Eviction, Small Claims, Probate.* www.clerk.indian-river.org
Civil Records: Access: Mail, in person, online. Both court and visitors may perform in person searches. Search fee: $1.50 per name per year. Court makes copy: $1.00 per page. Required to search: name, years to search; also helpful: address. Civil cases indexed by defendant, plaintiff. Civil records on computer since 1984, prior on microfiche. Online access to county recordings index is free at www.clerk.indian-river.org/recordssearch/ori.asp. Records go back to 1983. Full access to court records is via the clerk's subscription service. Fee is $200.00 per month. For information about free and fee access, call Gary at 772-567-8000 x1216. Mail turnaround time 2 days.
Criminal Records: Access: Mail, in person, online. Both court and visitors may perform in person searches. Search fee: $1.50 per name per year. Court makes copy: $1.00 per page. Required to search: name, years to search, DOB; also helpful: address, SSN, race, sex. Criminal records on computer (Felony since 1986, Misdemeanor since 1983), both archived since 1925. Online access to criminal records is same as civil. Mail turnaround time 2 days.
General Information: Public access terminal available. No juvenile, child abuse or sexual battery

records released. Will not fax documents. Certification fee: $1.50. Payee: Clerk of Circuit Court. Only cashiers checks and money orders accepted. Prepayment required. SASE helpful.

Jackson County

Circuit & County Courts PO Box 510, Marianna, FL 32447; phone: 850-482-9552; fax: 850-482-7849; hours 8AM-4:30PM (CST). *Felony, Misdemeanor, Civil, Eviction, Small Claims, Probate.* www.jacksonclerk.com
Civil Records: Access: Fax, mail, in person, online. Both court and visitors may perform in person searches. Search fee: $1.50 per name per year. Court makes copy: $1.00 per page; same fee for self serve. Required to search: name, years to search; also helpful: address. Civil cases indexed by defendant, plaintiff. Civil records go back to 1900; computerized records go back to 1989. Access an index of judgments, liens, recorded documents at www.myfloridacounty.com. Fees involved to order copies; save $1.50 per record by becoming a subscriber. Mail turnaround time 1-5 days.
Criminal Records: Access: Fax, mail, in person. Both court and visitors may perform in person searches. Search fee: $1.50 per name per year. Court makes copy: $1.00 per page; same fee for self serve. Required to search: name, years to search, DOB; also helpful: address, SSN, race, sex. Criminal records go back to 1900; computerized records since 1989. Mail turnaround time 1-5 days.
General Information: Public access terminal goes back to 1989. No juvenile, child abuse or sexual battery records released. Will fax documents $3.00 1st page, $1.00 each add'l. Certification fee: $1.50. Payee: Clerk of Circuit Court. Personal checks or Visa, MC accepted. Prepayment required. SASE helpful.

Jefferson County

Circuit & County Courts Jefferson County Courthouse, Rm 10, Monticello, FL 32344; phone: 850-342-0218; fax: 850-342-0222; hours 8AM-5PM (EST). *Felony, Misdemeanor, Civil, Eviction, Small Claims, Probate.* www.myjeffersoncounty.com
Civil Records: Access: Mail, in person, online. Only the court performs in person searches; visitors may not. Search fee: $1.50 per name per year. Court makes copy: $1.00 per page. Required to search: name, years to search; also helpful: address. Civil cases indexed by defendant, plaintiff. Civil records on computer since 7/90, prior on dockets. Access an index of judgments, liens, recorded documents at www.myfloridacounty.com, for 01/1/73 to current. Fees involved to order copies; save $1.50 per record by becoming a subscriber. Mail turnaround time 1 week.
Criminal Records: Access: Fax, mail, in person. Only the court performs in person searches; visitors may not. Search fee: $1.50 per name per year. Court makes copy: $1.00 per page. Required to search: name, years to search, DOB; also helpful: address, SSN, race, sex. Criminal records on computer since 1989, prior on microfiche from 1969 to 1980, archived since 1950s, prior to 1950 on dockets. Mail turnaround time 1 week.
General Information: No public access terminal. No juvenile, child abuse or sexual battery records released. Fee to fax documents is $2.00 per page. Certification fee: $1.50. Payee: Clerk of Circuit Court. Personal checks accepted. Credit cards accepted if in person, surcharges apply. Prepayment required.

Lafayette County

Circuit & County Courts PO Box 88, Mayo, FL 32066; phone: 386-294-1600; fax: 386-294-4231; 8AM-5PM (EST). *Felony, Misdemeanor, Civil, Eviction, Small Claims, Probate.*
Civil Records: Access: Phone, mail, fax, in person, online. Both court and visitors may perform in person searches. No search fee. Court makes copy:

$1.00 per page. Required to search: name, years to search; also helpful: address. Civil cases indexed by defendant, plaintiff. Civil records on computer since 1997, on books back to early 1900s. Access an index of judgments, liens, recorded documents at www.myfloridacounty.com. Fees involved to order copies; save $1.50 per record by becoming a subscriber. Mail turnaround time 5-7 days.
Criminal Records: Access: Phone, mail, fax, in person. Both court and visitors may perform in person searches. Search fee: $1.50 per name per yr. Court makes copy: $1.00 per page. Required to search: name, years to search, DOB; also helpful: address, SSN, race, sex. Criminal records computerized since 1989. Mail turnaround 5-7 days.
General Information: Public access terminal available. No juvenile, child abuse or sexual battery records released. Certification fee: $1.50. Payee: Clerk of Circuit Court. Personal checks accepted. Prepayment and SASE required.

Lake County

Circuit & County Courts PO Box 7800, 550 W Main St, Tavares, FL 32778; phone: 352-742-4100; criminal phone: 352-742-4126(Felony) 352-742-4128(Misdemeanor); civil phone: 352-742-4145 County; 352-742-4148 Circuit; probate phone: 352-742-4122; fax: 352-742-4166; hours 8:30AM-5PM (EST). *Felony, Misdemeanor, Civil, Eviction, Small Claims, Probate.*
www.lakecountyclerk.org/default1.asp
Civil Records: Access: Fax, mail, in person, online. Both court and visitors may perform in person searches. Search fee: $1.50 per name per year. Court makes copy: $1.00 per page. Required to search: name, years to search. Civil cases indexed by defendant, plaintiff. Civil records on computer since 1984, county civil on index books since 11/51, circuit civil since 1888.
Online access to Clerk of Court records is free at www.lakecountyclerk.org/services.asp?subject=Online_Court_Records. County civil records go back to 1985; Circuit records go back to 9/84. Also, previous 2-weeks civil records and divorces on a private site at http://extra.orlandosentinel.com/publicrecords/search.asp. Mail turnaround time 7-10 days.
Criminal Records: Access: Fax, mail, in person, online. Both court and visitors may perform in person searches. Search fee: $1.50 per name per year. Court makes copy: $1.00 per page. Required to search: name, years to search, DOB; also helpful: SSN, sex. Criminal records on computer since 1989, archived since 1888. Some on index books. Online access is the same as civil, see above. Mail turnaround time 7-10 days.
General Information: Public access terminal has criminal back to 1989 and civil back to 1985. Expunged & sealed records will not be released. No mental health, juvenile, child abuse or sexual battery records released. Will fax documents for $1.00 per page. Certification fee: $1.50. Payee: Clerk of Circuit Court. Personal checks accepted. Prepayment required. SASE helpful.

Lee County

Circuit & County Courts PO Box 2469, Ft Myers, FL 33902; phone: 239-335-2283; hours 7:45AM-5PM (EST). *Felony, Misdemeanor, Civil, Eviction, Small Claims, Probate, Traffic.*
www.leeclerk.org
Civil Records: Access: Mail, online, in person. Both court and visitors may perform in person searches. Search fee: $1.50 per name per year. Court makes copy: $1.00 per page. Required to search: name, years to search. Civil cases indexed by defendant, plaintiff. Civil records on computer since 1988, prior on microfilm and dockets. Access records free at www.leeclerk.org/court_inquiry_disclaimer.htm. Online records go back to 1988. Includes traffic, felony, misdemeanor, civil, small claims and probate. Access an index of judgments, liens, recorded documents at www.leeclerk.org or

www.myfloridacounty.com. Search free but fees involved to order certified copies; save the per-record copy fee by becoming a subscriber; sub fee is $25.00 per month. Mail turnaround time 5 days.
Criminal Records: Access: Mail, online, in person. Both court and visitors may perform in person searches. Search fee: $1.50 per name per year. Court makes copy: $1.00 per page. Required to search: name, years to search, DOB; also helpful: address, SSN, race, sex. Criminal records on computer-(Felony since 1978, Misdemeanor since 1986), prior on microfilm. Online access to criminal records is the same as civil. Mail turnaround time 5 days.
General Information: Public access terminal goes back to 1990. No juvenile, child abuse or sexual offense records released. Will not fax documents. Certification fee: $1.50 per document. Payee: Clerk of Circuit Court. Personal checks accepted. Prepayment and SASE required.

Leon County

Circuit & County Courts PO Box 726, Tallahassee, FL 32302; phone: 850-577-4000; criminal phone: 850-577-4070; civil phone: 850-577-4170; probate phone: 850-577-4180; hours 8:30AM-5PM (EST). *Felony, Misdemeanor, Civil, Eviction, Small Claims, Probate.* www.clerk.leon.fl.us
Civil Records: Access: Mail, online, in person. Both court and visitors may perform in person searches. Search fee: $1.50 per name per year. Court makes copy: $1.00 per page. Required to search: name, years to search; also helpful: address. Civil cases indexed by defendant, plaintiff. Civil records on computer since 8/86, prior on docket books. Also, you may search cases and "High Profile Cases" (re: Election 2000) at www.clerk.leon.fl.us under "Search Court Databases." Registration required. Access an index of judgments, liens, recorded documents at www.myfloridacounty.com. Fees involved to order copies; save $1.50 per record by becoming a subscriber. Mail turnaround time 1-5 days.
Criminal Records: Access: Mail, online, in person. Both court and visitors may perform in person searches. Search fee: $1.50 per name per year. Court makes copy: $1.00 per page. Required to search: name, years to search, DOB; also helpful: address, SSN, race, sex. Criminal records on computer since 1976, on microfiche since 1937, archived since late 1800s/early 1900s. Online access to criminal records is the same as civil. Mail turnaround time 1-5 days.
General Information: Public access terminal goes back to 1990. No juvenile, child abuse or sexual battery records released. Certification fee: $1.50. Payee: Clerk of Circuit Court. Personal checks accepted. Prepayment required. SASE helpful.

Levy County

Circuit & County Courts PO Box 610, Bronson, FL 32621; criminal phone: 352-486-5256; civil phone: 352-486-5277; probate phone: 352-486-5459; 8AM-5PM (EST). *Felony, Misdemeanor, Civil, Eviction, Small Claims, Probate.*
www.levyclerk.com
Civil Records: Access: Mail, in person, online. Both court and visitors may perform in person searches. Search fee: $1.50 per name per year. Court makes copy: $1.00 per page; same fee for self serve. Required to search: name, years to search; also helpful: address. Civil cases indexed by defendant, plaintiff. Civil records on computer from 1986, microfiche to 1981 (in process), prior on docket books. Access an index of judgments, liens, recorded documents is at www.myfloridacounty.com. Fees involved to order copies; save $1.50 per record by becoming a subscriber. Mail turnaround time 1-2 days.
Criminal Records: Access: Mail, in person. Both court and visitors may perform in person searches. Search fee: $1.50 per name per year. Court makes copy: $1.00 per page; same fee for self serve. Required to search: name, years to search, DOB, signed release; also helpful: address, SSN, race, sex.

Criminal records on computer from 1986 to present, prior on docket books. Mail turnaround 2-3 days.

General Information: Public access terminal has civil records back to 1986. No juvenile, child abuse or sexual battery records released. Certification fee: $1.50. Payee: Clerk of Circuit Court. Business checks accepted. Prepayment and SASE required.

Liberty County

Circuit & County Courts PO Box 399, Bristol, FL 32321; phone: 850-643-2215; probate phone: same; fax: 850-643-2866; hours 8AM-5PM (EST). *Felony, Misdemeanor, Civil, Eviction, Small Claims, Probate.* www.libertyclerk.com

Civil Records: Access: Mail, in person, online. Both court and visitors may perform in person searches. Search fee: $1.50 per name per year. Court makes copy: $1.00 per page. Required to search: name, years to search; also helpful: address. Civil cases indexed by defendant, plaintiff. Civil records on docket books. Access an index of judgments, liens, and civil court-related documents at www.myfloridacount y.com. Fees involved to order copies; save $1.50 per record by becoming a subscriber. Mail turnaround time 1 week.

Criminal Records: Access: Mail, in person. Both court and visitors may perform in person searches. Search fee: $1.50 per name per year. Court makes copy: $1.00 per page. Required to search: name, years to search, DOB; also helpful: address, SSN, race, sex. Criminal records on docket books. Mail turnaround time 1 week.

General Information: Public access terminal has criminal back to 1998 and civil back to 2002. No juvenile, child abuse or sexual battery records released. Certification fee: $1.50. Payee: Clerk of Circuit Court. Business checks accepted. Prepayment and SASE required.

Madison County

Circuit & County Courts PO Box 237, Madison, FL 32341; phone: 850-973-1500; fax: 850-973-2059; hours 8AM-5PM (EST). *Felony, Misdemeanor, Civil, Eviction, Small Claims, Probate.*

Civil Records: Access: Phone, mail, in person, online. Both court and visitors may perform in person searches. Search fee: $1.50 per name per year. Court makes copy: $1.00 per page; same fee for self serve. Required to search: name, years to search; also helpful: address. Civil cases indexed by defendant, plaintiff. Civil records on computer since 1988, prior on docket books. Access an index of judgments, liens, recorded documents at www.myfloridacounty.com. Fees involved to order copies; save $1.50 per record by becoming a subscriber. Mail turnaround time 1-3 days.

Criminal Records: Access: Phone, mail, in person. Both court and visitors may perform in person searches. Search fee: $1.50 per name per year. Court makes copy: $1.00 per page; same fee for self serve. Required to search: name, years to search, DOB; also helpful: address, SSN, race, sex. Criminal records on computer since 1988, prior on docket books. Mail turnaround time 1-3 days.

General Information: No public access terminal. No juvenile, child abuse or sexual battery records released. Certification fee: $1.50. Payee: Clerk of Circuit Court. Personal checks accepted. Prepayment required. SASE requested.

Manatee County

Circuit & County Courts PO Box 25400, Bradenton, FL 34206; phone: 941-749-1800; criminal phone: 941-741-4019; civil phone: 941-741-4025; probate phone: 941-741-4021; criminal fax: 941-741-4082; civil records fax: 941-741-4093; probate fax: 941-741-4093; hours 8:30AM-5PM (EST). *Felony, Misdemeanor, Civil, Eviction, Small Claims, Probate.* www.manateeclerk.com

Civil Records: Access: Phone, fax, mail, online, in person, email. Both court and visitors may perform

in person searches. Search fee: $1.50 per name per year. Court makes copy: $1.00 per page. Self serve copy fee: $1.00 per page. Required to search: name, years to search; also helpful: address. Civil cases indexed by defendant, plaintiff. Civil records on computer since 9/80, prior on microfilm back to 1972. A subscription online service is $50 plus $60 per user fee advance; for sign-up information visit the website. Also, court records at Circuit clerk's office are free at www.manateeclerk.com/mp a/cvweb.asp. Access an index of judgments, liens, recordings at www.myfloridacounty.com. Fees involved to order copies; save $1.50 per record by becoming a subscriber. Mail turnaround 2 days.

Criminal Records: Access: Phone, fax, mail, online, in person, email. Both court and visitors may perform in person searches. Search fee: $1.50 per name per year. Court makes copy: $1.00 per page. Self serve copy fee: $1.00 per page. Required to search: name, years to search, DOB; also helpful: address, charge, race, sex. Criminal records on computer since 1981, prior on docket books back to 1972. Online access to criminal records is the same as civil. Mail turnaround time 2 days.

General Information: Public access terminal has criminal back to 1981 and civil back to 9/1980. No juvenile, adoption, child abuse or sexual battery victim records released. Will fax documents for $1.00 per page. Certification fee: $1.50. Payee: Clerk of Circuit Court. Personal checks or Visa, MC accepted. Prepayment required. SASE helpful.

Marion County

Circuit & County Courts PO Box 1030, Ocala, FL 34478; phone: 352-620-3892 (cty civ); criminal phone: 352-620-3861; civil phone: 352-620-3891 (Circ); probate phone: 352-620-3874; criminal fax: 352-840-5668; civil records fax: 352-620-3300; hours 8AM-5PM (EST). *Felony, Misdemeanor, Civil, Eviction, Small Claims, Probate.* www.marioncountyclerk.org

Civil Records: Access: Fax, mail, in person, online. Both court and visitors may perform in person searches. Search fee: $1.50 per name per year. Court makes copy: $1.00 per page. Required to search: name, years to search; also helpful: address. Civil cases indexed by defendant, plaintiff. Civil records on computer since 1983, on microfiche since 1958. Online access to county clerk civil records is free at www.marioncountyclerk.org/. Click on Case Search found on left side under Courts. Access an index of judgments, liens, recorded documents at www.myfloridacounty.com. Fees involved to order copies; save $1.50 per record by becoming a subscriber. Mail turnaround time 1-2 weeks.

Criminal Records: Access: Fax, mail, in person. Both court and visitors may perform in person searches. Search fee: $1.50 per name per year. Court makes copy: $1.00 per page. Required to search: name, years to search, DOB; also helpful: address, SSN, race, sex. Criminal records on computer. Felonies since 1984, on microfiche from 1950 to 1979, prior on index cards. Misdemeanors since 1983, on microfiche from 1900 to 1982, archived since 1900s, prior on index cards. Mail turnaround time 1-2 weeks.

General Information: Public access terminal goes back to 1983. No juvenile records released. Will fax documents to local or toll free line, otherwise fee involved. Certification fee: $1.50. Payee: Clerk of Court. Personal checks accepted. In person requester may use credit card, surcharge applies. Prepayment required. SASE requested.

Martin County

Circuit & County Courts PO Box 9016, Stuart, FL 34995; criminal phone: 772-288-5576; civil phone: 772-288-5717; probate phone: 772-288-5540; criminal fax: 772-288-5990; civil records fax: 772-288-5991; probate fax: 772-221-2388; hours 8AM-5PM (EST). *Felony, Misdemeanor, Civil, Eviction, Small Claims, Probate.* http://clerk-web.martin.fl.us/ClerkWeb

Civil Records: Access: Phone, fax, mail, online, in person. Both court and visitors may perform in person searches. Search fee: $1.50 per name per year. Court makes copy: $1.00 per page. Required to search: name, years to search; also helpful: address. Civil cases indexed by defendant, plaintiff. Civil records on computer since 10/86, prior on microfiche, microfilm and archived. Online access to civil case information on the records division database is free at http://clerk-web.martin.fl.us/wb_or1. Also includes small claims, recordings, other document types. Mail turnaround time 1 week.

Criminal Records: Access: Phone, fax, mail, in person, online. Both court and visitors may perform in person searches. Search fee: $1.50 per name per year prior to 1990. Court makes copy: $1.00 per page. Required to search: name, years to search, DOB; also helpful: address, SSN. Criminal records on computer. Felonies since 1986, on microfiche since 1956, prior on index cards and docket books. Misdemeanors since 1985, on microfiche since 1973, prior on index cards and docket books. Criminal and civil records are available through dial in modem for a nominal fee contract with the Clerk. This is the same access mode that government agencies may use free upon request. Mail turnaround time 1 week.

General Information: Public access terminal has criminal back to 1989 and civil back to 1984. No juvenile, child abuse or sexual battery records released. Will fax documents $1.25 per page. Certification fee: $1.50. Payee: Clerk of Circuit Court. Personal checks accepted. Prepayment required.

Miami - Dade County

See Dade County.

Monroe County

Circuit & County Courts Clerk of the Court, 500 Whitehead St, Key West, FL 33040; phone: 305-294-4641 x3342; fax: 305-295-3623; hours 8:30AM-5PM (EST). *Felony, Misdemeanor, Civil, Eviction, Small Claims, Probate.* www.co.monroe.fl.us

Civil Records: Access: Mail, fax, in person, online. Both court and visitors may perform in person searches. Search fee: $1.50 per name per year. Court makes copy: $1.00 per page. Required to search: name, years to search; also helpful: address. Civil cases indexed by defendant, plaintiff. Civil records on computer since 1983, on microfiche since 1972, prior on docket books. Some records purged after 2 years. Probate from 1972. Online access to civil cases is free at www.clerk-of-the-court.com/searchCiv ilCases.asp. Subscription is required for viewing full document library. Mail turnaround 1-2 weeks.

Criminal Records: Access: Mail, fax, in person, online. Both court and visitors may perform in person searches. Search fee: $1.50 per name per year. Court makes copy: $1.00 per page. Required to search: name, years to search, DOB; also helpful: address, SSN, race, sex. Criminal records (pending felony and misdemeanors) on computer, others since 1992, non-pending on microfiche since 1945. Online access to criminal records is free at www.clerk-of-the-court.com/searchCriminalCases.asp. Includes traffic cases online. Subscription is required for viewing full document library. Mail turnaround time 1-2 weeks.

General Information: Public access terminal goes back to 1982. No juvenile, child abuse or sexual battery records released. Fee to fax documents is $1.00 per page. Certification fee: $1.50. Payee: Clerk of Circuit Court. Personal checks accepted. Prepayment required. SASE helpful.

Nassau County

Circuit & County Courts PO Box 456, 76347 Veterans Way, Fernandina Beach, FL 32035; criminal phone: 904-548-4607; civil phone: 904-548-4600; probate phone: 904-548-4600; fax: 904-548-4529; hours 8:30AM-5PM (EST). *Felony, Misdemeanor, Civil, Eviction, Small Claims, Probate.* www.nassauclerk.com

Civil Records: Access: Phone, fax, mail, in person, online. Only the court performs in person searches; visitors may not. Search fee: $1.50 per name per year. Court makes copy: $1.00 per page. Required to search: name, years to search; also helpful: address. Civil cases indexed by defendant, plaintiff. Civil records on computer since 1993, on microfiche since 1982, prior on docket books. Access an index of judgments, sentences, county commitments, uniform state commitments, disposition notices and nolle prosequi only at www.myfloridacounty.com. Fees involved to order copies; save $1.50 per record by becoming a subscriber. Mail turnaround time 1 week.

Criminal Records: Access: Phone, fax, mail, in person, online. Only the court performs in person searches; visitors may not. Search fee: $1.50 per name per year. Court makes copy: $1.00 per page. Required to search: name, years to search, DOB; also helpful: address, SSN, race, sex. Criminal records on computer since 1985, on microfiche since 1982, prior on docket books. Limited criminal records online; see civil section above. Note: Past 5 years only can be done on the phone. Mail turnaround time 1 week.

General Information: No public access terminal. No juvenile, child abuse or sexual battery records released. Will fax documents for $1.00 per page. Certification fee: $1.50. Payee: Clerk of Circuit Court. Personal checks accepted. Prepayment and SASE required.

Okaloosa County

Circuit & County Courts 1250 N Eglin Pky, Shalimar, FL 32579; phone: 850-651-7200; fax: 850-651-7230; hours 8AM-5PM (CST). *Felony, Misdemeanor, Civil, Eviction, Small Claims, Probate.*
www.clerkofcourts.cc

Civil Records: Access: Mail, online, in person. Both court and visitors may perform in person searches. Search fee: $1.50 per year per name; Certificates $6.00. Court makes copy: $1.00 per page. Required to search: name, years to search; also helpful: address. Civil cases indexed by defendant, plaintiff. Civil records on computer from 6/86; archives from 1915; prior on microfilm. 3 options available. Access to the full online system (civil, probate, traffic) requires monthly fee of $100.00. For more information, call 850-689-5821. Also, civil records are free at www.clerkofcourts.cc/orsearch/pubchoice.asp Records go back to 1/86. Search civil index by defendant or plaintiff, date, or file type. Note: Access an index of judgments, liens, recorded documents back to 1/1983 at www.myfloridacounty.com. Fees involved to order copies; save $1.50 per record by becoming a subscriber. Mail turnaround time 1 day.

Criminal Records: Access: Mail, online, in person. Both court and visitors may perform in person searches. Search fee: $1.50 per year per name; Certificates $6.00. Court makes copy: $1.00 per page. Required to search: name, years to search, DOB; also helpful: address, SSN, race, sex. Criminal records on computer from 1/89; archives from 1915; prior on microfilm. Access to the full online system (civil, probate, traffic) requires monthly fee of $100.00. For more information, call 850-689-5821. Both felony and misdemeanor indexes can be searched. Also, the county clerk has placed traffic misdemeanor records free on the Internet at www.clerkofcourts.cc/pa/pa.urd/pamw6500.display Mail turnaround time 1 day to 1 week.

General Information: Public access terminal has criminal back to 1/1989 and civil back to 6/1986. No juvenile, child abuse or sexual battery records released. Will fax documents for $1.00 per page. Certification fee: $1.50 per page. Payee: Clerk of Circuit Court. Personal checks accepted. Prepayment and SASE required.

Okeechobee County

Circuit & County Courts 304 NW 2nd St, Rm 101, Okeechobee, FL 34972; phone: 863-763-2131; hours 8:30AM-5PM (EST). *Felony, Misdemeanor, Civil, Eviction, Small Claims, Probate.*

Civil Records: Access: Mail, in person. Both court and visitors may perform in person searches. Search fee: $1.50 per name per year. Court makes copy: $1.00 per page. Required to search: name, years to search; also helpful: address. Civil cases indexed by defendant, plaintiff. Civil records on computer since 1990, on index cards from 1983 to 1988. Mail turnaround time for criminal: 2 weeks; civil 1-2 weeks.

Criminal Records: Access: Mail, in person. Both court and visitors may perform in person searches. Search fee: $1.50 per name per year. Court makes copy: $1.00 per page. Required to search: name, years to search, DOB; also helpful: address, SSN, race, sex. Criminal records on computer since 1989, on index cards from 1932 to 1988. Mail turnaround time for criminal: 2 weeks; civil 1-2 weeks.

General Information: Public access terminal has criminal back to 1985 and civil back to 2000. No juvenile, child abuse or sexual battery records released. Certification fee: $1.50. Payee: Clerk of Circuit Court. Personal checks accepted. Prepayment and SASE required.

Orange County

Circuit & County Courts PO Box 4994 (425 N Orange Ave), Orlando, FL 32801-1544; phone: 407-836-2060; hours 8AM-5PM (EST). *Felony, Misdemeanor, Civil, Eviction, Small Claims, Probate.* http://orangeclerk.ocfl.net
Note: Mail requests should use room numbers; civil circuit-310; civil county-350; crim circuit-210; crim county-250.

Civil Records: Access: Mail, online, in person, email. Both court and visitors may perform in person searches. Search fee: $1.50 per name per year. Court makes copy: $1.00 per page. Required to search: name, years to search. Civil cases indexed by defendant, plaintiff. Civil records are on computer as follows: Circuit civil-1992; Domestic civil-1992; Probate-1993; Traffic-1980. The Teleclerk countywide remote online system has been replaced by the free iclerk system at http://orangeclerk1.onetgov.net/. Set your browser "privacy" to "low." Use "public" as username and password. For more information, call 407-836-2060. Also, previous 2-weeks civil records on a private site at http://extra.orlandosentinel.com/publicrecords/search.asp. Note: This court also accepts email requests. Mail turnaround 2 days.

Criminal Records: Access: Mail, online, in person, email. Both court and visitors may perform in person searches. Search fee: $1.50 per name per year. Court makes copy: $1.00 per page. Required to search: name, years to search, DOB. Criminal records on computer go back to 1990; prior records go back to 1987. The Teleclerk countywide remote online system has been replaced by the free iclerk system at http://orangeclerk1.onetgov.net. Note: This court also accepts email requests. Mail turnaround time 2 days.

General Information: Public access terminal goes back to 2000. (Available in Records Management Division.) No sex-related or adoption records released. Certification fee: $1.50. Payee: Orange County Clerk of Courts. Personal checks accepted from Orange County only. Prepayment required. SASE helpful.

Orange County

County Court - Apopka Branch 1111 N Rock Springs Rd, Apopka, FL 32712; phone: 407-836-2007; fax: 407-654-1031; hours 8AM-5PM (EST). *Misdemeanor, Civil Actions Under $15,000, Eviction, Small Claims.* http://orangeclerk.ocfl.net
Note: Records maintained at Orlando office.

Civil Records: Access: Mail, online, in person. Both court and visitors may perform in person searches. Search fee: $1.50 per name per year. Court makes copy: $1.00 per page. Required to search: name, years to search. Civil cases indexed by defendant, plaintiff. Pending civil records on computer. All dockets on microfilm or microfiche; some records on index cards. The Teleclerk countywide remote online system has been replaced by the free iclerk system at http://orangeclerk1.onetgov.net. Set your browser "privacy" to "low." Use "public" as username and password. Probate records available. Also, previous 2-weeks civil records on a private site at http://extra.orlandosentinel.com/publicrecords/search.asp. Mail turnaround time 2 days.

Criminal Records: Access: Mail, online, in person. Both court and visitors may perform in person searches. Search fee: $1.50 per name. Court makes copy: $1.00 per page. Required to search: name, years to search, DOB; also helpful: SSN. Criminal records (Pending) on computer. All dockets on microfilm or microfiche. Some records on index cards. Online access to criminal records is the same as civil. Mail turnaround time 2 days.

General Information: Public use terminal available. No sex related or adoption records released. Certification fee: $2.50. Payee: Clerk of County Court. No Personal checks accepted. Prepayment required. SASE helpful.

County Court - NE Orange Division 450 N Lakemont Ave, Winter Park, FL 32792; phone: 407-671-1116; fax: 407-671-4837; hours 7:30AM-5:30PM (EST). *Misdemeanor, Civil Actions Under $15,000, Eviction, Small Claims.*
http://orangeclerk.ocfl.net

Civil Records: Access: Phone, mail, online, in person. Only the court performs in person searches; visitors may not. Search fee: $1.50 per name per year. Court makes copy: $1.00 per page. Required to search: name, years to search. Civil cases indexed by defendant, plaintiff. Civil records (Pending) on computer. All dockets on microfilm or microfiche. The Teleclerk countywide remote online system has been replaced by the free Iclerk system at http://orangeclerk1.onetgov.net. Set your browser "privacy" to "low." Use "public" as username and password. Also, previous 2-weeks civil records on private site at http://extra.orlandosentinel.com/publicrecords/search.asp. Mail turnaround time 2 days.

Criminal Records: Access: Phone, mail, online, in person. Only the court performs in person searches; visitors may not. Search fee: $1.50 per name per year. Court makes copy: $1.00 per page. Required to search: name, years to search, DOB; also helpful: SSN. Criminal records (Pending) on computer. All dockets on microfilm or microfiche. Online access to criminal records is the same as civil. Mail turnaround time 2 days.

General Information: No public access terminal. No sex related or adoption records released. Will fax documents to local or toll-free number. Certification fee: $1.50. Payee: Clerk of County Court. Only cashiers checks and money orders accepted. Prepayment required. SASE helpful.

County Court #3 Clerk of Courts, 475 W Story Rd, Ocoee, FL 34761; phone: 407-836-2007; fax: 407-667-6241; hours 8AM-5PM (EST). *Misdemeanor, Civil Actions Under $15,000, Eviction, Small Claims.* http://orangeclerk.ocfl.net

Civil Records: Access: Mail, online, in person. Both court and visitors may perform in person searches. Search fee: $5.00 per name. Court makes copy: $1.50 per page. Required to search: name, years to search. Civil cases indexed by defendant, plaintiff. Civil records go back to 1890; on computer back to 1990. All dockets are on microfilm or microfiche. The Teleclerk countywide remote online system has been replaced by the free iclerk system at http://orangeclerk1.onetgov.net/. Set your browser "privacy" to "low. Use "public" as username and password. For more information, call 407-836-2060. Also, previous 2-weeks civil records on a private site at http://extra.orlandosentinel.com/publicrecords/search.asp. Mail turnaround time 2 days depending on file.

Criminal Records: Access: Mail, online, in person. Both court and visitors may perform in person searches. Search fee: $5.00 per name. Court makes copy: $1.50 per page. Required to search: name, years to search, DOB; also helpful: SSN. Criminal records go back to 1890; on computer back to 1990. All dockets are on microfilm or microfiche. Online access to criminal records is the same as civil. Mail turnaround time 2 days depending on file.

General Information: Public use terminal available. No sex related or adoption records released. Certification fee: $2.00 per page. Payee: Clerk of County Court. Personal checks or Visa, MC accepted. Accepted for civil payments only. Prepayment required. SASE helpful.

Osceola County

Circuit Court - Civil 2 Courthouse Sq, Kissimmee, FL 34741; phone: 407-343-3500; probate phone: 407-343-3506; fax: 407-343-3652; hours 8:30AM-5PM (EST). *Civil Actions Over $5,000, Probate.* www.ninja9.org

Civil Records: Access: Mail, in person, online. Both court and visitors may perform in person searches. Search fee: $1.50 per name per year per division. Court makes copy: $1.00 per page. Required to search: name, years to search. Civil cases indexed by defendant, plaintiff. Civil records on computer from 1990, on docket books from 1800s to 1990. Online access to court records on the Clerk of Circuit Court database are free at www.osceolaclerkcourt.org/genrlmnu.htm. Also, access an index of judgments, liens, recorded documents at www.myfloridacounty.com. Fees involved to order copies; save $1.50 per record by becoming a subscriber. Also, previous 2-weeks civil records on a private site at http://extra.orlandosentinel.com/publicrecords/search.asp. Mail turnaround time 1-2 days.

General Information: Public terminal has only civil records back to 1990. No appeal records released. Will fax documents if prepaid. Certification fee: $1.50. Payee: Clerk of Court. Business checks accepted. Prepayment and SASE required.

County Court - Civil 2 Courthouse Sq, #2000, Kissimmee, FL 34741; phone: 407-343-3500; hours 8:30AM-5PM (EST). *Eviction, Small Claims.* www.osceolaclerk.com

Civil Records: Access: Mail, in person, online. Both court and visitors may perform in person searches. Search fee: $1.50 per name per year per division. Court makes copy: $1.00 per page. Required to search: name, years to search. Civil cases indexed by defendant, plaintiff. Civil records on computer from 1991, on index cards from 1972 to 1991, on docket books from 1800s to 1972. Online access to court records on the Clerk of Circuit Court database are free at www.osceolaclerkcourt.org. Mail turnaround time 1 week.

General Information: Public terminal has only civil records back to 1990. No juvenile records released. Will fax documents if prepaid. Certification fee: $1.50. Payee: Clerk of Court. Business checks accepted. Prepayment required. SASE helpful.

Circuit & County Courts - Criminal Division 2 Courthouse Square, Kissimmee, FL 34741; phone: 407-343-3543; fax: 407-343-3552; hours 8:30AM-5PM (EST). *Felony, Misdemeanor.* www.osceolaclerk.com

Note: Misdemeanors can be reached at 407-343-3555.

Criminal Records: Access: Mail, in person, online. Both court and visitors may perform in person searches. Search fee: $1.50 per name per year. Court makes copy: $1.00 per page; same fee for self serve. Required to search: name, years to search, DOB, SSN. Criminal records on computer back to 1990, on index since 1978, prior on docket books from 1800s to 1978. Online access to criminal records is free at www.osceolaclerkcourt.org/search.htm. Includes

party index and case summary searching. Search inmates at www.osceola.org/index.cfm?lsFuses=inmates. Note: Both the court and visitors may perform in person searches as long as the case occurred 1990 or after. Mail turnaround 1 week.

General Information: Public terminal has only criminal records back to 1990. No juvenile or sealed records released. Will fax documents to local or toll free line. Certification fee: $1.50. Payee: Money orders payable to Clerk of the Court. Business checks accepted. Credit cards accepted; a surcharge is added. Prepayment required. SASE requested.

Palm Beach County

Circuit Court - Civil Division PO Box 4667, West Palm Beach, FL 33402; phone: 561-355-2986; fax: 561-355-4643; hours 8AM-5PM (EST). *Civil.* www.pbcountyclerk.com

Civil Records: Access: Phone, mail, online, in person. Both court and visitors may perform in person searches. Search fee: $1.50 per name per year. Court makes copy: $1.00 per page. Required to search: name, years to search; also helpful: address. Civil cases indexed by defendant, plaintiff. Civil records (Circuit) on computer from 1982, prior records on microfiche and dockets. County on computer from 1987, prior on microfilm. Access to the countywide is free. Civil index goes back to '88. Records also include probate, traffic and domestic. Contact Rowtera Simmons at 561-355-4277 for information. Also, access 15th judicial circuit records at http://web3172.co.palm-beach.fl.us. Registration and password is required. Service may be discontinued. Note: Also, civil records only are free at http://courtcon.co.palm-beach.fl.us/pls/jiwp/ck_public_qry_main.cp_main_idx. Mail turnaround time 1 week.

General Information: Public terminal has only civil records back to 2000. No juvenile, child abuse or sexual battery records released. Certification fee: $1.50. Payee: Clerk of Circuit Court. Personal checks accepted. Prepayment and SASE required.

County Court - Civil Division 205 N Dixie Hwy, West Palm Beach, FL 33402; phone: 561-355-2500; fax: 561-355-4643; hours 8AM-5PM (EST). *Eviction, Small Claims.* www.pbcountyclerk.com

Civil Records: Access: Mail, online, in person. Both court and visitors may perform in person searches. Search fee: $1.50 per name per year. Court makes copy: $1.00 per page. Required to search: name, years to search; also helpful: address. Civil cases indexed by defendant, plaintiff. Civil records (Circuit) on computer from 1982, prior records on microfiche and dockets. County on computer from 1987, prior on microfilm. Access to the countywide remote online system requires $145 setup and $65 per month fees. Civil index goes back to '88. Records also include probate, traffic and domestic. Contact M. McArthur at 561-355-6846 for information. Mail turnaround time 1 week.

General Information: Public terminal has only civil records back to 2000. No juvenile, child abuse or sexual battery records released. Certification fee: $1.50. Payee: Clerk of Circuit Court. Personal checks accepted. Prepayment and SASE required.

Circuit & County Courts - Criminal Division 205 N Dixie Hwy, West Palm Beach, FL 33401; phone: 561-355-2519; fax: 561-355-3802; hours 8AM-5PM (EST). *Felony, Misdemeanor.* www.pbcountyclerk.com

Note: Faxes can only be received by state agencies.

Criminal Records: Access: Phone, fax, mail, online, in person. Both court and visitors may perform in person searches. Search fee: $1.50 per name per year. Court makes copy: $1.00 per page. Required to search: name, years to search, DOB, aliases. Criminal records on computer & microfiche (some files) from 1970s, archived from 1920s. Access to the countywide criminal online system requires $145 setup and $65 per month fee. Records also include probate, traffic and domestic. Contact Mr.

McArthur for information. Also, access to 15th judicial circuit records is at http://web3172.co.palm-beach.fl.us. Registration and password is required. Mail turnaround 1 day.

General Information: Public terminal has only criminal records. No juvenile, child abuse or sexual battery records released. Certification fee: $1.50. Payee: Clerk of Circuit Court. Personal checks accepted. Prepayment required.

Circuit Court - Probate Division PO Box 4238, 205 N Dixie Hwy, Rm 4.2200, West Palm Beach, FL 33402; phone: 561-355-2900; hours 8AM-5PM (EST). *Probate.* www.pbcountyclerk.com

Note: Online access to 15th judicial circuit records is available at http://web3172.co.palm-beach.fl.us. Registration and password is required.

Pasco County

Circuit & County Courts - Civil Division 38053 Live Oak Ave, Dade City, FL 33523; phone: 352-521-4482; probate phone: 352-521-4217; hours 8:30AM-5PM (EST). *Civil, Eviction, Small Claims, Probate.* www.pascoclerk.com

Civil Records: Access: Mail, online, in person. Both court and visitors may perform in person searches. Search fee: $1.50 per name per year. Court makes copy: $1.00 per page. Required to search: name, years to search. Civil cases indexed by defendant, plaintiff. Civil records on computer from 1985, on docket cards and docket books from 1900s. Online access to Clerk of Court records via the Internet is a subscription service. Monthly fees are involved. Probate records also available. Call 352-521-4274, ext 4767 for more information. Note: Access an index of judgments, liens, recorded documents at www.myfloridacounty.com. Fees involved to order copies; save $1.50 per record by becoming a subscriber. Mail turnaround time 2-4 days.

General Information: Public terminal has only civil records back to 3/1985. No adoption records released. Certification fee: $1.50. Payee: Clerk of Court. Personal checks accepted. Prepayment required.

Circuit & County Courts - Criminal Division 38053 Live Oak Ave, Dade City, FL 33523-3894; phone: 352-521-4504; hours 8:30AM-5PM (EST). *Felony, Misdemeanor.* www.jud6.org

Criminal Records: Access: Mail, online, in person. Both court and visitors may perform in person searches. Search fee: $1.50 per name per year. Court makes copy: $1.00 per page. Required to search: name, years to search, address, DOB; also helpful: SSN. Criminal records on computer since 1978. Access to the countywide criminal online system requires $100 deposit, $50 annual fee and $10 monthly minimum. There is a $.10 per screen charge. The system is open 24 hours daily. Search by name or case number. Call 352-521-4201 for more information. Mail turnaround time 2-4 days.

General Information: Public terminal has only criminal records back to 1979. No confidential, sealed or juvenile records released. Certification fee: $1.50. Payee: Clerk of Courts. Personal checks accepted. Out of state personal checks not accepted. Local residents may use credit card. Prepayment required.

Pinellas County

Circuit & County Courts - Civil Division 315 Court St, Rm170, Clearwater, FL 33756; phone: 727-464-3267; fax: 727-464-4070; hours 8AM-5PM (EST). *Civil, Eviction, Small Claims, Probate.* www.jud6.org

Civil Records: Access: Fax, mail, online, in person. Both court and visitors may perform in person searches. Search fee: $1.50 per name per year. Court makes copy: $1.00 per page. Required to search: name, years to search. Civil cases indexed by defendant, plaintiff. Civil records on computer from 1980, on microfiche from 1900s to 1982, older data in warehouse. Access to the countywide civil online system requires $60 fee plus $5.00 a month and $.05 per screen over 100. Index goes back to 1972. Contact Sue Maskeny at 727-464-3779 for information. Includes probate and traffic records. Also, you can access the clerk's criminal and other data as a free non-subscriber at https://pubtitles.co.pinellas.fl.us/login/loginx.jsp. However, you are on the clock and may be booted if you overuse the system. Note: Also, access an index of judgments, liens, recorded documents at www.myfloridacounty.com. Fees involved to order copies; save $1.50 per record by becoming a subscriber. Mail turnaround time 1 week.

General Information: Public terminal has only civil records back to 1972. No adoption or juvenile records released. Will fax documents $1.00 per page. Certification fee: $1.50. Payee: Clerk of the Court. Personal checks accepted. Prepayment required. SASE helpful.

County Court - Criminal Division 14250
49th St N, Clearwater, FL 34622-2831; phone: 727-464-7000; fax: 727-464-7040; hours 8AM-5PM (EST). *Misdemeanor.*
www.jud6.org
Criminal Records: Access: Mail, online, in person. Both court and visitors may perform in person searches. Search fee: $1.50 per name per year. Court makes copy: $1.00 per page. Required to search: name, years to search; also helpful: address, DOB, SSN. Criminal records on computer since 10/77, prior on index books. Prior to 1993 on microfilm. Access to the countywide criminal online system requires $60 fee plus $5.00 a month and $.05 per screen over 100. Criminal index goes back to 1972. Contact Sue Maskeny at 727-464-3779 for information. Also, you can access the clerk's criminal and other data as a free non-subscriber at https://pubtitles.co.pinellas.fl.us/login/loginx.jsp. However, you are on the clock and may be booted if you overuse the system. Mail turnaround time 3-5 days.

General Information: Public terminal has only criminal records. No sealed or non-arrested case records released. Certification fee: $1.50. Payee: Clerk of Courts. Personal checks accepted. Prepayment required.

Criminal Justice Center Circuit Criminal
Court Records, 14250 49th St N, Clearwater, FL 34622; phone: 727-464-6793; fax: 727-464-6233; hours 8AM-5PM (EST). *Felony.*
www.jud6.org
Criminal Records: Access: Fax, mail, online, in person. Both court and visitors may perform in person searches. Search fee: $1.50 per name per year. Court makes copy: $1.00 per page. Required to search: name, years to search, DOB. Criminal records on computer from 1977, on microfilm from 1912 to 1976, on docket books from 1912. Access to the countywide criminal online system requires $60 fee plus $5.00 a month and $.05 per screen over 100. Criminal index goes back to 1972. Contact Sue Maskeny at 727-464-3779 for information. Also, you can access the clerk's criminal and other data as a free non-subscriber at https://pubtitles.co.pinellas.fl.us/login/loginx.jsp. However, you are on the clock and may be booted if you overuse the system. Mail turnaround time 1 week.

General Information: Public terminal has only criminal records back to 1977. Will fax documents $1.00 per page. Certification fee: $1.50. Payee: Clerk of Circuit Court. Personal checks accepted. Prepayment required.

Polk County

Circuit Court - Civil Division PO Box 9000,
Drawer CC2, Bartow, FL 33831-9000; phone: 863-534-4488; probate phone: 863-534-4478; fax: 863-534-7707; hours 8AM-5PM (EST). *Civil Actions Over $15,000, Probate.*
www.polk-county.net/clerk/clerk.html

Civil Records: Access: Phone, mail, online, in person. Both court and visitors may perform in person searches. Search fee: $1.50 per name per year. Court makes copy: $1.00 per page if image on computer. Required to search: name. Civil cases indexed by defendant, plaintiff. Civil Records on computer since 1978; on microfiche from 1800s to 1978. Free internet access to limited records is at www.polkcountyclerk.net/public_records/public_index.html. Complete access to the database requires $150 setup fee, but there is no monthly fees. Call 863-534-7575 for more information. Mail turnaround time 2-3 days.

General Information: Public terminal has only civil records. No sex related cases, adoption, confidential, victims or child abuse records released. Will fax documents to local or toll free line. Certification fee: $1.50. Payee: Clerk of Court. Personal checks accepted. Prepayment and SASE required.

County Court - Civil Division PO Box 9000,
Drawer CC12, Bartow, FL 33830-9000; phone: 863-534-4556; fax: 863-534-4045; hours 8AM-5PM (EST). *Civil Actions Under $15,000, Eviction, Small Claims.*
www.polkcountyclerk.net
Civil Records: Access: Phone, mail, online, in person. Both court and visitors may perform in person searches. No search fee. Court makes copy: $1.00 per page. Required to search: name, years to search. Civil cases indexed by defendant, plaintiff. Civil records on computer from 1983, on microfiche from 1961 to 1995. Case index information back to 1983 is free from the County Clerk's website at www.polkcountyclerk.net. Mail turnaround time 1-5 days.

General Information: Public terminal has only civil records. Certification fee: $1.50. Payee: Clerk of Court. Checks, cash, cashiers checks and money orders accepted. Prepayment and SASE required.

Circuit & County Courts - Felony
Division PO Box 9000, Drawer CC9, Bartow, FL 33830; phone: 863-534-4000; fax: 863-534-4137; hours 8AM-5PM (EST). *Felony.*
www.polk-county.net/clerk/clerk.html
Criminal Records: Access: Phone, mail, in person. Both court and visitors may perform in person searches. Search fee: $1.50 per name. Court makes copy: $1.00 per page. Required to search: name, years to search, DOB; also helpful: SSN. Criminal records on computer-felonies since 1977, misdemeanors purged periodically. Both on microfiche and archived since 1800s. Mail turnaround time varies. Indicate on request when record is needed.

General Information: Public terminal has only criminal records back to 1977. No sex related cases, victims or child abuse released. Certification fee: $1.50 per page. Payee: Clerk of Circuit Court. Personal checks accepted. Prepayment required.

Circuit & County Courts - Misdemeanor
Division PO Box 9000, Drawer CC10, Bartow, FL 33831-9000; phone: 863-534-4446; fax: 863-534-4137; hours 8AM-5PM (EST). *Misdemeanor, Traffic.*
www.polkcountyclerk.net
Criminal Records: Access: Mail, in person. Both court and visitors may perform in person searches. Search fee: 3 year search: $4.10; lifetime: $5.10. Court makes copy: $1.00 per page. Required to search: name, years to search, DOB; also helpful: SSN. Criminal records on computer: felonies since 1977, misdemeanors purged periodically. Both on microfiche and archived since 1800s. Mail turnaround time varies. Indicate on request when record is needed.

General Information: Public terminal has only criminal records back to 1977. No sex related cases, victims or child abuse released. Certification fee: $1.50 per cert. Payee: Clerk of Circuit Court. Personal checks accepted. Prepayment required.

Putnam County

Circuit & County Courts - Civil Division
PO Box 758, Palatka, FL 32178; phone: 386-329-0361; probate phone: 386-329-0251; fax: 386-329-0888; hours 8:30AM-5PM (EST). *Civil, Eviction, Small Claims, Probate.*
Civil Records: Access: Mail, fax, in person, email. Both court and visitors may perform in person searches. Search fee: $1.50 per name per year. Court makes copy: $1.00 per page. Self serve copy fee: $.15 per page. Required to search: name, years to search. Civil cases indexed by defendant, plaintiff. Civil records on computer from 1984, on microfiche from 1973 to 1984, on index cards and docket books from 1900s to 1973. Access to the countywide remote online system requires $400 setup fee and $40. monthly charge plus $.05 per minute over 20 hours. Civil records go back to 1984. System includes criminal and real property records. Contact Putnam County IT Dept to register. Note: Access an index of judgments, liens, recorded documents at www.myfloridacounty.com. Fees involved to order copies; save $1.50 per record by becoming a subscriber. Mail turnaround time 2-3 days.

General Information: Public terminal has only civil records back to 1984. No juvenile or incompetency records released. Fee to fax documents is $2.25 per page. Certification fee: $1.50. Payee: Clerk of Court. Personal checks accepted. Prepayment required. SASE requested.

Circuit & County Courts - Criminal
Division PO Box 758, Palatka, FL 32178; phone: 386-329-0255; fax: 386-329-1223; hours 8:30AM-5PM (EST). *Felony, Misdemeanor.*
Criminal Records: Access: Mail, fax, in person, email. Both court and visitors may perform in person searches. Search fee: $1.50 per name per year. Court makes copy: $1.00 per page. Self serve copy fee: $.15 per page. Required to search: name, years to search; also helpful: DOB. Criminal records on computer from 1988, in files from 1930s to 1988. Access to the countywide criminal online system requires $400 setup fee and $40. monthly charge plus $.05 per minute over 20 hours. Criminal records go back to 1972. System includes civil and real property records. Contact Ryel Christiansen to register. Mail turnaround time 2-3 days.

General Information: Public terminal has only criminal records back to 1972. No juvenile records released. Fee to fax documents is $2.25 per page. Certification fee: $1.50. Payee: Clerk of Circuit Court. Personal checks accepted. Prepayment required.

Santa Rosa County

Circuit & County Courts - Civil Division
PO Box 472, Milton, FL 32572; phone: 850-623-0135; hours 8AM-4:30PM (CST). *Civil, Eviction, Small Claims, Probate.*
www.santarosaclerk.com
Civil Records: Access: Fax, mail, in person, online. Both court and visitors may perform in person searches. Search fee: $1.50 per name per year. Court makes copy: $1.00 per page. Required to search: name, years to search. Civil cases indexed by defendant, plaintiff. Civil records (Circuit) on computer from 1990, archived and on docket books from 1900s. County on computer from 1989, on microfiche from 1900s, on docket books from early 1900s. Access an index of judgments, liens, and court records free at http://oncoreweb.srcco l.com/srccol/party5.asp or search at www.myfloridacounty.com where fees involved to order copies; save $1.50 per record by becoming a subscriber. Mail turnaround time ASAP.

General Information: Public terminal has only civil records back to 1991. No adoption records released. Will fax documents $2.00 per page. Certification fee: $1.50 per document. Payee: Clerk of Courts. Personal checks accepted. Prepayment and SASE required.

Circuit & County Courts - Criminal Division PO Box 472, Milton, FL 32572; phone: 850-983-1972; fax: 850-626-5705; hours 8AM-4:30PM (CST). *Felony, Misdemeanor.* www.santarosaclerk.com/
Note: Misdemeanor phone number is 850-983-1990.
Criminal Records: Access: Mail, fax, in person, online. Both court and visitors may perform in person searches. Search fee: $1.00 per name per year. Court makes copy: $1.00 per page. Required to search: name, years to search, DOB; also helpful: SSN. Criminal records on computer back to 1989; felonies on index cards from 1925, misdemeanors on docket books from 1900s. Access an index of judgments, liens, and court records free at http://oncoreweb.srccol.com/oncoreweb4101/Search.aspx Mail turnaround time 1 week.
General Information: Public terminal has only criminal records back to 1984. No records released before sentencing. Fee to fax documents is $2.00 per page. Certification fee: $1.50 per page. Payee: Clerk's Office (include Division/Department name). Personal checks accepted. Prepayment and SASE required.

Sarasota County

Circuit & County Courts - Civil PO Box 3079, Sarasota, FL 34230; phone: 941-983-4630; fax: 850-983-1990; hours 8:30AM-5PM (EST). *Civil, Eviction, Small Claims, Probate.*
www.sarasotaclerk.com
Civil Records: Access: Mail, online, in person. Both court and visitors may perform in person searches. Search fee: $1.50 per name per year. Court makes copy: $1.00 per page. Required to search: name, years to search. Civil cases indexed by defendant, plaintiff. Civil records on computer from 1983, circuit & county on docket books from 1900s to 1983. Civil and DV case records from the Clerk of Circuit Court database are free online at www.clerk.co.sarasota.fl.us/srqapp/civilinq.asp. Probate court records are at www.clerk.co.sarasota.fl.us/srqapp/probinq.asp.
Note: Access an index of judgments, liens, recorded documents at www.myfloridacounty.com. Fees involved to order copies; save $1.50 per record by becoming a subscriber. Mail turnaround time 1 week.
General Information: Public terminal has only civil records back to 1984. No adoption, mental health, or sealed records released. Certification fee: $1.50. Payee: Clerk of Circuit Court. Personal checks accepted. Credit cards will be accepted as of 07/97. Prepayment required. SASE helpful.

Circuit & County Courts - Criminal PO Box 3079, Sarasota, FL 34230; phone: 941-861-7400; hours 8:30AM-5PM (EST). *Felony, Misdemeanor.*
www.sarasotaclerk.com
Criminal Records: Access: Phone. mail, online, in person. Both court and visitors may perform in person searches. Search fee: $1.50 per name per year. Court makes copy: $1.00 per page. Required to search: name, years to search, DOB, SSN. Criminal records on computer since 1983, (circuit) on docket books from 1900s to 1983, (county) on docket books from 1960s to 1983. Criminal and traffic case records from the Clerk of the Circuit Court database are free online at http://clerk.co.sarasota.fl.us/cvdisclaim.htm. Civil, probate and domestic records are also available. Mail turnaround time 1 week.
General Information: Public terminal has only criminal records back to 1995. No juvenile records released. Certification fee: $1.50 per document. Payee: Clerk of Circuit Court. Personal checks accepted. Prepayment required. SASE helpful.

Seminole County

Circuit & County Courts - Civil Division PO Box 8099, 301 N Park Ave, Sanford, FL 32772; phone: 407-665-4330; civil phone: 407-665-4366; probate phone: 407-665-4374; fax: 407-330-7193; hours 8AM-4:30PM (EST). *Civil, Eviction, Small Claims, Probate.*
Civil Records: Access: Mail, in person, online. Both court and visitors may perform in person searches. Search fee: $1.50 per name per year. Court makes copy: $1.00 per page. Required to search: name, years to search. Civil cases indexed by defendant, plaintiff. Civil records on computer since 1986, on microfiche since 1913. Access to the County Clerk's online records is free at www.seminoleclerk.org/OfficialRecords. Search by name, clerk's file number, or book & page. Also, previous 2-weeks civil records on a private site at http://extra.orlandosentinel.com/publicrecords/search.asp. Mail turnaround time 1 week.
General Information: Public terminal has only civil records back to 1986. No confidential files pursuant to law or sealed records released. Certification fee: $1.50 per document. Payee: Clerk of the Circuit Court. Personal checks accepted. Prepayment and SASE required.

Circuit & County Courts - Criminal Division 301 N Park Ave, Sanford, FL 32771; phone: 407-665-4450; fax: 407-665-4545; hours 8AM-4:30PM (EST). *Felony, Misdemeanor.*
www.seminoleclerk.org
Criminal Records: Access: Mail, in person. Both court and visitors may perform in person searches. Search fee: $1.50 per name per year. Court makes copy: $1.00 per page. Required to search: name, years to search, DOB; also helpful: race, sex. Criminal records on computer since 1983; prior on microfiche. Mail turnaround time 2-4 days for felonies, no set time for misdemeanors.
General Information: Public terminal has only criminal records. No records of investigations which have not resulted in an arrest released. Local faxes $1.00 per page; out of state faxes $2.00 per page. Certification fee: $6.00 to prepare plus $1.50 per document. Payee: Clerk of Courts. Local personal and company checks allowed. Prepayment required.

St. Johns County

Circuit & County Courts - Civil Division PO Drawer 300, St Augustine, FL 32085-0300; phone: 904-819-3600; probate phone: 904-819-3654; fax: 904-819-3661; hours 8AM-5PM (EST). *Civil, Eviction, Small Claims, Probate.*
www.co.st-johns.fl.us
Civil Records: Access: Fax, mail, online, in person. Both court and visitors may perform in person searches. Search fee: $1.50 per name per year. Court makes copy: $1.00 per page. Required to search: name, years to search. Civil cases indexed by defendant, plaintiff. Civil records on computer from 1984, on microfiche from 1976 to 1986, on docket books from 1820 to 1983. County on computer from 1991, microfiche from 1983 to 1991, docket books from 1820 to 1983. Access to the countywide remote online system requires $200 setup fee plus a monthly fee of $50. Searching is by name or case number. Call Mark Dearing at 904-819-3610 for more information. Also, access the county Clerk of Circuit Court recording database free at http://doris.clk.co.st-johns.fl.us/oncoreweb/Search.aspx Note: Access an index of judgments, liens, recorded documents at www.myfloridacounty.com. Fees involved to order copies; save $1.50 per record by becoming a subscriber at $25.00 per month. Mail turnaround time 4-5 days.
General Information: Public terminal has only civil records back to 1986. No confidential or sealed records released. Fee to fax documents: $2.00 per page. Certification fee: $1.50. Payee: Clerk of Circuit Court. Personal checks or Visa, MC accepted. Prepayment and SASE required.

Circuit & County Courts - Criminal Division PO Drawer 300, St Augustine, FL 32085-0300; phone: 904-819-3615; fax: 904-819-3666; hours 8AM-5PM (EST). *Felony, Misdemeanor.*
www.co.st-johns.fl.us
Criminal Records: Access: Fax, mail, online, in person. Both court and visitors may perform in person searches. Search fee: $1.50 per name per year. Court makes copy: $1.00 per page. Required to search: name, years to search, DOB; also helpful: address, SSN. Criminal Records on computer. Felony since 1986, Misdemeanor since 1984. Felony on log books from 1950 to 1984. Access to the countywide criminal online system requires $200 setup fee plus a monthly fee of $50. Searching is by name or case number. Call Mark Dearing at 904-819-3611 for more information. Mail turnaround time 4-5 days.
General Information: Public terminal has only criminal records. No juvenile or sexual offense records released. Fee to fax documents is $1.00 per page. Certification fee: $1.50. Payee: Clerk of Circuit Court. Personal checks or Visa, MC accepted. Prepayment required. Escrow/billing accounts available to government agencies. SASE required.

St. Lucie County

Circuit & County Courts - Civil Division PO Drawer 700, 218 S 2nd St, Ft Pierce, FL 34954; phone: 772-462-6976 (Circuit); civil phone: 772-785-5880 (County); criminal fax: 772-462-1774; civil fax: 772-462-1998; hours 8AM-5PM (EST). *Civil, Eviction, Small Claims.*
www.slcclerkofcourt.com/circuitcivil/circuitcivil.htm
Note: Small claims phone is 772-785-5880; Small Claims and County Civil files and microfiche are located at the Courthouse Annex, 250 NW County Club Dr, Pt St. Lucie, FL 34986.
Civil Records: Access: Mail, in person, online. Both court and visitors may perform in person searches. Search fee: $1.50 per name per year. Court makes copy: $1.00 per page; same fee for self serve. Required to search: name, years to search. Civil cases indexed by defendant, plaintiff. Circuit records on computer back to 1992. Circuit on microfiche from 1981 to 1992, County from 1981 to 1992. Circuit on docket books from 1900s to 1981, County from 1900s to 1981. Online access to civil records at http://public.slcclerkofcourt.com. Case tracking and bond record tracking are available. Access an index of judgments, liens, recorded documents at www.myfloridacounty.com. Fees involved to order copies; save $1.50 per record by becoming a subscriber. Mail turnaround time 1 day.
General Information: Public terminal has only civil records. No sealed cases or adoption records released. Will fax documents to local or toll free line. Certification fee: $1.50 per document. Payee: Clerk of Court. Personal checks accepted; drivers license & photo ID required. Prepayment required.

Circuit & County Courts - Criminal Division PO Drawer 700, 218 S 2nd St, Ft Pierce, FL 34954; phone: 772-462-6900; fax: 772-462-2833; hours 8AM-5PM (EST). *Felony, Misdemeanor.*
www.slcclerkofcourt.com/felony/felony.htm
Note: County Misdemeanor and criminal traffic phone is 772-462-6954 or 772-462-6958; fax number is 772)-462-6868.
Criminal Records: Access: Fax, mail, in person, online. Both court and visitors may perform in person searches. Search fee: $1.50 per name per year. Court makes copy: $1.00 per page. Required to search: name, years to search, DOB, signed release; also helpful: address, SSN, race, sex. Criminal records on computer back to 1982, on microfiche to 1960, on books prior to 1900s. Online access to bonds, traffic and misdemeanor records is free at http://public.slcclerkofcourt.com. Online records go back to 7/6/1992. Felony records only available to government agencies. Mail turnaround time 1-2 weeks; fax turnaround time 1-5 days.

General Information: Public terminal has only criminal records back to 1983. No sealed or expunged records released. Fee to fax documents is $2.00 per page. Certification fee: $1.50. Payee: Clerk of Court. Only cashiers checks and money orders accepted. Prepayment required.

Probate Court PO Box 700, c/o Clerk of Circ. Ct, Probate Dept, 415 S 2nd St, Clerk of Circ. Ct, Probate Dept, Ft Pierce, FL 34954; phone: 772-462-6920; fax: 772-462-6984; hours 8AM-5PM (EST). *Probate.*
www.slcclerkofcourt.com/probate/probate.htm

Sumter County

Circuit & County Courts - Civil Division
209 N Florida St, Bushnell, FL 33513; phone: 352-793-0211; fax: 352-568-6608; hours 8:30AM-5PM (EST). *Civil, Eviction, Small Claims, Probate.*
Civil Records: Access: Fax, mail, in person, online. Both court and visitors may perform in person searches. Search fee: $1.50 per name per year. Court makes copy: $1.00 per page. Required to search: name, years to search. Civil cases indexed by defendant, plaintiff. Civil records go back to 1800s; on computer go back to 12/1999; in docket books from 1986 to 11/30/99 (circuit only). Access an index of judgments, liens, recorded documents at www.myfloridacounty.com. Fees involved to order copies; save $1.50 per record by becoming a subscriber. Faxes accepted if only pre-paid. Mail turnaround time 1 week; phone turnaround is 30 min to 1 hour.
General Information: No public access terminal. No juvenile or adoption records released. Will fax documents $1.00 per page. Certification fee: $1.50 per document. Payee: Clerk of Circuit Court. No personal checks accepted. VISA and MC accepted in person. Prepayment required. SASE requested.

Circuit & County Courts - Criminal Division 209 N Florida St, Bushnell, FL 33513; phone: 352-793-0211; fax: 352-568-6608; hours 8:30AM-5PM (EST). *Felony, Misdemeanor.*
Criminal Records: Access: Mail, in person. Both court and visitors may perform in person searches. Search fee: $1.50 per name per year. Court makes copy: $1.00 per page. Required to search: name, years to search, DOB. Criminal records (circuit) on computer since 2000, on index books from 1965 to 1999, prior in vaults. County on computer since 1982, on microfiche from 1960 to 1982, on docket books since early 1900s. Mail turnaround time 1 week.
General Information: No public access terminal. No juvenile records released. Fee to fax documents is $1.00 per page. Certification fee: $1.50. Payee: Clerk of Court. Only cashiers checks and money orders accepted. Prepayment required. SASE requested.

Suwannee County

Circuit & County Courts 200 S Ohio Ave, Live Oak, FL 32060; phone: 386-362-0500; probate phone: 386-362-0560; fax: 386-362-0567; probate fax: 386-362-0548; hours 8:30AM-5PM (EST). *Felony, Misdemeanor, Civil, Eviction, Small Claims, Probate.*
www.suwclerk.org/index2.html
Civil Records: Access: Mail, in person, online. Both court and visitors may perform in person searches. Search fee: $1.50 per name per year. Fee is per index. Court makes copy: $1.00 per page; same fee for self serve. Required to search: name, years to search; also helpful: address. Civil cases indexed by defendant, plaintiff. Civil records on computer from 1983, archived from 1859 to 1983. Access to County Clerk of Circuit Court records is at www.suwclerk.org/public.html. Note: Written requests require prepayment. Mail turnaround time 1 week.
Criminal Records: Access: Mail, in person, online. Both court and visitors may perform in person searches. Search fee: $1.50 per name per year. Fee is per index. Court makes copy: $1.00 per page; same fee for self serve. Required to search: name, years to

search, DOB, signed release; also helpful: address. Criminal records on computer from 1983, archived from 1859 to 1983. Access to County Clerk of Circuit Court records is at www.suwclerk.org/public.html. Criminal records may be temporarily unavailable. Note: Written requests require prepayment. Mail turnaround time 1 week.
General Information: No public access terminal. No juvenile or adoption records released. Will fax documents for $3.00 1st page plus $.50 each add'l. Certification fee: $1.50. Payee: Suwannee Court Clerk. Personal checks accepted. Prepayment and SASE required.

Taylor County

Circuit & County Courts PO Box 620, Perry, FL 32348; phone: 850-838-3506; probate phone: x 15; fax: 850-838-3549; hours 8AM-5PM (EST). *Felony, Misdemeanor, Civil, Eviction, Small Claims, Probate.*
Civil Records: Access: Mail, in person, online. Only the court performs in person searches; visitors may not. Search fee: $1.50 per name per year. Self serve copy fee: $1.00 per page. Required to search: name, years to search. Civil cases indexed by defendant, plaintiff. Civil records on computer back to 1982; on index from 1973 to 1991, prior on index books to 1856. Access an index of judgments, liens, recorded documents at www.myfloridacounty.com. Fees involved to order copies; save $1.50 per record by becoming a subscriber. Mail turnaround time 1 week.
Criminal Records: Access: Mail, in person. Only the court performs in person searches; visitors may not. Search fee: $1.50 per name per year. Self serve copy fee: $1.00 per page. Required to search: name, years to search, DOB; also helpful: SSN, race, sex. Criminal records on computer back to 1982; on index from 1973 to 1991, prior on index books to 1950. Mail turnaround time 1 week.
General Information: No public access terminal. No juvenile records released. Will fax documents for $1.00 per fax plus copy cost. Certification fee: $1.50. Payee: Taylor County Clerk of Court. Business checks accepted. Prepayment required. SASE helpful.

Union County

Circuit & County Courts Courthouse, Rm 103, Lake Butler, FL 32054; phone: 386-496-3711; fax: 386-496-1718; hours 8AM-5PM (EST). *Felony, Misdemeanor, Civil, Eviction, Small Claims, Probate.* http://circuit8.org
Civil Records: Access: Fax, mail, in person, online. Only the court performs in person searches; visitors may not. Search fee: $1.50 per name per year. Court makes copy: $1.00 per page; same fee for self serve. Required to search: name, years to search. Civil cases indexed by defendant, plaintiff. Civil records on docket books from 1921. Access an index of judgments, liens, recorded documents at www.myfloridacounty.com. Fees involved to order copies; save $1.50 per record by becoming a subscriber. Mail turnaround time 2-3 days.
Criminal Records: Access: Fax, mail, in person, online. Only the court performs in person searches; visitors may not. Search fee: $1.50 per name per year. Court makes copy: $1.00 per page; same fee for self serve. Required to search: name, years to search, DOB; also helpful: SSN. Criminal records on docket books from 1921. Access the circuit-wide criminal quick lookup at http://circuit8.org/golem/gencrim.html. Account and password is required; restricted usage. Mail turnaround time 2-3 days.
General Information: No public access terminal. No juvenile records released. Will fax documents $1.00 per page. Certification fee: $1.50. Payee: Clerk of Court. Personal checks accepted. Prepayment required. SASE preferred.

Volusia County

Circuit & County Courts - Civil Division
PO Box 6043, De Land, FL 32721; phone: 386-736-5915; probate phone: 386-736-5914; fax: 386-822-5711; hours 8AM-4:30PM (EST). *Civil, Eviction, Small Claims, Probate.*
www.clerk.org
Civil Records: Access: Fax, mail, online, in person. Both court and visitors may perform in person searches. Search fee: $1.50 per name per year. Court makes copy: $1.00 per page. Required to search: name, years to search. Civil cases indexed by defendant, plaintiff. Civil records on computer from 1986, on docket books from 1863 to 1986. Access to the countywide remote online system requires $100 setup fee plus a $25 monthly fee. Windows required. Search by name or case number. Call Thom White 386-822-5004 for more information. Criminal, probate and traffic records are also available. Also, Access an index of judgments, liens, recorded documents at www.myfloridacounty.com. Fees involved to order copies; save $1.50 per record by becoming a subscriber. Note: Also, previous 2-weeks civil records on a private site at http://extra.orlandosentinel.com/publicrecords/search.asp. Mail turnaround time 1-2 weeks.
General Information: Public terminal has only civil records back to 1986. No sealed records released. Fee to fax documents is $1.00 per page. Certification fee: $1.50. Payee: Clerk of Circuit Court. Personal checks accepted. Prepayment required. SASE requested.

Circuit & County Courts - Criminal Division PO Box 6043, De Land, FL 32721-6043; phone: 386-736-5915; fax: 386-740-5175; hours 8AM-4:30PM (EST). *Felony, Misdemeanor.*
www.clerk.org
Criminal Records: Access: Mail, online, in person. Both court and visitors may perform in person searches. Search fee: $1.50 per name per year. Court makes copy: $1.00 per page. Required to search: name, years to search, DOB; also helpful: SSN, race, sex. Criminal records 1982 to present on computer, on microfiche from 1856 to 1988, on docket books prior to 1983. Two access methods are available. Access to the Clerk of Circuit Courts database of Citation Violations and 24-hour Arrest Reports is free at www.clerk.org/index.html. Access to the countywide criminal online system requires $125 setup fee plus a $25 monthly fee. Windows required. Search by name or case number back to 1988. Call 904-822-5710 for more information. Civil, probate and traffic records are also available. Mail turnaround time up to 1 week.
General Information: Public terminal has only criminal records. No confidential, sexual battery and juvenile records released. Will fax documents $1.00 per page. Certification fee: $1.50. Payee: Clerk of Court. Personal and out of state checks accepted with proper ID. Prepayment and SASE required.

Wakulla County

Circuit & County Courts 3056 Crawfordville Hwy, Crawfordville, FL 32327; phone: 850-926-0905; criminal phone: 850-926-0359; civil phone: 850-926-0323; criminal fax: 850-926-0936; civil fax: 850-926-0938; hours 8AM-5PM (EST). *Felony, Misdemeanor, Civil, Eviction, Small Claims, Probate.* www.wakullaclerk.com/
Note: Felony/Misdemeanor court can be reached at 850-926-0324.
Civil Records: Access: Phone, fax, mail, in person, online. Both court and visitors may perform in person searches. Search fee: $1.50 per name per year. Court makes copy: $1.00 per page. Required to search: name, years to search. Civil cases indexed by defendant, plaintiff. Civil records on computer since 1990, on docket books from 1800s. Access an index of judgments, liens, recorded documents at www.myfloridacounty.com. Fees involved to order copies; save $1.50 per record by becoming a

subscriber. Faxes must be pre-paid. Mail turnaround time 3-4 days.

Criminal Records: Access: Fax, mail, in person. Both court and visitors may perform in person searches. Search fee: $1.50 per name per year. Court makes copy: $1.00 per page. Required to search: name, years to search, DOB; also helpful: SSN. Criminal records on computer since 1990, on docket books from 1800s. Visitors may review docket books, only court performs name searches. Faxes must be pre-paid. Mail turnaround time 3-4 days.

General Information: No public access terminal. No juvenile, adoption records released. Fee to fax documents is $1.00 per page. Certification fee: $1.50. Payee: Clerk of Court. Personal checks accepted. Prepayment required. SASE helpful.

Walton County

Circuit & County Courts PO Box 1260, De Funiak Springs, FL 32435; phone: 850-892-8115; criminal fax: 850-892-8017; civil fax: 850-892-7551; probate fax: 850-892-7551; hours 8AM-4:30PM (CST). *Felony, Misdemeanor, Civil, Eviction, Small Claims, Probate.*
www.co.walton.fl.us/clerk/
Note: Probate is a separate index at this same address.
Civil Records: Access: Fax, mail, online, in person. Only the court performs in person searches; visitors may not. Search fee: $1.50 per name per year. Court makes copy: $1.00 per page; same fee for self serve. Required to search: name, years to search.

Civil cases indexed by defendant, plaintiff. Civil records on computer from 1988, on dockets from 1900s. Website offers access to final judgments or orders only on closed cases. Mail turnaround time same day if received before 3PM.

Criminal Records: Access: Fax, mail, online, in person. Only the court performs in person searches; visitors may not. Search fee: $1.50 per name per year. Court makes copy: $1.00 per page; same fee for self serve. Required to search: name, years to search, DOB. Criminal records on computer from 1988, on dockets from 1900s. Websites offers access to felony judgments of guilt. Mail turnaround time 24 hours.

General Information: Public terminal has only civil records back to mid-1980s. No sealed, expunged, or pre-sentence investigation records released. Will fax documents $1.00 per page. Certification fee: $1.50 per instrument. Payee: Clerk of Courts. Personal checks accepted. Prepayment required. SASE helpful.

Washington County

Circuit & County Courts PO Box 647, Chipley, FL 32428-0647; phone: 850-638-6285; probate phone: 850-638-6008; fax: 850-638-6297; hours 8AM-4PM (CST). *Felony, Misdemeanor, Civil, Eviction, Small Claims, Probate.*
Civil Records: Access: Phone, fax, mail, in person, online. Both court and visitors may perform in person searches. Search fee: $1.50 per name per

year. Court makes copy: $1.00 per page; same fee for self serve. Required to search: name, years to search. Civil cases indexed by defendant, plaintiff. Civil records on computer from 1985; on docket books from 1940. Access an index of judgments, liens, recorded documents at www.myfloridacounty.com. Fees involved to order copies; save $1.50 per record by becoming a subscriber. Mail turnaround time 1 day.

Criminal Records: Access: Phone, fax, mail, in person. Only the court performs in person searches; visitors may not. Search fee: $1.50 per name per year. Court makes copy: $1.00 per page; same fee for self serve. Required to search: name, years to search. Criminal records on computer back to 1981, on docket books from 1900. Mail turnaround time 1 day.

General Information: Public terminal has only civil records back to 1980. No adoption or juvenile records released. Will fax documents to local or toll free line. Certification fee: $1.50. Payee: Clerk of Court. Business checks accepted. Local personal checks accepted. Prepayment required. SASE requested.

Florida Recording Offices

ORGANIZATION: 67 counties, 67 recording offices. The recording officer is Clerk of the Circuit Court. All transactions are recorded in the "Official Record," a grantor/grantee index. Some counties will search by type of transaction while others will return everything on the index. 57 counties are in the Eastern Time Zone (EST) and 10 are in the Central Time Zone (CST).

REAL ESTATE RECORDS: Any name searched in the "Official Records" will usually include all types of liens and property transfers for that name. Most counties will perform searches. In addition to the usual $1.00 per page copy fee, certification of documents usually cost $1.50 per document. Tax records are located at the Property Appraiser Office.

Note that a number of counties make their real estate records available online.

UCC RECORDS: Financing statements are filed at the state level, and real estate related collateral at the Clerk of the Circuit Court. Until 1/2002, farm related financing was also filed at the clerk's office. All but a few counties will perform UCC searches. Use search request form UCC-11. Search fees are usually $1.50 per debtor name per year searched and include all lien and real estate transactions on record. Copies usually cost $1.00 per page.

TAX LIEN RECORDS: Federal tax liens on personal property of businesses are filed with the Secretary of State. All other federal and state tax liens on personal property are filed with the county Clerk of Circuit Court. Usually tax liens on personal property are filed in the same index with UCC financing statements and real estate transactions. Most counties will perform a tax lien as part of a UCC search. Copies usually cost $1.00 per page.

OTHER LIENS: Judgments, hospital, mechanics, sewer, ambulance.

ONLINE ACCESS: There are numerous county agencies that provide online access to records, but the statewide system MyFlorida.com predominates. My Florida offers free access to the over 60 counties Circuit Clerks of Court recorded document indexes including real estate records liens, judgments, marriages, and deaths at www.myfloridacounty.com/services/officialrecords_intro.shtml. Fees involved to order copies; save $1.50 per record by becoming a subscriber. Subscription fee is $120.00 per year, plus monthly transaction fees for copies.

Since October 1, 2002, any person preparing or filing a document for recording in the Official Record may not include a Social Security Number in such document unless required by law. The Clerk of the Circuit Court cannot place an image or copy of the following documents on a publicly available Internet website for general public display: Military discharges; Death certificates; Court files, records or papers relating to Family Law, Juvenile Law, or Probate Law cases.

Any person has the right to request the Clerk/County Recorder to redact/remove his Social Security Number from an image or copy of an Official Record that has been placed on such Clerk/County Recorder's publicly available Internet website.

Alachua County

County Clerk of the Circuit Court, PO Box 600, Gainesville, FL 32602. 352-374-3625; fax-352-491-4649; hours: 8:15AM-5PM www.clerk-alachua-fl.org

Records indexed on a public use terminal back to 1970. Office will perform a UCC and Tax lien search but public must search other records themselves. Search fee $1.50 per name per year. Copy fee $1.00 per page. Cert fee- $1.50 per doc plus copy fee. Payee- Alachua County Clerk of Circuit Court. **Online access to Property Appraiser, Real Estate, Lien, Vital Statistic, Recording, Traffic Citation records:** Access to the Clerk of Courts recording database is free at www.alachuaclerk.org. Index goes back to 1971. Records go back to 1990. Also, search the County Appraiser's Property Search page free online at www.acpafl.org. Sales search and GIS search also here. Also search ancient records - pre-1940 plats, pre-1970 marriages, deeds, transcriptions and more - free at www.clerk-alachua-fl.org/archive/default.cfm. Search traffic citations at www.co.alachua.fl.us/traffic/. Access an index of recorded documents at www.myfloridacounty.com. Fees involved to order copies; save $1.50 per record by becoming a subscriber. Also, search tax roll data free at www.actcfl.org/collectmax/collect30.asp. **Other phones:** Treasurer- 352-374-3605; Appraiser/Auditor- 352-374-5230; Finance Director- 352-374-3605. **Property tax/Assessor-** 12 S E 1st St, Gainesville, FL 32601; not known.

Baker County

County Clerk of the Circuit Court, 339 E. MacClenny Ave, MacClenny, FL 32063. 904-259-0208; fax-904-259-4176; hours: 8:30AM-5PM

Will not search real estate records. Will search UCC records, but not tax liens. UCC search per debtor name- $1.50 per name per year. Copy fee $1.00 per page. Cert fee- $1.50 per doc plus copy fee. Payee- Baker County Clerk of Circuit Court. **Online access to Real Estate, Lien, Recording, Property records:** Access an index of recorded documents at www.myfloridacounty.com. Fees involved to order copies; save $1.50 per record by becoming a subscriber. Also, search for property data for free at www.emapsplus.com/FLBaker/maps/. Choose to search by owner. **Other phones:** Treasurer- 904-259-6880; Appraiser/Auditor- 904-259-3191; Elections- 904-259-6339.

Bay County

County Clerk of the Circuit Court, PO Box 2269, Panama City, FL 32402. 850-747-5104; fax-850-747-5199; hours: 8AM-4:30PM www.baycoclerk.com

All records in one index. Records indexed on a public use terminal back to 1987. Only the public may search. Copy fee $1.00 per page. Cert fee- $1.50 per doc plus copy fee. Payee- Bay County Clerk of Circuit Court. **Online access to Property Tax, Real Estate, Tax Lien, Recording, Appraiser, Property Sale records:** Access to the Clerk of the Circuit Court Recordings database is free at www.baycoclerk.com/index.cfm. Records go back to 1/1987. Search the property appraiser database free at www.qpublic.net/bay/ or at www.qpublic.net/bay/search1.html; search the tax collector data at http://bctc.elementaldata.com/disclaimer.asp. Assessor database is free online at www.qpublic.net/bay/search.html. Access an index of recorded documents at www.myfloridacounty.com. Fees involved to order copies; save $1.50 per record by

becoming a subscriber. **Other phones:** Appraiser/Auditor- 850-784-4095. **Property tax/Assessor-** 658 Mulberry Ave, Panama City, FL 32401; 850-784-4095.

Bradford County

County Clerk of the Circuit Court, PO Drawer B, Starke, FL 32091. RE & UCC recording phone-904-966-6283; fax-904-964-4454; hours: 8AM-5PM

All records in one index. Records indexed on a public use terminal back to 1986. Only the public may search. Copy fee $1.00 per page. Cert fee- $1.50 per doc plus copy fee. Payee- Bradford County Clerk of Circuit Court. **Online access to Real Estate, Appraisal, Deed, Judgment, Marriage, Lien, Court records:** Access to the recorders database is free at www.mybradfordcounty.com. Click on "Official Records." Also, search the property appraiser database at www.bradfordappraiser.com/Search_F.asp. Access an index of recorded documents at www.myfloridacounty.com. Fees involved to order copies; save $1.50 per record by becoming a subscriber. **Other phones:** Treasurer- 904-966-6246; Appraiser/Auditor- 904-964-6280; Elections- 904-966-6236; Vital Records- 904-966-7383. **Property tax/Assessor-** 904-966-6217.

Brevard County

County Clerk of the Circuit Court, PO Box 2767, Titusville, FL 32781. 321-264-5244, 264-5350; fax-321-264-5246; hours: 8AM-5PM www.brevardclerk.us

Only the public may search. Copy fee $1.00 per page. Cert fee- $1.oo per page plus $1.50 per instrument. Payee- Brevard County Clerk of Circuit Court. **Online access to Real Estate, Lien, Marriage, Recording, Tax Sale, Property Appraiser,**

Personal Property records: Access to the clerk's tax lien (1981-95), land records (1995 to present) and indexed records from 1981 to 9/30/1995 are at www.clerk.co.brevard.fl.us/pages/pubrec9.htm. Registration and a password is now required; application fee is $5.00. Marriage records also available; access is free. Search most wanted and arrests at www.sheriff.co.brevard.fl.us under "Departments." Pproperty tax, sales and personal property records at http://brevardpropertyappraiser.com/asp/disclaimer.asp. Also, tax deed sales are listed free at www.clerk.co.brevard.fl.us/taxdeed/taxdeed.HTM. For "public use" the clerk offers a public system at http://webfyi.clerk.co.brevard.fl.us/netfyi/instruct.html that includes plats, traffic, courts and more. **Other phones:** Appraiser/Auditor- 321-264-6700. **Property tax/Assessor-** 321-264-6700.

Broward County

Director of County Records, 115 S Andrews Ave, Rm 114; Records Division, Fort Lauderdale, FL 33301. RE & UCC recording phone-954-357-7281; fax-954-357-7267; hours: 7:30AM-5PM www.broward.org/records
Office personnel or visitors may perform searches. Search fee $1.00 per name. UCC search per debtor name- $1.50 per name per year. Copy fee $1.00 per page. Cert fee- $1.50 per doc plus copy fee. Payee- Broward County Board of County Commissioners. **Online access to Property, Appraiser, Real Estate, Lien, Recording, Occ. License, Most Wanted, Arrest, Missing, Sex Offender, Vendor Payment records:** Access to the county records Public Search database 1978-present is free at http://205.166.161.12/oncoreV2/. Also, search the occupational license database at http://bcegov2.broward.org/olsearch/olsearch.asp. Also, search the sheriff's multiple databases at www.sheriff.org. Also, search property tax data for free at http://bcegov.co.broward.fl.us/revenue/nameform.htm. Search appraiser records at www.bcpa.net/index.cfm?page=search. Search vendor payments at www.broward.org/Guests/vendor.htm. **Other phones:** Treasurer- 954-357-7235; Appraiser/Auditor- 954-357-6908; Elections- 954-357-7050; Vital Records- Birth 954-467-4413/Death records 954-467-4424. **Property tax/Assessor-** 954-357-6904.

Calhoun County

County Clerk of the Circuit Court, 20859 SE Central Ave, Rm 130, Blountstown, FL 32424. RE & UCC recording phone-850-674-4545; fax-850-674-5553; hours: 8AM-4PM www.calhounclerk.com
Records indexed on computer back to 09/85. Office personnel or visitors may perform searches. Will not perform tax lien searches. Copy fee $1.00 per page. Cert fee- $1.50 per doc plus copy fee. Payee- Calhoun County Clerk of Circuit Court. **Online access to Real Estate, Lien, Deed, Judgment, Recording records:** Access an index of recorded documents at www.myfloridacounty.com. Fees involved to order copies; save $1.50 per record by becoming a subscriber. **Other phones:** Appraiser/Auditor- 850-674-8242. **Property tax/Assessor-** same address as above. 850-674-8242.

Charlotte County

County Clerk of the Circuit Court, PO Box 510156, Punta Gorda, FL 33951-0156. 941-637-2245; fax-941-637-2172; hours: 8AM-5PM www.co.charlotte.fl.us
All records in one index. Records indexed on a public use terminal back to 1977. Office personnel (by written request only) or visitors may perform searches. Search fee $1.50 per name per year. Copy fee $1.00 per page. Cert fee- $1.50 per doc plus copy fee. Payee- Clerk of Circuit Court. **Online access to Property Appraiser, Real Estate, Lien, Recording, Property Sale, Arrest, Most Wanted, Sex Offender records:** Property records are free at www.ccappraiser.com/record.asp. Sales records

are also here and at the tax collector database, free at www.cctaxcol.com/record.asp?. Search sheriff data at www.ccso.org/localcrime/crimedatabase.cfm. Bulk database record purchases, by year, are also available. Access an index of recorded documents at www.myfloridacounty.com. Fees involved to order copies; save $1.50 per record by becoming a subscriber. **Other phones:** Appraiser/Auditor- 941-743-1488. **Property tax/Assessor-** 18500 Murdock Cir, Punta Gorda, FL 33946; not known.

Citrus County

County Clerk of the Circuit Court, 110 N. Apopka Ave. Rm 101, Inverness, FL 34450-4299. 352-341-6475; fax-352-341-6477; hours: 8AM-5PM www.clerk.citrus.fl.us
All records in one index. Office personnel or visitors may perform searches. Search fee $1.50 per name per year. Copy fee $1.00 per page. Cert fee- $1.50 per doc plus copy fee. Payee- Citrus County Clerk of Circuit Court. **Online access to Property Appraiser, Real Estate, Lien, Deed, Marriage, Recording, Property Tax, Sex Offender, Personal Property, Probate, Military Discharge, Tax Deed Sale records:** Free access to the recorded records at http://24.129.131.20/search.asp?cabinet=opr. Search property tax records for free at http://citrustaxcollector.governmax.com. Search property appraiser records free at www.pa.citrus.fl.us/ccpaask.html. Also, download land sales data free at www.pa.citrus.fl.us/sales_download.html. Access recorded documents index-www.myfloridacounty.com. Tax deed sales-www.clerk.citrus.fl.us. Fees involved to order copies; save $1.50 per record by becoming a subscriber. Also, search sheriff sex offender list at www.sheriffcitrus.org/SexOffenders/SexOffPred.htm. Search arrests at www.sheriffcitrus.org/ArrestReport/arrests.aspx. **Other phones:** Appraiser/Auditor- 352-637-6600. **Property tax/Assessor-** 210 N Apopka Ave, #200, Inverness, Fl 34450; 352-341-6600.

Clay County

County Clerk of the Circuit Court, PO Box 698, Green Cove Springs, FL 32043-0698. 904-284-6317, R/E recording phone-904-284-6362, UCC recording phone-904-284-6362; fax-904-278-3641; hours: 8:30AM-4:30PM www.clayclerk.com
No search fee for general index. Will help lookup real estate records in official records, but no title searches. UCC search (including tax liens) per debtor name- $1.50 per name per year. Separate federal/state combined tax lien search- $1.00 per year per debtor. Copy fee $1.00 per page. Cert fee- $1.50 per doc plus copy fee. Payee- Clay County Clerk of Circuit Court. **Online access to Appraiser, Real Estate, Lien, Recording, Tangible Personal Property, Property Tax, Most Wanted, Sex Offender records:** The county clerk of circuit court allows free online access to recording records at http://clerk.co.clay.fl.us/oncoreweb/. This replaces the commercial system. Records go back to 1990. Also, access property appraiser records free at www.ccpao.com/ccpao.asp?page=search; tangible property at www.ccpao.com/tpp/default.htm; account # required. Treasurer RE & tangible personal property at www.claycountytax.com/Tax_Searchr/porr.html. Also, access an index of recorded documents at www.myfloridacounty.com. Fees involved to order copies; save $1.50 per record by becoming a subscriber. Also, search sex offenders and most wanted at http://claysheriff.com. **Other phones:** Appraiser/Auditor- 904-284-6320. **Property tax/Assessor-** PO Box 38, Green Cove Springs, FL 32043-0038 www.ccpao.com/tpp/default.htm; 904-284-6305, assessor fax- 904-284-2923.

Collier County

County Clerk of the Circuit Court, PO Box 413044, Naples, FL 34101-3044. 239-732-2646, R/E recording phone-239-732-2606, UCC recording phone-239-732-

2606; fax-239-774-8003; hours: 8AM-5PM (No recording after 4:30PM) www.clerk.collier.fl.us
All records in one index. Records indexed on a public use terminal back to 1981. Office will perform a UCC and Tax lien search but public must search other records themselves. General index search fee $1.50 per name per year. Copy fee $1.00 per page. Cert fee- $1.50 per doc plus copy fee. Payee- Collier County Clerk of Circuit Court. **Online access to Property Appraiser, Real Estate, Lien, UCC, Vital Statistic, Recording, Tax Sale, Wanted, Missing Person, Property Tax records:** Access to records on the Property Appraiser database are free at www.collierappraiser.com/Disclaimer.asp. The sheriff's wanted and missing persons lists are at www.colliersheriff.org. Access to clerk of courts court records, lien, real estate, UCCs and vital records is free at www.clerk.collier.fl.us/clerkspubliac/Default.htm. Lending agency data is available. Also search property tax rolls at www.colliertax.com/Search.asp. Tax deeds sales data is free at www.clerk.collier.fl.us/OfficialRecords/Tax_Deeds/Tax%20Deeds.htm. Also, access recorded document index at www.myfloridacounty.com. Fees involved to order copies; save $1.50 per record by becoming a subscriber. **Other phones:** Treasurer- 239-732-6179; Appraiser/Auditor- 239-774-8175; Elections- 239-732-8450; Vital Records- 239-732-8205. **Property tax/Assessor-** same address as above. 239-732-8141.

Columbia County

County Clerk of the Circuit Court, PO Box 2069, Lake City, FL 32056-2069. 386-758-1342, R/E recording phone-386-758-1053, UCC recording phone-386-758-1053; fax-386-758-1337; hours: 8AM-5PM http://www2.myfloridacounty.com/wps/wcm/connect/columbiaclerk
All records in one index. Records indexed on a public use terminal back to 1987. Office personnel or visitors may perform searches. Search fee $1.50 per name per year. Will not search real estate records. Copy fee $1.00 per page. Cert fee- $1.50 per doc plus copy fee. Payee- Columbia County Clerk of Circuit Court. **Online access to Real Estate, Lien, Recording, Probate, Property Tax, Appraiser, GIS, Occ License records:** Access to the Clerk of Circuit Courts recording database index is free at www.columbiaclerk.com. Click on Order Official Records. Search by name, book/page, file number of document type. This is a www.myfloridacounty.com website; fees are involved to order copies; save $1.50 per record by becoming a subscriber. Search property appraiser records free at http://columbia.floridapa.com/GIS/Search_F.asp. Also, search the tax rolls and occupational licenses for free at www.columbiataxcollector.com/collectmax/collect30.asp. **Other phones:** Treasurer- 386-758-1042; Appraiser/Auditor- 386-758-1087; Elections- 386-758-1028; Vital Records- 386-758-1150. **Property tax/Assessor-** 135 NE Hernando, Lake City, FL 32055; 386-758-1077.

Dade County

County Clerk of the Circuit Court, 22 N.W. 1st St, Miami, FL 33128. 305-275-1155; fax-305-372-7775; hours: 9AM-4PM www.miami-dadeclerk.com/dadecoc/
Records indexed on computer. Office personnel or visitors may perform searches. General index search fee $1.50 per year. Copy fee $1.00 per page. Cert fee- $1.50 per doc plus copy fee. Payee- Dade County Clerk of Circuit Court. **Online access to Real Estate, Recording, Judgment, Lien, Marriage, Tax Deed Sale, Property Appraiser, Property Tax records:** 3 sources available. Record access to 11 databases requires $125 initial setup fee & minimum $52 monthly fee for 208 minutes, $.25 ea. add'l minute. Records date back to 1975. Contact 305-596-8148 for info. 2nd service recorder only. Fee is $50 per month, at www.miami-dadeclerk.com/dadecoc/Premier_Services.asp. Third,

recorder records are free at www.miami-dadeclerk.com/public-records/pubsearch.asp. Property search GIS site free at www.emapsplus.com/FLDade/maps/. Tax Collector records, free at www.co.miami-dade.fl.us/proptax/. Search property at http://gisims2.co.miami-dade.fl.us/MyHome/propmap.asp. Tax deed sales: www.miami-dadeclerk.com/tax-deeds/home.asp. Also, www.miamidade.gov/public-records records search site. **Other phones:** Appraiser/Auditor- 305-375-5447. **Property tax/Assessor-** 305-375-4099.

De Soto County

County Clerk of the Circuit Court, 115 E. Oak St, Arcadia, FL 34266. RE & UCC recording phone-863-993-4876; fax-863-993-4669; hours: 8AM-4:45PM
Separate indices to search. Records indexed on a public use terminal back to 1983. Office will perform a UCC search but public must search other records themselves. UCC search per debtor name- $1.50 per name per year. Separate federal/state combined tax lien search- $1.00 per year. Copy fee $1.00 per page. Cert fee- $1.50 per doc plus copy fee. Payee- De Soto County Clerk of Circuit Court. **Online access to Real Estate, Lien, Recording, Property Tax, Inmate, Wanted records:** Access an index of recorded documents at www.myfloridacounty.com. Fees involved to order copies; save $1.50 per record by becoming a subscriber. Also, access the property appraiser data free at http://qpublic.net/desoto/search.html. Also, access to the tax collector data is free at www.qpublic.net/dctc/search.html. Search the sheriff's inmate list at http://65.40.25.25/Sheriff.htm Search the most wanted list at www.desotosheriff.com/mostwanted.htm. **Other phones:** Appraiser/Auditor- 863-993-4866. **Property tax/Assessor-** same address as above. 863-993-4866.

Dixie County

County Clerk of the Circuit Court, PO Box 1206, Cross City, FL 32628. RE & UCC recording phone-352-498-1200; fax-352-498-1201; hours: 9AM-N,1-5PM
All records in one index. Only the public may search. Copy fee $1.00 per page. Cert fee- $1.50 per doc, includes copy fee. Payee- Dixie County Clerk of Circuit Court. **Online access to Real Estate, Lien, Recording, Assessor, Property records:** Access an index of recorded documents at www.myfloridacounty.com. Fees involved to order copies; save $1.50 per record by becoming a subscriber. Also, access assessor's property data free at http://dixiefl.patriotproperties.com/default.asp. **Other phones:** Appraiser/Auditor- 352-498-1212; Elections-352-498-1216. **Property tax/Assessor-** PO Box 260, Cross City, FL 32628; 352-498-1212.

Duval County

County Clerk of the Circuit Court, 330 E. Bay St #103; Courthouse, Jacksonville, FL 32202. 904-630-2043; fax-904-630-2959; hours: 8:30AM-4:30PM
Online access to the state recorders' meta-search site is free at www.myfloridacounty.com. Click on Official Records. Separate indices to search. Records indexed on a public use terminal back to 1985. Office personnel or visitors may perform searches. Search fee $1.50 per name per year. Will not search real estate records. Copy fee $1.00 per page. Cert fee- $1.00 per doc plus copy fee. Payee- Duval County Clerk of Circuit Court. **Online access to Property Appraiser, Real Estate, Lien, Recording, Grantor/Grantee, Vital Statistic, Occ. License, Inmate records:** Access to the Clerk of Circuit Court and City of Jacksonville Official Records with grantor/grantee index is free at http://205.173.32.5/OnCoreWeb/Search.aspx. Search the tax collector real estate data at http://tc.coj.net/realestate/. Also, search County Property Appraiser records for Duval County and City of Jacksonville at http://apps2.coj.net/pao. Search occupational licenses for free at http://tc.coj.net/occlicense/; Tangible property at

http://tc.coj.net/tpproperty/ Access an index of recorded documents at www.myfloridacounty.com. Fees involved to order copies; save $1.50 per record by becoming a subscriber. Access inmate information at-www.jaxsheriff.com/inmatesearch/(xhreii55bpunkk3iuhlbth2o)/default.aspx. **Other phones:** Treasurer- 904-630-2068; Appraiser/Auditor- 904-630-2020.

Escambia County

Clerk of the Circuit Court, 223 Palafox Pl; Old Courthouse, Pensacola, FL 32501. RE & UCC recording phone-850-595-3930; fax-850-595-4827; hours: 8AM-5PM www.clerk.co.escambia.fl.us
All records in one index. Records indexed on a public use terminal back to 1982. Office personnel or visitors may perform searches. Search fee $1.50 per name per year. Copy fee $1.00 per page. Cert fee- $1.50 per doc plus copy fee. Payee- Escambia Clerk of Circuit Court. **Online access to Property Appraiser, Real Estate, Grantor/Grantee, Lien, Recording, Vital Statistic, Property Tax, Tax Sale records:** Access to the Clerk of Court Public Records database is free at www.clerk.co.escambia.fl.us/public_records.html. This includes grantor/grantee index and marriage, traffic, court records, tax sales. Also, access to the tax collector's Property Tax Inquiry database is free at www.chrisjones.org/Search/. Click on ECTC Online then on "Cyber-Tax." Tax sale info also available. Also, search the property appraiser real estate records at www.escpa.org/Search/. Access an index of Recorded documents at www.myfloridacounty.com. Fees involved to order copies; save $1.50 per record by becoming subscriber. Also, Sheriff's office sexual offenders, etc found at www.escambiaso.com/investigations.htm. **Other phones:** Treasurer- 850-436-5200; Appraiser/Auditor- 850-434-2735. **Property tax/Assessor-** 850-434-2735.

Flagler County

County Clerk of the Circuit Court, PO Box 787; Recording Division, Bunnell, FL 32110. 386-437-7433; fax-386-437-7374; hours: 8AM-4:30PM www.flaglerclerk.com
All records in one index. Records indexed on a public use terminal back to 1988; overall index goes back to 1917; also on microfilm. Search fee $1.50 per name per year unless otherwise indicated. Will search for any real estate records in general index. Tax lien search fee- $1.00 per debtor plus $1.00 per year. Copy fee $1.00 per page. Cert fee- $1.50 per doc plus copy fee. Payee- Flagler County Clerk of Circuit Court. No credit cards accepted. **Online access to Property Appraiser, Recording, Real Estate, Lien, Deed, Probate, Judgment, Marriage, Death, Military Discharge, Most Wanted, Sex Offender, Property Sale records:** Search recording records free at www.flaglerclerk.com/oncoreweb/Search.aspx. Also, recording index on CD-rom for $51.52; for info, call Vickie Hunter- 386-437-7396. Also, search appraiser property info free at www.qpublic.net/flagler/search.html. Check sales at www.qpublic.net/flagler/flaglersearch.html. Also, access to state recorders' meta-search site is free at www.myflaglerclerk.com. Click on Official Records. Also, sheriff's most wanted and sex offender lists are at www.myfcso.com/fcso/. Access an index of recorded documents at www.myfloridacounty.com. Fees involved to order copies; save $1.50 per record by becoming a subscriber. **Other phones:** Treasurer- 386-437-7414; Appraiser/Auditor- 386-437-7450; Elections- 386-437-7447. **Property tax/Assessor-** 386-437-7450.

Franklin County

County Clerk of the Circuit Court, 33 Market St #203, Apalachicola, FL 32320. 850-653-8861 x108 or x109; fax-850-653-2261; hours: 8:30AM-4:30PM www.franklinclerk.com
There is also an office at Carrabelle Annex,1647 Hwy 98 E, Carrabelle, FL 32322; 850-697- 3263. All

records in one index. Records indexed on a public use terminal back to 1968. Only the public may search. Copy fee $1.00 per page. Cert fee- $1.50 per doc plus copy fee. Payee- Franklin County Clerk of Circuit Court. **Online access to Real Estate, Lien, Recording records:** Access an index of recorded documents at www.myfloridacounty.com. Fees involved to order copies; save $1.50 per record by becoming a subscriber. **Other phones:** Treasurer- 850-653-8861; Appraiser/Auditor- 850-653-9236; Elections- 850-653-9520. **Property tax/Assessor-** same address as above. 850-653-9323.

Gadsden County

County Clerk of the Circuit Court, PO Box 1649, Quincy, FL 32353-1649. 850-875-8601; fax-850-875-8612; hours: 8:30AM-5PM www.clerk.co.gadsden.fl.us
All records in one index. Records indexed on a public use terminal back to 1985. Office personnel or visitors may perform searches. Search fee $1.50 per name. Copy fee $1.00 per page. Cert fee- $1.50 per doc plus copy fee. Payee- Gadsden County Clerk of Circuit Court. **Online access to Real Estate, Recording, Judgment, Deed, Lien, Vital Statistic, Property Appraiser records:** Access to official records index is free at www.clerk.co.gadsden.fl.us/OfficialRecords/. Index records go back to 1985. Provides index numbers only. Also, access to the property appraiser database is free at www.qpublic.net/gadsden/search.html. Also, search tax collector records at www.gadsdentaxcollector.com/collectmax/collect30.asp. Search property sales at www.qpublic.net/gadsden/gadsdensearch.html. No name searching. **Other phones:** Appraiser/Auditor- 850-627-7168. **Property tax/Assessor-** 850-627-7168.

Gilchrist County

County Clerk of the Circuit Court, PO Box 37, Trenton, FL 32693. RE & UCC recording phone-352-463-3170; fax-352-463-3166; hours: 8:30AM-5PM www.co.gilchrist.fl.us/cophone
All records in one index. Records indexed on a public use terminal back to 1983. Only the public may search. Copy fee $1.00 per page. Cert fee- $1.50 per doc plus copy fee. Payee- Gilchrist County Clerk of Circuit Court. **Online access to Real Estate, Property Appraiser, Lien, Recording, Deed, Judgment, Marriage, Death records:** Access to the property appraiser database is free at www.qpublic.net/gilchrist/search.html. Also, sales searches are at www.gcpaonline.net; click on Search. Access an index of recorded documents at http://mygilchristcounty.com or www.myfloridacounty.com. Fees involved to order copies; save $1.50 per record by becoming a subscriber. **Other phones:** Appraiser/Auditor- 352-463-3190; Elections- 352-463-3194. **Property tax/Assessor-** 352-463-3190.

Glades County

County Clerk of the Circuit Court, PO Box 10, Moore Haven, FL 33471. RE & UCC recording phone-863-946-6010; fax-863-946-0560; hours: 8AM-5PM http://gladesclerk.com/
All records in one index. Records indexed on computer back to 1/1989. Office personnel or visitors may perform searches. Search fee $1.50 per name per year. Copy fee $1.00 per page. Cert fee- $1.50 per doc plus copy fee. Payee- Glades County Clerk of Circuit Court. **Online access to Real Estate, Lien, Recording records:** Access an index of recorded documents at www.myfloridacounty.com. Fees involved to order copies; save $1.50 per record by becoming a subscriber. **Other phones:** Appraiser/Auditor- 863-946-6025.

Gulf County

County Clerk of the Circuit Court, 1000 Cecil G. Costin, Sr. Blvd. Rm. 148, Port St. Joe, FL 32456. 850-229-6112, R/E recording phone-850-229-6113, UCC

recording phone-850-229-6113; fax-850-229-6174; hours: 9AM-5PM www.gulfclerk.com
All records in one index. Records indexed on a public use terminal back to 1986. Only the public may search. Copy fee $1.00 per page. Cert fee-$1.00 per doc plus copy fee. Payee- Gulf County Clerk of Circuit Court. **Online access to Real Estate, Lien, Deed, Judgment, Marriage, Death, Recording records:** Access an index of recorded documents at www.myfloridacounty.com. Fees involved to order copies; save $1.50 per record by becoming a subscriber. **Other phones:** Treasurer- 850-229-6116; Appraiser/Auditor- 850-229-6115; Elections- 850-229-6117; Vital Records- 850-227-1276. **Property tax/Assessor-** 1000 Cecil G. Costin, Sr. Blvd., Port St. Joe, FL 32456; 850-229-6115.

Hamilton County

County Clerk of the Circuit Court, 207 NE 1st St; Rm 106, Jasper, FL 32052. RE & UCC recording phone-386-792-1288; fax-386-792-3524; hours: 8:30AM-4:30PM
All records in one index. Records indexed on a public use terminal back to 1984. Office will perform a UCC search but public must search other records themselves. UCC search per debtor name- $1.50 per name per ,year. Copy fee $1.00 per page. Cert fee- $1.50 per doc plus copy fee. Payee- Hamilton County Clerk of Circuit Court. **Online access to Real Estate, Lien, Recording records:** Access an index of recorded documents at www.myfloridacounty.com. Fees involved to order copies; save $1.50 per record by becoming a subscriber. **Other phones:** Treasurer- 386-792-1288; Appraiser/Auditor- 386-792-1284; Elections- 386-792-1426; Vital Records- 386-792-1288. **Property tax/Assessor-** same address as above. 386-792-2791.

Hardee County

County Clerk of the Circuit Court, PO Drawer 1749, Wauchula, FL 33873. 863-773-4174; fax-863-773-3295; hours: 8AM-5PM; 8AM-4PM Recording hours www.hardeeclerk.com
All records in one index. Office personnel or visitors may perform searches. Search fee $1.50 per name per year. Will search UCC records and tax liens. Copy fee $1.00 per page. Cert fee- $1.50 per doc plus copy fee. Payee- Hardee County Clerk of Circuit Court. **Online access to Real Estate, Recording, Lien, Property Appraiser, Most Wanted, Arrest, Inmate, Warrant records:** Access an index of recorded documents at www.myfloridacounty.com. Fees involved to order copies; save $1.50 per record by becoming a subscriber. Also, online assess to the property appraiser data free at www.hardeecounty.net/cfaps/appraiser/propform.cfm. Also, search the sheriff's most wanted, inmate, arrest, warrant and missing person lists at www.hardeeso.com. **Other phones:** Appraiser/Auditor- 863-773-2196. **Property tax/Assessor-** 863-773-9144.

Hendry County

Clerk of the Circuit Court, PO Box 1760, La Belle, FL 33975-1760. 863-675-5217; fax-863-675-5238; hours: 8:30AM-5PM www.hendryclerk.org
All records in one index. Records indexed on a public use terminal back to 1980. Only the public may search. General index search fee $1.00 per year. Real estate owner, mortgage, and property transfer searches available. Copy fee $1.00 per page. Cert fee- $1.50 per doc plus copy fee. Payee- Hendry County Clerk of Circuit Court. **Online access to Real Estate, Lien, Recording records:** Access an index of recorded documents at www.myfloridacounty.com. Also, access the property appraiser database at www.hendryprop.com/GIS/Search_F.asp. Also, Official Records Database found at http://64.45.229.253/offrec/ormain.htm - Has images from April 12, 1990 – Book 450 Page 1 to latest available. Web records are updated once a week. **Property tax/Assessor-** 863-675-5270.

Hernando County

County Clerk of the Circuit Court, 20 N. Main, Rm 215, Brooksville, FL 34601. 352-540-6768; fax-352-754-4243; hours: 8AM-5PM www.clerk.co.hernando.fl.us
All records in one index. Records indexed on a public use terminal back to 1983. Office personnel or visitors may perform searches. Search fee $1.50 per name per page. Copy fee $1.00 per page. Cert fee- $1.50 per doc plus copy fee. Payee- Hernando County Clerk of Circuit Court. **Online access to Property Appraiser, Real Estate, Lien, Marriage, Recording, Most Wanted, Arrest records:** Access to the clerk's Official Records database is now free at www.clerk.co.hernando.fl.us/disclaimer.asp. Your browser must be Javascript enabled. Includes recordings, marriages, and court records. Also, the county now offers 2 levels of the Public Inquiry System Property Appraiser Real Estate database - Easy Search and Real Time Search - free at www.co.hernando.fl.us/pa/propsearch.htm. Search by owner, address, or parcel key. Also, access an index of recorded documents at www.myfloridacounty.com. Fees involved to order copies; save $1.50 per record by becoming a subscriber. Search sheriff's most wanted and arrests (back to 1995) lists at www.hcso.hernando.fl.us. **Other phones:** Treasurer- 352-754-4190; Appraiser/Auditor- 352-754-4190.

Highlands County

County Clerk of the Circuit Court, 590 S. Commerce Ave, Sebring, FL 33870. Main phone & R/E recording-863-402-6590; UCC recording phone-800-822-5436; hours: 8AM-5PM www.clerk.co.highlands.fl.us
All records in one index. Only the public may search. Copy fee $1.00 per page. Cert fee- $1.50 per doc plus copy fee. Payee- Clerk of Court. **Online access to Property Appraiser, Personal Property, Real Estate, Lien, Recording records:** Property appraiser records are free at www.appraiser.co.highlands.fl.us/search.html; tangible personal property records are available. Also, online access to the recorders' meta-search site is at www.myflorida.com. Click on Official Records. Free search; fee for documents. Also, online access to deeds, mortgages, judgments from the county recording database are free at www.clerk.co.highlands.fl.us/official/search.html. Records go back to 1983. Also, county tax collector database for personal property and real estate is free at www.collector.co.highlands.fl.us/search/index.html. **Other phones:** Treasurer- 863-402-6685; Appraiser/Auditor- 863-402-6661; Elections- 863-402-6654; Vital Records- 863-402-6040. **Property tax/Assessor-** 863-402-6659.

Hillsborough County

County Clerk of the Circuit Court, PO Box 3249, Tampa, FL 33601-1110. 813-276-8100 x4367, R/E recording phone-813-276-8100, UCC recording phone-813-276-8100; fax-813-276-2114; hours: 8AM-5PM www.hillsclerk.com
All records in one index. Records indexed on computer back to 1965. Only the public may search. General index search fee $1.00 per year. Copy fee $1.00 per page. Cert fee- $1.50 per doc plus copy fee. Payee- Hillsborough County Clerk of Circuit Court. **Online access to Property Appraiser, Personal Property, Real Estate, Lien, Deed, Recording, Warrant, Inmate, Repo/Impound records:** Property appraiser records are free at www.hcpafl.org/disclaimer.html. Receive owner data, legal, sales, value summaries. The clerk's recordings index can be searched free at http://publicrecord.hillsclerk.com. Also, access recorded document index at www.myfloridacounty.com; fees involved to order copies; subscribers save $1.50 per record. Call 813-276-8100 x4444 for info. Also, search sheriff's warrants, inmates, repo data free at www.hcso.tampa.fl.us/Page_Headers/online.htm. Images of official records from 1990 to current day are at www.hillsclerk.com. **Other phones:** Appraiser/Auditor- 813-272-6100.

Holmes County

County Clerk of the Circuit Court, PO Box 397, Bonifay, FL 32425. 850-547-1102, R/E recording phone-850-547-1100, UCC recording phone-850-547-1100; fax-850-547-6630; hours: 8AM-4PM www.holmesclerk.com
All records in one index. Records indexed on a public use terminal back to 1982. Only the public may search. Copy fee $1.00 per page. Cert fee-$1.50 per doc plus copy fee. Payee- Holmes County Clerk of Circuit Court. **Online access to Real Estate, Lien, Recording records:** Access an index of recorded documents at www.myfloridacounty.com. Fees involved to order copies; save $1.50 per record by becoming a subscriber. **Other phones:** Treasurer- 850-547-1115; Appraiser/Auditor- 850-547-1113; Elections- 850-547-1107. **Property tax/Assessor-** 300 N Waukesha St, Bonifay, FL 32425; 850-547-1100.

Indian River County

County Clerk of the Circuit Court, PO Box 1028, Vero Beach, FL 32961-1028. 772-770-5185 x184; fax-772-770-5008; hours: 8:30AM-5PM www.clerk.indian-river.org
All records in one index. Office personnel or visitors may perform searches. Search fee $1.00 plus $1.00 per yr. Copy fee $1.00 per page. Cert fee- $1.50 per doc plus copy fee. Payee- Indian River County Clerk of Circuit Court. **Online access to Property Appraiser, Real Estate, Lien, Vital Statistic, Inmate, Criminal History records:** Appraiser information is free, but only some of the recording office information is. Appraiser records are free at http://ircpa.irene.net/search.html. Also, access to Clerk of the Circuit Court recording indices are free at www.clerk.indian-river.org/recordssearch/ori.asp.
Records go back to 1983. Sheriff's data on inmates and criminal histories at www.ircsheriff.org/programs.cfm. Full real estate, lien and court and vital records from the Clerk of the Circuit Court is at their fee site; subscriptions start $100 per month, increasing with amount of access. For info about free and fee access, call 772-567-8000 x216. **Other phones:** Appraiser/Auditor- 772-567-8188; Vital Records- 772-567-8000. **Property tax/Assessor-** 925 14th Lane, Vero Beach, FL 32960; not known.

Jackson County

County Clerk of the Circuit Court, PO Drawer 510, Marianna, FL 32447. RE & UCC recording phone-850-482-9552; fax-850-482-7849; hours: 8AM-4:30PM www.jacksonclerk.com
All records in one index. Only the public may search. Copy fee $1.00 per page. Cert fee- $1.50 per doc plus copy fee. Payee- Jackson County Clerk of Circuit Court. **Online access to Real Estate, Lien, Recording, Marriage, Probate, Property Tax records:** Access to the Clerk of Circuit Court Official Records database is free at www.jacksonclerk.com. Images will go back to 5/1996. Also, search property tax data for free at www.jacksoncountytaxcollector.com/SearchSelect.aspx Access an index of recorded documents at www.myfloridacounty.com. Fees involved to order copies; save $1.50 per record by becoming a subscriber. **Other phones:** Treasurer- 850-482-9653; Appraiser/Auditor- 850-482-9646; Elections- 850-482-9652; Vital Records- 850-482-9552 (marriage only). **Property tax/Assessor-** 850-482-9646.

Jefferson County

County Clerk of the Circuit Court, Courthouse; Rm 10, Monticello, FL 32344. 850-342-0218 x27, R/E recording phone-850-342-0218 x 227, UCC recording phone-850-342-0218 x 227; fax-850-342-0222; hours: 8AM-5PM http://co.jefferson.fl.us
All records in one index. Records indexed on a public use terminal back to 1973. Only the public may search. General index search fee $1.00 per year per name. Separate federal tax lien search-$1.00 per debtor per year; state lien- $2.00 per debtor. Copy fee $1.00 per page. Cert fee- $1.50

per doc plus copy fee. Payee- Jefferson County Clerk of Circuit Court. **Online access to Property, Real Estate, Lien, Recording records:** Access to the Property Appraiser database is free at http://qpublic.net/jefferson/search.html. Sales searches are also available. Also, online access to recordings database is free at www.myjeffersoncounty.com. Also, search the tax collector database free at www.jeffersoncountytaxcollector.com/SearchSelect.aspx. Access an index of recorded documents at www.myfloridacounty.com. Fees involved to order copies; save $1.50 per record by becoming a subscriber. **Other phones:** Treasurer- 850-342-0218 x 232; Appraiser/Auditor- 850-997-3356; Elections- 850-997-3348. **Property tax/Assessor-** 150 N Jefferson, Monticello, FL 32344; 850-997-3356.

Lafayette County

County Clerk of the Circuit Court, PO Box 88, Mayo, FL 32066. 386-294-1600; fax-386-294-4231; hours: 8AM-5PM www.lafayetteclerk.com
Only the public may search. Copy fee $1.00 per page. Cert fee- $1.50 per doc plus copy fee. Payee- Lafayette County Clerk of Circuit Court. **Online access to Real Estate, Lien, Recording records:** Access an index of recorded documents at www.myfloridacounty.com. Fees involved to order copies; save $1.50 per record by becoming a subscriber. **Other phones:** Treasurer- 386-294-1961; Appraiser/Auditor- 386-294-1991. **Property tax/Assessor-** 386-294-1991.

Lake County

County Clerk of the Circuit Court, PO Box 7800, Tavares, FL 32778-7800. RE & UCC recording phone-352-253-2600; fax-352-253-2616; hours: 8:30AM-5PM (Recording hours: 8:30AM-4:30PM) www.lakecountyclerk.org
All records in one index. Records indexed on a public use terminal back to 1974. Office personnel or visitors may perform searches. General index search fee $1.00 per name/year. UCC search per debtor name- $1.50 per name per year. S. Copy fee $1.00 per page. Cert fee- $1.50 per doc plus copy fee. Payee- Lake County Clerk of Circuit Court. **Online access to Property Appraiser, Recording, Real Estate, Lien, Marriage, Death, Divorce records:** new official records database is free online at www.lakecountyclerk.org/services.asp?subject=Online_Official_Records. Records go as far back as 1974. Includes court records. Also, records on the County Property Assessor database are free at www.lakecopropappr.com/property_search.asp. Also, marriage records back to 11/2000 are at www.lakecountyclerk.org/departments.asp?subject=Marriage_Licenses. Also, access to state recorders' meta-search site is free at www.myfloridacounty.com. Click on Official records. Also, private site has previous 2 weeks real estate, marriage, divorce records at http://extra.orlandosentinel.com/publicrecords/search.asp. **Other phones:** Treasurer- 352-742-9808; Appraiser/Auditor- 352-343-9748; Elections- 352-343-9734; Vital Records- 352-589-6424; Tax Collector- 352-343-9622. **Property tax/Assessor-** 317 W Main St, Tavares, FL 32778; 352-343-9748.

Lee County

County Clerk of the Circuit Court, PO Box 2278, Fort Myers, FL 33902-2278. 239-335-2283; hours: 8AM-5PM http://leeclerk.org/index.asp
There is also a Cape Coral Branch Office - Lee County Gov't Ctr., 1039 SE 9th PL, Cape Coral, FL 33990. All records in one index. General search fee $1.00 per year. Real estate owner, mortgage, and property transfer searches available. Will search UCC records; search includes tax liens if requested. UCC search per debtor name- $1.50 per name per year. Copy fee $1.00 per page. Cert fee- $1.50 per doc plus copy fee. Payee- Lee County Clerk of Circuit Court. **Online access to Property Appraiser, Real Estate, Occ. License, Lien, Recording, Judgment, Business or Personal Tangible Property, Vessel, Vehicle records:** Access most tax, vehicle, and occupation-

related databases free at www.leetc.com/home.asp. Also, search the recorders index free at http://leeclerk.org/SearchOfficialRecords.htm but obtain certified copies at the Clerk's office or order certified copies online and search County Official Records at www.myfloridacounty.com and click on Order Official Records. Search tangible business property at www.leepa.org/Tangible/Business%20Search.htm. The online property information inquiry is at www.leepa.org/Queries/SearchCriteria.htm. **Other phones:** Appraiser/Auditor- 239-335-6150. **Property tax/Assessor-** 239-339-6100.

Leon County

County Clerk of the Circuit Court, PO Box 726, Tallahassee, FL 32302. 850-577-4030, R/E recording phone-850-577-4050; fax-850-577-4235; hours: 8:30AM-5PM www.clerk.leon.fl.us
Online records at www.clerk.leon.fl.us MAY have ID information removed; some records MAY have been removed from this online service, though this is rare. All records in one index. Records indexed on a public use terminal back to 1984. Only the public may search. Copy fee $1.00 per page. Cert fee- $1.50 per doc plus copy fee. Payee- Leon County Clerk of Circuit Court. **Online access to Property Appraiser, Real Estate, Lien, Marriage, Recording, Foreclosure, Contractor, Most Wanted records:** Real Estate, lien, and foreclosure records from the County Clerk are free at www.clerk.leon.fl.us. Lending agency information is also available. Also, access to full document images requires user name and password, plus $100 per month. Property Appraiser database records free at www.co.leon.fl.us/propappr/search.cfm. Access recorded documents index free at www.myfloridacounty.com. Fees involved to order copies. Search contractors lists at www.leonpermits.org/contractors/. Search tax collector rolls at http://dta.co.leon.fl.us/tax/default.asp. Marriages are at http://cvweb.clerk.leon.fl.us/index_marriage.html. **Other phones:** Appraiser/Auditor- 850-488-6102. **Assessor-** same address as above. 850-488-6102.

Levy County

County Clerk of the Circuit Court, PO Drawer 610, Bronson, FL 32621. RE & UCC recording phone-352-486-5229; hours: 8AM-5PM www.levyclerk.com
All records in one index. Records indexed on a public use terminal back to 1983. Only the public may name search. Real estate owner, mortgage, and property transfer records available if you provide book and page number; fee is $1.00 per page. Copy fee $1.00 per page. Cert fee- $1.50 per doc plus copy fee. Payee- Levy County Clerk of Circuit Court. **Online access to Real Estate, Lien, Recording, Property Tax, Property Appraiser, Warrant records:** Access the recording database free at http://levyclerk.com/scripts/LevyClerk.exe?K. Search by name, book/page, file number or document type. Access an index of recorded documents at www.myfloridacounty.com. Fees involved to order copies; save $1.50 per record by becoming a subscriber. Also, search county warrants list for free at www.levyso.com. Also, access to the property appraiser data is free at www.qpublic.net/levy/search.html. Also, search tax collector data free at www.levytaxcollector.com/collectmax/collect30.asp. **Other phones:** Appraiser/Auditor- 352-486-5222; Elections- 352-486-5163; Vital recs- 352-486-5274.

Liberty County

County Clerk of the Circuit Court, PO Box 399, Bristol, FL 32321. 850-643-2215; fax-850-643-2866; hours: 8AM-5PM www.libertyclerk.com
All records in one index. Records indexed on a public use terminal back to 1990. Only the public may search. Copy fee $1.00 per page. Cert fee- $1.50 per doc plus copy fee. Payee- Liberty County Clerk of Circuit Court. **Online access to Real Estate, Lien, Recording records:** Access an index of recorded documents at www.myfloridacounty.com. Fees involved to order copies; save $1.50 per record by becoming a subscriber.

Other phones: Treasurer- 850-643-2442; Appraiser/Auditor- 850-643-2279. **Property tax/Assessor-** 850-643-2279.

Madison County

County Clerk of the Circuit Court, PO Box 237, Madison, FL 32341-0237. 850-973-1500, R/E recording phone-850-973-1500 x27, UCC recording phone-850-973-1500 x27; fax-850-973-2059; hours: 8AM-5PM www.madisonclerk.com
All records in one index. Records indexed on a public use terminal back to 1990. Only the public may search. Copy fee $1.00 per page. Cert fee- $1.50 per doc plus copy fee. Payee- Madison County Clerk of Circuit Court. **Online access to Real Estate, Lien, Recording, Property, Appraiser, Sale records:** Access an index of recorded documents at www.myfloridacounty.com. Fees involved to order copies; save $1.50 per record by becoming a subscriber. Official Records indexes are for past 10 years. Also, access appraiser's property cards and sale databases free at www.madisonpa.com/GIS/Search_F.asp. **Other phones:** Treasurer- 850-973-1500; Appraiser/Auditor- 850-973-6133; Elections- 850-973-6507. **Property tax/Assessor-** 850-973-6133.

Manatee County

County Clerk of the Circuit Court, PO Box 25400, Bradenton, FL 34206. 941-741-4041, R/E recording phone-941-741-4040 or 4041; fax-941-741-4082; hours: 8:30AM-5PM www.manateeclerk.com
All records in one index. Office personnel or visitors may perform searches. General index search fee $1.00 per year per name. Copy fee $1.00 per page. Cert fee- $1.50 per doc plus copy fee. Payee- Manatee County Clerk of Circuit Court. **Online access to Property Appraiser, Real Estate, Lien, Recording, Deed, Judgment, Death, Marriage, Condominium, Foreclosure Sale, Tax Deed Sale, Most Wanted records:** Search and view real estate and recordings records free from the Clerk of Circuit Court and Comptroller's database at www.manateeclerk.com. Also, access an index of recorded documents at www.myfloridacounty.com. Fees involved to order copies. Also, Appraiser records are free at www.manateepao.com. Tax deed sales at www.clerkofcourts.com/Sales/TaxDeeds/taxdeed.pdf. Also, property tax records are at www.taxcollector.com/dataaccess/design/1owner.asp. Search foreclosure sales at www.manateeclerk.com. **Other phones:** Treasurer- 941-748-4800; Appraiser/Auditor- 941-748-8208; Elections- 941-741-3823; Vital Records- 941-748-0747. **Property tax/Assessor-** PO Box 1000, Bradenton, FL 34206; 941-748-8208.

Marion County

County Clerk of the Circuit Court, PO Box 1030, Ocala, FL 34478-1030. RE & UCC recording phone-352-620-3925; fax-352-620-3930; hours: 8AM-5PM www.marioncountyclerk.org
All records in one index. Records indexed on a public use terminal back to 1989. Office personnel or visitors may perform searches. Search fee $1.00 per name per year. Copy fee $1.00 per page. Cert fee- $1.50 per doc plus copy fee. Payee- Marion County Clerk of Circuit Court. **Online access to Property Appraiser, Real Estate, Recording, Tax Collector, Tax Deed Sale, Inmate, Sex Offender, Deed, Lien, Judgment, Death, Marriage records:** Tax collector data is free at http://mariontaxcollector.governmax.com/collectmax/collect30.asp. Also search recorder records free at http://216.255.240.38/wb_or1/or_sch_1.asp Access an index of recorded documents at www.myfloridacounty.com. Fees involved to order copies; save $1.50 per record by becoming a subscriber. Also, search the sheriff's jail inmate database at www.marionso.com:8000/search.asp. Also, acc3ess property data via the GIS mapping site at www.marioncountyfl.org/IS251/GISWEB/gis_home.htm. Click on County Interactive map, then the red ?. **Other phones:** Appraiser/Auditor- 352-368-8300.

Martin County

County Clerk of the Circuit Court, PO Box 9016, Stuart, FL 34995. RE & UCC recording phone-772-288-5554; fax-772-223-7920; hours: 8AM-5PM www.martin.fl.us/GOVT

772-288-5552 is the direct telephone number for index search requests. Office personnel or visitors may perform searches. General index search fee $1.00 per name per year.$1.50-UCCs,Searchs not Guaranteed. Copy fee $1.00 per page. Cert fee-$1.50 per doc plus copy fee. Payee- Clerk of Circuit Court. **Online access to Property Appraiser, Real Estate, Lien, Recording, Personal Property records:** Access to the clerk of the circuit court recordings database are free at http://clerk-web.martin.fl.us/wb_or1. Also, records on the county property appraiser database are free at http://paoweb.martin.fl.us. Choose from "Online Property Searches." Personal property searches are also available. County tax collector data files are free at http://taxcol.martin.fl.us/advsrch_home.asp. Also, online access to the state recorders' meta-search site is free at www.myfloridacounty.com. **Other phones:** Treasurer- 772-288-5595; Appraiser/Auditor- 772-288-5608; Elections- 772-288-5637. **Property tax/Assessor-** 772-288-5608.

Monroe County

County Clerk of the Circuit Court, PO Box 1980, Key West, FL 33041-1980. 305-292-3540, R/E recording phone-305-292-3507; fax-305-295-3623; hours: 8:30AM-5PM www.co.monroe.fl.us

All records in one index. Records indexed on a public use terminal back to 1996. Office personnel or visitors may perform searches. General index search fee $1.50 per name per year. Will not search real estate records. Copy fee $1.00 per page. Cert fee- $1.50 per doc plus copy fee. Payee- Monroe County Clerk of Circuit Court. **Online access to Real Estate, Recording, Deed, Lien, Property Tax, Occ. License, Arrest, Inmate, Warrant records:** Access to the clerk of circuit courts database is free at www.clerk-of-the-court.com/searchOfficialRecords.asp. Also, access to property appraiser data is free at www.mcpafl.org/datacenter/mapdisc.asp? Also, search property tax and occupational licenses free at www.monroetaxcollector.com/collectmax/collect30.asp. Also, search warrant lists at http://www2.keysso.net/WebWarrants/WebWarrantsA.htm; arrests at www.keysso.net. **Other phones:** Treasurer- 305-292-3420; Vital Records- 305-292-3507; Tax Collector- 305-245-5000. **Property tax/Assessor-** same address as above. not known.

Nassau County

County Clerk of the Circuit Court, 76347 Veterans Way, Yulee, FL 32035. 904-548-4600; fax-904-548-4549; hours: 8:30AM-5PM; Recording Hours: 9AM-4PM) www.nassauclerk.com

All records in one index. Records indexed on a public use terminal back to 1982. Office personnel or visitors may perform searches. Search fee $1.00 per name per year. Copy fee $1.00 per page. Cert fee- $1.50 per doc plus copy fee. Payee- Nassau County Clerk of Circuit Court. **Online access to Real Estate, Lien, Recording records:** Access an index of recorded documents at www.myfloridacounty.com. Fees involved to order copies; save $1.50 per record by becoming a subscriber. Also, the recorders database is free at www.nassauclerk.org/OfficialRecords/. **Other phones:** Appraiser/Auditor- 904-491-7300. **Property tax/Assessor-** same address as above. 904-491-7300.

Okaloosa County

County Clerk of the Circuit Court, PO Drawer 1359, Crestview, FL 32536. 850-689-5847, R/E recording phone-850-689-5041, UCC recording phone-850-689-5041; fax-850-689-5886; hours: 8AM-5PM www.clerkofcourts.cc

Access an index of recorded documents at www.myfloridacounty.com. Fees involved to order copies; save $1.50 per record by becoming a subscriber. All records in one index. Records indexed on a public use terminal back to 1983. Office will perform a UCC search but public must search other records themselves. Search fee $1.00 per name per year. Copy fee $1.00 per page. Cert fee-$1.50 per doc plus copy fee. Payee- Okaloosa County Clerk of Circuit Court. **Online access to Property Appraiser, Real Estate, Lien, Recording, Vital Statistic, Property Tax, Occ. License records:** Several databases are available. Access to Okaloosa County online system requires a monthly usage fee of $100. No addresses listed. Lending agency, traffic and domestic records are. For info, contact Don Howard at 850-689-5821. Access the clerk's land and official records for free at www.clerkofcourts.cc/orsearch/disclaimer.htm; includes access to marriage, civil court, traffic records. Access tax collector data at http://okaloosa.governmax.com/collectmax/search_collect.asp?. Property Appraiser records are online at http://qpublic.net/okaloosa/search1.html; sales & sales lists are at www.okaloosapa.com. Also, online access to the state recorders' meta-search site is free at www.myfloridacounty.com. **Other phones:** Treasurer-850-689-5801; Appraiser/Auditor- 850-689-5900; Elections- 850-651-7272.

Okeechobee County

County Clerk of the Circuit Court, 304 N.W. 2nd St; Rm 101, Okeechobee, FL 34972. 863-763-2131, R/E recording phone-863-763-0239, UCC recording phone-863-763-0239; hours: 8:30AM-5PM www.clerk.co.okeechobee.fl.us

All records in one index. Records indexed on a public use terminal back to Dec 1, 1970. Office personnel may perform searches. No record searches by phone. General index search fee $1.50 per name per year. Copy fee $1.00 per page. Cert fee- $1.50 per doc plus copy fee. Payee-Okeechobee County Clerk of Circuit Court. **Online access to Property, Recording, Appraiser, GIS, Personal Property, Property Sale records:** Search the statewide recording database via www.myfloridacounty.com. There is a fee to order. Also, access to the property appraiser database is free at www.okeechobeepa.com/GIS/Search_F.asp. Also search property on GIS site at www.emapsplus.com/FLOkeechobee/maps/. **Other phones:** Treasurer- 863-763-3421; Appraiser/Auditor-863-763-4422; Elections- 863-763-4014; Vital Records- 863-462-5819. **Property tax/Assessor-** 307 NW 5th Ave #A, Okeechobee, FL 34972; 863-763-4422.

Orange County

County Comptroller, PO Box 38; Official Records Dept., Orlando, FL 32802-0038. RE & UCC recording phone-407-836-5115; fax-407-836-5120; hours: 7:30AM-4:30PM www.occompt.com

All records in one index. Records indexed on a public use terminal. Only the public may search. General index search fee $1.50 per name per year. Copy fee $1.00 per page. Cert fee- $1.50 per doc plus copy fee. Payee- Orange County Comptroller. **Online access to Property Appraiser, Recording, Real Estate, Lien, Vital Statistic, Land Sale, Personal Property, Property Tax, Contractor records:** Real Estate, Lien, and Marriage records on the county Comptroller database are free at www.occompt.com/2002/records.html. Lending Agency data available. Also, private site has previous 2 weeks real estate, marriage, divorce records at http://extra.orlandosentinel.com/publicrecords/search.asp. Also, the appraiser property records are free at www.ocpafl.org/docs/disclaimer.html; at this site, click on "Record Searches." Also search personal property and residential sales records. Also, search property tax data at www.ocpafl.org/docs/disclaimer.html. Search contractor licenses: www.orangecountyfl.net/ebuilding/ContractorSearch/ContractorSearch.asp. **Other phones:** Treasurer- 407-836-5715; Appraiser/Auditor- 407-836-5000;

Elections- 407-836-2070; Vital Records- 407-623-1182. **Property tax/Assessor-** 407-836-5044.

Osceola County

County Clerk of the Circuit Court, 2 Courthouse Sq, #2000, Kissimmee, FL 34741-5491. 407-343-3500 x3517, R/E recording phone-407-343-3517, UCC recording phone-407-343-3517; fax-407-343-3534; hours: 8:30AM-5PM; 8:30AM-4PM Recording hours www.osceolaclerk.com

All records in one index. Records indexed on a public use terminal back to 1986. Office will perform a UCC search but public must search other records themselves. Search fee $1.50 per name per year. Copy fee $1.00 per page. Cert fee-$1.50 per doc plus copy fee. Payee- Osceola County Clerk of Circuit Court. **Online access to Real Estate, Property Tax, Appraiser, Occ. License, Inmate, Appraiser, Recording records:** Search recorded documents at www.myfloridacounty.com. Fees involved to order copies; save $1.50 per record by becoming a subscriber. Occupation licenses and tax collector data is free 7.5

Property appraiser records are free at www.osceolataxcollector.com/collectmax/collect30.asp?sid=E584F1A07F8540DE97C9BCBC22D10842. To purchase database call 407-343-3700. Data comes as 8mm data cartridges, CD-ROM. Fees vary; tax roll data is $75.00. Also, recording/land records are online at http://osceolarecorder.governmax.com/recordmax/recordd40.asp. Search inmate list at www.osceola.org/index.cfm?lsFuses=inmates. **Other phones:** Appraiser/Auditor- 407-343-3700; Elections-407-343-3900; Vital Records- 407-343-2000. **Property tax/Assessor-** 407-343-4000.

Palm Beach County

County Clerk of the Circuit Court, PO Box 4177, West Palm Beach, FL 33402. 561-355-2991, R/E recording phone-561-355-2932, UCC recording phone-561-355-2932; fax-561-355-2633; hours: 8AM-5PM www.pbcountyclerk.com

A subscription full-index online records system and CD-Roms of indexes are available. All records in one index. Records indexed on computer back to 1968. Office personnel or visitors may perform searches. General search fee $1.50 per name per year. Separate federal/state combined tax lien search-$1.00 per year. Copy fee $1.00 per page. Cert fee-$1.50 per doc plus copy fee. Payee- Palm Beach County Clerk of Circuit Court. **Online to Property Appraiser, Real Estate, Deed, Lien, Judgment, Recording, Vital Statistic, Property Tax, Personal Property, Occ License, Warrant, Sexual Predator, Sheriff Booking records:** Access recording database free at www.pbcountyclerk.com/records_home.html. Records go back to 1968; images back to 1968; includes marriage records 1979 to present. Also, search real estate, property tax, personal property data at www.co.palm-beach.fl.us/tc_pubaccess/default.asp. Search sheriff bookings at www.pbso.org/blotter/criteria.cfm. Search warrants & sex predators at www.pbso.org/index.cfm?fa=crimestoppers. Also, property appraiser records are free at www.co.palm-beach.fl.us/papa. Search tax deeds at www.pbcountyclerk.com/dt_web2/or_sch_1.asp. Search occupational licenses at www.co.palm-beach.fl.us/tc_pubaccess/occ/occ_search.asp. **Other phones:** Appraiser/Auditor- 561-355-2866; Elections-561-355-2650; Vital Records- 561-653-2350. **Property tax/Assessor-** 301 N Olive Ave, West Palm Beach, Fl 33401; 561-355-2866.

Pasco County

County Clerk of the Circuit Court, 38053 Live Oak Ave, Rm 205, Dade City, FL 33523-3894. 352-521-4469 or 4408, R/E recording phone-352-521-4469; hours: 8:30AM-5PM www.pascoclerk.com

All records in one index. Search fee $1.50 per name. Real estate owner, mortgage, and property transfer searches available. Will search UCC records. Copy fee $1.00 per page. Cert fee- $1.50 per doc plus copy fee. Payee- Pasco County Clerk of Circuit Court. **Online access to Property Appraiser, Real Estate, Lien, Vital Statistic, Recording, Occ License, Personal Property, Wanted, Sexual Predator, Contractor/Permit records:** Several sources available. Access to real estate, liens, marriage records requires $25 annual fee plus a $50 deposit. Billing rate is $.05 per minute, $.03 evenings. For information, call 352-521-4529. Also, free access to indexes at www.pascoclerk.com. Click on "records." Access an index of recorded documents at www.myfloridacounty.com. Fees involved to order copies. Search sheriff's wanted and sex predators at http://pascosheriff.com. Also, property appraiser data is free at http://appraiser.pascogov.com w/ sales data & maps. Search tax records and occupational licenses at http://taxcollector.pascogov.com/search/prclsearch.asp. Contractors/permit at http://opal.pascocountyfl.net/. **Other phones:** Appraiser/Auditor- 352-521-4433. **Property tax/Assessor-** 352-521-4433.

Pinellas County

County Clerk of the Circuit Court, 315 Court St; Rm 150, Clearwater, FL 33756. 727-464-4876; fax-727-464-4383; hours: 8AM-5PM http://pinellasclerk.org Index: Many indices. Records indexed on a public use terminal back to 1987. Office will perform a UCC search but public must search other records themselves. Search fee $1.50. Limited real estate owner, mortgage, and property transfer searches available; book and page number must be provided. Copy fee $1.00 per page. Cert fee- $1.50 per doc plus copy fee. Payee- Pinellas County Clerk of Circuit Court. **Online access to Property Appraiser, Real Estate, Lien, Judgment, Recording, Traffic/Boating Fine, Tax Collector, Personal Property, Tax Deed Sale, Accident Report records:** Assessor/property records are free at http://pao.co.pinellas.fl.us/search2.html. Also, recording records are no longer at http://clerk.co.pinellas.fl.us. Tax deed sales lists are at http://pubtitlet.co.pinellas.fl.us/servlet/taxdeed.saledates.DM79. Search most wanted at www.co.pinellas.fl.us/sheriff/csprofiles.htm. Also, access recorded document index at www.myfloridacounty.com. Fees involved to order copies. Also, search tax collector data free at www.visualgov.com/pinellascounty/. Accident reports-http://stockton.pcsonet.com/Crash%20Reports/policy.htm. **Other phones:** Appraiser/Auditor- 727-464-3207. **Property tax/Assessor-** same address as above. 727-464-3207.

Polk County

County Clerk of the Circuit Court, PO Box 9000 Drawer CC-8, Bartow, FL 33831-9000. RE & UCC recording phone-863-534-4516; fax-863-534-4008; hours: 8AM-4:30PM www.polkcountyclerk.net Separate indices to search. Records indexed on computer from 1990 forward, 1989 back on microfilm. Office personnel or visitors may perform searches. Search fee $1.50 per name. Copy fee $1.00 per page. Cert fee- $1.50 per doc plus copy fee. Payee- Clerk of Circuit Court. **Online access to Property Appraiser, Real Estate, Lien, Vital Statistic, Recording, Personal Property, Occ License Account, Tax Collector, Tax Deed Sale, Warrant, Most Wanted records:** Search the county clerk database at www.polkcountyclerk.net/public_records/public_index.html for free court records, deeds, mortgages, plats, marriages, resolutions. For copies of documents, call 863-534-4524. Fee is $1.00 per page. Also, appraiser property and personal property records are free at www.polkpa.org. Also, search occupational license accounts at http://198.31.196.18/occupational_search/. Also, search tax deed sales at www.polkcountyclerk.net/Taxdeed/Taxdeed_Sale.html. Search the sheriff's warrant and most wanted lists at www.polksheriff.org/wanted/. **Other phones:** Appraiser/Auditor- 863-534-4777. **Property tax/Assessor-** 255 N Wilson Ave, Barton, FL 33830; 863-534-4777.

Putnam County

County Clerk of the Circuit Court, PO Box 758, Palatka, FL 32178-0758. 386-329-0361, R/E recording phone-386-329-0256, UCC recording phone-386-329-0256; fax-386-329-0889; hours: 8:30AM-5PM www.putnam-fl.com/clk/ All records in one index. Records indexed on a public use terminal back to 10/1983. Only the public may search. Copy fee $1.00 per page. Cert fee- $1.50 per doc plus copy fee. Payee- Putnam County Clerk of Circuit Court. **Online access to Real Estate, Lien, Recording, Tax Appraiser, Property, GIS, Occ License, Warrant, Jail Log, Most Wanted records:** Access to the county clerk database requires a $400 setup fee and monthly charge of $40 plus $.05 per minute over 20 hours. Includes civil court records and real property records back to 10/1983. For info, call 904-329-0353. Also, access an index of recorded documents at www.myfloridacounty.com. Fees involved to order copies. The sheriff's warrants, jail, most wanted lists are at www.pcso.us. Also, search property data on the GIS site at www.emapsplus.com/FLPutnam/maps/. Also, search the online tax rolls at www.putnam-fl.com/app/disclaimer.htm. No name searching. Also, search the treasurer's tax rolls and occupational licensing at www.putnam-fl.com/txc/onlineinquiry.htm. **Other phones:** Appraiser/Auditor- 386-329-0286; Elections- 386-329-0455; Vital Records- 386-329-0420. **Property tax/Assessor-** same address.

Santa Rosa County

County Clerk of the Circuit Court, PO Box 472, Milton, FL 32572. RE & UCC recording phone-850-983-1966; fax-850-983-1991; hours: 8AM-4:30PM www.santarosaclerk.com All records in one index. Will not search real estate records. Will search UCC records; search includes tax liens if requested. UCC search per debtor name- $1.50 per year, 5 year maximum. Separate federal tax lien search- $1.00 per year, 5 year maximum. Separate state tax lien search- $1.00 per year, 5 year maximum. Separate federal or state or combined tax lien search- $1.00 per year, 5 year maximum. Copy fee $1.00 per page. Cert fee- $1.50 per doc plus copy fee. Payee- Santa Rosa County Clerk of Circuit Court. **Online access to Property Appraiser, Real Estate, Lien, Deed, Recording, Marriage, Death, Judgment, Tax Collector, Fugitive records:** Access to the Clerk's index of recorded documents is at http://oncoreweb.srccol.com/oncoreweb/. Or, go to www.myflorida.com where you may search the index free; fees involved to order copies or view images. Also, access to the appraiser property records is free at www.srcpa.org/property.html or at the main Property Appraiser page at www.srcpa.org click on "Record Search." Search for fugitives at www.santarosasheriff.com/fugitives.shtml. Also, search the real estate tax collector data for free at http://santarosataxcollector.governmax.com/collectmax/collect30.asp; occupational licenses at http://santarosataxcollector.governmax.com/collectmax/search_collect.asp?l_nm=occlic_bus_name&sid. **Other phones:** Treasurer- 850-983-1950; Appraiser/Auditor- 850-983-1880; Elections- 850-983-1900; Clerk of Courts-Research Dept- 850-983-1970. **Property tax/Assessor-** 850-983-1880.

Sarasota County

County Clerk of the Circuit Court, PO Box 3079, Sarasota, FL 34230. RE & UCC recording phone-941-861-7400; 8:30AM-5PM www.sarasotaclerk.com All records in one index. Records indexed on a public use terminal back to 1983. Only the public may search. Copy fee $1.00 per page. Cert fee- $1.50 per doc plus copy fee. Payee- Sarasota County Clerk of Circuit Court. **Online access to Real Estate, Lien, Vital Statistic, Recording, Property Appraiser, Personal Property, records:** Access to the Clerk of Circuit Court recordings database are free at www.sarasotaclerk.com. Includes civil, criminal, and traffic court indexes. Also search indexes

at www.sarasotaclerk.com. Marriage licenses may be searched; probate also available. Access an index of recorded documents at www.myfloridacounty.com. Fees involved to order copies. Also, search tax collector http://sarasotataxcollector.governmax.com/collectmax/collect30.asp. Also, property appraiser data is free at www.sarasotaproperty.net/scpa_record_search.asp; includes subdivision/condominium sales. Search sheriff arrests back 30 days at www.sarasotasheriff.org/arrests.asp. **Other phones:** Appraiser/Auditor- 941-861-8200; Elections- 941-861-8600; Vital Records- 941-316-1043.

Seminole County

Clerk of the Circuit Court, PO Box 8099-Attn Recording Dept, Sanford, FL 32772-8099. 407-665-4336, R/E recording phone-407-665-4409, UCC recording phone-407-665-4409; fax-407-330-7193; hours: 8AM-4:30PM www.seminoleclerk.org All records in one index. Only the public may search. Copy fee $1.00 per page. Cert fee- $1.50 per doc plus copy fee. Payee- Seminole County Clerk of Circuit Court. **Online access to Property Appraiser, Real Estate, Lien, Recording, Marriage, Divorce records:** The county clerk of circuit court's recordings database is free at http://officialrecords.seminoleclerk.org/NV_Records/. Property appraisal records free at www.scpafl.org/pls/web/web_main.main. Also a map search. Also, private site has previous 2 weeks real estate, marriage, divorce records at http://extra.orlandosentinel.com/publicrecords/search.asp. Also, search tax collector personal property and real estate records free at www.seminoletax.org/TaxSearch.htm. Also, sheriff's felon, offender, and sex offender lists are at www.seminolesheriff.org. **Other phones:** Appraiser/Auditor- 407-665-7502; Elections- 407-65-7709.

St. Johns County

County Clerk of the Circuit Court, 4010 Lewis Speedway, St. Augustine, FL 32095. 904-819-3600, R/E recording phone-904-819-3632, UCC recording phone-904-819-3632; fax-904-819-3661; hours: 8AM-5PM (No recording after 4:15PM) www.co.st-johns.fl.us Real estate record owner and property searches available. Will search UCC records, tax liens included if requested. UCC search per debtor name- $1.50 per name per year. Separate federal/state combined tax lien search- $1.00 per debtor year. Copy fee $1.00 per page. Cert fee- $1.50 per doc plus copy fee. Payee- St. Johns County Clerk of Circuit Court. **Online access to Property Appraiser, Real Estate, Lien, Recording, Civil, Probate, UCC, Property Tax, Occ. License, Most Wanted, Sex Offender records:** Access to the county Clerk of Circuit Court recording database is free at www.co.st-johns.fl.us/Const-Officers/Clerk-of-Court/doris/searchdocs.asp. Search by name, parcel ID, instrument type. Includes civil and probate records, UCCs. Access an index of recorded documents at www.myfloridacounty.com. Fees involved to order copies; save $1.50 per record by becoming a subscriber. Also, sheriff sex offender and wanted lists are at www.co.st-johns.fl.us/Const-Officers/Sheriff/index.html. Also, online access to the county property appraiser database is free at www.sjcpa.us/Disclaimer%20for%20as400.htm. Also, search property tax and occ. licenses for free at http://stjohnstaxcollector.governmax.com. **Other phones:** Appraiser/Auditor- 904-823-2200; Elections- 904-823-2238.

St. Lucie County

County Clerk of the Circuit Court, PO Box 700, Fort Pierce, FL 34954. Main phone & R/E recording-772-462-6928, UCC recording phone-772-462-6927; fax-772-462-1283; hours: 8AM-5PM www.stlucieco.gov All records in one index. Records indexed on a public use terminal back to 1992. Office personnel or visitors may perform searches. General index search fee $1.00 per year. Copy fee $1.00 per page. Real estate copy- $1.50 per page. Cert fee- $1.50 per doc plus copy fee. Payee- St. Lucie County Clerk of Circuit Court. **Online access to Property Appraiser, Real Estate, Lien, Recording, Marriage, Fictitious Name, Personal Property, GIS records:** Access to the clerk of circuit courts database of recordings, deeds, liens, mortgages, marriages, fictitious names is free at http://public.slcclerkofcourt.com. Business searching is also available for a small fee. Access an index of recorded documents at www.myfloridacounty.com. Fees involved to order copies. Also search property data free at www.emapsplus.com/FLStLucie/maps/. Also, property appraiser records are free online at www.paslc.org. Click on "Real estate" or "Personal property" to get search options. Also, search property tax rolls for free at http://216.77.1.194/tc/tax es/quick_tax.asp. **Other phones:** 772-462-1476; Appraiser/Auditor- 772-462-1000; Vital Records- 772-462-3800. **Property tax/Assessor-** 2300 Virginia Ave, Ft. Pierce, FL 34982; 772-462-1650.

Sumter County

County Clerk of the Circuit Court, 209 N. Florida St; Rm 106, Bushnell, FL 33513. 352-793-0215; fax-352-793-0218; 8:30AM-5PM www.sumterclerk.com
All records in one index. Records indexed on a public use terminal back to 1979. Office personnel or visitors may perform searches. Search fee $1.50 per name per year. Copy fee $1.00 per page. Cert fee- $1.50 per page plus copy fee. Payee- Sumter County Clerk of Circuit Court. **Online access to Real Estate, Lien, Recording, Property Tax, Occ License records:** Access an index of recorded documents at www.myfloridacounty.com. Fees involved to order copies; save $1.50 per record by becoming a subscriber. Also, search tax collector and occupational licenses for free at http://sumtertaxcollector.governmax.com/collectmax/co llect30.asp. **Other phones:** Appraiser/Auditor- 352-793-0210.

Suwannee County

County Clerk of the Circuit Court, 200 S. Ohio Ave, Live Oak, FL 32064. RE & UCC recording phone-386-362-0554; fax-386-362-0532; hours: 8:30AM-4:45PM www.suwclerk.org
All records in one index. Records indexed on a public use terminal back to 1/1/1983. Office personnel or visitors may perform searches. General search fee $1.00 per year per name. Will not search real estate records. Will search UCC records, tax liens not included in UCC search. UCC search per debtor name- $1.50 per name per year. Copy fee $1.00 per page. Cert fee- $1.50 per doc plus copy fee. Payee- Suwannee County Clerk of Circuit Court. **Online access to Real Estate, Lien, Deed, Recording, Property Tax, Marriage, GIS, Inmate, Most Wanted records:** Access of the county clerk of circuit database index is free at www.suwclerk.org/public.html. This directs you to the statewide database; search index free; subscription required for documents. Also, search the tax collector database free at www.suwanneecountytax.com/coll ectmax/collect30.asp. Also, search property data on th4e GIS-mapping site at www.emapsplus.com/FLSuwannee/maps/. Also, search sheriff's most wanted and inmate lists at www.suwanneesheriff.com. **Other phones:** Treasurer- 386-364-3414; Appraiser/Auditor- 386-362-1385; Elections- 386-362-2616; Vital Records- 386-362-0554.

Taylor County

County Clerk of the Circuit Court, PO Box 620, Perry, FL 32348. RE & UCC recording phone-850-838-3506; fax-850-838-3549; hours: 8AM-5PM www.taylorclerk.com
Only the public may search. Copy fee $1.00 per page. Cert fee- $1.50 per doc plus copy fee. Payee- Taylor County Clerk of Circuit Court. **Online access to Recording, Deed, Lien, Judgment, County Commissioner records:** Access an index of recorded documents at www.myfloridacounty.com. Fees involved to order copies; save $1.50 per record by becoming a subscriber. Also, access to county commission records is free at http://taco.perryfl.com/search.htm. Online records go back to 1988. **Other phones:** Treasurer- 850-838-3517; Appraiser/Auditor- 850-838-3511; Elections- 850-838-3515; Vital Records- 850-838-3506. **Property tax/Assessor-** 850-838-3517.

Union County

County Clerk of the Circuit Court, State Rd 100; Courthouse Rm 103, Lake Butler, FL 32054. 386-496-3711; fax-386-496-1718; hours: 8AM-5PM
Records indexed on a public use terminal back to 1983. Office personnel or visitors may perform searches. Real estate owner, mortgage, and property transfer searches available. Will search UCC records, search includes tax liens. UCC search per debtor name- $1.50 per name per year. Separate federal/state combined tax lien search- $1.00 per debtor per year. Copy fee $1.00 per page. Cert fee- $1.50 per doc plus copy fee. Payee- Union County Clerk of Circuit Court. **Online access to Real Estate, Lien, Recording, Property, GIS records:** Access an index of recorded documents at www.myfloridacounty.com. Fees involved to order copies; save $1.50 per record by becoming a subscriber. Also, search the GIS-mapping site for property data for free at www.emapsplus.com/FLUnion/maps/. **Other phones:** Treasurer- 386-496-1026; Appraiser/Auditor- 386-496-3431; Elections- 386-496-2236. **Property tax/Assessor-** 386-496-3331.

Volusia County

County Clerk of the Circuit Court, PO Box 6043, Deland, FL 32721. RE & UCC recording phone-386-736-5912; fax-386-740-5197; hours: 8AM-4:30PM www.clerk.org/index.html
A private site has previous 2 weeks real estate, marriage, divorce records at http://ext ra.orlandosentinel.com/publicrecords/search.asp. All records in one index. Records indexed on a public use terminal back to 1996. Only the public may search. Copy fee $1.00 per page. Cert fee- $1.50 per doc plus copy fee. Payee- Volusia County Clerk of Circuit Court. **Online access to Property Appraiser, Real Estate, Lien, Vital Statistic, Recording, Citation Violation, Arrest, Property Sale, GIS, Inmate, Tax Deed Sale, Court, Personal Property records:** Recording data is free at www.clerk.org/index.html. Click on Public Records. Recorder indices go back to 3/1996; soon back to 1990. Arrest ledger, tax deed sales and citations also at this website. County also offers full real estate, lien, court and vital records on a commercial site; set up is $100 with $25 monthly. For info, contact clerk. Search the inmate list free at http://volusia.org/correctio ns/search_page.htm. Access index of recorded documents at www.myfloridacounty.com; see section introduction. Also, search property appraiser database free at http://webserver.vcgov.org/vc_search.html. Also

search property records free at www.emapsplus.com/FLVolusia/maps/. **Other phones:** Appraiser/Auditor- 386-736-5902. **Property tax/Assessor-** 123 W Indiana, Deland, FL 32724.

Wakulla County

County Clerk of the Circuit Court, 3056 Crawfordville Hwy; Wakulla County Court House, Crawfordville, FL 32327. 850-926-0905, R/E recording phone-850-926-0326, UCC recording phone-850-926-0326; fax-850-926-0938; 8AM-4PM www.wakullaclerk.com
All records in one index. Records indexed on a public use terminal back to 1990. Only the public may search. Office may perform a separate federal and/or state tax lien search- $1.00 per year per name. Copy fee $1.00 per page. Cert fee- $1.50 per doc plus copy fee. Payee- Wakulla County Clerk of Circuit Court. **Online access to Real Estate, Lien, Recording records:** Access an index of recorded documents at www.myfloridacounty.com. Fees involved to order copies; save $1.50 per record by becoming a subscriber. **Other phones:** Treasurer- 850-926-3371; Appraiser/Auditor- 850-926-3271.

Walton County

County Clerk of the Circuit Court, PO Box 1260, De Funiak Springs, FL 32433. RE & UCC recording phone-850-892-8115; fax-850-892-7551; hours: 8AM-4PM www.co.walton.fl.us/clerk
Records indexed on a public use terminal back to 1976. Copy fee $1.00 per page. Cert fee- $1.50 per doc plus copy fee. Payee- Walton County Clerk of Circuit Court. **Online access to Real Estate, Lien, Vital Statistic, Grantor/Grantee, Property Tax records:** Records back to 1/1976 on County Clerk database are free at www.co.walton.fl.us/clerk/orse arch/Default.aspx. This takes the place of the old commercial system. Also, property appraiser records are free at www.qpublic.net/walton/search1.html. Also, search tax collector data free at http://fl-walton-taxcollector.governmaxa.com/collectmax/collect30.asp. **Other phones:** Treasurer- 850-892-8121; Appraiser/Auditor- 850-892-8123. **Property tax/Assessor-** 850-892-8121.

Washington County

County Clerk of the Circuit Court, PO Box 647, Chipley, FL 32428. RE & UCC recording phone-850-638-6285; fax-850-638-6059; hours: 8AM-4PM
All records in one index. Records indexed on a public use terminal back to 1980. Only the public may search. Copy fee $1.00 per page. Cert fee- $1.50 per doc plus copy fee. Payee- Washington County Clerk of Circuit Court. **Online access to Recording, Deed, Judgment, Lien, Appraiser, Property Tax, Property Sale records:** Access an index of recorded documents at www.mywashingtoncounty.com. Fees involved to order copies; save $1.50 per record by becoming a subscriber. Also, search the property appraiser sales and tax records for free at www.qpublic.net/washin gton/index-pa-search.html. Also, search the tax collector records for free at www.qpublic.net/wctc/index-tc-search.html. **Other phones:** Treasurer- 850-638-6205; Appraiser/Auditor- 850-638-6205; Elections- 850-638-6230; Vital Records- 850-638-6230. **Property tax/Assessor-** 850-638-6275..

Florida County Locator

You will usually be able to find the city name in the City/County Cross Reference below. In that case, it is a simple matter to determine the county from the cross reference. However, only the official US Postal Service city names are included in this index. There are an additional 40,000 place names that people use in their addresses. Therefore, we have also included a ZIP/City Cross Reference immediately following the City/County Cross Reference.

If you know the ZIP Code but the city name does not appear in the City/County Cross Reference index, look up the ZIP Code in the ZIP/City Cross Reference, find the city name, then look up the city name in the City/County Cross Reference. For example, you want to know the county for an address of Menands, NY 12204. There is no "Menands" in the City/County Cross Reference. The ZIP/City Cross Reference shows that ZIP Codes 12201-12288 are for the city of Albany. Looking back in the City/County Cross Reference, Albany is in Albany County.

Florida City/County Cross Reference

ABMPS Dade
ALACHUA Alachua
ALFORD (32420) Jackson(95), Washington(4)
ALTAMONTE SPRINGS Seminole
ALTHA Calhoun
ALTOONA (32702) Lake(83), Marion(16)
ALTURAS Polk
ALVA (33920) Lee(85), Hendry(14)
ANNA MARIA Manatee
ANTHONY Marion
APALACHICOLA Franklin
APOLLO BEACH Hillsborough
APOPKA (32703) Orange(79), Seminole(20)
APOPKA Orange
ARCADIA De Soto
ARCHER (32618) Alachua(73), Levy(26)
ARGYLE Walton
ARIPEKA Pasco
ASTATULA Lake
ASTOR (32102) Lake(83), Volusia(16)
ATLANTIC BEACH Duval
AUBURNDALE Polk
AVON PARK (33825) Highlands(98), Polk(1)
AVON PARK Highlands
BABSON PARK Polk
BAGDAD Santa Rosa
BAKER (32531) Okaloosa(97), Santa Rosa(2)
BALM Hillsborough
BARBERVILLE Volusia
BARTOW Polk
BASCOM Jackson
BAY PINES Pinellas
BELL Gilchrist
BELLE GLADE Palm Beach
BELLEAIR BEACH Pinellas
BELLEAIR SHORES Pinellas
BELLEVIEW Marion
BEVERLY HILLS Citrus
BIG PINE KEY Monroe
BLOUNTSTOWN Calhoun
BOCA GRANDE Lee
BOCA RATON Palm Beach
BOKEELIA Lee
BONIFAY (32425) Holmes(90), Washington(9)
BONITA SPRINGS (34134) Lee(89), Collier(10)
BONITA SPRINGS Lee
BOSTWICK Putnam
BOWLING GREEN (33834) Hardee(75), Manatee(18), Polk(6)
BOYNTON BEACH Palm Beach
BRADENTON Manatee
BRADENTON BEACH Manatee
BRADLEY Polk
BRANDON Hillsborough
BRANFORD (32008) Suwannee(66), Gilchrist(25), Lafayette(6), Dixie(1)
BRISTOL Liberty
BRONSON Levy

BROOKER (32622) Bradford(82), Alachua(17)
BROOKSVILLE Hernando
BROOKSVILLE Pasco
BRYANT Palm Beach
BRYCEVILLE Nassau
BUNNELL Flagler
BUSHNELL Sumter
CALLAHAN Nassau
CAMPBELLTON Jackson
CANAL POINT (33438) Palm Beach(62), Martin(37)
CANAL POINT Palm Beach
CANDLER Marion
CANTONMENT Escambia
CAPE CANAVERAL Brevard
CAPE CORAL Lee
CAPTIVA Lee
CARRABELLE Franklin
CARYVILLE (32427) Washington(93), Holmes(6)
CASSADAGA Volusia
CASSELBERRY Seminole
CEDAR KEY Levy
CENTER HILL Sumter
CENTURY Escambia
CHATTAHOOCHEE Gadsden
CHIEFLAND Levy
CHIPLEY Washington
CHOKOLOSKEE Collier
CHRISTMAS Orange
CITRA Marion
CLARCONA Orange
CLARKSVILLE Calhoun
CLEARWATER Pinellas
CLEARWATER BEACH Pinellas
CLERMONT (34714) Lake(95), Polk(4)
CLERMONT Lake
CLEWISTON (33440) Hendry(98), Palm Beach(1)
COCOA Brevard
COCOA BEACH Brevard
COLEMAN Sumter
COPELAND Collier
CORTEZ Manatee
COTTONDALE (32431) Jackson(79), Washington(20)
CRAWFORDVILLE Wakulla
CRESCENT CITY Putnam
CRESTVIEW (32539) Okaloosa(89), Walton(10)
CRESTVIEW Okaloosa
CROSS CITY Dixie
CRYSTAL BEACH Pinellas
CRYSTAL RIVER Citrus
CRYSTAL SPRINGS Pasco
CYPRESS Jackson
DADE CITY (33523) Pasco(83), Hernando(16)
DADE CITY Pasco
DANIA Broward
DAVENPORT (33896) Polk(89), Osceola(10)
DAVENPORT Polk
DAY Lafayette

DAYTONA BEACH Volusia
DE LEON SPRINGS Volusia
DEBARY Volusia
DEERFIELD BEACH Broward
DEFUNIAK SPRINGS Walton
DELAND (32720) Volusia(86), Lake(13)
DELAND Volusia
DELRAY BEACH Palm Beach
DELTONA Volusia
DESTIN Okaloosa
DOCTORS INLET Clay
DOVER Hillsborough
DUNDEE Polk
DUNEDIN Pinellas
DUNNELLON (34431) Marion(81), Levy(18)
DUNNELLON Citrus
DUNNELLON Marion
DURANT Hillsborough
EAGLE LAKE Polk
EARLETON Alachua
EAST PALATKA Putnam
EASTLAKE WEIR Marion
EASTPOINT Franklin
EATON PARK Polk
EBRO (32437) Washington(88), Bay(11)
EDGEWATER Volusia
EGLIN AFB Okaloosa
ELFERS Pasco
ELKTON St. Johns
ELLENTON Manatee
ENGLEWOOD (34223) Sarasota(75), Charlotte(24)
ENGLEWOOD Charlotte
ENGLEWOOD Sarasota
ESTERO Lee
EUSTIS Lake
EVERGLADES CITY Collier
EVINSTON Alachua
FAIRFIELD Marion
FEDHAVEN Polk
FELDA Hendry
FELLSMERE Indian River
FERNANDINA BEACH Nassau
FERNDALE Lake
FLAGLER BEACH Flagler
FLEMING ISLAND Clay
FLORAHOME Putnam
FLORAL CITY Citrus
FORT LAUDERDALE Broward
FORT MC COY Marion
FORT MEADE Polk
FORT MYERS (33917) Lee(98), Charlotte(1)
FORT MYERS Lee
FORT MYERS BEACH Lee
FORT OGDEN De Soto
FORT PIERCE St. Lucie
FORT WALTON BEACH Okaloosa
FORT WHITE Columbia
FOUNTAIN Bay
FREEPORT Walton
FROSTPROOF Polk
FRUITLAND PARK Lake
GAINESVILLE Alachua

GENEVA Seminole
GEORGETOWN Putnam
GIBSONTON Hillsborough
GLEN SAINT MARY Baker
GLENWOOD Volusia
GOLDENROD Seminole
GONZALEZ Escambia
GOODLAND Collier
GOTHA Orange
GRACEVILLE (32440) Jackson(86), Holmes(13)
GRAHAM Bradford
GRAND ISLAND Lake
GRAND RIDGE (32442) Jackson(90), Calhoun(9)
GRANDIN Putnam
GRANT Brevard
GREEN COVE SPRINGS (32043) Clay(98), Putnam(1)
GREENSBORO Gadsden
GREENVILLE (32331) Madison(58), Jefferson(22), Taylor(19)
GREENWOOD Jackson
GRETNA Gadsden
GROVELAND Lake
GULF BREEZE (32561) Santa Rosa(54), Escambia(45)
GULF BREEZE Santa Rosa
GULF HAMMOCK Levy
HAINES CITY Polk
HALLANDALE Broward
HAMPTON (32044) Bradford(93), Alachua(6)
HAROLD Santa Rosa
HASTINGS St. Johns
HAVANA Gadsden
HAWTHORNE (32640) Alachua(58), Putnam(41)
HERNANDO Citrus
HIALEAH Dade
HIGH SPRINGS (32643) Alachua(61), Gilchrist(27), Columbia(10)
HIGH SPRINGS Alachua
HIGHLAND CITY Polk
HILLIARD Nassau
HOBE SOUND Martin
HOLDER Citrus
HOLIDAY Pasco
HOLLISTER Putnam
HOLLYWOOD Broward
HOLMES BEACH Manatee
HOLT (32564) Santa Rosa(87), Okaloosa(12)
HOMELAND Polk
HOMESTEAD Dade
HOMOSASSA Citrus
HOMOSASSA SPRINGS Citrus
HORSESHOE BEACH Dixie
HOSFORD Liberty
HOWEY IN THE HILLS Lake
HUDSON Pasco
HURLBURT FIELD Okaloosa
IMMOKALEE (34142) Collier(96), Lee(1), Hendry(1)
IMMOKALEE Collier

INDIALANTIC Brevard
INDIAN LAKE ESTATES Polk
INDIAN ROCKS BEACH Pinellas
INDIANTOWN Martin
INGLIS (34449) Levy(92), Citrus(7)
INTERCESSION CITY Osceola
INTERLACHEN Putnam
INVERNESS Citrus
ISLAMORADA Monroe
ISLAND GROVE Alachua
ISTACHATTA Hernando
JACKSONVILLE (32234) Duval(72),
    Clay(23), Nassau(3)
JACKSONVILLE Duval
JACKSONVILLE St. Johns
JACKSONVILLE BEACH Duval
JASPER Hamilton
JAY Santa Rosa
JENNINGS Hamilton
JENSEN BEACH Martin
JUPITER (33478) Palm Beach(93),
    Martin(6)
JUPITER Palm Beach
KATHLEEN (33849) Polk(93), Pasco(6)
KENANSVILLE Osceola
KEY BISCAYNE Dade
KEY COLONY BEACH Monroe
KEY LARGO Monroe
KEY WEST Monroe
KEYSTONE HEIGHTS (32656) Clay(83),
    Bradford(16)
KILLARNEY Orange
KINARD Calhoun
KISSIMMEE (34747) Osceola(98),
    Orange(1)
KISSIMMEE (34759) Polk(81), Osceola(18)
KISSIMMEE Osceola
LA CROSSE Alachua
LABELLE (33935) Hendry(82), Glades(17)
LABELLE Hendry
LACOOCHEE Pasco
LADY LAKE (32159) Lake(73), Sumter(26)
LADY LAKE (32162) Sumter(66),
    Marion(33)
LADY LAKE Lake
LAKE ALFRED Polk
LAKE BUTLER (32054) Union(88),
    Bradford(11)
LAKE CITY (32055) Columbia(97),
    Suwannee(2)
LAKE CITY Columbia
LAKE COMO Putnam
LAKE GENEVA Clay
LAKE HAMILTON Polk
LAKE HARBOR Palm Beach
LAKE HELEN Volusia
LAKE MARY Seminole
LAKE MONROE Seminole
LAKE PANASOFFKEE Sumter
LAKE PLACID Highlands
LAKE WALES Polk
LAKE WORTH Palm Beach
LAKELAND (33810) Polk(98),
    Hillsborough(1)
LAKELAND Polk
LAMONT (32336) Jefferson(65),
    Madison(19), Taylor(15)
LANARK VILLAGE Franklin
LAND O LAKES Pasco
LARGO Pinellas
LAUREL Sarasota
LAUREL HILL (32567) Walton(66),
    Okaloosa(33)
LAWTEY (32058) Bradford(96), Union(3)
LECANTO Citrus
LEE Madison
LEESBURG Lake
LEHIGH ACRES Lee
LITHIA (33547) Hillsborough(97), Polk(2)
LIVE OAK Suwannee
LLOYD Jefferson
LOCHLOOSA Alachua

LONG KEY Monroe
LONGBOAT KEY (34228) Sarasota(62),
    Manatee(37)
LONGWOOD Seminole
LORIDA Highlands
LOUGHMAN Polk
LOWELL Marion
LOXAHATCHEE Palm Beach
LULU Columbia
LUTZ (33559) Hillsborough(57), Pasco(42)
LYNN HAVEN Bay
MACCLENNY Baker
MAITLAND (32751) Orange(78),
    Seminole(21)
MAITLAND Orange
MALABAR Brevard
MALONE Jackson
MANASOTA Manatee
MANGO Hillsborough
MARATHON Monroe
MARATHON SHORES Monroe
MARCO ISLAND Collier
MARIANNA Jackson
MARY ESTHER Okaloosa
MASCOTTE Lake
MAYO Lafayette
MC ALPIN Suwannee
MC DAVID Escambia
MC INTOSH Marion
MELBOURNE Brevard
MELBOURNE BEACH Brevard
MELROSE (32666) Putnam(52),
    Alachua(18), Bradford(16), Clay(12)
MERRITT ISLAND Brevard
MEXICO BEACH Bay
MIAMI Dade
MIAMI BEACH Dade
MICANOPY (32667) Alachua(65),
    Marion(34)
MICCOSUKEE CPO Leon
MID FLORIDA Seminole
MIDDLEBURG Clay
MIDWAY Gadsden
MILLIGAN Okaloosa
MILTON Santa Rosa
MIMS (32754) Brevard(91), Volusia(8)
MINNEOLA Lake
MIRAMAR BEACH Walton
MOLINO Escambia
MONTICELLO (32344) Jefferson(98),
    Leon(1)
MONTICELLO Jefferson
MONTVERDE Lake
MOORE HAVEN Glades
MORRISTON (32668) Levy(81), Marion(18)
MOSSY HEAD Walton
MOUNT DORA (32757) Lake(93),
    Orange(6)
MOUNT DORA Lake
MOUNT DORA Seminole
MOUNT PLEASANT Gadsden
MULBERRY Polk
MURDOCK Charlotte
MYAKKA CITY Manatee
NALCREST Polk
NAPLES (34119) Collier(98), Lee(1)
NAPLES Collier
NEPTUNE BEACH Duval
NEW PORT RICHEY Pasco
NEW SMYRNA BEACH Volusia
NEWBERRY (32669) Alachua(79),
    Gilchrist(18), Levy(2)
NICEVILLE (32578) Okaloosa(92),
    Walton(7)
NICEVILLE Okaloosa
NICHOLS Polk
NOBLETON Hernando
NOCATEE De Soto
NOKOMIS Sarasota
NOMA Holmes
NORTH FORT MYERS (33917) Lee(98),
    Charlotte(1)

NORTH FORT MYERS Lee
NORTH PALM BEACH Palm Beach
NORTH PORT Sarasota
O BRIEN Suwannee
OAK HILL Volusia
OAKLAND Orange
OCALA Marion
OCHOPEE (34141) Collier(65), Dade(28),
    Monroe(5)
OCKLAWAHA Marion
OCOEE Orange
ODESSA (33556) Hillsborough(74),
    Pasco(25)
OKAHUMPKA Lake
OKEECHOBEE (34972) Okeechobee(98),
    Osceola(1)
OKEECHOBEE (34974) Okeechobee(89),
    Martin(3), Glades(3), Highlands(3)
OKEECHOBEE Okeechobee
OLD TOWN Dixie
OLDSMAR Pinellas
OLUSTEE Baker
ONA (33865) Hardee(97), De Soto(2)
ONECO Manatee
OPA LOCKA Dade
ORANGE CITY Volusia
ORANGE LAKE Marion
ORANGE PARK (32073) Clay(98),
    Duval(1)
ORANGE PARK Clay
ORANGE SPRINGS Marion
ORLANDO Brevard
ORLANDO Orange
ORMOND BEACH (32174) Volusia(98),
    Flagler(1)
ORMOND BEACH Volusia
OSPREY Sarasota
OSTEEN Volusia
OTTER CREEK Levy
OVERSTREET Gulf
OVIEDO Seminole
OXFORD (34484) Sumter(98), Marion(1)
OZONA Pinellas
PAHOKEE Palm Beach
PAISLEY Lake
PALATKA Putnam
PALM BAY Brevard
PALM BEACH Palm Beach
PALM BEACH GARDENS Palm Beach
PALM CITY (34990) Martin(95), St.
    Lucie(4)
PALM CITY Martin
PALM COAST Flagler
PALM HARBOR Pinellas
PALMDALE Glades
PALMETTO Manatee
PANACEA (32346) Wakulla(87),
    Franklin(12)
PANAMA CITY (32413) Bay(88),
    Walton(11)
PANAMA CITY Bay
PANAMA CITY BEACH (32413) Bay(88),
    Walton(11)
PANAMA CITY BEACH Bay
PARRISH Manatee
PATRICK A F B Brevard
PAXTON Walton
PENNEY FARMS Clay
PENSACOLA Escambia
PERRY Taylor
PIERSON Volusia
PINELAND Lee
PINELLAS PARK Pinellas
PINETTA Madison
PLACIDA Charlotte
PLANT CITY Hillsborough
PLYMOUTH Orange
POINT WASHINGTON Walton
POLK CITY Polk
POMONA PARK Putnam
POMPANO BEACH Broward

PONCE DE LEON (32455) Holmes(83),
    Walton(16)
PONTE VEDRA BEACH St. Johns
PORT CHARLOTTE Charlotte
PORT ORANGE Volusia
PORT RICHEY Pasco
PORT SAINT JOE (32456) Gulf(88),
    Bay(11)
PORT SAINT JOE Gulf
PORT SAINT LUCIE St. Lucie
PORT SALERNO Martin
PUNTA GORDA (33955) Charlotte(82),
    Lee(17)
PUNTA GORDA Charlotte
PUTNAM HALL Putnam
QUINCY Gadsden
RAIFORD (32083) Union(77), Bradford(22)
RAIFORD Union
REDDICK Marion
RIVER RANCH Polk
RIVERVIEW Hillsborough
ROCKLEDGE Brevard
ROSELAND Indian River
ROSEMARY BEACH (32461) Bay(50),
    Walton(50)
ROTONDA WEST Charlotte
RUSKIN Hillsborough
SAFETY HARBOR Pinellas
SAINT AUGUSTINE St. Johns
SAINT CLOUD Osceola
SAINT JAMES CITY Lee
SAINT LEO Pasco
SAINT MARKS Wakulla
SAINT PETERSBURG Pinellas
SALEM Taylor
SAN ANTONIO Pasco
SAN MATEO Putnam
SANDERSON Baker
SANFORD Seminole
SANIBEL Lee
SANTA ROSA BEACH Walton
SARASOTA (34243) Manatee(85),
    Sarasota(14)
SARASOTA Sarasota
SATELLITE BEACH Brevard
SATSUMA Putnam
SCOTTSMOOR Brevard
SEBASTIAN Brevard
SEBASTIAN Indian River
SEBRING Highlands
SEFFNER Hillsborough
SEMINOLE Pinellas
SEVILLE Volusia
SHADY GROVE Taylor
SHALIMAR Okaloosa
SHARPES Brevard
SILVER SPRINGS Marion
SNEADS Jackson
SOPCHOPPY Wakulla
SORRENTO Lake
SOUTH BAY Palm Beach
SOUTH FLORIDA Broward
SPARR Marion
SPRING HILL Hernando
STARKE (32091) Bradford(89), Clay(10)
STEINHATCHEE (32359) Dixie(62),
    Taylor(37)
STUART Martin
SUGARLOAF SHORES Monroe
SUMATRA Liberty
SUMMERFIELD Marion
SUMMERLAND KEY Monroe
SUMTERVILLE Sumter
SUN CITY Hillsborough
SUN CITY CENTER Hillsborough
SUNNYSIDE (32461) Bay(50), Walton(50)
SUWANNEE Dixie
SYDNEY Hillsborough
TALLAHASSEE Leon
TALLEVAST Manatee
TAMPA Hillsborough
TANGERINE Orange

TARPON SPRINGS Pinellas
TAVARES Lake
TAVERNIER Monroe
TELOGIA Liberty
TERRA CEIA Manatee
THONOTOSASSA Hillsborough
TITUSVILLE Brevard
TRENTON (32693) Gilchrist(64), Levy(35)
TRILBY Pasco
UMATILLA (32784) Lake(68), Marion(31)
VALPARAISO Okaloosa
VALRICO Hillsborough
VENICE Sarasota
VENUS (33960) Highlands(86), Glades(13)
VERNON (32462) Washington(71),
   Bay(17), Walton(10)

VERO BEACH Indian River
WABASSO Indian River
WACISSA Jefferson
WAKULLA SPRINGS Leon
WALDO (32694) Alachua(96), Bradford(3)
WAUCHULA Hardee
WAUSAU Washington
WAVERLY Polk
WEBSTER (33597) Sumter(84),
   Hernando(15)
WEIRSDALE (32195) Marion(83), Lake(16)
WELAKA Putnam
WELLBORN (32094) Suwannee(94),
   Columbia(5)
WEST PALM BEACH Palm Beach
WESTON Broward

WESTVILLE (32464) Holmes(63),
   Walton(36)
WEWAHITCHKA Calhoun
WEWAHITCHKA Gulf
WHITE SPRINGS (32096) Hamilton(52),
   Columbia(41), Suwannee(6)
WILDWOOD Sumter
WILLISTON (32696) Levy(91), Marion(8)
WIMAUMA (33598) Hillsborough(96),
   Manatee(2)
WINDERMERE Orange
WINTER BEACH Indian River
WINTER GARDEN (34787) Orange(96),
   Lake(3)
WINTER GARDEN Orange
WINTER HAVEN Polk

WINTER PARK (32792) Orange(68),
   Seminole(31)
WINTER PARK Orange
WINTER SPRINGS Seminole
WOODVILLE Leon
WORTHINGTON SPRINGS Union
YALAHA Lake
YANKEETOWN Levy
YOUNGSTOWN (32466) Bay(95),
   Washington(3), Calhoun(1)
YULEE Nassau
ZELLWOOD Orange
ZEPHYRHILLS (33540) Pasco(98),
   Hillsborough(1)
ZEPHYRHILLS Pasco
ZOLFO SPRINGS Hardee

Florida ZIP/City Cross Reference

32003-32003	ORANGE PARK	32127-32127	PORT ORANGE	32329-32329	APALACHICOLA
32004-32004	PONTE VEDRA BEACH	32128-32128	DAYTONA BEACH	32330-32330	GREENSBORO
32006-32006	FLEMING ISLAND	32129-32129	PORT ORANGE	32331-32331	GREENVILLE
32007-32007	BOSTWICK	32130-32130	DE LEON SPRINGS	32332-32332	GRETNA
32008-32008	BRANFORD	32131-32131	EAST PALATKA	32333-32333	HAVANA
32009-32009	BRYCEVILLE	32132-32132	EDGEWATER	32334-32334	HOSFORD
32011-32011	CALLAHAN	32133-32133	EASTLAKE WEIR	32335-32335	SUMATRA
32013-32013	DAY	32134-32134	FORT MC COY	32336-32336	LAMONT
32024-32025	LAKE CITY	32135-32135	PALM COAST	32337-32337	LLOYD
32026-32026	RAIFORD	32136-32136	FLAGLER BEACH	32340-32341	MADISON
32030-32030	DOCTORS INLET	32137-32137	PALM COAST	32343-32343	MIDWAY
32033-32033	ELKTON	32138-32138	GRANDIN	32344-32345	MONTICELLO
32034-32035	FERNANDINA BEACH	32139-32139	GEORGETOWN	32346-32346	PANACEA
32038-32038	FORT WHITE	32140-32140	FLORAHOME	32347-32348	PERRY
32040-32040	GLEN SAINT MARY	32141-32141	EDGEWATER	32350-32350	PINETTA
32041-32041	YULEE	32142-32142	PALM COAST	32351-32351	QUINCY
32042-32042	GRAHAM	32145-32145	HASTINGS	32352-32352	MOUNT PLEASANT
32043-32043	GREEN COVE SPRINGS	32147-32147	HOLLISTER	32352-32353	QUINCY
32044-32044	HAMPTON	32148-32149	INTERLACHEN	32355-32355	SAINT MARKS
32046-32046	HILLIARD	32151-32151	FLAGLER BEACH	32356-32356	SALEM
32050-32050	MIDDLEBURG	32157-32157	LAKE COMO	32357-32357	SHADY GROVE
32052-32052	JASPER	32158-32159	LADY LAKE	32358-32358	SOPCHOPPY
32053-32053	JENNINGS	32160-32160	LAKE GENEVA	32359-32359	STEINHATCHEE
32054-32054	LAKE BUTLER	32162-32162	LADY LAKE	32360-32360	TELOGIA
32055-32056	LAKE CITY	32164-32164	PALM COAST	32361-32361	WACISSA
32058-32058	LAWTEY	32168-32170	NEW SMYRNA BEACH	32362-32362	WOODVILLE
32059-32059	LEE	32173-32176	ORMOND BEACH	32395-32399	TALLAHASSEE
32060-32060	LIVE OAK	32177-32178	PALATKA	32400-32406	PANAMA CITY
32061-32061	LULU	32179-32179	OCKLAWAHA	32407-32407	PANAMA CITY BEACH
32062-32062	MC ALPIN	32180-32180	PIERSON	32408-32409	PANAMA CITY
32063-32063	MACCLENNY	32181-32181	POMONA PARK	32410-32410	MEXICO BEACH
32064-32064	LIVE OAK	32182-32182	ORANGE SPRINGS	32411-32413	PANAMA CITY
32065-32065	ORANGE PARK	32183-32183	OCKLAWAHA	32413-32413	PANAMA CITY BEACH
32066-32066	MAYO	32185-32185	PUTNAM HALL	32417-32417	PANAMA CITY
32067-32067	ORANGE PARK	32187-32187	SAN MATEO	32420-32420	ALFORD
32068-32068	MIDDLEBURG	32189-32189	SATSUMA	32421-32421	ALTHA
32071-32071	O BRIEN	32190-32190	SEVILLE	32422-32422	ARGYLE
32072-32072	OLUSTEE	32192-32192	SPARR	32423-32423	BASCOM
32073-32073	ORANGE PARK	32193-32193	WELAKA	32424-32424	BLOUNTSTOWN
32079-32079	PENNEY FARMS	32195-32195	WEIRSDALE	32425-32425	BONIFAY
32080-32080	SAINT AUGUSTINE	32198-32198	DAYTONA BEACH	32426-32426	CAMPBELLTON
32082-32082	PONTE VEDRA BEACH	32200-32232	JACKSONVILLE	32427-32427	CARYVILLE
32083-32083	RAIFORD	32233-32233	ATLANTIC BEACH	32428-32428	CHIPLEY
32084-32086	SAINT AUGUSTINE	32234-32239	JACKSONVILLE	32430-32430	CLARKSVILLE
32087-32087	SANDERSON	32240-32240	JACKSONVILLE BEACH	32431-32431	COTTONDALE
32091-32091	STARKE	32241-32247	JACKSONVILLE	32432-32432	CYPRESS
32092-32092	SAINT AUGUSTINE	32250-32250	JACKSONVILLE BEACH	32433-32433	DEFUNIAK SPRINGS
32094-32094	WELLBORN	32254-32260	JACKSONVILLE	32434-32434	MOSSY HEAD
32095-32095	SAINT AUGUSTINE	32266-32266	NEPTUNE BEACH	32435-32435	DEFUNIAK SPRINGS
32096-32096	WHITE SPRINGS	32267-32297	JACKSONVILLE	32437-32437	EBRO
32097-32097	YULEE	32301-32304	TALLAHASSEE	32438-32438	FOUNTAIN
32099-32099	JACKSONVILLE	32305-32305	WAKULLA SPRINGS	32439-32439	FREEPORT
32100-32100	DAYTONA BEACH	32305-32308	TALLAHASSEE	32440-32440	GRACEVILLE
32102-32102	ASTOR	32309-32309	MICCOSUKEE CPO	32442-32442	GRAND RIDGE
32105-32105	BARBERVILLE	32309-32318	TALLAHASSEE	32443-32443	GREENWOOD
32110-32110	BUNNELL	32320-32320	APALACHICOLA	32444-32444	LYNN HAVEN
32111-32111	CANDLER	32321-32321	BRISTOL	32445-32445	MALONE
32112-32112	CRESCENT CITY	32322-32322	CARRABELLE	32446-32448	MARIANNA
32113-32113	CITRA	32323-32323	LANARK VILLAGE	32449-32449	KINARD
32114-32123	DAYTONA BEACH	32324-32324	CHATTAHOOCHEE	32449-32449	WEWAHITCHKA
32123-32123	PORT ORANGE	32326-32327	CRAWFORDVILLE	32452-32452	NOMA
32124-32127	DAYTONA BEACH	32328-32328	EASTPOINT	32453-32453	OVERSTREET

32454-32454	POINT WASHINGTON
32455-32455	PONCE DE LEON
32456-32457	PORT SAINT JOE
32459-32459	SANTA ROSA BEACH
32460-32460	SNEADS
32461-32461	SUNNYSIDE
32461-32461	ROSEMARY BEACH
32462-32462	VERNON
32463-32463	WAUSAU
32464-32464	WESTVILLE
32465-32465	WEWAHITCHKA
32466-32466	YOUNGSTOWN
32500-32526	PENSACOLA
32530-32530	BAGDAD
32531-32531	BAKER
32533-32533	CANTONMENT
32534-32534	PENSACOLA
32535-32535	CENTURY
32536-32536	CRESTVIEW
32537-32537	MILLIGAN
32538-32538	PAXTON
32539-32539	CRESTVIEW
32540-32541	DESTIN
32542-32542	EGLIN AFB
32544-32544	HURLBURT FIELD
32547-32549	FORT WALTON BEACH
32550-32550	MIRAMAR BEACH
32559-32559	PENSACOLA
32560-32560	GONZALEZ
32561-32562	GULF BREEZE
32563-32563	HAROLD
32563-32563	GULF BREEZE
32564-32564	HOLT
32565-32565	JAY
32566-32566	GULF BREEZE
32567-32567	LAUREL HILL
32568-32568	MC DAVID
32569-32569	MARY ESTHER
32570-32572	MILTON
32573-32576	PENSACOLA
32577-32577	MOLINO
32578-32578	NICEVILLE
32579-32579	SHALIMAR
32580-32580	VALPARAISO
32581-32582	PENSACOLA
32583-32583	MILTON
32588-32588	NICEVILLE
32589-32589	PENSACOLA
32600-32614	GAINESVILLE
32615-32616	ALACHUA
32617-32617	ANTHONY
32618-32618	ARCHER
32619-32619	BELL
32621-32621	BRONSON
32622-32622	BROOKER
32625-32625	CEDAR KEY
32626-32626	CHIEFLAND
32627-32627	GAINESVILLE
32628-32628	CROSS CITY
32631-32631	EARLETON
32633-32633	EVINSTON
32634-32634	FAIRFIELD

Zip Range	City
32635-32635	GAINESVILLE
32639-32639	GULF HAMMOCK
32640-32640	HAWTHORNE
32641-32641	GAINESVILLE
32643-32643	HIGH SPRINGS
32644-32644	CHIEFLAND
32648-32648	HORSESHOE BEACH
32653-32653	GAINESVILLE
32654-32654	ISLAND GROVE
32655-32655	HIGH SPRINGS
32656-32656	KEYSTONE HEIGHTS
32658-32658	LA CROSSE
32662-32662	LOCHLOOSA
32663-32663	LOWELL
32664-32664	MC INTOSH
32666-32666	MELROSE
32667-32667	MICANOPY
32668-32668	MORRISTON
32669-32669	NEWBERRY
32680-32680	OLD TOWN
32681-32681	ORANGE LAKE
32683-32683	OTTER CREEK
32686-32686	REDDICK
32692-32692	SUWANNEE
32693-32693	TRENTON
32694-32694	WALDO
32696-32696	WILLISTON
32697-32697	WORTHINGTON SPRINGS
32701-32701	ALTAMONTE SPRINGS
32702-32702	ALTOONA
32703-32704	APOPKA
32706-32706	CASSADAGA
32707-32707	CASSELBERRY
32708-32708	WINTER SPRINGS
32709-32709	CHRISTMAS
32710-32710	CLARCONA
32712-32712	APOPKA
32713-32713	DEBARY
32714-32717	ALTAMONTE SPRINGS
32718-32718	CASSELBERRY
32719-32719	WINTER SPRINGS
32720-32721	DELAND
32722-32722	GLENWOOD
32723-32724	DELAND
32725-32725	DELTONA
32726-32727	EUSTIS
32728-32728	DELTONA
32730-32730	CASSELBERRY
32732-32732	GENEVA
32733-32733	GOLDENROD
32735-32735	GRAND ISLAND
32736-32736	EUSTIS
32738-32739	DELTONA
32744-32744	LAKE HELEN
32745-32745	MOUNT DORA
32745-32745	MID FLORIDA
32746-32746	LAKE MARY
32747-32747	LAKE MONROE
32750-32750	LONGWOOD
32751-32751	MAITLAND
32752-32752	LONGWOOD
32753-32753	DEBARY
32754-32754	MIMS
32756-32757	MOUNT DORA
32759-32759	OAK HILL
32762-32762	OVIEDO
32763-32763	ORANGE CITY
32764-32764	OSTEEN
32765-32766	OVIEDO
32767-32767	PAISLEY
32768-32768	PLYMOUTH
32771-32773	SANFORD
32774-32774	ORANGE CITY
32775-32775	SCOTTSMOOR
32776-32776	SORRENTO
32777-32777	TANGERINE
32778-32778	TAVARES
32779-32779	LONGWOOD
32780-32783	TITUSVILLE
32784-32784	UMATILLA
32789-32790	WINTER PARK
32791-32791	LONGWOOD
32792-32793	WINTER PARK
32794-32794	MAITLAND
32795-32795	LAKE MARY
32796-32796	TITUSVILLE
32798-32798	ZELLWOOD
32799-32799	MID FLORIDA
32800-32899	ORLANDO
32901-32902	MELBOURNE
32903-32903	INDIALANTIC
32904-32904	MELBOURNE
32905-32911	PALM BAY
32912-32919	MELBOURNE
32920-32920	CAPE CANAVERAL
32922-32924	COCOA
32925-32925	PATRICK A F B
32926-32927	COCOA
32931-32932	COCOA BEACH
32934-32936	MELBOURNE
32937-32937	SATELLITE BEACH
32940-32941	MELBOURNE
32948-32948	FELLSMERE
32949-32949	GRANT
32950-32950	MALABAR
32951-32951	MELBOURNE BEACH
32952-32954	MERRITT ISLAND
32955-32956	ROCKLEDGE
32957-32957	ROSELAND
32958-32958	SEBASTIAN
32959-32959	SHARPES
32960-32969	VERO BEACH
32970-32970	WABASSO
32971-32971	WINTER BEACH
32976-32978	SEBASTIAN
33001-33001	LONG KEY
33002-33002	HIALEAH
33004-33004	DANIA
33008-33009	HALLANDALE
33010-33018	HIALEAH
33019-33029	HOLLYWOOD
33030-33035	HOMESTEAD
33036-33036	ISLAMORADA
33037-33037	KEY LARGO
33039-33039	HOMESTEAD
33040-33041	KEY WEST
33042-33042	SUMMERLAND KEY
33043-33043	BIG PINE KEY
33044-33044	SUGARLOAF SHORES
33045-33045	KEY WEST
33050-33050	MARATHON
33051-33051	KEY COLONY BEACH
33052-33052	MARATHON SHORES
33054-33056	OPA LOCKA
33060-33069	POMPANO BEACH
33070-33070	TAVERNIER
33071-33071	POMPANO BEACH
33081-33081	HOLLYWOOD
33082-33082	SOUTH FLORIDA
33083-33084	HOLLYWOOD
33090-33092	HOMESTEAD
33093-33097	POMPANO BEACH
33100-33102	MIAMI
33103-33104	ABMPS
33107-33148	MIAMI
33149-33149	KEY BISCAYNE
33150-33154	MIAMI
33154-33154	MIAMI BEACH
33155-33239	MIAMI
33239-33239	MIAMI BEACH
33242-33299	MIAMI
33300-33326	FORT LAUDERDALE
33327-33327	WESTON
33327-33394	FORT LAUDERDALE
33401-33407	WEST PALM BEACH
33408-33408	NORTH PALM BEACH
33409-33410	WEST PALM BEACH
33410-33410	PALM BEACH GARDENS
33411-33422	WEST PALM BEACH
33424-33426	BOYNTON BEACH
33427-33429	BOCA RATON
33430-33430	BELLE GLADE
33431-33434	BOCA RATON
33435-33437	BOYNTON BEACH
33438-33438	CANAL POINT
33439-33439	BRYANT
33440-33440	CLEWISTON
33441-33443	DEERFIELD BEACH
33444-33448	DELRAY BEACH
33454-33454	LAKE WORTH
33455-33455	HOBE SOUND
33458-33458	JUPITER
33459-33459	LAKE HARBOR
33460-33464	LAKE WORTH
33464-33464	BOCA RATON
33465-33467	LAKE WORTH
33468-33469	JUPITER
33470-33470	LOXAHATCHEE
33471-33471	MOORE HAVEN
33474-33474	BOYNTON BEACH
33475-33475	HOBE SOUND
33476-33476	PAHOKEE
33477-33478	JUPITER
33480-33480	PALM BEACH
33481-33481	BOCA RATON
33482-33484	DELRAY BEACH
33486-33488	BOCA RATON
33491-33491	CANAL POINT
33493-33493	SOUTH BAY
33496-33499	BOCA RATON
33503-33503	BALM
33504-33504	BAY PINES
33508-33511	BRANDON
33513-33513	BUSHNELL
33514-33514	CENTER HILL
33521-33521	COLEMAN
33523-33523	DADE CITY
33524-33524	CRYSTAL SPRINGS
33525-33526	DADE CITY
33527-33527	DOVER
33530-33530	DURANT
33534-33534	GIBSONTON
33537-33537	LACOOCHEE
33538-33538	LAKE PANASOFFKEE
33539-33544	ZEPHYRHILLS
33547-33547	LITHIA
33548-33549	LUTZ
33550-33550	MANGO
33556-33556	ODESSA
33558-33559	LUTZ
33563-33567	PLANT CITY
33568-33569	RIVERVIEW
33570-33570	RUSKIN
33571-33571	SUN CITY CENTER
33572-33572	APOLLO BEACH
33573-33573	SUN CITY CENTER
33574-33574	SAINT LEO
33575-33575	RUSKIN
33576-33576	SAN ANTONIO
33583-33584	SEFFNER
33585-33585	SUMTERVILLE
33586-33586	SUN CITY
33587-33587	SYDNEY
33592-33592	THONOTOSASSA
33593-33593	TRILBY
33594-33595	VALRICO
33597-33597	WEBSTER
33598-33598	WIMAUMA
33600-33697	TAMPA
33700-33743	SAINT PETERSBURG
33744-33744	BAY PINES
33747-33747	SAINT PETERSBURG
33755-33767	CLEARWATER
33767-33767	CLEARWATER BEACH
33769-33769	CLEARWATER
33770-33771	LARGO
33772-33772	SEMINOLE
33773-33774	LARGO
33775-33776	SEMINOLE
33777-33777	LARGO
33777-33777	SEMINOLE
33778-33779	LARGO
33780-33782	PINELLAS PARK
33783-33784	SAINT PETERSBURG
33785-33785	INDIAN ROCKS BEACH
33786-33786	BELLEAIR BEACH
33801-33815	LAKELAND
33820-33820	ALTURAS
33821-33821	ARCADIA
33823-33823	AUBURNDALE
33825-33826	AVON PARK
33827-33827	BABSON PARK
33830-33831	BARTOW
33834-33834	BOWLING GREEN
33835-33835	BRADLEY
33836-33837	DAVENPORT
33838-33838	DUNDEE
33839-33839	EAGLE LAKE
33840-33840	EATON PARK
33841-33841	FORT MEADE
33842-33842	FORT OGDEN
33843-33843	FROSTPROOF
33844-33845	HAINES CITY
33846-33846	HIGHLAND CITY
33847-33847	HOMELAND
33848-33848	INTERCESSION CITY
33849-33849	KATHLEEN
33850-33850	LAKE ALFRED
33851-33851	LAKE HAMILTON
33852-33852	LAKE PLACID
33853-33853	LAKE WALES
33854-33854	FEDHAVEN
33855-33855	INDIAN LAKE ESTATES
33856-33856	NALCREST
33857-33857	LORIDA
33858-33858	LOUGHMAN
33859-33859	LAKE WALES
33860-33860	MULBERRY
33862-33862	LAKE PLACID
33863-33863	NICHOLS
33864-33864	NOCATEE
33865-33865	ONA
33867-33867	RIVER RANCH
33868-33868	POLK CITY
33870-33872	SEBRING
33873-33873	WAUCHULA
33875-33876	SEBRING
33877-33877	WAVERLY
33880-33888	WINTER HAVEN
33890-33890	ZOLFO SPRINGS
33896-33897	DAVENPORT
33898-33898	LAKE WALES
33900-33903	FORT MYERS
33903-33903	NORTH FORT MYERS
33904-33904	CAPE CORAL
33905-33908	FORT MYERS
33909-33910	CAPE CORAL
33911-33913	FORT MYERS
33914-33915	CAPE CORAL
33916-33917	FORT MYERS
33917-33917	NORTH FORT MYERS
33918-33918	FORT MYERS
33918-33918	NORTH FORT MYERS
33919-33919	FORT MYERS
33920-33920	ALVA
33921-33921	BOCA GRANDE
33922-33922	BOKEELIA
33923-33923	BONITA SPRINGS
33924-33924	CAPTIVA
33925-33925	CHOKOLOSKEE
33926-33926	COPELAND
33927-33927	PUNTA GORDA
33928-33928	ESTERO
33929-33929	EVERGLADES CITY
33930-33930	FELDA
33931-33932	FORT MYERS BEACH
33933-33933	GOODLAND
33934-33934	IMMOKALEE
33935-33935	LABELLE
33936-33936	LEHIGH ACRES
33937-33937	MARCO ISLAND
33938-33938	MURDOCK
33939-33942	NAPLES
33943-33943	OCHOPEE
33944-33944	PALMDALE
33945-33945	PINELAND
33946-33946	PLACIDA
33947-33947	ROTONDA WEST

33948-33949 PORT CHARLOTTE	34228-34228 LONGBOAT KEY	34487-34487 HOMOSASSA	34711-34715 CLERMONT
33950-33951 PUNTA GORDA	34229-34229 OSPREY	34488-34489 SILVER SPRINGS	34729-34729 FERNDALE
33952-33954 PORT CHARLOTTE	34230-34243 SARASOTA	34491-34492 SUMMERFIELD	34731-34731 FRUITLAND PARK
33955-33955 PUNTA GORDA	34250-34250 TERRA CEIA	34498-34498 YANKEETOWN	34734-34734 GOTHA
33956-33956 SAINT JAMES CITY	34251-34251 MYAKKA CITY	34601-34605 BROOKSVILLE	34736-34736 GROVELAND
33957-33957 SANIBEL	34260-34260 MANASOTA	34606-34608 SPRING HILL	34737-34737 HOWEY IN THE HILLS
33959-33959 BONITA SPRINGS	34264-34264 ONECO	34609-34610 BROOKSVILLE	34739-34739 KENANSVILLE
33960-33960 VENUS	34265-34266 ARCADIA	34611-34611 SPRING HILL	34740-34740 KILLARNEY
33961-33964 NAPLES	34267-34267 FORT OGDEN	34613-34614 BROOKSVILLE	34741-34747 KISSIMMEE
33965-33965 FORT MYERS	34268-34268 NOCATEE	34615-34630 CLEARWATER	34748-34749 LEESBURG
33969-33969 MARCO ISLAND	34269-34269 ARCADIA	34634-34635 BELLEAIR SHORES	34753-34753 MASCOTTE
33970-33972 LEHIGH ACRES	34270-34270 TALLEVAST	34635-34635 INDIAN ROCKS BEACH	34755-34755 MINNEOLA
33975-33975 LABELLE	34272-34272 LAUREL	34636-34636 ISTACHATTA	34756-34756 MONTVERDE
33980-33981 PORT CHARLOTTE	34274-34275 NOKOMIS	34637-34639 LAND O LAKES	34758-34759 KISSIMMEE
33982-33983 PUNTA GORDA	34276-34278 SARASOTA	34640-34649 LARGO	34760-34760 OAKLAND
33990-33993 CAPE CORAL	34280-34282 BRADENTON	34652-34656 NEW PORT RICHEY	34761-34761 OCOEE
33994-33994 FORT MYERS	34284-34285 VENICE	34660-34660 OZONA	34762-34762 OKAHUMPKA
33999-34120 NAPLES	34286-34289 NORTH PORT	34661-34661 NOBLETON	34769-34773 SAINT CLOUD
34133-34136 BONITA SPRINGS	34292-34293 VENICE	34664-34666 PINELLAS PARK	34777-34778 WINTER GARDEN
34137-34137 COPELAND	34295-34295 ENGLEWOOD	34667-34667 HUDSON	34785-34785 WILDWOOD
34138-34138 CHOKOLOSKEE	34420-34421 BELLEVIEW	34668-34668 PORT RICHEY	34786-34786 WINDERMERE
34139-34139 EVERGLADES CITY	34423-34429 CRYSTAL RIVER	34669-34669 HUDSON	34787-34787 WINTER GARDEN
34140-34140 GOODLAND	34430-34434 DUNNELLON	34673-34673 PORT RICHEY	34788-34789 LEESBURG
34141-34141 OCHOPEE	34436-34436 FLORAL CITY	34674-34674 HUDSON	34797-34797 YALAHA
34142-34143 IMMOKALEE	34442-34442 HERNANDO	34677-34677 OLDSMAR	34945-34951 FORT PIERCE
34145-34146 MARCO ISLAND	34445-34445 HOLDER	34679-34679 ARIPEKA	34952-34953 PORT SAINT LUCIE
34201-34212 BRADENTON	34446-34446 HOMOSASSA	34680-34680 ELFERS	34954-34954 FORT PIERCE
34215-34215 CORTEZ	34447-34447 HOMOSASSA SPRINGS	34681-34681 CRYSTAL BEACH	34956-34956 INDIANTOWN
34216-34216 ANNA MARIA	34448-34448 HOMOSASSA	34682-34685 PALM HARBOR	34957-34958 JENSEN BEACH
34217-34217 BRADENTON BEACH	34449-34449 INGLIS	34688-34689 TARPON SPRINGS	34972-34974 OKEECHOBEE
34218-34218 HOLMES BEACH	34450-34453 INVERNESS	34690-34692 HOLIDAY	34979-34982 FORT PIERCE
34219-34219 PARRISH	34460-34461 LECANTO	34692-34692 TARPON SPRINGS	34983-34988 PORT SAINT LUCIE
34220-34221 PALMETTO	34464-34465 BEVERLY HILLS	34695-34695 SAFETY HARBOR	34990-34991 PALM CITY
34222-34222 ELLENTON	34470-34483 OCALA	34697-34698 DUNEDIN	34992-34992 PORT SALERNO
34223-34224 ENGLEWOOD	34484-34484 OXFORD	34705-34705 ASTATULA	34994-34997 STUART

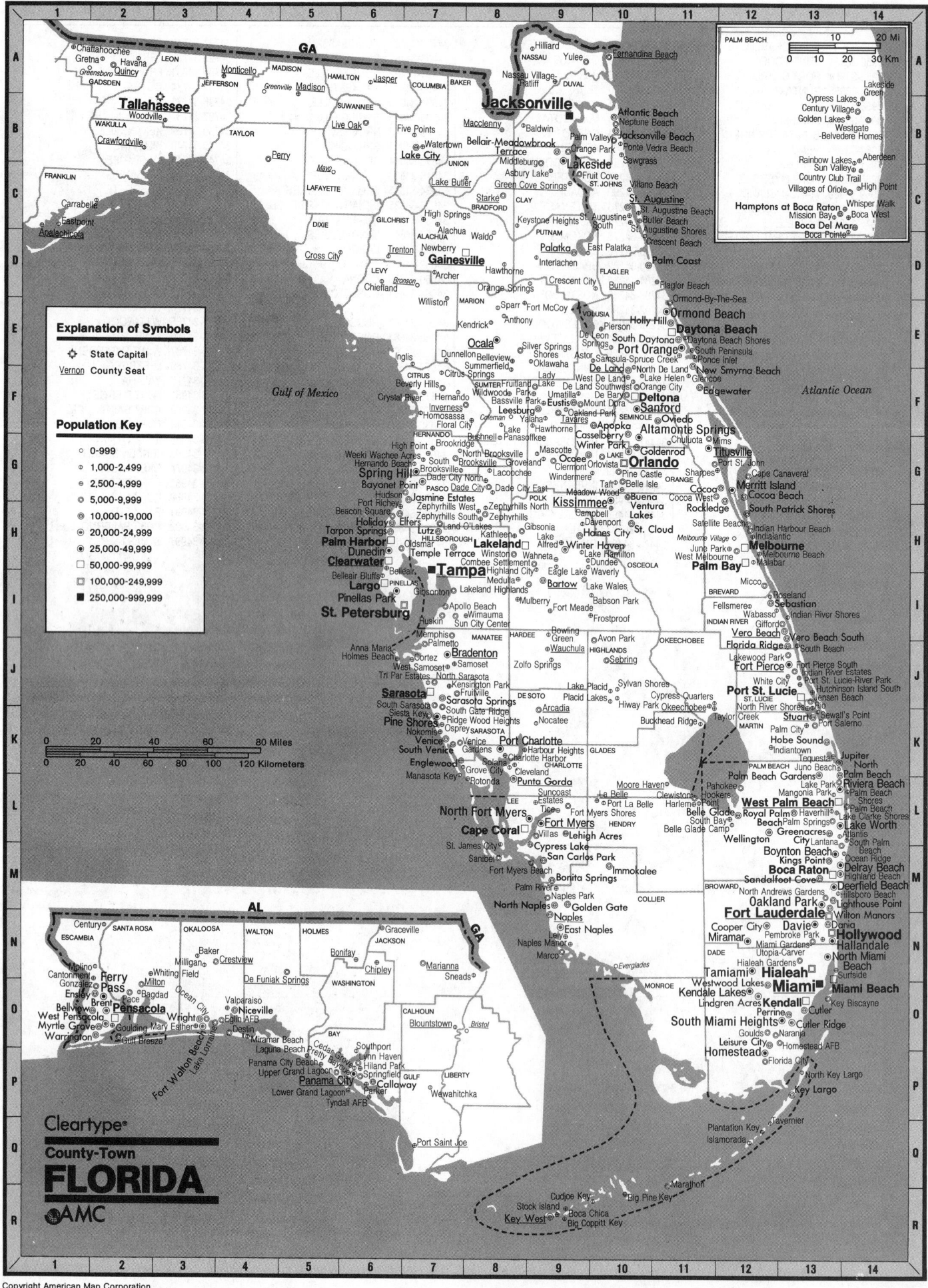

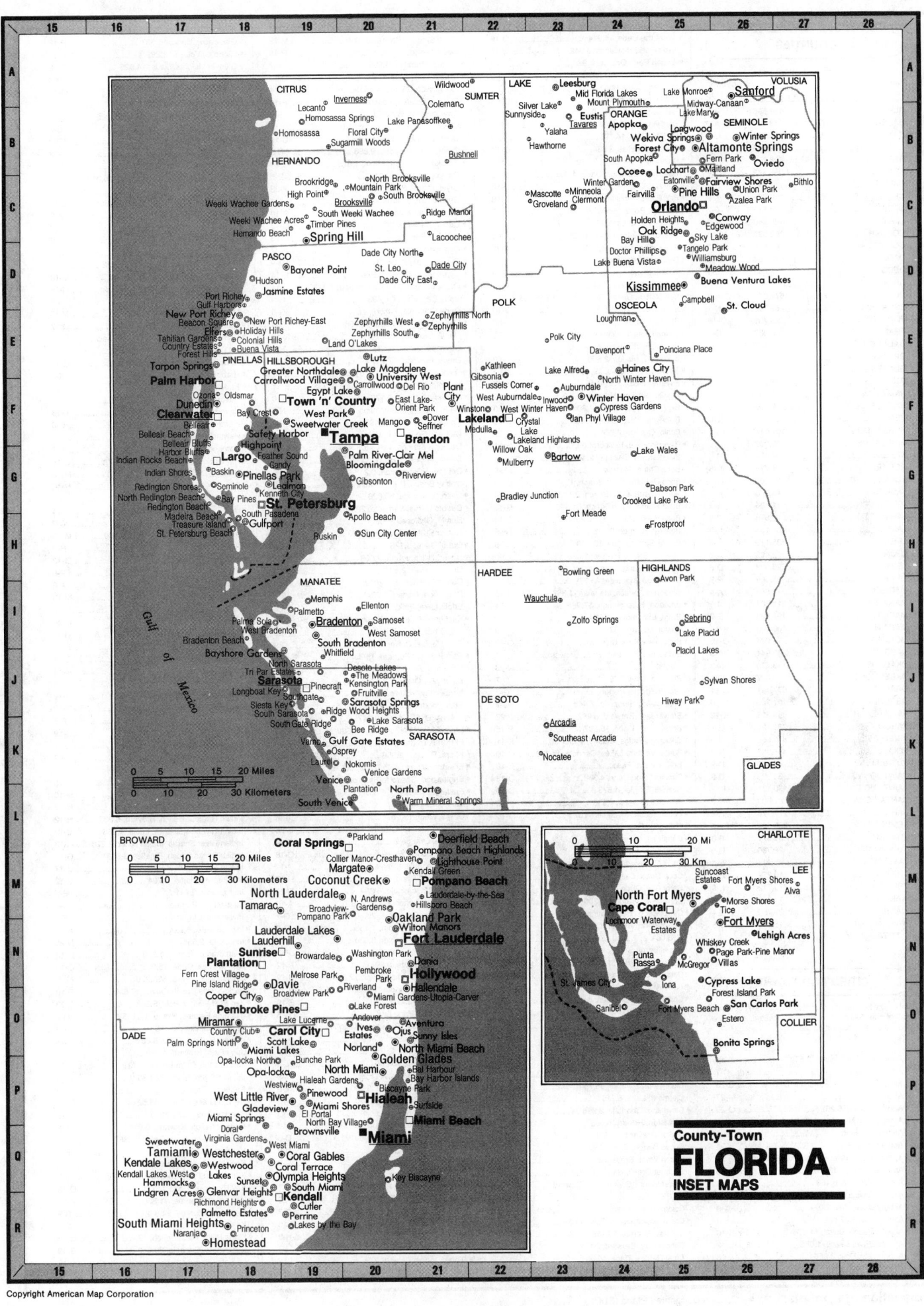

County-Town
FLORIDA
INSET MAPS

COUNTIES

(67 Counties)

Name of County	Population	Location on Map
ALACHUA	181,596	D-7
BAKER	18,486	A-7
BAY	126,994	O-5
BRADFORD	22,515	C-8
BREVARD	398,978	I-11
BROWARD	1,255,488	M-11
CALHOUN	11,011	O-7
CHARLOTTE	110,975	L-8
CITRUS	93,515	F-7
CLAY	105,986	C-8
COLLIER	152,099	M-10
COLUMBIA	42,613	A-7
DADE	1,937,094	N-11
DESOTO	23,865	J-8
DIXIE	10,585	C-5
DUVAL	672,971	A-9
ESCAMBIA	262,798	N-1
FLAGLER	28,701	D-10
FRANKLIN	8,967	C-1
GADSDEN	41,105	A-1
GILCHRIST	9,667	C-6
GLADES	7,591	K-10
GULF	11,504	P-7
HAMILTON	10,930	A-5
HARDEE	19,499	I-8
HENDRY	25,773	L-10
HERNANDO	101,115	G-7
HIGHLANDS	68,432	J-10
HILLSBOROUGH	834,054	H-7
HOLMES	15,778	N-5
INDIAN RIVER	90,208	I-11
JACKSON	41,375	N-6
JEFFERSON	11,296	A-3
LAFAYETTE	5,578	C-5
LAKE	152,104	E-9
LEE	335,113	L-8
LEON	192,493	A-3
LEVY	25,923	D-6
LIBERTY	5,569	P-7
MADISON	16,569	A-4
MANATEE	211,707	I-8
MARION	194,833	E-7
MARTIN	100,900	K-12
MONROE	78,024	O-10
NASSAU	43,941	A-8
OKALOOSA	143,776	N-3
OKEECHOBEE	29,627	I-11
ORANGE	677,491	G-11
OSCEOLA	107,728	H-10
PALM BEACH	863,518	K-12
PASCO	281,131	G-7
PINELLAS	851,659	I-6
POLK	405,382	G-9
PUTNAM	65,070	D-9
SAINT JOHNS	83,829	C-9
SAINT LUCIE	150,171	J-12
SANTA ROSA	81,608	N-2
SARASOTA	277,776	K-8
SEMINOLE	287,529	F-10
SUMTER	31,577	F-8
SUWANNEE	26,780	B-5
TAYLOR	17,111	B-4
UNION	10,252	B-7
VOLUSIA	370,712	E-9
WAKULLA	14,202	B-2
WALTON	27,760	N-4
WASHINGTON	16,919	O-5
TOTAL	12,937,926	

CITIES AND TOWNS

Note: The first name is that of the city or town, second, that of the county in which it is located, then the population and location on the map.

- • Aberdeen, Palm Beach, 2,572 .... B-14
- Alachua, Alachua, 4,529 .... C-7
- Altamonte Springs, Seminole, 34,879 .... B-25
- • Alva, Lee, 1,036 .... M-27
- • Andover, Dade, 6,251 .... O-20
- Anna Maria, Manatee, 1,744 .... J-6
- Anthony, Marion E-8
- Apalachicola, Franklin, 2,602 .... C-1
- • Apollo Beach, Hillsborough, 6,025 .... I-7
- Apopka, Orange, 13,512 .... G-10
- Arcadia, DeSoto, 6,488 .... K-9
- Archer, Alachua, 1,372 .... D-7
- • Asbury Lake, Clay, 2,072 .... C-9
- • Astor, Lake, 1,273 .... E-9
- Atlantic Beach, Duval, 11,636 .... B-10
- Atlantis, Palm Beach, 1,653 .... L-13
- Auburndale, Polk, 8,858 .... F-23
- • Aventura, Dade, 14,914 .... O-19
- Avon Park, Highlands, 8,042 .... J-10
- • Azalea Park, Orange, 8,926 .... C-26
- • Babson Park, Polk, 1,125 .... I-9
- • Bagdad, Santa Rosa, 1,457 .... O-2
- Baker, Okaloosa N-3
- Bal Harbour, Dade, 3,045 .... O-19
- Baldwin, Duval, 1,450 .... B-9
- Bartow, Polk, 14,716 .... I-9
- • Baskin, Pinellas, 3,834 .... G-17
- • Bassville Park, Lake, 2,752 .... F-9
- Bay Harbor Islands, Dade, 4,703 .... O-19
- • Bay Hill, Orange, 5,346 .... D-10
- • Bay Pines, Pinellas, 4,171 .... C-18
- • Bayonet Point, Pasco, 21,860 .... G-7
- • Bayshore Gardens, Manatee, 17,062 .... J-19
- • Beacon Square, Pasco, 6,265 .... G-6
- • Bee Ridge, Sarasota, 6,406 .... K-20
- • Bellair-Meadowbrook Terrace, Clay, 15,606 .... B-9
- Belle Glade, Palm Beach, 16,177 .... L-12
- • Belle Glade Camp, Palm Beach, 1,616 .... L-12
- Belle Isle, Orange, 5,272 .... G-10
- Belleair, Pinellas, 3,968 .... H-6
- Belleair Beach, Pinellas, 2,070 .... F-3
- Belleair Bluffs, Pinellas, 2,128 .... I-6
- Belleview, Marion, 2,666 .... E-8
- • Bellview, Escambia, 19,386 .... O-2
- • Beverly Hills, Citrus, 6,163 .... F-7
- • Big Coppitt Key, Monroe, 2,388 .... R-9
- • Big Pine Key, Monroe, 4,206 .... R-10
- Biscayne Park, Dade, 3,068 .... P-19
- • Bithlo, Orange, 4,834 .... C-27
- • Bloomingdale, Hillsborough, 13,912 .... G-21
- Blountstown, Calhoun, 2,404 .... O-7
- Boca Chica, Monroe R-9
- • Boca Del Mar, Palm Beach, 17,754 .... C-13
- • Boca Pointe, Palm Beach, 2,147 .... C-14
- Boca Raton, Palm Beach, 61,492 .... M-13
- • Boca West, Palm Beach, 2,847 .... C-14
- Bonifay, Holmes, 2,612 .... N-6
- • Bonita Springs, Lee, 13,600 .... M-9
- Bowling Green, Hardee, 1,836 .... I-9
- Boynton Beach, Palm Beach, 46,194 .... M-13
- Bradenton, Manatee, 43,779 .... J-7
- Bradenton Beach, Manatee, 1,657 .... I-18
- • Brandon, Hillsborough, 57,985 .... F-21
- • Brent, Escambia, 21,624 .... O-2
- Bristol, Liberty, 937 .... O-8
- • Broadview Park, Broward, 6,109 .... O-18
- • Broadview-Pompano Park, Broward, 5,230 .... N-23
- Bronson, Levy, 875 .... D-7
- • Brookridge, Hernando, 2,805 .... G-7
- Brooksville, Hernando, 7,440 .... G-7
- • Browardale, Broward, 6,257 .... P-23
- • Brownsville, Dade, 15,607 .... P-18
- • Buckhead Ridge, Glades, 1,279 .... K-11
- • Buena Ventura Lakes, Osceola, 14,148 .... G-10
- Buena Vista, Pasco E-18
- • Bunche Park, Dade, 4,388 .... O-18
- Bunnell, Flagler, 1,873 .... D-10
- Bushnell, Sumter, 1,998 .... F-8
- • Butler Beach, St. Johns, 3,377 .... D-10
- Callaway, Bay, 12,253 .... P-6
- • Campbell, Osceola, 3,884 .... H-10
- Cantonment, Escambia N-2
- Cape Canaveral, Brevard, 8,014 .... G-12
- Cape Coral, Lee, 74,991 .... L-8
- • Carol City, Dade, 53,331 .... O-18
- Carrabelle, Franklin, 1,200 .... C-2
- • Carrollwood, Hillsborough, 7,195 .... E-20
- • Carrollwood Village, Hillsborough, 15,051 .... E-19
- Casselberry, Seminole, 18,911 .... F-10
- Cedar Grove, Bay, 1,479 .... P-6
- Century, Escambia, 1,989 .... N-2
- • Century Village, Palm Beach, 8,363 .... B-14
- • Charlotte Harbor, Charlotte, 3,327 .... K-8
- • Charlotte Park, Charlotte, 2,225 .... K-8
- Chattahoochee, Gadsden, 4,382 .... A-1
- Chiefland, Levy, 1,917 .... D-6
- Chipley, Washington, 3,866 .... O-6
- • Chuluota, Seminole, 1,441 .... G-11
- • Citrus Springs, Citrus, 2,213 .... F-7
- Clearwater, Pinellas, 98,784 .... H-6
- Clermont, Lake, 6,910 .... G-9
- • Cleveland, Charlotte, 2,896 .... K-8
- Clewiston, Hendry, 6,085 .... L-11
- Cocoa, Brevard, 17,722 .... G-11
- Cocoa Beach, Brevard, 12,123 .... G-12
- • Cocoa West, Brevard, 6,160 .... G-11
- Coconut Creek, Broward, 27,485 .... M-20
- • Collier Manor-Cresthaven, Broward, 7,322 .... N-19
- Colonial Hills, Pasco E-18
- • Combee Settlement, Polk, 5,463 .... H-9
- • Conway, Orange, 13,159 .... C-26
- Cooper City, Broward, 20,791 .... N-12
- Coral Gables, Dade, 40,091 .... P-18
- Coral Springs, Broward, 79,443 .... M-19
- • Coral Terrace, Dade, 23,255 .... P-18
- • Cortez, Manatee, 4,509 .... J-7
- • Country Club, Dade, 3,408 .... O-18
- • Country Club Trail, Palm Beach, 4,599 .... C-14
- Country Estates, Pasco E-18
- Crawfordville, Wakulla B-2
- • Crescent Beach, St. Johns, 1,081 .... D-10
- Crescent City, Putnam, 1,859 .... D-10
- Crestview, Okaloosa, 9,886 .... N-3
- • Crooked Lake Park, Polk, 1,575 .... G-24
- Cross City, Dixie, 2,041 .... D-5
- • Crystal Lake, Polk, 5,300 .... F-23
- Crystal River, Citrus, 4,044 .... F-7
- • Cudjoe Key, Monroe, 1,714 .... R-10
- • Cutler, Dade, 16,201 .... O-13
- • Cutler Ridge, Dade, 21,268 .... O-13
- • Cypress Gardens, Polk, 9,188 .... F-24
- • Cypress Lake, Lee, 10,491 .... M-9
- • Cypress Lakes, Palm Beach, 1,260 .... B-14
- • Cypress Quarters, Okeechobee, 1,343 .... J-11
- Dade City, Pasco, 5,633 .... G-8
- Dade City East, Pasco G-8
- • Dade City North, Pasco, 3,058 .... G-8
- Dania, Broward, 13,024 .... N-13
- Davenport, Polk, 1,529 .... H-9
- Davie, Broward, 47,217 .... N-13
- Daytona Beach, Volusia, 61,921 .... E-11
- Daytona Beach Shores, Volusia, 2,335 .... E-11
- • De Bary, Volusia, 7,176 .... F-10
- De Funiak Springs, Walton, 5,120 .... N-5
- De Land, Volusia, 16,491 .... F-11
- • De Land Southwest, Volusia, 1,249 .... F-9
- • De Leon Springs, Volusia, 1,481 .... E-10
- Deerfield Beach, Broward, 46,325 .... M-13
- • Del Rio, Hillsborough, 8,248 .... F-20
- Delray Beach, Palm Beach, 47,181 .... M-13
- • Deltona, Volusia, 50,828 .... F-10
- • Desoto Lakes, Sarasota, 2,807 .... J-20
- Destin, Okaloosa, 8,080 .... O-4
- • Doctor Phillips, Orange, 7,963 .... D-11
- • Doral, Dade, 3,126 .... Q-18
- • Dover, Hillsborough, 2,606 .... F-21
- Dundee, Polk, 2,335 .... H-9
- Dunedin, Pinellas, 34,012 .... H-6
- Dunnellon, Marion, 1,624 .... E-7
- Eagle Lake, Polk, 1,758 .... H-9
- • East Lake-Orient Park, Hillsborough, 6,171 .... F-20
- • East Naples, Collier, 22,951 .... C-9
- • East Palatka, Putnam, 1,989 .... D-9
- • Eastpoint, Franklin, 1,577 .... C-1
- Eatonville, Orange, 2,170 .... C-25
- Edgewater, Volusia, 15,337 .... F-11
- Edgewood, Orange, 1,062 .... C-25
- • Eglin AFB, Okaloosa, 8,347 .... O-4
- • Egypt Lake, Hillsborough, 14,580 .... F-19
- El Portal, Dade, 2,457 .... P-18
- • Elfers, Pasco, 12,356 .... G-6
- • Ellenton, Manatee, 2,573 .... I-20
- • Englewood, Charlotte/Sarasota, 15,025 .... K-7
- • Ensley, Escambia, 16,362 .... O-2
- • Estero, Lee, 3,177 .... O-26
- Eustis, Lake, 12,967 .... F-6
- • Fairview Shores, Orange, 13,192 .... C-25
- Fairvilla, Orange C-24
- • Feather Sound, Pinellas, 2,690 .... G-18
- Fellsmere, Indian River, 2,179 .... I-12
- Fern Crest Village, Broward N-17
- • Fern Park, Seminole, 8,294 .... B-25
- Fernandina Beach, Nassau, 8,765 .... A-10
- • Ferry Pass, Escambia, 26,301 .... O-2
- • Five Points, Columbia, 1,136 .... B-7
- Flagler Beach, Flagler, 3,820 .... D-11
- • Floral City, Citrus, 2,609 .... F-8
- Florida City, Dade, 5,806 .... P-12
- • Florida Ridge, Indian River, 12,218 .... I-12
- • Forest City, Seminole, 10,638 .... B-25
- Forest Hills, Pasco E-18
- • Forest Island Park, Lee, 5,988 .... O-25
- Fort Lauderdale, Broward, 149,377 .... N-13
- Fort McCoy, Marion E-8
- Fort Meade, Polk, 4,976 .... H-9
- Fort Myers, Lee, 45,206 .... L-9
- • Fort Myers Beach, Lee, 9,284 .... M-9
- • Fort Myers Shores, Lee, 5,460 .... L-9
- Fort Pierce, St. Lucie, 36,830 .... J-12
- • Fort Pierce North, St. Lucie, 5,833 .... J-13
- • Fort Pierce South, St. Lucie, 5,320 .... J-13
- Fort Walton Beach, Okaloosa, 21,471 .... O-3
- Frostproof, Polk, 2,808 .... I-9
- • Fruit Cove, St. Johns, 5,904 .... C-9
- Fruitland Park, Lake, 2,754 .... F-9
- • Fruitville, Sarasota, 9,808 .... J-7
- • Fussels Corner, Polk, 3,840 .... F-23
- Gainesville, Alachua, 84,770 .... D-7
- • Gandy, Pinellas, 3,164 .... G-18
- • Gibsonia, Polk, 5,168 .... H-9
- • Gibsonton, Hillsborough, 7,706 .... I-7
- • Gifford, Indian River, 6,278 .... I-13
- • Gladeview, Dade, 15,637 .... P-18
- • Glencoe, Volusia, 2,282 .... F-11
- • Glenvar Heights, Dade, 14,823 .... Q-18
- • Golden Gate, Collier, 14,148 .... M-9
- • Golden Glades, Dade, 25,474 .... O-19
- • Golden Lakes, Palm Beach, 3,867 .... B-14
- • Goldenrod, Orange/Seminole, 12,362 .... G-10
- • Gonzalez, Escambia, 7,669 .... O-2
- • Goulding, Escambia, 4,159 .... O-2
- • Goulds, Dade, 7,284 .... O-12
- Graceville, Jackson, 2,675 .... N-6
- • Greater Northdale, Hillsborough, 16,318 .... E-6
- Green Cove Springs, Clay, 4,497 .... C-9
- Greenacres City, Palm Beach, 18,683 .... L-13
- Gretna, Gadsden, 1,981 .... A-2
- • Grove City, Charlotte, 2,374 .... K-7
- Groveland, Lake, 2,300 .... G-9
- Gulf Breeze, Santa Rosa, 5,530 .... O-2
- • Gulf Gate Estates, Sarasota, 11,622 .... K-19
- Gulf Harbors, Pasco D-18
- Gulfport, Pinellas, 11,727 .... H-18
- Haines City, Polk, 11,683 .... H-9
- Hallandale, Broward, 30,996 .... N-13
- • Hammocks, Dade, 10,897 .... Q-17
- • Hamptons at Boca Raton, Palm Beach, 11,686 .... C-14
- • Harbor Bluffs, Pinellas, 2,659 .... G-17
- • Harbour Heights, Charlotte, 2,523 .... K-8
- • Harlem, Hendry, 2,826 .... L-11
- Havana, Gadsden, 1,654 .... A-2
- Haverhill, Palm Beach, 1,058 .... L-13
- Hawthorne, Alachua, 1,305 .... D-8
- • Hawthorne, Lake, 1,804 .... F-9
- • Hernando, Citrus, 2,103 .... F-7
- • Hernando Beach, Hernando, 1,767 .... C-19
- Hialeah, Dade, 188,004 .... M-13
- Hialeah Gardens, Dade, 7,713 .... M-13
- • High Point, Hernando, 2,814 .... G-7
- • High Point, Palm Beach, 2,288 .... C-14
- High Springs, Alachua, 3,144 .... C-7
- Highland Beach, Palm Beach, 3,209 .... M-13
- • Highland City, Polk, 1,919 .... H-9
- • Highpoint, Pinellas, 13,818 .... G-18
- • Hiland Park, Bay, 3,865 .... P-6
- Hilliard, Nassau, 1,751 .... A-8
- Hillsboro Beach, Broward, 1,748 .... M-13
- • Hobe Sound, Martin, 11,507 .... K-13
- • Holden Heights, Orange, 4,387 .... C-25
- • Holiday, Pasco, 19,360 .... H-6
- Holiday Hills, Pasco E-18
- Holly Hill, Volusia, 11,141 .... E-11
- Hollywood, Broward, 121,697 .... N-13
- Holmes Beach, Manatee, 4,810 .... J-6
- Homestead, Dade, 26,866 .... O-12
- • Homestead AFB, Dade, 5,153 .... O-13
- • Homosassa, Citrus, 2,113 .... F-7
- • Homosassa Springs, Citrus, 6,271 .... B-19
- Hookers Point, Hendry L-11
- • Hudson, Pasco, 7,344 .... G-7
- • Hutchinson Island South, St. Lucie, 3,893 .... J-13
- • Immokalee, Collier, 14,120 .... M-10
- Indialantic, Brevard, 2,844 .... H-12
- Indian Harbour Beach, Brevard, 6,933 .... H-12
- • Indian River Estates, St. Lucie, 4,858 .... J-13
- Indian River Shores, Indian River, 2,278 .... I-13
- Indian Rocks Beach, Pinellas, 3,963 .... G-17
- Indian Shores, Pinellas, 1,405 .... G-17
- • Indiantown, Martin, 4,794 .... K-12
- Inglis, Levy, 1,241 .... E-7
- Interlachen, Putnam, 1,160 .... D-9
- Inverness, Citrus, 5,797 .... F-7
- • Inwood, Polk, 6,824 .... F-23
- • Iona, Lee, 9,565 .... N-25
- • Islamorada, Monroe, 1,220 .... Q-12
- • Ives Estates, Dade, 13,531 .... O-19
- Jacksonville, Duval, 635,230 .... B-9
- Jacksonville Beach, Duval, 17,839 .... B-10
- • Jan Phyl Village, Polk, 5,308 .... F-23
- • Jasmine Estates, Pasco, 17,136 .... G-7
- Jasper, Hamilton, 2,099 .... A-6
- • Jensen Beach, Martin, 9,884 .... J-13
- • June Park, Brevard, 4,080 .... H-12
- Juno Beach, Palm Beach, 2,121 .... K-13
- Jupiter, Palm Beach, 24,986 .... K-13
- • Kathleen, Polk, 2,743 .... H-8
- • Kendale Lakes, Dade, 48,524 .... O-12
- • Kendall, Dade, 87,271 .... O-13
- • Kendall Green, Broward, 3,815 .... M-19
- • Kendall Lakes West, Dade, 6,038 .... Q-17
- Kendrick, Marion E-8
- Kenneth City, Pinellas, 4,462 .... G-18
- • Kensington Park, Sarasota, 3,026 .... J-7
- • Key Biscayne, Dade, 8,854 .... O-13
- • Key Largo, Monroe, 11,336 .... P-13
- Key West, Monroe, 24,832 .... R-9
- Keystone Heights, Clay, 1,315 .... C-8
- • Kings Point, Palm Beach, 12,422 .... M-13
- Kissimmee, Osceola, 30,050 .... G-10
- La Belle, Hendry, 2,703 .... L-10

Explanation of symbols: •– Census Designated Place (CDP)

Explanation of symbols: ● – Census Designated Place (CDP)

General Help Numbers:

Governor's Office

203 State Capitol
Atlanta, GA 30334
www.ganet.org/governor/
index_flash.html

404-656-1776
Fax 404-657-7332
8AM-4:30PM

Attorney General's Office

40 Capitol Square SW
Atlanta, GA 30334-1300
www.law.state.ga.us

404-656-3300
Fax 404-651- 9325
8AM-5PM

Legislative Records

State Capitol
General Assembly of Georgia
Atlanta, GA 30334
www.legis.state.ga.us

404-656-5040
Fax 404-656-5043
8:30AM-4:30PM

State Archives

Archives & History Department
5800 Jonesboro Rd.
Atlanta, GA 30260
www.sos.state.ga.us/archives/

678-364-3700
Fax 678-364-3856
8 AM - 4:45 PM

State Specifics:

Capital:

Atlanta
Fulton County

Time Zone:

EST

Number of Counties:

159

Population:

8,829,383

Web Site:

www.georgia.gov

State Agencies

Criminal Records

Georgia Bureau of Investigation, Attn: GCIC, PO Box 370748, Decatur, GA 30037-0748 (Courier: 3121 Panthersville Rd, Decatur, GA 30034); 404-244-2639, 404-244-8417-Fax; 8AM-4PM.

www.ganet.org/gbi

GCIC is the central criminal records repository for the State. (Note: anyone with a signed release may make a record request at any local law enforcement office and the statewide record will be provided. Fees for this may vary; the maximum fee is $20.00.)

Records are available from 1972 forward. It takes 1-3 days before new records are available for inquiry. Records are normally destroyed after court order. 70% of all arrests in database have final dispositions recorded, 81% for those arrests within last 5 years.

Searching: Records are available here to employers, government agencies including licensing agencies, and adoption and foster care providers. 100% of arrest records are fingerprint supported. Include the following in your request-name, set of fingerprints, date of birth, sex, race, Social Security Number. Certain law enforcement agencies, who are online, and local agencies may

access and retrieve records for investigative/background purposes. These agencies have the option of requesting a signed release from subject or including a set of fingerprints. The following data is not released: juvenile records, traffic ticket information or out-of-state or federal charges. Information released includes arrest, disposition, and custodial information for offenses designated as fingerprintable by the State AG. Records without dispositions are released.

Access by: mail, in person, online.

Fee & Payment: Fee is $15.00 per name. If statutes require a FBI check, both state and FBI require one set of fingerprint cards, a total search fee of $24.00 per name is required plus the fingerprints. Agencies may establish an account. Fee payee: Georgia Bureau of Investigations. Prepayment required. Money orders are accepted. No credit cards accepted.

Mail search: Turnaround time: 7 to 10 days. No SASE is required.

In person search: In-person requests are returned by mail in about 14 days.

Online search: There are three searchable databases found at www.cscj.org/crimjustinfo. They are for parolees, sexual offenders, and inmates. There is no online access to the criminal records database.

Statewide Court Records

Administrative Office of the Courts, 244 Washington St SW, #300, Atlanta, GA 30334; 404-656-5171, 404-651-6449-Fax; 8:30AM-5PM.

www.georgiacourts.org

Except for certain online research capabilities, all court record access must be done at the local level.

Access by: online.

Online search: Supreme Court docket information and opinions are available from the web, but there is no online access available statewide for trial courts, although statewide access is being planned. A certified copy of a Supreme Court Opinion can be purchased online for $5.00 at http://www2.s tate.ga.us/Courts/Supreme/main_pp.html.

Sexual Offender Registry

Georgia Bureau of Investigations, GCIC - Sexual Offender Registry, PO Box 370748, Decatur, GA 30037-0748 (Courier address: 3121 Panthersville Rd, Decatur, GA 30037); 404-270-8465, 404-244-2600 (24 Hour Line to GBI), 404-270-8452-Fax; 8AM-4PM.

www.ganet.org/gbi/disclaim.html

The website outlines which offenders are in the searchable database at the website.

Records are available from 7/01/96 for information pertaining to sex offenders who have been released from prison, placed on probation, parole, or supervised release after July 1, 1996. It takes 1-3 days before new records are available for inquiry. Records are normally destroyed after 10 years unless more than one prior or who have been convicted of an aggravated offense such as aggravated child molestation, will remain on the registry for life.

Searching: As of July 1, 1999, sexual offenders who have more than one prior conviction for an offense listed in O.C.G.A. § 42-1-12, or who have been convicted of an aggravated offense such as aggravated child molestation, will remain on the registry for life.

Access by: mail, in person, online.

Fee & Payment: There is no fee.

Mail search: Turnaround time: 7 to 10 days.

In person search: In person requests are returned by mail in about 14 days if lists are involved.

Online search: Records may be searched at www.ganet.org/gbi/sorsch.cgi. Earliest records go back to 07/01/96. Searches may be conducted for sex offenders, absconders, and predators.

Incarceration Records

Georgia Department of Corrections, Inmate Records Office - 6th Fl, East Tower, 2 Martin Luther King, Jr. Drive, S.E., Atlanta, GA 30334-4900; 404-656-4569, 404-463-6232-Fax; 8AM-4:30PM.

www.dcor.state.ga.us

Records are available on current and former inmates. It takes 1-3 days before new records are available for inquiry. Records are normally destroyed after 15 years.

Searching: Include the following in your request-name; DOB, Inmate number or SSN are helpful. Location, physical identifiers, conviction information, release dates, and inmate number are released.

Access by: mail, phone, fax, in person, online.

Fee & Payment: There is a $10.00 fee for PEN PAK certification.

Mail search: Turnaround time: 7 to 14 days. This is for PEN PAK only. Request is sent to Sec of State's office for certification. No SASE is required. Requests in writing must be on letterhead.

Phone search: Only general "public" information is released over the phone.

Fax search: Records are available by fax.

In person search: You may make your record request in person; use the agency form. Results are available in two days.

Online search: The website has an extensive array of search capabilities. Also, a private company offers free web access to DOC records at www.vinelink.com/index.jsp.

Corporation Records, Limited Partnership, Limited Liability Partnerships, Limited Liability Company Records

Sec of State - Corporation Division, Record Searches, 315 W Tower, #2 ML King Drive, Atlanta, GA 30334-1530; 404-656-2817, 9AM-5PM.

www.sos.state.ga.us/corporations

Trade Names, Fictitious Names, Assumed Names and DBAs are found at the county level.

Records are available from the 1960s, and earlier if the filer has moved records from the county level to the state level. Indexes are maintained on microfilm and document imaging systems. New records are available for inquiry immediately.

Searching: Date of incorporation, officer names, current status and registered name and address available at website. Copies and/or certificates can be ordered by mail or from the web.

Access by: mail, in person, online.

Fee & Payment: There is no fee for a website search; there is a $10.00 fee for a Certificate of Existence (good standing) or certified copies. Fee payee: Secretary of State. Prepayment required. Web requests must be paid by credit card. Personal checks accepted. Credit cards accepted: MasterCard, Visa, AmEx.

Mail search: Turnaround time: 1 week. No SASE is required.

In person search: Immediate records only if expedited service fees paid.

Online search: Records are available from the corporation database on the Internet site above. The corporate database can be searched by entity name or registered agent for no fee. Document Image and certificates available for a $10.00 fee at www.ganet.org/services/corp/corpsearch.shtml. Other services include name reservation, filing procedures, downloading of forms/applications.

Expedited service: Expedited service is available for mail and in person searches. Turnaround time: 24 hours. Add $50.00 per entity.

Trademarks/Servicemarks

Secretary of State, Trademark Division, 2 Martin Luther King, Room 315, W Tower, Atlanta, GA 30334; 404-656-2861, 404-657-6380-Fax; 8AM-5PM.

www.sos.state.ga.us/corporations/trademarks.htm

Applications and filing instructions can be obtained at the website.

Records are available from the beginning of the Division and are maintained on computer. It takes 24 hours before new records are available for inquiry.

Searching: Records are permanently retained. Include the following in your request-registration number. Search by mark name or description or by owner name or by goods and services. Will not expedite requests.

Access by: mail, in person, online.

Fee & Payment: $10.00 per record. Fee payee: Secretary of State Prepayment required. Personal checks accepted. No credit cards accepted.

Mail search: Turnaround time: 2 to 3 days. No SASE is required.

In person search: They will take your request in person, but they will mail back the records.

Online search: A record database is searchable from the website at www.sos.state.ga.us/corporations/marksearch.htm. Search by registration #, mark name, description, connection, owner, or classification.

Uniform Commercial Code

Superior Court Clerks' Cooperative Authority, 1875 Century Blvd, #100, Atlanta, GA 30345; 404-327-9058, 404-327-7877-Fax; 8:30AM-5PM.

www.gsccca.org

High volume, ongoing requesters can open a "search account" and receive expedited service.

Records are available from 1-1-95, indexed on computer. It takes 3-4 days before new records are available for inquiry.

Searching: All uniform commercial code filings are filed at the county level. As of January 1, 1995, new UCC filings are indexed statewide (older filings are only available at the county). Submit a UCC-11 to the address above to search new filings. Include the following in your request-debtor name, Social Security or federal employer number. All tax liens are filed at the county level only.

Access by: mail, fax, in person, online.

Fee & Payment: Uncertified copies made by searcher are $.25 each. Certified copies are also available at the county level for $2.50 for first page. Fee payee: GSCCCA. Prepayment required. Personal checks accepted. Credit cards accepted.

Mail search: Turnaround time: 1 day. No SASE is required.

Fax search: However, this is only available to established accounts.

In person search: Simple requests may be processed while you wait.

Online search: Online name searching is available free at the website. Also search by secured party, tax payer ID, date, or file number. For certified searches, there is a monthly charge of $9.95 and a $.25 fee per image. Billing is monthly. The system is open 24 hours daily. The website also includes real estate indexes and images, lien index, and notary index.

Other access: The entire UCC Central Index System can be purchased on a daily, weekly, biweekly basis. For more information, contact the Director's office.

Expedited service: Expedited service is available online. Add $25.00 per search.

Federal and State Tax Liens

Records not maintained by a state level agency.

All tax liens are filed at the county level.

Sales Tax Registrations

Taxpayer Services Division, Registration and Licensing Section, PO 49512, Atlanta, GA 30359-1512; 404-417-4490 (Registration), 404-417-6601 (General Info), 404-651-9490-Fax; 8AM-4:30PM.

www.etax.dor.ga.gov

Check unclaimed funds at www.etax.dor.ga.gov/unclaimed/new.shtml.

Records are available for all active accounts, which are kept on computer. Inactive accounts are on microfilm. It takes 10 business days before new records are available for inquiry.

Searching: This agency will confirm that a business is registered and active, but will not provide further information without consent. Include the following in your request-tax permit number or business name.

Access by: mail, phone, in person.

Fee & Payment: Fee is $1.00 per page, if copies needed.

Mail search: Turnaround time: 2 weeks. Please give reason for request. Requests in writing will be honored if over two.

Phone search: No fee for telephone request.

In person search: No fee for request. Generally, the information is returned by mail in two weeks.

Birth Certificates

Department of Human Resources, Vital Records Unit, 2600 Skyland Dr NE, Atlanta, GA 30319; 404-679-4701, 877-572-6343 (Credit Card Line), 404-679-4730-Fax; 8AM-4:45PM.

http://health.state.ga.us/programs/vitalrecords/index.asp

Request forms may be printed from the web page.

Records are available from 1919 to present. It takes 1 month before new records are available for inquiry. Records are indexed on inhouse computer.

Searching: For investigative purposes or distant relatives, a notarized, signed release from person of record is required. Include the following in your request-full name, names of parents, mother's maiden name, date of birth, place of birth. If born after 2003 the it is suggested to include the Hospital Name with the request.

Access by: mail, phone, fax, in person, online.

Fee & Payment: The fee is $10.00 per record. Add $5.00 per name requested for second copies. Multi year searches are $10.00 per ten years or portions thereof. Credit card fee is $12.50 Fee payee: Georgia Department of Human Resources. Prepayment required. Major credit cards accepted.

Mail search: Turnaround time: 10 weeks or more. No SASE is required.

Phone search: See expedited services.

Fax search: Same criteria as phone searching.

In person search: Turnaround time is usually 30 minutes.

Online search: Records may be ordered online through an approved vendor - www.vitalchek.com. The credit card fee applies.

Expedited service: Expedited service is available for mail, phone and fax searches. Turnaround time: overnight delivery. Add $17.50 for overnight service plus use of credit card fee required.

Death Records

Department of Human Resources, Vital Records Unit, 2600 Skyland Dr NE, Atlanta, GA 30319; 404-679-4701, 877-572-6343 (Credit Card Line), 404-679-4730-Fax; 8AM-4:45PM.

http://health.state.ga.us/programs/vitalrecords/index.asp

A request form may be downloaded from the web page.

Records are available from 1919 to present. It takes 1 month before new records are available for inquiry. Records are indexed on inhouse computer.

Searching: Death certificates are available to the general public. Cause of death is released to next of kin only. Include the following in your request-full name, date of death, place of death. Age at death, sex and race are helpful.

Access by: mail, phone, fax, in person, online.

Fee & Payment: The fee is $10.00 per name. Add $5.00 per name for second copies. Multi year searches are $10.00 per 10 years or portions thereof. Credit card fee is $12.50 Fee payee: Georgia Department of Human Resources. Prepayment required. Major credit cards accepted.

Mail search: Turnaround time: 3 to 4 weeks. No SASE is required.

Phone search: See expedited services.

Fax search: Same criteria as phone searching.

In person search: Turnaround time 30 minutes.

Online search: Records may be ordered online through an approved vendor - www.vitalchek.com. The credit card fee applies.

Other access: The death index is available for the years 1919-1998 on microfiche for $50.00.

Expedited service: Expedited service is available for mail, phone and fax searches. Turnaround time: overnight delivery. Add $17.50 for overnight delivery, plus include credit card fee.

Marriage Certificates

Department of Human Resources, Vital Records Unit, 2600 Skyland Dr NE, Atlanta, GA 30319; 404-679-4701, 877-572-6343 (Credit Card Line), 404-679-4730-Fax; 8AM-4:45PM.

http://health.state.ga.us/programs/vitalrecords/index.asp

This agency will do search to identify the county of record and issue a certificate, but cannot issue a copy of the original record. Certified copies are only available at the county level.

Records are available from 1952 on. Prior to 1952, records must be obtained from the county probate office. It takes 1 month. before new records are available for inquiry. Records are indexed on inhouse computer.

Searching: Certified copies of marriage licenses are available to the general public; but copies of the marriage application are only issued to bride and groom. Records may not be ordered via e-mail. Include the following in your request-full names of husband and wife, date of marriage, place or county of marriage.

Access by: mail, phone, fax, in person.

Fee & Payment: The search fee is $10.00 per name. Add $5.00 per name requested for second copies. Multi-year search are $10.00 per ten years or portions thereof. Credit card fee is $12.50 Fee payee: Georgia Department of Human Resources. Prepayment required. Major credit cards accepted.

Mail search: Turnaround time: 3 to 4 weeks. No SASE is required.

Phone search: See expedited services.

Fax search: Same criteria as phone searches.

In person search: Turnaround time 30 minutes.

Other access: The marriage index is available on microfiche for $50.00, the set includes the years 1964-1998.

Expedited service: Expedited service is available for mail, phone and fax searches. Turnaround time: overnight delivery. Add $17.50 for express delivery plus the credit card surcharge.

Divorce Records

Department of Human Resources, Vital Records Unit, 2600 Skyland Dr NE, Atlanta, GA 30319; 404-679-4701, 877-572-6343 (Credit Card Line), 404-679-4730-Fax; 8AM-4:45PM.

http://health.state.ga.us/programs/vitalrecords/index.asp

Divorce records are found at the county of issue. However, this agency will do search to identify the county of record and issue a certificate, but cannot issue a copy of the original record. Certified copies are only available at the county level.

Records are available 1952.

Access by: mail, phone, fax, in person.

Fee & Payment: The fee is $10.00, $5.00 for a second copy. Credit card fee is $12.50 Fee payee: GA Department of Human Resources. Personal checks accepted. Major credit cards accepted.

Mail search: Records are available by mail.

Phone search: See expedited services.

Fax search: Same criteria as phone searches.

In person search: Search of index availability immediately.

Other access: Divorce microfiche indexes are available to the public, sold in complete set for the years 1919-1998 for $50.00.

Expedited service: Expedited service is available for fax and phone searches. Add $17.50 for express delivery plus the credit card use fee.

Workers' Compensation Records

State Board of Workers Compensation, 270 Peachtree St, NW, Atlanta, GA 30303-1299; 404-656-3875, 8AM-4:30PM.

www.sbwc.georgia.gov

Records are available from 1995. Records are maintained for 10 years. Records are indexed on inhouse computer.

Searching: Must have a court order signed by a judge to obtain records from this agency unless you are a party to the case. Include the following in your request-claimant name, Social Security Number.

Access by: mail.

Fee & Payment: The agency will bill for required fees. Fee payee: State Board of Workers Compensation. Personal checks accepted. No credit cards accepted.

Mail search: Turnaround time: 2 to 3 weeks. The fee is $25.00 for the first 10 pages plus $.50 per page for over 10 pages. Certification for a document is $25.00. No SASE is required. No fee for mail request.

Driver Records

Department of Driver Services, Driver's Services Section, MVR Unit, PO Box 80447, Conyers, GA 30013 (Courier address: 2206 East View Parkway, Conyers, GA 30013); 678-413-8441, 8AM-3:30PM.

www.dmvs.ga.gov

Copies of tickets are not available from a central depository. It is recommended you go directly to the issuing court.

Records are available for either a 3 year record or a 7 year record. Accident involvement is shown if the driver was cited. The driver's address is part of the record. It takes ten days or more before new records are available for inquiry.

Searching: Georgia has strict rules concerning driver record access. If an individual requests a driving record on another, the driver's notarized signature is needed (except for court subpoena). Large requesters must have "bulk-user certificates" on file. The driver's full name, DOB and license number are required. Direct questions to mvr@dmvs.ga.gov.

Access by: mail, in person, online.

Fee & Payment: $5.00 for a 3 year period; $7.00 for a 7 year period. Fee payee: Department of Motor Vehicle Safety Prepayment required. No credit cards or personal checks accepted.

Mail search: Turnaround time: 2 weeks. No SASE is required.

In person search: Walk-in requesters may receive up to three records while waiting, additional requests are processed overnight. Walk-in requests are also available at most driver's license offices.

Online search: Through the coordinated efforts of the GA Department of Motor Vehicle Safety and the Georgia Technology Authority, driving records are now available via the Internet for "certified users, including insurance, employers, and car rental companies. Requesters must complete several applications and user agreement forms. The fees are $5.00 for a three-year record and $7.00 for a seven-year record. For further information,   visit: https://online.dmvs.ga.gov/mvr/cert.asp.

Other access: Georgia no long offers magnetic tape processing for high volume users.

Expedited service: Has no regular policy for expediting requests.

Vehicle Ownership, Vehicle Identification

Department of Motor Vehicle Safety, Motor Vehicle Services - Research, PO Box 740381, Atlanta, GA 30374-0381; 404-362-6500, 404-362-2729-Fax; 8AM-4:30PM.

www.dmvs.ga.gov

Records are available from 2000 forward. New records are available for inquiry immediately. Records are normally destroyed after 5 years.

Searching: Records are not open to the general public and are restricted to authorized (notarized) agents or individuals, judgment creditor, tax collector, law enforcement officials, license dealers, etc. There is an online access mode for only GA licensed dealers. Include the following in your request-statement of reason for requests, fee; must be on letterhead. Records are only released to casual requesters with notarized consent of the subject

Access by: mail, in person, online.

Fee & Payment: Fees: $5.00 per record for VIN and title histories; $.50 for a title or tag search computer print-out. Certified tag or title record is $10.00. Lien information is considered part of the title history. There is a full charge for a "no record found." Fee payee: Department of Motor Vehicle Safety. Prepayment required. Personal checks accepted. No credit cards accepted.

Mail search: Turnaround time: 2 weeks. A SASE is requested.

In person search: Turnaround time is while you wait.

Online search: Online access available to Georgia dealers only; registration is required.

Expedited service: Will expedite if you provide a court date that indicates that the request must be received in a timely manner.

Accident Reports

Department of Motor Vehicle Safety, Accident Reporting Section, PO Box 80447, Conyers, GA 30013; 678-413-8647, 678-413-8584-Fax; 8AM-4:30PM.

Records are available for 10 years to present. It takes 30 days or less before new records are available for inquiry. Records are normally destroyed after 10 years.

Searching: Only persons involved in the accident or their legal representative may obtain a copy, unless the subject has given written permission. Include the following in your request-full name, date of accident, location of accident.

Access by: mail, in person.

Fee & Payment: The fee for a report is $5.00. There is no charge for a "no record found." Fee payee: Department of Motor Vehicle Safety. Prepayment required. Cash, money orders, certified checks, and cashier's checks are all accepted. No credit cards or personal checks accepted.

Mail search: Turnaround time: 1 week to 10 days. No SASE is required.

In person search: Request must be in writing. Turnaround time is within the hour.

Expedited service: Does not offer expedited service.

Vessel Ownership, Vessel Registration

Georgia Dept of Natural Resources, Boat Registration Office, PO Box 105310, Atlanta, Georgia 30348-5310; 770-414-3337, 770-414-3344-Fax; 8AM-4:30PM.

www.gadnr.org

Liens are at the county level and will not show on records at this location.

Records are available from 1986 to present. Records are indexed on microfiche from 1986 to 1993 and on computer from 1994 to present. All motorized boats must be registered. All sailboats 12 ft or longer must be registered. It takes 30-45 days before new records are available for inquiry.

Searching: Either the name, registration # or hull # must be submitted.

Access by: mail, phone, fax, in person.

Fee & Payment: There is no search fee.

Mail search: Turnaround time: 1 to 2 weeks. No SASE is required.

Phone search: Verification only.

Fax search: Same criteria as mail searching.

In person search: Simple requests may be processed while you wait.

Voter Registration

Secretary of State, Elections Division, 2 Martin Luther King Dr SE, Suite 1104, Atlanta, GA 30334; 404-656-2871, 888-265-1115, 404-651-9531-Fax; 8AM-5PM.

www.sos.state.ga.us/elections

Data entry to the database is done at the county level.

Records are available from 1995, on computer. Data is keyed in by county personnel onto the state computer. It takes minutes before new records are available for inquiry.

Searching: Records may be ordered as a flat file in ASCII format directly from the website. Include the following in your request-full name, Social Security Number if available, date of birth, phone number of requester. All requests must be in writing. Records may be requested at county level, also. The following data is not released: Social Security Numbers or bulk information or lists for commercial purposes.

Access by: mail, phone, fax, online.

Fee & Payment: There is no fee for individual requests. Copies are $.25 per page. There are fees to purchase the database, and these fees can be found at the website. Fee payee: Secretary of State Prepayment required. Personal checks accepted.

Mail search: Turnaround time: 3 to 5 business days. No SASE is required.

Phone search: Interactive phone service via the toll-free number provides district and precinct information.

Fax search: Fax searching of statutes is available.

Online search: Name and DOB needed to search registration information at the website. Go to "Poll Locator." The results will provide address and district-precinct information, no SSNs released.

Other access: CDs, Internet files, disks, and paper lists are available for purchase for non-commercial purposes. Look at the website for pricing.

GED Certificates

GED Testing Service, 1800 Century Pl #555, Atlanta, GA 30345; 404-679-1644, 8:30AM-4:30PM M-F.

www.dtae.org

It takes 4 to 6 weeks before new records are available for inquiry.

Searching: Include the following in your request-a signed release, name, year and location of test, date of birth, and Social Security Number.

Access by: mail, in person.

Fee & Payment: The fee for a verification or for a copy of a transcript is $5.00 per record. A duplicate diploma is $8.00. Fee payee: GED Testing Services. Prepayment required. Money orders are accepted. No credit cards accepted.

Mail search: Turnaround time: 2 weeks. No SASE is required.

In person search: Records may only be picked up between 12 noon to 4PM Tues. through Fri.

Hunting and Fishing License Information

Access to Records is Restricted.

Department of Natural Resources, Hunting & Fishing Licenses, 2189 Northlake Pkwy, Bldg 10, #108, Tucker, GA 30084; 770-414-3333, 770-414-3344-Fax; 8AM-4:30PM.

http://georgiawildlife.dnr.state.ga.us

The request must be in writing and cite that under the Georgia Open Records Act you request that a search be done. The database may not be current for non-resident licenses and license purchases made via the website.

Georgia State Licensing Agencies

For details about the agency responsible for licensing/certifying/registering an item below or in the Agency Quick Finder section, match an item's number with the number of the agency in the *Licensing Agency Information* section.

Georgia Licenses Searchable Online

Acupuncturist #23	www.medicalboard.state.ga.us/bdsearch/index.html
Air Conditioning Contr. #9	https://secure.sos.state.ga.us/myverification/
Architect #15	https://secure.sos.state.ga.us/myverification/
Athletic Agent #13	https://secure.sos.state.ga.us/myverification/
Athletic Trainer #16	https://secure.sos.state.ga.us/myverification/
Auctioneer/Auction Dealer #13	https://secure.sos.state.ga.us/myverification/
Audiologist #16	https://secure.sos.state.ga.us/myverification/
Bank #17	www.ganet.org/dbf/other_institutions.html
Barber/Barber Shop #19	https://secure.sos.state.ga.us/myverification/
Charity #26	www.sos.state.ga.us/securities/charitysearch.htm
Check Casher/Seller #17	www.ganet.org/dbf/other_institutions.html
Chiropractor #18	https://secure.sos.state.ga.us/myverification/
Cosmetologist/Cosmetology Shop #19	https://secure.sos.state.ga.us/myverification/
Counselor #10	https://secure.sos.state.ga.us/myverification/
Credit Union #17	www.ganet.org/dbf/other_institutions.html
Dentist / Dental Hygienist #20	https://secure.sos.state.ga.us/myverification/
Detox Specialist #23	www.medicalboard.state.ga.us/bdsearch/index.html
Dietitian #2	https://secure.sos.state.ga.us/myverification/
Drug Whlse/Retail/Mfg (Hospital) #31	www.ganet.org/dbf/other_institutions.html
EDP - Electronic Data Processor #17	https://secure.sos.state.ga.us/myverification/
Electrical Contractor #9	https://secure.sos.state.ga.us/myverification/
Embalmer #13	https://secure.sos.state.ga.us/myverification/
Engineer #11	https://secure.sos.state.ga.us/myverification/
Esthetician #19	https://secure.sos.state.ga.us/myverification/
Family Therapist #10	https://secure.sos.state.ga.us/myverification/
Forester #36	https://secure.sos.state.ga.us/myverification/
Funeral Director/Apprentice #13	https://secure.sos.state.ga.us/myverification/
Funeral Establishment #13	https://secure.sos.state.ga.us/myverification/
Geologist #29	https://secure.sos.state.ga.us/myverification/
Hearing Aid Dealer/Dispenser #21	https://secure.sos.state.ga.us/myverification/
Holding Company/Rep. Office #17	www.ganet.org/dbf/other_institutions.html
Insurance Adjuster #8	www.inscomm.state.ga.us/AGENTS/agentstatus.asp
Insurance Agent / Counselor #8	www.inscomm.state.ga.us/AGENTS/agentstatus.asp
Interior Designer #15	https://secure.sos.state.ga.us/myverification/
Landscape Architect #25	https://secure.sos.state.ga.us/myverification/
Lobbyist #22	www.ethics.state.ga.us
Lobbyist Organization #22	www.ethics.state.ga.us
Low Voltage Contractor #9	https://secure.sos.state.ga.us/myverification/
Manicurist #19	https://secure.sos.state.ga.us/myverification/
Marriage Counselor #10	https://secure.sos.state.ga.us/myverification/
Medical Doctor #23	www.medicalboard.state.ga.us/bdsearch/index.html
Mortgage Institution #17	www.ganet.org/dbf/mortgage.html
Nail Care #19	https://secure.sos.state.ga.us/myverification/
Notary Public #3	www.gsccca.org/search/notary/search.asp
Nuclear Pharmacist #31	https://secure.sos.state.ga.us/myverification/
Nurse-LPN #2	https://secure.sos.state.ga.us/myverification/
Nurse-RN #28	https://secure.sos.state.ga.us/myverification/
Nursing Home Administrator #16	https://secure.sos.state.ga.us/myverification/
Occupational Therapist/Assistant #2	https://secure.sos.state.ga.us/myverification/
Optician, Dispensing #21	https://secure.sos.state.ga.us/myverification/
Optometrist #21	https://secure.sos.state.ga.us/myverification/
Osteopathic Physician #23	www.medicalboard.state.ga.us/bdsearch/index.html
Perfusionist #23	www.medicalboard.state.ga.us/bdsearch/index.html
Pesticide Applicator #4	www.kellysolutions.com/ga/Applicators/index.htm
Pesticide Contr./Employee #4	www.kellysolutions.com/ga/Applicators/index.htm
Pharmacist #31	https://secure.sos.state.ga.us/myverification/
Pharmacy School, Clinic Researcher #31	https://secure.sos.state.ga.us/myverification/
Physical Therapist/Therapist Asst #2	https://secure.sos.state.ga.us/myverification/
Physician Assistant #23	www.medicalboard.state.ga.us/bdsearch/index.html
Plumber Journeyman/Contractor #9	https://secure.sos.state.ga.us/myverification/

Podiatrist #33 .... https://secure.sos.state.ga.us/myverification/
Poison Pharmacist #31 .... https://secure.sos.state.ga.us/myverification/
Private Detective #13 .... https://secure.sos.state.ga.us/myverification/
Psychologist #16 .... https://secure.sos.state.ga.us/myverification/
Public Accountant-CPA #14 .... https://secure.sos.state.ga.us/myverification/
Public Adjuster #8 .... www.inscomm.state.ga.us/AGENTS/agentstatus.asp
Real Estate Agent/Saller #27 .... www.grec.state.ga.us/clsweb/realestate.aspx
Real Estate Appraiser #27 .... www.grec.state.ga.us/clsweb/appraiser.aspx
Real Estate Broker #27 .... www.grec.state.ga.us/clsweb/realestate.aspx
Real Estate Community Assn. Mgr. #27 .... www.grec.state.ga.us
Rebuilder (Motor Vehicle) #13 .... https://secure.sos.state.ga.us/myverification/
Respiratory Care Practitioner #23 .... www.medicalboard.state.ga.us/bdsearch/index.html
Salvage Pool Operator #13 .... https://secure.sos.state.ga.us/myverification/
Salvage Yard Dealer #13 .... https://secure.sos.state.ga.us/myverification/
School Librarian #12 .... https://secure.sos.state.ga.us/myverification/
Security Guard/Agency #13 .... https://secure.sos.state.ga.us/myverification/
Social Worker #10 .... https://secure.sos.state.ga.us/myverification/
Speech-Language Pathologist #16 .... https://secure.sos.state.ga.us/myverification/
Surplus Line Broker #8 .... www.inscomm.state.ga.us/AGENTS/agentstatus.asp
Surveyor, Land #11 .... https://secure.sos.state.ga.us/myverification/
Teacher #7 .... https://www.gapsc.com/certification/lookup.asp
Used Car Dealer / Car Parts Dist. #13 .... https://secure.sos.state.ga.us/myverification/
Utility Contractor #9 .... https://secure.sos.state.ga.us/myverification/
Veterinarian/Veterinary Technician #37 .... https://secure.sos.state.ga.us/myverification/
Waste Water System Operator #24 .... https://secure.sos.state.ga.us/myverification/
Waste Water Laboratory Analyst #24 .... https://secure.sos.state.ga.us/myverification/
Water Distribution System Operator #24 .... https://secure.sos.state.ga.us/myverification/
Water Laboratory Operator #24 .... https://secure.sos.state.ga.us/myverification/
Water Operator Class 1-4 #24 .... https://secure.sos.state.ga.us/myverification/

Georgia Licensing Quick Finder

Acupuncturist #23 404-657-6490
Air Conditioning Contr. #9 478-207-1416
Amusement Ride Inspector #32 404-679-0687
Animal Technician #37 478-207-1686
Architect #15 478-207-1401
Athletic Agent #13 478-207-1460
Athletic Trainer #16 478-207-1670
Attorney #30 404-527-8700
Auctioneer/Auction Dealer #13 478-207-1460
Audiologist #16 478-207-1670
Bank #17 770-986-1633
Barber/Barber Shop #19 478-207-1430
Cemetery #26 404-656-3920
Charity #26 404-656-3920
Check Casher/Seller #17 770-986-1633
Chiropractor #18 478-207-1686
Coin-operated Machine #6 404-417-4490
Cosmetologist/Cosmetology Shop #19 478-207-1430
Counselor #10 478-207-1670
Court Reporter #1 404-656-6422
Credit Union #17 770-986-1637
Dental Hygienist #20 478-207-1686
Dentist #20 478-207-1686
Detox Specialist #23 404-656-3913
Dietitian #2 478-207-1620
Drug Whlse/Retail/Mfg (Hospital) #31 .. 478-207-1686
EDP - Electronic Data Processor #17 .. 770-986-1633
Electrical Contractor #9 478-207-1416
Embalmer #13 478-207-1460
Emergency Medical Technician #34 404-679-0547
Engineer #11 478-207-1450
Esthetician #19 478-207-1430
Family Therapist #10 478-207-1670
Forester #36 478-207-1401
Funeral Director/Apprentice #13 478-207-1460
Funeral Establishment #13 478-207-1460
Geologist #29 478-207-1401
Hearing Aid Dealer/Dispenser #21 478-207-1686
Holding Company/Representative Office #17
.... 770-986-1633

Insurance Adjuster #8 404-656-2101
Insurance Agent #8 404-656-2101
Insurance Counselor #8 404-656-2101
Interior Designer #15 478-207-1401
Investment Advisor (Firm) #26 404-656-3920
Landfill Inspector/Operator #5 404-362-2696
Landscape Architect #25 478-207-1401
Liquor Control #6 404-417-4490
Lobbyist #22 404-463-1980
Lobbyist Organization #22 404-463-1980
Low Voltage Contractor #9 478-207-1416
Manicurist #19 478-207-1430
Marriage Counselor #10 478-207-1670
Medical Doctor #23 404-657-6489
Mortgage Institution #17 770-986-1269
Nail Care #19 478-207-1430
Notary Public #3 404-327-6023
Nuclear Pharmacist #31 478-207-1686
Nurse-LPN #2 478-207-1620
Nurse-RN #28 478-207-1640
Nursing Home Administrator #16 478-207-1670
Occupational Therapist/Assistant #2 .. 478-207-1620
Optician, Dispensing #21 478-207-1686
Optometrist #21 478-207-1686
Osteopathic Physician #23 404-657-6489
Perfusionist #23 404-463-2292
Pesticide Applicator #4 404-656-4958
Pesticide Contr./Employee #4 404-656-4958
Pharmacist #31 478-207-1686
Pharmacy School, Clinic Researcher #31
.... 478-207-1686
Physical Therapist/Therapist Asst #2 .. 478-207-1620
Physician Assistant #23 404-657-4688
Plumber Journeyman/Contr. #9 478-207-1416
Podiatrist #33 478-207-1686
Poison Pharmacist #31 478-207-1686
Private Detective #13 478-207-1460
Psychologist #16 478-207-1670
Public Accountant-CPA #14 478-207-1401
Public Adjuster #8 404-656-2101

Real Estate Agent/Sales #27 404-656-3916
Real Estate Appraiser #27 404-656-3916
Real Estate Broker #27 404-656-3916
Real Estate Community Assn. Mgr. #27 404-656-3916
Rebuilder (Motor Vehicle) #13 478-207-1460
Respiratory Care Practitioner #23 404-656-3914
Salvage Pool Operator #13 478-207-1460
Salvage Yard Dealer #13 478-207-1460
School Administrator/Supervisor #7 ... 404-657-9000
School Bus Driver #35 678-413-8400
School Counselor #7 404-657-9000
School Librarian #12 478-207-1401
School Media Specialist #7 404-657-9000
School Social Worker #7 404-657-9000
Securities Salesperson/Dealer #26 404-656-3920
Security Guard/Agency #13 478-207-1460
Shorthand Court Reprtr/Stenomask #1. 404-656-6422
Social Worker #10 478-207-1670
Speech-Language Pathologist #16 478-207-1670
Surplus Line Broker #8 404-656-2101
Surveyor, Land #11 478-207-1450
Teacher #7 404-657-9000
Timber Dealer/Processor #4 404-656-4958
Tobacco Seller #6 404-417-4490
Truck Driver #35 678-413-8400
Used Car Dealer #13 478-207-1460
Used Car Parts Dist. #13 478-207-1460
Utility Contractor #9 478-207-1416
Veterinarian/Veterinary Technician #37 478-207-1686
Veterinary Faculty #37 478-207-1686
Waste Water Collection System Operator #24
.... 912-207-1460
Waste Water Industrial Operator #24 . 912-207-1460
Waste Water Laboratory Analyst #24 .. 912-207-1460
Waste Water Operator 1-4 #24 912-207-1460
Water Distribution System Op. #24 912-207-1460
Water Laboratory Operator #24 912-207-1460
Water Operator Class 1-4 #24 912-207-1460

1 Clerk of the Board, Board of Court Reporting, 244 Washington St SW, #300, Atlanta, GA 30334; 404-656-6422, Fax: 404-651-6449. www.georgiacourts.org/agencies/bcr Email: reisss@gaaoc.us

2 Examining Boards Division, Board of Examiners of Licensed Practical Nurses, 237 Coliseum Dr, Macon, GA 31217; 478-207-1620, Fax: 478-207-1633. www.sos.state.ga.us/plb/lpn Search Database at https://secure.sos.state.ga.us/myverification/

3 Clerks Authority, Notary Public Division, 1875 Century Blvd #100, Atlanta, GA 30345; 404-327-6023, Fax: 404-327-7887. www.gsccca.or g/Projects/aboutnp.asp Search Database at www.gsccca.org/search/notary/search.asp

4 Department of Agriculture, Pesticide Division, 19 MLK Jr. Dr, SW, Rm 550, Atlanta, GA 30334; 404-656-4958, Fax: 404-657-8378. www.agr.state.ga.us Search Database at www.kellysolutions.com/ga/Applicators/index.htm

5 Dept of Natural Resources, Environmental Protection Division, 4244 International Pky, #104, Atlanta, GA 30354; 404-362-2696, Fax: 404-362-2693. www.state.ga.us/dnr/environ/

6 Department of Revenue, Centralized Taxpayer Regis., 1800 Century Center RL NE, PO Box 49512, Atlanta, GA 30359-1512; 404-417-4490.

7 Georgia Professional Standards Commission, Teacher Certification, 2 PeachTree St. #6000, Atlanta, GA 30303; 404-657-9000. www.gapsc.com/teachercertification.asp Note: To check teacher status, the SSN is required.

8 Licensing Division, Insurance Commissioner's Office, 2 Martin Luther King Jr Dr, West Tower, #908, Atlanta, GA 30334; 404-656-2101, Fax: 404-656-0874. www.gainsurance.org Search Database at www.inscomm.state.g a.us/AGENTS/agentstatus.asp

9 State Construction Industry Licensing Board, 237 Coliseum Dr, Macon, GA 31217; 478-207-1416, Fax: 478-207-1425. www.sos.state.ga.us/plb/construct Email: ckhouser@sos.state.ga.us Search Database at https://secure.sos.state.ga.us/myverification/ Note: They sell rosters for $25.00.

10 Examining Boards Division, Board of Prof. Counselors, Social Workers, & Marriage/Family Therapists, 237 Coliseum Dr, Macon, GA 31217; 478-207-1670, Fax: 478-207-1676. www.sos.state.ga.us/plb/counselors Search at https://secure.sos.state.ga.us/myverification/

11 Examining Boards Division, Professional Engineers & Land Surveyors Board, 237 Coliseum Dr, Macon, GA 31217-3858; 478-207-1450, Fax: 478-207-1456. www.sos.state.ga.us/plb/pels/ Email: pels@sos.state.ga.us Search Database at https://secure.sos.state.ga.us/m yverification/ Note: They sell rosters for $25.00.

12 Examining Boards Division, Board for the Cert. of Librarians, 237 Coliseum Dr, Macon, GA 31217-3858; 478-207-1400, Fax: 478-207-1410. www.sos.state.ga.us/plb/librarians Search at https://secure.sos.state.ga.us/myverification/

13 Professional Licensing, Licensing Boards, 237 Coliseum Dr, Macon, GA 31217; 478-207-1460, Fax: 478-207-1468.

www.sos.state.ga.us/plb Search Database at https://secure.sos.state.ga.us/myverification/

14 Examining Boards Division, Board of Accountancy, 237 Coliseum Dr, Macon, GA 31217-3858; 478-207-1400, Fax: 478-207-1410. www.sos.state.ga.us/plb/accountancy Search Database at https://secure.sos.state.ga.us/myverification/

15 Examining Boards Division, Board of Architects and Interior Designers, 237 Coliseum Dr, Macon, GA 31217; 478-207-1400, Fax: 478-207-1410. www.sos.state.ga.us/a rchitects Search Database at https://secure.sos.state.ga.us/myverification/

16 Examining Boards Division, State Examining Board-Medical, 237 Coliseum Dr, Macon, GA 31217; 478-207-1670, Fax: 478-207-1676. www.sos.state.ga.us/plb/ Search Database at https://secure.sos.state.ga.us/myverification/

17 Dept of Banking and Finance, Regulated Institutions, 2990 Brandywine Rd #200, Atlanta, GA 30341; 770-986-1633, Fax: 770-986-1654. www.ganet.org/dbf/dbf.html Search Database at www.ganet.org/dbf/regulated_institutions.html

18 Examining Boards Division, Board of Chiropractic Examiners, 237 Coliseum Dr, Macon, GA 31217; 478-207-1686, Fax: 478-207-1699. www.sos.state.ga.us/plb/chiro Search Database at https://secure.sos.state.ga.us/myverification/

19 Examining Boards Division, Board of Cosmetology, 237 Coliseum Drive, Macon, GA 31217; 478-207-1430, Fax: 478-207-1442. www.sos.state.ga.us/plb/barber_cosmet Search at https://secure.sos.state.ga.us/myverification/

20 Examining Boards Division, Board of Dentistry, 237 Coliseum Drive, Macon, GA 31217-3858; 478-207-1686, Fax: 478-207-1699. www.sos.state.ga.us/plb/dentistry Search at https://secure.sos.state.ga.us/myverification/

21 Examining Boards Division, Board of Hearing Aid Dispensers, Board of Dispensing Opticians, Examiners in Optometry, 237 Coliseum Dr, Macon, GA 31217; 478-207-1686, Fax: 478-207-1699. www.sos.state.ga.us/plb/opticians Search at https://secure.sos.state.ga.us/myverification/

22 State Ethics Commission, 205 Jesse Hill Jr Dr, #478 East Tower, Atlanta, GA 30334; 404-463-1980, Fax: 404-463-1988. www.ethics.state.ga.us Email: ethics@ethics.state.ga.us Search Database at www.ethics.state.ga.us At the website, choose type of Lobbyist lists to examine.

23 Examining Boards Division, Composite Board of Medical Examiners, 2 Peachtree St, 10th Fl, Atlanta, GA 30303; 404-656-3913, Fax: 404-656-9723. www.medicalboard.state.ga.us Search Database at www.medicalboard.state.g a.us/bdsearch/index.html

24 Examining Boards Division, Water & Wastewater Treatment Plant Operators & Laboratory Analysts, 237 Coliseum Dr, Macon, GA 31217; 404-207-1460, Fax: 404-207-1468. www.sos.state.ga.us/plb/water Search Database at https://secure.sos.state .ga.us/myverification/ Note: Verification Letter from Board $25.00 fee, https://www.sos.state.ga.u s/plb/water/download-forms.htm. For Excel format "Roster Request Form".

25 Examining Boards Division, Board of Landscape Architects, 237 Coliseum Dr, Macon, GA 31217-3858; 478-207-1400, Fax: 478-207-1410. www.sos.state.ga.us/plb/landscape Search Database at https://secure.sos.state.ga.us/myverification/

26 Securities & Business Regulation, Office of Secretary of State, 2 Martin Luther King Jr Dr, West Tower, #802, Atlanta, GA 30334-1530; 404-656-3920, Fax: 404-657-8410. www.sos.state.ga.us/securities Email: securities@sos.state.ga.us Search Database at www.sos.state.ga.us/securities

27 Real Estate Commission/Appraiser Board, 229 Peachtree St NE, International Tower, #1000, Atlanta, GA 30303-1605; 404-656-3916, Fax: 404-656-6650. www.grec.state.ga.us Email: grecmail@grec.state.ga.us Real estate companies to be on main website soon; click on Consumer Information. Also search for appraisers www.asc.gov/content/category1/appr_by_state.asp

28 Examining Boards Division, Board of Nursing, 237 Coliseum Dr, Macon, GA 30217-3858; 478-207-1640, Fax: 478-207-1660. www.sos.state.ga.us/plb/rn Search Database at https://secure.sos.state.ga.us/myverification/

29 Examining Boards Division, Board of Registration for Professional Geologists, 237 Coliseum Dr, Macon, GA 31217-3858; 478-207-1400, Fax: 478-207-1410. www.sos.state.ga.us/plb/geologists/ Search Database at https://secure.sos.state.ga.us/myverification/

30 State Bar of Georgia, 104 Marietta St NW #100, Atlanta, GA 30303; 404-527-8700, Fax: 404-527-8717. www.gabar.org

31 Examining Boards Division, Board of Pharmacy, 237 Coliseum Dr, Macon, GA 31217; 478-207-1686, Fax: 478-207-1699. www.sos.state.ga.us/plb/pharmacy Search at https://secure.sos.state.ga.us/myverification/

32 Department of Labor, Safety Engineering Division, 1700 Century Circle NE, Atlanta, GA 30345; 404-679-0687, Fax: 404-679-5818. www.dol.state.ga.us/

33 Examining Boards Division, Board of Podiatry Examiners, 237 Coliseum Dr, Macon, GA 31217; 478-207-1676, Fax: 478-207-1699. www.sos.state.ga.us/plb/podiatry Search data at https://secure.sos.state.ga.us/myverification/

34 Emergency Medical Svcs, 2600 Skyland Dr, Atlanta, GA 30319; 404-679-0547, Fax: 404-679-0526. www.health.state.ga.us/

35 Department of Public Safety, Department of Driver Services, PO Box 80447, Atlanta, GA 30013; 678-413-8400. www.state.ga.us/gsp/

36 Examining Boards Division, Board of Regis. for Foresters, 237 Coliseum Dr, Macon, GA 31217; 478-207-1400, Fax: 478-207-1410. www.sos.state.ga.us/plb/foresters Search at https://secure.sos.state.ga.us/myverification/

37 Examining Boards Division, Board of Veterinary Medicine, 237 Coliseum Dr, Macon, GA 31217; 478-207-1686, Fax: 478-207-1699. www.sos.state.ga.us/plb/veterinary Search at https://secure.sos.state.ga.us/myverification/

Georgia Federal Courts

The following list indicates the district and division name for each county in the state. If the bankruptcy court location is different from the district court, then the location of the bankruptcy court appears in parentheses.

County/Court Cross Reference

County	District	Division
Appling	Southern	Brunswick (Savannah)
Atkinson	Southern	Waycross (Savannah)
Bacon	Southern	Waycross (Savannah)
Baker	Middle	Albany/Americus (Macon)
Baldwin	Middle	Macon
Banks	Northern	Gainesville
Barrow	Northern	Gainesville
Bartow	Northern	Rome
Ben Hill	Middle	Albany/Americus (Macon)
Berrien	Middle	Valdosta (Columbus)
Bibb	Middle	Macon
Bleckley	Middle	Macon
Brantley	Southern	Waycross (Savannah)
Brooks	Middle	Thomasville (Columbus)
Bryan	Southern	Savannah
Bulloch	Southern	Statesboro (Augusta)
Burke	Southern	Augusta
Butts	Middle	Macon
Calhoun	Middle	Albany/Americus (Macon)
Camden	Southern	Brunswick (Savannah)
Candler	Southern	Statesboro (Augusta)
Carroll	Northern	Newnan
Catoosa	Northern	Rome
Charlton	Southern	Waycross (Savannah)
Chatham	Southern	Savannah
Chattahoochee	Middle	Columbus
Chattooga	Northern	Rome
Cherokee	Northern	Atlanta
Clarke	Middle	Athens (Macon)
Clay	Middle	Columbus
Clayton	Northern	Atlanta
Clinch	Middle	Valdosta (Columbus)
Cobb	Northern	Atlanta
Coffee	Southern	Waycross (Savannah)
Colquitt	Middle	Thomasville (Columbus)
Columbia	Southern	Augusta
Cook	Middle	Valdosta (Columbus)
Coweta	Northern	Newnan
Crawford	Middle	Macon
Crisp	Middle	Albany/Americus (Macon)
Dade	Northern	Rome
Dawson	Northern	Gainesville
De Kalb	Northern	Atlanta
Decatur	Middle	Thomasville (Columbus)
Dodge	Southern	Dublin (Augusta)
Dooly	Middle	Macon
Dougherty	Middle	Albany/Americus (Macon)
Douglas	Northern	Atlanta
Early	Middle	Albany/Americus (Macon)
Echols	Middle	Valdosta (Columbus)
Effingham	Southern	Savannah
Elbert	Middle	Athens (Macon)
Emanuel	Southern	Statesboro (Augusta)
Evans	Southern	Statesboro (Augusta)
Fannin	Northern	Gainesville
Fayette	Northern	Newnan
Floyd	Northern	Rome
Forsyth	Northern	Gainesville
Franklin	Middle	Athens (Macon)
Fulton	Northern	Atlanta
Gilmer	Northern	Gainesville
Glascock	Southern	Augusta
Glynn	Southern	Brunswick (Savannah)
Gordon	Northern	Rome
Grady	Middle	Thomasville (Columbus)
Greene	Middle	Athens (Macon)
Gwinnett	Northern	Atlanta
Habersham	Northern	Gainesville
Hall	Northern	Gainesville
Hancock	Middle	Macon
Haralson	Northern	Newnan
Harris	Middle	Columbus
Hart	Middle	Athens (Macon)
Heard	Northern	Newnan
Henry	Northern	Atlanta
Houston	Middle	Macon
Irwin	Middle	Valdosta (Columbus)
Jackson	Northern	Gainesville
Jasper	Middle	Macon
Jeff Davis	Southern	Brunswick (Savannah)
Jefferson	Southern	Augusta
Jenkins	Southern	Statesboro (Augusta)
Johnson	Southern	Dublin (Augusta)
Jones	Middle	Macon
Lamar	Middle	Macon
Lanier	Middle	Valdosta (Columbus)
Laurens	Southern	Dublin (Augusta)
Lee	Middle	Albany/Americus (Macon)
Liberty	Southern	Savannah
Lincoln	Southern	Augusta
Long	Southern	Brunswick (Savannah)
Lowndes	Middle	Valdosta (Columbus)
Lumpkin	Northern	Gainesville
Macon	Middle	Macon
Madison	Middle	Athens (Macon)
Marion	Middle	Columbus
McDuffie	Southern	Augusta
McIntosh	Southern	Brunswick (Savannah)
Meriwether	Northern	Newnan
Miller	Middle	Albany/Americus (Macon)
Mitchell	Middle	Albany/Americus (Macon)
Monroe	Middle	Macon
Montgomery	Southern	Dublin (Augusta)
Morgan	Middle	Athens (Macon)
Murray	Northern	Rome
Muscogee	Middle	Columbus
Newton	Northern	Atlanta
Oconee	Middle	Athens (Macon)
Oglethorpe	Middle	Athens (Macon)
Paulding	Northern	Rome

Peach	Middle	Macon
Pickens	Northern	Gainesville
Pierce	Southern	Waycross (Savannah)
Pike	Northern	Newnan
Polk	Northern	Rome
Pulaski	Middle	Macon
Putnam	Middle	Macon
Quitman	Middle	Columbus
Rabun	Northern	Gainesville
Randolph	Middle	Columbus
Richmond	Southern	Augusta
Rockdale	Northern	Atlanta
Schley	Middle	Albany/Americus (Macon)
Screven	Southern	Statesboro (Augusta)
Seminole	Middle	Thomasville (Columbus)
Spalding	Northern	Newnan
Stephens	Northern	Gainesville
Stewart	Middle	Columbus
Sumter	Middle	Albany/Americus (Macon)
Talbot	Middle	Columbus
Taliaferro	Southern	Augusta
Tattnall	Southern	Statesboro (Augusta)
Taylor	Middle	Columbus
Telfair	Southern	Dublin (Augusta)
Terrell	Middle	Albany/Americus (Macon)

Thomas	Middle	Thomasville (Columbus)
Tift	Middle	Valdosta (Columbus)
Toombs	Southern	Statesboro (Augusta)
Towns	Northern	Gainesville
Treutlen	Southern	Dublin (Augusta)
Troup	Northern	Newnan
Turner	Middle	Albany/Americus (Macon)
Twiggs	Middle	Macon
Union	Northern	Gainesville
Upson	Middle	Macon
Walker	Northern	Rome
Walton	Middle	Athens (Macon)
Ware	Southern	Waycross (Savannah)
Warren	Southern	Augusta
Washington	Middle	Macon
Wayne	Southern	Brunswick (Savannah)
Webster	Middle	Albany/Americus (Macon)
Wheeler	Southern	Dublin (Augusta)
White	Northern	Gainesville
Whitfield	Northern	Rome
Wilcox	Middle	Macon
Wilkes	Southern	Augusta
Wilkinson	Middle	Macon
Worth	Middle	Albany/Americus (Macon)

Standards for Federal Courts: Search fee is $26.00 per item (one party name or case number). Copy fee is $.50 per page. Certification fee is $9.00 per document, double for exemplification, if available. All fees standard unless noted in profile. Mail Search: always enclose a stamped self addressed envelope unless otherwise noted. Most courts accept fax requests or will suggest a copying/search vendor. Before releasing records, all courts require prepayment, unless noted.

Open records are located at the court unless otherwise noted. District courts index by defendant and plaintiff as well as by case number. Bankruptcy courts usually index by debtor and case number. While most courts now have their indexes on computer, many may still maintain index card files as well.

Courts offering internet access via CM-ECF or older RACER, PACER, or Web-PACER systems charge $.08 per page fee unless noted as free. Where PACER is available, the universal sign-up number is 800-676-6856. Find PACER and the US Party/Case Index at http://pacer.psc.uscourts.gov.

US District Court

Middle District of Georgia

Albany/Americus Division Court Clerk, 201 W Broad Ave, Albany, GA 31701 (also use mail address for courier delivery), 229-430-8432, Fax-229-430-8538. Hours- 8:30AM-5PM. www.gamd.uscourts.gov

Counties: Baker, Ben Hill, Calhoun, Crisp, Dougherty, Early, Lee, Miller, Mitchell, Schley, Sumter, Terrell, Turner, Webster, Worth. Ben Hill and Crisp were transferred from the Macon Division as of 10/1997.

Searches & Indexing: Results do not include SSN or DOB. Both computer and card indexes maintained; on computer back to 1991 New cases in the index immediately after filing date. Records purged never. District-wide searches available for files after 1/91.

Fee & Payment: Pay by money order, cashier check, in-state business check. No personal checks. Payee: Clerk, USDC. Prepayment required.

Phone Search: Only docket information is available by phone.

Mail Search: search usually completed- 24 hours. Include SASE for return.

In Person Search: Fee charged if court performs your search. No self-serve copier available.

E-Services: ECF replaces PACER whose records did go back to 1/1991. New records online after 1 day. ECF at www.gamd.uscourts.gov/CMECF.htm

Athens Division Court Clerk, PO Box 1106, Athens, GA 30603 (courier address: 115 E Hancock Ave, Athens, GA 30601), 706-227-1094, Fax-706-546-2190. Hours- 8:30AM-5PM. www.gamd.uscourts.gov

Counties: Clarke, Elbert, Franklin, Greene, Hart, Madison, Morgan, Oconee, Oglethorpe, Walton. Closed cases before 4/1997 are located in the Macon Division.

Searches & Indexing: Results do not include SSN or DOB. Both computer and card indexes maintained; computer back to 1990. New cases in the index 2 days after filing date. Records purged never.

Fee & Payment: Pay by Visa/MC/AmEx/ Discover, money order, cashier check, business check. No personal checks. Payee: US District Court.

Phone Search: No searching by telephone.

Mail Search: search usually completed- 1 day. Include SASE for return.

In Person Search: Fee charged if court performs your search. No self-serve copier available.

E-Services: ECF replaces PACER whose records did go back to 1/1991. New records online after 1 day. ECF at www.gamd.uscourts.gov/CMECF.htm

Columbus Division Court Clerk, PO Box 124, Columbus, GA 31902 (courier address: Rm 216, 120 12th St, Columbus, GA 31901), 706-649-7816. 8:30AM-4:30PM. www.gamd.uscourts.gov

Counties: Chattahoochee, Clay, Harris, Marion, Muscogee, Quitman, Randolph, Stewart, Talbot, Taylor.

Searches & Indexing: Results do not include SSN or DOB. Both computer and card indexes maintained. New cases in the index immediately after filing date. Records purged never.

Fee & Payment: Pay by Visa/MC/AmEx/ Discover, money order, cashier check, business check. No personal checks. Payee: Clerk, US Courts. Prepayment required.

Phone Search: Only docket information is available by phone.

Mail Search: search usually completed- 2 days. Include SASE for return.

In Person Search: Fee charged if court performs your search. No self-serve copier available.

E-Services: ECF replaces PACER whose records did go back to 1/1991. New records online after 1 day. ECF at www.gamd.uscourts.gov/CMECF.htm

Macon Division Court Clerk, PO Box 128, Macon, GA 31202-0128 (courier address: 475 Mulberry, Suite 216, Macon, GA 31201), 478-752-3497, Fax-478-752-3496. Hours- 8AM-5PM. www.gamd.uscourts.gov

Counties: Baldwin, Ben Hill, Bibb, Bleckley, Butts, Crawford, Crisp, Dooly, Hancock, Houston, Jasper, Jones, Lamar, Macon, Monroe, Peach, Pulaski, Putnam, Twiggs, Upson, Washington, Wilcox, Wilkinson. Athens Division cases closed before 4/1997 are also located here.

Searches & Indexing: Results include last 4 SSN digits, also birth year. Both computer and card indexes maintained. New cases in the index immediately after filing date. Records purged never. Records after 1/91 can be searched from any court in this district.

Fee & Payment: Pay by money order, cashier check, business check. No personal checks. Payee: US Courts. Will fax documents $3.00 per page.

Phone Search: Only docket information is available by phone.

Mail Search: search usually completed- 2 days. Include SASE for return.

In Person Search: Fee charged if court performs your search. No self-serve copier available.

E-Services: ECF replaces PACER whose records did go back to 1/1991. New records online after 1 day. ECF at www.gamd.uscourts.gov/CMECF.htm

Thomasville Division c/o Valdosta Division, PO Box 68, Valdosta, GA 31601 (courier address: Rm 212, 401 N Patterson, Valdosta, GA 31603), 229-226-3651; 229-242-3616 Valdosta, Fax-229-244-9547. 8AM-5PM. www.gamd.uscourts.gov

Counties: Brooks, Colquitt, Decatur, Grady, Seminole, Thomas. No criminal cases can be searched at this court, but trials held at Valdosta; see Macon Division for records.

Searches & Indexing: Cases indexed by and case number. Results do not include SSN or DOB. Records purged never. Open records located at Valdosta Division.

Fee & Payment: Pay by Visa/MC/AmEx/ Discover, money order, cashier's, business or personal check.

Phone Search: No searching by telephone.

Mail Search: search usually completed- 48 hours. Include SASE for return.

In Person Search: permitted. No self-serve copier available.

E-Services: ECF replaces PACER whose records did go back to 1/1991. New records online after 1 day. ECF at www.gamd.uscourts.gov/CMECF.htm

Valdosta Division Court Clerk, PO Box 68, Valdosta, GA 31603 (courier address: Rm 212, 401 N Patterson, Valdosta, GA 31601), 229-242-3616, Fax-229-244-9547. Hours- 8AM-5PM. www.gamd.uscourts.gov

Counties: Berrien, Clinch, Cook, Echols, Irwin, Lanier, Lowndes, Tift. No criminal cases can be

searched at this court, but trials held at Valdosta; see Macon Division for records.

Searches & Indexing: Results do not include SSN or DOB. Computer index maintained. New cases in the index immediately after filing date. Records purged never.

Fee & Payment: Pay by Visa/MC/AmEx/ Discover, money order, cashier's, business or personal check. Payee: US Courts. Prepayment required.

Phone Search: Docket data available by phone.

Mail Search: search usually completed- 24 hours. SASE not required.

In Person Search: Fee charged if court performs your search. Self-serve copier available - - current fee is not known - per page.

E-Services: ECF replaces PACER whose records did go back to 1/1991. New records online after 1 day. ECF at www.gamd.uscourts.gov/CMECF.htm

US Bankruptcy Court

Middle District of Georgia

Columbus Division Court Clerk, PO Box 2147, Columbus, GA 31902 (courier address: 901 Front Ave, 1 Arsenal Pl, Columbus, GA 31902), 706-649-7837, Fax-706-649-7845. Hours- 8:30AM-5PM. www.gamb.uscourts.gov

Counties: Berrien, Brooks, Chattahoochee, Clay, Clinch, Colquitt, Cook, Decatur, Echols, Grady, Harris, Irwin, Lanier, Lowndes, Marion, Muscogee, Quitman, Randolph, Seminole, Stewart, Talbot, Taylor, Thomas, Tift. This court has records for the Thomasville and Valdosta branches, also Chapter 11 & 12 records for the Albany branch.

Searches & Indexing: Include any alias names for debtor in search request. Results include last 4 SSN digits. Computer index maintained. New cases in the index immediately after filing date. Records purged every 12 months.

Fee & Payment: Pay by money order, cashier check, business check. No personal checks. Payee: Clerk, Bankruptcy Court. Prepayment required.

Phone Search: Docket information available by phone. Voice Case Information Service available, call VCIS at 800-211-3015 or 912-752-8183.

Mail Search: search usually completed- 2-3 days. Include SASE for return.

In Person Search: Fee charged if court performs your search. No self-serve copier available.

E-Services: PACER online at http://pacer.gamb.uscourts.gov. PACER records go back to 3/1990, some back to 1985. New records online after 1 day. ECF at https://ecf.gamb.uscourts.gov. May not be complete, as yet; read disclaimer at ECF site. **Opinions Online:** www.gamb.uscourts.gov/opinions.htm. **Other Online Access:** Calendars free at www.gamb.uscourts.gov/cgi-bin/crtcals.cgi.

Macon Division Court Clerk, PO Box 1957, Macon, GA 31201 (courier address: 433 Cherry St, Macon, GA 31202), 478-752-3506, Fax-478-752-8157. Hours- 8:30AM-5PM. www.gamb.uscourts.gov

Counties: Baldwin, Baker, Ben Hill, Bibb, Bleckley, Butts, Calhoun, Clarke, Crawford, Crisp, Dooly, Dougherty, Early, Elbert, Franklin, Greene,

Hancock, Hart, Houston, Jasper, Jones, Lamar, Lee, Macon, Madison, Miller, Mitchell, Monroe, Morgan, Oconee, Oglethorpe, Peach, Pulaski, Putnam, Schley, Sumter, Terrell, Turner, Twiggs, Upson, Walton, Washington, Webster, Wilcox, Wilkinson, Worth. This court has records for the Athens branch as well as Chapter 7 & 13 records from the Albany branch. This branch also has criminal records for Valdosta and Thomasville Divisions.

Searches & Indexing: Include any alias names for debtor in search request. Results include last 4 SSN digits. Computer index maintained. New cases in the index 1-2 days after filing date.

Fee & Payment: Pay by money order, cashier check, business check. No personal checks. Payee: Clerk, US Bankruptcy Court. Prepayment required.

Phone Search: This court will only search for basic information by phone; limit is 3 searches per phone call. Voice Case Information Service available, call VCIS at 800-211-3015 or 478-752-8183.

Mail Search: search usually completed- 5 days. Include SASE for return.

In Person Search: Fee charged if court performs your search. No self-serve copier available.

E-Services: PACER online at http://pacer.gamb.uscourts.gov. PACER records go back to 3/1990, some back to 1985. New records online after 1 day. ECF at https://ecf.gamb.uscourts.gov. May not be complete, as yet; read disclaimer at ECF site. **Opinions Online:** www.gamb.uscourts.gov/opinions.htm. **Other Online Access:** Calendars free at www.gamb.uscourts.gov/cgi-bin/crtcals.cgi.

US District Court

Northern District of Georgia

Atlanta Division Court Clerk, 2211 US Courthouse, 75 Spring St SW, Atlanta, GA 30303-3361 (also use mail address for courier delivery), 404-215-1600, records rm- 404-215-1660, crim dockets- 404-331-4227, civil dockets- 404-331-6613. Hours- 8AM-4:45PM. www.gand.uscourts.gov

Counties: Cherokee, Clayton, Cobb, De Kalb, Douglas, Fulton, Gwinnett, Henry, Newton, Rockdale.

Searches & Indexing: Results include last 4 SSN digits. Computer index maintained. New cases in the index 1 day after filing date. Records purged schedule varies.

Fee & Payment: Pay by no business or personal checks accepted. Payee: Clerk, US District Court. Prepayment required.

Phone Search: Only docket information is available by phone.

Mail Search: search usually completed- 5-10 working days. SASE not required.

In Person Search: Fee charged if court performs your search. No self-serve copier available.

E-Services: ECF replaces PACER. Document images available. PACER records go back to 8/1992. New records online after 1 day. ECF at https://ecf.gand.uscourts.gov

Gainesville Division Court Clerk, Federal Bldg, Rm 201, 121 Spring St SE, Gainesville, GA 30501 (also use mail address for courier delivery), 678-450-2760. Hours- 8AM-4:45PM. www.gand.uscourts.gov

Counties: Banks, Barrow, Dawson, Fannin, Forsyth, Gilmer, Habersham, Hall, Jackson, Lumpkin, Pickens, Rabun, Stephens, Towns, Union, White.

Searches & Indexing: Results do not include SSN or DOB. Computer index maintained. New cases in the index 24 hours after filing date. Records purged schedule varies.

Fee & Payment: Pay by no business or personal checks accepted. Law firm checks accepted. Payee: Clerk, US District Court. Prepayment required.

Phone Search: No searching by telephone.

Mail Search: search usually completed- 24 hours. Include SASE for return.

In Person Search: Fee charged if court performs your search. No self-serve copier available.

E-Services: ECF replaces PACER. Document images available. PACER records go back to 8/1992. New records online after 1 day. ECF at https://ecf.gand.uscourts.gov

Newnan Division Court Clerk, PO Box 939, Newnan, GA 30264 (courier address: 18 Greenville St, #352, Newnan, GA 30263), 678-423-3060. www.gand.uscourts.gov

Counties: Carroll, Coweta, Fayette, Haralson, Heard, Meriwether, Pike, Spalding, Troup.

Searches & Indexing: Results include last 4 SSN digits, also birth year. Computer index maintained. New cases in the index immediately after filing date. Records purged schedule varies.

Fee & Payment: Pay by no business or personal checks accepted. Law firm checks accepted. Payee: Clerk, US District Court. Prepayment required.

Phone Search: Only docket information is available by phone.

Mail Search: search usually completed- 2 days. SASE not required.

In Person Search: Fee charged if court performs your search. No self-serve copier available.

E-Services: ECF replaces PACER. Document images available. PACER records go back to 8/1992. New records online after 1 day. ECF at https://ecf.gand.uscourts.gov

Rome Division Court Clerk, PO Box 1186, Rome, GA 30162-1186 (courier address: 600 E 1st St, Rm 304, Rome, GA 30161), 706-378-4060, Hours- 8AM-5PM. www.gand.uscourts.gov

Counties: Bartow, Catoosa, Chattooga, Dade, Floyd, Gordon, Murray, Paulding, Polk, Walker, Whitfield.

Searches & Indexing: Results include last 4 SSN digits. Computer, microfiche and card indexes maintained. Records prior to 1978 on index cards. New cases in the index immediately after filing date. Records purged schedule varies.

Fee & Payment: Pay by no business or personal checks accepted. Attorney checks accepted. Payee: Clerk, US District Court. Prepayment required.

Phone Search: Only docket information showing if a suit has been filed, date of filing, and if case is pending or closed is released via phone.

Mail Search: search usually completed- 24 hours. Include SASE for return.

In Person Search: Fee charged if court performs your search. No self-serve copier available.

E-Services: ECF replaces PACER. Document images available. PACER records go back to 8/1992. New records online after 1 day. ECF at https://ecf.gand.uscourts.gov

US Bankruptcy Court

Northern District of Georgia

Atlanta Division Court Clerk, 1340 US Courthouse, 75 Spring St SW, Atlanta, GA 30303-3361 (also use mail address for courier delivery), 404-215-1000, records rm- 404-215-1169. Hours- 8AM-4PM. www.ganb.uscourts.gov

Counties: Cherokee, Clayton, Cobb, DeKalb, Douglas, Fulton, Gwinnett, Henry, Newton, Rockdale.

Searches & Indexing: Results include last 4 SSN digits. Computer, microfiche and card indexes maintained. New cases in the index 1-2 days after filing date. Records purged never.

Fee & Payment: Pay by money order, cashier check, business check. No personal checks. Payee: Clerk, US Bankruptcy Court. Prepayment required.

Phone Search: Docket information available by phone. Voice Case Information Service available, call VCIS at 800-510-8284 or 404-730-2866.

Mail Search: search usually completed- 1-2 days. Include SASE for return.

In Person Search: permitted. No self-serve copier available - $.50 per page.

E-Services: ECF replaces PACER whose records did go back to 8/1986. New records online after 1 day. ECF at http://ecf.ganb.uscourts.gov **Opinions Online:** www.ganb.uscourts.gov/judges/opn/opn_index.php.

Gainesville Division Court Clerk, 121 Spring St SE, Rm 120, Gainesville, GA 30501 (also use mail address for courier delivery), 678-450-2700. Hours- 8AM-4PM. www.ganb.uscourts.gov

Counties: Banks, Barrow, Dawson, Fannin, Forsyth, Gilmer, Habersham, Hall, Jackson, Lumpkin, Pickens, Rabun, Stephens, Towns, Union, White.

Searches & Indexing: Court maintains index cards on older cases. Results include last 4 SSN digits. Both computer and card indexes maintained. New cases in the index immediately after filing date. Records purged never.

Fee & Payment: Pay by money order, cashier's or personal check. No debtor's checks accepted. Payee: Clerk, US Bankruptcy Court. Prepayment required.

Phone Search: Docket information available via phone. Voice Case Information Service available, call VCIS at 800-510-8284 or 404-730-2866.

Mail Search: search usually completed- 1-2 days. Include SASE for return.

In Person Search: permitted. No self-serve copier available.

E-Services: ECF replaces PACER whose records did go back to 8/1986. New records online after 1 day. ECF at http://ecf.ganb.uscourts.gov **Opinions Online:** www.ganb.uscourts.gov/judges/opn/opn_index.php.

Newnan Division Clerk of Court, PO Box 2328, Newnan, GA 30264 (courier address: Rm 220, 18 Greenville St, Newnan, GA 30263), 678-423-3000. Hours- 8AM-4PM. www.ganb.uscourts.gov

Counties: Carroll, Coweta, Fayette, Haralson, Heard, Meriwether, Pike, Spalding, Troup.

Searches & Indexing: Results include last 4 SSN digits. Card and microfiche indexes maintained. New cases in the index 1 day after filing date. Records purged never.

Fee & Payment: Pay by money order, cashier's or personal check. No debtor's checks accepted. Payee: Clerk, US Bankruptcy Court. Prepayment required.

Phone Search: Only docket information is available by phone, no charge if case number is provided. Debtor's address and social security number not released. Voice Case Information Service available, call VCIS at 800-510-8284 or 404-730-2866.

Mail Search: search usually completed- 1-2 days. SASE not required.

In Person Search: permitted. No self-serve copier available.

E-Services: ECF replaces PACER whose records did go back to 8/1986. New records online after 1 day. ECF at http://ecf.ganb.uscourts.gov **Opinions Online:** www.ganb.uscourts.gov/judges/opn/opn_index.php.

Rome Division Clerk of Court, 600 E 1st St, Rm 339, Rome, GA 30161-3187 (also use mail address for courier delivery), 706-378-4000. Hours- 8AM-4PM. www.ganb.uscourts.gov

Counties: Bartow, Catoosa, Chattooga, Dade, Floyd, Gordon, Murray, Paulding, Polk, Walker, Whitfield.

Searches & Indexing: Results include last 4 SSN digits. A card index is maintained. New cases in the index 24 hours after filing date. Records purged never.

Fee & Payment: Pay by money order, cashier's or personal check. Payee: Clerk, US Bankruptcy Court. Prepayment required.

Phone Search: Docket information available by phone. Voice Case Information Service available, call VCIS at 800-510-8284 or 404-730-2866.

Mail Search: search usually completed- 1-2 days. Include SASE for return.

In Person Search: Fee charged if court performs your search. No self-serve copier available.

E-Services: ECF replaces PACER whose records did go back to 8/1986. New records online after 1 day. ECF at http://ecf.ganb.uscourts.gov **Opinions Online:** www.ganb.uscourts.gov/judges/opn/opn_index.php.

US District Court

Southern District of Georgia

Augusta Division Court Clerk, PO Box 1130, Augusta, GA 30903 (courier address: 500 E Ford St, 1st Fl, Augusta, GA), 706-849-4400. Hours- 8:30AM-5PM. www.gasd.uscourts.gov

Counties: Burke, Columbia, Dodge, Glascock, Jefferson, Johnson, Laurens, Lincoln, McDuffie, Montgomery, Richmond, Taliaferro, Telfair, Treutlen, Warren, Wheeler, Wilkes.

Searches & Indexing: Records alphabetically indexed and stored by chronological case number order. Holds records for the unstaffed Dublin Division. Results do not include SSN or DOB. Computer index maintained. New cases in the index immediately after filing date.

Fee & Payment: Pay by money order, cashier's or personal check. Payee: US Courts. Prepayment required.

Phone Search: Docket information available via phone.

Mail Search: search usually completed- 1-2 weeks. Include SASE for return.

In Person Search: Fee charged if court performs your search. No self-serve copier available.

E-Services: ECF replaces PACER. Document images available. PACER records go back to 6/1995. New records online after 1 day. ECF at https://ecf.gasd.uscourts.gov **Other Online Access:** Opinions and calendars on PACER.

Brunswick Division Court Clerk, PO Box 1636, Brunswick, GA 31521 (courier address: Rm 220, 801 Gloucester St, Brunswick, GA 31520), 912-280-1330, Fax-912-280-1331. Hours- 8:30AM-5PM. www.gasd.uscourts.gov

Counties: Appling, Camden, Glynn, Jeff Davis, Long, McIntosh, Wayne.

Searches & Indexing: Results do not include SSN or DOB. Computer index back one and one-half years is maintained; prior records indexed on microfiche. New cases in the index immediately after filing date.

Fee & Payment: Pay by money order, cashier's or personal check. Payee: Clerk, US District Court. Prepayment required.

Phone Search: Only docket information is available by phone.

Mail Search: search usually completed- 2 days. Include SASE for return.

In Person Search: Fee charged if court performs your search. No self-serve copier available.

E-Services: ECF replaces PACER. Document images available. PACER records go back to 6/1995. New records online after 1 day. ECF at https://ecf.gasd.uscourts.gov **Other Online Access:** Opinions and calendars on PACER.

Savannah Division Court Clerk, PO Box 8286, Savannah, GA 31412 (courier address: Rm 306, 125 Bull St, Savannah, GA 31401), 912-650-4020, Fax-912-650-4030. Hours- 8:30AM-5PM. www.gasd.uscourts.gov

Counties: Atkinson, Bacon, Bulloch, Brantley, Bryan, Candler, Charlton, Chatham, Coffee, Effingham, Emanuel, Evans, Jenkins, Liberty, Pierce, Screven, Tattnall, Toombs, Ware. Holds records for unstaffed Statesboro and Waycross Divisions.

Searches & Indexing: Results do not include SSN or DOB. Computer index back to 1992 maintained; prior records on microfiche. New cases in the index immediately after filing date.

Fee & Payment: Pay by money order, cashier's or personal check. Payee: Clerk, US District Court. Prepayment required.

Phone Search: Only docket information is available by phone.

Mail Search: search usually completed- 1-2 days. SASE not required.

In Person Search: Fee charged if court performs your search. No self-serve copier available.

E-Services: ECF replaces PACER. Document images available. PACER records go back to 6/1995. New records online after 1 day. ECF at https://ecf.gasd.uscourts.gov **Other Online Access:** Opinions and calendars on PACER.

US Bankruptcy Court

Southern District of Georgia

Augusta Division Court Clerk, PO Box 1487, Augusta, GA 30903 (courier address: 933 Broad St - 3rd Fl, Augusta, GA 30901), 706-724-2421. Hours- 8:30AM-5PM. www.gas.uscourts.gov

Counties: Bulloch, Burke, Candler, Columbia, Dodge, Emanuel, Evans, Glascock, Jefferson, Jenkins, Johnson, Laurens, Lincoln, McDuffie, Montgomery, Richmond, Screven, Taliaferro, Tattnall, Telfair, Toombs, Treutlen, Warren, Wheeler, Wilkes.

Searches & Indexing: Court handles files for Statesboro, Dublin, and Augusta divisions. Results include last 4 SSN digits. Computer index maintained. New cases in the index 24 hours after filing date. Records purged yearly. District-wide searches available here back to 1986.

Fee & Payment: Pay by money order, cashier check, business check. No personal checks. Payee: Clerk, US Bankruptcy Court. Prepayment required.

Phone Search: If case number is provided via phone, all docket information will be released.

Mail Search: search usually completed- 7 days. Include SASE for return.

In Person Search: Fee charged if court performs your search. No self-serve copier available.

E-Services: ECF replaces PACER and RACER. Document images available. PACER records go back to 8/1986. ECF at https://ecf.gasb.uscourts.gov **Opinions Online:** http://pacer.gasb.uscourts.gov/bkcyorders/dtSearch.html. **Other Online Access:** Court now participates in the US party case index. Calendars free at http://pacer.gasb.uscourts.gov/calendar/.

Savannah Division Court Clerk, PO Box 8347, Savannah, GA 31412 (courier address: Rm 213, 125 Bull St, Savannah, GA 31412), 912-650-4100, records rm- 912-650-4107. Hours- 8:30AM-5PM. www.gas.uscourts.gov

Counties: Appling, Atkinson, Bacon, Brantley, Bryan, Camden, Charlton, Chatham, Coffee, Effingham, Glynn, Jeff Davis, Liberty, Long, McIntosh, Pierce, Ware, Wayne.

Searches & Indexing: Cases also indexed by SSN. Court handles files for Waycross, Brunswick and Savannah divisions. Results include last 4 SSN digits. Computer index maintained. New cases in the index immediately after filing date. Records purged every 6 months. District-wide searches available here back to 8/1985.

Fee & Payment: Pay by money order, cashier check, business check. No personal checks. Payee: Clerk, US Bankruptcy Court. Prepayment required.

Phone Search: Phone search is limited to information on computer.

Mail Search: search usually completed- 3 days. SASE not required.

In Person Search: Fee charged if court performs your search. No self-serve copier available.

E-Services: ECF replaces PACER and RACER. Document images available. PACER records go back to 1988. New records online after 1 day. ECF at https://ecf.gasb.uscourts.gov **Opinions Online:** http://pacer.gasb.uscourts.gov/bkcyorders/dtSearch.html. **Other Online Access:** Court now participates in the US party case index. Calendars free at http://pacer.gasb.uscourts.gov/calendar/.

Georgia County Courts

Court	Jurisdiction	No. of Courts	How Organized
Superior Courts*	General	100	49 Circuits
State Courts*	Limited	69	69 Counties
Combined Courts*		43	
Magistrate Courts*	Limited	159	By County
Combined Superior/ Magistrate Court*		17	
Civil Courts*	Limited	2	Bibb, Richmond
County Recorder's Courts	Limited	4	Chatham, DeKalb, Gwinnett, Muscogee
Municipal Courts	Municipal	474	Includes City Court of Atlanta
Probate Courts*	Probate	159	By County
Juvenile Courts	Special	159	By County

* Profiled in this Sourcebook.

Court	CIVIL								
	Tort	Contract	Real Estate	Min. Claim	Max. Claim	Small Claims	Estate	Eviction	Domestic Relations
Superior Courts*	X	X	X	$0	No Max	X		X	X
State Courts*	X	X		$0	No Max	X		X	
Combined Courts*	X	X		$0	No Max	$0		X	
Magistrate Courts*	X	X		$0	$15,000	$15,000		X	
Combined Superior/ Magistrate Court*									
Civil Courts*	X	X		$0	$7500	$7500			
Recorder's Courts									
Municipal Courts									
Probate Courts*							X		
Juvenile Courts									

Court	CRIMINAL				
	Felony	Misdemeanor	DWI/DUI	Preliminary Hearing	Juvenile
Superior Courts*	X	X	X	X	
State Courts*		X	X	X	
Combined Courts*				X	
Magistrate Courts*		X		X	
Combined Superior/ Magistrate Court*			X	X	
Civil Courts*				X	
Recorder's Courts		X	X	X	
Municipal Courts		X	X	X	
Probate Courts*		X	X	X	
Juvenile Courts					X

ADMINISTRATION   Court Administrator, 244 Washington St SW, Suite 550, Atlanta, GA, 30334; 404-656-5171, Fax: 404-651-6449. www.georgiacourts.org/aoc/index.html

COURT STRUCTURE   Georgia's Superior Courts are arranged in 49 circuits of general jurisdiction, and these assume the role of a State Court if the county does not have one. The 69 State Courts, like Superior Courts, can conduct jury trials, but are limited jurisidiction. Each county has a Probate, a Juvenile, and a Magistrate Court; the latter has jurisdiction over civil actions under $15,000, also one type of misdemeanor related to passing bad checks.

Magistrate Courts also issue arrest warrants and set bond on all felonies. Magistrate Courts also have jurisdiction for bad checks, arrest warrants, preliminary hearings, and county ordinance violations. Probate courts can, in certain cases, issue search and arrest warrants, and hear miscellaneous misdemeanors.

ONLINE ACCESS   Supreme Court docket information and opinions are available from the web. A certified copy of a Supreme Court Opinion can be purchased online for $5.00 at www2.state.ga.us/Courts/Supreme/main_pp.html. A limited number of courts offer Internet access to court records, but there is no online access available statewide, although statewide access is being planned.

ADDITIONAL INFORMATION   In many Georgia counties the courts will not perform criminal record searches, and, in many cases, will not do civil record searches. An in person search or the use of a record retriever is advised.

The Georgia Crime Information Center is the felony criminal history state repository.

Magistrate Courts also have jurisdiction for bad checks, arrest warrants, preliminary hearings, and county ordinance violations.

Appling County

Superior & State Court PO Box 269, 69 Tippins St #103, Baxley, GA 31513; phone: 912-367-8126; fax: 912-367-8180; hours 8AM-5PM (EST). *Felony, Misdemeanor, Civil.*
Civil Records: Access: In person only. Visitors must perform in person searches themselves. Court makes copy: $.25 for first page, $.10 each add'l. Required to search: name, years to search. Civil cases indexed by defendant, plaintiff. Civil records on docket books back to 1800s.
Criminal Records: Access: In person only. Visitors must perform in person searches themselves. Court makes copy: $.25 for 1st page, $.10 each add'l. Required to search: name, years to search, DOB; SSN helpful. Crim records on docket books back to 1800s.
General Information: Public terminal has only civil records back to 1996. No juvenile, adoption, sealed, sexual, mental health or expunged records released. Certification fee: $2.50 plus $.50 per page after first. Payee: Court Clerk. Personal checks accepted.

Magistrate Court P O Box 366, 72 Tippins St, Baxley, GA 31515; phone: 912-367-8116, 367-8117; fax: 912-367-8182; hours 8:30AM-5PM *Civil Actions Under $15,000, Eviction, Small Claims.*

Probate Court 83 S Oak St #A, Baxley, GA 31513; phone: 912-367-8114; fax: 912-367-8114; hours 8:30AM-5PM (EST). *Probate.*

Atkinson County

Superior Court PO Box 6, South Main, Courthouse Square, Pearson, GA 31642; phone: 912-422-3343; fax: 912-422-7025; hours 8AM-5PM (EST). *Felony, Misdemeanor, Civil.*
Civil Records: Access: In person only. Visitors must perform in person searches themselves. Court makes copy: $.50 per page. Self serve copy fee: $.25 per page. Required to search: name, years to search. Civil cases indexed by defendant. Civil records in docket books back to 1919.
Criminal Records: Access: In person only. Visitors must perform in person searches themselves. Court makes copy: $.50 per page. Self serve copy fee: $.25 per page. Required to search: name, years to search. Criminal records in docket books back to 1919.
General Information: Public use terminal not available. No juvenile, adoption, sealed, sexual, mental health or expunged records released. Certification fee: $2.50 plus $.50 per page after first. Payee: Clerk of Superior Court. Personal checks accepted. Prepayment required.

Magistrate Court PO Box 674, Pearson, GA 31642; phone: 912-422-7158; fax: 912-422-7989; hours 8AM-5PM (EST). *Civil Actions Under $15,000, Eviction, Small Claims.*

Probate Court PO Box 855, Pearson, GA 31642; phone: 912-422-3552; fax: 912-422-7842; hours 8AM-5PM (EST). *Probate.*

Bacon County

Superior Court PO Box 376, Alma, GA 31510; phone: 912-632-4915; probate phone: 912-632-7661; fax: 912-632-6545; hours 9AM-5PM (EST). *Felony, Misdemeanor, Civil.*
Civil Records: Access: Mail, in person. Both court and visitors may perform in person searches. No search fee. Court makes copy: $1.00 per page. Self serve copy fee: $.25 per page. Required to search: name, years to search. Civil cases indexed by defendant, plaintiff. Civil records on index from 1970, archived to 1918, computerized since 2000. Mail turnaround time 1 week.
Criminal Records: Access: Mail, in person. Both court and visitors may perform in person searches. No search fee. Court makes copy: $1.00 per page. Self serve copy fee: $.25 per page. Required to search: name, years to search, DOB; also helpful: SSN, race, sex. Criminal records on index from 1970, archived to 1918, computerized since 2000. Mail turnaround time 1 week.
General Information: Public terminal goes back to 2000. No juvenile, adoption, sealed, sexual, mental health, expunged or first offender records released. Will fax documents. Certification fee: $2.50 plus $.50 per page after. Pay: Clerk of Superior Court. Personal checks accepted. Prepayment SASE required.

Magistrate Court Box 389, 205 W 15th St, Courthouse #100, Alma, GA 31510; phone: 912-632-5961; civil phone: 912-632-7661; probate phone: 912-632-7661; fax: 912-632-7662; hours 9AM-5PM (EST). *Civil Actions Under $15,000, Eviction, Small Claims, Probate.*

Probate Court PO Box 389, 502 W 12th St, Alma, GA 31510; phone: 912-632-7661; fax: 912-632-7662; hours 9AM-5PM (EST). *Probate.*

Baker County

Superior Court PO Box 10, Governmental Bldg, Newton, GA 39870; phone: 229-734-3004; fax: 229-734-7770; hours 9AM-5PM (EST). *Felony, Misdemeanor, Civil.*
Civil Records: Access: In person only. Visitors must perform in person searches themselves. Court makes copy: $.25 per page. Required to search: name, years to search. Civil cases indexed by defendant. Civil records on index from 1850.
Criminal Records: Access: In person only. Visitors must perform in person searches themselves. Court makes copy: $.25 per page. Required to search: name, years to search, DOB; SSN helpful. Criminal records on index from 1850.
General Information: Public terminal has only civil records back to 1995. No juvenile, adoption, sealed, sexual or expunged records released. Certification fee: $2.50 plus $.50 per page after first. Payee: Court Clerk. Personal checks accepted. Prepayment required.

Magistrate Court PO Box 548, Newton, GA 39870; phone: 229-734-3009; fax: 229-734-8822; probate fax: same; hours 9AM-5PM (EST). *Civil Actions Under $15,000, Eviction, Small Claims.*

Probate Court PO Box 548, Newton, GA 39870; phone: 229-734-3007; fax: 229-734-8822; hours 9AM-5PM M-W & F; 9AM-N Th (EST). *Probate.* https://www.gaprobate.org/counties/baker/index.html

Baldwin County

Superior & State Court PO Drawer 987, Milledgeville, GA 31059-0987; phone: 478-445-4007; fax: 478-445-6039; hours 8:30AM-5PM (EST). *Felony, Misdemeanor, Civil.*
Civil Records: Access: In person only. Visitors must perform in person searches themselves. Court makes copy: $.25 per page. Required to search: name, years to search. Civil cases indexed by defendant, plaintiff. Civil records on docket from 1861; on computer back to 1996.
Criminal Records: Access: In person only. Visitors must perform in person searches themselves. Court makes copy: $.25 per page. Required to search: name, years to search. Criminal records on docket from 1861; on computer back to 1996.
General Information: Public terminal goes back to 1998. No juvenile, adoption, sealed, sexual, mental health or expunged records released. Certification fee: $2.50 plus $.50 per page after first. Personal checks accepted. Prepayment required.

Magistrate Court 121 N Wilkenson, #107, Milledgeville, GA 31061; phone: 478-445-4446; fax: 478-445-5918; hours 8:30AM-5PM (EST). *Civil Actions Under $15,000, Eviction, Small Claims.*

Probate Court 121 N Wilkinson St, #109, Milledgeville, GA 31061; phone: 478-445-4807; fax: 478-445-5178; hours 8:30AM-5PM *Probate.* https://www.gaprobate.org/counties/baldwin/index.html

Banks County

Superior Court PO Box 337, 144 Yonah Homer Rd #8, Homer, GA 30547; phone: 706-677-6240; fax: 706-677-6294; hours 8:00AM-5PM (EST). *Felony, Misdemeanor, Civil.*
Civil Records: Access: In person only. Visitors must perform in person searches themselves. Court makes copy: $.25 per page. Required to search: name, years to search. Civil cases indexed by defendant, plaintiff. Civil records on docket from 1960.
Criminal Records: Access: In person only. Visitors must perform in person searches themselves. Court makes copy: $.25 per page. Required to search: name, years to search, DOB. Criminal records on docket from 1960.
General Information: Public terminal goes back to 2000. No juvenile, adoption, sealed, sexual, mental health or expunged records released. Certification fee: $3.75 per doc. Payee: Clerk of Superior Court. Personal checks accepted. Prepayment required.

Magistrate Court 144 Yonah Homer Rd #10, Homer, GA 30547-2614; phone: 706-677-6270; fax: 706-677-6215; hours 8:30AM-5PM (EST). *Civil Actions Under $15,000, Eviction, Small Claims.*

Probate Court 144 Yonah Homer Rd,#7, Homer, GA 30547; phone: 706-677-6250; fax: 706-677-2337; hours 8AM-5PM (EST). *Probate.*
https://www.gaprobate.org/counties/banks/index.html

Barrow County

Superior Court PO Box 1280, Winder, GA 30680; phone: 770-307-3035; fax: 770-867-4800; hours 8AM-5PM *Felony, Misdemeanor, Civil.*
Civil Records: Access: In person only. Visitors must perform in person searches themselves. Court makes copy: $1.00 per page. Self serve copy fee: $.25 per page. Required to search: name, years to search. Civil cases indexed by defendant, plaintiff. Civil records on computer from 1990, docket from 1915.
Criminal Records: Access: In person only. Visitors must perform in person searches themselves. Court makes copy: $1.00 per page. Self serve copy fee: $.25 per page. Required to search: name, years to search, DOB. Criminal records on computer from 1990, docket from 1915.
General Information: Public terminal has criminal back to 1992 and civil back to 1990. No juvenile, adoption, sealed, sexual, mental health or expunged records released. Certification fee: $2.50 plus $.50 per page after first. Payee: Clerk of Superior Court. Business checks accepted. Prepayment required.

Magistrate Court 30 N Broad St, #227, Winder, GA 30680; phone: 770-307-3050; fax: 770-868-1440; hours 8AM-5PM (EST). *Civil Actions Under $15,000, Eviction, Small Claims.*

Probate Court Barrow County Courthouse, 30 N Broad St, Winder, GA 30680; phone: 770-307-3045; fax: 770-307-4470; hours 8AM-4;30PM *Probate.*
https://www.gaprobate.org/counties/barrow/index.html

Bartow County

Superior Court 135 W Cherokee Ave, #233, Cartersville, GA 30120; phone: 770-387-5025; fax: 770-387-5611; hours 8AM-5PM (EST). *Felony, Misdemeanor, Civil.*
Civil Records: Access: In person only. Visitors must perform in person searches themselves. Court makes copy: $.25 per page. Required to search: name, years to search. Civil cases indexed by defendant, plaintiff. Civil records on computer from 9/92, on books from 1900s.
Criminal Records: Access: In person only. Visitors must perform in person searches themselves. Court makes copy: $.25 per page. Required to search: name, years to search, DOB, SSN, signed release. Criminal records on computer for 10 years, prior on books.
General Information: No public access terminal. No juvenile, adoptions or sealed records released. Certification fee: $2.50 plus $.25 each add'l page.

Payee: Clerk of Superior Court. Personal checks accepted. Prepayment required.

Magistrate Court 135 W Cherokee Ave, #225, Cartersville, GA 30120; phone: 770-387-5070; fax: 770-387-5073; hours 7AM-5:30PM (EST). *Civil Actions Under $15,000, Eviction, Small Claims, Misdemeanors.* www.bartowcourt.com

Probate Court 135 W Cherokee, #243A, Cartersville, GA 30120; phone: 770-387-5075; fax: 770-387-5074; hours 8AM-5PM (EST). *Probate.*
https://www.gaprobate.org/counties/bartow/index.html

Ben Hill County

Superior Court PO Box 1104, 115 S Sheridan, Fitzgerald, GA 31750; phone: 229-426-5135; fax: 229-426-5487; hours 8:30AM-4:30PM (EST). *Felony, Misdemeanor, Civil.*
Civil Records: Access: In person only. Visitors must perform in person searches themselves. Court makes copy: $1.00 per page. Self serve copy fee: $.25 per page. Required to search: name, years to search. Civil cases indexed by defendant. Civil records computerized since 1994, archived from 1907.
Criminal Records: Access: In person only. Visitors must perform in person searches themselves. Court makes copy: $1.00 per page. Self serve copy fee: $.25 per page. Required to search: name, years to search, signed release; also helpful: DOB, SSN. Criminal records computerized since 1994, archived from 1907. **General Info:** No public access terminal. No juvenile, adoption, sealed, sexual, mental health or expunged records released. Certification fee: $2.00 plus $.50 per page. Payee: Clerk. Personal checks accepted. Prepayment required.

Magistrate Court Box 1163, 255 Appomattox Rd, Fitzgerald, GA 31750; phone: 229-426-5141; fax: 229-426-5123; hours 8:30AM-4:30PM *Civil Actions Under $15,000, Eviction, Small Claims.*

Probate Court 111 S Sheridan St, Fitzgerald, GA 31750; phone: 229-426-5137; fax: 229-426-5486; hours 8:30AM-4:30PM (EST). *Probate.*

Berrien County

Superior Court 101 E Marion Ave, #3, Nashville, GA 31639; phone: 229-686-5506; fax: 229-543-1032; hours 8AM-4:30PM (EST). *Felony, Misdemeanor, Civil.*
Civil Records: Access: Mail, in person. Both court and visitors may perform in person searches. No search fee. Court makes copy: $.25 per page; same fee for self serve. Required to search: name, years to search. Civil cases indexed by defendant, plaintiff. Civil records on docket back to 1800. Mail turnaround time same day.
Criminal Records: Access: Mail, in person. Both court and visitors may perform in person searches. No search fee. Court makes copy: $.25 per page; same fee for self serve. Required to search: name, years to search, DOB; also helpful: SSN, race, sex. Criminal records on docket back to 1800. Mail turnaround time same day.
General Information: No public access terminal. No juvenile, adoption, sealed, sexual, mental health or expunged records released. Certification fee: $2.50 plus $.50 per page after first. Payee: Court Clerk. Personal checks accepted, prepayment-SASE required

Magistrate Court PO Box 267, 115 S Davis St, Nashville, GA 31639; phone: 229-686-7019; fax: 229-686-6328; hours 8:30AM-4:30PM (EST). *Civil Actions Under $15,000, Eviction, Small Claims.*

Probate Court 205 N Jefferson St, Nashville, GA 31639; phone: 229-686-5213; fax: 229-686-9495; hours 8AM-4:30-M-FRI (EST). *Probate.*
https://www.gaprobate.org/counties/berrien/index.html

Bibb County

Superior Court PO Box 1015, 275 2nd St, Rm 216, Macon, GA 31202; phone: 478-621-6527; fax: 478-621-5823; hours 8:30AM-5PM *Felony, Civil.*

Civil Records: Access: Mail, in person, online. Both court and visitors may perform in person searches. Search fee: $10.00 per name. Court makes copy: $1.00 per page. Required to search: name, years to search. Civil cases indexed by defendant, plaintiff. Civil records on computer from 1993, on books from 1823. Court calendars online at www.co.bibb.ga.us/CalendarDirectory/CalendarDirectory.asp. Mail turnaround time same day.
Criminal Records: Access: Mail, in person, online. Both court and visitors may perform in person searches. Search fee: $10.00 per name. Court makes copy: $1.00 per page. Self serve copy fee: $.25 per page. Required to search: name, years to search, DOB, signed release; also helpful: SSN. Criminal records on computer since 1989. Superior court calendars at www.co.bibb.ga.us/CalendarDirectory/CalendarDirectory.asp. Mail turnaround time same day.
General Information: Public terminal has only civil records back to 1995. No adoption or sealed records released. Certification fee: $2.50 plus $.50 per page after first. Payee: Superior Court Clerk. Only cashiers checks and money orders accepted. Prepayment required.

State Court PO Box 5086, Macon, GA 31213-7199; phone: 478-621-6676; fax: 478-621-6326; hours 8AM-5PM (EST). *Misdemeanor, Civil.* www.co.bibb.ga.us
Civil Records: Access: Mail, in person, online. Both court and visitors may perform in person searches. No search fee. Court makes copy: $.50 per page; same fee for self serve. Required to search: name, years to search. Civil cases indexed by defendant, plaintiff. Civil records on computer from 1989, docket from 1952. Civil court calendars are searchable online at www.co.bibb.ga.us/StateCourtClerk/Civil/Default.htm. Website will have access to full court record indexes in future. Usually 1 day turnaround time.
Criminal Records: Access: Mail, in person. Both court and visitors may perform in person searches. No search fee. Court makes copy: $.50 per page; same fee for self serve. Required to search: name, years to search, DOB; also helpful: SSN, race, sex. Criminal records on computer from 1989, docket from 1945. Mail Usually one day turnaround time.
General Information: Public terminal has criminal back to 1989 and civil back to 1990. No juvenile, adoption, sealed, sexual, mental health or expunged records released. Will fax to toll-free line if 5 pages or less, otherwise documents mailed. Certification fee: $2.50 per page. Exemplification is an add'l $5.00 per page. Payee: Bibb State Court Clerk. Business checks accepted. Prepayment and SASE required.

Civil & Magistrate Court 601 Mulberry, #101, Bibb County Courthouse, Macon, GA 31201; phone: 478-621-6495; criminal phone: 478-621-6505; civil phone: 478-621-6495; criminal fax: 478-621-6497; civil fax: 478-621-5861; hours 8AM-5PM (EST). *Civil Actions Under $25,000, Eviction, Small Claims.* www.bibbcourt.com Note: Searchable database not yet available for this jurisdiction.

Probate Court 207 Bibb County Courthouse, PO Box 6518, Macon, GA 31208-6518; phone: 478-621-6494; fax: 478-621-6686; hours 8AM-5PM (EST). *Probate.* www.co.bibb.ga.us

Bleckley County

Superior Court 306 SE 2nd St, Cochran, GA 31014; phone: 478-934-3210; fax: 478-934-6671; hours 8:30AM-5PM *Felony, Misdemeanor, Civil.*
Civil Records: Access: In person only. Visitors must perform in person searches themselves. Court makes copy: $.25 per page. Required to search: name, years to search. Civil cases indexed by defendant, plaintiff. Civil records archived from 1913.
Criminal Records: Access: In person only. Visitors must perform in person searches themselves. Court makes copy: $.25 per page. Required to search: name, years to search, DOB; SSN helpful. Criminal records archived from 1913, docket from 1913.

General Information: Public terminal has only civil records back to 1995. No juvenile, adoption, sealed, sexual, mental health or expunged records released. Certification fee: $2.50 plus $.50 per page after first. Payee: Clerk of the Superior Court. Personal checks not accepted. Prepayment required.

Magistrate Court 306 2nd St SE, Cochran, GA 31014; phone: 478-934-3202; fax: 478-934-7826; hours 8:30AM-5PM (EST). *Civil Actions Under $15,000, Eviction, Small Claims.*

Probate Court 306 SE 2nd St, Cochran, GA 31014; 478-934-3204; 8:30AM-5PM *Probate.* https://www.gaprobate.org/counties/bleckley/index.html

Brantley County

Superior Court PO Box 1067, 117 Brantley St, Nahunta, GA 31553; phone: 912-462-6280; fax: 912-462-6247; hours 8AM-5PM (EST). *Felony, Misdemeanor, Civil.*
Civil Records: Access: In person only. Visitors must perform in person searches themselves. Court makes copy: $.25 per page. Required to search: name, years to search. Civil cases indexed by defendant, plaintiff. Civil records on dockets from 1920; computerized records go back 1998.
Criminal Records: Access: In person only. Visitors must perform in person searches themselves. Court makes copy: $.25 per page. Required to search: name, years to search, DOB, SSN, signed release. Criminal records on dockets from 1920.
General Information: No juvenile, adoption, sealed, 1st offenders, expunged or confidential records released. Certification fee: $2.50 plus $.50 per page after first. Payee: Superior Court Clerk. Personal checks accepted. Prepayment required.

Magistrate Court PO Box 998, 117 Brantley St, Nahunta, GA 31553; phone: 912-462-6780; fax: 912-462-6897; hours 8AM-4:30PM (EST). *Civil Actions Under $15,000, Eviction, Small Claims.*

Probate Court PO Box 207, 117 Brantley St, Nahunta, GA 31553; phone: 912-462-5192; fax: 912-462-8360; hours 8AM-5PM (EST). *Probate.*

Brooks County

Superior Court PO Box 630, Quitman, GA 31643; phone: 229-263-4747/5150; fax: 229-263-5050; hours 8AM-5PM *Felony, Misdemeanor, Civil.* http://southernjudicialcircuit.com
Civil Records: Access: In person, phone if specific date is known. Visitors must perform in person searches themselves. Court makes copy: $.25 per page. Self serve copy fee: $1.00 per page. Required to search: name, years to search. Civil cases indexed by defendant, plaintiff. Civil records in books to 1857.
Criminal Records: Access: In person only. Visitors must perform in person searches themselves. Court makes copy: $.25 per page. Self serve copy fee: $1.00 per page. Required to search: name, years to search, DOB; SSN helpful. Crim records in books to 1857.
General Information: Public terminal has only civil records back to 1/1993. No juvenile, adoption, sealed, sexual, mental health or expunged records released. Will fax documents to local or toll free line. Certification fee: $2.50 plus $.50 per page after first. Payee: Clerk Superior Court. Business checks accepted. Prepayment required.

Magistrate Court PO Box 387, 400 E Courtland Ave, Quitman, GA 31643; phone: 229-263-9989; probate phone: 229-263-5567; criminal/civil fax: 229-263-7847; hours 8AM-5PM (EST). *Civil Actions Under $15,000, Eviction, Small Claims.*
Note: Court also has jurisdiction for bad checks, arrest warrants, preliminary hearings, garnishments, and county ordinance violations.

Probate Court PO Box 665, One Screven St, Quitman, GA 31643; phone: 229-263-5567; fax: 229-263-5058; hours 8AM-5PM (EST). *Probate.*

Bryan County

Superior & State Court PO Box 670, Pembroke, GA 31321; phone: 912-653-3872; criminal phone: 912-653-7785 felonies; civil phone: 912-653-3874; criminal fax: 912-653-3870; civil fax: 912-653-5255; hours 8AM-5PM (EST). *Felony, Misdemeanor, Civil.*
Civil Records: Access: In person only. Visitors must perform in person searches themselves. Court makes copy: $.25 per page; same fee for self serve. Required to search: name, years to search. Civil cases indexed by defendant, plaintiff. Civil records on dockets from 1960, recent records are computerized since 9/93.
Criminal Records: Access: In person only. Visitors must perform in person searches themselves. Court makes copy: $.25 per page; same fee for self serve. Required to search: name, years to search, DOB; SSN helpful. Criminal records on dockets from 1960, recent records are computerized since 9/93.
General Information: Public terminal goes back to 1993. No juvenile, adoption, sealed, sexual, mental health or expunged records released. Will fax specific case file for $2.00 1st page, $1.00 each add'l, must be pre-paid. Certification fee: $2.50 per page. Payee: Clerk of Superior & State Court. Personal checks accepted. Prepayment required.

Magistrate Court Box 670, Pembroke, GA 31321; phone: 912-653-3860; fax: 912-653-5254; hours 8AM-5PM (EST). *Civil Actions Under $15,000, Eviction, Small Claims.*

Probate Court PO Box 418, Pembroke, GA 31321; phone: 912-653-3856; fax: 912-653-3845; hours 8:30AM-12, 1-5PM (EST). *Probate.* www.georgiacourts.org

Bulloch County

Superior & State Court Judicial Annex Bldg, 20 Siebald St, Statesboro, GA 30458; phone: 912-764-9009; fax: 912-764-5953; hours 8:00AM-5PM (EST). *Felony, Misdemeanor, Civil.*
Civil Records: Access: In person only. Both court and visitors may perform in person searches. No search fee. Court makes copy: $.25 per page; same fee for self serve. Required to search: name, years to search. Civil cases indexed by defendant. Civil records on computer from 1991, dockets back to 1796. Mail turnaround time 7 days.
Criminal Records: Access: In person only. Both court and visitors may perform in person searches. No search fee. Court makes copy: $.25 per page; same fee for self serve. Required to search: name, years to search. Criminal records on computer from 1991, dockets back to 1796.
General Information: Public terminal goes back to 1991. No juvenile, adoption, sexual, mental health or expunged records released. Certification fee: $2.50 plus doc. Payee: Court Clerk. Personal checks accepted. Prepayment required.

Magistrate Court Box 1004, Statesboro, GA 30459-1004; phone: 912-764-6458, 912-764-5050; fax: 912-489-6731; hours 8AM-5PM (EST). *Civil Actions Under $15,000, Eviction, Small Claims.*

Probate Court PO Box 1005, 2 N Main St #103, Statesboro, GA 30459; phone: 912-489-8749; fax: 912-764-8740; hours 8:00AM-5PM (EST). *Probate.* https://www.gaprobate.org/counties/bulloch/index.html

Burke County

Superior & State Court PO Box 803, 111 E 6th St, Rm 107, Waynesboro, GA 30830; phone: 706-554-2279; fax: 706-554-7887; hours 9AM-5PM (EST). *Felony, Misdemeanor, Civil.*
Civil Records: Access: In person only. Visitors must perform in person searches themselves. Court makes copy: $.25 per page. Required to search: name, years to search. Civil cases indexed by defendant. Civil records on minute books back to 1856, indexed on computer since 1996.

Criminal Records: Access: In person only. Visitors must perform in person searches themselves. Court makes copy: $.25 per page. Required to search: name, years to search, DOB; SSN helpful. Criminal records on minute books back to 1856, indexed on computer since 1996. **General Information:** No public access terminal. No juvenile, adoption, sexual, mental health or expunged records released. Certification fee: $2.50 plus $.50 per page after first. Payee: Clerk of Superior Court; personal check accepted, prepayment required.

Magistrate Court Box 401, 602 N Liberty St, Waynesboro, GA 30830; phone: 706-554-4281; fax: 706-554-8772; hours 8AM-5PM (EST). *Civil Actions Under $15,000, Eviction, Small Claims.*

Probate Court PO Box 322, 111 E 6th St, Waynesboro, GA 30830; phone: 706-554-3000; fax: 706-554-6693; hours 9AM-5PM (EST). *Probate.* https://www.gaprobate.org/counties/burke/index.html

Butts County

Superior Court PO Box 320, 26 3rd St, Jackson, GA 30233; phone: 770-775-8215; fax: 770-504-1359; 8AM-5PM *Felony, Misdemeanor, Civil.*
Civil Records: Access: In person, fax, mail. Visitors must perform in person searches themselves. Court makes copy: $.25 per page. Required to search: name, years to search. Civil cases indexed by defendant, plaintiff. Civil records on dockets from 1966, computerized since 1998. Mail turnaround 3-4 days.
Criminal Records: Access: In person, fax, mail. Visitors must perform in person searches themselves. Search fee: None. Court makes copy: $.25 per page. Required to search: name, years to search, signed release; also helpful: DOB, SSN, race, sex. Criminal records on dockets from 1966, computerized since 1998. Mail turnaround 3-4 days.
General Information: Public terminal has civil and criminal back to 1988. No juvenile, adoption, sexual, mental health or expunged records released. Certification fee: $2.50 plus $.50 per page. Payee: Clerk of Superior Court. Personal checks accepted. Prepayment and SASE required.

Magistrate Court Box 457, Jackson, GA 30233; phone: 770-775-8220; fax: 770-775-1954; hours 8AM-5PM (EST). *Civil Actions Under $15,000, Eviction, Small Claims.*

Probate Court 25 3rd St, #7, Jackson, GA 30233; phone: 770-775-8204; hours 8AM-5PM (EST). *Probate, Traffic.* https://www.gaprobate.org/counties/butts/index.html

Calhoun County

Superior Court PO Box 69, Morgan, GA 39866; phone: 229-849-2715; fax: 229-849-0072; hours 8AM-5PM (EST). *Felony, Misdemeanor, Civil.*
Civil Records: Access: Mail, in person. Both court and visitors may perform in person searches. Search fee: $5.00 per name. Court makes copy: $1.00 per page. Self serve copy fee: $.25 per page. Required to search: name, years to search. Civil cases indexed by defendant, plaintiff. Civil records on dockets back to 1854.
Criminal Records: Access: In person only. Both court and visitors may perform in person searches. Search fee: $5.00 per name. Court makes copy: $1.00 per page. Self serve copy fee: $.25 per page. Required to search: name, years to search, DOB. Criminal records on dockets back to 1854.
General Information: No public access terminal. No juvenile, adoption, sexual, mental health or expunged records released. Will fax $2.00 per page; no charge to toll-free numbers. Certification fee: $3.00. Payee: Superior Court Clerk. Personal checks accepted. Prepayment required.

Magistrate & Probate Court PO Box 87, 31 Court St #C, Morgan, GA 39866; phone: 229-849-2115, 849-2116; fax: 229-849-2117; hours 8AM-5PM (EST). *Civil Actions Under $15,000, Eviction, Small Claims, Probate.*

Camden County

Superior Court PO Box 550, 210 E 4th St, Woodbine, GA 31569; phone: 912-576-5631; fax: 912-576-5648; hours 9AM-5PM (EST). *Felony, Misdemeanor, Civil.*
Civil Records: Access: In person only. Visitors must perform in person searches themselves. Court makes copy: $1.00 per page. Self serve copy fee: $.25 per page. Required to search: name, years to search. Civil cases indexed by defendant, plaintiff. Civil records on computer from 1989, dockets from 1776.
Criminal Records: Access: In person only. Visitors must perform in person searches themselves. Court makes copy: $1.00 per page. Self serve copy fee: $.25 per page. Required to search: name, years to search, signed release; also helpful: DOB, SSN. Criminal records on computer from 1989, dockets from 1776.
General Information: Public terminal has criminal back to 1989 and civil back to 1991. No juvenile, adoption, sexual or expunged records released. Will not fax specific case file. Certification fee: $2.50 plus $.50 per page. Payee: Clerk of Superior Court. Personal checks accepted. Prepayment required.

Magistrate Court Box 386, 210 E 4th Street, Woodbine, GA 31569; phone: 912-576-5658; fax: 912-576-5658; hours 9AM-5PM (EST). *Civil Actions Under $15,000, Eviction, Small Claims.*
http://camdenmagcourt.com

Probate Court 210 E Fourth St, Courthouse Sq, Woodbine, GA 31569; phone: 912-576-3785; fax: 912-576-5484; probate fax: 912-576-7145; hours 9AM-5PM *Probate, Misdemeanor Drug, Traffic.*

Candler County

Superior & State Court PO Drawer 830, 355 Broad St, Metter, GA 30439; phone: 912-685-5257; probate phone: 912-685-2357; fax: 912-685-2946; hours 8:30AM-5PM *Felony, Misdemeanor, Civil.*
Civil Records: Access: Mail, in person. Visitors must perform in person searches themselves. Court makes copy: $.25 per page; same fee for self serve. Required to search: name, years to search. Civil cases indexed by defendant, plaintiff. Civil records on dockets from 1914. Mail turnaround time 2 days.
Criminal Records: Access: Mail, in person. Visitors must perform in person searches themselves. Court makes copy: $.25 per page; same fee for self serve. Required to search: name, years to search. Criminal records on dockets from 1914. Mail turnaround time 2 days.
General Information: Public terminal goes back to 1995. No juvenile, adoption, mental health, expunged or sealed records released. Will fax documents to local or toll free line. Certification fee: $2.00 plus $.50 per page. Payee: Clerk of Superior & State Court. Personal checks accepted. Prepayment required.

Magistrate Court 5 Courthouse Square, Metter, GA 30439; phone: 912-685-2888; fax: 912-685-3995; hours 8:30AM-N, 1-5PM (EST). *Civil Actions Under $15,000, Eviction, Small Claims.*

Probate Court Courthouse Square, Metter, GA 30439; phone: 912-685-2357; fax: 912-685-5130; hours 8:30AM-5PM (EST). *Probate.*
https://www.gaprobate.org/counties/candler/index.html

Carroll County

Superior & State Court PO Box 1620, Carrollton, GA 30112; phone: 770-214-3125; criminal phone: 770-830-5835 x2247/2239; civil phone: 770-830-5835 x2245/2246; probate phone: 770-830-5840; criminal/civil fax: 770-214-3125; hours 8AM-5PM *Felony, Misdemeanor, Civil.*
Civil Records: Access: Mail, in person. Both court and visitors may perform in person searches. Search fee: $5.00 per name. Court makes copy: $.25 per page. Required to search: name, years to search. Civil cases indexed by defendant, plaintiff. Civil records on computer from 1986, docket. Mail turnaround time 1 week.

Criminal Records: Access: Mail, in person. Both court and visitors may perform in person searches. Search fee: $5.00 per name. Court makes copy: $.25 per page. Required to search: name, years to search, DOB; also helpful: SSN, race, sex. Criminal records on computer from 1986 for State Court, but Superior Court records are not computerized. Mail turnaround time 1 week.
General Information: Public use terminal available. No juvenile, adoption, sexual, mental health or expunged records released. Certification fee: $2.50 plus $.50 per page after first. Payee: Clerk of Superior & State Court. Personal checks accepted. Prepayment and SASE required.

Magistrate Court 108 Courtyard Sq, Carrollton, GA 30117; phone: 770-830-5874; fax: 770-830-5851; hours 9AM-5PM (EST). *Misdemeanors, Civil Actions Under $15,000, Eviction, Small Claims.*

Probate Court PO Box 338, 311 Newnan St, Rm 204, Carrollton, GA 30112; phone: 770-830-5840; fax: 770-830-5995; 8AM-5PM (EST). *Probate.*
https://www.gaprobate.org/counties/carroll/index.html

Catoosa County

Superior Court 875 Lafayette St, Ringgold, GA 30736; phone: 706-935-4231; fax: 706-965-7431; hours 8:30AM-5PM *Felony, Misdemeanor, Civil.*
Civil Records: Access: In person only. Visitors must perform in person searches themselves. Court makes copy: $1.00 per page. Required to search: name, years to search. Civil cases indexed by defendant, plaintiff. Civil on dockets from 1800.
Criminal Records: Access: In person only. Visitors must perform in person searches themselves. Court makes copy: $1.00 per page. Required to search: name, years to search, DOB; SSN helpful. Criminal records on dockets from 1800.
General Information: No public access terminal. No juvenile, adoption, sexual, mental health or expunged records released. Certification fee: $2.50 plus $.50 per page after first. Payee: Superior Court - Court Clerk. Personal checks accepted. Prepayment required.

Magistrate Court 798 Lafayette St, Ringgold, GA 30736; phone: 706-935-3114; hours 9AM-N, 1-5PM (EST). *Civil Actions Under $15,00, Eviction, Small Claims.*

Probate Court 875 Lafayette St, Justice Bldg, Ringgold, GA 30736; phone: 706-935-3511; fax: 706-935-3519; hours 8:30AM-5PM M-F (EST). *Probate.* This court will not perform mail searches.

Charlton County

Superior Court PO Box 760, Courthouse, 100 S Third St, Folkston, GA 31537; phone: 912-496-2354; fax: 912-496-3882; hours 8:30AM-5PM (EST). *Felony, Misdemeanor, Civil.*
Civil Records: Access: In person only. Visitors must perform in person searches themselves. Court makes copy: $.25 per page. Required to search: name, years to search. Civil cases indexed by defendant. Civil records on index from 1954.
Criminal Records: Access: In person. Visitors must perform in person searches themselves. No search fee. Court makes copy: $.25 per page. Required to search: name, years to search, DOB, SSN. Criminal records on index from 1954.
General Information: No public access terminal. No juvenile, adoption, sexual, mental health or expunged records released. Will not fax documents. Certification fee: $2.50 plus $.50 per page after first. Payee: Court Clerk. Personal checks accepted.

Magistrate Court 100 B County St, Folkston, GA 31537; phone: 912-496-2617; fax: 912-496-2560; hours 9AM-4:30PM (EST). *Civil Actions Under $15,000, Eviction, Small Claims.*

Probate Court 100 S 3rd St, Folkston, GA 31537; phone: 912-496-2230; fax: 912-496-1156; hours 8AM-5PM (EST). *Probate.*
https://www.gaprobate.org/counties/charlton/index.html

Chatham County

Superior Court PO Box 10227, Savannah, GA 31412-0427; phone: 912-652-7197; criminal phone: 912-652-7209; civil phone: 912-652-7200; criminal/civil fax: 912-652-7380; hours 8AM-5PM (EST). *Felony, Civil.*
www.chathamcourts.org/chatcourts.html
Civil Records: Access: Mail, in person, online. Both court and visitors may perform in person searches. No search fee. Court makes copy: $.25 per page; same fee for self serve. Required to search: name, years to search. Civil cases indexed by defendant, plaintiff. Civil records on computer from 1984, archived back to 1900, dockets back to 1900s. Search county court civil records at www.chathamcounty.org/jims/. Mail turnaround time 1 week.
Criminal Records: Access: Mail, in person, online. Both court and visitors may perform in person searches. No search fee. Court makes copy: $.25 per page; same fee for self serve. Required to search: name, years to search, signed release; also helpful: DOB, SSN. Criminal records on computer from 1984, archived back to 1900, dockets back to 1900s. Search county court criminal records at www.chathamcounty.org/jims/. Mail turnaround time 1 week.
General Information: Public terminal goes back to 1984. No adoption records released. Will not fax documents. Certification fee: $2.00. Payee: Court Clerk. Personal checks accepted. Prepayment required. SASE requested.

State Court 133 Montgomery St, County Courthouse, Savannah, GA 31401; phone: 912-652-7224; fax: 912-652-7229; hours 8AM-5PM (EST). *Misdemeanor, Civil.* www.statecourt.org
Note: Search fines, tickets, and restitution records free at www.chathamcounty.org/jims/fines/default.asp.
Civil Records: Access: Mail, fax, in person, online. Both court and visitors may perform in person searches. Search fee: $3.00 per name. Court makes copy: $1.00 per page. Required to search: name, years to search, address. Civil cases indexed by defendant, plaintiff. Civil records on computer from 1983, prior on books. Search county civil dockets and records free at www.chathamcounty.org/jims/. Search by name or case number. Mail turnaround 2 days.
Criminal Records: Access: Mail, fax, in person, online. Both court and visitors may perform in person searches. Search fee: $3.00 per name. Court makes copy: $1.00 per page. Required to search: name, years to search. Criminal records on computer from 1983, prior on books. Search county criminal dockets and records free at www.chathamcounty.org/jims/. Mail turnaround time 2 days.
General Information: Public use terminal available. No first time criminal offender or sealed civil records released. Will fax documents for $.50 per page. Certification fee: $2.50 plus $.50 per page. Payee: Clerk of State Court. Only cashiers checks and money orders accepted. Prepayment and SASE required.

Magistrate Court 133 Montgomery St, Rm 303, 3rd Fl, Savannah, GA 31401; phone: 912-652-7181; fax: 912-652-7550; hours 8AM-5PM (EST). *Civil Actions Under $15,000, Eviction, Small Claims.*
www.chathamcourts.org/chatcourts.html
Note: Court also has jurisdiction for bad checks, arrest warrants, preliminary hearings, and county ordinance violations. Search dockets online at www.chathamcounty.org/jims/.

Probate Court 133 Montgomery St, Rm 509, Savannah, GA 31401; phone: 912-652-7265; fax: 912-652-7262; hours 8AM-5PM (EST). *Probate.*
www.chathamcourts.org/chatcourts.html

Chattahoochee County

Superior & Magistrate Court PO Box 120, Cusseta, GA 31805; phone: 706-989-3424; fax: 706-989-1508; hours 8AM-5PM (EST). *Felony, Misdemeanor, Civil, Eviction, Small Claims.*
Note: Magistrate Court is 706-989-3643.
Civil Records: Access: In person only. Visitors must perform in person searches themselves. Court

makes copy: $1.00 per page. Self serve copy fee: $.25 per page. Required to search: name, years to search. Civil cases indexed by defendant, plaintiff. Civil records on dockets from 1854.
Criminal Records: Access: In person only. Visitors must perform in person searches themselves. Court makes copy: $1.00 per page. Self serve copy fee: $.25 per page. Required to search: name, years to search, DOB; SSN helpful. Crim recs on dockets from 1854.
General Information: Public use terminal available. No juvenile, adoption, sexual, mental health or expunged records released. Certification fee: $2.50 plus $.50 per page after first. Payee: Court Clerk. Business checks accepted. Prepayment required.

Probate Court PO Box 119, Cusseta, GA 31805; phone: 706-989-3603; fax: 706-989-2015; hours 8AM-N, 1-5PM (EST). *Probate.*

Chattooga County

Superior & State Court PO Box 159, Summerville, GA 30747; phone: 706-857-0706; fax: 706-857-0686; hours 8:30AM-5PM (EST). *Felony, Misdemeanor, Civil, Eviction, Small Claims.*
Civil Records: Access: In person only. Visitors must perform in person searches themselves. Court makes copy: $.25 per page. Required to search: name, years to search. Civil cases indexed by defendant, plaintiff. Civil records on dockets from 1960.
Criminal Records: Access: In person only. Visitors must perform in person searches themselves. Court makes copy: $.25 per page. Required to search: name, years to search, DOB; SSN helpful. Criminal records on dockets from 1960.
General Information: Public use terminal available. No juvenile, adoption, sexual, mental health or expunged records released. Certification fee: $2.50 plus $.50 per page after first. Payee: Clerk of Court. Personal checks accepted. Prepayment required.

Magistrate Court 10017 Commerce St, Summerville, GA 30747; phone: 706-857-0711; fax: 706-857-0675; hours 9AM-5PM (EST). *Civil Actions Under $15,000, Eviction, Small Claims.*

Probate Court PO Box 467, 10035 Commerce St, Summerville, GA 30747; phone: 706-857-0709; fax: 706-857-0877; 8:30AM-N, 1-5PM *Probate.*
https://www.gaprobate.org/counties/chattooga/index.html

Cherokee County

Superior & State Court 90 North St, #G170, Canton, GA 30114; phone: 678-493-6501; hours 8AM-5PM (EST). *Felony, Misdemeanor, Civil.*
Note: This court location also handles juvenile records.
Civil Records: Access: In person only. Visitors must perform in person searches themselves. Court makes copy: $1.00 per page. Self serve copy fee: $.25 per page. Required to search: name. Civil cases indexed by defendant, plaintiff. Civil records on computer from 1990, archived 1900-1991, on dockets back to 1900.
Criminal Records: Access: In person only. Visitors must perform in person searches themselves. Court makes copy: $1.00 per page. Self serve copy fee: $.25 per page. Required to search: name, years to search, DOB; SSN helpful. Criminal records on computer from 1990, archived 1900-1990, on dockets back to 1900.
General Information: Public terminal goes back to 1991. No juvenile, adoption, sexual, mental health, expunged or confidential records released. Certification fee: $2.00 plus $.50 per add'l page. Payee: Clerk of Court. Only cashiers checks and money orders accepted. Prepayment required.

Magistrate Court 90 North St, #150, Canton, GA 30114; phone: 678-493-6431; hours 8:30AM-5PM (EST). *Civil Actions Under $15,000, Eviction, Small Claims.* www.cccourt.com
Note: Search the magistrate court database online at www.cccourt.com. Court also has jurisdiction for bad checks, arrest warrants, preliminary hearings, and county ordinance violations.

Probate Court 90 North St, Rm 340, Canton, GA 30114; phone: 678-493-6160; fax: 678-493-6170; hours 8AM-4;30PM (EST). *Probate.*
https://www.gaprobate.org/counties/cherokee/index.html

Clarke County

Superior & State Court PO Box 1805, Athens, GA 30603; phone: 706-613-3190; hours 8AM-5PM (EST). *Felony, Misdemeanor, Civil.*
http://athensclarke.allclerks.us
Note: Located at 325 E Washington, Rm 450, 30601. This court will perform no searches for the public.
Civil Records: Access: In person only. Visitors must perform in person searches themselves. Court makes copy: in-house copies are $.25 each; by mail is $1.00 per page. Required to search: name, years to search. Civil cases indexed by defendant, plaintiff. Civil records on computer from 1993, docket books from 1801.
Criminal Records: Access: In person only. Visitors must perform in person searches themselves. Court makes copy: in-house copies are $.25 each; by mail is $1.00 per page. Required to search: name, years to search, DOB. Criminal records on computer from 1993, docket books from 1801.
General Information: Public use terminal available. No juvenile, adoptions, sealed, sexual, mental health or expunged records released. Certification fee: $2.50 plus $.50 per page after first. Payee: County Clerk. Personal checks accepted. Prepayment required.

Magistrate Court PO Box 1868, 325 E Washington St, Athens, GA 30601; phone: 706-613-3310; fax: 706-613-3314; 8AM-5PM (EST). *Civil Actions Under $15,000, Eviction, Small Claims.*

Probate Court 325 E Washington St, #215, Athens, GA 30601; phone: 706-613-3320; fax: 706-613-3323; hours 8AM-5PM (EST). *Probate.*

Clay County

Superior Court PO Box 550, Ft Gaines, GA 39851; phone: 229-768-2631; fax: 229-768-3047; hours 8AM-4:30PM (EST). *Felony, Misdemeanor, Civil, Eviction.*
Civil Records: Access: In person only. Visitors must perform in person searches themselves. Court makes copy: $1.00 per page. Required to search: name, years to search. Civil cases indexed by defendant, plaintiff. Civil records on computer from 1990, on dockets from 1854.
Criminal Records: Access: In person only. Visitors must perform in person searches themselves. Court makes copy: $1.00 per page. Required to search: name, years to search. Criminal records on computer from 1990, on dockets from 1854.
General Information: Public terminal goes back to 1990. No juvenile, adoption, sexual, mental health or expunged records released. Certification fee: $3.00. Payee: Superior Court Clerk. Personal checks accepted. Prepayment required.

Magistrate Court PO Box 73, 210 S Washington St, Ft Gaines, GA 39851; phone: 229-768-2841; fax: 229-768-3047; hours 8AM-4:30PM (EST). *Civil Actions Under $15,000, Eviction, Small Claims.*

Probate Court PO Box 448, 210 S Washington, Ft Gaines, GA 39851; phone: 229-768-2445; fax: 229-768-2710; hours 8AM-4:30PM (EST). *Probate.*

Clayton County

Superior Court 9151 Tara Blvd, #ICL19, Jonesboro, GA 30236-4912; phone: 770-477-3405; hours 8AM-5PM (EST). *Felony, Civil.*
www.co.clayton.ga.us/superior_court/clerk_of_courts
Civil Records: Access: Mail, in person. Visitors must perform in person searches themselves. No search fee. Court makes copy: $1.00 per page by mail; $.25 per page walk-in. Required to search: name, years to search. Civil cases indexed by defendant. Civil records on docket books for all records, on computer from 1996, on microfilm from 1990, archived 1858-1982, on dockets to 1858. Court

calendars online at www.co.clayton.ga.us/courtcalendars/index.htm. Mail turnaround time 1 week.
Criminal Records: Access: Mail, in person. Visitors must perform in person searches themselves. No search fee. Court makes copy: $1.00 per page by mail; $.25 per page walk-in. Required to search: name, years to search, DOB; also helpful: SSN, race, sex. Criminal record keeping same as civil. Court calendars online at www.co.clayton.ga.us/courtcalendars/index.htm. Mail turnaround time 1 week.
General Information: Public terminal has only civil records back to 1996. No adoption, sexual, mental health or expunged records released. Certification fee: $2.00. Payee: Clerk of Superior Court. Only cashiers checks, money orders and attorney checks accepted. Prepayment required.

State Court 9151 Tara Blvd, #1CL181, Jonesboro, GA 30236; phone: 770-477-3388; fax: 770-472-8159; hours 8AM-5PM (EST). *Misdemeanor.*
www.co.clayton.ga.us/state_court/clerk_of_courts
Criminal Records: Access: In person only. Visitors must perform in person searches themselves. Court makes copy: $.25 per page. Required to search: name, years to search. Criminal records on computer from 1985.
General Information: Public terminal has only criminal records back to 1990. No juvenile, adoption, sexual, mental health or expunged records released. Certification fee: $2.50 plus $.50 per page after first. Payee: Court Clerk. Business checks accepted. Prepayment required.

Magistrate Court 9151 Tara Blvd, #2TC08, Jonesboro, GA 30236-4912; phone: 770-477-3444; fax: 770-473-5750; hours 8AM-5PM (EST). *Civil Actions Under $15,000, Eviction, Small Claims.*
www.co.clayton.ga.us/courts.htm

Probate Court 121 S McDonough St, Annex 3, Jonesboro, GA 30236-3694; phone: 770-477-3299; fax: 770-477-3306; hours 8AM-4:30PM (EST). *Probate.* www.co.clayton.ga.us/probate_court

Clinch County

Superior & State Court PO Box 433, Homerville, GA 31634; phone: 912-487-5854; fax: 912-489-3083; hours 8AM-5PM (EST). *Felony, Misdemeanor, Civil.*
Civil Records: Access: Mail, in person. Both court and visitors may perform in person searches. No search fee. Court makes copy: $.25 per page. Required to search: name, years to search. Civil cases indexed by defendant, plaintiff. Civil records on dockets from 1900. Mail turnaround time 1-3 days.
Criminal Records: Access: Mail, in person. Both court and visitors may perform in person searches. No search fee. Court makes copy: $.25 per page. Required to search: name, years to search, DOB; also helpful: SSN, race, sex. Criminal records on dockets from 1900. Mail turnaround time 1-2 days.
General Information: Public terminal goes back to 1998. No juvenile, adoption, sexual, mental health or expunged records released. Will fax documents for $3.00 per page. Certification fee: $3.00. Payee: Court Clerk. Personal checks accepted. Prepayment required. SASE requested.

Magistrate Court 100 Court Square, Homerville, GA 31634; phone: 912-487-2514; fax: 912-487-5507; hours 9AM-12;00- 1-5PM (EST). *Civil Actions Under $15,000, Eviction, Small Claims.*

Probate Court PO Box 364, 25 Court Sq, #F, Homerville, GA 31634; phone: 912-487-5523; fax: 912-487-3083; 9AM-12;00, 1-5PM (EST). *Probate.*

Cobb County

Superior Court PO Box 3370, Marietta, GA 30061; phone: 770-528-1300; hours 8AM-5PM (EST). *Felony, Misdemeanor, Civil.*
www.cobbgasupctclk.com/index.htm
Civil Records: Access: Online, in person. Visitors must perform in person searches themselves. Court makes copy: $.25 per page; same fee for self serve.

Required to search: name, years to search. Civil cases indexed by defendant, plaintiff. Civil records on computer from 1982, records on dockets from 1958. Civil or criminal indexes of Clerk of Superior Court are free at www.cobbgasupctclk.com/index.htm. Search by name, type or case number. Data updated Fridays.

Criminal Records: Access: Mail, online, in person. Visitors must perform in person searches themselves. No search fee. Court makes copy: $.25 per page; same fee for self serve. Required to search: name, years to search. Criminal records on computer from 1982, Records on dockets from 1958. Online access to criminal records is the same as civil. Mail turnaround time 1-3 days.

General Information: Public terminal goes back to 1982. No juvenile, adoption, sexual, mental health or expunged records released. Certification fee: $2.00 plus $.50 per page. Payee: Clerk of Superior Court. Personal checks accepted. Prepayment required.

State Court - Civil & Criminal Divisions

12 E Park Square, Marietta, GA 30090-9630; criminal phone: 770-528-1262; civil phone: 770-528-1203; criminal fax: 770-528-1268; civil fax: 770-528-1205; hours 8AM-5PM (EST). *Misdemeanor, Civil, Eviction.* www.cobbstatecourtclerk.com

Civil Records: Access: In person only. Both court and visitors may perform in person searches. Search fee: none unless record is offsite (pre-1998), then $7.00 per name. Court makes copy: $.25 per page. Required to search: name, years to search. Civil cases indexed by defendant, plaintiff. Civil records on computer since 3/10/97, docket books from 1965.

Criminal Records: Access: In person only. Both court and visitors may perform in person searches. Search fee: none unless record is offsite (pre-1996), then $7.00. Court makes copy: $.25 per page. Required to search: name, years to search, offense; also helpful: DOB. Criminal records on computer since 1981, docket books from 1965.

General Information: Public terminal has criminal back to 1981 and civil back to 3/10/97. No sealed records released. Certification fee: $3.00. Payee: State Court Clerk. No personal checks accepted. Prepayment required.

Magistrate Court 32 Waddell St, 3rd Fl, Marietta, GA 30090-9656; phone: 770-528-8900; hours 8AM-5PM (EST). *Civil Actions Under $15,000, Small Claims.* www.cobbcounty.org/judicial/magistrate/index.htm

Probate Court 32 Waddell St, Marietta, GA 30060; phone: 770-528-1990; fax: 770-528-1996; hours 8AM-4:30PM (EST). *Probate.* https://www.gaprobate.org/counties/cobb/index.html

Coffee County

Superior & State Court 101 S Peterson Ave, Douglas, GA 31533; phone: 912-384-2865; fax: 912-384-0291; hours 8:30AM-5PM (EST). *Felony, Misdemeanor, Civil.*

Civil Records: Access: In person only. Visitors must perform in person searches themselves. Court makes copy: $.25 per page. Required to search: name. Civil cases indexed by defendant, plaintiff. Civil records on dockets.

Criminal Records: Access: In person only. Visitors must perform in person searches themselves. Court makes copy: $.25 per page. Required to search: name, years to search. Criminal records on dockets.

General Information: No public access terminal. No juvenile, adoption, sexual, mental health or expunged records released. Certification fee: $3.00 per cert. Payee: Clerk Superior Court. Business checks accepted.

Magistrate Court 101 S Peterson Ave, Douglas, GA 31533; phone: 912-384-2983; criminal phone: 912-384-1381; fax: 912-383-0800; hours 8:30AM-5PM (EST). *Civil Actions Under $15,000, Eviction, Small Claims.* www.coffeemagcourt.com

Probate Court 101 S Peterson Ave, Douglas, GA 31533; phone: 912-384-5213; fax: 912-383-8116; hours 8:30AM-5PM (EST). *Probate, Civil.* https://www.gaprobate.org/counties/coffee/index.html

Colquitt County

Superior & State Court PO Box 2827, Moultrie, GA 31776; phone: 229-616-7420; criminal phone: 229-616-7423 Sup; 616-7064 state; civil phone: 229-616-7066 Sup; 616-7420 state; fax: 229-616-7029; hours 8AM-5PM (EST). *Felony, Misdemeanor, Civil.* http://southernjudicialcircuit.com

Civil Records: Access: In person only. Visitors must perform in person searches themselves. Court makes copy: $1.00 per page. Self serve copy fee: $.25 per page. Required to search: name, years to search. Civil cases indexed by defendant, plaintiff. Civil records go back to 1800s, civil records on dockets books, computerized records go back to 1999.

Criminal Records: Access: In person only. Visitors must perform in person searches themselves. Court makes copy: $1.00 per page. Self serve copy fee: $.25 per page. Required to search: name, years to search. Criminal records on dockets books; computerized records go back to 1999.

General Information: Public terminal goes back to 1999. No juvenile, adoption, sexual, mental health or expunged records released. Certification fee: $2.50. Payee: Court Clerk. Personal checks accepted. Prepayment required.

Magistrate Court PO Box 70, Moultrie, GA 31776; phone: 229-616-7450; fax: 229-616-7494; hours 8AM-5PM (EST). *Civil Actions Under $15,000, Eviction, Small Claims.*

Probate Court PO Box 264, Colquitt County Govt Bldg, 9 S Main St, Rm 108, Moultrie, GA 31776-0264; phone: 229-616-7415; fax: 229-616-7489; hours 8AM-5PM (EST). *Probate.* https://www.gaprobate.org/counties/colquitt/index.html

Columbia County

Superior Court PO Box 2930, Evans, GA 30809; phone: 706-312-7139; fax: 706-312-7152; hours 8AM-5PM (EST). *Felony, Misdemeanor, Civil.* Note: This court is located at 640 Ronald Reagan Dr in Evans, GA 30809.

Civil Records: Access: In person only. Visitors must perform in person searches themselves. Court makes copy: $.25 per page. Required to search: name, years to search. Civil cases indexed by plaintiff. Civil records on computer from 1987, prior on docket books.

Criminal Records: Access: In person only. Visitors must perform in person searches themselves. Court makes copy: $.25 per page. Required to search: name, years to search, DOB; SSN helpful. Criminal records on computer from 1987, prior on docket books.

General Information: Public use terminal available. No juvenile, adoption, sexual, mental health or expunged records released. Certification fee: $2.00 plus $.50 per page. Payee: Clerk of Superior Court. Personal checks not accepted. Prepayment required.

Magistrate Court PO Box 777, 640 Ronald Reagan Dr, Evans, GA 30809; phone: 706-868-3316; fax: 706-868-3314; 8AM-5PM (EST). *Civil Actions Under $15,000, Eviction, Small Claims.*

Probate Court PO Box 525, 1956 Appling Harlem Hwy, Appling, GA 30802; phone: 706-541-1254; fax: 706-541-4001; hours 8AM-4:30PM (EST). *Probate.*

Cook County

Superior Court 212 N Hutchinson Ave, Adel, GA 31620; phone: 229-896-7717; hours 8:30AM-4:30PM (EST). *Felony, Misdemeanor, Civil.*

Civil Records: Access: Phone, mail, in person. Both court and visitors may perform in person searches. Search fee: $10.00 per name, per 7 year period. Court makes copy: $1.00 per page. Self serve copy fee: $.25 per page. Required to search: name, years to search.

Civil cases indexed by defendant. Civil records on dockets books, microfilm. Mail turnaround time same day.

Criminal Records: Access: Mail, in person. Both court and visitors may perform in person searches. Search fee: $10.00 per name per 7 year period. Court makes copy: $1.00 per page. Self serve copy fee: $.25 per page. Required to search: name, years to search, DOB, signed release; also helpful: SSN, race, sex. Criminal records on dockets books, microfilm. Mail turnaround time same day.

General Information: No public access terminal. No juvenile, adoption, sexual, 1st offenders, mental health or expunged records released. Certification fee: $2.50 plus $.50 per page after first. Payee: Court Clerk.; business check accepted. prepayment required.

Magistrate Court 1000 County Farm Rd, Adel, GA 31620; phone: 229-896-3151; fax: 229-896-5186; hours 8AM-4:30PM (EST). *Civil Actions Under $15,000, Eviction, Small Claims.*

Probate Court 212 N Hutchinson Ave, Adel, GA 31620; phone: 229-896-3941; fax: 229-896-6083; hours 8:30AM-5PM *Probate, Misdemeanor Traffic.*

Coweta County

Superior Court PO Box 943, 200 Court Square, Newnan, GA 30264; phone: 770-254-2693/2695; fax: 770-254-3700; 8AM-5PM (EST). *Felony, Civil.*

Civil Records: Access: Mail, in person. Visitors must perform in person searches themselves. No search fee. Court makes copy: $.25 per page. Required to search: name, years to search. Civil cases indexed by defendant, plaintiff. Civil records on computer from 1990, dockets books to 1970.

Criminal Records: Access: In person only. Both court and visitors may perform in person searches. No search fee. Court makes copy: $.25 per page. Required to search: name, years to search, DOB; SSN helpful. Criminal records on docket books back to 1919. Can only conduct felony searches from 1990 to present.

General Information: Public terminal goes back to 1990. No juvenile, adoption, sexual, mental health or expunged records released. Certification fee: $2.50 plus $.50 per page after first. Payee: Clerk of Superior & State Court. Business checks accepted. Prepayment required.

State Court 9 E Broad St, Newnan, GA 30263; phone: 770-254-2699; fax: 770-254-3700; hours 8AM-5PM (EST). *Misdemeanor, Civil.* www.coweta.ga.us/Resources/stateclk.html

Civil Records: Access: Phone, in person. Both court and visitors may perform in person searches. Search fee: None, unless records are off-site (older than 4 years)- fee is $5.00. Court makes copy: $.25 per page. Required to search: name, years to search. Civil cases indexed by defendant, plaintiff. Civil records on computer from 1990, dockets bk to 1970.

Criminal Records: Access: Mail, in person. Both court and visitors may perform in person searches. Search fee: None, unless records are off-site (older than 4 years)- fee is $5.00. Court makes copy: $.25 per page. Required to search: name, years to search, DOB. Criminal records on docket books back to 1919; on computer from 1990. Can only conduct felony searches from 1990 to present. Mail turnaround time 2-3 days.

General Information: Public terminal goes back to 1990. No juvenile, adoption, sexual, mental health or expunged records released. Certification fee: $2.50 plus $.50 per page after first. Payee: Clerk of Superior & State Court. Only cashiers checks and money orders accepted. Prepayment and SASE required.

Magistrate Court 22-34 E Broad St, Newnan, GA 30263; phone: 770-254-2610; fax: 770-254-2614; hours 8AM-5PM (EST). *Civil Actions Under $15,000, Eviction, Small Claims.*

Probate Court 22 E Broad St, Newnan, GA 30263; phone: 770-254-2640; fax: 770-254-2648; hours 8AM-N, 1-5PM (EST). *Probate.* https://www.gaprobate.org/counties/coweta/index.html

Crawford County

Superior Court PO Box 1037, Roberta, GA 31058; phone: 478-836-3328; probate phone: 478-836-3313; fax: 478-836-9170; hours 9AM-5PM (EST). *Felony, Misdemeanor, Civil.*
Civil Records: Access: Mail, in person. Visitors must perform in person searches themselves. Search fee: Copy fees apply. Court makes copy: $1.00 per page. Self serve copy fee: $.25 per page. Required to search: name, years to search. Civil cases indexed by defendant, plaintiff. Civil records on dockets books to 1830, records computerized since 1998. Mail turnaround time 2 days.
Criminal Records: Access: Mail, in person. Visitors must perform in person searches themselves. Search fee: Copy fees apply. Court makes copy: $1.00 per page. Self serve copy fee: $.25 per page. Required to search: name, years to search, DOB; also helpful: SSN, race, sex. Criminal records on dockets books to 1830, records computerized since 1998. Mail turnaround time 2 days.
General Information: Public terminal goes back to 1998. No juvenile, adoption, sexual, mental health or expunged records released. Will fax documents for $2.50 per page, prepaid. Certification fee: $2.50 first page, $.50 ea add'l. Payee: Clerk of Superior Court. Personal checks accepted. Prepayment required.

Magistrate Court PO Box 568, Roberta, GA 31078; phone: 478-836-5804; fax: 478-836-4340; hours 9AM-5PM (EST). *Civil Actions Under $15,000, Eviction, Small Claims.*

Probate Court PO Box 1028, Roberta, GA 31078; phone: 478-836-3313; fax: 478-836-4111; hours 9AM-5PM (EST). *Probate.*
https://www.gaprobate.org/counties/crawford/index.html
Note: Traffic records here also.

Crisp County

Superior & Juvenile Court PO Box 747, Cordele, GA 31010-0747; phone: 229-276-2616; fax: 229-273-5750; hours 8:30AM-5PM (EST). *Felony, Misdemeanor, Civil Actions Over $15,000.*
Civil Records: Access: Mail, in person. Visitors must perform in person searches themselves. Court makes copy: $.25 per page; same fee for self serve. Required to search: name, years to search. Civil cases indexed by defendant. Civil records on docket books to 1905, computerized since 1994. Mail turnaround time 1-2 days.
Criminal Records: Access: Mail, in person. Visitors must perform in person searches themselves. Court makes copy: $.25 per page; same fee for self serve. Required to search: name, years to search; also helpful: SSN. Criminal records on docket books to 1905, computerized since 1994. Mail turnaround time 1-2 days.
General Information: Public terminal goes back to 1994. No juvenile, adoption, sexual, mental health or expunged records released. Fee to fax documents is $2.50 1st page, $1.00 each add'l. Certification fee: $2.00 plus $.50 per page. Cert fee includes copies. Payee: Clerk of Superior Court. Personal checks accepted. Prepayment and SASE required.

Magistrate Court 210 S 7th St, Rm 102, Cordele, GA 31015; phone: 229-276-2618; fax: 229-276-2634; hours 8:30AM-5PM (EST). *Civil Actions Under $15,000, Eviction, Small Claims.*

Probate Court 210 S 7th St, Rm 103, Cordele, GA 31015; phone: 229-276-2621; fax: 229-273-9184; hours 9AM-5PM (EST). *Probate.*
https://www.gaprobate.org/counties/crisp/index.html
Note: Mailing address is PO Box 26, Cordele GA 31010-0026

Dade County

Superior Court PO Box 417, Trenton, GA 30752; phone: 706-657-4778; Sm Claims 706-657-4113; probate phone: 706-657-4414; hours 8:30AM-5PM (EST). *Felony, Misdemeanor, Civil, Eviction, Small Claims.* www.gsccca.org/clerks

Civil Records: Access: Phone, fax, mail, in person. Both court and visitors may perform in person searches. No search fee. Court makes copy: $1.50 per page. Required to search: name, years to search. Civil cases indexed by defendant, plaintiff. Civil records on computer back to 1/1999; prior on docket books. Mail turnaround time 1 day.
Criminal Records: Access: Mail, fax, in person. Both court and visitors may perform in person searches. Search fee: $5.00 per name. Court makes copy: $1.50 per page. Required to search: name, years to search, DOB, signed release. Criminal records on computer back to 1/1999; prior on docket books to 1900's. Mail turnaround time 1 day.
General Information: Public terminal goes back to 1999. No juvenile, adoption, sexual, mental health or expunged records released. Fee to fax documents is $1.00 per page. Certification fee: $2.00 plus $.50 per page after first. Payee: Superior Court. Personal checks accepted. Prepayment required. SASE requested.

Magistrate Court PO Box 1263, 75 Case Ave, Trenton, GA 30752; phone: 706-657-4113; fax: 706-657-8618; hours 8AM-5PM (EST). *Civil Actions Under $15,000, Eviction, Small Claims.*

Probate Court PO Box 605, 75 Case Ave, Trenton, GA 30752; phone: 706-657-4414; fax: 706-657-4305; 8:30AM-12;00,1-5PM *Probate.*
https://www.gaprobate.org/counties/dade/index.html

Dawson County

Superior Court 25 Tucker Ave, #106, Dawsonville, GA 30534; phone: 706-344-3510; fax: 706-344-3511; hours 8AM-5PM (EST). *Felony, Misdemeanor, Civil.*
Civil Records: Access: Phone, mail, fax, in person. Visitors must perform in person searches themselves. No search fee. Court makes copy: $.25 per page; same fee for self serve. Required to search: name, years to search. Civil cases indexed by plaintiff. Civil records on computer back to 1994, prior in dockets books. Note: The court search only searches the computer index. Mail turnaround time 1 week.
Criminal Records: Access: mail, fax, in person. Visitors must perform in person searches themselves. No search fee. Court makes copy: $.25 per page; same fee for self serve. Required to search: name, years to search, DOB; also helpful: SSN, race, sex. Criminal records on computer back to 1994, prior in dockets books. Note: The court search only searches the computer index. Mail turnaround time 1 week.
General Information: Public use terminal available. No juvenile, adoption, sexual, mental health or expunged records released. Certification fee: $2.50. Payee: Superior Court. Prepayment required.

Magistrate Court 25 Tucker Ave #104, Dawsonville, GA 30534; phone: 706-344-3730; fax: 706-265-8480; hours 8AM-8PM (EST). *Civil Actions Under $15,000, Eviction, Small Claims.*

Probate Court 25 Tucker Ave, #102, Dawsonville, GA 30534; phone: 706-344-3580; fax: 706-265-6155; hours 8AM-5PM (EST). *Probate.*
https://www.gaprobate.org/counties/dawson/index.html

De Kalb County

Superior Court 556 N McDonough St, Decatur, GA 30030; phone: 404-371-2836; fax: 404-371-2635; hours 7:30AM-6PM (EST). *Felony, Misdemeanor, Civil.*
www.co.dekalb.ga.us/superior/index.htm
Civil Records: Access: In person, online. Visitors must perform in person searches themselves. Court makes copy: $1.00 per page. Required to search: name, years to search. Civil cases indexed by defendant, plaintiff. Civil records on computer from 1988, prior archived. Online access is free at www.ojs.dekalbga.org.
Criminal Records: Access: In person, online. Visitors must perform in person searches

themselves. Court makes copy: $1.00 per page. Self serve copy fee: $.25 per page. Required to search: name, years to search, DOB; also helpful: SSN, race, sex. Criminal records on computer from 1988, on microfilm from 1947. Online access is free at www.ojs.dekalbga.org. Jail and inmate records are also available.
General Information: Public use terminal available. No juvenile, adoption, sexual, mental health or expunged records released. Certification fee: $2.50 plus $.50 per page after first. Payee: Clerk of Superior Court. Personal checks accepted. Prepayment required.

State Court 556 N McDonough St, Decatur, GA 30030; phone: 404-371-2261; fax: 404-371-3064; hours 8:30AM-5PM (EST). *Misdemeanor, Civil.*
www.dekalbstatecourt.net
Civil Records: Access: Mail, in person, online. Visitors must perform in person searches themselves. No search fee. Court makes copy: $.50 per page. Required to search: name, years to search. Civil cases indexed by defendant, plaintiff. Civil records on docket books. Online access is free at www.ojs.dekalbga.org. Also, current court calendars free at www.dekalbstatecourt.net. Note: The court will perform limited searches. Mail turnaround time 7 days.
Criminal Records: Access: In person, online, mail. Both court and visitors may perform in person searches. No search fee. Court makes copy: $.50 per page. Required to search: name. Criminal records on docket books. Online access is free at www.ojs.dekalbga.org. Jail and inmate records also available. Also, current court calendars free at www.dekalbstatecourt.net. Mail turnaround time 7 days.
General Information: Public use terminal available. Certification fee: $5.00 per doc. Payee: Court Clerk. Only cashiers checks and money orders accepted. Prepayment required. SASE requested.

Magistrate Court 120 W Trinity Pl, Rm 210, Decatur, GA 30030; phone: 404-371-4766; hours 8:30AM-5PM (EST). *Civil Actions Under $15,000, Eviction, Small Claims.*
http://dekalbstatecourt.net
Note: Online access is available free at www.ojs.dekalbga.org. Court also has jurisdiction for bad checks, arrest warrants, preliminary hearings, and county ordinance violations.

Probate Court County Courthouse, 556 N McDonough St, Rm 1100, Decatur, GA 30030; phone: 404-371-2718; fax: 404-371-7055; hours 8:30AM-4:00PM (EST). *Probate.*

Decatur County

Superior & State Court PO Box 336, Bainbridge, GA 39818; phone: 229-248-3025; fax: 229-248-3029; hours 8AM-5PM (EST). *Felony, Misdemeanor, Civil.*
Civil Records: Access: In person only. Visitors must perform in person searches themselves. Court makes copy: $.25 per page; same fee for self serve. Required to search: name, years to search. Civil cases indexed by defendant, plaintiff. Civil records on docket books from 1823; computerized from 1996.
Criminal Records: Access: In person only. Visitors must perform in person searches themselves. Court makes copy: $.25 per page; same fee for self serve. Required to search: name, years to search, DOB; SSN helpful. Criminal records on docket books from 1823; computerized from 1996.
General Information: Public terminal has criminal back to 1996 and civil back to 1997. No juvenile, adoption, sexual, mental health or expunged records released. Certification fee: $2.50 plus $.50 per page. Payee: Court Clerk. No personal checks accepted. Prepayment required.

Magistrate Court 912 Spring Creek Rd, Box #3, Bainbridge, GA 39817; phone: 229-248-3014; fax: 229-248-3863; hours 9AM-5PM (EST). *Civil Actions Under $15,000, Eviction, Small Claims.*

Probate Court PO Box 234, Bainbridge, GA 39818; phone: 229-248-3016; fax: 229-248-3858; hours 9AM-5PM (EST). *Probate.*
https://www.gaprobate.org/counties/decatur/index.html

Dodge County

Superior Court PO Drawer 4276, 5401 Anson Ave, Eastman, GA 31023; phone: 478-374-2871; fax: 478-374-3035; hours 9AM-5PM (EST). *Felony, Misdemeanor, Civil.*
Civil Records: Access: In person only. Visitors must perform in person searches themselves. Court makes copy: $.25 per page. Required to search: name, years to search. Civil cases indexed by defendant. Civil records on docket books.
Criminal Records: Access: In person only. Visitors must perform in person searches themselves. Court makes copy: $.25 per page. Required to search: name, years to search, DOB, signed release; SSN helpful. Criminal records on docket books and computer.
General Information: No public access terminal. No juvenile, adoption, sexual, mental health or expunged records released. Certification fee: $2.00 plus $.50 per page after first. Payee: Court Clerk. Personal checks accepted. Prepayment required.

Magistrate Court 5018 Courthouse Cir, #202, Eastman, GA 31023; phone: 478-374-7243/8144; fax: 478-374-5716; hours 8:30AM-N; 1PM-4:30PM (EST). *Civil Actions Under $15,000, Eviction, Small Claims.*

Probate Court PO Box 514, 5401 Anson Ave, Eastman, GA 31023; phone: 478-374-3775/478-374-8152; fax: 478-374-9197; hours 9AM-N, 1-5PM (EST). *Probate.*

Dooly County

Superior Court PO Box 326, 104 Second st, Vienna, GA 31092-0326; phone: 229-268-4234; fax: 229-268-1427; hours 8:30AM-5PM (EST). *Felony, Misdemeanor, Civil.*
Civil Records: Access: Fax, mail, in person. Visitors must perform in person searches themselves. Court makes copy: $1.00 per page. Self serve copy fee: $.25 per page. Required to search: name, years to search. Civil cases indexed by defendant, plaintiff. Civil records on computer since 1995. Prefer to have public perform searches.
Criminal Records: Access: In person. Visitors must perform in person searches themselves. Court makes copy: $1.00 per page. Self serve copy fee: $.25 per page. Required to search: name, years to search, DOB, signed release; also helpful: SSN, race, sex. Criminal records on computer since 1995, docket books prior to 1857. Note: Prefer to have public to perform searches.
General Information: No public access terminal. No juvenile, adoption, sexual, mental health or expunged records released. Certification fee: $2.50. Payee: Dooly County Superior Court Clerk. Personal checks accepted. Prepayment required.

Magistrate Court PO Box 336, 209 D W Union St, Vienna, GA 31092; phone: 229-268-4324; fax: 229-268-3585; hours 8AM-N, 1-5PM (EST). *Civil Actions Under $15,000, Eviction, Small Claims.*

Probate Court 104 2nd St South, Vienna, GA 31092; phone: 229-268-4217 x1; fax: 229-268-6142; hours 8AM-5PM M,T,Th,F; 8:30AM-N W & Sat or by appointment (EST). *Probate, Misdemeanor, Traffic.* www.doolycountyprobate.com
Note: Misdemeanor records phone number is ext. 4.

Dougherty County

Superior & State Court PO Box 1827, 225 Pine Ave, #126, Albany, GA 31702; phone: 229-431-2198; fax: 229-878-3155; hours 8:30AM-5PM (EST). *Felony, Misdemeanor, Civil.*
www.albany.ga.us/doco/court_system.htm
Civil Records: Access: Online, in person. Visitors must perform in person searches themselves. Court makes copy: $1.00 per page. Self serve copy fee: $.25 per page. Required to search: name, years to search.

Civil cases indexed by defendant, plaintiff. Civil records on computer from 1992, overall records go back to 1854. Access pre-2003 civil and criminal court docket data free at www.albany.ga.us/doco/clerk_court_rec.htm. The same system permits access to probate, tax, deeds, death certificate records, and older civil/criminal records.
Criminal Records: Access: Online, in person. Visitors must perform in person searches themselves. Court makes copy: $1.00 per page. Self serve copy fee: $.25 per page. Required to search: name, years to search SSN. Criminal records on computer from 1992, overall records go back to 1854. Online access to criminal records is the same as civil.
General Information: Public terminal goes back to 1992. No juvenile, adoption, sexual, mental health or expunged records released. Certification fee: $3.00 for 1st page. Copy fee for add'l pages. Payee: Court Clerk. Personal checks accepted. Prepayment required.

Magistrate Court PO Box 1827, 225 Pine Ave, Rm 308, Albany, GA 31702; phone: 229-431-3216; fax: 229-434-2692; hours 8:30AM-5PM (EST). *Civil Actions Under $15,000, Eviction, Small Claims.*

Probate Court PO Box 1827, 225 Pine Ave, #123, Albany, GA 31702; phone: 229-431-2102; fax: 229-434-2694; hours 8:30AM-5PM (EST). *Probate.* https://www.gaprobate.org/counties/dougherty/index.html Note: Search the probate court index at www.albany.ga.us/doco/clerk_court_rec.htm.

Douglas County

Superior Court Douglas County Courthouse, 8700 Hospital Dr, Douglasville, GA 30134; phone: 770-920-7252; hours 8AM-5PM (EST). *Felony, Misdemeanor, Civil.*
Civil Records: Access: In person only. Visitors must perform in person searches themselves. Court makes copy: $1.00 per page. Self serve copy fee: $.25 per page. Required to search: name, years to search. Civil cases indexed by defendant, plaintiff. Civil records on computer from 1994, prior on docket books to 1871.
Criminal Records: Access: In person only. Visitors must perform in person searches themselves. Court makes copy: $1.00 per page. Self serve copy fee: $.25 per page. Required to search: name, years to search, DOB, signed release; SSN helpful. Criminal records on computer from 1994, prior on docket books to 1871.
General Information: Public terminal goes back to 1994. No juvenile, adoption, sexual, mental health or expunged records released. Certification fee: $2.50 plus $.50 per page. Payee: Clerk of Superior Court. Personal checks accepted. Prepayment required.

Magistrate Court 8700 Hospital Dr, Douglasville, GA 30134; phone: 770-920-7215; hours 8AM-5PM (EST). *Civil Actions Under $15,000, Eviction, Small Claims.*

Probate Court 8700 Hospital Dr, Douglasville, GA 30134; phone: 770-920-7249; fax: 770-920-7381; hours 8AM-5PM (EST). *Probate.*

Early County

Superior & State Court PO Box 849, Blakely, GA 39823; phone: 229-723-3033; fax: 229-723-4411; hours 8AM-5PM (EST). *Felony, Misdemeanor, Civil.*
Civil Records: Access: In person only. Visitors must perform in person searches themselves. Court makes copy: $1.00 per page. Self serve copy fee: $.25 per page. Required to search: name, years to search. Civil cases indexed by defendant, plaintiff. Civil records on dockets.
Criminal Records: Access: In person only. Visitors must perform in person searches themselves. Court makes copy: $1.00 per page. Self serve copy fee: $.25 per page. Required to search: name, years to search, DOB; SSN helpful. Criminal records on dockets.

General Information: No public access terminal. No juvenile, adoption, sexual, mental health or expunged records released. Certification fee: $2.50 plus $.50 per page after first. Payee: Court Clerk. Personal checks accepted. Prepayment required.

Magistrate Court Early County Courthouse, Rm D, 111 Court Sq, Blakely, GA 39823; phone: 229-723-3454 and 229-723-5492; fax: 229-723-5246; hours 8AM-5PM (EST). *Civil Actions Under $15,000, Eviction, Small Claims, Probate.*

Echols County

Superior Court PO Box 213, Statenville, GA 31648; phone: 229-559-5642; fax: 229-559-5792; hours 8AM-N, 1-4:30PM (EST). *Felony, Misdemeanor, Civil.*
http://southernjudicialcircuit.com
Civil Records: Access: In person only. Visitors must perform in person searches themselves. Court makes copy: $1.00 per page; same fee for self serve. Required to search: name, years to search. Civil cases indexed by defendant, plaintiff. Civil records on dockets books, computerized since 1995.
Criminal Records: Access: In person only. Visitors must perform in person searches themselves. Court makes copy: $1.00 per page; same fee for self serve. Required to search: name, years to search. Criminal records on dockets books, computerized since 1995.
General Information: Public terminal goes back to 1995. No juvenile, adoption, sexual, mental health or expunged records released. Certification fee: $2.00 1st page, $.50 each add'l page. Payee: Court Clerk. Personal checks accepted. Prepayment required.

Magistrate & Probate Court PO Box 118, 110 Hwy 94 East, Statenville, GA 31648; phone: 229-559-5526; fax: 229-559-8128; hours 8:00AM-4:30PM (EST). *Civil Actions Under $15,000, Eviction, Small Claims, Probate.*

Effingham County

Superior Court PO Box 387, Springfield, GA 31329; phone: 912-754-2146; probate phone: 912-754-2112; hours 8:30AM-5PM (EST). *Felony, Misdemeanor, Civil.*
Civil Records: Access: Mail, in person. Both court and visitors may perform in person searches. Search fee: $20.00 per name. Court makes copy: $.25 per page; same fee for self serve. Required to search: name, years to search. Civil cases indexed by defendant, plaintiff. Civil records on computer from 1991, dockets books. Mail turnaround time 3-5 days.
Criminal Records: Access: Mail, in person. Both court and visitors may perform in person searches. Search fee: $20.00 per name. Court makes copy: $.25 per page; same fee for self serve. Required to search: name, years to search, DOB; also helpful: SSN, race, sex. Criminal records on computer from 1991, dockets books. Mail turnaround time 3-5 days.
General Information: Public terminal goes back to 1991. No juvenile, adoption, sexual, mental health or expunged records released. Certification fee: $2.50 plus $.50 per add'l page,. Payee: Court Clerk. Business checks accepted. Prepayment and SASE required.

Magistrate Court PO Box 819, 901 Pine St, Springfield, GA 31329; phone: 912-754-2124/29/50; fax: 912-754-4893; 8AM-5PM *Civil Actions Under $15,000, Eviction, Small Claims.*
www.georgiacourts.org

Probate Court 901 Pine St, PO Box 387, Springfield, GA 31329; phone: 912-754-2112; fax: 912-754-3894; hours 8:30AM-5PM (EST). *Probate.*
https://www.gaprobate.org/counties/effingham/index.html

Elbert County

Superior & State Court PO Box 619, Elberton, GA 30635; phone: 706-283-2005; fax: 706-213-7286; hours 8AM-5PM (EST). *Felony, Misdemeanor, Civil.*

Civil Records: Access: Mail, in person. Visitors must perform in person searches themselves. No search fee. Court makes copy: $.50 per page. Self serve copy fee: $.50 per page. Required to search: name, years to search. Civil cases indexed by defendant, plaintiff. Civil records on computer from 1996 excluding felonies; docket books prior. Mail turnaround time 1 week.
Criminal Records: Access: Mail, in person. Visitors must perform in person searches themselves. No search fee. Court makes copy: $.50 per page. Self serve copy fee: $.50 per page. Required to search: name, years to search. Civil records on computer from 1996 excluding felonies; docket books prior. Mail turnaround time 1 week.
General Information: Public terminal goes back to 1996. No juvenile, adoption, sexual, mental health or expunged records released. Will fax documents for $2.50 1st page and $1.00 each add'l. Certification fee: $2.00 per cert. Payee: Clerk of Court. No personal checks accepted. Prepayment required.

Magistrate Court PO Box 763, 245 S Oliver St, Elberton, GA 30635; phone: 706-283-2027; fax: 706-283-2004; hours 8AM-5PM (EST). *Civil Actions Under $15,000, Eviction, Small Claims.*

Probate Court Elbert County Courthouse, Elberton, GA 30635; phone: 706-283-2016; fax: 706-283-9668; hours 8AM-5PM (EST). *Probate.*

Emanuel County

Superior & State Court PO Box 627, Swainsboro, GA 30401; phone: 478-237-8911; hours 8AM-5PM (EST). *Felony, Misdemeanor, Civil.*
Civil Records: Access: In person only. Visitors must perform in person searches themselves. Court makes copy: $1.00 per page. Self serve copy fee: $.25 per page. Required to search: name, years to search. Civil cases indexed by defendant, plaintiff. Civil records computerized since 1999, earlier on dockets books.
Criminal Records: Access: In person only. Visitors must perform in person searches themselves. Court makes copy: $1.00 per page. Self serve copy fee: $.25 per page. Required to search: name, years to search, DOB; SSN helpful. Criminal records computerized since 1999, earlier on dockets books.
General Information: No public access terminal. No juvenile, adoption, sexual, mental health or expunged records released. Certification fee: $2.50 plus $.50 per page. Payee: Court Clerk. Personal checks accepted. Prepayment required.

Magistrate Court 107 N Main St, Swainsboro, GA 30401; phone: 478-237-7278; fax: 478-237-9154; hours 8AM-5PM Fri-7:30-4:30 (EST). *Civil Actions Under $15,000, Eviction, Small Claims.*

Probate Court PO Box 70, Swainsboro, GA 30401; phone: 478-237-7091; fax: 478-237-2633; hours 8AM-5PM (EST). *Probate.*

Evans County

Superior & State Court PO Box 845, Claxton, GA 30417; phone: 912-739-3868; fax: 912-739-2504; hours 8AM-5PM (EST). *Felony, Misdemeanor, Civil.*
Civil Records: Access: In person only. Visitors must perform in person searches themselves. Court makes copy: $1.00 per page. Self serve copy fee: $.25 per page. Required to search: name, years to search. Civil cases indexed by defendant, plaintiff. Civil records on computer from 1989, dockets bookstore 1915.
Criminal Records: Access: In person only. Visitors must perform in person searches themselves. Court makes copy: $1.00 per page. Self serve copy fee: $.25 per page. Required to search: name, years to search, DOB; SSN helpful. Criminal records on computer from 1989, dockets books to 1915.
General Information: Public use terminal available. No juvenile, adoption, sexual, mental health or expunged records released. Certification fee: $2.50

plus $.50 per page after first. Payee: Court Clerk. Personal checks accepted. Prepayment required.

Magistrate Court Courthouse Annex, 7 Freeman St, Claxton, GA 30417; phone: 912-739-3745; fax: 912-739-8856; hours 8AM-5PM (EST). *Civil Actions Under $15,000, Eviction, Small Claims.*

Probate Court 123 W Main St, PO Box 852, Claxton, GA 30417; phone: 912-739-4080; fax: 912-739-4077; hours 8AM-N, 1-5PM (EST). *Probate.*
https://www.gaprobate.org/counties/effingham/index. html

Fannin County

Superior Court PO Box 1300, 420 W Main St, Blue Ridge, GA 30513; phone: 706-632-2039; probate phone: 706-632-3011; hours 9AM-5PM (EST). *Felony, Misdemeanor, Civil.*
http://9thjudicialdistrict-ga.org/dca9apphp.shtml
Civil Records: Access: In person only. Visitors must perform in person searches themselves. Court makes copy: $1.00 per page. Self serve copy fee: $.25 per page. Required to search: name, years to search. Civil cases indexed by defendant, plaintiff. Civil records on docket books back to the early 1900's.
Criminal Records: Access: In person only. Visitors must perform in person searches themselves. Court makes copy: $1.00 per page. Self serve copy fee: $.25 per page. Required to search: name, years to search, DOB, signed release; SSN helpful. Criminal records on docket books back to the early 1900's.
General Information: No public access terminal. No juvenile, adoption, or DD214 records released. Certification fee: $2.50 plus $.50 per page after first. Payee: Fannin County Court Clerk. Personal checks accepted. Prepayment required.

Magistrate Court 400 W Main St #202, Blue Ridge, GA 30513; phone: 706-632-5558; fax: 706-632-8236; hours 9AM-5PM (EST). *Civil Actions Under $15,000, Eviction, Small Claims, Misdemeanor.*

Probate Court 400 W Main St #204, Blue Ridge, GA 30513; phone: 706-632-3011; fax: 706-632-7167; hours 8AM-5PM (EST). *Probate.*

Fayette County

Superior Court PO Box 130, Fayetteville, GA 30214; phone: 770-716-4290; criminal phone: 770-716-4293; civil phone: 770-716-4294; hours 8AM-5PM (EST). *Felony, Misdemeanor, Civil.*
www.admin.co.fayette.ga.us
Note: The court will copy and mail specific documents for $1.00 per page.
Civil Records: Access: In person only. Visitors must perform in person searches themselves. Court makes copy: $.25 per page. Required to search: name, years to search. Civil cases indexed by defendant, plaintiff. Civil records on computer since 1989; prior records on dockets books.
Criminal Records: Access: In person only. Visitors must perform in person searches themselves. Court makes copy: $.25 per page. Required to search: name, years to search, DOB; SSN helpful. Criminal records on computer since 1989; prior records on dockets books.
General Information: Public use terminal available. No juvenile, adoption, sexual, mental health or expunged records released. Certification fee: $2.00 plus $.50 per page after first. Payee: Court Clerk. Only cashiers checks and money orders accepted. Prepayment required.

Magistrate Court 1 Center Dr, Fayetteville, GA 30214-8401; phone: 770-716-4230; fax: 770-716-4855; hours 8AM-5PM (EST). *Civil Actions Under $15,000, Eviction, Small Claims.*
Note: Court also has jurisdiction for bad checks, arrest warrants, and preliminary hearings.

Probate Court 1 Center Dr, Fayetteville, GA 30214; phone: 770-716-4224; fax: 770-716-4854; hours 8AM-5PM (EST). *Probate.*
https://www.gaprobate.org/counties/fayette/index.html

Floyd County

Superior Court PO Box 1110, #3 Government Plaza, #101, Rome, GA 30163; phone: 706-291-5190; probate phone: 706-291-5136; hours 8AM-5PM (EST). *Felony, Misdemeanor, Civil.*
www.floydsuperiorcourt.org
Civil Records: Access: Phone, in person. Visitors must perform in person searches themselves. Court makes copy: $.50 per page. Required to search: name, years to search. Civil cases indexed by defendant, plaintiff. Civil records on computer since 11/95; prior on docket books to 1833. Note: The court will only do a name search to determine if a case exists, then provides a case number.
Criminal Records: Access: In person only. Both court and visitors may perform in person searches. Court makes copy: $.50 per page. Required to search: name, years to search, signed release. Criminal records on computer since 1/96; prior on docket books back to 1833. Note: Court will only do a name search to determine if a case exists, then provides a case number.
General Information: Public terminal has criminal back to 1/1996 and civil back to 11/95. No juvenile, adoption, sexual, mental health or expunged records released. Will fax file copy for $1.00 per page. Certification fee: $2.00. Payee: Court Clerk. Personal checks not accepted. Prepayment required.

Magistrate Court 3 Government Plaza, Rm 227, 410 Tribute St, Rm 227, Rome, GA 30161; phone: 706-291-5250; fax: 706-291-5269; hours 8:45AM-4:45PM (EST). *Civil Actions Under $15,000, Eviction, Small Claims.*
Note: Copy fee is $.50 a page; certification is $2.00; will fax results for an add'l $.50 per page. Court also has jurisdiction for bad checks, arrest warrants, preliminary hearings, and county ordinance violations.

Probate Court 3 Government Plaza, #201, County Administrative Offices, Rome, GA 30161; phone: 706-291-5136/8; fax: 706-291-5189; hours 8AM-5:00PM (EST). *Probate.*

Forsyth County

Superior & State Court 100 Courthouse Square, Rm 010, Cumming, GA 30040; phone: 770-781-2120; fax: 770-886-2858; hours 8:30AM-5PM (EST). *Felony, Misdemeanor, Civil, Eviction, Small Claims.*
www.forsythco.com
Civil Records: Access: In person only. Visitors must perform in person searches themselves. Court makes copy: $.25 per page; same fee for self serve. Required to search: name, years to search. Civil cases indexed by defendant. Civil records on computer since 1996; prior records on docket books back to 1832.
Criminal Records: Access: In person only. Visitors must perform in person searches themselves. Court makes copy: $.25 per page; same fee for self serve. Required to search: name, years to search; SSN helpful. Criminal records on computer since late 1989.
General Information: Public terminal has criminal back to 1999 and civil back to 1980. No juvenile, adoption, sexual, mental health or expunged records released. Certification fee: $2.50 plus $.50 per page after first. Payee: Court Clerk. Personal checks accepted. Prepayment required.

Magistrate Court 121 Dahlonega St, Cumming, GA 30040; phone: 770-781-2211; fax: 770-844-7581; hours 8AM-4:30PM (EST). *Civil Actions Under $15,000, Eviction, Small Claims, Probate.*

Probate Court County Courthouse Annex, Rm 101, 112 W Maple St, Cumming, GA 30040; phone: 770-781-2140; fax: 770-886-2839; hours 8:30AM-5PM (EST). *Probate.*

Franklin County

Superior Court PO Box 70, Carnesville, GA 30521; phone: 706-384-2514; hours 8AM-5PM (EST). *Felony, Misdemeanor, Civil.*
Civil Records: Access: In person only. Visitors must perform in person searches themselves. Court makes copy: $1.00 per page. Self serve copy fee: $.25 per page. Required to search: name, years to search. Civil cases indexed by defendant, plaintiff. Civil records on computer since 2002; prior records on docket books.
Criminal Records: Access: In person only. Visitors must perform in person searches themselves. Court makes copy: $1.00 per page. Self serve copy fee: $.25 per page. Required to search: name, years to search, DOB; SSN helpful. Criminal records on computer since 2002; prior records on docket books.
General Information: Public terminal goes back to 2002. No juvenile, adoption, sexual, mental health or expunged records released. Certification fee: $2.50 for 1st page, $.50 each add'l. Payee: Court Clerk. Personal checks accepted. Prepayment required.

Magistrate Court PO Box 467, 156 Athens St, Carnesville, GA 30521; phone: 706-384-7473; fax: 706-384-4346; hours 8AM-5PM (EST). *Civil Actions Under $15,000, Eviction, Small Claims.*

Probate Court PO Box 207, 9592 Lavonia Rd, Carnesville, GA 30521; phone: 706-384-2403; fax: 706-384-2636; hours 8AM-5PM (EST). *Probate.*
https://www.gaprobate.org/counties/franklin/index.html
Note: This location also holds traffic misdemeanors and vital records.

Fulton County

Superior Court - Civil 136 Pryor St SW, Rm C-155, Superior Court Clerk, Atlanta, GA 30303; civil phone: 404-730-5344; fax: 404-302-8416; hours 8:30AM-5PM (EST). *Civil.*
www.fcclk.org
Civil Records: Access: In person only. Both court and visitors may perform in person searches. Search fee: varies. Court makes copy: $1.00 per page. Self serve copy fee: $.25 per page. Required to search: name, years to search. Civil cases indexed by defendant, plaintiff. Civil records on computer since 1972.
General Information: Public terminal goes back to 1972. No juvenile, adoption, sexual, mental health, sealed or expunged records released. Certification fee: $2.50 for 1st page; $.50 each add'l. Includes copy fee. Payee: Clerk of Fulton Superior Court. Personal checks accepted. Prepayment required.

Superior Court - Criminal 136 Pryor St SW, Rm 106, Atlanta, GA 30303; phone: 404-730-5770 Admin; criminal phone: 404-730-5248; fax: 404-302-8416; hours 8:30AM-5PM (EST). *Felony, Misdemeanor, Eviction.* www.fcclk.org
Note: File Rm phone- 404-730-5375
Criminal Records: Access: In person only. Visitors must perform in person searches themselves. Court makes copy: $1.00 per page. Required to search: name, years to search, DOB, SSN, signed release; charges helpful. Criminal records on computer from 1973. Note: Criminal record room, who process criminal record requests, will accept requests for specific cases only, but will not do name searches per se.
General Information: Public terminal has only criminal records back to 1974. No sealed or expunged records released. Will not fax specific case file. Certification fee: $2.50 for 1st page; $.50 each add'l, includes copies. Cert Dept. phone- 404-730-6872. Payee: Clerk of Superior Court. Personal checks accepted. Prepayment required.

State Court TG100 Justice Center Twr, 185 Central Ave SW, Atlanta, GA 30303; phone: 404-730-5000; criminal fax:; civil fax: 404-730-8141; hours 8:30AM-5PM (EST). *Misdemeanor, Civil.*
Civil Records: Access: In person only. Both court and visitors may perform in person searches.

Search fee: $15.00 if court performs search. Court makes copy: $1.00 per page. Required to search: name, years to search. Civil cases indexed by defendant, plaintiff. Civil records on computer from 1984, books back to 1982.
Criminal Records: Access: In person only. Both court and visitors may perform in person searches. Search fee: $15.00 if court performs search. Court makes copy: $1.00 per page. Required to search: name, years to search, DOB, signed release; SSN helpful, race, aliases, date of offense, sex, approximate arrest date. Criminal records on computer from 1984, books back to 1982.
General Information: No juvenile, adoption, sexual, mental health or expunged records released. Certification fee: $2.50 per page. Includes copy fee. Payee: Court Clerk. Business checks accepted. Prepayment required.

Magistrate Court 185 Central Ave SW, TG-700, Justice Ctr Tower, Atlanta, GA 30303; phone: 404-730-5045; criminal phone: 404-730-4752; hours 8:30AM-5PM (EST). *Civil Actions Under $15,000, Eviction, Small Claims.*
Note: Court also has jurisdiction for bad checks, arrest warrants, preliminary hearings, and county ordinance violations. Go to www.fultoncourtconnect.com for civil records.

Probate Court 136 Pryor St, # 230, Atlanta, GA 30303; phone: 404-730-4640; fax: 404-730-8283; hours 8:30AM-5PM (EST). *Probate.*
https://www.gaprobate.org/counties/fulton/index.html

Gilmer County

Superior Court #1 Westside Square, Ellijay, GA 30540; phone: 706-635-4462; fax: 706-635-1462; hours 8:30AM-5PM (EST). *Felony, Misdemeanor, Civil.*
http://9thjudicialdistrict-ga.org/dca9apphp.shtml
Civil Records: Access: In person only. Visitors must perform in person searches themselves. Court makes copy: $1.00 per page. Self serve copy fee: $.25 per page. Required to search: name, years to search. Civil cases indexed by defendant, plaintiff. Civil records on docket books computerized records since 1994.
Criminal Records: Access: In person only. Visitors must perform in person searches themselves. Court makes copy: $1.00 per page. Self serve copy fee: $.25 per page. Required to search: name, years to search, signed release; also helpful: DOB, SSN. Criminal records on docket books; computerized since 1994.
General Information: Public terminal goes back to 1994. No juvenile, adoption, sealed, sexual, mental health, expunged or sealed records released. Certification fee: $2.50 plus $.50 per page after first. Payee: Superior Court Clerk. Personal checks accepted. Prepayment required.

Magistrate Court 53 Sand St, Ellijay, GA 30540; phone: 706-635-2515; fax: 706-635-7756; hours 8:30AM-5PM (EST). *Civil Actions Under $15,000, Eviction, Small Claims.*

Probate Court 51 Sand St, Ellijay, GA 30540; phone: 706-635-4763; fax: 706-635-4761; hours 8:30AM-5PM (EST). *Probate.*
https://www.gaprobate.org/counties/gilmer/index.html

Glascock County

Superior Court PO Box 231, 62 E Main St, Gibson, GA 30810; phone: 706-598-2084; fax: 706-598-2577; hours 8AM-5PM M,Tu,Th,F; Wed 8AM-Noon (EST). *Felony, Misdemeanor, Civil.*
Civil Records: Access: In person only. Visitors must perform in person searches themselves. Court makes copy: $1.00 per page. Self serve copy fee: $.25 per page. Required to search: name, years to search. Civil cases indexed by defendant, plaintiff. Civil records on computer from 1991, records go back to 1990.
Criminal Records: Access: In person only. Visitors must perform in person searches themselves. Court makes copy: $1.00 per page. Self serve copy fee: $.25

per page. Required to search: name, years to search, DOB; SSN helpful. Criminal records on computer from 1991 records go back to 1990.
General Information: Public terminal goes back to 1991. (Public access in county cases only.) No juvenile, adoption, sexual, mental health or expunged records released. Will fax specific case file for $1.00 per page. Certification fee: $2.50 plus $.50 per page copy fee after first. Payee: Court Clerk. Personal checks accepted. Prepayment required.

Magistrate Court PO Box 201, 370 W Main St, Gibson, GA 30810; phone: 706-598-2013; fax: 706-598-3577; hours 8AM-5PM, M,T, Th,Fri, 8AM-N, W (EST). *Civil Actions Under $15,000, Eviction, Small Claims.*

Probate Court PO Box 277, 370 W Main St, Gibson, GA 30810; phone: 706-598-3241; fax: 706-598-2471; hours 8AM-N, 1-5PM-M,T,Th,Fri; 8am-Noon W (EST). *Probate.*

Glynn County

Superior Court PO Box 1355, Brunswick, GA 31521; phone: 912-554-7272; fax: 912-267-5625; hours 8AM-5PM (EST). *Felony, Civil.*
Civil Records: Access: Phone, fax, mail, in person. Both court and visitors may perform in person searches. No search fee. Court makes copy: $.25 per page. Required to search: name, years to search. Civil cases indexed by defendant, plaintiff. Civil records on computer back to 1987, archived and in docket books from 1800s. Mail turnaround time 1-3 days.
Criminal Records: Access: Phone, fax, mail, in person. Both court and visitors may perform in person searches. No search fee. Court makes copy: $.25 per page. Required to search: name, years to search, DOB, signed release; also helpful: SSN, race, sex. Criminal records on computer back to 1987, index back to 1800s. Mail turnaround time 1-3 days.
General Information: Public terminal goes back to 1987. No juvenile, adoption, sexual, mental health or expunged records released. Fee to fax documents is $5.00 per document. Certification fee: $2.50. Payee: Court Clerk. Personal checks accepted. Prepayment required. Will bill copy and cert fees. SASE requested.

State Court 701 "H" St, #104, Brunswick, GA 31520; phone: 912-554-7325; fax: 912-261-3849; hours 9AM-5PM (EST). *Misdemeanor, Civil.*
Civil Records: Access: In person only. Visitors must perform in person searches themselves. Court makes copy: $.25 per page. Required to search: name, years to search. Civil cases indexed by defendant. Civil records on dockets books to 1980; on computer back to 1994.
Criminal Records: Access: In person only. Visitors must perform in person searches themselves. Court makes copy: $.25 per page. Required to search: name, years to search. Criminal records on dockets books to 1979; on computer back to 1994.
General Information: Public terminal goes back to 1994. No juvenile, adoption, sexual, mental health or expunged records released. Certification fee: $2.00 plus $.50 per page. Payee: Clerk of State Court. Only cashiers checks and money orders accepted. Prepayment required.

Magistrate Court PO Box 1355, 701 H St, Brunswick, GA 31521; phone: 912-554-7250; fax: 912-267-5677; hours 8:00AM-5PM (EST). *Civil Actions Under $15,000, Eviction, Small Claims.*

Probate Court 701 H St, Box 302, Brunswick, GA 31520; phone: 912-554-7231; fax: 912-466-8001; hours 8:30AM-5PM (EST). *Probate, Civil, Small Claims.*
https://www.gaprobate.org/counties/glynn/index.html

Gordon County

Superior Court 100 Wall St, #102, Calhoun, GA 30701; phone: 706-629-9533; fax: 706-629-2139; hours 8:30AM-5PM (EST). *Felony, Misdemeanor, Civil.*
Civil Records: Access: Mail, in person. Both court and visitors may perform in person searches. No search fee. Court makes copy: $1.00 per page. Self serve copy fee: $.25 per page. Required to search: name, years to search. Civil cases indexed by defendant, plaintiff. Civil records on computer since 3/97; prior records on docket books. Mail turnaround time 1-2 days.
Criminal Records: Access: Mail, in person. Both court and visitors may perform in person searches. No search fee. Court makes copy: $1.00 per page. Self serve copy fee: $.25 per page. Required to search: name, years to search. Criminal records on computer since 3/97; prior records on docket books. Mail turnaround time 1-2 days.
General Information: Public terminal goes back to 1997. No sealed records released. Will not fax documents. Certification fee: $2.50. Payee: Superior Court Clerk. Personal checks accepted. Prepayment and SASE required.

Magistrate Court PO Box 1025, 100 Wall St, Calhoun, GA 30703; phone: 706-629-6818 x2270, x2271; criminal phone: 706-879-2271; civil phone: 706-879-2271; fax: 706-602-1751; hours 8:30AM-5PM (EST). *Misdemeanors, Civil Actions Under $15,000, Eviction, Small Claims.*

Probate Court PO Box 669, 100 S Wall St, Calhoun, GA 30703; phone: 706-629-7314; fax: 706-629-4698; hours 8:30AM-5PM (EST). *Probate.*
https://www.gaprobate.org/counties/gordon/index.html

Grady County

Superior Court 250 N Broad St, Box 8, Cairo, GA 39828; phone: 229-377-2912; fax: 229-377-7078; hours 8AM-5PM (EST). *Felony, Misdemeanor, Civil.*
Civil Records: Access: In person only. Both court and visitors may perform in person searches. No search fee. Court makes copy: $1.00 per page. Self serve copy fee: $.25 per page. Required to search: name, years to search. Civil cases indexed by defendant, plaintiff. Civil records on computer since 1993; prior records on docket books from 1906. Note: Court will assist visitors with searches.
Criminal Records: Access: In person only. Visitors must perform in person searches themselves. Court makes copy: $1.00 per page. Self serve copy fee: $.25 per page. Required to search: name, years to search. Criminal records on computer since 1993; prior records on docket books from 1906. Note: Court will assist visitors with searches.
General Information: Public terminal goes back to 1993. No juvenile or adoption records released. Certification fee: $2.00 per cert. Payee: Superior Court Clerk. Personal checks accepted. Prepayment required.

Magistrate Court 250 N Broad St, Box 2, Cairo, GA 39828; phone: 229-377-4132; fax: 229-377-4127; hours 8AM-5PM (EST). *Civil Actions Under $15,000, Eviction, Small Claims.*

Probate Court 250 N Broad St, Box #1, Courthouse, Cairo, GA 39828; phone: 229-377-4621; fax: 229-378-8052; hours 8AM-5PM (EST). *Probate.*
www.georgiacourts.org/courts/probate/grady

Greene County

Superior & Juvenile Court 113 N Main St, #109, Greensboro, GA 30642; phone: 706-453-3340; fax: 706-453-9179; hours 8AM-5PM (EST). *Felony, Misdemeanor, Civil, Eviction, Small Claims.*
Civil Records: Access: In person only. Visitors must perform in person searches themselves. Court makes copy: $.25 per page. Required to search: name, years to search. Civil cases indexed by defendant,

plaintiff. Overall records go back to 1700. Computerized records go back to 2000.
Criminal Records: Access: In person only. Visitors must perform in person searches themselves. Court makes copy: $.25 per page. Required to search: name, years to search; SSN helpful. Overall records go back to 1700. Computerized records go back to 2000.
General Information: No public access terminal. No juvenile or adoption records released. Certification fee: $2.50 per document. Payee: Superior Court Clerk. Personal checks accepted. Prepayment required.

Magistrate & Probate Court 113 N Main St, #113, Greensboro, GA 30642; phone: 706-453-3346; fax: 706-453-7649; hours 8AM-5PM (EST). *Civil Actions Under $15,000, Eviction, Small Claims, Probate.*
https://www.gaprobate.org/counties/greene/index.html

Gwinnett County

Superior & State Court PO Box 880 (75 Langley Dr), Lawrenceville, GA 30046; phone: 770-822-8100; hours 8AM-5PM (EST). *Felony, Misdemeanor, Civil, Eviction, Small Claims.*
www.gwinnettcourts.com/courts/Supcourt.htm
Civil Records: Access: Online, in person. Visitors must perform in person searches themselves. Court makes copy: $.25 per page. Required to search: name, years to search. Civil cases indexed by defendant, plaintiff. Civil records on computer from 1990, prior records on card index. Online access to court case party index is free at www.gwinnettcourts.com/misc/casendx.htm. Search by name or case number.
Criminal Records: Access: Online, in person. Visitors must perform in person searches themselves. Court makes copy: $.25 per page. Required to search: name, years to search. Criminal records on computer from 1990, prior records on card index. Online access to criminal records is the same as civil.
General Information: Public use terminal available. No sealed records released. Certification fee: $2.50 plus $.50 per page. Payee: Superior Court Clerk. Personal checks accepted. Prepayment required.

Magistrate Court 75 Langley Dr, Justice & Admin. Ctr, Lawrenceville, GA 30045-6900; phone: 770-822-8080; fax: 770-822-8075; hours 8AM-5PM (EST). *Civil Actions Under $15,000, Eviction, Small Claims.*
www.gwinnettcourts.com/courts/Magcourt.htm

Probate Court 75 Langley Dr, Justice & Admin Ctr, Lawrenceville, GA 30045; phone: 770-822-8250; fax: 770-822-8274; hours 8:AM-4:30PM (EST). *Probate.*
www.gwinnettcourts.com/courts/Procourt.htm

Habersham County

Superior & State Court 555 Monroe St, Unit 35, Clarkesville, GA 30523; phone: 706-754-2923; probate phone: 706-754-2013; hours 8AM-5PM (EST). *Felony, Misdemeanor, Civil.*
www.co.habersham.ga.us
Civil Records: Access: Mail, in person. Visitors must perform in person searches themselves. No search fee. Self serve copy fee: $.25 per page. Required to search: name, years to search. Civil cases indexed by defendant, plaintiff. Civil records on index books from 1819. Mail turnaround time 1-2 days.
Criminal Records: Access: Mail, in person. Visitors must perform in person searches themselves. No search fee. Self serve copy fee: $.25 per page. Required to search: name, years to search. Criminal records on index books from 1819. Mail turnaround time 1-2 days.
General Information: Public terminal goes back to 1992. No juvenile, adoption, sexual, mental health or expunged records released. Will fax documents to local or toll free line. Certification fee: $3.00 per document. Payee: Court Clerk. Personal checks accepted. Prepayment required.

Magistrate Court PO Box 580, 226 Grant St, Clarkesville, GA 30523; phone: 706-754-4871; criminal phone: 706-754-0126; civil phone: 706-754-4871; fax: 706-839-7093; hours 8;30AM-5PM (EST). *Civil Actions Under $15,000, Eviction, Small Claims.*
www.co.habersham.ga.us

Probate Court PO Box 625, 555 Monroe St, County Courthouse, Clarkesville, GA 30523; phone: 706-754-2013; fax: 706-754-5093; hours 8AM-5PM (EST). *Probate.*

Hall County

Superior & State Court PO Box 1336, Gainesville, GA 30503; phone: 770-531-7025; fax: 770-531-7070; hours 8AM-5PM (EST). *Felony, Misdemeanor, Civil.*
Civil Records: Access: In person only. Visitors must perform in person searches themselves. Court makes copy: $.25 per page. Required to search: name, years to search. Civil cases indexed by defendant, plaintiff. Civil records on computer back to 1989, dockets books from early 1900s in storage.
Criminal Records: Access: In person only. Visitors must perform in person searches themselves. Court makes copy: $.25 per page. Required to search: name, years to search. Criminal records on computer back to 1989, dockets books from early 1900s in storage.
General Information: Public terminal goes back to 7/1989. No juvenile, adoption, sexual, mental health or expunged records released. Certification fee: $2.00 plus $.50 per page. Payee: Court Clerk. Personal checks accepted. Prepayment required.

Magistrate Court PO Box 1435, 225 Green St, 2nd Fl, Gainesville, GA 30503; phone: 770-531-6912; fax: 770-531-6917; hours 8AM-5PM (EST). *Civil Actions Under $15,000, Eviction, Small Claims, Misdemeanors.*
www.hallcounty.org/judicial/#majistrate

Probate Court Hall County Courthouse, Rm 1000, 225 Green St, Gainesville, GA 30501; phone: 770-531-6923; fax: 770-531-4946; hours 8;30AM-4:30PM (EST). *Probate.*
www.hallcounty.org/judicial/#probate
Note: The search fee is $4.00 per record

Hancock County

Superior Court PO Box 451, Courthouse Sq, Sparta, GA 31087; phone: 706-444-6644; fax: 706-444-5685; hours 9AM-5PM (EST). *Felony, Misdemeanor, Civil.*
Civil Records: Access: Mail, in person. Visitors must perform in person searches themselves. Search fee: $5.00 per name. Court makes copy: $.25 per page. Required to search: name, years to search. Civil cases indexed by defendant, plaintiff. Civil records on docket books from 1991. Mail turnaround time 1 week.
Criminal Records: Access: Mail, in person. Visitors must perform in person searches themselves. Search fee: $5.00 per name. Court makes copy: $.25 per page. Required to search: name, years to search, DOB, signed release; also helpful: SSN, race, sex. Criminal records on books since 1991. Mail turnaround time 1 week.
General Information: Public use terminal available. (Terminal to have civil and criminal records soon.) No juvenile, adoptions, sealed, sexual, mental health or expunged records released. Certification fee: $2.50 per doc. Payee: Clerk of Superior Court. Personal checks accepted. Prepayment and SASE required.

Magistrate Court 603 Courthouse Square, Sparta, GA 31087; phone: 706-444-6234; fax: 706-444-6178; hours 9AM-5PM (EST). *Civil Actions Under $15,000, Eviction, Small Claims.*

Probate Court 601 Courthouse Square, Sparta, GA 31087; phone: 706-444-5343; fax: 706-444-8024; hours 8AM-5PM (EST). *Probate.*
https://www.gaprobate.org/counties/hancock/index.html

Haralson County

Superior Court Drawer 849, 4485 Georgia Hwy 120, Buchanan, GA 30113; phone: 770-646-2005; probate phone: 770-646-2008; fax: 770-646-8827; hours 8:30AM-5PM (EST). *Felony, Misdemeanor, Civil.*

Civil Records: Access: Mail, in person. Both court and visitors may perform in person searches. No search fee. Court makes copy: $.25 per page. Required to search: name, years to search. Civil cases indexed by defendant, plaintiff. Civil records on dockets books from the 1864. Mail turnaround time 1 week.

Criminal Records: Access: Mail, in person. Both court and visitors may perform in person searches. No search fee. Court makes copy: $.25 per page. Required to search: name, years to search, signed release. Criminal records on dockets books from the 1864. Mail turnaround time 1 week.

General Information: No public access terminal. No juvenile, adoption, sexual, mental health or expunged records released. Certification fee: $2.50 plus $.50 per page after first. Payee: Clerk of Superior Court. Personal checks accepted. Prepayment and SASE required.

Magistrate Court PO Box 1040, 4485 Hwy 120, Buchanan, GA 30113; phone: 770-646-2015; fax: 770-646-6627; hours 8:30AM-5PM (EST). *Civil Actions Under $15,000, Eviction, Small Claims.*

Probate Court PO Box 620, 4485 Georgia Hwy 20, Buchanan, GA 30113; phone: 770-646-2008; fax: 770-646-3419; hours 8:30AM-5PM (EST). *Probate.*
https://www.gaprobate.org/counties/haralson/index.html

Harris County

Superior Court PO Box 528, 102 N College, Hamilton, GA 31811; phone: 706-628-4944; fax: 706-628-7039; hours 8AM-5PM (EST). *Felony, Misdemeanor, Civil.*

Civil Records: Access: In person only. Visitors must perform in person searches themselves. Court makes copy: $.25 per page. Required to search: name, years to search. Civil cases indexed by defendant, plaintiff. Civil records on dockets books from 1900; on computer back to 1999.

Criminal Records: Access: In person only. Visitors must perform in person searches themselves. Court makes copy: $.25 per page. Required to search: name, years to search, DOB; also helpful: race, sex. Criminal records on dockets books from 1900; on computer back to 1999.

General Information: Public terminal goes back to 1999. Juvenile, adoption, sexual, mental health or expunged records are only released with a signed release. Certification fee: $2.50 plus $.50 per page after first. Payee: Court Clerk. No personal checks accepted. Prepayment required.

Magistrate Court PO Box 347, 102 N College St, Hamilton, GA 31811; phone: 706-628-4977; fax: 706-628-5416; hours 8AM-5PM (EST). *Civil Actions Under $15,000, Eviction, Small Claims.*
www.harrismagcourt.com
Note: Court also has jurisdiction for bad checks, arrest warrants, preliminary hearings, and county ordinance violations. Website may soon have court records available.

Probate Court PO Box 569, 102 N College St #116, Hamilton, GA 31811; phone: 706-628-5038; fax: 706-628-7322; hours 8AM-5PM (No longer close at noon) (EST). *Probate.*

Hart County

Superior Court PO Box 386, Hartwell, GA 30643; phone: 706-376-7189; fax: 706-376-1277; hours 8:30AM-5PM (EST). *Felony, Misdemeanor, Civil.*

Civil Records: Access: In person only. Visitors must perform in person searches themselves. Court makes copy: $1.00 per page. Self serve copy fee: $.25 per page. Required to search: name, years to search. Civil cases indexed by defendant, plaintiff. Civil records on computer back to 1997, dockets books from 1853.

Criminal Records: Access: In person only. Visitors must perform in person searches themselves. Court makes copy: $1.00 per page. Self serve copy fee: $.25 per page. Required to search: name, years to search, DOB; SSN helpful. Criminal records on computer back to 1997, dockets books from 1853.

General Information: Public terminal goes back to 1997. No juvenile, adoption, sexual, mental health or expunged records released. Certification fee: $2.50 plus $.50 per page after first. Payee: Clerk of Court. Personal checks accepted. Prepayment required.

Magistrate Court PO Box 698, 165 W Franklin, Hartwell, GA 30643; phone: 706-376-6817; fax: 706-376-6821; hours 8:30AM-5PM (EST). *Civil Actions Under $15,000, Eviction, Small Claims.*
www.hartmagcourt.com

Probate Court PO Box 1159, 185 W Franklin St, Hartwell, GA 30643; phone: 706-376-2565; fax: 706-376-9032; hours 8:30AM-5PM M-F (EST). *Probate, Misdemeanor Traffic.*
https://www.gaprobate.org/counties/hart/index.html
Note: Also handles births, deaths, marriages and firearm permits.

Heard County

Superior Court PO Box 249, 215 Court St, Franklin, GA 30217; phone: 706-675-3301; fax: 706-675-0819; hours 8:30AM-5PM (EST). *Felony, Misdemeanor, Civil.*

Civil Records: Access: In person only. Visitors must perform in person searches themselves. Court makes copy: $.25 per page. Required to search: name, years to search. Civil cases indexed by defendant, plaintiff. Civil records on docket books from 1800s.

Criminal Records: Access: In person only. Visitors must perform in person searches themselves. Court makes copy: $.25 per page. Required to search: name, years to search, DOB, signed release; SSN helpful. Criminal records on docket books from 1800s.

General Information: No public access terminal. No juvenile, adoptions, sealed, sexual, mental health or expunged records released. Will fax specific case file for $1.00 per page. Certification fee: $2.50 plus $.50 per page after first. Payee: Court Clerk. Personal checks accepted. Prepayment required.

Magistrate Court PO Box 395, Franklin, GA 30217; phone: 706-675-3002; fax: 706-675-0819; hours 8:30AM-5PM (EST). *Civil Actions Under $15,000, Eviction, Small Claims.*

Probate Court PO Box 478, 215 E Court Sq, Franklin, GA 30217; phone: 706-675-3353; fax: 706-675-0819; hours 8:30AM-5PM (EST). *Probate.*
https://www.gaprobate.org/counties/heard/index.html

Henry County

Superior Court One Courthouse Square, McDonough, GA 30253; phone: 770-954-2121; fax: 770-898-7573; hours 8AM-5PM (EST). *Felony, Misdemeanor, Civil.*

Civil Records: Access: Phone, mail, in person. Visitors must perform in person searches themselves. Court makes copy: $.25 per page. Required to search: name, years to search. Civil cases indexed by defendant, plaintiff. Civil records on dockets books from 1800s.

Criminal Records: Access: In person only. Visitors must perform in person searches themselves. Court makes copy: $.25 per page. Required to search: name, years to search, DOB, signed release; SSN helpful. Criminal records on dockets books from 1800s.

General Information: No public access terminal. No juvenile, adoption, sexual, mental health or expunged records released. No fee to fax documents. Certification fee: $2.50 plus $.50 per add'l page. Payee: Clerk of Superior Court. Personal checks accepted. Prepayment required.

Magistrate Court 30 Atlanta St, McDonough, GA 30253; phone: 770-954-2111; fax: 770-954-2144; hours 8AM-5PM (EST). *Civil Actions Under $15,000, Eviction, Small Claims.*

Probate Court 99 Sims St, McDonough, GA 30253; phone: 770-954-2303; fax: 770-954-2308; hours 8AM-4:30PM (EST). *Probate.*
https://www.gaprobate.org/counties/henry/index.html

Houston County

Superior Court 201 Perry Pky, Perry, GA 31069; phone: 478-218-4720; criminal phone: 478-218-4730; civil phone: 478-218-4740; fax: 478-218-4745; hours 8:30AM-5PM (EST). *Felony, Misdemeanor, Civil.*
www.houstoncountyga.org
Civil Records: Access: Phone, fax, mail, in person. Both court and visitors may perform in person searches. No search fee. Court makes copy: $.25 per page; same fee for self serve. Required to search: name, years to search. Civil cases indexed by defendant, plaintiff. Civil records on computer from 1984, dockets books back to 1823. Mail turnaround time 1-2 days.

Criminal Records: Access: Fax, mail, in person. Both court and visitors may perform in person searches. No search fee. Court makes copy: $.25 per page; same fee for self serve. Required to search: name, years to search, DOB; also helpful: SSN, race, sex. Criminal records on computer from 1984, dockets books back to 1823. Mail turnaround time 1-2 days.

General Information: Public terminal goes back to 1984. No juvenile, adoption, mental health or expunged records released. Will fax documents. Certification fee: $2.50 plus $.50 per page after first. Payee: Court Clerk. No personal checks accepted. Prepayment required.

State Court 202 Carl Vinson Pky, Warner Robins, GA 31088; phone: 478-542-2105; fax: 478-542-2077; hours 8AM-5PM (EST). *Misdemeanor, Civil.*
www.houstoncountyga.com
Note: The county recorder's office offers free online access to liens at www.houstoncountyga.com.
Civil Records: Access: Mail, fax, in person. Visitors must perform in person searches themselves. No search fee. Court makes copy: $.25 per page. Required to search: name, years to search. Civil cases indexed by defendant. Civil records on computer from 1987, dockets books from 1965.

Criminal Records: Access: In person only. Visitors must perform in person searches themselves. Court makes copy: $.25 per page. Required to search: name, years to search, DOB; SSN helpful. Criminal records on computer from 1987, dockets books from 1965.

General Information: No juvenile, adoption, sexual, mental health or expunged records released. Certification fee: $2.50 plus $.50 per page after first. Payee: Court Clerk. Only cashiers checks and money orders accepted. Prepayment required.

Magistrate Court 89 Cohen Walker Dr, Warner Robins, GA 31088; phone: 478-987-4695; fax: 478-987-5249; hours 8AM-5PM (EST). *Civil Actions Under $15,000, Eviction, Small Claims.*
http://georgiacourts.org/courts/magistrate/houston/

Probate Court PO Box 1801, 201 N Perry Pky, Perry, GA 31069; phone: 478-218-4710; fax: 478-218-4715; hours 8:30AM-4:30PM (EST). *Probate.*
www.houstoncountyga.org/probate_court.htm

Irwin County

Superior Court 113 N Irwin Ave, Ocilla, GA 31774; phone: 229-468-5356; fax: 229-468-9753; hours 8AM-5PM (EST). *Felony, Misdemeanor, Civil.*

Civil Records: Access: Phone, mail, in person. Visitors must perform in person searches themselves. No search fee. Court makes copy: $1.00 per page. Self serve copy fee: $.25 per page. Required to search: name, years to search. Civil cases indexed by defendant, plaintiff. Civil records on dockets books from 1870s, records are not computerized. Court will not do general record searches, the specific case file must be given. Mail turnaround time 2 days.

Criminal Records: Access: Phone, mail, in person. Visitors must perform in person searches themselves. No search fee. Court makes copy: $1.00 per page. Self serve copy fee: $.25 per page. Required to search: name, years to search, DOB, signed release; also helpful: SSN, race, sex. Criminal records on dockets books from 1900, records are not computerized. Court will not do general record searches, the specific case file must be given. Mail turnaround time 2 days.

General Information: Public use terminal available. No juvenile, adoption, sexual, mental health or expunged records released. Will fax documents for $2.50 1st page, $1.00 each add'l page. Certification fee: $2.50 plus $.50 per page after first. Payee: Court Clerk. Personal checks accepted. Prepayment required.

Magistrate Court 301 S Irwin Ave, #102, Ocilla, GA 31774; phone: 229-468-7671; fax: 229-468-8444; hours 8AM-5PM, M-Th, 8AM-N, Fri (EST). *Civil Actions Under $15,000, Eviction, Small Claims.*

Probate Court 301 S Irwin Ave, Ocilla, GA 31774; phone: 229-468-5138; fax: 229-468-5702; hours 8:00-12:00 - 1:00-5:00 (EST). *Probate.* https://www.gaprobate.org/counties/irwin/index.html

Jackson County

Superior & State Court PO Box 7, Jefferson, GA 30549; phone: 706-387-6255; criminal phone: 707-387-6254; civil phone: 707-387-6248; fax: 706-387-6273; hours 8AM-5PM (EST). *Felony, Misdemeanor, Civil.*

Civil Records: Access: In person only. Visitors must perform in person searches themselves. Self serve copy fee: $.25 per page. Required to search: name, years to search. Civil cases indexed by defendant, plaintiff. Civil records on computer from 1992, on dockets books from 1800s.

Criminal Records: Access: In person only. Visitors must perform in person searches themselves. Self serve copy fee: $.25 per page. Required to search: name, years to search, DOB; SSN helpful. Criminal records on computer from 1992, on dockets books from 1800s.

General Information: Public terminal goes back to 1992. No juvenile, adoption, sexual, mental health or expunged records released. Will fax specific case file to local or toll-free number only. Certification fee: $2.50 plus $.50 per page after first. Payee: Court Clerk. No personal checks accepted. Prepayment required.

Magistrate Court 5000 Jackson Parkway #230, Jefferson, GA 30549; phone: 706-335-6356; fax: 706-387-6369; hours 8AM-5PM (EST). *Civil Actions Under $15,000, Eviction, Small Claims.*

Probate Court 5000 Jackson Pky #140, Jefferson, GA 30549; phone: 706-367-6275; fax: 706-387-6285; hours 8:AM-5PM (EST). *Probate.* www.jacksoncountygov.com/ProbateCourt/ Note: Jackson County Probate does not handle civil and criminal records.

Jasper County

Superior Court 126 W Green St, #110, Monticello, GA 31064; phone: 706-468-4901; fax: 706-468-4946; hours 8AM-5PM (EST). *Felony, Misdemeanor, Civil.*

Civil Records: Access: In person only. Visitors must perform in person searches themselves. Court makes copy: $1.00 per page. Self serve copy fee: $.25 per page. Required to search: name, years to search. Civil cases indexed by defendant, plaintiff. Civil records on computer from 1990, dockets books from 1807.

Criminal Records: Access: In person only. Visitors must perform in person searches themselves. Court makes copy: $1.00 per page. Self serve copy fee: $.25

per page. Required to search: name, years to search, DOB; SSN helpful. Criminal records on computer from 1990, dockets books from 1807.

General Information: Public terminal has criminal back to 1992 and civil back to 1990. No juvenile, adoption, sexual, mental health or expunged records released. Will fax specific document for $2.50 per page. Certification fee: $2.50 plus $.50 per page after first. Payee: Court Clerk. Personal checks accepted. Prepayment required.

Magistrate Court 126 W Green St, #110, Monticello, GA 31064; phone: 706-468-4909; fax: 706-468-4946; hours 8:30AM-4:30PM (EST). *Civil Actions Under $15,000, Eviction, Small Claims.* www.jaspercourt.com Note: Access records online via the state system at www.gsccca.org. Court also has jurisdiction for bad checks, arrest warrants, preliminary hearings, and county ordinance violations.

Probate Court Jasper County Courthouse, 126 W Green St, #111, Monticello, GA 31064; phone: 706-468-4903; fax: 706-468-4926; hours 8AM-4:30PM (EST). *Probate.* https://www.gaprobate.org/counties/jasper/index.html

Jeff Davis County

Superior & State Court PO Box 429, Hazlehurst, GA 31539; phone: 912-375-6615; fax: 912-375-6637; hours 8AM-5PM (EST). *Felony, Misdemeanor, Civil.*

Civil Records: Access: Fax, mail, in person. Both court and visitors may perform in person searches. No search fee. Court makes copy: $.25 per page. Required to search: name, years to search. Civil cases indexed by defendant, plaintiff. Civil records on dockets books, limited records on computer back 3 years. Mail turnaround time 1 week; fax is immediate on finding results.

Criminal Records: Access: Fax, mail, in person. Both court and visitors may perform in person searches. Search fee: $3.00 per name. Court makes copy: $.25 per page. Required to search: name, years to search. Criminal records on dockets books. Mail turnaround time 1 week; fax is immediate on finding results.

General Information: No public access terminal. No juvenile, confidential, adoption or sealed records released. Fee to fax documents is $2.00 1st page, $1.00 each add'l. Certification fee: $2.50 plus $.50 per page after first. Payee: Court Clerk. Personal checks accepted. Prepayment required. SASE requested.

Magistrate Court PO Box 568, 14 Jeff Davis St, Hazlehurst, GA 31539; phone: 912-375-6630; fax: 912-375-6630; hours 8AM-5PM (EST). *Civil Actions Under $15,000, Eviction, Small Claims.* www.jeffdaviscourt.com

Probate Court PO Box 446, Hazlehurst, GA 31539; phone: 912-375-6626; fax: 912-375-0502; hours 9AM-5PM (EST). *Probate.*

Jefferson County

Superior & State Court PO Box 151, Louisville, GA 30434; phone: 478-625-7922; fax: 478-625-4037; hours 8AM-5PM (EST). *Felony, Misdemeanor, Civil.*

Civil Records: Access: Mail, in person. Both court and visitors may perform in person searches. No search fee. Court makes copy: $.25 per page. Required to search: name, years to search. Civil cases indexed by defendant, plaintiff. Civil records on dockets books from 1865; on computer back to 1995.

Criminal Records: Access: In person only. Both court and visitors may perform in person searches. No search fee. Court makes copy: $.25 per page. Required to search: name, years to search, DOB or SSN. Criminal records on dockets books from 1865; on computer back to 1995.

General Information: Public terminal goes back to 1995. No juvenile, adoption, sexual, mental health or expunged records released. Will fax documents. Certification fee: $2.50 plus $1.00 per add'l page:

Payee: Court Clerk. Personal checks accepted. Prepayment required.

Magistrate Court PO Box 749, 911 Clarks Mill Rd, Louisville, GA 30434; phone: 478-625-8834; fax: 478-625-4039; hours 8AM-5PM (EST). *Civil Actions Under $15,000, Eviction, Small Claims.* www.jeffersoncount.com

Probate Court PO Box 307, Louisville, GA 30434; phone: 478-625-3258; fax: 478-625-0245; probate fax: same; hours 8AM-5PM (EST). *Probate.* https://www.gaprobate.org/counties/jefferson/index.html

Jenkins County

Superior & State Court PO Box 659, Millen, GA 30442; phone: 478-982-4683; fax: 478-982-1274; hours 8:30AM-5PM (EST). *Felony, Misdemeanor, Civil.*

Civil Records: Access: In person only. Visitors must perform in person searches themselves. Court makes copy: $.25 per page; same fee for self serve. Required to search: name, years to search. Civil cases indexed by defendant. Civil records on dockets books.

Criminal Records: Access: In person only. Visitors must perform in person searches themselves. Court makes copy: $.25 per page; same fee for self serve. Required to search: name, years to search, DOB; SSN helpful. Criminal records on dockets books.

General Information: Public terminal goes back to 1990. No juvenile, adoption, sexual, mental health or expunged records released. Certification fee: $2.50 plus $.25 per page after first. Payee: Clerk of Court. Personal checks accepted. Prepayment required.

Magistrate Court PO Box 892, Winthrop Ave Courthouse Sq, Millen, GA 30442; phone: 478-982-5580; fax: 478-982-4911; hours 8:30AM-5PM (EST). *Civil Actions Under $15,000, Eviction, Small Claims.*

Probate Court PO Box 904, 611 E Winthrope Ave, Millen, GA 30442; phone: 478-982-5581; fax: 478-982-2829; hours 8:30AM-5PM (EST). *Probate.* https://www.gaprobate.org/counties/jenkins/index.html

Johnson County

Superior & Magistrate Court PO Box 321, Wrightsville, GA 31096; phone: 478-864-3484; fax: 478-864-1343; hours 9AM-5PM (EST). *Felony, Misdemeanor, Civil, Eviction, Small Claims.*

Civil Records: Access: In person only. Visitors must perform in person searches themselves. Court makes copy: $.25 per page. Required to search: name, years to search. Civil cases indexed by defendant, plaintiff. Civil records on computer from 1991, dockets books from 1859.

Criminal Records: Access: In person only. Visitors must perform in person searches themselves. Court makes copy: $.25 per page. Required to search: name, years to search, DOB; SSN helpful. Criminal records on computer from 1991, dockets books from 1859.

General Information: No public access terminal. No juvenile, adoption, sexual, mental health or expunged records released. Certification fee: $3.00 per cert. Payee: Court Clerk. Personal checks accepted. Prepayment required.

Probate Court PO Box 264, Wrightsville, GA 31096; phone: 478-864-3316; fax: 478-864-0528; hours 9AM-5PM (EST). *Probate.*

Jones County

Superior Court PO Box 39, 110 S Jefferson St, Gray, GA 31032; phone: 478-986-6671/6674""""; fax: 478-986-2030; hours 8:30AM-4:30PM (EST). *Felony, Misdemeanor, Civil Over $15,000.*

Civil Records: Access: In person only. Visitors must perform in person searches themselves. Court makes copy: $.50 per page. Required to search: name, years to search. Civil cases indexed by defendant, plaintiff. Civil records on computer since 1989, dockets books from 1800s. The court will fax records not requiring a search, $5.00 minimum.

Criminal Records: Access: In person only. Visitors must perform in person searches themselves. Court makes copy: $.50 per page. Required to search: name, years to search, signed release. Criminal records on docket books, computerized since 1995.

General Information: Public terminal goes back to 1995. No juvenile, adoption, sexual, mental health or expunged records released. Certification fee: $2.50 plus $.50 per page after first. Payee: Superior Court. Personal checks accepted. Prepayment required.

Magistrate Court PO Box 88, 110 S Jefferson St, Gray, GA 31032; phone: 478-986-5113; fax: 478-986-6536; hours 8:30AM-4:30PM (EST). *Civil Under $15,000, Small Claims, Eviction.*

Probate Court PO Box 1359, 110 S Jefferson St, Gray, GA 31032; phone: 478-986-6668; fax: 478-986-1715; hours 8:30AM-4:30PM (EST). *Probate, Traffic, Vital Records.*

Lamar County

Superior Court 326 Thomaston St, Box 7, Barnesville, GA 30204; phone: 770-358-5145; fax: 770-358-5814; hours 8AM-5PM (EST). *Felony, Misdemeanor, Civil.*

Civil Records: Access: In person only. Visitors must perform in person searches themselves. Court makes copy: $1.00 for first page, $.25 each add'l. Self serve copy fee: $.25 per page. Required to search: name, years to search. Civil cases indexed by defendant. Civil records on dockets books from 1921; on computer back to 9/2000.

Criminal Records: Access: In person only. Visitors must perform in person searches themselves. Court makes copy: $1.00 for first page, $.25 each add'l. Self serve copy fee: $.25 per page. Required to search: name, years to search, DOB, offense, date of offense; SSN helpful. Criminal records on dockets books from 1921; on computer back to 9/2000.

General Information: No public access terminal. No juvenile, adoption, sexual, mental health or expunged records released. Will not fax specific case file. Certification fee: $2.50 for 1st page. Payee: Court Clerk. Personal checks accepted. Prepayment required. Will bill copy fees.

Magistrate Court 121 Roberta Dr, #B, Barnesville, GA 30204; phone: 770-358-5154; fax: 770-358-5214; hours 8AM-N, 1-5PM (EST). *Civil Actions Under $15,000, Eviction, Small Claims.*

Probate Court 326 Thomaston St, Barnesville, GA 30204; phone: 770-358-5155; fax: 770-358-5348; hours 8AM-5PM (EST). *Probate, Misdemeanor, Traffic.*

Lanier County

Superior Court County Courthouse, 100 Main St, Lakeland, GA 31635; phone: 229-482-3594; fax: 229-482-8333; hours 8AM-N, 1-5PM (EST). *Felony, Misdemeanor, Civil.*

Civil Records: Access: In person only. Visitors must perform in person searches themselves. Court makes copy: $.25 per page. Required to search: name, years to search. Civil cases indexed by defendant, plaintiff. Civil records on dockets books from 1921; on computer back to 1995.

Criminal Records: Access: In person only. Visitors must perform in person searches themselves. Court makes copy: $.25 per page. Required to search: name, years to search, DOB, signed release. Criminal records on dockets books from 1921; on computer back to 1995.

General Information: No public access terminal. No juvenile, adoption, sexual, mental health or expunged records released. Certification fee: $3.00. Payee: Court Clerk. Personal checks accepted. Prepayment required.

Magistrate Court 100 Main St, #3, County Courthouse, Lakeland, GA 31635; phone: 229-482-2207; fax: 229-482-8333; 8AM-N; 1PM-5PM *Civil Actions Under $15,000, Eviction, Small Claims.*

Probate Court County Courthouse, 100 Main St, Lakeland, GA 31635; phone: 229-482-3668; fax: 229-482-8333; hours 8AM-N, 1-5PM (EST). *Probate.*
https://www.gaprobate.org/counties/lanier/index.html

Laurens County

Superior & Magistrate Court PO Box 2028, Dublin, GA 31040; phone: 478-272-3210; fax: 478-275-2595; hours 8:30AM-5:30PM (EST). *Felony, Misdemeanor, Civil, Eviction, Small Claims.*

Civil Records: Access: In person only. Visitors must perform in person searches themselves. Court makes copy: $.25 per page; same fee for self serve. Required to search: name, years to search. Civil cases indexed by defendant, plaintiff. Civil records on computer from 1992, dockets books from 1800s.

Criminal Records: Access: In person only. Visitors must perform in person searches themselves. Court makes copy: $.25 per page; same fee for self serve. Required to search: name, years to search; SSN helpful. Criminal records on computer from 1992, dockets books from 1800s.

General Information: Public terminal goes back to 1992. No juvenile, adoption, sexual, mental health or expunged records released. Certification fee: $2.50 plus $.50 per page after first. Payee: Court Clerk. Personal checks accepted. Prepayment required.

Probate Court PO Box 2098, 101 N Jefferson St, Courthouse, Rm 108, Dublin, GA 31040; phone: 478-272-2566; fax: 478-277-2932; hours 8:30AM-5:30PM (EST). *Probate.*
https://www.gaprobate.org/counties/laurens/index.html

Lee County

Superior Court PO Box 597, 100 Leslie Hwy, Leesburg, GA 31763; phone: 229-759-6918; fax: 229-759-6049; hours 8AM-5PM (EST). *Felony, Misdemeanor, Civil.*

Civil Records: Access: Mail, in person. Both court and visitors may perform in person searches. No search fee. Court makes copy: $1.00 per page, $.25 ea add'l. Self serve copy fee: $.25 per page. Required to search: name, years to search. Civil cases indexed by defendant, plaintiff. Civil records on docket books from 1850. Mail turnaround time 1 week.

Criminal Records: Access: Mail, in person. Both court and visitors may perform in person searches. Search fee: $5.00. Court makes copy: $1.00 per page, $.25 ea add'l. Self serve copy fee: $.25 per page. Required to search: name, years to search, DOB; also helpful: SSN, race, sex. Criminal records on docket books from 1850, computerized since 1996. Mail turnaround time 1 week.

General Information: No public access terminal. No juvenile, adoption, sexual, mental health or expunged records released. Will fax documents to local or toll free line. Certification fee: $2.00 per cert. Payee: Court Clerk. Personal checks accepted. Prepayment and SASE required.

Magistrate Court PO Box 522, 100 Leslie Hwy, Leesburg, GA 31763; phone: 229-759-6016; fax: 229-759-3303; hours 8AM-5PM (EST). *Civil Actions Under $15,000, Eviction, Small Claims.*

Probate Court PO Box 592, 100 Leslie Hwy, Leesburg, GA 31763; phone: 229-759-6005; fax: 229-759-3345; hours 8AM-5PM (EST). *Probate, Traffic.*

Liberty County

Superior & State Court PO Box 50, Hinesville, GA 31313-0050; phone: 912-876-3625; criminal phone: 912-876-7289; civil phone: 912-876-7276; fax: 912-876-7394; hours 8AM-5PM (EST). *Felony, Misdemeanor, Civil.*
www.libertyco.com

Civil Records: Access: Fax, mail, in person. Both court and visitors may perform in person searches. Search fee: $5.00. Court makes copy: $1.00 per page. Required to search: name, years to search, signed release. Civil cases indexed by defendant, plaintiff.

Civil records on computer from 1986, dockets books from 1700s. Mail turnaround time 1-3 days.

Criminal Records: Access: Mail, in person. Both court and visitors may perform in person searches. Search fee: $5.00 per name. Court makes copy: $1.00 per page. Required to search: name, years to search, DOB, signed release; also helpful: SSN, race, sex. Criminal records on computer from 1986, dockets books from 1700s. Mail turnaround time 1-3 days.

General Information: Public use terminal available. No juvenile, adoption, sexual, mental health or expunged records released. Will fax documents for $5.00 1st 5 pages, $1.00 each add'l page. Need prepaid account for fax retrieval. Certification fee: $2.50 plus $.50 per page after first. Payee: Court Clerk. Business checks accepted. Prepayment required.

Magistrate Court PO Box 912, 112 N Main St #103, Courthouse Annex, Hinesville, GA 31310; phone: 912-368-2063; fax: 912-876-2474; hours 8AM-Noon,1-5PM (EST). *Civil Actions Under $15,000, Eviction, Small Claims.*
www.libertyco.com

Probate Court PO Box 28, 112 N Main St, Rm 100, Hinesville, GA 31310; phone: 912-876-3635; fax: 912-876-3589; 8AM-5PM (EST). *Probate.*

Lincoln County

Superior Court PO Box 340, Lincolnton, GA 30817; phone: 706-359-5505; fax: 706-359-5027; hours 9AM-5PM (EST). *Felony, Misdemeanor, Civil.*

Civil Records: Access: In person only. Visitors must perform in person searches themselves. Court makes copy: $1.00 per page. Self serve copy fee: $.25 per page. Required to search: name, years to search. Civil cases indexed by defendant, plaintiff. Civil records on index books from 1796, computerized since 1992. There is no public terminal, must search in the books.

Criminal Records: Access: In person only. Visitors must perform in person searches themselves. Court makes copy: $1.00 per page. Self serve copy fee: $.25 per page. Required to search: name, years to search. Criminal records on index books from 1796, records are not computerized.

General Information: Public terminal goes back to 1990. No adoption or juvenile records released. Certification fee: $2.50. Payee: Superior Court Clerk. Personal checks accepted. Prepayment required.

Magistrate & Probate Court PO Box 205, 210 Humphrey St, Lincolnton, GA 30817; phone: 706-359-5519; probate phone: 706-359-5528; fax: 706-359-5520; hours 8AM-5PM (EST). *Civil Actions Under $15,000, Eviction, Small Claims, Probate.*

Note: Probate fax is 706-359-4729. Court also has jurisdiction for bad checks, arrest warrants, preliminary hearings, and county ordinance violations.

Long County

Superior & State Court PO Box 458, Ludowici, GA 31316; phone: 912-545-2123; fax: 912-545-2020; hours 8:30AM-5PM (EST). *Felony, Misdemeanor, Civil.*

Civil Records: Access: Mail, fax, in person. Both court and visitors may perform in person searches. Search fee: $5.00 per name. Court makes copy: $1.00 per page. Self serve copy fee: $.25 per page. Required to search: name, years to search. Civil cases indexed by defendant, plaintiff. Civil records on docket books, archived from 1921. Mail turnaround time 1 week.

Criminal Records: Access: Mail, fax, in person. Both court and visitors may perform in person searches. Search fee: $5.00 per name. Court makes copy: $1.00 per page. Self serve copy fee: $.25 per page. Required to search: name, years to search, DOB; also helpful: SSN, race, sex. Criminal records on docket books, archived from 1921. Mail turnaround time 1 week.

General Information: Public terminal goes back to 1993. No juvenile, adoption, sealed, sexual, mental health, expunged or confidential records released. Certification fee: $2.50 for 1st page, $.50 each add'l. Cert fee includes copies. Payee: Court Clerk. Business checks accepted. Prepayment and SASE required.

Magistrate & Probate Court PO Box 87, 49 McDonald St, Ludowici, GA 31316; phone: 912-545-2315; probate phone: 912-545-2131; fax: 912-545-2150; 8:30AM-4:30PM (EST). *Civil Actions Under $15,000, Eviction, Small Claims, Probate.*
Note: Court also has jurisdiction for bad checks, arrest warrants, preliminary hearings, and county ordinance violations. Use PO Box 426 for probate Court.

Lowndes County

Superior & State Court PO Box 1349, 108 E Central Ave, Valdosta, GA 31603; phone: 229-333-5127; fax: 229-333-7637; hours 8AM-5PM (EST). *Felony, Misdemeanor, Civil.*
http://southernjudicialcircuit.com
Civil Records: Access: Mail, in person. Both court and visitors may perform in person searches. Search fee: $3.00 per name for mail requests. Court makes copy: $.25 per page. Required to search: name, years to search. Civil cases indexed by defendant, plaintiff. Civil records on computer from 1990, prior on dockets books.
Criminal Records: Access: In person only. Visitors must perform in person searches themselves. Court makes copy: $.25 per page. Required to search: name, years to search, DOB; SSN helpful. Criminal records on computer back to 1984; prior on docket books.
General Information: Public terminal has criminal back to 1984 and civil back to 1990. No juvenile, adoption, sexual, mental health or expunged records released. Fee to fax documents is $.25 per page. Certification fee: $2.50 plus $.50 per page after 1st; $5.00 minimum. Payee: Court Clerk. Only cashiers checks and money orders accepted. Prepayment required.

Magistrate Court PO Box 1349, 108 E Central Ave, Valdosta, GA 31603; phone: 229-671-2610; fax: 229-671-3442; hours 8AM-5PM (EST). *Civil Actions Under $15,000, Eviction, Small Claims.*

Probate Court PO Box 72, 100 E Central Ave, Rm 105, Valdosta, GA 31603; phone: 229-333-5103; fax: 229-333-7646; hours 8AM-5PM (EST). *Probate.* www.lowndescounty.com

Lumpkin County

Superior, Juvenile & Magistrate Court 99 Courthouse Hill, #D, Dahlonega, GA 30533-0541; phone: 706-864-3736; hours 8AM-5PM (EST). *Felony, Misdemeanor, Civil, Eviction, Small Claims.*
Note: For Magistrate Court criminal records info, call 706-864-7760.
Civil Records: Access: In person only. Visitors must perform in person searches themselves. Court makes copy: $1.00 per page. Self serve copy fee: $.25 per page. Required to search: name, years to search; also helpful: address. Civil cases indexed by defendant, plaintiff. Civil records on computer from 1988, prior on dockets books to 1833.
Criminal Records: Access: In person only. Visitors must perform in person searches themselves. Court makes copy: $1.00 per page. Self serve copy fee: $.25 per page. Required to search: name, years to search, DOB; SSN helpful. Criminal records on computer from 1988, prior on dockets books to 1833.
General Information: Public use terminal available. No juvenile, adoption, sealed records released. Will not fax specific case file. Certification fee: $2.50 plus $.50 per page after first. Payee: Court Clerk. Personal checks accepted. Prepayment required.

Probate Court 99 Courthouse Hill, #C, Dahlonega, GA 30533; phone: 706-864-3847; hours 8AM-5PM (EST). *Probate, Traffic, Vital Records.*

Macon County

Superior Court PO Box 337, Oglethorpe, GA 31068; phone: 478-472-7661; fax: 478-472-4775; 8AM-5PM (EST). *Felony, Misdemeanor, Civil.*
Civil Records: Access: Mail, in person. Both court and visitors may perform in person searches. Court makes copy: $1.00 per page. Self serve copy fee: $.25 per page. Civil cases indexed by defendant, plaintiff. Civil records on dockets books from 1800s.
Criminal Records: Access: In person only. Both court and visitors may perform in person searches. Court makes copy: $1.00 per page. Self serve copy fee: $.25 per page. Criminal records on dockets books from 1800s.
General Information: Public use terminal available. No juvenile, adoption, sexual, mental health or expunged records released. Will fax documents for $2.00. Certification fee: $2.50 per page. Payee: Court Clerk. Business checks accepted. Prepayment required.

Magistrate Court PO Box 605, Oglethorpe, GA 31068; phone: 478-472-8509; fax: 478-472-5643; hours 8AM-N, 1-5PM (EST). *Civil Actions Under $15,000, Eviction, Small Claims.*

Probate Court PO Box 216, 100 Sumter St, Oglethorpe, GA 31068; phone: 478-472-7685; fax: 478-472-5643; 8AM-N, 1-5PM (EST). *Probate.*

Madison County

Superior Court PO Box 247, Danielsville, GA 30633; phone: 706-795-6310; fax: 706-795-2209; 8AM-5PM (EST). *Felony, Misdemeanor, Civil.*
Civil Records: Access: In person only. Visitors must perform in person searches themselves. Court makes copy: $.25 per page. Required to search: name, years to search. Civil cases indexed by defendant. Civil on computer since 7/96, archived since 1811.
Criminal Records: Access: In person only. Visitors must perform in person searches themselves. Court makes copy: $.25 per page. Required to search: name, years to search, DOB; SSN helpful. Criminal records on computer since 7/96, archived since 1811.
General Information: Public use terminal available. No juvenile, adoption, sexual, mental health or expunged records released. Certification fee: $2.50 plus $.50 per page after first. Payee: Court Clerk. No personal checks accepted. Prepayment required.

Magistrate Court PO Box 6, 91 Albany Ave, Danielsville, GA 30633; phone: 706-795-5679; fax: 706-795-2222; hours 8AM-5PM (EST). *Civil Actions Under $15,000, Eviction, Small Claims.*

Probate Court PO Box 207, 91 Albany Ave, Danielsville, GA 30633; phone: 706-795-6365; fax: 706-795-5933; hours 8AM-5PM (EST). *Probate.*

Marion County

Superior Court PO Box 41, Buena Vista, GA 31803; phone: 229-649-7321; fax: 229-649-7931; 8:30AM-5PM (EST). *Felony, Misdemeanor, Civil.*
Civil Records: Access: In person only. Visitors must perform in person searches themselves. Court makes copy: $.25 per page. Required to search: name, years to search. Civil cases indexed by defendant, plaintiff. Civil records on books.
Criminal Records: Access: In person only. Visitors must perform in person searches themselves. Court makes copy: $.25 per page. Required to search: name, years to search; SSN helpful. Criminal records on books.
General Information: No public access terminal. No juvenile, adoption, sexual, mental health or expunged records released. Certification fee: $2.50 plus $.50 per page after first. Payee: Court Clerk. Personal checks accepted. Prepayment required.

Magistrate & Probate Court PO Box 207, 100 N Broad St, Buena Vista, GA 31803; phone: 229-649-5542; fax: 229-649-2059; hours 8:30AM-5PM (EST). *Civil Under $15,000, Eviction, Small Claims, Probate.*

McDuffie County

Superior Court PO Box 158, 337 Main St, Rm 101, Thomson, GA 30824; phone: 706-595-2134; criminal phone: 706-595-2139; civil phone: 706-595-2138; probate phone: 706-595-2124; fax: 706-595-9150; hours 8AM-5PM (EST). *Felony, Misdemeanor, Civil.*
Civil Records: Access: In person only. Visitors must perform in person searches themselves. Court makes copy: $1.00 per page if court assists. Self serve copy fee: $.25 per page. Required to search: name, years to search. Civil cases indexed by defendant, plaintiff. Civil records on computer from 1991, dockets books from 1871.
Criminal Records: Access: In person only. Visitors must perform in person searches themselves. Court makes copy: $1.00 if court assists. Self serve copy fee: $.25 per page. Required to search: name, years to search, signed release; also helpful: DOB. Civil records on computer from 1991, dockets books from 1800s.
General Information: Public terminal goes back to 1991. No juvenile or adoption records released. Certification fee: $2.50 plus $.50 per page after first. Payee: Clerk Superior Court. Personal checks accepted. Prepayment required.

Magistrate Court PO Box 252, Thomson, GA 30824; phone: 706-597-2618; fax: 706-595-2041; hours 8AM-5PM (EST). *Civil Actions Under $15,000, Eviction, Small Claims.*

Probate Court PO Box 2028, 337 Main St, Rm 108, Thomson, GA 30824; phone: 706-595-2124; fax: 706-597-2644; hours 8AM-5PM *Probate.*

McIntosh County

Superior & State Court PO Box 1661, Darien, GA 31305; phone: 912-437-6641; fax: 912-437-6673; hours 8AM-4:30PM (EST). *Felony, Misdemeanor, Civil.*
Civil Records: Access: In person only. Visitors must perform in person searches themselves. Court makes copy: $.50 per page if helped by court. Self serve copy fee: $.25 per page. Required to search: name, years to search. Civil cases indexed by defendant, plaintiff. Civil records on computer from 1991.
Criminal Records: Access: In person only. Visitors must perform in person searches themselves. Court makes copy: $.50 per page if court assists. Self serve copy fee: $.25 per page. Required to search: name, years to search, DOB; SSN helpful. Criminal records on computer from 1991.
General Information: Public terminal goes back to 1990. No juvenile, adoption, sexual, or expunged records released. Certification fee: $2.50. Payee: Court Clerk. Personal checks accepted. Prepayment required.

Magistrate Court PO Box 459, Darien, GA 31305; phone: 912-437-4888; fax: 912-437-2768; hours 8AM-4:30PM (EST). *Civil Actions Under $15,000, Eviction, Small Claims.*

Probate Court PO Box 453, Darien, GA 31305; phone: 912-437-6636; fax: 912-437-6635; hours 8AM-5PM (EST). *Probate.*
www.darientel.net/~pcourt

Meriwether County

Superior Court PO Box 160, Greenville, GA 30222; phone: 706-672-4416; fax: 706-672-9465; hours 8:30AM-5PM (EST). *Felony, Misdemeanor, Civil.*
Note: This court will not do name searches.
Civil Records: Access: In person only. Visitors must perform in person searches themselves. Court makes copy: $1.00 per page. Self serve copy fee: $.25 per page. Required to search: name, years to search. Civil cases indexed by defendant, plaintiff. Civil records on microfilm and computer from 1990, prior on writ and minute books to 1827.

Criminal Records: Access: In person only. Visitors must perform in person searches themselves. Court makes copy: $1.00 per page. Self serve copy fee: $.25 per page. Required to search: name, years to search, DOB, SSN. Criminal records go back to 1827; on computer back to 1991.

General Information: Public terminal has criminal back to 1991 and civil back to 1990. No juvenile, adoption, sexual, mental health or expunged records released. Certification fee: $2.50 plus $.50 per page after first. Payee: Court Clerk. Business checks accepted. Prepayment required.

Magistrate Court PO Box 702, 124 N Court Sq, Greenville, GA 30222; phone: 706-672-1247; hours 8:30AM-N; 1PM-4:30PM (EST). *Civil Actions Under $15,000, Eviction, Small Claims.*

Probate Court PO Box 608, 100 Court Sq, Greenville, GA 30222; phone: 706-672-4952; probate phone: 706-672-1817; fax: 706-672-6660; hours 8:30AM-5PM (EST). *Probate.*

Miller County

Superior & State Court PO Box 66, Colquitt, GA 39837; phone: 229-758-4102; fax: 229-758-3865; hours 8AM-5PM (EST). *Felony, Misdemeanor, Civil.*

Civil Records: Access: In person only. Visitors must perform in person searches themselves. Court makes copy: $1.00 per page. Self serve copy fee: $.25 per page. Required to search: name, years to search. Civil cases indexed by defendant, plaintiff. Civil records on dockets books from 1800s, computerized from 1995.

Criminal Records: Access: In person only. Visitors must perform in person searches themselves. Court makes copy: $1.00 per page. Self serve copy fee: $.25 per page. Required to search: name, years to search. Criminal records on dockets books from 1800s, computerized from 1995.

General Information: Public terminal goes back to 1995. No juvenile or adoption records released. Certification fee: $2.50 plus $1.00 per page after first. Payee: Court Clerk. Business checks accepted. Prepayment required.

Magistrate & Probate Court 155 S 1st St, Box 1, Rm 110, Colquitt, GA 39837; phone: 229-758-4110; fax: 229-758-8133; hours 9AM-5PM (EST). *Civil Actions Under $15,000, Small Claims, Probate.*

Mitchell County

Superior & State Court PO Box 427, Camilla, GA 31730; phone: 229-336-2022; hours 8:30AM-5PM (EST). *Felony, Misdemeanor, Civil.*

Civil Records: Access: In person only. Visitors must perform in person searches themselves. Court makes copy: $.25 per page. Required to search: name, years to search. Civil cases indexed by defendant. Civil records on dockets books from 1800s.

Criminal Records: Access: In person only. Visitors must perform in person searches themselves. Court makes copy: $.25 per page. Required to search: name, years to search, DOB; SSN helpful. Criminal records on dockets books from 1800s.

General Information: No public access terminal. No juvenile, adoption, sexual, mental health or expunged records released. Certification fee: $2.50 plus $.50 per page after first. Payee: Court Clerk. Only cashiers checks and money orders accepted. Prepayment required.

Magistrate Court PO Box 626, Camilla, GA 31730-0626; phone: 229-336-2076/7; fax: 229-336-2039; hours 8:30AM-5PM (EST). *Civil Actions Under $15,000, Eviction, Small Claims.*

Probate Court PO Box 229, 11 W Beard St #102, Camilla, GA 31730; phone: 229-336-2016; fax: 229-336-2354; hours 8:30AM-5PM (EST). *Probate.* https://www.gaprobate.org/counties/mitchell/index.html

Monroe County

Superior Court PO Box 450, Forsyth, GA 31029; phone: 478-994-7022; fax: 478-994-7053; hours 8AM-5PM (EST). *Felony, Misdemeanor, Civil.*

Civil Records: Access: Mail, in person. Visitors must perform in person searches themselves. Court makes copy: $1.00 per page. Self serve copy fee: $.25 per page. Required to search: name, years to search. Civil cases indexed by defendant, plaintiff. Civil records on computer from 1986, dockets books from 1800s. Mail turnaround time 3 days.

Criminal Records: Access: Mail, in person. Both court and visitors may perform in person searches. No search fee. Court makes copy: $1.00 per page. Self serve copy fee: $.25 per page. Required to search: name, years to search, signed release. Criminal records on computer from 1989. Mail turnaround time 3 days.

General Information: Public use terminal available. No juvenile, adoption, sexual, mental health or expunged records released. Will not fax documents. Certification fee: $2.50 plus $.50 per page after first. Payee: Court Clerk. Personal checks accepted. Prepayment and SASE required.

Magistrate Court PO Box 974, 145 L Cary Bittick Dr, Justice Center, Forsyth, GA 31029; phone: 478-994-7018; fax: 478-994-7284; hours 9:00AM-5:00PM (EST). *Civil Actions Under $15,000, Eviction, Small Claims.* www.monroemagcourt.com

Probate Court PO Box 187, Courthouse, Rm 2, Forsyth, GA 31029; phone: 478-994-7036; fax: 478-994-7054; hours 8AM-5:00PM (EST). *Probate, Misdemeanor Traffic.*

Montgomery County

Superior Court PO Box 311, Mt Vernon, GA 30445; phone: 912-583-4401; hours 8AM-5PM (EST). *Felony, Misdemeanor, Civil.*

Civil Records: Access: In person only. Visitors must perform in person searches themselves. Court makes copy: $1.00 per page. Self serve copy fee: $.25 per page. Required to search: name, years to search. Civil cases indexed by defendant, plaintiff. Civil records on computer from 1993, dockets from 1793.

Criminal Records: Access: In person only. Visitors must perform in person searches themselves. Court makes copy: $1.00 per page. Self serve copy fee: $.25 per page. Required to search: name, years to search, DOB; SSN helpful. Criminal records on computer from 1993, on dockets from 1793.

General Information: Public terminal goes back to 1993. No juvenile or adoption records released. Certification fee: $2.50 per page. Payee: Superior Court Clerk. Personal checks accepted.

Magistrate Court PO Box 174, 400 Railroad Ave, Mt Vernon, GA 30445; phone: 912-583-2170; fax: 912-583-4343; hours 8:30AM-4:30PM *Civil Actions Under $15,000, Eviction, Small Claims.*

Probate Court PO Box 444, 400 Railroad Ave, Mt Vernon, GA 30445; phone: 912-583-2681; fax: 912-583-4343; hours 9AM-5PM (EST). *Probate, Misdemeanor Traffic.* https://www.gaprobate.org/counties/montgomery/index.html

Morgan County

Superior Court PO Box 130, 149 E Jefferson St, Madison, GA 30650; phone: 706-342-3605; fax: 706-343-6462; hours 9AM-5PM (EST). *Felony, Misdemeanor, Civil.*

Civil Records: Access: In person only. Visitors must perform in person searches themselves. Court makes copy: $1.00 per page. Self serve copy fee: $.25 per page. Required to search: name, years to search. Civil cases indexed by defendant, plaintiff. Civil records on computer from 1986, on dockets from 1900s.

Criminal Records: Access: In person only. Visitors must perform in person searches themselves. Court

makes copy: $1.00 per page. Self serve copy fee: $.25 per page. Required to search: name, years to search, signed release. Criminal records on computer from 1986, on dockets from 1900s.

General Information: Public use terminal available. No juvenile, adoption, sexual, mental health or expunged records released. Certification fee: $2.50 plus $.50 per page after first. Payee: Superior Court Clerk. Personal checks accepted. Prepayment required.

Magistrate Court PO Box 589, Madison, GA 30650; phone: 706-342-3088; fax: 706-343-6364; hours 9AM-5PM (EST). *Civil Actions Under $15,000, Eviction, Small Claims.* www.morganga.org

Note: Court also has jurisdiction for certain misdemeanors including bad checks, arrest warrants, preliminary hearings, and county ordinance violations.

Probate Court PO Box 857, 259 N 2nd St, Madison, GA 30650; phone: 706-343-6500; fax: 706-343-6465; hours 9AM-5PM (EST). *Probate.* This court also has Misdemeanor and Traffic cases.

Murray County

Superior Court PO Box 1000, 121 N Third Ave, Chatsworth, GA 30705; phone: 706-695-2932; fax: 706-517-9672; hours 8:30AM-5PM (EST). *Felony, Misdemeanor, Civil.*

Civil Records: Access: In person only. Visitors must perform in person searches themselves. Court makes copy: $.25 per page. Required to search: name, years to search. Civil cases indexed by defendant, plaintiff. Civil records on dockets from 1940, prior to 1940 archived; computerized records since 2000.

Criminal Records: Access: In person only. Visitors must perform in person searches themselves. Court makes copy: $.25 per page. Required to search: name, years to search, signed release. Criminal records on dockets from 1940, prior to 1940 archived; computerized records since 2000.

General Information: Public terminal goes back to 2000. No juvenile, adoption, sexual, mental health or expunged records released. Certification fee: $2.50 plus $.50 per page after first. Payee: Superior Court Clerk. Personal checks accepted. Prepayment required.

Magistrate Court 121 N 4th Ave, Chatsworth, GA 30705; phone: 706-695-3021; fax: 706-695-7525; hours 8AM-N, 1-5PM (EST). *Civil Actions Under $15,000, Eviction, Small Claims.*

Probate Court 115 Fort St, Chatsworth, GA 30705; phone: 706-695-3812; fax: 706-517-1340; hours 8:30AM-5PM (EST). *Probate.* https://www.gaprobate.org/counties/murray/index.html

Muscogee County

Superior & State Court PO Box 2145, Columbus, GA 31902; phone: 706-653-4351; fax: 706-653-4359; hours 8:30AM-5PM (EST). *Felony, Misdemeanor, Civil.*

Civil Records: Access: Mail, in person. Both court and visitors may perform in person searches. Search fee: $30.00 per name. Court makes copy: $.25 per page; same fee for self serve. Required to search: name, years to search. Civil cases indexed by defendant, plaintiff. Civil records on computer from 1989, on dockets from 1919 to 1989. Mail turnaround time 1 week.

Criminal Records: Access: Mail, in person. Both court and visitors may perform in person searches. Search fee: $30.00 per name. Court makes copy: $.25 per page; same fee for self serve. Required to search: name, years to search, DOB; also helpful: SSN. Criminal records on computer since 1989, on dockets from 1989 to 1957. Mail turnaround time 1 week.

General Information: Public terminal goes back to 1989. No adoption, sealed or first offender records released. Certification fee: $2.50 plus $.50 per page after first. Payee: Superior Court Clerk. Business checks accepted. Prepayment required. SASE requested.

Magistrate Court P O Box 1340, 100 10th St, Columbus, GA 31902; phone: 706-653-4390 ext1; fax: 706-653-4559; hours 10:30AM-N, 1-4PM *Civil Actions Under $15,000, Eviction, Small Claims.*

Probate Court PO Box 1340, 100 10th St, Columbus, GA 31902; phone: 706-653-4333; hours 8:30AM-4PM (EST). *Probate.*

Newton County

Superior Court 1132 Usher St, Rm 338, Covington, GA 30014; phone: 770-784-2035; probate phone: 770-784-2045; fax: 770-385-8930; hours 8AM-5PM *Felony, Misdemeanor, Civil.*
Civil Records: Access: Mail, in person. Visitors must perform in person searches themselves. Search fee: $1.00 (for mailing). Court makes copy: $.25 per page. Required to search: name, years to search. Civil cases indexed by defendant, plaintiff. Civil records on computer from 1991, on dockets from 1900s. Mail turnaround time two weeks.
Criminal Records: Access: Mail, in person. Visitors must perform in person searches themselves. Search fee: $1.00 (for mailing). Court makes copy: $.25 per page. Required to search: name, years to search, signed release. Criminal records on computer from 1991, on dockets from 1900s. Mail turnaround time 2 weeks.
General Information: Public terminal goes back to 1991. No adoption, sexual, mental health or expunged records released. Certification fee: $2.50 plus $.50 per page after first. Payee: Superior Court Clerk. Personal checks accepted. Prepayment required.

Magistrate & Probate Court 1132 Usher St, Rm 148, Covington, GA 30014; phone: 770-784-2045 or 770-784-2050; fax: 770-784-2145; hours 8AM-5PM (EST). *Civil Actions Under $15,000, Eviction, Small Claims, Probate.*

Oconee County

Superior & Magistrate Courts PO Box 1099, Watkinsville, GA 30677; phone: 706-769-3940; fax: 706-769-3948; hours 8AM-5PM (EST). *Felony, Misdemeanor, Civil, Eviction, Small Claims.*
Civil Records: Access: In person only. Visitors must perform in person searches themselves. Court makes copy: $.25 per page; same fee for self serve. Required to search: name, years to search. Civil cases indexed by defendant, plaintiff. Civil records on computer from 1989, on dockets from 1875.
Criminal Records: Access: In person only. Visitors must perform in person searches themselves. Court makes copy: $.25 per page; same fee for self serve. Required to search: name, years to search; also helpful: DOB, SSN. Criminal records on computer from 1989, on dockets from 1875.
General Information: Public terminal goes back to 1989. No juvenile, adoption, sexual, mental health or expunged records released. Certification fee: $2.50 plus $.50 per page after first. Payee: Superior Court Clerk. Personal checks accepted. Prepayment required.

Probate Court PO Box 54, 23 N Main St, Watkinsville, GA 30677; phone: 706-769-3936; fax: 706-769-3934; hours 8AM-5PM (EST). *Probate.*
www.oconeecounty.net

Oglethorpe County

Superior Court PO Box 68, Lexington, GA 30648; phone: 706-743-5731; fax: 706-743-5335; 8AM-5PM (EST). *Felony, Misdemeanor, Civil.*
www.gsccca.org/Clerks/default.asp
Civil Records: Access: Mail, in person. Visitors must perform in person searches themselves. Search fee: $25.00. Court makes copy: $1.00 per page. Self serve copy fee: $.25 per page. Required to search: name, years to search. Civil cases indexed by defendant. Civil records on computer from 1992, on dockets from 1900s.
Criminal Records: Access: In person only. Visitors must perform in person searches themselves. Court makes copy: $1.00 per page. Self serve copy fee: $.25

per page. Required to search: name, years to search, DOB; SSN helpful. Criminal records on computer from 1992, on dockets from 1900s.
General Information: Public terminal goes back to 1992. No juvenile or adoption records released. Will fax documents for $2.50 per page. Certification fee: $2.00 per cert. Payee: Superior Court Clerk. Personal checks accepted. Prepayment required.

Magistrate Court P O Box 356, 339 W Main St, Lexington, GA 30648; phone: 706-743-8321; fax: 706-743-3177; hours 8AM-N, 1-5PM (EST). *Civil Actions Under $15,000, Eviction, Small Claims.*

Probate Court PO Box 70, 111 W Main St, Lexington, GA 30648; phone: 706-743-5350; fax: 706-743-3514; hours 7:30AM-5PM (EST). *Probate.*
https://www.gaprobate.org/counties/oglethorpe/index.html

Paulding County

Superior Court 11 Courthouse Square, Rm G3, Dallas, GA 30132; phone: 770-443-7527; criminal phone: 770-505-6582; civil phone: 770-443-7529; fax: 770-505-3863; hours 8AM-5PM (EST). *Felony, Misdemeanor, Civil.*
Civil Records: Access: In person only. Visitors must perform in person searches themselves. Court makes copy: $1.00 per page. Self serve copy fee: $.25 per page. Required to search: name, years to search. Civil cases indexed by defendant, plaintiff. Civil records on computer from 1990, archived from 1850.
Criminal Records: Access: In person only. Visitors must perform in person searches themselves. Court makes copy: $1.00 per page. Self serve copy fee: $.25 per page. Required to search: name, years to search, DOB; SSN helpful. Criminal records on docket books.
General Information: No public access terminal. No juvenile, adoption, sexual, mental health or expunged records released. Certification fee: $2.50 plus $.50 per page after first. Payee: Court Clerk. Personal checks accepted. Prepayment required.

Magistrate Court 25 Courthouse Square, Rm 402, Dallas, GA 30132; phone: 770-443-7533; probate phone: 770-443-7541; hours 8AM-N, 1-5PM (EST). *Civil Actions Under $15,000, Eviction, Small Claims, Probate.* www.pauldingcourt.com

Probate Court 25 Courthouse Sq. Annex, Rm 102, Dallas, GA 30132; phone: 770-443-7541; fax: 770-443-7631; 8AM-N, 1-5PM (EST). *Probate.*
https://www.gaprobate.org/counties/paulding/index.html

Peach County

Superior Court PO Box 389, Ft Valley, GA 31030; phone: 478-825-5331; fax: 478-825-8662; hours 8:30AM-5PM *Felony, Misdemeanor, Civil.*
Civil Records: Access: Mail, in person. Both court and visitors may perform in person searches. No search fee. Court makes copy: $.25 per page; same fee for self serve. Required to search: name, years to search. Civil cases indexed by defendant, plaintiff. Civil records on computer back to 1997; on dockets from 1925. Mail turnaround time 1 week.
Criminal Records: Access: Mail, in person. Both court and visitors may perform in person searches. No search fee. Court makes copy: $.25 per page; same fee for self serve. Required to search: name, years to search, DOB; also helpful: SSN, race, sex. Criminal records on computer back to 1997; on dockets from 1925. Mail turnaround time 1 week.
General Information: No public access terminal. No juvenile, adoption, sexual, mental health or expunged records released. Certification fee: $3.00. Payee: Court Clerk. Personal checks accepted. Prepayment and SASE required.

Magistrate Court 700 Spruce St, Wing A, Ft Valley, GA 31030; phone: 478-825-2060; fax: 478-825-1893; hours 8AM-5PM (EST). *Civil Actions Under $15,000, Eviction, Small Claims.*

Probate Court PO Box 327, 205 W Church St, Ft Valley, GA 31030; phone: 478-825-2313; fax: 478-825-2678; hours 8AM-5PM (EST). *Probate.*

Pickens County

Superior Court 52 N Main St, #102, Jasper, GA 30143; criminal phone: 706-253-8764; civil phone: 706-253-8763; hours 8AM-5PM (EST). *Felony, Misdemeanor, Civil.*
http://9thjudicialdistrict-ga.org/dca9apphp.shtml
Civil Records: Access: In person only. Visitors must perform in person searches themselves. Court makes copy: $.25 per page. Self serve copy fee: $.25 per page. Required to search: name, years to search. Civil cases indexed by defendant, plaintiff. Civil records on computer from 1988, dockets from 1854.
Criminal Records: Access: In person only. Visitors must perform in person searches themselves. Court makes copy: $.25 per page. Self serve copy fee: $.25 per page. Required to search: name, years to search, DOB, signed release; SSN helpful. Criminal records on computer from 1988, dockets from 1854.
General Information: Public use terminal available. No juvenile, adoption, sexual, mental health or expunged records released. Certification fee: $2.50 plus $.50 per page after first. Cert fee includes copies. Payee: Court Clerk. Personal checks accepted. Prepayment required.

Magistrate Court 50 N Main St, #105, Jasper, GA 30143; phone: 706-253-8747; fax: 706-253-8750; hours 8AM-5PM (EST). *Civil Actions Under $15,000, Eviction, Small Claims.*

Probate Court 50 N Main St, #203, Jasper, GA 30143; phone: 706-253-8756; criminal phone: 706-253-8755; probate phone: 706-253-8757; fax: 706-253-8760; probate fax: same; hours 8AM-N, 1-5PM (EST). *Probate, Misdemeanor.*
https://www.gaprobate.org/counties/pickens/index.html
Note: Misdemeanors are limited to traffic and DNRs.

Pierce County

Superior & State Court PO Box 588, 312 Nichols St, Blackshear, GA 31516; phone: 912-449-2020; fax: 912-449-2106; hours 9AM-5PM (EST). *Felony, Misdemeanor, Civil.*
Civil Records: Access: In person only. Visitors must perform in person searches themselves. Court makes copy: $.25 per page; same fee for self serve. Required to search: name, years to search. Civil cases indexed by defendant. Civil records on computer from 1991, on index from 1800s.
Criminal Records: Access: In person only. Visitors must perform in person searches themselves. Court makes copy: $.25 per page; same fee for self serve. Required to search: name, years to search. Criminal records on computer from 1991, on index from 1800s.
General Information: Public terminal goes back to 1991. Certification fee: $2.50 for 1st page, $.50 each add'l. Payee: Superior Court Clerk. Personal checks accepted. Prepayment required.

Magistrate Court 312 Nichols St, #3, Blackshear, GA 31516-1926; phone: 912-449-2027, 449-2007; fax: 912-449-2103; 9AM-5PM *Civil Actions Under $15,000, Eviction, Small Claims.*

Probate Court PO Box 406, 312 Nichols St, Blackshear, GA 31516; phone: 912-449-2029; fax: 912-449-1417; hours 9AM-5PM (EST). *Probate.*

Pike County

Superior Court PO Box 10, Zebulon, GA 30295; phone: 770-567-2000; hours 8AM-5PM (EST). *Felony, Misdemeanor, Civil.*
Civil Records: Access: In person only. Visitors must perform in person searches themselves. Court makes copy: $.25 per page. Required to search: name, years to search. Civil cases indexed by defendant, plaintiff. Civil records on dockets books from 1823.
Criminal Records: Access: In person only. Visitors must perform in person searches themselves. Court makes copy: $.25 per page. Required to search: name, years to search. Criminal records on dockets books from 1823.
General Information: No public access terminal. No juvenile, adoption, sexual, mental health or

expunged records released. Certification fee: $2.50 plus $.50 per page after first. Payee: Court Clerk. Personal checks accepted. Prepayment required.

Magistrate Court PO Box 466, 77 Jackson St, Zebulon, GA 30295; phone: 770-567-2004; fax: 770-567-2023; 8AM-N, 1;30-5PM (EST). *Civil Actions Under $15,000, Eviction, Small Claims.*

Probate Court PO Box 324, 16001 Barnesville St, Zebulon, GA 30295; phone: 770-567-8734; fax: 770-567-2019; hours 8:30AM-Noon; 1PM-5PM (EST). *Probate.*

Polk County

Superior Court PO Box 948, 100 Proir St, Rm 106, Cedartown, GA 30125; phone: 770-749-2114; fax: 770-749-2148; hours 9AM-5PM (EST). *Felony, Misdemeanor, Civil.*
Civil Records: Access: In person only. Visitors must perform in person searches themselves. Court makes copy: $.25 per page; same fee for self serve. Required to search: name, years to search. Civil cases indexed by defendant, plaintiff. Civil records on computer from 1991, alpha indexes from 1930.
Criminal Records: Access: Mail, in person. Visitors must perform in person searches themselves. Court makes copy: $.25 per page; same fee for self serve. Required to search: name, years to search, DOB, signed release; also helpful: race, sex. Criminal records on computer from 1991, alpha indexes from 1930.
General Information: Public use terminal available. No juvenile, adoption, sexual, mental health or expunged records released. Fee to fax documents is $2.00 per page. Certification fee: $2.50 plus $.50 per page after first. Payee: Court Clerk. Personal checks accepted. Prepayment required.

Magistrate Court 100 Prior St, Courthouse 2, Cedartown, GA 30125; phone: 770-749-2187; civil phone: 770-749-2130; criminal fax: 770-749-2186; civil fax: 770-749-2189; 9AM-5PM (EST). *Civil Actions Under $15,000, Eviction, Small Claims.*
Note: Rockmart, GA office: 200 S Marble St, Rockmart, GA 30153; 770-684-4718. Court also has jurisdiction for bad checks, arrest warrants, preliminary hearings, and county ordinance violations.

Probate Court Polk County Courthouse, 100 Prior St Rm 102, Cedartown, GA 30125; phone: 770-749-2128/ 2129; fax: 770-749-2150; hours 9AM-4:45PM (EST). *Probate.*
www.polkcountygeorgia.us/courts.html
Note: This location also holds traffic and vital records.

Pulaski County

Superior Court PO Box 60, Hawkinsville, GA 31036; phone: 478-783-1911; fax: 478-892-3308; hours 8AM-5PM (EST). *Felony, Misdemeanor, Civil.*
Civil Records: Access: Mail, in person. Visitors must perform in person searches themselves. No search fee. Court makes copy: $1.00 per page. Self serve copy fee: $.25 per page. Required to search: name, years to search. Civil cases indexed by defendant, plaintiff. Civil records on computer from 1986, alpha index from early 1800s.
Criminal Records: Access: In person only. Visitors must perform in person searches themselves. Court makes copy: $1.00 per page. Self serve copy fee: $.25 per page. Required to search: name, years to search, signed release; also helpful: DOB, SSN. Criminal records on computer from 1986, alpha index from early 1800s.
General Information: Public terminal has criminal back to 1986 and civil back to 1989. No juvenile or adoption records released. Certification fee: $2.00 plus $.50 per page. Payee: Court Clerk. Personal checks accepted. Prepayment required.

Magistrate Court PO Box 667, Community Bldg, Lumpkin St, Hawkinsville, GA 31036; phone: 478-783-1357; fax: 478-783-0696; hours 8AM-

5PM (EST). *Civil Actions Under $15,000, Eviction, Small Claims.*

Probate Court 350 Commerce St, County Courthouse, PO Box 156, Hawkinsville, GA 31036; phone: 478-783-2061; fax: 478-783-9219; hours 8AM-5PM (EST). *Probate.*

Putnam County

Superior & State Court County Courthouse, 100 Jefferson Ave, Eatonton, GA 31024; phone: 706-485-4501 superior ct; 706-485-4056 state ct; fax: 706-485-2875; hours 8AM-5PM (EST). *Felony, Misdemeanor, Civil.*
Civil Records: Access: In person only. Visitors must perform in person searches themselves. Court makes copy: $1.00 per page. Self serve copy fee: $.25 per page. Required to search: name, years to search. Civil cases indexed by defendant, plaintiff. Civil records on computer since 1997; prior records on dockets to early 1900s.
Criminal Records: Access: In person only. Visitors must perform in person searches themselves. Court makes copy: $1.00 per page. Self serve copy fee: $.25 per page. Required to search: name, years to search, DOB; SSN helpful. Criminal records on computer since 1997; prior records on dockets to early 1930s.
General Information: Public terminal goes back to 1997. No juvenile, adoption, sexual, mental health or expunged records released. Will not fax specific case file. Certification fee: $2.50 plus $.50 per add'l page. Payee: Court Clerk. Personal checks accepted. Prepayment required.

Magistrate Court 108 S Madison Ave, #101, Eatonton, GA 31024; phone: 706-485-4306; fax: 706-484-1814; hours 8AM-5PM (EST). *Civil Actions Under $15,000, Eviction, Small Claims.*

Probate Court County Courthouse, 100 S Jefferson Ave, Eatonton, GA 31024; phone: 706-485-5476/9761; fax: 706-485-2515; hours 8AM-5PM (EST). *Probate.*
https://www.gaprobate.org/counties/putnam/index.html

Quitman County

Superior Court PO Box 307, Georgetown, GA 39854; phone: 229-334-2578; hours 8AM-N, 1-5PM (EST). *Felony, Misdemeanor, Civil.*
Civil Records: Access: In person only. Visitors must perform in person searches themselves. Court makes copy: $.50 per page; same fee for self serve. Required to search: name, years to search. Civil records go back to 1920s.
Criminal Records: Access: In person only. Visitors must perform in person searches themselves. Court makes copy: $.50 per page; same fee for self serve. Required to search: name, years to search, DOB; SSN helpful. Records go back to 1930s. The court asks mail requesters to mail the sheriff's office with a $10.00 fee and signed, notarized (subject) request.
General Information: Public terminal has criminal back to 2001 and civil back to 2002. No juvenile, adoption, sexual, mental health or expunged records released. Certification fee: $2.50 for 1st page, $.50 each add'l. Payee: Clerk of Superior Court. Personal checks accepted. Prepayment required.

Magistrate & Probate Court PO Box 7, 115 Main St, Georgetown, GA 39854; phone: 229-334-2224; fax: 229-334-6826; hours 8:AM-5PM (EST). *Civil Actions Under $15,000, Eviction, Small Claims, Probate.*

Rabun County

Superior Court 25 Courthouse Sq, #105, Clayton, GA 30525; phone: 706-782-3615; fax: 706-782-1391; hours 8:30AM-5PM (EST). *Felony, Misdemeanor, Civil.*
Civil Records: Access: Mail, in person. Visitors must perform in person searches themselves. No search fee. Court makes copy: $.25 per page. Self serve copy fee: $.25 per page. Required to search: name, years to search. Civil cases indexed by

defendant, plaintiff. Civil records on dockets from 1949; on computer since.
Criminal Records: Access: Mail, in person. Visitors must perform in person searches themselves. No search fee. Court makes copy: $.25 per page. Self serve copy fee: $.25 per page. Required to search: name, years to search, DOB, signed release; also helpful: SSN, race, sex. Criminal records on dockets from 1949; on computer since.
General Information: No public access terminal. No juvenile, adoption, sexual, mental health or expunged records released. Will fax documents for $.25 per copy. Payment must be made in advance. Certification fee: $2.50 for 1st page, $.50 each add'l. Payee: Court Clerk. Personal checks accepted. Prepayment required.

Magistrate Court 25 Courthouse Sq, #105, Clayton, GA 30525; phone: 706-782-2285; fax: 706-782-1391; hours 8:30AM-5PM (EST). *Civil Actions Under $15,000, Eviction, Small Claims.*

Probate Court 25 Courthouse Square, #215, Clayton, GA 30525; phone: 706-782-3614; fax: 706-782-9278; hours 8:30AM-5:00PM (EST). *Probate.* www.rabuncountygov.com/contactus.htm

Randolph County

Superior Court PO Box 98, Cuthbert, GA 39840; phone: 229-732-2216; fax: 229-732-5881; hours 8AM-5PM (EST). *Felony, Misdemeanor, Civil.*
Civil Records: Access: In person only. Visitors must perform in person searches themselves. Court makes copy: $1.00 per page. Self serve copy fee: $.25 per page. Required to search: name, years to search. Civil cases indexed by defendant. Civil records on index from 1835.
Criminal Records: Access: In person only. Visitors must perform in person searches themselves. Court makes copy: $1.00 per page. Self serve copy fee: $.25 per page. Required to search: name, years to search, DOB; SSN helpful. Criminal records on index from 1835.
General Information: Public terminal goes back to 2005. No juvenile, adoption, sexual, mental health or expunged records released. Certification fee: $2.00 plus $.50 per page after first. Payee: Court Clerk. Personal checks accepted. Prepayment required.

Magistrate Court PO Box 6, 113 W Pearl St, Cuthbert, GA 39840; phone: 229-732-6182; fax: 229-732-5635; 8AM-5PM; W 8AM-12;00 *Civil Actions Under $15,000, Eviction, Small Claims.*

Probate Court PO Box 424, 208 Court St, Cuthbert, GA 39840; phone: 229-732-2671; fax: 229-732-5781; hours 8AM-5PM (EST). *Probate.*

Richmond County

Superior Court 530 Greene St, Rm 503, Augusta, GA 30911; phone: 706-821-2460; fax: 706-821-2448; hours 8:30AM-5PM (EST). *Felony, Misdemeanor, Civil.*
www.augustaga.gov/departments/clerk_sup
Civil Records: Access: Mail, in person, online. Visitors must perform in person searches themselves. Court makes copy: $.25 per page. Required to search: name, years to search. Civil cases indexed by defendant, plaintiff. Civil records on docket books and microfilm from 1940s, real estate from 1986 on computer. Access court dockets free at www.augustaga.gov/WebDocket/ for records 2001 forward. Mail turnaround time 1 week.
Criminal Records: Access: Mail, in person, online. Visitors must perform in person searches themselves. Court makes copy: $.25 per page. Required to search: name, years to search. Criminal records on docket books and microfilm from 1940s, real estate from 1986 on computer. Access court dockets free at www.augustaga.gov/WebDocket/ for records 2001 forward. Mail turnaround time 1 week.
General Information: No public access terminal. No juvenile, adoption, sexual, mental health or expunged records released. Certification fee: $2.50 plus $.50 per page after first. Payee: Superior Court

Clerk. Business and local checks accepted. Prepayment required. SASE requested.

State Court 401 Walton Way, #218A, Augusta, GA 30911; phone: 706-821-1233; fax: 706-821-1218; 8:30AM-5PM (EST). *Misdemeanor, Civil.* www.augustaga.gov

Civil Records: Access: In person, online. Visitors must perform in person searches themselves. Court makes copy: $.25 per page. Required to search: name, years to search. Civil cases indexed by defendant, plaintiff. Civil records on docket books and microfilm from 1940s, prior archived; computerized records since 2001. Name search at www.augustaga.gov/WebDocket/.

Criminal Records: Access: In person only. Visitors must perform in person searches themselves. Court makes copy: $.25 per page. Required to search: name, years to search, DOB, SSN helpful. Criminal records on docket books and microfilm from 1940s, prior archived; computerized records since 2001.

General Information: Public terminal has criminal back to 1/2001 and civil back to 1999. No juvenile, adoption, sexual, mental health or expunged records released. Certification fee: $2.50 plus $.50 per page after first. Payee: Court Clerk. Only cashiers checks and money orders accepted. Prepayment required.

Civil & Magistrate Court 530 Greene St, Rm 705, Augusta, GA 30911; phone: 706-821-2370; fax: 706-821-2381; hours 8:30AM-5PM (EST). *Civil Actions Under $45,000, Eviction, Small Claims.* www.augustaga.gov/departments/civil_magistrate/home.asp

Note: Court does have some misdemeanor records that are city ordinance violations.

Civil Records: Access: Phone, mail, in person. Both court and visitors may perform in person searches. No search fee. Court makes copy: $.25 per page. Required to search: name, years to search. Civil cases indexed by defendant, plaintiff. Civil records on dockets back to 1972. Mail turnaround time 1 day.

General Information: No public access terminal. Certification fee: $5.00. Payee: Magistrate Court. Business checks accepted. Prepayment required. SASE requested.

Probate Court 530 Greene St, Rm 401, Augusta, GA 30911; phone: 706-821-2434; fax: 706-821-2442; hours 8:30AM-5PM (EST). *Probate.*

Rockdale County

Superior Court PO Box 937, 922 Court St, Conyers, GA 30012; phone: 770-929-4021; hours 8AM-4:45PM (EST). *Felony, Civil.*
Note: The court will not do searches, but will provide assistance for $11.00 per hour.

Civil Records: Access: In person only. Visitors must perform in person searches themselves. Court makes copy: $.25 per page; same fee for self serve. Required to search: name, years to search. Civil cases indexed by defendant, plaintiff. Civil records on computer back to 1993, in books from 1900.

Criminal Records: Access: In person only. Visitors must perform in person searches themselves. Court makes copy: $.25 per page; same fee for self serve. Required to search: name, case number. Criminal records on computer back to 1990, books from 1900.

General Information: Public terminal has criminal back to 1990 and civil back to 1993. No juvenile, adoption, sexual, mental health or expunged records released. Certification fee: $2.50 plus $.50 per page after first. Payee: Clerk Superior Court. Personal checks accepted. Prepayment required.

State Court PO Box 938, Conyers, GA 30012; phone: 770-929-4019; fax: 770-929-4110; hours 8AM-4:45PM (EST). *Misdemeanor, Civil.*

Civil Records: Access: In person only. Visitors must perform in person searches themselves. Court makes copy: $.25 per page. Required to search: name, years to search. Civil cases indexed by defendant, plaintiff. Civil records on computer from 1994, on dockets to 1994.

Criminal Records: Access: In person only. Visitors must perform in person searches themselves. Court makes copy: $.25 per page. Required to search: name, years to search. Criminal records on computer from 1990, on dockets from 1987-1990.

General Information: Public terminal goes back to 1994. No juvenile, adoption, sexual, mental health or expunged records released. Certification fee: $2.50 plus $.50 per page after first. Payee: Rockdale State Court. Business checks accepted. Prepayment required.

Magistrate Court PO Box 289, Conyers, GA 30012; phone: 770-929-4075; fax: 770-785-2496; hours 8:30AM-4:30PM (EST). *Civil Actions Under $15,000, Eviction, Small Claims.*

Probate Court 922 Court St NE, Rm 107, Conyers, GA 30012; phone: 770-929-4058; fax: 770-918-6502; 8:30AM-4:30PM (EST). *Probate.* https://www.gaprobate.org/counties/rockdale/index.html

Schley County

Superior Court PO Box 7, 14 S Broad St, Ellaville, GA 31806; phone: 229-937-5581; fax: 229-937-5588; hours 8AM-N,1-5PM (EST). *Felony, Misdemeanor, Civil.* www.gsccca.org/clerks

Civil Records: Access: In person only. Visitors must perform in person searches themselves. Court makes copy: $.25 per page; same fee for self serve. Required to search: name, years to search. Civil cases indexed by defendant. Civil records in books from 1885.

Criminal Records: Access: In person only. Visitors must perform in person searches themselves. Court makes copy: $.25 per page; same fee for self serve. Required to search: name, years to search, DOB, signed release; SSN helpful. Criminal records in books from 1934.

General Information: Public use terminal available. No adoption records released. Will not fax specific case file. Certification fee: $5.00 per document includes copies. Payee: Clerk Superior Court. Personal checks accepted. Prepayment required.

Magistrate Court PO Box 372, 14 Broad St, Ellaville, GA 31806; phone: 229-937-5581; fax: 229-937-5588; hours 9AM-5PM (closed at noon) (EST). *Civil Actions Under $15,000, Eviction, Small Claims.*

Probate Court PO Box 385, 14 S Broad St, Ellaville, GA 31806; phone: 229-937-2905; fax: 229-937-5588; hours 8:30AM-N, 1-5PM (EST). *Probate.* https://www.gaprobate.org/counties/schley/index.html

Screven County

Superior Court PO Box 156, 216 Mims Rd, Sylvania, GA 30467; phone: 912-564-2614; fax: 912-564-2622; hours 8AM-5PM (EST). *Felony, Misdemeanor, Civil.*

Civil Records: Access: In person only. Visitors must perform in person searches themselves. Court makes copy: $1.00 per page. Self serve copy fee: $.25 per page. Required to search: name, years to search. Civil cases indexed by defendant, plaintiff. Civil records on dockets.

Criminal Records: Access: In person only. Visitors must perform in person searches themselves. Court makes copy: $1.00 per page. Self serve copy fee: $.25 per page. Required to search: name, years to search, DOB; SSN helpful. Criminal records on dockets.

General Information: Public terminal goes back to 1991. No juvenile or adoption records released. Certification fee: $3.00 first page, $1.50 ea add'l. Payee: Court Clerk. Personal checks accepted. Prepayment required.

State Court PO Box 156, Sylvania, GA 30467; phone: 912-564-2614; fax: 912-564-2622; hours 8:00AM-5PM (EST). *Misdemeanor, Civil.*

Civil Records: Access: In person only. Visitors must perform in person searches themselves. Court

makes copy: $.25 per page. Required to search: name, years to search. Civil cases indexed by defendant, plaintiff. Civil records on dockets from 1793; computerized records since 1991.

Criminal Records: Access: In person only. Visitors must perform in person searches themselves. Court makes copy: $.25 per page. Required to search: name, years to search, DOB; SSN helpful. Criminal records on dockets from 1793; computerized records since 1991.

General Information: Public terminal goes back to 1991. No juvenile, adoption, sexual, mental health or expunged records released. Certification fee: $3.00 per cert. Payee: Court Clerk. Personal checks accepted. Prepayment required.

Magistrate Court PO Box 64, 216 Mims Rd, Sylvania, GA 30467; phone: 912-564-7375; fax: 912-564-5618; hours 8AM-5PM (EST). *Civil Actions Under $15,000, Eviction, Small Claims.*

Probate Court 216 Mims Rd, #107, Sylvania, GA 30467; phone: 912-564-2783; fax: 912-564-9139; hours 8AM-5PM (EST). *Probate.*

Seminole County

Superior Court PO Box 672, Main St, Donalsonville, GA 39845; phone: 229-524-2525; fax: 229-524-8883; hours 8:30AM-5PM (EST). *Felony, Misdemeanor, Civil.*

Civil Records: Access: Fax, in person. Both court and visitors may perform in person searches. Search fee: $1.00 per name per year. Court makes copy: $1.00 per page. Required to search: name, years to search. Civil cases indexed by defendant, plaintiff. Civil records on computer from 1994, on dockets from 1921.

Criminal Records: Access: Fax, mail, in person. Both court and visitors may perform in person searches. Search fee: $1.00 per name per year. Court makes copy: $1.00 per page. Required to search: name, years to search, DOB, signed release; also helpful: SSN, race, sex. Criminal records on computer from 1994, on dockets from 1921. Mail turnaround time 1 day.

General Information: No public access terminal. No juvenile, adoption, sexual, mental health or expunged records released. Will fax documents $1.00 per page. Certification fee: $2.50 per page. Payee: Court Clerk. Personal checks accepted. Prepayment and SASE required.

Magistrate & Probate Court Seminole County Courthouse, 200 S Knox Ave, Donalsonville, GA 39845; phone: 229-524-5256; fax: 229-524-8644; hours 8:30AM-5PM (EST). *Civil Actions Under $15,000, Eviction, Small Claims.* https://www.gaprobate.org/counties/seminole/index.html

Spalding County

Superior Court PO Box 1046, Griffin, GA 30224; phone: 770-467-4356; criminal phone: 770-467-4745; civil phone: 770-467-4746; fax: 770-467-4478; hours 8AM-5PM (EST). *Felony, Misdemeanor, Civil.*

Civil Records: Access: Mail, in person. Visitors must perform in person searches themselves. Court makes copy: $.25 per page. Required to search: name, years to search. Civil cases indexed by defendant, plaintiff. Civil records on computer from 1991, on dockets from 1852. Mail for specific case info only, the court will not do name searches. Mail turnaround time 2 days.

Criminal Records: Access: Mail, in person. Visitors must perform in person searches themselves. Court makes copy: $.25 per page. Required to search: name, years to search; also helpful: DOB, SSN, race, sex. Criminal records on computer from 1991, on dockets from 1852. Court will not do name searches, will only do specific case files. Mail turnaround time 2 days.

General Information: Public terminal goes back to 1991. No juvenile, adoption, sexual, mental health or expunged records released. Certification fee: $2.00

per document; $.50 per page. Payee: Court Clerk. Personal checks accepted. Prepayment and SASE required.

State Court PO Box 1046, Griffin, GA 30224; phone: 770-467-4356; criminal phone: 770-467-4745; civil phone: 770-467-4746; probate phone: 770-467-4340; fax: 770-467-4478; hours 8AM-5PM (EST). *Misdemeanor, Civil.*
Civil Records: Access: Mail, in person. Visitors must perform in person searches themselves. Court makes copy: $.25 per page. Required to search: name, years to search. Civil cases indexed by defendant, plaintiff. Civil records on computer back to 1995; prior records on dockets from 1852. Mail access only for specific cases; no name searching by the court.
Criminal Records: Access: Mail, in person. Visitors must perform in person searches themselves. Court makes copy: $.25 per page. Required to search: name, years to search, DOB; also helpful: SSN, race, sex. Criminal records on computer back to 1995; prior records on dockets from 1852. Mail access for specific case information only, no name searching by the court. Mail turnaround time 2 days.
General Information: Public terminal goes back to 1995. No juvenile, adoption, sexual, mental health or expunged records released. Certification fee: $2.00 per cert. Payee: Court Clerk. Business checks accepted. Prepayment and SASE required.

Magistrate Court 132 E Solomon St, Griffin, GA 30223; phone: 770-467-4320; fax: 770-467-0081; hours 8AM-5PM (EST). *Civil Actions Under $15,000, Eviction, Small Claims.*

Probate Court 132 E Solomon St, Griffin, GA 30223; phone: 770-467-4340; fax: 770-467-4243; hours 8AM-N, 1-5PM (EST). *Probate.*
https://www.gaprobate.org/counties/spalding/index.html

Stephens County

Superior Court 205 Alexander St N, #202, Toccoa, GA 30577; phone: 706-886-9496; fax: 706-886-5710; hours 8AM-5PM (EST). *Felony, Misdemeanor, Civil.*
Civil Records: Access: Mail, in person. Both court and visitors may perform in person searches. Search fee: $7.50 per name. Court makes copy: $1.00 per page. Self serve copy fee: $.25 per page. Required to search: name, years to search. Civil cases indexed by defendant, plaintiff. Civil records on computer back to 1988, on dockets from 1906.
Criminal Records: Access: In person only. Both court and visitors may perform in person searches. Search fee: $7.50 per name. Court makes copy: $1.00 per page. Self serve copy fee: $.25 per page. Required to search: name, years to search, DOB, signed release; SSN helpful. Criminal records on computer back to 1988, on dockets from 1906. Mail turnaround time 1 day.
General Information: Public terminal has criminal back to 1990 and civil back to 1988. No juvenile, adoption, sexual, mental health or expunged records released. Fee to fax documents pre-paid: $2.00 1st page, $1.00 each add'l. Certification fee: $2.50 plus $.50 per page after first. Payee: Court Clerk. Personal checks accepted. Prepayment required.

State Court 205 N Alexander St, Rm 202, County Government Bldg, Toccoa, GA 30577; phone: 706-886-3598/9496; fax: 706-886-5710; hours 8AM-5PM (EST). *Misdemeanor, Civil.*
Civil Records: Access: In person only. Visitors must perform in person searches themselves. Court makes copy: $1.00 per page. Self serve copy fee: $.25 per page. Required to search: name, years to search. Civil cases indexed by defendant, plaintiff. Civil records on computer back to 1991, on dockets from 1906.
Criminal Records: Access: In person only. Visitors must perform in person searches themselves. Court makes copy: $1.00 per page. Self serve copy fee: $.25 per page. Required to search: name, years to search, DOB; SSN helpful. Criminal records on computer back to 1990, on dockets from 1906.

General Information: Public terminal has criminal back to 1990 and civil back to 1991. No juvenile, adoption, sexual, mental health or expunged records released. Will not fax specific case file. Certification fee: $2.50 plus $.50 per page after first. Payee: Court Clerk. Personal checks accepted. Prepayment required.

Magistrate Court 205 N Alexander St, Rm 107, Toccoa, GA 30577; phone: 706-886-6205; fax: 706-886-5569; hours 8:30AM-5:00Pm (EST). *Civil Actions Under $15,000, Eviction, Small Claims.*

Probate Court 205 N Alexander, #108, Toccoa, GA 30577; phone: 706-886-2828; fax: 706-886-2631; hours 8AM-5PM M-F, closed for lunch hour (EST). *Probate.*

Stewart County

Superior Court PO Box 910, Main St, Lumpkin, GA 31815; phone: 229-838-6220; fax: 229-838-4505; hours 8AM-4:30PM (EST). *Felony, Misdemeanor, Civil.*
Civil Records: Access: In person only. Visitors must perform in person searches themselves. Court makes copy: $.50 per page. Self serve copy fee: $.25 per page. Required to search: name, years to search; also helpful: address. Civil cases indexed by defendant. Civil records in index books.
Criminal Records: Access: In person only. Visitors must perform in person searches themselves. Court makes copy: $.50 per page. Self serve copy fee: $.25 per page. Required to search: name, years to search; also helpful: address, DOB, SSN. Criminal records in index books to 1840s.
General Information: Public use terminal available. No juvenile, adoption, sexual, mental health or sealed records are released. Certification fee: $2.50 plus $.50 per page after first. Payee: Clerk of Superior Court. Personal checks accepted. Prepayment required.

Magistrate Court PO Box 712, 712 Broad St, Lumpkin, GA 31815; phone: 229-838-0505; fax: 229-838-0015; hours 8AM-5PM (EST). *Civil Actions Under $15,000, Eviction, Small Claims.*

Probate Court PO Box 876, Lumpkin, GA 31815; phone: 229-838-4394; fax: 229-838-9084; hours 8AM-N, 1-4:30PM (EST). *Probate.*
https://www.gaprobate.org/counties/stewart/index.html

Sumter County

State Court PO Box 333, Americus, GA 31709; phone: 229-928-4537; hours 9AM-5PM (EST). *Misdemeanor, Civil.*
Civil Records: Access: In person only. Visitors must perform in person searches themselves. Court makes copy: $.25 per page. Self serve copy fee: $.25 per page. Required to search: name, years to search. Civil cases indexed by defendant, plaintiff. Civil records on dockets from late 1800s.
Criminal Records: Access: In person only. Visitors must perform in person searches themselves. Court makes copy: $.25 per page. Self serve copy fee: $.25 per page. Required to search: name, years to search, DOB; SSN helpful. Criminal records on dockets from late 1800s.
General Information: No public access terminal. No juvenile, adoption, sealed, sexual, mental health or expunged records released. Certification fee: $2.50 plus $.50 per page. Certification only done if court performs makes the copy. Payee: Court Clerk. Prepayment required.

Magistrate Court PO Box 563, Americus, GA 31709; phone: 229-928-4524; fax: 229-928-4527; hours 9AM-5PM (EST). *Civil Actions Under $15,000, Eviction, Small Claims.*

Probate Court PO Box 246, 500 W Lamar St, Americus, GA 31709; phone: 229-928-4551; fax: 229-928-4622; hours 8AM-5PM (EST). *Probate.*

Talbot County

Superior Court PO Box 325, Talbotton, GA 31827; phone: 706-665-3239; fax: 706-665-8637; hours 9AM-5PM (EST). *Felony, Misdemeanor, Civil.*
Civil Records: Access: In person only. Visitors must perform in person searches themselves. Court makes copy: $.25 per page; same fee for self serve. Required to search: name, years to search. Civil cases indexed by defendant, plaintiff. Civil records on dockets from 1827.
Criminal Records: Access: In person only. Visitors must perform in person searches themselves. Court makes copy: $.25 per page; same fee for self serve. Required to search: name, years to search. Criminal records are computerized. Historical documents are indexed in docket books.
General Information: No public access terminal. No juvenile, adoption, sexual, mental health or expunged records released. Certification fee: $2.00 plus $.50 per page after first. Payee: Superior Court. Business checks accepted. Prepayment required.

Magistrate & Probate Court PO Box 157, s7 S Washington St, Talbotton, GA 31827; phone: 706-665-8866; fax: 706-665-8240; hours 8AM-5PM (EST). *Civil Actions Under $15,000, Eviction, Small Claims, Probate.*
https://www.gaprobate.org/counties/talbot/index.html

Taliaferro County

Superior Court PO Box 182, Crawfordville, GA 30631; phone: 706-456-2123; fax: 706-456-2749; hours 9AM-5PM (EST). *Felony, Misdemeanor, Civil.*
Civil Records: Access: In person only. Visitors must perform in person searches themselves. Court makes copy: $1.00 per page. Self serve copy fee: $.25 per page. Required to search: name, years to search. Civil cases indexed by defendant, plaintiff. Civil records on dockets from 1825.
Criminal Records: Access: In person only. Visitors must perform in person searches themselves. Court makes copy: $1.00 per page. Self serve copy fee: $.25 per page. Required to search: name, years to search, DOB; SSN helpful. Criminal records on dockets from 1825.
General Information: Public use terminal available. No juvenile, adoption, sexual, mental health or expunged records released. Certification fee: $2.00. Payee: Court Clerk. Personal checks accepted. Prepayment required.

Magistrate & Probate Court PO Box 264, 113 Monument St, Courthouse, Crawfordville, GA 30631; phone: 706-456-2253; hours 9AM-5PM (EST). *Civil Actions Under $15,000, Eviction, Small Claims, Probate, Misdemeanor Traffic.*

Tattnall County

Superior & State Court PO Box 39, Reidsville, GA 30453; phone: 912-557-6716; fax: 912-557-4861; hours 8AM-5PM (EST). *Felony, Misdemeanor, Civil.*
Civil Records: Access: In person only. Visitors must perform in person searches themselves. Court makes copy: $.25 per page; same fee for self serve. Required to search: name, years to search; also helpful: address. Civil cases indexed by defendant, plaintiff. Civil records on computer back to 1990; on dockets from 1800s.
Criminal Records: Access: In person only. Visitors must perform in person searches themselves. Court makes copy: $.25 per page; same fee for self serve. Required to search: name, years to search, DOB; SSN helpful. Criminal records on computer back to 1990; on dockets from 1800s.
General Information: Public terminal goes back to 1990. No juvenile, adoption, sexual, mental health or expunged records released. Certification fee: $3.00 1st page plus $.50 each add'l. Payee: Court Clerk. Business checks accepted. Prepayment required.

Magistrate Court PO Box 513, Reidsville, GA 30453; phone: 912-557-4372; fax: 912-557-3136; hours 8AM-5PM (EST). *Civil Actions Under $15,000, Eviction, Small Claims.*

Probate Court 111 N Main St, Reidsville, GA 30453; phone: 912-557-6719; fax: 912-557-3976; hours 8:30AM-5PM (EST). *Probate.*

Taylor County

Superior Court PO Box 248, Courthouse Sq, Butler, GA 31006; phone: 478-862-5594; fax: 478-862-5334; hours 8AM-5PM (EST). *Felony, Misdemeanor, Civil.*
Civil Records: Access: In person only. Both court and visitors may perform in person searches. Search fee: Copy fee only. Court makes copy: $1.00 per page. Self serve copy fee: $.25 per page. Required to search: name, years to search. Civil cases indexed by defendant, plaintiff. Civil records on computer from 1991, dockets from 1852.
Criminal Records: Access: In person only. Visitors must perform in person searches themselves. Court makes copy: $1.00 per page. Self serve copy fee: $.25 per page. Required to search: name, years to search, DOB; SSN helpful. Criminal records on computer from 1991, dockets from 1852.
General Information: Public terminal has only civil records back to 1995. No juvenile, adoption, sexual, mental health or expunged records released. Will fax specific case file for $2.50 per page. Certification fee: $2.50. Payee: Court Clerk. Personal checks accepted. Prepayment required.

Magistrate & Probate Court PO Box 536, 2 N Broad St, Butler, GA 31006; phone: 478-862-3357; fax: 478-862-9447; hours 8AM-5PM (EST). *Civil Actions Under $15,000, Eviction, Small Claims, Probate, Traffic.*
https://www.gaprobate.org/counties/taylor/index.html

Telfair County

Superior Court Courthouse, 128 Oak St, #2, McRae, GA 31055; phone: 229-868-6525; fax: 229-868-7956; hours 8:30AM-4:30PM (EST). *Felony, Misdemeanor, Civil.*
Civil Records: Access: Phone, mail, in person. Visitors must perform in person searches themselves. Court makes copy: $.25 per page; same fee for self serve. Required to search: name, years to search. Civil cases indexed by defendant. Civil records on dockets from early 1900s.
Criminal Records: Access: Phone, in person. Visitors must perform in person searches themselves. Court makes copy: $.25 per page; same fee for self serve. Required to search: name, years to search, DOB, signed release; also helpful: SSN, race, sex. Criminal records on dockets from early 1900s. Mail turnaround time 1 week.
General Information: No public access terminal. No juvenile, adoption, sexual, mental health or expunged records released. Certification fee: $3.00. Payee: Court Clerk. Personal checks accepted. Prepayment required. SASE requested.

Magistrate Court 128 E Oak St, #5, McRae, GA 31055; phone: 229-868-6772; fax: 229-868-6902; hours 8:00AM-4:30PM (EST). *Civil Actions Under $15,000, Eviction, Small Claims.*

Probate Court 128 E Oak St, #1, McRae, GA 31055; phone: 229-868-6038; probate phone: 229-868-7987; fax: 229-868-7620; hours 8:30AM-N, 1-4:30PM (EST). *Probate, Traffic.*

Terrell County

Superior Court PO Box 189, 513 S Main St, Dawson, GA 39842; phone: 229-995-2631; hours 8:30AM-5PM (EST). *Felony, Misdemeanor, Civil.*
Civil Records: Access: In person only. Visitors must perform in person searches themselves. Court makes copy: $1.00 per page. Self serve copy fee: $.25 per page. Required to search: name, years to search. Civil cases indexed by defendant. Civil records on computer from 1988, dockets books from 1900s.

Criminal Records: Access: In person only. Visitors must perform in person searches themselves. Court makes copy: $1.00 per page. Self serve copy fee: $.25 per page. Required to search: name, years to search, DOB, signed release; SSN helpful. Criminal records on computer from 1988, dockets books from 1900s.
General Information: Public terminal goes back to 1989. No juvenile, adoption, sexual, mental health or expunged records released. Certification fee: $2.50 plus $.50 per page after first. Payee: Court Clerk. Business checks accepted. Prepayment required.

Magistrate Court PO Box 793, Dawson, GA 39842; phone: 229-995-3757; fax: 229-995-4496; hours 8AM-5PM (EST). *Civil Actions Under $15,000, Eviction, Small Claims, Misdemeanors.*

Probate Court PO Box 67, 513 S Main St, Dawson, GA 39842; phone: 229-995-5515; fax: 229-995-4301; 8AM-N, 1-5PM (EST). *Probate.*
https://www.gaprobate.org/counties/terrell/index.html

Thomas County

Superior & State Court PO Box 1995, Thomasville, GA 31799; phone: 229-225-4108; fax: 229-225-4110; hours 8AM-5PM (EST). *Felony, Misdemeanor, Civil.* www.thomascoclerkofcourt.org
Civil Records: Access: In person only. Visitors must perform in person searches themselves. Court makes copy: $1.00 per page. Self serve copy fee: $.50 per page. Required to search: name, years to search. Civil cases indexed by defendant, plaintiff. Civil records on computer from 1989, archived from 1826.
Criminal Records: Access: In person only. Visitors must perform in person searches themselves. Court makes copy: $1.00 per page. Self serve copy fee: $.50 per page. Required to search: name, years to search, DOB; SSN helpful. Criminal records computerized since 1989.
General Information: Public terminal goes back to 1989. No juvenile, adoption, sexual, mental health or expunged records released. Will fax specific case file for $2.50 per fax. Certification fee: $2.00. Payee: Court Clerk. Personal checks accepted. Prepayment required.

Magistrate Court PO Box 879, 921 Smith Ave, Thomasville, GA 31799; phone: 229-225-3334; fax: 229-225-3342; hours 8AM-5PM (EST). *Civil Actions Under $15,000, Eviction, Small Claims.*

Probate Court PO Box 1582, Thomasville, GA 31799; phone: 229-225-4116; fax: 229-227-1698; hours 8AM-5PM (EST). *Probate.*

Tift County

Superior & State Court PO Box 354, Tifton, GA 31793; phone: 229-386-7810; fax: 229-386-7813; hours 8AM-5PM (EST). *Felony, Misdemeanor, Civil.*
Note: Call 229-786-7815 to reach the Superior Court.
Civil Records: Access: In person only. Visitors must perform in person searches themselves. Court makes copy: $.25 per page. Required to search: name, years to search. Civil cases indexed by defendant. Civil records on dockets books from 1905.
Criminal Records: Access: In person only. Visitors must perform in person searches themselves. Court makes copy: $.25 per page. Required to search: name, years to search, DOB; SSN helpful. Criminal records on dockets books from 1905.
General Information: Public terminal goes back to 2002. No juvenile, adoption, sexual, mental health or expunged records released. Certification fee: $2.50 plus $.50 per page after first. Payee: Court Clerk. Personal checks accepted. Prepayment required.

Magistrate Court PO Box 214, Tifton, GA 31793; phone: 229-386-7907; fax: 229-386-7978; hours 8AM-5PM (EST). *Civil Actions Under $15,000, Eviction, Small Claims.*

Probate Court PO Box 792, 225 Tift Ave, Rm 117, Tifton, GA 31793; phone: 229-386-7936, 229-386-7914; fax: 229-386-7926; hours 8AM-5PM (EST). *Probate.*

Toombs County

Superior & State Court PO Drawer 530, Lyons, GA 30436; phone: 912-526-3501; fax: 912-526-1004; hours 8:30AM-5PM (EST). *Felony, Misdemeanor, Civil.*
Civil Records: Access: In person only. Visitors must perform in person searches themselves. Court makes copy: $1.00 per page. Required to search: name, years to search. Civil cases indexed by defendant, plaintiff. Civil records on dockets books from 1908, on computer since 1995.
Criminal Records: Access: In person only. Visitors must perform in person searches themselves. Court makes copy: $1.00 per page. Required to search: name, years to search, DOB; SSN helpful. Criminal records on dockets books from 1908, on computer since 1995.
General Information: Public terminal goes back to 1995. No juvenile, adoption, sexual, mental health or expunged records released. Certification fee: $2.50 plus $1.00 per page after first. Payee: Court Clerk. No personal checks accepted. Prepayment required.

Magistrate Court PO Box 1460, 100 Courthouse Sq, Lyons, GA 30436; phone: 912-526-8984; fax: 912-526-8985; hours 8:30AM-5PM (EST). *Civil Actions Under $15,000, Eviction, Small Claims.*

Probate Court 100 Courthouse Sq, County Courthouse, PO Box 1370, Lyons, GA 30436; phone: 912-526-8696; fax: 912-526-1008; hours 8:30AM-5PM (EST). *Probate.*

Towns County

Superior Court 48 River St, #E, Hiawassee, GA 30546; phone: 706-896-2130; fax: 706-896-1772; hours 8:30AM-4:30PM (EST). *Felony, Misdemeanor, Civil.*
Civil Records: Access: In person only. Visitors must perform in person searches themselves. Court makes copy: $1.00 per page. Self serve copy fee: $.25 per page. Required to search: name, years to search. Civil cases indexed by plaintiff. Civil records on dockets books from 1923, records computerized 2002 forward.
Criminal Records: Access: In person only. Visitors must perform in person searches themselves. Court makes copy: $1.00 per page. Self serve copy fee: $.25 per page. Required to search: name, years to search, DOB, signed release; SSN helpful. Criminal records on docket books to 1945, indexed by defendant; records computerized 2002 forward.
General Information: No public access terminal. No juvenile, adoption, sexual, mental health or expunged records released. Certification fee: $2.50 per page. Payee: Court Clerk. Personal checks accepted. Prepayment required.

Magistrate & Probate Court 48 River St, #C, Hiawassee, GA 30546; phone: 706-896-3467; fax: 706-896-1772; 8:30AM-4:30PM. *Civil Actions Under $15,000, Eviction, Small Claims, Probate.*

Treutlen County

Superior & State Court PO Box 356, Soperton, GA 30457; phone: 912-529-4215; probate phone: 912-529-3342; hours 8AM-5PM (EST). *Felony, Misdemeanor, Civil.*
Civil Records: Access: Mail, in person. Both court and visitors may perform in person searches. No search fee. Court makes copy: $1.00 per page. Self serve copy fee: $.25 per page. Required to search: name, years to search. Civil cases indexed by defendant, plaintiff. Civil records on computer from 1991, dockets books from 1919. Mail turnaround time 1-2 days.
Criminal Records: Access: Mail, in person. Both court and visitors may perform in person searches. No search fee. Court makes copy: $1.00 per page. Self serve copy fee: $.25 per page. Required to search: name, years to search, DOB; also helpful: SSN, race, sex. Criminal records on computer from 1991,

dockets books from 1919. Mail turnaround time 1-2 days.

General Information: Public terminal goes back to 1990. No juvenile, adoption, sexual, mental health or expunged records released. Certification fee: $2.50 plus $.50 per page after first. Payee: Court Clerk. Personal checks accepted. Prepayment required.

Magistrate & Probate Court 114 2nd St S, Courthouse Annex, Soperton, GA 30457; phone: 912-529-3342; probate phone: 912-529-4320; fax: 912-529-6838; hours 8AM-5PM (EST). *Civil Under $15,000, Eviction, Small Claims, Probate.*

Troup County

Superior & State Court 900 Dallas St, LaGrange, GA 30240; phone: 706-883-1740; fax: 706-883-1724; hours 8AM-5PM (EST). *Felony, Misdemeanor, Civil.*
Civil Records: Access: In person only. Visitors must perform in person searches themselves. Court makes copy: $.25 per page. Required to search: name, years to search. Civil cases indexed by defendant, plaintiff. Civil records on computer from 1996, on docket books from 1940s.
Criminal Records: Access: In person only. Visitors must perform in person searches themselves. Court makes copy: $.25 per page. Required to search: name, years to search, DOB; SSN helpful. Criminal records on computer from 1996, on docket books from 1940s.
General Information: Public terminal goes back to 1996. No juvenile, adoption, sexual, mental health or expunged records released. Will not fax specific case file. Certification fee: $2.50 plus $.50 per page. Cert fee includes copies. Payee: Court Clerk. Personal checks accepted if local. Prepayment required.

Magistrate Court 119 Ridley Ave, #101, LaGrange, GA 30240; phone: 706-883-1695; fax: 706-883-1632; hours 8AM-5PM (EST). *Civil Actions Under $15,000, Eviction, Small Claims.*

Probate Court 900 Dallis St, County Admin. Bldg, LaGrange, GA 30240; phone: 706-883-1690; fax: 706-812-7933; hours 8AM-5PM (EST). *Probate.*
www.georgiacourts.org/
Note: Includes guardianship, administrations, custodial accounts, citations, mental health.

Turner County

Superior Court PO Box 106, 219 E College Ave, Ashburn, GA 31714; phone: 229-567-2011; fax: 229-567-0450; hours 8AM-5PM (EST). *Felony, Misdemeanor, Civil.*
Civil Records: Access: In person only. Visitors must perform in person searches themselves. Court makes copy: $1.00 per page. Self serve copy fee: $.25 per page. Required to search: name, years to search. Civil cases indexed by defendant, plaintiff. Civil records on docket books, archived from 1905.
Criminal Records: Access: In person only. Visitors must perform in person searches themselves. Court makes copy: $1.00 per page. Self serve copy fee: $.25 per page. Required to search: name, years to search, DOB, signed release; SSN helpful. Criminal records on docket books, archived from 1905.
General Information: No public access terminal. No juvenile, adoption, sexual, mental health or expunged records released. Certification fee: $2.50 plus $1.00 per page after first. Payee: Court Clerk. Personal checks not accepted. Prepayment required.

Magistrate Court 219 E College, Ashburn, GA 31714; phone: 229-567-3155; hours 9AM-4:30PM (EST). *Civil Actions Under $15,000, Eviction, Small Claims.*

Probate Court PO Box 2506, Ashburn, GA 31714-2506; phone: 229-567-2151; fax: 229-567-0358; hours 8AM-5PM, closed for lunch (EST). *Probate.*

Twiggs County

Superior Court PO Box 243, Jeffersonville, GA 31044; phone: 478-945-3350; fax: 478-945-6751; hours 8AM-5PM (EST). *Felony, Misdemeanor, Civil.*
Civil Records: Access: In person only. Visitors must perform in person searches themselves. Court makes copy: $.25 per page. Required to search: name, years to search. Civil cases indexed by defendant, plaintiff. Civil records on computer from 1991, dockets books to 1901.
Criminal Records: Access: In person only. Visitors must perform in person searches themselves. Court makes copy: $.25 per page. Required to search: name, years to search, DOB, signed release; SSN helpful. Criminal records on computer from 1991, dockets books to 1901.
General Information: Public terminal goes back to 1991. No juvenile, adoption, sexual, mental health or expunged records released. Certification fee: $2.50 plus $.50 per page after first. Payee: Court Clerk. Personal checks accepted. Prepayment required.

Magistrate Court PO Box 146, 425 N Railroad St #212, Jeffersonville, GA 31044; phone: 478-945-3428; fax: 478-945-2083; hours 9AM-5PM (EST). *Civil Actions Under $15,000, Eviction, Small Claims.*

Probate Court PO Box 186, 425 Railroad St N, Jeffersonville, GA 31044; phone: 478-945-3390/3252; fax: 478-945-6070; hours 9AM-5PM (EST). *Probate, Misdemeanor Traffic.*

Union County

Superior Court 114 Courthouse St, #5, Blairsville, GA 30512; phone: 706-439-6022; fax: 706-439-6026; hours 8AM-5PM (EST). *Felony, Misdemeanor, Civil.*
Civil Records: Access: In person only. Both court and visitors may perform in person searches. No search fee. Court makes copy: $.25 per page. Required to search: name, years to search. Civil cases indexed by defendant, plaintiff. Civil records on computer from 1993, on dockets from 1936.
Criminal Records: Access: In person only. Both court and visitors may perform in person searches. No search fee. Court makes copy: $.25 per page. Required to search: name, years to search, DOB, signed release; SSN helpful. Criminal records on docket books from 1930; computerized back to 1997.
General Information: Public terminal has criminal back to 1997 and civil back to 1993. No juvenile, adoption, sexual, mental health or expunged records released. Certification fee: $2.50 plus $.25 per page after first. Payee: Court Clerk. Personal checks accepted. Prepayment required.

Magistrate Court 114 Courthouse St, #10, Blairsville, GA 30512; phone: 706-439-6008; fax: 706-439-6104; hours 8AM-4:30PM (EST). *Civil Actions Under $15,000, Eviction, Small Claims.*

Probate Court 114 Courthouse St, #8, Blairsville, GA 30512; phone: 706-439-6006; fax: 706-439-6009; hours 8AM-4:30PM (EST). *Probate.*

Upson County

Superior Court PO Box 469, Thomaston, GA 30286; phone: 706-647-7835; probate phone: 706-647-7015; fax: 706-647-8999; hours 8AM-5PM (EST). *Felony, Misdemeanor, Civil.*
Civil Records: Access: Mail, in person. Visitors must perform in person searches themselves. Search fee: $5.00. Court makes copy: $1.00 per page. Self serve copy fee: $.25 per page. Required to search: name, years to search. Civil cases indexed by defendant, plaintiff. Civil records on dockets books from 1927; on computer back to 1990. Mail turnaround time 15 days.
Criminal Records: Access: Mail, in person. Visitors must perform in person searches themselves. Court makes copy: $1.00 per page. Self serve copy fee: $.25 per page. Required to search: name, years to search,

DOB; also helpful: SSN, race, sex. Criminal records on docket books from 1937; on computer back to 1990. Mail turnaround time 15 days.
General Information: Public terminal goes back to 1990. No juvenile, adoption, sexual, mental health or expunged records released. Certification fee: $2.50 plus $.50 per page after first. Payee: Court Clerk. Personal checks accepted. Prepayment required.

Magistrate Court PO Box 890, 305 S Hightower, Thomaston, GA 30286; phone: 706-647-6891; fax: 706-647-1248; hours 8AM-4:45PM (EST). *Civil Under $15,000, Eviction, Small Claims.*

Probate Court PO Box 906, 106 E Lee St, Thomaston, GA 30286; phone: 706-647-7015; fax: 706-646-3341; hours 8AM-5PM (EST). *Probate.*

Walker County

Superior & State Court PO Box 448, LaFayette, GA 30728; phone: 706-638-1772; fax: 706-638-1779; hours 8AM-5PM (EST). *Felony, Misdemeanor, Civil.*
Civil Records: Access: In person only. Visitors must perform in person searches themselves. Court makes copy: $1.00 per page. Self serve copy fee: $.25 per page. Required to search: name, years to search. Civil cases indexed by defendant, plaintiff. Civil records on dockets books from 1883; computerized since 2000.
Criminal Records: Access: In person only. Visitors must perform in person searches themselves. Court makes copy: $1.00 per page. Self serve copy fee: $.25 per page. Required to search: name, years to search, DOB; SSN helpful. Criminal records on dockets books from 1883.
General Information: No juvenile, adoption, sexual, mental health or expunged records released. Will not fax specific case file. Certification fee: $2.00. Payee: Court Clerk. Personal checks accepted.

Magistrate Court 102 Napier St, LaFayette, GA 30728; phone: 706-638-1217; fax: 706-638-1218; hours 8AM-5PM (EST). *Civil Actions Under $15,000, Eviction, Small Claims.*

Probate Court PO Box 436, 103 S Duke St, LaFayette, GA 30728; phone: 706-638-2852; fax: 706-638-2869; hours 8AM-5PM (EST). *Probate.*
www.walkercounty.org

Walton County

Superior Court PO Box 745, Monroe, GA 30655; phone: 770-267-1307; fax: 770-267-1441; 8:30AM-5PM (EST). *Felony, Misdemeanor, Civil.*
Civil Records: Access: In person only. Visitors must perform in person searches themselves. Court makes copy: $.25 per page. Required to search: name, years to search. Civil cases indexed by defendant, plaintiff. Civil records on computer from 1990, dockets books from 1900s.
Criminal Records: Access: In person only. Visitors must perform in person searches themselves. Court makes copy: $.25 per page. Required to search: name, years to search; also helpful: DOB, race, sex. Criminal records on computer from 1990, dockets books from 1900s.
General Information: Public use terminal available. No juvenile, adoption, sexual, mental health or expunged records released. Certification fee: $2.50 plus $.50 per page after first. Payee: Court Clerk. Personal checks accepted. Prepayment required.

Magistrate Court 303 S Hammond Dr #116, Monroe, GA 30655; phone: 770-267-1349; criminal/civil fax: 770-266-1512; hours 8:30AM-5PM (EST). *Civil Actions Under $15,000, Eviction, Small Claims, Criminal warrants, Bad check warrants, County ordinance violations.*

Probate Court 303 S Hammond Dr #118, Monroe, GA 30655; phone: 770-267-1345, 266-1751; fax: 770-267-1417; 8:30AM-5PM *Probate.*
https://www.gaprobate.org/counties/walton/index.html
Note: This location also has traffic and misdemeanor records.

Ware County

Superior & State Court PO Box 776, Waycross, GA 31502; phone: 912-287-4340; fax: 912-287-2498; hours 9AM-5PM (EST). *Felony, Misdemeanor, Civil.*

Civil Records: Access: In person only. Visitors must perform in person searches themselves. Court makes copy: $1.00 per page if court assists. Self serve copy fee: $.25 per page. Required to search: name, years to search. Civil cases indexed by defendant. Civil records on computer since 1995; prior records on dockets books from 1874.

Criminal Records: Access: In person only. Visitors must perform in person searches themselves. Court makes copy: $1.00 per page if court assists. Self serve copy fee: $.25 per page. Required to search: name, years to search, DOB; SSN helpful. Criminal records on computer since 1995; prior records on dockets books from 1874.

General Information: No public access terminal. No juvenile, adoption, sexual, mental health or expunged records released. Certification fee: $2.50 plus $.50 per page after first. Payee: Court Clerk. Personal checks accepted. Prepayment required.

Magistrate Court PO Box 17, 201 State St, Rm 102, Waycross, GA 31501; criminal phone: 912-287-4373; civil phone: 912-287-4375; fax: 912-287-4377; hours 9AM-5PM (EST). *Civil Actions Under $15,000, Eviction, Small Claims.*

Probate Court Ware County Courthouse, 800 Church St, #123, Waycross, GA 31501; phone: 912-287-4315/6; probate phone: 912-287-4316; fax: 912-287-4317; probate fax: same; hours 9AM-5PM (EST). *Probate.*

Warren County

Superior Court PO Box 227, 100 Main St, Warrenton, GA 30828; phone: 706-465-2262; fax: 706-465-0232; hours 8AM-5PM (EST). *Felony, Misdemeanor, Civil.*

Civil Records: Access: Mail, in person. Visitors must perform in person searches themselves. Court makes copy: $1.00 per page. Required to search: name, years to search. Civil cases indexed by defendant, plaintiff. Civil records on docket books to 1950.

Criminal Records: Access: Mail, in person. Visitors must perform in person searches themselves. Court makes copy: $1.00 per page. Required to search: name, years to search, DOB, signed release; also helpful: SSN, race, sex. Criminal records on docket books to 1950, computerized since 2000.

General Information: No public access terminal. No juvenile, adoption, sexual, mental health or expunged records released. Certification fee: $2.50 for 1st page, $.50 each add'l. Payee: Court Clerk. Only cashiers checks and money orders accepted. Prepayment required.

Magistrate Court PO Box 203, Warrenton, GA 30828; phone: 706-465-3123; fax: 706-465-1300; hours 8AM-N, 1-5PM (EST). *Civil Actions Under $15,000, Eviction, Small Claims.*

Probate Court PO Box 364, 100 Main St, Warrenton, GA 30828; phone: 706-465-2227; fax: 706-465-1347; hours 8AM-4:30PM (EST). *Probate.*

Washington County

Superior & State Court PO Box 231, Sandersville, GA 31082; phone: 478-552-3186; fax: 478-553-9969; hours 9AM-5PM (EST). *Felony, Misdemeanor, Civil.*

Civil Records: Access: Mail, in person. Visitors must perform in person searches themselves. Court makes copy: $1.00 per page. Self serve copy fee: $.25 per page. Required to search: name, years to search. Civil cases indexed by defendant, plaintiff. Civil records on dockets books to 1869. Mail turnaround time 2 days.

Criminal Records: Access: Mail, in person. Visitors must perform in person searches themselves. Court makes copy: $1.00 per page. Self serve copy fee: $.25 per page. Required to search: name, years to search. Criminal records on dockets books to 1869. Mail turnaround time 2 days.

General Information: Public terminal goes back to 1995. No juvenile, adoption, sexual, mental health or expunged records released. Will fax documents to local or toll free line, as long as copy fee paid. Certification fee: $2.50. Payee: Court Clerk. Personal checks not accepted. Prepayment required.

Magistrate Court PO Box 1053, 132 W Haynes St Rm 110, Sandersville, GA 31082; phone: 478-552-3591; fax: 478-552-4010; 9AM-5PM *Civil Actions Under $15,000, Eviction, Small Claims.*

Probate Court PO Box 669, 132 W Haynes ST #106, Sandersville, GA 31082; phone: 478-552-3304; fax: 478-552-7424; hours 9AM-N, 1-5PM (EST). *Probate.*

Wayne County

Superior & State Court PO Box 920, Jesup, GA 31598; phone: 912-427-5930; fax: 912-427-5939; hours 8:30AM-5PM (EST). *Felony, Misdemeanor, Civil.*

Civil Records: Access: In person only. Visitors must perform in person searches themselves. Court makes copy: $.25 per page; same fee for self serve. Required to search: name, years to search. Civil cases indexed by defendant, plaintiff. Civil records on computer, on docket books from 1810.

Criminal Records: Access: In person only. Visitors must perform in person searches themselves. Court makes copy: $.25 per page; same fee for self serve. Required to search: name, years to search, DOB. Criminal records on computer, on docket books from 1810.

General Information: Public terminal goes back to 1994. No juvenile, adoption, sexual, mental health or expunged records released. Certification fee: $2.50 plus $.50 per page after first. Payee: Superior Court Clerk. Personal checks accepted. Prepayment required.

Magistrate Court PO Box 27, 174 N Brunswick St, Jesup, GA 31598; phone: 912-427-5960; fax: 912-427-5944; 8:30AM-N; 1PM-5PM (EST). *Civil Actions Under $15,000, Eviction, Small Claims.*

Probate Court 174 N Brunswick St, Jesup, GA 31546; phone: 912-427-5940; fax: 912-427-5944; hours 8:30AM-5PM (EST). *Probate.*

Webster County

Superior Court PO Box 117, Preston, GA 31824; phone: 229-828-3525; fax: 229-828-6961; hours 8AM-4:30PM (EST). *Felony, Misdemeanor, Civil.*

Civil Records: Access: In person only. Visitors must perform in person searches themselves. Court makes copy: $.25 per page. Required to search: name, years to search. Civil cases indexed by defendant, plaintiff. Civil records on docket books from 1860; computerized records since 2000.

Criminal Records: Access: In person only. Visitors must perform in person searches themselves. Court makes copy: $.25 per page. Required to search: name, years to search, signed release. Criminal records on docket books from 1860; computerized records since 2000.

General Information: Public terminal goes back to 2000. No juvenile, adoption, sexual, mental health or expunged records released. Certification fee: $2.50 plus $.50 per page after 1st page. Payee: Clerk Superior Court. Personal checks accepted. Prepayment required.

Magistrate & Probate Court PO Box 135, 6330 Hamilton St, Rm101, Preston, GA 31824; phone: 229-828-3615; fax: 229-828-3616; hours 8:00AM-4:30PM (EST). *Civil Actions Under $15,000, Eviction, Small Claims, Probate.*

Note: This court will not give out SSN's. Court also has jurisdiction for bad checks, arrest warrants, preliminary hearings, and county ordinance violations

Wheeler County

Superior Court PO Box 38, Alamo, GA 30411; phone: 912-568-7137; hours 8AM-4PM (EST). *Felony, Misdemeanor, Civil.*

Civil Records: Access: In person only. Visitors must perform in person searches themselves. Court makes copy: $.25 per page; same fee for self serve. Required to search: name, years to search. Civil cases indexed by defendant. Civil records on docket books from 1913.

Criminal Records: Access: In person only. Visitors must perform in person searches themselves. Court makes copy: $.25 per page; same fee for self serve. Required to search: name, years to search. Criminal records on docket books from 1913.

General Information: No public access terminal. No juvenile or adoption records released. Certification fee: $2.50 plus $.50 per add'l page. Payee: Superior Court Clerk. Personal checks accepted. Prepayment required.

Magistrate & Probate Court PO Box 477, 119 W Pearl St, Alamo, GA 30411; phone: 912-568-7133; criminal fax: 912-568-1743; civil/probate fax is the same; 8AM-4PM (EST). *Civil Actions Under $15,000, Eviction, Small Claims, Probate.*

White County

Superior Court 59 S Main St, #B, Cleveland, GA 30528; phone: 706-865-2613; fax: 706-865-2613; hours 8:30AM-5PM (EST). *Felony, Misdemeanor, Civil.*

Civil Records: Access: In person only. Visitors must perform in person searches themselves. Court makes copy: $1.00 per page. Self serve copy fee: $.25 per page. Required to search: name, years to search. Civil cases indexed by defendant, plaintiff. Civil records on computer from 1996, on docket books from 1857. Will accept mail requests only if a case number is provided.

Criminal Records: Access: In person only. Visitors must perform in person searches themselves. Court makes copy: $1.00 per page. Self serve copy fee: $.25 per page. Required to search: name, years to search. Criminal records on computer from 1996, on docket books from 1857. Will accept mail requests only if a case number is provided.

General Information: Public terminal goes back to 1996. No juvenile, adoption, sexual, mental health or expunged records released. Will fax specific case file for $1.00 per page fax fee. Certification fee: $2.50 plus $.50 per page after first. Payee: Superior Court Clerk. Business checks accepted. Prepayment required.

Magistrate Court 59 S Main St, #D, Cleveland, GA 30528; phone: 706-865-6636; criminal phone: 706-865-2613; criminal/civil fax: 706-865-7738; hours 8:30AM-5PM (EST). *Civil Actions Under $15,000, Misdemeanor, Eviction, Small Claims.*

Probate Court 59 S Main St, #H, Cleveland, GA 30528; phone: 706-865-4141; fax: 706-865-1324; hours 8:30AM-5PM (EST). *Probate, Misdemeanor.*

Whitfield County

Superior Court PO Box 868, 300 W Crawford St, Dalton, GA 30722; phone: 706-275-7450; fax: 706-275-7456; hours 8AM-5PM (EST). *Felony, Misdemeanor, Civil.*

Civil Records: Access: In person only. Visitors must perform in person searches themselves. Court makes copy: $.50 per page. Required to search: name, years to search. Civil cases indexed by defendant, plaintiff. Civil records on computer from 1988, on docket books from 1852.

Criminal Records: Access: In person only. Visitors must perform in person searches themselves. Court makes copy: $.50 per page. Required to search: name, years to search, offense, date of offense. Criminal records on computer from 1988, on docket books from 1852.

General Information: Public use terminal available. No juvenile, adoption, sexual, mental health or expunged records released. Certification fee: $3.00 per cert. Payee: Superior Court Clerk. Business checks accepted. Prepayment required.

Magistrate Court PO Box 386, 210 N Thornton Ave, Dalton, GA 30722-0386; phone: 706-278-5052; fax: 706-278-8810; hours 8AM-5PM M-W, F; 9AM-5PM Th (EST). *Civil Actions Under $15,000, Eviction, Small Claims.* www.whitfieldcountyga.com/Magistrate%20Court/magistrate_court.htm

Probate Court 301 Crawford St, Dalton, GA 30720; phone: 706-275-7400; fax: 706-281-1735; hours 8AM-4:45PM (EST). *Probate.*

Wilcox County

Superior & Magistrate Courts 103 N Broad St, Abbeville, GA 31001; phone: 229-467-2442; probate phone: 229-467-2220; fax: 229-467-2886; hours 9AM-5PM (EST). *Felony, Misdemeanor, Civil, Eviction, Small Claims.*
Civil Records: Access: Mail, in person. Both court and visitors may perform in person searches. No search fee. Court makes copy: $1.00 per page. Self serve copy fee: $.25 per page. Required to search: name, years to search. Civil cases indexed by defendant, plaintiff. Civil records on computer since 1995; prior records on docket books from 1950s. Mail turnaround time 1 week.
Criminal Records: Access: Mail, in person. Both court and visitors may perform in person searches. No search fee. Court makes copy: $1.00 per page. Self serve copy fee: $.25 per page. Required to search: name, years to search, DOB; also helpful: SSN. Criminal records on computer since 1995; prior records on docket books from 1950s. Mail turnaround time 1 week.
General Information: Public use terminal available. No juvenile, adoption, sexual, mental health or expunged records released. Certification fee: $2.50 per page. Payee: Superior Court Clerk. Personal checks accepted. Prepayment required.

Probate Court 103 N Broad St, Abbeville, GA 31001; phone: 229-467-2220; fax: 229-467-2000; hours 9AM-5PM (EST). *Probate.*

Wilkes County

Superior Court 23 E Court St, Rm 205, Washington, GA 30673; phone: 706-678-2423; fax: 706-678-2115; hours 9AM-5PM (EST). *Felony, Misdemeanor, Civil.*
Civil Records: Access: In person only. Visitors must perform in person searches themselves. Court makes copy: $.25 per page. Self serve copy fee: $.25 per page. Required to search: name, years to search. Civil cases indexed by defendant, plaintiff. Civil records on docket books from 1700s, computerized from 1998.
Criminal Records: Access: In person only. Visitors must perform in person searches themselves. Court makes copy: $.25 per page. Self serve copy fee: $.25 per page. Required to search: name, years to search. Criminal records on docket books from 1700s, computerized from 1998.
General Information: Public terminal goes back to 1998. No juvenile or adoption records released. Certification fee: $2.50 plus $.50 per page after 1st. Payee: Superior Court Clerk. Personal checks accepted. Prepayment required.

Magistrate Court 23 E Court St, Rm 427, Washington, GA 30673; phone: 706-678-1881; fax: 706-678-1865; hours 8:30AM-5PM (EST). *Civil Actions Under $15,000, Eviction, Small Claims.*

Probate Court 23 E Court St, Rm 422, Washington, GA 30673; phone: 706-678-2523; fax: 706-678-4854; hours 8:30AM-5PM (EST). *Probate.*

Wilkinson County

Superior Court PO Box 250, Irwinton, GA 31042; phone: 478-946-2221; fax: 478-946-1497; 8AM-5PM (EST). *Felony, Misdemeanor, Civil.*
Civil Records: Access: In person only. Visitors must perform in person searches themselves. Court makes copy: $1.00 per page. Self serve copy fee: $.25 per page. Required to search: name, years to search. Civil cases indexed by defendant, plaintiff. Civil records on computer from 1991, on docket books from 1900s.
Criminal Records: Access: In person only. Visitors must perform in person searches themselves. Court makes copy: $1.00 per page. Self serve copy fee: $.25 per page. Required to search: name, years to search, DOB. Criminal records on computer from 1991, on docket books from 1900s.

General Information: Public terminal goes back to 1991. No juvenile, adoption, sexual, mental health or expunged records released. Certification fee: $2.50 per page. Payee: Superior Court Clerk. Personal checks accepted. Prepayment required.

Magistrate & Probate Court PO Box 201, 100 Bacon St, Irwinton, GA 31042; phone: 478-946-2222/2439; fax: 478-946-3810; hours 8AM-5PM (EST). *Civil Actions Under $15,000, Eviction, Small Claims, Probate.* www.wilkinsoncourt.com

Worth County

Superior & State Court 201 N Main St, Rm 13, Sylvester, GA 31791; phone: 229-776-8205; fax: 229-776-8237; hours 8AM-5PM (EST). *Felony, Misdemeanor, Civil, Small Claims.*
Civil Records: Access: In person only. Visitors must perform in person searches themselves. Court makes copy: $1.00 per page. Self serve copy fee: $.25 per page. Required to search: name, years to search. Civil cases indexed by defendant, plaintiff. Civil records computerized since 1995, on books since 1880, real estate records from 9/93.
Criminal Records: Access: In person only. Visitors must perform in person searches themselves. Court makes copy: $1.00 per page. Self serve copy fee: $.25 per page. Required to search: name, years to search; SSN helpful. Criminal records computerized since 1995.
General Information: Public terminal goes back to 1995. No juvenile, adoption, sexual, mental health or expunged records released. Will not fax specific case file. Certification fee: $2.00 per document. Payee: Superior Court Clerk. Personal checks accepted. Prepayment required.

Magistrate Court PO Box 64, 201 N Main St, Rm 21, Sylvester, GA 31791; phone: 229-776-8210; fax: 229-776-8245; hours 9AM-5PM (EST). *Civil Actions Under $15,000, Eviction, Small Claims.*
Note: All records are maintained at the Superior Court, not here.

Probate Court 201 N Main St, Rm 12, Sylvester, GA 31791; phone: 229-776-8207; fax: 229-776-1540; hours 8AM-5PM (EST). *Probate.* https://www.gaprobate.org/counties/worth/index.html

Georgia Recording Offices

ORGANIZATION: 159 counties, 159 recording offices. The recording officer is Clerk of Superior Court. All transactions are recorded in a "General Execution Docket." The entire state is in the Eastern Time Zone (EST).

REAL ESTATE RECORDS: Most counties will not perform real estate searches. Copy fees are the same as for UCC. Certification fees are usually $2.00-$2.50 per document - $1.00 for seal and $1.00 for stamp - plus $.50 per page.

UCC RECORDS: There is no central state agency office for UCC. Financing statements are filed only with the Clerk of Superior Court and one can file in any county. Their system, as of January 1, 1995, merges all new UCC filings into a central statewide database, and allows statewide searching for new filings only from any county office. However, filings prior to that date will remain at the county offices. Only a few counties will perform local UCC searches. Use search request form UCC-11 for local searches. Search fees vary from $2.50 to $25.00 per debtor name. UCC copies usually cost $.25 per page if you make it and $1.00 per page if the county makes it.

TAX LIEN RECORDS: All tax liens on personal property are filed with the county Clerk of Superior Court in a "General Execution Docket" (grantor/grantee) or "Lien Index." Most counties will not perform tax lien searches. Copy fees are the same as for UCC.

OTHER LIENS: Judgments, hospital, materialman, county tax, lis pendens, child support, labor, mechanics.

ONLINE ACCESS: The Georgia Superior Court Clerk's Cooperative Authority (GSCCCA) at www.gsccca.org/search offers free access to three state indices. The Real Estate Index contains property transactions from all counties since 01/01/99. The Lien Index includes liens filed on real and personal property. Throughput varies, but is generally from 01/10/2002. The UCC Index contains financing statement data from all counties since 1/1995, and can be searched by name, taxpayer ID, file date and file number. Additionally, the actual image of the corresponding UCC statement can be downloaded for a fee. Visit website for details.

Appling County

County Superior Court Clerk, PO Box 269, Baxley, GA 31513. 912-367-8126; fax-912-367-8180; hours: 8AM-5PM
All records in one index. Records indexed on a public use terminal back to 1996. Only the public may search. Copy fee $.25; real estate $.50 per page. Cert fee-$2.50 per cert plus copy fee. Payee-Appling County Clerk of the Superior Court. **Online access to RE Deed, Lien, UCC records:** See www.gsccca.org for Deed, Lien and UCC indexes. **Other phones:** Treasurer- 912-367-8100. **Property tax/Assessor-** same address. 912-367-8109.

Atkinson County

County Superior Court Clerk, PO Box 6, Pearson, GA 31642. 912-422-3343; fax-912-422-7025; hours: 8AM-N, 1-5PM
Only the public may search. Copy fee $.25 per page. Cert fee- $2.50 per cert plus copy fee. Payee-Atkinson County Clerk of the Superior Court. **Online access to RE Deed, UCC records:** See www.gsccca.org for Deed and UCC indexes. **Property tax/Assessor-** 912-422-7382.

Bacon County

County Superior Court Clerk, PO Box 376, Alma, GA 31510. RE & UCC recording phone-912-632-4915; fax-912-632-6545; hours: 9AM-5PM
Separate indices to search include real estate and liens. Only the public may search. Copy fee $1.00 per page. RE or tax lien copy- $.25 per page. Cert fee- $2.00 per doc, $.50 per page. Payee- Bacon County Clerk of the Superior Court. **Online access to RE Deed, Lien, UCC records:** See www.gsccca.org for Deed, Lien and UCC indexes. **Other phones:** Treasurer- 912-632-5214; Elections- 912-632-7661; Vital Records- 912-632-7661. **Property tax/Assessor-** 912-632-5215.

Baker County

County Superior Court Clerk, PO Box 10, Newton, GA 39870. 229-734-3004; fax-229-734-7770; hours: 9AM-5PM
Only the public may search. Copy fee $1.00 per page. Cert fee- $2.00 per cert plus copy fee. Payee-Baker County Clerk of the Superior Court. **Online access to RE Deed, Lien, UCC records:** See www.gsccca.org for Deed, Lien and UCC indexes. **Property tax/Assessor-** 229-734-3012.

Baldwin County

County Superior Court Clerk, PO Drawer 987, Milledgeville, GA 31059. 478-445-4007, R/E recording phone-478-445-4008, UCC recording phone-478-445-5754; fax-478-445-6039; hours: 8:30AM-5PM
www.baldwincountyga.com
Separate indices to search include deeds to1998, liens to 2004 on computer. Only the public may search. Copy fee $1.00 per page. RE record copy- $.25 per page. Cert fee- $2.50 per cert plus copy fee. Payee- Baldwin County Clerk of the Superior Court. **Online access to RE Deed, Lien, UCC records:** See www.gsccca.org for Deed, Lien and UCC indexes. **Other phones:** Treasurer- 478-434-4791; Appraiser/Auditor- 478-445-5300; Elections- 478-445-4526; Vital Records- 478-445-4807; Sheriff- 478-445-4893. **Property tax/Assessor-** 121 N. Wilkinson St. #114, Milledgeville, GA 31061; 478-453-5300.

Banks County

County Superior Court Clerk, 144 Yonah Homer Rd #8, Homer, GA 30547-2614. 706-677-6243, R/E recording phone-706-677-6240, UCC recording phone-706-677-6240; fax-706-677-6294; hours: 8AM-5PM
Only the public may search. Copy fee $1.00 per page. Cert fee- $3.75 per doc, $.50 per page. Payee- Banks County Clerk of the Superior Court. **Online to RE Deed, UCC, Lien recordss:** See www.gsccca.org for Deed, Lien, UCC indexes. **Other phones:** Treasurer- 706-677-6200; Elections- 706-677-6250. **Property tax/Assessor-** 706-677-2320.

Barrow County

County Superior Court Clerk, PO Box 1280, Winder, GA 30680. 770-307-3035; fax-770-867-4800; hours: 8AM-5PM
Separate indices to search include grantor/grantee, liens. Only the public may search. Copy fee $1.00 per page. Cert fee- $2.50 per doc, $.50 per page. Payee- Barrow County Clerk of the Superior Court. **Online access to RE Deed, Lien, UCC records:** See www.gsccca.org for Deed, Lien and UCC indexes. **Other phones:** Treasurer- 770-307-3106; Vital Records- 770-307-3035. **Property tax/Assessor-** 233 E Broad St, Winder, GA 30680; 770-307-3108.

Bartow County

County Superior Court Clerk, 135 W. Cherokee Ave.; #233, Cartersville, GA 30120. 770-387-5025; fax-770-387-5611 or 606-2389; hours: 8AM-5PM
Separate indices to search include liens, deeds, civil and criminal, plats; indexed by year and division. Records indexed on a public use terminal back to 1992. Only the public may search. Copy fee $.25 per page. Cert fee- $2.50 1st pg., $.25 each add'l pg includes copy fee. Payee- Bartow County Clerk of the Superior Court. **Online access to RE Deed, UCC, Lien records:** See www.gsccca.org for Deed, Lien and UCC indexes. **Property tax/Assessor-** 770-387-5090.

Ben Hill County

County Superior Court Clerk, PO Box 1104, Fitzgerald, GA 31750-1104. RE & UCC recording phone-229-426-5135; fax-229-426-5487; 8:30AM-4:30PM
Only the public may search. Copy fee $1.00 per page. Cert fee- $2.00 per doc plus copy fee. Payee-Ben Hill County Clerk of the Superior Court. **Online access to RE Deed, UCC, Lien records:** See www.gsccca.org for Deed, Lien and UCC indexes. **Other phones:** Elections- 229-426-5151. **Property tax/Assessor-** 229-426-5147.

Berrien County

County Superior Court Clerk, 101 E. Marion Ave. #3, Nashville, GA 31639. RE & UCC recording phone-229-686-5506; fax-229-543-1032; hours: 8AM-5PM
Record index not computerized. Only the public may search. Copy fee $1.00 per page. Cert fee- $2.50 per doc, $.50 per page includes copy fee. Payee- Berrien County Clerk of the Superior Court. **Online access to RE Deed, Lien, UCC:** See www.gsccca.org for Deed, Lien and UCC indexes. **Other phones:** Treasurer- 229-686-7461 (Tax Commissioner); Elections- 229-686-5213; Vital Records- 229-686-5213. **Property tax/Assessor-** PO Box 446, Nashville, GA 31639; 229-686-2149.

Bibb County

County Superior Court Clerk, PO Box 1015, Macon, GA 31202-1015. 478-621-6527; fax-478-621-6033; hours: 8:30AM-5PM
A convenient county online searching index page is at www.co.bibb.ga.us. All records in one index. Records indexed on a public use terminal back to 1996. Only the public may search. Real estate

record search fee- $10.00 per name. Copy fee $.25 per page. Cert fee- $2.50 per doc, $.50 per page. Payee- Bibb County Clerk of the Superior Court. **Online access to RE Deed, UCC, Property, Lien, Finance Statement, Property Tax, Ownership:** See www.gsccca.org for Deed and UCC indexes. Also, search land, financing statements and liens on the Superior Court clerk search page for free at http://68.109.200.12/resolution. Also, search the assessors' property tax records for free at www.qpublic.net/bibb/digest_search1.html. Also, search for property ownership for free at www.co.bibb.ga.us/engineering/property/search.htm. Also, search property info at www.co.bibb.ga.us/gisonline/advancedsearch.asp and Ad Valorem tax statements at www.co.bibb.ga.us/TaxBills/Searchpage.asp, **Other phones:** Treasurer- 478-621-6310. **Property tax/Assessor**- 478-742-2254.

Bleckley County

County Superior Court Clerk, 306 SE 2nd St, Cochran, GA 31014. 478-934-3210; fax-478-934-6671; hours: 8:30AM-5PM
Only the public may search. Copy fee $.25 per page. Cert fee- $2.50 1st pg., $.50 for every add'l pg. Payee- Bleckley County Clerk of the Superior Court. **Online access to RE Deed, Lien, UCC records:** See www.gsccca.org for Deed, Lien and UCC indexes. **Other phones:** Treasurer- 478-934-3200. **Property tax/Assessor**- 478-934-3209.

Brantley County

County Superior Court Clerk, PO Box 1067, Nahunta, GA 31553. 912-462-5635, R/E recording phone-912-462-7682; UCC recording phone-912-462-7682; fax-912-462-6427; hours: 8AM-5PM
Records indexed on computer. Only the public may search. Copy fee $1.00 per page. Cert fee- $2.00 per doc, $.50 per page. Payee- Brantley County Clerk of the Superior Court. **Online access to RE Deed, Lien, UCC records:** See www.gsccca.org for Deed, Lien and UCC indexes. **Other phones:** Treasurer- 912-462-5256; Elections- 912-462-6159; Vital Records- 912-462-5192. **Property tax/Assessor**- 912-462-5251.

Brooks County

County Superior Court Clerk, PO Box 630, Quitman, GA 31643. RE & UCC recording phone-229-263-4747; fax-229-263-5050; hours: 8AM-5PM
Separate indices to search include grantor/grantee real estate, tax liens, GED, hospital liens, federal tax liens. Records indexed on a public use terminal back to 1988. Only the public may search. Copy fee $1.00 per page. Cert fee- $2.50 per doc, $.50 per add'l page. Payee- Brooks County Clerk of the Superior Court. **Online access to RE Deed, Lien, UCC records:** See www.gsccca.org for Deed, Lien and UCC indexes. **Other phones:** Elections- 229-2635567; Vital Records- 229-263-7585. **Property tax/Assessor**- 229-263-7920.

Bryan County

County Superior Court Clerk, PO Box 670, Pembroke, GA 31321. 912-653-3872, R/E recording phone-912-653-3872 option #4, UCC recording phone-912-653-3872 option #4; fax-912-653-3805; hours: 8AM-5PM
County does NOT do any searches; see the online service. Only the public may search. Copy fee $1.00 per page. Cert fee- $2.50 per cert plus copy fee. Payee- Bryan County Clerk of the Superior Court. **Online access to RE Deed, UCC, Lien, Notary, Plat records:** See www.gsccca.org for Deed, Lien and UCC indexes. **Other phones:** Treasurer- 912-653-3839; Appraiser/Auditor- 912-653-3889; Elections- 912-653-3859; Vital Records- 912-653-3856. **Property tax/Assessor**- 912-653-3889.

Bulloch County

County Superior Court Clerk, 20 Siebald St; Judicial Annex, Statesboro, GA 30458. 912-764-9009; fax-912-764-5953; hours: 8AM-5PM www.bullochtaxassessors.org
All records in one index. Records indexed on a public use terminal back to 1991. Only the public may search. Copy fee $1.00 per page. Cert fee- $2.50 per cert plus copy fee. Payee- Bulloch County Clerk of the Superior Court. **Online access to RE Deed, Lien, UCC records:** See www.gsccca.org for Deed, Lien and UCC indexes. **Other phones:** Treasurer- 912-764-6285. **Property tax/Assessor**- 115 N Main St, Statesboro, GA 30458; 912-764-2181.

Burke County

County Superior Court Clerk, PO Box 803, Waynesboro, GA 30830-0803. RE & UCC recording phone-706-554-2279; fax-706-554-7887; hours: 9AM-5PM
Records indexed on a public use terminal back to 1996. Only the public may search. Copy fee $1.00 per page. RE or tax lien copy- $.25 per page. Cert fee- $2.00 per doc, $.50 per page plus copy fee. Payee- Burke County Clerk of the Superior Court. **Online access to RE Deed, UCC, Lien, Plat records:** See www.gsccca.org for Deed, Lien and UCC indexes. **Other phones:** Treasurer- 706-554-2324; Appraiser/Auditor- 706-554-2607; Elections- 706-554-7457; Vital Records- 706-554-3000. **Property tax/Assessor**- PO Box 46, Waynesboro, Ga 30830; 706-554-2607.

Butts County

County Superior Court Clerk, PO Box 320, Jackson, GA 30233. 770-775-8215; fax-770-504-1359; hours: 8AM-5PM
Only the public may search. Copy fee $1.00 per page. Cert fee- $2.50 per cert plus copy fee. Payee- Butts County Clerk of the Superior Court. **Online access to RE Deed, UCC, Lien records:** See www.gsccca.org for Deed, Lien and UCC indexes. **Other phones:** Treasurer- 770-775-8200. **Property tax/Assessor**- 770-775-8207.

Calhoun County

County Superior Court Clerk, PO Box 69, Morgan, GA 39866. 229-849-2715; fax-229-849-0072; hours: 8AM-5PM
All records in one index. Office personnel or visitors may perform searches. Search fee $1.00 per name. Will search real estate records. Will search UCC records. Will do tax lien search, but they do not maintain hard-copy records. Copy fee $1.00 per page. RE record copy- $.25 per page. Cert fee- $3.00 per doc plus copy fee. Payee- Calhoun County Clerk of the Superior Court. **Online access to RE Deed, UCC records:** See www.gsccca.org for Deed, and UCC indexes. **Other phones:** Treasurer- 229-849-2970; Elections- 229-849-2972; Vital Records- 229-849-2115. **Property tax/Assessor**- 229-849-4685.

Camden County

County Superior Court Clerk, PO Box 550, Woodbine, GA 31569-0550. 912-576-5651, UCC recording phone-915-576-5651; fax-912-576-5648; hours: 9AM-5PM
Only the public may search. Copy fee $.25 per page. Cert fee- $2.00 1st pg, $.50 each add'l. Payee- Camden County Clerk of the Superior Court. **Online access to RE Deed, Lien, UCC records:** See www.gsccca.org for Deed, Lien and UCC indexes. **Other phones:** Treasurer- 912-576-5601. **Property tax/Assessor**- 912-576-3241.

Candler County

County Superior Court Clerk, PO Drawer 830, Metter, GA 30439. 912-685-5257; fax-912-685-2946; hours: 8:30AM-5PM
All records in one index. Records indexed on a public use terminal back to 1997. Only the public may search. Copy fee $.25; tax lien or real estate $1.00 per page. Cert fee- $2.00 per doc, $.50 per page. Payee- Candler County Clerk of the Superior Court. **Online access to RE Deed, Lien, UCC records:** See www.gsccca.org for Deed, Lien and UCC indexes. **Other phones:** Treasurer- 912-685-5257; Elections- 912-685-6687; Vital Records- 912-685-2357. **Property tax/Assessor**- same address as above. 912-685-6346.

Carroll County

County Superior Court Clerk, PO Box 1620, Carrollton, GA 30112. RE & UCC recording phone-770-830-5830; fax-770-214-3584; hours: 8AM-5PM
Separate indices to search. Records indexed on a public use terminal back to 1976 for deeds, 1994 for liens/plats. Only the public may search. Copy fee $1.00 per page. Cert fee- $2.50 per cert plus copy fee. Payee- Carroll County Clerk of the Superior Court. **Online access to RE Deed, UCC, Notary, Public, Lien, Plats records:** See www.gsccca.org for Deed, Lien and UCC indexes. **Other phones:** Treasurer- 770-830-5801; Appraiser/Auditor- 770-830-5812; Elections- 770-830-5823; Vital Records- 770-836-6667. **Property tax/Assessor**- 423 College St, Carrollton, GA 30117; 770-830-5812.

Catoosa County

County Superior Court Clerk, 875 Lafayette St; Courthouse, Ringgold, GA 30736. 706-935-4231; fax-none; hours: 8:30AM-5PM
Only the public may search. Copy fee $1.00 per page. Cert fee- $2.50 per doc, $.50 per page. Payee- Catoosa County Clerk of the Superior Court. **Online access to RE Deed, Lien, UCC records:** See www.gsccca.org for Deed, Lien and UCC indexes. **Other phones:** Treasurer- 706-935-2500. **Property tax/Assessor**- 706-965-3772.

Charlton County

County Superior Court Clerk, PO Box 760, Folkston, GA 31537. 912-496-2354; fax-912-496-3882; hours: 8AM-5PM
Only the public may search. Copy fee $1.00 per page. Cert fee- $.50 per doc, plus $.50 per page. Payee- Charlton County Clerk of the Superior Court. **Online access to RE Deed, Lien, UCC records:** See www.gsccca.org for Deed, Lien and UCC indexes. **Property tax/Assessor**- 912-496-7437.

Chatham County

County Superior Court Clerk, PO Box 10227, Savannah, GA 31412. Main phone & R/E recording-912-652-7214, UCC recording 912-652-7219; fax-912-652-7380; 8AM-5PM www.chathamcourts.org
Separate indices to search include Civil, Criminal, Real Estate, Liens. Records indexed on computer. Only the public may search. Copy fee $.25 per page. Cert fee- $2.00 per doc + $.50 per page. Payee- Chatham County Clerk of the Superior Court. **Online access to RE Deed, Lien, UCC, Assessor records:** See www.gsccca.org for Deed, Lien and UCC indexes. Search the assessor database at www.chathamcounty.org/prc.html. **Other phones:** Elections- 912-652-7494; Vital Records- 912-356-2108. **Property tax/Assessor**- 912-652-7127.

Chattahoochee County

County Superior Court Clerk, PO Box 120, Cusseta, GA 31805-0120. RE & UCC recording phone-706-989-3424; fax-706-989-0396; hours: 8AM-5PM
Records indexed on computer back to 1993. Only the public may search. Copy fee $1.00 per page. Tax lien copy- $.25. Cert fee- $2.50 per cert plus copy fee. Payee- Chattahoochee County Clerk of the Superior Court. **Online access to RE Deed, Lien, UCC records:** See www.gsccca.org for Deed, Lien and UCC indexes. **Other phones:** Elections- 706-989-3602; Vital Records- 706-989-3603. **Property tax/Assessor**- 706-989-3249.

Chattooga County

County Superior Court Clerk, PO Box 159, Summerville, GA 30747. 706-857-0706; fax-706-857-0686; hours: 8:30AM-5PM

Only the public may search. Copy fee $.25 per page. Cert fee- $2.00 per doc, $.50 per page. Payee- Chattooga County Clerk of the Superior Court. **Online access to RE Deed, Lien, UCC records:** See www.gsccca.org for Deed, Lien and UCC indexes. **Other phones:** Treasurer- 706-857-0703. **Property tax/Assessor-** 706-857-3819.

Cherokee County

County Superior Court Clerk, 90 North St; #G-170, Canton, GA 30114. Main phone & R/E recording-678-493-6531, UCC recording phone-678-493-6527; hours: 8AM-5PM www.cherokeega.com
Only the public may search. Copy fee $1.00 per page. Cert fee- $2.00 per doc, $.50 per page. Payee- Cherokee County Clerk of the Superior Court. **Online access to Grantor/Grantee, Lien, RE Deed, UCC, Sex Offender, Inmate records:** See www.gsccca.org for Deed and UCC indexes. Also, access recording records free at http://deeds.cherokeega.com/Search.aspx. Also, search the sheriff's sex offender list at www.cherokeega-sheriff.org/offender/offender.htm. Also, search inmate info on private company website at www.vinelink.com/index.jsp. **Other phones:** Elections- 770-479-0407; Vital Records- 678-493-6160; Tax Assessor- 678-493-6120. **Property tax/Assessor-** 100 North St, #G-20, Canton, GA 30114; not known.

Clarke County

County Superior Court Clerk, PO Box 1805, Athens, GA 30603. 706-613-3196, R/E recording phone-706-613-3190; fax-706-613-3189; hours: 8AM-5PM
Separate indices to search include deeds, liens, plats, civil and criminal. Only the public may search. Copy fee $1.00 per page, $.25 self serve. Cert fee- $2.50 1st page plus $.50 each add'l page includes copy fee. Payee- Clerk of Superior Court. **Online access to RE Deed, UCC, Property records:** See www.gsccca.org for Deed and UCC indexes. Also, view property information for free at https://athens-clarke.ga.ezgov.com/ezproperty/review_search.jsp; however, no name searching. **Other phones:** Treasurer- 706-613-3040. **Property tax/Assessor-** 706-613-3140.

Clay County

County Superior Court Clerk, PO Box 550, Fort Gaines, GA 39851-0550. 229-768-2631; fax-229-768-3047; hours: 8AM-4:30PM
All records in one index. Only the public may search. Copy fee $1.00 per page. Cert fee- $3.00 1st pg, $.50 each add'l. Payee- Clay County Clerk of the Superior Court. **Online access to RE Deed, UCC, Lien records:** See www.gsccca.org for Deed, Lien and UCC indexes. **Other phones:** Treasurer- 229-768-3238; Elections- 229-768-2445; Vital Records- 229-768-2445; Tax Commissioner- 229-768-2915. **Property tax/Assessor-** PO Box 218, Fort Gaines, GA 39851; 229-768-2000.

Clayton County

County Superior Court Clerk, 9151 Tara Blvd; Rm 202, Jonesboro, GA 30236. 770-477-3395; fax-770-477-3490; hours: 8AM-5PM www.co.clayton.ga.us/superior_court/clerk_of_courts/
Separate indices to search include Ged, Real Estate, and hospital. Only the public may search. Copy fee $1.00 per page. RE or tax lien copy- $.25 per page. Cert fee- $2.00 per doc, $.50 per page. Payee- Clayton County Clerk of the Superior Court. **Online to Real Estate, UCC, Lien, Property Tax records:** See www.gsccca.org for Deed, Lien and UCC indexes. Also, assessor records for free at www.qpublic.net/clayton/search.html. **Other phones:** ; Tax Commissioner- 770-477-3311; Probate Court -770-477-3301. **Property tax/Assessor-** 770-447-3285.

Clinch County

County Superior Court Clerk, PO Box 433, Homerville, GA 31634. 912-487-5854, R/E recording phone-912-481-5854; fax-912-487-3083; hours: 8AM-5PM

Only the public may search. Copy fee $.25 per page. Cert fee- $3.00 per doc plus copy fee. Payee- Clinch County Clerk of the Superior Court. **Online access to RE Deed, Lien, UCC records:** See www.gsccca.org for Deed, Lien and UCC indexes. **Property tax/Assessor-** 912-487-2561.

Cobb County

County Superior Court Clerk, PO Box 3490, Marietta, GA 30061. 770-528-1363; fax-770-528-1325; hours: 8AM-5PM www.cobbgasupctclk.com
Only the public may search. Copy fee $1.00 per page. Cert fee- $2.00 1st pg, $.50 each add'l. Payee- Cobb County Clerk of the Superior Court. **Online access to Real Estate, Grantor/Grantee, UCC, Deed, Property Tax records:** Property records on the County Superior Court Clerk website are free at www.cobbgasupctclk.com/index.htm. Search by name, address, land description, instrument type, or book & page. You may also search court records. Also, see www.gsccca.org for online access to Deed and UCC indexes. Also, search property tax records for free at www.cobbtax.org. Click on "Property Taxes". No name searching. **Other phones:** Treasurer- 770-528-8600. **Property tax/Assessor-** 770-528-3100.

Coffee County

County Superior Court Clerk, 101 S. Peterson Ave.; Courthouse, Douglas, GA 31533. 912-384-2865, R/E recording phone-912-384-2865 x239, UCC recording phone-912-384-2865 x239; hours: 8:30AM-5PM
Only the public may search. Copy fee $1.00 per page. Cert fee- $3.00 per cert plus copy fee. Payee- Coffee County Clerk of the Superior Court. **Online access to RE Deed, Lien, UCC records:** See www.gsccca.org for Deed, Lien and UCC indexes. **Other phones:** Treasurer- 912-384-4799; Appraiser/Auditor- 912-384-2136; Elections- 912-384-5213 or 384-7018; Vital Records- 912-389-4458. **Property tax/Assessor-** 912-384-2136.

Colquitt County

County Superior Court Clerk, PO Box 2827, Moultrie, GA 31776-2827. 229-616-7420, R/E recording phone-229-616-7063; fax-229-616-7029; hours: 8AM-5PM
Only the public may search. Copy fee $1.00 per page. Cert fee- $2.00 per doc, $.50 per page. Payee- Colquitt County Clerk of the Superior Court. **Online access to RE Deed, UCC, Lien, Notary, Public records:** See www.gsccca.org for Deed, Lien and UCC indexes. **Property tax/Assessor-** 229-616-7425.

Columbia County

County Superior Court Clerk, PO Box 2930, Evans, GA 30809. 706-312-7139; hours: 8AM-5PM
Only the public may search. Copy fee $1.00 per page. Cert fee- $2.00 per doc, $.50 per page. Payee- Columbia County Clerk of the Superior Court. **Online access to RE Deed, UCC, Lien, records:** See www.gsccca.org for Deed, Lien and UCC indexes. **Property tax/Assessor-** 706-541-0920.

Cook County

County Superior Court Clerk, 212 N. Hutchinson Ave, Adel, GA 31620-2497. RE & UCC recording phone-229-896-7717; hours: 8:30AM-4:30PM
This agency only records real estate transactions, not UCC. Separate indices to search. Records indexed on a public use terminal. Only the public may search. Copy fee $1.00 per page. Cert fee- $2.00 per doc, $.50 per page includes copy fee. Payee- Cook County Clerk of the Superior Court. **Online access to RE Deed, Lien, UCC records:** See www.gsccca.org for Deed, Lien and UCC indexes. **Other phones:** Elections- 229-896-3941. **Property tax/Assessor-** 229-896-3665.

Coweta County

County Superior Court Clerk, 200 Court Sq; Courthouse, First Fl, Newnan, GA 30263. Main phone & R/E recording-770-254-2690, UCC recording phone-770-254-2696; fax-770-254-3700; hours: 8AM-5PM

Only the public may search. Copy fee $1.00 per page. Cert fee- $2.50 1st page, $.50 each add'l. Payee- Coweta County Clerk of the Superior Court. **Online access to RE Deed, UCC, Lien records:** See www.gsccca.org for Deed, Lien and UCC indexes. **Property tax/Assessor-** 770-254-2680.

Crawford County

County Superior Court Clerk, PO Box 1037, Roberta, GA 31078-1037. RE & UCC recording phone-478-836-3328; hours: 9AM-5PM
Separate indices to search include grantor, grantee, liens. Will not search real estate records. Will not search UCC records or tax liens. Copy fee $1.00 per page; $.25 self serve. Cert fee- $2.50 per doc plus $.50 per page. Payee- Crawford County Clerk of the Superior Court. **Online access to RE Deed, Lien, UCC records:** See www.gsccca.org for Deed, Lien and UCC indexes. **Other phones:** Treasurer- 478-836-3575; Appraiser/Auditor- 478-836-2800; Elections- 478-836-1877; Vital Records- 478-836-3313. **Property tax/Assessor-** PO Box 1054, Roberta, GA 31078; 478-836-2800.

Crisp County

County Superior Court Clerk, PO Box 747, Cordele, GA 31010-0747. RE & UCC recording phone-229-276-2616; fax-229-273-5730; hours: 8:30AM-5PM
Only the public may search. Copy fee $1.00 per page. Cert fee- $2.50 1st pg, $.50 each add'l. Payee- Crisp County Clerk of the Superior Court. **Online access to RE Deed, Lien, UCC records:** See www.gsccca.org for Deed, Lien and UCC indexes. **Other phones:** Treasurer- 229-276-2672; Appraiser/Auditor- 229-276-2635; Elections- 229-276-2611; Tax Commissioner- 229-276-2630. **Property tax/Assessor-** 229-276-2635.

Dade County

County Superior Court Clerk, PO Box 417, Trenton, GA 30752. RE & UCC recording phone-706-657-4778; fax-706-657-8284; hours: 8:30AM-5PM
Separate indices to search include deeds, liens, courts. Records indexed on a public use terminal back to 1999. Only the public may search. Copy fee $1.00 per page. Cert fee- $2.00 per doc, $.50 per page, plus copy fee. Payee- Dade County Clerk of Superior Court. **Online access to RE Deed, Lien, UCC records:** See www.gsccca.org for Deed, Lien and UCC indexes. **Other phones:** Treasurer- 706-657-4625; Appraiser/Auditor- 706-657-6341; Elections- 706-657-4414; Vital Records- 706-657-4414; Tax Commission- 706-657-7563; Small Claims -706-657-4113. **Property tax/Assessor-** 706-657-6341.

Dawson County

County Superior Court Clerk, 25 Tucker Ave, #106, Dawsonville, GA 30534-0222. 706-344-3510, R/E recording phone-706-344-3510 x229, UCC recording phone-706-344-3510 x227; fax-706-344-3511; hours: 8AM-5PM
Index: There are separate indices to search. Records indexed on a public terminal. Only the public may search. Copy fee $1.00 per page. Cert fee- $2.50 per doc, $.25 per page, plus copy fee. Payee- Dawson County Clerk of the Superior Court. **Online access to RE Deed, UCC, Lien records:** See www.gsccca.org for Deed, Lien and UCC indexes. Search the assessor property information for free at www.dawsontaxassessors.org/page2.html.

De Kalb County

County Superior Court Clerk, 556 N. McDonough St; Courthouse, Rm 208, Decatur, GA 30030. 404-371-2836, R/E recording phone-404-371-2836 x3741, UCC recording phone-404-371-2836 x3735; hours: 7:30AM-6PM
Records indexed on a public use terminal back to 1996. Office will perform a UCC search but public must search other records themselves. Office will not make your copies. Cert fee- $2.50 per doc, $.50 per page. Payee- De Kalb County Clerk of the Superior Court. **Online access to RE Deed, UCC,**

Property Tax, records: See www.gsccca.org for Deed and UCC indexes. Also, search tax commissioner property tax data for free at https://dklbweb.dekalbga.org/taxcommissioner/Property TaxMain2.htm. No name searching. Also, search the registered sex offender list at www.dekalbsheriff.org/regnames3.html. **Property tax/Assessor-** 404-371-4938.

Decatur County

County Superior Court Clerk, PO Box 336, Bainbridge, GA 39818. RE & UCC recording phone-229-248-3025; fax-229-248-3029; hours: 8AM-5PM
Separate indices to search include liens, UCC's, real estate. Records indexed on a public use terminal back to 1995 (UCC). Only the public may search. Copy fee $.25 per page. Cert fee- $2.00 per doc, $.50 per page includes copy fee. Payee- Decatur County Clerk of the Superior Court. **Online access to RE Deed, Lien, UCC records:** See www.gsccca.org for Deed, Lien and UCC indexes. **Other phones:** Treasurer- 229-248-3030; Appraiser/Auditor- 229-248-3008; Elections- 229-248-3021; Vital Records- 229-248-3055. **Property tax/Assessor-** PO Box 1106, Bainbridge, GA 39818; 229-248-3008.

Dodge County

County Superior Court Clerk, PO Box 4276, Eastman, GA 31023-4276. 478-374-2871; fax-478-374-3035; hours: 9AM-N,1-5PM
Only the public may search. Copy fee $1.00 per page. Real estate copy- $.25 per page. Cert fee- $2.50 per doc, plus $.50 per page. Payee- Dodge County Clerk of the Superior Court. **Online access to RE Deed, Lien, UCC records:** See www.gsccca.org for Deed, Lien and UCC indexes. **Other phones:** Treasurer- 478-374-3775; Elections- 478-378-8123; Vital Records- 478-374-3775. **Property tax/Assessor-** 478-374-8122.

Dooly County

County Superior Court Clerk, PO Box 326, Vienna, GA 31092-0326. RE & UCC recording phone-229-268-4234; fax-229-268-6142; hours: 8:30AM-5PM
Only the public may search. Copy fee $1.00 per page. Cert fee- $2.50 per doc, $1.00 per page. Payee- Dooly County Clerk of the Superior Court. **Online access to RE Deed, Lien, UCC records:** See www.gsccca.org for Deed, Lien and UCC indexes. **Other phones:** Treasurer- 229-268-4228. **Property tax/Assessor-** 229-268-4719.

Dougherty County

County Superior Court Clerk, PO Box 1827, Albany, GA 31701. RE & UCC recording phone-229-431-2198; fax-229-431-2850; hours: 8:30AM-5PM www.albany.ga.us
Only the public may search. Copy fee $1.00 per page. Cert fee- $2.00 per doc, $1.00 per page. Payee- Dougherty County Clerk of the Superior Court. **Online access to Real Estate, Personal Property, Tax, Court, Deed, Mortgage, Tax Assessor, Personal Property, UCC, Death, Divorce, Trade Name records:** Access to the clerk of courts Dept. of Deeds public menu is at www.albany.ga.us/doco/clerk_court_rec.htm. Click on "clerk of courts records." The tax records are at www.albany.ga.us/doco/Tax%20&%20Tag/tax_tag.ht m has personal property, deeds, assessments. Click on "County/City Tax Record System." Call 229-431-2130 during business hours for help navigating this system. Also, see www.gsccca.org for online access to Deed and UCC indexes. **Other phones:** Treasurer- 229-431-2130; Elections- 229-431-3247. **Property tax/Assessor-** 229-431-2130.

Douglas County

County Superior Court Clerk, 8700 Hospital Dr.; Douglas County Courthouse, Douglasville, GA 30134. 770-920-7252, R/E recording phone-770-920-7257, UCC recording phone-770-920-7449; fax-770-920-7561; hours: 8AM-5PM

Separate indices to search include real estate, liens, plats, UCC's. Records indexed on a public use terminal. Only the public may search. Copy fee $1.00 per page. RE or tax lien copy- $.50 per page. Cert fee- $2.50 1st 2 pages, $.50 each add'l. Payee- Douglas County Clerk of the Superior Court. **Online access to RE Deed, Lien, UCC records:** See www.gsccca.org for Deed, Lien and UCC indexes. **Other phones:** Appraiser/Auditor- 770-920-7228; Elections- 770-920-7236; Vital Records- 770-920-7249. **Property tax/Assessor-** same address as above. 770-920-7228.

Early County

County Superior Court Clerk, PO Box 849, Blakely, GA 39823. RE & UCC recording phone-229-723-3033; fax-229-723-4411; hours: 8AM-5PM
Only the public may search. Copy fee $1.00 per page. Cert fee- $2.50 per doc, $.50 per page. Payee- Early County Clerk of the Superior Court. **Online access to RE Deed, Lien, UCC records:** See www.gsccca.org for Deed, Lien and UCC indexes. **Other phones:** Treasurer- 229-723-4024. **Property tax/Assessor-** 229-723-3088.

Echols County

County Superior Court Clerk, PO Box 213, Statenville, GA 31648. RE & UCC recording phone-229-559-5642; fax-229-559-5792; hours: 8AM-N, 1-4:30PM
Separate indices to search include Platt, Lien, Deeds. Records indexed on a public use terminal back to 5/24/1993. Only the public may search. Copy fee $1.00 per page. Cert fee- $2.50 1st page, $.50 each add'l page. Payee- Echols County Clerk of the Superior Court. **Online access to RE Deed, Lien, UCC records:** See www.gsccca.org for Deed, Lien and UCC indexes. **Other phones:** Treasurer- 229-559-5253; Elections- 229-559-7526. **Property tax/Assessor-** PO Box 326, Statenville, GA 31648; 229-559-7370.

Effingham County

County Superior Court Clerk, PO Box 387, Springfield, GA 31329-0387. 912-754-2118, R/E recording phone-912-754-2145; hours: 8:30AM-5PM
All records in one index. Will not search real estate records. Will not search UCC records or tax liens. Copy fee $.25 per page. Cert fee- $2.00 per doc, $.50 per page. Payee- Effingham County Clerk of the Superior Court. **Online access to RE Deed, UCC, Lien records:** See www.gsccca.org for Deed, Lien and UCC indexes. **Other phones:** Elections- 912-754-2115; Vital Records- 912-754-2112; Tax Commissioner- 912-754-2121; Zoning -912-754-2128. **Property tax/Assessor-** PO Box 239, Springfield, GA 31329; 912-754-2125.

Elbert County

County Superior Court Clerk, PO Box 619, Elberton, GA 30635. RE & UCC recording phone-706-283-2005; fax-706-213-7286; hours: 8AM-5PM
Separate indices to search include Grantor/Grantee. Only the public may search. Copy fee $1.00 per page. Cert fee- $2.00 per doc, $.50 per page. Payee- Elbert County Clerk of the Superior Court. **Online access to RE Deed, UCC, Lien, Plat Recording records:** See www.gsccca.org for Deed, Lien and UCC indexes. **Other phones:** Treasurer- 706-283-2018; Elections- 706-283-2016. **Property tax/Assessor-** 706-283-2008.

Emanuel County

County Superior Court Clerk, PO Box 627, Swainsboro, GA 30401. RE & UCC recording phone-478-237-8911; fax-478-237-2173; hours: 8AM-5PM
Only the public may search. Copy fee $1.00 per page. Cert fee- $2.00 per doc, $.50 per page. Payee- Emanuel County Clerk of the Superior Court. **Online access to RE Deed, UCC records:** See www.gsccca.org for Deed and UCC indexes. **Other phones:** Treasurer- 478-237-3881. **Property tax/Assessor-** 478-237-3424.

Evans County

County Superior Court Clerk, PO Box 845, Claxton, GA 30417. RE & UCC recording phone-912-739-3868; fax-912-739-2504; hours: 8AM-5PM
Records indexed on computer back to 1989. Only the public may search. Copy fee $1.00 per page. Cert fee- $2.00 per doc, $.50 per page; includes copy fee. Payee- Evans County Clerk of the Superior Court. **Online access to RE Deed, Lien, UCC records:** See www.gsccca.org for Deed, Lien and UCC indexes. **Other phones:** Treasurer- 912-739-1147; Elections- 912-739-0708. **Property tax/Assessor-** 912-739-3424.

Fannin County

County Superior Court Clerk, PO Box 1300, Blue Ridge, GA 30513. RE & UCC recording phone-706-632-2039; hours: 9AM-5PM
Separate indices to search include civil, criminal, real estate. Only the public may search. Copy fee $1.00 per page; self serve $.25. Cert fee- $2.50 per doc, $.50 per page plus copy fee. Payee- Fannin County Clerk of the Superior Court. **Online access to RE Deed, Lien, UCC records:** See www.gsccca.org for Deed, Lien and UCC indexes. **Other phones:** Treasurer- 706-632-2645; Appraiser/Auditor- 706-632-5954; Elections- 706-632-7740; Vital Records- 706-623-3011. **Property tax/Assessor-** 706-632-5954.

Fayette County

County Superior Court Clerk, PO Box 130, Fayetteville, GA 30214. 770-716-4290, R/E recording phone-770-716-4291, UCC recording phone-770-716-4291; fax-770-716-4868; hours: 8AM-4:30PM www.admin.co.fayette.ga.us
Only the public may search. Copy fee $1.00 per page. Cert fee- $2.00 per doc, $.50 per page. Payee- Fayette County Clerk of the Superior Court. **Online access to Assessor, Real Estate, UCC, Lien records:** Records on the County Assessor database are free on the GIS-mapping site at www.fayettecountymaps.com/disclaimer.htm. See www.gsccca.org for Deed and UCC indexes. **Other phones:** ; Tax Commissioner- 770-461-3652. **Property tax/Assessor-** 770-460-5730 x5402.

Floyd County

County Superior Court Clerk, PO Box 1110, Rome, GA 30162-1110. Main phone & R/E recording-706-291-5158, UCC recording phone-706-291-5206; fax-706-233-0035; hours: 8AM-5PM
Separate indices to search include liens, UCCs. Records indexed on a public use terminal back to 10/1984. Only the public may search. Copy fee $1.00 per page. RE or tax lien copy- $.50 per page. Cert fee- $2.00 per doc, $.50 per page. Payee- Floyd County Clerk of the Superior Court. **Online access to RE Deed, Lien, UCC records:** See www.gsccca.org for Deed, Lien and UCC indexes. **Other phones:** Treasurer- 706-291-5148; Appraiser/Auditor- 706-291-5144; Elections- 706-291-5168; Tax Office- 706-291-5147. **Property tax/Assessor-** 706-291-5143.

Forsyth County

County Superior Court Clerk, 100 Courthouse Sq, Rm 010, Cumming, GA 30040. Main phone & R/E recording-770-781-2120, UCC recording phone-770-781-2120 x 2690 or 2681; fax-770-886-2858; hours: 8:30AM-5PM www.forsythco.com
Separate indices to search include real estate index back to1986, GED index back to 1991, plats index back to 1961, hospital lien index back to 12/30/2003. Records indexed on a public use terminal. Only the public may search. Copy fee $1.00 per page. Tax lien copy- $.25 per page. Cert fee- $2.50 per doc plus $.50 per page includes copy fee. Payee- Forsyth County Clerk of the Superior Court. **Online access to RE Deed, Lien, UCC records:** See www.gsccca.org for Deed, Lien and UCC indexes. **Other phones:** Treasurer- 770-781-2110; Appraiser/Auditor- 770-781-2106; Elections-

770-781-2118; Vital Records- 770-781-2140. **Property tax/Assessor**- 110 E Main St #260, Cumming, GA 30040; 770-781-2106.

Franklin County

County Superior Court Clerk, PO Box 70, Carnesville, GA 30521. Main phone & R/E recording-706-384-2514, UCC recording phone-706-384-4858; fax-706-384-4384; hours: 8AM-5PM
Records indexed on a public use terminal back to 1994, Deeds. Only the public may search. Copy fee $1.00 per page. Real estate copy- $.25 per page. Cert fee- $2.50 per doc, $.50 per page. Payee- Franklin County Clerk of the Superior Court. **Online access to RE Deed, Lien, UCC records:** See www.gsccca.org for Deed, Lien and UCC indexes. **Other phones:** Vital Records- 706-384-2403. **Property tax/Assessor**- 706-384-4896.

Fulton County

County Superior Court Clerk, 136 Pryor St, SW, Atlanta, GA 30303. Main phone & R/E recording-404-730-5371, UCC recording phone-404-730-5553; hours: 8:30AM-5PM www.fcclk.org
Separate indices to search include deed, lien, GED, business indexes, notice of commencement, federal tax liens, and plat indexes. Only the public may search. Copy fee $1.00 per page. Cert fee- $2.00 per doc, $.50 per page plus copy fee. Payee- Fulton County Clerk of the Superior Court. **Online access to RE Deed, Lien, UCC records:** See www.gsccca.org for Deed, Lien and UCC indexes. **Other phones:** Treasurer- 404-730-6100; Tax Lien Records- 404-730-5305; Copy requests -404-730-5286. **Property tax/Assessor**- 404-730-6440.

Gilmer County

County Superior Court Clerk, 1 West Side Sq; Courthouse, Box #30, Ellijay, GA 30540. RE & UCC recording phone-706-635-4462; fax-706-635-1462; hours: 8:30AM-5PM
Only the public may search. Copy fee $1.00 per page. Cert fee- $2.50 per doc, $.50 per page. Payee- Gilmer County Clerk of the Superior Court. **Online access to RE Deed, Lien, UCC records:** See www.gsccca.org for Deed, Lien and UCC indexes. **Other phones:** Treasurer- 706-635-4361. **Property tax/Assessor**- 706-635-2703.

Glascock County

County Superior Court Clerk, PO Box 231, Gibson, GA 30810. RE & UCC recording phone-706-598-2084; fax-706-598-2577; hours: 8AM-N,1-5PM
Records indexed on a public use terminal back to 1924. Only the public may search. Copy fee $.25 per page. Cert fee- $2.00 per doc, $.50 per page. Payee- Glascock County Clerk of the Superior Court. **Online to RE Deed, UCC, Lien records:** See www.gsccca.org for Deed, Lien and UCC indexes. **Other phones:** Treasurer- 706-598-2671; Elections- 706-598-3241. **Property tax/Assessor**- same address as above. 706-598-2863.

Glynn County

County Superior Court Clerk, PO Box 1355, Brunswick, GA 31521-1355. RE & UCC recording phone-912-554-7313; fax-912-267-5625; hours: 8:30AM-5PM
Separate indices to search include Property records, Liens, and Plats. Records indexed on a public use terminal back to 1/1995. Only the public may search. Copy fee $1.00 per page. RE or tax lien copy- $.25 per copy. Cert fee- $2.50 per doc, $.50 per page. Payee- Glynn County Clerk of the Superior Court. **Online access to Assessor, Property, Recording, UCC, Lien records:** Access the county assessor property tax records free on the GIS mapping website at http://glynn.binarybus.com. See www.gsccca.org for online access to Deed, Lien and UCC indexes. **Other phones:** Treasurer- 912-554-7120; Elections- 912-554-7060. **Property tax/Assessor**- 912-554-7093.

Gordon County

County Superior Court Clerk, 100 Wall St.; Courthouse, #102, Calhoun, GA 30701. RE & UCC recording phone-706-629-9533; fax-706-629-2139; hours: 8:30AM-5PM
Only the public may search. Copy fee $1.00 per page. RE or tax lien copy- $.50 per page. Cert fee- $2.50 per doc, $.50 per page. Payee- Gordon County Clerk of the Superior Court. **Online access to RE Deed, Lien, UCC records:** See www.gsccca.org for Deed, Lien and UCC indexes. **Other phones:** Treasurer- 706-629-9242; Elections- 706-629-7781; Vital Records- 706-629-7314. **Property tax/Assessor**- 706-629-6812.

Grady County

Superior Court Clerk, Box 8, 250 N. Broad St, Cairo, GA 39828. RE & UCC recording phone-229-377-2912; hours: 8:30AM-5PM
Records indexed on a public use terminal. Only the public may search. Copy fee $1.00 per page. RE or tax lien copy- $.25 per page. Cert fee- $2.00 per doc, $.50 per page. Payee- Grady County Clerk of the Superior Court. **Online access to RE Deed, Lien, UCC records:** See www.gsccca.org for Deed, Lien and UCC indexes. **Other phones:** ; Registrar- 229-377-1897.

Greene County

County Superior Court Clerk, 113 N Main St; Courthouse, #109, Greensboro, GA 30642-1107. 706-453-3340; fax-706-453-9179; hours: 8AM-5PM
Only the public may search. Copy fee $.25 per page. Cert fee- $2.50 1st page, $.25 each add'l. Payee- Greene County Clerk of the Superior Court. **Online access to RE Deed, UCC, Lien records:** See www.gsccca.org for Deed, Lien and UCC indexes. **Property tax/Assessor**- 706-453-3355.

Gwinnett County

County Superior Court Clerk, PO Box 880, Lawrenceville, GA 30046. RE & UCC recording phone-770-822-8100; hours: 8AM-5PM www.gwinnettcourts.com
Separate indices to search include real property index, court record index. Only the public may search. Copy fee $.25 per page. Cert fee- $2.50 1st page, $.50 per add'l page includes copy fee. Payee- Gwinnett County Clerk of the Superior Court. **Online access to Property, Deed, UCC, Plats, Lien records:** See www.gsccca.org for Deed, Plat and UCC indexes. Deed records go back to 1870; UCCs to1995. **Other phones:** Treasurer- 770-822-8000; Elections- 770-822-8787; Vital Records- 770-822-8250. **Property tax/Assessor**- 75 Langley Dr, Lawrenceville, GA 30045; 770-822-7233.

Habersham County

County Superior Court Clerk, 555 Monroe St, Unit 35, Clarkesville, GA 30523. RE & UCC recording phone-706-754-2923; fax-706-754-8779; hours: 8AM-5PM www.co.habersham.ga.us
Records indexed on a public use terminal back to 1972. Only the public may search. Copy fee $.25 per page. Cert fee- $2.50 1st page, $.50 add'l. Payee- Habersham County Clerk of the Superior Court. **Online access to RE Deed, UCC, Lien records:** See www.gsccca.org for Deed, Lien and UCC indexes. **Other phones:** Treasurer- 706-754-6264; Appraiser/Auditor- 706-754-2557; Elections- 706-754-2013; Vital Records- 706-754-2013. **Property tax/Assessor**- 706-754-2557.

Hall County

County Superior Court Clerk, PO Box 1336, Gainesville, GA 30503-1336. 770-531-7052, R/E recording phone-770-531-7058; fax-770-536-0702; hours: 8AM-5PM www.hallcounty.org
Only the public may search. Copy fee $1.00 per page. Cert fee- $2.00 per doc, $.50 per page. Payee- Hall County Clerk of the Superior Court. **Online access to RE Deed, UCC, Lien, Plat records:**

See www.gsccca.org for Deed, Lien and UCC indexes. **Other phones:** Treasurer- 770-531-6950. **Property tax/Assessor**- 770-531-6720.

Hancock County

County Superior Court Clerk, PO Box 451, Sparta, GA 31087. RE & UCC recording phone-706-444-6644; fax-706-444-5685; hours: 9AM-5PM
Separate indices to search include real estate, liens, UCC, civil, criminal. Records indexed on computer. Only the public may search. Search fee $5.00 per name. Copy fee $.25 per page. Cert fee- $2.50 1st page, $.50 each add'l includes copy fee. Payee- Hancock County Clerk of the Superior Court. **Online access to RE Deed, Lien, UCC records:** See www.gsccca.org for Deed, Lien and UCC indexes. **Other phones:** Treasurer- 706-444-5746; Elections- 706-444-5343; Vital Records- 706-444-5343. **Property tax/Assessor**- 602 3rd St, Sparta, GA 31087; 706-444-5721.

Haralson County

County Superior Court Clerk, PO Drawer 849, Buchanan, GA 30113. RE & UCC recording phone-770-646-2005; fax-770-646-2035; 8:30AM-5PM
Separate indices to search. Records indexed on a public use terminal back to 05/05. Only the public may search. Copy fee $1.00 per page. Cert fee- $2.00 per doc, $.50 per page plus copy fee. Payee- Haralson County Clerk of the Superior Court. **Online access to RE Deed, Lien, UCC records:** See www.gsccca.org for Deed, Lien and UCC indexes. **Other phones:** Treasurer- 770-646-2022; Appraiser/Auditor- 770-646-2022; Vital Records- 770-646-2008. **Property tax/Assessor**- 770-646-2022.

Harris County

County Superior Court Clerk, PO Box 528, Hamilton, GA 31811. RE & UCC recording phone-706-628-5570; fax-706-628-7039; hours: 8AM-5PM
Separate indices to search include several indices by year. Records indexed on a public use terminal back to 1999. Only the public may search. Copy fee $.25 per page. Cert fee- $2.50 per doc, $.50 per page plus copy fee. Payee- Harris County Clerk of the Superior Court. **Online access to RE Deed, Lien, UCC records:** See www.gsccca.org for Deed, Lien and UCC indexes. **Other phones:** Treasurer- 706-628-4958; Elections- 706-628-5210; Tax Commissioner- 706-628-4843. **Property tax/Assessor**- same address as above. 706-628-5171.

Hart County

County Superior Court Clerk, PO Box 386, Hartwell, GA 30643. RE & UCC recording phone-706-376-7189; fax-706-376-1277; hours: 8:30AM-5PM
Only the public may search. Copy fee $1.00 per page, $.25 self serve per page. Cert fee- $2.00 per doc, $.50 per page. Payee- Hart County Clerk of the Superior Court. **Online access to RE Deed, Lien, UCC records:** See www.gsccca.org for Deed, Lien and UCC indexes. **Other phones:** Treasurer- 706-376-2024; Appraiser/Auditor- 706-376-3997; Elections- 706-376-2565; Vital Records- 706-376-2565. **Property tax/Assessor**- 706-376-3997.

Heard County

County Superior Court Clerk, PO Box 249, Franklin, GA 30217. 706-675-3301; fax-706-675-0819; hours: 8:30AM-5PM
Only the public may search. Copy fee $1.00 per page. Real estate copy- $.25 per page. Cert fee- $2.50 per doc plus copy fee. Payee- Heard County Clerk of the Superior Court. **Online access to RE Deed, Lien, UCC records:** See www.gsccca.org for Deed, Lien and UCC indexes. **Property tax/Assessor**- 706-675-3786.

Henry County

County Superior Court Clerk, #1 Courthouse Sq, McDonough, GA 30253. RE & UCC recording phone-770-954-2121; hours: 8AM-5PM www.co.henry.ga.us

All records in one index. Records indexed on a public use terminal back to 1986. Only the public may search. Copy fee $1.00 per page. Cert fee- $2.50 1st page, $.50 each add'l. Payee- Henry County Clerk of the Superior Court. **Online access to RE Deed, UCC, Property Tax, Assessor records:** See www.gsccca.org for Deed, Lien and UCC indexes. Also, search property tax data free at https://hcwebb.boca.co.henry.ga.us/Henry_Tax/form.as p Also search tax assessor records for free at https://hcwebb.boca.co.henry.ga.us/Henry_Tax/index.ht ml. **Other phones:** Treasurer- 770-954-2470; Elections- 770-954-2069; Vital Records- 770-954-2303. **Property tax/Assessor-** 140 Henry Parkway, McDonough, Ga 30253; 770-954-2420.

Houston County

County Superior Court Clerk, 201 N Perry Pkwy, Perry, GA 31069. 478-987-2170, R/E recording 478-218-4720, UCC recording 478-218-4720; fax-478-987-3252; 8:30AM-5PM www.houstoncountyga.com
All records in one index. Records indexed on computer. Only the public may search. Copy fee $.25 per page. Cert fee- $2.50 per doc, $.50 per page. Payee- Houston County Clerk of the Superior Court. **Online to Assessor, RE, Plat, Lien records:** Access to the assessor's Mapguide database is free at www.assessors.houstoncountyga.org/. Download the Autodesk MapGuide viewer. Also, the clerks recording indices of plats, land records, liens is free at http://67.32.12.213/resolution/. Pre-1998 real estate and pre-1994 financing statements are also available. See www.gsccca for online access to Deed, Lien and UCC indexes. **Other phones:** Appraiser/Auditor- 478-218-4750; Elections- 478-987-1973; Vital Records- 478-218-4710; Marriage/Death/Birth Records- 478-218-4710; Divorce Records -478-218-4740. **Property tax/Assessor-** 478-218-4750.

Irwin County

County Superior Court Clerk, 301 S Irwin Ave #103, Ocilla, GA 31774. 229-468-5356; fax-229-468-9753; hours: 8AM-5PM
Separate indices to search include GE Dkt, minute book. Records indexed on computer back to 2004. Only the public may search. Copy fee $1.00 per page. Cert fee- $2.50 per doc, $.50 per page. Payee- Irwin County Clerk of the Superior Court. **Online access to RE Deed, UCC records:** See www.gsccca.org for Deed and UCC indexes. **Other phones:** Treasurer- 229-468-5505; Elections- 229-468-5894; Vital Records- 229-468-5138. **Property tax/Assessor-** 200 S Irwin Ave, Ocilla, GA 31774; 229-468-5514.

Jackson County

County Superior Court Clerk, PO Box 7, Jefferson, GA 30549. 706-387-6255, R/E recording phone-706-387-6258; fax-706-387-6273; hours: 8AM-5PM www.jacksoncountygov.com
All records in one index. Records indexed on a public use terminal back to 1988. Only the public may search. Copy fee $1.00 per page. Cert fee- $2.00 per doc, $.50 per page includes copy fee. Payee- Jackson County Clerk of the Superior Court. **Online access to RE Deed, Lien, Plats, UCC records:** See www.gsccca.org for Deed, Lien and UCC indexes. **Other phones:** Appraiser/Auditor- 706-367-6330; Elections- 706-367-6377; Vital Records- 706-387-6276. **Property tax/Assessor-** 67 Athens St, Jefferson, GA 30549.

Jasper County

County Superior Court Clerk, Courthouse, Monticello, GA 31064. 706-468-4901, R/E recording phone-706-468-4901 x226, UCC recording phone-706-468-4901 x226; fax-706-468-4946; hours: 8AM-5PM
Separate indices to search include lien, real estate. Records indexed on a public use terminal back to 1993. Only the public may search. Copy fee $1.00 per page. Cert fee- $2.50 per doc, plus $.50 per page, includes copy fee. Payee- Jasper County

Clerk of the Superior Court. **Online access to RE Deed, UCC, Lien records:** See www.gsccca.org for Deed, Lien and UCC indexes. **Other phones:** Treasurer- 706-468-4900; Appraiser/Auditor- 706-468-4904; Elections- 706-468-4903; Vital Records- 706-468-4903. **Property tax/Assessor-** 126 W Greene St #124, Monticello, GA 31064; 706-468-4904.

Jeff Davis County

County Superior Court Clerk, PO Box 429, Hazlehurst, GA 31539. RE & UCC recording phone-912-375-6615; fax-912-375-6637; hours: 8AM-5PM
All records in one index. Records indexed. Only the public may search. Copy fee $1.00 per page. Cert fee- $2.00 per doc, $.50 per page. Payee- Jeff Davis County Clerk of the Superior Court. **Online access to RE Deed, Lien, UCC records:** See www.gsccca.org for Deed, Lien and UCC indexes. **Other phones:** Treasurer- 912-375-6611; Appraiser/Auditor- 912-375-6624; Elections- 912-375-6625; Vital Records- 912375-6626. **Property tax/Assessor-** 912-375-6624.

Jefferson County

County Superior Court Clerk, PO Box 151, Louisville, GA 30434. 478-625-7922; fax-478-625-9589; hours: 9AM-5PM
Only the public may search. Copy fee $.25 per page. Cert fee- $2.50 per doc, plus $.50 per page. Payee- Jefferson County Clerk of the Superior Court. **Online access to RE Deed, Lien, UCC records:** See www.gsccca.org for Deed, Lien and UCC indexes. **Other phones:** Treasurer- 478-625-7736. **Property tax/Assessor-** 478-625-8209.

Jenkins County

County Superior Court Clerk, PO Box 659, Millen, GA 30442. RE & UCC recording phone-478-982-4683; fax-478-982-1274; hours: 8:30AM-1-5PM
Only the public may search. Copy fee $1.00 per page. RE or tax lien copy- $.25 per page. Cert fee- $2.50 per doc, plus copy fee. Payee- Jenkins County Clerk of the Superior Court. **Online access to RE Deed, Lien, UCC records:** See www.gsccca.org for Deed, Lien and UCC indexes. **Other phones:** Treasurer- 478-982-4925. **Property tax/Assessor-** 478-982-4939.

Johnson County

County Superior Court Clerk, PO Box 321, Wrightsville, GA 31096. 478-864-3484; fax-478-864-1343; hours: 9AM-5PM
Only the public may search. Copy fee $.25 per page. Cert fee- $3.00 per doc plus copy fee. Payee- Johnson County Clerk of the Superior Court. **Online access to RE Deed, Lien, UCC records:** See www.gsccca.org for Deed, Lien and UCC indexes. **Other phones:** Treasurer- 478-864-2565. **Property tax/Assessor-** 478-864-3325.

Jones County

County Superior Court Clerk, PO Box 39, Gray, GA 31032. 478-986-6671; fax-478-986-2030; hours: 8:30AM-4:30PM
Separate indices to search include grantors/grantee, liens. Records indexed on computer back to 1990 for deeds, back to July, 1991 for liens. Only the public may search. Copy fee $.50 per page. Cert fee- $2.50 per doc plus copy fee. Payee- Jones County Clerk of the Superior Court. **Online access to RE Deed, Lien, UCC records:** See www.gsccca.org for Deed, Lien and UCC indexes. **Other phones:** Treasurer- 478-986-6538; Tax Commissioner- 478-986-6538. **Property tax/Assessor-** 478-986-6300.

Lamar County

County Superior Court Clerk, 326 Thomaston St; Courthouse, Barnesville, GA 30204-1669. 770-358-5145; fax-770-358-5814; hours: 8AM-5PM
Only the public may search. Copy fee $1.00 1st page; $.25 each add'l. Cert fee- $2.50 per doc, $.50 per page. Payee- Lamar County Clerk of the

Superior Court. **Online access to RE Deed, Lien, UCC records:** See www.gsccca.org for Deed, Lien and UCC indexes. **Other phones:** Treasurer- 770-358-5162. **Property tax/Assessor-** 770-358-5161.

Lanier County

County Superior Court Clerk, 100 Main St; County Courthouse, Lakeland, GA 31635. 229-482-3594; fax-229-482-8333; hours: 8AM-N,1-5PM
Only the public may search. Copy fee $1.00 per page. Cert fee- $3.00 per cert plus copy fee. Payee- Lanier County Clerk of the Superior Court. **Online access to RE Deed, Lien, UCC records:** See www.gsccca.org for Deed, Lien and UCC indexes. **Other phones:** Treasurer- 229-482-3795. **Property tax/Assessor-** 229-482-2090.

Laurens County

County Superior Court Clerk, PO Box 2028, Dublin, GA 31040. RE & UCC recording phone-478-272-3210; fax-478-275-2595; hours: 8:30AM-5:30PM
Separate indices to search include deed, UCC, courts. Only the public may search. Copy fee $1.00 per page. Cert fee- $2.50 per doc, $.50 per page. Payee- Laurens County Clerk of the Superior Court. **Online access to RE Deed, Lien, UCC records:** See www.gsccca.org for Deed, Lien and UCC indexes. **Other phones:** Treasurer- 478-272-6994; Elections- 478-272-2566; Vital Records- 478-272-2051. **Property tax/Assessor-** 478-272-6443.

Lee County

County Superior Court Clerk, PO Box 49, Leesburg, GA 31763. RE & UCC recording phone-229-759-6018; fax-229-759-6049; hours: 8AM-5PM
Separate indices to search. Only the public may search. Copy fee $.25 per page. Cert fee- $2.00 per doc, $1.00 per page. Payee- Lee County Clerk of the Superior Court. **Online access to RE Deed, UCC, Lien records:** See www.gsccca.org for Deed, Lien and UCC indexes. **Other phones:** Treasurer- 229-759-6000. **Property tax/Assessor-** 229-759-6010.

Liberty County

County Superior Court Clerk, PO Box 50, Hinesville, GA 31310. RE & UCC recording phone-912-876-3625; fax-912-369-5463; hours: 8AM-5PM www.libertyco.com
Only the public may search. Copy fee $1.00 per page. Cert fee- $2.50 per doc, $.50 per page. Payee- Liberty County Clerk of the Superior Court. **Online access to RE Deed, UCC, Lien records:** See www.gsccca.org for Deed, Lien and UCC indexes. **Other phones:** Treasurer- 912-876-3389; Vital Records- 912-876-3625. **Property tax/Assessor-** 912-876-2823.

Lincoln County

County Superior Court Clerk, PO Box 340, Lincolnton, GA 30817. RE & UCC recording phone-706-359-5505; hours: 9AM-N, 1PM-5PM
Only the public may search. RE record copy- $1.00 per page. Cert fee- $2.00 per doc, $1.00 per page. Payee- Lincoln County Clerk of the Superior Court. **Online access to RE Deed, UCC records:** See www.gsccca.org for Deed and UCC indexes. **Other phones:** Appraiser/Auditor- 706-359-5502; Elections- 706-359-6126; Vital Records- 706-359-5528. **Property tax/Assessor-** 706-359-5502.

Long County

County Superior Court Clerk, PO Box 458, Ludowici, GA 31316. RE & UCC recording phone-912-545-2123; fax-912-545-2020; hours: 8:30AM-5PM
Separate indices to search include deeds, liens, plats, UCC's, hospital liens, GED. Records indexed on a public use terminal back to 1996 (deeds). Only the public may search. Copy fee $1.50 per page; self serve $.25. Cert fee- $2.50 1st page; $.50 each add'l includes copy fee. Payee- Long County Clerk of the Superior Court. **Online access to RE Deed, Lien, UCC records:** See www.gsccca.org for Deed, Lien and UCC indexes.

Other phones: Treasurer- 912-545-2127; Elections-912-545-2234; Vital Records- 912-545-2131; Sheriffs Dept.-912-545-2118. **Property tax/Assessor-** PO Box 642, Ludowici, GA 31316; 912-545-9111.

Lowndes County

County Superior Court Clerk, PO Box 1349, Valdosta, GA 31601-1349. Main phone & R/E recording-229-333-5125, UCC recording phone-229-333-5183; fax-229-333-7637; hours: 8AM-5PM
Separate indices to search include Deeds, liens, hospital liens. Records indexed on computer. Only the public may search. Copy fee $.25 per page. Cert fee- $2.00 per doc plus $.50 per page. Payee- Lowndes County Clerk of the Superior Court. **Online access to RE Deed, Lien, UCC records:** See www.gsccca.org for Deed, Lien and UCC indexes. **Other phones:** Treasurer- 229-671-2570. **Property tax/Assessor-** 229-671-2540.

Lumpkin County

County Superior Court Clerk, 99 Courthouse Hill, #D, Dahlonega, GA 30533-0541. RE & UCC recording phone-706-864-3736; fax-706-864-5298; hours: 8AM-5PM
Will not search real estate records. Will not search UCC records or tax liens. Copy fee $.25 per page. Cert fee- $2.50 per doc, $.50 per each add'l page plus copy fee. Payee- Lumpkin County Clerk of the Superior Court. **Online access to RE Deed, UCC, Lien records:** See www.gsccca.org for Deed, Lien and UCC indexes. **Other phones:** Treasurer- 706-864-3742; Appraiser/Auditor- 706-864-2433; Elections- 706-864-6279; Vital Records- 706-864-3847. **Property tax/Assessor-** 706-864-2433.

Macon County

County Superior Court Clerk, PO Box 337, Oglethorpe, GA 31068. RE & UCC recording phone-478-472-7661; fax-478-472-4775; hours: 8:30AM-5PM
All records in one index. Records indexed on a public use terminal. Only the public may search. Copy fee $1.00 per page if assisted: $.25 per page self serve. Cert fee- $2.00 per cert plus $.50 per page copy fee. Payee- Macon County Clerk of the Superior Court. **Online access to RE Deed, Lien, UCC records:** See www.gsccca.org for Deed, Lien and UCC indexes. **Other phones:** Treasurer- 478-472-7031; Appraiser/Auditor- 478-472-6560; Elections- 478-472-7685. **Property tax/Assessor-** PO Box 297, 122 Chatham St, Oglethorpe, GA 31068; 478-472-6560.

Madison County

County Superior Court Clerk, PO Box 247, Danielsville, GA 30633. 706-795-3352, R/E recording phone-706-795-6310, UCC recording phone-706-795-6310; fax-706-795-2209; hours: 8AM-5PM
Separate indices to search include liens, plats. Records indexed on computer. Only the public may search. Copy fee $1.00 per page. Cert fee- $2.50 per cert plus $.50 per page. Payee- Madison County Clerk of the Superior Court. **Online access to RE Deed, Lien, UCC records:** See www.gsccca.org for Deed, Lien and UCC indexes.

Marion County

County Superior Court Clerk, PO Box 41, Buena Vista, GA 31803. RE & UCC recording phone-229-649-7321; fax-229-649-7931; hours: 9AM-5PM
Only the public may search. Copy fee $1.00 per page. Cert fee- $2.50 per doc, $.50 per page. Payee- Marion County Clerk of the Superior Court. **Online access to RE Deed, Lien, UCC records:** See www.gsccca.org for Deed, Lien and UCC indexes. **Other phones:** Treasurer- 229-649-2603; Appraiser/Auditor- 229-649-5504; Elections- 229-649-2603; Vital Records- 229-649-5542. **Property tax/Assessor-** 229-649-5504.

McDuffie County

County Superior Court Clerk, PO Box 158, Thomson, GA 30824-0150. RE & UCC recording phone-706-595-2134; fax-706-595-9150; hours: 8AM-5PM
Separate indices to search include lien, plat & real estate in hard copy; UCC in separate online index, other electronic indexes can be searched in one index. Only the public may search. Copy fee $1.00 per page; self serve $.25. Cert fee- $2.00 per doc, $.50 per page includes copy fee. Payee- McDuffie County Clerk of the Superior Court. **Online access to RE Deed, Lien, UCC records:** See www.gsccca.org for Deed, Lien and UCC indexes. **Other phones:** Treasurer- 706-595-2100; Appraiser/Auditor- 706-595-2128; Elections- 706-595-2105; Vital Records- 706-595-2124. **Property tax/Assessor-** 706-595-2128.

McIntosh County

County Superior Court Clerk, PO Box 1661, Darien, GA 31305. RE & UCC recording phone-912-437-6641; fax-912-437-6673; hours: 8AM-4:30PM
Only the public may search. General copy fee $1.00 per page. RE or tax lien copy- $.50 per page. Cert fee- $2.00 per doc, $.50 per page. Payee- McIntosh County Clerk of the Superior Court. **Online to Deed (2000-present), Lien, UCC records:** Call 800-304-5175 to subscribe to UCCs and Deed indexes online service. See www.gsccca.org for online access to Deed, Lien and UCC indexes. **Other phones:** Treasurer- 912-437-6641; Appraiser/Auditor- 912-437-6663; Vital Records- 912-437-6636. **Property tax/Assessor-** 912-437-6663.

Meriwether County

County Superior Court Clerk, PO Box 160, Greenville, GA 30222-0160. RE & UCC recording phone-706-672-4416; fax-706-672-9465; hours: 8:30AM-5PM
Only the public may search. Copy fee $1.00 per page. Cert fee- $2.00 per doc, $.50 per page. Payee- Meriwether County Clerk of the Superior Court. **Online access to RE Deed, Lien, UCC records:** See www.gsccca.org for Deed, Lien and UCC indexes. **Other phones:** Treasurer- 706-672-4219; Appraiser/Auditor- 706-672-4222; Elections- 706-672-4952; Vital Records- 706-672-4974. **Property tax/Assessor-** 706-672-4222.

Miller County

County Superior Court Clerk, PO Box 66, Colquitt, GA 39837. RE & UCC recording phone-229-758-4102; fax-229-758-6585; hours: 9AM-5PM
Separate indices to search include deed, lien, hospital lien, civil and criminal. Only the public may search. Copy fee $1.00 per page. Cert fee- $2.50 per cert plus copy fee. Payee- Miller County Clerk of the Superior Court. **Online access to RE Deed, Lien, UCC records:** See www.gsccca.org for Deed, Lien and UCC indexes. **Other phones:** Treasurer- 229-758-4101; Appraiser/Auditor- 229-758-4100; Elections- 229-758-4118; Vital Records- 229-758-4110. **Property tax/Assessor-** 155 S First St, Colquitt, GA 39837; 229-758-4100.

Mitchell County

County Superior Court Clerk, PO Box 427, Camilla, GA 31730. RE & UCC recording phone-229-336-2022; fax-229-336-2003; hours: 8:30AM-5PM
Only the public may search. Copy fee $.25 per page. Cert fee- $2.50 1st page, $.50 each add'l. Payee- Mitchell County Clerk of the Superior Court. **Online access to RE Deed, Lien, UCC records:** See www.gsccca.org for Deed, Lien and UCC indexes. **Other phones:** Treasurer- 229-336-2010; Elections- 229-336-2016; Vital Records- 229-336-2016. **Property tax/Assessor-** 229-336-2005.

Monroe County

County Superior Court Clerk, PO Box 450, Forsyth, GA 31029-0450. 478-994-7022; fax-478-994-7053; hours: 8:30AM-4:30PM
Only the public may search. Copy fee $1.00 per page. Cert fee- $2.00 per doc, $.50 per page. Payee- Monroe County Clerk of the Superior Court. **Online access to RE Deed, UCC, Lien records:** See www.gsccca.org for Deed, Lien and UCC indexes. **Other phones:** Appraiser/Auditor- 478-994-7038; Elections- 478-994-7036; Vital Records- 478-994-7036. **Property tax/Assessor-** 478-994-7038.

Montgomery County

County Superior Court Clerk, PO Box 311, Mount Vernon, GA 30445. 912-583-4401; fax-912-583-4343; hours: 9AM-5PM
All records in one index. Records indexed on a public use terminal back to 1993. Only the public may search. Copy fee $1.00 per page. Cert fee- $2.00 per doc, $.50 per page. Payee- Clerk of Court. **Online access to RE Deed, Lien, UCC records:** See www.gsccca.org for Deed, Lien and UCC indexes. **Other phones:** Elections- 912-583-2681; Vital Records- 912-583-2681. **Property tax/Assessor-** 912-583-4131.

Morgan County

County Superior Court Clerk, PO Drawer 551, Madison, GA 30650. 706-342-3605; fax-706-343-6462; hours: 9AM-5PM
Temporary location; 259 2nd St. Madison, Ga.30650. Separate indices to search include real estate, liens, case management, UCC's. Records indexed on a public use terminal. Only the public may search. Copy fee $1.00 per page. Tax lien copy- $.25. Cert fee- $2.50 per doc, $.50 per page plus copy fee. Payee- Morgan County Clerk of the Superior Court. **Online access to RE Deed, Lien, UCC records:** See www.gsccca.org for Deed, Lien and UCC indexes. **Property tax/Assessor-** 706-342-0551.

Murray County

County Superior Court Clerk, PO Box 1000, Chatsworth, GA 30705. 706-695-2932; fax-706-517-9672; hours: 8:30AM-5PM
Only the public may search. Copy fee $.25 per page. Cert fee- $2.50 1st page; $.25 each add'l. Payee- Murray County Clerk of the Superior Court. **Online access to RE Deed, Lien, UCC records:** See www.gsccca.org for Deed, Lien and UCC indexes. **Other phones:** Treasurer- 706-695-3423. **Property tax/Assessor-** 706-695-2521.

Muscogee County

County Superior Court Clerk, PO Box 2145, Columbus, GA 31902-2145. 706-653-4358, R/E recording phone-706-653-4356, UCC recording phone-706-653-4356; fax-706-653-4359; 8:30AM-5PM
Only the public may search. Copy fee $.25 per page. Cert fee- $3.00 per cert $.50 add'l. Payee- Muscogee County Clerk of the Superior Court. **Online access to RE Deed, Lien, UCC records:** See www.gsccca.org for Deed, Lien and UCC indexes. **Other phones:** Treasurer- 706-653-4100. **Property tax/Assessor-** 706-653-4398.

Newton County

County Superior Court Clerk, 1132 Usher St, 3rd Fl; Newton County Judicial Ctr, Covington, GA 30014. 770-784-2035, R/E recording phone-770-784-2040, UCC recording phone-770-784-2040; fax-770-788-3717; hours: 8AM-5PM
Records indexed on a public use terminal. Only the public may search. Copy fee $1.00 per page. Cert fee- $2.50 1st page, $.50 each add'l. Payee- Newton County Clerk of the Superior Court. **Online access to RE Deed, Lien, UCC records:** See www.gsccca.org for Deed, Lien and UCC indexes. **Other phones:** Elections- 770-784-2055; Vital Records- 770-784-2045. **Property tax/Assessor-** same address as above. 770-784-2030.

Oconee County

County Superior Court Clerk, PO Box 1099, Watkinsville, GA 30677. 706-769-3940; fax-706-769-3948; hours: 8AM-5PM
Only the public may search. Copy fee $1.00 per page. Cert fee- $2.50 per doc, $.50 per page. Payee- Oconee County Clerk of the Superior Court. **Online access to RE Deed, UCC, Lien records:** See www.gsccca.org for Deed, Lien and UCC indexes. **Property tax/Assessor-** 706-769-3921.

Oglethorpe County

County Superior Court Clerk, PO Box 68, Lexington, GA 30648-0068. RE & UCC recording phone-706-743-5731; fax-706-743-5335; hours: 8AM-5PM
Separate indices to search include lien, court, real estate. Records indexed on a public use terminal back six years. Only the public may search. Copy fee $1.00 per page; $.25 self serve. Cert fee- $2.00 per doc, $.50 per page, plus copy fee. Payee- County Clerk of Superior Court. **Online access to Real Estate, Deed, UCC records:** County clerk UCC and real estate records avaialble by monthly subscription; fee- $9.95 plus $.25 per printed page. Guest accounts available. For info and to open an account, call 404-327-9058. Also, see www.gsccca.org for online access to Deed, Lien and UCC indexes. **Other phones:** Treasurer- 706-743-5270; Elections- 706-743-5350. **Property tax/Assessor-** PO Box 136, Lexington, GA 30648; 706-743-5166.

Paulding County

County Superior Court Clerk, 11 Courthouse Sq.; Rm G-2, Dallas, GA 30132. 770-443-7527, R/E recording phone-770-443-7528; hours: 8AM-5PM
Only the public may search. Copy fee $1.00 per page. Cert fee- $2.00 per doc, $.50 per page. Payee- Paulding County Clerk of the Superior Court. **Online access to RE Deed, Lien, UCC records:** See www.gsccca.org for Deed, Lien and UCC indexes. **Property tax/Assessor-** 770-443-7606.

Peach County

County Superior Court Clerk, PO Box 389, Fort Valley, GA 31030. 478-825-5331; fax-478-825-8662; hours: 8:30AM-5PM
Only the public may search. Copy fee $.25 per page. Cert fee- $2.50 per doc, $.50 per page, includes copy fee. Payee- Peach County Clerk of the Superior Court. **Online access to RE Deed, Lien, UCC records:** See www.gsccca.org for Deed, Lien and UCC indexes. **Other phones:** Treasurer- 478-825-2535. **Property tax/Assessor-** 478-825-5924.

Pickens County

County Superior Court Clerk, PO Box 130, Jasper, GA 30143. 706-253-8763, R/E recording phone-706-253-8766, UCC recording phone-706-253-8773; hours: 8AM-5PM
Separate indices to search include lis pendun book, hospital lien book, consolidated lien book, deed books. Records indexed on a public use terminal back to 1987. Only the public may search. Copy fee $1.00 per page. Real estate copy- $.25 per page. Cert fee- $2.50 1st page, $.50 each add'l page. Payee- Pickens County Clerk of the Superior Court. **Online access to RE Deed, Lien, UCC records:** See www.gsccca.org for Deed, Lien and UCC indexes. **Property tax/Assessor-** 706-253-8700.

Pierce County

County Superior Court Clerk, PO Box 588, Blackshear, GA 31516. RE & UCC recording phone-912-449-2020; fax-912-449-2106; hours: 9AM-5PM
Separate indices to search include real estate, plat index, lien index. Records indexed on a public use terminal back to 2003. Only the public may search. Copy fee $1.00 per page. RE or tax lien copy- $.50 per page. Cert fee- $2.50 per doc plus copy fee. Payee- Pierce County Clerk of the Superior Court. **Online to RE Deed, Lien, UCC records:** See www.gsccca.org for Deed, Lien and UCC. **Other**

phones: Appraiser/Auditor- 912-449-2025; Elections-912-449-2028. **Property Assessor-** 114 Strickland Ave #1, Blackshear, GA 21516; 912-449-2025.

Pike County

County Superior Court Clerk, PO Box 10, Zebulon, GA 30295. 770-567-2000; hours: 8AM-5PM
Separate indices to search include lien, plat, deeds. Record index not computerized. Only the public may search. Copy fee $1.00 per page. Cert fee- $2.00 per doc, $.50 per page includes copy fee. Payee- Pike County Clerk of the Superior Court. **Online access to RE Deed, UCC, Lien records:** See www.gsccca.org for Deed, Lien and UCC indexes.

Polk County

County Superior Court Clerk, PO Box 948, Cedartown, GA 30125. 770-749-2114; fax-770-749-2148; hours: 9AM-5PM
Only the public may search. Copy fee $.25 per page. Cert fee- $2.50 per page. Payee- Polk County Clerk of the Superior Court. **Online access to RE Deed, Lien, UCC records:** See www.gsccca.org for Deed, Lien and UCC indexes. **Other phones:** Treasurer- 770-749-2108. **Property tax/Assessor-** 770-749-2125.

Pulaski County

Superior Court Clerk, PO Box 60, Hawkinsville, GA 31036. RE & UCC recording phone-478-783-1911; fax-478-892-3308; hours: 8AM-5PM
Separate indices must be searched. Only the public may search. Copy fee $1.00 per page. Cert fee- $2.00 per doc, $.50 per page, includes copies. Payee- Pulaski County Clerk of the Superior Court. **Online access to RE Deed, Lien, UCC records:** See www.gsccca.org for Deed, Lien and UCC indexes. **Other phones:** Treasurer- 478-783-2811; Elections- 478-783-2061; Vital Records- 478-783-2061. **Property tax/Assessor-** Lumpkin St, Hawkinsville, GA 31036; 478-783-4154.

Putnam County

County Superior Court Clerk, 100 S Jefferson St; Courthouse, Eatonton, GA 31024-1087. RE & UCC recording phone-706-485-4501; fax-706-485-2875; hours: 8AM-5PM
All records in one index. Records indexed on a public use terminal back to 1992. Only the public may search. Copy fee $1.00 per page, $.25 self serve. Cert fee- $3.00 per doc plus $1.00 per page. Payee- Putnam County Clerk of the Superior Court. **Online access to RE Deed, UCC, Lien records:** See www.gsccca.org for Deed, Lien and UCC indexes. **Other phones:** Treasurer- 706-485-5441; Elections- 706-485-8683; Vital Records- 706-485-5476. **Property tax/Assessor-** 706-485-6376.

Quitman County

County Superior Court Clerk, PO Box 307, Georgetown, GA 39854. RE & UCC recording phone-229-334-2578; fax-229-334-3991; hours: 8AM-N, 1-5PM
Separate indices to search include deeds, liens, fed tax lien, etc. Only the public may search. Separate federal/state combined tax lien search- $10.00 per debtor. Copy fee $1.00 per page. RE or tax lien copy- $.25 per page. Cert fee- $2.50 1st pg., $.50 each add'l pg. Payee- Quitman County Clerk of the Superior Court. **Online access to RE Deed, Lien, UCC records:** See www.gsccca.org for Deed, Lien and UCC indexes. **Other phones:** Treasurer- 229-334-0903; Appraiser/Auditor- 229-334-2159; Elections-229-334-2224; Vital Records- 229-334-2224. **Property tax/Assessor-** PO Box 582, Georgetown, GA 39854; 229-334-2159.

Rabun County

County Superior Court Clerk, 25 Courthouse Sq #105, Clayton, GA 30525. RE & UCC recording phone-706-782-3615; fax-706-782-1391; hours: 8:30AM-5PM
Separate indices to search. Records indexed on a public use terminal back to 1993. Only the public

may search. Copy fee $1.00 per page; $.25 self serve. Cert fee- $2.50 1st page, $.25 each add'l page plus copy fee. Payee- Rabun County Clerk of the Superior Court. **Online access to RE Deed, Lien, UCC records:** See www.gsccca.org for Deed, Lien and UCC indexes. **Other phones:** Treasurer- 706-782-3813; Elections- 706-782-2657; Vital Records- 706-782-3614. **Property tax/Assessor-** same address as above. 706-782-5068.

Randolph County

County Superior Court Clerk, PO Box 98, Cuthbert, GA 39840. 229-732-2216; fax-229-732-5881; hours: 8AM-5PM
Only the public may search. Copy fee $.50 per page. Real estate copy- $.25 per page. Cert fee- $2.50 per doc plus copy fee. Payee- Randolph County Clerk of the Superior Court. **Online access to RE Deed, Lien, UCC records:** See www.gsccca.org for Deed, Lien and UCC indexes. **Other phones:** Treasurer- 229-732-6440. **Property tax/Assessor-** 229-732-2522.

Richmond County

County Superior Court Clerk, PO Box 2046, Augusta, GA 30903. 706-821-2460, R/E recording phone-706-821-2468, UCC recording phone-706-821-1296; fax-706-821-2448; hours: 8:30AM-5PM
Only the public may search. Copy fee $1.00 per page. Cert fee- $2.50 per doc, plus $50 per page. Payee- Richmond County Clerk of the Superior Court. **Online access to RE Deed, Lien, UCC records:** See www.gsccca.org for Deed, Lien and UCC indexes. **Other phones:** Treasurer- 706-821-2391. **Property tax/Assessor-** 706-821-2310.

Rockdale County

County Superior Court Clerk, PO Box 937, Conyers, GA 30012. Main phone & R/E recording-770-929-4068, UCC recording phone-770-929-4069; fax-770-860-0381; hours: 8:15AM-4:45PM
Only the public may search. Copy fee $1.00 per page. Cert fee- $2.50 per doc, $.50 per page. Payee- Rockdale County Clerk of the Superior Court. **Online access to RE Deed, UCC, Lien records:** See www.gsccca.org for Deed, Lien and UCC indexes. **Other phones:** Treasurer- 770-929-4009. **Property tax/Assessor-** 770-929-4024.

Schley County

County Superior Court Clerk, PO Box 7, Ellaville, GA 31806-0007. RE & UCC recording phone-229-937-5581; fax-229-937-5588; hours: 8AM-N,1-5PM
Separate indices to search. Only the public may search. Copy fee $.25 per page. Cert fee- $2.00 per doc, $.35 per page includes copy fee. Payee- Schley County Clerk of the Superior Court. **Online access to RE Deed, Lien, UCC, Plats records:** See www.gsccca.org for Deed, Lien and UCC indexes. **Other phones:** Appraiser/Auditor- 229-937-9169; Elections- 229-937-2905; Vital Records- 229-937-2905; Tax Commissioner- 229-937-2689. **Property tax/Assessor-** 229-937-9169.

Screven County

County Superior Court Clerk, PO Box 156, Sylvania, GA 30467. 912-564-2614; fax-912-564-2622; hours: 8AM-5PM
Only the public may search. Copy fee $.25 per page. Cert fee- $3.00 1st page; $1.50 each add'l page. Payee- Screven County Clerk of the Superior Court. **Online access to RE Deed, Lien, UCC records:** See www.gsccca.org for Deed, Lien and UCC indexes. **Property tax/Assessor-** 912-564-7918.

Seminole County

County Superior Court Clerk, PO Box 672, Donalsonville, GA 39845. RE & UCC recording phone-229-524-2525; fax-229-524-8883; hours: 9AM-5PM
All records in one index. Only the public may search. Copy fee $1.00 per page. Cert fee- $2.00 per doc, $.50 per page plus copy fee. Payee-

Seminole County Clerk of the Superior Court. **Online access to RE Deed, Lien, UCC records:** See www.gsccca.org for Deed, Lien and UCC indexes. **Other phones:** Vital Records- 229-524-5256. **Property tax/Assessor-** 229-524-5831.

Spalding County

County Superior Court Clerk, PO Box 1046, Griffin, GA 30224. 770-467-4356; hours: 8AM-5PM

All records in one index. Records indexed on a public use terminal back to 1984. Only the public may search. Copy fee $.25 per page. Cert fee- $2.00 per doc, $.50 per page. Payee- Spalding County Clerk of the Superior Court. **Online access to RE Deed, UCC, Lien records:** See www.gsccca.org for Deed, Lien and UCC indexes. Plats will soon be available. **Property tax/Assessor-** 770-228-9900 x350.

Stephens County

County Superior Court Clerk, 205 N. Alexander St, Rm 202; Stephens County Courthouse, Toccoa, GA 30577-2310. RE & UCC recording phone-706-886-9496; fax-706-886-5710; hours: 8AM-5PM

Separate indices to search include real estate documents, plats, liens. Records indexed on a public use terminal back to 1978 for deeds, 1988 for criminal and civil records. Only the public may search. Copy fee $1.00 per page. Cert fee- $2.50 1st page, $.50 each add'l. Payee- Stephens County Clerk of the Superior Court. **Online access to RE Deed, UCC, Lien records:** See www.gsccca.org for Deed, Lien and UCC indexes. **Other phones:** Elections- 706-886-8954; Vital Records- 706-886-2828. **Property tax/Assessor-** 205 N Alexander St, Rm 101, Toccoa, GA 30577; 706-886-4753.

Stewart County

County Superior Court Clerk, PO Box 910, Lumpkin, GA 31815-0910. 229-838-6220; fax-229-838-4505; hours: 8AM-4:30PM

Records indexed on a public use terminal back to 1996. Only the public may search. Copy fee $1.00 per page. RE or tax lien copy- $.25 per page. Cert fee- $2.50 per doc, $.50 per page. Payee- Stewart County Clerk of the Superior Court. **Online access to RE Deed, Lien, UCC records:** See www.gsccca.org for Deed, Lien and UCC indexes.

Sumter County

Superior Court Clerk, PO Box 333, Americus, GA 31709. RE & UCC recording phone-229-928-4537; hours: 9AM-5PM

Only the public may search. Copy fee $1.00 per page. Cert fee- $2.00 per doc, $.50 per page. Payee- Sumter County Clerk of the Superior Court. **Online access to RE Deed, UCC, Lien:** See www.gsccca.org for Deed, Lien and UCC indexes. **Other phones:** Appraiser/Auditor- 229-928-4513; Elections- 229-928-4580; Vital Records- 229-924-3637 (Health Dept). **Property tax/Assessor-** 229-928-4513.

Talbot County

County Superior Court Clerk, PO Box 325, Talbotton, GA 31827-0325. 706-665-3239; fax-706-665-8637; hours: 9AM-5PM

Only the public may search. Copy fee $1.00 per page. Cert fee- $2.00 per doc, $.50 per page. Payee- Talbot County Clerk of the Superior Court. **Online access to RE Deed, Lien, UCC records:** See www.gsccca.org for Deed, Lien and UCC indexes. **Other phones:** Treasurer- 706-665-3240. **Property tax/Assessor-** 706-665-3377.

Taliaferro County

County Superior Court Clerk, PO Box 182, Crawfordville, GA 30631. RE & UCC recording phone-706-456-2123; fax-706-456-2749; hours: 9AM-N, 1-5PM

Separate indices to search include Deeds, Liens, and Plats. Records indexed. Only the public may search. Copy fee$.25 per page. Cert fee- $2.00 per doc plus $.25 per page. Payee- Taliaferro County

Clerk of the Superior Court. **Online access to RE Deed, Lien, UCC records:** See www.gsccca.org for Deed, Lien and UCC indexes. **Other phones:** Elections- 706-456-2253; Vital Records- 706-456-2316. **Property tax/Assessor-** 706-456-2717.

Tattnall County

County Superior Court Clerk, PO Box 39, Reidsville, GA 30453. RE & UCC recording phone-912-557-6716; fax-912-557-4552; hours: 8AM-4:30PM

Separate indices to search include real estate, federal tax liens, GED for liens. Only the public may search. Copy fee $1.00 per page. Cert fee- $3.00 per cert plus copy fee. Payee- Tattnall County Clerk of the Superior Court. **Online access to RE Deed, Lien, UCC records:** See www.gsccca.org for Deed, Lien and UCC indexes. **Other phones:** Appraiser/Auditor- 912-557-4010; Probate Court- 912-557-6917. **Property tax/Assessor-** 912-557-4010.

Taylor County

County Superior Court Clerk, PO Box 248, Butler, GA 31006. RE & UCC recording phone-478-862-5594; fax-478-862-5334; hours: 8AM-5PM

Separate indices to search include grantor/grantee, hosp lien, GED. Only the public may search. Copy fee $1.00 per page. RE record copy- $.25 per page. Cert fee- $2.00 per doc, $.50 per page plus copy fee. Payee- Taylor County Clerk of the Superior Court. **Online access to RE Deed, Lien, UCC records:** See www.gsccca.org for Deed, Lien and UCC indexes. **Other phones:** Vital Records- 478-862-3357. **Property tax/Assessor-** 478-862-3802.

Telfair County

County Superior Court Clerk, 128 E Oak St, #2; Courthouse, McRae, GA 31055-1604. RE & UCC recording phone-229-868-6525; fax-229-868-7956; hours: 8:30AM-4:30PM

Only the public may search. Copy fee $.25 per page. Cert fee- $3.00 per doc plus $.25 per page. Payee- Telfair County Clerk of the Superior Court. **Online access to RE Deed, UCC records:** See www.gsccca.org for Deed and UCC. **Other phones:** Appraiser/Auditor- 229-868-2896; Elections- 229-868-6038. **Property tax/Assessor-** 229-868-6772.

Terrell County

County Superior Court Clerk, PO Box 189, Dawson, GA 39842. 229-995-2631; hours: 8:30AM-5PM

All records in one index. Records indexed on a public use terminal back to 1995. Only the public may search. Copy fee $1.00 per page. Cert fee- $3.00 1st page, $.50 each add'l. Payee- Terrell County Clerk of the Superior Court. **Online access to RE Deed, Lien, UCC records:** See www.gsccca.org for Deed, Lien and UCC indexes. **Other phones:** Treasurer- 229-995-5151. **Property tax/Assessor-** 229-995-5210.

Thomas County

County Superior Court Clerk, PO Box 1995, Thomasville, GA 31799. 229-225-4108; fax-229-225-4110; hours: 8AM-5PM www.thomascoclerkofcourt.org

Only the public may search. Copy fee $1.00 per page. Cert fee- $2.00 per cert plus copy fee. Payee- Thomas County Clerk of the Superior Court. **Online access to RE Deed, UCC, Lien records:** See www.gsccca.org for Deed, Lien and UCC indexes. **Other phones:** Treasurer- 229-225-4133; Appraiser/Auditor- 229-225-4133; Elections- 229-225-4101; Vital Records- 229-226-4241. **Property tax/Assessor-** 229-225-4133.

Tift County

County Superior Court Clerk, PO Box 354, Tifton, GA 31793. 229-386-7810; fax-229-386-7807; hours: 9AM-5PM

Only the public may search. Copy fee $.25 per page. Cert fee- $2.50 per cert plus copy fee. Payee- Tift County Clerk of the Superior Court. **Online**

access to RE Deed, Lien, UCC records: See www.gsccca.org for Deed, Lien and UCC indexes. **Property tax/Assessor-** 229-386-7840.

Toombs County

County Superior Court Clerk, PO Drawer 530, Lyons, GA 30436. RE & UCC recording phone-912-526-3501; fax-912-526-1015; hours: 8:30AM-5PM

All records in one index. Only the public may search. Copy fee $1.00 per page. Cert fee- $2.00 per doc, $.50 per page plus copy fee. Payee- Toombs County Clerk of the Superior Court. **Online access to RE Deed, Lien, UCC records:** See www.gsccca.org for Deed, Lien and UCC indexes. **Other phones:** Treasurer- 912-526-8575; Appraiser/Auditor- 912-526-6291; Elections- 912-526-8696. **Property tax/Assessor-** 912-526-6291.

Towns County

County Superior Court Clerk, 48 River St.; Courthouse, #E, Hiawassee, GA 30546. RE & UCC recording phone-706-896-2130; fax-706-896-1772; hours: 8:30AM-4:30PM

All records in one index. Only the public may search. Copy fee $1.00 per page. Cert fee- $2.00 per doc, $.50 per page includes copy fee. Payee- Towns County Clerk of the Superior Court. **Online access to Real Estate, Deed, UCC records:** See www.gsccca.org for Deed, Lien and UCC indexes. **Other phones:** Treasurer- 706-896-2276; Appraiser/Auditor- 706-896-3984; Elections- 706-896-4353; Vital Records- 706-896-3467. **Property tax/Assessor-** 706-896-3984.

Treutlen County

County Superior Court Clerk, PO Box 356, Soperton, GA 30457. RE & UCC recording phone-912-529-4215; fax-912-529-6737; hours: 8AM-5PM

Records indexed on a public use terminal back to 2000. Only the public may search. Copy fee $.25 per page. Cert fee- $2.00 per doc, $.50 per page. Payee- Treutlen County Clerk of the Superior Court. **Online access to RE Deed, Lien, UCC records:** See www.gsccca.org for Deed, Lien and UCC indexes. **Other phones:** Elections- 912-529-3098. **Property tax/Assessor-** 912-529-4343.

Troup County

County Superior Court Clerk, PO Box 866, LaGrange, GA 30241-0866. RE & UCC recording phone-706-883-1740; hours: 8AM-5PM

Only the public may search. Copy fee $1.00 per page. Cert fee- $2.50 per doc, $.50 per page. Payee- Troup County Clerk of the Superior Court. **Online access to RE Deed, Lien, UCC records:** See www.gsccca.org for Deed, Lien and UCC indexes. **Other phones:** Treasurer- 706-883-1620. **Property tax/Assessor-** 706-883-1625.

Turner County

County Superior Court Clerk, PO Box 106, Ashburn, GA 31714. RE & UCC recording phone-229-567-2011; fax-229-567-0450; hours: 8AM-5PM

Only the public may search. Copy fee $1.00 per page. Cert fee- $2.50 1st page, $.50 each add'l. Payee- Turner County Clerk. **Online access to RE Deed, UCC records:** See www.gsccca.org for Deed and UCC indexes. **Other phones:** Treasurer- 229-567-4313; Appraiser/Auditor- 229-567-2334. **Property tax/Assessor-** 229-567-2334.

Twiggs County

County Superior Court Clerk, PO Box 228, Jeffersonville, GA 31044-0228. RE & UCC recording phone-478-945-3350; fax-478-945-6751; hours: 8AM-5PM

Only the public may search. Copy fee $.25 per page. Cert fee- $2.00 per doc, $.50 per page. Payee- Twiggs County Clerk of the Superior Court. **Online access to RE Deed, UCC records:** See www.gsccca.org for Deed and UCC indexes. **Other phones:** Treasurer- 478-945-3629; Appraiser/Auditor- 478-945-3663; Elections- 478-945-

3639; Vital Records- 478-945-3390. **Property tax/Assessor-** 478-945-3663.

Union County

County Superior Court Clerk, 114 Courthouse St #5, Blairsville, GA 30512. 706-439-6022; fax-706-439-6026; hours: 8AM-5PM
Only the public may search. Copy fee $.25 per page. Cert fee- $2.50 per cert plus copy fee. Payee-Union County Clerk of the Superior Court. **Online access to RE Deed, Lien, UCC records:** See www.gsccca.org for Deed, Lien and UCC indexes. **Other phones:** Treasurer- 706-439-6000. **Property tax/Assessor-** 706-439-6011.

Upson County

County Superior Court Clerk, PO Box 469, Thomaston, GA 30286. 706-647-7835; fax-706-647-8999; hours: 8AM-5PM
Separate indices to search include land records, liens, plats. Records indexed on computer back to 1998. Only the public may search. Copy fee $1.00 per page. Cert fee- $2.50 per doc, $.50 per page, plus copy fee. Payee- County Clerk of Superior Court. **Online access to RE Deed, Lien, UCC records:** See www.gsccca.org for Deed, Lien and UCC indexes. **Other phones:** Elections- 706-647-7015. **Property tax/Assessor-** same address as above. 706-647-8176.

Walker County

County Superior Court Clerk, PO Box 448, La Fayette, GA 30728. 706-638-1742, R/E recording phone-706-638-1780, UCC recording phone-706-638-1757; fax-706-638-1779; hours: 8AM-5PM
Separate indices to search. Records indexed on computer back to 1993. Only the public may search. Copy fee $1.00 per page. Cert fee- $2.00 per cert plus copy fee. Payee- Walker County Clerk of the Superior Court. **Online access to RE Deed, Lien, UCC records:** See www.gsccca.org for Deed, Lien and UCC indexes. **Other phones:** Treasurer- 706-638-2929; Elections- 706-638-4349. **Property tax/Assessor-** PO Box 1604, LaFayette, GA 30728; 706-638-2929.

Walton County

County Superior Court Clerk, 303 S. Hammond Dr #335, Monroe, GA 30655. RE & UCC phone-770-267-1307; fax-770-267-1441; hours: 8:30AM-5PM
Separate indices to search include real estate, grantor/grantee, plats, liens. Only the public may search. Copy fee $1.00 per page. Cert fee- $2.50 1st page, $.50 each add'l page plus copy fee. Payee- Walton County Clerk of the Superior Court. **Online access to RE Deed, UCC, Lien records:** See www.gsccca.org for Deed, Lien and UCC. **Property tax/Assessor-** 303 S. Hammond Dr #335, Monroe, GA 30655; 770-267-1352.

Ware County

County Superior Court Clerk, PO Box 776, Waycross, GA 31502-0776. 912-287-4340; fax-912-287-2498; hours: 9AM-5PM
Only the public may search. Copy fee $1.00 per page. Cert fee- $2.50 per cert plus copy fee. Payee-Ware County Clerk of the Superior Court. **Online access to RE Deed, Lien, UCC records:** See www.gsccca.org for Deed, Lien and UCC indexes. **Other phones:** Treasurer- 912-287-4305. **Property tax/Assessor-** 912-287-4383.

Warren County

County Superior Court Clerk, PO Box 227, Warrenton, GA 30828. RE & UCC recording phone-706-465-2262; fax-706-465-0232; hours: 8AM-N, 1-5PM
Separate indices to search include books, deeds, plat, UCCs indices. Records indexed on computer. Only the public may search. Copy fee $1.00 per page. RE or tax lien copy- $.25 per page. Cert fee-$2.50 per doc, $.50 add'l. Payee- Warren County Clerk of the Superior Court. **Online access to RE Deed, Lien, UCC records:** See www.gsccca.org for

Deed, Lien and UCC indexes. **Other phones:** Treasurer- 706-465-2171. **Property tax/Assessor-** 706-465-3321.

Washington County

County Superior Court Clerk, PO Box 231, Sandersville, GA 31082-0231. RE & UCC recording phone-478-552-3186; fax-478-553-9969; hours: 9AM-5PM
Separate indices to search. Records indexed on a public use terminal back to 1995. Only the public may search. Copy fee $1.00, if real estate $.25 per page. Cert fee- $2.00 per doc, $.50 per page. Payee- Washington County Clerk of the Superior Court. **Online access to RE Deed, Lien, UCC records:** See www.gsccca.org for Deed, Lien and UCC indexes. **Property tax/Assessor-** 478-552-2937.

Wayne County

County Superior Court Clerk, PO Box 920, Jesup, GA 31598-0920. RE & UCC recording phone-912-427-5930; fax-912-427-5939; hours: 8:30AM-5PM
Only the public may search. Copy fee $.25 per page. Cert fee- $2.00 per doc, $.50 per page. Payee- Wayne County Clerk of the Superior Court. **Online access to RE Deed, Lien, UCC records:** See www.gsccca.org for Deed, Lien and UCC indexes. **Other phones:** Treasurer- 706-427-5900. **Property tax/Assessor-** 912-427-5920.

Webster County

County Superior Court Clerk, PO Box 117, Preston, GA 31824. 229-828-3525; fax-229-828-6961; hours: 8AM-N, 12:30-4:30PM
Records indexed on a public use terminal back to 2002. Only the public may search. Copy fee $.25 per page. Cert fee- $2.50 1st page, $.50 each add'l. Payee- Webster County Clerk of the Superior Court. **Online access to RE Deed, UCC, Lien records:** See www.gsccca.org for Deed, Lien and UCC indexes. **Property tax/Assessor-** 229-828-3690.

Wheeler County

County Superior Court Clerk, PO Box 38, Alamo, GA 30411-0038. RE & UCC recording phone-912-568-7137; fax-912-568-7453; hours: 8AM-4PM
Separate indices to search include deeds, liens, plats. Only the public may search. Copy fee $1.00 per page; self serve $.25. Cert fee- $2.00 per doc, $.50 per page plus copy fee. Payee- Wheeler County Clerk of the Superior Court. **Online access to RE Deed, Lien, UCC records:** See www.gsccca.org for Deed, Lien and UCC indexes. **Other phones:** Treasurer- 912-568-7131; Elections- 912-568-7133; Vital Records- 912-568-7161. **Property tax/Assessor-** PO Box 149, Alamo, GA 30411; 912-568-7924.

White County

County Superior Court Clerk, 59 S. Main St; Courthouse, #B, Cleveland, GA 30528. RE & UCC recording phone-706-865-2613; fax-706-865-2613; hours: 8:30AM-5PM
Index: Indices are searchable by year. Records indexed on a public use terminal back to 1998. Only the public may search. Copy fee $1.00 per page. Cert fee- $2.50 per doc, $.50 per page, includes copy fee. Payee- White County Clerk of the Superior Court. **Online to RE Deed, Lien, UCC records:** See www.gsccca.org for Deed, Lien and UCC indexes. **Other phones:** Treasurer- 706-865-2225; Appraiser/Auditor- 706-865-5328; Elections-706-865-4141; Vital Records- 706-865-4141; **Property tax/Assessor-** 59 S. Main St #E, Cleveland, GA 30528; 706-865-5328.

Whitfield County

County Superior Court Clerk, PO Box 868, Dalton, GA 30722. 706-275-7450; fax-706-275-7456; hours: 8AM-5PM
Only the public may search. Copy fee $.25 per page. Cert fee- $3.00 per cert plus copy fee. Payee-Whitfield County Clerk of the Superior Court.

Online access to Assessor, Property Tax, RE Deed, Lien, UCC, Sex Offender records: See www.gsccca.org for Deed, Lien and UCC indexes. Also, access to property tax data is available free at www.whitfieldcountyga.com/GIS/Public/searchassessor.asp. A subscription service is also available for professions who require full property data. Also, a sex offender search is online at www.whitfieldcountyga.com/wcso/searchsexoffender.asp. **Other phones:** Treasurer- 706-275-7510. **Property tax/Assessor-** 706-275-7410.

Wilcox County

County Superior Court Clerk, 103 N Broad StCourthouse; Courthouse, Abbeville, GA 31001-1000. RE & UCC recording phone-229-467-2442; fax-229-467-2886; hours: 9AM-5PM
Separate indices to search include deed, lien, UCC, plat. Records indexed on a public use terminal back to 1993. Only the public may search. Copy fee $1.00 per page. Real estate or tax lien record copy- $.25 per page. Cert fee- $2.50 per doc, $.50 per add'l page, includes copy fee. Payee- County Clerk of Superior Court. **Online access to RE Deed, UCC, Lien, Plat records:** See www.gsccca.org for Deed, Lien and UCC indexes. **Other phones:** Treasurer- 229-467-2010; Appraiser/Auditor- 229-467-2028; Elections- 229-467-2300; Vital Records- 229-467-2220. **Property tax/Assessor-** 103 N. Broad St., Abbeville, GA 31001; 229-467-2428.

Wilkes County

County Superior Court Clerk, 23 E. Court St; Rm 205, Washington, GA 30673. RE & UCC recording phone-706-678-2423; fax-706-678-2115; hours: 9AM-5PM
Separate indices to search include deed, lien, plat. Records indexed on computer back to 1997. Only the public may search. Copy fee $.25 per page. Cert fee- $2.00 per doc and $.50 per page. Payee-Wilkes County Superior Court Clerk. **Online to RE Deed, Lien, UCC records:** See www.gsccca.org for Deed, UCC indexes, liens and plats. **Other phones:** Elections- 706-678-2523; Vital Records- 706-678-2523. **Property tax/Assessor-** 23 E Court St, Rm 202, Washington, GA 30673; 706-678-7732.

Wilkinson County

County Superior Court Clerk & Juvenile Court, PO Box 250, Irwinton, GA 31042-0250. RE & UCC recording phone-478-946-2221; fax-478-946-1497; hours: 8AM-5PM
Separate indices to search include liens, real estate, civil and criminal. Records indexed on a public use terminal back to 1989. Only the public may search. Copy fee $1.00 per page; self serve $.25. Cert fee- $2.00 per doc, $.50 per page plus copy fee. Payee- Wilkinson County Clerk of the Superior Court. **Online access to RE Deed, Lien, UCC records:** See www.gsccca.org for Deed, Lien and UCC indexes. **Other phones:** Treasurer- 478-946-2236; Appraiser/Auditor- 478-946-2076; Elections-478-946-2188; Vital Records- 478-946-2222; Tax Commisioner- 478-946-2232. **Property tax/Assessor-** PO Box 189, Irwinton, GA 31042 478-946-2076.

Worth County

County Superior Court Clerk, 201 N. Main St; Courthouse, Rm 13, Sylvester, GA 31791. RE & UCC recording phone-229-776-8205; fax-229-776-8237; hours: 8AM-5PM
Separate indices to search include books 1988-1993, books 1917-1988, liens, computer. Records indexed on computer back to 1996. Only the public may search. Copy fee $1.00 per page; self serve $.25. Cert fee- $2.50 per doc, $.50 per page, plus copy fee. Payee- Worth County Clerk of the Superior Court. **Online access to RE Deed, Lien, UCC records:** See www.gsccca.org for Deed, Lien and UCC indexes. **Other phones:** Elections- 229-776-8208; Vital Records- 229-776-8207; Tax Office- 229-776-8204. **Property tax/Assessor-** 229-776-8203.

Georgia County Locator

You will usually be able to find the city name in the City/County Cross Reference below. In that case, it is a simple matter to determine the county from the cross reference. However, only the official US Postal Service city names are included in this index. There are an additional 40,000 place names that people use in their addresses. Therefore, we have also included a ZIP/City Cross Reference immediately following the City/County Cross Reference.

If you know the ZIP Code but the city name does not appear in the City/County Cross Reference index, look up the ZIP Code in the ZIP/City Cross Reference, find the city name, then look up the city name in the City/County Cross Reference. For example, you want to know the county for an address of Menands, NY 12204. There is no "Menands" in the City/County Cross Reference. The ZIP/City Cross Reference shows that ZIP Codes 12201-12288 are for the city of Albany. Looking back in the City/County Cross Reference, Albany is in Albany County.

Georgia City/County Cross Reference

ABBEVILLE Wilcox
ACWORTH (30102) Cherokee(53), Bartow(25), Cobb(21),
ACWORTH (30101) Cobb(71), Paulding(23), Bartow(4)
ADAIRSVILLE (30103) Bartow(66), Gordon(25), Floyd(8)
ADEL Cook
ADRIAN (31002) Emanuel(54), Johnson(25), Laurens(14), Treutlen(6)
AILEY Montgomery
ALAMO (30411) Wheeler(69), Laurens(30)
ALAPAHA (31622) Berrien(95), Irwin(4)
ALBANY (31701) Dougherty(96), Lee(3)
ALBANY (31705) Dougherty(89), Worth(5), Mitchell(4)
ALBANY (31721) Dougherty(87), Lee(8), Baker(2), Terrell(1)
ALBANY Dougherty
ALLENHURST (31301) Liberty(76), Long(23)
ALLENTOWN Wilkinson
ALMA (31510) Bacon(95), Pierce(4)
ALPHARETTA (30005) Fulton(81), Forsyth(18)
ALPHARETTA Fulton
ALSTON Montgomery
ALTO (30510) Habersham(62), Banks(30), Hall(6)
ALTO Habersham
AMBROSE Coffee
AMERICUS (31719) Sumter(91), Schley(8)
AMERICUS Sumter
ANDERSONVILLE (31711) Macon(80), Sumter(16), Schley(2)
APPLING Columbia
ARABI (31712) Crisp(82), Turner(11), Worth(6)
ARAGON (30104) Polk(72), Floyd(24), Bartow(3)
ARGYLE Clinch
ARLINGTON (39813) Calhoun(58), Early(40)
ARMUCHEE (30105) Floyd(67), Chattooga(32)
ARNOLDSVILLE (30619) Oglethorpe(91), Oconee(8)
ASHBURN (31714) Turner(96), Worth(2)
ATHENS (30601) Clarke(95), Madison(3), Jackson(1)
ATHENS (30606) Clarke(88), Oconee(11)
ATHENS (30607) Jackson(59), Clarke(40)
ATHENS Clarke
ATLANTA (30339) Cobb(96), Fulton(3)
ATLANTA (30338) De Kalb(98), Fulton(1)
ATLANTA (30360) De Kalb(79), Gwinnett(20)
ATLANTA (30324) Fulton(83), De Kalb(16)
ATLANTA (30349) Fulton(65), Clayton(34)
ATLANTA (30350) Fulton(97), De Kalb(2)
ATLANTA (30354) Fulton(91), Clayton(8)
ATLANTA De Kalb
ATLANTA Fulton
ATTAPULGUS Decatur

AUBURN (30011) Barrow(78), Gwinnett(21)
AUBURN Barrow
AUGUSTA (30907) Columbia(73), Richmond(26)
AUGUSTA (30909) Richmond(98), Columbia(1)
AUGUSTA Columbia
AUGUSTA Richmond
AUSTELL (30168) Cobb(90), Douglas(9)
AVERA (30803) Jefferson(92), Glascock(7)
AVONDALE ESTATES De Kalb
AXSON (31624) Atkinson(68), Coffee(23), Ware(8)
BACONTON Mitchell
BAINBRIDGE Decatur
BALDWIN Banks
BALL GROUND (30107) Cherokee(80), Pickens(14), Forsyth(4)
BARNESVILLE (30204) Lamar(95), Upson(3)
BARNEY Brooks
BARTOW (30413) Jefferson(71), Washington(27), Johnson(1)
BARWICK Brooks
BAXLEY Appling
BELLVILLE Evans
BERLIN Colquitt
BETHLEHEM (30620) Barrow(73), Gwinnett(19), Walton(6)
BISHOP (30621) Oconee(73), Morgan(26)
BLACKSHEAR Pierce
BLAIRSVILLE (30512) Union(98), Fannin(1)
BLAIRSVILLE Union
BLAKELY (39823) Early(97), Miller(2)
BLOOMINGDALE (31302) Chatham(55), Effingham(44)
BLUE RIDGE (30513) Fannin(89), Gilmer(10)
BLUFFTON (31724) Clay(89), Early(10)
BLUFFTON (39824) Early(54), Clay(45)
BLYTHE (30805) Burke(54), Richmond(45)
BOGART (30622) Oconee(61), Clarke(30), Jackson(8)
BOLINGBROKE Monroe
BONAIRE Houston
BONEVILLE McDuffie
BOSTON (31626) Thomas(82), Brooks(17)
BOSTWICK Morgan
BOWDON (30108) Carroll(95), Heard(4)
BOWDON JUNCTION Carroll
BOWERSVILLE Hart
BOWMAN (30624) Elbert(74), Hart(14), Madison(10)
BOX SPRINGS (31801) Talbot(58), Marion(39), Muscogee(1)
BRASELTON (30517) Jackson(63), Gwinnett(14), Hall(13), Barrow(8)
BREMEN (30110) Haralson(92), Carroll(7)
BRINSON (39825) Decatur(90), Seminole(9)
BRINSON Decatur
BRISTOL (31518) Appling(56), Pierce(26), Wayne(14), Bacon(2)

BRONWOOD Terrell
BROOKFIELD Tift
BROOKLET Bulloch
BROOKS (30205) Spalding(52), Fayette(47)
BROXTON (31519) Coffee(97), Jeff Davis(2)
BRUNSWICK Glynn
BUCHANAN (30113) Haralson(87), Polk(12)
BUCKHEAD (30625) Morgan(95), Putnam(4)
BUENA VISTA (31803) Marion(94), Schley(4)
BUFORD (30519) Gwinnett(93), Hall(6)
BUFORD Gwinnett
BUTLER Taylor
BYROMVILLE Dooly
BYRON (31008) Peach(67), Crawford(23), Houston(9)
CADWELL Laurens
CAIRO Grady
CALHOUN (30701) Gordon(98), Floyd(1)
CALHOUN Gordon
CALVARY Grady
CAMAK Warren
CAMILLA (31730) Mitchell(98), Decatur(1)
CANON (30520) Hart(60), Franklin(39)
CANTON Cherokee
CARLTON (30627) Madison(71), Oglethorpe(28)
CARNESVILLE (30521) Franklin(96), Banks(3)
CARROLLTON Carroll
CARTERSVILLE Bartow
CASSVILLE Bartow
CATAULA Harris
CAVE SPRING Floyd
CECIL Cook
CEDAR SPRINGS Early
CEDARTOWN (30125) Polk(98), Floyd(1)
CENTERVILLE Houston
CHATSWORTH Murray
CHAUNCEY (31011) Dodge(98), Laurens(1)
CHERRYLOG (30522) Gilmer(57), Fannin(42)
CHESTER (31012) Dodge(89), Bleckley(9), Laurens(1)
CHESTNUT MOUNTAIN Hall
CHICKAMAUGA (30707) Walker(97), Catoosa(2)
CHULA (31733) Tift(54), Irwin(44)
CISCO Murray
CLARKDALE Cobb
CLARKESVILLE (30523) Habersham(89), Rabun(10)
CLARKSTON De Kalb
CLAXTON (30417) Evans(89), Tattnall(10)
CLAYTON (30525) Rabun(98), Towns(1)
CLERMONT (30527) Hall(89), White(10)
CLEVELAND (30528) White(96), Lumpkin(3)
CLIMAX Decatur
CLINCHFIELD Houston

CLYO Effingham
COBB Sumter
COBBTOWN (30420) Tattnall(92), Candler(6)
COCHRAN (31014) Bleckley(85), Twiggs(11), Dodge(2)
COCHRAN Putnam
COHUTTA Whitfield
COLBERT (30628) Madison(93), Oglethorpe(6)
COLEMAN (39836) Clay(68), Randolph(31)
COLEMAN (31736) Randolph(80), Clay(19)
COLLINS Tattnall
COLQUITT (31737) Miller(96), Baker(2)
COLQUITT (39837) Miller(80), Early(13), Decatur(3), Baker(2)
COLUMBUS Muscogee
COMER (30629) Madison(91), Oglethorpe(8)
COMMERCE (30530) Jackson(41), Banks(26), Madison(22), Franklin(9)
COMMERCE Jackson
CONCORD Pike
CONLEY (30288) De Kalb(52), Clayton(47)
CONLEY Clayton
CONYERS (30012) Rockdale(97), De Kalb(1)
CONYERS (30013) Rockdale(93), Newton(6)
CONYERS Rockdale
COOLIDGE (31738) Thomas(88), Colquitt(11)
COOSA Floyd
CORDELE Crisp
CORNELIA Habersham
COTTON Mitchell
COVINGTON (30014) Newton(89), Walton(9)
COVINGTON Newton
CRANDALL Murray
CRAWFORD Oglethorpe
CRAWFORDVILLE (30631) Taliaferro(91), Wilkes(7), Greene(1)
CRESCENT McIntosh
CULLODEN (31016) Monroe(52), Upson(28), Crawford(14), Lamar(4)
CUMMING (30040) Forsyth(95), Cherokee(4)
CUMMING Forsyth
CUSSETA (31805) Chattahoochee(98), Stewart(1)
CUTHBERT (39840) Randolph(89), Calhoun(10)
CUTHBERT Randolph
DACULA (30019) Gwinnett(98), Walton(1)
DACULA Gwinnett
DAHLONEGA Lumpkin
DAISY Evans
DALLAS (30157) Paulding(98), Cobb(1)
DALLAS Paulding
DALTON Whitfield
DAMASCUS (31741) Early(73), Baker(19), Miller(6)
DAMASCUS (39841) Early(95), Miller(2), Baker(1)

DANIELSVILLE (30633) Madison(98), Franklin(1)
DANVILLE (31017) Twiggs(76), Wilkinson(19), Bleckley(4)
DARIEN McIntosh
DAVISBORO Washington
DAWSON (39842) Terrell(93), Calhoun(6)
DAWSON Terrell
DAWSONVILLE (30534) Dawson(86), Lumpkin(10), Forsyth(2)
DE SOTO (31743) Sumter(65), Lee(34)
DEARING (30808) McDuffie(97), Warren(2)
DECATUR De Kalb
DEMOREST Habersham
DENTON (31532) Jeff Davis(97), Coffee(2)
DEWY ROSE (30634) Elbert(55), Hart(44)
DEXTER Laurens
DILLARD Rabun
DIXIE Brooks
DOERUN (31744) Colquitt(66), Worth(29), Mitchell(4)
DONALSONVILLE Seminole
DOUGLAS Coffee
DOUGLASVILLE (30134) Douglas(62), Paulding(37)
DOUGLASVILLE Douglas
DOVER Screven
DRY BRANCH (31020) Twiggs(95), Bibb(4)
DU PONT (31630) Clinch(74), Echols(25)
DUBLIN Laurens
DUDLEY (31022) Laurens(97), Bleckley(1), Dodge(1)
DULUTH (30097) Gwinnett(48), Fulton(45), Forsyth(5)
DULUTH Fulton
DULUTH Gwinnett
EAST ELLIJAY Gilmer
EASTANOLLEE (30538) Stephens(72), Franklin(27)
EASTMAN Dodge
EATONTON Putnam
EDEN Effingham
EDISON (39846) Calhoun(95), Clay(4)
ELBERTON (30635) Elbert(98), Hart(1)
ELKO Houston
ELLABELL (31308) Bryan(77), Bulloch(22)
ELLAVILLE (31806) Schley(90), Macon(8)
ELLENTON Colquitt
ELLENWOOD (30294) De Kalb(42), Clayton(34), Henry(23)
ELLENWOOD Gwinnett
ELLERSLIE Harris
ELLIJAY (30536) Gilmer(98), Dawson(1)
ELLIJAY Gilmer
EMERSON Bartow
ENIGMA (31749) Berrien(65), Tift(32), Irwin(1)
EPWORTH Fannin
ESOM HILL Polk
ETON Murray
EVANS Columbia
EXPERIMENT Spalding
FAIRBURN (30213) Fulton(86), Fayette(13)
FAIRMOUNT (30139) Gordon(60), Pickens(33), Bartow(5)
FARGO (31631) Clinch(78), Charlton(13), Echols(8)
FARMINGTON Oconee
FAYETTEVILLE (30215) Fayette(92), Clayton(7)
FAYETTEVILLE Fayette
FELTON Haralson
FITZGERALD (31750) Ben Hill(86), Irwin(13)
FLEMING Liberty
FLINTSTONE Walker
FLOVILLA Butts
FLOWERY BRANCH Hall
FOLKSTON (31537) Charlton(93), Camden(6)
FOREST PARK Clayton
FORSYTH Monroe

FORT BENNING (31905) Chattahoochee(59), Muscogee(40)
FORT BENNING Muscogee
FORT GAINES Clay
FORT OGLETHORPE Catoosa
FORT STEWART (31314) Liberty(97), Bryan(1)
FORT STEWART Liberty
FORT VALLEY (31030) Peach(76), Crawford(20), Macon(2), Houston(1)
FORTSON (31808) Harris(65), Muscogee(34)
FOWLSTOWN Decatur
FRANKLIN Heard
FRANKLIN SPRINGS Franklin
FUNSTON Colquitt
GAINESVILLE (30506) Hall(95), Forsyth(4)
GAINESVILLE Hall
GARFIELD (30425) Emanuel(38), Bulloch(38), Jenkins(23)
GAY Meriwether
GENEVA Talbot
GEORGETOWN (39854) Clay(51), Quitman(48)
GEORGETOWN (31754) Quitman(89), Clay(11)
GIBSON (30810) Glascock(86), Warren(11), Jefferson(1)
GILLSVILLE (30543) Hall(59), Banks(24), Jackson(15)
GIRARD (30426) Burke(81), Screven(18)
GLENN Heard
GLENNVILLE (30427) Tattnall(98), Long(1)
GLENWOOD (30428) Wheeler(73), Laurens(26)
GOOD HOPE (30641) Walton(82), Morgan(16)
GORDON (31031) Wilkinson(65), Twiggs(21), Baldwin(7), Jones(5)
GOUGH Burke
GRACEWOOD Richmond
GRANTVILLE (30220) Meriwether(54), Coweta(45)
GRAY Jones
GRAYSON Gwinnett
GRAYSVILLE Catoosa
GREENSBORO Greene
GREENVILLE (30222) Meriwether(98), Troup(1)
GRIFFIN (30224) Spalding(91), Pike(6), Lamar(2)
GRIFFIN Spalding
GROVETOWN (30813) Columbia(95), Richmond(4)
GUYTON Effingham
HADDOCK (31033) Jones(86), Baldwin(13)
HAGAN Evans
HAHIRA (31632) Lowndes(58), Cook(41)
HAMILTON Harris
HAMPTON (30228) Henry(60), Clayton(34), Spalding(4)
HARALSON Coweta
HARDWICK Baldwin
HARLEM (30814) Columbia(98), McDuffie(1)
HARRISON Washington
HARTSFIELD Colquitt
HARTWELL Hart
HAWKINSVILLE (31036) Pulaski(86), Houston(13)
HAZLEHURST (31539) Jeff Davis(94), Appling(4)
HELEN White
HELENA (31037) Telfair(88), Wheeler(9), Dodge(1)
HEPHZIBAH (30815) Richmond(79), Burke(20)
HIAWASSEE Towns
HIGH SHOALS Morgan
HILLSBORO (31038) Jasper(74), Jones(23), Putnam(2)
HINESVILLE (31313) Liberty(98), Long(1)

HINESVILLE Liberty
HIRAM (30141) Paulding(96), Cobb(3)
HOBOKEN Brantley
HOGANSVILLE (30230) Troup(64), Heard(17), Meriwether(17), Coweta(1)
HOLLY SPRINGS Cherokee
HOMER Banks
HOMERVILLE Clinch
HORTENSE (31543) Wayne(50), Brantley(43), Glynn(5)
HOSCHTON (30548) Jackson(78), Gwinnett(10), Barrow(8), Hall(2)
HOWARD Taylor
HULL (30646) Madison(97), Jackson(1), Clarke(1)
IDEAL Macon
ILA Madison
INMAN Fayette
IRON CITY (39859) Seminole(96), Miller(3)
IRWINTON Wilkinson
IRWINVILLE Irwin
JACKSON (30233) Butts(82), Monroe(10), Henry(3), Lamar(2)
JACKSONVILLE Telfair
JAKIN Early
JASPER (30143) Pickens(98), Cherokee(1)
JEFFERSON Jackson
JEFFERSONVILLE (31044) Twiggs(98), Wilkinson(1)
JEKYLL ISLAND Glynn
JEKYLL ISLAND BRANCH Glynn
JENKINSBURG (30234) Butts(84), Henry(14)
JERSEY Walton
JESUP Wayne
JEWELL (31045) Warren(96), Hancock(3)
JONESBORO (30236) Clayton(94), Henry(5)
JONESBORO (30238) Clayton(94), Fayette(5)
JONESBORO Clayton
JULIETTE (31046) Monroe(88), Jones(11)
JUNCTION CITY Talbot
KATHLEEN Houston
KENNESAW Cobb
KEYSVILLE (30816) Burke(73), Jefferson(26)
KINGS BAY Camden
KINGSLAND Camden
KINGSTON (30145) Bartow(56), Floyd(43)
KITE (31049) Johnson(60), Emanuel(39)
KNOXVILLE Crawford
LA FAYETTE Walker
LAGRANGE (30240) Troup(98), Heard(1)
LAGRANGE Troup
LAKE PARK (31636) Lowndes(60), Echols(39)
LAKELAND Lanier
LAKEMONT Rabun
LAVONIA (30553) Franklin(63), Hart(36)
LAWRENCEVILLE Gwinnett
LEARY (31762) Baker(50), Calhoun(50)
LEARY (39862) Calhoun(96), Baker(3)
LEBANON Cherokee
LEESBURG Lee
LENOX (31637) Cook(88), Colquitt(5), Berrien(3), Tift(1)
LESLIE (31764) Sumter(92), Lee(7)
LEXINGTON Oglethorpe
LILBURN Gwinnett
LILLY Dooly
LINCOLNTON (30817) Lincoln(96), McDuffie(1), Wilkes(1)
LINDALE (30147) Floyd(94), Polk(5)
LITHIA SPRINGS Douglas
LITHONIA De Kalb
LIZELLA (31052) Bibb(55), Crawford(44)
LOCUST GROVE (30248) Henry(93), Spalding(4), Butts(1)
LOGANVILLE (30052) Walton(57), Gwinnett(40), Rockdale(1)
LOGANVILLE Gwinnett

LOOKOUT MOUNTAIN (30750) Walker(66), Dade(33)
LOUISVILLE (30434) Jefferson(96), Burke(3)
LOUVALE Stewart
LOVEJOY Clayton
LUDOWICI (31316) Long(98), Liberty(1)
LULA (30554) Hall(59), Banks(40)
LUMBER CITY (31549) Telfair(82), Wheeler(17)
LUMPKIN Stewart
LUTHERSVILLE Meriwether
LYERLY Chattooga
LYONS (30436) Toombs(89), Emanuel(5), Tattnall(5)
MABLETON Cobb
MACON (31210) Bibb(90), Monroe(9)
MACON (31211) Bibb(58), Jones(41)
MACON (31217) Bibb(51), Twiggs(37), Jones(10)
MACON (31220) Bibb(80), Monroe(19)
MACON Bibb
MADISON (30650) Morgan(93), Greene(5), Walton(1)
MANASSAS Tattnall
MANCHESTER (31816) Meriwether(90), Talbot(9)
MANOR Ware
MANSFIELD (30055) Jasper(49), Newton(44), Morgan(5)
MANSFIELD Jasper
MARBLE HILL (30148) Pickens(70), Dawson(29)
MARIETTA Cobb
MARSHALLVILLE Macon
MARTIN (30557) Franklin(55), Stephens(44)
MATTHEWS Jefferson
MAUK (31058) Taylor(47), Marion(45), Schley(6)
MAXEYS Oglethorpe
MAYSVILLE (30558) Jackson(53), Banks(46)
MC CAYSVILLE Fannin
MC INTYRE Wilkinson
MC RAE Telfair
MCDONOUGH (30252) Henry(98), Rockdale(1)
MCDONOUGH Henry
MEANSVILLE (30256) Pike(57), Upson(40), Lamar(2)
MEIGS (31765) Mitchell(42), Thomas(33), Colquitt(24)
MELDRIM Effingham
MENLO (30731) Chattooga(60), Walker(25), Dade(14)
MERIDIAN McIntosh
MERSHON (31551) Pierce(58), Bacon(41)
MESENA Warren
METTER Candler
MIDLAND (31820) Muscogee(65), Harris(34)
MIDVILLE (30441) Burke(49), Emanuel(49), Jenkins(1)
MIDWAY Liberty
MILAN (31060) Dodge(76), Telfair(23)
MILLEDGEVILLE (31061) Baldwin(94), Putnam(3), Wilkinson(1), Hancock(1)
MILLEDGEVILLE Baldwin
MILLEN (30442) Jenkins(93), Burke(4), Screven(1)
MILLWOOD (31552) Ware(67), Atkinson(28), Coffee(4)
MILNER (30257) Lamar(87), Pike(12)
MINERAL BLUFF Fannin
MITCHELL (30820) Glascock(47), Warren(45), Washington(6)
MOLENA (30258) Pike(72), Upson(27)
MONROE Walton
MONTEZUMA (31063) Dooly(67), Macon(32)
MONTICELLO Jasper

MONTROSE (31065) Laurens(87), Bleckley(8), Wilkinson(3)
MOODY A F B Lowndes
MORELAND Coweta
MORGAN Calhoun
MORGANTON (30560) Fannin(83), Union(16)
MORRIS (39867) Clay(83), Randolph(8), Quitman(5), Stewart(2)
MORRIS (31767) Quitman(60), Clay(29), Randolph(4), Stewart(4)
MORROW Clayton
MORVEN Brooks
MOULTRIE Colquitt
MOUNT AIRY Habersham
MOUNT BERRY Floyd
MOUNT VERNON Montgomery
MOUNT ZION Carroll
MOUNTAIN CITY Rabun
MURRAYVILLE (30564) Lumpkin(61), Hall(33), White(5)
MUSELLA (31066) Crawford(94), Monroe(3), Bibb(2)
MYSTIC Irwin
NAHUNTA (31553) Brantley(97), Charlton(2)
NASHVILLE Berrien
NAYLOR (31641) Lowndes(78), Lanier(21)
NELSON Cherokee
NEWBORN (30056) Jasper(56), Newton(22), Morgan(20)
NEWBORN Newton
NEWINGTON (30446) Screven(67), Effingham(32)
NEWNAN Coweta
NEWTON Baker
NICHOLLS (31554) Coffee(67), Bacon(22), Ware(9)
NICHOLSON (30565) Jackson(85), Madison(14)
NORCROSS (30092) Gwinnett(97), Fulton(2)
NORCROSS Gwinnett
NORMAN PARK (31771) Colquitt(97), Worth(2)
NORRISTOWN Emanuel
NORTH METRO Gwinnett
NORWOOD Warren
NUNEZ Emanuel
OAKFIELD Worth
OAKMAN Gordon
OAKWOOD Hall
OCHLOCKNEE (31773) Thomas(79), Grady(18), Colquitt(1)
OCILLA Irwin
OCONEE Washington
ODUM (31555) Wayne(85), Appling(14)
OFFERMAN Pierce
OGLETHORPE Macon
OLIVER Screven
OMAHA Stewart
OMEGA (31775) Colquitt(58), Tift(24), Worth(17)
ORCHARD HILL Spalding
OXFORD (30054) Newton(84), Walton(15)
OXFORD Newton
PALMETTO (30268) Fulton(81), Coweta(18)
PARROTT (31777) Terrell(81), Webster(18)
PARROTT (39877) Webster(81), Terrell(18)
PATTERSON (31557) Pierce(95), Appling(3)
PAVO (31778) Brooks(69), Thomas(28), Colquitt(1)
PEACHTREE CITY Fayette
PEARSON (31642) Atkinson(91), Coffee(5), Clinch(2)
PELHAM (31779) Mitchell(82), Grady(16)
PEMBROKE (31321) Bryan(54), Bulloch(45)

PENDERGRASS (30567) Jackson(74), Hall(25)
PERKINS (30822) Jenkins(96), Burke(3)
PERRY (31069) Houston(97), Peach(2)
PINE LAKE De Kalb
PINE MOUNTAIN (31822) Harris(67), Troup(24), Meriwether(8)
PINE MOUNTAIN VALLEY Harris
PINEHURST Dooly
PINEVIEW (31071) Wilcox(94), Pulaski(5)
PITTS (31072) Crisp(52), Wilcox(47)
PLAINFIELD Dodge
PLAINS (31780) Sumter(74), Webster(25)
PLAINVILLE (30733) Gordon(93), Floyd(6)
POOLER Chatham
PORTAL (30450) Bulloch(98), Emanuel(1)
PORTERDALE Fayette
PORTERDALE Newton
POULAN Worth
POWDER SPRINGS (30127) Cobb(80), Paulding(19)
POWDER SPRINGS Cobb
PRESTON Webster
PULASKI Candler
PUTNEY Dougherty
QUITMAN Brooks
RABUN GAP Rabun
RANGER (30734) Gordon(76), Pickens(23)
RAY CITY (31645) Berrien(51), Lowndes(26), Lanier(22)
RAYLE (30660) Wilkes(80), Oglethorpe(16), Taliaferro(3)
REBECCA (31783) Turner(60), Irwin(30), Ben Hill(9)
RED OAK Fulton
REDAN De Kalb
REGISTER (30452) Bulloch(97), Evans(1)
REIDSVILLE Tattnall
RENTZ Laurens
RESACA (30735) Gordon(63), Murray(22), Whitfield(14)
REX (30273) Clayton(92), Henry(7)
REYNOLDS (31076) Macon(69), Taylor(30)
RHINE (31077) Dodge(94), Telfair(5)
RICEBORO (31323) Liberty(94), McIntosh(5)
RICHLAND (31825) Webster(74), Stewart(24)
RICHMOND HILL Bryan
RINCON Effingham
RINGGOLD (30736) Catoosa(97), Walker(2)
RISING FAWN (30738) Dade(69), Walker(30)
RIVERDALE (30296) Clayton(81), Fulton(11), Fayette(6)
RIVERDALE Clayton
ROBERTA Crawford
ROCHELLE Wilcox
ROCK SPRING (30739) Walker(82), Catoosa(17)
ROCKLEDGE Laurens
ROCKMART (30153) Polk(65), Paulding(30), Haralson(4)
ROCKY FACE (30740) Whitfield(87), Walker(12)
ROCKY FORD (30455) Screven(98), Jenkins(1)
ROME Floyd
ROOPVILLE (30170) Heard(62), Carroll(37)
ROSSVILLE (30741) Walker(66), Catoosa(33)
ROSWELL (30075) Fulton(82), Cobb(15), Cherokee(1)
ROSWELL Fulton
ROYSTON (30662) Franklin(56), Hart(27), Madison(14), Elbert(1)
RUPERT (31081) Taylor(96), Macon(1), Schley(1)
RUTLEDGE Morgan
RYDAL (30171) Bartow(79), Gordon(20)

SAINT GEORGE Charlton
SAINT MARYS Camden
SAINT SIMONS ISLAND Glynn
SALE CITY (31784) Mitchell(95), Colquitt(4)
SANDERSVILLE Washington
SAPELO ISLAND McIntosh
SARDIS Burke
SARGENT Coweta
SASSER Terrell
SAUTEE NACOOCHEE (30571) White(97), Habersham(2)
SAVANNAH Chatham
SCOTLAND Telfair
SCOTTDALE De Kalb
SCREVEN Wayne
SEA ISLAND Glynn
SEA ISLAND BRANCH Glynn
SENOIA (30276) Coweta(82), Meriwether(12), Fayette(5)
SEVILLE Wilcox
SHADY DALE Jasper
SHANNON Floyd
SHARON Taliaferro
SHARPSBURG Coweta
SHELLMAN (31786) Randolph(95), Terrell(2), Calhoun(1)
SHELLMAN (39886) Randolph(63), Calhoun(34), Terrell(1)
SHILOH (31826) Talbot(63), Harris(36)
SILOAM Greene
SILVER CREEK (30173) Floyd(92), Polk(7)
SMARR Monroe
SMITHVILLE (31787) Lee(60), Sumter(39)
SMYRNA Cobb
SNELLVILLE (30039) Gwinnett(95), De Kalb(2), Rockdale(1)
SNELLVILLE Gwinnett
SOCIAL CIRCLE (30025) Walton(74), Newton(25)
SOCIAL CIRCLE Walton
SOPERTON (30457) Treutlen(94), Montgomery(3), Emanuel(1)
SPARKS Cook
SPARTA (31087) Hancock(95), Baldwin(3), Washington(1)
SPRINGFIELD Effingham
STAPLETON (30823) Warren(50), Jefferson(48)
STATENVILLE Echols
STATESBORO Bulloch
STATHAM (30666) Barrow(66), Oconee(25), Jackson(7)
STEPHENS Oglethorpe
STILLMORE Emanuel
STOCKBRIDGE (30281) Henry(88), Rockdale(5), Clayton(5)
STOCKTON (31649) Lanier(77), Echols(17), Clinch(5)
STONE MOUNTAIN (30087) De Kalb(57), Gwinnett(42)
STONE MOUNTAIN De Kalb
SUCHES (30572) Union(75), Fannin(24)
SUGAR VALLEY (30746) Gordon(96), Walker(3)
SUMMERTOWN Emanuel
SUMMERVILLE (30747) Chattooga(96), Walker(3)
SUMNER Worth
SUNNY SIDE Spalding
SURRENCY Appling
SUWANEE (30024) Gwinnett(72), Forsyth(25), Fulton(2)
SUWANEE Gwinnett
SWAINSBORO Emanuel
SYCAMORE (31790) Turner(98), Irwin(1)
SYLVANIA Screven
SYLVESTER (31791) Worth(98), Dougherty(1)
TALBOTTON Talbot
TALKING ROCK (30175) Pickens(62), Gilmer(37)

TALLAPOOSA Haralson
TALLULAH FALLS Rabun
TALMO (30575) Jackson(74), Hall(25)
TARRYTOWN (30470) Montgomery(83), Treutlen(16)
TATE Pickens
TAYLORSVILLE (30178) Bartow(81), Polk(17), Paulding(1)
TEMPLE (30179) Carroll(50), Paulding(32), Haralson(17)
TENNGA Murray
TENNILLE (31089) Washington(98), Johnson(1)
THE ROCK (30285) Upson(61), Pike(20), Lamar(18)
THOMASTON Upson
THOMASVILLE (31792) Thomas(97), Grady(2)
THOMASVILLE Thomas
THOMSON (30824) McDuffie(96), Warren(1), Columbia(1)
TIFTON Tift
TIGER Rabun
TIGNALL (30668) Wilkes(82), Lincoln(17)
TOCCOA (30577) Stephens(69), Franklin(22), Habersham(6), Banks(1)
TOCCOA Stephens
TOOMSBORO Wilkinson
TOWNSEND McIntosh
TRENTON Dade
TRION (30753) Chattooga(77), Walker(22)
TUCKER (30084) De Kalb(78), Gwinnett(21)
TUCKER De Kalb
TUNNEL HILL (30755) Whitfield(53), Catoosa(46)
TURIN Coweta
TURNERVILLE Habersham
TWIN CITY (30471) Emanuel(85), Bulloch(13), Candler(1)
TY TY (31795) Worth(56), Tift(43)
TYBEE ISLAND Chatham
TYRONE Fayette
UNADILLA (31091) Dooly(98), Houston(1)
UNION CITY Fulton
UNION POINT (30669) Greene(88), Oglethorpe(10)
UPATOI (31829) Muscogee(71), Harris(28)
UVALDA (30473) Toombs(61), Montgomery(38)
VALDOSTA (31605) Lowndes(97), Brooks(2)
VALDOSTA Lowndes
VALONA McIntosh
VARNELL Whitfield
VIDALIA (30474) Toombs(87), Montgomery(11), Emanuel(1)
VIDALIA Toombs
VIENNA (31092) Dooly(96), Crisp(3)
VILLA RICA (30180) Carroll(70), Douglas(20), Paulding(8)
WACO (30182) Carroll(62), Haralson(37)
WADLEY Jefferson
WALESKA Cherokee
WALTHOURVILLE Liberty
WARESBORO Ware
WARM SPRINGS (31830) Meriwether(96), Harris(3)
WARNER ROBINS Houston
WARRENTON Warren
WARTHEN Washington
WARWICK (31796) Worth(98), Crisp(1)
WASHINGTON Wilkes
WATKINSVILLE (30677) Oconee(96), Greene(3)
WAVERLY Camden
WAVERLY HALL (31831) Talbot(55), Harris(44)
WAYCROSS (31503) Ware(94), Brantley(4), Pierce(1)
WAYCROSS Ware
WAYNESBORO Burke

WAYNESVILLE (31566) Brantley(56), Camden(38), Glynn(4)
WEST GREEN (31567) Jeff Davis(58), Coffee(41)
WEST POINT (31833) Troup(70), Harris(29)
WESTON Webster
WHIGHAM Grady
WHITE (30184) Bartow(70), Cherokee(29)
WHITE OAK Camden

WHITE PLAINS (30678) Greene(96), Hancock(1), Taliaferro(1)
WHITESBURG (30185) Carroll(95), Douglas(4)
WILDWOOD Dade
WILEY Rabun
WILLACOOCHEE (31650) Coffee(70), Atkinson(28)
WILLIAMSON (30292) Pike(68), Spalding(31)

WINDER (30680) Barrow(98), Oconee(1)
WINSTON Douglas
WINTERVILLE (30683) Clarke(60), Oglethorpe(37), Madison(2)
WOODBINE Camden
WOODBURY Meriwether
WOODLAND Talbot
WOODSTOCK (30188) Cherokee(97), Cobb(2)
WOODSTOCK Cherokee

WRAY (31798) Irwin(50), Coffee(41), Ben Hill(7)
WRENS Jefferson
WRIGHTSVILLE (31096) Johnson(84), Washington(10), Laurens(5)
YATESVILLE (31097) Upson(89), Lamar(7), Monroe(3)
YOUNG HARRIS (30582) Towns(78), Union(21)
ZEBULON (30295) Pike(97), Lamar(2)

Georgia ZIP/City Cross Reference

Note: In 2003, a number of Georgia Zip Codes were changed. This change affected 31 Zip Codes (listed below) beginning with 317. These 31 Zip Codes now begin with 398. The locations (and county in parenthesis) are: ARLINGTON (Calhoun), ATTAPULGUS (Decatur), BAINBRIDGE (Decatur), BLAKELY (Early), BLUFFTON (Clay), BRINSON (Decatur), BRONWOOD (Terrell), CAIRO (Grady), CALVARY (Grady), CEDAR SPRINGS (Early), CLIMAX (Decatur), COLEMAN (Randolph), COLQUITT (Miller), CUTHBERT (Randolph), DAMASCUS (Early), DAWSON (Terrell), DONALSONVILLE (Seminole), EDISON (Calhoun), FORT GAINES (Clay), FOWLSTOWN (Decatur), GEORGETOWN (Quitman), IRON CITY (Seminole), JAKIN (Early), LEARY (Calhoun), MORGAN (Calhoun), MORRIS (Quitman), NEWTON (Baker), PARROTT (Terrell), SASSER (Terrell), SHELLMAN (Randolph), WHIGHAM (Grady). There is one new Zip Code for Atlanta - 39901.

30001-30001 AUSTELL	30090-30090 MARIETTA	30161-30165 ROME	30248-30248 LOCUST GROVE
30002-30002 AVONDALE ESTATES	30091-30093 NORCROSS	30168-30168 AUSTELL	30249-30249 LOGANVILLE
30003-30003 NORCROSS	30094-30094 CONYERS	30169-30169 CANTON	30250-30250 LOVEJOY
30004-30005 ALPHARETTA	30095-30099 DULUTH	30170-30170 ROOPVILLE	30251-30251 LUTHERSVILLE
30006-30008 MARIETTA	30101-30102 ACWORTH	30171-30171 RYDAL	30252-30253 MCDONOUGH
30009-30009 ALPHARETTA	30103-30103 ADAIRSVILLE	30172-30172 SHANNON	30254-30254 NEWNAN
30010-30010 NORCROSS	30104-30104 ARAGON	30173-30173 SILVER CREEK	30255-30255 MANSFIELD
30011-30011 AUBURN	30105-30105 ARMUCHEE	30174-30174 SUWANEE	30256-30256 MEANSVILLE
30012-30013 CONYERS	30106-30106 AUSTELL	30175-30175 TALKING ROCK	30257-30257 MILNER
30014-30016 COVINGTON	30107-30107 BALL GROUND	30176-30176 TALLAPOOSA	30258-30258 MOLENA
30017-30017 GRAYSON	30108-30108 BOWDON	30177-30177 TATE	30259-30259 MORELAND
30018-30018 JERSEY	30109-30109 BOWDON JUNCTION	30178-30178 TAYLORSVILLE	30260-30260 MORROW
30019-30019 DACULA	30110-30110 BREMEN	30179-30179 TEMPLE	30261-30261 LAGRANGE
30020-30020 CLARKDALE	30111-30111 CLARKDALE	30180-30180 VILLA RICA	30262-30262 NEWBORN
30021-30021 CLARKSTON	30112-30112 CARROLLTON	30182-30182 WACO	30263-30265 NEWNAN
30022-30023 ALPHARETTA	30113-30113 BUCHANAN	30183-30183 WALESKA	30266-30266 ORCHARD HILL
30024-30024 SUWANEE	30114-30115 CANTON	30184-30184 WHITE	30267-30267 OXFORD
30025-30025 SOCIAL CIRCLE	30116-30119 CARROLLTON	30185-30185 WHITESBURG	30268-30268 PALMETTO
30026-30026 DULUTH	30120-30121 CARTERSVILLE	30187-30187 WINSTON	30269-30269 PEACHTREE CITY
30026-30026 NORTH METRO	30122-30122 LITHIA SPRINGS	30188-30189 WOODSTOCK	30270-30270 PORTERDALE
30027-30027 CONLEY	30123-30123 CASSVILLE	30195-30199 DULUTH	30270-30270 PEACHTREE CITY
30028-30028 CUMMING	30124-30124 CAVE SPRING	30201-30202 ALPHARETTA	30271-30271 NEWNAN
30029-30029 DULUTH	30125-30125 CEDARTOWN	30203-30203 AUBURN	30272-30272 RED OAK
30029-30029 NORTH METRO	30126-30126 MABLETON	30204-30204 BARNESVILLE	30273-30273 REX
30030-30037 DECATUR	30127-30127 POWDER SPRINGS	30205-30205 BROOKS	30274-30274 RIVERDALE
30038-30038 LITHONIA	30128-30128 CUMMING	30206-30206 CONCORD	30275-30275 SARGENT
30039-30039 SNELLVILLE	30129-30129 COOSA	30207-30208 CONYERS	30276-30276 SENOIA
30040-30041 CUMMING	30130-30131 CUMMING	30209-30210 COVINGTON	30277-30277 SHARPSBURG
30042-30046 LAWRENCEVILLE	30132-30132 DALLAS	30211-30211 DACULA	30278-30278 SNELLVILLE
30047-30048 LILBURN	30133-30135 DOUGLASVILLE	30212-30212 EXPERIMENT	30279-30279 SOCIAL CIRCLE
30049-30049 ELLENWOOD	30136-30136 DULUTH	30213-30213 FAIRBURN	30281-30281 STOCKBRIDGE
30049-30049 LAWRENCEVILLE	30137-30137 EMERSON	30214-30215 FAYETTEVILLE	30284-30284 SUNNY SIDE
30050-30051 FOREST PARK	30138-30138 ESOM HILL	30216-30216 FLOVILLA	30285-30285 THE ROCK
30052-30052 LOGANVILLE	30139-30139 FAIRMOUNT	30217-30217 FRANKLIN	30286-30286 THOMASTON
30054-30054 OXFORD	30140-30140 FELTON	30218-30218 GAY	30287-30287 MORROW
30055-30055 MANSFIELD	30141-30141 HIRAM	30219-30219 GLENN	30288-30288 CONLEY
30056-30056 NEWBORN	30142-30142 HOLLY SPRINGS	30220-30220 GRANTVILLE	30289-30289 TURIN
30057-30057 LITHIA SPRINGS	30143-30143 JASPER	30221-30221 GRAYSON	30290-30290 TYRONE
30058-30058 LITHONIA	30144-30144 KENNESAW	30222-30222 GREENVILLE	30291-30291 UNION CITY
30059-30059 MABLETON	30145-30145 KINGSTON	30223-30224 GRIFFIN	30292-30292 WILLIAMSON
30060-30069 MARIETTA	30146-30146 LEBANON	30226-30226 LILBURN	30293-30293 WOODBURY
30070-30070 PORTERDALE	30147-30147 LINDALE	30227-30227 LAWRENCEVILLE	30294-30294 ELLENWOOD
30071-30071 NORCROSS	30148-30148 MARBLE HILL	30228-30228 HAMPTON	30295-30295 ZEBULON
30072-30072 PINE LAKE	30149-30149 MOUNT BERRY	30229-30229 HARALSON	30296-30296 RIVERDALE
30073-30073 POWDER SPRINGS	30150-30150 MOUNT ZION	30230-30230 HOGANSVILLE	30297-30298 FOREST PARK
30074-30074 REDAN	30151-30151 NELSON	30232-30232 INMAN	30301-30399 ATLANTA
30075-30077 ROSWELL	30152-30152 KENNESAW	30233-30233 JACKSON	30401-30401 SWAINSBORO
30078-30078 SNELLVILLE	30153-30153 ROCKMART	30234-30234 JENKINSBURG	30410-30410 AILEY
30079-30079 SCOTTDALE	30154-30154 DOUGLASVILLE	30235-30235 JERSEY	30411-30411 ALAMO
30080-30082 SMYRNA	30155-30155 DULUTH	30236-30238 JONESBORO	30412-30412 ALSTON
30083-30083 STONE MOUNTAIN	30156-30156 KENNESAW	30239-30239 ALPHARETTA	30413-30413 BARTOW
30084-30085 TUCKER	30157-30157 DALLAS	30240-30241 LAGRANGE	30414-30414 BELLVILLE
30086-30088 STONE MOUNTAIN	30158-30159 NORTH METRO	30243-30246 LAWRENCEVILLE	30415-30415 BROOKLET
30089-30089 DECATUR	30160-30160 KENNESAW	30247-30247 LILBURN	30417-30417 CLAXTON

30420-30420	COBBTOWN
30421-30421	COLLINS
30423-30423	DAISY
30424-30424	DOVER
30425-30425	GARFIELD
30426-30426	GIRARD
30427-30427	GLENNVILLE
30428-30428	GLENWOOD
30429-30429	HAGAN
30434-30434	LOUISVILLE
30436-30436	LYONS
30438-30438	MANASSAS
30439-30439	METTER
30441-30441	MIDVILLE
30442-30442	MILLEN
30445-30445	MOUNT VERNON
30446-30446	NEWINGTON
30447-30447	NORRISTOWN
30448-30448	NUNEZ
30449-30449	OLIVER
30450-30450	PORTAL
30451-30451	PULASKI
30452-30452	REGISTER
30453-30453	REIDSVILLE
30454-30454	ROCKLEDGE
30455-30455	ROCKY FORD
30456-30456	SARDIS
30457-30457	SOPERTON
30458-30461	STATESBORO
30464-30464	STILLMORE
30466-30466	SUMMERTOWN
30467-30467	SYLVANIA
30470-30470	TARRYTOWN
30471-30471	TWIN CITY
30473-30473	UVALDA
30474-30475	VIDALIA
30477-30477	WADLEY
30499-30499	REIDSVILLE
30501-30501	GAINESVILLE
30502-30502	CHESTNUT MOUNTAIN
30503-30507	GAINESVILLE
30510-30510	ALTO
30511-30511	BALDWIN
30512-30512	BLAIRSVILLE
30513-30513	BLUE RIDGE
30514-30514	BLAIRSVILLE
30515-30515	BUFORD
30516-30516	BOWERSVILLE
30517-30517	BRASELTON
30518-30519	BUFORD
30520-30520	CANON
30521-30521	CARNESVILLE
30522-30522	CHERRYLOG
30523-30523	CLARKESVILLE
30525-30525	CLAYTON
30527-30527	CLERMONT
30528-30528	CLEVELAND
30529-30530	COMMERCE
30531-30531	CORNELIA
30533-30533	DAHLONEGA
30534-30534	DAWSONVILLE
30535-30535	DEMOREST
30536-30536	ELLIJAY
30537-30537	DILLARD
30538-30538	EASTANOLLEE
30539-30539	EAST ELLIJAY
30540-30540	ELLIJAY
30541-30541	EPWORTH
30542-30542	FLOWERY BRANCH
30543-30543	GILLSVILLE
30544-30544	DEMOREST
30545-30545	HELEN
30546-30546	HIAWASSEE
30547-30547	HOMER
30548-30548	HOSCHTON
30549-30549	JEFFERSON
30552-30552	LAKEMONT
30553-30553	LAVONIA
30554-30554	LULA
30555-30555	MC CAYSVILLE
30557-30557	MARTIN
30558-30558	MAYSVILLE
30559-30559	MINERAL BLUFF
30560-30560	MORGANTON
30562-30562	MOUNTAIN CITY
30563-30563	MOUNT AIRY
30564-30564	MURRAYVILLE
30565-30565	NICHOLSON
30566-30566	OAKWOOD
30567-30567	PENDERGRASS
30568-30568	RABUN GAP
30571-30571	SAUTEE NACOOCHEE
30572-30572	SUCHES
30573-30573	TALLULAH FALLS
30575-30575	TALMO
30576-30576	TIGER
30577-30577	TOCCOA
30580-30580	TURNERVILLE
30581-30581	WILEY
30582-30582	YOUNG HARRIS
30596-30596	ALTO
30597-30597	DAHLONEGA
30598-30598	TOCCOA
30599-30599	COMMERCE
30601-30613	ATHENS
30619-30619	ARNOLDSVILLE
30620-30620	BETHLEHEM
30621-30621	BISHOP
30622-30622	BOGART
30623-30623	BOSTWICK
30624-30624	BOWMAN
30625-30625	BUCKHEAD
30627-30627	CARLTON
30628-30628	COLBERT
30629-30629	COMER
30630-30630	CRAWFORD
30631-30631	CRAWFORDVILLE
30633-30633	DANIELSVILLE
30634-30634	DEWY ROSE
30635-30635	ELBERTON
30638-30638	FARMINGTON
30639-30639	FRANKLIN SPRINGS
30641-30641	GOOD HOPE
30642-30642	GREENSBORO
30643-30643	HARTWELL
30645-30645	HIGH SHOALS
30646-30646	HULL
30647-30647	ILA
30648-30648	LEXINGTON
30650-30650	MADISON
30655-30656	MONROE
30660-30660	RAYLE
30662-30662	ROYSTON
30663-30663	RUTLEDGE
30664-30664	SHARON
30665-30665	SILOAM
30666-30666	STATHAM
30667-30667	STEPHENS
30668-30668	TIGNALL
30669-30669	UNION POINT
30671-30671	MAXEYS
30673-30673	WASHINGTON
30677-30677	WATKINSVILLE
30678-30678	WHITE PLAINS
30680-30680	WINDER
30683-30683	WINTERVILLE
30701-30703	CALHOUN
30705-30705	CHATSWORTH
30707-30707	CHICKAMAUGA
30708-30708	CISCO
30710-30710	COHUTTA
30711-30711	CRANDALL
30719-30722	DALTON
30724-30724	ETON
30725-30725	FLINTSTONE
30726-30726	GRAYSVILLE
30728-30728	LA FAYETTE
30730-30730	LYERLY
30731-30731	MENLO
30732-30732	OAKMAN
30733-30733	PLAINVILLE
30734-30734	RANGER
30735-30735	RESACA
30736-30736	RINGGOLD
30738-30738	RISING FAWN
30739-30739	ROCK SPRING
30740-30740	ROCKY FACE
30741-30741	ROSSVILLE
30742-30742	FORT OGLETHORPE
30746-30746	SUGAR VALLEY
30747-30747	SUMMERVILLE
30750-30750	LOOKOUT MOUNTAIN
30751-30751	TENNGA
30752-30752	TRENTON
30753-30753	TRION
30755-30755	TUNNEL HILL
30756-30756	VARNELL
30757-30757	WILDWOOD
30802-30802	APPLING
30803-30803	AVERA
30805-30805	BLYTHE
30806-30806	BONEVILLE
30807-30807	CAMAK
30808-30808	DEARING
30809-30809	EVANS
30810-30810	GIBSON
30811-30811	GOUGH
30812-30812	GRACEWOOD
30813-30813	GROVETOWN
30814-30814	HARLEM
30815-30815	HEPHZIBAH
30816-30816	KEYSVILLE
30817-30817	LINCOLNTON
30818-30818	MATTHEWS
30819-30819	MESENA
30820-30820	MITCHELL
30821-30821	NORWOOD
30822-30822	PERKINS
30823-30823	STAPLETON
30824-30824	THOMSON
30828-30828	WARRENTON
30830-30830	WAYNESBORO
30833-30833	WRENS
30900-30999	AUGUSTA
31001-31001	ABBEVILLE
31002-31002	ADRIAN
31003-31003	ALLENTOWN
31004-31004	BOLINGBROKE
31005-31005	BONAIRE
31006-31006	BUTLER
31007-31007	BYROMVILLE
31008-31008	BYRON
31009-31009	CADWELL
31010-31010	CORDELE
31011-31011	CHAUNCEY
31012-31012	CHESTER
31013-31013	CLINCHFIELD
31014-31014	COCHRAN
31015-31015	CORDELE
31016-31016	CULLODEN
31017-31017	DANVILLE
31018-31018	DAVISBORO
31019-31019	DEXTER
31020-31020	DRY BRANCH
31021-31021	DUBLIN
31022-31022	DUDLEY
31023-31023	EASTMAN
31024-31024	EATONTON
31025-31025	ELKO
31026-31026	COCHRAN
31026-31026	EATONTON
31027-31027	DUBLIN
31028-31028	CENTERVILLE
31029-31029	FORSYTH
31030-31030	FORT VALLEY
31031-31031	GORDON
31032-31032	GRAY
31033-31033	HADDOCK
31034-31034	HARDWICK
31035-31035	HARRISON
31036-31036	HAWKINSVILLE
31037-31037	HELENA
31038-31038	HILLSBORO
31039-31039	HOWARD
31040-31040	DUBLIN
31041-31041	IDEAL
31042-31042	IRWINTON
31044-31044	JEFFERSONVILLE
31045-31045	JEWELL
31046-31046	JULIETTE
31047-31047	KATHLEEN
31049-31049	KITE
31050-31050	KNOXVILLE
31051-31051	LILLY
31052-31052	LIZELLA
31054-31054	MC INTYRE
31055-31055	MC RAE
31057-31057	MARSHALLVILLE
31058-31058	MAUK
31059-31059	MILLEDGEVILLE
31060-31060	MILAN
31061-31062	MILLEDGEVILLE
31063-31063	MONTEZUMA
31064-31064	MONTICELLO
31065-31065	MONTROSE
31066-31066	MUSELLA
31067-31067	OCONEE
31068-31068	OGLETHORPE
31069-31069	PERRY
31070-31070	PINEHURST
31071-31071	PINEVIEW
31072-31072	PITTS
31073-31073	PLAINFIELD
31075-31075	RENTZ
31076-31076	REYNOLDS
31077-31077	RHINE
31078-31078	ROBERTA
31079-31079	ROCHELLE
31081-31081	RUPERT
31082-31082	SANDERSVILLE
31083-31083	SCOTLAND
31084-31084	SEVILLE
31085-31085	SHADY DALE
31086-31086	SMARR
31087-31087	SPARTA
31088-31088	WARNER ROBINS
31089-31089	TENNILLE
31090-31090	TOOMSBORO
31091-31091	UNADILLA
31092-31092	VIENNA
31093-31093	WARNER ROBINS
31094-31094	WARTHEN
31095-31095	WARNER ROBINS
31096-31096	WRIGHTSVILLE
31097-31097	YATESVILLE
31098-31099	WARNER ROBINS
31106-31199	ATLANTA
31200-31299	MACON
31301-31301	ALLENHURST
31302-31302	BLOOMINGDALE
31303-31303	CLYO
31304-31304	CRESCENT
31305-31305	DARIEN
31307-31307	EDEN
31308-31308	ELLABELL
31309-31309	FLEMING
31310-31310	HINESVILLE
31312-31312	GUYTON
31313-31313	HINESVILLE
31314-31315	FORT STEWART
31316-31316	LUDOWICI
31318-31318	MELDRIM
31319-31319	MERIDIAN
31320-31320	MIDWAY
31321-31321	PEMBROKE
31322-31322	POOLER
31323-31323	RICEBORO
31324-31324	RICHMOND HILL
31326-31326	RINCON
31327-31327	SAPELO ISLAND
31328-31328	TYBEE ISLAND
31329-31329	SPRINGFIELD
31331-31331	TOWNSEND
31332-31332	VALONA
31333-31333	WALTHOURVILLE
31400-31499	SAVANNAH
31501-31503	WAYCROSS
31510-31510	ALMA

31512-31512 AMBROSE	31721-31721 ALBANY	31811-31811 HAMILTON
31513-31515 BAXLEY	31722-31722 BERLIN	31812-31812 JUNCTION CITY
31516-31516 BLACKSHEAR	31723-31723 BLAKELY	31814-31814 LOUVALE
31518-31518 BRISTOL	31724-31724 BLUFFTON	31815-31815 LUMPKIN
31519-31519 BROXTON	31725-31725 BRINSON	31816-31816 MANCHESTER
31520-31521 BRUNSWICK	31726-31726 BRONWOOD	31820-31820 MIDLAND
31522-31522 SAINT SIMONS ISLAND	31727-31727 BROOKFIELD	31821-31821 OMAHA
31523-31525 BRUNSWICK	31728-31728 CAIRO	31822-31822 PINE MOUNTAIN
31527-31527 JEKYLL ISLAND	31729-31729 CALVARY	31823-31823 PINE MOUNTAIN VALLEY
31527-31527 JEKYLL ISLAND BRANCH	31730-31730 CAMILLA	31824-31824 PRESTON
31532-31532 DENTON	31732-31732 CEDAR SPRINGS	31825-31825 RICHLAND
31533-31535 DOUGLAS	31733-31733 CHULA	31826-31826 SHILOH
31537-31537 FOLKSTON	31734-31734 CLIMAX	31827-31827 TALBOTTON
31539-31539 HAZLEHURST	31735-31735 COBB	31829-31829 UPATOI
31542-31542 HOBOKEN	31736-31736 COLEMAN	31830-31830 WARM SPRINGS
31543-31543 HORTENSE	31737-31737 COLQUITT	31831-31831 WAVERLY HALL
31544-31544 JACKSONVILLE	31738-31738 COOLIDGE	31832-31832 WESTON
31545-31546 JESUP	31739-31739 COTTON	31833-31833 WEST POINT
31547-31547 KINGS BAY	31740-31740 CUTHBERT	31836-31836 WOODLAND
31548-31548 KINGSLAND	31741-31741 DAMASCUS	31900-31904 COLUMBUS
31549-31549 LUMBER CITY	31742-31742 DAWSON	31905-31905 FORT BENNING
31550-31550 MANOR	31743-31743 DE SOTO	31906-31994 COLUMBUS
31551-31551 MERSHON	31744-31744 DOERUN	31995-31995 FORT BENNING
31552-31552 MILLWOOD	31745-31745 DONALSONVILLE	31997-31999 COLUMBUS
31553-31553 NAHUNTA	31746-31746 EDISON	39813-39813 ARLINGTON
31554-31554 NICHOLLS	31747-31747 ELLENTON	39815-39815 ATTAPULGUS
31555-31555 ODUM	31749-31749 ENIGMA	39817-39819 BAINBRIDGE
31556-31556 OFFERMAN	31750-31750 FITZGERALD	39823-39823 BLAKELY
31557-31557 PATTERSON	31751-31751 FORT GAINES	39824-39824 BLUFFTON
31558-31558 SAINT MARYS	31752-31752 FOWLSTOWN	39825-39825 BRINSON
31560-31560 SCREVEN	31753-31753 FUNSTON	39826-39826 BRONWOOD
31561-31561 SEA ISLAND	31754-31754 GEORGETOWN	39827-39828 CAIRO
31561-31561 SEA ISLAND BRANCH	31756-31756 HARTSFIELD	39829-39829 CALVARY
31562-31562 SAINT GEORGE	31757-31758 THOMASVILLE	39832-39832 CEDAR SPRINGS
31563-31563 SURRENCY	31759-31759 IRON CITY	39834-39834 CLIMAX
31564-31564 WARESBORO	31760-31760 IRWINVILLE	39836-39836 COLEMAN
31565-31565 WAVERLY	31761-31761 JAKIN	39837-39837 COLQUITT
31566-31566 WAYNESVILLE	31762-31762 LEARY	39840-39840 CUTHBERT
31567-31567 WEST GREEN	31763-31763 LEESBURG	39841-39841 DAMASCUS
31568-31568 WHITE OAK	31764-31764 LESLIE	39842-39842 DAWSON
31569-31569 WOODBINE	31765-31765 MEIGS	39845-39845 DONALSONVILLE
31598-31599 JESUP	31766-31766 MORGAN	39846-39846 EDISON
31601-31606 VALDOSTA	31767-31767 MORRIS	39851-39851 FORT GAINES
31620-31620 ADEL	31768-31768 MOULTRIE	39852-39852 FOWLSTOWN
31622-31622 ALAPAHA	31769-31769 MYSTIC	39854-39854 GEORGETOWN
31623-31623 ARGYLE	31770-31770 NEWTON	39859-39859 IRON CITY
31624-31624 AXSON	31771-31771 NORMAN PARK	39861-39861 JAKIN
31625-31625 BARNEY	31772-31772 OAKFIELD	39862-39862 LEARY
31626-31626 BOSTON	31773-31773 OCHLOCKNEE	39866-39866 MORGAN
31627-31627 CECIL	31774-31774 OCILLA	39867-39867 MORRIS
31629-31629 DIXIE	31775-31775 OMEGA	39870-39870 NEWTON
31630-31630 DU PONT	31776-31776 MOULTRIE	39877-39877 PARROTT
31631-31631 FARGO	31777-31777 PARROTT	39885-39885 SASSER
31632-31632 HAHIRA	31778-31778 PAVO	39886-39886 SHELLMAN
31634-31634 HOMERVILLE	31779-31779 PELHAM	39897-39897 WHIGHAM
31635-31635 LAKELAND	31780-31780 PLAINS	39901-39901 ATLANTA
31636-31636 LAKE PARK	31781-31781 POULAN	
31637-31637 LENOX	31782-31782 PUTNEY	
31638-31638 MORVEN	31783-31783 REBECCA	
31639-31639 NASHVILLE	31784-31784 SALE CITY	
31641-31641 NAYLOR	31785-31785 SASSER	
31642-31642 PEARSON	31786-31786 SHELLMAN	
31643-31643 QUITMAN	31787-31787 SMITHVILLE	
31645-31645 RAY CITY	31788-31788 MOULTRIE	
31646-31646 SAINT GEORGE	31789-31789 SUMNER	
31647-31647 SPARKS	31790-31790 SYCAMORE	
31648-31648 STATENVILLE	31791-31791 SYLVESTER	
31649-31649 STOCKTON	31792-31792 THOMASVILLE	
31650-31650 WILLACOOCHEE	31793-31794 TIFTON	
31698-31699 VALDOSTA	31795-31795 TY TY	
31699-31699 MOODY A F B	31796-31796 WARWICK	
31700-31708 ALBANY	31797-31797 WHIGHAM	
31709-31710 AMERICUS	31798-31798 WRAY	
31711-31711 ANDERSONVILLE	31799-31799 THOMASVILLE	
31712-31712 ARABI	31801-31801 BOX SPRINGS	
31713-31713 ARLINGTON	31803-31803 BUENA VISTA	
31714-31714 ASHBURN	31804-31804 CATAULA	
31715-31715 ATTAPULGUS	31805-31805 CUSSETA	
31716-31716 BACONTON	31806-31806 ELLAVILLE	
31717-31718 BAINBRIDGE	31807-31807 ELLERSLIE	
31719-31719 AMERICUS	31808-31808 FORTSON	
31720-31720 BARWICK	31810-31810 GENEVA	

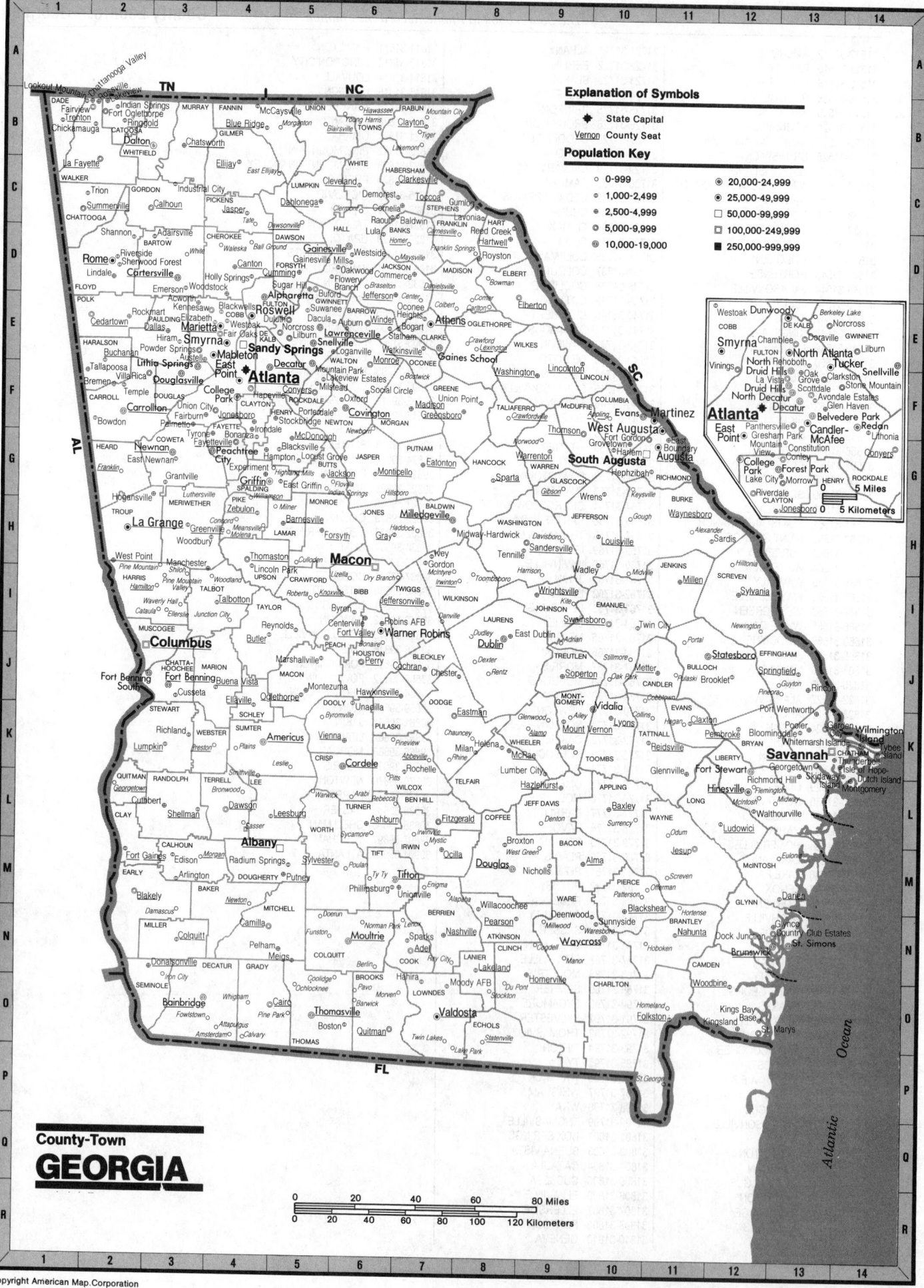

County-Town
GEORGIA

Explanation of Symbols

✦ State Capital
Vernon County Seat

Population Key

○ 0-999
⊕ 1,000-2,499
⊕ 2,500-4,999
⊕ 5,000-9,999
⊕ 10,000-19,000

⊛ 20,000-24,999
⊛ 25,000-49,999
□ 50,000-99,999
□ 100,000-249,999
■ 250,000-999,999

Explanation of symbols: ●– Census Designated Place (CDP)

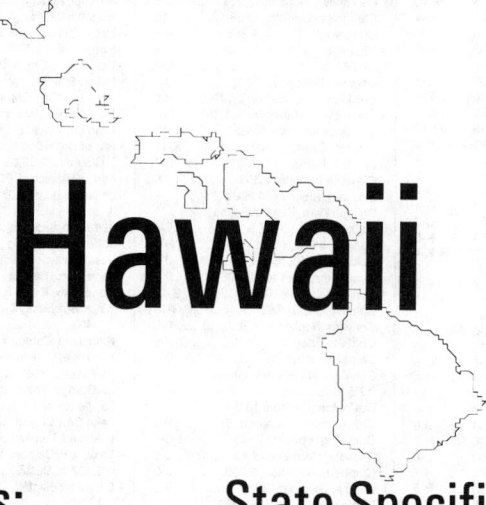

Hawaii

General Help Numbers:

Governor's Office
State Capitol 808-586-0034
415 S Beretania St Fax 808-586-0006
Honolulu, HI 96813 7:45AM-5PM
http://gov.state.hi.us

Attorney General's Office
425 Queen St 808-586-1500
Honolulu, HI 96813 Fax 808-586-1239
www.state.hi.us/ag 7:45AM-4:30PM

Legislative Records
Hawaii Legislature
415 S Beretania St 808-587-0700
Honolulu, HI 96813 Fax 808-586-3584
www.capitol.hawaii.gov 9AM-5PM

State Archives
Iolani Palace Grounds 808-586-0329
Honolulu, HI 96813 Fax 808-586-0330
www.state.hi.us/dags/archives 9AM-4PM

State Specifics:

Capital: Honolulu
Honolulu County

Time Zone: HT (Hawaii Standard Time)

Number of Counties: 4

Population: 1,262,840

Web Site: www.state.hi.us

State Agencies

Criminal Records

Hawaii Criminal Justice Data Center, Criminal Record Request, 465 S King St, Room 101, Honolulu, HI 96813; 808-587-3106, 8AM-4PM.

www.state.hi.us/hcjdc

Records are available from the 1930's. It takes 1 to 20 days before new records are available for inquiry. Records are indexed on in an electronic statewide repository of criminal history records. 89% of all arrests in database have final dispositions recorded, 81% for those arrests within last 5 years.

Searching: Include the following in your request- any aliases. Also helpful are gender, date of birth, Social Security Number. Submission of fingerprints is an option. 99% of the records are fingerprint-supported. Only records with convictions are released to the public. Records without dispositions are not released.

Access by: mail, in person.

Fee & Payment: The search fee for a name-based criminal record search is $15.00. A fingerprint-based search is $25.00. A public access printout, available only in-person at this office or at main police stations, is $10.00. Certification fee: $10.00. Fee payee: Director of Finance, State of Hawaii. Prepayment required. Money orders and cashiers' checks are the only acceptable methods of payment. No credit cards accepted.

Mail search: Turnaround time: 3 to 5 days. A SASE is requested.

In person search: The public may access conviction information by computer on-site. Thee is no fee to view the record, but $10.00 for a computer printout.

Statewide Court Records

Administrative Director of Courts, 417 S. King St, Honolulu, HI 96813; 808-539-4900, 808-539-4909 (Public Affairs Office), 808-539-4855-Fax; 7:45AM-4:30PM.

www.courts.state.hi.us/index.jsp

Access by: online.

Online search: Free online access to Circuit Court and Family Court records is available at www.courts.state.hi.us (click on "Search Court

Records"). Search by name or case number. These records are not considered "official" for FCRA compliant searches. The system is open daily - 3:30 a.m. to 12:00 midnight, Hawaii Standard Time. Also, opinions from the appellate court are available from the home web page site.

Sexual Offender Registry

Hawaii Criminal Justice Data Center, Sexual Offender Registry, 465 S King St, Room 101, Honolulu, HI 96813; 808-587-3106, 8AM-4PM.

http://sexoffenders.hawaii.gov/index.html

Information regarding covered offenders is permitted pursuant to Chapter 846E. Public access to this information is based solely on the fact of each offender's criminal conviction and is not based on an estimate of the offender's level of dangerousness.

Searching: The following information about offenders is available to the public: name, prior names, aliases, photograph, residence address, personal vehicles(s) driven, street name of employment, college/university affiliation, and crime for which convicted.

Access by: in person, online.

In person search: Information is available at Public Access locations at the HCJDC and main county police stations, including the Kona police station.

Online search: Search at http://sexoffenders.hawaii.gov/search.jsp?. Search by name or ZIP Code.

Incarceration Records

Hawaii Department of Public Safety, Inmate Classification, 919 Ala Moana Blvd #401, Honolulu, HI 96814; 808-587-2567, 808-587-2586-Fax; 7:45AM-4:30PM.

www.hawaii.gov/hcjdc

Records are available on current and former inmates. Some older records were lost when a new computer system was installed. It takes 1 to 20 days before new records are available for inquiry.

Searching: Include the following in your request-name; DOB and SSN helpful. There is no fee. Records are considered public information.

Access by: mail, phone.

Mail search: Turnaround time: 1-2 days. A SASE is helpful.

Phone search: Limited information available by telephone.

Corporation, Trade Name, Limited Partnership, Assumed Name, Trademarks/Servicemarks, Limited Liability Company, Limited Liability Partnerships

Business Registration Division, PO Box 40, Honolulu, HI 96810 (Courier address: 335 Merchant St, 2nd Fl, Honolulu, HI 96813); 808-586-2727, 808-586-2733-Fax; 7:45AM-4:30PM.

www.businessregistrations.com

Records are available from 1859 to present for active entities, 1900 to present for inactive entities. New records are available for inquiry immediately.

Searching: There are no access restrictions. Records are open to the public. Include the following in your request-full name of business. In addition to the articles of incorporation, corporation records include the following information: Annual Reports, Officers, Directors, DBAs, Prior (merged) names, Inactive and Reserved names.

Access by: mail, phone, fax, in person, online.

Fee & Payment: There is no search fee. The copy fee is $.25 per page. Fee payee: Business Registration Division. Prepayment required. Personal checks accepted. Credit cards accepted ($1.00 minimum charge).

Mail search: Turnaround time: 2 weeks. A SASE is requested.

Phone search: They will confirm data over the phone or let you know how many copies to prepay.

Fax search: Same criteria as mail searches.

In person: Turnaround time is while you wait.

Online search: Online access to business names is available through the Internet at www.businessregistrations.com. There are no fees, the system is open 24 hours. For assistance during business hours, call 808-586-2727. Tax license searching is available free at www.ehawaiigov.org/serv/taxpayer. Search by name, ID number of DBA name.

Other access: Bulk data can be purchased online through ehawaiigov.com. Visit the website or call 808-587-4220 for more information.

Uniform Commercial Code, Federal and State Tax Liens, Real Estate Recordings

UCC Division, Bureau of Conveyances, PO Box 2867, Honolulu, HI 96803 (Courier address: Dept. of Land & Natural Resources, 1151 Punchbowl St, Honolulu, HI 96813); 808-587-0154, 808-587-4380-Fax; 7:45AM-4:30PM.

www.state.hi.us/dlnr/bc/bc.html

Records are available from 1845. Records are on microfiche from 1976 through 02/28/02. It takes 1 day before new records are available for inquiry.

Searching: Use search request form UCC-11. Include the following in your request-debtor name. A UCC record does not include tax liens; a separate search is required.

Access by: mail, in person, online.

Fee & Payment: Fees are $25.00 per debtor name plus $5.00 for each financing statement and statement of assignment reported. Copies cost $1.00 per page. Fee payee: Bureau of Conveyances. Prepayment required. An initial fee of $25.00 must be paid in advance, additional fees will be invoiced. Personal checks accepted. No credit cards accepted.

Mail search: Turnaround time: 1 week. A SASE is requested.

In person search: There is self-service in the public reference room.

Online search: Search the indices from 1976 forward at http://132.160.239.151/boc/. Search by grantor, grantee, business name. Includes real estate recordings.

Sales Tax Registrations

State does not impose sales tax.

Birth Certificates

State Department of Health, Vital Records Section, PO Box 3378, Honolulu, HI 96801 (Courier address: 1250 Punchbowl St, Room 103, Honolulu, HI 96813); 808-586-4533, 7:45AM-2:30PM.

www.hawaii.gov/health/vital-records

Records are primarily limited to family members and spouse.

Records are available from mid 1800's to present. It takes 10-20 days before new records are available for inquiry. Records are indexed on inhouse computer.

Searching: Must have a signed release from person of record or immediate family member. Include the following in your request-full name, names of parents, mother's maiden name, date of birth, place of birth, relationship to person of record, reason for information request. An applicant/requestor must provide the information needed to 1) establish his/her direct and tangible interest in the record and 2) locate the desired record. Records forms are available from the webpage.

Access by: mail, in person, online.

Fee & Payment: Fees are $10.00 for first copy and $4.00 for each subsequent copy of same record. Fee payee: State Department of Health. Prepayment required. Money orders, certified checks, and cashier's checks are accepted. No credit cards accepted.

Mail search: Turnaround time: 4 to 6 weeks. No SASE is required.

In person search: Turnaround time is 10 days or more.

Online search: Records may requested from https://www.ehawaiigov.org/doh/vitrec/html/down.html. The turnaround time is the same as mail requests.

Expedited service: Expedited service is available for mail searches. Turnaround time: 5 to 7 days. You must enclose a return pre-paid, self-addressed envelope.

Death Records

State Department of Health, Vital Records Section, PO Box 3378, Honolulu, HI 96801 (Courier address: 1250 Punchbowl St, Room 103, Honolulu, HI 96813); 808-586-4533, 7:45AM-2:30PM.

www.hawaii.gov/health/vital-records

Records are primarily limited to family members and spouse.

Records are available from mid 1800's on, but early records are not complete. It takes 10-20 days before new records are available for inquiry. Records are indexed on inhouse computer.

Searching: Must have a signed release from immediate family member. Include the following in your request-full name, date of death, place of death, names of parents, relationship to person of record, reason for information request. An applicant/requestor must provide the information needed to 1) establish his/her direct and tangible interest in the record and 2) locate the desired record. Records forms are available from the webpage.

Access by: mail, in person.

Fee & Payment: The fee is $10.00 per record and $4.00 for each subsequent copy of same record. Fee payee: State Department of Health. Prepayment required. Cashier's checks and money orders accepted. No credit cards accepted.

Mail search: Turnaround time: 4 to 6 weeks.

In person search: Turnaround time is 10 days or more.

Expedited service: Expedited service is available for mail searches. Turnaround time: 5 to 7 days. You must enclose a return pre-paid, self-addressed envelope.

Marriage Certificates

State Department of Health, Vital Records Section, PO Box 3378, Honolulu, HI 96801 (Courier address: 1250 Punchbowl St, Room 103, Honolulu, HI 96813); 808-586-4533, 7:45AM-2:30PM.   www.hawaii.gov/health/vital-records

Records are primarily limited to family members and spouse.

Records are available from mid 1800's to present. It takes 3-5 days before new records are available for inquiry. Records are indexed on inhouse computer.

Searching: Must have a signed release from person of record or immediate family member. Include the following in your request-names of husband and wife, wife's maiden name, date of marriage, place or county of marriage, names of parents, relationship to person of record, reason for information request. An applicant/requestor must provide the information needed to 1) establish his/her direct and tangible interest in the record and 2) locate the desired record. Records forms are available from the webpage.

Access by: mail, in person, online.

Fee & Payment: Fee is $10.00 per record and $4.00 for subsequent copy of same record. Fee payee: State Department of Health. Prepayment required. Cashier's check and money orders accepted. No credit cards accepted.

Mail search: Turnaround time: 4 to 6 weeks. No SASE is required.

In person search: Turnaround time is 10 days or more.

Online search: Records may requested from https://www.ehawaiigov.org/doh/vitrec/html/down.html. The turnaround time is the same as mail requests.

Expedited service: Expedited service is available for mail searches. Turnaround time: 5 to 7 days. You must enclose a return pre-paid, self-addressed envelope.

Divorce Records

State Department of Health, Vital Records Section, PO Box 3378, Honolulu, HI 96801 (Courier: 1250 Punchbowl St, Room 103, Honolulu, HI 96813); 808-586-4533, 7:45AM-2:30PM.

www.hawaii.gov/health/vital-records

Records are primarily limited to family members and spouse.

Records are available from July 1951 to Dec 2002. Prior records and those from Jan. 2003 forward are held by the clerk of the court granting the decree.

It takes 10-20 days before new records are available for inquiry. Records are indexed on manually.

Searching: Must have a signed release from person of record or immediate family member. Include the following in your request-names of husband and wife, date of divorce, place of divorce, relationship to person of record, reason for information request. An applicant/requestor must provide the information needed to 1) establish his/her direct and tangible interest in the record and 2) locate the desired record. Records forms are available from the webpage.

Access by: mail, in person.

Fee & Payment: The fee is $10.00 per record and $4.00 each additional copy of same record. Fee payee: State Department of Health. Prepayment required. Cashier's check and money orders accepted. No credit cards accepted.

Mail search: Turnaround time: 4 to 6 weeks.

In person search: Results are mailed. Turnaround time is 10 days or more.

Expedited service: Expedited service is available for mail searches. Turnaround time: 5 to 7 days. You must enclose a return pre-paid, self-addressed envelope.

Workers' Compensation Records

Labor & Industrial Relations, Disability Compensation Division, 830 Punchbowl St, Room 209, Honolulu, HI 96813; 808-586-9174, 808-586-9219-Fax; 7:45AM-4:30PM.

http://hawaii.gov/labor/dcd

Records are available for the past 8 years. Prior records are in the State Archives but still must be requested through the Disability Compensation Division. It takes 2 to 7 days from receipt before new records are available for inquiry. Records are indexed on inhouse computer. Records are normally destroyed after 40 years.

Searching: Must have a signed release from injured party or HI circuit court order signed by a judge. Include the following in your request-claimant name, Social Security Number, claim number.

Access by: mail, fax, in person.

Fee & Payment: There is no search fee, copy fee is $.05 per page. Fee payee: Director of Finance. Prepayment required. Personal checks accepted. No credit cards accepted.

Mail search: Turnaround time: 6 to 12 weeks. A SASE is requested.

Fax search: Same criteria as mail searches.

In person search: In person requests only saves mail time; results are mailed.

Driver Records

Traffic Violations Bureau, Abstract Section, 1111 Alakea St, 2nd Fl, Honolulu, HI 96813; 808-538-5530, 808-961-7470 (Hawaii Court), 808-244-2800 (Maui Court), 808-246-3330 (Kauai Court), 808-538-5520-Fax; 7:45AM-9:PM.

www.hawaii.gov/dot/highways

The TVB issues two types of abstracts. The Public Abstract shows moving violation convictions, but not juvenile records unless signed for. The Court Abstract shows all action, whether convicted or dismissed.

Searching: The Public Abstract is given to insurers and employers. Casual requesters can obtain records; however, personal information is not released. Include the following in your request-photo ID. The driver's full name, DOB and either license number or SSN are needed when ordering. The webpage for the courts is www.courts.state.hi.us/index.jsp.

Access by: mail, in person, online.

Fee & Payment: The fee is $7.00 per request. There is a full charge even if no record is found. Copies of tickets are only available from the court where ticket was issued. The fees are $1.00 for first copy, $.50 each additional copy. Fee payee: District Court Prepayment required. The state requires a money order or cashier's check for mail-in requests; in-person requesters may use cash, credit cards, or business checks. Personal checks not accepted. Visa/MC and JCB accepted.

Mail search: Turnaround time: 2 - 5 days.

In person search: Walk-in requests can be processed in five to twenty minutes at any county district traffic court or at the Traffic Violations Bureau Office in Honolulu.

Online search: Online ordering by DPPA complaint requesters is available from the state-designated entity - Hawaii Information Consortium (HIC). The record fee is $9.00 per record, plus a $75.00 annual subscribtion fee is required. Record requests are accepted via FTP. Results, if clear, are returned via FTP. Results with hits on convictions on the record are returned on paper. Visit their website at http://pahoehoe.ehawaii.gov/portal/subscriber.html or call HIC at 808-587-4220 for more information.

Other access: Magnetic tape ordering is available in Hawaii for frequent or large orders. The fee is $9.00 per request. Turnaround time is 48 hours. Call HIC at 808-587-4220 for details.

Expedited service: Will expedite delivery if a pre-paid envelope is provided.

Vehicle Ownership, Vehicle Identification

Access to Records is Restricted.

Accident Reports

Records not maintained by a state level agency.

Accident reports are not available from the state. Records are maintained at the county level at the police departments and are only available to those involved.

Vessel Ownership, Vessel Registration

Land & Natural Resources, Division of Boating & Recreation, 333 Queen St Rm 300, Honolulu, HI 96813; 808-587-1970, 808-587-1977-Fax; 7:45AM-4:30PM.

www.hawaii.gov/dlnr/dbor/dbor.html

Records are available 1950s, computerized since 1994, and on microfiche from 1987 to 1994. It takes 30 days or less before new records are available for inquiry.

Searching: Requests must be made in writing and must include a statement revealing the purpose for which the information will be used. Name or hull ID number or registration number is required for search. The following data is not released: addresses or phone numbers.

Access by: mail, fax, in person.

Fee & Payment: There is no search fee.

Mail search: Turnaround time: 1 to 2 days. No SASE is required.

Fax search: Same criteria as mail searching.

In person search: Turnaround time is usually the same day.

Voter Registration
Access to Records is Restricted.

Office of Elections, Voter Registration, 802 Lehua Ave, Honolulu, HI 96782; 808-453-8683, 808-453-6006-Fax; 7:45AM-4:30PM.

www.hawaii.gov/elections

Voter information is maintained by the County Clerks. Here are contact numbers. City and County of Honolulu 808-523-4293; County of Hawaii 808-961-8277; County of Maui 808-270-7749; County of Kauai 808-241-6350. The Federal Help America Vote Act of 2002 (HAVA) law requires implementation of a central, computerized, statewide voter registration system by 01/01/2006.

GED Certificates (Diplomas)

Community Education, ATR - Adult Education, 475 22nd Ave, Bldg 302, Rm 124, Honolulu, HI 96816; 808-735-8371, 808-735-8375-Fax; 8AM-4PM.

High school diplomas, not GED certificates, are issued to qualified individuals. While this agency issues diplomas, there are also many school systems in Hawaii that do so as well. This agency is in the process of compiling a statewide database.

Searching: If this agency does not have the record, they will assist the requester in locating the school that issued the diploma. Include the following in your request-signed release, date of birth, Social Security Number. Knowing the approximate date and location of the test is helpful. The requirements are for both verifications and copies of transcripts.

Access by: mail, fax, in person.

Fee & Payment: There is no fee for a fax verification form this agency. However, depending on the other record location site, fees may be charged.

Mail search: Turnaround time: 5 to 10 days. A SASE is required.

Fax search: Same criteria as mail search.

In person search: Same criteria as mail search.

Hunting and Fishing License Information
Access to Records is Restricted.

Land & Natural Resources Department, Kalanimokui Bldg, 1151 Punchbowl St, Honolulu, HI 96813; 808-587-0100 (Fishing), 808-587-0166 (Hunting), 7:45AM-4:30PM.

www.state.hi.us/dlnr

Fishing information is kept by the Aquatic Resources Division; Hunting information by the Division of Forestry & Wildlife. 808-587-0115 is fax for Fishing; 808-587-0160 is fax for Hunting. Limited record information is released to the public. Generally, this department's information is only released to law enforcement agencies. There is no "search engine" here.

Hawaii State Licensing Agencies

For details about the agency responsible for licensing/certifying/registering an item below or in the Agency Quick Finder section, match an item's number with the number of the agency in the *Licensing Agency Information* section.

Licenses Searchable Online

Acupuncturist #4	www.ehawaiigov.org/serv/pvl
Architect #19	www.ehawaiigov.org/serv/pvl
Auction #42	www.ehawaiigov.org/serv/pvl
Bank/Bank Agencies/Offices #28	www.hawaii.gov/dcca/areas/dfi/regulate/regulate/
Barber Shop #5	www.ehawaiigov.org/serv/pvl
Barber/Barber Apprentice #5	www.ehawaiigov.org/serv/pvl
Beauty Instructor #5	www.ehawaiigov.org/serv/pvl
Beauty Operator/School/Shop #5	www.ehawaiigov.org/serv/pvl
Cemetery #42	www.ehawaiigov.org/serv/pvl
Certified Public Accountant - CPA #21	www.ehawaiigov.org/serv/pvl
Chiropractor #6	www.ehawaiigov.org/serv/pvl
Collection Agency #42	www.ehawaiigov.org/serv/pvl
Condominium Hotel Operator #34	www.ehawaiigov.org/serv/pvl
Condominium Managing Agent #34	www.ehawaiigov.org/serv/pvl
Contractor #27	www.ehawaiigov.org/serv/pvl
Credit Union #28	www.hawaii.gov/dcca/areas/dfi/regulate/regulate/
Dental Hygienist #7	www.ehawaiigov.org/serv/pvl
Dentist #7	http://pahoehoe.ehawaii.gov/pvl/app
Drug (Prescription) Dist./Whlse. #16	www.ehawaiigov.org/serv/pvl
Elected Officials Financial Disclosure #41	www.state.hi.us/ethics/noindex/pubrec.htm
Electrician #29	www.ehawaiigov.org/serv/pvl
Electrologist #42	www.ehawaiigov.org/serv/pvl
Elevator Mechanic #29	www.ehawaiigov.org/serv/pvl
Emergency Medical Personnel #13	www.ehawaiigov.org/serv/pvl
Employment Agency #42	www.ehawaiigov.org/serv/pvl
Engineer #19	www.ehawaiigov.org/serv/pvl
Escrow Company #28	www.hawaii.gov/dcca/areas/dfi/regulate/regulate/
Financial Services Loan Company #28	www.hawaii.gov/dcca/areas/dfi/regulate/regulate/
Hearing Aid Dealer/Fitter #30	www.ehawaiigov.org/serv/pvl
Insurance Adjuster #31	www.ehawaiigov.org/serv/hils
Insurance Agent/Producer / Solicitor #31	www.ehawaiigov.org/serv/hils
Landscape Architect #19	www.ehawaiigov.org/serv/pvl
Lobbyist #41	www.state.hi.us/ethics/noindex/pubrec.htm
Marriage & Family Therapist #42	www.ehawaiigov.org/serv/pvl
Massage Therapist/Establishment #42	www.ehawaiigov.org/serv/pvl
Mechanic #42	www.ehawaiigov.org/serv/pvl
Medical Doctor #13	www.ehawaiigov.org/serv/pvl
Mortgage Broker/Solicitor #42	www.ehawaiigov.org/serv/pvl
Motor Vehicle Dealer/Broker/Seller/Repair #42	www.ehawaiigov.org/serv/pvl
Naturopathic Physician #10	www.ehawaiigov.org/serv/pvl
Nurse #14	www.ehawaiigov.org/serv/pvl
Nursing Home Administrator #12	www.ehawaiigov.org/serv/pvl
Occupational Therapist #17	www.ehawaiigov.org/serv/pvl
Optician, Dispensing #8	www.ehawaiigov.org/serv/pvl
Optometrist #11	www.ehawaiigov.org/serv/pvl
Osteopathic Physician #13	www.ehawaiigov.org/serv/pvl
Pest Control Field Rep./Operator #32	www.ehawaiigov.org/serv/pvl
Pharmacist / #16	www.ehawaiigov.org/serv/pvl
Physical Therapist #17	www.ehawaiigov.org/serv/pvl
Physician Assistant #13	www.ehawaiigov.org/serv/pvl
Pilot, Port #42	www.ehawaiigov.org/serv/pvl
Plumber #29	www.ehawaiigov.org/serv/pvl
Podiatrist #13	www.ehawaiigov.org/serv/pvl
Private Detective / Detective/Inv. Agency #18	www.ehawaiigov.org/serv/pvl
Psychologist #20	www.ehawaiigov.org/serv/pvl
Public Accountant - PA #21	www.ehawaiigov.org/serv/pvl
Real Estate Agent/Broker/Sales #34	www.ehawaiigov.org/serv/pvl

Real Estate Appraiser #9 ....www.ehawaiigov.org/serv/pvl
Savings & Loan Association #28 ....www.hawaii.gov/dcca/areas/dfi/regulate/regulate/
Savings Bank #28 ....www.hawaii.gov/dcca/areas/dfi/regulate/regulate/
Security Guard/Agency #18 ....www.ehawaiigov.org/serv/pvl
Social Worker #42 ....www.ehawaiigov.org/serv/pvl
Speech Pathologist/Audiologist #22 ....www.ehawaiigov.org/serv/pvl
Surveyor, Land #19 ....www.ehawaiigov.org/serv/pvl
Timeshare #42 ....www.ehawaiigov.org/serv/pvl
Travel Agency #42 ....www.ehawaiigov.org/serv/pvl
Trust Company #28 ....www.hawaii.gov/dcca/areas/dfi/regulate/regulate/
Veterinarian #23...www.ehawaiigov.org/serv/pvl

Hawaii Licensing Quick Finder

Acupuncturist #4 808-586-3000
Airport-related Occupation #37 808-836-6533
Architect #19 808-586-3000
Attorney #38 808-537-1868
Auction #42 808-586-2699
Bank/Bank Agencies/Offices #28 808-586-2820
Barber Shop #5...808-586-3000
Barber/Barber Apprentice #5.................808-586-3000
Beauty Instructor #5 808-586-3000
Beauty Operator/School/Shop #5.........808-586-3000
Boxer #24 808-586-2701
Boxing Manager / Matchmaker #24 808-586-2701
Boxing Physician / Second #24 808-586-2701
Boxing Professional (Promoter) #24 808-586-2701
Boxing Timekeeper/Judge/Referee #24 808-586-2701
Cable Franchise #26 808-586-2620
Cemetery #42 808-586-2699
Certified Public Accountant - CPA #21.808-586-3000
Chiropractor #6...808-586-3000
Clinical Lab Technician #40...................808-453-6653
Clinical Lab Cytotechnologist #40 808-453-6653
Clinical Lab Director #40 808-453-6653
Clinical Lab Technologist/Spec. #40 808-453-6653
Collection Agency #42 808-586-2699
Condominium Hotel Operator #34 808-587-3222
Condominium Managing Agent #34 808-587-3222
Contractor #27 808-586-3000
Credit Union #28 808-586-2820
Dental Hygienist #7..................................808-586-3000
Dentist #7...808-586-3000
Drivers License #39 808-532-7730
Drug (Prescription) Dist./Whlse. #16 808-586-2694
Educational Administrator #35 808-586-3392
Elected Officials Financial Disclosure #41
....808-587-0460

Electrician #29...808-586-3000
Electrologist #42.......................................808-586-2699
Elevator Mechanic #29............................808-586-3000
Embalmer #15...808-586-8000
Emergency Medical Personnel #13 808-586-3000
Employment Agency #42 808-586-2699
Engineer #19 808-586-3000
Escrow Company #28 808-586-2820
Financial Services Loan Company #28 808-586-2820
Hearing Aid Dealer/Fitter #30................808-586-3000
Insurance Adjuster #31 808-586-2788
Insurance Agent #31................................808-586-2788
Insurance Producer / Solicitor #31 808-586-2788
Investment Advisor/Rep. #25 808-586-2730
Landscape Architect #19........................808-586-3000
Lobbyist #41 808-587-0460
Marine License, Commercial #36..........808-587-0100
Marriage & Family Therapist #42 808-586-2693
Massage Therapist/Establishment #42 808-586-2699
Mechanic #42 808-586-2701
Medical Doctor #13..................................808-586-3000
Mortgage Broker/Solicitor #42..............808-586-3000
Motor Vehicle Dealer/Broker/Seller #42 808-586-2699
Motor Vehicle Repair Dealer #42 808-586-2699
Naturopathic Physician #10...................808-586-3000
Notary Public #3 808-586-1216
Nuclear Medicine Technologist #33 808-586-4700
Nurse #14 808-586-3000
Nurses' Aide #14 808-586-3000
Nursing Home Administrator #12 808-586-3000
Occupational Therapist #17 808-586-2698
Optician, Dispensing #8 808-586-3000
Optometrist #11 808-586-2694
Osteopathic Physician #13.....................808-586-3000
Pest Control Field Rep./Operator #32..808-586-3000

Pesticide Applicator #2...........................808-973-9409
Pesticide Applicator, Private #2 808-973-9424
Pesticide Dealer #2 808-973-9413
Pesticide Product #2 808-973-9414
Pharmacist / Pharmacy #16....................808-586-2694
Physical Therapist #17............................808-586-2694
Physician Assistant #13 808-586-3000
Pilot, Port #42 808-586-2699
Plumber #29 808-586-3000
Podiatrist #13..808-586-2708
Private Detective #18 808-586-3000
Private Detective/Investigation Agency #18
....808-586-3000
Psychologist #20......................................808-586-3000
Public Accountant - PA #21 808-586-3000
Radiation Therapist #33..........................808-586-4700
Radiographer #33.....................................808-586-4700
Real Estate Agent/Broker/Sales #34 ...808-587-3222
Real Estate Appraiser #9 808-586-3000
Sanitarian #15 808-586-4576
Savings & Loan Association #28 808-586-2820
Savings Bank #28 808-586-2820
Securities Salesperson #25 808-586-2730
Security Guard/Agency #18 808-586-2700
Shorthand Reporter #1............................808-539-4226
Social Worker #42 808-586-2696
Speech Pathologist/Audiologist #22 808-586-3000
Surveyor, Land #19 808-586-3000
Tattoo Artist #15 808-586-8000
Taxi Certifications #39.............................808-532-7730
Teacher #35 808-586-3392
Timeshare #42 808-586-2699
Travel Agency #42 808-586-2699
Trust Company #28 808-586-2820
Veterinarian #23.......................................808-586-3000

Hawaii Licensing Agency Information

1 Board of Certified Shorthand Reporters, 777 Punchbowl St, Honolulu, HI 96813; 808-539-4226, Fax: 808-539-4149. Email: csrhi@maui.net

2 Department of Agriculture, 1428 S. King St., Honolulu, HI 96814; 808-973-9401, Fax: 808-973-9418. www.hawaiiag.org/hdoa
Email: hdoa.info@hawaii.gov

3 Department of Attorney General, Notary Public Office, 425 Queen St, Honolulu, HI 96813; 808-586-1216, Fax: 808-586-1205.
www.state.hi.us/ag/notary_unit.htm

4 Department of Commerce & Consumer Affairs, Board of Acupuncture, PO Box 3469 (335 Merchant St., 96813), Honolulu, HI 96801; 808-586-2698, Fax: 808-586-2689. www.hawaii.gov/dcca/areas/pvl/boards/acupuncture/
Email: acupuncture@dcca.hawaii.gov
Search Database at www.ehawaiigov.org/serv/pvl

5 Department of Commerce & Consumer Affairs, Board of Barbering & Cosmetology, PO Box 3469 (1010 Richards St, 96813), Honolulu, HI 96801; 808-586-2696. Email: barber_cosm@dcca.hawaii.gov
Search Database at www.ehawaiigov.org/serv/pvl
Note: Rosters are available for sale, however do not include personal info or addresses.

6 Department of Commerce & Consumer Affairs, Board of Chiropractic Examiners, PO Box 3469 (335 Merchant St., 96813), Honolulu, HI 96801; 808-586-2698, Fax: 808-586-2689. www.hawaii.gov/dcca/areas/pvl/boards/chiropractor/
Email: chiropractor@dcca.hawaii.gov
Search Database at www.ehawaiigov.org/serv/pvl

7 Department of Commerce & Consumer Affairs, Board of Dental Examiners, PO Box 3469 (1010 Richards St 96813), Honolulu, HI 96801; 808-586-2702. www.hawaii.gov/dcca/areas/pvl/boards/dentist/ Email: dental@dcca.hawaii.gov
Search Database at www.ehawaiigov.org/serv/pvl

8 Department of Commerce & Consumer Affairs, Dispensing Optician Program, PO Box 3469 (1010 Richards St, 96813), Honolulu, HI 96801; 808-586-3000, Fax: 808-586-3031.
Email: optician@dcca.state.hi.us
Search Database at www.ehawaiigov.org/serv/pvl

9 Department of Commerce & Consumer Affairs, Professional & Vocational Licensing, Attn:REA, PO Box 3469, Honolulu, HI 96801; 808-586-2704.
www.hawaii.gov/dcca/areas/pvl/programs/realestateappraiser/ Email: appraiser@dcca.state.hi.us
Search Database at www.ehawaiigov.org/serv/pvl

10 Department of Commerce & Consumer Affairs, Board of Examiners in Naturopathy, PO Box 3469 (1010 Richards St, 96813), Honolulu, HI 96801; 808-586-2704, Fax: 808-586-3031.
Email: naturopathy@dcca.state.hi.us
Search Database at www.ehawaiigov.org/serv/pvl

11 Department of Commerce & Consumer Affairs, Board of Examiners in Optometry, PO Box 3469 (335 Merchant St. 3rd Fl, 96813), Honolulu, HI 96801; 808-586-2694. www.hawaii.gov/dcca/areas/pvl/boards/optometry/ Email: optometry@dcca.state.hi.us Search Database at www.ehawaiigov.org/serv/pvl

12 Department of Commerce & Consumer Affairs, Nursing Home Administrators Program, PO Box 3469 (335 Merchant St, 96813), Honolulu, HI 96801; 808-586-2695. www.hawaii.gov/dcca/areas/pvl/programs/nursing home/ Email: nursing_home@dcca.hawaii.gov Search Database at www.ehawaiigov.org/serv/pvl

13 Department of Commerce & Consumer Affairs, Board of Medical Examiners, PO Box 3469 (335 Merchant, 96813), Honolulu, HI 96801; 808-586-2708. www.hawaii.gov/dcca/areas/pvl/boards/medical/ Email: medical@dcca.hawaii.gov Search Database at www.ehawaiigov.org/serv/pvl

14 Department of Commerce & Consumer Affairs, Board of Nursing, PO Box 3469 (335 Merchant St, 96813), Honolulu, HI 96801; 808-586-2695. www.hawaii.gov/dcca/areas/pvl/boards/nursing/ Email: nursing@dcca.hawaii.gov Search Database at www.ehawaiigov.org/serv/pvl

15 Department of Health, Sanitation Branch, 591 Ala Moana Blvd, Honolulu, HI 96813; 808-586-8000, Fax: 808-586-8040. www.hawaii.gov/doh Email: san_info@ehsdmail.health.state.hi.us

16 Department of Commerce & Consumer Affairs, Board of Pharmacy, PO Box 3469 (335 Merchant St. 3rd Fl, 96813), Honolulu, HI 96801; 808-586-2694. www.hawaii.gov/dcca/areas/pvl/boards/pharmacy/ Email: pharmacy@dcca.state.hi.us Search Database at www.ehawaiigov.org/serv/pvl

17 Department of Commerce & Consumer Affairs, Board of Physical Therapy, PO Box 3469 (335 Merchant St. 3rd Fl, 96813), Honolulu, HI 96801; 808-586-2694. www.hawaii.gov/dcca/are as/pvl/boards/physicaltherapy/ Email: phys_therapy@dcca.state.hi.us Search Database at www.ehawaiigov.org/serv/pvl

18 Department of Commerce & Consumer Affairs, Board of Private Detectives & Guards, PO Box 3469 (335 Merchant St, 96813), Honolulu, HI 96801; 808-586-2705, Fax: 808-586-2689. www.hawaii.gov/dcca/areas/pvl/boards/private/ Email: detective@dcca.hawaii.gov Search Database at www.ehawaiigov.org/serv/pvl

19 Department of Commerce & Consumer Affairs, Architects & Surveyors, Board of Prof. Engineers, PO Box 3469 (1010 Richards St, 96813), Honolulu, HI 96801; 808-586-2702. www.hawaii.gov/dcca/areas/pvl/boards/engineer/ Email: easla@dcca.hawaii.gov Search Database at www.ehawaiigov.org/serv/pvl

20 Department of Commerce & Consumer Affairs, Board of Psychology, PO Box 3469 (335 Merchant St Rm 301, 96813), Honolulu, HI 96801; 808-586-2693. www.hawaii.gov/dcca/are as/pvl/boards/psychology/ Email: psychology@hawaii.gov Search Database at www.ehawaiigov.org/serv/pvl

21 Department of Commerce & Consumer Affairs, Board of Public Accountancy, PO Box 3469 (1010 Richards St, 96813), Honolulu, HI 96801; 808-586-2696, Fax: 808-586-2874. www.hawaii.gov/dcca/areas/pvl/boards/accountan cy/ Email: accountancy@dcca.hawaii.gov Search Database at www.ehawaiigov.org/serv/pvl Note: Search for CPA or PA. Also, they do sell/provide lists or other means of verification at (1) www.ehawaii.gov/pvllistbuilder (2) www.ehawaii.gov/subscription/html/.

22 Department of Commerce & Consumer Affairs, Board of Speech Pathology & Audiology, PO Box 3469 (335 Merchant St Rm 301, 96813), Honolulu, HI 96801; 808-586-2701. www.hawaii.gov/dcca/pvl Email: speech@dcca.hawaii.gov Search Database at www.ehawaiigov.org/serv/pvl

23 Department of Commerce & Consumer Affairs, Board of Veterinary Examiners, PO Box 3469 (1010 Richards St, 96813), Honolulu, HI 96801; 808-586-2696. www.hawaii.gov/dcca/areas/pvl/boards/veterinary/ Email: veterinary@dcca.hawaii.gov Search Database at www.ehawaiigov.org/serv/pvl Note: Rosters are available for sale, however do not include personal info or addresses.

24 Department of Commerce & Consumer Affairs, Boxing Commission, PO Box 3469 (1010 Richards St, 96813), Honolulu, HI 96801; 808-586-2701, Fax: 808-586-2689. www.hawaii.gov/dcca/areas/pvl/boards/boxing/ Email: boxing@dcca.state.hi.us

25 Department of Commerce & Consumer Affairs, Business Registration Division, Securities Compliance Branch, PO Box 3469 (1010 Richards St, 96813), Honolulu, HI 96801; 808-586-2722, Fax: 808-586-2733. www.hawaii.gov/dcca/ocp/

26 Department of Commerce & Consumer Affairs, Cable TV Division, PO Box 541, Honolulu, HI 96809; 808-586-2620, Fax: 808-586-2625. www.hawaii.gov/dcca/catv

27 Department of Commerce & Consumer Affairs, Contractors License Board, PO Box 3469 335 Merchant St. (96813), Honolulu, HI 96801; 808-586-2700, Fax: 808-586-3031. www.hawaii.gov/dcca/areas/pvl/boards/contractor/ Email: contractor@dcca.hawaii.gov Search Database at www.ehawaiigov.org/serv/pvl

28 Department of Commerce & Consumer Affairs, Division of Financial Institutions, PO Box 2054 (335 Merchant St Rm 221), Honolulu, HI 96805; 808-586-2820, Fax: 808-586-2818. www.hawaii.gov/dcca/dfi Email: dfi@dcca.hawaii.gov   Search database at www.hawaii.gov/dcca/areas/dfi/regulate/regulate

29 Dept of Commerce & Consumer Affairs, Board of Electricians, Plumbers & Elevator Mechanics Licensing, PO Box 3469 (335 Merchant St., 96813), Honolulu, HI 96801; 808-586-2705. www.hawaii.gov/dcca/areas/pvl/boards/electrician/ Email: elect_plumb@dcca.hawaii.gov Search Database at www.ehawaiigov.org/serv/pvl

30 Dept. of Commerce & Consumer Affairs, Hearing Aid Dealers & Fitters Program, PO Box 3469 (335 Merchant St., 96813), Honolulu, HI 96801; 808-586-2698, Fax: 808-586-2689. www.hawaii.gov/dcca/areas/pvl/programs/hearing/

Email: hearingaid@dcca.hawaii.gov Search Database at www.ehawaiigov.org/serv/pvl

31 Department of Commerce & Consumer Affairs, Insurance Division, Licensing Branch, 335 Merchant St #333, Honolulu, HI 96813; 808-586-2790, Fax: 808-587-6714. www.ehawaiigov.org   Email: inslic@dcca.hawaii.gov Search Database at www.ehawaiigov.org/serv/hils

32 Department of Commerce & Consumer Affairs, Pest Control Board, PO Box 3469 (335 Merchant St, 96813), Honolulu, HI 96801; 808-586-2705. Email: pest_control@dcca.hawaii.gov Search Database at www.ehawaiigov.org/serv/pvl

33 Department of Health, Radiologic Technology Board, 591 Ala Moana Blvd, Honolulu, HI 96813-4921; 808-586-4700, Fax: 808-586-5838. Email: rtakata@sdmail.health.state.hi.us

34 Department of Commerce & Consumer Affairs, Real Estate Commission, 335 Merchant Street Rm 333, Honolulu, HI 96813; 808-586-2643. www.state.hi.us/hirec Email: hirec@dcca.state.hi.us Search Database at www.ehawaiigov.org/serv/pvl

35 Department of Education, Board of Education, PO Box 2360, Honolulu, HI 96804; 808-586-3332, Fax: 808-586-3433.

36 Department of Land & Natural Resources, Division of Aquatic Resources, 1151 Punch Bowl St Rm 330, Honolulu, HI 96813; 808-587-0100, Fax: 808-587-0115. www.state.hi.us/dlnr/dar Email: dlnr_aquatics@exec.state.hi.us

37 Department of Transportation, Airports Division, Airport District Manager, 300 Rodgers Blvd. # 12, Honolulu, HI 96819-1897; 808-836-6533, Fax: 808-836-6682. www.state.hi.us/dot/airports

38 Hawaii State Bar Association, 1132 Bishop St #906, Honolulu, HI 96813-2814; 808-537-1868, Fax: 808-521-7936. www.hsba.org

39 Motor Vehicle Licensing Division, City Square Driver License, 1199 Dillingham St Rm A101, Honolulu, HI 96817; 808-532-7730, Fax: 808-832-2904. School Bus and Regular Bus Drivers are now part of the general "commercial drivers' license." No longer something that can be verified separately.

40 Department of Health, Laboratory Licensing, 2725 Waimano Home Rd, Pearl City, HI 96782; 808-453-6653, Fax: 808-453-6662.

41 State Ethics Commission, 1001 Bishop St, Pacific Tower #970, Honolulu, HI 96813; 808-587-0460, Fax: 808-587-0470. www.state.hi.us/ethics Email: ethics@hawaiiethics.org   Search Database at www.state.hi.us/ethics/noindex/pubrec.htm

42 Department of Commerce & Consumer Affairs, Professional & Vocational Licensing Div-Programs, 335 Merchant St, 3rd Fl, Honolulu, HI 96813; 808-587-3295. www.state.hi.us/dcca/pvl/ Search Database at www.ehawaiigov.org/serv/pvl.

Hawaii Federal Courts

The following list indicates the district and division name for each county in the state.

County/Court Cross Reference

Hawaii .... Honolulu
Honolulu .... Honolulu
Kalawao .... Honolulu
Kauai .... Honolulu
Maui .... Honolulu

US District Court

Honolulu Division Court Clerk, 300 Ala Moana Blvd, Rm C-338, Honolulu, HI 96850 (also use mail address for courier delivery), 808-541-1300 x8, crim dockets- 808-541-1301, civil dockets- 808-541-1297, Fax-808-541-1303. Hours- 8:30AM-4PM. www.hid.uscourts.gov

Counties: All counties.

Searches & Indexing: Results do not include SSN or DOB. Computer, microfiche and card indexes maintained. New cases in the index immediately after filing date. Records purged never.

Fee & Payment: Pay by money order, cashier's or personal check. Payee: Clerk, US District Court. Prepayment required.

Phone Search: No searching by telephone.

Mail Search: search usually completed- 1 week. Include SASE for return.

In Person Search: Fee charged if court performs your search. No self-serve copier available.

E-Services: PACER online at http://pacer.hid.uscourts.gov. PACER records go back to 10/1991. New records online after 1 day. ECF at https://ecf.hid.uscourts.gov. ECF may still be in testing stage; if so, do not use. **Other Online Access:** Daily calendar at www.hid.uscourts.gov/calendar.

US Bankruptcy Court

Honolulu Division Court Clerk, 1132 Bishop St, Suite 250-L, Honolulu, HI 96813 (also use mail address for courier delivery), 808-522-8100, Fax-800-522-8120. Hours- 8AM-4PM. www.hib.uscourts.gov

Counties: All counties.

Searches & Indexing: Results include last 4 SSN digits. Both computer and card indexes maintained. New cases in the index 24 hours after filing date.

Fee & Payment: Pay by money order, cashier's or personal check. No debtor's checks accepted. Payee: Bankruptcy Court. Prepayment required.

Phone Search: Only docket information is available by phone. Voice Case Information Service available, call VCIS at 808-522-8122.

Mail Search: search usually completed- 2 weeks. Include SASE for return.

In Person Search: Fee charged if court performs your search. Self-serve copier available - $.10 per page.

E-Services: PACER records go back to 1987. New records online after 1 day. ECF at https://ecf.hib.uscourts.gov **Opinions Online:** www.hib.uscourts.gov/opinions/index_opinions.htm. **Other Online Access:** Calendars are at www.hib.uscourts.gov/calendars/index_calendars.htm.

Standards for Federal Courts: Search fee is $26.00 per item (one party name or case number). Copy fee is $.50 per page. Certification fee is $9.00 per document, double for exemplification, if available. All fees standard unless noted in profile. Mail Search: always enclose a stamped self addressed envelope unless otherwise noted. Most courts accept fax requests or will suggest a copying/search vendor. Before releasing records, all courts require prepayment, unless noted.

Open records are located at the court unless otherwise noted. District courts index by defendant and plaintiff as well as by case number. Bankruptcy courts usually index by debtor and case number. While most courts now have their indexes on computer, many may still maintain index card files as well.

Courts offering internet access via CM-ECF or older RACER, PACER, or Web-PACER systems charge $.08 per page fee unless noted as free. Where PACER is available, the universal sign-up number is 800-676-6856. Find PACER and the US Party/Case Index at http://pacer.psc.uscourts.gov.

Hawaii County Courts

Court	Jurisdiction	No. of Courts	How Organized
Circuit Courts*	General	4	4 Circuits
District Courts*	Limited	7	4 Circuits

* Profiled in this Sourcebook.

	CIVIL								
Court	Tort	Contract	Real Estate	Min. Claim	Max. Claim	Small Claims	Estate	Eviction	Domestic Relations
Circuit Courts*	X	X	X	$5000/ $10,000	No Max		X		X
District Courts*	X	X	X	$0	$20,000	$3500		X	

	CRIMINAL				
Court	Felony	Misdemeanor	DWI/DUI	Preliminary Hearing	Juvenile
Circuit Courts*	X	X	X		X
District Courts*		X	X	X	

ADMINISTRATION   Administrative Director of Courts, Judicial Branch, 417 S King St, Honolulu, HI, 96813; 808-539-4900, Fax: 808-539-4855. www.courts.state.hi.us/index.jsp

COURT STRUCTURE   Hawaii's trial level is comprised of Circuit Courts (with Family Courts) and District Courts. These trial courts function in four judicial circuits: First (Oahu), Second (Maui/Molokai/Lanai), Third (Hawaii County), and Fifth (Kauai/Niihau). The Fourth Circuit was merged with the Third in 1943.

Circuit Courts are general jurisdiction and handle all jury trials, felony cases, and civil cases over $20,000, also probate and guardianship. The District Court handles criminal cases punishable by a fine and/or less then 1-yr imprisonment and some civil cases up to $20,000, also landlord/tenant and DUI cases.

ONLINE ACCESS   Free online access to all Circuit Court and family court records, and civil records from the District courts is available at the website www.courts.state.hi.us (click on "Search Court Records"). Search by name or case number. These records are not considered "official" for FCRA compliant searches. Most courts have access back to mid 1980's. Also, opinions from the Appellate Court are available from the home page url.

ADD'L INFORMATION   Most Hawaii state courts offer a public access terminal to search records at the courthouse.

Civil cases down to $5000 minimum are found at the Circuit Court if a jury is involved.

Hawaii County

3rd Circuit Court Legal Documents Section PO Box 1007, Hilo, HI 96721-1007; phone: 808-961-7404; fax: 808-961-7416; hours 7:45AM-4:30PM (HT). *Felony, Misdemeanor, Civil Actions Over $5,000, Probate.*
www.courts.state.hi.us
Civil Records: Access: Mail, fax, in person, online. Both court and visitors may perform in person searches. Search fee: $5.00 per name. Court makes copy: $1.00 for first page, $.50 each add'l. A microfilm copy is $1.00 per page. Required to search: name, years to search. Civil cases indexed by defendant, plaintiff. Civil records on computer from 1988, index card system prior to 1988. Free record searching at www.courts.state.hi.us/index.jsp. Click on "Search Court Records." Search by name or case number. Records go back to early 1900s. Mail turnaround time 2 days depending upon staff coverage.
Criminal Records: Access: Mail, fax, in person, online. Both court and visitors may perform in person searches. Search fee: $5.00 per name. Court makes copy: $1.00 for first page, $.50 each add'l. Microfilm copy is $1.00 per page. Required to search: name, years to search. Criminal records on computer

from 1988, index card system prior to 1988. Online access to criminal records is same as civil. Mail turnaround time normally 2 days.
General Information: Public use terminal available. No adoption, juvenile, dependencies, confidential records released without court's approval. Will fax documents to local or toll free line. Certification fee: $2.00. Payee: Clerk, 3rd Circuit Court. Personal checks accepted. Prepayment and SASE required.

District Court PO Box 4879, Hilo, HI 96720; phone: 808-961-7470; fax: 808-961-7447; hours 7:45AM-4:30PM (HT). *Misdemeanor, Civil Actions Under $20,000, Eviction, Small Claims.*
www.courts.state.hi.us/index.jsp
Civil Records: Access: Phone, fax, mail, in person, online. Both court and visitors may perform in person searches. Search fee: $5.00 per name. Court makes copy: $1.00 for first page, $.50 each add'l. Off site storage- usual copy fees plus $5.00. Required to search: name, years to search, case number; also helpful: address. Civil cases indexed by defendant. Civil records on ledgers from statehood. Free record searching at www.courts.state.hi.us/index.jsp. Click on "Search Court Records." Mail turnaround time 1 week.
Criminal Records: Access: Phone, fax, mail, in person, online. Both court and visitors may perform

in person searches. Search fee: $5.00 per name. Court makes copy: $1.00 for first page, $.50 each add'l. Off-site storage- usual copy fees plus $5.00. Required to search: name, years to search, case number; also helpful: address, DOB, SSN. Criminal records on computer since 3/1996. Free record searching at www.courts.state.hi.us/index.jsp. Click on "Search Court Records." Mail turnaround time 1 week.
General Information: Public terminal has only criminal records back to 3/1996. No family court records released. Will fax documents $2.00 1st page, $1.00 each add'l. Extra fee for out of state faxing. Certification fee: $2.00. Payee: Clerk of the District Court. Personal checks or Visa, MC accepted. Prepayment required. SASE requested.

Honolulu County

1st Circuit Court Legal Documents Branch, 777 Punchbowl St, 1st Fl, Honolulu, HI 96813; phone: 808-539-4300; fax: 808-539-4314; hours 7:45AM-4:30PM (HT). *Felony, Civil Actions Over $5,000, Probate, Family.*
www.courts.state.hi.us/index.jsp
Civil Records: Access: Mail, in person, online. Both court and visitors may perform in person searches. Search fee: $5.00 per name. Court makes copy: $1.00

for first page, $.50 each add'l. Microfilm service fee $5.00 and $1.00 per page copy fee. Required to search: name, years to search. Civil cases indexed by defendant, plaintiff. Records on computer from 1983, on microfiche and archived from 1900. Free record searching at www.courts.state.hi.us/index.jsp. Click on "Search Court Records." Search by name or case number. Mail turnaround time same day.

Criminal Records: Access: Mail, in person, online. Both court and visitors may perform in person searches. Search fee: $5.00 per name. Court makes copy: $1.00 for first page, $.50 each add'l. Microfilm service fee $5.00; cost of copies $1.00 per page. Required to search: name, years to search, DOB; also helpful: SSN. Records on computer from 1983, on microfiche and archived from 1900. Online access is the same as civil. Mail turnaround time same day.

General Information: Public use terminal available. No adoptions, paternity or sealed records released. Certification fee: $2.00 per cert. Payee: 1st Circuit Court. Business checks accepted. Prepayment and SASE required.

District Court - Civil Division
1111 Alakea St, 3rd Fl, Honolulu, HI 96813; phone: 808-538-5151; fax: 808-538-5444; hours 7:45AM-4:15PM (HT). *Civil Actions Under $20,000, Eviction, Small Claims.*
www.courts.state.hi.us/index.jsp

Civil Records: Access: Phone, mail, in person, online. Both court and visitors may perform in person searches. Search fee: $5.00 per name. Required to search: name, years to search. Free record searching at www.courts.state.hi.us/index.jsp. Click on "Search Court Records." Mail turnaround time 1 week.

General Information: Public terminal has civil records back to 1990. No sealed records released. Call for fax fee. No certification fee. Payee: District Court of the 1st Circuit. Personal checks or Visa, MC, Discover accepted. Prepayment and SASE required.

District Court - Criminal Division
1111 Alakea St, 7rd Fl, Judicial Services, Honolulu, HI 96813; phone: 808-538-5100; fax: 808-538-5111; hours 8AM-4:15PM (HT). *Misdemeanor, Traffic.*
www.courts.state.hi.us/index.jsp

Criminal Records: Access: Fax, mail, in person, online. Only the court performs in person searches; visitors may not. Search fee: $5.00 per name. No copy fee. Required to search: name, years to search, SSN, signed release, aliases; also helpful: address, DOB. Free record searching at www.courts.state.hi.us/index.jsp. Click on "Search Court Records." Mail turnaround time 1 week.

General Information: No sealed records released. No certification fee. Payee: District Court of the 1st Judicial Circuit. Business checks accepted. Prepayment and SASE required.

Kauai County

5th Circuit Court
3059 Umi St Rm, #101, Lihue, HI 96766; phone: 808-246-3300; fax: 808-246-3310; hours 7:45AM-4:30PM (HT). *Felony, Misdemeanor, Civil Actions Over $20,000, Probate.*
www.courts.state.hi.us

Civil Records: Access: Mail, in person, online. Both court and visitors may perform in person searches. Search fee: $5.00 per name. Court makes copy: $1.00 for first page, $.50 each add'l. Required to search: name, years to search. Civil cases indexed by plaintiff & defendant. Civil records on computer from 1987, microfiche from 1960. Free record searching at www.courts.state.hi.us/index.jsp. Click on "Search Court Records." Search by name or case number. Mail turnaround time approx. 1 week.

Criminal Records: Access: Mail, in person, online. Both court and visitors may perform in person searches. Search fee: $5.00 per name. Court makes copy: $1.00 for first page, $.50 each add'l. Required to search: name, years to search, DOB; also helpful: SSN. Criminal records on computer from 1987, microfiche from 1960. Online access same as civil. Mail turnaround time approx. 1 week.

General Information: No public access terminal. No juvenile, dependencies records released. Certification fee: $2.00. Payee: 5th Circuit Court. Only cashiers checks, money orders or cash accepted. Prepayment and SASE required.

District Court of the 5th Circuit - Civil
4357 Rice St, #101, Lihue, HI 96766; phone: 808-246-3301; fax: 808-241-7103; hours 7:45AM-4:30PM (HT). *Civil Actions Under $20,000, Eviction, Small Claims.*
www.courts.state.hi.us/index.jsp

Civil Records: Access: Phone, fax, mail, in person, online. Both court and visitors may perform in person searches. Search fee: $5.00 per case. Court makes copy: $1.00 for first page, $.50 each add'l. Required to search: name, years to search. Civil cases indexed by defendant, on index cards. Free record searching at www.courts.state.hi.us/index.jsp. Click on "Search Court Records." Mail turnaround time 1-7 days.

General Information: No public access terminal. No juvenile records released. Will fax documents for $2.00 1st page, $1.00 each add'l. No certification fee. Payee: District Court of the Fifth Judicial Circuit. Personal in-state checks accepted; no third party checks. Visa, MasterCard accepted. Prepayment required. SASE requested.

District Court of the 5th Circuit - Criminal
3059 Umi St, Rm 111, Lihue, HI 96766; phone: 808-246-3330; fax: 808-246-3309; hours 7:45AM-4:30PM (HT). *Misdemeanor.*
www.courts.state.hi.us/index.jsp

Criminal Records: Access: Phone, fax, mail, in person, online. Only the court performs in person searches; visitors may not. Search fee: $10.00. Court makes copy: $1.00 for first page, $.50 each add'l. Required to search: name, years to search, DOB; also helpful: SSN. Free record searching at www.courts.state.hi.us/index.jsp. Click on "Search Court Records." Mail turnaround time 1 week.

General Information: Will fax documents for $2.00 1st page, $1.00 each add'l page. Certification fee: $2.00 per cert. Payee: District Court.

Maui County

2nd Circuit Court
2145 Main St, #106, Wailuku, HI 96793; phone: 808-244-2969; fax: 808-244-2932; hours 7:45AM-4:30PM (HT). *Felony, Misdemeanor, Civil Actions Over $5,000, Probate.*
www.courts.state.hi.us

Note: This court also covers the counties of Lanai and Molokai.

Civil Records: Access: Mail, in person, online. Both court and visitors may perform in person searches. Search fee: $5.00 per name. Court makes copy: file marked pages are $1.00 per page; non-file marked are $.50. Required to search: name, years to search. Civil cases indexed by defendant, plaintiff. Civil records on computer from 10/88, some prior on microfiche. Access Circuit Court & family court records free at www.courts.state.hi.us/index.jsp. Click on "Search Court Records." Records go back to 1984. Mail turnaround time 1 week.

Criminal Records: Access: Mail, in person, online. Both court and visitors may perform in person searches. Search fee: $5.00 per name. Court makes copy: file marked pages $1.00 per page; non-file marked are $.50. Required to search: name, years to search; also helpful: DOB, SSN. Criminal records on computer from 10/88, some prior on microfiche. Online access to criminal records is same as civil. Mail turnaround time 1 week.

General Information: Public use terminal available. No juvenile or paternity records released. Fee to fax documents is $5.00 1st page, $2.00 each add'l in USA; $2.00 for first and $1.00 each add'l in Hawaii. Certification fee: $2.00 per cert. Payee: Clerk, 2nd Circuit Court. Personal checks accepted. Prepayment and SASE required.

Lanai District Court
PO Box 631376, Lanai City, HI 96763; phone: 808-565-6447; fax: 808-565-7543; hours 7:45AM-4:30PM (HT). *Misdemeanor, Civil Actions Under $20,000, Eviction, Small Claims.*
www.courts.state.hi.us/index.jsp

Civil Records: Access: Mail, online, in person. Only the court performs in person searches; visitors may not. Search fee: $5.00 per search. Court makes copy: $1.00 for first page, $.50 each add'l. Required to search: name, years to search. Civil cases indexed by defendant, plaintiff. Civil records on index and docket books back to statehood. Free record searching at www.courts.state.hi.us/index.jsp. Click on "Search Court Records." Records go back to 12/03. Mail turnaround time 2-3 weeks.

Criminal Records: Access: Mail, in person, online. Only the court performs in person searches; visitors may not. Search fee: $5.00 per search. Court makes copy: $1.00 for first page, $.50 each add'l. Required to search: name, years to search; also helpful: DOB, SSN. Criminal records on computer since 1997. Online access to criminal records is same as civil. Mail turnaround time 2-3 weeks.

General Information: Certification fee: $1.00. Payee: Lanai District Court. Personal checks accepted. Credit cards accepted if paid through Wailuku Dist. Court. Prepayment required.

Molokai District Court
PO Box 284, Kaunakakai, HI 96748; phone: 808-553-1100, 553-5451; fax: 808-553-3374; hours 7:45AM-4:30PM (HT). *Misdemeanor, Civil Actions Under $20,000, Eviction, Small Claims.*
www.courts.state.hi.us

Civil Records: Access: In person, online. Only the court performs in person searches; visitors may not. Court makes copy: $1.00 for first page, $.50 each add'l. Required to search: name, years to search. Civil cases indexed by defendant, plaintiff, on index and docket books back to statehood. Free record searching at www.courts.state.hi.us/index.jsp. Click on "Search Court Records."

Criminal Records: Access: In person, online. Only the court performs in person searches; visitors may not. Search fee: $5.00 per name. Court makes copy: $1.00 for first page, $.50 each add'l. Required to search: name, years to search, DOB, SSN. Criminal records on computer since 1980. Online access to criminal records is same as civil.

General Information: No juvenile or paternity records released. Certification fee: $5.00 per cert. Payee: Molokai District Court. Business checks accepted. Prepayment required.

Wailuku District Court
2145 Main St, #137, Wailuku, HI 96793; phone: 808-244-2800; fax: 808-244-2849; hours 7:45AM-4:30PM (HT). *Misdemeanor, Civil Actions Under $20,000, Eviction, Small Claims.*
www.courts.state.hi.us

Civil Records: Access: Mail, in person, online. Only the court performs in person searches; visitors may not. Search fee: $5.00 per name. Court makes copy: $1.00 for first page, $.50 each add'l. Required to search: name, years to search; also helpful: address. Civil cases indexed by defendant, plaintiff. Civil records on index and docket books. Free record searching at www.courts.state.hi.us/index.jsp. Click on "Search Court Records." Mail turnaround time 2-3 weeks.

Criminal Records: Access: Mail, in person, online. Only the court performs in person searches; visitors may not. Search fee: $5.00 per name. Court makes copy: $1.00 for first page, $.50 each add'l. Required to search: name, years to search, DOB, SSN. Criminal records on computer since 1980. Online access to criminal records is same as civil. Mail turnaround time 2-3 weeks.

General Information: Will fax documents $5.00 1st page, $2.00 each add'l. Within HI; $2.00 1st page, $1.00 each add'l. No certification fee. Payee: District Court 2nd Circuit. Personal checks or Visa, MC accepted. Prepayment and SASE required.

Hawaii Recording Office

ORGANIZATION: All UCC financing statements, tax liens, and real estate documents are filed centrally with the Bureau of Conveyances located in Honolulu. The entire state is in the Hawaii Time Zone (HT).

Bureau of Conveyances

Bureau of Conveyances, PO Box 2867, Honolulu, HI 96803. 808-587-0154, R/E recording phone-808-587-0134; fax-808-587-4380; hours: 7:45AM-4:30PM www.hawaii.gov/dlnr/bc

Office will perform a UCC search but public must search other records themselves. Will not search real estate records. UCC search per debtor name- $25.00 minimum; Add'l charges for found records. Copy fee $1.00 per page. Cert fee- $1.00 per page. Payee- Bureau of Conveyances. **Online access to Property records:** Property records on the Hawaii County property assessor records are free at www.hawaiipropertytax.com. Also, search Honolulu real estate records at www.honolulupropertytax.com. No name searching. Maui Assessor Property records are free at www.mauipropertytax.com. Indices to all documents recorded in the Bureau of Conveyances from 1976 to current are online at http://132.160.239.151/boc/. Certified copies of documents may also be ordered. **Other phones:** Land Court- 808-587-0138. **Property tax/Assessor-** 842 Bethel St, Honolulu, HI 96813; 808-527-5541/5511.

Hawaii County Locator

You will usually be able to find the city name in the City/County Cross Reference below. In that case, it is a simple matter to determine the county from the cross reference. However, only the official US Postal Service city names are included in this index. There are an additional 40,000 place names that people use in their addresses. Therefore, we have also included a ZIP/City Cross Reference immediately following the City/County Cross Reference.

If you know the ZIP Code but the city name does not appear in the City/County Cross Reference index, look up the ZIP Code in the ZIP/City Cross Reference, find the city name, then look up the city name in the City/County Cross Reference. For example, you want to know the county for an address of Menands, NY 12204. There is no "Menands" in the City/County Cross Reference. The ZIP/City Cross Reference shows that ZIP Codes 12201-12288 are for the city of Albany. Looking back in the City/County Cross Reference, Albany is in Albany County.

Hawaii City/County Cross Reference

AIEA Honolulu
ANAHOLA Kauai
BARBERS POINT Honolulu
BARBERS POINT N A S Honolulu
CAMP H M SMITH Honolulu
CAPTAIN COOK Hawaii
ELEELE Kauai
EWA BEACH Honolulu
FORT SHAFTER Honolulu
HAIKU Maui
HAKALAU Hawaii
HALEIWA Honolulu
HANA Maui
HANALEI Kauai
HANAMAULU Kauai
HANAPEPE Kauai
HAUULA Honolulu
HAWAII NATIONAL PARK Hawaii
HAWI Hawaii
HICKAM AFB Honolulu
HILO Hawaii
HOLUALOA Hawaii
HONAUNAU Hawaii
HONOKAA Hawaii
HONOLULU Honolulu

HONOMU Hawaii
HOOLEHUA Maui
KAAAWA Honolulu
KAHUKU Honolulu
KAHULUI Maui
KAILUA Honolulu
KAILUA KONA Hawaii
KALAHEO Kauai
KALAUPAPA Maui
KAMUELA Hawaii
KANEOHE Honolulu
KAPAA Kauai
KAPAAU Hawaii
KAPOLEI Honolulu
KAUMAKANI Kauai
KAUNAKAKAI Maui
KEAAU Hawaii
KEALAKEKUA Hawaii
KEALIA Kauai
KEAUHOU Hawaii
KEKAHA Kauai
KIHEI Maui
KILAUEA Kauai
KOLOA Kauai
KUALAPUU Maui

KULA Maui
KUNIA Honolulu
KURTISTOWN Hawaii
LAHAINA Maui
LAIE Honolulu
LANAI CITY Maui
LAUPAHOEHOE Hawaii
LAWAI Kauai
LIHUE Kauai
M C B H KANEOHE BAY Honolulu
MAKAWAO Maui
MAKAWELI Kauai
MAUNALOA Maui
MILILANI Honolulu
MOUNTAIN VIEW Hawaii
NAALEHU Hawaii
NINOLE Hawaii
OCEAN VIEW Hawaii
OOKALA Hawaii
PAAUHAU Hawaii
PAAUILO Hawaii
PAHALA Hawaii
PAHOA Hawaii
PAIA Maui
PAPAALOA Hawaii

PAPAIKOU Hawaii
PEARL CITY Honolulu
PEARL HARBOR Honolulu
PEPEEKEO Hawaii
PRINCEVILLE Kauai
PUKALANI Maui
PUUNENE Maui
SCHOFIELD BARRACKS Honolulu
TAMC Honolulu
TRIPLER ARMY MEDICAL CTR Honolulu
VOLCANO Hawaii
WAHIAWA Honolulu
WAIALUA Honolulu
WAIANAE Honolulu
WAIKOLOA Hawaii
WAILUKU Maui
WAIMANALO Honolulu
WAIMEA Kauai
WAIPAHU Honolulu
WAKE ISLAND Honolulu
WHEELER ARMY AIRFIELD Honolulu

ZIP/City Cross Reference

96701-96701 AIEA
96703-96703 ANAHOLA
96704-96704 CAPTAIN COOK
96705-96705 ELEELE
96706-96706 EWA BEACH
96707-96707 KAPOLEI
96708-96708 HAIKU
96709-96709 KAPOLEI
96710-96710 HAKALAU
96712-96712 HALEIWA
96713-96713 HANA
96714-96714 HANALEI
96715-96715 HANAMAULU
96716-96716 HANAPEPE
96717-96717 HAUULA
96718-96718 HAWAII NATIONAL PARK
96719-96719 HAWI
96720-96721 HILO
96722-96722 PRINCEVILLE
96725-96725 HOLUALOA
96726-96726 HONAUNAU
96727-96727 HONOKAA
96728-96728 HONOMU
96729-96729 HOOLEHUA
96730-96730 KAAAWA
96731-96731 KAHUKU

96732-96733 KAHULUI
96734-96734 KAILUA
96737-96737 OCEAN VIEW
96738-96738 WAIKOLOA
96739-96739 KEAUHOU
96740-96740 KAILUA KONA
96741-96741 KALAHEO
96742-96742 KALAUPAPA
96743-96743 KAMUELA
96744-96744 KANEOHE
96745-96745 KAILUA KONA
96746-96746 KAPAA
96747-96747 KAUMAKANI
96748-96748 KAUNAKAKAI
96749-96749 KEAAU
96750-96750 KEALAKEKUA
96751-96751 KEALIA
96752-96752 KEKAHA
96753-96753 KIHEI
96754-96754 KILAUEA
96755-96755 KAPAAU
96756-96756 KOLOA
96757-96757 KUALAPUU
96759-96759 KUNIA
96760-96760 KURTISTOWN
96761-96761 LAHAINA

96762-96762 LAIE
96763-96763 LANAI CITY
96764-96764 LAUPAHOEHOE
96765-96765 LAWAI
96766-96766 LIHUE
96767-96767 LAHAINA
96768-96768 MAKAWAO
96769-96769 MAKAWELI
96770-96770 MAUNALOA
96771-96771 MOUNTAIN VIEW
96772-96772 NAALEHU
96773-96773 NINOLE
96774-96774 OOKALA
96775-96775 PAAUHAU
96776-96776 PAAUILO
96777-96777 PAHALA
96778-96778 PAHOA
96779-96779 PAIA
96780-96780 PAPAALOA
96781-96781 PAPAIKOU
96782-96782 PEARL CITY
96783-96783 PEPEEKEO
96784-96784 PUUNENE
96785-96785 VOLCANO
96786-96786 WAHIAWA
96788-96788 PUKALANI

96789-96789 MILILANI
96790-96790 KULA
96791-96791 WAIALUA
96792-96792 WAIANAE
96793-96793 WAILUKU
96795-96795 WAIMANALO
96796-96796 WAIMEA
96797-96797 WAIPAHU
96800-96850 HONOLULU
96853-96853 HICKAM AFB
96854-96854 WHEELER ARMY
             AIRFIELD
96857-96857 SCHOFIELD BARRACKS
96858-96858 FORT SHAFTER
96859-96859 TRIPLER ARMY MED CTR
96859-96859 TAMC
96860-96860 PEARL HARBOR
96861-96861 CAMP H M SMITH
96862-96862 BARBERS POINT N A S
96862-96862 BARBERS POINT
96863-96863 M C B H KANEOHE BAY
96898-96898 WAKE ISLAND

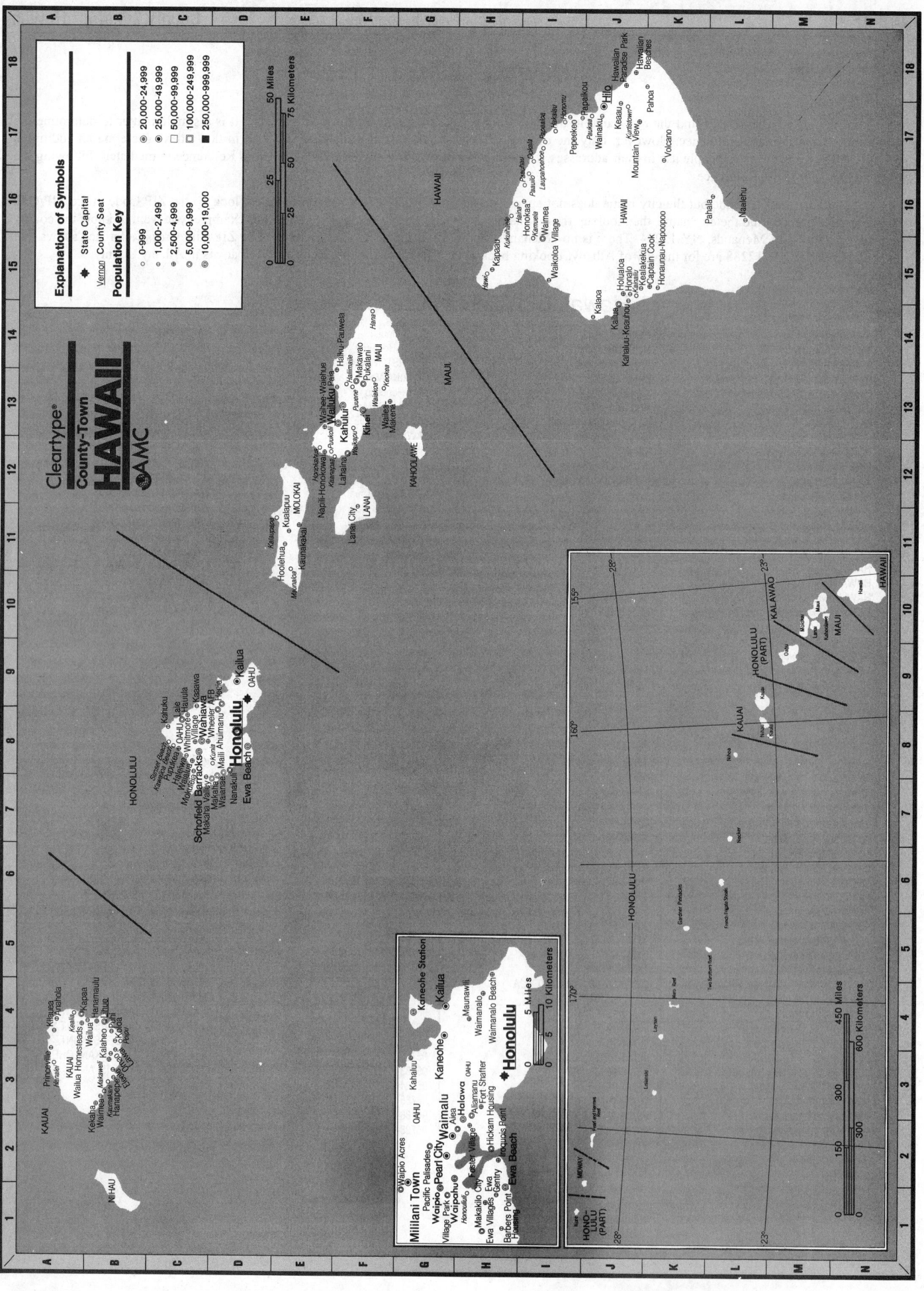

COUNTIES

(5 Counties)

Name of County	Population	Location on Map
HAWAII	120,317	G-16
HONOLULU	836,231	B-7
KALAWAO	130	D-11
KAUAI	51,177	A-2
MAUI	100,374	G-13
TOTAL	1,108,229	

CITIES AND TOWNS

Note: The first name is that of the city or town, second, that of the county in which it is located, then the population and location on the map.

- Ahuimanu, Honolulu, 8,387 .... D-8
- Aiea, Honolulu, 8,906 .... H-2
- Aliamanu, Honolulu, 8,835 .... H-3
- Anahola, Kauai, 1,181 .... A-4
- Barbers Point Housing, Honolulu, 2,218 ...... H-1
- Captain Cook, Hawaii, 2,595 .... J-15
- Eleele, Kauai, 1,489 .... B-3
- Ewa Beach, Honolulu, 14,315 .... D-8
- Ewa Gentry, Honolulu, 1,992 .... H-1
- Ewa Villages, Honolulu, 3,780 .... H-1
- Fort Shafter, Honolulu, 2,952 .... H-3
- Foster Village, Honolulu H-2
- Haiku-Pauwela, Maui, 4,509 .... F-13
- Halawa, Honolulu, 13,408 .... H-2
- Haleiwa, Honolulu, 2,442 .... C-8
- Hanamaulu, Kauai, 3,611 .... B-4
- Hanapepe, Kauai, 1,395 .... B-3
- Hauula, Honolulu, 3,479 .... C-8
- Hawaiian Beaches, Hawaii, 2,846 .... J-18
- Hawaiian Paradise Park, Hawaii, 3,389 ..... J-17
- Heeia, Honolulu, 5,010 .... D-9
- Hickam Housing, Honolulu, 6,553 .... H-2
- Hilo, Hawaii, 37,808 .... J-17
- Holualoa, Hawaii, 3,834 .... J-15
- Honalo, Hawaii, 1,926 .... J-15
- Honaunau-Napoopoo, Hawaii, 2,373 .... K-15
- Honokaa, Hawaii, 2,186 .... I-16
- Honolulu, Honolulu, 365,272 .... D-9
- Hoolehua, Maui E-11
- Iroquois Point, Honolulu, 4,188 .... H-2
- Kaaawa, Honolulu, 1,138 .... C-8
- Kahaluu, Honolulu, 3,068 .... G-3
- Kahaluu-Keauhou, Hawaii, 1,990 .... J-15
- Kahuku, Honolulu, 2,063 .... C-8
- Kahului, Maui, 16,889 .... F-13
- Kailua, Hawaii, 9,126 .... J-14

- Kailua, Honolulu, 36,818 .... D-9
- Kalaheo, Kauai, 3,592 .... B-3
- Kalaoa, Hawaii, 4,490 .... J-14
- Kaneohe, Honolulu, 35,448 .... G-4
- Kaneohe Station, Honolulu, 11,662 .... G-4
- Kapaa, Kauai, 8,149 .... A-4
- Kapaau, Hawaii, 1,083 .... H-15
- Kaunakakai, Maui, 2,658 .... E-11
- Keaau, Hawaii, 1,584 .... J-17
- Kealakekua, Hawaii, 1,453 .... J-15
- Kekaha, Kauai, 3,506 .... B-3
- Kihei, Maui, 11,107 .... F-13
- Kilauea, Kauai, 1,685 .... A-4
- Koloa, Kauai, 1,791 .... B-4
- Kualapuu, Maui, 1,661 .... E-11
- Lahaina, Maui, 9,073 .... F-12
- Laie, Honolulu, 5,577 .... C-8
- Lanai City, Maui, 2,400 .... F-11
- Lawai, Kauai, 1,787 .... B-3
- Lihue, Kauai, 5,536 .... B-4
- Maili, Honolulu, 6,059 .... D-8
- Makaha, Honolulu, 7,990 .... C-7
- Makaha Valley, Honolulu, 1,012 .... C-7
- Makakilo City, Honolulu, 9,828 .... H-1
- Makawao, Maui, 5,405 .... F-13
- Maunawili, Honolulu, 4,847 .... H-4
- Mililani Town, Honolulu, 29,359 .... G-2
- Mokuleia, Honolulu, 1,776 .... C-8
- Mountain View, Hawaii, 3,075 .... J-17
- Naalehu, Hawaii, 1,027 .... L-16
- Nanakuli, Honolulu, 9,575 .... D-8
- Napili-Honokowai, Maui, 4,332 .... E-12
- Omao, Kauai, 1,142 .... B-3
- Pacific Palisades, Honolulu G-2
- Pahala, Hawaii, 1,520 .... L-16
- Pahoa, Hawaii, 1,027 .... K-18
- Paia, Maui, 2,091 .... F-13
- Papaikou, Hawaii, 1,634 .... I-17
- Pearl City, Honolulu, 30,993 .... G-2
- Pepeekeo, Hawaii, 1,813 .... I-17
- Princeville, Kauai, 1,244 .... A-3
- Puhi, Kauai, 1,210 .... B-4
- Pukalani, Maui, 5,879 .... F-13
- Pupukea, Honolulu, 4,111 .... C-8
- Schofield Barracks, Honolulu, 19,597 .... C-8
- Village Park, Honolulu, 7,407 .... G-1
- Volcano, Hawaii, 1,516 .... K-16
- Wahiawa, Honolulu, 17,386 .... C-8
- Waialua, Honolulu, 3,943 .... C-8
- Waianae, Honolulu, 8,758 .... D-7
- Waihee-Waiehue, Maui, 4,004 .... E-13
- Waikoloa Village, Hawaii, 2,248 .... I-15
- Wailea-Makena, Maui, 3,799 .... F-13
- Wailua, Kauai, 2,018 .... B-4
- Wailua Homesteads, Kauai, 3,870 .... A-4

- Wailuku, Maui, 10,688 .... E-13
- Waimalu, Honolulu, 29,967 .... H-2
- Waimanalo, Honolulu, 3,508 .... H-4
- Waimanalo Beach, Honolulu, 4,185 .... H-5
- Waimea, Hawaii, 5,972 .... I-15
- Waimea, Kauai, 1,840 .... B-3
- Wainaku, Hawaii, 1,243 .... J-17
- Waipahu, Honolulu, 31,435 .... G-2
- Waipio, Honolulu, 11,812 .... G-2
- Waipio Acres, Honolulu, 5,304 .... D-8
- Wheeler AFB, Honolulu, 2,600 .... D-8
- Whitmore Village, Honolulu, 3,373 .... C-8

Explanation of symbols: ●– Census Designated Place (CDP)

General Help Numbers:

Governor's Office
PO Box 83720
Boise, ID 83720-0034
http://www2.state.id.us/gov/index.htm

208-334-2100
Fax 208-334-2175
8AM-6PM

Attorney General's Office
PO Box 83720
Boise, ID 83720-0010
http://www2.state.id.us/ag

208-334-2400
Fax 208-334-2530
8AM-5PM

Legislative Records
PO Box 83720
Boise, ID 83720-0054
http://www2.state.id.us/legislat/legislat.html

208-334-2475
Fax 208-334-2125
8AM-5PM

State Archives
Historical Library & Archives
450 N 4th Street
Boise, ID 83702-6027
http://idahohistory.net

208-334-3356
Fax 208-334-3198
9AM-5PM

State Specifics:

Capital:
Boise
Ada County

Time Zone:
MST*

* Idaho's ten northwestern-most counties are PST:
They are: Benewah, Bonner, Boundary, Clearwater,
Idaho, Kootenai, Latah, Lewis, Nez Perce, Shoshone.

Number of Counties:
44

Population:
1,393,262

Web Site:
www.state.id.us

State Agencies

Criminal Records

State Repository, Bureau of Criminal Identification, PO Box 700, Meridian, ID 83680-0700 (Courier address: 700 S Stratford Dr, Meridian, ID 83642); 208-884-7130, 208-884-7193-Fax; 8AM-4PM.

www.isp.state.id.us

A signed release is not required, but suggested; see below.

Records are available from 1960 on. It takes about 3 days before new records are available for inquiry. Records are normally destroyed after subject reaches 99th year. 66% of all arrests in database have final dispositions recorded, and at least 56% for those arrests within last 5 years.

Searching: Include the following in your request-name, DOB. SSN and alias will aid in identification. Fingerprints are optional but may be required to establish positive identification. Fingerprint searches take 5-7 days. 100% of records are fingerprint-supported. A record of an arrest without disposition after 12 months from date of arrest will only be given if signed release presented. Requests without the release will receive only records with dispositions.

Access by: mail, in person.

Fee & Payment: The $10.00 fee per person is applicable for either a name search or a fingerprint search. Fee payee: Idaho State Police Prepayment required. Cashier check or money order is preferred form of payment. No credit cards accepted.

Mail search: Turnaround time: 10 to 15 days.

In person search: You may request information in person, but results are still mailed.

Statewide Court Records

Administrative Director of the Courts, Clerk of the Courts, PO Box 83720, Boise, ID 83720-0101 (Courier: 451 W State St, Boise, ID 83720); 208-334-2246, 208-334-2146-Fax; 9AM-5PM.

www.isc.idaho.gov

Except for certain online research capabilities, all trial court record access must be done at the local level. For tribal court information, visit www.isc.idaho.gov/tribalmn.htm.

Access by: online.

Online search: Although appellate and supreme court opinions are available from the web, there is no statewide computer system offering external access. ISTARS is a statewide intra-court/intra-agency system for all counties, enabling all courts to provide public access terminals on-site.

Sexual Offender Registry

State Repository, Central Sexual Offender Registry, PO Box 700, Meridian, ID 83680-0700 (Courier: 700 S Stratford Dr, Meridian, ID 83642); 208-884-7305, 208-884-7193-Fax; 8AM-5PM.

www.isp.state.id.us

Records are available from 07/01/93. It takes about 3 days before new records are available for inquiry.

Searching: Any person may inquire by submitting a completed SOR-4 Form to the central registry or a local sheriff. Photos may be requested using SOR-5 Form. Include the following in your request-name and either DOB or address. Requests may be made on a named individual or a list of registered sex offenders by ZIP Code or county.

Access by: mail, in person, online.

Fee & Payment: There is a $5.00 fee, plus an additional $5.00 if photo needed, unless the request is made via online. Fee payee: BCI. Prepayment required. Cashier check or money order is preferred form of payment. But personal checks are accepted. No credit cards accepted.

Mail search: Turnaround time: 5 to 7 days.

In person search: You may request information from this agency or from any local sheriff's office.

Online search: Access from the web page is available to the public. Inquires can be made by name, address, or by county or ZIP Code.

Incarceration Records

Idaho Department of Corrections, Records Bureau, 1299 N. Orchard Street, Suite 110, Boise, ID 83706; 208-658-2000, 208-327-7444-Fax; 8AM-5PM.

www.corrections.state.id.us

Records are available on current and former inmates. It takes about 3 days before new records are available for inquiry. Records are normally destroyed after 2 years if probation only and not convicted of sex crime. All other records not destroyed but sent to state storage.

Searching: Include the following in your request-first and last name. DOB, SSN, DOC number are helpful.

Access by: mail, phone, fax, in person, online.

Fee & Payment: Cost is $2.00 for pulling from state storage, if required. Copies are $.10 per page after 5 pages.

Mail search: Turnaround time: 5 to 7 days. Requests in writing must be specific about information requested. Use SASE or you will be charged for postage.

Phone search: Limited searching by phone, "is subject there or not." **Fax search:** Only if just needing an inmate location.

In person search: The public has right to view records in person upon making a written request to schedule an appointment with records custodian.

Online search: This database search at https://www.accessidaho.org/public/corr/offender/search.html provides information about offenders currently under Idaho Department of Correction jurisdiction: those incarcerated, on probation, or on parole. Names of individuals who have served time and satisfied their sentence will appear - their convictions will not. Also, a private company offers free web access to Idaho DOC at www.vinelink.com/index.jsp.

Corporation Records, Limited Partnerships, Trademarks/Servicemarks, Limited Liability Companies, Limited Liability Partnerships, Assumed Names

Secretary of State, Corporation Division, PO Box 83720, Boise, ID 83720-0080 (Courier address: 700 W Jefferson, Boise, ID 83720); 208-334-2301, 208-334-2080-Fax; 8AM-5PM.

www.idsos.state.id.us

Effective 1/1/97, fictitious or assumed names are found at this office. (Previously they were recorded at the county level.) Not-for-profits records are located here, also.

Records are available for all entities. It takes 24 hours before new records are available for inquiry. Records are indexed on inhouse computer.

Searching: Ongoing requesters should establish a pre-paid account. Include the following in your request-full name of business, specific records that you need copies of. In addition to the articles of incorporation, corporation records include the following information: Annual Reports, Officers, Directors, Prior names, filing status and Reserved names, and Filing History. Cross reference of owners/officers is not avail.

Access by: mail, phone, fax, in person, online.

Fee & Payment: There is no search fee. The fee for copies is $.25 per page. Certification is $10.00 as is a Certification of Existence. Fee payee: Secretary of State. Prepayment required. Personal checks accepted. Major credit cards accepted.

Mail search: Turnaround time: 1 to 2 days. No SASE is required.

Phone search: There is a limit of 3 entities per call.

Fax search: Copies cost an additional $.50 each if returned by fax.

In person search: Call first to make an appointment so that they can pull file.

Online search: Business Entity Searches at www.accessidaho.org/public/sos/corp/search.html?SearchFormstep=crit. This is a free Internet service open 24 hours daily. Includes not-for-profit entities.

Other access: There are a variety of formats and media available for bulk purchase requesters. Requesters can subscribers to a monthly CD update.

Expedited service: Expedited service is available for mail, phone and in person searches. Turnaround time: 1 day. Add $20.00 per document.

Uniform Commercial Code, Federal and State Tax Liens

UCC Division, Secretary of State, PO Box 83720, Boise, ID 83720-0080 (Courier address: 700 W Jefferson, Boise, ID 83720); 208-334-3191, 208-334-2847-Fax; 8AM-5PM.

www.idsos.state.id.us

Records are available from 1967. It takes 1 to 2 days before new records are available for inquiry. Records are indexed on inhouse computer.

Searching: The search includes federal tax liens, farm filings, and seed and labor filings. There is also an agricultural commodity lien search. Federal tax liens on individuals are filed at the county level. Include the following in your request-debtor name. For state tax liens that closed prior to 01/07/98, one must search at the county. On that date, the state took over the filing and database of state tax liens.

Access by: mail, phone, fax, in person, online.

Fee & Payment: UCC information search request is $12.00 per name. Copies are $1.00 per page if no file number given and $.25 per page if file name given. Other fees involved for other filings. Fee payee: Secretary of State. Prepayment is not required, but preferred. Personal checks accepted. No credit cards accepted.

Mail search: Turnaround time: 1 to 2 days. No SASE is required. **Phone search:** They will tell whether a filing exists. **Fax search:** There is an additional fee of $.50 per page.

In person search: You may request information in person, time permitting.

Online search: There is a free limited search at https://www.accessidaho.org/secure/sos/liens/search.html. We recommend professional searchers to subscribe to the extensive commercial service at this site. There is a $75 annual fee and possible transaction fees.

Other access: A summary data file on current filing is available on CD.

Expedited service: An expedited search is available for an additional $10.00.

Sales Tax Registrations

Revenue Operations Division, Records Management, PO Box 36, Boise, ID 83722 (Courier address: 800 Park, Boise, ID 83722); 208-334-7660, 208-334-7792 (Records Management), 208-334-7650-Fax; 8AM-5:00PM.

http://tax.idaho.gov/SalesUseTaxRate.htm

Records are available from 1983. The agency maintains records on computer since 1998 and on microfiche from 1983 to present. It takes 90 days before new records are available for inquiry. Records are normally destroyed after 3 years.

Searching: This agency will only confirm that a business is registered if a tax permit number is provided. They will provide no other information. The only information released is that within public domain. They will also search if provided with a tax permit number, a DBA or an EIN.

Access by: mail, phone, fax, in person, online.

Fee & Payment: There is no search fee, but there is a fee for postage for mail requests or for faxing. Fee payee: ISTC, PO Box 36, Boise, ID 83732. Prepayment required. Personal checks accepted. No credit cards accepted.

Mail search: Turnaround time: 1 to 10 days. The copy fee is $.10 per page, after 20 pages. No SASE is required. **Phone search:** No fee for telephone request. Only general information is released. **Fax search:** The fee is $1.00 per page. Turnaround time 24 hours.

In person search: Copy fees apply.

Online search: Email requests are accepted at rmcmichael@tax.state.id.us.

Birth Certificates

Vital Records, PO Box 83720, Boise, ID 83720-0036 (Courier: 450 W State St, 1st Floor, Boise, ID 83702); 208-334-5988, 208-389-9096-Fax; 8AM-5PM.   www.healthandwelfare.idaho.gov

Records are available on computer from July 1911 to present. It takes 2 weeks before new records are available for inquiry.

Searching: Records are confidential for 100 years. Only immediate family or legal representative may receive records as well as those who have a notarized release from persons of record or an immediate family member. Include the following in your request-full name, names of parents, mother's maiden name, date of birth, city of birth, relationship to person of record, reason for information request. Also include a copy of a photo ID and sign the request. The following data is not released: adoption records or sealed records.

Access by: mail, fax.

Fee & Payment: Requesters must include their signature and a copy of a driver's license or photo ID. Fee is $13.00 per name, add $13.00 per name requested for additional copies. Fee payee: Vital Records. Prepayment required. Credit cards accepted for fax requests only. Personal checks accepted. Major credit cards accepted.

Mail search: Turnaround time: 2 to 3 weeks. No SASE is required. **Fax search:** See Expedited Service.

Expedited service: Expedited service is available for fax requests. The fee is $23.50 plus cost of return by FedEx or mail. Requests received by noon (MT) will be processed within 2 working days if requesting Federal Express delivery; otherwise 1 week turnaround.

Death Records

Vital Records, PO Box 83720, Boise, ID 83720-0036 (Courier: 450 W State St, 1st Floor, Boise, ID 83702); 208-334-5988, 208-389-9096-Fax; 8AM-5PM. www.healthandwelfare.idaho.gov

Records are available from July 1911 to present. It takes 2 weeks before new records are available for inquiry. Records are indexed on microfilm, inhouse computer.

Searching: Records are confidential for 50 years and are available only to immediate family members or legal representatives or a person who has a notarized release from persons of record or an immediate family member. Include the following in your request-full name, date of death, city of death, relationship to person of record, reason for information request.

Access by: mail, fax, online.

Fee & Payment: Include a copy of your driver's license or photo ID and signature with request. The fee is $13.00 per name or additional copy. Fee payee: Vital Records. Prepayment required. Credit cards are accepted with fax requests only. Personal checks accepted. Major credit cards accepted.

Mail search: Turnaround time: 2 to 3 weeks. No SASE is required. **Fax search:** See Expedited Services.

Online search: The agency has made the death index of records older than 50 available at http://abish.byui.edu/specialCollections/fhc/Death/searchForm.cfm. There is no fee. **Expedited service:** Expedited service is available for fax requests. The fee is $23.50 plus cost of return by FedEx.

Marriage Certificates

Vital Records, PO Box 83720, Boise, ID 83720-0036 (Courier address: 450 W State St, 1st Floor, Boise, ID 83702); 208-334-5988, 208-389-9096-Fax; 8AM-5PM.

www.healthandwelfare.idaho.gov

Records are available from May 1947 to present. It takes 4 to 6 weeks before new records are available for inquiry.

Searching: Records are confidential for 50 years. Only immediate family members and legal representatives may obtain recent records, others may obtain records with a notarized release from a family member or person of record. Include the following in your request-names of husband and wife, date of marriage, city of marriage, relationship.

Access by: mail, fax.

Fee & Payment: Include a copy of a photo ID or driver's license and a signature with request. The fee is $13.00 per name and per each additional copy. Fee payee: Vital Records. Prepayment required. Credit cards accepted with fax requests only. Personal checks accepted. Major credit cards accepted.

Mail search: Turnaround time: 2 to 3 weeks. No SASE is required.

Fax search: See Expedited Services.

Expedited service: Expedited service is available for fax requests. The fee is $23.50 plus cost of return by FedEx, Postal Express, or Priority Mail.

Divorce Records

Vital Records, PO Box 83720, Boise, ID 83720-0036 (Courier address: 450 W State St, 1st Floor, Boise, ID 83702); 208-334-5988, 208-389-9096-Fax; 8AM-5PM.

www.healthandwelfare.idaho.gov

This agency only maintains certificates of divorce; copies of decrees are available through the court system.

Records are available from May 1947 to present. New records are available for inquiry immediately. Records are indexed on microfilm, inhouse computer.

Searching: Records are confidential for 50 years and are available only to immediate family members, legal representatives, and a person with a notarized signed release from persons of record or immediate family. Include the following in your request-names of husband and wife, date of divorce, city of divorce, relationship.

Access by: mail, fax.

Fee & Payment: Include a copy of a driver's license or photo ID and include a signature with request. The fee is $13.00 per name. Fee payee: Vital Records. Prepayment required. Credit cards are accepted with fax requests only. Personal checks accepted. Major credit cards accepted.

Mail search: Turnaround time: 2 to 3 weeks. No SASE is required.

Fax search: See Expedited Services.

Expedited service: Expedited service is available for fax requests. The fee is $23.50 plus cost of return by FedEx, Postal Express, or Priority Mail.

Workers' Compensation Records

Industrial Commission of Idaho, Attn: Records Management, PO Box 83720, Boise, ID 83720; 208-334-6000, 208-334-2321-Fax; 8AM-5PM.

http://www2.state.id.us/iic

RMR-1 is used by parties on an open claim. RMR-2 is used by employers and prospective employers subject to ADA. RMR-3 is used by employers and prospective employers not subject to ADA. RMR-4 is subject's release for other parties.

Records are available from 1917 on. New records are available for inquiry immediately. Records are indexed on microfilm, inhouse computer. Records are normally destroyed after microfilming.

Searching: RMR-2 form requires notarized signature. If not subject to ADA, then form RMR-3 is used which requires non-notarized signature. Include the following in your request-claimant name, Social Security Number, date of accident and claim number. The following data is not released: psychiatric information.

Access by: mail, phone, fax, in person.

Fee & Payment: Copy costs depend upon file size which are those that exceed 100 copied pages or 50 microfilmed pages. Larger files cost $.05 per page on paper and $.15 per page on microfilm plus labor. If file is off site, shipping fees of $2.00 per file apply. Fee payee: Industrial Commission. Charges that total under $5.00 are waived. Personal checks accepted but no credit cards.

Mail search: Turnaround time: 3 days. There is a charge for postage. A SASE is required.

Phone search: Limited data is given via phone.

Fax search: Fax searching available, except RMR-2 Form.

In person search: One may request information in person. However, not all files are available the same day because some files are not on site and must be ordered from storage.

Driver Records

Idaho Transportation Department, Driver's Services, PO Box 34, Boise, ID 83731-0034 (Courier address: 3311 W State, Boise, ID 83703); 208-334-8736, 208-334-8739-Fax; 8:30AM-5PM.

www.itd.idaho.gov/dmv

Records are available for at least 3 years for moving violations, DUIs and suspensions. Accidents are not shown on the record. It takes 1 day from receipt before new records are available for inquiry. Records are normally destroyed after 7 years and archived to tape.

Searching: Personal information is not released to casual requesters unless the requestor claims a valid authorization. A request form is available at www.itd.idaho.gov/dmv/DriverServices/3120.pdf. The driver's license number and DOB are used for the primary search. If no record is found, a secondary search is performed using the name and DOB, or name and license number. The following data is not released: Social Security Numbers, medical information, signature, address.

Access by: mail, fax, in person, online.

Fee & Payment: The fee is $4.00 per record. Convenience fees are added for online and batch searches. Fee payee: Idaho Transportation Department. Prepayment required. Ongoing requesters can set up an account. Personal checks accepted. Credit cards accepted: MasterCard, Visa.

Mail search: Turnaround time: 3 to 5 days: Mail-in requesters are asked to use the state form. No SASE is required.

Fax search: Fax requests for records are accepted, if paid by a credit card or by account. Call 208-334-8761 to set up an account.

In person search: Walk-in requesters may receive up to ten records while they wait, the rest are processed overnight.

Online search: Idaho offers online access (CICS) to the driver license files through its portal provider, Access Idaho. Fee is $5.50 per record. For more information, call 208-332-0102 or visit www.accessidaho.org.

Other access: Idaho offers bulk retrieval of basic drivers license information with a signed contract. For information, call 208-334-860.

Vehicle Ownership, Vehicle Identification, Vessel Ownership

Idaho Transportation Department, Vehicle Services, PO Box 34, Boise, ID 83731-0034 (Courier address: 3311 W State St, Boise, ID 83707); 208-334-8773, 208-334-8663, 208-334-8542-Fax; 8:30AM-5PM.

www.itd.idaho.gov/dmv/vehicleservices/vs.htm

Model year vessels 2000 or newer that have either a motor or are longer than 12 feet must be titled. If a lien is placed on a model year older than 2000, then that vessel must be titled.

Records are available from 1981. It takes 1 day before new records are available for inquiry.

Searching: Personal information is not released to casual requesters unless the requestor claims a valid authorization. Use of the request form is suggested (found at www.itd.idaho.gov/dmv/VehicleServices/3374.pdf). Submit the name, VIN, license plate number for search, current address is also helpful. The following data is not released: Social Security Numbers or medical records.

Access by: mail, fax, in person, online.

Fee & Payment: The fee is $4.00 for current title with lien information or for a registration search. A complete title history (using the microfilm) is $8.00. Convenience fees are added for online and batch searches. Fee payee: Idaho Transportation Department. Prepayment required. Motor vehicle record accounts may be established by calling 208-334-8761. Personal checks accepted. Credit cards accepted: MasterCard, Visa.

Mail search: Turnaround time: 5 to 10 days. Information request forms are available. No SASE is required. **Fax search:** You may fax a request with a major credit card. Results, except for title history records, can returned by fax to local or toll-fee number for no additional fee. Turnaround time is three days.

In person search: You may request information in person here or at any County Assessor auto licensing location statewide.

Online search: Idaho offers online and batch access to registration and title files through its portal provider, Access Idaho. Records are $5.50 each or $3.50 for a lien search for subscribers. For more information, call 208-332-0102 or visit www.accessidaho.org.

Other access: Idaho offers bulk retrieval of registration, ownership, and vehicle information with a signed contract. For more information, call 208-334-8601.

Accident Reports

Idaho Transportation Department, Traffic and Highway Safety-Accident Records, PO Box 7129, Boise, ID 83707-1129 (Courier address: 3311 W State St, Boise, ID 83707); 208-334-8100, 208-334-4430-Fax; 8AM-12:00PM; 1PM-5PM.

Records are available from 1970's (on microfilm) to present. It takes 1 day for electronic reports, 3 months if paper before new records are available for inquiry. Records are normally destroyed after microfilming.

Searching: Include the following in your request-full name, date of accident, location of accident, driver's license number.

Access by: mail, phone, fax, in person.

Fee & Payment: The fee is $4.00 per report plus handling and tax. Fee payee: Idaho Transportation Department, Financial Control. Do not send a check with a request, you will be billed. Personal checks accepted. No credit cards accepted.

Mail search: Turnaround time: 2 weeks. A SASE is requested.

Phone search: No fee for telephone request. Fee charged if copies sent. Turnaround time is 2 weeks. **Fax search:** Turnaround time 2 weeks.

In person search: It is suggested that walk-in requesters call first before going to department should the state have to locate the records on microfilm.

Other access: Computer files may be purchased with prepaid deposit plus computer charges. However, the file will not contain addresses, citation information, or drivers' license numbers and other personal information. Annual databases may be purchased.

Vessel Registration

Idaho Parks & Recreation, PO Box 83720, Boise, ID 83720-0065 (Courier address: 5657 Warm Springs, Boise, ID 83712); 208-334-4180 x306, 208-334-2639-Fax; 8AM-5PM.

www.idahoparks.org

Liens are not recorded on registration and must be searched with either UCCs or at the DOT where vessels are titled.

Records are available from 1987 to present. Older records are available, but to search them, you must know the registration #. Records are indexed on computer. All boats with motors and/or sails must be registered.

Searching: Registration records are open to the public. Phone numbers and addresses are not released. To search, provide one of the following: owner's name, hull #, or registration #.

Access by: mail, phone, fax, in person.

Fee & Payment: There is no search fee.

Mail search: Turnaround time: 10 working days. No SASE is required.

Phone search: Name searching is permitted by telephone. **Fax search:** Searching by fax for pre-approved accounts.

In person search: Counter service available.

Voter Registration
Access to Records is Restricted.

State Elections Office, Sec of State, 700 W Jefferson #203, Boise, ID 83720; 208-334-2852, 208-334-2282 (Fax).

www.idahovotes.gov

Records are maintained by the County Clerks. The counties will generally release name, address, and voting precinct on individual request. Lists may be purchased, but not for commercial purposes. However, the Federal Help America Vote Act of 2002 (HAVA) law requires implementation of a central, computerized, statewide voter registration system by 01/01/2006. The state will comply.

GED Certificates

Department of Education, GED Testing, PO Box 83720, Boise, ID 83720-0027; 208-332-6980, 208-334-4664-Fax; 8AM-5PM. www.sde.state.id.us

It takes 1 week before new records are available for inquiry.

Searching: Include the following in your request-SSN, date of birth. A signed release is necessary for copies of transcripts or for scores. Will not expedite requests.

Access by: mail, phone, fax, in person.

Fee & Payment: There is a $5.00 fee for a copy of a transcript. There is no fee for a verification.

Mail search: Turnaround time: 2 to 3 days. No SASE is required.

Phone search: No fee for telephone request. Verification only over the phone.

Fax search: Turnaround time is 1 day, but only for a verification, not for a transcript.

In person search: Information is released immediately.

Hunting and Fishing License Information

ID Department of Fish & Game, Licenses Division, PO Box 25, Boise, ID 83707-0025 (Courier: 1075 Park Blvd, Boise, ID 83707); 208-334-2592, 208-334-3736 (Enforcement Office), 208-334-2148-Fax; 8AM-5PM.

http://fishandgame.idaho.gov

The license division says that if you want an individual name, you must call the Enforcement Office. This office will not release individual records with addresses, they will only confirm is there is a license issued.

Records are available from January 1992 to present. It takes 1 to 2 days before new records are available for inquiry.

Searching: Name searches are not done. Use of their request form is required. Include notarized signature of the subject and copy of valid ID of the requester.

Access by: mail, phone, in person.

Fee & Payment: There is no fee unless the search is extensive.

Mail search: Turnaround time: variable. No SASE is required.

Phone search: They will only confirm.

In person search: Turnaround time: variable.

Idaho State Licensing Agencies

For details about the agency responsible for licensing/certifying/registering an item below or in the Agency Quick Finder section, match an item's number with the number of the agency in the *Licensing Agency Information* section.

Idaho Licenses Searchable Online

Applicator, Commercial/Private #20	www.agri.state.id.us/Categories/Pesticides/licensing/licenseLookUp.php
Athletic Trainer #30	www.accessidaho.org/public/bomed/license/search.html
Attorney #29	http://www2.state.id.us/isb/mem/attorney_roster.asp
Chemigator #20	www.agri.state.id.us/Categories/Pesticides/licensing/licenseLookUp.php
Collection Agency/Collector #21	http://finance.idaho.gov/CollectionAgencyLicence.aspx
Community Action Program #27	www.puc.state.id.us/consumer/helplist.pdf
Contractor, Public Works #31	www.accessidaho.org/public/dbs/pubworks/search.html
Crematory #3	https://www.ibol.idaho.gov/eIBOLPublic/LPRBrowserI.aspx
Dental Hygienist #13	http://www2.state.id.us/isbd/search.htm
Dentist #13	http://www2.state.id.us/isbd/search.htm
Dietitian #30	www.accessidaho.org/public/bomed/license/search.html
Elections & Campaign Disclosure #28	www.idsos.state.id.us/notary/npindex.htm
Engineer #17	http://www2.state.id.us/ipels/pelsnumb.htm
Funeral Director #3	https://www.ibol.idaho.gov/eIBOLPublic/LPRBrowserI.aspx
Funeral Director Trainee #3	https://www.ibol.idaho.gov/eIBOLPublic/LPRBrowserI.aspx
Funeral Establishment #3	https://www.ibol.idaho.gov/eIBOLPublic/LPRBrowserI.aspx
Geologist #18	http://www2.state.id.us/ibpg/search.htm
Guide #15	http://www2.state.id.us/oglb/oglbhome.htm
Insurance Agent Licensure Exam #24	www.doi.state.id.us/Insurance/search.aspx
Insurance Agent/Corp./Partnership #24	www.doi.state.id.us/Insurance/search.aspx
Insurance Broker #24	www.doi.state.id.us/Insurance/search.aspx
Insurer, Domestic/Mutual/Foreign #24	www.doi.state.id.us/Insurance/search.aspx
Lobbyist #28	www.idsos.state.id.us/elect/lobbyist/lobinfo.htm
Medical Doctor #30	www.accessidaho.org/public/bomed/license/search.html
Medical Resident #30	www.accessidaho.org/public/bomed/license/search.html
Medical, Temporary #30	www.accessidaho.org/public/bomed/license/search.html
Mortgage Broker/Banker #21	http://finance.idaho.gov/MortgageLicense.aspx
Mortgage Company #21	http://finance.idaho.gov/MortgageLicense.aspx
Mortician/Mortician Resid't Trainee #3	https://www.ibol.idaho.gov/eIBOLPublic/LPRBrowserI.aspx
Notary Public #28	www.idsos.state.id.us/notary/npindex.htm
Occupational Therapist/Assistant #30	www.accessidaho.org/public/bomed/license/search.html
Oral Surgeon #13	http://www2.state.id.us/isbd/search.htm
Orthodontist #13	http://www2.state.id.us/isbd/search.htm
Osteopathic Physician #30	www.accessidaho.org/public/bomed/license/search.html
Outfitter #15	http://www2.state.id.us/oglb/oglbhome.htm
Pesticide Appl./Operator/Dealer/Mfg #6	www.agri.state.id.us/agresource/_agtechlookup/querylic.asp
Physical Therapist/Assistant #30	www.accessidaho.org/public/bomed/license/search.html
Physician Assistant #30	www.accessidaho.org/public/bomed/license/search.html
Polysomnography Tech./Trainee #30	www.accessidaho.org/public/bomed/license/search.html
Polysomnography Technologist #30	www.accessidaho.org/public/bomed/license/search.html
Public Accountant Firm #12	http://www2.state.id.us/boa/HTM/firmsearch.htm
Public Accountant-CPA #12	http://www2.state.id.us/boa/HTM/accountantsearch.htm
Public Accountant-LPA #12	http://www2.state.id.us/boa/HTM/accountantsearch.htm
Real Estate Agent/Broker/Company #34	www.accessidaho.org/public/irec/licensing/search.html
Real Estate Appraiser #19	www.asc.gov/content/category1/appr_by_state.asp
Respiratory Therapist #30	www.accessidaho.org/public/bomed/license/search.html
Securities Broker/Seller/Issuer #21	http://finance.idaho.gov/SecuritiesLicence.aspx
Surveyor, Land #17	http://www2.state.id.us/ipels/pelsnumb.htm
Temporary Medical #30	www.accessidaho.org/public/bomed/license/search.html
Utility Pay Station #27	www.puc.state.id.us/consumer/paystations.htm

Idaho Licensing Quick Finder

Applicator, Commercial/Private #20	208-332-8500
Aquaculture, Commercial #20	208-332-8500
Architect #19	208-334-3233
Artificial Inseminator #20	208-332-8500
Asbestos Worker #10	208-334-2129
Athletic Trainer #30	208-327-7000
Attorney #29	208-344-4500
Bakery #11	208-327-7499
Bank #21	208-332-8005
Barber School Instructor #19	208-334-3233
Barber/Barber Shop/Barber School #19	208-334-3233
Bed & Breakfast #11	208-327-7499
Beekeeper #20	208-332-8500
Beer & Wine License,Whlse./Retail #25	208-884-7060
Boiler Inspector #10	208-334-2129
Boiler Safety Code #10	208-334-2129
Bottling Plant #11	208-327-7499
Boxer #32	208-221-6534
Boxing/Wrestling Event #32	208-221-6534
Boxing/Wrestling Professional #32	208-221-6534
Brewery #25	208-884-7060
Brokerage Dealer #12	208-334-2490
Building Inspector #10	208-334-3896
Chemigator #20	208-332-8500
Child Care Institution/Agency #7	208-334-5700
Child Care Licensee #7	208-334-5700
Chiropractor #19	208-334-3233
Clinical Laboratory Registration #2	208-334-2235
Clinical Nurse Specialist #14	208-334-3110 X21
Collection Agency/Collector #21	208-332-8002
Commission Merchant #20	208-332-8500
Commodity Dealer #20	208-332-8500
Communication Disorders School Specialist #5	208-332-6800
Community Action Program #27	208-334-0300
Construction Manager #31	208-334-4057
Consumer Loan Company & Credit Sale #21	208-332-8002
Contractor, Public Works #31	208-334-4057
Controlled Substance Registrant #16	208-334-2356
Cosmetologist/Cosmetology Salon #19	208-334-3233
Cosmetology School/Instructor #19	208-334-3233
Counselor #19	208-334-3233
Counselor, Professional #19	208-334-3233
Credit Union #21	208-332-8003
Crematory #3	208-334-3233
Dairy Farm/Dairy Prod't Processor#20	208-332-8500
Day Care Center Inspector #11	208-327-7499
Day Care Center/Home #7	208-334-5700
Dental Hygienist #13	208-334-2369
Dentist / Dental Assistant #13	208-334-2369
Denturist #19	208-334-3233
Dietitian #30	208-327-7000
Driller, Rotary #26	208-287-4800
Drug Mfg./Repackager/Whlse. #16	208-334-2356
Drug Outlet (i.e. Nursing Home) #16	208-334-2356
Drug Sales, Non-Pharmacy (i.e. Grocery Store) #16	208-334-2356
Egg Distributor/Grader #20	208-332-8500
Elections & Campaign Disclosure #28	208-334-2852
Electrical Apprentice/Journeyman #10	208-334-2183
Electrical Inspector/Contractor #10	208-334-2183
Electrolysis #19	208-334-3233
Elevator Installation/Repairmen #10	208-334-2129
Emergency Medical Technician #9	208-334-4000
Engineer #17	208-334-3860
Environmental Health Specialist #19	208-334-3233
Esthetician #19	208-334-3233
Euthanasia Agency #1	208-332-8588
Euthanasia Technician #1	208-332-8588
Exceptional Child School Program Advisor #5	208-332-6800
Farm Produce Dealer/Broker #20	208-332-8500
Feed Manufacturer, Commercial #20	208-332-8500
Fertilizer Manufacturer,Commer'l #20	208-332-8500
Finance Company #21	208-332-8002
Fire Inspector #23	208-334-4370
Fire Sprinkler Fitter #23	208-334-4370
Fire Sprinkler System Contractor #23	208-334-4370
Fireworks License #23	208-334-4370
Fishing, Commercial #22	208-334-3717
Florist/Nurseryman #20	208-332-8620
Food Establishment Studied #11	208-327-7499
Food Processing/Mfg. Plant #11	208-327-7499
Food Warehouse, Cold Storage #11	208-327-7499
Foster Home #7	208-334-5700
Funeral Director #3	208-334-3233
Funeral Director Trainee #3	208-334-3233
Funeral Establishment #3	208-334-3233
Fur Buyer #22	208-334-3717
Game Farm (commercial wildlife) #22	208-334-3717
Geologist #18	208-334-2268
Grocery Store #11	208-327-7499
Guide #15	208-327-7380
Hearing Aid Dealer/Fitter #19	208-334-3233
Horse Racing Event/Occupation #33	208-884-7080
Hospital (Child or Elderly) #8	208-334-6626
Insurance Agent LicenseExam #24	208-334-4250
Insurance Agent/Corp./Partn'rship #24	208-334-4250
Insurance Broker #24	208-334-4250
Insurer, Domestic/Mutual/Foreign/Alien #24	208-334-4250
Intermediate Care Facility for the Mentally Retarded #8	208-334-6626
Investment Advisor #21	208-332-8004
Landscape Architect #19	208-334-3233
Liquor License, Retail #25	208-884-7060
Livestock Auction Market #20	208-332-8500
Livestock Brand #25	208-884-7070
Loan Agent #12	208-334-2490
Loan Collection Officer #12	208-334-2490
Lobbyist #28	208-334-2852
Logging #10	208-334-3950
Mammography #2	208-334-2235
Manufactured Commerc'l Building #10	208-334-3896
Manufactured Homes & Housing #10	208-334-3896
Manufactured Housing Dealer/Broker/Mfg. #10	208-334-3896
Medical Doctor #30	208-327-7000
Medical Resident #30	208-327-7000
Medical, Temporary #30	208-327-7000
Midwife Nurse #14	208-334-3110 X21
Milk & Dairy Product Storage/Hauling/Handling #20	208-332-8500
Mine Safety Training #10	208-334-2129
Mixer-Loader #20	208-332-8500
Mortgage Broker/Banker #21	208-332-8002
Mortgage Company #21	208-332-8002
Mortician/Mortician Resident Trainee #3	208-334-3233
Notary Public #28	208-334-2300
Nurse #14	208-334-3110 X21
Nurse Anesthetist #14	208-334-3110 X21
Nurse Practition'r-Div/Medicaid#14	208-334-3110 x21
Nurse-LPN #14	208-334-3110 X21
Nursing Assistant #14	800-748-2480
Nursing Care (Skilled) Facility #8	208-334-6626
Nursing Home Administrator #19	208-334-3233
Occupational Therapist/Assistant #30	208-327-7000
Optometrist #19	208-334-3233
Oral Surgeon #13	208-334-2369
Organic Certification #20	208-332-8620
Orthodontist #13	208-334-2369
Osteopathic Physician #30	208-327-7000
Outfitter #15	208-327-7380
Paramedic (EMT) #9	208-334-4000
Pest Control Consultant #6	208-332-8600
Pesticide Applicator/Oprt/Dealer/Mfg #6	208-332-8600
Pharmacist/Pharmacist Intern/Preceptor #16	208-334-2356
Pharmacy Mail Svc. #16	208-334-2356
Pharmacy/Drug Store #16	208-334-2356
Physical Therapist/Assistant #30	208-327-7000
Physician Assistant #30	208-327-7000
Plumbing Apprentice/Journeyman #10	208-334-3442
Plumbing Inspector/Contractor #10	208-334-3442
Podiatrist #19	208-334-3233
Police (Peace) Officer #25	208-884-7250
Polysomnography Technician/Trainee #30	208-327-7000
Polysomnography Technologist #30	208-327-7000
Psychologist #19	208-334-3233
Public Accountant-CPA #12	208-334-2490
Public Accountant-LPA #12	208-334-2490
Public Commodity Warehouse #20	208-332-8500
Real Estate Agent/Broker/Cmpny #34	208-334-3285
Real Estate Appraiser #19	208-334-3233
Recreational Vehicle Manufacturer #10	208-334-3896
Rehabilitation Facility #8	208-334-6626
Residential Care Administrator #19	208-334-3233
Residential Care Facility #8	208-334-6626
Residential School #7	208-334-5700
Respiratory Therapist #30	208-327-7000
Restaurant Sanitation Standard #11	208-327-7499
Savings & Loan Association #21	208-332-8005
School Counselor #5	208-332-6800
School Nurse #5	208-332-6800
School Principal/Superintendent #5	208-332-6800
Securities Broker/Dealer/Seller/Issuer #21	208-332-8004
Seed Company #20	208-332-8620
Septic System Permit #11	208-327-7499
Septic Tank Pumper #11	208-327-7499
Shooting Preserve #22	208-334-3717
Shorthand Reporter #4	208-334-2517
Social Worker #19	208-334-3233
Soil & Plant Amendment Mfg. #20	208-332-8620
Solicitor (Financial) #21	208-332-8002
Special Education Director #5	208-332-6800
Subdivision Approval #11	208-327-7499
Substance Abuse Treatment Center #7	208-334-5700
Subsurface Sewage License #11	208-327-7499
Surveyor, Land #17	208-334-3860
Swimming Pool Operator #11	208-327-7499
Taxidermist #22	208-334-3717
Teacher #5	208-332-6800
Temporary Medical #30	208-327-7000
Trapper/Junior Trapper #22	208-334-3717
Trust Company #21	208-332-8005
Utility Pay Station #27	208-334-0300
Utility Regulation Gas/Water/Power/Phone #27	208-334-0300
Veterinarian/Veterinary Technician #1	208-332-8588
Veterinary Drug Outlet/Technician #16	208-334-2356
Water Laboratory #2	208-334-2235
Water Rights Examiner #26	208-287-4800
Water Well Driller #26	208-287-4800
Weighmaster #20	208-332-8500
Winery #25	208-884-7060
Wrestler #32	208-221-6534
X-ray Equipment #2	208-334-2235

Idaho Licensing Agency Information

1 Board of Veterinary Medicine, PO Box 7249, Boise, ID 83707; 208-332-8588, Fax: 208-334-4062.   Email: sjensen@agri.state.id.us

2 Bureau of Laboratories, 2220 Old Penitentiary Rd, Boise, ID 83712; 208-334-2235, Fax: 208-334-2382.

3 Bureau of Occupational Licenses, Mortician Board of Examiners, 1109 Main St, #220, Boise, ID 83702-5642; 208-334-3233, Fax: 208-334-3945.   https://www.ibol.idaho.gov/
Email: ibol@ibol.state.id.us
Search Database at https://www.ibol.idaho.go v/eIBOLPublic/LPRBrowserI.aspx

4 Certified Shorthand Reporters Board, 3350 Americana Terrace #243, Boise, ID 83706; 208-334-2517, Fax: 208-334-5211.
Email: modedo@ibpq.state.id.us

5 Department of Education, Teacher Certification, PO Box 83720, Boise, ID 83720-0027; 208-332-6800, Fax: 208-334-2094.
www.sde.state.id.us/certification
Email: kpotter@sde.state.id.us

6 Department of Agriculture, Pesticides Division - Licensing, 2270 Old Penitentiary Rd, Boise, ID 83712; 208-332-8600, Fax: 208-334-3547.
www.agri.state.id.us
Email: ar_app_licensing@agri.state.id.us
Search Database at www.agri.state.id.us/agr esource/_agtechlookup/querylic.asp

7 Department of Health & Welfare, Division of Family and Community Services, 450 W State St, 5th Fl, Boise, ID 83720;
208-334-5700, Fax: 208-332-7331.
http://www2.state.id.us/dhw/facs/index_facs.htm

8 Department of Health & Welfare, Bureau of Facility Standards, PO Box 83720 (450 W. State St, 10th Fl), Boise, ID 83720-0036; 208-334-6626, Fax: 208-334-6558.
http://www2.state.id.us/dhw/

9 Department of Health & Welfare, Bureau of Emergency Medical Services, 590 W Washington, Boise, ID 83702;
208-334-4000, Fax: 208-334-4015.
http://www2.state.id.us/dhw/index.htm

10 Division of Building Safety, 1090 E. Watertower St., Meridian, ID 83642; 208-334-3950, Fax: 208-334-2683; Elect. 208-855-2165; Plumb. 208-855-9339.
http://www2.state.id.us/dbs/dbs_index.html
Email: swallace@dbs.state.id.us

11 Environmental Health Department, Bakery & Related Licensing, 707 N Armstrong Place, Boise, ID 83704; 208-327-7499, Fax: 208-327-8553.
www.cdhd.org/index.cfm

12 Board of Accountancy, 1109 Main #470, Boise, ID 83702-0002; 208-334-2490, Fax: 208-334-2615.   http://www2.state.id.us/boa
Email: isba@boa.state.id.us
Search Database at http://www2.state.id.us/boa

13 Board of Dentistry, PO Box 83720 (708 1/2 W. Franklin St), Boise, ID 83720-0021; 208-334-2369, Fax: 208-334-3247.
http://www2.state.id.us/isbd
Email: smiller@isbd.state.id.us
Search Database at
http://www2.state.id.us/isbd/search.htm

14 Board of Nursing, 280 N 8th St #210, Boise, ID 83720; 208-334-3110, Fax: 208-334-3262.
http://www2.state.id.us/ibn/ibnhome.htm
Email: lcoley@ibn.state.id.us

15 Board of Outfitters & Guides, 1365 N Orchard St, Rm 172, Boise, ID 83706; 208-327-7380, Fax: 208-327-7382.
http://www2.state.id.us/oglb/oglbhome.htm
Email: dsangrey@oglb.state.id.us
Search Database at
http://www2.state.id.us/oglb/oglbhome.htm   Note: Scroll to the bottom of the page to find the appropriate links for searching.

16 Board of Pharmacy, 3380 Americana Terr #320, PO Box 83720, Boise, ID 83720-0067; 208-334-2356, Fax: 208-334-3536.
www.state.id.us/bop
Email: rmarkuson@bop.state.id.us   Note: List are available for $53.00 each; written request and prepayment required. Applications are available online.

17 Board of Professional Engineers & Surveyors, 5535 W Overland Rd, Boise, ID 83705; 208-373-7210, Fax: 208-373-7213.
http://www2.state.id.us/ipels/index.htm
Email: dcurtis@ipels.state.id.us
Search Database at
http://www2.state.id.us/ipels/pelsnumb.htm

18 Board of Professional Geologists, P.O. Box 83720, Boise, ID 83720-0033; 208-334-2268.
http://www2.state.id.us/ibpg/
Email: ibpg@ibpg.state.id.us
Search Database at
http://www2.state.id.us/ibpg/search.htm

19 Bureau of Occupational Licenses, 1109 Main St, Owyhee Plaza, #220, Boise, ID 83702; 208-334-3233, Fax: 208-334-3945.
http://www2.state.id.us/ibol/
Email: ibol@ibol.state.id.us

20 Department of Agriculture, Inspections/Registrations, 2270 Old Penitentiary Rd, Boise, ID 83712; 208-332-8500, Fax: 208-334-2170.   www.agri.state.id.us

21 Department of Finance, Financial Bureau, 700 W State St, 2nd Fl, Boise, ID 83720-0031; 208-332-8000, Fax: 208-332-8098.
http://finance.idaho.gov/
Email: finance@fin.state.id.us

22 Department of Fish & Game, PO Box 25, Boise, ID 83707; 208-334-3700, Fax: 208-334-2114.   http://www2.state.id.us/fishgame
Email: idfginfo@idfg.state.id.us

23 Department of Insurance, State Fire Marshall, 700 W State St, 3rd Fl, Boise, ID 83720-0043; 208-334-4370, Fax: 208-334-4375.
www.doi.state.id.us/sfm/firemars.aspx
Email: mlarson@doi.state.id.us

24 Department of Insurance, 700 W State St 3rd floor, Boise, ID 83720-0043; 208-334-4250, Fax: 208-334-4398.
www.doi.state.id.us
Search Database at
www.doi.state.id.us/insurance/search.asp

25 State Police, PO Box 700, Meridian, ID 83680-0700; 208-884-7000, Fax: 208-884-7090.
www.isp.state.id.us

26 Department of Water Resources, 322 E Front St (PO Box 83720), Boise, ID 83720-0098; 208-287-4800, Fax: 208-287-6700.
www.idwr.state.id.us
Email: dlarsen@idwr.state.id.us

27 Public Utilities Commission, 472 W Washington St, Boise, ID 83702; 208-334-0300, Fax: 208-334-3762.
www.puc.state.id.us

28 Secretary of State, 700 W Jefferson #203, Boise, ID 83720-0800; 208-334-2300, Fax: 208-334-2282.
www.idsos.state.id.us
Email: sosinfo@idsos.state.id.us

29 State Bar, PO Box 895, Boise, ID 83701; 208-334-4500, Fax: 208-334-4515.
http://www2.state.id.us/isb/
Search Database at http://www2.state.id.u s/isb/mem/attorney_roster.asp

30 Board of Medicine, PO Box 83720 (1755 Westgate Dr), Boise, ID 83720-0058; 208-327-7000, Fax: 208-327-7005.
www.bom.state.id.us
Email: info@bom.state.id.us   Search Database at
www.accessidaho.org/public/bomed/license/search .html

31 Division of Building Safety, Public Works Contractors Board, 1090 E Watertower St, Meridian, ID 83642;
208-334-4057, Fax: 208-855-9666.
http://www2.state.id.us/dbs/dbs_index.html

32 State Athletic Department, 800 Park Blvd Plaza 4, PO Box 36, Boise, ID 83722-0410; 208-221-6534, Fax: 208-334-7844.

33 Horse Racing Commission, 700 Stratford Dr, Meridian, ID 83642; 208-884-7080, Fax: 208-884-7098.   www.in.gov/ihrc/
Email: ardie.noyes@isp.state.id.us

34 Real Estate Commission, 633 N 4th St, Boise, ID 83720-0077; 208-334-3285, Fax: 208-334-2050.   www.idahorealestatecommission.com
Email: djones@irec.state.id.us
Search Database at www.accessidaho.org/publ ic/irec/licensing/search.html.

Idaho Federal Courts

The following list indicates the district and division name for each county in the state. If the bankruptcy court location is different from the district court, then the location of the bankruptcy court appears in parentheses.

County/Court Cross Reference

County	Court		County	Court
Ada	Boise		Gem	Boise
Adams	Boise		Gooding	Boise
Bannock	Pocatello		Idaho	Pocatello (Moscow)
Bear Lake	Pocatello		Jefferson	Pocatello
Benewah	Coeur d' Alene		Jerome	Boise
Bingham	Pocatello		Kootenai	Coeur d' Alene
Blaine	Boise		Latah	Moscow
Boise	Boise		Lemhi	Pocatello
Bonner	Coeur d' Alene		Lewis	Moscow
Bonneville	Pocatello		Lincoln	Boise
Boundary	Coeur d' Alene		Madison	Pocatello
Butte	Pocatello		Minidoka	Boise
Camas	Boise		Nez Perce	Moscow
Canyon	Boise		Oneida	Pocatello
Caribou	Pocatello		Owyhee	Boise
Cassia	Boise		Payette	Boise
Clark	Pocatello		Power	Pocatello
Clearwater	Moscow		Shoshone	Coeur d' Alene
Custer	Pocatello		Teton	Pocatello
Elmore	Boise		Twin Falls	Boise
Franklin	Pocatello		Valley	Boise
Fremont	Pocatello		Washington	Boise

Standards for Federal Courts: Search fee is $26.00 per item (one party name or case number). Copy fee is $.50 per page. Certification fee is $9.00 per document, double for exemplification, if available. All fees standard unless noted in profile. Mail Search: always enclose a stamped self addressed envelope unless otherwise noted. Most courts accept fax requests or will suggest a copying/search vendor. Before releasing records, all courts require prepayment, unless noted.

Open records are located at the court unless otherwise noted. District courts index by defendant and plaintiff as well as by case number. Bankruptcy courts usually index by debtor and case number. While most courts now have their indexes on computer, many may still maintain index card files as well.

Courts offering internet access via CM-ECF or older RACER, PACER, or Web-PACER systems charge $.08 per page fee unless noted as free. Where PACER is available, the universal sign-up number is 800-676-6856. Find PACER and the US Party/Case Index at http://pacer.psc.uscourts.gov.

US District Court

District of Idaho

Boise Division Court Clerk, MSC 039, Federal Bldg, 550 W Fort St, Rm 400, Boise, ID 83724 (also use mail address for courier delivery), 208-334-1361, 800-448-6172, Fax-208-334-9362. Hours- 8AM-5PM. www.id.uscourts.gov

Counties: Ada, Adams, Blaine, Boise, Camas, Canyon, Cassia, Elmore, Gem, Gooding, Jerome, Lincoln, Minidoka, Owyhee, Payette, Twin Falls, Valley, Washington.

Searches & Indexing: Results do not include SSN or DOB. Both computer and card indexes maintained; computer back to 1990; images back to 1999. New cases in the index immediately after filing date.

Fee & Payment: Pay by money order, cashier's or personal check. No credit cards. Payee: US District Court Clerk. Prepayment required for large requests.

Phone Search: All public information is released via phone.

Mail Search: search usually completed- 1 week. SASE not required.

In Person Search: Fee charged if court performs your search. Copying available from Court Copy Service, a private vendor. No self-serve copier available.

E-Services: No PACER access to this court. ECF at https://ecf.idd.uscourts.gov **Other Online Access:** The old, free RACER system no longer updated. Court now participate in the US party case index. Also view calendars at www.id.uscourts.gov/Calendar_DC_Public.htm.

Coeur d' Alene Division c/o Boise Division, MSD 039, Federal Bldg, 550 W Fort St, Rm 400, Boise, ID 83724 (also use mail address for courier delivery), 208-334-1361, Fax-208-334-9386. Hours- 8AM-5PM. www.id.uscourts.gov

Counties: Benewah, Bonner, Boundary, Kootenai, Shoshone.

Searches & Indexing: Cases indexed by name and case number. Results do not include SSN or DOB. Computer index back to 1992 maintained. New cases in the index within 7 days after filing date. Records purged varies. Open records located at Boise Division.

Fee & Payment: Pay by money order, cashier's or personal check.

Phone Search: No searching by telephone.

Mail Search: search usually completed- 24-48 hours. Include SASE for return.

In Person Search: permitted. No self-serve copier available.

E-Services: No PACER access to this court. ECF at https://ecf.idd.uscourts.gov **Other Online Access:** The old, free RACER system no longer updated. Court now participate in the US party case index. Also view calendars at www.id.uscourts.gov/Calendar_DC_Public.htm.

Moscow Division c/o Boise Division, PO Box 039, Federal Bldg, 550 W Fort St, Boise, ID 83724 (also use mail address for courier delivery), 208-334-1074, Fax-208-883-1576. Hours- 8AM-5PM. www.id.uscourts.gov

Counties: Clearwater, Latah, Lewis, Nez Perce.

Searches & Indexing: Cases indexed by and case number. Index on computer back to 2000. Open records located at Boise Division.

Fee & Payment: Pay by money order, cashier's or personal check.

Phone Search: No searching by telephone.

Mail Search: search usually completed- 24-48 hours. Include SASE for return.

In Person Search: permitted. Self-serve copier available - $.10 per page.

E-Services: No PACER access to this court. ECF at https://ecf.idd.uscourts.gov **Other Online Access:** The old, free RACER system no longer updated. Court now participate in the US party case index. Also view calendars at www.id.uscourts.gov/Calendar_DC_Public.htm.

Pocatello Division c/o Boise Division, 801 E Sherman, Pocatello, ID 83201 (also use mail address for courier delivery), 208-334-1074 1-800-448-6172. www.id.uscourts.gov

Counties: Bannock, Bear Lake, Bingham, Bonneville, Butte, Caribou, Clark, Custer, Franklin, Fremont, Idaho, Jefferson, Lemhi, Madison, Oneida, Power, Teton.

Searches & Indexing: Cases indexed by and case number. Open records located at Boise Division.

Fee & Payment: Pay by no business or personal checks accepted.

Phone Search: No searching by telephone.

Mail Search: search usually completed- 48 hours. Include SASE for return.

In Person Search: permitted. No self-serve copier available.

E-Services: No PACER access to this court. ECF at https://ecf.idd.uscourts.gov **Other Online Access:** The old, free RACER system is no longer updated. Court now participate in the US party case index. Also view calendars at www.id.uscourts.gov/Calendar_DC_Public.htm.

US Bankruptcy Court

District of Idaho

Boise Division Court Clerk, MSC 042, US Courthouse, 550 W Fort St, Rm 400, Boise, ID 83724 (also use mail address for courier delivery), 208-334-1074, Fax-208-334-9362. Hours- 8AM-5PM. www.id.uscourts.gov

Counties: Ada, Adams, Blaine, Boise, Camas, Canyon, Cassia, Elmore, Gem, Gooding, Jerome, Lincoln, Minidoka, Owyhee, Payette, Twin Falls, Valley, Washington.

Searches & Indexing: Results include SSN. Computer index maintained. New cases in the index immediately after filing date. Records purged immediately when case closed.

Fee & Payment: Pay by no business or personal checks accepted. Prepayment required.

Phone Search: Only docket information is available by phone. Voice Case Information Service available, call VCIS at 208-334-9386.

Mail Search: search usually completed- 24 hours. SASE not required.

In Person Search: Fee charged if court performs your search. Make search and copy arrangements with private vendor Court Copy Services, 208-334-9463. No self-serve copier available.

E-Services: No PACER online. No PACER access to this court. ECF at https://ecf.idd.uscourts.gov **Opinions Online:** www.id.uscourts.gov/cfCourt/decisions/bk_decisionlist.cfm. Also, search archived bankruptcy cases at www.id.uscourts.gov/cfCourt/CourtArchives/Archive_SearchForm.cfm. **Other Online Access:** The old, free RACER system is no longer updated. Court now participate in the US party case index. Also view calendars at www.id.uscourts.gov/Calendar_DC_Public.htm.

Coeur d' Alene - Nothern Division Court Clerk, 205 N 4th St, 2nd Fl, Coeur d'Alene, ID 83814 (also use mail address for courier delivery), 208-664-4925, Fax-208-765-0270. Hours- 8AM-5PM. www.id.uscourts.gov

Counties: Benewah, Bonner, Boundary, Kootenai, Shoshone.

Searches & Indexing: Results do not include SSN or DOB. Computer and paper indexes maintained. New cases in the index immediately after filing date. Records purged immediately when case closed.

Fee & Payment: Pay by money order, cashier check, business check. No personal checks. Payee: US Bankruptcy Court. Prepayment required.

Phone Search: Only docket information is available by phone. Voice Case Information Service available, call VCIS at 208-334-9386.

Mail Search: search usually completed- 24 hours. Include SASE for return.

In Person Search: Fee charged if court performs your search. No self-serve copier available.

E-Services: No PACER online. No PACER access to this court. ECF at https://ecf.idd.uscourts.gov **Opinions Online:** www.id.uscourts.gov/cfCourt/decisions/bk_decisionlist.cfm. Also, search archived bankruptcy cases at www.id.uscourts.gov/cfCourt/CourtArchives/Archive_SearchForm.cfm. **Other Online Access:** The old, free RACER system is no longer updated. Court now participate in the US party case index. Also view calendars at www.id.uscourts.gov/Calendar_DC_Public.htm.

Moscow - Northern Division Court Clerk, 220 E 5th St, Rm 304, Moscow, ID 83843 (also use mail address for courier delivery), 208-882-7612, Fax-208-883-1576. Hours- 8AM-5PM. www.id.uscourts.gov

Counties: Clearwater, Idaho, Latah, Lewis, Nez Perce.

Searches & Indexing: Results include last 4 SSN digits only. Computer index maintained. New cases in the index immediately after filing date. Records purged immediately when case closed.

Fee & Payment: Pay by money order, cashier check, business check. No personal checks. Payee: US Bankruptcy Court. Prepayment required.

Phone Search: Only docket information is available by phone. Voice Case Information Service available, call VCIS at 208-334-9386.

Mail Search: search usually completed- 1 week. Include SASE for return.

In Person Search: Fee charged if court performs your search. No self-serve copier available.

E-Services: No PACER online. No PACER access to this court. ECF at https://ecf.idd.uscourts.gov **Opinions Online:** www.id.uscourts.gov/cfCourt/decisions/bk_decisionlist.cfm. Also, search archived bankruptcy cases at www.id.uscourts.gov/cfCourt/CourtArchives/Archive_SearchForm.cfm. **Other Online Access:** The old, free RACER system is no longer updated. Court now participate in the US party case index. Also view calendars at www.id.uscourts.gov/Calendar_DC_Public.htm.

Pocatello Division Court Clerk, 801 E Sherman, Pocatello, ID 83201 (also use mail address for courier delivery), 208-478-4123, Fax-208-478-4106. Hours- 8AM-5PM. www.id.uscourts.gov

Counties: Bannock, Bear Lake, Bingham, Bonneville, Butte, Caribou, Clark, Custer, Franklin, Fremont, Jefferson, Lemhi, Madison, Oneida, Power, Teton.

Searches & Indexing: Results do not include SSN or DOB. Computer index maintained. New cases in the index immediately after filing date. Records purged immediately when case closed. No cases may have been sent to Federal Records Center.

Fee & Payment: Pay by money order, cashier check, business check. No personal checks. Payee: US Bankruptcy Court. Copy service will bill after first order. Copy service faxes results $.50 per page.

Phone Search: Only docket information is available by phone. Voice Case Information Service available, call VCIS at 208-334-9386.

Mail Search: search usually completed- 24 hours. Include SASE for return.

In Person Search: Fee charged if court performs your search. No self-serve copier available.

E-Services: No PACER online. No PACER access to this court. ECF at https://ecf.idd.uscourts.gov **Opinions Online:** www.id.uscourts.gov/cfCourt/decisions/bk_decisionlist.cfm. Also, search archived bankruptcy cases at www.id.uscourts.gov/cfCourt/CourtArchives/Archive_SearchForm.cfm. **Other Online Access:** The old, free RACER system is no longer updated. Court now participate in the US party case index. Also view calendars at www.id.uscourts.gov/Calendar_DC_Public.htm.

Idaho County Courts

Court	Jurisdiction	No. of Courts	How Organized
District Courts*	General	Comb.	7 Districts
Magistrates Division*	Limited	2	7 Districts
Combined Courts*		44	

* Profiled in this Sourcebook.

Court	CIVIL								
	Tort	Contract	Real Estate	Min. Claim	Max. Claim	Small Claims	Estate	Eviction	Domestic Relations
District Courts*	X	X	X	$0	No Max				
Magistrates Division*	X	X	X	$0	$10,000	$4000	X	X	X

Court	CRIMINAL				
	Felony	Misdemeanor	DWI/DUI	Preliminary Hearing	Juvenile
District Courts*	X	X	X	X	
Magistrates. Division*			X	X	X

ADMINISTRATION — Administrative Director of Courts, Supreme Court Building, PO Box 83720, Boise, ID, 83720-0101; 208-334-2246, Fax: 208-334-2146. www.isc.idaho.gov//

COURT STRUCTURE — District judges hear felony criminal cases and civil actions if the amount involved is more than $10,000, and appeals of decisions of the Magistrate Division. The Magistrate Division hears probate matters, divorce proceedings, juvenile proceedings, initial felony proceedings through the preliminary hearing, criminal misdemeanors, infractions, civil cases when the amount in dispute does not exceed $10,000, and cases in Small Claims Court, established for disputes of $4,000 or less.

ONLINE ACCESS — Although appellate and supreme court opinions are available from the web site, but there is no statewide computer system offering external access. ISTARS is a statewide intra-court/intra-agency system run and managed by the State Supreme Court. All counties are on ISTARS, and all courts provide public access terminals on-site.

ADDITIONAL INFORMATION — A statewide court administrative rule states that record custodians do not have a duty to "compile or summarize information contained in a record, nor ... to create new records for the requesting party." Under this rule, some courts will not perform searches.

Many courts require a signed release for employment record searches.

A detailed description of the court rules regarding access to records may be found in Idaho Court Administrative Rule 32.

Ada County

Ada County Criminal Court 200 W Front St, Rm 1190, Boise, ID 83702-5931; phone: 208-287-6900; criminal phone: x2; fax: 208-287-6919; hours 8AM-5PM (MST). *Felony, Misdemeanor, Traffic.* http://www2.state.id.us/fourthjudicial
Criminal Records: Access: Mail, in person. Both court and visitors may perform in person searches. No search fee. Court makes copy: $1.00 per page. Required to search: name, years to search; also helpful: address, DOB, SSN. Criminal records on computer from 1985, microfiche from 1983, docket books to statehood. Mail turnaround 1-2 weeks.
General Information: Public terminal available. No alcohol level or confidential evaluation records released. Will fax documents to local or toll free line. Certification fee: $1.50. Payee: Ada County. Personal checks accepted. Prepayment and SASE required.

District & Magistrate Courts 200 W Front, Rm 1155, Boise, ID 83702-5931; phone: 208-287-6900; fax: 208-287-6919; hours 8AM-5PM (MST). *Civil, Eviction, Small Claims, Probate.*

http://www2.state.id.us/fourthjudicial
Civil Records: Access: Mail, in person. Both court and visitors may perform in person searches. No search fee. Court makes copy: $1.00 per page. Required to search: name, years to search; also helpful: address. Civil cases indexed by defendant, plaintiff, on computer since 1985, microfiche and docket books from 1860s. Mail turnaround time 1-7 days.
Criminal Records: Access: Mail, in person. Both court and visitors may perform in person searches. No search fee. Court makes copy: $1.00 per page. Required to search: name, years to search; also helpful: address, DOB, SSN. Criminal records on computer since 1985, microfiche and docket books from 1860s. Mail turnaround time 1-7 days.
General Information: Public terminal has criminal back to 1980 and civil back to 1994. No juvenile, adoption, child protection records released. Will fax documents to local or toll free line. Certification fee: $1.50 per page. Payee: Ada County. Personal checks accepted. Prepayment and SASE required.

Adams County

District & Magistrate Courts PO Box 48, Council, ID 83612; phone: 208-253-4561/4233; fax: 208-253-4880; hours 8AM-5PM (MST). *Felony, Misdemeanor, Civil, Eviction, Small Claims, Probate.*
Civil Records: Access: Fax, mail, in person. Both court and visitors may perform in person searches. No search fee. Court makes copy: $1.00 per page; same fee for self serve. Required to search: name, years to search. Civil cases indexed by defendant, plaintiff, on computer back to 1993, microfiche from 1972, docket books from 1911. Mail turnaround time 2 days.
Criminal Records: Access: Fax, mail, in person. Both court and visitors may perform in person searches. No search fee. Court makes copy: $1.00 per page; same fee for self serve. Required to search: name, years to search, signed release, DOB or SSN. Criminal records on computer back to 1993, microfiche from 1972, docket books from 1911. Include DOB and/or SSN. Mail turnaround 2 days.

General Information: Public terminal goes back to 1993. No juvenile, sealed cases records released. Will fax documents $4.00 per page. Certification fee: $1.00. Payee: Adams County. Personal checks accepted. Prepayment required. SASE requested.

Bannock County

District & Magistrate Courts 624 E Center, Rm 220, Pocatello, ID 83201; phone: 208-236-7351; criminal phone: 208-236-7352; civil phone: 208-236-7350; probate phone: 208-236-7351; fax: 208-236-7013; hours 8AM-5PM (MST). *Felony, Misdemeanor, Civil, Eviction, Small Claims, Probate.*

www.co.bannock.id.us/clkcrt1.htm

Note: The phone number for Misdemeanors is 208-236-7272.

Civil Records: Access: Fax, mail, in person. Both court and visitors may perform in person searches. Search fee: None, unless extensive research involved. Court makes copy: $1.00 per page. Required to search: name, years to search. Civil cases indexed by defendant, plaintiff, on computer from 1986, on docket books from 1970s. Mail turnaround time 1 day to 2 weeks.

Criminal Records: Access: Fax, mail, in person. Both court and visitors may perform in person searches. Search fee: None, unless extensive research involved. Court makes copy: $1.00 per page. Required to search: name, years to search; also helpful: DOB, SSN. Criminal records on computer from 1986, on docket books from 1970s. Mail turnaround time 1 day to 2 weeks.

General Information: Public terminal goes back to 1995. No adoption, mental, juvenile, termination, domestic violence records released. Will fax documents $1.00 per page. Certification fee: $1.50 per page. Payee: Bannock County District Court. Personal checks accepted. No credit cards. Prepayment and SASE required.

Bear Lake County

District & Magistrate Courts PO Box 190, Paris, ID 83261; phone: 208-945-2208 x6; fax: 208-945-2780; hours 8:30AM-5PM (MST). *Felony, Misdemeanor, Civil, Eviction, Small Claims, Probate.*

Civil Records: Access: Fax, mail, in person. Only the court performs in person searches; visitors may not. No search fee. Court makes copy: $1.00 per page; same fee for self serve. Required to search: name, years to search. Civil cases indexed by defendant, plaintiff, on computer back to 1991, docket books from early 1900s. Mail turnaround time 2-3 days.

Criminal Records: Access: Fax, mail, in person. Only the court performs in person searches; visitors may not. No search fee. Court makes copy: $1.00 per page; same fee for self serve. Required to search: name, years to search, DOB; also helpful: SSN, signed release. Criminal records on computer back to 1991, docket books from early 1900s. Mail turnaround time 2-3 days.

General Information: No public access terminal. No juvenile, CPA, divorce records released. Will fax documents $1.00 per page. Certification fee: $1.50 per document. Payee: Clerk of Court. Business checks accepted. Prepayment and SASE required.

Benewah County

District & Magistrate Courts Courthouse, 701 College Ave, St Maries, ID 83861; phone: 208-245-3241; fax: 208-245-3046; hours 9AM-5PM (PST). *Felony, Misdemeanor, Civil, Eviction, Small Claims, Probate.*

Civil Records: Access: Fax, mail, in person. Only the court performs in person searches; visitors may not. Search fee: $5.00 per name. Court makes copy: $1.00 per page. Required to search: name, years to search. Civil cases indexed by defendant, plaintiff, on computer from 1991, index cards and docket books from early 1900s. Court planning online access later

in 2005. Note: Fax requests must include copy of fees check. Mail turnaround time 3 days.

Criminal Records: Access: Mail, fax, in person. Only the court performs in person searches; visitors may not. Search fee: $5.00 per name. If printout required $.15 per page. Court makes copy: $1.00 per page. Required to search: name, years to search. Criminal records on computer from 1991, index cards and docket books from early 1900s. Court planning online access later in 2005. Note: Fax requests must include copy of fees check. Mail turnaround time 3-5 days.

General Information: No public access terminal. No juvenile, adoptions, mental commitments or sealed records released. No fee to fax documents if search fee paid. Certification fee: $1.00 per seal. Payee: Clerk of Court. Personal checks accepted. Prepayment and SASE required.

Bingham County

District & Magistrate Courts 501 N Maple St, #402, Blackfoot, ID 83221-1700; phone: 208-785-8040 X3154-Dist, X3121-Magis; criminal phone: X3118, X3117 or X3122; civil phone: X3123 or X3124; probate phone: X3123 or X3124; fax: 208-785-3167; 8AM-N, 1-5PM (MST). *Felony, Misdemeanor, Civil, Eviction, Small Claims, Probate.*

Note: Direct phone for District Ct is 2087-785-8057. Small Claims phone X3120.

Civil Records: Access: Phone, fax, mail, in person. Both court and visitors may perform in person searches. No search fee. Court makes copy: $1.00 per page. Required to search: name, years to search; also helpful: address. Civil cases indexed by defendant, plaintiff, on computer from 1989, from microfiche from 1865. Mail turnaround time 1-2 weeks.

Criminal Records: Access: Phone, fax, mail, in person. Visitors must perform in person searches themselves. No search fee. Court makes copy: $1.00 per page. Required to search: name, years to search, signed release; also helpful: address, DOB, SSN. Criminal records on computer from 1989, from microfiche from 1865. Mail turnaround time 1-2 weeks.

General Information: Public terminal goes back to 1989. No juvenile, adoption, mental records released. Will fax documents for $1.25 per page. Certification fee: $1.00 per page. Payee: Clerk of Court. Personal checks accepted. Prepayment and SASE required.

Blaine County

District & Magistrate Courts 201 2nd Ave S, #106, Hailey, ID 83333; phone: 208-788-5548; fax: 208-788-5527; hours 9AM-5PM (MST). *Felony, Misdemeanor, Civil, Eviction, Small Claims, Probate.*

Note: The Magistrate Court (Misdemeanor, Small Claims, Eviction, Probate) is in #106; Magistrate Court phone is 208-788-5525; fax 208-788-5527.

Civil Records: Access: In person only. Visitors must perform in person searches themselves. Court makes copy: $1.00 per page. Required to search: name, years to search. Civil cases indexed by defendant, plaintiff, on computer from 1992.

Criminal Records: Access: In person only. Visitors must perform in person searches themselves. Court makes copy: $1.00 per page. Required to search: name, years to search, DOB, SSN. Criminal records on computer since 1988.

General Information: Public terminal goes back to 1992. No juvenile records released. Certification fee: $1.00 per document. Payee: Clerk of Court. Personal checks accepted. Prepayment required.

Boise County

District & Magistrate Courts PO Box 126, Idaho City, ID 83631; phone: 208-392-4452; fax: 208-392-6712; hours 8AM-5PM (MST). *Felony, Misdemeanor, Civil, Eviction, Small Claims, Probate.*

Civil Records: Access: In person only. Visitors must perform in person searches themselves. Court makes copy: $1.00 per page. Required to search: name, years to search. Civil cases indexed by defendant, plaintiff, on computer from 6/90, on docket books from 1863.

Criminal Records: Access: In person only. Visitors must perform in person searches themselves. Court makes copy: $1.00 per page. Required to search: name, years to search, SSN; also helpful: DOB. Criminal records on computer from 6/90, on docket books from 1863.

General Information: Public use terminal available. No juvenile, adoption records released. Certification fee: $1.50 per page. Payee: Boise County. Personal checks accepted. Prepayment required.

Bonner County

District & Magistrate Courts 215 S 1st Ave, Bonner Courthouse, Sandpoint, ID 83864; phone: 208-265-1432; fax: 208-265-1447; hours 9AM-5PM (PST). *Felony, Misdemeanor, Civil, Eviction, Small Claims, Probate.*

Civil Records: Access: In person only. Visitors must perform in person searches themselves. Court makes copy: $1.00 per page; same fee for self serve. Required to search: name, years to search; also helpful: address. Civil cases indexed by defendant, plaintiff, on computer from 1990, index and docket books from 1907.

Criminal Records: Access: In person only. Visitors must perform in person searches themselves. Court makes copy: $1.00 per page; same fee for self serve. Required to search: name, years to search; also helpful: address, DOB, SSN. Criminal records on computer from 1990, index and docket books from 1907.

General Information: Public terminal goes back to 1990. No juvenile records released. Will fax specific case file for $3.00 per page. Certification fee: $1.00. Payee: Bonner County Clerk. Personal checks accepted. Prepayment required.

Bonneville County

District & Magistrate Courts 605 N Capital, Idaho Falls, ID 83402; phone: 208-529-1350 x6; fax: 208-529-1300; hours 8AM-5PM (MST). *Felony, Misdemeanor, Civil, Eviction, Small Claims, Probate.*

www.co.bonneville.id.us

Civil Records: Access: Phone, mail, in person. Visitors must perform in person searches themselves. No search fee. Court makes copy: $1.00 per page. Self serve copy fee: $.10 per page. Required to search: name, years to search, case type. Civil cases indexed by defendant, plaintiff, on computer from civil from 1991. Docket books by case number ongoing. Actual case records are archived before 10/91.

Criminal Records: Access: Phone, mail, in person. Visitors must perform in person searches themselves. No search fee. Court makes copy: $1.00 per page. Self serve copy fee: $.10 per page. Required to search: name, years to search, DOB, signed release; also helpful: SSN, offense. Criminal misdemeanor records on computer from 1983, felony on computer from 1991, civil from 1991. Criminal on microfiche from 1977, civil from 1923. Docket books by case number ongoing. Actual case records are archived before 10/91.

General Information: Public terminal goes back to 1991. No child protective, protection orders, juvenile, sanity, or termination records released. Certification fee: $1.00 per page. Payee: Bonneville County. Personal checks accepted. Prepayment required.

Boundary County

District & Magistrate Courts Boundary County Courthouse, PO Box 419, Bonners Ferry, ID 83805; phone: 208-267-5504; fax: 208-267-7814; hours 9AM-5PM (PST). *Felony, Misdemeanor, Civil, Eviction, Small Claims, Probate.*

Civil Records: Access: In person only. Visitors must perform in person searches themselves. Court makes copy: $1.00 per page. Required to search: name, years to search; also helpful: address. Civil cases indexed by defendant, plaintiff, on computer from 1989; by case number, index books, cards or microfiche by name from early 1900s.

Criminal Records: Access: In person only. Visitors must perform in person searches themselves. Court makes copy: $1.00 per page. Required to search: name, years to search, SSN; also helpful: DOB. Criminal records on computer from 1989; by case number, index books, cards or microfiche by name from early 1900s.

General Information: Public terminal goes back to 1989. No sealed records released. Certification fee: $1.00 per page. Payee: Clerk of Court. Personal checks accepted. Prepayment required.

Butte County

District & Magistrate Courts 326 W Grand Ave, Arco, ID 83213; phone: 208-527-8259; fax: 208-527-3448; hours 9AM-N; 1PM-5PM (MST). *Felony, Misdemeanor, Civil, Eviction, Small Claims, Probate.*

Civil Records: Access: Phone, fax, mail, in person. Both court and visitors may perform in person searches. No search fee. Court makes copy: $1.00 per page. Self serve copy fee: $.10 per page. Required to search: name, years to search; also helpful: address. Civil cases indexed by defendant, plaintiff, on computer from 1989, archives prior. Docket books by case number from early 1910s. Mail time 1 week.

Criminal Records: Access: Phone, fax, mail, in person. Both court and visitors may perform in person searches. No search fee. Court makes copy: $1.00 per page. Self serve copy fee: $.10 per page. Required to search: name, years to search; also helpful: address, DOB, SSN. Criminal records on computer from 1992 archives prior. Docket books by case number from early 1910s. Mail time 1 week.

General Information: No public access terminal. No juvenile records released. Fee to fax documents is $1.00 per page. Certification fee: $1.00 per page. Payee: Butte County Magistrate Court. Personal checks accepted. Prepayment and SASE required.

Camas County

District & Magistrate Courts PO Box 430, Fairfield, ID 83327; phone: 208-764-2238; fax: 208-764-2349; hours 8:30AM-N, 1-5PM (MST). *Felony, Misdemeanor, Civil, Eviction, Small Claims, Probate.*

Civil Records: Access: Mail, in person. Both court and visitors may perform in person searches. No search fee. Court makes copy: $1.00 per page; same fee for self serve. Required to search: name, years to search; also helpful: address. Civil cases indexed by defendant, plaintiff. Civil records from archives from 1917. Register of actions by case number. Mail turnaround time same day.

Criminal Records: Access: Mail, in person. Both court and visitors may perform in person searches. No search fee. Court makes copy: $1.00 per page; same fee for self serve. Required to search: name, years to search; also helpful: address, DOB, SSN. Criminal records from archives from 1917. Register of actions by case number. Mail turnaround 1 day.

General Information: Public terminal has criminal back to 1994 and civil back to 1994. No juvenile or domestic violence records released. Will fax documents to local or toll free line. Certification fee: $1.00. Payee: Camas County Courthouse. Personal checks accepted. Prepayment and SASE required.

Canyon County

District & Magistrate Courts 1115 Albany, Caldwell, ID 83605; criminal phone: 208-454-7571; civil phone: 208-454-7570; fax: 208-454-7525; hours 8:30AM-5PM (MST). *Felony, Misdemeanor, Civil, Eviction, Small Claims, Probate.* www.the3rdjudicialdistrict.com

Note: Small claims phone is 208-454-7577

Civil Records: Access: In person only. Visitors must perform in person searches themselves. Court makes copy: $1.00 per page. Self serve copy fee: $.50 per page. Required to search: name, years to search. Civil cases indexed by defendant, plaintiff, on computer from 1989, microfiche from 1800s, and docket books. A daily court calendar is at www.the3rdjudicialdistrict.com.

Criminal Records: Access: In person only. Visitors must perform in person searches themselves. Court makes copy: $1.00 per page. Self serve copy fee: $.50 per page. Required to search: name, years to search; also helpful: DOB. Criminal records on computer from 1989, microfiche from 1800s, and docket books. A daily court calendar is at www.the3rdjudicialdistrict.com.

General Information: Public terminal goes back to 1989. No adoption, mental, domestic violence records not released. Certification fee: $1.00 per page. Payee: Clerk of Court. Only cashiers checks and money orders accepted. Prepayment required.

Caribou County

District & Magistrate Courts 159 S Main, Soda Springs, ID 83276; phone: 208-547-4342; fax: 208-547-4759; hours 9AM-5PM (MST). *Felony, Misdemeanor, Civil, Eviction, Small Claims, Probate.*

Civil Records: Access: Phone, fax, mail, in person. Both court and visitors may perform in person searches. No search fee. Court makes copy: $1.00 per page. Required to search: name, years to search. Civil cases indexed by defendant, plaintiff, on computer from 1989, from 1930 archived in vault. Mail turnaround time up to 1 week.

Criminal Records: Access: Phone, fax, mail, in person. Both court and visitors may perform in person searches. No search fee. Court makes copy: $1.00 per page. Required to search: name, years to search, DOB, SSN; also helpful: address. Criminal records on computer from 1989, from 1930 archived in vault. Mail turnaround time up to 1 week.

General Information: Public terminal goes back to 1989. No adoption, guardianship records released. Will fax documents $2.00 1st page, $1.00 each add'l. Certification fee: $1.50. Payee: Clerk of Court. Business checks accepted. Out of state checks not accepted. Prepayment and SASE required.

Cassia County

District & Magistrate Courts 1459 Overland, Burley, ID 83318; phone: 208-878-7351 Magistrate; 878-4367 Dist; criminal phone: 208-878-4367; civil phone: 208-878-4367; probate phone: 208-878-7351; fax: 208-878-1003; hours 8:30AM-5PM (MST). *Felony, Misdemeanor, Civil, Eviction, Small Claims, Probate.* http://cassiacounty.org/judicial/index.htm

Note: Probate is a separate index at this same address.

Civil Records: Access: Phone, fax, mail, in person. Both court and visitors may perform in person searches. No search fee. Court makes copy: $1.00 per page. Self serve copy fee: $1.00 per page if court's document; $.15 in not. Required to search: name, years to search; address helpful. Civil cases indexed by defendant, plaintiff, on computer from 1990, archives from 1900s. Mail turnaround 1-2 days.

Criminal Records: Access: Fax, mail, in person. Both court and visitors may perform in person searches. No search fee. Court makes copy: $1.00 per page. Self serve copy fee: $1.00 per page if court's document; $.15 in not. Required to search: name, years to search; also helpful: address, DOB, SSN. Criminal records on computer from 1990, archives from 1900s. Mail turnaround time 1-2 days.

General Information: Public terminal goes back to 1990. No juvenile, adoption, mental commitment, child protection records released. Will fax documents $2.50 per page. Certification fee: $1.50 per page. Payee: Clerk of Court. Personal checks accepted. Prepayment and SASE required.

Clark County

District & Magistrate Courts PO Box 205, DuBois, ID 83423; phone: 208-374-5402; fax: 208-374-5609; hours 9AM-5PM (MST). *Felony, Misdemeanor, Civil, Eviction, Small Claims, Probate.*

Civil Records: Access: In person only. Both court and visitors may perform in person searches. No search fee. Self serve copy fee: $1.00 per page. Required to search: name, years to search; also helpful: address. Civil cases indexed by defendant, plaintiff, on computer from 1985, on microfiche for civil judgments and from archives from 1919.

Criminal Records: Access: In person only. Visitors must perform in person searches themselves. Self serve copy fee: $1.00 per page. Required to search: name, years to search; also helpful: address, DOB, SSN. Criminal records on computer from 1985, on microfiche for civil judgments and from archives from 1919.

General Information: Public terminal goes back to 10 years. No juvenile, adoption records released. Will not fax documents. Certification fee: $1.00 per page. Payee: Clerk of Court. Personal checks accepted. Prepayment required.

Clearwater County

District & Magistrate Courts PO Box 586, Orofino, ID 83544; phone: 208-476-5596; fax: 208-476-5159; hours 8AM-5PM (PST). *Felony, Misdemeanor, Civil, Eviction, Small Claims, Probate.*

Civil Records: Access: Phone, fax, mail, in person. Only the court performs in person searches; visitors may not. No search fee. Court makes copy: $1.00 per page. Required to search: name, years to search. Civil cases indexed by defendant, plaintiff, on computer from 8/91, in docket books prior to 1911. Mail turnaround time 7 days.

Criminal Records: Access: Phone, fax, mail, in person. Only the court performs in person searches; visitors may not. No search fee. Court makes copy: $1.00 per page. Required to search: name or case number, years to search. Criminal records on computer from 8/91, in docket books prior to 1911. Mail turnaround time 7 days.

General Information: No public access terminal. No juvenile, domestic violence, adoption, social records released. Will fax documents $1.00 per page. Certification fee: $1.00. Payee: Clerk of Court. Business checks accepted. Prepayment required. SASE requested.

Custer County

District & Magistrate Courts PO Box 385, Challis, ID 83226; phone: 208-879-2359; fax: 208-879-6412; hours 8AM-5PM (MST). *Felony, Misdemeanor, Civil, Eviction, Small Claims, Probate.*

Civil Records: Access: Phone, mail, in person. Both court and visitors may perform in person searches. Search fee: $5.00 per name. Court makes copy: $1.00 per page. Required to search: name, years to search. Civil cases indexed by defendant. Civil records on computer from 1989, archived from early 1900s. Mail turnaround time 1 week.

Criminal Records: Access: Phone, mail, in person. Both court and visitors may perform in person searches. Search fee: $5.00 per name. Court makes copy: $1.00 per page. Required to search: name, years to search, DOB, signed release; also helpful: SSN. Criminal records on computer from 1989, archived from early 1900s. Mail turnaround time 1 week.

General Information: Public terminal goes back to 1989. No juvenile, adoption records released. Will not fax documents. Certification fee: $1.00 per page. Payee: Custer County. Personal checks accepted. Prepayment required.

Elmore County

District & Magistrate Courts 150 S 4th E, #5, Mountain Home, ID 83647; phone: 208-587-2133 x208; fax: 208-587-2134; hours 9AM-5PM (MST). *Felony, Misdemeanor, Civil, Eviction, Small Claims, Probate.*

Civil Records: Access: In person only. Visitors must perform in person searches themselves. Court makes copy: $1.00 per page. Required to search: name; also helpful: years to search. Civil cases indexed by defendant, plaintiff, on computer from 1992, on microfiche from 1972, archived from early 1900s.

Criminal Records: Access: In person only. Visitors must perform in person searches themselves. Court makes copy: $1.00 per page. Required to search: name, DOB, signed release; also helpful: years to search, SSN. Criminal records on computer from 1992, on microfiche from 1972, archived from early 1900s.

General Information: Public use terminal available. No juvenile, adoption, domestic violence, mental commitment records released. Will fax specific case file for $1.00 per page. Certification fee: $1.00 per page. Payee: Elmore County. Personal checks accepted. Prepayment required.

Franklin County

District & Magistrate Courts 39 W Oneida, Preston, ID 83263; phone: 208-852-0877; fax: 208-852-2926; hours 9AM-5PM (MST). *Felony, Misdemeanor, Civil, Eviction, Small Claims, Probate.*

Civil Records: Access: Phone, fax, mail, in person. Both court and visitors may perform in person searches. Search fee: $5.00 per name. Fee is for years prior to 1990. No fee for 1990 to present. Court makes copy: $1.00 per page. Required to search: name, years to search. Civil cases indexed by defendant, plaintiff, on computer from 1987, microfiche from 1983, archived from 1920. Mail turnaround time 2-3 days.

Criminal Records: Access: Phone, fax, mail, in person. Both court and visitors may perform in person searches. Search fee: $5.00 per name. Fee is for years prior to 1990. No fee for 1990 to present. Court makes copy: $1.00 per page. Required to search: name, years to search; also helpful: DOB, SSN. Criminal records on computer from 1987, microfiche from 1977, archived from 1920. Mail turnaround time 2-3 days.

General Information: Public terminal goes back to 1984. No adoption records released. No fee to fax documents. Local faxing only. Certification fee: $1.00 per cert. Payee: Clerk of Court. Personal checks accepted. Prepayment and SASE required.

Fremont County

District & Magistrate Courts 151 W 1st N, St Anthony, ID 83445; phone: 208-624-7401; fax: 208-624-4607; hours 9AM-5PM (MST). *Felony, Misdemeanor, Civil, Eviction, Small Claims, Probate.*

Civil Records: Access: Phone, fax, mail, in person. Both court and visitors may perform in person searches. No search fee. Court makes copy: $1.00 per page; same fee for self serve. Required to search: name, years to search; also helpful: address. Civil cases indexed by defendant, plaintiff, on computer back to 1990, microfiche for last 20 years, prior archives. Thursday is the best day for in person searches. Mail turnaround time 1 week.

Criminal Records: Access: Fax, mail, in person. Both court and visitors may perform in person searches. No search fee. Court makes copy: $1.00 per page; same fee for self serve. Required to search: name, years to search, DOB; also helpful: SSN. Criminal records on computer back to 1990, microfiche for last 20 years, prior archives. Note: Thursday is the best day for in person searches. Mail turnaround time 1 week.

General Information: Public terminal goes back to 1990. No adoption or juvenile records released. Fee to fax documents is $2.00 per page. Certification fee: $1.00 per page. Payee: Clerk of Court. Personal checks accepted. Prepayment and SASE required.

Gem County

District & Magistrate Courts 415 E Main St, Emmett, ID 83617; phone: 208-365-4561-District 208-365-4221-Magistrate, fax: 208-365-6172; hours 8AM-5PM (MST). *Felony, Misdemeanor, Civil, Eviction, Small Claims, Probate.* www.co.gem.id.us/judicial/default.htm

Civil Records: Access: Mail, in person. Both court and visitors may perform in person searches. Search fee: $5.00 per name. Court makes copy: $.05 per page. Required to search: name, years to search; also helpful: address. Civil cases indexed by defendant, plaintiff, on computer from 1990, on microfiche and archived from 1916. Mail turnaround time 10 days.

Criminal Records: Access: Mail, in person. Both court and visitors may perform in person searches. Search fee: $5.00 per name per court. Court makes copy: $.05 per page. Required to search: name, years to search, DOB, SSN; also helpful: address. Criminal records on computer from 1990, on microfiche and archived from 1972. Mail turnaround time 10 days.

General Information: Public terminal goes back to 1990. No juvenile, adoption records or domestic violence released. Will fax documents to local or toll free line. Certification fee: $1.00 plus $.50 per page. Payee: Gem County. Personal checks accepted. Prepayment and SASE required.

Gooding County

District & Magistrate Courts PO Box 27, Gooding, ID 83330; criminal phone: 208-934-4861; civil phone: 208-934-4261; fax: 208-934-4408; hours 8AM-5PM (MST). *Felony, Misdemeanor, Civil, Eviction, Small Claims, Probate.*

Note: Magistrate Court can be reached at 208-934-4261. Magistrate Court address is PO Box 477. Only felony records are available at District Court.

Civil Records: Access: Phone, fax, mail, in person. Visitors must perform in person searches themselves. Court makes copy: $1.00 per page. Required to search: name, years to search. Civil cases indexed by defendant, plaintiff, on computer from 1994, on microfiche, docket books from 1860s.

Criminal Records: Access: In person only. Visitors must perform in person searches themselves. Court makes copy: $1.00 per page. Required to search: name, years to search, DOB, SSN. Criminal records on computer from 1994, on microfiche, docket books from 1860s.

General Information: Public use terminal available. No juvenile, adoption, domestic violence records released. Fee to fax documents is $1.00 per page. Certification fee: $1.00. Payee: Gooding County Clerk. Personal checks accepted. Prepayment and SASE required.

Idaho County

District & Magistrate Courts 320 W Main, Grangeville, ID 83530; phone: 208-983-2776; fax: 208-983-2376; hours 8:30AM-5PM (PST). *Felony, Misdemeanor, Civil, Eviction, Small Claims, Probate.*

Civil Records: Access: Phone, fax, mail, in person. Only the court performs in person searches; visitors may not. No search fee. Court makes copy: $1.00 per page. Required to search: name, years to search. Civil cases indexed by defendant, plaintiff, on computer from 1989, on microfiche and archived from late 1800s. Mail turnaround time same week.

Criminal Records: Access: Phone, fax, mail, in person. Only the court performs in person searches; visitors may not. No search fee. Court makes copy: $1.00 per page. Required to search: name, years to search. Criminal records on computer from 1989, on microfiche and archived from late 1800s. Mail turnaround time same week.

General Information: No domestic violence, juvenile, adoption, termination records released. Will fax documents for $1.00 per page. Certification fee: only charge for copies. Payee: Idaho County. Personal checks accepted. Prepayment required.

Jefferson County

District & Magistrate Courts PO Box 71, Rigby, ID 83442; phone: 208-745-7736; fax: 208-745-6636; hours 9AM-5PM (MST). *Felony, Misdemeanor, Civil, Eviction, Small Claims, Probate.*

Note: Information is on the public access computer; please use this before requesting the clerks' assistance

Civil Records: Access: In person only. Both court and visitors may perform in person searches. No search fee. Court makes copy: $1.00 per page. Required to search: name, years to search. Civil cases indexed by defendant, plaintiff. Civil records archived from early 1900s; on computer back to 8/1992.

Criminal Records: Access: In person only. Both court and visitors may perform in person searches. No search fee. Court makes copy: $1.00 per page. Required to search: name, years to search, DOB. Criminal records archived from early 1900s; on computer back to 8/1992.

General Information: Public terminal goes back to 8/1992. No juvenile, adoption, some domestic records released. Will fax specific case file $3.00 per page, limit 10 pages. Certification fee: $1.00 per page. Payee: Clerk of Court. Personal checks accepted. Prepayment required.

Jerome County

District & Magistrate Courts 300 N Lincoln St, Jerome, ID 83338; phone: 208-324-8811; fax: 208-324-2719; hours 8:30AM-5PM (MST). *Felony, Misdemeanor, Civil, Eviction, Small Claims, Probate.*

Civil Records: Access: Fax, mail, in person. Both court and visitors may perform in person searches. No search fee. Court makes copy: $1.00 per page; same fee for self serve. Required to search: name, years to search. Civil cases indexed by defendant, plaintiff, on computer from 1989, prior on microfiche back to 1919. Mail turnaround 2 days.

Criminal Records: Access: Fax, mail, in person. Visitors must perform in person searches themselves. No search fee. Court makes copy: $1.00 per page; same fee for self serve. Required to search: name, years to search, address, DOB, SSN. Criminal records on computer from 1989, civil from 1988, prior on microfiche back to 1919. Note: Will not do background searches. Mail turnaround time 2 days.

General Information: Public use terminal available. No juvenile records released. Will fax documents $3.00 1st page, $2.50 each add'l. Certification fee: $1.50 per page. Payee: Clerk of Court. Personal checks accepted. Prepayment and SASE required.

Kootenai County

District & Magistrate Court PO Box 9000, 324 W Garden Ave, Coeur d'Alene, ID 83816-9000; phone: 208-446-1180; criminal phone: 208-446-1170; civil phone: 208-446-1160; probate phone: 208-446-1160; fax: 208-446-1188; hours 9AM-5PM (PST). *Felony, Misdemeanor, Civil, Eviction, Small Claims, Probate.* www.co.kootenai.id.us/departments/districtcourt

Civil Records: Access: Mail, in person. Visitors must perform in person searches themselves. Court makes copy: $1.00 per page. Required to search: name, years to search. Civil cases indexed by defendant, plaintiff, on computer from 1989, on microfiche from 1881, archived from 1819. Mail turnaround time in 2 days.

Criminal Records: Access: Mail, in person. Visitors must perform in person searches themselves. Court makes copy: $1.00 per page. Required to search: name, years to search; also helpful: DOB, SSN. Criminal records on computer from 1989, on microfiche from 1881, archived from 1819. Mail turnaround time in 2 days.

General Information: Public terminal goes back to 1989. No sealed, adoption, parental termination, mentally incapacitated records released. Will fax documents to local or toll free line. Certification fee: $1.00. Payee: Clerk of Court. Personal checks accepted. Credit cards accepted through Official Payments 800-533-0743. Prepayment required.

Latah County

District & Magistrate Courts PO Box 8068, Moscow, ID 83843; phone: 208-883-2255; fax: 208-883-2259; hours 8:30AM-5PM M-W, 8AM-5PM Th,F (PST). *Felony, Misdemeanor, Civil, Eviction, Small Claims, Probate.*
Civil Records: Access: Phone, fax, mail, in person. Both court and visitors may perform in person searches. Search fee: $4.00 per name. Court makes copy: $1.00 per page. Required to search: name, years to search; also helpful: address. Civil cases indexed by defendant, plaintiff, on computer from 1986, archived from 5/1888. Mail turnaround time 1-2 days.
Criminal Records: Access: Phone, fax, mail, in person. Both court and visitors may perform in person searches. Search fee: $4.00 per name. Court makes copy: $1.00 per page. Required to search: name, years to search; also helpful: address, DOB, SSN. Criminal records on computer from 1986, archived from 5/1888. Mail turnaround time 1-2 days.
General Information: Public terminal goes back to 1992. No adoption, juvenile records released. Will fax documents to local or toll free line. Certification fee: $1.00 per page. Payee: Clerk of Court. Personal checks accepted. Prepayment required.

Lemhi County

District & Magistrate Courts 206 Courthouse Dr, Salmon, ID 83467; phone: 208-756-2815; criminal phone: x225; civil phone: x225; probate phone: x242; criminal fax: 208-756-8424; civil fax: 208-756-8424; probate fax: 208-756-4673; hours 8AM-5PM (MST). *Felony, Misdemeanor, Civil, Eviction, Small Claims, Probate.*
Civil Records: Access: Phone, fax, mail, in person. Both court and visitors may perform in person searches. Search fee: $5.00 per name. Court makes copy: $1.00 per page; same fee for self serve. Required to search: name, years to search; also helpful: address. Civil cases indexed by defendant, plaintiff, on computer from 1991, on microfiche from 1964, archives from 1869. Mail turnaround time 1-3 days.
Criminal Records: Access: Phone, fax, mail, in person. Both court and visitors may perform in person searches. Search fee: $5.00 per name. Court makes copy: $1.00 per page; same fee for self serve. Required to search: name, years to search; also helpful: address, DOB, SSN. Criminal records on computer from 1991, on microfiche from 1964, archives from 1869. Mail turnaround time 1 day.
General Information: Public terminal goes back to 1991. No PSI, sealed records released. Fee to fax documents is $1.00 per page. Certification fee: $1.00 per document and $.50 per page. Payee: Lemhi County Clerk. Personal checks accepted. Prepayment required. SASE requested.

Lewis County

District & Magistrate Courts 510 Oak St, Rm 1, PO Box 39, Nezperce, ID 83543; phone: 208-937-2251; fax: 208-937-9233; 9AM-5PM *Felony, Misdemeanor, Civil, Eviction, small claims, Probate.*
Civil Records: Access: Phone, fax, mail, in person. Both court and visitors may perform in person searches. No search fee. Court makes copy: $1.00 per page. Required to search: name, years to search. Civil cases indexed by defendant, plaintiff, on computer from 1991, archived from late 1911. Mail turnaround time 1 week.
Criminal Records: Access: Phone, fax, mail, in person. Both court and visitors may perform in person searches. No search fee. Court makes copy:

$1.00 per page. Required to search: name, years to search; also helpful: DOB, SSN. Criminal records on computer from 1991, archived from late 1911. Mail turnaround time 1 week.
General Information: No public access terminal. No juvenile, adoption records released. Will fax documents $1.00 per page. Certification fee: $1.00. Payee: Clerk of Court. Two-party checks not accepted. Prepayment and SASE required.

Lincoln County

District & Magistrate Courts 111 W B St, Shoshone, ID 83352; phone: 208-886-2173; fax: 208-886-2458; hours 8:30AM-5PM (MST). *Felony, Misdemeanor, Civil, Eviction, Small Claims, Probate.*
Civil Records: Access: In person, mail, fax. Both court and visitors may perform in person searches. No search fee. Court makes copy: $1.00 per page. Required to search: name, years to search. Civil cases indexed by defendant, plaintiff, on computer from 1992, archives from 1800s. Mail turnaround time 5 days.
Criminal Records: Access: In person, mail, fax. Both court and visitors may perform in person searches. No search fee. Court makes copy: $1.00 per page. Required to search: name, years to search; also helpful: DOB, SSN. Criminal records on computer from 1992, archives from 1800s. Mail turnaround time 5 days.
General Information: Public terminal goes back to 1995. No juvenile, domestic violence, sealed records released. Certification fee: $1.00. Payee: Lincoln County Courts. Personal checks accepted. Prepayment and SASE required.

Madison County

District & Magistrate Courts PO Box 389, Rexburg, ID 83440; phone: 208-356-9383; fax: 208-356-5425; hours 9AM-5PM (MST). *Felony, Misdemeanor, Civil, Eviction, Small Claims, Probate.*
Civil Records: Access: In person only. Both court and visitors may perform in person searches. Court makes copy: $1.00 per page. Required to search: name, years to search; also helpful: address. Civil cases indexed by defendant, plaintiff, on computer from 1991, microfiche and archives from early 1900s.
Criminal Records: Access: In person only. Visitors must perform in person searches themselves. Court makes copy: $1.00 per page. Required to search: name, years to search; also helpful: address, DOB, SSN. Criminal records on computer from 1991, microfiche and archives from early 1900s.
General Information: Public terminal goes back to 1991. No juvenile records released. Certification fee: $1.00. Payee: Clerk of Court. Personal checks accepted. Prepayment required.

Minidoka County

District & Magistrate Courts PO Box 368, Rupert, ID 83350; phone: 208-436-9041 (Dist) 436-7186 (Magis); fax: 208-436-5857; chours 8:30AM-5PM (MST). *Felony, Misdemeanor, Civil, Eviction, Small Claims, Probate.*
Civil Records: Access: Fax, mail, in person. Both court and visitors may perform in person searches. No search fee. Court makes copy: $1.00 per page. Required to search: name, years to search. Civil cases indexed by defendant, plaintiff, on computer from 1989, archives from early 1900s. Mail turnaround time 1-3 days.
Criminal Records: Access: Fax, mail, in person. Both court and visitors may perform in person searches. No search fee. Court makes copy: $1.00 per page. Required to search: name, years to search, DOB, SSN, signed release. Criminal records on computer from 1989, archives from early 1900s. Mail turnaround time 1-3 days.
General Information: Public terminal goes back to 1989. Juvenile records released with a signed release. Will fax documents $.50 per page. Certification fee:

$1.00 per document. Payee: Clerk of Court. Personal checks accepted. Prepayment required.

Nez Perce County

District & Magistrate Court PO Box 896, 1230 Main St, Lewiston, ID 83501; phone: 208-799-3040; fax: 208-799-3058; hours 8AM-5PM (PST). *Felony, Misdemeanor, Civil, Eviction, Small Claims, Probate.*
www.co.nezperce.id.us/clerk/clerk.htm
Civil Records: Access: Phone, fax, mail, in person. Both court and visitors may perform in person searches. No search fee. Court makes copy: $1.00 per page. Required to search: name; also helpful: years to search. Civil cases indexed by defendant, plaintiff, on computer from 1990, microfiche from 1970 and archives from late 1800s. Mail turnaround time- 10 day waiting period.
Criminal Records: Access: Phone, fax, mail, in person. Both court and visitors may perform in person searches. No search fee. Court makes copy: $1.00 per page. Required to search: name, DOB; also helpful: years to search, aliases, SSN. Criminal records on computer from 1990, microfiche from 1970 and archives from late 1800s. Mail turnaround time- 10 day waiting period.
General Information: Public terminal goes back to 1983. Will fax documents $1.00 per doc $1.00 1st page, plus (if long-distance) $.50 each add'l minute. Certification fee: $1.00 per doc. Payee: Clerk of Court. Personal checks accepted. No credit cards. Prepayment and SASE required.

Oneida County

District & Magistrate Courts 10 Court St, Malad City, ID 83252; phone: 208-766-4116; fax: 208-766-2990; hours 9AM-5PM (MST). *Felony, Misdemeanor, Civil, Eviction, Small Claims, Probate.*
Note: Probate is a separate index at the same address.
Civil Records: Access: Phone, fax, mail, in person. Both court and visitors may perform in person searches. No search fee. Court makes copy: $1.00 per page; same fee for self serve. Required to search: name, years to search; also helpful: address. Civil cases indexed by case number, defendant, plaintiff. Civil records on computer from 7/90, archives from 1886. Mail turnaround time 1-2 days.
Criminal Records: Access: Phone, fax, mail, in person. Both court and visitors may perform in person searches. No search fee. Court makes copy: $1.00 per page; same fee for self serve. Required to search: name, years to search; also helpful: address, DOB, SSN. Criminal records on computer from 7/90, archives from 1886. Mail turnaround time 1-2 days.
General Information: No public access terminal. No juvenile, adoption records released. Will fax documents $1.00 per page. Certification fee: $1.00 per page. Payee: Clerk of Court. Personal checks accepted. Prepayment required. SASE requested.

Owyhee County

District & Magistrate Courts-I Courthouse, PO Box 128, Murphy, ID 83650; phone: 208-495-2806; fax: 208-495-1226; hours 8:30AM-5PM (MST). *Felony, Misdemeanor, Civil, Eviction, Small Claims, Probate.*
http://owyheecounty.net/court/index.htm
Civil Records: Access: Mail, in person. Only the court performs in person searches; visitors may not. Search fee: $5.00 per name found. Court makes copy: $1.00 per page. Required to search: name, years to search. Civil cases indexed by defendant, plaintiff, on computer from 1992, archives from 1800s. Mail turnaround time 5-10 days, longer if records archived.
Criminal Records: Access: Fax, mail, in person. Only the court performs in person searches; visitors may not. Search fee: $5.00 per name found. Court makes copy: $1.00 per page. Required to search: name, years to search; also helpful: DOB. Criminal records on computer from 1992, archives

from 1800s. Signed release required for search of juvenile records. Mail turnaround time 5-10 days, longer if records archived.

General Information: No public access terminal. No adoption, juvenile (except for some that are open), domestic violence records released. Fee to fax documents is $1.00 per page (copies) and $5.00 per document. Certification fee: $1.00 per page. Payee: Owyhee County. Only cashiers checks and money orders accepted. Prepayment required. Mail requests: Include $.37 for return postage.

Homedale Magistrate Court

31 W Wyoming, Homedale, ID 83628-3402; phone: 208-337-4540; fax: 208-337-3035; hours 8:30AM-5PM (MST). *Misdemeanor, Civil Actions Under $10,000, Eviction, Small Claims.*

Civil Records: Access: Mail, in person. Only the court performs in person searches; visitors may not. No search fee. Court makes copy: $1.00 per page. Required to search: name, years to search; also helpful: address. Civil cases indexed by defendant. Civil records on computer from 1992, archives from 1975. Mail turnaround time 2 days.

Criminal Records: Access: Mail, in person. Only the court performs in person searches; visitors may not. No search fee. Court makes copy: $1.00 per page. Required to search: name, years to search; also helpful: address, DOB, SSN. Criminal records on computer from 1992, archives from 1975. Mail turnaround time 2 days.

General Information: No public access terminal. No juvenile or mental records released. Will fax documents $5.00 each 1st 2 pages, $2.00 pages 3-10; $.75 each add'l. Certification fee: $1.00 per page. Payee: Clerk of Court. Prepayment required.

Payette County

District & Magistrate Courts 1130 3rd Ave N, #104, Payette, ID 83661; phone: 208-642-6000 (Dist) 642-6010(Magis); fax: 208-642-6011; hours 9AM-5PM (MST). *Felony, Misdemeanor, Civil, Eviction, Small Claims, Probate.* Note: Rm 104 - District Court; Rm 106 - Magistrate Court

Civil Records: Access: Fax, mail, in person. Both court and visitors may perform in person searches. Search fee: $5.00 per name. Court makes copy: $1.00 per page; same fee for self serve. Required to search: name, years to search; also helpful: address. Civil cases indexed by defendant, plaintiff, on computer back to 1992, prior on microfiche or archived from 1917. Mail turnaround time 1 day.

Criminal Records: Access: Fax, mail, in person. Both court and visitors may perform in person searches. Search fee: $5.00 per name. Court makes copy: $1.00 per page; same fee for self serve. Required to search: name, years to search, signed release; also helpful: address, DOB, SSN. Criminal records on computer back to 1992, prior microfiche or archived from 1917. Mail turnaround time 1 day.

General Information: Public terminal goes back to 1992. No juvenile, adoption records released. Will fax documents $3.00 1st page, $.50 each add'l. Certification fee: $1.00. Payee: Clerk of Court. Personal checks accepted. Prepayment and SASE required.

Power County

District & Magistrate Courts 543 Bannock Ave, American Falls, ID 83211; phone: 208-226-7611 (Dist) 226-7618(Magistrate); fax: 208-226-7612; 9AM-5PM (MST). *Felony, Misdemeanor, Civil, Eviction, Small Claims, Probate.*

Civil Records: Access: Phone, fax, mail, in person. Both court and visitors may perform in person searches. Search fee: $5.00 per name found. Court makes copy: $1.00 per page; same fee for self serve. Required to search: name, years to search. Civil cases indexed by defendant and plaintiff. Civil records on computer from 1994, prior archived from 1913. Mail turnaround time 3-10 days.

Criminal Records: Access: Phone, fax, mail, in person. Both court and visitors may perform in person searches. Search fee: $5.00 per name found. Court makes copy: $1.00 per page; same fee for self serve. Required to search: name, years to search, signed release, DOB, SSN, signed release. Criminal records on computer from 1988, prior archived from 1913. Mail turnaround time 10 days.

General Information: Public terminal has criminal back to 1988 and civil back to 1994. No juvenile, mental commitment records released. Fee to fax documents is $1.00 per page. Certification fee: $1.50 per cert. Payee: Power County Magistrate Court. Accepts cashier check or money order only. Prepayment and SASE required.

Shoshone County

District & Magistrate Courts 700 Bank St, Wallace, ID 83873; phone: 208-752-1266; fax: 208-753-0921; 9AM-5PM *Felony, Misdemeanor, Civil, Eviction, Small Claims, Probate.*

Civil Records: Access: Phone, fax, mail, in person. Both court and visitors may perform in person searches. No search fee. Court makes copy: $1.00 per page. Required to search: name, years to search; also helpful: address. Civil cases indexed by defendant, plaintiff, on computer from 1988, archived from late 1880s. Juvenile case information not available by fax. Mail turnaround time 1-2 days.

Criminal Records: Access: Phone, mail, in person. Both court and visitors may perform in person searches. No search fee. Court makes copy: $1.00 per page. Required to search: name, years to search; also helpful: address, DOB, SSN. Criminal records on computer from 1988, archived from late 1880s. Mail turnaround time 1-2 days.

General Information: Public terminal goes back to 6/1995. No special proceeding, juvenile records released. Will fax documents $2.00 1st page, $1.00 each add'l. Add $1.00 1st page if long distance. Certification fee: $1.00. Payee: Clerk of Court. Personal checks accepted. Prepayment and SASE required.

Teton County

District & Magistrate Courts 89 N Main, #5, Driggs, ID 83422; phone: 208-354-2239; hours 9AM-5PM (MST). *Felony, Misdemeanor, Civil, Eviction, Small Claims, Probate.*
Note: Address and telephone given above are for District Court. If you wish to access only the Magistrate Court and call 208-354-2239.

Civil Records: Access: Phone, fax, mail, in person. Both court and visitors may perform in person searches. Search fee: $5.00 per name. Court makes copy: $1.00 per page; same fee for self serve. Required to search: name, years to search; also helpful: address. Civil cases indexed by defendant, plaintiff, on computer from 1992, archives from 1974, I-Star since 1992. Mail turnaround time 3 days.

Criminal Records: Access: Phone, fax, mail, in person. Both court and visitors may perform in person searches. Search fee: $5.00 per name. Court makes copy: $1.00 per page; same fee for self serve. Required to search: name, years to search; also helpful: address, DOB, SSN. Criminal records on computer from 1992, archives from 1974, I-Star since 1993. The court only performs research on Fridays. Mail turnaround time 1-7 days.

General Information: Public terminal goes back to 1992. No juvenile, DV records released. Will fax documents $2.00 per page. Certification fee: $1.00. Payee: Clerk of Court. Personal checks accepted. Prepayment and SASE required.

Twin Falls County

District & Magistrate Courts PO Box 126, Twin Falls, ID 83303-0126; phone: 208-736-4013; fax: 208-736-4155; hours 8AM-5PM (MST). *Felony, Misdemeanor, Civil, Eviction, Small Claims, Probate.*

Civil Records: Access: In person only. Visitors must perform in person searches themselves. Court makes copy: $1.00 per page. Required to search: name, years to search; also helpful: address. Civil cases indexed by defendant, on computer from 12/1989, archives from early 1900s.

Criminal Records: Access: In person only. Visitors must perform in person searches themselves. Court makes copy: $1.00 per page. Required to search: name, years to search; also helpful: address, DOB, SSN. Criminal records on computer from 12/1989, archives from 1951 felonies, 1970 for misdemeanors.

General Information: Public terminal goes back to 12/1989. No adoption, termination, juvenile records released. Will fax specific case file $2.50 per page. Certification fee: $1.00 per page. Payee: Court Services. Personal checks accepted. Prepayment required.

Valley County

District & Magistrate Courts-I PO Box 1350, Cascade, ID 83611; phone: 208-382-7178; fax: 208-382-7184; hours 8AM-5PM (MST). *Felony, Misdemeanor, Civil, Eviction, Small Claims, Probate.*
Note: A Courthouse Annex in McCall handles Misdemeanors, Small Claims and Juvenile. However, the McCall Court does not do background checks and forwards its closed cases to the court in Cascade.

Civil Records: Access: Phone, fax, mail, in person. Both court and visitors may perform in person searches. Search fee: $5.00. Court makes copy: $1.00 per page. Self serve copy fee: $.15 per page. Required to search: name, years to search; also helpful: address. Civil cases indexed by defendant, plaintiff, on computer from 1990, microfiche and archives from early 1900s. Mail turnaround time 1-3 days.

Criminal Records: Access: Phone, fax, mail, in person. Both court and visitors may perform in person searches. Search fee: $5.00. Court makes copy: $1.00 per page. Self serve copy fee: $.15 per page. Required to search: name, years to search; also helpful: address, DOB, SSN. Criminal records on computer from 1990, microfiche and archives from early 1900s. Mail turnaround time 1-3 days.

General Information: Public terminal goes back to 1990. No juvenile records released. No fee to fax documents. Certification fee: $1.00 per document. Payee: Valley County. Two-party checks not accepted. Prepayment and SASE required.

Washington County

District & Magistrate Courts PO Box 670, Weiser, ID 83672; phone: 208-414-2092; fax: 208-414-3925; hours 8:30AM-5PM (MST). *Felony, Misdemeanor, Civil, Eviction, Small Claims, Probate.* www.the3rdjudicialdistrict.com
Note: This court will only perform searches for probate records, and these requests must be in writing. Turnaround time on probate records is 3-10 days.

Civil Records: Access: In person, mail. Visitors must perform in person searches themselves. No search fee. Court makes copy: $1.00 per page; same fee for self serve. Required to search: name. Civil cases indexed by defendant, plaintiff, on computer from 2/90, archives from late 1800s.

Criminal Records: Access: In person only. Visitors must perform in person searches themselves. Court makes copy: $1.00 per page; same fee for self serve. Required to search: name, years to search, DOB. Criminal records on computer from 2/90, archives from late 1800s.

General Information: Public terminal goes back to 2/1990. No juvenile, adoption, hospitalization, child protection-termination of parental rights records released. Certification fee: $1.00. Payee: Washington County. Business checks accepted if local. Prepayment required.

Idaho Recording Offices

ORGANIZATION: 44 counties, 44 recording offices. The recording officer is County Recorder. Many counties utilize a grantor/grantee index containing all transactions recorded with them. 34 counties are in the Mountain Time Zone (MST), and the uppermost 10 are in the Pacific Time Zone (PST).

REAL ESTATE RECORDS: Most counties will not perform real estate name searches. Certification of copies usually costs $1.00 per document.

UCC RECORDS: Financing statements are filed at the state level except for real estate related filings. All counties will perform UCC searches. Use search request form UCC-4. Search fees are usually $6.00 per debtor name for a listing of filings and $12.00 per debtor name for a listing plus copies at no additional charge. Separately ordered copies usually cost $1.00 per page.

TAX LIEN RECORDS: Until 07/01/98, state tax liens were filed at the local county recorder. Now they are filed with the Secretary of State who has all active case files. Federal tax liens on personal property of businesses are filed with the Secretary of State. Other federal tax liens are filed with the county recorder. Some counties will perform a combined tax lien search for $5.00 while others will not perform tax lien searches.

OTHER LIENS: Judgments, hospital, labor, mechanics.

ONLINE ACCESS: Two counties have web access to assessor records. The Secretary of State's office offers online access to UCCs.

Ada County

County Clerk & Recorder, 200 W Front St, Rm 1207, Boise, ID 83702. 208-287-6845, UCC recording phone-208-287-6855; fax-208-287-6459; hours: 8:30AM-4:30PM

Will not search real estate records. Will search UCC records; search includes tax liens if requested. UCC info request only per debtor name- $6.00. UCC search & copy request per debtor name- $12.00. Separate federal or state tax lien search- $5.00 per debtor. Separate federal/state combined tax lien search- $10.00 per debtor. Copy fee $1.00 per page after 10 pages. Cert fee- $1.00 per doc plus copy fee. Payee- Ada County Clerk & Recorder. **Online access to Assessor, Property, Inmate records:** Search the property assessor database for property data for free at www.adacountyassessor.org. Click on "Online Property Information System". No name searching. Also, search inmate info on private company website at www.vinelink.com/index.jsp. **Other phones:** Treasurer- 208-287-6800; Elections- 208-287-6860; Vital Records- 208-334-5980. **Property tax/Assessor-** 208-287-7200.

Adams County

County Clerk & Recorder, PO Box 48, Council, ID 83612. 208-253-4561; fax-208-253-4880; hours: 8AM-N, 1-5PM

All records in one index. Office will perform a UCC search but public must search other records themselves. Search fee $6.00. Copy fee $1.00 per page. Cert fee- $1.00 per cert plus copy fee. Payee- Adams County Clerk and Recorder. **Other phones:** Treasurer- 208-253-4263. **Property tax/Assessor-** PO Box 46, Council, ID 83612; 208-253-4271.

Bannock County

County Clerk & Recorder, 624 E. Center; Courthouse, Rm 211, Pocatello, ID 83201. RE & UCC recording phone-208-236-7340; fax-208-236-7345; hours: 8AM-5PM

All records in one index. Records indexed on computer. Office will perform a UCC and Tax lien search but public must search other records themselves. Search fee $6.00. Copy fee $1.00 per page. Cert fee- $1.00 per page. Payee- Bannock County Clerk and Recorder. **Online access to Real Estate Recording, Deed records:** Access recording office land data at www.etitlesearch.com; registration required, fee based on usage. **Property tax/Assessor-** 208-236-7260.

Bear Lake County

County Clerk & Recorder, PO Box 190, Paris, ID 83261. RE & UCC recording phone-208-945-2212 x5; fax-208-945-2780; hours: 8:30AM-5PM

Separate indices to search include mortgage, assignments, deed books. Records may be computerized in late 2005. Office will perform a UCC search but public must search other records themselves. UCC info request only per debtor name- $6.00. UCC search & copy request per debtor name- $12.00. Separate federal/state combined tax lien search- $5.00 per debtor. Copy fee $1.00 per page. Cert fee- $1.00 per doc plus copy fee. Payee- Bear Lake County Clerk and Recorder. **Other phones:** Treasurer- 208-945-2130 x7; Elections- 208-945-2212 x5; Vital Records- 208-945-2212 x5. **Property tax/Assessor-** same address as above. 208-945-2155 x4.

Benewah County

County Clerk & Recorder, 701 College, St. Maries, ID 83861. RE & UCC recording phone-208-245-3212; fax-208-245-9152; hours: 9AM-5PM

Separate indices to search. Records indexed on computer back to 1986. Only the public may search. Copy fee $1.00 per page plus tax. Cert fee- $1.00 per cert plus copy fee. Payee- Benewah County Clerk and Recorder. **Online access to Real Estate Recording, Deed records:** Access recording office land data at www.etitlesearch.com; registration required, fee based on usage. **Other phones:** Treasurer- 208-245-2421; Elections- 208-245-3212. **Property tax/Assessor-** same address 208-245-2821.

Bingham County

County Clerk & Recorder, 501 N. Maple #205, Blackfoot, ID 83221. 208-785-5005, R/E recording phone-208-785-5005 x3163, UCC recording phone-208-785-5005 x3157; fax-208-785-4131; hours: 8AM-5PM

All records in one index. Records indexed on computer. Only the public may search. Copy fee $1.00 per page. Cert fee- $1.00 per page plus copy fee. Payee- Bingham County Clerk and Recorder. **Online access to Real Estate Recording, Deed records:** Access recording office land data at www.etitlesearch.com; registration required, fee based on usage. **Other phones:** Treasurer- 208-785-5005 x3090; Appraiser/Auditor- 208-785-5005 x3024; Elections- 208-785-5005 x3164; Vital Records- 208-334-5988. **Property tax/Assessor-** 208-785-5005 x3017.

Blaine County

County Clerk & Recorder, 206 1st Ave. South #200, Hailey, ID 83333. RE & UCC recording phone-208-788-5505; fax-208-788-5501; hours: 9AM-5PM www.co.blaine.id.us

All records in one index by name. Office personnel or visitors may perform searches. UCC info request only per debtor name- $6.00. UCC search & copy request per debtor name- $12.00. Tax lien search fee- $5.00 per debtor. Copy fee $1.00 per page. Cert fee- $1.00 per cert plus copy fee. Payee- Blaine County Recorder. **Online access to Real Estate Recording, Deed records:** Access recording office land data at www.etitlesearch.com; registration required, fee based on usage. **Other phones:** Treasurer- 208-788-5530; Appraiser/Auditor- 208-788-5535; Elections- 208-788-5510. **Property tax/Assessor-** 219 1st Ave S #101, Hailey, ID 83333; 208-788-5535.

Boise County

County Clerk & Recorder, PO Box 1300, Idaho City, ID 83631. RE & UCC recording phone-208-392-4431; fax-208-392-4473; hours: 8AM-5PM

Only the public may search. Copy fee $1.00 per page. Cert fee- $1.50 per doc plus copy fee. Payee- Boise County Clerk and Recorder. **Other phones:** Treasurer- 208-392-4441; Appraiser/Auditor- 208-392-4415; Elections- 208-392-4431; **Property tax/Assessor-** same address 208-392-4415.

Bonner County

County Clerk & Recorder, 215 S. First, Sandpoint, ID 83864. 208-265-1432, R/E recording phone-208-265-1490, UCC recording phone-208-265-1490; fax-208-265-1447; hours: 9AM-5PM

Separate indices to search. Records indexed on a public use terminal back to 1992. Only the public may search. Copy fee $1.00 per page. Cert fee- $1.00 per cert plus copy fee. Payee- Bonner County Clerk and Recorder. **Online access to Real Estate Recording, Deed records:** Access recording office land data at www.etitlesearch.com; registration required, fee based on usage. **Other phones:** Treasurer- 208-265-1433; Elections- 208-265-1490. **Property tax/Assessor-** 127 S 1st Ave #2, Sandpoint, ID 83864; 208-265-1440.

Bonneville County

County Clerk & Recorder, 605 N. Capital Ave, Idaho Falls, ID 83402-3582. 208-529-1350 #9, R/E recording phone-208-529-1350 x1350, UCC recording phone-208-529-1350x1350; fax-208-529-1311; hours: 8AM-5PM www.co.bonneville.id.us

All records in one index. Records indexed on a public use terminal back to 1994. Office personnel or visitors may perform searches. Will not search real estate records. UCC info request only per debtor name- $6.00. UCC search & copy request per debtor name- $12.00. Separate federal/state combined tax lien search- $5.00 per debtor. Copy fee $1.00 per page. Cert fee- $1.00 per cert plus copy fee. Payee- Bonneville County. **Online access to Real Estate Recording, Deed records:** Access recording office land data at www.etitlesearch.com; registration required, fee based on usage. **Other phones:** Treasurer- 208-529-1350 x1380; Appraiser/Auditor- 208-529-1350 x1361; Elections- 208-529-1350 x1363; Vital Records- 208-529-1350 x1350. **Property tax/Assessor-** same address as above. 208-529-1350 x1320.

Boundary County

County Clerk & Recorder, PO Box 419, Bonners Ferry, ID 83805. RE & UCC recording phone-208-267-2242; fax-208-267-7814; hours: 9AM-5PM www.boundary-idaho.com

All records in one index. Records indexed on a public use terminal back to 1986. Office will perform a UCC search but public must search other records themselves. UCC info request only per debtor name- $6.00. UCC search & copy request per debtor name- $12.00. Copy fee $1.00 per page. Cert fee- $1.00 per cert plus copy fee. Payee- Boundary County Clerk and Recorder. **Online access to Real Estate Recording, Deed records:** Access recording office land data at www.etitlesearch.com; registration required, fee based on usage. **Other phones:** Treasurer- 208-267-3291; Appraiser/Auditor- 208-267-3301; Elections- 208-267-2242; Vital Records- 208-267-2242. **Property tax/Assessor-** PO Box 57, Bonners Ferry, ID 83805; 208-267-3301.

Butte County

County Clerk & Recorder, PO Box 737, Arco, ID 83213. Main phone & R/E recording-208-527-3021, UCC recording phone-208-527-3012; fax-208-527-3295; hours: 9AM-5PM

Separate indices to search include books, scanner, microfilm. Records indexed on a by-appointment public use terminal back to 1983. Only the public may search. Copy fee $1.00 per page. Cert fee- $2.50 per page plus copy fee. Payee- Butte County Clerk and Recorder. **Online access to Real Estate Recording, Deed records:** Access recording office land data at www.etitlesearch.com; registration required, fee based on usage. **Other phones:** Treasurer- 208-527-3047. **Property tax/Assessor-** 208-527-8288.

Camas County

County Clerk & Recorder, PO Box 430, Fairfield, ID 83327-0430. RE & UCC recording phone-208-764-2242; fax-208-764-2349; hours: 8:30AM-N, 1-5PM

Separate indices to search include books. Record index not computerized. Office personnel or visitors may perform searches. Search fee $6.00 per name. Will not search real estate records. Copy fee $1.00 per page. Cert fee- $1.00 per cert plus copy fee. Payee- Camas County Clerk and Recorder. **Online access to Real Estate Recording, Deed records:** Access recording office land data at www.etitlesearch.com; registration required, fee based on usage. **Other phones:** Treasurer- 208-764-2126; Appraiser/Auditor- 208-764-2370; Elections- 208-764-2242; Vital Records- 208-764-2242. **Property tax/Assessor-** 505 Soldier Rd, Fairfield, ID 83327; 208-764-2370.

Canyon County

County Recorder, 1115 Albany St, Caldwell, ID 83605. RE & UCC recording phone-208-454-7556; fax-208-454-6689; 8:30AM-5PM www.canyoncounty.org

All records in one index. General index search fee $5.00 per name. Will search real estate records. Will search UCC records, tax liens not included in UCC search. UCC info request only per debtor name- $6.00. UCC search & copy request per debtor name- $12.00. Copies included in search fee. RE or tax lien copy- $1.00 per page. Cert fee- $1.00 per doc plus $1.00 per page. Payee- Canyon County Recorder. **Online access to Assessor, Property records:** Access to the Assessor and Treasurer's databases requires $35 registration/setup fee and 150 yearly fee. For subscription information, email clane@canyoncounty.org or call 208-454-7401 or visit the website. **Other phones:** Treasurer- 208-454-7354; Elections- 208-454-7562; Vital Records- 208-334-5980. **Property tax/Assessor-** 1115 Albany St, Caldwell, ID 83605; 208-454-7431.

Caribou County

County Clerk & Recorder, PO Box 775, Soda Springs, ID 83276-0775. RE & UCC recording phone-208-547-4324; fax-208-547-4759; hours: 9AM-5PM

All records in one index. Records indexed on a public use terminal back to 1998. Office will perform a UCC search but public must search other records themselves. UCC info request only per debtor name- $13.48 per hour. Copy fee $1.00 per page. Cert fee- $1.00 per cert plus copy fee. Payee- Caribou County Clerk and Recorder. **Other phones:** Treasurer- 208-547-3726. **Property tax/Assessor-** same address as above. 208-547-4749.

Cassia County

County Clerk & Recorder, 1459 Overland Ave, Rm 105, Burley, ID 83318. RE & UCC recording phone-208-878-5240; fax-208-878-1003; hours: 8:30AM-5PM

Separate indices to search include 3 systems, depending upon year of document. Only the public may search. Copy fee $1.00 per page. Fax back-$2.50 per doc, payment in advance. Cert fee- $1.00 per doc plus copy fee. Payee- Cassia County Recorder. **Other phones:** Treasurer- 208-878-7202; Appraiser/Auditor- 208-878-3540; Elections- 208-878-5240; Vital Records- 208-878-5240. **Property tax/Assessor-** 203 E 15th St, Burley, ID 83318; 208-878-3540.

Clark County

County Clerk & Recorder, PO Box 205, Dubois, ID 83423. 208-374-5304; fax-208-374-5609; hours: 9AM-5PM

Only the public may search. Copy fee $.25 per page. Cert fee- $1.00 per page. Payee- Clark County Clerk and Recorder. **Online access to Real Estate Recording, Deed records:** Access recording office land data at www.etitlesearch.com; registration required, fee based on usage. **Property tax/Assessor-** 208-374-5404.

Clearwater County

County Clerk & Recorder, PO Box 586, Orofino, ID 83544-0586. RE & UCC recording phone-208-476-5615; fax-208-476-9315; hours: 8AM-5PM www.clearwatercounty.org

All records in one index. All current records available. Only the public may search. Copy fee $1.00 per page. Cert fee- $1.00 per cert plus copy fee. Payee- Clearwater County Clerk and Recorder. **Other phones:** Treasurer- 208-476-5213; Appraiser/Auditor- 208-476-7042; Elections- 208-476-5615; Vital Records- 208-476-5615. **Property tax/Assessor-** PO Box 626, Orofino, ID 83544; 208-476-7042.

Custer County

County Clerk & Recorder, PO Box 385, Challis, ID 83226. 208-879-2360; fax-208-879-5246; hours: 8AM-5PM

All records in one index. Records indexed on computer back to 11/1998. Office will perform a UCC search but public must search other records themselves. Search fee $1.00 per page copy fee. Copy fee $1.00 per page. Cert fee- $1.00 per doc, plus copy fee. Payee- Custer County Clerk and Recorder. **Online access to Real Estate Recording, Deed records:** Access recording office land data at www.etitlesearch.com; registration required, fee based on usage. **Other phones:** Treasurer- 208-879-2330; Elections- 208-879-2360; Vital Records- 208-879-2360. **Property tax/Assessor-** PO Box 547, Challis, ID 83226; 208-879-2325.

Elmore County

County Clerk & Recorder, 150 S. 4th East; ##3, Mountain Home, ID 83647-3097. RE & UCC recording phone-208-587-2130; fax-208-587-2159; hours: 9AM-5PM www.elmoreco.org

Records indexed on a public use terminal back to 4/15/1998. Only the public may search. General copy fee $6.00 per name/document. RE or tax lien copy- $1.00 per page. Cert fee- $1.00 per cert plus copy fee. Payee- Elmore County. **Other phones:** Treasurer- 208-587-2138; Appraiser/Auditor- 208-587-2126; Elections- 208-587-2130; Vital Records- 208-587-2130. **Property tax/Assessor-** same address as above. 208-587-2126.

Franklin County

County Clerk & Recorder, 39 W. Oneida, Preston, ID 83263. RE & UCC recording phone-208-852-1090; fax-208-852-1094; hours: 9AM-5PM

All records in one index. Records indexed on a public use terminal back to 1993. Office will perform a UCC search but public must search other records themselves. Search fee $12.00. Copy fee $1.00 per page. Cert fee- $1.00 per document. Payee- Franklin County Clerk and Recorder. **Online access to Real Estate Recording, Deed records:** Access recording office land data at www.etitlesearch.com; registration required, fee based on usage. **Other phones:** Treasurer- 208-852-1095; Appraiser/Auditor- 208-852-1091; Elections- 208-852-1090; Vital Records- 208-852-1090. **Property tax/Assessor-** same address as above. 208-852-1091.

Fremont County

County Clerk & Recorder, 151 W. 1st N. Rm12, St. Anthony, ID 83445. RE & UCC recording phone-208-624-3148; fax-208-624-7335; hours: 8AM-5PM www.co.fremont.id.us/departments/index.htm

All records in one index. Records indexed on a public use terminal back to 7/1986. Only the public may search. Copy fee $1.00 per page. Cert fee- $1.00 per cert plus copy fee. Payee- Fremont County Clerk and Recorder. **Online access to Real Estate Recording, Deed records:** Access recording office land data at www.etitlesearch.com; registration required, fee based on usage. **Other phones:** Treasurer- 208-624-3361; Appraiser/Auditor- 208-624-7984; Elections- 208-624-7332; Vital Records- 208-624-3148; Commissioners- 208-624-4271. **Property tax/Assessor-** same address as above. 208-624-7894.

Gem County

County Clerk & Recorder, 415 E. Main, Emmett, ID 83617. RE & UCC recording phone-208-365-4561; fax-208-365-7795; hours: 8AM-5PM

Index: Indices by instrument type. Office will perform a UCC search but public must search other records themselves. UCC info request only per debtor name- $6.00. Search and copies-$12.00. Separate federal/state combined tax lien search-$5.00 per debtor. Copy fee $1.00 per page. Cert fee- $1.00 per instrument plus copy fee. Payee- Gem County Clerk and Recorder. **Other phones:**

Treasurer- 208-365-3272; Appraiser/Auditor- 208-365-2982; Elections- 208-365-4561; Vital Records- 208-334-5980. **Property tax/Assessor-** same address as above. 208-365-2982.

Gooding County

County Clerk & Recorder, PO Box 417, Gooding, ID 83330. RE & UCC recording phone-208-934-4841; fax-208-934-5085; hours: 9AM-5PM
Index: All records prior to 1997 are in books or on microfilm. Records indexed on a public use terminal back to 1997. Office will perform a UCC search but public must search other records themselves. Tax liens not included in UCC search. UCC info request only per debtor name- $12.00. Copy fee $1.00 per page. Cert fee- $1.00 per page plus copy fee. Payee- Gooding County Clerk and Recorder. **Other phones:** Treasurer- 208-935-5673; Elections- 208-934-4841. **Property tax/Assessor-** 208-934-5666.

Idaho County

County Clerk & Recorder, 320 W. Main; Rm 5, Grangeville, ID 83530. 208-983-2751; fax-208-983-1428; hours: 8:30AM-5PM www.idahocounty.org
All records in one index. Office will perform a UCC search but public must search other records themselves. UCC info request only per debtor name- $6.00. UCC search & copy request per debtor name- $12.00. Copy fee $1.00 per page. Cert fee- $1.00 per page plus copy fee. Payee- Idaho County Recorder. **Other phones:** Treasurer- 208-983-2801. **Property tax/Assessor-** 208-983-2742.

Jefferson County

County Clerk & Recorder, PO Box 275, Rigby, ID 83442. RE & UCC recording phone-208-745-7756; fax-208-745-6636; hours: 9AM-5PM
Records indexed on computer. Only the public may search. Cert fee- $1.00 per page. Payee-Jefferson County Clerk and Recorder. **Online access to Real Estate Recording, Deed records:** Access recording office land data at www.etitlesearch.com; registration required, fee based on usage. **Other phones:** Treasurer- 208-745-9219. **Property tax/Assessor-** 208-745-9215.

Jerome County

County Clerk & Recorder, 300 N. Lincoln; Courthouse, Rm 301, Jerome, ID 83338. 208-324-8811, R/E recording phone-208-324-8811 x114, UCC recording phone-208-324-8811 x114; fax-208-324-2719; hours: 8:30AM-4:30PM
Separate indices to search in computer or on microfiche. Records indexed on a public use terminal back to 1/1/1990. Office personnel or visitors may perform searches. Search fee $5.00 per name. Copy fee $1.00 per page. Cert fee- $1.00 per cert plus copy fee. Payee- Jerome County Clerk and Recorder. **Online access to Real Estate Recording, Deed records:** Access recording office land data at www.etitlesearch.com; registration required, fee based on usage. **Other phones:** Treasurer- 208-324-7594; Appraiser/Auditor- 208-324-7507 x138; Elections- 208-324-8811 x113. **Property tax/Assessor-** same address as above. 208-324-7508 X139.

Kootenai County

Recorder, PO Box 9000, Coeur d'Alene, ID 83816-9000. 208-446-1480; hours: 9AM-5PM www.co.kootenai.id.us/departments/recorder/
All records in one index. Records indexed on a public use terminal back to 1990. Only the public may search. Copy fee $1.00 per page. Non-standard forms $4.00 add'l. Cert fee- $1.00 per cert plus copy fee. Payee- Kootenai County Recorder's Office. **Online access to Plats, Surveys, CPF's, Parcel records:** Access to the county mapping/recording database is free at www.co.kootenai.id.us/departments/mapping. No name searching. **Other phones:** Treasurer- 208-446-1005 x1005. **Property tax/Assessor-** 208-446-1500 x1500.

Latah County

County Clerk & Recorder, PO Box 8068, Moscow, ID 83843-0568. RE & UCC recording phone-208-882-8580 x3379; fax-208-883-7203; hours: 8AM-5PM www.latah.id.us
All records in one index. Records indexed on a public use terminal back to 1986. Only the public may search. Copy fee $1.00 per page. Cert fee- $1.00 per doc plus copy fee. Payee- Latah County Recorder. **Other phones:** Treasurer- 208-882-8580 x3343; Appraiser/Auditor- 208-882-8580 x3516; Elections- 208-883-2278; Vital Records- 208-334-5980 (Boise). **Property tax/Assessor-** same address as above. 208-882-8580 x3306.

Lemhi County

County Clerk & Recorder, 206 Courthouse Drive, Salmon, ID 83467. RE & UCC recording phone-208-756-2815 x224; fax-208-756-8424; hours: 8AM-5PM
Separate indices to search include deeds, mortgages, assignments, agreements, marriages, releases, mining claims, leases. Records indexed on a public use terminal back to 1984. Office will perform a UCC search but public must search other records themselves. UCC info request only per debtor name- $6.00. UCC search & copy request per debtor name- $12.00. Copy fee $1.00 per page. Cert fee- $1.00 per cert plus copy fee. Payee- Lemhi County Clerk and Recorder. **Other phones:** Treasurer- 208-756-2816 x227; Appraiser/Auditor- 208-756-3116 x236; Elections- 208-756-2815 x221; Vital Records- 208-756-2815 x224. **Property tax/Assessor-** same address as above. 208-756-3116 x236.

Lewis County

County Clerk & Recorder, 510 Oak St RM 1, Nezperce, ID 83543. 208-937-2661; fax-208-937-9234; hours: 9AM-5PM
All records in one index. Only the public may search. Copy fee $1.00 per page. Cert fee- $1.00 per cert plus copy fee. Payee- Lewis County Clerk and Recorder. **Other phones:** Treasurer- 208-937-2341; Elections- 208-937-2661. **Property tax/Assessor-** same address as above. 208-937-2261.

Lincoln County

County Clerk & Recorder, 111 W. B St, Shoshone, ID 83352-5364. RE & UCC recording phone-208-886-7641; fax-208-886-2798; hours: 8:30AM-5PM
Separate indices to search include books, disks and computer. Records indexed on computer back to 1989. Only the public may search. Copy fee $1.00 per page. Cert fee- $1.00 per cert plus copy fee. Payee- Lincoln County Clerk and Recorder. **Other phones:** Treasurer- 208-886-7681; Appraiser/Auditor- 208-886-2161; Elections- 208-886-7641; Vital Records- 208-886-7641. **Property tax/Assessor-** same address as above. 208-886-2161.

Madison County

County Clerk & Recorder, PO Box 389, Rexburg, ID 83440. 208-359-6200 x1, R/E recording phone-208-356-3662, UCC recording phone-208-356-3662; fax-208-356-8396; hours: 9AM-5PM www.co.madison.id.us
Separate indices to search. Records indexed on a public use terminal back to 1987. Office will perform a UCC search but public must search other records themselves. Search fee $6.00 per name. Copy fee $1.00 per page. Cert fee- $1.00 per cert plus copy fee. Payee- Madison County Clerk and Recorder. **Online access to Real Estate Recording, Deed records:** Access recording office land data at www.etitlesearch.com; registration required, fee based on usage. **Other phones:** Treasurer- 208-356-6871. **Property tax/Assessor-** same address as above. 208-356-3071.

Minidoka County

County Clerk & Recorder, PO Box 368, Rupert, ID 83350-0474. 208-436-9511; fax-208-436-0737; hours: 8:30AM-5PM www.minidoka.id.us
Separate indices to search include books, card, computer, microfiche. Office will perform a UCC search but public must search other records themselves. UCC info request only per debtor name- $6.00. UCC search & copy request per debtor name- $12.00. Copy fee $1.00 per page. Cert fee- $1.00 per cert plus copy fee. Payee- Minidoka County Recorder. **Other phones:** Treasurer- 208-436-7188; Appraiser/Auditor- 208-436-7181; Elections- 208-436-9511; Vital Records- 208-334-5980. **Property tax/Assessor-** 702 G St, Rupert, ID 83350; 208-436-7181.

Nez Perce County

County Clerk & Recorder, PO Box 896, Lewiston, ID 83501-0896. RE & UCC recording phone-208-799-3020; fax-208-799-3070; hours: 8AM-5PM www.co.nezperce.id.us
Index: Books, and Computer. Records indexed on a public use terminal back to 1984. Office will perform a UCC search but public must search other records themselves. Search fee $12.00. Copy fee $1.00 per page. Cert fee- $1.00 per cert plus copy fee. Payee- Nez Perce County Auditor and Recorder. **Other phones:** Treasurer- 208-799-3030; Elections- 208-799-3023; Vital Records- 208-799-3020. **Property tax/Assessor-** same address as above. 208-799-3010.

Oneida County

County Clerk & Recorder, 10 Court St, Malad, ID 83252. 208-766-4116 x100, R/E recording phone-208-76-4116 x100/101/102, UCC recording phone-208-76-4116 x100/101/102; fax-208-766-2448; hours: 9AM-5PM
Separate indices to search include deeds, mortgages, judgments, liens and contracts. Only the public may search. Copy fee $1.00 per page. Cert fee- $1.00 per cert plus copy fee. Payee- Oneida County Clerk and Recorder. **Other phones:** Treasurer- 208-766-2962; Appraiser/Auditor- 208-766-4116 x109, 106 or 116; Elections- 208-76-4116 x100 or 102. **Property tax/Assessor-** 208-766-2954.

Owyhee County

County Clerk & Recorder, PO Box 128, Murphy, ID 83650. RE & UCC recording phone-208-495-2421; fax-208-495-1173; hours: 8:30AM-5PM
All records in one index. Records indexed on a public use terminal back to 1999. Office will perform a Tax lien search but public must search other records themselves. Search fee $6.00. Copy fee $1.00 per page. Cert fee- $1.00 per page plus copy fee. Payee- Owyhee County Clerk and Recorder. **Other phones:** Treasurer- 208-495-1158; Appraiser/Auditor- 208-495-2817; Elections- 208-495-2421; Vital Records- 208-495-2421. **Property tax/Assessor-** same address as above. 208-495-2817.

Payette County

County Clerk & Recorder, 1130 3rd Ave. North, #104, Payette, ID 83661. RE & UCC recording phone-208-642-6000; fax-208-642-6011; hours: 9AM-5PM www.payettecounty.org
All records in one index. Office will perform a UCC search but public must search other records themselves. UCC info request only per debtor name- $6.00. UCC search & copy request per debtor name- $12.00. Copy fee $1.00 per page. Cert fee- $1.00 per cert plus copy fee. Payee- Payette County Clerk and Recorder. **Other phones:** Treasurer- 208-642-6005; Appraiser/Auditor- 208-642-6012; Elections- 208-642-6000. **Property tax/Assessor-** 1130 3rd Ave N #103, Payette, ID 83661; 208-642-6012.

Power County

County Clerk & Recorder, 543 Bannock, American Falls, ID 83211. RE & UCC recording phone-208-226-7611; fax-208-226-7612; hours: 9AM-5PM www.co.power.id.us
All records in one index. Office will perform a UCC search but public must search other records themselves. Search fee $6.00. Copy fee $.50 per page. Cert fee- $1.00 per cert plus copy fee. Payee-Power County Clerk and Recorder. **Online access to Real Estate Recording, Deed records:** Access recording office land data at www.etitlesearch.com; registration required, fee based on usage. **Other phones:** Treasurer- 208-226-7614; Elections- 208-226-7611; Vital Records- 208-226-7611. **Property tax/Assessor-** same address as above. 208-226-7616.

Shoshone County

County Clerk & Recorder, 700 Bank St; Courthouse, #120, Wallace, ID 83873-2348. RE & UCC recording phone-208-752-1264; fax-208-753-2711; hours: 9AM-5PM
Separate indices to search. Records indexed on a public use terminal back to 12/1984. Office will perform a UCC search but public must search other records themselves. Search fee $11.00 per name. Copy fee $1.00 per page. Cert fee- $1.00 per doc plus copy fee. Payee- Shoshone County Clerk and Recorder. **Online access to Real Estate Recording, Deed records:** Access recording office land data at www.etitlesearch.com; registration required, fee based on usage. **Other phones:** Treasurer- 208-752-1261; Appraiser/Auditor- 208-752-1202; Elections- 208-752-1264; Vital Records- 208-752-1264. **Property tax/Assessor-** same address as above. 208-752-1202.

Teton County

County Clerk & Recorder, 89 N. Main #1, Driggs, ID 83422. RE & UCC recording phone-208-354-2905; fax-208-354-8410; hours: 9AM-5PM
All records in one index. Real estate owner, mortgage, and property transfer searches available. Will search UCC records, search includes tax liens. UCC info request only per debtor name- $5.00. UCC search & copy request per debtor name- $5.00. Separate federal tax lien search- $6.00 per debtor. Separate state tax lien search- $6.00 per debtor. Copy fee $1.00 per page. Cert fee- $1.50 per cert plus copy fee. Payee- Teton County Clerk and Recorder. **Online access to Real Estate Recording, Deed records:** Access recording office land data at www.etitlesearch.com; registration required, fee based on usage. **Other phones:** Treasurer- 208-354-2254; Appraiser/Auditor- 208-354-3507; Elections- 208-354-2905. **Property tax/Assessor-** 208-354-3507.

Twin Falls County

County Clerk & Recorder, PO Box 126, Twin Falls, ID 83303-0126. RE & UCC recording phone-208-736-4004; fax-208-736-4182; hours: 8AM-5PM www.twinfallscounty.org
Index: Pre-1991 indices on microfilm or binders. Began scanning images on computer in 1991. Only the public may search. Copy fee $1.00 per page. Cert fee- $1.00 per cert plus copy fee. Payee- Twin Falls County Clerk and Recorder. **Online access to Real Estate Recording, Deed records:** Access recording office land data at www.etitlesearch.com; registration required, fee based on usage. **Other phones:** Treasurer- 208-736-4008; Elections- 208-736-4004; Vital Records- 208-334-5980. **Property tax/Assessor-** 208-736-4010.

Valley County

County Clerk & Recorder, PO Box 1350, Cascade, ID 83611-1350. 208-382-7100; fax-208-382-7107; hours: 9AM-5PM
Only the public may search. Copy fee $1.00 per page. Cert fee- $1.00 per cert plus copy fee. Payee-Valley County Clerk and Recorder. **Online access to Real Estate Recording, Deed records:** Access recording office land data at www.etitlesearch.com; registration required, fee based on usage. **Other phones:** Treasurer- 208-382-7110. **Property tax/Assessor-** 208-382-7126.

Washington County

County Clerk & Recorder, PO Box 670, Weiser, ID 83672-0670. 208-549-2092, R/E recording phone-208-414-2092, UCC recording phone-208-414-2092; fax-208-549-3925; hours: 8:30AM-5PM
Separate indices to search include Deeds back to 1958. Records indexed on computer back to 1987. Only the public may search. Copy fee $1.00 per page. Cert fee- $1.00 per doc plus copy fee. Payee-Washington County Clerk and Recorder. **Other phones:** Treasurer- 208-414-0324; Appraiser/Auditor- 208-414-2000; Elections- 208-414-2092; Vital Records- 208-414-2092 (1907-1911 only); Vital Statistics (Boise, ID)- 288-334-5988. **Property tax/Assessor-** same address as above. 208-414-2000..

Idaho County Locator

You will usually be able to find the city name in the City/County Cross Reference below. In that case, it is a simple matter to determine the county from the cross reference. However, only the official US Postal Service city names are included in this index. We have also included a ZIP/City Cross Reference immediately following the City/County Cross Reference. If you know the ZIP Code but the city name does not appear in the City/County Cross Reference index, look up the ZIP Code in the ZIP/City Cross Reference, find the city name, then look up the city name in the City/County Cross Reference.

Idaho City/County Cross Reference

ABERDEEN Bingham
AHSAHKA Clearwater
ALBION Cassia
ALMO Cassia
AMERICAN FALLS Power
ARBON Power
ARCO Butte
ARIMO Bannock
ASHTON Fremont
ATHOL (83801) Kootenai(87), Bonner(12)
ATLANTA Elmore
ATOMIC CITY Bingham
AVERY Shoshone
BANCROFT Caribou
BANKS Boise
BASALT Bingham
BAYVIEW (83803) Kootenai(93), Bonner(6)
BELLEVUE Blaine
BERN Bear Lake
BLACKFOOT Bingham
BLANCHARD Bonner
BLISS Gooding
BLOOMINGTON Bear Lake
BOISE (83716) Ada(69), Boise(28), Elmore(2)
BOISE Ada
BONNERS FERRY Boundary
BOVILL Latah
BRUNEAU Owyhee
BUHL Twin Falls
BURLEY Cassia
CALDER Shoshone
CALDWELL (83607) Canyon(94), Payette(4), Gem(1)
CALDWELL Canyon
CAMBRIDGE Washington
CAREY Blaine
CAREYWOOD Bonner
CARMEN Lemhi
CASCADE Valley
CASTLEFORD Twin Falls
CATALDO (83810) Kootenai(97), Shoshone(2)
CHALLIS (83226) Custer(98), Lemhi(1)
CHESTER Fremont
CLARK FORK Bonner
CLARKIA Shoshone
CLAYTON Custer
CLIFTON Franklin
COBALT Lemhi
COCOLALLA Bonner
COEUR D ALENE Kootenai
COLBURN Bonner
CONDA Caribou
COOLIN Bonner
CORRAL Camas
COTTONWOOD Idaho
COUNCIL Adams
CRAIGMONT Lewis
CULDESAC (83524) Nez Perce(96), Lewis(3)
DAYTON Franklin
DEARY Latah
DECLO Cassia
DESMET Benewah
DIETRICH Lincoln
DINGLE Bear Lake
DONNELLY Valley
DOVER Bonner
DOWNEY Bannock

DRIGGS Teton
DUBOIS Clark
EAGLE Ada
EASTPORT Boundary
EDEN Jerome
ELBA Cassia
ELK CITY Idaho
ELK RIVER Clearwater
ELLIS (83235) Custer(82), Lemhi(17)
EMMETT Gem
FAIRFIELD Camas
FELT Teton
FENN Idaho
FERDINAND Idaho
FERNWOOD (83830) Benewah(94), Shoshone(5)
FILER Twin Falls
FIRTH Bingham
FISH HAVEN Bear Lake
FORT HALL Bingham
FRANKLIN Franklin
FRUITLAND Payette
FRUITVALE Adams
GARDEN VALLEY Boise
GENESEE (83832) Latah(67), Nez Perce(32)
GENEVA Bear Lake
GEORGETOWN Bear Lake
GIBBONSVILLE Lemhi
GLENNS FERRY Elmore
GOODING Gooding
GRACE Caribou
GRAND VIEW Owyhee
GRANGEVILLE Idaho
GREENCREEK Idaho
GREENLEAF Canyon
HAGERMAN (83332) Gooding(82), Twin Falls(17)
HAILEY Blaine
HAMER Jefferson
HAMMETT (83627) Elmore(98), Owyhee(1)
HANSEN Twin Falls
HARRISON Kootenai
HARVARD Latah
HAYDEN Kootenai
HAZELTON Jerome
HEADQUARTERS Clearwater
HEYBURN (83336) Minidoka(72), Cassia(27)
HILL CITY Camas
HOLBROOK Oneida
HOMEDALE Owyhee
HOPE Bonner
HORSESHOE BEND (83629) Boise(91), Gem(8)
HOWE Butte
HUSTON Canyon
IDAHO CITY Boise
IDAHO FALLS Bonneville
INDIAN VALLEY (83632) Adams(90), Washington(9)
INKOM Bannock
IONA Bonneville
IRWIN Bonneville
ISLAND PARK Fremont
JEROME (83338) Jerome(98), Gooding(1)
JULIAETTA (83535) Latah(92), Nez Perce(7)
KAMIAH (83536) Idaho(68), Lewis(31)
KELLOGG Shoshone

KENDRICK (83537) Nez Perce(76), Latah(23)
KETCHUM (83340) Blaine(98), Custer(1)
KIMBERLY Twin Falls
KING HILL Elmore
KINGSTON Shoshone
KOOSKIA Idaho
KOOTENAI Bonner
KUNA (83634) Ada(95), Canyon(4)
LACLEDE Bonner
LAKE FORK Valley
LAPWAI Nez Perce
LAVA HOT SPRINGS Bannock
LEADORE (83464) Lemhi(98), Clark(1)
LEMHI Lemhi
LENORE (83541) Nez Perce(52), Clearwater(47)
LETHA Gem
LEWISTON Nez Perce
LEWISVILLE Jefferson
LOWMAN Boise
LUCILE Idaho
MACKAY Custer
MACKS INN Fremont
MALAD CITY Oneida
MALTA Cassia
MARSING Owyhee
MAY (83253) Lemhi(86), Custer(13)
MC CALL (83638) Valley(96), Adams(2)
MC CAMMON Bannock
MCCALL (83638) Valley(96), Adams(2)
MEDIMONT Kootenai
MELBA (83641) Canyon(50), Owyhee(41), Ada(8)
MENAN (83434) Jefferson(91), Madison(8)
MERIDIAN Ada
MESA Adams
MIDDLETON Canyon
MIDVALE Washington
MINIDOKA Minidoka
MONTEVIEW Jefferson
MONTPELIER Bear Lake
MOORE Butte
MORELAND Bingham
MOSCOW Latah
MOUNTAIN HOME Elmore
MOUNTAIN HOME A F B Elmore
MOYIE SPRINGS Boundary
MULLAN Shoshone
MURPHY Owyhee
MURRAY Shoshone
MURTAUGH (83344) Twin Falls(78), Cassia(21)
NAMPA (83687) Canyon(98), Ada(1)
NAMPA Canyon
NAPLES Boundary
NEW MEADOWS (83654) Adams(98), Idaho(1)
NEW PLYMOUTH Payette
NEWDALE (83436) Madison(57), Teton(28), Fremont(13)
NEZPERCE Lewis
NORDMAN Bonner
NORTH FORK Lemhi
NOTUS Canyon
OAKLEY Cassia
OLA Gem
OLDTOWN Bonner
OROFINO Clearwater
OSBURN Shoshone

OVID Bear Lake
PALISADES Bonneville
PARIS Bear Lake
PARKER Fremont
PARMA (83660) Canyon(89), Payette(10)
PAUL (83347) Lincoln(73), Jerome(18), Minidoka(8)
PAYETTE Payette
PECK Nez Perce
PICABO Blaine
PIERCE Clearwater
PINEHURST Shoshone
PINGREE Bingham
PLACERVILLE Boise
PLUMMER Benewah
POCATELLO (83202) Bannock(96), Bingham(3)
POCATELLO (83204) Bannock(94), Power(5)
POCATELLO Bannock
POLLOCK (83547) Idaho(80), Adams(20)
PONDERAY Bonner
PORTHILL Boundary
POST FALLS Kootenai
POTLATCH Latah
PRESTON Franklin
PRIEST RIVER Bonner
PRINCETON Latah
RATHDRUM Kootenai
REUBENS (83548) Nez Perce(65), Lewis(34)
REXBURG Madison
RICHFIELD Lincoln
RIGBY Jefferson
RIGGINS Idaho
RIRIE (83443) Bonneville(54), Jefferson(45)
ROBERTS Jefferson
ROCKLAND Power
ROGERSON Twin Falls
RUPERT Minidoka
SAGLE Bonner
SAINT ANTHONY Fremont
SAINT CHARLES Bear Lake
SAINT MARIES (83861) Benewah(88), Kootenai(11)
SALMON Lemhi
SAMUELS Bonner
SANDPOINT Bonner
SANTA Benewah
SHELLEY (83274) Bingham(98), Bonneville(1)
SHOSHONE Lincoln
SHOUP Lemhi
SILVERTON Shoshone
SMELTERVILLE Shoshone
SODA SPRINGS (83276) Caribou(91), Bear Lake(8)
SPALDING Nez Perce
SPENCER Clark
SPIRIT LAKE (83869) Kootenai(73), Bonner(26)
SPRINGFIELD Bingham
SQUIRREL Fremont
STANLEY Custer
STAR (83669) Ada(90), Canyon(9)
STITES Idaho
STONE Oneida
SUGAR CITY (83448) Madison(76), Fremont(23)

SUN VALLEY Blaine
SWAN VALLEY Bonneville
SWANLAKE Bannock
SWEET (83670) Gem(92), Boise(7)
TENDOY Lemhi
TENSED Benewah
TERRETON Jefferson

TETON (83451) Fremont(64), Madison(35)
TETONIA Teton
THATCHER Franklin
TROY Latah
TWIN FALLS Twin Falls
UCON Bonneville
VICTOR Teton

VIOLA Latah
WALLACE Shoshone
WARREN Idaho
WAYAN (83285) Caribou(50), Bonneville(49)
WEIPPE Clearwater
WEISER Washington

WENDELL Gooding
WESTON Franklin
WHITE BIRD Idaho
WILDER Canyon
WINCHESTER Lewis
WORLEY Kootenai
YELLOW PINE Valley

Idaho ZIP/City Cross Reference

ZIP Range	City	ZIP Range	City	ZIP Range	City	ZIP Range	City
83201-83202	POCATELLO	83327-83327	FAIRFIELD	83531-83531	FENN	83672-83672	WEISER
83203-83203	FORT HALL	83328-83328	FILER	83533-83533	GREENCREEK	83676-83676	WILDER
83204-83209	POCATELLO	83330-83330	GOODING	83534-83534	HEADQUARTERS	83677-83677	YELLOW PINE
83210-83210	ABERDEEN	83332-83332	HAGERMAN	83535-83535	JULIAETTA	83680-83680	MERIDIAN
83211-83211	AMERICAN FALLS	83333-83333	HAILEY	83536-83536	KAMIAH	83686-83687	NAMPA
83212-83212	ARBON	83334-83334	HANSEN	83537-83537	KENDRICK	83700-83799	BOISE
83213-83213	ARCO	83335-83335	HAZELTON	83538-83538	COTTONWOOD	83801-83801	ATHOL
83214-83214	ARIMO	83336-83336	HEYBURN	83539-83539	KOOSKIA	83802-83802	AVERY
83215-83215	ATOMIC CITY	83337-83337	HILL CITY	83540-83540	LAPWAI	83803-83803	BAYVIEW
83217-83217	BANCROFT	83338-83338	JEROME	83541-83541	LENORE	83804-83804	BLANCHARD
83218-83218	BASALT	83340-83340	KETCHUM	83542-83542	LUCILE	83805-83805	BONNERS FERRY
83220-83220	BERN	83341-83341	KIMBERLY	83543-83543	NEZPERCE	83806-83806	BOVILL
83221-83221	BLACKFOOT	83342-83342	MALTA	83544-83544	OROFINO	83808-83808	CALDER
83223-83223	BLOOMINGTON	83343-83343	MINIDOKA	83545-83545	PECK	83809-83809	CAREYWOOD
83226-83226	CHALLIS	83344-83344	MURTAUGH	83546-83546	PIERCE	83810-83810	CATALDO
83227-83227	CLAYTON	83346-83346	OAKLEY	83547-83547	POLLOCK	83811-83811	CLARK FORK
83228-83228	CLIFTON	83347-83347	PAUL	83548-83548	REUBENS	83812-83812	CLARKIA
83229-83229	COBALT	83348-83348	PICABO	83549-83549	RIGGINS	83813-83813	COCOLALLA
83230-83230	CONDA	83349-83349	RICHFIELD	83551-83551	SPALDING	83814-83816	COEUR D ALENE
83231-83231	MOORE	83350-83350	RUPERT	83552-83552	STITES	83821-83821	COOLIN
83232-83232	DAYTON	83352-83352	SHOSHONE	83553-83553	WEIPPE	83822-83822	OLDTOWN
83233-83233	DINGLE	83353-83354	SUN VALLEY	83554-83554	WHITE BIRD	83823-83823	DEARY
83234-83234	DOWNEY	83355-83355	WENDELL	83555-83555	WINCHESTER	83824-83824	DESMET
83235-83235	ELLIS	83401-83406	IDAHO FALLS	83601-83601	ATLANTA	83825-83825	DOVER
83236-83236	FIRTH	83415-83415	IDAHO FALLS	83602-83602	BANKS	83826-83826	EASTPORT
83237-83237	FRANKLIN	83420-83420	ASHTON	83604-83604	BRUNEAU	83827-83827	ELK RIVER
83238-83238	GENEVA	83421-83421	CHESTER	83605-83607	CALDWELL	83830-83830	FERNWOOD
83239-83239	GEORGETOWN	83422-83422	DRIGGS	83610-83610	CAMBRIDGE	83832-83832	GENESEE
83241-83241	GRACE	83423-83423	DUBOIS	83611-83611	CASCADE	83833-83833	HARRISON
83243-83243	HOLBROOK	83424-83424	FELT	83612-83612	COUNCIL	83834-83834	HARVARD
83244-83244	HOWE	83425-83425	HAMER	83615-83615	DONNELLY	83835-83835	HAYDEN
83245-83245	INKOM	83427-83427	IONA	83616-83616	EAGLE	83836-83836	HOPE
83246-83246	LAVA HOT SPRINGS	83428-83428	IRWIN	83617-83617	EMMETT	83837-83837	KELLOGG
83250-83250	MC CAMMON	83429-83429	ISLAND PARK	83619-83619	FRUITLAND	83839-83839	KINGSTON
83251-83251	MACKAY	83431-83431	LEWISVILLE	83620-83620	FRUITVALE	83840-83840	KOOTENAI
83252-83252	MALAD CITY	83433-83433	MACKS INN	83622-83622	GARDEN VALLEY	83841-83841	LACLEDE
83253-83253	MAY	83434-83434	MENAN	83623-83623	GLENNS FERRY	83842-83842	MEDIMONT
83254-83254	MONTPELIER	83435-83435	MONTEVIEW	83624-83624	GRAND VIEW	83843-83843	MOSCOW
83255-83255	MOORE	83436-83436	NEWDALE	83626-83626	GREENLEAF	83845-83845	MOYIE SPRINGS
83256-83256	MORELAND	83437-83437	PALISADES	83627-83627	HAMMETT	83846-83846	MULLAN
83260-83260	OVID	83438-83438	PARKER	83628-83628	HOMEDALE	83847-83847	NAPLES
83261-83261	PARIS	83440-83441	REXBURG	83629-83629	HORSESHOE BEND	83848-83848	NORDMAN
83262-83262	PINGREE	83442-83442	RIGBY	83630-83630	HUSTON	83849-83849	OSBURN
83263-83263	PRESTON	83443-83443	RIRIE	83631-83631	IDAHO CITY	83850-83850	PINEHURST
83271-83271	ROCKLAND	83444-83444	ROBERTS	83632-83632	INDIAN VALLEY	83851-83851	PLUMMER
83272-83272	SAINT CHARLES	83445-83445	SAINT ANTHONY	83633-83633	KING HILL	83852-83852	PONDERAY
83274-83274	SHELLEY	83446-83446	SPENCER	83634-83634	KUNA	83853-83853	PORTHILL
83276-83276	SODA SPRINGS	83447-83447	SQUIRREL	83635-83635	LAKE FORK	83854-83854	POST FALLS
83277-83277	SPRINGFIELD	83448-83448	SUGAR CITY	83636-83636	LETHA	83855-83855	POTLATCH
83278-83278	STANLEY	83449-83449	SWAN VALLEY	83637-83637	LOWMAN	83856-83856	PRIEST RIVER
83280-83280	STONE	83450-83450	TERRETON	83638-83638	MC CALL	83857-83857	PRINCETON
83281-83281	SWANLAKE	83451-83451	TETON	83638-83638	MCCALL	83858-83858	RATHDRUM
83283-83283	THATCHER	83452-83452	TETONIA	83639-83639	MARSING	83860-83860	SAGLE
83285-83285	WAYAN	83454-83454	UCON	83641-83641	MELBA	83861-83861	SAINT MARIES
83286-83286	WESTON	83455-83455	VICTOR	83642-83642	MERIDIAN	83862-83862	SAMUELS
83287-83287	FISH HAVEN	83460-83460	REXBURG	83643-83643	MESA	83864-83864	SANDPOINT
83301-83301	TWIN FALLS	83462-83462	CARMEN	83644-83644	MIDDLETON	83865-83865	COLBURN
83302-83302	ROGERSON	83463-83463	GIBBONSVILLE	83645-83645	MIDVALE	83866-83866	SANTA
83303-83303	TWIN FALLS	83464-83464	LEADORE	83647-83647	MOUNTAIN HOME	83867-83867	SILVERTON
83311-83311	ALBION	83465-83465	LEMHI	83648-83648	MOUNTAIN HOME A F B	83868-83868	SMELTERVILLE
83312-83312	ALMO	83466-83466	NORTH FORK	83650-83650	MURPHY	83869-83869	SPIRIT LAKE
83313-83313	BELLEVUE	83467-83467	SALMON	83651-83651	NAMPA	83870-83870	TENSED
83314-83314	BLISS	83468-83468	TENDOY	83654-83654	NEW MEADOWS	83871-83871	TROY
83316-83316	BUHL	83469-83469	SHOUP	83655-83655	NEW PLYMOUTH	83872-83872	VIOLA
83318-83318	BURLEY	83501-83501	LEWISTON	83656-83656	NOTUS	83873-83873	WALLACE
83320-83320	CAREY	83520-83520	AHSAHKA	83657-83657	OLA	83874-83874	MURRAY
83321-83321	CASTLEFORD	83522-83522	COTTONWOOD	83660-83660	PARMA	83876-83876	WORLEY
83322-83322	CORRAL	83523-83523	CRAIGMONT	83661-83661	PAYETTE	83877-83877	POST FALLS
83323-83323	DECLO	83524-83524	CULDESAC	83666-83666	PLACERVILLE	83888-83888	SANDPOINT
83324-83324	DIETRICH	83525-83525	ELK CITY	83669-83669	STAR		
83325-83325	EDEN	83526-83526	FERDINAND	83670-83670	SWEET		
83326-83326	ELBA	83530-83530	GRANGEVILLE	83671-83671	WARREN		

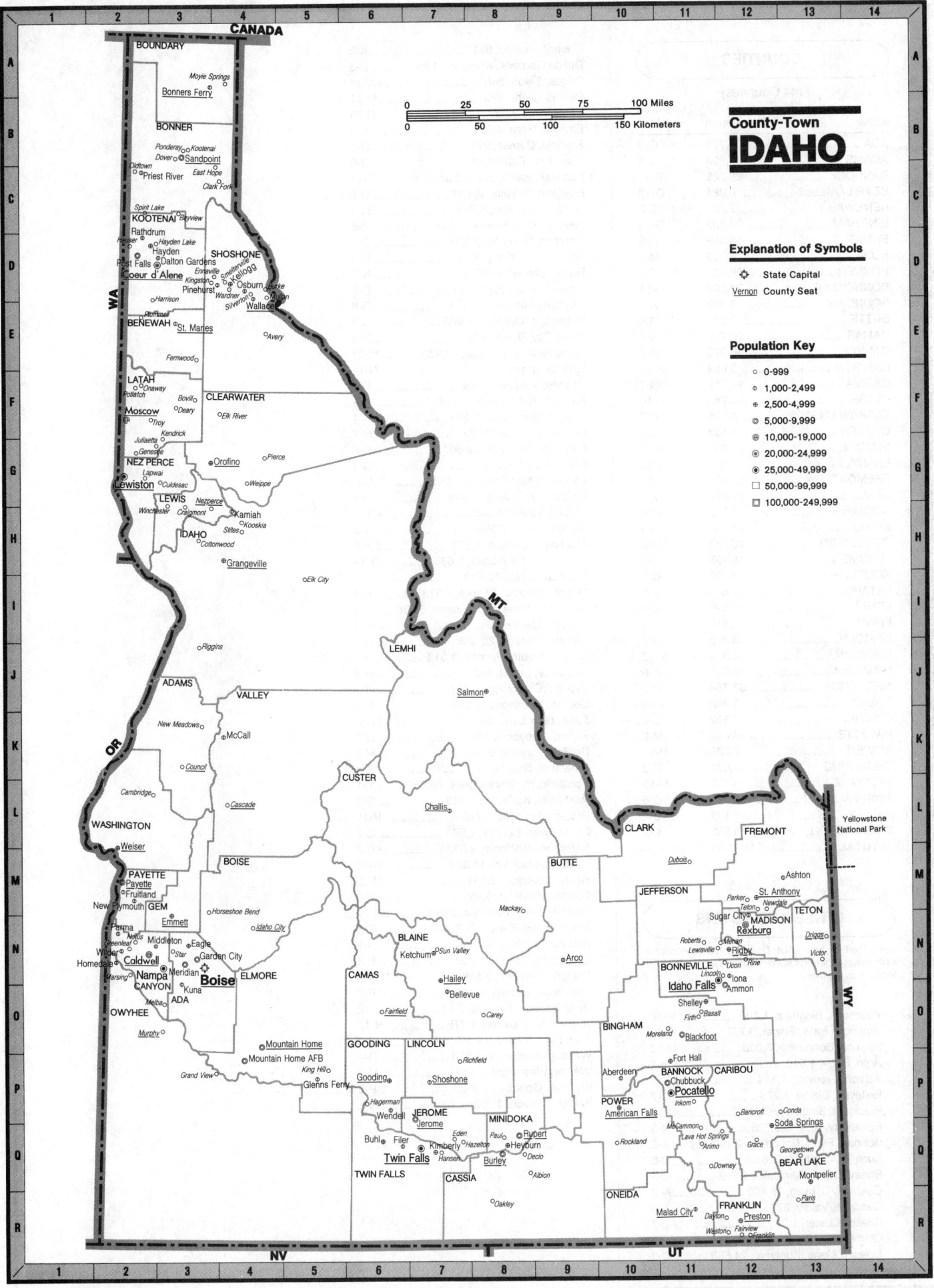

County-Town
IDAHO

Explanation of Symbols

◇ State Capital
Vernon County Seat

Population Key

∘ 0-999
⊕ 1,000-2,499
⊕ 2,500-4,999
⊙ 5,000-9,999
⊛ 10,000-19,000
⊚ 20,000-24,999
⊙ 25,000-49,999
□ 50,000-99,999
▣ 100,000-249,999

Explanation of symbols: •– Census Designated Place (CDP)

Illinois

General Help Numbers:

Governor's Office
207 State House
Springfield, IL 62706
http://www.illinois.gov/gov/

217-782-6830
Fax 217-524-0897
8:30AM-5PM

Attorney General's Office
500 S 2nd St
Springfield, IL 62706
www.ag.state.il.us

217-782-1090
Fax 217-524-4701
8:45AM-4:45PM

Legislative Records
Illinois General Assembly
House (or Senate) Bills Division
Springfield, IL 62706
www.legis.state.il.us

217-782-3944
217-782-7017
Fax 217-524-6059
8AM-4:30PM

State Archives
Archives Division
Norton Bldg, Capitol Complex
Springfield, IL 62756
www.sos.state.il.us/departments
/archives/archives.html

217-782-4682
Fax 217-524-3930
8AM-4:30PM M-F,
8AM-3:30PM SA

State Specifics:

Capital:　　　　　　　Springfield
　　　　　　　　　　　Sangamon County

Time Zone:　　　　　　　　CST

Number of Counties:　　　　102

Population:　　　　　12,713,634

Web Site:　　http://www100.state.il.us

State Agencies

Criminal Records

Illinois State Police, Bureau of Identification, 260 N Chicago St, Joliet, IL 60432-4075; 815-740-5216 x5184, 815-740-5215-Fax; 8AM-4PM M-F.

www.isp.state.il.us

Records are available from 1930's on. It takes 1 to 5 days before new records are available for inquiry. Records are indexed on microfilm, index cards, inhouse computer. 61% of all arrests in database have final dispositions recorded, 67% for those arrests within last 5 years.

Searching: Requester must use the Uniform Conviction Information Form ISP6-405B. Personal requests are honored per Illinois statute.

100% of arrest records are fingerprint supported. Include the following in your request-name, date of birth, sex, race. Fingerprint cards are an option; a fingerprint search using Form ISP6-404B is recommended in order to assure proper identification. All forms can be ordered (but not downloaded) at the website. The following data is not released: records with warrants only, juvenile records unless juvenile convicted by an adult court of law. No records are released without a disposition of conviction.

Access by: mail, in person, online.

Fee & Payment: The search fee is $16.00 per form. A fingerprint search is $20.00. Fee payee: Illinois State Police. Prepayment required. Modem

users and ongoing UCIA requesters must prepay for records in groups of 35 at a time. Personal checks accepted. No credit cards accepted.

Mail search: Turnaround time: 3 to 4 weeks. No SASE is required.

In person search: An in person search saves mailing time only.

Online search: Online access costs $10.00 per name. Upon signing an interagency agreement with ISP and establishing an escrow account, users can submit inquiries by email. Responses are sent back in 24 to 48 hours by either email or fax.

Statewide Court Records

Administrative Office of Courts, 222 N. LaSalle - 13th Floor, Chicago, IL 60601; 312-793-3250, 312-793-1335-Fax; 8AM-5PM.

www.state.il.us/court

Except for certain online research capabilities, all court record access must be done at the local level.

Access by: online.

Online search: The web page offers access to supreme and appellate opinions. There is no statewide public online system for local court records. A few Circuit Courts offer online access. A vendor, Judici.com, offers free searching for a few counties with a fee service for multi-county searching.

Sexual Offender Registry

Illinois State Police, SOR Unit, 400 Iles Park Place, #300, Springfield, IL 62703-2978; 217-785-0653, 8AM-4PM. www.isp.state.il.us/sor

Persons required to register as Sex Offenders are persons who have been charged of an offense listed in Illinois Compiled Statutes 730 ILCS 150/2(B). It takes 1 to 5 days before new records are available for inquiry.

Searching: Illinois Compiled Statutes (730 ILCS 152/115 (a) and (b)) mandate that the Illinois State Police ("ISP") establish and maintain a statewide Sex Offender Database, accessible on the Internet. A status field indicates if offender listed as "COMPLIANT" are in good standing with the Sex Offender Registration Laws. Offenders listed as "NON-COMPLIANT" have failed to maintain accurate registration information.

Access by: online.

Online search: The website provides an online listing of sex offenders required to register in the State of Illinois. The database is updated daily and allows searching by name, city, county, and ZIP Code. Note: the City of Chicago provides its own search site at http://12.17.79.4.

Incarceration Records

Illinois Department of Corrections, Public Information Office, PO Box 19277, Springfield, IL 62794-9277 (Courier: 1301 Concordia Court, Springfield, IL 62794); 217-522-2666 x2008, 217-522-3568-Fax; 8:30AM-5PM.

www.idoc.state.il.us

Offender information is available to the general public and private organizations. Records are available on current and former inmates, except online is current only. It takes 1 to 5 days before new records are available for inquiry.

Searching: Records are never destroyed, but are archived. Include the following in your request-full name and DOB, IBOC #, gender, race helpful. For a online search, you can provide name or DOB or IDOC #. Location, conviction information, physical identifiers, and release dates are reported.

Access by: mail, phone, online.

Mail search: Turnaround time: 1 to 2 weeks. No SASE is required. **Phone search:** Name searching available by phone.

Online search: Click on Inmate Search at the website. Also, a private company offers free web access at www.vinelink.com/index.jsp. Includes state, DOC, and county jails.

Corporation, Limited Partnership, Trade Names, Assumed Name, Limited Liability Company Records

Department of Business Services, Corporate Department, 330 Howlett Bldg, 3rd Floor, Copy Section, Springfield, IL 62756 (Courier address: 501 S 2nd St, Springfield, IL 62756); 217-782-7880, 217-782-9521 (Name Availability), 217-524-5248 (Expedited Srv), 217-524-8008 (Nmae Availability), 217-782-4528-Fax; 8AM-4:30PM.

www.ilsos.net

Records are available from mid-1800's on. Closed records are stored at the State Archives. Only limited information is available for corporations dissolved before 1986. New records are available for inquiry immediately. Records are indexed on inhouse computer.

Searching: Records are on micro-film from 1984. In-house computer has name of agent, state and date of incorporation, etc. Include the following in your request-full name of business, corporation file number. In addition to the articles of incorporation, corporation records include the following information: Annual Reports, Officers, Directors, Prior (merged) names, Assumed names, and Inactive names.

Access by: mail, phone, fax, in person, online.

Fee & Payment: The search fee is $5.00 per name. Certification is $10.00 which includes search fee. Copies are $.50 per page after the initial $5.00. Fee payee: Secretary of State. Prepayment required. There is an additional $.50 charge to use a credit card. Personal checks and MasterCard, Visa, Discover accepted.

Mail search: Turnaround time: 5 to 7 days. A SASE is requested.

Phone search: Expedited copy service is available using a credit card.

Fax search: Limited information can be requested by fax.

In person search: Turnaround time: variable.

Online search: The website gives free access to corporate and LLC records at www.cybe rdriveillinois.com/departments/business_services/c orpstart.html. A commercial access program is also available. Fees vary. Potential users must submit in writing the purpose of the request. Submit your request to become involved in this program to the Director's Office.

Other access: List or bulk file purchases are available. Contact the Director's office for details.

Expedited service: Expedited service is available for mail, phone and fax searches. Turnaround time: 24 hours. Add $50.00 per business name for a certified copy and $20.00 for a Good Standing or abstract of corporate record.

Uniform Commercial Code, Federal Tax Liens

Secretary of State, UCC Division, 2nd & Edwards St, Howlett Bldg, Room 350 West, Springfield, IL 62756; 217-782-7518, 8AM-4:30PM.

www.cyberdriveillinois.com

Records are available from 1962. Records are computerized since 1972, as digital images since 2000. It takes 48 hours before new records are available for inquiry.

Searching: Use search request form UCC-11. Request searches for federal tax liens on businesses since 1988 separately with a fee of $5.00. Federal tax liens on individuals and all state tax liens are filed at the county level. Include the following in your request-debtor name and address. Records are not reported on searches one year after lapsing.

Access by: mail, in person.

Fee & Payment: A UCC search is $10.00 per debtor name. A federal tax lien search only is available for $5.00 plus $.50 per page of copies. Copies are $1.00 per page. Fee payee: Secretary of State. Prepayment required. Personal checks and MasterCard, Visa, Discover accepted.

Mail search: Turnaround time: 48 hours. A SASE is requested.

In person search: view documents at no charge.

Other access: The entire database can be purchased and This agency offers a CD update service for $250 per month.

State Tax Liens

Records not maintained by a state level agency.

All state tax liens are filed at the county.

Sales Tax Registrations

Revenue Department, Taxpayer Services, PO Box 19041, Springfield, IL 62794-9041 (Courier address: 101 W Jefferson, Springfield, IL 62702); 800-732-8866, 217-782-3336, 217-782-4217-Fax; 8AM-5PM.

www.iltax.com/Businesses

Records are available for all active businesses with the state, records can go back to the 1930s.

Searching: This agency will only confirm that a business is registered and if registered as a retailer or reseller. They provide no other information. Since the report contains the SSN of the owner, the report is only returned to the owner. Include the following in your request-tax number or business name. The state tax permit or federal tax ID is also helpful.

Access by: mail, phone, in person.

Fee & Payment: The fee is $5.00 per return.

Mail search: Turnaround time: 7 to 10 days. A SASE is requested.

Phone search: Will do up to 5 confirmations at a time.

In person search: Turnaround time: variable.

Birth Certificates

IL Department of Public Health, Division of Vital Records, 605 W Jefferson St, Springfield, IL 62702-5097; 217-782-6554, 217-782-6553 (Instructions), 217-523-2648-Fax; 8:30AM-5PM

www.idph.state.il.us/vitalrecords/index.htm

Records are available from 1916 to present. It takes up to one month before new records are available for inquiry. Records are indexed on microfiche, inhouse computer.

Searching: Birth records are not considered public records. Copies are available to subject if 18 years old, parents, or legal guardian (with court order). Include the following in your request-full name, date of birth, place of birth, relationship to person of record, names of parents, mother's maiden name, signature of requester and photo ID with daytime phone. Place of birth can be city or county. Include name of hospital, if known. The following data is not released: sealed records.

Access by: mail, phone, fax, in person, online.

Fee & Payment: Fees are $10.00 per name for a computer abstract and $15.00 per name for a certified copy of original. Add $2.00 for each additional copy. Add $8.50 service fee to use a credit card. Fee payee: Illinois Department of Public Health. Prepayment required. Personal checks accepted. Major credit cards accepted.

Mail search: Turnaround time: 15 days. No SASE is required.

Phone search: Use of credit card is required for extra fee of $8.50. Normal turnaround time is 2 days.

Fax search: Same criteria as phone searching.

In person search: Turnaround time less than 1/2 hour, must show picture ID.

Online search: Records may requested from www.vitalchek.com, a state-endorsed vendor. Also, detailed instructions are at the website above. Requests are processed within 2 days.

Expedited service: Expedited service is available for mail, phone and fax searches. Add $8.50 for using a credit card, $14.50 for express delivery.

Death Records

IL Department of Public Health, Division of Vital Records, 605 W Jefferson St, Springfield, IL 62702-5097; 217-782-6554, 217-782-6553 (Instructions), 217-523-2648-Fax; 8:30AM-4PM.

www.idph.state.il.us/vitalrecords/index.htm

Records are available from 1916 to present. New records are available for inquiry immediately. Records are indexed on microfiche.

Searching: Death records are not considered public documents. Copies are available to person with property rights and or an interest in the record. Once records are 20 years old, they are open for genealogical searches. Include the following in your request-full name, date of death, place of death, relationship to person of record, parents' names, reason for request, photo ID and signature of requester.

Access by: mail, fax, in person, online.

Fee & Payment: Fees are $17.00 for a certified Death Certificate, or $10.00 if for genealogy (archived) records. Fee payee: Illinois Department of Public Health. Prepayment required. Personal checks accepted. Major credit cards accepted.

Mail search: Turnaround time: 8 to 10 weeks. No SASE is required.

Fax search: See expedited service.

In person search: There is one day waiting period. If ordered by 2PM, will be available the next day after 10AM.

Online search: Records may requested from www.vitalchek.com, a state-endorsed vendor. Detailed instructions are at the website above. Also, the state archives database of Illinois Death Certificates 1916-1950 is available free at www.cyberdriveillinois.com/departments/archives/genealogy/forms/idphdeathsrch.html.

Expedited service: Expedited service is available for mail, online, and fax searches. The fee is $8.50 for the credit card use and $14.50 for express

delivery. If you send your request in by express delivery, they will turnaround in two days.

Marriage Certificates, Divorce Records

Records not maintained by a state level agency.

State will verify marriage or divorce from 1962-present, but will not issue certificate. Verification requests must be in writing and there is a fee of $5.00 per event requested. Records of marriage and divorce are found at the county of issue.

There is a free online search of a statewide Marriage Index for 1763-1900 found at the Illinois State Archives website at www.cyberdriveillinois.com/departments/archives/marriage.html.

Workers' Compensation Records

IL Workers' Compensation Commission, 100 W Randolph, 8th Floor, Chicago, IL 60601; 312-814-6611, 8:30AM-5PM.

www.iwcc.il.gov

The website lists cases that are up for a hearing status.

Records are available on computer from 1982 to present, on microfiche from 1927 to 1981. Settled file copies are stored in Springfield, but must be requested from Chicago. Data is indexed by name and file number. It takes 3 months before new records are available for inquiry. Records are indexed on file folders. Records are normally destroyed after five years.

Searching: Include the following in your request-claimant name, Social Security Number, date of accident. Include case number and company name.

Access by: mail, phone, in person, online.

Fee & Payment: There is no charge for a small file. For "large files," the office will contact you and suggest you use a record retrieval service. If your request is large enough to warrant the use of a copy service, the service will have its own fees that must be paid by you. Personal checks are accepted.

Mail search: Turnaround time: 2 weeks. Send a name as well as any other information you may have, such as company name and date of accident, to determine if any files exist. A SASE is requested.

Phone search: Information about a case is accessed by the file number. The staff will do a name search if you have enough information for them to do so.

In person search: There are several public access terminals available in the office.

Online search: Case information status for active cases only is available at the webpage. Click on the IIC box on the right side of the screen.

Driver Records

Abstract Information Unit, Drivers Services Department, 2701 S Dirksen Prky, Springfield, IL 62723; 217-782-2720, 8AM-4:30PM.

www.sos.state.il.us

No personal identifiable information is provided on record unless requester is exempt. Exempt requesters include business representatives with a legitimate business need (e.g. insurance, financial institutions, employers, etc.).

Records are available for 4 years for moving violations; 7 years for suspension; lifetime for DWI. Commercial Driver records can go back 10 years for serious violations. It takes 2 weeks before new records are available for inquiry.

Searching: Non-exempt requesters, with no consent, may receive records without personal information, but there is a 10 day waiting period while the state notifies the subject. Include the following in your request-full name, date of birth, sex. Exempt requesters qualify per DPPA guidelines and receive full record information.

Access by: mail, in person, online.

Fee & Payment: The fee is $12.00 per record, which includes certification. There is a full charge for a "no record found." Fee payee: Secretary of State. Prepayment required. Personal checks accepted. No credit cards accepted.

Mail search: Turnaround time: 10 days. No SASE is required.

In person search: Up to five requests will be processed immediately if requester meets the access requirement (see above). Requests are available from any full-time Driver Services Facility statewide.

Online search: A program for high volume, approved users may be available. Records are $12.00 each. Call 217-785-2384 for further information.

Other access: Overnight cartridge batch processing may be available to high volume users (there is a 200 request minimum per day). Call 217-785-2384 for more information.

Vehicle Ownership, Vehicle Identification

Vehicle Services Department, Vehicle Record Inquiry, 501 S 2nd Street #408, Springfield, IL 62756; 217-782-6992, 217-524-0122-Fax; 8AM-4:30PM.

www.sos.state.il.us

Records are available generally for 10 years to present. It takes 1 to 2 weeks before new records are available for inquiry. Records are normally destroyed after 10 years.

Searching: Personal information is not released for non-business purposes. Bulk sales are not permitted for solicitation purposes. Include the following in your request-name, reason for search. Records are open to "Exempt" requesters include courts, law enforcement, legal representatives (including licensed IL PIs) the insurance industry and others designated per DPPA. A non-exempt requester receives data without personal information.

Access by: mail, fax, in person.

Fee & Payment: The fee is $5.00 per record search. Fee payee: Secretary of State. Prepayment required. Personal checks and MasterCard, Visa, Discover accepted.

Mail search: Turnaround time: 4 to 7 days. You may search by mail, but there is a 10 day delay if the requester is not "exempt." A SASE is requested.

Fax search: Fax requests are accepted for approved accounts.

In person search: Walk-in requesters may retrieve data immediately; however, if requester is not exempt there is a 10 day delay.

Other access: This agency will sell customized, bulk requests upon approval of purpose and with a signed contract. Contact the Data Processing Division in Room 400.

Accident Reports (Crash Reports)

Illinois State Police, Patrol Records Unit, 500 Iles Park Place, Ste 200, Springfield, IL 62703-2982; 217-785-0614, 217-785-2325-Fax; 8AM-5PM.

www.isp.state.il.us

To request report if crash occurred on IL Tollway System, send check or money order payable to: IL Toll Highway Authority, Attn: State Police District 15, One Authority Drive, Downers Grove, IL 60515.

Records are available from 1976 to present. It takes 2-4 weeks before new records are available for inquiry. Records are normally destroyed after 2 years but maintained on microfilm for 50 years.

Searching: If the accident was not investigated by the State Police, then the requestors must contact the local law enforcement authority that did the investigation. Crash reports are considered public record and are available without restriction. Items needed by the requester include date, names of drivers involved, report number, and an exact location.

Access by: mail, phone, in person, online.

Fee & Payment: The fee is $5.00 per report or $20.00 for a reconstruction report. Add $1.00 if ordered online. Fee payee: Illinois State Police. Prepayment required. Personal checks accepted. No credit cards accepted.

Mail search: Turnaround time: 7 to 10 days. If requester provides prepaid express envelope & label, the request will be returned quicker. A SASE is requested.

Phone search: You may call to get information, but copies of records are only released with written requests.

In person search: Turnaround time is immediate if report is on file.

Online search: Records can be requested and paid for online via E-Pay at the webpage. Visit www.isp.state.il.us/traffic/crashreports.cfm. The fee is $6.00 per report.

Vessel Ownership
Vessel Registration

Department of Natural Resources, One Natural Resources Way, Springfield, IL 62702; 800-382-1696, 217-557-0180, 217-782-5016-Fax; 8:30AM-5PM.

http://dnr.state.il.us

Lien information will show on the history report.

Records are available from 1982 to the present. Snow mobile records are also available. Records are indexed on computer. All boats must be titled and registered unless if only used on a private lake. It takes 8 weeks before new records are available for inquiry. Records are normally destroyed after 4 years.

Searching: Include the following in your request- name or hull ID or registration #. Include reason for request. To search,

Access by: mail, phone.

Fee & Payment: There is a $5.00 fee for any search, including a title history search. Fee payee: IL Dept of Natural Resources. Prepayment required. Personal checks accepted. No credit cards accepted.

Mail search: Turnaround time: 4 to 6 weeks. No SASE is required.

Phone search: They will give very limited name search and verification information, time permitting.

Other access: Bulk data may be released via a FOIA request. Write for details.

Voter Registration
Access to Records is Restricted.

IL State Board of Elections, 1020 S Spring, Springfield, IL 62704; 217-782-4141, 217-782-5959-Fax; 8AM-4:30PM.

www.elections.state.il.us

The data is not considered public record at the state level and is only available in bulk format to political committees and government agencies. Records are "overlaid" three to four rimes a year. County Clerks control the information at the local level. However, the Federal Help America Vote Act of 2002 (HAVA) law requires implementation of a central, computerized, statewide voter registration system by 01/01/2006. The state will comply.

GED Certificates
Access to Records is Restricted.

Illinois Community College Board, GED Testing, 401 East Capitol, Springfield, IL 62701; 217-785-0123, 217-558-6700-Fax; 8AM-5PM.

This agency has recently taken over responsibility of the GED records and is putting into place a statewide search service. Until completed (early 2006), all GED information requests must be accessed from the county agency where the test was taken. Most counties require a signed consent and prefer not to do a "yes or name" verification but instead supply a transcript copy for a fee.

Hunting and Fishing License Information
Access to Records is Restricted.

IL Dept of Natural Resources, License Section, PO Box 19459, Springfield, IL 62794; 217-782-2965, 217-782-5016-Fax; 8:30AM-5PM.

http://dnr.state.il.us

They are just now creating a central database. At this time, records are not available. The vendors hold license records for years prior to 2002. Vendors can be searched at http://dnr.state.il.us/admin/systems/vendor.htm

Illinois State Licensing Agencies

For details about the agency responsible for licensing/certifying/registering an item below or in the Agency Quick Finder section, match an item's number with the number of the agency in the *Licensing Agency Information* section.

Illinois Licenses Searchable Online

Acupuncturist #11	https://www.idfpr.com/dpr/licenselookup/default.asp
Alarm Contractor #11	https://www.idfpr.com/dpr/licenselookup/default.asp
Amusement Attraction #5	www.state.il.us/agency/idol/Listings/Carnlist.htm
Amusement Ride #5	www.state.il.us/agency/idol/Listings/Carnlist.htm
Architect #11	https://www.idfpr.com/dpr/licenselookup/default.asp
Armed Security Agent/Agency #11	https://www.idfpr.com/dpr/licenselookup/default.asp
Asbestos Contractor #17	www.idph.state.il.us/
Athletic Trainer #11	https://www.idfpr.com/dpr/licenselookup/default.asp
ATM Privately Owned #29	www.obre.state.il.us/CBT/REGENTY/ATMREG.pdf
Attorney #1	www.iardc.org/lawyersearch.asp
Auctioneer #29	www.obrelookupclear.state.il.us/default.asp
Audiologist #11	https://www.idfpr.com/dpr/licenselookup/default.asp
Bank #29	www.obrelookupclear.state.il.us/default.asp
Barber #11	https://www.idfpr.com/dpr/licenselookup/default.asp
Basic classr'm Training Course #11	https://www.idfpr.com/dpr/licenselookup/default.asp
Bilingual Teacher, Transitional #28	https://isbes1.isbe.net/otis
Bull Ride #5	www.state.il.us/agency/idol/Listings/Carnlist.htm
Bungee Jump #5	www.state.il.us/agency/idol/Listings/Carnlist.htm
Carnival #5	www.state.il.us/agency/idol/Listings/Carnlist.htm
Check Seller/Distributor #29	www.obrelookupclear.state.il.us/default.asp
Chiropractor #11	https://www.idfpr.com/dpr/licenselookup/default.asp
Collection Agency #11	https://www.idfpr.com/dpr/licenselookup/default.asp
Controlled Substance Registrant #11	https://www.idfpr.com/dpr/licenselookup/default.asp
Corporate Fiduciary #29	www.obre.state.il.us/CBT/REGENTY/usa.asp?State=N
Cosmetologist #11	https://www.idfpr.com/dpr/licenselookup/default.asp
Counselor/Clinical Prof. Counselor #11	https://www.idfpr.com/dpr/licenselookup/default.asp
CPA- Public Accountant #11	https://www.idfpr.com/dpr/licenselookup/default.asp
Dentist/Dental Hygienist #11	https://www.idfpr.com/dpr/licenselookup/default.asp
Design Firm #11	https://www.idfpr.com/dpr/licenselookup/default.asp
Dietitian/Nutrition Counselor #11	https://www.idfpr.com/dpr/licenselookup/default.asp
Doctor/Physician #11	https://www.idfpr.com/dpr/licenselookup/default.asp
Drug Distributor, Wholesale #11	https://www.idfpr.com/dpr/licenselookup/default.asp
Early Childhood Teacher #28	https://isbes1.isbe.net/otis
Engineer, Structural #11	https://www.idfpr.com/dpr/licenselookup/default.asp
Engineer/Engineer Intern #11	https://www.idfpr.com/dpr/licenselookup/default.asp
Environmental Health Practitioner #11	https://www.idfpr.com/dpr/licenselookup/default.asp
Esthetician #11	https://www.idfpr.com/dpr/licenselookup/default.asp
Euthanasia Tech #11	https://www.idfpr.com/dpr/licenselookup/default.asp
Firearms Trainer #11	https://www.idfpr.com/dpr/licenselookup/default.asp
Funeral Director/Embalmer #11	https://www.idfpr.com/dpr/licenselookup/default.asp
Geologist #11	https://www.idfpr.com/dpr/licenselookup/default.asp
Go-kart track #5	www.state.il.us/agency/idol/Listings/Carnlist.htm
HMO/PPA #4	www.ins.state.il.us/PPA/PPA_list.asp
Home Inspector #29	www.obrelookupclear.state.il.us/default.asp
Home Medical Equip Provider #11	https://www.idfpr.com/dpr/licenselookup/default.asp
Insurance Producer #4	http://neonwebh.cmcf.state.il.us:8080/ins/imsfor
Interior Designer #11	https://www.idfpr.com/dpr/licenselookup/default.asp
Landscape Architect #11	https://www.idfpr.com/dpr/licenselookup/default.asp
Lead Contractor #17	http://app.idph.state.il.us/Envhealth/Lead/Leadcnt.asp
Lead Risk Assessor/Inspect./Supvr #17	http://app.idph.state.il.us/Envhealth/lead/Leadinsp.asp
Lead Training Provider #17	http://app.idph.state.il.us/Envhealth/lead/Leadinsp.asp
Liquor License, Retail/Dist./Mfg. #25	http://www2.state.il.us/lcc/license_search.asp
Lobbyist #14	www.cyberdriveillinois.com/departments/index/lobbyist/home.html
Locksmith #11	https://www.idfpr.com/dpr/licenselookup/default.asp

Long Term Care Insurance Co #4	http://neonwebh.cmcf.state.il.us:8080/ins/imsfor
Marriage & Family Therapist #11	https://www.idfpr.com/dpr/licenselookup/default.asp
Massage Therapist #11	https://www.idfpr.com/dpr/licenselookup/default.asp
Medical Corporation #11	https://www.idfpr.com/dpr/licenselookup/default.asp
Medical Doctor #11	https://www.idfpr.com/dpr/licenselookup/default.asp
Mortgage Banker/Broker #29	www.obre.state.il.us/MBLookup/MBList.htm
Nail Technician #11	https://www.idfpr.com/dpr/licenselookup/default.asp
Naprapath #11	https://www.idfpr.com/dpr/licenselookup/default.asp
Notary Public #14	www.cyberdriveillinois.com/departments/index/notary/home.html
Nurse #11	https://www.idfpr.com/dpr/licenselookup/default.asp
Nursing Home Administrator #17	www.medicare.gov/Nursing/Overview.asp
Occupational Therapist #11	https://www.idfpr.com/dpr/licenselookup/default.asp
Optometrist #11	https://www.idfpr.com/dpr/licenselookup/default.asp
Orthotist #11	https://www.idfpr.com/dpr/licenselookup/default.asp
Osteopathic Physician #11	https://www.idfpr.com/dpr/licenselookup/default.asp
Pawnbroker #29	www.obrelookupclear.state.il.us/default.asp
Pedorthist #11	https://www.idfpr.com/dpr/licenselookup/default.asp
Perfusionist #11	https://www.idfpr.com/dpr/licenselookup/default.asp
Pest Control Technician/Business #17	www.idph.state.il.us/
Pesticide Applicator #17	www.idph.state.il.us/
Pharmacist/Pharmacy #11	https://www.idfpr.com/dpr/licenselookup/default.asp
Physical Therapist #11	https://www.idfpr.com/dpr/licenselookup/default.asp
Physician Assistant #11	https://www.idfpr.com/dpr/licenselookup/default.asp
Podiatrist #11	https://www.idfpr.com/dpr/licenselookup/default.asp
Polygraph Examiner #11	https://www.idfpr.com/dpr/licenselookup/default.asp
Private Detective #11	https://www.idfpr.com/dpr/licenselookup/default.asp
Private Security Contractor #11	https://www.idfpr.com/dpr/licenselookup/default.asp
Psychologist #11	https://www.idfpr.com/dpr/licenselookup/default.asp
Psychology Business #11	https://www.idfpr.com/dpr/licenselookup/default.asp
Public Accountant-CPA #11	https://www.idfpr.com/dpr/licenselookup/default.asp
Real Estate Agent/Broker/Seller #29	www.obrelookupclear.state.il.us/default.asp
Real Estate Appraiser #29	www.obrelookupclear.state.il.us/default.asp
Respiratory Care Practitioner #11	https://www.idfpr.com/dpr/licenselookup/default.asp
Roofer #11	https://www.idfpr.com/dpr/licenselookup/default.asp
Roofing Contractor #11	https://www.idfpr.com/dpr/licenselookup/default.asp
Savings & Loan Association #29	www.obrelookupclear.state.il.us/default.asp
Savings Bank #29	www.obrelookupclear.state.il.us/default.asp
Securities Salesperson/Dealer #16	www.nasd.com/web/idcplg?IdcService=SS_GET_PAGE&nodeId=6
Security Force #11	https://www.idfpr.com/dpr/licenselookup/default.asp
Security Guard Firm/Agency #11	https://www.idfpr.com/dpr/licenselookup/default.asp
Sewage System Contractor #17	www.idph.state.il.us/
Shorthand Reporter #11	https://www.idfpr.com/dpr/licenselookup/default.asp
Ski Lift, Tram #5	www.state.il.us/agency/idol/Listings/Carnlist.htm
Social Worker #11	https://www.idfpr.com/dpr/licenselookup/default.asp
Special Teacher #28	https://isbes1.isbe.net/otis
Speech-Language Pathologist #11	https://www.idfpr.com/dpr/licenselookup/default.asp
Stock Broker #16	www.nasd.com/web/idcplg?IdcService=SS_GET_PAGE&nodeId=6
Substitute Teacher #28	https://isbes1.isbe.net/otis
Surgical Technician #11	https://www.idfpr.com/dpr/licenselookup/default.asp
Surveyor, Land #11	https://www.idfpr.com/dpr/licenselookup/default.asp
Teacher #28	https://isbes1.isbe.net/otis
Timeshare/Land Sales #29	www.obrelookupclear.state.il.us/default.asp
Trust Company #29	www.obre.state.il.us/CBT/REGENTY/Institution.asp?Inst=2
Veterinarian #11	https://www.idfpr.com/dpr/licenselookup/default.asp
Water Well & Pump Installer/Contr. #17	www.idph.state.il.us/
Water Well Contractor/IDPH #17	www.idph.state.il.us/

Illinois Licensing Quick Finder

Accident Reconstruction Specialist #19 217-782-4540
Acupuncturist #11 217-785-0800
Alarm Contractor #11 217-785-0800
Alcohol Abuse Counselor #21 217-698-8110
Ambulance Service #13 217-785-2080
Amusement Attraction #5 217-782-9347
Amusement Ride #5 217-782-9347
Animal Breeder #6 217-785-3423
Aquaculturist #6 217-785-3423
Architect #11 217-785-0800
Armed Security Agent/Agency #11 217-785-0800
Asbestos Contractor #17 217-782-3517
Athletic Trainer #11 217-785-0800
ATM Privately Owned #29 312-793-3000
Attorney #1 217-522-6838
Auctioneer #29 312-793-8704
Auctioneer, Vehicle #30 217-782-7817
Audiologist #11 217-785-0800
Automotive Parts Recycler #30 217-782-7817
Basic Classroom Training Course #11 .. 217-785-0800
Bank #29 312-793-3000
Barber #11 217-785-0800
Bilingual Teacher, Transitional #28 800-845-8749
Bingo Operation #18 217-785-5864
Blacksmith #26 312-814-2600
Blaster #7 217-782-4970
Boat Operator #6 217-782-2138
Boiler Inspector #10 217-782-2696
Boxing/Wrestling Event/Professn'l #11 . 217-785-0800
Breath Analyzer Operator #13 217-782-1571
Bull Ride #5 217-782-9347
Bungee Jump #5 217-782-9347
Business Broker #16 217-785-4923
Business Opportunity #16 217-785-7371
Carnival #5 217-782-9347
Charitable Game #18 217-785-5864
Check Seller/Distributor #29 312-793-3000
Child Care Facility #2 217-785-2688
Chiropractor #11 217-785-0800
Coal Mine Worker #8 217-782-6791
Collection Agency #11 217-785-0800
Controlled Substance Registrant #11 ... 217-785-0800
Coroner (County) #19 217-782-4540
Corporate Fiduciary #29 312-793-3000
Correction Officer (County) #19 217-782-4540
Cosmetologist #11 217-785-0800
Counselor/Clinical Prof. Counsel'r #11. 217-785-0800
CPA - Public Accountant #11 217-785-0800
Criminal Electronic Surveillance Officer #19 217-782-4540
Cross-Connection Control Device Inspector #24 217-782-1020
Day Care #2 217-785-2688
Dentist/Dental Hygienist #11 217-785-0800
Design Firm #11 217-785-0800
Dietitian/Nutrition Counselor #11 217-785-0800
Distribution System (Public) Operator #24 217-782-9720
Doctor/Physician #11 217-785-0800
Driving Instructor #7 847-437-3953
Drug Distributor, Wholesale #11 217-785-0800
Early Childhood Teacher #28 800-845-8749
Emergency Medical Technician #13 217-785-2080
Employee Leasing Company #4 217-782-6366
Employment Agency #23 312-793-2810
Engineer/ Engineer Intern #11 217-785-0800
Engineer, Structural #11 217-785-0800
Environmental Health Practitioner #11 .. 217-785-0800
Esthetician #11 217-785-0800
Euthanasia Technician #11 217-785-0800
Explosive Magazine Storage #8 217-782-9976
Explosive, General Use #8 217-782-9976
Firearms Regulation (Firearm Owner's Reg.) #27 217-782-7980
Firearms Trainer #11 217-785-0800
Fish Dealer #6 217-785-3423
Fisherman, Commercial #6 217-785-3423
Food Processing Plant/Warehouse #13 217-785-2439
Food Service Sanitation Manager #13. 217-785-2439
Funeral Director/Embalmer #11 217-785-0800
Fur Buyer/Tanner/Dyer #6 217-785-3423
Gambling Addiction Counselor #21 217-698-8110
Gambling Employee #20 312-814-4702
Geologist #11 217-785-0800
Go-kart track #5 217-782-9347
Hearing Instrument Dispenser #15 217-782-4733
Hearing Screening Technician #15 217-782-4733
HMO #4 217-782-6366
Home Health Aide #13 217-782-7412
Home Health Care Agency #13 217-782-7412
Home Inspector #29 217-782-3000
Home Medical Equip Provider #11 217-785-0800
Horseshoer #26 312-814-2600
Hospital #13 217-782-7412
Hunting Area Operator #6 217-785-3423
Industrial Radiographer #9 217-785-9913
Insurance Producer #4 217-782-6366
Interior Designer #11 217-785-0800
Investment Adviser #16 217-785-4929
Investment Adviser Rep, #16 217-557-4609
Laboratory Analysis Technician #13 217-785-8820
Land Sale #11 217-785-0800
Landfill Chief Operator #24 217-782-9877
Landscape Architect #11 217-785-0800
Lead Contractor #17 217-782-3517
Lead Risk Assessor/Inspector/Supervisor #17 217-782-3517
Lead Training Provider #17 217-782-3517
Liquor License, Retail/Dist./Mfg. #25 ... 312-814-3930
Loan Broker #16 217-785-4923
Lobbyist #14 217-782-0705
Locksmith #11 217-785-0800
Long-term Care Insurer #4 217-782-6366
Marriage & Family Therapist #11 217-785-0800
Massage Therapist #11 217-785-0800
Medical Corporation #11 217-785-0800
Medical Doctor #11 217-785-0800
Mental Health Counselor #21 217-698-8110
Mine Engineer/Foreman #8 217-782-6791
Mine Rescue Supervisor/Assistant #8 . 217-782-6791
Mine Supervisor #8 217-782-6791
Mortgage Banker/Broker #29 217-793-1409
Motor Vehicle Dealer, New #30 217-782-7817
Nail Technician #11 217-785-0800
Naprapath #11 217-785-0800
Notary Public #14 217-782-0705
Nuclear Medicine Technologist #9 217-785-9913
Nurse #11 217-785-0800
Nurses' Aide #13 217-785-5133
Nursing Agency #23 .. 312-793-1718 or 312-793-2810
Nursing Home #12 217-782-1200
Nursing Home Administrator #17 217-782-0514
Occupational Aide #12 217-782-1200
Occupational Therapist #11 217-785-0800
Optometrist #11 217-785-0800
Orthotist #11 217-785-0800
Osteopathic Physician #11 217-785-0800
Pari-Mutuel Employee #26 312-814-2600
Pawnbroker #29 312-793-3000
Pedorthist #11 217-785-0800
Perfusionist #11 217-785-0800
Pest Control Technician/Business #17 217-782-4674
Pesticide Applicator #17 217-782-5830
Pharmacist/Pharmacy #11 217-785-0800
Physical Aide #12 217-782-1200
Physical Therapist #11 217-785-0800
Physician Assistant #11 217-785-0800
Plumber #17 217-782-4977
Plumber Apprentice #13 217-785-1153
Podiatrist #11 217-785-0800
Polygraph - Deception Detection Examiner #11 217-785-0800
Private Detective #11 217-785-0800
Private Security Contractor #11 217-785-0800
Psychologist #11 217-785-0800
Psychology Business #11 217-785-0800
Public Accountant-CPA #11 217-785-0800
Pull Tab Operator #18 217-785-5864
Racetrack #26 312-814-2600
Radiation Therapist #10 217-785-9913
Radiographer #10 217-785-9913
Radon Measurement Specialist #10 217-785-9935
Real Estate Agent/Broker/Sales #29 ... 312-793-8704
Real Estate Appraiser #29 312-793-8704
Rehabilitation Aide #12 217-782-1200
Respiratory Care Practitioner #11 217-785-0800
Restaurant & Retail Food Store #17 217-785-2439
Riverboat Employee #20 312-814-4702
Roofer #11 217-785-0800
Roofing Contractor #11 217-785-0800
Salvage Firm #13 217-785-2439
Savings & Loan Association #29 217-782-9043
Savings Bank #29 217-782-9043
School Business Official #28 800-845-8749
School Guidance Counselor #28 800-845-8749
School Media Specialist/Librarian #28 .. 800-845-8749
School Nurse #28 800-845-8749
School Principal/Super./Admin. #28 800-845-8749
School Psychologist #28 800-845-8749
Scrap Processor #30 217-782-7817
Security Force #11 217-785-0800
Security Guard Firm #11 217-785-0800
Securities Salesperson/Dealer #16 217-782-2256
Sewage System Contractor #17 217-782-5830
Sheriff Law Enforcement Officer #19 ... 217-782-4540
Shorthand Reporter #11 217-785-0800
Ski Lift, Tram #5 217-782-9347
Social Worker #11 217-785-0800
Special Teacher #28 800-845-8749
Speech-Language Pathologist #11 217-785-0800
Stock Broker #16 217-782-2256
Substance Abuse Counselor #21 217-698-8110
Substitute Teacher #28 800-845-8749
Surgical Technician #11 217-785-0800
Surveyor, Land #11 217-785-0800
Tanning Facility #17 217-785-2439
Taxidermist #6 217-785-3423
Teacher #28 800-845-8749
Timber Buyer #3 217-782-6431
Timeshare #11 217-785-0800
Timeshare/Land Sales #29 312-793-8704
Trust Company #29 312-793-3000
Underground Shot Firer #8 217-782-6791
Used Vehicle Dealer #30 217-782-7817
Vehicle Rebuilder/Repair #30 217-782-7817
Veterinarian #11 217-785-0800
Vision Screening Technician #15 217-782-4733
Waste Water Plant Operator #24 217-782-9720
Water Supply Operator #24 217-782-9720
Water Well & Pump InstallContr. #17 .. 217-782-5830
Water Well Contractor/IDPH #17 217-782-5830
Weighing & Measuring Device Serviceman #22 217-782-3817

Illinois Licensing Agency Information

1 Attorney Registration & Disciplinary Commission of Supreme Court of IL, 1 N. Old Capitol Plaza #333, Springfield, IL 62701; 217-522-6838, Fax: 217-522-2417.
www.iardc.org
Search Database at
www.iardc.org/lawyersearch.asp

2 Department of Children & Family Services, 406 E Monroe St, Springfield, IL 62701; 217-785-2509, Fax: 217-785-1052.
www.state.il.us/dcfs

3 Department of Natural Resources, Division of Forest Services, 1 Natural Resources Way, Springfield, IL 62702; 217-782-6431, Fax: 217-785-8405.
www.dnr.state.il.us

4 Department of Insurance, 320 W Washington, Springfield, IL 62767-0001; 217-782-4515, Fax: 217-782-5020.
www.ins.state.il.us
Email: director@ins.state.il.us

5 Department of Labor, Carnival & Amusement Ride Safety Division, 1 West Old State Capitol Plaza, #300, Springfield, IL 62701; 217-782-9347, Fax: 217-782-0596.
www.state.il.us/agency/idol/
Search Database at
www.state.il.us/agency/idol/Listings/Carnlist.htm

6 Dept of Natural Resources, Commercial Permits, One Natural Resources Way, Springfield, IL 62702-1271; 217-785-3423, Fax: 217-782-5016.
http://dnr.state.il.us

7 Secretary of State, Commercial Driver Training, 650 Roppolo Dr, Elk Grove, IL 60007; 847-437-3953, Fax: 847-437-3911.
www.cyberdriveillinois.com/

8 Department of Natural Resources, Office of Mine & Minerals, One Natural Resources Way, Springfield, IL 62702-1271; 217-782-6791, Fax: 217-524-4819.
http://dnr.state.il.us/mines/

9 Emergency Management Agency, 1035 Outer Park Dr, Springfield, IL 62704; 217-785-9900, Fax: 217-785-9962.
www.state.il.us/iema/
Email: webmaster@iema.state.il.us

10 State Fire Marshall, 1035 Stevenson Dr, Springfield, IL 62703; 217-785-0969, Fax: 217-782-1062.
www.state.il.us/osfm

11 Department of Prof. Regulation, Professions/Occupations/Entities, 320 W Washington, 3rd Fl, Springfield, IL 62786; 217-785-0800, Fax: 217-782-7645. www.dpr.state.il.us
Email: netinfo@dpr084rl.state.il.us
Search Database at https://www.idfpr.com/dpr/licenselookup/default.asp

12 Department of Public Aid, Bureau of Long-Term Care, 201 S. Grand Ave, Springfield, IL 62763-0001; 217-782-1200, Fax: 217-524-7114.
www.dpaillinois.com/
Email: aidd2011@mail.idpa.state.il.us

13 Department of Public Health, Education & Training Section, 525 W Jefferson St 4th Fl, Springfield, IL 62761; 217-782-4977, Fax: 217-782-3987.
www.idph.state.il.us

14 Secretary of State, Index Department, 111 E Monroe St, Springfield, IL 62756; 217-782-7017, Fax: 217-524-0930.
www.cyberdriveillinois.com/departments/index/home.html

15 Department of Public Health, Division of Health Assessment & Screening, 500 E. Monroe, 1st Floor, Springfield, IL 62701; 217-782-4733, Fax: 217-557-5324.
www.idph.state.il.us
Email: gtanner@idph.state.il.us

16 Secretary of State, Securities Department, 520 S 2nd St, Lincoln Tower, #200, Springfield, IL 62701; 217-782-2256, Fax: 217-524-2172.
www.cyberdriveillinois.com/departments/securities/home.html
Search Database at
www.nasd.com/web/idcplg?IdcService=SS_GET_PAGE&nodeId=6

17 Department of Public Health, Environmental Health, 525 W Jefferson St, 3rd Fl, Springfield, IL 62761; 217-782-5830, Fax: 217-785-0253.
www.idph.state.il.us
Email: mailus@idph.state.il.us

18 Department of Revenue, Bingo Division, 101 W Jefferson, Springfield, IL 62702; 217-785-5864, Fax: 217-557-4398.
www.iltax.com

19 Law Enforcement & Standards Training Board, 600 S 2nd St, #300, Springfield, IL 62704; 217-782-4540, Fax: 217-524-5350.
www.ptb.state.il.us
Email: ptb@pop.state.il.us

20 Gaming Board, 160 N Lasalle #300, Chicago, IL 60601; 312-814-4700, Fax: 312-814-4602.
www.igb.state.il.us

21 Counselor Certification Dept, IAODAPCA, 1305 Wabash Ave #L, Springfield, IL 62704-4938; 217-698-8110, Fax: 217-698-8234.
www.iaodapca.org
Email: IAODAPCA@aol.com.

22 Department of Agriculture, State Fairgrounds, PO Box 19281, Springfield, IL 62794-9281; 217-782-2172, Fax: 217-524-7801.
www.agr.state.il.us

23 Department of Labor, State of Illinois Bldg., 160 N LaSalle, 13th Fl, #C1300, Chicago, IL 60601; 312-793-2800, Fax: 312-793-5257.
www.state.il.us/agency/idol
Email: idol@pop.state.il.us

24 Environmental Protection Agency, PO Box 19276 (1021 N Grand Ave E), Springfield, IL 62794-9276; 217-782-1020, Fax: 217-782-0075.
www.epa.state.il.us/water/index.html

25 Freedom of Information Compliance Officer, Liquor Control Commission, 100 W Randolph, #5-300, Chicago, IL 60601; 312-814-2206, Fax: 312-814-2241.
www.state.il.us/lcc/default.htm
Email: ilcc_info@mail.state.il.us
Search Database at
http://www2.state.il.us/lcc/license_search.asp

26 Racing Board, 100 W Randolph, #11-100, Chicago, IL 60601; 312-814-2600, Fax: 312-814-5062.
www.state.il.us/agency/irb
Email: irb@pop.state.il.us

27 State Police, FOID, 100 Iles Park Pl, Springfield, IL 62708; 217-782-7980, Fax: 217-782-9139.
www.isp.state.il.us

28 Division of Professional Certification, Board of Education, 100 N 1st St, Springfield, IL 62777; 800-845-8749, 217 782-4321, Fax: 217 524-4928.
www.isbe.state.il.us/teachers/
Search Database at https://isbes1.isbe.net/otis

29 Office of Banks & Real Estate, Bureaus of Res. Finance; Banks & Trusts; Real Estate Professions, 500 E Monroe, Springfield, IL 62701-1509; 217-782-3000, Fax: 217-524-5941.
www.obre.state.il.us/AGENCY/licenseinfo.htm
Email: obr_webmaster@pop.state.il.us
Search Database at
www.obrelookupclear.state.il.us/default.asp

30 Secretary of State, Vehicle Services, Dealers/Remitters, Howlett Bldg, Rm 069, Springfield, IL 62756; 217-782-7817, Fax: 217-524-0120.
www.sos.state.il.us
Email: secwhite@ccgate.sos.state.il.us

Illinois Federal Courts

The following list indicates the district and division name for each county in the state. If the bankruptcy court location is different from the district court, then the location of the bankruptcy court appears in parentheses.

County/Court Cross Reference

County	District	Division
Adams	Central	Springfield
Alexander	Southern	Benton
Bond	Southern	East St Louis
Boone	Northern	Rockford
Brown	Central	Springfield
Bureau	Central	Peoria
Calhoun	Southern	East St Louis
Carroll	Northern	Rockford
Cass	Central	Springfield
Champaign	Central	Danville/Urbana (Danville)
Christian	Central	Springfield
Clark	Southern	Benton (East St Louis)
Clay	Southern	Benton (East St Louis)
Clinton	Southern	East St Louis
Coles	Central	Danville/Urbana (Danville)
Cook	Northern	Chicago (Eastern)
Crawford	Southern	Benton (East St Louis)
Cumberland	Southern	Benton
De Kalb	Northern	Rockford
De Witt	Central	Springfield
Douglas	Central	Danville/Urbana (Danville)
Du Page	Northern	Chicago (Eastern)
Edgar	Central	Danville/Urbana (Danville)
Edwards	Southern	Benton
Effingham	Southern	Benton (East St Louis)
Fayette	Southern	East St Louis
Ford	Central	Danville/Urbana (Danville)
Franklin	Southern	Benton
Fulton	Central	Peoria
Gallatin	Southern	Benton
Greene	Central	Springfield
Grundy	Northern	Chicago (Eastern)
Hamilton	Southern	Benton
Hancock	Central	Peoria
Hardin	Southern	Benton
Henderson	Central	Rock Island (Peoria)
Henry	Central	Rock Island (Peoria)
Iroquois	Central	Danville/Urbana (Danville)
Jackson	Southern	Benton
Jasper	Southern	Benton (East St Louis)
Jefferson	Southern	Benton
Jersey	Southern	East St Louis
Jo Daviess	Northern	Rockford
Johnson	Southern	Benton
Kane	Northern	Chicago (Eastern)
Kankakee	Central	Danville/Urbana (Danville)
Kendall	Northern	Chicago (Eastern)
Knox	Central	Peoria
La Salle	Northern	Chicago (Eastern)
Lake	Northern	Chicago (Eastern)
Lawrence	Southern	Benton (East St Louis)
Lee	Northern	Rockford
Livingston	Central	Peoria (Danville)
Logan	Central	Springfield
Macon	Central	Danville/Urbana (Spmgfld)
Macoupin	Central	Springfield
Madison	Southern	East St Louis
Marion	Southern	East St Louis
Marshall	Central	Peoria
Mason	Central	Springfield
Massac	Southern	Benton
McDonough	Central	Peoria
McHenry	Northern	Rockford
McLean	Central	Peoria (Springfield)
Menard	Central	Springfield
Mercer	Central	Rock Island (Peoria)
Monroe	Southern	East St Louis
Montgomery	Central	Springfield
Morgan	Central	Springfield
Moultrie	Central	Danville/Urbana (Danville)
Ogle	Northern	Rockford
Peoria	Central	Peoria
Perry	Southern	Benton
Piatt	Central	Danville/Urbana (Danville)
Pike	Central	Springfield
Pope	Southern	Benton
Pulaski	Southern	Benton
Putnam	Central	Peoria
Randolph	Southern	East St Louis
Richland	Southern	Benton (East St Louis)
Rock Island	Central	Rock Island (Peoria)
Saline	Southern	Benton
Sangamon	Central	Springfield
Schuyler	Central	Springfield
Scott	Central	Springfield
Shelby	Central	Springfield
St. Clair	Southern	East St Louis
Stark	Central	Peoria
Stephenson	Northern	Rockford
Tazewell	Central	Peoria
Union	Southern	Benton
Vermilion	Central	Danville/Urbana (Danville)
Wabash	Southern	Benton
Warren	Central	Rock Island (Peoria)
Washington	Southern	East St Louis (Benton)
Wayne	Southern	Benton
White	Southern	Benton
Whiteside	Northern	Rockford
Will	Northern	Chicago (Eastern)
Williamson	Southern	Benton
Winnebago	Northern	Rockford
Woodford	Central	Peoria

Standards for Federal Courts: Search fee is $26.00 per item (one party name or case number). Copy fee is $.50 per page. Certification fee is $9.00 per document, double for exemplification, if available. All fees standard unless noted in profile. Mail Search: always enclose a stamped self addressed envelope unless otherwise noted. Most courts accept fax requests or will suggest a copying/search vendor. Before releasing records, all courts require prepayment, unless noted.

Open records are located at the court unless otherwise noted. District courts index by defendant and plaintiff as well as by case number. Bankruptcy courts usually index by debtor and case number. While most courts now have their indexes on computer, many may still maintain index card files as well.

Courts offering internet access via CM-ECF or older RACER, PACER, or Web-PACER systems charge $.08 per page fee unless noted as free. Where PACER is available, the universal sign-up number is 800-676-6856. Find PACER and the US Party/Case Index at http://pacer.psc.uscourts.gov.

US District Court

Central District of Illinois

Peoria Division US District Clerk Office, 309 Federal Bldg, 100 NE Monroe St, Peoria, IL 61602 (also use mail address for courier delivery), 309-671-7117, Fax-309-671-0780. Hours- 8AM-5PM. www.ilcd.uscourts.gov

Counties: Bureau, Fulton, Hancock, Knox, Livingston, McDonough, McLean, Marshall, Peoria, Putnam, Stark, Tazewell, Woodford.

Searches & Indexing: Results do not include SSN or DOB. Both computer and card indexes maintained; computer back to 1992. New cases in the index immediately after filing date. Records purged after 5-7 years. District-wide searches available for civil cases from 11/1989; criminal from 4/1992.

Fee & Payment: Pay by credit cards, money order, cashier check, law firm check. No personal or business checks accepted. Payee: Clerk, US District Court. Prepayment required.

Phone Search: No searching by telephone.

Mail Search: search usually completed- 1-2 weeks. Include SASE for return.

In Person Search: Fee charged if court performs your search. No self-serve copier available.

E-Services: ECF replaces PACER whose records did go back to 1995. New records online after 1 day. ECF at https://ecf.ilcd.uscourts.gov Opinions Online: www.ilcd.uscourts.gov/orders&opinions.htm.

Rock Island Division US District Clerk Office, Rm 40, US Court House, 211 19th St, Rock Island, IL 61201 (also use mail address for courier delivery), 309-793-5778, Fax-309-793-5878. Hours- 8AM-5PM. www.ilcd.uscourts.gov

Counties: Henderson, Henry, Mercer, Rock Island, Warren.

Searches & Indexing: Results do not include SSN or DOB; court will confirm them if asked. Computer index maintained. New cases in the index immediately after filing date. Records purged after 5-7 years. District-wide searches

available for civil cases from 11/1989; criminal from 4/1992.

Fee & Payment: Pay by money order, cashier check, business check. No personal checks. Payee: Clerk of US District Court. Prepayment required.

Phone Search: All information not sealed is available via phone.

Mail Search: search usually completed- 1-2 days. Include SASE for return.

In Person Search: Fee charged if court performs your search. No self-serve copier available.

E-Services: ECF replaces PACER whose records did go back to 1995. New records online after 1 day. ECF at https://ecf.ilcd.uscourts.gov Opinions Online: www.ilcd.uscourts.gov/orders&opinions.htm.

Springfield Division Clerk of Court, 151 US Courthouse, 600 E Monroe, Springfield, IL 62701 (also use mail address for courier delivery), 217-492-4020, Fax-217-492-4028. Hours- 8AM-5PM. www.ilcd.uscourts.gov

Counties: Adams, Brown, Cass, Christian, De Witt, Greene, Logan, Macoupin, Mason, Menard, Montgomery, Morgan, Pike, Sangamon, Schuyler, Scott, Shelby.

Searches & Indexing: Results do not include SSN or DOB; court will confirm them if asked. Both computer and card indexes maintained; civil on computer back to 1988; criminal to 1992. New cases in the index immediately after filing date. Records purged after 5-7 years. District-wide searches available for civil cases from 11/1989; criminal from 1992.

Fee & Payment: Pay by money order, cashier check, business check. No personal checks. Payee: US District Court Clerk. Prepayment required.

Phone Search: No searching by telephone.

Mail Search: search usually completed- 1 week. SASE not required.

In Person Search: Fee charged if court performs your search. Self-serve copier available - $.50 per page.

E-Services: ECF replaces PACER whose records did go back to 1995. New records online after 1 day. ECF at https://ecf.ilcd.uscourts.gov Opinions Online: www.ilcd.uscourts.gov/orders&opinions.htm.

Urbana Division Court Clerk, 201 S Vine, Rm 218, Urbana, IL 61802 (also use mail address for courier delivery), 217-373-5830, Fax-217-373-5830. Hours- 8AM-5PM. www.ilcd.uscourts.gov

Counties: Champaign, Coles, Douglas, Edgar, Ford, Iroquois, Kankakee, Macon, Moultrie, Piatt, Vermilion.

Searches & Indexing: Results do not include SSN or DOB. Both computer and card indexes maintained; computer index goes back to 1989. New cases in the index immediately after filing date. Records purged after 5-7 years. District-wide searches available here for civil records from 11/1989; criminal from 4/1992.

Fee & Payment: Pay by money order, cashier check, business check. No personal checks. Payee: Clerk, US District Court. Prepayment required.

Phone Search: Only docket information available by phone.

Mail Search: search usually completed- 1 week. Include SASE for return.

In Person Search: Fee charged if court performs your search. No self-serve copier available - $.50 per page.

E-Services: ECF replaces PACER whose records did go back to 1995. New records online after 1 day. ECF at https://ecf.ilcd.uscourts.gov Opinions Online: www.ilcd.uscourts.gov/orders&opinions.htm.

US Bankruptcy Court

Central District of Illinois

Danville Division Court Clerk, 201 N Vermilion #130, Danville, IL 61832-4733 (also use mail address for courier delivery), 217-431-4820, Fax-217-431-2694. Hours- 7:30AM-4:30PM. www.ilcb.uscourts.gov

Counties: Champaign, Coles, Douglas, Edgar, Ford, Iroquois, Kankakee, Livingston, Moultrie, Piatt, Vermilion.

Searches & Indexing: Results include last 4 SSN digits. Computer index maintained. After 4/04 all records on computer only. New cases in the index 24 hours after filing date. Records purged immediately when case closed.

Fee & Payment: Pay by money order, cashier check, business check. No personal checks. Payee: US Bankruptcy Court. Prepayment required. Will fax documents for fee depending on where.

Phone Search: Docket information available via phone. Voice Case Information Service available, call VCIS at 800-827-9005 or 217-492-4550.

Mail Search: search usually completed- 1-2 days. Include SASE for return.

In Person Search: Fee charged if court performs your search. No self-serve copier available.

E-Services: PACER online at http://pacer.ilcb.uscourts.gov for pre-2004 cases. PACER records go back to 1989-90. New records online after 1 day. ECF at https://ecf.ilcb.uscourts.gov Opinions Online: www.ilcb.uscourts.gov/Opinions/opinions.asp. Other Online Access: Hearing calendars free at https://ecf.ilcb.uscourts.gov/cgi-bin/PublicCalendar.pl.

Peoria Division Court Clerk, Rm 216, 100 NE Monroe, Peoria, IL 61602 (also use mail address for courier delivery), 309-671-7035, Fax-309-671-7076. Hours- 8AM-5PM. www.ilcb.uscourts.gov

Counties: Bureau, Fulton, Hancock, Henderson, Henry, Knox, Marshall, McDonough, Mercer, Peoria, Putnam, Rock Island, Stark, Tazewell, Warren, Woodford.

Searches & Indexing: Results include last 4 SSN digits. Computer index maintained. New cases in the index 24 hours after filing date. Records purged immediately when case closed.

Fee & Payment: Pay by money order, cashier check, business check. No personal checks. Payee: US Bankruptcy Court. Will invoice for copy fees only.

Phone Search: Voice Case Information Service available, call VCIS at 800-827-9005 or 217-492-4550.

Mail Search: search usually completed- 1-2 days. Include SASE for return. You may fax for a fee quote.

In Person Search: Fee charged if court performs your search. No self-serve copier available.

E-Services: PACER online at http://pacer.ilcb.uscourts.gov for pre-2004 cases. PACER records go back to 1989-90. New records online after 1 day. ECF at https://ecf.ilcb.uscourts.gov **Opinions Online:** www.ilcb.uscourts.gov/Opinions/opinions.asp. **Other Online Access:** Hearing calendars free at https://ecf.ilcb.uscourts.gov/cgi-bin/PublicCalendar.pl.

Springfield Division Court Clerk, 600 E Monroe St, 226 US Courthouse, Springfield, IL 62701 (also use mail address for courier delivery), 217-492-4551, Fax-217-492-4556. Hours- 8AM-5PM. www.ilcb.uscourts.gov

Counties: Adams, Brown, Cass, Christian, De Witt, Greene, Logan, Macon, Macoupin, Mason, McLean, Menard, Montgomery, Morgan, Pike, Sangamon, Schuyler, Scott, Shelby.

Searches & Indexing: Results include last 4 SSN digits. Computer index maintained. After 4/12/04 all records on computer only. New cases in the index 24 hours after filing date. Records purged immediately when case closed.

Fee & Payment: Pay by money order, cashier check, business check. No personal checks. Payee: US Bankruptcy Court. Will invoice for copy fees only.

Phone Search: Voice Case Information Service available, call VCIS at 800-827-9005 or 217-492-4550.

Mail Search: search usually completed- 2-3 days. Include SASE for return.

In Person Search: Fee charged if court performs your search. No self-serve copier available.

E-Services: PACER online at http://pacer.ilcb.uscourts.gov for pre-2004 cases. PACER records go back to 1989-90. New records online after 1 day. ECF at https://ecf.ilcb.uscourts.gov **Opinions Online:** www.ilcb.uscourts.gov/Opinions/opinions.asp. **Other Online Access:** Hearing calendars free at https://ecf.ilcb.uscourts.gov/cgi-bin/PublicCalendar.pl.

US District Court

Northern District of Illinois

Chicago (Eastern) Division Court Clerk, 20th Fl, 219 S Dearborn St, Chicago, IL 60604 (also use mail address for courier delivery), 312-435-5698, records rm- 312-435-5699, 312-435-5863, Fax-312-554-8512. Hours- 8:30AM-4:30PM; phone inquires 8:15-5PM. www.ilnd.uscourts.gov

Counties: Cook, Du Page, Grundy, Kane, Kendall, Lake, La Salle, Will.

Searches & Indexing: Results do not include SSN or DOB. Computer index back to 2005 maintained; also on microfiche. New cases in the index 2 days after filing date. Records purged varies.

Fee & Payment: Pay by Visa/MC (in person only), money order, cashier's or personal check. No checks accepted for criminal bail. Payee: Clerk, US District Court. Prepayment required.

Phone Search: Only docket information available by phone. Phone inquiries may be made from 8:15AM-5PM.

Mail Search: search usually completed- 2 days. Include SASE for return.

In Person Search: Fee charged if court performs your search. Self-serve copier available - $.25 per page.

E-Services: ECF replaces PACER whose records did go back to 1988. New records online after 1 day. ECF at https://ecf.ilnd.uscourts.gov **Opinions Online:** www.ilnd.uscourts.gov/RACER2/index.html. **Other Online Access:** Online ruling data at www.nysd.uscourts.gov/courtweb/public.htm.

Rockford (Western) Division Court Clerk, Rm 211, 211 S Court St, Rockford, IL 61101 (also use mail address for courier delivery), 815-987-4355, Fax-815-987-4291. Hours- 8:30AM-4:30PM; phone inquires 8:15-5PM. www.ilnd.uscourts.gov

Counties: Boone, Carroll, De Kalb, Jo Daviess, Lee, McHenry, Ogle, Stephenson, Whiteside, Winnebago.

Searches & Indexing: Results do not include SSN or DOB. Computer index maintained. New cases in the index 1-3 days after filing date. Records purged varies.

Fee & Payment: Pay by money order, cashier's or personal check. Payee: Clerk, US District Court. Prepayment required.

Phone Search: No searching by telephone.

Mail Search: search usually completed- 1-2 days. Any indictments, pending information, case numbers and docket sheets (if specifically requested) are released. SASE not required.

In Person Search: permitted. No self-serve copier available.

E-Services: ECF replaces PACER whose records did go back to 1988. New records online after 1 day. ECF at https://ecf.ilnd.uscourts.gov **Opinions Online:** www.ilnd.uscourts.gov/RACER2/index.html. **Other Online Access:** Online ruling data at www.nysd.uscourts.gov/courtweb/public.htm.

US Bankruptcy Court

Northern District of Illinois

Chicago (Eastern) Division Court Clerk, 219 S Dearborn St, Chicago, IL 60604-1802 (also use mail address for courier delivery), 312-435-5694, records rm- 312-435-5862, Fax-312-408-7750. Hours- 9AM-4:30PM. www.ilnb.uscourts.gov

Counties: Cook, Du Page, Grundy, Kane, Kendall, La Salle, Lake, Will.

Searches & Indexing: Results include last 4 SSN digits. Computer index maintained. New cases in the index 1 day after filing date. Records purged never.

Fee & Payment: Pay by money order, cashier check, business check. No personal checks. Payee: Clerk, US Bankruptcy Court. Prepayment required.

Phone Search: If case number is provided by phone, any docket sheet data is released via phone Voice Case Information Service available, call VCIS at 888-232-6814 or 312-408-5089.

Mail Search: search usually completed- 1 week. Include SASE for return.

In Person Search: Fee charged if court performs your search. Copying available via Ikon Copy Svc, 312-913-9508. Self-serve copier available - $.28 per page.

E-Services: Access to PACER/RACER is available at the website. Document images available. PACER records go back to 7/1993. New records online after 1 day. ECF at https://ecf.ilnb.uscourts.gov **Other Online Access:** Case Image Viewing is available from 5AM to 11:59 p.m. CST at www.ilnb.uscourts.gov/casenotice.htm. Access fee is $.08 per page.

Rockford Division Court Clerk, Rm 110, 211 S Court St, Rockford, IL 61101 (also use mail address for courier delivery), 815-987-4350, Fax-815-987-4205. Hours- 9AM-4:30PM. www.ilnb.uscourts.gov

Counties: Boone, Carroll, De Kalb, Jo Daviess, Lee, McHenry, Ogle, Stephenson, Whiteside, Winnebago.

Searches & Indexing: Cases indexed by debtor, creditors, and case number. Results include last 4 SSN digits. Computer index back to 1994 maintained. New cases in the index immediately after filing date.

Fee & Payment: Pay by money order, cashier's or personal check. No debtor's checks accepted. Payee: Clerk, US Bankruptcy Court.

Phone Search: Only docket information is available by phone. Voice Case Information Service available, call VCIS at 888-232-6814.

Mail Search: search usually completed- 10 days. Include SASE for return.

In Person Search: Fee charged if court performs your search. No self-serve copier available.

E-Services: Access to PACER/RACER is available at the website. Document images available. PACER records go back to 1992. New records online after 1 day. ECF at https://ecf.ilnb.uscourts.gov **Other Online Access:** Case Image Viewing is available from 5AM to 11:59PM CST at www.ilnb.uscourts.gov/casenotice.htm. Access fee is $.08 per page.

US District Court

Southern District of Illinois

Benton Division Court Clerk, 301 W Main St, Benton, IL 62812 (also use mail address for courier delivery), 618-439-7760. Hours- 9AM-4:30PM. www.ilsd.uscourts.gov

Counties: Alexander, Clark, Clay, Crawford, Cumberland, Edwards, Effingham, Franklin, Gallatin, Hamilton, Hardin, Jackson, Jasper, Jefferson, Johnson, Lawrence, Massac, Perry, Pope, Pulaski, Richland, Saline, Union, Wabash, Wayne, White, Williamson. Cases may also be allocated to the Benton Division.

Searches & Indexing: Name and date required to search for records. Results do not include SSN or DOB. Computer, microfiche and card indexes maintained. New cases in the index immediately after filing date. Records purged as deemed necessary.

Fee & Payment: Pay by money order, cashier's or personal check. Payee: Clerk, US District Court. Except in an emergency, prepayment required.

Phone Search: Docket information available via phone.

Mail Search: search usually completed- 2 days. Include SASE for return.

In Person Search: Fee charged if court performs your search. Self-serve copier available - $.50 per page.

E-Services: ECF replaces PACER whose records did go back to 1985. New records online after 1 day. ECF at https://ecf.ilsd.uscourts.gov **Opinions Online:** www.ilsd.uscourts.gov/opinions.cfm.

East St Louis Division Court Clerk, PO Box 249, East St Louis, IL 62202 (courier address: 750 Missouri Ave, East St Louis, IL 62201), 618-482-9371, records rm- 618-482-9371. Hours- 9AM-4:30PM. www.ilsd.uscourts.gov

Counties: Bond, Calhoun, Clinton, Fayette, Jersey, Madison, Marion, Monroe, Randolph, St. Clair, Washington. Cases for these counties may also be allocated to the Benton Division.

Searches & Indexing: Name and date required to search for records. Results do not include SSN or DOB. Computer, microfiche and card indexes maintained, computer back to 1990. New cases in the index immediately after filing date. Records purged as deemed necessary.

Fee & Payment: Pay by money order, cashier's or personal check. Payee: Clerk, US District Court. Except in an emergency, prepayment required.

Phone Search: Docket information available via phone.

Mail Search: search usually completed- 2 days. Include SASE for return.

In Person Search: Fee charged if court performs your search. You may make copies only if arrangement made with bonded vendor. No self-serve copier available - $.50 per page.

E-Services: ECF replaces PACER whose records did go back to 1985. New records online after 1 day. ECF at https://ecf.ilsd.uscourts.gov **Opinions Online:** www.ilsd.uscourts.gov/opinions.cfm.

US Bankruptcy Court

Southern District of Illinois

Benton Division Court Clerk, 301 W Main, Benton, IL 62812 (also use mail address for courier delivery), 618-435-2200. Hours- 8AM-4:30PM. www.ilsb.uscourts.gov

Counties: Alexander, Edwards, Franklin, Gallatin, Hamilton, Hardin, Jackson, Jefferson, Johnson, Massac, Perry, Pope, Pulaski, Randolph, Saline, Union, Wabash, Washington, Wayne, White, Williamson.

Searches & Indexing: Results do not include SSN or DOB. New cases in the index immediately after filing date. Records purged as deemed necessary.

Fee & Payment: Pay by Visa/MC, money order, cashier check, business check. No personal checks accepted. Payee: Clerk, US Bankruptcy Court. Prepayment required.

Phone Search: Voice Case Information Service available, call VCIS at 800-726-5622 or 618-482-9365.

Mail Search: search usually completed- within 1-2 days. Include SASE for return.

In Person Search: Fee charged if court performs your search. No self-serve copier available.

E-Services: ECF replaces PACER whose records did go back to 1/1989. New records online immediately. ECF at https://ecf.ilsb.uscourts.gov **Opinions Online:** www.ilsb.uscourts.gov/search_main/opinionsearch.asp.

East St Louis Division Court Clerk, 750 Missouri Ave, East St Louis, IL 62201 (also use mail address for courier delivery), 618-482-9400. Hours- 8AM-4:30PM. www.ilsb.uscourts.gov

Counties: Bond, Calhoun, Clark, Clay, Clinton, Crawford, Cumberland, Effingham, Fayette, Jasper, Jersey, Lawrence, Madison, Marion, Monroe, Richland, St. Clair.

Searches & Indexing: Results do not include SSN or DOB. Records also indexed on microfiche. New cases in the index immediately after filing date. Records purged as deemed necessary. District-wide searches available here.

Fee & Payment: Pay by Visa/MC, money order, cashier's or personal check. No debtor's checks accepted. Payee: Clerk, US Bankruptcy Court. Prepayment required.

Phone Search: Voice Case Information Service available, call 800-726-5622 or 618-482-9365.

Mail Search: search usually completed- within 1-2 days. SASE required.

In Person Search: Fee charged if court performs your search. No self-serve copier available.

E-Services: ECF replaces PACER whose records did go back to 1/1989. New records online after 1 day. ECF at https://ecf.ilsb.uscourts.gov **Opinions Online:** www.ilsb.uscourts.gov/search_main/opinionsearch.asp.

Illinois County Courts

Court	Jurisdiction	No. of Courts	How Organized
Circuit Courts*	General	106	22 Circuits

* Profiled in this Sourcebook.

	CIVIL								
Court	Tort	Contract	Real Estate	Min. Claim	Max. Claim	Small Claims	Estate	Eviction	Domestic Relations
Circuit Courts*	X	X	X	$0	No Max	$5000	X	X	X

	CRIMINAL				
Court	Felony	Misdemeanor	DWI/DUI	Preliminary Hearing	Juvenile
Circuit Courts*	X	X	X	X	X

ADMINISTRATION Administrative Office of Courts, 222 N LaSalle 13th Floor, Chicago, IL, 60601; 312-793-3250, Fax: 312-793-1335. www.state.il.us/court/

COURT STRUCTURE Illinois is divided into 22 judicial circuits; 3 are single county: Cook, Du Page (18th Circuit) and Will (12th Circuit). The other 19 circuits consist of 2 or more contiguous counties. The Circuit Court of Cook County is the largest unified court system in the world. Its 2300-person staff handles approximately 2.4 million cases each year. The civil part of the various Circuit Courts in Cook County is divided as follows: under $30,000 are "civil cases" and over $30,000 are "civil law division cases."

Probate is handled by the Circuit Court in all counties.

ONLINE ACCESS While there is no statewide public online system available, other than appellate and supreme court opinions from the web site. A number of Illinois Circuit Courts offer online access, many through a vendor at www.judici.com.

ADDITIONAL INFORMATION The search fee is set by statute and has three levels based on the county population. The higher the population, the larger the fee. In most courts, both civil and criminal data is on computer from the same starting date. In most Illinois courts the search fee is charged on a per name per year basis.

Adams County

Circuit Court 521 Vermont St, Quincy, IL 62301; phone: 217-277-2100; probate phone: 217-277-2108; fax: 217-277-2116; hours 8:15AM-4:30PM (CST). *Felony, Misdemeanor, Civil, Eviction, Small Claims, Probate.*
www.co.adams.il.us
Civil Records: Access: Phone, mail, fax, in person, online, email. Both court and visitors may perform in person searches. Search fee: $6.00 per name. Fee is $10.00 for years prior to 1987. Court makes copy: $.50 each. Required to search: name, years to search. Civil cases indexed by defendant, plaintiff. Civil records on computer from 1987, books and index cards from 1920. Online access to 8th Circuit Clerk of Court records is free at www.judici.com/courts/cases/case_search.jsp?court=IL001025J. Search by name, case or docket number back to 1987. Mail turnaround 2-3 days.
Criminal Records: Access: Phone, mail, fax, in person, online, email. Both court and visitors may perform in person searches. Search fee: $6.00 per name. Fee is $10.00 for years prior to 1987. Court makes copy: $.50 each. Required to search: name, years to search, DOB. Criminal records on computer from 1987, books and index cards from 1920. Online access to criminal records is the same as civil. The county inmate list and warrant list is at the home page. Mail turnaround 2-3 days.
General Information: Public use terminal available. No juvenile or adoption records released. Certification fee: $6.00. Payee: Clerk of Circuit Court. Personal checks accepted. Prepayment and SASE required.

Alexander County

Circuit Court 2000 Washington Ave, Cairo, IL 62914; phone: 618-734-0107; fax: 618-734-7003; hours 8AM-N-1-4PM (CST). *Felony, Misdemeanor, Civil, Eviction, Small Claims, Probate.*
Civil Records: Access: Fax, mail, in person. Only the court performs in person searches; visitors may not. Search fee: $6.00 per name per year. Court makes copy: $2.00 for first page, $.50 each add'l. Required to search: name, years to search. Civil cases indexed by defendant, plaintiff. Civil records on computer from 1987, books and index cards from 1800s. Mail turnaround time 1 day.
Criminal Records: Access: Fax, mail, in person. Only the court performs in person searches; visitors may not. Search fee: $6.00 per name per year. Court makes copy: $2.00 for first page, $.50 each add'l. Required to search: name. Criminal records on computer from 1987, books and index cards from 1800s. Mail turnaround time 1 day.
General Information: No public access terminal. No juvenile or adoption records released. Will fax documents to local or toll free line. Certification fee: $6.00 per cert. Payee: Clerk of Circuit Court. Business checks accepted but no personal checks or credit cards. Prepayment and SASE required.

Bond County

Circuit Court 200 W College Ave, Greenville, IL 62246; phone: 618-664-3208; fax: 618-664-2257; hours 8AM-4:30PM (CST). *Felony, Misdemeanor, Civil, Small Claims, Probate.*
www.johnkking.com

Civil Records: Access: Mail, in person, online. Both court and visitors may perform in person searches. Search fee: $5.00 per name per year. Court makes copy: $.50 per page; same fee for self serve. Required to search: name, years to search. Civil cases indexed by defendant, plaintiff. Civil records on computer back to 1/87 (and are limited); in index books from 1900s. Online access is same as criminal, see below. Mail turnaround time 1 day.
Criminal Records: Access: Mail, in person, online. Both court and visitors may perform in person searches. Search fee: $5.00 per name per year. Court makes copy: $.50 per page; same fee for self serve. Required to search: name, years to search, DOB. Criminal records on computer back to 1964; index books from 1900s. Online access is free at www.judici.com/courts/cases/index.jsp?court=IL003015J. Premium/fee service is also available. Mail turnaround time 1-2 weeks.
General Information: Public terminal has criminal back to 1964 and civil back to 1987. No juvenile or adoption records released. Will not fax documents. Certification fee: $5.00. Payee: Clerk of Circuit Court. Personal checks accepted. Prepayment and SASE required.

Boone County

Circuit Court 601 N Main, #303, Belvidere, IL 61008; phone: 815-544-0371; hours 8:30AM-5PM (CST). *Felony, Misdemeanor, Civil, Eviction, Small Claims, Probate.*
www.boonecountyil.org/deptframeset.htm
Civil Records: Access: Mail, in person, online. Both court and visitors may perform in person searches.

Search fee: $6.00 per name per year. Court makes copy: $2.00 for 1st page, $.50 each add'l. Required to search: name, years to search. Civil cases indexed by defendant, plaintiff. Civil records on computer since 8/1993, on index books from 1800s. Search cases free online at www.judici.com/courts/cases/case_search.jsp?court=IL004015J. Also, a more convenient premium fee service is available. Mail turnaround time 1-2 days.

Criminal Records: Access: Mail, in person, online. Both court and visitors may perform in person searches. Search fee: $6.00 per name per year. Court makes copy: $2.00 for 1st page, $.50 each add'l. Required to search: name, years to search, DOB. Records on computer since 8/1993, on index books from 1800s. Online access is the same as civil. Mail turnaround time 1-2 days.

General Information: Public terminal goes back to 8/1993. No juvenile or adoption records released. Certification fee: $6.00 per document. Payee: Clerk of Circuit Court. Personal checks may be accepted. Prepayment and SASE required.

Brown County

Circuit Court Brown County Courthouse, 200 Court St, Rm 5, Mt Sterling, IL 62353; phone: 217-773-2713; fax: 217-773-3648; hours 8:30AM-4:30PM (CST). *Felony, Misdemeanor, Civil, Eviction, Small Claims, Probate.*

Civil Records: Access: Phone, fax, mail, in person. Both court and visitors may perform in person searches. Search fee: $4.00 per name per year. Court makes copy: $.35 per page. Required to search: name, years to search. Civil cases indexed by defendant, plaintiff. Civil records on computer since 1994, on index books from 1830s. Mail turnaround time 1 week.

Criminal Records: Access: Phone, fax, mail, in person. Both court and visitors may perform in person searches. Search fee: $4.00 per name per year. Court makes copy: $.35 per page. Required to search: name, years to search, DOB, signed release. Criminal records on computer since 1994, on index books from 1830s. Mail turnaround time 1 week.

General Information: Public terminal has criminal back to 1994 and civil back to 1994. No juvenile or adoption records released. Will fax documents $3.00 per page. Certification fee: $2.00. Payee: Clerk of Circuit Court. Only cashiers checks and money orders accepted. Prepayment and SASE required.

Bureau County

Circuit Court 702 S Main, Princeton, IL 61356; phone: 815-872-2001; fax: 815-872-0027; hours 8AM-4PM (CST). *Felony, Misdemeanor, Civil, Eviction, Small Claims, Probate.*
www.bccirclk.gov
Civil Records: Access: Online, in person. Both court and visitors may perform in person searches. Search fee: $4.00 per name per year. Court makes copy: $.50 per page. Required to search: name, years to search. Civil cases indexed by defendant, plaintiff. Civil records on computer from 8/1988, prior on index books. Online access to judicial circuit records is free at www.bccirclk.gov/remote.htm. Click on "JIMS". Index includes dates, defendants, record sheets and dispositions and goes back to 8/1988.

Criminal Records: Access: Mail, in person, online. Both court and visitors may perform in person searches. Search fee: $6.00 per name per year. Court makes copy: $.50 per page. Required to search: name, years to search, DOB. Criminal records on computer from 8/1988, prior on index books. Online access to criminal records is the same as civil. Mail turnaround time 1 week.

General Information: Public use terminal available. No juvenile or adoption records released. Fee to fax documents is $2.00 1st pg; $1.00 each add'l. Certification fee: $6.00. Payee: Bureau County Circuit Clerk. Personal checks accepted. Prepayment and SASE required.

Calhoun County

Circuit Court PO Box 486, Hardin, IL 62047; phone: 618-576-2451; fax: 618-576-9541; hours 8:30AM-4:30PM (CST). *Felony, Misdemeanor, Civil, Eviction, Small Claims, Probate.*
Note: Probate is a separate index at this same address.
Civil Records: Access: Phone, fax, mail, in person. Both court and visitors may perform in person searches. Search fee: $6.00 per name. Court makes copy: $2.00 for first page. $.50 per page, pages 2-19; $.25 each add'l page; same fee for self serve. Required to search: name, years to search. Civil cases indexed by defendant, plaintiff. Civil records on index books from 1800s, computerized since 7/98. Mail turnaround time 1 day.

Criminal Records: Access: Phone, fax, mail, in person. Both court and visitors may perform in person searches. Search fee: $6.00 per name. Court makes copy: $2.00 for first page. $.50 per page, pages 2-19; $.25 each add'l page; same fee for self serve. Required to search: name, years to search, DOB. Criminal records on index books from 1800s, computerized since 7/98. Mail turnaround time 1 day.

General Information: No public access terminal. No juvenile or adoption records released. No fee to fax documents. Certification fee: $2.00. Payee: Clerk of Circuit Court. Only cashiers checks and money orders accepted. Prepayment and SASE required.

Carroll County

Circuit Court 301 N Main St, PO Box 32, Mt Carroll, IL 61053; phone: 815-244-0230; fax: 815-244-3869; hours 8:30AM-4:30PM (CST). *Felony, Misdemeanor, Civil, Eviction, Small Claims, Probate.*

Civil Records: Access: Mail, in person, online. Both court and visitors may perform in person searches. Search fee: $6.00 per name per year. Court makes copy: $2.00 for first page, $.50 each add'l. Required to search: name, years to search. Civil cases indexed by defendant. Civil records on computer from 1988, prior on index books. Access is free to civil, small claims, probate and traffic records at www.judici.com/courts/index.jsp?court=IL008015J. Records go back to 1988. Mail turnaround time 2-3 days.

Criminal Records: Access: Mail, in person, online. Both court and visitors may perform in person searches. Search fee: $6.00 per name per year. Court makes copy: $2.00 for first page, $.50 each add'l. Required to search: name, years to search, DOB. Criminal records on computer from 1988, prior on index books. Criminal records access is free at www.judici.com/courts/index.jsp?court=IL008015J. Records go back to 1988. Mail turnaround time 2-3 days.

General Information: Public terminal goes back to 1988. No juvenile, mental health or adoption records released. Will not fax documents. Certification fee: $10.00 per doc. Payee: Clerk of Circuit Court. Local personal checks accepted. Prepayment and SASE required.

Cass County

Circuit Court PO Box 203, Virginia, IL 62691; phone: 217-452-7225; hours 8:30AM-4:30PM (CST). *Felony, Misdemeanor, Civil, Eviction, Small Claims, Probate.*

Civil Records: Access: Mail, in person. Visitors must perform in person searches themselves. Search fee: $6.00 per name per year, for search conducted by staff. Court makes copy: $1.00 for first page, $.50 each add'l. Required to search: name, years to search. Civil cases indexed by defendant, plaintiff. Civil records on index books from 1800s. Mail turnaround time 1-2 weeks.

Criminal Records: Access: Mail, in person. Visitors must perform in person searches themselves. Search fee: $6.00 per name per year, for search performed by staff. Court makes copy: $1.00 for first page, $.50 each add'l. Required to search: name, years

to search, DOB; also helpful: SSN. Criminal records on index books from 1800s, on computer back to 1998. Mail turnaround time 1-2 weeks.

General Information: Public terminal goes back to 8/8/98. No juvenile or adoption records released. Will not fax documents. Certification fee: $5.00 for up to 19 pages. Payee: Cass County Circuit Clerk. Personal checks accepted. No credit cards accepted. Prepayment and SASE required.

Champaign County

Circuit Court 101 E Main, Urbana, IL 61801; criminal phone: 217-384-3727; civil phone: 217-384-3725; fax: 217-384-3879; hours 8:30AM-4:30PM (CST). *Felony, Misdemeanor, Civil, Eviction, Small Claims, Probate.*
www.cccircuitclerk.com
Civil Records: Access: Mail, online, in person. Both court and visitors may perform in person searches. Search fee: $4.00 per name per year. Court makes copy: $1.50 1st page, $.50 add'l page. Required to search: name, years to search. Civil cases indexed by defendant, plaintiff. Civil records on computer from 1986, index books from 1800s. Access to the circuit clerk's case query online system formerly called PASS is now free at https://secure.jtsmith.com/clerk/clerk.asp. Online case records go back to '92. Mail turnaround time 1-2 weeks.

Criminal Records: Access: Mail, online, in person. Both court and visitors may perform in person searches. Search fee: $4.00 per name per year. Court makes copy: $1.50 1st page, $.50 add'l page. Required to search: name, years to search; also helpful: DOB, SSN. Criminal records on computer from 1988, index books from 1800s. Online access to criminal records is the same as civil. Mail turnaround time 1-2 weeks.

General Information: Public use terminal available. No juvenile or adoption records released. Will fax documents for $1.00 1st page, $.50 ea add'l. Certification fee: $2.00. Payee: Clerk of Circuit Court. Personal checks accepted. Prepayment and SASE required.

Christian County

Circuit Court PO Box 617, Taylorville, IL 62568; phone: 217-824-4966; fax: 217-824-5030; hours 8AM-4PM (CST). *Felony, Misdemeanor, Civil, Eviction, Small Claims, Probate.*
Civil Records: Access: Phone, mail, in person. Both court and visitors may perform in person searches. Search fee: $5.00 per name per year. Court makes copy: $1.00 for first page, $.50 each add'l. Required to search: name; also helpful: years to search. Civil cases indexed by defendant, plaintiff. Civil records on computer from 1988, index books from 1840. Mail turnaround time 1-2 days.

Criminal Records: Access: Phone, mail, in person. Both court and visitors may perform in person searches. Search fee: $5.00 per name per year. Court makes copy: $1.00 for first page, $.50 each add'l. Required to search: name; also helpful: years to search, DOB. Criminal records on computer from 1988, index books from 1840. Mail turnaround time 1-2 days.

General Information: Public terminal goes back to 1988. No juvenile or adoption records released. Will fax documents to toll free or local number. Certification fee: $2.00. Payee: Clerk of Circuit Court. Business checks accepted. Prepayment and SASE required.

Clark County

Circuit Court PO Box 187, Marshall, IL 62441; phone: 217-826-2811; criminal phone: 217-826-2811; hours 8AM-4PM (CST). *Felony, Misdemeanor, Civil, Eviction, Small Claims, Probate.*
Civil Records: Access: Mail, in person. Both court and visitors may perform in person searches. Search fee: $6.00 per name per year. Court makes

copy: $2.00 for first page, $.50 each add'l. After 20 pages, fee is $.25 per page. Required to search: name, years to search; also helpful: address. Civil cases indexed by defendant, plaintiff. Civil records on computer from 1989, index books from 1800s. Mail turnaround time 1 week.

Criminal Records: Access: Mail, in person. Both court and visitors may perform in person searches. Search fee: $6.00 per name per year. Court makes copy: $2.00 for first page, $.50 each add'l. $.25 per page after 20. Required to search: name, years to search, DOB, signed release; also helpful: address, SSN. Criminal records on computer from 1989, index books from 1800s. Mail turnaround time 1 week.

General Information: Public use terminal available. No juvenile, maternity, or adoption records released. Certification fee: $6.00. Payee: Clerk of Circuit Court. Only cashiers checks and money orders accepted. Prepayment and SASE required.

Clay County

Circuit Court PO Box 100, Louisville, IL 62858; phone: 618-665-3523; fax: 618-665-3543; hours 8AM-4PM (CST). *Felony, Misdemeanor, Civil, Eviction, Small Claims, Probate.*

Civil Records: Access: Fax, mail, in person. Both court and visitors may perform in person searches. Search fee: $5.00 per name. Fee is $5.00 per year prior to 1988. Court makes copy: $1.00 for first page, $.50 each add'l 19; $.25 each thereafter. Required to search: name, years to search. Civil cases indexed by defendant. Civil records on computer from 1988, index books from 1850s. Mail turnaround time 2-3 days.

Criminal Records: Access: Fax, mail, in person. Both court and visitors may perform in person searches. Search fee: $5.00 per name. Fee is $5.00 per year prior to 1988. Court makes copy: $1.00 for first page, $.50 each add'l 19; $.25 each add'l. Required to search: name, years to search; also helpful: DOB. Criminal records on computer from 1988, index books from 1850s. Mail turnaround time 2-3 days.

General Information: Public terminal goes back to 1988. No juvenile or adoption records released. Will fax documents for $1.00 1st page, $.50 each add'l. Certification fee: $6.00. Payee: Clerk of Circuit Court. No personal checks accepted. Prepayment and SASE required.

Clinton County

Circuit Court County Courthouse, PO Box 407, Carlyle, IL 62231; phone: 618-594-2464; hours 8AM-4PM (CST). *Felony, Misdemeanor, Civil, Eviction, Small Claims, Probate.*

Civil Records: Access: Mail, in person. Both court and visitors may perform in person searches. Search fee: $10.00 per name. Fee is for 10 year search. Court makes copy: $.50 per page. Required to search: name, years to search. Civil cases indexed by defendant, plaintiff. Civil records on computer from 1988, index books from 1825. Mail turnaround time 2-4 days.

Criminal Records: Access: Mail, in person. Both court and visitors may perform in person searches. Search fee: $10.00 per name. Flat fee for 10 year search. Court makes copy: $.50 per page. Required to search: name, years to search, DOB. Criminal records on computer from 1988, index books from 1825. Mail turnaround time 2-4 days.

General Information: Public terminal goes back to 1988. No juvenile or adoption records released. Will not fax documents. Certification fee: $6.00 per document. Payee: Clerk of Circuit Court. Personal checks accepted. Prepayment and SASE required.

Coles County

Circuit Court PO Box 48, Charleston, IL 61920; phone: 217-348-0516; fax: 217-348-7324; hours 8:30AM-4:30PM (CST). *Felony, Misdemeanor, Civil, Eviction, Small Claims, Probate.*

Civil Records: Access: Fax, mail, in person, online. Both court and visitors may perform in person searches. Search fee: $6.00 per name per year. Court makes copy: $2.00 1st page, $.50 each add'l. Required to search: name, years to search. Civil cases indexed by defendant, plaintiff. Civil records on computer from 1989, index books from 1800s. Access is free to civil, small claims, probate and traffic records at www.judici.com/courts/index.jsp?court=IL015025 J, to 1989. Mail turnaround 1 day or same day.

Criminal Records: Access: Fax, mail, in person, online. Both court and visitors may perform in person searches. Search fee: $6.00 per name. Court makes copy: $2.00 1st page; $.50 per page. Required to search: name, years to search, DOB; also helpful: SSN. Criminal records on computer from 1989, index books from 1800s. Criminal records access is free at www.judici.com/courts/index.jsp?court=IL015025 J Mail turnaround time 1-2 days.

General Information: Public terminal has civil and criminal back to 1989. No juvenile or adoption records released. Will fax documents to local or toll free line. Certification fee: $6.00. Payee: Clerk of Circuit Court. Personal checks accepted. Prepayment and SASE required.

Cook County

Circuit Court - Criminal Division 2650 S California Ave, #526, Chicago, IL 60608; phone: 773-869-2965 records; 773-869-3140 Admin; criminal phone: 773-869-3677 Admin only; fax: 773-869-4511; hours 8:30AM-4:30PM (CST). *Felony.* www.cookcountyclerkofcourt.org

Note: Records Dept on 5th Fl. Cases are heard in six district courts within the county and each court also has a central index. This location houses felony records only, but both felony and misdemeanor are on this division's computer system.

Criminal Records: Access: Mail, Fax, in person. Both court and visitors may perform in person searches. Search fee: $9.00 per name per year. Court makes copy: $2.00 for first page, $.50 each add'l. $.25 per page after 20. Required to search: name, years to search, DOB; also helpful: SSN. Criminal records on computer since 1964; prior records on microfiche from 1800s. A search or record request form is online at http://198.173.15.31/forms/pdf_files/CriminalForm.pdf. No hard copies of misdemeanors here; you must get them from the branch where they are heard. Note: Fax requests must be prepaid. Mail turnaround time 7-10 days. Pre-2003 records are in archives and may take add'l 2-3 days to process.

General Information: Public terminal has criminal records back to 1985. (Multiple terminals in the lobby - includes felony and all misdemeanors from branches.) No juvenile or adoption records released. Certification fee: $9.00 per doc. Payee: Clerk of Circuit Court. Personal checks accepted with drivers license number. Prepayment and SASE required.

Circuit Court - Chicago District 1 50 W Washington, Rm 601, Chicago, IL 60602; phone: 312-603-5030; criminal phone: 312-603-4641; civil phone: 312-603-5145; probate phone: 312-603-6441; hours 8:30AM-4:30PM (CST). *Misdemeanor, Civil Action Under $100,000, Eviction, Small Claims, Probate.* www.cookcountyclerkofcourt.org

Note: Cases heard in 6 district courts within the county. Each court has a central index, but all case files wind up here. Probate is a separate division in Rm 1202.

Civil Records: Access: Phone, mail, online, in person. Both court and visitors may perform in person searches. Search fee: $9.00 per year. Court makes copy: $2.00 for first page, $.50 each add'l. Self serve copy fee: $.50 per page. Required to search: name, years to search. Civil cases indexed by defendant, plaintiff. Civil records on computer from 1983, index books from 1800s.

Search full case dockets free at www.cookcountyclerkofcourt.org/terms/full_docket_search/index.htm. Limited case snapshots are also online at www.cookcountyclerkofcourt.org/Terms/terms.htm. Search by name, number, or date. Data includes parties (up to 3), attorneys, case type, filing date, the ad damnum (amount of damages sought), division/district, and most current court date. An online search request form is at http://198.173.15.31/forms/pdf_files/CivilForm.pdf. Note: Court calls/calendars for 4 days at http://198.173.15.31/onlinecases/courtcall/CCsearchindex.asp. Phone inquiries to court to check case status only. Mail turnaround time 1 week.

Criminal Records: Access: Phone, mail, in person. Visitors must perform in person searches themselves. Search fee: $9.00 per year. Court makes copy: $2.00 for first page, $.50 each add'l. Self serve copy fee: $.50 per page. Required to search: name, years to search, DOB. Download criminal records search request form at http://198.173.15.31/forms/pdf_files/CriminalForm.pdf. Note: Search misdemeanors in person in Rm 1006. Phone inquiries to court to check case status only. Mail turnaround time 1 week.

General Information: Public terminal goes back to 1985. No juvenile or adoption records released. Certification fee: $9.00 per doc. Payee: Clerk of Circuit Court. On personal checks write your social security and driver's license numbers. Prepayment and SASE required.

Bridgeview District 5 10220 S 76th Ave, Rm 121, Bridgeview Court Bldg, Bridgeview, IL 60453; phone: 708-974-6500; criminal phone: 708-974-6421; hours 8:30-4:30PM (CST). *Felony, Misdemeanor, Civil Action Under $100,000, Eviction, Small Claims.* www.cookcountyclerkofcourt.org

Note: Alsip, Bedford Pk, Bridgeview, Burbank, Countryside, Evergreen Pk, Forest View, Hickory Hills, Hinsdale, Hodgkins, Hometown, Justice, Lagrange, Lemont, Lyons, McCook, Oak Lawn, Orland Hills, Palos Park, Stickney, Summit, West Haven, Willow Springs, Worth.

Civil Records: Access: Mail, online, in person. Visitors must perform in person searches themselves. Search fee: $9.00 per name this division. Court makes copy: $2.00 for first page, $.50 each add'l. Required to search: name, years to search. Civil cases indexed by defendant, plaintiff. Civil records computerized since 1985, microfiche to early 1970s. Online case information is available; see Circuit Court - Chicago Division for details. Mail turnaround time varies.

Criminal Records: Access: Mail, in person. Visitors must perform in person searches themselves. Search fee: $9.00 per name per division. Court makes copy: $2.00 for first page, $.50 each add'l. Required to search: name. Criminal records computerized since 1985, prior on microfiche to early 1970s. Felony mail requests- download criminal search request form at http://198.173.15.31/forms/pdf_files/CriminalForm.pdf; mail to Clerk of Circuit Court, Criminal Div - Records, 2650 S California, Chicago, IL 60608, 773-869-3147. Misdemeanor records (county-wide) are also located at Circuit Court - Chicago District 1, Richard J. Daley Ctr, 50 W. Washington Ave, Rm 1006, Chicago, IL 60602. Mail turnaround time varies.

General Information: Public terminal goes back to 1985. Certification fee: $9.00 per doc. Payee: Clerk of Circuit Court. On personal checks write your social security and driver's license numbers. No credit cards. SASE required.

Markham District 6 16501 S Kedzie Pkwy, Rm 119, Markham, IL 60426-5509; phone: 708-210-4551, 210-4553, 210-4455; criminal phone: 708-210-4588; hours 8:30AM-4:30PM (CST). *Felony, Misdemeanor, Civil Action Under $30,000, Eviction, Small Claims, Traffic.* www.cookcountyclerkofcourt.org

Note: Blue Is, Burnham, Calumet, Chicago Hgts, Crestwood, Crete, Dixmoor, Dolton, Flossmoor, Glenwood, Harvey, Hazelcrest, Homewood, Lansing, Lynwood, Markham, Matteson, Midlothian, Oak Forest, Posen, Riverdale, Robbins, Sauk Village, Tinley Pk.

Civil Records: Access: Mail, online, in person. Visitors must perform in person searches themselves. Search fee: $9.00 per name this division. Court makes copy: $2.00 for first page, $.50 each add'l. Self serve copy fee: $.25 per page. Required to search: name. Civil cases indexed by defendant, plaintiff. Civil records computerized since 1989. Online case information is available; see Circuit Court - Chicago Division for details.

Criminal Records: Access: Mail, in person. Visitors must perform in person searches themselves. Search fee: $9.00 per name this division. Court makes copy: $2.00 for first page, $.50 each add'l. Self serve copy fee: $.25 per page. Required to search: name, years to search. Misdemeanor records go back 10 years. Felony mail requests- download criminal search request form at http://198.173.15.31/forms/pdf_files/CriminalForm.pdf; mail to Clerk of Circuit Court, Criminal Div - Records, 2650 S California, Chicago, IL 60608, 773-869-3147. Misdemeanor records (county-wide) are also located at Circuit Court - Chicago District 1, Richard J. Daley Ctr, 50 W. Washington Ave, Rm 1006, Chicago, IL 60602. Mail turnaround time 2 weeks.

General Information: Public terminal has criminal back to 1985 and civil back to 1985. Will not fax documents. Certification fee: $9.00 per doc includes copies. Payee: Clerk of Circuit Court. On personal checks write your social security and driver's license numbers. No credit cards. Prepayment and SASE required.

Maywood District 4 1500 S Maybrook Dr, Rm 236, Maywood, IL 60153-2410; phone: 708-865-6040; criminal phone: 708-865-5517; civil phone: 708-865-5187; hours 8:30AM-4:30PM (CST). *Felony, Misdemeanor, Civil Action Under $100,000, Eviction, Small Claims.*

www.cookcountyclerkofcourt.org

Note: Bellwood, Berkeley, Berwyn, Broadview, Brookfield, Cicero, Elmwood Park, Forest Park, Franklin Park, Hillside, La Grange Park, Maywood, Melrose Park, Northlake, North Riverside, Oak Park, River Forest, River Grove, Riverside, Stone Park, Westchester.

Civil Records: Access: Mail, online, in person. Visitors must perform in person searches themselves. Search fee: $9.00 per name per division. Court makes copy: $2.00 for first page, $.50 each add'l. Required to search: name; also helpful: years to search. Civil cases indexed by defendant, plaintiff. Civil records computerized since 1982, docket books to 1970s, prior archived. Online case information is available; see Circuit Court - Chicago Division for details. Mail turnaround time varies.

Criminal Records: Access: Mail, in person. Visitors must perform in person searches themselves. Search fee: $9.00 per name per division. Court makes copy: $2.00 for first page, $.50 each add'l. Required to search: name, years to search, DOB. Felony mail requests- download criminal search request form at http://198.173.15.31/forms/pdf_files/CriminalForm.pdf; mail to Clerk of Circuit Court, Criminal Div - Records, 2650 S California, Chicago, IL 60608, 773-869-3147. Misdemeanor records (county-wide) are also located at Circuit Court - Chicago District 1, Richard J. Daley Ctr, 50 W. Washington Ave, Rm 1006, Chicago, IL 60602. Mail turnaround time varies.

General Information: Public use terminal available. Certification fee: $9.00 per doc. Payee: Clerk of Circuit Court. On personal checks write your social security and driver's license numbers. No credit cards. Prepayment and SASE required.

Rolling Meadows District 3 2121 Euclid Ave, Rolling Meadows, IL 60008-1566; phone: 847-818-3000; criminal phone: 847-818-2928; civil phone: 847-818-2300; fax: 847-818-2706; hours 8:30AM-4:30PM (CST). *Felony, Misdemeanor, Civil Action Under $100,000, Eviction, Small Claims.*

www.cookcountyclerkofcourt.org

Note: Arlington Hgts, Barrington, Bartlett, Bensonville, Buffalo Grove, Elgin, Elk Grove Village, Hanover Pk, Harwood Hgts, Inverness, Mt. Prospect, Norridge, Palatine, Prospect Hgts, Rolling Meadows, Roselle, Rosemont, Schaumburg, Schiller Pk, Wheeling.

Civil Records: Access: Mail, online, in person. Visitors must perform in person searches themselves. Search fee: $9.00 per name this division only. Court makes copy: $2.00 for first page, $.50 each add'l to 19 pgs. Required to search: name; also helpful: years to search. Civil cases indexed by defendant, plaintiff. Civil records are computerized since 1986. Online case information is available; see Circuit Court - Chicago Division for details. Mail turnaround time varies.

Criminal Records: Access: Fax, mail, in person. Visitors must perform in person searches themselves. Search fee: $9.00 per name this division only. Court makes copy: $2.00 for first page, $.50 each add'l to 19 pgs. Required to search: name, years to search; also helpful: DOB, SSN. Felony mail requests- download criminal search request form at http://198.173.15.31/forms/pdf_files/CriminalForm.pdf; mail to Clerk of Circuit Court, Criminal Div - Records, 2650 S California, Chicago, IL 60608, 773-869-3147. Misdemeanor records (county-wide) are also located at Circuit Court - Chicago District 1, Richard J. Daley Ctr, 50 W. Washington Ave, Rm 1006, Chicago, IL 60602. **Note:** Fax requests accepted from companies only. Mail turnaround time varies.

General Information: Public terminal goes back to 1984. Certification fee: $9.00 per doc. Payee: Clerk of Circuit Court. On personal checks write your social security and driver's license numbers. No credit cards. SASE required.

Skokie District 2 Skokie Court Bldg, Rm 136, 5600 Old Orchard Rd, Skokie, IL 60076-1023; phone: 847-470-7250; hours 8:30AM-4:30PM (CST). *Felony, Misdemeanor, Civil Action Under $100,000, Eviction, Small Claims.*

www.cookcountyclerkofcourt.org

Note: Deerfield, Des Plaines, Evanston, Glencoe, Glenview, Golf, Kenilworth, Lincolnwood, Morton Grove, Niles, Northbrook, Northfield, Park Ridge, Prospect Heights, Skokie, Wilmette, Winnetka.

Civil Records: Access: Phone, mail, online, in person. Visitors must perform in person searches themselves. Search fee: $9.00 per name per year. Court makes copy: $2.00 for 1st page, $.50 each add'l. Required to search: name, years to search. Civil cases indexed by defendant, plaintiff. Civil records computerized since 1983. Online case information is available; see Circuit Court - Chicago Division for details. Mail turnaround time 1-3 weeks.

Criminal Records: Access: Mail, in person. Both court and visitors may perform in person searches. Search fee: $9.00 per name per year; will only do 1 or 2 names per request. Court makes copy: $2.00 for 1st page, $.50 each add'l. Required to search: name, years to search; also helpful: DOB, SSN. Felony mail requests- download criminal search request form at http://198.173.15.31/forms/pdf_files/CriminalForm.pdf; mail to Clerk of Circuit Court, Criminal Div - Records, 2650 S California, Chicago, IL 60608, 773-869-3147. Misdemeanor records (county-wide) are also located at Circuit Court - Chicago District 1, Richard J. Daley Ctr, 50 W. Washington Ave, Rm 1006, Chicago, IL 60602. Mail turnaround time 1 week to 1 month.

General Information: Public terminal goes back to 1988. (2 terminals at Info booth and 2 in Rm 136.) All records are public. Certification fee: $9.00 per doc. Payee: Clerk of Circuit Court. On personal checks write your social security and driver's license numbers. No credit cards. Prepayment required.

Crawford County

Circuit Court PO Box 655, Robinson, IL 62454-0655; phone: 618-544-3512; fax: 618-546-5628; hours 8AM-4PM (CST). *Felony, Misdemeanor, Civil, Eviction, Small Claims, Probate.*

Civil Records: Access: Fax, mail, in person. Both court and visitors may perform in person searches. Search fee: $4.00 per name per year. Court makes copy: $1.00 for first page, $.50 each add'l; same fee for self serve. Required to search: name, years to search. Civil cases indexed by defendant, plaintiff. Civil records on computer from 1989, index books from 1800s. Mail turnaround time 2-4 days.

Criminal Records: Access: Fax, mail, in person. Both court and visitors may perform in person searches. Search fee: $4.00 per name per year. Court makes copy: $1.00 for first page, $.50 each add'l; same fee for self serve. Required to search: name, years to search, DOB. Criminal records on computer from 1989, index books from 1800s. Mail turnaround time up to 1 week.

General Information: Public terminal goes back to 1992. No juvenile or adoption records released. Will fax documents $2.00 1st page, $.25 each add'l. Certification fee: $5.00. Payee: Circuit Clerk. Personal checks accepted. Prepayment and SASE required.

Cumberland County

Circuit Court PO Box 145, Toledo, IL 62468; phone: 217-849-3601; fax: 217-849-2655; hours 8AM-4PM (CST). *Felony, Misdemeanor, Civil, Eviction, Small Claims, Probate.*

Civil Records: Access: Phone, fax, mail, in person. Both court and visitors may perform in person searches. Search fee: $6.00 per name per year. Court makes copy: $2.00 for 1st page, $.50 per page next 19, then $.25 per page. Required to search: name, years to search. Civil cases indexed by defendant, plaintiff. Civil records on computer from 1990, index books from 1885. Mail turnaround time up to 1 week.

Criminal Records: Access: Phone, fax, mail, in person. Both court and visitors may perform in person searches. Search fee: $6.00 per name per year. Court makes copy: $2.00 for 1st page, $.50 per page next 19, then $.25 per page. Required to search: name, years to search; also helpful: DOB, SSN. Criminal records on computer from 1990, index books from 1885. Mail turnaround time up to 1 week.

General Information: Public use terminal available. No juvenile or adoption records released. Will fax documents. Certification fee: $10.00. Payee: Clerk of Circuit Court. Only cashiers checks and money orders accepted. Prepayment and SASE required.

De Kalb County

Circuit Court 133 W State St, Sycamore, IL 60178; criminal phone: 815-895-7138; civil phone: 815-895-7131; fax: 815-895-7140; hours 8:30AM-4:30PM (CST). *Felony, Misdemeanor, Civil, Eviction, Small Claims, Probate.*

www.co.kane.il.us/judicial

Civil Records: Access: Mail, in person, online. Both court and visitors may perform in person searches. Search fee: $4.00 per name per year. Court makes copy: $1.00 for first page, $.50 each add'l. After 20 pages, copies $.25 each. Required to search: name, years to search; also helpful: address. Civil cases indexed by defendant, plaintiff. Civil records on computer since 1987, records go back to 1858. Online access to court records is via a internet subscription system. Fee is $240 per year for this county or $300 for Will, Madison, Sangamon, Winnebago, Kane, Kendall, DeKalb courts. For info, email bmulticourt@janojustice.com or call 866-511-2892. Mail turnaround time 2 weeks.

Criminal Records: Access: Mail, in person, online. Both court and visitors may perform in person searches. Search fee: $4.00 per name per year. Court makes copy: $1.00 for first page, $.50 each add'l. After 20 pages $.25 each. Required to search: name, years to search, signed release; also helpful: address, DOB. Criminal records on computer since 9/91, on index books back 60 years. Online access to court records is via a internet subscription system. Fee is $240 per year for this county or $300 for Will, Madison, Sangamon, Winnebago, Kane, Kendall, DeKalb courts. For info, email bmulticourt@janojustice.com or call 866-511-2892. Mail turnaround time 2 weeks.

General Information: Public use terminal available. No juvenile or adoption records released. Certification fee: $5.00. Payee: DeKalb County Circuit Clerk. Personal checks or Visa, MC accepted. Accepted in person only. Prepayment and SASE required.

De Witt County

Circuit Court 201 Washington St, Clinton, IL 61727; phone: 217-935-2195; fax: 217-935-3310; hours 8:30AM-4:30PM (CST). *Felony, Misdemeanor, Civil, Eviction, Small Claims, Probate.*

Civil Records: Access: Mail, fax, in person. Both court and visitors may perform in person searches. Search fee: $4.00 per name per year. Court makes copy: $2.00 for first page, $.50 each add'l, if over 20 then $.25 per pg. Self serve copy fee: $.25 per page. Required to search: name, years to search. Civil cases indexed by defendant. Civil records on computer from 1989, index books from 1839. Mail turnaround time 1-2 weeks.

Criminal Records: Access: Mail, fax, in person. Both court and visitors may perform in person searches. Search fee: $4.00 per name per year. Court makes copy: $2.00 for first page, $.50 each add'l up to 20; $.25 each add'l. Self serve copy fee: $.25 per page. Required to search: name, years to search, DOB. Criminal records on computer from 1989, index books from 1839. Mail turnaround time 1-2 weeks.

General Information: Public terminal goes back to 1989. No juvenile or adoption records released. Will fax documents to local or toll free line. Certification fee: $10.00 per document. Payee: Clerk of Circuit Court. Only cashiers checks and money orders accepted. Prepayment and SASE required.

Douglas County

Circuit Court PO Box 50, Tuscola, IL 61953; phone: 217-253-2352; criminal phone: 217-253-2353 -Traffic; hours 8:30AM-4:30PM (CST). *Felony, Misdemeanor, Civil, Eviction, Small Claims, Probate.*

Civil Records: Access: Phone, fax, mail, in person. Both court and visitors may perform in person searches. Search fee: $5.00 per name per year. Court makes copy: $1.00 for first page, $.50 each add'l. $.25 per pg after 20 pages. Required to search: name, years to search. Civil cases indexed by defendant, plaintiff. Civil records on computer from 1989, index books from 1859. Mail turnaround time 1 week.

Criminal Records: Access: Mail, in person. Both court and visitors may perform in person searches. Search fee: $5.00 per name per year. Court makes copy: $1.00 for first page, $.50 each add'l. $.25 per page after 20. Required to search: name, years to search: also helpful: DOB, SSN. Criminal records on computer from 1989, index books from 1859. Mail turnaround time 1 week.

General Information: Public terminal goes back to 1989. No juvenile or adoption records released. Will fax documents $5.00 for 1st 4 pages; $1.00 each add'l. Certification fee: $2.00. Payee: Douglas County Circuit Clerk. Personal checks accepted. Prepayment and SASE required.

Du Page County

Circuit Court 505 N County Farm Rd, Wheaton, IL 60187; phone: 630-407-8700; criminal phone: 630-682-7080/630-407-8600; civil phone: 630-682-7100; fax: 630-682-7082; hours 8:30AM-4:30PM (CST). *Felony, Misdemeanor, Civil, Eviction, Small Claims, Probate.*
www.co.dupage.il.us/courtclerk

Civil Records: Access: Mail, in person. Both court and visitors may perform in person searches. Search fee: $6.00 per name per year. Court makes copy: $2.00 for first page, $.50 each add'l. Required to search: name, years to search. Civil cases indexed by defendant, plaintiff. Civil records online from 1976, microfilm records back to 1939, index records back to 1839. All document files after 1/92 are on optical disk. Mail turnaround time 1 week.

Criminal Records: Access: Mail, in person. Both court and visitors may perform in person searches. Search fee: $6.00 per name per year. Court makes copy: $2.00 for first page, $.50 each add'l. Required to search: name, years to search, DOB. Criminal records online from 1976, microfilm records back to 1939, index records back to 1839. All document files after 1/01/92 are on optical disk. Mail turnaround time 1 week.

General Information: Public terminal goes back to 1976. No juvenile or adoption records released. Certification fee: $6.00 per doc. Payee: Clerk of Circuit Court. Personal checks and Visa/MC accepted. Prepayment and SASE required.

Edgar County

Circuit Court County Courthouse, 115 W Court, Paris, IL 61944; phone: 217-466-7447; fax: 217-466-7443; hours 8AM-4PM (CST). *Felony, Misdemeanor, Civil, Eviction, Small Claims, Probate.*

Civil Records: Access: Phone, mail, in person. Both court and visitors may perform in person searches. Search fee: $4.00 per name per year. Court makes copy: $2.00 first page; $.50 per page thereafter. Required to search: Name, years to search. Civil cases indexed by defendant, plaintiff. Civil records on computer from 1992, index books from 1823.

Criminal Records: Access: In person only. Both court and visitors may perform in person searches. Search fee: $4.00 per name per year. Court makes copy: $2.00 first page; $.50 each add'l. Required to search: Name, years to search, DOB. Criminal records on computer from 1992, index books from 1880. Mail turnaround time 1 week.

General Information: Public terminal goes back to 1992-3. No juvenile or adoption records released. Will not fax documents. Certification fee: $2.00 per cert. Payee: Circuit Clerk. Personal checks accepted. Prepayment and SASE required.

Edwards County

Circuit Court County Courthouse, Albion, IL 62806; phone: 618-445-2016; fax: 618-445-4943; hours 8AM-4PM (CST). *Felony, Misdemeanor, Civil, Eviction, Small Claims, Probate.*

Civil Records: Access: Mail, in person. Both court and visitors may perform in person searches. Search fee: $4.00 per name per year. Court makes copy: $.50 per page; same fee for self serve. Required to search: name, years to search. Civil cases indexed by defendant. Civil records on computer from 1988, books and index cards from 1815. Mail turnaround time 1 week.

Criminal Records: Access: Mail, in person. Both court and visitors may perform in person searches. Search fee: $4.00 per name per year. Court makes copy: $.50 per page; same fee for self serve. Required to search: name, years to search, DOB. Criminal records on computer from 1988, index books from 1815. Mail turnaround time 1 week.

General Information: Public terminal goes back to 1988. No juvenile or adoption records released. Will fax documents to local or toll-free number for $2.00 per page. Certification fee: $2.00. Payee: Clerk of Circuit Court. Only cashiers checks and money orders accepted. Prepayment and SASE required.

Effingham County

Circuit Court PO Box 586, 100 E Jefferson, Effingham, IL 62401; phone: 217-342-4065; fax: 217-342-6183; hours 8AM-4PM (CST). *Felony, Misdemeanor, Civil, Small Claims, Probate.*

Civil Records: Access: Mail, in person. Both court and visitors may perform in person searches. Search fee: $5.00 per name; also $5.00 per year if prior to 1988; $5.00 per page for computer generated info. Court makes copy: $1.00 for 1st page, $.50 each add'l. $.25 per page after 20. Required to search: name, years to search; also helpful: address. Civil cases indexed by defendant, plaintiff. Civil records on computer from 1988, index books from 1800s. Mail turnaround time 1 week.

Criminal Records: Access: Mail, in person. Both court and visitors may perform in person searches. Search fee: $5.00 per name; also $5.00 per year if prior to 1988; $5.00 per page for computer generated info. Court makes copy: $1.00 for 1st page, $.50 each add'l. $.25 per page after 20. Required to search: name, years to search, DOB; also helpful: address. Criminal records on computer from 1988, index books from 1800s. Mail turnaround time 1 week.

General Information: Public terminal goes back to 1988. No juvenile or adoption records released. Will not fax documents. Certification fee: $6.00 per document. Payee: Effingham County Circuit Clerk. Business checks accepted. Prepayment and SASE required.

Fayette County

Circuit Court 221 S 7th St, Vandalia, IL 62471; phone: 618-283-5009; criminal phone: 618-283-4490; hours 8AM-4PM (CST). *Felony, Misdemeanor, Civil, Eviction, Small Claims, Probate.*

Civil Records: Access: Phone, mail, fax, in person. Both court and visitors may perform in person searches. Search fee: $5.00 per name per year. Court makes copy: $1.00 for first page, $.50 each add'l. Self serve copy fee: $.25 per page. Required to search: name, years to search. Civil cases indexed by defendant. Civil records on computer from 1988, index books from 1800s. Mail turnaround time 1 month.

Criminal Records: Access: Phone, mail, fax, in person. Both court and visitors may perform in person searches. Search fee: $5.00 per name per year. Court makes copy: $1.00 for first page, $.50 each add'l. Self serve copy fee: $.25 per page. Required to search: name, years to search, DOB. Criminal records on computer from 1988, index books from 1800s. Mail turnaround time 1 month.

General Information: Public terminal has criminal back to 1989 and civil back to 1989. No juvenile, impounded or adoption records released. Certification fee: $2.00. Payee: Clerk of Circuit Court. Business checks accepted. Prepayment and SASE required.

Ford County

Circuit Court 200 W State St, Paxton, IL 60957; phone: 217-379-2641; fax: 217-379-3445; hours 8:30AM-4:30PM (CST). *Felony, Misdemeanor, Civil, Eviction, Small Claims, Probate.*

Civil Records: Access: Mail, fax, in person. Both court and visitors may perform in person searches. Search fee: $4.00 per name per year. Court makes copy: $1.00 for first page, $.50 each add'l; after 20 pages then $.25 per page; same fee for self serve. Required to search: name, years to search. Civil cases indexed by defendant. Civil records on index books from 1800s; on computer back to 3/2000. Mail turnaround time 2 days.

Criminal Records: Access: Mail, fax, in person. Both court and visitors may perform in person searches. Search fee: $4.00 per name per year. Court makes copy: $1.00 for first page, $.50 each add'l; after 20 pages $.25 each; same fee for self serve. Required to search: name, years to search, DOB (signed release if for juvenile). Criminal records on index books from 1800s; on computer back to 3/2000. Mail turnaround time 2 days.

General Information: Public terminal goes back to 3/2000. (Civil and criminal records back to 1980s may be available.) No juvenile or adoption records released. Will fax documents to local or toll free line. Certification fee: $5.00 per certification. Payee: Clerk of Circuit Court. Personal checks accepted. Prepayment and SASE required.

Franklin County

Circuit Court County Courthouse, PO Box 485, Benton, IL 62812; phone: 618-439-2011; fax: 618-439-4119; hours 8AM-4PM (CST). *Felony, Misdemeanor, Civil, Small Claims, Probate, Entry and Detainer, Traffic.*

Note: Traffic 618-438-6731.

Civil Records: Access: Fax, mail, in person. Both court and visitors may perform in person searches. Search fee: $4.00 per name per year. Court makes copy: $1.00 for first page, $.50 each add'l. Required to search: name, years to search. Civil cases indexed by defendant, plaintiff. Civil records on computer from 1987, index books from 1843. Mail turnaround time 1 week.

Criminal Records: Access: Fax, mail, in person. Both court and visitors may perform in person searches. Search fee: $4.00 per name per year. Court makes copy: $1.00 for first page, $.50 each add'l. Required to search: name, years to search, DOB. Criminal records on computer from 1987, index books from 1843. Mail turnaround time 1 week.

General Information: Public terminal goes back to 1987. No juvenile or adoption records released. Will not fax documents. Certification fee: $5.00 per cert. Payee: Franklin County Circuit Clerk. Only cashiers checks and money orders accepted. Prepayment and SASE required.

Fulton County

Circuit Court PO Box 152, Lewistown, IL 61542; phone: 309-547-3041; fax: 309-547-3674; hours 8AM-4PM (CST). *Felony, Misdemeanor, Civil, Eviction, Small Claims, Probate.*

Civil Records: Access: Phone, mail, fax, in person. Both court and visitors may perform in person searches. Search fee: $5.00 per name per year. Court makes copy: $1.00 first page, $.50 each add'l; $.15 each after 19 pgs. Required to search: name, years to search. Civil cases indexed by defendant, plaintiff. Civil records on computer back to 1990, index books from 1900. Mail turnaround time 2-3 days.

Criminal Records: Access: Mail, in person. Both court and visitors may perform in person searches. Search fee: $5.00 per name per year. Court makes copy: $1.00 first page, $.50 each add'l; $.15 each after 19 pgs. Required to search: name, years to search; also helpful: DOB. Criminal records on computer back to 1990, index books from 1879. Mail turnaround time 1-2 days; older, archived records require add'l 2-3 days.

General Information: Public terminal goes back to 1992. No juvenile, impounded or adoption records released. Certification fee: $3.00. Payee: Fulton County Circuit Clerk. Business checks accepted. Prepayment and SASE required.

Gallatin County

Circuit Court County Courthouse, PO Box 249, Shawneetown, IL 62984; phone: 618-269-3140; fax: 618-269-4324; hours 8AM-N, 1-4PM (CST). *Felony, Misdemeanor, Civil, Eviction, Small Claims, Probate.*

Civil Records: Access: Fax, mail, in person. Both court and visitors may perform in person searches. Search fee: $6.00 per name, per year. Court makes copy: $.25 per page. Required to search: name, years to search. Civil cases indexed by defendant. Civil records on index books from 1800s; computerized records since 1992. Mail turnaround time 1 week.

Criminal Records: Access: Fax, mail, in person. Both court and visitors may perform in person

searches. Search fee: $6.00 per name, per year. Court makes copy: $.25 per page. Required to search: name, years to search, DOB, signed release. Criminal records on index books from 1800s; computerized records since 1992. Mail turnaround time 1 week.

General Information: Public terminal goes back to 1999. No juvenile or adoption records released. Will fax documents $1.00 per page. Certification fee: $2.00 per cert. Payee: Clerk of Circuit Court. Business checks accepted. No credit cards. Prepayment and SASE required.

Greene County

Circuit Court 519 N Main, County Courthouse, Carrollton, IL 62016; phone: 217-942-3421; fax: 217-942-5431; hours 8AM-4PM (CST). *Felony, Misdemeanor, Civil, Eviction, Small Claims, Probate.*

Civil Records: Access: Phone, mail, in person. Both court and visitors may perform in person searches. Search fee: $5.00 per name. Court makes copy: $.25 per page; same fee for self serve. Required to search: name, years to search. Civil cases indexed by defendant, plaintiff. Civil records on index books from 1830s; computerized since 2000. Mail turnaround time 1-2 days.

Criminal Records: Access: Phone, fax, mail, in person. Both court and visitors may perform in person searches. Search fee: $5.00 per name. Court makes copy: $.25 per page; same fee for self serve. Required to search: name, years to search, DOB. Criminal records on index books from 1875; computerized since 2000. No felonies by phone. Include signed release with felony search requests. Mail turnaround time 1-2 days.

General Information: Public terminal goes back to 2000. No juvenile or adoption records released. Will fax documents for $.25 per page. Certification fee: $3.00. Payee: Clerk of Circuit Court. Personal checks accepted. Prepayment and SASE required.

Grundy County

Circuit Court PO Box 707, Morris, IL 60450; phone: 815-941-3256; fax: 815-941-3265; hours 8AM-4:30PM (CST). *Felony, Misdemeanor, Civil, Eviction, Small Claims, Probate.*

Civil Records: Access: Mail, in person. Both court and visitors may perform in person searches. Search fee: $5.00 per name per year. Court makes copy: $2.00 1st page; $.50 each add'l page. Self serve copy fee: $.50 per page. Required to search: name, years to search. Civil cases indexed by defendant, plaintiff. Civil records on computer back to 1988. Online access to judicial circuit records should be in early 2006 (or when funding available) for local attorney firms and retrievers. Mail turnaround time 1-2 days.

Criminal Records: Access: Mail, in person. Both court and visitors may perform in person searches. Search fee: $5.00 per name per year. Court makes copy: $2.00 1st page; $.50 each add'l page. Self serve copy fee: $.50 per page. Required to search: name, years to search, DOB, signed release. Criminal records on computer back to 1988. Mail turnaround time 1-2 days.

General Information: No public access terminal. No juvenile or adoption records released. Will not fax documents. Certification fee: $4.00 per document. Payee: Clerk of Circuit Court. Personal checks accepted. Prepayment and SASE required.

Hamilton County

Circuit Court County Courthouse, McLeansboro, IL 62859; phone: 618-643-3224; fax: 618-643-3455; hours 8AM-4:30PM (CST). *Felony, Misdemeanor, Civil, Eviction, Small Claims, Probate.*

Note: Probate is a separate index at this address.

Civil Records: Access: Mail, in person. Both court and visitors may perform in person searches. Search fee: $4.00 per name per year. Court makes copy: $.50 per page; same fee for self serve. Required

to search: name, years to search. Civil cases indexed by defendant, plaintiff. Civil records on index books from 1800s; computer records go back to 1990. Mail turnaround time 1-2 days.

Criminal Records: Access: Mail, in person. Both court and visitors may perform in person searches. Search fee: $4.00 per name per year. Court makes copy: $.50 per page; same fee for self serve. Required to search: name, years to search, DOB. Criminal records on index books from 1800s; computer records go back to 1990. Mail turnaround time 1-2 days.

General Information: Public use terminal available. No juvenile or adoption records released. Will fax documents. Certification fee: $5.00. Payee: Clerk of Circuit Court. No personal checks accepted. Prepayment and SASE required.

Hancock County

Circuit Court PO Box 189, 500 Main St, #8, Carthage, IL 62321; phone: 217-357-2616; fax: 217-357-2231; hours 8AM-4PM (CST). *Felony, Misdemeanor, Civil, Eviction, Small Claims, Probate.*

Civil Records: Access: Phone, fax, mail, in person. Both court and visitors may perform in person searches. Search fee: $5.00 per name per year. Court makes copy: $2.00 for first page, $.50 each add'l. Required to search: name, years to search. Civil cases indexed by defendant, plaintiff. Civil records on computer from 1992, index books from 1800s. Note: For phone and fax searches, they will only search to determine if a record exists. Mail turnaround time 1 week.

Criminal Records: Access: Phone, fax, mail, in person. Both court and visitors may perform in person searches. Search fee: $5.00 per name per year. Court makes copy: $2.00 for first page, $.50 each add'l. Required to search: name, years to search, DOB; also helpful: SSN. Criminal records on computer from 1990, index books from 1970, archived to 1800s. Note: For phone and fax searches, they will only search to determine if a record exists. Mail turnaround time 1 week.

General Information: No public access terminal. No juvenile or adoption records released. Will fax documents no fee. Certification fee: $3.00. Payee: Clerk of Circuit Court. Personal checks accepted, if local bank. Prepayment and SASE required.

Hardin County

Circuit Court PO Box 308, Main & Market Sts, County Courthouse, Elizabethtown, IL 62931; phone: 618-287-2735; fax: 618-287-2713; hours 8AM-4PM (CST). *Felony, Misdemeanor, Civil, Eviction, Small Claims, Probate.*

Civil Records: Access: Mail, fax, in person. Both court and visitors may perform in person searches. Search fee: $6.00 per name per year. Court makes copy: $1.00 for 1st page; $.50 each add'l. Required to search: name, years to search. Civil cases indexed by defendant, plaintiff. Civil records on computer back to 9/1992; on index books from 1800s. Mail turnaround time 1 week.

Criminal Records: Access: Mail, fax, in person. Both court and visitors may perform in person searches. Search fee: $6.00 per name per year. Court makes copy: $1.00 for 1st page; $.50 each add'l. Required to search: name, years to search, DOB. Criminal records on computer back to 9/1992; on index books from 1800s. Mail turnaround time 1 week.

General Information: No public access terminal. No juvenile or adoption records released. Fee to fax documents is $2.00 for 1st 2 pages; $.50 each add'l page. Certification fee: $6.00 per document; certified judgment is $10.00. Payee: Circuit Clerk. Business checks, cashiers checks and money orders accepted. Prepayment and SASE required.

Henderson County

Circuit Court County Courthouse, PO Box 546, Oquawka, IL 61469; phone: 309-867-3121; fax: 309-867-3207; hours 8AM-4PM (CST). *Felony, Misdemeanor, Civil, Eviction, Small Claims, Probate.*
Civil Records: Access: Phone, mail, in person. Both court and visitors may perform in person searches. Search fee: $5.00 per name per year. Court makes copy: $2.00 plus $.50 each add'l page till 20, then $.25 per page. Required to search: name, years to search. Civil cases indexed by defendant, plaintiff. Civil records on computer from 1991, index books from 1800s. Mail turnaround time 1 day to 1 week.
Criminal Records: Access: Phone, mail, in person. Both court and visitors may perform in person searches. Search fee: $5.00 per name per year. Court makes copy: $2.00 plus $.50 each for 1st 20 pages, then $.25 per page. Required to search: name, years to search; also helpful: SSN. Criminal records on computer from 1991, index books from 1800s. Mail turnaround time 1 day to 1 week.
General Information: Public terminal goes back to 1991. No juvenile or adoption records released. Will not fax documents. Certification fee: $3.00 1st page plus $.50 each add'l. Payee: Clerk of Circuit Court. Personal checks accepted. Prepayment and SASE required.

Henry County

Circuit Court 307 W Center St, Henry County Courthouse, Cambridge, IL 61238; phone: 309-937-3572; fax: 309-937-3990; hours 8AM-4:30PM (CST). *Felony, Misdemeanor, Civil, Eviction, Small Claims, Probate.*
Note: Probate is a separate index at this same address.
Civil Records: Access: Mail, in person, online. Both court and visitors may perform in person searches. Search fee: $6.00 per name per year. Court makes copy: $1.50 for first page, $.50 each add'l. Required to search: name, years to search. Civil cases indexed by defendant. Civil records on computer from 1989, index books from 1800s. Access is free to civil, small claims, probate and traffic records at www.judici.com/courts/index.jsp?court=IL037015 J. Mail turnaround time 2 weeks.
Criminal Records: Access: Mail, in person, online. Both court and visitors may perform in person searches. Search fee: $6.00 per name per year. Court makes copy: $1.50 for first page, $.50 each add'l. Required to search: name, middle initial, years to search, DOB; also helpful-last known address. Criminal records on computer from 1989, index books from 1800s. Criminal records access is free at www.judici.com/courts/index.jsp?court=IL037015 J. Mail turnaround time 2 weeks.
General Information: Public terminal goes back to 1989. No juvenile or adoption records released. Will fax documents to local or toll free line. Certification fee: $4.00 per page; Exemplifications are $6.00. Payee: Clerk of Circuit Court. Only cashiers checks and money orders accepted. Prepayment required.

Iroquois County

Circuit Court 550 S 10th St, Watseka, IL 60970; phone: 815-432-6950 (-6952 Traf); fax: 815-432-6953; hours 8:30AM-4:30PM (CST). *Felony, Misdemeanor, Civil, Eviction, Small Claims, Probate.*
www.judici.com/courts/index.jsp?court=IL038025J
Civil Records: Access: Fax, mail, in person, online. Both court and visitors may perform in person searches. Search fee: $6.00 per name per year. Court makes copy: $.50 per page. Required to search: name, years to search. Civil cases indexed by defendant. Civil records on index books from 1900, computerized since 1989. Search cases free online at www.judici.com/courts/cases/case_search.jsp?court=IL038025J. Also, a more convenient premium fee service is available. Mail turnaround time 1-2 days.

Criminal Records: Access: Fax, mail, in person, online. Both court and visitors may perform in person searches. Search fee: $6.00 per name per year. Court makes copy: $.50 per page. Required to search: name, years to search, DOB. Criminal records on index books from 1820, computerized since 1993. Online access is same as civil, see above. Mail turnaround time 1-2 days.
General Information: Public use terminal available. No juvenile or adoption records released. Fee to fax documents is $6.00 per document. Certification fee: $2.00. Payee: Clerk of Circuit Court. Personal checks accepted. Prepayment and SASE required.

Jackson County

Circuit Court PO Drawer 730, 1001 Walnut, County Courthouse, Murphysboro, IL 62966; phone: 618-687-7300; hours 8AM-4PM (CST). *Felony, Misdemeanor, Civil, Eviction, Small Claims, Probate.*
www.circuitclerk.co.jackson.il.us
Civil Records: Access: Mail, in person, online. Both court and visitors may perform in person searches. Search fee: $4.00 per name per year. Court makes copy: $1.00 1st page, $.50 each add'l. Required to search: name, years to search. Civil cases indexed by defendant, plaintiff. Civil records on computer from 1986, index books from 1860. Access civil, small claims, and traffic records free at http://circuitclerk.co.jackson.il.us/. Also, premiums service subscription with full info is available $77 per 6-months. Probate records are free at www.iltrails.org/jackson/prodex.htm. Mail turnaround time 1-2 weeks.
Criminal Records: Access: Mail, in person, online. Both court and visitors may perform in person searches. Search fee: $4.00 per name per year. Court makes copy: $1.00 1st page, $.50 each add'l. Required to search: name, years to search. Criminal records on computer from 1986, index books from 1860. Criminal records access is free at http://circuitclerk.co.jackson.il.us/. Click on "Case information." Also, premiums service subscription with full info is available $77 per 6-months. Mail turnaround time 1-2 weeks.
General Information: Public terminal goes back to 1970. No juvenile or adoption records released. May fax documents if not busy. Certification fee: $10.00 per doc. Payee: Circuit Clerk. Personal checks accepted. No credit cards. Prepayment and SASE required.

Jasper County

Circuit Court 100 W Jourdan St, Newton, IL 62448; phone: 618-783-2524; fax: 618-783-8621; hours 8AM-4PM (CST). *Felony, Misdemeanor, Civil, Eviction, Small Claims, Probate.*
Note: Probate is a separate index at this same address.
Civil Records: Access: Mail, in person. Both court and visitors may perform in person searches. Search fee: $5.00 per name. Court makes copy: $1.00 1st page; $.50 each add'l. Required to search: name, years to search; also helpful: address. Civil cases indexed by defendant, plaintiff. Civil records on computer from 1988, index books from 1835. Mail turnaround time 1 week.
Criminal Records: Access: Mail, in person. Both court and visitors may perform in person searches. Search fee: $5.00 per name. Court makes copy: $1.00 1st page; $.50 each add'l. Required to search: name, years to search, DOB, sex, signed release. Criminal records on computer from 1988, index books from 1835. Mail turnaround time 1 week.
General Information: No public access terminal. No juvenile or adoption records released. Fee to fax documents is $2.00 per document. Certification fee: $6.00 per cert. Payee: Clerk of Circuit Court. Personal checks accepted. Prepayment and SASE required.

Jefferson County

Circuit Court PO Box 1266, Mt Vernon, IL 62864; phone: 618-244-8008; fax: 618-244-8029; hours 8AM-5PM (CST). *Felony, Misdemeanor, Civil, Eviction, Small Claims, Probate.*
Civil Records: Access: Phone, fax, mail, in person. Both court and visitors may perform in person searches. Search fee: $8.00. Court makes copy: $.25 per page. Required to search: name, years to search. Civil cases indexed by defendant. Civil records on computer back to 1988, index books from 1800s. Fax requests must be followed by original by mail before being processed. Mail turnaround time 1-2 weeks.
Criminal Records: Access: Phone, fax, mail, in person. Both court and visitors may perform in person searches. Search fee: $8.00. Court makes copy: $.25 per page. Required to search: name, years to search, DOB, SSN. Criminal records on computer back to 1988, index books from 1800s. Mail turnaround time 1-2 weeks.
General Information: Public terminal goes back to 1988. Sealed records not released. Will fax documents $.25 per page plus phone charge. No certification fee. Payee: Clerk of Circuit Court. Only cashiers checks and money orders accepted. Prepayment and SASE required.

Jersey County

Circuit Court 201 W Pearl St, Jerseyville, IL 62052; phone: 618-498-5571; fax: 618-498-6128; hours 8:30AM-4:30PM (CST). *Felony, Misdemeanor, Civil, Eviction, Small Claims, Probate.*
Civil Records: Access: Fax, mail, in person. Both court and visitors may perform in person searches. Search fee: $5.00 per name. Court makes copy: $.50 per page. Required to search: name, years to search. Civil cases indexed by defendant. Civil records on computer from 1991, index books from 1800s. Mail turnaround time 1 week.
Criminal Records: Access: Fax, mail, in person. Both court and visitors may perform in person searches. Search fee: $5.00 per name. Court makes copy: $.50 per page. Required to search: name, years to search, DOB. Criminal records on computer back to 1991, index books from 1800s. Mail turnaround time 1 week.
General Information: No public access terminal. No juvenile or adoption records released. Will fax documents. Certification fee: $2 for 1st 2 pages; $.50 each add'l. Payee: Clerk of Circuit Court. Personal checks accepted. Prepayment and SASE required.

Jo Daviess County

Circuit Court 330 N Bench St, Galena, IL 61036; phone: 815-777-2295/0037; criminal phone: 815-777-2295; civil phone: 815-777-0037; probate phone: 815-777-0037; hours 8AM-4PM (CST). *Felony, Misdemeanor, Civil, Eviction, Small Claims, Probate.*
Civil Records: Access: Mail, in person, online. Visitors must perform in person searches themselves. No search fee. Court makes copy: $.50 per page; same fee for self serve. Required to search: name, years to search. Civil cases indexed by defendant, plaintiff. Civil records on computer since 1992, on index books from 1960; will and probate back to 1850. Access is free to civil, small claims, probate and traffic records at www.judici.com/courts/index.jsp?court=IL043015 J. Note: Clerk accepts mail requests to perform a probate search for $6.00, paid in advance. Mail turnaround time 1 week.
Criminal Records: Access: Mail, in person, online. Both court and visitors may perform in person searches. Search fee: $6.00 per name. Fee is for 1992 to present. Prior to 1992 $6.00 per name per year. Court makes copy: $.50 per page; same fee for self serve. Required to search: name, years to search, DOB. Criminal records on computer since 1992, on index books from 1960. Online access to criminal

records is free at www.judici.com/courts/index.jsp?court=IL043015 J. Mail turnaround time 1 week.
General Information: Public terminal goes back to 1992. No juvenile or adoption records released. Will fax documents for copy fee charge, if to toll- free line. Certification fee: $10.00 per cert includes copies. Payee: Circuit Clerk. Business checks accepted. Prepayment and SASE required.

Johnson County

Circuit Court PO Box 517, Vienna, IL 62995; phone: 618-658-4751; fax: 618-658-2908; hours 8AM-4PM (CST). *Felony, Misdemeanor, Civil, Eviction, Small Claims, Probate.*
Civil Records: Access: Mail, in person. Both court and visitors may perform in person searches. Search fee: $6.00 per name per year. Court makes copy: $.50 per page; same fee for self serve. Required to search: name, years to search. Civil cases indexed by defendant, plaintiff. Civil records on computer from 1987, index books from 1930s. Mail turnaround time 1 week.
Criminal Records: Access: Mail, in person. Both court and visitors may perform in person searches. Search fee: $6.00 per name per year. Court makes copy: $.50 per page; same fee for self serve. Required to search: name, years to search, DOB. Criminal records on computer from 1987, index books from 1930s. Mail turnaround time 1 week.
General Information: Public terminal goes back to 1987. No juvenile or adoption records released. Will fax documents with advance payment. Certification fee: $10.00 per certification. Payee: Circuit Clerk. Business checks accepted. Prepayment and SASE required.

Kane County

Circuit Court PO Box 112, Geneva, IL 60134; phone: 630-232-3413; fax: 630-208-2172; hours 8:30AM-4:30PM M,T,Th,F; open til 7PM Wed (CST). *Felony, Misdemeanor, Civil, Eviction, Small Claims, Probate.*
www.cic.co.kane.il.us
Civil Records: Access: Phone, fax, mail, in person, online. Both court and visitors may perform in person searches. Search fee: $4.00 per name per year. Court makes copy: $2.00 for 1st page, $.50 each next 19, then $.25 each add'l. Required to search: name, years to search. Civil cases indexed by defendant, plaintiff. Civil records on computer from 1986, index books from 1800s. Online access to court records is via an internet subscription system. Fee is $240 per year for this county or $300 for Will, Madison, Sangamon, Winnebago, Kane, Kendall, DeKalb courts. For info, email multicourt@janojustice.com or call 866-511-2892. Mail turnaround time 2 days.
Criminal Records: Access: Phone, fax, mail, in person, online. Both court and visitors may perform in person searches. Search fee: $4.00 per name per year. Court makes copy: $2.00 for 1st page, $.50 each next 19, then $.25 each add'l. Required to search: name, years to search, DOB. Criminal records on computer from 1986, index books from 1800s. Online access to court records is via an internet subscription system. Fee is $240 per year for this county or $300 for Will, Madison, Sangamon, Winnebago, Kane, Kendall, DeKalb courts. For info, email multicourt@janojustice.com or call 866-511-2892. Mail turnaround time 2 days.
General Information: Public terminal goes back to 1986. (More than one terminals are available.) No juvenile, mental health or adoption records released. Will fax documents $2.00 1st page, $.50 each add'l. Certification fee: $4.00. Judgment orders certification fee $10.00. Payee: Clerk of Circuit Court. Personal checks or Visa, MC, Discover accepted. Prepayment and SASE required.

Kankakee County

Circuit Court 450 E Court St, County Courthouse, Kankakee, IL 60901; phone: 815-937-2905; fax: 815-939-8830; hours 8:30AM-4:30PM (CST). *Felony, Misdemeanor, Civil, Eviction, Small Claims, Probate.*
Civil Records: Access: Mail, in person. Both court and visitors may perform in person searches. Search fee: $5.00 per name per year. Court makes copy: $2.00 for first page, $.50 each add'l. Required to search: name, years to search. Civil cases indexed by defendant, plaintiff. Civil records on computer from 1990, index books from 1800s. Mail turnaround time 1-2 weeks.
Criminal Records: Access: Mail, in person. Both court and visitors may perform in person searches. Search fee: $5.00 per name per year. Court makes copy: $2.00 for first page, $.50 each add'l. Required to search: name, years to search, DOB. Criminal records on computer from 1990, index books from 1800s. Mail turnaround time 1-2 weeks.
General Information: Public terminal goes back to 1990. No juvenile, impounded, mental health, expunged or adoption records released. Will not fax documents. Certification fee: $5.00 per certification. Payee: Clerk of Circuit Court. Personal checks accepted. Prepayment and SASE required.

Kendall County

Circuit Court PO Drawer M, 807 W John St, Yorkville, IL 60560; phone: 630-553-4183; criminal hours 630-553-4184; civil phone: 630-553-4183; hours 8AM-4:30PM (CST). *Felony, Misdemeanor, Civil, Eviction, Small Claims, Probate.*
Note: Traffic/DUI at 630-553-4185.
Civil Records: Access: Mail, in person, online. Both court and visitors may perform in person searches. Search fee: $6.00 per name per year. Court makes copy: $2.00 for first page, $.50 each add'l. $4.00 per page when hard copy printouts when cases are maintained on an automated medium. Required to search: name, years to search. Civil cases indexed by defendant, plaintiff. Civil records on computer since 1992, on index books from 1800s. Online access to court records is via a internet subscription system. Fee is $240 per year for this county or $300 for Will, Madison, Sangamon, Winnebago, Kane, Kendall, DeKalb courts. For info, email bmulticourt@janojustice.com or call 866-511-2892. Mail turnaround time 2-3 days.
Criminal Records: Access: Mail, in person, online. Both court and visitors may perform in person searches. Search fee: $6.00 per name per year. Court makes copy: $2.00 for first page, $.50 each add'l. $4.00 per page when hard copy printouts when cases are maintained on an automated medium. Required to search: name, years to search, DOB. Criminal records on computer since 1992, on index books from 1800s. Online access to court records is via a internet subscription system. Fee is $240 per year for this county or $300 for Will, Madison, Sangamon, Winnebago, Kane, Kendall, DeKalb courts. For info, email bmulticourt@janojustice.com or call 866-511-2892. Mail turnaround time 2-3 days.
General Information: Public terminal goes back to 1993. No juvenile or adoption records released. Certification fee: $4.00. Payee: Clerk of Circuit Court. Only cashiers checks and money orders accepted. Prepayment and SASE required.

Knox County

Circuit Court County Courthouse, Galesburg, IL 61401; phone: 309-345-3817; hours 8:30AM-4:30PM (CST). *Felony, Misdemeanor, Civil, Eviction, Small Claims, Probate.*
Civil Records: Access: Fax, mail, in person. Both court and visitors may perform in person searches. Search fee: $5.00 per year per name. Court makes copy: $2.00 for first page, $.50 each add'l. Required to search: name, years to search. Civil cases indexed by defendant, plaintiff. Civil records on index books from 1800s. Mail turnaround time 1 week.

Criminal Records: Access: Fax, mail, in person. Both court and visitors may perform in person searches. Search fee: $5.00 per year per name. Court makes copy: $2.00 for first page, $.50 each add'l. Required to search: name, years to search, DOB, sex. Criminal records on index books from 1800s. Mail turnaround time 1 week.
General Information: Public use terminal available. No juvenile or adoption records released. Will fax documents same as copy schedule. Certification fee: $3.00. Payee: Clerk of Circuit Court. Personal checks accepted. Prepayment required.

La Salle County

Circuit Court - Civil Division PO Box 617, 111 W Madison St, Ottawa, IL 61350-0617; criminal phone: 815-434-8271; civil phone: 815-434-8671; fax: 815-433-9198; hours 8AM-4:30PM (CST). *Civil, Eviction, Small Claims, Probate.*
Civil Records: Access: Online, in person. Both court and visitors may perform in person searches. No search fee. Court makes copy: $2.00 for 1st page, $1.00 each add'l. Required to search: name, years to search. Civil cases indexed by defendant, plaintiff. Some records on computer since late 1980s; prior records on index books from 1800s. Online access to Judicial Circuit records requires a $200 setup fee (waived for not-for-profits) and $.10 per minute usage fee. Call Clerk's office at 815-434-8671 for details.

General Information: Public terminal has only civil records back to 1984. No juvenile or adoption records released. Will not fax documents. Certification fee: $2.00. Payee: Clerk of Circuit Court. Personal checks or Visa, MC accepted. Prepayment required.

Circuit Court - Criminal Division 707 Etna Rd, #141, Ottawa, IL 61360; phone: 815-434-8271; civil phone: 815-434-8671; fax: 815-434-8299; hours 8AM-4:30PM (CST). *Felony, Misdemeanor.*
www.lasallecounty.com
Criminal Records: Access: In person, online. Visitors must perform in person searches themselves. Search fee: None. Court makes copy: $2.00 for first page, $1.00 each add'l. Required to search: name, years to search; also helpful: DOB. Online access to Judicial Circuit records requires a $200 setup fee (waived for not-for-profits) and $.10 per minute usage fee. Call the Clerk's office at 815-434-8671 for details.
General Information: Public terminal has only criminal records back to 1984. No juvenile or adoption records released. No fee to fax documents. Certification fee: $2.00. Payee: Clerk of Circuit Court. Personal checks or Visa, MC accepted. Prepayment and SASE required.

Lake County

Circuit Court 18 N County St, Waukegan, IL 60085; phone: 847-377-3600 (Admin.); criminal phone: 847-377-3211; civil phone: 847-377-3211; fax: 847-377-3249; hours 8:30AM-5PM (CST). *Felony, Misdemeanor, Civil, Eviction, Small Claims, Probate.*
www.19thcircuitcourt.state.il.us
Civil Records: Access: Mail, in person. Both court and visitors may perform in person searches. Search fee: $6.00 per name per year. Court makes copy: $2.00 for 1st pg, $.50 each add'l to 19, then $.25 ea; same fee for self serve. Required to search: name, years to search. Civil cases indexed by defendant, plaintiff. Civil records on computer or microfiche from 1968, index books from 1800s. Mail turnaround time 1-2 days.
Criminal Records: Access: Mail, in person. Both court and visitors may perform in person searches. Search fee: $6.00 per name per year. Court makes copy: $2.00 for 1st pg, $.50 each add'l to 19, then $.25 ea; same fee for self serve. Required to search: name, years to search, DOB. Criminal records on

computer or microfiche from 1968, index books from 1800s. Mail turnaround time 1-2 days.

General Information: Public use terminal available. No juvenile or adoption records released. Certification fee: $6.00. Payee: Circuit Clerk. No personal checks accepted. Discover cards accepted (in person only). Prepayment and SASE required.

Lawrence County

Circuit Court County Courthouse, 1100 State St, Lawrenceville, IL 62439; phone: 618-943-2815; fax: 618-943-5205; hours 8AM-4PM (CST). *Felony, Misdemeanor, Civil, Eviction, Small Claims, Probate.*

Note: Probate is a separate index at this same address.

Civil Records: Access: Mail, in person. Both court and visitors may perform in person searches. Search fee: $4.00 per name per year. Court makes copy: $1.00 for first page, $.50 each add'l; after 20 pages, will copy for $.25 per page. Required to search: name, years to search, address. Civil cases indexed by defendant, plaintiff. Civil records on computer from 10/99, index books from 1800s. Mail turnaround time 2-3 days.

Criminal Records: Access: Mail, in person. Both court and visitors may perform in person searches. Search fee: $4.00 per name per year. Court makes copy: $1.00 for first page, $.50 each add'l; after 20 pages $.25 per page. Required to search: name, years to search, address, DOB, SSN, signed release. Criminal records on computer from 10/99, index books from 1800s. Mail turnaround time 2-3 days.

General Information: No public access terminal. No juvenile or adoption records released. Will fax documents for $1.00 1st page, $.50 each add'l; after 20 pages, will copy for $.25 per page. Certification fee: $5.00. Payee: Clerk of Circuit Court. Only cashiers checks and money orders accepted. Prepayment and SASE required.

Lee County

Circuit Court 309 S Galena, #320, Dixon, IL 61021; phone: 815-284-5234; hours 8:00AM-4:30PM (CST). *Felony, Misdemeanor, Civil, Eviction, Small Claims, Probate.*

Civil Records: Access: Mail, in person, online. Both court and visitors may perform in person searches. Search fee: $6.00 per name per year. Court makes copy: $2.00 for 1st page; $.50 each add'l. Required to search: name, years to search. Civil cases indexed by defendant, plaintiff. Civil records on computer from 1989, index books from 1800s. Access is free to civil, small claims, probate and traffic records at www.judici.com/courts/index.jsp?court=IL052025 J. Mail turnaround time 1 week.

Criminal Records: Access: Mail, in person, online. Both court and visitors may perform in person searches. Search fee: $6.00 per name per year. Court makes copy: $2.00 for 1st page; $.50 each add'l. Required to search: name, years to search, DOB; also helpful: SSN. Criminal records on computer from 1989, index books from 1800s. Criminal records access is free at www.judici.com/courts/index.jsp?court=IL052025 J. Mail turnaround time 1 week.

General Information: Public terminal goes back to 8/1989. No juvenile, impounded or adoption records released. Certification fee: $2.00 per cert. Payee: Clerk of Circuit Court. Personal checks accepted. Visa/MC accepted in person only. Prepayment and SASE required.

Livingston County

Circuit Court 112 W Madison St, Pontiac, IL 61764; phone: 815-844-2602; criminal phone: x1; civil phone: x2; probate phone: x3; fax: 815-844-2322; hours 8AM-4:30PM (CST). *Felony, Misdemeanor, Civil, Eviction, Small Claims, Probate.*

Note: Probate in a separate index at this same address.

Civil Records: Access: Mail, in person, online. Both court and visitors may perform in person searches. Search fee: $5.00 per name per year. Court makes copy: $1.00 for 1st pg; $.50 per pg, pages 2-19; $.25 each add'l page. Self serve copy fee: $.25 per page. Required to search: name, years to search; also helpful: address. Civil cases indexed by defendant, plaintiff. Civil records on computer from 1989 (child support since 1988), index books from 1837. Search probate index 1837-1958 at www.cyberdriveillinois.com/departments/archives/pontiac.html. Mail turnaround time 3-5 days.

Criminal Records: Access: Mail, in person. Both court and visitors may perform in person searches. Search fee: $4.00 per name per year. Court makes copy: $1.00 for 1st pg; $.50 per pg, pages 2-19; $.25 each add'l. Self serve copy fee: $.25 per page. Required to search: name, years to search, DOB, SSN; also helpful: address. Criminal records on computer from 1989, index books from 1837. Note: Signed release required for juvenile cases. Mail turnaround time 3-5 days.

General Information: Public terminal goes back to 1989. No juvenile, impound or adoption records released. Fee to fax documents is $3.00 per fax. Certification fee: $2.00 per document. Payee: Livingston County Circuit Clerk. Personal checks accepted. Prepayment and SASE required.

Logan County

Circuit Court County Courthouse, PO Box 158, Lincoln, IL 62656; criminal phone: 217-735-2376/2377; civil phone: 217-732-1163; criminal fax: 217-732-1231; civil fax: 217-732-1232; hours 8:30AM-4:30PM (CST). *Felony, Misdemeanor, Civil, Eviction, Small Claims, Probate.*

www.co.logan.il.us/circuit_clerk

Civil Records: Access: Mail, fax, in person, online. Both court and visitors may perform in person searches. Search fee: $5.00 per name per year. Court makes copy: $2.00 for first page, $.50 each add'l. After 20 pages, the fee is $.25 per page. Required to search: name, years to search. Civil cases indexed by defendant, plaintiff. Civil records on computer back to 1990, index books from 1857. Online access to civil, small claims, probate and traffic records is free at http://co.logan.il.us/circuit_clerk/. Click on search court cases. A subscription premium service with full records is available. Mail turnaround time 1 week.

Criminal Records: Access: Mail, fax, in person, online. Both court and visitors may perform in person searches. Search fee: $5.00 per name per year. Court makes copy: $2.00 for first page, $.50 each add'l. $.25 per page after 20. Required to search: name, years to search, DOB; also helpful: sex. Criminal records on computer back to 1990, index books from 1857. Access to criminal records is same as civil. Mail turnaround time 1 week.

General Information: Public terminal goes back to 1989. No juvenile or adoption records released. Certification fee: $5.00 per doc. Payee: Carla Bender, Circuit Clerk. Business or personal checks or credit cards accepted. Prepayment required.

Macon County

Circuit Court 253 E Wood St, Decatur, IL 62523; criminal phone: 217-421-0272; civil phone: 217-424-1454; probate phone: 217-424-1455; hours 8AM-4:30PM (CST). *Felony, Misdemeanor, Civil, Eviction, Small Claims, Probate.*

www.court.co.macon.il.us

Civil Records: Access: Phone, fax, mail, online, in person. Both court and visitors may perform in person searches. Search fee: $6.00 per name per year. Court makes copy: $2.00 for first page, $.50 each add'l. Required to search: name, years to search; also helpful: address. Civil cases indexed by defendant, plaintiff. Civil records on computer from 1989, index books from 1800s. Access to court records is free at www.court.co.macon.il.us/Templates/SearchCaseInfo.htm. Search docket information back to 04/96. Includes traffic, probate, family, small claims. Mail turnaround time 1 week.

Criminal Records: Access: Fax, mail, online, in person. Both court and visitors may perform in person searches. Search fee: $6.00 per name per year. Court makes copy: $2.00 for first page, $.50 each add'l. Required to search: name, years to search; also helpful: address, DOB, SSN. Criminal records on computer from 1989, index books from 1800s. Access to court records is free online at www.court.co.macon.il.us/Templates/SearchCaseInfo.htm. Search docket information back to 04/96. Mail turnaround time 1 week.

General Information: Public terminal goes back to 1989. No juvenile or adoption records released. Will fax documents to local or toll free line, if not certified copy. Certification fee: $2.00 per cert. Payee: Macon County Circuit Clerk. Business and personal checks accepted. No credit cards. Prepayment and SASE required.

Macoupin County

Circuit Court PO Box 197, Carlinville, IL 62626; phone: 217-854-3211; fax: 217-854-7361; hours 8:30AM-4:30PM (CST). *Felony, Misdemeanor, Civil, Eviction, Small Claims, Probate.*

Civil Records: Access: Mail, in person. Both court and visitors may perform in person searches. Search fee: $6.00 per name per year. Court makes copy: $2.00 for first page, $.50 each add'l; $.25 for 20+ pages. Required to search: name, years to search. Civil cases indexed by defendant, plaintiff. Civil records on computer from 1994, index books from 1837. Mail turnaround time 1 month to 6 weeks.

Criminal Records: Access: Mail, in person. Both court and visitors may perform in person searches. Search fee: $6.00 per name per year. Court makes copy: $2.00 for first page, $.50 each add'l; $.25 for 20+ pages. Required to search: name, years to search; also helpful: DOB, SSN. Criminal records on computer from 1994, index books from 1837. Mail turnaround time 1 month to 6 weeks.

General Information: Public terminal goes back to 1994. No juvenile or adoption records released. Will fax documents for same fee structure as copy fees. Certification fee: $6.00. Payee: Mike Mathis Circuit Clerk. Personal checks accepted. Prepayment and SASE required.

Madison County

Circuit Court 155 N Main St, Edwardsville, IL 62025; phone: 618-692-6240; fax: 618-692-0676; hours 8:30AM-4:30PM (CST). *Felony, Misdemeanor, Civil, Eviction, Small Claims, Probate.*

www.co.madison.il.us

Civil Records: Access: Mail, in person, online. Both court and visitors may perform in person searches. Search fee: $6.00 per name per year. Court makes copy: $2.00 for 1st pg; $.50 per pg for pgs 2-19; $.25 ea add'l pg. Required to search: name, years to search. Civil cases indexed by defendant, plaintiff. Civil records on computer from 1990, index books from 1800s. Online access to court records is via a internet subscription system. Fee is $240 per year for this county or $300 for Will, Sangamon, Madison, Winnebago, Kane, Kendall, DeKalb courts. For info, email bmulticourt@janojustice.com or call 866-511-2892. Mail turnaround time 2-3 days.

Criminal Records: Access: Mail, in person, online. Both court and visitors may perform in person searches. Search fee: $6.00 per name per year. Court makes copy: $2.00 for 1st page; $.50 each for pgs 2-19; $.25 ea add'l pg. Required to search: name, years to search, DOB. Criminal records on computer from 1990, index books from 1800s. Online access to court records is via a internet subscription system. Fee is $240 per year for this county or $300 for Will, Sangamon, Madison, Winnebago, Kane, Kendall, DeKalb courts. For info, email bmulticourt@janojustice.com or call 866-511-2892. Mail turnaround time 2-3 days.

General Information: Public terminal goes back to 1990. No juvenile, mental health, adoption records released. Will fax documents to local or toll free line. Certification fee: $6.00. Payee: Clerk of Circuit Court. Personal checks accepted. Prepayment and SASE required.

Marion County

Circuit Court PO Box 130, 100 E Main, Salem, IL 62881; phone: 618-548-3856; hours 8AM-4PM (CST). *Felony, Misdemeanor, Civil, Eviction, Small Claims, Probate.*
Civil Records: Access: In person only. Visitors must perform in person searches themselves. Court makes copy: $1.00 for 1st page, $.50 each add'l. Required to search: name, years to search. Civil cases indexed by defendant, plaintiff. Civil records on computer from 1988, index books from 1800s.
Criminal Records: Access: In person only. Visitors must perform in person searches themselves. Court makes copy: $1.00 for 1st page, $.50 each add'l. Required to search: name, years to search; also helpful: DOB, SSN. Criminal records on computer from 1988, index books from 1800s.
General Information: Public terminal goes back to 1988. No juvenile or adoption records released. Certification fee: $6.00 per doc. Payee: Clerk of Circuit Court. Only cashiers checks and money orders accepted. Prepayment required. Will bill to attorneys.

Marshall County

Circuit Court PO Box 328, Lacon, IL 61540-0328; phone: 309-246-6435; fax: 309-246-2173; hours 8:30AM-N, 1-4:30PM (CST). *Felony, Misdemeanor, Civil, Eviction, Small Claims, Probate.*
Civil Records: Access: Mail, in person. Both court and visitors may perform in person searches. Search fee: $6.00 per name per year. Court makes copy: $.50 per page. Required to search: name, years to search. Civil cases indexed by defendant, plaintiff. Civil records on computer from 1988, microfiche since 1964, index books from 1800s. Mail turnaround time 1 week.
Criminal Records: Access: Mail, in person. Both court and visitors may perform in person searches. Search fee: $6.00 per name per year. Court makes copy: $.50 per page. Required to search: name, years to search, DOB. Criminal records on computer from 1988, microfiche since 1964, index books from 1800s. Mail turnaround time 1 week.
General Information: Public terminal goes back to 1988. No juvenile or adoption records released. Will fax documents to local or toll free line. Certification fee: $4.00. Payee: Clerk of Circuit Court. Personal checks accepted. Prepayment and SASE required.

Mason County

Circuit Court 125 N Plum, Havana, IL 62644; phone: 309-543-6619; fax: 309-543-4214; hours 8AM-4PM (CST). *Felony, Misdemeanor, Civil, Eviction, Small Claims, Probate.*
www.masoncountyil.org
Civil Records: Access: Mail, in person. Both court and visitors may perform in person searches. Search fee: $4.00 per name per year. Court makes copy: $1.00 for first page, $.50 each add'l. Required to search: name, years to search. Civil cases indexed by defendant, plaintiff. Civil records on computer from 1989, index books from 1800s. Mail turnaround time 1 week.
Criminal Records: Access: Mail, in person. Both court and visitors may perform in person searches. Search fee: $4.00 per name per year. Court makes copy: $1.00 for first page, $.50 each add'l. Required to search: name, years to search, DOB. Criminal records on computer from 1989, index books from 1800s. Mail turnaround time 1 week.
General Information: Public terminal goes back to 1989. No juvenile or adoption records released. Will fax documents for $5.00 per fax. Certification fee: $2.50 per cert. Payee: Clerk of Circuit Court. Only cashiers checks and money orders accepted. Prepayment and SASE required.

Massac County

Circuit Court PO Box 152, Courthouse Sq, Metropolis, IL 62960; phone: 618-524-9359; fax: 618-524-4850; hours 8AM-N, 1-4PM (CST). *Felony, Misdemeanor, Civil, Eviction, Small Claims, Probate.*
Civil Records: Access: Mail, in person. Both court and visitors may perform in person searches. Search fee: $6.00 per name per year. Court makes copy: $.10 per page. Required to search: name, years to search. Civil cases indexed by defendant. Civil records on computer from 1986, index books from 1800s. Mail turnaround time 5 business days.
Criminal Records: Access: Mail, in person. Both court and visitors may perform in person searches. Search fee: $6.00 per name per year. Court makes copy: $.10 per page. Required to search: name, years to search, DOB, signed release. Criminal records on computer from 1986, index books from 1800s. Mail turnaround time 5 business days.
General Information: Public terminal goes back to 1986. No juvenile or adoption records released. Certification fee: $3.00. Payee: Clerk of Circuit Court. Only cashiers checks and money orders accepted. Prepayment and SASE required.

McDonough County

Circuit Court County Courthouse, #1 Courthouse Sq, Macomb, IL 61455; phone: 309-837-4889; fax: 309-833-4493; hours 8AM-4PM (CST). *Felony, Misdemeanor, Civil, Eviction, Small Claims, Probate.*
Civil Records: Access: Phone, fax, mail, in person. Both court and visitors may perform in person searches. Search fee: $5.00 per name per year. Court makes copy: $2.00 1st pg; $.50 each add'l 19 pgs; $.25 over 20 pgs. Required to search: name, years to search. Civil cases indexed by defendant, plaintiff. Civil records on computer from 1991, index books from 1800s. Mail turnaround time 1 week.
Criminal Records: Access: Phone, fax, mail, in person. Both court and visitors may perform in person searches. Search fee: $5.00 per name per year. Court makes copy: $2.00 1st pg; $.50 each add'l 19 pages; $.25 each over 20. Required to search: name, years to search; also helpful: SSN. Criminal records on computer from 1991, index books from 1800s. Mail turnaround time 1 week.
General Information: Public terminal has criminal back to 1985 and civil back to 1990. No juvenile or adoption records released. Fee to fax documents is $2.00 per page. Certification fee: $3.00. Payee: Clerk of Circuit Court. Personal checks accepted. Prepayment and SASE required.

McHenry County

Circuit Court 2200 N Seminary Ave, Woodstock, IL 60098; phone: 815-334-4307; fax: 815-338-8583; hours 8AM-4:30PM (CST). *Felony, Misdemeanor, Civil, Eviction, Small Claims, Probate.*
www.mchenrycircuitclerk.org
Civil Records: Access: Phone, fax, mail, online, in person. Both court and visitors may perform in person searches. Search fee: $6.00 per name per year. Court makes copy: $1.00 for first page, $.50 each add'l. Required to search: name, years to search. Civil cases indexed by defendant, plaintiff. Civil records on computer from 1991, index books from 1800s. Access to records on the remote online system requires $750 license fee and $53.50 access fee, plus $50 per month. Records date back to 1991 with Civil, criminal, probate, traffic, and domestic records. For more info, call 815-334-4193. Mail turnaround time 1 week; criminal requests processed same day.
Criminal Records: Access: Phone, fax, mail, online, in person. Both court and visitors may perform in person searches. Search fee: $6.00 per name per year. Court makes copy: $1.00 for first page, $.50 each add'l. Required to search: name, years to search, DOB; also helpful: SSN. Criminal records on computer from 1990, index books from 1800s. Access to records on the remote online system requires $750 license fee and $53.50 access fee, plus $50 per month. Records date back to 1990 with civil, criminal, probate, traffic, and domestic records. For more info, call 815-334-4193. Note: Phone searches are limited to one only. Mail turnaround time 1 week; criminal requests processed same day.
General Information: Public terminal goes back to 1992. No juvenile or adoption records released. Certification fee: $6.00 per doc. Payee: Clerk of Circuit Court. Personal checks or Visa, MC, Discover accepted. Prepayment and SASE required.

McLean County

Circuit Court Attn: Clerk, PO Box 2420, Bloomington, IL 61702-2420; phone: 309-888-5301; criminal phone: 309-888-5321; civil phone: 309-888-5341; hours 8:30AM-4:30PM (CST). *Felony, Misdemeanor, Civil, Eviction, Small Claims, Probate.*
www.mcleancountyil.gov
Civil Records: Access: Mail, in person, online. Both court and visitors may perform in person searches. Search fee: $6.00 per name per year. Court makes copy: $2.00 for first page, $.50 each add'l. Required to search: name, years to search. Civil cases indexed by defendant, plaintiff. Civil records on computer from 1991, index books from 1800s. Public access is free   at www.mcleancountyil.gov/circuitclerk/PA_main.htm. Mail turnaround time 10 days.
Criminal Records: Access: Mail, in person, online. Both court and visitors may perform in person searches. Search fee: $6.00 per name per year. Court makes copy: $2.00 for first page, $.50 each add'l. Required to search: name, years to search, DOB; also helpful: address, SSN. Criminal records on computer from 1991, index books from 1800s. Public access is free   at www.mcleancountyil.gov/circuitclerk/PA_main.htm. Mail turnaround time 10 days.
General Information: Public terminal has only criminal records back to 1991. No juvenile or adoption records released. Certification fee: $6.00. Payee: McLean County Circuit Clerk. Personal checks accepted. Prepayment and SASE required.

Menard County

Circuit Court PO Box 466, Petersburg, IL 62675; phone: 217-632-2615; hours 8:30AM-4:30PM (CST). *Felony, Misdemeanor, Civil, Eviction, Small Claims, Probate.*
Civil Records: Access: Mail, in person. Both court and visitors may perform in person searches. Search fee: $6.00 per name per year. Court makes copy: $1.00 for first page, $.50 each add'l. Required to search: name, years to search. Civil cases indexed by defendant. Civil records on computer from 3/1994, on index books from 1839. Mail turnaround time 2 days.
Criminal Records: Access: Mail, in person. Both court and visitors may perform in person searches. Search fee: $6.00 per name per year. Court makes copy: $1.00 for first page, $.50 each add'l. Required to search: name, years to search, DOB. Criminal records on computer from 3/1994, on index books from 1839. Mail turnaround time 2 days.
General Information: No public access terminal. No juvenile or adoption records released. Certification fee: $2.00. Payee: Clerk of Circuit Court. Only cashiers checks and money orders accepted. Prepayment and SASE required.

Mercer County

Circuit Court PO Box 175, Aledo, IL 61231; phone: 309-582-7122; fax: 309-582-7121; hours 8AM-4PM (CST). *Felony, Misdemeanor, Civil, Eviction, Small Claims, Probate.*
www.mercercountyil.org

Civil Records: Access: Fax, mail, in person, online. Both court and visitors may perform in person searches. No search fee. Court makes copy: $.50 per page; same fee for self serve. Required to search: name, years to search. Civil cases indexed by defendant, plaintiff. Civil records on computer from 1988, index books from 1800s. Access is free to civil, small claims, probate and traffic records at www.judici.com/courts/index.jsp?court=IL066015 J. Mail turnaround time 2-3 days.

Criminal Records: Access: Phone, fax, mail, in person, online. Both court and visitors may perform in person searches. Search fee: $5.00 per name per year. Court makes copy: $.50 per page; same fee for self serve. Required to search: name, years to search, DOB. Criminal records on computer from 1988, index books from 1800s. Criminal records access is free at www.judici.com/courts/index.jsp?court=IL066015 J. Mail turnaround time 2-3 days.

General Information: Public terminal goes back to 1988. No juvenile or adoption records released. Fee to fax documents is $1.00 per page. Certification fee: $5.00 per cert, includes copies. Payee: Clerk of Circuit Court. Business checks accepted. Prepayment and SASE required.

Monroe County

Circuit Court 100 S Main St, Waterloo, IL 62298; phone: 618-939-8681; criminal phone: x273; civil phone: x274; probate phone: x274; fax: 618-939-1929; hours 8AM-4:30PM (CST). *Felony, Misdemeanor, Civil, Eviction, Small Claims, Probate.*

Civil Records: Access: Phone, fax, mail, in person. Both court and visitors may perform in person searches. Search fee: $6.00 per name per year. Court makes copy: $1.00 for first page, $.50 each add'l. If over 20 pages, fee is $.25 per page. Self serve copy fee: $.20 per page. Required to search: name, years to search, DOB. Civil cases indexed by defendant, plaintiff. Civil records on computer from 1992, index books from 1818. Mail turnaround time 1 week.

Criminal Records: Access: Phone, fax, mail, in person. Both court and visitors may perform in person searches. Search fee: $6.00 per name per year. Court makes copy: $1.00 for first page, $.50 each add'l. If over 20 pages, $.25 per page. Self serve copy fee: $.20 per page. Required to search: name, years to search, DOB. Criminal records on computer from 1992, index books from 1818. Mail turnaround time 1 week.

General Information: Public terminal goes back to 1992. No juvenile or adoption records released. No fee to fax documents. Certification fee: $5.00 per cert. Payee: Circuit Clerk. Business checks accepted. SASE required.

Montgomery County

Circuit Court County Courthouse, PO Box C, Hillsboro, IL 62049; phone: 217-532-9546; criminal phone: 217-532-9547; civil phone: 217-532-9546; probate phone: 217-532-9545; fax: 217-532-9614; hours 8AM-4PM (CST). *Felony, Misdemeanor, Civil, Eviction, Small Claims, Probate.* www.montgomeryco.com/circlerk.htm

Civil Records: Access: Mail, online, in person. Both court and visitors may perform in person searches. Search fee: $5.00 per name per year. Court makes copy: $.50 per page. Self serve copy fee: $.25 per page. Required to search: name, years to search. Civil cases indexed by defendant, plaintiff. Civil records on computer from 1988, index books from 1821, microfiche (probate only) since 1939. Online access to court records is at www.courts.montgomery.k12.il.us/CaseInfo.htm. Mail turnaround time 1 week.

Criminal Records: Access: Mail, online, in person. Both court and visitors may perform in person searches. Search fee: $5.00 per name per year. Court makes copy: $.50 per page. Self serve copy fee: $.25 per page. Required to search: name, years to search, DOB. Criminal records on computer from 1988,

index books from 1821, microfiche (probate only) since 1939. Online access to court records is at www.courts.montgomery.k12.il.us/CaseInfo.htm. Mail turnaround time 1 week.

General Information: Public terminal goes back to 1988. No juvenile or adoption records released. Will not fax documents. Certification fee: $10.00 per doc. Payee: Clerk of Circuit Court. Only cashiers checks and money orders accepted. Prepayment and SASE required.

Morgan County

Circuit Court PO Box 1120, 300 W State St, Jacksonville, IL 62650; phone: 217-243-5419; fax: 217-243-2009; hours 8:30AM-4:30PM (CST). *Felony, Misdemeanor, Civil, Eviction, Small Claims, Probate.* www.morgancounty-il.com

Note: Probate is a separate index at this same address.

Civil Records: Access: Mail, in person. Both court and visitors may perform in person searches. Search fee: $5.00 per name per year. Court makes copy: $1.50 first page, $.50 each add'l; same fee for self serve. Required to search: name, years to search. Civil cases indexed by defendant and plaintiff. Civil records on computer from 1990, index books from mid 1800s. Mail turnaround time 1 week.

Criminal Records: Access: Mail, in person. Both court and visitors may perform in person searches. Search fee: $5.00 per name per year. Court makes copy: $1.50 first page, $.50 each add'l; same fee for self serve. Required to search: name, years to search, DOB. Criminal records on computer from 1990, index books from mid 1800s. Mail turnaround time 1 week.

General Information: Public terminal goes back to 1990. No juvenile or adoption records released. Will fax documents for $1.50 1st page, $.50 each add'l. Certification fee: $4.00 per document. Payee: Clerk of Circuit Court. Only cashiers checks and money orders accepted. Prepayment and SASE required.

Moultrie County

Circuit Court 10 S Main, #7, Moultrie County Courthouse, Sullivan, IL 61951; phone: 217-728-4622; fax: 217-728-7833; hours 8:30AM-N, 1-4:30PM (CST). *Felony, Misdemeanor, Civil, Eviction, Small Claims, Probate.* www.circuit-clerk.moultrie.il.us

Civil Records: Access: Mail, in person. Both court and visitors may perform in person searches. Search fee: $4.00 per name per year. Court makes copy: $.50 per page. Required to search: name, years to search. Civil cases indexed by defendant. Civil records on computer from 1990, index books from 1850. Mail turnaround time 1 week.

Criminal Records: Access: Mail, in person. Both court and visitors may perform in person searches. Search fee: $4.00 per name per year. Court makes copy: $.50 per page. Required to search: name, years to search, DOB. Criminal records on computer from 1990, index books from 1850. Mail turnaround time 1 week.

General Information: No public access terminal. No juvenile or adoption records released. If necessary, will fax documents for $2.00 per page fax fee. Certification fee: $2.00 per cert. Payee: Clerk of Circuit Court. Business checks accepted. Prepayment and SASE required.

Ogle County

Circuit Court PO Box 337, Oregon, IL 61061; phone: 815-732-1130; criminal phone: 815-732-1140; civil phone: 815-732-1130; hours 8:30AM-4:30PM (CST). *Felony, Misdemeanor, Civil, Eviction, Small Claims, Probate.* www.oglecounty.org/marty/circuitclerk.html

Civil Records: Access: Mail, in person, online. Both court and visitors may perform in person searches. Search fee: $6.00 per name per year. Court makes copy: $2.00 for first page, $.50 each add'l. $.25 per page after 20. Required to search: name, years to

search. Civil cases indexed by defendant, plaintiff. Civil records on computer back to 1994; prior records on microfiche last 10 years, index books from 1836. Access is free to civil, small claims, probate and traffic records at www.oglecounty.org. Click on "Search for Case Information." Mail turnaround time 2-3 weeks.

Criminal Records: Access: Mail, online, in person. Both court and visitors may perform in person searches. Search fee: $6.00 per name per year. Court makes copy: $2.00 for first page, $.50 each add'l. $.25 per page after 20. Required to search: name, years to search, DOB. Criminal records on computer back to 1989; prior records on microfiche last 10 years, index books from 1836. Criminal records access is free at www.oglecounty.org. Click on "Search for Case Information." Mail turnaround time 2-3 weeks.

General Information: Public terminal has criminal back to 1989 and civil back to 1994. No juvenile or adoption records released. Will not fax documents. Certification fee: $10.00 per document. Payee: Clerk of Circuit Court. Only cashiers checks and money orders accepted. Prepayment and SASE required.

Peoria County

Circuit Court 324 Main St, Peoria, IL 61602; phone: 309-672-6953; fax: 309-677-6228; hours 8:30AM-5PM (CST). *Felony, Misdemeanor, Civil, Eviction, Small Claims, Probate.*

Civil Records: Access: Phone, mail, in person. Both court and visitors may perform in person searches. Search fee: $6.00 per name per year. Court makes copy: $2.00 for first page, $.50 each add'l. Required to search: name, years to search. Civil cases indexed by defendant, plaintiff. Civil records on computer from 1986 (traffic), from 1987 (civil), archived from 1800s. Mail turnaround time 1 week.

Criminal Records: Access: Phone, mail, in person. Both court and visitors may perform in person searches. Search fee: $6.00 per name per year, Add'l $10.00 to mail. Court makes copy: $2.00 for first page, $.50 each add'l. Required to search: name, years to search, DOB; also helpful: SSN. Criminal records on computer from 1978, archived from 1800s. Mail turnaround time 1 week.

General Information: Public terminal goes back to 1979. No juvenile or adoption records released. Certification fee: $6.00 per doc. Payee: Clerk of Circuit Court. Personal checks or Visa, MC accepted. Prepayment and SASE required.

Perry County

Circuit Court PO Box 219, Pinckneyville, IL 62274; phone: 618-357-6726; hours 8AM-4PM (CST). *Felony, Misdemeanor, Civil, Eviction, Small Claims, Probate.*

Note: Probate is a separate index at this same address.

Civil Records: Access: Mail, in person. Both court and visitors may perform in person searches. Search fee: $4.00 per name per year. Court makes copy: $1.00 for 1st page; $.50 for next 19 pages; $.25 per page thereafter. Required to search: name, years to search. Civil cases indexed by defendant, plaintiff. Civil records on computer from 1990, index books from 1800s. Mail turnaround time up to 1 week.

Criminal Records: Access: Mail, in person. Both court and visitors may perform in person searches. Search fee: $4.00 per name per year. Court makes copy: $1.00 for 1st page; $.50 for next 19 pages; $.25 each add'l. Required to search: name, years to search; also helpful: DOB. Criminal records on computer from 1990, index books from 1800s. Mail turnaround time up to 1 week.

General Information: Public terminal goes back to 1990. No juvenile or adoption records released. Will not fax documents. Certification fee: $2.00. Payee: Clerk of Circuit Court. Only cashiers checks and money orders accepted. Prepayment and SASE required.

Piatt County

Circuit Court PO Box 288, Monticello, IL 61856; phone: 217-762-4966; fax: 217-762-8394; probate fax: same; hours 8:30AM-4:30PM (CST). *Felony, Misdemeanor, Civil, Eviction, Small Claims, Probate.*
www.chittendensuperiorcourt.com
Civil Records: Access: Phone, fax, mail, in person. Both court and visitors may perform in person searches. No search fee. Court makes copy: $1.00 for first page, $.50 each add'l. Required to search: name, years to search. Civil cases indexed by defendant, plaintiff. Civil records on computer since 1988, index books from 1800s. Mail turnaround time 2-3 days.
Criminal Records: Access: Phone, fax, mail, in person. Both court and visitors may perform in person searches. No search fee. Court makes copy: $1.00 for first page, $.50 each add'l. Required to search: name, years to search, DOB; also helpful: SSN. Criminal records on computer since 1988, index books from 1800s. Mail turnaround time 2-3 days.
General Information: No public access terminal. No juvenile or adoption records released. Will fax documents $2.00 1st page, $1.00 each add'l. Certification fee: $1.00 plus $.50 each add'l page. Payee: Clerk of Circuit Court. Business checks accepted. Prepayment required.

Pike County

Circuit Court Pike County Courthouse, 100 E Washington St, Pittsfield, IL 62363; phone: 217-285-6612; fax: 217-285-4726; hours 8:30AM-4:30PM (CST). *Felony, Misdemeanor, Civil, Eviction, Small Claims, Probate.*
Civil Records: Access: Mail, in person, online. Both court and visitors may perform in person searches. Search fee: $6.00 per name per year. Court makes copy: $2.00 for first page, $.50 each add'l. $.25 per page after 19 pages. Self serve copy fee: $.25 per page. Required to search: name, years to search. Civil cases indexed by defendant, plaintiff. Civil records on computer since 1992, index books from 1800s. Access is free to civil, small claims, probate and traffic records at www.judici.com/courts/index.jsp?court=IL075015J. Mail turnaround time ASAP.
Criminal Records: Access: Mail, in person, online. Both court and visitors may perform in person searches. Search fee: $6.00 per name per year. Court makes copy: $2.00 for first page, $.50 each add'l. $.25 per page after 19. Self serve copy fee: $.25 per page. Required to search: name, years to search; also helpful: SSN. Criminal records on computer since 1992, index books from 1800s. Criminal records access is free at www.judici.com/courts/index.jsp?court=IL075015J. Mail turnaround time ASAP.
General Information: Public terminal has criminal back to 1992 and civil back to 1992. No juvenile or adoption records released. Will fax documents of civil searches only. Certification fee: $6.00 per document includes copies; $10.00 for judgment. Payee: Circuit Clerk. No personal checks accepted; money order or cash only. Prepayment and SASE required.

Pope County

Circuit Court PO Box 438, Golconda, IL 62938; phone: 618-683-3941; fax: 618-683-3018; hours 8AM-4PM (CST). *Felony, Misdemeanor, Civil, Eviction, Small Claims, Probate.*
Civil Records: Access: Phone, fax, mail, in person. Both court and visitors may perform in person searches. Search fee: $6.00 per name per year. Court makes copy: $.25 per page; same fee for self serve. Required to search: name, years to search. Civil cases indexed by defendant. Civil records on computer from 1989, index books from 1800s. Mail turnaround time 2-3 days.
Criminal Records: Access: Phone, fax, mail, in person. Both court and visitors may perform in person searches. Search fee: $6.00 per name per year. Court makes copy: $.25 per page; same fee for self serve. Required to search: name, years to search, DOB. Criminal records on computer from 1989, index books from 1800s. Mail turnaround time 2-3 days.
General Information: Public terminal goes back to 1989. No juvenile or adoption records released. Will fax documents $.50 per page. Certification fee: $6.00. Payee: Circuit Clerk. Business checks accepted. Prepayment and SASE required.

Pulaski County

Circuit Court PO Box 88, 500 Illinois Ave, Rm C, Mound City, IL 62963; phone: 618-748-9300; fax: 618-748-9329; hours 8AM-N, 1-4PM (CST). *Felony, Misdemeanor, Civil, Eviction, Small Claims, Probate.*
Civil Records: Access: Mail, in person. Both court and visitors may perform in person searches. Search fee: $6.00 per name. Court makes copy: $1.00 for first page, $.50 each add'l. If over 20 pages, fee is $.25 per copy. Required to search: name, years to search. Civil cases indexed by defendant, plaintiff. Civil records on computer since 1989, on books prior. Mail turnaround time 1 week.
Criminal Records: Access: Mail, in person. Both court and visitors may perform in person searches. Search fee: $6.00 per name per year. Court makes copy: $1.00 for first page, $.50 each add'l. If over 20 pages, $.25 per copy. Required to search: name, years to search, signed release; also helpful: DOB, SSN. Criminal records on computer since 1989, on books prior. Mail turnaround time 1 week.
General Information: No public access terminal. No juvenile, adoption records released. Certification fee: $6.00 per doc. Payee: Clerk of Circuit Court. Only cashiers checks and money orders accepted. Prepayment and SASE required.

Putnam County

Circuit Court 120 N 4th St, Hennepin, IL 61327; phone: 815-925-7016; fax: 815-925-7492; hours 9AM-4PM (CST). *Felony, Misdemeanor, Civil, Eviction, Small Claims, Probate.*
Civil Records: Access: Mail, in person. Both court and visitors may perform in person searches. Search fee: $5.00 per name. Fee is per 5 years searched. Court makes copy: $.50 per page. $.25 per page after 20. Required to search: name, years to search. Civil cases indexed by defendant. Civil records on computer from 1991, index books from 1836. Mail turnaround time 3 days.
Criminal Records: Access: Mail, in person. Both court and visitors may perform in person searches. Search fee: $5.00 per name. Fee is per 5 years searched. Court makes copy: $.50 per page. $.25 per page after 20. Required to search: name, years to search, DOB. Criminal records on computer from 1991, index books from 1836. Note: No criminal searches performed on Thursdays. Mail turnaround time 3 days.
General Information: Public use terminal available. No juvenile or adoption records released. Certification fee: $2.00. Payee: Clerk of Circuit Court. Only cashiers checks and money orders accepted. Prepayment and SASE required.

Randolph County

Circuit Court County Courthouse, Rm 302, Chester, IL 62233; phone: 618-826-5000 X194; fax: 618-826-3761; hours 8AM-4PM (CST). *Felony, Misdemeanor, Civil, Eviction, Small Claims, Probate.*
Civil Records: Access: Mail, in person. Both court and visitors may perform in person searches. Search fee: $4.00 per name per year. Court makes copy: $.25 per page. Required to search: name, years to search. Civil cases indexed by defendant, plaintiff. Civil records on computer from 1992, index books from 1800s. Visitors can search both. Mail turnaround time 1-2 days.
Criminal Records: Access: Mail, in person. Both court and visitors may perform in person searches.

self serve. Required to search: name, years to search, DOB. Criminal records on computer from 1989, index books from 1800s. Mail turnaround time 2-3 days.
General Information: Public terminal goes back to 1989. No juvenile or adoption records released. Will fax documents $.50 per page. Certification fee: $6.00. Payee: Circuit Clerk. Business checks accepted. Prepayment and SASE required.

Search fee: $4.00 per name per year. Court makes copy: $.25 per page. Required to search: name, years to search, DOB. Criminal records on computer from 1992, index books from 1800s. Visitors can search both. Mail turnaround time 1-2 days.
General Information: Public terminal goes back to 1992. No juvenile or adoption records released. Certification fee: $2.00 for seal and $1.00 1st page and $.50 each add'l page. Payee: Clerk of Circuit Court. Business checks accepted. Prepayment and SASE required.

Richland County

Circuit Court 103 W Main, #21, Olney, IL 62450; phone: 618-392-2151; fax: 618-392-5041; hours 8AM-4PM (CST). *Felony, Misdemeanor, Civil, Eviction, Small Claims, Probate.*
Civil Records: Access: Phone, mail, fax, in person. Both court and visitors may perform in person searches. Search fee: $4.00 per name per year. Court makes copy: $1.00 for first page, $.50 each add'l. Required to search: name, years to search. Civil cases indexed by defendant. Civil records on index books from 1867; on computer back to 1999. Mail turnaround time 1-2 weeks.
Criminal Records: Access: Mail, in person. Both court and visitors may perform in person searches. Search fee: $4.00 per name per year. Court makes copy: $1.00 for first page, $.50 each add'l. Required to search: name, years to search, DOB. Criminal records on index books from 1867; on computer back to 1986. Mail turnaround time 1-2 weeks.
General Information: Public terminal goes back to 1999. No juvenile or adoption records released. Will fax documents for $0.25 per page. Certification fee: $5.00 per certification. Payee: Clerk of Circuit Court. Only cashiers checks and money orders accepted. Prepayment and SASE required.

Rock Island County

Circuit Court PO Box 5230, 210 15th St, Rock Island, IL 61204-5230; phone: 309-786-4451; fax: 309-786-3029; hours 8AM-4:30PM (CST). *Felony, Misdemeanor, Civil, Eviction, Small Claims, Probate.*
www.co.rock-island.il.us/CirClk.asp?id=279
Civil Records: Access: Mail, online, in person. Both court and visitors may perform in person searches. Search fee: $6.00 per name per year. Court makes copy: $2.00 for 1st page, $.50 each add'l. Required to search: name, years to search. Civil cases indexed by defendant, plaintiff. Civil records on computer from 1989, index books from 1950s. Full access to court records on the remote online system requires $300 setup fee plus a $1.00 per minute for access. Civil, criminal, probate, traffic, and domestic records can be accessed by name or case number. Also, access to civil, small claims, probate and traffic records is free at www.judici.com/courts/cases/index.jsp?court=IL081025J. Mail turnaround time 1 week.
Criminal Records: Access: Mail, online, in person. Both court and visitors may perform in person searches. Search fee: $6.00 per name per year. Court makes copy: $2.00 for 1st page, $.50 each add'l; $.25 each after 19 pages. Required to search: name, years to search, DOB. Criminal records on computer from 1989, index books from 1950s. Online access to criminal records is the same as civil - there are two methods. Mail turnaround time 1 week.
General Information: Public terminal goes back to 5/1989. No juvenile or adoption records released. Will not fax documents. Certification fee: $6.00 per document. Payee: Circuit Clerks Office. Money orders accepted. Prepayment and SASE required.

Saline County

Circuit Court County Courthouse, Harrisburg, IL 62946; phone: 618-253-5096; fax: 618-25303904; hours 8AM-4PM (CST). *Felony, Misdemeanor, Civil, Eviction, Small Claims, Probate.*

Civil Records: Access: Fax, mail, in person. Both court and visitors may perform in person searches. Search fee: $5.00 per name per year. Court makes copy: $1.00 for first page, $.50 each add'l. Required to search: name, years to search. Civil cases indexed by defendant, plaintiff. Civil records on computer back to 1986, index books archived from 1886. Mail turnaround time 1-2 weeks.

Criminal Records: Access: Fax, mail, in person. Both court and visitors may perform in person searches. Search fee: $5.00 per name per year. Court makes copy: $1.00 for first page, $.50 each add'l. Required to search: name, years to search, DOB. Criminal records on computer back to 1986, index books archived from 1800s. Mail turnaround time 1-2 weeks.

General Information: Public use terminal available. No juvenile or adoption records released. Fee to fax documents is $2.00 1st page, $1.00 each add'l. Certification fee: $5.00. Payee: Clerk of Circuit Court. Business checks accepted. Prepayment and SASE required.

Sangamon County

Circuit Court 200 S 9th St, Rm 405, Springfield, IL 62701; phone: 217-753-6674; fax: 217-753-6665; hours 8:30AM-4:30PM (CST). *Felony, Misdemeanor, Civil, Eviction, Small Claims, Probate.*
www.co.sangamon.il.us/court
Civil Records: Access: Fax, mail, in person, online. Both court and visitors may perform in person searches. Search fee: $4.00 per name per year. Court makes copy: $2.00 for first page, $.50 each add'l. $.25 per page after 19. Required to search: name, years to search. Civil cases indexed by defendant, plaintiff. Civil records on computer from 1982, index books from 1800s. Online access to court records is via a internet subscription system. Fee is $240 per year for this county or $300 for Will, Madison, Sangamon, Winnebago, Kane, Kendall, DeKalb courts. For info, email bmulticourt@janojustice.com or call 866-511-2892. Mail turnaround time 1-2 weeks.

Criminal Records: Access: Fax, mail, in person, online. Both court and visitors may perform in person searches. Search fee: $4.00 per name per year. Court makes copy: $2.00 for first page, $.50 each add'l. $.25 per page after 19. Required to search: name, years to search, DOB. Criminal records on computer from 1982, index books from 1800s. Online access to court records is via a internet subscription system. Fee is $240 per year for this county or $300 for Will, Madison, Sangamon, Winnebago, Kane, Kendall, DeKalb courts. For info, email bmulticourt@janojustice.com or call 866-511-2892. Mail turnaround time 1-2 weeks.

General Information: Public use terminal available. No juvenile, mental health, adoption records released. No fee to fax documents. Certification fee: $4.00. Payee: Circuit Clerk. Personal checks accepted. Prepayment and SASE required.

Schuyler County

Circuit Court PO Box 80, Rushville, IL 62681; phone: 217-322-4633; fax: 217-322-6164; hours 8AM-4PM (CST). *Felony, Misdemeanor, Civil, Eviction, Small Claims, Probate.*
Civil Records: Access: Mail, in person. Both court and visitors may perform in person searches. Search fee: $6.00 per name per year. Court makes copy: $2.00 for first page, $.50 each add'l. $.25 after 20. Required to search: name, years to search. Civil cases indexed by defendant. Civil records on computer from 1988, index books from 1800s. Mail turnaround time 1 week.

Criminal Records: Access: Mail, in person. Both court and visitors may perform in person searches. Search fee: $6.00 per name per year. Court makes copy: $2.00 for first page, $.50 each add'l. $.25 per page after 20. Required to search: name, years to search, DOB. Criminal records on computer from

1988, index books from 1800s. Mail turnaround time 1 week.

General Information: No public access terminal. No juvenile or adoption records released. Fee to fax documents is $1.00 per page. Certification fee: $10.00. Payee: Clerk of Circuit Court. Only cashiers checks and money orders accepted. Prepayment and SASE required.

Scott County

Circuit Court 35 E Market St, Winchester, IL 62694; phone: 217-742-5217; fax: 217-742-5853; hours 8AM-N, 1-4PM (CST). *Felony, Misdemeanor, Civil, Eviction, Small Claims, Probate.*
Civil Records: Access: Mail, in person. Both court and visitors may perform in person searches. Search fee: $6.00 per name per year. Court makes copy: $1.00 for first page, $.50 each add'l. After 20 pages, copies $.25 each. Required to search: name, years to search. Civil cases indexed by defendant, plaintiff. Civil records on index books from 1800s. Mail turnaround time 1 week.

Criminal Records: Access: Mail, in person. Both court and visitors may perform in person searches. Search fee: $6.00 per name per year. Court makes copy: $1.00 for first page, $.50 each add'l. After 20 pages $.25 each. Required to search: name, years to search, DOB. Criminal records on index books from 1800s. Mail turnaround time 1 week.

General Information: No public access terminal. No juvenile or adoption records released. Will not fax documents. Certification fee: $2.00. Payee: Clerk of Circuit Court. Only cashiers checks and money orders accepted. Prepayment and SASE required.

Shelby County

Circuit Court County Courthouse, PO Box 469, Shelbyville, IL 62565; phone: 217-774-4212; fax: 217-774-4109; hours 8AM-4PM (CST). *Felony, Misdemeanor, Civil, Eviction, Small Claims, Probate.*
Civil Records: Access: Fax, mail, in person. Both court and visitors may perform in person searches. Search fee: $5.00 per name per year. Court makes copy: $1.00 for first page, $.50 each add'l. Self serve copy fee: $.25 per page. Required to search: name, years to search. Civil cases indexed by defendant, plaintiff. Civil records on computer from 1988, index books from 1848. Mail turnaround time 1-2 weeks.

Criminal Records: Access: Fax, mail, in person. Both court and visitors may perform in person searches. Search fee: $5.00 per name per year. Court makes copy: $1.00 for first page, $.50 each add'l. Self serve copy fee: $.25 per page. Required to search: name, years to search, DOB. Criminal records on computer from 1988, index books from 1848. Mail turnaround time 1-2 weeks.

General Information: Public terminal goes back to 1988. No juvenile or adoption records released. Will fax documents for $5.00 per name or year. Certification fee: $10.00 per document for add'l pages. Payee: Circuit Clerk. Prepayment and SASE required.

St. Clair County

Circuit Court 10 Public Square, Belleville, IL 62220-1623; phone: 618-277-6832; criminal phone: x4 for felony; probate phone: x2307; fax: 618-825-2742; hours 8AM-4PM (CST). *Felony, Misdemeanor, Civil, Eviction, Small Claims, Probate.*
Civil Records: Access: Mail, in person. Both court and visitors may perform in person searches. Search fee: $6.00 per name per year. Court makes copy: $2.00 for first page, $.50 each add'l. $.25 per pg after 19. Required to search: name, years to search; also helpful: address. Civil cases indexed by defendant, plaintiff. Civil records on computer from 1990, microfiche from 1800s. Mail turnaround time 1-2 days.

Criminal Records: Access: Mail, in person. Both court and visitors may perform in person searches.

Search fee: $6.00 per name per year. Court makes copy: $2.00 for first page, $.50 each add'l. $.25 per page after 19. Required to search: name, years to search, DOB. Criminal records on computer from 1990, microfiche from 1800s. Mail turnaround time 1-2 days.

General Information: Public use terminal available. No juvenile or adoption records released. Will not fax documents. Certification fee: $6.00. Payee: Clerk of Circuit Court. Personal Checks not excepted. Prepayment and SASE required.

Stark County

Circuit Court 130 W Main St, Toulon, IL 61483; phone: 309-286-5941; fax: 309-286-4039; hours 8:30AM-4:30PM (CST). *Felony, Misdemeanor, Civil, Eviction, Small Claims, Probate.*
Civil Records: Access: Mail, in person. Both court and visitors may perform in person searches. Search fee: $6.00 per name per year. Court makes copy: $1.00 for first page, $.50 each add'l. Required to search: name, years to search. Civil cases indexed by defendant. Civil records on index books from 1800s. Mail turnaround time 2-3 days.

Criminal Records: Access: Mail, in person. Both court and visitors may perform in person searches. Search fee: $6.00 per name per year. Court makes copy: $1.00 for first page, $.50 each add'l. Required to search: name, years to search, DOB. Criminal records on index books from 1800s. Mail turnaround time 2-3 days.

General Information: Public terminal has criminal back to 2000 and civil back to 2001. No juvenile or adoption records released. Certification fee: $4.00. Payee: Clerk of Circuit Court. Personal checks accepted. Prepayment and SASE required.

Stephenson County

Circuit Court 15 N Galena Ave, Freeport, IL 61032; phone: 815-235-8266; criminal fax: 815-233-1576; civil fax: 815-235-8262; hours 8:30AM-4:30PM (CST). *Felony, Misdemeanor, Civil, Eviction, Small Claims, Probate.*
www.judici.com
Civil Records: Access: Mail, in person, online. Both court and visitors may perform in person searches. Search fee: $6.00 per name per year. Court makes copy: $2.00 for first page, $.50 each add'l; same fee for self serve. Required to search: name, years to search. Civil cases indexed by defendant, plaintiff. Civil records on computer from 8/1989, index books from 1875. Access is free to civil, small claims, probate and traffic records at www.judici.com/courts/index.jsp?court=IL089015J. Mail turnaround time 5-15 days.

Criminal Records: Access: Mail, in person, online. Both court and visitors may perform in person searches. Search fee: $6.00 per name per year. Court makes copy: $2.00 for first page, $.50 each add'l; same fee for self serve. Required to search: name, years to search, DOB. Criminal records on computer from 8/1989, index books from 1875. Criminal records access is free at www.judici.com/courts/index.jsp?court=IL089015J. Mail turnaround time 5-15 days.

General Information: Public terminal goes back to 1989. No juvenile or adoption records released. Certification fee: $10.00. Payee: Clerk of Circuit Court. Business checks accepted. Prepayment and SASE required.

Tazewell County

Circuit Court Courthouse, 4th & Court Sts, Pekin, IL 61554; phone: 309-477-2214; hours 8:30AM-5PM (CST). *Felony, Misdemeanor, Civil, Small Claims, Probate.*
Civil Records: Access: Mail, in person. Both court and visitors may perform in person searches. Search fee: $6.00 per name per year. Court makes copy: $2.00 for first page, $.50 each add'l. After 20 pages, $.25 per page. Required to search: name, years to search. Civil cases indexed by defendant, plaintiff.

Civil records on computer from 2/89 index books from 1800s. Mail turnaround time 3-4 days.

Criminal Records: Access: Mail, in person. Both court and visitors may perform in person searches. Search fee: $6.00 per name per year. Court makes copy: $2.00 for first page, $.50 each add'l. $.25 per page after 20. Required to search: name, years to search, DOB, signed release. Criminal records on computer from 2/89 index books from 1800s. Mail turnaround time 3-4 days.

General Information: Public terminal goes back to 2/1989. No juvenile or adoption records released. Certification fee: $6.00. Payee: Clerk of Circuit Court. Only cashiers checks and money orders accepted. Prepayment and SASE required.

Union County

Circuit Court Union County Courthouse, 309 W Market, Rm 101, Jonesboro, IL 62952; phone: 618-833-5913; fax: 618-833-5223; hours 8AM-N,1-4PM (CST). *Felony, Misdemeanor, Civil, Eviction, Small Claims, Probate.*

Civil Records: Access: Fax, mail, in person, online. Both court and visitors may perform in person searches. Search fee: $6.00 per name per year. Court makes copy: $2.00 first page, $.50 2-19th copy, $.25 thereafter. Required to search: name, years to search. Civil cases indexed by defendant, plaintiff. Civil records on computer from 1986, index books from 1800s. Access is free to civil, small claims, probate and traffic records at www.judici.com/courts/index.jsp?court=IL091015 J. Note: Public can only search paper records up to 1986. Only court personnel have access to computer records. Mail turnaround time 1 week.

Criminal Records: Access: Fax, mail, in person, online. Both court and visitors may perform in person searches. Search fee: $6.00 per name per year. Court makes copy: $2.00 first page, $.50 each add'l 19 pages; $.25 each over 20. Required to search: name, years to search; also helpful: DOB. Criminal records on computer from 1986, index books from 1800s. Criminal records access is free at www.judici.com/courts/index.jsp?court=IL091015 J. Note: In person criminal record search procedures are the same as civil. Mail turnaround time 1 week.

General Information: No public access terminal. No juvenile or adoption records released. Fee to fax documents is $5.00. Certification fee: $5.00 per doc. Payee: Lorraine Moreland, Circuit Clerk. Business checks accepted. No personal checks or credit cards. Prepayment and SASE required.

Vermilion County

Circuit Court 7 N Vermilion, Danville, IL 61832; phone: 217-554-7700; probate phone: 217-554-7731; fax: 217-554-7728; hours 8:30AM-4:30PM (CST). *Felony, Misdemeanor, Civil, Eviction, Small Claims, Probate.*
www.co.vermilion.il.us
Civil Records: Access: Phone, mail, in person, online. Both court and visitors may perform in person searches. Search fee: $6.00 per name per year. Court makes copy: $2.00 for 1st page, $.50 each add'l. Self serve copy fee: $.10 per page. Required to search: name, years to search. Civil cases indexed by defendant, plaintiff. Civil records on computer from 1989; microfilm from 3/1949 to 5/1989; index books from 1800s. Search the index at www.judici.com/courts/cases/case_search.jsp?court=IL092015J. Records are current to 1989. Mail turnaround time 2-3 days.

Criminal Records: Access: Phone, mail, in person, online. Both court and visitors may perform in person searches. Search fee: $6.00 per name per year. Court makes copy: $2.00 for 1st page, $.50 each add'l. Self serve copy fee: $.10 per page. Required to search: name, years to search, DOB; also helpful: SSN. Criminal records on computer from 1989; microfilm from 3/1949 to 5/1989; index books from 1800s. Search the index at www.judici.com/courts/cases/case_search.jsp?court=IL092015J. Records are current to 1989. Mail turnaround time 1 week.

General Information: Public terminal goes back to 1989. No juvenile, impounded, mental health or adoption records released. Certification fee: $5.00 per doc. Payee: Clerk of Circuit Court. Business checks accepted. Prepayment and SASE required.

Wabash County

Circuit Court PO Box 997, 401 Market St, Mt Carmel, IL 62863; phone: 618-262-5362; fax: 618-263-4441; hours 8AM-5PM (CST). *Felony, Misdemeanor, Civil, Eviction, Small Claims, Probate.*

Civil Records: Access: Mail, in person. Both court and visitors may perform in person searches. Search fee: $4.00 per name per year. Court makes copy: $.50 each for 1st 20 pages; $.25 each add'l. Self serve copy fee: $.25 per page. Required to search: name, years to search. Civil cases indexed by defendant, plaintiff. Civil records on computer from 1988, index books from 1800s. Mail turnaround time 5 days.

Criminal Records: Access: Mail, in person. Both court and visitors may perform in person searches. Search fee: $4.00 per name per year. Court makes copy: $.50 each 1st 20 pages; $.25 each add'l. Self serve copy fee: $.25 per page. Required to search: name, years to search, DOB. Criminal records on computer from 1988, index books from 1800s. Mail turnaround time 5 days.

General Information: Public terminal goes back to 1988. No juvenile or adoption records released. Will fax if all fees prepaid. Certification fee: $5.00. Payee: Clerk of Circuit Court. Only cashiers checks and money orders accepted. Prepayment and SASE required.

Warren County

Circuit Court 100 W Broadway, Monmouth, IL 61462; phone: 309-734-5179; criminal phone: x302; civil phone: x304; probate phone: x306; fax: 309-734-4151; hours 8AM-4:30PM (CST). *Felony, Misdemeanor, Civil, Eviction, Small Claims, Probate.*

Civil Records: Access: Mail, in person. Both court and visitors may perform in person searches. Search fee: $5.00 per name per year. Court makes copy: $2.00 1st page; $.50 each add'l page. Required to search: name, years to search. Civil cases indexed by defendant. Civil records on computer from 2000, index books from 1800s. Mail turnaround time 7-10 days.

Criminal Records: Access: Mail, in person. Both court and visitors may perform in person searches. Search fee: $5.00 per name per year. Court makes copy: $2.00 1st page; $.50 each add'l page. Required to search: name, years to search, DOB. Criminal records on computer from 2000, index books from 1800s. Mail turnaround time 7-10 days.

General Information: Public terminal goes back to 1999. No juvenile or adoption records released. Will fax documents uncertified. Certification fee: $3.00. Payee: Clerk of Circuit Court. Only cashiers checks and money orders accepted. Prepayment and SASE required.

Washington County

Circuit Court 101 E St Louis St, Nashville, IL 62263; phone: 618-327-4800 X305; fax: 618-327-3583; hours 8AM-4PM (CST). *Felony, Misdemeanor, Civil, Eviction, Small Claims, Probate.*

Civil Records: Access: Mail, in person. Both court and visitors may perform in person searches. Search fee: $5.00 per name per year. Court makes copy: $1.00 per page. Self serve copy fee: $.50 per page. Required to search: name, years to search. Civil cases indexed by defendant, plaintiff. Civil records on computer since 1998; 1988 for child support; prior records on index books from 1800s. Mail turnaround time 3-5 days.

Criminal Records: Access: Mail, in person. Both court and visitors may perform in person searches. Search fee: $5.00 per name per year. Court makes copy: $1.00 per page. Self serve copy fee: $.50 per page. Required to search: name, years to search; also helpful: DOB. Criminal records on computer since 1998; 1988 for child support; prior records on index books from 1800s. Mail turnaround time 3-5 days.

General Information: Public terminal goes back to 1997. No juvenile or adoption records released. Will fax documents to local or toll free line. Certification fee: $3.00 per document. Payee: Washington County Circuit Clerk. No personal checks accepted. Prepayment required. Will bill to attorneys. SASE required.

Wayne County

Circuit Court County Courthouse, 307 E Main St, Fairfield, IL 62837; phone: 618-842-7684; fax: 618-842-2556; hours 8AM-4:30PM (CST). *Felony, Misdemeanor, Civil, Small Claims, Probate.*

Civil Records: Access: Mail, fax, in person. Both court and visitors may perform in person searches. Search fee: $4.00 per name per year. Court makes copy: $1.00 1st page, $.50 each add'l; same fee for self serve. Required to search: name, years to search. Civil cases indexed by defendant, plaintiff. Civil records on computer back to 11/88, index books from 1800s. Mail turnaround time 1 week.

Criminal Records: Access: Mail, fax, in person. Both court and visitors may perform in person searches. Search fee: $4.00 per name per year. Court makes copy: $1.00 1st page, $.50 each add'l; same fee for self serve. Required to search: name, years to search, DOB. Criminal records computerized back 1/1990. Mail turnaround time 1 week.

General Information: Public terminal goes back to 1988. No juvenile or adoption records released. Will fax documents. Certification fee: $5.00 per certification. Payee: Clerk of Circuit Court. Only cashiers checks and money orders accepted. Prepayment and SASE required.

White County

Circuit Court PO Box 310, 301 E Main, County Courthouse, Carmi, IL 62821; phone: 618-382-2321 x4; fax: 618-382-2322; hours 8AM-4PM (CST). *Felony, Misdemeanor, Civil, Small Claims, Probate.*

Civil Records: Access: Fax, mail, in person. Both court and visitors may perform in person searches. Search fee: $4.00 per name per year. Court makes copy: $.50 per page; same fee for self serve. Required to search: name, years to search. Civil cases indexed by defendant, plaintiff. Civil records on computer from 1991, index books from 1800s. Mail turnaround time 1-2 weeks.

Criminal Records: Access: Fax, mail, in person. Both court and visitors may perform in person searches. Search fee: $4.00 per name per year. Court makes copy: $.50 per page; same fee for self serve. Required to search: name, years to search; also helpful: DOB. Criminal records on computer from 1991, index books from 1800s. Mail turnaround time 1-2 weeks.

General Information: Public terminal goes back to 1991. No juvenile or adoption records released. Will fax documents $2.00 per page. Certification fee: $5.00 per document. Payee: Clerk of Circuit Court. Personal checks accepted. Prepayment and SASE required.

Whiteside County

Circuit Court 200 E Knox St, Morrison, IL 61270-2698; phone: 815-772-5188; fax: 815-772-5187; hours 8:30AM-4:30PM (CST). *Felony, Misdemeanor, Civil, Eviction, Small Claims, Probate.*

Civil Records: Access: Phone, fax, mail, in person, online. Both court and visitors may perform in person searches. Search fee: $6.00 per name. Court makes copy: $.25 per page. Required to search: name, years to search. Civil cases indexed by defendant. Civil records on computer from 1989, index books from 1800s. Access is free to civil, small claims, probate and traffic records at www.judici.com/courts/cases/case_search.jsp?court=IL098015J. Mail turnaround time 1 week.

Criminal Records: Access: Phone, fax, mail, in person, online. Both court and visitors may perform in person searches. Search fee: $6.00 per name. Court makes copy: $.25 per page. Required to search: name, years to search, DOB. Criminal records on computer from 1988, index books from 1800s. Access to criminal records is the same as civil. Mail turnaround time 1 week.

General Information: Public use terminal available. No juvenile or adoption records released. No fee to fax documents. Local faxing only. Certification fee: $4.00. Payee: Clerk of Circuit Court. Personal checks accepted. Prepayment and SASE required.

Will County

Circuit Court 14 W Jefferson St, #212, Joliet, IL 60432; phone: 815-727-8592; probate phone: 815-730-7242; fax: 815-727-8896; probate fax: 815-730-7160; hours 8:30AM-4:30PM (CST). *Felony, Misdemeanor, Civil, Eviction, Small Claims, Probate.*

www.willcountycircuitcourt.com

Civil Records: Access: Fax, mail, in person, online. Both court and visitors may perform in person searches. Search fee: $4.00 per name per year. Court makes copy: $2.00 for first page, $.50 each add'l. Required to search: name, years to search. Civil cases indexed by defendant, plaintiff. Civil records on computer from 1989, index books from 1800s. Online access to court records is via a internet subscription system. Fee is $240 per year for Will County or $300 for Will,Sangamon,Madison,Winnebago,Kane,Kendall,DeKalb courts. For info, email benright@willcountyillinois.com or call 815-727-8592. Mail turnaround time 48 hours.

Criminal Records: Access: Fax, mail, in person, online. Both court and visitors may perform in person searches. Search fee: $4.00 per name per year. Court makes copy: $2.00 for first page, $.50 each add'l. Required to search: name, years to search, DOB. Criminal records on computer from 1989, index books from 1800s. Online access to court records is via a internet subscription system. Fee is $240 per year for Will County or $300 for Will,Sangamon,Madison,Winnebago,Kane,Kendall,DeKalb courts. For info, email

benright@willcountyillinois.com or call 815-727-8592. Note: Only attorneys can fax in requests. Mail turnaround time 2 weeks.

General Information: Public terminal goes back to 10 years. No juvenile, adoption, mental health records released. Will not fax documents. Certification fee: $4.00. Payee: Pamela J McGuire Clerk of Circuit Court. Only cashiers checks and money orders accepted. Prepayment and SASE required.

Williamson County

Circuit Court 200 W Jefferson St, Marion, IL 62959; phone: 618-997-1301 X153; hours 8AM-4PM (CST). *Felony, Misdemeanor, Civil, Eviction, Small Claims, Probate.*

Civil Records: Access: Mail, in person. Both court and visitors may perform in person searches. Search fee: $4.00 per name per year. Court makes copy: $1.00 for first page, $.50 each add'l. Required to search: name, years to search. Civil cases indexed by defendant, plaintiff. Civil records on computer from 7/86, index books from 1800s. Mail turnaround time 1 week.

Criminal Records: Access: Mail, in person. Both court and visitors may perform in person searches. Search fee: $4.00 per name per year. Court makes copy: $1.00 for first page, $.50 each add'l. Required to search: name, years to search, DOB. Criminal records on computer from 7/86, index books from 1800s. Mail turnaround time 1 week.

General Information: Public use terminal available. No juvenile or adoption records released. Certification fee: $2.00. Payee: Clerk of Circuit Court. Business checks accepted. Prepayment and SASE required.

Winnebago County

Circuit Court 400 W State St, Rockford, IL 61101; phone: 815-987-3031 (records); criminal phone: 815-987-3079/3175; civil phone: 815-987-2510; fax: 815-987-3012; hours 8AM-5PM (CST). *Felony, Misdemeanor, Civil, Eviction, Small Claims, Probate.*

www.cc.co.winnebago.il.us

Note: Criminal records is in Rm 108. Civil is Rm 104.

Civil Records: Access: Phone, mail, in person, online. Both court and visitors may perform in person searches. Search fee: $6.00 per page. Court makes copy: $2.00 for first page, $.50 each add'l. After 20 pgs, fee is $.25 per pg. Required to search: name, years to search. Civil cases indexed by

defendant, plaintiff. Civil records on computer back to 1983; prior records on index books from 1800s. Online access to court records is free at www.cc.co.winnebago.il.us/caseinfo.asp?P=I; Registration, username and password required. Includes Civil, Probate, Traffic but not juvenile back to 1980s. Call Craig at 815-987-2532 for information. Mail turnaround time 1 week.

Criminal Records: Access: Phone, mail, in person, online. Both court and visitors may perform in person searches. Search fee: $6.00 per name per year. Court makes copy: $2.00 for first page, $.50 each add'l. $.25 per page after 20. Required to search: name, years to search, DOB. Criminal records on computer back to 1983; prior records on index books from 1800s. Access criminal records online same as civil. Mail turnaround time 1 week.

General Information: Public terminal has criminal back to 1985 and civil back to 1980. No juvenile, mental or adoption records released. Will fax documents to local or toll free line. Certification fee: $8.00 per doc. Payee: Clerk of Circuit Court. Personal checks accepted. No credit cards. Prepayment and SASE required.

Woodford County

Circuit Court PO Box 284, 115 N Main, County Courthouse #201, Eureka, IL 61530; phone: 309-467-3312; hours 8AM-5PM (CST). *Felony, Misdemeanor, Civil, Eviction, Small Claims, Probate.*

Civil Records: Access: Mail, in person. Both court and visitors may perform in person searches. Search fee: $5.00 per name per year. Court makes copy: $.50 per page. Required to search: name, years to search. Civil cases indexed by defendant, plaintiff. Civil records on computer from 1990, index books from 1800s. Mail turnaround time 2-3 days.

Criminal Records: Access: Mail, in person. Both court and visitors may perform in person searches. Search fee: $5.00 per name per year. Court makes copy: $.50 per page. Required to search: name, years to search, DOB. Criminal records on computer from 1990, index books from 1800s. Mail turnaround time 2-3 days.

General Information: Public terminal goes back to 1990. No juvenile or adoption records released. Certification fee: $4.00. Cert fee includes copies. Payee: Woodford County Circuit Clerk. Personal checks accepted. Prepayment and SASE required.

Illinois Recording Offices

ORGANIZATION: 102 counties, 103 recording offices. Cook County had separate offices for real estate recording and UCC filing until June 30, 2001. As of that date the UCC filing office only searches for -- and no longer takes new -- UCC filings. The recording officer is Recorder of Deeds. Many counties utilize a grantor/grantee index containing all transactions. The entire state is in the Central Time Zone (CST).

REAL ESTATE RECORDS: Most counties will not perform real estate searches. Cost of certified copies varies widely, but many counties charge the same as the cost of recording the document. Tax records are usually located at the Treasurer's Office.

UCC RECORDS: Financing statements are filed at the state level except for real estate related filings which are filed with the County Recorder. (See above regarding Cook County.) Most counties will perform UCC searches. Use search request form UCC-11. Search fees are usually $10.00 per debtor name/address combination. Copies usually cost $1.00 per page.

TAX LIEN RECORDS: Federal tax liens on personal property of businesses are filed with the Secretary of State. Other federal and all state tax liens on personal property are filed with the County Recorder. Some counties will perform tax lien searches for $5.00-$10.00 per name (state and federal are separate searches in many of these counties) and $1.00 per page of copy.

OTHER LIENS: Judgments, mechanics, contractor, medical, lis pendens, oil & gas, mobile home.

ONLINE ACCESS: A limited number of counties offer online access. There is no statewide system.

Adams County

County Recorder, 507 Vermont St #110, Quincy, IL 62301. RE & UCC recording phone-217-277-2125; hours: 8:30AM-4:30PM
All records in one index. Only the public may search. Copy fee $1.00 per page. Cert fee- $12.00 per cert + $1.00 per page after 4 pages. Payee- Adams County Clerk/Recorder. **Online access to Assessor, Real Estate records:** Access property data free at www.emapsplus.com/ILAdams/maps/ including name searching. **Other phones:** Treasurer- 217-277-2248; Elections- 217-277-2157; Vital Records- 217-277-2158. **Property tax/Assessor-** 217-277-2136.

Alexander County

County Recorder, 2000 Washington Ave, Cairo, IL 62914. RE & UCC recording phone-618-734-7000; fax-618-734-7002; hours: 8AM-N, 1-4PM
Separate indices to search include mortgages, deeds, deaths, births, marriages, releases, misc, liens. Records indexed on computer back to 1990. Only the public may search. Copy fee $1.00 per page. Cert fee- $5.00 per cert plus copy fee. Payee- Alexander County Recorder. **Other phones:** Treasurer- 618-734-7009; Elections- 618-734-7000; Vital Records- 618-734-7000. **Property tax/Assessor-** same address as above. 618-734-7011.

Bond County

County Recorder, 203 W. College Ave, Greenville, IL 62246. 618-664-0449; fax-618-664-9414; hours: 8AM-4PM
Separate indices to search include Grantor/Grantee. Records indexed on a public use terminal back to 4/15/2005. Only the public may search. Copy fee $1.00 per page. Cert fee- $25.00 1st 4 pages, $1.00 each add'l page. Payee- Bond County Recorder. **Other phones:** Treasurer- 618-664-0618; Elections- 618-664-0449; Vital Records- 618-664-0449. **Property tax/Assessor-** same address as above. 618-664-2848.

Boone County

County Recorder, 601 N. Main St; #202, Belvidere, IL 61008. 815-544-3103; fax-815-547-8701; hours: 8:30AM-5PM www.boonecountyil.org
Records indexed on a public use terminal back to 1990. Office will perform a UCC search but public must search other records themselves. UCC search per debtor name/address- $10.00. Copy fee $1.00 per page. Cert fee- Same as original recording fee. Payee- Boone County Recorder. **Online access to Real Estate, Property Tax, Land Sale records:** Access land data on commercial site - PropertyMax - at http://booneilpropertymax.governmaxa.com/propertymax/rover30.asp. Subscription packages from $10.00 per month. Search property by owner, address, parcel #, property description, or GIS map. **Other phones:** Treasurer- 815-544-2666; Elections- 815-544-3103; Vital Records- 815-544-3103. **Property tax/Assessor-** 601 N Main St #103, Belvidere, IL 61008; 815-544-2958.

Brown County

County Recorder, Courthouse - Rm4; #1 Court St, Mount Sterling, IL 62353-1285. RE & UCC recording phone-217-773-3421; fax-217-773-2233; hours: 8:30AM-4:30PM
All records in one index. Record index not computerized. Office will perform a UCC search but public must search other records themselves. Search fee $13.00. Copy fee $1.00 per page. Cert fee- $48.00 per cert, plus $1.00 per addtl page. Payee- Brown County Recorder. **Other phones:** Treasurer- 217-773-3133; Elections- 217-773-3421; Vital Records- 217-773-3421. **Property tax/Assessor-** 217-773-3415.

Bureau County

County Recorder, 700 S. Main St.; Courthouse, Princeton, IL 61356. RE & UCC recording phone-815-875-3239; fax-815-879-4803; hours: 8AM-4PM
Separate indices to search include grantor/grantee, tract, federal or state tax liens, unemployment tax, retailers tax, public aid liens, child support liens. Records indexed on a public use terminal back to 8/1986. Office will perform a UCC search but public must search other records themselves. Search fee $10.00 per name for UCC. Copy fee $.50 per page. Cert fee- $12.00 per cert includes copy fee. Payee- Bureau County Recorder. **Other phones:** Treasurer- 815-875-3241; Elections- 815-875-2014; Vital Records- 815-875-3239. **Property tax/Assessor-** same address, 815-875-6478.

Calhoun County

County Clerk & Recorder, PO Box 187, Hardin, IL 62047. 618-576-2351; fax-618-576-2895; hours: 8:30AM-4:30PM
Separate indices to search include Grantor/Grantee, Tract index. Records indexed on computer back to 1992. Office will perform a UCC and Tax lien search but public must search other records themselves. Search fee $10.00. Copy fee $.50 per page. Cert fee- $2.00 per cert plus copy fee. Payee- Calhoun County Clerk and Recorder. **Other phones:** Treasurer- 618-576-2421; Elections- 618-576-2351; Vital Records- 618-576-2351. **Property tax/Assessor-** 618-576-8041.

Carroll County

County Recorder, PO Box 152, Mount Carroll, IL 61053. 815-244-0223; fax-815-244-3709; hours: 8:30AM-4:30AM
Only the public may search. Copy fee $2.00 per page. Cert fee- Same as original recording fee. Payee- Carroll County Recorder. **Other phones:** Treasurer- 815-244-0243. **Property tax/Assessor-** 815-244-0238.

Cass County

County Recorder, 100 E Springfield St, Virginia, IL 62691. 217-452-7217; fax-217-452-7219; hours: 8:30AM-4:30PM
Only the public may search. Copy fee $1.00 per page. Cert fee- $35.00 add'l $1.00 per page. Payee- Cass County Recorder. **Other phones:** Treasurer- 217-452-7721. **Property tax/Assessor-** 217-452-7249.

Champaign County

County Recorder, 1776 E. Washington, Urbana, IL 61802. 217-384-3774; fax-217-344-1663; hours: 8AM-4:30PM
All records in one index. Records indexed on computer. Office will perform a UCC and Tax lien search but public must search other records themselves. Search fee $10.00. General copy fee $1.50 per page. RE record copy- $1.50 per page. Cert fee- $12.00 per cert + $1.00 per page after 4 pages. Payee- Champaign County Recorder. **Online access to Recording, Real Estate, Deed, Lien records:** Recorder office data by subscription on either the Laredo system using subscription and fees or the Tapestry System using credit card, https://tapestry.fidlar.com/tapsearch.aspx; $3.99 search; $.50 per image. **Other phones:** Treasurer- 217-384-3743. **Property tax/Assessor-** 217-384-3760.

Christian County

County Recorder, PO Box 647, Taylorville, IL 62568. RE & UCC recording phone-217-824-4960; fax-217-824-5105; hours: 8AM-4PM

All records in one index. Records indexed on a public use terminal back to 1990. Office will perform a UCC search but public must search other records themselves. UCC search per debtor name/address- $10.00. Copy fee $1.00 per page. Cert fee- $31.00 per cert plus copy fee. Payee-Christian County Recorder. **Online access to Real Estate, Recorder, Deed, Lien, UCC records:** Recorder office data by subscription on either the Laredo system using subscription and fees or the Tapestry System using credit card, https://tapestry.fidlar.com/tapsearch.aspx; $3.99 search; $.50 per image. From 1990 to present . **Other phones:** Treasurer- 217-824-4889; Elections- 217-824-4969; Vital Records- 217-824-4969. **Property tax/Assessor-** 217-824-5900.

Clark County

County Recorder, Courthouse, Marshall, IL 62441. RE & UCC recording phone-217-826-8311; hours: 8AM-4PM www.clarkcountyil.org

Separate indices to search include grantor/grantee, mortgagor/mortgagee, financing statements, misc, liens, O&G lease, O&G assign, memo of judgments. Office will perform a UCC search but public must search other records themselves. Will not search real estate records. UCC search per debtor name/address- $10.00. Copy fee $1.00 per page. RE or tax lien copy- $.50 per page. Cert fee- $14.00 per cert plus copy fee. Payee- Clark County Recorder. **Other phones:** Treasurer- 217-826-5721; Elections- 217-826-8311; Vital Records- 217-826-8311. **Property tax/Assessor-** 501 Archer Ave, Marshall, IL 62441; 217-826-5815.

Clay County

County Recorder, PO Box 160, Louisville, IL 62858-0160. RE & UCC recording phone-618-665-3626; fax-618-665-3607; hours: 8AM-4PM

All records in one index. General index search fee $10.00 per name. Real estate owner, mortgage, and property transfer searches available. Will search UCC records and tax liens. UCC search per debtor name- $10.00 per name per 5 yrs. Separate federal tax lien search- $5.00 per debtor. Separate state tax lien search- $5.00 per debtor. Copy fee $1.00 per page. Cert fee- $20.00 per document includes copy fee. Payee- Clay County Recorder. **Other phones:** Treasurer- 618-665-3727; Elections- 618-665-3626; Vital Records- 618-665-3626. **Property tax/Assessor-** 618-665-3370.

Clinton County

County Recorder, PO Box 308, Carlyle, IL 62231. Main phone & R/E recording-618-594-2464, UCC recording phone-618-594-0142; fax-618-594-0195; hours: 8AM-4PM www.clintonco.org

All records in one index. Office will perform a tax lien search but public must search other records themselves. Tax lien search fee-$10.00 per debtor. Copy fee $1.00 per page. Cert fee- $6.00 per cert plus copy fee. Payee- Clinton County Recorder. **Online access to Recording, Real Estate, Deed, Lien records:** Recorder office data by subscription on either the Laredo system using subscription and fees or the Tapestry System using credit card, https://tapestry.fidlar.com/tapsearch.aspx; $3.99 search; $.50 per image. Index back to 1988; images to 1992. **Other phones:** Treasurer- 618-594-2464; Elections- 618-594-2464; Vital Records- 618-594-2464. **Property tax/Assessor-** 618-594-3221.

Coles County

County Recorder, 651 Jackson Ave, Rm 122, Charleston, IL 61920. RE & UCC recording phone-217-348-7325; fax-217-348-7337; hours: 8:30AM-4:30PM

Separate indices to search include grantor/grantee, morgagor/mortgagee. Records indexed on a public use terminal back to 12/1/78. Only the office personnel may search. Copy fee $5.00 per instrument up to 10 pages, $1.00 each add'l page. Cert fee- $5.00 per cert plus copy fee. Payee-Coles County Recorder. **Online access to Real Estate, Recorder, Lien, UCC, Deed records:** Records on the recorder's database are free at www.landaccess.com/proi/county.jsp?county=ilcoles . **Other phones:** Treasurer- 217-348-0511; Elections- 217-348-0524; Vital Records- 217-348-0501. **Property tax/Assessor-** 217-348-0508.

Cook County

Recorder of Deeds, 118 N. Clark St; Rm 120, Chicago, IL 60602-1387. 312-603-7524, R/E recording phone-312-603-5066; fax-312-603-5063; hours: 9AM-5PM www.ccrd.info

All records in one index. Records indexed on computer. Office personnel or visitors may perform searches. Search fee $10.00. General copy fee $1.00 per page. Tax lien copy- $6.00 per document. Cert fee- $6.00 per page plus copy fee. Payee- Cook County Recorder. **Online access to Property Tax records:** . **Other phones:** Treasurer- 312-603-4436; Vital Records- 312-603-7790. **Property tax/Assessor-** same address as above. 312-443-7550.

Cook County Recorder

County Recorder, 118 N. Clark St. #120; Rm 230, Chicago, IL 60602. 312-603-5134, 312-603-5050, R/E recording phone-312-603-5066, UCC recording phone-312-603-5050; fax-312-603-5063; hours: 8AM-4:55PM www.ccrd.info

There are no filings recorded at this office after June 30, 2001. Only records prior to this date can be searched. All records in one index. Records indexed on a public use terminal back to 1985. Office will perform a UCC and Tax lien search but public must search other records themselves. Search fee $5.00. Copy fee $1.00 per page. Cert fee- double the uncertified doc cost. Payee- Cook County Recorder. **Online access to Real Estate, Recorder, Deed, Grantor/Grantee, Heir, Inmate, Wanted Sex Offender records:** Search Grantor/Grantee index and locate property data at www.ccrd.info. Fee for documents. Search DIMS database of recordings since 10/1985; registration and fees apply. Includes Treasurer's Current Year Tax System (APIN) and DuPagerecorder. Sign-up information is at www.ccrd.info/CCRD/il031/index.jsp. Also, you may purchase the real estate transfer list; $100 per year on disk ($50 if you pick-up at agency.). Also, search the treasurer's heirs database free at www.cookcountytreasurer.com/inheritance.aspx?ntopicid=238. Also, you may search assessor data free at www.cookcountyassessor.com/startsearch.html, however, there is no name searching. **Other phones:** Treasurer- 312-443-4436. **Property tax/Assessor-** same address as above. 312-443-7550.

Crawford County

County Recorder, PO Box 616, Robinson, IL 62454-0602. RE & UCC recording phone-618-546-1212; fax-618-546-0140; hours: 8AM-4PM http://crawfordcountycentral.com/coclerk/

Separate indices to search include grantor/grantee. Records indexed on a public use terminal back to 1980. Office personnel or visitors may perform searches. Search fee $10.00 per name. Copy fee $1.00 per page. Cert fee- $13.00 per cert includes copy fee. Payee- Crawford County Recorder. **Other phones:** Treasurer- 618-544-2614; Elections- 618-546-2590; Vital Records- 618-546-1212. **Property tax/Assessor-** same address as above. 618-544-8221.

Cumberland County

County Recorder, PO Box 146, Toledo, IL 62468. RE & UCC recording phone-217-849-2631; fax-217-849-2968; hours: 8AM-4PM

All records in one index. Records indexed on a public use terminal back to 1990. Office will perform a UCC search but public must search other records themselves. Search fee $10.00. Copy fee $.50 per page. Cert fee- $12.00 per cert plus copy fee. Payee- Cumberland County Recorder. **Other phones:** Treasurer- 217-849-2321; Elections- 217-849-2631; Vital Records- 217-849-2631. **Property tax/Assessor-** same address. 217-849-3831.

De Kalb County

County Recorder, 110 E. Sycamore St, Sycamore, IL 60178. 815-895-7156; fax-815-895-7148; hours: 8:30AM-4:30PM

All records in one index. Records indexed on a public use terminal back to 1987. Office will perform a UCC search but public must search other records themselves. Search fee $10.00 per name. Tax liens not included in UCC search. Copy fee $1.00 per page. Cert fee- $39.00 1st 4 pages, $1.00 each add'l page. Payee- De Kalb County Recorder. **Online access to Real Estate, Lien records:** The De Kalb County online system requires a $350 subscription fee, with a per minute charge of $.25, $.50 if printing. Records date back to 1980. Lending agency information is available. For further information, contact Sheila Larson at 815-895-7152. **Other phones:** Treasurer- 815-895-7112. **Property tax/Assessor-** same address. 815-895-7120.

De Witt County

County Recorder, PO Box 439, Clinton, IL 61727-0439. RE & UCC recording phone-217-935-2119; fax-217-935-4596; hours: 8:30AM-4:30PM

Separate indices to search include Grantor/Grantee, Lot and section. Only the public may search. Copy fee $1.00 per page. RE record copy- $.50 per page. Cert fee- $2.50 per doc plus copy fee. Payee- De Witt County Recorder. **Other phones:** Treasurer- 217-935-2359; Appraiser/Auditor- 217-935-2242; Elections- 217-935-2119; Vital Records- 217-935-2119. **Property tax/Assessor-** 217-935-2242.

Douglas County

County Recorder, PO Box 467, Tuscola, IL 61953-0467. RE & UCC recording phone-217-253-4410; fax-217-253-2233; hours: 8:30AM-4:30PM

All records in one index. Office will perform a UCC search but public must search other records themselves. Search fee $10.00. General copy fee $1.00 per page. RE record copy- $2.00 per document. Cert fee- $8.00 per cert plus copy fee. Payee- Douglas County Recorder. **Other phones:** Treasurer- 217-253-4011; Elections- 217-253-2411; Vital Records- 217-253-2411. **Property tax/Assessor-** same address as above. 217-253-3031.

Du Page County

County Recorder, PO Box 936, Wheaton, IL 60189. RE & UCC recording phone-630-407-5400; fax-630-407-5300; hours: 8AM-4:30PM www.dupageco.org/recorder/

All records in one index. Records indexed on computer back to 1976. Office will perform a UCC search but public must search other records themselves. UCC search per debtor name/address- $10.00. Copy fee $1.00 per page. RE or tax lien copy- $.50 per page. Cert fee- $5.00 per cert plus copy fee. Payee- Du Page County Recorder. **Online access to Real Estate, Lien, Tax Assessor records:** For access to the Du Page County database one must lease a live interface telephone line from a carrier to establish a connection. There is a fee of $.05 per transaction. Records date back to 1977. For info, contact Fred Kieltcka at 630-682-7030. Free internet access may soon be available. Access to sheriff's sex offenders, most wanted, and deadbeat parents lists are free at www.co.dupage.il.us/sheriff/. Search Wayne Township property records at www.waynetownshipassessor.com/disclaimer.html Search Bloomingdale Township property records at www.bloomingdaletownshipassessor.com/OPID/opid.asp. Search Wheatland Township records at www.wheatlandtownship.com/Assessor/disclaim.html.

No name searching in either Town. **Other phones:** Treasurer- 630-407-5900; Elections- 630-407-5600; Vital Records- 630-407-5500. **Property tax/Assessor-** 630-407-5858.

Edgar County

County Clerk and Recorder, 115 W. Court St, Rm J, Paris, IL 61944-1785. RE & UCC recording phone-217-466-7433; fax-217-466-7430; hours: 8AM-4PM www.edgarcounty-il.gov
All records in one index since 01/01/94. Records indexed on computer since 01/01/94. Search fee $10.00. Limited real estate owner, mortgage, and property transfer searches available. Tax liens not included in UCC search, must be searched separate. Copy fee $1.00 per page. Cert fee- $12.00 1st 4 pages; $1.00 each add'l. Payee- Edgar County Recorder. **Other phones:** Treasurer- 217-466-7446; Elections- 217-466-7433; Vital Records- 217-466-7433. **Property tax/Assessor-** 111 N Central, Paris, IL 61944; 217-466-7418.

Edwards County

County Recorder, 50 E. Main St; Courthouse, Albion, IL 62806-1294. RE & UCC recording phone-618-445-2115; fax-618-445-4941; hours: 8AM-4PM
Separate indices to search include grantor/grantee, tract, entry book. General index search fee $10.00 per name. Copy fee $1.00 per copy. Cert fee- $10.00 per cert plus copy fee. Payee- Edwards County Recorder. **Other phones:** Treasurer- 618-445-3581; Elections- 618-445-2115; Vital Records- 618-445-2115. **Property tax/Assessor-** same address as above. 618-445-3591.

Effingham County

County Clerk & Recorder, PO Box 628, Effingham, IL 62401-0628. RE & UCC recording phone-217-342-6535; fax-217-342-3577; hours: 8AM-4PM http://co.effingham.il.us
All records in one index. Office will perform a UCC search but public must search other records themselves. Search fee $10.00 per debtor. Copy fee $1.00 document up to 4 pages. Cert fee- $12.00 per cert plus copy fee. Payee- Effingham County Clerk and Recorder. **Other phones:** Treasurer- 217-342-6844; Elections- 217-342-6535; Vital Records- 217-342-6535. **Property tax/Assessor-** 101 N. 4th St #302, Effingham, IL 62401; 217-324-6711.

Fayette County

County Recorder, PO Box 401, Vandalia, IL 62471-0401. RE & UCC recording phone-618-283-5000; fax-618-283-5004; hours: 8AM-4PM
Separate indices to search include grantor/grantee by date. Only the public may search. Copy fee $1.00 per page. Cert fee- $12.00 for 1st 4 pages includes 1st 4 copy pages. Payee- Fayette County Recorder. **Other phones:** Treasurer- 618-283-5022; Elections- 618-283-5000; Vital Records- 618-283-5000. **Property tax/Assessor-** 221 S. 7th St, Vandalia, IL 62471; 618-283-5020.

Ford County

County Recorder, 200 W. State St; Rm 101, Paxton, IL 60957. RE & UCC recording phone-217-379-2721; fax-217-379-3258; hours: 8:30AM-4:30PM www.prairienet.org
All records in one index. Record index not computerized. Only the public may search. Copy fee $1.00 per page. Cert fee- $5.00 per cert plus copy fee. Payee- Ford County Recorder. **Other phones:** Treasurer- 217-379-2532; Elections- 217-379-2721; Vital Records- 217-379-2721. **Property tax/Assessor-** 217-379-4132.

Franklin County

County Clerk & Recorder, PO Box 607, Benton, IL. 62812. RE & UCC recording phone-618-438-3221; fax-618-435-3405; hours: 8AM-4PM
Separate indices to search include grantor/grantee, mortgagors/mortgagees, miscellaneous, federal lien tax notice, retailer's occupation tax lien, judgment, military, state income tax lien, mechanic lien, corporation, oil & gas leases. Records indexed on a public use terminal back to 1990. Only the public may search. Tax liens not included in UCC search. Must have written request for searches. UCC search per debtor name/address- $10.00. Copy fee $1.00 per page. Must have a written request for copies with money included. RE record copy- $.50 per page. Tax lien copy-$10.00 per name. Cert fee- $1.00 per cert plus copy fee. Payee- Franklin County Clerk & Recorder. **Other phones:** Treasurer- 618-438-7311; Elections- 618-438-3403; Vital Records- 618-438-3221. **Property tax/Assessor-** 202 W Main, Benton, IL 62812; 618-438-4331.

Fulton County

County Recorder, PO Box 226, Lewistown, IL 61542. 309-547-3041, R/E recording phone-309-547-3041 x43, UCC recording phone-309-547-3041 x43; hours: 8AM-4PM www.fultonco.org
Office will perform a UCC search but public must search other records themselves. UCC search per debtor name/address- $10.00. Copy fee $1.00 per page. Cert fee- $5.00 per doc plus copy fee. Payee-Fulton County Recorder. **Online access to Recording, Real Estate, Deed, Lien records:** Recorder office data by subscription on either the Laredo system using subscription and fees or the Tapestry System using credit card, https://tapestry.fidlar.com/tapsearch.aspx; $3.99 search; $.50 per image. **Other phones:** Treasurer- 309-547-3041 x25; Elections- 309-547-3041 x704; Vital Records- 309-547-3041 x 42. **Property tax/Assessor-** 309-547-3041 x58.

Gallatin County

County Recorder, PO Box 550, Shawneetown, IL 62984. RE & UCC recording phone-618-269-3025; fax-618-269-3343; hours: 8AM-4PM
Separate indices to search include grantor/grantee. Records indexed on computer 3/91. Only the public may search. Copy fee $1.00 per page. RE record copy- $.25 per page. Cert fee- $10.00 per cert plus copy fee. Payee- Gallatin County Recorder. **Online access to Property records:** Search for property information on the GIS-mapping site for free at www.co.gallatin.mt.us/GIS/index.htm. No name searching. **Other phones:** Treasurer- 618-269-3022; Appraiser/Auditor- 618-269-3791; Elections- 618-269-3025; Vital Records- 618-269-3025. **Property tax/Assessor-** PO Box 640, Shawneetown, IL 62984; 618-269-3791.

Greene County

County Recorder, 519 N. Main St; Courthouse, Carrollton, IL 62016-1033. RE & UCC recording phone-217-942-5443; fax-217-942-9323; hours: 8AM-4PM
All records in one index. Records indexed on a public use terminal back to 1997. Only the public may search. Copy fee $.25 per page. Cert fee- $44.00 per cert includes copy fee. Payee- Greene County Recorder. **Other phones:** Treasurer- 217-942-5124; Elections- 217-942-5443; Vital Records- 217-942-5443. **Property tax/Assessor-** same address as above. 217-942-6412.

Grundy County

County Recorder, PO Box 675, Morris, IL 60450-0675. 815-941-3224; fax-815-942-2222; hours: 8AM-4:30PM
Separate indices to search. Records indexed on a public use terminal back to 1989 (names). Office will perform a tax lien search but public must search other records themselves. Search fee $10.00 per name. Copy fee $1.00 per page. Cert fee- Same as original recording fee includes copy fee. Payee- Grundy County Recorder. **Other phones:** Treasurer- 815-941-3215; Elections- 815-941-3221; Vital Records- 815-941-3222. **Property tax/Assessor-** 815-941-3269.

Hamilton County

County Recorder, Courthouse, 100 S Jackson St; Rm 2, McLeansboro, IL 62859-1489. 618-643-2721; hours: 8AM-4:30PM
All records in one index. Will search real estate records. Will search UCC records and tax liens. UCC search per debtor name/address- $10.00. Tax lien search fee $10.00 per search. Separate federal tax lien search- $10.00 per debtor. Separate state tax lien search- $10.00 per debtor. Federal/state combined tax lien search- $20.00 per debtor. Copy fee $1.00 per page. Cert fee- $5.00 1st 4 pages; $1.00 each add'l. Payee- Hamilton County Recorder. **Other phones:** Treasurer- 618-643-3313; Elections- 618-643-2721; Vital Records- 618-643-2721. **Property tax/Assessor-** 100 S Jackson, 3rd Fl Courthouse, McLeansboro, IL 62859; 618-643-3971.

Hancock County

County Recorder, PO Box 39, Carthage, IL 62321-0039. RE & UCC recording phone-217-357-3911; fax-none; hours: 8AM-4PM
Index: a. Office will perform a UCC search but public must search other records themselves. UCC search per debtor name/address- $10.00. Copy fee $.50 per copy if off computer; $1.00 per page if off microfiche. Cert fee- $15.00 per doc plus copy fee. Payee- Hancock County Recorder. **Other phones:** Treasurer- 217-357-2624; Appraiser- 217-357-3519; Elections- 217-357-3911; Vital Records- 217-357-3911. **Property tax/Assessor-** PO Box 444, Carthage, Il 62321; 217-357-2615.

Hardin County

County Recorder, PO Box 187, Elizabethtown, IL 62931. RE & UCC recording phone-618-287-2251; fax-618-287-2661; hours: 8AM-4PM
Office personnel or visitors may perform searches. Search fee $10.00 per name. Copy fee $1.00 per document. Cert fee- $5.00 per cert plus copy fee. Payee- Hardin County Recorder. **Other phones:** Treasurer- 618-287-2053; Elections- 618-287-2251; Vital Records- 618-287-2251; Circuit Clerk- 618-287-2735; Other Fax -618-287-2661. **Property tax/Assessor-** PO Box 119, Elizabethtown, IL 62931; 618-287-3551.

Henderson County

County Recorder, PO Box 308, Oquawka, IL 61469-0308. RE & UCC recording phone-309-867-2911; fax-309-867-2033; hours: 8AM-4PM
Index: More than 1 index. Record index not computerized. Only the public may search. Copy fee $.50 per page. Cert fee- $12.00 per cert plus copy fee. Payee- Henderson County Recorder. **Other phones:** Treasurer- 309-867-3121; Appraiser/Auditor- 309-867-3291; Elections- 309-867-2911; Vital Records- 309-867-2911. **Property tax/Assessor-** PO Box 342, Oquawka, IL 61469; 309-867-3291.

Henry County

County Recorder, 307 W Center St; Henry County Courthouse, Cambridge, IL 61238. 309-937-3486; fax-309-937-2796; hours: 8AM-4:30PM www.henrycty.com/recorder/index.html
All records in one index. Records indexed on a public use terminal back to 1990. Only the public may search. Copy fee $.50 per page. Cert fee- $41.00 1st 4 pages includes copy fee. Payee-Henry County Recorder. **Online access to Assessor records:** Access to the assessor database is free at www.henrycty.com/assessor/search.asp. Also, the county most wanted/fugitive list is at www.henrycty.com/sheriff/fugitives.html. **Other phones:** Treasurer- 309-937-3576; Elections- 309-937-3492; Vital Records- 309-937-3575. **Property tax/Assessor-** same address as above. 309-937-3570.

Iroquois County

County Recorder, 1001 E. Grant St, Watseka, IL 60970. 815-432-6962; fax-815-432-3894; hours: 8:30AM-4:30PM
All records in one index. Records indexed on a public use terminal back to 7/2001. Only the public may search. Copy fee $3.00 1st 4 pages, $1.00 each add'l. Cert fee- $5.00 per cert plus copy fee. Payee- Iroquois County Recorder. **Other phones:** Treasurer- 815-432-6985; Elections- 815-432-6960; Vital Records- 815-432-6960. **Property tax/Assessor-** same address as above. 815-432-6978.

Jackson County

County Recorder, 1001 Walnut, The Courthouse, Murphysboro, IL 62966. 618-687-7360; 8AM-4PM
Only the public may search except UCC. Will search UCC records prior to 7/2001 only. UCC search per debtor name/address- $10.00. Copy fee $.50 per page. Cert fee- $21.50 per document. Payee-Jackson County Recorder. **Other phones:** Treasurer- 618-687-3555. **Property tax/Assessor-** 20 S 10th Street, Murphysboro, IL 62966; 618-687-7220.

Jasper County

County Recorder, 204 W Washington St #2, Newton, IL 62448. RE & UCC recording phone-618-783-3124; fax-618-783-4137; hours: 8AM-4PM
Separate indices to search include books. Record index not computerized. Office personnel or visitors may perform searches. Search fee $10.00 per name. Will not search real estate records. Copy fee $.50 per page. Cert fee- $5.00 cert includes copy fee. Payee- Jasper County Recorder. **Other phones:** Treasurer- 618-783-3211; Elections- 618-783-3124; Vital Records- 618-783-3124. **Property tax/Assessor-** same address as above. 618-783-8042.

Jefferson County

County Recorder, 100 S. 10th St, Rm 105; Courthouse, Mount Vernon, IL 62864. 618-244-8020; hours: 8AM-5PM
Send SASE if requesting specific documents. All records in one index. Only the public may search, except UCC. UCC search per debtor name/address- $10.00. Copy fee $1.00 per page. Cert fee- $5.00 per cert plus copy fee. Payee-Jefferson County Recorder. **Other phones:** Treasurer- 618-244-8010. **Property tax/Assessor-** 618-244-8016.

Jersey County

County Recorder, 200 N Lafayette #2, Jerseyville, IL 62052. RE & UCC recording phone-618-498-5571 x117/8; fax-618-498-7823; hours: 8:30AM-4:30PM
All records in one index. Records indexed on computer back to June 1, 1985. Office will perform a UCC search but public must search other records themselves. UCC search per debtor name/address- $10.00. Copy fee $2.00 per page. Cert fee- $10.00 per cert includes copy fee. Payee-Jersey County Recorder. **Other phones:** Treasurer- 618-498-5571 x110; Elections- 618-498-5571 x112; Vital Records- 618-498-5571 x113. **Property tax/Assessor-** same address as above. 618-498-5571 x126.

Jo Daviess County

County Recorder, 330 N. Bench St, Galena, IL 61036. RE & UCC recording phone-815-777-9694; fax-815-777-3688; hours: 8AM-4PM www.jodaviess.org
All records in one index. Records indexed on a public use terminal back to 1989. Only the public may search. Copy fee $.50 per page. Cert fee- Same as original recording fee. Payee- Jo Daviess County Recorder. **Other phones:** Treasurer- 815-777-0355; Elections- 815-777-0161; Vital Records- 815-777-0161. **Property tax/Assessor-** same address as above. 815-777-1016, assessor fax- 815-777-9422.

Johnson County

County Recorder, PO Box 96, Vienna, IL 62995. RE & UCC recording phone-618-658-3611; fax-618-658-2908; hours: 8AM-N,1-4PM
All records in one index. General index search fee $10.00 per book/name. Will search real estate records. Will search UCC records and tax liens. UCC search per debtor book/name- $10.00. Separate federal tax lien search- $10.00 per debtor. Separate state tax lien search- $10.00 per debtor. Copy fee $1.00 per document. Cert fee- $7.00 per cert plus copy fee. Payee- Johnson County Recorder. **Other phones:** Treasurer- 618-658-8042; Elections- 618-658-3611; Vital Records- 618-658-3611. **Property tax/Assessor-** PO Box 337, Vienna, IL 62995; 618-658-8010.

Kane County

County Recorder, PO Box 71, Geneva, IL 60134. RE & UCC recording phone-630-232-5935; fax-630-232-5945; hours: 8:30AM-4:30PM www.co.kane.il.us
Office will perform a UCC search but public must search other records themselves. UCC search per debtor name/address- $10.00. Copy fee $1.00 per page. Payee- Kane County Recorder. **Online access to Real Estate records:** Search property tax info free at www.co.kane.il.us/treasurer/. Search by parcel number only; no name searching. **Other phones:** Treasurer- 630-232-3565. **Property tax/Assessor-** 630-232-3818.

Kankakee County

County Recorder, 189 E. Court St, Kankakee, IL 60901. RE & UCC recording phone-815-937-2980; fax-815-937-3657; hours: 8:30AM-4:30PM
All records in one index. Records indexed on a public use terminal back to 1992. Only the public may search. General copy fee $1.00 per page. RE record copy- $.25 per page. Cert fee- Same as original recording fee plus copy fee. Payee-Kankakee County Recorder. **Other phones:** Treasurer- 815-937-2960; Elections- 815-937-2990; Vital Records- 815-937-2990. **Property tax/Assessor-** same address as above. 815-937-2945.

Kendall County

County Recorder, 111 W. Fox St, Yorkville, IL 60560. RE & UCC recording phone-630-553-4112; fax-630-553-5283; hours: 8AM-4:30PM
Records indexed in books and microfilm from 1993 and before. Only the public may search. Copy fee $.50 per page. Cert fee- $27.00 for 1st 4 pages; $1.00 each add'l page plus copy fee. Payee-Kendall County Recorder. **Online access to Real Estate records:** Search property information at www.co.kendall.il.us/cidnet/public.htm. Search tax information by name or parcel number. **Other phones:** Treasurer- 630-553-4124; Appraiser/Auditor- 630-553-4146; Elections- 630-553-4105; Vital Records- 630-553-4105. **Property tax/Assessor-** 630-553-4146.

Knox County

County Recorder, 200 S. Cherry, County Courthouse, Galesburg, IL 61401. 309-345-3818; fax-309-343-3842; hours: 8:30AM-4:30PM
Office will perform a UCC search but public must search other records themselves. UCC search per debtor name/address- $10.00. Copy fee $.25 per page. Cert fee- $18.00 per 4 pages. Payee- Knox County Recorder. **Other phones:** Treasurer- 309-345-3863; Elections- 309-345-3815. **Property tax/Assessor-** 309-345-3806.

La Salle County

County Recorder, PO Box 189, Ottawa, IL 61350. RE & UCC recording -815-434-8226; fax-815-434-8260; hours: 8AM-4:30PM
www.lasallecounty.org/Final/contents2.htm
All records in one index. Records indexed on a public use terminal back to 7/1982. Only the public may search. Copy fee $1.00 per page. Cert fee- $10.00 per doc plus copy fee. Payee- La Salle

County Recorder. **Online access to Real Estate, Assessor records:** Assessor/property records on the County Assessor database are online at www.lasallecounty.org/cidnet/asrpfull.htm. Registration and password required; there is a $200.00 per year fee, plus per minute charges. For information, phone 815-434-8233. Also, last 2 years assessment data can be accessed online free at www.lasallecounty.org/contents3.htm. Parcel number is required. **Other phones:** Treasurer- 815-434-8220; Elections- 815-434-8202; Vital Records- 815-434-8202. **Property tax/Assessor-** same address as above. 815-434-8280.

Lake County

County Recorder, 18 N. County St; Courthouse - 2nd Fl, Waukegan, IL 60085-4358. RE & UCC recording phone-847-377-2575; fax-847-625-7200; hours: 8:30AM-5PM www.co.lake.il.us/recorder
Office will perform a UCC search but public must search other records themselves. UCC search per debtor name/address- $10.00. Copy fee $1.00 per page. Cert fee- $1.00 per page plus copy fee. Payee- Lake County Recorder. **Online access to Real Estate records:** Search the tax assessor's database at www.co.lake.il.us/assessor/assessments/default.asp. No name searching. **Other phones:** Treasurer- 847-377-2323; Elections- 847-377-3610; Vital Records- 847-377-3610. **Property tax/Assessor-** 847-377-2050.

Lawrence County

County Recorder, 1100 State St, Courthouse, Lawrenceville, IL 62439. RE & UCC recording phone-618-943-5126; fax-618-943-5205; hours: 9AM-5PM
All records in one index. Records indexed on computer back to 1987. Only the public may search. Copy fee $1.00 per page. Cert fee- $12.00 per doc, same as fee charged. Payee- Lawrence County Recorder. **Other phones:** Treasurer- 618-943-2016; Elections- 618-943-2346; Vital Records- 618-943-2346. **Property tax/Assessor-** 1106 Jefferson, Lawrenceville, IL 62439; 618-943-2719.

Lee County

County Recorder, PO Box 329, Dixon, IL 61021-0329. 815-288-3309; fax-815-288-6492; hours: 8:30AM-4:30PM
All records in one index. Office will perform a UCC search but public must search other records themselves. UCC search per debtor name/address- $16.00. Copy fee $1.00 per page. Cert fee- Same as original recording fee includes copy fee. Payee-Lee County Recorder. **Other phones:** Treasurer- 815-288-4477. **Property tax/Assessor-** same address as above. 815-288-4483.

Livingston County

County Recorder, 112 W. Madison; Courthouse, Pontiac, IL 61764-1871. RE & UCC recording phone-815-844-2006; fax-815-842-1844; hours: 8AM-4:30PM www.livingstoncounty-il.org
Separate indices to search include land tract books, as well as computer scanned documents. Only the public may search. Office will show public how to look up. Copy fee $1.00 per page. Cert fee- $5.00 per doc plus copy fee. Payee- Livingston County Recorder. **Other phones:** Treasurer- 815-844-2306; Elections- 815-842-9318; Vital Records- 815-844-2006. **Property tax/Assessor-** 110 W Water #2, Pontiac, IL 61764; 815-844-7214.

Logan County

County Recorder, PO Box 278, Lincoln, IL 62656. RE & UCC recording -217-732-4148; fax-217-732-6064; 8:30am-4:30pm www.co.logan.il.us/county_clerk/
Separate indices to search include Grantor/Grantee. Records indexed on a public use terminal back to 1984. Office will perform a UCC search but public must search other records themselves. Search fee $10.00. Copy fee $1.00 per page. RE or tax lien copy- $.25 per page. Cert fee-

$30.00 per doc, plus copy fee. Payee- Logan County Recorder. **Online access to Real Estate records:** Search the tax assessor database at http://loganilpropertymax.governmaxa.com/propertyma x/rover30.asp?sid=671F91267FEE4E1CA02DA85876 98C606. **Other phones:** Treasurer- 217-732-3761; Elections- 217-732-4148; Vital Records- 217-732-4148. **Property tax/Assessor-** 122 N Mclean St, Lincoln, IL 62656; 217-732-9635.

Macon County

County Recorder, 141 S. Main St, Rm 201, Decatur, IL 62523-1293. RE & UCC recording phone-217-424-1359; fax-217-428-2908; hours: 8:30AM-4:30PM Index: Computer and Tract index. Records indexed on a public use terminal back to 4/1985. Only the public may search. Copy fee $1.00 per page. Cert fee- $10.00 per page plus copy fee. Payee- Macon County Recorder. **Other phones:** Treasurer- 217-424-1426; Elections- 217-424-1309; Vital Records- 217-424-1305. **Property tax/Assessor-** same address as above. 217-424-1364.

Macoupin County

County Recorder, PO Box 107, Carlinville, IL 62626. 217-854-3214; fax-217-854-7347; 8:30AM-4:30PM Records indexed on computer back to 2001. Only the public may search. Copy fee $1.00 per page. Cert fee- $10.00 per cert plus copy fee. Payee- Macoupin County Recorder. **Other phones:** Treasurer- 217-854-4014. **Property tax/Assessor-** 217-854-8281.

Madison County

County Recorder, PO Box 308, Edwardsville, IL 62025-0308. Main phone & R/E recording-618-296-4775, UCC recording phone-618-296-4777; fax-618-692-9843; hours: 8AM-5PM www.co.madison.il.us All records in one index. Records indexed on a public use terminal back to June, 1985. Office will perform a UCC search but public must search other records themselves. Search fee $10.00 per name. Copy fee $1.00 per page. Cert fee- $12.00 per doc + $1 per page beyond 4 plus copy fee. Payee- Madison County Recorder. **Online access to Recording, Real Estate, Deed, Lien records:** Recorder office data by subscription on either the Laredo system using subscription and fees or the Tapestry System using credit card, https://tapestry.fidlar.com/tapsearch.aspx; $3.99 search; $.50 per image. **Other phones:** Treasurer- 618-692-6260; Appraiser/Auditor- 618-296-4569; Elections-618-296-4682; Vital Records- 618-296-4685. **Property tax/Assessor-** 157 N Main St #229, Edwardsville, IL 62025; 618-692-6270.

Marion County

County Recorder, PO Box 637, Salem, IL 62881. 618-548-3400, R/E recording phone-618-548-3852, UCC recording phone-618-548-3852; fax-618-548-2226; hours: 8AM-4PM All records in one index. Records indexed on a public use terminal back to 10/1985. Office will perform a UCC search but public must search other records themselves. UCC search per debtor name- $10.00. Copy fee $1.00 per page; $.50 each add'l. Cert fee- $12.00 per cert and $1.00 per page plus copy fee. Payee- Marion County Recorder. **Other phones:** Treasurer- 618-548-3858; Elections-618-548-3400; Vital Records- 618-548-3850. **Property tax/Assessor-** 100 E Main St, Rm 101, Salem, IL 62881; 618-548-3853.

Marshall County

County Recorder, PO Box 328, Lacon, IL 61540. RE & UCC recording phone-309-246-6325; fax-309-246-3667; hours: 8:30AM-4:30PM All records in one index. Records indexed on a public use terminal back to 1988. Office will perform a UCC search but public must search other records themselves. Copy fee $1.00 per page. Cert fee- $25.00-1st 4 pages, $1.00 per add'l page. Payee- Marshall County Recorder. **Other phones:**

Treasurer- 309-246-6085; Elections- 309-246-6325; Vital Records- 309-246-6325. **Property tax/Assessor-** same address as above. 309-246-2350.

Mason County

County Recorder, PO Box 77, Havana, IL 62644. RE & UCC recording phone-309-543-6661; fax-309-543-2085; hours: 8AM-4PM All records in one index. Records indexed on a public use terminal back to 1986. Office will perform a UCC search but public must search other records themselves. UCC search per debtor name/address- $10.00. Copy fee $.25 per page. Cert fee- $5.00 per doc plus copy fee. Payee- Mason County Recorder. **Other phones:** Treasurer- 309-543-3359; Elections- 309-543-6661; Vital Records- 309-543-6661. **Property tax/Assessor-** 125 N Plum, Havana, IL 62644; 309-543-4775.

Massac County

County Recorder, PO Box 429, Metropolis, IL 62960. RE & UCC recording phone-618-524-5213; fax-618-524-8514; hours: 8AM-4PM All records in one index; Liens were separate before 1996. Will not search real estate records. Will not search UCC records or tax liens. Copy fee $1.00 per page. Real estate or tax lien record copy- $.25 per page. Cert fee- $5.00 per cert plus copy fee. Payee- Massac County Recorder. **Other phones:** Treasurer- 618-524-5121; Elections- 618-524-5213; Vital Records- 618-524-5213. **Property tax/Assessor-** 618-524-9632.

McDonough County

County Recorder, 1 Courthouse Sq, Macomb, IL 61455. RE & UCC recording phone-309-833-2474; fax-309-836-3368; hours: 8AM-4PM Separate indices to search include tracs. Only the public may search. Copy fee $1.50 per page. Cert fee- Same as original recording fee. Payee- McDonough County Recorder. **Other phones:** Treasurer- 309-833-2032; Elections- 309-833-4649; Vital Records- 309-833-2474. **Property tax/Assessor-** same address as above. 309-833-5305.

McHenry County

County Recorder, 2200 N. Seminary Ave; Rm A280, Woodstock, IL 60098. 815-334-4110, UCC recording phone-217-782-7518; fax-815-338-9612; hours: 8AM-4:30PM www.co.mchenry.il.us/countydpt/recorder Separate indices to search. Records indexed on a public use terminal back to 9/1/1979. Office personnel or visitors may perform searches. Search fee $10.00 per name. Copy fee $1.50 1st page, $.50 each add'l. Cert fee- $12.00 for 1st 4 pages, $1.00 each add'l page plus copy fee. Payee- McHenry County Recorder. **Online access to Assessor/Treasurer, Property, Foreclosure, Recording, Deed, Lien records:** Records on the County Treasurer Inquiry site are free at http://taxweb2k.co.mchenry.il.us/cidnet/publictreasurer. htm. The sheriff's foreclosure list is free at www.co.mchenry.il.us. Also, recorder office data by subscription on either the Laredo system using subscription and fees or the Tapestry System using credit card, https://tapestry.fidlar.com/tapsearch.aspx; $3.99 search; $.50 per image. **Property tax/Assessor-** same address as above. not known.

McLean County

County Recorder, PO Box 2400, Bloomington, IL 61702-2400. RE & UCC recording phone-309-888-5170; fax-309-888-5927; hours: 8AM-4:30PM www.mcleancountyil.gov Only the public may search. Copy fee $1.00 per page. Cert fee- $18.00 1st 4 pg, then $1.00. Payee- McLean County Recorder. **Online access to Recorder, Deed, UCC, Lien, Immigration List, Assessor, Property, Treasurer Tax Bill, Assumed Name, Elected Official records:** Access to recorder official records and UCCs is free at www.mcleancountyil.gov/resolution/. Also, access

assessor county parcel and mobile home lots free at www.mcleancountyil.gov/tax/; no name searching. Access Township of Normal assessor database free at www.normaltownship.org/assessor/parcelsearch.php. No name searching; parcel number or address required. Access immigration records at www.mcleancountyil.gov/CircuitClerk/imgrecs/imgrec s.html. Also, search the assumed named list at www.mcleancountyil.gov/CountyClerk/CountyClerkA ssumedNamesMain.asp. Search election officials by precinct at the website. **Other phones:** Treasurer- 309-888-5180; Elections- 309-888-5190. **Property tax/Assessor-** 309-888-5130.

Menard County

County Recorder, PO Box 465, Petersburg, IL 62675. 217-632-2415, R/E recording phone-217-632-3201, UCC recording phone-217-632-3201; fax-217-632-4301; hours: 8:30AM-4:30PM All records in one index. Only the public may search. Copy fee $1.00 per page. Cert fee- $9.00 per doc plus copy fee. Payee- Menard County Recorder. **Other phones:** Treasurer- 217-632-2333; Appraiser/Auditor- 217-632-4461; Elections- 217-632-3201; Vital Records- 217-632-3201. **Property tax/Assessor-** same address as above. 217-632-4461.

Mercer County

County Recorder, PO Box 66, Aledo, IL 61231. RE & UCC recording phone-309-582-7021; fax-309-582-7022; hours: 8AM-4PM All records in one index. Records indexed on a public use terminal back to 9/1997. Office will perform a UCC search but public must search other records themselves. UCC search per debtor name/address- $10.00. Copy fee $1.00 per page from computer; $.50 per page from old books. Cert fee- fee to cert same as recording fee. Payee- Mercer County Recorder. **Other phones:** Treasurer- 309-582-2524; Elections- 309-582-7021; Vital Records- 309-582-7021. **Property tax/Assessor-** 100 S.E. 3rd St, Aledo, IL 61231; 309-582-7814.

Monroe County

County Recorder, 100 S. Main; Courthouse, Waterloo, IL 62298-1399. 618-939-8681; fax-618-939-5905; hours: 8AM-4:30PM Only the public may search. Copy fee $1.00 per page. Cert fee- $2.50 per doc plus copy fee. Payee- Monroe County Recorder. **Online access to Recording, Real Estate, Deed, Lien records:** Recorder office data by subscription on either the Laredo system using subscription and fees or the Tapestry System using credit card, https://tapestry.fidlar.com/tapsearch.aspx; $3.99 search; $.50 per image. **Other phones:** Treasurer- 618-939-8681 x213. **Property tax/Assessor-** 618-939-8681 x211.

Montgomery County

County Recorder, 1 Courthouse Sq; PO Box 595, Hillsboro, IL 62049-0595. RE & UCC recording phone-217-532-9535; fax-217-532-9581; hours: 8AM-4PM www.montgomeryco.com Separate indices to search include Tract-1822-1990, Grantor/Grantee, Computer-ACS land rec 1991-now. Records indexed on computer back to 1991. Only the public may search. Copy fee $1.00 per page. Cert fee- $29.00 per doc plus copy fee. Payee- Montgomery County Recorder. **Other phones:** Treasurer- 217-532-9521; Elections- 217-532-9530; Vital Records- 217-532-9537. **Property tax/Assessor-** same address. 217-532-9595.

Morgan County

County Recorder, PO Box 1387, Jacksonville, IL 62651. RE & UCC recording phone-217-243-8581; fax-217-243-8368; hours: 8:30AM-4:30PM All records in one index. Records indexed on a public use terminal back to 4/1987. Office will perform a UCC and Tax lien search but public must search other records themselves. Search fee

$10.00. Copy fee $1.00 per page. Cert fee- $5.00 per doc, plus copy fee. Payee- Morgan County Recorder. **Online access to Real Estate Recording, Deed records:** Access recording office land data at www.etitlesearch.com; registration required, fee based on usage. **Other phones:** Treasurer- 217-243-8581; Elections- 217-243-8581; Vital Records- 217-243-8581. **Property tax/Assessor-** 217-243-8557.

Moultrie County

County Recorder, 10 S Main, #6; Courthouse, Sullivan, IL 61951. RE & UCC recording phone-217-728-4389; fax-217-728-8178; hours: 8:30AM-4:30PM
All records in one index. Records indexed on a public use terminal back to 1/1/92. Office will perform a UCC search but public must search other records themselves. Search fee $10.00 per name. Copy fee $1.00 per page. Cert fee- $14.00 per cert plus copy fee. Payee- Moultrie County Recorder. **Other phones:** Treasurer- 217-728-4032; Elections- 217-728-4389; Vital Records- 217-728-4389. **Property tax/Assessor-** 10 S Main #10, Sullivan, IL 61951; 217-728-4951.

Ogle County

County Recorder, PO Box 357, Oregon, IL 61061. 815-732-1115 x269/1, R/E recording phone-815-732-1115 x269/270/271, UCC recording phone-815-732-1115 x269/270/271; hours: 8:30AM-4:30PM
Separate indices to search include Grantor/Grantee. Records indexed on a public use terminal back to 10/1/1984. Office will perform a UCC and Tax lien search but public must search other records themselves. Search fee $10.00. Copy fee $1.00 per page. Payee- Ogle County Recorder. **Online access to Land, Recorder, Deed, UCC records:** Access to recorder data is free at www.landaccess.com/proi/county.jsp?county=ilogle, . **Other phones:** Treasurer- 815-732-1100 x202/201/310 & 286; Elections- 815-732-1110 x012/213/281/214 & 215; Vital Records- 815-732-1110 x012/213/281/214 & 215. **Property tax/Assessor-** same address as above. 815-732-1150 x239, 256, 257, 258 & 305.

Peoria County

County Recorder, 324 Main St; County Courthouse, Rm G04, Peoria, IL 61602. RE & UCC recording phone-309-672-6090; fax-309-677-6202; hours: 9AM-5PM www.co.peoria.il.us/
Separate indices to search. Records indexed on a public use terminal back to 1988. Office will perform a UCC search but public must search other records themselves. Will not search real estate records. UCC search per debtor name/address- $10.00. Copy fee $.50 per page. Cert fee- Same as current recording fee plus copy fee. Payee- Peoria County Recorder. **Online access to Assessor, Property, Recording, Deed records:** Access tax assessor records at www.co.peoria.il.us/frame.php?destination=209.251.115.194%2Fassessor%2Frealasp1.asp. Also, the recorder's office has a subscription service with web access; call recorder for details. **Other phones:** Treasurer- 309-672-6065. **Property tax/Assessor-** same address as above. 309-672-6910.

Perry County

County Recorder, PO Box 438, Pinckneyville, IL 62274. RE & UCC recording phone-618-357-5116; fax-618-357-3194; hours: 8AM-4PM www.perrycountyil.org
All records in one index. Records indexed on a public use terminal back to 1987. Only the office personnel may search. Search fee $10.00 per name. Copy fee $3.00 per document. Cert fee- $5.00 per doc plus copy fee. Payee- Perry County Recorder. **Other phones:** Treasurer- 618-357-5002; Elections- 618-357-5116; Vital Records- 618-357-5116. **Property tax/Assessor-** PO Box 177, Pinchneyville, IL 63374; 618-357-2209.

Piatt County

County Recorder, PO Box 558, Monticello, IL 61856-0558. RE & UCC recording phone-217-762-9487; fax-217-762-7563; hours: 8:30AM-4:30PM www.piattcounty.org
All records in one index. Records indexed on a public use terminal back to 1/1/1988. Only the public may search. General copy fee $1.00 per page. RE or tax lien copy- $.50 per page. Cert fee- $8.00 per file plus $.50 per page up to 8 copies. Payee- Piatt County Recorder. **Other phones:** Treasurer- 217-762-4866; Elections- 217-762-9487; Vital Records- 217-762-9487. **Property tax/Assessor-** same address as above. 217-762-4266.

Pike County

County Recorder, 100 E. Washington St.; Courthouse, Pittsfield, IL 62363. RE & UCC recording phone-217-285-6812; fax-217-285-5820; hours: 8:30AM-4PM
All records in one index. Records indexed on a public use terminal back to 1990. Office will perform a UCC and Tax lien search but public must search other records themselves. Search fee $10.00. Copy fee $1.00 per page. Cert fee- $10.00 per doc plus copy fee. Payee- Pike County Recorder. **Other phones:** Treasurer- 217-285-4218; Elections- 217-285-6812; Vital Records- 217-285-6812. **Property tax/Assessor-** same address as above. 217-285-2382.

Pope County

County Recorder, PO Box 216, Golconda, IL 62938. 618-683-4466; fax-618-683-4466; hours: 8AM-N, 1-4PM
Separate indices to search. Record index not computerized. Office personnel or visitors may perform searches. Search fee $10.00 per name. Copy fee $.25 per page. Cert fee- $5.00 per cert includes copy fee. Payee- Pope County Recorder. **Other phones:** Treasurer- 618-683-5501. **Property tax/Assessor-** PO Box 579, Golconda, IL 62938; 618-683-6231.

Pulaski County

County Recorder, PO Box 118, Mound City, IL 62963. 618-748-9360; fax-618-748-9305; 8AM-N, 1-4PM
Separate indices to search. Records indexed on computer back to 1990. Only the office personnel may search. Search fee $10.00 per name. Will not do a federal or state tax lien search. Copy fee $.50 per page. Cert fee- $7.00 per doc plus copy fee. Payee- Pulaski County Recorder. **Other phones:** Treasurer- 618-748-9322. **Property tax/Assessor-** 500 Illinois Ave, Rm F, Mound City, IL 62963; 618-748-9321.

Putnam County

County Recorder, PO Box 236, Hennepin, IL 61327. RE & UCC recording phone-815-925-7129; fax-815-925-7549; hours: 9AM-4PM
Separate indices; Entry Book, Grantor/Grantee, Tract index, Fed & State Tax lien, LisPendens, Memo of Judgmts. Office personnel or visitors may perform searches. Search fee $10.00. Will not search real estate records. Copy fee $1.00 per page. RE or tax lien copy- $.50 per page. Cert fee- $27.00 per doc; includes 4 pages, $1.00 each add'l page. Payee- Putnam County Recorder. **Other phones:** Treasurer- 815-925-7226; Appraiser/Auditor-815-925-7238; Elections- 815-925-7129; Vital Records- 815-925-7129. **Property tax/Assessor-** 815-925-7238.

Randolph County

County Recorder, 1 Taylor St, Rm 202, Chester, IL 62233-0309. 618-826-5000 x191, R/E recording phone-618-826-5000 x117, UCC recording phone-618-826-5000 x117; fax-618-826-3750; hours: 8AM-4PM
Separate indices to search include deeds, mtgs, judgments, UCCs. Records indexed on a public use terminal back to 1989. Only the public may search. Copy fee $.50 per page. Cert fee- $26.00

for 4 pages, $.50 each add'l page. Payee-Randolph County Recorder. **Online access to Recording, Real Estate, Deed, Lien records:** Recorder office data by subscription on either the Laredo system using subscription and fees or the Tapestry System using credit card, https://tapestry.fidlar.com/tapsearch.aspx; $3.99 search; $.50 per image. Images back to 1995; index to 1989. **Other phones:** Treasurer- 618-826-5000 x224; Elections- 618-826-5000 x116; Vital Records- 618-826-5000 x112. **Property tax/Assessor-** same address as above. 618-826-5000 x192.

Richland County

County Recorder, 103 W. Main; Courthouse, Olney, IL 62450. 618-392-3111; fax-618-393-4005; hours: 8AM-4PM
Separate indices to search include grantor/grantee. Record index not computerized. Office will perform a UCC search with UCC1, but public must search other records themselves. UCC search per debtor name/address- $10.00. UCC copy fee $2.00 per page. Real estate or tax lien record copy-$6.00 per document. Cert fee- call for information. Payee- Richland County Recorder. **Other phones:** Treasurer- 618-392-8341; Elections- 618-392-3111; Vital Records- 618-392-3111. **Property tax/Assessor-** same address as above. 618-395-4387.

Rock Island County

County Recorder, PO Box 3067, Rock Island, IL 61204. 309-558-3360; fax-309-558-3642; hours: 8AM-4:30PM www.co.rock-island.il.us
Records indexed on a public use terminal back to 1982. Only the public may search. Copy fee $1.00 per page. RE or tax lien copy- $.25 per page; $2.00 each if mailed. Cert fee- Does not certify. Payee-Rock Island County Recorder. **Online access to Property, Assessor, Recording, Real Estate, Deed, Lien records:** Recorder office data by subscription on either the Laredo system using subscription and fees or the Tapestry System using credit card, https://tapestry.fidlar.com/tapsearch.aspx; $3.99 search; $.50 per image. Index back to 1982, images 1992. Also, Moline Town assessor records are free at www.molinetownship.com/OnlineSearch/Search.asp. No name searching. Also, for certified copy of vital records go to http://ricoclerk.revealed.net/. **Other phones:** Treasurer- 309-786-4451. **Property tax/Assessor-** 309-786-4451.

Saline County

County Recorder, 10 E. Poplar, #17, Harrisburg, IL 62946. 618-253-8197, R/E recording phone-618-253-3073, UCC recording phone-618-253-3073; fax-618-252-3073; hours: 8AM-4PM
Separate indices to search include grantor/grantee. Records indexed on computer back to 2004. Office will perform a UCC search but public must search other records themselves. UCC search per debtor name/address- $10.00. General copy fee $1.00; tax lien $.50 per page. Real estate records other than deeds- $.50 per page. Cert fee- $12.00 per doc includes copy fee. Payee- Saline County Recorder. **Other phones:** Treasurer- 618-253-6915; Elections-618-253-8197; Vital Records- 618-253-8197. **Property tax/Assessor-** 618-252-0691.

Sangamon County

County Recorder, PO Box 669, Springfield, IL 62705-0669. 217-535-3150; fax-217-535-3159; hours: 8:30AM-5PM www.co.sangamon.il.us
All records in one index. Records indexed on a public use terminal back to 1994. Only the office personnel may search. Search fee $10.00 per name. Copy fee $1.00 per page. RE or tax lien copy- $2.00 1st page, $.50 each add'l. Cert fee- $26.00 per cert includes copy fee. Payee-Sangamon County Recorder. **Online access to Recording, Real Estate, Deed, Lien records:** Recorder office data by subscription on either the Laredo system using subscription and fees or the Tapestry System using credit card,

https://tapestry.fidlar.com/tapsearch.aspx; $3.99 search; $.50 per image. Records go back to 1992. **Other phones:** Treasurer- 217-753-6800. **Property tax/Assessor-** 200 S 9th St, Rm 210, Springfield, IL 62705; 217-753-6615.

Schuyler County

County Recorder, PO Box 200, Rushville, IL 62681. RE & UCC recording phone-217-322-4734; fax-217-322-6164; hours: 8AM-4PM
Separate indices to search include entry book, grantor/grantee, tract, state and federal lien books. Office will perform a UCC search but public must search other records themselves. Search fee $10.00 per name. Copy fee $1.00 per page. RE or tax lien copy- $.50 per page. Cert fee- $7.00 per cert plus copy fee. Payee- Schuyler County Recorder. **Other phones:** Treasurer- 217-322-3830; Elections- 217-322-4734; Vital Records- 217-322-4734. **Property tax/Assessor-** 217-322-4432.

Scott County

County Recorder, Courthouse, Winchester, IL 62694. RE & UCC recording phone-217-742-3178; fax-217-742-5853; hours: 8AM-4PM
All records in one index. Record index not computerized. Office personnel or visitors may perform searches. Search fee $10.00. Real estate owner, mortgage, and property transfer searches available. Copy fee $1.00 per page. Cert fee- $24.00 per cert plus copy fee. Payee- Scott County Recorder. **Other phones:** Treasurer- 217-742-3368; Elections- 217-742-3178; Vital Records- 217-742-3178. **Property tax/Assessor-** 217-742-5751.

Shelby County

County Recorder, PO Box 230, Shelbyville, IL 62565. 217-774-4421; fax-217-774-5291; hours: 8AM-4PM
All records in one index. Records indexed on a public use terminal back to 9/1990. Only the public may search. Copy fee $1.00 per page. Cert fee- $34.00 per cert plus copy fee. Payee- Shelby County Recorder. **Other phones:** Treasurer- 217-774-3841; Elections- 217-774-4421; Vital Records- 217-774-4421. **Property tax/Assessor-** same address as above. 217-774-5579.

St. Clair County

County Recorder, PO Box 543, Belleville, IL 62220. 618-277-6600, UCC recording phone-618-277-6600 x2484; hours: 8:30AM-5PM www.stclaircountyrecorder.com
Will not search real estate records. Will search UCC records, tax liens not included in UCC search. UCC search per debtor name/address- $13.00. Tax lien search fee- $11.00 per debtor. Copy fee $1.00 per page. RE or tax lien copy- $2.00 per page. Payee- St. Clair County Recorder. **Online access to Recorder, Grantor/Grantee, Real Estate, Divorce, Lien, Judgment records:** Access to the recorder records is free at www.stclaircountyrecorder.com/cgi-bin/display.cgi?file=search. Three search methods are available. **Other phones:** Treasurer- 618-277-6600 x2448; Elections- 770-531-6600 x2363. **Property tax/Assessor-** 618-277-6600 x2509.

Stark County

County Recorder, PO Box 97, Toulon, IL 61483. RE & UCC recording phone-309-286-5911; fax-309-286-4039; hours: 8:30AM-4:30PM www.starkcourt.org
All records in one index. Office will perform a UCC search but public must search other records themselves. Search fee $10.00 per name. Copy fee $.50 per page. Cert fee- $5.00 per copy plus copy fee. Payee- Stark County Recorder. **Online access to Unclaimed Fund records:** Access the county clerk of courts unclaimed funds database at www.starkcourt.org (click on "Unclaimed Funds"). File is in pdf format. **Other phones:** Treasurer- 309-286-5901; Elections- 309-286-5911; Vital Records- 309-286-5911. **Property tax/Assessor-** PO Box 386, Toulon, IL 61483; 309-286-7172.

Stephenson County

County Recorder, 15 N. Galena Ave, #1, Freeport, IL 61032. 815-235-8385; fax-none; 8:30AM-4:30PM
Separate indices to search. Records indexed on a public use terminal back to 1985. Only the office personnel may search. Search fee $10.00 per name. Copy fee $1.00 per page. Cert fee- $12.00 per cert plus copy fee after 4 pages. Payee-Stephenson County Recorder. **Other phones:** Treasurer- 815-235-8264. **Property tax/Assessor-** same address as above. 815-235-8260.

Tazewell County

County Recorder, PO Box 36, Pekin, IL 61555-0036. 309-477-2210; fax-309-477-2321; hours: 8:30AM-5PM www.tazewell.com
All records in one index. Office will perform a UCC search but public must search other records themselves. UCC search per debtor name- $15.00. Copy fee $.50 per page. $1.00 per page to fax. Cert fee- $12.00 1st 4 pages; $1.00 each add'l page, includes copy fee. Payee- Tazewell County Recorder. **Other phones:** Treasurer- 309-477-2284. **Property tax/Assessor-** 11 S 4th St, McKenzie Bldg, Pekin, IL 61554; 309-477-2275.

Union County

County Recorder, 309 W. Market, Jonesboro, IL 62952. 618-833-5711; fax-618-833-8712; hours: 8AM-4PM
Record index not computerized. Only the public may search. Copy fee $.50 per page. Cert fee- $5.00 per cert plus copy fee. Payee- Union County Recorder. **Other phones:** Treasurer- 618-833-5621. **Property tax/Assessor-** 618-833-8051.

Vermilion County

County Recorder, 6 N. Vermilion St, Danville, IL 61832-5877. 217-554-6041; fax-217-554-6047; hours: 8AM-4:30PM
Separate indices to search include books, microfilm, tract cards, computer. Records indexed on computer back to 7/1987. Office will perform a UCC search but public must search other records themselves. Search fee $10.00. Copy fee $1.00 1st page; $.50 each add'l. Cert fee- $12.00 per cert up to 4 pages, $1.00 for add'l pages per doc, plus copy fee. Payee- County Recorder. **Online access to Real Estate, Recorder, Lien, UCC, Deed records:** Access to real estate records is free at www.landaccess.com/proi/county.jsp?county=ilvermilion. **Other phones:** Treasurer- 217-554-6081. **Property tax/Assessor-** same address as above. 217-554-1941.

Wabash County

County Recorder, PO Box 277, Mount Carmel, IL 62863. RE & UCC recording phone-618-262-4561; hours: 8AM-5PM
All records in one index. Records indexed on computer, no images. Back to 1857. Office will perform a UCC search but public must search other records themselves. UCC search per debtor name/address- $10.00. Separate federal tax lien search- $5.00 per debtor. Copy fee $1.00 per page. RE or tax lien copy- $.50 per page. Cert fee- $12.00 1st 4 pg, then $1.00. Payee- Wabash County Recorder. **Other phones:** Treasurer- 618-262-5262; Elections- 618-262-4561; Vital Records- 618-262-4561. **Property tax/Assessor-** same address as above. 618-262-4463.

Warren County

County Recorder, 100 W Broadway; Courthouse, Monmouth, IL 61462-1797. 309-734-8592; fax-309-734-7406; hours: 8AM-4:30PM
Separate indices to search include tracts, computer. Records indexed on a public use terminal back to 1986. Office will perform a UCC search but public must search other records themselves. UCC search per debtor name/address- $10.00. Copy fee $.50 per page. Payee- Warren County Recorder. **Other phones:** Treasurer- 309-734-8536; Elections- 309-734-4612; Vital Records- 309-734-8592. **Property**

tax/Assessor- same address as above. 309-734-8561.

Washington County

County Recorder, 101 E. St. Louis St; County Courthouse, Nashville, IL 62263-1105. RE & UCC recording phone-618-327-4800 x300; fax-618-327-3582; hours: 8AM-4PM
Separate indices to search. Records indexed on a public use terminal back to 10/2001. Office will perform a UCC search. UCC search per debtor name/address- $10.00. Copy fee $1.00 per page. Cert fee- $5.00 per cert plus $1.00 per page plus copy fee. Payee- Washington County Recorder. **Other phones:** Treasurer- 618-327-4800 x315; Elections- 618-327-4800 x300; Vital Records- 618-327-4800 x300. **Property tax/Assessor-** same address as above. 618-327-4800 x325.

Wayne County

County Recorder, PO Box 187, Fairfield, IL 62837. RE & UCC recording phone-618-842-5182; fax-618-842-6427; 8AM-4:30PM http://assessor.wayne.il.us
Records indexed between 1886 and May, 1988 are book indexes, from June, 1988 to present on computer. Office personnel or visitors may perform searches. Search fee $10.00 per name. Copy fee $1.00 per page. Cert fee- $5.00 per cert plus copy fee. Payee- Wayne County Recorder. **Online access to Assessor, Property records:** Records on the Wayne Township Assessor Office database are free at http://assessor.wayne.il.us/OPID.html. Also, you may subscribe to the advanced search feature for a fee. Access includes legal, assessment, sales history, buildings and other information. **Other phones:** Treasurer- 618-842-5087; Elections- 618-842-5182; Vital Records- 618-842-5182. **Property tax/Assessor-** PO Box 384, Fairfield, IL 62837; 618-842-2582.

White County

County Recorder, PO Box 339, Carmi, IL 62821. RE & UCC recording phone-618-382-7211;: 8AM-4PM
All records in one index. Office will perform a UCC search but public must search other records themselves. Search fee $10.00. Copy fee $2.00 per page. Cert fee- $18.00 1st 4 pg, then $1.00. Payee- White County Recorder. **Other phones:** Treasurer- 618-382-8122; Elections- 618-382-7211; Vital Records- 618-382-7211. **Property tax/Assessor-** 618-382-721182-2332.

Whiteside County

County Recorder, 200 E. Knox, Morrison, IL 61270. 815-772-5241, R/E recording phone-815-772-5192, UCC recording phone-815-772-5192; fax-815-772-5244; hours: 8:30AM-4:30PM www.whiteside.org
Separate indices to search include entry book, grantor/grantee, tract index. Only the public may search. Copy fee $.50 per page. Payee- Whiteside County Recorder. **Other phones:** Treasurer- 815-772-5196; Vital Records- 815-772-5189. **Property tax/Assessor-** same address as above. 815-772-5195.

Will County

County Recorder, 58 E Clinton, #100, Joliet, IL 60432. 815-740-4637; fax-815-740-4697; 8:30AM-4:30PM
Record index not computerized. Only the public may search. Copy fee $1.00 per page. Cert fee-Same as original recording fee. Payee- Will County Recorder. **Online access to Assessor, Appraiser, Property, Voter Registration, Deed, Lien, Mortgage records:** Access to the Recorder's real estate and lien records is free at www.willcountydata.com/rec/searchselect.htm Access to voter registration data is free at https://www.willcountydata.com/voterstatus/Voter_lookup_input.htm. Assessor has free parcel number inquiry at http://66.158.72.248:2080/cics/cwba/ccalm03; no name searching. Also, access to Town of Manhattan assessor records is free at www.manhattantownship.net. No name searching.

Williamson County

County Recorder, PO Box 1108, Marion, IL 62959-1108. 618-997-1301 X121, R/E recording phone-618-997-1301 x 121; fax-618-993-2071; hours: 8AM-4PM

Separate indices to search include mortgage, deed, miscellaneous. Records indexed on computer back to 1992. Search fee $10.00 per name. Copy fee $1.00 per page. Cert fee- $5.00 per cert plus copy fee. Payee- Williamson County Recorder. **Other phones:** Treasurer- 618-997-1301 x129; Elections- 618-997-1301 x102; Vital Records- 618-997-1301 x102. **Property tax/Assessor-** 200 W Jefferson, Marion, IL 62959; 618-997-1301 x164.

Winnebago County

County Recorder, 404 Elm St, Rm 405, Rockford, IL 61101. 815-987-3100, R/E recording phone-815-987-3010; fax-815-961-3261; hours: 8AM-4PM www.co.winnebago.il.us

Separate indices to search include computer, books to 1993. Records indexed on a public use terminal back to 1980. Search fee $5.00 unless otherwise indicated. UCC search per debtor name/address- $13.75. Copy fee $.25 per page. Cert fee- $25.00 add'l $1.00 per page, includes copies. Payee-Winnebago County Recorder. **Online access to Property, UCC, Assessor, Court records:** Access county property and court data by subscription at www.co.winnebago.il.us; registration and $10.00 per month fee required. Access land and UCC free at www.landaccess.com/proi/county.jsp?county=ilwinnebago. **Other phones:** Treasurer- 815-987-3010; Elections- 815-987-3086; Vital Records- 815-987-3050. **Property tax/Assessor-** 404 Elm St, Rockford, IL 61101; 815-987-3025.

Woodford County

County Recorder, 115 N. Main; Courthouse, Rm 202, Eureka, IL 61530-1273. RE & UCC recording phone-309-467-2822; fax-309-467-7391; hours: 8AM-5PM

Records indexed on a public use terminal back to 1986. Only the public may search. Copy fee $1.00 per page. Cert fee- $38 per first 4 pages, $1.00 per page after 4. Payee- Woodford County Recorder. **Other phones:** Treasurer- 309-467-4621; Elections- 309-467-2822; Vital Records- 309-467-2822. **Property tax/Assessor-** 309-467-3708.

Illinois County Locator

You will usually be able to find the city name in the City/County Cross Reference below. In that case, it is a simple matter to determine the county from the cross reference. However, only the official US Postal Service city names are included in this index. There are an additional 40,000 place names that people use in their addresses. Therefore, we have also included a ZIP/City Cross Reference immediately following the City/County Cross Reference.

If you know the ZIP Code but the city name does not appear in the City/County Cross Reference index, look up the ZIP Code in the ZIP/City Cross Reference, find the city name, then look up the city name in the City/County Cross Reference. For example, you want to know the county for an address of Menands, NY 12204. There is no "Menands" in the City/County Cross Reference. The ZIP/City Cross Reference shows that ZIP Codes 12201-12288 are for the city of Albany. Looking back in the City/County Cross Reference, Albany is in Albany County.

Illinois City/County Cross Reference

ABINGDON (61410) Knox(97), Warren(2)
ADAIR McDonough
ADDIEVILLE Washington
ADDISON Du Page
ADRIAN Hancock
AKIN Franklin
ALBANY Whiteside
ALBERS Clinton
ALBION Edwards
ALDEN McHenry
ALEDO Mercer
ALEXANDER (62601) Morgan(93), Sangamon(6)
ALEXIS (61412) Mercer(83), Warren(16)
ALGONQUIN (60102) McHenry(82), Kane(17)
ALHAMBRA Madison
ALLENDALE Wabash
ALLERTON (61810) Vermilion(71), Douglas(14), Edgar(12), Champaign(1)
ALMA Marion
ALPHA Henry
ALSEY Scott
ALSIP Cook
ALTAMONT (62411) Effingham(98), Fayette(1)
ALTO PASS (62905) Union(79), Jackson(20)
ALTON (62002) Madison(98), Macoupin(1)
ALTONA (61414) Knox(68), Henry(31)
ALVIN Vermilion
AMBOY Lee
AMF OHARE Cook
ANCHOR (61720) McLean(91), Ford(8)
ANCONA Livingston
ANDALUSIA Rock Island
ANDOVER Henry
ANNA Union
ANNAPOLIS (62413) Crawford(93), Clark(6)
ANNAWAN Henry
ANTIOCH Lake
APPLE RIVER Jo Daviess
ARCOLA (61910) Douglas(86), Coles(13)
ARENZVILLE (62611) Cass(83), Morgan(16)
ARGENTA Macon
ARLINGTON Bureau
ARLINGTON HEIGHTS Cook
ARMINGTON (61721) Tazewell(92), Logan(7)
ARMSTRONG Vermilion
AROMA PARK Kankakee
ARROWSMITH McLean
ARTHUR (61911) Douglas(54), Moultrie(41), Coles(4)
ASHKUM Iroquois
ASHLAND (62612) Cass(76), Morgan(22)
ASHLEY (62808) Washington(81), Jefferson(18)
ASHMORE Coles
ASHTON (61006) Lee(78), Ogle(21)
ASSUMPTION (62510) Christian(86), Shelby(13)
ASTORIA Fulton

ATHENS (62613) Menard(95), Logan(3)
ATKINSON Henry
ATLANTA (61723) Logan(98), McLean(1)
ATWATER Macoupin
ATWOOD (61913) Douglas(64), Piatt(34), Moultrie(1)
AUBURN Sangamon
AUGUSTA (62311) Hancock(90), Schuyler(5), Adams(3)
AURORA (60504) Du Page(76), Kane(12), Will(9), Kendall(2)
AURORA Du Page
AURORA Kane
AVA Jackson
AVISTON (62216) Clinton(97), Madison(2)
AVON (61415) Fulton(80), Warren(19)
BAILEYVILLE (61007) Ogle(69), Stephenson(30)
BALDWIN Randolph
BARDOLPH McDonough
BARNHILL Wayne
BARRINGTON (60010) Lake(57), Cook(36), McHenry(4)
BARRINGTON Lake
BARRY (62312) Pike(85), Adams(14)
BARSTOW Rock Island
BARTELSO Clinton
BARTLETT (60103) Du Page(50), Cook(49)
BASCO Hancock
BATAVIA Kane
BATCHTOWN Calhoun
BATH Mason
BAYLIS (62314) Pike(76), Adams(22)
BEARDSTOWN Cass
BEASON (62512) Logan(93), De Witt(6)
BEAVERVILLE (60912) Kankakee(56), Iroquois(43)
BECKEMEYER Clinton
BEDFORD PARK Cook
BEECHER (60401) Will(97), Kankakee(2)
BEECHER CITY (62414) Effingham(63), Fayette(27), Shelby(9)
BELKNAP (62908) Massac(53), Johnson(46)
BELLE RIVE (62810) Jefferson(95), Hamilton(2), Wayne(1)
BELLEVILLE St. Clair
BELLFLOWER McLean
BELLMONT Wabash
BELLWOOD Cook
BELVIDERE Boone
BEMENT Piatt
BENLD Macoupin
BENSENVILLE Du Page
BENSON Woodford
BENTON Franklin
BERKELEY Cook
BERWICK Warren
BERWYN Cook
BETHALTO Madison
BETHANY (61914) Moultrie(97), Macon(2)
BIG ROCK (60511) Kane(94), De Kalb(5)
BIGGSVILLE Henderson
BINGHAM Fayette

BIRDS Lawrence
BISHOP HILL Henry
BISMARCK Vermilion
BLACKSTONE Livingston
BLANDINSVILLE (61420) McDonough(91), Hancock(8)
BLOOMINGDALE Du Page
BLOOMINGTON McLean
BLUE ISLAND Cook
BLUE MOUND (62513) Macon(76), Christian(23)
BLUFF SPRINGS Cass
BLUFFS (62621) Scott(94), Morgan(5)
BLUFORD (62814) Jefferson(98), Wayne(1)
BOLES Johnson
BOLINGBROOK (60440) Will(97), Du Page(2)
BOLINGBROOK Will
BONDVILLE Champaign
BONE GAP Edwards
BONFIELD Kankakee
BONNIE Jefferson
BOODY Macon
BOURBONNAIS Kankakee
BOWEN (62316) Hancock(97), Adams(2)
BRACEVILLE (60407) Grundy(51), Will(47)
BRADFORD (61421) Stark(58), Bureau(34), Marshall(6)
BRADLEY Kankakee
BRAIDWOOD Will
BREESE Clinton
BRIDGEPORT Lawrence
BRIDGEVIEW Cook
BRIGHTON (62012) Jersey(46), Macoupin(45), Madison(7)
BRIMFIELD Peoria
BRISTOL Kendall
BROADLANDS (61816) Champaign(97), Douglas(2)
BROADVIEW Cook
BROCTON (61917) Edgar(95), Douglas(4)
BROOKFIELD Cook
BROOKPORT (62910) Massac(96), Pope(3)
BROUGHTON Hamilton
BROWNING (62624) Schuyler(97), Fulton(2)
BROWNS (62818) Wabash(61), Edwards(38)
BROWNSTOWN Fayette
BRUSSELS Calhoun
BRYANT Fulton
BUCKINGHAM (60917) Kankakee(90), Livingston(8)
BUCKLEY Iroquois
BUCKNER Franklin
BUDA Bureau
BUFFALO Sangamon
BUFFALO GROVE (60089) Lake(57), Cook(42)
BUFFALO PRAIRIE Rock Island
BULPITT Christian
BUNCOMBE (62912) Johnson(55), Union(44)

BUNKER HILL Macoupin
BURBANK Cook
BUREAU Bureau
BURLINGTON Kane
BURNSIDE Hancock
BURNT PRAIRIE (62820) White(86), Wayne(13)
BUSHNELL McDonough
BUTLER Montgomery
BYRON Ogle
CABERY (60919) Kankakee(43), Ford(31), Livingston(25)
CACHE Alexander
CAIRO Alexander
CALEDONIA (61011) Boone(70), Winnebago(29)
CALHOUN Richland
CALUMET CITY Cook
CAMARGO Douglas
CAMBRIA Williamson
CAMBRIDGE Henry
CAMDEN Schuyler
CAMERON Warren
CAMP GROVE Marshall
CAMP POINT Adams
CAMPBELL HILL (62916) Jackson(77), Randolph(12), Perry(10)
CAMPUS Livingston
CANTON Fulton
CANTRALL Sangamon
CAPRON Boone
CARBON CLIFF Rock Island
CARBONDALE (62902) Jackson(70), Williamson(27)
CARBONDALE Jackson
CARLINVILLE Macoupin
CARLOCK (61725) McLean(70), Woodford(29)
CARLYLE Clinton
CARMAN Henderson
CARMI White
CAROL STREAM Cook
CAROL STREAM Du Page
CARPENTERSVILLE Kane
CARRIER MILLS (62917) Saline(88), Williamson(11)
CARROLLTON Greene
CARTERVILLE Williamson
CARTHAGE Hancock
CARY (60013) McHenry(94), Lake(5)
CASEY (62420) Clark(85), Cumberland(11), Coles(1)
CASEYVILLE St. Clair
CASTLETON Stark
CATLIN Vermilion
CAVE IN ROCK Hardin
CEDAR POINT La Salle
CEDARVILLE Stephenson
CENTRALIA (62801) Marion(67), Clinton(22), Washington(6), Jefferson(4)
CERRO GORDO (61818) Piatt(77), Macon(22)
CHADWICK (61014) Carroll(82), Whiteside(17)

CHAMBERSBURG (62323) Pike(91), Brown(8)
CHAMPAIGN Champaign
CHANA Ogle
CHANDLERVILLE (62627) Cass(71), Mason(28)
CHANNAHON (60410) Will(94), Grundy(5)
CHAPIN (62628) Morgan(87), Scott(12)
CHARLESTON Coles
CHATHAM Sangamon
CHATSWORTH Livingston
CHEBANSE (60922) Kankakee(62), Iroquois(37)
CHENOA (61726) McLean(94), Livingston(5)
CHERRY Bureau
CHERRY VALLEY (61016) Winnebago(88), Boone(11)
CHESTER Randolph
CHESTERFIELD (62630) Macoupin(97), Greene(1)
CHESTNUT Logan
CHICAGO Cook
CHICAGO HEIGHTS Cook
CHICAGO RIDGE Cook
CHILLICOTHE (61523) Peoria(97), Marshall(2)
CHRISMAN Edgar
CHRISTOPHER Franklin
CICERO Cook
CISCO (61830) Piatt(70), Macon(29)
CISNE Wayne
CISSNA PARK Iroquois
CLARE De Kalb
CLAREMONT (62421) Richland(97), Crawford(1), Lawrence(1)
CLARENDON HILLS Du Page
CLAY CITY (62824) Clay(95), Wayne(4)
CLAYTON (62324) Adams(97), Brown(2)
CLAYTONVILLE Iroquois
CLIFTON Iroquois
CLINTON De Witt
COAL CITY Grundy
COAL VALLEY (61240) Rock Island(75), Henry(24)
COATSBURG Adams
COBDEN Union
COELLO Franklin
COFFEEN Montgomery
COLCHESTER (62326) McDonough(97), Hancock(2)
COLETA Whiteside
COLFAX McLean
COLLINSVILLE (62234) Madison(90), St. Clair(9)
COLLISON Vermilion
COLMAR McDonough
COLONA Henry
COLP Williamson
COLUMBIA (62236) Monroe(94), St. Clair(5)
COLUSA Hancock
COMPTON Lee
CONCORD Morgan
CONGERVILLE (61729) Woodford(96), McLean(3)
COOKSVILLE McLean
CORDOVA Rock Island
CORNELL Livingston
CORNLAND Logan
CORTLAND De Kalb
COTTAGE HILLS Madison
COULTERVILLE (62237) Randolph(46), Washington(27), Perry(26)
COUNTRY CLUB HILLS Cook
COWDEN (62422) Shelby(74), Fayette(25)
CREAL SPRINGS (62922) Williamson(71), Johnson(28)
CRESCENT CITY Iroquois
CRESTON Ogle
CRETE Will
CREVE COEUR Tazewell

CROPSEY (61731) McLean(67), Ford(31), Livingston(1)
CROSSVILLE White
CRYSTAL LAKE McHenry
CUBA Fulton
CULLOM (60929) Livingston(89), Ford(10)
CUTLER (62238) Perry(95), Randolph(4)
CYPRESS (62923) Johnson(85), Pulaski(8), Union(5)
DAHINDA Knox
DAHLGREN (62828) Hamilton(97), Wayne(2)
DAKOTA Stephenson
DALE Hamilton
DALLAS CITY (62330) Hancock(93), Henderson(6)
DALTON CITY (61925) Macon(57), Moultrie(42)
DALZELL Bureau
DANA (61321) La Salle(87), Livingston(4), Woodford(4), Marshall(3)
DANFORTH Iroquois
DANVERS (61732) McLean(63), Tazewell(36)
DANVILLE Vermilion
DARIEN Du Page
DAVIS (61019) Stephenson(65), Winnebago(34)
DAVIS JUNCTION (61020) Ogle(94), Winnebago(5)
DAWSON Sangamon
DE KALB De Kalb
DE LAND Piatt
DE SOTO (62924) Jackson(80), Williamson(19)
DECATUR Macon
DEER CREEK Tazewell
DEER GROVE (61243) Whiteside(89), Bureau(5), Lee(5)
DEERE CO GROUP CLAIMS Rock Island
DEERFIELD (60015) Lake(95), Cook(4)
DEERFIELD Cook
DEKALB De Kalb
DELAVAN Tazewell
DENNISON (62423) Clark(90), Edgar(9)
DEPUE Bureau
DES PLAINES Cook
DEWEY (61840) Champaign(97), Ford(2)
DEWITT De Witt
DIETERICH (62424) Effingham(90), Jasper(9)
DIVERNON Sangamon
DIX (62830) Jefferson(95), Marion(4)
DIXON (61021) Lee(91), Ogle(8)
DOLTON Cook
DONGOLA (62926) Union(90), Pulaski(9)
DONNELLSON (62019) Montgomery(52), Bond(47)
DONOVAN Iroquois
DORSEY (62021) Madison(93), Macoupin(6)
DOVER Bureau
DOW Jersey
DOWELL Jackson
DOWNERS GROVE Du Page
DOWNS McLean
DU BOIS (62831) Washington(91), Perry(8)
DU QUOIN (62832) Perry(96), Jackson(3)
DUNDAS (62425) Richland(86), Jasper(13)
DUNDEE Kane
DUNFERMLINE Fulton
DUNLAP Peoria
DUPO St. Clair
DURAND Winnebago
DWIGHT (60420) Livingston(93), Grundy(6)
EAGARVILLE Macoupin
EARLVILLE (60518) La Salle(72), De Kalb(22), Lee(4)
EAST ALTON Madison
EAST CARONDELET (62240) St. Clair(97), Monroe(2)
EAST DUBUQUE Jo Daviess

EAST GALESBURG Knox
EAST LYNN Vermilion
EAST MOLINE Rock Island
EAST PEORIA (61611) Tazewell(86), Woodford(13)
EAST SAINT LOUIS St. Clair
EASTON Mason
EDDYVILLE Pope
EDELSTEIN (61526) Peoria(90), Marshall(8), Stark(1)
EDGEWOOD (62426) Effingham(58), Clay(37), Fayette(4)
EDINBURG Christian
EDWARDS Peoria
EDWARDSVILLE Madison
EFFINGHAM Effingham
EL PASO (61738) Woodford(96), McLean(2)
ELBURN Kane
ELCO Alexander
ELDENA Lee
ELDORADO (62930) Saline(98), Gallatin(1)
ELDRED Greene
ELEROY Stephenson
ELGIN (60120) Kane(56), Cook(43)
ELGIN Du Page
ELGIN Kane
ELIZABETH (61028) Jo Daviess(98), Carroll(1)
ELIZABETHTOWN (62931) Hardin(82), Gallatin(17)
ELK GROVE VILLAGE (60007) Cook(96), Du Page(3)
ELK GROVE VILLAGE Cook
ELKHART Logan
ELKVILLE Jackson
ELLERY (62833) Edwards(56), Wayne(43)
ELLIOTT Ford
ELLIS GROVE Randolph
ELLISVILLE Fulton
ELLSWORTH McLean
ELMHURST Du Page
ELMWOOD Peoria
ELMWOOD PARK Cook
ELSAH Jersey
ELVASTON Hancock
ELWIN Macon
ELWOOD Will
EMDEN (62635) Tazewell(94), Logan(5)
EMINGTON Livingston
EMMA White
ENERGY Williamson
ENFIELD (62835) White(94), Hamilton(5)
EOLA Du Page
EQUALITY (62934) Gallatin(68), Saline(31)
ERIE (61250) Whiteside(94), Henry(5)
ESMOND (60129) Ogle(53), De Kalb(46)
ESSEX (60935) Kankakee(98), Will(1)
EUREKA Woodford
EVANSTON Cook
EVANSVILLE Randolph
EVERGREEN PARK Cook
EWING (62836) Franklin(98), Jefferson(1)
FAIRBURY (61739) Livingston(97), McLean(2)
FAIRFIELD Wayne
FAIRMOUNT Vermilion
FAIRVIEW Fulton
FAIRVIEW HEIGHTS St. Clair
FARINA (62838) Fayette(55), Clay(29), Marion(13), Effingham(1)
FARMER CITY (61842) De Witt(89), McLean(9), Piatt(1)
FARMERSVILLE Montgomery
FARMINGTON (61531) Fulton(92), Peoria(5), Knox(1)
FENTON (61251) Whiteside(95), Rock Island(5)
FERRIS Hancock
FIATT Fulton
FIDELITY Jersey
FIELDON (62031) Jersey(97), Greene(2)

FILLMORE Montgomery
FINDLAY Shelby
FISHER (61843) Champaign(94), McLean(5)
FITHIAN Vermilion
FLANAGAN Livingston
FLAT ROCK (62427) Crawford(93), Lawrence(6)
FLORA Clay
FLOSSMOOR Cook
FOOSLAND (61845) Champaign(76), Ford(14), McLean(9)
FOREST CITY Mason
FOREST PARK Cook
FORREST Livingston
FORRESTON Ogle
FORSYTH Macon
FORT SHERIDAN Lake
FOWLER Adams
FOX LAKE Lake
FOX RIVER GROVE (60021) McHenry(96), Lake(3)
FOX VALLEY Du Page
FRANKFORT Will
FRANKFORT HEIGHTS Franklin
FRANKLIN (62638) Morgan(98), Macoupin(1)
FRANKLIN GROVE (61031) Lee(96), Ogle(3)
FRANKLIN PARK Cook
FRANKLIN PARK Du Page
FREDERICK Schuyler
FREEBURG St. Clair
FREEMAN SPUR Williamson
FREEPORT Stephenson
FULTON Whiteside
FULTS Monroe
GALATIA (62935) Saline(97), Hamilton(1)
GALATIA Saline
GALENA Jo Daviess
GALESBURG Knox
GALT Whiteside
GALVA (61434) Henry(97), Knox(1)
GARDEN PRAIRIE (61038) Boone(89), McHenry(10)
GARDNER Grundy
GAYS (61928) Moultrie(75), Coles(16), Shelby(7)
GEFF Wayne
GENESEO Henry
GENEVA Kane
GENOA De Kalb
GEORGETOWN Vermilion
GERLAW Warren
GERMAN VALLEY (61039) Stephenson(69), Ogle(30)
GERMANTOWN Clinton
GIBSON CITY (60936) Ford(98), Champaign(1)
GIFFORD Champaign
GILBERTS Kane
GILLESPIE Macoupin
GILMAN Iroquois
GILSON Knox
GIRARD (62640) Macoupin(89), Montgomery(10)
GLADSTONE Henderson
GLASFORD (61533) Peoria(82), Fulton(17)
GLEN CARBON Madison
GLEN ELLYN Du Page
GLENARM Sangamon
GLENCOE Cook
GLENDALE HEIGHTS Du Page
GLENVIEW Cook
GLENVIEW NAS Cook
GLENWOOD Cook
GODFREY (62035) Madison(87), Jersey(12)
GOLCONDA (62938) Pope(90), Hardin(5), Massac(4)
GOLDEN Adams
GOLDEN EAGLE Calhoun

GOLDEN GATE Wayne
GOLF Cook
GOOD HOPE McDonough
GOODFIELD Woodford
GOODWINE Iroquois
GOREVILLE (62939) Johnson(92), Williamson(4), Union(3)
GORHAM Jackson
GRAFTON Jersey
GRAND CHAIN (62941) Pulaski(61), Massac(38)
GRAND RIDGE La Salle
GRAND TOWER Jackson
GRANITE CITY Madison
GRANT PARK (60940) Kankakee(95), Will(4)
GRANTSBURG (62943) Johnson(76), Massac(19), Pope(4)
GRANVILLE Putnam
GRAYMONT Livingston
GRAYSLAKE Lake
GRAYVILLE (62844) White(57), Edwards(42)
GREAT LAKES Lake
GREEN VALLEY Tazewell
GREENFIELD (62044) Greene(87), Macoupin(12)
GREENUP Cumberland
GREENVIEW Menard
GREENVILLE Bond
GRIDLEY (61744) McLean(91), Livingston(8)
GRIGGSVILLE Pike
GROVELAND Tazewell
GURNEE Lake
HAGARSTOWN Fayette
HAMBURG Calhoun
HAMEL Madison
HAMILTON Hancock
HAMLETSBURG Pope
HAMMOND (61929) Piatt(97), Moultrie(2)
HAMPSHIRE (60140) Kane(98), De Kalb(1)
HAMPTON Rock Island
HANNA CITY Peoria
HANOVER Jo Daviess
HANOVER PARK (60133) Cook(57), Du Page(42)
HARDIN Calhoun
HARMON (61042) Lee(98), Whiteside(1)
HARRISBURG Saline
HARRISTOWN Macon
HARTFORD Madison
HARTSBURG (62643) Montgomery(60), Logan(40)
HARVARD McHenry
HARVEL (62538) Montgomery(83), Christian(16)
HARVEY Cook
HARWOOD HEIGHTS Cook
HAVANA (62644) Mason(94), Fulton(5)
HAZEL CREST Cook
HEBRON McHenry
HECKER Monroe
HENDERSON Knox
HENNEPIN Putnam
HENNING Vermilion
HENRY Marshall
HERALD White
HEROD (62947) Saline(43), Hardin(31), Pope(25)
HERRICK (62431) Shelby(53), Fayette(46)
HERRIN Williamson
HERSCHER (60941) Kankakee(96), Iroquois(2), Ford(1)
HETTICK Macoupin
HEYWORTH (61745) McLean(96), De Witt(3)
HICKORY HILLS Cook
HIDALGO Jasper
HIGHLAND (62249) Madison(94), Clinton(4)
HIGHLAND PARK Lake

HIGHWOOD Lake
HILLSBORO Montgomery
HILLSDALE Rock Island
HILLSIDE Cook
HILLVIEW Greene
HINCKLEY De Kalb
HINDSBORO (61930) Douglas(81), Coles(18)
HINES Cook
HINSDALE (60527) Du Page(91), Cook(8)
HINSDALE Du Page
HOFFMAN Clinton
HOFFMAN ESTATES Cook
HOLCOMB Ogle
HOMER (61849) Champaign(84), Vermilion(15)
HOMETOWN Cook
HOMEWOOD Cook
HOOPESTON (60942) Vermilion(91), Iroquois(8)
HOOPPOLE Henry
HOPEDALE Tazewell
HOPKINS PARK Kankakee
HOYLETON Washington
HUDSON (61748) McLean(98), Woodford(1)
HUEY Clinton
HULL (62343) Pike(89), Adams(10)
HUMBOLDT Coles
HUME Edgar
HUNTLEY (60142) McHenry(76), Kane(23)
HUNTSVILLE Schuyler
HURST Williamson
HUTSONVILLE Crawford
ILLINOIS CITY (61259) Rock Island(98), Mercer(1)
ILLIOPOLIS (62539) Sangamon(94), Macon(5)
INA (62846) Jefferson(98), Franklin(1)
INDIANOLA (61850) Vermilion(98), Edgar(1)
INDUSTRY (61440) McDonough(97), Schuyler(2)
INGLESIDE Lake
INGRAHAM (62434) Jasper(84), Clay(15)
IOLA Clay
IPAVA Fulton
IROQUOIS Iroquois
IRVING Montgomery
IRVINGTON Washington
ISLAND LAKE (60042) Lake(51), McHenry(48)
ITASCA Du Page
IUKA Marion
IVESDALE (61851) Champaign(89), Piatt(8), Douglas(2)
JACKSONVILLE Morgan
JACOB Jackson
JANESVILLE Cumberland
JEFFERSON BANK Peoria
JERSEYVILLE Jersey
JEWETT (62436) Jasper(59), Cumberland(40)
JOHNSONVILLE Wayne
JOHNSTON CITY Williamson
JOLIET Will
JONESBORO Union
JOPPA Massac
JOY (61260) Mercer(94), Rock Island(5)
JUNCTION Gallatin
JUSTICE Cook
KAMPSVILLE (62053) Calhoun(97), Pike(2)
KANE (62054) Greene(58), Jersey(41)
KANEVILLE Kane
KANKAKEE Kankakee
KANSAS (61933) Edgar(85), Clark(12), Coles(2)
KARBERS RIDGE Hardin
KARNAK (62956) Pulaski(50), Massac(48)
KASBEER Bureau

KEENES (62851) Wayne(65), Jefferson(27), Marion(7)
KEENSBURG Wabash
KEITHSBURG (61442) Mercer(95), Henderson(4)
KELL (62853) Marion(98), Jefferson(1)
KEMPTON (60946) Ford(81), Livingston(18)
KENILWORTH Cook
KENNEY (61749) De Witt(72), Logan(15), Macon(12)
KENT (61044) Stephenson(65), Jo Daviess(35)
KEWANEE Henry
KEYESPORT (62253) Bond(59), Clinton(37), Fayette(3)
KILBOURNE Mason
KINCAID Christian
KINDERHOOK Pike
KINGS Ogle
KINGSTON (60145) De Kalb(93), Boone(6)
KINGSTON MINES Peoria
KINMUNDY (62854) Marion(97), Clay(1), Fayette(1)
KINSMAN (60437) Grundy(97), La Salle(2)
KIRKLAND (60146) De Kalb(89), Boone(8), Ogle(1), Winnebago(1)
KIRKWOOD (61447) Warren(92), Henderson(7)
KNOXVILLE Knox
LA FAYETTE (61449) Knox(53), Stark(46)
LA GRANGE Cook
LA GRANGE PARK Cook
LA HARPE (61450) Hancock(56), McDonough(41), Henderson(1)
LA MOILLE (61330) Bureau(52), Lee(47)
LA PLACE Piatt
LA PRAIRIE (62346) Adams(63), Schuyler(22), Hancock(14)
LA ROSE Marshall
LA SALLE La Salle
LACON Marshall
LADD Bureau
LAFOX Kane
LAKE BLUFF Lake
LAKE FOREST Lake
LAKE FORK Logan
LAKE IN THE HILLS McHenry
LAKE VILLA Lake
LAKE ZURICH Lake
LAKEWOOD Shelby
LANARK Carroll
LANCASTER Wabash
LANE De Witt
LANSING Cook
LATHAM (62543) Logan(82), Macon(17)
LAURA (61451) Peoria(92), Stark(7)
LAWNDALE Logan
LAWRENCEVILLE Lawrence
LE ROY McLean
LEAF RIVER (61047) Ogle(96), Winnebago(2), Stephenson(1)
LEBANON St. Clair
LEE (60530) Lee(56), De Kalb(43)
LEE CENTER Lee
LELAND (60531) La Salle(64), De Kalb(35)
LEMONT (60439) Cook(51), Du Page(44), Will(4)
LENA (61048) Stephenson(96), Jo Daviess(3)
LENZBURG (62255) St. Clair(92), Washington(7)
LEONORE La Salle
LERNA (62440) Coles(72), Cumberland(27)
LEWISTOWN Fulton
LEXINGTON McLean
LIBERTY Adams
LIBERTYVILLE Lake
LIMA Adams
LINCOLN Logan
LINCOLN'S NEW SALEM Menard

LINCOLNSHIRE Lake
LINCOLNWOOD Cook
LINDENWOOD Ogle
LISLE Du Page
LITCHFIELD (62056) Montgomery(93), Macoupin(6)
LITERBERRY Morgan
LITTLE YORK (61453) Warren(87), Henderson(12)
LITTLETON (61452) Schuyler(83), McDonough(16)
LIVERPOOL Fulton
LIVINGSTON Madison
LOAMI Sangamon
LOCKPORT Will
LODA (60948) Iroquois(95), Ford(4)
LOGAN Franklin
LOMAX Henderson
LOMBARD Du Page
LONDON MILLS (61544) Fulton(86), Knox(13)
LONG GROVE Lake
LONG POINT Livingston
LONGVIEW (61852) Champaign(82), Douglas(17)
LOOGOOTEE Fayette
LORAINE (62349) Adams(94), Hancock(5)
LOSTANT (61334) La Salle(89), Putnam(9)
LOUISVILLE Clay
LOVEJOY St. Clair
LOVES PARK (61111) Winnebago(97), Boone(2)
LOVES PARK Winnebago
LOVINGTON (61937) Moultrie(94), Macon(3), Piatt(1)
LOWDER Sangamon
LOWPOINT Woodford
LUDLOW (60949) Champaign(90), Ford(9)
LYNDON Whiteside
LYNN CENTER (61262) Henry(92), Mercer(7)
LYONS Cook
MACEDONIA (62860) Franklin(88), Hamilton(11)
MACHESNEY PARK Winnebago
MACKINAW Tazewell
MACOMB McDonough
MACON Macon
MAEYSTOWN Monroe
MAGNOLIA (61336) Putnam(96), Marshall(3)
MAHOMET Champaign
MAKANDA (62958) Jackson(69), Williamson(15), Union(14)
MALDEN Bureau
MALTA De Kalb
MANCHESTER Scott
MANHATTAN Will
MANITO (61546) Mason(83), Tazewell(16)
MANLIUS Bureau
MANSFIELD (61854) Piatt(95), McLean(4)
MANTENO (60950) Kankakee(98), Will(1)
MAPLE PARK (60151) Kane(81), De Kalb(18)
MAPLETON Peoria
MAQUON Knox
MARENGO McHenry
MARIETTA (61459) Fulton(60), McDonough(39)
MARINE Madison
MARION Williamson
MARISSA (62257) St. Clair(70), Washington(27), Randolph(1)
MARK Putnam
MARKHAM Cook
MAROA Macon
MARSEILLES La Salle
MARSHALL (62441) Clark(98), Edgar(1)
MARTINSVILLE (62442) Clark(98), Crawford(1)
MARTINTON Iroquois
MARYVILLE Madison

MASCOUTAH St. Clair
MASON (62443) Effingham(90), Clay(9)
MASON CITY Mason
MATHERVILLE Mercer
MATTESON Cook
MATTOON Coles
MAUNIE White
MAYWOOD Cook
MAZON Grundy
MC CLURE (62957) Alexander(65), Union(34)
MC CONNELL Stephenson
MC HENRY McHenry
MC LEAN (61754) McLean(96), Logan(3)
MC LEANSBORO Hamilton
MC NABB Putnam
MCHENRY (60051) McHenry(89), Lake(10)
MCHENRY Cook
MCHENRY McHenry
MECHANICSBURG (62545) Sangamon(63), Christian(36)
MEDIA (61460) Henderson(95), Warren(4)
MEDINAH Du Page
MEDORA (62063) Jersey(58), Macoupin(41)
MELROSE PARK Cook
MELVIN (60952) Ford(95), Livingston(4)
MENARD Randolph
MENDON (62351) Adams(85), Hancock(14)
MENDOTA (61342) La Salle(97), Bureau(1), Lee(1)
MEREDOSIA (62665) Morgan(95), Scott(2), Cass(2)
MERNA McLean
METAMORA Woodford
METCALF Edgar
METROPOLIS Massac
MICHAEL Calhoun
MIDDLETOWN (62666) Logan(85), Menard(14)
MIDLOTHIAN Cook
MILAN Rock Island
MILFORD Iroquois
MILL SHOALS White
MILLBROOK Kendall
MILLCREEK Union
MILLEDGEVILLE (61051) Carroll(94), Ogle(3), Whiteside(2)
MILLER CITY Alexander
MILLINGTON Kendall
MILLSTADT St. Clair
MILMINE Piatt
MILTON Pike
MINERAL Bureau
MINIER Tazewell
MINONK (61760) Woodford(93), Marshall(6)
MINOOKA (60447) Grundy(48), Kendall(26), Will(24)
MOBIL OIL CREDIT CORP Du Page
MODE Shelby
MODESTO (62667) Macoupin(98), Morgan(1)
MODOC Randolph
MOKENA Will
MOLINE Rock Island
MOMENCE Kankakee
MONEE Will
MONMOUTH Warren
MONROE CENTER (61052) Ogle(94), Winnebago(2), De Kalb(2)
MONTGOMERY (60538) Kendall(61), Kane(38)
MONTGOMERY WARD Du Page
MONTICELLO Piatt
MONTROSE (62445) Jasper(55), Cumberland(33), Effingham(11)
MOOSEHEART Kane
MORO Madison
MORRIS Grundy
MORRISON Whiteside

MORRISONVILLE (62546) Christian(90), Montgomery(9)
MORTON Tazewell
MORTON GROVE Cook
MOSSVILLE Peoria
MOUND CITY Pulaski
MOUNDS Pulaski
MOUNT AUBURN (62547) Christian(97), Macon(2)
MOUNT CARMEL Wabash
MOUNT CARROLL (61053) Carroll(92), Jo Daviess(7)
MOUNT ERIE Wayne
MOUNT MORRIS Ogle
MOUNT OLIVE (62069) Macoupin(97), Montgomery(2)
MOUNT PROSPECT Cook
MOUNT PULASKI Logan
MOUNT STERLING Brown
MOUNT VERNON Jefferson
MOWEAQUA (62550) Shelby(63), Christian(36)
MOZIER Calhoun
MT ZION Macon
MUDDY Saline
MULBERRY GROVE (62262) Bond(87), Fayette(11), Montgomery(1)
MULKEYTOWN Franklin
MUNCIE Vermilion
MUNDELEIN Lake
MURDOCK Douglas
MURPHYSBORO Jackson
MURRAYVILLE Morgan
NACHUSA Lee
NAPERVILLE (60565) Du Page(65), Will(34)
NAPERVILLE (60564) Will(81), Du Page(18)
NAPERVILLE Du Page
NASHVILLE Washington
NASON Jefferson
NATIONAL STOCK YARDS St. Clair
NAUVOO Hancock
NEBO (62355) Pike(62), Calhoun(37)
NELSON Lee
NEOGA (62447) Cumberland(87), Shelby(11), Coles(1)
NEPONSET (61345) Bureau(97), Stark(2)
NEW ATHENS (62264) St. Clair(97), Monroe(2)
NEW BADEN (62265) Clinton(91), St. Clair(8)
NEW BEDFORD Bureau
NEW BERLIN Sangamon
NEW BOSTON Mercer
NEW BURNSIDE (62967) Johnson(88), Williamson(11)
NEW CANTON Pike
NEW DOUGLAS (62074) Madison(90), Bond(4), Macoupin(3), Montgomery(1)
NEW HAVEN (62867) Gallatin(59), White(40)
NEW HOLLAND (62671) Logan(95), Mason(4)
NEW LENOX Will
NEW MEMPHIS Clinton
NEW SALEM Pike
NEW WINDSOR (61465) Mercer(88), Henry(11)
NEWARK (60541) Kendall(91), Grundy(6), La Salle(2)
NEWMAN (61942) Douglas(91), Edgar(8)
NEWTON (62448) Jasper(97), Richland(2)
NIANTIC Macon
NILES Cook
NILWOOD Macoupin
NIOTA Hancock
NOBLE (62868) Richland(94), Clay(4), Wayne(1)
NOKOMIS (62075) Montgomery(95), Christian(4)
NORA Jo Daviess

NORMAL McLean
NORRIS Fulton
NORRIS CITY (62869) White(94), Gallatin(3), Hamilton(1)
NORTH AURORA Kane
NORTH CHICAGO Lake
NORTH HENDERSON (61466) Mercer(96), Warren(2)
NORTHBROOK Cook
O FALLON St. Clair
OAK FOREST Cook
OAK LAWN Cook
OAK PARK Cook
OAKDALE (62268) Washington(94), Perry(5)
OAKFORD (62673) Cass(51), Menard(48)
OAKLAND (61943) Coles(78), Douglas(14), Edgar(6)
OAKLEY Macon
OAKWOOD Vermilion
OBLONG (62449) Crawford(90), Jasper(8)
OCONEE (62553) Shelby(50), Christian(29), Montgomery(20)
ODELL Livingston
ODIN Marion
OGDEN (61859) Champaign(88), Vermilion(11)
OGLESBY La Salle
OHIO (61349) Bureau(77), Lee(21), Cass(1)
OHLMAN Montgomery
OKAWVILLE Washington
OLIVE BRANCH Alexander
OLMSTED Pulaski
OLNEY Richland
OLYMPIA FIELDS Cook
OMAHA Gallatin
ONARGA Iroquois
ONEIDA Knox
OPDYKE Jefferson
OPHEIM Henry
OPHIEM Henry
OQUAWKA Henderson
ORANGEVILLE Stephenson
ORAVILLE Jackson
OREANA Macon
OREGON Ogle
ORIENT Franklin
ORION (61273) Henry(83), Rock Island(16)
ORLAND PARK Cook
OSCO Henry
OSWEGO Kendall
OTTAWA La Salle
OWANECO (62555) Christian(91), Macon(8)
OZARK Johnson
PALATINE (60074) Cook(98), Lake(1)
PALATINE Cook
PALESTINE Crawford
PALMER Christian
PALMYRA Macoupin
PALOMA Adams
PALOS HEIGHTS Cook
PALOS HILLS Cook
PALOS PARK Cook
PANA (62557) Christian(92), Shelby(5), Montgomery(1)
PANAMA Montgomery
PAPINEAU Iroquois
PARIS Edgar
PARK FOREST (60466) Cook(54), Will(45)
PARK RIDGE Cook
PARKERSBURG Richland
PATOKA (62875) Marion(94), Fayette(5)
PATTERSON Greene
PAW PAW Lee
PAWNEE (62558) Sangamon(88), Christian(8), Montgomery(2)
PAXTON (60957) Ford(96), Champaign(2)
PAYSON Adams
PEARL (62361) Pike(97), Calhoun(2)

PEARL CITY (61062) Stephenson(96), Jo Daviess(2)
PECATONICA (61063) Winnebago(91), Stephenson(8)
PEKIN Tazewell
PENFIELD (61862) Champaign(79), Vermilion(20)
PEORIA Peoria
PEORIA HEIGHTS Peoria
PEOTONE (60468) Will(97), Kankakee(2)
PERCY (62272) Randolph(80), Perry(19)
PERKS Pulaski
PERRY Pike
PERU (61354) La Salle(98), Bureau(1)
PESOTUM Champaign
PETERSBURG Menard
PHILO Champaign
PIASA (62079) Macoupin(66), Jersey(33)
PIERRON Bond
PINCKNEYVILLE Perry
PIPER CITY (60959) Ford(93), Livingston(5)
PITTSBURG Williamson
PITTSFIELD Pike
PLAINFIELD (60544) Will(98), Kendall(1)
PLAINVIEW Macoupin
PLAINVILLE Adams
PLANO Kendall
PLATO CENTER Kane
PLEASANT HILL (62366) Pike(98), Calhoun(1)
PLEASANT PLAINS Sangamon
PLYMOUTH (62367) Hancock(50), McDonough(41), Schuyler(7)
POCAHONTAS (62275) Bond(68), Madison(22), Clinton(8)
POLO Ogle
POMONA Jackson
PONTIAC Livingston
POPLAR GROVE Boone
PORT BYRON Rock Island
POSEN Cook
POTOMAC Vermilion
PRAIRIE CITY McDonough
PRAIRIE DU ROCHER (62277) Randolph(57), Monroe(42)
PREEMPTION Mercer
PRINCETON Bureau
PRINCEVILLE (61559) Peoria(97), Stark(2)
PROPHETSTOWN (61277) Whiteside(80), Henry(19)
PROSPECT HEIGHTS Cook
PULASKI Pulaski
PUTNAM (61560) Putnam(93), Bureau(4), Marshall(2)
QUINCY Adams
RADOM Washington
RALEIGH Saline
RAMSEY (62080) Fayette(92), Montgomery(6), Shelby(1)
RANKIN (60960) Vermilion(72), Ford(21), Iroquois(3), Champaign(2)
RANSOM (60470) La Salle(90), Grundy(6), Livingston(2)
RANTOUL Champaign
RAPIDS CITY Rock Island
RARITAN Henderson
RAYMOND (62560) Montgomery(90), Macoupin(9)
RED BUD (62278) Randolph(68), Monroe(31)
REDDICK (60961) Kankakee(83), Livingston(13), Grundy(2)
REDMON Edgar
RENAULT Monroe
REYNOLDS (61279) Rock Island(73), Mercer(26)
RICHMOND McHenry
RICHTON PARK Cook
RICHVIEW (62877) Washington(97), Jefferson(2)

RIDGE FARM (61870) Vermilion(95), Edgar(4)
RIDGWAY Gallatin
RIDOTT Stephenson
RINARD Wayne
RINGWOOD McHenry
RIO (61472) Knox(98), Mercer(1)
RIVER FOREST Cook
RIVER GROVE Cook
RIVERDALE Cook
RIVERSIDE Cook
RIVERTON Sangamon
ROANOKE Woodford
ROBBINS Cook
ROBERTS (60962) Ford(97), Livingston(2)
ROBINSON Crawford
ROCHELLE (61068) Ogle(97), Lee(1)
ROCHESTER (62563) Sangamon(96), Christian(3)
ROCK CITY Stephenson
ROCK FALLS Whiteside
ROCK ISLAND Rock Island
ROCKBRIDGE (62081) Greene(98), Jersey(2)
ROCKFORD (61102) Winnebago(98), Ogle(1)
ROCKFORD (61114) Winnebago(96), Boone(3)
ROCKFORD Winnebago
ROCKPORT Pike
ROCKTON Winnebago
ROCKWOOD (62280) Jackson(58), Randolph(41)
ROLLING MEADOWS Cook
ROME Peoria
ROMEOVILLE Will
ROODHOUSE (62082) Greene(88), Scott(9), Morgan(1)
ROSAMOND (62083) Christian(61), Montgomery(38)
ROSCOE (61073) Winnebago(98), Boone(1)
ROSELLE (60172) Du Page(81), Cook(18)
ROSEVILLE (61473) McDonough(69), Warren(30)
ROSICLARE Hardin
ROSSVILLE Vermilion
ROUND LAKE Lake
ROXANA Madison
ROYAL Champaign
ROYALTON Franklin
RUSHVILLE Schuyler
RUSSELL Lake
RUTLAND (61358) La Salle(75), Marshall(24)
SADORUS (61872) Champaign(90), Douglas(9)
SAILOR SPRINGS Clay
SAINT ANNE (60964) Kankakee(93), Iroquois(6)
SAINT AUGUSTINE (61474) Knox(93), Warren(5), Fulton(1)
SAINT CHARLES Kane
SAINT DAVID Fulton
SAINT ELMO (62458) Fayette(91), Effingham(8)
SAINT FRANCISVILLE (62460) Lawrence(89), Wabash(10)
SAINT JACOB Madison
SAINT JOSEPH Champaign
SAINT LIBORY St. Clair
SAINT PETER Fayette
SAINTE MARIE Jasper
SALEM Marion
SAN JOSE (62682) Mason(82), Tazewell(9), Logan(8)
SANDOVAL (62882) Marion(92), Clinton(7)
SANDWICH (60548) De Kalb(77), La Salle(19), Kendall(3)
SAUNEMIN Livingston
SAVANNA Carroll
SAVOY Champaign

SAWYERVILLE Macoupin
SAYBROOK McLean
SCALES MOUND Jo Daviess
SCHAUMBURG Cook
SCHELLER (62883) Jefferson(62), Franklin(29), Perry(7)
SCHILLER PARK Cook
SCIOTA (61475) McDonough(87), Warren(11)
SCIOTO MILLS Stephenson
SCIOTO MILLSX Stephenson
SCOTT AIR FORCE BASE St. Clair
SCOTTVILLE Macoupin
SEATON (61476) Mercer(88), Henderson(10), Warren(1)
SEATONVILLE Bureau
SECOR Woodford
SENECA (61360) La Salle(83), Grundy(16)
SERENA La Salle
SESSER Franklin
SEWARD Winnebago
SEYMOUR Champaign
SHABBONA De Kalb
SHANNON (61078) Carroll(84), Stephenson(8), Ogle(7)
SHATTUC Clinton
SHAWNEETOWN Gallatin
SHEFFIELD Bureau
SHELBYVILLE Shelby
SHELDON Iroquois
SHERIDAN La Salle
SHERMAN Sangamon
SHERRARD Mercer
SHIPMAN Macoupin
SHIRLAND Winnebago
SHIRLEY McLean
SHOBONIER (62885) Fayette(95), Marion(4)
SHUMWAY (62461) Effingham(93), Shelby(6)
SIBLEY Ford
SIDELL (61876) Vermilion(84), Edgar(15)
SIDNEY Champaign
SIGEL (62462) Cumberland(59), Shelby(39), Effingham(1)
SILVIS Rock Island
SIMPSON (62985) Johnson(86), Pope(13)
SIMS Wayne
SKOKIE Cook
SMITHBORO Bond
SMITHFIELD Fulton
SMITHSHIRE (61478) Warren(94), Henderson(5)
SMITHTON St. Clair
SOLON MILLS McHenry
SOMONAUK (60552) De Kalb(58), La Salle(41)
SORENTO (62086) Bond(81), Montgomery(16), Madison(1)
SOUTH BELOIT (61080) Winnebago(96), Boone(3)
SOUTH ELGIN Kane
SOUTH HOLLAND Cook
SOUTH PEKIN Tazewell
SOUTH ROXANA Madison
SOUTH WILMINGTON Grundy
SPARLAND (61565) Marshall(95), Peoria(4)
SPARTA Randolph
SPEER Stark
SPRING GROVE (60081) McHenry(79), Lake(20)
SPRING VALLEY Bureau
SPRINGERTON (62887) White(78), Hamilton(21)
SPRINGFIELD Sangamon
STANDARD Putnam
STANDARD CITY Macoupin
STANFORD McLean
STAUNTON (62088) Macoupin(85), Madison(14)
STEELEVILLE Randolph

STEGER (60475) Will(56), Cook(43)
STERLING (61081) Whiteside(98), Lee(1)
STEWARD (60553) Lee(98), De Kalb(1)
STEWARDSON Shelby
STILLMAN VALLEY (61084) Ogle(95), Winnebago(4)
STOCKLAND Iroquois
STOCKTON Jo Daviess
STONE PARK Cook
STONEFORT (62987) Saline(57), Williamson(34), Pope(7)
STONINGTON Christian
STOY Crawford
STRASBURG Shelby
STRAWN (61775) Livingston(90), Ford(9)
STREAMWOOD Cook
STREATOR (61364) La Salle(91), Livingston(8)
STRONGHURST Henderson
SUBLETTE Lee
SUGAR GROVE Kane
SULLIVAN Moultrie
SUMMER HILL Pike
SUMMERFIELD St. Clair
SUMMIT ARGO Cook
SUMNER (62466) Lawrence(88), Crawford(6), Richland(5)
SUTTER (62373) Hancock(94), Adams(5)
SYCAMORE (60178) De Kalb(97), Kane(2)
TABLE GROVE (61482) Fulton(52), Knox(25), McDonough(21)
TALLULA Menard
TAMAROA Perry
TAMMS Alexander
TAMPICO (61283) Whiteside(49), Bureau(48), Henry(2)
TAYLOR RIDGE Rock Island
TAYLOR SPRINGS Montgomery
TAYLORVILLE Christian
TECHNY Cook
TENNESSEE (62374) McDonough(58), Hancock(41)
TEUTOPOLIS (62467) Effingham(86), Jasper(8), Cumberland(5)
TEXICO (62889) Jefferson(69), Marion(30)
THAWVILLE (60968) Iroquois(56), Ford(41), Livingston(1)
THAYER Sangamon
THEBES Alexander
THOMASBORO Champaign
THOMPSONVILLE (62890) Franklin(67), Williamson(24), Saline(6), Hamilton(1)
THOMSON Carroll
THORNTON Cook
TILDEN Randolph
TILTON Vermilion
TIMEWELL (62375) Brown(97), Adams(2)
TINLEY PARK (60477) Cook(95), Will(4)
TISKILWA Bureau
TOLEDO Cumberland
TOLONO Champaign
TOLUCA Marshall
TONICA (61370) La Salle(98), Putnam(1)
TOPEKA Mason
TOULON (61483) Stark(61), Henry(38)
TOVEY Christian
TOWANDA McLean
TOWER HILL Shelby
TREMONT Tazewell
TRENTON (62293) Clinton(73), St. Clair(16), Madison(9)
TRILLA (62469) Cumberland(76), Coles(23)
TRIUMPH La Salle
TRIVOLI (61569) Peoria(97), Fulton(2)
TROY Madison
TROY GROVE La Salle
TUNNEL HILL Johnson
TUSCOLA Douglas
ULLIN (62992) Pulaski(97), Alexander(2)
UNION McHenry
UNION HILL Kankakee

UNITY Alexander
URBANA Champaign
URSA Adams
UTICA La Salle
VALIER Franklin
VALMEYER Monroe
VAN ORIN Bureau
VANDALIA Fayette
VARNA Marshall
VENEDY Washington
VENICE (62090) Madison(97), St. Clair(2)
VERGENNES Jackson
VERMILION Edgar
VERMONT (61484) McDonough(64), Fulton(34), Schuyler(1)
VERNON (62892) Marion(90), Fayette(9)
VERNON HILLS Lake
VERONA Grundy
VERSAILLES Brown
VICTORIA Knox
VIENNA Johnson
VILLA GROVE (61956) Douglas(95), Champaign(4)
VILLA PARK Du Page
VILLA RIDGE Pulaski
VIOLA Mercer
VIRDEN (62690) Macoupin(89), Montgomery(5), Sangamon(4)
VIRGIL Kane
VIRGINIA Cass
WADSWORTH Lake
WAGGONER (62572) Macoupin(58), Montgomery(41)
WALNUT (61376) Bureau(92), Lee(7)
WALNUT HILL (62893) Marion(57), Jefferson(42)
WALSH Randolph
WALSHVILLE Montgomery
WALTONVILLE Jefferson
WAPELLA De Witt
WARREN (61087) Jo Daviess(98), Stephenson(1)
WARRENSBURG Macon
WARRENVILLE Du Page
WARSAW (62379) Hancock(95), Adams(4)
WASCO Kane
WASHBURN (61570) Woodford(77), Marshall(22)
WASHINGTON Tazewell
WATAGA Knox
WATERLOO (62298) Monroe(92), St. Clair(7)
WATERMAN De Kalb
WATSEKA Iroquois
WATSON Effingham
WAUCONDA Lake
WAUKEGAN Lake
WAVERLY (62692) Morgan(76), Sangamon(23)
WAYNE (60184) Du Page(59), Kane(40)
WAYNE CITY (62895) Wayne(95), Hamilton(4)
WAYNESVILLE De Witt
WEDRON La Salle
WELDON (61882) De Witt(91), Macon(7)
WELLINGTON Iroquois
WENONA (61377) Marshall(88), La Salle(11)
WEST BROOKLYN Lee
WEST CHICAGO (60185) Du Page(98), Kane(1)
WEST CHICAGO Du Page
WEST FRANKFORT (62896) Franklin(94), Williamson(5)
WEST LIBERTY Jasper
WEST POINT Hancock
WEST SALEM (62476) Edwards(77), Wabash(19), Lawrence(1), Richland(1)
WEST UNION Clark
WEST YORK (62478) Clark(55), Crawford(44)
WESTCHESTER Cook

WESTERN SPRINGS Cook
WESTERVELT Shelby
WESTFIELD (62474) Clark(90), Coles(9)
WESTMONT Du Page
WESTVILLE Vermilion
WHEATON Du Page
WHEELER (62479) Jasper(97),
    Effingham(2)
WHEELING (60090) Cook(98), Lake(1)
WHITE HALL Greene
WHITE HEATH (61884) Piatt(77),
    Champaign(22)
WHITTINGTON Franklin
WILLIAMSFIELD (61489) Knox(89),
    Peoria(10)

WILLIAMSVILLE (62693) Sangamon(88),
    Logan(11)
WILLISVILLE Perry
WILLOW HILL Jasper
WILLOW SPRINGS Cook
WILLOWBROOK (60527) Du Page(91),
    Cook(8)
WILMETTE Cook
WILMINGTON (60481) Will(98), Grundy(1)
WILSONVILLE Macoupin
WINCHESTER (62694) Scott(86),
    Morgan(13)
WINDSOR (61957) Shelby(93), Moultrie(6)
WINFIELD Du Page
WINNEBAGO Winnebago

WINNETKA Cook
WINSLOW Stephenson
WINTHROP HARBOR Lake
WITT Montgomery
WOLF LAKE Union
WONDER LAKE McHenry
WOOD DALE Du Page
WOOD RIVER Madison
WOODHULL (61490) McDonough(47),
    Henry(47), Knox(4)
WOODLAND Iroquois
WOODLAWN Jefferson
WOODRIDGE Du Page
WOODSON Morgan
WOODSTOCK McHenry

WOOSUNG Ogle
WORDEN Madison
WORTH Cook
WRIGHTS Greene
WYANET Bureau
WYOMING (61491) Stark(96), Marshall(3)
XENIA (62899) Clay(96), Marion(3)
YALE (62481) Jasper(97), Cumberland(2)
YATES CITY Knox
YORKVILLE Kendall
ZEIGLER Franklin
ZION Lake

Illinois ZIP/City Cross Reference

60000-60000	PALATINE
60001-60001	ALDEN
60002-60002	ANTIOCH
60004-60006	ARLINGTON HEIGHTS
60007-60007	ELK GROVE VILLAGE
60008-60008	ROLLING MEADOWS
60009-60009	ELK GROVE VILLAGE
60010-60011	BARRINGTON
60012-60012	CRYSTAL LAKE
60013-60013	CARY
60014-60014	CRYSTAL LAKE
60015-60015	DEERFIELD
60016-60019	DES PLAINES
60020-60020	FOX LAKE
60021-60021	FOX RIVER GROVE
60022-60022	GLENCOE
60025-60025	GLENVIEW
60026-60026	GLENVIEW NAS
60029-60029	GOLF
60030-60030	GRAYSLAKE
60031-60031	GURNEE
60033-60033	HARVARD
60034-60034	HEBRON
60035-60035	HIGHLAND PARK
60037-60037	FORT SHERIDAN
60038-60038	PALATINE
60039-60039	CRYSTAL LAKE
60040-60040	HIGHWOOD
60041-60041	INGLESIDE
60042-60042	ISLAND LAKE
60043-60043	KENILWORTH
60044-60044	LAKE BLUFF
60045-60045	LAKE FOREST
60046-60046	LAKE VILLA
60047-60047	LAKE ZURICH
60048-60048	LIBERTYVILLE
60049-60049	LONG GROVE
60050-60050	MC HENRY
60050-60050	MCHENRY
60051-60051	MC HENRY
60051-60051	MCHENRY
60053-60053	MORTON GROVE
60055-60055	PALATINE
60056-60056	MOUNT PROSPECT
60060-60060	MUNDELEIN
60061-60061	VERNON HILLS
60062-60062	NORTHBROOK
60063-60063	DEERFIELD
60064-60064	NORTH CHICAGO
60065-60065	NORTHBROOK
60067-60067	PALATINE
60068-60068	PARK RIDGE
60069-60069	LINCOLNSHIRE
60070-60070	PROSPECT HEIGHTS
60071-60071	RICHMOND
60072-60072	RINGWOOD
60073-60073	ROUND LAKE
60074-60074	PALATINE
60075-60075	RUSSELL
60076-60077	SKOKIE
60078-60078	PALATINE
60079-60079	WAUKEGAN
60080-60080	SOLON MILLS
60081-60081	SPRING GROVE
60082-60082	TECHNY
60083-60083	WADSWORTH
60084-60084	WAUCONDA
60085-60085	WAUKEGAN
60086-60086	NORTH CHICAGO
60087-60087	WAUKEGAN
60088-60088	GREAT LAKES
60089-60089	BUFFALO GROVE
60090-60090	WHEELING
60091-60091	WILMETTE
60092-60092	LIBERTYVILLE
60093-60093	WINNETKA
60094-60095	PALATINE
60096-60096	WINTHROP HARBOR
60097-60097	WONDER LAKE
60098-60098	WOODSTOCK
60099-60099	ZION
60100-60100	CAROL STREAM
60101-60101	ADDISON
60102-60102	ALGONQUIN
60103-60103	BARTLETT
60104-60104	BELLWOOD
60105-60106	BENSENVILLE
60107-60107	STREAMWOOD
60108-60108	BLOOMINGDALE
60109-60109	BURLINGTON
60110-60110	CARPENTERSVILLE
60111-60111	CLARE
60112-60112	CORTLAND
60113-60113	CRESTON
60114-60114	ADDISON
60115-60115	DE KALB
60115-60115	DEKALB
60116-60116	CAROL STREAM
60117-60117	BLOOMINGDALE
60118-60118	DUNDEE
60119-60119	ELBURN
60120-60122	ELGIN
60122-60122	CAROL STREAM
60123-60123	ELGIN
60125-60125	CAROL STREAM
60126-60126	ELMHURST
60128-60128	CAROL STREAM
60129-60129	ESMOND
60130-60130	FOREST PARK
60131-60131	FRANKLIN PARK
60132-60132	CAROL STREAM
60133-60133	HANOVER PARK
60134-60134	GENEVA
60135-60135	GENOA
60136-60136	GILBERTS
60137-60138	GLEN ELLYN
60139-60139	GLENDALE HEIGHTS
60140-60140	HAMPSHIRE
60141-60141	HINES
60142-60142	HUNTLEY
60143-60143	ITASCA
60144-60144	KANEVILLE
60145-60145	KINGSTON
60146-60146	KIRKLAND
60147-60147	LAFOX
60148-60148	LOMBARD
60149-60149	MONTGOMERY WARD
60150-60150	MALTA
60151-60151	MAPLE PARK
60152-60152	MARENGO
60153-60153	MAYWOOD
60154-60154	WESTCHESTER
60155-60155	CAROL STREAM
60155-60155	BROADVIEW
60156-60156	LAKE IN THE HILLS
60157-60157	MEDINAH
60158-60158	CAROL STREAM
60159-60159	SCHAUMBURG
60160-60161	MELROSE PARK
60162-60162	HILLSIDE
60163-60163	BERKELEY
60164-60164	MELROSE PARK
60165-60165	STONE PARK
60168-60168	SCHAUMBURG
60170-60170	PLATO CENTER
60171-60171	RIVER GROVE
60172-60172	ROSELLE
60173-60173	SCHAUMBURG
60174-60175	SAINT CHARLES
60176-60176	SCHILLER PARK
60177-60177	SOUTH ELGIN
60178-60178	SYCAMORE
60179-60179	HOFFMAN ESTATES
60180-60180	UNION
60181-60181	VILLA PARK
60182-60182	VIRGIL
60183-60183	WASCO
60184-60184	WAYNE
60185-60186	WEST CHICAGO
60187-60187	WHEATON
60188-60188	CAROL STREAM
60189-60189	WHEATON
60190-60190	WINFIELD
60191-60191	WOOD DALE
60192-60196	SCHAUMBURG
60197-60199	CAROL STREAM
60201-60209	EVANSTON
60251-60251	PALATINE
60296-60297	MCHENRY
60301-60304	OAK PARK
60305-60305	RIVER FOREST
60351-60351	CAROL STREAM
60352-60352	MOBIL OIL CREDIT CORP
60353-60353	CAROL STREAM
60398-60398	FRANKLIN PARK
60399-60399	BENSENVILLE
60401-60401	BEECHER
60402-60402	BERWYN
60406-60406	BLUE ISLAND
60407-60407	BRACEVILLE
60408-60408	BRAIDWOOD
60409-60409	CALUMET CITY
60410-60410	CHANNAHON
60411-60412	CHICAGO HEIGHTS
60415-60415	CHICAGO RIDGE
60416-60416	COAL CITY
60417-60417	CRETE
60419-60419	DOLTON
60420-60420	DWIGHT
60421-60421	ELWOOD
60422-60422	FLOSSMOOR
60423-60423	FRANKFORT
60424-60424	GARDNER
60425-60425	GLENWOOD
60426-60426	HARVEY
60428-60428	MARKHAM
60429-60429	HAZEL CREST
60430-60430	HOMEWOOD
60431-60436	JOLIET
60437-60437	KINSMAN
60438-60438	LANSING
60439-60439	LEMONT
60440-60440	BOLINGBROOK
60441-60441	LOCKPORT
60442-60442	MANHATTAN
60443-60443	MATTESON
60444-60444	MAZON
60445-60445	MIDLOTHIAN
60446-60446	ROMEOVILLE
60447-60447	MINOOKA
60448-60448	MOKENA
60449-60449	MONEE
60450-60450	MORRIS
60451-60451	NEW LENOX
60452-60452	OAK FOREST
60453-60454	OAK LAWN
60455-60455	BRIDGEVIEW
60456-60456	HOMETOWN
60457-60457	HICKORY HILLS
60458-60458	JUSTICE
60459-60459	BURBANK
60460-60460	ODELL
60461-60461	OLYMPIA FIELDS
60462-60462	ORLAND PARK
60463-60463	PALOS HEIGHTS
60464-60464	PALOS PARK
60465-60465	PALOS HILLS
60466-60466	PARK FOREST
60467-60467	ORLAND PARK
60468-60468	PEOTONE
60469-60469	POSEN
60470-60470	RANSOM
60471-60471	RICHTON PARK
60472-60472	ROBBINS
60473-60473	SOUTH HOLLAND
60474-60474	SOUTH WILMINGTON
60475-60475	STEGER
60476-60476	THORNTON
60477-60477	TINLEY PARK
60478-60478	COUNTRY CLUB HILLS
60479-60479	VERONA
60480-60480	WILLOW SPRINGS
60481-60481	WILMINGTON
60482-60482	WORTH
60490-60490	BOLINGBROOK
60491-60491	LOCKPORT
60499-60499	BEDFORD PARK
60501-60501	SUMMIT ARGO

60502-60507 AURORA	60921-60921 CHATSWORTH	61051-61051 MILLEDGEVILLE	61283-61283 TAMPICO
60510-60510 BATAVIA	60922-60922 CHEBANSE	61052-61052 MONROE CENTER	61284-61284 TAYLOR RIDGE
60511-60511 BIG ROCK	60924-60924 CISSNA PARK	61053-61053 MOUNT CARROLL	61285-61285 THOMSON
60512-60512 BRISTOL	60926-60926 CLAYTONVILLE	61054-61054 MOUNT MORRIS	61299-61299 ROCK ISLAND
60513-60513 BROOKFIELD	60927-60927 CLIFTON	61057-61057 NACHUSA	61301-61301 LA SALLE
60514-60514 CLARENDON HILLS	60928-60928 CRESCENT CITY	61058-61058 NELSON	61310-61310 AMBOY
60515-60516 DOWNERS GROVE	60929-60929 CULLOM	61059-61059 NORA	61311-61311 ANCONA
60517-60517 WOODRIDGE	60930-60930 DANFORTH	61060-61060 ORANGEVILLE	61312-61312 ARLINGTON
60518-60518 EARLVILLE	60931-60931 DONOVAN	61061-61061 OREGON	61313-61313 BLACKSTONE
60519-60519 EOLA	60932-60932 EAST LYNN	61062-61062 PEARL CITY	61314-61314 BUDA
60520-60520 HINCKLEY	60933-60933 ELLIOTT	61063-61063 PECATONICA	61315-61315 BUREAU
60521-60523 HINSDALE	60934-60934 EMINGTON	61064-61064 POLO	61316-61316 CEDAR POINT
60525-60525 LA GRANGE	60935-60935 ESSEX	61065-61065 POPLAR GROVE	61317-61317 CHERRY
60526-60526 LA GRANGE PARK	60936-60936 GIBSON CITY	61067-61067 RIDOTT	61318-61318 COMPTON
60527-60527 HINSDALE	60938-60938 GILMAN	61068-61068 ROCHELLE	61319-61319 CORNELL
60527-60527 WILLOWBROOK	60939-60939 GOODWINE	61070-61070 ROCK CITY	61320-61320 DALZELL
60530-60530 LEE	60940-60940 GRANT PARK	61071-61071 ROCK FALLS	61321-61321 DANA
60531-60531 LELAND	60941-60941 HERSCHER	61072-61072 ROCKTON	61322-61322 DEPUE
60532-60532 LISLE	60942-60942 HOOPESTON	61073-61073 ROSCOE	61323-61323 DOVER
60534-60534 LYONS	60944-60944 HOPKINS PARK	61074-61074 SAVANNA	61324-61324 ELDENA
60536-60536 MILLBROOK	60945-60945 IROQUOIS	61075-61075 SCALES MOUND	61325-61325 GRAND RIDGE
60537-60537 MILLINGTON	60946-60946 KEMPTON	61076-61076 SCIOTO MILLS	61326-61326 GRANVILLE
60538-60538 MONTGOMERY	60948-60948 LODA	61076-61076 SCIOTO MILLSX	61327-61327 HENNEPIN
60539-60539 MOOSEHEART	60949-60949 LUDLOW	61077-61077 SEWARD	61328-61328 KASBEER
60540-60540 NAPERVILLE	60950-60950 MANTENO	61078-61078 SHANNON	61329-61329 LADD
60541-60541 NEWARK	60951-60951 MARTINTON	61079-61079 SHIRLAND	61330-61330 LA MOILLE
60542-60542 NORTH AURORA	60952-60952 MELVIN	61080-61080 SOUTH BELOIT	61331-61331 LEE CENTER
60543-60543 OSWEGO	60953-60953 MILFORD	61081-61081 STERLING	61332-61332 LEONORE
60544-60544 PLAINFIELD	60954-60954 MOMENCE	61084-61084 STILLMAN VALLEY	61333-61333 LONG POINT
60545-60545 PLANO	60955-60955 ONARGA	61085-61085 STOCKTON	61334-61334 LOSTANT
60546-60546 RIVERSIDE	60956-60956 PAPINEAU	61087-61087 WARREN	61335-61335 MC NABB
60548-60548 SANDWICH	60957-60957 PAXTON	61088-61088 WINNEBAGO	61336-61336 MAGNOLIA
60549-60549 SERENA	60959-60959 PIPER CITY	61089-61089 WINSLOW	61337-61337 MALDEN
60550-60550 SHABBONA	60960-60960 RANKIN	61091-61091 WOOSUNG	61338-61338 MANLIUS
60551-60551 SHERIDAN	60961-60961 REDDICK	61100-61110 ROCKFORD	61340-61340 MARK
60552-60552 SOMONAUK	60962-60962 ROBERTS	61111-61111 LOVES PARK	61341-61341 MARSEILLES
60553-60553 STEWARD	60963-60963 ROSSVILLE	61112-61114 ROCKFORD	61342-61342 MENDOTA
60554-60554 SUGAR GROVE	60964-60964 SAINT ANNE	61115-61115 MACHESNEY PARK	61344-61344 MINERAL
60555-60555 WARRENVILLE	60966-60966 SHELDON	61125-61126 ROCKFORD	61345-61345 NEPONSET
60556-60556 WATERMAN	60967-60967 STOCKLAND	61130-61132 LOVES PARK	61346-61346 NEW BEDFORD
60557-60557 WEDRON	60968-60968 THAWVILLE	61201-61206 ROCK ISLAND	61348-61348 OGLESBY
60558-60558 WESTERN SPRINGS	60969-60969 UNION HILL	61230-61230 ALBANY	61349-61349 OHIO
60559-60559 WESTMONT	60970-60970 WATSEKA	61231-61231 ALEDO	61350-61350 OTTAWA
60560-60560 YORKVILLE	60973-60973 WELLINGTON	61232-61232 ANDALUSIA	61353-61353 PAW PAW
60561-60561 DARIEN	60974-60974 WOODLAND	61233-61233 ANDOVER	61354-61354 PERU
60563-60567 NAPERVILLE	61001-61001 APPLE RIVER	61234-61234 ANNAWAN	61356-61356 PRINCETON
60568-60568 AURORA	61006-61006 ASHTON	61235-61235 ATKINSON	61358-61358 RUTLAND
60570-60570 HINSDALE	61007-61007 BAILEYVILLE	61236-61236 BARSTOW	61359-61359 SEATONVILLE
60572-60572 AURORA	61008-61008 BELVIDERE	61237-61237 BUFFALO PRAIRIE	61360-61360 SENECA
50585-60586 AURORA	61010-61010 BYRON	61238-61238 CAMBRIDGE	61361-61361 SHEFFIELD
60597-60597 FOX VALLEY	61011-61011 CALEDONIA	61239-61239 CARBON CLIFF	61362-61362 SPRING VALLEY
60598-60598 AURORA	61012-61012 CAPRON	61240-61240 COAL VALLEY	61363-61363 STANDARD
60599-60599 FOX VALLEY	61013-61013 CEDARVILLE	61241-61241 COLONA	61364-61364 STREATOR
60600-60626 CHICAGO	61014-61014 CHADWICK	61242-61242 CORDOVA	61367-61367 SUBLETTE
60627-60627 RIVERDALE	61015-61015 CHANA	61243-61243 DEER GROVE	61368-61368 TISKILWA
60628-60634 CHICAGO	61016-61016 CHERRY VALLEY	61244-61244 EAST MOLINE	61369-61369 TOLUCA
60635-60635 ELMWOOD PARK	61017-61017 COLETA	61249-61249 DEERE CO GROUP CLAIMS	61370-61370 TONICA
60636-60649 CHICAGO	61018-61018 DAKOTA	61250-61250 ERIE	61371-61371 TRIUMPH
60650-60650 CICERO	61019-61019 DAVIS	61251-61251 FENTON	61372-61372 TROY GROVE
60651-60665 CHICAGO	61020-61020 DAVIS JUNCTION	61252-61252 FULTON	61373-61373 UTICA
60666-60666 AMF OHARE	61021-61021 DIXON	61254-61254 GENESEO	61374-61374 VAN ORIN
60667-60701 CHICAGO	61024-61024 DURAND	61256-61256 HAMPTON	61375-61375 VARNA
60706-60706 HARWOOD HEIGHTS	61025-61025 EAST DUBUQUE	61257-61257 HILLSDALE	61376-61376 WALNUT
60707-60707 ELMWOOD PARK	61027-61027 ELEROY	61258-61258 HOOPPOLE	61377-61377 WENONA
60712-60712 LINCOLNWOOD	61028-61028 ELIZABETH	61259-61259 ILLINOIS CITY	61378-61378 WEST BROOKLYN
60714-60714 NILES	61030-61030 FORRESTON	61260-61260 JOY	61379-61379 WYANET
60799-60799 CHICAGO	61031-61031 FRANKLIN GROVE	61261-61261 LYNDON	61401-61402 GALESBURG
60803-60803 ALSIP	61032-61032 FREEPORT	61262-61262 LYNN CENTER	61410-61410 ABINGDON
60804-60804 CICERO	61036-61036 GALENA	61263-61263 MATHERVILLE	61411-61411 ADAIR
60805-60805 EVERGREEN PARK	61037-61037 GALT	61264-61264 MILAN	61412-61412 ALEXIS
60827-60827 RIVERDALE	61038-61038 GARDEN PRAIRIE	61265-61266 MOLINE	61413-61413 ALPHA
60901-60902 KANKAKEE	61039-61039 GERMAN VALLEY	61270-61270 MORRISON	61414-61414 ALTONA
60910-60910 AROMA PARK	61041-61041 HANOVER	61272-61272 NEW BOSTON	61415-61415 AVON
60911-60911 ASHKUM	61042-61042 HARMON	61273-61273 ORION	61416-61416 BARDOLPH
60912-60912 BEAVERVILLE	61043-61043 HOLCOMB	61274-61274 OSCO	61417-61417 BERWICK
60913-60913 BONFIELD	61044-61044 KENT	61275-61275 PORT BYRON	61418-61418 BIGGSVILLE
60914-60914 BOURBONNAIS	61045-61045 KINGS	61276-61276 PREEMPTION	61419-61419 BISHOP HILL
60915-60915 BRADLEY	61046-61046 LANARK	61277-61277 PROPHETSTOWN	61420-61420 BLANDINSVILLE
60917-60917 BUCKINGHAM	61047-61047 LEAF RIVER	61278-61278 RAPIDS CITY	61421-61421 BRADFORD
60918-60918 BUCKLEY	61048-61048 LENA	61279-61279 REYNOLDS	61422-61422 BUSHNELL
60919-60919 CABERY	61049-61049 LINDENWOOD	61281-61281 SHERRARD	61423-61423 CAMERON
60920-60920 CAMPUS	61050-61050 MC CONNELL	61282-61282 SILVIS	61424-61424 CAMP GROVE

61425-61425	CARMAN
61426-61426	CASTLETON
61427-61427	CUBA
61428-61428	DAHINDA
61430-61430	EAST GALESBURG
61431-61431	ELLISVILLE
61432-61432	FAIRVIEW
61433-61433	FIATT
61434-61434	GALVA
61435-61435	GERLAW
61436-61436	GILSON
61437-61437	GLADSTONE
61438-61438	GOOD HOPE
61439-61439	HENDERSON
61440-61440	INDUSTRY
61441-61441	IPAVA
61442-61442	KEITHSBURG
61443-61443	KEWANEE
61447-61447	KIRKWOOD
61448-61448	KNOXVILLE
61449-61449	LA FAYETTE
61450-61450	LA HARPE
61451-61451	LAURA
61452-61452	LITTLETON
61453-61453	LITTLE YORK
61454-61454	LOMAX
61455-61455	MACOMB
61458-61458	MAQUON
61459-61459	MARIETTA
61460-61460	MEDIA
61462-61462	MONMOUTH
61465-61465	NEW WINDSOR
61466-61466	NORTH HENDERSON
61467-61467	ONEIDA
61468-61468	OPHEIM
61468-61468	OPHIEM
61469-61469	OQUAWKA
61470-61470	PRAIRIE CITY
61471-61471	RARITAN
61472-61472	RIO
61473-61473	ROSEVILLE
61474-61474	SAINT AUGUSTINE
61475-61475	SCIOTA
61476-61476	SEATON
61477-61477	SMITHFIELD
61478-61478	SMITHSHIRE
61479-61479	SPEER
61480-61480	STRONGHURST
61482-61482	TABLE GROVE
61483-61483	TOULON
61484-61484	VERMONT
61485-61485	VICTORIA
61486-61486	VIOLA
61488-61488	WATAGA
61489-61489	WILLIAMSFIELD
61490-61490	WOODHULL
61491-61491	WYOMING
61501-61501	ASTORIA
61516-61516	BENSON
61517-61518	BRIMFIELD
61519-61519	BRYANT
61520-61520	CANTON
61523-61523	CHILLICOTHE
61524-61524	DUNFERMLINE
61525-61525	DUNLAP
61526-61526	EDELSTEIN
61528-61528	EDWARDS
61529-61529	ELMWOOD
61530-61530	EUREKA
61531-61531	FARMINGTON
61532-61532	FOREST CITY
61533-61533	GLASFORD
61534-61534	GREEN VALLEY
61535-61535	GROVELAND
61536-61536	HANNA CITY
61537-61537	HENRY
61539-61539	KINGSTON MINES
61540-61540	LACON
61541-61541	LA ROSE
61542-61542	LEWISTOWN
61543-61543	LIVERPOOL
61544-61544	LONDON MILLS
61545-61545	LOWPOINT
61546-61546	MANITO
61547-61547	MAPLETON
61548-61548	METAMORA
61550-61550	MORTON
61552-61552	MOSSVILLE
61553-61553	NORRIS
61554-61558	PEKIN
61559-61559	PRINCEVILLE
61560-61560	PUTNAM
61561-61561	ROANOKE
61562-61562	ROME
61563-61563	SAINT DAVID
61564-61564	SOUTH PEKIN
61565-61565	SPARLAND
61567-61567	TOPEKA
61568-61568	TREMONT
61569-61569	TRIVOLI
61570-61570	WASHBURN
61571-61571	WASHINGTON
61572-61572	YATES CITY
61600-61607	PEORIA
61610-61610	CREVE COEUR
61611-61611	EAST PEORIA
61612-61615	PEORIA
61616-61616	PEORIA HEIGHTS
61625-61644	PEORIA
61649-61649	JEFFERSON BANK
61650-61656	PEORIA
61701-61710	BLOOMINGTON
61720-61720	ANCHOR
61721-61721	ARMINGTON
61722-61722	ARROWSMITH
61723-61723	ATLANTA
61724-61724	BELLFLOWER
61725-61725	CARLOCK
61726-61726	CHENOA
61727-61727	CLINTON
61728-61728	COLFAX
61729-61729	CONGERVILLE
61730-61730	COOKSVILLE
61731-61731	CROPSEY
61732-61732	DANVERS
61733-61733	DEER CREEK
61734-61734	DELAVAN
61735-61735	DEWITT
61736-61736	DOWNS
61737-61737	ELLSWORTH
61738-61738	EL PASO
61739-61739	FAIRBURY
61740-61740	FLANAGAN
61741-61741	FORREST
61742-61742	GOODFIELD
61743-61743	GRAYMONT
61744-61744	GRIDLEY
61745-61745	HEYWORTH
61747-61747	HOPEDALE
61748-61748	HUDSON
61749-61749	KENNEY
61750-61750	LANE
61751-61751	LAWNDALE
61752-61752	LE ROY
61753-61753	LEXINGTON
61754-61754	MC LEAN
61755-61755	MACKINAW
61756-61756	MAROA
61758-61758	MERNA
61759-61759	MINIER
61760-61760	MINONK
61761-61761	NORMAL
61764-61764	PONTIAC
61769-61769	SAUNEMIN
61770-61770	SAYBROOK
61771-61771	SECOR
61772-61772	SHIRLEY
61773-61773	SIBLEY
61774-61774	STANFORD
61775-61775	STRAWN
61776-61776	TOWANDA
61777-61777	WAPELLA
61778-61778	WAYNESVILLE
61790-61790	NORMAL
61791-61799	BLOOMINGTON
61801-61803	URBANA
61810-61810	ALLERTON
61811-61811	ALVIN
61812-61812	ARMSTRONG
61813-61813	BEMENT
61814-61814	BISMARCK
61815-61815	BONDVILLE
61816-61816	BROADLANDS
61817-61817	CATLIN
61818-61818	CERRO GORDO
61820-61826	CHAMPAIGN
61830-61830	CISCO
61831-61831	COLLISON
61832-61832	DANVILLE
61833-61833	TILTON
61834-61834	DANVILLE
61839-61839	DE LAND
61840-61840	DEWEY
61841-61841	FAIRMOUNT
61842-61842	FARMER CITY
61843-61843	FISHER
61844-61844	FITHIAN
61845-61845	FOOSLAND
61846-61846	GEORGETOWN
61847-61847	GIFFORD
61848-61848	HENNING
61849-61849	HOMER
61850-61850	INDIANOLA
61851-61851	IVESDALE
61852-61852	LONGVIEW
61853-61853	MAHOMET
61854-61854	MANSFIELD
61855-61855	MILMINE
61856-61856	MONTICELLO
61857-61857	MUNCIE
61858-61858	OAKWOOD
61859-61859	OGDEN
61862-61862	PENFIELD
61863-61863	PESOTUM
61864-61864	PHILO
61865-61865	POTOMAC
61866-61868	RANTOUL
61870-61870	RIDGE FARM
61871-61871	ROYAL
61872-61872	SADORUS
61873-61873	SAINT JOSEPH
61874-61874	SAVOY
61875-61875	SEYMOUR
61876-61876	SIDELL
61877-61877	SIDNEY
61878-61878	THOMASBORO
61880-61880	TOLONO
61882-61882	WELDON
61883-61883	WESTVILLE
61884-61884	WHITE HEATH
61910-61910	ARCOLA
61911-61911	ARTHUR
61912-61912	ASHMORE
61913-61913	ATWOOD
61914-61914	BETHANY
61917-61917	BROCTON
61919-61919	CAMARGO
61920-61920	CHARLESTON
61924-61924	CHRISMAN
61925-61925	DALTON CITY
61928-61928	GAYS
61929-61929	HAMMOND
61930-61930	HINDSBORO
61931-61931	HUMBOLDT
61932-61932	HUME
61933-61933	KANSAS
61936-61936	LA PLACE
61937-61937	LOVINGTON
61938-61938	MATTOON
61940-61940	METCALF
61941-61941	MURDOCK
61942-61942	NEWMAN
61943-61943	OAKLAND
61944-61944	PARIS
61949-61949	REDMON
61951-61951	SULLIVAN
61953-61953	TUSCOLA
61955-61955	VERMILION
61956-61956	VILLA GROVE
61957-61957	WINDSOR
62001-62001	ALHAMBRA
62002-62002	ALTON
62006-62006	BATCHTOWN
62009-62009	BENLD
62010-62010	BETHALTO
62011-62011	BINGHAM
62012-62012	BRIGHTON
62013-62013	BRUSSELS
62014-62014	BUNKER HILL
62015-62015	BUTLER
62016-62016	CARROLLTON
62017-62017	COFFEEN
62018-62018	COTTAGE HILLS
62019-62019	DONNELLSON
62021-62021	DORSEY
62022-62022	DOW
62023-62023	EAGARVILLE
62024-62024	EAST ALTON
62025-62026	EDWARDSVILLE
62027-62027	ELDRED
62028-62028	ELSAH
62030-62030	FIDELITY
62031-62031	FIELDON
62032-62032	FILLMORE
62033-62033	GILLESPIE
62034-62034	GLEN CARBON
62035-62035	GODFREY
62036-62036	GOLDEN EAGLE
62037-62037	GRAFTON
62040-62040	GRANITE CITY
62044-62044	GREENFIELD
62045-62045	HAMBURG
62046-62046	HAMEL
62047-62047	HARDIN
62048-62048	HARTFORD
62049-62049	HILLSBORO
62050-62050	HILLVIEW
62051-62051	IRVING
62052-62052	JERSEYVILLE
62053-62053	KAMPSVILLE
62054-62054	KANE
62056-62056	LITCHFIELD
62058-62058	LIVINGSTON
62059-62059	LOVEJOY
62060-62060	MADISON
62061-62061	MARINE
62062-62062	MARYVILLE
62063-62063	MEDORA
62065-62065	MICHAEL
62067-62067	MORO
62069-62069	MOUNT OLIVE
62070-62070	MOZIER
62071-62071	NATIONAL STOCK YARDS
62074-62074	NEW DOUGLAS
62075-62075	NOKOMIS
62076-62076	OHLMAN
62077-62077	PANAMA
62078-62078	PATTERSON
62079-62079	PIASA
62080-62080	RAMSEY
62081-62081	ROCKBRIDGE
62082-62082	ROODHOUSE
62083-62083	ROSAMOND
62084-62084	ROXANA
62085-62085	SAWYERVILLE
62086-62086	SORENTO
62087-62087	SOUTH ROXANA
62088-62088	STAUNTON
62089-62089	TAYLOR SPRINGS
62090-62090	VENICE
62091-62091	WALSHVILLE
62092-62092	WHITE HALL
62093-62093	WILSONVILLE
62094-62094	WITT
62095-62095	WOOD RIVER
62097-62097	WORDEN
62098-62098	WRIGHTS
62201-62207	EAST SAINT LOUIS

62208-62208	FAIRVIEW HEIGHTS	62321-62321	CARTHAGE	62448-62448	NEWTON	62612-62612	ASHLAND

Zip	City	Zip	City	Zip	City	Zip	City
62208-62208	FAIRVIEW HEIGHTS	62321-62321	CARTHAGE	62448-62448	NEWTON	62612-62612	ASHLAND
62214-62214	ADDIEVILLE	62323-62323	CHAMBERSBURG	62449-62449	OBLONG	62613-62613	ATHENS
62215-62215	ALBERS	62324-62324	CLAYTON	62450-62450	OLNEY	62615-62615	AUBURN
62216-62216	AVISTON	62325-62325	COATSBURG	62451-62451	PALESTINE	62617-62617	BATH
62217-62217	BALDWIN	62326-62326	COLCHESTER	62452-62452	PARKERSBURG	62618-62618	BEARDSTOWN
62218-62218	BARTELSO	62327-62327	COLMAR	62454-62454	ROBINSON	62621-62621	BLUFFS
62219-62219	BECKEMEYER	62328-62328	QUINCY	62458-62458	SAINT ELMO	62622-62622	BLUFF SPRINGS
62220-62223	BELLEVILLE	62329-62329	COLUSA	62459-62459	SAINTE MARIE	62624-62624	BROWNING
62224-62224	MASCOUTAH	62330-62330	DALLAS CITY	62460-62460	SAINT FRANCISVILLE	62625-62625	CANTRALL
62225-62225	SCOTT AIR FORCE BASE	62332-62332	PITTSFIELD	62461-62461	SHUMWAY	62626-62626	CARLINVILLE
62226-62226	BELLEVILLE	62334-62334	ELVASTON	62462-62462	SIGEL	62627-62627	CHANDLERVILLE
62230-62230	BREESE	62336-62336	FERRIS	62463-62463	STEWARDSON	62628-62628	CHAPIN
62231-62231	CARLYLE	62338-62338	FOWLER	62464-62464	STOY	62629-62629	CHATHAM
62232-62232	CASEYVILLE	62339-62339	GOLDEN	62465-62465	STRASBURG	62630-62630	CHESTERFIELD
62233-62233	CHESTER	62340-62340	GRIGGSVILLE	62466-62466	SUMNER	62631-62631	CONCORD
62234-62234	COLLINSVILLE	62341-62341	HAMILTON	62467-62467	TEUTOPOLIS	62633-62633	EASTON
62236-62236	COLUMBIA	62343-62343	HULL	62468-62468	TOLEDO	62634-62634	ELKHART
62237-62237	COULTERVILLE	62344-62344	HUNTSVILLE	62469-62469	TRILLA	62635-62635	EMDEN
62238-62238	CUTLER	62345-62345	KINDERHOOK	62471-62471	VANDALIA	62638-62638	FRANKLIN
62239-62239	DUPO	62346-62346	LA PRAIRIE	62473-62473	WATSON	62639-62639	FREDERICK
62240-62240	EAST CARONDELET	62347-62347	LIBERTY	62474-62474	WESTFIELD	62640-62640	GIRARD
62241-62241	ELLIS GROVE	62348-62348	LIMA	62475-62475	WEST LIBERTY	62642-62642	GREENVIEW
62242-62242	EVANSVILLE	62349-62349	LORAINE	62476-62476	WEST SALEM	62643-62643	HARTSBURG
62243-62243	FREEBURG	62351-62351	MENDON	62477-62477	WEST UNION	62644-62644	HAVANA
62244-62244	FULTS	62352-62352	MILTON	62478-62478	WEST YORK	62649-62649	HETTICK
62245-62245	GERMANTOWN	62353-62353	MOUNT STERLING	62479-62479	WHEELER	62650-62651	JACKSONVILLE
62246-62246	GREENVILLE	62354-62354	NAUVOO	62480-62480	WILLOW HILL	62655-62655	KILBOURNE
62247-62247	HAGARSTOWN	62355-62355	NEBO	62481-62481	YALE	62656-62656	LINCOLN
62248-62248	HECKER	62356-62356	NEW CANTON	62501-62501	ARGENTA	62659-62659	LINCOLN'S NEW SALEM
62249-62249	HIGHLAND	62357-62357	NEW SALEM	62510-62510	ASSUMPTION	62660-62660	LITERBERRY
62250-62250	HOFFMAN	62358-62358	NIOTA	62511-62511	ATWATER	62661-62661	LOAMI
62252-62252	HUEY	62359-62359	PALOMA	62512-62512	BEASON	62662-62662	LOWDER
62253-62253	KEYESPORT	62360-62360	PAYSON	62513-62513	BLUE MOUND	62663-62663	MANCHESTER
62254-62254	LEBANON	62361-62361	PEARL	62514-62514	BOODY	62664-62664	MASON CITY
62255-62255	LENZBURG	62362-62362	PERRY	62515-62515	BUFFALO	62665-62665	MEREDOSIA
62256-62256	MAEYSTOWN	62363-62363	PITTSFIELD	62517-62517	BULPITT	62666-62666	MIDDLETOWN
62257-62257	MARISSA	62365-62365	PLAINVILLE	62518-62518	CHESTNUT	62667-62667	MODESTO
62258-62258	MASCOUTAH	62366-62366	PLEASANT HILL	62519-62519	CORNLAND	62668-62668	MURRAYVILLE
62259-62259	MENARD	62367-62367	PLYMOUTH	62520-62520	DAWSON	62670-62670	NEW BERLIN
62260-62260	MILLSTADT	62370-62370	ROCKPORT	62521-62527	DECATUR	62671-62671	NEW HOLLAND
62261-62261	MODOC	62372-62372	SUMMER HILL	62530-62530	DIVERNON	62672-62672	NILWOOD
62262-62262	MULBERRY GROVE	62373-62373	SUTTER	62531-62531	EDINBURG	62673-62673	OAKFORD
62263-62263	NASHVILLE	62374-62374	TENNESSEE	62532-62532	ELWIN	62674-62674	PALMYRA
62264-62264	NEW ATHENS	62375-62375	TIMEWELL	62533-62533	FARMERSVILLE	62675-62675	PETERSBURG
62265-62265	NEW BADEN	62376-62376	URSA	62534-62534	FINDLAY	62676-62676	PLAINVIEW
62266-62266	NEW MEMPHIS	62378-62378	VERSAILLES	62535-62535	FORSYTH	62677-62677	PLEASANT PLAINS
62268-62268	OAKDALE	62379-62379	WARSAW	62536-62536	GLENARM	62681-62681	RUSHVILLE
62269-62269	O FALLON	62380-62380	WEST POINT	62537-62537	HARRISTOWN	62682-62682	SAN JOSE
62271-62271	OKAWVILLE	62401-62401	EFFINGHAM	62538-62538	HARVEL	62683-62683	SCOTTVILLE
62272-62272	PERCY	62410-62410	ALLENDALE	62539-62539	ILLIOPOLIS	62684-62684	SHERMAN
62273-62273	PIERRON	62411-62411	ALTAMONT	62540-62540	KINCAID	62685-62685	SHIPMAN
62274-62274	PINCKNEYVILLE	62413-62413	ANNAPOLIS	62541-62541	LAKE FORK	62686-62686	STANDARD CITY
62275-62275	POCAHONTAS	62414-62414	BEECHER CITY	62543-62543	LATHAM	62688-62688	TALLULA
62277-62277	PRAIRIE DU ROCHER	62415-62415	BIRDS	62544-62544	MACON	62689-62689	THAYER
62278-62278	RED BUD	62417-62417	BRIDGEPORT	62545-62545	MECHANICSBURG	62690-62690	VIRDEN
62279-62279	RENAULT	62418-62418	BROWNSTOWN	62546-62546	MORRISONVILLE	62691-62691	VIRGINIA
62280-62280	ROCKWOOD	62419-62419	CALHOUN	62547-62547	MOUNT AUBURN	62692-62692	WAVERLY
62281-62281	SAINT JACOB	62420-62420	CASEY	62548-62548	MOUNT PULASKI	62693-62693	WILLIAMSVILLE
62282-62282	SAINT LIBORY	62421-62421	CLAREMONT	62549-62549	MT ZION	62694-62694	WINCHESTER
62283-62283	SHATTUC	62422-62422	COWDEN	62550-62550	MOWEAQUA	62695-62695	WOODSON
62284-62284	SMITHBORO	62423-62423	DENNISON	62551-62551	NIANTIC	62700-62796	SPRINGFIELD
62285-62285	SMITHTON	62424-62424	DIETERICH	62552-62552	OAKLEY	62801-62801	CENTRALIA
62286-62286	SPARTA	62425-62425	DUNDAS	62553-62553	OCONEE	62803-62803	HOYLETON
62288-62288	STEELEVILLE	62426-62426	EDGEWOOD	62554-62554	OREANA	62805-62805	AKIN
62289-62289	SUMMERFIELD	62427-62427	FLAT ROCK	62555-62555	OWANECO	62806-62806	ALBION
62292-62292	TILDEN	62428-62428	GREENUP	62556-62556	PALMER	62807-62807	ALMA
62293-62293	TRENTON	62431-62431	HERRICK	62557-62557	PANA	62808-62808	ASHLEY
62294-62294	TROY	62432-62432	HIDALGO	62558-62558	PAWNEE	62809-62809	BARNHILL
62295-62295	VALMEYER	62433-62433	HUTSONVILLE	62560-62560	RAYMOND	62810-62810	BELLE RIVE
62296-62296	VENEDY	62434-62434	INGRAHAM	62561-62561	RIVERTON	62811-62811	BELLMONT
62297-62297	WALSH	62435-62435	JANESVILLE	62563-62563	ROCHESTER	62812-62812	BENTON
62298-62298	WATERLOO	62436-62436	JEWETT	62565-62565	SHELBYVILLE	62814-62814	BLUFORD
62301-62306	QUINCY	62438-62438	LAKEWOOD	62567-62567	STONINGTON	62815-62815	BONE GAP
62310-62310	ADRIAN	62439-62439	LAWRENCEVILLE	62568-62568	TAYLORVILLE	62816-62816	BONNIE
62311-62311	AUGUSTA	62440-62440	LERNA	62570-62570	TOVEY	62817-62817	BROUGHTON
62312-62312	BARRY	62441-62441	MARSHALL	62571-62571	TOWER HILL	62818-62818	BROWNS
62313-62313	BASCO	62442-62442	MARTINSVILLE	62572-62572	WAGGONER	62819-62819	BUCKNER
62314-62314	BAYLIS	62443-62443	MASON	62573-62573	WARRENSBURG	62820-62820	BURNT PRAIRIE
62316-62316	BOWEN	62444-62444	MODE	62574-62574	WESTERVELT	62821-62821	CARMI
62318-62318	BURNSIDE	62445-62445	MONTROSE	62601-62601	ALEXANDER	62822-62822	CHRISTOPHER
62319-62319	CAMDEN	62446-62446	MOUNT ERIE	62610-62610	ALSEY	62823-62823	CISNE
62320-62320	CAMP POINT	62447-62447	NEOGA	62611-62611	ARENZVILLE	62824-62824	CLAY CITY

62825-62825	COELLO
62827-62827	CROSSVILLE
62828-62828	DAHLGREN
62829-62829	DALE
62830-62830	DIX
62831-62831	DU BOIS
62832-62832	DU QUOIN
62833-62833	ELLERY
62834-62834	EMMA
62862-62862	MILL SHOALS
62863-62863	MOUNT CARMEL
62864-62864	MOUNT VERNON
62865-62865	MULKEYTOWN
62866-62866	NASON
62867-62867	NEW HAVEN
62868-62868	NOBLE
62869-62869	NORRIS CITY
62870-62870	ODIN
62871-62871	OMAHA
62872-62872	OPDYKE
62874-62874	ORIENT
62875-62875	PATOKA
62876-62876	RADOM
62877-62877	RICHVIEW
62878-62878	RINARD
62879-62879	SAILOR SPRINGS
62880-62880	SAINT PETER
62881-62881	SALEM
62882-62882	SANDOVAL
62883-62883	SCHELLER
62884-62884	SESSER
62885-62885	SHOBONIER
62886-62886	SIMS
62887-62887	SPRINGERTON
62888-62888	TAMAROA
62889-62889	TEXICO
62890-62890	THOMPSONVILLE
62891-62891	VALIER
62892-62892	VERNON
62893-62893	WALNUT HILL

62835-62835	ENFIELD
62836-62836	EWING
62837-62837	FAIRFIELD
62838-62838	FARINA
62839-62839	FLORA
62840-62840	FRANKFORT HEIGHTS
62841-62841	FREEMAN SPUR
62842-62842	GEFF
62843-62843	GOLDEN GATE
62894-62894	WALTONVILLE
62895-62895	WAYNE CITY
62896-62896	WEST FRANKFORT
62897-62897	WHITTINGTON
62898-62898	WOODLAWN
62899-62899	XENIA
62901-62903	CARBONDALE
62905-62905	ALTO PASS
62906-62906	ANNA
62907-62907	AVA
62908-62908	BELKNAP
62909-62909	BOLES
62910-62910	BROOKPORT
62912-62912	BUNCOMBE
62913-62913	CACHE
62914-62914	CAIRO
62915-62915	CAMBRIA
62916-62916	CAMPBELL HILL
62917-62917	CARRIER MILLS
62918-62918	CARTERVILLE
62919-62919	CAVE IN ROCK
62920-62920	COBDEN
62921-62921	COLP
62922-62922	CREAL SPRINGS
62923-62923	CYPRESS
62924-62924	DE SOTO
62926-62926	DONGOLA
62927-62927	DOWELL
62928-62928	EDDYVILLE
62929-62929	ELCO
62930-62930	ELDORADO

62844-62844	GRAYVILLE
62845-62845	HERALD
62846-62846	INA
62847-62847	IOLA
62848-62848	IRVINGTON
62849-62849	IUKA
62850-62850	JOHNSONVILLE
62851-62851	KEENES
62852-62852	KEENSBURG
62931-62931	ELIZABETHTOWN
62932-62932	ELKVILLE
62933-62933	ENERGY
62934-62934	EQUALITY
62935-62935	GALATIA
62938-62938	GOLCONDA
62939-62939	GOREVILLE
62940-62940	GORHAM
62941-62941	GRAND CHAIN
62942-62942	GRAND TOWER
62943-62943	GRANTSBURG
62944-62944	HAMLETSBURG
62945-62945	GALATIA
62946-62946	HARRISBURG
62947-62947	HEROD
62948-62948	HERRIN
62949-62949	HURST
62950-62950	JACOB
62951-62951	JOHNSTON CITY
62952-62952	JONESBORO
62953-62953	JOPPA
62954-62954	JUNCTION
62955-62955	KARBERS RIDGE
62956-62956	KARNAK
62957-62957	MC CLURE
62958-62958	MAKANDA
62959-62959	MARION
62960-62960	METROPOLIS
62961-62961	MILLCREEK
62962-62962	MILLER CITY
62963-62963	MOUND CITY

62853-62853	KELL
62854-62854	KINMUNDY
62855-62855	LANCASTER
62856-62856	LOGAN
62857-62857	LOOGOOTEE
62858-62858	LOUISVILLE
62859-62859	MC LEANSBORO
62860-62860	MACEDONIA
62861-62861	MAUNIE
62964-62964	MOUNDS
62965-62965	MUDDY
62966-62966	MURPHYSBORO
62967-62967	NEW BURNSIDE
62969-62969	OLIVE BRANCH
62970-62970	OLMSTED
62971-62971	ORAVILLE
62972-62972	OZARK
62973-62973	PERKS
62974-62974	PITTSBURG
62975-62975	POMONA
62976-62976	PULASKI
62977-62977	RALEIGH
62979-62979	RIDGWAY
62982-62982	ROSICLARE
62983-62983	ROYALTON
62984-62984	SHAWNEETOWN
62985-62985	SIMPSON
62987-62987	STONEFORT
62988-62988	TAMMS
62990-62990	THEBES
62991-62991	TUNNEL HILL
62992-62992	ULLIN
62993-62993	UNITY
62994-62994	VERGENNES
62995-62995	VIENNA
62996-62996	VILLA RIDGE
62997-62997	WILLISVILLE
62998-62998	WOLF LAKE
62999-62999	ZEIGLER

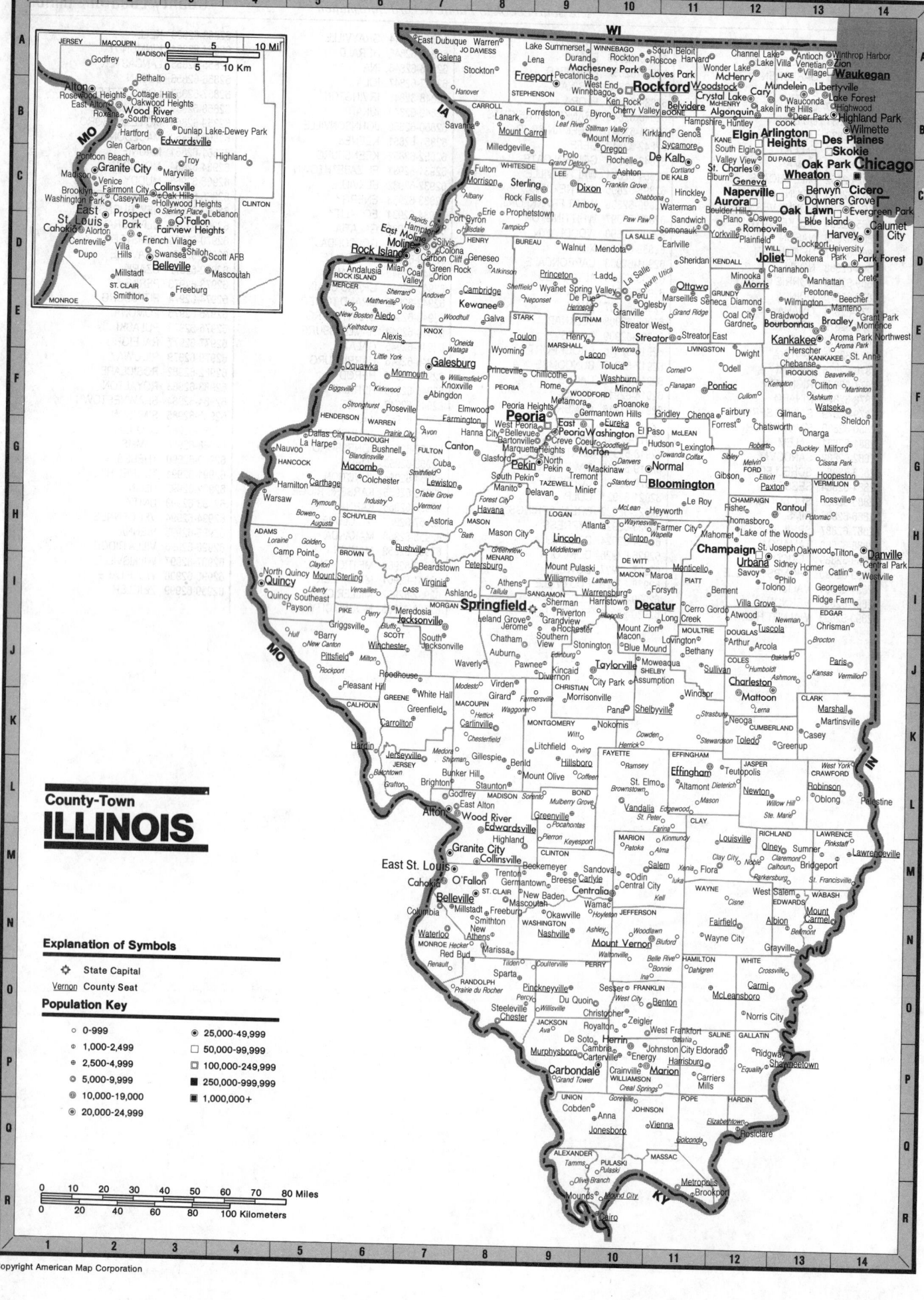

County-Town
ILLINOIS

Explanation of Symbols

⬦ State Capital

Vernon County Seat

Population Key

○ 0-999	⊛ 25,000-49,999
◌ 1,000-2,499	□ 50,000-99,999
⊕ 2,500-4,999	▫ 100,000-249,999
◔ 5,000-9,999	■ 250,000-999,999
◉ 10,000-19,000	■ 1,000,000+
⊜ 20,000-24,999	

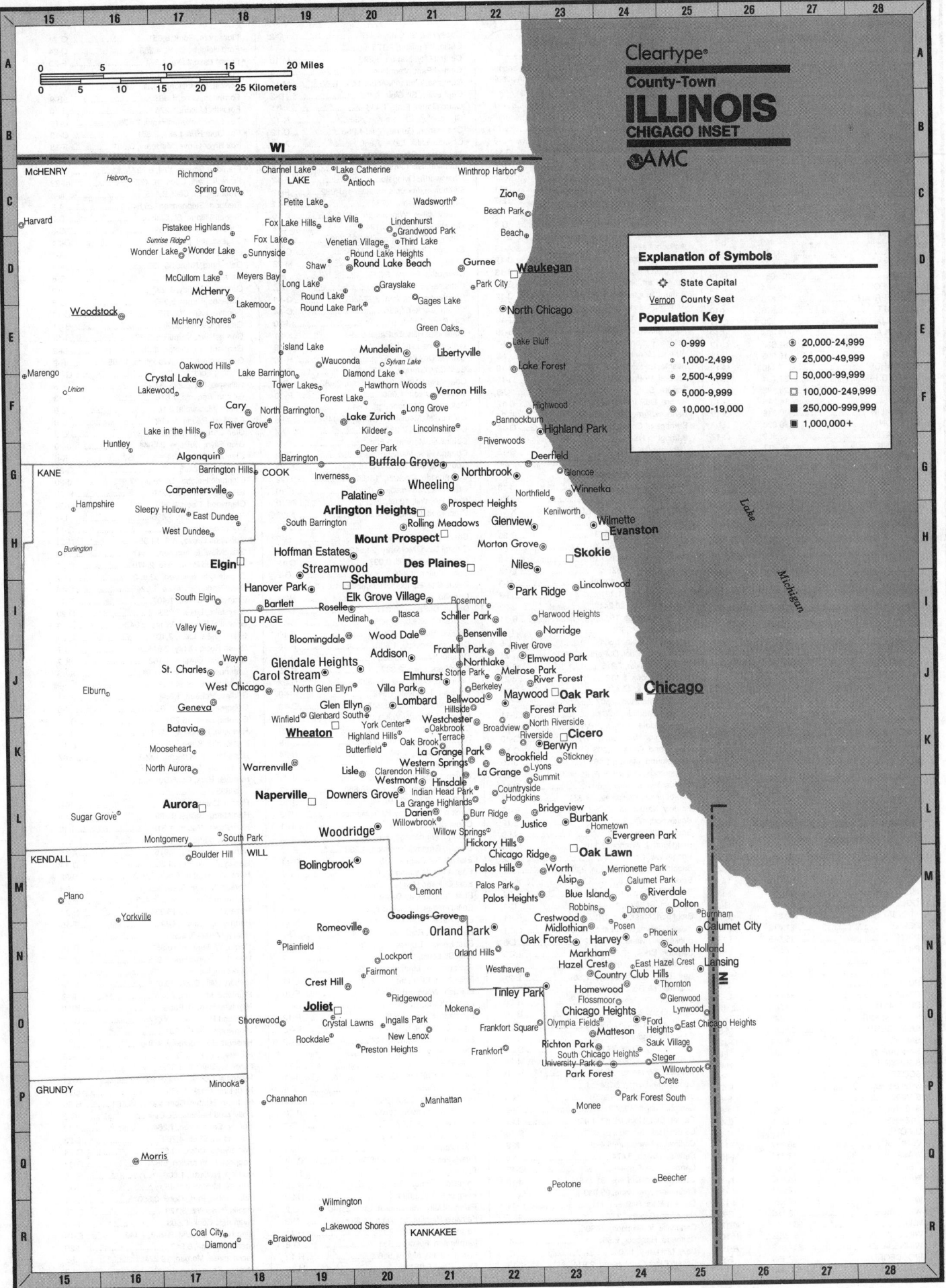

Cleartype®
County-Town
ILLINOIS
CHIGAGO INSET
◈AMC

Explanation of Symbols

◈ State Capital
Vernon County Seat

Population Key

○ 0-999	◉ 20,000-24,999
◔ 1,000-2,499	◉ 25,000-49,999
◑ 2,500-4,999	☐ 50,000-99,999
◕ 5,000-9,999	☐ 100,000-249,999
◉ 10,000-19,000	■ 250,000-999,999
	■ 1,000,000+

0   5   10   15   20 Miles
0   5   10   15   20   25 Kilometers

Explanation of symbols: • – Census Designated Place (CDP)

Jerseyville, Jersey, 7,382 .... K-7
Johnston City, Williamson, 3,706 .... P-11
Joliet, Will, 76,836 .... D-13
Jonesboro, Union, 1,728 .... Q-10
Justice, Cook, 11,137 .... L-22
Kankakee, Kankakee, 27,575 .... E-13
Ken Rock, Winnebago B-10
Kenilworth, Cook, 2,402 .... H-23
Kewanee, Henry, 12,969 .... E-8
Kildeer, Lake, 2,257 .... F-20
Kincaid, Christian, 1,353 .... J-9
Kirkland, DeKalb, 1,011 .... B-11
Knoxville, Knox, 3,243 .... F-7
La Grange, Cook, 15,362 .... K-22
La Grange Highlands, Cook L-21
La Grange Park, Cook, 12,861 .... K-22
La Harpe, Hancock, 1,407 .... G-5
La Salle, La Salle, 9,717 .... D-10
Lacon, Marshall, 1,986 .... E-9
Ladd, Bureau, 1,283 .... D-10
Lake Barrington, Lake, 3,855 .... F-19
Lake Bluff, Lake, 5,513 .... E-22
• Lake Catherine, Lake, 1,515 .... C-19
Lake Forest, Lake, 17,836 .... B-13
• Lake Summerset, Stephenson/Winnebago, 1,296 .... A-9
Lake Villa, Lake, 2,857 .... A-13
Lake Zurich, Lake, 14,947 .... F-19
Lake in the Hills, McHenry, 5,866 .... B-12
• Lake of the Woods, Champaign, 2,748 .... H-12
Lakemoor, Lake/McHenry, 1,322 .... D-18
Lakewood, McHenry, 1,609 .... F-17
• Lakewood Shores, Will, 1,606 .... R-19
Lanark, Carroll, 1,382 .... B-8
Lansing, Cook, 28,086 .... N-25
Lawrenceville, Lawrence, 4,897 .... M-14
Le Roy, McLean, 2,777 .... H-11
Lebanon, St. Clair, 3,688 .... D-3
Leland Grove, Sangamon, 1,679 .... I-9
Lemont, Cook, 7,348 .... M-21
Lena, Stephenson, 2,605 .... A-8
Lewistown, Fulton, 2,572 .... G-7
Lexington, McLean, 1,809 .... G-11
Libertyville, Lake, 19,174 .... A-13
Lichtfield, Montgomery K-9
Lincoln, Logan, 15,418 .... H-9
Lincolnshire, Lake, 4,931 .... F-21
Lincolnwood, Cook, 11,365 .... I-23
Lindenhurst, Lake, 8,038 .... C-20
Lisle, DuPage, 19,512 .... K-20
Litchfield, Montgomery, 6,883 .... K-4
Lockport, Will, 9,401 .... D-13
Lombard, DuPage, 39,408 .... J-20
Long Creek, Macon, 1,250 .... I-10
Long Grove, Lake, 4,740 .... F-20
• Long Lake, Lake, 2,888 .... D-19
Louisville, Clay, 1,098 .... M-12
Loves Park, Winnebago, 15,462 .... A-10
Lovington, Moultrie, 1,143 .... J-11
Lynwood, Cook, 6,535 .... O-25
Lyons, Cook, 9,828 .... K-22
Machesney Park, Winnebago, 19,033 .... A-10
Mackinaw, Tazewell, 1,331 .... G-9
Macomb, McDonough, 19,952 .... G-6
Macon, Macon, 1,282 .... J-10
Madison, Limestone/Madison, 4,629 .... C-1
Mahomet, Champaign, 3,103 .... H-12
Manhattan, Will, 2,059 .... D-13
Manito, Mason, 1,711 .... G-8
Manteno, Kankakee, 3,488 .... E-13
Marengo, McHenry, 4,768 .... F-15
Marion, Williamson, 14,545 .... P-10
Marissa, St. Clair, 2,375 .... N-8
Markham, Cook, 13,136 .... N-24
Maroa, Macon, 1,602 .... I-10
Marquette Heights, Tazewell, 3,077 .... G-9
Marseilles, La Salle, 4,811 .... E-11
Marshall, Clark, 3,555 .... K-14
Martinsville, Clark, 1,161 .... K-13
Maryville, Madison, 2,576 .... C-3
Mascoutah, St. Clair, 5,511 .... N-8
Mason City, Mason, 2,323 .... H-9
Matteson, Cook, 11,378 .... O-23
Mattoon, Coles, 18,441 .... J-12
Maywood, Cook, 27,139 .... J-22
McCullom Lake, McHenry, 1,033 .... D-18
McHenry, McHenry, 16,177 .... A-12
McHenry Shores, McHenry E-18
McLeansboro, Hamilton, 2,677 .... O-12
• Medinah, DuPage, 2,512 .... I-20
Melrose Park, Cook, 20,859 .... J-22
Mendota, La Salle, 7,018 .... D-10
Meredosia, Morgan, 1,134 .... I-6
Merrionette Park, Cook, 2,065 .... M-24
Metamora, Woodford, 2,520 .... F-9
Metropolis, Massac, 6,734 .... R-11
Meyers Bay, Lake D-19
Midlothian, Cook, 14,372 .... N-23
Milan, Rock Island, 5,831 .... D-6
Milford, Iroquois, 1,512 .... G-14
Milledgeville, Carroll, 1,076 .... B-8
Millstadt, St. Clair, 2,566 .... N-7
Minier, Tazewell, 1,155 .... G-10
Minonk, Woodford, 1,982 .... F-10
Minooka, Grundy/Will, 2,561 .... D-12
Mokena, Will, 6,128 .... D-13
Moline, Rock Island, 43,202 .... D-7
Momence, Kankakee, 2,968 .... E-14
Monee, Will, 1,044 .... P-23
Monmouth, Warren, 9,489 .... F-6
Montgomery, Kane/Kendall, 4,267 .... L-17
Monticello, Piatt, 4,549 .... I-11
Mooseheart, Kane K-17
Morris, Grundy, 10,270 .... D-12
Morrison, Whiteside, 4,363 .... C-8
Morrisonville, Christian, 1,113 .... K-9
Morton, Tazewell, 13,799 .... G-9
Morton Grove, Cook, 22,408 .... H-23
Mound City, Pulaski, 765 .... R-10
Mounds, Pulaski, 1,407 .... R-10
Mount Carmel, Wabash, 8,287 .... N-13
Mount Carroll, Carroll, 1,726 .... B-8
Mount Morris, Ogle, 2,919 .... B-9
Mount Olive, Macoupin, 2,126 .... L-8
Mount Prospect, Cook, 53,170 .... H-21
Mount Pulaski, Logan, 1,610 .... I-10
Mount Sterling, Brown, 1,922 .... I-6
Mount Vernon, Jefferson, 16,988 .... N-11
Mount Zion, Macon, 4,522 .... I-11
Moweaqua, Christian/Shelby, 1,785 .... J-10
Mundelein, Lake, 21,215 .... E-20
Murphysboro, Jackson, 9,176 .... P-9
Naperville, DuPage/Will, 85,351 .... C-12
Nashville, Washington, 3,202 .... N-9
Nauvoo, Hancock, 1,108 .... G-4
Neoga, Cumberland, 1,678 .... K-12
New Athens, St. Clair, 2,010 .... N-8
New Baden, Clinton/St. Clair, 2,602 .... M-9
New Lenox, Will, 9,627 .... O-21
Newton, Jasper, 3,154 .... L-12
Niles, Cook, 28,284 .... H-22
Nokomis, Montgomery, 2,534 .... K-10
Normal, McLean, 40,023 .... G-10
Norridge, Cook, 14,459 .... I-23
Norris City, White, 1,341 .... O-12
North Aurora, Kane, 5,940 .... K-17
North Barrington, Lake, 1,787 .... F-19
North Chicago, Lake, 34,978 .... E-22
North Glen Ellyn, DuPage J-20
North Lake, Cook J-21
North Pekin, Tazewell, 1,556 .... G-9
North Quincy, Adams I-4
North Riverside, Cook, 6,005 .... K-22
Northbrook, Cook, 32,308 .... G-22
Northfield, Cook, 4,635 .... G-23
Northlake, Cook, 12,505 .... J-21
Oak Brook, Cook/DuPage, 9,178 .... K-21
Oak Forest, Cook, 26,203 .... N-23
Oak Hills, St. Clair C-3
Oak Lawn, Cook, 56,182 .... C-13
Oak Park, Cook, 53,648 .... C-13
Oakbrook Terrace, DuPage, 1,907 .... K-21
Oakwood, Vermilion, 1,533 .... H-13
Oakwood Heights, Madison B-2
Oakwood Hills, McHenry, 1,498 .... E-18
Oblong, Crawford, 1,616 .... L-13
Odell, Livingston, 1,030 .... F-12
Odin, Marion, 1,150 .... M-10
O'Fallon, St. Clair, 16,073 .... D-3
Oglesby, La Salle, 3,619 .... E-10
Okawville, Washington, 1,274 .... N-9
Olney, Richland, 8,664 .... M-13
Olympia Fields, Cook, 4,248 .... O-23
Onarga, Iroquois, 1,281 .... F-13
Oquawka, Henderson, 1,442 .... F-6
Oregon, Ogle, 3,891 .... B-10
Orion, Henry, 1,821 .... D-7
Orland Hills, Cook, 5,510 .... N-22
Orland Park, Cook, 35,720 .... N-22
Oswego, Kendall, 3,876 .... C-12
Ottawa, La Salle, 17,451 .... D-11
Palatine, Cook, 39,253 .... G-20
Palestine, Crawford, 1,619 .... L-14
Palos Heights, Cook, 11,478 .... M-22
Palos Hills, Cook, 17,803 .... M-22
Palos Park, Cook, 4,199 .... M-22
Pana, Christian, 5,796 .... K-10
Paris, Edgar, 8,987 .... J-14
Park City, Lake, 4,677 .... D-22
Park Forest, Cook/Will, 24,656 .... D-14
Park Forest South, Cook/Will P-24
Park Ridge, Cook, 36,175 .... I-22
Pawnee, Sangamon, 2,384 .... J-9
Paxton, Ford, 4,289 .... G-13
Payson, Adams, 1,114 .... I-5
Pecatonica, Winnebago, 1,760 .... A-9
Pekin, Peoria/Tazewell, 32,254 .... G-9
Peoria, Peoria, 113,504 .... F-9
Peoria Heights, Peoria/Tazewell/Woodford, 6,930 .... F-9
Peotone, Will, 2,947 .... E-13
Peru, La Salle, 9,302 .... E-10
Petersburg, Menard, 2,261 .... I-8
Petite Lake, Lake C-19
Philo, Champaign, 1,028 .... I-12
Phoenix, Cook, 2,217 .... N-24
Pinckneyville, Perry, 3,372 .... O-9
• Pistakee Highlands, McHenry, 3,848 .... C-18
Pittsfield, Pike, 4,231 .... J-6
Plainfield, Will, 4,557 .... D-12
Plano, Kendall, 5,104 .... C-12
Pleasant Hill, Pike, 1,030 .... J-6
Polo, Ogle, 2,514 .... B-9
Pontiac, Livingston, 11,428 .... F-11
Pontoon Beach, Madison, 4,013 .... C-2
Port Byron, Rock Island, 1,002 .... D-7
Posen, Cook, 4,226 .... N-24
• Preston Heights, Will, 2,750 .... O-19
Princeton, Bureau, 7,197 .... D-9
Princeville, Peoria, 1,421 .... F-8
Prophetstown, Whiteside, 1,749 .... C-8
Prospect Heights, Cook, 15,239 .... G-21
Quincy, Adams, 39,681 .... I-4
Quincy Southeast, Adams I-4
Rantoul, Champaign, 17,212 .... H-12
Red Bud, Randolph, 2,918 .... N-8
Richmond, McHenry, 1,016 .... C-18
Richton Park, Cook, 10,523 .... O-23
Ridgewood, Will O-20
Ridgway, Gallatin, 1,103 .... P-12
River Forest, Cook, 11,669 .... J-22
River Grove, Cook, 9,961 .... J-22
Riverdale, Cook, 13,671 .... M-24
Riverside, Cook, 8,774 .... K-22
Riverton, Sangamon, 2,638 .... I-9
Riverwoods, Lake, 2,868 .... G-22
Roanoke, Woodford, 1,910 .... F-10
Robbins, Cook, 7,498 .... M-23
Robinson, Crawford, 6,740 .... L-14
Rochelle, Ogle, 8,769 .... C-10
Rochester, Sangamon, 2,676 .... J-9
Rock Falls, Whiteside, 9,654 .... C-9
Rock Island, Rock Island, 40,552 .... D-6
Rockdale, Will, 1,709 .... O-19
Rockford, Winnebago, 139,426 .... B-10
Rockton, Winnebago, 2,928 .... A-10
Rolling Meadows, Cook, 22,591 .... H-20
• Rome, Peoria, 1,902 .... F-9
Romeoville, Will, 14,074 .... D-13
Roodhouse, Greene, 2,139 .... J-7
Roscoe, Winnebago, 2,079 .... A-10
Roselle, Cook/DuPage, 20,819 .... I-20
Rosemont, Cook, 3,995 .... I-22
Roseville, Warren, 1,151 .... F-6
• Rosewood Heights, Madison, 4,821 .... B-2
Rosiclare, Hardin, 1,378 .... Q-12
Rossville, Vermilion, 1,334 .... H-14
Round Lake, Lake, 3,550 .... D-20
Round Lake Beach, Lake, 16,434 .... D-20
Round Lake Heights, Lake, 1,251 .... D-20
Round Lake Park, Lake, 4,045 .... E-20
Roxana, Madison, 1,562 .... B-2
Royalton, Franklin, 1,191 .... O-10
Rushville, Schuyler, 3,229 .... H-6
Saint Anne, Kankakee, 1,153 .... E-14
Saint Charles, DuPage/Kane, 22,501 .... C-12
Saint Elmo, Fayette, 1,473 .... L-11
Saint Joseph, Champaign, 2,052 .... H-13
Salem, Marion, 7,470 .... M-10
Sandoval, Marion, 1,535 .... M-10
Sandwich, DeKalb/Kendall, 5,567 .... D-11
Sauk Village, Cook/Will, 9,926 .... O-25
Savanna, Carroll, 3,819 .... B-8
Savoy, Champaign, 2,674 .... I-12
Schaumburg, Cook/DuPage, 68,586 .... I-20
Schiller Park, Cook, 11,189 .... I-22
• Scott AFB, St. Clair, 7,245 .... D-3
Seneca, Grundy/La Salle, 1,878 .... E-11
Sesser, Franklin, 2,087 .... O-10
Shaw, Lake D-19
Shawneetown, Gallatin, 1,575 .... P-12
Shelbyville, Shelby, 4,943 .... K-11
Sheldon, Iroquois, 1,109 .... F-14
Sheridan, La Salle, 1,288 .... D-11
Sherman, Sangamon, 2,080 .... I-9
Shiloh, St. Clair, 2,655 .... D-3
Shorewood, Will, 6,264 .... O-18
Sidney, Champaign, 1,027 .... I-13
Silvis, Rock Island, 6,926 .... D-7
Skokie, Cook, 59,432 .... B-13
Sleepy Hollow, Kane, 3,241 .... H-17
Smithton, St. Clair, 1,587 .... N-8
Somonauk, DeKalb/La Salle, 1,263 .... D-11
South Barrington, Cook, 2,937 .... H-19
South Beloit, Winnebago, 4,072 .... A-10
South Chicago Heights, Cook, 3,597 .... O-24
South Elgin, Kane, 7,474 .... B-12
South Holland, Cook, 22,105 .... N-24
South Jacksonville, Morgan, 3,187 .... J-7
South Park, Kane L-17
South Pekin, Tazewell, 1,184 .... G-9
South Roxana, Madison, 1,961 .... B-2
Southern View, Sangamon, 1,906 .... J-9
Sparta, Randolph, 4,853 .... O-8
Spring Grove, McHenry, 1,066 .... C-18
Spring Valley, Bureau, 5,246 .... E-10
Springfield, Sangamon, 105,227 .... I-9
Staunton, Macoupin, 4,806 .... L-8
Steeleville, Randolph, 2,059 .... O-9
Steger, Cook/Will, 8,584 .... P-24
Sterling, Whiteside, 15,132 .... C-9
Stickney, Cook, 5,678 .... K-23
Stockton, Jo Daviess, 1,871 .... A-8
Stone Park, Cook, 4,383 .... J-22
Stonington, Christian, 1,006 .... J-10
Streamwood, Cook, 30,987 .... H-19
Streator, La Salle/Livingston, 14,121 .... E-11
Streator East, La Salle E-11
Streator West, La Salle E-11
Sugar Grove, Kane, 2,005 .... L-16
Sullivan, Moultrie, 4,354 .... J-11
Summit, Cook, 9,971 .... L-22
Sumner, Lawrence, 1,083 .... M-13
Sunnyside, McHenry, 1,529 .... D-18
Swansea, St. Clair, 8,201 .... D-2
Sycamore, DeKalb, 9,708 .... B-11
Taylorville, Christian, 11,133 .... J-10
Teutopolis, Effingham, 1,417 .... L-12
Third Lake, Lake, 1,248 .... D-20
Thomasboro, Champaign, 1,250 .... H-12
Thornton, Cook, 2,778 .... N-24
Tilton, Vermilion, 2,729 .... H-14
Tinley Park, Cook/Will, 37,121 .... O-23
Toledo, Cumberland, 1,199 .... K-12
Tolono, Champaign, 2,605 .... I-12
Toluca, Marshall, 1,315 .... F-10
Toulon, Stark, 1,328 .... E-8
Tower Lakes, Lake, 1,333 .... F-19
Tremont, Tazewell, 2,088 .... G-9
Trenton, Clinton, 2,481 .... M-9
Troy, Madison, 6,046 .... C-3
Tuscola, Douglas, 4,155 .... I-12
University Park, Cook/Will, 6,204 .... D-23
Urbana, Champaign, 36,344 .... H-12
Valley View, Kane C-12
Vandalia, Fayette, 6,114 .... L-10
• Venetian Village, Lake, 3,133 .... A-13
Venice, Madison, 3,571 .... C-2
Vernon Hills, Lake, 15,319 .... F-21
Vienna, Johnson, 1,446 .... Q-11
Villa Grove, Douglas, 2,734 .... I-12
Villa Hills, St. Clair D-2
Villa Park, DuPage, 22,253 .... J-21
Virden, Macoupin/Sangamon, 3,635 .... J-8
Virginia, Cass, 1,767 .... I-7
Wadsworth, Lake, 1,826 .... C-21
Walnut, Bureau, 1,463 .... D-9
Wamac, Clinton/Marion/Washington, 1,501 .... N-10
Warren, Jo Daviess, 1,550 .... A-8
Warrensburg, Macon, 1,274 .... I-10
Warrenville, DuPage, 11,333 .... K-19
Warsaw, Hancock, 1,882 .... H-4
Washburn, Marshall/Woodford, 1,075 .... F-10
Washington, Tazewell, 10,099 .... G-9
Washington Park, St. Clair, 7,431 .... C-2
Waterloo, Monroe, 5,072 .... N-7
Waterman, DeKalb, 1,074 .... C-11
Watseka, Iroquois, 5,424 .... F-14
Wauconda, Lake, 6,294 .... B-13
Waukegan, Lake, 69,392 .... A-13
Waverly, Morgan, 1,402 .... J-8
Wayne, DuPage/Kane, 1,541 .... H-4
Wayne City, Wayne, 1,099 .... N-11
West Chicago, DuPage, 14,796 .... J-18
West Dundee, Kane, 3,728 .... H-17
West End, Winnebago B-10
West Frankfort, Franklin, 8,526 .... O-11
• West Peoria, Peoria, 5,314 .... G-9
West Salem, Edwards, 1,042 .... M-13
Westchester, Cook, 17,301 .... K-22
Western Springs, Cook, 11,984 .... K-21
Westhaven, Cook N-22
Westmont, DuPage, 21,228 .... L-21
Westville, Vermilion, 3,387 .... I-14
Wheaton, DuPage, 51,464 .... C-13
Wheeling, Cook/Lake, 29,911 .... G-21
White Hall, Greene, 2,814 .... J-7
Williamsville, Sangamon, 1,140 .... I-9
Willow Springs, Cook/DuPage, 4,509 .... L-22
Willowbrook, DuPage, 8,598 .... L-21
• Willowbrook, Will, 1,808 .... P-25
Wilmette, Cook, 26,690 .... B-14
Wilmington, Will, 4,743 .... E-13
Winchester, Scott, 1,769 .... J-7
Windsor, Shelby, 1,143 .... J-11
Winfield, DuPage, 7,096 .... K-19
Winnebago, Winnebago, 1,840 .... B-10
Winnetka, Cook, 12,174 .... G-23
Winthrop Harbor, Lake, 6,240 .... A-13
Wonder Lake, McHenry, 1,024 .... D-17
• Wonder Lake, McHenry, 6,664 .... A-12
Wood Dale, DuPage, 12,425 .... I-21
Wood River, Madison, 11,490 .... L-7
Woodridge, DuPage/Will, 26,256 .... L-20
Woodstock, McHenry, 14,353 .... A-12
Worth, Cook, 11,208 .... M-23
Wyanet, Bureau, 1,017 .... D-9
Wyoming, Stark, 1,462 .... E-8
• York Center, DuPage, 4,818 .... K-20
Yorkville, Kendall, 3,925 .... D-12
Zeigler, Franklin, 1,746 .... O-10
Zion, Lake, 19,775 .... A-13

Explanation of symbols: •– Census Designated Place (CDP)

Indiana

General Help Numbers:

Governor's Office
200 W. Washington St.
Indianapolis, IN 46204-2797
www.in.gov/gov

317-232-4567
Fax 317-232-3443
8AM-5PM

Attorney General's Office
302 W Washington
Indianapolis, IN 46204
www.in.gov/attorneygeneral

317-232-6201
Fax 317-232-7979
8:30AM-5PM

Legislative Records
Legislative Services Agency
200 W Washington, Room 301
Indianapolis, IN 46204-2789
www.in.gov/legislative

317-232-9856
8:15AM-4:45PM

State Archives
Commission on Public Records
6440 E 30th St
Indianapolis, IN 46219
www.in.gov/icpr

317-591-5222
Fax 317-591-5324
8AM-4:30PM

State Specifics:

Capital: Indianapolis
                                Marion County

Time Zone: EST*
* Indiana's eleven northwestern-most counties are CST:
They are: Gibson, Jasper, Laporte, Lake, Newton, Porter, Posey, Spencer, Starke,
Vanderburgh, Warrick.

Number of Counties: 92

Population: 6,237,659

Web Site: www.state.in.us

State Agencies

Criminal Records

Indiana State Police, Central Records, IGCN - 100 N Senate Ave, Rm N302, Indianapolis, IN 46204; 317-232-5424, 317-233-8813-Fax; 8AM-4PM.

www.IN.gov/isp

Records are available from 1935. It takes 10 days before new records are available for inquiry. Records are indexed on inhouse computer. Records are normally destroyed after 99 years. Approximately 25% of all arrests in database have final dispositions recorded, over 50% for those arrests within last 5 years. This agency now is notified when charges are made after fingerprints are submitted.

Searching: The release of records is governed by IC 10-13-3-27. A "Limited Criminal History" is available to designated entities including employers, licensing agencies, schools, and certain other designates. Use State Form 8053. Include the following in your request-full name, date of birth, sex, race. Submitting fingerprints is an option, but if requesting record on oneself. 100% of the records are fingerprint-supported. Record will show all activity, including arrests, dismissals, and convictions. But, if a charge is over a year old with no disposition, then the record will not be released.

Access by: mail, in person, online.

Fee & Payment: The fee for employers is $7.00 per name for a limited criminal history, and if no fingerprints used. The fee for a fingerprint search is $10.00. If subject requests own record, fee is $10.00, and this is for a FULL record. Fee payee: State of Indiana. Prepayment required. Ongoing requesters (20 records per months for 3 months) may open a monthly billing account. Cash, money orders, and certified checks accepted. No bills over $10.00 accepted; credit cards accepted online only.

Mail search: Turnaround time: Two weeks. Use State Form 8053, which can be downloaded from www.in.gov/isp/lch/LCHrequest.pdf.

In person search: Requester must have picture ID, turnaround time is 15-20 minutes, but the full record is mailed out 4 days later.

Online search: The standard online search fee is $16.32 at www.in.gov/isp/lch/. Subcribers to accessIndiana can obtain records for $15.00 per search or for no charge if you are statuatorily exempt, or $7.00 if you have a government exemption.

Statewide Court Records

State Court Administrator, 200 W Washington St, #1080, Indianapolis, IN 46204; 317-232-2542, 317-233-6586-Fax; 8:30AM-4:30PM.

www.in.gov/judiciary

Except for certain online research capabilities, all court record access must be done at the local level.

Access by: online.

Online search: The website gives free access to an index of docket information for Supreme, Appeals, and Tax Court cases. There is no statewide trial court records service available.

Sexual Offender Registry

Sex and Violent Offender Directory Manager, Indiana Criminal Justice Institute, One North Capitol, Suite 1000, Indianapolis, IN 46204-2038; 317-232-1233, 317-232-4979 (Fax) .

https://secure.in.gov/serv/cji_sor

Indiana law requires the Indiana Criminal Justice Institute to maintain a directory of individuals who have been convicted of one or more of the sex and violent offenses requiring registration with local sheriff departments.

Records are available from 04/01/89.

Searching: While this state agency will help requesters to a point, most searchers are directed to the local sheriffs' offices or to the web page.

Access by: mail, phone, in person, online.

Mail search: Turnaround time: 3 - 5 days.

Phone search: Limited phone searching is available.

In person search: No searching in person at this agency, but you may search at any of the local sheriff's offices in the state.

Online search: The website has a searching capabilities by name and city or county. Email questions to svod@cji.state.in.us. Also, an excellent search site is maintained by the Indiana Sheriff's Association at www.indianasheriffs.org/default.asp.

Incarceration Records

Indiana Department of Corrections, IGCS, Supervisor of Records, Room E-334, 302 W. Washington Street, Indianapolis, IN 46204; 317-232-5765, 317-232-5728-Fax; 8AM-4:30PM.

www.in.gov/indcorrection

Records are available on current and former inmates. It takes 10 days before new records are available for inquiry. Records are normally destroyed after 10 years.

Searching: Computerized records go back to 1989. Include the following in your request-first and last name; the DOB and SSN helpful. To search online provide either full name or inmate number. Location, DOC number, physical identifiers, sentencing and conviction information, and release dates are released.

Access by: mail, phone, fax, online.

Fee & Payment: Fee is $.10 per page. Fee payee: Department of Corrections Prepayment required. Personal checks not accepted.

Mail search: Turnaround time: 5 to 10 working days.

Phone search: Limited searching available by phone.

Fax search: Fax requests are accepted.

Online search: At the website, click on Offender Search.

Corporation, Limited Partnerships, Fictitious Name, Assumed Name, Limited Liability Company, Limited Liability Partnerships

Corporation Division, Secretary of State, 302 W Washington St, Room E018, Indianapolis, IN 46204; 317-232-6576, 317-233-3387-Fax; 8AM-5:30PM   www.in.gov/sos

This agency also holds Agricultural Cooperative and Business Trust records.

Records are available for all active entities and most inactives. It takes 1-3 days after receipt before new records are available for inquiry. Records are indexed on microfilm, inhouse computer, and paper.

Searching: There are no restrictions, all information is public record. Include the following in your request-full name of business, specific records that you need copies of. Other records available include: Annual or Bi-annual Reports, Officers (when applicable), Prior (merged) names, Inactive and Reserved names, Assumed Business names, and Registered Agent and address.

Access by: mail, phone, in person, online.

Fee & Payment: There is no search fee. Copies cost $1.00 per page plus $15.00 for document certification. Due & Diligent Searches may be ordered for information that cannot be found initially. Fee payee: Secretary of State. Will invoice. The state has pre-paid accounts for filing only. Personal checks accepted. Credit cards accepted online.

Mail search: Turnaround time: 3 to 5 days. No pre-payments accepted for mail requests. Due & Diligent searches take 10 business days. A SASE is welcomed.

Phone search: Limited verification information is available.

In person search: Requests submitted by noon are ready by noon the next day. Requests after 12 noon are ready within 2 business days.

Online search: You can conduct Business Entity Name Searches, Name Availability Checks and acquire official Certificates of Existence or Authorization at the website. The site also gives access to UCC records. Frequent users of Business Services Online should subscribe to accessIndiana at www.ai.org/ai/business/.

Other access: Monthly lists of all new businesses are available online, as are bulk data and specialized searches. Look for Special Business Entity Search Orders at the website.

Trademarks/Servicemarks

Secretary of State, Trademark Division, 302 W Washington St, IGC-South, Room E018, Indianapolis, IN 46204; 317-232-6540, 317-233-3675-Fax; 8:AM-4:30PM.

www.in.gov/sos/business/trademarks.html

These records are considered public and are available with no restrictions.

Records are available for active trademarks. It takes 2 to 3 days before new records are available for inquiry. Records are normally destroyed after 3 years after expiration of mark.

Searching: Search   requires trademark/servicemark name or file ID number. It generally takes 2 to 3 days to search for logo/designs, but name of mark searches can be done immediately. If you have the file ID number, it will help. Cannot search by owner of trademark.

Access by: mail, phone, fax, in person, online.

Mail search: Turnaround time: 2 to 3 days. A SASE is requested.

Phone search: Limited searching by telephone; will do 2 or 3 names only.

Fax search: Limited searching by fax; will do 2 or 3 names only.

In person search: You may request information in person, however, the search clerk is not available full-time.

Online search: www.in.gov/apps/sos/trademarks. This database contains information regarding the status of all trademarks on file with the state of Indiana. Access is free.

Uniform Commercial Code

UCC Division, Secretary of State, 302 West Washington St, Room E-018, Indianapolis, IN 46204; 317-233-3984, 317-233-3387-Fax; 8AM-5:30PM.

www.in.gov/sos/business/ucc.html

Records are available 1964, indexed on computer. It takes up to 3 days before new records are available for inquiry.

Searching: Use the state request form. All tax liens are filed at the county level. Include the following in your request-debtor name or initial financing statement number.

Access by: mail, in person, online.

Fee & Payment: The search fee of $5.00 per debtor name, which includes all copies. Fee payee: Secretary of State. Personal checks accepted. No credit cards accepted.

Mail search: Turnaround time: 2 days.

In person search: Turnaround time is 2 days

Online search: You may browse lien records at https://secure.in.gov/sos/bus_service/online_ucc/browse/default.asp. There is no charge. An official search may be performed for $4.40. If requester is subscriber to AccessIndiana then fee to obtain record is $3.00. Plans are underway to offer filing services also. Bulk downloads and special orders are available online.

Federal and State Tax Liens

Records not maintained by a state level agency.

All tax liens are found at the county level.

Sales Tax Registrations

IN Dept of Revenue, Sales Tax Registrations, PO Box 7218, Indianapolis, IN 46207; 317-233-4015, 317-232-2103-Fax; 8AM-4:30PM.

www.in.gov/dor

Searching: This agency will only confirm whether a company is registered. No other information will be given about the company. The database is not available for purchase. Include the following in your request-legal name and address or Indiana Tax ID or Federal Tax ID.

Access by: mail, phone.

Mail search: Turnaround time: 4 to 6 weeks. No fee for mail request.

Phone search: No fee for telephone request. This is very limited, only one search permitted.

Birth Certificates

State Department of Health, Vital Records Office, PO Box 7125, Indianapolis, IN 46206-7125 (Courier address: 2 N. Meridian, Indianapolis, IN 46204); 317-233-2700, 317-233-7210-Fax; 8:15AM-4:45PM.

www.in.gov/isdh/index.htm

The information is also available at each local county health department.

Records are available from October 1907 on and are computerized since 1978. It takes 12 weeks before new records are available for inquiry. Records are indexed on microfilm, index cards, books (volumes).

Searching: Must have a signed release from person of record or be immediate family member or show direct need. Include the following in your request-full name, names of parents, mother's maiden name, date of birth, place of birth, relationship to person of record, reason for information request.

Access by: mail, phone, fax, in person, online.

Fee & Payment: Search is $10.00 per name. If exact date of birth is not known there is an additional fee of $10.00 for each 5 years searched. Add $4.00 per name requested for each additional copy of same record. Fee payee: Indiana State Department of Health. Prepayment required. Personal checks accepted. Major credit cards accepted.

Mail search: Turnaround time: 3 to 4 weeks. Must include a copy of a signature ID with your request. No SASE is required.

Phone search: Searching by telephone. Available from VitalChek at 866-601-0891 (approved third party vendor).

Fax search: See expedited service.

In person search: Only available between 10AM-2PM, it takes about 30 minutes to process the request.

Online search: Records may be ordered online via the website, but the requester must still fax a photo copy of an ID before the record request is processed. Also, records may requested from www.vitalchek.com, a state-endorsed vendor.

Expedited service: Expedited service is available for mail, online and fax searches. Turnaround time: 3 to 5 days. The expedited service requires use of a credit card (extra $12.95) and a $15.50 payment for overnight service.

Death Records

State Department of Health, Vital Records Office, PO Box 7125, Indianapolis, IN 46206-7125 (Courier address: 2 N. Meridian, Indianapolis, IN 46204); 317-233-2700, 317-233-7210-Fax; 8:15AM-4:45PM.

www.in.gov/isdh/index.htm

Records are available from 1900 on. It takes 12 weeks before new records are available for inquiry. Records are indexed on microfilm, index cards, books (volumes).

Searching: This index is not for public review. You must have a signed release from immediate family member. Include a copy of your photo ID with your request. Include the following in your request-full name, date of death, place of death, relationship to person of record, reason for information request.

Access by: mail, phone, fax, in person, online.

Fee & Payment: Fee is $8.00 per name. If exact date of death is not known, there is a $8.00 fee for each 5 years searched. Add $4.00 per name requested for each additional copy of same record. Fee payee: Indiana State Department of Health. Prepayment required. Personal checks accepted. Major credit cards accepted.

Mail search: Turnaround time: 1 month. No SASE is required.

Phone search: Searching by telephone. Available from VitalChek at 866-601-0891 (approved third party vendor).

Fax search: See expedited service.

In person search: Available from 10AM-2PM.

Online search: Records may requested from www.vitalchek.com, a state-endorsed vendor.

Expedited service: Expedited service is available for fax searches. Turnaround time: 3 to 5 days. The expedited service requires use of a credit card (extra $12.95) and a $15.50 payment for overnight service.

Marriage Certificates, Divorce Records

Records not maintained by a state level agency.

Marriage and divorce records are found at county of issue. This agency tells us that the index can also be found at the Indiana State Library.

Workers' Compensation Records

Workers Compensation Board, 402 W Washington St, Room W196, Indianapolis, IN 46204-2753; 317-232-3808, 317-233-5493-Fax; 8AM-4:30PM.

www.in.gov/workcomp/index.html

Claims information for disputes that require a hearing are available online, those are the only online records available.

Records are available for past 9 years. It takes 48 hours before new records are available for inquiry. Records are indexed on inhouse computer. Records are normally destroyed after 12 years.

Searching: Must have a notarized authorization release from claimant or a subpoena to obtain records from this agency. Requests are reviewed by the Executive Secretary who decides whether to release the information. Include the following in

your request-claimant name, Social Security Number, date of accident, reason for information request.

Access by: mail.

Fee & Payment: Copies are $.10 per page, there is no search fee. Fee payee: Workers Compensation Board. Personal checks accepted. No credit cards accepted.

Mail search: Turnaround time: variable. A SASE is required.

Driver Records

BMV-Driving Records, 100 N Senate Ave, Indiana Government Center North, Room N405, Indianapolis, IN 46204; 317-232-6000 x2, 8:15AM-4:30PM. www.IN.gov/bmv

Copies of tickets are available at the address listed above for a fee of $8.00 per ticket.

Records are available for 7 years (10 years if requested) for moving violations, DWIs and suspensions. Accidents reported to the state police appear on the record. It takes 1-3 weeks before new records are available for inquiry.

Searching: Personal information is not disclosed to casual requesters. Further, a driver's SSN, driver's license number or Federal ID number is not disclosed to all non-governmental requesters. Include the following in your request-State Form 48430, ID of requester. The license number or name and DOB are required when ordering.

Access by: mail, in person, online.

Fee & Payment: The fee is $4.00 per record (except for online requests), $8.00 for a complete history. Add $4.00 for certification. Turnaround time is 4 to 6 weeks for histories. Fee payee: Bureau of Motor Vehicles. Prepayment required. Personal checks accepted. No credit cards accepted.

Mail search: Turnaround time: 5 to 7 days. No SASE is required.

In person search: Up to ten requests are processed at one time for a walk-in requester at the Customer Service Center located at 531 Virginia Ave, Indianapolis or at any of the Regional Service Centers.

Online search: Access Indiana Information Network (AIIN) is the state owned interactive information and communication system which provides batch and interactive access to driving records. There is an annual $50.00 fee. Online access costs $6.00 per record. For more information, call AIIN at 317-233-2010 or go to www.in.gov.

Vehicle Ownership, Vehicle Identification, Vessel Ownership, Vessel Registration

Bureau of Motor Vehicles, Records, 100 N Senate Ave, Room N404, Indianapolis, IN 46204; 317-233-2513 (Titles), 317-233-6000 (Registration), 8:15AM-4:45PM.

www.in.gov/bmv

Records are available for 3 years on computer and up to ten years on microfilm. All motor boats that were valued over $3,000 when new must be titled and registered. It takes minutes before new records are available for inquiry.

Searching: Casual requesters can obtain records, but no personal information is released on subjects without consent. Vehicle owner's SSN, driver's license number, and Federal ID number cannot be disclosed to all non-governmental requesters. There are five types of records available for search; title inquiry, title history, registration inquiry, registration history, and registration copy. The title history will show liens. The title inquiry will show current listed lienholder, also.

Access by: mail, in person, online.

Fee & Payment: For vehicle, the fee is $4.00 per "inquiry" and $8.00 per "history." For watercraft, the fee is $4.00 for all title and registration searches. Certification is an additional $4.00. Fee payee: Bureau of Motor Vehicles. Prepayment required. Personal checks accepted. No credit cards accepted.

Mail search: Turnaround time: within 2 weeks. No SASE is required.

In person search: The walk-in address for the Customer Service Center is 531 Virginia Ave, Indianapolis. There are several other locations in the state that will process requests Turnaround time depends on availability of personnel. Title histories are not provided on an immediate basis, they must be returned by mail or picked up later.

Online search: The Access Indiana Information network (AIIN) at 317-233-2010 is the state appointed vendor. Visit www.in.gov for more information. Search the Indiana Bureau of Motor Vehicles database for title and lien information by VIN number, title number, or social security number. Salvage titles included. The fee is $5.00 per record plus an annual fee of $50.00.

Other access: Bulk record requests are not available from Indiana.

Accident Reports

State Police Department, Vehicle Crash Records Sections, Room N301, Indiana Government Center, Indianapolis, IN 46204; 317-232-8286, 317-232-0652-Fax; 8AM-4PM.

The only reports released are those of the officers. Indiana operator report forms are not released.

Records are available from 20 years to present. Older records are archived on microfiche. It takes 2 hours to 2 weeks before new records are available for inquiry.

Searching: Include the following in your request-full name, date of accident, location of accident.

Access by: mail, phone, in person.

Fee & Payment: The fee is $3.00 per report. If you are requesting all reports on a per-name basis, there is a $6.81 per hour search fee in addition. Fee payee: Indiana State Police. Prepayment required. Personal checks accepted. No credit cards accepted.

Mail search: Turnaround time: 10 days. No SASE is required.

Phone search: You can phone to see if a report is on file before the fee is sent.

In person search: Normal turnaround time is while you wait. If you are requesting all accidents on a "name," this request should be in writing and will take longer.

Other access: For information about bulk file purchasing, contact the Data Section at 317-232-8289.

Voter Registration

Access to Records is Restricted.

Election Division, 302 Washington, Room E-204, Indianapolis, IN 46204-2767; 317-232-3939, 317-233-6793-Fax; 8AM-4:30PM.

www.IN.gov/sos/elections

This agency will not sell records for commercial or investigative reasons, but will sell data in bulk format for political purposes for $5,000. In general, the Circuit Court has records locally. Campaign finance reports are searchable at the website, which is full of good information about elections in IN.

GED Certificates

Division of Adult Education, GED Testing, State House Rm 229, Indianapolis, IN 46204-2798; 317-232-0522, 317-233-0859-Fax; 8AM-4:30PM.

www.doe.state.in.us/adulted

The suggested Release Form is available online at the website. This agency also releases diplomas and transcripts of scores.

It takes six weeks before new records are available for inquiry.

Searching: To search, all of the following are required: a signed release, name, year of test, date of birth, SSN, city of test, and a phone number where you can be reached.

Access by: mail, fax.

Fee & Payment: There is no fee. Email requests are accepted, but, like all requests, a signed release is required.

Mail search: Turnaround time: 5 to 7 days. Records are available by mail.

Fax search: Records are available by fax.

Hunting and Fishing License Information

Records not maintained by a state level agency.

The records are not released to the public. Attorneys may obtain records only if hunting or fishing laws have been broken. This agency and accessindiana will not do look-ups on the system and will not make lists available.

Indiana State Licensing Agencies

For details about the agency responsible for licensing/certifying/registering an item below or in the Agency Quick Finder section, match an item's number with the number of the agency in the *Licensing Agency Information* section.

Indiana Licenses Searchable Online

Acupuncturist #9	https://extranet.in.gov/WebLookup/Search.aspx
Alcoholic Bev. Dealer/Manufacturer #1	www.in.gov/ai/appfiles/atc-license-lookup/
Alcoholic Bev. Dist./Retail/Employee #1	www.in.gov/ai/appfiles/atc-license-lookup/
Appraiser, Residential/General #18	https://extranet.in.gov/WebLookup/Search.aspx
Appraiser, Trainee/Temp #18	https://extranet.in.gov/WebLookup/Search.aspx
Architect #18	https://extranet.in.gov/WebLookup/Search.aspx
Asbestos Contractor #4	www.in.gov/idem/air/compliance/index.html
Asbestos Disposal Mgr/Worker #4	www.in.gov/idem/air/compliance/index.html
Asbestos Inspector/Spvr./Designer #4	www.in.gov/idem/air/compliance/index.html
Asbestos Training Course Provider #4	www.in.gov/idem/air/compliance/index.html
Athletic Trainer #9	https://extranet.in.gov/WebLookup/Search.aspx
Attorney #15	http://hostpub.courts.state.in.us/HostPublisher/rollatty/roa1_inp.jsp
Auctioneer #18	https://extranet.in.gov/WebLookup/Search.aspx
Audiologist #9	https://extranet.in.gov/WebLookup/Search.aspx
Bailbondsman/Agent #7	www.in.gov/idoi/bailbond/
Barber/Barber Instructor #18	https://extranet.in.gov/WebLookup/Search.aspx
Boxer #18	https://extranet.in.gov/WebLookup/Search.aspx
Boxing Occupation #18	https://extranet.in.gov/WebLookup/Search.aspx
Child Care Center #10	www.in.gov/apps/fssa/carefinder/
Child Care Home/Provider #10	www.in.gov/apps/fssa/carefinder/
Chiropractor #9	https://extranet.in.gov/WebLookup/Search.aspx
Clinical Nurse Specialist #9	https://extranet.in.gov/WebLookup/Search.aspx
Collection Agency #19	www.in.gov/serv/sos_securities
Cosmetologist #18	https://extranet.in.gov/WebLookup/Search.aspx
CPA-Public Accountant #18	https://extranet.in.gov/WebLookup/Search.aspx
Dental Anesthetist #9	https://extranet.in.gov/WebLookup/Search.aspx
Dental Hygienist #9	https://extranet.in.gov/WebLookup/Search.aspx
Dentist #9	https://extranet.in.gov/WebLookup/Search.aspx
Dietitian #9	https://extranet.in.gov/WebLookup/Search.aspx
Electrologist #18	https://extranet.in.gov/WebLookup/Search.aspx
Embalmer #18	https://extranet.in.gov/WebLookup/Search.aspx
Engineer #18	https://extranet.in.gov/WebLookup/Search.aspx
Engineering Intern #18	https://extranet.in.gov/WebLookup/Search.aspx
Environmental Health Specialist #9	https://extranet.in.gov/WebLookup/Search.aspx
Esthetician #18	https://extranet.in.gov/WebLookup/Search.aspx
Funeral/Cemetery Director #18	https://extranet.in.gov/WebLookup/Search.aspx
Hazardous Waste Facility/Handler #5	www.in.gov/idem/land/permits/lists/index.html
Health Services Administrator #9	https://extranet.in.gov/WebLookup/Search.aspx
Hearing Aid Dealer #9	https://extranet.in.gov/WebLookup/Search.aspx
Hypnotist #9	https://extranet.in.gov/WebLookup/Search.aspx
Insurance Agent/Consultant #7	www.in.gov/idoi/agent_licensing/
Investment Advisor #19	www.in.gov/serv/sos_securities
Landscape Architect #18	https://extranet.in.gov/WebLookup/Search.aspx
Loan Broker #19	www.in.gov/serv/sos_securities
Lottery Retailer #16	www.in.gov/hoosierlottery/games/retailerlocator.asp
Manicurist #18	https://extranet.in.gov/WebLookup/Search.aspx
Marriage & Family Therapist #9	https://extranet.in.gov/WebLookup/Search.aspx
Medical Doctor #9	https://extranet.in.gov/WebLookup/Search.aspx
Medical Residency Permit #9	https://extranet.in.gov/WebLookup/Search.aspx
Mental Health Counselor #9	https://extranet.in.gov/WebLookup/Search.aspx
Midwife Nurse #9	https://extranet.in.gov/WebLookup/Search.aspx
Notary Public #17	www.ai.org/serv/sos_notary
Nurse #9	https://extranet.in.gov/WebLookup/Search.aspx
Nurse Midwife #9	https://extranet.in.gov/WebLookup/Search.aspx

Nurse-RN/LPN #9	https://extranet.in.gov/WebLookup/Search.aspx
Nursing Home Administrator #9	https://extranet.in.gov/WebLookup/Search.aspx
Occupational Therapist #9	https://extranet.in.gov/WebLookup/Search.aspx
Occupational Therapy Assistant #9	https://extranet.in.gov/WebLookup/Search.aspx
Optometrist #9	https://extranet.in.gov/WebLookup/Search.aspx
Optometrist Drug Certification #9	https://extranet.in.gov/WebLookup/Search.aspx
Osteopathic Physician #9	https://extranet.in.gov/WebLookup/Search.aspx
Pharmacist/Pharmacist Intern #9	https://extranet.in.gov/WebLookup/Search.aspx
Pharmacy Technician #9	https://extranet.in.gov/WebLookup/Search.aspx
Physical Therapist/Therapist Asst #9	https://extranet.in.gov/WebLookup/Search.aspx
Physician #9	https://extranet.in.gov/WebLookup/Search.aspx
Physician Assistant #9	https://extranet.in.gov/WebLookup/Search.aspx
PI Company Employee #18	https://extranet.in.gov/WebLookup/Search.aspx
Placement Officer #14	http://mustang.doe.state.in.us/TEACH/teach_inq.cfm
Plumber #18	https://extranet.in.gov/WebLookup/Search.aspx
Plumbing Contractor #18	https://extranet.in.gov/WebLookup/Search.aspx
Podiatrist #9	https://extranet.in.gov/WebLookup/Search.aspx
Polygraph Examiner #21	www.indianapolygraphassociation.com/members.html#top
Private Detective #18	https://extranet.in.gov/WebLookup/Search.aspx
Psychologist #9	https://extranet.in.gov/WebLookup/Search.aspx
Public Accountant #18	https://extranet.in.gov/WebLookup/Search.aspx
Real Estate Agent/Broker/Seller #18	https://extranet.in.gov/WebLookup/Search.aspx
Real Estate Appraiser #18	https://extranet.in.gov/WebLookup/Search.aspx
Recovery Agent #7	www.in.gov/idoi/bailbond/
Respiratory Care Practitioner #9	https://extranet.in.gov/WebLookup/Search.aspx
School Administrator/Principal #14	http://mustang.doe.state.in.us/TEACH/teach_inq.cfm
School Counselor #14	http://mustang.doe.state.in.us/TEACH/teach_inq.cfm
School Director #14	http://mustang.doe.state.in.us/TEACH/teach_inq.cfm
School Nurse #14	http://mustang.doe.state.in.us/TEACH/teach_inq.cfm
Securities Broker/Dealer #19	www.in.gov/serv/sos_securities
Securities Sales Agent #19	www.in.gov/serv/sos_securities
Shampoo Operator #18	https://extranet.in.gov/WebLookup/Search.aspx
Social Worker #9	https://extranet.in.gov/WebLookup/Search.aspx
Social Worker, Clinical #9	https://extranet.in.gov/WebLookup/Search.aspx
Solid Waste Facility #5	www.in.gov/idem/land/permits/lists/index.html
Speech Pathologist #9	https://extranet.in.gov/WebLookup/Search.aspx
Surveyor, Land #18	https://extranet.in.gov/WebLookup/Search.aspx
Teacher #14	http://mustang.doe.state.in.us/TEACH/teach_inq.cfm
Veterinarian #9	https://extranet.in.gov/WebLookup/Search.aspx
Veterinary Tech #9	https://extranet.in.gov/WebLookup/Search.aspx
Waste Tire Processor/Transporter #5	www.in.gov/idem/land/permits/lists/index.html
Yard Waste Composting Facility #5	www.in.gov/idem/land/permits/lists/index.html

Indiana Licensing Quick Finder

Acupuncturist #9 ... 317-232-2960
Alcoholic Bev. Dealer/Manufacturer #1 . 317-232-2430
Alcoholic Bev. Dist./Retailer/Employee #1
... 317-232-2430
Animal (Dead) Rendering #2 ... 317-227-0300
Appraiser, Residential/General #18 ... 317-232-2980
Appraiser, Trainee/Temp #18 ... 317-232-2980
Architect #18 ... 317-232-2980
Asbestos Contractor #4 ... 317-232-4861
Asbestos Disposal Manager/Worker #4 317-232-8232
Asbestos Inspector/Supvr./Designer #4 317-232-8232
Asbestos Management Planner #4 ... 317-232-8232
Asbestos Training Course Provider #4 . 317-232-8219
Athletic Trainer #9 ... 317-232-2960
Attorney #15 ... 317-232-5861
Auctioneer #18 ... 317-232-2980
Audiologist #9 ... 317-232-2960
Bailbondsman/Agent #7 ... 317-232-5249
Bank & Trust Company #6 ... 317-232-5846
Barber/Barber Instructor #18 ... 317-232-2980
Boiler & Pressure Vessel Inspector #8 . 317-232-1921

Boxer #18 ... 317-232-2980
Boxing Occupation #18 ... 317-232-2980
Brands, Livestock #2 ... 317-227-0300
Building & Loan #6 ... 317-232-5851
Check Casher #6 ... 317-232-3955
Child Care Center #10 ... 317-232-4469
Child Care Home/Provider #10 ... 317-232-4521
Chiropractor #9 ... 317-232-2960
Clinical Nurse Specialist #9 ... 317-232-2960
Collection Agency #19 ... 317-232-0093
Consumer Credit Grantor #6 ... 317-232-5849
Cosmetologist #18 ... 317-232-2980
CPA-Public Accountant #18 ... 317-232-2980
Credit Union #6 ... 317-232-5851
Dairy-related Occupation #2 ... 317-227-0300
Dental Anesthetist #9 ... 317-232-2960
Dental Hygienist #9 ... 317-232-2960
Dentist #9 ... 317-232-2960
Dietitian #9 ... 317-232-2960
Electrologist #18 ... 317-232-2980
Elevator Safety Contractor #8 ... 317-232-6609

Embalmer #18 ... 317-232-2980
Emergency Medical Technician #11 317-233-6545
Engineer #18 ... 317-232-2980
Engineering Intern #18 ... 317-232-2980
Environmental Health Specialist #9 . 317-232-2960
Esthetician #18 ... 317-232-2980
Funeral/Cemetery Director #18 ... 317-232-2980
Grain Bank/Warehouse #12 ... 317-232-1358
Grain Buyer #12 ... 317-232-1360
Hazardous Waste Facility/Handler #5 ... 317-232-8603
Health Services Administrator #9 ... 317-232-2960
Hearing Aid Dealer #9 ... 317-232-2960
Horse Racing Occupation #13 ... 317-233-3119
Hypnotist #9 ... 317-232-2960
Insurance Adjuster #7 ... 317-232-2414
Insurance Agent/Consultant #7 ... 317-232-2414
Investment Advisor #19 ... 317-232-6681
Landscape Architect #18 ... 317-232-2980
Lead Contractor #4 ... 317-232-4861
Lead Inspector #4 ... 317-233-6514
Lead Project Designer #4 ... 317-233-6514

Lead Project Supervisor/Assessor #4 ... 317-233-6514
Lead Training Course Provider #4 317-232-8219
Lead Worker #4 317-233-6514
Lender #6 317-232-3955
Livestock Dealer/market #2 317-227-0300
Livestock Transportation #2 317-227-0300
Loan Broker #19 317-232-6681
Lottery Retailer #16 317-264-4800
Manicurist #18 317-232-2980
Manufactured Home Builder #8 317-232-1408
Marriage & Family Therapist #9 317-232-2960
Meat & Poultry #2 317-227-0300
Medical Doctor #9 317-232-2960
Medical Residency Permit #9 317-232-2960
Mental Health Counselor #9 317-232-2960
Midwife Nurse #9 317-232-2960
Money Transmitter #6 317-232-3955
Notary Public #17 317-232-6542
Nurse #9 317-232-2960
Nurse Midwife #9 317-232-2960
Nurse-RN/LPN #9 317-232-2960
Nursing Home Administrator #9 317-232-2960
Occupational Therapist #9 317-232-2960

Occupational Therapy Assistant #9 317-232-2960
Optometrist #9 317-232-2960
Optometrist Drug Certification #9 317-232-2960
Osteopathic Physician #9 317-232-2960
Pawnbroker #6 317-232-3955
Pesticide Applicator #3 765-494-1594
Pesticide Technician/Consultant #3 765-494-1594
Pharmacist/Pharmacist Intern #9 317-232-2960
Pharmacy Technician #9 317-232-2960
Physical Therapist/Therapist Asst #9 ... 317-233-2960
Physician #9 317-232-2960
Physician Assistant #9 317-232-2960
PI Company Employee #18 317-232-2980
Placement Officer #14 317-232-9010
Plumber /Plumbing Contractor #18 317-232-2980
Podiatrist #9 317-232-2960
Polygraph Examiner #21 317-232-8263
Private Detective #18 317-232-2980
Psychologist #9 317-232-2960
Public Accountant #18 317-232-2980
Radiologic Technologist #20 317-233-7565
Real Estate Agent/Broker/Seller #18 ... 317-232-2980
Real Estate Appraiser #18 317-232-2980

Recovery Agent #7 317-232-5249
Respiratory Care Practitioner #9 317-232-2960
School Administrator/Principal #14 317-232-9010
School Counselor #14 317-232-9010
School Director #14 317-232-9010
School Nurse #14 317-232-9010
Securities Broker/Dealer #19 317-232-6690
Securities Sales Agent #19 317-232-6690
Shampoo Operator #18 317-232-2980
Social Worker #9 317-232-2960
Social Worker, Clinical #9 317-232-2960
Solid Waste Facility #5 317-232-8603
Speech Pathologist #9 317-232-2960
Surveyor, Land #18 317-232-2980
Teacher #14 317-232-9010
Underground Storage Tank #8 317-233-3560
Veterinarian #9 317-232-2960
Veterinary Tech #9 317-232-2960
Warehouse, Agricultural, etc. #12 317-232-1358
Waste Tire Processor/Transporter #5.. 317-232-8603
Waste Water Treatment Plant Operator #5
.... 317-232-8666
Yard Waste Composting Facility #5 317-232-8603

Indiana Licensing Agency Information

1 Alcohol and Tobacco Commission, 302 W Washington St, Rm E114, Indianapolis, IN 46204; 317-233-3940, Fax: 317-234-1520.
www.in.gov/atc
Email: kchew@atc.state.in.us
Search Database at www.in.gov/ai/appfiles/atc-license-lookup/

2 Licensing & Compliance, Board of Animal Health, 805 Beachway Dr #50, Indianapolis, IN 46224; 317-227-0300, Fax: 317-227-0330.
www.state.in.us/boah/
Email: dderrer@boah.in.gov

3 Department of Biochemistry, Office of Indiana State Chemist, Purdue University,175 S. University Street, West Lafayette, IN 47907-2063; 765-494-1492, Fax: 765-494-4331.
www.isco.purdue.edu
Email: walshm@isco.purdue.edu

4 Department of Environmental Management, Asbestos/Lead Program, 100 N. Senate Ave, Indianapolis, IN 46204-6015; 317-233.3257, Fax: 317-232-8406.
www.IN.gov/idem/
Search Database at www.in.gov/idem/air/compliance/index.html

5 Department of Environmental Management, Office of Land Quality, PO Box 6015, Indianapolis, IN 46204-6015; 317-232-8603, Fax: 317-232-2403.
www.in.gov/idem/land/
Email: webmaster@dem.state.in.us
Search Database at www.in.gov/idem/land/permits/lists/index.html

6 Department of Financial Institutions, 30 S Meridian St #300, Indianapolis, IN 46204-2759; 317-232-3955, Fax: 317-232-7655.
www.dfi.state.in.us

7 Department of Insurance, 311 W Washington St #300, Indianapolis, IN 46204-2787; 317-232-2385, Fax: 317-232-5251.
www.in.gov/idoi
Email: doi@state.in.us

8 Fire & Building Services, 402 W Washington St, IGS-S, Rm E241, Indianapolis, IN 46204; 317-232-2222, Fax: 317-232-0146.
www.in.gov/sema/osfm/

9 Health Professions Bureau, 402 W Washington St Rm W066, Indianapolis, IN 46204-2758; 317-232-2960, Fax: 317-233-4236.
www.ai.org/hpb Email: kburch@hpb.state.in.us
Search Database at
https://extranet.in.gov/WebLookup/Search.aspx
Note: To search online, you have to subscribe to AIIN. For more info on AIIN, visit www.state.in.us/premium/about.html.

10 Family and Social Services Administration, Bureau of Child Development, 402 W. Washington St., Rm W386, Indianapolis, IN 46201; 317-232-1144.
www.in.gov/fssa/carefinder/
Email: cbigsbee2@fssa.state.in.us/
Search Database at
www.in.gov/apps/fssa/carefinder/

11 Emergency Medical Svcs, EMS Certification, 302 W Washington St, IGCS #E208, Indianapolis, IN 46204; 317-233-6545, Fax: 317-233-8394.
www.in.gov/sema/ems Note: The toll free number EMS number is 800-666-7784.

12 Grain Buyers & Warehouse Licensing Agency, 150 W Market St, Rm 416, Indianapolis, IN 46204-2810; 317-232-1356, Fax: 317-232-1362.
www.IN.gov/igbwla/
Email: dhenry@commerce.state.in.us Note: Confidentiality Clause in governing statute prevents giving listing of licensees.

13 Horse Racing Licensing, 150 W Market St, Indianapolis, IN 46204; 317-233-3119, Fax: 317-233-4470.
www.IN.gov/ihrc/
Email: hrc@state.in.us

14 Professional Standards Board, 101 W Ohio St, #300, Indianapolis, IN 46204; 317-232-9010, 1-866-542-3672, Fax: 317-232-9023.
Email: helpdesk@psb.state.in.us

15 Clerk of the Indiana Supreme Court, Roll of Attoneys Clerk, 217 State House, 200 W Washington St, Indianapolis, IN 46204; 317-232-1930, Fax: 317-232-8365.
www.IN.gov/judiciary/
Search Database at http://hostpub.courts.state.in.us/HostPublisher/rollatty/roa1_inp.jsp

16 Lottery Commission of Indiana, 201 S Capitol Av #1100, Indianapolis, IN 46225; 317-264-4800, Fax: 317-264-4908.
www.in.gov/hoosierlottery
Email: playersupport@hoosierlottery.com

17 Business Services Division - Notary, Office of Secretary of State, Statehouse, #201, Indianapolis, IN 46204; 317-232-6542, Fax: 317-233-3283.
www.in.gov/sos/notary/
Email: notary@sos.in.gov
Search Database at www.ai.org/serv/sos_notary

18 Professional Licensing Agency, Boards & Commissions, 402 W Washington St, Rm W072, Indianapolis, IN 46204; 317-232-2980, Fax: 317-232-2312.
www.IN.gov/pla/
Email: jsmall@hpb.in.gov Search Database at https://extranet.in.gov/WebLookup/Search.aspx

19 Secretary of State, Securities Division, 302 W Washington Rm E-111, Indianapolis, IN 46204; 317-232-6681, Fax: 317-233-3675.
www.in.gov/sos/securities/index.html
Search Database at
www.in.gov/serv/sos_securities

20 Division of End. & Radiologic Health, Board of Health, 2 N Meridian St, 5F, Indianapolis, IN 46204-3010; 317-233-7150, Fax: 317-233-7154.

21 State Police, 100 N Senate Ave, Government Center N, #302, Indianapolis, IN 46204-2259; 317-232-8263.
www.indianapolygraphassociation.com
Search Database at
www.indianapolygraphassociation.com/members.html#top.

Indiana Federal Courts

The following list indicates the district and division name for each county in the state. If the bankruptcy court location is different from the district court, then the location of the bankruptcy court appears in parentheses.

County/Court Cross Reference

County	District	Division
Adams	Northern	Fort Wayne
Allen	Northern	Fort Wayne
Bartholomew	Southern	Indianapolis
Benton	Northern	Lafayette (Hammond at Lafayette)
Blackford	Northern	Fort Wayne
Boone	Southern	Indianapolis
Brown	Southern	Indianapolis
Carroll	Northern	Lafayette (Hammond at Lafayette)
Cass	Northern	South Bend
Clark	Southern	New Albany
Clay	Southern	Terre Haute
Clinton	Southern	Indianapolis
Crawford	Southern	New Albany
Daviess	Southern	Evansville
DeKalb	Northern	Fort Wayne
Dearborn	Southern	New Albany
Decatur	Southern	Indianapolis
Delaware	Southern	Indianapolis
Dubois	Southern	Evansville
Elkhart	Northern	South Bend
Fayette	Southern	Indianapolis
Floyd	Southern	New Albany
Fountain	Southern	Indianapolis
Franklin	Southern	Indianapolis
Fulton	Northern	South Bend
Gibson	Southern	Evansville
Grant	Northern	Fort Wayne
Greene	Southern	Terre Haute
Hamilton	Southern	Indianapolis
Hancock	Southern	Indianapolis
Harrison	Southern	New Albany
Hendricks	Southern	Indianapolis
Henry	Southern	Indianapolis
Howard	Southern	Indianapolis
Huntington	Northern	Fort Wayne
Jackson	Southern	New Albany
Jasper	Northern	Lafayette (Hammond at Lafayette)
Jay	Northern	Fort Wayne
Jefferson	Southern	New Albany
Jennings	Southern	New Albany
Johnson	Southern	Indianapolis
Knox	Southern	Terre Haute
Kosciusko	Northern	South Bend
La Porte	Northern	South Bend
LaGrange	Northern	Fort Wayne
Lake	Northern	Hammond (Hammond. at Gary)
Lawrence	Southern	New Albany
Madison	Southern	Indianapolis
Marion	Southern	Indianapolis
Marshall	Northern	South Bend
Martin	Southern	Evansville
Miami	Northern	South Bend
Monroe	Southern	Indianapolis
Montgomery	Southern	Indianapolis
Morgan	Southern	Indianapolis
Newton	Northern	Lafayette (Hammond at Lafayette)
Noble	Northern	Fort Wayne
Ohio	Southern	New Albany
Orange	Southern	New Albany
Owen	Southern	Terre Haute
Parke	Southern	Terre Haute
Perry	Southern	Evansville
Pike	Southern	Evansville
Porter	Northern	Hammond (Hammond. at Gary)
Posey	Southern	Evansville
Pulaski	Northern	South Bend
Putnam	Southern	Terre Haute
Randolph	Southern	Indianapolis
Ripley	Southern	New Albany
Rush	Southern	Indianapolis
Scott	Southern	New Albany
Shelby	Southern	Indianapolis
Spencer	Southern	Evansville
St. Joseph	Northern	South Bend
Starke	Northern	South Bend
Steuben	Northern	Fort Wayne
Sullivan	Southern	Terre Haute
Switzerland	Southern	New Albany
Tippecanoe	Northern	Lafayette (Hammond at Lafayette)
Tipton	Southern	Indianapolis
Union	Southern	Indianapolis
Vanderburgh	Southern	Evansville
Vermillion	Southern	Terre Haute
Vigo	Southern	Terre Haute
Wabash	Northern	South Bend
Warren	Northern	Lafayette (Hammond at Lafayette)
Warrick	Southern	Evansville
Washington	Southern	New Albany
Wayne	Southern	Indianapolis
Wells	Northern	Fort Wayne
White	Northern	Lafayette (Hammond at Lafayette)
Whitley	Northern	Fort Wayne

Standards for Federal Courts: Search fee is $26.00 per item (one party name or case number). Copy fee is $.50 per page. Certification fee is $9.00 per document, double for exemplification, if available. All fees standard unless noted in profile. Mail Search: always enclose a stamped self addressed envelope unless otherwise noted. Most courts accept fax requests or will suggest a copying/search vendor. Before releasing records, all courts require prepayment, unless noted.

Open records are located at the court unless otherwise noted. District courts index by defendant and plaintiff as well as by case number. Bankruptcy courts usually index by debtor and case number. While most courts now have their indexes on computer, many may still maintain index card files as well.

Courts offering internet access via CM-ECF or older RACER, PACER, or Web-PACER systems charge $.08 per page fee unless noted as free. Where PACER is available, the universal sign-up number is 800-676-6856. Find PACER and the US Party/Case Index at http://pacer.psc.uscourts.gov.

US District Court

Northern District of Indiana

Fort Wayne Division Court Clerk, Rm 1108, Federal Bldg, 1300 S Harrison St, Fort Wayne, IN 46802 (also use mail address for courier delivery), 260-423-3000. Hours- 9AM-4PM. www.innd.uscourts.gov

Counties: Adams, Allen, Blackford, DeKalb, Grant, Huntington, Jay, Lagrange, Noble, Steuben, Wells, Whitley.

Searches & Indexing: Results do not include SSN or DOB. Both computer and card indexes maintained; computer index goes back to 1991. New cases in the index 1-2 days after filing date. Records purged as deemed necessary.

Fee & Payment: Pay by money order, cashier's or personal check. No credit cards. Payee: Clerk, US District Court. Prepayment required.

Phone Search: Only case names and numbers is released via phone.

Mail Search: search usually completed- 3 days. Include SASE for return.

In Person Search: Fee charged if court performs your search. Only the court may search the card index. No self-serve copier available.

E-Services: ECF replaces PACER whose records did go back to 1994. New records online after 1 day. ECF at https://ecf.innd.uscourts.gov **Opinions Online:** www.innd.uscourts.gov/opinions.asp.

Hammond Division Court Clerk, Rm 101, 507 State St, Hammond, IN 46320 (also use mail address for courier delivery), 219-852-6500. Hours- 9AM-4PM. www.innd.uscourts.gov

Counties: Lake, Porter.

Searches & Indexing: Results do not include SSN or DOB. Computer index back to 1992 maintained. New cases in the index 1-3 days after filing date. Records purged as deemed necessary.

Fee & Payment: Pay by money order, cashier's or personal check. Payee: Clerk, US District Court. Prepayment required. No credit cards.

Phone Search: Only docket information is available by phone.

Mail Search: search usually completed- 1 week. Include SASE for return.

In Person Search: Fee charged if court performs your search. No self-serve copier available.

E-Services: ECF replaces PACER whose records did go back to 1994. New records online immediately. ECF at https://ecf.innd.uscourts.gov **Opinions Online:** www.innd.uscourts.gov/opinions.asp.

Lafayette Division Court Clerk, PO Box 1498, Lafayette, IN 47902 (courier address: 230 N 4th St, Lafayette, IN 47901), 765-420-6250. Hours- 9AM-4PM. www.innd.uscourts.gov

Counties: Benton, Carroll, Jasper, Newton, Tippecanoe, Warren, White.

Searches & Indexing: Results do not include SSN or DOB. Computer index maintained; microfiche index available. New cases in the index 24 hours after filing date. Records purged as deemed necessary.

Fee & Payment: Pay by money order, cashier's or personal check. Payee: Clerk, US District Court. Prepayment required.

Phone Search: Only docket information is available by phone.

Mail Search: search usually completed- 3 days. Include SASE for return.

In Person Search: Fee charged if court performs your search. No self-serve copier available.

E-Services: ECF replaces PACER whose records did go back to 1994. New records online after 1 day. ECF at https://ecf.innd.uscourts.gov **Opinions Online:** www.innd.uscourts.gov/opinions.asp.

South Bend Division Court Clerk, Rm 102, 204 S Main, South Bend, IN 46601 (also use mail address for courier delivery), 574-246-8000, Fax-574-246-8002. Hours- 9AM-4PM. www.innd.uscourts.gov

Counties: Cass, Elkhart, Fulton, Kosciusko, La Porte, Marshall, Miami, Pulaski, St. Joseph, Starke, Wabash.

Searches & Indexing: Results include last 4 SSN digits, also birth year. Computer index maintained. New cases in the index 2 days after filing date. Records purged as deemed necessary.

Fee & Payment: Pay by money order, cashier's or personal check. Payee: Clerk, US District Court. Prepayment required.

Phone Search: Only docket information is available by phone.

Mail Search: search usually completed- 3 days. Include SASE for return.

In Person Search: Fee charged if court performs your search. No self-serve copier available.

E-Services: ECF replaces PACER whose records did go back to 1994. New records online after 1 day. ECF at https://ecf.innd.uscourts.gov **Opinions Online:** www.innd.uscourts.gov/opinions.asp.

US Bankruptcy Court

Northern District of Indiana

Fort Wayne Division Court Clerk, PO Box 2547, Fort Wayne, IN 46801-2547 (courier address: 1188 Federal Bldg, 1300 S Harrison St, Fort Wayne, IN 46802), 260-420-5100. Hours- 9AM-4PM. www.innb.uscourts.gov

Counties: Adams, Allen, Blackford, DeKalb, Grant, Huntington, Jay, Lagrange, Noble, Steuben, Wells, Whitley.

Searches & Indexing: Cases indexed by debtor, creditors, and case number. Results include last 4 SSN digits. Computer index back to 9/2003 maintained. A card index of debtor names is also maintained. New cases in the index 24 hours after filing date. Records purged every 6 months. Records in closed cases are only kept locally for a brief period; date of filing and date of closing are factors in determining when a case is shipped.

Fee & Payment: Pay by money order, cashier's or personal check. No debtor's checks accepted. Payee: Clerk, US Bankruptcy Court. Prepayment required.

Phone Search: Only docket information is available by phone. Voice Case Information Service available, call VCIS at 800-755-8393 or 574-236-8814.

Mail Search: search usually completed- 5 day maximum. Include SASE for return.

In Person Search: Fee charged if court performs your search. No self-serve copier available.

E-Services: ECF replaces PACER whose records did go back to 1992. New records online after 1 day. ECF at https://ecf.innb.uscourts.gov **Opinions Online:** www.innb.uscourts.gov/opinions/. **Other Online Access:** Judges calendars at www.innb.uscourts.gov/courtcal.htm.

Hammond at Gary Division US Bankruptcy Clerk, 5400 Federal Plaza, Hammond, IN 46320 (also use mail address for courier delivery), 219-852-3480. Hours- 9AM-4PM. www.innb.uscourts.gov

Counties: Lake, Porter.

Searches & Indexing: Cases indexed by debtor, creditors, and case number. Results include last 4 SSN digits. Computer index back to 9/2002 maintained. New cases in the index 24 hours after filing date. Records in closed cases are only kept locally for a brief period based on filing date and closing date, about 6 months.

Fee & Payment: Pay by Visa/MC, money order, cashier's or personal check. No debtor's checks/credit cards accepted. Payee: Clerk, US Bankruptcy Court. Prepayment required.

Phone Search: Only docket information is available by phone. Voice Case Information Service available, call VCIS at 800-755-8393.

Mail Search: search usually completed- 5 day maximum. Include SASE for return.

In Person Search: Fee charged if court performs your search. Self-serve copier available - $.15 per page.

E-Services: ECF replaces PACER whose records did go back to 1992. New records online after 1 day. ECF at https://ecf.innb.uscourts.gov **Opinions Online:** www.innb.uscourts.gov/opinions/. **Other Online Access:** Judges calendars at www.innb.uscourts.gov/courtcal.htm.

Hammond at Lafayette Division c/o Fort Wayne Division, PO Box 2547, Fort Wayne, IN 46801-2547 (courier address: US Court House, 1300 S Harrison St, Fort Wayne, IN 46802), 260-420-5100. Hours- 9AM-4PM. www.innb.uscourts.gov

Counties: Benton, Carroll, Jasper, Newton, Tippecanoe, Warren, White. All files for the Hammond Division at Lafayette are physically kept in the Fort Wayne office. All papers pertaining to Hammond Division at Lafayette cases after the initial filing, including claims, should be sent to the Fort Wayne office.

Searches & Indexing: Cases indexed by debtor, collector, and case number. Results include last 4 SSN digits. Records purged every 6 months. Open records located at Ft. Wayne Division.

Fee & Payment: Pay by money order, cashier's or personal check. No business checks accepted.

Phone Search: Voice Case Information Service available, call VCIS at 800-755-8393 or 574-236-8814.

Mail Search: search usually completed- 5 days. Include SASE for return.

In Person Search: permitted. No self-serve copier available.

E-Services: ECF replaces PACER whose records did go back to 1992. New records online after 1 day. ECF at https://ecf.innb.uscourts.gov **Opinions Online:** www.innb.uscourts.gov/opinions/. **Other Online Access:** Judges calendars at www.innb.uscourts.gov/courtcal.htm.

South Bend Division Court Clerk, PO Box 7003, South Bend, IN 46634-7003 (courier address: 401 S Michigan St, South Bend, IN 46601), 574-968-2100. Hours- 9AM-4PM. www.innb.uscourts.gov

Counties: Cass, Elkhart, Fulton, Kosciusko, La Porte, Marshall, Miami, Pulaski, St. Joseph, Starke, Wabash.

Searches & Indexing: Cases indexed by debtor, creditors, and case number. Results include last 4 SSN digits. Computer index back to 9/2002 maintained. New cases in the index 24 hours after filing date. Records purged every 6 months. Records in closed cases are only kept locally for a brief period. Records shipped to Chicago FRC semi-annually; date of filing and date of closing are factors in determining when a case is shipped.

Fee & Payment: Pay by Visa/MC, money order, cashier's or personal check. No debtor's checks accepted. Payee: Clerk, US Bankruptcy Court. Prepayment required.

Phone Search: Only docket information is available by phone. Voice Case Information Service available, call VCIS at 800-755-8393 or 574-968-2275.

Mail Search: search usually completed- 5 day maximum. Include SASE for return.

In Person Search: Fee charged if court performs your search. Self-serve copier available - $.15 per page.

E-Services: ECF replaces PACER whose records did go back to 1992. New records online after 1 day. ECF at https://ecf.innb.uscourts.gov **Opinions Online:** www.innb.uscourts.gov/opinions/. **Other Online Access:** Judges calendars at www.innb.uscourts.gov/courtcal.htm.

US District Court

Southern District of Indiana

Evansville Division Court Clerk, 304 Federal Bldg, 101 NW Martin Luther King Blvd, Evansville, IN 47708 (also use mail address for courier delivery), 812-434-6410, records rm- 812-434-6410, Fax-812-434-6418. Hours- 8:30AM-5PM. www.insd.uscourts.gov

Counties: Daviess, Dubois, Gibson, Martin, Perry, Pike, Posey, Spencer, Vanderburgh, Warrick.

Searches & Indexing: Cases prior to 1992 indexed by name only on index cards. Results include SSN or DOB for criminal cases; civil includes only last 4 SSN digits. New cases in the index immediately after filing date.

Fee & Payment: Pay by money order, cashier's or personal check. Payee: Clerk, US District Court. Prepayment required. Court search covers a period of 10 years.

Phone Search: No searching by telephone.

Mail Search: search usually completed- 24 hours. SASE not required.

In Person Search: Fee charged if court performs your search. No self-serve copier available.

E-Services: ECF at https://ecf.insd.uscourts.gov **Other Online Access:** Search case records free at www.insd.uscourts.gov/casesearch.htm; Criminal goes back to 1994; civil 1991-2002. Court now participate in the US party case index.

Indianapolis Division Clerk of Court, Rm 105, 46 E Ohio St, Indianapolis, IN 46204 (also use mail address for courier delivery), 317-229-3700, Fax-317-229-3959. Hours- 8:30AM-5PM. www.insd.uscourts.gov

Counties: Bartholomew, Boone, Brown, Clinton, Decatur, Delaware, Fayette, Fountain, Franklin, Hamilton, Hancock, Hendricks, Henry, Howard, Johnson, Madison, Marion, Monroe, Montgomery, Morgan, Randolph, Rush, Shelby, Tipton, Union, Wayne.

Searches & Indexing: Computer index maintained. New cases in the index immediately after filing date. Records purged never. District-wide searches available here back to 1996.

Fee & Payment: Pay by Visa/MC, money order, business checks. No personal checks. Payee: Clerk, US District Court. Prepayment required.

Phone Search: Only information on the docket sheet face is released via phone.

Mail Search: search usually completed- 1-2 days. SASE not required.

In Person Search: Fee charged if court performs your search. No self-serve copier available.

E-Services: No PACER access to this court. ECF at https://ecf.insd.uscourts.gov **Other Online Access:** Search case records free at www.insd.uscourts.gov/casesearch.htm; Criminal goes back to 1994; civil 1991-2002. Court now participate in the US party case index.

New Albany Division Court Clerk, Rm 210, 121 W Spring St, New Albany, IN 47150 (also use mail address for courier delivery), 812-542-4510, Fax-812-542-4515. Hours- 8AM-4:30PM. www.insd.uscourts.gov

Counties: Clark, Crawford, Dearborn, Floyd, Harrison, Jackson, Jefferson, Jennings, Lawrence, Ohio, Orange, Ripley, Scott, Switzerland, Washington.

Searches & Indexing: Results do not include SSN or DOB. Computer index back to 7/2002 maintained. A card index also maintained. New cases in the index immediately after filing date. Files may also be in Indianapolis or Evansville Divisions.

Fee & Payment: Pay by money order, cashier's or personal check. Payee: Clerk, US District Court. Prepayment required. No credit cards.

Phone Search: No searching by telephone.

Mail Search: search usually completed- 1-2 days. Include SASE for return.

In Person Search: Fee charged if court performs your search. No self-serve copier available.

E-Services: No PACER access to this court. ECF at https://ecf.insd.uscourts.gov **Other Online Access:** Search case records free at www.insd.uscourts.gov/casesearch.htm; Criminal goes back to 1994; civil 1991-2002. Court now participate in the US party case index.

Terre Haute Division Court Clerk, 210 Federal Bldg, Terre Haute, IN 47808 (also use mail address for courier delivery), 812-234-9484, Fax-812-238-1831. Hours- 8:30AM-5PM. www.insd.uscourts.gov

Counties: Clay, Greene, Knox, Owen, Parke, Putnam, Sullivan, Vermillion, Vigo.

Searches & Indexing: Results do not include SSN or DOB. Computer index maintained back to 1993. New cases in the index immediately after filing date.

Fee & Payment: Pay by money order, cashier's or personal check. Payee: Clerk, US District Court. Prepayment required.

Phone Search: All information not sealed is available via phone.

Mail Search: search usually completed- 1 week. Include SASE for return.

In Person Search: Fee charged if court performs your search. No self-serve copier available.

E-Services: No PACER access to this court. ECF at https://ecf.insd.uscourts.gov **Other Online Access:** Search case records free at www.insd.uscourts.gov/casesearch.htm; Criminal goes back to 1994; civil 1991-2002. Court now participate in the US party case index.

US Bankruptcy Court

Southern District of Indiana

Evansville Division Court Clerk, 352 Federal Building, 101 NW Martin Luther King Blvd, Evansville, IN 47708 (also use mail address for courier delivery), 812-434-6470, Fax-812-434-6471. 8:30AM-5PM. www.insb.uscourts.gov

Counties: Daviess, Dubois, Gibson, Martin, Perry, Pike, Posey, Spencer, Vanderburgh, Warrick.

Searches & Indexing: Results include SSN. Computer index back to 10/12/04 maintained. New cases in the index 1-2 days after filing date. Records purged every 3 months.

Fee & Payment: Pay by money order, cashier's or personal check. No debtor's checks accepted. Payee: Clerk, US Bankruptcy Court. Prepayment required.

Phone Search: Only docket information is available by phone. Voice Case Information Service available, call VCIS at 800-335-8003.

Mail Search: search usually completed- 10 days. Include SASE for return.

In Person Search: Fee charged if court performs your search. Self-serve copier available - $.50 per page.

E-Services: PACER at www.insb.uscourts.gov. Click on "Case Search." Registration and fees required. Document images available. The free case lookup system is no longer found. PACER records go back to 1988. New records online after 1 day. ECF at https://ecf.insb.uscourts.gov **Opinions Online:** http://pacer.insb.uscourts.gov/public/default.asp. Includes judge calendars as well. **Other Online Access:** Court now participate in the US party case index.

Indianapolis Division Court Clerk, PO Box 44978, Indianapolis, IN 46244 (courier address: US Courthouse, Rm 116, 46 E Ohio St, Indianapolis, IN 46204), 317-229-3800, records rm- 317-229-3842, Fax-317-229-3801. Hours- 8:30AM-5PM. www.insb.uscourts.gov

Counties: Bartholomew, Boone, Brown, Clinton, Decatur, Delaware, Fayette, Fountain, Franklin, Hamilton, Hancock, Hendricks, Henry, Howard, Johnson, Madison, Marion, Monroe, Montgomery, Morgan, Randolph, Rush, Shelby, Tipton, Union, Wayne.

Searches & Indexing: Results include last 4 SSN digits. Computer index back to 10/12/04 maintained. Records stored electronically since 1986. New cases in the index 48 hours after filing date. Records purged every 3 months.

Fee & Payment: Pay by money order, cashier's or personal check. No debtor's checks accepted. Payee: Clerk, US Bankruptcy Court (SDIN).

Phone Search: Only docket information is available by phone. Voice Case Information Service available, call VCIS at 800-335-8003.

Mail Search: search usually completed- 1 day. Include SASE for return.

In Person Search: Fee charged if court performs your search. No self-serve copier available.

E-Services: PACER at www.insb.uscourts.gov. Click on "Case Search." Registration and fees required. Document images available. The free case lookup system is no longer found. PACER records go back to 1988. New records online after 1 day. ECF at https://ecf.insb.uscourts.gov **Opinions Online:** http://pacer.insb.uscourts.gov/public/default.asp. Includes judge calendars as well. **Other Online Access:** Court now participate in the US party case index.

New Albany Division Court Clerk, US Courthouse, Rm 110, 121 W Spring St, New Albany, IN 47150 (also use mail address for courier delivery), 812-452-4540, Fax-812-542-4541. 8:30AM-5PM. www.insb.uscourts.gov

Counties: Clark, Crawford, Dearborn, Floyd, Harrison, Jackson, Jefferson, Jennings, Lawrence, Ohio, Orange, Ripley, Scott, Switzerland, Washington.

Searches & Indexing: Results include last 4 SSN digits. Computer index back to 10/12/04 maintained. New cases in the index 48 hours after filing date. Records purged every 3 months.

Fee & Payment: Pay by money order, cashier's or personal check. No debtor's checks accepted. Payee: Clerk, US Bankruptcy Court (SDIN).

Phone Search: Only docket information is available by phone. Voice Case Information Service available, call VCIS at 800-335-8003.

Mail Search: search usually completed- 1-2 days. Include SASE for return.

In Person Search: Fee charged if court performs your search. No self-serve copier available.

E-Services: PACER at www.insb.uscourts.gov. Click on "Case Search." Registration and fees required. Document images available. The free

case lookup system is no longer found. PACER records go back to 1988. New records online after 1 day. ECF at https://ecf.insb.uscourts.gov **Opinions Online:** http://pacer.insb.uscourts.gov/public/default.asp. Includes judge calendars as well. **Other Online Access:** Court now participate in the US party case index.

Terre Haute Division Court Clerk, Federal Bldg Rm 207, 30 N 7th St, Terre Haute, IN 47808 (also use mail address for courier delivery), 812-238-1550, Fax-812-238-1831. Hours- 8:30AM-5PM. www.insb.uscourts.gov

Counties: Clay, Greene, Knox, Owen, Parke, Putnam, Sullivan, Vermillion, Vigo.

Searches & Indexing: Results include last 4 SSN digits. Computer index back to 10/12/04 maintained. Records stored electronically since 1986. New cases in the index 48 hours after filing date. Records purged every 3 months.

Fee & Payment: Pay by money order, cashier's or personal check. No debtor's checks accepted. Payee: Clerk, US Bankruptcy Court. Prepayment required. Search fee charged if a detailed search is required.

Phone Search: Only docket information is available by phone. Voice Case Information Service available, call VCIS at 800-335-8003.

Mail Search: search usually completed- 1 day. Include SASE for return.

In Person Search: Fee charged if court performs your search. No self-serve copier available.

E-Services: PACER at www.insb.uscourts.gov. Click on "Case Search." Registration and fees required. Document images available. The free case lookup system is no longer found. PACER records go back to 1988. New records online after 1 day. ECF at https://ecf.insb.uscourts.gov **Opinions Online:** http://pacer.insb.uscourts.gov/public/default.asp. Includes judge calendars as well. **Other Online Access:** Court now participate in the US party case index.

Indiana County Courts

Court	Jurisdiction	No. of Courts	How Organized
Circuit Courts*	General	24	88 Circuits
Superior Courts*	General	4	
Combined Courts*		68	
County Courts*	Limited	Comb	
Combined Circuit/County*		4	
City Courts	Limited	48	
Small Claims -Marion County	Special	9	
Town Courts	Municipal	27	
Probate Court	Special	1	St. Joseph County

* Profiled in this Sourcebook.

Court	CIVIL								
	Tort	Contract	Real Estate	Min. Claim	Max. Claim	Small Claims	Estate	Eviction	Domestic Relations
Circuit Courts*	X	X	X	$0	No Max	$3000	X		X
Superior Courts*	X	X	X	$0	No Max	$3000	X		X
County Courts*	X	X	X	$0	$10,000	$3000		X	X
City Courts	X	X		$0	$2500			X	X
Small Claims - Marion County						$3000			
Town Courts									X
Probate Court							X		

Court	CRIMINAL				
	Felony	Misdemeanor	DWI/DUI	Preliminary Hearing	Juvenile
Circuit Courts*	X	X	X	X	X
Superior Courts*	X	X	X	X	X
County Courts*	X	X	X	X	
City Courts		X	X	X	
Small Claims - Marion County					
Town Courts		X	X	X	
Probate Court					X

ADMINISTRATION State Court Administrator, 115 W Washington St, #1080, Indianapolis, IN, 46204; 317-232-2542, Fax: 317-232-8372. www.in.gov/judiciary

COURT STRUCTURE There are 92 judicial circuits with Circuit Courts or Combined Circuit and Superior Courts. In addition, there are 48 City Courts and 27 Town Courts. County courts are gradually being restructured into divisions of the Superior Courts. Note that Small Claims in Marion County are heard at the township and records are maintained at that level.

ONLINE ACCESS There is no statewide trial court records service available. However, the web site above gives free access to an index of docket information for Supreme, Appeals, and Tax Court cases.

ADDITIONAL INFORMATION The Circuit Court Clerk/County Clerk in a county is the same individual and is responsible for keeping all county judicial records. However, we recommend that, when requesting a record, the request indicate which court heard the case (Circuit, Superior, or County). Many courts are no longer performing searches, especially criminal searches, based on a 7/8/96 statement by the State Board of Accounts.

State statute sets the certification fee as $1.00 per document plus copy fee and $1.00 per page for copies.

Adams County

Circuit & Superior Court 112 S 2nd St, Decatur, IN 46733; phone: 260-724-5309; fax: 260-724-5313; 8AM-4:30PM *Felony, Misdemeanor, Civil, Eviction, Small Claims, Probate.*

Civil Records: Access: In person only. Visitors must perform in person searches themselves. Court makes copy: $1.00 per page. Required to search: name, years to search. Civil cases indexed by defendant, plaintiff. Civil records on computer from 1992, archived from 1876. Some records on index cards.

Criminal Records: Access: In person only. Visitors must perform in person searches themselves. Court makes copy: $1.00 per page. Required to search: name, years to search, DOB; SSN helpful. Criminal records on computer from 1992, archived from 1876. Some records on index cards.

General Information: Public terminal goes back to 1979. (Limited data available.) No juvenile, adoption, mental health or sealed records released. Will fax specific case file for $1.00 per page. Certification fee: $1.00 per page. Payee: Adams County Clerk. Only cashiers checks and money orders accepted. Prepayment required.

Allen County

Circuit & Superior Court 715 S Calhoun St, Rm 201, Courthouse, Attn: Clerk of Allen County, Ft Wayne, IN 46802; phone: 260-449-7245; fax: 260-449-7929; hours 8AM-4:30PM (EST). *Felony, Misdemeanor, Civil, Eviction, Small Claims, Probate.*

www.co.allen.in.us

Note: Misdemeanor & Traffic phone- 260-449-7175; Small claims phone- 260-449-7130; Court Admin.- 260-449-7566.

Civil Records: Access: In person only. Visitors must perform in person searches themselves. Court makes copy: $1.00 per page. Required to search: name, years to search. Civil cases indexed by defendant, plaintiff. Recent civil cases on computer back to 11/1995; prior records on microfiche, archived and index from 1824.

Criminal Records: Access: In person only. Visitors must perform in person searches themselves. Court makes copy: $1.00 per page. Required to search: name, years to search. Felony cases on computer back to 2/1994; prior records on microfiche, archived and index from 1824.

General Information: Public terminal has criminal back to 2/1994 and civil back to 1/1995. No juvenile, adoption or sealed records released. Will not fax specific case file. Certification fee: $1.00 per page. Payee: Clerk of Allen Circuit Court. Business checks accepted. Prepayment required.

Bartholomew County

Circuit & Superior Court PO Box 924, Columbus, IN 47202-0924; phone: 812-379-1600; fax: 812-379-1675; hours 8AM-5PM (EST). *Felony, Misdemeanor, Civil, Eviction, Small Claims, Probate.* www.bartholomewco.com

Civil Records: Access: In person, online. Visitors must perform in person searches themselves. Court makes copy: $.25 per page; same fee for self serve. Required to search: name. Civil cases indexed by plaintiff. Civil records on computer from 1985, on microfilm from 1920. An online subscription service is at https://www.doxpop.com/prod/welcome.jsp. Fees involved. Records date from 05/85. A limited free search of open cases is available.

Criminal Records: Access: Fax, mail, in person, online. Visitors must perform in person searches themselves. No search fee. Court makes copy: $.25 per page; same fee for self serve. Required to search: name, years to search, DOB; also helpful: SSN, race, sex. Criminal records on computer from 1985, on microfilm from 1920. Online access to criminal

records is the same as civil. Mail turnaround time 1 day.

General Information: Public terminal goes back to 1985. No juvenile, mental health, adoption or sealed released. All searches 1985 to present. Will fax specific case file requests $5.00 per page; no fee to toll-free number. Certification fee: $1.00 per page. Payee: Bartholomew County Clerk. Personal checks accepted. Prepayment and SASE required.

Benton County

Circuit Court 706 E 5th St, #37, Fowler, IN 47944-1556; phone: 765-884-0930; fax: 765-884-0322; hours 8:30AM-4PM (EST). *Felony, Misdemeanor, Civil, Eviction, Small Claims, Probate.*

Civil Records: Access: In person only. Visitors must perform in person searches themselves. Court makes copy: $1.00 per page. Required to search: name, years to search. Civil cases indexed by defendant, plaintiff. Civil records on computer from 1992, on index books from 1860.

Criminal Records: Access: Mail, in person, fax. Visitors must perform in person searches themselves. Search fee: $5.00 per name; send search requests to attention of Vickie Harvey in Clerk's office. Court makes copy: $1.00 per page. Required to search: name, years to search, DOB. Criminal records on computer from 1992, on index books from 1860. Mail turnaround time 2-3 days.

General Information: Public terminal goes back to 1992. No juvenile, mental, adoption or sealed released. Will fax documents to local or toll free line. Certification fee: $1.00. Payee: Benton County Clerk. Only cashiers checks and money orders accepted. Prepayment and SASE required.

Blackford County

Circuit & Superior Court 110 W Washington St, Hartford City, IN 47348; phone: 765-348-1130; fax: 765-348-7234; hours 8AM-4PM (EST). *Felony, Misdemeanor, Civil, Eviction, Small Claims, Probate.*

Civil Records: Access: Fax, mail, in person. Visitors must perform in person searches themselves. No search fee. Court makes copy: $1.00 per page. Required to search: name, years to search. Civil cases indexed by defendant, plaintiff. Civil records on computer from 1991, on index from 1800. Mail turnaround time 1 week.

Criminal Records: Access: Fax, mail, in person. Visitors must perform in person searches themselves. No search fee. Court makes copy: $1.00 per page. Required to search: name, years to search, DOB; also helpful: SSN. court records on computer from 1991, on index from 1800. Mail turnaround time 1 week.

General Information: Public terminal goes back to 1991. No juvenile, mental, adoption or sealed released. Fee to fax documents is $1.00 per page. Certification fee: $2.00 per cert. Payee: Clerk of Blackford County. Business and personal checks accepted. Prepayment required.

Boone County

Circuit & Superior Court I & II Rm 212, Courthouse Sq, Lebanon, IN 46052; phone: 765-482-3510; hours 7AM-4PM (EST). *Felony, Misdemeanor, Civil, Eviction, Small Claims, Probate.*

www.bccn.boone.in.us/bccn/Boone_Clerk.html

Civil Records: Access: Mail, in person. Both court and visitors may perform in person searches. No search fee. Court makes copy: $1.00 per page. Required to search: name, years to search. Civil cases indexed by defendant, plaintiff. Civil records on index from 1900. Mail turnaround time 1 week.

Criminal Records: Access: Mail, in person. Both court and visitors may perform in person searches. No search fee. Court makes copy: $1.00 per page. Required to search: name, years to search; also

helpful: SSN. Criminal records on index from 1900. Mail turnaround time 1 week.

General Information: Public terminal has criminal back to 1994 and civil back to 2002. No juvenile, mental, adoption or sealed released. Will fax documents to local or toll free line. Certification fee: $2.00 per cert. Payee: Boone County Clerk. Business checks accepted. Prepayment and SASE required.

Brown County

Circuit Court Box 85, Nashville, IN 47448; phone: 812-988-5510; fax: 812-988-5562; hours 8AM-4PM (EST). *Felony, Misdemeanor, Civil, Eviction, Small Claims, Probate.*

Civil Records: Access: In person, online. Visitors must perform in person searches themselves. Court makes copy: $1.00 per page; same fee for self serve. Required to search: name, years to search. Civil cases indexed by defendant, plaintiff. Civil records on open cases on computer from 1993, in entry books from early 1800s. Pre-2005 records not indexed by SSN, but SSNs can be viewed. Fee access to civil records back to 1993 is by subscription at https://www.doxpop.com/prod/welcome.jsp; free access limited to only current open cases.

Criminal Records: Access: In person, online. Visitors must perform in person searches themselves. Court makes copy: $1.00 per page; same fee for self serve. Required to search: name, years to search, DOB; also helpful: SSN. Criminal records on open cases on computer from 1993, in entry books from early 1800s. Pre-2005 records not indexed by SSN, but SSNs can be viewed. Fee access to civil records back to 1993 is by subscription at www.doxpop.com/prod/welcome.jsp; free access limited to only current open cases.

General Information: Public terminal goes back to 1993. No juvenile, mental, adoption or sealed records released. Will not fax back documents. Certification fee: $1.00. Payee: County Clerk. Personal checks accepted. Prepayment required.

Carroll County

Circuit & Superior Court Courthouse, 101 W Main, Delphi, IN 46923; phone: 765-564-4485; fax: 765-564-1835; hours 8AM-5PM M,T,Th,F; 8AM-N Wed (EST). *Felony, Misdemeanor, Civil, Eviction, Small Claims, Probate.*

Civil Records: Access: In person only. Visitors must perform in person searches themselves. Court makes copy: $1.00 per page. Required to search: name, years to search. Civil cases indexed by defendant, plaintiff. Civil records archived from 1981, on index from 1828.

Criminal Records: Access: In person only. Visitors must perform in person searches themselves. Court makes copy: $1.00 per page. Required to search: name, years to search. Criminal records archived from 1981, on index from 1828.

General Information: No public access terminal. No juvenile, mental, adoption or sealed released. Certification fee: $1.00. Payee: Carroll County Clerk. Personal checks not accepted. Prepayment required.

Cass County

Circuit & Superior Court 200 Court Park, Logansport, IN 46947; phone: 574-753-7730; hours 8AM-4PM (EST). *Felony, Misdemeanor, Civil, Eviction, Small Claims, Probate.*

Civil Records: Access: Mail, in person. Both court and visitors may perform in person searches. No search fee. Court makes copy: $1.00 per page. Required to search: name, years to search. Civil cases indexed by defendant, plaintiff. Civil records on computer from 1989, on index from 1830s. Mail turnaround time 2 weeks.

Criminal Records: Access: Mail, in person. Both court and visitors may perform in person searches. No search fee. Court makes copy: $1.00 per page. Required to search: name, years to search, DOB; also helpful: SSN, signed release. Criminal records on computer from 1989, on index from 1830s. Mail turnaround time 2 weeks.

General Information: Public terminal goes back to 1989. No juvenile, mental, adoption or sealed released. Will fax documents for $1.00 per page. Certification fee: $3.00. Payee: Cass County Clerk. Personal checks not accepted; use money order. Prepayment required. SASE requested.

Clark County

Circuit, Superior & County Court 501 E Court, Rm 137, Jeffersonville, IN 47130; phone: 812-285-6244; hours 8:30AM-4:30PM M-F; 8:30-N Sat (EST). *Felony, Misdemeanor, Civil, Eviction, Small Claims, Probate.*

www.clarkprosecutor.org/html/courts/courts.htm

Civil Records: Access: In person only. Visitors must perform in person searches themselves. Court makes copy: $1.00 per page. Required to search: name, years to search; also helpful: address. Civil cases indexed by defendant, plaintiff. Civil records on computer since 8/92, on index cards from 1900.

Criminal Records: Access: In person only. Visitors must perform in person searches themselves. Court makes copy: $1.00 per page. Required to search: name, years to search; also helpful: DOB, SSN. Criminal records on computer since 8/92, on index cards from 1900.

General Information: Public terminal has criminal back to 1992 and civil back to 1993. No juvenile, mental, adoption or sealed released. Certification fee: $1.00 per cert. Payee: County Clerk. Business checks accepted. Prepayment required.

Clay County

Circuit & Superior Court 609 E National Ave, #213, Brazil, IN 47834; hours 8AM-4PM (EST). *Felony, Misdemeanor, Civil, Eviction, Small Claims, Probate.*

Civil Records: Access: Mail, in person. Visitors must perform in person searches themselves. Court makes copy: $1.00 per page; same fee for self serve. Required to search: name, years to search; also helpful: address. Civil cases indexed by defendant, plaintiff. Civil records on index from 1850; on computer back to 1995. Mail turnaround time 1 week.

Criminal Records: Access: Mail, in person. Visitors must perform in person searches themselves. Court makes copy: $1.00 per page; same fee for self serve. Required to search: name, years to search, address, DOB; also helpful-SSN, signed release. Criminal records on index from 1850; on computer back to 1995. Mail turnaround time 1 week.

General Information: No public access terminal. No juvenile, mental, adoption or sealed released. Certification fee: $1.00. Payee: County Clerk. Business checks accepted. Prepayment and SASE required.

Clinton County

Circuit & Superior Court 265 Courthouse Square, Frankfort, IN 46041; phone: 765-659-6335; hours 8AM-4PM M-Th,8AM-5PM F; 8/AM-12PM Thur (EST). *Felony, Misdemeanor, Civil, Eviction, Small Claims, Probate.*

Civil Records: Access: In person, online. Visitors must perform in person searches themselves. Court makes copy: $1.00 per page. Required to search: name, years to search. Civil cases indexed by defendant, plaintiff. Civil records on computer from 1991, on microfiche and index from 1900s. An online subscription service is at https://www.doxpop.com/prod/welcome.jsp. Fees involved. Records date from 01/91. A limited free search of open cases is available.

Criminal Records: Access: In person, online. Visitors must perform in person searches themselves. No search fee. Court makes copy: $1.00 per page. Required to search: name, years to search, signed release; also helpful: DOB. Criminal records on computer from 1991, on microfiche and index

from 1900s. Online access to criminal records is the same as civil.

General Information: Public terminal goes back to 1991. No juvenile, mental, adoption or sealed released. Will not fax documents. Certification fee: $1.00 per page. Payee: County Clerk. Business checks accepted. Prepayment required.

Crawford County

Circuit Court Box 375, English, IN 47118; phone: 812-338-2565; fax: 812-338-2507; hours 8AM-4PM M,F; 8AM-6PM T-Th (EST). *Felony, Misdemeanor, Civil, Eviction, Small Claims, Probate.*

Civil Records: Access: In person only. Visitors must perform in person searches themselves. Court makes copy: $1.00 per page. Self serve copy fee: $.50 per page. Required to search: name, years to search. Civil cases indexed by defendant, plaintiff. Civil records on index from 1900s.

Criminal Records: Access: Fax, mail, in person. Only the court performs in person searches; visitors may not. Search fee: $5.00 per name. Court makes copy: $1.00 per page. Self serve copy fee: $.50 per page. Required to search: name, years to search, DOB, SSN, signed release. Criminal records on index from 1900s. Mail turnaround time 1 week.

General Information: No public access terminal. No juvenile, mental, adoption or sealed released. No fee to fax documents. Certification fee: $2.00 per document. Payee: County Clerk. Business checks accepted. Prepayment and SASE required.

Daviess County

Circuit & Superior Court PO Box 739, Washington, IN 47501; phone: 812-254-8660; criminal phone: 812-254-8669; civil phone: 812-254-8664; probate phone: 812-254-8664; fax: 812-254-8698; 8AM-4PM (EST). *Felony, Misdemeanor, Civil, Eviction, Small Claims, Probate.*

Civil Records: Access: Mail, in person, online. Both court and visitors may perform in person searches. No search fee. Court makes copy: $1.00 per page. Required to search: name, years to search. Civil cases indexed by defendant, plaintiff. Civil records on index from 1900s; recent on computer since 1993. An online subscription service is at https://www.doxpop.com/prod/welcome.jsp. Fees involved. Records date from 02/94. A limited free search of open cases is available. Mail turnaround time varies.

Criminal Records: Access: Mail, in person, online. Both court and visitors may perform in person searches. No search fee. Court makes copy: $1.00 per page. Required to search: name, years to search. Criminal records on index from 1900s; recent on computer since 1993. Online access to criminal records is the same as civil. Mail turnaround time varies.

General Information: Public use terminal available. No juvenile, mental, adoption or sealed records released. Certification fee: $1.00 per cert. Payee: Daviess County Clerk. Business checks accepted. Prepayment and SASE required.

Dearborn County

Circuit & Superior Court Courthouse, 215 W High St, Lawrenceburg, IN 47025; phone: 812-537-8867; fax: 812-532-2021; hours 8:30AM-4:30PM (EST). *Felony, Misdemeanor, Civil, Eviction, Small Claims, Probate.*

www.dearborncounty.org/datafiles/judges.html

Civil Records: Access: In person only. Visitors must perform in person searches themselves. Court makes copy: $1.00 per page. Required to search: name, years to search. Civil cases indexed by defendant, plaintiff. Civil records on computer from 1992, on index from 1970s.

Criminal Records: Access: In person only. Visitors must perform in person searches themselves. Court makes copy: $1.00 per page. Required to search: name, years to search, DOB; SSN helpful. Criminal

records on computer from 1992, on index from 1970s, archived to 1930.

General Information: Public terminal goes back to 2000. No juvenile, mental, adoption or sealed records released. Certification fee: $1.00 per cert. Payee: Circuit Court Clerk. Only cashiers checks and money orders accepted. Prepayment required.

Decatur County

Circuit & Superior Court 150 Courthouse Square, #244, Greensburg, IN 47240; phone: 812-663-8223/8642; fax: 812-662-6627; hours 8AM-4PM, 8AM-5PM F (EST). *Felony, Misdemeanor, Civil, Eviction, Small Claims, Probate.*

www.decaturcounty.in.gov

Civil Records: Access: In person only. Visitors must perform in person searches themselves. Court makes copy: $1.00 per page; same fee for self serve. Required to search: name, years to search. Civil cases indexed by defendant, plaintiff. Civil records on index from 1823; on computer back to 1998.

Criminal Records: Access: In person only. Visitors must perform in person searches themselves. Court makes copy: $1.00 per page; same fee for self serve. Required to search: name, years to search, DOB; SSN helpful. Criminal records on index from 1823; on computer back to 1998.

General Information: Public terminal goes back to 1998. No juvenile, mental, adoption or sealed released. Will fax specific case file if situation warrants. Certification fee: $1.00 per page. Payee: Decatur County Clerk. Personal checks accepted. Prepayment required.

DeKalb County

Circuit & Superior Court PO Box 230, Auburn, IN 46706; phone: 260-925-0912; fax: 260-925-5126; hours 8:30AM-4:30PM (EST). *Felony, Misdemeanor, Civil, Eviction, Small Claims, Probate.*

Civil Records: Access: In person only. Visitors must perform in person searches themselves. Court makes copy: $1.00 per page; same fee for self serve. Required to search: name, years to search. Civil cases indexed by defendant, plaintiff. Civil records on computer back to 1987, on index from 1913.

Criminal Records: Access: In person only. Visitors must perform in person searches themselves. Court makes copy: $1.00 per page; same fee for self serve. Required to search: name, years to search, DOB. Criminal records on computer back to 1987, on index from 1913. Will send case files if case number known.

General Information: Public terminal goes back to 1987. No juvenile, mental, adoption or sealed released. Certification fee: $1.00. Payee: Court Clerk. Only cashiers checks and money orders accepted. Prepayment required.

Delaware County

Circuit Court Box 1089, Muncie, IN 47308; phone: 765-747-7726; fax: 765-747-7768; hours 8:30AM-4:30PM (EST). *Felony, Misdemeanor, Civil, Small Claims, Probate.* www.dcclerk.org

Civil Records: Access: Fax, mail, in person, online. Both court and visitors may perform in person searches. No search fee. Court makes copy: $.10 per page. Required to search: name, years to search. Civil cases indexed by defendant, plaintiff. Civil records on computer from 1989, on microfiche, archived and on index from 1800. An online subscription service is at https://www.doxpop.com/prod/welcome.jsp. Fees involved. Records date from 01/89. A limited free search of open cases is available.

Criminal Records: Access: In person, online. Visitors must perform in person searches themselves. No search fee. Court makes copy: $.10 per page. Required to search: name, years to search, DOB, SSN. Criminal records on computer from 1989, on microfiche, archived and on index from 1800. Online access to criminal records from 1850 to 1950 only is free at www.munpl.org/Main_Page

s/documents.htm, the Muncie Public Library website. Also, an online subscription service is at www.doxpop.com. Fees involved. Records date from 01/89. A limited free search of open cases is available. Mail turnaround time 1-2 days.

General Information: Public terminal goes back to 1989. No juvenile, mental, adoption or sealed released. Fee to fax documents is $2.00. Certification fee: $1.00. Payee: Delaware County Clerk. Business checks accepted. Prepayment required.

Dubois County

Circuit & Superior Court 1 Courthouse Square, Jasper, IN 47546; phone: 812-481-7035; fax: 812-481-7030; hours 8AM-4PM (EST). *Felony, Misdemeanor, Civil, Eviction, Small Claims, Probate.*

Civil Records: Access: In person only. Visitors must perform in person searches themselves. Court makes copy: $.25 per page. Required to search: name; also helpful: years to search. Civil cases indexed by defendant, plaintiff. Civil records on computer from 8\93, on index books from 1930.

Criminal Records: Access: In person only. Visitors must perform in person searches themselves. Court makes copy: $.25 per page. Required to search: name; also helpful: years to search. Criminal records on computer from 8\93, on index books from 1930.

General Information: Public terminal goes back to 1993. No juvenile, mental, adoption or sealed records released. Certification fee: $1.00. Payee: Court Clerk. Personal checks accepted. Prepayment required.

Elkhart County

Elkhart Superior Courts 1, 2, 5, 6 315 S 2nd St, Elkhart, IN 46516; phone: 574-523-2233/2305/2007; fax: 574-523-2323; hours 8AM-4PM T-F, 8AM-5PM M (EST). *Felony, Misdemeanor, Civil, Eviction, Small Claims, Probate.* www.elkhartcountyindiana.com/administrative/clerk.html

Civil Records: Access: In person, online. Visitors must perform in person searches themselves. Court makes copy: $1.00 per page. Required to search: name, years to search. Civil cases indexed by defendant, plaintiff. Civil records archived from 1830; on computer since 1996. Some records on index books. An online subscription service is at https://www.doxpop.com/prod/welcome.jsp. Fees involved. Records date from 01/92. A limited free search of open cases is available.

Criminal Records: Access: In person, online. Visitors must perform in person searches themselves. Court makes copy: $1.00 per page. Required to search: name, years to search, DOB; also helpful: SSN. Criminal records archived from 1830; on computer since 1996. Some records on index books. Online access to criminal records is the same as civil.

General Information: Public use terminal available. No juvenile, mental, adoption or sealed records released. Certification fee: $2.00. Payee: Court Clerk. Personal checks not accepted. Prepayment required.

Goshen Circuit & Superior Courts 3, 4 Courthouse, 101 N Main St, Goshen, IN 46526; phone: 574-535-6431; fax: 574-535-6471; hours 8AM-5PM M, 8AM-4PM T-F (EST). *Felony, Misdemeanor, Civil, Eviction, Small Claims, Probate.* www.elkhartcountyindiana.com/administrative/clerk.html

Note: Includes Circuit Court (Rm 204) and Superior Court 3 (Rm 205, 535-6438) and 4 (Rm 105, 535-6403).

Civil Records: Access: In person, online. Visitors must perform in person searches themselves. Court makes copy: $1.00 per page. Required to search: name, years to search. Civil cases indexed by defendant, plaintiff. Civil records archived from 1830; on computer since 1996. Some records on index books. An online subscription service is at https://www.doxpop.com/prod/welcome.jsp. Fees involved; $39.00 per month. Records date from

01/92. A limited free search of open cases is available.

Criminal Records: Access: In person, online. Visitors must perform in person searches themselves. No search fee. Court makes copy: $1.00 per page. Required to search: name, years to search, DOB; also helpful: SSN. Criminal records archived from 1830; on computer since 1996. Some records on index books. Online access to criminal records is the same as civil.

General Information: Public terminal goes back to 1996. No juvenile, mental, adoption or sealed records released. Will not fax documents. Certification fee: $1.00 per cert. Payee: Court Clerk. No personal checks accepted. Prepayment required.

Fayette County

Circuit & Superior Court PO Box 607, Connersville, IN 47331-0607; phone: 765-825-1813; hours 8:30AM-4PM (5PM on Wed) (EST). *Felony, Misdemeanor, Civil, Eviction, Small Claims, Probate.* www.co.fayette.in.us

Civil Records: Access: In person only. Visitors must perform in person searches themselves. Court makes copy: $1.00 per page. Required to search: name, years to search. Civil cases indexed by defendant, plaintiff. Civil records on computer from 1988 (Circuit), 1992 (Superior).

Criminal Records: Access: In person only. Visitors must perform in person searches themselves. Court makes copy: $1.00 per page. Required to search: name, years to search. Criminal records on computer from 1988 (Circuit), 1992 (Superior).

General Information: Public use terminal available. No juvenile, mental, adoption or sealed released. Certification fee: $1.00. Payee: Fayette County Clerk. Only cashiers checks and money orders accepted. Prepayment required.

Floyd County

Circuit, Superior & County Court Box 1056, City County Bldg, New Albany, IN 47150; phone: 812-948-5414; criminal phone: 812-948-2765; civil phone: 812-948-5412; probate phone: 812-948-5411; fax: 812-948-4711; hours 8AM-4PM (EST). *Felony, Misdemeanor, Civil, Eviction, Small Claims, Probate.*

Note: Probate is a separate index at this same address.

Civil Records: Access: Mail, in person, online. Visitors must perform in person searches themselves. Court makes copy: $.10 per page; same fee for self serve. Required to search: name, years to search. Civil cases indexed by defendant, plaintiff. Civil records on computer from 1988, archived from 1978, on index from 1819. Online access is the same as criminal, see below. Mail turnaround 1-2 days.

Criminal Records: Access: Mail, in person. Visitors must perform in person searches themselves. Search fee: $5.00. Court makes copy: $.10 per page; same fee for self serve. Required to search: name, years to search; also helpful: SSN. Criminal records on computer from 1988, archived from 1978, on index from 1819. Access to court records is free at www.floydcounty.in.gov/court_rec_menu.asp. Name search or view calendars or case summaries. Mail turnaround time 1-2 days.

General Information: Public terminal goes back to 1988. No juvenile, mental, adoption or sealed released. Will not fax documents. Certification fee: $1.00 per page. Payee: Court Clerk. Personal checks accepted. Prepayment and SASE required.

Fountain County

Circuit Court Box 183, Covington, IN 47932; phone: 765-793-2192; fax: 765-793-5002; hours 8AM-4PM (EST). *Felony, Misdemeanor, Civil, Eviction, Small Claims, Probate.*

Civil Records: Access: Mail, in person. Both court and visitors may perform in person searches. No search fee. Court makes copy: $1.00 per page; same fee for self serve. Required to search: name, years to search. Civil cases indexed by defendant, plaintiff.

Civil records on computer from 1995. Mail turnaround time 1-2 days if records after 1989, 4-5 days if prior.

Criminal Records: Access: Mail, in person. Both court and visitors may perform in person searches. No search fee. Court makes copy: $1.00 per page; same fee for self serve. Required to search: name, years to search. Criminal records on computer from 1995. Mail turnaround time 1-2 days if records after 1989, 4-5 days if prior.

General Information: Public terminal goes back to 1995. No juvenile, mental, adoption or sealed released. Will not fax documents. Certification fee: $2.00. Payee: Court Clerk. Personal checks not accepted. Prepayment and SASE required.

Franklin County

Circuit Court 459 Main, Brookville, IN 47012; phone: 765-647-5111; fax: 765-647-3224; hours 8:30AM-4PM (EST). *Felony, Misdemeanor, Civil, Eviction, Small Claims, Probate.*

Civil Records: Access: In person only. Visitors must perform in person searches themselves. Court makes copy: $1.00 per page. Required to search: name, years to search. Civil cases indexed by defendant, plaintiff. Civil records on index.

Criminal Records: Access: In person only. Visitors must perform in person searches themselves. Court makes copy: $1.00 per page. Required to search: name, years to search. Criminal records on index.

General Information: No public access terminal. No juvenile, mental, adoption or sealed released. Certification fee: $1.00. Payee: Court Clerk. Personal checks accepted. Prepayment required.

Fulton County

Circuit Court 815 Main St, PO Box 524, Rochester, IN 46975; phone: 574-223-2911; criminal phone: 574-223-2911; civil phone: 574-223-7714; probate phone: 574-223-7715; fax: 574-223-8304; hours 8AM-4PM M-Th, 8AM-5PM F (EST). *Felony, Misdemeanor, Civil, Eviction, Small Claims, Probate.*

Civil Records: Access: Mail, in person. Both court and visitors may perform in person searches. No search fee. Court makes copy: $1.00 per page. Required to search: name, years to search. Civil cases indexed by defendant, plaintiff. Civil records on computer from 1989, on microfiche, archived and on index from 1845. Mail turnaround time 3-4 days.

Criminal Records: Access: Mail, in person. Both court and visitors may perform in person searches. No search fee. Court makes copy: $1.00 per page. Required to search: name, years to search. Criminal records on computer from 1989, on microfiche, archived and on index from 1845. Mail turnaround time 3-4 days.

General Information: Public terminal goes back to 10 years. No juvenile, mental, adoption or sealed released. Will fax documents for $4.00 per page. Certification fee: $1.00. Payee: Court Clerk. Business checks accepted. Prepayment and SASE required.

Gibson County

Circuit & Superior Court Courthouse, PO Box 630, Princeton, IN 47670; phone: 812-386-6474; fax: 812-385-5025; hours 8AM-4PM (CST). *Felony, Misdemeanor, Civil, Eviction, Small Claims, Probate.*

Civil Records: Access: In person only. Visitors must perform in person searches themselves. Court makes copy: $.35 per page uncertified. Required to search: name, years to search. Civil cases indexed by defendant, plaintiff. Civil records on computer 1/1996 for Superior; 2/1/2000 for Circuit. On microfiche from 1940, on index from 1813.

Criminal Records: Access: In person only. Visitors must perform in person searches themselves. Court makes copy: $.35 per page uncertified. Required to search: name, years to search. Criminal records on computer 1/1996 for Superior; 2/1/2000 for Circuit. On microfiche from 1940, on index from 1813.

General Information: Public terminal goes back to 1/1996 for superior; 2/2000 for Circuit. No juvenile, mental, adoption or sealed records released. Will not fax specific case file. Certification fee: $1.00 per page includes copy fee. Payee: Court Clerk. Only cashiers checks and money orders accepted. Prepayment required.

Grant County

Circuit & Superior Court Courthouse 101 E 4th St, Marion, IN 46952; phone: 765-668-8121; fax: 765-668-6541; hours 8AM-4PM (EST). *Felony, Misdemeanor, Civil, Eviction, Small Claims, Probate.*
www.grantcounty.net
Note: Probate is in a separate index at this address.
Civil Records: Access: In person only. Visitors must perform in person searches themselves. Court makes copy: $.10 per page; same fee for self serve. Required to search: name, years to search; also helpful: address. Civil cases indexed by defendant, plaintiff. Civil records on computer from 1989, on index from 1881.
Criminal Records: Access: In person only. Visitors must perform in person searches themselves. Court makes copy: $.10 per page; same fee for self serve. Required to search: name, years to search; also helpful: DOB, SSN. Criminal records on computer from 1989, on index from 1881.
General Information: Public terminal goes back to 7/1989. No juvenile, adoption, mental health or sealed records released. Will fax specific case file for $1.00 per page fee. Certification fee: $1.00 per certification. Payee: Court Clerk. Personal checks accepted. Prepayment required.

Greene County

Circuit & Superior Court PO Box 229, Bloomfield, IN 47424; phone: 812-384-8532; fax: 812-384-8458; hours 8AM-4PM (EST). *Felony, Misdemeanor, Civil, Eviction, Small Claims, Probate.*
Civil Records: Access: In person only. Visitors must perform in person searches themselves. Court makes copy: $1.00 per page. Required to search: name, years to search. Civil cases indexed by defendant, plaintiff. Civil records on computer back to 1989, all other records in books.
Criminal Records: Access: In person only. Visitors must perform in person searches themselves. Court makes copy: $1.00 per page. Required to search: name, years to search. Criminal records on computer back to 1989; prior in books.
General Information: No public access terminal. No juvenile, mental, adoption or sealed released. Certification fee: $1.00. Payee: Court Clerk. Only cashiers checks and money orders accepted. Prepayment required.

Hamilton County

Circuit & Superior Court One Hamilton County Square, #106, Noblesville, IN 46060-2233; phone: 317-776-9629; fax: 317-776-9727; hours 8AM-4:30PM (EST). *Felony, Misdemeanor, Civil, Eviction, Small Claims, Probate.*
www.co.hamilton.in.us
Civil Records: Access: In person only. Visitors must perform in person searches themselves. Court makes copy: $.50 per page; same fee for self serve. Required to search: name, years to search. Civil cases indexed by defendant, plaintiff. Civil indices on computer from 1987, on index from 1840s.
Criminal Records: Access: In person only. Visitors must perform in person searches themselves. Court makes copy: $.50 per page; same fee for self serve. Required to search: name, years to search. Criminal records on computer from 1987, on index from 1840s.
General Information: Public terminal goes back to mid-1986. No juvenile, mental, adoption or sealed released. Will not fax specific case file. Certification fee: $1.00 plus $.50 per page. Payee: Court Clerk. Business checks accepted. Prepayment required.

Hancock County

Circuit & Superior Court 9 E Main St, Rm 201, Greenfield, IN 46140; phone: 317-477-1109; fax: 317-477-1163; hours 8AM-4PM (EST). *Felony, Misdemeanor, Civil, Eviction, Small Claims, Probate.*
Civil Records: Access: In person only. Both court and visitors may perform in person searches. No search fee. Court makes copy: $1.00 per page for case history, otherwise $.25 per page. Self serve copy fee: $.25 per page. Required to search: name, years to search. Civil cases indexed by defendant, plaintiff. Civil records on computer from 7/88, on index and archived from 1883.
Criminal Records: Access: In person only. Both court and visitors may perform in person searches. No search fee. Court makes copy: $1.00 per page for case history, otherwise $.25 per page. Self serve copy fee: $.25 per page. Required to search: name, years to search, DOB; SSN helpful. Criminal records on computer from 7/88, on index and archived from 1883.
General Information: Public use terminal available. No juvenile, mental, adoption or sealed released. Certification fee: $1.00. Payee: Court Clerk. Only cashier checks or money orders accepted. Prepayment required.

Harrison County

Circuit Court 300 N Capitol, Corydon, IN 47112; phone: 812-738-4289; criminal phone: 812-738-8149; civil phone: 812-738-4289; probate phone: 812-738-4289; criminal fax: 812-738-2459; civil fax: 812-738-3126; probate fax: 812-738-3126; hours 8AM-4:30PM (EST). *Civil, Eviction, Probate.*
Civil Records: Access: In person only. Visitors must perform in person searches themselves. Court makes copy: $1.00 per page; same fee for self serve. Required to search: name, years to search. Civil cases indexed by defendant, plaintiff. Civil records on index from 1900. Court personnel will only do record searching when they have time; strongly urge using a retriever.
Criminal Records: Access: In person. Visitors must perform in person searches themselves. Court makes copy: $1.00 per page; same fee for self serve. Required to search: name, years to search, DOB; also helpful-SSN. Criminal records on index from 1900; on computer back to 1992. Court personnel only do record searching when they have time; suggest to use a retriever.
General Information: No public access terminal. No juvenile, mental, adoption or sealed released. Fee to fax documents is $1.00 per page. Certification fee: $1.00 per document. Payee: Court Clerk. Only cashiers checks and money orders accepted. Prepayment required.

Superior Court 1445 Gardner Ln, #3126, Corydon, IN 47112; phone: 812-738-8149; fax: 812-738-2459; hours 8AM-4:30PM (EST). *Felony, Misdemeanor, Small Claims.*
Civil Records: Access: In person only. Visitors must perform in person searches themselves. Court makes copy: $1.00 per page; same fee for self serve. Required to search: name, years to search. Civil cases indexed by defendant, plaintiff. Civil records on index from 1976; on computer back to 1992.
Criminal Records: Access: In person only. Visitors must perform in person searches themselves. Court makes copy: $1.00 per page; same fee for self serve. Required to search: name, years to search, DOB; also helpful-SSN. Criminal records on index from 1976; on computer back to 1992.
General Information: Public terminal goes back to 1992; indexes only. No juvenile, mental, adoption or sealed released. Will not fax specific case file. Certification fee: $1.00 per document. Payee: Court Clerk. Only cashiers checks and money orders accepted. Prepayment required.

Hendricks County

Circuit & Superior Court PO Box 599, Danville, IN 46122; phone: 317-745-9231; fax: 317-745-9306; hours 8AM-4PM (EST). *Felony, Misdemeanor, Civil, Eviction, Small Claims, Probate.*
Civil Records: Access: In person only. Visitors must perform in person searches themselves. Court makes copy: $1.00 per page. Required to search: name, years to search. Civil cases indexed by defendant, plaintiff. Civil records on computer since late 1992, on index from 1800s. Will do mail request if out of state; turnaround time is 72-hrs.
Criminal Records: Access: In person only. Visitors must perform in person searches themselves. Court makes copy: $1.00 per page. Required to search: name, years to search; also helpful: DOB, SSN. Criminal records on computer since late 1992, on index from 1800s. Will do mail request if out of state; turnaround time is 72-hrs.
General Information: Public terminal goes back to 9/1992. No juvenile, mental, adoption or sealed released. Certification fee: $1.00. Payee: Court Clerk. Business checks accepted. Prepayment required.

Henry County

Circuit & Superior Courts I & II PO Box B, New Castle, IN 47362; phone: 765-529-6401; fax: 765-521-7046; hours 8AM-4PM (EST). *Felony, Misdemeanor, Civil, Eviction, Small Claims, Probate.*
Civil Records: Access: In person only. Visitors must perform in person searches themselves. Court makes copy: $1.00 per page. Required to search: name, years to search. Civil cases indexed by plaintiff. Civil records on computer from 2003, archived from 1979, on index from 1976.
Criminal Records: Access: In person only. Visitors must perform in person searches themselves. Court makes copy: $1.00 per page. Required to search: name, years to search. Criminal records on computer from 2003, archived from 1979, on index from 1976.
General Information: Public terminal goes back to 2/1991. No juvenile, mental, protective orders, adoption or any other confidential records. Will not fax specific case file. Certification fee: $1.00 per document. Payee: Henry County Clerk. Only cashiers checks and money orders accepted. Prepayment required.

Howard County

Circuit & Superior Court PO Box 9004, Kokomo, IN 46904; phone: 765-456-2204; criminal phone: 765-456-2000; civil phone: 765-456-2000; criminal/civil fax: 765-456-2267; hours 8AM-4PM (EST). *Felony, Misdemeanor, Civil, Eviction, Small Claims, Probate.* http://co.howard.in.us/clerk1
Note: Small claims pnone-765-456-2204.
Civil Records: Access: In person, online. Visitors must perform in person searches themselves. Court makes copy: $.20 per page from printed records. Self serve copy fee: $.20 per page. Required to search: name, years to search. Civil cases indexed by defendant, plaintiff. Civil records on computer since 1994, on microfiche from early 1800s. An online subscription service is at https://www.doxpop.com/prod/welcome.jsp. Fees involved. Records date from 07/94. A limited free search of open cases is available.
Criminal Records: Access: In person, online. Visitors must perform in person searches themselves. Search fee: None. Court makes copy: $.20 per page from printed records. Self serve copy fee: $.20 per page. Required to search: name, years to search; also helpful: DOB, SSN. Criminal records on computer since 1992, on microfiche from early 1800s. Online access to criminal records is same as civil.
General Information: Public terminal goes back to 1994. No juvenile, mental, adoption or sealed records released. Certification fee: $1.00. Payee: County Clerk. Only cashiers checks and money orders accepted. Prepayment required.

Huntington County

Circuit & Superior Court PO Box 228, Huntington, IN 46750; phone: 260-358-4817; fax: 260-358-4880; hours 8AM-4:30PM (EST). *Felony, Misdemeanor, Civil, Eviction, Small Claims, Probate.*

Civil Records: Access: Fax, phone, mail, in person. Both court and visitors may perform in person searches. No search fee. Court makes copy: $1.00 per page. Required to search: name, years to search. Civil cases indexed by defendant, plaintiff. Civil records on computer from 1990, on microfiche from 1970, on index and archived from 1800s.

Criminal Records: Access: In person only. Visitors must perform in person searches themselves. Court makes copy: $1.00 per page. Required to search: name, years to search. Criminal records on computer from 1990, on microfiche from 1970, on index and archived from 1800s.

General Information: Public terminal goes back to 1990. No juvenile, mental, adoption or sealed released. Will fax documents to local or toll free line. Certification fee: $1.00 per cert. Payee: County Clerk. Personal checks not accepted. Prepayment required.

Jackson County

Circuit Court PO Box 318, Brownstown, IN 47220; phone: 812-358-6117; criminal phone: 812-358-6116; civil phone: 812-358-6116; probate phone: 812-358-6133; fax: 812-358-6187; hours 8AM-4:30PM (EST). *Felony, Misdemeanor, Civil, Eviction, Small Claims, Probate.*

Note: Will not perform searches for private companies.

Civil Records: Access: Fax, mail, in person. Both court and visitors may perform in person searches. Search fee: $5.00 per name. Court makes copy: $1.00 per page; same fee for self serve. Required to search: name, years to search. Civil cases indexed by defendant, plaintiff. Civil records on computer from 1989, on index from 1800s.

Criminal Records: Access: In person only. Visitors must perform in person searches themselves. Court makes copy: $1.00 per page; same fee for self serve. Required to search: name, years to search; also helpful: DOB, SSN. Criminal records on computer from 1989, on index from 1800s. Note: Will recommend local document retrievers to do searches for you.

General Information: Public terminal goes back to 1989. No juvenile, mental, adoption or sealed released. Will fax documents $5.00 per doc; no fee to toll-free number. Certification fee: $1.00 per document. Payee: Jackson County Clerk. No personal checks accepted. Prepayment and SASE required.

Superior Court PO Box 788, Seymour, IN 47274; phone: 812-522-9676; fax: 812-523-6065; hours 8AM-4:30PM (EST). *Felony, Misdemeanor, Civil, Eviction, Small Claims.*

Civil Records: Access: Mail, in person. Visitors must perform in person searches themselves. No search fee. Court makes copy: $1.00 per page; same fee for self serve. Required to search: name, years to search. Civil cases indexed by defendant, plaintiff. Civil records on computer from 1989, on index from 1800s.

Criminal Records: Access: In person only. Visitors must perform in person searches themselves. Court makes copy: $1.00 per page; same fee for self serve. Required to search: name, years to search; also helpful: DOB, SSN. Criminal records on computer from 1989, on index from 1800s.

General Information: No public access terminal. No juvenile, mental, adoption or sealed released. Will fax documents $5.00 per doc; no fee to toll-free number. Certification fee: $1.00 per page. Payee: Jackson County Clerk. Only cashiers checks and money orders accepted. Prepayment required.

Jasper County

Circuit Court 115 W Washington, Rensselaer, IN 47978; phone: 219-866-4941; criminal phone: 219-866-4926/4921; civil phone: 219-866-4926/4921; probate phone: 218-866-4929; hours 8AM-4PM (CST). *Felony, Misdemeanor, Civil, Eviction, Small Claims, Probate.*

Note: This court also handles juvenile, paternity and adoption.

219-866-4909 Traffic; 219-866-4928 Child Support

Civil Records: Access: Mail, in person. Both court and visitors may perform in person searches. No search fee. Court makes copy: $.50 per page. Required to search: name, years to search. Civil cases indexed by defendant, plaintiff. County records on computer from 1976, circuit from 1989. Some records on index from 1900s. Mail turnaround time 1 day.

Criminal Records: Access: Mail, in person. Both court and visitors may perform in person searches. No search fee. Court makes copy: $.50 per page. Required to search: name, years to search; also helpful: DOB, SSN. County records on computer from 1976, circuit from 1989. Some records on index from 1900s. Mail turnaround time 1 day.

General Information: Public terminal goes back to 1989. No juvenile, mental, adoption or sealed released. Certification fee: $.50 per page. Payee: Jasper County Clerk. Business checks accepted. Prepayment and SASE required.

Superior Court 115 W Washington St, #103, Rensselaer, IN 47978; phone: 219-866-4971; criminal phone: 21-866-4922/4912; civil phone: 21-866-4922/4912; probate phone: 219-866-4912; hours 8AM-4PM (CST). *Felony, Misdemeanor, Civil, Probate.*

Civil Records: Access: Mail, in person. Both court and visitors may perform in person searches. No search fee. Court makes copy: $.50 per page. Non-case related copies are $.10 per page; same fee for self serve. Required to search: name, years to search. Civil cases indexed by defendant, plaintiff. County records on computer from 1976, circuit from 1989. Some records on index from 1800s. Mail turnaround time 1 day to 1 week.

Criminal Records: Access: Mail, in person. Both court and visitors may perform in person searches. No search fee. Court makes copy: $.50 per page. Non-case related copies are $.10 per page; same fee for self serve. Required to search: name, years to search. County records on computer from 1976, circuit from 1989. Some records on index from 1800s. Mail turnaround time 1 day to 1 week.

General Information: Public terminal goes back to 1989. No juvenile, mental, adoption or sealed released. Certification fee: $1.00 per page includes copy fee. Payee: County Clerk. Only cashiers checks and money orders accepted. Prepayment and SASE required.

Jay County

Circuit & Superior Court Courthouse, Portland, IN 47371; phone: 260-726-4951; hours 8:30AM-4:30PM (EST). *Felony, Misdemeanor, Civil, Eviction, Small Claims, Probate.*

www.co.jay.in.us

Civil Records: Access: In person, online. Visitors must perform in person searches themselves. No search fee. Court makes copy: $1.00 per page. Required to search: name, years to search; also helpful: address. Civil cases indexed by defendant, plaintiff. Civil records on computer from 8\94, prior on microfiche from 1979, on index books from 1900. An online subscription service is at https://www.doxpop.com/prod/welcome.jsp. Fees involved. Records date from 03/94. A limited free search of open cases is available.

Criminal Records: Access: Mail, in person, online. Visitors must perform in person searches themselves. No search fee. Court makes copy: $1.00 per page. Required to search: name, years to search, DOB; also helpful: SSN, address. Criminal records on computer from 8\94, prior on microfiche from 1979, on index books from 1900. Online access to criminal records is the same as civil.

General Information: Public terminal goes back to 1994. No juvenile, mental, adoption or sealed records released. Certification fee: $1.00 per page. Payee: Court Clerk. Personal and business checks accepted. No credit cards. Prepayment and SASE required.

Jefferson County

Circuit & Superior Court Courthouse, 300 E Main St, Rm 203, Madison, IN 47250; phone: 812-265-8923; fax: 812-265-8950; hours 8AM-4PM (EST). *Felony, Misdemeanor, Civil, Eviction, Small Claims, Probate.*

Civil Records: Access: In person only. Visitors must perform in person searches themselves. Court makes copy: $1.00 per page; same fee for self serve. Required to search: name, years to search. Civil cases indexed by plaintiff, defendant. Civil records on index from 1975, computerized since 1995.

Criminal Records: Access: In person only. Visitors must perform in person searches themselves. Court makes copy: $1.00 per page; same fee for self serve. Required to search: Name, years to search, address, DOB, SSN. Criminal records on index from 1975, computerized since 1995.

General Information: Public terminal goes back to 1976. No juvenile, mental, adoption or sealed released. Certification fee: $1.00 per page. Payee: County Clerk. Only cashiers checks and money orders accepted. Prepayment required.

Jennings County

Circuit Court Courthouse, PO Box 385, Vernon, IN 47282; phone: 812-352-3082; probate phone: 812-352-3070; hours 8AM-4PM (EST). *Felony, Misdemeanor, Civil, Eviction, Small Claims, Probate.*

Civil Records: Access: In person only. Visitors must perform in person searches themselves. Court makes copy: $.25 per page; same fee for self serve. Required to search: name, years to search. Civil cases indexed by defendant, plaintiff. Civil records on index from 1930; computerized since 2000.

Criminal Records: Access: In person only. Visitors must perform in person searches themselves. Court makes copy: $.25 per page; same fee for self serve. Required to search: name, years to search, DOB; SSN helpful. Criminal records on index from 1930; computerized since 2000.

General Information: Public terminal goes back to 10/2000. No juvenile, mental, adoption or sealed released. Certification fee: $1.00. Payee: County Clerk. Personal checks accepted. Prepayment required.

Johnson County

Circuit & Superior Court Courthouse, PO Box 368, Franklin, IN 46131; phone: 317-736-3708; criminal phone: 317-736-3986; civil phone: 317-736-3708; probate phone: 317-736-3913; fax: 317-736-3749; hours 8AM-4:30PM (EST). *Felony, Misdemeanor, Civil, Eviction, Small Claims, Probate.*

Civil Records: Access: Phone, fax, mail, in person, online. Both court and visitors may perform in person searches. No search fee. Court makes copy: $1.00 per page. Self serve copy fee: $.50 per page. Required to search: name, years to search. Civil cases indexed by defendant, plaintiff. Civil records on computer back 10 years. An online subscription service is at https://www.doxpop.com/prod/welcome.jsp. Fees involved. Records date from 08/89. A limited free search of open cases is available. Mail turnaround time 1-2 days.

Criminal Records: Access: Phone, fax, mail, in person, online. Both court and visitors may perform in person searches. No search fee. Court makes copy: $1.00 per page. Self serve copy fee: $.50 per page. Required to search: name, years to search; also helpful: DOB, SSN. Criminal records on computer back 15 years. Online access is the same as civil. Mail turnaround time 1-2 days.

General Information: Public terminal goes back to 1989. No juvenile, mental, adoption or sealed released. Long distance fee for faxing only. Certification fee: $1.00 per page. Payee: County Clerk. Business checks accepted. Prepayment required.

Knox County

Circuit & Superior Court 101 N 7th St, Vincennes, IN 47591; phone: 812-885-2521; fax: 312-895-4929; hours 8AM-4PM (EST). *Felony, Misdemeanor, Civil, Eviction, Small Claims, Probate.*

Civil Records: Access: Mail, in person. Visitors must perform in person searches themselves. No search fee. Court makes copy: $1.00 per page; same fee for self serve. Required to search: name, years to search. Civil cases indexed by defendant, plaintiff. Civil records on index books from 1800s. Mail turnaround time 1 week.

Criminal Records: Access: Mail, in person. Visitors must perform in person searches themselves. No search fee. Court makes copy: $1.00 per page; same fee for self serve. Required to search: name, years to search. Criminal records on index books from 1800s. Mail turnaround time 1 week.

General Information: No public access terminal. No juvenile, mental, adoption or sealed released. Will fax documents for no fee. Certification fee: $1.00 per page. Payee: Knox County Clerk. Personal checks accepted. Prepayment required.

Kosciusko County

Circuit & Superior Court 121 N Lake, Warsaw, IN 46580; phone: 574-372-2331; criminal phone: 574-372-2457 (1st), 372-2453 (2nd & 3rd); civil phone: 574-372-2331; probate phone: 574-372-2330; fax: 574-372-2338; hours 8AM-4:30PM (EST). *Felony, Misdemeanor, Civil, Eviction, Small Claims, Probate.*

Note: Probate records on same computer system, but actual index is separate.

Civil Records: Access: Fax, in person. Both court and visitors may perform in person searches. No search fee. Court makes copy: $.05 per page, $1.00 minimum. Required to search: name, years to search. Civil cases indexed by defendant, plaintiff. Civil records on computer from 10/1/93, general index from 1908.

Criminal Records: Access: Fax, in person. Both court and visitors may perform in person searches. No search fee. Court makes copy: $.05 per page, $1.00 minimum. Required to search: name, years to search; also helpful-DOB, SSN. DL#. Criminal records on computer from 10/1/93, general index from 1908.

General Information: Public terminal goes back to 1993. No juvenile, mental, adoption or sealed released. Will fax documents to toll free number only. Certification fee: $1.00 per certification. Payee: County Clerk. Personal checks accepted. Prepayment required.

La Porte County

Circuit & Superior Court 813 Lincolnway, La Porte, IN 46350; phone: 219-326-6808; fax: 219-326-6626; hours 8:00AM-4PM (CST). *Felony, Misdemeanor, Civil, Eviction, Probate.*

Note: Microfilm department is at phone extension 435.

Civil Records: Access: In person, fax. Visitors must perform in person searches themselves. Search fee: $1.00 per page. Court makes copy: $1.00 per page; same fee for self serve. Required to search: name, years to search. Civil cases indexed by defendant, plaintiff. Civil records on microfiche and index from 1900.

Criminal Records: Access: In person, fax. Visitors must perform in person searches themselves. Search fee: $1.00 per page. Court makes copy: $1.00

per page; same fee for self serve. Required to search: name, years to search. Criminal records on microfiche and index from 1900.

General Information: Public terminal goes back to 10 years. No juvenile, mental, adoption or sealed released. Will fax documents if all fees are prepaid. Certification fee: $1.00 per page. Payee: Court Clerk. Business checks accepted. Prepayment required.

LaGrange County

Circuit & Superior Court 105 N Detroit St, Courthouse, LaGrange, IN 46761; phone: 260-463-3442; fax: 260-463-2187; hours 8AM-4PM Tu-Fri, 8AM-5PM Mon (EST). *Felony, Misdemeanor, Civil, Eviction, Small Claims, Probate.*

Civil Records: Access: Phone, mail, in person. Visitors must perform in person searches themselves. No search fee. Court makes copy: $1.00 per page. Required to search: name, years to search. Civil cases indexed by defendant, plaintiff. Civil records on computer from 1990, on books from 1900. Mail turnaround time 1-2 days from 1/1/90; 30 days if prior to 1/1990.

Criminal Records: Access: Phone, mail, in person. Visitors must perform in person searches themselves. No search fee. Court makes copy: $1.00 per page. Required to search: name, years to search; also helpful: DOB, SSN. Criminal records on computer from 1990, on books from 1900. Mail turnaround time 1-2 days from 1/1/90; 30 days if prior to 1/1/90.

General Information: Public terminal goes back to 1991. No juvenile, mental, adoption or sealed released. Certification fee: $1.00 per cert. Payee: LaGrange County Clerk. Personal checks accepted. Prepayment required. SASE requested.

Lake County

Circuit & Superior Court 2293 N Main St, Courthouse, Crown Point, IN 46307; phone: 219-755-3460; criminal phone: 219-755-3477; civil phone: 219-755-3462; probate phone: 219-755-3468; criminal fax: 219-755-3781; civil fax: 219-755-3520; hours 8:30AM-4PM (CST). *Felony, Misdemeanor, Civil, Eviction, Small Claims, Probate.*

www.lakecountyin.org/portal/media-type/html/group/superior-court/page/default.psml

Note: Telephone of traffic, D-felonies, and misdemeanors is 219-755-3620.

Civil Records: Access: Mail, fax, in person, online. Both court and visitors may perform in person searches. No search fee. Court makes copy: $1.00 per page. Self serve copy fee: $1.00 per page. Required to search: name, years to search; also helpful: address. Civil cases indexed by defendant, plaintiff. Civil records go back to 1920s; on microfiche back to 1983; on computer back to 1990s. Online searching for County Clerk records is available at web page. Note: Fax requests must be on letterhead. Mail turnaround time 1 week.

Criminal Records: Access: Mail, in person, online. Both court and visitors may perform in person searches. Search fee: $7.00. Court makes copy: $1.00 per page. Required to search: name, years to search, DOB, SSN; also helpful: address. Criminal records go back to 1900s; on microfiche back to 1983; on computer back to 1990s. Online searching for County Clerk records available at website. Note: Search requests for background checks are forwarded to the County Bureau of Identification, 219-755-3316. Authorization required. Mail turnaround time 1 week.

General Information: Public terminal goes back to 1990. No juvenile, mental, adoption or sealed released. Will fax documents for $1.00 per page add'l fee. Certification fee: $1.00 per page. Payee: Lake County Clerk. Business checks accepted. Prepayment required.

Lawrence County

Circuit, Superior & County Court 31 Courthouse, 916 15th St, Rm 31, Bedford, IN 47421; phone: 812-275-7543; fax: 812-277-2024; hours 8:30AM-4:30PM (EST). *Felony, Misdemeanor, Civil, Eviction, Small Claims, Probate.*

Note: Superior Court I is located at 1410 I St, 812-275-3124. Superior Court II is located at 1420 I St, 812-275-4161. All small claims are filed in Superior II.

Civil Records: Access: In person only. Visitors must perform in person searches themselves. Court makes copy: $1.00 per page. Required to search: name, years to search. Civil cases indexed by plaintiff. Civil records on computer from 1987, on index from 1817.

Criminal Records: Access: In person only. Visitors must perform in person searches themselves. Court makes copy: $1.00 per page. Required to search: name, years to search, DOB; SSN helpful. Criminal records on computer from 1987, on index from 1817.

General Information: Public terminal goes back to 1987. No juvenile, mental, adoption or sealed released. Certification fee: $1.00 per cert. Payee: Lawrence County Clerk. Only cashiers checks and money orders accepted. Prepayment required.

Madison County

Circuit, Superior & County Court PO Box 1277, Anderson, IN 46015-1277; phone: 765-641-9443; probate phone: 765-641-9467; fax: 765-640-4203; hours 8AM-4PM (EST). *Felony, Misdemeanor, Civil, Eviction, Small Claims, Probate.*

http://madisoncty.com/courts/index.html

Civil Records: Access: In person only. Visitors must perform in person searches themselves. Court makes copy: $1.00 per page. Required to search: name, years to search. Civil cases indexed by defendant. Civil records on microfiche and archived from 1950, on index from 1900.

Criminal Records: Access: In person only. Visitors must perform in person searches themselves. Court makes copy: $1.00 per page. Required to search: name, years to search, signed release. Criminal records on microfiche and archived from 1950, on index from 1900.

General Information: Public terminal has only criminal records back to 1900. No juvenile, mental, adoption or sealed released. Certification fee: $1.00. Payee: County Clerk. Business checks accepted. Prepayment required.

Marion County

Circuit & Superior Court 200 E Washington St, Indianapolis, IN 46204; phone: 317-327-4740; criminal phone: 317-327-4733; civil phone: 317-327-4733; probate phone: 317-327-4718; fax: 317-327-3893; hours 8AM-4:30PM (EST). *Felony, Misdemeanor, Civil, Probate.*

www.indygov.org/clerk

Note: The Municipal Court of Marion County, once separate, is now part of Superior Court. All records were merged.

Civil Records: Access: Mail, online, in person. Both court and visitors may perform in person searches. No search fee. Court makes copy: $1.00 per page; same fee for self serve. Required to search: name, years to search. Civil cases indexed by defendant, plaintiff. Civil records on computer back to 1981, on microfiche, archived and on index from 1912. Small claims records are held by the township in which they were filed; the phone numbers are listed below. Perform an online name search for free at www.civicnet.net. There is a $7.50 charge assessed to view each Case Summary. Online records go back to 1991. Mail turnaround time 1-2 days.

Criminal Records: Access: Mail, online, in person. Both court and visitors may perform in person searches. Search fee: $10.00 per name. Court makes copy: $1.00 per page; same fee for self serve.

Required to search: name, years to search, DOB; also helpful: SSN. Criminal records on computer back to 1981, on microfiche, archived and on index from 1912. Small claims records are held by the township in which they were filed; the phone numbers are listed below. Access to online criminal records at https://www.civicnet.net/criminal/ requires a subscription or you may search at rate of $4.50 per name and pay with credit card. Criminal records go back to 1988. Mail turnaround time 1-2 days.
General Information: Public use terminal available. No juvenile, mental, adoption or sealed released. Certification fee: $1.00. Payee: County Clerk. Personal checks accepted. Prepayment required.

Marshall County

Circuit & Superior Court 1 & 2 211 W Madison St, Plymouth, IN 46563; phone: 574-936-8922; fax: 574-936-8893; hours 8AM-4PM (EST). *Felony, Misdemeanor, Civil, Eviction, Small Claims, Probate.*

Civil Records: Access: In person, online. Visitors must perform in person searches themselves. Court makes copy: $1.00 per page; same fee for self serve. Required to search: name, years to search; also helpful: address. Civil cases indexed by defendant, plaintiff. Civil records on computer from 1989, on microfiche, archived and on index from 1835. An online subscription service is at https://www.doxpop.com/prod/welcome.jsp/prod/welcome.jsp. Fees involved. Records date from 09/88. A limited free search of open cases is available.
Criminal Records: Access: In person, online. Visitors must perform in person searches themselves. Court makes copy: $1.00 per page; same fee for self serve. Required to search: name, years to search, signed release; also helpful: address, DOB, SSN. Criminal records on computer from 1989, on microfiche, archived and on index from 1835. Online access to criminal records is the same as civil.
General Information: Public terminal has criminal back to 1988 and civil back to 1991. No juvenile, mental, adoption or sealed released. Will fax specific case file requests for $5.00 first page;$1.00 each addl, not to exceed $10.00. Certification fee: $2.00. Payee: County Clerk. Business checks accepted. Prepayment required.

Martin County

Circuit Court PO Box 120 (111 Main St), Shoals, IN 47581; phone: 812-247-3651; fax: 812-247-2791; hours 8AM-4PM (EST). *Felony, Misdemeanor, Civil, Eviction, Small Claims, Probate.*

Civil Records: Access: Mail, fax, in person. Both court and visitors may perform in person searches. No search fee. Court makes copy: $1.00 per page. Required to search: name, years to search. Civil cases indexed by defendant, plaintiff. Civil records on index books. Mail turnaround time 4 days.
Criminal Records: Access: Mail, fax, in person. Both court and visitors may perform in person searches. No search fee. Court makes copy: $1.00 per page. Required to search: name, years to search, DOB or SSN. Criminal records on index books. Mail turnaround time 4 days.
General Information: No public access terminal. No juvenile, mental, adoption, or sealed records released. Will fax documents to local or toll free line. Certification fee: $2.00 per certification. Payee: County Clerk. Business checks accepted. Prepayment required.

Miami County

Circuit & Superior Court PO Box 184, Peru, IN 46970; phone: 765-472-3901; fax: 765-472-1778; hours 8AM-4PM (EST). *Felony, Misdemeanor, Civil, Eviction, Small Claims, Probate.*
Civil Records: Access: Fax, mail, in person, online. Both court and visitors may perform in person

searches. Search fee: $10.00 per name per page. Court makes copy: $1.00 per page; same fee for self serve. Required to search: name, years to search. Civil cases indexed by defendant, plaintiff. Civil records on computer back to 4/1998, archived from 1900s. Some records on docket books by case number and alpha. An online subscription service is at https://www.doxpop.com/prod/welcome.jsp. Fees involved. Records date from 03/98. A limited free search of open cases is available. Mail turnaround time 1-2 days.
Criminal Records: Access: Fax, mail, in person, online. Both court and visitors may perform in person searches. Search fee: $10.00 per name per page. Court makes copy: $1.00 per page; same fee for self serve. Required to search: name, years to search, DOB, SSN, signed release. Criminal records on computer back to 4/1998; archived from 1900s. Some records on docket books by case number and alpha. Online access to criminal records is the same as civil. Mail turnaround time 1-2 days.
General Information: Public use terminal available. No juvenile, mental, adoption, or sealed released. Will fax documents $1.00 per page; no fee for toll free or local call. Certification fee: $1.00. Payee: Miami County Clerk. Personal checks accepted. Prepayment required.

Monroe County

Circuit Court PO Box 547, Bloomington, IN 47402; phone: 812-349-2614; fax: 812-349-2610; hours 8AM-4PM (EST). *Felony, Misdemeanor, Civil, Eviction, Small Claims, Probate.*
www.co.monroe.in.us
Civil Records: Access: Mail, fax, in person, online. Both court and visitors may perform in person searches. No search fee. Court makes copy: $1.00 per page; same fee for self serve. Required to search: name, years to search. Civil cases indexed by defendant, plaintiff. Civil records on computer from 1993. Some records on docket books by case number and alpha. In the process of putting records on microfilm. An online subscription service is at https://www.doxpop.com/prod/welcome.jsp. Fees involved. Records date from 08/93. A limited free search of open cases is available. Mail turnaround time 48 hours.
Criminal Records: Access: Mail, fax, in person, online. Both court and visitors may perform in person searches. No search fee. Court makes copy: $1.00 per page; same fee for self serve. Required to search: name, years to search, DOB; also helpful: SSN. Criminal records on computer from 1993. Some records on docket books by case number and alpha. In the process of putting records on microfilm. Online access to criminal records is the same as civil. Mail turnaround time 48 hours.
General Information: Public terminal goes back to 8/1993. No juvenile, mental, adoption or sealed released. Fee to fax documents is $1.00 per page. Certification fee: $1.00 per page. Payee: Monroe County Clerk. Personal checks accepted. Prepayment required.

Montgomery County

Circuit, Superior & County Court PO Box 768, Crawfordsville, IN 47933; phone: 765-364-6430; fax: 765-364-6355; hours 8:30AM-4:30PM (EST). *Felony, Misdemeanor, Civil, Eviction, Small Claims, Probate.*
www.montgomeryco.net/
Note: Probate is a separate index at this same address.
Civil Records: Access: Phone, fax, mail, in person, online. Both court and visitors may perform in person searches. No search fee. Court makes copy: $1.00 per page; same fee for self serve. Required to search: name, years to search. Civil cases indexed by defendant, plaintiff. Civil records on computer from 1990, some on microfiche and docket books, and archived from 1800s. An online subscription service is at https://www.doxpop.com/prod/welcome.jsp. Fees involved. Records date from 01/90. A limited free search of open cases is available. Note:

Indicate type(s) of cases sought in mail search request. Mail turnaround time 1 week.
Criminal Records: Access: Mail, fax, in person, online. Both court and visitors may perform in person searches. No search fee. Court makes copy: $1.00 per page; same fee for self serve. Required to search: name, years to search, DOB; also helpful: SSN. Criminal records on computer from 1990, some on microfiche and docket books, and archived from 1800s. Online access to criminal records is the same as civil. Mail turnaround time 1 week.
General Information: Public terminal goes back to 1990. No juvenile, mental, adoption or sealed released. Will fax documents $1.00 per page plus $3.25 fax fee. Certification fee: $2.00 per page includes copy fee. Payee: Montgomery County Clerk. Business checks accepted. Prepayment and SASE required.

Morgan County

Circuit & Superior Court PO Box 1556, Martinsville, IN 46151; phone: 765-342-1025; fax: 765-342-1111; hours 8AM-4PM (EST). *Felony, Misdemeanor, Civil, Eviction, Small Claims, Probate.*
Civil Records: Access: In person only. Visitors must perform in person searches themselves. Court makes copy: $.05 per page. Required to search: name, years to search. Civil cases indexed by defendant, plaintiff. Civil records archived from 1970; on computer back to 1993. Some records on index cards. In some instances, limited information is given over the phone if the docket number is known.
Criminal Records: Access: In person only. Visitors must perform in person searches themselves. Court makes copy: $.05 per page. Required to search: name, years to search, DOB; SSN helpful, signed release. Criminal records archived from 1970; on microfilm 1992-95, on computer back to 1993.
General Information: Public terminal goes back to 1995. No juvenile, mental, adoption or sealed released. Certification fee: $1.00 per page. Payee: Morgan County Clerk. Personal checks accepted; no credit cards. Prepayment required.

Newton County

Circuit & Superior Court PO Box 49, Kentland, IN 47951; phone: 219-474-6081; hours 8AM-4PM (CST). *Felony, Misdemeanor, Civil, Eviction, Small Claims, Probate.*
Civil Records: Access: Mail, in person. Both court and visitors may perform in person searches. Search fee: $3.00 per name. Court makes copy: $.25 per page; same fee for self serve. Required to search: name, years to search. Civil cases indexed by defendant, plaintiff. Civil records on index from 1937, partial on microfiche; on computer back to 1996. Mail turnaround time 1-2 weeks.
Criminal Records: Access: Mail, in person. Both court and visitors may perform in person searches. Search fee: $3.00 per name. Court makes copy: $.25 per page; same fee for self serve. Required to search: name, years to search, DOB, signed release; also helpful: SSN. Criminal records on index from 1937, partial on microfiche; on computer back to 1996. Mail turnaround time 1-2 weeks.
General Information: Public terminal goes back to 1995. No juvenile, mental, adoption or sealed records released. Will fax documents to local or toll free line. Certification fee: $1.25. Payee: Clerk of Newton Circuit Court. Business checks accepted. Prepayment and SASE required.

Noble County

Circuit, Superior I & Superior II Court 101 N Orange St, Albion, IN 46701; phone: 260-636-2736; fax: 260-636-4000; hours 8AM-4PM (EST). *Felony, Misdemeanor, Civil, Eviction, Small Claims, Probate.*
Note: Clerk's office manages records for all three courts. Circuit Court phone is 260-636-2128.

Civil Records: Access: In person only. Visitors must perform in person searches themselves. Court makes copy: $1.00 per page. Required to search: name, years to search. Civil cases indexed by defendant, plaintiff. Civil records on index cards and docket books to 1856; on computer back to 1992. Court will accept genealogy search requests by mail.

Criminal Records: Access: Fax, mail, in person. Visitors must perform in person searches themselves. Court makes copy: $1.00 per page. Required to search: name, years to search; also helpful: DOB, SSN. Criminal records on index cards and docket books to 1856; on computer back to 1992. Criminal record searches are 10-year only. Mail turnaround time 1 week.

General Information: Public terminal goes back to 1992. (Court will assist in instructing users for genealogy purposes.) No juvenile, mental, adoption or sealed released. Will not fax documents. Certification fee: $1.00 per certification. Payee: Noble County Clerk. No personal checks accepted. Prepayment required.

Ohio County

Circuit & Superior Court PO Box 185, Rising Sun, IN 47040; phone: 812-438-2610; fax: 812-438-1215; hours 9AM-4PM M,T,Th,F 9AM-N Sat (EST). *Felony, Misdemeanor, Civil, Eviction, Small Claims, Probate.*

Civil Records: Access: In person only. Both court and visitors may perform in person searches. No search fee. Court makes copy: $1.00 per page. Required to search: name, years to search. Civil cases indexed by defendant, plaintiff. Civil records archived from 1844; on computer back to 8/1999.

Criminal Records: Access: In person only. Visitors must perform in person searches themselves. Court makes copy: $1.00 per page. Required to search: name, years to search. Criminal records on computer back to 8/1999.

General Information: Public use terminal available. No juvenile, mental, adoption or sealed released. Fee to fax documents is $3.00 1st page, $1.00 each add'l paid in advance. Certification fee: $2.00. Payee: Ohio County Clerk. Prepayment required.

Orange County

Circuit Court Courthouse, Court St, Paoli, IN 47454; phone: 812-723-2649; fax: 812-723-0239; hours 8AM-4PM (EST). *Felony, Civil, Eviction, Small Claims, Probate.*

Note: Probate is a separate index at this same address. See County Superior Court for misdemeanors and Class D (minor) felonies.

Civil Records: Access: Mail, fax, in person. Both court and visitors may perform in person searches. No search fee. Court makes copy: $1.00 per page. Self serve copy fee: $.10 per page. Required to search: name, years to search. Civil cases indexed by defendant, plaintiff. Civil records archived from 1874. Some records on docket books. Mail turnaround time 2 weeks.

Criminal Records: Access: Mail, fax, in person. Both court and visitors may perform in person searches. No search fee. Court makes copy: $1.00 per page. Self serve copy fee: $.10 per page. Required to search: name, years to search. Criminal records archived from 1874. Some records on docket books. Mail turnaround time 2 weeks.

General Information: No public access terminal. No juvenile, mental, adoption or sealed released. Will fax documents. Certification fee: $1.00 per document. Payee: Orange Circuit Clerk. Only cashiers checks and money orders accepted. Prepayment and SASE required.

County Superior Court 205 E Main St, Paoli, IN 47454; phone: 812-723-3322; fax: 812-723-5839; hours 8AM-N, 1-4PM (EST). *Felony (Class D), Misdemeanor.*

Criminal Records: Access: In person. Both court and visitors may perform in person searches. No

search fee. Court makes copy: $1.00 per page. Required to search: name, years to search. Criminal records archived from 1874. Some records on docket books. Note: Direct mail search requests to the Circuit and County Court.

General Information: No public access terminal. No juvenile, mental, adoption or sealed released. Certification fee: $1.00 per doc. Only cashiers checks and money orders accepted. Prepayment required.

Owen County

Circuit Court PO Box 146, Courthouse, Spencer, IN 47460; phone: 812-829-5015; fax: 812-829-5147; 8AM-4PM (EST). *Felony, Misdemeanor, Civil, Eviction, Small Claims, Probate.*

Civil Records: Access: In person only. Visitors must perform in person searches themselves. Court makes copy: $1.00 per page; same fee for self serve. Required to search: name, years to search. Civil cases indexed by defendant, plaintiff. Civil records archived from 1800s. Some records on docket books.

Criminal Records: Access: In person only. Visitors must perform in person searches themselves. Court makes copy: $1.00 per page; same fee for self serve. Required to search: name, years to search. Criminal records archived from 1800s. Some records on docket books.

General Information: No public access terminal. No juvenile, mental, adoption or sealed records released. Certification fee: $1.00 per page. Payee: Owen County Clerk. Business checks accepted. Prepayment required.

Parke County

Circuit Court 116 W High St, Rm 204, Rockville, IN 47872; phone: 765-569-5132; probate phone: 765-569-3521; fax: 765-569-4222; hours 8AM-4PM (EST). *Felony, Misdemeanor, Civil, Eviction, Small Claims, Probate.*

Civil Records: Access: In person only. Visitors must perform in person searches themselves. Self serve copy fee: $1.00 per page. Required to search: name, years to search. Civil cases indexed by defendant, plaintiff. Civil records archived from 1880s. Some records on docket books.

Criminal Records: Access: In person only. Visitors must perform in person searches themselves. Self serve copy fee: $1.00 per page. Required to search: name, years to search. Criminal records archived from 1880s. Some records on docket books.

General Information: No public access terminal. No juvenile, mental, adoption or sealed released. Certification fee: $2.00. Payee: Parke County Clerk. Personal checks not accepted. Prepayment required.

Perry County

Circuit Court 2219 Payne St, #219, Courthouse, Tell City, IN 47586; phone: 812-547-3741; hours 8AM-4PM (EST). *Felony, Misdemeanor, Civil, Eviction, Small Claims, Probate.*

Civil Records: Access: In person only. Both court and visitors may perform in person searches. No search fee. Court makes copy: $.50 per page. Required to search: name, years to search. Civil cases indexed by defendant, plaintiff. Civil records archived from 1900s. Some records on dockets.

Criminal Records: Access: In person only. Both court and visitors may perform in person searches. No search fee. Court makes copy: $.50 per page. Required to search: name, years to search. Criminal records archived from 1900s. Some records on dockets.

General Information: Public terminal goes back to 1997. No juvenile, mental, adoption or sealed released. Certification fee: $1.00 per cert. Payee: Perry County Clerk. Business checks accepted. Prepayment required.

Pike County

Circuit Court PO Box 407, Petersburg, IN 47567; phone: 812-354-6026; probate phone: 812-354-6025; fax: 812-354-3552; probate fax: 812-354-6369; 8AM-4PM (EST). *Felony, Misdemeanor, Civil, Eviction, Small Claims, Probate.*

Civil Records: Access: In person only. Both court and visitors may perform in person searches. No search fee. Court makes copy: $1.00 per page; same fee for self serve. Required to search: name, years to search. Civil cases indexed by defendant, plaintiff. Civil records archived from 1817. Some records on docket books and index file; on computer since 7/99.

Criminal Records: Access: In person only. Both court and visitors may perform in person searches. No search fee. Court makes copy: $1.00 per page; same fee for self serve. Required to search: name, years to search, DOB. Criminal records archived from 1817. Some records on docket books and index file; on computer since 7/99.

General Information: No public access terminal. No juvenile, mental, adoption or sealed released. Certification fee: $1.00 per cert. Payee: Pike County Clerk. Only cashiers checks and money orders accepted. Prepayment required.

Porter County

Circuit Court Records Division, Courthouse, 16 E Lincolnway, Rm 217, Valparaiso, IN 46383-5659; phone: 219-465-3453; fax: 219-465-3592; hours 8:30AM-4:30PM (CST). *Felony, Misdemeanor, Civil, Eviction, Small Claims, Probate.*

www.porterco.org/

Note: Eviction and small claims are in Rm 211, 219-465-3413.

Civil Records: Access: Mail, in person. Both court and visitors may perform in person searches. No search fee. Court makes copy: $1.00 per page; same fee for self serve. Required to search: name, years to search. Civil cases indexed by defendant, plaintiff. Civil records on computer index from 1990. Circuit Court records kept from 1844, Superior Court records from 1895. Probate records from Circuit Court kept from 1853, Superior Court from 1900. Mail turnaround time 1-2 weeks.

Criminal Records: Access: Mail, in person. Both court and visitors may perform in person searches. No search fee. Court makes copy: $1.00 per page; same fee for self serve. Required to search: name, years to search. Criminal records on computer index since 1990. Circuit Court criminal records kept from 1877, Superior Court from 1895. Mail turnaround time 1-2 weeks.

General Information: Public terminal goes back to 2000. No juvenile, mental, adoption or sealed released. Certification fee: $1.00 per document. Payee: Porter County Clerk. Only cashiers checks and money orders accepted. Prepayment and SASE required.

Superior Court 3560 Willow Creek Dr, Portage, IN 46368; phone: 219-759-2501; 8:30AM-4:30PM (CST). *Misdemeanor, Civil, Small Claims, Probate.*

Civil Records: Access: Mail, in person. Both court and visitors may perform in person searches. No search fee. Court makes copy: $2.00 per page. Required to search: name, years to search. Civil cases indexed by defendant, plaintiff. Civil records on computer since 1991; prior records on manual index. Mail turnaround time 1 week.

Criminal Records: Access: Mail, in person. Both court and visitors may perform in person searches. No search fee. Court makes copy: $2.00 per page. Required to search: name, years to search; also helpful: DOB, SSN. Criminal records on computer since 1991; prior records on manual index. Mail turnaround time 1 week.

General Information: Public terminal goes back to 1997. No juvenile, mental, adoption or sealed records released. Fee to fax documents is $.79 per page. Certification fee: $1.00 per cert. Payee: Porter County Clerk. Only cashiers checks and money orders accepted. Prepayment required.

Posey County

Circuit & Superior Court PO Box 606, 300 Main St, Mount Vernon, IN 47620-0606; phone: 812-838-1306; criminal phone: 812-838-8367; civil phone: 812-838-8368; probate phone: 812-838-1306; fax: 812-838-1307; hours 8AM-4PM (CST). *Felony, Misdemeanor, Civil, Eviction, Small Claims, Probate.*

http://members.sigecom.net/pcc

Civil Records: Access: In person only. Visitors must perform in person searches themselves. Court makes copy: $1.00 per page. Required to search: name, years to search; also helpful: address. Civil cases indexed by defendant, plaintiff. Civil records on computer since 8/88, prior on docket books.

Criminal Records: Access: In person only. Visitors must perform in person searches themselves. Court makes copy: $1.00 per page. Required to search: name, years to search; also helpful: DOB, SSN. Criminal records on computer since 8/88, prior on docket books.

General Information: Public use terminal available. (Available in Superior Court.) No juvenile, mental, adoption or sealed released. Certification fee: $1.00. Payee: Posey County Clerk. Only cashiers checks and money orders accepted. Prepayment required.

Pulaski County

Circuit Court 112 E Main, Rm 230, Winamac, IN 46996; phone: 574-946-3313; fax: 574-946-4953; hours 8AM-4PM (EST). *Felony, Civil, Probate.*

Note: Civil suits, eviction and small claims are managed by the Superior Court.

Civil Records: Access: In person only. Visitors must perform in person searches themselves. Court makes copy: $.50 per page. Required to search: name, years to search. Civil cases indexed by defendant. Civil records archived from 1850s. Some records on docket books. On computer back to 2000.

Criminal Records: Access: In person only. Visitors must perform in person searches themselves. Court makes copy: $.50 per page. Required to search: name, years to search; SSN helpful. Criminal records archived from 1850s. Some records on docket books. On computer back to 1998.

General Information: Public use terminal available. No juvenile, mental, adoption or sealed records released. Certification fee: $2.00 per cert. Payee: Pulaski County Clerk. Only cashiers checks and money orders accepted. Prepayment required.

Superior Court 110 E Meridian, Winamac, IN 46996; phone: 574-946-3371; fax: 574-946-3573; hours 8AM-4PM (EST). *Misdemeanor, Civil, Eviction, Small Claims, Traffic.*

Note: Add'l current civil records can be found at the Circuit Court. The advantage this court offers is that it will do limited phone index searches and the Circuit Court will not.

Civil Records: Access: Phone, in person. Visitors must perform in person searches themselves. Search fee: None. Court makes copy: $.50 per page. Required to search: name, years to search. Civil cases indexed by defendant. Most records go back a maximum of two years; older records found at Circuit Court Clerk office.

Criminal Records: Access: Phone, in person. No criminal searching at this court. Search fee: None. Court makes copy: $.50 per page. Required to search: Name only. Misdemeanor records go back a maximum of two years; older records found at Circuit Court Clerk office. Clerk will do short, usually single name searches for no fee over the phone.

General Information: Public terminal goes back to 1996. No juvenile, mental, adoption or sealed records released. Certification fee: $2.00. Payee: Pulaski County. Only cashiers checks and money orders accepted. Prepayment required.

Putnam County

Circuit & Superior Court PO Box 546, Greencastle, IN 46135; phone: 765-653-2648; probate phone: 765-653-2649; fax: 765-653-8405; hours 8AM-4PM (EST). *Felony, Misdemeanor, Civil, Eviction, Small Claims, Probate.*

Civil Records: Access: Mail, in person, online. Visitors must perform in person searches themselves. Court makes copy: $1.00 per page. Required to search: name, years to search. Civil cases indexed by defendant, plaintiff. Civil records on index books from 1991, archived from 1800s. Some records on docket books. An online subscription service is at https://www.doxpop.com/prod/welcome.jsp. Fees involved. Records date from 01/92. A limited free search of open cases is available.

Criminal Records: Access: In person, online. Visitors must perform in person searches themselves. Court makes copy: $1.00 per page. Required to search: name, years to search; also helpful: DOB, SSN. Criminal records on index books from 1991, archived from 1800s. Some records on docket books. Online access to criminal records is the same as civil. Mail turnaround time 1 week.

General Information: Public terminal goes back to 1998 Circuit; 1993 Superior. No juvenile, mental, adoption or sealed released. Certification fee: $1.00. Payee: Putnam County Clerk. Business checks accepted. Prepayment required.

Randolph County

Circuit & Superior Court PO Box 230 Courthouse, Winchester, IN 47394-0230; phone: 765-584-7070 X231; fax: 765-584-2958; hours 8AM-4PM (EST). *Felony, Misdemeanor, Civil, Eviction, Small Claims, Probate.*

Civil Records: Access: Fax, mail, in person, online. Visitors must perform in person searches themselves. No search fee. Court makes copy: $1.00 per page; same fee for self serve. Required to search: name, years to search. Civil cases indexed by defendant, plaintiff. Civil records archived from early 1800s, computerized from 1994. Records on docket books and microfiche. An online subscription service is at https://www.doxpop.com/prod/welcome.jsp. Fees involved. Records date from 03/94. A limited free search of open cases is available. Mail turnaround time 3 days.

Criminal Records: Access: Fax, mail, in person, online. Visitors must perform in person searches themselves. No search fee. Court makes copy: $1.00 per page; same fee for self serve. Required to search: name, years to search. Criminal records archived from early 1800s, computerized since 1994. Records on docket books and microfiche. Online access to criminal records is the same as civil. Mail turnaround time 3 days.

General Information: Public terminal goes back to 6/1994. No juvenile, mental, adoption or sealed released. Will fax documents $4.00 for 1st page, $.75 each add'l. Certification fee: $1.00. Payee: Randolph County Clerk. Checks and money orders accepted. Prepayment and SASE required.

Ripley County

Circuit Court PO Box 177, Versailles, IN 47042; phone: 812-689-6115; hours 8AM-4PM (EST). *Felony, Misdemeanor, Civil, Eviction, Small Claims, Probate.*

Civil Records: Access: Phone, mail, in person. Both court and visitors may perform in person searches. No search fee. Court makes copy: $1.00 per page. Required to search: name, years to search. Civil cases indexed by defendant, plaintiff. Civil records on computer since 1993, archived from 1800s. Some records on docket books. Mail turnaround time 1 week.

Criminal Records: Access: Mail, in person. Both court and visitors may perform in person searches. No search fee. Court makes copy: $1.00 per page. Required to search: name, years to search, DOB, signed release; also helpful: SSN. Criminal records on computer since 1993, archived from 1800s. Some records on docket books. Mail turnaround time 1 week.

General Information: Public use terminal available. No juvenile, mental, adoption or sealed records released. Will fax documents for $1.00 per page. Payments must be mailed in first. Certification fee: $3.00. Payee: Clerk of Ripley Circuit Court. Personal checks accepted. Prepayment required.

Rush County

Circuit & Superior Court PO Box 429, Rushville, IN 46173; phone: 765-932-2086; fax: 765-932-4165; hours 8AM-4PM (EST). *Felony, Misdemeanor, Civil, Eviction, Small Claims, Probate.*

Note: This office will not conduct general searches, but will pull files if the specific case number is given.

Civil Records: Access: In person only. Visitors must perform in person searches themselves. Court makes copy: $1.00 per page; same fee for self serve. Required to search: name, years to search. Civil cases indexed by defendant, plaintiff. Civil records archived from 1822. Some records on docket books.

Criminal Records: Access: In person only. Visitors must perform in person searches themselves. Court makes copy: $1.00 per page; same fee for self serve. Required to search: name, years to search, DOB; SSN, cause number helpful. Criminal records archived from 1822. Some records on docket books. Court will only search the status of an open case, and you need to provide the case number of it.

General Information: No public access terminal. No juvenile, mental, adoption or sealed records released. Certification fee: $1.00 per unit. Payee: Rush County Clerk. Business checks accepted. Prepayment required.

Scott County

Circuit & Superior Court 1 E McClain Ave, #120, Scottsburg, IN 47170; phone: 812-752-8420; fax: 812-752-5459; hours 8:30AM-4:30PM (EST). *Felony, Misdemeanor, Civil, Eviction, Small Claims, Probate.*

Civil Records: Access: In person only. Visitors must perform in person searches themselves. Court makes copy: $1.00 per page. Required to search: name, years to search; also helpful: address. Civil cases indexed by defendant, plaintiff. Civil records on computer from 2/90, on docket books from 1970.

Criminal Records: Access: In person only. Visitors must perform in person searches themselves. Court makes copy: $1.00 per page. Required to search: name, years to search; also helpful: DOB, SSN. Criminal records on computer from 2/90, on docket books from 1970.

General Information: Public terminal goes back to 1990. No juvenile, mental, adoption or sealed released. Certification fee: $2.00 per cert. Payee: Scott County Clerk. Business checks accepted. Prepayment required.

Shelby County

Circuit & Superior Court 407 S Harrison St, Shelbyville, IN 46176; phone: 317-392-6350; hours 8AM-4PM (EST). *Felony, Misdemeanor, Civil, Eviction, Small Claims, Probate.*

Civil Records: Access: In person only. Visitors must perform in person searches themselves. Court makes copy: $1.00 per page. Required to search: name, years to search. Civil cases indexed by defendant, plaintiff. Civil records on computer since 7/95.

Criminal Records: Access: In person only. Visitors must perform in person searches themselves. Court makes copy: $1.00 per page. Required to search: name, years to search. Criminal records on computer since 7/95.

General Information: Public use terminal available. No juvenile, mental, adoption or sealed released. Certification fee: $1.00. Payee: Clerk of Court. Personal checks not accepted. Prepayment required.

Spencer County

Circuit Court PO Box 12, Rockport, IN 47635; phone: 812-649-6027; fax: 812-649-6030; hours 8AM-4PM (CST). *Felony, Misdemeanor, Civil, Eviction, Small Claims, Probate.*
Note: Probate is a separate index at this same address
Civil Records: Access: In person, online. Visitors must perform in person searches themselves. Court makes copy: $1.00 per page; same fee for self serve. Required to search: name, years to search. Civil cases indexed by defendant, plaintiff. Civil records archived from early 1900s. Some records on docket books. Child support cases on computer. Starting 2/02 all new cases are computerized. Fee access to civil records back to 2002 is by subscription at www.doxpop.com/prod/welcome.jsp, free access limited to only current open cases.
Criminal Records: Access: In person, online. Visitors must perform in person searches themselves. Court makes copy: $1.00 per page; same fee for self serve. Required to search: name, years to search. Criminal records archived from early 1900s. Some records on docket books. Starting 2/02 all new cases are computerized. Fee access to criminal records back to 2002 is by subscription at www.doxpop.com/prod/welcome.jsp; free access limited to only current open cases.
General Information: Public terminal goes back to 2002. No juvenile, mental, adoption or sealed released. Will fax specific case file requests for no fee once all other fees are paid. Certification fee: $1.00 per document. Payee: Spencer Circuit Court. Only cashiers checks and money orders accepted. Prepayment required.

St. Joseph County

Circuit & Superior Court 101 S Main St, South Bend, IN 46601; phone: 574-235-9635; fax: 574-235-9838; 8AM-4:30PM EST *Felony, Misd., Civil, Eviction, Small Claims, Probate.*
Civil Records: Access: Mail, in person. Both court and visitors may perform in person searches. No search fee. Court makes copy: $.05 per page. Required to search: name, years to search. Civil cases indexed by defendant, plaintiff. Civil records on general index from 1962, computerized since 1992. Mail turnaround time within 48 hours.
Criminal Records: Access: In person only. Visitors must perform in person searches themselves. Court makes copy: $.05 per page. Required to search: name, years to search; also helpful: address, DOB, SSN. Criminal records on general index from 1962, computerized since 1984.
General Information: Public use terminal available. No juvenile, mental, adoption or sealed released. Certification fee: $1.00. Payee: St Joseph County Clerk. Business checks accepted. Prepayment and SASE required.

Starke County

Circuit Court PO Box 395, Courthouse, Knox, IN 46534; phone: 574-772-9128; probate phone: 574-772-9162; fax: 574-772-9169; hours 8:30AM-4PM (CST). *Felony, Misdemeanor, Civil, Eviction, Small Claims, Probate.*
Civil Records: Access: In person only. Both court and visitors may perform in person searches. Court makes copy: $1.00 per page. Required to search: name, years to search. Civil cases indexed by defendant, plaintiff. Civil records archived from 1850s. Some records on docket books.
Criminal Records: Access: In person only. Both court and visitors may perform in person searches. Court makes copy: $1.00 per page. Required to search: name, years to search, DOB; SSN helpful. Criminal records archived from 1850s. Some records on docket books.
General Information: No public access terminal. No juvenile, mental, adoption or sealed released. Certification fee: $2.00. Payee: Clerk of Stark Circuit Court. Business checks accepted. Prepayment required.

Steuben County

Circuit & Superior Court Courthouse, 55 S Public Square, Angola, IN 46703; phone: 260-668-1000 X2240; hours 8AM-4:30PM (EST). *Felony, Misdemeanor, Civil, Eviction, Small Claims, Probate.*
Civil Records: Access: In person only. Visitors must perform in person searches themselves. Court makes copy: $1.00 per page. Required to search: name, years to search. Civil cases indexed by defendant, plaintiff. Civil records archived from 1800s. Some records on docket books.
Criminal Records: Access: In person only. Visitors must perform in person searches themselves. Court makes copy: $1.00 per page. Required to search: name, years to search. Criminal records archived from 1800s, computerized since 6/94. Some records on docket books.
General Information: Public use terminal available. No juvenile, mental, adoption, some probate, or sealed released. Certification fee: $2.00. Payee: Steuben County Clerk. Only cashiers checks and money orders accepted. Prepayment required.

Sullivan County

Circuit & Superior Court Courthouse, Rm 304, PO Box 370, Sullivan, IN 47882-0370; phone: 812-268-4657; probate phone: 812-268-4411; fax: 812-268-4870; hours 8AM-4PM (EST). *Felony, Misdemeanor, Civil, Eviction, Small Claims, Probate.*
Civil Records: Access: In person, online. Visitors must perform in person searches themselves. Court makes copy: $1.00 per page; same fee for self serve. Required to search: name, years to search; also helpful: address. Civil cases indexed by defendant, plaintiff. Civil records on docket books or general index from late 1850's; computerized from 1999. An online subscription service is at https://www.doxpop.com/prod/welcome.jsp. Fees involved. Records date from 6/98. A limited free search of open cases is available.
Criminal Records: Access: In person, online. Visitors must perform in person searches themselves. Court makes copy: $1.00 per page; same fee for self serve. Required to search: name, years to search, DOB, signed release; also helpful: address, SSN. Criminal records on docket books or general index from late 1850's; computerized from 1999. Online access to criminal records is same as civil.
General Information: Public terminal goes back to 1991. No juvenile, mental, adoption or sealed released. Certification fee: $1.00 per page. Payee: Sullivan County. No personal checks accepted; business check okay. No credit cards. Prepayment required.

Switzerland County

Circuit & Superior Court Courthouse, 212 W Main St, Vevay, IN 47043; phone: 812-427-3175; fax: 812-427-2017; hours 8AM-3:30PM M-W & F; 8AM-N Th (EST). *Felony, Misdemeanor, Civil, Eviction, Small Claims, Probate.*
Civil Records: Access: in person only. Visitors must perform in person searches themselves. Court makes copy: first 4 pages free, $1.00 for 5th page, then $.25 each add'l; same fee for self serve. Required to search: name, years to search, DOB. Civil cases indexed by defendant, plaintiff. Civil records archived from 1900s. All records on docket books or general index.
Criminal Records: Access: In person only. Visitors must perform in person searches themselves. Court makes copy: first 4 pages free, $1.00 for 5th page, then $.25 each add'l; same fee for self serve. Required to search: name, years to search, DOB. Criminal records archived from 1900s. All records on docket books or general index.
General Information: Public use terminal available. No juvenile, mental, adoption or sealed records released. Certification fee: $1.00 per page. Payee:

Switzerland County Clerk. Only cash, cashiers checks and money orders accepted.

Tippecanoe County

Circuit, Superior & County Court PO Box 1665, Lafayette, IN 47902; phone: 765-423-9326; probate phone: 765-423-9343; fax: 765-423-9194; hours 8AM-4:30PM (EST). *Felony, Misdemeanor, Civil, Eviction, Small Claims, Probate.*
www.tippecanoe.in.gov
Civil Records: Access: In person, mail, online. Visitors must perform in person searches themselves. Court makes copy: $1.00 per page. Self serve copy fee: $.05 per page. Required to search: name, years to search. Civil cases indexed by defendant, plaintiff. Civil records on computer from 1987, on microfiche from 1900. Some records on index and docket books. Online access to court records through CourtView are free online at www.tippecanoe.in.gov/court/pa.htm.
Criminal Records: Access: In person, mail, online. Visitors must perform in person searches themselves. Court makes copy: $1.00 per page. Self serve copy fee: $.05 per page. Required to search: name, years to search; also helpful: DOB, SSN, sex, signed release. Criminal records on computer from 1987, on microfiche from 1900. Some records on index and docket books. Online access to criminal records is the same as civil.
General Information: Public terminal goes back to mid 1980s. No juvenile, mental, adoption or sealed released. Will fax documents for $2.00 per page. Certification fee: $1.00. Payee: Tippecanoe County Clerk. Business checks accepted. Prepayment required.

Tipton County

Circuit Court Tipton County Courthouse, Tipton, IN 46072; phone: 765-675-2795; fax: 765-675-4103; hours 8AM-4PM M,T,Th, (till noon W); 8AM-5PM F (EST). *Felony, Misdemeanor, Civil, Eviction, Small Claims, Probate.*
Civil Records: Access: In person only. Visitors must perform in person searches themselves. Court makes copy: $1.00 per page; same fee for self serve. Required to search: name, years to search. Civil cases indexed by defendant, plaintiff. Civil records on card file and archived from 1930s.
Criminal Records: Access: In person only. Visitors must perform in person searches themselves. Court makes copy: $1.00 per page; same fee for self serve. Required to search: name, years to search. Criminal records on card file and archived from 1930s.
General Information: No public access terminal. No juvenile, mental, adoption or sealed released. Certification fee: $1.00. Payee: Tipton County Clerk. Personal checks accepted. Prepayment required.

Union County

Circuit Court 26 W Union St, Liberty, IN 47353; phone: 765-458-6121; fax: 765-458-5263; hours 8AM-4PM (EST). *Felony, Misdemeanor, Civil, Eviction, Small Claims, Probate.*
Civil Records: Access: In person only. Both court and visitors may perform in person searches. No search fee. Court makes copy: $.25 per page. Required to search: name, years to search. Civil cases indexed by defendant, plaintiff. Civil records archived from 1821. Some records on docket books or entry books.
Criminal Records: Access: In person only. Both court and visitors may perform in person searches. Search fee: None. Court makes copy: $.25 per page. Required to search: name, years to search; also helpful: DOB, SSN. Criminal records archived from 1821. Some records on docket books or entry books.
General Information: No public access terminal. No juvenile, mental, adoption or sealed records released. Certification fee: $2.00 per cert. Payee: Union County Clerk. Only cashiers checks and money orders accepted. Prepayment required.

Vanderburgh County

Circuit & Superior Court PO Box 3356, Civic Ctr Courts Bldg - Rm 216, Evansville, IN 47732-3356; phone: 812-435-5160; criminal phone: 812-435-5169; civil phone: 812-435-5722; probate phone: 812-435-5377; fax: 812-435-5849; hours 7:30AM-4:30PM (CST). *Felony, Misdemeanor, Civil, Eviction, Small Claims, Probate.*
www.vanderburghgov.org/home/index.asp?page=64
Civil Records: Access: In person only. Visitors must perform in person searches themselves. Court makes copy: $1.00 per page. Required to search: name, years to search. Civil cases indexed by defendant, plaintiff. Civil records on computer back to 1991, archived from 1900s. Some records on index books.
Criminal Records: Access: In person only. Visitors must perform in person searches themselves. Court makes copy: $1.00 per page. Required to search: name, years to search, DOB, SSN. Criminal records on computer back to 1991, archived from 1900s. Some records on index books.
General Information: Public terminal goes back to 1991. (Terminal closes at 4PM.) No juvenile, mental, adoption or sealed released. Certification fee: $1.00. Payee: Vanderburgh County Clerk. Business checks accepted. Prepayment required.

Vermillion County

Circuit Court PO Box 10, Newport, IN 47966-0010; phone: 765-492-3500; fax: 765-492-5001; hours 8AM-4PM (EST). *Felony, Misdemeanor, Civil, Eviction, Small Claims, Probate.*
Civil Records: Access: mail, in person. Both court and visitors may perform in person searches. No search fee. Court makes copy: $1.00 per page. Required to search: name. Civil cases indexed by defendant, plaintiff. Records on computer go back to 1994; archived from 1824. Some records on docket books.
Criminal Records: Access: In person only. Both court and visitors may perform in person searches. No search fee. Court makes copy: $1.00 per page. Required to search: name. Records on computer go back to 1994; archived from 1825. Some records on docket books.
General Information: No public access terminal. No juvenile, mental, adoption or sealed released. Certification fee: $2.00. Payee: Vermillion County Clerk. Business checks accepted. Prepayment required.

Vigo County

Circuit Court PO Box 8449, Courthouse, 2nd Fl, Terre Haute, IN 47807-8449; phone: 812-462-3211; hours 8AM-4PM (EST). *Felony, Misdemeanor, Civil, Eviction, Small Claims, Probate.*
http://vigocountyin.com
Civil Records: Access: In person, online. Visitors must perform in person searches themselves. Court makes copy: $1.00 per page. Required to search: name, years to search. Civil cases indexed by defendant, plaintiff. Civil records on index books; on computer back to 8/1996. An online subscription service is at https://www.doxpop.com/prod/welcome.jsp. Fees involved. Records date from 04/96. A limited free search of open cases is available.
Criminal Records: Access: In person, online. Visitors must perform in person searches themselves. No search fee. Court makes copy: $1.00 per page. Required to search: name, years to search; also helpful: DOB, SSN. Criminal records on index books; on computer back to 8/1996. Online access to criminal records is the same as civil.
General Information: Public terminal goes back to 1996. No juvenile, mental, adoption or sealed released. Certification fee: $1.00 per cert. Payee: Vigo County Clerk. Only cashiers checks and money orders accepted. No credit cards. Prepayment required.

Wabash County

Circuit & Superior Court 69 W Hill St, Wabash, IN 46992; phone: 260-563-0661 X230; fax: 260-569-1352; hours 8AM-4PM (EST). *Felony, Misdemeanor, Civil, Eviction, Small Claims, Probate.*
Civil Records: Access: In person, online. Visitors must perform in person searches themselves. Court makes copy: $1.00 per page. Required to search: name, years to search. Civil cases indexed by defendant, plaintiff. Civil records archived from 1800s; on computer since 1989. Some judgments on fee books. An online subscription service is at https://www.doxpop.com/prod/welcome.jsp. Fees involved. Records date from 08/89. A limited free search of open cases is available.
Criminal Records: Access: In person, online. Visitors must perform in person searches themselves. Court makes copy: $1.00 per page. Required to search: name, years to search, DOB; also helpful: SSN. Criminal records archived from 1800s; on computer since 1989. Some judgments on fee books. Online access to criminal records is the same as civil.
General Information: Public use terminal available. No juvenile, mental, adoption or sealed records released. Certification fee: $1.00. Payee: Wabash County Clerk. Business checks accepted. Prepayment required.

Warren County

Circuit Court 125 N Monroe, #11, Williamsport, IN 47993; phone: 765-762-3510; fax: 765-762-7251; hours 8AM-4PM (EST). *Felony, Misdemeanor, Civil, Eviction, Small Claims, Probate.*
Civil Records: Access: In person only. Both court and visitors may perform in person searches. No search fee. Court makes copy: $1.00 per page. Required to search: name, years to search. Civil cases indexed by defendant, plaintiff. Civil records archived from 1828. Some records on docket books.
Criminal Records: Access: In person only. Both court and visitors may perform in person searches. No search fee. Court makes copy: $1.00 per page. Required to search: name, years to search, DOB; SSN helpful. Criminal records archived from 1828. Some records on docket books.
General Information: No public access terminal. No juvenile, mental, adoption or sealed released. Fee to fax specific is $1.00 per page. Certification fee: $1.00 per cert. Payee: Warren County Clerk. Personal checks accepted. Prepayment required.

Warrick County

Circuit & Superior Court One County Square, #200, Boonville, IN 47601; phone: 812-897-6160; hours 8AM-4PM (CST). *Felony, Misdemeanor, Civil, Eviction, Small Claims, Probate.*
Civil Records: Access: In person only. Both court and visitors may perform in person searches. No search fee. Court makes copy: $1.00 per page. Required to search: name, years to search. Civil cases indexed by defendant, plaintiff. Civil records on computer from 1987, archived from 1900s. Some records on index books.
Criminal Records: Access: In person only. Both court and visitors may perform in person searches. No search fee. Court makes copy: $1.00 per page. Required to search: name, years to search; also helpful: DOB, SSN. Criminal records on computer from 1987, archived from 1900s. Some records on index books.
General Information: Public terminal goes back to 1987. No juvenile, mental, adoption or sealed released. Will not fax back case files. Certification fee: $1.00 per cert. Payee: Warrick County Clerk. Business checks accepted. Prepayment required.

Washington County

Circuit & Superior Court Courthouse, 99 Public Sq, #102, Salem, IN 47167; phone: 812-883-1634; civil phone: 812-883-5748; probate phone: 812-883-5748; fax: 812-883-8108; hours 8:30AM-4PM M-Th, 8:30AM-6PM F (EST). *Felony, Misdemeanor, Civil, Small Claims, Probate.*
Note: Will only return calls to toll-free numbers.
Civil Records: Access: In person only. Visitors must perform in person searches themselves. Court makes copy: $1.00 per page. Self serve copy fee: $1.00 per page. Required to search: name, years to search; also helpful: address. Civil cases indexed by defendant, plaintiff. Civil records on books, archived from 1820. Some records on docket books.
Criminal Records: Access: In person only. Both court and visitors may perform in person searches. No search fee. Court makes copy: $1.00 per page. Self serve copy fee: $1.00 per page. Required to search: name, years to search, DOB; also helpful: address, SSN. Criminal index on computer from 1980, docket books and archived from 1820.
General Information: No public access terminal. No juvenile, mental, adoption or sealed released; no information given out via telephone. Will not fax specific case file. Certification fee: $1.00. Payee: Washington County Clerk. Only cashiers checks and money orders accepted. Prepayment required.

Wayne County

Circuit & Superior Court Courthouse, 301 E Main St, Richmond, IN 47374; phone: 765-973-9200; criminal phone: 765-973-9218 Circ Ct; civil phone: 765-973-9221 Circ Ct; criminal/civil fax: 765-973-9490; hours 8:30AM-5PM M; 8:30AM-4:30PM T-F (EST). *Felony, Misdemeanor, Civil, Eviction, Small Claims, Probate.*
www.co.wayne.in.us/courts
Note: Circuit clerk- 765-973-9266; Superior Ct #1- 765-973-9259; Superior Ct #2- 765-973-9260; Small claims- 765-973-9202.
Civil Records: Access: Mail, fax, in person, online. Visitors must perform in person searches themselves. No search fee. Court makes copy: $1.00 per page. Required to search: name, years to search. Civil cases indexed by defendant, plaintiff. Civil records on computer from 4/90, circuit on microfiche from 1957, superior on microfiche from 1960 to 1971, all archived from 1800s. Some records on dockets. Access records via subscription service at https://www.doxpop.com/prod/welcome.jsp. Fees involved. Records date from 3/90; a limited free search of open cases is available. Note: Fax request must be on letterhead. Mail turnaround time 1 week.
Criminal Records: Access: Mail, fax, in person, online. Both court and visitors may perform in person searches. No search fee. Court makes copy: $1.00 per page. Required to search: name, years to search, fax request on letterhead. Criminal records on computer from 4/90, circuit on microfiche from 1957, superior on microfiche from 1960 to 1971, all archived from 1800s. Some records on dockets. Online access to criminal records is the same as civil. Note: Fax request must be on letterhead. Mail turnaround time 1 week.
General Information: Public terminal goes back to 1990. No juvenile, mental, adoption or sealed released. Will not fax documents. Certification fee: $1.00 per cert. Payee: Wayne County Clerk. Personal checks accepted. Prepayment and SASE required.

Wells County

Circuit & Superior Court 102 W Market, Rm 201, Bluffton, IN 46714; phone: 260-824-6479; probate phone: 260-824-6480; fax: 260-824-6559; probate fax: same; hours 8AM-4:30PM (EST). *Civil, Probate.*
Civil Records: Access: In person only. Visitors must perform in person searches themselves. Court makes copy: $1.00 per page; same fee for self serve. Required to search: name, years to search. Civil cases

indexed by defendant, plaintiff. Civil records archived from 1837. Some records on docket books.

Criminal Records: Access: In person only. Visitors must perform in person searches themselves. Court makes copy: $1.00 per page; same fee for self serve. Required to search: name, years to search, DOB; SSN helpful. Criminal records archived from 1837. Some records on docket books.

General Information: No public access terminal. No juvenile, mental, adoption or sealed released. Will not fax specific case file. Certification fee: $1.00. Payee: Wells County Clerk. Personal checks accepted. Prepayment required.

White County

Circuit Court PO Box 350, 110 N Main, Monticello, IN 47960; phone: 574-583-7032; fax: 574-583-1532; hours 8AM-4PM (EST). *Civil, Probate.*

Civil Records: Access: In person only. Visitors must perform in person searches themselves. Court makes copy: $1.00 per page; same fee for self serve. Required to search: name, years to search. Civil cases indexed by defendant, plaintiff. Civil records on indexes and files, some records on docket books back to 1950s.

General Information: No public access terminal. No juvenile, mental, adoption or sealed released.

Certification fee: $1.00. Payee: White County Clerk. Personal checks accepted. Prepayment required.

Superior Court PO Box 1005, 110 N Main, Monticello, IN 47960; phone: 574-583-9520; criminal phone: 574-583-9520; civil phone: 574-583-7032; criminal fax: 574-583-2437; civil fax: 574-583-1532; hours 8AM-4PM (EST). *Felony, Misdemeanor, Eviction, Small Claims.*

Civil Records: Access: In person only. Both court and visitors may perform in person searches. No search fee. Court makes copy: $1.00 per page. Required to search: name, years to search. Civil cases indexed by defendant, plaintiff. Civil records on indexes and files, some records on docket books. Note: Court will search only if a date is provided

Criminal Records: Access: In person only. Visitors must perform in person searches themselves. No search fee. Court makes copy: $1.00 per page. Required to search: name, years to search. Criminal records on indexes and files, some records on docket books. Note: Court will criminal search only if a date is provided.

General Information: No public access terminal. No juvenile, mental, adoption or sealed released. Will fax specific case file. Certification fee: $1.00 per page. Payee: White County Clerk. Personal checks accepted. Prepayment required.

Whitley County

Circuit & Superior Court 101 W Van Buren, Rm 10, Columbia City, IN 46725; phone: 260-248-3102; fax: 260-248-3137; hours 8AM-4:30PM (EST). *Felony, Misdemeanor, Civil, Eviction, Small Claims, Probate.*

Civil Records: Access: In person only. Visitors must perform in person searches themselves. Court makes copy: $1.00 per page. Required to search: name, years to search. Civil cases indexed by defendant, plaintiff. Civil records on computer from 1999. Some records on docket books.

Criminal Records: Access: In person only. Visitors must perform in person searches themselves. Court makes copy: $1.00 per page. Required to search: name; years to search; also helpful: DOB. Criminal records on computer from 1999. Some records on docket books back to 1900.

General Information: Public terminal goes back to 1993 (Circuit); 1988 (Superior). No juvenile, mental, adoption or sealed released. Certification fee: $1.00. Payee: Whitley County Clerk. Only cashiers checks and money orders accepted. Prepayment required..

Indiana Recording Offices

ORGANIZATION: 92 counties, 92 recording offices. The recording officer is County Recorder (Circuit Clerk for state tax liens on personal property). Many counties utilize a "Miscellaneous Index" for tax and other liens. 81 counties are in the Eastern Time Zone (EST), and 11 are in the Central Time Zone (CST).

REAL ESTATE RECORDS: Most counties will not perform real estate name searches. Copies usually cost $1.00 per page, and certification usually costs $5.00 per document.

UCC RECORDS: Financing statements are filed at the state level, except for real estate related collateral, which are filed with the County Recorder. However, prior to 07/2001, consumer goods collateral were also filed at the County Recorder and these older records can be searched there. Starting 07/2002, farm collateral will change from local to state centralized filing. All counties will perform UCC searches. Use search request form UCC-11. Search fees are usually $8.00 per debtor name and $5.00 for each add'l name. Copies are usually included in the search fee. Most counties also charge $.50 for a financing statement reported on a search.

TAX LIEN RECORDS: All federal tax liens on personal property are filed with the County Recorder. State tax liens on personal property are filed with the Circuit Clerk, who is in a different office from the Recorder. Refer to the County Court section for information about Indiana Circuit Courts. Most counties will not perform tax lien searches.

OTHER LIENS: Judgments, mechanics, hospital, sewer, utility, innkeeper.

ONLINE ACCESS: A growing number of agencies offer online access. The most notable is the subscription service offered by Marion County at www.civicnet.net

Adams County

County Recorder, 313 W. Jefferson, Rm 240; Adams County Service Complex, Decatur, IN 46733. RE & UCC recording phone-260-724-5343; fax-260-724-5344; hours: 8AM-4:30PM
Records indexed on a public use terminal back to 1999. Only the public may search. Copies included in search fee. RE record copy- $1.00 per page. Cert fee- $5.00 per doc plus copy fee. Payee-Adams County Recorder. **Other phones:** Treasurer-260-724-5353; Auditor- 260-724-5300. **Property tax/Assessor-** 260-724-5301.

Allen County

County Recorder, 1 E. Main St; City County Bldg, Rm 206, Fort Wayne, IN 46802-1890. RE & UCC recording phone-260-449-7165; fax-260-449-3261; hours: 8AM-4:30PM
Only the public may search. Copy fee $1.00 per page. Cert fee- $5.00 per doc. Payee- Allen County Recorder. **Other phones:** Treasurer- 260-428-7693; Elections- 260-449-7329; Vital Records-260-449-7147. **Property Assessor-** 260-428-7123.

Bartholomew County

County Recorder, PO Box 1121, Columbus, IN 47202-1121. 812-379-1520; fax-812-375-5440; hours: 8AM-5PM www.bartholomewco.com
Separate indices to search include deeds, mortgages, releases, miscellaneous. Records indexed on a public use terminal back to 1985. Only the public may search. Copy fee $1.00 per page. Cert fee- $5.00 per doc plus copy fee. Payee-Bartholomew County Recorder. **Online access to Property, GIS records:** Access to PAGIS, the county Public Access Geographic Information System, is free at www.bartholomewco.com/login.phtml; you must have an email for free registration. **Other phones:** Treasurer- 812-379-1530; Elections- 812-379-1604; Vital Records- 812-379-1550. **Property tax/Assessor-** 440 3rd St #201 (county), #202 (city), Columbus, IN 47201; 812-379-1505.

Benton County

County Recorder, 706 E. 5th St; #24, Fowler, IN 47944-1556. RE & UCC recording phone-765-884-1630; fax-765-884-2013; hours: 8:30AM-4PM
Separate indices to search include Mtg, Deed, Computer, and Misc. Only the public may search. Copies included in search fee. RE or tax lien copy-$1.00 per page. Cert fee- $5.00 per doc plus copy fee. Payee- Benton County Recorder. **Other phones:** Treasurer- 765-884-1070; Elections- 765-884-0930; Vital Records- 765-884-1728. **Property tax/Assessor-** same address. 765-884-1205.

Blackford County

County Recorder, 110 W. Washington St; Courthouse, Hartford City, IN 47348. RE & UCC recording phone-765-348-2207; fax-765-348-7222; hours: 8AM-4PM
Separate indices to search include computer, books. Records indexed on computer back to 1992. Office will perform a UCC search but public must search other records themselves. UCC search per debtor name- $8.00; $5.00 each add'l. Copy fee $1.00 per page. Cert fee- $5.00 per doc plus copy fee. Payee- Blackford County Recorder. **Other phones:** Treasurer- 765-348-2504; Elections-765-348-1130; Vital Records- 765-348-2207. **Property tax/Assessor-** same address. 765-348-1707.

Boone County

County Recorder, 202 Courthouse Sq, Lebanon, IN 46052. 765-482-3070, R/E recording phone-765-482-2940; hours: 8AM-4PM
All records in one index. Office will perform a UCC search but public must search other records themselves. Search fee $8.00. Copy fee $1.00 per page. Cert fee- $5.00 per doc + $1.00 per copy. Payee- Boone County Recorder. **Other phones:** Treasurer- 765-482-2880; Elections- 765-482-3510. **Property tax/Assessor-** 765-482-0140.

Brown County

County Recorder, PO Box 86, Nashville, IN 47448. RE & UCC recording phone-812-988-5462; fax-812-988-5520; hours: 8AM-4PM
Office will perform a UCC search but public must search other records themselves. UCC search per debtor name- $8.00; $5.00 each add'l. Copies included in search fee. RE or tax lien copy- $1.00 per page. Cert fee- $5.00 per doc plus copy fee. Payee- Brown County Recorder. **Other phones:** Treasurer- 812-988-5458. **Property tax/Assessor-** 812-988-5466.

Carroll County

County Recorder, 101 W. Main St; Court House, Delphi, IN 46923-1522. RE & UCC recording phone-765-564-2124; fax-765-564-2576; hours: 8AM-5PM M,T,Th,F; 8AM-N W
Office will perform a UCC search but public must search other records themselves. Search fee $8.00; $5.00 each add'l. Copies included in search fee. RE record copy- $1.00 per page. Cert fee- $5.00 per doc plus copy fee. Payee- Carroll County Recorder. **Other phones:** Treasurer- 765-564-3446; Elections- 765-564-4485; Vital Records- 765-564-3420. **Property tax/Assessor-** 765-564-3444.

Cass County

County Recorder, 102 Cass County Gov't Bldg., Logansport, IN 46947. 574-753-7810; fax-574-753-0712; hours: 8AM-4PM M-TH; 8AM-5PM F www.in-map.net/counties/CASS/recorder/
All records in one index. Only the public may search. Copies included in search fee. RE or tax lien copy- $1.00 per page. Cert fee- $5.00 per doc plus copy fee. Payee- Cass County Recorder. **Other phones:** Treasurer- 574-753-7720. **Property tax/Assessor-** 574-753-7720.

Clark County

County Recorder, 501 E. Court Ave, Rm 105, Jeffersonville, IN 47130. 812-285-6236; hours: 8:30AM-4:30PM
Office will perform a UCC search but public must search other records themselves. UCC search per debtor name- $8.00,$5.00 add'l. Copies included in search fee. RE or tax lien copy- $1.00 per page. Cert fee- $6.00 per doc; no fee to certify UCCs. Payee- Clark County Recorder. **Other phones:** Treasurer- 812-285-6205. **Property tax/Assessor-** 812-285-6224.

Clay County

County Recorder, 609 E National Ave.; Courthouse, Rm 111, Brazil, IN 47834. RE & UCC recording phone-812-448-9005; fax-812-446-5095; hours: 8AM-4PM www.claycountyin.gov
Separate indices to search include deed, mortgage, miscellaneous, UCC, tax lien, old age, veteran. Records indexed on a public use terminal back to

1991; deeds back to 1953. Office will perform a UCC search but public must search other records themselves. UCC search per debtor name- $8.00; $5.00 each add'l., includes copy fee. Copy fee $1.00 per page. Cert fee- $5.00 per doc plus copy fee. Payee- Clay County Recorder. **Other phones:** Treasurer- 812-448-9009; Elections- 812-448-9023; Vital Records- 812-448-9018. **Property tax/Assessor-** 609 E National Ave, 1st Fl, Rm 105, Brazil, IN 47834; 812-448-9013.

Clinton County

County Recorder, 270 Courthouse Sq, Frankfort, IN 46041-1957. RE & UCC recording phone-765-659-6320; fax-765-659-6391; hours: 8AM-4PM M W F; 8AM-N Th

Separate indices to search include searches by date. Records indexed on a public use terminal back to August 1995. Only the public may search. Copies included in search fee. Copy larger that 9 X 14 1/2-$2.00 per page. Real estate or tax lien record copy- $1.00 per page. Cert fee- $5.00 per doc plus copy fee. Payee- Clinton County Recorder. **Other phones:** Treasurer- 765-659-6325; Elections- 765-659-6335; Vital Records- 765-659-6385. **Property tax/Assessor-** 765-659-6315.

Crawford County

County Recorder, PO Box 214, English, IN 47118-0214. RE & UCC recording phone-812-338-2615; fax-812-338-2507; hours: 8AM-4PM M & F; 8AM-6PM T & Th; Closed W

Separate indices to search include deed, mortgage, misc, survey, UCC's. Records indexed on a public use terminal. Only the public may search. Copies included in search fee. RE record copy- $1.00 per page. Cert fee- $5.00 per doc plus copy fee. Payee-Crawford County Recorder. **Other phones:** Treasurer- 812-338-2651. **Property tax/Assessor-** 812-338-2402.

Daviess County

County Recorder, PO Box 793, Washington, IN 47501. 812-254-8675; fax-812-254-8647; hours: 8AM-4PM

Separate indices to search include mortgages, deeds, miscellaneous. Only the public may search. Copies included in search fee. RE or tax lien copy- $1.00 per page. Cert fee- $5.00 per doc; $5.00 to certify UCCs plus copy fee. Payee- Daviess County Recorder. **Other phones:** Treasurer- 812-254-8677. **Property tax/Assessor-** 200 E Walnut St, Washington, IN 47501; 812-254-8660.

Dearborn County

County Recorder, 215 B, W. High St, Lawrenceburg, IN 47025. RE & UCC recording phone-812-537-8837; fax-none; hours: 8:30AM-4:30PM

Only the public may search. Copies included in search fee. RE record copy- $1.00 per page. Cert fee- $5.00 per doc plus copy fee. Payee- Dearborn County Recorder. **Other phones:** Treasurer- 812-537-8811. **Property tax/Assessor-** 812-537-8809.

Decatur County

County Recorder, 150 Courthouse Sq; #121, Greensburg, IN 47240. RE & UCC recording phone-812-663-4681; fax-812-663-2407; hours: 8AM-4PM (F open until 5PM)

All records in one index. Records indexed on computer back to 2003. Office will perform a UCC search but public must search other records themselves. Search fee $8.00; $5.00 each add'l. Copy fee $1.00 per page. Cert fee- $5.00 per doc plus copy fee. Payee- Decatur County Recorder. **Other phones:** Treasurer- 812-663-4190; Appraiser/Auditor- 812-663-2570; Elections- 812-663-8223; Vital Records- 812-663-8301. **Property tax/Assessor-** same address. 812-663-4868.

DeKalb County

County Recorder, PO Box 810, Auburn, IN 46706. RE & UCC recording phone-260-925-2112; fax-260-925-5126; hours: 8:30AM-4:30PM

All records in one index. Records indexed on a public use terminal back to 12/5/1995. Office will perform a UCC search but public must search other records themselves. Search fee $8.00. Copies included in search fee. RE record copy- $1.00 per page. Cert fee- $5.00 per doc. Payee- DeKalb County Recorder. **Other phones:** Treasurer- 260-925-2712; Elections- 260-925-0912; Vital Records-260-925-2220. **Property/Assessor-** 260-925-1824.

Delaware County

County Recorder, PO Box 1008, Muncie, IN 47308. 765-747-7804; fax-765-284-1875; hours: 8:30AM-4:30PM

Office will perform a UCC search but public must search other records themselves. UCC search per debtor name- $8.00; $5.00 each add'l. Copies included in search fee. RE or tax lien copy- $1.00 per page. Cert fee- $5.00 per doc; no fee to certify UCCs. Payee- Delaware County Recorder. **Other phones:** Treasurer- 765-747-7808; Vital Records- 765-747-7804. **Property tax/Assessor-** 765-747-7715.

Dubois County

County Recorder, 1 Courthouse Sq, Rm 101, Jasper, IN 47546. RE & UCC recording phone-812-481-7067; fax-812-481-7044; hours: 8AM-4PM

Index: Books and Computers. Only the public may search. Copy fee $1.00 per page. Cert fee- $5.00 per page plus copy fee. Payee- Dubois County Recorder. **Other phones:** Treasurer- 812-481-7080. **Property tax/Assessor-** 812-481-7010.

Elkhart County

County Recorder, PO Box 837, Goshen, IN 46527. 574-535-6754; R/E recording phone-574-535-6756; hours: 8AM-5PM M, 8AM-4PM T- F www.elkhartcountygov.com/administrative

Records indexed on a public use terminal back to 1990. Only the public may search. Copy fee $1.00 per page. Cert fee- $5.00 per doc plus copy fee. Payee- Elkhart County Recorder. **Online access to Real Estate, Lien, Tax Assessor records:** Access Elkhart County records for an annual fee of $50. plus a minimum of $20. per month of use. The minimum fee allows for 2 hours access, and add'l use is billed at $10 per hour. Lending agency information available. For information, call at 574-535-6777. **Other phones:** Treasurer- 574-535-6759; Elections- 574-535-6469; Vital Records- 574-523-2107; Voter Registration- 574-535-6775. **Property tax/Assessor-** 574-535-6702.

Fayette County

County Recorder, 401 N Central Ave, Connersville, IN 47331. 765-825-3051; fax-none; hours: 8:30AM-4PM www.co.fayette.in.us

Index: pre-1994 records indices include UCC, Deed, Mortgage, Miscellaneous. Records indexed on a public use terminal back to 1994. Office will perform a UCC search but public must search other records themselves. UCC search per debtor name- $8.00; $5.00 each add'l. Copies included in search fee. RE or tax lien copy- $1.00 per page. Cert fee- $5.00 per doc plus copy fee. Payee- Fayette County Recorder. **Online access to Property, Assessor records:** Access assessor property data free at www.co.fayette.in.us/auditor.htm. **Other phones:** Treasurer- 765-825-1013; Elections- 765-825-1813; Recorder- 765-825-3051; Health Dept -765-825-4013. **Property tax/Assessor-** 111 W 4th St, Connersville, IN 47331; 765-825-4931.

Floyd County

County Recorder, PO Box 878, New Albany, IN 47151-0878. RE & UCC recording phone-812-948-5430; fax-812-949-7727; hours: 8AM-4PM

All records in one index. Records indexed on a public use terminal back to 1990. Only the public may search. State tax liens at county clerk's office. Copy fee $1.00 per page. Cert fee- $5.00 per doc plus copy fee. Payee- Floyd County Recorder. **Online access to Recording, Real Estate records:** Computerized versions of microfiche cards will be on the internet sometime in 2004; call clerk at 812-948-5430 for update information. **Other phones:** Treasurer- 812-948-5477; Elections- 812-948-5419; Vital Records- 812-948-4726. **Property tax/Assessor-** 812-948-5420.

Fountain County

County Recorder, PO Box 55, Covington, IN 47932. RE & UCC recording phone-765-793-2431; fax-765-793-6211; hours: 8AM-4PM

Records indexed on a public use terminal back to 6/1992. Only the public may search. Copies included in search fee. RE or tax lien copy- $1.00 per page. Cert fee- $5.00 per doc plus copy fee. Payee- Fountain County Recorder. **Other phones:** Treasurer- 765-793-3691; Elections- 765-793-2192; Vital Records- 765-793-3035. **Property tax/Assessor-** 765-793-3481.

Franklin County

County Recorder, 459 Main St, Brookville, IN 47012-1486. RE & UCC recording phone-765-647-5131; hours: 8:30AM-4PM

Office will perform a UCC search but public must search other records themselves. UCC search per debtor name- $8.00; $5.00 each add'l. Copy fee $1.00 per page. Cert fee- $5.00 per doc plus copy fee. Payee- Franklin County Recorder. **Other phones:** Treasurer- 765-647-5121; Elections- 765-647-5111; Vital Records- 765-647-4322. **Property tax/Assessor-** 765-647-4921.

Fulton County

County Recorder, 125 E 9th St, Rochester, IN 46975. RE & UCC recording phone-574-223-2914; fax-574-223-4734; hours: 8AM-4PM (F 8AM-5PM)

Separate indices by instrument number and by book & page number. Records indexed on a public use terminal back to 5/13/1996. Office will perform a UCC search but public must search other records themselves. UCC search per debtor name- $8.00; $5.00 each add'l. Copies included in search fee. Real estate record or tax lien record copy- $1.00 per page. Cert fee- $5.00 per doc plus copy fee. Payee- Fulton County Recorder. **Other phones:** Treasurer- 574-223-7705; Vital Records- 574-223-2881. **Property tax/Assessor-** 574-223-2801.

Gibson County

County Recorder, PO Box 1078, Princeton, IN 47670. RE & UCC recording phone-812-385-3332; fax-812-386-9502; hours: 8AM-4PM

Index: Pre-7/1987 records in books. Records indexed on computer. Only the public may search. Copy fee $1.00 per page. Cert fee- $5.00 per doc plus copy fee. Payee- Gibson County Recorder. **Other phones:** Treasurer- 812-385-2540; Appraiser/Auditor- 812-385-4927; Elections- 812-385-8401; Vital Records- 812-385-3831. **Property tax/Assessor-** 812-385-5286.

Grant County

County Recorder, 401 S. Adams St, Marion, IN 46953. 765-651-2421, R/E recording phone-765-668-8871, UCC recording phone-765-668-8871; hours: 8AM-4PM www.grantcounty.net

Records indexed on a public use terminal back to 1990. Office will perform a UCC search but public must search other records themselves. UCC search per debtor name- $8.00; $5.00 each add'l. Copies included in search fee. RE or tax lien copy- $1.00 per page. Cert fee- $5.00 per doc; no fee to certify UCCs. Payee- Grant County Recorder. **Online access to Recorder, Deed, UCC, Mortgage, Assessor, Property Tax, Voter Registration records:** Access to recorder data is free at http://recorder.grant.in.uinquire.us/. Click on "Recorder Information." Tax information is free at http://auditor.grant.in.uinquire.us/. Click on "Tax Information." Access to assessor property information is free at http://assessor.grant.in.uinquire.us/. Click on "Property Information." Also, voter registration is at http://voters.grant.in.uinquire.us/nxweb.exe;

registration, login, and password required. **Other phones:** Treasurer- 765-668-8871; Appraiser/Auditor- 765-668-8871; Elections- 765-668-8871; Vital Records- 765-668-8871. **Property tax/Assessor-** 765-668-8871.

Greene County

County Recorder, PO Box 309, Bloomfield, IN 47424. 812-384-2020, R/E recording phone-812-384-2020 & 812-384-2023, UCC recording phone-812-384-2021 & 812-384-2023; fax-812-384-2044; hours: 8AM-4PM www.co.greene.in.us
Records indexed books prior to 11/18/2002, after 11/18/2002 maintained in one index. Office will perform a UCC search but public must search other records themselves. UCC search per debtor name- $8.00; $5.00 each add'l. Copy fee $1.00 per page. Cert fee- $5.00 per doc plus copy fee. Payee- Greene Co. Recorder. **Other phones:** Treasurer- 812-384-4378; Elections- 812-384-2015; Vital Records- 812-384-2016. **Property tax/Assessor-** same address as above. 812-384-2003.

Hamilton County

County Recorder, 33 N. 9th St, #309; Courthouse, Noblesville, IN 46060. Main phone & R/E recording-317-776-9618, UCC recording phone-317-776-9688; fax-317-776-8200; hours: 8AM-4:30PM http://recordersoffice.hamilton-co.org/
Records indexed on a public use terminal back to 1990. Only the public may search. Copy fee $1.00 per page. Cert fee- $5.00 per doc plus copy fee. Payee- Hamilton County Recorder. **Online access to Inmate, Offender records:** Search inmate information for free on private company website at www.hamiltoncountyauditor.org/realestate/. **Other phones:** Treasurer- 317-776-9620. **Property tax/Assessor-** 317-776-9614.

Hancock County

County Recorder, 9 E. Main St; Courthouse, Rm 204, Greenfield, IN 46140. 317-462-1142, UCC recording phone-317-477-1142; hours: 8AM-4PM www.hancockcoingov.org/recorder
Records indexed on a public use terminal. Only the public may search. Copies included in search fee. RE or tax lien copy- $1.00 per page. Cert fee- $5.00 per doc plus copy fee. Payee- Hancock County Recorder. **Online access to Sale Disclosure records:** Access to the assessor's sales disclosure data is free at www.hancockcoingov.org/assessor/sales_disclosure_search.asp. **Other phones:** Treasurer- 317-462-1152; Elections- 317-477-1171; Vital Records- 317-477-1125. **Property tax/Assessor-** 317-477-1102.

Harrison County

County Recorder, 300 Capitol Ave; Courthouse, Rm 204, Corydon, IN 47112. RE & UCC recording phone-812-738-3788; fax-812-738-1153; hours: 8AM-4PM M,T,Th,F; 8AM-N W & Sat
Records indexed on computer. Office will perform a UCC search but public must search other records themselves. UCC search per debtor name- $8.00; $5.00 each add'l name. Copy fee $1.00 per page. Cert fee- $5.00 per doc plus copy fee. Payee- Harrison County Recorder. **Other phones:** Treasurer- 812-738-2348; Elections- 812-738-3126; Vital Records- 812-738-3237. **Property tax/Assessor-** 812-738-4280.

Hendricks County

County Recorder, 355 S Washington, Danville, IN 46122. RE & UCC recording phone-317-745-9224; hours: 8AM-4PM www.co.hendricks.in.us
All records in one index. Office personnel or visitors may perform searches. Will not search real estate or tax lien records. UCC search per debtor name- $8.00; $5.00 each add'l. Copies included in search fee. RE or tax lien copy- $1.00 per page. Cert fee- $5.00 per doc plus copy fee. Payee- Hendricks County Recorder. **Online access to Property, GIS-Mapping records:** Access to county property data on the GIS mapping site is free at http://in32.plexisgroup.com/map/index.html. Click on "Query" to select query by owner name. **Other phones:** Treasurer- 317-745-9220; Appraiser/Auditor- 317-745-9206. **Property/Assessor-** 317-745-9207.

Henry County

County Recorder, PO Box K, New Castle, IN 47362. RE & UCC recording phone-765-529-4304; fax-765-521-7017; hours: 8AM-4PM
Records indexed on a public use terminal back to 1991. Office personnel or visitors may perform searches. Will not search real estate or tax lien records. Will search UCC records if you use UCC info form. UCC search per debtor name- $8.00; $5.00 each add'l. Copy fee $1.00 per page. Cert fee- $5.00 per doc plus copy fee. Payee- Henry County Recorder. **Other phones:** Treasurer- 765-529-4404; Elections- 765-529-6401; Vital Records- 765-521-7058; Auditor- 765-529-2800. **Property tax/Assessor-** 765-529-2104.

Howard County

County Recorder, PO Box 733, Kokomo, IN 46903-0733. 765-456-2210; fax-765-456-2056; hours: 8AM-4PM
Records indexed on a public use terminal back to May, 1998. Only the public may search. Copy fee $1.00 per page. Cert fee- $5.00 per doc plus copy fee. Payee- Howard County Recorder. **Other phones:** Treasurer- 317-456-2213. **Property tax/Assessor-** 317-456-2211.

Huntington County

County Recorder, 201 N. Jefferson St.; Rm 101, Huntington, IN 46750-2841. RE & UCC recording phone-260-358-4848; hours: 8AM-4:30PM
Office personnel or visitors may perform searches. Will not search real estate records. Will search UCC records. Will not do federal tax lien search. UCC search per debtor name- $8.00; $5.00 each add'l. Copy fee $1.00 per page. Cert fee- $5.00 per doc plus copy fee. Payee- Huntington County Recorder. **Other phones:** Treasurer- 260-358-4860. **Property tax/Assessor-** 260-358-4802.

Jackson County

County Recorder, PO Box 75, Brownstown, IN 47220. 812-358-6113; hours: 8AM-4:30PM
Records indexed on a public use terminal back to 1991. Office will perform a UCC search but public must search other records themselves. UCC search per debtor name- $8.00; $5.00 each add'l. Copies included in search fee. RE or tax lien copy- $1.00 per page. Cert fee- $5.00 per doc plus copy fee. Payee- Jackson County Recorder. **Other phones:** Treasurer- 812-358-6125. **Property tax/Assessor-** 812-358-6111.

Jasper County

County Recorder, 115 W. Washington, Courthouse Box 4, Rensselaer, IN 47978-2891. 219-866-4923, R/E recording phone-219-866-4930 (Auditor), UCC recording phone-219-866-4923 (Recorder); hours: 8AM-4PM
Separate indices to search include deeds, mtgs, misc, psf, UCCs. Only the public may search. Copies included in search fee. RE record copy- $1.00 per page. Cert fee- $5.00 per doc plus copy fee. Payee- Jasper County Recorder. **Other phones:** Treasurer- 219-866-4938. **Property tax/Assessor-** 219-866-4914.

Jay County

County Recorder, 120 W. Main St, Portland, IN 47371. RE & UCC recording phone-260-726-6940; hours: 8:30AM-4:30PM
All records in one index. Records indexed on a public use terminal back to Jan 1997. Office will perform a UCC search but public must search other records themselves. Search fee $8.00 for 1st, $5.00 each add'l. Copies included in search fee. RE or tax lien copy- $1.00 per page. Cert fee- $5.00 per cert plus $1.00 copy fee per page. Payee- Jay County Recorder. **Other phones:** Treasurer- 260-726-6925. **Property tax/Assessor-** 260-726-6929.

Jefferson County

County Recorder, 300 E Main St; Courthouse - Rm 104, Madison, IN 47250. RE & UCC recording phone-812-265-8902; hours: 8AM-4PM
Separate indices to search include pre 1999, deeds, mortgages, misc. May be searched at Room 104. Office will perform a UCC search but public must search other records themselves. UCC search per debtor name- $8.00; $5.00 each add'l. Copy fee $1.00 per page. Cert fee- $5.00 per doc plus copy fee. Payee- Jefferson County Recorder. **Other phones:** Treasurer- 812-265-8910; Elections- 812-265-8926; Health Dept- 812-273-1942. **Property tax/Assessor-** 300 E Main St, Rm 102, Courthouse, Madison, IN 47250; 812-265-8905.

Jennings County

County Recorder, PO Box 397, Vernon, IN 47282-0397. RE & UCC recording phone-812-352-3053; fax-812-352-3000; hours: 8AM-4PM
Separate indices to search include UCC's. Records indexed on a public use terminal back to October, 1991. Office will perform a UCC search but public must search other records themselves. UCC search per debtor name- $8.00; $5.00 each add'l. Copies included in search fee. RE record copy- $1.00 per page. Cert fee- $5.00 per doc plus copy fee. Payee- Jennings County Recorder. **Other phones:** Treasurer- 812-352-3060; Appraiser/Auditor- 812-352-3021; Elections- 812-352-3080; Vital Records- 812-352-3024; Auditors Phones- 812-352-3016; Clerks Phone -812-352-3070. **Property tax/Assessor-** 812-352-3013.

Johnson County

County Recorder, PO Box 489, Franklin, IN 46131. RE & UCC recording phone-317-736-3718; fax-317-736-4776; hours: 8AM-4:30PM
Records indexed on a public use terminal back to 1994. Only the public may search. Copies included in search fee. RE record copy- $1.00 per page. Cert fee- $5.00 per doc plus copy fee. Payee- Johnson County Recorder. **Other phones:** Treasurer- 317-736-3711; Elections- 317-736-3789; Vital Records- 317-736-3775; Assessor County- 317-736-3715. **Property tax/Assessor-** 317-736-3030.

Knox County

County Recorder, 101 N 7th St, Courthouse, Vincennes, IN 47591. 812-885-2508; fax-812-886-2414; hours: 8AM-4PM
Records indexed on a public use terminal back to 2002. Office will perform a UCC search but public must search other records themselves. UCC search per debtor name-$8.00; $5.00 each add'l. Copies included in search fee. RE or tax lien copy- $1.00 per page; to copy & fax to toll-free number- $2.00; $3.00 to non-toll-free number. Cert fee- $5.00 per doc plus copy fee. Payee- Knox County Recorder. **Other phones:** Treasurer- 812-885-2506. **Property tax/Assessor-** 812-885-2513.

Kosciusko County

County Recorder, 100 W. Center St; Courthouse Rm 14, Warsaw, IN 46580. RE & UCC recording phone-574-372-2360; fax-574-372-2469; hours: 8AM-4:30PM http://kcgov.com/countyOfficeSelect.asp
All records in one index. Office personnel or visitors may perform searches. Will not search real estate records. Will search UCC records. Will not do federal tax lien search. UCC search per debtor name- $8.00; $5.00 each add'l. Copies included in search fee. RE record copy- $1.00 per copy. Cert fee- $5.00 per cert plus copy fee. Payee- Kosciusko County Recorder. **Online access to Property, GIS Mapping records:** Recorded documents are not online. But access to property records on the searchable GIS mapping site is free at http://kcgov.com/application/gis/viewer.htm. Click on

"Search" to get to name search mode. **Other phones:** Treasurer- 574-372-2370; Elections- 574-372-2329; Vital Records- 574-372-2329. **Property tax/Assessor-** 100 W Center, Warsaw, IN 46580; 574-372-2310.

La Porte County

County Recorder, 813 Lincolnway, La Porte, IN 46350-3488. 219-326-6808, R/E recording phone-219-326-6808 x257, UCC recording phone-219-326-6808 x380; fax-219-326-0828; hours: 8AM-4PM (Recording hours 8AM-3PM) www.laportecounty.org
All records in one index. Will not search real estate records. Will search UCC records, tax liens not included in UCC search. UCC search per debtor name- $8.00; $5.00 each add'l. Copies included in search fee. RE or tax lien copy- $1.00 per page. Cert fee- $5.00 per doc plus copy fee. Payee- La Porte County Recorder. **Online access to Recording, Real Estate, Deed, Lien records:** Recorder office data by subscription on either the Laredo system using subscription and fees or the Tapestry System using credit card, https://tapestry.fidlar.com/tapsearch.aspx; $3.99 search; $.50 per image. Index back to 8/1988; images to 8/1999. **Other phones:** Treasurer- 219-326-6808 x490; Elections- 219-326-6808 x242; Vital Records- 219-326-6808 x200. **Property tax/Assessor-** 219-326-6808 x233.

LaGrange County

County Recorder, PO Box 214, LaGrange, IN 46761. RE & UCC recording phone-260-499-6320; hours: 8AM-5PM M; 8AM-4PM T-F www.lagrangecounty.org
Will not search real estate records. Will search UCC records, but not tax liens. UCC search per debtor name- $8.00; $5.00 each add'l. Copies included in search fee. RE record copy- $1.00 per page. Cert fee- $5.00 per doc plus copy fee. Payee- LaGrange County Recorder. **Other phones:** Treasurer- 260-499-6316. **Property tax/Assessor-** 260-499-6319.

Lake County

County Recorder, 2293 N Main St; Bldg. A, 2nd Fl, Crown Point, IN 46307. 219-755-3730; fax-219-755-3257; hours: 8:30AM-4:30PM
All records in one index. Records indexed on computer back to1995. Office personnel or visitors may perform searches. Search fee $8.00; $5.00 each add'l. Copies included in search fee. RE record copy- $1.00 per page. Cert fee- $5.00 per doc plus copy fee. Payee- Lake County Recorder. **Online access to Assessor, Property Tax records:** Access property tax data online at www.lakecountyin.org/index.jsp; click on "online property tax information" and follow links. Search free as Guest, but no name searching. Subscription service allows name searching; sub fee is $19.95 per month. **Other phones:** Treasurer- 219-755-3760. **Property tax/Assessor-** 219-755-3100.

Lawrence County

County Recorder, 916 15th St, Rm 21; Rm 21, Bedford, IN 47421. RE & UCC recording phone-812-275-3245; fax-812-275-4138; hours: 8:30AM-4:30PM
Records indexed on computer back to 12/1994. Only the office personnel may search. UCC search per debtor name- $8.00; $5.00 each add'l. Copies included in search fee. RE record copy- $1.00 per page. Cert fee- $5.00 per doc plus copy fee. Payee- Lawrence County Recorder. **Other phones:** Treasurer- 812-275-2431; Appraiser/Auditor- 812-275-3111. **Property tax/Assessor-** 812-275-5695.

Madison County

County Recorder, 16 E. 9th St, Anderson, IN 46016. 765-641-9618, R/E recording phone-765-641-9615, UCC recording phone-765-608-7828; fax-765-641-9617; hours: 8AM-4PM
All records in one index. Records indexed on a public use terminal back to 11/1989. Office will perform a UCC search but public must search other records themselves. Search fee $8.00. Copy fee $1.00 per page. Cert fee- $5.00 per doc plus

copy fee. Payee- Madison County Recorder. **Other phones:** Treasurer- 765-641-9645; Elections- 765-641-9459; Vital Records- 765-641-9433. **Property tax/Assessor-** 765-641-9401.

Marion County

County Recorder, 200 E. Washington; City-County Bldg, #721, Indianapolis, IN 46204. 317-327-4020, R/E recording phone-317-327-4018, UCC recording phone-317-327-4015; fax-317-327-3942; 8AM-4:30PM www.indygov.org/eGov/County/Recorder/home.htm
All records in one index. Records indexed on a public use terminal back to 1964. Office will perform a UCC search but public must search other records themselves. Search fee $8.00; $5.00 each add'l. Copies included in search fee. RE or tax lien copy- $1.00 per page. Cert fee- $5.00 per doc plus copy fee. Payee- Marion County Recorder. **Online access to Real Estate, Lien, Deed, UCC, Inmate records:** Access to Marion County online records requires a $200 set up fee, plus an escrow balance of at least $100 must be maintained. add'l charges are $.25 per minute, $.05 display charge for 1st page; $.05 each add'l page. Records date back to 1964; images from 1964. Federal tax liens and UCC information are available. For information, contact Mike Kerner at 317-327-4587. Also, acquire recording information on customized CD-rom and in specialized online reports. Also, access recording office land data at www.etitlesearch.com; registration required, fee based on usage. Also, search inmate info on private company website at www.vinelink.com/index.jsp. **Other phones:** Treasurer- 317-327-4040; Auditor- 317-327-4646. **Property tax/Assessor-** 317-327-4907.

Marshall County

County Recorder, 112 W. Jefferson St; Rm 201, Plymouth, IN 46563. RE & UCC recording phone-574-935-8515; fax-574-935-5099; hours: 8AM-4PM
All records in one index. Records indexed on a public use terminal back to 7/1996. Office will perform a UCC search but public must search other records themselves. Search fee $8.00. Copy fee $1.00 per page. Cert fee- $5.00 per doc plus copy fee. Payee- Marshall County Recorder. **Other phones:** Treasurer- 574-935-8518. **Property tax/Assessor-** same address as above. 574-935-8525.

Martin County

County Recorder, PO Box 147, Shoals, IN 47581. RE & UCC recording phone-812-247-2420; fax-812-247-2756; hours: 8AM-4PM
All records in one index. Will not search real estate records. Will not search UCC records or tax liens. Copy fee $1.00 per page. Cert fee- $5.00 per doc plus copy fee. Payee- Martin County Recorder. **Other phones:** Treasurer- 812-247-3701. **Property tax/Assessor-** 111 Main St, Shoals, IN 47581; 812-247-2070.

Miami County

County Recorder, 25 N. Broadway #205, Peru, IN 46970. 765-472-3901; fax-765-472-1412; hours: 8AM-4PM
Records indexed on a public use terminal back to 1990. Office will perform a UCC search but public must search other records themselves. UCC search per debtor name- $8.00;$5.00 add'l. Copies included in search fee. RE or tax lien copy- $1.00 per page. Cert fee- $5.00 per doc plus copy fee. Payee- Miami County Recorder.

Monroe County

County Recorder, PO Box 1634, Bloomington, IN 47402. RE & UCC recording phone-812-349-2520; hours: 8AM-4PM www.co.monroe.in.us/recorder/index.htm
There are two assessors; one county and one township. Separate indices to search deeds, mortgages, misc. All indices computerized since 05/91; images available on computer since 05/99. Office personnel only does UCC searches, visitors must

perform searches for all other documents. No search fee except for UCC search. Will search UCC records. Will not do federal tax lien search. UCC search per debtor name-$8.00 1st name; $5.00 each add'l name per search. Copy fee $1.00 per page. Cert fee- $5.00 per cert plus copy fee. Payee- Monroe County Recorder. **Other phones:** Treasurer- 812-349-2530; Elections- 812-349-2615; Vital Records- 812-349-2543. **Property tax/Assessor-** 812-349-2502.

Montgomery County

County Recorder, PO Box 865, Crawfordsville, IN 47933. 765-364-6415; fax-765-364-6404; hours: 8AM-4PM
Office will perform a UCC search but public must search other records themselves. UCC search per debtor name- $8.00; $5.00 each add'l. Copies included in search fee. RE or tax lien copy- $1.00 per page. Cert fee- $5.00 per doc plus copy fee. Payee- Montgomery County Recorder. **Other phones:** Treasurer- 765-364-6410. **Property tax/Assessor-** 765-364-6420.

Morgan County

County Recorder, PO Box 1653, Martinsville, IN 46151. RE & UCC recording phone-765-342-1077; hours: 8AM-4PM (8AM-5PM F)
All records in one index. Office will perform a UCC search but public must search other records themselves. Search fee $8.00; $5.00 each add'l. Copy fee $1.00 per page. Cert fee- $5.00 per doc plus copy fee. Payee- Morgan County Recorder. **Other phones:** Treasurer- 765-342-1048; Elections- 765-342-1029; Vital Records- 765-342-6621. **Property tax/Assessor-** same address as above. 765-342-1065.

Newton County

County Recorder, 201 N 3rd St, Kentland, IN 47951. 219-474-6081; hours: 8AM-4PM
Mortgage searches available. Will search UCC records. Will not do federal tax lien search. UCC search per debtor name- $8.00; $5.00 each add'l. Copies included in search fee. RE or tax lien copy- $1.00 per page. Cert fee- $5.00 per doc plus copy fee. Payee- Newton County Recorder. **Other phones:** Treasurer- 219-474-6081. **Property tax/Assessor-** 219-474-6081.

Noble County

County Recorder, 101 N. Orange St, Rm 210, Albion, IN 46701. RE & UCC recording phone-260-636-2672; fax-260-636-3264; hours: 8AM-4PM www.noblecountyrecorder.com
Separate indices to search include deeds, mortgages, miscellaneous, bonds, discharges. Office will perform a UCC search but public must search other records themselves. UCC search per debtor name- $5.00 per search. Copies included in search fee. RE or tax lien copy- $1.00 per page. Cert fee- $5.00 per doc plus copy fee. Payee- Noble County Recorder. **Other phones:** Treasurer- 260-636-2644. **Property tax/Assessor-** same address as above. 260-636-2297.

Ohio County

County Recorder, 413 Main St; Courthouse, Rising Sun, IN 47040. RE & UCC recording phone-812-438-3369; fax-812-438-4590; hours: 9AM-4PM M,T,Th,F; 9AM-12 Sat; Closed Wed
Office will perform a UCC search but public must search other records themselves. UCC search per debtor name- $8.00; $5.00 each add'l. State tax liens in Clerk's office. Copies included in search fee. RE or tax lien copy- $1.00 per page. Cert fee- $5.00 1st pg, $1.00 each add'l. Payee- Ohio County Recorder. **Other phones:** Treasurer- 812-438-2724; Elections- 812-438-2610; Vital Records- 812-438-2551. **Property tax/Assessor-** 812-438-3264.

Orange County

County Recorder, 205 E Main St #8, Paoli, IN 47454. 812-723-7114; fax-none; hours: 8AM-4PM
Records indexed on a public use terminal back to 1993, deeds only back to 1955. Office will perform a UCC search but public must search other records themselves. UCC search per debtor name- $8.00; $5.00 each add'l. UCC copy fee included in search fee. RE record copy- $1.00 per page. Tax lien copy- $.50. Cert fee- $5.00 per doc plus copy fee. Payee- Orange County Recorder. **Property tax/Assessor-** 812-723-3600.

Owen County

County Recorder, Courthouse, Spencer, IN 47460. 812-829-5013; fax-812-829-5014; hours: 8AM-4PM
Separate indices to search include deeds, mortgages, miscellaneous, UCC files. Office will perform a UCC search but public must search other records themselves. UCC search per debtor name- $8.00; $5.00 each add'l. Copies included in search fee. RE or tax lien copy- $1.00 per page. Cert fee- $5.00 per doc plus copy fee. Payee- Owen County Recorder. **Other phones:** Treasurer- 812-829-5011. **Property tax/Assessor-** 812-829-5018.

Parke County

County Recorder, 116 W. High St.; Rm 102, Rockville, IN 47872-1787. RE & UCC recording phone-765-569-3419; fax-765-569-4037; hours: 8AM-4PM
Office will perform a UCC search but public must search other records themselves. UCC search per debtor name- $8.00; $5.00 each add'l. Copies included in search fee. RE record copy- $1.00 per page. Cert fee- $5.00 per doc plus copy fee. Payee- Parke County Recorder. **Other phones:** Treasurer- 765-569-3437. **Property tax/Assessor-** 765-569-4036.

Perry County

County Recorder, 2219 Payne St, Rm W2, Tell City, IN 47586-2830. RE & UCC recording phone-812-547-4261; fax-812-547-6428; hours: 8AM-4PM
All records in one index. Office will perform a UCC search but public must search other records themselves. UCC search per debtor name- $8.00; $5.00 each add'l. Copy fee $1.00 per page. Copy fee for UCC included in search fee. Cert fee- $5.00 per doc plus copy fee. Payee- Perry County Recorder. **Other phones:** Treasurer- 812-547-4816; Elections- 812-547-3741; Vital Records- 812-547-2746. **Property tax/Assessor-** same address as above. 812-547-5531.

Pike County

County Recorder, 801 E Main St; Courthouse, Petersburg, IN 47567-1298. 812-354-6747; fax-812-354-9431; hours: 8AM-4PM
Separate indices to search include deed, mortgage, miscellaneous. Records indexed on computer back to 1/1994. Office will perform a UCC search but public must search other records themselves. UCC search per debtor name- $8.00; $5.00 each add'l. Copy fee $1.00 per page. Cert fee- $5.00 per doc plus copy fee. Payee- Pike County Recorder. **Other phones:** Treasurer- 812-354-6363; Elections- 812-354-6025; Vital Records- 812-354-8797. **Property tax/Assessor-** same address as above. 812-354-6584.

Porter County

County Recorder, 155 Indiana Ave; #210, Valparaiso, IN 46383. Main & R/E recording Recording phone-219-465-3465, UCC recording phone-219-465-3374; fax-219-465-3850; hours: 8:30AM-4:30PM
All records in one index. Records indexed on computer back to 1992. Only the public may search. We don't have state tax liens. They are in the county clerk's office. Copy fee $1.00 per page. Cert fee- $5.00 per doc plus copy fee. Payee- Porter County Recorder. **Other phones:** Treasurer-

219-465-3470. **Property tax/Assessor-** 219-465-3460.

Posey County

County Recorder, 126 E 3rd St #215, Mount Vernon, IN 47620. RE & UCC recording phone-812-838-1314; fax-812-838-8563; hours: 8AM-4PM
Separate indices to search include deeds, grantor/grantee, mortgages, mortgagor/mortgage, etc. Records indexed on computer back to May, 1993. Office will perform a UCC search but public must search other records themselves. UCC search fee is $8.00 for 1 name, $5.00 each additional name. Copies included in search fee. RE or tax lien copy- $1.00 per page. Cert fee- $5.00 per doc plus copy fee. Payee- Posey County Recorder. **Other phones:** Treasurer- 812-838-1316; Elections- 812-838-1339; Vital Records- 812-838-8561. **Property tax/Assessor-** same address as above. 812-838-1309.

Pulaski County

County Recorder, 112 E Main St; Courthouse - Rm 220, Winamac, IN 46996. RE & UCC recording phone-574-946-3844; hours: 8AM-4PM
All records in one index. Will not search real estate records. Will search UCC records. Will not do a state tax lien search. UCC search per debtor name- $8.00; $5.00 each add'l. Copies included in search fee. RE or tax lien copy- $1.00 per page. Cert fee- $5.00 per doc plus copy fee. Payee- Pulaski County Recorder. **Other phones:** Treasurer- 574-946-3632; Elections- 574-946-3313; Vital Records- 574-946-6080. **Property tax/Assessor-** 112 E Main St, Winamac, IN 46996; 574-946-3845.

Putnam County

County Recorder, Courthouse Sq; Rm 25, Greencastle, IN 46135. 765-653-5613; fax-765-653-2378; hours: 8AM-4PM
All records in one index. Only the public may search. Copy fee $1.00 per page. Cert fee- $5.00 per doc plus copy fee. Payee- Putnam County Recorder. **Other phones:** Treasurer- 765-653-4510. **Property tax/Assessor-** 765-653-4312.

Randolph County

County Recorder, 100 S Main St; Courthouse, Rm 101, Winchester, IN 47394-1899. RE & UCC recording phone-765-584-7300; hours: 8AM-4PM
All records in one index. Will not search real estate records. Will search UCC records. Will not do federal tax lien search. UCC search per debtor name-$8.00; $5.00 for each add'l name. Copies included in search fee. RE or tax lien copy- $1.00 per page. Cert fee- $5.00 per doc plus copy fee. Payee- Randolph County Recorder. **Other phones:** Treasurer- 765-584-0704; Appraiser/Auditor- 765-584-7407; Elections- 765-584-1155; Vital Records- 765-584-1155. **Property tax/Assessor-** 100 S Main St, Rm 103, Winchester, IN 47394; 765-584-2427.

Ripley County

County Recorder, PO Box 404, Versailles, IN 47042. RE & UCC recording phone-812-689-5808; fax-812-689-0048; hours: 8AM-4PM
All records in one index. Index on computer back to 1989. Will search UCC records, but not tax liens or real estate. UCC search per debtor name- $8.00 per search; $5.00 per add'l name on same form. Copies included in search fee. RE or tax lien copy- $1.00 per page. Cert fee- $5.00 per doc plus copy fee. Payee- Ripley County Recorder. **Other phones:** Treasurer- 812-689-6352. **Property tax/Assessor-** PO Box 382, Versailles, IN 47042; 812-689-5656.

Rush County

County Recorder, Courthouse, Rm 208, Rushville, IN 46173. 765-932-2388; hours: 8AM-4PM
Office will perform a UCC search but public must search other records themselves. Search fee $8.00; $5.00 each add'l. Copy fee $1.00 per page. Cert

fee- $5.00 per doc plus copy fee. Payee- Rush County Recorder. **Other phones:** Treasurer- 765-932-2386. **Property tax/Assessor-** 765-932-3242.

Scott County

County Recorder, 1 E. McClain St, #100, Scottsburg, IN 47170. 812-752-8442; fax-812-752-2678; hours: 8:30AM-4:30PM
Records indexed on a public use terminal back to 1992. Office will perform a UCC search but public must search other records themselves. UCC search per debtor name- $8.00; $5.00 each add'l. Copy fee $1.00 per page. UCC copy fee included in search fee. Cert fee- $5.00 per doc plus copy fee. Payee- Scott County Recorder. **Other phones:** Treasurer- 812-752-8414. **Property tax/Assessor-** 1 E. McClain St, #150, Scottsburg, IN 47170; 812-752-8436.

Shelby County

County Recorder, 407 S. Harrison; Courthouse, Shelbyville, IN 46176. RE & UCC recording phone-317-392-6370; fax-317-392-6393; hours: 8AM-4PM
Office will perform a UCC search but public must search other records themselves. UCC search per debtor name- $8.00; $5.00 each add'l. Copies included in search fee. RE record copy- $1.00 per page. Cert fee- $5.00 per doc plus copy fee. Payee- Shelby County Recorder. **Other phones:** Treasurer- 317-392-6375. **Property tax/Assessor-** 317-392-5481.

Spencer County

County Recorder, 200 Main; Courthouse, Rockport, IN 47635. 812-649-6013; fax-812-649-6005; hours: 8AM-4PM
Office will perform a UCC search but public must search other records themselves. UCC search per debtor name- $8.00; $5.00 each add'l. Copies included in search fee. Self serve copy $.50 per page. RE record copy- $1.00 per page. Cert fee- $5.00 per doc plus copy fee. Payee- Spencer County Recorder. **Other phones:** Treasurer- 812-649-4556. **Property tax/Assessor-** 812-649-2381.

St. Joseph County

County Recorder, 227 W Jefferson; Rm 321, South Bend, IN 46601. RE & UCC recording phone-574-235-9525; fax-574-235-5170; hours: 8AM-4:30PM
Records indexed on computer from 1991 to present, prior in index books. Only the public may search, except UCC. UCC search per debtor name- $8.00; $5.00 each add'l. Copy fee $1.00 per page. Cert fee- $5.00 per doc, copy fee extra. Payee- St. Joseph County Recorder. **Online access to Recording, Real Estate, Deed, Lien, Most Wanted records:** Recorder office data by subscription on either the Laredo system using subscription and fees or the Tapestry System using credit card, https://tapestry.fidlar.com/tapsearch.aspx; $3.99 search; $.50 per image. Index back to 12/1992; images 1998 to 2005. **Other phones:** Treasurer- 574-235-9531; Elections- 574-235-9635; Vital Records- 574-235-6719. **Property tax/Assessor-** 574-235-9523.

Starke County

County Recorder, PO Box 1, Knox, IN 46534. 574-772-9110, R/E recording phone-574-772-9109, UCC recording phone-574-772-9109; fax-574-772-9178; hours: 8:30AM-4PM
Office will perform a UCC search but public must search other records themselves. UCC search per debtor name- $8.00; $5.00 each add'l. Copies included in search fee. RE record copy- $1.00 per page. Cert fee- $5.00 per doc plus copy fee. Payee- Starke County Recorder. **Other phones:** Treasurer- 574-772-9113. **Property tax/Assessor-** 574-772-9107.

Steuben County

County Recorder, PO Box 397, Angola, IN 46703. RE & UCC recording phone-260-668-1000 x1700; fax-260-665-8483; hours: 8AM-4:30PM

All records in one index. Records indexed on a public use terminal back to 1994. Office will perform a UCC search but public must search other records themselves. Search fee $8.00; $5.00 each add'l. Copies included in search fee. RE or tax lien copy- $1.00 per page. Cert fee- $5.00 per doc plus copy fee. Payee- Steuben County Recorder. **Other phones:** Treasurer- 260-668-1000 x1900; Elections- 260-668-1000 x2220; Vital Records- 260-668-1000 x1500. **Property tax/Assessor-** 260-668-1000 x1000.

Sullivan County

County Recorder, 100 Court House Sq, Rm 205, Sullivan, IN 47882-1565. 812-268-4844; fax-812-268-0521; hours: 8AM-4PM
All records in one index. Records indexed on a public use terminal back to 8/2/2004. Office will perform a UCC search but public must search other records themselves. UCC search per debtor name- $8.00; $5.00 each add'l. Copy fee $1.00 per page. Cert fee- $5.00 per doc plus copy fee. Payee- Sullivan County Recorder. **Other phones:** Treasurer- 812-268-6410; Vital Records- 812-268-4029. **Property tax/Assessor-** 812-268-4657.

Switzerland County

County Recorder, 212 W Main; Courthouse, Vevay, IN 47043. 812-427-2544; hours: 8AM-3:30PM
Separate indices to search include deeds, mortgages, liens, misc. Only the public may search. Copy fee $1.00 per copy. Cert fee- $5.00 per doc plus copy fee. Payee- Switzerland County Recorder. **Other phones:** Treasurer- 812-427-3369; Auditor- 812-427-3302. **Property tax/Assessor-** same address as above. 812-427-3379.

Tippecanoe County

County Recorder, 20 N. 3rd St, Lafayette, IN 47901. Main phone & R/E recording-765-423-9352, UCC recording phone-765-423-9353; fax-765-423-9158; 8AM-4:30PM http://county.tippecanoe.in.us
Office will perform a UCC search and federal tax lien but public must search other records themselves. General search fee $1.00 per page found. UCC search per debtor name- $5.00 per name + $3.00 supplemental per season. Copies included in search fee. RE or tax lien copy- $1.00 per page. Cert fee- $5.00 per doc plus copy fee. Payee- Tippecanoe County Recorder. **Property tax/Assessor-** 765-423-9255.

Tipton County

County Recorder, 101 E. Jefferson St.; Courthouse, Tipton, IN 46072. 765-675-4614; fax-765-675-3893; hours: 8AM-4PM
Records indexed on computer back to 5/ 1996. Only the public may search. Copy fee $1.00 per page. Cert fee- $5.00 per doc plus copy fee. Payee- Tipton County Recorder. **Other phones:** Treasurer- 765-675-2742; Appraiser/Auditor- 765-675-2724. **Property tax/Assessor-** same address. 765-675-2465.

Union County

County Recorder, 26 W. Union St, Liberty, IN 47353. RE & UCC recording phone-765-458-5434; fax-765-458-5263; hours: 8AM-4PM
Separate indices to search. Record index not computerized. Office will perform a UCC search but public must search other records themselves. UCC search per debtor name- $8.00; $5.00 each add'l. Copies included in search fee. RE or tax lien copy- $1.00 per page. Cert fee- $5.00 per doc plus copy fee. Payee- Union County Recorder. **Other phones:** Treasurer- 317-458-6491. **Property tax/Assessor-** 317-458-5331.

Vanderburgh County

County Recorder, PO Box 1037, Evansville, IN 47708. RE & UCC recording phone- 812-435-5215; fax-812-435-5580; 8-4:30 www.assessor.evansville.net

Office will perform a UCC search but public must search other records themselves. UCC search per debtor name- $8.00; $5.00 each add'l. Copy fee $1.00 per page. No UCC copy fee. Cert fee- $5.00 per doc plus copy fee. Payee- Vanderburgh County Recorder. **Online access to Property records:** Records on the County Assessor Property database are free at www.assessor.evansville.net/disclaim.htm. **Other phones:** Treasurer- 812-435-5248; Elections- 812-435-5160; Vital Records- 812-435-5681. **Property tax/Assessor-** 812-435-5273.

Vermillion County

County Recorder, PO Box 145, Newport, IN 47966-0145. 765-492-5003; fax-765-492-5000- auditor; hours: 8AM-4PM
Separate indices to search include mortgages and misc. deeds, imaged by instrument number. Records indexed on computer back to 1994. Office will perform a UCC search but public must search other records themselves. UCC search per debtor name- $8.00,1st,$5.00 add'l. Copy fee $1.00 per page. Cert fee- $5.00 per doc plus $1.00 per page, plus copy fee. Payee- Vermillion County Recorder. **Property tax/Assessor-** 765-492-5004.

Vigo County

County Recorder, 199 Oak St, Terre Haute, IN 47807. RE & UCC recording phone-812-462-3301; fax-812-232-2219; 8-4 www.vigocounty.org/recorder/
Separate indices to search include deeds, mortgages, misc. Only the office personnel may search. Search fee $8.00. Copy fee $1.00 per page, also $1.00 per page fax back. Cert fee- $5.00 per doc plus copy fee. Payee- Vigo County Recorder. **Online access to Assessor, Property, Tax Sale records:** Search Vigo County property information by parcel, name or address at www.vigocounty.org/assessor/. **Other phones:** Treasurer- 812-462-3251; Vital Records- 812-462-2442. **Property tax/Assessor-** 189 Oak Street, Terre haute, IN 47807; 812-462-3358.

Wabash County

County Recorder, One W. Hill St.; Courthouse, Wabash, IN 46992. RE & UCC recording phone-260-563-0661 x253; hours: 8AM-4PM
All records in one index. Records indexed on a public use terminal back to 1/1/2004. Only the public may search. Copies included in search fee. RE or tax lien copy- $1.00 per page. Cert fee- $5.00 per doc plus $1.00 per page copy fee. Payee- Wabash County Recorder. **Other phones:** Treasurer- 260-563-0661 x259. **Property tax/Assessor-** 260-563-0661 x227.

Warren County

County Recorder, 125 N. Monroe; Courthouse - #10, Williamsport, IN 47993-1162. 765-762-3174; fax-765-762-7222; hours: 8AM-4PM
Separate indices to search include computer & books. Records indexed on a public use terminal back to 1/1/1997. Only the public may search. Copy fee $1.00 per page. Cert fee- $5.00 per doc plus copy fee. Payee- Warren County Recorder. **Other phones:** Treasurer- 765-762-3562; Elections- 765-762-3510. **Property/Assessor-** 765-762-4528.

Warrick County

County Recorder, PO Box 285, Boonville, IN 47601. RE & UCC recording phone-812-897-6165; fax-812-897-6168; hours: 8AM-4PM www.warrickcounty.gov/departments/recorder.htm
Records indexed on computer, books and aperture cards. Office will perform a UCC search but public must search other records themselves. UCC search per debtor name- $8.00; $5.00 each add'l. Copy fee $1.00 per page. Cert fee- $5.00 per doc plus copy fee. Payee- Warrick County Recorder. **Online access to Assessor, Property, Tax Bill records:** Access to the assessors property tax data is free at www.pvdnetwork.com/Search/Search.asp. Also,

access to tax bill records is free at www.pvdnetwork.com/Search/TaxSearch.asp. **Other phones:** Treasurer- 812-897-6166; Elections- 812-897-6161. **Property tax/Assessor-** 812-897-6125.

Washington County

County Recorder, Courthouse, Salem, IN 47167. 812-883-4001; fax-812-883-4020; hours: 8:30AM-4PM (F 8:30AM-6PM)
Separate indices to search include deed, mortgage, misc., UCC's, veteran discharge, cemetery all before 1997. Records indexed on computer back to October, 1996. Only the public may search. Copy fee $1.00 per page. Cert fee- $5.00 per doc plus copy fee. Payee- Washington County Recorder. **Other phones:** Treasurer- 812-883-3307. **Property tax/Assessor-** 812-883-4000.

Wayne County

County Recorder, 401 E Main St; County Admin. Bldg, Richmond, IN 47374. RE & UCC recording phone-765-973-9235; fax-765-973-9341; 8:30AM-5PM M; (4:30 PM T-F) www.co.wayne.in.us/offices
Office will perform a UCC search but public must search other records themselves. UCC search fee $8.00; $5.00 each add'l entry found. Copy fee $1.00 per page. Cert fee- $5.00 per doc plus copy fee. Payee- Wayne County Recorder. **Online access to Property, Assessor, Marriage records:** Access to the county property records database is free at http://prc.co.wayne.in.us. Marriage records are being added irregularly to the website at www.co.wayne.in.us/marriage/retrieve.cgi. Records are from 1811 forward, with recent years being added. **Other phones:** Treasurer- 765-973-9238; Elections- 765-973-9226; Vital Records- 765-973-9245. **Property tax/Assessor-** 765-973-9254.

Wells County

County Recorder, 102 W Market St; Courthouse #203, Bluffton, IN 46714. RE & UCC recording phone-260-824-6507; fax-260-824-1238; hours: 8AM-4:30PM www.wellscounty.org
Office will perform a UCC search but public must search other records themselves. UCC search per debtor name- $8.00; $5.00 each add'l. Copies included in search fee. Real estate or tax lien record copy- $1.00 per page. Cert fee- $5.00 per doc plus copy fee. Payee- Wells County Recorder. **Other phones:** Treasurer- 260-824-6514; Appraiser/Auditor- 260-824-6476; Elections- 260-824-6482; Vital Records- 260-824-6489; Auditor- 260-824-6474. **Property tax/Assessor-** 260-824-6476.

White County

County Recorder, PO Box 127, Monticello, IN 47960. 574-583-5912; fax-574-583-1521; hours: 8AM-4PM
Records indexed on computer back to 1988. Only the public may search. Copy fee $1.00 per page. Cert fee- $6.00 per doc plus copy fee. Payee- White County Recorder. **Property tax/Assessor-** 574-583-7755.

Whitley County

County Recorder, 220 W Van Buren St #206; County Gov't Ctr, Columbia City, IN 46725. RE & UCC recording phone-260-248-3106; fax-260-248-3163; hours: 8AM-4:30PM M-Th; 8AM-6PM F
Separate indices to search include mortgage, deed, UCC, misc. Office will perform a UCC search but public must search other records themselves. UCC search per debtor name- $8.00; $5.00 each add'l. Copy fee $1.00 per page. UCC copy fee- none. Cert fee- $5.00 per doc plus copy fee. Payee- Whitley County Recorder. **Other phones:** Treasurer- 260-248-3105; Elections- 260-248-3102. **Property tax/Assessor-** 260-248-3109.

Indiana County Locator

You will usually be able to find the city name in the City/County Cross Reference below. In that case, it is a simple matter to determine the county from the cross reference. However, only the official US Postal Service city names are included in this index. There are an additional 40,000 place names that people use in their addresses. Therefore, we have also included a ZIP/City Cross Reference immediately following the City/County Cross Reference.

If you know the ZIP Code but the city name does not appear in the City/County Cross Reference index, look up the ZIP Code in the ZIP/City Cross Reference, find the city name, then look up the city name in the City/County Cross Reference. For example, you want to know the county for an address of Menands, NY 12204. There is no "Menands" in the City/County Cross Reference. The ZIP/City Cross Reference shows that ZIP Codes 12201-12288 are for the city of Albany. Looking back in the City/County Cross Reference, Albany is in Albany County.

Indiana City/County Cross Reference

ADVANCE Boone
AKRON (46910) Fulton(58), Kosciusko(31), Miami(9)
ALAMO Montgomery
ALBANY (47320) Delaware(92), Randolph(7)
ALBION Noble
ALEXANDRIA (46001) Madison(97), Delaware(2)
AMBIA (47917) Warren(51), Benton(48)
AMBOY (46911) Miami(89), Wabash(10)
AMO Hendricks
ANDERSON (46017) Madison(96), Delaware(3)
ANDERSON Madison
ANDREWS (46702) Huntington(91), Wabash(8)
ANGOLA Steuben
ARCADIA Hamilton
ARCOLA Allen
ARGOS (46501) Marshall(96), Fulton(3)
ARLINGTON (46104) Rush(98), Shelby(1)
ASHLEY (46705) DeKalb(70), Steuben(29)
ATHENS Fulton
ATLANTA (46031) Hamilton(62), Tipton(37)
ATTICA (47918) Fountain(81), Warren(17), Tippecanoe(1)
ATWOOD Kosciusko
AUBURN (46706) DeKalb(98), Allen(1)
AURORA Dearborn
AUSTIN (47102) Scott(85), Jackson(14)
AVILLA (46710) Noble(96), DeKalb(3)
AVOCA Lawrence
AVON Hendricks
BAINBRIDGE Putnam
BARGERSVILLE (46106) Johnson(96), Morgan(3)
BATESVILLE (47006) Franklin(58), Ripley(40)
BATH (47010) Franklin(69), Union(30)
BATTLE GROUND (47920) Tippecanoe(79), White(14), Carroll(6)
BEDFORD Lawrence
BEECH GROVE Marion
BELLMORE Parke
BENNINGTON (47011) Switzerland(55), Ohio(44)
BENTONVILLE Fayette
BERNE Adams
BETHLEHEM Clark
BEVERLY SHORES Porter
BICKNELL Knox
BIPPUS Huntington
BIRDSEYE (47513) Dubois(78), Crawford(15), Perry(4), Orange(1)
BLANFORD Vermillion
BLOOMFIELD Greene
BLOOMINGDALE Parke
BLOOMINGTON (47404) Monroe(98), Owen(1)
BLOOMINGTON Monroe
BLUFFTON (46714) Wells(96), Adams(3)
BOGGSTOWN (46110) Shelby(94), Johnson(5)

BOONE GROVE Porter
BOONVILLE (47601) Warrick(98), Spencer(1)
BORDEN (47106) Clark(90), Washington(5), Floyd(4)
BOSTON Wayne
BOSWELL (47921) Benton(81), Warren(18)
BOURBON (46504) Marshall(96), Kosciusko(3)
BOWLING GREEN (47833) Owen(51), Clay(48)
BRADFORD Harrison
BRANCHVILLE Perry
BRAZIL (47834) Clay(89), Vigo(6), Parke(4)
BREMEN (46506) Marshall(88), St. Joseph(11)
BRIDGETON Parke
BRIMFIELD Noble
BRINGHURST Carroll
BRISTOL Elkhart
BRISTOW Perry
BROOK (47922) Newton(94), Jasper(5)
BROOKLYN Morgan
BROOKSTON (47923) White(87), Carroll(12)
BROOKVILLE Franklin
BROWNSBURG Hendricks
BROWNSTOWN Jackson
BROWNSVILLE (47325) Union(78), Fayette(19), Wayne(2)
BRUCEVILLE Knox
BRYANT (47326) Jay(96), Adams(2)
BUCK CREEK Tippecanoe
BUCKSKIN Gibson
BUFFALO White
BUNKER HILL Miami
BURKET Kosciusko
BURLINGTON Carroll
BURNETTSVILLE (47926) White(67), Carroll(29), Cass(2)
BURNEY Decatur
BURROWS Carroll
BUTLER DeKalb
BUTLERVILLE Jennings
CAMBRIDGE CITY (47327) Wayne(94), Henry(4)
CAMBY (46113) Morgan(55), Marion(29), Hendricks(15)
CAMDEN (46917) Carroll(98), Cass(1)
CAMPBELLSBURG (47108) Washington(91), Orange(8)
CANAAN (47224) Jefferson(98), Switzerland(1)
CANNELBURG Daviess
CANNELTON Perry
CARBON (47837) Parke(66), Clay(33)
CARLISLE Sullivan
CARMEL Hamilton
CARTERSBURG Hendricks
CARTHAGE (46115) Rush(94), Hancock(5)
CAYUGA Vermillion
CEDAR GROVE Franklin
CEDAR LAKE Lake

CELESTINE Dubois
CENTERPOINT (47840) Clay(95), Putnam(4)
CENTERVILLE Wayne
CENTRAL Harrison
CHALMERS White
CHANDLER Warrick
CHARLESTOWN Clark
CHARLOTTESVILLE (46117) Hancock(89), Henry(10)
CHESTERTON Porter
CHRISNEY Spencer
CHURUBUSCO (46723) Whitley(63), Allen(23), Noble(12)
CICERO Hamilton
CLARKS HILL (47930) Tippecanoe(73), Montgomery(14), Clinton(11)
CLARKSBURG Decatur
CLARKSVILLE Clark
CLAY CITY (47841) Clay(98), Owen(1)
CLAYPOOL Kosciusko
CLAYTON (46118) Hendricks(97), Morgan(2)
CLEAR CREEK Monroe
CLIFFORD Bartholomew
CLINTON Vermillion
CLOVERDALE (46120) Putnam(74), Owen(20), Morgan(4)
COAL CITY (47427) Owen(86), Clay(13)
COALMONT Clay
COATESVILLE (46121) Hendricks(56), Putnam(43)
COLBURN Tippecanoe
COLFAX (46035) Clinton(69), Boone(26), Montgomery(3)
COLUMBIA CITY (46725) Whitley(96), Noble(2)
COLUMBUS (47201) Bartholomew(95), Brown(4)
COLUMBUS Bartholomew
COMMISKEY (47227) Jennings(80), Jefferson(19)
CONNERSVILLE Fayette
CONVERSE (46919) Grant(53), Miami(37), Howard(8), Wabash(1)
CORTLAND Jackson
CORUNNA (46730) DeKalb(97), Noble(2)
CORY (47846) Clay(98), Vigo(1)
CORYDON Harrison
COVINGTON (47932) Fountain(89), Warren(5), Vermillion(4)
CRAIGVILLE (46731) Wells(90), Adams(9)
CRANDALL Harrison
CRANE Martin
CRAWFORDSVILLE Montgomery
CROMWELL (46732) Noble(57), Kosciusko(42)
CROSS PLAINS Ripley
CROTHERSVILLE (47229) Jackson(89), Jennings(10)
CROWN POINT (46307) Lake(98), Porter(1)
CROWN POINT Lake

CULVER (46511) Marshall(77), Starke(10), Fulton(10), Pulaski(1)
CUTLER (46920) Carroll(98), Clinton(1)
CYNTHIANA (47612) Posey(79), Gibson(20)
DALE (47523) Spencer(37), Dubois(33), Warrick(29)
DALEVILLE (47334) Delaware(98), Henry(1)
DANA Vermillion
DANVILLE Hendricks
DARLINGTON Montgomery
DAYTON Tippecanoe
DECATUR Adams
DECKER Knox
DEEDSVILLE Miami
DELONG Fulton
DELPHI Carroll
DEMOTTE (46310) Jasper(82), Newton(17)
DENHAM Pulaski
DENVER (46926) Miami(95), Cass(3)
DEPAUW Harrison
DEPUTY (47230) Jefferson(91), Jennings(8)
DERBY Perry
DILLSBORO (47018) Dearborn(97), Ohio(2)
DONALDSON Marshall
DUBLIN Wayne
DUBOIS (47527) Dubois(97), Orange(1)
DUGGER (47848) Sullivan(96), Greene(3)
DUNKIRK (47336) Jay(63), Blackford(20), Delaware(16)
DUNREITH Henry
DUPONT (47231) Jefferson(74), Jennings(25)
DYER Lake
EARL PARK (47942) Benton(96), Newton(3)
EARL PARK Benton
EAST CHICAGO Lake
EAST ENTERPRISE Switzerland
EATON (47338) Delaware(98), Blackford(1)
ECKERTY Crawford
ECONOMY Wayne
EDINBURGH (46124) Johnson(54), Bartholomew(26), Shelby(19)
EDWARDSPORT (47528) Knox(98), Sullivan(1)
ELBERFELD (47613) Warrick(91), Gibson(7)
ELIZABETH (47117) Harrison(97), Floyd(2)
ELIZABETHTOWN (47232) Bartholomew(69), Jennings(30)
ELKHART Elkhart
ELLETTSVILLE Monroe
ELNORA (47529) Daviess(96), Greene(3)
ELWOOD (46036) Madison(91), Tipton(7)
EMINENCE Morgan
EMISON Knox
ENGLISH (47118) Crawford(67), Orange(27), Perry(5)
ETNA GREEN (46524) Kosciusko(97), Marshall(2)

EVANSTON Spencer
EVANSVILLE (47712) Vanderburgh(86), Posey(13)
EVANSVILLE Vanderburgh
FAIR OAKS (47943) Jasper(55), Newton(45)
FAIRBANKS Sullivan
FAIRLAND Shelby
FAIRMOUNT (46928) Grant(97), Madison(2)
FALMOUTH (46127) Rush(75), Fayette(24)
FARMERSBURG (47850) Sullivan(76), Vigo(23)
FARMLAND Randolph
FERDINAND (47532) Dubois(69), Spencer(27), Perry(2)
FILLMORE Putnam
FINLY Hancock
FISHERS Hamilton
FLAT ROCK (47234) Shelby(92), Bartholomew(7)
FLORA (46929) Carroll(91), Howard(8)
FLORENCE Switzerland
FLOYDS KNOBS (47119) Floyd(95), Clark(4)
FOLSOMVILLE Warrick
FONTANET Vigo
FOREST Clinton
FORT BRANCH Gibson
FORT RITNER Lawrence
FORT WAYNE (46818) Allen(98), Whitley(1)
FORT WAYNE Allen
FORTVILLE (46040) Hancock(73), Hamilton(19), Madison(6)
FOUNTAIN CITY (47341) Wayne(97), Randolph(2)
FOUNTAINTOWN (46130) Shelby(72), Hancock(27)
FOWLER Benton
FOWLERTON Grant
FRANCESVILLE (47946) Pulaski(83), Jasper(15)
FRANCISCO Gibson
FRANKFORT (46041) Clinton(98), Carroll(1)
FRANKLIN Johnson
FRANKTON Madison
FREDERICKSBURG (47120) Washington(97), Harrison(2)
FREEDOM Owen
FREELANDVILLE Knox
FREETOWN (47235) Jackson(71), Brown(28)
FREMONT Steuben
FRENCH LICK (47432) Orange(87), Dubois(11), Martin(1)
FRIENDSHIP Ripley
FULDA Spencer
FULTON Fulton
GALVESTON (46932) Cass(90), Howard(5), Miami(4)
GARRETT DeKalb
GARY (46403) Lake(98), Porter(1)
GARY Lake
GAS CITY Grant
GASTON (47342) Delaware(97), Grant(1)
GENEVA (46740) Adams(93), Wells(4), Jay(2)
GENTRYVILLE (47537) Spencer(68), Warrick(31)
GEORGETOWN (47122) Floyd(62), Harrison(37)
GLENWOOD (46133) Fayette(57), Rush(42)
GOLDSMITH Tipton
GOODLAND (47948) Newton(72), Jasper(15), Benton(12)
GOSHEN Elkhart
GOSPORT (47433) Owen(72), Monroe(16), Morgan(10)
GRABILL Allen

GRAMMER Bartholomew
GRANDVIEW Spencer
GRANGER (46530) St. Joseph(95), Elkhart(4)
GRANTSBURG Crawford
GRASS CREEK Fulton
GRAYSVILLE Sullivan
GREENCASTLE (46135) Putnam(98), Parke(1)
GREENFIELD Hancock
GREENS FORK Wayne
GREENSBORO Henry
GREENSBURG Decatur
GREENTOWN Howard
GREENVILLE (47124) Floyd(74), Harrison(25)
GREENWOOD Johnson
GRIFFIN (47616) Posey(85), Gibson(14)
GRIFFITH Lake
GRISSOM AFB Miami
GRISSOM ARB Miami
GROVERTOWN (46531) Starke(97), Marshall(2)
GUILFORD Dearborn
GWYNNEVILLE Shelby
HAGERSTOWN (47346) Wayne(96), Henry(3)
HAMILTON (46742) Steuben(84), DeKalb(15)
HAMLET (46532) Starke(60), La Porte(39)
HAMMOND Lake
HANNA La Porte
HANOVER Jefferson
HARDINSBURG (47125) Orange(56), Washington(43)
HARLAN Allen
HARMONY Clay
HARRODSBURG Monroe
HARTFORD CITY Blackford
HARTSVILLE (47244) Bartholomew(74), Decatur(25)
HATFIELD Spencer
HAUBSTADT (47639) Gibson(76), Vanderburgh(21), Warrick(1)
HAYDEN Jennings
HAZLETON (47640) Gibson(70), Pike(29)
HEBRON (46341) Porter(79), Lake(17), Jasper(1)
HELMSBURG Brown
HELTONVILLE (47436) Lawrence(92), Monroe(7)
HEMLOCK Howard
HENRYVILLE (47126) Clark(95), Washington(3), Scott(1)
HIGHLAND Lake
HILLISBURG Clinton
HILLSBORO (47949) Fountain(97), Montgomery(2)
HILLSDALE Vermillion
HOAGLAND (46745) Allen(97), Adams(2)
HOBART (46342) Lake(98), Porter(1)
HOBBS Tipton
HOLLAND (47541) Dubois(74), Pike(18), Warrick(4), Spencer(2)
HOLTON Ripley
HOMER Rush
HOPE Bartholomew
HOWE LaGrange
HUDSON (46747) Steuben(77), LaGrange(13), DeKalb(8)
HUNTERTOWN (46748) Allen(96), DeKalb(2), Noble(1)
HUNTINGBURG (47542) Dubois(97), Pike(2)
HUNTINGTON Huntington
HURON Lawrence
HYMERA Sullivan
IDAVILLE (47950) White(91), Carroll(8)
INDIANAPOLIS (46229) Marion(92), Hancock(7)
INDIANAPOLIS (46234) Marion(67), Hendricks(32)

INDIANAPOLIS (46239) Marion(98), Hancock(1)
INDIANAPOLIS (46256) Marion(93), Hamilton(6)
INDIANAPOLIS (46259) Marion(91), Shelby(4), Johnson(3)
INDIANAPOLIS (46278) Marion(94), Hendricks(5)
INDIANAPOLIS Hamilton
INDIANAPOLIS Marion
INGALLS Madison
INGLEFIELD Vanderburgh
IRELAND Dubois
JAMESTOWN (46147) Boone(91), Hendricks(8)
JASONVILLE (47438) Greene(70), Clay(24), Sullivan(5)
JASPER Dubois
JEFFERSONVILLE Clark
JONESBORO Grant
JONESVILLE Bartholomew
JUDSON Parke
KEMPTON (46049) Tipton(91), Clinton(8)
KENDALLVILLE Noble
KENNARD Henry
KENTLAND Newton
KEWANNA (46939) Fulton(93), Pulaski(6)
KEYSTONE Wells
KIMMELL Noble
KINGMAN (47952) Fountain(84), Parke(15)
KINGSBURY La Porte
KINGSFORD HEIGHTS La Porte
KIRKLIN (46050) Clinton(73), Boone(22), Tipton(3)
KNIGHTSTOWN (46148) Henry(84), Rush(15)
KNIGHTSVILLE Clay
KNOX Starke
KOKOMO (46901) Howard(98), Miami(1)
KOKOMO Howard
KOLEEN Greene
KOUTS Porter
KURTZ Jackson
LA CROSSE (46348) La Porte(98), Porter(1)
LA FONTAINE (46940) Wabash(87), Huntington(8), Grant(3)
LA PORTE La Porte
LACONIA Harrison
LADOGA (47954) Montgomery(94), Putnam(4)
LAFAYETTE Tippecanoe
LAGRANGE (46761) LaGrange(95), Steuben(4)
LAGRO Wabash
LAKE CICOTT Cass
LAKE STATION Lake
LAKE VILLAGE Newton
LAKETON Wabash
LAKEVILLE (46536) St. Joseph(92), Marshall(7)
LAMAR Spencer
LANDESS Grant
LANESVILLE (47136) Harrison(81), Floyd(18)
LAOTTO (46763) Noble(85), DeKalb(14)
LAPAZ Marshall
LAPEL Madison
LAPORTE La Porte
LARWILL (46764) Whitley(92), Noble(7)
LAUREL Franklin
LAWRENCEBURG Dearborn
LEAVENWORTH (47137) Crawford(96), Perry(2)
LEBANON Boone
LEESBURG Kosciusko
LEITERS FORD Fulton
LEO Allen
LEOPOLD Perry
LEROY Lake
LEWIS (47858) Vigo(48), Clay(37), Sullivan(14)

LEWISVILLE (47352) Rush(52), Henry(46), Fayette(1)
LEXINGTON (47138) Jefferson(52), Scott(46)
LIBERTY (47353) Union(94), Franklin(5)
LIBERTY CENTER (46766) Wells(98), Huntington(1)
LIBERTY MILLS Wabash
LIGONIER (46767) Noble(96), Elkhart(1), LaGrange(1)
LINCOLN CITY Spencer
LINDEN (47955) Montgomery(97), Tippecanoe(2)
LINN GROVE Adams
LINTON Greene
LITTLE YORK Washington
LIZTON Hendricks
LOGANSPORT (46947) Cass(98), Carroll(1)
LOOGOOTEE (47553) Martin(79), Daviess(20)
LOSANTVILLE (47354) Randolph(72), Henry(16), Delaware(6), Wayne(4)
LOWELL Lake
LUCERNE (46950) Cass(96), Fulton(3)
LYNN Randolph
LYNNVILLE (47619) Warrick(92), Gibson(6)
LYONS Greene
MACKEY Gibson
MACY (46951) Miami(70), Fulton(29)
MADISON (47250) Jefferson(96), Ripley(2), Switzerland(1)
MAGNET Perry
MANILLA (46150) Rush(92), Shelby(7)
MARENGO (47140) Orange(53), Crawford(46)
MARIAH HILL Spencer
MARION Grant
MARKLE (46770) Wells(73), Huntington(26)
MARKLEVILLE (46056) Madison(82), Hancock(14), Henry(3)
MARSHALL Parke
MARTINSVILLE Morgan
MARYSVILLE (47141) Clark(92), Scott(7)
MATTHEWS Grant
MAUCKPORT Harrison
MAXWELL Hancock
MAYS Rush
MC CORDSVILLE (46055) Hancock(75), Hamilton(24)
MECCA Parke
MEDARYVILLE (47957) Pulaski(89), Jasper(10)
MEDORA (47260) Jackson(98), Lawrence(1)
MELLOTT Fountain
MEMPHIS Clark
MENTONE (46539) Kosciusko(91), Fulton(6), Marshall(2)
MEROM Sullivan
MERRILLVILLE Lake
METAMORA Franklin
MEXICO Miami
MIAMI Miami
MICHIGAN CITY (46360) La Porte(94), Porter(5)
MICHIGAN CITY La Porte
MICHIGANTOWN Clinton
MIDDLEBURY (46540) Elkhart(90), LaGrange(9)
MIDDLETOWN (47356) Henry(92), Madison(5), Delaware(2)
MIDLAND Greene
MILAN Ripley
MILFORD (46542) Kosciusko(95), Elkhart(4)
MILL CREEK La Porte
MILLERSBURG (46543) Elkhart(71), LaGrange(27), Noble(1)
MILLHOUSEN Decatur

MILLTOWN (47145) Crawford(96), Washington(3)

MILROY (46156) Rush(95), Decatur(4)

MILTON (47357) Wayne(71), Fayette(22), Madison(5)

MISHAWAKA St. Joseph

MITCHELL Lawrence

MODOC (47358) Randolph(98), Wayne(1)

MONGO LaGrange

MONON (47959) White(87), Jasper(9), Pulaski(2)

MONROE Adams

MONROE CITY Knox

MONROEVILLE (46773) Allen(89), Adams(10)

MONROVIA Morgan

MONTEREY (46960) Pulaski(62), Starke(30), Fulton(6)

MONTEZUMA Parke

MONTGOMERY Daviess

MONTICELLO (47960) White(88), Carroll(11)

MONTMORENCI Tippecanoe

MONTPELIER (47359) Blackford(87), Wells(11)

MOORELAND (47360) Henry(94), Wayne(3), Randolph(1)

MOORES HILL Dearborn

MOORESVILLE (46158) Morgan(90), Hendricks(9)

MORGANTOWN (46160) Brown(53), Morgan(29), Johnson(16)

MOROCCO Newton

MORRIS Ripley

MORRISTOWN (46161) Shelby(74), Hancock(17), Rush(7)

MOUNT AYR Newton

MOUNT PLEASANT Perry

MOUNT SAINT FRANCIS Floyd

MOUNT SUMMIT Henry

MOUNT VERNON Posey

MULBERRY (46058) Clinton(97), Tippecanoe(2)

MUNCIE Delaware

MUNSTER Lake

NABB (47147) Clark(42), Scott(31), Jefferson(25)

NAPOLEON Ripley

NAPPANEE (46550) Elkhart(84), Kosciusko(10), Marshall(4)

NASHVILLE (47448) Brown(98), Monroe(1)

NEBRASKA Jennings

NEEDHAM (46162) Johnson(57), Shelby(42)

NEW ALBANY Floyd

NEW CARLISLE (46552) La Porte(56), St. Joseph(43)

NEW CASTLE Henry

NEW GOSHEN Vigo

NEW HARMONY Posey

NEW HAVEN Allen

NEW LEBANON Sullivan

NEW LISBON Henry

NEW MARKET Montgomery

NEW MIDDLETOWN Harrison

NEW PALESTINE (46163) Hancock(94), Shelby(4)

NEW PARIS Elkhart

NEW POINT Decatur

NEW RICHMOND (47967) Montgomery(92), Tippecanoe(7)

NEW ROSS (47968) Montgomery(86), Boone(8), Hendricks(4)

NEW SALISBURY Harrison

NEW TRENTON Franklin

NEW WASHINGTON Clark

NEW WAVERLY Cass

NEWBERRY (47449) Greene(93), Daviess(5), Martin(1)

NEWBURGH Warrick

NEWPORT Vermillion

NEWTOWN Fountain

NINEVEH (46164) Brown(69), Johnson(30)

NOBLESVILLE Hamilton

NORMAN (47264) Jackson(72), Lawrence(24), Monroe(3)

NORTH JUDSON (46366) Starke(96), Pulaski(3)

NORTH LIBERTY (46554) St. Joseph(97), La Porte(3)

NORTH MANCHESTER (46962) Wabash(94), Kosciusko(5)

NORTH SALEM (46165) Hendricks(98), Putnam(1)

NORTH VERNON Jennings

NORTH WEBSTER Kosciusko

NOTRE DAME St. Joseph

OAKFORD Howard

OAKLAND CITY (47660) Gibson(85), Pike(13)

OAKTOWN (47561) Knox(93), Sullivan(6)

OAKVILLE Delaware

ODON Daviess

OLDENBURG Franklin

ONWARD Cass

OOLITIC Lawrence

ORA Starke

ORESTES Madison

ORLAND (46776) Steuben(76), LaGrange(23)

ORLEANS (47452) Orange(82), Lawrence(16)

OSCEOLA (46561) St. Joseph(87), Elkhart(12)

OSGOOD Ripley

OSSIAN (46777) Wells(93), Allen(3), Adams(2)

OSSIAN Steuben

OSSIAN Wells

OTISCO Clark

OTTERBEIN (47970) Benton(45), Warren(34), Tippecanoe(18)

OTWELL (47564) Pike(87), Dubois(12)

OWENSBURG Greene

OWENSVILLE Gibson

OXFORD Benton

PALMYRA (47164) Harrison(72), Washington(27)

PAOLI Orange

PARAGON (46166) Morgan(89), Owen(10)

PARIS CROSSING (47270) Jennings(93), Jefferson(6)

PARKER CITY (47368) Randolph(84), Delaware(15)

PATOKA Gibson

PATRICKSBURG Owen

PATRIOT Switzerland

PAXTON Sullivan

PEKIN (47165) Washington(96), Clark(1), Floyd(1)

PENCE Warren

PENDLETON (46064) Madison(94), Hancock(4)

PENNVILLE (47369) Jay(95), Blackford(4)

PERRYSVILLE Vermillion

PERSHING Wayne

PERU (46970) Miami(93), Cass(3), Wabash(2)

PETERSBURG Pike

PETROLEUM Wells

PIERCETON (46562) Kosciusko(85), Noble(8), Whitley(6)

PIERCEVILLE Ripley

PIMENTO (47866) Vigo(96), Sullivan(3)

PINE VILLAGE (47975) Warren(93), Benton(6)

PITTSBORO (46167) Hendricks(98), Boone(1)

PLAINFIELD Hendricks

PLAINVILLE Daviess

PLEASANT LAKE Steuben

PLEASANT MILLS Adams

PLYMOUTH Marshall

POLAND (47868) Owen(83), Clay(13), Putnam(2)

PONETO Wells

PORTAGE Porter

PORTLAND Jay

POSEYVILLE (47633) Posey(93), Gibson(4), Vanderburgh(1)

PRAIRIE CREEK Vigo

PRAIRIETON Vigo

PREBLE Adams

PRINCETON Gibson

PUTNAMVILLE Putnam

QUINCY (47456) Owen(60), Morgan(35), Putnam(2)

RAGSDALE Knox

RAMSEY Harrison

REDKEY (47373) Jay(82), Randolph(17)

REELSVILLE Putnam

REMINGTON (47977) Jasper(79), Benton(19), White(1)

RENSSELAER Jasper

REYNOLDS White

RICHLAND Spencer

RICHMOND Wayne

RIDGEVILLE (47380) Randolph(91), Jay(8)

RILEY Vigo

RISING SUN Ohio

ROACHDALE (46172) Putnam(97), Montgomery(2)

ROANN (46974) Wabash(61), Miami(38)

ROANOKE (46783) Huntington(50), Allen(39), Whitley(8), Wells(2)

ROCHESTER Fulton

ROCKFIELD Carroll

ROCKPORT Spencer

ROCKVILLE Parke

ROLLING PRAIRIE La Porte

ROME Perry

ROME CITY Noble

ROMNEY (47981) Tippecanoe(88), Montgomery(11)

ROSEDALE (47874) Parke(51), Vigo(33), Clay(14)

ROSELAWN Newton

ROSSVILLE (46065) Clinton(59), Carroll(40)

ROYAL CENTER (46978) Cass(93), Pulaski(3), White(3)

RUSHVILLE Rush

RUSSELLVILLE (46175) Putnam(89), Parke(7), Montgomery(3)

RUSSIAVILLE (46979) Howard(83), Clinton(10), Tipton(3), Carroll(1)

SAINT ANTHONY Dubois

SAINT BERNICE Vermillion

SAINT CROIX (47576) Perry(95), Crawford(4)

SAINT JOE DeKalb

SAINT JOHN Lake

SAINT MARY OF THE WOODS Vigo

SAINT MEINRAD (47577) Spencer(93), Perry(6)

SAINT PAUL (47272) Decatur(69), Shelby(28), Rush(2)

SALAMONIA Jay

SALEM Washington

SAN PIERRE (46374) Starke(95), Pulaski(3)

SANDBORN (47578) Knox(81), Greene(17)

SANDFORD Vigo

SANTA CLAUS Spencer

SARATOGA Randolph

SCHERERVILLE Lake

SCHNEIDER Lake

SCHNELLVILLE Dubois

SCIPIO Jennings

SCOTLAND Greene

SCOTTSBURG (47170) Scott(84), Washington(14)

SEDALIA Clinton

SEELYVILLE Vigo

SELLERSBURG (47172) Clark(92), Floyd(7)

SELMA Delaware

SERVIA Wabash

SEYMOUR (47274) Jackson(93), Bartholomew(3), Jennings(2)

SHARPSVILLE (46068) Tipton(90), Howard(9)

SHELBURN Sullivan

SHELBY Lake

SHEPARDSVILLE Vigo

SHERIDAN (46069) Hamilton(68), Boone(27), Clinton(4)

SHIPSHEWANA LaGrange

SHIRLEY (47384) Henry(72), Hancock(27)

SHOALS Martin

SIDNEY Kosciusko

SILVER LAKE (46982) Kosciusko(75), Wabash(20), Fulton(3)

SIMS Grant

SMITHVILLE Monroe

SOLSBERRY (47459) Greene(87), Owen(11)

SOMERSET Wabash

SOMERVILLE Gibson

SOUTH BEND St. Joseph

SOUTH MILFORD LaGrange

SOUTH WHITLEY (46787) Whitley(91), Kosciusko(7)

SPENCER Owen

SPENCERVILLE (46788) Allen(64), DeKalb(35)

SPICELAND Henry

SPRINGPORT (47386) Henry(97), Delaware(2)

SPRINGVILLE (47462) Lawrence(82), Greene(8), Monroe(8)

SPURGEON Pike

STANFORD Monroe

STAR CITY (46985) Pulaski(96), White(3)

STATE LINE Warren

STAUNTON Clay

STENDAL Pike

STILESVILLE (46180) Morgan(56), Hendricks(43)

STINESVILLE Monroe

STOCKWELL Tippecanoe

STRAUGHN (47387) Henry(98), Fayette(1)

STROH LaGrange

SULLIVAN Sullivan

SULPHUR Crawford

SULPHUR SPRINGS Henry

SUMAVA RESORTS Newton

SUMMITVILLE (46070) Madison(94), Delaware(3), Grant(2)

SUNMAN (47041) Ripley(61), Dearborn(38)

SWAYZEE (46986) Grant(98), Howard(1)

SWEETSER Grant

SWITZ CITY Greene

SYRACUSE (46567) Kosciusko(96), Elkhart(3)

TALBOT Benton

TANGIER Parke

TASWELL (47175) Crawford(92), Orange(7)

TAYLORSVILLE Bartholomew

TEFFT Jasper

TELL CITY Perry

TEMPLETON Benton

TENNYSON (47637) Warrick(87), Spencer(12)

TERRE HAUTE Vigo

THAYER Newton

THORNTOWN Boone

TIPPECANOE (46570) Marshall(88), Fulton(11)

TIPTON Tipton

TOBINSPORT Perry

TOPEKA (46571) LaGrange(98), Noble(1)

TRAFALGAR (46181) Johnson(84), Brown(15)

TROY (47588) Spencer(89), Perry(10)

TUNNELTON Lawrence
TWELVE MILE (46988) Cass(97), Fulton(2)
TYNER Marshall
UNDERWOOD (47177) Scott(57), Clark(42)
UNION CITY (47390) Randolph(95), Jay(4)
UNION MILLS (46382) La Porte(98), Lake(1)
UNIONDALE Wells
UNIONVILLE (47468) Monroe(59), Brown(40)
UNIVERSAL Vermillion
UPLAND (46989) Grant(96), Blackford(2), Delaware(1)
URBANA Wabash
VALLONIA (47281) Jackson(58), Washington(41)
VALPARAISO Porter
VAN BUREN (46991) Grant(85), Huntington(12), Wells(2)
VEEDERSBURG Fountain
VELPEN (47590) Pike(86), Dubois(13)
VERNON Jennings
VERSAILLES Ripley
VEVAY (47043) Switzerland(97), Jefferson(2)

VINCENNES Knox
WABASH Wabash
WADESVILLE Posey
WAKARUSA (46573) Elkhart(74), St. Joseph(25)
WALDRON (46182) Shelby(81), Rush(18)
WALKERTON (46574) St. Joseph(38), Marshall(22), Starke(21), La Porte(17)
WALLACE Fountain
WALTON Cass
WANATAH La Porte
WARREN (46792) Huntington(82), Wells(17)
WARSAW Kosciusko
WASHINGTON Daviess
WATERLOO (46793) DeKalb(98), Steuben(1)
WAVELAND (47989) Montgomery(81), Parke(15), Putnam(3)
WAWAKA Noble
WAYNETOWN (47990) Montgomery(86), Fountain(13)
WEBSTER Wayne
WEST BADEN SPRINGS Orange
WEST COLLEGE CORNER (47003) Franklin(86), Union(13)

WEST HARRISON (47060) Dearborn(72), Franklin(27)
WEST LAFAYETTE Tippecanoe
WEST LEBANON Warren
WEST MIDDLETON Howard
WEST NEWTON Marion
WEST TERRE HAUTE Vigo
WESTFIELD Hamilton
WESTPHALIA Knox
WESTPOINT Tippecanoe
WESTPORT (47283) Decatur(92), Bartholomew(4), Jennings(2)
WESTVILLE (46391) La Porte(76), Porter(23)
WHEATFIELD Jasper
WHEATLAND Knox
WHEELER Porter
WHITELAND Johnson
WHITESTOWN Boone
WHITING Lake
WILKINSON (46186) Hancock(96), Henry(3)
WILLIAMS (47470) Lawrence(97), Martin(2)
WILLIAMSBURG (47393) Wayne(71), Randolph(28)

WILLIAMSPORT Warren
WILLOW BRANCH Hancock
WINAMAC Pulaski
WINCHESTER Randolph
WINDFALL (46076) Tipton(94), Howard(5)
WINGATE (47994) Montgomery(77), Fountain(18), Tippecanoe(3)
WINONA LAKE Kosciusko
WINSLOW Pike
WOLCOTT (47995) White(96), Jasper(2)
WOLCOTTVILLE (46795) LaGrange(89), Noble(9)
WOLFLAKE Noble
WOODBURN Allen
WORTHINGTON (47471) Greene(81), Owen(18)
WYATT St. Joseph
YEOMAN Carroll
YODER (46798) Allen(92), Wells(7)
YORKTOWN Delaware
YOUNG AMERICA Cass
ZANESVILLE Allen
ZIONSVILLE (46077) Boone(91), Hamilton(7), Marion(1)

Indiana ZIP/City Cross Reference

ZIP	City
46001-46001	ALEXANDRIA
46011-46018	ANDERSON
46030-46030	ARCADIA
46031-46031	ATLANTA
46032-46033	CARMEL
46034-46034	CICERO
46035-46035	COLFAX
46036-46036	ELWOOD
46037-46038	FISHERS
46039-46039	FOREST
46040-46040	FORTVILLE
46041-46041	FRANKFORT
46044-46044	FRANKTON
46045-46045	GOLDSMITH
46046-46046	HILLISBURG
46047-46047	HOBBS
46048-46048	INGALLS
46049-46049	KEMPTON
46050-46050	KIRKLIN
46051-46051	LAPEL
46052-46052	LEBANON
46055-46055	MC CORDSVILLE
46056-46056	MARKLEVILLE
46057-46057	MICHIGANTOWN
46058-46058	MULBERRY
46060-46062	NOBLESVILLE
46063-46063	ORESTES
46064-46064	PENDLETON
46065-46065	ROSSVILLE
46067-46067	SEDALIA
46068-46068	SHARPSVILLE
46069-46069	SHERIDAN
46070-46070	SUMMITVILLE
46071-46071	THORNTOWN
46072-46072	TIPTON
46074-46074	WESTFIELD
46075-46075	WHITESTOWN
46076-46076	WINDFALL
46077-46077	ZIONSVILLE
46082-46082	CARMEL
46102-46102	ADVANCE
46103-46103	AMO
46104-46104	ARLINGTON
46105-46105	BAINBRIDGE
46106-46106	BARGERSVILLE
46107-46107	BEECH GROVE
46110-46110	BOGGSTOWN
46111-46111	BROOKLYN
46112-46112	BROWNSBURG
46113-46113	CAMBY
46114-46114	CARTERSBURG
46115-46115	CARTHAGE
46117-46117	CHARLOTTESVILLE
46118-46118	CLAYTON
46120-46120	CLOVERDALE
46121-46121	COATESVILLE
46122-46122	DANVILLE
46123-46123	AVON
46124-46124	EDINBURGH
46125-46125	EMINENCE
46126-46126	FAIRLAND
46127-46127	FALMOUTH
46128-46128	FILLMORE
46129-46129	FINLY
46130-46130	FOUNTAINTOWN
46131-46131	FRANKLIN
46133-46133	GLENWOOD
46135-46135	GREENCASTLE
46140-46140	GREENFIELD
46142-46143	GREENWOOD
46144-46144	GWYNNEVILLE
46146-46146	HOMER
46147-46147	JAMESTOWN
46148-46148	KNIGHTSTOWN
46149-46149	LIZTON
46150-46150	MANILLA
46151-46151	MARTINSVILLE
46154-46154	MAXWELL
46155-46155	MAYS
46156-46156	MILROY
46157-46157	MONROVIA
46158-46158	MOORESVILLE
46160-46160	MORGANTOWN
46161-46161	MORRISTOWN
46162-46162	NEEDHAM
46163-46163	NEW PALESTINE
46164-46164	NINEVEH
46165-46165	NORTH SALEM
46166-46166	PARAGON
46167-46167	PITTSBORO
46168-46168	PLAINFIELD
46170-46170	PUTNAMVILLE
46171-46171	REELSVILLE
46172-46172	ROACHDALE
46173-46173	RUSHVILLE
46175-46175	RUSSELLVILLE
46176-46176	SHELBYVILLE
46180-46180	STILESVILLE
46181-46181	TRAFALGAR
46182-46182	WALDRON
46183-46183	WEST NEWTON
46184-46184	WHITELAND
46186-46186	WILKINSON
46187-46187	WILLOW BRANCH
46200-46298	INDIANAPOLIS
46301-46301	BEVERLY SHORES
46302-46302	BOONE GROVE
46303-46303	CEDAR LAKE
46304-46304	CHESTERTON
46307-46308	CROWN POINT
46310-46310	DEMOTTE
46311-46311	DYER
46312-46312	EAST CHICAGO
46319-46319	GRIFFITH
46320-46320	HAMMOND
46321-46321	MUNSTER
46322-46322	HIGHLAND
46323-46327	HAMMOND
46340-46340	HANNA
46341-46341	HEBRON
46342-46342	HOBART
46345-46345	KINGSBURY
46346-46346	KINGSFORD HEIGHTS
46347-46347	KOUTS
46348-46348	LA CROSSE
46349-46349	LAKE VILLAGE
46350-46350	LA PORTE
46350-46350	LAPORTE
46351-46352	LA PORTE
46352-46352	LAPORTE
46355-46355	LEROY
46356-46356	LOWELL
46360-46361	MICHIGAN CITY
46365-46365	MILL CREEK
46366-46366	NORTH JUDSON
46367-46367	LA PORTE
46368-46368	PORTAGE
46371-46371	ROLLING PRAIRIE
46372-46372	ROSELAWN
46373-46373	SAINT JOHN
46374-46374	SAN PIERRE
46375-46375	SCHERERVILLE
46376-46376	SCHNEIDER
46377-46377	SHELBY
46379-46379	SUMAVA RESORTS
46380-46380	TEFFT
46381-46381	THAYER
46382-46382	UNION MILLS
46383-46385	VALPARAISO
46390-46390	WANATAH
46391-46391	WESTVILLE
46392-46392	WHEATFIELD
46393-46393	WHEELER
46394-46394	WHITING
46399-46399	LOWELL
46400-46404	GARY
46405-46405	LAKE STATION
46406-46409	GARY
46410-46411	MERRILLVILLE
46501-46501	ARGOS
46502-46502	ATWOOD
46504-46504	BOURBON
46506-46506	BREMEN
46507-46507	BRISTOL
46508-46508	BURKET
46510-46510	CLAYPOOL
46511-46511	CULVER
46513-46513	DONALDSON
46514-46517	ELKHART
46524-46524	ETNA GREEN
46526-46528	GOSHEN
46530-46530	GRANGER
46531-46531	GROVERTOWN
46532-46532	HAMLET
46534-46534	KNOX
46536-46536	LAKEVILLE
46537-46537	LAPAZ
46538-46538	LEESBURG
46539-46539	MENTONE
46540-46540	MIDDLEBURY
46542-46542	MILFORD
46543-46543	MILLERSBURG
46544-46546	MISHAWAKA
46550-46550	NAPPANEE
46552-46552	NEW CARLISLE
46553-46553	NEW PARIS
46554-46554	NORTH LIBERTY
46555-46555	NORTH WEBSTER
46556-46556	NOTRE DAME
46561-46561	OSCEOLA
46562-46562	PIERCETON
46563-46563	PLYMOUTH
46565-46565	SHIPSHEWANA
46566-46566	SIDNEY
46567-46567	SYRACUSE
46570-46570	TIPPECANOE
46571-46571	TOPEKA
46572-46572	TYNER
46573-46573	WAKARUSA
46574-46574	WALKERTON
46580-46582	WARSAW
46590-46590	WINONA LAKE
46595-46595	WYATT
46600-46699	SOUTH BEND

46701-46701	ALBION
46702-46702	ANDREWS
46703-46703	ANGOLA
46704-46704	ARCOLA
46705-46705	ASHLEY
46706-46706	AUBURN
46710-46710	AVILLA
46711-46711	BERNE
46713-46713	BIPPUS
46714-46714	BLUFFTON
46720-46720	BRIMFIELD
46721-46721	BUTLER
46723-46723	CHURUBUSCO
46725-46725	COLUMBIA CITY
46730-46730	CORUNNA
46731-46731	CRAIGVILLE
46732-46732	CROMWELL
46733-46733	DECATUR
46737-46737	FREMONT
46738-46738	GARRETT
46740-46740	GENEVA
46741-46741	GRABILL
46742-46742	HAMILTON
46743-46743	HARLAN
46744-46744	OSSIAN
46745-46745	HOAGLAND
46746-46746	HOWE
46747-46747	HUDSON
46748-46748	HUNTERTOWN
46750-46750	HUNTINGTON
46755-46755	KENDALLVILLE
46759-46759	KEYSTONE
46760-46760	KIMMELL
46761-46761	LAGRANGE
46763-46763	LAOTTO
46764-46764	LARWILL
46765-46765	LEO
46766-46766	LIBERTY CENTER
46767-46767	LIGONIER
46769-46769	LINN GROVE
46770-46770	MARKLE
46771-46771	MONGO
46772-46772	MONROE
46773-46773	MONROEVILLE
46774-46774	NEW HAVEN
46776-46776	ORLAND
46777-46777	OSSIAN
46778-46778	PETROLEUM
46779-46779	PLEASANT LAKE
46780-46780	PLEASANT MILLS
46781-46781	PONETO
46782-46782	PREBLE
46783-46783	ROANOKE
46784-46784	ROME CITY
46785-46785	SAINT JOE
46786-46786	SOUTH MILFORD
46787-46787	SOUTH WHITLEY
46788-46788	SPENCERVILLE
46789-46789	STROH
46790-46790	OSSIAN
46791-46791	UNIONDALE
46792-46792	WARREN
46793-46793	WATERLOO
46794-46794	WAWAKA
46795-46795	WOLCOTTVILLE
46796-46796	WOLFLAKE
46797-46797	WOODBURN
46798-46798	YODER
46799-46799	ZANESVILLE
46800-46899	FORT WAYNE
46901-46904	KOKOMO
46910-46910	AKRON
46911-46911	AMBOY
46912-46912	ATHENS
46913-46913	BRINGHURST
46914-46914	BUNKER HILL
46915-46915	BURLINGTON
46916-46916	BURROWS
46917-46917	CAMDEN
46919-46919	CONVERSE
46920-46920	CUTLER
46921-46921	DEEDSVILLE
46922-46922	DELONG
46923-46923	DELPHI
46925-46925	DENHAM
46926-46926	DENVER
46928-46928	FAIRMOUNT
46929-46929	FLORA
46930-46930	FOWLERTON
46931-46931	FULTON
46932-46932	GALVESTON
46933-46933	GAS CITY
46935-46935	GRASS CREEK
46936-46936	GREENTOWN
46937-46937	HEMLOCK
46938-46938	JONESBORO
46939-46939	KEWANNA
46940-46940	LA FONTAINE
46941-46941	LAGRO
46942-46942	LAKE CICOTT
46943-46943	LAKETON
46944-46944	LANDESS
46945-46945	LEITERS FORD
46946-46946	LIBERTY MILLS
46947-46947	LOGANSPORT
46950-46950	LUCERNE
46951-46951	MACY
46952-46953	MARION
46957-46957	MATTHEWS
46958-46958	MEXICO
46959-46959	MIAMI
46960-46960	MONTEREY
46961-46961	NEW WAVERLY
46962-46962	NORTH MANCHESTER
46965-46965	OAKFORD
46967-46967	ONWARD
46968-46968	ORA
46970-46970	PERU
46971-46971	GRISSOM AFB
46971-46971	GRISSOM ARB
46974-46974	ROANN
46975-46975	ROCHESTER
46977-46977	ROCKFIELD
46978-46978	ROYAL CENTER
46979-46979	RUSSIAVILLE
46980-46980	SERVIA
46982-46982	SILVER LAKE
46983-46983	SIMS
46984-46984	SOMERSET
46985-46985	STAR CITY
46986-46986	SWAYZEE
46987-46987	SWEETSER
46988-46988	TWELVE MILE
46989-46989	UPLAND
46990-46990	URBANA
46991-46991	VAN BUREN
46992-46992	WABASH
46994-46994	WALTON
46995-46995	WEST MIDDLETON
46996-46996	WINAMAC
46998-46998	YOUNG AMERICA
47001-47001	AURORA
47003-47003	WEST COLLEGE CORNER
47006-47006	BATESVILLE
47010-47010	BATH
47011-47011	BENNINGTON
47012-47012	BROOKVILLE
47016-47016	CEDAR GROVE
47017-47017	CROSS PLAINS
47018-47018	DILLSBORO
47019-47019	EAST ENTERPRISE
47020-47020	FLORENCE
47021-47021	FRIENDSHIP
47022-47022	GUILFORD
47023-47023	HOLTON
47024-47024	LAUREL
47025-47025	LAWRENCEBURG
47030-47030	METAMORA
47031-47031	MILAN
47032-47032	MOORES HILL
47033-47033	MORRIS
47034-47034	NAPOLEON
47035-47035	NEW TRENTON
47036-47036	OLDENBURG
47037-47037	OSGOOD
47038-47038	PATRIOT
47039-47039	PIERCEVILLE
47040-47040	RISING SUN
47041-47041	SUNMAN
47042-47042	VERSAILLES
47043-47043	VEVAY
47060-47060	WEST HARRISON
47102-47102	AUSTIN
47104-47104	BETHLEHEM
47106-47106	BORDEN
47107-47107	BRADFORD
47108-47108	CAMPBELLSBURG
47110-47110	CENTRAL
47111-47111	CHARLESTOWN
47112-47112	CORYDON
47114-47114	CRANDALL
47115-47115	DEPAUW
47116-47116	ECKERTY
47117-47117	ELIZABETH
47118-47118	ENGLISH
47119-47119	FLOYDS KNOBS
47120-47120	FREDERICKSBURG
47122-47122	GEORGETOWN
47123-47123	GRANTSBURG
47124-47124	GREENVILLE
47125-47125	HARDINSBURG
47126-47126	HENRYVILLE
47129-47129	CLARKSVILLE
47130-47134	JEFFERSONVILLE
47135-47135	LACONIA
47136-47136	LANESVILLE
47137-47137	LEAVENWORTH
47138-47138	LEXINGTON
47139-47139	LITTLE YORK
47140-47140	MARENGO
47141-47141	MARYSVILLE
47142-47142	MAUCKPORT
47143-47143	MEMPHIS
47144-47144	JEFFERSONVILLE
47145-47145	MILLTOWN
47146-47146	MOUNT SAINT FRANCIS
47147-47147	NABB
47150-47151	NEW ALBANY
47160-47160	NEW MIDDLETOWN
47161-47161	NEW SALISBURY
47162-47162	NEW WASHINGTON
47163-47163	OTISCO
47164-47164	PALMYRA
47165-47165	PEKIN
47166-47166	RAMSEY
47167-47167	SALEM
47170-47170	SCOTTSBURG
47172-47172	SELLERSBURG
47174-47174	SULPHUR
47175-47175	TASWELL
47177-47177	UNDERWOOD
47199-47199	JEFFERSONVILLE
47201-47203	COLUMBUS
47220-47220	BROWNSTOWN
47222-47222	BURNEY
47223-47223	BUTLERVILLE
47224-47224	CANAAN
47225-47225	CLARKSBURG
47226-47226	CLIFFORD
47227-47227	COMMISKEY
47228-47228	CORTLAND
47229-47229	CROTHERSVILLE
47230-47230	DEPUTY
47231-47231	DUPONT
47232-47232	ELIZABETHTOWN
47234-47234	FLAT ROCK
47235-47235	FREETOWN
47236-47236	GRAMMER
47240-47240	GREENSBURG
47243-47243	HANOVER
47244-47244	HARTSVILLE
47245-47245	HAYDEN
47246-47246	HOPE
47247-47247	JONESVILLE
47249-47249	KURTZ
47250-47250	MADISON
47260-47260	MEDORA
47261-47261	MILLHOUSEN
47262-47262	NEBRASKA
47263-47263	NEW POINT
47264-47264	NORMAN
47265-47265	NORTH VERNON
47270-47270	PARIS CROSSING
47272-47272	SAINT PAUL
47273-47273	SCIPIO
47274-47274	SEYMOUR
47280-47280	TAYLORSVILLE
47281-47281	VALLONIA
47282-47282	VERNON
47283-47283	WESTPORT
47302-47308	MUNCIE
47320-47320	ALBANY
47322-47322	BENTONVILLE
47324-47324	BOSTON
47325-47325	BROWNSVILLE
47326-47326	BRYANT
47327-47327	CAMBRIDGE CITY
47330-47330	CENTERVILLE
47331-47331	CONNERSVILLE
47334-47334	DALEVILLE
47335-47335	DUBLIN
47336-47336	DUNKIRK
47337-47337	DUNREITH
47338-47338	EATON
47339-47339	ECONOMY
47340-47340	FARMLAND
47341-47341	FOUNTAIN CITY
47342-47342	GASTON
47344-47344	GREENSBORO
47345-47345	GREENS FORK
47346-47346	HAGERSTOWN
47348-47348	HARTFORD CITY
47351-47351	KENNARD
47352-47352	LEWISVILLE
47353-47353	LIBERTY
47354-47354	LOSANTVILLE
47355-47355	LYNN
47356-47356	MIDDLETOWN
47357-47357	MILTON
47358-47358	MODOC
47359-47359	MONTPELIER
47360-47360	MOORELAND
47361-47361	MOUNT SUMMIT
47362-47362	NEW CASTLE
47366-47366	NEW LISBON
47367-47367	OAKVILLE
47368-47368	PARKER CITY
47369-47369	PENNVILLE
47370-47370	PERSHING
47371-47371	PORTLAND
47373-47373	REDKEY
47374-47375	RICHMOND
47380-47380	RIDGEVILLE
47381-47381	SALAMONIA
47382-47382	SARATOGA
47383-47383	SELMA
47384-47384	SHIRLEY
47385-47385	SPICELAND
47386-47386	SPRINGPORT
47387-47387	STRAUGHN
47388-47388	SULPHUR SPRINGS
47390-47390	UNION CITY
47392-47392	WEBSTER
47393-47393	WILLIAMSBURG
47394-47394	WINCHESTER
47396-47396	YORKTOWN
47401-47408	BLOOMINGTON
47420-47420	AVOCA
47421-47421	BEDFORD
47424-47424	BLOOMFIELD
47426-47426	CLEAR CREEK
47427-47427	COAL CITY
47429-47429	ELLETTSVILLE
47430-47430	FORT RITNER
47431-47431	FREEDOM
47432-47432	FRENCH LICK
47433-47433	GOSPORT
47434-47434	HARRODSBURG

ZIP Range	Place	ZIP Range	Place	ZIP Range	Place	ZIP Range	Place
47435-47435	HELMSBURG	47555-47555	MAGNET	47830-47830	BELLMORE	47925-47925	BUFFALO
47436-47436	HELTONVILLE	47556-47556	MARIAH HILL	47831-47831	BLANFORD	47926-47926	BURNETTSVILLE
47437-47437	HURON	47557-47557	MONROE CITY	47832-47832	BLOOMINGDALE	47928-47928	CAYUGA
47438-47438	JASONVILLE	47558-47558	MONTGOMERY	47833-47833	BOWLING GREEN	47929-47929	CHALMERS
47439-47439	KOLEEN	47559-47559	MOUNT PLEASANT	47834-47834	BRAZIL	47930-47930	CLARKS HILL
47441-47441	LINTON	47561-47561	OAKTOWN	47836-47836	BRIDGETON	47931-47931	COLBURN
47443-47443	LYONS	47562-47562	ODON	47837-47837	CARBON	47932-47932	COVINGTON
47445-47445	MIDLAND	47564-47564	OTWELL	47838-47838	CARLISLE	47933-47939	CRAWFORDSVILLE
47446-47446	MITCHELL	47567-47567	PETERSBURG	47840-47840	CENTERPOINT	47940-47940	DARLINGTON
47448-47448	NASHVILLE	47568-47568	PLAINVILLE	47841-47841	CLAY CITY	47941-47941	DAYTON
47449-47449	NEWBERRY	47573-47573	RAGSDALE	47842-47842	CLINTON	47942-47942	EARL PARK
47451-47451	OOLITIC	47574-47574	ROME	47845-47845	COALMONT	47943-47943	FAIR OAKS
47452-47452	ORLEANS	47575-47575	SAINT ANTHONY	47846-47846	CORY	47944-47944	FOWLER
47453-47453	OWENSBURG	47576-47576	SAINT CROIX	47847-47847	DANA	47946-47946	FRANCESVILLE
47454-47454	PAOLI	47577-47577	SAINT MEINRAD	47848-47848	DUGGER	47948-47948	GOODLAND
47455-47455	PATRICKSBURG	47578-47578	SANDBORN	47849-47849	FAIRBANKS	47949-47949	HILLSBORO
47456-47456	QUINCY	47579-47579	SANTA CLAUS	47850-47850	FARMERSBURG	47950-47950	IDAVILLE
47457-47457	SCOTLAND	47580-47580	SCHNELLVILLE	47851-47851	FONTANET	47951-47951	KENTLAND
47458-47458	SMITHVILLE	47581-47581	SHOALS	47852-47852	GRAYSVILLE	47952-47952	KINGMAN
47459-47459	SOLSBERRY	47584-47584	SPURGEON	47853-47853	HARMONY	47954-47954	LADOGA
47460-47460	SPENCER	47585-47585	STENDAL	47854-47854	HILLSDALE	47955-47955	LINDEN
47462-47462	SPRINGVILLE	47586-47586	TELL CITY	47855-47855	HYMERA	47957-47957	MEDARYVILLE
47463-47463	STANFORD	47587-47587	TOBINSPORT	47856-47856	JUDSON	47958-47958	MELLOTT
47464-47464	STINESVILLE	47588-47588	TROY	47857-47857	KNIGHTSVILLE	47959-47959	MONON
47465-47465	SWITZ CITY	47590-47590	VELPEN	47858-47858	LEWIS	47960-47960	MONTICELLO
47467-47467	TUNNELTON	47591-47591	VINCENNES	47859-47859	MARSHALL	47962-47962	MONTMORENCI
47468-47468	UNIONVILLE	47596-47596	WESTPHALIA	47860-47860	MECCA	47963-47963	MOROCCO
47469-47469	WEST BADEN SPRINGS	47597-47597	WHEATLAND	47861-47861	MEROM	47964-47964	MOUNT AYR
47470-47470	WILLIAMS	47598-47598	WINSLOW	47862-47862	MONTEZUMA	47965-47965	NEW MARKET
47471-47471	WORTHINGTON	47601-47601	BOONVILLE	47863-47863	NEW GOSHEN	47966-47966	NEWPORT
47490-47490	BLOOMINGTON	47610-47610	CHANDLER	47864-47864	NEW LEBANON	47967-47967	NEW RICHMOND
47501-47501	WASHINGTON	47611-47611	CHRISNEY	47865-47865	PAXTON	47968-47968	NEW ROSS
47512-47512	BICKNELL	47612-47612	CYNTHIANA	47866-47866	PIMENTO	47969-47969	NEWTOWN
47513-47513	BIRDSEYE	47613-47613	ELBERFELD	47868-47868	POLAND	47970-47970	OTTERBEIN
47514-47514	BRANCHVILLE	47614-47614	FOLSOMVILLE	47869-47869	PRAIRIE CREEK	47971-47971	OXFORD
47515-47515	BRISTOW	47615-47615	GRANDVIEW	47870-47870	PRAIRIETON	47973-47973	PENCE
47516-47516	BRUCEVILLE	47616-47616	GRIFFIN	47871-47871	RILEY	47974-47974	PERRYSVILLE
47519-47519	CANNELBURG	47617-47617	HATFIELD	47872-47872	ROCKVILLE	47975-47975	PINE VILLAGE
47520-47520	CANNELTON	47618-47618	INGLEFIELD	47874-47874	ROSEDALE	47976-47976	EARL PARK
47521-47521	CELESTINE	47619-47619	LYNNVILLE	47875-47875	SAINT BERNICE	47977-47977	REMINGTON
47522-47522	CRANE	47620-47620	MOUNT VERNON	47876-47876	SAINT MARY OF THE WOODS	47978-47978	RENSSELAER
47523-47523	DALE	47629-47630	NEWBURGH			47980-47980	REYNOLDS
47524-47524	DECKER	47631-47631	NEW HARMONY	47877-47877	SANDFORD	47981-47981	ROMNEY
47525-47525	DERBY	47633-47633	POSEYVILLE	47878-47878	SEELYVILLE	47982-47982	STATE LINE
47527-47527	DUBOIS	47634-47634	RICHLAND	47879-47879	SHELBURN	47983-47983	STOCKWELL
47528-47528	EDWARDSPORT	47635-47635	ROCKPORT	47880-47880	SHEPARDSVILLE	47984-47984	TALBOT
47529-47529	ELNORA	47637-47637	TENNYSON	47881-47881	STAUNTON	47985-47985	TANGIER
47530-47530	EMISON	47638-47638	WADESVILLE	47882-47882	SULLIVAN	47986-47986	TEMPLETON
47531-47531	EVANSTON	47639-47639	HAUBSTADT	47884-47884	UNIVERSAL	47987-47987	VEEDERSBURG
47532-47532	FERDINAND	47640-47640	HAZLETON	47885-47885	WEST TERRE HAUTE	47988-47988	WALLACE
47535-47535	FREELANDVILLE	47647-47647	BUCKSKIN	47901-47905	LAFAYETTE	47989-47989	WAVELAND
47536-47536	FULDA	47648-47648	FORT BRANCH	47906-47907	WEST LAFAYETTE	47990-47990	WAYNETOWN
47537-47537	GENTRYVILLE	47649-47649	FRANCISCO	47909-47909	LAFAYETTE	47991-47991	WEST LEBANON
47541-47541	HOLLAND	47654-47654	MACKEY	47916-47916	ALAMO	47992-47992	WESTPOINT
47542-47542	HUNTINGBURG	47660-47660	OAKLAND CITY	47917-47917	AMBIA	47993-47993	WILLIAMSPORT
47545-47545	IRELAND	47665-47665	OWENSVILLE	47918-47918	ATTICA	47994-47994	WINGATE
47546-47549	JASPER	47666-47666	PATOKA	47920-47920	BATTLE GROUND	47995-47995	WOLCOTT
47550-47550	LAMAR	47670-47671	PRINCETON	47921-47921	BOSWELL	47996-47996	WEST LAFAYETTE
47551-47551	LEOPOLD	47683-47683	SOMERVILLE	47922-47922	BROOK	47997-47997	YEOMAN
47552-47552	LINCOLN CITY	47700-47750	EVANSVILLE	47923-47923	BROOKSTON		
47553-47553	LOOGOOTEE	47801-47814	TERRE HAUTE	47924-47924	BUCK CREEK		

County-Town
INDIANA

Copyright American Map Corporation

COUNTIES

(92 Counties)

Name of County	Population	Location on Map
ADAMS	31,095	E-11
ALLEN	300,836	C-10
BARTHOLOMEW	63,657	L-8
BENTON	9,441	F-3
BLACKFORD	14,067	F-10
BOONE	38,147	H-6
BROWN	14,080	L-7
CARROLL	18,809	F-6
CASS	38,413	E-6
CLARK	87,777	O-9
CLAY	24,705	K-4
CLINTON	30,974	G-6
CRAWFORD	9,914	P-6
DAVIESS	27,533	N-4
DE KALB	35,324	B-11
DEARBORN	38,835	L-11
DECATUR	23,645	L-9
DELAWARE	119,659	H-10
DUBOIS	36,616	O-4
ELKHART	156,198	B-8
FAYETTE	26,015	J-10
FLOYD	64,404	P-8
FOUNTAIN	17,808	H-4
FRANKLIN	19,580	K-11
FULTON	18,840	D-7
GIBSON	31,913	P-1
GRANT	74,169	F-9
GREENE	30,410	L-4
HAMILTON	108,936	H-7
HANCOCK	45,527	I-8
HARRISON	29,890	P-7
HENDRICKS	75,717	I-6
HENRY	48,139	I-10
HOWARD	80,827	F-7
HUNTINGTON	35,427	E-9
JACKSON	37,730	M-7
JASPER	24,960	C-4
JAY	21,512	F-11
JEFFERSON	29,797	N-10
JENNINGS	23,661	M-9
JOHNSON	88,109	K-7
KNOX	39,884	O-2
KOSCIUSKO	65,294	C-8
LA PORTE	107,066	B-6
LAGRANGE	29,477	A-10
LAKE	475,594	C-3
LAWRENCE	42,836	N-6
MADISON	130,669	G-9
MARION	797,159	I-7
MARSHALL	42,182	C-7
MARTIN	10,369	N-5
MIAMI	36,897	E-8
MONROE	108,978	L-6
MONTGOMERY	34,436	H-5
MORGAN	55,920	K-6
NEWTON	13,551	D-3
NOBLE	37,877	B-9
OHIO	5,315	M-11
ORANGE	18,409	N-6
OWEN	17,281	K-5
PARKE	15,410	I-4
PERRY	19,107	P-5
PIKE	12,509	O-3
PORTER	128,932	C-4
POSEY	25,968	Q-1
PULASKI	12,643	D-5
PUTNAM	30,315	J-5
RANDOLPH	27,148	H-11
RIPLEY	24,616	L-10
RUSH	18,129	J-10
SAINT JOSEPH	247,052	B-6
SCOTT	20,991	N-9
SHELBY	40,307	J-8
SPENCER	19,490	Q-4
STARKE	22,747	C-6
STEUBEN	27,446	B-11
SULLIVAN	18,993	M-3
SWITZERLAND	7,738	M-11
TIPPECANOE	130,598	F-4
TIPTON	16,119	H-7
UNION	6,976	J-11
VANDERBURGH	165,058	Q-2
VERMILLION	16,773	I-3
VIGO	106,107	K-3
WABASH	35,069	D-8
WARREN	8,176	G-3
WARRICK	44,920	P-4
WASHINGTON	23,717	N-7
WAYNE	71,951	I-11
WELLS	25,948	E-10
WHITE	23,265	E-5
WHITLEY	27,651	D-10
TOTAL	5,544,159	

CITIES AND TOWNS

Note: The first name is that of the city or town, second, that of the county in which it is located, then the population and location on the map.

Akron, Fulton, 1,001 .... D-8
Albany, Delaware/Randolph, 2,357 .... G-11
Albion, Noble, 1,823 .... C-10
Alexandria, Madison, 5,709 .... H-9
Anderson, Madison, 59,459 .... H-9
Andrews, Huntington, 1,118 .... E-9
Angola, Steuben, 5,824 .... A-11
Arcadia, Hamilton, 1,468 .... H-8
Ardmore, St. Joseph A-7
Argos, Marshall, 1,642 .... C-7
Attica, Fountain, 3,457 .... G-4
Auburn, De Kalb, 9,379 .... C-11
Aurora, Dearborn, 3,825 .... M-12
Austin, Scott, 4,310 .... N-9
Avilla, Noble, 1,366 .... C-11
Bargersville, Johnson, 1,681 .... K-7
Batesville, Franklin/Ripley, 4,720 .... L-11
Bedford, Lawrence, 13,817 .... N-6
Beech Grove, Marion, 13,383 .... J-8
Berne, Adams, 3,559 .... F-12
Bicknell, Knox, 3,357 .... N-3
Black Oak, Lake B-3
Bloomfield, Greene, 2,592 .... M-5
Bloomington, Monroe, 60,633 .... L-6
Bluffton, Wells, 9,020 .... E-11
Boonville, Warrick, 6,724 .... Q-4
Bourbon, Marshall, 1,672 .... C-8
Brazil, Clay, 7,640 .... K-4
Bremen, Marshall, 4,725 .... B-8
• Bright, Dearborn, 3,945 .... L-12
Bristol, Elkhart, 1,133 .... A-9
Broadview, Monroe L-6
Brooklyn, Morgan, 1,162 .... K-7
Brookston, White, 1,804 .... F-5
Brookville, Franklin, 2,529 .... K-11
Brownsburg, Hendricks, 7,628 .... I-7
Brownstown, Jackson, 2,872 .... M-8
Bunker Hill, Miami, 1,010 .... F-8
Butler, De Kalb, 2,601 .... B-12
Cambridge City, Wayne, 2,091 .... I-11
Cannelton, Perry, 1,786 .... R-5
Carmel, Hamilton, 25,380 .... I-8
Cayuga, Vermillion, 1,083 .... I-3
Cedar Lake, Lake, 8,885 .... C-3
Centerville, Wayne, 2,398 .... I-12
Chandler, Warrick, 3,099 .... Q-3
Charlestown, Clark, 5,889 .... O-9
Chesterfield, Delaware/Madison, 2,730 .... H-9
Chesterton, Porter, 9,124 .... B-4
Churubusco, Whitley, 1,781 .... C-10
Cicero, Hamilton, 3,268 .... H-8
Clarksville, Clark, 19,833 .... P-9
Clermont, Marion, 1,678 .... I-7
Clinton, Vermillion, 5,040 .... J-3
Cloverdale, Putnam, 1,681 .... K-5
Columbia City, Whitley, 5,706 .... D-10
Columbus, Bartholomew, 31,802 .... L-8
Connersville, Fayette, 15,550 .... J-11
Converse, Grant/Miami, 1,144 .... F-9
Corydon, Harrison, 2,661 .... P-8
Covington, Fountain, 2,747 .... H-3
Crawfordsville, Montgomery, 13,584 .... H-5
Crothersville, Jackson, 1,687 .... N-9
Crown Point, Lake, 17,728 .... B-3
Culver, Marshall, 1,404 .... C-7
Cumberland, Hancock/Marion, 4,557 .... I-8
Dale, Spencer, 1,553 .... Q-5
Daleville, Delaware, 1,681 .... H-10
Danville, Hendricks, 4,345 .... J-6
Darmstadt, Vanderburgh, 1,346 .... Q-2
De Motte, Jasper, 2,482 .... C-4
Decatur, Adams, 8,644 .... E-12
Delphi, Carroll, 2,531 .... F-6
Dillsboro, Dearborn, 1,200 .... M-11
Dunkirk, Blackford/Jay, 2,739 .... G-11
• Dunlap, Elkhart, 5,705 .... B-8
Dyer, Lake, 10,923 .... B-3
East Chicago, Lake, 33,892 .... A-3
Eaton, Delaware, 1,614 .... G-10
Edgewood, Madison, 2,057 .... H-9
Edinburgh, Bartholomew/Johnson, 4,536 .... L-8
Elkhart, Elkhart, 43,627 .... A-8
Ellettsville, Monroe, 3,275 .... L-6
Elwood, Madison/Tipton, 9,494 .... G-9
Englewood, Lawrence N-6
English, Crawford, 614 .... P-6
Evansville, Vanderburgh, 126,272 .... Q-2
• Fairland, Shelby, 1,348 .... J-8
Fairmount, Grant, 3,130 .... G-9
Fairview Park, Vermillion, 1,446 .... J-3
Farmersburg, Sullivan, 1,159 .... L-3
Farmland, Randolph, 1,412 .... H-11
Ferdinand, Dubois, 2,318 .... P-5
Fishers, Hamilton, 7,508 .... I-8
Flora, Carroll, 2,179 .... F-6
Fort Branch, Gibson, 2,447 .... P-2
Fort Wayne, Allen, 173,072 .... D-11
Fortville, Hancock, 2,690 .... I-9
Fowler, Benton, 2,333 .... F-4
Frankfort, Clinton, 14,754 .... G-6
Franklin, Johnson, 12,907 .... K-8
Frankton, Madison, 1,736 .... H-9
Fremont, Steuben, 1,407 .... A-12
French Lick, Orange, 2,087 .... O-6
• Galena, Floyd, 1,231 .... P-8
Galveston, Cass, 1,609 .... F-7
Garrett, De Kalb, 5,349 .... C-11
Gary, Lake, 116,646 .... B-3
Gas City, Grant, 6,296 .... G-9
Geneva, Adams, 1,280 .... F-12
Georgetown, Floyd, 2,092 .... P-8
• Georgetown, St. Joseph, 3,993 .... A-7
Goodland, Newton, 1,033 .... E-4
Goshen, Elkhart, 23,797 .... B-9
• Granger, St. Joseph, 20,241 .... A-7
Greencastle, Putnam, 8,984 .... J-5
Greendale, Dearborn, 3,881 .... L-12
Greenfield, Hancock, 11,657 .... J-9
Greensburg, Decatur, 9,286 .... K-10
Greentown, Howard, 2,172 .... G-8
Greenwood, Johnson, 26,265 .... J-8
Griffith, Lake, 17,916 .... B-3
• Grissom AFB, Cass/Miami, 4,271 .... F-7
• Gulivoire Park, St. Joseph, 2,788 .... A-7
Hagerstown, Wayne, 1,835 .... I-11
Hammond, Lake, 84,236 .... B-3
Hanover, Jefferson, 3,610 .... N-10
Hartford City, Blackford, 6,960 .... G-10
Haubstadt, Gibson, 1,455 .... P-2
Hebron, Porter, 3,183 .... C-4
• Hidden Valley, Dearborn, 2,116 .... L-12
Highland, Lake, 23,696 .... B-3
• Highland, Vanderburgh, 3,508 .... Q-2
Hobart, Lake, 21,822 .... B-4
Home Place, Hamilton I-8
Hope, Bartholomew, 2,171 .... L-9
Huntertown, Allen, 1,330 .... C-11
Huntingburg, Dubois, 5,242 .... P-5
Huntington, Huntington, 16,389 .... E-10
• Indian Heights, Howard, 3,669 .... G-8
Indianapolis, Marion, 731,327 .... I-8
Jasonville, Greene, 2,200 .... L-4
Jasper, Dubois, 10,030 .... P-5
Jeffersonville, Clark, 21,841 .... P-9
Jonesboro, Grant, 2,073 .... G-9
Kendallville, Noble, 7,773 .... B-11
Kentland, Newton, 1,798 .... E-3
Kingsford Heights, La Porte, 1,486 .... B-6
Knightstown, Henry, 2,048 .... J-10
Knox, Starke, 3,705 .... C-6
Kokomo, Howard, 44,962 .... G-8
• Koontz Lake, Marshall/Starke, 1,615 .... B-6
Kouts, Porter, 1,603 .... C-5
La Porte, La Porte, 21,507 .... B-6
Ladoga, Montgomery, 1,124 .... I-5
Lafayette, Tippecanoe, 43,764 .... G-5
Lagrange, Lagrange, 2,382 .... A-10
• Lake Dalecarlia, Lake, 1,276 .... C-3
Lake Station, Lake, 13,899 .... B-4
• Lakes of the Four Seasons, Lake/Porter, 6,556 .... C-4
Lapel, Madison, 1,742 .... H-9
Lawrence, Marion, 26,763 .... I-8
Lawrenceburg, Dearborn, 4,375 .... M-12
Lebanon, Boone, 12,059 .... H-6
Leo, Allen C-11
Liberty, Union, 2,051 .... J-12
Ligonier, Noble, 3,443 .... B-9
Linton, Greene, 5,814 .... M-4
Liverpool, Lake B-4
Logansport, Cass, 16,812 .... E-7
Long Beach, La Porte, 2,044 .... A-5
Loogootee, Martin, 2,884 .... N-5
Lowell, Lake, 6,430 .... C-3
Lydick, St. Joseph A-7
Lynn, Randolph, 1,183 .... H-12
Madison, Jefferson, 12,006 .... N-10
Marion, Grant, 32,618 .... F-9
Markle, Huntington/Wells, 1,208 .... E-10
Martinsville, Morgan, 11,677 .... K-7
• Melody Hill, Vanderburgh, 2,932 .... Q-3
Meridian Hills, Marion, 1,728 .... I-7
Merrillville, Lake, 27,257 .... B-3
• Mexico, Miami, 1,003 .... E-8
Michigan City, La Porte, 33,822 .... A-5
Middlebury, Elkhart, 2,004 .... A-9
Middletown, Henry, 2,333 .... H-10
Milan, Ripley, 1,529 .... L-11
Milford, Kosciusko, 1,388 .... B-9
Mishawaka, St. Joseph, 42,608 .... A-8
Mitchell, Lawrence, 4,669 .... N-6
Monon, White, 1,585 .... E-5
Monroeville, Allen, 1,232 .... D-12
Montezuma, Parke, 1,134 .... I-3
Monticello, White, 5,237 .... E-5
Montpelier, Blackford, 1,880 .... F-11
Mooresville, Morgan, 5,541 .... J-7
Morocco, Newton, 1,044 .... D-3
Mount Vernon, Posey, 7,217 .... Q-1
Mulberry, Clinton, 1,262 .... G-6
Muncie, Delaware, 71,035 .... H-10
Munster, Lake, 19,949 .... B-3
Nappanee, Elkhart/Kosciusko, 5,510 .... B-8
Nashville, Brown, 873 .... L-7
New Albany, Floyd, 36,322 .... P-9
New Carlisle, St. Joseph, 1,446 .... A-6
New Castle, Henry, 17,753 .... I-10
New Chicago, Lake, 2,066 .... B-4
New Elliot, Lake B-3
New Haven, Allen, 9,320 .... D-11
• New Paris, Elkhart, 1,007 .... B-9
New Pekin, Washington, 1,095 .... O-8
New Whiteland, Johnson, 4,097 .... K-8
Newburgh, Warrick, 2,880 .... Q-3
Newport, Vermillion, 627 .... I-3
Noblesville, Hamilton, 17,655 .... H-8
North Judson, Starke, 1,582 .... C-5
North Liberty, St. Joseph, 1,366 .... B-7
North Manchester, Wabash, 6,383 .... D-9
• North Terre Haute, Vigo, 4,331 .... K-3
North Vernon, Jennings, 5,311 .... M-9
• Oak Park, Clark, 5,630 .... P-9
Oakland City, Gibson, 2,810 .... P-3
Odon, Daviess, 1,475 .... N-4
Ogden Dunes, Porter, 1,499 .... B-4
Oolitic, Lawrence, 1,424 .... M-6
Orleans, Orange, 2,083 .... N-6
Osceola, St. Joseph, 1,999 .... A-8
Osgood, Ripley, 1,688 .... L-10
Ossian, Wells, 2,428 .... E-11
Otterbein, Benton/Tippecanoe, 1,291 .... G-4
Owensville, Gibson, 1,053 .... P-2
Oxford, Benton, 1,273 .... F-4
Paoli, Orange, 3,542 .... O-6
Parker City, Randolph, 1,323 .... H-11
Pendleton, Madison, 2,309 .... I-9
Peru, Miami, 12,843 .... E-8
Petersburg, Pike, 2,449 .... O-4
Pierceton, Kosciusko, 1,030 .... D-9
Plainfield, Hendricks, 10,433 .... J-7
Plymouth, Marshall, 8,303 .... C-7
Portage, Porter, 29,060 .... B-4
Porter, Porter, 3,118 .... B-4
Portland, Jay, 6,483 .... G-12
Poseyville, Posey, 1,089 .... P-2
Princes Lakes, Johnson, 1,055 .... K-8
Princeton, Gibson, 8,127 .... P-2
Redkey, Jay, 1,383 .... G-11
Remington, Jasper, 1,247 .... E-4
Rensselaer, Jasper, 5,045 .... E-4
Richmond, Wayne, 38,705 .... I-12
Rising Sun, Ohio, 2,311 .... M-12
Roanoke, Huntington, 1,018 .... D-10
Rochester, Fulton, 5,969 .... D-7
Rockport, Spencer, 2,315 .... R-4
Rockville, Parke, 2,706 .... J-4
Rome City, Noble, 1,138 .... B-10
Ross, Lake B-3
Rossville, Clinton, 1,175 .... G-6
Rushville, Rush, 5,533 .... J-10
Saint John, Lake, 4,921 .... B-3
Saint Paul, Decatur/Shelby, 1,032 .... K-9
Salem, Washington, 5,619 .... O-8
Schererville, Lake, 19,926 .... B-3
Scottsburg, Scott, 5,334 .... N-9
Seelyville, Vigo, 1,090 .... K-4
Sellersburg, Clark, 5,745 .... P-9
Seymour, Jackson, 15,576 .... M-8
Shadeland, Tippecanoe, 1,674 .... G-5
Shelburn, Sullivan, 1,147 .... L-3
Shelbyville, Shelby, 15,336 .... K-9
Sheridan, Hamilton, 2,046 .... H-7
Shoals, Martin, 853 .... N-5
• Simonton Lake, Elkhart, 3,554 .... A-8
Smith Valley, Johnson J-7
South Bend, St. Joseph, 105,511 .... A-7
• South Haven, Porter, 6,112 .... B-4
South Whitley, Whitley, 1,482 .... D-9
Southport, Marion, 1,969 .... J-8
Speedway, Marion, 13,092 .... I-7
Spencer, Owen, 2,609 .... L-5
Sullivan, Sullivan, 4,663 .... L-3
Summitville, Madison, 1,010 .... G-9
Swayzee, Grant, 1,059 .... F-9
Syracuse, Kosciusko, 2,729 .... B-9
• Taylorsville, Bartholomew, 1,044 .... L-8
Tell City, Perry, 8,088 .... Q-5
Terre Haute, Vigo, 57,483 .... K-3
Thorntown, Boone, 1,506 .... H-6
Tipton, Tipton, 4,751 .... G-8
Trail Creek, La Porte, 2,463 .... A-5
• Tri-Lakes, Whitley, 3,299 .... C-10
Union City, Randolph, 3,612 .... H-12
Upland, Grant, 3,295 .... G-10
Valparaiso, Porter, 24,414 .... B-4
Veedersburg, Fountain, 2,192 .... H-4
Vernon, Jennings, 370 .... M-9
Versailles, Ripley, 1,791 .... M-11
Vevay, Switzerland, 1,393 .... N-11
Vincennes, Knox, 19,859 .... N-3
Wabash, Wabash, 12,127 .... E-9
Wakarusa, Elkhart, 1,667 .... B-8
Walkerton, St. Joseph, 2,061 .... B-6
Walton, Cass, 1,053 .... F-7
Warren, Huntington, 1,185 .... F-10
Warren Park, Marion, 1,763 .... I-8
Warsaw, Kosciusko, 10,968 .... C-9
Washington, Daviess, 10,838 .... N-4
Waterloo, De Kalb, 2,040 .... B-11
West Glen Park, Lake B-3
West Lafayette, Tippecanoe, 25,907 .... G-5
West Terre Haute, Vigo, 2,495 .... K-3
Westfield, Hamilton, 3,304 .... H-8
Westport, Decatur, 1,478 .... L-10
Westville, La Porte, 5,255 .... B-5
Whiteland, Johnson, 2,446 .... K-8
Whiting, Lake, 5,155 .... A-3
Williamsport, Warren, 1,798 .... G-4
Winamac, Pulaski, 2,262 .... D-6
Winchester, Randolph, 5,095 .... H-12
Winona Lake, Kosciusko, 4,053 .... C-9
Woodburn, Allen, 1,321 .... D-12
Worthington, Greene, 1,473 .... L-5
Yorktown, Delaware, 4,106 .... H-10
Zionsville, Boone, 5,281 .... I-7

Explanation of symbols: •– Census Designated Place (CDP)

General Help Numbers:

Governor's Office

State Capitol Bldg
Des Moines, IA 50319
www.governor.state.ia.us/

515-281-5211
Fax 515-281-6611
8AM-4:30PM

Attorney General's Office

Hoover Bldg
1305 E Walnut St
Des Moines, IA 50319
www.state.ia.us/government/ag

515-281-5164
Fax 515-281-4209
8AM-4:30PM

Legislative Records

Legislative Information Office
State Capitol
Des Moines, IA 50319
www.legis.state.ia.us

515-281-5129
Fax 515-281-8027
8AM-4:30PM

State Archives

Library/Archives
600 E. Locust
Des Moines, IA 50319-0290
www.iowahistory.org

515-281-5111
Fax 515-282-0502
9AM-4:30PM TU-SAT
Open Mondays June-Aug

State Specifics:

Capital:

Des Moines
Polk County

Time Zone:

CST

Number of Counties:

99

Population:

2,954,451

Web Site:

www.iowa.gov/state/main/index.html

State Agencies

Criminal Records

Division of Criminal Investigations, Bureau of Identification, Wallace State Office Bldg, 502 E. 9th, Des Moines, IA 50319-0041; 515-281-4776, 515-242-6876-Fax; 8AM-4:30PM.

www.state.ia.us/government/dps/dci/crimhist.htm

Iowa law requires employers to pay the fee for potential employees record checks. (This is normal operating procedure when and employer uses a pre-employment screening company in compliance with FCRA.)

Records are available until the person is 80 years old or passes away. There is a computerized index going back to 1935. 100% of arrest records are fingerprint supported. It takes up to 10 days before new records are available for inquiry. Records are indexed on in house computer (100%). Records

are normally destroyed after 4 years if there is no disposition. 91% of all arrests in database have final dispositions recorded, 91% for those arrests within last 5 years.

Searching: A signed release or waiver is not required, nor are fingerprints. If a waiver is included, the report will show any arrest over 18 months old without a disposition, otherwise not. Include the following in your request-full name, date of birth, sex. The Social Security Number and middle name are helpful. Be sure to give the full name. Request form is required for each surname. Form can be obtained from the website, by fax, mail, or in person. A signed release by subject entitles requester to all records including those without dispositions (up to 4 years old). If the subject's signed release is not presented, then no

arrest records over 18 months old without dispositions are released.

Access by: mail, in person.

Fee & Payment: The fee for a record search is $13.00 for mail back, $15.00 for fax back, and $10.00 for in person searches. Fee payee: Iowa Division of Criminal Investigation. Payment is required unless account established. Personal checks accepted. Credit cards accepted: MasterCard, Visa.

Mail search: Turnaround time: 2 to 5 days or so. No SASE is required.

In person search: Records may be ordered and received in person.

Other access: Although this agency does not offer online access, there is online free access to the statewide Iowa Judicial System courts database at www.judicial.state.ia.us/online_records/.

Expedited service: Expedited service is available for fax searches. Account is required, request must be prepaid or a credit card is required. Turnaround time: 1 to 3 days. Add $2.00 per record to receive back by fax.

Statewide Court Records

Clerk of Supreme Court, Judicial Branch Bldg, 111 East Court Ave, Des Moines, IA 50319; 515-281-5911, 515-242-6164-Fax; 8AM-4:30PM.

www.judicial.state.ia.us

Access by: mail, fax, online.

Mail search: The search consists of the free webpage lookup. Written requests will be honored, if search is not extensive.

Fax search: Fax requests for basic information are accepted.

Online search: Criminal, civil, probate, traffic and appellate information is available from all 99 Iowa counties at www.judicial.state.ia.us/online_re cords/. There is no fee for basic information, and a pay system is available for more detailed requests. Name searches are available on a statewide or specific county basis. Although records are updated daily, the historical records offered are not from the same starting date on a county-by-county basis. Also, from the home page one may access supreme and appellate court opinions.

Other access: The state Law Library (515-281-5124) has case information. A list of licensed attorneys may be purchased from the Client Security Commission (515-725-8029).

Sexual Offender Registry

Division of Criminal Investigations, SOR Unit, Wallace State Office Bldg, Des Moines, IA 50319; 515-281-8716, 515-281-4898-Fax; 8AM-4:30PM.

www.iowasexoffenders.com

The Iowa Sex Offender Registry became law on July 1, 1995 and is found in Chapter 692A Code of Iowa.

Records are available from 07/01/95, if online back to 1999. It takes up to 2 days before new records are available for inquiry.

Searching: Include the following in your request-date of birth, address if known, SSN helpful. This office will not permit walk-in requesters, it is suggested to visit the local police of sheriff office.

Access by: mail, online.

Mail search: Turnaround time: 1 to 2 days. No SASE is required.

Online search: The website contains the majority of sex offenders registered in Iowa. Instant access is available.

Incarceration Records

Iowa Department of Corrections, 420 Watson Powell Jr. Way,, Des Moines, IA 50309-1639; 515-242-5708, 515-281-4062 (Second fax number), 515-281-7345-Fax; 8AM-4:30PM.

www.doc.state.ia.us

Records are available on current and former inmates. It takes up to 10 days before new records are available for inquiry. Records are normally destroyed after Never.

Searching: Computer records go back to 1986. Include the following in your request-full name and DOB or SSN. Location, physical identifiers, county of conviction, and conviction information details are released. Deeper records - sentencing information - are also available; please include details of reason for request. The following data is not released: medical or home address data.

Access by: mail, phone, fax, in person, online.

Fee & Payment: Search fee is $12.00 per hour plus postage fee. Copy fee is $.15 per page. Fee payee: Treasurer, State of Iowa, Dept. of Corrections. Prepayment required. Personal checks accepted. No credit cards accepted.

Mail search: Turnaround time: 1 to 10 days. Turnaround time on archived records is significantly longer. No SASE is required.

Phone search: Name searching for basic information is available by phone.

Fax search: Requesters may fax to number above.

In person search: Limited counter service is available.

Online search: Click on Public Info for an inmate search. This site seems to be under construction at times.

Other access: Bulk records are not available, but should be in the future.

Corporation, Limited Liability Company, Fictitious Name, Limited Partnership, Trademarks/Servicemarks

Secretary of State - Corporation Division, 321 E 12th Street, 1st Floor, Lucas Bldg, Des Moines, IA 50319; 515-281-5204, 515-242-5953-Fax; 8AM-4:30PM.

www.sos.state.ia.us

Records are available from the late 1800s. New records are available for inquiry immediately. Records are indexed on microfilm, inhouse computer, on-line.

Searching: Include the following in your request-full name of business or filing number, specific records that you need copies of. In addition to the articles of incorporation, the following information is released: Annual/Biennial Reports, Officers, Directors, DBAs, Prior (merged) names, Inactive and Reserved names.

Access by: mail, phone, fax, in person, online.

Fee & Payment: A Good Standing is $5.00. Copies are $1.00 each, certification is an additional $5.00 per document set. Fee payee: Secretary of State. Prepayment required. A charge account may be established for ongoing requesters. Call 515-281-5204 for more details. Personal checks accepted. Credit cards accepted: MasterCard, Visa.

Mail search: Turnaround time: 2 to 3 days. A SASE is requested. No fee for mail request.

Phone search: No fee for telephone request. You are restricted to 3 requests per call.

Fax search: Add $1.00 for each page that is faxed. Turnaround time is 2 days.

In person search: No fee for request.

Online search: For free searching, go to www.sos.state.ia.us/corp/corp_search.asp.

Other access: This agency will sell the records in database format. Call the number listed above and ask for Karen Ubaldo for more information.

Uniform Commercial Code, Federal Tax Liens

UCC Division, Secretary of State, 1st Floor, Lucas Bldg, Des Moines, IA 50319; 515-281-5204, 515-242-5953 (Other Fax Line), 515-242-6556-Fax; 8AM-4:30PM.

www.sos.state.ia.us

Records are available from 1966 and are computerized. All current records are on optical disk. It takes 1 to 3 days before new records are available for inquiry.

Searching: Use search request form UCC-11. Specify if you also want federal tax liens and include another search fee. Federal tax liens on individuals and all state tax liens are filed at the county level. Include the following in your request-debtor name or filing number. Copies of filings may be requested at time of search, but do not ask for copies with your initial request unless you have a charge account.

Access by: mail, phone, fax, in person, online.

Fee & Payment: The fee is $5.00 per debtor name, $6.00 for federal liens. Copies are $1.00 per page. Fee payee: Secretary of State. Prepayment required. Personal checks accepted. Credit cards accepted: MasterCard, Visa.

Mail search: Turnaround time: 1 to 2 days. A SASE is requested.

Phone search: A telephone search is available with a prepaid or charge account, or with credit card.

Fax search: Turnaround time usually same day, fee is $1.00 per page.

In person search: Simple requests may be processed while you wait.

Online search: All computerized information on or before June 30, 2001 is available online at www.sos.state.ia.us/Ucc_Search/UccOld_Search.h tml. There is no fee at this "UCC Archive" site. For computerized records online from July 1, 2001 to present, you may search at www.sos.stat e.ia.us/UCC_Search/UCC_Search.asp.

State Tax Liens

Records not maintained by a state level agency.

Records are found at the county recorder's offices.

Sales Tax Registrations

Department of Revenue, Taxpayer Services, Hoover State Office Bldg, Des Moines, IA 50306; 515-281-3114, 515-242-6487-Fax; 8AM-4PM.

www.state.ia.us/tax

Records are available for 3 years. Records are indexed on computer, microfiche. Records are normally destroyed after 3 years.

Searching: This agency will provide any information found on the face of the Tax Permit-business name, business address, and tax permit number. Information not released includes telephone numbers, tax liabilities, taxes collected, officers, federal ID#s, etc. Include the following in your request-business name. They will also search by tax permit number. Requests are accepted by email at idrf@idrf.state.ia.us.

Access by: mail, phone, fax.

Fee & Payment: There is no search fee; however, there is a $5.00 copy fee per document. Fee payee: Treasurer State of Iowa. Prepayment required. Personal checks accepted. No credit cards accepted.

Mail search: Turnaround time: 14 to 21 days. No SASE is required.

Phone search: Limited information is available by phone.

Fax search: Records are available by fax.

Other access: The agency will provide the database on lists, fees vary from $20.00 to $45.00.

Birth Certificates

Iowa Department of Public Health, Bureau of Vital Records, 321 E 12th St, Lucas Bldg, Des Moines, IA 50319-0075; 515-281-4944, 515-281-5871 (Message Recording), 7AM-4:45PM.

www.idph.state.ia.us

All vital records are open for inspection at the county level, usually for a $15.00 fee.

Records are available from 1880 to present. It takes 30 days to 6 weeks before new records are available for inquiry. Records are indexed on microfiche, inhouse computer.

Searching: Adoption records are not released. Include the following in your request-full name, names of parents, mother's maiden name, date of birth, place of birth, relationship to person of record, reason for information request. Must have copy of a photo ID (mail) or a photo ID (in person) to search.

Access by: mail, phone, in person.

Fee & Payment: The search fee is $15.00 per index searched. There is an additional $5.50 fee to use a credit card. For records 1880 to 1915, a $15.00 per year fee is charged. Fee payee: Iowa Department of Public Health. Prepayment required. Personal checks accepted. Major credit cards accepted.

Mail search: Turnaround time: within 1 month.

Phone search: Records are available by phone with use of credit card.

In person search: Same day service is not available. Turnaround time is 48 hours.

Expedited service: Expedited mail service is available for phone searches. Add $11.00 per package for faster shipping. Must use a credit card which is an extra $5.50. Normal turnaround time is 10-14 days.

Death Records

Iowa Department of Public Health, Vital Records, 321 E 12th St, Lucas Bldg, Des Moines, IA 50319-0075; 515-281-4944, 515-281-5871 (Message Recording), 7AM-4:45PM.

www.idph.state.ia.us

Records are available from 1880 to present. From 1880 to 1895 there is no index, the county of occurrence must be submitted with request. It takes up to 60 days before new records are available for inquiry. Records are indexed on microfiche, inhouse computer.

Searching: Include the following in your request-full name, date of death, place of death,

relationship to person of record, reason for information request. Must have a copy of a photo ID (mail) or a photo ID (in person) to search.

Access by: mail, phone, in person.

Fee & Payment: The search fee is $15.00 per index searched. There is an additional $5.50 fee when using a credit card. If searching 1880-1895, an additional $15.00 per year required. Fee payee: Iowa Department of Public Health. Prepayment required. Personal checks accepted. Major credit cards accepted.

Mail search: Turnaround time: within 1 month.

Phone search: Record requests are available by phone with use of credit card. Family history searches not accepted over the phone.

In person search: Same day service in not available. Turnaround time is 48 hours.

Expedited service: Expedited mail service is available phone searches. Add fee for express delivery. Also, be sure to include the extra credit card fee. Turnaround time is 7-10 days.

Marriage Certificates

Iowa Department of Public Health, Vital Records, 321 E 12th St, Lucas Bldg, Des Moines, IA 50319-0075; 515-281-4944, 515-281-5871 (Message Recording), 7AM-4:45PM.

www.idph.state.ia.us

Records are available from 1880. Records from 1880 to 1915 have to be searched by year. 1916 forward are indexed. It takes up 2 week2 before new records are available for inquiry. Records are indexed on microfiche, inhouse computer.

Searching: Include the following in your request-names of husband and wife, date of marriage, place or county of marriage.

Access by: mail, phone, in person.

Fee & Payment: The search fee is $15.00 per record. There is an additional $5.50 fee when using a credit card. If searching 1880-1915, an additional $15.00 per year required. Fee payee: Iowa Department of Public Health. Prepayment required. Personal checks accepted. Major credit cards accepted.

Mail search: Turnaround time: within 1 month.

Phone search: Record requests are available by phone with use of credit card. Family history searches not accepted by phone.

In person search: Same day service is not available. Turnaround time is 48 hours.

Expedited service: Expedited mail service is available for phone searches. Add fee for express delivery. Also, there is an additional $5.50 for use of credit card. Turnaround time is 7-10 days.

Divorce Records

Records not maintained by a state level agency.

Divorce records are found at the county court issuing the decree. In general, records are available from 1880.

Workers' Compensation Records

Iowa Workforce Development, Division of Workers' Compensation, 1000 E Grand Ave, Des Moines, IA 50319; 515-281-5387, 515-281-6501-Fax; 8AM-4:30PM.

www.iowaworkforce.org/wc

Regular, ongoing requesters may apply for charge accounts.

Records are available from 1985 to present. It takes 2 weeks before new records are available for inquiry.

Searching: Include the following in your request-claimant name, Social Security Number, place of employment at time of accident. Older records may take as long as 6 weeks to research.

Access by: mail, fax, in person.

Fee & Payment: The search fee is $24.00 per hour, with a $6.00 minimum. Photo copies are $.50 per page, fax copies $.75 per page. Fee payee: Workers' Compensation. Prepayment required. Personal checks accepted. No credit cards accepted.

Mail search: Turnaround time: 3 to 5 days. A SASE is requested.

Fax search: Fax requests accepted.

In person search: Files are available for personal viewing only if requested in advance.

Other access: This agency sells its entire database or can sell data transmissions of pages ($.045 per page).

Driver Records

Department of Transportation, Driver Service Records Section, PO Box 9204, Des Moines, IA 50306-9204 (Courier address: Park Fair Mall, 100 Euclid, Des Moines, IA 50306); 515-244-9124, 800-532-1121 (Iowa only), 515-237-3152-Fax; 8AM-4:30PM.

www.dot.state.ia.us/mvd

Copies of tickets can be requested from this address for $.50 per copy.

Records are available for 5 to 7 years for moving violations; 12 years for DWIs; 3 to 7 years after closed for suspensions. The driver's address is shown on the record. Accidents are listed, but fault is not shown. It takes 2 to 3 days before new records are available for inquiry. Records are normally destroyed after 5 years.

Searching: Casual requesters receive records without personal information, unless written consent of the subject is presented. Will not expedite requests. Include the following in your request-full name, driver's license number, date of birth.

Access by: mail, fax, in person, online.

Fee & Payment: The fee for certified mail-in or walk-in requests is $5.50 per record. Electronic records are $8.50 each. There is no charge for a no record found. Fee payee: Treasurer, State of Iowa. Prepayment required. Personal checks accepted. No credit cards accepted.

Mail search: Turnaround time: 5 to 10 days. An account can be established for on-going requesters. No SASE is required.

Fax search: Pre-approved accounts may be able to fax to IowaAccess, but not to this agency.

In person search: The public access terminal is no longer available. Records must be ordered from personnel.

Online search: The state requires that all ongoing requesters/users access records via IowaAccess. The fee is $8.50 per record, the service is interactive or batch. Requesters must be approved and open an account. The records contain personal information, so requesters must comply with DPPA. For more information, contact IowaAccess at 515-323-3468 or 866-492-3468.

Vehicle Ownership, Vehicle Identification

Department of Transportation, Office of Vehicle Services, PO Box 9278, Des Moines, IA 50306-9278 (Courier address: Park Fair Mall, 100 Euclid, Des Moines, IA 50306); 515-237-3148, 515-237-3049, 515-237-3181-Fax; 8AM-4:30PM.

www.dot.state.ia.us/mvd

Vehicle lien information is not maintained by this department.

Records are available for 7 years for title; for 3 years for registration. Records are normally destroyed after 7 years.

Searching: Vehicle registration information is released to casual requesters, but personal information is not given without written consent of the subject. The state is in compliance with DPPA. Records may be accessed by VIN, name, title no. and plate - subject to DPPA and Iowa Code 321.11.

Access by: mail, fax, in person, online.

Fee & Payment: Fees: $.50 per certified record. Computer printout is $1.00. Record search-$2.70 per quarter hour or fraction thereof. Fee payee: Iowa Department of Transportation. Prepayment required. Personal checks accepted. No credit cards accepted.

Mail search: Turnaround time: within 30 days. No SASE is required.

Fax search: Fax searching available.

In person search: You may request information in person, but results may still be mailed, depending on workload.

Online search: Online access is available to dealers, Iowa licensed investigators and security companies. There is no fee. All accounts must register and be pre-approved. Write to the Office of Motor Vehicle, explaining purpose/use of records.

Other access: Iowa makes the entire vehicle file or selected data available for purchase. Weekly updates are also available for those purchasers. Requesters subject to DPPA requirements. For more information, call 515-237-3110.

Accident Reports

Department of Transportation, Office of Driver Services, Park Fair Mall, 100 Euclid, Des Moines, IA 50306; 515-244-9124, 800-532-1121, 515-239-1837-Fax; 8AM-4:30PM.

www.dot.state.ia.us/mvd/ods/index.htm

County sheriffs in Iowa are authorized to furnish copies of officer accident reports, but not all do.

Records are available for five years. It takes three days before new records are available for inquiry. Records are normally destroyed after 5 years.

Searching: Accident reports are available only to the person involved in accident or the person's insurance company or attorney. Include the following in your request-full name, date of accident, location of accident. Will not expedite requests.

Access by: mail, fax, in person.

Fee & Payment: The fee is $4.00 per officer report. Fee payee: Treasurer, State of Iowa. Prepayment required. The state allows regular, ongoing requesters to open a deposit account. Personal checks accepted. No credit cards accepted.

Mail search: Turnaround time: 2 to 3 weeks. No SASE is required.

Fax search: Same criteria as mail searches.

In person search: Turnaround time for walk-in requesters is generally immediate.

Vessel Ownership, Vessel Registration

Records not maintained by a state level agency.

Vessels are registered at the county level.

Voter Registration

Secretary of State, Voter Registration Division, Lucas State Office Building, 1st Fl, Des Moines, IA 50319; 515-281-5752, 515-242-5953-Fax; 8AM-4:30PM.

www.sos.state.ia.us

Records are available for active records. It takes two weeks before new records are available for inquiry.

Searching: E-mail requests to sos@sos.state.ia.us. The following data is not released: SSNs, DLs, or bulk information or lists for commercial purposes.

Access by: mail, phone, fax, in person.

Fee & Payment: There is no fee to view a single record. Lists may be purchased.

Mail search: Mail requests are accepted.

Phone search: Will only confirm.

Fax search: Fax requests are accepted if request list is short.

In person search: Records may be viewed.

Other access: Information is available on cartridge, disk or CD for political purposes only. Data can be sorted by any field on the registration file. Fees are determined by cost of production, but in general are $1.45 per thousand.

GED Certificates

Department of Education, GED Records, Grimes State Office Building, Des Moines, IA 50319-0146; 515-281-7308, 515-281-3636, 515-281-6544-Fax; 8AM-5PM.

It takes 1 month before new records are available for inquiry.

Searching: Include the following in your request-Social Security Number, date of birth. A signed release form is required for a copy of a diploma or transcript. The year and city of test are also helpful.

Access by: mail, phone, fax, in person.

Fee & Payment: There is a $5.00 fee for a copy of a transcript or a diploma, $3.00 for a second transcript. There is no fee for a verification. Fee payee: IA Department of Education. Prepayment required. Money orders are accepted. No credit cards or personal checks accepted.

Mail search: Turnaround time: 1 to 3 days. A SASE is requested.

Phone search: Limited information is available.

Fax search: They will return verification data by fax to local or toll-free numbers.

In person search: Limited information given across-the-counter.

Other access: There are several different statewide GED databases available.

Hunting and Fishing License Information

Department of Natural Resources, Wallace Building, 502 E 9th Street, Des Moines, IA 50319-0034; 515-242-5818, 515-281-8895-Fax; 8AM-4PM.

www.state.ia.us

Records are available from 2000 on computer, prior years on microfiche. Records are normally destroyed after 15 years.

Searching: Include the following in your request-full name, date of birth, Social Security Number. This agency only maintains records for deer (except bow & free landowners) and turkey.

Access by: mail, phone, fax, in person.

Fee & Payment: There is no charge for a search of one electronic record for personal use. Lists will incur a fee based on length and how search must be done. Fee payee: Iowa Department of Natural Resources. Personal checks accepted.

Mail search: Turnaround time: 7 days. No SASE is required.

Phone search: You may call for information.

Fax search: Fax requests accepted with signature of the requester.

In person search: You may request information in person.

Other access: Bulk data is released on CD, call for details.

Iowa State Licensing Agencies

For details about the agency responsible for licensing/certifying/registering an item below or in the Agency Quick Finder section, match an item's number with the number of the agency in the *Licensing Agency Information* section.

Iowa Licenses Searchable Online

Acupuncturist #14	www.docboard.org/ia/df/iasearch.htm
Anesthesiologist #14	www.docboard.org/ia/df/iasearch.htm
Architect #10	www.state.ia.us/government/com/prof/search/index.html
Bank #4	www.idob.state.ia.us
Debt Management Company #4	www.idob.state.ia.us/license/lic_default.htm
Delayed Deposit Service Business #4	www.idob.state.ia.us/license/lic_default.htm
Doctor #14	www.docboard.org/ia/df/iasearch.htm
Engineer #10	www.state.ia.us/government/com/prof/search/index.html
Excursion Gambling Boat #19	www.iowa.gov/irgc/
Finance Company #4	www.idob.state.ia.us/license/lic_default.htm
Hypnotist #14	www.docboard.org/ia/df/iasearch.htm
Landscape Architect #10	www.state.ia.us/government/com/prof/search/index.html
Lobbyist #8	www.legis.state.ia.us/Lobbyist.html
Medical Doctor #14	www.docboard.org/ia/df/iasearch.htm
Money Transmitter #4	www.idob.state.ia.us/license/lic_default.htm
Mortgage Banker/Broker #4	www.idob.state.ia.us/license/lic_default.htm
Mortgage Loan Service #4	www.idob.state.ia.us/license/lic_default.htm
Notary Public #21	www.sos.state.ia.us/notaries/notary_search.asp
Nurse, Nurse LPN #15	www.state.ia.us/nursing/Licensure.html
Nurse, Advance Regist'd Practice #15	www.state.ia.us/nursing/Licensure.html
Optometrist #22	www.arbo.org/index.php?action=findanoptometrist
Orthopedic Doctor #14	www.docboard.org/ia/df/iasearch.htm
Osteopathic Physician #14	www.docboard.org/ia/df/iasearch.htm
Pari-Mutuel Race Track Enclosure #19	www.iowa.gov/irgc/
Pediatrician #14	www.docboard.org/ia/df/iasearch.htm
Pesticide Dealer/Applicator #3	www.kellysolutions.com/ia/dealers/index.asp
Psychiatrist #14	www.docboard.org/ia/df/iasearch.htm
Real Estate Agent/Broker/Sales #10	www.state.ia.us/government/com/prof/search/index.html
Real Estate Appraiser #23	www.state.ia.us/government/com/prof/search/index.html
Surveyor, Land #10	www.state.ia.us/government/com/prof/search/index.html

Iowa Licensing Quick Finder

Acupuncturist #14	515-281-5171
Adoption Investigator #18	515-281-5584
Alcoholic Beverage Retail/Whlse./Mfg. #5	515-281-7430
Amusement Ride Inspection #27	515-281-5415
Anesthesiologist #14	515-281-5171
Appraiser #10	515-281-7393
Architect #10	515-281-7393
Asbestos Abatement Contractor/Worker/Inspector #27	515-281-6175
Asbestos Project Designer/Mgmt. Planner #27	515-281-6175
Athletic Agent #21	515-281-5204
Athletic Trainer #22	515-281-4401
Attorney #11	515-281-5911
Audiologist #22	515-281-6959
Bail Enforcement Agent #25	515-281-7610
Bank #4	515-281-4014
Barber #22	515-281-6959
Boiler Inspector #27	515-281-6533
Bus Driver #28	515-237-3079
Chiropractor #22	515-281-4287
Contractor #27	515-242-5870
Controlled Substance Registrant #16	515-281-5944
Cosmetologist #22	515-281-4416
Cosmetology Instructor #22	515-281-4416
Cosmetology Salon/School #22	515-281-4416
Credit Union #6	515-281-6514
Crematory #22	515-281-4287
Day Care #17	515-283-9106
Debt Management Company #4	515-281-4014
Delayed Deposit Service Business #4	515-281-4014
Dental Hygienist #13	515-281-5047
Dentist #13	515-281-5047
Dietitian #22	515-281-6959
Doctor #14	515-281-5171
Drug Distributor/Whlse./Mfg. #16	515-281-5944
Electrologist #22	515-281-4416
Elevator Inspection #27	515-281-5415
Emergency Med. Tech-Paramedic #27	515-281-3239
Engineer #10	515-281-4126
Esthetician #22	515-281-4416
Esthetician #24	515-281-4416
Excursion Gambling Boat #19	515-281-7352
Family Foster Care #17	515-283-9106
Finance Company #4	515-281-4014
First Response Paramedic #27	515-281-4958
Funeral Director/Home #22	515-281-4287
Group Foster Care #17	515-283-9106
Hearing Aid Dispenser/Dealer #22	515-281-4416
Hypnotist #14	515-281-5171
Instructional School #21	515-281-5204
Instructor, Com. College or Voc./Tech. School #12	515-281-5849
Insurance Agency /Company #7	515-281-7367
Insurance Producer #7	515-281-7757
Landfill Operator #20	515-281-5918
Landscape Architect #10	515-281-4126
Lobbyist #8	515-281-5381
Lottery Retailer #26	515-281-7900
Manicurist #24	515-281-4416
Manicurist/Nail Technician #22	515-281-4416
Marriage & Family Therapist #22	515-281-4422
Massage Therapist #22	515-281-6959
Medical Doctor #14	515-281-5171
Mental Health Counselor #22	515-281-4422
Money Transmitter #4	515-281-4014
Mortgage Banker/Broker #4	515-281-4014
Mortgage Loan Service #4	515-281-4014
Mortuary Science #22	515-281-4287
Nail Technologist #24	515-281-4416
Notary Public #21	515-281-5204
Nuclear Medicine Technologist #9	515-725-0306
Nurse - Nurse LPN #15	515-281-3255
Nurse,Advance Regist'd Practice #15	515-281-3255
Nursing Home Administrator #22	515-281-4401
Occupational Therapist/Assistant #22	515-281-4401
Optometrist #22	515-281-4287
Orthopedic Doctor #14	515-281-5171
Osteopathic Physician #14	515-281-5171
Pari-Mutuel Race Track Enclosure #19	515-281-7352
Pediatrician #14	515-281-5171
Pesticide Dealer/Applicator #3	515-281-5601
Pharmacist/Pharmacist Tech/Intern#16	515-281-5944

Pharmacy #16	515-281-5944	
Physical Therapist/Assistant #22	515-281-4401	
Physician Assistant #22	515-281-4401	
Podiatrist #22	515-281-4287	
Post-Secondary School #21	515-281-5204	
Private Investigator/Security Guard #25	515-281-7610	
Psychiatrist #14	515-281-5171	
Psychologist #22	515-281-4401	
Public Accountant-CPA #10	515-281-4126	
Radiation Therapist #9	515-281-4942	
Radioactive Material #9	515-281-3478	
Radiographer, Medical #9	515-725-0306	
Radon Measurement Specialist #9	515-281-4928	
Radon Mitigation Specialist #9	515-281-4928	
Real Estate Agent/Broker/Sales #10	515-281-7393	
Real Estate Appraiser #23	515-281-7393	
Respiratory Therapist #22	515-281-4287	
School Coach / Counselor #12	515-281-5849	
School Principal/Superintendent #12	515-281-5849	
Securities Agent/Broker/Dealer #7	515-281-4441	
Sheep Dealer #2	515-281-8601	
Shorthand Reporter #11	515-725-8029	
Social Worker #22	515-281-4422	
Solid Waste Operator #20	515-281-5918	
Speech Pathologist/Audiologist #22	515-281-6959	
Surveyor, Land #10	515-281-4126	
Tattoo Artist #22	515-281-8074	
Taxi Driver #28	515-237-3079	
Teacher #12	515-281-5849	
Transient Merchant #21	515-281-5204	
Travel Agency #21	515-281-5204	
Truck Driver #28	515-237-3079	
Veterinarian / Veterin'yTechnician #2	515-281-8617	
Voting Booth/Equipment #1	515-281-0145	
Waste Water Lagoon/Treatment Operator #20	515-725-0284	
Water Distribution Operator #20	515-725-0284	
Water Treatment Operator #20	515-725-0284	
Well Driller #20	515-725-0284	

Iowa Licensing Agency Information

1 Attn: Sandy Steinbach, Secretary of State's Office, Board of Voting Systems Examiners, Hoover Bldg, 2nd Fl, Des Moines, IA 50319; 515-281-0145, Fax: 515-242-5953. www.sos.state.ia.us

2 Department of Agriculture, Animal Industry Bureau, CP & RA, E 9th & Grand Ave, Wallace Bldg, 2nd Fl, Des Moines, IA 50319; 515-281-5305, Fax: 515-281-4282. www.agriculture.state.ia.us/animalIndustry.htm

3 Department of Agriculture, Pesticide Division, Wallace State Office Bldg, Des Moines, IA 50319; 515-281-5601, Fax: 515-242-6497. www.agriculture.state.ia.us/pesticidebureau.htm Email: chuck.eckermann@idals.state.ia.us Search Database at www.kellysolutions.com/ia/dealers/index.asp

4 Department of Commerce, Iowa Division of Banking, 200 E Grand Ave, Des Moines, IA 50309; 515-281-4014, Fax: 515-281-4862. www.idob.state.ia.us Email: www.idob.state.ia.us/./email/email_form.asp Search Database at www.idob.state.ia.us/license/lic_default.htm

5 Department of Commerce, Alcoholic Beverage Division, 1918 SE Hulsizer Ave, Ankeny, IA 50021; 515-281-7432, Fax: 515-281-7375. www.iowaabd.com Email: freund@iowaabd.com

6 Department of Commerce, Credit Union Division, 200 E Grand Ave #370, Des Moines, IA 50309; 515-281-6514, Fax: 515-281-7595. www.iacudiv.state.ia.us

7 IA Insurance Division, 330 Maple St, Des Moines, IA 50319-0065; 515-281-5705, Fax: 515-281-3059. www.iid.state.ia.us Email: producer.licensing@iid.state.ia.us

8 Lobby1st Registration, Chief Clerk of the House, Statehouse, Des Moines, IA 50319; 515-281-5381. www.legis.state.ia.us/ Search Database at www.legis.state.ia.us/Lobbyist.html Note: You may also search at http://coolice.legis.state.ia.us/Cool-ICE/default.asp?Category=Matt&Service=Lobby.

9 Department of Public Health, Bureau of Radiological Health, Lucas State Office Bldg 5th Fl, 321 E 12th St, Des Moines, IA 50319; 515-281-3478, Fax: 515-281-4529. http://idph.state.ia.us/

10 Department of Commerce, Professional Licensing Div., 1920 SE Hulsizer Ave, Ankeny, IA 50021; 515-281-7393, Fax: 515-281-7411. www.state.ia.us/proflic Search Database at www.state.ia.us/government/com/prof/search/

11 Supreme Court Clerk's Office, Legal Boards, 1111 E Court Ave, Des Moines, IA 50319; 515-281-5911, Fax: 515-242-6164. www.judicial.state.ia.us/regs

12 Department of Education, Board of Education Examiners, Grimes State Office Bldg, Des Moines, IA 50319-0147; 515-281-5849, Fax: 515-281-7669. www.state.ia.us/educate/programs/boee

13 Board of Dental Examiners, 400 SW 8th St, #D, Des Moines, IA 50309-4687; 515-281-5157, Fax: 515-281-7969. www.state.ia.us/dentalboard Email: ibde@bon.state.ia.us Note: Telephone verifications accepted, call 515-281-5047.

14 Board of Medical Examiners, 400 SW 8th #C, Des Moines, IA 50309-4686; 515-281-5171, Fax: 515-242-5908. www.docboard.org/ia Email: ibme@bon.state.ia.us Search Database at www.docboard.org/ia/df/iasearch.htm Note: Automated phone system verifications, call 515-281-5171. There is also direct access to their database (for a fee) at https://www.info.state.ia.us/sing/medicalmain.htm.

15 Board of Nursing, River Point Business Park, 400 SW 8th St. #B, Des Moines, IA 50309-4685; 515-281-3255, Fax: 515-281-4825. www.state.ia.us/nursing/ Email: ibon@bon.state.ia.us Search Database at www.state.ia.us/nursing/Licensure.html Note: Rosters available. Forms available at www.state.ia.us/nursing/, select general info.

16 Board of Pharmacy Examiners, 400 SW 8th St. # E, Des Moines, IA 50308; 515-281-5944, Fax: 515-281-4609. www.state.ia.us/ibpe

17 Department of Human Services, Adult & Family Services, Hoover State Office Bldg, 5th Fl, Des Moines, IA 50319-0114; 515-281-5521, Fax: 515-281-4597. www.dhs.state.ia.us

18 Department of Human Services, Divison of B.D.P.S., 1305 E Walnut, Des Moines, IA 50319-0114; 515-281-5584, Fax: 515-242-6036.

19 Department of Inspections & Appeals, Racing & Gaming Commission, 717 E Court Av #B, Des Moines, IA 50309; 515-281-7352, Fax: 515-242-6560. www.iowa.gov/irgc/ Search Database at www.iowa.gov/irgc/

20 Department of Natural Resources, 502 E 9th St, Wallace State Office Bldg, Des Moines, IA 50319-0034; 515-281-5918, Fax: 515-281-6794. www.iowadnr.com. Email: elonda.bacon@dnr.state.ia.us

21 Secretary of State, Lucas Bldg, 1st Fl, 321 E. 12th St., Des Moines, IA 50319; 515-281-5204, Fax: 515-242-5953 or 6556. www.sos.state.ia.us Email: sos@sos.state.ia.us

22 Department of Public Health, Division of Professional Licensing, Lucas State Office Bldg 321 E 12th St, Des Moines, IA 50319; 515-281-7074, Fax: 515-281-3121. www.idph.state.ia.us/licensure

23 Real Estate Appraiser Board, 1918 SE Hulsizer, Ankeny, IA 50021-3941; 515-281-7393, Fax: 515-281-7411. www.state.ia.us/government/com/prof/appraiser/home.html Email: IAPP@max.state.ia.us Search Database at www.state.ia.us/government/com/prof/search/

24 Bureau of Professional Licensure, Board of Cosmetology Arts & Sciences Examiners, 321 E 12th St, Lucas State Office Bldg 5th Fl, Des Moines, IA 50319-0075; 515-281-4416, Fax: 515-281-3121. www.idph.state.ia.us/licensure

25 Department of Public Safety, Wallace State Office Bldg, Des Moines, IA 50319; 515-281-7610, Fax: 515-281-8921. www.dps.state.ia.us Email: piinfo@dps.state.ia.us

26 Department of Revenue & Finance, Lottery Board, 2015 Grand Av, Des Moines, IA 50312; 515-281-7900, Fax: 515-281-7882. www.ialottery.com Email: Web.Master@ilot.state.ia.us

27 Division of Labor, Workforce Development, 1000 E Grand Ave, Des Moines, IA 50319-0209; 515-281-6175, Fax: 515-281-7995. www.iowaworkforce.org

28 Department of Transportation, Motor Vehicle Division, Office of Driver Svcs, PO Box 9204, 100 Euclid, Park Fair Mall, Des Moines, IA 50306-9204; 515-237-3079, Fax: 515-237-3152. www.dot.state.ia.us/mvd/ods/ Email: ods@dot.iowa.gov

Iowa Federal Courts

The following list indicates the district and division name for each county in the state. If the bankruptcy court location is different from the district court, then the location of the bankruptcy court appears in parentheses.

Iowa County/Court Cross Reference

County	District	Division
Adair	Southern	Council Bluffs (Des Moines)
Adams	Southern	Council Bluffs (Des Moines)
Allamakee	Northern	Cedar Rapids
Appanoose	Southern	Des Moines (Central)
Audubon	Southern	Council Bluffs (Des Moines)
Benton	Northern	Cedar Rapids
Black Hawk	Northern	Cedar Rapids
Boone	Southern	Des Moines (Central)
Bremer	Northern	Cedar Rapids
Buchanan	Northern	Cedar Rapids
Buena Vista	Northern	Sioux Cty (Cedar Rapids)
Butler	Northern	Sioux Cty (Cedar Rapids)
Calhoun	Northern	Sioux Cty (Cedar Rapids)
Carroll	Northern	Sioux Cty (Cedar Rapids)
Cass	Southern	Council Bluffs (Des Moines)
Cedar	Northern	Cedar Rapids
Cerro Gordo	Northern	Cedar Rapids
Cherokee	Northern	Sioux Cty (Cedar Rapids)
Chickasaw	Northern	Cedar Rapids
Clarke	Southern	Council Bluffs (Des Moines)
Clay	Northern	Sioux Cty (Cedar Rapids)
Clayton	Northern	Cedar Rapids
Clinton	Southern	Council Bluffs (Des Moines)
Crawford	Northern	Sioux Cty (Cedar Rapids)
Dallas	Southern	Des Moines (Central)
Davis	Southern	Des Moines (Central)
Decatur	Southern	Council Bluffs (Des Moines)
Delaware	Northern	Cedar Rapids
Des Moines	Southern	Des Moines (Central)
Dickinson	Northern	Sioux Cty (Cedar Rapids)
Dubuque	Northern	Cedar Rapids
Emmet	Northern	Sioux Cty (Cedar Rapids)
Fayette	Northern	Cedar Rapids
Floyd	Northern	Cedar Rapids
Franklin	Northern	Sioux Cty (Cedar Rapids)
Fremont	Southern	Council Bluffs (Des Moin
Greene	Southern	Des Moines (Central)
Grundy	Northern	Cedar Rapids
Guthrie	Southern	Des Moines (Central)
Hamilton	Northern	Sioux Cty (Cedar Rapids)
Hancock	Northern	Sioux Cty (Cedar Rapids)
Hardin	Northern	Cedar Rapids
Harrison	Southern	Council Bluffs (Des Moines)
Henry	Southern	Davenport (Des Moines)
Howard	Northern	Cedar Rapids
Humboldt	Northern	Sioux Cty (Cedar Rapids)
Ida	Northern	Sioux Cty (Cedar Rapids)
Iowa	Northern	Cedar Rapids
Jackson	Northern	Cedar Rapids
Jasper	Southern	Des Moines (Central)
Jefferson	Southern	Des Moines (Central)
Johnson	Southern	Davenport (Des Moines)
Jones	Northern	Cedar Rapids
Keokuk	Southern	Des Moines (Central)
Kossuth	Northern	Sioux Cty (Cedar Rapids)
Lee	Southern	Davenport (Des Moines)
Linn	Northern	Cedar Rapids
Louisa	Southern	Davenport (Des Moines)
Lucas	Southern	Council Bluffs (Des Moines)
Lyon	Northern	Sioux Cty (Cedar Rapids)
Madison	Southern	Des Moines (Central)
Mahaska	Southern	Des Moines (Central)
Marion	Southern	Des Moines (Central)
Marshall	Southern	Des Moines (Central)
Mills	Southern	Council Bluffs (Des Moines)
Mitchell	Northern	Cedar Rapids
Monona	Northern	Sioux Cty (Cedar Rapids)
Monroe	Southern	Des Moines (Central)
Montgomery	Southern	Council Bluffs (Des Moines)
Muscatine	Southern	Davenport (Des Moines)
O'Brien	Northern	Sioux Cty (Cedar Rapids)
Osceola	Northern	Sioux Cty (Cedar Rapids)
Page	Southern	Council Bluffs (Des Moines)
Palo Alto	Northern	Sioux Cty (Cedar Rapids)
Plymouth	Northern	Sioux Cty (Cedar Rapids)
Pocahontas	Northern	Sioux Cty (Cedar Rapids)
Polk	Southern	Des Moines (Central)
Pottawattamie	Southern	Council Bluffs (Des Moines)
Poweshiek	Southern	Des Moines (Central)
Ringgold	Southern	Council Bluffs (Des Moines)
Sac	Northern	Sioux Cty (Cedar Rapids)
Scott	Southern	Davenport (Des Moines)
Shelby	Southern	Council Bluffs (Des Moines)
Sioux	Northern	Sioux Cty (Cedar Rapids)
Story	Southern	Des Moines (Central)
Tama	Northern	Cedar Rapids
Taylor	Southern	Council Bluffs (Des Moines)
Union	Southern	Council Bluffs (Des Moines)
Van Buren	Southern	Davenport (Des Moines)
Wapello	Southern	Des Moines (Central)
Warren	Southern	Des Moines (Central)
Washington	Southern	Davenport (Des Moines)
Wayne	Southern	Council Bluffs (Des Moines)
Webster	Northern	Sioux Cty (Cedar Rapids)
Winnebago	Northern	Sioux Cty (Cedar Rapids)
Winneshiek	Northern	Cedar Rapids
Woodbury	Northern	Sioux Cty (Cedar Rapids)
Worth	Northern	Sioux Cty (Cedar Rapids)
Wright	Northern	Sioux Cty (Cedar Rapids)

Standards for Federal Courts: Search fee is $26.00 per item (one party name or case number). Copy fee is $.50 per page. Certification fee is $9.00 per document, double for exemplification, if available. All fees standard unless noted in profile. Mail Search: always enclose a stamped self addressed envelope unless otherwise noted. Most courts accept fax requests or will suggest a copying/search vendor. Before releasing records, all courts require prepayment, unless noted.

Open records are located at the court unless otherwise noted. District courts index by defendant and plaintiff as well as by case number. Bankruptcy courts usually index by debtor and case number. While most courts now have their indexes on computer, many may still maintain index card files as well.

Courts offering internet access via CM-ECF or older RACER, PACER, or Web-PACER systems charge $.08 per page fee unless noted as free. Where PACER is available, the universal sign-up number is 800-676-6856. Find PACER and the US Party/Case Index at http://pacer.psc.uscourts.gov.

US District Court

Northern District of Iowa

Cedar Rapids (Eastern) Division Clerk of Court, 101 1st St SE, Rm 313, Cedar Rapids, IA 52401 (also use mail address for courier delivery), 319-286-2300, Fax-319-286-2301. Hours- 8AM-4:30PM. www.iand.uscourts.gov

Counties: Allamakee, Benton, Black Hawk, Bremer, Buchanan, Cedar, Chickasaw, Clayton, Delaware, Dubuque, Fayette, Floyd, Grundy, Hardin, Howard, Iowa, Jackson, Jones, Linn, Mitchell, Tama, Winneshiek.

Searches & Indexing: Results do not include SSN or DOB. Computer index maintained. New cases in the index immediately after filing date.

Fee & Payment: Pay by money order, cashier's or personal check. Payee: Clerk, US District Court. Prepayment required.

Phone Search: Anything public record is released via phone, but only for one name per call.

Mail Search: search usually completed- 1-2 days. SASE required.

In Person Search: Fee charged if court performs your search. No self-serve copier available.

E-Services: PACER online at http://pacer.iand.uscourts.gov. PACER records go back to 11/1992. New records online after 1 day. ECF at https://ecf.iand.uscourts.gov **Opinions Online:** www.iand.uscourts.gov. Click on Decisions/Opinions and Jury Verdicts.

Sioux City (Western) Division Court Clerk, Rm 301, Federal Bldg, 320 6th St, Sioux City, IA 51101 (also use mail address for courier delivery), 712-233-3900. Hours- 8AM-5PM. www.iand.uscourts.gov

Counties: Buena Vista, Butler, Calhoun, Carroll, Cerro Gordo, Cherokee, Clay, Crawford, Dickinson, Emmet, Franklin, Hamilton, Hancock,

Humboldt, Ida, Kossuth, Lyon, Monona, O'Brien, Osceola, Palo Alto, Plymouth, Pocahontas, Sac, Sioux, Webster, Winnebago, Woodbury, Worth, Wright. This court also has records for the Ft. Dodge, Independence, and Mason City Divisions, but not Green, Boone or Marshall counties. Court is held occasionally held at Ft. Dodge, but records are here at Sioux City.

Searches & Indexing: Results do not include SSN or DOB. Computer index back to 1995 maintained. New cases in the index immediately after filing date.

Fee & Payment: Pay by money order, cashier's or personal check. No credit cards. Payee: Clerk, US District Court. Prepayment required.

Phone Search: Only docket information available by phone.

Mail Search: search usually completed- 2-3 days. Include SASE for return.

In Person Search: Fee charged if court performs your search. No self-serve copier available.

E-Services: PACER online at http://pacer.iand.uscourts.gov. PACER records go back to 11/1992. New records online after 1 day. ECF at https://ecf.iand.uscourts.gov **Opinions Online:** www.iand.uscourts.gov. Click on Decisions/Opinions and Jury Verdicts.

US Bankruptcy Court

Northern District of Iowa

Cedar Rapids (Eastern) Division Court Clerk, PO Box 74890, Cedar Rapids, IA 52407-4890 (courier address: 8th Fl, 425 2nd St SE, Cedar Rapids, IA 52401), 319-286-2200, Fax-319-286-2280. Hours- 8AM-4:30PM. www.ianb.uscourts.gov

Counties: Allamakee, Benton, Black Hawk, Bremer, Buchanan, Cedar, Chickasaw, Clayton, Delaware, Dubuque, Fayette, Floyd, Grundy, Howard, Iowa, Jackson, Jones, Linn, Mitchell, Tama, Winneshiek. Also has electronic records of cases from the Sioux City Division.

Searches & Indexing: Cases indexed by debtor, creditors, and case number. Court also handles records for Sioux City division. Results include last 4 SSN digits. Computer index maintained. New cases in the index immediately after filing date. District-wide searches available here back to 1988.

Fee & Payment: Pay by Visa/MC, money order, cashier check, business check. No personal checks. Law firm checks accepted if in-state. Payee: Clerk, US Bankruptcy Court. Prepayment required.

Phone Search: Only minimal information released via phone; not all docket information is released. Voice Case Information Service available, call 800-249-9859 or 319-362-9906.

Mail Search: search usually completed- 2 days. Include SASE for return.

In Person Search: permitted. Self-serve copier available - $.25 per page.

E-Services: ECF replaces PACER. Document images available. ECF at https://ecf.ianb.uscourts.gov **Opinions Online:** www.ianb.uscourts.gov/decframe.html. **Other Online Access:** Calendars free at www.ianb.uscourts.gov/cal/index.html.

Sioux City (Western) Division Court Clerk, PO Box 3857, Sioux City, IA 51102-3857 (courier address: Federal Bldg., 320 6th St, Sioux City, IA 51101), 712-233-3939, Fax-712-233-3942. 8AM-4:30PM. www.ianb.uscourts.gov

Counties: Buena Vista, Calhoun, Carroll, Cerro Gordo, Cherokee, Clay, Crawford, Dickinson, Emmet, Floyd, Franklin, Hamilton, Hancock, Hardin, Humboldt, Ida, Kossuth, Lyon, Mitchell, Monona, O'Brien, Osceola, Palo Alto, Plymouth, Pocahontas, Sac, Sioux, Webster, Winnebago, Woodbury, Worth, Wright. Case records are also available electronically at the Cedar Rapids Division.

Searches & Indexing: Cases indexed by debtor, creditors, and case number. Results include last 4 SSN digits. Computer index maintained. New cases in the index immediately after filing date. District-wide searches available here back to 1988.

Fee & Payment: Pay by Visa/MC, money order, cashier check, business check. No personal checks. Law firm checks accepted if in-state. Payee: Clerk, US Bankruptcy Court. Prepayment required.

Phone Search: Only minimal information released via phone; not all docket information is released. Voice Case Information Service available, call VCIS at 800-249-9859 or 319-362-9906.

Mail Search: search usually completed- 2 days. Include SASE for return.

In Person Search: permitted. Self-serve copier available - $.10 per page.

E-Services: ECF replaces PACER. Document images available. ECF at https://ecf.ianb.uscourts.gov **Opinions Online:** www.ianb.uscourts.gov/decframe.html. **Other Online Access:** Calendars free at www.ianb.uscourts.gov/cal/index.html.

US District Court

Southern District of Iowa

Council Bluffs (Western) Division Court Clerk, PO Box 307, Council Bluffs, IA 51502 (courier address: Rm 313, 8 S 6th St, Council Bluffs, IA 51502), 712-328-0283, Fax-712-328-1241. Hours- 7:30AM-11:30AM M-W; N-4PM Fri. www.iasd.uscourts.gov

Counties: Audubon, Cass, Fremont, Harrison, Mills, Montgomery, Page, Pottawattamie, Shelby.

Searches & Indexing: Results do not include SSN or DOB. Computer index back to 1990 maintained. New cases in the index immediately after filing date. Records purged 3 years after case closed.

Fee & Payment: Pay by Visa/MC/Discover, money order, cashier's or personal check. Payee: Clerk, US District Court. Search fee is charged if the clerk's staff is required to spend more than 5 minutes searching. Will fax documents for $3.00 for up to 9 pages, $5.00 if more, plus copy fee.

Phone Search: All information available is released via phone.

Mail Search: search usually completed- 2-3 days. SASE required.

In Person Search: Fee charged if court performs your search. Self-serve copier - $.50 per page.

E-Services: ECF replaces PACER. Document images available. PACER records go back to mid 1989. New records online after 1 day. ECF at https://ecf.iasd.uscourts.gov. Required as of 4/2005. **Opinions Online:** www.iasd.us courts.gov/iasd/opinions.nsf/main/page. **Other Online Access:** Court calendars free at www.iasd.uscourts.gov/iasd/judgecal.nsf/main/page.

Davenport (Eastern) Division

Court Clerk, 211 19th St, Rock Island, IA 61201 (courier address: Rm 215, 131 E 4th St (Temporary Address), Davenport, IA 52801), 309-786-6615 or 563-322-3223, Fax-309-786-7532. www.iasd.uscourts.gov

Counties: Henry, Johnson, Lee, Louisa, Muscatine, Scott, Van Buren, Washington. Court is temporarily located at US District Court in Rock Island, Illinois, and will return to 131 E 4th St in Davenport, IA in 2006.

Searches & Indexing: Civil cases are handled here. Results do not include SSN or DOB. Both computer and card indexes maintained. New cases in the index 1 day after filing date. Records purged every 2 years.

Fee & Payment: Pay by money order, cashier's or personal check. Payee: Clerk, US District Court. Will bill fees. Will fax back for $3.00 up to 9 pages; $5.00 if more, plus copy fees.

Phone Search: Docket information available via phone.

Mail Search: search usually completed- week-10 days. SASE required.

In Person Search: Fee charged if court performs your search. Self-serve copier available - $.10 per page.

E-Services: ECF replaces PACER. Document images available. PACER records go back to mid 1989. New records online after 1 day. ECF at https://ecf.iasd.uscourts.gov. Required as of 4/2005. **Opinions Online:** www.iasd.uscou rts.gov/iasd/opinions.nsf/main/page. **Other Online Access:** Court calendars free at www.iasd.uscourts.gov/iasd/judgecal.nsf/main/page.

Des Moines (Central) Division

Court Clerk, PO Box 9344, Des Moines, IA 50306-9344 (courier address: 123 E. Walnut St, Rm 300, Des Moines, IA 50306), 515-284-6248, Fax-515-284-6418. Hours- 8AM-5PM. www.iasd.uscourts.gov

Counties: Adair, Adams, Appanoose, Boone, Clarke, Clinton, Dallas, Davis, Decatur, Des Moines, Greene, Guthrie, Jasper, Jefferson, Keokuk, Lucas, Madison, Mahaska, Marion, Marshall, Monroe, Polk, Poweshiek, Ringgold, Story, Taylor, Union, Wapello, Warren, Wayne.

Searches & Indexing: Results do not include SSN or DOB. Computer index maintained. Records stored by date filed and closed. New cases in the index immediately after filing date.

Fee & Payment: Pay by money order, cashier's or personal check, credit card. Payee: Clerk, US District Court. Court will bill. Will fax back for $3.00 up to 9 pages; $5.00 if more, plus copy fee.

Phone Search: No searching by telephone.

Mail Search: search usually completed- 1-2 days. SASE required.

In Person Search: Fee charged if court performs your search. Only the clerk can conduct criminal searches. No self-serve copier available.

E-Services: ECF replaces PACER. Document images available. PACER records go back to mid 1989. New records online immediately. ECF at https://ecf.iasd.uscourts.gov. Required as of 4/2005. **Opinions Online:** www.iasd.usc ourts.gov/iasd/opinions.nsf/main/page. **Other Online Access:** Court calendars free at www.iasd.uscourts.gov/iasd/judgecal.nsf/main/page.

US Bankruptcy Court

Southern District of Iowa

Des Moines Division Court Clerk, PO Box 9264, Des Moines, IA 50306-9264 (courier address: 300 US Courthouse Annex, 110 E Court Ave, Des Moines, IA 50309), 515-284-6230, Fax-515-284-6404. Hours- 8AM-5PM. www.iasb.uscourts.gov

Counties: Adair, Adams, Appanoose, Audubon, Boone, Cass, Clarke, Clinton, Dallas, Davis, Decatur, Des Moines, Fremont, Greene, Guthrie, Harrison, Henry, Jasper, Jefferson, Johnson, Keokuk, Lee, Louisa, Lucas, Madison, Mahaska, Marion, Marshall, Mills, Monroe, Montgomery, Muscatine, Page, Polk, Pottawattamie, Poweshiek, Ringgold, Scott, Shelby, Story, Taylor, Union, Van Buren, Wapello, Warren, Washington, Wayne.

Searches & Indexing: Results include last 4 SSN digits. Computer index maintained. New cases in the index immediately after filing date. Records purged every 6 months.

Fee & Payment: Pay by money order, cashier check, business check. No personal checks. Payee: CopyCat Photocopy Center.

Phone Search: Information released via phone is: name, case number, chapter date file, assets, attorney, attorney's telephone number, trustee, judge, status and discharge. Information is available from June 1987. Voice Case Information Service available, call VCIS at 888-219-5534 or 515-284-6427.

Mail Search: search usually completed- 3-4 working days. Include SASE for return.

In Person Search: Fee charged if court performs your search. No self-serve copier available.

E-Services: New CM/ECF online system access only. PACER records go back to 6/1987. New records online after 1 day. ECF at https://ecf.iasb.uscourts.gov **Other Online Access:** The RACER system has been replaced by the ECF/PACER system. Access fee is $.08 per page.

Iowa County Courts

Court	Jurisdiction	No. of Courts	How Organized
District Courts*	General	100	8 Districts

* Profiled in this Sourcebook.

Court	CIVIL								
	Tort	Contract	Real Estate	Min. Claim	Max. Claim	Small Claims	Estate	Eviction	Domestic Relations
District Courts*	X	X	X	$0	No Max	$4000	X	X	X

Court	CRIMINAL				
	Felony	Misdemeanor	DWI/DUI	Preliminary Hearing	Juvenile
District Courts*	X	X	X	X	X

ADMINISTRATION
State Court Administrator, Judicial Branch Bldg, 1111 East Court Ave, Des Moines, IA, 50319; 515-281-5241, Fax: 515-242-0014. www.judicial.state.ia.us

COURT STRUCTURE
The District Court is the court of general jurisdiction. Effective 7/1/95, the Small Claims limit increased to $4000 from $3000.

Vital records were moved from courts to the County Recorder's office in each county.

ONLINE ACCESS
Criminal, civil, probate, traffic and appellate information is now available from all 99 counties in Iowa at www.judicial.state.ia.us/online_records. There is no fee for basic information, and a pay system is offered for more detailed requests. Name searches are available on a statewide or specific county basis. While this is an excellent site with much information, there is one important consideration to keep in mind. Although records are updated daily, the historical records offered are not from the same starting date on a county-by-county basis. Also, from the home page one may access supreme and apppellate court opinions.

ADDITIONAL INFORMATION
In most courts, the Certification Fee is $10.00 plus copy fee. Copy Fee is $.50 per page. Most courts do not do searches and recommend either in person searches or use of a record retriever.

Courts that accept written search requests usually require an SASE.

Most courts have a Public access terminal for access to that court's records.

Adair County

5th District Court PO Box L, Greenfield, IA 50849; phone: 641-743-2445; fax: 641-743-2974; hours 8AM-4:30PM (CST). *Felony, Misdemeanor, Civil, Eviction, Small Claims, Probate.*
www.judicial.state.ia.us/district/district5
Civil Records: Access: In person, online. Both court and visitors may perform in person searches. Court makes copy: $.50 per page; same fee for self serve. Required to search: name, years to search. Civil cases indexed by defendant, plaintiff. Civil records on docket books from late 1800s, computerized since 11/1996. Civil, probate, and appellate information is at www.judicial.state.ia.us/online_records.
Criminal Records: Access: In person, online. Visitors must perform in person searches themselves. Court makes copy: $.50 per page; same fee for self serve. Required to search: name, years to search, DOB, signed release; also helpful: SSN. Criminal records on docket books from late 1800s, computerized since 11/1996. Criminal, traffic, and appellate information is online at www.judicial.state.ia.us/online_records.
General Information: Public terminal goes back to 1997. No juvenile, sealed, dissolution of marriage, mental health domestic abuse or deferred records released. Certification fee: $10.00. Payee: Clerk of Court. Personal checks accepted. Prepayment required.

Adams County

5th District Court Courthouse, PO Box 484, Corning, IA 50841; phone: 641-322-4711; fax: 641-322-4523; probate fax: same; hours 8AM-4:30PM (CST). *Felony, Misdemeanor, Civil, Eviction, Small Claims, Probate.*
www.judicial.state.ia.us/district/district5
Civil Records: Access: In person, online. Visitors must perform in person searches themselves. Court makes copy: $.50 per page. Required to search: name, years to search. Civil cases indexed by defendant, plaintiff. Civil records on docket books from late 1800s, on computer back to 11/96. Civil, probate, and appellate information is at www.judicial.state.ia.us/online_records.
Criminal Records: Access: In person, online. Visitors must perform in person searches themselves. Court makes copy: $.50 per page. Required to search: name, years to search, signed release. Criminal records on docket books from late 1800s, on computer back to 11/96. Criminal, traffic, and appellate information is online at www.judicial.state.ia.us/online_records.
General Information: Public terminal has only civil records back to 1996. No sealed, dissolution of marriage, mental health, sealed or expunged records released. Certification fee: $10.00. Payee: Clerk of Court. Personal checks accepted. Prepayment required.

Allamakee County

1st District Court PO Box 248, Waukon, IA 52172; phone: 563-568-6351; fax: 563-568-6353; hours 8AM-4:30PM Monday - Friday (CST). *Felony, Misdemeanor, Civil, Eviction, Small Claims, Probate.*
www.judicial.state.ia.us/district/district1
Civil Records: Access: In person, online. Visitors must perform in person searches themselves. Court makes copy: $.50 per page; same fee for self serve. Required to search: name, years to search. Civil cases indexed by defendant, plaintiff. All judgments on computer back to 4/1997; on index books back to 1880, probate back to 1852. Civil, probate, and appellate information is at www.judicial.state.ia.us/online_records.
Criminal Records: Access: In person, online. Visitors must perform in person searches themselves. No search fee. Court makes copy: $.50 per page; same fee for self serve. Required to search: name, years to search, signed release. Criminal records on docket books from 1800s; on computer back to 4/1997. Criminal, traffic, and appellate information is online at www.judicial.state.ia.us/online_records.
General Information: Public terminal goes back to 4/1997. No juvenile, adoption, sealed, pending dissolution of marriage, mental health, domestic abuse or deferred records released. Certification fee: $10.00. Payee: Clerk of Court. Personal checks accepted. Prepayment required.

Appanoose County

8th District Court PO Box 400, Centerville, IA 52544; phone: 641-856-6101; fax: 641-856-2282; hours 8AM-4:30 PM (CST). *Felony, Misdemeanor, Civil, Eviction, Small Claims, Probate.*
www.judicial.state.ia.us/district/district8
Civil Records: Access: In person, online. Visitors must perform in person searches themselves. Court makes copy: $.50 per page. Required to search: name, years to search. Civil cases indexed by defendant, plaintiff. Civil records on docket books from 1847, on computer back to 2/96. Civil, probate, and appellate data at www.judicial.state.ia.us/online_records.
Criminal Records: Access: In person, online. Visitors must perform in person searches themselves. Court makes copy: $.50 per page. Required to search: name, years to search, signed release. Criminal records on docket books from 1847, on computer back to 2/96. Criminal, traffic, and appellate information is online at www.judicial.state.ia.us/online_records.
General Information: Public terminal goes back to 1996. No juvenile, sealed, dissolution of marriage, mental health, domestic abuse or deferred records released. Certification fee: $10.00. Payee: Clerk of Court. Personal checks or Visa/MC accepted. Prepayment required.

Audubon County

4th District Court 318 Leroy St, #6, Audubon, IA 50025; phone: 712-563-4275; fax: 712-563-4276; hours 8AM-4:30PM (CST). *Felony, Misdemeanor, Civil, Eviction, Small Claims, Probate.*
www.judicial.state.ia.us/district/district4
Civil Records: Access: In person, online. Visitors must perform in person searches themselves. Court makes copy: $.50 per page. Required to search: name, years to search; also helpful: address. Civil cases indexed by defendant, plaintiff. Civil records on docket books from 1930s, computerized since 1996. Civil, probate, and appellate information is at www.judicial.state.ia.us/online_records.
Criminal Records: Access: In person, online. Visitors must perform in person searches themselves. Court makes copy: $.50 per page. Required to search: name, years to search; also helpful: DOB, SSN, address. Criminal records on docket books from late 1800s. Criminal, traffic, and appellate information is online at www.judicial.state.ia.us/online_records.
General Information: Public terminal goes back to 11/1996. No juvenile, sealed, dissolution of marriage, mental health, domestic abuse or deferred records released. Certification fee: $10.00 per doc includes copies. Payee: Clerk of Court. Prepayment required.

Benton County

6th District Court PO Box 719, Vinton, IA 52349; phone: 319-472-2766; fax: 319-472-2747; hours 8AM-4:30PM (CST). *Felony, Misdemeanor, Civil, Eviction, Small Claims, Probate.*
www.judicial.state.ia.us/district/district6
Civil Records: Access: In person, online. Visitors must perform in person searches themselves. Court makes copy: $.50 per page; same fee for self serve. Required to search: name, years to search. Civil cases indexed by defendant, plaintiff. Civil records on original record books from 1800s, index is on computer since 6/95. Civil, probate, and appellate information is at www.judicial.state.ia.us/online_records.
Criminal Records: Access: In person, online. Visitors must perform in person searches themselves. No search fee. Court makes copy: $.50 per page; same fee for self serve. Required to search: name, years to search. Criminal records on original record books from 1800s, index is on computer since 6/95. Criminal, traffic, and appellate information is online at www.judicial.state.ia.us/online_records.
General Information: Public terminal goes back to 1995. No juvenile, sealed, dissolution of marriage,

mental health, domestic abuse or deferred records released. Certification fee: $10.00 per document. Payee: Clerk of Court. Personal checks accepted. Prepayment required.

Black Hawk County

1st District Court 316 E 5th St, Waterloo, IA 50703; phone: 319-833-3331; probate phone: x 1856; fax: 319-833-3251; hours 8AM-4:30PM (CST). *Felony, Misdemeanor, Civil, Eviction, Small Claims, Probate.*
www.judicial.state.ia.us/district/district1
Civil Records: Access: In person, online. Visitors must perform in person searches themselves. Court makes copy: $.50 per page. Required to search: name, years to search. Civil cases indexed by defendant, plaintiff. Civil records on computer from 1992, docket books from early 1900s. Civil, probate, and appellate information is at www.judicial.state.ia.us/online_records.
Criminal Records: Access: In person, online. Visitors must perform in person searches themselves. No search fee. Court makes copy: $.50 per page. Required to search: name, years to search; also helpful: DOB, SSN. Criminal records on computer from 1992, docket books from early 1900s. Criminal, traffic, and appellate information is online at www.judicial.state.ia.us/online_records.
General Information: Public terminal goes back to 1992. No juvenile, sealed, dissolution of marriage, mental health, domestic abuse or deferred records released. Certification fee: $10.00. Payee: District Court. Personal checks accepted. Prepayment required.

Boone County

2nd District Court 201 State St, Boone, IA 50036; phone: 515-433-0561; fax: 515-433-0563; hours 8AM-4:30PM (CST). *Felony, Misdemeanor, Civil, Eviction, Small Claims, Probate.*
www.judicial.state.ia.us/district/district2
Civil Records: Access: In person, online. Visitors must perform in person searches themselves. Court makes copy: $.50 per page. Required to search: name, years to search. Civil cases indexed by defendant, plaintiff. Civil records on docket books from 1890s; computerized records go back to 1996. Civil, probate, and appellate information is at www.judicial.state.ia.us/online_records.
Criminal Records: Access: In person, online. Visitors must perform in person searches themselves. Court makes copy: $.50 per page. Required to search: name, years to search, offense, date of offense. Criminal records on docket books from 1890s; computerized records go back to 1996. Criminal, traffic, and appellate information is online at www.judicial.state.ia.us/online_records.
General Information: Public terminal goes back to 1996. No juvenile, sealed, dissolution of marriage, mental health, domestic abuse or deferred records released. Certification fee: $10.00. Payee: Clerk of Court. Personal checks accepted. Prepayment required.

Bremer County

2nd District Court PO Box 328, Waverly, IA 50677; phone: 319-352-5661; fax: 319-352-1054; hours 8AM-4:30PM (CST). *Felony, Misdemeanor, Civil, Eviction, Small Claims, Probate.*
www.co.bremer.ia.us
Civil Records: Access: In person, online. Visitors must perform in person searches themselves. Court makes copy: $.50 per page; same fee for self serve. Required to search: name, years to search. Civil cases indexed by defendant, plaintiff. Civil records on computer since 7/97; prior records on docket books from 1900's. Civil, probate, and appellate information is at www.judicial.state.ia.us/online_records.
Criminal Records: Access: In person, online. Visitors must perform in person searches themselves. Court makes copy: $.50 per page; same fee for self serve. Required to search: name, years to

search. Criminal records go back to 1900's; computerized records go back to 1996. Criminal, traffic, and appellate information is online at www.judicial.state.ia.us/online_records.
General Information: Public terminal goes back to 1998. No juvenile, sealed, dissolution of marriage, mental health, domestic abuse or deferred records released. Will fax specific of $2.00 per page. Certification fee: $10.00. Payee: Clerk of Court. Personal checks or Visa, MC accepted. Prepayment required.

Buchanan County

1st District Court PO Box 259, Independence, IA 50644; phone: 319-334-2196; fax: 319-334-7455; hours 8AM-4:30PM (CST). *Felony, Misdemeanor, Civil, Eviction, Small Claims, Probate.*
www.judicial.state.ia.us/district/district1/
Note: Probate is in a separate index at this address.
Civil Records: Access: In person, online. Both court and visitors may perform in person searches. Court makes copy: $.50 per page. Self serve copy fee: none. Required to search: name, years to search. Civil cases indexed by defendant, plaintiff. Civil records on docket books from 1800s; computerized since 1996. Civil, probate, and appellate information is at www.judicial.state.ia.us.
Criminal Records: Access: Mail, in person, online. Both court and visitors may perform in person searches. No search fee. Court makes copy: $.50 per page. Self serve copy fee: none. Required to search: name, years to search. Criminal records on docket books from 1800s; computerized since 1996. Criminal, traffic, and appellate information is online at www.judicial.state.ia.us. Mail turnaround time 2 days.
General Information: Public terminal goes back to 1985. No juvenile, sealed, dissolution of marriage, mental health, domestic abuse or deferred records released. Will fax specific case file requests; fee is $.50 per page. Certification fee: $10.00 per document. Payee: Clerk of Court. Personal checks or Visa, MC accepted. Prepayment and SASE required.

Buena Vista County

3rd District Court PO Box 1186, Storm Lake, IA 50588; phone: 712-749-2546; fax: 712-749-2700; hours 8AM-4:30PM (CST). *Felony, Misdemeanor, Civil, Eviction, Small Claims, Probate.*
www.judicial.state.ia.us/district/district3
Civil Records: Access: In person, online. Visitors must perform in person searches themselves. Court makes copy: $.50 per page. Required to search: name, years to search. Civil cases indexed by defendant, plaintiff. Civil records on index cards from early 1900s; on computer back to 1996. Civil, probate, and appellate information is at www.judicial.state.ia.us/online_records.
Criminal Records: Access: In person, online. Visitors must perform in person searches themselves. Court makes copy: $.50 per page. Required to search: name, years to search. Criminal records on index cards from early 1900s; on computer back to 1994. Criminal, traffic, and appellate information is online at www.judicial.state.ia.us/online_records.
General Information: Public terminal goes back to 1995. No juvenile, sealed, dissolution of marriage, mental health, domestic abuse or deferred records released. Certification fee: $10.00 per document. Payee: Clerk of Court. Personal checks accepted. Prepayment required.

Butler County

2nd District Court PO Box 307, Allison, IA 50602; phone: 319-267-2487; fax: 319-267-2488; hours 9AM-3:30PM (CST). *Felony, Misdemeanor, Civil, Eviction, Small Claims, Probate.*
www.judicial.state.ia.us/district/district2

Civil Records: Access: In person, online. Visitors must perform in person searches themselves. Court makes copy: $.50 per page; same fee for self serve. Required to search: name, years to search. Civil cases indexed by defendant, plaintiff. Civil records on docket books from 1800s, on computer back to 4/97. Civil, probate, and appellate information is at www.judicial.state.ia.us/online_records.

Criminal Records: Access: In person, online. Visitors must perform in person searches themselves. Court makes copy: $.50 per page; same fee for self serve. Required to search: name, years to search. Criminal records on docket books from 1800s, on computer back to 4/97. Criminal, traffic, and appellate information is online at www.judicial.state.ia.us/online_records.

General Information: Public terminal goes back to 4/1997. No juvenile, sealed, dissolution of marriage, mental health, domestic abuse or deferred records released. Will fax documents $1.00 per page. Certification fee: $10.00. Payee: Clerk of Court. Personal checks accepted. Prepayment required.

Calhoun County

2nd District Court 416 Fourth St #5, Rockwell City, IA 50579; phone: 712-297-8122; fax: 712-297-5082; hours 8AM-4:30PM (CST). *Felony, Misdemeanor, Civil, Eviction, Small Claims, Probate.*
www.judicial.state.ia.us/district/district2
Civil Records: Access: In person, online. Visitors must perform in person searches themselves. Court makes copy: $.50 per page. Required to search: name, years to search. Civil cases indexed by defendant, plaintiff. Civil records on docket books from 1880s, computerized since 7/97. Civil, probate, and appellate information is at www.judicial.state.ia.us/online_records.

Criminal Records: Access: In person, online. Visitors must perform in person searches themselves. No search fee. Court makes copy: $.50 per page. Required to search: name, years to search, DOB, signed release; also helpful: SSN. Criminal records on docket books from 1880s, computerized since 7/97. Criminal, traffic, and appellate data at www.judicial.state.ia.us/online_records.

General Information: Public terminal goes back to 7/1997. No juvenile, sealed, pending dissolution of marriage, mental health, domestic abuse or deferred records released. Will fax specific case file requests for $1.00 per page. Certification fee: $10.00 per document. Payee: Clerk of the Court. Personal checks or Visa, MC accepted. Prepayment required.

Carroll County

2nd District Court PO Box 867, Carroll, IA 51401; phone: 712-792-4327; fax: 712-792-4328; hours 8AM-4:30PM (CST). *Felony, Misdemeanor, Civil, Eviction, Small Claims, Probate.*
www.judicial.state.ia.us/district/district2
Civil Records: Access: In person, online. Visitors must perform in person searches themselves. Court makes copy: $.50 per page. Self serve copy fee: $.25 per page. Required to search: name, years to search. Civil cases indexed by defendant, plaintiff. Civil records on index books from 1800s; computerized records go back to 1993 on a limited basis. Everything from 9/1997 to present. Civil, probate, and appellate data at www.judicial.state.ia.us/online_records.

Criminal Records: Access: In person, online. Visitors must perform in person searches themselves. No search fee. Court makes copy: $.50 per page. Self serve copy fee: $.25 per page. Required to search: name, years to search. Criminal records on computer from 6/1993, index books from 1800s. Criminal, traffic, and appellate information is online at www.judicial.state.ia.us/online_records.

General Information: Public terminal goes back to 1997. No juvenile, sealed, dissolution of marriage, mental health, domestic abuse or deferred records released. Will fax specific case file requests for $1.00 per page. Certification fee: $10.00. Payee: Clerk of

Court. Personal checks accepted. Credit cards accepted. Prepayment required.

Cass County

4th District Court 5 W 7th St, Courthouse, Atlantic, IA 50022; phone: 712-243-2105; fax: 712-243-4661; hours 8AM-4:30PM (CST). *Felony, Misdemeanor, Civil, Eviction, Small Claims, Probate.*
www.judicial.state.ia.us/district/district4
Civil Records: Access: In person, online. Visitors must perform in person searches themselves. Court makes copy: $.25 per page. Required to search: name, years to search. Civil cases indexed by defendant, plaintiff. Civil records on docket books from early 1900s; on computer back to 11/1996. Civil, probate, and appellate information is at www.judicial.state.ia.us/online_records.

Criminal Records: Access: In person, online. Visitors must perform in person searches themselves. Court makes copy: $.25 per page. Required to search: name, years to search, signed release; also helpful: DOB, SSN. Criminal records on docket books from 1880s; on computer back to 11/1996. Criminal, traffic, and appellate information is online at www.judicial.state.ia.us/online_records.

General Information: Public terminal goes back to 11/96. No juvenile, sealed, dissolution of marriage, mental health, domestic abuse or deferred records released. Certification fee: $10.00. Payee: Clerk of Court. Personal checks accepted. Prepayment required.

Cedar County

7th District Court 400 Cedar St, Attn: Cedar County Clerk of Court, Tipton, IA 52772; phone: 563-886-2101; fax: 563-886-3594; hours 8AM-4:30PM (CST). *Felony, Misdemeanor, Civil, Eviction, Small Claims, Probate.*
www.judicial.state.ia.us/district/district7
Civil Records: Access: In person, online. Visitors must perform in person searches themselves. Court makes copy: $.50 per page; same fee for self serve. Required to search: name, years to search. Civil cases indexed by defendant, plaintiff. Civil records on computer since 12/1996; on microfiche and docket books from 1839. Civil, probate, and appellate information is at www.judicial.state.ia.us/online_records.

Criminal Records: Access: In person, online. Visitors must perform in person searches themselves. Court makes copy: $.50 per page; same fee for self serve. Required to search: name, years to search; also helpful: DOB, SSN, signed release. Criminal records on computer since 7/1992; on microfiche and docket books from 1839. Criminal, traffic, and appellate information is online at www.judicial.state.ia.us/online_records.

General Information: Public terminal has criminal back to 7/1992 and civil back to 10/1996. No juvenile, sealed, dissolution of marriage, mental health, domestic abuse or deferred records released. Certification fee: $10.00 per doc. Payee: Clerk of Court. Only cashiers checks and money orders accepted. Prepayment required.

Cerro Gordo County

2nd District Court 220 W Washington, Mason City, IA 50401; phone: 641-424-6431; hours 8AM-4:30PM (CST). *Felony, Misdemeanor, Civil, Eviction, Small Claims, Probate.*
www.judicial.state.ia.us/district/district2
Civil Records: Access: In person, online. Visitors must perform in person searches themselves. Court makes copy: $.50 per page. Required to search: name, years to search. Civil cases indexed by defendant, plaintiff. Civil records on computer since 1996: prior records on docket books from early 1900s. Civil, probate, and appellate information is at www.judicial.state.ia.us/online_records.

Criminal Records: Access: In person, online. Visitors must perform in person searches

themselves. Court makes copy: $.50 per page. Required to search: name, years to search; also helpful: DOB, SSN. Criminal records on computer since 4/95; prior records on index cards from 1977. Criminal, traffic, and appellate information is online at www.judicial.state.ia.us/online_records.

General Information: Public terminal has criminal back to 1995 and civil back to 1996. No Sealed, dissolution of marriage, mental health, domestic abuse or deferred records released. Certification fee: $10.00 per doc. Payee: Clerk of Court. Personal checks and Visa/MC accepted. Prepayment required.

Cherokee County

3rd District Court 520 W Main St, Cherokee, IA 51012; phone: 712-225-6744; probate phone: 712-225-6744; fax: 712-225-6749; hours 8AM-4:30PM (CST). *Felony, Misdemeanor, Civil, Eviction, Small Claims, Probate.*
www.judicial.state.ia.us/district/district3
Civil Records: Access: In person, online. Visitors must perform in person searches themselves. Court makes copy: $.50 per page. Required to search: name, years to search. Civil cases indexed by defendant, plaintiff. Civil records on docket books from 1800s, indexed on computer since 1997. Civil, probate, and appellate information is at www.judicial.state.ia.us/online_records.

Criminal Records: Access: In person, online. Visitors must perform in person searches themselves. Court makes copy: $.50 per page. Required to search: name, years to search. Criminal records index is computerized since 1997. Criminal, traffic, and appellate information is online at www.judicial.state.ia.us/online_records.

General Information: Public terminal goes back to 1997. No juvenile, sealed, dissolution of marriage, mental health, domestic abuse or deferred records released. Certification fee: $10.00. Payee: Clerk of Court. Personal checks accepted. Prepayment required.

Chickasaw County

1st District Court County Courthouse, 8 E Prospect, New Hampton, IA 50659; phone: 641-394-2106; fax: 641-394-5106; hours 8AM-4:30PM (CST). *Felony, Misdemeanor, Civil, Eviction, Small Claims, Probate.*
www.judicial.state.ia.us/district/district1
Civil Records: Access: In person, online. Visitors must perform in person searches themselves. Court makes copy: $.50 per page 1st 10; $.25 per each add'l. Required to search: name, years to search. Civil cases indexed by defendant, plaintiff. Civil records on docket books from late 1800s; on computer back to 1996. Civil, probate, and appellate information is at www.judicial.state.ia.us/online_records.

Criminal Records: Access: In person, online. Visitors must perform in person searches themselves. Court makes copy: $.50 per page, $.25 per page after first 10. Required to search: name, years to search, signed release. Criminal records on docket books from late 1800s; on computer back to 1996. Criminal, traffic, and appellate information is online at www.judicial.state.ia.us/online_records.

General Information: Public terminal goes back to 1996. No juvenile, sealed, dissolution of marriage, adoption, mental health, domestic abuse or deferred records released. Certification fee: $10.00 per doc. Payee: Clerk of District Court. Personal checks and Visa/MC accepted. Prepayment required.

Clarke County

5th District Court 100 S Main St, Clarke County Courthouse, Osceola, IA 50213; phone: 641-342-6096; fax: 641-342-2463; hours 8AM-4:30PM (CST). *Felony, Misdemeanor, Civil, Eviction, Small Claims, Probate.*
www.judicial.state.ia.us/district/district5
Civil Records: Access: In person, online. Both court and visitors may perform in person searches. Court makes copy: $.50 per page. Required to search: name, years to search. Civil cases indexed by defendant,

plaintiff. Civil records on docket books from early 1900s, on computer back to 7/96. Civil, probate, and appellate information is at www.judicial.state.ia.us/online_records.
Criminal Records: Access: In person, online. Both court and visitors may perform in person searches. No search fee. Court makes copy: $.50 per page. Required to search: name, years to search; also helpful: SSN. Criminal records on docket books from early 1900s, on computer back to 7/96. Criminal, traffic, and appellate information is online at www.judicial.state.ia.us/online_records.
General Information: Public use terminal available. No juvenile, sealed, dissolution of marriage, mental health, domestic abuse or deferred records released. Certification fee: $10.00. Payee: Clerk of Court. Personal checks accepted. Prepayment required.

Clay County

3rd District Court Courthouse, 215 W 4th St, Spencer, IA 51301; phone: 712-262-4335; hours 8 AM-4:30 PM (CST). *Felony, Misdemeanor, Civil, Eviction, Small Claims, Probate.*
www.judicial.state.ia.us/district/district3
Civil Records: Access: In person, online. Visitors must perform in person searches themselves. Court makes copy: $.50 per page; same fee for self serve. Required to search: name, years to search. Civil cases indexed by defendant, plaintiff. Civil records on microfilm from to 1972 to 1995, docket books from 1800s, on computer back to 8/18/97. Civil, probate, and appellate information is at www.judicial.state.ia.us/online_records.
Criminal Records: Access: In person, online. Visitors must perform in person searches themselves. Court makes copy: $.50 per page; same fee for self serve. Required to search: name, years to search. Criminal records on microfilm from to 1972 to 1995, docket books from 1800s, on computer back to 1/7/97. Criminal, traffic, and appellate information at www.judicial.state.ia.us/online_records.
General Information: Public terminal has criminal back to 8/18/97 and civil back to 1/7/1997. No juvenile, sealed, pending dissolution of marriage, mental health, sealed domestic abuse or deferred records released. Certification fee: $10.00. Payee: Clerk of Court. Personal checks or Visa, MC accepted.

Clayton County

1st District Court PO Box 418, Clayton County Courthouse, Elkader, IA 52043; phone: 563-245-2204; fax: 563-245-1175; hours 8AM-4:30PM (CST). *Felony, Misdemeanor, Civil, Eviction, Small Claims, Probate.*
www.judicial.state.ia.us/district/district1
Civil Records: Access: In person, online. Visitors must perform in person searches themselves. Court makes copy: $.50 per page; same fee for self serve. Required to search: name, years to search. Civil cases indexed by defendant, plaintiff. Civil records on docket books from late 1880s, on computer back to 4/97. Civil, probate, and appellate information is at www.judicial.state.ia.us/online_records.
Criminal Records: Access: In person, online. Visitors must perform in person searches themselves. Court makes copy: $.50 per page; same fee for self serve. Required to search: name, years to search. Criminal records on docket books from late 1880s, on computer back to 4/97. Criminal, traffic, and appellate information is online at www.judicial.state.ia.us/online_records.
General Information: Public use terminal available. No juvenile unless child is age 10 or older and offense is considered a public offense, sealed, dissolution of marriage, mental health, domestic abuse or deferred records released. Certification fee: $10.00. Payee: Clerk of Court. Personal checks accepted. Prepayment required.

Clinton County

7th District Court PO Box 2957, Courthouse, Clinton, IA 52733; phone: 563-243-6213; criminal phone: x4140; civil phone: x4236; probate phone: x4234; criminal fax: 563-243-3655; civil records probate hours 8AM-4:30PM (CST). *Felony, Misdemeanor, Civil, Eviction, Small Claims, Probate.*
www.judicial.state.ia.us/district/district7
Civil Records: Access: In person, online. Visitors must perform in person searches themselves. Court makes copy: $.50 per page. Required to search: name, years to search. Civil cases indexed by defendant. Civil records on computer since 1993, on docket books prior. Civil, probate, and appellate information is at www.judicial.state.ia.us/online_records.
Criminal Records: Access: In person, online. Visitors must perform in person searches themselves. No search fee. Court makes copy: $.50 per page. Required to search: name, years to search, DOB, signed release. Criminal records on computer since 1980, on docket books prior. Criminal, traffic, and appellate information is online at www.judicial.state.ia.us/online_records.
General Information: Public terminal goes back to 1993. No juvenile, adoption, sealed, dissolution of marriage before decree, mental health, domestic abuse or deferred records released. Will not fax documents. Certification fee: $10.00 per document. Payee: Clerk of Court. Personal checks or Visa, MC accepted. Prepayment required.

Crawford County

3rd District Court 1202 Broadway, Denison, IA 51442; phone: 712-263-2242; fax: 712-263-573; hours 8AM-4:30PM (CST). *Felony, Misdemeanor, Civil, Eviction, Small Claims, Probate.*
www.judicial.state.ia.us/district/district3
Civil Records: Access: In person, online. Visitors must perform in person searches themselves. Court makes copy: $.50 per page; same fee for self serve. Required to search: name, years to search. Civil cases indexed by defendant, plaintiff. Civil records available since 1937, on docket books from 1869, on computer back to 9/2/97, Small Claims ro 3/6/97, Probate to 5/8/97. Civil, probate, and appellate information is at www.judicial.state.ia.us/online_records.
Criminal Records: Access: In person, online. Visitors must perform in person searches themselves. Court makes copy: $.50 per page; same fee for self serve. Required to search: name, years to search. Criminal records available since 1937, on docket books from 1869, on computer back to 10/96, Traffic to 1/16/96. Criminal, traffic, and appellate information is online at www.judicial.state.ia.us/online_records.
General Information: Public use terminal available. No juvenile, sealed, dissolution of marriage, mental health, domestic abuse or deferred records released. Certification fee: $10.00. Payee: Clerk of Court. Personal checks accepted. Prepayment required.

Dallas County

5th District Court 801 Court St, Adel, IA 50003; phone: 515-993-5816; criminal phone: 515-993-5816; civil phone: 515-993-6856; probate phone: 515-993-6856; criminal fax: 515-993-6991; civil fax: 515-993-4752; probate fax: 515-993-4752; hours 8AM-4:30PM (CST). *Felony, Misdemeanor, Civil, Eviction, Small Claims, Probate.*
www.judicial.state.ia.us/district/district5/
Note: Probate records are in a separate index.
Civil Records: Access: In person, mail, online. Visitors must perform in person searches themselves. No search fee. Court makes copy: $.50 per page. Self serve copy fee: $.10 per page. Required to search: name, years to search. Civil cases indexed by defendant, plaintiff. Civil records on docket books from 1800s; computerized records since 1996. Civil, probate, and appellate information is at

www.judicial.state.ia.us/online_records. Mail turnaround time 1 week.
Criminal Records: Access: In person, mail, online. Visitors must perform in person searches themselves. No search fee. Court makes copy: $.50 per page. Self serve copy fee: $.10 per page. Required to search: name, years to search. Criminal records on docket books from 1800s; computerized records since 1994. Criminal, traffic, and appellate information at www.judicial.state.ia.us/online_records. Mail turnaround time 1 week.
General Information: Public terminal goes back to 1996. No juvenile, sealed, mental health, domestic abuse or deferred records released. Will fax documents, no fee. Certification fee: $10.00. Payee: Clerk of Court. Personal checks accepted.

Davis County

8th District Court Davis County Courthouse, Bloomfield, IA 52537; phone: 641-664-2011; fax: 641-664-2041; hours 8AM-4:30PM (CST). *Felony, Misdemeanor, Civil, Eviction, Small Claims, Probate.*
www.judicial.state.ia.us/district/district8
Civil Records: Access: In person, online. Visitors must perform in person searches themselves. Court makes copy: $.50 per page. Required to search: name, years to search. Civil cases indexed by defendant, plaintiff. Civil records on docket books from late 1800s; computerized since 1997. Civil, probate, and appellate information is at www.judicial.state.ia.us/online_records.
Criminal Records: Access: In person, online. Visitors must perform in person searches themselves. Court makes copy: $.50 per page. Required to search: name, years to search, DOB. Criminal records on docket books from late 1800s; computerized since 1997. Criminal, traffic, and appellate information is online at www.judicial.state.ia.us/online_records.
General Information: Public terminal goes back to 1997. No juvenile, sealed, dissolution of marriage, mental health, domestic abuse or deferred records released. Certification fee: $10.00 per document. Payee: Clerk of Court. Personal checks accepted. Prepayment required.

Decatur County

5th District Court 207 N Main St, Leon, IA 50144; phone: 641-446-4331; fax: 641-446-3759; hours 8AM-4:30PM (CST). *Felony, Misdemeanor, Civil, Eviction, Small Claims, Probate.*
www.judicial.state.ia.us/district/district5/
Note: Probate is a separate index at this same address.
Civil Records: Access: In person, online. Visitors must perform in person searches themselves. Court makes copy: $.50 per page. Required to search: name, years to search. Civil cases indexed by defendant, plaintiff. Civil records on docket books since 1880; on computer back to 1996. Civil, probate, and appellate data at www.judicial.state.ia.us/online_records.
Criminal Records: Access: In person, online. Visitors must perform in person searches themselves. No search fee. Court makes copy: $.50 per page. Required to search: name, years to search, DOB or SSN. Criminal records on docket books since 1880; on computer back to 1996. Criminal, traffic, and appellate information is online at www.judicial.state.ia.us/online_records.
General Information: Public terminal goes back to 1996. No juvenile, sealed, dissolution of marriage, mental health, domestic abuse or deferred records released. Will not fax documents. Certification fee: $10.00 per document. Payee: Clerk of Court. Personal checks accepted. Prepayment required.

Delaware County

District Court Delaware County Courthouse, PO Box 527, Manchester, IA 52057; phone: 563-927-4942; fax: 563-927-3074; hours 8AM-4:30PM (CST). *Felony, Misdemeanor, Civil, Eviction, Small Claims, Probate.*

Civil Records: Access: In person, online. Visitors must perform in person searches themselves. Court makes copy: $.50 per page. Required to search: name, years to search. Civil cases indexed by defendant, plaintiff. Civil records on docket books from late 1800s; on computer back to 1996. Civil, probate, and appellate information is at www.judicial.state.ia.us/online_records.

Criminal Records: Access: In person, online. Visitors must perform in person searches themselves. Court makes copy: $.50 per page. Required to search: name, years to search. Criminal records on docket books from late 1800s; on computer back to 1996. Criminal, traffic, and appellate information is online at www.judicial.state.ia.us/online_records.

General Information: Public terminal goes back to 1996. No juvenile, sealed, dissolution of marriage, mental health, domestic abuse or deferred records released. Certification fee: $10.00 per doc. Payee: Clerk of Court. Personal checks and Visa/MC accepted. Prepayment required.

Des Moines County

8th District Court 513 Main St, PO Box 158, Burlington, IA 52601; phone: 319-753-8262/8262; fax: 319-753-8253; hours 8AM-4:30PM (CST). *Felony, Misdemeanor, Civil, Eviction, Small Claims, Probate.*
www.judicial.state.ia.us/district/district8/
Note: City of Des Moines is not located here; see Polk county.

Civil Records: Access: In person, online. Visitors must perform in person searches themselves. Court makes copy: $.50 per page; same fee for self serve. Required to search: name, years to search; also helpful: address. Civil cases indexed by defendant, plaintiff. Civil records on computer from 7/1992, docket books prior. Civil, probate, and appellate information is at www.judicial.state.ia.us/online_records.

Criminal Records: Access: In person, online. Visitors must perform in person searches themselves. No search fee. Court makes copy: $.50 per page; same fee for self serve. Required to search: name, years to search, aliases; also helpful: DOB, SSN. Criminal records on computer from 7/1992, docket books prior. Criminal, traffic, and appellate data at www.judicial.state.ia.us/online_records. Records go back to 1992.

General Information: Public terminal goes back to 1992. No juvenile, sealed, dissolution of marriage, mental health, domestic abuse or deferred records released. Certification fee: $10.00. Payee: Clerk of Court. Personal checks or Visa, MC accepted. Prepayment required.

Dickinson County

3rd District Court PO Drawer O-N, Spirit Lake, IA 51360; phone: 712-336-1138; fax: 712-336-4005; hours 8AM-4:30PM (CST). *Felony, Misdemeanor, Civil, Eviction, Small Claims, Probate.*
www.judicial.state.ia.us/district/district3
Civil Records: Access: In person, online. Visitors must perform in person searches themselves. Court makes copy: $.50 per page; same fee for self serve. Required to search: name, years to search. Civil cases indexed by defendant, plaintiff. Early information on microfiche, docket books from 1800s; computerized back to 1992. Civil, probate, and appellate information is at www.judicial.state.ia.us/online_records.

Criminal Records: Access: In person, online. Visitors must perform in person searches themselves. Court makes copy: $.50 per page; same fee for self serve. Required to search: name, years to search. Criminal records early information on microfiche, docket books from 1800s; computerized back to 1992. Criminal, traffic, and appellate information is online at www.judicial.state.ia.us/online_records.

General Information: Public terminal has criminal back to 1993 and civil back to 1995. No juvenile, sealed, dissolution of marriage, mental health, domestic abuse or deferred records released. Certification fee: $10.00. Payee: Clerk of Court. Personal checks accepted. Prepayment required.

Dubuque County

1st District Court PO Box 1220, Dubuque, IA 52004-1220; phone: 563-589-4418; hours 8AM-4:30PM (CST). *Felony, Misdemeanor, Civil, Eviction, Small Claims, Probate.*
www.judicial.state.ia.us/district/district1
Civil Records: Access: In person, online. Visitors must perform in person searches themselves. Court makes copy: $.50 per page; same fee for self serve. Required to search: name, years to search. Civil cases indexed by defendant, plaintiff. Civil records on computer since 7/1994, on docket books from 1900s. Civil, probate, and appellate information is at www.judicial.state.ia.us/online_records.

Criminal Records: Access: In person, online. Visitors must perform in person searches themselves. No search fee. Court makes copy: $.50 per page; same fee for self serve. Required to search: name, years to search; also helpful: DOB, SSN. Criminal records on computer since 7/1994, on docket books from 1900s. Criminal, traffic, and appellate data at www.judicial.state.ia.us/online_records.

General Information: Public terminal goes back to 1994. No juvenile, sealed, dissolution of marriage, mental health, domestic abuse or expunged records released. Will not fax documents. Certification fee: $10.00 per document. Payee: Clerk of District Court. Local checks or Visa, MC accepted. Prepayment required.

Emmet County

3rd District Court Emmet County, 609 1st Ave N, Estherville, IA 51334; phone: 712-362-3325; hours 8AM-4:30PM (CST). *Felony, Misdemeanor, Civil, Eviction, Small Claims, Probate.*
www.judicial.state.ia.us/district/district3
Civil Records: Access: In person, online. Visitors must perform in person searches themselves. Court makes copy: $.50 per page. Required to search: name, years to search. Civil cases indexed by defendant, plaintiff. Civil records on docket books from 1900s, on computer back to 2/96. Civil, probate, and appellate information is at www.judicial.state.ia.us/online_records.

Criminal Records: Access: In person, online. Visitors must perform in person searches themselves. Court makes copy: $.50 per page. Required to search: name, years to search. Criminal records on docket books from 1900s, on computer back to 2/96. Criminal, traffic, and appellate information is online at www.judicial.state.ia.us/online_records.

General Information: Public terminal goes back to 1997. No juvenile, sealed, dissolution of marriage, mental health, domestic abuse or deferred records released. Certification fee: $10.00 per doc. Payee: Clerk of Court. Personal checks and Visa/MC accepted. Prepayment required.

Fayette County

Fayette County District Court PO Box 458, West Union, IA 52175; phone: 563-422-5694; fax: 563-422-3137; hours 8AM-N, 4:30PM (CST). *Felony, Misdemeanor, Civil, Eviction, Small Claims, Probate, Traffic.*
Civil Records: Access: In person, online. Visitors must perform in person searches themselves. Court makes copy: $.50 per page. Required to search: name, years to search. Civil cases indexed by defendant, plaintiff. Civil records on docket books from 1900s, on computer back to 8/96. Civil, probate, and appellate information is at www.judicial.state.ia.us/online_records.

Criminal Records: Access: In person, online. Visitors must perform in person searches themselves. No search fee. Court makes copy: $.50

per page. Required to search: name, years to search. Criminal records on docket books from 1900s; 1940-1960 on CD-ROM, on computer back to 8/96. Criminal, traffic, and appellate information is online at www.judicial.state.ia.us/online_records.

General Information: Public terminal goes back to 1996. No juvenile, sealed, dissolution of marriage, mental health, domestic abuse or deferred records released. Certification fee: $10.00 per doc. Payee: Clerk of Court. Personal checks and Visa/MC accepted. Prepayment required.

Floyd County

2nd District Court 101 S Main St, Charles City, IA 50616; phone: 641-228-7777; fax: 641-228-7772; hours 8AM-4:30PM (CST). *Felony, Misdemeanor, Civil, Eviction, Small Claims, Probate.*
www.judicial.state.ia.us/district/district2
Civil Records: Access: In person, online. Visitors must perform in person searches themselves. Court makes copy: $.50 per page; same fee for self serve. Required to search: name, years to search. Civil cases indexed by defendant, plaintiff. Civil records in docket books, are computerized since 1996. Civil, probate, and appellate information is at www.judicial.state.ia.us/online_records.

Criminal Records: Access: In person, online. Visitors must perform in person searches themselves. Court makes copy: $.50 per page; same fee for self serve. Required to search: name, years to search, DOB, signed release; also helpful: SSN. Criminal records in docket books, are computerized since 1996. Criminal, traffic, and appellate information is online at www.judicial.state.ia.us/online_records.

General Information: Public terminal goes back to 5/1996. No juvenile, sealed, dissolution of marriage, mental health, domestic abuse or deferred records released. Will not fax documents. Certification fee: $10.00. Payee: Clerk of Court. Personal checks accepted. Credit cards accepted. Prepayment required.

Franklin County

2nd Judicial District Court 12 1st Ave NW, PO Box 28, Hampton, IA 50441; phone: 641-456-5626; fax: 641-456-5628; hours 8AM-4PM (CST). *Felony, Misdemeanor, Civil, Eviction, Small Claims, Probate.*
www.judicial.state.ia.us/district/district2
Civil Records: Access: In person, online. Visitors must perform in person searches themselves. Court makes copy: $.50 per page. Required to search: name, years to search. Civil cases indexed by defendant, plaintiff. Civil records on microfiche and/or microfilm from 1860 to 1984, on docket books from 1984 to present. Civil, probate, and appellate information is at www.judicial.state.ia.us/online_records.

Criminal Records: Access: In person, online. Visitors must perform in person searches themselves. Court makes copy: $.50 per page. Required to search: name, years to search. Criminal records on microfiche and/or microfilm from 1860 to 1984, on docket books from 1984 to present. Criminal, traffic, and appellate information is online at www.judicial.state.ia.us/online_records.

General Information: Public terminal goes back to 4/97. No juvenile, sealed, dissolution of marriage, mental health, domestic abuse or deferred records released. Will fax specific case file requests for $1.00 per page. Certification fee: $10.00 per doc. Payee: Clerk of District Court. Personal checks or Visa, MC accepted. Credit cards accepted for traffic fees only. Prepayment required.

Fremont County

4th District Court PO Box 549, Sidney, IA 51652; phone: 712-374-2232; fax: 712-374-3330; hours 8:00AM-4:30PM (CST). *Felony, Misdemeanor, Civil, Eviction, Small Claims, Probate.*
www.judicial.state.ia.us/district/district4

Civil Records: Access: In person, online. Visitors must perform in person searches themselves. Court makes copy: $.50 per page; same fee for self serve. Required to search: name. Civil cases indexed by defendant, plaintiff. Computerized from 11/96, civil records in docket books and microfiche from the 1930's. Civil, probate, and appellate information is at www.judicial.state.ia.us/online_records.

Criminal Records: Access: In person, online. Visitors must perform in person searches themselves. No search fee. Court makes copy: $.50 per page; same fee for self serve. Required to search: name. Computerized from 11/96, criminal records in docket books and microfiche from the 1930's. Criminal, traffic, and appellate information is online at www.judicial.state.ia.us/online_records.

General Information: Public terminal goes back to 11/1996. No juvenile, sealed, pending, mental health, domestic abuse or expunged records released. Will not fax documents. Certification fee: $10.00 per document. Payee: Clerk of Court. Personal checks accepted. Prepayment required.

Greene County

2nd District Court Greene County Courthouse, 114 N Chestnut, Jefferson, IA 50129; phone: 515-386-2516; fax: 515-386-2321; probate fax: same; hours 8AM-4:30PM (CST). *Felony, Misdemeanor, Civil, Eviction, Small Claims, Probate.*
www.judicial.state.ia.us/district/district2
Civil Records: Access: In person, online. Visitors must perform in person searches themselves. Court makes copy: $.50 per page; same fee for self serve. Required to search: name, years to search. Civil cases indexed by defendant, plaintiff. Civil records on microfiche from 1981 back to establishment of court, docket books from 1800s, on computer back to 7/97. Civil, probate, and appellate information is at www.judicial.state.ia.us/online_records.

Criminal Records: Access: In person, online. Visitors must perform in person searches themselves. Court makes copy: $.50 per page; same fee for self serve. Required to search: name, years to search. Criminal records on microfiche from 1981 back to establishment of court, docket books from 1800s, on computer back to 7/97. Criminal, traffic, and appellate information is online at www.judicial.state.ia.us/online_records.

General Information: Public terminal goes back to 7/1997. No juvenile, sealed, dissolution of marriage, mental health, domestic abuse or deferred records released. Will fax for $1.00 per page. Certification fee: $10.00. Payee: Clerk of Court. Personal checks or Visa, MC accepted. Credit cards accepted for traffic fees only. Prepayment required.

Grundy County

1st District Court Grundy County Courthouse, 706 G Ave, Grundy Center, IA 50638; phone: 319-824-5229; fax: 319-824-3447; hours 8AM-4:30PM (CST). *Felony, Misdemeanor, Civil, Eviction, Small Claims, Probate.*
www.grundycounty.org/clerkofcourt/index.asp
Civil Records: Access: In person, online. Visitors must perform in person searches themselves. Court makes copy: $.50 per page. Required to search: name, years to search. Civil cases indexed by defendant, plaintiff. Civil records on docket books from 1881, on computer back to 4/97. Civil, probate, and appellate data at www.judicial.state.ia.us/online_records. Records complete back to 4/97.

Criminal Records: Access: In person, online. Visitors must perform in person searches themselves. Court makes copy: $.50 per page. Required to search: name, years to search. Criminal records on docket books from 1881, on computer back to 4/97. Criminal, traffic, and appellate information is online at www.judicial.state.ia.us/online_records.

General Information: Public terminal goes back to 1997. No pending, confidential, juvenile, sealed, dissolution of marriage, mental health, or expunged records released. Certification fee: $10.00. Payee:

Clerk of Court. Personal checks or Visa, MC accepted. Prepayment required.

Guthrie County

5th District Court Courthouse, 200 N 5th St, Guthrie Center, IA 50115; phone: 641-747-3415; hours 8AM-4:30PM (CST). *Felony, Misdemeanor, Civil, Eviction, Small Claims, Probate.*
www.judicial.state.ia.us/district/district5
Civil Records: Access: In person, online. Visitors must perform in person searches themselves. Court makes copy: $.50 per page. Required to search: name, years to search. Civil cases indexed by defendant, plaintiff. Civil records on computer since 11/96; prior records on docket books from 1880s. Civil, probate, and appellate information is at www.judicial.state.ia.us/online_records.

Criminal Records: Access: In person, online. Visitors must perform in person searches themselves. Court makes copy: $.50 per page. Required to search: name, years to search. Criminal records on computer since 11/96; prior records on docket books from 1880s. Criminal, traffic, and appellate information is online at www.judicial.state.ia.us/online_records.

General Information: Public terminal goes back to 1996. No juvenile, sealed, dissolution of marriage, mental health, domestic abuse or deferred records released. Certification fee: $10.00. Payee: Clerk of Court. Personal checks accepted. Prepayment required.

Hamilton County

2nd District Court Courthouse, PO Box 845, Webster City, IA 50595; phone: 515-832-9600; fax: 515-832-9519; probate fax: same; hours 8:30AM-4:30PM (CST). *Felony, Misdemeanor, Civil, Eviction, Small Claims, Probate.*
www.judicial.state.ia.us/district/district2
Civil Records: Access: In person, online. Visitors must perform in person searches themselves. Court makes copy: $.50 per page. Required to search: name, years to search. Civil cases indexed by defendant, plaintiff. Civil records on microfiche from 1939, docket books from 1880s. Civil, probate, and appellate information is at www.judicial.state.ia.us/online_records.

Criminal Records: Access: In person, online. Visitors must perform in person searches themselves. Court makes copy: $.50 per page. Required to search: name, years to search. Criminal records go back to 1996. Criminal, traffic, and appellate information is online at www.judicial.state.ia.us/online_records.

General Information: Public use terminal available. No juvenile, sealed, dissolution of marriage, mental health, domestic abuse records released. Will fax specific case file requests for $1.00 per page. Certification fee: $10.00. Payee: Clerk of Court. Personal checks accepted. Credit cards accepted. Prepayment required.

Hancock County

2nd District Court 855 State St, Garner, IA 50438; phone: 641-923-2532; fax: 641-923-3521; hours 9AM-3:30PM (CST). *Felony, Misdemeanor, Civil, Eviction, Small Claims, Probate.*
www.judicial.state.ia.us/district/district2
Civil Records: Access: In person, online. Visitors must perform in person searches themselves. Court makes copy: $.50 per page. Required to search: name, years to search. Civil cases indexed by defendant, plaintiff. Civil records on docket books from 1880s; on computer since 1997. Civil, probate, and appellate information is at www.judicial.state.ia.us/online_records.

Criminal Records: Access: In person, online. Visitors must perform in person searches themselves. Court makes copy: $.50 per page. Required to search: name, years to search. Criminal records on docket books from 1880s; on computer since 1997. Criminal, traffic, and appellate data at www.judicial.state.ia.us/online_records.

General Information: Public terminal goes back to 1997. No juvenile, sealed, dissolution of marriage, mental health, domestic abuse or deferred records released. Certification fee: $10.00. Payee: Clerk of Court. Personal checks accepted. Prepayment required.

Hardin County

2nd District Court PO Box 495, Courthouse, Eldora, IA 50627; phone: 641-858-2328; fax: 641-858-2320; hours 8AM-4:30PM (CST). *Felony, Misdemeanor, Civil, Eviction, Small Claims, Probate.*
www.judicial.state.ia.us/district/district2
Civil Records: Access: In person, online. Visitors must perform in person searches themselves. Court makes copy: $.50 per page. Required to search: name, years to search. Civil cases indexed by defendant, plaintiff. Civil records on docket books from 1880s, on computer back to 2/96. Civil, probate, and appellate information is at www.judicial.state.ia.us/online_records.

Criminal Records: Access: In person, online. Visitors must perform in person searches themselves. Court makes copy: $.50 per page. Required to search: name, years to search. Criminal records on docket books from 1880s, on computer back to 2/96. Criminal, traffic, and appellate information is online at www.judicial.state.ia.us/online_records.

General Information: Public terminal goes back to 1996. No juvenile, sealed, dissolution of marriage, mental health, domestic abuse or deferred records released. Certification fee: $10.00 per doc. Payee: Clerk of Court. Personal checks and Visa/MC accepted. Prepayment required.

Harrison County

District Court Court House, Logan, IA 51546; phone: 712-644-2665; fax: 712-644-2615; hours 8:30AM-3:30PM (CST). *Felony, Misdemeanor, Civil, Eviction, Small Claims, Probate.*
Note: Probate is a separate office at this same address.
Civil Records: Access: In person, online. Visitors must perform in person searches themselves. Court makes copy: $.25 per page. Required to search: name, years to search. Civil cases indexed by defendant, plaintiff. Civil records on computer since 11/96; prior on docket books since 1840s in Clerk's office. Recent death and birth certificates on microfiche. Civil, probate, and appellate information is at www.judicial.state.ia.us/online_records.

Criminal Records: Access: In person, online. Visitors must perform in person searches themselves. No search fee. Court makes copy: $.25 per page. Required to search: name, years to search. Criminal records on computer since 11/96, prior on docket books from 1840s in Clerk's office. Criminal, traffic, and appellate information is online at www.judicial.state.ia.us/online_records.

General Information: Public use terminal available. No juvenile, sealed, confidential, dissolution of marriage, mental health, domestic abuse or deferred records released. Will not fax documents. Certification fee: $10.00 per document. Payee: Clerk of Court. Personal checks accepted. Prepayment required.

Henry County

8th District Court Clerk of Court, PO Box 176, Mount Pleasant, IA 52641; criminal phone: 319-385-3150/319-385-4203; civil phone: 319-385-2632; probate phone: 319-385-2632; criminal fax: 319-385-4203; civil fax: 319-385-4144; probate fax: 319-385-4144; hours 8AM-4:30PM (CST). *Felony, Misdemeanor, Civil, Eviction, Small Claims, Probate.*
www.judicial.state.ia.us/district/district8/
Note: Probate is a separate index at this same address.
Civil Records: Access: In person, online. Visitors must perform in person searches themselves. Court makes copy: $.50 per page; same fee for self serve.

Required to search: name, years to search. Civil cases indexed by defendant, plaintiff. Civil records on docket books from 1880s, on computer back to 10/1986. Civil, probate, and appellate information is at www.judicial.state.ia.us/online_records.
Criminal Records: Access: In person, online. Visitors must perform in person searches themselves. No search fee. Court makes copy: $.50 per page; same fee for self serve. Required to search: name, years to search, DOB; also helpful: address, SSN. Criminal records on docket books from early 1900s, on computer back to 2/96. Criminal, traffic, and appellate information is online at www.judicial.state.ia.us/online_records.
General Information: Public use terminal available. No juvenile, sealed, mental health, domestic abuse or deferred records released. Certification fee: $10.00 per certification. Payee: Clerk of Court. Personal checks accepted. Prepayment required.

Howard County

1st District Court Courthouse, 137 N Elm St, Cresco, IA 52136; phone: 563-547-2661; hours 8AM-4:30PM (CST). *Felony, Misdemeanor, Civil, Eviction, Small Claims, Probate.*
www.judicial.state.ia.us/district/district1
Civil Records: Access: In person, online. Visitors must perform in person searches themselves. Court makes copy: $.50 per page. Required to search: name, years to search. Civil cases indexed by defendant, plaintiff. Civil records on docket books from 1900s, on computer back to 4/97. Civil, probate, and appellate information is at www.judicial.state.ia.us/online_records.
Criminal Records: Access: In person, online. Visitors must perform in person searches themselves. Court makes copy: $.50 per page. Required to search: name, years to search, DOB. Criminal records on docket books from 1900s, on computer back to 4/97. Criminal, traffic, and appellate information is online at www.judicial.state.ia.us/online_records.
General Information: Public terminal goes back to 1997. No juvenile, sealed, pending, mental health, domestic abuse or deferred records released. Certification fee: $10.00 per doc. Payee: Clerk of Court. Personal checks accepted. Prepayment required.

Humboldt County

2nd District Court PO Box 100, Dakota City, IA 50529; phone: 515-332-1806; fax: 515-332-7100; hours 9AM-3:30PM (CST). *Felony, Misdemeanor, Civil, Eviction, Small Claims, Probate.*
www.judicial.state.ia.us/district/district2
Civil Records: Access: In person, online. Visitors must perform in person searches themselves. Court makes copy: $.50 per page. Required to search: name, years to search. Civil cases indexed by defendant, plaintiff. Civil records on docket books from early 1900s; computerized records since 7/97. Civil, probate, and appellate information is at www.judicial.state.ia.us/online_records.
Criminal Records: Access: In person, online. Visitors must perform in person searches themselves. Court makes copy: $.50 per page. Required to search: name, years to search. Criminal records on docket books from early 1900s; computerized records since 7/97. Criminal, traffic, and appellate information is online at www.judicial.state.ia.us/online_records.
General Information: Public terminal goes back to 7/1997. No juvenile, sealed, dissolution of marriage, mental health, domestic abuse or deferred records released. Certification fee: $10.00 per doc. Payee: Clerk of Court. Personal checks and Visa/MC accepted. Prepayment required.

Ida County

3rd District Court Courthouse, 401 Moorehead St, Ida Grove, IA 51445; phone: 712-364-2628; fax: 712-364-2699; hours 8AM-4:30PM T,Th,F (CST). *Felony, Misdemeanor, Civil, Eviction, Small Claims,*

Probate.
www.judicial.state.ia.us/district/district3
Civil Records: Access: In person, online. Visitors must perform in person searches themselves. Court makes copy: $.50 per page. Required to search: name, years to search. Civil cases indexed by defendant, plaintiff. Civil records on docket books from early 1800s, computerized since 7/97. Civil, probate, and appellate information is at www.judicial.state.ia.us/online_records.
Criminal Records: Access: In person, online. Visitors must perform in person searches themselves. Court makes copy: $.50 per page. Required to search: name, years to search. Criminal records on docket books from early 1800s, computerized since 7/97. Criminal, traffic, and appellate information is online at www.judicial.state.ia.us/online_records.
General Information: Public terminal goes back to 7/1997. No juvenile, sealed, dissolution of marriage, mental health, domestic abuse or deferred records released. Certification fee: $10.00 per doc. Payee: Clerk of Court. Personal checks and Visa/MC accepted. Prepayment required.

Iowa County

6th District Court PO Box 266, Marengo, IA 52301; phone: 319-642-3914; hours 8AM-4:30PM (CST). *Felony, Misdemeanor, Civil, Eviction, Small Claims, Probate.*
www.judicial.state.ia.us/district/district6
Civil Records: Access: In person, online. Visitors must perform in person searches themselves. Court makes copy: $.50 per page. Required to search: name, years to search. Civil cases indexed by defendant, plaintiff. Civil records on docket books from early 1800s; on computer back to 2/97. Civil, probate, and appellate information is at www.judicial.state.ia.us/online_records.
Criminal Records: Access: Mail, in person, online. Visitors must perform in person searches themselves. No search fee. Court makes copy: $.50 per page. Required to search: name, years to search. Criminal records on docket books from early 1800s; on computer back to 2/1997. Criminal, traffic, and appellate information is online at www.judicial.state.ia.us/online_records. Mail Turnaround is as time permits.
General Information: Public terminal goes back to 2/1997. No juvenile, sealed, dissolution of marriage, mental health, domestic abuse or deferred records released. Certification fee: $10.00 per doc. Payee: Clerk of Court. Personal checks and Visa/MC accepted. Prepayment required.

Jackson County

7th District Court 201 W Platt, Maquoketa, IA 52060; phone: 563-652-4946; fax: 563-652-2708; hours 8AM-4:30PM (CST). *Felony, Misdemeanor, Civil, Eviction, Small Claims, Probate.*
www.judicial.state.ia.us/district/district7/
Note: Probate is a separate index at this same address.
Civil Records: Access: In person, online. Visitors must perform in person searches themselves. Court makes copy: $.50 per page. Required to search: name, years to search. Civil cases indexed by defendant, plaintiff. Civil records on computer since 1994, on docket books from 1900s. Civil, probate, and appellate information is at www.judicial.state.ia.us/online_records.
Criminal Records: Access: In person, online. Visitors must perform in person searches themselves. No search fee. Court makes copy: $.50 per page. Required to search: name, years to search, DOB; also helpful: SSN. Criminal records on computer since 1994, on docket books from 1900s. Criminal, traffic, and appellate information is online at www.judicial.state.ia.us/online_records.
General Information: Public terminal has criminal back to 1993 and civil back to 1997. No juvenile, sealed, dissolution of marriage, mental health, domestic abuse or deferred records released. Certification fee: $10.00 per document. Payee: Clerk

of Court. Personal checks accepted. Prepayment required.

Jasper County

5th District Court 101 1st St N, Rm 104, Newton, IA 50208; phone: 641-792-3255; criminal phone: 641-792-9161; civil phone: 641-792-3255; probate phone: 641-792-3255; fax: 641-792-2818; hours 8AM-4:30PM (CST). *Felony, Misdemeanor, Civil, Eviction, Small Claims, Probate.*
www.judicial.state.ia.us/district/district5/
Note: Probate is a separate index at this same address.
Civil Records: Access: In person, online. Visitors must perform in person searches themselves. Court makes copy: $.50 per page; same fee for self serve. Required to search: name, years to search. Civil cases indexed by defendant, plaintiff. Civil records on computer since 1994, docket books from 1900s. Civil, probate, and appellate information is at www.judicial.state.ia.us/online_records. Note: Court will pull file if given case number.
Criminal Records: Access: In person, online. Visitors must perform in person searches themselves. No search fee. Court makes copy: $.50 per page; same fee for self serve. Required to search: name, years to search. Criminal records on computer since 1994, docket books from 1900s. Criminal, traffic, and appellate information is online at www.judicial.state.ia.us/online_records. Note: Court will pull file if given case number.
General Information: Public terminal goes back to 1994. No juvenile, sealed, dissolution of marriage, mental health, or deferred records released. Juvenile delinquency is public record, not CINA< FINA termination of adoption. Will not fax documents. Certification fee: $10.00 per document includes copies. Payee: Clerk of Court. Personal checks accepted. Prepayment required.

Jefferson County

8th District Court PO Box 984, Fairfield, IA 52556; phone: 641-472-3454; fax: 641-472-9472; hours 8AM-4:30PM M-F (CST). *Felony, Misdemeanor, Civil, Eviction, Small Claims, Probate.*
www.judicial.state.ia.us/district/district8
Civil Records: Access: In person, online. Visitors must perform in person searches themselves. Court makes copy: $.25 per page. Required to search: name, years to search. Civil cases indexed by defendant, plaintiff. Civil records on docket books from 1800s, on computer back to 2/96. Civil, probate, and appellate information is at www.judicial.state.ia.us/online_records.
Criminal Records: Access: In person, online. Visitors must perform in person searches themselves. Court makes copy: $.25 per page. Required to search: name, years to search, DOB. Criminal records on docket books from 1800s, on computer back to 2/96. Criminal, traffic, and appellate information is online at www.judicial.state.ia.us/online_records.
General Information: Public terminal goes back to 1/1996. No juvenile, sealed, dissolution of marriage, mental health, domestic abuse or deferred records released. Will fax documents $1.00 per page. Certification fee: $10.00 per doc. Payee: Clerk of Court. Personal checks and Visa/MC accepted. Prepayment required.

Johnson County

6th District Court PO Box 2510, Iowa City, IA 52244; phone: 319-356-6060; hours 8AM-4:30PM (CST). *Felony, Misdemeanor, Civil, Eviction, Small Claims, Probate.*
www.judicial.state.ia.us/district/district6
Civil Records: Access: In person, online. Visitors must perform in person searches themselves. Court makes copy: $.50 per page; same fee for self serve. Required to search: name, years to search. Civil cases indexed by defendant, plaintiff. Civil records on docket books and microfilm from 1880s, on computer

back to 4/93. Civil, probate, and appellate data at www.judicial.state.ia.us/online_records.
Criminal Records: Access: In person, online. Visitors must perform in person searches themselves. No search fee. Court makes copy: $.50 per page; same fee for self serve. Required to search: name, years to search; also helpful: address, DOB, SSN. Criminal records on docket books and microfilm from 1880s, on computer back to 4/93. Criminal, traffic, and appellate information is online at www.judicial.state.ia.us/online_records.
General Information: Public terminal goes back to 1994. No juvenile, sealed, dissolution of marriage, mental health, domestic abuse or deferred records released. Certification fee: $10.00. Payee: Clerk of Court. Personal checks accepted. Prepayment required.

Jones County

6th District Court PO Box 19, Attn: Clerk of District Court, Anamosa, IA 52205; phone: 319-462-4341; hours 8AM-4:30PM (CST). *Felony, Misdemeanor, Civil, Eviction, Small Claims, Probate.*
www.judicial.state.ia.us/district/district6
Civil Records: Access: In person, online. Visitors must perform in person searches themselves. Court makes copy: $.50 per page. Required to search: name, years to search. Civil cases indexed by defendant, plaintiff. Civil records on docket books from mid 1800s; dockets on computer back to 6/1997. Civil, probate, and appellate information is at www.judicial.state.ia.us/online_records.
Criminal Records: Access: In person, online. Visitors must perform in person searches themselves. Court makes copy: $.50 per page. Required to search: name, years to search. Criminal records on docket books from early 1900s; dockets on computer back to 11/1996. Criminal, traffic, and appellate information is online at www.judicial.state.ia.us/online_records.
General Information: Public terminal has criminal back to 1996 and civil back to 1997. No juvenile, sealed, dissolution of marriage (prior to decree), mental health or deferred records released. Certification fee: $10.00. Payee: Clerk of Court. Personal checks accepted. Prepayment required.

Keokuk County

8th District Court 101 S Main, Courthouse, Sigourney, IA 52591; phone: 641-622-2210; fax: 641-622-2171; hours 8AM-4:30PM (CST). *Felony, Misdemeanor, Civil, Eviction, Small Claims, Probate.*
www.judicial.state.ia.us/district/district8
Civil Records: Access: In person, online. Visitors must perform in person searches themselves. Court makes copy: $.25 per page. Required to search: name, years to search. Civil cases indexed by defendant, plaintiff. Records on docket books from 1888; computer back to 2/1997. Civil, probate, and appellate information is at www.judicial.state.ia.us/online_records.
Criminal Records: Access: In person, online. Visitors must perform in person searches themselves. Court makes copy: $.25 per page. Required to search: name, years to search. Criminal records on docket books from 1888; on computer back to 2/1997. Criminal, traffic, and appellate data at www.judicial.state.ia.us/online_records.
General Information: Public terminal goes back to 2/1997. No juvenile, sealed, dissolution of marriage, mental health, domestic abuse or deferred records released. Certification fee: $10.00 per doc. Payee: Clerk of Court. Personal checks accepted. No credit cards. Prepayment required.

Kossuth County

3rd District Court Kossuth County Courthouse, 114 W State St, Algona, IA 50511; phone: 515-295-3240; hours 8AM-4:30PM (CST). *Felony, Misdemeanor, Civil, Eviction, Small Claims, Probate.*

www.judicial.state.ia.us/district/district3
Civil Records: Access: In person, online. Visitors must perform in person searches themselves. Court makes copy: $.50 per page. Required to search: name, years to search. Civil cases indexed by defendant, plaintiff. Civil records on computer since 9/97; prior records on dockets. Civil, probate, and appellate information is at www.judicial.state.ia.us/online_records.
Criminal Records: Access: In person, online. Visitors must perform in person searches themselves. No search fee. Court makes copy: $.50 per page. Required to search: name, years to search. Criminal records on computer since 9/97; prior records on dockets. Criminal, traffic, and appellate information is online at www.judicial.state.ia.us/online_records.
General Information: Public terminal goes back to 9/1997. No juvenile, sealed, dissolution of marriage, mental health, domestic abuse or deferred records released. Certification fee: $10.00 per doc. Payee: Clerk of Court. Personal checks and Visa/MC accepted. Prepayment required.

Lee County

8th District Court PO Box 1443, Ft Madison, IA 52627; criminal phone: 319-372-4553; civil phone: 319-372-3523; hours 8AM-4:30PM (CST). *Felony, Misdemeanor, Civil, Eviction, Small Claims, Probate.*
www.judicial.state.ia.us/district/district8
Civil Records: Access: In person, online. Visitors must perform in person searches themselves. Court makes copy: $.50 per page. Required to search: name, years to search. Civil cases indexed by defendant, plaintiff. Civil records on docket books from early 1800s; computerized from 1996. Civil, probate, and appellate information is at www.judicial.state.ia.us/online_records.
Criminal Records: Access: In person, online. Visitors must perform in person searches themselves. Court makes copy: $.50 per page. Required to search: name, years to search. Criminal records on docket books from early 1800s; computerized from 1996. Criminal, traffic, and appellate information is online at www.judicial.state.ia.us/online_records.
General Information: Public terminal goes back to 1996. No juvenile, sealed, pending dissolution of marriage, mental health, domestic abuse or deferred records released. Certification fee: $10.00. Payee: Clerk of Court. Personal checks accepted. Prepayment required.

Linn County

District Court Linn County Courthouse, PO Box 1468, Cedar Rapids, IA 52406-1468; phone: 319-398-3411; fax: 319-398-3449; hours 8AM-4:30PM (CST). *Felony, Misdemeanor, Civil, Eviction, Small Claims, Probate.*
Civil Records: Access: In person, online. Visitors must perform in person searches themselves. Court makes copy: $.50 per page. Required to search: name, years to search. Civil cases indexed by defendant, plaintiff. Civil records on computer from 1995, docket books from early 1900s. Civil, probate, and appellate information is at www.judicial.state.ia.us/online_records.
Criminal Records: Access: In person, online. Visitors must perform in person searches themselves. Court makes copy: $.50 per page. Required to search: name, years to search; also helpful: address, DOB. Criminal records on computer since 1993. Criminal, traffic, and appellate information is online at www.judicial.state.ia.us/online_records.
General Information: Public use terminal available. No juvenile, sealed, pending dissolution of marriage, mental health, domestic abuse or deferred records released. Certification fee: $10.00. Payee: Clerk of Court. Personal checks accepted. Prepayment required.

Louisa County

8th District Court PO Box 268, Wapello, IA 52653; phone: 319-523-4541; fax: 319-523-4542; hours 8AM-4:30PM (CST). *Felony, Misdemeanor, Civil, Eviction, Small Claims, Probate.*
www.judicial.state.ia.us/district/district8
Civil Records: Access: In person, online. Both court and visitors may perform in person searches. Court makes copy: $.25 per page. Required to search: name, years to search. Civil cases indexed by defendant, plaintiff. Civil records on docket books from 1920s, on computer since 2/97. Civil, probate, and appellate information is at www.judicial.state.ia.us/online_records.
Criminal Records: Access: In person, online. Both court and visitors may perform in person searches. No search fee. Court makes copy: $.50 per page. Required to search: name, years to search, DOB, signed release; also helpful: SSN. Criminal records on docket books from 1920s, on computer since 2/97. Criminal, traffic, and appellate information is online at www.judicial.state.ia.us/online_records.
General Information: Public terminal goes back to 2/1997. No juvenile, sealed, dissolution of marriage, mental health, domestic abuse or deferred records released. Certification fee: $10.00. Payee: Clerk of Court. Personal checks accepted. Prepayment required.

Lucas County

5th District Court Courthouse, 916 Braden, Chariton, IA 50049; phone: 641-774-4421; fax: 641-774-8669; hours 8AM-4:30PM M-F (CST). *Felony, Misdemeanor, Civil, Eviction, Small Claims, Probate.*
www.judicial.state.ia.us/district/district5
Civil Records: Access: In person, online. Visitors must perform in person searches themselves. Court makes copy: $.50 per page; same fee for self serve. Required to search: name, years to search. Civil cases indexed by defendant, plaintiff. Civil records on docket books from 1880s; on computer back to 1997. Civil, probate, and appellate information is at www.judicial.state.ia.us/online_records. Mail turnaround time-as time permits.
Criminal Records: Access: In person, online. Visitors must perform in person searches themselves. No search fee. Court makes copy: $.50 per page; same fee for self serve. Required to search: name, years to search, signed release; also helpful: SSN. Criminal records on docket books from 1880s; on computer back to 1997. Criminal, traffic, and appellate information is online at www.judicial.state.ia.us/online_records.
General Information: Public terminal goes back to 2/1997. No juvenile, adoption, sealed, dissolution of marriage, mental health, domestic abuse or deferred records released. Will fax specific case file requests for $1.00 per page. Certification fee: $10.00 per certification. Payee: Clerk of District Court. Personal checks or Visa, MC accepted. Prepayment required.

Lyon County

3rd District Court Courthouse, Rock Rapids, IA 51246; phone: 712-472-2623; fax: 712-472-2422; hours 8AM-4:30PM (CST). *Felony, Misdemeanor, Civil, Eviction, Small Claims, Probate.*
www.judicial.state.ia.us/district/district3
Civil Records: Access: In person, online. Visitors must perform in person searches themselves. Court makes copy: $.50 per page. Required to search: name, years to search. Civil cases indexed by defendant, plaintiff. Civil records on docket books from 1880s, on computer back to 9/97. Civil, probate, and appellate information is at www.judicial.state.ia.us/online_records.
Criminal Records: Access: In person, online. Visitors must perform in person searches themselves. Court makes copy: $.50 per page. Required to search: name, years to search. Criminal records on docket books from 1880s, on computer

back to 9/97. Criminal, traffic, and appellate data at www.judicial.state.ia.us/online_records.

General Information: Public terminal goes back to 1997. No juvenile, sealed, dissolution of marriage, mental health, domestic abuse or deferred records released. Certification fee: $10.00 per doc. Payee: Clerk of Court. Personal checks and Visa/Mc accepted. Prepayment required.

Madison County

5th District Court PO Box 152, Winterset, IA 50273; phone: 515-462-4451; fax: 515-462-9825; hours 8AM-4:30PM (CST). *Felony, Misdemeanor, Civil, Eviction, Small Claims, Probate.*
www.judicial.state.ia.us/district/district5
Civil Records: Access: In person, online. Visitors must perform in person searches themselves. Court makes copy: $.50 per page. Required to search: name, years to search. Civil cases indexed by plaintiff. Civil records on docket books from 1880s; computerized records since 1996. Civil, probate, and appellate information is at www.judicial.state.ia.us/online_records.
Criminal Records: Access: In person, online. Visitors must perform in person searches themselves. Court makes copy: $.50 per page. Required to search: name, years to search; also helpful: DOB. Criminal records on docket books from 1880s; computerized records since 1996. Misdemeanors from 1974 to present. Criminal, traffic, and appellate information is online at www.judicial.state.ia.us/online_records.
General Information: Public terminal goes back to 1996. No juvenile, sealed, dissolution of marriage, mental health, domestic abuse of deferred records released. Certification fee: $10.00 per doc. Payee: Clerk of Court. Personal checks accepted. No credit cards. Prepayment required.

Mahaska County

8th District Court Courthouse, 106 S 1st St, Oskaloosa, IA 52577; phone: 641-673-7786; fax: 641-672-1256; hours 8AM-4:30PM (CST). *Felony, Misdemeanor, Civil, Eviction, Small Claims, Probate.*
www.judicial.state.ia.us/district/district8
Civil Records: Access: In person, online. Visitors must perform in person searches themselves. Court makes copy: $.50 per page. Docket copy $1.00 per page. Required to search: name, years to search. Civil cases indexed by defendant, plaintiff. Civil records on docket books from 1880s; computerized records since 1995. Civil, probate, and appellate information is at www.judicial.state.ia.us/online_records.
Criminal Records: Access: In person, online. Visitors must perform in person searches themselves. Court makes copy: $.50 per page. Docket copy fee $1.00 per page. Required to search: name, years to search. Criminal records on docket books from 1880s; computerized records since 1995. Criminal, traffic, and appellate information is online at www.judicial.state.ia.us/online_records.
General Information: Public use terminal available. No juvenile, sealed, dissolution of marriage, mental health, domestic abuse or deferred records released. Certification fee: $10.00. Payee: Clerk of Court. Personal checks accepted. Prepayment required.

Marion County

5th District Court PO Box 497, Knoxville, IA 50138; phone: 641-828-2207; probate phone: Ext 4; fax: 641-828-7580; hours 8AM-4:30PM (CST). *Felony, Misdemeanor, Civil, Eviction, Small Claims, Probate.*
www.judicial.state.ia.us/district/district5
Civil Records: Access: In person, online. Visitors must perform in person searches themselves. Court makes copy: $.50 per page; same fee for self serve. Required to search: name, years to search. Civil cases indexed by defendant, plaintiff. Civil records on computer since 1992, docket books from 1896. Civil, probate, and appellate information is at www.judicial.state.ia.us/online_records.

Criminal Records: Access: In person, online. Visitors must perform in person searches themselves. Court makes copy: $.50 per page; same fee for self serve. Required to search: name, years to search. Criminal records on computer since 1992, docket books from 1896. Criminal, traffic, and appellate information is online at www.judicial.state.ia.us/online_records.
General Information: Public terminal has criminal back to 1993 and civil back to 1994. Delinquencies are public, not CINA, FINA, Termination or adoptions. No juvenile, sealed, dissolution of marriage, or mental health records released. Certification fee: $10.00. Payee: Clerk of Court. Personal checks accepted. Prepayment required.

Marshall County

2nd District Court Courthouse, 17 E Main St, Marshalltown, IA 50158; phone: 641-754-1603; fax: 641-754-1600; hours 8AM-4:30PM (CST). *Felony, Misdemeanor, Civil, Eviction, Small Claims, Probate.*
www.judicial.state.ia.us/district/district2
Civil Records: Access: In person, online. Visitors must perform in person searches themselves. Court makes copy: $.50 per page; same fee for self serve. Required to search: name, years to search. Civil cases indexed by defendant, plaintiff. Civil records on computer since 6/1994, docket books from late 1800s. Civil, probate, and appellate information is at www.judicial.state.ia.us/online_records.
Criminal Records: Access: In person, online. Visitors must perform in person searches themselves. Court makes copy: $.50 per page; same fee for self serve. Required to search: name, years to search; also helpful: DOB, SSN. Criminal records on computer since 8/1992, docket books from late 1800s. Criminal, traffic, and appellate information is online at www.judicial.state.ia.us/online_records.
General Information: Public terminal has criminal back to 8/1992 and civil back to 1994. No juvenile, sealed, pending dissolution of marriage, mental health, sealed domestic abuse and deferred records released. Certification fee: $10.00 per document. Payee: Clerk of Court. Personal checks accepted. Credit cards accepted. Prepayment required.

Mills County

4th District Court 418 Sharp St, Courthouse, Glenwood, IA 51534; phone: 712-527-4880; fax: 712-527-4936; hours 8AM-4:30PM (CST). *Felony, Misdemeanor, Civil, Eviction, Small Claims, Probate.*
www.judicial.state.ia.us/district/district4
Civil Records: Access: In person, online. Both court and visitors may perform in person searches. Court makes copy: $.50 per page; same fee for self serve. Required to search: name, years to search. Civil cases indexed by defendant, plaintiff. Civil records on docket books since 1880s; computerized records since 02/96. Civil, probate, and appellate information is at www.judicial.state.ia.us/online_records.
Criminal Records: Access: In person, online. Both court and visitors may perform in person searches. No search fee. Court makes copy: $.50 per page; same fee for self serve. Required to search: name, years to search, DOB; also helpful: SSN. Criminal records on docket books since 1880s; computerized records since 2/96. Criminal, traffic, and appellate information is online at www.judicial.state.ia.us/online_records.
General Information: Public terminal goes back to 2/1996. No juvenile, sealed, dissolution of marriage, mental health, domestic abuse or deferred records released. Certification fee: $10.00. Payee: Clerk of Court. Personal checks accepted. Prepayment required.

Mitchell County

2nd District Court 508 State St, Osage, IA 50461; phone: 641-732-3726; fax: 641-732-3728; hours 9AM-3:30PM (CST). *Felony, Misdemeanor, Civil, Eviction, Small Claims, Probate.*
www.judicial.state.ia.us/district/district2

Civil Records: Access: In person, online. Visitors must perform in person searches themselves. Court makes copy: $.50 per page; same fee for self serve. Required to search: name, years to search. Civil cases indexed by defendant, plaintiff. Civil records on docket books from 1880s, computerized since 1997. Civil, probate, and appellate information is at www.judicial.state.ia.us/online_records.
Criminal Records: Access: In person, online. Visitors must perform in person searches themselves. No search fee. Court makes copy: $.50 per page; same fee for self serve. Required to search: name, years to search, signed release. Criminal records on docket books from 1880s, computerized since 1997. Criminal, traffic, and appellate information is online at www.judicial.state.ia.us/online_records.
General Information: Public terminal goes back to 4/1997. No juvenile, sealed, dissolution of marriage, mental health, domestic abuse or deferred records released. Will not fax documents. Certification fee: $10.00 per document. Payee: Clerk of Court. Personal checks accepted. Prepayment required.

Monona County

3rd District Court 610 Iowa Ave, Attn: Clerk of Court, Onawa, IA 51040; phone: 712-423-2491; hours 8AM-4:30PM (CST). *Felony, Misdemeanor, Civil, Eviction, Small Claims, Probate.*
www.judicial.state.ia.us/district/district3
Civil Records: Access: In person, online. Visitors must perform in person searches themselves. Court makes copy: $.50 per page. Required to search: name, years to search. Civil cases indexed by defendant, plaintiff. Civil records on computer since 7/97; prior records on microfiche and docket books from 1880s. Civil, probate, and appellate information is at www.judicial.state.ia.us/online_records.
Criminal Records: Access: In person, online. Visitors must perform in person searches themselves. No search fee. Court makes copy: $.50 per page. Required to search: name, years to search. Criminal records on computer since 7/97; prior records on microfiche and docket books from 1880s. Criminal, traffic, and appellate information is online at www.judicial.state.ia.us/online_records.
General Information: Public use terminal available. No juvenile, sealed, dissolution of marriage, mental health, or deferred records released. Certification fee: $10.00. Payee: Clerk of Court. Personal checks accepted. Prepayment required.

Monroe County

8th District Court Courthouse, 10 Benton Ave E, Albia, IA 52531; phone: 641-932-5212; fax: 641-932-3245; hours 8AM-4:30PM (CST). *Felony, Misdemeanor, Civil, Eviction, Small Claims, Probate.*
www.judicial.state.ia.us/district/district8
Civil Records: Access: In person, online. Visitors must perform in person searches themselves. Court makes copy: $.50 per page. Required to search: name, years to search. Civil cases indexed by defendant, plaintiff. Civil records on docket books from late 1800s, on computer back to 2/97. Civil, probate, and appellate information is at www.judicial.state.ia.us/online_records.
Criminal Records: Access: In person, online. Visitors must perform in person searches themselves. Court makes copy: $.50 per page. Required to search: name, years to search, DOB, signed release; also helpful: SSN. Criminal records on docket books from late 1800s, on computer back to 2/97. Criminal, traffic, and appellate information is online at www.judicial.state.ia.us/online_records.
General Information: Public terminal goes back to 1997. No juvenile, sealed, dissolution of marriage, mental health, domestic abuse or deferred records released. Certification fee: $10.00 per doc. Payee: Clerk of Court. Personal checks or Visa/MC accepted. Prepayment required.

Montgomery County

4th District Court PO Box 469, Red Oak, IA 51566; phone: 712-623-4986; hours 8:30AM-4:30PM (CST). *Felony, Misdemeanor, Civil, Eviction, Small Claims, Probate.*
www.judicial.state.ia.us/district/district4
Civil Records: Access: In person, online. Visitors must perform in person searches themselves. Court makes copy: $.25 per page. Required to search: name, years to search. Civil cases indexed by defendant, plaintiff. Civil records on docket books from 1940, microfiche prior, on computer back to 6/96. Civil, probate, and appellate information is at www.judicial.state.ia.us/online_records.
Criminal Records: Access: In person, online. Visitors must perform in person searches themselves. No search fee. Court makes copy: $.25 per page. Required to search: name, years to search. Criminal records on docket books from 1940, microfiche prior, on computer back to 6/96. Criminal, traffic, and appellate information is online at www.judicial.state.ia.us/online_records.
General Information: Public use terminal available. No juvenile, sealed, dissolution of marriage, mental health or deferred records released. Certification fee: $10.00. Payee: Clerk of Court. Personal checks accepted. Prepayment required.

Muscatine County

7th District Court PO Box 8010, Courthouse, Muscatine, IA 52761; phone: 563-263-6511; criminal phone: 563-263-2447; fax: 563-264-3622; hours 8AM-4:30PM (CST). *Felony, Misdemeanor, Civil, Eviction, Small Claims, Probate.*
www.judicial.state.ia.us/district/district7
Civil Records: Access: In person, online. Visitors must perform in person searches themselves. Court makes copy: $.50 per page. Required to search: name, years to search. Civil cases indexed by defendant, plaintiff. Civil records on docket books, on computer since 10/95. Civil, probate, and appellate data at www.judicial.state.ia.us/online_records.
Criminal Records: Access: In person, online. Visitors must perform in person searches themselves. Court makes copy: $.50 per page. Required to search: name, years to search. Criminal Records are computerized since 4/94. Criminal, traffic, and appellate information is online at www.judicial.state.ia.us/online_records.
General Information: Public use terminal available. No juvenile, sealed, dissolutions of marriage, mental health, domestic abuse or deferred records released. Certification fee: $10.00. Payee: Clerk of Court. Personal checks accepted. Prepayment required.

O'Brien County

3rd District Court Courthouse, Criminal Records, Primghar, IA 51245; phone: 712-757-3255; fax: 712-957-2965; hours 8AM-4:30PM (CST). *Felony, Misdemeanor, Civil, Eviction, Small Claims, Probate.*
www.judicial.state.ia.us/district/district3
Civil Records: Access: In person, online. Visitors must perform in person searches themselves. Court makes copy: $.50 per page; same fee for self serve. Required to search: name, years to search. Civil cases indexed by defendant, plaintiff. Civil records on docket books from late 1800s; computerized since 1997. Civil, probate, and appellate information is at www.judicial.state.ia.us/online_records.
Criminal Records: Access: In person, online. Visitors must perform in person searches themselves. No search fee. Court makes copy: $.50 per page; same fee for self serve. Required to search: name, years to search; also helpful: DOB, SSN. Criminal records on docket books from late 1800s; computerized since 1997. Criminal, traffic, and appellate information is online at www.judicial.state.ia.us/online_records.
General Information: Public terminal goes back to 9/1997. No juvenile, sealed, dissolution of marriage, mental health records released. Certification fee:

$10.00. Payee: Clerk of Court. Personal checks accepted. Prepayment required.

Osceola County

3rd District Court Courthouse, Criminal Records, Sibley, IA 51249; phone: 712-754-3595; fax: 712-754-2480; probate fax: same; hours 8AM-4:30PM (may be closed Monday & Wednesday) (CST). *Felony, Misdemeanor, Civil, Eviction, Small Claims, Probate.*
www.judicial.state.ia.us/district/district3
Civil Records: Access: In person, online. Visitors must perform in person searches themselves. Court makes copy: $.50 per page. Required to search: name, years to search. Civil cases indexed by defendant, plaintiff. Civil records on docket books from 1883; on computer back to 1997. Civil, probate, and appellate information is at www.judicial.state.ia.us/online_records.
Criminal Records: Access: In person, online. Visitors must perform in person searches themselves. No search fee. Court makes copy: $.50 per page. Required to search: name, years to search. Criminal records on docket books from 1883; on computer back to 1997. Criminal, traffic, and appellate information is online at www.judicial.state.ia.us/online_records.
General Information: Public terminal goes back to 9/1997. No juvenile, sealed, dissolution of marriage, mental health, domestic abuse or deferred records released. Certification fee: $10.00. Payee: Clerk of Court. Personal checks accepted. Prepayment required.

Page County

4th District Court 112 E Main, Box 263, Clarinda, IA 51632; phone: 712-542-3214; fax: 712-542-5460; hours 8AM-4:30PM (CST). *Felony, Misdemeanor, Civil, Eviction, Small Claims, Probate.*
www.judicial.state.ia.us/district/district4/
Civil Records: Access: In person, online. Visitors must perform in person searches themselves. Court makes copy: $.25 per page; same fee for self serve. Required to search: name, years to search. Civil cases indexed by defendant, plaintiff. Civil records on docket books; on computer back to 1995. Probate records are a separate index Civil, probate, and appellate information is at www.judicial.state.ia.us/online_records.
Criminal Records: Access: In person, online. Visitors must perform in person searches themselves. No search fee. Court makes copy: $.25 per page; same fee for self serve. Required to search: name, years to search, DOB, SSN, signed release. Criminal records on docket books; on computer back to 1995. Criminal, traffic, and appellate data at www.judicial.state.ia.us/online_records.
General Information: Public terminal goes back to 1995. No juvenile, sealed dissolution of marriage, mental health or deferred records released. Will fax specific case file requests for $2.00. Certification fee: $10.00. Payee: Clerk of District Court. Personal checks accepted. Prepayment required.

Palo Alto County

3rd District Court PO Box 387, Emmetsburg, IA 50536; phone: 712-852-3603; hours 8AM-4:30PM (CST). *Felony, Misdemeanor, Civil, Eviction, Small Claims, Probate.*
www.judicial.state.ia.us/district/district3
Civil Records: Access: In person, online. Visitors must perform in person searches themselves. Court makes copy: $.50 per page. Required to search: name, years to search. Civil cases indexed by defendant, plaintiff. Civil records on docket books from 1800s; computerized from 1997. Civil, probate, and appellate information is at www.judicial.state.ia.us/online_records.
Criminal Records: Access: In person, online. Visitors must perform in person searches themselves. Court makes copy: $.50 per page. Required to search: name, years to search, DOB,

SSN. Criminal records on docket books from 1800s; computerized from 1997. Criminal, traffic, and appellate information is online at www.judicial.state.ia.us/online_records.
General Information: Public terminal goes back to 1997. No juvenile, sealed, dissolution of marriage, mental health, domestic abuse or deferred records released. Certification fee: $10.00 per doc. Payee: Clerk of Court. Personal checks and Visa/MC accepted. Prepayment required.

Plymouth County

3rd Judicial District Plymouth County Clerk of District Court, 215 Fourth Ave SE, Courthouse, Le Mars, IA 51031; phone: 712-546-4215; hours 8AM-4:30PM (CST). *Felony, Misdemeanor, Civil, Eviction, Small Claims, Probate.*
www.judicial.state.ia.us/district/district3
Civil Records: Access: In person, online. Visitors must perform in person searches themselves. Court makes copy: $.50 per page. Required to search: name, years to search. Civil cases indexed by defendant, plaintiff. Civil records on docket books from 1895 to 11/92, docket cards from 11/92 to 7/97, on computer back to 7/97. Civil, probate, and appellate data at www.judicial.state.ia.us/online_records.
Criminal Records: Access: In person, online. Visitors must perform in person searches themselves. Court makes copy: $.50 per page. Required to search: name, years to search. Criminal records on docket books from 1895 to 11/92, docket cards from 11/92 to 7/97, on computer back to 7/97. Criminal, traffic, and appellate information is online at www.judicial.state.ia.us/online_records.
General Information: Public terminal goes back to 1997. No juvenile, (sealed, dissolution of marriage), mental health, domestic abuse or deferred records released. Will fax specific case file requests for $.50 per page. Certification fee: $10.00. Payee: Clerk of Court. Personal checks accepted. Prepayment required.

Pocahontas County

2nd District Court Courthouse, 99 Court Square, Pocahontas, IA 50574; phone: 712-335-4208; fax: 712-335-5045; hours 9AM-3:30PM (public hours) (CST). *Felony, Misdemeanor, Civil, Eviction, Small Claims, Probate.*
www.judicial.state.ia.us/district/district2
Civil Records: Access: In person, online. Visitors must perform in person searches themselves. Court makes copy: $.50 per page. Required to search: name, years to search. Civil cases indexed by defendant, plaintiff. Civil records on docket books from 1880s, on computer back to 7/97. Civil, probate, and appellate information is at www.judicial.state.ia.us/online_records.
Criminal Records: Access: In person, online. Visitors must perform in person searches themselves. Court makes copy: $.50 per page. Required to search: name, years to search, DOB. Criminal records on docket books from 1880s, on computer back to 7/97. Criminal, traffic, and appellate information is online at www.judicial.state.ia.us/online_records.
General Information: Public terminal goes back to 7/1997. No juvenile, sealed, dissolution of marriage, mental health, domestic abuse or deferred records released. Certification fee: $10.00. Payee: Clerk of Court. Personal checks accepted. Prepayment required.

Polk County

District Court 500 Mulberry St, Rm 201, Des Moines, IA 50309; phone: 515-286-3772; criminal fax: 515-323-5250; civil fax: 515-286-3172; hours 8AM-4:30PM (CST). *Felony, Misdemeanor, Civil, Eviction, Small Claims, Probate.*
Civil Records: Access: Mail, in person, online. Visitors must perform in person searches themselves. Search fee: Turnaround time 1 week. Court makes copy: $.50 per page. Required to search: name, years to search; also helpful: address. Civil

cases indexed by defendant, plaintiff. Civil records on computer back to 1990; docket books and index cards from 1880s and microfilm prior to 1970. Civil, probate, and appellate information is at www.judicial.state.ia.us/online_records. Note: Mail search requests are not recommended.
Criminal Records: Access: Mail, in person, online. Visitors must perform in person searches themselves. Court makes copy: $.50 per page. Required to search: name, years to search, address, DOB; also helpful: SSN. Criminal records on computer back to 1990; docket books and index cards from 1880s and microfilm prior to 1970. Criminal, traffic, and appellate information is online at www.judicial.state.ia.us/online_records. Note: Mail search requests are not recommended. Mail turnaround time 1 week.
General Information: Public terminal goes back to 1991. No juvenile, child, sealed, pending, mental health, expunged, domestic abuse or deferred records released. Certification fee: $10.00 per doc. Payee: Clerk of Court. Personal checks accepted. Credit cards accepted: Visa. Prepayment required.

Pottawattamie County

4th District Court 227 S 6th St, Council Bluffs, IA 51501; phone: 712-328-5604; hours 8:30AM-4:30PM (CST). *Felony, Misdemeanor, Civil, Eviction, Small Claims, Probate.*
www.judicial.state.ia.us/district/district4
Civil Records: Access: In person, mail, online. Visitors must perform in person searches themselves. Court makes copy: $.25 per page. Required to search: name, years to search. Civil cases indexed by defendant, plaintiff. Civil records on computer from 1978, index books prior. Records are being microfilmed as load permits. Civil, probate, and appellate information is at www.judicial.state.ia.us/online_records. Mail turnaround time in 2 days.
Criminal Records: Access: In person, online. Visitors must perform in person searches themselves. Court makes copy: $.25 per page. Required to search: name, years to search. Criminal records on computer from 1978, index books prior. Records are being microfilmed as load permits. Criminal, traffic, and appellate information is online at www.judicial.state.ia.us/online_records.
General Information: Public use terminal available. No juvenile, sealed, pending dissolution of marriage, mental health, domestic abuse or deferred records released. Certification fee: $10.00. Payee: Clerk of Court. Personal checks accepted. Prepayment required.

Poweshiek County

8th District Court PO Box 218, Montezuma, IA 50171; phone: 641-623-5644; fax: 641-623-5320; hours 8AM-4:30PM (CST). *Felony, Misdemeanor, Civil, Eviction, Small Claims, Probate.*
www.judicial.state.ia.us/district/district8
Civil Records: Access: In person, online. Visitors must perform in person searches themselves. Court makes copy: $.50 per page. Required to search: name, years to search. Civil cases indexed by defendant, plaintiff. Civil records on index cards from 1980, docket books from early 1900s, computer since 7/95. Civil, probate, and appellate information is at www.judicial.state.ia.us/online_records.
Criminal Records: Access: In person, online. Visitors must perform in person searches themselves. Court makes copy: $.50 per page. Required to search: name, years to search. Criminal records on computer since 1995, index cards since 1980, docket books from early 1900s. Criminal, traffic, and appellate information is online at www.judicial.state.ia.us/online_records.
General Information: Public use terminal available. No juvenile, sealed, pending, dissolution of marriage, mental health, domestic abuse or deferred records released. Certification fee: $10.00. Payee: Clerk of Court. Personal checks accepted. Prepayment required.

Ringgold County

5th District Court PO Box 523, 109 W Madison, Mount Ayr, IA 50854; phone: 641-464-3234; fax: 641-464-2478; hours 8AM-4:30PM (CST). *Felony, Misdemeanor, Civil, Small Claims, Probate, Traffic.*
www.judicial.state.ia.us/district/district5
Civil Records: Access: In person, online. Visitors must perform in person searches themselves. Court makes copy: $.50 per page. Required to search: name, years to search. Civil cases indexed by defendant, plaintiff. Civil records on docket books; on computer back to 11/06. Civil, probate, and appellate information is at www.judicial.state.ia.us/online_records.
Criminal Records: Access: In person, online. Visitors must perform in person searches themselves. Court makes copy: $.50 per page. Required to search: name, years to search. Criminal records on docket books; on computer back to 11/96. Criminal, traffic, and appellate information is online at www.judicial.state.ia.us/online_records.
General Information: Public terminal goes back to 11/96. No CINA, juvenile, sealed, pending dissolution of marriage, mental health or expunged records released. Certification fee: $10.00. Payee: Clerk of Court. Personal checks accepted.

Sac County

2nd District Court PO Box 368, Sac City, IA 50583; phone: 712-662-7791; fax: 712-662-7978; hours 8AM-4:30PM (CST). *Felony, Misdemeanor, Civil, Eviction, Small Claims, Probate.*
www.judicial.state.ia.us/district/district2
Civil Records: Access: In person, online. Visitors must perform in person searches themselves. Court makes copy: $.50 per page. Required to search: name. Civil cases indexed by defendant, plaintiff. Civil records go back to 1888; on computer back to 7/1997. Civil, probate, and appellate information is at www.judicial.state.ia.us/online_records.
Criminal Records: Access: In person, online. Visitors must perform in person searches themselves. No search fee. Court makes copy: $.50 per page. Required to search: name, approximate date. Criminal records go back to 1888; on computer back to 7/1997. Criminal, traffic, and appellate data at www.judicial.state.ia.us/online_records. Note: Court may assist in search, if necessary.
General Information: Public use terminal available. No juvenile, sealed, pending dissolution of marriage, mental health, domestic abuse or deferred records released. Will not fax documents. Certification fee: $10.00. Payee: Clerk of Court. Personal checks accepted. Prepayment required.

Scott County

7th District Court 416 W 4th St, Davenport, IA 52801; phone: 563-326-8786; hours 8AM-4:30PM (CST). *Felony, Misdemeanor, Civil, Eviction, Small Claims, Probate.*
Civil Records: Access: In person, online. Visitors must perform in person searches themselves. Court makes copy: $.50 per page. Required to search: name, years to search. Civil cases indexed by defendant, plaintiff. Civil records on computer back to 11/1993, docket books prior. Civil, probate, and appellate data at www.judicial.state.ia.us/online_records.
Criminal Records: Access: In person, online. Visitors must perform in person searches themselves. Court makes copy: $.50 per page. Required to search: name, years to search, DOB; also helpful: SSN. Criminal records on computer back to 1992, printouts and docket books prior. Criminal, traffic, and appellate information is online at www.judicial.state.ia.us/online_records.
General Information: Public terminal goes back to 1992. No juvenile, sealed, dissolution of marriage, mental health, domestic abuse or deferred records released. Certification fee: $10.00 per doc. Payee: Clerk of Court. Personal checks and Visa/MC accepted. Prepayment required.

Shelby County

4th District Court PO Box 431, Harlan, IA 51537; phone: 712-755-5543; fax: 712-755-2667; hours 8:30AM-3:30PM (CST). *Felony, Misdemeanor, Civil, Eviction, Small Claims, Probate.*
www.shco.org
Note: The court will not perform name searches.
Civil Records: Access: In person, online. Visitors must perform in person searches themselves. Court makes copy: $.25 per page. Required to search: name, years to search. Civil cases indexed by defendant, plaintiff. Civil records on original files back to 1969, microfilm prior, on computer back to 10/95. Civil, probate, and appellate information is at www.judicial.state.ia.us/online_records.
Criminal Records: Access: In person, online. Visitors must perform in person searches themselves. No search fee. Court makes copy: $.25 per page. Required to search: name, years to search; also helpful: DOB. Criminal records on original files back to 1980, microfilm prior, on computer back to 10/95. Criminal, traffic, and appellate information is online at www.judicial.state.ia.us/online_records.
General Information: Public use terminal available. No juvenile, sealed, dissolution of marriage, mental health, domestic abuse or deferred records released. Will fax specific case file requests for $2.00 plus $.25 per page. Certification fee: $10.00. Payee: Clerk of Court. Personal checks accepted. Prepayment required.

Sioux County

3rd District Court PO Box 47, Courthouse, Orange City, IA 51041; phone: 712-737-2286; fax: 712-737-8908; hours 8AM-4:30PM (CST). *Felony, Misdemeanor, Civil, Eviction, Small Claims, Probate.*
www.judicial.state.ia.us/district/district3
Civil Records: Access: In person, online. Visitors must perform in person searches themselves. Court makes copy: $.50 per page. Required to search: name, years to search. Civil cases indexed by defendant, plaintiff. Civil records on docket books from 1800s; computerized records since 9/97. Civil, probate, and appellate info is at www.judicial.state.ia.us/online_records.
Criminal Records: Access: In person, online. Visitors must perform in person searches themselves. Court makes copy: $.50 per page. Required to search: name, years to search, signed release. Criminal records on docket books from 1800s; computerized records since 9/97. Criminal, traffic, and appellate information is online at www.judicial.state.ia.us/online_records.
General Information: Public terminal goes back to 1997. No juvenile, sealed, dissolution of marriage, mental health, domestic abuse or deferred records released. Certification fee: $10.00 per doc. Payee: Clerk of Court. Personal checks or Visa/MC accepted. Prepayment required.

Story County

2nd District Court PO Box 408, 1315 S B Ave, Nevada, IA 50201; phone: 515-382-7410; hours 8AM-4:30PM (CST). *Felony, Misdemeanor, Civil, Probate.*
www.judicial.state.ia.us/district/district2/
Note: Also has a branch in Ames that handles minor misdemeanors, traffic, and small claims.
Civil Records: Access: In person, online. Visitors must perform in person searches themselves. Court makes copy: $.50 per page. Required to search: name, years to search. Civil cases indexed by defendant, plaintiff. Civil records on docket books from 1900s; on computer back to 1995. Civil, probate, and appellate information is at www.judicial.state.ia.us/online_records.
Criminal Records: Access: In person, online. Visitors must perform in person searches themselves. No search fee. Court makes copy: $.50

per page. Required to search: name, years to search. Criminal records on computer since 1992, prior on docket books. Criminal, traffic, and appellate data at www.judicial.state.ia.us/online_records.

General Information: Public use terminal available. No sealed, pending dissolution of marriage, mental health, or expunged records released. Will not fax documents. Certification fee: $10.00 per cert. Payee: Clerk of Court. Personal checks accepted. Prepayment required.

Ames Associate District Court PO Box 748, 515 Clark St, Ames, IA 50010; phone: 515-239-5140; hours 8AM-4:30PM (CST). *Misdemeanor (Minor), Small Claims, Eviction.*
www.judicial.state.ia.us/district/district2/
Note: A branch of the District Court in Nevada.
Civil Records: Access: In person, online. Visitors must perform in person searches themselves. Court makes copy: $.50 per page; same fee for self serve. Required to search: name, years to search. Civil cases indexed by defendant, plaintiff. Civil records on computer back to 1995. Civil, probate, and appellate information is at www.judicial.state.ia.us/online_records.
Criminal Records: Access: In person, online. Visitors must perform in person searches themselves. Court makes copy: $.50 per page; same fee for self serve. Required to search: name, approx date of offense. Criminal records on computer since 1992, prior on docket books. Criminal, traffic, and appellate information is online at www.judicial.state.ia.us/online_records.
General Information: Public terminal has criminal back to 3/1995 and civil back to 7/1995. No sealed or expunged records released. Will not fax documents. Certification fee: $10.00. Payee: Clerk of Court. Personal checks accepted. Prepayment required.

Tama County

6th Judicial District Court PO Box 306, Toledo, IA 52342; phone: 641-484-3721; fax: 641-484-6403; hours 8AM-4:30PM (CST). *Felony, Misdemeanor, Civil, Eviction, Small Claims, Probate.*
www.judicial.state.ia.us/district/district6
Civil Records: Access: In person, online. Visitors must perform in person searches themselves. Court makes copy: $.50 per page; same fee for self serve. Required to search: name, years to search. Civil cases indexed by defendant, plaintiff. Civil records on docket books from 1880s; computerized records since 1997. Magistrate dockets to 1972, prior to 1972, Justice of the Peace. Civil, probate, and appellate data at www.judicial.state.ia.us/online_records.
Criminal Records: Access: In person, online. Visitors must perform in person searches themselves. No search fee. Court makes copy: $.50 per page; same fee for self serve. Required to search: name, years to search. Criminal records on docket books from 1880s; computerized records since 1995. Magistrate dockets to 1972, prior to 1972, Justice of the Peace. Criminal, traffic, and appellate data at www.judicial.state.ia.us/online_records.
General Information: Public terminal has only traffic records back to 1995. No juvenile, sealed, dissolution of marriage, mental health, domestic abuse or deferred records released. Will not fax documents. Certification fee: $10.00. Payee: Clerk of Court. Personal checks accepted. Prepayment required.

Taylor County

5th District Court Courthouse, Bedford, IA 50833; phone: 712-523-2095; fax: 712-523-2936; hours 8AM-4:30PM (CST). *Felony, Misdemeanor, Civil, Eviction, Small Claims, Probate.*
www.judicial.state.ia.us/district/district5
Civil Records: Access: In person, online. Visitors must perform in person searches themselves. Court makes copy: $.50 per page; same fee for self serve. Required to search: name, years to search. Civil cases indexed by defendant, plaintiff. Civil records on

computer since 11/01/96; prior to 1880s. Civil, probate, and appellate information is at www.judicial.state.ia.us/online_records.
Criminal Records: Access: In person, online. Visitors must perform in person searches themselves. Court makes copy: $.50 per page; same fee for self serve. Required to search: name, years to search. Criminal records on computer since 11/01/96; prior to 1880s. Criminal, traffic, and appellate data at www.judicial.state.ia.us/online_records.
General Information: Public use terminal available. No juvenile, sealed, dissolution of marriage, mental health, domestic abuse or deferred records released. Will fax specific case file requests to local or toll free line. Certification fee: $10.00. Payee: Clerk of Court. Personal checks accepted. Prepayment required.

Union County

5th District Court Courthouse, Creston, IA 50801; phone: 641-782-7315; fax: 641-782-8241; hours 8AM-4:30PM (CST). *Felony, Misdemeanor, Civil, Eviction, Small Claims, Probate.*
www.judicial.state.ia.us/district/district5
Civil Records: Access: In person, mail, online. Visitors must perform in person searches themselves. No search fee. Court makes copy: $.50 per page; same fee for self serve. Required to search: name, years to search. Civil cases indexed by defendant, plaintiff. Civil records on docket books from 1900s; computerized back to 10/1996. Civil, probate, and appellate information is at www.judicial.state.ia.us/online_records. Mail turnaround time 1-2 days.
Criminal Records: Access: In person, mail, online. Visitors must perform in person searches themselves. No search fee. Court makes copy: $.50 per page; same fee for self serve. Required to search: name, years to search. Criminal records on docket books from 1900s; computerized back to 10/1996. Criminal, traffic, and appellate information is online at www.judicial.state.ia.us/online_records. Mail turnaround time 1-2 days.
General Information: Public terminal goes back to 10/1996. No juvenile cases less than 10 years, sealed, pending dissolution of marriage, mental health, or deferred records released. No fee to fax documents. Certification fee: $10.00. Payee: Clerk of Court. Personal checks accepted. Prepayment required.

Van Buren County

8th District Court Courthouse Criminal Records, Keosauqua, IA 52565; phone: 319-293-3108; fax: 319-293-3811; hours 8AM-4:30PM (CST). *Felony, Misdemeanor, Civil, Eviction, Small Claims, Probate.*
www.judicial.state.ia.us/district/district8
Civil Records: Access: In person, online. Visitors must perform in person searches themselves. Court makes copy: $.50 per page; same fee for self serve. Required to search: name, years to search. Civil cases indexed by defendant, plaintiff. Civil records on docket books from 1837, computerized since 1997. Civil, probate, and appellate information back to 1997 is at www.judicial.state.ia.us/online_records.
Criminal Records: Access: In person, online. Visitors must perform in person searches themselves. Court makes copy: $.50 per page; same fee for self serve. Required to search: name, years to search, DOB. Criminal records on docket books from 1837, computerized since 1997. Criminal, traffic, and appellate information is online at www.judicial.state.ia.us/online_records.
General Information: Public terminal has criminal back to 1997 and civil back to 1997. (Probate is also on terminal, but in separate index if prior to 1997.) No sealed, mental health, or sealed records released; will release un-sealed juvenile, marriage dissolution or DA records if after July, 2000. Certification fee: $10.00. Payee: Clerk of Court. Personal checks accepted. Prepayment required.

Wapello County

8th District Court 101 W 4th, Ottumwa, IA 52501; phone: 641-683-0060; hours 8AM-4:30PM (CST). *Felony, Misdemeanor, Civil, Eviction, Small Claims, Probate.*
www.judicial.state.ia.us/district/district8/
Note: SSNs are only maintained on a confidential sheet not available to the public.
Civil Records: Access: In person, online. Visitors must perform in person searches themselves. Court makes copy: $.50 per page. Required to search: name, years to search. Civil cases indexed by defendant, plaintiff. Civil records on computer back to 5/1994; docket books prior. Civil, probate, and appellate information is at www.judicial.state.ia.us/online_records.
Criminal Records: Access: In person, online. Visitors must perform in person searches themselves. Court makes copy: $.50 per page. Required to search: name, years to search, DOB; also helpful: SSN. Criminal records on computer back to 5/1994; docket books prior. Criminal, traffic, and appellate information is online at www.judicial.state.ia.us/online_records.
General Information: Public terminal goes back to 1995. No juvenile, sealed, dissolution of marriage, mental health, domestic abuse or deferred records released. Certification fee: $10.00 per doc. Payee: Clerk of Court. Personal checks and Visa/MC accepted. Prepayment required.

Warren County

5th District Court PO Box 379, Indianola, IA 50125; phone: 515-961-1033; criminal phone: 515-961-1033; civil phone: 515-961-1027; probate phone: 515-961-1037; fax: 515-961-1071; hours 8AM-4:30PM (CST). *Felony, Misdemeanor, Civil, Eviction, Small Claims, Probate.*
www.judicial.state.ia.us/district/district5
Civil Records: Access: In person, online. Visitors must perform in person searches themselves. Court makes copy: $.50 per page; same fee for self serve. Required to search: name, years to search. Civil cases indexed by defendant, plaintiff. Civil records on computer back to 10/1995; prior on docket books to 1925. Civil, probate, and appellate information is at www.judicial.state.ia.us/online_records.
Criminal Records: Access: In person, online. Visitors must perform in person searches themselves. No search fee. Court makes copy: $.50 per page; same fee for self serve. Required to search: name, years to search. Criminal records on computer back to 10/1995; prior on docket books to 1945. Criminal, traffic, and appellate information is online at www.judicial.state.ia.us/online_records.
General Information: Public terminal goes back to 1995. No juvenile, sealed, dissolution of marriage, mental health, domestic abuse or deferred records released. Will not fax documents. Certification fee: $10.00. Payee: Clerk of Court. Personal checks accepted. Credit cards accepted. Prepayment required.

Washington County

8th District Court PO Box 391, Washington, IA 52353; phone: 319-653-7741; fax: 319-653-7787; hours 8AM-4:30PM (CST). *Felony, Misdemeanor, Civil, Eviction, Small Claims, Probate.*
www.judicial.state.ia.us/district/district8
Civil Records: Access: In person, online. Visitors must perform in person searches themselves. Court makes copy: $.50 per page. Required to search: name, years to search. Civil cases indexed by defendant, plaintiff. Civil records on computer back to 1997, microfilm from 1940, docket books since court inception. Civil, probate, and appellate information is at www.judicial.state.ia.us/online_records.
Criminal Records: Access: In person, online. Visitors must perform in person searches themselves. Court makes copy: $.50 per page. Required to search: name, years to search. Criminal records on computer back to 1997, microfilm from 1940, docket books since court inception. Criminal,

traffic, and appellate information is online at www.judicial.state.ia.us/online_records.
General Information: Public terminal goes back to 1997. No juvenile, sealed, mental health, domestic abuse or deferred records released. Certification fee: $10.00 per doc. Payee: Clerk of Court. Personal checks accepted. Prepayment required.

Wayne County

5th District Court PO Box 424, Corydon, IA 50060; phone: 641-872-2264; fax: 641-872-2431; hours 8AM-4:30PM (CST). *Felony, Misdemeanor, Civil, Eviction, Small Claims, Probate.*
www.judicial.state.ia.us/district/district5
Civil Records: Access: In person, online. Visitors must perform in person searches themselves. Court makes copy: $.50 per page. Required to search: name, years to search. Civil cases indexed by defendant, plaintiff. Civil records on dockets from 1890, on computer back to 2/97. Civil, probate, and appellate data at www.judicial.state.ia.us/online_records.
Criminal Records: Access: In person, online. Visitors must perform in person searches themselves. Court makes copy: $.50 per page. Required to search: name, years to search, DOB. Criminal records on dockets from 1890, on computer back to 2/97. Criminal, traffic, and appellate data at www.judicial.state.ia.us/online_records.
General Information: Public terminal goes back to 2/1997. No juvenile, sealed, mental health, domestic abuse or deferred records released. Certification fee: $10.00. Payee: Clerk of Court. Personal checks accepted. Prepayment required.

Webster County

2nd District Court 701 Central Ave, Courthouse, Ft Dodge, IA 50501; phone: 515-576-7115; fax: 515-576-0555; probate fax: same; hours 8AM-4:30PM (CST). *Felony, Misdemeanor, Civil, Eviction, Small Claims, Probate.*
www.judicial.state.ia.us/district/district2
Civil Records: Access: In person, online. Visitors must perform in person searches themselves. Court makes copy: $.50 per page. Required to search: name, years to search. Civil cases indexed by defendant, plaintiff. Civil records on docket books from 1800s, on computer since 1995. Civil, probate, and appellate information is at www.judicial.state.ia.us/online_records.
Criminal Records: Access: In person, online. Visitors must perform in person searches themselves. Court makes copy: $.50 per page. Required to search: name, years to search, signed release. Criminal records on docket books from 1800s, on computer since 1995. Criminal, traffic, and appellate information is online at www.judicial.state.ia.us/online_records.
General Information: Public use terminal available. No juvenile, sealed, dissolution of marriage, mental health, domestic abuse or deferred records released. Certification fee: $10.00. Payee: Clerk of Court. Personal checks accepted. Prepayment required.

Winnebago County

2nd District Court 126 S Clark, Box 468, Forest City, IA 50436; phone: 641-585-4520; fax: 641-585-2615; hours 9AM-3:30PM (CST). *Felony, Misdemeanor, Civil, Eviction, Small Claims, Probate.*
www.judicial.state.ia.us/district/district2
Civil Records: Access: In person, online. Visitors must perform in person searches themselves. Court makes copy: $.50 per page; same fee for self serve. Required to search: name, years to search; also helpful: address. Civil cases indexed by defendant, plaintiff. Civil records on dockets from 1880s; on computer since 9/1997. Civil, probate, and appellate data at www.judicial.state.ia.us/online_records.
Criminal Records: Access: In person, online. Visitors must perform in person searches themselves. No search fee. Court makes copy: $.50

per page; same fee for self serve. Required to search: name, years to search; also helpful: address, DOB, aliases, offense, date of offense. Criminal records on dockets from 1940s; on computer since 9/1997. Criminal, traffic, and appellate information is online at www.judicial.state.ia.us/online_records.
General Information: Public terminal goes back to 9/1997. No juvenile, pending or dismissed dissolution of marriage, mental health, criminal deferred or substance abuse records released. Domestic abuse law change states that parts of the file may be public, depending on Judge's order. Certification fee: $10.00 per document. Payee: Clerk of Court. Personal checks or Visa, MC accepted. Prepayment required.

Winneshiek County

1st District Court 201 W Main St, Decorah, IA 52101; phone: 563-382-2469; fax: 563-382-0603; hours 8AM-4:30PM (CST). *Felony, Misdemeanor, Civil, Eviction, Small Claims, Probate.*
www.judicial.state.ia.us/district/district1
Civil Records: Access: In person, online. Visitors must perform in person searches themselves. Court makes copy: $.50 per page. Self serve copy fee: $.25 per page. Required to search: name, years to search. Civil cases indexed by defendant, plaintiff. Civil records on computer since 1992, docket books since 1860s. Civil, probate, and appellate information is at www.judicial.state.ia.us/online_records.
Criminal Records: Access: In person, online. Visitors must perform in person searches themselves. Court makes copy: $.50 per page. Self serve copy fee: $.25 per page. Required to search: name, years to search, signed release. Criminal records on computer since 1991, docket books since 1860s. Criminal, traffic, and appellate information at www.judicial.state.ia.us/online_records.
General Information: Public terminal has criminal back to 1991 and civil back to 1992. No juvenile, sealed, mental health, domestic abuse or deferred records released. Certification fee: $10.00 per document. Payee: Clerk of Court. Personal checks accepted. Prepayment required.

Woodbury County

3rd District Court Woodbury County Courthouse, 620 Douglas, Rm 101, Sioux City, IA 51101-1248; phone: 712-279-6611; fax: 712-279-6021; hours 8AM-4:30PM (CST). *Felony, Civil, Eviction, Probate.*
www.judicial.state.ia.us/district/district3
Civil Records: Access: In person, online. Visitors must perform in person searches themselves. Court makes copy: $.50 per page. Required to search: name, years to search. Civil cases indexed by defendant, plaintiff. Civil records on index books from early 1900; on computer from 7/95. Civil, probate, and appellate information is at www.judicial.state.ia.us/online_records.
Criminal Records: Access: In person, online. Visitors must perform in person searches themselves. Court makes copy: $.50 per page. Required to search: name, years to search. Criminal records on index books from early 1900; on computer from 10/95. Criminal, traffic, and appellate data at www.judicial.state.ia.us/online_records.
General Information: Public terminal has criminal back to 10/1995 and civil back to 7/1995. (Terminal has probate record index back to 7/1995.) No sealed, adoption, substance abuse, pending, or mental health records released. Certification fee: $10.00. Payee: Clerk of Court. Personal checks accepted. Prepayment required.

Associate District Court 407 7th St, County Clerk at Law Enforcement Ctr, Sioux City, IA 51101; phone: 712-279-6624; fax: 712-279-9564; hours 8AM-4:30PM (CST). *Misdemeanor, Civil, Eviction, Small Claims.*
Civil Records: Access: In person, online. Visitors must perform in person searches themselves. Court makes copy: $.50 per page; same fee for self serve.

Required to search: name, years to search. Civil cases indexed by defendant, plaintiff. Civil records on docket books from early 1900; on computer from 7/95. Civil, probate, and appellate information is at www.judicial.state.ia.us/online_records.
Criminal Records: Access: In person, online. Visitors must perform in person searches themselves. Court makes copy: $.50 per page; same fee for self serve. Required to search: name, years to search. Criminal Records indexed on computer since 1992; on computer from 7/92. Criminal, traffic, and appellate information is online at www.judicial.state.ia.us/online_records.
General Information: Public terminal goes back to 1992. No juvenile records released. Certification fee: $10.00. Payee: Clerk of Court. Personal checks accepted. Prepayment required.

Worth County

2nd District Court 1000 Central Ave, Northwood, IA 50459; phone: 641-324-2840; fax: 641-324-2360; hours 9AM-3:30PM (CST). *Felony, Misdemeanor, Civil, Eviction, Small Claims, Probate.*
www.judicial.state.ia.us/district/district2/
Civil Records: Access: In person, online. Visitors must perform in person searches themselves. Court makes copy: $.50 per page. Required to search: name, years to search. Civil cases indexed by defendant, plaintiff. Civil records on computer and docket books, on computer back to 4/97. Civil, probate, and appellate information is at www.judicial.state.ia.us/online_records.
Criminal Records: Access: In person, online. Visitors must perform in person searches themselves. No search fee. Court makes copy: $.50 per page. Required to search: name, years to search. Criminal records on computer and docket books, on computer back to 4/97. Criminal, traffic, and appellate information is online at www.judicial.state.ia.us/online_records.
General Information: Public terminal goes back to 4/1997. No juvenile, sealed, dissolution of marriage, mental health, domestic abuse, dismissed, or deferred records released. Will fax specific case file requests. Certification fee: $10.00 per doc. Payee: Clerk of Court. Personal checks and Visa/MC accepted. Prepayment required.

Wright County

2nd District Court PO Box 306, Clarion, IA 50525; phone: 515-532-3113; fax: 515-532-2343; hours 9AM-3:30PM (CST). *Felony, Misdemeanor, Civil, Eviction, Small Claims, Probate.*
www.judicial.state.ia.us/district/district2/
Note: Probate is separate index at this same address
Civil Records: Access: In person, online. Visitors must perform in person searches themselves. Court makes copy: $.50 per page; same fee for self serve. Required to search: name, years to search. Civil cases indexed by defendant, plaintiff. Civil records on docket books from 1880; on computer since 1997. Civil, probate, and appellate information is at www.judicial.state.ia.us/online_records.
Criminal Records: Access: In person, online. Visitors must perform in person searches themselves. No search fee. Court makes copy: $.50 per page; same fee for self serve. Required to search: name, years to search; also helpful: DOB, SSN. Criminal records on docket books from 1880s; on computer since 1997. Criminal, traffic, and appellate information is online at www.judicial.state.ia.us/online_records.
General Information: Public terminal goes back to 1997. No juvenile, sealed, dissolution of marriage, mental health, domestic abuse or deferred records released. Will fax specific case file requests for $2.00 fee. Certification fee: $20.00 per document. Payee: Clerk of Court. Personal checks accepted. Prepayment required.

Iowa Recording Offices

ORGANIZATION: 99 counties, 100 recording offices. Lee County has two recording offices. The recording officer is the County Recorder. Many counties utilize a grantor/grantee index containing all transactions recorded with them. See the notes under the county for how to determine which office is appropriate to search. The entire state is in the Central Time Zone (CST).

REAL ESTATE RECORDS: Most counties are hesitant to perform real estate searches, but some will provide a listing from the grantor/grantee index with the understanding that it is not certified in the sense that a title search is. Certification of copies usually costs $2.00-5.00 per document.

UCC RECORDS: Financing statements are filed at the state level except for real estate related collateral, which are filed with the County Recorder. However, prior to 07/2001, consumer goods were also filed at the County Recorder and these older records can be searched there. Most Iowa counties will perform UCC searches; see county profiles for exceptions. Use search request form UCC-11. Search fees are usually $5.00 per debtor name ($6.00 if the standard UCC-11 form is not used). Copies usually cost $1.00 per page.

TAX LIEN RECORDS: Federal tax liens on personal property of businesses are filed with the Secretary of State. Other federal and all state tax liens on personal property are filed with the County Recorder. County search practices vary widely, but most provide some sort of tax lien search for $6.00 per name.

OTHER LIENS: Home improvement, job service.

ONLINE ACCESS: As yet there is no fully operational statewide access to county recorder data, however 87-plus counties' land records are available at http://iowalandrecords.org after you register. New in 2005, this County Land Record Information System offers free searching and pdf images of deeds, liens, even UCCs and judgments, though this state-sponsored service may begin charging at any time. There is also features for monitoring for new documents and saving documents.

Assessor records for 55 counties plus cities of Ames, Cedar Rapids, Dubuque, Iowa City, and Souix City are available free at www.iowaassessors.com. A statewide Property Tax lookup and payment page is at www.iowatreasurers.org/county_locator.cfm?ID=1. First, select the county, then follow prompts to the search page where you can first look-up the name, then parcel info.

Adair County

County Recorder, 400 Public Sq; Courthouse, Greenfield, IA 50849. 641-743-2411; fax-641-743-2565; hours: 8AM-4:30PM
Only the public may search. Copy fee $1.00 per page. Cert fee- $5.00 per doc plus copy fee. Payee-Adair County Recorder. **Online access to Assessor, Property records:** Access assessor property and sales data is free at www.iowaassessors.com. **Other phones:** Treasurer- 641-743-2312; Elections- 641-743-2546; Vital Records- 641-743-2411. **Property tax/Assessor-** 641-745-2531.

Adams County

County Recorder, PO Box 28, Corning, IA 50841. RE & UCC recording phone-641-322-3744; fax-641-322-3744; hours: 8:30AM-4:30PM
Index: Pre-1990 indices are deeds, mortgages, miscellaneous. Records indexed on computer back to 4/1988. Office will perform a UCC search but public must search other records themselves. UCC search (on proper form) per debtor name- $5.00. Tax lien search- $6.00 per debtor. Copy fee $1.00 per page. RE record copy-$. 25 per page. Cert fee- $5.00 per doc plus copy fee. Payee- Adams County Recorder. **Online access to Real Estate, Deed, Lien, UCC, Judgment records:** Access land records available at http://iowalandrecords.org after registering. Free 2004-2005 index searching; images to be added; site may begin charging at any time. **Other phones:** Treasurer- 641-322-3210; Elections- 641-322-3340; Vital Records- 641-322-3744; Clerk of Court-641-322-4711. **Property tax/Assessor-** PO Box 28, Corning, IA 50841; 641-322-4312.

Allamakee County

County Recorder, 110 Allamakee St; Courthouse, Waukon, IA 52172-1794. RE & UCC recording phone-563-568-2364; fax-319-568-6419; hours: 8AM-4PM

Records indexed on computer back to 1983. Only the public may search. Separate federal/state combined tax lien search- $6.00 per document. Copy fee $1.00 per page. RE record copy- $.50 per page. Cert fee- $5.00 per doc plus copy fee. Payee-Allamakee County Recorder. **Online access to Real Estate, Deed, Lien, UCC, Judgment, Assessor, Property records:** Access land records at http://iowalandrecords.org after registering. Free searching and pdf images of deeds, liens, UCCs, judgments; may begin charging at any time. Monitor for new documents and save documents. 77 counties now enrolled. Also, for UCC since 2001 centralized at www.sos.state.ia.us/uccsearch for the State of Iowa. Access to the assessor database of property and sales data is free at www.iowaassessors.com. **Other phones:** Treasurer- 563-568-3793. **Property tax/Assessor-** 563-568-3145.

Appanoose County

County Recorder, Courthouse, Centerville, IA 52544. RE & UCC recording phone-641-856-6103; fax-641-856-8023; hours: 8:30AM-4:30PM
All records in one index. Records indexed on a public use terminal back to 7/1/2001. Office personnel or visitors may perform searches. Search fee $5.00. Copy fee $1.00, if real estate $.25 per page. Cert fee- $5 per doc, plus copy fee. Will not certify UCCs. Payee- Appanoose County Recorder. **Online access to Real Estate, Deed, Lien, UCC, Judgment records:** Access land records may be available at http://iowalandrecords.org after registering. Free searching and pdf images of deeds, liens, UCCs, judgments; may begin charging at any time. Monitor for new documents and save documents. **Other phones:** Treasurer- 641-856-3097; Vital Records- 641-856-6103. **Property tax/Assessor-** 641-437-4529.

Audubon County

County Recorder, 318 Leroy St. #7, Audubon, IA 50025-1255. RE & UCC recording phone-712-563-2119; fax-712-563-4766; hours: 8AM-4:30PM
Office will perform a tax lien search but public must search other records themselves. Separate federal/state combined tax lien search- $6.00 per debtor. Copy fee $1.00 per page. Cert fee- $5.00. Payee- Audubon County Recorder of Deeds. **Other phones:** Treasurer- 712-563-2293; Vital Records- 712-563-2119. **Property tax/Assessor-** 712-563-3418.

Benton County

County Recorder, Courthouse, Vinton, IA 52349. 319-472-3309; fax-319-472-3309; hours: 8AM-4:30PM
All records in one index. Records indexed on a public use terminal back to 7/1/2001. Only the public may search. Copy fee $.50 per page. Cert fee- $5.00 per doc plus copy fee. Payee- Benton County Recorder. **Online access to Real Estate, Deed, Lien, UCC, Judgment records:** Access land records at http://iowalandrecords.org after registering. Free searching and pdf images of deeds, liens, UCCs, judgments; may begin charging at any time. Monitor for new documents and save documents. **Other phones:** Treasurer- 319-472-2450; Elections- 319-472-2365; Vital Records- 319-472-3309. **Property tax/Assessor-** same address as above. 319-472-5211.

Black Hawk County

County Recorder, 316 E. 5th St; Courthouse, Rm 208, Waterloo, IA 50703-4774. 319-833-3171, R/E recording phone-319-833-3012, UCC recording phone-319-833-3012; fax-319-833-3170; hours: 8AM-5PM
Office will perform a UCC search but public must search other records themselves. UCC search per debtor name- $5.00. Copy fee $1.00 per page. RE record copy- $.75 per page. Cert fee- $5.00 per doc plus copy fee. Payee- Black Hawk County

Recorder. **Online access to Assessor, Property records:** Access to the assessor database of property and sales data is free at www.iowaassessors.com. **Other phones:** Treasurer- 319-833-3013; Elections- 319-833-3007; Vital Records- 319-833-3012. **Property tax/Assessor-** 319-833-3006.

Boone County

County Recorder, 201 State St, Boone, IA 50036-3987. RE & UCC recording phone-515-433-0514; fax-515-432-8102; 8AM-4:30PM www.co.boone.ia.us
All records in one index. Records indexed on a public use terminal back to 1995. Office will perform a Tax lien search but public must search other records themselves. Copy fee $1.00 per page. RE record copy- $.50 per page. Cert fee- $5.00 per doc plus copy fee. Payee- Boone County Recorder. **Online access to Assessor, Property, Real Estate, Deed, Lien, UCC, Judgment records:** Access to the assessor database of property and sales data is free at www.iowaassessors.com. Also, access land records at http://iowalandrecords.org after registering. Free searching and pdf images of deeds, liens, UCCs, judgments; may begin charging at any time. Monitor for new documents and save documents. **Other phones:** Treasurer- 515-433-0510; Elections- 515-433-0502; Vital Records- 515-433-0514. **Property tax/Assessor-** 515-433-0508.

Bremer County

County Recorder, 415 E Bremer Ave, Waverly, IA 50677. RE & UCC recording phone-319-352-0401; fax-319-352-0518; hours: 8AM-4:30PM
General index search performed by phone is free; otherwise search fee is $5.00. Copy fee $1.00 per page. RE record copy- $.50 per page. Cert fee- $5.00 per cert plus copy fee. Payee- Bremer County Recorder. **Online access to Assessor, Property records:** Access to the assessor database of property and sales data is free at www.iowaassessors.com. **Other phones:** Treasurer- 319-352-0242; Elections- 319-352-0340; Vital Records- 319-352-0401. **Assessor-** 319-352-0145.

Buchanan County

County Recorder, PO Box 298, Independence, IA 50644-0298. RE & UCC recording phone-319-334-4259; fax-319-334-7453; hours: 8AM-4:30PM
All records in one index. Records indexed on computer back to 1994. Office will perform a UCC search but public must search other records themselves. Search fee $5.00 per name. Copy fee $1.00 per page. RE record copy- $.50 per page. Tax lien copy-$5.00 per page. Cert fee- $5.00 per cert plus copy fee. Payee- Buchanan County Recorder. **Other phones:** Treasurer- 319-334-4340; Elections- 319-334-4109; Vital Records- 319-334-4259. **Property tax/Assessor-** PO Box 388, Independence, IA 50644; 319-334-2706.

Buena Vista County

County Recorder, PO Box 454, Storm Lake, IA 50588. 712-749-2539; fax-712-749-2539; 8AM-4:30PM
Office will perform a UCC search but public must search other records themselves. UCC search per debtor name- $5.00. Copy fee $1.00 per page. RE record copy- $.50 per page. Cert fee- $5.00 1st page, $.50 each add'l. Payee- Buena Vista County Recorder. **Online access to Property, Assessor, Real Estate, Deed, Lien, UCC, Judgment, Ag Sale, Inmate, Accident, Incident records:** Access land records at http://iowalandrecords.org after registering. Free searching and pdf images of deeds, liens, UCCs, judgments; may begin charging at any time. Monitor for new documents and save documents. Also, search the property assessor and Ag sales databases for free at www.co.buena-vista.ia.us/assessors/. No name searching. Also, search the jail inmates list for free at www.bvsheriff.com/jailroster/index.html. Also, search accident/incident reports for free at www.bvsheriff.com/accident-incident/index.html. **Other phones:** Treasurer- 712-749-5533. **Property tax/Assessor-** 712-749-2543.

Butler County

County Recorder, PO Box 346, Allison, IA 50602. 319-267-2735; fax-319-267-2675; hours: 8AM-4PM
Office personnel or visitors may perform searches. Search fee $5.00 per name. Will not search real estate records. Copy fee $1.00 per page. RE record copy- $.50 per page. Tax lien copy- $2.50. Cert fee- $10.00 per doc plus copy. Payee- Butler County Recorder. **Property tax/Assessor-** 319-267-2264.

Calhoun County

County Recorder, 416 4th St. #3; Calhoun County Courthouse, Rockwell City, IA 50579. RE & UCC recording phone-712-297-8121; 8:30AM-4:30PM www.calhouncountyiowa.com/recorders_office.htm
Will not search real estate records. Will do fixture filing document number UCC record searches only. Tax liens not included in UCC search. UCC search per debtor name- $5.00. UCC search request using non-standard form (per name)- $6.00. Tax lien search fee- $5.00 per debtor. Separate federal tax lien search- $5.00 per debtor. Separate federal/state combined tax lien search- $6.00 per debtor. Copy fee $.25 per page, $1.00 minimum. Cert fee- $5.00 per doc plus copy fee. Payee- Calhoun County Recorder. **Online access to Treasurer, Property, Death, Assessor, Real Estate Sale records:** Access to the treasurers property database is free at https://www.iowatreasurers.net/propertytax/index.php. Also, access to Death records for genealogists is free at www.rootsweb.com/~usgenweb/ia/calhoun/death.htm. Access to the assessor database of property and sales data is free at www.iowaassessors.com and at http://calhoun.iowaassessors.com/search.php?mode=search. **Other phones:** Treasurer- 712-297-7111; Vital Records- 712-297-8121. **Property tax/Assessor-** 416 4th St. #6, Rockwell City, IA; 712-297-7500.

Carroll County

County Recorder, PO Box 782, Carroll, IA 51401-0782. RE & UCC recording phone-712-792-3328; fax-712-792-9493; hours: 8AM-4:30PM
Office will perform a UCC search but public must search other records themselves. Search fee $6.00 per name. Copy fee $1.00 per page. RE record copy- $.50 per page. Cert fee- $5.00 per doc plus copy fee. Payee- Carroll County Recorder of Deeds. **Online access to Assessor, Property records:** Access to the assessor database of property and sales data is free at www.iowaassessors.com. **Other phones:** Treasurer- 712-792-1200; Vital Records- 712-792-3328. **Property tax/Assessor-** 712-792-9973.

Cass County

County Recorder, 5 W. 7th, Atlantic, IA 50022-1492. 712-243-1692; fax-712-243-6660; 8AM-4:30PM
Only the public may search. Copy fee $1.00 per page. Cert fee- $5.00 per doc plus copy fee. Payee- Cass County Recorder. **Online access to Real Estate, Deed, Lien, UCC, Judgment records:** Access land records at http://iowalandrecords.org after registering. Free searching and pdf images of deeds, liens, UCCs, judgments; may begin charging at any time. Monitor for new documents and save documents. **Other phones:** Treasurer- 712-243-5503; Elections- 712-243-4570; Vital Records- 712-243-1692. **Property tax/Assessor-** 712-243-2005.

Cedar County

County Recorder, 400 Cedar St; Courthouse, Tipton, IA 52772-1752. RE & UCC recording phone-563-886-2230; fax-563-886-2120; hours: 8AM-4PM
Separate indices to search include searching by years 1984-1995, 1996-2000, 2001-2004, current year and current month. Record index not computerized. Only the public may search. General copy fee $1.00; real estate record- $.25 per page, $1.00 minimum. Cert fee- $5.00 per doc plus copy fee. Payee- Cedar County Recorder. **Online access to Real Estate, Deed, Lien, UCC, Judgment records:** Access land records may be available at http://iowalandrecords.org after registering.

Free searching and pdf images of deeds, liens, UCCs, judgments; may begin charging at any time. Monitor for new documents and save documents. **Other phones:** Treasurer- 563-886-2557; Elections- 563-886-3168; Vital Records- 563-886-2230. **Property tax/Assessor-** 563-886-6413.

Cerro Gordo County

County Recorder, 220 N. Washington, Mason City, IA 50401. RE & UCC recording phone-641-421-3056; fax-641-421-3154; 8-4:30 www.co.cerro-gordo.ia.us
All records in one index. Records indexed on a public use terminal back to 1987. Only the public may search. RE record copy- $.50 per page. Tax lien copy- $5.00 for fed lien/$.50 per state. Cert fee- $5.00 per doc plus copy fee. Payee- Cerro Gordo County Recorder of Deeds. **Online access to Real Estate, Property, Assessor records:** Access to the County and Mason City property records is free at www.co.cerro-gordo.ia.us/parcel_inquiry/parcel_inquiry.cfm. No name searching. Also, access to the assessor database of property and sales data is free at www.iowaassessors.com. **Other phones:** Treasurer- 641-421-3037; Elections- 641-421-3027; Vital Records- 641-421-3062. **Property tax/Assessor-** same address. 641-421-3065 (county); -3061 (city).

Cherokee County

County Recorder, Drawer G, Cherokee, IA 51012. RE & UCC recording phone-712-225-6735; fax-712-225-6754; hours: 8AM-4:30PM
All records in one index. Records indexed on a public use terminal back to 1988. Office personnel or visitors may perform searches. Search fee $5.00. Copy fee $.50 per page. Cert fee- $5.00 per doc plus copy fee. Payee- Cherokee County Recorder of Deeds. **Online access to Land, Deed, Lien, UCC, Judgment records:** Access land records may be available at http://iowalandrecords.org after registering. Free searching and pdf images of deeds, liens, UCCs, judgments; may begin charging at any time. Monitor for new documents and save documents. **Other phones:** Treasurer- 712-225-6740; Appraiser/Auditor- 712-225-6701; Elections- 712-225-6704; Vital Records- 712-225-6735. **Property tax/Assessor-** 712-225-6701.

Chickasaw County

County Recorder, PO Box 14, New Hampton, IA 50659. RE & UCC recording phone-641-394-2336; fax-641-394-2816; hours: 8:30AM-4:30PM www.chickasawcoia.org/Recorder
All records in one index. Office personnel or visitors may perform searches. Search fee $6.00 per debtor. Copy fee $.50 per page. Cert fee- $5.00 per doc, plus $.50 each add'l pg. Payee- Chickasaw County Recorder. **Online access to Real Estate, Deed, Lien, UCC, Judgment, Assessor, Property records:** Access land records at http://iowalandrecords.org after registering. Free searching and pdf images of deeds, liens, UCCs, judgments; may begin charging at any time. Monitor for new documents and save documents. Access to the assessor database of property and sales data is free at www.iowaassessors.com. **Other phones:** Treasurer- 641-394-2107; Elections- 641-394-2100; Vital Records- 641-394-2336. **Property tax/Assessor-** PO Box 94, 8 E Prospect St, New Hampton, IA 50659; 641-394-2813.

Clarke County

County Recorder, 100 S Main, Courthouse, Osceola, IA 50213. 641-342-3313; fax-641-342-3313; 8:30am-4:30pm www.clarkecountyia.org/recorder/index.html
All records in one index. Records indexed on a public use terminal back to 1998. Only the public may search. Copy fee $.50 per page. Cert fee- $5.00 per doc plus $1.00 per page copy fee. Payee- Clarke County Recorder. **Online access to Assessor, Property records:** Access to the assessor property and sales data is free at www.iowaassessors.com. **Other phones:** Treasurer- 641-342-3311. **Property Assessor-** 641-342-3817.

Clay County

County Recorder, 300 W. 4th St, #3; Admin. Bldg, Spencer, IA 51301-3806. RE & UCC recording phone-712-262-1081; fax-712-264-3983; hours: 8AM-4:30PM www.co.clay.ia.us
Office will perform a tax lien search but public must search other records themselves. Search fee $5.00 per debtor. Copy fee $1.00 per page. Cert fee- $5.00 per doc plus copy fee. Payee- Clay County Recorder of Deeds. **Online access to Real Estate, Recording, Grantor/Grantee, Lien, Judgment, UCC, Tax Sale Certificate, Mortgage, Assessor, Property records:** At the main website, click to choose database to search; name search on all except the real estate/tax inquiry. Also, access land records at http://iowalandrecords.org after registering. Free searching and pdf images of deeds, liens, UCCs, judgments; may begin charging at any time. Monitor for new documents and save documents. Also, access to the assessor database of property and sales data is free at www.iowaassessors.com. **Other phones:** Treasurer- 712-262-2179; Appraiser/Auditor- 712-262-1986; Elections- 712-262-1569; Vital Records- 712-262-1081. **Property tax/Assessor-** 712-262-1986.

Clayton County

County Recorder, PO Box 278, Elkader, IA 52043. RE & UCC recording phone-563-245-2710; fax-319-245-2353; 8AM-4:30PM www.claytoncountyiowa.net
All records in one index. Records indexed on a public use terminal back to 6/1992. Only the public may search. Copy fee $1.00 per page. Cert fee- $5.00 per doc plus copy fee. Payee- Clayton County Recorder. **Other phones:** Treasurer- 563-245-1807; Appraiser/Auditor- 563-245-2533; Elections- 563-245-1106; Vital Records- 563-245-2710; Clerk of Court- 563-245-2204. **Property tax/Assessor-** 563-245-2533.

Clinton County

County Recorder, PO Box 2957, Clinton, IA 52733-2957. 563-244-0565 x0544, R/E recording phone-563-244-0565, UCC recording phone-563-244-0565; fax-563-242-8412; hours: 8AM-4:30PM www.clintoncountyiowa.com
All records in one index. Records indexed on a public use terminal back to 1988. Only the public may search. Copy fee $1.00 per page. Cert fee- $5.00 per doc plus copy fee. Payee- Clinton County Recorder of Deeds. **Online access to Assessor, Property records:** Access to the assessor database of property and sales data is free at www.iowaassessors.com. **Other phones:** Treasurer- 563-242-0573; Elections- 563-244-0568; Vital Records- 563-244-0565 /0544. **Property tax/Assessor-** same address as above. 563-242-0569.

Crawford County

County Recorder, 1202 Broadway, Denison, IA 51442. RE & UCC recording phone-712-263-3643; fax-712-263-3413; hours: 8AM-4:30PM http://crawfordcounty.org
All records in one index. Records indexed on computer from 1989 to present, prior indexes are all separate: land deed, land mortgages, town deeds, town mortgages, misc. Office personnel will only search tax liens, otherwise visitors must perform searches. Federal and state combined tax lien search fee-$6.00 per debtor. Copy fee $.25 per page. Cert fee- $5.00 per doc plus $1.00 per page copy fee. Payee- Crawford County Recorder. **Online access to Real Estate, Deed, Lien, UCC, Judgment records:** Access land records at http://iowalandrecords.org after registering. Free searching and pdf images of deeds, liens, UCCs, judgments; may begin charging at any time. Monitor for new documents and save documents. **Other phones:** Treasurer- 712-263-2648; Elections- 712-263-3045; Vital Records- 712-263-3643; no info given over the phone. **Property tax/Assessor-** 712-263-3447.

Dallas County

County Recorder, PO Box 38, Adel, IA 50003-0038. RE & UCC recording phone-515-993-5804; fax-515-933-5970; hours: 8AM-4:30PM
Office personnel or visitors may perform searches. Search fee $6.00 per name. Copy fee $1.00 per page. RE record copy- $.50 per page. Cert fee- $5.00 per doc plus copy fee. Payee- Dallas County Recorder. **Online access to Assessor, Property records:** Access to the assessor database of property and sales data is free at www.iowaassessors.com. **Other phones:** Treasurer- 515-993-5808; Vital Records- 515-993-5804. **Property tax/Assessor-** 515-993-5802.

Davis County

County Recorder, 100 Courthouse Sq #7, Bloomfield, IA 52537. RE & UCC recording phone-641-664-2321; fax-641-664-3082; hours: 7:30AM-4:30PM www.daviscountyrecorder.org
All records in one index. Records indexed on a public use terminal back to 1950. Office will perform a UCC search but public must search other records themselves. Search fee $5.00. Copy fee $1.00 per page. RE record copy- $.30 per page. Cert fee- $5.00 per doc plus copy fee. Payee- Davis County Recorder. **Online access to Real Estate, Assessor, Property Tax, Deed, Lien, UCC, Judgment records:** Access land records at http://iowalandrecords.org after registering. Free searching and pdf images of deeds, liens, UCCs, judgments; may begin charging at any time. Monitor for new documents and save documents. Also, access to county real estate data is free on the GIS system at www.daviscountyassessor.org/pmc/. Also, access to the assessor database of property and sales data is free at www.iowaassessors.com. **Other phones:** Treasurer- 641-664-2155; Elections- 641-664-2101; Vital Records- 641-664-2321. **Property tax/Assessor-** 641-664-3101.

Decatur County

County Recorder, 207 N. Main St, Leon, IA 50144. 641-446-4322; fax-641-446-7159; 8AM-4:30PM
Office personnel or visitors may perform searches. Search fee $5.00 per name. Will not search real estate records. Copy fee $1.00, if real estate $.25 per page. Cert fee- $4.00 per cert plus copy fee. Payee- Decatur County Recorder. **Property tax/Assessor-** 641-446-4314.

Delaware County

County Recorder, 301 E Main; Courthouse, Manchester, IA 52057. 563-927-4665; fax-319-927-3641; hours: 8AM-4:30PM
All records in one index. Records indexed on computer back to 1980. Office personnel or visitors may perform searches. Search fee $7.00 per name. Will not search UCC records. Copy fee $1.00 per page. RE record copy- $.25 per page. Cert fee- $5.00 per doc plus copy fee. Payee- Delaware County Recorder. **Other phones:** Treasurer- 563-927-2845. **Property tax/Assessor-** 563-927-2526.

Des Moines County

County Recorder, PO Box 277, Burlington, IA 52601-0277. RE & UCC recording phone-319-753-8221; fax-319-753-8721; hours: 8AM-4:30PM www.co.des-moines.ia.us/
Separate indices to search include computer and legal books. Records indexed on a public use terminal back to 1992. Office personnel or visitors may perform searches. Search fee $6.00 per name. Will not search real estate records. General copy fee $1.00 per page. RE record copy- $1.00 per page if on microfilm; $2.00 if faxed. Cert fee- $5.00 per doc plus copy fee. Payee- Des Moines County Recorder. **Online access to Assessor, Property records:** Access to the assessor database of property and sales data is free at www.iowaassessors.com. **Other phones:** Treasurer- 319-753-8252; Appraiser/Auditor- 319-753-8255; Elections- 319-753-

8266; Vital Records- 319-753-8221; Motor Vehicle- 319-753-8273. **Property tax/Assessor-** same address as above. 319-753-8224.

Dickinson County

County Recorder, PO Box O.E., Spirit Lake, IA 51360. RE & UCC recording phone-712-336-1495; fax-712-336-2677; hours: 8AM-4:30PM
Records indexed on computer back to 1993. Only the public may search. Copy fee $1.00 per page. Tax lien copy- $5.00 per page. Cert fee- $5.00 per doc plus copy fee. Payee- Dickinson County Recorder. **Online access to Assessor, Property records:** Access to the assessor database of property and sales data is free at www.iowaassessors.com. **Other phones:** Treasurer- 712-336-1205; Vital Records- 712-336-1495. **Assessor-** 712-336-2687.

Dubuque County

County Recorder, 720 Central #9; Courthouse, Dubuque, IA 52001. RE & UCC recording phone-563-589-4434; fax-319-589-4484; hours: 8:30AM-5PM www.dubuquecounty.org
Records indexed on a public use terminal back to 1988. Office will perform a UCC search but public must search other records themselves. Search fee $5.00. Copy fee $1.00 per page. Cert fee- $2.00 per doc plus copy fee. Payee- Dubuque County Recorder. **Online access to Assessor, Property records:** Access to the assessor database of property and sales data is free at www.iowaassessors.com. **Other phones:** Treasurer- 563-589-4436; Elections- 563-589-4458; Vital Records- 563-589-4434. **Property tax/Assessor-** 563-589-4432.

Emmet County

County Recorder, 609 1st Ave North, Estherville, IA 51334. RE & UCC recording phone-712-362-4115; fax-712-362-7454; hours: 8AM-4:30PM
All records in one index. Only the public may search. General copy fee $1.00 per page. RE record copy- $.50 per page. Cert fee- $5.00 per doc plus copy fee. Payee- Emmet County Recorder. **Online access to Real Estate, Assessor, Property records:** Access to real estate records on the county database are free at www.emmet.org/pmc. Also, the GIS mapping database may be searched. Includes parcel report, survey section grid, parcel maps, and more. Search the "Parcel Data" link by owner name, parcel ID, or address. Search Page or Disclaimer Page is: www.record32@netins.net. Also, access to the assessor database of property and sales data is free at www.iowaassessors.com. **Other phones:** Treasurer- 712-362-3824; Appraiser/Auditor- 712-362-2609; Elections- 712-362-4261; Vital Records- 712-362-4115; Clerk of Court- 712-362-3325. **Property tax/Assessor-** 712-362-2609.

Fayette County

County Recorder, PO Box 226, West Union, IA 52175-0226. 563-422-3687; fax-563-422-3739; hours: 8AM-4PM www.fayettecounty.ia.com
All records in one index. Records indexed on a public use terminal back to 1985. Office personnel or visitors may perform searches. Search fee $5.00 per name. Will not search real estate records. Copy fee $1.00 per page. RE record copy- $.50 per page. Cert fee- $5.00 per cert plus $.50 per page copy fee. Payee- Fayette County Recorder. **Online access to Most Wanted, Assessor, Property records:** Search for Fayette County most wanted at www.fayettecountysheriff.com/mostwanted.htm. Access to the assessor database of property and sales data is free at www.iowaassessors.com. **Other phones:** Treasurer- 563-422-3787; Elections- 563-422-3497; Vital Records- 563-422-3680. **Property tax/Assessor-** PO Box 167, West Union, IA; 563-422-3397.

Floyd County

County Recorder, 101 S Main; Courthouse, Charles City, IA 50616. RE & UCC recording phone-641-257-6154; fax-641-228-6458; hours: 8AM-4:30PM www.floydcoia.org

All records in one index. Only the public may search. Copy fee $.50 per page, $1.00 per page to fax. Cert fee- $5.00 per doc plus copy fee. Payee- Floyd County Recorder. **Online access to Assessor, Property, Real Estate, Deed, Lien, UCC, Judgment records:** Also, access to the assessor database of property and sales data is free at www.iowaassessors.com. Also, access land records at http://iowalandrecords.org after registering. Free searching and pdf images of deeds, liens, UCCs, judgments; may begin charging at any time. Monitor for new documents and save documents. **Other phones:** Treasurer- 641-257-6118; Elections- 641-257-6131; Vital Records- 641-257-6154. **Property tax/Assessor-** same address as above. 641-257-6152.

Franklin County

County Recorder, PO Box 26, Hampton, IA 50441. 641-456-5675; fax-641-456-6009; hours: 8AM-4PM
All records in one index, After 1985. Records indexed on a public use terminal back to 10/1/2001. Only the public may search. Copy fee $1.00, if real estate $.25 per page. Cert fee- $5.00 per doc plus copy fee. Payee- Franklin County Recorder. **Online access to Real Estate, Deed, Lien, UCC, Judgment records:** Access land records at http://iowalandrecords.org after registering. Free searching and pdf images of deeds, liens, UCCs, judgments; may begin charging at any time. Monitor for new documents and save documents. **Other phones:** Treasurer- 641-456-5678; Elections- 641-456-5622. **Property tax/Assessor-** 641-456-5118.

Fremont County

County Recorder, PO Box 295, Sidney, IA 51652. RE & UCC recording phone-712-374-2315; fax-712-374-2826; hours: 8AM-4:30PM www.co.fremont.ia.us
All records in one index. Records indexed on a public use terminal back to 1984. Office will perform a UCC search but public must search other records themselves. Search fee $6.00. Copy fee $1.00 per page. RE or tax lien copy- $.50 per page. Cert fee- $5.00 per doc plus copy fee. Payee- Fremont County Recorder. **Online access to Real Estate, Deed, Lien, UCC, Judgment records:** Access land records at http://iowalandrecords.org after registering. Free searching and pdf images of deeds, liens, UCCs, judgments; may begin charging at any time. Monitor for new documents and save documents. **Other phones:** Treasurer- 712-374-2122; Elections- 712-374-2031; Vital Records- 712-374-2315. **Property tax/Assessor-** PO Box 760, Sidney, IA 51652; 712-374-2631.

Greene County

County Recorder, 114 N. Chestnut; Courthouse, Jefferson, IA 50129. RE & UCC recording phone-515-386-5670; fax-515-386-5274; hours: 8AM-4:30PM
All records in one index alpha. Office will perform a UCC or tax line search but public must search other records themselves. UCC search per debtor name- $5.00. Separate federal/state combined tax lien search- $6.00 per debtor. Copy fee $1.00, if real estate $.25 per page. $1.25 per page if mailed. Cert fee- $5.00 per doc plus copy fee. Payee- Greene County Recorder. **Online access to Assessor, Property, Real Estate, Deed, Lien, UCC, Judgment records:** Access to the assessor database of property and sales data is free at www.iowaassessors.com. Also, access land records at http://iowalandrecords.org after registering. Free searching and pdf images of deeds, liens, UCCs, judgments; may begin charging at any time. Monitor for new documents and save documents. **Other phones:** Treasurer- 515-386-5675; Appraiser/Auditor- 515-386-5680; Elections- 515-386-5680; Vital Records- 515-386-5670. **Assessor-** same address as above. 515-386-5660.

Grundy County

County Recorder, 706 G Ave, Grundy Center, IA 50638-1447. RE & UCC recording phone-319-824-3234; fax-319-824-3017; hours: 8AM-4:30PM

Office will perform a UCC search but public must search other records themselves. Search fee $6.00 per name. Copy fee $1.00 per page. Cert fee- $5.00 per doc plus copy fee. Payee- Grundy County Recorder. **Online access to Assessor, Property records:** Access to the assessor database of property and sales data is free at www.iowaassessors.com. **Other phones:** Treasurer- 319-824-3412; Elections- 319-824-3122; Vital Records- 319-824-3234. **Assessor-** 319-824-6216.

Guthrie County

County Recorder, 200 N. 5th; Courthouse, Guthrie Center, IA 50115. RE & UCC recording phone-641-747-3412; fax-641-747-3081; hours: 8AM-4:30PM
All records in one index. Records indexed on computer back to 1987. Only the public may search. General copy fee $5.00, if real estate $.25 per page. Cert fee- $5.00 per doc plus copy fee. Payee- Guthrie County Recorder. **Online access to Assessor, Property records:** Access to the assessor database of property and sales data is free at www.iowaassessors.com. **Other phones:** Treasurer- 641-747-3414; Appraiser/Auditor- 641-747-3319; Elections- 641-747-3619; Vital Records- 641-747-3412. **Property tax/Assessor-** same address as above. 641-747-3319.

Hamilton County

County Recorder, PO Box 126, Webster City, IA 50595-0126. 515-832-9535; fax-515-832-8620; hours: 8AM-4:30PM
Office personnel or visitors may perform searches. Search fee $6.00 per name. Copy fee $1.00 per page. RE record copy- $.50 per page. Cert fee- $5.00 1st page, $.50 each add'l. Payee- Hamilton County Recorder. **Online access to Assessor, Property, Real Estate, Deed, Lien, UCC, Judgment records:** Access to the assessor database of property and sales data is free at www.iowaassessors.com. Also, access land records at http://iowalandrecords.org after registering. Free searching and pdf images of deeds, liens, UCCs, judgments; may begin charging at any time. Monitor for new documents and save documents. **Other phones:** Treasurer- 515-832-9542. **Property tax/Assessor-** 515-832-9505.

Hancock County

County Recorder, 855 State St, Garner, IA 50438. Main phone & R/E recording-641-923-2464, UCC recording phone-641-923-2404; fax-641-923-3912; 8AM-4PM
Only the public may search. Copy fee $1.00 per page. RE or tax lien copy- $.50 per page. Cert fee- $5.00 per doc plus copy fee. Payee- Hancock County Recorder. **Other phones:** Treasurer- 641-923-3122; Appraiser/Auditor- 641-923-2269; Vital Records- 641-923-2464. **Assessor-** 641-923-2269.

Hardin County

County Recorder, PO Box 443, Eldora, IA 50627. 641-939-8178; fax-641-939-8245; hours: 8AM-4:30PM
Office will perform a UCC search but public must search other records themselves. UCC search per debtor name- $5.00. UCC search request using non-standard form (per name)- $6.00. Copy fee $1.00, if real estate $.25 per page. Cert fee- $5.00 per cert plus copy fee. Payee- Hardin County Recorder. **Other phones:** Treasurer- 641-939-8226; Appraiser/Auditor- 641-939-8230; Drivers License- 641-939-8328. **Assessor-** 641-939-8100.

Harrison County

County Recorder, Courthouse, Logan, IA 51546. RE & UCC recording phone-712-644-2545; fax-712-644-3157; hours: 8AM-4:30PM
Office personnel or visitors may perform searches. Search fee $5.00 per name. Will not search real estate records. Copy fee $1.00 per page. RE record copy- $.50 per page. Cert fee- $5.00 per doc plus copy fee. Payee- Harrison County Recorder. **Online access to Assessor, Property records:** Access to the assessor database of property and sales data is free at www.iowaassessors.com. **Other phones:** Treasurer-

712-644-2750; Elections- 712-644-2401; Vital Records- 712-644-2545. **Assessor-** 712-644-3101.

Henry County

County Recorder, PO Box 106, Mount Pleasant, IA 52641. 319-385-0765; fax-319-385-3601; hours: 8AM-4:30PM
All records in one index. Records indexed on a public use terminal back to 1984. Office will perform a UCC search but public must search other records themselves. UCC search per debtor name- $5.00. Copy fee $.50 per page. Cert fee- $5.00 per page plus copy fee. Payee- Henry County Recorder. **Other phones:** Treasurer- 319-385-0763; Elections- 319-385-0756; Vital Records- 319-385-0765. **Property tax/Assessor-** PO Box 149, Mt. Pleasant, IA 52641; 319-385-0750.

Howard County

County Recorder, 137 N Elm; Court House, Cresco, IA 52136. 563-547-3621; fax-319-547-1103; hours: 8AM-4:30PM
Office personnel or visitors may perform searches. Search fee $5.00 per name. Copy fee $1.00 per page. RE or tax lien copy- $.50 per page. Cert fee- $5.00 per doc plus copy fee. Payee- Howard County Recorder. **Online access to Real Estate, Deed, Lien, UCC, Judgment records:** Access land records at http://iowalandrecords.org after registering. Free searching and pdf images of deeds, liens, UCCs, judgments; may begin charging at any time. Monitor for new documents and save documents. **Other phones:** Treasurer- 563-547-3860; Vital Records- 563-547-3621. **Property tax/Assessor-** 563-547-3409.

Humboldt County

County Recorder, PO Box 100, Dakota City, IA 50529-0100. 515-332-3693; fax-515-332-1738; 8-4:30PM
Separate indices to search. Records indexed on a public use terminal back to 7/1/1997. Only the public may search. General copy fee $1.00 per page. Real estate or tax lien record copy- $.25 per page. Cert fee- $5.00 1st page, $1.00 each add'l, plus copy fee. Payee- Humboldt County Recorder. **Other phones:** Treasurer- 515-332-1681; Elections- 515-332-1571; Vital Records- 515-332-3693. **Assessor-** same address as above. 515-332-1463.

Ida County

County Recorder, 401 Moorehead; Courthouse, Ida Grove, IA 51445. RE & UCC recording phone-712-364-2220; fax-712-364-3939; hours: 8AM-4:30PM
Office personnel or visitors may perform searches. Search fee $5.00 per name. Will not search real estate records. Copy fee $.25 per page. Cert fee- $5.00 per doc plus copy fee. Payee- Ida County Recorder. **Other phones:** Treasurer- 712-364-2287; Elections- 712-364-2620; Vital Records- 712-364-2220. **Property tax/Assessor-** 712-364-3622.

Iowa County

County Recorder, PO Box 185, Marengo, IA 52301. RE & UCC recording phone-319-642-3622; fax-319-642-5562; hours: 7:30AM-4:30PM www.co.iowa.ia.us/recorder.htm
All records in one index. Records indexed on a public use terminal back to 1992. Only the public may search. Copy fee $1.00 per page. Cert fee- $5.00 per doc & $2.00 per page. Payee- Iowa County Recorder. **Online access to Real Estate, Grantor/Grantee, Assessor, Property records:** Access real estate records free at http://65.240.48.153/index.html. Access to the assessor database of property and sales data is free at www.iowaassessors.com. **Other phones:** Treasurer- 319-642-3672; Elections- 319-642-3923; Vital Records- 319-642-3622. **Assessor-** 319-642-3851.

Jackson County

County Recorder, 201 W. Platt; Courthouse, Maquoketa, IA 52060. RE & UCC recording phone-563-652-2504; fax-563-652-6460; hours: 8AM-4:30PM www.jacksoncountyiowa.com

Records indexed on computer back to 1987. Only the public may search. RE record copy- $.50 per page. Cert fee- $5.00 and $1.00 per page for real estate filings, Vital records cert $15.00 each. Payee- Jackson County Recorder. **Online access to Land, Deed, Lien, UCC, Judgment records:** Access land records may be available at http://iowalandrecords.org after registering. Free searching and pdf images of deeds, liens, UCCs, judgments; may begin charging at any time. Monitor for new documents and save documents. **Other phones:** Treasurer- 563-652-5649; Elections- 563-652-3144; Vital Recs- 563-652-2504. **Assessor-** 563-652-4935.

Jasper County

County Recorder, PO Box 665, Newton, IA 50208. 641-792-5442, R/E recording phone-647-792-5442, UCC recording phone-647-792-5442; fax-641-791-3680; hours: 8AM-5PM
All records in one index. Office will perform a UCC search but public must search other records themselves. UCC search per debtor name- $5.00. UCC search request using non-standard form (per name)- $6.00. Copy fee $1.00 per page. Fee to fax back- $2.00 per page. Cert fee- $5.00 per doc, up to 10 pages, $.25 each add'l page plus copy fee. Payee- Jasper County Recorder. **Online access to Assessor, Property records:** Access to the assessor database of property and sales data is free at www.iowaassessors.com. **Other phones:** Treasurer- 641-792-6115; Elections- 641-792-7350; Vital Records- 647-792-5442. **Property tax/Assessor-** same address as above. 641-792-6195.

Jefferson County

County Recorder, 51 W. Briggs, Fairfield, IA 52556-2820. 641-472-4331, R/E recording phone-641-472-2840, UCC recording phone-641-472-2840; fax-641-472-2597; hours: 8AM-4:30PM
All records in one index. Will not search real estate records. Will search UCC records; search includes tax liens if requested. UCC search per debtor name- $5.00. UCC search request using non-standard form (per name)- $6.00. State tax lien searches are uncertified and performed at no charge. Separate federal tax lien search- $6.00 per debtor. Separate state tax lien search-No charge. Separate federal/state combined tax lien search- $6.00 per debtor. Copy fee $1.00 per page. RE record copy- $.50 per page. Cert fee- $2.00 per doc plus $.50 per page. Payee- Jefferson County Recorder. **Online access to Assessor, Property records:** Access to the assessor database of property and sales data is free at www.iowaassessors.com. Statewide recorder's website to be ready 7/1/2005 at www.clris.com. **Other phones:** Treasurer- 641-472-2349; Appraiser/Auditor-641-472-2840; Vital Records- 641-472-2840. **Property tax/Assessor-** PO Box 308, Fairfield, Fairfield, IA 52556-0308; 641-472-2849.

Johnson County

County Recorder, 913 S. Dubuque St, #202, Iowa City, IA 52240-4207. 319-356-6093; fax-319-339-6181; hours: 8AM-4PM M,W,F; 8AM-5:30PM T,Th www.johnson-county.com
Office will perform a UCC search but public must search other records themselves. Search fee $5.00 per name. Copy fee $1.00, if real estate $.25 per page. Cert fee- $2.00 per doc plus copy fee. Payee- Johnson County Recorder. **Online access to Assessor, Property records:** Access to assessor property and sales data is free at www.johnson-ia-assessor.org/pmc/default.asp?pid=. Also, access to Iowa City assessor and property data is free at http://iowacity.iowaassessors.com. **Other phones:** Treasurer- 319-356-6087; Elections- 319-356-6004; Vital recs- 319-356-6093. **Assessor-** 319-356-6078.

Jones County

County Recorder, 500 W Main; Courthouse, Rm 116, Anamosa, IA 52205-1632. RE & UCC recording phone-319-462-2477; fax-319-462-5802; hours: 8AM-4:30PM www.co.jones.ia.us/recorder.html

Index: Pre-199e records in a number of indices. Owner, mortgage, and property transfer self-searches available. Will search UCC records, but not tax liens. UCC search per debtor name- $5.00. Copy fee $1.00 per page. Real estate or tax lien record copy- $.50 per page. Cert fee- $5.00 per doc plus copy fee. Payee- Jones County Recorder. **Other phones:** Treasurer- 319-462-3550; Elections- 319-462-2282; Vital Records- 319-462-2477. **Assessor-** 500 W Main St, Anamosa, IA 52205; 319-462-2671.

Keokuk County

County Recorder, 101 S. Main St.; Courthouse, Sigourney, IA 52591. RE & UCC recording phone-641-622-2540; fax-641-622-3789; hours: 8AM-4:30PM www.keokukcountyia.com
All records in one index. Office personnel or visitors may perform searches. Search fee $5.00. Will not search real estate records. Copy fee $1.00 per page. Cert fee- $5.00 1st page; $1.00 each add'l page. Payee- Keokuk County Recorder. **Online access to Real Estate, Deed, Lien, UCC, Judgment, Assessor, Property records:** Access land records at http://iowalandrecords.org after registering. Free searching and pdf images of deeds, liens, UCCs, judgments; may begin charging at any time. Monitor for new documents and save documents. Access to the assessor database of property and sales data is free at www.iowaassessors.com. **Other phones:** Treasurer- 641-622-2421; Elections- 641-622-2320; Vital Records- 641-622-2540. **Assessor-** 641-622-2560.

Kossuth County

County Recorder, 114 W. State, Algona, IA 50511. 515-295-5660; fax-515-295-3071; hours: 8AM-4PM
Only the public may search. Copy fee $1.00 per page. RE record copy- $.50 per page. Tax lien copy- $5.00 per page. Cert fee- $5.00 1st page, $2.50 each add'l. Payee- Kossuth County Recorder. **Online access to Assessor, Property, Real Estate, Deed, Lien, UCC, Judgment records:** Access to the assessor database of property and sales data is free at www.iowaassessors.com. Also, access land records at http://iowalandrecords.org after registering. Free searching and pdf images of deeds, liens, UCCs, judgments; may begin charging at any time. Monitor for new documents and save documents. **Other phones:** Treasurer- 515-295- 3404. **Property tax/Assessor-** 515-295-3857.

Lee County (Northern District)

County Recorder, PO Box 322, Fort Madison, IA 52627-0322. RE & UCC recording phone-319-372-4662; fax-319-372-7033; hours: 8:30AM-4:30PM www.leecounty.org
All records in one index. Records indexed on a public use terminal back to 1984. Office personnel or visitors may perform searches. Will not search real estate records. Will search UCC records, tax liens not included in UCC search. UCC search per debtor name- $5.00. Separate federal tax lien search- $6.00 per debtor. This agency will not do a state tax lien search. Copy fee $1.00 per page. RE record copy- $.35 per page. Cert fee- $5.00 per cert plus copy fee. Payee- Lee County Recorder. **Online access to Real Estate, Deed, Lien, UCC, Judgment records:** Access land records at http://iowalandrecords.org after registering. Free searching and pdf images of deeds, liens, UCCs, judgments; may begin charging at any time. Monitor for new documents and save documents. **Other phones:** Treasurer- 319-372-3405; Elections- 319-372-3705; Vital Records- 319-372-4662. **Property tax/Assessor-** 319-372-6302.

Lee County (Southern District)

County Recorder, PO Box 160, Keokuk, IA 52632. RE & UCC recording phone-319-524-1126; fax-319-524-1544; hours: 8:30AM-4:30PM www.leecounty.org
All records in one index. Records indexed on a public use terminal back to 1984. Office will perform a UCC or tax line search but public must search other records themselves. UCC search

request must be on correct form. UCC search per debtor name- $5.00. Separate federal tax lien search- $6.00 per debtor. Copy fee $1.00 per page. RE record copy- $.35 per page. Cert fee- $5.00 per doc plus copy fee. Payee- Lee County Recorder. **Online access to Real Estate, Deed, Lien, UCC, Judgment records:** Access land records at http://iowalandrecords.org after registering. Free searching and pdf images of deeds, liens, UCCs, judgments; may begin charging at any time. Monitor for new documents and save documents. **Other phones:** Treasurer- 319-524-1550; Appraiser/Auditor- 319-524-2482; Elections- 319-524-2482; Vital Records- 319-524-1126. **Property tax/Assessor-** 319-524-1375.

Linn County

County Recorder, PO Box 1406, Cedar Rapids, IA 52406-1406. RE & UCC recording phone-319-892-5420; fax-319-892-5459; hours: 8AM-5PM www.linncountyrecorder.com
All records in one index. Records indexed on a public use terminal back to 1975. Office will perform a UCC search but public must search other records themselves. UCC search per debtor name- $5.00. Copy fee $1.00 per page. Cert fee- $5.00 per doc, plus copy fee. Payee- Linn County Recorder. **Online access to Assessor, Property, Real Estate, Deed, Lien, UCC, Judgment records:** Access to the assessor database of property and sales data is free at www.iowaassessors.com. Also, access to City of Cedar Rapids property information is free at www.cedar-rapids-assessor.org/pmc/. No name searching. Access county land records at http://iowalandrecords.org after registering. Free searching and pdf images of deeds, liens, UCCs, judgments; may begin charging at any time. Monitor for new documents and save documents. **Other phones:** Treasurer- 319-892-5550; Elections- 319-892-5400; Vital Records- 319-892-5445. **Property tax/Assessor-** same address as above. 319-892-5220.

Louisa County

County Recorder, PO Box 264, Wapello, IA 52653-0264. 319-523-5361; fax-319-523-5364; 8-4:30PM
Office will perform a UCC search but public must search other records themselves. UCC search per debtor name- $6.00, $5.00 for add'l page. Copy fee $1.00 per page. Cert fee- $5.00 per cert plus copy fee. Payee- Louisa County Recorder.

Lucas County

County Recorder, 916 Braden, Courthouse, Chariton, IA 50049. 641-774-2413; fax-641-774-1619; hours: 8AM-4PM
Only the public may search. Copy fee $1.00 per page. RE or tax lien copy- $.25 per page. Cert fee- $5.00 per doc plus $1.00 per page. Payee- Lucas County Recorder. **Other phones:** Treasurer- 641-774-5213. **Property tax/Assessor-** 641-774-4411.

Lyon County

County Recorder, 206 Second Ave; Courthouse, Rock Rapids, IA 51246. RE & UCC recording phone-712-472-2381; fax-712-472-2381; hours: 8AM-4:30PM
Office personnel or visitors may perform searches. Search fee $6.00 per name. Will not search real estate records. Copy fee $1.00 per page. Cert fee- $5.00 per doc plus copy fee. Payee- Lyon County Recorder. **Online access to Assessor, Property records:** Access to the assessor database of property and sales data is free at www.iowaassessors.com. **Other phones:** Treasurer- 712-472-3703; Elections- 712-472-3713; Vital Records- 712-472-2381. **Property tax/Assessor-** 712-472-3592.

Madison County

County Recorder, PO Box 152, Winterset, IA 50273-0152. RE & UCC recording phone-515-462-3771; fax-515-462-5881; 8AM-4:30PM www.madisoncoia.us
All records in one index. Records indexed on a public use terminal back to 1987. Office personnel or visitors may perform searches. Will not search real estate records. UCC search per debtor name-

$5.00. UCC search request using non-standard form (per name)- $6.00. Federal tax lien search- $6.00; $5.00 for state tax lien. Copy fee $.50 per page. Cert fee- $5.00 per doc plus copy fee. Payee- Madison County Recorder. **Online access to Assessor, Property records:** Access to the assessor database of property and sales data is free at www.iowaassessors.com. **Other phones:** Treasurer- 515-462-1542; Elections- 515-462-3914; Vital Records- 515-462-3771. **Property tax/Assessor-** 515-462-4303.

Mahaska County

County Recorder, 106 S.1st. St; Courthouse, Oskaloosa, IA 52577. RE & UCC recording phone-641-673-8187; hours: 8AM-4:30PM

Only the public may search. Copy fee $1.00 per page. Cert fee- $10.00 per doc plus copy fee. Payee- Mahaska County Recorder. **Online access to Assessor, Property records:** Access to the assessor database of property and sales data is free at www.iowaassessors.com. **Other phones:** Treasurer- 641-673-5482; Vital Records- 641-673-8187. **Property tax/Assessor-** 641-673-5805.

Marion County

County Recorder, 214 E. Main St., Knoxville, IA 50138. RE & UCC recording phone-641-828-2211; fax-641-828-3538; hours: 8AM-4:30PM

Records indexed on a public use terminal back to 1986. Will not search real estate records. May search UCC records. UCC search includes tax liens if requested. UCC search per debtor name- $5.00. UCC search request using non-standard form (per name)- $6.00. Separate federal/state combined tax lien search- $6.00 per debtor. Copy fee $1.00 per page. Cert fee- $5.00 per doc plus copy fee. Payee- Marion County Recorder. **Online access to Assessor, Property records:** Access to the assessor database of property and sales data is free at www.iowaassessors.com. **Other phones:** Treasurer- 641-828-2202; Vital Records- 641-828-2211. **Property tax/Assessor-** 641-828-2215.

Marshall County

County Recorder, PO Box 573, Marshalltown, IA 50158-0573. 641-754-6355, R/E recording phone-641-754-6323; fax-641-754-6349; hours: 8AM-4:30PM www.co.marshall.ia.us

All records in one index. Records indexed on a public use terminal back to 7/1983. Office will perform a UCC search but public must search other records themselves. Search fee $6.00. Copy fee $.50. per page. Cert fee- $5.00 per doc plus copy fee. Payee- Marshall County Recorder. **Online access to Assessor, Property records:** Access to the assessor's property record card system is free at www.co.marshall.ia.us/departments/assessor/disclaimer_html. Also, access to the assessor database of property and sales data is free at www.iowaassessors.com. **Other phones:** Treasurer- 641-754-6366; Elections- 641-754-6302; Vital Records- 641-754-6355; Auditor- 641-754-6323. **Property tax/Assessor-** 1 E. Main St., Marshalltown, IA 50158; 641-754-6305.

Mills County

County Recorder, 418 Sharp St; Courthouse, Glenwood, IA 51534. 712-527-9315; fax-712-527-1507; hours: 8AM-4:30PM

Office will perform a UCC search but public must search other records themselves. UCC search per debtor name- $5.00. Copy fee $1.00 per page. Cert fee- $5.00 per doc plus copy fee. Payee- Mills County Recorder. **Online access to Assessor, Property, Real Estate, Deed, Lien, UCC, Judgment records:** Access to the assessor database of property and sales data is free at www.iowaassessors.com. Also, access land records at http://iowalandrecords.org after registering. Free searching and pdf images of deeds, liens, UCCs, judgments; may begin charging at any time. Monitor for new documents and save documents. **Other phones:** Treasurer- 712-527-4419. **Property tax/Assessor-** 712-527-4883.

Mitchell County

County Recorder, 508 State St, Osage, IA 50461-1250. RE & UCC recording phone-641-732-5861; fax-641-732-5218; hours: 8AM-4:30PM

Records indexed on computer from July, 2000 to present, prior to July, 2000 indexed in books. Office will perform a UCC search but public must search other records themselves. UCC search per debtor name- $5.00. UCC search request using non-standard form (per name)- $6.00. Copy fee $.50 per page. Cert fee- $5.00 per doc plus copy fee. Payee- Mitchell County Recorder. **Online access to Real Estate, Deed, Lien, UCC, Judgment records:** Access land records at http://iowalandrecords.org after registering. Free searching and pdf images of deeds, liens, UCCs, judgments; may begin charging at any time. Monitor for new documents and save documents. **Other phones:** Treasurer- 641-732-5861. **Property tax/Assessor-** same address as above. 641-732-5861.

Monona County

County Recorder, PO Box 53, Onawa, IA 51040. RE & UCC recording phone-712-423-2575; fax-712-423-3034; hours: 8AM-4:30PM

Only the public may search. Copy fee $1.00 per page. RE record copy- $.50 per page. Cert fee- $5.00 per page. Payee- Monona County Recorder. **Online access to Assessor, Property records:** Access to the assessor database of property and sales data is free at www.iowaassessors.com. **Other phones:** Treasurer- 712-423-2271; Elections- 712-423-2191; Vital Records- 712-423-2575. **Assessor-** 712-423-2271.

Monroe County

County Recorder, 10 Benton Ave. East; Courthouse, Albia, IA 52531. 641-932-5164; fax-641-932-2863; hours: 8AM-4PM

Real estate owner, mortgage, and property transfer searches available. Will search UCC records, but not tax liens. UCC search per debtor name- $5.00. UCC search request using non-standard form (per name)- $6.00. Copy fee $1.00 per page, $.25 self serve. Cert fee- $5.00 per doc plus $.25 per page. Payee- Monroe County Recorder. **Other phones:** Treasurer- 641-932-5011. **Property tax/Assessor-** 641-932-2180.

Montgomery County

County Recorder, PO Box 469, Red Oak, IA 51566. RE & UCC recording phone-712-623-4363; fax-712-623-8915; hours: 8AM-4:30PM

Records indexed on a public use terminal back to 1987. Only the public may search. Copy fee $1.00 per page. RE record copy- $.50 per page. Cert fee- $5.00 per cert plus copy fee. Payee- Montgomery County Recorder. **Online access to Assessor, Property, Real Estate, Deed, Lien, UCC, Judgment records:** Access to the assessor database of property and sales data is free at www.iowaassessors.com. Also, access land records at http://iowalandrecords.org after registering. Free searching and pdf images of deeds, liens, UCCs, judgments; may begin charging at any time. Monitor for new documents and save documents. **Other phones:** Treasurer- 712-623-2392; Appraiser/Auditor- 712-623-4171; Elections- 712-623-5127; Vital Records- 712-623-4363. **Property tax/Assessor-** 712-623-4171.

Muscatine County

County Recorder, 401 E. 3rd St; Courthouse, Muscatine, IA 52761-4166. RE & UCC recording phone-563-263-7741; fax-563-263-7248; hours: 8AM-4:30PM www.co.muscatine.ia.us

Office personnel or visitors may perform searches. Search fee $6.00 per name. Copy fee $1.00 per page; fee to fax back- $1.50 per page. Federal Tax lien copy- $5.00 per page. Cert fee- $5.00 per doc plus copy fee. Payee- Muscatine County Recorder. **Online access to Property, GIS-mapping, Assessor records:** Access to property data on the GIS service is free at www.magic-gis.org/pmc/main.asp?page=query. No name searching. Access to the assessor database of

property and sales data is free at www.iowaassessors.com. **Other phones:** Treasurer- 563-263-7113; Elections- 563-263-5821; Vital Records- 563-263-7741. **Assessor-** 563-263-7061.

O'Brien County

County Recorder, PO Box 340, Primghar, IA 51245-0340. RE & UCC recording phone-712-957-3045; fax-712-957-3046; hours: 8AM-4:30PM www.obriencounty.com/government/recorder.htm

Will do verbal record searches on computer back to 1988, but will not guarantee results. All records in one index. Will not search real estate records. Will not search UCC records. Will search tax liens. Federal/state combined tax lien search fee- $5.00 per page. Copy fee $1.00 per page. RE record copy- $.50 per page or $1.00 per page in older books. Cert fee- $5.00 per doc plus copy fee. Payee- O'Brien County Recorder. **Other phones:** Treasurer- 712-957-3210 or 4185; Elections- 712-957-3225; Vital Records- 712-957-3045; Clerk of Court- 712-957-3255. **Property tax/Assessor-** PO Box 446, Primghar, IA 51245; 712-957-3205.

Osceola County

County Recorder, 300 7th St; Courthouse, Sibley, IA 51249-1695. RE & UCC recording phone-712-754-3345; fax-712-754-3743; hours: 8AM-4:30PM

All records in one index. Records indexed on a public use terminal back to 1985. Office will perform a UCC search but public must search other records themselves. Search fee $6.00 per name. Copy fee $1.00 per page. Cert fee- $5.00 per cert plus copy fee. Payee- Osceola County Recorder. **Online access to Real Estate, Deed, Lien, UCC, Judgment records:** Access land records at http://iowalandrecords.org after registering. Free searching and pdf images of deeds, liens, UCCs, judgments; may begin charging at any time. Monitor for new documents and save documents. **Other phones:** Treasurer- 712-754-3217; Elections- 712-754-2241; Vital Records- 712-754-3345; Assessor- 712-754-3438. **Assessor-** same address as above. 712-754-3438.

Page County

County Recorder, 112 E. Main St.; Courthouse, Clarinda, IA 51632. 712-542-3130; fax-712-542-3636; hours: 8AM-4:30PM

Office personnel or visitors may perform searches. Search fee $11.00 per name. Will not search UCC records. Copy fee $1.00 per page. RE record copy- $.50 per page. Tax lien copy- $5.00 per page. Cert fee- $5.00 per doc plus copy fee. Payee- Page County Recorder. **Online access to Land, Deed, Lien, UCC, Judgment records:** Access land records may be available at http://iowalandrecords.org after registering. Free searching and pdf images of deeds, liens, UCCs, judgments; may begin charging at any time. Monitor for new documents and save documents. **Other phones:** Treasurer- 712-542-5322. **Property tax/Assessor-** 712-542-2516.

Palo Alto County

County Recorder, PO Box 248, Emmetsburg, IA 50536. RE & UCC recording phone-712-852-3701; fax-712-852-3704; hours: 8AM-4PM

All records in one index. Records indexed on a public use terminal back to 1984. Only the public may search. Copy fee $.50 per page. Cert fee- $5.00 per cert + $.50 per page. Payee- Palo Alto County Recorder. **Online access to Real Estate, Deed, Lien, UCC, Judgment, Assessor, Property records:** Access land records at http://iowalandrecords.org after registering. Free searching and pdf images of deeds, liens, UCCs, judgments; may begin charging at any time. Monitor for new documents and save documents. Access to the assessor database of property and sales data is free at www.iowaassessors.com. **Other phones:** Treasurer- 712-852-3844; Elections- 712-852-2924; Vital Records- 712-852-3701. **Property tax/Assessor-** 712-852-3823.

Plymouth County

County Recorder, 215 4th Ave. SE; Courthouse, Le Mars, IA 51031. 712-546-4020; hours: 8AM-5PM
Will not search real estate records. Will search UCC records, tax liens not included in UCC search. UCC search per debtor name- $5.00. UCC search request using non-standard form (per name)- $6.00. Tax lien search fee- $6.00 per debtor. Separate federal tax lien search- $6.00 per debtor. Separate state tax lien search- $6.00 per debtor. Copy fee $1.00 per page. Cert fee- $5.00 per certification; add'l $.50 per page. Payee- Plymouth County Recorder. **Online access to Assessor, Property, Real Estate, Deed, Lien, UCC, Judgment records:** Access to the assessor database of property and sales data is free at www.iowaassessors.com. Also, access land records at http://iowalandrecords.org after registering. Free searching and pdf images of deeds, liens, UCCs, judgments; may begin charging at any time. Monitor for new documents and save documents. **Other phones:** Treasurer- 712-546-4020.

Pocahontas County

County Recorder, 99 Court Sq, Pocahontas, IA 50574-1621. RE & UCC recording phone-712-335-4404; fax-712-335-4502; hours: 8AM-4PM
Separate indices to search include deeds, mortgage, miscellaneous. Records indexed on computer back to 1991. Office personnel or visitors may perform searches. Office will perform very limited searches; may search for a name for free. UCC or tax lien search per debtor name- $6.00. Copy fee $1.00, if real estate $.25 per page. Cert fee- $5.00 per cert plus copy fee. Payee-Pocahontas County Recorder. **Online access to Land, Deed, Lien, UCC, Judgment records:** Access land records may be available at http://iowalandrecords.org after registering. Free searching and pdf images of deeds, liens, UCCs, judgments; may begin charging at any time. Monitor for new documents and save documents. **Other phones:** Treasurer- 712-335-4334; Vital Records- 712-335-4404. **Property tax/Assessor-** same address as above. 712-335-5016.

Polk County

County Recorder, 111 Court Ave, Rm 250; County Admin. Bldg., Des Moines, IA 50309. Main phone & R/E recording-515-286-3160, UCC recording phone-515-286-2241; fax-515-323-5393; hours: 8AM-4:30PM http://recorder.co.polk.ia.us
All records in one index. Records indexed on a public use terminal. Office personnel or visitors may perform searches. Will not search real estate records. Will search UCC records on computer, tax liens not included in UCC search. UCC search per debtor name- $5.00. Separate federal/state combined tax lien search- $11.00 per debtor. Copy fee $.50 per page. Cert fee- $5.00 per doc plus copy fee. Payee- Polk County Recorder. **Online access to Assessor, Property, Real Estate Sale, Recording, Deed, Lien, UCC records:** Access to the Recorder's Index Search is free at http://216.81.134.113/resolution/. Also includes trade names, financing statements, and plats as well as recordings. Also, access to the Polk County assessor database is free at www.assess.co.polk.ia.us/web/basic/search.html.
Search by property or by sales. Also, download resi., commercial, or agricultural data free at www.assess.co.polk.ia.us/web/basic/exports.html. Also, access to the assessor database of property and sales data is free at www.iowaassessors.com. **Other phones:** Treasurer- 515-286-3041; Elections- 515-286-3247; Vital Records- 515-286-3781. **Property tax/Assessor-** 111 Court St #195, Des Moines, IA 50309; 515-286-3014, assessor fax- 515-286-3386.

Pottawattamie County

County Recorder, 227 S. Sixth St, Council Bluffs, IA 51501. RE & UCC recording phone-712-328-5612; fax-712-328-4738; hours: 8AM-4PM www.pottcounty.com

Records indexed on computer back to 1989. Office will perform a UCC search but public must search other records themselves. Search fee $5.00 per name. Copy fee $1.00 per page. Cert fee- $5.00 per doc plus copy fee. Payee- Pottawattamie County Recorder. **Online access to Real Estate, Property, Residential Sale, Assessor records:** Records on the County Courthouse/Council Bluffs property database are free at www.pottco.org. Search by owner name, address, or parcel number. Records since 7/1/89, images since 10/20/2002. Also, access to the assessor database of property and sales data is free at www.iowaassessors.com. **Other phones:** Treasurer- 712-328-5627; Elections- 712-328-5700 (Auditor); Vital Records- 712-328-5612; Recorder's Office Info Line- 712-328-5725. **Property tax/Assessor-** 712-328-5617.

Poweshiek County

County Recorder, PO Box 656, Montezuma, IA 50171-0656. RE & UCC recording phone-641-623-5434; fax-641-623-2875; hours: 8AM-4PM
All records in one index. Only the public may search. Copy fee $.50 per page, $2.00 if mailed. Cert fee- $5.00 per doc plus copy fee. Payee-Poweshiek County Recorder. **Online access to Assessor, Property records:** Access to the assessor database of property and sales data is free at www.iowaassessors.com. **Other phones:** Treasurer- 641-623-5128; Elections- 641-623-5434; Vital Records- 641-623-5434. **Assessor-** PO Box 516, Montezuma, IA 50171-0516; 641-623-5445.

Ringgold County

County Recorder, 109 W Madison #204, Mount Ayr, IA 50854. RE & UCC recording phone-641-464-3231; fax-641-464-2568; hours: 8AM-4PM
Office personnel or visitors may perform searches. Search fee $6.00 per name. Copy fee $1.00 per page. RE record copy- $.50 per page. Cert fee- $6.00 per doc plus copy fee. Payee- Ringgold County Recorder. **Other phones:** Treasurer- 641-464-3230; Vital Records- 641-464-3231. **Property tax/Assessor-** 641-464-3233.

Sac County

County Recorder, 100 NW State St., Sac City, IA 50583. RE & UCC recording phone-712-662-7789; fax-712-662-6298; hours: 8AM-4:30PM www.saccounty.org
Separate indices to search include computer, index books. Records indexed on computer back to 1990. Only the public may search. Copy fee $.50 per page. Cert fee- $5.00 per cert plus copy fee. Payee- Sac County Recorder. **Online access to Real Estate, Deed, Lien, UCC, Judgment records:** Assessor's property records are online for a small fee; contact the Auditors Office at 712-662-7310 or visit www.saccounty.org/features/gis.asp. Also, access land records at http://iowalandrecords.org after registering. Free searching and pdf images of deeds, liens, UCCs, judgments; live from 1/2004; may begin charging at any time. Monitor for new documents and save documents. **Other phones:** Treasurer- 712-662-7411; Appraiser/Auditor- 712-662-7310; Elections- 712-662-7310; Vital Records- 712-662-7789. **Property tax/Assessor-** same address as above. 712-662-4492, assessor fax- 712-662-7358.

Scott County

County Recorder, 428 Western Ave; 5th Fl, Davenport, IA 52801-1187. RE & UCC recording phone-563-326-8621; fax-563-328-3225; hours: 8AM-4:30PM www.scottcountyiowa.com
Separate indices to search include affidavits, Articles of Corp. Liens, Lands, Trade Names, Plats. Records indexed on a public use terminal back to 1989. Only the public may search. Copy fee $1.00 per page. Cert fee- $5.00 per doc plus copy fee. Payee- Scott County Recorder. **Online access to Assessor, Property, Real Estate, Deed, Lien, UCC, Judgment, Restaurant Inspection, Most Wanted, Sheriff Sale records:** Access land records at

http://iowalandrecords.org after registering. Free searching and pdf images of deeds, liens, UCCs, judgments; may begin charging at any time. Monitor for new documents and save documents. Also, access to assessor property records is free at www.scottcountyiowa.com/assessor/query.asp. Access to the assessor database of property and sales data is free at www.scottcountyiowa.com. Sheriff sales lists free at www.scottcountyiowa.com/sheriff/sales.php. **Other phones:** Treasurer- 563-326-8664; Elections- 563-326-8631; Vital Records- 563-326-8650. **Assessor-** same address as above. 563-326-8635.

Shelby County

County Recorder, PO Box 67, Harlan, IA 51537-0067. RE & UCC recording phone-712-755-5640; fax-712-755-7556; hours: 8AM-4:30PM www.shco.org
All records in one index. Records indexed on a public use terminal. Office personnel or visitors may perform searches. Search fee $5.00 per name. Will not search real estate records. Copy fee $1.00 per page. Cert fee- $5.00 per doc plus copy fee. Payee-Shelby County Recorder. **Online access to Real Estate Recording, Assessor, Property, Deed, Lien, UCC, Judgment records:** Access land records at http://iowalandrecords.org after registering. Free searching and pdf images of deeds, liens, UCCs, judgments; may begin charging at any time. Monitor for new documents and save documents. Also, access to the assessor database of property and sales data is free at http://shelby.iowaassessors.com. Also, access recording office land data at www.etitlesearch.com; registration required, fee based on usage. Also, access to the county GIS parcel search is free at http://maps.shco.org/pmc/main.asp?page=query. You can do a name search, fees involved. Call 870-856-3055 for subscription info. **Other phones:** Treasurer- 712-755-5898; Elections- 712-755-3831; Vital Records- 712-755-5640. **Property tax/Assessor-** same address as above. 712-755-5718.

Sioux County

County Recorder, PO Box 48, Orange City, IA 51041. RE & UCC recording phone-712-737-2229; fax-712-737-2230; 8AM-4:30PM www.siouxcounty.org
All records in one index. Will not search real estate records. Will search UCC records, tax liens not included in UCC search. UCC search per debtor name- $5.00. UCC search request using non-standard form (per name)- $6.00. Tax lien search fee- $6.00 per debtor. Copy fee $1.00 per page; if real estate $.25 per page. Cert fee- $2.00 per page includes copy fee. Payee- Sioux County Recorder. **Online access to Property Tax records:** Search the treasurer's property tax records online by subscription; for information please contact Micah Van Maanen at 712-737-6818, http://siouxcounty.org/treasurer.htm. **Other phones:** Treasurer- 712-737-3505; Appraiser/Auditor- 712-737-4274; Elections- 712-737-2216; Vital Records- 712-737-2229. **Property tax/Assessor-** PO Box 48, Orange City, IA 51041; 712-737-4274.

Story County

County Recorder, PO Box 55, Nevada, IA 50201-0055. RE & UCC recording phone-515-382-7230; fax-515-382-7326; hours: 8AM-5PM (No recording after 3:30PM) www.storycounty.com/departments.html
All records in one index. Records indexed on a public use terminal back to 1976. Office will perform a UCC and Tax lien search but public must search other records themselves. Search fee $5.00. Copy fee $1.00 per page. Cert fee- $5.00 per doc plus copy fee. Payee- Story County Recorder. **Online access to Assessor, Property Tax, Grantor/Grantee, Deed, Mortgage, UCC, Sheriff Sale, Most Wanted records:** Records on the county assessor database are free at www.storyassessor.org/pmc/. No name searching. Also, land records on the recorder's database are free at https://www.landaccess.com. Also, City of Ames property assessor data is free at www.amesassessor.org/pmc/ but no name searching. Also, the sheriff's sale and most wanted lists are at

www.storycounty.com/SheriffWeb.nsf/index.htm.
Also, access to the assessor database of property and sales data is free at www.iowaassessors.com. **Other phones:** Treasurer- 515-382-7330; Appraiser/Auditor- 515-382-7322; Elections- 515-382-7217; Vital Records- 515-382-7237; Deputy Assessor- 515-382-7322. **Property tax/Assessor-** same address as above. 515-382-7320.

Tama County

County Recorder, PO Box 82, Toledo, IA 52342. 641-484-3320; fax-641-484-5127; hours: 8AM-4:30PM
Office will perform a UCC search but public must search other records themselves. UCC search per debtor name- $5.00. Copy fee $1.00 per page. Cert fee- $5.00 per doc plus $.25 per page. Payee- Tama County Recorder. **Online access to Assessor, Property records:** Access to the assessor database of property and sales data is free at www.iowaassessors.com. **Other phones:** Treasurer- 641-484-3141. **Assessor-** 641-484-3545.

Taylor County

County Recorder, 405 Jefferson St.; Courthouse, Bedford, IA 50833. 712-523-2275; fax-712-523-2274; hours: 8AM-4:30PM
Only the public may search. Copy fee $1.00 per page. Cert fee- $2.00 per page plus copy fee. Payee- Taylor County Recorder. **Other phones:** Treasurer- 712-523-2080. **Assessor-** 712-523-2444.

Union County

County Recorder, 300 N. Pine St, Creston, IA 50801. 641-782-1725; fax-641-782-1709; 8:30AM-4:30PM
Office personnel or visitors may perform searches. Search fee $6.00 per name. Will not search tax liens. Copy fee $1.00 per page. RE or tax lien copy- $.50 per page. Cert fee- $5.00 per doc plus $.50 per page. Payee- Union County Recorder. **Other phones:** Treasurer- 641-782-1710. **Property tax/Assessor-** 641-782-1735.

Van Buren County

County Recorder, PO Box 455, Keosauqua, IA 52565. RE & UCC recording phone-319-293-3240; fax-319-293-6327; hours: 8AM-4:30PM
All records in one index. Records indexed on a public use terminal back to 7/1/1988. Only the public may search. Copy fee $1.00, if real estate $.25 per page. Cert fee- $2.50 per doc plus copy fee. Payee- Van Buren County Recorder. **Online access to Real Estate, Deed, Lien, UCC, Judgment records:** Access land records at http://iowalandrecords.org after registering. Free searching and pdf images of deeds, liens, UCCs, judgments; may begin charging at any time. Monitor for new documents and save documents. **Other phones:** Treasurer- 319-293-3110; Elections- 319-293-3129; Vital Records- 319-293-3240. **Property tax/Assessor-** same address as above. 319-293-3001.

Wapello County

County Recorder, 101 W. 4th St, Ottumwa, IA 52501. RE & UCC recording phone-641-683-0045; fax-641-683-0019; hours: 8AM-4:30PM
Office personnel or visitors may perform searches. Search fee $6.00 per name. Will not search real estate records. Copy fee $1.00 per page. Cert fee- $5.00 per doc plus copy fee. Payee- Wapello County Recorder. **Other phones:** Treasurer- 641-683-0040; Vital Records- 641-683-0045. **Property tax/Assessor-** 641-683-0088.

Warren County

County Recorder, 301 N Buxton, #109, Indianola, IA 50125. 515-961-1089; hours: 8AM-4:30PM
All records in one index. Records indexed on a public use terminal back to 1991. Office will perform a UCC search but public must search other records themselves. Mail requests must include a SASE. Search per debtor name- $5.00. Copy fee $1.00 per page. Cert fee- $5.00 per doc plus copy fee. Payee- Warren County Recorder. **Online access to Assessor, Property records:** Access to the assessor database of property and sales data is free at www.iowaassessors.com. **Other phones:** Treasurer- 515-961-1110. **Property tax/Assessor-** 515-961-1010.

Washington County

County Recorder, PO Box 889, Washington, IA 52353-0889. RE & UCC recording phone-319-653-7727; hours: 8AM-4:30PM
All records in one index. Records indexed on plats. Mortgage searches available, uncertified scan of computer index. Will not search UCC records, but will search tax liens. Tax lien search fee- $6.00 per debtor. General copy fee $1.00. Real estate copy-minimum $1.00 + $.40 per page. UCC fee- $5.00 per doc + copy fee of $.40 per page. Payee- Washington County Recorder. **Online access to Assessor, Property records:** Access to the assessor database of property and sales data is free at www.iowaassessors.com. **Other phones:** Treasurer- 319-653-7726; Elections- 319-653-7777; Vital Records- 319-653-7727. **Assessor-** 319-653-7709.

Wayne County

County Recorder, PO Box 435, Corydon, IA 50060. RE & UCC recording phone-641-872-1676; fax-641-872-2843; hours: 8AM-4PM
Separate indices to search include deeds, mortgages, mortgage release, contracts, miscellaneous. Records indexed on a public use terminal back to 1988. Only the public may search, but office can assist. General copy fee $.25 per page. UCC record copy- $1.00 per page. Cert fee- $5.00 1st page; $1.00 each add'l page, plus copy fee. Payee- Wayne County Recorder. **Online access to Land, Deed, Lien, UCC, Judgment records:** Access land records available at http://iowalandrecords.org after registering. Free searching and pdf images; may begin charging at any time. **Other phones:** Treasurer- 641-872-2515; Vital Records- 641-872-1676. **Property tax/Assessor-** same address as above. 641-872-2663.

Webster County

County Recorder, PO Box 1253, Fort Dodge, IA 50501. RE & UCC recording phone-515-576-2401; fax-515-574-3723; hours: 8AM-4:30PM
www.webstercountyia.org
Records indexed on a public use terminal back to 1994. Office will perform a UCC search but public must search other records themselves. UCC search per debtor name- $5.00. UCC search request using non-standard form (per name)- $6.00. Copy fee $1.00; tax lien copy- $1.00 per page state; $5.00 per page federal. Cert fee- $6.00 per doc plus copy fee. Payee- Webster County Recorder. **Online access to Assessor, Property, Real Estate, Deed, Lien, UCC, Judgment records:** Access to the assessor database of property and sales data is free at www.iowaassessors.com. Also, property data is free at www.webstercountyia.org Also, access land records at http://iowalandrecords.org after registering. Free searching and pdf images of deeds, liens, UCCs, judgments; may begin charging at any time. Monitor for new documents and save documents. **Other phones:** Treasurer- 515-576-2731; Elections- 515-573-7175; Vital Records- 515-576-2401. **Property tax/Assessor-** 515-576-4721.

Winnebago County

County Recorder, 126 S. Clark St #1; Courthouse, Forest City, IA 50436-1706. RE & UCC recording phone-641-585-2094; fax-641-585-1094; hours: 8AM-4:30PM
All records in one index. Records indexed on a public use terminal back to February, 1995. Only the public may search. Copy fee $.50 per page. Cert fee- $5.00 per doc plus copy fee. Payee- Winnebago County Recorder. **Online access to Assessor, Property records:** Access to the assessor database of property and sales data is free at www.iowaassessors.com. **Other phones:** Treasurer- 641-585-2322; Appraiser/Auditor- 641-585-3412; Vital Records- 641-585-2094. **Property tax/Assessor-** same address as above. 641-585-2163.

Winneshiek County

County Recorder, 201 W. Main St, Decorah, IA 52101. 563-382-3486; fax-319-387-4083; hours: 8AM-4PM
Office personnel or visitors may perform searches. Search fee $6.00 per name. Will not search real estate records. Copy fee $1.00 per page. Cert fee- $2.00 per doc plus copy fee. Payee- Winneshiek County Recorder. **Online access to Assessor, Property records:** Access to the assessor database of property and sales data is free at www.iowaassessors.com. **Other phones:** Treasurer- 563-382-3753; Vital Records- 563-382-3486. **Assessor-** 563-382-5356.

Woodbury County

County Auditor & Recorder, 620 Douglas St; Rm 106, Sioux City, IA 51101. RE & UCC recording phone-712-279-6528; fax-712-233-8946; 8AM-4:30PM
All records in one index. Records indexed on computer from 6/94 to present, prior to 6/94 in books. Only the public may search. Copy fee $.50 per page. If copies are background is black with white letters $1.00 per page. Cert fee- $5.00 per doc plus copy fee. Payee- Woodbury County Auditor & Recorder. **Online access to Assessor, Property, Real Estate, Deed, Lien, UCC, Judgment records:** Access to the assessor database of property and sales data is free at www.iowaassessors.com. Also, search Sioux City property data for free at http://sidwellmaps.com/website/siouxcity/eula1.asp. No name searching. Also, access land records at http://iowalandrecords.org after registering. Free searching and pdf images of deeds, liens, UCCs, judgments; may begin charging at any time. Monitor for new documents and save documents. **Other phones:** Treasurer- 712-279-6495; Elections- 712-279-6465; Vital Records- 712-279-6266. **Property tax/Assessor-** 620 Douglas St, Courthouse 701, Sioux City, IA 51101; 712-279-6505 or 712-279-6535.

Worth County

County Recorder, 1000 Central Ave, Northwood, IA 50459. RE & UCC recording phone-641-324-2734; fax-641-324-3682; hours: 8AM-4PM
Records indexed on a public use terminal back to 1994. Only the public may search. General copy fee $1.00 per page. RE record copy- $.50 per page in person, $1.00 per page if mailed, $1.50 per page if faxed. Cert fee- $5.00 per doc plus copy fee. Payee- Worth County Recorder. **Online access to Land, Deed, Lien, UCC, Judgment records:** Access land records at http://iowalandrecords.org after registering. Free searching and pdf images of deeds, liens, UCCs, judgments; may begin charging at any time. Monitor for new documents and save documents. **Other phones:** Treasurer- 641-324-2942; Elections- 641-324-2316; Vital Records- 641-324-2734. **Assessor-** same address as above. 641-324-1198.

Wright County

County Recorder, PO Box 187, Clarion, IA 50525. RE & UCC recording phone-515-532-3204; fax-515-532-2669; hours: 8AM-4PM
www.wrightcounty.org/county_offices.htm
Office personnel or visitors may perform searches. Search fee $6.00 per name. Copy fee $1.00 per page. RE record copy- $.50 per page. Cert fee- $5.00 per doc plus copy fee. Payee- Wright County Recorder. **Online access to Real Estate, Deed, Lien, UCC, Judgment records:** Access land records at http://iowalandrecords.org after registering. Free searching and pdf images of deeds, liens, UCCs, judgments; may begin charging at any time. Monitor for new documents and save documents. **Other phones:** Treasurer- 515-532-2691. **Assessor-** 515-532-3737.

Iowa County Locator

You will usually be able to find the city name in the City/County Cross Reference below. In that case, it is a simple matter to determine the county from the cross reference. However, only the official US Postal Service city names are included in this index. We have also included a ZIP/City Cross Reference immediately following the City/County Cross Reference.

Iowa City/County Cross Reference

A C NIELSEN CO Clinton
ACKLEY (50601) Hardin(71), Franklin(11), Butler(9), Grundy(7)
ACKWORTH Warren
ADAIR (50002) Adair(68), Guthrie(30), Audubon(1)
ADEL Dallas
AFTON Union
AGENCY Wapello
AINSWORTH Washington
AKRON Plymouth
ALBERT CITY (50510) Buena Vista(84), Pocahontas(15)
ALBIA Monroe
ALBION Marshall
ALBURNETT Linn
ALDEN (50006) Hardin(84), Franklin(14)
ALEXANDER (50420) Franklin(84), Wright(10), Story(4)
ALGONA Kossuth
ALLEMAN Polk
ALLENDORF Osceola
ALLERTON Wayne
ALLISON Butler
ALPHA Fayette
ALTA Buena Vista
ALTA VISTA (50603) Chickasaw(85), Howard(13)
ALTON (51003) Sioux(98), Plymouth(1)
ALTOONA Polk
ALVORD Lyon
AMANA (52203) Iowa(84), Johnson(14)
AMANA Iowa
AMES (50014) Story(96), Boone(3)
AMES Story
ANAMOSA Jones
ANDOVER Clinton
ANDREW Jackson
ANITA (50020) Cass(87), Adair(6), Audubon(5)
ANKENY Polk
ANTHON Woodbury
APLINGTON (50604) Butler(85), Grundy(14)
ARCADIA Carroll
ARCHER O'Brien
AREDALE (50605) Butler(69), Franklin(30)
ARGYLE Lee
ARION Crawford
ARISPE Union
ARLINGTON (50606) Fayette(94), Clayton(5)
ARMSTRONG (50514) Emmet(79), Kossuth(20)
ARNOLDS PARK Dickinson
ARTHUR (51431) Ida(87), Sac(12)
ASHTON (51232) Osceola(76), Lyon(19), O'Brien(2)
ASPINWALL Crawford
AT AND T Pottawattamie
ATALISSA (52720) Muscatine(78), Cedar(21)
ATKINS Benton
ATLANTIC (50022) Cass(98), Audubon(1)
AUBURN (51433) Sac(59), Calhoun(39), Carroll(1)
AUDUBON Audubon
AURELIA (51005) Cherokee(87), Buena Vista(12)
AURORA (50607) Buchanan(60), Fayette(39)
AUSTINVILLE Butler

AVOCA (51521) Pottawattamie(91), Shelby(8)
AYRSHIRE (50515) Palo Alto(81), Clay(18)
BADGER (50516) Webster(88), Humboldt(11)
BAGLEY (50026) Guthrie(71), Greene(28)
BALDWIN (52207) Jackson(90), Clinton(9)
BANCROFT Kossuth
BARNES CITY (50027) Mahaska(97), Poweshiek(2)
BARNUM Webster
BARTLETT Fremont
BATAVIA (52533) Jefferson(71), Wapello(28)
BATTLE CREEK (51006) Ida(90), Woodbury(9)
BAXTER Jasper
BAYARD (50029) Guthrie(96), Greene(3)
BEACON Mahaska
BEACONSFIELD Ringgold
BEAMAN (50609) Grundy(73), Marshall(20), Tama(5)
BEAVER Boone
BEDFORD Taylor
BELLE PLAINE (52208) Benton(93), Iowa(3), Tama(1)
BELLEVUE Jackson
BELMOND Wright
BENNETT Cedar
BENTON Ringgold
BERNARD (52032) Dubuque(59), Jackson(36), Jones(4)
BERWICK Polk
BETTENDORF Scott
BEVINGTON Madison
BIG ROCK Scott
BIRMINGHAM (52535) Van Buren(96), Jefferson(3)
BLAIRSBURG (50034) Hamilton(85), Wright(14)
BLAIRSTOWN (52209) Benton(96), Iowa(3)
BLAKESBURG (52536) Wapello(88), Monroe(9), Davis(2)
BLANCHARD Page
BLENCOE (51523) Monona(95), Harrison(4)
BLOCKTON (50836) Taylor(90), Ringgold(9)
BLOOMFIELD (52537) Davis(95), Wapello(4)
BLUE GRASS (52726) Scott(91), Muscatine(8)
BODE (50519) Humboldt(71), Kossuth(28)
BONAPARTE Van Buren
BONDURANT Polk
BOONE Boone
BOONEVILLE Dallas
BOUTON (50039) Dallas(96), Boone(3)
BOXHOLM Boone
BOYDEN (51234) Sioux(97), Lyon(2)
BRADDYVILLE Page
BRADFORD Franklin
BRADGATE (50520) Humboldt(95), Pocahontas(4)
BRANDON Buchanan
BRAYTON (50042) Audubon(92), Cass(7)
BREDA (51436) Carroll(75), Sac(13), Crawford(10)
BRIDGEWATER (50837) Adair(74), Cass(18), Adams(6)
BRIGHTON (52540) Jefferson(50), Washington(49)

BRISTOW Butler
BRITT Hancock
BRONSON Woodbury
BROOKLYN Poweshiek
BRUNSVILLE Plymouth
BRYANT Clinton
BUCKEYE Hardin
BUCKINGHAM Tama
BUFFALO Scott
BUFFALO CENTER (50424) Winnebago(88), Kossuth(11)
BURLINGTON Des Moines
BURNSIDE Webster
BURR OAK Winneshiek
BURT Kossuth
BUSSEY (50044) Marion(73), Mahaska(19), Monroe(7)
CALAMUS Clinton
CALLENDER Webster
CALMAR (52132) Winneshiek(86), Howard(13)
CALUMET O'Brien
CAMANCHE Clinton
CAMBRIDGE (50046) Story(81), Polk(18)
CANTRIL Van Buren
CARBON Adams
CARLISLE (50047) Warren(87), Polk(12)
CARNARVON Sac
CARPENTER Mitchell
CARROLL Carroll
CARSON Pottawattamie
CARTER LAKE Pottawattamie
CASCADE (52033) Dubuque(70), Jones(30)
CASEY (50048) Guthrie(73), Adair(26)
CASTALIA (52133) Winneshiek(72), Fayette(27)
CASTANA Monona
CEDAR Mahaska
CEDAR FALLS (50613) Black Hawk(97), Grundy(1)
CEDAR FALLS Black Hawk
CEDAR RAPIDS Linn
CENTER JUNCTION Jones
CENTER POINT (52213) Linn(90), Benton(7), Scott(1)
CENTERVILLE Appanoose
CENTRAL CITY Linn
CHAPIN Franklin
CHARITON Lucas
CHARLES CITY Floyd
CHARLOTTE (52731) Clinton(91), Jackson(8)
CHARTER OAK Crawford
CHATSWORTH Sioux
CHELSEA (52215) Tama(83), Poweshiek(17)
CHEROKEE Cherokee
CHESTER Howard
CHILLICOTHE Wapello
CHURDAN (50050) Greene(95), Calhoun(3), Carroll(1)
CHURDAN Greene
CINCINNATI Appanoose
CLARE (50524) Webster(94), Pocahontas(2), Humboldt(1)
CLARENCE (52216) Cedar(86), Jones(13)
CLARINDA Page
CLARION Wright
CLARKSVILLE Butler
CLEAR LAKE Cerro Gordo

CLEARFIELD (50840) Taylor(80), Ringgold(19)
CLEGHORN (51014) Cherokee(98), O'Brien(1)
CLEMONS Marshall
CLERMONT (52135) Fayette(97), Clayton(2)
CLIMBING HILL Woodbury
CLINTON Clinton
CLIO Wayne
CLIVE (50325) Polk(87), Dallas(12)
CLUTIER Tama
COGGON (52218) Linn(86), Delaware(13)
COIN Page
COLESBURG (52035) Clayton(71), Delaware(18), Dubuque(10)
COLFAX Jasper
COLLEGE SPRINGS Page
COLLINS (50055) Story(69), Jasper(28), Marshall(2)
COLO Story
COLUMBIA Marion
COLUMBUS CITY Louisa
COLUMBUS JUNCTION (52738) Louisa(95), Washington(4)
COLWELL Floyd
CONESVILLE (52739) Louisa(65), Muscatine(34)
CONRAD (50621) Grundy(92), Marshall(7)
CONROY Iowa
COON RAPIDS (50058) Carroll(80), Guthrie(11), Audubon(5), Greene(3)
COOPER Greene
CORALVILLE Johnson
CORNING (50841) Adams(94), Taylor(5)
CORRECTIONVILLE (51016) Woodbury(93), Ida(6)
CORWITH (50430) Hancock(64), Kossuth(29), Humboldt(2), Wright(2)
CORYDON Wayne
COULTER Franklin
COUNCIL BLUFFS (51503) Pottawattamie(98), Mills(1)
COUNCIL BLUFFS Pottawattamie
CRAIG Plymouth
CRAWFORDSVILLE (52621) Washington(69), Louisa(29), Henry(1)
CRESCENT Pottawattamie
CRESCO (52136) Howard(92), Winneshiek(7)
CRESTON (50801) Union(96), Adair(1), Adams(1)
CROMWELL Union
CRYSTAL LAKE Hancock
CUMBERLAND (50843) Cass(96), Adams(3)
CUMMING (50061) Warren(60), Madison(15), Dallas(11), Polk(11)
CURLEW Palo Alto
CUSHING (51018) Woodbury(60), Ida(39)
CYLINDER Palo Alto
DAKOTA CITY Humboldt
DALLAS Marion
DALLAS CENTER Dallas
DANA (50064) Greene(94), Boone(6)
DANBURY (51019) Woodbury(79), Ida(8), Monona(6), Crawford(5)
DANVILLE (52623) Des Moines(91), Henry(8)
DAVENPORT Scott
DAVIS CITY Decatur
DAWSON Dallas

DAYTON (50530) Webster(96), Boone(3)
DE SOTO Dallas
DE WITT Clinton
DECATUR Decatur
DECORAH Winneshiek
DEDHAM (51440) Carroll(97), Audubon(2)
DEEP RIVER (52222) Poweshiek(73), Iowa(26)
DEFIANCE (51527) Shelby(84), Crawford(16)
DELAWARE Delaware
DELHI Delaware
DELMAR (52037) Clinton(93), Jackson(6)
DELOIT Crawford
DELPHOS Ringgold
DELTA (52550) Keokuk(98), Mahaska(1)
DENISON Crawford
DENMARK Lee
DENVER Bremer
DERBY (50068) Wayne(64), Lucas(35)
DES MOINES (50320) Polk(89), Warren(10)
DES MOINES Polk
DEWAR Black Hawk
DEXTER (50070) Dallas(34), Guthrie(25), Madison(23), Adair(17)
DIAGONAL (50845) Ringgold(97), Union(2)
DICKENS (51333) Clay(97), Dickinson(2)
DIKE Grundy
DIXON Scott
DOLLIVER Emmet
DONAHUE Scott
DONNELLSON Lee
DOON (51235) Lyon(96), Sioux(3)
DORCHESTER (52140) Allamakee(94), Winneshiek(5)
DOUDS (52551) Van Buren(96), Davis(3)
DOUGHERTY (50433) Cerro Gordo(53), Floyd(18), Franklin(18), Butler(9)
DOW CITY Crawford
DOWS (50071) Wright(53), Franklin(46)
DRAKESVILLE (52552) Davis(94), Wapello(5)
DUBUQUE Dubuque
DUMONT (50625) Butler(92), Franklin(7)
DUNCOMBE (50532) Webster(94), Hamilton(4)
DUNDEE Delaware
DUNKERTON Black Hawk
DUNLAP (51529) Harrison(81), Crawford(8), Monona(6), Shelby(2)
DURANGO Dubuque
DURANT (52747) Cedar(63), Scott(24), Muscatine(12)
DYERSVILLE (52040) Dubuque(94), Delaware(5)
DYSART (52224) Tama(71), Benton(27)
EAGLE GROVE (50533) Wright(96), Humboldt(2), Webster(1)
EARLHAM (50072) Madison(77), Dallas(22)
EARLING Shelby
EARLVILLE Delaware
EARLY Sac
EDDYVILLE (52553) Wapello(47), Mahaska(41), Monroe(11)
EDGEWOOD (52042) Clayton(75), Delaware(24)
ELBERON (52225) Tama(82), Benton(17)
ELDON (52554) Wapello(88), Davis(4), Jefferson(3), Van Buren(2)
ELDORA (50627) Hardin(95), Grundy(4)
ELDRIDGE Scott
ELGIN (52141) Fayette(71), Clayton(28)
ELK HORN (51531) Shelby(86), Audubon(13)
ELKADER Clayton
ELKHART Polk
ELKPORT Clayton
ELLIOTT (51532) Montgomery(55), Pottawattamie(38), Cass(6)
ELLSTON (50074) Ringgold(97), Union(2)

ELLSWORTH (50075) Hamilton(88), Pocahontas(11)
ELMA (50628) Howard(97), Mitchell(2)
ELWOOD Clinton
ELY (52227) Linn(97), Johnson(2)
EMERSON (51533) Mills(68), Montgomery(31)
EMMETSBURG Palo Alto
EPWORTH Dubuque
ESSEX (51638) Page(97), Montgomery(2)
ESTHERVILLE (51334) Emmet(98), Dickinson(1)
EVANSDALE Black Hawk
EVERLY (51338) Clay(82), Dickinson(17)
EXIRA (50076) Audubon(98), Guthrie(1)
EXLINE Appanoose
FAIRBANK (50629) Buchanan(44), Fayette(28), Black Hawk(15), Bremer(10)
FAIRFAX (52228) Linn(80), Benton(11), Johnson(7)
FARLEY Dubuque
FARMERSBURG Clayton
FARMINGTON (52626) Van Buren(75), Lee(24)
FARNHAMVILLE (50538) Calhoun(91), Webster(8)
FARRAGUT Fremont
FAYETTE Fayette
FENTON (50539) Kossuth(81), Palo Alto(18)
FERGUSON Marshall
FERTILE (50434) Cerro Gordo(87), Worth(11)
FESTINA Winneshiek
FLORIS Davis
FLOYD Floyd
FONDA (50540) Pocahontas(82), Calhoun(14), Buena Vista(1), Sac(1)
FONDA Pocahontas
FONTANELLE Adair
FOREST CITY (50436) Winnebago(91), Hancock(8)
FORT ATKINSON (52144) Winneshiek(78), Fayette(12), Chickasaw(8)
FORT DODGE Webster
FORT MADISON Lee
FOSTORIA Clay
FREDERICKSBURG (50630) Chickasaw(92), Bremer(7)
FREDERIKA Bremer
FREMONT (52561) Mahaska(73), Keokuk(15), Benton(11)
FRUITLAND Muscatine
GALT Wright
GALVA (51020) Ida(66), Sac(17), Cherokee(15)
GARBER Clayton
GARDEN CITY Hardin
GARDEN GROVE Decatur
GARNAVILLO Clayton
GARNER Hancock
GARRISON Benton
GARWIN (50632) Tama(83), Marshall(16)
GENEVA Franklin
GEORGE Lyon
GIBSON (50104) Keokuk(82), Poweshiek(12), Mahaska(5)
GIFFORD Hardin
GILBERT Story
GILBERTVILLE Black Hawk
GILLETT GROVE Clay
GILMAN (50106) Marshall(71), Jasper(15), Tama(9), Poweshiek(3)
GILMORE CITY (50541) Pocahontas(50), Humboldt(49)
GLADBROOK (50635) Tama(94), Marshall(5)
GLENWOOD Mills
GLIDDEN (51443) Carroll(98), Greene(1)
GOLDFIELD (50542) Wright(80), Humboldt(19)
GOODELL Hancock

GOOSE LAKE Clinton
GOWRIE (50543) Webster(94), Greene(5)
GRAETTINGER (51342) Palo Alto(81), Emmet(18)
GRAFTON (50440) Worth(98), Mitchell(1)
GRAND JUNCTION (50107) Greene(95), Boone(3)
GRAND MOUND Clinton
GRAND RIVER (50108) Decatur(90), Clarke(8)
GRANDVIEW Louisa
GRANGER (50109) Polk(61), Dallas(38)
GRANT Montgomery
GRANVILLE (51022) Sioux(59), O'Brien(39)
GRAVITY Taylor
GRAY Audubon
GREELEY (52050) Delaware(87), Clayton(12)
GREEN MOUNTAIN Marshall
GREENE (50636) Butler(83), Floyd(16)
GREENFIELD Adair
GREENVILLE Clay
GRIMES (50111) Polk(95), Dallas(4)
GRINNELL (50112) Poweshiek(89), Jasper(10)
GRINNELL Poweshiek
GRISWOLD (51535) Cass(52), Pottawattamie(47)
GRUNDY CENTER Grundy
GRUVER Emmet
GUERNSEY (52221) Poweshiek(88), Iowa(11)
GUTHRIE CENTER Guthrie
GUTTENBERG (52052) Clayton(93), Dubuque(6)
HALBUR Carroll
HALE Jones
HAMBURG Fremont
HAMLIN (50117) Audubon(98), Guthrie(1)
HAMPTON Franklin
HANCOCK Pottawattamie
HANLONTOWN (50444) Worth(80), Cerro Gordo(18), Winnebago(1)
HANSELL Franklin
HARCOURT (50544) Webster(98), Greene(1)
HARDY Humboldt
HARLAN Shelby
HARPER Keokuk
HARPERS FERRY Allamakee
HARRIS (51345) Osceola(94), Dickinson(5)
HARTFORD Warren
HARTLEY (51346) O'Brien(89), Osceola(6), Clay(4)
HARTWICK (52232) Poweshiek(85), Iowa(14)
HARVEY Marion
HASTINGS Mills
HAVELOCK (50546) Pocahontas(97), Palo Alto(2)
HAVERHILL Marshall
HAWARDEN Sioux
HAWKEYE Fayette
HAYESVILLE Keokuk
HAZLETON Buchanan
HEDRICK (52563) Keokuk(67), Wapello(31), Jefferson(1)
HENDERSON (51541) Mills(71), Pottawattamie(19), Montgomery(9)
HIAWATHA Linn
HIGHLANDVILLE Winneshiek
HILLS Johnson
HILLSBORO (52630) Van Buren(55), Henry(26), Lee(17)
HINTON Plymouth
HOLLAND Grundy
HOLSTEIN (51025) Ida(86), Cherokee(7), Woodbury(5)
HOLY CROSS (52053) Dubuque(83), Clayton(16)
HOMESTEAD (52236) Iowa(98), Johnson(2)

HONEY CREEK Pottawattamie
HOPKINTON (52237) Delaware(94), Dubuque(3), Jones(1)
HORNICK (51026) Woodbury(75), Monona(24)
HOSPERS (51238) Sioux(64), O'Brien(35)
HOUGHTON Lee
HUBBARD (50122) Hardin(98), Story(1)
HUDSON (50643) Black Hawk(93), Grundy(6)
HULL Sioux
HUMBOLDT (50548) Humboldt(98), Webster(1)
HUMESTON (50123) Wayne(78), Lucas(10), Decatur(8), Clarke(1)
HUXLEY (50124) Story(93), Polk(6)
IDA GROVE Ida
IMOGENE (51645) Fremont(53), Mills(36), Page(6), Montgomery(2)
INDEPENDENCE Buchanan
INDIANOLA Warren
INWOOD (51240) Lyon(90), Sioux(9)
IONIA (50645) Chickasaw(97), Floyd(2)
IOWA CITY Johnson
IOWA FALLS (50126) Hardin(97), Franklin(2)
IRA Jasper
IRETON (51027) Sioux(81), Plymouth(18)
IRWIN Shelby
JACKSON JUNCTION Winneshiek
JAMAICA (50128) Guthrie(63), Greene(24), Dallas(12)
JANESVILLE (50647) Bremer(54), Black Hawk(45)
JEFFERSON Greene
JESUP (50648) Buchanan(90), Black Hawk(9)
JEWELL Hamilton
JOHNSTON Polk
JOICE (50446) Worth(81), Winnebago(19)
JOLLEY Calhoun
KALONA (52247) Washington(66), Johnson(33)
KAMRAR Hamilton
KANAWHA (50447) Hancock(76), Wright(23)
KELLERTON (50133) Ringgold(97), Decatur(2)
KELLEY (50134) Story(78), Boone(21)
KELLOGG Jasper
KENSETT Worth
KENT (50850) Adams(50), Union(49)
KEOKUK Lee
KEOSAUQUA Van Buren
KEOTA (52248) Keokuk(72), Washington(27)
KESLEY Butler
KESWICK (50136) Keokuk(95), Iowa(3)
KEYSTONE Benton
KILLDUFF Jasper
KIMBALLTON (51543) Audubon(84), Shelby(15)
KINGSLEY (51028) Plymouth(82), Woodbury(17)
KINROSS Keokuk
KIRKMAN Shelby
KIRKVILLE Wapello
KIRON (51448) Crawford(65), Sac(18), Ida(15)
KLEMME (50449) Cerro Gordo(65), Hancock(34)
KNIERIM Calhoun
KNOXVILLE Marion
LA MOTTE (52054) Jackson(97), Dubuque(2)
LA PORTE CITY (50651) Black Hawk(93), Benton(6)
LACONA (50139) Warren(69), Lucas(20), Marion(9)
LADORA Iowa
LAKE CITY (51449) Calhoun(96), Carroll(3)
LAKE MILLS (50450) Winnebago(94), Worth(5)
LAKE PARK Dickinson

LAKE VIEW Sac
LAKOTA Kossuth
LAMONI (50140) Decatur(91), Ringgold(8)
LAMONT (50650) Buchanan(71), Fayette(26), Delaware(2)
LANESBORO Carroll
LANGWORTHY Jones
LANSING Allamakee
LARCHWOOD Lyon
LARRABEE (51029) Cherokee(95), O'Brien(4)
LATIMER Franklin
LAUREL (50141) Marshall(53), Jasper(46)
LAURENS (50554) Pocahontas(96), Palo Alto(2), Buena Vista(1)
LAWLER (52154) Chickasaw(94), Howard(5)
LAWTON Woodbury
LE CLAIRE Scott
LE GRAND Marshall
LE MARS Plymouth
LEDYARD Kossuth
LEHIGH Webster
LEIGHTON (50143) Mahaska(97), Marion(2)
LELAND Winnebago
LENOX (50851) Taylor(77), Adams(11), Union(8), Ringgold(2)
LEON Decatur
LESTER Lyon
LETTS (52754) Louisa(77), Muscatine(22)
LEWIS (51544) Cass(77), Pottawattamie(22)
LIBERTY CENTER Warren
LIBERTYVILLE (52567) Jefferson(83), Van Buren(16)
LIDDERDALE Carroll
LIME SPRINGS Howard
LINCOLN Tama
LINDEN (50146) Dallas(88), Guthrie(11)
LINEVILLE (50147) Wayne(85), Marion(14)
LINN GROVE (51033) Buena Vista(60), Clay(39)
LISBON (52253) Linn(71), Cedar(13), Jones(10), Johnson(4)
LISCOMB (50148) Marshall(88), Grundy(11)
LITTLE CEDAR Mitchell
LITTLE ROCK (51243) Lyon(91), Osceola(8)
LITTLE SIOUX (51545) Harrison(89), Monona(10)
LITTLEPORT Clayton
LIVERMORE (50558) Humboldt(54), Kossuth(45)
LOCKRIDGE (52635) Jefferson(74), Henry(25)
LOGAN Harrison
LOHRVILLE (51453) Calhoun(91), Carroll(7), Greene(1)
LONE ROCK Kossuth
LONE TREE (52755) Johnson(87), Louisa(10), Muscatine(1)
LONG GROVE (52756) Scott(98), Clinton(1)
LORIMOR (50149) Union(68), Madison(31)
LOST NATION Clinton
LOVILIA (50150) Monroe(98), Marion(1)
LOW MOOR Clinton
LOWDEN (52255) Cedar(97), Clinton(2)
LU VERNE (50560) Kossuth(81), Humboldt(18)
LUANA (52156) Clayton(83), Allamakee(16)
LUCAS (50151) Lucas(55), Warren(43), Clarke(1)
LUTHER Boone
LUXEMBURG Dubuque
LUZERNE (52257) Benton(98), Iowa(1)
LYNNVILLE (50153) Jasper(91), Mahaska(5), Poweshiek(2)
LYTTON (50561) Calhoun(58), Sac(41)
MACEDONIA Pottawattamie

MACKSBURG (50155) Madison(94), Adair(4), Union(1)
MADRID (50156) Boone(96), Polk(2), Dallas(1)
MAGNOLIA Harrison
MALCOM Poweshiek
MALLARD (50562) Palo Alto(88), Pocahontas(11)
MALOY Ringgold
MALVERN Mills
MANCHESTER Delaware
MANILLA (51454) Crawford(70), Shelby(29)
MANLY (50456) Worth(96), Cerro Gordo(3)
MANNING (51455) Carroll(85), Crawford(7), Audubon(5), Shelby(1)
MANSON (50563) Calhoun(81), Pocahontas(15), Webster(2)
MAPLETON (51034) Monona(92), Woodbury(5), Crawford(1)
MAQUOKETA (52060) Jackson(98), Clinton(1)
MARATHON Buena Vista
MARBLE ROCK Floyd
MARCUS (51035) Cherokee(93), Plymouth(5)
MARENGO (52301) Iowa(98), Benton(1)
MARION Linn
MARNE (51552) Cass(78), Shelby(20), Pottawattamie(1)
MARQUETTE Clayton
MARSHALLTOWN Marshall
MARTELLE (52305) Jones(86), Linn(13)
MARTENSDALE Warren
MARTINSBURG Keokuk
MASON CITY Cerro Gordo
MASONVILLE (50654) Delaware(64), Buchanan(35)
MASSENA (50853) Cass(96), Adams(3)
MATLOCK Sioux
MAURICE Sioux
MAXWELL (50161) Story(58), Polk(40), Jasper(1)
MAY CITY Osceola
MAYNARD Fayette
MC CALLSBURG (50154) Story(90), Hardin(9)
MC CAUSLAND Scott
MC CLELLAND Pottawattamie
MC GREGOR Clayton
MC INTIRE Mitchell
MECHANICSVILLE (52306) Cedar(78), Jones(21)
MEDIAPOLIS Des Moines
MELBOURNE (50162) Marshall(97), Jasper(2)
MELCHER Marion
MELROSE (52569) Monroe(68), Appanoose(17), Wayne(9), Lucas(3)
MELVIN (51350) Osceola(96), O'Brien(3)
MENLO (50164) Guthrie(70), Adair(29)
MERIDEN Cherokee
MERRILL Plymouth
MESERVEY (50457) Cerro Gordo(51), Hancock(22), Franklin(18), Wright(8)
MIDDLE AMANA Iowa
MIDDLETOWN Des Moines
MILES (52064) Jackson(93), Clinton(6)
MILFORD Dickinson
MILLERSBURG Iowa
MILLERTON Wayne
MILO Warren
MILTON (52570) Van Buren(84), Davis(15)
MINBURN Dallas
MINDEN Pottawattamie
MINEOLA Mills
MINGO (50168) Jasper(95), Polk(4)
MISSOURI VALLEY (51555) Harrison(80), Pottawattamie(19)
MITCHELLVILLE (50169) Polk(81), Jasper(18)
MODALE Harrison
MONDAMIN Harrison

MONMOUTH (52309) Jackson(74), Jones(25)
MONONA (52159) Clayton(75), Allamakee(24)
MONROE (50170) Jasper(87), Marion(12)
MONTEZUMA (50171) Poweshiek(98), Mahaska(1)
MONTEZUMA Poweshiek
MONTICELLO Jones
MONTOUR Tama
MONTPELIER Muscatine
MONTROSE Lee
MOORHEAD (51558) Monona(92), Harrison(7)
MOORLAND (50566) Webster(98), Calhoun(1)
MORAVIA (52571) Appanoose(90), Monroe(9)
MORLEY Jones
MORNING SUN (52640) Louisa(74), Des Moines(25)
MORRISON Grundy
MOSCOW (52760) Muscatine(62), Cedar(37)
MOULTON (52572) Appanoose(92), Davis(7)
MOUNT AUBURN Benton
MOUNT AYR Ringgold
MOUNT PLEASANT (52641) Henry(96), Washington(2)
MOUNT STERLING Van Buren
MOUNT UNION (52644) Henry(70), Des Moines(29)
MOUNT VERNON Linn
MOVILLE Woodbury
MURRAY (50174) Clarke(97), Union(2)
MUSCATINE (52761) Muscatine(96), Louisa(2)
MYSTIC Appanoose
NASHUA (50658) Chickasaw(85), Floyd(12), Bremer(2)
NEMAHA Sac
NEOLA (51559) Pottawattamie(96), Harrison(3)
NEVADA Story
NEW ALBIN Allamakee
NEW HAMPTON Chickasaw
NEW HARTFORD (50660) Butler(84), Grundy(15)
NEW LIBERTY (52765) Scott(87), Cedar(12)
NEW LONDON (52645) Henry(86), Des Moines(13)
NEW MARKET (51646) Taylor(97), Page(2)
NEW PROVIDENCE (50206) Hardin(88), Marshall(7), Story(4)
NEW SHARON (50207) Mahaska(98), Poweshiek(1)
NEW VIENNA (52065) Dubuque(89), Delaware(10)
NEW VIRGINIA (50210) Warren(91), Clarke(8)
NEWELL (50568) Buena Vista(90), Sac(8)
NEWHALL Benton
NEWTON Jasper
NICHOLS (52766) Muscatine(93), Johnson(6)
NODAWAY (50857) Adams(76), Taylor(19), Montgomery(3)
NORA SPRINGS (50458) Floyd(64), Cerro Gordo(31), Mitchell(4)
NORTH BUENA VISTA Clayton
NORTH ENGLISH (52316) Iowa(88), Keokuk(11)
NORTH LIBERTY Johnson
NORTH WASHINGTON Chickasaw
NORTHBORO (51647) Page(80), Fremont(19)
NORTHWOOD Worth
NORWALK Warren
NORWAY (52318) Benton(75), Iowa(24)
NUMA Appanoose

OAKDALE Johnson
OAKLAND Pottawattamie
OAKVILLE (52646) Louisa(53), Des Moines(46)
OCHEYEDAN Osceola
ODEBOLT Sac
OELWEIN Fayette
OGDEN Boone
OKOBOJI Dickinson
OLDS Henry
OLIN (52320) Jones(93), Cedar(6)
OLLIE (52576) Keokuk(98), Jefferson(1)
ONAWA Monona
ONSLOW Jones
ORAN Fayette
ORANGE CITY Sioux
ORCHARD (50460) Mitchell(75), Floyd(24)
ORIENT Adair
OSAGE Mitchell
OSCEOLA Clarke
OSKALOOSA Mahaska
OSSIAN (52161) Winneshiek(84), Fayette(15)
OTHO Webster
OTLEY (50214) Marion(98), Jasper(1)
OTO Woodbury
OTTOSEN (50570) Humboldt(60), Kossuth(37), Pocahontas(1)
OTTUMWA Wapello
OXFORD (52322) Johnson(97), Iowa(2)
OXFORD JUNCTION (52323) Jones(83), Clinton(7), Linn(4), Cedar(4)
OYENS Plymouth
PACIFIC JUNCTION Mills
PACKWOOD (52580) Jefferson(95), Keokuk(4)
PALMER Pocahontas
PALO (52324) Linn(85), Benton(14)
PANAMA (51562) Shelby(97), Harrison(2)
PANORA Guthrie
PARKERSBURG (50665) Butler(76), Grundy(23)
PARNELL (52325) Iowa(85), Johnson(14)
PATON (50217) Greene(79), Boone(14), Webster(5)
PATTERSON Madison
PAULLINA (51046) O'Brien(96), Cherokee(3)
PELLA (50219) Marion(94), Mahaska(5)
PEOSTA Dubuque
PERCIVAL Fremont
PERRY (50220) Dallas(93), Boone(5)
PERSHING Marion
PERSIA (51563) Harrison(97), Shelby(2)
PERU (50222) Madison(98), Clarke(1)
PETERSON (51047) Clay(70), Buena Vista(16), Cherokee(9), O'Brien(4)
PIERSON (51048) Woodbury(71), Cherokee(28)
PILOT GROVE Lee
PILOT MOUND Boone
PISGAH Harrison
PLAINFIELD (50666) Bremer(73), Butler(26)
PLANO (52581) Appanoose(95), Wayne(4)
PLEASANT VALLEY Scott
PLEASANTVILLE (50225) Marion(71), Warren(28)
PLOVER Pocahontas
PLYMOUTH (50464) Cerro Gordo(77), Worth(20), Mitchell(2)
POCAHONTAS Pocahontas
POLK CITY (50226) Polk(97), Boone(2)
POMEROY (50575) Calhoun(66), Pocahontas(33)
POPEJOY Franklin
PORTSMOUTH (51565) Shelby(79), Harrison(20)
POSTVILLE (52162) Allamakee(55), Clayton(32), Winneshiek(8), Fayette(3)
PRAIRIE CITY (50228) Jasper(96), Polk(1), Marion(1)
PRAIRIEBURG Linn

PRESCOTT (50859) Adams(97), Adair(2)
PRESTON (52069) Jackson(94), Clinton(5)
PRIMGHAR O'Brien
PRINCETON Scott
PROLE (50229) Warren(89), Madison(10)
PROMISE CITY Wayne
PROTIVIN Howard
PULASKI Davis
QUASQUETON Buchanan
QUIMBY Cherokee
RADCLIFFE (50230) Hardin(70), Hamilton(27), Story(1)
RAKE Winnebago
RALSTON Carroll
RANDALIA Fayette
RANDALL Hamilton
RANDOLPH (51649) Fremont(98), Mills(1)
RAYMOND Black Hawk
READLYN Bremer
REASNOR Jasper
RED OAK Montgomery
REDDING Ringgold
REDFIELD (50233) Dallas(88), Guthrie(11)
REINBECK (50669) Grundy(90), Tama(7), Black Hawk(1)
REMBRANDT Buena Vista
REMSEN (51050) Plymouth(98), Cherokee(1)
RENWICK (50577) Humboldt(69), Wright(30)
RHODES (50234) Marshall(77), Jasper(22)
RICEVILLE (50466) Howard(51), Mitchell(48)
RICHLAND (52585) Keokuk(59), Washington(30), Jefferson(9)
RICKETTS Crawford
RIDGEWAY Winneshiek
RINARD Calhoun
RINGSTED (50578) Emmet(93), Palo Alto(3), Kossuth(3)
RIPPEY (50235) Greene(91), Boone(5), Dallas(2)
RIVERSIDE (52327) Washington(68), Johnson(28), Louisa(2)
RIVERTON Fremont
ROBINS Linn
ROCK FALLS Cerro Gordo
ROCK RAPIDS Lyon
ROCK VALLEY (51247) Sioux(98), Lyon(1)
ROCKFORD (50468) Floyd(86), Cerro Gordo(13)
ROCKWELL Cerro Gordo
ROCKWELL CITY Calhoun
RODMAN Palo Alto
RODNEY (51051) Monona(92), Woodbury(7)
ROLAND (50236) Story(97), Hamilton(2)
ROLFE (50581) Pocahontas(98), Palo Alto(1)
ROME Henry
ROSE HILL (52586) Mahaska(92), Keokuk(7)
ROWAN (50470) Wright(96), Franklin(3)
ROWLEY Buchanan
ROYAL Clay
RUDD (50471) Floyd(94), Mitchell(5)
RUNNELLS (50237) Polk(92), Jasper(4), Marion(2)
RUSSELL (50238) Lucas(92), Wayne(7)
RUTHVEN (51358) Palo Alto(80), Clay(19)
RUTLAND Humboldt
RYAN Delaware
SABULA (52070) Jackson(89), Clinton(10)
SAC CITY Sac
SAINT ANSGAR (50472) Mitchell(95), Worth(4)
SAINT ANTHONY (50239) Marshall(87), Story(12)
SAINT CHARLES (50240) Warren(60), Madison(39)
SAINT DONATUS Jackson
SAINT LUCAS Fayette
SAINT MARYS Warren

SAINT OLAF Clayton
SAINT PAUL Lee
SALEM (52649) Henry(86), Lee(13)
SALIX Woodbury
SANBORN O'Brien
SCARVILLE Winnebago
SCHALLER (51053) Sac(91), Ida(6), Buena Vista(2)
SCHLESWIG (51461) Crawford(94), Ida(5)
SCOTCH GROVE Jones
SCRANTON (51462) Greene(97), Carroll(2)
SEARSBORO (50242) Poweshiek(94), Jasper(5)
SELMA (52588) Van Buren(73), Davis(25), Jefferson(1)
SERGEANT BLUFF Woodbury
SEYMOUR (52590) Wayne(90), Appanoose(9)
SHAMBAUGH Page
SHANNON CITY (50861) Union(76), Ringgold(23)
SHARPSBURG Taylor
SHEFFIELD (50475) Franklin(76), Cerro Gordo(23)
SHELBY (51570) Shelby(56), Pottawattamie(36), Harrison(6)
SHELDAHL Polk
SHELDON (51201) O'Brien(89), Sioux(9)
SHELL ROCK Butler
SHELLSBURG Benton
SHENANDOAH (51603) Page(85), Fremont(14)
SHENANDOAH Page
SHERRILL (52073) Dubuque(97), Clayton(2)
SIBLEY Osceola
SIDNEY Fremont
SIGOURNEY Keokuk
SILVER CITY (51571) Mills(53), Pottawattamie(46)
SIOUX CENTER Sioux
SIOUX CITY (51109) Woodbury(87), Plymouth(12)
SIOUX CITY Woodbury
SIOUX RAPIDS (50585) Buena Vista(71), Clay(28)
SLATER (50244) Story(72), Polk(25), Boone(2)
SLOAN (51055) Woodbury(66), Monona(33)
SMITHLAND (51056) Woodbury(92), Monona(7)
SOLDIER Monona
SOLON Johnson
SOMERS (50586) Calhoun(89), Webster(10)
SOUTH AMANA Iowa
SOUTH ENGLISH Keokuk
SPENCER Clay
SPERRY Des Moines
SPILLVILLE Winneshiek
SPIRIT LAKE Dickinson
SPRAGUEVILLE Jackson
SPRINGBROOK Jackson
SPRINGVILLE Linn
STACYVILLE Mitchell
STANHOPE Hamilton
STANLEY (50671) Fayette(72), Buchanan(27)
STANTON Montgomery
STANWOOD Cedar
STATE CENTER (50247) Marshall(94), Story(5)
STEAMBOAT ROCK (50672) Hardin(91), Grundy(8)
STOCKPORT (52651) Van Buren(93), Jefferson(6)
STOCKTON (52769) Scott(66), Muscatine(31), Henry(1)
STORM LAKE Buena Vista
STORY CITY (50248) Story(87), Hamilton(10), Boone(2)

STOUT Grundy
STRATFORD (50249) Hamilton(77), Webster(14), Boone(7)
STRAWBERRY POINT (52076) Clayton(95), Delaware(3), Fayette(1)
STRUBLE Plymouth
STUART (50250) Guthrie(74), Adair(25)
SULLY Jasper
SUMNER (50674) Bremer(72), Fayette(21), Chickasaw(6)
SUPERIOR Dickinson
SUTHERLAND (51058) O'Brien(95), Clay(2), Cherokee(1)
SWALEDALE Cerro Gordo
SWAN (50252) Warren(68), Marion(31)
SWEA CITY Kossuth
SWEDESBURG Henry
SWISHER (52338) Johnson(94), Linn(5)
TABOR (51653) Fremont(64), Mills(35)
TAINTOR Mahaska
TAMA Tama
TEEDS GROVE Clinton
TEMPLETON (51463) Carroll(98), Audubon(1)
TENNANT Shelby
TERRIL (51364) Dickinson(75), Clay(16), Emmet(8)
THAYER (50254) Union(97), Clarke(3)
THOMPSON Winnebago
THOR (50591) Humboldt(84), Webster(15)
THORNBURG Keokuk
THORNTON (50479) Cerro Gordo(89), Franklin(10)
THURMAN Fremont
TIFFIN Johnson
TINGLEY Ringgold
TIPTON Cedar
TITONKA (50480) Kossuth(94), Hancock(3), Winnebago(1)
TODDVILLE Linn
TOETERVILLE Mitchell
TOLEDO Tama
TORONTO Clinton
TRACY (50256) Marion(75), Mahaska(24)
TRAER Tama
TREYNOR Pottawattamie
TRIPOLI Bremer
TROY MILLS Linn
TRUESDALE Buena Vista
TRURO (50257) Madison(69), Warren(16), Clarke(14)
TURIN Monona
UDELL Appanoose
UNDERWOOD Pottawattamie
UNION (50258) Hardin(78), Marshall(20), Grundy(1)
UNIONVILLE (52594) Appanoose(68), Davis(31)
UNIVERSITY PARK Mahaska
URBANA Benton
URBANDALE (50323) Polk(59), Dallas(40)
URBANDALE Polk
UTE (51060) Monona(85), Crawford(14)
VAIL Crawford
VAN HORNE Benton
VAN METER (50261) Dallas(55), Madison(44)
VAN WERT Decatur
VARINA Pocahontas
VENTURA (50482) Cerro Gordo(87), Hancock(12)
VICTOR (52347) Iowa(79), Poweshiek(20)
VILLISCA (50864) Montgomery(85), Page(9), Taylor(2), Cass(1)
VINCENT Webster
VINING Tama
VINTON Benton
VIOLA Linn
VOLGA Clayton
WADENA (52169) Fayette(95), Clayton(4)
WALCOTT (52773) Scott(98), Muscatine(1)
WALFORD Benton
WALKER (52352) Linn(98), Buchanan(1)

WALL LAKE (51466) Sac(93), Carroll(3), Crawford(3)
WALLINGFORD Emmet
WALNUT (51577) Pottawattamie(74), Shelby(24)
WAPELLO Louisa
WASHINGTON Washington
WASHTA (51061) Cherokee(79), Ida(19)
WATERLOO Black Hawk
WATERVILLE Allamakee
WATKINS Benton
WAUCOMA (52171) Fayette(70), Chickasaw(15), Winneshiek(13)
WAUKEE Dallas
WAUKON (52172) Allamakee(98), Winneshiek(1)
WAVERLY Bremer
WAYLAND (52654) Henry(84), Washington(14)
WEBB (51366) Clay(92), Buena Vista(7)
WEBSTER (52355) Keokuk(94), Iowa(5)
WEBSTER CITY Hamilton
WELDON (50264) Decatur(66), Clarke(33)
WELLMAN (52356) Washington(78), Johnson(11), Iowa(8)
WELLSBURG (50680) Grundy(98), Hardin(1)
WELTON Clinton
WESLEY (50483) Kossuth(78), Hancock(21)
WEST AMANA Iowa
WEST BEND (50597) Kossuth(55), Palo Alto(41), Humboldt(1)
WEST BRANCH (52358) Cedar(84), Johnson(15)
WEST BURLINGTON Des Moines
WEST CHESTER Washington
WEST DES MOINES (50266) Polk(75), Dallas(25)
WEST DES MOINES Polk
WEST GROVE Davis
WEST LIBERTY Muscatine
WEST POINT (52656) Lee(98), Henry(1)
WEST UNION Fayette
WESTFIELD Plymouth
WESTGATE Fayette
WESTPHALIA Shelby
WESTSIDE (51467) Crawford(72), Carroll(27)
WEVER (52658) Lee(87), Des Moines(12)
WHAT CHEER (50268) Keokuk(93), Mahaska(6)
WHEATLAND (52777) Clinton(94), Cedar(5)
WHITING Monona
WHITTEMORE (50598) Kossuth(76), Palo Alto(23)
WHITTEN Hardin
WILLIAMS (50271) Hamilton(91), Wright(8)
WILLIAMSBURG Iowa
WILLIAMSON Lucas
WILTON (52778) Muscatine(56), Cedar(43)
WINFIELD (52659) Henry(84), Louisa(15)
WINTERSET Madison
WINTHROP Buchanan
WIOTA Cass
WODEN (50484) Winnebago(49), Hancock(47), Kossuth(3)
WOODBINE Harrison
WOODBURN (50275) Clarke(86), Lucas(13)
WOODWARD (50276) Dallas(72), Boone(27)
WOOLSTOCK (50599) Wright(80), Hamilton(19)
WORTHINGTON (52078) Dubuque(79), Delaware(20)
WYOMING Jones
YALE (50277) Guthrie(84), Dallas(15)
YARMOUTH Des Moines
YORKTOWN Page
ZEARING Story
ZWINGLE (52079) Dubuque(50), Jackson(50)

Iowa ZIP/City Cross Reference

50001-50001	ACKWORTH
50002-50002	ADAIR
50003-50003	ADEL
50005-50005	ALBION
50006-50006	ALDEN
50007-50007	ALLEMAN
50008-50008	ALLERTON
50009-50009	ALTOONA
50010-50014	AMES
50015-50015	ANKENY
50020-50020	ANITA
50021-50021	ANKENY
50022-50022	ATLANTIC
50023-50023	ANKENY
50025-50025	AUDUBON
50026-50026	BAGLEY
50027-50027	BARNES CITY
50028-50028	BAXTER
50029-50029	BAYARD
50030-50030	BEACONSFIELD
50031-50031	BEAVER
50032-50032	BERWICK
50033-50033	BEVINGTON
50034-50034	BLAIRSBURG
50035-50035	BONDURANT
50036-50037	BOONE
50038-50038	BOONEVILLE
50039-50039	BOUTON
50040-50040	BOXHOLM
50041-50041	BRADFORD
50042-50042	BRAYTON
50043-50043	BUCKEYE
50044-50044	BUSSEY
50046-50046	CAMBRIDGE
50047-50047	CARLISLE
50048-50048	CASEY
50049-50049	CHARITON
50050-50050	CHURDAN
50051-50051	CLEMONS
50052-50052	CLIO
50054-50054	COLFAX
50055-50055	COLLINS
50056-50056	COLO
50057-50057	COLUMBIA
50058-50058	COON RAPIDS
50059-50059	COOPER
50060-50060	CORYDON
50061-50061	CUMMING
50062-50062	DALLAS
50063-50063	DALLAS CENTER
50064-50064	DANA
50065-50065	DAVIS CITY
50066-50066	DAWSON
50067-50067	DECATUR
50068-50068	DERBY
50069-50069	DE SOTO
50070-50070	DEXTER
50071-50071	DOWS
50072-50072	EARLHAM
50073-50073	ELKHART
50074-50074	ELLSTON
50075-50075	ELLSWORTH
50076-50076	EXIRA
50077-50077	CHURDAN
50078-50078	FERGUSON
50101-50101	GALT
50102-50102	GARDEN CITY
50103-50103	GARDEN GROVE
50104-50104	GIBSON
50105-50105	GILBERT
50106-50106	GILMAN
50107-50107	GRAND JUNCTION
50108-50108	GRAND RIVER
50109-50109	GRANGER
50110-50110	GRAY
50111-50111	GRIMES
50112-50112	GRINNELL
50115-50115	GUTHRIE CENTER
50116-50116	HAMILTON
50117-50117	HAMLIN
50118-50118	HARTFORD
50119-50119	HARVEY
50120-50120	HAVERHILL
50122-50122	HUBBARD
50123-50123	HUMESTON
50124-50124	HUXLEY
50125-50125	INDIANOLA
50126-50126	IOWA FALLS
50127-50127	IRA
50128-50128	JAMAICA
50129-50129	JEFFERSON
50130-50130	JEWELL
50131-50131	JOHNSTON
50132-50132	KAMRAR
50133-50133	KELLERTON
50134-50134	KELLEY
50135-50135	KELLOGG
50136-50136	KESWICK
50137-50137	KILLDUFF
50138-50138	KNOXVILLE
50139-50139	LACONA
50140-50140	LAMONI
50141-50141	LAUREL
50142-50142	LE GRAND
50143-50143	LEIGHTON
50144-50144	LEON
50145-50145	LIBERTY CENTER
50146-50146	LINDEN
50147-50147	LINEVILLE
50148-50148	LISCOMB
50149-50149	LORIMOR
50150-50150	LOVILIA
50151-50151	LUCAS
50152-50152	LUTHER
50153-50153	LYNNVILLE
50154-50154	MC CALLSBURG
50155-50155	MACKSBURG
50156-50156	MADRID
50157-50157	MALCOM
50158-50158	MARSHALLTOWN
50160-50160	MARTENSDALE
50161-50161	MAXWELL
50162-50162	MELBOURNE
50163-50163	MELCHER
50164-50164	MENLO
50165-50165	MILLERTON
50166-50166	MILO
50167-50167	MINBURN
50168-50168	MINGO
50169-50169	MITCHELLVILLE
50170-50170	MONROE
50171-50172	MONTEZUMA
50173-50173	MONTOUR
50174-50174	MURRAY
50177-50177	GRINNELL
50197-50198	KNOXVILLE
50201-50201	NEVADA
50206-50206	NEW PROVIDENCE
50207-50207	NEW SHARON
50208-50208	NEWTON
50210-50210	NEW VIRGINIA
50211-50211	NORWALK
50212-50212	OGDEN
50213-50213	OSCEOLA
50214-50214	OTLEY
50216-50216	PANORA
50217-50217	PATON
50218-50218	PATTERSON
50219-50219	PELLA
50220-50220	PERRY
50221-50221	PERSHING
50222-50222	PERU
50223-50223	PILOT MOUND
50225-50225	PLEASANTVILLE
50226-50226	POLK CITY
50227-50227	POPEJOY
50228-50228	PRAIRIE CITY
50229-50229	PROLE
50230-50230	RADCLIFFE
50231-50231	RANDALL
50232-50232	REASNOR
50233-50233	REDFIELD
50234-50234	RHODES
50235-50235	RIPPEY
50236-50236	ROLAND
50237-50237	RUNNELLS
50238-50238	RUSSELL
50239-50239	SAINT ANTHONY
50240-50240	SAINT CHARLES
50241-50241	SAINT MARYS
50242-50242	SEARSBORO
50243-50243	SHELDAHL
50244-50244	SLATER
50246-50246	STANHOPE
50247-50247	STATE CENTER
50248-50248	STORY CITY
50249-50249	STRATFORD
50250-50250	STUART
50251-50251	SULLY
50252-50252	SWAN
50253-50253	TAINTOR
50254-50254	THAYER
50255-50255	THORNBURG
50256-50256	TRACY
50257-50257	TRURO
50258-50258	UNION
50259-50259	GIFFORD
50261-50261	VAN METER
50262-50262	VAN WERT
50263-50263	WAUKEE
50264-50264	WELDON
50265-50266	WEST DES MOINES
50268-50268	WHAT CHEER
50269-50269	WHITTEN
50271-50271	WILLIAMS
50272-50272	WILLIAMSON
50273-50273	WINTERSET
50274-50274	WIOTA
50275-50275	WOODBURN
50276-50276	WOODWARD
50277-50277	YALE
50278-50278	ZEARING
50300-50321	DES MOINES
50322-50323	URBANDALE
50325-50325	CLIVE
50327-50397	DES MOINES
50398-50398	WEST DES MOINES
50401-50402	MASON CITY
50420-50420	ALEXANDER
50421-50421	BELMOND
50423-50423	BRITT
50424-50424	BUFFALO CENTER
50426-50426	CARPENTER
50427-50427	CHAPIN
50428-50428	CLEAR LAKE
50430-50430	CORWITH
50431-50431	COULTER
50432-50432	CRYSTAL LAKE
50433-50433	DOUGHERTY
50434-50434	FERTILE
50435-50435	FLOYD
50436-50436	FOREST CITY
50438-50438	GARNER
50439-50439	GOODELL
50440-50440	GRAFTON
50441-50441	HAMPTON
50444-50444	HANLONTOWN
50446-50446	JOICE
50447-50447	KANAWHA
50448-50448	KENSETT
50449-50449	KLEMME
50450-50450	LAKE MILLS
50451-50451	LAKOTA
50452-50452	LATIMER
50453-50453	LELAND
50454-50454	LITTLE CEDAR
50455-50455	MC INTIRE
50456-50456	MANLY
50457-50457	MESERVEY
50458-50458	NORA SPRINGS
50459-50459	NORTHWOOD
50460-50460	ORCHARD
50461-50461	OSAGE
50464-50464	PLYMOUTH
50465-50465	RAKE
50466-50466	RICEVILLE
50467-50467	ROCK FALLS
50468-50468	ROCKFORD
50469-50469	ROCKWELL
50470-50470	ROWAN
50471-50471	RUDD
50472-50472	SAINT ANSGAR
50473-50473	SCARVILLE
50475-50475	SHEFFIELD
50476-50476	STACYVILLE
50477-50477	SWALEDALE
50478-50478	THOMPSON
50479-50479	THORNTON
50480-50480	TITONKA
50481-50481	TOETERVILLE
50482-50482	VENTURA
50483-50483	WESLEY
50484-50484	WODEN
50501-50501	FORT DODGE
50510-50510	ALBERT CITY
50511-50511	ALGONA
50514-50514	ARMSTRONG
50515-50515	AYRSHIRE
50516-50516	BADGER
50517-50517	BANCROFT
50518-50518	BARNUM
50519-50519	BODE
50520-50520	BRADGATE
50521-50521	BURNSIDE
50522-50522	BURT
50523-50523	CALLENDER
50524-50524	CLARE
50525-50526	CLARION
50527-50527	CURLEW
50528-50528	CYLINDER
50529-50529	DAKOTA CITY
50530-50530	DAYTON
50531-50531	DOLLIVER
50532-50532	DUNCOMBE
50533-50533	EAGLE GROVE
50535-50535	EARLY
50536-50536	EMMETSBURG
50538-50538	FARNHAMVILLE
50539-50539	FENTON
50540-50540	FONDA
50541-50541	GILMORE CITY
50542-50542	GOLDFIELD
50543-50543	GOWRIE
50544-50544	HARCOURT
50545-50545	HARDY
50546-50546	HAVELOCK
50548-50548	HUMBOLDT
50551-50551	JOLLEY
50552-50552	KNIERIM
50553-50553	FONDA
50554-50554	LAURENS
50556-50556	LEDYARD
50557-50557	LEHIGH
50558-50558	LIVERMORE
50559-50559	LONE ROCK
50560-50560	LU VERNE
50561-50561	LYTTON
50562-50562	MALLARD
50563-50563	MANSON
50565-50565	MARATHON
50566-50566	MOORLAND
50567-50567	NEMAHA
50568-50568	NEWELL
50569-50569	OTHO
50570-50570	OTTOSEN
50571-50571	PALMER
50573-50573	PLOVER
50574-50574	POCAHONTAS
50575-50575	POMEROY
50576-50576	REMBRANDT
50577-50577	RENWICK
50578-50578	RINGSTED
50579-50579	ROCKWELL CITY
50580-50580	RODMAN

ZIP	City	ZIP	City	ZIP	City	ZIP	City
50581-50581	ROLFE	50677-50677	WAVERLY	51050-51050	REMSEN	51454-51454	MANILLA
50582-50582	RUTLAND	50680-50680	WELLSBURG	51051-51051	RODNEY	51455-51455	MANNING
50583-50583	SAC CITY	50681-50681	WESTGATE	51052-51052	SALIX	51458-51458	ODEBOLT
50585-50585	SIOUX RAPIDS	50682-50682	WINTHROP	51053-51053	SCHALLER	51459-51459	RALSTON
50586-50586	SOMERS	50700-50706	WATERLOO	51054-51054	SERGEANT BLUFF	51460-51460	RICKETTS
50587-50587	RINARD	50707-50707	EVANSDALE	51055-51055	SLOAN	51461-51461	SCHLESWIG
50588-50588	STORM LAKE	50799-50799	WATERLOO	51056-51056	SMITHLAND	51462-51462	SCRANTON
50590-50590	SWEA CITY	50801-50801	CRESTON	51057-51057	STRUBLE	51463-51463	TEMPLETON
50591-50591	THOR	50830-50830	AFTON	51058-51058	SUTHERLAND	51465-51465	VAIL
50592-50592	TRUESDALE	50831-50831	ARISPE	51059-51059	TURIN	51466-51466	WALL LAKE
50593-50593	VARINA	50833-50833	BEDFORD	51060-51060	UTE	51467-51467	WESTSIDE
50594-50594	VINCENT	50835-50835	BENTON	51061-51061	WASHTA	51501-51503	COUNCIL BLUFFS
50595-50595	WEBSTER CITY	50836-50836	BLOCKTON	51062-51062	WESTFIELD	51510-51510	CARTER LAKE
50597-50597	WEST BEND	50837-50837	BRIDGEWATER	51063-51063	WHITING	51519-51519	AT AND T
50598-50598	WHITTEMORE	50839-50839	CARBON	51100-51111	SIOUX CITY	51520-51520	ARION
50599-50599	WOOLSTOCK	50840-50840	CLEARFIELD	51201-51201	SHELDON	51521-51521	AVOCA
50601-50601	ACKLEY	50841-50841	CORNING	51230-51230	ALVORD	51523-51523	BLENCOE
50602-50602	ALLISON	50842-50842	CROMWELL	51231-51231	ARCHER	51525-51525	CARSON
50603-50603	ALTA VISTA	50843-50843	CUMBERLAND	51232-51232	ASHTON	51526-51526	CRESCENT
50604-50604	APLINGTON	50844-50844	DELPHOS	51234-51234	BOYDEN	51527-51527	DEFIANCE
50605-50605	AREDALE	50845-50845	DIAGONAL	51235-51235	DOON	51528-51528	DOW CITY
50606-50606	ARLINGTON	50846-50846	FONTANELLE	51237-51237	GEORGE	51529-51529	DUNLAP
50607-50607	AURORA	50847-50847	GRANT	51238-51238	HOSPERS	51530-51530	EARLING
50608-50608	AUSTINVILLE	50848-50848	GRAVITY	51239-51239	HULL	51531-51531	ELK HORN
50609-50609	BEAMAN	50849-50849	GREENFIELD	51240-51240	INWOOD	51532-51532	ELLIOTT
50611-50611	BRISTOW	50850-50850	KENT	51241-51241	LARCHWOOD	51533-51533	EMERSON
50612-50612	BUCKINGHAM	50851-50851	LENOX	51242-51242	LESTER	51534-51534	GLENWOOD
50613-50614	CEDAR FALLS	50852-50852	MALOY	51243-51243	LITTLE ROCK	51535-51535	GRISWOLD
50616-50616	CHARLES CITY	50853-50853	MASSENA	51244-51244	MATLOCK	51536-51536	HANCOCK
50619-50619	CLARKSVILLE	50854-50854	MOUNT AYR	51245-51245	PRIMGHAR	51537-51537	HARLAN
50620-50620	COLWELL	50857-50857	NODAWAY	51246-51246	ROCK RAPIDS	51540-51540	HASTINGS
50621-50621	CONRAD	50858-50858	ORIENT	51247-51247	ROCK VALLEY	51541-51541	HENDERSON
50622-50622	DENVER	50859-50859	PRESCOTT	51248-51248	SANBORN	51542-51542	HONEY CREEK
50623-50623	DEWAR	50860-50860	REDDING	51249-51249	SIBLEY	51543-51543	KIMBALLTON
50624-50624	DIKE	50861-50861	SHANNON CITY	51250-51250	SIOUX CENTER	51544-51544	LEWIS
50625-50625	DUMONT	50862-50862	SHARPSBURG	51301-51301	SPENCER	51545-51545	LITTLE SIOUX
50626-50626	DUNKERTON	50863-50863	TINGLEY	51330-51330	ALLENDORF	51546-51546	LOGAN
50627-50627	ELDORA	50864-50864	VILLISCA	51331-51331	ARNOLDS PARK	51548-51548	MC CLELLAND
50628-50628	ELMA	50936-50981	DES MOINES	51333-51333	DICKENS	51549-51549	MACEDONIA
50629-50629	FAIRBANK	51001-51001	AKRON	51334-51334	ESTHERVILLE	51550-51550	MAGNOLIA
50630-50630	FREDERICKSBURG	51002-51002	ALTA	51338-51338	EVERLY	51551-51551	MALVERN
50631-50631	FREDERIKA	51003-51003	ALTON	51340-51340	FOSTORIA	51552-51552	MARNE
50632-50632	GARWIN	51004-51004	ANTHON	51341-51341	GILLETT GROVE	51553-51553	MINDEN
50633-50633	GENEVA	51005-51005	AURELIA	51342-51342	GRAETTINGER	51554-51554	MINEOLA
50634-50634	GILBERTVILLE	51006-51006	BATTLE CREEK	51343-51343	GREENVILLE	51555-51555	MISSOURI VALLEY
50635-50635	GLADBROOK	51007-51007	BRONSON	51344-51344	GRUVER	51556-51556	MODALE
50636-50636	GREENE	51008-51008	BRUNSVILLE	51345-51345	HARRIS	51557-51557	MONDAMIN
50637-50637	GREEN MOUNTAIN	51009-51009	CALUMET	51346-51346	HARTLEY	51558-51558	MOORHEAD
50638-50638	GRUNDY CENTER	51010-51010	CASTANA	51347-51347	LAKE PARK	51559-51559	NEOLA
50640-50640	HANSELL	51011-51011	CHATSWORTH	51349-51349	MAY CITY	51560-51560	OAKLAND
50641-50641	HAZLETON	51012-51012	CHEROKEE	51350-51350	MELVIN	51561-51561	PACIFIC JUNCTION
50642-50642	HOLLAND	51014-51014	CLEGHORN	51351-51351	MILFORD	51562-51562	PANAMA
50643-50643	HUDSON	51015-51015	CLIMBING HILL	51354-51354	OCHEYEDAN	51563-51563	PERSIA
50644-50644	INDEPENDENCE	51016-51016	CORRECTIONVILLE	51355-51355	OKOBOJI	51564-51564	PISGAH
50645-50645	IONIA	51017-51017	CRAIG	51357-51357	ROYAL	51565-51565	PORTSMOUTH
50647-50647	JANESVILLE	51018-51018	CUSHING	51358-51358	RUTHVEN	51566-51566	RED OAK
50648-50648	JESUP	51019-51019	DANBURY	51360-51360	SPIRIT LAKE	51570-51570	SHELBY
50649-50649	KESLEY	51020-51020	GALVA	51363-51363	SUPERIOR	51571-51571	SILVER CITY
50650-50650	LAMONT	51022-51022	GRANVILLE	51364-51364	TERRIL	51572-51572	SOLDIER
50651-50651	LA PORTE CITY	51023-51023	HAWARDEN	51365-51365	WALLINGFORD	51573-51573	STANTON
50652-50652	LINCOLN	51024-51024	HINTON	51366-51366	WEBB	51574-51574	TENNANT
50653-50653	MARBLE ROCK	51025-51025	HOLSTEIN	51401-51401	CARROLL	51575-51575	TREYNOR
50654-50654	MASONVILLE	51026-51026	HORNICK	51430-51430	ARCADIA	51576-51576	UNDERWOOD
50655-50655	MAYNARD	51027-51027	IRETON	51431-51431	ARTHUR	51577-51577	WALNUT
50657-50657	MORRISON	51028-51028	KINGSLEY	51432-51432	ASPINWALL	51578-51578	WESTPHALIA
50658-50658	NASHUA	51029-51029	LARRABEE	51433-51433	AUBURN	51579-51579	WOODBINE
50659-50659	NEW HAMPTON	51030-51030	LAWTON	51436-51436	BREDA	51591-51591	RED OAK
50660-50660	NEW HARTFORD	51031-51031	LE MARS	51437-51437	CARNARVON	51593-51593	HARLAN
50661-50661	NORTH WASHINGTON	51033-51033	LINN GROVE	51439-51439	CHARTER OAK	51601-51603	SHENANDOAH
50662-50662	OELWEIN	51034-51034	MAPLETON	51440-51440	DEDHAM	51630-51630	BLANCHARD
50664-50664	ORAN	51035-51035	MARCUS	51441-51441	DELOIT	51631-51631	BRADDYVILLE
50665-50665	PARKERSBURG	51036-51036	MAURICE	51442-51442	DENISON	51632-51632	CLARINDA
50666-50666	PLAINFIELD	51037-51037	MERIDEN	51443-51443	GLIDDEN	51636-51636	COIN
50667-50667	RAYMOND	51038-51038	MERRILL	51444-51444	HALBUR	51637-51637	COLLEGE SPRINGS
50668-50668	READLYN	51039-51039	MOVILLE	51445-51445	IDA GROVE	51638-51638	ESSEX
50669-50669	REINBECK	51040-51040	ONAWA	51446-51446	IRWIN	51639-51639	FARRAGUT
50670-50670	SHELL ROCK	51041-51041	ORANGE CITY	51447-51447	KIRKMAN	51640-51640	HAMBURG
50671-50671	STANLEY	51044-51044	OTO	51448-51448	KIRON	51645-51645	IMOGENE
50672-50672	STEAMBOAT ROCK	51045-51045	OYENS	51449-51449	LAKE CITY	51646-51646	NEW MARKET
50673-50673	STOUT	51046-51046	PAULLINA	51450-51450	LAKE VIEW	51647-51647	NORTHBORO
50674-50674	SUMNER	51047-51047	PETERSON	51451-51451	LANESBORO	51648-51648	PERCIVAL
50675-50675	TRAER	51048-51048	PIERSON	51452-51452	LIDDERDALE	51649-51649	RANDOLPH
50676-50676	TRIPOLI	51049-51049	QUIMBY	51453-51453	LOHRVILLE	51650-51650	RIVERTON

Zip Range	City	Zip Range	City	Zip Range	City	Zip Range	City
51651-51651	SHAMBAUGH	52169-52169	WADENA	52334-52334	SOUTH AMANA	52621-52621	CRAWFORDSVILLE
51652-51652	SIDNEY	52170-52170	WATERVILLE	52335-52335	SOUTH ENGLISH	52623-52623	DANVILLE
51653-51653	TABOR	52171-52171	WAUCOMA	52336-52336	SPRINGVILLE	52624-52624	DENMARK
51654-51654	THURMAN	52172-52172	WAUKON	52337-52337	STANWOOD	52625-52625	DONNELLSON
51655-51655	BARTLETT	52175-52175	WEST UNION	52338-52338	SWISHER	52626-52626	FARMINGTON
51656-51656	YORKTOWN	52201-52201	AINSWORTH	52339-52339	TAMA	52627-52627	FORT MADISON
51693-51693	SHENANDOAH	52202-52202	ALBURNETT	52340-52340	TIFFIN	52630-52630	HILLSBORO
52001-52004	DUBUQUE	52203-52204	AMANA	52341-52341	TODDVILLE	52631-52631	HOUGHTON
52030-52030	ANDREW	52205-52205	ANAMOSA	52342-52342	TOLEDO	52632-52632	KEOKUK
52031-52031	BELLEVUE	52206-52206	ATKINS	52343-52343	TORONTO	52635-52635	LOCKRIDGE
52032-52032	BERNARD	52207-52207	BALDWIN	52344-52344	TROY MILLS	52637-52637	MEDIAPOLIS
52033-52033	CASCADE	52208-52208	BELLE PLAINE	52345-52345	URBANA	52638-52638	MIDDLETOWN
52035-52035	COLESBURG	52209-52209	BLAIRSTOWN	52346-52346	VAN HORNE	52639-52639	MONTROSE
52036-52036	DELAWARE	52210-52210	BRANDON	52347-52347	VICTOR	52640-52640	MORNING SUN
52037-52037	DELMAR	52211-52211	BROOKLYN	52348-52348	VINING	52641-52641	MOUNT PLEASANT
52038-52038	DUNDEE	52212-52212	CENTER JUNCTION	52349-52349	VINTON	52642-52642	ROME
52039-52039	DURANGO	52213-52213	CENTER POINT	52350-52350	VIOLA	52644-52644	MOUNT UNION
52040-52040	DYERSVILLE	52214-52214	CENTRAL CITY	52351-52351	WALFORD	52645-52645	NEW LONDON
52041-52041	EARLVILLE	52215-52215	CHELSEA	52352-52352	WALKER	52646-52646	OAKVILLE
52042-52042	EDGEWOOD	52216-52216	CLARENCE	52353-52353	WASHINGTON	52647-52647	OLDS
52043-52043	ELKADER	52217-52217	CLUTIER	52354-52354	WATKINS	52648-52648	PILOT GROVE
52044-52044	ELKPORT	52218-52218	COGGON	52355-52355	WEBSTER	52649-52649	SALEM
52045-52045	EPWORTH	52219-52219	PRAIRIEBURG	52356-52356	WELLMAN	52650-52650	SPERRY
52046-52046	FARLEY	52220-52220	CONROY	52357-52357	WEST AMANA	52651-52651	STOCKPORT
52047-52047	FARMERSBURG	52221-52221	GUERNSEY	52358-52358	WEST BRANCH	52652-52652	SWEDESBURG
52048-52048	GARBER	52222-52222	DEEP RIVER	52359-52359	WEST CHESTER	52653-52653	WAPELLO
52049-52049	GARNAVILLO	52223-52223	DELHI	52361-52361	WILLIAMSBURG	52654-52654	WAYLAND
52050-52050	GREELEY	52224-52224	DYSART	52362-52362	WYOMING	52655-52655	WEST BURLINGTON
52052-52052	GUTTENBERG	52225-52225	ELBERON	52400-52499	CEDAR RAPIDS	52656-52656	WEST POINT
52053-52053	HOLY CROSS	52226-52226	ELWOOD	52501-52501	OTTUMWA	52657-52657	SAINT PAUL
52054-52054	LA MOTTE	52227-52227	ELY	52530-52530	AGENCY	52658-52658	WEVER
52055-52055	LITTLEPORT	52228-52228	FAIRFAX	52531-52531	ALBIA	52659-52659	WINFIELD
52056-52056	LUXEMBURG	52229-52229	GARRISON	52533-52533	BATAVIA	52660-52660	YARMOUTH
52057-52057	MANCHESTER	52230-52230	HALE	52534-52534	BEACON	52701-52701	ANDOVER
52060-52060	MAQUOKETA	52231-52231	HARPER	52535-52535	BIRMINGHAM	52720-52720	ATALISSA
52064-52064	MILES	52232-52232	HARTWICK	52536-52536	BLAKESBURG	52721-52721	BENNETT
52065-52065	NEW VIENNA	52233-52233	HIAWATHA	52537-52537	BLOOMFIELD	52722-52722	BETTENDORF
52066-52066	NORTH BUENA VISTA	52235-52235	HILLS	52538-52538	WEST GROVE	52725-52725	BIG ROCK
52068-52068	PEOSTA	52236-52236	HOMESTEAD	52540-52540	BRIGHTON	52726-52726	BLUE GRASS
52069-52069	PRESTON	52237-52237	HOPKINTON	52542-52542	CANTRIL	52727-52727	BRYANT
52070-52070	SABULA	52240-52240	IOWA CITY	52543-52543	CEDAR	52728-52728	BUFFALO
52071-52071	SAINT DONATUS	52241-52241	CORALVILLE	52544-52544	CENTERVILLE	52729-52729	CALAMUS
52072-52072	SAINT OLAF	52242-52246	IOWA CITY	52548-52548	CHILLICOTHE	52730-52730	CAMANCHE
52073-52073	SHERRILL	52247-52247	KALONA	52549-52549	CINCINNATI	52731-52731	CHARLOTTE
52074-52074	SPRAGUEVILLE	52248-52248	KEOTA	52550-52550	DELTA	52732-52733	CLINTON
52075-52075	SPRINGBROOK	52249-52249	KEYSTONE	52551-52551	DOUDS	52734-52734	A C NIELSEN CO
52076-52076	STRAWBERRY POINT	52250-52250	KINROSS	52552-52552	DRAKESVILLE	52736-52736	CLINTON
52077-52077	VOLGA	52251-52251	LADORA	52553-52553	EDDYVILLE	52737-52737	COLUMBUS CITY
52078-52078	WORTHINGTON	52252-52252	LANGWORTHY	52554-52554	ELDON	52739-52739	CONESVILLE
52079-52079	ZWINGLE	52253-52253	LISBON	52555-52555	EXLINE	52742-52742	DE WITT
52099-52099	DUBUQUE	52254-52254	LOST NATION	52556-52557	FAIRFIELD	52745-52745	DIXON
52101-52101	DECORAH	52255-52255	LOWDEN	52560-52560	FLORIS	52746-52746	DONAHUE
52130-52130	ALPHA	52257-52257	LUZERNE	52561-52561	FREMONT	52747-52747	DURANT
52131-52131	BURR OAK	52301-52301	MARENGO	52562-52562	HAYESVILLE	52748-52748	ELDRIDGE
52132-52132	CALMAR	52302-52302	MARION	52563-52563	HEDRICK	52749-52749	FRUITLAND
52133-52133	CASTALIA	52305-52305	MARTELLE	52565-52565	KEOSAUQUA	52750-52750	GOOSE LAKE
52134-52134	CHESTER	52306-52306	MECHANICSVILLE	52566-52566	KIRKVILLE	52751-52751	GRAND MOUND
52135-52135	CLERMONT	52307-52307	MIDDLE AMANA	52567-52567	LIBERTYVILLE	52752-52752	GRANDVIEW
52136-52136	CRESCO	52308-52308	MILLERSBURG	52568-52568	MARTINSBURG	52753-52753	LE CLAIRE
52140-52140	DORCHESTER	52309-52309	MONMOUTH	52569-52569	MELROSE	52754-52754	LETTS
52141-52141	ELGIN	52310-52310	MONTICELLO	52570-52570	MILTON	52755-52755	LONE TREE
52142-52142	FAYETTE	52312-52312	MORLEY	52571-52571	MORAVIA	52756-52756	LONG GROVE
52143-52143	FESTINA	52313-52313	MOUNT AUBURN	52572-52572	MOULTON	52757-52757	LOW MOOR
52144-52144	FORT ATKINSON	52314-52314	MOUNT VERNON	52573-52573	MOUNT STERLING	52758-52758	MC CAUSLAND
52146-52146	HARPERS FERRY	52315-52315	NEWHALL	52574-52574	MYSTIC	52759-52759	MONTPELIER
52147-52147	HAWKEYE	52316-52316	NORTH ENGLISH	52575-52575	NUMA	52760-52760	MOSCOW
52149-52149	HIGHLANDVILLE	52317-52317	NORTH LIBERTY	52576-52576	OLLIE	52761-52761	MUSCATINE
52150-52150	JACKSON JUNCTION	52318-52318	NORWAY	52577-52577	OSKALOOSA	52765-52765	NEW LIBERTY
52151-52151	LANSING	52319-52319	OAKDALE	52580-52580	PACKWOOD	52766-52766	NICHOLS
52154-52154	LAWLER	52320-52320	OLIN	52581-52581	PLANO	52767-52767	PLEASANT VALLEY
52155-52155	LIME SPRINGS	52321-52321	ONSLOW	52583-52583	PROMISE CITY	52768-52768	PRINCETON
52156-52156	LUANA	52322-52322	OXFORD	52584-52584	PULASKI	52769-52769	STOCKTON
52157-52157	MC GREGOR	52323-52323	OXFORD JUNCTION	52585-52585	RICHLAND	52771-52771	TEEDS GROVE
52158-52158	MARQUETTE	52324-52324	PALO	52586-52586	ROSE HILL	52772-52772	TIPTON
52159-52159	MONONA	52325-52325	PARNELL	52588-52588	SELMA	52773-52773	WALCOTT
52160-52160	NEW ALBIN	52326-52326	QUASQUETON	52590-52590	SEYMOUR	52774-52774	WELTON
52161-52161	OSSIAN	52327-52327	RIVERSIDE	52591-52591	SIGOURNEY	52776-52776	WEST LIBERTY
52162-52162	POSTVILLE	52328-52328	ROBINS	52593-52593	UDELL	52777-52777	WHEATLAND
52163-52163	PROTIVIN	52329-52329	ROWLEY	52594-52594	UNIONVILLE	52778-52778	WILTON
52164-52164	RANDALIA	52330-52330	RYAN	52595-52595	UNIVERSITY PARK	52800-52809	DAVENPORT
52165-52165	RIDGEWAY	52331-52331	SCOTCH GROVE	52601-52601	BURLINGTON		
52166-52166	SAINT LUCAS	52332-52332	SHELLSBURG	52619-52619	ARGYLE		
52168-52168	SPILLVILLE	52333-52333	SOLON	52620-52620	BONAPARTE		

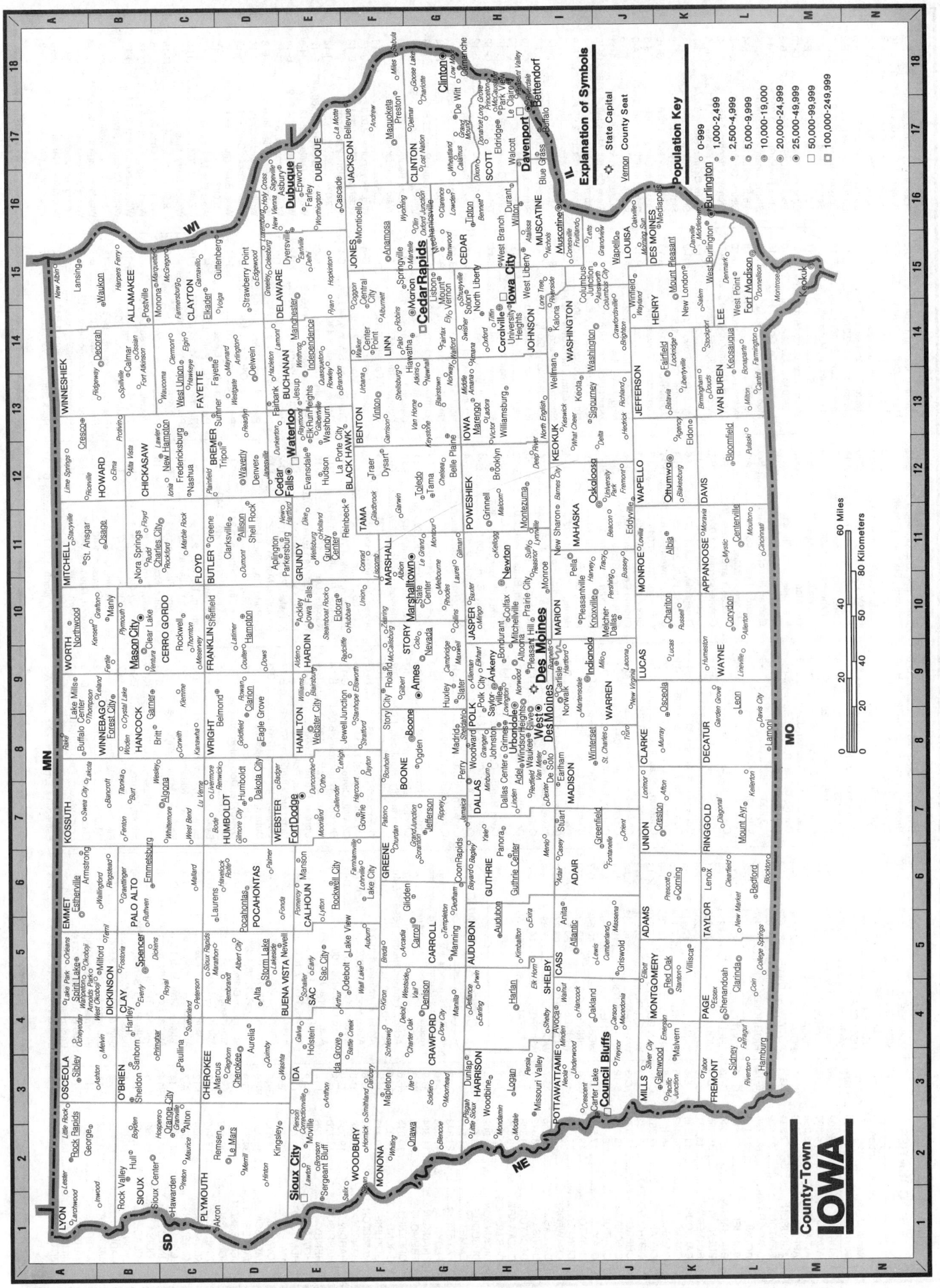

County-Town
IOWA

Explanation of Symbols

✪ State Capital

⊛ *Vernon* County Seat

Population Key

○ 0-999
⊙ 1,000-2,499
⊚ 2,500-4,999
⊛ 5,000-9,999
⊕ 10,000-19,000
⊗ 20,000-24,999
◉ 25,000-49,999
□ 50,000-99,999
▢ 100,000-249,999

COUNTIES

(99 Counties)

Name of County	Population	Location on Map
ADAIR	8,409	I-6
ADAMS	4,866	J-5
ALLAMAKEE	13,855	B-14
APPANOOSE	13,743	K-10
AUDUBON	7,334	G-5
BENTON	22,429	F-12
BLACK HAWK	123,798	E-12
BOONE	25,186	F-7
BREMER	22,813	C-12
BUCHANAN	20,844	D-13
BUENA VISTA	19,965	D-4
BUTLER	15,731	C-10
CALHOUN	11,508	E-5
CARROLL	21,423	G-5
CASS	15,128	I-5
CEDAR	17,381	G-15
CERRO GORDO	46,733	C-9
CHEROKEE	14,098	C-3
CHICKASAW	13,295	B-12
CLARKE	8,287	J-8
CLAY	17,585	B-4
CLAYTON	19,054	C-14
CLINTON	51,040	G-16
CRAWFORD	16,775	G-3
DALLAS	29,755	G-7
DAVIS	8,312	K-11
DECATUR	8,338	K-8
DELAWARE	18,035	D-14
DES MOINES	42,614	J-15
DICKINSON	14,909	B-4
DUBUQUE	86,403	E-16
EMMET	11,569	A-5
FAYETTE	21,843	C-13
FLOYD	17,058	C-10
FRANKLIN	11,364	C-9
FREMONT	8,226	K-3
GREENE	10,045	F-6
GRUNDY	12,029	E-10
GUTHRIE	10,935	H-6
HAMILTON	16,071	E-8
HANCOCK	12,638	B-8
HARDIN	19,094	E-9
HARRISON	14,730	G-3
HENRY	19,226	J-14
HOWARD	9,809	B-12
HUMBOLDT	10,756	C-7
IDA	8,365	E-3
IOWA	14,630	G-12
JACKSON	19,950	F-16
JASPER	34,795	G-9
JEFFERSON	16,310	J-13
JOHNSON	96,119	H-14
JONES	19,444	F-15
KEOKUK	11,624	I-12
KOSSUTH	18,591	A-7
LEE	38,687	K-14
LINN	168,767	F-14
LOUISA	11,592	J-15
LUCAS	9,070	J-9
LYON	11,952	A-1
MADISON	12,483	I-7
MAHASKA	21,522	I-11
MARION	30,001	I-10
MARSHALL	38,276	F-10
MILLS	13,202	J-3
MITCHELL	10,928	A-10
MONONA	10,034	F-2
MONROE	8,114	J-10
MONTGOMERY	12,076	J-4
MUSCATINE	39,907	I-5
O'BRIEN	15,444	B-3
OSCEOLA	7,267	A-3
PAGE	16,870	K-4
PALO ALTO	10,669	B-5
PLYMOUTH	23,388	C-1
POCAHONTAS	9,525	D-5
POLK	327,140	G-8
POTTAWATTAMIE	82,628	I-2
POWESHIEK	19,033	G-11
RINGGOLD	5,420	K-6
SAC	12,324	E-4
SCOTT	150,979	H-16
SHELBY	13,230	I-4
SIOUX	29,903	B-1
STORY	74,252	F-9
TAMA	17,419	F-11
TAYLOR	7,114	K-5
UNION	12,750	J-6
VAN BUREN	7,676	K-13
WAPELLO	35,687	J-12
WARREN	36,033	J-8
WASHINGTON	19,612	I-14
WAYNE	7,067	K-9
WEBSTER	40,342	D-7
WINNEBAGO	12,122	A-8
WINNESHIEK	20,847	A-13
WOODBURY	98,276	E-2
WORTH	7,991	A-9
WRIGHT	14,269	C-8
TOTAL	2,776,755	

CITIES AND TOWNS

Note: The first name is that of the city or town, second, that of the county in which it is located, then the population and location on the map.

Ackley, Franklin/Hardin, 1,696 .. E-10
Adel, Dallas, 3,304 .... H-8
Akron, Plymouth, 1,450 .... C-1
Albia, Monroe, 3,870 .... K-11
Algona, Kossuth, 6,015 .... B-7
Allison, Butler, 1,000 .... D-11
Alta, Buena Vista, 1,820 .... D-4
Alton, Sioux, 1,063 .... D-11
Altoona, Polk, 7,191 .... H-9
Ames, Story, 47,198 .... G-9
Anamosa, Jones, 5,100 .... F-15
Anita, Cass, 1,068 .... I-6
Ankeny, Polk, 18,482 .... H-9
Aplington, Butler, 1,034 .... D-11
Armstrong, Emmet, 1,025 .... A-6
Asbury, Dubuque, 2,013 .... D-16
Atlantic, Cass, 7,432 .... I-5
Audubon, Audubon, 2,524 .... H-5
Aurelia, Cherokee, 1,034 .... D-4
Avoca, Pottawattamie, 1,497 .... I-4
Bedford, Taylor, 1,528 .... L-6
Belle Plaine, Benton, 2,834 .... G-12
Bellevue, Jackson, 2,239 .... E-17
Belmond, Wright, 2,500 .... C-9
Bettendorf, Scott, 28,132 .... H-17
Bloomfield, Davis, 2,580 .... L-12
Blue Grass, Scott, 1,214 .... I-17
Bondurant, Polk, 1,584 .... H-9
Boone, Boone, 12,392 .... F-8
Britt, Hancock, 2,133 .... B-8
Brooklyn, Poweshiek, 1,439 .... H-12
Buffalo, Scott, 1,260 .... I-17
Buffalo Center, Winnebago, 1,081 .... A-8
Burlington, Des Moines, 27,208 .... K-16
Calmar, Winneshiek, 1,026 .... B-13
Camanche, Clinton, 4,436 .... G-18
Carlisle, Polk/Warren, 3,241 .... I-9
Carroll, Carroll, 9,579 .... F-5
Carter Lake, Pottawattamie, 3,200 .... I-3
Cascade, Dubuque/Jones, 1,812 .... E-16
Cedar Falls, Black Hawk, 34,298 .... D-12
Cedar Rapids, Linn, 108,751 .... G-14
Center Point, Linn, 1,693 .... F-14
Centerville, Appanoose, 5,936 .. L-11
Central City, Linn, 1,063 .... F-14
Chariton, Lucas, 4,616 .... K-10
Charles City, Floyd, 7,878 .... B-11
Cherokee, Cherokee, 6,026 .... D-3
Clarinda, Page, 5,104 .... L-5
Clarion, Wright, 2,703 .... D-8
Clarksville, Butler, 1,382 .... D-11
Clear Lake, Cerro Gordo, 8,183 .... B-9
Clinton, Clinton, 29,201 .... G-18
Clive, Polk, 7,462 .... H-8
Colfax, Jasper, 2,462 .... H-10
Columbus Junction, Louisa, 1,616 .... I-15
Coon Rapids, Carroll, 1,266 .... G-6
Coralville, Johnson, 10,347 .... H-14
Corning, Adams, 1,806 .... K-6
Corydon, Wayne, 1,675 .... L-10
Council Bluffs, Pottawattamie, 54,315 .... I-3
Cresco, Howard, 3,669 .... A-13
Creston, Union, 7,911 .... J-7
Dakota City, Humboldt, 1,024 .... D-7
Dallas Center, Dallas, 1,454 .... H-8
Davenport, Scott, 95,333 .... H-17
De Soto, Dallas, 1,033 .... I-8
De Witt, Clinton, 4,514 .... G-17
Decorah, Winneshiek, 8,063 .... B-14
Denison, Crawford, 6,604 .... G-4
Denver, Bremer, 1,600 .... D-12
Des Moines, Polk, 193,187 .... H-9
Dubuque, Dubuque, 57,546 .... E-17
Dunlap, Harrison, 1,251 .... G-3
Durant, Cedar/Muscatine/Scott, 1,549 .... H-16
Dyersville, Delaware/Dubuque, 3,703 .... E-15
Dysart, Tama, 1,230 .... F-12
Eagle Grove, Wright, 3,671 .... D-8
Earlham, Madison, 1,157 .... I-7
Eddyville, Mahaska/Monroe/ Wapello, 1,010 .... J-11
Eldon, Wapello, 1,070 .... K-13
Eldora, Hardin, 3,038 .... E-10
Eldridge, Scott, 3,378 .... H-17
Elk Run Heights, Black Hawk, 1,088 .... E-12
Elkader, Clayton, 1,510 .... C-15
Emmetsburg, Palo Alto, 3,940 .... B-6
Epworth, Dubuque, 1,297 .... E-16
Estherville, Emmet, 6,720 .... A-5
Evansdale, Black Hawk, 4,638 . E-12
Fairbank, Buchanan/Fayette, 1,018 .... D-13
Fairfield, Jefferson, 9,768 .... K-13
Farley, Dubuque, 1,354 .... E-16
Fayette, Fayette, 1,317 .... C-14
Forest City, Hancock/ Winnebago, 4,430 .... B-9
Fort Dodge, Webster, 25,894 .... E-7
Fort Madison, Lee, 11,618 .... L-15
Fredericksburg, Chickasaw, 1,011 .... C-12
Garner, Hancock, 2,916 .... B-9
George, Lyon, 1,066 .... A-2
Glenwood, Mills, 4,571 .... J-3
Glidden, Carroll, 1,099 .... F-6
Gowrie, Webster, 1,028 .... F-7
Greene, Butler, 1,142 .... C-11
Greenfield, Adair, 2,074 .... I-6
Grimes, Polk, 2,653 .... H-8
Grinnell, Poweshiek, 8,902 .... H-11
Griswold, Cass, 1,049 .... J-5
Grundy Center, Grundy, 2,491 . E-11
Guthrie Center, Guthrie, 1,614 ... H-6
Guttenberg, Clayton, 2,257 .... C-15
Hamburg, Fremont, 1,248 .... L-3
Hampton, Franklin, 4,133 .... D-10
Harlan, Shelby, 5,148 .... H-4
Hartley, O'Brien, 1,632 .... B-4
Hawarden, Sioux, 2,439 .... C-1
Hiawatha, Linn, 4,986 .... F-14
Holstein, Ida, 1,449 .... E-3
Hudson, Black Hawk, 2,037 .... E-12
Hull, Sioux, 1,724 .... B-2
Humboldt, Humboldt, 4,438 .... D-7
Huxley, Story, 2,047 .... G-9
Ida Grove, Ida, 2,357 .... E-4
Independence, Buchanan, 5,972 .... E-13
Indianola, Warren, 11,340 .... I-9
Iowa City, Johnson, 59,738 .... H-14
Iowa Falls, Hardin, 5,424 .... E-10
Jefferson, Greene, 4,292 .... G-7
Jesup, Buchanan, 2,121 .... E-13
Jewell Junction, Hamilton, 1,106 .... E-9
Johnston, Polk, 4,702 .... H-8
Kalona, Washington, 1,942 .... I-14
Keokuk, Lee, 12,451 .... L-15
Keosauqua, Van Buren, 1,020 .. L-13
Keota, Keokuk, 1,000 .... I-13
Kingsley, Plymouth, 1,129 .... D-2
Knoxville, Marion, 8,232 .... I-10
La Porte City, Black Hawk, 2,128 .... E-13
Lake City, Calhoun, 1,841 .... F-6
Lake Mills, Winnebago, 2,143 .... A-9
Lake View, Sac, 1,303 .... E-5
Lamoni, Decatur, 2,319 .... L-8
Lansing, Allamakee, 1,007 .... A-15
Laurens, Pocahontas, 1,550 .... C-5
Le Claire, Scott, 2,734 .... H-18
Le Mars, Plymouth, 8,454 .... D-2
Lenox, Adams/Taylor, 1,303 .... K-6
Leon, Decatur, 2,047 .... L-8
Lisbon, Linn, 1,452 .... G-15
Logan, Harrison, 1,401 .... H-3
Madrid, Boone, 2,395 .... G-8
Malvern, Mills, 1,210 .... K-3
Manchester, Delaware, 5,137 .. E-14
Manly, Worth, 1,349 .... B-10
Manning, Carroll, 1,484 .... G-5
Manson, Calhoun, 1,844 .... E-6
Mapleton, Monona, 1,294 .... F-3
Maquoketa, Jackson, 6,111 .... F-17
Marcus, Cherokee, 1,171 .... C-3
Marengo, Iowa, 2,270 .... G-13
Marion, Linn, 20,403 .... F-14
Marshalltown, Marshall, 25,178 .... F-11
Mason City, Cerro Gordo, 29,040 .... B-10
Mechanicsville, Cedar, 1,012 ... G-15
Mediapolis, Des Moines, 1,637 .... J-16
Melcher-Dallas, Marion, 1,302 .. J-10
Milford, Dickinson, 2,170 .... A-5
Missouri Valley, Harrison, 2,888 .... H-3
Mitchellville, Polk, 1,670 .... H-9
Monona, Clayton, 1,520 .... B-15
Monroe, Jasper, 1,739 .... I-10
Montezuma, Poweshiek, 1,651 .... H-12
Monticello, Jones, 3,522 .... F-15
Mount Ayr, Ringgold, 1,796 .... L-7
Mount Pleasant, Henry, 8,027 ... K-14
Mount Vernon, Linn, 3,657 .... G-15
Moville, Woodbury, 1,306 .... E-2
Muscatine, Muscatine, 22,881 ... I-16
Nashua, Chickasaw, 1,476 .... C-12
Nevada, Story, 6,009 .... G-9
New Hampton, Chickasaw, 3,660 .... C-12
New London, Henry, 1,922 .... K-15
New Sharon, Mahaska, 1,136 .... I-11
Newell, Buena Vista, 1,089 ....
Newton, Jasper, 14,789 .... H-10
Nora Springs, Floyd, 1,505 .... B-10
North Liberty, Johnson, 2,926 ... H-14
Northwood, Worth, 1,940 .... A-10
Norwalk, Warren, 5,726 .... I-9
Oakland, Pottawattamie, 1,496 .... I-4
Odebolt, Sac, 1,158 .... E-4
Oelwein, Fayette, 6,493 .... D-13
Ogden, Boone, 1,909 .... G-8
Onawa, Monona, 2,936 .... F-2
Orange City, Sioux, 4,940 .... C-2
Osage, Mitchell, 3,439 .... B-11
Osceola, Clarke, 4,164 .... K-8
Oskaloosa, Mahaska, 10,632 .... I-11
Ottumwa, Wapello, 24,488 .... K-12
Panora, Guthrie, 1,100 .... H-7
• Park View, Scott, 2,192 .... H-17
Parkersburg, Butler, 1,804 .... D-11
Paullina, O'Brien, 1,134 .... C-3
Pella, Marion, 9,270 .... I-11
Perry, Dallas, 6,652 .... G-7
Pleasant Hill, Polk, 3,671 .... H-9
Pleasantville, Marion, 1,536 .... I-10
Pocahontas, Pocahontas, 2,085 .... D-6
Polk City, Polk, 1,908 .... H-8
Postville, Allamakee/Clayton, 1,472 .... B-14
Prairie City, Jasper, 1,360 .... H-10
Preston, Jackson, 1,025 .... F-17
Primghar, O'Brien, 950 .... B-3
Red Oak, Montgomery, 6,264 .... K-4
Reinbeck, Grundy, 1,605 .... E-11
Remsen, Plymouth, 1,513 .... C-2
Rock Rapids, Lyon, 2,601 .... A-2
Rock Valley, Sioux, 2,540 .... B-2
Rockwell, Cerro Gordo, 1,008 .. C-10
Rockwell City, Calhoun, 1,981 .... E-6
Roland, Story, 1,035 .... F-9
Sac City, Sac, 2,492 .... E-5
Sanborn, O'Brien, 1,345 .... B-3
• Saylorville, Polk, 2,709 .... H-9
Sergeant Bluff, Woodbury, 2,772 .... E-1
Sheffield, Franklin, 1,174 .... C-10
Sheldon, O'Brien/Sioux, 4,937 ... B-3
Shell Rock, Butler, 1,385 .... D-11
Shenandoah, Fremont/Page, 5,572 .... K-4
Sibley, Osceola, 2,815 .... A-3
Sidney, Fremont, 1,253 .... L-3
Sigourney, Keokuk, 2,111 .... I-13
Sioux Center, Sioux, 5,074 .... B-2
Sioux City, Woodbury, 80,505 .... E-1
Slater, Story, 1,268 .... G-9
Solon, Johnson, 1,050 .... G-15
Spencer, Clay, 11,066 .... B-5
Spirit Lake, Dickinson, 3,871 .... A-5
Springville, Linn, 1,068 .... F-15
St. Ansgar, Mitchell, 1,063 .... A-11
State Center, Marshall, 1,248 ... G-10
Storm Lake, Buena Vista, 8,769 . D-4
Story City, Story, 2,959 .... F-9
Strawberry Point, Clayton, 1,357 .... D-14
Stuart, Adair/Guthrie, 1,522 .... I-7
Sumner, Bremer, 2,078 .... C-13
Tama, Tama, 2,697 .... G-12
Tipton, Cedar, 2,998 .... G-16
Toledo, Tama, 2,380 .... G-12
Traer, Tama, 1,552 .... F-12
Tripoli, Bremer, 1,188 .... C-12
University Heights, Johnson, 1,042 .... H-14
Urbandale, Polk, 23,500 .... H-8
Villisca, Montgomery, 1,332 .... K-5
Vinton, Benton, 5,103 .... F-13
Walcott, Muscatine/Scott, 1,356 .... H-16
Wapello, Louisa, 2,013 .... J-15
Washburn, Black Hawk E-12
Washington, Washington, 7,074 .... I-14
Waterloo, Black Hawk, 66,467 . E-12
Waukee, Dallas, 2,512 .... H-8
Waukon, Allamakee, 4,019 .... B-14
Waverly, Bremer, 8,539 .... D-12
Webster City, Hamilton, 7,894 .... E-8
Wellman, Washington, 1,085 .... I-14
West Branch, Cedar, 1,908 .... H-15
West Burlington, Des Moines, 3,083 .... K-15
West Des Moines, Dallas/ Polk, 31,702 .... H-8
West Liberty, Muscatine, 2,935 .... H-15
West Point, Lee, 1,079 .... L-15
West Union, Fayette, 2,490 .... C-14
Williamsburg, Iowa, 2,174 .... H-13
Wilton, Cedar/Muscatine, 2,577 .... H-16
Windsor Heights, Polk, 5,190 .... H-8
Winfield, Henry, 1,051 .... J-15
Winterset, Madison, 4,196 .... I-8
Woodbine, Harrison, 1,500 .... H-3
Woodward, Dallas, 1,197 .... G-8

Explanation of symbols: •– Census Designated Place (CDP)

Kansas

General Help Numbers:

Governor's Office

State Capitol Bldg, Room 212S   785-296-3232
Topeka, KS 66612-1590   Fax 785-296-7973
http://www.ksgovernor.org   8AM-5PM

Attorney General's Office

Memorial Hall   785-296-2215
120 SW 10th Ave   Fax 785-296-6296
Topeka, KS 66612-1597   8AM-5PM
http://www.accesskansas.org/ksag/

Legislative Records

Kansas State Library, Capitol Bldg   785-296-2149
300 SW 10th Ave   Fax 785-296-6650
Topeka, KS 66612   8AM-5PM
www.kslegislature.org

State Archives

Library and Archives Division   785-272-8681
6425 SW 6th Ave   Fax 785-272-8682
Topeka, KS 66615-1099   9AM-4:30PM M-SA
www.kshs.org

State Specifics:

Capital: Topeka
Shawnee County

Time Zone: CST*

* Kansas' five western-most counties are MST:
They are: Greeley, Hamilton, Kearny, Sherman, Wallace,

Number of Counties: 105

Population: 2,735,502

Website: www.accesskansas.org

State Agencies

Criminal Records

Kansas Bureau of Investigation, Criminal Records Division, 1620 SW Tyler, Crim. History Record Sec., Topeka, KS 66612-1837; 785-296-8200, 785-368-7162-Fax; 8AM-5PM.

www.accesskansas.org/kbi

Agencies dealing with children, the elderly or disabled clientele may qualify for reduced fees for record checks. These accounts are known as Caretaker accounts.

Records are available from 1939 to present. It takes up to 4 days before new records are available for inquiry. Records are indexed on Kansas Central Repository database, which is synchronized with the automated fingerprint ID system database. Records are normally destroyed after court-ordered expungement or after subject reaches 100 years of age. 50% of all arrests in database have final dispositions recorded, 57% for those arrests within last 5 years.

Searching: The criminal history information maintained by the KBI includes felony and misdemeanor arrests, prosecution data, court dispositions and information of incarceration in state-operated confinement facilities. Include the following in your request-full name, sex, race, date of birth, Social Security Number. Each request must be on a separate "Records Check Request Form.". Fingerprints are optional. Approximately 85% of records are fingerprint supported. Turnaround time may be several weeks if the record is not currently automated; approximately 46% of records are automated. The following data is not released: expunged records, non-convictions or juvenile records except to Criminal justice agencies and agencies required by law. Records of arrests within the past 12 months are also released when the records of disposition have not yet been received. Records release include court convictions for violations of Kansas law that are felonies or class A or class B misdemeanors as well as municipal ordinances or county resolutions that are equivalent to class A or class B misdemeanors under state statute. Class C misdemeanor assaults are also part of the database.

Access by: mail, fax, online.

Fee & Payment: Fees: $17.50 for a name check online; $20.00 by mail; $30.00 for fingerprint search. Add $10.00 for certification. If a "caregiver" fee is $12.50 for online name check and fingerprint check is $20.00. Fee payee: KBI Records Fees Fund. Prepayment required. Personal checks and credit cards are accepted.

Mail search: Turnaround time: 2 to 4 weeks. A SASE is requested.

Fax search: Prior arrangement is required, same criteria as mail.

Online search: Anyone may obtain non-certified criminal records online at www.accesskansas.org/kbi/criminalhistory/. The system is also available for premium subscribers of accessKansas. The fee is $17.50 per record; credit cards accepted online. The system is unavailable between the hours of midnight and 4 AM daily. A Kansas "Most Wanted" list is available at www.accesskansas.org/kbi/mw.htm.

Statewide Court Records

Judicial Administrator, Kansas Judicial Center, 301 SW 10th St, Topeka, KS 66612-1507; 785-296-3229, 785-296-1028-Fax; 8AM-5PM.

www.kscourts.org

There is no statewide access to all county trial courts.

Access by: phone, online.

Phone search: For information on appellate cases, call the Clerk of the Appellate Court at the number listed above.

Online search: The website above offers free online access to published opinions of the Supreme and Appellate courts, as well as case information for the Appellate courts. Five counties have record index acess from www.accesskansas.org. Fees are involved.

Sexual Offender Registry

Kansas Bureau of Investigation, Offender Registration, 1620 SW Tyler, Topeka, KS 66612; 785-296-8200, 785-296-6781-Fax; 8AM-5PM.

https://www.accesskansas.org/ssrv-registered-offender/index.do

There are over 3,100 offenders registered in the state. Records are available from 4/14/1994 forward. It takes 10 working days before new records are available for inquiry.

Searching: Further information on any registered offender in the file can be obtained from the sheriff's office in the registrant's county of residence. Include the following in your request-name, DOB. SSN is helpful.

Access by: mail, fax, in person, online.

Mail search: Turnaround time: 1 to 2 days. A SASE is requested.

Fax search: Prior arrangement is required, same criteria as mail.

In person search: Search in person at this office or at local sheriff offices in the state.

Online search: Searching is available at the website. All open registrants are searchable.

Incarceration Records

Kansas Department of Corrections, Public Information Officer, 900 SW Jackson, 4th floor, Topeka, KS 66612-1284; 785-296-3310, 785-296-0014-Fax; 8AM-5PM.

http://docnet.dc.state.ks.us

General questions can be sent to kdocpub@kdoc.dc.state.ks.us.

Records are available on current and former inmates. It takes up to 4 days before new records

are available for inquiry. Records are normally destroyed after 30 years.

Searching: Include the following in your request-full name. The date of birth and Social Security Number are helpful. Location, KDOC number, physical identifiers, sentencing and conviction information, disciplinary record, and custody or supervision level are released. The following data is not released: medical, mental health, substance abuse

Access by: mail, phone, fax, online.

Mail search: Turnaround time: 2 to 4 weeks. SASE is required.

Phone search: Name searching permitted.

Fax search: Same criteria as mail.

Online search: Web access to the database known as KASPER gives information on offenders who are: currently incarcerated; under post-incarceration supervision; and, who have been discharged from a sentence. The database does not have information available about inmates sent to Kansas under the provisions of the interstate compact agreement. Go to http://docnet.dc.state.ks.us/kasper2/kasperexpl.htm.

Corporation, Limited Partnerships, Limited Liability Company Records

Secretary of State, Memorial Hall, 1st Floor, 120 SW 10th Ave, Topeka, KS 66612-1594; 785-296-4564, 785-296-4570-Fax; 8AM-5PM.

www.kssos.org/main.html

Records are available since the applicable laws have been in effect. All Annual Reports are on microfilm at the Historical Society. New records are available for inquiry immediately. Records are indexed on inhouse computer.

Searching: Items not released include confidential annual report balance sheets and copies of extensions. Include the following in your request-full name of business, specific records that you need copies of. Records include articles of incorporation, all amendments and Annual Reports,

Access by: mail, phone, fax, in person, online.

Fee & Payment: There is no search fee. Plain copies are $1.00 per page. A certificate of good standing is $15.00, $12.50, if electronic. A letter of good standing is $10.00. Fee payee: Secretary of State. Prepayment required. Prepaid accounts are available. Personal checks accepted. Credit cards accepted: MasterCard, Visa.

Mail search: Turnaround time: 2 to 3 days. No SASE is required.

Phone search: General information is given without charge.

Fax search: Items can be returned by fax for an additional $2.00 for the first page and $1.00 each additional page.

In person search: No fee for request.

Online search: Free entity searching is available at www.accesskansas.org/apps/corporations.html. Search by individual or company name, key word, date, or organizational number. There is no fee to search records, but there is a fee to order copies of certificates of good standings.

Trademarks/Servicemarks

Secretary of State, Trademarks/Servicemarks Division, 120 SW 10th Ave, Rm 100, Topeka, KS 66612-1240; 785-296-4564, 785-296-4570-Fax; 8AM-5PM. www.kssos.org

Records are available from the 1950s, all on computer. It takes 2 to 3 days before new records are available for inquiry.

Searching: All information recorded is available to the public. However, Kansas law prohibits the use of names and/or addresses derived from public record for solicitation purposes. Include the following in your request-trademark/servicemark name, number of owner. The search provides the names and addresses of owners, date of filing, and class code of filing.

Access by: mail, phone, fax, in person.

Fee & Payment: There is no search fee. Copies are $1.00 per page. Certification is $15.00 plus the copy fees. Fee payee: Secretary of State. Prepayment required. The Secretary of State's office offers prepaid accounts for all regular, ongoing requesters. Personal checks accepted. Credit cards accepted: MasterCard, Visa.

Mail search: Turnaround time: 1 to 2 days. A mail request must include the name of trademark/servicemark and/or the owner's name. No SASE is required. No fee for mail request.

Phone search: No fee for telephone request. They will give you limited information from the computer index.

Fax search: Turnaround time 24 hours.

In person search: No fee for request.

Other access: For bulk file purchase call Ann at 785-296-6271.

Uniform Commercial Code, Federal and State Tax Liens

Secretary of State - UCC Searches, Memorial Hall, 1st Fl, 120 SW 10th Ave, Topeka, KS 66612; 785-296-4564, 785-296-3659-Fax; 8AM-5PM.

www.kssos.org/business/business_ucc.html

Records are available from 1966 on computer, from 1966 to present on microfiche with exception of electronic filings. These images available from July 30, 2001.

Searching: Use search request form UCC-II. The search includes federal tax liens on businesses. Federal tax liens on individuals can be filed here or at county, all state tax liens are filed at the county level. Include the following in your request-debtor name. You must order copies to receive collateral information. No collateral data is given over the phone.

Access by: mail, phone, fax, in person, online.

Fee & Payment: The search fee is $20.00 per name, $10.00 if searched online, and copies are $1.00 per page. Fee payee: Secretary of State. Prepayment required. Personal checks accepted. Credit cards accepted: MasterCard, Visa.

Mail search: Turnaround time: 3 days. The search is done on the name exactly as presented. If there is a possibility of a variation, each variation must be submitted. A SASE is requested.

Phone search: Search costs $20.00 per debtor name.

Fax search: Same criteria as mail searching. You can have information returned by fax for an additional $2.00 for the first page and $1.00 each additional page.

In person search: Unless extensive list given, data available while you wait.

Online search: Online service is provided by accessKansas at www.accesskansas.org. The system is open 24 hours daily. There is an annual fee. UCC records are $10.00 per record. This is the same online system used for corporation records. For more information, call at 800-4-KANSAS.

Other access: Records in a bulk or database format is available from accessKansas.com.

Sales Tax Registrations

Access to Records is Restricted.

Kansas Department of Revenue, Record Requests, Docking State Office Bldg, 915 SW Harrison, Topeka, KS 66625-3570; 785-296-3081, 785-296-7928-Fax; 8AM-5PM.

www.ksrevenue.org

Sales tax registration information is considered confidential and not public record.

Birth Certificates

Kansas Department of Health & Environment, Office of Vital Statistics, 1000 SW Jackson, #120, Topeka, KS 66612-2221; 785-296-1400, 785-296-3253 (Phone Credit Card Orders), 785-357-4332-Fax; 8AM-5PM.

www.kdhe.state.ks.us/vital

Vital records are not considered public records in Kansas. Uncertified copies or verifications are not provided to the public. Birth certificates began being filed with the Office July 1, 1911.

Records are available from July 1911 to present. Delayed birth registrations from the late-1800s are available. It takes approximately 2 weeks before new records are available for inquiry. Records are indexed on microfiche, inhouse computer. Records are normally destroyed after (records kept indefinitely).

Searching: Must have a signed release from person of record or have direct interest for personal or property right. You must also include photocopy of your government-issued photo ID (DL, for instance). Include the following in your request-full name, names of parents, mother's maiden name, date of birth, place of birth, relationship to person of record, reason for information request. Include a daytime phone number.

Access by: mail, phone, fax, in person, online.

Fee & Payment: The fee is $12.00 for first certified copy, includes search of 5 years. Additional fee required for additional years searched. Add $7.00 for each additional copy of same record. Fee payee: Vital Statistics. Prepayment required. There is an additional $9.00 VitalChek fee with the use of a credit card. Personal checks accepted. Major credit cards accepted.

Mail search: Turnaround time: 5-10 business days. Include copy of your government-issued photo ID. A SASE is requested.

Phone search: You must use a credit card for an additional $9.00 fee. Turnaround time is within 3 business days. Phone service hours are from 8am to 4pm.

Fax search: The fee must include $9.00 for use of a credit card. Turnaround time is within 3 business days.

In person search: Available 9AM to 4PM. You must complete an application and provide your photo ID. Turnaround time: 20 to 30 minutes.

Online search: Records may be ordered online via a state designated vendor VitalChek at www.vitalchek.com.

Expedited service: Expedited service is available for credit card searches through VitalChek. Turnaround time: 3 to 5 days. Overnight mail services for return of documents is available for $22.50 plus credit card fee and record fee. Requests may require up to 24 business hours to process.

Death Records

Kansas State Department of Health & Environment, Office of Vital Statistics, 1000 SW Jackson, #120, Topeka, KS 66612-2221; 785-296-1400, 785-296-3253 (Phone Credit Card Orders), 785-357-4332-Fax; 8AM-5PM.

www.kdhe.state.ks.us/vital

Vital records are not considered public records in Kansas. Uncertified copies or verifications are not provided to the public.

Records are available from July 1, 1911 to present. New records are available for inquiry immediately. Records are indexed on microfiche, inhouse computer. Records are normally destroyed after (records kept indefinitely).

Searching: Must have a signed release from immediate family member or show direct interest for personal or property right. You must also include photocopy of your government-issued photo ID (DL, for instance). Include the following in your request-full name, date of death, place of death, relationship to person of record, reason for information request. Please include a daytime phone number.

Access by: mail, phone, fax, in person, online.

Fee & Payment: The fee is $13.00 for first certified copy, includes search of 5 years. Additional fee required for additional years searched. Add $8.00 for each additional copy of same record. Fee payee: Vital Statistics. Prepayment required. Money orders are accepted. There is a $9.00 VitalChek fee for the use of a credit card. Personal checks accepted. Major credit cards accepted.

Mail search: Turnaround time: 5-10 business days. Must include a personal ID. A SASE is requested.

Phone search: Use a credit card required for an additional $9.00 fee. Turnaround time is within 3 business days.

Fax search: Same criteria as phone searches.

In person search: Available 9AM to 4PM. Must complete an application and provide your personal photo ID. Turnaround time: 20 to 30 minutes.

Online search: Records may be ordered online via a state designated vendor VitalChek at www.vitalchek.com.

Expedited service: Expedited service is available for credit card searches through VitalChek. Turnaround time: 3 to 5 days. Overnight mail services for return of documents is available for $22.50 plus credit card fee and record fee. Requests may require up to 24 business hours to process.

Marriage Certificates

Kansas State Department of Health & Environment, Office of Vital Statistics, 1000 SW Jackson, #120, Topeka, KS 66612-2221; 785-296-1400, 785-296-3253 (Phone Credit Card Orders), 785-357-4332-Fax; 8AM-5PM.

www.kdhe.state.ks.us/vital

Vital records are not considered public records in Kansas. Uncertified copies or verifications are not provided to the public.

Records are available from May 1, 1913 to present. Records prior to 1913 are found at county of issue. Records are computerized from 1993. It takes 2 months before new records are available for inquiry. Records are indexed on microfiche, inhouse computer. Records are normally destroyed after (records kept indefinitely).

Searching: Must have a signed release from person of record or have direct interest in personal or property right. You must also include photocopy of your government-issued photo ID (DL, for instance). Include the following in your request-names of husband and wife, date of marriage, place or county of marriage, relationship to person of record, reason for information request, wife's maiden name. Include a daytime phone number.

Access by: mail, phone, fax, in person, online.

Fee & Payment: The fee is $12.00 for first certified copy, includes search of 5 years. Additional fee required for additional years searched. Add $7.00 for each additional copy of same record. Fee payee: Vital Statistics. Prepayment required. Money orders are accepted. Personal checks accepted. Major credit cards accepted.

Mail search: Turnaround time: 5-10 business days. Must include a personal ID number. A SASE is requested.

Phone search: You must use a credit card for an additional $9.00 fee. Turnaround time is within 3 business days.

Fax search: Same criteria as phone searches.

In person search: You must complete an application and provide your photo ID. Available 9AM to 4PM. Turnaround time 20 to 30 minutes.

Online search: Records may be ordered online via a state designated vendor VitalChek at www.vitalchek.com.

Expedited service: Expedited service is available for credit card searches through VitalChek. Turnaround time: 3 to 5 days. Overnight mail services for return of documents is available for $22.50 plus credit card fee and record fee. Requests may require up to 24 business hours to process.

Divorce Records

Kansas State Department of Health & Environment, Office of Vital Statistics, 1000 SW Jackson, #120, Topeka, KS 66612-2221; 785-296-1400, 785-296-3253 (Phone Credit Card Orders), 785-357-4332-Fax; 8AM-5PM.

www.kdhe.state.ks.us/vital

The agency will issue a divorce certificate, but a copy of the decree must be ordered from the county of issue. Vital records are not considered public records in Kansas. Uncertified copies or verifications are not provided to the public.

Records are available from July 1, 1951 to present. Records prior to July 1, 1951 are found at county of issue. It takes the second month after the divorce is filed before new records are available for inquiry. Records are indexed on microfiche, inhouse computer. Records are normally destroyed after (records kept indefinitely).

Searching: Must have a signed release from person of record or show direct interest in personal or property right. You must also include photocopy of your government-issued photo ID (DL, for instance). Include the following in your request-names of husband and wife, date of divorce, county of divorce, relationship to person of record, reason for information request. Include your daytime telephone number.

Access by: mail, phone, fax, in person, online.

Fee & Payment: The fee is $12.00 for first certified copy, includes search of 5 years. Additional fee required for additional years searched. Add $7.00 for each additional copy of same record. Fee payee: Vital Statistics. Prepayment required. Money orders are accepted. Personal checks accepted. Major credit cards accepted.

Mail search: Turnaround time: 5-10 business days. A SASE is requested.

Phone search: Must use a credit card for an additional $9.00 fee. Turnaround time is within 3 business days.

Fax search: Same criteria as phone searches.

In person search: You must complete an application and provide your photo ID. Available 9AM to 4PM. Turnaround time is 20-30 minutes.

Online search: Records may be ordered online via a state designated vendor VitalChek at www.vitalchek.com.

Expedited service: Expedited service is available for credit card searches through VitalChek. Turnaround time: 3 to 5 days. Overnight mail services for return of documents is available for $22.50 plus credit card fee and record fee. Requests may require up to 24 business hours to process.

Workers' Compensation Records

Human Resources Department, Workers Compensation Division, 800 SW Jackson, Suite 600, Topeka, KS 66612-1227; 785-296-6762, 785-291-3430-Fax; 8AM-5PM.

www.dol.ks.gov/index.html

Records are available from the mid-1970's on. New records are available for inquiry immediately. Records are indexed on inhouse computer, file folders.

Searching: Information not released includes financial information submitted by employer, peer review records, and records related to safety inspections. Medical records are only released to those authorized by law, and are not open to the general public. Include the following in your request-claimant name, SSN, signed release. All requests must be on Division Forms. The forms are available from the web or can be faxed. Employers may receive medical records if a job has been conditionally offered and there is a signed release by the subject.

Access by: mail, phone, fax, in person.

Fee & Payment: There is no search fee.

Mail search: Turnaround time: 1 week to 10 days. No SASE is required.

Phone search: Some records are available for verification by phone.

Fax search: Fax searching available.

In person search: Requests maintained off premises will take 2 days to obtain.

Driver Records, Accident Reports

Department of Revenue, Driver Control Bureau, PO Box 12021, Topeka, KS 66612-2021 (Courier address: Docking State Office Building, 915 Harrison, Rm 100, Topeka, KS 66612); 785-296-3671, 785-296-6851-Fax; 8AM-4:45PM.

www.ksrevenue.org/vehicle.htm

Records are available for 3 years for minor violations and lifetime for DWIs. The state does not record speeding violations of 10 mph or less over in a 55 to 75 speed zone. It takes 2 to 21 days before new records are available for inquiry. Records are normally destroyed after 4 to 6 years, depending on violation, records then are microfilmed.

Searching: Permissible use requesters should use Form TR/DL 302. Casual requesters must secure written consent from subject before any records are released and use Form TR/DL 301. Include the following in your request-full name, DOB. License #. The driver license number and either full name or DOB are required when ordering a driving record. The driver's address will show on the record. For an accident report, include the full name, DOB and/or VIN number, and date of accident. The following data is not released: medical information.

Access by: mail, in person, online.

Fee & Payment: The fee is $6.00 for a walk-in or mail-in request for a driving record. An accident report is available for $6.00 per page and copies of tickets $6.00 each. Fee payee: Department of Revenue. Prepayment required. Personal checks accepted. No credit cards accepted.

Mail search: Turnaround time: 2 to 5 days. A SASE is requested.

In person search: Walk-in requests are usually processed within 30 minutes. Local law enforcement agencies may also honor driving record requests at a higher cost.

Online search: Kansas has contracted with the AccessKansas (800-452-6727) to service all electronic media requests of driver license histories at www.accesskansas.org. The fee per record is $6.00 for batch requests or $6.50 for immediate inquiry. There is an initial $75 subscription fee and an annual $60 fee. The system is open 24 hours a day, 7 days a week. Batch requests are available at 7:30 am (if ordered by 10 pm the previous day).

Vehicle Ownership, Vehicle Identification

Division of Vehicles, Title and Registration Bureau, 915 Harrison, Rm 155, Topeka, KS 66626-0001; 785-296-3621, 785-296-3852-Fax; 8AM-4:45PM.

www.ksrevenue.org/vehicle.htm

Records are available from approximately 1940. Older records are on microfiche, on microfilm from 1970-1987, and computerized since 1988. It takes 8 weeks from application date before new records are available for inquiry.

Searching: Casual requesters can only obtain records with consent of subject. Records are restricted from purchase for the purpose of obtaining address mail lists for selling property or services. Include the following in your request-Form TR/DL302.

Access by: mail, in person, online.

Fee & Payment: The fee for a title/registration verification depends on the request mode, noted as below. Fee payee: Kansas Department of Revenue. Prepayment required. Personal checks accepted. No credit cards accepted.

Mail search: Turnaround time: 2 days. The fee for a title or registration verification is $6.00. The fee for a title application copy of a vehicle title history is $10.00. A SASE is requested.

In person search: Inquires are processed while you wait; however, requests must include form mentioned above. Same fees as by mail.

Online search: Online batch inquires are $6.00 per record; online interactive requests are $6.50 per record. Visit www.accesskansas.org for a complete description of accessKansas (800-452-6727), the state authorized vendor. There is an initial $75 subscription fee and an annual $60 fee to access records from AccessKansas.

Other access: This agency has several programs available to sell data in bulk format. Contact Donnita Thomas at the Dept of Revenue's Bureau of Policy and Research.

Vessel Ownership, Vessel Registration

Kansas Department of Wildlife & Parks, Boat Registration, 512 SE 25th Ave, Pratt, KS 67124-8174; 620-672-5911, 620-672-3013-Fax; 8AM-5PM M-F.

www.kdwp.state.ks.us

Liens must be searched at the county level.

Records are available from 1967 to present. Records are indexed on computer. Titles are not required. All motorized or sailboats must be registered. It takes 1 week before new records are available for inquiry. Records are normally destroyed after 3 years.

Searching: All requests must be submitted in writing with specific reason given for the request. No information is released for solicitation purposes. Include the following in your request-name, either KA# or hull #, and name of person making request.

Access by: mail, fax, in person.

Fee & Payment: There is no search fee, unless extensive searching is requested.

Mail search: Turnaround time: 1-3 days. No SASE is required.

Fax search: Same criteria as mail searching.

In person search: Inquires are processed while you wait; however, requests must be in writing.

Voter Registration

Access to Records is Restricted.

Secretary of State - Elections Division, Memorial Hall, 1st Floor, 120 SW 10th Ave, Topeka, KS 66612-1594; 785-296-4564, 785-291-3051-Fax; 8AM-5PM.

www.kssos.org

Individual records must be searched at the county level. This agency will sell the database on disk or CD only for political purposes. However, the Federal Help America Vote Act of 2002 (HAVA) law requires implementation of a central, computerized, statewide voter registration system by 01/01/2006. The state will comply.

GED Certificates

Kansas Board of Regents, GED Records, 1000 SW Jackson St #520, Topeka, KS 66612-1368; 785-296-3191, 785-296-0983-Fax; 8AM-4:30PM.

www.kansasregents.org

It takes 3 weeks before new records are available for inquiry.

Searching: Include the following in your request-name at time of test, DOB, SSN, signed release and requester phone number. Also include the date of the test.

Access by: mail, in person.

Fee & Payment: There is a $10.00 fee for a verification, transcript, or a duplicate diploma. Fee payee: Kansas Board of Regents. Prepayment required. Cash and money orders are accepted. Personal checks not accepted. No credit cards accepted.

Mail search: Turnaround time: 1 week. No SASE is required.

In person search: Walk-in requests are accepted from 10AM until 3PM.

Hunting and Fishing License Information

Dept of Wildlife & Parks, Licensing and Permits, 512 SE 25th Ave, Pratt, KS 67124-8174; 620-672-5911, 620-672-3013-Fax; 8AM-5PM.

www.kdwp.state.ks.us

The database of fishing licenses consists only of those licenses issued by this agency. There are many vendors throughout the state that also issue licenses and their data is not forwarded to this agency.

Records are available for 2 years. Boat statistics are available. It takes 1 month before new records are available for inquiry. Records are indexed on hard copy, most of the time. Records are normally destroyed after 3 years.

Searching: You can get big game information only. Requester must indicate what information is required and its intended use. Requests for information to be used for the sale of products or services will not be answered. Include the following in your request-full name, date of birth. Request may require an Open Records Certification to be completed. Suggest to call first.

Access by: mail, in person.

Fee & Payment: You must have Department approval. The agency reserves the right to recover costs for voluminous requests.

Mail search: Turnaround time: 1 to 3 days. No SASE is required.

In person search: You may request information in person.

Kansas State Licensing Agencies

Kansas Licenses Searchable Online

Alcohol/Drug Counselor #3	www.ksbsrb.org/verification.html
Architect #14	www.accesskansas.org/roster-search/index.html
Athletic Trainer #10	www.ksbha.org
Body Piercer #6	www.accesskansas.org/kboc
Charity Organization #27	www.kscharitycheck.org/search.asp
Chiropractor #10	www.ksbha.org
Cosmetologist / Cosmetology Facility #6	www.accesskansas.org/kboc/
Counselor, Professional #3	www.ksbsrb.org/verification.html
Crematories #11	www.accesskansas.org/ksbma/listings.html
Dental Hygienist #19	www.accesskansas.org/dental-verification/index.html
Dentist #19	www.accesskansas.org/dental-verification/index.html
Electrologist #6	www.accesskansas.org/kboc/
Embalmer #11	www.accesskansas.org/ksbma/listings.html
Engineer #14	www.accesskansas.org/roster-search/index.html
Esthetician #6	www.accesskansas.org/kboc/
Funeral Dir./Assist. Dir./Establishment #11	www.accesskansas.org/ksbma/listings.html
Geologist #14	www.accesskansas.org/roster-search/index.html
Insurance Agent #22	http://towerii.ksinsurance.org/agent/agent.jsp?pagnam=agentsearch
Insurance Company #22	http://towerii.ksinsurance.org/agent/agency.jsp?pagnam=agencysearch
Landscape Architect #14	www.accesskansas.org/roster-search/index.html
Lobbyist #27	www.kssos.org/elections/elections_lobbyists.html
Marriage & Family Therapist #3	www.ksbsrb.org/verification.html
Medical Doctor #10	www.ksbha.org
Nail Technician #6	www.accesskansas.org/kboc/
Nurse #12	https://www.accesskansas.org/app/nursing/verification/
Occupational Therapist/Assistant #10	www.ksbha.org
Optometrist #26	www.arbo.org/index.php?action=findanoptometrist
Osteopathic Physician #10	www.ksbha.org
Permanent Cosmetic Technician #6	www.accesskansas.org/kboc/
Pharmacist #13	https://www.accesskansas.org/pharmacy_verification/index.html
Physical Therapist/Assistant #10	www.ksbha.org
Physician Assistant #10	www.ksbha.org
Podiatrist #10	www.ksbha.org
Private Investigator #23	https://www.accesskansas.org/kbi-pi-verify/index.html
Psychologist #3	www.ksbsrb.org/verification.html
Psychologist, Masters Level #3	www.ksbsrb.org/verification.html
Public Accountant-CPA #4	www.ksboa.org/permit_list.htm
Real Estate Agent/Salesperson/Broker #31	https://www.accesskansas.org/krec/verification/index.html
Real Estate Appraiser #28	www.accesskansas.org
Respiratory Therapist #10	www.ksbha.org
Social Worker #3	www.ksbsrb.org/verification.html
Surveyor, Land #14	www.accesskansas.org/roster-search/index.html
Tanning Facility #6	www.accesskansas.org/kboc/
Tattoo Artist #6	www.accesskansas.org/kboc/
Teacher #7	www.ksbe.state.ks.us/cert/cert_search.html
Veterinarian #15	www.accesskansas.org/veterinary/listing.html

Kansas Licensing Quick Finder

Abstractor #1	620-544-2311	
Adult Care Home Administrator #16	785-296-0061	
Alcohol Vendor #20	785-296-7015	
Alcohol/Drug Counselor #3	785-296-3240	
Ambulance Attendant / Service #8	785-296-7299	
Animal Facility Inspector #2	785-296-2326	
Architect #14	785-296-3054	
Athletic Trainer #10	785-296-7413	
Attorney #18	785-296-8409	
Audiologist #16	785-296-0061	
Barber / Barber Shop #5	785-296-2211	
Barber College #5	785-296-2211	
Body Piercer #6	785-296-3155	
Charity Organization #27	800-432-2310	
Child Care Attendant #30	785-296-1270	
Chiropractor #10	785-296-7413	
Contractor, General #21	785-368-8222	
Cosmetologist/Cosmetic Facility #6	785-296-3155	
Cosmetology School Instructor #6	785-296-3155	
Counselor, Professional #3	785-296-3240	
Crematories #11	785-296-3980	
Dentist / Dental Hygienist #19	785-296-6400	
Dietitian #16	785-296-0061	
Drug Tax Stamp #20	785-368-8222	
Electrologist #6	785-296-3155	
Embalmer #11	785-296-3980	
Emergency Medical Technician #8	785-296-7299	
Engineer #14	785-296-3054	
Esthetician #6	785-296-3155	
Fundraiser/Prof. Solicitor #27	800-432-2310	
Funeral Director/Assistant Financial Director #11	785-296-3980	
Funeral Establishment Branch Establishments #11	785-296-3980	
Geologist #14	785-296-3054	
Hearing Aid Dispenser #9	316-263-0774	
Home Health Aide #16	785-296-6877	
Insurance Agent #22	785-296-7859	
Insurance Company #22	785-296-7859	

Investment Advisor #29	785-296-3307
Landscape Architect #14	785-296-3054
Livestock Inspector #2	785-296-2326
Lobbyist #27	785-296-3488
Marriage & Family Therapist #3	785-296-3240
Medical Doctor #10	785-296-7413
Medication Aide #16	785-296-6877
Nail Technician #6	785-296-3155
Notary Public #27	785-296-2239
Nurse #12	785-296-4929
Nurses' Aide #16	785-296-6877
Nursing Home Administrator #16	785-296-0061
Occupational Therapist/Assistant #10	785-296-7413
Optometrist #26	785-832-9986
Osteopathic Physician #10	785-296-7413
Permanent Cosmetic Technician #6	785-296-3155
Pesticide Applicator / Dealer #24	785-296-2263
Pharmacist #13	785-296-8420
Physical Therapist/Assistant #10	785-296-7413
Physician Assistant #10	785-296-7413
Podiatrist #10	785-296-7413
Private Investigator #23	785-296-4436
Psychologist #3	785-296-3240
Psychologist, Masters Level #3	785-296-3240
Public Accountant-CPA #4	785-296-2162
Racing & Wagering Equipment/Services #25	785-296-5800
Racing Facility Owner/Manager #25	785-296-5800
Racing Occupation #25	785-296-5800
Real Estate Agent/Seller/Broker #31	785-296-3411
Real Estate Appraiser #28	785-271-3373
Respiratory Therapist #10	785-296-7413
Salon #5	785-296-2211
School Administrator/Counselor #7	785-296-2288
School Library Media Specialist #7	785-296-2288
School Nurse #7	785-296-2288
Securities Agent #29	785-296-3307
Securities Broker/Dealer #29	785-296-3307
Shorthand Reporter #17	785-296-3299
Social Worker #3	785-296-3240
Special Investigator #2	785-296-2326
Speech/Language Pathologist #16	785-296-0061
Surveyor, Land #14	785-296-3054
Tanning Facility #6	785-296-3155
Tattoo Artist #6	785-296-3155
Teacher #7	785-296-2288
Tobacco Registration #20	785-296-7015
Veterinarian #15	785-456-8781

Kansas Licensing Agency Information

1 Abstracters Board of Examiners, 521 S. Main - PO Box 549, Hugoton, KS 67951-0549; 620-544-2311, Fax: 620-544-8029. Email: glen@pld.com

2 Animal Health Department, 708 S Jackson, Topeka, KS 66603-3714; 785-296-2326, Fax: 785-296-1765. www.accesskansas.org/kahd/

3 Behavioral Sciences Regulatory Board, 712 S Kansas, Topeka, KS 66603; 785-296-3240, Fax: 785-296-3112. www.ksbsrb.org/
Email: leslie.allen@bsrb.state.ks.us Search Database at www.ksbsrb.org/verification.html

4 Board of Accountancy, 900 SW Jackson #556, Topeka, KS 66612-1239; 785-296-2162, Fax: 785-291-3501. www.ksboa.org
Email: info@ksboa.state.ks.us Search Database at www.ksboa.org/permit_list.htm

5 Board of Barbering, 700 SW Jackson #1002, Topeka, KS 66603; 785-296-2211, Fax: 785-368-7071. Email: barber@yahoo.com

6 Board of Cosmetology, 714 SW Jackson #100, Topeka, KS 66603; 785-296-3155, Fax: 785-296-3002. www.ink.org/public/kboc
Search Database at www.accesskansas.org/kboc/

7 Board of Education, 120 SE 10th Ave, Topeka, KS 66612-1182; 785-296-3201, Fax: 785-296-7933. www.ksbe.state.ks.us/Welcome.html
Search Database at www.ksbe.state.ks.us/cert/cert_search.html Check status and verify via telephone at 785-296-2288.

8 Board of Emergency Medical Services, Landon State Office Building 900SW Jackson #10315, Topeka, KS 66603-3826; 785-296-7296, Fax: 785-296-6212. www.ksbems.org

9 Board of Examiners for Hearing Aid Dispensers, 600 N St Francis, Wichita, KS 67201-0252; 316-263-0774, Fax: 316-264-2681.
Email: sherry@mid-stateslabs.com

10 Board of Healing Arts, 235 S Topeka Blvd, Topeka, KS 66603-3068; 785-296-7413, Fax: 785-296-0852. www.ksbha.org Email: cabbot@ink.org

11 Board of Mortuary Arts, 700 SW Jackson, #904, Topeka, KS 66603-3733; 785-296-3980, Fax: 785-296-0891. www.accesskansas.org/ksbma
Email: bomal@ksbma.state.ks.us Search Database at www.accesskansas.org/ksbma/listings.html

12 Board of Nursing, Landon State Office Bldg. 900 SW Jackson, Rm 1051, Topeka, KS 66612-1230; 785-296-4929, Fax: 785-296-3929. www.ksbn.org Email: info@ksbn.state.ks.us

Search Database at https://www.accesskansas.org/app/nursing/verification/ Registered users of INK can subscribe and get license verifications for $.25; Non-subscribers fee is $1.00 each.

13 Board of Pharmacy, 900 Jackson, Landon State Office Bldg, Rm 560, Topeka, KS 66612-1231; 785-296-4056, Fax: 785-296-8420.
www.accesskansas.org/pharmacy/
Email: pharmacy@pharmacy.state.ks.us
Search Database at https://www.accesskansas.org/pharmacy_verification/index.html

14 Board of Technical Professions, 900 SW Jackson, Rm 507, Topeka, KS 66612-1257; 785-296-3053. www.accesskansas.org/ksbtp/
Search Database at www.accesskansas.org/roster-search/index.html

15 Board of Veterinary Examiners, PO Box 242 (1003 Lincoln), Wamego, KS 66547-0242; 785-456-8781, Fax: 785-456-8782. www.accesskansas.org/veterinary/ Search Database at www.accesskansas.org/veterinary/listing.html

16 Department of Health & Environment, Bureau of Health Facilities, 1000 SW Jackson #200, Topeka, KS 66612-1290; 785-296-1240, Fax: 785-296-3075. www.kdhe.state.ks.us/hoc/index.html
Email: mpetty@kdhe.state.ks.us

17 Clerk of Appellate Court, 301 S.W. 10th Avenue Rm. 374, Topeka, KS 66612-1507; 785-296-3229, Fax: 785-296-1028.
www.kscourts.org Email: green@kscourts.org

18 Clerk of the Supreme Court, 301 SW 10th Ave, Rm 374, Topeka, KS 66612; 785-296-8409, Fax: 785-296-1028. www.kscourts.org
Email: registration@kscourts.org

19 Dental Board, 900 SW Jackson St Rm 564S, Topeka, KS 66612-1220; 785-296-6400, Fax: 785-296-3116. www.accesskansas.org/kdb
Email: info@dental.state.ks.us
Search Database at www.accesskansas.org/dental-verification/index.html

20 Department of Revenue, Alcoholic Beverage Control, 915 SW Harrison St, Rm 214, Topeka, KS 66625-3512; 785-296-7015, Fax: 785-296-7185. www.ksrevenue.org/abc.htm
Email: abc@kdor.state.ks.us

21 Dept of Revenue, Robert B Docking, State Office Bldg, 915 SW Harrison St, Topeka, KS 66625-0001; 785-368-8222. www.ksrevenue.org

22 Insurance Department, 420 SW 9th, Topeka, KS 66612-1678; 785-296-7859, Fax: 785-368-

7019. www.ksinsurance.org Search Database at www.ksinsurance.org/company/main.html

23 Bureau of Investigation, Private Detective Licensing Unit, 1620 SW Tyler, Topeka, KS 66612-1837; 785-296-4436, Fax: 785-296-6781. www.accesskansas.org/kbi/
Email: corrina.clements@kbi.state.ks.us Search Database at https://www.accesskansas.org/kbi-pi-verify/index.html

24 Department of Agriculture, Records Ctr, 109 SW 9th St, Topeka, KS 66612; 785-296-2263, Fax: 785-296-0673. www.accesskansas.org/kda

25 Racing Commission, 700 SW Harrison, #420, Topeka, KS 66603-3754; 785-296-5800, Fax: 785-296-0900. www.accesskansas.org/krc
Email: kracing@ynetworks.com

26 Board of Examiners in Optometry, 3109 W. 6th St. #D, Lawrence, KS 66049; 785-832-9986, Fax: 785-832-9986. www.kssbeo.com
Email: kssbeo@terraworld.net Search Database at www.arbo.org/index.php?action=findanoptometrist

27 Office of Secretary of State, Memorial Hall, 1st Floor, 120 SW 10th Av, Topeka, KS 66612-1594; 785-296-4564. www.kssos.org/main.html
Email: kssos@kssos.org

28 Office of the Commissioner of Banks, Real Estate Appraisal Board, 1100 SW Wanamaker #104, Topeka, KS 66604-3805; 785-271-3373, Fax: 785-271-3370.
www.accesskansas.org/kreab
Email: kreab@cjnetworks.com
Search Database at www.accesskansas.org

29 Securities Commissioner of Kansas, 618 S Kansas 2nd Fl, Topeka, KS 66603-3804; 785-296-3307, Fax: 785-296-6872.
www.securities.state.ks.us
Email: securities@securities.state.ks.us

30 Child Care Licensing & Registration, 1000 SW Jackson #200, Topeka, KS 66612; 785-296-1240, Fax: 785-296-0803. www.kdhe.state.ks.us/bcclr/

31 Real Estate Commission, Licensing Board, 3 Townsite Plaza #200, 120 SE 6th, Topeka, KS 66603-3511; 785-296-3411, Fax: 785-296-1771. www.accesskansas.org/krec/
Email: krec@krec.state.ks.us Search Database at https://www.accesskansas.org/krec/verification/index.html Search results limited to 15 results at one time if a general name or city search is requested.

Kansas Federal Courts

The following list indicates the district and division name for each county in the state. If the bankruptcy court location is different from the district court, then the location of the bankruptcy court appears in parentheses.

County/Court Cross Reference

County	Court		County	Court		County	Court
Allen	Topeka		Greeley	Wichita		Osborne	Wichita
Anderson	Topeka		Greenwood	Wichita		Ottawa	Topeka
Atchison	Kansas City		Hamilton	Wichita		Pawnee	Wichita
Barber	Wichita		Harper	Wichita		Phillips	Wichita
Barton	Wichita		Harvey	Wichita		Pottawatomie	Topeka
Bourbon	Kansas City		Haskell	Wichita		Pratt	Wichita
Brown	Kansas City		Hodgeman	Wichita		Rawlins	Wichita
Butler	Wichita		Jackson	Topeka		Reno	Wichita
Chase	Topeka		Jefferson	Wichita		Republic	Topeka
Chautauqua	Wichita		Jewell	Topeka		Rice	Wichita
Cherokee	Kansas City		Johnson	Kansas City		Riley	Topeka
Cheyenne	Wichita		Kearny	Wichita		Rooks	Wichita
Clark	Wichita		Kingman	Wichita		Rush	Wichita
Clay	Topeka		Kiowa	Wichita		Russell	Wichita
Cloud	Topeka		Labette	Kansas City		Saline	Topeka
Coffey	Topeka		Lane	Wichita		Scott	Wichita
Comanche	Kansas City (Wichita)		Leavenworth	Kansas City		Sedgwick	Wichita
Cowley	Wichita		Lincoln	Topeka		Seward	Wichita
Crawford	Kansas City		Linn	Kansas City		Shawnee	Topeka
Decatur	Wichita		Logan	Wichita		Sheridan	Wichita
Dickinson	Topeka		Lyon	Topeka		Sherman	Wichita
Doniphan	Kansas City		Marion	Topeka		Smith	Wichita
Douglas	Topeka		Marshall	Kansas City		Stafford	Wichita
Edwards	Wichita		McPherson	Wichita		Stanton	Wichita
Elk	Wichita		Meade	Wichita		Stevens	Wichita
Ellis	Wichita		Miami	Kansas City		Sumner	Wichita
Ellsworth	Wichita		Mitchell	Topeka		Thomas	Wichita
Finney	Wichita		Montgomery	Wichita		Trego	Wichita
Ford	Wichita		Morris	Topeka		Wabaunsee	Topeka
Franklin	Topeka		Morton	Wichita		Wallace	Wichita
Geary	Topeka		Nemaha	Kansas City		Washington	Topeka
Gove	Wichita		Neosho	Topeka		Wichita	Wichita
Graham	Wichita		Ness	Wichita		Wilson	Topeka
Grant	Wichita		Norton	Wichita		Woodson	Topeka
Gray	Wichita		Osage	Topeka		Wyandotte	Kansas City

Standards for Federal Courts: Search fee is $26.00 per item (one party name or case number). Copy fee is $.50 per page. Certification fee is $9.00 per document, double for exemplification, if available. All fees standard unless noted in profile. Mail Search: always enclose a stamped self addressed envelope unless otherwise noted. Most courts accept fax requests or will suggest a copying/search vendor. Before releasing records, all courts require prepayment, unless noted.

Open records are located at the court unless otherwise noted. District courts index by defendant and plaintiff as well as by case number. Bankruptcy courts usually index by debtor and case number. While most courts now have their indexes on computer, many may still maintain index card files as well.

Courts offering internet access via CM-ECF or older RACER, PACER, or Web-PACER systems charge $.08 per page fee unless noted as free.

Where PACER is available, the universal sign-up number is 800-676-6856. Find PACER and the US Party/Case Index at http://pacer.psc.uscourts.gov.

US District Court

District of Kansas

Kansas City Division Clerk of Court, 500 State Ave, Kansas City, KS 66101 (also use mail address for courier delivery), 913-551-6719, Fax-913-551-6942. Hours- 9AM-4:30PM. www.ksd.uscourts.gov

Counties: Atchison, Bourbon, Brown, Cherokee, Crawford, Doniphan, Johnson, Labette, Leavenworth, Linn, Marshall, Miami, Nemaha, Wyandotte.

Searches & Indexing: Results do not include SSN or DOB. Computer, microfiche and card indexes maintained, computer back to 1995. New cases in the index immediately after filing date. Records purged never.

Fee & Payment: Pay by Visa/MC, money order, cashier's, business or personal check. Payee: Clerk, US District Court. No search fee is charged unless certification is required. All certification searches conducted by the Wichita office.

Phone Search: Only docket information is released via phone if you have a case number.

Mail Search: search usually completed- 5-7 days. SASE not required.

In Person Search: permitted. No self-serve copier available.

E-Services: ECF replaces PACER whose records did go back to 1991. New records online after 1 day. ECF at https://ecf.ksd.uscourts.gov

Topeka Division Clerk, US District Court, Rm 490, 444 SE Quincy, Topeka, KS 66683 (also use mail address for courier delivery), 785-295-2610.   Hours-   9AM-4:30PM. www.ksd.uscourts.gov

Counties: Allen, Anderson, Chase, Clay, Cloud, Coffey, Dickinson, Douglas, Franklin, Geary, Jackson, Jewell, Lincoln, Lyon, Marion, Mitchell, Morris, Neosho, Osage, Ottawa, Pottawatomie, Republic, Riley, Saline, Shawnee, Wabaunsee, Washington, Wilson, Woodson.

Searches & Indexing: In a search, a full name, case number and a date are very helpful. Results do not include SSN or DOB. Both computer and card indexes maintained. New cases in the index 24 hours after filing date. Records purged never.

Fee & Payment: Pay by money order, cashier's or personal check. Payee: Clerk of US District Court. Prepayment required.

Phone Search: Docket information available via phone.

Mail Search: search usually completed- 2 days. Include SASE for return.

In Person Search: Fee charged if court performs your search. In person searchers may search free on computer No self-serve copier available.

E-Services: ECF replaces PACER whose records did go back to 1991. New records online after 1 day. ECF at https://ecf.ksd.uscourts.gov

Wichita Division Court Clerk, 204 US Courthouse, 401 N Market, Wichita, KS 67202-2096 (also use mail address for courier delivery), 316-269-6491.   Hours-   9AM-4:30PM. www.ksd.uscourts.gov

Counties: All counties in Kansas. Cases may be heard from counties in the other division.

Searches & Indexing: Results do not include SSN or DOB. Both computer and card indexes maintained. Criminal records indexed on computer back to 1994; civil to 1990. Earlier indexes on microfiche, index cards. New cases in the index immediately after filing date. Records purged never. District-wide searches available here.

Fee & Payment: Pay by credit cards, personal or business checks. Payee: Clerk, US District Court. Prepayment required.

Phone Search: No searching by telephone.

Mail Search: search usually completed- 7 working days. Include SASE for return.

In Person Search: Fee charged if court performs your search. No self-serve copier available.

E-Services: ECF replaces PACER whose records did go back to 1991. New records online after 1 day. ECF at https://ecf.ksd.uscourts.gov

US Bankruptcy Court

District of Kansas

Kansas City Division Court Clerk, 500 State Ave, #161 US Courthouse, Kansas City, KS 66101 (also use mail address for courier delivery), 913-551-6732, Fax-913-551-6715. Hours- 9AM-4PM. www.ksb.uscourts.gov

Counties: Atchison, Bourbon, Brown, Cherokee, Comanche, Crawford, Doniphan, Johnson, Labette, Leavenworth, Linn, Marshall, Miami, Nemaha, Wyandotte.

Searches & Indexing: Approximate year of filing will also help in a search. Results include last 4 SSN digits. Computer index maintained. New cases in the index 1 day after filing date. Records purged every 6 months. District-wide searches from 1989 forward available here; master listing for pre-1989 cases available from Topeka Office.

Fee & Payment: Pay by money order, cashier check only. No debtor's personal checks accepted. Payee: Clerk of US Bankruptcy Court. Prepayment required.

Phone Search: Only docket information is available by phone. Voice Case Information Service available, call VCIS at 800-827-9028 or 316-269-6668.

Mail Search: search usually completed- 1-2 days. Include SASE for return.

In Person Search: Fee charged if court performs your search. Self-serve copier available - $.25 per page.

E-Services: ECF replaces PACER whose records did go back to 1988. New records online after 1 day. ECF at https://ecf.ksb.uscourts.gov. Document images available. **Other Online Access:** Motion dockets and calendars free at www.ksb.uscourts.gov/motion.html.

Topeka Division Court Clerk, 240 US Courthouse, 444 SE Quincy, Topeka, KS 66683 (also use mail address for courier delivery), 785-295-2750, Fax-785-295-2964. Hours- 9AM-4PM. www.ksb.uscourts.gov

Counties: Allen, Anderson, Chase, Clay, Cloud, Coffey, Dickinson, Douglas, Franklin, Geary, Jackson, Jewell, Lincoln, Lyon, Marion, Mitchell, Morris, Neosho, Osage, Ottawa, Pottawatomie, Republic, Riley, Saline, Shawnee, Wabaunsee, Washington, Wilson, Woodson.

Searches & Indexing: Results include last 4 SSN digits. Computer index maintained. New cases in the index 1 day after filing date. Records purged every 6 months.

Fee & Payment: Pay by money order, cashier's or personal check. No debtor's checks accepted.

Payee: Clerk, US Bankruptcy Court. Prepayment required.

Phone Search: Only docket information is available by phone. Voice Case Information Service available, call VCIS at 800-827-9028 or 316-269-6668.

Mail Search: search usually completed- 1 week. SASE not required.

In Person Search: Fee charged if court performs your search. Self-serve copier available - $.25 per page.

E-Services: ECF replaces PACER whose records did go back to 1988. New records online after 1 day. ECF at https://ecf.ksb.uscourts.gov. Document images available. **Other Online Access:** Motion dockets and calendars free at www.ksb.uscourts.gov/motion.html.

Wichita Division Court Clerk, 167 US Courthouse, 401 N Market, Wichita, KS 67202 (also use mail address for courier delivery), 316-269-6486, Fax-316-269-6181. Hours- 9AM-4PM. www.ksb.uscourts.gov

Counties: Barber, Barton, Butler, Chautauqua, Cheyenne, Clark, Comanche, Cowley, Decatur, Edwards, Elk, Ellis, Ellsworth, Finney, Ford, Gove, Graham, Grant, Gray, Greeley, Greenwood, Hamilton, Harper, Harvey, Haskell, Hodgeman, Jefferson, Kearny, Kingman, Kiowa, Lane, Logan, McPherson, Meade, Montgomery, Morton, Ness, Norton, Osborne, Pawnee, Phillips, Pratt, Rawlins, Reno, Rice, Rooks, Rush, Russell, Scott, Sedgwick, Seward, Sheridan, Smith, Stafford, Stanton, Stevens, Sumner, Thomas, Trego, Wallace, Wichita.

Searches & Indexing: Results include SSN. Computer and microfiche indexes maintained. New cases in the index 1 day after filing date. Records purged every 6 months. District-wide searches from 1989 forward available here.

Fee & Payment: Pay by money order, cashier's or personal check. Payee: Clerk, US Bankruptcy Court. Prepayment required.

Phone Search: Only attorneys, trustees, hearing dates and file dates released via phone. Voice Case Information Service available, call VCIS at 800-827-9028 or 316-269-6668.

Mail Search: search usually completed- 3-4 working days. SASE not required.

In Person Search: permitted. Self-serve copier available - $.25 per page.

E-Services: ECF replaces PACER whose records did go back to 1988. New records online after 1 day. ECF at https://ecf.ksb.uscourts.gov. Document images available. **Other Online Access:** Motion dockets and calendars free at www.ksb.uscourts.gov/motion.html.

Kansas County Courts

Court	Jurisdiction	No. of Courts	How Organized
District Courts*	General	109	31 Districts
Municipal Courts	Municipal	350	

* Profiled in this Sourcebook.

Court	CIVIL								
	Tort	Contract	Real Estate	Min. Claim	Max. Claim	Small Claims	Estate	Eviction	Domestic Relations
District Courts*	X	X	X	$0	No Max	$1800	X	X	
Municipal Courts									

Court	CRIMINAL				
	Felony	Misdemeanor	DWI/DUI	Preliminary Hearing	Juvenile
District Courts*	X	X	X	X	X
Municipal Courts			X		

ADMINISTRATION

Judicial Administrator, Kansas Judicial Center, 301 SW 10th St, Topeka, KS, 66612; 785-296-3229, Fax: 785-296-1028. www.kscourts.org

COURT STRUCTURE

The District Court is the court of general jurisdiction. There are 110 courts in 31 districts in 105 counties. If an individual in Municipal Court wants a jury trial, the request must be filed de novo in a District Court.

ONLINE ACCESS

Commercial online access is available for District Court Records in 4 counties – Franklin, Johnson, Sedgwick, Shawnee, and Wyandotte - through Access Kansas, part of the Information Network of Kansas (INK) Services. A user may access INK at www.accesskansas.org or via a dial-up system. The INK subscription fee is $75.00, and the annual renewal fee is $60.00. There is no per minute connect charge, but there is a transaction fee. Other information from INK includes Drivers License, Title, Registration, Lien, and UCC searches. For additional information or a registration packet, call 800-4-KANSAS (800-452-6727).

The Kansas Appellate Courts offer free online access to case information at www.kscourts.org. Published opinions from the Appellate and Supreme courts are also available.

ADDITIONAL INFORMATION

Five counties - Cowley, Crawford, Labette, Montgomery, and Neosho - have two hearing locations but only one record center, which is the location included in this Sourcebook.

Many Kansas courts do not do criminal record searches and will refer any criminal requests to the Kansas Bureau of Investigation. The Kansas Legislature's Administrative Order 156 (Fall, 2000) allows Courts to charge up to $12.00 per hour for search services, though courts may set their own search fees, if any.

Allen County

District Court PO Box 630, 1 N Washington St, Iola, KS 66749; phone: 620-365-1425; fax: 620-365-1429; hours 8AM-5PM *Felony, Misdemeanor, Civil, Eviction, Small Claims, Probate.*
Civil Records: Access: Fax, mail, in person. Both court and visitors may perform in person searches. Search fee: $12.00 per hour. Court makes copy: $.50 per page. Required to search: name, years to search. Civil cases indexed by defendant, plaintiff; on computer from 1993, manual index from 1800s.
Criminal Records: Access: None. No criminal searching at this court. Search fee: $12.00 per hour. Court makes copy: $.50 per page. Criminal records on computer from 1993, manual index from 1800s. All criminal searches are referred to the KBI unless a case number is provided. The fees described here for criminal records only pertain if a case # given.
General Information: Public terminal has only civil records back to 1993. No juvenile (under the age of 15), mental health, sealed or expunged records released. Accepts requests via email, but cannot return results by email. Fee to fax documents is $1.00 per page. Certification fee: $1.00. Payee: Clerk of Court. Personal checks accepted. Prepayment & SASE required.

Anderson County

District Court PO Box 305, Garnett, KS 66032; phone: 785-448-6886; fax: 785-448-3230; hours 8AM-N, N-4PM (CST). *Felony, Misdemeanor, Civil, Eviction, Small Claims, Probate.*
www.kscourts.org/dstcts/4dstct.htm
Civil Records: Access: Fax, mail, in person, online. Both court and visitors may perform in person searches. Search fee: $12.00 per hour. Court makes copy: $.25 per page; same fee for self serve. Required to search: name, years to search. Civil cases indexed by defendant, plaintiff; on computer from 1977, index books from 1800s. Current court calendars are free online at www.kscourts.org/dstcts/4andckt.htm. Also, access to probate court records is free at www.kscourts.org/dstcts/4anprrec.htm Mail turnaround time-3 days.
Criminal Records: Access: Fax, mail, in person, online. Visitors must perform in person searches themselves. Search fee: $12.00 per hour. Court makes copy: $.25 per page; same fee for self serve. Required to search: name, years to search. Criminal records on computer from 1977, index books from 1800s. Online access to criminal calendars is the same as civil. Note: For criminal record searches, the court urges requesters to contact the KS

Bureau of Investigations. Mail turnaround time within 3 days.
General Information: Public terminal goes back to 1977. (Terminal includes probate, marriage, etc. This court is not on statewide system.) No juvenile, mental health, sealed or expunged records released. Will fax documents $2.00 1st page, $.50 each add'l. Certification fee: $1.00 per document. Payee: District Court. Personal checks accepted. SASE required.

Atchison County

District Court PO Box 408, Atchison, KS 66002; phone: 913-367-7400; fax: 913-367-1171; hours 8AM-5PM (CST). *Felony, Misdemeanor, Civil, Eviction, Small Claims, Probate.*
Civil Records: Access: Fax, mail, in person. Both court and visitors may perform in person searches. Search fee: $12.00 per hour. Court makes copy: $.25 per page. Required to search: name, years to search. Civil cases indexed by defendant, plaintiff; on computer from 1991, index books from 1900s, archives from 1860s. Mail turnaround time 1-5 days.
Criminal Records: Access: In person only. Both court and visitors may perform in person searches. Search fee: $12.00 per hour if court assists. Court

makes copy: $.25 per page. Required to search: name, years to search; SSN helpful. Criminal records on computer from 1991, index books from 1900s, archives from 1860s. Mail turnaround 1-5 days.

General Information: Public terminal goes back to 1990. No juvenile, mental health, sealed or expunged records released. Will fax documents for $1.25 per page. Certification fee: $1.00. Payee: District Court. Personal checks accepted. Prepayment and SASE required.

Barber County

District Court 118 E Washington, Medicine Lodge, KS 67104; phone: 620-886-5639; fax: 620-886-5854; hours 8AM-N,1-5PM (CST). *Felony, Misdemeanor, Civil, Eviction, Small Claims, Probate.*

Civil Records: Access: In person only. Visitors must perform in person searches themselves. Court makes copy: $.25 per page. Required to search: name, years to search. Civil cases indexed by defendant, plaintiff; on computer from 1990, microfiche from 1900-1976, index cards from 1800s.

Criminal Records: Access: In person only. Visitors must perform in person searches themselves. Court makes copy: $.25 per page. Required to search: name, years to search, SSN; also helpful: DOB. Criminal records on computer from 1990, microfiche from 1900-1976, index cards from 1800s.

General Information: Public terminal goes back to 1990. No juvenile, mental health, sealed or expunged records released. Certification fee: $1.00 per cert. Payee: District Court. Personal checks accepted. Prepayment required.

Barton County

District Court 1400 Main, Rm 306, Great Bend, KS 67530; phone: 620-793-1856; fax: 620-793-1860; hours 8AM-5PM (CST). *Felony, Misdemeanor, Civil, Eviction, Small Claims, Probate.*

Civil Records: Access: Fax, mail, in person. Both court and visitors may perform in person searches. Search fee: $12.00 per hour. Court makes copy: $.35 per page; $.50 for microfilm copies. Required to search: name, years to search. Civil cases indexed by defendant, plaintiff; on computer 1990, microfiche and archives from 1800s, index from 1987. Mail turnaround time 3 days.

Criminal Records: Access: Fax, mail, in person. Both court and visitors may perform in person searches. Search fee: $12.00 per hour. Court makes copy: $.35 per page; $.50 for microfilm copies. Required to search: name, years to search. Criminal records on computer 1990, microfiche and archives from 1800s, index from 1987. Note: Screening firm and employment-related searches and bulk requests will be referred to the state criminal record agency. Mail turnaround time 3 days.

General Information: Public terminal goes back to 1990. No juvenile, mental health, sealed or expunged records released. No fee to fax documents. No certification fee. Payee: Clerk of Court. Personal checks accepted. Prepayment and SASE required.

Bourbon County

District Court PO Box 868, Ft Scott, KS 66701; phone: 620-223-0780; criminal phone: 620-223-1838; civil phone: 620-223-0780; probate phone: 620-223-1380; fax: 620-223-5303; hours 8:30AM-4:30PM (CST). *Felony, Misdemeanor, Civil, Eviction, Small Claims, Probate.*

Civil Records: Access: In person only. Visitors must perform in person searches themselves. Court makes copy: $.25 per page. Self serve copy fee: $.10 per page. Required to search: name, years to search. Civil cases indexed by defendant, plaintiff; on computer since 1990, index on computer since 1985.

Criminal Records: Access: In person only. Visitors must perform in person searches themselves. Court makes copy: $.25 per page. Self serve copy fee: $.10 per page. Required to search: name, years to search;

SSN helpful. Criminal records on computer since 1990, index on computer since 1985.

General Information: Public terminal goes back to 20 years. No juvenile, mental health, sealed or expunged records released. Will not fax specific case file. Certification fee: $1.00 per document. Payee: Clerk of Court. Personal checks accepted. Prepayment required.

Brown County

District Court PO Box 417, Hiawatha, KS 66434; phone: 785-742-7481; fax: 785-742-3506; hours 8AM-5PM (CST). *Felony, Misdemeanor, Civil, Eviction, Small Claims, Probate.*

Civil Records: Access: Phone, fax, mail, in person. Both court and visitors may perform in person searches. Search fee: $12.00 per hour. Court makes copy: $.50 for 1st page, $.25 each add'l. Required to search: name, years to search. Civil cases indexed by defendant, plaintiff; on computer from 1982, microfiche from 1900s, index books from 1900s. Mail turnaround time 1-2 days.

Criminal Records: Access: Phone, fax, mail, in person. Both court and visitors may perform in person searches. Search fee: $12.00 per hour. Court makes copy: $.50 for first page, $.25 each add'l. Required to search: name, years to search; also helpful: SSN. Criminal records on computer from 1982, microfiche and index books from 1900s. Mail turnaround time 1-2 days.

General Information: Public terminal goes back to 1982. No juvenile, mental health, sealed or expunged records released. Fee to fax documents is $1.00 per page. Certification fee: $1.00 per document. Payee: District Court. Personal checks accepted. Prepayment and SASE required.

Butler County

District Court 201 W Pine, #101, El Dorado, KS 67042; phone: 316-322-4370; fax: 316-321-9486; hours 8AM-5PM (CST). *Felony, Misdemeanor, Civil, Eviction, Small Claims, Probate.*

Civil Records: Access: In person only. Visitors must perform in person searches themselves. Court makes copy: $.50 per page; same fee for self serve. Required to search: name, years to search. Civil cases indexed by defendant, plaintiff; on computer from 1992, index cards from 1800s.

Criminal Records: Access: In person, fax. Visitors must perform in person searches themselves. Search fee: $12.00 per hour. Court makes copy: $.50 per page; same fee for self serve. Required to search: name, years to search, SSN. Criminal records on computer from 1992, index cards from 1800s.

General Information: Public terminal goes back to 1992. No juvenile, mental health, sealed or expunged records released. Will fax documents to local or toll free line. Certification fee: $1.00 per page. Payee: Clerk of District Court. Personal checks accepted. Prepayment required.

Chase County

District Court PO Box 529, Cottonwood Falls, KS 66845; phone: 620-273-6319; fax: 620-273-6890; hours 8AM-5PM (CST). *Felony, Misdemeanor, Civil, Eviction, Small Claims, Probate.*

Civil Records: Access: In person only. Visitors must perform in person searches themselves. Court makes copy: $.50 per page. Required to search: name, years to search. Civil cases indexed by defendant, plaintiff; on computer from late 1990, microfiche from 1860, index books from 1860; visitors may search the printed index desk copy.

Criminal Records: Access: In person only. Visitors must perform in person searches themselves. Court makes copy: $.50 per page. Required to search: name, years to search. Criminal records on computer from late 1990, microfiche from 1860, index books from 1860; visitors may search the printed index desk copy.

General Information: Public terminal goes back to 1991. No juvenile, mental health, sealed or expunged

records released. Certification fee: $2.00 per cert. Payee: District Court. Personal checks accepted. No credit cards. Prepayment required.

Chautauqua County

District Court 215 N Chautauqua, PO Box 306, Sedan, KS 67361; phone: 620-725-5870; fax: 620-725-3027; hours 8:00AM-4:30PM (CST). *Felony, Misdemeanor, Civil, Eviction, Small Claims, Probate.*

www.14thjudicialdistrict-ks.org

Civil Records: Access: Mail, in person. Both court and visitors may perform in person searches. Search fee: $12.00 per hour. Court makes copy: $.25 per page; same fee for self serve. Required to search: name, years to search. Civil cases indexed by defendant, plaintiff; on computer from 1990, archives from 1950, index cards from 1870. Mail turnaround time 1-2 weeks.

Criminal Records: Access: Mail, in person. Both court and visitors may perform in person searches. Search fee: $12.00 per hour. Court makes copy: $.25 per page; same fee for self serve. Required to search: name, years to search; also helpful: DOB. Criminal records on computer from 1990, archives from 1950, index cards from 1870. Mail turnaround time 1-2 weeks.

General Information: Public terminal goes back to 1990. No juvenile, mental health, sealed or expunged records released. Will fax documents. Certification fee: $1.00 per certification. Payee: District Court. Personal checks accepted. SASE required.

Cherokee County

District Court PO Box 189, Columbus, KS 66725; phone: 620-429-3880; fax: 620-429-1130; hours 8AM-5PM (CST). *Felony, Misdemeanor, Civil, Eviction, Small Claims, Probate.*

Civil Records: Access: Mail, fax, in person. Visitors must perform in person searches themselves. Search fee: $12.00 per hour. Court makes copy: $.25 page. Required to search: name, years to search. Civil cases indexed by defendant, plaintiff; on computer back 14 years, index books from 1867. Mail turnaround time 3 days.

Criminal Records: Access: Mail, fax, in person. Visitors must perform in person searches themselves. Search fee: $12.00 per hour. Court makes copy: $.25 per page. Required to search: name, years to search; also helpful: SSN. Criminal records on computer back 14 years, index books from 1867. Mail turnaround time 3 days.

General Information: Public terminal goes back to 1995. No juvenile, mental health, sealed or expunged records released. Will not fax documents. Certification fee: $1.25 per page includes copy. Payee: District Court. Personal checks accepted; 14-day hold. No credit cards. Prepayment required.

Cheyenne County

District Court PO Box 646, St Francis, KS 67756; phone: 785-332-8850; fax: 785-332-8851; hours 8AM-N,1-5PM (CST). *Felony, Misdemeanor, Civil, Eviction, Small Claims, Probate.*

Note: Probate records on a separate index.

Civil Records: Access: Fax, mail, in person. Both court and visitors may perform in person searches. No search fee. Court makes copy: $.25 per page; same fee for self serve. Required to search: name, years to search. Civil cases indexed by defendant, plaintiff; on strip index from 1989, index cards from 1870. Mail turnaround time 2 days.

Criminal Records: Access: Fax, mail, in person. Both court and visitors may perform in person searches. No search fee. Court makes copy: $.25 per page; same fee for self serve. Required to search: name, years to search. Criminal records on strip index from 1989, index cards from 1870. Mail turnaround time 2 days.

General Information: No public access terminal. No juvenile, adoptions, mental health, sealed or expunged records released. Will fax documents $1.00

per page unless toll free line used. Certification fee: $1.00 per cert. Payee: Clerk of Court. Personal checks accepted. Prepayment required.

Clark County

District Court PO Box 790, Ashland, KS 67831; phone: 620-635-2753; fax: 620-635-2155; hours 8AM-5PM (CST). *Felony, Misdemeanor, Civil, Eviction, Small Claims, Probate.*
www.kscourts.org/dstcts/16dstct.htm
Civil Records: Access: Mail, fax, in person. Both court and visitors may perform in person searches. Search fee: $12.00 per hour. Court makes copy: $.25 per page; same fee for self serve. Required to search: name, years to search. Civil cases indexed by defendant, plaintiff; on computer from 1992 (Child support only), microfiche and archives from 1800s, index cards from 1800s. Mail turnaround 1 day.
Criminal Records: Access: Mail, fax, in person. Both court and visitors may perform in person searches. Search fee: $12.00 per hour; may be no fee if short name search. Court makes copy: $.25 per page; same fee for self serve. Required to search: name, years to search; also helpful: SSN. Criminal records on index cards. Mail turnaround time 1 day.
General Information: Public use terminal available. No juvenile, mental health, sealed or expunged records released. Will fax documents. Certification fee: $1.00. Payee: District Court. Personal checks accepted. Prepayment and SASE required.

Clay County

District Court PO Box 203, Clay Center, KS 67432; phone: 785-632-3443; fax: 785-632-2651; hours 8AM-5PM (CST). *Felony, Misdemeanor, Civil, Eviction, Small Claims, Probate.*
Civil Records: Access: Mail, in person. Visitors must perform in person searches themselves. Search fee: $12.00 per hour. Court makes copy: $.25 per page. Required to search: name, years to search. Civil cases indexed by defendant, plaintiff; on computer from 7/1994, index books from late 1800s. Mail turnaround time 2 days.
Criminal Records: Access: Mail, in person. Visitors must perform in person searches themselves. Search fee: $12.00 per hour. Court makes copy: $.25 per page. Required to search: name. Criminal records on computer from 7/1994, index books from late 1800s. Mail turnaround time 2 days.
General Information: Public use terminal available. No juvenile, adoption, mental health, sealed or expunged records released. Will fax documents for $2.00 per page. Certification fee: $1.00. Payee: Clerk of District Court. Personal checks accepted. Prepayment and SASE required.

Cloud County

District Court 811 Washington, Concordia, KS 66901; phone: 785-243-8124; fax: 785-243-8188; hours 8:00AM-5PM (CST). *Felony, Misdemeanor, Civil, Eviction, Small Claims, Probate.*
www.kscourts.org/dstcts/12dstct.htm
Civil Records: Access: Phone, fax, mail, in person. Visitors must perform in person searches themselves. Search fee: $12.00 per hour. Court makes copy: $.25 per page. Required to search: name, years to search. Civil cases indexed by defendant, plaintiff. Civil records in print indexes from 1992, index books prior to '92. Mail turnaround 3-4 days.
Criminal Records: Access: Fax, mail, in person. Both court and visitors may perform in person searches. Search fee: $12.00 per hour. Court makes copy: $.25 per page. Required to search: name, years to search; also helpful: SSN. Criminal records in print indexes from 1992, index books prior to 1992. Mail turnaround time 3-4 days.
General Information: Public terminal goes back to 1994. No juvenile, mental health, sealed or expunged records released. Will fax documents $2.00 per page. Certification fee: $1.00 per page. Payee: Clerk of Court. Personal checks accepted. Prepayment and SASE required.

Coffey County

District Court PO Box 330, Burlington, KS 66839; phone: 620-364-8628; fax: 620-364-8535; hours 8AM-4PM (CST). *Felony, Misdemeanor, Civil, Eviction, Small Claims, Probate.*
www.kscourts.org/dstcts/4dstct.htm
Civil Records: Access: Mail, fax, in person, email, online. Both court and visitors may perform in person searches. Search fee: $12.00 per hour. Court makes copy: $.25 per page; same fee for self serve. Required to search: name, years to search. Civil cases indexed by defendant, plaintiff; on computer back to 1800s. Current court calendars at www.franklincos.org/4thdistrict/coffeybydate.html. Probate and marriage records are accessible at this website. Also, access to probate court records is free at www.kscourts.org/dstcts/4coprrec.htm. Mail turnaround time 3 days.
Criminal Records: Access: Mail, fax, in person, email. Both court and visitors may perform in person searches. Search fee: $12.00 per hour. Court makes copy: $.25 per page; same fee for self serve. Required to search: name, years to search, DOB. Criminal records on computer back to 1800s. Online access to criminal court calendar is the same as civil, but records or index are not online. Mail turnaround time 3 days.
General Information: Public use terminal available. No juvenile, mental health, sealed or expunged records released. Fee to fax documents is $2.00 1st page; $.50 each add'l. Certification fee: $1.00. Payee: Clerk of District Court. Personal checks accepted. Prepayment and SASE required.

Comanche County

District Court PO Box 722, Coldwater, KS 67029; phone: 620-582-2182; fax: 620-582-2603; hours 8AM-5PM (CST). *Felony, Misdemeanor, Civil, Eviction, Small Claims, Probate.*
www.kscourts.org/dstcts/16dstct.htm
Civil Records: Access: In person only. Both court and visitors may perform in person searches. No search fee. Court makes copy: $.25 per page; same fee for self serve. Required to search: name, years to search. Civil cases indexed by defendant, plaintiff; on computer since 1992 (child support only), index cards from 1886.
Criminal Records: Access: In person only. Both court and visitors may perform in person searches. No search fee. Court makes copy: $.25 per page; same fee for self serve. Required to search: name, years to search; SSN helpful. Criminal records on index cards from 1886.
General Information: Public use terminal available. No juvenile, mental health, sealed or expunged records released. Will fax specific case file for $1.00 per page. Certification fee: $1.00 per page. Payee: District Court. Personal checks accepted. Prepayment required.

Cowley County

Arkansas City District Court PO Box 1152, Arkansas City, KS 67005; phone: 620-441-4520; fax: 620-442-7213; hours 8AM-N,1-4PM (CST). *Felony, Misdemeanor, Civil, Eviction, Small Claims, Probate.*
Note: This court covers the southern part of the county. Many felony records are kept at Winfield.
Civil Records: Access: Mail, in person. Both court and visitors may perform in person searches. Search fee: $12.00 per hour. Court makes copy: $.50 per page. Required to search: name, years to search. Civil cases indexed by defendant, plaintiff. Civil records from 1977. This Court facility has only been in existence since 1977, so no records prior to that date, index cards only. Computer records commencing 1994. Mail turnaround time 1 week.
Criminal Records: Access: Mail, in person. Both court and visitors may perform in person searches. Search fee: $12.00. Court makes copy: $.50 per page. Required to search: name, years to search, SSN. Criminal records from 1977. This Court facility has

only been in existence since 1977, so no records prior to that date. Computer records commencing 1994. Mail turnaround time 1 week.
General Information: Public terminal goes back to 1994. No juvenile, mental health, sealed or expunged records released. Will fax documents; free up to 4 pages then $1.00 per add'l page. Certification fee: $1.00 per page. Payee: Clerk of Court. Personal checks accepted. Prepayment required. SASE helpful.

Winfield District Court PO Box 472, Winfield, KS 67156; phone: 620-221-5470; fax: 620-221-1097; hours 8AM-N,1-4PM (CST). *Felony, Misdemeanor, Civil, Eviction, Small Claims, Probate.*
Note: This court covers northern part of county.
Civil Records: Access: Fax, mail, in person. Both court and visitors may perform in person searches. Search fee: $12.00 per hour. Court makes copy: $.50 per page. Required to search: name, years to search. Civil cases indexed by defendant, plaintiff; on computer since 1994, index cards from 1874. Mail turnaround time 1 week.
Criminal Records: Access: Fax, mail, in person. Both court and visitors may perform in person searches. Search fee: $12.00 per hour. Court makes copy: $.50 per page. Required to search: name, years to search. Criminal records on computer since 1994, index cards from 1874. Mail turnaround 1 week.
General Information: Public terminal goes back to 1994. No juvenile, mental health, sealed or expunged records released. Certification fee: $1.00 per cert. Payee: Clerk of Court. Personal checks accepted. No credit cards. Prepayment required.

Crawford County

Girard District Court PO Box 69, Girard, KS 66743; phone: 620-724-6211; fax: 620-724-4987; hours 8AM-5PM (CST). *Felony, Misdemeanor, Civil, Probate.*
Note: Records on computer are maintained here for the Pittsburg District Court as well since 8/92. For prior cases, search both courts separately.
Civil Records: Access: Fax, mail, in person. Both court and visitors may perform in person searches. Search fee: $12.00 per hour. Court makes copy: $.25 per page. Required to search: name, years to search. Civil cases indexed by defendant, plaintiff; on computer since 8/1992, microfiche from 1977, index cards from 1977. Mail turnaround time 3 days.
Criminal Records: Access: Phone, fax, in person. Both court and visitors may perform in person searches. Search fee: $12.00 per hour. Court makes copy: $.25 per page. Required to search: name, years to search. Criminal records on computer since 8/1992, microfiche from 1977, index cards from 1977. Employment/work-related inquires are referred to the Kansas Bureau of Investigation. Mail turnaround time 3 days.
General Information: Public terminal goes back to 1977. No juvenile, mental health, sealed or expunged records released. Will fax documents $2.50 per page. Certification fee: $1.00. Payee: Clerk of Court. Personal checks accepted. Prepayment and SASE required.

Pittsburg District Court 602 N Locust, Pittsburg, KS 66762; phone: 620-231-0391; fax: 620-231-0316; hours 8AM-5PM (CST). *Misdemeanor, Civil, Eviction, Small Claims, Probate.*
Note: Records back to 8/92 can be searched at Girard District Court as well; Girard and Pittsburg share a computer system. For cases prior to 8/92, search both courts separately.
Civil Records: Access: Fax, mail, in person. Both court and visitors may perform in person searches. Search fee: $12.00 per hour. Court makes copy: $.25 per page; same fee for self serve. Required to search: name, years to search. Civil cases indexed by defendant, plaintiff; on computer since 8/1992, microfiche from 1977, index cards from 1977. Mail turnaround time 3 days.

Criminal Records: Access: Mail, in person. Both court and visitors may perform in person searches. Search fee: $12.00 per hour. Court makes copy: $.25 per page; same fee for self serve. Required to search: name, years to search. Criminal records on computer since 8/1992, microfiche from 1977, index cards from 1977. Employment/work-related mail inquires are referred to the Kansas Bureau of Investigation. Note: Mail requests must be on courts form, call court for form and they will fax it to you. Mail turnaround time 3 days.

General Information: Public terminal goes back to 8/1992. No juvenile, mental health, sealed or expunged records released. Will fax documents $2.50 per page. Certification fee: $1.00. Payee: Clerk of Court. Personal checks accepted. Prepayment and SASE required.

Decatur County

District Court PO Box 89, Oberlin, KS 67749; phone: 785-475-8107; fax: 785-475-8170; hours 8AM-5PM (CST). *Felony, Misdemeanor, Civil, Eviction, Small Claims, Probate.*

Civil Records: Access: In person only. Visitors must perform in person searches themselves. Court makes copy: $.25 per page. Required to search: name, years to search. Civil cases indexed by defendant, plaintiff; on index books from 1870.

Criminal Records: Access: In person only. Visitors must perform in person searches themselves. Court makes copy: $.25 per page. Required to search: name, years to search. Criminal records on index books from 1870.

General Information: Public terminal goes back to 2004. No adoption, juvenile, mental health, sealed or expunged records released. Certification fee: $1.00. Payee: Clerk of District Court. Prepayment required.

Dickinson County

District Court PO Box 127, Abilene, KS 67410; phone: 785-263-3142; fax: 785-263-4407; hours 9AM-5PM (CST). *Felony, Misdemeanor, Civil, Eviction, Small Claims, Probate.*

Civil Records: Access: Mail, fax, in person, email. Both court and visitors may perform in person searches. Search fee: $12.00 per hour. Court makes copy: $1.00 for first 4 pages; $.25 per add'l page; same fee for self serve. Required to search: name, years to search. Civil cases indexed by defendant, plaintiff; on computer since 7/92, on index books prior. Mail Civil turnaround 3 days.

Criminal Records: Access: In person only. Visitors must perform in person searches themselves. Court makes copy: $1.00 for first 4 pages; $.25 per add'l page; same fee for self serve. Required to search: name, years to search; also helpful: SSN. Criminal records on computer since 7/92, on index books prior. Will search only if case number is provided. Direct search requests to KBI. Mail turnaround time 1 week.

General Information: Public terminal goes back to 7/1992. No juvenile, mental health, sealed or expunged records released. Will fax documents for $1.00 per page. Certification fee: $1.00 per document. Payee: Clerk of District Court. Personal checks accepted. Prepayment and SASE required.

Doniphan County

District Court PO Box 295, Troy, KS 66087; phone: 785-985-3582; fax: 785-985-2402; hours 8AM-5PM (CST). *Felony, Misdemeanor, Civil, Eviction, Small Claims, Probate.*

Civil Records: Access: Phone, fax, mail, in person. Both court and visitors may perform in person searches. Search fee: $12.00 per hour. Court makes copy: $.50 for 1st page, $.25 each add'l. Self serve copy fee: $.25 per page. Required to search: name, years to search. Civil cases indexed by defendant, plaintiff; on computer since 1992; index cards from 1856. Mail turnaround time 1-2 days.

Criminal Records: Access: Phone, fax, mail, in person. Both court and visitors may perform in

person searches. Search fee: $12.00 per hour. Court makes copy: $.50 for first page, $.25 each add'l. Self serve copy fee: $.25 per page. Required to search: name, years to search; also helpful: address, DOB. Criminal records on computer since 1992; index cards from 1852. Mail turnaround time 1-2 days.

General Information: Public terminal goes back to 1992. No juvenile, mental health, sealed or expunged records released. Fee to fax documents is $2.00 per page. Certification fee: $1.00 per document. Payee: Clerk of Court. Personal checks accepted. Prepayment and SASE required.

Douglas County

District Court 111 E 11th St, Rm 144, Lawrence, KS 66044-2966; phone: 785-832-5258/5256; fax: 785-832-5258; hours 8AM-N, 1:15-4PM (CST). *Felony, Misdemeanor, Civil, Eviction, Small Claims, Probate.*

www.douglas-county.com/District_Court/dc.asp
Civil Records: Access: Phone, fax, mail, in person, online. Both court and visitors may perform in person searches. Search fee: $12.00 per hour. Court makes copy: $.25 per page. Required to search: name, years to search. Civil cases indexed by defendant, plaintiff; on index cards from 1863, archived from 1865 on film, indexed on computer since 1989. Internet access to the new court records system will require registration, password, and yearly fee; Online records go back to 1986. You will have to call the District Court for sign-up info. Note: All written requests must include a phone number. Mail turnaround time 3 days.

Criminal Records: Access: Phone, fax, mail, in person, online. Both court and visitors may perform in person searches. Search fee: $12.00 per hour. Court makes copy: $.25 per page. Required to search: name, years to search; also helpful: DOB, SSN. Criminal records on computer from 1989, index cards 1860, archived from 1865. Online access to criminal records is the same as civil. Note: All other background check requests must be in writing. Mail turnaround time 3 days.

General Information: Public terminal goes back to 1995. No juvenile, mental health, sealed or expunged records released. Will fax documents for $2.00 per document. Certification fee: $1.00 per cert. Authentications- $2.00 each. Payee: Clerk of Court. Personal checks accepted. Prepayment required.

Edwards County

District Court PO Box 232, Kinsley, KS 67547; phone: 620-659-2442; fax: 602-659-2998; hours 8AM-5PM (CST). *Felony, Misdemeanor, Civil, Eviction, Small Claims, Probate.*

www.kscourts.org/dstcts/24dstct.htm
Civil Records: Access: Mail, in person. Both court and visitors may perform in person searches. Search fee: $12.00 per hour. Court makes copy: $.25 per page. Required to search: name, years to search. Civil cases indexed by defendant, plaintiff; on index books from 1800s.

Criminal Records: Access: In person only. Visitors must perform in person searches themselves. Court makes copy: $.25 per page. Required to search: name, years to search. Criminal records on index books from 1800s.

General Information: Public terminal goes back to 10/2002. No juvenile, adoption, mental health, sealed or expunged records released. Will fax documents to local or toll free line. Certification fee: $1.00. Payee: Clerk District Court. Personal checks accepted. Prepayment and SASE required.

Elk County

District Court PO Box 306, Howard, KS 67349; phone: 620-374-2370; fax: 620-374-3531; hours 8AM-4:30PM (CST). *Felony, Misdemeanor, Civil, Eviction, Small Claims, Probate.*

Civil Records: Access: Mail, in person. Both court and visitors may perform in person searches. Search fee: Depending on difficulty, clerk may charge

$12 per hr search fee. Court makes copy: $.50 per page. Self serve copy fee: $.50 per page. Required to search: name, years to search. Civil cases indexed by defendant, plaintiff; on index books from 1907. Mail turnaround time 1-2 days.

Criminal Records: Access: Mail, in person. Both court and visitors may perform in person searches. Search fee: Depending on difficulty, clerk may charge $12 per hr search fee. Court makes copy: $.50 per page. Self serve copy fee: $.50 per page. Required to search: name, years to search. Criminal records on index books from 1907; on computer back to 1984. Mail turnaround time 1-2 days.

General Information: Public terminal goes back to 1984. No juvenile, mental health, sealed or expunged records released. Fee to fax documents is $2 plus $.50 per page. Certification fee: $1.00 per document. Payee: Clerk of District Court. Personal checks accepted. Prepayment required.

Ellis County

District Court PO Box 8, Hays, KS 67601; phone: 785-628-9415; fax: 785-628-8415; hours 8AM-5PM (CST). *Felony, Misdemeanor, Civil, Eviction, Small Claims, Probate.*

www.23rdjudicial.org
Civil Records: Access: Mail, in person. Both court and visitors may perform in person searches. Search fee: $12.00 per hour. Court makes copy: $.25 per page. Required to search: name, years to search. Civil cases indexed by defendant, plaintiff; on computer from 1991, microfiche from 1900s, index cards from 1800s, archives from 1800s.

Criminal Records: Access: In person only. Visitors must perform in person searches themselves. Court makes copy: $.25 per page. Required to search: name, years to search. Criminal records on computer from 1991, microfiche from 1900s, index cards from 1800s, archives from 1800s.

General Information: Public terminal goes back to 1991. No juvenile, mental health, sealed or expunged records released. Will fax documents for $.50 1st page, $.25 each add'l page. Certification fee: $1.00 per cert. Payee: Clerk of Court. Personal checks accepted. Prepayment and SASE required.

Ellsworth County

District Court 210 N Kansas, Ellsworth, KS 67439-3118; phone: 785-472-3832; fax: 785-472-5712; hours 8AM-5PM (CST). *Felony, Misdemeanor, Civil, Eviction, Small Claims, Probate.*

Civil Records: Access: Phone, fax, mail, in person. Both court and visitors may perform in person searches. No search fee. Court makes copy: $.35 per page. Required to search: name, years to search. Civil cases indexed by defendant, plaintiff; on computer from 1994, microfiche from 1900s, books from late 1800s. Mail turnaround time 1-2 days.

Criminal Records: Access: Phone, fax, mail, in person. Both court and visitors may perform in person searches. No search fee. Court makes copy: $.35 per page. Required to search: name, years to search; also helpful: SSN. Criminal records on computer from 1994, microfiche from 1900s, books from late 1800s. Mail turnaround time 1-2 days.

General Information: No public access terminal. No juvenile, mental health, sealed or expunged records released. Will fax documents $.50 per page. No certification fee. Payee: District Court. Personal checks accepted. Prepayment and SASE required.

Finney County

District Court PO Box 798, Garden City, KS 67846; criminal phone: 620-271-6132; civil phone: 620-271-6121; fax: 620-271-6140; hours 8AM-4:30PM (CST). *Felony, Misdemeanor, Civil, Eviction, Small Claims, Probate.*

Civil Records: Access: In person only. Visitors must perform in person searches themselves. Court makes copy: $.25 per page, $1.00 minimum. Self serve copy fee: $.25 per page. Required to search:

name, years to search. Civil cases indexed by defendant, plaintiff; on computer from 1991, microfiche from 1900s, index books from 1900s.

Criminal Records: Access: In person only. Visitors must perform in person searches themselves. Court makes copy: $.25 per page, $1.00 minimum. Self serve copy fee: $.25 per page. Required to search: name, years to search. Criminal records on computer from 1991, microfiche from 1900s, index books from 1900s.

General Information: Public terminal goes back to 1991. No juvenile, Mental health, sealed or expunged records released. Certification fee: $1.00 per page. Payee: District Court. Personal checks accepted. Prepayment required.

Ford County

District Court 101 W Spruce, Dodge City, KS 67801; phone: 620-227-4609; criminal phone: 620-227-4608; civil phone: 620-227-4610; probate phone: 620-277-4606; fax: 620-227-6799; hours 8AM-5PM (CST). *Felony, Misdemeanor, Civil, Eviction, Small Claims, Probate.*
www.kscourts.org/dstcts/16dstct.htm
Civil Records: Access: In person only. Both court and visitors may perform in person searches. No search fee. Court makes copy: $.25 per page. Self serve copy fee: $.10 per page. Required to search: case number. Civil cases indexed by defendant, plaintiff; on computer back to 10/1991, microfiche/film from 1900s, index books from 1900s. Mail turnaround time 3 days.
Criminal Records: Access: In person only. Both court and visitors may perform in person searches. No search fee. Court makes copy: $.25 per page. Self serve copy fee: $.10 per page. Required to search: case number. Criminal records on computer back to 10/1991, microfiche/film from 1900s, index books from 1900s.
General Information: Public terminal goes back to 10/1991. No juvenile, mental health, sealed or expunged records released. Fee to fax specific case file is $1.00 per page. Certification fee: $1.00 per document. Payee: Clerk of District Court. Personal checks accepted. Prepayment required.

Franklin County

District Court PO Box 637 (301 S Main), Ottawa, KS 66067; phone: 785-242-6000; fax: 785-242-5970; hours 8AM-12, 1PM-4PM (CST). *Felony, Misdemeanor, Civil, Eviction, Small Claims, Probate.*
www.kscourts.org/dstcts/4dstct.htm
Civil Records: Access: Mail, fax, in person, online. Both court and visitors may perform in person searches. Search fee: $12.00 per hour. Court makes copy: $.25 per page. Required to search: name, years to search. Civil cases indexed by defendant, plaintiff; on computer back to 1979, index books from 1800s. Index online through Access Kansas; see www.accesskansas.org for subscription information. Current court calendars are free at www.franklincoks.org/4thdistrict/franklinbydate.html. Also, access to probate court records is free at www.kscourts.org/dstcts/4frprrec.htm.
Criminal Records: Access: In person, online. Visitors must perform in person searches themselves. Court makes copy: $.25 per page. Required to search: name, years to search, SSN. Criminal records on computer back to 1980, index books from 1800s. Online access to criminal calendars is the same as civil. Mail turnaround time 3-5 days.
General Information: Public use terminal available. No juvenile, mental health, sealed or expunged records released. Will fax documents to local or toll free line. Certification fee: $1.00. Payee: Clerk of District Court. Personal checks accepted. Prepayment and SASE required.

Geary County

District Court PO Box 1147, Junction City, KS 66441; phone: 785-762-5221; fax: 785-762-4420; hours 8AM-5PM (CST). *Felony, Misdemeanor, Civil, Eviction, Small Claims, Probate.*
Civil Records: Access: Mail, in person, email. Both court and visitors may perform in person searches. Search fee: $12.00 per hour. Court makes copy: $.25 per page, $1.00 minimum. Required to search: name, years to search. Civil cases indexed by defendant, plaintiff; on computer from 1992, microfiche, index books and archives from 1894. Mail turnaround time 3 days.
Criminal Records: Access: Mail, in person, email. Both court and visitors may perform in person searches. Search fee: $12.00 per hour. Court makes copy: $.25 per page, $1.00 minimum. Required to search: name, years to search; also helpful: SSN. Criminal records on computer from 1992, microfiche, index books and archives from 1894. Mail turnaround time 3 days.
General Information: Public terminal goes back to 1992. No juvenile, adoption, mental health, sealed or expunged records released. Fee to fax documents is $2.00 per page. Certification fee: $1.00. Payee: Clerk of Court. Personal checks accepted. Prepayment required.

Gove County

District Court PO Box 97, Gove, KS 67736; phone: 785-938-2310; fax: 785-938-2312; hours 8AM-N, 1-5PM (CST). *Felony, Misdemeanor, Civil, Eviction, Small Claims, Probate.*
Civil Records: Access: Fax, mail, in person. Both court and visitors may perform in person searches. Search fee: $12.00 per hour. Court makes copy: $.25 per page; same fee for self serve. Required to search: name, years to search. Civil cases indexed by defendant, plaintiff; on computer from 1992, index books from 1890 through present. Mail turnaround time 1-2 days.
Criminal Records: Access: Fax, mail, in person. Both court and visitors may perform in person searches. Search fee: $12.00 per hour. Court makes copy: $.25 per page; same fee for self serve. Required to search: name, years to search. Criminal records on computer from 1992, index books from 1890 through present. Mail turnaround time 1-2 days.
General Information: No public access terminal. No juvenile, mental health, sealed or expunged records released. Fee to fax documents is $1.00 per page. Certification fee: $1.00. Payee: Clerk of District Court. Personal checks accepted. Prepayment and SASE required.

Graham County

District Court 410 N Pomeroy, Hill City, KS 67642; phone: 785-421-3458; fax: 785-421-5463; probate fax: 785-421-5463; hours 8AM-5PM (CST). *Felony, Misdemeanor, Civil, Eviction, Small Claims, Probate.*
Note: Probate is a separate index at this same address.
Civil Records: Access: In person only. Visitors must perform in person searches themselves. Court makes copy: $.25 per page. Civil cases indexed by defendant, plaintiff; on index books from 1880s; computerized records go back to 2004.
Criminal Records: Access: Mail, in person. Visitors must perform in person searches themselves. Search fee: $12.00 per hour. Court makes copy: $.25 per page. Required to search: name, years to search, DOB; also helpful: SSN, signed release. Criminal records on index books from 1880s; computerized records go back to 2004.
General Information: No public access terminal. No juvenile, mental health, sealed or expunged records released. Will fax documents to local or toll free line. Certification fee: $1.00 per instrument. Payee: Clerk of District Court. Personal checks accepted. Prepayment required.

Grant County

District Court 108 S Glenn, Ulysses, KS 67880; phone: 620-356-1526; fax: 620-353-2131; hours 8:30AM-5PM (CST). *Felony, Misdemeanor, Civil, Eviction, Small Claims, Probate.*
Civil Records: Access: Mail, in person. Visitors must perform in person searches themselves. Search fee: $12.80 per hour. Court makes copy: $.50 per page; same fee for self serve. Required to search: name, years to search. Civil cases indexed by defendant, plaintiff; on computer from 1977, microfiche index from 1880s. Mail turnaround time same day.
Criminal Records: Access: Mail, in person. Visitors must perform in person searches themselves. Search fee: $12.80 per hour. Court makes copy: $.50 per page; same fee for self serve. Required to search: name, years to search. Criminal records on computer from 1977, microfiche index from 1880s. The court refers all searchers to the state Bureau of investigations, including in-person searchers. Mail turnaround time same day.
General Information: Public use terminal available. No juvenile, mental health, sealed or expunged records released. Will not fax documents. Certification fee: $1.00. Payee: District Court. Personal checks accepted. Prepayment and SASE required.

Gray County

District Court PO Box 487, Cimarron, KS 67835; phone: 620-855-3812; fax: 620-855-7037; hours 8AM-5PM (CST). *Felony, Misdemeanor, Civil, Eviction, Small Claims, Probate.*
www.kscourts.org/dstcts/16dstct.htm
Civil Records: Access: Fax, mail, in person. Visitors must perform in person searches themselves. Search fee: $12.00 per hour. Court makes copy: $.50 per page. Self serve copy fee: $.25 per page. Required to search: name; also helpful: years to search. Civil cases indexed by defendant, plaintiff; on computer from 1990, index books from 1800s. Fax requests must be pre-paid.
Criminal Records: Access: Fax, mail, in person. Visitors must perform in person searches themselves. Search fee: $12.00 per hour. Court makes copy: $.50 per page. Self serve copy fee: $.25 per page. Required to search: name, years to search; also helpful: address, DOB. Criminal records on computer from 1990, index books from 1800s. Fax requests must be pre-paid.
General Information: Public terminal goes back to 1990. No juvenile, mental health, sealed or expunged records released. Will fax documents for $1.00 per page. Certification fee: $1.00. Payee: Clerk of District Court. Personal checks accepted. Prepayment required.

Greeley County

District Court PO Box 516, Tribune, KS 67879; phone: 620-376-4292; hours 8AM-N, 1-5PM (MST). *Felony, Misdemeanor, Civil, Eviction, Small Claims, Probate.*
Civil Records: Access: In person only. Visitors must perform in person searches themselves. Court makes copy: $.50 per page. Required to search: name. Civil cases indexed by defendant, plaintiff; on hardcopy index from beginning. Mail turnaround time 3 working days.
Criminal Records: Access: In person only. Visitors must perform in person searches themselves. No search fee. Court makes copy: $.50 per page. Required to search: name, also helpful: SSN. Criminal records on hardcopy index from beginning.
General Information: Public terminal goes back to 1986. No juvenile, mental health, sealed or expunged records released. Will fax documents for $1.00 per page. Certification fee: $1.00 per page. Payee: Clerk of the District Court. Personal checks accepted. Prepayment required.

Greenwood County

District Court 311 N Main, Eureka, KS 67045; phone: 620-583-8153; fax: 620-583-6818; hours 8AM-5PM (CST). *Felony, Misdemeanor, Civil, Eviction, Small Claims, Probate.*
Civil Records: Access: Mail, in person. Both court and visitors may perform in person searches. Search fee: $12.00 per hour if search is conducted by court personnel. Court makes copy: $.50 per page. Required to search: name, years to search. Civil cases indexed by defendant, plaintiff; on computer from 1993, index cards from 1800s. Mail turnaround time 1-3 days.
Criminal Records: Access: Mail, in person. Both court and visitors may perform in person searches. Search fee: $12.00 per hour if search is performed by court personnel. Court makes copy: $.50 per page. Required to search: name, years to search. Criminal records on computer from 1993, index cards from 1800s. Mail turnaround time 1-3 days.
General Information: Public use terminal available. No juvenile, mental health, sealed or expunged records released. Will fax documents to local or toll free line. Certification fee: $1.00. Payee: Clerk of Court. Personal checks accepted. Prepayment and SASE required.

Hamilton County

District Court PO Box 745, Syracuse, KS 67878; phone: 620-384-5159; fax: 620-384-7806; hours 8AM-5PM (MST). *Felony, Misdemeanor, Civil, Eviction, Small Claims, Probate.*
Civil Records: Access: In person only. Visitors must perform in person searches themselves. Court makes copy: $.25 per page; same fee for self serve. Required to search: name, years to search. Civil cases indexed by defendant, plaintiff; on computer from 1985, microfiche, archives and index cards from 1880s.
Criminal Records: Access: In person only. Visitors must perform in person searches themselves. Court makes copy: $.25 per page; same fee for self serve. Required to search: name, years to search. Criminal records on computer from 1985, microfiche, archives and index cards from 1880s.
General Information: Public terminal goes back to 1985. No juvenile, mental health, sealed or expunged records released. Will fax specific case file for $1.00 per page. Certification fee: $1.00. Payee: Clerk of District Court. Personal checks accepted. Prepayment required.

Harper County

District Court PO Box 467, Anthony, KS 67003; phone: 620-842-3721; fax: 620-842-6025; hours 8AM-N, 1-5PM (CST). *Felony, Misdemeanor, Civil, Eviction, Small Claims, Probate.*
Civil Records: Access: In person only. Both court and visitors may perform in person searches. Court makes copy: $.25 per page. Required to search: name, years to search. Civil cases indexed by defendant, plaintiff; on computer from 1976, microfiche, index books and archives from 1887.
Criminal Records: Access: In person only. Visitors must perform in person searches themselves. Court makes copy: $.25 per page. Required to search: name, years to search, SSN. Criminal records on computer from 1976, microfiche, index books and archives from 1887.
General Information: Public terminal goes back to 1995. No juvenile, mental health, sealed or expunged records released. Will fax documents $1.00 per page. Certification fee: $1.00 per cert. Payee: Clerk of District Court. Personal checks accepted. Prepayment required.

Harvey County

District Court PO Box 665, Newton, KS 67114-0665; phone: 316-284-6890; criminal phone: 316-284-6896; civil phone: 316-284-6894; probate phone: 316-284-6892; fax: 316-283-4601; hours 9AM-5PM (CST). *Felony, Misdemeanor, Civil, Eviction, Small Claims, Probate.*
Civil Records: Access: Mail, fax, in person, email. Both court and visitors may perform in person searches. Search fee: $12.00 per hour. Court makes copy: $.50 per page; same fee for self serve. Required to search: name, years to search. Civil cases indexed by defendant, plaintiff; on index books from 1800s; on computer back to mid 1970s. Mail turnaround time 3-5 days.
Criminal Records: Access: Mail, fax, in person. Both court and visitors may perform in person searches. Search fee: $12.00 per name. Court makes copy: $.50 per page; same fee for self serve. Required to search: name, years to search, DOB; also helpful-SSN, signed release. Criminal records computerized since 1960s, archived from 1800s. Call KBI for thorough search. Mail turnaround time 3-5 days.
General Information: Public use terminal available. No juvenile, mental health, sealed or expunged records released. Certification fee: $1.00. Payee: Clerk of District Court. Personal checks accepted. Prepayment required. SASE helpful.

Haskell County

District Court PO Box 146, Sublette, KS 67877; phone: 620-675-2671; fax: 620-675-8599; hours 8AM-5PM (CST). *Felony, Misdemeanor, Civil, Eviction, Small Claims, Probate.*
Civil Records: Access: Phone, mail, fax, in person. Both court and visitors may perform in person searches. Search fee: $12.00 per hour. Court makes copy: $.25 per page. Self serve copy fee: $.25 per page. Required to search: name, years to search. Civil cases indexed by defendant, plaintiff; on computer from 1990, index books from 1874.
Criminal Records: Access: In person only. Visitors must perform in person searches themselves. Court makes copy: $.25 per page. Self serve copy fee: $.25 per page. Required to search: name, years to search. Criminal records on computer from 1990, index books from 1874.
General Information: Public terminal has criminal back to 1990 and civil back to 1990. No juvenile, mental health, sealed or expunged records released. Will fax documents for $.25 per page plus $3.00. Certification fee: $1.00. Payee: Clerk of District Court. Personal checks accepted. Prepayment required.

Hodgeman County

District Court PO Box 187, Jetmore, KS 67854; phone: 620-357-6522; fax: 620-357-6216; hours 8:30AM-5PM (CST). *Felony, Misdemeanor, Civil, Eviction, Small Claims, Probate.*
www.kscourts.org/dstcts/24dstct.htm
Note: Probate is a separate index at this same address.
Civil Records: Access: Phone, fax, mail, in person. Both court and visitors may perform in person searches. Search fee: $12.00 per hour. Court makes copy: $.25 per page. Required to search: name, years to search. Civil cases indexed by defendant, plaintiff; on index cards and books from 1800s. Mail turnaround time 1-2 days.
Criminal Records: Access: In person only. Visitors must perform in person searches themselves. Court makes copy: $.25 per page. Required to search: name, years to search; SSN helpful. Criminal records on index cards and books from 1800s.
General Information: No public access terminal. No juvenile, mental health, sealed or expunged records released. Will fax documents $.50 per page. Certification fee: $1.00 per page. Payee: Clerk of Court. Personal checks accepted. Prepayment required. Must prepay for mail and fax.

Jackson County

District Court 400 New York Ave, #311, Holton, KS 66436; phone: 785-364-2191; fax: 785-364-3804; hours 8AM-4:30PM (CST). *Felony, Misdemeanor, Civil, Eviction, Small Claims, Probate.*
Civil Records: Access: In person only. Visitors must perform in person searches themselves. Court makes copy: $.25 per page; same fee for self serve. Required to search: name, years to search. Civil cases indexed by defendant, plaintiff; on index cards from 1800s, recent records computerized.
Criminal Records: Access: In person only. Visitors must perform in person searches themselves. Court makes copy: $.25 per page; same fee for self serve. Required to search: name, years to search. Criminal records on index cards from 1800s, recent records computerized.
General Information: Public terminal goes back to 1850s. No juvenile, mental health, sealed or expunged records released. Certification fee: $1.00. Payee: Clerk of District Court. Personal checks accepted. Prepayment required.

Jefferson County

District Court PO Box 327, Oskaloosa, KS 66066; phone: 785-863-2461; fax: 785-863-2369; hours 8AM-4:30PM (CST). *Felony, Misdemeanor, Civil, Eviction, Small Claims, Probate.*
Civil Records: Access: In person only. Visitors must perform in person searches themselves. Court makes copy: $.25 per page. Required to search: name, years to search. Civil cases indexed by defendant, plaintiff; on computer since 1/77, on index books from 1855.
Criminal Records: Access: In person only. Visitors must perform in person searches themselves. Court makes copy: $.25 per page. Required to search: name, years to search; SSN helpful. Criminal records on index books from 1855, computerized since 1/77.
General Information: Public use terminal available. No juvenile, mental health, sealed or expunged records released. Certification fee: $1.00. Payee: District Court. Personal checks accepted. Prepayment required.

Jewell County

District Court 307 N Commercial, Mankato, KS 66956; phone: 785-378-4030; fax: 785-378-4035; hours 8AM-5PM (CST). *Felony, Misdemeanor, Civil, Eviction, Small Claims, Probate.*
www.kscourts.org/dstcts/12dstct.htm
Civil Records: Access: Phone, fax, mail, in person. Both court and visitors may perform in person searches. Search fee: $12.00 per hour. Court makes copy: $.25 per page. Required to search: name, years to search. Civil cases indexed by defendant, plaintiff; on index books from 1871. Mail turnaround time 2-7 days.
Criminal Records: Access: Phone, fax, mail, in person. Both court and visitors may perform in person searches. Search fee: $12.00 per hour. Court makes copy: $.25 per page. Required to search: name, years to search. Criminal records on index books from 1871. Mail turnaround time 2-7 days.
General Information: Public terminal goes back to 1995. No juvenile, mental health, sealed or expunged records released. Will fax documents $3.00 per page. Certification fee: $1.00. Payee: District Court. Personal checks accepted. Prepayment and SASE required.

Johnson County

District Court 100 N Kansas, Olathe, KS 66061; phone: 913-715-3500; criminal phone: 913-715-3460; civil phone: 913-715-3400; fax: 913-715-3481; hours 8:30AM-4PM (CST). *Felony, Misdemeanor, Civil, Eviction, Small Claims, Probate.*
http://rta.jocogov.org
Note: Search requests should be made to the Records Center, phone 913-715-3480.

Civil Records: Access: In person, online. Both court and visitors may perform in person searches. Search fee: $12.00 per hour. Court makes copy: $.50 per page. Copy fee for records prior to 1997 $10.00 flat fee. Required to search: name, years to search. Civil cases indexed by defendant, plaintiff; on computer from 1980, microfiche, archives and index prior. Index online through Access Kansas; includes marriages, civil and criminal courts; see www.accesskansas.org for subscription information. Mail turnaround time 1-2 days if current records; 1-2 weeks for very old document.
Criminal Records: Access: In person, online. Both court and visitors may perform in person searches. Search fee: $12.00 per hour. Court makes copy: $.50 per page; records prior to 1997 $10.00 flat fee. Required to search: name, years to search. Criminal records on computer from 1980, microfiche, archives and index prior. Access to criminal records online is same as civil.
General Information: Public terminal goes back to 1968. No juvenile, mental health, sealed or expunged records released. No employment searches. Will fax documents $2.50 per page. Certification fee: $1.00 per cert. Payee: Clerk of the District Court. Only cashiers checks and money orders accepted. Prepayment required.

Kearny County

District Court PO Box 64, Lakin, KS 67860; phone: 620-355-6481; fax: 620-355-7462; hours 8AM-N,1-5PM (CST). *Felony, Misdemeanor, Civil, Eviction, Small Claims, Probate.*
Civil Records: Access: Mail, in person. Visitors must perform in person searches themselves. Search fee: $12.00 per hour; but court will only search if you provide a case number. Court makes copy: $.25 per page; same fee for self serve. Required to search: name, years to search. Civil cases indexed by defendant, plaintiff; on computer from 1991, index books from 1900s. A case number must be provided with mail search requests. Mail turnaround time 3 days.
Criminal Records: Access: Mail, in person. Visitors must perform in person searches themselves. Search fee: $12.00 per hour, but court will only search if you provide a case number. Court makes copy: $.25 per page; same fee for self serve. Required to search: name, years to search. Criminal records on computer from 1991, index books from 1900s. A case number must be provided with mail search requests. Mail turnaround time 3 days.
General Information: Public terminal goes back to 6/1991. No juvenile, mental health, adoption, sealed or expunged records released. Will fax documents for $1.00 per page prepaid. Certification fee: $1.00. Payee: District Court. Personal checks accepted. Prepayment and SASE required.

Kingman County

District Court PO Box 495 (130 N Spruce St), Kingman, KS 67068; phone: 620-532-5151; fax: 620-532-2952; hours 8AM-N, 1-5PM (CST). *Felony, Misdemeanor, Civil, Eviction, Small Claims, Probate.*
Civil Records: Access: Mail, fax, in person. Both court and visitors may perform in person searches. Search fee: $12.00 per hour. Court makes copy: $.25 per page; same fee for self serve. Required to search: name, years to search. Civil cases indexed by defendant, plaintiff; on computer from 1990, microfiche, archives and index cards from 1800s. Mail turnaround time 1-2 days.
Criminal Records: Access: Mail, fax, in person. Both court and visitors may perform in person searches. Search fee: $12.00 per hour. Court makes copy: $.25 per page; same fee for self serve. Required to search: name, years to search; also helpful: case type. Criminal records on computer from 1990, microfiche, archives and index cards from 1800s. Mail turnaround time 1-2 days.
General Information: Public terminal goes back to 1980s. No juvenile, mental health, sealed or

expunged records released. Fee to fax documents is $1.00 per page. Certification fee: $1.00 per pleading. Payee: Clerk of Court. Personal checks accepted. Prepayment and SASE required.

Kiowa County

District Court 211 E Florida, Greensburg, KS 67054; phone: 620-723-3317; fax: 620-723-2970; probate fax: same; hours 8AM-5PM (CST). *Felony, Misdemeanor, Civil, Eviction, Small Claims, Probate.*
www.kscourts.org/dstcts/16dstct.htm
Civil Records: Access: Fax, mail, in person. Both court and visitors may perform in person searches. Search fee: $12.00 per hour. Court makes copy: $.25 per page. Required to search: name, years to search. Civil cases indexed by defendant, plaintiff. Civil records archived and on index books from 1800s; computerized back to 1980. Mail turnaround time 7 days.
Criminal Records: Access: Fax, mail, in person. Both court and visitors may perform in person searches. Search fee: $12.00 per hour. Court makes copy: $.25 per page. Required to search: name, years to search, signed release; also helpful: DOB. Criminal records archived and on index books from 1800s; computerized back to 1940. Mail turnaround time 7 days.
General Information: Public use terminal available. No juvenile, mental health, sealed or expunged records released. Fee to fax documents is $1.00 per page. Certification fee: $1.00. Payee: Clerk of District Court. Personal checks accepted. Prepayment and SASE required.

Labette County

District Court 201 S Central, Parsons, KS 67357; phone: 620-421-4120; fax: 620-421-3633; hours 8AM-5PM (CST). *Felony, Misdemeanor, Civil, Eviction, Small Claims, Probate.*
Civil Records: Access: Mail, in person. Both court and visitors may perform in person searches. No search fee. Court makes copy: $.25 per page. Required to search: name, years to search. Civil cases indexed by defendant, plaintiff; on computer from 1992, index books from 1874. Mail turnaround time 1-2 days.
Criminal Records: Access: Mail, in person. Both court and visitors may perform in person searches. Search fee: $12.00 per hr; $6.00 min. Court makes copy: $.25 per page. Required to search: name, years to search. Criminal records on computer from 1992, index books from 1874. Mail turnaround time 1-2 days.
General Information: Public terminal goes back to 1992. No juvenile, adoption, mental health, sealed or expunged records released. Certification fee: $1.00 per cert. Payee: Clerk of District Court. Personal checks accepted. Prepayment and SASE required.

District Court Courthouse, 501 Merchant, 3rd Fl, Oswego, KS 67356; phone: 620-795-4533 x245; fax: 620-795-3056; hours 8AM-5PM (CST). *Felony, Misdemeanor, Civil, Eviction, Small Claims, Probate.*
Civil Records: Access: In person only. Visitors must perform in person searches themselves. Court makes copy: $.25 per page; same fee for self serve. Required to search: name, years to search. Civil cases indexed by defendant, plaintiff; on computer since 1992.
Criminal Records: Access: In person only. Visitors must perform in person searches themselves. No search fee. Court makes copy: $.25 per page; same fee for self serve. Required to search: name, years to search; also helpful: DOB, SSN. Criminal records on computer since 1992.
General Information: Public terminal goes back to 1994. no juvenile, adoption, mental health, sealed or expunged records released. Will fax documents, fee is $2.00 for 1st page, $.50 each add'l. Certification fee: $1.00 per certification. Payee: Clerk of District Court. Personal checks accepted. Prepayment required.

Lane County

District Court PO Box 188, Dighton, KS 67839; phone: 620-397-2805; fax: 620-397-5526; hours 8AM-5PM (CST). *Felony, Misdemeanor, Civil, Eviction, Small Claims, Probate.*
www.kscourts.org/dstcts/24dstct.htm
Civil Records: Access: Mail, in person. Both court and visitors may perform in person searches. Search fee: $12.00 per hour. Court makes copy: $.25 per page. Required to search: name, years to search. Civil cases indexed by defendant, plaintiff; on computer since 1993; prior records from 1800s. Mail turnaround time 1-2 weeks.
Criminal Records: Access: Mail, in person. Visitors must perform in person searches themselves. Search fee: $12.00 per name. Court makes copy: $.25 per page. Required to search: name, years to search; also helpful: SSN. Criminal records on computer since 1993; prior records from 1800s. Mail turnaround time 1-2 weeks.
General Information: No public access terminal. No juvenile, mental health, sealed or expunged records released. Certification fee: $1.00 per page. Payee: Clerk of Court. Personal checks accepted. Prepayment and SASE required.

Leavenworth County

District Court 601 S 3rd St, Leavenworth, KS 66048; phone: 913-684-0700; criminal phone: 913-684-0704; civil phone: 913-684-0701; fax: 913-684-0492; hours 8AM-5PM (CST). *Felony, Misdemeanor, Civil, Eviction, Small Claims, Probate.*
Civil Records: Access: Mail, in person. Both court and visitors may perform in person searches. Search fee: $12.00 per hour, if extensive. Court makes copy: $.25 per page. Required to search: name, years to search. Civil cases indexed by defendant, plaintiff; on computer from 1990, microfiche to 1952 and index books from 1901. Mail turnaround time 3-4 days.
Criminal Records: Access: Mail, in person. Both court and visitors may perform in person searches. Search fee: $12.00 per hour, if extensive. Court makes copy: $.25 per page. Required to search: name, years to search; also helpful: SSN. Criminal records on computer from 1990, microfiche and index books from 1960. Mail turnaround time 3-4 days.
General Information: Public terminal goes back to 1980. No juvenile, mental health, sealed or expunged records released. Will fax documents if local call. Certification fee: $1.00 per page. Payee: Clerk of District Court. Personal checks accepted. SASE required.

Lincoln County

District Court 216 E Lincoln Ave, Lincoln, KS 67455; phone: 785-524-4057; fax: 785-524-3204; hours 8AM-12, 1-5PM (CST). *Felony, Misdemeanor, Civil, Eviction, Small Claims, Probate.*
www.kscourts.org/dstcts/12dstct.htm
Civil Records: Access: Fax, mail, in person. Only the court performs in person searches; visitors may not. No search fee. Court makes copy: $.25 per page. Required to search: name; also helpful: years to search. Civil cases indexed by defendant, plaintiff. All records on computer.
Criminal Records: Access: In person only. Only the court performs in person searches; visitors may not. No search fee. Court makes copy: $.25 per page. Required to search: name; also helpful: years to search, DOB, SSN. Criminal records on computer since 1980, on index cards from 1880. Will search 1 name by phone only, maybe.
General Information: No public access terminal. No juvenile, mental health, sealed or expunged records released. Will fax documents $3.00 per page. Certification fee: $1.00. Payee: Clerk of Court. Personal checks accepted. Prepayment required.

Linn County

District Court PO Box 350, 318 Chestnut St, Mound City, KS 66056-0350; phone: 913-795-2660; fax: 913-795-2004; hours 8AM-4:30PM (CST). *Felony, Misdemeanor, Civil, Eviction, Small Claims, Probate.*

Civil Records: Access: In person only. Visitors must perform in person searches themselves. Court makes copy: $.25 per page. Required to search: name, years to search. Civil cases indexed by defendant, plaintiff; on computer from 1990, archives and index books from 1854.

Criminal Records: Access: In person only. Visitors must perform in person searches themselves. Court makes copy: $.25 per page. Required to search: name, years to search. Criminal records on computer from 1990, archives and index books from 1886.

General Information: Public terminal has criminal back to 1975 and civil back to 1800s. No juvenile, mental health, sealed or expunged records released. Will not fax specific case file. Certification fee: $1.25. Payee: Clerk of District Court. Personal checks accepted. Prepayment required.

Logan County

District Court 710 W 2nd St, Oakley, KS 67748-1233; phone: 785-672-3654; fax: 785-672-3517; hours 8:30AM-N, 1-5PM (CST). *Felony, Misdemeanor, Civil, Eviction, Small Claims, Probate.*

Civil Records: Access: In person only. Visitors must perform in person searches themselves. Court makes copy: $.25 per page. Required to search: name; also helpful: years to search. Civil cases indexed by defendant, plaintiff; on computer from 1927, index cards from 1887.

Criminal Records: Access: In person only. Visitors must perform in person searches themselves. Court makes copy: $.25 per page. Required to search: name; SSN helpful, years to search. Criminal records on computer from 1927 index cards from 1887.

General Information: Public use terminal available. No juvenile, mental health, sealed or expunged records released. Certification fee: $1.00. Payee: Clerk of District Court. Personal checks accepted. Prepayment required.

Lyon County

District Court 430 Commercial St, Emporia, KS 66801; phone: 620-341-3281; fax: 620-341-3497; hours 8AM-4PM (CST). *Felony, Misdemeanor, Civil, Eviction, Small Claims, Probate.*
www.lyoncounty.org/DistrictCourt.htm

Civil Records: Access: Fax, mail, in person. Both court and visitors may perform in person searches. Search fee: $12.00 per hour. Court makes copy: $.50 per page; same fee for self serve. Required to search: name, years to search. Civil cases indexed by defendant, plaintiff. Records maintained since 1859. Mail turnaround time 3 days maximum.

Criminal Records: Access: Fax, mail, in person. Both court and visitors may perform in person searches. Search fee: $12.00 per hour. Court makes copy: $.50 per page; same fee for self serve. Required to search: name, years to search. Records maintained since 1859. Mail turnaround time 3 days maximum.

General Information: Public terminal goes back to 1998. No mental health, sealed or expunged records released. Will fax documents $1.00 per page. Certification fee: $2.00 per document. Payee: Clerk of District Court. Personal checks accepted. Prepayment required.

Marion County

District Court PO Box 298, Marion, KS 66861; phone: 620-382-2104; fax: 620-382-2259; hours 8AM-5PM; 9AM-5PM open to public (CST). *Felony, Misdemeanor, Civil, Eviction, Small Claims, Probate.*

Civil Records: Access: In person only. Visitors must perform in person searches themselves. Court makes copy: $1.00 per page; $.25 each after 1st 4.

Required to search: name, years to search. Civil cases indexed by defendant, plaintiff; on computer from 7/1992, on index cards from 1800s.

Criminal Records: Access: In person only. Visitors must perform in person searches themselves. Court makes copy: $1.00 per page; $.25 each after 1st 4. Required to search: name, years to search. Criminal records on computer from 7/1992, on index cards from 1800s.

General Information: Public terminal goes back to 1992. No juvenile, mental health, sealed or expunged records released. Will not fax specific case file. Certification fee: $1.00 per cert. Payee: District Court. Personal checks accepted. Prepayment required.

Marshall County

District Court PO Box 149, 1201 Broadway, Office #5, Marysville, KS 66508; phone: 785-562-5301; fax: 785-562-2458; hours 8AM-5PM; Search hours: 8:30AM-4:30PM (CST). *Felony, Misdemeanor, Civil, Eviction, Small Claims, Probate.*

Note: Actual marriage licenses from 1860 through June 18, 1942 may be viewed and copied from 1:00PM - 4:00PM. Records are located in old historical courthouse located next door at 1207 Broadway.

Civil Records: Access: Fax, mail, in person. Both court and visitors may perform in person searches. Search fee: $12.00 per hour. Court makes copy: $.50 for 1st page, $.25 each add'l; same fee for self serve. Required to search: name, years to search. Civil cases indexed by defendant, plaintiff; on computer from 1980, microfiche from 1977 (earlier records on roll-marriage licenses on computer index 1860s, forward/naturalizations on computer index). Mail turnaround time 1-2 days.

Criminal Records: Access: Fax, mail, in person. Both court and visitors may perform in person searches. Search fee: $12.00 per hour. Court makes copy: $.50 for first page, $.25 each add'l; same fee for self serve. Required to search: name, years to search. Criminal records on computer from 1986, microfiche from 1977. Mail turnaround time 1-2 days.

General Information: Public terminal has criminal back to 1982 and civil back to 1980. No juvenile, offender under 14 years of age, no child in need of care, mental health, sealed or expunged records released. Will fax documents for $2.00 1st page, $1.00 each add'l. Prepayment required. Certification fee: $1.00. Payee: Clerk of Court. Personal checks accepted. Prepayment and SASE required.

McPherson County

District Court PO Box 1106, McPherson, KS 67460; phone: 620-241-3422; fax: 620-241-1372; hours 8AM-5PM (CST). *Felony, Misdemeanor, Civil, Eviction, Small Claims, Probate.*

Civil Records: Access: Mail, in person. Both court and visitors may perform in person searches. Search fee: $12.00 per hour. Court makes copy: $.50 per page. Required to search: name, years to search. Civil cases indexed by defendant, plaintiff; on microfilm from 1953, index cards from 1900s. Mail turnaround time 1-3 days.

Criminal Records: Access: Mail, in person. Both court and visitors may perform in person searches. Search fee: $12.00 per hour. Court makes copy: $.50 per page. Required to search: name, years to search; also helpful: SSN. Criminal records on microfilm from 1953, index cards from 1900s. Mail turnaround time 1-3 days.

General Information: Public terminal goes back to 1980s. No juvenile, mental health, sealed or expunged records released. Will fax documents for $1.00 per page. Certification fee: $1.00. Payee: District Court. Personal checks accepted. Prepayment and SASE required.

Meade County

Meade County District Court PO Box 623, Meade, KS 67864; phone: 620-873-8750; fax: 620-873-8759; hours 8AM-5PM (CST). *Felony, Misdemeanor, Civil, Eviction, Small Claims, Probate.*
www.kscourts.org/dstcts/16dstct.htm

Note: All employment background checks requested by mail, phone, or fax are referred to the KBI (state agency for criminal records).

Civil Records: Access: Fax, mail, in person. Both court and visitors may perform in person searches. Search fee: $12.00 per hour. Court makes copy: $.25 per page. Required to search: name, years to search. Civil cases indexed by defendant, plaintiff; on computer from 1990, index cards from 1896.

Criminal Records: Access: In person only. Both court and visitors may perform in person searches. Search fee: $12.00 per hour. Court makes copy: $.25 per page. Required to search: name, years to search. Criminal records on computer from 1990, index cards from 1896. Mail turnaround time 1-2 days.

General Information: Public terminal goes back to 1996. No juvenile, mental health, sealed or expunged records released. Will fax documents for $2.00 1st page, $.50 each add'l page. Certification fee: $1.00 per page. Payee: Clerk of Court. Personal checks accepted. Prepayment and SASE required.

Miami County

District Court PO Box 187, Paola, KS 66071; phone: 913-294-3326; fax: 913-294-2535; hours 8AM-4:30PM (CST). *Felony, Misdemeanor, Civil, Eviction, Small Claims, Probate.*

Civil Records: Access: In person only. Both court and visitors may perform in person searches. No search fee. Court makes copy: $.50 per page. Self serve copy fee: $.25 per page. Required to search: name, years to search. Civil cases indexed by defendant, plaintiff; on computer from 1984, index cards from 1890s.

Criminal Records: Access: In person only. Both court and visitors may perform in person searches. No search fee. Court makes copy: $.50 per page. Self serve copy fee: $.25 per page. Required to search: name, years to search; SSN helpful. Criminal records on computer from 1984, index cards from 1890s.

General Information: Public terminal goes back to 1987. No juvenile, mental health, sealed or expunged records released. Will fax specific document for $.50 per page. Certification fee: $1.00 per page. Payee: District Court. Personal checks accepted. Prepayment required.

Mitchell County

District Court 115 S Hersey, Beloit, KS 67420; phone: 785-738-3753; fax: 785-738-4101; hours 8AM-5PM (CST). *Felony, Misdemeanor, Civil, Eviction, Small Claims, Probate.*
www.kscourts.org/dstcts/12dstct.htm

Note: Probate is a separate index at this same address

Civil Records: Access: Mail, in person. Both court and visitors may perform in person searches. Search fee: $12.00 per hour. Court makes copy: $.25 per page; same fee for self serve. Required to search: name, years to search. Civil cases indexed by defendant, plaintiff; on index cards from 1876. Mail turnaround time 1-2 days.

Criminal Records: Access: Mail, in person. Both court and visitors may perform in person searches. Search fee: $12.00 per hour. Court makes copy: $.25 per page; same fee for self serve. Required to search: name, years to search. Criminal records on index cards from 1977, archived to 1870. Mail turnaround time 1-2 days.

General Information: No public access terminal. No juvenile, mental health, sealed or expunged records released. Will fax documents. Certification fee: $1.00 per page. Payee: Clerk of Court. Personal checks accepted. Prepayment and SASE required.

Montgomery County

Independence District Court 300 E Main St, #201, Independence, KS 67301; phone: 620-330-1070; fax: 620-331-6120; hours 8AM-5PM (CST). *Felony, Misdemeanor, Civil, Eviction, Small Claims, Probate.*

Civil Records: Access: Fax, mail, in person. Both court and visitors may perform in person searches. Search fee: $12.00 per hour. $6.00 minimum. Court makes copy: $.25 per page. Required to search: name, years to search. Civil cases indexed by defendant, plaintiff; on computer since 1992, on microfiche from 1870-1930, archives 1930-1992, index cards from 1870. This court covers civil cases for the northern part of the county. It is suggested to search both courts. Mail turnaround time 72 hours.

Criminal Records: Access: Fax, mail, in person. Both court and visitors may perform in person searches. Search fee: $12.00 per hour. $6.00 minimum. Court makes copy: $.25 per page. Required to search: name, years to search; also helpful: SSN. Criminal records on computer since 1992, on microfiche from 1870-1930, archives 1930-1992, index cards from 1870. Mail turnaround time 72 hours.

General Information: Public terminal goes back to 1993. No juvenile, adoptions, mental health, sealed or expunged records released. Will fax documents for $5.00 1st page, $1.00 each add'l. Certification fee: $1.00. Payee: Clerk of Court. Personal checks accepted; no credit cards. Prepayment required.

Coffeyville District Court 102 W 7th St, #A, Coffeyville, KS 67337; phone: 620-251-1060; fax: 620-251-2734; hours 8:30AM-N, 1:00-4:30PM (CST). *Civil, Eviction, Small Claims, Probate.*

Note: This court covers civil cases for the southern part of the county, although cases can be filed in either court. It is recommended to search both courts

Civil Records: Access: Fax, mail, in person. Both court and visitors may perform in person searches. Search fee: $12.80 per hour; $6.00 minimum. Court makes copy: $.25 per page. Required to search: name, years to search. Civil cases indexed by defendant, plaintiff; on computer back to 1992, on paper, fiche, etc. since 1924. Mail turnaround time 72 hours.

General Information: No public access terminal. No juvenile, mental health, sealed, adoption, or expunged records released. Fee to fax documents is $1.00 per page. Certification fee: $1.00 per page. Payee: Clerk of Court. Personal checks accepted. Prepayment required. SASE requested.

Morris County

District Court County Courthouse, Council Grove, KS 66846; phone: 620-767-6838; fax: 620-767-6488; hours 9AM-5PM (CST). *Felony, Misdemeanor, Civil, Eviction, Small Claims, Probate.*

Civil Records: Access: Fax, mail, in person. Both court and visitors may perform in person searches. Search fee: $12.00 per hour. Court makes copy: $.25 per page. Required to search: name, years to search. Civil cases indexed by defendant, plaintiff; on computer since 1992, on microfiche, archives and index cards from 1860. Mail turnaround time 1-2 days.

Criminal Records: Access: Fax, mail, in person. Both court and visitors may perform in person searches. Search fee: $12.00 per hour. Court makes copy: $.25 per page. Required to search: name, years to search. Criminal records on computer since 1992, on microfiche, archives and index cards from 1860. Mail turnaround time 1-2 days.

General Information: Public terminal goes back to 1992. Will fax documents $1.00 per page. Certification fee: $1.00. Payee: Clerk of Court. Personal checks accepted. Prepayment and SASE required.

Morton County

District Court PO Box 825, Elkhart, KS 67950; phone: 620-697-2563; fax: 620-697-4289; hours 8AM-N, 1-5PM (CST). *Felony, Misdemeanor, Civil, Eviction, Small Claims, Probate.*

Civil Records: Access: Mail, fax, in person. Both court and visitors may perform in person searches. Search fee: $12.80 per hour. Court makes copy: $.25 per page. Required to search: name, years to search. Civil cases indexed by defendant, plaintiff; on computer from 1992, index cards from 1800s. Mail turnaround time same day.

Criminal Records: Access: In person only. Visitors must perform in person searches themselves. Court makes copy: $.25 per page. Required to search: name, years to search. Criminal records on computer from 1977, index cards from 1800s.

General Information: Public terminal has criminal back to 1977 and civil back to 1992. No juvenile, mental health, sealed or expunged records released. Fee to fax documents: $2.50 1st pg.; $.50 each add'l. Certification fee: $1.00 per certification. Payee: Clerk of Court. Two party checks not accepted. Prepayment required.

Nemaha County

District Court PO Box 213, Seneca, KS 66538; phone: 785-336-2146; fax: 785-336-6450; hours 8AM-5PM (CST). *Felony, Misdemeanor, Civil, Eviction, Small Claims, Probate.*

Civil Records: Access: Phone, mail, in person. Both court and visitors may perform in person searches. Search fee: $12.00 per hour. Court makes copy: $.25 per page; same fee for self serve. Required to search: name, years to search. Civil cases indexed by defendant, plaintiff; on computer from 1977, index cards from 1870. Mail turnaround time 1-2 days.

Criminal Records: Access: In person only. Visitors must perform in person searches themselves. Court makes copy: $.25 per page; same fee for self serve. Required to search: name, years to search, SSN. Criminal records on computer from 1977, index cards from 1870.

General Information: Public terminal goes back to 1977. No juvenile, mental health, sealed or expunged records released. Will fax documents for $2.00 1st page, $1.00 each add'l. Certification fee: $1.00. Payee: Clerk of District Court. Business checks accepted. Prepayment and SASE required.

Neosho County

Chanute District Court 102 S Lincoln, PO Box 889, Chanute, KS 66720; phone: 620-431-5700; fax: 620-431-5710; hours 8AM-5PM (CST). *Felony, Misdemeanor, Civil, Eviction, Small Claims.*

Note: This is a branch court of Erie.

Civil Records: Access: Mail, in person. Both court and visitors may perform in person searches. Search fee: $12.00 per hour. Court makes copy: $.50 per page. Required to search: name, years to search. Civil cases indexed by defendant, plaintiff; on computer since 1993; prior back to 1955.

Criminal Records: Access: In person only. Both court and visitors may perform in person searches. Search fee: $12.00 per hour per name. Court makes copy: $.50 per page. Required to search: name, years to search. Criminal records on computer since 1993; prior back to 1955. Mail turnaround time 1-3 days.

General Information: Public terminal goes back to 1993. No juvenile, mental health, sealed or expunged records released. Fee to fax documents is $1.00 per page. Certification fee: $1.00 per cert. Payee: Clerk of District Court. Personal checks accepted. Prepayment required.

Erie District Court Neosho County Courthouse, PO Box 19, Erie, KS 66733; phone: 620-244-3831; criminal phone: 620-431-5700; fax: 620-244-3830; hours 8AM-N, 1-4:30PM (CST). *Felony, Misdemeanor, Civil, Eviction, Small Claims, Probate.*

Note: This is the main court for the county.

Ness County

District Court PO Box 445, Ness City, KS 67560; phone: 785-798-3693; fax: 785-798-3348; hours 8AM-5PM (CST). *Felony, Misdemeanor, Civil, Eviction, Small Claims, Probate.*

Note: Probate is a separate index at this same address.

Civil Records: Access: Fax, mail, in person. Both court and visitors may perform in person searches. Search fee: $12.00 per hour. Court makes copy: $.25 per page; same fee for self serve. Required to search: name, years to search. Civil cases indexed by defendant, plaintiff; on index books from 1885.

Criminal Records: Access: In person only. Visitors must perform in person searches themselves. Court makes copy: $.25 per page; same fee for self serve. Required to search: name, years to search. Criminal records on index books from 1885.

General Information: Public terminal goes back to 2003. No juvenile, mental health, sealed or expunged records released. Fee to fax documents is $1.00 per page. Certification fee: $1.00 per page. Payee: Clerk of Court. Personal checks accepted. Prepayment required.

Norton County

District Court PO Box 70, Norton, KS 67654; phone: 785-877-5720; fax: 785-877-5722; hours 8AM-5PM (CST). *Felony, Misdemeanor, Civil, Eviction, Small Claims, Probate.*

Civil Records: Access: Mail, in person. Both court and visitors may perform in person searches. Search fee: $12.00 per hour. Court makes copy: $.25 per page; same fee for self serve. Required to search: name, years to search. Civil cases indexed by defendant, plaintiff; on index from 1900s. Mail turnaround time 1 week.

Criminal Records: Access: Mail, in person. Visitors must perform in person searches themselves. Search fee: $12.00 per hour. Court makes copy: $.25 per page; same fee for self serve. Required to search: name, years to search. Criminal records on index from 1900s. Mail turnaround time 1 week.

General Information: Public terminal goes back to 2004. No juvenile, mental health, sealed or expunged records released. Will fax documents to local or toll free line. Certification fee: $1.00. Payee: Clerk of District Court. Personal checks accepted. Prepayment and SASE required.

Osage County

District Court PO Box 549, Lyndon, KS 66451; phone: 785-828-4514; fax: 785-828-4704; hours 8AM-N,1-4PM (CST). *Felony, Misdemeanor, Civil, Eviction, Small Claims, Probate.*
www.franklincoks.org/4thdistrict/index

Civil Records: Access: In person, online. Visitors must perform in person searches themselves. Court makes copy: $.25 per page. Required to search: name,

Civil Records: Access: Fax, mail, in person. Both court and visitors may perform in person searches. Search fee: $12.00 per hour. Court makes copy: $.50 per page. Required to search: name, years to search. Civil cases indexed by defendant, plaintiff; on index cards from 1900s; on computer back to 1993. Mail turnaround time 1-3 days.

Criminal Records: Access: Mail, in person. Visitors must perform in person searches themselves. Search fee: $12.00 per record. Court makes copy: $.50 per page. Required to search: name, years to search, DOB. Criminal records on index cards from 1900s; on computer back to 1993. Limited mail searches are okay, lists should be sent to the central state agency. Searches for employment, credit or the like are referred to KBI. Mail turnaround time 1-3 days.

General Information: Public terminal goes back to 1993. No juvenile, mental health, sealed or expunged records released. Fee to fax documents is $1.00 per page. Certification fee: $1.00. Payee: Clerk of Court. Personal checks accepted. Prepayment and SASE required.

years to search. Civil cases indexed by defendant, plaintiff; on computer from 1980. Current court calendars are free online at www.franklincoks.org/4thdistrict/osagebydate.html. Also, access to old probate court and marriage records is free at www.kscourts.org/dstcts/4osprrec.htm. Also, case information is soon to be available at www.franklincoks.org/4thdistrict/index.

Criminal Records: Access: In person, online. Visitors must perform in person searches themselves. Search fee: $12.00 per hour. Court makes copy: $.25 per page. Required to search: name, years to search. Criminal records on computer from 1980. Online access to criminal records is the same as civil.

General Information: Public terminal has criminal back to 1980 and civil back to 1980. No juvenile, mental health, sealed or expunged records released. Certification fee: $1.00. Payee: Clerk of Court. Business checks accepted. Prepayment required.

Osborne County

District Court PO Box 160, 423 W Main, Osborne, KS 67473; phone: 785-346-5911; fax: 785-346-5992; hours 8AM-N, 1-5PM (CST). *Felony, Misdemeanor, Civil, Eviction, Small Claims, Probate.*

Civil Records: Access: In person only. Visitors must perform in person searches themselves. Court makes copy: $.25 per page. Self serve copy fee: $.10 per page. Required to search: name, years to search. Civil cases indexed by defendant, plaintiff; on microfiche from 1872-1980, index books from 1981, index cards from 1872.

Criminal Records: Access: In person, fax, mail. Both court and visitors may perform in person searches. Search fee: $12.00 per hr. Court makes copy: $.25 per page. Self serve copy fee: $.10 per page. Required to search: name, years to search; also helpful: SSN. Criminal records on microfiche from 1872-1980, index books from 1981, index cards from 1872. Mail turnaround time 3 days.

General Information: No public access terminal. No juvenile, mental health, sealed or expunged records released. Certification fee: $1.00 per doc. Payee: Clerk of District Court. Personal checks accepted. Prepayment required. SASE requested.

Ottawa County

District Court 307 N Concord, Minneapolis, KS 67467; phone: 785-392-2917; fax: 785-392-3626; hours 8AM-N;1-5PM (CST). *Felony, Misdemeanor, Civil, Eviction, Small Claims, Probate.*

Civil Records: Access: Mail, fax, in person. Both court and visitors may perform in person searches. Search fee: $9.00 per hour. Court makes copy: $.25 per page; same fee for self serve. Required to search: name, years to search. Civil cases indexed by defendant, plaintiff; on index from 1800s; computerized records since 1990.

Criminal Records: Access: In person only. Both court and visitors may perform in person searches. No search fee. Court makes copy: $.25 per page; same fee for self serve. Required to search: name, years to search; SSN helpful. Criminal records on index from 1800s; computerized records since 1990.

General Information: Public terminal has criminal back to 1999 and civil back to 2000. No juvenile, mental health, sealed or expunged records released. Certification fee: $2.00 per doc. Payee: Clerk of District Court. Personal checks accepted. Prepayment required.

Pawnee County

District Court PO Box 270, Larned, KS 67550; phone: 620-285-6937; fax: 620-285-3665; hours 8AM-5PM (CST). *Felony, Misdemeanor, Civil, Eviction, Small Claims, Probate.* www.kscourts.org/dstcts/24dstct.htm

Civil Records: Access: Fax, mail, in person. Both court and visitors may perform in person searches.

Search fee: $12.00 an hour. Court makes copy: $.25 per page; same fee for self serve. Required to search: name, years to search. Civil cases indexed by defendant, plaintiff; on computer from 1991, index cards from 1900s. Mail turnaround time 1 day.

Criminal Records: Access: Fax, mail, in person. Visitors must perform in person searches themselves. Search fee: $12.00 an hour. Court makes copy: $.25 per page; same fee for self serve. Required to search: name, years to search; also helpful: SSN. Criminal records on computer from 1991, index cards from 1900s. Mail turnaround time 1-2 days.

General Information: No public access terminal. No juvenile, mental health, sealed or expunged records released. Will fax documents $.50 per page. Certification fee: $1.00 per page. Payee: Clerk of District Court. Personal checks accepted; no credit cards. Prepayment required.

Phillips County

District Court PO Box 564, Phillipsburg, KS 67661; phone: 785-543-6830; fax: 785-543-6832; hours 8AM-5PM (CST). *Felony, Misdemeanor, Civil, Eviction, Small Claims, Probate.*

Civil Records: Access: Mail, in person. Visitors must perform in person searches themselves. Search fee: $12.00 per hour. Court makes copy: $.25 per page. Self serve copy fee: $.10 per page. Required to search: name, years to search. Civil cases indexed by defendant, plaintiff; on index from 1900s; on computer back to 1994. Mail turnaround time 2 days.

Criminal Records: Access: Mail, in person. Visitors must perform in person searches themselves. Search fee: $12.00 per hour. Court makes copy: $.25 per page. Self serve copy fee: $.10 per page. Required to search: name, years to search; also helpful: DOB, SSN. Criminal records on index from 1900s; on computer back to 1994. Mail turnaround time 2 days.

General Information: Public terminal goes back to 2/2004. No juvenile, mental health, sealed or expunged records released. Will fax documents for $.50 per page. Certification fee: $1.00 per cert. Payee: Clerk of District Court. Personal checks accepted. Prepayment required.

Pottawatomie County

District Court PO Box 129, Westmoreland, KS 66549; phone: 785-457-3392; fax: 785-457-2107; hours 8AM-4:30PM (CST). *Felony, Misdemeanor, Civil, Eviction, Small Claims, Probate.*

Civil Records: Access: In person only. Visitors must perform in person searches themselves. Court makes copy: $.25 per page. Required to search: name, years to search. Civil cases indexed by defendant, plaintiff. Civil records computerized since 1998, on microfiche from 1800s, index from 1800s.

Criminal Records: Access: In person only. Visitors must perform in person searches themselves. Court makes copy: $.25 per page. Required to search: name, years to search; SSN helpful. Criminal records computerized since 1998, on microfiche from 1800s, index from 1800s.

General Information: Public terminal goes back to 1999. No juvenile, mental health, sealed or expunged records released. Certification fee: $2.00 per doc. Payee: Clerk of District Court. Personal checks accepted, no credit cards. Prepayment required.

Pratt County

District Court PO Box 984, Pratt, KS 67124; phone: 620-672-4100; fax: 620-672-2902; hours 8AM-N, 1-5PM (CST). *Felony, Misdemeanor, Civil, Eviction, Small Claims, Probate.* www.prattcounty.org

Civil Records: Access: Mail, fax, in person. Both court and visitors may perform in person searches. Search fee: $12.00 per hour. Court makes copy: $.25 per page. Required to search: name, years to search. Civil cases indexed by defendant, plaintiff; on

computer back to 1988, microfiche, archives, index from 1878. Mail turnaround time 48 hours.

Criminal Records: Access: Mail, fax, in person. Both court and visitors may perform in person searches. Search fee: $12.00 per hour. Court makes copy: $.25 per page. Required to search: name, years to search, DOB; also helpful: SSN, signed release. Criminal records on computer back to 1988, microfiche, archives, index from 1878. Mail turnaround time 1-2 days.

General Information: Public terminal goes back to 1988. No juvenile, mental health, sealed or expunged records released. Fee to fax documents is $1.00 per page. Certification fee: $1.00 per item. Payee: Clerk of District Court. Personal checks accepted. Prepayment and SASE required.

Rawlins County

District Court 607 Main, #F, Atwood, KS 67730; phone: 785-626-3465; fax: 785-626-3350; hours 9AM-5PM (CST). *Felony, Misdemeanor, Civil, Eviction, Small Claims, Probate.*

Civil Records: Access: In person only. Visitors must perform in person searches themselves. Court makes copy: $.25 per page. Required to search: name, years to search. Civil cases indexed by defendant, plaintiff; on index from 1900s.

Criminal Records: Access: In person only. Visitors must perform in person searches themselves. Court makes copy: $.25 per page. Required to search: name, years to search. Criminal records on index from 1900s. This agency refers requesters to the Kansas Bureau of Investigations.

General Information: Public terminal goes back to 3/2004. No juvenile, mental health, sealed or expunged records released. Certification fee: $1.00. Payee: Clerk of District Court. Only in state checks accepted. Prepayment required.

Reno County

District Court 206 W 1st, Hutchinson, KS 67501; phone: 620-694-2956; fax: 620-694-2958; hours 8AM-N, 1-5PM (CST). *Felony, Misdemeanor, Civil, Eviction, Small Claims, Probate.*

Civil Records: Access: Mail, in person. Both court and visitors may perform in person searches. Search fee: $1.00 per 5 minutes. Court makes copy: $.25 per page. Required to search: name, years to search. Civil cases indexed by defendant, plaintiff; on computer from 1992, index cards from 1900s. Mail turnaround time 3-5 days (in-state); 3-10 days (out-of-state).

Criminal Records: Access: Mail, in person. Both court and visitors may perform in person searches. Search fee: $1.00 per 5 minutes. Court makes copy: $.25 per page. Required to search: name, years to search, DOB, signed release; also helpful: address, SSN. Criminal records on computer from 1992, index cards from 1900s. Mail turnaround time 3-5 days (in-state); 3-10 days (out-of-state).

General Information: Public terminal goes back to 2003. No mental health, juvenile (some), sealed or expunged records released. Certification fee: $1.00. Payee: Clerk of District Court. Personal checks accepted. Prepayment and SASE required.

Republic County

District Court PO Box 8, Belleville, KS 66935; phone: 785-527-7234; fax: 785-527-5029; hours 8AM-5PM (CST). *Felony, Misdemeanor, Civil, Eviction, Small Claims, Probate.* www.kscourts.org/dstcts/12dstct.htm

Note: Probate is a separate index at the same address.

Civil Records: Access: Mail, in person. Both court and visitors may perform in person searches. Search fee: $12.00 per hour. Court makes copy: $.25 per page. Required to search: name, years to search. Civil cases indexed by defendant, plaintiff; on computer from 1990, index cards from 1869 for probate.

Criminal Records: Access: In person only. Visitors must perform in person searches themselves. Court makes copy: $.25 per page. Required to search: name, years to search. Criminal records on computer from 1990, index cards from 1869 for probate. **General Information:** No public access terminal. No juvenile, mental health, sealed or expunged records released. Will fax documents to local or toll free line or for $3.00 per page. Certification fee: $1.00 per document. Payee: Clerk of Court. Personal checks accepted. Prepayment and SASE required.

Rice County

District Court 101 W Commercial, Lyons, KS 67554; phone: 620-257-2383; fax: 620-257-3826; hours 8:00AM-5PM (CST). *Felony, Misdemeanor, Civil, Eviction, Small Claims, Probate.*
Civil Records: Access: Fax, mail, in person. Both court and visitors may perform in person searches. Search fee: $12.00 per hour. Court makes copy: $1.00 for first page, $.25 each add'l; same fee for self serve. Required to search: name, years to search. Civil cases indexed by defendant, plaintiff; on computer from 1980, index cards from 1880. Mail turnaround time 3 days.
Criminal Records: Access: Fax, mail, in person. Visitors must perform in person searches themselves. Search fee: $12.00 per hour. Court makes copy: $1.00 for first page, $.25 each add'l; same fee for self serve. Required to search: name, years to search; also helpful: SSN. Criminal records on computer from 1980, index cards from 1880. All criminal searches are referred to the KBI, 1620 SW Tyler, Topeka KS 66601. Mail turnaround time 1-3 days.
General Information: Public terminal goes back to 1980s. No juvenile, mental health, sealed or expunged records released. Fee to fax documents is $.50 per page. No certification fee. Payee: Clerk of Court. Personal checks accepted. Prepayment and SASE required.

Riley County

District Court PO Box 158, Manhattan, KS 66505-0158; phone: 785-537-6364; hours 8:30AM-5PM (CST). *Felony, Misdemeanor, Civil, Eviction, Small Claims, Probate.*
Civil Records: Access: In person only. Visitors must perform in person searches themselves. Court makes copy: $.25 per page. Required to search: name, years to search. Civil cases indexed by defendant, plaintiff; on computer back to 10/93; prior records in index journals.
Criminal Records: Access: In person only. Visitors must perform in person searches themselves. Court makes copy: $.25 per page. Required to search: name, years to search; also helpful: DOB, SSN. Criminal records on computer back to 1986, microfiche, archives and index cards from 1900s.
General Information: Public terminal goes back to 1980. No mental health, sealed or expunged records released. Certification fee: $1.00. Payee: Clerk of Court. Personal checks accepted. Prepayment required.

Rooks County

District Court 115 N Walnut, PO Box 532, Stockton, KS 67669; phone: 785-425-6718; fax: 785-425-6568; hours 8AM-5PM (CST). *Felony, Misdemeanor, Civil, Eviction, Small Claims, Probate.*
Civil Records: Access: Mail, in person. Both court and visitors may perform in person searches. Search fee: $12.00 per hour. Court makes copy: $.25 per page; same fee for self serve. Required to search: name, years to search. Civil cases indexed by defendant, plaintiff; on index cards from 1888; on computer since. Mail turnaround time 1-3 days.
Criminal Records: Access: In person only. Both court and visitors may perform in person searches. Court makes copy: $.25 per page; same fee for self serve. Required to search: name, years to search; also helpful: DOB, SSN. Criminal records on index cards

from 1888; on computer since. The court personnel will not do criminal record searches for the public. **General Information:** Public use terminal available. No juvenile, adoption, mental health, sealed or expunged records released. Fee to fax documents is $2.50 1st page and $1.50 ea add'l. Certification fee: $2.00. Payee: Clerk of Court. Personal checks accepted. Prepayment and SASE required.

Rush County

District Court PO Box 387, La Crosse, KS 67548; phone: 785-222-2718; fax: 785-222-2748; hours 8AM-5PM (CST). *Felony, Misdemeanor, Civil, Eviction, Small Claims, Probate.*
www.kscourts.org/dstcts/24dstct.htm
Note: Probate is a separate index at this same address.
Civil Records: Access: Phone, fax, mail, in person. Both court and visitors may perform in person searches. Search fee: $12.00 per hour. Court makes copy: $.25 per page; same fee for self serve. Required to search: name, years to search. Civil cases indexed by defendant, plaintiff; on computer from 4/1994, on index from 1800s. Mail turnaround time 3 days.
Criminal Records: Access: In person only. Visitors must perform in person searches themselves. Court makes copy: $.25 per page; same fee for self serve. Required to search: name, years to search; SSN helpful. Criminal records on computer from 4/1994, on index from 1800s.
General Information: Public terminal goes back to 2003. No juvenile, mental health, sealed or expunged records released. Will fax documents for $.50 per page. Certification fee: $1.00 per page. Payee: Clerk of District Court. Personal checks accepted. Prepayment and SASE required.

Russell County

District Court PO Box 876, Russell, KS 67665; phone: 785-483-5641; fax: 785-483-2448; hours 8AM-5PM (CST). *Felony, Misdemeanor, Civil, Eviction, Small Claims, Probate.*
Civil Records: Access: Fax, mail, in person. Both court and visitors may perform in person searches. Search fee: $12.00 per hour. Court makes copy: $.50 per page; same fee for self serve. Required to search: name, years to search. Civil cases indexed by defendant, plaintiff; on computer from 1990, index cards from 1900s. Mail turnaround time 3 days.
Criminal Records: Access: Fax, mail, in person. Both court and visitors may perform in person searches. Search fee: $12.00 per hour. Court makes copy: $.50 per page; same fee for self serve. Required to search: name, years to search, DOB. Criminal records on computer from 1990, index cards from 1900s. Mail turnaround time 3 days.
General Information: Public terminal goes back to 1990. No juvenile, mental health, sealed or expunged records released. Fee to fax documents is $.50 per page. No certification fee. Payee: Clerk of Court. Personal checks accepted. Prepayment and SASE required.

Saline County

District Court PO Box 1760, Salina, KS 67402-1760; phone: 785-309-5831; fax: 785-309-5845; hours 8AM-5PM (CST). *Felony, Misdemeanor, Civil, Eviction, Small Claims, Probate.*
Civil Records: Access: Mail, in person. Both court and visitors may perform in person searches. Search fee: $12.00 per hour. Court makes copy: $.25 per page. Required to search: name, years to search, address. Civil cases indexed by defendant, plaintiff; on computer from 1990, index from early 1900s. Mail turnaround time 1 week.
Criminal Records: Access: Mail, in person. Both court and visitors may perform in person searches. Search fee: $12.00 per hour. Court makes copy: $.25 per page. Required to search: name, years to search, address, DOB, SSN, signed release. Criminal records on computer from 1990, index from early 1900s. Mail turnaround time 1 week.

General Information: Public use terminal available. No juvenile, mental health, sealed or expunged records released. Certification fee: $1.00. Payee: Clerk of District Court. Personal checks accepted. Prepayment required.

Scott County

District Court 303 Court, Scott City, KS 67871; phone: 620-872-7208; fax: 620-872-3683; hours 8AM-N, 1-5PM (CST). *Felony, Misdemeanor, Civil, Eviction, Small Claims, Probate.*
Civil Records: Access: Mail, in person. Both court and visitors may perform in person searches. Court makes copy: $.25 per page. Required to search: name, years to search. Civil cases indexed by defendant, plaintiff; on computer back to 1992, index cards from 1980s.
Criminal Records: Access: In person only. Visitors must perform in person searches themselves. Court makes copy: $.25 per page. Required to search: name, years to search, DOB. Criminal records on computer back to 1992, index cards from 1980s.
General Information: Public terminal goes back to 1992. No juvenile, mental health, sealed or expunged records released. Fee to fax documents is $1.00 per page. Certification fee: $1.00. Payee: Clerk of Court. Personal checks accepted. Prepayment and SASE required.

Sedgwick County

District Court 525 N Main, Wichita, KS 67203; phone: 316-660-5800; criminal phone: 316-660-5719; civil phone: 316-660-5719; probate phone: 316-660-5721; fax: 316-660-5784; hours 8AM-4PM (CST). *Felony, Misdemeanor, Civil, Eviction, Small Claims, Probate.*
www.dc18.org/
Note: Phone numbers above are for records department; direct numbers for the divisions are: criminal-316-660-5720 (fax-660-5777); civil-316-660-5690 (fax-660-5775).
Civil Records: Access: Fax, mail, online, in person. Both court and visitors may perform in person searches. Search fee: $12.00 per hour. Fee charged if more than 15 minutes. Court makes copy: $.25 per page; same fee for self serve. Required to search: name, years to search. Civil cases indexed by defendant, plaintiff; on computer from 1983, microfiche from 1982, archives from 1977 and index cards from 1900s. Access to civil, judgment and marriage records is by remote online system AccessKansas; requires a $225 setup fee, $49 monthly fee and small transaction fee. The system also includes probate, traffic, domestic, and criminal cases. For more information, call 316-383-7563 or visit www.accesskansas.org/online-services.html. Note: Email record requests to micro@dc18.org Mail turnaround time 7-10 days.
Criminal Records: Access: Online, in person. Visitors must perform in person searches themselves. Court makes copy: $.25 per page; same fee for self serve. Required to search: name, years to search. Criminal records on computer from 1983, microfiche from 1982, archives from 1977 and index cards from 1900s. Online access to criminal records is the same as civil.
General Information: Public use terminal available. No juvenile, adoption, mental health, sealed or expunged records released. Will fax documents $5.00 1st page, $2.00 each add'l. Certification fee: $1.00 per cert. Payee: Clerk of Court. Personal checks accepted. Prepayment and SASE required.

Seward County

District Court 415 N Washington, #103, Liberal, KS 67901; phone: 620-626-3375; criminal phone: 620-626-3234; civil phone: 620-626-3391; probate phone: 620-626-3232; fax: 620-626-3302; hours 8:30AM-5PM (CST). *Felony, Misdemeanor, Civil, Eviction, Small Claims, Probate.*

Note: Court will do searches on occasion, fee is $12.00 per hour. The Small Claims Court can be reached at 620-626-3232.

Civil Records: Access: In person only. Visitors must perform in person searches themselves. Court makes copy: $.25 per page; same fee for self serve. Required to search: name, years to search. Civil cases indexed by defendant, plaintiff; on computer back to 1977, index from 1900s.

Criminal Records: Access: In person only. Visitors must perform in person searches themselves. Court makes copy: $.25 per page; same fee for self serve. Required to search: name, years to search; SSN helpful. Criminal records on computer back to 1977, index from 1900s.

General Information: Public terminal goes back to 1977. No juvenile, mental health, sealed or expunged records released. Will fax specific case file for $2.00 1st page; $.50 each add'l page. Certification fee: $1.25. Payee: Clerk of District Court. Personal checks accepted. Prepayment required.

Shawnee County

District Court 200 E 7th Rm 209, Topeka, KS 66603; phone: 785-233-8200 X4327; criminal phone: x5157; civil phone: x5158; probate phone: x4358; criminal fax: 785-291-4908; civil fax: 785-291-4911; probate fax: 785-291-4911; hours 8AM-5PM (CST). *Felony, Misdemeanor, Civil, Eviction, Small Claims, Probate.*
www.shawneecourt.org

Civil Records: Access: Fax, mail, in person, online. Both court and visitors may perform in person searches. Search fee: $12.00 per hour. Court makes copy: $.50 per page. Required to search: name, years to search. Civil cases indexed by defendant, plaintiff; on computer from 1980, microfiche from 1950, archives and index from 1800s. Index online through INK of Kansas. See www.ink.org for subscription information. Also, access to county court records is free at www.shawneecourt.org/doe/index.html. Also, online access to court record images is free at www.shawneecourt.org/img_temp.htm. Also find "viewing restricted" domestic documents here. Also, daily dockets lists free at www.shawneecourt.org/docket/. Mail turnaround time 3-4 days.

Criminal Records: Access: Fax, mail, in person, online. Both court and visitors may perform in person searches. Search fee: $12.00 per hour. Court makes copy: $.50 per page. Required to search: name, years to search, DOB. Criminal records on computer from 1980, microfiche from 1950, archives and index from 1800s. Online access to criminal records is the same as civil. Mail turnaround time 3-4 days.

General Information: Public use terminal available. No juvenile, mental health, sealed or expunged records released. Will fax documents to local or toll free line. Certification fee: $2.25 for Authentication; $1.25 for certification. Payee: Clerk of District Court. Personal checks accepted. Prepayment required.

Sheridan County

District Court PO Box 753, Hoxie, KS 67740; phone: 785-675-3451; fax: 785-675-2256; hours 8AM-N, 1PM-5PM (CST). *Felony, Misdemeanor, Civil, Eviction, Small Claims, Probate.*
Note: Probate records prior to 2004 are on a separate index.

Civil Records: Access: Phone, fax, mail, in person. Both court and visitors may perform in person searches. Search fee: $12.00 per hour. Court makes copy: $.25 per page; same fee for self serve. Required to search: name, years to search. Civil cases indexed by defendant, plaintiff; on strip index from 1885. Mail requests require use of a special form. Mail turnaround time 1-2 days.

Criminal Records: Access: Phone, fax, mail, in person. Both court and visitors may perform in person searches. Search fee: $12.00 per hour. Court makes copy: $.25 per page; same fee for self serve. Required to search: name, years to search, signed release. Criminal records on computer back to 2004;

partial computer records back to 1995; on strip index from 1885. Mail turnaround time 1-2 days.

General Information: Public terminal goes back to 2004. No juvenile, mental health, sealed or expunged records released. Will fax documents to local or toll free line. Certification fee: $1.00 per page includes copies. Payee: Clerk of Court. Personal checks accepted. Prepayment and SASE required.

Sherman County

District Court 813 Broadway, Rm 201, Goodland, KS 67735; phone: 785-899-4850; fax: 785-899-4858; hours 8:30AM-5PM (MST). *Felony, Misdemeanor, Civil, Eviction, Small Claims, Probate.*

Civil Records: Access: In person only. Visitors must perform in person searches themselves. Court makes copy: $.25 per page. Required to search: name, years to search. Civil cases indexed by defendant, plaintiff; on docket books from 1900s.

Criminal Records: Access: In person only. Visitors must perform in person searches themselves. Court makes copy: $.25 per page. Required to search: name, years to search; SSN helpful. Criminal records on docket books from 1900s.

General Information: Public use terminal available. No juvenile, mental health, sealed or expunged records released. Certification fee: $1.00. Payee: Clerk of District Court. Personal checks accepted. Prepayment required.

Smith County

District Court PO Box 273, Smith Center, KS 66967; phone: 785-282-5140/41; fax: 785-282-5145; hours 8AM-5PM (CST). *Felony, Misdemeanor, Civil, Eviction, Small Claims, Probate.*

Civil Records: Access: In person only. Visitors must perform in person searches themselves. Court makes copy: $.25 per page; same fee for self serve. Required to search: name, years to search. Civil cases indexed by defendant, plaintiff; on index cards from 1873.

Criminal Records: Access: In person only. Visitors must perform in person searches themselves. Court makes copy: $.25 per page; same fee for self serve. Required to search: name, years to search; SSN helpful. Criminal records on index cards from 1873.

General Information: Public terminal has criminal back to - not known and civil back to 1873. No juvenile, mental health, sealed or expunged records released. Certification fee: $1.00. Payee: Clerk of Court. Personal checks accepted. Prepayment required.

Stafford County

District Court PO Box 365, St John, KS 67576; phone: 620-549-3295; fax: 620-549-3298; hours 8AM-5PM (CST). *Felony, Misdemeanor, Civil, Eviction, Small Claims, Probate.*
www.staffordcounty.org

Civil Records: Access: Phone, mail, fax, in person, email. Both court and visitors may perform in person searches. Search fee: $12.00 per hour, 15 minutes minimum. Court makes copy: $.25 per page. Required to search: name, years to search. Civil cases indexed by defendant, plaintiff; on computer from 1988, microfiche and index from 1900s.

Criminal Records: Access: In person only. Visitors must perform in person searches themselves. Court makes copy: $.25 per page. Required to search: name, years to search. Criminal records on computer from 1988, microfiche and index from 1900s. All mail request must go to the Kansas Bureau of Investigations.

General Information: Public terminal goes back to 1988. No juvenile, mental health, sealed or expunged records released. Will not fax documents. Certification fee: no cert fee. Payee: Clerk of District Court. Personal checks accepted. Prepayment and SASE required.

Stanton County

District Court PO Box 913, Johnson, KS 67855; phone: 620-492-2180; fax: 620-492-6410; hours 8AM-5PM (CST). *Felony, Misdemeanor, Civil, Eviction, Small Claims, Probate.*

Civil Records: Access: Phone, fax, mail, in person. Both court and visitors may perform in person searches. Search fee: $12.00 per hour. Court makes copy: $.25 per page. Required to search: name, years to search. Civil cases indexed by defendant, plaintiff; on computer from 1977, index from 1887. Mail turnaround time 1-3 days.

Criminal Records: Access: Phone, fax, mail, in person. Both court and visitors may perform in person searches. Search fee: $12.00 per hour. Court makes copy: $.25 per page. Required to search: name, years to search, DOB, SSN. Criminal records on computer from 1977, index from 1887. Mail turnaround time 1-3 days.

General Information: Public use terminal available. No juvenile, mental health, sealed or expunged records released. Will fax documents $2.50 1st page, $.50 each add'l. Certification fee: $1.00 per cert. Payee: Clerk of District Court. Personal checks accepted. Prepayment and SASE required.

Stevens County

District Court 200 E 6th, Hugoton, KS 67951; phone: 620-544-2484; fax: 620-544-2528; hours 8AM-5PM Closed noon-1PM (CST). *Felony, Misdemeanor, Civil, Eviction, Small Claims, Probate.*

Civil Records: Access: Mail, fax, in person. Both court and visitors may perform in person searches. Search fee: $12.50 per hour. Court makes copy: $.25 per page; same fee for self serve. Required to search: name, years to search. Civil cases indexed by defendant, plaintiff; on computer, microfiche, archives and index from 1887. Mail turnaround time 3 days.

Criminal Records: Access: Mail, fax, in person. Visitors must perform in person searches themselves. No search fee. Court makes copy: $.25 per page; same fee for self serve. Required to search: name, years to search; also helpful: SSN. Criminal records on computer from 1991, microfiche, archives and index from 1887. Mail turnaround time 1-3 days.

General Information: Public terminal has criminal back to 1991 approximately and civil back to 1887. No juvenile, mental health, sealed or expunged records released. Fee to fax documents is $3.00 plus $.25 per page. Certification fee: $1 per page. Payee: Clerk of District Court. Personal checks accepted. Prepayment required. Must prepay for fax and mail. SASE required.

Sumner County

District Court PO Box 399, County Courthouse, Wellington, KS 67152; phone: 620-326-5936; probate phone: 620-399-1042; fax: 620-326-5365; hours 8AM-N, 1-5PM (CST). *Felony, Misdemeanor, Civil, Eviction, Small Claims, Probate.*
Note: Court will not perform searches for "employment purposes" nor do they perform lien searches. The court prefers that you summit requests on their request form.

Civil Records: Access: Mail, fax, in person. Both court and visitors may perform in person searches. Search fee: $12.00 per hour. Court makes copy: $.25 per page. Required to search: name, years to search. Civil cases indexed by defendant, plaintiff; on computer back to 1991, index cards from 1800s for probate. Mail turnaround time 1-3 days.

Criminal Records: Access: Mail, fax, in person. Both court and visitors may perform in person searches. Search fee: $12.00 per hour. Court makes copy: $.25 per page. Required to search: name, years to search; also helpful: case number. Criminal records on computer back to 1991, index cards from 1800s for probate. Mail turnaround time 1-3 days.

General Information: Public terminal goes back to 1991. No juvenile, mental health, sealed or expunged records released. Will fax documents for $1.00 per page up to 10 pages. Certification fee: $2.00. Payee: Clerk of Court. Personal checks accepted. Prepayment required.

Thomas County

District Court PO Box 805, Colby, KS 67701; phone: 785-462-4540; fax: 785-460-2291; hours 8:30AM-5PM (CST). *Felony, Misdemeanor, Civil, Eviction, Small Claims, Probate.*

Civil Records: Access: Fax, mail, in person. Both court and visitors may perform in person searches. Search fee: $12.00 per hour. Court makes copy: $.25 per page. Required to search: name, years to search. Civil cases indexed by defendant, plaintiff; on index from 1887. Mail turnaround time 72 hours if KBI does search.

Criminal Records: Access: Fax, mail, in person. Both court and visitors may perform in person searches. Search fee: $12.00 per hour. Court makes copy: $.25 per page. Required to search: name, years to search, DOB, sex; also helpful: SSN. Criminal records on index from 1887. Mail turnaround time 72 hours if KBI does search

General Information: Public terminal goes back to 1996. No juvenile, mental health, sealed or expunged records released. Will fax documents $1.00 per page. Certification fee: $1.00 per page. Payee: Clerk. Personal checks accepted. Prepayment and SASE required.

Trego County

District Court 216 N Main, Wakeeney, KS 67672; phone: 785-743-2148; fax: 785-743-2726; hours 8:30AM-5PM (CST). *Felony, Misdemeanor, Civil, Eviction, Small Claims, Probate.*

Civil Records: Access: Phone, mail, fax, in person. Both court and visitors may perform in person searches. Search fee: $12.00 per hour. Court makes copy: $.25 per page; same fee for self serve. Required to search: name, years to search. Civil cases indexed by defendant, plaintiff; on computer since 1996; prior records on card index. Mail turnaround time 1-2 days.

Criminal Records: Access: Mail, in person. Only the court performs in person searches; visitors may not. Search fee: $12.00 per hour. Court makes copy: $.25 per page; same fee for self serve. Required to search: name, years to search; also helpful: DOB, SSN, sex. Criminal records on computer since 1996; prior records on card index. Mail turnaround time 1-2 days.

General Information: Public terminal goes back to 1996. No juvenile, mental health, sealed or expunged records released. Fee to fax documents is $2.00 1st page; $.50 each add'l page. Certification fee: $1.00 per page. Payee: Clerk of Court. Personal checks accepted. Prepayment and SASE required.

Wabaunsee County

District Court Courthouse, PO Box 278, Alma, KS 66401; phone: 785-765-2406; fax: 785-765-2487; hours 8AM-4:30PM (CST). *Felony, Misdemeanor, Civil, Eviction, Small Claims, Probate.*

Civil Records: Access: In person only. Visitors must perform in person searches themselves. Court makes copy: $.50 per page. Required to search: name, years to search. Civil cases indexed by defendant, plaintiff; on book index from 1800s; on computer back to 1996.

Criminal Records: Access: In person only. Visitors must perform in person searches themselves. Court makes copy: $.50 per page. Required to search: name, years to search; SSN helpful. Criminal records on book index from 1800s; on computer back to 1996.

General Information: Public terminal goes back to 1996. No juvenile, mental health, sealed or expunged records released. Certification fee: $1.25. Payee: Clerk of District Court. Personal checks accepted. Prepayment required.

Wallace County

District Court PO Box 8, Sharon Springs, KS 67758; phone: 785-852-4289; fax: 785-852-4271; hours 8AM-N,1-5PM (MST). *Felony, Misdemeanor, Civil, Eviction, Small Claims, Probate.*

Civil Records: Access: Mail, in person, fax. Visitors must perform in person searches themselves. Search fee: $12.00 per hour. Court makes copy: $.25 per page; same fee for self serve. Required to search: name; also helpful: years to search. Civil cases indexed by defendant, plaintiff; on index from 1887. By mail/fax only if requested for a particular case, court will not do name searches.

Criminal Records: Access: In person only. Visitors must perform in person searches themselves. Court makes copy: $.25 per page; same fee for self serve. Required to search: name; also helpful: years to search. Criminal records on index from 1887.

General Information: No public access terminal. No juvenile offender (under 14 years old), juvenile in need of care, adoption, mental health, sealed or expunged records released. Will fax documents to local or toll free line. Certification fee: $1.00 per page. Payee: Clerk of Court. Personal checks accepted. Prepayment required.

Washington County

District Court Courthouse, 214 C St, Washington, KS 66968; phone: 785-325-2381; fax: 785-325-2557; hours 8AM-N,1-5PM (CST). *Felony, Misdemeanor, Civil, Eviction, Small Claims, Probate.* www.kscourts.org/dstcts/12dstct.htm

Civil Records: Access: Fax, mail, in person. Visitors must perform in person searches themselves. No search fee. Court makes copy: $.25 per page; same fee for self serve. Required to search: name, years to search. Civil cases indexed by defendant, plaintiff; on card index from 1887; on computer back to 1995.

Criminal Records: Access: In person only. Visitors must perform in person searches themselves. Court makes copy: $.25 per page; same fee for self serve. Required to search: name, years to search. Criminal records on card index from 1887; on computer back to 1995.

General Information: No public access terminal. No juvenile, mental health, sealed or expunged records released. Fee to fax documents is $3.00 per page. Certification fee: $1.00 per document. Payee: Clerk of Court. Personal checks accepted. Prepayment and SASE required.

Wichita County

District Court PO Box 968, 206 S 4th St, Leoti, KS 67861; phone: 620-375-4454; fax: 620-375-2999; hours 8AM-5PM (CST). *Felony, Misdemeanor, Civil, Eviction, Small Claims, Probate.*

Note: This court is not in Wichita, KS. Wichita, KS is in Sedgwick County.

Civil Records: Access: Mail, in person. Both court and visitors may perform in person searches. Search fee: $12.00 per hour. Court makes copy: $.20 per page; same fee for self serve. Required to search: name, years to search. Civil cases indexed by defendant, plaintiff; on computer back to 1986, on index from 1900.

Criminal Records: Access: In person only. Visitors must perform in person searches themselves. Court makes copy: $.20 per page; same fee for self serve. Required to search: name. Criminal records on computer back to 1986, on index from 1900. Note: Criminal records are through the KBI.

General Information: Public terminal goes back to 1986. No juvenile, mental health, sealed or expunged records released. Certification fee: $1.00. Payee: Clerk of District Court. Personal checks accepted. Prepayment and SASE required.

Wilson County

District Court PO Box 300, Fredonia, KS 66736; phone: 620-378-4533; fax: 620-378-4531; hours 8AM-5PM (CST). *Felony, Misdemeanor, Civil, Eviction, Small Claims, Probate.*

Civil Records: Access: Fax, mail, in person. Both court and visitors may perform in person searches. Search fee: $12.00 per hour. Court makes copy: $.50 per page; same fee for self serve. Required to search: name, years to search. Civil cases indexed by defendant, plaintiff; on computer since 1993, index cards from 1864. Mail turnaround time 1-3 weeks.

Criminal Records: Access: In person only. Visitors must perform in person searches themselves. No search fee. Court makes copy: $.50 per page; same fee for self serve. Required to search: name, years to search; also helpful: SSN. Criminal records on computer since 1993, index cards from 1864.

General Information: Public terminal goes back to 1993. No juvenile, mental health, sealed or expunged records released. Will fax documents for $1.00 per page. Certification fee: $1.00 per page. Payee: Clerk of Court. Personal checks accepted. Prepayment and SASE required.

Woodson County

District Court PO Box 228, Yates Center, KS 66783; phone: 620-625-8610; fax: 620-625-8674; hours 8AM-5PM (CST). *Felony, Misdemeanor, Civil, Eviction, Small Claims, Probate.*

Civil Records: Access: Fax, mail, in person. Both court and visitors may perform in person searches. Search fee: $12.00 per hour. Court makes copy: $.50 per page; same fee for self serve. Required to search: name, years to search. Civil cases indexed by defendant, plaintiff; on index from 1880s, on computer since 1993. Mail turnaround time 1 day.

Criminal Records: Access: In person only. Visitors must perform in person searches themselves. Court makes copy: $.50 per page; same fee for self serve. Required to search: name, years to search. Criminal records on index from 1880s, on computer since 1993. Refer phone inquires to KBI at 785-296-8200.

General Information: Public terminal goes back to 1993. No juvenile (under age 14 years), mental health, sealed or expunged records released. Fee to fax documents is $1.00 per page. Certification fee: $1.00 per certification. Payee: District Court. Business checks accepted. Prepayment and SASE required.

Wyandotte County

District Court 710 N 7th St, Kansas City, KS 66101; criminal phone: 913-573-2905; civil phone: 913-573-2901/2811; probate phone: 913-573-4136; criminal fax: 913-573-8177; civil fax: 913-573-4134; hours 8AM-5PM (CST). *Felony, Misdemeanor, Civil, Eviction, Small Claims, Probate.*

Civil Records: Access: Phone, mail, online, in person. Both court and visitors may perform in person searches. Court makes copy: $.25 per page. Required to search: name, years to search. Civil cases indexed by defendant, plaintiff; on computer from 1975, microfiche, archives and index from 1900s. Access to the remote online system is available at www.accesskansas.org. Fees are involved.

Criminal Records: Access: Online, in person. Visitors must perform in person searches themselves. Court makes copy: $.25 per page. Required to search: name, years to search, DOB, SSN. Criminal records on computer from 1972, microfiche, archives and index from early 1900s. Online access to criminal records is the same as civil. Note: Refer phone inquires to KBI at 785-296-8200.

General Information: Public use terminal available. No juvenile, mental health, sealed or expunged records released. Certification fee: $1.00. Payee: Clerk of District Court. Personal checks accepted. Prepayment and SASE required.

Kansas Recording Offices

ORGANIZATION: 105 counties, 105 recording offices. The recording officer is Register of Deeds. Many counties utilize a "Miscellaneous Index" for tax and other liens, separate from real estate records. 100 counties are in the Central Time Zone (CST) and 5 are in the Mountain Time Zone (MST).

REAL ESTATE RECORDS: Most counties will not perform real estate searches, although some will do as an accommodation with the understanding that they are not "certified." Some counties will also do a search based upon legal description to determine owner. Copy fees vary, and certification fees are usually $1.00 per document. Tax records are located at the Appraiser's Office.

UCC RECORDS: Financing statements are filed at the state level, except for real estate related collateral, which are filed with the Register of Deeds. However, prior to 07/2001, consumer goods collateral were also filed at the Register of Deeds and these older records can be searched there. All counties will perform UCC searches. Use search request form UCC-3. Search fees are usually $15.00 per debtor name. Copies usually cost $1.00 per page.

TAX LIEN RECORDS: Federal tax liens on personal property of businesses are filed with the Secretary of State. Other federal tax liens and all state tax liens on personal property are filed with the county Register of Deeds. Most counties automatically include tax liens on personal property with a UCC search. Tax liens on personal property may usually be searched separately for $8.00 per name.

OTHER LIENS: Mechanics, harvesters, lis pendens, threshers.

ONLINE ACCESS: A few counties have online access to recorder records; there is no statewide system.

Allen County

County Register of Deeds, 1 N. Washington Ave, Iola, KS 66749. RE & UCC recording phone-620-365-1412; fax-620-365-1414; 8AM-5PM www.ksrods.org
Records indexed on computer from 1995 to present, all records are also indexed to books also. Office will perform a UCC search but public must search other records themselves. (If a prepaid fee of $13.00 per hour is paid, they will search real estate records also). Search fee $15.00 per name. Copy fee $1.00 per page if faxed, $.50 per page if mailed plus postage. Cert fee- $1.00 per doc plus copy fee. Payee- Allen County Register of Deeds. **Other phones:** Treasurer- 620-365-1409; Appraiser/Auditor- 620-365-1415; Elections- 620-365-1407; Vital Records- 785-296-1400 (Topeka); Clerk of District Court (Marriage, etc.)- 620-365-1425; City of Iola Clerk (Birth & Death before 1911) -620-365-4910. **Assessor-** same address. 620-365-1415.

Anderson County

County Register of Deeds, 100 E 4th St; Courthouse, Garnett, KS 66032-1503. RE & UCC recording phone-785-448-3715; fax-785-448-3275; hours: 8AM-5PM
Separate indices to search include deed, mortgage, D & G books, misc. Records indexed on a public use terminal back to 1997. Office personnel or visitors may perform searches. Search fee $15.00 per name. Copy fee $1.00 per page. Cert fee-$1.00 per page plus copy fee. Payee- Anderson County Register of Deeds. **Online access to Marriage records:** Access to marriage records is by alpha search for free at www.kscourts.org/dstcts/4anmarec.htm. **Other phones:** Treasurer- 785-448-5824; Appraiser/Auditor-785-448-6844; Elections- 785-448-6841. **Property tax/Assessor-** same address. 785-448-6844.

Atchison County

County Register of Deeds, 423 N. 5th St.; Courthouse, Atchison, KS 66002-1861. RE & UCC recording phone-913-367-2568; fax-913-367-8441; 8:30-5PM
Records indexed on computer back to 1996. Office will perform a UCC search but public must search other records themselves. Search fee $15.00. Copy fee $1.00 per page. RE record copy- $.50 per page. Cert fee- $1.00 per page plus copy fee. Payee- Atchison County Register of Deeds. **Other phones:** Treasurer- 913-367-5332; Appraiser/Auditor- 913-367-4400; Elections- 913-367-1653; Vital Records- 913-367-1653. **Property tax/Assessor-** 913-367-4400.

Barber County

County Register of Deeds, 120 E. Washington St; Courthouse, Medicine Lodge, KS 67104. 620-886-3981; fax-620-886-5045; hours: 8:30AM-5PM
Records indexed on a public use terminal back to 1990. Office personnel or visitors may perform searches. Search fee $15.00 per name. Will search real estate records on a limited basis. Copy fee $1.00 per page. RE record copy- $.25 per page standard; fee may vary. Cert fee- $1.00 per cert plus copy fee. Payee- Barber County Register of Deeds. **Other phones:** Treasurer- 620-886-3775; Appraiser/Auditor- 620-886-3723; Elections- 620-886-3961. **Property tax/Assessor-** 620-886-3795.

Barton County

County Register of Deeds, 1400 Main St; Courthouse, #205, Great Bend, KS 67530-4037. RE & UCC recording phone-620-793-1849; fax-620-793-1981; hours: 8AM-5PM www.bartoncounty.org
Records indexed on a public use terminal back to 1998. Office will perform a UCC search but public must search other records themselves. Search fee $15.00. Copy fee $1.00 per page. Cert fee- $1.00 per cert plus copy fee. Payee- Barton County Register of Deeds. **Online access to Assessor, Property records:** Access to the County Property value list by address and name is at www.bartoncounty.org/propvals.pdf. **Other phones:** Treasurer- 620-793-1827; Appraiser/Auditor- 620-793-1821; Elections- 620-793-1835; Vital Records- 620-793-1870. **Property tax/Assessor-** same address as above. 620-793-1821.

Bourbon County

County Register of Deeds, 210 S. National, Fort Scott, KS 66701. RE & UCC recording phone-620-223-3800 x17; fax-620-223-5241; hours: 8:30AM-4:30PM
All records in one index. Search fee $15.00. Will not search real estate records. Copy fee $1.00 per page. Tax lien copy- $.25 per page. Cert fee- $1.00 per cert plus copy fee. Payee- Bourbon County Register of Deeds. **Other phones:** Treasurer- 620-223-3800 x15; Vital Records- 620-223-3800x14. **Property tax/Assessor-** same address as above. 620-223-3800 x16.

Brown County

County Register of Deeds, 601 Oregon; Courthouse, Hiawatha, KS 66434. RE & UCC recording phone-785-742-3741; fax-785-742-3255; hours: 8AM-5PM www.brown.kansasgov.com
Record index not computerized. Only the public may search. General index search fee $10.00 per hour. Copy fee $1.00 per page. RE record copy-$.30 per page. Cert fee- $1.00 per cert plus copy fee. Payee- Brown County Register of Deeds. **Other phones:** Treasurer- 785-742-2051; Appraiser/Auditor- 785-742-7232; Elections- 785-742-2581. **Property tax/Assessor-** 785-742-7232.

Butler County

County Register of Deeds, 205 W. Central; Courthouse, #104, El Dorado, KS 67042. Main phone & R/E recording-316-322-4113, UCC recording phone-316-322-4111; fax-316-321-1011; hours: 8AM-5PM www.bucoks.com
Separate indices to search include land books, Grantee/Grantor book, and Computer. Records indexed on a public use terminal back to 1993. Office will perform a UCC and Tax lien search but public must search other records themselves. Search fee $15.00. Copy fee $1.00 per page. Cert fee- $1.00 per cert plus copy fee. Payee- Butler County Register of Deeds. **Online access to Appraiser, Real Estate Value records:** Access to the appraiser's Real Estate Market Values data is free at www.bucoks.com/depts/appr/values/values.htm. No name searching. **Other phones:** Treasurer- 316-322-4210; Appraiser/Auditor- 316-322-4220; Elections-316-322-4233; Vital Records- 785-296-1400 (State of Kansas). **Property tax/Assessor-** 316-321-4220.

Chase County

County Register of Deeds, PO Box 529, Cottonwood Falls, KS 66845-0529. RE & UCC recording phone-620-273-6398; fax-620-273-6617; hours: 8AM-5PM
Separate indices to search include UCC and numerical land. Search fee $5.00 per name unless otherwise indicated. UCC or tax lien search per debtor name- $15.00. Copy fee $1.00 per page. Cert fee- $1.00 per cert plus $.50 per page copy fee. Payee- Chase County Register of Deeds. **Other phones:** Treasurer- 620-273-6493; Appraiser/Auditor- 620-273-6306; Elections- 620-273-6423; Vital Records- 620-273-6398. **Property tax/Assessor-** same address. 620-273-6423.

Chautauqua County

County Register of Deeds, 215 N. Chautauqua; Courthouse, Sedan, KS 67361. 620-725-5830; fax-620-725-5831; hours: 8AM-N,1-4PM

Record index not computerized. Office personnel or visitors may perform searches. Search fee $8.00 per name. Will not search real estate records. UCC search per debtor name- $15.00. Copy fee $1.00 per page. RE or tax lien copy- $.50-$1.00 per page. Cert fee- $1.00 per cert plus copy fee. Payee-Chautauqua County Register of Deeds. **Other phones:** Treasurer- 620-725-3666. **Property tax/Assessor-** 620-725-3127.

Cherokee County

County Register of Deeds, PO Box 228, Columbus, KS 66725. RE & UCC recording phone-620-429-3777; fax-620-429-1362; hours: 9AM-5PM
Records indexed on a public use terminal back to 4/1/2005. Office will perform a UCC and Tax lien search but public must search other records themselves. Search fee $15.00. Copy fee $1.00 per page. Cert fee- $1.00 per cert plus copy fee. Payee-Cherokee County Register of Deeds. **Other phones:** Treasurer- 620-429-2418; Appraiser/Auditor-620-429-3984; Elections- 620-429-8043. **Property tax/Assessor-** 620-429-3984.

Cheyenne County

County Register of Deeds, PO Box 907, St. Francis, KS 67756-0907. RE & UCC recording phone-785-332-8820; fax-785-332-8825; hours: 8AM-N,1-5PM
Record index not computerized. Office personnel or visitors may perform searches. Search fee $15.00 per name. Will not search real estate records. Copy fee $1.00 per page. RE record copy- $.35 per page. Cert fee- $1.00 per cert plus copy fee. Payee-Cheyenne County Register of Deeds. **Other phones:** Treasurer- 785-332-8810; Appraiser/Auditor-785-332-8830; Elections- 785-332-8800; Vital Records- 785-332-8850. **Assessor-** 785-332-8830.

Clark County

County Register of Deeds, PO Box 222, Ashland, KS 67831-0222. RE & UCC recording phone-620-635-2812; fax-620-635-2393; hours: 8:30AM-4:30PM
Separate indices to search in books; index not computerized. Only the public may search. Copy fee $1.00 per page. RE record copy- $.25 per page, plus postage. Cert fee- $1.00 per cert plus copy fee. Payee- Clark County Register of Deeds. **Other phones:** Treasurer- 620-635-2745; Appraiser/Auditor-620-635-2142; Elections- 620-635-2813. **Property tax/Assessor-** 620-635-2142.

Clay County

County Register of Deeds, PO Box 63, Clay Center, KS 67432. 785-632-3811; fax-785-632-2736; 8AM-5PM
Records indexed on a public use terminal back to 1997. Office personnel or visitors may perform searches. Search fee $15.00 per name. Copy fee $1.00 per page. RE or tax lien copy- $.50 per page. Cert fee- $1.00 per cert plus copy fee. Payee- Clay County Register of Deeds. **Other phones:** Treasurer- 785-632-3282. **Property tax/Assessor-** 785-632-2800.

Cloud County

County Register of Deeds, PO Box 96, Concordia, KS 66901-0096. RE & UCC recording phone-785-243-8121; fax-785-243-8123; hours: 8AM-4:30PM www.cloudcountyks.org
All records in one index. Office personnel or visitors may perform searches. Search fee $15.00 per name. Will not search real estate records. Will search UCC records, search includes tax liens. Copy fee $1.00 per page. Cert fee- $3.00 per cert includes copy fee. Payee- Cloud County Register of Deeds. **Online access to Assessor, Property records:** Access to assessor property data is free at www.cloudcountyks.org/V2RunLev2.asp?submit1=O K. You may search by registering or without. **Other phones:** Treasurer- 785-243-8115; Appraiser/Auditor-785-243-8100; Elections- 785-243-8110; State Office-785-296-1401. **Property tax/Assessor-** 811 Washington St, Concordia, KS 66901; 785-243-8100.

Coffey County

County Register of Deeds, 110 S 6th St, Rm 205 - Courthouse, Burlington, KS 66839. 620-364-2423; fax-620-364-8975; 8AM-5PM www.coffeycountyks.org
Separate indices to search include deed, mortgage, misc or oil & gas books. All documents are indexed by legal description or in misc books, if. Will not search real estate records. Will search UCC records, search includes tax liens. UCC search per debtor name- $15.00. Copy fee $1.00 per page. RE record copy- $.50 per page. Cert fee- $1.00 per cert plus copy fee. Payee- Coffey County Register of Deeds. **Online access to Marriage records:** Access to marriage records is by alpha search up to 1/18/2001 for free at www.kscourts.org/dstcts/4os marec.htm. **Other phones:** Treasurer- 620-364-5532. **Property tax/Assessor-** 620-364-8426.

Comanche County

County Register of Deeds, PO Box 576, Coldwater, KS 67029-0576. RE & UCC recording phone-620-582-2152; fax-620-582-2390; hours: 9AM-N,1-5PM
Separate indices to search include tract, and grantor/grantee. Records indexed on computer back to 1/2/2005. Office will perform a UCC search but public must search other records themselves. Tax liens included in UCC search. UCC search per debtor name- $15.00. Copy fee $1.00 per page. Cert fee- $1.00 per cert plus copy fee. Payee- Comanche County Register of Deeds. **Other phones:** Treasurer- 620-582-2964; Appraiser/Auditor- 620-582-2544; Elections- 620-582-2361. **Property tax/Assessor-** 620-582-2544.

Cowley County

County Register of Deeds, PO Box 741, Winfield, KS 67156-0471. 620-221-5461; fax-620-221-5463; hours: 8AM-N,1-5PM
All records in one index. Office will perform a UCC search, including tax liens, but public must search other records themselves. UCC search per debtor name- $15.00. Copy fee $1.00 per page. Cert fee- $1.00 per cert, includes copy fee. Payee-Cowley County Register of Deeds. **Other phones:** Treasurer- 620-221-5412. **Assessor-** 620-221-5430.

Crawford County

County Register of Deeds, PO Box 44, Girard, KS 66743. RE & UCC recording phone-620-724-8218; fax-620-724-8823; hours: 8:30AM-4:30PM
Record index not computerized. Office will perform a UCC search but public must search other records themselves. UCC search per debtor name- $15.00. Copy fee $1.00 per page. RE record copy- $.25 per page. Cert fee- $1.00 per cert plus copy fee. Payee- Crawford County Register of Deeds. **Other phones:** Treasurer- 620-724-8222. **Property tax/Assessor-** 620-724-6431.

Decatur County

County Register of Deeds, PO Box 167, Oberlin, KS 67749-0167. RE & UCC recording phone-785-475-8105; fax-785-475-8150; hours: 8AM-N,1-5PM
Separate indices to search include numeric, real estate descriptions, and Miscellaneous-other. Record index not computerized. Only the public may search. Copy fee $.25 per page. Cert fee- $1.00 per cert plus copy fee. Payee- Decatur County Register of Deeds. **Other phones:** Treasurer-785-475-8103; Appraiser/Auditor- 785-475-8109; Elections- 785-475-8102; Vital Records- 785-475-8105; Clerk of District Court- 785-475-8107; Decatur County Clerk -785-475-8102. **Assessor-** PO Box 28, Oberlin, KS 67749-0028; 785-475-8109.

Dickinson County

County Register of Deeds, PO Box 517, Abilene, KS 67410. RE & UCC recording phone-785-263-3073; fax-785-263-0428; hours: 8AM-5PM
Separate indices to search include deed, mortgage, misc. Records indexed on a public use terminal back to 2000. Office personnel or visitors may perform searches. UCC search per debtor name-$15.00. Separate federal/state combined tax lien search- $8.00 per debtor. Copy fee $.50 per page. UCC copy $1.00 per page. Cert fee- $1.00 per cert plus copy fee. Payee- Dickinson County Register of Deeds. **Online access to Property, Assessor records:** Access to county property tax data is free at www.dickinson.kansasgov.com/disclaimerlev2.asp
Other phones: Treasurer- 785-263-3231; Vital Records- 785-263-3073. **Property tax/Assessor-** 1st and Buckey Sts, Courthouse, Abilene, KS 67410; 785-263-4418.

Doniphan County

County Register of Deeds, PO Box 73, Troy, KS 66087. RE & UCC recording phone-785-985-3932; fax-785-985-3723; 8AM-5PM www.dpcountyks.com
All records in one index. Office personnel or visitors may perform searches. Search fee $15.00 per search. Copy fee $.50 per page. Cert fee- $1.00 per cert plus copy fee. Payee- Doniphan County Register of Deeds. **Other phones:** Treasurer- 785-985-3831; Appraiser/Auditor- 785-985-3977; Elections- 785-985-3513. **Property tax/Assessor-** 785-985-3977.

Douglas County

County Register of Deeds, 1100 Massachusetts; Courthouse, Lawrence, KS 66044-3097. 785-832-5283, R/E recording phone-785-832-5282; fax-785-330-2807; hours: 8AM-5PM www.douglas-county.com
All records in one index. Search fee $15.00 per name. Will not search real estate records. Copy fee $.50 per page. UCC copy $1.00 per page. Cert fee-$1.00 per cert plus copy fee. Payee- Douglas County Register of Deeds. **Online access to Appraiser, Real Estate, Recording, Deed, Lien, Voter Registration records:** Two non-government sites provide free access to County Assessor. Records. County Property Appraiser records at www.douglas-county.com/value/disclaimer.asp. Property valuations at http://old.hometown.lawrence.com/valuation/valuation.cgi. Check voter registration names at www.douglas-county.com/clerk/regvoters.asp. Also, Register of Deeds Records data is by subscription; for info and subscription call 785-832-5183. **Other phones:** Treasurer- 785-841-7700; Appraiser/Auditor- 785-832-5290; Elections- 785-832-5147. **Property tax/Assessor-** same address as above. 785-841-7700 x107, assessor fax- 785-841-0021.

Edwards County

County Register of Deeds, PO Box 264, Kinsley, KS 67547-0264. 620-659-3131; fax-620-659-2583; hours: 8AM-5PM
Office personnel or visitors may perform searches. Search fee $15.00. Copy fee $1.00 per page. Cert fee- $1.00 per cert, copy not included. Payee-Edwards County Register of Deeds. **Other phones:** Treasurer- 620-659-3132. **Property tax/Assessor-** 312 Massachusetts, Kinsley, KS 67547; 620-659-3000.

Elk County

County Register of Deeds, PO Box 476, Howard, KS 67349-0476. RE & UCC recording phone-620-374-2472; fax-620-374-2771; hours: 8AM-4:30PM
Separate indices to search include mortgages, affidavits. Record index not computerized. Office will perform a tax lien search but public must search other records themselves. Copy fee $1.00 per page. RE record copy- $.25 per page. Cert fee-$1.00 per cert plus copy fee. Payee- Elk County Register of Deeds. **Other phones:** Treasurer- 620-374-2256; Appraiser/Auditor- 620-374-2832; Elections- 620-374-2490; Vital Records- 620-374-2370. **Property tax/Assessor-** 620-374-2832.

Ellis County

County Register of Deeds, PO Box 654, Hays, KS 67601. 785-628-9450, R/E recording phone-785-628-9452; fax-785-628-9451; hours: 8AM-5PM www.ksrods.org

All records in one index. Search fee $15.00 per debtor. Will search real estate records. Will search UCC records; search includes tax liens if requested. Copy fee $1.00 per page. RE record copy- $.25 per page. Cert fee- $1.00 per cert plus copy fee. Payee- Ellis County Register of Deeds. **Other phones:** Treasurer- 785-628-9466; Appraiser/Auditor- 785-628-9400; Elections- 785-628-9410; Vital Records- 785-628-9450; Second Line- 785-628-9452. **Property tax/Assessor-** 1204 Fort St, Hays, KS 67601; 785-628-9400.

Ellsworth County

County Register of Deeds, 210 N. Kansas #7; Courthouse, Ellsworth, KS 67439-3110. 785-472-3022; fax-785-472-4912; hours: 8AM-5PM
All records in one index. Records indexed on computer back to 1995. Office personnel or visitors may perform searches. Search fee $15.00. Copy fee $1.00 per page. Cert fee- $1.00 per cert plus$.25 copy fee. Payee- Ellsworth County Register of Deeds. **Other phones:** Treasurer- 785-472-4152. **Property tax/Assessor-** 785-472-3165.

Finney County

County Register of Deeds, PO Box M, Garden City, KS 67846. RE & UCC recording phone-620-272-3520; fax-620-272-3624; 8-5PM www.finneycounty.org
All records in one index. Records indexed on a public use terminal back to 1989. Office personnel or visitors may perform searches. Search fee $15.00 per name. Copy fee $1.00 per sheet. RE or tax lien copy- $.25 per page. Cert fee- $1.00 per cert plus copy fee. Payee- Finney County Register of Deeds. **Other phones:** Treasurer- 620-373-3526; Appraiser/Auditor- 620-272-3585; Elections- 620-272-3523. **Property tax/Assessor-** PO Box 873, Garden City, KS 67846; 620-272-3517.

Ford County

County Register of Deeds, PO Box 1352, Dodge City, KS 67801-1352. Main phone & R/E recording-620-227-4565, UCC recording phone-620-227-4568; fax-620-227-4566; hours: 9AM-5PM
Separate indices to search include deeds, mortgage, mortgage release, oil & gas, oil & gas assign and release, and miscellaneous. Only the public may search. Copy fee $.50 per page. Fax back- $1.00 each. Cert fee- $1.00 per cert plus copy fee. Payee- Ford County Register of Deeds. **Other phones:** Treasurer- 620-227-4535; Appraiser/Auditor- 620-227-4570; Elections- 620-227-4553. **Property tax/Assessor-** 620-227-4516.

Franklin County

County Register of Deeds, 315 S. Main; Courthouse, Rm 103, Ottawa, KS 66067-2335. 785-229-3440; fax-785-229-3441; hours: 8AM-4:30PM
All records in one index. Records indexed on a public use terminal back to 1993. Office will perform a UCC and Tax lien search but public must search other records themselves. Search fee $15.00. Copy fee $1.00 per page. RE record copy- $.25 per page after the first. Cert fee- $1.00 per cert and $.25 per page. Payee- Franklin County Register of Deeds. **Online access to Marriage records:** Access to county marriage records is by alpha search for free at www.kscourts.org/dstcts/4frmarec.htm. **Other phones:** Treasurer- 785-229-3450; Elections- 785-229-3410; Vital Records- 785-229-6000. **Property tax/Assessor-** same address as above. 785-229-3420.

Geary County

County Register of Deeds, PO Box 927, Junction City, KS 66441-2591. 785-238-5531; fax-785-762-2642; hours: 8:30AM-5PM
Record index not computerized. Only the public may search. Copy fee $1.00 per page. Tax lien copy- $.25. Cert fee- $1.00 per cert plus copy fee. Payee- Geary County Register of Deeds. **Other phones:** Treasurer- 785-238-3912. **Property tax/Assessor-** 785-238-4407.

Gove County

County Register of Deeds, PO Box 116, Gove, KS 67736. RE & UCC recording phone-785-938-4465; fax-785-938-4486; hours: 8AM-Noon, 12:30PM 4:30PM
Records indexed on a public use terminal back 2 years. Office personnel or visitors may perform searches. Search fee $15.00 per name. Separate federal/state combined tax lien search available. Copy fee $1.00 per page. RE record copy- $.50 per page. Cert fee- $1.00 per cert plus copy fee. Payee- Gove County Register of Deeds. **Other phones:** Treasurer- 785-938-2275; Appraiser/Auditor- 785-938-2301; Elections- 785-938-2300; Vital Records- 785-938-4465. **Property tax/Assessor-** PO Box 128, Gove, KS 67736; 785-938-2301.

Graham County

County Register of Deeds, 410 N. Pomeroy, Hill City, KS 67642. 785-421-2551; fax-785-421-2784; hours: 8AM-5PM
Record index not computerized. Office will perform a UCC search but public must search other records themselves. Copy fee $1.00 per page. Cert fee- $1.00 per cert plus copy fee. Payee- Graham County Register of Deeds. **Other phones:** Treasurer- 785-674-2331. **Property tax/Assessor-** 785-674-2196.

Grant County

County Register of Deeds, 108 S. Glenn, Lower Level; Courthouse, Ulysses, KS 67880. RE & UCC recording phone-620-356-1538; fax-620-356-5379; 9AM-5PM
Office will perform a UCC search but public must search other records themselves. Search fee $15.00. Copy fee $1.00 per page. Cert fee- $1.00 per cert plus copy fee. Payee- Grant County Register of Deeds. **Other phones:** Treasurer- 620-356-1551; Appraiser/Auditor- 620-356-3362; Elections- 620-356-1335. **Property tax/Assessor-** 620-356-3362.

Gray County

County Register of Deeds, PO Box 487, Cimarron, KS 67835-0487. 620-855-3835; fax-620-855-3107; hours: 8AM-5PM
Separate indices to search include range index and city index. Office personnel or visitors may perform searches. Search fee $15.00 per name. Copy fee $.50 per page. Fax fee $1.00 per page. Cert fee- $1.00 per cert plus copy fee. Payee- Gray County Register of Deeds. **Other phones:** Treasurer- 620-855-3861; Appraiser/Auditor- 620-855-3858; Elections- 620-855-3618. **Property tax/Assessor-** same address as above. 620-855-3858.

Greeley County

County Register of Deeds, PO Box 12, Tribune, KS 67879. 620-376-4275; fax-620-376-2294; hours: 9AM-5PM
All records in one index. Will not search real estate records. Will search UCC records, search includes tax liens. UCC search per debtor name- $15.00. Separate federal/state combined tax lien search-$8.00 per debtor. Copy fee $1.00 per page. Cert fee- $1.00 per doc plus copy fee. Payee- Greeley County Register of Deeds. **Other phones:** Treasurer- 620-376-4413. **Property tax/Assessor-** 620-376-4057.

Greenwood County

County Register of Deeds, 311 N Main; Courthouse, Eureka, KS 67045-1311. 620-583-8162; fax-620-583-8178; hours: 8AM-5PM
Record index not computerized. Office personnel or visitors may perform searches. Search fee $15.00 per name. Will not search real estate records. Copy fee $1.00 per page. Tax lien copy- $.50. Cert fee- $1.00 per cert plus copy fee. Payee- Greenwood County Register of Deeds. **Other phones:** Treasurer- 620-583-8146. **Property tax/Assessor-** 620-583-7431.

Hamilton County

County Register of Deeds, PO Box 1167, Syracuse, KS 67878. RE & UCC recording phone-620-384-6925; fax-620-384-5853; hours: 8AM-N, 1-4:30PM
All records in one index. Office will perform a UCC search but public must search other records themselves. Search fee $15.00. Copy fee $.25 per page, UCC copies $1.00 per page. Cert fee- $1.00 per doc plus copy fee. Payee- Hamilton County Register of Deeds. **Other phones:** Treasurer- 620-384-5522; Appraiser/Auditor- 620-384-5451.

Harper County

County Register of Deeds, 201 N Jennings; Courthouse, Anthony, KS 67003. RE & UCC recording phone-620-842-5336; fax-620-842-3455; hours: 8AM-N,1-5PM www.harpercountyks.gov
Will search real estate by record owner as a courtesy. Will search UCC records, search includes tax liens. UCC search per debtor name- $15.00. Copy fee $1.00 per page. Cert fee- $1.00 per cert plus copy fee. Payee- Harper County Register of Deeds. **Other phones:** Treasurer- 620-842-5191; Elections- 620-842-5555. **Property tax/Assessor-** same address as above. 620-842-3718.

Harvey County

County Register of Deeds, PO Box 687, Newton, KS 67114-0687. RE & UCC recording phone-316-284-6950; fax-316-284-6951; hours: 8AM-5PM
Separate indices to search include tract books. Records indexed on a public use terminal back 6 months. Office personnel (only with an information request) or visitors may perform searches. Search fee $15.00 per name. Copy fee $1.00 per page. Cert fee- $1.00 per cert plus copy fee. Payee- Harvey County Register of Deeds. **Other phones:** Treasurer- 316-284-6976; Appraiser/Auditor- 316-284-6815; Elections- 316-284-6842. **Property tax/Assessor-** 316-284-6815.

Haskell County

County Register of Deeds, PO Box 656, Sublette, KS 67877. 620-675-8343; hours: 9AM-N,1-5PM
Separate indices to search include deeds, mortgages, misc. Records indexed on a public use terminal. They are working on going all the way back to the beginning. Office personnel or visitors may perform searches. Search fee $15.00 per name. Copy fee $1.00 per instrument. Cert fee- $1.00 per cert plus copy fee. Payee- Haskell County Register of Deeds. **Other phones:** Treasurer- 620-675-2265. **Property tax/Assessor-** 620-675-8269.

Hodgeman County

County Register of Deeds, PO Box 505, Jetmore, KS 67854-0505. 620-357-8536; fax-620-357-6161; hours: 9AM-N, 1-5PM
Separate indices to search include city and rural in two different books. Record index not computerized. Office personnel will perform small searches or visitors may perform searches. UCC search per debtor name- $15.00. Separate federal/state combined tax lien search- $8.00 per debtor. Copy fee $1.00 per page. Cert fee- $1.00 per cert plus copy fee. Payee- Hodgeman County Register of Deeds. **Other phones:** Treasurer- 620-357-6236. **Property tax/Assessor-** 620-357-8366.

Jackson County

County Register of Deeds, 415 New York; Courthouse, Rm 203, Holton, KS 66436. RE & UCC recording phone-785-364-3591; fax-785-364-3420; hours: 8AM-4:30PM
Separate indices to search include land tract index and computer. Records indexed on a public use terminal back to 1988. Office personnel or visitors may perform searches. Search fee $15.00 per lien. Copy fee $1.00 per page. RE record copy- $.25 per page after the first. Cert fee- $1.00 per cert plus copy fee. Payee- Jackson County Register of

Deeds. **Other phones:** Treasurer- 785-364-3791; Appraiser/Auditor- 785-364-5256; Elections- 785-364-5200. **Property tax/Assessor-** 785-364-5256.

Jefferson County

County Register of Deeds, PO Box 352, Oskaloosa, KS 66066-0352. RE & UCC recording phone-785-863-2243; fax-785-863-2602; hours: 8AM-6:30PM M; 8AM-4PM T-F www.jfcountyks.com
All records in one index. Records indexed on computer back to 1997. Only the public may search. General index search fee $10.00 per hour. Copy fee $1.00 per page. Cert fee- $1.00 per cert plus copy fee. Payee- Jefferson County Register of Deeds. **Other phones:** Treasurer- 785-863-2691; Appraiser/Auditor- 785-863-2552; Elections- 785-863-2272. **Property tax/Assessor-** 785-863-2080.

Jewell County

County Register of Deeds, 307 N. Commercial St; Courthouse, Mankato, KS 66956-2093. RE & UCC recording phone-785-378-4070; fax-785-378-4075; hours: 8:30AM-N, 1-4:30PM
Separate indices to search. Record index not computerized. Office personnel or visitors may perform searches. General index search fee $5.00 per hour. Separate federal/state combined tax lien search- $15.00. Copy fee $1.00 per page. Cert fee- $1.00 per cert plus copy fee. Payee- Jewell County Register of Deeds. **Other phones:** Treasurer- 785-378-4090; Appraiser/Auditor- 785-378-4000; Elections- 785-378-4020. **Property tax/Assessor-** 785-378-4000.

Johnson County

County Register of Deeds, PO Box 700, Olathe, KS 66051. 913-715-2300 x5375; fax-913-715-2310; hours: 8AM-5PM www.jocoks.com
Records indexed on a public use terminal back to 1987. Office personnel or visitors may perform searches. Search fee $8.00 per name. Will not search real estate records. UCC search per debtor name- $20.00. Copy fee $1.00 per page. RE record copy- $.50 per page. Tax lien copy- $.25 per page. Cert fee- $1.00 per cert plus copy fee. Payee-Johnson County Register of Deeds. **Online access to Property Appraiser, Tax Sale, Land, Marriage records:** Records on the Johnson County Kansas Land Records database are free at http://appraiser.jocogov.org/disclaimer.htm. At the bottom of the Disclaimer page, click on "Yes". No name searching. Also, search the tax sales list for free at www.jocoks.com/countyclerk/taxsale/salenone.htm.
Marriages are accessible via the Accesskansas subscription service at www.accesskansas.org. **Other phones:** Treasurer- 913-715-2600. **Property tax/Assessor-** 913-829-9500.

Kearny County

County Register of Deeds, PO Box 42, Lakin, KS 67860. RE & UCC recording phone-620-355-6241; fax-620-355-7382; hours: 8AM-5PM
Records indexed on computer back to 1999. Office personnel or visitors may perform searches. Search fee $15.00 per name. Will not search real estate records. Copy fee $1.00 per page. RE record copy- $.25 per page. Cert fee- $1.00 per cert plus copy fee. Payee- Kearny County Register of Deeds. **Other phones:** Treasurer- 620-355-6372; Appraiser/Auditor- 620-355-6427; Elections- 620-355-6422. **Property tax/Assessor-** 620-355-6427.

Kingman County

County Register of Deeds, 130 N Spruce, Kingman, KS 67068. RE & UCC recording phone-620-532-3211; fax-620-532-2037; hours: 8AM-N,1-5PM
Record index not computerized. Office personnel or visitors may perform searches. Search fee $8.00 per name. Will not search real estate records. UCC search per debtor name- $15.00. Copy fee $1.00 per page. Cert fee- $1.00 per cert plus copy fee. Payee- Kingman County Register of Deeds. **Other phones:** Treasurer- 620-532-3461; Appraiser/Auditor-

620-532-2256; Elections- 620-532-2521. **Property tax/Assessor-** 620-532-2256.

Kiowa County

County Register of Deeds, 211 E Florida, Greensburg, KS 67054. 620-723-2441; fax-620-723-1033; 8:30AM-N, 1-5PM
www.kiowacounty.us/register_deeds.html
All records in one index. Office personnel or visitors may perform searches. Search fee $15.00. Copy fee $1.00 per page. Cert fee- $1.00 per cert plus copy fee. Payee- Kiowa County Register of Deeds. **Other phones:** Treasurer- 620-723-2681; Appraiser/Auditor- 620-723-3301. **Property tax/Assessor-** 620-723-3366.

Labette County

County Register of Deeds, 521 Merchant; Courthouse, Oswego, KS 67356. RE & UCC recording phone-620-795-4931; fax-620-795-2928; hours: 8:30AM-5PM
Separate indices to search include legal. Records indexed on computer back to 1999. Office will perform a UCC search but public must search other records themselves. UCC search per debtor name- $15.00. Copy fee $1.00 per page. RE record copy- $.25 per page. Cert fee- $1.50 per cert plus copy fee. Payee- Labette County Register of Deeds. **Other phones:** Treasurer- 620-795-2918; Appraiser/Auditor- 620-795-2548; Elections- 620-795-2138. **Property tax/Assessor-** 620-795-2548.

Lane County

County Register of Deeds, PO Box 805, Dighton, KS 67839-0805. RE & UCC recording phone-620-397-2803; fax-620-397-5937; hours: 8AM-N,1-5PM
Separate indices to search include mortgage, deed, assign, misc indexes. Office personnel or visitors may perform searches. Search fee $15.00 per debtor. Real estate owner, mortgage, and property transfer searches available. Copy fee $1.00 per page. Cert fee- $2.00 per cert plus copy fee. Payee- Lane County Register of Deeds. **Other phones:** Treasurer- 620-397-2802; Appraiser/Auditor- 620-397-2804; Elections- 620-397-5356. **Property tax/Assessor-** same address as above. 620-397-2804.

Leavenworth County

County Register of Deeds, 300 Walnut, Rm 103; Courthouse, Leavenworth, KS 66048. RE & UCC recording phone-913-684-0424; fax-913-684-0406; hours: 8AM-5PM
All records in one index. Records indexed on a public use terminal back to 1995. Only the office personnel may search. Search fee $8.00 per name. Will not search real estate records. UCC search per debtor name- $15.00. Copy fee $1.00 for 1st page; $.50 each add'l. Cert fee- $1.00 per cert plus copy fee. Payee- Leavenworth County Register of Deeds. **Other phones:** Treasurer- 913-684-0430; Appraiser/Auditor- 913-684-0440; Elections- 913-684-0421. **Property tax/Assessor-** 913-684-0440.

Lincoln County

County Register of Deeds, 216 E. Lincoln, Lincoln, KS 67455-2056. 785-524-4657; fax-785-524-5008; hours: 8AM-N,12:30-4:30PM
Separate indices to search include mtgs, deeds, misc. Records indexed on computer back to 1980. Office will perform a UCC search but public must search other records themselves. Search fee $15.00. Copy fee $1.00 per page. RE or tax lien copy- $.35 per page. Cert fee- $1.00 per cert plus copy fee. Payee- Lincoln County Register of Deeds. **Other phones:** Treasurer- 785-524-4190; Appraiser/Auditor- 785-524-4958; Elections- 785-524-4757.

Linn County

County Register of Deeds, PO Box 350, Mound City, KS 66056-0350. 913-795-2226, R/E recording phone-913-352-2226, UCC recording phone-913-352-2226; fax-913-795-2889; hours: 8AM-N, 12:30-4:30PM

Office personnel or visitors may perform searches. Search fee $8.00 per name. Will not search real estate records. UCC search per debtor name- $15.00. Copy fee $1.00 per page. RE record copy- $1.50 1st page, $.15 each add'l. Cert fee- $1.00 per cert plus copy fee. Payee- Linn County Register of Deeds. **Other phones:** Treasurer- 913-795-2227. **Property tax/Assessor-** 913-795-2536.

Logan County

County Register of Deeds, 710 W. 2nd St; Courthouse, Oakley, KS 67748. RE & UCC recording phone-785-672-4224; fax-785-672-3517; hours: 8AM-5PM
Record index not computerized. Office personnel or visitors may perform searches. Search fee $15.00 per name. Will not search real estate records. Copy fee $1.00 per page. RE or tax lien copy- $.25 per page, $1.00 per page mailed or faxed. Cert fee- $1.00 per cert plus copy fee. Payee- Logan County Register of Deeds. **Other phones:** Treasurer- 785-672-3216; Appraiser/Auditor- 785-672-4821; Elections- 785-672-4244; County Clerk- 785-672-4244. **Property tax/Assessor-** 785-672-4821.

Lyon County

County Register of Deeds, 430 Commercial St, Emporia, KS 66801. RE & UCC recording phone-620-341-3241; fax-620-341-3438; hours: 8AM-5PM www.lyoncounty.org
Record index not computerized. Office personnel or visitors may perform searches. Search fee $15.00 per name. Copy fee $1.00 per page. Cert fee- $1.00 per cert plus copy fee. Payee- Lyon County Register of Deeds.

Marion County

County Register of Deeds, PO Box 158, Marion, KS 66861-0158. 620-382-2151; fax-620-382-3420; hours: 8:30AM-5PM
Separate indices to search include numerical indexes. Will not search real estate records. Will search UCC records; search includes tax liens if requested. UCC search per debtor name- $15.00. Copy fee $1.00 per page. RE record copy- $.25 per page; $.50 if on microfilm. Tax lien copy- $.50 per page. Cert fee- $1.00 per cert plus copy fee. Payee- Marion County Register of Deeds. **Other phones:** Treasurer- 620-382-2180; Appraiser/Auditor- 620-382-3778; Elections- 620-382-2185. **Property tax/Assessor-** 620-382-3715.

Marshall County

County Register of Deeds, PO Box 391, 1201 Broadway; Courthouse, Marysville, KS 66508. RE & UCC recording phone-785-562-3226; fax-785-562-5685; hours: 8:30AM-5PM
Separate indices to search include Range 6,7,8,9,10. All city indexes separate. Office will perform a UCC search but public must search other records themselves. Limited searches only on real estate. Search fee $6.00 per debtor. UCC search per debtor name- $15.00. Copy fee $1.00 per page. Cert fee- $2.00 per cert includes copy fee. Payee- Marshall County Register of Deeds. **Other phones:** Treasurer- 785-562-5363; Appraiser/Auditor- 785-562-3301; Elections- 785-562-5361. **Property tax/Assessor-** same address as above. 785-562-3301.

McPherson County

County Register of Deeds, PO Box 86, McPherson, KS 67460. RE & UCC recording phone-620-241-5050; fax-620-245-0749; hours: 8AM-5PM www.mcphersoncountyks.us
Index: Searchable by document Type. Records indexed on a public use terminal back to 1997. Office will perform a UCC search but public must search other records themselves. Search fee $15.00. Copy fee $1.00 1st copy, $.50 each add'l page. Cert fee- $1.00 per cert plus copy fee. Payee-McPherson County Register of Deeds. **Online access to Real Estate Recoding, Deed records:** Access recording office land data at

www.etitlesearch.com; registration required, fee based on usage. **Other phones:** Treasurer- 620-241-3664; Appraiser/Auditor- 620-241-5870; Elections- 620-241-3656. **Property tax/Assessor-** P O Box 530, McPherson, KS 67460; 620-241-5870.

Meade County

County Register of Deeds, PO Box 399, Meade, KS 67864-0399. 620-873-8705, R/E recording phone-602-873-8705; fax-620-873-8707; hours: 8AM-5PM
All records in one index. Office personnel or visitors may perform searches. Search fee $15.00 per name. Will not do "detailed" real estate record searches. Copy fee $1.00 per page if mailed out. RE record copy- $.50 per page. Cert fee- $1.00 per cert plus copy fee. Payee- Meade County Register of Deeds. **Other phones:** Treasurer- 620-873-8740; Appraiser/Auditor- 620-873-8710; Elections- 620-873-8700. **Property tax/Assessor-** PO Box 278, Meade, KS 67864-0278; 620-873-8710.

Miami County

County Register of Deeds, 201 S. Pearl St. #101, Paola, KS 66071. 913-294-3716; fax-913-294-9515; hours: 8AM-4:30PM
Office will perform a UCC search but public must search other records themselves. UCC search per debtor name- $15.00. Copy fee $1.00 per page. Cert fee- $1.00 per cert plus copy fee. Payee- Miami County Register of Deeds. **Other phones:** Treasurer- 913-294-2353. **Property tax/Assessor-** 913-294-9311.

Mitchell County

County Register of Deeds, PO Box 6, Beloit, KS 67420. 785-738-3854; fax-785-738-5844; hours: 8:30AM-5PM
Record index not computerized. Office personnel or visitors may perform searches. Search fee $8.00 per name. UCC search per debtor name- $15.00. Must use nat'l request form. Copy fee $1.00 per page. Cert fee- $1.00 per cert plus copy fee. Payee- Mitchell County Register of Deeds. **Other phones:** Treasurer- 785-738-3411. **Property tax/Assessor-** 785-738-5061.

Montgomery County

County Register of Deeds, PO Box 647, Independence, KS 67301. 620-330-1140; fax-620-330-1144; hours: 8:30AM-5PM
Record index not computerized. Office personnel or visitors may perform searches. Search fee $15.00 per name. Will not search real estate records. Copy fee $1.00 per page. Cert fee- $1.00 per cert plus copy fee. Payee- Montgomery County Register of Deeds. **Other phones:** Treasurer- 620-331-3040. **Property tax/Assessor-** 620-331-4510.

Morris County

County Register of Deeds, Courthouse, Council Grove, KS 66846. 620-767-5614; fax-620-767-6712; hours: 8AM-5PM
All records in one index. Records indexed on a public use terminal back to 1994. Only the public may search. Copy fee $1.00 per page. Cert fee- $1.00 per page includes copy. Payee- Morris County Register of Deeds. **Other phones:** Treasurer- 620-767-5617; Appraiser/Auditor- 620-767-5533; Elections- 620-767-5518. **Property tax/Assessor-** 501 W Main St, Council Grove, KS 66846; 620-767-5617.

Morton County

County Register of Deeds, PO Box 756, Elkhart, KS 67950-0756. RE & UCC recording phone-620-697-2561; fax-620-697-4386; hours: 9AM-5PM
Records indexed on a public use terminal back to 1991. Office personnel or visitors may perform searches. Search fee $8.00 per name. Will not search real estate records. UCC search per debtor name- $15.00. Copy fee $1.00 per page. Cert fee- $1.00 per doc $.25 per page. Payee- Morton County Register of Deeds. **Other phones:** Treasurer-

620-697-2560; Appraiser/Auditor- 620-697-2106; Elections- 620-697-2157. **Property tax/Assessor-** 620-697-2106.

Nemaha County

County Register of Deeds, PO Box 186, Seneca, KS 66538. RE & UCC recording phone-785-336-2120; fax-785-336-3373; hours: 8AM-4:30PM
All records in one index. Office personnel or visitors may perform searches. Search fee $8.00 per debtor. UCC search per debtor name- $15.00. Copy fee $1.00 per page. RE record copy- $.50 per page. Tax lien copy- $.25 per page. Cert fee- $1.00 per cert plus copy fee. Payee- Nemaha County Register of Deeds. **Other phones:** Treasurer- 785-336-2106. **Property tax/Assessor-** 785-336-2179.

Neosho County

County Register of Deeds, PO Box 138, Erie, KS 66733-0138. 620-244-3858; fax-620-244-3860; hours: 8AM-4:30PM
Office will perform a UCC search but public must search other records themselves. UCC search per debtor name- $15.00. Separate federal/state combined tax lien search- $8.00 per debtor. Copy fee $.25 per page; $1.00 per page for UCC and fax back service. Cert fee- $1.00 per cert plus copy fee. Payee- Neosho County Register of Deeds. **Other phones:** Treasurer- 620-244-3800; Elections- 620-244-3811. **Property tax/Assessor-** PO Box 184, Erie, KS 66733-0184; 620-244-3821, assessor fax- 620-244-3867.

Ness County

County Register of Deeds, PO Box 127, Ness City, KS 67560. 785-798-3127; fax-785-798-3829; hours: 8AM-N, 1PM-5PM
Record index not computerized. Office personnel or visitors may perform searches. Search fee $15.00 per name. Will not search real estate records. Copy fee $1.00 per page. Cert fee- $2.00 for 1st 2 pages. Payee- Ness County Register of Deeds. **Property tax/Assessor-** 785-798-2777.

Norton County

County Register of Deeds, PO Box 70, Norton, KS 67654. RE & UCC recording phone-785-877-5765; fax-785-877-5703; hours: 8AM-N, 1-5PM www.nortoncountyks.org
Separate indices to search include numerical books (5), grantor/grantee, miscellaneous index books, city books. Records indexed on computer back to 1999. Office personnel or visitors may perform searches. Search fee $15.00 per name. Copy fee $1.00 per page. Cert fee- $1.00 per cert plus copy fee. Payee- Norton County Register of Deeds. **Other phones:** Treasurer- 785-877-5795; Appraiser/Auditor- 785-877-5700; Elections- 785-877-5710. **Property tax/Assessor-** 785-877-5700.

Osage County

County Register of Deeds, PO Box 265, Lyndon, KS 66451-0265. 785-828-4523; fax-785-828-3648; hours: 8AM-5PM www.osageco.org
Separate indices to search include numerical land, UCCs, power of attorneys, military discharges. Office personnel (time permitting) or visitors may perform searches. Will not search real estate records. Will search UCC records time; search includes tax liens if requested. UCC search per debtor name- $15.00; includes 1st 10 copy pages free. Copy fee $1.00 per page. copy- $1.00 for 1st page & $.25 per add'l page. Cert fee- $1.00 per page plus copy fee. Payee- Osage County Register of Deeds. **Online access to Appraiser, Property records:** Online access to property appraiser is free at www.osageco.org/MV2Base.asp?VarCN=34. There are two levels- public and registered user. The latter can see sales information as well as property data. **Other phones:** Treasurer- 913-828-4923. **Property tax/Assessor-** 717 Topeka Ave, Lyndon, KS 66451; 913-828-3124.

Osborne County

County Register of Deeds, PO Box 160, Osborne, KS 67473-0160. 785-346-2452; fax-785-346-5252; hours: 8:30AM-N, 1-5PM www.osbornecounty.org
Records indexed on computer back to 1996. Office personnel or visitors may perform searches. General index search fee $7.00 per hour. UCC search per debtor name- $15.00. UCC copy fee $1.00 per page. RE record copy- $.25 per page plus postage. Cert fee- $1.00 per cert plus copy fee. Payee- Osborne County Register of Deeds. **Online access to Property, Appraiser records:** Access to property appraisal land data is free at www.osbornecounty.org. Search field is at bottom right of page. CAMA Records found at www.osbornecounty.org. **Other phones:** Treasurer- 785-346-2251; Appraiser/Auditor- 785-346-2310; Elections- 785-346-2431. **Property tax/Assessor-** 785-346-2310.

Ottawa County

County Register of Deeds, 307 N Concord; Courthouse - #220, Minneapolis, KS 67467-2140. RE & UCC recording phone-785-392-2078; fax-785-392-3605; hours: 8AM-N, 1-5PM www.ottawacounty.org
Separate indices to search include numeric by legal desc., general by name. Search fee $15.00 per name. Will not search real estate records. Federal/state combined tax lien search- $8.00 per debtor. Copy fee $.25 per page. Cert fee- $1.00 per cert plus copy fee. Payee- Ottawa County Register of Deeds. **Online access to Appraiser, Property Tax records:** Access to the appraiser property data is free at www.ottawacounty.org/index.asp?DocumentID=283. **Other phones:** Treasurer- 785-392-3129; Appraiser/Auditor- 785-392-3037; Elections- 785-392-2279. **Property tax/Assessor-** same address as above. 785-392-3037.

Pawnee County

County Register of Deeds, 715 Broadway St.; Courthouse, 2nd Fl, Larned, KS 67550-3097. RE & UCC recording phone-620-285-3276; fax-620-285-3802; hours: 8:30AM-5PM
Separate indices to search include land index and reception index. Records being indexed on computer. No search fee for general index. Will look up last deed of record and do a simple name search. Will search UCC records. UCC search includes tax liens if requested. UCC search per debtor name- $15.00. Separate federal/state combined tax lien search- $5.00 per debtor, copy fee is $1.00 per page (mail or fax). Copy fee $1.00 per page. Cert fee- $1.00 per cert plus copy fees. Payee- Pawnee County. **Other phones:** Treasurer- 620-285-3746; Appraiser/Auditor- 620-285-2915; Elections- 620-285-3721; Vital Records- 620-285-6937. **Property tax/Assessor-** 715 Broadway, 2nd Fl, Larned, KS 67550; 620-285-2915.

Phillips County

County Register of Deeds, 310 State St; Courthouse, Phillipsburg, KS 67661. 785-543-6875; fax-785-999-9999; hours: 8AM-5PM
All records in one index. Record index not computerized. Office personnel or visitors may perform searches. Search fee $15.00. General copy fee $1.00 per page. RE record copy- $.25 per page. Cert fee- $1.00 per cert plus copy fee. Payee- Phillips County Register of Deeds. **Other phones:** Treasurer- 785-543-6895. **Property tax/Assessor-** 785-543-6810.

Pottawatomie County

County Register of Deeds, PO Box 186, Westmoreland, KS 66549. 785-457-3471; fax-785-457-3577; hours: 8AM-4:30PM www.pottcounty.org
All records in one index. Records indexed. Only the public may search. Copy fee $1.00 per page. RE record copy- $.50 per copy. Cert fee- $1.50 per cert plus copy fee. Payee- Pottawatomie County Register of Deeds. **Other phones:** Treasurer- 785-457-3681. **Property tax/Assessor-** 785-457-3500.

Pratt County

County Register of Deeds, PO Box 873, Pratt, KS 67124. RE & UCC recording phone-620-672-4140; fax-620-672-9541; hours: 8AM-N,1-5PM www.prattcounty.org
Separate indices to search include tract indexes by legal description and cross grantor/grantee indexes by name. Records indexed on computer back to 1995. Only the public may search. Copy fee $1.00 per page. RE record copy- $.50 per page. Tax lien copy- $.25 per page. Cert fee- $1.00 per cert plus copy fee. Payee- Pratt County Register of Deeds. **Other phones:** Treasurer- 620-672-4116; Appraiser/Auditor- 620-672-4112; Elections- 620-672-4110; District Court (probates & state tax liens)- 620-672-4100. **Property tax/Assessor-** same address as above. 620-672-4112.

Rawlins County

County Register of Deeds, PO Box 201, Atwood, KS 67730. RE & UCC recording phone-785-626-3172; fax-785-626-9481; hours: 9AM-N,1-5PM
Record index not computerized. Office personnel or visitors may perform searches. Search fee $15.00 per name. Will not search real estate records. Copy fee $1.00 per page. Cert fee- $1.00 per page. Payee- Rawlins County Register of Deeds. **Other phones:** Treasurer- 785-626-3331. **Property tax/Assessor-** 785-626-3101.

Reno County

County Register of Deeds, 206 W. First, Hutchinson, KS 67501. 620-694-2942; fax-620-694-2944; hours: 8AM-5PM
Record index not computerized. Office personnel or visitors may perform searches. Search fee $8.00 per name. Will not search real estate records. UCC search per debtor name- $15.00. Copy fee $1.00 per page. Cert fee- $1.00 per cert plus copy fee. Payee- Reno County Register of Deeds. **Other phones:** Treasurer- 620-694-2938. **Property tax/Assessor-** 620-694-2915.

Republic County

County Register of Deeds, 1815 M St. #3, Belleville, KS 66935. 785-527-7238; fax-785-527-2659; hours: 8AM-5PM
Record index not computerized. Office personnel or visitors may perform searches. Search fee $15.00 per name. Will not search real estate records. Copy fee $.25 per page. Cert fee- $1.00 per cert plus copy fee. Payee- Republic County Register of Deeds. **Other phones:** Treasurer- 785-527-5691. **Property tax/Assessor-** 785-527-5691.

Rice County

County Register of Deeds, 101 W. Commercial, Lyons, KS 67554. RE & UCC recording phone-620-257-2931; fax-620-257-3039; hours: 8AM-5PM
Separate indices to search include deeds, mortgage, O&G records, misc and numerical indexes. Records indexed on computer back to 1998. Only the public may search. Copy fee $1.00 per page. Cert fee- $1.00 per cert plus copy fee. Payee- Rice County Register of Deeds. **Other phones:** Treasurer- 620-257-2852. **Property tax/Assessor-** 620-257-3611.

Riley County

County Register of Deeds, 5th & Humboldt Sts.; 110 Courthouse Plaza, Manhattan, KS 66502-6018. RE & UCC recording phone-785-537-6340; fax-785-537-6343; hours: 8AM-5PM www.rileycountyks.gov/
All records in one index. Office personnel or visitors may perform searches. Search fee $15.00. Will not search real estate records, unless minor in nature. Will search UCC records, search includes tax liens. Copy fee $1.00 per page. Cert fee- $1.00 per cert, plus copy fee. Payee- Riley County Register of Deeds. **Other phones:** Treasurer- 785-537-6320; Appraiser/Auditor- 785-537-6310. **Property tax/Assessor-** same address. 785-537-6310.

Rooks County

County Register of Deeds, 115 N. Walnut St., Stockton, KS 67669. 785-425-6291; fax-785-425-6497; hours: 8AM-N,1-5PM
All records in one index. Will not search real estate records. Will search UCC records, tax liens not included in UCC search. UCC search per debtor name- $15.00. Separate federal/state combined tax lien search- $8.00 per debtor. Copy fee $1.00 per page. Cert fee- $1.00 per cert plus copy fee. Payee- Rooks County Register of Deeds. **Other phones:** Treasurer- 785-425-6291. **Property tax/Assessor-** 785-425-6262.

Rush County

County Register of Deeds, PO Box 117, La Crosse, KS 67548. 785-222-3312; fax-785-222-3559; hours: 8:30AM-N, 1-5PM
Records indexed on a public use terminal back to April, 2003. Office will perform a UCC search with written request only, but public must search other records themselves. UCC search per debtor name- $15.00. Copy fee $1.00 per page. Cert fee- $2.00 per cert plus copy fee. Payee- Rush County Register of Deeds. **Other phones:** Treasurer- 785-222-3416. **Property tax/Assessor-** 785-222-2659.

Russell County

County Register of Deeds, PO Box 191, Russell, KS 67665. RE & UCC recording phone-785-483-4612; fax-785-483-5725; hours: 8AM-5PM
Records indexed on a public use terminal back to 1995. Books back to 1966. Office personnel or visitors may perform searches. Search fee $15.00 per name. Will not search real estate records. Copy fee $1.00 per page. RE or tax lien copy- $.50 per page. Cert fee- $1.00 per cert plus copy fee. Payee- Russell County Register of Deeds. **Other phones:** Treasurer- 785-483-2251; Appraiser/Auditor- 785-483-5551; Elections- 785-483-4641. **Property tax/Assessor-** 785-483-5551.

Saline County

County Register of Deeds, PO Box 5040, Salina, KS 67402-5040. 785-309-5855; fax-785-309-5856; hours: 8AM-5PM www.co.saline.ks.us
Office personnel or visitors may perform searches. Search fee $15.00 per name. Will not search real estate records. General copy fee $1.00 each; real estate is $.25 per page. Cert fee- $1.00 per cert plus copy fee. Payee- Saline County Register of Deeds. **Other phones:** Treasurer- 785-309-5860. **Property tax/Assessor-** 785-309-5800.

Scott County

County Register of Deeds, 303 Court St.; Courthouse, Scott City, KS 67871. RE & UCC recording phone-620-872-3155; fax-620-872-7145; hours: 8AM-5PM www.scott.kansasgov.com
All records in one index. Records indexed on a public use terminal back to 1989. Office personnel or visitors may perform searches. Separate federal/state combined tax lien search- $8.00 per debtor. Copy fee $1.00 per page. RE record copy- $.25 per page. Cert fee- $1.00 per cert plus copy fee. Payee- Scott County Register of Deeds. **Other phones:** Treasurer- 620-872-2640; Appraiser/Auditor- 620-872-5446; Elections- 620-872-2420. **Property tax/Assessor-** same address. 620-872-5446.

Sedgwick County

County Register of Deeds, PO Box 3326, Wichita, KS 67201-3326. RE & UCC recording phone-316-660-9400; fax-316-383-8066; hours: 8AM-5PM www.sedgwickcounty.org/deeds/
Only the public may search. Search fee $15.00 per name. Copy fee $1.00 per page. Cert fee- $1.00 per cert plus copy fee. Payee- Sedgwick County Register of Deeds. **Online access to Real Estate, Lien, Recorder, Assessor, Property Sale, Property Tax, Treasurer, Delinquent Tax, Marriage, Probate records:** Access to the exhaustive County online system (all departments) require a $225 set up fee, $49 monthly fee and a per transaction fee of $.09. For information on this and county record access generally, call Cindy Kirkland at 316-660-9860. Also, access recorder deeds free at https://rod.sedgwickcounty.org. Also, search property appraisal/tax data at www.sedgwickcounty.org/realpropertyinfo/realproperty.html. Also, access marriage, courts, probate records with sub at www.accesskansas.org. **Other phones:** Treasurer- 316-660-9100; Appraiser/Auditor- 316-660-9110; Elections- 316-660-7100; County Clerk- 316-660-9200. **Property tax/Assessor-** 316-660-9110.

Seward County

County Register of Deeds, 415 N. Washington, #105; Courthouse, Liberal, KS 67901. Main phone & R/E recording-620-626-3220, UCC recording phone-620-626-3223; fax-620-626-3362; hours: 8AM-5PM www.seward.kansasgov.com
Separate numerical indices to search include city, township. This office will do limited real estate searches. Tax lien or UCC search (request in writing) per debtor name- $15.00. Copy fee $1.00 per page. Cert fee- $1.00 per cert plus copy fee. Payee- Seward County Register of Deeds. **Other phones:** Treasurer- 620-626-3219; Appraiser/Auditor- 620-626-3252; Elections- 620-626-3201; Vital Records- 913-296-1400. **Property/Assessor-** 415 N Washington St, Liberal, KS 67901; 620-626-3252.

Shawnee County

County Register of Deeds, 200 E. 7th St; #108, Topeka, KS 66603-3932. Main phone & R/E recording-785-233-8200 x4020, UCC recording phone-785-233-8200 x4021; fax-785-291-4950; hours: 8AM-4:30PM www.co.shawnee.ks.us
Separate indices to search include grantee/grantor, numerical, computer & books (depending on age of document). Office will perform a UCC search, tax liens included in UCC search, but public must search other records themselves. Search fee $15.00 per name. Copy fee $1.50 per page. Cert fee- $1.00 per doc plus copy fee. Payee- Shawnee County Register of Deeds. **Online access to Property Appraiser, Personal Property records:** Search residential or commercial property appraisal data at www.co.shawnee.ks.us/Appraiser/appr_home.shtm. Search residential by name; commercial by address. **Other phones:** Treasurer- 785-233-8200 x5161; Appraiser/Auditor- 785-233-2882 x6000; Elections- 785-266-0285. **Property tax/Assessor-** 785-233-8200 x5151.

Sheridan County

County Register of Deeds, PO Box 899, Hoxie, KS 67740-0899. 785-675-3741; fax-785-675-3050; hours: 8AM-N,1-5PM
Record index not computerized. Office personnel or visitors may perform searches. Search fee $15.00 per name. Will not search real estate records. Copy fee $1.00 per page. Cert fee- $1.00 per cert plus copy fee. Payee- Sheridan County Register of Deeds. **Other phones:** Treasurer- 785-675-3622. **Property tax/Assessor-** 785-675-3932.

Sherman County

County Register of Deeds, 813 Broadway; Rm 104, Goodland, KS 67735-3097. RE & UCC recording phone-785-899-4845; fax-785-899-4848; hours: 8AM-N,1-3PM www.sherman.kansasgov.com
Separate indices to search include numeric, grantor/grantee, misc., mortgagor/mortgagee. Office will perform a UCC search but public must search other records themselves. UCC search per debtor name- $15.00. Copy fee $1.00 per page. Cert fee- $1.00 per cert includes copy fee. Payee- Sherman County Register of Deeds. **Other phones:** Treasurer- 785-899-4810; Appraiser/Auditor- 785-899-4825; Elections- 785-899-4800. **Property tax/Assessor-** 813 Broadway, Rm 302, Goodland, KS 67735; 785-899-4825, assessor fax- 785-899-4830.

Smith County

County Register of Deeds, 218 S. Grant, Smith Center, KS 66967. RE & UCC recording phone-785-282-5160; fax-785-282-6257; hours: 8AM-N, 1-5PM

All records in one index. Office personnel or visitors may perform searches. General index search fee $8.00 per name. UCC search per debtor name- $15.00. UCC copy fee $2.00 per page. RE record copy- $1.00 per page. Cert fee- $1.00 per page. Payee- Smith County Register of Deeds. **Other phones:** Treasurer- 785-282-5170; Appraiser/Auditor- 785-282-5100; Elections- 785-282-5110. **Property tax/Assessor-** same address as above. 785-282-5100.

Stafford County

County Register of Deeds, 209 N. Broadway; Stafford County Courthouse, St. John, KS 67576. 620-549-3505; fax-620-549-3481; hours: 8AM-N,1-5PM

Records indexed on a public use terminal back to 2003. Office personnel or visitors may perform searches. Search fee $5.00 per name. Will not search real estate records. UCC search per debtor name- $15.00. Copy fee $1.00 per page. Cert fee- $1.00 per cert + copy fee. Payee- Stafford County Register of Deeds. **Other phones:** Treasurer- 620-549-3508; Appraiser/Auditor- 620-549-3540. **Property tax/Assessor-** 620-549-3540.

Stanton County

County Register of Deeds, PO Box 716, Johnson, KS 67855. 620-492-2190; fax-620-492-2688; hours: 8:30AM-N, 1-5PM

Record index not computerized. Office personnel or visitors may perform searches. Search fee $8.00 per name. Will not search real estate records. UCC search per debtor name- $15.00. Copy fee $1.00 per page. RE record copy- $1.00 1st page, then $.50 per page. Tax lien copy- $.15 per copy. Cert fee- $1.00 per cert plus copy fee. Payee- Stanton County Register of Deeds. **Other phones:** Treasurer- 620-492-2160. **Property/Assessor-** 620-492-6896.

Stevens County

County Register of Deeds, 200 E. 6th, Hugoton, KS 67951. RE & UCC recording phone-620-544-2630; fax-620-544-4081; hours: 9AM-5PM

Record index not computerized. Office will perform a UCC search but public must search other records themselves. UCC search per debtor name- $15.00. Copy fee $1.00 per page. RE record copy- $.25 per page. Cert fee- $1.00 per cert plus copy fee. Payee- Stevens County Register of Deeds. **Other phones:** Treasurer- 620-544-2542; Appraiser/Auditor- 620-544-2693; Elections- 620-544-2541. **Property tax/Assessor-** 620-544-2993.

Sumner County

County Register of Deeds, PO Box 469, Wellington, KS 67152. RE & UCC recording phone-620-326-2041; fax-620-326-8172; hours: 8AM-5PM

Records indexed on a public use terminal back to 1998. Office personnel or visitors may perform searches. Search fee $8.00 per name. UCC search per debtor name- $15.00. Copy fee $1.00 per page. Tax lien copy- $.25 per page. Cert fee- $1.00 per cert plus copy fee. Payee- Sumner County Register of Deeds. **Other phones:** Treasurer- 620-326-3371; Appraiser/Auditor- 620-326-8986; Elections- 620-326-3395. **Property tax/Assessor-** 620-326-8986.

Thomas County

County Register of Deeds, 300 N. Court, Colby, KS 67701. 785-460-4535, R/E recording phone-785-462-4535, UCC recording phone-785-462-4535; fax-785-460-4512; hours: 8AM-N, 1PM-5PM

Office personnel or visitors may perform searches. Search fee $8.00 per name. UCC search per debtor name- $15.00. Copy fee $1.00, real estate is $.25 per page. Cert fee- $1.00 per cert plus copy fee. Payee- Thomas County Register of Deeds. **Other phones:** Treasurer- 785-462-4520; Elections- 785-462-4500. **Property tax/Assessor-** 785-462-4525.

Trego County

County Register of Deeds, 216 Main, WaKeeney, KS 67672-2189. RE & UCC recording phone-785-743-6622; fax-785-743-2461; hours: 8:30AM-5PM

Records indexed on a public use terminal back to 7/15/1992. Office will perform a UCC search but public must search other records themselves. Search fee $15.00. Copy fee $1.00 per page. RE record copy- $1.00 1st page, $.25 each add'l. Cert fee- $1.00 per cert plus copy fee. Payee- Trego County Register of Deeds. **Other phones:** Treasurer- 785-743-2001; Appraiser/Auditor- 785-743-5758; Elections- 785-743-5773. **Property tax/Assessor-** same address as above. 785-743-5758.

Wabaunsee County

County Register of Deeds, PO Box 278, Alma, KS 66401-0278. RE & UCC recording phone-785-765-3822; fax-785-765-3824; hours: 8AM-4:30PM www.wabaunsee.kansasgov.com

Separate indices to search include numerical, misc, and UCC. Only the public may search. Copy fee $1.00 per page. RE record copy- $.50 per page. Cert fee- $1.00 per cert plus $.50 per page. Payee- Wabaunsee County Register of Deeds. **Online access to Property Tax, Treasurer, Property, Assessor records:** Access to the treasurer's property tax data is free at www.wabaunsee.kansasgov.com/TaxSearch.asp. Also, access to the assessor parcel search data is at www.wabaunsee.kansasgov.com/v2loginreg.asp; registration is asked for, but you may search basic data for free. To subscribe, phone 785-765-3508. **Other phones:** Treasurer- 785-765-3812; Appraiser/Auditor-785-765-3508; Elections- 785-765-2421; Vital Records- 785-765-3822. **Property tax/Assessor-** same address as above. 785-765-3508.

Wallace County

County Register of Deeds, PO Box 10, Sharon Springs, KS 67758-9998. RE & UCC recording phone-785-852-4283; fax-785-852-4783; hours: 8AM-N, 1-5PM

Index: UCCs in a separate index. Record index not computerized. Office will perform a UCC search and/or tax liens but public must search other records themselves. UCC search per debtor name-$15.00. Copy fee $.25 per page. UCC copies are $1.00 per page. Cert fee- $1.00 per cert plus copy fee. Payee- Wallace County Register of Deeds. **Other phones:** Treasurer- 785-852-4281; Appraiser/Auditor- 785-852-4206; Elections- 785-852-4282. **Property tax/Assessor-** 785-852-4206.

Washington County

County Register of Deeds, 214 C St; Courthouse, Washington, KS 66968-1928. RE & UCC recording phone-785-325-2286; fax-785-325-2830; hours: 8AM-5PM www.washingtonks.net/

All records in one index. Office personnel or visitors may perform searches. Search fee $15.00 unless otherwise indicated. Will give real estate information at no charge. Will search UCC records, search includes tax liens. Separate federal/state combined tax lien search- $8.00 per debtor. Copy fee $1.00 per page. RE record copy- $.25 per page; from old bound books- $.50 per page. Cert fee-$1.00 per cert includes copy fee. Payee-Washington County Register of Deeds. **Other phones:** Treasurer- 785-325-2461; Appraiser/Auditor-785-325-2236; Elections- 785-325-2974; Vital Records- 785-296-1400 (Topeka, KS). **Property tax/Assessor-** 214 C St, Washington, KS 66968; 785-325-2236.

Wichita County

County Register of Deeds, PO Box 472, Leoti, KS 67861-0472. RE & UCC recording phone-620-375-2733; fax-316-375-4350; hours: 8AM-N,1-5PM

Separate indices to search include Platt or City Platt. Record index not computerized. Office will perform a UCC search but must search other records themselves. Search fee $15.00. Copy fee $1.00 per page. Cert fee- $1.00 per page includes copy fee. Payee- Wichita County Register of Deeds. **Other phones:** Treasurer- 620-375-2713; Appraiser/Auditor- 620-375-4242; Elections- 620-375-2731. **Property tax/Assessor-** 620-375-4242.

Wilson County

County Register of Deeds, Courthouse; Rm 106, Fredonia, KS 66736-1396. RE & UCC recording phone-620-378-3662; fax-620-378-4762; hours: 8:30AM-5PM

All records in one index. Records indexed on a public use terminal back to 2002. Office personnel or visitors may perform searches. Search fee $15.00. Copy fee $1.00 per page. Cert fee- $1.00 per cert plus copy fee. Payee- Wilson County Register of Deeds. **Property tax/Assessor-** 620-378-2187.

Woodson County

County Register of Deeds, 105 W. Rutledge, Rm 101, Yates Center, KS 66783-1499. 620-625-8635; fax-620-625-8670; hours: 8AM-N,1-5PM www.woodsoncounty.net

Office personnel or visitors may perform searches. Search fee $8.00 per name. Will not search real estate records. UCC search per debtor name- $15.00. Copy fee $1.00 per page. RE or tax lien copy- $.50 per page. Cert fee- $1.00 per cert plus copy fee. Payee- Woodson County Register of Deeds. **Other phones:** Treasurer- 620-625-8650. **Property tax/Assessor-** 620-625-8600.

Wyandotte County

County Register of Deeds, 710 N. 7th St.; Courthouse, Kansas City, KS 66101-3084. RE & UCC recording phone-913-573-2841; fax-913-321-3075; hours: 8AM-5PM

Records indexed on a public use terminal back to 1991. Office personnel or visitors may perform searches. Search fee $15.00 per name. Will not search real estate records. Copy fee $1.00 per page. RE record copy- $1.00 1st page, $.50 each add'l. Tax lien copy- $.50 per page. Cert fee- $1.00 per cert plus copy fee. Payee- Wyandotte County Register of Deeds. **Online access to Real Estate, Lien, Property Appraisal, Personal Property, Recording, Deed, Judgment records:** County records are online and property tax records are on dial-up. The property dial-up services requires a $20 set up fee, $5 monthly minimum and $.05 each transaction. Lending agency info also available. Contact Louise Sachen 913-573-2885 for signup. Also, Register has online subscription services named Laredo and Tapestry; index goes back to 1975, images to 1991. Tapestry accepts credit card searches $3.99 a search, $.50 per image. Also, Judgments and Liens via subscription at www.accesskansas.org. Records from the County Treasurer Tax database are free at https://www.accesskansas.org/apps/wyandotteProperty Tax. Name search for personal property only; property searches require street number/ name; no name searching. **Other phones:** Treasurer- 913-573-2823; Appraiser/Auditor- 913-573-2889; Elections- 913-334-1414. **Property tax/Assessor-** 913-287-2641.

Kansas County Locator

You will usually be able to find the city name in the City/County Cross Reference below. In that case, it is a simple matter to determine the county from the cross reference. However, only the official US Postal Service city names are included in this index. There are an additional 40,000 place names that people use in their addresses. Therefore, we have also included a ZIP/City Cross Reference immediately following the City/County Cross Reference.

If you know the ZIP Code but the city name does not appear in the City/County Cross Reference index, look up the ZIP Code in the ZIP/City Cross Reference, find the city name, then look up the city name in the City/County Cross Reference. For example, you want to know the county for an address of Menands, NY 12204. There is no "Menands" in the City/County Cross Reference. The ZIP/City Cross Reference shows that ZIP Codes 12201-12288 are for the city of Albany. Looking back in the City/County Cross Reference, Albany is in Albany County.

City/County Cross Reference

ABBYVILLE Reno
ABILENE Dickinson
ADA (67414) Ottawa(94), Lincoln(5)
ADMIRE Lyon
AGENDA Republic
AGRA Phillips
ALBERT (67511) Barton(56), Rush(43)
ALDEN (67512) Rice(90), Reno(9)
ALEXANDER (67513) Rush(90),
   Pawnee(9)
ALLEN Lyon
ALMA Wabaunsee
ALMENA (67622) Norton(98), Phillips(1)
ALTA VISTA (66834) Wabaunsee(52),
   Morris(19), Jackson(17), Geary(10)
ALTAMONT Labette
ALTON (67623) Osborne(96), Smith(3)
ALTOONA Wilson
AMERICUS Lyon
AMES Cloud
ANDALE Sedgwick
ANDOVER Butler
ANTHONY Harper
ARCADIA (66711) Crawford(96),
   Bourbon(3)
ARCADIA Bourbon
ARGONIA (67004) Sumner(86), Harper(12)
ARKANSAS CITY Cowley
ARLINGTON Reno
ARMA Crawford
ARNOLD (67515) Ness(75), Trego(24)
ASHLAND Clark
ASSARIA (67416) Saline(97),
   McPherson(2)
ATCHISON (66002) Atchison(93),
   Leavenworth(5), Jefferson(1)
ATHOL Smith
ATLANTA (67008) Cowley(69), Butler(30)
ATTICA (67009) Harper(97), Barber(2)
ATWOOD Rawlins
AUBURN (66402) Shawnee(98), Osage(1)
AUGUSTA Butler
AURORA Cloud
AXTELL (66403) Marshall(93), Nemaha(6)
BAILEYVILLE (66404) Nemaha(94),
   Marshall(5)
BALDWIN CITY (66006) Douglas(95),
   Franklin(4)
BARNARD (67418) Lincoln(91), Mitchell(8)
BARNES (66933) Washington(93), Riley(6)
BARTLETT Labette
BASEHOR Leavenworth
BAXTER SPRINGS Cherokee
BAZINE Ness
BEATTIE Marshall
BEAUMONT Butler
BEAVER Barton
BEELER (67518) Ness(74), Lane(25)
BELLE PLAINE Sumner
BELLEVILLE Republic
BELOIT (67420) Mitchell(97), Cloud(1)
BELPRE (67519) Edwards(90),
   Pawnee(10)
BELVIDERE Kiowa

BELVUE (66407) Wabaunsee(70),
   Pottawatomie(29)
BENDENA Doniphan
BENEDICT Wilson
BENNINGTON Ottawa
BENTLEY Sedgwick
BENTON (67017) Butler(89), Sedgwick(10)
BERN Nemaha
BERRYTON (66409) Shawnee(91),
   Douglas(6), Osage(2)
BEVERLY (67423) Lincoln(98), Ellsworth(1)
BIRD CITY Cheyenne
BISON Rush
BLUE MOUND (66010) Linn(96),
   Bourbon(2)
BLUE RAPIDS (66411) Marshall(97),
   Riley(2)
BLUFF CITY (67018) Harper(91),
   Sumner(8)
BOGUE Graham
BONNER SPRINGS (66012)
   Wyandotte(65), Leavenworth(34)
BREMEN (66412) Marshall(93),
   Washington(6)
BREWSTER (67732) Thomas(59),
   Sherman(32), Rawlins(7)
BRONSON (66716) Bourbon(94), Allen(5)
BROOKVILLE (67425) Saline(58),
   Ellsworth(40), Lincoln(1)
BROWNELL (67521) Ness(89), Trego(10)
BUCKLIN (67834) Ford(92), Clark(6)
BUCYRUS (66013) Johnson(52),
   Miami(47)
BUFFALO (66717) Wilson(96), Woodson(3)
BUHLER (67522) Reno(91), Harvey(8)
BUNKER HILL Russell
BURDEN Cowley
BURDETT (67523) Pawnee(92),
   Hodgeman(7)
BURDICK (66838) Morris(93), Marion(4),
   Chase(1)
BURLINGAME (66413) Osage(95),
   Lyon(3), Wabaunsee(1)
BURLINGTON Coffey
BURNS (66840) Butler(58), Marion(36),
   Chase(5)
BURR OAK Jewell
BURRTON (67020) Harvey(58), Reno(37),
   Sedgwick(3)
BUSHTON (67427) Rice(81), Ellsworth(16),
   Barton(2)
BYERS (67021) Pratt(94), Stafford(5)
CALDWELL Sumner
CAMBRIDGE Cowley
CANEY Montgomery
CANTON (67428) McPherson(93),
   Marion(6)
CARBONDALE Osage
CARLTON Dickinson
CASSODAY Butler
CATHARINE Ellis
CAWKER CITY (67430) Mitchell(75),
   Jewell(17), Osborne(4), Smith(2)
CEDAR Smith

CEDAR POINT (66843) Chase(97),
   Marion(2)
CEDAR VALE (67024) Chautauqua(77),
   Cowley(22)
CENTERVILLE (66014) Anderson(52),
   Linn(47)
CENTRALIA Nemaha
CHANUTE (66720) Neosho(96), Wilson(3)
CHAPMAN Dickinson
CHASE Rice
CHAUTAUQUA Chautauqua
CHENEY (67025) Sedgwick(72),
   Kingman(26)
CHEROKEE Crawford
CHERRYVALE (67335) Montgomery(87),
   Labette(12)
CHETOPA (67336) Labette(75),
   Cherokee(24)
CIMARRON (67835) Gray(73), Finney(22),
   Hodgeman(3)
CIRCLEVILLE Jackson
CLAFLIN (67525) Barton(96), Rice(3)
CLAY CENTER (67432) Clay(98),
   Ottawa(1)
CLAYTON (67629) Norton(81), Decatur(18)
CLEARVIEW CITY Johnson
CLEARWATER (67026) Sedgwick(96),
   Sumner(3)
CLIFTON (66937) Washington(83),
   Clay(16)
CLYDE (66938) Cloud(80),
   Washington(11), Republic(4), Clay(3)
COATS (67028) Pratt(60), Kiowa(25),
   Barber(13)
CODELL Rooks
COFFEYVILLE (67337) Montgomery(95),
   Labette(4)
COLBY Thomas
COLDWATER (67029) Comanche(97),
   Kiowa(2)
COLLYER (67631) Trego(73), Graham(22),
   Gove(3), Sheridan(1)
COLONY (66015) Anderson(79),
   Coffey(20)
COLUMBUS Cherokee
COLWICH Sedgwick
CONCORDIA (66901) Cloud(97),
   Republic(2)
CONWAY SPRINGS (67031) Sumner(96),
   Sedgwick(3)
COOLIDGE Hamilton
COPELAND (67837) Haskell(55), Gray(39),
   Meade(5)
CORNING Nemaha
COTTONWOOD FALLS Chase
COUNCIL GROVE (66846) Morris(94),
   Lyon(4)
COURTLAND (66939) Republic(92),
   Jewell(7)
COYVILLE Wilson
CRESTLINE Cherokee
CUBA (66940) Republic(98),
   Washington(1)
CUMMINGS Atchison

CUNNINGHAM (67035) Kingman(71),
   Pratt(18), Reno(9)
DAMAR (67632) Rooks(73), Graham(26)
DANVILLE Harper
DE SOTO Johnson
DEARING Montgomery
DEERFIELD (67838) Kearny(62),
   Finney(37)
DELIA Jackson
DELPHOS (67436) Ottawa(84), Cloud(15)
DENISON (66419) Jackson(87),
   Jefferson(12)
DENNIS Labette
DENNIS THE MENACE Sedgwick
DENTON Doniphan
DERBY Sedgwick
DEXTER Cowley
DIGHTON (67839) Lane(92), Gove(6)
DODGE CITY Ford
DORRANCE (67634) Russell(98),
   Barton(1)
DOUGLASS (67039) Butler(97), Cowley(1)
DOVER Shawnee
DOWNS (67437) Osborne(95), Smith(4)
DRESDEN (67635) Decatur(70),
   Sheridan(29)
DURHAM Marion
DWIGHT (66849) Morris(63), Geary(36)
EASTON Leavenworth
EDGERTON (66021) Johnson(71),
   Miami(26), Douglas(2)
EDMOND (67636) Norton(82), Graham(17)
EDNA Labette
EDSON Sherman
EDWARDSVILLE Wyandotte
EFFINGHAM Atchison
EL DORADO Butler
ELBING Butler
ELK CITY (67344) Montgomery(65),
   Chautauqua(21), Elk(13)
ELK FALLS Elk
ELKHART Morton
ELLINWOOD (67526) Barton(94), Rice(4),
   Stafford(1)
ELLIS (67637) Ellis(87), Trego(12)
ELLSWORTH Ellsworth
ELMDALE Chase
ELSMORE Allen
ELWOOD Doniphan
EMMETT (66422) Pottawatomie(54),
   Jackson(45)
EMPORIA Lyon
ENGLEWOOD Clark
ENSIGN (67841) Gray(80), Ford(19)
ENTERPRISE Dickinson
ERIE Neosho
ESBON Jewell
ESKRIDGE Wabaunsee
EUDORA (66025) Douglas(76),
   Johnson(22)
EUREKA Greenwood
EVEREST (66424) Brown(89),
   Atchison(10)
FAIRVIEW Brown

FALL RIVER (67047) Greenwood(67), Elk(20), Wilson(11)
FALUN (67442) Saline(97), McPherson(2)
FARLINGTON Crawford
FLORENCE Marion
FONTANA Miami
FORD Ford
FORMOSO (66942) Jewell(98), Republic(1)
FORT DODGE Ford
FORT LEAVENWORTH Leavenworth
FORT RILEY Geary
FORT SCOTT Bourbon
FOSTORIA Pottawatomie
FOWLER (67844) Meade(80), Ford(13), Gray(5)
FRANKFORT (66427) Marshall(97), Pottawatomie(2)
FRANKLIN Crawford
FREDONIA Wilson
FREEPORT (67049) Harper(90), Sumner(10)
FRONTENAC Crawford
FULTON (66738) Bourbon(97), Linn(2)
GALENA Cherokee
GALESBURG Neosho
GALVA McPherson
GARDEN CITY Finney
GARDEN PLAIN Sedgwick
GARDNER Johnson
GARFIELD Pawnee
GARLAND Bourbon
GARNETT Anderson
GAS Allen
GAYLORD (67638) Smith(98), Osborne(1)
GEM (67734) Thomas(52), Rawlins(47)
GENESEO (67444) Rice(65), Ellsworth(34)
GEUDA SPRINGS (67051) Sumner(83), Cowley(16)
GIRARD Crawford
GLADE (67639) Phillips(96), Rooks(3)
GLASCO (67445) Cloud(92), Ottawa(7)
GLEN ELDER (67446) Mitchell(91), Jewell(8)
GODDARD Sedgwick
GOESSEL Marion
GOFF Nemaha
GOODLAND Sherman
GORHAM (67640) Russell(73), Ellis(26)
GOVE Gove
GRAINFIELD (67737) Gove(75), Sheridan(25)
GRANTVILLE Jefferson
GREAT BEND (67530) Barton(98), Stafford(1)
GREELEY (66033) Anderson(62), Franklin(35), Linn(2)
GREEN (67447) Clay(61), Riley(38)
GREENLEAF Washington
GREENSBURG Kiowa
GREENWICH Sedgwick
GRENOLA (67346) Elk(75), Chautauqua(25)
GRIDLEY (66852) Coffey(82), Greenwood(10), Woodson(6)
GRINNELL (67738) Gove(73), Sheridan(26)
GYPSUM (67448) Saline(47), McPherson(26), Dickinson(22), Marion(3)
HADDAM (66944) Washington(96), Republic(3)
HALSTEAD Harvey
HAMILTON Greenwood
HANOVER Washington
HANSTON (67849) Hodgeman(97), Ness(2)
HARDTNER Barber
HARLAN Smith
HARPER (67058) Harper(97), Kingman(2)
HARTFORD (66854) Lyon(78), Coffey(21)
HARVEYVILLE (66431) Wabaunsee(91), Shawnee(8)

HAVANA (67347) Montgomery(67), Chautauqua(32)
HAVEN Reno
HAVENSVILLE (66432) Pottawatomie(78), Jackson(20), Nemaha(1)
HAVILAND (67059) Kiowa(75), Edwards(16), Pratt(7)
HAYS Ellis
HAYSVILLE Sedgwick
HAZELTON (67061) Barber(68), Harper(31)
HEALY (67850) Lane(84), Scott(10), Gove(4)
HEPLER (66746) Crawford(91), Bourbon(8)
HERINGTON (67449) Dickinson(81), Morris(17)
HERNDON (67739) Rawlins(95), Decatur(4)
HESSTON Harvey
HIAWATHA Brown
HIGHLAND Doniphan
HILL CITY Graham
HILLSBORO Marion
HILLSDALE Miami
HOISINGTON Barton
HOLCOMB (67851) Finney(95), Kearny(2), Scott(1)
HOLLENBERG Washington
HOLTON (66436) Jackson(97), Atchison(2)
HOLYROOD (67450) Ellsworth(84), Barton(14), Russell(1)
HOME Marshall
HOPE (67451) Dickinson(98), Marion(1)
HORTON (66439) Brown(84), Jackson(10), Atchison(5)
HOWARD Elk
HOXIE (67740) Sheridan(97), Graham(2)
HOYT (66440) Jackson(98), Shawnee(1)
HUDSON Stafford
HUGOTON Stevens
HUMBOLDT Allen
HUNTER (67452) Lincoln(54), Mitchell(45)
HUTCHINSON Reno
INDEPENDENCE Montgomery
INGALLS (67853) Gray(90), Finney(9)
INMAN (67546) McPherson(86), Rice(6), Reno(5)
IOLA Allen
ISABEL (67065) Barber(59), Pratt(38), Kingman(1)
IUKA Pratt
JAMESTOWN (66948) Cloud(81), Republic(18)
JENNINGS (67643) Decatur(94), Sheridan(5)
JETMORE Hodgeman
JEWELL Jewell
JOHNSON (67855) Stanton(96), Grant(2), Morton(1)
JUNCTION CITY Geary
KALVESTA Finney
KANOPOLIS Ellsworth
KANORADO (67741) Sherman(95), Cheyenne(2), Wallace(1)
KANSAS CITY (66109) Wyandotte(97), Leavenworth(2)
KANSAS CITY Wyandotte
KECHI Sedgwick
KENDALL (67857) Hamilton(55), Kearny(44)
KENSINGTON (66951) Smith(75), Phillips(24)
KINCAID (66039) Anderson(89), Allen(10)
KINGMAN (67068) Kingman(98), Reno(1)
KINGSDOWN (67858) Ford(90), Clark(9)
KINSLEY (67547) Edwards(97), Hodgeman(1)
KIOWA Barber
KIRWIN (67644) Phillips(91), Smith(5), Rooks(3)
KISMET Seward
LA CROSSE Rush

LA CYGNE Linn
LA HARPE Allen
LAKE CITY Barber
LAKIN Kearny
LAMONT Greenwood
LANCASTER Atchison
LANE Franklin
LANSING Leavenworth
LARNED (67550) Pawnee(97), Stafford(1)
LATHAM (67072) Butler(87), Cowley(12)
LAWRENCE (66044) Douglas(92), Jefferson(4), Leavenworth(3)
LAWRENCE Douglas
LE ROY Coffey
LEAVENWORTH Leavenworth
LEBANON (66952) Smith(98), Jewell(1)
LEBO (66856) Coffey(70), Osage(29)
LECOMPTON Douglas
LEHIGH Marion
LENEXA Johnson
LENORA (67645) Norton(73), Graham(26)
LEON Butler
LEONARDVILLE Riley
LEOTI (67861) Wichita(96), Logan(3)
LEVANT Thomas
LEWIS Edwards
LIBERAL Seward
LIBERTY (67351) Montgomery(85), Labette(14)
LIEBENTHAL Rush
LINCOLN Lincoln
LINCOLNVILLE (66858) Marion(97), Chase(2)
LINDSBORG (67456) McPherson(89), Saline(10)
LINN Washington
LINWOOD Leavenworth
LITTLE RIVER Rice
LOGAN (67646) Phillips(78), Rooks(9), Graham(7), Norton(4)
LONG ISLAND Phillips
LONGFORD (67458) Clay(83), Ottawa(15)
LONGTON (67352) Elk(96), Chautauqua(3)
LORRAINE Ellsworth
LOST SPRINGS (66859) Marion(86), Morris(13)
LOUISBURG Miami
LOUISVILLE Pottawatomie
LUCAS (67648) Russell(75), Osborne(18), Lincoln(6)
LUDELL Rawlins
LURAY (67649) Russell(65), Osborne(34)
LYNDON Osage
LYONS Rice
MACKSVILLE (67557) Stafford(59), Pratt(19), Pawnee(14), Edwards(6)
MADISON (66860) Greenwood(58), Lyon(41)
MAHASKA (66955) Washington(98), Republic(1)
MAIZE Sedgwick
MANCHESTER Dickinson
MANHATTAN (66503) Riley(98), Pottawatomie(1)
MANHATTAN Riley
MANKATO Jewell
MANTER (67862) Stanton(75), Morton(24)
MAPLE CITY Cowley
MAPLE HILL Wabaunsee
MAPLETON (66754) Bourbon(96), Linn(3)
MARIENTHAL Wichita
MARION Marion
MARQUETTE (67464) McPherson(75), Ellsworth(24)
MARYSVILLE Marshall
MATFIELD GREEN Chase
MAYETTA Jackson
MAYFIELD Sumner
MC CONNELL A F B Sedgwick
MC CRACKEN (67556) Rush(67), Ellis(16), Ness(15)

MC CUNE (66753) Crawford(96), Labette(4)
MC DONALD (67745) Rawlins(75), Cheyenne(25)
MC FARLAND Wabaunsee
MC LOUTH (66054) Jefferson(69), Leavenworth(30)
MCCONNELL AFB Sedgwick
MCPHERSON McPherson
MEADE Meade
MEDICINE LODGE Barber
MELVERN Osage
MENTOR Saline
MERIDEN (66512) Jefferson(90), Jackson(6), Shawnee(3)
MILAN Sumner
MILFORD Geary
MILTON (67106) Sumner(62), Sedgwick(35), Kingman(2)
MILTONVALE (67466) Cloud(60), Ottawa(25), Clay(14)
MINNEAPOLIS Ottawa
MINNEOLA (67865) Ford(65), Clark(34)
MISSION Johnson
MOLINE (67353) Elk(75), Chautauqua(24)
MONTEZUMA (67867) Gray(96), Meade(3)
MONUMENT (67747) Logan(90), Thomas(9)
MORAN (66755) Allen(98), Bourbon(1)
MORGANVILLE Clay
MORLAND Graham
MORRILL Brown
MORROWVILLE Washington
MOSCOW Stevens
MOUND CITY Linn
MOUND VALLEY Labette
MOUNDRIDGE (67107) McPherson(68), Harvey(31)
MOUNT HOPE (67108) Sedgwick(59), Reno(40)
MULBERRY Crawford
MULLINVILLE Kiowa
MULVANE (67110) Sedgwick(68), Sumner(30), Cowley(1)
MUNDEN Republic
MURDOCK Kingman
MUSCOTAH (66058) Jackson(66), Atchison(33)
NARKA (66960) Republic(97), Washington(2)
NASHVILLE (67112) Kingman(86), Barber(13)
NATOMA (67651) Osborne(66), Rooks(26), Ellis(5), Russell(1)
NEAL Greenwood
NEKOMA (67559) Rush(84), Pawnee(15)
NEODESHA (66757) Wilson(92), Montgomery(7)
NEOSHO FALLS (66758) Coffey(54), Woodson(40), Anderson(2), Allen(1)
NEOSHO RAPIDS (66864) Lyon(90), Coffey(9)
NESS CITY Ness
NETAWAKA (66516) Jackson(78), Brown(21)
NEW ALBANY Wilson
NEW ALMELO Norton
NEW CAMBRIA (67470) Saline(89), Ottawa(10)
NEW CENTURY Johnson
NEWTON (67114) Harvey(95), Butler(2), Marion(1)
NICKERSON Reno
NIOTAZE Chautauqua
NORCATUR (67653) Decatur(70), Norton(29)
NORTH NEWTON Harvey
NORTON Norton
NORTONVILLE (66060) Jefferson(51), Atchison(48)
NORWAY Republic

NORWICH (67118) Kingman(94), Sedgwick(2), Harper(1), Sumner(1)
OAKHILL (67472) Clay(70), Ottawa(29)
OAKLEY (67748) Logan(83), Thomas(11), Gove(4)
OBERLIN (67749) Decatur(98), Rawlins(1)
ODIN Barton
OFFERLE (67563) Edwards(56), Ford(38), Hodgeman(4)
OGALLAH (67656) Trego(92), Graham(7)
OGDEN Riley
OKETO Marshall
OLATHE Johnson
OLMITZ Barton
OLPE Lyon
OLSBURG Pottawatomie
ONAGA (66521) Pottawatomie(94), Nemaha(5)
ONEIDA Nemaha
OPOLIS Crawford
OSAGE CITY Osage
OSAWATOMIE (66064) Miami(96), Franklin(3)
OSBORNE Osborne
OSKALOOSA Jefferson
OSWEGO (67356) Labette(98), Cherokee(1)
OTIS (67565) Rush(87), Barton(10), Russell(1)
OTTAWA Franklin
OVERBROOK (66524) Osage(58), Douglas(28), Shawnee(9), Franklin(2)
OVERLAND PARK Johnson
OXFORD (67119) Sumner(67), Cowley(32)
OZAWKIE Jefferson
PALCO (67657) Rooks(60), Graham(37), Trego(2)
PALMER (66962) Washington(88), Clay(11)
PAOLA Miami
PARADISE (67658) Russell(67), Osborne(32)
PARK (67751) Gove(69), Sheridan(30)
PARKER (66072) Linn(94), Miami(4)
PARSONS (67357) Labette(93), Neosho(6)
PARTRIDGE Reno
PAWNEE ROCK (67567) Barton(61), Pawnee(24), Stafford(9), Rush(5)
PAXICO Wabaunsee
PEABODY (66866) Marion(93), Harvey(5)
PECK (67120) Sedgwick(70), Sumner(29)
PENOKEE Graham
PERRY Jefferson
PERU Chautauqua
PFEIFER Ellis
PHILLIPSBURG Phillips
PIEDMONT (67122) Greenwood(65), Elk(34)
PIERCEVILLE Finney
PIQUA Woodson
PITTSBURG (66762) Crawford(97), Cherokee(2)
PLAINS (67869) Meade(86), Seward(13)
PLAINVILLE Rooks
PLEASANTON Linn
PLEVNA Reno
POMONA Franklin
PORTIS (67474) Osborne(72), Smith(27)
POTTER Atchison
POTWIN Butler
POWHATTAN Brown

PRAIRIE VIEW (67664) Phillips(92), Norton(7)
PRATT Pratt
PRESCOTT Linn
PRETTY PRAIRIE (67570) Reno(90), Kingman(9)
PRINCETON Franklin
PROTECTION (67127) Comanche(88), Clark(11)
QUENEMO Osage
QUINTER (67752) Gove(91), Sheridan(8)
RAGO Kingman
RAMONA (67475) Marion(63), Dickinson(36)
RANDALL Jewell
RANDOLPH Riley
RANSOM (67572) Ness(81), Trego(18)
RANTOUL (66079) Franklin(94), Miami(5)
RAYMOND Rice
READING (66868) Lyon(88), Osage(10)
REDFIELD Bourbon
REPUBLIC Republic
REXFORD (67753) Thomas(63), Sheridan(30), Rawlins(5)
RICHFIELD Morton
RICHMOND (66080) Franklin(77), Anderson(22)
RILEY Riley
RIVERTON Cherokee
ROBINSON (66532) Brown(72), Doniphan(27)
ROCK (67131) Cowley(98), Butler(1)
ROLLA (67954) Morton(74), Stevens(25)
ROSALIA Butler
ROSE HILL (67133) Butler(98), Sedgwick(1)
ROSSVILLE (66533) Shawnee(97), Jackson(3)
ROXBURY McPherson
ROZEL Pawnee
RUSH CENTER (67575) Rush(96), Pawnee(3)
RUSSELL (67665) Russell(98), Barton(1)
RUSSELL SPRINGS Logan
SABETHA (66534) Nemaha(92), Brown(7)
SAINT FRANCIS Cheyenne
SAINT GEORGE Pottawatomie
SAINT JOHN (67576) Stafford(96), Pratt(3)
SAINT MARYS (66536) Pottawatomie(94), Wabaunsee(2), Shawnee(2)
SAINT PAUL Neosho
SALINA Saline
SATANTA (67870) Haskell(78), Grant(16), Seward(5)
SAVONBURG (66772) Allen(97), Bourbon(2)
SAWYER (67134) Pratt(89), Barber(10)
SCAMMON Cherokee
SCANDIA Republic
SCHOENCHEN Ellis
SCOTT CITY (67871) Scott(97), Finney(1)
SCRANTON Osage
SEDAN Chautauqua
SEDGWICK (67135) Harvey(60), Sedgwick(39)
SELDEN (67757) Sheridan(57), Decatur(38), Thomas(4)
SENECA Nemaha
SEVERY (67137) Greenwood(88), Elk(11)
SEWARD Stafford
SHARON (67138) Barber(97), Harper(2)

SHARON SPRINGS Wallace
SHAWNEE Johnson
SHAWNEE MISSION Johnson
SHIELDS (67874) Lane(86), Gove(13)
SILVER LAKE (66539) Shawnee(97), Jackson(2)
SIMPSON Mitchell
SMITH CENTER Smith
SMOLAN Saline
SOLDIER (66540) Jackson(96), Nemaha(3)
SOLOMON (67480) Dickinson(59), Saline(20), Ottawa(19)
SOUTH HAVEN Sumner
SOUTH HUTCHINSON Reno
SPEARVILLE (67876) Ford(91), Hodgeman(8)
SPIVEY Kingman
SPRING HILL (66083) Johnson(62), Miami(37)
STAFFORD Stafford
STARK (66775) Neosho(98), Bourbon(1)
STERLING (67579) Rice(81), Reno(18)
STILWELL Johnson
STOCKTON Rooks
STRONG CITY Chase
STUDLEY (67759) Sheridan(89), Graham(10)
STUTTGART Phillips
SUBLETTE (67877) Haskell(93), Seward(6)
SUMMERFIELD Marshall
SUN CITY Barber
SYCAMORE Montgomery
SYLVAN GROVE (67481) Lincoln(96), Russell(3)
SYLVIA Reno
SYRACUSE (67878) Hamilton(85), Stanton(14)
TALMAGE Dickinson
TAMPA Marion
TECUMSEH Shawnee
TESCOTT (67484) Ottawa(80), Saline(15), Lincoln(3)
THAYER (66776) Neosho(82), Wilson(15)
TIMKEN (67582) Rush(98), Pawnee(1)
TIPTON (67485) Osborne(53), Mitchell(46)
TONGANOXIE Leavenworth
TOPEKA (66615) Shawnee(87), Wabaunsee(12)
TOPEKA (66617) Shawnee(90), Jefferson(8)
TOPEKA Shawnee
TORONTO (66777) Woodson(87), Greenwood(11), Wilson(1)
TOWANDA Butler
TREECE Cherokee
TRIBUNE Greeley
TROY Doniphan
TURON (67583) Reno(49), Pratt(41), Stafford(9)
TURON Pratt
TYRO Montgomery
UDALL (67146) Cowley(93), Sumner(6)
ULYSSES (67880) Grant(98), Kearny(1)
UNIONTOWN Bourbon
UTICA (67584) Ness(56), Gove(23), Lane(10), Trego(9)
VALLEY CENTER (67147) Sedgwick(97), Harvey(2)
VALLEY FALLS (66088) Jefferson(97), Atchison(2)
VASSAR Osage

VERMILLION (66544) Marshall(95), Nemaha(4)
VICTORIA Ellis
VIOLA Sedgwick
VIRGIL (66870) Greenwood(97), Woodson(2)
VLIETS Marshall
WA KEENEY (67672) Trego(96), Graham(3)
WAKARUSA (66546) Shawnee(86), Osage(13)
WAKEFIELD (67487) Clay(90), Dickinson(7), Geary(2)
WALDO (67673) Russell(82), Osborne(17)
WALDRON Harper
WALKER Ellis
WALLACE (67761) Wallace(70), Logan(26), Wichita(2)
WALNUT (66780) Bourbon(78), Crawford(20), Neosho(1)
WALTON (67151) Harvey(89), Marion(10)
WAMEGO (66547) Pottawatomie(88), Wabaunsee(11)
WATERVILLE (66548) Marshall(95), Washington(2), Riley(1)
WATHENA Doniphan
WAVERLY (66871) Coffey(96), Osage(3)
WEBBER Jewell
WEIR Cherokee
WELDA (66091) Anderson(97), Franklin(2)
WELLINGTON Sumner
WELLS Ottawa
WELLSVILLE (66092) Franklin(66), Miami(25), Douglas(7)
WESKAN (67762) Wallace(98), Greeley(1)
WEST MINERAL Cherokee
WESTMORELAND Pottawatomie
WESTPHALIA (66093) Anderson(56), Coffey(43)
WETMORE (66550) Nemaha(80), Jackson(10), Brown(8)
WHEATON (66551) Pottawatomie(98), Marshall(1)
WHITE CITY (66872) Morris(96), Geary(3)
WHITE CLOUD (66094) Doniphan(98), Brown(1)
WHITEWATER (67154) Butler(94), Harvey(5)
WHITING Jackson
WICHITA (67230) Sedgwick(96), Butler(3)
WICHITA Sedgwick
WILLIAMSBURG (66095) Franklin(88), Anderson(10)
WILMORE (67155) Comanche(84), Kiowa(15)
WILSEY Morris
WILSON (67490) Ellsworth(82), Russell(10), Lincoln(6)
WINCHESTER (66097) Jefferson(98), Leavenworth(1)
WINDOM (67491) McPherson(77), Rice(22)
WINFIELD Cowley
WINONA (67764) Logan(88), Thomas(11)
WOODBINE Dickinson
WOODSTON Rooks
WRIGHT Ford
YATES CENTER Woodson
YODER Reno
ZENDA (67159) Kingman(83), Harper(16)
ZURICH (67676) Rooks(90), Ellis(9)

Kansas ZIP/City Cross Reference

ZIP	City	ZIP	City	ZIP	City	ZIP	City
66002-66002	ATCHISON	66403-66403	AXTELL	66712-66712	ARMA	66871-66871	WAVERLY
66006-66006	BALDWIN CITY	66404-66404	BAILEYVILLE	66713-66713	BAXTER SPRINGS	66872-66872	WHITE CITY
66007-66007	BASEHOR	66406-66406	BEATTIE	66714-66714	BENEDICT	66873-66873	WILSEY
66008-66008	BENDENA	66407-66407	BELVUE	66716-66716	BRONSON	66901-66901	CONCORDIA
66010-66010	BLUE MOUND	66408-66408	BERN	66717-66717	BUFFALO	66930-66930	AGENDA
66012-66012	BONNER SPRINGS	66409-66409	BERRYTON	66720-66720	CHANUTE	66931-66931	AMES
66013-66013	BUCYRUS	66411-66411	BLUE RAPIDS	66724-66724	CHEROKEE	66932-66932	ATHOL
66014-66014	CENTERVILLE	66412-66412	BREMEN	66725-66725	COLUMBUS	66933-66933	BARNES
66015-66015	COLONY	66413-66413	BURLINGAME	66727-66727	COYVILLE	66935-66935	BELLEVILLE
66016-66016	CUMMINGS	66414-66414	CARBONDALE	66728-66728	CRESTLINE	66936-66936	BURR OAK
66017-66017	DENTON	66415-66415	CENTRALIA	66732-66732	ELSMORE	66937-66937	CLIFTON
66018-66018	DE SOTO	66416-66416	CIRCLEVILLE	66733-66733	ERIE	66938-66938	CLYDE
66019-66019	CLEARVIEW CITY	66417-66417	CORNING	66734-66734	FARLINGTON	66939-66939	COURTLAND
66020-66020	EASTON	66418-66418	DELIA	66735-66735	FRANKLIN	66940-66940	CUBA
66021-66021	EDGERTON	66419-66419	DENISON	66736-66736	FREDONIA	66941-66941	ESBON
66023-66023	EFFINGHAM	66420-66420	DOVER	66738-66738	FULTON	66942-66942	FORMOSO
66024-66024	ELWOOD	66422-66422	EMMETT	66739-66739	GALENA	66943-66943	GREENLEAF
66025-66025	EUDORA	66423-66423	ESKRIDGE	66740-66740	GALESBURG	66944-66944	HADDAM
66026-66026	FONTANA	66424-66424	EVEREST	66741-66741	GARLAND	66945-66945	HANOVER
66027-66027	FORT LEAVENWORTH	66425-66425	FAIRVIEW	66741-66741	ARCADIA	66946-66946	HOLLENBERG
66030-66030	GARDNER	66426-66426	FOSTORIA	66742-66742	GAS	66948-66948	JAMESTOWN
66031-66031	NEW CENTURY	66427-66427	FRANKFORT	66743-66743	GIRARD	66949-66949	JEWELL
66032-66032	GARNETT	66428-66428	GOFF	66746-66746	HEPLER	66951-66951	KENSINGTON
66033-66033	GREELEY	66429-66429	GRANTVILLE	66748-66748	HUMBOLDT	66952-66952	LEBANON
66035-66035	HIGHLAND	66431-66431	HARVEYVILLE	66749-66749	IOLA	66953-66953	LINN
66036-66036	HILLSDALE	66432-66432	HAVENSVILLE	66751-66751	LA HARPE	66955-66955	MAHASKA
66039-66039	KINCAID	66433-66433	MARYSVILLE	66753-66753	MC CUNE	66956-66956	MANKATO
66040-66040	LA CYGNE	66434-66435	HIAWATHA	66754-66754	MAPLETON	66958-66958	MORROWVILLE
66041-66041	LANCASTER	66436-66436	HOLTON	66755-66755	MORAN	66959-66959	MUNDEN
66042-66042	LANE	66438-66438	HOME	66756-66756	MULBERRY	66960-66960	NARKA
66043-66043	LANSING	66439-66439	HORTON	66757-66757	NEODESHA	66961-66961	NORWAY
66044-66047	LAWRENCE	66440-66440	HOYT	66758-66758	NEOSHO FALLS	66962-66962	PALMER
66048-66048	LEAVENWORTH	66441-66441	JUNCTION CITY	66759-66759	NEW ALBANY	66963-66963	RANDALL
66049-66049	LAWRENCE	66442-66442	FORT RILEY	66760-66760	OPOLIS	66964-66964	REPUBLIC
66050-66050	LECOMPTON	66449-66449	LEONARDVILLE	66761-66761	PIQUA	66966-66966	SCANDIA
66051-66051	OLATHE	66450-66450	LOUISVILLE	66762-66762	PITTSBURG	66967-66967	SMITH CENTER
66052-66052	LINWOOD	66451-66451	LYNDON	66763-66763	FRONTENAC	66968-66968	WASHINGTON
66053-66053	LOUISBURG	66501-66501	MC FARLAND	66767-66767	PRESCOTT	66970-66970	WEBBER
66054-66054	MC LOUTH	66502-66506	MANHATTAN	66769-66769	REDFIELD	67001-67001	ANDALE
66056-66056	MOUND CITY	66507-66507	MAPLE HILL	66770-66770	RIVERTON	67002-67002	ANDOVER
66058-66058	MUSCOTAH	66508-66508	MARYSVILLE	66771-66771	SAINT PAUL	67003-67003	ANTHONY
66060-66060	NORTONVILLE	66509-66509	MAYETTA	66772-66772	SAVONBURG	67004-67004	ARGONIA
66061-66063	OLATHE	66510-66510	MELVERN	66773-66773	SCAMMON	67005-67005	ARKANSAS CITY
66064-66064	OSAWATOMIE	66512-66512	MERIDEN	66775-66775	STARK	67008-67008	ATLANTA
66066-66066	OSKALOOSA	66514-66514	MILFORD	66776-66776	THAYER	67009-67009	ATTICA
66067-66067	OTTAWA	66515-66515	MORRILL	66777-66777	TORONTO	67010-67010	AUGUSTA
66070-66070	OZAWKIE	66516-66516	NETAWAKA	66778-66778	TREECE	67012-67012	BEAUMONT
66071-66071	PAOLA	66517-66517	OGDEN	66779-66779	UNIONTOWN	67013-67013	BELLE PLAINE
66072-66072	PARKER	66518-66518	OKETO	66780-66780	WALNUT	67015-67015	BELVIDERE
66073-66073	PERRY	66520-66520	OLSBURG	66781-66781	WEIR	67016-67016	BENTLEY
66075-66075	PLEASANTON	66521-66521	ONAGA	66782-66782	WEST MINERAL	67017-67017	BENTON
66076-66076	POMONA	66522-66522	ONEIDA	66783-66783	YATES CENTER	67018-67018	BLUFF CITY
66077-66077	POTTER	66523-66523	OSAGE CITY	66801-66801	EMPORIA	67019-67019	BURDEN
66078-66078	PRINCETON	66524-66524	OVERBROOK	66830-66830	ADMIRE	67020-67020	BURRTON
66079-66079	RANTOUL	66526-66526	PAXICO	66833-66833	ALLEN	67021-67021	BYERS
66080-66080	RICHMOND	66527-66527	POWHATTAN	66834-66834	ALTA VISTA	67022-67022	CALDWELL
66083-66083	SPRING HILL	66528-66528	QUENEMO	66835-66835	AMERICUS	67023-67023	CAMBRIDGE
66085-66085	STILWELL	66531-66531	RILEY	66838-66838	BURDICK	67024-67024	CEDAR VALE
66086-66086	TONGANOXIE	66532-66532	ROBINSON	66839-66839	BURLINGTON	67025-67025	CHENEY
66087-66087	TROY	66533-66533	ROSSVILLE	66840-66840	BURNS	67026-67026	CLEARWATER
66088-66088	VALLEY FALLS	66534-66534	SABETHA	66842-66842	CASSODAY	67028-67028	COATS
66090-66090	WATHENA	66535-66535	SAINT GEORGE	66843-66843	CEDAR POINT	67029-67029	COLDWATER
66091-66091	WELDA	66536-66536	SAINT MARYS	66845-66845	COTTONWOOD FALLS	67030-67030	COLWICH
66092-66092	WELLSVILLE	66537-66537	SCRANTON	66846-66846	COUNCIL GROVE	67031-67031	CONWAY SPRINGS
66093-66093	WESTPHALIA	66538-66538	SENECA	66849-66849	DWIGHT	67032-67032	CALDWELL
66094-66094	WHITE CLOUD	66539-66539	SILVER LAKE	66850-66850	ELMDALE	67035-67035	CUNNINGHAM
66095-66095	WILLIAMSBURG	66540-66540	SOLDIER	66851-66851	FLORENCE	67036-67036	DANVILLE
66097-66097	WINCHESTER	66541-66541	SUMMERFIELD	66852-66852	GRIDLEY	67037-67037	DERBY
66100-66112	KANSAS CITY	66542-66542	TECUMSEH	66853-66853	HAMILTON	67038-67038	DEXTER
66113-66113	EDWARDSVILLE	66543-66543	VASSAR	66854-66854	HARTFORD	67039-67039	DOUGLASS
66115-66160	KANSAS CITY	66544-66544	VERMILLION	66855-66855	LAMONT	67041-67041	ELBING
66200-66201	SHAWNEE MISSION	66545-66545	VLIETS	66856-66856	LEBO	67042-67042	EL DORADO
66201-66201	MISSION	66546-66546	WAKARUSA	66857-66857	LE ROY	67045-67045	EUREKA
66202-66222	SHAWNEE MISSION	66547-66547	WAMEGO	66858-66858	LINCOLNVILLE	67047-67047	FALL RIVER
66222-66222	MISSION	66548-66548	WATERVILLE	66859-66859	LOST SPRINGS	67049-67049	FREEPORT
66223-66251	SHAWNEE MISSION	66549-66549	WESTMORELAND	66860-66860	MADISON	67050-67050	GARDEN PLAIN
66251-66251	OVERLAND PARK	66550-66550	WETMORE	66861-66861	MARION	67051-67051	GEUDA SPRINGS
66262-66283	SHAWNEE MISSION	66551-66551	WHEATON	66862-66862	MATFIELD GREEN	67052-67052	GODDARD
66283-66283	OVERLAND PARK	66552-66552	WHITING	66863-66863	NEAL	67053-67053	GOESSEL
66285-66285	SHAWNEE MISSION	66554-66554	RANDOLPH	66864-66864	NEOSHO RAPIDS	67054-67054	GREENSBURG
66285-66285	LENEXA	66555-66555	MARYSVILLE	66865-66865	OLPE	67055-67055	GREENWICH
66286-66286	SHAWNEE MISSION	66600-66699	TOPEKA	66866-66866	PEABODY	67056-67056	HALSTEAD
66286-66286	SHAWNEE	66701-66701	FORT SCOTT	66868-66868	READING	67057-67057	HARDTNER
66401-66401	ALMA	66710-66710	ALTOONA	66869-66869	STRONG CITY	67058-67058	HARPER
66402-66402	AUBURN	66711-66711	ARCADIA	66870-66870	VIRGIL	67059-67059	HAVILAND

67060-67060 HAYSVILLE	67401-67402 SALINA	67546-67546 INMAN	67733-67733 EDSON
67061-67061 HAZELTON	67410-67410 ABILENE	67547-67547 KINSLEY	67734-67734 GEM
67062-67062 HESSTON	67414-67414 ADA	67548-67548 LA CROSSE	67735-67735 GOODLAND
67063-67063 HILLSBORO	67416-67416 ASSARIA	67550-67550 LARNED	67736-67736 GOVE
67065-67065 ISABEL	67417-67417 AURORA	67552-67552 LEWIS	67737-67737 GRAINFIELD
67066-67066 IUKA	67418-67418 BARNARD	67553-67553 LIEBENTHAL	67738-67738 GRINNELL
67067-67067 KECHI	67420-67420 BELOIT	67554-67554 LYONS	67739-67739 HERNDON
67068-67068 KINGMAN	67422-67422 BENNINGTON	67556-67556 MC CRACKEN	67740-67740 HOXIE
67070-67070 KIOWA	67423-67423 BEVERLY	67557-67557 MACKSVILLE	67741-67741 KANORADO
67071-67071 LAKE CITY	67425-67425 BROOKVILLE	67559-67559 NEKOMA	67743-67743 LEVANT
67072-67072 LATHAM	67427-67427 BUSHTON	67560-67560 NESS CITY	67744-67744 LUDELL
67073-67073 LEHIGH	67428-67428 CANTON	67561-67561 NICKERSON	67745-67745 MC DONALD
67074-67074 LEON	67429-67429 CARLTON	67562-67562 ODIN	67747-67747 MONUMENT
67101-67101 MAIZE	67430-67430 CAWKER CITY	67563-67563 OFFERLE	67748-67748 OAKLEY
67102-67102 MAPLE CITY	67431-67431 CHAPMAN	67564-67564 OLMITZ	67749-67749 OBERLIN
67103-67103 MAYFIELD	67432-67432 CLAY CENTER	67565-67565 OTIS	67751-67751 PARK
67104-67104 MEDICINE LODGE	67436-67436 DELPHOS	67566-67566 PARTRIDGE	67752-67752 QUINTER
67105-67105 MILAN	67437-67437 DOWNS	67567-67567 PAWNEE ROCK	67753-67753 REXFORD
67106-67106 MILTON	67438-67438 DURHAM	67568-67568 PLEVNA	67755-67755 RUSSELL SPRINGS
67107-67107 MOUNDRIDGE	67439-67439 ELLSWORTH	67569-67569 TURON	67756-67756 SAINT FRANCIS
67108-67108 MOUNT HOPE	67441-67441 ENTERPRISE	67570-67570 PRETTY PRAIRIE	67757-67757 SELDEN
67109-67109 MULLINVILLE	67442-67442 FALUN	67572-67572 RANSOM	67758-67758 SHARON SPRINGS
67110-67110 MULVANE	67443-67443 GALVA	67573-67573 RAYMOND	67759-67759 STUDLEY
67111-67111 MURDOCK	67444-67444 GENESEO	67574-67574 ROZEL	67761-67761 WALLACE
67112-67112 NASHVILLE	67445-67445 GLASCO	67575-67575 RUSH CENTER	67762-67762 WESKAN
67114-67114 NEWTON	67446-67446 GLEN ELDER	67576-67576 SAINT JOHN	67764-67764 WINONA
67117-67117 NORTH NEWTON	67447-67447 GREEN	67577-67577 SEWARD	67801-67801 DODGE CITY
67118-67118 NORWICH	67448-67448 GYPSUM	67578-67578 STAFFORD	67831-67831 ASHLAND
67119-67119 OXFORD	67449-67449 HERINGTON	67579-67579 STERLING	67834-67834 BUCKLIN
67120-67120 PECK	67450-67450 HOLYROOD	67581-67581 SYLVIA	67835-67835 CIMARRON
67122-67122 PIEDMONT	67451-67451 HOPE	67582-67582 TIMKEN	67836-67836 COOLIDGE
67123-67123 POTWIN	67452-67452 HUNTER	67583-67583 TURON	67837-67837 COPELAND
67124-67124 PRATT	67454-67454 KANOPOLIS	67584-67584 UTICA	67838-67838 DEERFIELD
67127-67127 PROTECTION	67455-67455 LINCOLN	67585-67585 YODER	67839-67839 DIGHTON
67128-67128 RAGO	67456-67456 LINDSBORG	67601-67601 HAYS	67840-67840 ENGLEWOOD
67131-67131 ROCK	67457-67457 LITTLE RIVER	67621-67621 AGRA	67841-67841 ENSIGN
67132-67132 ROSALIA	67458-67458 LONGFORD	67622-67622 ALMENA	67842-67842 FORD
67133-67133 ROSE HILL	67459-67459 LORRAINE	67623-67623 ALTON	67843-67843 FORT DODGE
67134-67134 SAWYER	67460-67460 MCPHERSON	67625-67625 BOGUE	67844-67844 FOWLER
67135-67135 SEDGWICK	67463-67463 MANCHESTER	67626-67626 BUNKER HILL	67846-67846 GARDEN CITY
67137-67137 SEVERY	67464-67464 MARQUETTE	67627-67627 CATHARINE	67849-67849 HANSTON
67138-67138 SHARON	67465-67465 MENTOR	67628-67628 CEDAR	67850-67850 HEALY
67140-67140 SOUTH HAVEN	67466-67466 MILTONVALE	67629-67629 CLAYTON	67851-67851 HOLCOMB
67142-67142 SPIVEY	67467-67467 MINNEAPOLIS	67630-67630 CODELL	67853-67853 INGALLS
67143-67143 SUN CITY	67468-67468 MORGANVILLE	67631-67631 COLLYER	67854-67854 JETMORE
67144-67144 TOWANDA	67469-67469 ENTERPRISE	67632-67632 DAMAR	67855-67855 JOHNSON
67146-67146 UDALL	67470-67470 NEW CAMBRIA	67634-67634 DORRANCE	67856-67856 KALVESTA
67147-67147 VALLEY CENTER	67472-67472 OAKHILL	67635-67635 DRESDEN	67857-67857 KENDALL
67149-67149 VIOLA	67473-67473 OSBORNE	67636-67636 EDMOND	67858-67858 KINGSDOWN
67150-67150 WALDRON	67474-67474 PORTIS	67637-67637 ELLIS	67859-67859 KISMET
67151-67151 WALTON	67475-67475 RAMONA	67638-67638 GAYLORD	67860-67860 LAKIN
67152-67152 WELLINGTON	67476-67476 ROXBURY	67639-67639 GLADE	67861-67861 LEOTI
67154-67154 WHITEWATER	67478-67478 SIMPSON	67640-67640 GORHAM	67862-67862 MANTER
67155-67155 WILMORE	67479-67479 SMOLAN	67641-67641 HARLAN	67863-67863 MARIENTHAL
67156-67156 WINFIELD	67480-67480 SOLOMON	67642-67642 HILL CITY	67864-67864 MEADE
67159-67159 ZENDA	67481-67481 SYLVAN GROVE	67643-67643 JENNINGS	67865-67865 MINNEOLA
67200-67220 WICHITA	67482-67482 TALMAGE	67644-67644 KIRWIN	67867-67867 MONTEZUMA
67221-67221 MC CONNELL A F B	67483-67483 TAMPA	67645-67645 LENORA	67868-67868 PIERCEVILLE
67221-67221 MCCONNELL AFB	67484-67484 TESCOTT	67646-67646 LOGAN	67869-67869 PLAINS
67223-67236 WICHITA	67485-67485 TIPTON	67647-67647 LONG ISLAND	67870-67870 SATANTA
67240-67240 DENNIS THE MENACE	67487-67487 WAKEFIELD	67648-67648 LUCAS	67871-67871 SCOTT CITY
67251-67278 WICHITA	67488-67488 WELLS	67649-67649 LURAY	67874-67874 SHIELDS
67301-67301 INDEPENDENCE	67490-67490 WILSON	67650-67650 MORLAND	67876-67876 SPEARVILLE
67330-67330 ALTAMONT	67491-67491 WINDOM	67651-67651 NATOMA	67877-67877 SUBLETTE
67332-67332 BARTLETT	67492-67492 WOODBINE	67652-67652 NEW ALMELO	67878-67878 SYRACUSE
67333-67333 CANEY	67501-67504 HUTCHINSON	67653-67653 NORCATUR	67879-67879 TRIBUNE
67334-67334 CHAUTAUQUA	67505-67505 SOUTH HUTCHINSON	67654-67654 NORTON	67880-67880 ULYSSES
67335-67335 CHERRYVALE	67510-67510 ABBYVILLE	67656-67656 OGALLAH	67882-67882 WRIGHT
67336-67336 CHETOPA	67511-67511 ALBERT	67657-67657 PALCO	67901-67905 LIBERAL
67337-67337 COFFEYVILLE	67512-67512 ALDEN	67658-67658 PARADISE	67950-67950 ELKHART
67340-67340 DEARING	67513-67513 ALEXANDER	67659-67659 PENOKEE	67951-67951 HUGOTON
67341-67341 DENNIS	67514-67514 ARLINGTON	67660-67660 PFEIFER	67952-67952 MOSCOW
67342-67342 EDNA	67515-67515 ARNOLD	67661-67661 PHILLIPSBURG	67953-67953 RICHFIELD
67344-67344 ELK CITY	67516-67516 BAZINE	67663-67663 PLAINVILLE	67954-67954 ROLLA
67345-67345 ELK FALLS	67517-67517 BEAVER	67664-67664 PRAIRIE VIEW	
67346-67346 GRENOLA	67518-67518 BEELER	67665-67665 RUSSELL	
67347-67347 HAVANA	67519-67519 BELPRE	67667-67667 SCHOENCHEN	
67349-67349 HOWARD	67520-67520 BISON	67669-67669 STOCKTON	
67351-67351 LIBERTY	67521-67521 BROWNELL	67670-67670 STUTTGART	
67352-67352 LONGTON	67522-67522 BUHLER	67671-67671 VICTORIA	
67353-67353 MOLINE	67523-67523 BURDETT	67672-67672 WA KEENEY	
67354-67354 MOUND VALLEY	67524-67524 CHASE	67673-67673 WALDO	
67355-67355 NIOTAZE	67525-67525 CLAFLIN	67674-67674 WALKER	
67356-67356 OSWEGO	67526-67526 ELLINWOOD	67675-67675 WOODSTON	
67357-67357 PARSONS	67529-67529 GARFIELD	67676-67676 ZURICH	
67360-67360 PERU	67530-67530 GREAT BEND	67701-67701 COLBY	
67361-67361 SEDAN	67543-67543 HAVEN	67730-67730 ATWOOD	
67363-67363 SYCAMORE	67544-67544 HOISINGTON	67731-67731 BIRD CITY	
67364-67364 TYRO	67545-67545 HUDSON	67732-67732 BREWSTER	

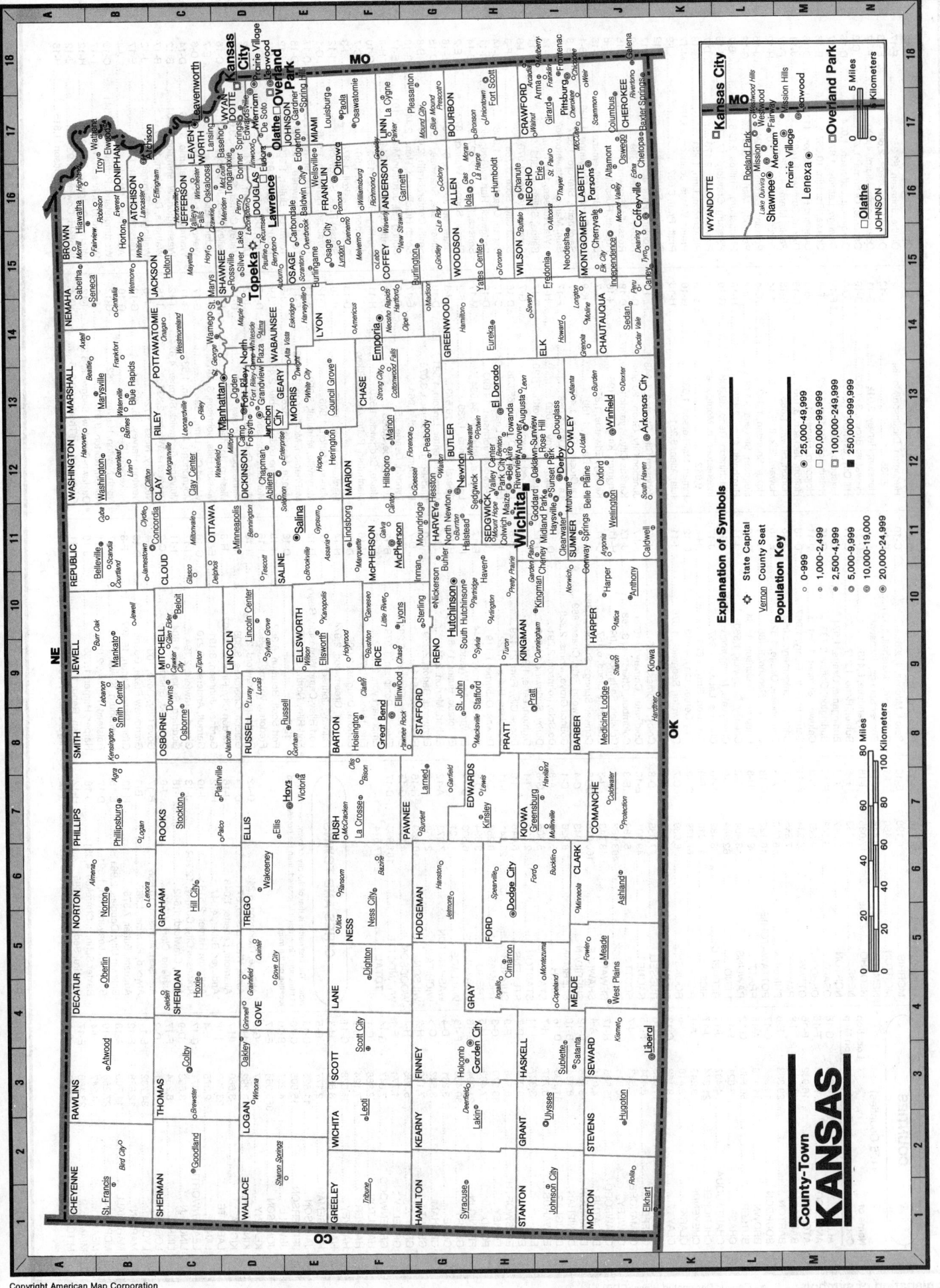

County-Town
KANSAS

Copyright American Map Corporation

COUNTIES
(105 Counties)

Name of County	Population	Location on Map
ALLEN	14,638	G-16
ANDERSON	7,803	F-16
ATCHISON	16,932	B-16
BARBER	5,874	I-8
BARTON	29,382	E-8
BOURBON	14,966	G-17
BROWN	11,128	A-15
BUTLER	50,580	G-12
CHASE	3,021	F-13
CHAUTAUQUA	4,407	J-14
CHEROKEE	21,374	J-17
CHEYENNE	3,243	A-1
CLARK	2,418	I-6
CLAY	9,158	C-12
CLOUD	11,023	C-10
COFFEY	8,404	F-15
COMANCHE	2,313	J-7
COWLEY	36,915	I-12
CRAWFORD	35,568	H-17
DECATUR	4,021	A-4
DICKINSON	18,958	D-12
DONIPHAN	8,134	B-16
DOUGLAS	81,798	D-16
EDWARDS	3,787	H-7
ELK	3,327	I-14
ELLIS	26,004	D-7
ELLSWORTH	6,586	E-9
FINNEY	33,070	G-3
FORD	27,463	H-5
FRANKLIN	21,994	E-16
GEARY	30,453	D-14
GOVE	3,231	D-4
GRAHAM	3,543	C-5
GRANT	7,159	H-2
GRAY	5,396	H-4
GREELEY	1,774	E-1
GREENWOOD	7,847	G-14
HAMILTON	2,388	G-1
HARPER	7,124	J-9
HARVEY	31,028	H-11
HASKELL	3,886	H-3
HODGEMAN	2,177	G-5
JACKSON	11,525	C-15
JEFFERSON	15,905	C-16
JEWELL	4,251	B-10
JOHNSON	355,054	E-17
KEARNY	4,027	G-2
KINGMAN	8,292	H-9
KIOWA	3,660	I-7
LABETTE	23,693	I-16
LANE	2,375	E-4
LEAVENWORTH	64,371	C-17
LINCOLN	3,653	D-9
LINN	8,254	F-17
LOGAN	3,081	D-2
LYON	34,732	E-14
MARION	12,888	F-12
MARSHALL	11,705	A-13
McPHERSON	27,268	F-11
MEADE	4,247	I-4
MIAMI	23,466	E-17
MITCHELL	7,203	C-9
MONTGOMERY	38,816	I-15
MORRIS	6,198	E-13
MORTON	3,480	A-14
NEMAHA	10,446	A-14
NEOSHO	17,035	D-17
NESS	4,033	F-5
NORTON	5,947	A-5
OSAGE	15,248	E-15
OSBORNE	4,867	C-8
OTTAWA	5,634	C-11
PAWNEE	7,555	G-7
PHILLIPS	6,590	A-6
POTTAWATOMIE	16,128	C-13
PRATT	9,702	H-8
RAWLINS	3,404	A-2
RENO	62,389	G-9
REPUBLIC	6,482	A-10
RICE	10,610	F-9
RILEY	67,139	C-13
ROOKS	6,039	C-7
RUSH	3,842	E-7
RUSSELL	7,835	D-8
SALINE	49,301	E-10
SCOTT	5,289	E-3
SEDGWICK	403,662	H-11
SEWARD	18,743	I-3
SHAWNEE	160,976	D-15
SHERIDAN	3,043	C-4
SHERMAN	6,926	C-1
SMITH	5,078	A-8
STAFFORD	5,365	G-8
STANTON	2,333	I-1
STEVENS	5,048	I-2
SUMNER	25,841	I-11
THOMAS	8,258	C-3
TREGO	3,694	D-5
WABAUNSEE	6,603	D-14
WALLACE	1,821	D-1
WASHINGTON	7,073	A-12
WICHITA	2,758	E-2
WILSON	10,289	H-15
WOODSON	4,116	G-15
WYANDOTTE	161,993	D-17
TOTAL	**2,477,574**	

CITIES AND TOWNS

Note: The first name is that of the city or town, second, that of the county in which it is located, then the population and location on the map.

Abilene, Dickinson, 6,242 — D-12
Alma, Wabaunsee, 871 — D-14
Altamont, Labette, 1,048 — J-16
Andover, Butler, 4,047 — H-12
Anthony, Harper, 2,516 — J-10
Arkansas City, Cowley, 12,762 — J-13
Arma, Crawford, 1,542 — I-18
Ashland, Clark, 1,032 — J-6
Atchison, Atchison, 10,656 — B-17
Atwood, Rawlins, 1,388 — B-3
Augusta, Butler, 7,876 — H-13
Baldwin City, Douglas, 2,961 — E-16
Basehor, Leavenworth, 1,591 — D-17
Baxter Springs, Cherokee, 4,351 — J-18
Bel Aire, Sedgwick, 3,695 — H-12
Belle Plaine, Sumner, 1,649 — I-12
Belleville, Republic, 2,517 — B-11
Beloit, Mitchell, 4,066 — C-10
Blue Rapids, Marshall, 1,131 — B-13
Bonner Springs, Johnson/Wyandotte, 6,413 — D-17
Buhler, Reno, 1,277 — G-11
Burlingame, Osage, 1,074 — E-15
Burlington, Coffey, 2,735 — F-15
Caldwell, Sumner, 1,351 — J-11
• Camp Forsyth, Geary, 1,967 — D-13
Caney, Montgomery, 2,062 — J-15
Carbondale, Osage, 1,526 — E-15
Chanute, Neosho, 9,488 — H-16
Chapman, Dickinson, 1,264 — D-12
Cherryvale, Montgomery, 2,464 — I-15
Chetopa, Labette, 1,357 — J-17
Cimarron, Gray, 1,626 — H-5
Clay Center, Clay, 4,613 — C-12
Clearwater, Sedgwick, 1,875 — I-11
Coffeyville, Montgomery, 12,917 — J-16
Colby, Thomas, 5,396 — C-3
Coldwater, Comanche, 939 — J-7
Columbus, Cherokee, 3,268 — J-17
Colwich, Sedgwick, 1,091 — H-11
Concordia, Cloud, 6,167 — C-11
Conway Springs, Sumner, 1,384 — I-11
Cottonwood Falls, Chase, 889 — F-13
Council Grove, Morris, 2,228 — E-14
De Soto, Johnson, 2,291 — D-17
Derby, Sedgwick, 14,699 — I-12
Dighton, Lane, 1,361 — F-4
Dodge City, Ford, 21,129 — H-5
Douglass, Butler, 1,722 — I-12
Downs, Osborne, 1,119 — C-9
Edgerton, Johnson, 1,244 — E-17
Edwardsville, Wyandotte, 3,979 — D-17
El Dorado, Butler, 11,504 — H-13
Elkhart, Morton, 2,318 — J-1
Ellinwood, Barton, 2,329 — F-9
Ellis, Ellis, 1,814 — D-7
Ellsworth, Ellsworth, 2,294 — E-9
Elwood, Doniphan, 1,079 — B-17
Emporia, Lyon, 25,512 — F-14
Erie, Neosho, 1,276 — H-16
Eudora, Douglas, 3,006 — D-17
Eureka, Greenwood, 2,974 — G-14
Fairway, Johnson, 4,173 — L-17
Fort Riley-Camp Whiteside, Geary — D-13
• Fort Riley North, Geary/Riley, 12,848 — D-13
Fort Scott, Bourbon, 8,362 — H-18
Fredonia, Wilson, 2,599 — I-15
Frontenac, Crawford, 2,588 — I-18
Galena, Cherokee, 3,308 — J-18
Garden City, Finney, 24,097 — H-3
Gardner, Johnson, 3,191 — E-17
Garnett, Anderson, 3,210 — G-16
Girard, Crawford, 2,794 — I-17
Goddard, Sedgwick, 1,804 — I-11
Goodland, Sherman, 4,983 — C-2
Gove City, Gove, 103 — D-4
Grandview Plaza, Geary, 1,233 — D-13
Great Bend, Barton, 15,427 — F-8
Greensburg, Kiowa, 1,792 — I-7
Halstead, Harvey, 2,015 — G-11
Harper, Harper, 1,735 — J-10
Haven, Reno, 1,198 — H-11
Hays, Ellis, 17,767 — E-7
Haysville, Sedgwick, 8,364 — I-11
Herington, Dickinson/Morris, 2,685 — E-12
Hesston, Harvey, 3,012 — G-11
Hiawatha, Brown, 3,603 — B-16
Hill City, Graham, 1,835 — C-6
Hillsboro, Marion, 2,704 — F-12
Hoisington, Barton, 3,182 — F-8
Holcomb, Finney, 1,400 — G-3
Holton, Jackson, 3,196 — C-15
Horton, Brown, 1,885 — B-16
Howard, Elk, 815 — I-14
Hoxie, Sheridan, 1,342 — C-4
Hugoton, Stevens, 3,179 — J-2
Humboldt, Allen, 2,178 — H-16
Hutchinson, Reno, 39,308 — G-10
Independence, Montgomery, 9,942 — I-15
Inman, McPherson, 1,035 — G-10
Iola, Allen, 6,351 — H-16
Jetmore, Hodgeman, 850 — G-6
Johnson City, Stanton, 1,348 — I-1
Junction City, Geary, 20,604 — D-13
Kansas City, Wyandotte, 149,767 — D-18
Kingman, Kingman, 3,196 — H-10
Kinsley, Edwards, 1,875 — H-7
Kiowa, Barber, 1,160 — J-9
La Crosse, Rush, 1,427 — F-7
La Cygne, Linn, 1,066 — F-17
Lakin, Kearny, 2,060 — G-2
Lansing, Leavenworth, 7,120 — C-17
Larned, Pawnee, 4,490 — G-7
Lawrence, Douglas, 65,608 — D-16
Leavenworth, Leavenworth, 38,495 — C-17
Leawood, Johnson, 19,693 — E-17
Lenexa, Johnson, 34,034 — E-17
Leoti, Wichita, 1,738 — E-2
Liberal, Seward, 16,573 — J-3
Lincoln Center, Lincoln, 1,381 — D-10
Lindsborg, McPherson, 3,076 — F-11
Louisburg, Miami, 1,964 — F-17
Lyndon, Osage, 964 — E-15
Lyons, Rice, 3,688 — F-9
Maize, Sedgwick, 1,520 — H-11
Manhattan, Pottawatomie/Riley, 37,712 — D-13
Mankato, Jewell, 1,037 — B-10
Marion, Marion, 1,906 — F-12
Marysville, Marshall, 3,359 — B-13
McPherson, McPherson, 12,422 — F-11
Meade, Meade, 1,526 — I-4
Medicine Lodge, Barber, 2,453 — J-8
Merriam, Johnson, 11,821 — L-17
Midland Park, Sedgwick — H-11
Minneapolis, Ottawa, 1,983 — D-11
Mission, Johnson, 9,504 — L-17
Mission Hills, Johnson, 3,446 — L-17
Mound City, Linn, 789 — F-17
Moundridge, McPherson, 1,531 — F-11
Mulvane, Sedgwick/Sumner, 4,674 — I-11
Neodesha, Wilson, 2,837 — H-15
Ness City, Ness, 1,724 — F-6
Newton, Harvey, 16,700 — H-11
Nickerson, Reno, 1,137 — G-10
North Newton, Harvey, 1,262 — H-11
Norton, Norton, 3,017 — A-5
• Oaklawn-Sunview, Sedgwick, 3,240 — H-11
Oakley, Logan/Thomas, 2,045 — D-4
Oberlin, Decatur, 2,197 — B-4
Ogden, Riley, 1,494 — D-13
Olathe, Johnson, 63,352 — E-17
Osage City, Osage, 2,689 — E-15
Osawatomie, Miami, 4,590 — F-17
Osborne, Osborne, 1,778 — C-8
Oskaloosa, Jefferson, 1,074 — D-16
Oswego, Labette, 1,870 — J-17
Ottawa, Franklin, 10,667 — E-16
Overland Park, Johnson, 111,790 — D-18
Oxford, Sumner, 1,143 — J-11
Paola, Miami, 4,698 — F-17
Park City, Sedgwick, 5,050 — H-12
Parsons, Labette, 11,924 — I-16
Peabody, Marion, 1,349 — F-12
Phillipsburg, Phillips, 2,828 — A-6
Pittsburg, Crawford, 17,775 — I-18
Plainville, Rooks, 2,173 — C-7
Pleasanton, Linn, 1,231 — G-18
Prairie Village, Johnson, 23,186 — M-17
Pratt, Pratt, 6,687 — H-8
Riverview, Sedgwick — H-11
Roeland Park, Johnson, 7,706 — L-17
Rose Hill, Butler, 2,399 — I-12
Rossville, Shawnee, 1,052 — D-15
Russell, Russell, 4,781 — D-8
Sabetha, Brown/Nemaha, 2,341 — A-15
Saint Francis, Cheyenne, 1,495 — B-1
Saint John, Stafford, 1,357 — G-8
Saint Marys, Pottawatomie/Wabaunsee, 1,791 — D-14
Salina, Saline, 42,303 — E-11
Satanta, Haskell, 1,073 — I-3
Scott City, Scott, 3,785 — F-3
Sedan, Chautauqua, 1,306 — J-14
Sedgwick, Harvey/Sedgwick, 1,438 — H-11
Seneca, Nemaha, 2,027 — A-14
Sharon Springs, Wallace, 872 — D-2
Shawnee, Johnson, 37,993 — L-16
Silver Lake, Shawnee, 1,390 — D-15
Smith Center, Smith, 2,016 — B-8
South Hutchinson, Reno, 2,444 — G-10
Spring Hill, Johnson/Miami, 2,191 — E-17
Stafford, Stafford, 1,344 — H-9
Sterling, Rice, 2,115 — G-10
Stockton, Rooks, 1,507 — C-7
Sublette, Haskell, 1,378 — I-3
Sunset Park, Sedgwick — I-12
Syracuse, Hamilton, 1,606 — G-1
Tonganoxie, Leavenworth, 2,347 — D-17
Topeka, Shawnee, 119,883 — D-15
Towanda, Butler, 1,289 — H-12
Tribune, Greeley, 918 — F-1
Troy, Doniphan, 1,073 — B-17
Ulysses, Grant, 5,474 — H-2
Valley Center, Sedgwick, 3,624 — H-11
Valley Falls, Jefferson, 1,253 — C-16
Victoria, Ellis, 1,157 — E-7
Wakeeney, Trego, 2,161 — D-6
Wamego, Pottawatomie, 3,706 — D-14
Washington, Washington, 1,304 — B-12
Wathena, Doniphan, 1,160 — B-17
Wellington, Sumner, 8,411 — I-11
Wellsville, Franklin, 1,563 — E-16
West Plains, Meade — I-4
Westmoreland, Pottawatomie, 541 — C-13
Westwood, Johnson, 1,772 — L-17
Wichita, Sedgwick, 304,011 — H-11
Winfield, Cowley, 11,931 — J-12
Yates Center, Woodson, 1,815 — H-15

Explanation of symbols: • – Census Designated Place (CDP)

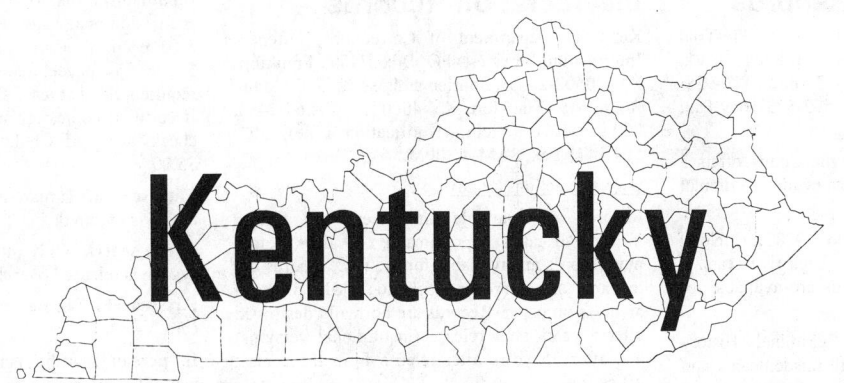

General Help Numbers:

Governor's Office
700 Capitol Ave, Room 100
Frankfort, KY 40601
http://gov.state.ky.us

502-564-2611
Fax 502-564-2517
7:30AM-5PM

Attorney General's Office
700 Capitol Ave, Ste. 118
Frankfort, KY 40601
www..law.state.ky.us

502-696-5300
Fax 502-564-2894
8AM-5PM

Legislative Records
Kentucky General Assembly, Research Commission
700 Capitol Ave, Room 300
Frankfort, KY 40601
www.lrc.state.ky.us

502-564-8100
Fax 502-564-6543
8AM-4:30PM

State Archives
300 Coffee Tree Rd
Frankfort, KY 40601
www.kdla.ky.gov/index.htm

502-564-8300
Fax 502-564-5773
8AM-4PM T-SA

State Specifics:

Capital:
Frankfort
Franklin County

Time Zone:
EST*

* Kentucky's forty western-most counties are CST: They are: Adair, Allen, Ballard, Barren, Breckinridge, Butler, Caldwell, Calloway, Carlisle, Christian, Clinton, Crittenden, Cumberland, Daviess, Edmonson, Fulton, Graves, Grayson, Hancock, Hart, Henderson, Hickman, Hopkins, Livingstone, Logan, Marshall, McCracken, McLean, Metcalfe, Monroe, Muhlenberg, Ohio,Russell, Simpson, Todd, Trigg, Union, Warren, Wayne, and Webster.

Number of Counties:
120

Population:
4,145,922

Web Site:
www.kentucky.gov/

State Agencies

Criminal Records

Kentucky State Police, Criminal Identification and Records Branch, 1250 Louisville Rd, Frankfort, KY 40601; 502-227-8713, 502-226-7422-Fax; 8AM-4PM.

www.kentuckystatepolice.org

Interestingly, local Kentucky courts will not do criminal searches. They refer all requesters to the Administrative Office of Courts in Frankfort, KY; phone 502-573-2350. This office will also suggest to check the court system.

Records are available from 1952 on for criminal records. It takes a minimum of 30 days before new records are available for inquiry. Records are indexed on inhouse computer, fingerprint cards.

Nearly 75% of records are automated. 100% of arrest records are fingerprint supported. 69% of all arrests in database have final dispositions recorded, 59% for those arrests within last 5 years.

Searching: Records are available to all requesters as long as a signed release is submitted. Special forms are suggested for certain employment purposes such as nursing, schools, lottery, EMT, YMCA, daycare, and adoptive/foster parent background searches. Include the following in your request-signed release from subject, full name, date of birth, Social Security Number, reason for information request. Fingerprints are not requested. The special forms may be downloaded from the webpage. Statistical information about criminal offenses and accidents

is available from 1971 on. The following data is not released: juvenile records. Records without dispositions, including pending and dismissed cases, are not released.

Access by: mail, in person.

Fee & Payment: The fee is $10.00 per name. Fee payee: Kentucky State Treasurer. Prepayment required. Personal checks accepted. No credit cards accepted.

Mail search: Turnaround time: 2 to 3 weeks. A SASE is requested.

In person search: Turnaround time is while you wait. There is a limit of 5 searches.

Statewide Court Records

Administrative Office of the Courts, Pre-Trial Services Records Unit, 100 Millcreek Park, Frankfort, KY 40601; 502-573-1682, 800-928-6381 (Set-up Account), 502-573-1669-Fax; 7:30AM-5PM. www.kycourts.net

The Administrative Office of the Courts offers a service of providing statewide criminal background checks.

Records are available back to 1978 for felony convictions, and misdemeanors back five years. It takes 1 day before new records are available for inquiry.

Searching: Their CourtNet Criminal History database contains records of all misdemeanor and traffic cases for at least the last five years, and felonies dating back to 1978 and it contains information from all 120 counties. Include the following in your request-name, DOB and SSN if known. The required Release Form is available from the AOC, call the number above.

Access by: mail, fax, in person, online.

Fee & Payment: Fee is $10.00 per record request, $15.00 if by fax. Fee payee: State Treasurer of Kentucky Personal checks accepted. Prepaid accounts are offered.

Mail search: Turnaround time: 3-7 days. A SASE is required.

Fax search: A pre-paid search request is permitted.

In person search: Walk-in hours are above, drive-through until 10:30PM.

Online search: Searching is limited. You may search six days of daily court calendars by county for free at http://dockets.kycourts.net/. From the website above search Supreme Court docket info and search Appellate opinions.

Sexual Offender Registry

Kentucky State Police, Criminal Identification and Records Branch, 1250 Louisville Rd, Frankfort, KY 40601; 502-227-8700, 866-564-5652 (Alert Line), 502-226-7419-Fax; 8AM-4PM.

http://kspsor.state.ky.us

The Alert Line is open 24 hours daily. Sex offenders must register their location for a minimum of ten years or a maximum of their lifetime, depending on crime.

Records are available from 7/15/94 forward (convictions) or incarcerated or sentenced if after July 15, 1998.

Searching: Only offenders convicted of statutorily covered crimes who are convicted after July 15, 1994 or incarcerated or sentenced after July 15, 1998 are listed.

Access by: phone, online.

Phone search: The Alert Line provides up-to-date information. Provide your telephone number and up to three ZIP Codes to monitor. You will be notified if registered sex offender is moving into one of the ZIP Code areas that you entered, and directed to the website for more information.

Online search: Access is available via the website. Search by Last Name, City, ZIP, or County.

Incarceration Records

Kentucky Department of Corrections, Offender Information Services, PO Box 2400, Frankfort, KY 40602-2400 (Courier address: 275 E. Main, Room 619, Frankfort, KY 40602); 502-564-2433, 800-511-1670 (Victim Notification Line), 502-564-1471-Fax; 8AM-4:30PM.

www.corrections.ky.gov

Records are available on current and former inmates. It takes approximately 30 days before new records are available for inquiry. Records are indexed on computer back to 1981; prior in archives on paper. Records are normally destroyed after 5 years after release (institutional versions) and after 75 years after release from the central office file.

Searching: Include the following in your request-full name. DOB and SSN are helpful. Index does not include alias or other names used. Location, physical identifiers, conviction and sentencing information, and release dates are reported.

Access by: mail, fax, online.

Fee & Payment: Copy fee is $.10 per page. There is no search fee. Fee payee: Kentucky Treasurer Prepayment required Personal checks accepted. Credit cards accepted.

Mail search: Turnaround time: 1 to 2 weeks. Older, archived records require a longer turnaround time. A SASE or postage is requested.

Fax search: Can request via fax.

Online search: The website provides current inmate information on the Kentucky Online Offender Lookup (KOOL) system as a service to the public. It can take as long as 120 days for the data to be current. Also, a private company offers free web access at www.vinelink.com/index.jsp. Include state, DOC, and county jails

Other access: The IT Department has the database on CD available for $50.00; call 502-564-4360.

Expedited service: Will expedite processing if reason is given for delivering the record in a timely manner.

Corporation, Limited Partnerships, Assumed Name, Limited Liability Company Records

Secretary of State, Corporate Records, PO Box 718, Frankfort, KY 40602-0718 (Courier address: 700 Capitol Ave, Room 156, Frankfort, KY 40601); 502-564-2848, 502-564-4075-Fax; 8AM-4:30PM.

www.sos.state.ky.us

Records are available from the 1977 forward on computer index. Hard copies are on microfilm. Records inactive by 1976 are archived and it takes 2 weeks to research. New records are available for inquiry immediately. Records are normally destroyed after they have been microfilmed.

Searching: Computer records contain name, dates, current registered agent and initial incorporators and initial directors. They do contain current lists of officers and directors when available. Include the following in your request-full name of business.

Access by: mail, phone, fax, in person, online.

Fee & Payment: There is no search fee, but there is a $5.00 certification fee. Copies are $5.00

(minimum) for up to first to 10 pages, and $.10 per each additional page. Pages can be certified for $.50 each. A Certificate of Good Standing is $10.00. Fee payee: Secretary of State. Prepayment required. Send at least $5.00 in the mail for copies. If certified copies are needed, call first. Personal checks accepted. Credit cards accepted, minimum $5.00.

Mail search: Turnaround time: 2 to 3 days. No SASE is required.

Phone search: Only information on the computer system is released over the phone.

Fax search: Fax requests accepted with a credit card.

In person search: Turnaround time while you wait. If you order 5 or more, they will mail the records to you.

Online search: The Internet site, open 24 hours, has a searchable database with over 340,000 KY businesses. The site also offers downloading of filing forms.

Other access: Monthly lists of new corporations are available for $50.00 per month.

Trademarks/Servicemarks

Secretary of State, Trademarks Section, 700 Capitol Ave, Suite 152, Frankfort, KY 40601; 502-564-2848 x442, 502-564-1484-Fax; 8AM-4:30PM.

http://sos.ky.gov

It takes minutes before new records are available for inquiry. Records are indexed on original documents on file in the office and online access to database. Records are normally destroyed after three years.

Searching: Include the trademark/servicemark name or applicant name or certification number. Also, wordmark and description helps.

Access by: mail, phone, fax, in person, online.

Fee & Payment: There is no fee.

Mail search: Turnaround time: 1 week. A SASE is requested.

Phone search: Ask for Johnna Ballinger.

Fax search: Fax requests accepted.

In person search: Turnaround time while you wait.

Online search: Free, searchable database at www.kysos.com/trademarks/tmstart.asp.

Uniform Commercial Code

UCC Branch, Secretary of State, PO Box 1470, Frankfort, KY 40601; 502-564-3490, 502-564-5687-Fax; 8AM-4:30PM.

http://sos.ky.gov/business/ucc

The state adopted Revised Article 9 effective July 1, 2001.

It takes 24 hours before new records are available for inquiry.

Searching: The Secretary of State maintains a searchable index for all active UCC records that provides for the retrieval of a record by the name of the debtor and by the file number of the initial financing statement to which the record relates. Include the following in your request-full debtor name. No partial name searches are permitted, except at website. The agency advises requesters to use Form UCC-11.

Access by: mail, fax, in person, online.

Fee & Payment: $5.00 for a certified search. $.10 per page for copies of UCC records. Ongoing requesters may open a pre-paid account with a $250 deposit. Fee payee: KY State Treasurer. Personal checks accepted. No credit cards accepted.

Mail search: Turnaround time: 1-3 business days. Full names are required.

Fax search: Only pre-paid, approved account may order by fax.

In person search: The physical address is Room 153 of the Capitol. Turnaround time while you wait. If you order extensive records, they will mail the results to you.

Online search: UCC record searching is offered free of charge at the website. Search by debtor name, or file number. SSNs are withheld from the online system. Pre-paid accounts may be established for those requiring copies or certified documents.

Federal and State Tax Liens

Records not maintained by a state level agency.

All tax liens are at the county level.

Sales Tax Registrations

Revenue Cabinet, Tax Compliance Department, Sales Tax Section, Station 53, PO Box 181, Frankfort, KY 40602-0181 (Courier address: 200 Fair Oaks, Bldg 2, Frankfort, KY 40602); 502-564-5170, 502-564-2041-Fax; 8AM-4:30PM.

http://revenue.ky.gov

This agency will only confirm if a tax permit exists. The agency will NOT confirm if a business is registered. They will provide no other information.

Records are available from the 1970's. Records are indexed on computer from 1996 to present, and on microfilm from 1985 to 1995.

Searching: Include the following in your request-tax permit number.

Access by: mail, in person.

Mail search: Turnaround time: 2 to 3 months. A SASE is requested. No fee for mail request.

In person search: No fee for request.

Birth Certificates

Department for Public Health, Vital Statistics, 275 E Main St - IE-A, Frankfort, KY 40621-0001; 502-564-4212, 877- 817-3632 (Order), 502-227-0032-Fax; 8AM-4PM.

http://chfs.ky.gov/dph/vital

Records are available from 1911 to present. It takes 1 month before new records are available for inquiry. Records are indexed on microfiche, inhouse computer, books (volumes).

Searching: Include the following in your request-full name, names of parents, mother's maiden name, date of birth, place of birth. Provide a daytime phone number.

Access by: mail, phone, fax, in person, online.

Fee & Payment: Searches are $10.00 per name. Add $10.50 if using a credit card. Fee payee: Kentucky State Treasurer. Prepayment required.

Personal checks accepted. Major credit cards accepted.

Mail search: Turnaround time: 3 to 4 weeks. No SASE is required.

Phone search: Must use a credit card (add $10.50 fee) for a phone request. Turnaround time is 3 to 5 days.

Fax search: Order by fax from fax 877-435-5584. Use of credit card required.

In person search: Turnaround time 1 1/2 hour.

Online search: Records may be ordered online via a state designated vendor at www.vitalchek.com.

Expedited service: Expedited service is available for mail, phone, online and fax orders. Turnaround time: overnight delivery. Add $12.75 per package for shipping. Also, be sure to include extra credit card use fee.

Death Records

Department for Public Health, Vital Statistics, 275 E Main St - IE-A, Frankfort, KY 40621-0001; 502-564-4212, 877- 817-3632 (Order), 502-227-0032-Fax; 8AM-3PM.

http://chfs.ky.gov/dph/vital

Records are available from 1911 on. It takes 1 month before new records are available for inquiry. Records are indexed on microfiche, inhouse computer, books (volumes).

Searching: Include the following in your request-full name, date of death, place of death. Provide a daytime phone number.

Access by: mail, phone, fax, in person, online.

Fee & Payment: The fee is $6.00 per name. Fee payee: Kentucky State Treasurer. Prepayment required. Personal checks accepted. Major credit cards accepted.

Mail search: Turnaround time: 3 to 4 weeks. No SASE is required.

Phone search: Must use a credit card (add $10.50 fee) to make phone request. Turnaround time is 2-3 days.

Fax search: Order by fax from fax 877-435-5584. Use of credit card required.

In person search: Turnaround time 1 1/2 hour.

Online search: In cooperation with the University of Kentucky, there is a searchable death index at http://ukcc.uky.edu:80/~vitalrec/. This is for non-commercial use only. Records are from 1911 through 1992. Also, there is a free genealogy site at http://vitals.rootsweb.com/ky/death/search.cgi. Death Indexes from 1911-2000 are available. You may search by surname, given name, place of death, residence, or year. Records may be ordered online via a state designated vendor at www.vitalchek.com.

Expedited service: Expedited service is available for mail, phone, online and fax orders. Turnaround time: overnight delivery. Add $12.75 per package for shipping. Also, be sure to include extra credit card use fee.

Marriage Certificates

Department for Public Health, Vital Statistics, 275 E Main St - IE-A, Frankfort, KY 40621-0001; 502-564-4212, 877- 817-3632 (Order), 502-227-0032-Fax; 8AM-3PM.

http://chfs.ky.gov/dph/vital

Records are available from June 1958 to present. It takes 1 to 2 months before new records are available for inquiry. Records are indexed on microfiche, inhouse computer, books (volumes).

Searching: Copies of marriage certificates prior to June 1958 may be obtained from the County Clerk in the county where the license was issued. Include the following in your request-names of husband and wife, date of marriage, place or county of marriage. Must also include where marriage license was obtained and a daytime phone number.

Access by: mail, phone, fax, in person, online.

Fee & Payment: The fee is $6.00 per name. Fee payee: Kentucky State Treasurer. Prepayment required. Personal checks accepted. Major credit cards accepted.

Mail search: Turnaround time: 3 to 4 weeks. No SASE is required.

Phone search: Must use a credit card (add $10.50 fee) for a phone request. Turnaround time is 3 to 5 days.

Fax search: Order by fax from fax 877-435-5584. Use of credit card required.

In person search: Turnaround time 1 1/2 hour.

Online search: In cooperation with the University of Kentucky, a searchable index is available on the Internet at http://ukcc.uky.edu:80/~vitalrec/. The index runs from 1973 through 1993. This is for non-commercial use only. Records may be ordered online via a state designated vendor at www.vitalchek.com.

Other access: Contact Libraries and Archives.

Expedited service: Expedited service is available for mail, phone, online and fax orders. Turnaround time: overnight delivery. Add $12.75 per package for shipping. Also, be sure to include extra credit card use fee.

Divorce Records

Department for Public Health, Vital Statistics, 275 E Main St - IE-A, Frankfort, KY 40621-0001; 502-564-4212, 877- 817-3632 (Order), 502-227-0032-Fax; 8AM-3PM.

http://chfs.ky.gov/dph/vital

Records are available from June, 1958 to present. It takes 1 to 2 months before new records are available for inquiry. Records are indexed on microfiche, inhouse computer, books (volumes).

Searching: Records of divorce proceedings are available from the Clerk of the Circuit Court that granted the decree. Include the following in your request-names of husband and wife, date of divorce, place of divorce. Provide a daytime phone number.

Access by: mail, phone, fax, in person, online.

Fee & Payment: The fee is $6.00 per name. Fee payee: Kentucky State Treasurer. Prepayment required. Personal checks accepted. Major credit cards accepted.

Mail search: Turnaround time: 3 to 4 weeks. No SASE is required.

Phone search: Must use a credit card (add $10.50 fee) for a phone request. Turnaround time 3-5 days.

Fax search: Order by fax from fax 877-435-5584. Use of credit card required.

In person search: Turnaround time 1 1/2 hour.

Online search: In cooperation with the University of Kentucky, there is a searchable index on the

Internet at http://ukcc.uky.edu:80/~vitalrec/. This is for non-commercial use only. The index is for 1973-1993. Records may be ordered online via a state designated vendor at www.vitalchek.com.

Other access: Contact Libraries and Archives.

Expedited service: Expedited service is available for mail, phone, online and fax orders. Turnaround time: overnight delivery. Add $12.75 per package for shipping. Also, be sure to include extra credit card use fee.

Workers' Compensation Records

Kentucky Office of Workers' Claims, Prevention Park, 657 To Be Announced Ave, Frankfort, KY 40601; 502-564-5550, 502-564-5732-Fax; 8AM-4:30PM.

http://labor.ky.gov/dwc

Records are available from 1982 to present on computer. New records are available for inquiry immediately. Records are normally destroyed after 75 years.

Searching: Must have a signed release from claimant only for copies of first report. Otherwise, information is open to the public per KRS 61.870 through 61.884. Include the following in your request-claimant name, Social Security Number, date of accident, place of employment at time of accident. The following data is not released: Social Security Numbers, addresses or personal information (height, weight, sex, eye color, etc.).

Access by: mail, phone, fax, in person.

Fee & Payment: Fees are $.50 per page from microfilm and photocopies are $.10 per page. Fee payee: Kentucky State Treasurer. Payment may be submitted at the time records are picked up. Otherwise, an invoice will be mailed at the end of the month. Personal checks accepted. No credit cards accepted.

Mail search: Turnaround time: 2 to 4 weeks. Requests are processed in order by the date received. A SASE is requested.

Phone search: Some data available via phone.

Fax search: Fax requests are processed by date of receipt same as requests that are mailed.

In person search: The office will have the records ready for you if you call ahead first and make an appointment.

Other access: A listing of file contents may be requested. Call for details.

Expedited service: If requesting agency provides account number for FedEx, then documents will be expedited.

Driver Records

Division of Driver Licensing, KY Transportation Cabinet, 200 Mero Street, Frankfort, KY 40622; 502-564-6800 x2250, 502-564-5787-Fax; 8AM-4:30PM.

www.kytc.state.ky.us/drlic

Requests for copies of tickets must be submitted in writing to Cabinets Record Custodian, Department of Administrative Services, at the address listed above. There is a $.10 fee per document.

Records are available for 3 years for moving violations, DWIs and suspensions. Accidents are not reported on 3 years records. It takes 5 to 10 days before new records are available for inquiry. Records are normally destroyed after five years.

Searching: Casual requesters can obtain record information, but personal information is "cloaked" unless written consent by subject is provided. A request form is found at http://transportation.ky.gov/kytci-forms/tc_94_3/tc943.html. The SSN or DL, the full name and DOB are needed when ordering. The driver's address is not included as part of the search report without a release from the driver.

Access by: mail, in person, online.

Fee & Payment: The fee is $3.00 per record, $4.50 if online. Fee payee: Kentucky State Treasurer. Credit cards accepted. Business checks accepted.

Mail search: Turnaround time: 3 days.

In person search: Walk-in requesters may receive records immediately at the address listed above or at any one of 11 field offices in the state.

Online search: There are 2 systems. Permissible use requesters who need personal information can order by batch, minimum order is 150 requests per batch. Input received by 3 PM will be available the next morning. Fee is $4.50 per record and billing is monthly. Call for details to subscribe. Records without personal information can be obtained at http://dhr.ky.gov/DHRWeb/. The same $4.50 fee applies and up to 50 records can be ordered and received immediately.

Vehicle Ownership, Vehicle Identification, Vessel Ownership, Vessel Registration

Department of Motor Vehicles, Division of Motor Vehicle Licensing, PO Box 2014, Frankfort, KY 40622; 502-564-3298, 502-564-2737 (Questions), 502-564-1686-Fax; 8AM-4:30PM.

www.kytc.state.ky.us

The state adopted all 14 permissible uses per DPPA guidelines.

Records are available from 1989 to present for title histories (VTRs). Vessel registration from 1985. Prior vessel records are kept by Circuit Clerks. Only motorized vessels must be titled and registered. It takes 1-4 weeks before new records are available for inquiry. Records are indexed on microfiche and computer. Records are normally destroyed after 20 years.

Searching: Vehicle and ownership records are not to the public without consent of subject. Vendors must submit either TC96-16 or TC96-325 when requesting data. This agency will not do a search by name and DOB only, must have DL. Also, will not search by SSN.

Access by: mail, in person, online.

Fee & Payment: The fee is $2.00 per record request. The state reports current lien information. There is a full charge for a "no record found." Fee payee: Kentucky State Treasurer Prepayment required. Cash and money orders are accepted. Personal checks accepted. No credit cards accepted.

Mail search: Turnaround time: 5 to 10 days. A SASE is requested.

In person search: Turnaround time is while you wait (typically, 15 minutes to 1 hour).

Online search: Online access costs $2.00 per record. The online mode is interactive. Title, lien and registration searches are available. Records include those for mobile homes. For more information, contact Gale Warfield at 502-564-4076.

Other access: Kentucky has the ability to supply customized bulk delivery of vehicle registration information. The request must be in writing with the intended use outlined. For more information, call 502-564-3298.

Expedited service: Expedited service is available for walk-ins only. You must set up an account. For more information, call 502-564-5301.

Accident Reports

State Police, Criminal Ident. & Records Branch, 1250 Louisville Rd, Frankfort, KY 40601; 502-226-2169, 502-226-7418-Fax; 8AM-4:30PM.

www.kentuckystatepolice.org

Records are available for past 5 years. It takes less than 1 day before new records are available for inquiry.

Searching: Requests must be made through "open records." Statistical detailed listing of accidents at specific locations without personal identifying information is available for a fee with a written request. For more information phone 502-226-2169 for details. Search requirements include the date, driver's name and location.

Access by: mail, fax, in person.

Fee & Payment: The charge is $.10 per page. Fee payee: KY State Treasurer. Prepayment required. Personal checks accepted. No credit cards accepted.

Mail search: Turnaround time: 1 to 2 weeks. A SASE is requested.

Fax search: Fax requests accepted.

In person search: Counter service is available.

Other access: Specific accident statistics may be obtained by phoning the statistics coordinator.

Voter Registration

State Board of Elections, 140 Walnut, Frankfort, KY 40601; 502-573-7100, 502-573-4369-Fax; 8AM-4:30PM.

http://elect.ky.gov/registrationinfo

Call or fax to request a copy of the agency's request form. Bulk data is available for political purposes or specific research purposes only. For individual searches, it is best to go to the county level.

Searching: The agency will provide verification of records and voting histories upon receipt of a written request (using their form). For questions, contact kim.bagwell@ky.gov. The SSN or DOB is required when doing a verification. The following data is not released: Social Security Numbers, bulk information or information to ineligible persons, pursuant to state statutes.

Access by: mail, fax, in person, online.

Fee & Payment: There is no search fee. There is a $.10 per page copy fee.

Mail search: Turnaround time: 3 business days. Turnaround time is longer for information exempted by statute.

Fax search: Records are available by fax.

In person search: Records may be ordered (with written request) and picked up in person. Law allows for 3 business day turnaround.

Online search: The agency offers a voter information status search at http://cdc.ky.gov/VICWeb/index.jsp. First name, last name and DOB are required.

Other access: Data is available on CD-Rom, labels or lists for eligible persons, pursuant to state statutes

GED Certificates

Kentucky Adult Education, GED Program, 1024 Capital Center Drive, Frankfort, KY 40601; 502-573-5114 x2, 502-573-5436-Fax; 8AM-4:30PM.

http://adulted.state.ky.us

It takes 4 weeks after test before new records are available for inquiry.

Searching: To verify or to get copy of transcript or diploma, all of the following is required: a signed release, name, date/year of test, date of birth, SSN, and city of test.

Access by: mail, in person.

Fee & Payment: The fee for verification or a copy of transcript or duplicate diplomas is $5.00 each. Fee payee: KY State Treasurer. Prepayment required. Money orders are accepted, personal checks are not. No credit cards accepted.

Mail search: Turnaround time: 1 week or less. No SASE is required.

In person search: In person searchers must bring a photo ID. Turnaround time is same day.

Hunting and Fishing License Information

Fish & Wildlife Resources Department, Division of Administrative Services, 1 Game Farm Rd, Arnold Mitchell Bldg, Frankfort, KY 40601; 502-564-4224, 502-564-0506-Fax; 8AM-4:30PM.

www.fw.ky.gov

A database has been created, starting in 1996. Records are not released without written request and for good reason. Records are not available for commercial mail lists. Older records are archived in boxes. Record retrieval extremely difficult.

Records are available for the past two years (actual copies). Prior records are archived and not readily available. It takes 16 days before new records are available for inquiry. Records are indexed on hard copy. Records are normally destroyed after 5 years, in general.

Searching: Requests must be in writing and addressed to the Commissioner's Office. The general public cannot receive records, beyond the type of license issued. Include the following in your request-full name, Social Security Number. By law, the agency will respond to all search requests within three days.

Access by: mail, fax, in person.

Fee & Payment: Fees are $.10 per page plus cost of postage. Prepayment required. Personal checks accepted.

Mail search: Turnaround time: 3 days. Records are available by mail.

Fax search: Records may be requested by fax.

In person search: Limited information available in person, extensive lists will be mailed.

Kentucky State Licensing Agencies

For details about the agency responsible for licensing/certifying/registering an item below or in the Agency Quick Finder section, match an item's number with the number of the agency in the *Licensing Agency Information* section.

Kentucky Licenses Searchable Online

Addiction Psychiatrist MD #41	http://weba.state.ky.us/genericsearch/LicenseSearch.asp?AGY=5
Alcohol/Drug Counselor #15	https://web1.ky.gov/OnPPub/Verification.aspx
Anesthesiologist #41	http://weba.state.ky.us/genericsearch/LicenseSearch.asp?AGY=5
Architect #7	http://kybera.com/roster.shtml
Art Therapist #15	https://web1.ky.gov/OnPPub/Verification.aspx
Athlete Agent #15	https://web1.ky.gov/OnPPub/Verification.aspx
Athletic Trainer, Medical #41	http://weba.state.ky.us/genericsearch/LicenseSearch.asp?AGY=5
Attorney #2	www.kybar.org/Default.aspx?tabid=26
Auctioneer, Livestock, Limited #4	http://weba.state.ky.us/genericsearch/LicenseSearch.asp?AGY=3
Auctioneer, Tobacco, Limited #4	http://weba.state.ky.us/genericsearch/LicenseSearch.asp?AGY=3
Auctioneer/Auctioneer Apprentice #4	http://weba.state.ky.us/genericsearch/LicenseSearch.asp?AGY=3
Audiologist #15	https://web1.ky.gov/OnPPub/Verification.aspx
Bank #18	http://dfi.ky.gov/scr/ifs/old/fi/
Check Casher #18	http://dfi.ky.gov/scr/ifs/default.asp?div=cs
Counselor, Pastoral #15	https://web1.ky.gov/OnPPub/Verification.aspx
Counselor, Professional #15	https://web1.ky.gov/OnPPub/Verification.aspx
CPA #3	http://web1.ky.gov/GenSearch/LicenseSearch.aspx?AGY=7
CPA Company #3	http://web1.ky.gov/GenSearch/LicenseSearch.aspx?AGY=6
Credit Union #18	http://dfi.ky.gov/scr/ifs/old/fi/
Dental Hygienist #6	http://dentistry.ky.gov/
Dental Laboratory #6	http://dentistry.ky.gov/
Dentist #6	http://dentistry.ky.gov/
Dietitian/Nutritionist #15	https://web1.ky.gov/OnPPub/Verification.aspx
Drinking Water System Operator #29	www.water.ky.gov/optcert/
EDP Servicer #18	http://dfi.ky.gov/scr/ifs/old/fi/
Engineer #39	http://kyboels.ky.gov/SearchRoster.asp
Engineer/Land Surveyor Firm #39	http://kyboels.ky.gov/SearchRoster.asp
Geologist #15	https://web1.ky.gov/OnPPub/Verification.aspx
Hearing Instrument Specialist #15	https://web1.ky.gov/OnPPub/Verification.aspx
Home Health Aid #9	https://ssla.state.ky.us/KBN/kbnknar.asp
Insurance Agent #21	www.doi.state.ky.us/kentucky/search/agent/
Insurance CE Provider #21	www.doi.state.ky.us/kentucky/search/provider/
Insurance Company/Insurer #21	www.doi.state.ky.us/kentucky/search/company/
Interior Designer #7	www.kybera.com/idlist.shtml
Investment Advisor/Company #18	http://dfi.ky.gov/scr/ifs/old/sec/
Legislative Employer of Lobbyists #40	http://klec.ky.gov/reports/employersagents.htm
Loan Company, Comm./Industrial #18	http://dfi.ky.gov/whoweregulate/Small%20Industrial%20Loan%20Recap.pdf
Lobbyist #40	http://klec.ky.gov/reports/employersagents.htm
Marriage & Family Therapist #15	https://web1.ky.gov/OnPPub/Verification.aspx
Medical Doctor/Surgeon #41	http://weba.state.ky.us/genericsearch/LicenseSearch.asp?AGY=5
Medical Specialist MD #41	http://weba.state.ky.us/genericsearch/LicenseSearch.asp?AGY=5
Midwife Nurse #9	https://ssla.state.ky.us/KBN/kbnknar.asp
Mortgage Broker #18	http://dfi.ky.gov/scr/ifs/default.asp?div=cs
Mortgage Loan Company #18	http://dfi.ky.gov/scr/ifs/default.asp?div=cs
Nurse Anesthetist #9	https://ssla.state.ky.us/KBN/kbnknar.asp
Nurse Clinical Specialist #9	https://ssla.state.ky.us/KBN/kbnknar.asp
Nurse Work Permit #9	https://ssla.state.ky.us/KBN/KBNssn.asp?TYPE=TP&APP=
Nurse-RN/LPN #9	https://ssla.state.ky.us/KBN/kbnknar.asp
Nurses Aide #9	https://ssla.state.ky.us/KBN/kbnknar.asp
Nursing Home Administrator #15	https://web1.ky.gov/OnPPub/Verification.aspx
Occupational Therapist/Assistant #15	https://web1.ky.gov/OnPPub/Verification.aspx
Ophthalmic Dispenser/Apprentice #10	https://kyeasupt1.state.ky.us/OPB/BrdWebSearch.asp?BRD=11
Optician/Optician Apprentice #10	https://kyeasupt1.state.ky.us/OPB/BrdWebSearch.asp?BRD=11
Optometrist #11	http://weba.state.ky.us/GenericSearch/LicenseSearch.asp?AGY=8
Osteopathic Physician #41	http://weba.state.ky.us/GenericSearch/LicenseSearch.asp?AGY=8
Physical Therapist #38	http://weba.state.ky.us/genericsearch/LicenseSearch.asp?AGY=5
Physical Therapist Assistant #38	http://weba.state.ky.us/genericsearch/LicenseSearch.asp?AGY=4

Physician Assistant #41 ....http://weba.state.ky.us/genericsearch/LicenseSearch.asp?AGY=5
Private Investigator #15 ....https://web1.ky.gov/OnPPub/Verification.aspx
Proprietary Education School #15 ....https://web1.ky.gov/OnPPub/Verification.aspx
Psychiatrist MD #41 ....http://weba.state.ky.us/genericsearch/LicenseSearch.asp?AGY=5
Psychologist #15 ....https://web1.ky.gov/OnPPub/Verification.aspx
Public Accountant Company #3 ....http://web1.ky.gov/GenSearch/LicenseSearch.aspx?AGY=6
Public Accountant-CPA #3 ....http://web1.ky.gov/GenSearch/LicenseSearch.aspx?AGY=7
Radiation Operator #44 ....http://weba.state.ky.us/genericsearch/LicenseSearch.asp?AGY=5
Real Estate Agent/Broker/Sales #33 ....http://weba.state.ky.us/realestate/LicenseeLookUp.asp
Real Estate Appraiser #32 ....www.kreab.ky.gov/
Real Estate Brokerage/Firm #33 ....http://weba.state.ky.us/realestate/FirmLookUp.asp
Retired LPN #9 ....http://kbn.ky.gov/onlinesrvs/retired.htm
Savings & Loan #18 ....http://dfi.ky.gov/scr/ifs/old/fi/
School Administrator #25 ....www.kyepsb.net
School Guidance Counselor #25 ....www.kyepsb.net
School Media Librarian #25 ....www.kyepsb.net
School Nurse #25 ....www.kyepsb.net
School Social Worker/Psychologist #25 ....www.kyepsb.net
Securities Agent #18 ....http://dfi.ky.gov/scr/ifs/old/sec/
Securities Broker/Dealer #18 ....http://dfi.ky.gov/scr/ifs/old/sec/
Securities, Agent of Issuer #18 ....http://dfi.ky.gov/scr/ifs/old/sec/
Sexual Assault Nurse Examiner #9 ....https://ssla.state.ky.us/KBN/kbnknar.asp
Social Worker #15 ....https://web1.ky.gov/OnPPub/Verification.aspx
Speech-Language Pathologist #15 ....https://web1.ky.gov/OnPPub/Verification.aspx
Surveyor, Land #39 ....http://kyboels.ky.gov/SearchRoster.asp
Teacher #25 ....www.kyepsb.net
Trust Company #18 ....http://dfi.ky.gov/scr/ifs/old/fi/
Veterinarian #15 ....https://web1.ky.gov/OnPPub/Verification.aspx
Waste Water System Operator #29 ....www.water.ky.gov/optcert/
Water Well Driller #29 ....www.water.ky.gov/gw/gwdb/

Kentucky Licensing Quick Finder

Addiction Psychiatrist MD #41 502-429-8046
Agent of Issuer, Securities #18 502-573-3390
Alcohol/Drug Counselor #15 ....502-564-3296 x226
Ambulance Provider #14 502-564-8963
Anesthesiologist #41 502-429-8046
Animal Technician #15 502-564-3296
Architect #7 859-246-2069
Art Therapist #15 ....502-564-3296 x230
Athlete Agent #15 ....502-564-3296 x222
Athletic Trainer, Medical #41 502-429-8046
Attorney #2 502-564-3795
Auctioneer, Livestock, or Tobacco #4 ..502-429-7145
Auctioneer/Auctioneer Apprentice #4 ..502-429-7145
Bank #18 502-573-3390
Barber #5 502-429-7148
Blacksmith #31 859-246-2040
Boiler Contractor/Insp./Installer #26 502-573-0373
Broker/Dealer Agent #18 502-573-3390
Building Inspector #26 502-564-8090
Check Casher #18 502-573-3390
Check Seller/Casher #18 502-573-3390
Child Care Facility #13 502-564-2800
Chiropractor #35 270-651-2522
Compost Operator #24 502-565-6716
Coroner #17 859-622-1328
Cosmetologist #37 502-564-4262
Counselor, Pastoral #15 ....502-564-3296 x226
Counselor, Professional #15 ....502-564-3296 x226
Credit Union #18 502-573-3390
Dental Hygienist #6 502-429-7280
Dental Laboratory #6 502-429-7280
Dental Laboratory Technician #6 502-429-7280
Dentist #6 502-429-7280
Dialysis Technician #9 ....502-429-3300 x290
Dietitian/Nutritionist #15 ....502-564-3296 x227
Drinking Water Treatment/Dist. System Operator #29
....502-564-3410

Driver Training Instructor #42 502-226-7404
Drug Manufacturer/Wholesaler #12 502-573-1580
EDP Servicer #18 502-573-3390
Electrical Contractor #26 502-573-0382
Electrical Inspector #26 502-573-0382
Elevator Inspector #26 502-573-0382
Embalmer #36 502-241-3918
EMS Instructor #14 502-564-8963
EMT, Basic #14 502-564-8963
EMT, First Response #14 502-564-8963
Engineer #39 502-573-2680
Engineer/Land Surveyor Firm #39 502-573-2680
Exterminator #16 502-573-0282
Fire Alarm System Inspector #26 502-573-0382
Fire Protection Sprinkler Installer #26 ..502-564-3626
Fire Suppression System Inspect'r #26 .502-564-8090
Fishing, Commercial #20 800-858-1549
Funeral Director #36 502-241-3918
Fur Buyer/Processor #20 800-858-1549
Geologist #15 ....502-564-3296 x227
Guide, Hunting & Fishing #20 800-858-1549
Health Care Facility #13 502-564-2800
Hearing Instrument Special't #15 .502-564-3296 x240
Home Health Aid #9 502-429-3300
Horse Claimer #31 859-246-2040
Horse Farm Manager/Agent #31 859-246-2040
Horse Owner/Trainer/Asst. Trainer #31 .829-246-2040
Horse Racing Occupation #31 859-246-2040
Horse Racing Official/Authorized Agent #31
....859-246-2040
Horse Veterinarian/Veterinary Asst #31 859-246-2040
Horse Veterinary Dental Tech. #31 859-246-2040
HVAC Contractor #26 502-564-1436
HVAC Journeyman/Master/Mech.#26 ...502-564-1436
Insurance Adjuster #21 502-564-3630
Insurance Agent #21 502-564-3630
Insurance CE Provider #21 502-564-3630

Insurance Company/Insurer #21 502-564-3630
Insurance Consultant/Solicitor #21 502-564-3630
Interior Designer #7 859-246-2069
Interpreters for the Deaf #15 ....502-564-3296 x239
Investment Advisor/Company #18 502-573-3390
Investment Advisor/Representative #18 502-573-3390
Jockey Agent #31 859-246-2040
Jockey/Jockey Apprentice #31 859-246-2040
Lake Operator #20 800-858-1549
Landfarm Operator #24 502-564-6716
Landfill Operator/Manager #24 502-564-6716
Law Enforcement Training Instr. #17 859-622-1328
Legislative Employers of Lobbyists #40 502-573-2863
Liquor License #1 502-564-4850
Loan Company, Comm./Industrial #18 .502-573-3390
Lobbyist #40 502-573-2863
Malt Beverage Distributor #1 502-564-4850
Marriage & Family Therapist #15 .502-564-3296 x239
Medical Doctor/Surgeon #41 502-429-8046
Medical Specialist MD #41 502-429-8046
Midwife Nurse #9 502-429-3300
Milk Sampler/Weigher/Tester #43 859-257-2785
Mine Safety Instructor #22 502-573-0140
Miner #22 502-573-0140
Mining Blaster #22 502-573-0140
Mining Fire Boss #22 502-573-0140
Mining Inspector/Foreman #22 502-573-0140
Mortgage Broker #18 502-573-3390
Mortgage Loan Company #18 502-573-3390
Nail Technician #37 502-564-4262
Notary Public #30 502-564-3490
Nurse Anesthetist #9 502-429-3300
Nurse Clinical Specialist #9 502-429-3300
Nurse Work Permit #9 502-429-3300
Nurse-RN/LPN #9 502-429-3300
Nurses Aide #9 502-429-3300
Nurses' Aide Instructor #9 502-329-7048

Nursing Home Administrator #15 . 502-564-3296 x222
Occupational Therapist/Assistant #15 .. 502-564-3296
Ophthalmic Dispenser/Optician/Apprentice #10
.... 502-564-3296 x227
Optometrist #11 859-246-2744
Osteopathic Physician #41 502-429-8046
Paramedic #14 502-564-8963
Pari-Mutuel Employee #31 859-246-2040
Pesticide Applicator / Dealer #16 502-573-0282
Pharmacist #12 502-573-1580
Pharmacy #12 502-573-1580
Physical Therapist #38 502-327-8497
Physical Therapist Assistant #38 502-327-8497
Physician Assistant #41 502-429-8046
Plans & Specifications Inspector #26 ... 502-564-8090
Plumber #26 502-573-0397
Podiatrist #27 270-759-0007
Police Officer #17 859-622-132
Polygraph Examiner/ Trainee #28 502-564-4756
Private Investigator #15 502-564-3296

Property Valuation Administrator #34 .. 502-564-8338
Proprietary Education School #15 502-564-4233
Psychiatrist MD #41 502-429-8046
Psychologist #15 .... 502-564-3296 x225
Public Accountant-CPA #3 502-595-3037
Racetrack Occupation (vendors, etc.) #31
.... 859-246-2040
Racing Vendor/Vendor Employee #31 .. 859-246-2040
Radiation Operator #44 502-564-3700
Radiation Producing Machine #44 502-564-3700
Radioactive Material Licensee #44 502-564-3700
Real Estate Agent/Broker/Sales #33 502-429-7250
Real Estate Appraiser #32 859-543-8943
Real Estate Brokerage/Firm #33 502-429-7250
Rehabilitation Counselor #23 502-564-4440
Retired LPN #9 502-429-3300
Sanitarian #8 502-564-7398
Savings & Loan #18 502-573-3390
School Administrator #25 502-564-4606
School Bus Driver #19 502-564-4718

School Guidance Counselor #25 502-564-4606
School Media Librarian #25 502-564-4606
School Nurse #25 502-564-4606
School Social Worker/Psychologist #25 502-564-4606
Securities Agent #18 502-573-3390
Securities Broker/Dealer #18 502-573-3390
Septic System Installer, Onsite #8 502-564-4856
Sexual Assault Nurse Examiner #9 502-429-3300
Social Worker #15 .... 502-564-3296 x230
Speech-Language Pathologist/Audiologist #15
.... 502-564-3296 x240
Stable Employee #31 859-246-2040
Surveyor, Land #39 502-573-2680
Taxidermist #20 800-858-1549
Teacher #25 502-564-4606
Trust Company #18 502-573-3390
Veterinarian #15 .... 502-564-3296 x223
Waste Water System Operator #29 502-564-3410
Water Well Driller #29 502-564-3410

Kentucky Licensing Agency Information

1 Alcoholic Beverage Control Department, 1003 Twilight Trail, #A2, Frankfort, KY 40601; 502-564-4850, Fax: 502-564-1442.

2 Bar Association, 514 W Main St, Frankfort, KY 40601-1883; 502-564-3795, Fax: 502-564-3225. www.kybar.org
Email: webmaster@kybar.org   Search Database at www.kybar.org/Default.aspx?tabid=26

3 Board of Accountancy, 332 W Broadway, #310, Louisville, KY 40202; 502-595-3037, Fax: 502-595-4281.
http://cpa.ky.gov/
Email: debby.abell@mail.state.ky.us
Search Database at http://cpa.ky.gov/

4 Board of Auctioneers, 9112 Leesgate Rd #5, Louisville, KY 40222-5089; 502-429-7145, Fax: 502-429-7147.   http://auctioneers.ky.gov
Email: auctioneers@mail.state.ky.us

5 Board of Barbering, 9114 Leesgate Rd, #6, Louisville, KY 40222-5055; 502-429-7148, Fax: 502-429-7149.

6 Board of Dentistry, 10101 Linn Station Rd, #540, Louisville, KY 40223; 502-429-7280, Fax: 502-429-7282.   http://dentistry.ky.gov/
Search Database at http://dentistry.ky.gov/

7 Board of Examiners & Registration of Architects, 301 E Main St #860, Lexington, KY 40507; 859-246-2069, Fax: 859-246-2431.
http://kybera.com/   Email: kybera@iglou.com
Search Database at http://kybera.com/roster.shtml

8 Department for Public Health, Registered Sanitarian Examining Committee, 275 E Main, 2nd Fl E, HS 2EA, Frankfort, KY 40621; 502-564-7398, Fax: 502-564-6533.
http://chs.state.ky.us/publichealth/registered_sanitariancontent.htm
Email: guy.delius@mail.state.ky.us

9 Board of Nursing, 312 Whittington Pky, #300, Louisville, KY 40222-5172; 502-429-3300, Fax: 502-329-7011.   http://kbn.ky.gov
Email: kbn.webmaster@mail.state.ky.us
Search Database at
https://ssla.state.ky.us/KBN/kbnknar.asp   Note: SSN required to search; there is $1.00 fee per name. Bulk data downloads also available, go to https://secure.kentucky.gov/portal/registration.aspx

10 Division of Occupations and Professions, Board of Ophthalmic Dispensers, PO Box 1360, Frankfort, KY 40602; 502-564-3296 x227, Fax: 502-564-4818.
http://occupations.ky.gov/ophthalmicdispensers/
Search Database at
https://kyeasupt1.state.ky.us/OPB/BrdWebSearch.asp?BRD=11 Note: You may also search ophthamoloy licenses at
http://weba.state.ky.us/genericsearch/LicenseSearch.asp?AGY=5.

11 Board of Optometric Examiners, 301 E Main St #850, Lexington, KY 40507-1578; 859-246-2744, Fax: 859-246-2746.
http://optometry.ky.gov/
Email: ky.optometry@mail.state.ky.us
Search Database at
http://weba.state.ky.us/GenericSearch/LicenseSearch.asp?AGY=8

12 Board of Pharmacy, 23 Millcreek Park, Frankfort, KY 40601; 502-573-1580, Fax: 502-573-1582.
http://pharmacy.ky.gov/   Note: Oral verification is limited to status and expiration date. Requests for add'l information must be in writing accompanied by a $5.00 fee. Copies of disciplinary orders/detailed searches may be more costly.

13 Division of Licensing & Regulations, Cabinet for Health Services, CHR Bldg, 5th Fl East, Frankfort, KY 40621-0001; 502-564-2800, Fax: 502-564-6546.
http://chs.state.ky.us/
Email: fparrish@mail.state.ky.us

14 Board of Emergency Medical Services, 2545 Lawrenceburg Rd, Frankfort, KY 40621; 502-564-8963, Fax: 502-564-4687.
www.kbems.org

15 Department of Administration, Division of Occupations & Professions, PO Box 1360, Frankfort, KY 40602; 502-564-3296, Fax: 502-564-4818.
http://finance.ky.gov/ourcabinet/caboff/OAS/op/

16 Department of Agriculture, Division of Pesticide Regulation, 107 Corporate Dr, Frankfort, KY 40601; 502-573-0282, Fax: 502-573-0303.
www.kyagr.com
Email: BillyRay.Smith@kyagr.com

17 Department of Criminal Justice Training, 521 Lancaster Ave,, Richmond, KY 40475; 859-622-1328, Fax: 859-622-2740.
http://docjt.jus.state.ky.us/
Email: pops@docjt.jus.state.ky.us

18 Department of Financial Institutions, Division of Law & Regulatory Compliance, 1025 Capitol Center Dr #200, Frankfort, KY 40601; 502-573-3390, Fax: 502-573-8787.
www.dfi.state.ky.us
Email: Becky.Mills@mail.state.ky.us
Search Database at
http://dfi.ky.gov/whoweregulate.htm

19 Department of Education, Pupil Transportation, 500 Mero St 15th Fl, Frankfort, KY 40601; 502-564-4718, Fax: 502-564-9574.
www.kde.state.ky.us

20 Department of Fish & Wildlife, 1 Game Farm Rd, Frankfort, KY 40601; 800-858-1549, Fax: 502-564-9136.
www.kdfwr.state.ky.us

21 Department of Insurance, Licensing Division, PO Box 517, 215 W Main St (40601), Frankfort, KY 40602-0517; 502-564-3630.
www.doi.state.ky.us/kentucky/
Email: Randy.Donahue@mail.state.ky.us
Search Database at www.doi.state.ky.us/kentucky

22 Department of Mines & Minerals, PO Box 2244, Frankfort, KY 40602-2244; 502-573-0140, Fax: 502-573-0152.
http://dmm.ppr.ky.gov/
Email: JohnFranklin@mail.state.ky.us

23 Department of Vocational Rehabilitation, 209 St Clair St, Frankfort, KY 40601; 502-564-4440, Fax: 502-564-6742.
http://ovr.ky.gov/index.htm
Email: flemingb@ihdi.uky.edu

24 Division of Waste Management, 14 Reilly Rd, Frankfort, KY 40601; 502-564-6716, Fax: 502-564-4049. www.waste.ky.gov
Email: ron.gruzesky@ky.gov

25 Education Professional Standards Board, 100 Airport Rd 3rd Fl, Frankfort, KY 40601; 502-564-4606, Fax: 502-564-7080.
www.kyepsb.net   Email: sherry.paul@ky.gov
Search Database at www.kyepsb.net

26 Department of Housing, Buildings, and Construction, 101 Sea Hero Rd, #100, Frankfort, KY 40601; 502-573-0373.
www.state.ky.us/agencies/cppr/dhbc/
Email: charlene.slemp@mail.state.ky.us

27 Kentucky Board of Podiatry, 908 B South 12th St, Murray, KY 42071-2949; 270-759-0007, Fax: 270-753-0684.

28 State Police, Polygraph Unit, 1250 Louisville Rd, Frankfort, KY 40601; 502-564-4756, Fax: 502-226-2191.
www.kentuckystatepolice.org
Email: kpayne@mail.state.ky.us

29 Division of Water, Natural Resources & Environmental Protection, 14 Reilly Rd, Frankfort Office Park, Frankfort, KY 40601; 502-564-3410, Fax: 502-564-9720.
www.water.ky.gov

30 Office of Secretary of State, Notary Commissions, PO Box 718, Frankfort, KY 40602-0821; 502-564-3490 x413, Fax: 502-564-4075.
www.kysos.com/admin/notary/mainpage.asp
Email: Kbagwell@mail.sos.state.ky.us

31 Kentucky Racing Commission, 4063 Iron Works Pike, Lexington, KY 40511; 859-246-2040, Fax: 859-246-2039.
http://krc.ppr.ky.gov/

32 Real Estate Appraisers Board, 2480 Fortune Dr #120, Lexington, KY 40509; 859-543-8943, Fax: 859-543-0028. www.kreab.ky.gov/
Email: larry.disney@ky.gov
Search Database at www.kreab.ky.gov

33 Real Estate Commission, 10200 Linn Station Rd, #201, Louisville, KY 40223; 502-429-7250, Fax: 502-429-7246.
http://krec.ky.gov
Email: krecweb@uky.edu
Search Database at http://krec.ky.gov

34 Department of Property Taxation, Revenue Cabinet, 200 Fair Oaks Lane, Frankfort, KY 40620; 502-564-8338, Fax: 502-564-8368.
Email: revweb@mail.state.ky.us

35 Board of Chiropractic Examiners, 209 S Green St (PO Box 183), Glasgow, KY 42142-0183; 270-651-2522, Fax: 270-651-8784.
Email: kychiro@glasgow-ky.com

36 Board of Embalmers & Funeral Directors, PO Box 324, Crestwood, KY 40014; 502-241-3918, Fax: 502-241-4297.

37 Board of Hairdressers & Cosmetologists, 111 St James Court #A, Frankfort, KY 40601; 502-564-4262, Fax: 502-564-0481.

38 Board of Physical Therapy, 9110 Leesgate Rd, #6, Louisville, KY 40222-5159; 502-327-8497, Fax: 502-423-0934. http://pt.ky.gov
Email: kybpt@ky.gov   Search data at http://weba.state.ky.us/genericsearch/LicenseSearch.asp?AGY=4

39 Professional Engineers & Land Surveyors, Board of Licensure, 160 Democrat Dr, Frankfort, KY 40601; 502-573-2680, Fax: 502-573-6687.
http://kyboels.state.ky.us/
Email: larry.perkins@mail.state.ky.us
Search Database at http://kyboels.ky.gov/SearchRoster.asp

40 Legislative Ethics Commission, 22 Mill Creek Park, Frankfort, KY 40601; 502-573-2863, Fax: 502-573-2929.
www.lrc.state.ky.us/otherweb/ethics/
Search Database at
www.lrc.state.ky.us/otherweb/ethics/

41 Board of Medical Licensure, 310 Whittington Pky, #1B, Louisville, KY 40222; 502-429-8046, Fax: 502-429-9923.
www.kbml.org   Search Database at http://weba.state.ky.us/genericsearch/LicenseSearch.asp?AGY=5 Note: Use the fee dialup service only if you have a license or certification number.

42 State Police Driver Testing Section, 1240 Airport RD, Frankfort, KY 40601; 502-226-7404, Fax: 502-226-7412.

43 Division of Regulatory Services, 103 Regulatory Service Bldg, Lexington, KY 40546-0275; 859-257-2785, Fax: 859-323-9931.
www.rs.uky.edu
Email: cthompso@ca.uky.edu

44 Radiation Health & Toxic Agents Branch, Department of Public Health, 275 E Main St, Frankfort, KY 40621; 502-564-3700, Fax: 502-564-1492.
http://publichealth.state.ky.us/radiation.htm

Kentucky Federal Courts

The following list indicates the district and division name for each county in the state. If the bankruptcy court location is different from the district court, then the location of the bankruptcy court appears in parentheses.

County/Court Cross Reference

County	District	Division
Adair	Western	Bowling Green (Louisville)
Allen	Western	Bowling Green (Louisville)
Anderson	Eastern	Frankfort (Lexington)
Ballard	Western	Paducah (Louisville)
Barren	Western	Bowling Green (Louisville)
Bath	Eastern	Lexington
Bell	Eastern	London (Lexington)
Boone	Eastern	Covington (Lexington)
Bourbon	Eastern	Lexington
Boyd	Eastern	Ashland (Lexington)
Boyle	Eastern	Lexington
Bracken	Eastern	Covington (Lexington)
Breathitt	Eastern	Lexington
Breckinridge	Western	Louisville
Bullitt	Western	Louisville
Butler	Western	Bowling Green (Louisville)
Caldwell	Western	Paducah (Louisville)
Calloway	Western	Paducah (Louisville)
Campbell	Eastern	Covington (Lexington)
Carlisle	Western	Paducah (Louisville)
Carroll	Eastern	Frankfort (Lexington)
Carter	Eastern	Ashland (Lexington)
Casey	Western	Bowling Green (Louisville)
Christian	Western	Paducah (Louisville)
Clark	Eastern	Lexington
Clay	Eastern	London (Lexington)
Clinton	Western	Bowling Green (Louisville)
Crittenden	Western	Paducah (Louisville)
Cumberland	Western	Bowling Green (Louisville)
Daviess	Western	Owensboro (Louisville)
Edmonson	Western	Bowling Green (Louisville)
Elliott	Eastern	Ashland (Lexington)
Estill	Eastern	Lexington
Fayette	Eastern	Lexington
Fleming	Eastern	Lexington
Floyd	Eastern	Pikeville (Lexington)
Franklin	Eastern	Frankfort (Lexington)
Fulton	Western	Paducah (Louisville)
Gallatin	Eastern	Covington (Lexington)
Garrard	Eastern	Lexington
Grant	Eastern	Covington (Lexington)
Graves	Western	Paducah (Louisville)
Grayson	Western	Owensboro (Louisville)
Green	Western	Bowling Green (Louisville)
Greenup	Eastern	Ashland (Lexington)
Hancock	Western	Owensboro (Louisville)
Hardin	Western	Louisville
Harlan	Eastern	London (Lexington)
Harrison	Eastern	Lexington
Hart	Western	Bowling Green (Louisville)
Henderson	Western	Owensboro (Louisville)
Henry	Eastern	Frankfort (Lexington)
Hickman	Western	Paducah (Louisville)
Hopkins	Western	Owensboro (Louisville)
Jackson	Eastern	London (Lexington)
Jefferson	Western	Louisville
Jessamine	Eastern	Lexington
Johnson	Eastern	Pikeville (Lexington)
Kenton	Eastern	Covington (Lexington)
Knott	Eastern	Pikeville (Lexington)
Knox	Eastern	London (Lexington)
Larue	Western	Louisville
Laurel	Eastern	London (Lexington)
Lawrence	Eastern	Ashland (Lexington)
Lee	Eastern	Lexington
Leslie	Eastern	London (Lexington)
Letcher	Eastern	Pikeville (Lexington)
Lewis	Eastern	Ashland (Lexington)
Lincoln	Eastern	Lexington
Livingston	Western	Paducah (Louisville)
Logan	Western	Bowling Green (Louisville)
Lyon	Western	Paducah (Louisville)
Madison	Eastern	Lexington
Magoffin	Eastern	Pikeville (Lexington)
Marion	Western	Louisville
Marshall	Western	Paducah (Louisville)
Martin	Eastern	Pikeville (Lexington)
Mason	Eastern	Covington (Lexington)
McCracken	Western	Paducah (Louisville)
McCreary	Eastern	London (Lexington)
McLean	Western	Owensboro (Louisville)
Meade	Western	Louisville
Menifee	Eastern	Lexington
Mercer	Eastern	Lexington
Metcalfe	Western	Bowling Green (Louisville)
Monroe	Western	Bowling Green (Louisville)
Montgomery	Eastern	Lexington
Morgan	Eastern	Ashland (Lexington)
Muhlenberg	Western	Owensboro (Louisville)
Nelson	Western	Louisville
Nicholas	Eastern	Lexington
Ohio	Western	Owensboro (Louisville)
Oldham	Western	Louisville
Owen	Eastern	Frankfort (Lexington)
Owsley	Eastern	London (Lexington)
Pendleton	Eastern	Covington (Lexington)
Perry	Eastern	Lexington
Pike	Eastern	Pikeville (Lexington)
Powell	Eastern	Lexington
Pulaski	Eastern	London (Lexington)
Robertson	Eastern	Covington (Lexington)
Rockcastle	Eastern	London (Lexington)
Rowan	Eastern	Ashland (Lexington)
Russell	Western	Bowling Green (Louisville)
Scott	Eastern	Lexington
Shelby	Eastern	Frankfort (Lexington)
Simpson	Western	Bowling Green (Louisville)
Spencer	Western	Louisville
Taylor	Western	Bowling Green (Louisville)
Todd	Western	Bowling Green (Louisville)
Trigg	Western	Paducah (Louisville)
Trimble	Eastern	Frankfort (Lexington)
Union	Western	Owensboro (Louisville)
Warren	Western	Bowling Green (Louisville)
Washington	Western	Louisville
Wayne	Eastern	London (Lexington)
Webster	Western	Owensboro (Louisville)
Whitley	Eastern	London (Lexington)
Wolfe	Eastern	Lexington
Woodford	Eastern	Lexington

Standards for Federal Courts: Search fee is $26.00 per item (one party name or case number). Copy fee is $.50 per page. Certification fee is $9.00 per document, double for exemplification, if available. All fees standard unless noted in profile. Mail Search: always enclose a stamped self addressed envelope unless otherwise noted. Most courts accept fax requests or will suggest a copying/search vendor. Before releasing records, all courts require prepayment, unless noted.

Open records are located at the court unless otherwise noted. District courts index by defendant and plaintiff as well as by case number. Bankruptcy courts usually index by debtor and case number. While most courts now have their indexes on computer, many may still maintain index card files as well.

Courts offering internet access via CM-ECF or older RACER, PACER, or Web-PACER systems charge $.08 per page fee unless noted as free. Where PACER is available, the universal sign-up number is 800-676-6856. Find PACER and the US Party/Case Index at http://pacer.psc.uscourts.gov.

US District Court

Eastern District of Kentucky

Ashland Division Court Clerk, Suite 336, 1405 Greenup Ave, Ashland, KY 41101 (also use mail address for courier delivery), 606-329-8652. Hours- 8:30AM-5PM. www.kyed.uscourts.gov

Counties: Boyd, Carter, Elliott, Greenup, Lawrence, Lewis, Morgan, Rowan.

Searches & Indexing: Lexington Division has district master index. Results do not include SSN or DOB. Both computer and card indexes maintained; computer index back to 1992. New cases in the index 1-2 days after filing date. Records purged never.

Fee & Payment: Pay by money order, cashier's or personal check. Payee: Clerk, USDC. Prepayment required.

Phone Search: Only docket information from active cases is released via phone.

Mail Search: search usually completed- 1-2 days. SASE not required.

In Person Search: Fee charged if court performs your search. No self-serve copier available.

E-Services: ECF replaces PACER whose records did go back to 9/1991. New records online after 1 day. ECF at https://ecf.kyed.uscourts.gov **Other Online Access:** For calendars, click on "Hearing Schedule" at www.kyed.uscourts.gov.

Covington Division Clerk of Court, 35 W 5th St, US Courthouse, Rm 289, Covington, KY 41011 (also use mail address for courier delivery), 859-392-7925.   Hours-   8:30AM-5PM. www.kyed.uscourts.gov

Counties: Boone, Bracken, Campbell, Gallatin, Grant, Kenton, Mason, Pendleton, Robertson.

Searches & Indexing: Results do not include SSN or DOB. Both computer and card indexes maintained. New cases in the index immediately after filing date. Records purged never.

Fee & Payment: Pay by money order, cashier's or personal check. Payee: Clerk, US District Court. Prepayment required.

Phone Search: No searching by telephone.

Mail Search: search usually completed- 48 hours. Turnaround time for written requests varies. Include SASE for return.

In Person Search: Fee charged if court performs your search. No self-serve copier available.

E-Services: ECF replaces PACER whose records did go back to 9/1991. New records online after 1 day. ECF at https://ecf.kyed.uscourts.gov **Other Online Access:** For calendars, click on "Hearing Schedule" at www.kyed.uscourts.gov.

Frankfort Division Court Clerk, Rm 313, 330 W Broadway, Frankfort, KY 40601 (also use mail address for courier delivery), 502-223-5225. Hours- 8:30AM-5PM. www.kyed.uscourts.gov

Counties: Anderson, Carroll, Franklin, Henry, Owen, Shelby, Trimble.

Searches & Indexing: Results do not include SSN or DOB. Both computer and card indexes maintained; on computer back to 1/1993. New cases in the index immediately after filing date. Records purged never.

Fee & Payment: Pay by money order, cashier's or personal check. Payee: Clerk, US District Court. Prepayment required.

Phone Search: Only docket information is available by phone.

Mail Search: search usually completed- 1-2 days. SASE not required.

In Person Search: Fee charged if court performs your search. No self-serve copier available.

E-Services: ECF replaces PACER whose records did go back to 9/1991. New records online after 1 day. ECF at https://ecf.kyed.uscourts.gov **Other Online Access:** For calendars, click on "Hearing Schedule" at www.kyed.uscourts.gov.

Lexington Division Court Clerk, PO Box 3074, Lexington, KY 40588 (courier address: Rm 206, 101 Barr St, Lexington, KY 40588-3074), 859-233-2503.   Hours-   8:30AM-5PM. www.kyed.uscourts.gov

Counties: Bath, Bourbon, Boyle, Breathitt, Clark, Estill, Fayette, Fleming, Garrard, Harrison, Jessamine, Lee, Lincoln, Madison, Menifee, Mercer, Montgomery, Nicholas, Perry, Powell, Scott, Wolfe, Woodford.

Searches & Indexing: Results do not include SSN or DOB. Computer and card indexes maintained; computer back to 10/1992. New cases in the index 24 hours after filing date. Records purged never.

Fee & Payment: Pay by money order, cashier's or personal check. Payee: Clerk, USDC. Prepayment required.

Phone Search: Only docket information from active cases is released via phone.

Mail Search: search usually completed- 2-3 weeks. SASE not required.

In Person Search: Fee charged if court performs your search. No self-serve copier available.

E-Services: ECF replaces PACER whose records did go back to 10/1992. New records online after 1 day. ECF at https://ecf.kyed.uscourts.gov **Other Online Access:** For calendars, click on "Hearing Schedule" at www.kyed.uscourts.gov.

London Division Court Clerk, PO Box 5121, London, KY 40745-5121 (courier address: 124 US Courthouse, 310 S Main, London, KY 40741),

606-877-7910.   Hours-   8:30AM-5PM. www.kyed.uscourts.gov

Counties: Bell, Clay, Harlan, Jackson, Knox, Laurel, Leslie, McCreary, Owsley, Pulaski, Rockcastle, Wayne, Whitley.

Searches & Indexing: Results do not include SSN or DOB. Computer index back to 3/2003 maintained. New cases in the index 1 day after filing date. Records purged never.

Fee & Payment: Pay by money order, cashier's, business or personal check. Payee: Clerk, USDC. Prepayment required.

Phone Search: Only docket information is available by phone.

Mail Search: search usually completed- 1 day. Include SASE for return.

In Person Search: Fee charged if court performs your search. No self-serve copier available.

E-Services: ECF replaces PACER whose records did go back to 9/1991. New records online after 1 day. ECF at https://ecf.kyed.uscourts.gov **Other Online Access:** For calendars, click on "Hearing Schedule" at www.kyed.uscourts.gov.

Pikeville Division Office of the Clerk, 203 Federal Bldg, 110 Main St, Pikeville, KY 41501 (also use mail address for courier delivery), 606-437-6160. 8AM-5PM. www.kyed.uscourts.gov

Counties: Floyd, Johnson, Knott, Letcher, Magoffin, Martin, Pike.

Searches & Indexing: Results do not include SSN or DOB. Computer index maintained. New cases in the index immediately after filing date. Records purged never.

Fee & Payment: Pay by money order, cashier's or personal check. Payee: Clerk, US District Court. Prepayment required except for Kentucky attorneys.

Phone Search: Only date of filing and case status is released via phone.

Mail Search: search usually completed- 24 hours. SASE not required.

In Person Search: Fee charged if court performs your search. Self-serve copier available - $.50; if from computer at front counter, $.10 per page.

E-Services: ECF replaces PACER whose records did go back to 9/1991. New records online after 1 day. ECF at https://ecf.kyed.uscourts.gov **Other Online Access:** For calendars, click on "Hearing Schedule" at www.kyed.uscourts.gov.

US Bankruptcy Court

Eastern District of Kentucky

Lexington Division Court Clerk, PO Box 1111, Lexington, KY 40589-1111 (courier address: Community Trust Bldg, Suite 202, 100 E Vine St, Lexington, KY 40507), 859-233-2608. Hours- 8:30AM-4PM. www.kyeb.uscourts.gov

Counties: Anderson, Bath, Bell, Boone, Bourbon, Boyd, Boyle, Bracken, Breathitt, Campbell, Carroll, Carter, Clark, Clay, Elliott, Estill, Fayette, Fleming, Floyd, Franklin, Gallatin, Garrard, Grant, Greenup, Harlan, Harrison, Henry, Jackson, Jessamine, Johnson, Kenton, Knott, Knox, Laurel, Lawrence, Lee, Leslie, Letcher, Lewis, Lincoln, Madison, Magoffin, Martin, Mason, McCreary, Menifee, Mercer, Montgomery, Morgan, Nicholas, Owen, Owsley, Pendleton, Perry, Pike, Powell,

Pulaski, Robertson, Rockcastle, Rowan, Scott, Shelby, Trimble, Wayne, Whitley, Wolfe, Woodford.

Searches & Indexing: Results include last 4 SSN digits only. Computer index only. New cases in the index 3 days after filing date.

Fee & Payment: Pay by money order, cashier check, business check. No personal checks. Payee: Clerk, US Bankruptcy Court. Prepayment required excluding pauper filings.

Phone Search: Only docket information is available by phone. Voice Case Information Service available, call VCIS at 800-998-2650 or 859-233-2650.

Mail Search: search usually completed- 5 days. Include SASE for return.

In Person Search: Fee charged if court performs your search. Self-serve copier - $.15 per page.

E-Services: ECF replaces PACER whose records did go back to 7/1992. ECF at https://ecf.kyeb.uscourts.gov **Opinions Online:** www.kyeb.uscourts.gov/opin/queryopin.asp. **Other Online Access:** Access calendars free at www.kyeb.uscourts.gov/calendar.htm

US District Court

Western District of Kentucky

Bowling Green Division Court Clerk, US District Court, 241 E Main St, Rm 120, Bowling Green, KY 42101-2175 (also use mail address for courier delivery), 270-389-2500, Fax-270-393-2519. Hours- 8:30AM-5PM. www.kywd.uscourts.gov

Counties: Adair, Allen, Barren, Butler, Casey, Clinton, Cumberland, Edmonson, Green, Hart, Logan, Metcalfe, Monroe, Russell, Simpson, Taylor, Todd, Warren.

Searches & Indexing: Results do not include SSN or DOB. Both computer and card indexes maintained. New cases in the index 1-2 days after filing date.

Fee & Payment: Pay by money order, cashier's or personal check. Payee: Clerk, US District Court. Prepayment required.

Phone Search: Only docket information is available by phone.

Mail Search: search usually completed- 1-2 days. Include SASE for return.

In Person Search: Fee charged if court performs your search. Self-serve copier - $.50 per page.

E-Services: Court is converting online WebPACER/PACER service over to ECF. PACER records go back to 1992. New records online after 1 day. ECF at https://ecf.kywd.uscourts.gov **Opinions Online:** www.kywd.uscourts.gov/judicialOpinionsSearch.php. **Other Online Access:** Calendars at www.kywd.uscourts.gov/CourtCalendars.php.

Louisville Division Clerk, US District Court, 601 Broadway, Rm106, Louisville, KY 40202 (also use mail address for courier delivery), 502-625-3500, records rm- 502-625-3550, Fax-502-625-3880. Hours- 8:30AM-4:30PM. www.kywd.uscourts.gov

Counties: Breckinridge, Bullitt, Hardin, Jefferson, Larue, Marion, Meade, Nelson, Oldham, Spencer, Washington.

Searches & Indexing: Results include last 4 SSN digits. Computer, microfiche and card indexes maintained. Records on index cards 1938-1979. Records indexed on microfiche 1979 to 4/92. Records after 4/92 on the automated system. New cases in the index immediately after filing date. District-wide searches available here for cases back to 1938.

Fee & Payment: Pay by money order, cashier's or personal check. Payee: Clerk, US District Court. Prepayment required.

Phone Search: Only docket information is available by phone.

Mail Search: search usually completed- 5-10 working days. Include SASE for return.

In Person Search: Fee charged if court performs your search. No self-serve copier available.

E-Services: Court is converting online WebPACER/PACER service over to ECF. PACER records go back to 1992. New records online after 1 day. ECF at https://ecf.kywd.uscourts.gov **Opinions Online:** www.kywd.uscourts.gov/judicialOpinionsSearch.php. **Other Online Access:** Calendars at www.kywd.uscourts.gov/CourtCalendars.php.

Owensboro Division Court Clerk, Federal Bldg, Rm 126, 423 Frederica St, Owensboro, KY 42301 (also use mail address for courier delivery), 270-689-4400, Fax-207-689-4419. Hours- 8AM-4:30PM. www.kywd.uscourts.gov

Counties: Daviess, Grayson, Hancock, Henderson, Hopkins, McLean, Muhlenberg, Ohio, Union, Webster.

Searches & Indexing: Court needs the correct name, date and/or criminal or civil case number to search. Results do not include SSN or DOB. Computer index maintained back to 1992. New cases in the index 1-2 days after filing date.

Fee & Payment: Pay by money order, cashier's, business or personal check. Payee: Clerk, US District Court. Court will only bill to in-state searchers.

Phone Search: Only docket information is available by phone.

Mail Search: search usually completed- 1 week. SASE not required.

In Person Search: Fee charged if court performs your search. Self-serve copier - $.50 per page.

E-Services: Court is converting online WebPACER/PACER service over to ECF. PACER records go back to 1992. New records online after 1 day. ECF at https://ecf.kywd.uscourts.gov **Opinions Online:** www.kywd.uscourts.gov/judicialOpinionsSearch.php. **Other Online Access:** Calendars at www.kywd.uscourts.gov/CourtCalendars.php.

Paducah Division Court Clerk, 501 Broadway, Ste127, Paducah, KY 42001 (also use mail address for courier delivery), 270-415-6400, Fax-270-415-6419. Hours- 8:30AM-5PM. www.kywd.uscourts.gov

Counties: Ballard, Caldwell, Calloway, Carlisle, Christian, Crittenden, Fulton, Graves, Hickman, Livingston, Lyon, McCracken, Marshall, Trigg.

Searches & Indexing: Results do not include SSN or DOB. Both computer and card indexes maintained; computer goes back to 1992. New cases in the index 1-2 days after filing date.

Fee & Payment: Pay by Visa/MC, money order, cashier's or personal check. Payee: Clerk, US District Court. Prepayment required.

Phone Search: Only docket information is available by phone.

Mail Search: search usually completed- 3-4 working days. Include SASE for return. You may fax for a fee quote.

In Person Search: Fee charged if court performs your search. Self-serve copier - $.50 per page.

E-Services: Court is converting online WebPACER/PACER service over to ECF. PACER records go back to 1992. New records online after 1 day. ECF at https://ecf.kywd.uscourts.gov **Opinions Online:** www.kywd.uscourts.gov/judicialOpinionsSearch.php. **Other Online Access:** Calendars at www.kywd.uscourts.gov/CourtCalendars.php.

US Bankruptcy Court

Western District of Kentucky

Louisville Division Court Clerk, 450 US Courthouse, 601 W Broadway, Louisville, KY 40202 (also use mail address for courier delivery), 502-627-5700. Hours- 8:30AM-4:30PM. www.kywb.uscourts.gov

Counties: Adair, Allen, Ballard, Barren, Breckinridge, Bullitt, Butler, Caldwell, Calloway, Carlisle, Casey, Christian, Clinton, Crittenden, Cumberland, Daviess, Edmonson, Fulton, Graves, Grayson, Green, Hancock, Hardin, Hart, Henderson, Hickman, Hopkins, Jefferson, Larue, Livingston, Logan, Lyon, Marion, Marshall, McCracken, McLean, Meade, Metcalfe, Monroe, Muhlenberg, Nelson, Ohio, Oldham, Russell, Simpson, Spencer, Taylor, Todd, Trigg, Union, Warren, Washington, Webster.

Searches & Indexing: Results include last 4 SSN digits only. New cases in the index immediately after filing date. District-wide searches available here; maintains records for all district divisions.

Fee & Payment: Pay by Visa/MC, money order, cashier check, business check. No personal checks. Payee: Clerk, US Bankruptcy Court. Prepayment required. Will fax back in emergency, $.50 per page.

Phone Search: Only basic case information is available by phone. Voice Case Information Service available, call VCIS at 800-263-9385 or 502-627-5660.

Mail Search: search usually completed- 2 days. Include SASE for return.

In Person Search: Fee charged if court performs your search. Self-serve copier available - $.15 per page.

E-Services: ECF replaces PACER whose records did go back to 7/1992. New records online after 1 day. ECF at https://ecf.kywb.uscourts.gov **Opinions Online:** www.kywb.uscourts.gov/opinions/main.php.

Kentucky County Courts

Court	Jurisdiction	No. of Courts	How Organized
Circuit Courts*	General	19	57 Judicial Circuits
District Courts*	Limited	19	60 Judicial Districts
Combined*		102	

* Profiled in this Sourcebook.

Court	CIVIL								
	Tort	Contract	Real Estate	Min. Claim	Max. Claim	Small Claims	Estate	Eviction	Domestic Relations
Circuit Courts*	X	X	X	$4000	No Max				X
District Courts*	X	X	X	$0	$4000	$1500	X	X	X

Court	CRIMINAL				
	Felony	Misdemeanor	DWI/DUI	Preliminary Hearing	Juvenile
Circuit Courts*	X				
District Courts*		X	X	X	X

ADMINISTRATION

Administrative Office of Courts, Pre-Trial Services Records Unit, 100 Mill Creek Park, Frankfort, KY, 40601; 502-573-1682, Fax: 502-573-1669. www.kycourts.net

COURT STRUCTURE

The Circuit Court is the court of general jurisdiction and the District Court is the limited jurisdiction court. Most of Kentucky's counties combined the courts into one location and records are co-mingled. Circuit courts have jurisdiction over cases involving capital offenses and felonies, divorces, adoptions, terminations of parental rights, land dispute title problems and contested probates of will. Juvenile matters, city and county ordinances, misdemeanors, traffic offenses, probate of wills, felony preliminary hearings, and civil cases involving $4,000 or less are heard in District Court. Ninety percent of all Kentuckians involved in court proceedings appear in District Court.

ONLINE ACCESS

There are statewide, online computer systems called SUSTAIN and KyCourts available for internal judicial/state agency use only, and KY Bar attorneys may register to use the KCOJ court records data at www.kycourts.net/CourtRecordsKBA/. No courts offer online access to records. However, you may search daily court calendars by county for free at http://dockets.kycourts.net. Also, you may search online for open dockets (limited) of the supreme court at the home page.

ADDITIONAL INFORMATION

Until 1978, county judges handled all cases; therefore, in many cases, District and Circuit Court records go back only to 1978. Records prior to that time are archived.

The Administrative Office of the Courts offers a service of providing statewide criminal background checks. They provide the record via fax, standard mail, walk-in or drive-thru service. Their CourtNet Criminal History database contains records of all misdemeanor and traffic cases for at least the last five years, and felonies dating back to 1978 and it contains information from all 120 counties. The required Release Form is available from the AOC at the number above. A check or money order for the Search Fee of $10.00 per requested individual, $15.00 if requested by fax. All accounts must set-up a prepaid bank. A SASE must accompany the request.

Adair County

Circuit & District Court 500 Public Square, #6, Columbia, KY 42728; phone: 270-384-2626; fax: 270-384-4299; hours 8AM-4PM (CST). *Felony, Misdemeanor, Civil, Eviction, Small Claims, Probate.*

Civil Records: Access: In person only. Visitors must perform in person searches themselves. Court makes copy: $.25 per page; same fee for self serve. Required to search: name, years to search. Civil records on computer since 6/1993, prior records on docket books since 1978.

Criminal Records: Access: Mail, in person. Visitors must perform in person searches themselves. No search fee. Court makes copy: $.25 per page; same fee for self serve. Required to search: name, years to search, SSN. Criminal records on computer since 6/1993, prior records on docket books since 1978. Mail requests must be made to Pretrial Services, 100 Millcreek Pk, Frankfort KY 40601, 800-928-6381 Mail turnaround time same day.

General Information: Public terminal goes back to 6/1993. No adoption, mental, juvenile, or sealed records released. No certification fee. Payee: Circuit Clerk. Personal checks accepted. Prepayment and SASE required.

Allen County

Circuit & District Court Box 477, Scottsville, KY 42164; phone: 270-237-3561; hours 8AM-4:30PM (CST). *Felony, Misdemeanor, Civil, Eviction, Small Claims, Probate.*

Civil Records: Access: In person only. Visitors must perform in person searches themselves. Court makes copy: $.25 per page. Required to search: name, years to search. Civil cases indexed by defendant, plaintiff. Civil records on computer since 1992, records on index cards from 1980 to 1992, prior records on books.

Criminal Records: Access: In person only. Visitors must perform in person searches themselves. Court makes copy: $.25 per page. Required to search: name, years to search; SSN helpful. Criminal records on computer back to 1992, records on index cards from 1978 to 1992, prior records on books. Court recommends that criminal search requests be directed to the State of Kentucky AOC, 502-573-2350.

General Information: Public terminal goes back to 9/1992. No adoption, mental, juvenile, or sealed records released. Certification fee: $5.00 per doc. Payee: Circuit Clerk. Local personal checks accepted. Prepayment required.

Anderson County

Circuit Court 151 S Main St, Courthouse, Lawrenceburg, KY 40342; phone: 502-839-3508; fax: 502-839-4995; hours 8:30AM-5PM (EST). *Felony, Civil Actions Over $4,000.*

Civil Records: Access: In person only. Only the court performs in person searches; visitors may not. Court makes copy: $.25 per page. Required to search: name, years to search. Civil cases indexed by defendant, plaintiff. Civil records on computer since 8/1994, prior records on docket books since 1978.

Criminal Records: Access: In person only. Only the court performs in person searches; visitors may not. Court makes copy: $.25 per page. Required to search: name, years to search; also helpful: DOB, SSN. Criminal records may be on computer back to 1994. All record requests are referred to the state agency at 800-928-6381.

General Information: No public access terminal. No adoption, mental, juvenile, or sealed records released. Certification fee: $5.00 per doc. Payee: Clerk of Circuit Court. Personal checks accepted. Prepayment required.

District Court 151 S Main, Lawrenceburg, KY 40342; phone: 502-839-5445; fax: 502-839-4995; hours 8:30AM-N, 1-5PM M-Th; 8:30AM-6PM F (EST). *Misdemeanor, Civil Actions Under $4,000, Eviction, Small Claims, Probate.*

Civil Records: Access: In person only. Both court and visitors may perform in person searches. Court makes copy: $1.00 per page. Required to search: name, years to search. Civil cases indexed by defendant, plaintiff. Civil records on computer since 8/1994, prior records on index cards back to 1978.

Criminal Records: Access: None. Both court and visitors may perform in person searches. Court makes copy: $1.00 per page. Required to search: name, years to search; also helpful: DOB, SSN. Criminal records on computer back to 1994; prior records on index cards back to 1978. The court will not do searches and offers no means to look up a name in an index; there is no way to get the case number. All requests are referred to Pre-trial Services at 800-928-6381.

General Information: Public terminal has criminal back to 1994 and civil back to 8/1994. No adoption, mental, juvenile, or sealed records released. Certification fee: $5.00 per doc. Payee: Anderson County District Court. Business checks accepted. Prepayment required.

Ballard County

Circuit & District Court Box 265, Wickliffe, KY 42087; phone: 270-335-5123; fax: 270-335-3849; hours 8AM-4PM (CST). *Felony, Misdemeanor, Civil, Eviction, Small Claims, Probate.*

Civil Records: Access: In person only. Both court and visitors may perform in person searches. Court makes copy: $.25 per page; same fee for self serve. Required to search: name, years to search. Civil cases indexed by defendant, plaintiff. Civil records on computer since 1992, prior records on books to 1978. Mail turnaround time 7 days.

Criminal Records: Access: In person only. Visitors must perform in person searches themselves. Court makes copy: $.25 per page; same fee for self serve. Required to search: name, years to search, DOB. Criminal records on computer since 1992, prior records on books to 1978.

General Information: Public terminal goes back to 1992. No adoption, mental, juvenile, or sealed records released. Fee to fax documents is $2.00 1st page, $1.00 each addl. Certification fee: $5.00 per document. Payee: Circuit Clerk. Only cashiers checks and money orders accepted. Prepayment required.

Barren County

Circuit & District Court PO Box 1359, Glasgow, KY 42142-1359; phone: 270-651-3763; fax: 270-651-6203; hours 8AM-4:30PM (CST). *Felony, Misdemeanor, Civil, Eviction, Small Claims, Probate.*

Civil Records: Access: In person only. Visitors must perform in person searches themselves. Court makes copy: $.25 per page; same fee for self serve. Required to search: name, years to search. Civil cases indexed by defendant, plaintiff. Civil records on computer back to 10/1991, prior records on index books since 1800s.

Criminal Records: Access: In person only. Visitors must perform in person searches themselves. Court makes copy: $.25 per page; same fee for self serve. Required to search: name, years to search, DOB; SSN helpful. Criminal records on computer back to 10/1991, prior records on index books since 1800s. Criminal record search requests should be directed to AOC Pre-Trial Services in Frankfort, 800-928-6381.

General Information: Public terminal goes back to 10/1991. No adoption, mental, juvenile, or sealed records released. Will not fax specific case file. Certification fee: $5.00 per document. Payee: Circuit Clerk. Personal checks accepted. Prepayment required.

Bath County

Circuit & District Court Box 558, Owingsville, KY 40360; phone: 606-674-2186 X6821; fax: 606-674-3996; hours 8AM-4PM (EST). *Felony, Misdemeanor, Civil, Eviction, Small Claims, Probate.*

Civil Records: Access: In person only. Visitors must perform in person searches themselves. Court makes copy: $.25 per page; same fee for self serve. Required to search: name, years to search. Civil cases indexed by defendant, plaintiff. Civil records computerized since 1994, on docket books since 1978, prior records archived.

Criminal Records: Access: In person only. Visitors must perform in person searches themselves. Court makes copy: $.25 per page; same fee for self serve. Required to search: name, years to search, DOB, SSN. Criminal records computerized since 1994, on docket books since 1978, prior records archived.

General Information: Public terminal goes back to 1994. No adoption, mental, juvenile, or sealed records released. Certification fee: $5.00 per doc. Payee: Circuit Clerk. Personal checks accepted. Prepayment required.

Bell County

Circuit & District Court Box 307, Pineville, KY 40977; phone: 606-337-2942; probate phone: 606-337-9900; fax: 606-337-8850; hours 8:30AM-4PM (EST). *Felony, Misdemeanor, Civil, Eviction, Small Claims, Probate.*

Civil Records: Access: Phone, mail, in person. Both court and visitors may perform in person searches. No search fee. Court makes copy: $.25 per page; same fee for self serve. Required to search: name, years to search. Civil cases indexed by defendant, plaintiff. Civil records on computer since 8/91, prior records on docket books since 1978.

Criminal Records: Access: In person only. Visitors must perform in person searches themselves. Court

makes copy: $.25 per page; same fee for self serve. Required to search: name, years to search. Criminal records on computer since 8/91, prior records on docket books since 1978. Direct written criminal records checks to Pretrial Services Records Division, 100 Millcreek Pk, Frankfort, KY, 40601; for info call 502-573-1682 or 800-928-6381

General Information: Public terminal goes back to 8/1991. No adoption, mental, juvenile, or sealed records released. will fax documents, $2.00 for 1st page, $1.00 each add'l page. Certification fee: $5.00. Payee: Circuit Clerk. Personal checks accepted. Prepayment and SASE required.

Boone County

Circuit & District Court 6025 Rogers Ln, #141, Burlington, KY 41005; phone: 859-334-2286; criminal phone: 859-334-3536 District; civil phone: 859-334-2287 District; fax: 859-334-3650; hours 8:30AM-4:30PM (EST). *Felony, Misdemeanor, Civil, Eviction, Small Claims, Probate.*

Civil Records: Access: Mail, in person. Both court and visitors may perform in person searches. No search fee. Court makes copy: $.25 per page. Required to search: name, years to search. Civil cases indexed by defendant, plaintiff. Civil records on computer since 7/1990, on index card file since 1978, prior records on books.

Criminal Records: Access: In person only. Visitors must perform in person searches themselves. Court makes copy: $.25 per page. Required to search: name, years to search, DOB; SSN helpful. Criminal records on computer since 7/1990, on index card file since 1978, prior records on books.

General Information: No adoption, mental, juvenile, or sealed records released. Fee to fax documents is $3.00 per page. Certification fee: $5.00 per doc. Payee: Circuit Clerk. Only cashiers checks and money orders accepted. Prepayment and SASE required.

Bourbon County

Circuit & District Court Box 740, Paris, KY 40361; phone: 859-987-2624; fax: 859-987-6049; hours 8:30AM-4:30PM T-Th, 8:30AM-6PM M (EST). *Felony, Misdemeanor, Civil, Eviction, Small Claims, Probate.*

Civil Records: Access: In person only. Visitors must perform in person searches themselves. Court makes copy: $.25 per page; same fee for self serve. Required to search: name, years to search. Civil cases indexed by defendant, plaintiff. Civil records on computer since 11/1991, prior records on books.

Criminal Records: Access: In person only. Visitors must perform in person searches themselves. Court makes copy: $.25 per page; same fee for self serve. Required to search: name, years to search; SSN helpful. Criminal records on computer since 11/1991, prior records on books.

General Information: Public terminal goes back to 1991. No adoption, mental, juvenile, or sealed records released. Certification fee: $5.00. Payee: Circuit Clerk. Personal checks accepted. Prepayment required.

Boyd County

Circuit & District Court Box 694, Catlettsburg, KY 41129-0694; phone: 606-739-4131; fax: 606-739-6330; hours 8:30AM-4PM (EST). *Felony, Misdemeanor, Civil, Eviction, Small Claims, Probate.*

Civil Records: Access: In person only. Visitors must perform in person searches themselves. Court makes copy: $.25 per page. Required to search: name, years to search. Civil cases indexed by defendant, plaintiff. Civil records on computer since 1991, prior records on index cards since 1975.

Criminal Records: Access: In person only. Visitors must perform in person searches themselves. Court makes copy: $.25 per page. Required to search: name, years to search; also helpful: DOB, SSN. Criminal records on computer since 1991, on index cards since 1978; misdemeanor & traffic from 1987.

General Information: Public terminal goes back to 1991. No adoption, mental, juvenile, or sealed records released. Certification fee: $5.00 per doc. Payee: Circuit Clerk. Personal checks accepted. Prepayment required.

Boyle County

Circuit Court Courthouse, 321 Main St, Danville, KY 40422; phone: 859-239-7442; fax: 859-239-7000; hours 8AM-4PM (EST). *Felony, Civil Actions Over $4,000.*

Civil Records: Access: Fax, mail, in person. Both court and visitors may perform in person searches. No search fee. Court makes copy: $.25 per page; same fee for self serve. Required to search: name, years to search. Civil cases indexed by defendant, plaintiff. Civil records on computer since 8/91, prior records on index cards. Note that civil case records do not contain SSN or DOBs. Therefore a truly accurate search cannot be done at this court, per the court.

Criminal Records: Access: In person only. Visitors must perform in person searches themselves. Court makes copy: $.25 per page; same fee for self serve. Required to search: name, years to search, DOB, SSN. Criminal records on computer since 8/91, prior records on index cards. This office will not perform criminal name checks.

General Information: Public terminal goes back to 8/1991. No adoption, mental, juvenile, or sealed records released. Will fax civil record searches only, $1.00 per page. Certification fee: $5.00. Payee: Circuit Clerk. No personal checks accepted. Prepayment and SASE required.

District Court Courthouse, 3rd Fl, Danville, KY 40422; phone: 859-239-7362; civil phone: 859-239-7394; fax: 859-239-7807; hours 8AM-4:30PM (EST). *Misdemeanor, Civil Actions Under $4,000, Eviction, Small Claims, Probate.*

Civil Records: Access: Mail, fax, in person. Both court and visitors may perform in person searches. No search fee. Court makes copy: $.25 per page. Required to search: name, years to search. Civil cases indexed by defendant, plaintiff. Civil records on computer since 8/91, prior records on index cards since 1977. Mail turnaround time 3-4 days.

Criminal Records: Access: Mail, fax, in person. Both court and visitors may perform in person searches. No search fee. Court makes copy: $.25 per page. Required to search: name, DOB, SSN. Criminal records on computer since 8/91; prior records on card index. Mail turnaround time 3-4 days.

General Information: Public terminal goes back to 8/1991. No adoption, mental, juvenile, or sealed records released. Fee to fax documents is $2.00 per page. Certification fee: $5.00 per doc. Payee: District Clerk. Personal checks accepted. Prepayment and SASE required.

Bracken County

Circuit & District Court PO Box 205, Brooksville, KY 41004-0205; phone: 606-735-3328; fax: 606-735-3900; hours 8AM-4PM M,T,Th,F, 8:30AM-N W & Sat (EST). *Felony, Misdemeanor, Civil, Eviction, Small Claims, Probate.*

Civil Records: Access: Mail, in person. Both court and visitors may perform in person searches. No search fee. Court makes copy: $.25 per page; same fee for self serve. Required to search: name, years to search. Civil cases indexed by defendant, plaintiff. Civil records on computer since 1993, prior records on docket books since the 1800s.

Criminal Records: Access: In person only. Visitors must perform in person searches themselves. Court makes copy: $.25 per page; same fee for self serve. Required to search: name, years to search. Criminal records on computer since 1993, prior records on docket books since the 1800s.

General Information: Public terminal goes back to 8/1992. No adoption, mental, juvenile, or sealed records released. Will not fax documents. Certification fee: $5.00 per document. Payee: Circuit Clerk. Prepayment and SASE required.

Breathitt County

Circuit & District Court 1137 Main St, Jackson, KY 41339; phone: 606-666-5768; fax: 606-666-4893; hours 8AM-4PM M,T,Th,F; 8AM-N W; 9AM-N Sat (EST). *Felony, Misdemeanor, Civil, Eviction, Small Claims, Probate.*

Civil Records: Access: Mail, in person. Both court and visitors may perform in person searches. No search fee. Court makes copy: $.25 per page. Required to search: name, years to search. Civil cases indexed by defendant, plaintiff. Civil records in files since 1987. Mail turnaround time 2-3 days.

Criminal Records: Access: Mail, in person. Both court and visitors may perform in person searches. No search fee. Court makes copy: $.25 per page. Required to search: name, years to search, DOB, SSN, signed release. Criminal records in files since 1987. Mail turnaround time 2-3 days.

General Information: Public terminal goes back to 1995. No adoption, mental, juvenile, or sealed records released. Certification fee: $5.00 per certification. Payee: Circuit Clerk. Personal checks accepted. Prepayment and SASE required.

Breckinridge County

Circuit & District Court PO Box 111, Hardinsburg, KY 40143; phone: 270-756-2239; fax: 270-756-1129; hours 8AM-4PM (CST). *Felony, Misdemeanor, Civil, Eviction, Small Claims, Probate.*

Civil Records: Access: In person only. Visitors must perform in person searches themselves. Court makes copy: $.25 per page. Required to search: name, years to search. Civil cases indexed by defendant, plaintiff. Civil records on computer back to 8/1994, on index cards since 1978, prior records on docket books since the 1800s.

Criminal Records: Access: In person only. Visitors must perform in person searches themselves. Court makes copy: $.25 per page. Required to search: name, years to search, DOB, SSN. Criminal records on computer back to 8/1994, on index cards since 1978, prior records on docket books since the 1800s.

General Information: Public use terminal available. No adoption, mental, juvenile, or sealed records released. Certification fee: $5.00. Payee: Circuit Clerk. Personal checks accepted. Prepayment required.

Bullitt County

Circuit & District Court Box 746, Shephardsville, KY 40165; phone: 502-543-7104; fax: 502-543-7158; hours 8AM-4PM (EST). *Felony, Misdemeanor, Civil, Eviction, Small Claims, Probate.*

Civil Records: Access: In person only. Visitors must perform in person searches themselves. Court makes copy: $.25 per page; same fee for self serve. Required to search: name. Civil cases indexed by defendant, plaintiff. Civil records on computer since 11/91, prior records on index cards since the 1800s.

Criminal Records: Access: In person only. Visitors must perform in person searches themselves. Court makes copy: $.25 per page; same fee for self serve. Required to search: name, years to search, DOB, SSN. Criminal records on computer since 11/91, prior records on index cards since the 1800s.

General Information: Public terminal goes back to 11/91. No adoption, mental, juvenile, or sealed records released. Fee to fax case file is $1.00 per page. Certification fee: $5.00. Payee: Circuit Clerk. Personal checks accepted. Prepayment required.

Butler County

Circuit & District Court Box 625, Morgantown, KY 42261; phone: 270-526-5631; fax: 270-526-6763; hours 8AM-4:30PM M-F; 9AM-N Sat (CST). *Felony, Misdemeanor, Civil, Eviction, Small Claims, Probate.*

Civil Records: Access: Mail, in person. No search fee. Court makes copy: $.25 per page. Required to search: name, years to search. Civil cases indexed by defendant, plaintiff. Civil records on computer since 1993, prior records on index cards since the 1800s. Mail turnaround time 1 week.

Criminal Records: Access: Mail, in person. Both court and visitors may perform in person searches. No search fee. Court makes copy: $.25 per page. Required to search: name, years to search, DOB; also helpful: SSN. Criminal records on computer since 1993, prior records on index cards since the 1800s, easily accessible from 1978. Mail turnaround time 1 week.

General Information: Public terminal goes back to 1993. No adoption, mental, juvenile, or sealed records released. No certification fee. Payee: Circuit Clerk. Personal checks accepted. Prepayment and SASE required.

Caldwell County

Circuit & District Court 105 W Court Sq, Princeton, KY 42445; phone: 270-365-6884; fax: 270-365-9171; hours 8AM-4PM (CST). *Felony, Misdemeanor, Civil, Eviction, Small Claims, Probate.*

www.sangamoncountycircuitclerk.org

Civil Records: Access: Mail, fax, in person, online. Visitors must perform in person searches themselves. No search fee. Court makes copy: $.25 per page. Copy request must include postage; same fee for self serve. Required to search: name, years to search. Civil cases indexed by defendant, plaintiff. Civil records on index cards; on computer back to 9/94. Online access by subscription available at www.janojustice.com/products/magnus_dot_com/cm.htm. Email sales@janojustice.com to fees and set-up.

Criminal Records: Access: In person, online. Visitors must perform in person searches themselves. No search fee. Court makes copy: $.25 per page. Copy request must include postage; same fee for self serve. Required to search: name, years to search, DOB; also helpful: SSN. Criminal records on index cards; on computer back to 9/94. Online access by subscription is same as civil. Mail turnaround time 2 days.

General Information: Public terminal goes back to 9/1994. No adoption, mental, juvenile, or sealed records released. Fee to fax documents is $2.00 for 1st page, $1.00 each add'l. Certification fee: $5.00 per document. Payee: Circuit Clerk. Personal checks accepted. Prepayment and SASE required.

Calloway County

Circuit & District Court 312 N 4th St, Murray, KY 42071; phone: 270-753-2714; fax: 270-759-9822; hours 8AM-4:30PM (CST). *Felony, Misdemeanor, Civil, Eviction, Small Claims, Probate.*

Note: Circuit court civil and criminal phone number is 270-753-2773.

Civil Records: Access: Mail, in person. Both court and visitors may perform in person searches. No search fee. Court makes copy: $.25 per page; same fee for self serve. Required to search: name, years to search. Civil cases indexed by defendant, plaintiff. Civil records on computer since 6/92, on index cards since 1978. Prior to 1978 records are archived in Frankfort.

Criminal Records: Access: In person only. Visitors must perform in person searches themselves. Court makes copy: $.25 per page; same fee for self serve. Required to search: name, years to search, DOB; SSN helpful. Criminal records on computer since 6/92, on index cards since 1978. Prior to 1978 records are archived in Frankfort.

General Information: Public terminal goes back to 1978. No adoption, mental, juvenile, or sealed records released. Certification fee: $5.00. Payee: Circuit Clerk. Personal checks accepted. Prepayment and SASE required.

Campbell County

Circuit Court 330 York St Rm 8, Newport, KY 41071; phone: 859-292-6314; probate phone: 859-292-6305; hours 8:30AM-4PM (EST). *Felony, Civil Actions Over $4,000.*
www.kycourts.net/clerks/campbellclerk.shtm
Note: Probate address is 600 Columbia St.
Civil Records: Access: In person only. Visitors must perform in person searches themselves. Court makes copy: $.25 per page. Required to search: name, years to search. Civil cases indexed by defendant, plaintiff. Civil records on computer since 1992, prior records on index cards since 1978.
Criminal Records: Access: In person only. Visitors must perform in person searches themselves. Court makes copy: $.25 per page. Required to search: name, years to search; SSN helpful. Criminal records on computer since 1992, prior records on index cards since 1978.
General Information: Public terminal goes back to 1992. No adoption, mental, juvenile, or sealed records released. Will not fax specific case file. Certification fee: $5.00 per document. Payee: Campbell Circuit Court. Personal checks accepted. Prepayment required.

District Court 600 Columbia St, Newport, KY 41071-1816; phone: 859-292-6305; fax: 859-292-6593; hours 8:30AM-4PM (EST). *Misdemeanor, Civil Actions Under $4,000, Eviction, Small Claims, Probate.*
www.kycourts.net/clerks/campbellclerk.shtm
Civil Records: Access: Mail, in person. Both court and visitors may perform in person searches. Search fee: $10.00 (probate searches only). Court makes copy: $.25 per page; same fee for self serve. Required to search: name, years to search. Civil cases indexed by defendant, plaintiff. Civil records on computer back to 1992, prior records on index cards to 1978.
Criminal Records: Access: In person only. Visitors must perform in person searches themselves. Court makes copy: $.25 per page; same fee for self serve. Required to search: name, years to search. Criminal records on computer back to 1992, prior records on index cards to 1978.
General Information: Public terminal goes back to 1992. No adoption, mental, juvenile, or sealed records released. Will not fax documents. Certification fee: $5.00 per document. Payee: Campbell Circuit Clerk. Business checks accepted. Prepayment and SASE required.

Carlisle County

Circuit & District Court Box 337, Bardwell, KY 42023; phone: 270-628-5425; fax: 270-628-5456; hours 8AM-4PM (CST). *Felony, Misdemeanor, Civil, Eviction, Small Claims, Probate.*
Civil Records: Access: Phone, fax, mail, in person. Both court and visitors may perform in person searches. No search fee. Court makes copy: $.25 per page; same fee for self serve. Required to search: name, years to search. Civil cases indexed by defendant, plaintiff. Civil records on computer since 5/1993, records on docket books since 1978, prior records archived. Mail turnaround time 1-5 days.
Criminal Records: Access: Phone, fax, mail, in person. Both court and visitors may perform in person searches. No search fee. Court makes copy: $.25 per page; same fee for self serve. Required to search: name, years to search. Criminal records on computer since 5/1993, records on docket books since 1978, prior records archived. Mail turnaround time 1-5 days.
General Information: Public terminal goes back to 1993. No adoption, mental, juvenile, or sealed records released. Will fax documents for $2.00 per page. Certification fee: $5.00. Payee: Circuit Clerk. Personal checks accepted. Prepayment and SASE required.

Carroll County

Circuit & District Court 802 Clay St, Carrollton, KY 41008; phone: 502-732-4305; fax: 502-732-8138; hours 8AM-4:30PM (EST). *Felony, Misdemeanor, Civil, Eviction, Small Claims, Probate.*
Civil Records: Access: In person only. Visitors must perform in person searches themselves. Court makes copy: $.25 per page. Required to search: name, years to search. Civil cases indexed by defendant, plaintiff. Civil records on computer since 1994, on docket books since 1980. Records before 1980 are archived in Frankfort.
Criminal Records: Access: In person only. Visitors must perform in person searches themselves. Court makes copy: $.25 per page. Required to search: name, years to search, DOB; SSN helpful. Criminal records on computer since 1994, on docket books since 1980. Records before 1980 are archived in Frankfort.
General Information: Public terminal goes back to 1994. No adoption, mental, juvenile, or sealed records released. Will not fax specific case file. Certification fee: $5.00 per cert. Payee: Circuit Clerk. Personal checks accepted. Prepayment required.

Carter County

Circuit Court 100 E Main St, Grayson, KY 41143; phone: 606-474-5191; fax: 606-474-8826; hours 8:30AM-4PM M-F; 9AM-N Sat (EST). *Felony, Civil Actions Over $4,000.*
Civil Records: Access: Mail, in person. Both court and visitors may perform in person searches. No search fee. Court makes copy: $.25 per page. Required to search: name, years to search. Civil cases indexed by defendant, plaintiff. Civil records on computer since 1994, records archived since 1978, prior records are archived.
Criminal Records: Access: In person only. Both court and visitors may perform in person searches. No search fee. Court makes copy: $.25 per page. Required to search: name, years to search, DOB, SSN. Criminal records on computer since 1994, records archived since 1978, prior records are archived. Mail turnaround time 1-2 days.
General Information: Public use terminal available. No adoption, mental, juvenile, or sealed records released. Will not fax documents. Certification fee: $5.00 per doc. Payee: Carter County Circuit Clerk. Prepayment and SASE required.

District Court Courthouse, Rm 203, 300 W Main, Grayson, KY 41143; phone: 606-474-6572; fax: 606-474-8584; hours 8AM-4PM (EST). *Misdemeanor, Civil Actions Under $4,000, Eviction, Small Claims, Probate.*
Civil Records: Access: Mail, in person. Both court and visitors may perform in person searches. Court makes copy: $.25 per page. Required to search: name, years to search. Civil cases indexed by defendant, plaintiff. Civil records on computer since 1994, prior records on index cards.
Criminal Records: Access: In person only. Visitors must perform in person searches themselves. Court makes copy: $.25 per page. Required to search: name, years to search, DOB; SSN helpful. Criminal records on computer since 1994, prior records on index cards.
General Information: Public terminal goes back to 4/94. No adoption, mental, juvenile, or sealed records released. Certification fee: $5.00. Payee: District Clerk. Personal checks accepted. Prepayment and SASE required.

Casey County

Circuit & District Court PO Box 147, Liberty, KY 42539; phone: 606-787-6510; fax: 606-787-2497; hours 8AM-4:30PM M, Tu & F, 8AM-4PM W-Th, 8AM-N Sat (EST). *Felony, Misdemeanor, Civil, Eviction, Small Claims, Probate.*
Note: This court asks all pre-trial record requests go to the Administrative office of the Courts in Frankfort.
Civil Records: Access: In person only. Visitors must perform in person searches themselves. Court

makes copy: $.25 per page; same fee for self serve. Required to search: name, years to search. Civil cases indexed by defendant, plaintiff. Civil records on index cards since 1978, prior records archived, computerized from 1995.
Criminal Records: Access: In person only. Visitors must perform in person searches themselves. Court makes copy: $.25 per page; same fee for self serve. Required to search: name, years to search, DOB, SSN. Criminal records on index cards since 1978, prior records archived, computerized from 1995.
General Information: Public terminal goes back to 1995. No adoption, mental, juvenile, or sealed records released. Certification fee: $5.00. Payee: Circuit Clerk. Personal checks accepted. Prepayment required.

Christian County

Circuit & District Court Christian County Justice Ctr, 100 Justice Way, Hopkinsville, KY 42240; phone: 270-889-6539; fax: 270-889-6564; hours 8AM-4:30PM (CST). *Felony, Misdemeanor, Civil, Eviction, Small Claims, Probate.*
Note: Fax number above is for District Court.
Civil Records: Access: Mail, in person. Both court and visitors may perform in person searches. Court makes copy: $.25 per page. Required to search: name, years to search. Civil cases indexed by defendant, plaintiff. Civil records on computer since 1991, prior records on index cards since 1978.
Criminal Records: Access: In person only. Visitors must perform in person searches themselves. Court makes copy: $.25 per page. Required to search: name, years to search; also helpful: DOB, SSN. Criminal records on computer since 1991, prior records on index cards since 1978. Note: Searchers must fill out request form, state reason why copies are needed, and provide copy of ID or drivers license.
General Information: Public use terminal available. No adoption, mental, juvenile, or sealed records released. Certification fee: $5.00 per document. Payee: Circuit Clerk. Personal checks accepted. Prepayment and SASE required.

Clark County

Circuit Court Box 687, Winchester, KY 40392; phone: 859-737-7264; hours 8AM-4PM (EST). *Felony, Civil Actions Over $4,000.*
Civil Records: Access: Mail, in person. Visitors must perform in person searches themselves. Court makes copy: $.25 per page. Required to search: name, years to search; also helpful: address. Civil cases indexed by defendant, plaintiff. Civil records on computer since 1989, on index cards since 1950, prior records archived since the 1700s.
Criminal Records: Access: In person only. Visitors must perform in person searches themselves. Court makes copy: $.25 per page. Required to search: name, years to search; also helpful: address, DOB, SSN. Criminal records on computer since 1989, on index cards since 1950, prior records archived since the 1700s.
General Information: Public terminal goes back to 1989. No adoption, mental, juvenile, or sealed records released. Certification fee: $5.00 per doc. Payee: Circuit Clerk. Personal checks accepted. Prepayment and SASE required.

District Court PO Box 687, Winchester, KY 40392-0687; phone: 859-737-7141; probate phone: 859-737-7141; fax: 859-737-7005; probate fax: same; hours 8AM-4PM (EST). *Misdemeanor, Civil Actions Under $4,000, Eviction, Small Claims, Probate.*
Civil Records: Access: Mail, in person. Both court and visitors may perform in person searches. No search fee. Court makes copy: $.25 per page; same fee for self serve. Required to search: name, years to search. Civil cases indexed by defendant, plaintiff. Civil records on computer since 1989, on docket books since 1978, prior records on archived. Mail turnaround time 1-3 days.

Criminal Records: Access: Mail, in person. Both court and visitors may perform in person searches. No search fee. Court makes copy: $.25 per page; same fee for self serve. Required to search: name, years to search; also helpful: DOB, SSN. Criminal records on computer since 1989, on docket books since 1978, prior records on archived. Mail turnaround time 1-3 days.

General Information: Public terminal goes back to 1986. No adoption, mental, juvenile, or sealed records released. Certification fee: $5.00. Payee: District Clerk. Personal checks accepted. Prepayment and SASE required.

Clay County

Circuit & District Court 316 Main St #108, Manchester, KY 40962; phone: 606-598-3663; fax: 606-598-4047; hours 7:30AM-4:30PM (EST). *Felony, Misdemeanor, Civil, Eviction, Small Claims, Probate.*

Civil Records: Access: In person only. Visitors must perform in person searches themselves. Court makes copy: $.25 per page. Required to search: name, years to search. Civil cases indexed by defendant, plaintiff. Civil records on computer back to 1992, on index cards since 1978, records through 1986 in archives.

Criminal Records: Access: In person only. Visitors must perform in person searches themselves. Court makes copy: $.25 per page. Required to search: name, years to search, DOB; SSN helpful. Criminal records on computer back to 1992, on index cards since 1978, records through 1986 in archives.

General Information: Public terminal goes back to 1992. No adoption, mental, juvenile, or sealed records released. Certification fee: $5.00 per doc. Payee: Circuit Clerk. Personal checks accepted. Prepayment required.

Clinton County

Circuit & District Court Courthouse 2nd Fl, 100 S Cross St, Albany, KY 42602; phone: 606-387-6424; fax: 606-387-8154; hours 8AM-4:30PM M-F; 8AM-N Sat (CST). *Felony, Misdemeanor, Civil, Eviction, Small Claims, Probate.*

Civil Records: Access: Phone, mail, in person. Both court and visitors may perform in person searches. No search fee. Court makes copy: $.25 per page. Required to search: name, years to search. Civil cases indexed by defendant, plaintiff. Civil records on computer since 8/92, on docket books since 1978, prior records archived to 1865. Mail turnaround time 5 days.

Criminal Records: Access: Phone, mail, in person. Visitors must perform in person searches themselves. No search fee. Court makes copy: $.25 per page. Required to search: name, years to search, SSN; also helpful: DOB. Criminal records on computer since 8/92, on docket books since 1978, prior records archive to 1865. Note: Will search pre-1992 records, or they can order it from the state archives. Mail turnaround time 5 days.

General Information: Public terminal goes back to 8/1992. No adoption, mental, juvenile, or sealed records released. Certification fee: $5.00 per doc. Payee: Circuit Clerk. Personal checks accepted. Prepayment and SASE required.

Crittenden County

Circuit & District Court 107 S Main, Marion, KY 42064; phone: 270-965-4200 (and) 270-965-4046; hours 8AM-4:30PM (CST). *Felony, Misdemeanor, Civil, Eviction, Small Claims, Probate, Traffic.*

Civil Records: Access: Mail, in person. Visitors must perform in person searches themselves. Court makes copy: $.25 per page. Required to search: name, years to search. Civil cases indexed by defendant, plaintiff. Civil records on index cards since 1977; on computer back to 9/94.

Criminal Records: Access: In person only. Visitors must perform in person searches themselves. Court

makes copy: $.25 per page. Required to search: name, years to search. Circuit criminal records on index cards since 1977; on computer back to 9/94; District Criminal 1994 to present.

General Information: Public terminal goes back to 9/1994. No adoption, mental, juvenile, or sealed records released. Fee to fax documents is $2.00 1st page; $1.00 each add'l. Certification fee: $5.00. Payee: Circuit Clerk. Personal checks not accepted. Prepayment and SASE required.

Cumberland County

Circuit & District Court Box 395, Burkesville, KY 42717; phone: 270-864-2611; fax: na/; hours 8AM-4PM (CST). *Felony, Misdemeanor, Civil, Eviction, Small Claims, Probate.*

Civil Records: Access: In person only. Visitors must perform in person searches themselves. Court makes copy: $.25 per page. Required to search: name, years to search. Civil cases indexed by defendant, plaintiff. Civil records on computer back to 6/93, on docket cards from 1978, prior records archived.

Criminal Records: Access: In person only. Visitors must perform in person searches themselves. No search fee. Court makes copy: $.25 per page. Required to search: name, years to search, DOB; SSN helpful. Criminal records on computer back to 6/93, on docket cards from 1978, prior records archived.

General Information: Public terminal goes back to 6/1993. No adoption, mental, juvenile, or sealed records released. Fee to fax documents is $2.00 and $1.00 per page. Certification fee: $5.00 per doc. Payee: Circuit Clerk. Personal checks accepted. Prepayment required.

Daviess County

Circuit & District Court Box 277, 100 E Second St, Owensboro, KY 42302; phone: 270-687-7330 (Circuit Crim); criminal phone: 270-687-7329 (Circuit Crim); 270-687-7200 (District Crim); civil phone: 270-687-7220 (Circuit Civil); 270-687-7205 (District Civil); probate phone: 270-687-7207; hours 8AM-4PM (CST). *Felony, Misdemeanor, Civil, Eviction, Small Claims, Probate.*

Civil Records: Access: In person only. Visitors must perform in person searches themselves. Court makes copy: $.25 per page. Required to search: name, years to search. Civil cases indexed by defendant, plaintiff. Civil records on computer since 4/91, on index cards since 1978, prior records on docket books since 1809. Search in person only on Tuesday or Thursday.

Criminal Records: Access: In person only. Visitors must perform in person searches themselves. Court makes copy: $.25 per page. Required to search: name, years to search, DOB, SSN. Criminal records on computer since 4/91, on index cards since 1978, prior records on docket books since 1809. Search in person only on Tuesday or Thursday.

General Information: Public use terminal available. No adoption, mental, juvenile, or sealed records released. Certification fee: $5.00. Payee: Circuit Clerk. Business checks accepted. Prepayment required.

Edmonson County

Circuit & District Court Box 739, 110 Cross Main St, Brownsville, KY 42210; phone: 270-597-2584; probate phone: 270-597-3918; fax: 270-597-2884; hours 8AM-4:30PM M-W,F; 8AM-N Th,S (CST). *Felony, Misdemeanor, Civil, Eviction, Small Claims, Probate.*

Civil Records: Access: In person only. Visitors must perform in person searches themselves. Court makes copy: $.25 per page; same fee for self serve. Required to search: name, years to search, address. Civil cases indexed by defendant, plaintiff. Civil records computerized since 1995, on index cards and docket books from 1800s.

Criminal Records: Access: In person only. Visitors must perform in person searches themselves. Court makes copy: $.25 per page; same fee for self serve.

Required to search: name, years to search, DOB, SSN. Criminal records computerized since 1995, on index cards and docket books from 1800s.

General Information: Public terminal goes back to 1995. No adoption, mental, juvenile, or sealed records released. Certification fee: $5.00. Payee: Circuit Clerk. Personal checks accepted. Prepayment required.

Elliott County

Circuit & District Court PO Box 788, Sandy Hook, KY 41171; phone: 606-738-5238; fax: 606-738-6962; hours 8AM-4PM M-F; 9AM-N Sat (EST). *Felony, Misdemeanor, Civil, Eviction, Small Claims, Probate.*

Civil Records: Access: In person only. Both court and visitors may perform in person searches. No search fee. Court makes copy: $.25 per page; same fee for self serve. Required to search: name, years to search. Civil cases indexed by defendant, plaintiff. Civil records on computer since 10/1992, prior records on index cards since 1978.

Criminal Records: Access: In person only. Both court and visitors may perform in person searches. No search fee. Court makes copy: $.25 per page; same fee for self serve. Required to search: name, years to search; SSN helpful. Criminal records on computer since 10/1992, prior records on index cards since 1978. Mail requests for criminal searches may be made to the state AOC.

General Information: Public terminal goes back to 10/1992. No adoption, mental, juvenile, or sealed records released. Will fax specific case file for $2.00 1st page; $1.00 each add'l. Certification fee: $5.00 per doc. Payee: Circuit Clerk. Personal checks accepted. Prepayment required.

Estill County

Circuit & District Court 130 Main St, Rm 207, Irvine, KY 40336; phone: 606-723-3970; fax: 606-723-1158; hours 8AM-4PM (EST). *Felony, Misdemeanor, Civil, Eviction, Small Claims, Probate.*

Note: Probate index is separate at this same address.

Civil Records: Access: Phone, fax, mail, in person. Both court and visitors may perform in person searches. No search fee. Court makes copy: $.25 per page; same fee for self serve. Required to search: name, years to search. Civil cases indexed by defendant, plaintiff. Civil records on index cards back to 1965; on computer back to 1994. Mail turnaround time 2-4 days.

Criminal Records: Access: Phone, fax, mail, in person. Both court and visitors may perform in person searches. No search fee. Court makes copy: $.25 per page; same fee for self serve. Required to search: name, years to search, DOB, SSN. Criminal records on computer back to 1994. Mail turnaround time 2-4 days.

General Information: Public terminal goes back to 1994. No adoption, mental, juvenile, or sealed records released. Fee to fax documents is $1.00 per page. Certification fee: $5.00 per document includes copy fee. Payee: Circuit Clerk. Personal checks accepted. Prepayment and SASE required.

Fayette County

Circuit Court - Criminal & Civil Divisions 120 N Limestone, Lexington, KY 40507; criminal phone: 859-246-2224; civil phone: 859-246-2141; fax: 859-246-2146; hours 8:30AM-4:30PM (EST). *Felony, Civil Actions Over $4,000.* www.kycourts.net/Courts/FayetteCourtsNS.shtm

Civil Records: Access: Mail, in person. Both court and visitors may perform in person searches. Search fee: $5.00 per name. Court makes copy: $.25 per page. Required to search: name, years to search. Civil cases indexed by defendant, plaintiff. Civil records on computer since 4/1993, on index cards since 1978, prior records on books and archived. Mail turnaround time 1-2 days.

Criminal Records: Access: Mail, in person. Both court and visitors may perform in person searches. Search fee: $5.00 per name. Court makes copy: $.25 per page. Required to search: name, years to search; also helpful: DOB, SSN. Criminal records on computer since 4/1993, on index cards since 1978, prior records on books and archived. Mail turnaround time 1-2 days.

General Information: Public terminal goes back to 1993. No adoption, juvenile, mental, or sealed records released. Certification fee: $5.00 per doc. Payee: Fayette County Circuit Clerk. No personal checks accepted. Prepayment and SASE required.

District Court - Criminal & Civil 150 N Limestone #D112, Lexington, KY 40507; criminal phone: 859-246-2228; civil phone: 859-246-2240; fax: 859-246-2146; hours 8AM-4PM (EST). *Misdemeanor, Civil Actions Under $4,000, Eviction, Small Claims, Probate.*
www.kycourts.net/Courts/FayetteCourtsNS.shtm
Civil Records: Access: Mail, in person. Both court and visitors may perform in person searches. Search fee: $5.00 per name. Court makes copy: $.25 per page. Required to search: name, years to search. Civil cases indexed by defendant, plaintiff. Civil records on computer since 1992, prior records on index cards since 1977.

Criminal Records: Access: In person only. Visitors must perform in person searches themselves. Court makes copy: $.25 per page. Required to search: name, years to search, DOB; SSN helpful. Criminal records on computer since 1977.

General Information: Public terminal goes back to 1992. No adoption, mental, juvenile, or sealed records released. Certification fee: $1.00 per cert. Payee: District Clerk. Personal checks accepted. Prepayment and SASE required.

Fleming County

Circuit & District Court Courthouse 100 Court Square, Flemingsburg, KY 41041; phone: 606-845-7011; fax: 606-849-2400; hours 8AM-4:30PM (EST). *Felony, Misdemeanor, Civil, Eviction, Small Claims, Probate.*
Civil Records: Access: Phone, fax, mail, in person. Both court and visitors may perform in person searches. No search fee. Court makes copy: $.25 per page; same fee for self serve. Required to search: name, years to search. Civil cases indexed by defendant, plaintiff. Civil records on computer since 5/1994, prior records on index cards since 1978.

Criminal Records: Access: In person only. Both court and visitors may perform in person searches. No search fee. Court makes copy: $.25 per page; same fee for self serve. Required to search: name, years to search, DOB; SSN helpful. Criminal records on computer since 5/1994, prior records on index cards since 1978. Mail turnaround time 1-2 days.

General Information: Public terminal goes back to 4/1994. No adoption, mental, juvenile, or sealed records released. Fee to fax documents is $1.00 per page. Certification fee: $5.00. Payee: Circuit Clerk. Personal checks accepted. Prepayment and SASE required.

Floyd County

Circuit Court 127 S Lake Dr, Prestonsburg, KY 41653-3368; phone: 606-889-1658; fax: 606-889-1666; hours 8AM-4PM (EST). *Felony, Civil Actions Over $4,000.*
Civil Records: Access: Mail, in person. Both court and visitors may perform in person searches. No search fee. Court makes copy: $.25 per page. Self serve copy fee: no charge if paper provided. Required to search: name, years to search. Civil cases indexed by defendant, plaintiff. Civil records on computer since 9/1991, prior records on index cards since 1978. Mail turnaround time 2-4 days.

Criminal Records: Access: Mail, in person. Both court and visitors may perform in person searches. No search fee. Court makes copy: $.25 per page. Self serve copy fee: no charge if paper provided. Required

to search: name, years to search, DOB, SSN. Criminal records on computer since 9/1991, prior records on index cards since 1978. Mail turnaround time 2-4 days.

General Information: Public terminal goes back to 1991. No adoption, mental, juvenile, or sealed records released. Will fax documents for $2.00 1st page; $1.00 per add'l page. Certification fee: $5.00. Payee: Clerk of Circuit Court. Personal checks accepted. Prepayment and SASE required.

District Court 127 S Lake Dr, Prestonsburg, KY 41653; criminal phone: 606-889-1672; civil phone: 606-889-1650; probate phone: 606-886-2124; fax: 606-889-1652; hours 8AM-4PM (EST). *Misdemeanor, Small Claims, Probate.*
Note: Small claims: 606-886-2124
Criminal Records: Access: Phone, mail, in person. Only the court performs in person searches; visitors may not. No search fee. Court makes copy: $.25 per page. Required to search: name, years to search; also helpful: SSN. Criminal records on computer since 1991, prior records in index cards since 1989. Records are only kept for five years in this office. Mail turnaround time 2-4 days.

General Information: No public access terminal. No adoption, mental, juvenile, or sealed records released. Certification fee: $5.00. Payee: Floyd District Court. Personal checks accepted. Prepayment and SASE required.

Franklin County

Circuit Court Box 678, 214 St Clair St, Frankfort, KY 40602; phone: 502-564-8380; criminal phone: 502-573-2350/Adm; fax: 502-564-8188; hours 8AM-4:30PM (EST). *Felony, Civil Actions Over $4,000.*
www.kycourts.net/Counties/Franklin.asp?County=Franklin
Note: Criminal records located at; 100 Mill Creek Park, Frankfort KY 40601- walk-in 7am-3pm or drive thru 7am -10pm
Civil Records: Access: In person only. Visitors must perform in person searches themselves. Court makes copy: $10.00 per document. Required to search: name, years to search. Civil cases indexed by defendant, plaintiff. Civil records on computer since 1990, prior records on index cards since 1978.

Criminal Records: Access: Mail, in person. Visitors must perform in person searches themselves. Search fee: $10.00 per name. Court makes copy: $10.00 per document. Required to search: name, years to search, DOB, SSN. Criminal records on computer since 1990, prior records on index cards since 1978. All requests are referred to the state Administrator's Office of Courts. Mail turnaround time 2-3 days.

General Information: No public access terminal. No adoption, mental, juvenile, or sealed records released. Will fax documents $15.00. Certification fee: $5.00 per doc. Payee: Circuit Clerk. Personal checks accepted. Prepayment and SASE required.

District Court Box 678, Frankfort, KY 40601; phone: 502-564-7013; fax: 502-564-8188; hours 8AM-4:30PM (EST). *Misdemeanor, Civil Actions Under $4,000, Eviction, Small Claims, Probate.*
Civil Records: Access: In person only. Visitors must perform in person searches themselves. Court makes copy: $.25 per page. Required to search: name, years to search. Civil cases indexed by defendant, plaintiff. Civil records on computer since 1990, records on index cards since 1978, prior records archived.
Criminal Records: Access: In person only. Visitors must perform in person searches themselves. Court makes copy: $.25 per page. Required to search: name, years to search, DOB. Criminal records on computer since 1990, records on index cards since 1978, prior records archived.

General Information: Public terminal goes back to 1990. No adoption, mental, juvenile, or sealed records released. Certification fee: $5.00 per doc. Payee:

Franklin Circuit Clerk. Personal checks accepted. Prepayment required.

Fulton County

Circuit & District Court Box 198, Hickman, KY 42050; phone: 270-236-3944; fax: 270-236-3729; hours 8AM-4PM (CST). *Felony, Misdemeanor, Civil, Eviction, Small Claims, Probate.*
Note: 6 days of the court docket information can be found at www.kycourts.com.
Civil Records: Access: Mail, in person. Both court and visitors may perform in person searches. Court makes copy: $.25 per page; same fee for self serve. Required to search: name, years to search. Civil cases indexed by defendant, plaintiff. Civil records on index from 1980, computerized from 1995, and archived since 1843.

Criminal Records: Access: In person only. Visitors must perform in person searches themselves. Court makes copy: $.25 per page; same fee for self serve. Required to search: name, years to search. Criminal records on index from 1980, computerized from 1995, and archived since 1843.

General Information: Public terminal goes back to 1978. No adoption, mental, juvenile, or sealed records released. Certification fee: $5.00. Payee: Circuit Clerk. Personal checks accepted. Prepayment and SASE required.

Gallatin County

Circuit Court Box 256, 100 Main St, Warsaw, KY 41095; phone: 859-567-5241; fax: 859-567-7420; hours 8AM-4:30PM M,T,Th,F; closed W (EST). *Felony, Civil Actions Over $4,000.*
Civil Records: Access: Mail, in person. Both court and visitors may perform in person searches. No search fee. Court makes copy: $.25 per page; same fee for self serve. Required to search: name, years to search. Civil cases indexed by defendant, plaintiff. Civil records go back to 1990. Computerized records go to 1993. Mail turnaround time 4 days.

Criminal Records: Access: Mail, in person. Both court and visitors may perform in person searches. No search fee. Court makes copy: $.25 per page; same fee for self serve. Required to search: name, years to search; also helpful: SSN. Criminal records go back to 1990. Computerized records to 1993. Mail turnaround time 4 days.

General Information: Public terminal goes back to 1995. No adoption, mental, juvenile, or sealed records released. Will fax documents for $2.00 per page, $3.00 per document. Certification fee: $5.00 per cert. Payee: Circuit Clerk. Personal checks accepted. Prepayment and SASE required.

District Court Box 256, Warsaw, KY 41095; phone: 859-567-2388; probate phone: 859-567-2388 x1; fax: 859-567-7420; probate fax: 859-567-1492; hours 8AM-4:30PM T,Th,F; 8AM-6PM M; 8AM-N Sat (EST). *Misdemeanor, Civil Actions Under $4,000, Eviction, Small Claims, Probate.*
Civil Records: Access: Fax, mail, in person. Both court and visitors may perform in person searches. No search fee. Court makes copy: $.25 per page; same fee for self serve. Required to search: name, years to search. Civil cases indexed by defendant, plaintiff. Civil records on computer since 10/1994, prior records on index cards since 1978. Mail turnaround time 1-2 days.

Criminal Records: Access: Fax, mail, in person. Both court and visitors may perform in person searches. No search fee. Court makes copy: $.25 per page; same fee for self serve. Required to search: name, years to search, DOB; also helpful: SSN. Criminal records on computer since 10/1994, prior records on index cards since 1978. Mail turnaround time 1-2 days.

General Information: Public terminal goes back to 10/1994. No adoption, mental, juvenile, or sealed records released. Fee to fax documents is $2.00 per page and $3.00 per document. Certification fee: $5.00

per doc. Payee: District Clerk. Personal checks accepted. Prepayment required.

Garrard County

Circuit & District Court 7 Public Square, Courthouse Annex, Lancaster, KY 40444; phone: 859-792-6032; fax: 859-792-6414; hours 8AM-4PM M,T,Th,F, 8AM-N Wed & Sat (EST). *Felony, Misdemeanor, Civil, Eviction, Small Claims, Probate.*

Note: Circuit Clerk can be reached at 859-792-2961.

Civil Records: Access: In person only. Visitors must perform in person searches themselves. Court makes copy: $.25 per page. Required to search: name, years to search. Civil cases indexed by defendant, plaintiff. Civil records in index since 1978.

Criminal Records: Access: In person only. Visitors must perform in person searches themselves. Court makes copy: $.25 per page. Required to search: name, years to search; also helpful: address, DOB, SSN. Criminal records in index since 1978.

General Information: Public use terminal available. No adoption, mental, juvenile, or sealed records released. Certification fee: $5.00 per doc. Payee: Circuit Clerk. Personal checks accepted. Prepayment required.

Grant County

Circuit & District Court Courthouse 101 N Main, Williamstown, KY 41097; phone: 859-824-4467 (Circuit) 859-823-5251 (District); fax: 859-824-0183; hours 8AM-4PM (EST). *Felony, Misdemeanor, Civil, Eviction, Small Claims, Probate.*

Civil Records: Access: In person only. Visitors must perform in person searches themselves. Court makes copy: $.25 per page. Required to search: name, years to search. Civil cases indexed by defendant, plaintiff. Civil records on computer back to 1992, prior records on index cards for District Court since 1978; Circuit Court since 1993.

Criminal Records: Access: In person only. Visitors must perform in person searches themselves. Court makes copy: $.25 per page. Required to search: name, years to search, DOB; SSN helpful. Criminal records on computer back to 1992, prior records on index cards since 1988.

General Information: Public terminal goes back to 7/1992. No adoption, mental, juvenile, or sealed records released. Will fax specific docket for $2.00 for 1st page; $1.00 each add'l page. Certification fee: $5.00. Payee: Circuit Clerk. Personal checks accepted. Prepayment required.

Graves County

Circuit & District Court Courthouse 100 E Broadway, Mayfield, KY 42066; phone: 270-247-1733; fax: 270-247-7358; hours 8AM-4:30PM (CST). *Felony, Misdemeanor, Civil, Eviction, Small Claims, Probate.*

Civil Records: Access: In person only. Visitors must perform in person searches themselves. Court makes copy: $.25 per page. Required to search: name, years to search. Civil cases indexed by defendant, plaintiff. Civil records on computer since 6/1994, prior records on index cards since 1978.

Criminal Records: Access: In person only. Visitors must perform in person searches themselves. Court makes copy: $.25 per page. Required to search: name, years to search, DOB; SSN helpful. Criminal records on computer since 6/1994, prior records on index cards since 1978.

General Information: Public terminal goes back to 6/1994. No adoption, mental, juvenile, or sealed records released. Will fax specific case file $3.00 plus $1.00 per page if specific case docket requested. Certification fee: $5.00 per doc. Payee: Circuit Clerk. Personal checks accepted. Prepayment required.

Grayson County

Circuit & District Court 125 E White Oak, Leitchfield, KY 42754; phone: 270-259-3040; fax: 270-259-9866; hours 8AM-4:30PM T,W,F; 8AM-5:30PM M,Th (CST). *Felony, Misdemeanor, Civil, Eviction, Small Claims, Probate.*

Civil Records: Access: Mail, in person. Both court and visitors may perform in person searches. Search fee: $10.00 per name. Court makes copy: $.25 per page. Required to search: name, years to search. Civil cases indexed by defendant, plaintiff. Civil records on computer since 5/94, prior records on index cards since 1978. Mail turnaround time 5 days.

Criminal Records: Access: Mail, in person. Both court and visitors may perform in person searches. Search fee: $10.00. Court makes copy: $.25 per page. Required to search: name, years to search; also helpful: DOB, SSN. Criminal records on computer since 5/94, prior records on index cards since 1978. Mail turnaround time 2 days.

General Information: Public terminal goes back to 5/1994. No adoption, mental, juvenile, or sealed records released. Certification fee: $5.00. Payee: Circuit Clerk. Personal checks accepted. Prepayment and SASE required.

Green County

Circuit & District Court 203 W Court St, Greensburg, KY 42743; phone: 270-932-5631; fax: 270-932-6468; hours 8AM-4PM M-W, F; 8AM-12:30PM Sat (EST). *Felony, Misdemeanor, Civil, Eviction, Small Claims, Probate.*

Civil Records: Access: Fax, mail, in person. Both court and visitors may perform in person searches. No search fee. Court makes copy: $.25 per page. Required to search: name, years to search; also helpful: address. Civil cases indexed by defendant, plaintiff. Civil records on index cards and computer since 1978. Mail turnaround time 1-2 days.

Criminal Records: Access: Fax, mail, in person. Both court and visitors may perform in person searches. No search fee. Court makes copy: $.25 per page. Required to search: name, years to search; also helpful: address, DOB, SSN. Criminal records on index cards and computer since 1978. Mail turnaround time 1-2 days.

General Information: Public use terminal available. No adoption, mental, juvenile, or sealed records released. No fee to fax documents; will fax to toll-free numbers only. No certification fee. Payee: Circuit Clerk. Personal checks accepted. Prepayment and SASE required.

Greenup County

Circuit & District Court Courthouse Annex, 301 Main St, Greenup, KY 41144; phone: 606-473-9869; fax: 606-473-7388; hours 9AM-4:30PM M-F (EST). *Felony, Misdemeanor, Civil, Eviction, Small Claims, Probate.*

Civil Records: Access: In person only. Both court and visitors may perform in person searches. Court makes copy: $.25 per page; same fee for self serve. Required to search: name, years to search. Civil cases indexed by defendant, plaintiff. Civil records on computer since 1990, prior records on index cards since 1978.

Criminal Records: Access: In person only. Visitors must perform in person searches themselves. Court makes copy: $.25 per page; same fee for self serve. Required to search: name, years to search, DOB; SSN helpful. Criminal records on computer since 1990, prior records on index cards since 1978.

General Information: Public terminal goes back to 1990. No adoption, mental, juvenile, or sealed records released. Certification fee: $5.00. Payee: Circuit Clerk. Personal checks accepted. Prepayment required.

Hancock County

Circuit & District Court Courthouse, PO Box 250, Hawesville, KY 42348; phone: 270-927-8144; fax: 270-927-8629; hours 8AM-4PM M,T,W,F; 8AM-5:30PM Th (CST). *Felony, Misdemeanor, Civil, Eviction, Small Claims, Probate.*

Civil Records: Access: In person only. Both court and visitors may perform in person searches. No search fee. Court makes copy: $.25 per page. Required to search: name, years to search. Civil cases indexed by defendant, plaintiff. Civil records on computer since 8/1994, prior records on index cards.

Criminal Records: Access: In person only. Both court and visitors may perform in person searches. No search fee. Court makes copy: $.25 per page. Required to search: name, years to search, DOB; SSN helpful. Criminal records on computer since 8/1994, prior records on index cards. Court recommends that you do searches through the state AOC in Frankfort.

General Information: Public terminal goes back to 8/1994. No adoption, mental, juvenile, or sealed records released. Fee to fax specific case file is $2.00 for 1st page; $1.00 each add'l. Certification fee: $5.00 per doc. Payee: Circuit Clerk. Personal checks accepted. Prepayment required.

Hardin County

Circuit & District Court Hardin County Justice Ctr, 120 E Dixie Ave, Elizabethtown, KY 42701; phone: 270-766-5000; fax: 270-766-5243; hours 8AM-4:30PM (EST). *Felony, Misdemeanor, Civil, Eviction, Small Claims, Probate.*

Civil Records: Access: In person only. Visitors must perform in person searches themselves. Court makes copy: $.25 per page. Required to search: name, years to search. Civil cases indexed by defendant, plaintiff. Civil records on computer since 3/28/94, prior records on index cards since 1978.

Criminal Records: Access: In person only. Visitors must perform in person searches themselves. Court makes copy: $.25 per page. Required to search: name, years to search, DOB. Criminal records on computer since 3/28/94, prior records on index cards since 1978.

General Information: Public terminal goes back to 1994. No adoption, mental, juvenile, motor vehicle or sealed records released. Will fax specific document for $2.00 per page, payable in advance by money order only. Certification fee: $5.00 per doc. Payee: Circuit Clerk. Money orders only accepted. Prepayment required.

Radcliff District Court 220 Freedom Way, Radcliff, KY 40160; phone: 270-351-1299/4799; fax: 270-351-1301; hours 8:30AM-12, 12:30-4PM (EST). *Probate, Eviction.*

Harlan County

Circuit & District Court Box 190, Harlan, KY 40831; phone: 606-573-2680; fax: 606-573-5895; hours 8AM-4:30PM (EST). *Felony, Misdemeanor, Civil, Eviction, Small Claims, Probate.*

Civil Records: Access: In person only. Visitors must perform in person searches themselves. Court makes copy: $.25 per page. Required to search: name, years to search. Civil cases indexed by defendant, plaintiff. Civil records on computer since 8/1991, on index cards since 1978, records prior to 1991 are archived in Frankfort.

Criminal Records: Access: In person only. Visitors must perform in person searches themselves. Court makes copy: $.25 per page. Required to search: name, years to search, DOB; SSN helpful. Criminal records on computer since 8/1991, on index cards since 1978, records prior to 1991 archived in Frankfort.

General Information: Public terminal goes back to 8/2001. No adoption, mental, juvenile, sealed or domestic violence records released. Will fax specific case file for $2.00 1st page, $1.00 each add'l. Certification fee: $5.00 per document. Payee: Circuit Clerk. Only local personal checks accepted. Prepayment required.

Harrison County

Circuit & District Court 115 Court St #1, Cynthiana, KY 41031; phone: 859-234-1914; fax: 859-234-6787; hours 8:30AM-4:30PM M-F, 9AM-12PM Sat (EST). *Felony, Misdemeanor, Civil, Eviction, Small Claims, Probate.*
Civil Records: Access: Mail, in person. Both court and visitors may perform in person searches. No search fee. Court makes copy: $.25 per page; same fee for self serve. Required to search: name, years to search. Civil cases indexed by defendant, plaintiff. Civil records on index cards since 1978 (circuit only); on computer back to 1995; others back to 1953.
Criminal Records: Access: In person only. Visitors must perform in person searches themselves. Court makes copy: $.25 per page; same fee for self serve. Required to search: name, years to search, DOB; SSN helpful. Criminal records on index cards since 1978 (circuit only); on computer back to 1995; others back to 1953.
General Information: Public terminal goes back to 1995. No adoption, mental, juvenile, or sealed records released. Certification fee: $5.00. Payee: Circuit Clerk. Personal checks accepted. Prepayment and SASE required.

Hart County

Circuit & District Court Box 248, Munfordville, KY 42765; phone: 270-524-5181; hours 8AM-4PM M-F (CST). *Felony, Misdemeanor, Civil, Eviction, Small Claims, Probate.*
Civil Records: Access: In person only. Visitors must perform in person searches themselves. Court makes copy: $.25 per page. Required to search: name, years to search; also helpful: address. Civil cases indexed by defendant, plaintiff. Civil records on index cards since 1978, computerized since 3/95.
Criminal Records: Access: In person only. Visitors must perform in person searches themselves. Court makes copy: $.25 per page. Required to search: name, years to search, DOB, SSN; also helpful: address. Criminal records on index cards since 1978, computerized since 3/95.
General Information: Public use terminal available. No adoption, mental, juvenile, or sealed records released. Certification fee: $5.00. Payee: Circuit Clerk. Business checks accepted. Prepayment required.

Henderson County

Circuit & District Court PO Box 675, Henderson, KY 42420; phone: 270-826-2405/1566; fax: 270-831-2710; hours 8AM-6PM M; 8AM-4:30PM T-F (CST). *Felony, Civil Actions Over $4,000.*
Civil Records: Access: In person only. Visitors must perform in person searches themselves. Court makes copy: $.25 per page; same fee for self serve. Required to search: name, years to search. Civil cases indexed by defendant, plaintiff. Civil records on computer from 3/1991, records on index cards from 1978 to 3/1991.
Criminal Records: Access: In person only. Visitors must perform in person searches themselves. Court makes copy: $.25 per page; same fee for self serve. Required to search: name, years to search, DOB. Criminal records on computer from 3/1991, records on index cards from 1978 to 3/1991.
General Information: Public terminal goes back to 1991. No adoption, mental, juvenile, or sealed records released. Certification fee: $5.00. Payee: Circuit Clerk. Personal checks accepted. Prepayment required.

Henry County

Circuit & District Court PO Box 359, 30 Main St, New Castle, KY 40050; phone: 502-845-7551 dist; 502-845-2868 Circ; fax: 502-845-2969; hours 8AM-4:30PM (EST). *Felony, Misdemeanor, Civil, Eviction, Small Claims, Probate.*
Civil Records: Access: In person only. Visitors must perform in person searches themselves. Court

makes copy: $.25 per page; same fee for self serve. Required to search: name, years to search. Civil cases indexed by defendant, plaintiff. Civil records on computer since 5/1994, records on docket books since 1800s.
Criminal Records: Access: In person only. Visitors must perform in person searches themselves. Court makes copy: $.25 per page; same fee for self serve. Required to search: name, years to search; SSN helpful. Criminal records on computer since 5/1994, records on docket books since 1800s.
General Information: Public terminal goes back to 5/1994. No adoption, mental, juvenile, or sealed records released. Certification fee: $5.00 per doc. Payee: Circuit Clerk. Personal checks accepted. Prepayment required.

Hickman County

Circuit & District Court 109 S Washington St, Clinton, KY 42031; phone: 270-653-3901; fax: 270-653-3989; hours 8AM-4PM (CST). *Felony, Misdemeanor, Civil, Eviction, Small Claims, Probate.*
Civil Records: Access: Mail, in person. Both court and visitors may perform in person searches. No search fee. Court makes copy: $.25 per page. Required to search: name, years to search. Civil cases indexed by defendant, plaintiff. Civil records on computer from 6/94 to present, on index from 1978 to 6/94. If court does search, request must be in writing. Mail turnaround time same day.
Criminal Records: Access: Mail, in person. Both court and visitors may perform in person searches. No search fee. Court makes copy: $.25 per page. Required to search: name, years to search, DOB; also helpful: SSN. Criminal records on computer from 6/94 to present, on index from 1978 to 6/94. Requests must be in writing. Mail turnaround time same day.
General Information: Public terminal goes back to 6/1994. No adoption, mental, juvenile, or sealed records released. Fee to fax documents is $2.00 1st pg; $1.00 each add'l. Certification fee: $5.00 per certification. Payee: Circuit Clerk. Personal checks accepted. Prepayment and SASE required.

Hopkins County

Circuit & District Court Courthouse 30 S Main St, Madisonville, KY 42431; criminal phone: 270-824-7501; civil phone: 270-824-7502; probate phone: 270-824-7500; fax: 270-824-7032; hours 7:30AM-4PM (CST). *Felony, Misdemeanor, Civil, Eviction, Small Claims, Probate.*
Civil Records: Access: In person only. Visitors must perform in person searches themselves. Court makes copy: $.25 per page; same fee for self serve. Required to search: name, years to search. Civil cases indexed by defendant, plaintiff. Civil records on computer back to 6/1991; on index cards from 1978 to 1991.
Criminal Records: Access: In person only. Visitors must perform in person searches themselves. Court makes copy: $.25 per page; same fee for self serve. Required to search: name, years to search, signed release; also helpful: DOB, SSN. Criminal records on computer back to 6/1991, on index cards from 1978 to 1991, archived since 1800s.
General Information: Public terminal goes back to 1992. No adoption, mental, juvenile, or sealed records released. Will not fax specific case file. Certification fee: $5.00. Payee: Circuit Clerk. Personal checks accepted. Prepayment required.

Jackson County

Circuit Court PO Box 84, McKee, KY 40447; phone: 606-287-7783; criminal phone: 606-287-8651; civil phone: 606-287-7783; criminal/civil fax: 606-287-3277; hours 8AM-4PM M-F 8AM-N Sat (EST). *Felony, Civil Actions Over $4,000.*
Civil Records: Access: Fax, mail, in person. Both court and visitors may perform in person searches. No search fee. Court makes copy: $.25 per page; same

fee for self serve. Required to search: name, years to search; also helpful: address. Civil cases indexed by defendant, plaintiff. Civil records on computer from 5/1993 to present, on index cards from 1978 to 1993. Mail turnaround time 2 days.
Criminal Records: Access: Fax, mail, in person. Both court and visitors may perform in person searches. No search fee. Court makes copy: $.25 per page; same fee for self serve. Required to search: name, years to search, DOB; also helpful: SSN. Criminal records on computer from 5/1993 to present, on index cards from 1990 to 1993. Mail turnaround time 2 days.
General Information: Public terminal goes back to 1993. No adoption, mental, juvenile, or sealed records released. Fee to fax documents is $1.00 per page. Certification fee: $5.00 per certification. Payee: Jackson County Circuit Clerk. Personal checks accepted. Prepayment and SASE required.

District Court PO Box 84, McKee, KY 40447; phone: 606-287-8651; fax: 606-287-3277; hours 8AM-4PM M-F; 8AM-N Sat (EST). *Misdemeanor, Civil Actions Under $4,000, Eviction, Small Claims, Probate.*
Civil Records: Access: Fax, mail, in person. Both court and visitors may perform in person searches. No search fee. Court makes copy: $.25 per page; same fee for self serve. Required to search: name, years to search. Civil cases indexed by defendant, plaintiff. Civil records on computer back to 5/1993, on index cards from 1978. Mail turnaround time 1 week.
Criminal Records: Access: Fax, mail, in person. Both court and visitors may perform in person searches. No search fee. Court makes copy: $.25 per page; same fee for self serve. Required to search: name, years to search, DOB; also helpful: SSN. Criminal records on computer back to 5/1993; on index cards from 1990. Mail turnaround time 1 week.
General Information: Public terminal goes back to 5/1993. No adoption, mental, juvenile, or sealed records released. Certification fee: $5.00. Payee: Jackson County District Clerk. Personal checks accepted. Prepayment and SASE required.

Jefferson County

Circuit Court 700 W Jefferson St, Circuit Clerk, Louisville, KY 40202; phone: 502-595-4932; criminal phone: 502-595-3009; fax: 502-595-4128. *Felony, Civil Actions over $4,000.*
Civil Records: Access: In person only. Visitors must perform in person searches themselves. Court makes copy: $.25 per page. Required to search: name, years to search. Civil cases indexed by defendant, plaintiff. Civil records on computer from 1991, prior in index cards.
Criminal Records: Access: In person only. Visitors must perform in person searches themselves. No search fee. Court makes copy: $.25 per page. Required to search: name, years to search. Civil records on computer from 1991, prior in index cards.
General Information: Public terminal goes back to 1991. No adoption or sealed records released. Certification fee: $5.00 per doc. Payee: Circuit Clerk. Personal checks accepted. Prepayment required.

District Court 600 W Jefferson St, Hall of Justice, Louisville, KY 40202; phone: 502-595-3064; criminal phone: 502-595-3042; civil phone: 502-595-3015; fax: 502-595-4629. *Misdemeanor, Civil Actions under $4,000, Eviction, Small Claims, Probate.*
Civil Records: Access: Phone, in person. Visitors must perform in person searches themselves. No search fee. Court makes copy: $.25 per page. Required to search: name, years to search. Civil cases indexed by defendant, plaintiff. Civil records on computer back to 1988; index cards 1978 to 1988.
Criminal Records: Access: In person only. Visitors must perform in person searches themselves. No search fee. Court makes copy: $.25 per page. Required to search: name, years to search. Criminal

records on computer back to 1988; on index cards 1978 to 1988.

General Information: Public terminal goes back to 1988. No adoption, mental, juvenile, or sealed records released. Certification fee: $5.00 per doc. Payee: Circuit Clerk. Personal checks accepted. Credit cards accepted for District Criminal Traffic only. Prepayment required.

Jessamine County

Circuit Court 107 N Main St, Nicholasville, KY 40356; phone: 859-885-4531; hours 8AM-4:30PM M-W, F; 8AM-12PM Th (EST). *Felony, Civil Actions Over $4,000.*
Civil Records: Access: Mail, in person. Visitors must perform in person searches themselves. No search fee. Court makes copy: $.25 per page. Required to search: name, years to search. Civil cases indexed by defendant, plaintiff. Civil records on computer from 6/1992 to present, on index cards from 1978 to 1992. Mail turnaround time 1-2 days.
Criminal Records: Access: Mail, in person. Visitors must perform in person searches themselves. No search fee. Court makes copy: $.25 per page. Required to search: name, years to search, DOB; also helpful: SSN. Criminal records on computer from 6/1992 to present, on index cards from 1978 to 1992. Mail turnaround time 1-2 days.
General Information: Public terminal goes back to 6/1992. No adoption, mental, juvenile, or sealed records released. Certification fee: $5.00 per doc. Payee: Jessamine Circuit Clerk. Personal checks accepted. Prepayment and SASE required.

District Court 107 N Main St, Nicholasville, KY 40356; phone: 859-887-1005; fax: 859-887-0425; hours 8AM-4:30PM M-W; 8AM-N Th; 8AM-4:30PM F (EST). *Misdemeanor, Civil Actions Under $4,000, Eviction, Small Claims, Probate.*
Civil Records: Access: Mail, in person. Both court and visitors may perform in person searches. No search fee. Court makes copy: $.25 per page. Required to search: name, years to search. Civil cases indexed by defendant, plaintiff. Civil records on computer since 1992, on file cards prior. Mail turnaround time 2-4 days.
Criminal Records: Access: Mail, in person. Both court and visitors may perform in person searches. No search fee. Court makes copy: $.25 per page. Required to search: name, years to search; also helpful: DOB, SSN. Criminal records on computer since 1992, on file cards prior. Mail turnaround time 2-4 days.
General Information: Public terminal goes back to 1992. No adoption, mental, juvenile, or sealed records released. Certification fee: $5.00 per doc. Payee: District Clerk. Personal checks accepted. Prepayment and SASE required.

Johnson County

Circuit & District Court Box 1405, Paintsville, KY 41240; phone: 606-788-7054; fax: 606-788-7053; hours 8AM-4:30PM; 8:30AM-N Sat Driver's license only (EST). *Felony, Misdemeanor, Civil, Eviction, Small Claims, Probate.*
Civil Records: Access: Phone, mail, in person. Visitors must perform in person searches themselves. No search fee. Court makes copy: $.25 per page; same fee for self serve. Required to search: name, years to search. Civil cases indexed by defendant, plaintiff. Civil records on computer since 9/88, on index cards from 1978 to 1988, books from 1843 to 1978. From 1988 and prior files are at the archives in Frankfort.
Criminal Records: Access: In person only. Visitors must perform in person searches themselves. Court makes copy: $.25 per page; same fee for self serve. Required to search: name, years to search, DOB, SSN. Criminal records on computer since 9/88, on index cards from 1978 to 1988, books from 1843 to 1978. From 1988 and prior files are at the archives in Frankfort. Court will not conduct searches. Contact AOC for statewide search by mail.

General Information: Public terminal goes back to 10/1988. No adoption, mental, juvenile, or sealed records released. Will not fax documents. Certification fee: $5.00 per document. Payee: Circuit Clerk. Personal checks accepted. Prepayment and SASE required.

Kenton County

Circuit Court PO Box 669, 230 Madison Ave, Covington, KY 41011; phone: 859-292-6521; fax: 859-292-6611; hours 8AM-4:30PM (EST). *Felony, Civil Actions Over $4,000.*
www.aoc.state.ky.us/kenton
Civil Records: Access: Mail, in person. Both court and visitors may perform in person searches. No search fee. Court makes copy: $.25 per page. Required to search: name, years to search. Civil cases indexed by defendant, plaintiff. Civil records on computer back to 6/12/89, on index cards from 1800s.
Criminal Records: Access: In person only. Visitors must perform in person searches themselves. Court makes copy: $.25 per page. Required to search: name, years to search, DOB or SSN. Criminal records on computer back to 4/27/90.
General Information: Public terminal has criminal back to 4/27/90 and civil back to 6/12/89. No adoption, mental, juvenile, or sealed records released. Will not fax documents. Video of hearings are $15.00; turnaround time 7-14 days. Certification fee: $5.00 per certification. Payee: Kenton Circuit Clerk. Prepayment and SASE required.

District Court 230 Madison Ave, 3rd Fl, Covington, KY 41011; phone: 859-292-6523; fax: 859-292-6611; hours 7AM-5PM (EST). *Misdemeanor, Civil Actions Under $4,000, Eviction, Small Claims, Probate.*
www.aoc.state.ky.us/kenton
Civil Records: Access: Mail, in person. Only the court performs in person searches; visitors may not. No search fee. Court makes copy: $.25 per page. Required to search: name, years to search. Civil cases indexed by defendant, plaintiff. Civil records on computer from 6/9/89 to present, on index cards from 1985.
Criminal Records: Access: In person only. Visitors must perform in person searches themselves. Court makes copy: $.25 per page. Required to search: name, years to search DOB; SSN helpful. Criminal records on computer from 5/20/91 to present, index cards held since 1996.
General Information: Public terminal has only criminal records. No adoption, mental, juvenile, or sealed records released. Fee to fax documents is $3.00 per document. Certification fee: $5.00 per document. Payee: District Clerk. Business checks accepted. Prepayment and SASE required.

Knott County

Circuit & District Court PO Box 1317, Hindman, KY 41822; phone: 606-785-5021; hours 8AM-4PM; 8AM-N Sat (EST). *Felony, Misdemeanor, Civil, Eviction, Small Claims, Probate.*
Civil Records: Access: Fax, mail, in person. Visitors must perform in person searches themselves. No search fee. Court makes copy: $.15 per page. Required to search: name, years to search. Civil cases indexed by defendant, plaintiff. Civil records in index files, computerized since 11/94. Mail turnaround time 2-4 days.
Criminal Records: Access: Phone, fax, mail, in person. Visitors must perform in person searches themselves. No search fee. Court makes copy: $.15 per page. Required to search: name, years to search, DOB; also helpful: SSN. Criminal records in index files; on computer back to 11/1994. Mail turnaround time 2-4 days.
General Information: Public terminal goes back to 11/94. No adoption, mental, juvenile, or sealed records released. Will fax documents to local or toll free line. Certification fee: $5.00. Payee: Circuit

Clerk. Personal checks accepted. Prepayment and SASE required.

Knox County

Circuit & District Court PO Box 760, 401 Court Sq #202, Barbourville, KY 40906; phone: 606-546-3075 (Circ. Ct), 546-3232 (Dist); fax: 606-546-7949; hours 8AM-4:30PM M-F; 8:30AM-N Sat (EST). *Felony, Misdemeanor, Civil, Eviction, Small Claims, Probate.*
Civil Records: Access: In person only. Visitors must perform in person searches themselves. Court makes copy: $.25 per page. Required to search: name, years to search. Civil cases indexed by defendant, plaintiff. Civil records go back to 1978; on computer back to 7/92.
Criminal Records: Access: In person only. Visitors must perform in person searches themselves. Court makes copy: $.25 per page. Required to search: name, years to search, DOB; SSN helpful. Criminal records go back to 1978; on computer back to 7/92.
General Information: Public terminal goes back to 7/1992. No adoption, mental, juvenile, or sealed records released. Certification fee: $5.00 per doc. Payee: Circuit Clerk. Personal checks accepted. Prepayment required.

Larue County

Circuit & District Court PO Box 191, 209 W High St, Courthouse Annex, Hodgenville, KY 42748; phone: 270-358-3421; fax: 270-358-3731; hours 8AM-4PM (EST). *Felony, Misdemeanor, Civil, Eviction, Small Claims, Probate.*
Civil Records: Access: In person only. Both court and visitors may perform in person searches. No search fee. Court makes copy: $.25 per page; same fee for self serve. Required to search: name, years to search. Civil cases indexed by defendant, plaintiff. Civil records on computer since 1995.
Criminal Records: Access: In person only. Both court and visitors may perform in person searches. No search fee. Court makes copy: $.25 per page; same fee for self serve. Required to search: name, years to search, DOB; SSN helpful. Criminal records on computer since 1995.
General Information: Public terminal goes back to 1995. No adoption, mental, juvenile, or sealed records released. No fee to fax specific case file. No certification fee. Payee: Circuit Clerk. Personal checks accepted. Prepayment required.

Laurel County

Circuit & District Court Box 1798, London, KY 40743-1798; phone: 606-864-2863; probate phone: 606-864-7445; fax: 606-864-8264; hours 8AM-4:30PM (EST). *Felony, Misdemeanor, Civil, Eviction, Small Claims, Probate.*
Civil Records: Access: In person only. Visitors must perform in person searches themselves. Court makes copy: $.25 per page. Required to search: name, years to search. Civil cases indexed by defendant, plaintiff. Civil records on computer from 7/94, and index books from 1992.
Criminal Records: Access: In person only. Visitors must perform in person searches themselves. Court makes copy: $.25 per page. Required to search: name, years to search, DOB, SSN. Criminal records on computer from 7/94, and index books from 1987.
General Information: Public terminal goes back to 1994. No adoption, mental, juvenile, or sealed records released. Certification fee: $5.00. Payee: Circuit Clerk. Personal checks accepted. Prepayment required.

Lawrence County

Circuit & District Court Courthouse, PO Box 212, Louisa, KY 41230; phone: 606-638-4215; fax: 606-638-0264; hours 8:30AM-4:30PM M-F, 8:30AM-N Sat (EST). *Felony, Misdemeanor, Civil, Eviction, Small Claims, Probate.*
Civil Records: Access: Mail, fax, in person. Both court and visitors may perform in person searches.

No search fee. Court makes copy: $.25 per page. Required to search: name, years to search. Civil cases indexed by defendant, plaintiff. Civil records on computer from 11/94, index cards from 1978. Mail turnaround time within 1 week.

Criminal Records: Access: Mail, in person. Both court and visitors may perform in person searches. No search fee. Court makes copy: $.25 per page. Required to search: name, years to search; also helpful: DOB, SSN. Criminal records on computer from 11/94, index cards from 1978. Mail turnaround time within 1 week.

General Information: Public terminal goes back to 1995. No adoption, mental, juvenile, or sealed records released. Fee to fax documents is $2.00 per page. Certification fee: $5.00 per doc. Payee: Circuit Clerk. Personal checks accepted. Prepayment and SASE required.

Lee County

Circuit & District Court Box E, Beattyville, KY 41311; phone: 606-464-8400; fax: 606-464-0144; hours 8AM-4PM M-F; 8:30AM-11:30AM Sat (EST). *Felony, Misdemeanor, Civil, Eviction, Small Claims, Probate.*

Civil Records: Access: In person only. Visitors perform in person searches themselves. Court makes copy: $.25 per page. Required to search: name, years to search. Civil cases indexed by defendant, plaintiff. Civil records on computer from 9/94 to present, on index cards from 1978.

Criminal Records: Access: In person only. Visitors must perform in person searches themselves. Court makes copy: $.25 per page. Required to search: name, years to search; DOB; SSN helpful. Criminal records on computer from 9/94 to present, on index cards from 1978.

General Information: Public terminal goes back to 9/1994. No adoption, mental, juvenile, or sealed records released. Certification fee: $5.00 per doc. Payee: Circuit Clerk. Only cashiers checks, money orders and attorney checks accepted. Prepayment required.

Leslie County

Circuit & District Court Box 1750, Hyden, KY 41749; phone: 606-672-2505; probate phone: 606-672-2503; fax: 606-672-5128; hours 8AM-4PM M-gaF; 8AM-N Sat (EST). *Felony, Misdemeanor, Civil, Eviction, Small Claims, Probate.*

Civil Records: Access: In person only. Visitors must perform in person searches themselves. Court makes copy: $.25 per page. Required to search: name, years to search. Civil cases indexed by plaintiff. Civil records on computer and index books.

Criminal Records: Access: In person only. Visitors must perform in person searches themselves. Court makes copy: $.25 per page. Required to search: name, years to search; also helpful: address, DOB, SSN. Criminal records on computer and index books.

General Information: Public use terminal available. No adoption, mental, juvenile, or sealed records released. Certification fee: $5.00. Payee: Circuit Clerk. Personal checks accepted. Prepayment required.

Letcher County

Circuit & District Court 156 W Main St, #201, Whitesburg, KY 41858; phone: 606-633-7559/8810; fax: 606-633-5864; hours 8:30AM-4PM M-F; 8:30AM-12PM first Sat of month (EST). *Felony, Misdemeanor, Civil, Eviction, Small Claims, Probate.*

Civil Records: Access: Fax, mail, in person. Both court and visitors may perform in person searches. No search fee. Court makes copy: $.25 per page. Required to search: name, years to search; also helpful: address. Civil cases indexed by defendant, plaintiff. Civil records on computer go back to 11/1991; on index books from 1986 to 1991. Files maintained in office. Records from 1985 to 1800s in archives in Frankfort.

Criminal Records: Access: In person only. Visitors must perform in person searches themselves. Court makes copy: $.25 per page. Required to search: name, years to search, DOB, SSN; also helpful: address. Criminal records on computer go back to 11/1991; on index cards from 1986 to 1991. Files maintained in office. Records from 1985 to 1800s in archives in Frankfort. Contact AOC 800-928-6381 for statewide search by mail.

General Information: Public use terminal available. No adoption, mental, juvenile, or sealed records released. Fee to fax documents is $2.00 1st page, $1.00 each add'l. Certification fee: $5.00. Payee: Circuit Clerk. Personal checks accepted. Prepayment and SASE required.

Lewis County

Circuit & District Court PO Box 70, Vanceburg, KY 41179; phone: 606-796-3053; fax: 606-796-3030; hours 8AM-4:30PM M,T,Th,F 8:30-N W,Sat (EST). *Felony, Misdemeanor, Civil, Eviction, Small Claims, Probate.*

Civil Records: Access: Phone, mail, in person. Both court and visitors may perform in person searches. No search fee. Court makes copy: $.25 per page; same fee for self serve. Required to search: name, years to search. Civil cases indexed by defendant, plaintiff. Computerized from 1994, civil records on index cards back to 1955. Mail turnaround time within 1 week.

Criminal Records: Access: Mail, in person. Both court and visitors may perform in person searches. No search fee. Court makes copy: $.25 per page; same fee for self serve. Required to search: name, years to search, DOB; also helpful: SSN. Computerized from 1994, criminal records on index cards back to 1960s. Mail turnaround time within 1 week.

General Information: Public terminal goes back to 1994. No adoption, mental, juvenile, or sealed records released. Certification fee: $5.00. Payee: Circuit Clerk. Personal checks accepted. Prepayment and SASE required.

Lincoln County

Circuit & District Court 101 E Main, Stanford, KY 40484; phone: 606-365-2535; fax: 606-365-3389; hours 8AM-4PM; 9AM-N Sat (EST). *Felony, Misdemeanor, Civil, Eviction, Small Claims, Probate.*

Civil Records: Access: In person only. Visitors must perform in person searches themselves. Court makes copy: $.25 per page. Required to search: name, years to search. Civil cases indexed by defendant, plaintiff. Civil records on computer from 5/94, index cards prior, archived from 1978 to 1900.

Criminal Records: Access: In person only. Visitors must perform in person searches themselves. Court makes copy: $.25 per page. Required to search: name, years to search; SSN helpful. Criminal records on computer from 5/94, index cards prior, archived from 1978 to 1900.

General Information: Public use terminal available. No adoption, mental, juvenile, or sealed records released. No certification fee. Payee: Circuit Clerk. Personal checks accepted. Prepayment required.

Livingston County

Circuit & District Court PO Box 160, Smithland, KY 42081; phone: 270-928-2172; fax: 270-928-2976; hours 8AM-6PM M 8AM-4PM T-F (CST). *Felony, Misdemeanor, Civil, Eviction, Small Claims, Probate.*

Civil Records: Access: In person only. Visitors must perform in person searches themselves. Court makes copy: $.25 per page. Required to search: name, years to search. Civil cases indexed by defendant, plaintiff. Civil records on computer from 1993 to present, index cards prior, archived from 1799 to 1851.

Criminal Records: Access: In person only. Visitors must perform in person searches themselves. Court makes copy: $.25 per page. Required to search: name, years to search, DOB; SSN helpful. Criminal records on computer from 1993 to present, index cards prior, archived from 1799 to 1851.

General Information: Public terminal goes back to 1993. No adoption, mental, juvenile, or sealed records released. Certification fee: $5.00. Payee: Circuit Clerk. Personal checks accepted. Prepayment required.

Logan County

Circuit Court Box 420, W 4th St, Russellville, KY 42276-0420; phone: 270-726-2424; fax: 270-726-7893; hours 8AM-4:30PM M-Th; 8AM-5PM F (CST). *Felony, Civil Actions Over $4,000.*

Civil Records: Access: In person only. Visitors must perform in person searches themselves. Court makes copy: $.25 per page; same fee for self serve. Required to search: name, years to search. Civil cases indexed by defendant, plaintiff. Civil records on computer from 4/1992 to present, on index card from 1978 to 1992.

Criminal Records: Access: In person only. Visitors must perform in person searches themselves. Court makes copy: $.25 per page; same fee for self serve. Required to search: name, years to search, DOB, SSN. Criminal records on computer from 4/1992 to present, on index card from 1978 to 1992.

General Information: Public terminal goes back to 1992. No adoptions, mental, juvenile or sealed records released. Certification fee: $5.00. Payee: Circuit Clerk. Only cashiers checks and money orders accepted. Prepayment required.

District Court Box 420, Russellville, KY 42276; phone: 270-726-3107; probate phone: 270-726-3108; fax: 270-726-7893; hours 8AM-4:30PM (CST). *Misdemeanor, Civil Actions Under $4,000, Eviction, Small Claims, Probate.*

Civil Records: Access: In person only. Visitors must perform in person searches themselves. Court makes copy: $.25 per page; same fee for self serve. Required to search: name, years to search. Civil cases indexed by defendant, plaintiff. Civil records on computer since 1992, index cards from 1978 to 1992.

Criminal Records: Access: In person only. Visitors must perform in person searches themselves. Court makes copy: $.25 per page; same fee for self serve. Required to search: name, years to search, DOB; SSN helpful. Criminal records on computer since 1992, index cards from 1978 to 1991.

General Information: Public terminal goes back to 1992. No adoption, mental, juvenile, or sealed records released. Certification fee: $5.00. Payee: Logan District Clerk. Personal checks accepted. Prepayment required.

Lyon County

Circuit & District Court Box 565, Eddyville, KY 42038; phone: 270-388-7231 Circ Ct; 270-388-2727 Dist Ct; fax: 270-388-9135; hours 8AM-4PM (CST). *Felony, Misdemeanor, Civil, Eviction, Small Claims, Probate.*

Note: This court also handles domestic violence, traffic, and juvenile cases.

Civil Records: Access: In person only. Visitors must perform in person searches themselves. Court makes copy: $.25 per page. Required to search: name, years to search. Civil cases indexed by defendant, plaintiff. Civil records on computer from 11/94 to present, on index cards from 1978 to 1994.

Criminal Records: Access: In person only. Visitors must perform in person searches themselves. Court makes copy: $.25 per page. Required to search: name, years to search, DOB; SSN helpful. Criminal records on computer from 11/94 to present. Circuit court records are on index cards from 1978 to 1994, but not District court records.

General Information: Public terminal goes back to 1995. No adoption, mental, juvenile, or sealed records released. Certification fee: $5.00 per doc. Payee: Circuit Clerk. Personal checks not accepted. Prepayment required.

Madison County

Circuit Court PO Box 813, 101 W Main St, County Courthouse, Richmond, KY 40476-0813; phone: 859-624-4793; fax: 859-625-0598; hours 8AM-4PM (EST). *Felony, Civil Actions Over $4,000.*
www.kycourts.net/Circuit/Circuit_Intro.shtm
Civil Records: Access: In person only. Visitors must perform in person searches themselves. Court makes copy: $.25 per page; same fee for self serve. Required to search: name, years to search. Civil cases indexed by defendant, plaintiff. Civil records on computer back to 10/1990 to present, on index cards from 1978 to 1990.
Criminal Records: Access: In person only. Visitors must perform in person searches themselves. Court makes copy: $.25 per page; same fee for self serve. Required to search: name, years to search; also helpful: DOB, SSN. Criminal records on computer back to 10/1990 to present, on index cards from 1978 to 1990. Contact AOC for statewide searches by mail.
General Information: Public terminal goes back to 10/90. No adoption, mental, juvenile, or sealed records released. Certification fee: $5.00. Payee: Madison Circuit Clerk. Personal checks accepted. Prepayment required.

District Court Madison Hall of Justice, 351 W Main St, Richmond, KY 40475; phone: 859-624-4722; fax: 859-624-4746; hours 8AM-4PM (EST). *Misdemeanor, Civil Actions Under $4,000, Eviction, Small Claims, Probate.*
Civil Records: Access: Fax, mail, in person. Visitors must perform in person searches themselves. No search fee. Court makes copy: $.25 per page. Required to search: name, years to search. Civil cases indexed by defendant, plaintiff. Civil records go back to 11/90; computerized records go back to 11/90.
Criminal Records: Access: In person only. Visitors must perform in person searches themselves. Court makes copy: $.25 per page. Required to search: name, years to search, DOB; SSN helpful. Criminal records go back to 11/90; computerized records go back to 11/90.
General Information: Public terminal goes back to 1991. No adoption, mental, juvenile, or sealed records released. Fee to fax documents is $2.00 per page. Certification fee: $5.00 per doc. Payee: District Court. Personal checks accepted. Prepayment and SASE required.

Magoffin County

Circuit & District Court Box 147, Salyersville, KY 41465; phone: 606-349-2215; fax: 606-349-2209; hours 8AM-4PM (EST). *Felony, Misdemeanor, Civil, Eviction, Small Claims, Probate.*
Civil Records: Access: Fax, mail, in person. Both court and visitors may perform in person searches. No search fee. Court makes copy: $.25 per page; same fee for self serve. Required to search: name, years to search. Civil cases indexed by defendant, plaintiff. Civil records on computer from 3/1993 to present, on index cards from 1978 to 1993. Cases before 1990 are in archives. Mail turnaround time 3 days.
Criminal Records: Access: Fax, mail, in person. Both court and visitors may perform in person searches. No search fee. Court makes copy: $.25 per page; same fee for self serve. Required to search: name, years to search, DOB; also helpful: SSN. Criminal records on computer from 3/1993 to present, on index cards from 1978 to 1993. Cases before 1990 are in archives. Mail turnaround time 3 days.
General Information: Public terminal goes back to 1993. No adoption, mental, juvenile, or sealed records released. Fee to fax documents is $2.00 for 1st page, $1.00 each add'l. Certification fee: $5.00; Seal $1.00 extra. Payee: Circuit Clerk. Personal checks accepted. Prepayment and SASE required.

Marion County

Circuit & District Court 120 W Main St, #6, Lebanon, KY 40033; phone: 270-692-2681; fax: 270-692-3097; hours 8:30AM-4:30PM; 8:30AM-N Sat (EST). *Felony, Misdemeanor, Civil, Eviction, Small Claims, Probate.*
Civil Records: Access: In person only. Visitors must perform in person searches themselves. Court makes copy: $.25 per page. Required to search: name, years to search. Civil cases indexed by defendant, plaintiff. Civil records on computer from 5/1993 to present, on index cards from 1978 to 1993.
Criminal Records: Access: In person only. Visitors must perform in person searches themselves. Court makes copy: $.25 per page. Required to search: name, years to search; SSN helpful. Criminal records on computer from 5/1993 to present, on index cards from 1978 to 1993.
General Information: Public terminal goes back to 1993. No adoption, mental, juvenile, or sealed records released. Certification fee: $5.00. Payee: Circuit Clerk. Personal checks accepted. Prepayment required.

Marshall County

Circuit & District Court 80 Judicial Dr, Unit #101, Benton, KY 42025; phone: 270-527-3883/1721; probate phone: 270-527-1721; fax: 270-527-5865; hours 8AM-4:30PM (CST). *Felony, Misdemeanor, Civil, Eviction, Small Claims, Probate.*
Civil Records: Access: Phone, fax, mail, in person. Both court and visitors may perform in person searches. No search fee. Court makes copy: $.25 per page; same fee for self serve. Required to search: name, years to search. Civil cases indexed by defendant, plaintiff. Civil records on computer since 8/1992 to present, on index books from 1978 to 1992. Mail turnaround time 3 days.
Criminal Records: Access: Phone, fax, mail, in person. Both court and visitors may perform in person searches. No search fee. Court makes copy: $.25 per page; same fee for self serve. Required to search: name, years to search, DOB; also helpful: SSN. Criminal records on computer since 8/1992 to present, on index books from 1978 to 1992. Mail turnaround time 3 days.
General Information: Public terminal has only civil records back to 8/1992. No adoption, mental, juvenile, or sealed records released. Fee to fax documents is $2.00 for 1st page, $1.00 each add'l. Certification fee: $5.00 per cert. Payee: Circuit Clerk. Personal checks accepted. Prepayment and SASE required.

Martin County

Circuit & District Court Box 430, Inez, KY 41224; phone: 606-298-3508; fax: 606-298-4202; hours 8AM-4PM except 1st & 3rd Th 8AM-7PM (EST). *Felony, Misdemeanor, Civil, Eviction, Small Claims, Probate.*
Civil Records: Access: Mail, in person. Both court and visitors may perform in person searches. No search fee. Court makes copy: $.25 per page. Return postage required. Required to search: name, years to search. Civil cases indexed by defendant, plaintiff. Civil records on computer since 4/1994, District on index books since 1987, Circuit on index books since 1978, prior records on docket books.
Criminal Records: Access: In person only. Visitors must perform in person searches themselves. Court makes copy: $.25 per page. Return postage required. Required to search: name, years to search; also helpful: DOB, SSN. Criminal records on computer since 4/1994, District on index books since 1987, Circuit on index books since 1978, prior records on docket books.
General Information: Public terminal goes back to 4/1994. No adoption, mental, juvenile, or sealed records released. Certification fee: $5.00 per doc. Payee: Circuit Clerk. Personal checks accepted. Prepayment and SASE required.

Mason County

Circuit Court 100 W 3rd St, Maysville, KY 41056; phone: 606-564-4340; fax: 606-564-0932; hours 8:30AM-4:30PM (EST). *Felony, Civil Actions Over $4,000.*
www.kycourts.net
Civil Records: Access: In person only. Visitors must perform in person searches themselves. Court makes copy: $.25 per page. Required to search: name, years to search. Civil cases indexed by defendant, plaintiff. Civil records on computer back to 4/1994, records on index books since 1929, prior records archived from 1798.
Criminal Records: Access: In person only. Visitors must perform in person searches themselves. Court makes copy: $.25 per page. Required to search: name, years to search, DOB. Criminal records on computer back to 4/1994, records on index books since 1929, prior records archived from 1798.
General Information: Public terminal goes back to 1994. No adoption, mental, juvenile, or sealed records released. Will not fax specific case file. Certification fee: $5.00 per cert includes copies. Payee: Kentucky State Treasurer. Personal checks or money order accepted. Prepayment required.

District Court 100 W 3rd St, Maysville, KY 41056; phone: 606-564-4011; fax: 606-564-0932; hours 8:30AM-4:30PM (EST). *Misdemeanor, Civil Actions Under $4000, Eviction, Small Claims, Probate.*
Civil Records: Access: In person only. Visitors must perform in person searches themselves. Court makes copy: $.25 per page; same fee for self serve. Required to search: name, years to search. Civil cases indexed by defendant, plaintiff. Civil records on computer since 4/1994, prior records on index books from 1978.
Criminal Records: Access: In person only. Visitors must perform in person searches themselves. Court makes copy: $.25 per page; same fee for self serve. Required to search: name, years to search. Criminal records on computer since 4/1994, prior records on index books from 1983.
General Information: Public terminal goes back to 1994. No adoption, mental, juvenile, or sealed records released. Will not fax specific case file. Certification fee: $5.00 per cert. Payee: Kentucky State Treasurer. Personal checks accepted. Prepayment required.

McCracken County

Circuit Court Box 1455, 301 S 6th St, Paducah, KY 42002-1455; phone: 270-575-7280; hours 8:30AM-4:30PM M, 8:30AM-4:30PM T-F (CST). *Felony, Civil Actions Over $4,000.*
Note: Visitors may only search from 2PM-4PM on Thursday.
Civil Records: Access: In person. Both court and visitors may perform in person searches. No search fee. Court makes copy: $.25 per page. Required to search: name, years to search. Civil cases indexed by defendant, plaintiff. Civil records on computer since 9/1991, prior records on index cards since 1978. Mail turnaround time same day.
Criminal Records: Access: In person. Both court and visitors may perform in person searches. No search fee. Court makes copy: $.25 per page. Required to search: name, years to search; also helpful: DOB. Criminal records on computer since 9/1991, prior records on index cards since 1978.
General Information: Public terminal goes back to 1991. No adoption, mental, juvenile, or sealed records released. Certification fee: $5.00. Payee: Circuit Clerk. Personal checks accepted. Prepayment required.

District Court Box 1436, Paducah, KY 42002; phone: 270-575-7270; fax: 270-575-7029; hours 8:30AM-4:30PM (CST). *Misdemeanor, Civil Actions Under $4,000, Eviction, Small Claims, Probate.*
Civil Records: Access: In person only. Visitors must perform in person searches themselves. Court makes copy: $.25 per page. Required to search: name,

years to search. Civil cases indexed by defendant, plaintiff. Civil records on computer since 9/91, on index books since 1978, prior records archived from the 1900s. Visitors may search only from 2PM to 4PM on Thursday.
Criminal Records: Access: In person only. Visitors must perform in person searches themselves. Court makes copy: $.25 per page. Required to search: name, years to search; SSN helpful. Criminal records on computer since 9/91, on index books since 1982, prior records archived from the 1900s.
General Information: Public terminal goes back to 1992. No adoption, mental, juvenile, or sealed records released. Certification fee: $5.00. Payee: District Clerk. Personal checks accepted. Prepayment required.

McCreary County

Circuit & District Court Box 40, Whitley City, KY 42653; phone: 606-376-5041; fax: 606-376-8844; hours 8:30AM-4:30PM (EST). *Felony, Misdemeanor, Civil, Eviction, Small Claims, Probate.*
Civil Records: Access: Mail, in person. Both court and visitors may perform in person searches. No search fee. Court makes copy: $.25 per page; same fee for self serve. Required to search: name, years to search; also helpful: address. Civil cases indexed by defendant, plaintiff. Civil records go back to 1992; on computer back to 1995.
Criminal Records: Access: In person only. Both court and visitors may perform in person searches. No search fee. Court makes copy: $.25 per page; same fee for self serve. Required to search: name, years to search, DOB, SSN; also helpful: address. Criminal records go back to 1992; on computer back to 1995. Court directs criminal search requests to Pretrial Svcs in Frankfort, 800-928-6381.
General Information: Public use terminal available. No adoption, mental, juvenile, or sealed records released. Certification fee: $5.00 per document. Payee: Circuit Clerk. Personal checks accepted. Prepayment required.

McLean County

Circuit & District Court Box 145 (210 E Main St), Calhoun, KY 42327; phone: 270-273-3966; criminal fax: 270-273-5918; civil/probate fax is the same; hours 8AM-4:30PM M-F; open till 6PM F (CST). *Felony, Misdemeanor, Civil, Eviction, Small Claims, Probate.*
Civil Records: Access: Mail, in person. Both court and visitors may perform in person searches. No search fee. Court makes copy: $.25 per page. Required to search: name, years to search. Civil cases indexed by defendant, plaintiff. Civil records on computer since 1991, prior records on index cards since 1978.
Criminal Records: Access: In person only. Both court and visitors may perform in person searches. Court makes copy: $.25 per page. Required to search: name, years to search, DOB; SSN helpful. Criminal records on computer since 1991, prior records on index cards since 1978. Note: The court refers all written requests to the Administrative Office of Courts in Frankfort.
General Information: Public terminal goes back to 1991. No adoption, mental, juvenile, or sealed records released. Will fax documents to local or toll free line. Certification fee: $5.00 per document includes copies. Payee: Circuit Clerk. Personal checks accepted. Prepayment required.

Meade County

Circuit & District Court Courthouse 516 Fairway Dr, Brandenburg, KY 40108; phone: 270-422-4961; fax: 270-422-2147; hours 8AM-4:30AM daily; til 6:30PM Th (EST). *Felony, Misdemeanor, Civil, Eviction, Small Claims, Probate.*
Note: Court asks all record requests go to the AOC office in Frankfort.

Civil Records: Access: In person, mail, fax. Visitors must perform in person searches themselves. Court makes copy: $.25 per page; same fee for self serve. Required to search: name, years to search. Civil cases indexed by defendant, plaintiff. Civil records on computer since 2/95, prior on index cards.
Criminal Records: Access: In person only. Visitors must perform in person searches themselves. Court makes copy: $.25 per page; same fee for self serve. Required to search: name, years to search. Criminal records on computer since 2/95, prior on index cards.
General Information: Public terminal goes back to 2/1995. No adoption, mental, juvenile, or sealed records released. Will not fax documents. Certification fee: $5.00. Payee: Circuit Clerk. Personal checks accepted. Prepayment required.

Menifee County

Circuit & District Court Box 172, Frenchburg, KY 40322; phone: 606-768-2461; fax: 606-768-2462; hours 8:30AM-4PM (EST). *Felony, Misdemeanor, Civil, Eviction, Small Claims, Probate.*
Civil Records: Access: In person only. Visitors must perform in person searches themselves. Court makes copy: $.25 per page. Required to search: name, years to search. Civil cases indexed by defendant, plaintiff. Civil records on index cards from 1978 to 1994.
Criminal Records: Access: In person only. Visitors must perform in person searches themselves. Court makes copy: $.25 per page. Required to search: name, years to search. Criminal records on index cards from 1978 to 1994.
General Information: Public terminal goes back to 1995. No adoption, mental, juvenile, or sealed records released. Certification fee: $5.00. Payee: Circuit Clerk. Prepayment required.

Mercer County

Circuit & District Court Courthouse, 224 Main St S, Harrodsburg, KY 40330-1696; phone: 859-734-6306; criminal phone: 859-734-6307; civil phone: 859-734-6305; probate phone: 859-734-6305; fax: 859-734-9159; hours 8AM-4:30PM (EST). *Felony, Misdemeanor, Civil, Eviction, Small Claims, Probate.*
Note: Circuit Civil & Criminal 859-734-6306.
Civil Records: Access: In person only. Visitors must perform in person searches themselves. Court makes copy: $.25 per page; same fee for self serve. Required to search: name, years to search. Civil cases indexed by defendant, plaintiff. Civil records on computer back to 1993; prior in index books.
Criminal Records: Access: In person only. Visitors must perform in person searches themselves. Court makes copy: $.25 per page; same fee for self serve. Required to search: name, years to search; also helpful: DOB, SSN. Criminal records on computer back to 1993; prior in index books.
General Information: Public terminal goes back to 1991. No adoption, mental, juvenile, or sealed records released. Certification fee: $5.00. Payee: Circuit Clerk. Personal checks accepted. Prepayment required.

Metcalfe County

Circuit & District Court Box 485, Edmonton, KY 42129; phone: 270-432-3663; fax: 270-432-4437; hours 8AM-4PM (CST). *Felony, Misdemeanor, Civil, Eviction, Small Claims, Probate.*
Civil Records: Access: Phone, fax, mail, in person. Both court and visitors may perform in person searches. No search fee. Court makes copy: $.25 per page; same fee for self serve. Required to search: name, years to search. Civil cases indexed by defendant, plaintiff. Civil records on computer back to 1992, prior on index cards since 1978. Mail turnaround time 1-2 days.
Criminal Records: Access: Phone, fax, mail, in person. Both court and visitors may perform in

person searches. No search fee. Court makes copy: $.25 per page; same fee for self serve. Required to search: name, years to search, DOB, SSN, signed release. Criminal records on computer back to 1992, prior records on index cards since 1980. Mail turnaround time 1-2 days.
General Information: Public terminal has criminal back to 1982 and civil back to 1978. No adoption, mental, juvenile, or sealed records released. Fee to fax documents is $2.00 1st page; $1.00 each add'l. Certification fee: $5.00 per doc. Payee: Circuit Clerk. Personal checks accepted. Prepayment and SASE required.

Monroe County

Circuit & District Court 200 N Main St #B, Tompkinsville, KY 42167; phone: 270-487-5480; fax: 270-487-0068; hours 8AM-4PM (CST). *Felony, Misdemeanor, Civil, Eviction, Small Claims, Probate.*
Civil Records: Access: Phone, mail, in person. Both court and visitors may perform in person searches. No search fee. Court makes copy: $.25 per page; same fee for self serve. Required to search: name, years to search. Civil cases indexed by defendant, plaintiff. Civil records kept in files.
Criminal Records: Access: In person only. Both court and visitors may perform in person searches. No search fee. Court makes copy: $.25 per page; same fee for self serve. Required to search: name, years to search. Criminal records kept in files. Mail turnaround time 1 week.
General Information: Public terminal goes back to 1995. No adoption, mental, juvenile, or sealed records released. Certification fee: $5.00. Payee: Circuit Clerk. Personal checks accepted. Prepayment and SASE required.

Montgomery County

Circuit & District Court PO Box 327, 1 Court St, Courthouse, Mt Sterling, KY 40353; phone: 859-498-5966; fax: 859-498-9341; hours 8:30AM-4PM (EST). *Felony, Misdemeanor, Civil, Eviction, Small Claims, Probate.*
Civil Records: Access: Mail, in person. Both court and visitors may perform in person searches. No search fee. Court makes copy: $.25 per page. Required to search: name, years to search. Civil cases indexed by defendant, plaintiff. Civil records on computer since 8/1991, on index cards from 1978-1991, prior records on docket books. Mail turnaround time 3 days.
Criminal Records: Access: In person only. Visitors must perform in person searches themselves. Court makes copy: $.25 per page. Required to search: name, years to search. Criminal records on computer since 8/1991, on index cards from 1978-1991, prior records on docket books.
General Information: Public terminal goes back to 8/1991. No adoption, mental, juvenile, or sealed records released. Certification fee: $5.00. Payee: Circuit Clerk. Personal checks accepted. Prepayment required.

Morgan County

Circuit & District Court Box 85, West Liberty, KY 41472; phone: 606-743-3763; criminal fax: 606-743-2633; civil/probate fax is the same; hours 8AM-4PM (EST). *Felony, Misdemeanor, Civil, Eviction, Small Claims, Probate.*
Civil Records: Access: Mail, in person. Both court and visitors may perform in person searches. No search fee. Court makes copy: $.25 per page; same fee for self serve. Required to search: name, years to search. Civil cases indexed by defendant, plaintiff. Civil records on computer back to 9/1993; index books back to 1921. Mail turnaround time 1 day.
Criminal Records: Access: Mail, in person. Both court and visitors may perform in person searches. No search fee. Court makes copy: $.25 per page; same fee for self serve. Required to search: name, years to search. Criminal records on computer back to 9/1993;

index books back to 1921. Mail turnaround time 1 day.

General Information: Public terminal goes back to 9/1992. No adoption, mental, juvenile, or sealed records released. Will fax documents if they have time and you pay $2.00 1st page, $1.00 each add'l. Certification fee: $5.00 per document. Payee: Circuit Clerk. Personal checks accepted. Prepayment required.

Muhlenberg County

Circuit Court PO Box 776, Greenville, KY 42345; phone: 270-338-4850 (Felony); fax: 270-338-0177; hours 8AM-4PM (CST). *Felony, Civil Actions Over $4,000.*

Note: Direct mail felony record requests to state AOC.

Civil Records: Access: In person only. Visitors must perform in person searches themselves. Court makes copy: $.25 per page. Required to search: name, years to search. Civil cases indexed by defendant, plaintiff. Civil records on computer since 5/1992, records on index since 1978, records archived if before 1985.

Criminal Records: Access: In person only. Visitors must perform in person searches themselves. Court makes copy: $.25 per page. Required to search: name, years to search, SSN; also helpful: DOB. Criminal records on computer since 5/1992, records on index since 1978, records archived if before 1985.

General Information: Public terminal goes back to 1992. No adoption, mental, juvenile, or sealed records released. Certification fee: $5.00. Payee: Circuit Clerk. Personal checks accepted. Prepayment required.

District Court Box 776, Greenville, KY 42345; phone: 270-338-0995; fax: 270-338-0177; hours 8AM-4PM (CST). *Misdemeanor, Civil Actions Under $4,000, Eviction, Small Claims, Probate.*

Civil Records: Access: In person only. Both court and visitors may perform in person searches. Court makes copy: $.25 per page. Self serve copy fee: none. Required to search: name, years to search. Civil cases indexed by defendant, plaintiff. Civil records on computer since 1992, on index books from 1978, archived if before 1985.

Criminal Records: Access: In person only. Visitors must perform in person searches themselves. Court makes copy: $.25 per page. Self serve copy fee: none. Required to search: name, years to search. Criminal records on computer since 1992, on index books from 1978, archived if before 1985. The court recommends all requesters go to the State Administrative Office of the Courts.

General Information: Public use terminal available. No adoption, mental, juvenile, or sealed records released. Certification fee: $5.00 per document. Payee: District Clerk. Personal checks accepted. Prepayment required.

Nelson County

Circuit & District Court Box 845, Bardstown, KY 40004; phone: 502-348-3648; hours 8:30AM-4:30PM (EST). *Felony, Misdemeanor, Civil, Eviction, Small Claims, Probate.*

Civil Records: Access: Mail, in person. Both court and visitors may perform in person searches. No search fee. Court makes copy: $.25 per page. Required to search: name, years to search. Civil cases indexed by defendant, plaintiff. Civil records on computer since 1990, on index since 1978, prior records archived from 1940. Mail turnaround time 2 weeks.

Criminal Records: Access: Mail, in person. Both court and visitors may perform in person searches. No search fee. Court makes copy: $.25 per page. Required to search: name, years to search, DOB; also helpful: SSN. Criminal records on computer since 1990, on index since 1978, prior records archived from 1940. Mail turnaround time 2 weeks.

General Information: Public terminal goes back to 1990. No adoption, mental, juvenile, domestic violence or sealed records released. Certification fee:

$5.00. Payee: Circuit Clerk. Personal checks accepted. Prepayment required.

Nicholas County

Circuit & District Court PO Box 109, Carlisle, KY 40311; phone: 859-289-2336; fax: 859-289-6141; hours 8:30AM-4:30PM M-F (EST). *Felony, Misdemeanor, Civil, Eviction, Small Claims, Probate.*

Civil Records: Access: Fax, mail, in person. Both court and visitors may perform in person searches. No search fee. Court makes copy: $.25 per page. Required to search: name, years to search, written request. Civil cases indexed by defendant, plaintiff. Civil records on computer since 3/1993, prior records on index cards. Mail turnaround time 1-2 days.

Criminal Records: Access: Fax, mail, in person. Both court and visitors may perform in person searches. No search fee. Court makes copy: $.25 per page. Required to search: name, years to search, written request. Criminal records on computer since 3/1993, prior records on index cards. Mail turnaround time 1-2 days.

General Information: Public terminal has criminal back to - not known and civil back to 1993. No adoption, mental, juvenile, or sealed records released. No fee to fax documents. Certification fee: $5.00. Payee: Circuit Clerk. Personal checks accepted. Prepayment and SASE required.

Ohio County

Circuit & District Court PO Box 67, 130 E Washington, #300, Hartford, KY 42347; phone: 270-298-3671; fax: 270-298-9565; hours 8:30AM-4:30PM (CST). *Felony, Misdemeanor, Civil, Eviction, Small Claims, Probate.*

Civil Records: Access: In person only. Visitors must perform in person searches themselves. Court makes copy: $.25 per page. Required to search: name, years to search. Civil cases indexed by defendant, plaintiff. Civil records on computer since 10/91, Circuit court on index books since 1800s, District court on index books since 1987, prior records archived.

Criminal Records: Access: In person only. Visitors must perform in person searches themselves. Court makes copy: $.25 per page. Required to search: name, years to search. Criminal records on computer since 10/91, Circuit court on index books since 1800s, District court on index books since 1987, prior records archived.

General Information: Public terminal goes back to 1992. No adoption, mental, juvenile, or sealed records released. Certification fee: $5.00 per doc. Payee: Circuit Clerk. No personal checks accepted. Prepayment required.

Oldham County

Circuit & District Court 100 W Main St, La Grange, KY 40031; phone: 502-222-9837; probate phone: 502-222-5621; fax: 502-222-3047; probate fax: 502-222-3047; hours 8AM-4PM (EST). *Felony, Misdemeanor, Civil, Eviction, Small Claims, Probate.*

Note: Criminal record requests are referred to the Administrative office of the Courts in Frankfort.

Civil Records: Access: In person only. Visitors must perform in person searches themselves. Court makes copy: $.25 per page. Required to search: name, years to search. Civil cases indexed by defendant, plaintiff. Civil records on computer since 1991, on index books since 1978, prior records archived since 1800s.

Criminal Records: Access: In person only. Visitors must perform in person searches themselves. Court makes copy: $.25 per page. Required to search: name, years to search; SSN helpful. Circuit criminal records on computer since 1991, District criminal back to 1983, on index books since 1978.

General Information: Public terminal goes back to 9/1991. No adoption, mental, juvenile, or sealed records released. Will fax specific file data for $2.00

per doc plus $1.00 per page. Certification fee: $5.00. Payee: Circuit Clerk. Personal checks accepted. Prepayment required.

Owen County

Circuit & District Court Box 473, Owenton, KY 40359; phone: 502-484-2232; fax: 502-484-0625; hours 8AM-4PM (EST). *Felony, Misdemeanor, Civil, Eviction, Small Claims, Probate.*

Civil Records: Access: Fax, mail, in person. Both court and visitors may perform in person searches. No search fee. Court makes copy: $.25 per page; same fee for self serve. Required to search: name, years to search. Civil cases indexed by defendant, plaintiff. Civil records on computer since 1992, prior records on index books since 1946. Cases before 1978 transferred to state archives. Mail turnaround time 1 week.

Criminal Records: Access: Fax, mail, in person. Both court and visitors may perform in person searches. No search fee. Court makes copy: $.25 per page; same fee for self serve. Required to search: name, years to search, DOB, SSN. Criminal records on computer since 1992, prior records on index books since 1946. Cases before 1978 transferred to state archives. Court suggests statewide search through A.O.C. at 502-573-2350. Mail turnaround time 1 week.

General Information: Public terminal goes back to 1978. No adoption, mental, juvenile, or sealed records released. Certification fee: $5.00. Payee: Circuit Clerk. Personal checks accepted. Prepayment required.

Owsley County

Circuit & District Court Box 130 (N Court St), Booneville, KY 41314; phone: 606-593-6226; probate phone: 606-593-6529; fax: 606-593-6343; hours 8AM-4PM M-F, 8AM-N Sat (EST). *Felony, Misdemeanor, Civil, Eviction, Small Claims, Probate.*

Civil Records: Access: In person only. Visitors must perform in person searches themselves. Court makes copy: $.25 per page. Required to search: name, years to search. Civil cases indexed by defendant, plaintiff. Civil records on computer since 10/1994, prior records on index cards since 1967.

Criminal Records: Access: In person only. Visitors must perform in person searches themselves. Court makes copy: $.25 per page. Required to search: name, years to search, DOB or SSN. Criminal records on computer since 10/1994, prior records on index cards since 1967.

General Information: Public terminal goes back to 1994. No adoption, mental, juvenile, or sealed records released. Will fax results $2.00 1st page; $1.00 ea add'l. Certification fee: $5.00. Payee: Circuit Clerk. Personal checks accepted. Prepayment required.

Pendleton County

Circuit & District Court PO Box 69, 223 Main St, Falmouth, KY 41040; phone: 859-654-3347; fax: 859-654-3405; hours 8AM-4PM (EST). *Felony, Misdemeanor, Civil, Eviction, Small Claims, Probate.*

Civil Records: Access: Mail, in person. Both court and visitors may perform in person searches. Court makes copy: $.25 per page. Required to search: name, years to search. Civil cases indexed by defendant, plaintiff. Civil records on computer since 7/1994, prior records on index books since 1978.

Criminal Records: Access: In person only. Both court and visitors may perform in person searches. Court makes copy: $.25 per page. Required to search: name, years to search. Criminal records on computer since 7/1994, prior records on index books since 1978.

General Information: Public use terminal available. No adoption, mental, juvenile, or sealed records released. Certification fee: $5.00. Payee: Circuit

Clerk. Personal checks accepted. Prepayment required.

Perry County

Circuit Court Box 7433, Hazard, KY 41701; phone: 606-435-6000; fax: 606-435-6143; hours 8AM-4PM (EST). *Felony, Civil Actions Over $4,000.*
Civil Records: Access: In person only. Visitors must perform in person searches themselves. No search fee. Court makes copy: $.25 per page. Required to search: name, years to search. Civil cases indexed by defendant, plaintiff. Civil records on computer since 10/1991, prior records on index cards since 1978.
Criminal Records: Access: In person only. Visitors must perform in person searches themselves. Court makes copy: $.25 per page. Required to search: name, years to search. Criminal records on computer since 10/1991, prior records on index cards since 1978.
General Information: Public terminal goes back to 1992. No adoption, mental, juvenile, or sealed records released. Certification fee: $5.00 per doc. Payee: Circuit Clerk. Personal checks accepted. Prepayment required.

District Court PO Box 7433, Hazard, KY 41702; phone: 606-435-6002; fax: 606-435-6143; hours 8AM-4PM (EST). *Misdemeanor, Civil Actions Under $4,000, Eviction, Small Claims, Probate.*
Civil Records: Access: In person. No search fee. Court makes copy: $.25 per page. Required to search: name, years to search. Civil cases indexed by defendant, plaintiff. Civil records on computer since 1991, records on index books since 1978, prior records archived since 1900s.
Criminal Records: Access: In person. Visitors must perform in person searches themselves. No search fee. Court makes copy: $.25 per page. Required to search: name, years to search. Criminal records on computer since 1991, records on index books since 1978, prior records archived since 1900s.
General Information: Public use terminal available. No adoption, mental, juvenile, or sealed records released. Certification fee: $5.00. Payee: District Clerk. Personal checks accepted. Prepayment required.

Pike County

Circuit & District Court PO Box 1002, Pikeville, KY 41502; phone: 606-433-7557; fax: 606-433-7044; hours 8AM-4:30PM (EST). *Felony, Misdemeanor, Civil, Eviction, Small Claims, Probate.*
Civil Records: Access: Mail, in person. Both court and visitors may perform in person searches. Court makes copy: $.25 per page. Required to search: name, years to search. Civil cases indexed by defendant, plaintiff. Civil records on computer since 3/1994, prior records on index cards from 1978.
Criminal Records: Access: In person only. Both court and visitors may perform in person searches. Court makes copy: $.25 per page. Required to search: name, years to search. Criminal records on computer since 3/1994, prior records on index cards from 1978. Mail turnaround time 3 days.
General Information: Public terminal goes back to 3/1994. No adoption, mental, juvenile, or sealed records released. Will not fax documents. Certification fee: $5.00 per doc. Payee: Circuit Clerk. Personal checks accepted. Prepayment and SASE required.

Powell County

Circuit & District Court Box 578, Stanton, KY 40380; phone: 606-663-4141; criminal phone: 606-663-4142; criminal fax: 606-663-2710; civil/probate fax is the same; hours 8AM-4PM M,T,W,F, 8AM-N Th & Sat (EST). *Felony, Misdemeanor, Civil, Eviction, Small Claims, Probate.*
Civil Records: Access: Mail, in person. Both court and visitors may perform in person searches. No search fee. Court makes copy: $.25 per page; same fee

for self serve. Required to search: name, years to search. Civil cases indexed by defendant, plaintiff. Civil records on computer since 1993, prior records on index cards since 1978.
Criminal Records: Access: In person only. Visitors must perform in person searches themselves. Court makes copy: $.25 per page; same fee for self serve. Required to search: name, years to search, DOB; SSN helpful. Criminal records on computer since 1993, prior records on index cards since 1978. This office will not provide criminal record checks.
General Information: Public terminal goes back to 1993. No adoption, mental, juvenile, or sealed records released. Will not fax documents. Certification fee: $5.00 per certification. Payee: Circuit Clerk. Personal checks not accepted; money orders preferred. Prepayment and SASE required.

Pulaski County

Circuit & District Court Box 664, 100 N Maine, Courthouse Sq 3rd Fl, Somerset, KY 42502; phone: 606-677-4029; fax: 606-677-4002; hours 8AM-4:30PM M-F, 8AM-N Sat (EST). *Felony, Misdemeanor, Civil, Eviction, Small Claims, Probate.*
Civil Records: Access: In person only. Visitors must perform in person searches themselves. Court makes copy: $.25 per page; same fee for self serve. Required to search: name, years to search. Civil cases indexed by defendant, plaintiff. Civil records on computer since 1991, prior records on index books from 1978.
Criminal Records: Access: In person only. Visitors must perform in person searches themselves. Court makes copy: $.25 per page; same fee for self serve. Required to search: name, years to search. Criminal records on computer since 1991, prior records on index books from 1978.
General Information: Public terminal goes back to 1977. No adoption, mental, juvenile, or sealed records released. Certification fee: $5.00. Payee: Circuit Clerk. Personal checks accepted. Prepayment required.

Robertson County

Circuit & District Court PO Box 63, 211 Court St, Mt Olivet, KY 41064; phone: 606-724-5993; fax: 606-724-5721; hours 8:30AM-4:30PM (EST). *Felony, Misdemeanor, Civil, Eviction, Small Claims, Probate.*
Civil Records: Access: In person only. Visitors must perform in person searches themselves. Court makes copy: $.25 per page. Required to search: name, years to search. Civil cases indexed by defendant, plaintiff. Civil records on computer to 1995, previous on index cards.
Criminal Records: Access: In person only. Visitors must perform in person searches themselves. Court makes copy: $.25 per page. Required to search: name, years to search; also helpful: DOB, SSN. Criminal records on computer to 1995, previous on index cards.
General Information: Public terminal goes back to 1995. No adoption, mental, juvenile, or sealed records released. Certification fee: $5.00 per doc. Payee: Circuit Clerk. Personal checks accepted. Prepayment required.

Rockcastle County

Circuit & District Court Courthouse Annex, 1st Fl, 205 E Main St, Rm 102, Mt Vernon, KY 40456; phone: 606-256-2581; hours 8AM-4PM M-W & F; 8AM-6PM Th; 8:30AM-N Sat (EST). *Felony, Misdemeanor, Civil, Eviction, Small Claims, Probate.*
Civil Records: Access: In person only. Visitors must perform in person searches themselves. Court makes copy: $.25 per page; same fee for self serve. Required to search: name, years to search. Civil cases indexed by defendant, plaintiff. Civil records on computer since 1991, index cards from 1978 to 1990, prior are archived at Frankfort.

Criminal Records: Access: In person only. Visitors must perform in person searches themselves. Court makes copy: $.25 per page; same fee for self serve. Required to search: name, years to search, DOB; SSN helpful. Criminal Records from 1991 to present are available. A form is available to request a criminal history through AOC Retrieval Services. This court provides the form via mail if you provide them a SASE.
General Information: Public terminal goes back to 1991. No adoption, mental, juvenile, or sealed records released. Will not fax documents. Certification fee: $5.00 per document. Payee: Circuit Clerk. Personal checks accepted. Prepayment required.

Rowan County

Circuit & District Court 627 E Main, Morehead, KY 40351-1398; phone: 606-784-4574; fax: 606-784-1899; hours 8:30AM-4:30PM M-F 8:30AM-12PM SAT (EST). *Felony, Misdemeanor, Civil, Eviction, Small Claims, Probate.*
www.kycourts.net
Civil Records: Access: In person only. Visitors must perform in person searches themselves. Court makes copy: $.50 per page. Required to search: name, years to search. Civil cases indexed by defendant, plaintiff. Civil records on computer from 1991, index cards from 1989, archived from 1900.
Criminal Records: Access: In person only. Visitors must perform in person searches themselves. Court makes copy: $.50 per page. Required to search: name, years to search. Criminal records on computer from 1991, index cards from 1989, archived from 1900.
General Information: Public use terminal available. No adoption, mental, juvenile, or sealed records released. No certification fee. Payee: Circuit Clerk. Only cashiers checks and money orders accepted. Prepayment required.

Russell County

Circuit & District Court 410 Monument Square, #203, Jamestown, KY 42629; phone: 270-343-2185; probate phone: 270-343-2185; fax: 270-343-5808; probate fax: same; hours 7:30AM-5PM (CST). *Felony, Misdemeanor, Civil, Eviction, Small Claims, Probate.*
Civil Records: Access: In person only. Visitors must perform in person searches themselves. Court makes copy: $.25 per page; same fee for self serve. Required to search: name, years to search. Civil cases indexed by defendant, plaintiff. Civil records on computer from 8/1994, index cards from 1978-1994, prior archived at Frankfort.
Criminal Records: Access: In person only. Visitors must perform in person searches themselves. Court makes copy: $.25 per page; same fee for self serve. Required to search: name, years to search. Criminal records on computer from 8/1994, index cards from 1978-1994, prior archived at Frankfort.
General Information: Public terminal goes back to 1994. No adoption, mental, juvenile, or sealed records released. Certification fee: $5.00. Payee: Circuit Clerk. Personal checks accepted. Prepayment required.

Scott County

Circuit & District Court 119 N Hamilton, Georgetown, KY 40324; phone: 502-863-0474; fax: 502-863-9089; hours 8:30-4:30PM (EST). *Felony, Misdemeanor, Civil, Eviction, Small Claims, Probate.*
Civil Records: Access: Mail, in person. Both court and visitors may perform in person searches. No search fee. Court makes copy: $.25 per page; same fee for self serve. Required to search: name, years to search. Civil cases indexed by defendant, plaintiff. Civil records on computer since 1992, index cards from 1978 to 1992, in books prior. Mail turnaround time varies.
Criminal Records: Access: Mail, in person. Both court and visitors may perform in person searches. No search fee. Court makes copy: $.25 per page; same

fee for self serve. Required to search: name, years to search; also helpful: SSN. Criminal records on computer since 1992, index cards from 1978 to 1992, in books prior. Mail turnaround time varies.

General Information: Public terminal goes back to 1992. No adoption, mental, juvenile, paternity and domestic violence records released. Certification fee: $5.00. Payee: Circuit Clerk. Personal checks accepted. Prepayment and SASE required.

Shelby County

Circuit & District Court 501 Main St, Shelbyville, KY 40065; phone: 502-633-1287; civil phone: 502-633-4736 (Dist Ct); fax: 502-633-0146; hours 8:30AM-4:30PM (EST). *Felony, Misdemeanor, Civil, Eviction, Small Claims, Probate.*

Note: Fax for misdemeanor clerk is 502-633-6421.

Civil Records: Access: Fax, mail, in person. Both court and visitors may perform in person searches. No search fee. Court makes copy: $.25 per page. Required to search: name, years to search. Civil cases indexed by defendant, plaintiff. Civil records on computer back to 1991; index cards from 1978 to 1991.

Criminal Records: Access: In person only. Visitors must perform in person searches themselves. Court makes copy: $.25 per page. Required to search: name, years to search, DOB. Criminal records on computer back to 1991; index cards from 1978 to 1991.

General Information: Public terminal goes back to 1991. No adoption, mental, juvenile, or sealed records released. Certification fee: $5.00 per doc. Payee: Circuit Clerk. Personal checks accepted. Prepayment and SASE required.

Simpson County

Circuit & District Court Box 261, Franklin, KY 42135-0261; phone: 270-586-8910/4241; fax: 270-586-0265; hours 8AM-4PM (CST). *Felony, Misdemeanor, Civil, Eviction, Small Claims, Probate.*

www.kycourts.net/Clerks/SimpsonClerk.shtm

Civil Records: Access: In person. Both court and visitors may perform in person searches. No search fee. Court makes copy: $.25 per page. Required to search: name, years to search. Civil cases indexed by defendant, plaintiff. Civil records on computer since 11/92, manual prior to 1978.

Criminal Records: Access: In person. Visitors must perform in person searches themselves. No search fee. Court makes copy: $.25 per page. Required to search: name, years to search, DOB, SSN. Criminal records on computer since 11/92, card index back to 1978.

General Information: Public use terminal available. No adoption, mental, juvenile, or sealed records released. Certification fee: $5.00. Payee: Circuit Clerk. Only cashiers checks and money orders accepted. Prepayment required.

Spencer County

Circuit & District Court Box 282, Taylorsville, KY 40071; phone: 502-477-3220; fax: 502-477-9368; hours 7:45AM-4PM (EST). *Felony, Misdemeanor, Civil, Eviction, Small Claims, Probate.*

Civil Records: Access: Mail, in person. Visitors must perform in person searches themselves. Court makes copy: $.25 per page; same fee for self serve. Required to search: name, years to search. Civil cases indexed by defendant, plaintiff. Civil records on computer from 8/94 to present, index cards from 1978 to 1994. Mail turnaround time 1-4 days.

Criminal Records: Access: Mail, in person. Visitors must perform in person searches themselves. Court makes copy: $.25 per page; same fee for self serve. Required to search: name, years to search, DOB; also helpful: SSN. Criminal records on computer from 8/94 to present, index cards from 1978 to 1994. Mail turnaround time 1-4 days.

General Information: Public terminal goes back to 1997. No adoption, mental, juvenile, or sealed records released. Certification fee: $5.00. Payee: Circuit Clerk. Personal checks accepted. Prepayment and SASE required.

Taylor County

Circuit & District Court 203 N Court Courthouse, Campbellsville, KY 42718; phone: 270-465-6686; fax: 270-789-4356; hours 8AM-4:30PM (EST). *Felony, Misdemeanor, Civil, Eviction, Small Claims, Probate.*

Civil Records: Access: In person only. Both court and visitors may perform in person searches. Court makes copy: $.25 per page. Self serve copy fee: $.15 per page. Required to search: name, years to search. Civil cases indexed by defendant, plaintiff. Civil records on computer from 1993 to present, index cards from 1978 to 1993.

Criminal Records: Access: In person only. Visitors must perform in person searches themselves. Court makes copy: $.25 per page. Self serve copy fee: $.15 per page. Required to search: name, years to search, DOB, SSN. Criminal records on computer from 1993 to present, index cards from 1978 to 1993.

General Information: Public terminal goes back to mid-1993. No adoption, mental, juvenile, or sealed records released. Certification fee: $5.00 per doc. Payee: Circuit Clerk. Personal checks accepted. Prepayment required.

Todd County

Circuit & District Court Box 337, 202 E Washington St, Elkton, KY 42220; phone: 270-265-2343 Circ Ct; 270-265-5631 Dist Ct; fax: 270-265-2122; hours 8AM-4:30PM (CST). *Felony, Misdemeanor, Civil, Eviction, Small Claims, Probate.*

Civil Records: Access: In person only. Visitors must perform in person searches themselves. Court makes copy: $.25 per page. Required to search: name, years to search. Civil cases indexed by defendant, plaintiff. Civil records on computer since 1/1993, index cards from 1978-1993, index books prior to 1978.

Criminal Records: Access: In person only. Visitors must perform in person searches themselves. Court makes copy: $.25 per page. Required to search: name, years to search. Criminal records on computer since 1/1993, index cards from 1978-1993, index books prior to 1978.

General Information: Public terminal goes back to 1993. No adoption, mental, juvenile, or sealed records released. Certification fee: $5.00 per doc. Payee: Circuit Clerk. Personal checks accepted. Prepayment required.

Trigg County

Circuit & District Court Box 673, Cadiz, KY 42211; phone: 270-522-6270; probate phone: 270-522-7070; fax: 270-522-5828; hours 8AM-4PM (CST). *Felony, Misdemeanor, Civil, Eviction, Small Claims, Probate.*

Note: District Court can be reached at 270-522-7070. Probate is a separate index at this same address.

Civil Records: Access: In person only. Visitors must perform in person searches themselves. Court makes copy: $.25 per page; same fee for self serve. Required to search: name, years to search. Civil cases indexed by defendant, plaintiff. Civil records on computer from 4/1993 to present, index cards from 1978 to 1993.

Criminal Records: Access: In person only. Visitors must perform in person searches themselves. Court makes copy: $.25 per page; same fee for self serve. Required to search: name, years to search, DOB; SSN helpful. Criminal records on computer from 4/1993 to present, index cards from 1978 to 1993.

General Information: Public terminal goes back to 4/1993. No adoption, mental, juvenile, or sealed records released. Will not fax specific case file. Certification fee: $5.00 per document. Payee: Circuit Clerk. Only cashiers checks and money orders accepted. Prepayment required.

Trimble County

Circuit & District Court Box 248, Bedford, KY 40006; phone: 502-255-3213, 502-255-3525 (District); criminal phone: 502-255-3213; civil phone: 502-255-3525; probate phone: 502-255-3525; criminal fax: 502-255-4953; civil fax: 502-255-3525; probate fax: 502-255-3525; hours 8AM-4:30PM M,T,Th,F 8AM-N Sat (EST). *Felony, Misdemeanor, Civil, Eviction, Small Claims, Probate.*

Probate records in separate index at this same address.

Civil Records: Access: Mail, in person. Both court and visitors may perform in person searches. No search fee. Court makes copy: $.25 per page; same fee for self serve. Required to search: name, years to search. Civil cases indexed by defendant, plaintiff. Civil records on computer and in folders from 1993 to present, folders 1978 to 1992, archives prior to 1978. Mail turnaround time 2-4 days.

Criminal Records: Access: In person only. Visitors must perform in person searches themselves. Court makes copy: $.25 per page; same fee for self serve. Required to search: name, years to search, DOB; SSN helpful. Criminal records on computer and in folders from 1993 to present, folders 1978 to 1992, archives prior to 1978.

General Information: Public terminal goes back to 1993. No adoption, mental, juvenile, or sealed records released. Will not fax documents. Certification fee: $5.00 per document includes copies. Payee: Circuit Clerk. Only cashiers checks and money orders accepted. Prepayment and SASE required.

Union County

Circuit & District Court PO Box 59, Morganfield, KY 42437; phone: 270-389-0800/0804; criminal fax: 270-389-9887; civil/probate fax is the same; hours 8AM-4PM (CST). *Felony, Misdemeanor, Civil, Eviction, Small Claims, Probate.*

Note: No searches performed on Thursday. Circuit Court phone-270-389-1811

Civil Records: Access: Mail, in person. Both court and visitors may perform in person searches. Court makes copy: $.25 per page. Required to search: name, years to search. Civil cases indexed by defendant, plaintiff. Civil records on computer since 6/1994 (new records only); prior on index cards and archived.

Criminal Records: Access: In person only. Visitors must perform in person searches themselves. Court makes copy: $.25 per page. Required to search: name, years to search, DOB, SSN. Criminal records on computer since 6/1994 (new records only); prior on index cards and archived. Contact AOC for statewide search by mail; criminal requests to be acquired through Pre-Trial Svcs in Frankfort.

General Information: Public terminal goes back to 6/1994. No adoption, mental, juvenile, or sealed records released. Will not fax documents. Certification fee: $5.00 per document. Payee: Circuit Clerk. Business checks accepted. Prepayment and SASE required.

Warren County

Circuit & District Court 1001 Center St #102, Bowling Green, KY 42101-2184; phone: 270-746-7400; fax: 270-746-7501; hours 8:AM-4:30PM (CST). *Felony, Misdemeanor, Civil, Eviction, Small Claims, Probate.*

Civil Records: Access: In person only. Visitors must perform in person searches themselves. Court makes copy: $.25 per page; same fee for self serve. Required to search: name, years to search. Civil cases indexed by defendant, plaintiff. Civil records on computer since 1989.

Criminal Records: Access: In person only. Visitors must perform in person searches themselves. Court makes copy: $.25 per page; same fee for self serve. Required to search: name, years to search; also helpful: DOB, SSN. Criminal records on computer since 1990.

General Information: Public terminal has criminal back to 1990 and civil back to 1989. No adoption, mental, juvenile, or sealed records released. Certification fee: $5.00. Payee: Circuit Clerk. Personal checks accepted. Prepayment required.

Washington County

Circuit & District Court PO Box 346, Springfield, KY 40069; phone: 859-336-3761; fax: 859-336-9824; hours 8AM-4:30PM; 8:30-12 on Sat (EST). *Felony, Misdemeanor, Civil, Eviction, Small Claims, Probate.*

Civil Records: Access: In person only. Both court and visitors may perform in person searches. No search fee. Court makes copy: $.25 per page; same fee for self serve. Required to search: name, years to search. Civil cases indexed by defendant, plaintiff. Civil records on computer, index cards and archived. Return postage required if specific documents asked to be mailed.

Criminal Records: Access: In person only. Both court and visitors may perform in person searches. No search fee. Court makes copy: $.25 per page; same fee for self serve. Required to search: name, years to search, DOB. Criminal records on computer, index cards and archived. Mail requests must be made to Pretrial Services, 100 Millcreek Park, Frankfort, KY 40602, 800-928-6381

General Information: Public use terminal available. No adoption, mental, juvenile, or sealed records released. Certification fee: $5.00. Payee: Circuit Clerk. Personal checks accepted. Prepayment required.

Wayne County

Circuit & District Court 109 N Main St, Monticello, KY 42633-1458; phone: 606-348-5841; fax: 606-348-4225; hours 8AM-4:15PM M-F; 8:30AM-N Sat (CST). *Felony, Misdemeanor, Civil, Eviction, Small Claims, Probate.*

Civil Records: Access: Mail, in person. Visitors must perform in person searches themselves. No search fee. Court makes copy: $.25 per page. Required to search: name, years to search. Civil cases indexed by defendant, plaintiff. Civil records on computer from 10/92 to present, index cards from 1978 to 1992. Mail turnaround time 5 days.

Criminal Records: Access: Mail, in person. Visitors must perform in person searches themselves. No search fee. Court makes copy: $.25 per page. Required to search: name, years to search; also helpful: DOB, SSN. Criminal records on computer from 10/92 to present, index cards from 1978 to 1992. Mail turnaround time 5 days.

General Information: Public terminal goes back to 1993. No adoption, mental, juvenile, or sealed records released. Certification fee: $5.00 per doc. Payee: Circuit Clerk. Personal checks accepted. Prepayment and SASE required.

Webster County

Circuit & District Court Box 290, 25 US Hwy 41A South, Dixon, KY 42409; phone: 270-639-9160; probate phone: 270-639-9300; fax: 270-639-6757; hours 8AM-4PM (CST). *Felony, Misdemeanor, Civil, Eviction, Small Claims, Probate.*

Civil Records: Access: Fax, mail, in person. Both court and visitors may perform in person searches. No search fee. Court makes copy: $.25 per page; same fee for self serve. Required to search: name, years to search. Civil cases indexed by defendant, plaintiff. Civil records in office from 1987 to present, prior records are at Frankfort archives. Mail turnaround time 1 day.

Criminal Records: Access: Fax, mail, in person. Both court and visitors may perform in person searches. No search fee. Court makes copy: $.25 per page; same fee for self serve. Required to search: name, years to search. Circuit criminal records in office from 1987 to present, prior records are at Frankfort archives; District Court to 1999. Mail turnaround time 1 day.

General Information: Public terminal goes back to 6/94. No adoption, mental, juvenile, or sealed records released. Fee to fax documents is $2.00 for 1st page, $1.00 each add'l. Certification fee: $5.00. Payee: Circuit Clerk. Personal checks accepted. Prepayment and SASE required.

Whitley County

Corbin Circuit & District Court 805 S Main St #10, Corbin, KY 40701; phone: 606-523-1085; fax: 606-523-2049; hours 8AM-4PM (EST). *Felony, Misdemeanor, Civil, Eviction, Small Claims, Probate.*

Civil Records: Access: In person only. Visitors must perform in person searches themselves. Court makes copy: $.25 per page. Required to search: name, years to search. Civil cases indexed by defendant, plaintiff. Civil records on computer from 1993 to present, index books prior.

Criminal Records: Access: In person only. Visitors must perform in person searches themselves. Court makes copy: $.25 per page. Required to search: name, years to search. Criminal records on computer from 1993 to present, index books prior.

General Information: Public terminal goes back to 1993. No adoption, mental, juvenile or sealed records released. Certification fee: $5.00. Payee: Whitley District Court. Personal checks accepted. Prepayment required.

Williamsburg Circuit & District Court Box 329, Williamsburg, KY 40769; phone: 606-549-2973; fax: 606-549-3393; hours 8AM-4PM (EST). *Felony, Misdemeanor, Civil, Eviction, Small Claims, Probate.*

Note: Circuit court can be reached at 606-549-2973. District court can be reached at 606-549-5162.

Civil Records: Access: In person only. Visitors must perform in person searches themselves. Court makes copy: $.25 per page. Required to search: name, years to search. Civil cases indexed by defendant, plaintiff. Civil records on computer from 1993 to present, index cards from 1978 to 1993.

Criminal Records: Access: In person only. Visitors must perform in person searches themselves. Court makes copy: $.25 per page. Required to search: name, years to search; also helpful: DOB, SSN. Criminal records on computer from 1993 to present, index cards from 1978 to 1993.

General Information: Public terminal goes back to 1993. No adoption, mental, juvenile, or sealed records released. Certification fee: $5.00 per doc. Payee: Whitley Circuit Clerk. Personal checks accepted. Prepayment required.

Wolfe County

Circuit & District Court Box 296, Campton, KY 41301; phone: 606-668-3736; fax: 606-668-3198; hours 8:30AM-4:30PM (EST). *Felony, Misdemeanor, Civil, Eviction, Small Claims, Probate.*

www.kycourts.net/clerks/wolfeclerk.shtm

Civil Records: Access: Mail, in person. Both court and visitors may perform in person searches. No search fee. Court makes copy: $.25 per page; same fee for self serve. Required to search: name, years to search. Civil cases indexed by defendant, plaintiff. Civil records on computer from 1992 to present, index books prior. Mail turnaround time same day.

Criminal Records: Access: Mail, in person. Both court and visitors may perform in person searches. No search fee. Court makes copy: $.25 per page; same fee for self serve. Required to search: name, years to search; also helpful: DOB, SSN. Criminal records on computer from 1992 to present, index books prior. Mail requests should be directed to Pretrial Services, 100 Millcreek Park, Frankfort, KY 40601, 502-573-2350. Mail turnaround time same day.

General Information: Public use terminal available. No adoption, mental, juvenile, or sealed records released. Certification fee: $5.00. Payee: Circuit Clerk. Personal checks accepted. Prepayment and SASE required.

Woodford County

Circuit & District Court 130 Court St, Versailles, KY 40383; phone: 859-873-3711; fax: 859-879-8531; hours 8AM-4PM M-Th; 8AM-6PM F (EST). *Felony, Misdemeanor, Civil, Eviction, Small Claims, Probate.*

Civil Records: Access: In person only. Visitors must perform in person searches themselves. Court makes copy: $.25 per page. Required to search: name, years to search. Civil cases indexed by defendant, plaintiff. Civil records on computer from 2/91 to present, index cards from 1978 to 1991.

Criminal Records: Access: In person only. Visitors must perform in person searches themselves. Court makes copy: $.25 per page. Required to search: name, years to search; SSN helpful. Criminal records on computer from 2/91 to present, index cards from 1978 to 1991.

General Information: Public terminal goes back to 1991. No adoption, mental, juvenile, or sealed records released. Certification fee: $5.00. Payee: Circuit Clerk. Personal checks accepted. Prepayment required.

Kentucky Recording Offices

ORGANIZATION: 120 counties, 122 recording offices. The recording officer is County Clerk. Kenton County has two recording offices. Jefferson County has a separate office for UCC filing until June 30, 2001; that office now only searches for filings up to that date. 80 counties are in the Eastern Time Zone (EST) and 40 are in the Central Time Zone (CST). Many offices are open until Noon on Saturdays.

REAL ESTATE RECORDS: Most counties will not perform real estate searches. Copy fees vary. Certification fee is usually $5 per document. Tax records are maintained by the Property Valuation Administrator, designated "Assessor" in this section.

UCC RECORDS: Under revised Article 9, Kentucky changes from a "local filing state" to a "central filing state" with the Secretary of State's office. Collateral on non-resident debtors were always filed at the state level. Real estate related UCCs are still found at the County Clerk's offcie. Many counties will not perform UCC searches. Use search request form UCC-11. Search fees are usually $5.00 per debtor name. Copy fees vary widely.

TAX LIEN RECORDS: All federal and state tax liens on personal property are filed with the County Clerk, often in an "Encumbrance Book." Most counties will not perform tax lien searches.

OTHER LIENS: Judgments, motor vehicle, mechanics, lis pendens, bail bond

ONLINE ACCESS: Five counties offer free access to assessor or real estate records. Several other counties offer commercial systems. There is no statewide system.

Adair County

County Clerk, 424 Public Sq, Columbia, KY 42728. RE & UCC recording phone-270-384-2801; fax-270-384-4805; hours: 7:30AM-4PM
Only the public may search. Copy fee $1.00 per page. Cert fee- $5.00 per cert plus copy fee. Payee-Adair County Clerk. **Other phones:** Elections- 270-384-2801; Vital Records- 270-384-2801.

Allen County

County Clerk, 201 W. Main St, Rm 6, Scottsville, KY 42164. RE & UCC recording phone-270-237-3706; fax-270-237-9206; 8AM-4:30PM, 8AM-N Sat
All records in one index. Office will perform a UCC search but public must search other records themselves. Search fee $5.00. Copy fee $.25 per page. Cert fee- $5.00 per doc plus copy fee. Payee-Allen County Clerk. **Property tax/Assessor-** same address as above. 270-237-3711.

Anderson County

County Clerk, 151 S. Main, Lawrenceburg, KY 40342. RE & UCC recording phone-502-839-3041; fax-502-839-3043; hours: 8:30AM-5PM M-Th; 8:30AM-6PM F
All records in one index. Records indexed on computer back to 1/1/1967. Only the public may search. Copy fee $.25 per page. Cert fee- $5.00 per doc plus copy fee. Payee- Anderson County Clerk. **Other phones:** Treasurer- 502-839-3471; Appraiser/Auditor- 502-839-4061; Elections- 502-839-3041; Vital Records- 502-564-4212. **Property tax/Assessor-** 502-839-4061.

Ballard County

County Clerk, PO Box 145, Wickliffe, KY 42087. RE & UCC recording phone-270-335-5168; fax-270-335-3081; hours: 8AM-4PM M-F; 8AM-5:30PM Last Friday of month
Mortgage searches available. Will search UCC records; search includes tax liens if requested. UCC search per debtor name- $5.00. Separate federal tax lien search- $5.00 per debtor. Separate state tax lien search- $5.00 per debtor. Copy fee $.50 per page. Cert fee- $5.00 per cert plus copy fee. Payee-Ballard County Clerk. **Other phones:** Treasurer- 270-335-5176; Elections- 270-335-5168; Vital Records- 270-335-5123. **Property tax/Assessor-** 270-335-3400.

Barren County

County Clerk, 117 N Public Sq #1A, Glasgow, KY 42141-2869. RE & UCC recording phone-270-651-5200; fax-270-651-1083; hours: 8AM-4:30AM
Index: Indexed by Yrs, Alpha. Records indexed on a public use terminal back to 1988. Office will perform a UCC search but public must search other records themselves. Search fee $5.00. Copy fee $1.00, if real estate $.25 per page. Cert fee- $6.00 per cert plus copy fee. Payee- Barren County Clerk. **Other phones:** Treasurer- 270-651-3338; Elections- 270-651-5200. **Property tax/Assessor-** same address as above. 270-651-2026.

Bath County

County Clerk, PO Box 609, Owingsville, KY 40360. 606-674-2613; fax-606-674-9526; hours: 8AM-4PM
Address for UCC is Secretary of State, UCC Branch, PO Box 1470, 700 Capital Ave #153, Frankfort, KY 40601. 502-564-2848. Only the public may search. Copy fee $1.00 per page. Cert fee- $3.50 per doc plus copy fee. Payee- Bath County Clerk. **Property tax/Assessor-** 606-674-6382.

Bell County

County Clerk, PO Box 157, Pineville, KY 40977. RE & UCC recording phone-606-337-6143; fax-606-337-5415; hours: 8AM-4PM M-F; 8AM-N Sat
All records in one index. Office will perform a UCC search but public must search other records themselves. Search fee $5.00 per name. Copy fee $2.00 per page. Cert fee- $5.00 per cert plus copy fee. Payee- Bell County Clerk. **Other phones:** Treasurer- 606-337-2497; Elections- 606-337-6143. **Property tax/Assessor-** 606-337-2720.

Boone County

County Clerk, PO Box 874, Burlington, KY 41005. 859-334-2137; fax-859-334-2193; hours: 8:30AM-4:30PM M, W-F; 8:30AM-6PM T
www.boonecountyclerk.com
Office will perform a UCC search but public must search other records themselves. Copy fee $1.00 per page. RE record copy- $.50 per page. Cert fee- $3.50 per cert plus copy fee. Payee- Boone County Clerk. **Online access to Real Estate, Lien, UCC, Assessor, Marriage records:** Access the county clerk database through eCCLIX, a fee-based service; $200.00 sign-up and $65.00 monthly. Records go back to 1989; images to 1998. For information, see the website or call 502-266-9445. **Other phones:** Treasurer- 859-334-2150. **Property tax/Assessor-** 859-334-2236.

Bourbon County

County Clerk, PO Box 312, Paris, KY 40362-0312. RE & UCC recording phone-859-987-2142; fax-859-987-5660; 8:30AM-4:30PM M-Th; 8:30AM-6PM F
Index: Indexes are 1786-1982, 1982-1989, 1989-present. Records indexed on a public use terminal back to 1989. Only the public may search. UCC copy fee $2.00 per page, self serve $.25 per page. Real estate or tax lien record copy- $3.50 per doc. Cert fee- $5.00 per cert plus copy fee. Payee-Bourbon County Clerk. **Other phones:** Treasurer- 859-987-2139; Elections- 859-987-2142; Vital Records- 502-564-4212. **Property tax/Assessor-** same address as above. 859-987-2152.

Boyd County

County Clerk, PO Box 523, Catlettsburg, KY 41129. 606-739-5116; fax-606-739-6357; hours: 8:30AM-4PM Main Office; 9AM-4:30PM
Records indexed on computer back to 1979. Only the public may search. Copy fee $.50 per page. Cert fee- $5.00 per doc includes copy fee. Payee-Boyd County Clerk. **Online access to Real Estate, Lien records:** Access to the County Clerk online records requires a $10 monthly usage fee. The system operates 24 hours daily; records date back to 1/1979. Lending agency information is available. For information, contact Doris Stephen Hallan-Clerk or Kathy Fisher at 606-739-5116. **Other phones:** Treasurer- 606-739-4242. **Property tax/Assessor-** 606-739-5173.

Boyle County

County Clerk, 321 W. Main St.; Rm 123, Danville, KY 40422-1837. RE & UCC recording phone-859-238-1112; fax-859-238-1114; hours: 8:30AM-5PM M; 8:30AM-4PM T-F
Search fee $1.00 for computer page. Copy fee $1.00 per page. RE record copy- $.50 per page. Cert fee- $5.00 per cert plus copy fee. Payee-Boyle County Clerk. **Other phones:** Treasurer- 859-238-1118; Vital Records- 502-564-4212 (Frankfort, KY). **Property tax/Assessor-** 859-238-1104.

Bracken County

County Clerk, PO Box 147, Brooksville, KY 41004-0147. RE & UCC recording 606-735-2952; fax-606-735-2687; 8AM-4PM M,T,Th,F; 8AM-N W,Sat
Only the public may search. Copy fee $.25 per page. Cert fee- $5.00 per cert plus copy fee. Payee-Bracken County Clerk. **Other phones:** Treasurer- 606-735-2125; Appraiser/Auditor- 606-735-2228;

Elections- 606-735-2952606-735-2952. **Property tax/Assessor-** 606-735-2228.

Breathitt County

County Clerk, 1137 Main St, Jackson, KY 41339. RE & UCC recording phone-606-666-3810; fax-606-666-3807; hours: 8AM-4PM M,T,Th,F; 8AM-N W; 9AM-N Sat

Office personnel or visitors may perform searches. Search fee $5.00 per name. Will only search real estate records if deed book and page number provided. Will not search tax liens. UCC search per debtor name- $5.00. Copy fee $1.00 per page. RE record copy- $.50 per page. Cert fee- $5.00 per record. Payee- Breathitt County Clerk. **Other phones:** Treasurer- 606-666-4268; Elections- 606-666-3810.

Breckinridge County

County Clerk, PO Box 538, Hardinsburg, KY 40143. Main phone & R/E recording-270-756-6166, UCC recording phone-270-756-2246; fax-270-756-1569; hours: 8AM-4PM, 8AM-N Sat

Separate indices to search include deeds, mortgages, leases, misc. Only the public may search. Copy fee $1.00 per page. Cert fee- $5.00 per cert plus $.25 per page. Payee- Breckinridge County Clerk. **Other phones:** Treasurer- 270-756-2269; Elections- 270-756-2246. **Property tax/Assessor-** PO Box 516, Hardinsburg, KY 40143; 270-756-5154.

Bullitt County

County Clerk, PO Box 6, Shepherdsville, KY 40165-0006. RE & UCC recording phone-502-543-2513; fax-502-543-9121; hours: 8AM-4PM M,T,W,F; 8AM-6PM Th www.bullittcountyclerk.ky.gov

Office will perform a UCC search but public must search other records themselves. UCC search per debtor name- $5.00. General copy fee $5.00 per doc. RE or tax lien copy- $.30 per page walk-in or $1.50 per page by mail. Cert fee- $5.00 per cert plus copy fee. Payee- Bullitt County Clerk. **Other phones:** Treasurer- 502-543-2262; Elections- 502-543-2513; Vital Records- 502-543-2415; Tax Collector-502-543-2514. **Property/Assessor-** 502-543-7480.

Butler County

County Clerk, PO Box 449, Morgantown, KY 42261. 270-526-5676; fax-270-526-2658; hours: 8AM-4:30PM

Records indexed on computer back to 1993. Only the public may search. Copy fee $.25 per page. Cert fee- $5.00 per cert plus copy fee. Payee- Butler County Clerk. **Other phones:** Treasurer- 270-526-3433. **Property tax/Assessor-** PO Box 538, Morgantown, KY 42261; 270-526-3455.

Caldwell County

County Clerk, 100 E Market St, Rm 23; Courthouse - Rm 3, Princeton, KY 42445. RE & UCC recording phone-270-365-6754; fax-270-365-7447; hours: 8AM-4PM

All records in one index. Records indexed on computer. Office personnel or visitors may perform searches. Will not search real estate records. Will search UCC records, but not tax liens. UCC search per debtor name- $5.00. Copy fee $1.00, if real estate $.25 per page. Cert fee- $5.00 per cert includes copy fee. Payee- Caldwell County Clerk. **Other phones:** Treasurer- 270-365-9776; Elections-270-365-6754. **Property/Assessor-** 270-365-7227.

Calloway County

County Clerk, 101 S. 5th St, Murray, KY 42071-2569. 270-753-3923; fax-270-759-9611; hours: 8AM-4:30PM

All records in one index. Records indexed on a public use terminal back to 11/1987. Office will perform a UCC search but public must search other records themselves. Search fee $5.00 per name. Copy fee $1.00 per page. RE or tax lien copy- $.50 per page. Cert fee- 5.00 per cert plus copy fee. Payee- Calloway County Clerk. **Property tax/Assessor-** 270-753-3482.

Campbell County

County Clerk, 4th & York Sts; Courthouse, Newport, KY 41071. 859-292-3850, R/E recording phone-859-292-3845; fax-859-292-3887; hours: 8:30AM-6PM M; 8:30AM-4PM T-F; 9AM-N Sat

Separate indices to search include deeds, mortgages, misc, business org, articles of inc, state & federal tax liens, probate, mechanics liens, court orders, fiscal court. Records indexed on a public use terminal back to 1995. Office will perform a UCC search but public must search other records themselves. UCC search per debtor name- $5.00. Copy fee $1.00 per page. RE or tax lien copy- $.50 per page. Cert fee- $5.00 1st 3 pages; $.25 each add'l page plus copy fee. Payee- Campbell County Clerk. **Online access to Property, Appraiser records:** Access to the Property Valuation Administrator property value is free at http://campbellpropertymax.governmax.com/propertymax/rover30.asp. **Other phones:** Treasurer- 859-292-3838; Appraiser/Auditor- 859-292-3871; Elections-859-292-3885. **Property tax/Assessor-** 330 York St, Newport, KY 41071; 859-292-3871.

Carlisle County

County Clerk, PO Box 176, Bardwell, KY 42023. RE & UCC recording phone-270-628-3233; fax-270-628-0191; hours: 8:30AM-4PM

All records in one index. Only the public may search. Copy fee $.10 per page. Cert fee- $5.00 per cert, copies not included. Payee- Carlisle County Clerk. **Other phones:** Treasurer- 270-628-3922. **Property tax/Assessor-** 270-628-5498.

Carroll County

County Clerk, 440 Main St; Court House, Carrollton, KY 41008. RE & UCC recording phone-502-732-7005; fax-502-732-7007; hours: 8:30-6PM M; 8:30AM-4:30PM T,W,Th,F

Separate indices to search include marriage licenses, wills on computer; land records, mortgages, tax liens & UCC's on computer back to 1990. Other indexes prior to 1990. Office will perform a UCC search but public must search other records themselves. UCC search per debtor name- $5.00. Copy fee $.25 per page. Cert fee- $5.00 per cert plus copy fee. Payee- Carroll County Clerk. **Other phones:** Treasurer- 502-732-7000; Elections- 502-732-7005; Vital Records- 502-564-4212. **Property tax/Assessor-** same address as above. 502-732-5448.

Carter County

County Clerk, 300 W. Main St, Rm 232, Grayson, KY 41143. RE & UCC recording phone-606-474-5188; fax-606-474-6883; hours: 8:30AM-4PM; 8:30AM-N Sat

Records indexed on a public use terminal back to 1975. Office will perform a UCC search but public must search other records themselves. Search fee $5.00. Copy fee $.50 per page. Cert fee- $5.00 per doc plus copy fee. Payee- Carter County Clerk. **Other phones:** Treasurer- 606-474-9551; Elections-606-474-5188; Vital Records- 606-474-5188. **Property tax/Assessor-** 606-474-5663.

Casey County

County Clerk, Box 310, Liberty, KY 42539. RE & UCC recording phone-606-787-6471; fax-606-787-9155; hours: 8AM-4:30PM M-F; 8AM-N Sat

Separate indices to search include multiple volumes. Records indexed on a public use terminal. Office will perform a UCC search but public must search other records themselves. UCC search per debtor name- $5.00. Copy fee $.25 per page. Cert fee- $5.00 per cert plus copy fee. Payee- Casey County Clerk. **Other phones:** Treasurer- 606-787-6154; Appraiser/Auditor- 606-787-7621; Elections- 606-787-6471; Vital Records- 606-787-6471. **Property tax/Assessor-** 606-787-7621.

Christian County

County Clerk, 511 S. Main, Hopkinsville, KY 42240. 270-887-4105, R/E recording phone-270-887-4109; fax-270-887-4186; hours: 8AM-4PM M-W; 8AM-6PM Th; 8AM-4:30PM Fri

Index: Various separate indices to search. Office will perform a UCC search but public must search other records themselves. UCC search per debtor name- $5.00. Copy fee $.25 per page. Cert fee- $5.00 per cert plus copy fee. Payee- Christian County Clerk. **Online access to Property, Assessor records:** Access property data by subscription at http://christianpva.com/wps-html/TaxRoll/; fees starts as low as $50 for 60 records. **Other phones:** Treasurer- 270-887-4103; Appraiser/Auditor- 270-887-4115; Elections- 270-887-4105. **Property tax/Assessor-** PO Box 96, Hopkinsville, KY 42240; 270-887-4115.

Clark County

County Clerk, PO Box 4060, Winchester, KY 40392. 859-745-0280, R/E recording phone-859-745-0282; fax-859-745-4251; hours: 8AM-5PM M; 8AM-4PM T-F

Office will perform a UCC search but public must search other records themselves. UCC search per debtor name- $5.00. Copy fee $.25 per page. Cert fee- $5.00 per cert plus copy fee. Payee- Clark County Clerk. **Other phones:** Treasurer- 859-745-0200; Elections- 859-745-0280; Vital Records- 859-745-0282. **Property tax/Assessor-** 859-745-0270.

Clay County

County Clerk, 102 Richmond Rd #101, Manchester, KY 40962. 606-598-2544; fax-606-599-0603; hours: 8AM-4:30PM; 8AM-N Sat

Records indexed on computer back to 1990; deed and mortgage records go back 30 years. Only the public may search. Copy fee $.50 per page. Cert fee- $5.00 per cert plus copy fee. Payee- Clay County Clerk. **Other phones:** Treasurer- 606-598-2071. **Property tax/Assessor-** 606-598-3832.

Clinton County

County Clerk, 212 Washington St; Courthouse, Albany, KY 42602. RE & UCC recording phone-606-387-5943; fax-606-387-5258; hours: 8AM-4:30PM; 8AM-N Sat

All records in one index. Records indexed on a public use terminal back to 1930. Only the public may search. Copy fee $1.00 per page. Cert fee- $3.50 per cert plus copy fee. Payee- Clinton County Clerk. **Other phones:** Treasurer- 606-387-5234; Elections- 606-387-5943; Vital Records- 606-387-5943. **Property tax/Assessor-** 606-387-5938.

Crittenden County

County Clerk, 107 S. Main; Courthouse, #203, Marion, KY 42064. RE & UCC recording phone-270-965-3403; fax-270-965-3447; hours: 8AM-4:30PM M,T,Th,F; 8AM-N W,Sat

All records in one index. Records indexed on a public use terminal back to 1843. Office personnel or visitors may perform searches. Search fee $5.00 per name. Copy fee $.50 per page. Cert fee- $5.00 per doc includes copy fee. Payee- Crittenden County Clerk. **Other phones:** Treasurer- 270-965-5251; Elections- 270-965-3404. **Property tax/Assessor-** same address. 270-965-4598.

Cumberland County

County Clerk, PO Box 275, Burkesville, KY 42717. RE & UCC recording phone-270-864-3726; fax-270-864-5884; hours: 8AM-4:30PM; 8AM-N Sat

Records indexed on a public use terminal back to 1969. Office will perform a UCC search but public must search other records themselves. Search fee $5.00. Copy fee $.50 per page. Cert fee- $3.50 per cert plus copy fee. Payee- Cumberland County Clerk. **Other phones:** Treasurer- 270-864-3444; Elections- 270-864-3726. **Property tax/Assessor-** 270-864-5161.

Daviess County

County Clerk, PO Box 609, Owensboro, KY 42302. 270-685-8420, R/E recording phone-270-685-8434; fax-270-685-2431; hours: 8AM-4PM M-Th; 8AM-6PM F www.daviessky.org
All records in one index. Records indexed on a public use terminal back to 1990. Office will perform a UCC search but public must search other records themselves. Search fee $5.00 per name. Copy fee $.25 per page. Cert fee- $5.00 per cert includes copy fee. Payee- Daviess County Clerk. **Other phones:** Treasurer- 270-685-8424; Elections- 270-685-8434. **Property tax/Assessor-** 270-685-8474.

Edmonson County

County Clerk, PO Box 830, Brownsville, KY 42210-0830. RE & UCC recording phone-270-597-2624; fax-270-597-9714; hours: 8AM-5PM M,T,W,F; 8AM-N Sat
Only the public may search. Copy fee $.50 per page. Cert fee- $5.00 per cert plus copy fee. Payee-Edmonson County Clerk. **Other phones:** Treasurer- 270-597-2819; Elections- 270-597-2624; Vital Records- 270-597-2624. **Property tax/Assessor-** 270-597-2381.

Elliott County

County Clerk, PO Box 225, Sandy Hook, KY 41171-0225. RE & UCC recording phone-606-738-5421; fax-606-738-4462; hours: 8AM-4PM; 9AM-N Sat
Record index not computerized. Only the public may search, but clerk searches UCC. Tax liens not included in UCC search. UCC search per debtor name- $5.00. Copy fee $1.00 per page. Real estate or tax lien record copy- $.50 per sheet. Cert fee-$5.00 per page plus copy fee. Payee- Elliott County Clerk. **Other phones:** Treasurer- 606-738-5821; Elections- 606-738-5421; Vital Records- 606-738-5421. **Property tax/Assessor-** 606-738-5090.

Estill County

County Clerk, PO Box 59, Irvine, KY 40336. 606-723-5156; fax-606-723-5108; hours: 8AM-N, 1-4PM M,T,Th,F; 8AM-Noon W,Sat
All records in one index. Records indexed on a public use terminal back to 1808. Only the public may search. Copy fee $.25 per page. Cert fee-$5.00 per cert includes copy fee. Payee- Estill County Clerk. **Other phones:** Treasurer- 606-723-4822; Elections- 606-723-5156. **Property tax/Assessor-** 606-723-4569.

Fayette County

County Clerk, 162 E. Main St, Lexington, KY 40507-1334. 859-253-3344; hours: 8AM-4:30PM
All records in one index. Office personnel searches UCC, all other indices searched by public. UCC search per debtor name- $5.00. Copy fee $.50 per page. Cert fee- $5.00 for doc, includes copies. Payee- Fayette County Clerk. **Online access to Property, Crime Map records:** Search property evaluations at www.pvdnetwork.com/PVDNet.asp?SiteID=116. Also, search the interactive crime map at http://crimewatch.lfucg.com. **Other phones:** Treasurer- 859-258-3300. **Property tax/Assessor-** 166 N Martin Luther King Blvd, Lexington, KY 40507; 859-254-2722.

Fleming County

County Clerk, Court Sq, Rm 101, Flemingsburg, KY 41041. RE & UCC recording phone-606-845-8461; fax-606-845-0212; hours: 8:30AM-4:30PM M-F; 8:30AM-N Sat
Office will perform a UCC search but public must search other records themselves. UCC search per debtor name- $5.00. Copy fee $1.00 per page. RE or tax lien copy- $2.00 per page. Cert fee- $5.00 per cert plus copy fee. Payee- Fleming County Clerk. **Other phones:** Treasurer- 606-845-8801;

Elections- 606-845-8461; Vital Records- 606-845-8461. **Property tax/Assessor-** 606-845-8801.

Floyd County

County Clerk, PO Box 1089, Prestonsburg, KY 41653-5089. 606-886-3816; fax-606-886-8089; hours: 8AM-4:30PM M,T,W,Th; 8AM-6PM F;9AM-N Sat
Separate indices to search include hard copy, computer. Records indexed on a public use terminal back to 1985. Only the public may search. Copy fee $.25 per page. Cert fee- $5.00 per doc plus copy fee. Payee- Floyd County Clerk. **Property tax/Assessor-** 606-886-9622.

Franklin County

County Clerk, PO Box 338, Frankfort, KY 40602. 502-875-8703, R/E recording phone-502-875-8710; fax-502-875-8718; hours: 8AM-4:30PM www.franklincountyclerk.org
All records in one index. Records indexed on a public use terminal back to 1980. Office will perform a UCC search but public must search other records themselves. Search fee $5.00. Copy fee $1.00 per page, if real estate $.25 per page. Cert fee- $5.00 per doc, plus copy fee. Payee-Franklin County Clerk. **Other phones:** Treasurer- 502-875-8747; Elections- 502-875-8704; Vital Records- 502-564-4212. **Property tax/Assessor-** 502-875-8780.

Fulton County

County Clerk, PO Box 126, Hickman, KY 42050. 270-236-2727; fax-270-236-3373; hours: 8AM-4PM
Office personnel or visitors may perform searches. Search fee $5.00 per name. Copy fee $1.00 per page. Cert fee- $5.00 per cert plus copy fee. Payee-Fulton County Clerk. **Other phones:** Treasurer- 270-236-2594. **Property tax/Assessor-** 270-236-2548.

Gallatin County

County Clerk, PO Box 1309, Warsaw, KY 41095. RE & UCC recording phone-859-567-5411; fax-859-567-5444; hours: 8AM-5PM M; 8AM-4:30PM T-F; 8AM-12 Sat
Separate indices to search. Records indexed on a public use terminal back to November, 1998. Book indexes prior to 1998. Only the public may search. Copy fee $2.00, if real estate or tax lien $.25 per page. Cert fee- $5.00 per cert includes copy fee. Payee- Gallatin County Clerk. **Other phones:** Treasurer- 859-567-5691; Elections- 859-567-5411; Vital Records- 859-567-5411. **Property tax/Assessor-** PO Box 883, Warsaw, KY 41095; 859-567-5621.

Garrard County

County Clerk, 15 Public Sq, #5; Courthouse Bldg., Lancaster, KY 40444. RE & UCC recording phone-859-792-3071; fax-859-792-6751; hours: 8AM-4PM M,T,Th,F; 8AM-N W,Sat
Berea, KY addresses may be in Madison County, and parts of Crab Orchard are in Lincoln County. Office personnel or visitors may perform searches. Search fee $5.00 per name. Copy fee $5.00 per document. Cert fee- $5.00 per cert plus copy fee. Payee-Garrard County Clerk. **Other phones:** Treasurer- 859-792-4178; Appraiser/Auditor- 859-792-3291; Elections- 859-792-3071; Vital Records- 859-792-3071. **Property tax/Assessor-** 859-792-3291.

Grant County

County Clerk, 107 N Main St; Courthouse Annex, Rm 15, Williamstown, KY 41097. 859-824-3321; fax-859-824-3367; hours: 8:30AM-4PM M-F; 8:30AM-N Sat
All records in one index. Will not search real estate records. Will search UCC records, but not tax liens. UCC search per debtor name- $5.00. Copy fee $.25 per record. Cert fee- $5.00 per cert, includes copies. Payee- Grant County Clerk. **Other phones:** Treasurer- 859-824-7561. **Property tax/Assessor-** 101 N Main St, Williamstown, KY 41097; 859-824-6511.

Graves County

County Clerk, Courthouse, Mayfield, KY 42066. 270-247-1676, R/E recording phone-270-247-1697; fax-270-247-1274; hours: 8AM-4:30PM M-Th; 8AM-6PM F
Office will perform a UCC search but public must search other records themselves. UCC search per debtor name- $5.00. Copy fee $2.00, if tax lien or real estate $.50 per page. Cert fee- $5.00 per doc plus copy fee. Payee- Graves County Clerk. **Other phones:** Treasurer- 270-247-3626; Elections- 270-247-1676. **Property tax/Assessor-** 270-247-3301.

Grayson County

County Clerk, 10 Public Sq, Leitchfield, KY 42754. main phone- 270-259-5295, UCC recording phone-270-259-3201; fax-270-230-0881; hours: 8AM-4PM M,T,W; 8AM-N Th,Sat; 8AM-5PM F
Separate indices to search include UCC, Deeds. Records indexed on computer back to 1986. Only the public may search. Court will check computer only. Search fee $5.00 per debtor. Will not search real estate records. Will search UCC records, but not tax liens. Copy fee $.25 per page. Cert fee- $5.00 per cert plus copy fee. Payee- Grayson County Clerk. **Other phones:** Treasurer- 270-259-5000; Elections- 270-259-3201; Vital Records- 270-259-5295; Deed Room-270-259-5295-. **Property tax/Assessor-** 270-259-4838.

Green County

County Clerk, 203 W. Court St, Greensburg, KY 42743. 270-932-5386; fax-270-932-6241; hours: 8AM-4PM M-W,F; 8AM-N Th,Sat
All records in one index. Records indexed on computer. Only the public may search. Copy fee $1.50 per instrument; $.50 per page generally. Cert fee- $5.00 per cert plus copy fee. Payee- Green County Clerk. **Other phones:** Treasurer- 270-932-4024. **Property tax/Assessor-** 270-932-7518.

Greenup County

County Clerk, PO Box 686, Greenup, KY 41144-0686. RE & UCC recording phone-606-473-7396; fax-606-473-5354; hours: 9AM-4:30PM
Index: Pre-1993 records on separate indices by doc type. Records indexed on computer back to 1993. Office will perform a UCC search but public must search other records themselves. UCC search per debtor name- $5.00. Copy fee $.50 per page. Cert fee- $5.00 per cert plus copy fee. Payee- Greenup County Clerk. **Other phones:** Treasurer- 606-473-5350; Elections- 606-473-7396; Vital Records- 606-473-7396. **Property tax/Assessor-** Main St, Courthouse, Rm209, Greenup, KY 41144; 606-473-9984.

Hancock County

County Clerk, PO Box 146, Hawesville, KY 42348. RE & UCC recording phone-270-927-6117; fax-270-927-8639; hours: 8AM-4PM M-W,F; 8AM-5:30PM Th
Only the public may search. Cert fee- $5.00 per cert plus copy fee. Payee- Hancock County Clerk. **Other phones:** Treasurer- 270-927-8101; Elections- 270-927-6117. **Property/Assessor-** 270-927-6846.

Hardin County

County Clerk, PO Box 1030, Elizabethtown, KY 42702. Main phone & R/E recording-270-765-2171, UCC recording phone-270-765-4116; fax-270-765-6193; hours: 8AM-4:30PM www.hccoky.org
Separate indices to search include grantor, grantee. Records indexed on a public use terminal back to 1982 for deeds, 1975 for mortgages. Only the public may search. Copy fee $.25 per page. Cert fee- $5.00 per doc included copy fee; $6.00 if to be returned by mail. Payee- Hardin County Clerk. **Online access to Recording, Will, Deed, Mortgage, Real Estate, Marriage, Assumed Name records:** Access the Clerk's permanent and temporary records search page free at www.hccoky.org/recordsearch/. Deeds go back to 1982; mortgages to 1975; most other

records all available. **Other phones:** Treasurer- 270-765-2350; Appraiser/Auditor- 270-765-2129; Elections- 270-765-6762; Vital Records- 270-765-2171. **Property tax/Assessor-** PO Box 70, #14 Public Sq, 2nd Fl, Elizabethtown, KY 42702; 270-765-2129.

Harlan County

County Clerk, PO Box 670, Harlan, KY 40831-0670. RE & UCC recording phone-606-573-3636; fax-606-573-0064; hours: 8:30AM-4:30PM M-W & F; 8:30AM-6PM Th
All records in one index. Records indexed on a public use terminal back to 1978. Office will perform a UCC search but public must search other records themselves. UCC search per debtor name- $5.00. Copy fee $1.00 per page. RE or tax lien copy- $.50 per page. Cert fee- $5.00 per cert plus copy fee. Payee- Harlan County Clerk. **Other phones:** Treasurer- 606-573-4771. **Property tax/Assessor-** 606-573-1990.

Harrison County

County Clerk, 313 Oddville Rd, Cynthiana, KY 41031. 859-234-7130, R/E recording phone-859-235-0513; fax-859-234-8049; hours: 8:30AM-4:30PM M T W F; 8:30AM-6PM T Th
Deed Room phone 859-235-0513. Records indexed on computer from 1985 to present, prior to 1985 they are in book indexes. Office will perform a UCC search but public must search other records themselves. Search fee $3.00 per name. Copy fee $.25 per page. Cert fee- $5.00 per doc includes copy fee. Payee- Harrison County Clerk. **Other phones:** Treasurer- 859-234-7136. **Property tax/Assessor-** 859-234-7113.

Hart County

County Clerk, PO Box 277, Munfordville, KY 42765. RE & UCC recording phone-270-524-2751; fax-270-524-0458; hours: 8AM-4PM (8AM-N Sat)
Only the public may search. Copy fee $1.00 per page. Cert fee- $3.50 per cert plus copy fee. Payee-Hart County Clerk. **Other phones:** Treasurer- 270-524-9474. **Property tax/Assessor-** 270-524-2321.

Henderson County

County Clerk, PO Box 374, Henderson, KY 42419-0374. RE & UCC recording phone-270-826-3906; fax-270-826-9677; hours: 8AM-4:30PM M-Th; 8AM-6PM Fri
Records indexed on a public use terminal back to 1992 to present. Only the public may search. Copy fee $.50 per file. RE or tax lien copy- $.25 per page. Cert fee- $5.00 per cert includes copy fee. Payee- Henderson County Clerk. **Other phones:** Treasurer- 270-826-3233; Appraiser/Auditor- 270-826-6024; Elections- 270-826-3906. **Property tax/Assessor-** PO Box 2003, Henderson, KY 42419; 270-827-6024.

Henry County

County Clerk, PO Box 615, New Castle, KY 40050-0615. 502-845-5705; fax-502-845-5708; hours: 8AM - 5PM; M ; 8AM-4PM,T,W,Th F
All records in one index. All records indexed on computer since 08/01/1996. Only the public may search. Copy fee $.25 per page; $.10 self serve. per page. Cert fee- $5.00. Payee- Henry County Clerk. **Other phones:** Treasurer- 502-845-5707. **Property tax/Assessor-** 23 S Property Rd, New Castle, KY 40050; 502-845-5740.

Hickman County

County Clerk, 110 E Clay; Courthouse, Clinton, KY 42031-1296. 270-653-2131; fax-270-653-4248; hours: 8:30AM-4PM
Separate indices to search include deeds, mortgages, liens, wills, orders. Records indexed on a public use terminal back to 1962. Only the public may search. Copy fee $.25 per page. Cert fee- $5.00 per cert plus copy fee. Payee- Hickman County Clerk. **Other phones:** Treasurer- 270-653-

6195; Elections- 270-653-2131; Vital Records- 270-653-6110. **Property tax/Assessor-** 270-653-5521.

Hopkins County

County Clerk, 10 S Main St, Madisonville, KY 42431. Main phone & R/E recording-270-821-7361, UCC recording phone-270-821-7361 x508; fax-270-825-7000; hours: 8AM-4PM
Separate indices to search include deeds, mortgages, encumbrances, leases and POA, wills, articles of veterans discharge, plats, fixture filings, misc, marriages, county court orders. Office will perform a UCC search but public must search other records themselves. UCC search per debtor name- $5.00. Copy fee $.50 per page; fax copy $1.00 per page. Cert fee- $5.00 plus copy fee. Payee- Hopkins County Clerk. **Other phones:** Treasurer- 270-825-2666. **Property tax/Assessor-** 25 E Center St, Madisonville, KY 42431; 270-825-3092.

Jackson County

County Clerk, PO Box 339, McKee, KY 40447. 606-287-7800; fax-606-287-4505; hours: 8AM-4PM; 8:30AM-N Sat
Records indexed on computer back to 1856. Only the public may search. Copy fee $.25 per page. Cert fee- $5.00 per cert plus copy fee. Payee-Jackson County Clerk. **Other phones:** Treasurer-606-287-8562. **Property tax/Assessor-** 606-287-7634.

Jefferson County Clerk

County Clerk, PO Box 35339, Louisville, KY 40232-5339. 502-574-6427, R/E recording phone-502-574-6220; fax-502-574-6041; hours: 8AM-4:30PM www.countyclerk.jefferson.ky.us/vip/
All records in one index. Records indexed on a public use terminal back to 1993 UCCs,1993-2003 title liens. Office will perform a UCC search but public must search other records themselves. Copy fee $2.00 per file number. Cert fee- $5.00 per cert plus copy fee. Payee- Jefferson County Clerk. **Online access to Property, Assessor, Voter Registration records:** Access to the county property valuation administrator's assessment roll is free at www.pvalouky.org. Also, to access voter registration go to http://cdc.ky.gov/VICWeb/index.jsp. **Property tax/Assessor-** 502-574-6380.

Jefferson County Recorder

County Clerk, 527 W Jefferson St, #105, Louisville, KY 40202. 502-574-5706, R/E recording phone-502-574-5785, UCC recording phone-502-574-6130; fax-502-574-5566; hours: 8AM-4:45PM www.countyclerk.jefferson.ky.us/vip/
Office will perform a UCC search but public must search other records themselves. UCC search per debtor name- $5.00. Payee- Jefferson County Clerk. **Online access to Land records:** Online land records system found at www.jccorecords.ky.gov/.

Jessamine County

County Clerk, 101 N. Main St, Nicholasville, KY 40356-1270. RE & UCC recording phone-859-885-4161; fax-859-885-5837; hours: 8AM-5PM M; 8AM-4PM T,W,F; 8AM-N Th; 9AM-N Sat
Only the public may search. Copy fee $1.00 per page. Payee- Jessamine County Clerk. **Other phones:** Treasurer- 859-885-4500; Elections- 859-885-4161. **Property tax/Assessor-** 859-885-4931.

Johnson County

County Clerk, 230 Court St.#124 Courthouse, Paintsville, KY 41240. 606-789-2557; fax-606-789-2559; hours: 8AM-4:30PM, 8:30AM-N Sat
Index: Indexed by Years. Only the public may search. Copy fee $.25 per page. Cert fee- $5.00 per cert plus copy fee. Payee- Johnson County Clerk. **Property tax/Assessor-** 606-789-2564.

Kenton County (1st District)

County Clerk, PO Box 1109, Covington, KY 41012. 859-392-1600, R/E recording phone-859-392-1653, UCC recording phone-859-392-1650; fax-859-392-1639; hours: 8:30AM-4PM M-Th; 8:30AM-6PM F www.kentonpva.com
Office will perform a UCC search but public must search other records themselves. UCC search per debtor name- $5.00. Copy fee $1.00, if real estate $.25 per page. Cert fee- $5.00 per cert plus copy fee. Payee- Kenton County Clerk. **Online access to Property Appraiser records:** Access the county Property Valuation database at www.kentonpva.com. Click on "Property Data." Search free by using "Guest Access." For full, professional property data you may subscribe; fee for user name/ password is $50. per month . **Other phones:** Treasurer- 859-392-1420; Elections- 859-392-1620; Vital Records- 859-392-1650 (Marriage Only). **Property tax/Assessor-** 859-392-1750.

Kenton County (2nd District)

County Clerk, PO Box 38, Independence, KY 41051. 859-392-1692, R/E recording phone-859-392-1619; fax-859-392-1681; hours: 8:30AM-4PM M,T,Th,F; 8:30AM-6PM W www.kentonpva.com
2nd District includes property south of Banklick Creek. 1st District includes property north of Banklick Creek. All records in one index. Only the public may search. General copy fee $1.00 per page. RE or tax lien copy- $.50 per page. Cert fee- $5.00 per cert plus copy fee. Payee- Kenton County Clerk. **Online access to Property Appraiser records:** Access the county Property Valuation database at www.kentonpva.com. Click on "Property Data." Search for free by using "Guest Access." For full, professional property data you may subscribe; fee for user name/ password is $50. per month . **Other phones:** Treasurer- 859-392-1420. **Property tax/Assessor-** 859-392-1750.

Knott County

County Clerk, PO Box 446, Hindman, KY 41822. 606-785-5651; fax-606-785-0996; hours: 8AM-4PM, 8AM-N Sat
Office personnel or visitors may perform searches. Search fee $5.00 per name. Copy fee $1.00, if real estate $.25 per page. Cert fee- $5.50 per cert plus copy fee. Payee- Knott County Clerk. **Other phones:** Treasurer- 606-785-5592. **Property tax/Assessor-** 606-785-5569.

Knox County

County Clerk, 401 Court Sq; #102, Barbourville, KY 40906. RE & UCC recording phone-606-546-3568; fax-606-546-3589; hours: 8:30AM-4PM
Office will perform a UCC search but public must search other records themselves. UCC search per debtor name- $5.00. Copy fee $1.00 per page. Cert fee- $5.00 per cert plus copy fee. Payee- Knox County Clerk. **Other phones:** Treasurer- 606-546-6192; Elections- 606-546-3568; Vital Records- 606-564-4212. **Property tax/Assessor-** 606-546-4113.

Larue County

County Clerk, 209 W. High St., Hodgenville, KY 42748. 270-358-3544; fax-270-358-4528; hours: 8AM-4:30PM M,T,Th,F; 8AM-N W,Sat
Separate indices to search include Grantor/Grantee, Tract index. Records indexed on a public use terminal back to 1985. Only the public may search. Copy fee $1.00 per page. Cert fee- $3.50 per page includes copy fee. Payee- Larue County Clerk. **Other phones:** Treasurer- 270-358-4400. **Property tax/Assessor-** 270-358-4202.

Laurel County

County Clerk, 101 S. Main, Rm 203; Courthouse, London, KY 40741. 606-864-5158; fax-606-864-7369; hours: 8AM-4:30PM; 8:30AM-N Sat
Only the public may search. Copy fee $2.00, if tax lien or real estate $.50 per page. Cert fee- $5.00

per cert plus copy fee. Payee- Laurel County Clerk. **Online to Property Appraiser records:** Access county Property Valuation database free at www.pvdnetwork.com/PVDNet.asp?SiteID=107. **Property tax/Assessor**- 606-864-2889.

Lawrence County

County Clerk, 122 S. Main Cross St, Louisa, KY 41230. Main phone & R/E recording-606-638-4108, UCC recording phone-606-638-0504; fax-606-638-0638; hours: 8:30AM-4PM; 8:30AM-N Sat
Records indexed on computer from 2000-2005, before 2000 in index books. Only the public may search. Copy fee .50 per page. Cert fee- $5.00 per cert includes copy fee. Payee- Lawrence County Clerk. **Other phones:** Treasurer- 606-638-4102; Appraiser/Auditor- 606-638-4743; Elections- 606-638-4108; Vital Records- 606-638-4188. **Property tax/Assessor**- same address as above. 606-638-4743.

Lee County

County Clerk, PO Box 551, Beattyville, KY 41311. RE & UCC recording phone-606-464-4115; fax-606-464-4102; hours: 8AM-4PM
Office personnel or visitors may perform searches. Search fee $5.00 per name. Will not search tax liens. Copy fee .25 per page. Cert fee- $5.00 per cert plus copy fee. Payee- Lee County Clerk. **Other phones:** Treasurer- 606-464-4100; Elections- 606-464-4115; Vital Records- 606-464-4115; 2nd Main Number- 606-464-4116. **Property tax/Assessor**- 606-464-4105.

Leslie County

County Clerk, PO Box 916, Hyden, KY 41749-0916. RE & UCC recording phone-606-672-2193; fax-606-672-4264; hours: 8AM-5PM; 8AM-N Sat
Records indexed on a public use terminal. Only the public may search. Copy fee .50 per page. Cert fee- $5.00 per cert plus copy fee. Payee- Leslie County Clerk. **Other phones:** Treasurer- 606-672-3901; Elections- 606-672-2995; Vital Records- 606-672-2193. **Property tax/Assessor**- 606-672-2456.

Letcher County

County Clerk, 156 Main St. #102, Whitesburg, KY 41858. 606-633-2432; fax-606-632-9282; hours: 8:30AM-4PM; 8:30AM-N 1st Sat of month
Records indexed on a public use terminal back to 1849. Only the public may search. Copy fee .50 per page. Cert fee- $5.00 per cert plus copy fee. Payee- Letcher County Clerk. **Property tax/Assessor**- 606-633-2182.

Lewis County

County Clerk, PO Box 129, Vanceburg, KY 41179-0129. RE & UCC recording phone-606-796-3062; fax-606-796-6511; hours: 8:30AM-4:30PM M T Th F; 8:30AM-N Wed
Separate indices to search include deeds, mortgages, release, assignments and enc indexed grantor/grantee. Leases & right of way have their own separate index, misc fixture filings, delinquent tax have separate indexes in front of each book. Record index not computerized. Only the public may search. Copy fee .50 per document. Cert fee- $5.50 per cert plus copy fee. Payee- Shirley A. Hinton, Lewis County Clerk. **Other phones:** Treasurer- 606-796-2722; Elections- 606-796-2311; Vital Records- 606-796-3062. **Property tax/Assessor**- PO Box 490, Vanceburg, KY 41179; 606-796-2622.

Lincoln County

County Clerk, 102 E. Main; Courthouse, Stanford, KY 40484. 606-365-4570, R/E recording phone-606-365-4520; fax-606-365-4572; hours: 8AM-4PM M-F; 9AM-N Sat
Only the public may search. Copy fee $2.00, if real estate or tax lien .25 per page. Cert fee- $5.00 per cert plus copy fee. Payee- Lincoln County Clerk.

Other phones: Treasurer- 606-365-4590; Elections- 606-365-4570. **Property tax/Assessor**- 606-365-4550.

Livingston County

County Clerk, PO Box 400, Smithland, KY 42081-0400. RE & UCC recording phone-270-928-2162; fax-270-928-2162; hours: 8AM-4PM; 8AM-6PM M
All records in one index. Only the public may search. Copy fee .25 per page. Cert fee- $5.00 per cert plus copy fee. Payee- Livingston County Clerk. **Other phones:** Vital Records- 270-928-2162. **Property tax/Assessor**- PO Box 77, Smithland, KY 42081; 270-928-2524.

Logan County

County Clerk, PO Box 358, Russellville, KY 42276-0358. RE & UCC recording phone-270-726-6061; fax-270-726-4355; hours: 8:30AM-4:30PM
Office personnel or visitors may perform searches. Search fee $5.00 per name. Will not search real estate records. Copy fee .25 per page. Cert fee- $5.00 per cert plus copy fee. Payee- Logan County Clerk. **Other phones:** Treasurer- 270-726-2167. **Property tax/Assessor**- 270-726-8334.

Lyon County

County Clerk, PO Box 310, Eddyville, KY 42038. RE & UCC recording phone-270-388-2331; fax-270-388-0634; hours: 8:30AM-4PM
Office will perform a UCC search but public must search other records themselves. UCC search per debtor name- $5.00. Copy fee $1.00 per page. Cert fee- $3.50 per cert plus copy fee. Payee- Lyon County Clerk. **Other phones:** Treasurer- 270-388-7193; Elections- 270-388-2331. **Property tax/Assessor**- 270-388-7271.

Madison County

County Clerk, 101 W. Main St; County Court House, Richmond, KY 40475-1415. 859-624-4704; fax-859-624-8474; hours: 8AM-4PM M-F; 8AM-6:30PM Th
Office will perform a UCC search but public must search other records themselves. UCC search per debtor name- $5.00. Copy fee $1.00 per page. Cert fee- $10.00 per cert. Payee- Madison County Clerk. **Property tax/Assessor**- 859-624-4704.

Magoffin County

County Clerk, PO Box 530, Salyersville, KY 41465. RE & UCC recording phone-606-349-2216; fax-606-349-2328; hours: 8:30AM-4PM; 8:30AM-N Sat
Record index not computerized. Only the public may search. Copy fee $1.00 per page. Cert fee- $5.00 per page includes copy fee. Payee- Magoffin County Clerk. **Other phones:** Treasurer- 606-349-2313; Elections- 606-349-6194; Vital Records- 606-349-2216. **Property tax/Assessor**- 606-349-6198.

Marion County

County Clerk, 120 W Main St; Courthouse, #3, Lebanon, KY 40033. 270-692-2651; fax-270-692-9811; hours: 8:30AM-4:30PM; 8:30AM-N Sat
All records in one index. Office will perform a UCC search but public must search other records themselves. UCC search per debtor name- $5.00. Copy fee .25 per page. Cert fee- $5.00 per doc includes copy fee. Payee- Marion County Clerk. **Other phones:** Treasurer- 270-692-3451. **Property tax/Assessor**- same address as above. 270-692-3401.

Marshall County

County Clerk, 1101 Main St; Courthouse, Benton, KY 42025. 270-527-4740; fax-270-527-4738; hours: 8AM-4:30PM
Only the public may search. Copy fee $1.00 per page. Tax lien copy- .50 per page. Cert fee- $5.00 per cert plus copy fee. Payee- Marshall County Clerk. **Property tax/Assessor**- 270-527-4728.

Martin County

County Clerk, PO Box 460, Inez, KY 41224-0485. RE & UCC recording phone-606-298-2810; fax-606-298-0143; hours: 8AM-5PM; 8AM-N Sat
All records in one index. Records indexed on a public use terminal back to 1988. Only the public may search. Copy fee .50 per page. Cert fee- $5.00 per cert plus copy fee. Payee- Martin County Clerk. **Other phones:** Treasurer- 606-298-2800; Elections- 606-298-2810; Vital Records- 606-298-7752. **Property tax/Assessor**- 606-298-2808.

Mason County

County Clerk, PO Box 234, Maysville, KY 41056. 606-564-3341; fax-606-564-8979; hours: 9AM-5PM; 9-11:30AM Sat
Office will perform a UCC search but public must search other records themselves. UCC search per debtor name- $5.00. Copy fee .25 per page. Cert fee- $5.00 per cert plus copy fee. Payee- Mason County Clerk. **Other phones:** Treasurer- 606-564-6381. **Property tax/Assessor**- 606-564-3700.

McCracken County

County Clerk, PO Box 609, Paducah, KY 42002-0609. 270-444-4700; fax-270-444-4704; hours: 8:30AM-4:30PM (M open until 5:30PM)
Only the public may search. Copy fee .50 per page. Cert fee- $5.00 per cert plus copy fee. Payee- McCracken County Clerk. **Other phones:** Treasurer- 270-444-4725. **Property tax/Assessor**- 270-444-4712.

McCreary County

County Clerk, PO Box 699, Whitley City, KY 42653. 606-376-2411; fax-606-376-3898; hours: 8:30AM-4:30PM M-F; 9AM-N Sat
Office will perform a UCC search but public must search other records themselves. UCC search per debtor name- $5.00. Copy fee $1.00 per page. Cert fee- $3.50 per cert plus copy fee. Payee- McCreary County Clerk. **Property tax/Assessor**- 606-376-2514.

McLean County

County Clerk, PO Box 57, Calhoun, KY 42327-0057. RE & UCC recording phone-270-273-3082; fax-270-273-5084; hours: 8AM-4:30PM; 9AM-N Sat
Index: Pre-1995 records indexed in separate books. Office will perform a UCC search but public must search other records themselves. UCC search per debtor name- $5.00. Copy fee .25 per page. Cert fee- $5.00 per instrument plus copy fee. Payee- McLean County Clerk. **Other phones:** Treasurer- 270-273-9964; Elections- 270-273-3082. **Property tax/Assessor**- PO Box 246, Calhoun, KY 42327-0246; 270-273-3291.

Meade County

County Clerk, PO Box 614, Brandenburg, KY 40108. 270-422-2152; fax-270-422-2158; hours: 8AM-4:30PM; 9AM-N Sat
Separate indices to search include grantor/grantee. Records indexed on computer back to 1967. Office will perform a UCC search but public must search other records themselves. UCC search per debtor name- $5.00. Copy fee .10 per page. Cert fee- $5.00 per cert includes copy fee. Payee- Meade County Clerk. **Property tax/Assessor**- same address as above. 270-422-2178.

Menifee County

County Clerk, PO Box 123, Frenchburg, KY 40322-0123. RE & UCC recording phone-606-768-3512; fax-606-768-6738; hours: 8:30AM-4PM M,T,W,F; 8:30-11:30AM Th,Sat
All records in one index. Only the public may search. Copy fee .25 per page. Cert fee- $5.00 per doc plus copy fee. Payee- Menifee County Clerk. **Other phones:** Treasurer- 606-768-2931; Elections- 606-768-3512; Vital Records- 606-768-3512. **Property**

tax/Assessor- PO Box 36, Frenchburg, KY 40322; 606-768-3514.

Mercer County

County Clerk, PO Box 426, Harrodsburg, KY 40330. 859-734-6313; fax-859-734-6309; hours: 8AM-4:30PM
Office will perform a UCC search but public must search other records themselves. UCC search per debtor name- $5.00. Separate federal/state combined tax lien search- $5.00 per debtor. Copy fee $.50 per page. Cert fee- $5.00 per cert plus copy fee. Payee- Mercer County Clerk. **Property tax/Assessor-** 859-734-6330.

Metcalfe County

County Clerk, PO Box 25, Edmonton, KY 42129. 270-432-4821; fax-270-432-5176; hours: 8AM-4PM
All records in one index. Records indexed on a public use terminal back to 1973. Only the public may search. Copy fee $.25 per page. Cert fee- $5.00 per cert includes copy fee. Payee- Metcalfe County Clerk. **Other phones:** Treasurer- 270-432-3181. **Property tax/Assessor-** 270-432-3162.

Monroe County

County Clerk, 200 N. Main St. #D, Tompkinsville, KY 42167-1548. RE & UCC recording phone-270-487-5471; fax-270-487-5976; hours: 8AM-4:30PM M-F; 8AM-N Sat
All records in one index. Search fee $5.00 per name. Will not search real estate, UCC or tax lien records. Copy fee $.25 per page. Cert fee- $5.00 per cert plus copy fee. Payee- Monroe County Clerk. **Other phones:** Treasurer- 270-487-5505; Elections- 270-487-5471; Vital Records- 270-487-8821. **Property tax/Assessor-** 200 N Main St #A, Tompkinsville, KY 42167; 270-487-6401.

Montgomery County

County Clerk, PO Box 414, Mount Sterling, KY 40353. RE & UCC recording phone-859-498-8700; fax-859-498-8729; hours: 8:30AM-4PM M-TH; 8:30-6PM F
Alternate fax number is 859-498-8738. Separate indices to search include grantor/grantee. Records indexed on computer from 1990 to present and 1796-1899, books from 1900-1989. Will not search real estate records. Will search UCC records and tax liens. UCC search per debtor name- $5.00. Copy fee $.25 per page. Cert fee- $5.00 per cert includes copy fee. Payee- Montgomery County Clerk. **Other phones:** Treasurer- 859-498-8703; Elections- 859-498-8700; Vital Records- 859-498-8700. **Property tax/Assessor-** 44 W Main St, Mt Sterling, KY 40353; 859-498-8710.

Morgan County

County Clerk, PO Box 26, West Liberty, KY 41472. RE & UCC recording phone-606-743-3949; fax-606-743-2111; hours: 8AM-4PM; 8AM-N Sat
Separate indices to search include all records before 1978, marriage records are separate. Records indexed on a public use terminal back to January, 2005. Only the public may search. Copy fee $1.00 per page. RE or tax lien copy- $.50 per page. Cert fee- $5.00 per cert includes copy fee. Payee- Morgan County Clerk. **Other phones:** Treasurer- 606-743-3195; Appraiser/Auditor- 606-743-3349; Elections- 606-743-3949; Vital Records- 606-743-3949. **Property tax/Assessor-** same address as above. 606-743-3349.

Muhlenberg County

County Clerk, PO Box 525, Greenville, KY 42345. 270-338-1441; fax-270-338-1774; hours: 8AM-4PM; 8AM-6PM F
Record copy fee-$.25 per page; $5.00 to fax back. $1.00 for research per book. Separate indices to search. Records indexed on computer back to 1984. Office will perform a UCC search but public must search other records themselves. UCC search per debtor name- $5.00. Cert fee- $5.00 per cert includes

copy fee. Payee- Muhlenberg County Clerk. **Property tax/Assessor-** 270-338-4664.

Nelson County

County Clerk, PO Box 312, Bardstown, KY 40004. Main phone & R/E recording-502-348-1830, UCC recording phone-502-348-1828; fax-502-348-1822; hours: 8:30AM-4:30PM M-F; 8AM-11:45AM Sat
Records indexed on a public use terminal back to 1/1/1984. Office will perform a UCC search but public must search other records themselves. Search fee $5.00. Copy fee $.25 per page. Cert fee- $5.00 per cert plus copy fee. Payee- Nelson County Clerk. **Other phones:** Treasurer- 502-348-1800; Appraiser/Auditor- 502-348-1810; Elections- 502-348-1829; Vital Records- 502-564-4212. **Property tax/Assessor-** same address as above. 502-348-1810.

Nicholas County

County Clerk, PO Box 227, Carlisle, KY 40311. 859-289-3730; fax-859-289-3709; hours: 8AM-4:30PM; 8-11:30AM Sat
Office personnel or visitors may perform searches. Search fee $5.00 per name. Copy fee $1.00 per page. Cert fee- $5.00 per cert plus copy fee. Payee- Nicholas County Clerk. **Other phones:** Treasurer- 859-289-3725; Elections- 859-289-3730. **Property tax/Assessor-** 859-289-3735.

Ohio County

County Clerk, PO Box 85, Hartford, KY 42347. 270-298-4422; fax-270-298-4425; hours: 8AM-4:30PM M-Th; 8AM-6PM F; 8AM-N Sat
Only the public may search. Copy fee $.25 per page. Cert fee- $5.00 per cert plus copy fee. Payee- Ohio County Clerk. **Property tax/Assessor-** 270-298-3692.

Oldham County

County Clerk, 100 W. Jefferson St, LaGrange, KY 40031. RE & UCC recording phone-502-222-9311; fax-502-222-3208; hours: 8:30AM-4PM M-W,F; 8:30AM-6PM Th http://oldhamcounty.state.ky.us
Office will perform a UCC search but public must search other records themselves. UCC search per debtor name- $5.00. Copies included in search fee. Cert fee- $5.00 per cert plus copy fee. Payee- Oldham County Clerk. **Online access to Real Estate, Lien, UCC, Assessor, Marriage records:** Access to the database is through eCCLIX database, a fee-based service; $200.00 sign-up & $65.00 monthly. Records go back, to 1980. UCC images to 2/97. Real estate instruments back to 1/95. Marriages back to 1980. For information, see the website http://oldhamcounty.state.ky.us/ecclix.stm or call 502-266-9445. **Other phones:** Elections- 502-222-0047. **Property tax/Assessor-** 502-222-9320.

Owen County

County Clerk, 135 W Bryan St, Owenton, KY 40359-0338. RE & UCC recording phone-502-484-2213; fax-502-484-1002; hours: 8AM-4PM M T TH F; 8AM-N Sat; Closed Wed.
All records in one index. Only the public may search. Copy fee $.25 per page. Cert fee- $5.00 per instrument, plus copy fee. Payee- Owen County Clerk. **Other phones:** Treasurer- 502-484-3557; Elections- 502-484-2213; Vital Records- 502-484-2213. **Property tax/Assessor-** 502-484-5172.

Owsley County

County Clerk, PO Box 500, Booneville, KY 41314. 606-593-5735; fax-606-593-5737; hours: 8AM-4PM; 8AM-12 Sat
All records in one index. Records indexed on a public use terminal. Only the public may search. Cert fee- $6.00 per cert includes copy fee. Payee- Owsley County Clerk. **Other phones:** Treasurer- 606-593-6202; Elections- 606-593-5735. **Property tax/Assessor-** 606-593-6265.

Pendleton County

County Clerk, PO Box 112, Falmouth, KY 41040. RE & UCC recording phone-859-654-3380; fax-859-654-5600; hours: 8:30AM-4PM M-F; 8:30AM-N Sat
Separate indices to search include wills, deeds, mortgages, articles in incorporation, mechanic liens, etc. Records indexed on computer back to 10/1/2004. Only the public may search. Copy fee $.25 per page. Cert fee- $5.00 per cert plus copy fee. Payee- Pendleton County Clerk. **Other phones:** Treasurer- 859-654-4321; Appraiser/Auditor- 859-654-3380; Elections- 859-654-3380. **Property tax/Assessor-** 233 Main St, Rm 4, Falmouth, KY 41040; 859-654-6055.

Perry County

County Clerk, PO Box 150, Hazard, KY 41702. RE & UCC recording phone-606-436-4614; fax-606-439-0557; hours: 8AM-4PM
Will fax back for $1.00 per page. Separate indices to search include grantor, grantee, cclix (computer). Records indexed on a public use terminal back to 8/1999. Office will perform a UCC search but public must search other records themselves. Will check to see if name exists. UCC search per debtor name- $5.00. Copy fee $.50 per page. Cert fee- $5.00 per cert plus copy fee. Payee- Perry County Clerk. **Other phones:** Treasurer- 606-436-1816; Elections- 606-436-3090. **Property tax/Assessor-** 606-436-4914.

Pike County

County Clerk, PO Box 631, Pikeville, KY 41502-0631. 606-432-6240, R/E recording phone-606-432-6208; fax-606-432-6222; hours: 8:30AM-4:30 M,T,W,Th; 8:30-6PM F; 8:30AM-N Sat.
Separate indices to search include deeds, mortgages, will, liens, art of inc. Records indexed on a public use terminal back to 1988. Office will perform a UCC search but public must search other records themselves. UCC search per debtor name- $5.00. Copy fee $.50 per page. Cert fee- $5.00 per cert includes copy fee. Payee- Pike County Clerk. **Other phones:** Elections- 606-432-6205; Vital Records- 606-432-6211. **Property tax/Assessor-** 146 Main St, #303, Pikeville, KY 41502; 606-432-6201.

Powell County

County Clerk, PO Box 548, Stanton, KY 40380. RE & UCC recording phone-606-663-6444; fax-606-663-6406; hours: 9AM-4PM M-W; 9AM-N Th; 9AM-4PM F; 9AM-N Sat
Only the public may search. Copy fee $.25; real estate $.10 per page. Cert fee- $5.00 per cert plus copy fee. Payee- Powell County Clerk. **Other phones:** Treasurer- 606-663-2834; Appraiser/Auditor- 606-663-4184; Vital Records- 502-564-4212. **Property tax/Assessor-** 606-663-4184.

Pulaski County

County Clerk, PO Box 724, Somerset, KY 42502. 606-679-3652, R/E recording phone-606-679-2042, UCC recording phone-606-679-2042; fax-606-678-0073; hours: 8AM-4:30PM
Office will perform a UCC search but public must search other records themselves. UCC search per debtor name- $5.00. Copy fee $.50 per page. Cert fee- $5.00 per cert plus copy fee. Payee- Pulaski County Clerk. **Other phones:** Treasurer- 606-679-1311; Elections- 606-679-3652; Vital Records- 606-679-3652. **Property tax/Assessor-** 606-679-1812.

Robertson County

County Clerk, PO Box 75, Mount Olivet, KY 41064. 606-724-5212; fax-606-724-5022; hours: 8:30-N, 1-4PM M,T,Th,F; 8:30AM-N W, Sat
All records in one index. Records indexed on computer back to 1967. Only the public may search. Copy fee $.10 per page. Cert fee- $6.50 per cert, up to 3 pages. Payee- Robertson County

Clerk. Other phones: Treasurer- 606-724-5403. **Property tax/Assessor**- 606-724-5213.

Rockcastle County

County Clerk, 205 E Main St #6, Mount Vernon, KY 40456. 606-256-2831; fax-606-256-4302; hours: 8:30-4PM; 8:30-N Sat

Separate indices to search include deeds, mortgages; like documents in single indices. Office will perform a UCC search but public must search other records themselves. UCC search per debtor name- $5.00. Copy fee $.25 per page. Cert fee- $5.00 per doc plus copy fee. Payee- Rockcastle County Clerk. **Other phones:** Treasurer- 606-256-3623. **Property/Assessor**- 606-256-4194.

Rowan County

County Clerk, 627 E. Main St; Courthouse - 2nd Fl, Morehead, KY 40351. RE & UCC recording phone-606-784-5212; fax-606-784-2923; hours: 8AM-4PM M-TH; 8AM-6PM F

All records in one index. Office will perform a UCC search but public must search other records themselves. Search fee $5.00 per debtor. Copy fee $1.00, real estate is $.25 per copy. Cert fee- $5.00 per cert, copy fee included. Payee- Rowan County Clerk. **Other phones:** Treasurer- 606-784-4211; Vital Records- 502-564 4212. **Property tax/Assessor**- 606-784-5512.

Russell County

County Clerk, PO Box 579, Jamestown, KY 42629-0579. 270-343-2125; fax-270-343-4700; hours: 8AM-4PM; 8-11AM Sat

Separate indices to search include grantor/grantee. Record index not computerized. Only the public may search. Copy fee $.25 per page. Cert fee- $5.00 per cert includes copy fee. Payee- Russell County Clerk. **Other phones:** Treasurer- 270-343-2112. **Property tax/Assessor**- 270-343-4395.

Scott County

County Clerk, 101 E Main St; Courthouse, Georgetown, KY 40324-1794. 502-863-7875; fax-502-863-7898; hours: 8:30AM-4:30PM M-Th; 8:30AM-6PM F

All records in one index. Records indexed on a public use terminal back to May, 1993. Office will perform a UCC search but public must search other records themselves. UCC search per debtor name- $5.00. Copy fee $1.00 per page. Cert fee- $5.00 per cert includes copy fee. Payee- Scott County Clerk. **Other phones:** Treasurer- 502-863-7850. **Property tax/Assessor**- same address as above. 502-863-7885.

Shelby County

County Clerk, PO Box 819, Shelbyville, KY 40066-0819. RE & UCC recording phone-502-633-4410, UCC recording phone-502-513-0265; fax-502-633-7887; hours: 8:30AM-4:30PM M,T,W,F; 8:30AM-6PM Th www.shelbycountyclerk.com

Office will perform a UCC search but public must search other records themselves. Copy fee $1.00 per page. RE record copy- $.10 per page. Cert fee- $5.00 per cert plus copy fee. Payee- Shelby County Clerk. **Online access to Real Estate, Deed, Recording records:** Access is via the eCCLIX subscription system at www.shelbycountyclerk.com/ecclix.stm. Images go back to 1998; index to 1995. Sign-up fee is $100 plus $65 per month for unlimited access. For more information, phone 502-266-9445 or email sales@softwaremanagementinc.com. **Other phones:** Treasurer- 502-633-1220; Elections- 502-633-4410; Vital Records- 502-564-4212. **Property tax/Assessor**- 502-633-4403.

Simpson County

County Clerk, PO Box 268, Franklin, KY 42135-0268. 270-586-8161; fax-270-586-6464; hours: 8AM-4PM www.simpsoncountyclerk.ky.gov

Office will perform a UCC search but public must search other records themselves. UCC search per debtor name- $5.00. Copy fee $.50 per page. Cert fee- $5.00 per cert plus copy fee. Payee- Simpson County Clerk. **Other phones:** Treasurer- 502-586-7184. **Property tax/Assessor**- 502-586-4261.

Spencer County

County Clerk, PO Box 544, Taylorsville, KY 40071. 502-477-3215; fax-502-477-3216; hours: 8AM-4:30PM M-F; 8AM-11:30 Sat

Office will perform a UCC search but public must search other records themselves. UCC search per debtor name- $5.00. Copy fee $.25 per page. Cert fee- $5.00 per cert plus copy fee. Payee- Spencer County Clerk. **Other phones:** Treasurer- 502-477-3211. **Property tax/Assessor**- 502-477-3207.

Taylor County

County Clerk, 203 N. Court St; ## 5, Campbellsville, KY 42718-2298. RE & UCC recording phone-270-465-6677; fax-270-789-1144; hours: 8AM-4:30PM M-Th; 8AM-5PM F

Only the public may search. Cert fee- $5.00. Payee- Taylor County Clerk. **Other phones:** Treasurer- 270-789-1008. **Property tax/Assessor**- 270-465-5811.

Todd County

County Clerk, PO Box 307, Elkton, KY 42220. 270-265-2363; fax-270-265-2588; hours: 8AM-4:30PM

Separate indices to search include Book and Computer. Records indexed on a public use terminal back to 7/2003. Only the public may search. Copy fee $.25 per page. Cert fee- $5.00 per cert plus copy fee. Payee- Todd County Clerk. **Other phones:** Treasurer- 270-265-2451. **Property tax/Assessor**- 270-265-5614.

Trigg County

County Clerk, PO Box 1310, Cadiz, KY 42211. 270-522-6661; fax-270-522-6662; hours: 8AM-4PM

All records in one index. Only the public may search. Copy fee $1.00 per page. Cert fee- $5.00 per cert plus copy fee. Payee- Trigg County Clerk. **Other phones:** Treasurer- 270-522-8459; Elections- 270-522-6661. **Property/Assessor**- 270-522-3271.

Trimble County

County Clerk, PO Box 262, Bedford, KY 40006-0262. RE & UCC recording phone-502-255-7174; fax-502-255-7045; hours: 8:30AM-4:30PM M,T,Th,F; 8:30AM-N Sat

All records in one index. Records indexed on computer. Only the public may search. Copy fee $.25 per page. Cert fee- $5.00 per cert plus copy fee. Payee- Trimble County Clerk. **Other phones:** Elections- 502-255-7174; Vital Records- 502-255-7174. **Property tax/Assessor**- 502-255-3592.

Union County

County Clerk, PO Box 119, Morganfield, KY 42437-0119. 270-389-1334; fax-270-389-9135; hours: 8AM-4PM

Office will perform a UCC search but public must search other records themselves. UCC search per debtor name- $5.00. Copy fee $.50 per page. Cert fee- $5.00 per cert. Payee- Union County Clerk. **Property tax/Assessor**- 270-389-1933.

Warren County

County Clerk, PO Box 478, Bowling Green, KY 42102-0478. RE & UCC recording phone-270-842-9416; fax-270-843-5319; hours: 8:30AM-4:30PM http://warrencounty.state.ky.us

All records in one index. Records indexed on computer. Office will perform a UCC search but public must search other records themselves. Search fee $5.00. Copy fee $.50 per page. Cert fee- $5.00 per cert plus copy fee. Payee- Warren County Clerk. **Online access to Real Estate, Lien, UCC, Assessor, Marriage records:** Access the county clerk database through eCCLIX, a fee-based

service; $200.00 sign-up and $65.00 monthly. Records go back to 1989; images to 1998. For information, see the website or call 502-266-9445. **Other phones:** Treasurer- 270-842-5805; Elections- 270-842-5306; Vital Records- 270-842-9416. **Property tax/Assessor**- same address as above. 270-842-3268.

Washington County

County Clerk, PO Box 446, Springfield, KY 40069. 859-336-5425; fax-859-336-5408; hours: 9AM-4:30PM; 9AM-N Sat

All records in one index. Records indexed on a public use terminal back to 1960. Only the public may search. Copy fee $.25 per page. Cert fee- $5.00 per cert plus copy fee. Payee- Washington County Clerk. **Other phones:** Elections- 859-336-5425. **Property tax/Assessor**- 859-336-5420.

Wayne County

County Clerk, PO Box 565, Monticello, KY 42633. RE & UCC recording phone-606-348-6661; fax-606-348-8303; hours: 8AM-4:30PM; 8AM-N Sat

Separate indices to search include computer, book, and print-out. Records indexed on a public use terminal. Office will perform a UCC search but public must search other records themselves. Tax liens not included in UCC search. UCC search per debtor name- $5.00. Copy fee $.25 per page. Cert fee- $5.00 per cert includes copy fee. Payee- Wayne County Clerk. **Other phones:** Treasurer- 606-348-8411; Elections- 606-348-6661; Vital Records- 606-348-6661. **Property tax/Assessor**- 109 N. Main St, Monticello, KY 42633; 606-348-6621.

Webster County

County Clerk, PO Box 19, Dixon, KY 42409-0019. RE & UCC recording phone-270-639-7006; fax-270-639-7029; hours: 8AM-4PM M; 8AM-4PM T-F

Office personnel or visitors may perform searches. Search fee $5.00 per name. Will not search real estate records. Copy fee $.25; real estate or tax lien $.50 per page. Cert fee- $5.00 per cert. Payee- Webster County Clerk. **Other phones:** Treasurer- 270-639-5042. **Property tax/Assessor**- 270-639-7016.

Whitley County

County Clerk, PO Box 8, Williamsburg, KY 40769. RE & UCC recording phone-606-549-6002; fax-606-549-2790; hours: 7:30AM-4PM; 7:30AM-N Sat

Office will perform a UCC search but public must search other records themselves. UCC search per debtor name- $3.50. Copy fee $.50 per page; fax back $2.50 per page. RE record copy- $.25 per page. Cert fee- $5.00 per cert plus copy fee. Payee- Whitley County Clerk. **Property tax/Assessor**- 606-549-6008.

Wolfe County

County Clerk, PO Box 400, Campton, KY 41301. RE & UCC recording phone-606-668-3515; fax-606-668-3367; 8AM-4PM M,T,Th,F; 8AM-N W & Sat

Office will perform a UCC search but public must search other records themselves. UCC search per debtor name- $5.00. Copy fee $1.00 per page. Payee- Wolfe County Clerk. **Other phones:** Treasurer- 606-668-4060; Appraiser/Auditor- 606-668-6925; Elections- 606-668-3515; Vital Records- 606-668-4212. **Property tax/Assessor**- 606-668-6923.

Woodford County

County Clerk, 103 S Main St; Courthouse - Rm 120, Versailles, KY 40383. RE & UCC recording phone-859-873-3421; fax-859-873-6985; hours: 8AM-4PM M,T,W,Th; 8AM-5:45PM F

Separate indices to search include cott index, chattel mortgages, taxes, etc. Record index not computerized. Only the public may search. Copy fee $.25 per page. Cert fee- $5.00 per cert plus copy fee. Payee- Woodford County Clerk. **Other phones:** Treasurer- 859-873-6122; Elections- 859-873-3421. **Property tax/Assessor**- 120 S Main, Versailles, KY 40383; 859-873-4101.

Kentucky County Locator

You will usually be able to find the city name in the City/County Cross Reference below. In that case, it is a simple matter to determine the county from the cross reference. However, only the official US Postal Service city names are included in this index. There are an additional 40,000 place names that people use in their addresses. Therefore, we have also included a ZIP/City Cross Reference immediately following the City/County Cross Reference.

If you know the ZIP Code but the city name does not appear in the City/County Cross Reference index, look up the ZIP Code in the ZIP/City Cross Reference, find the city name, then look up the city name in the City/County Cross Reference.

Kentucky City/County Cross Reference

AARON (42601) Clinton(97), Russell(2)
ABERDEEN Butler
ACORN Pulaski
ADAIRVILLE (42202) Logan(98), Simpson(1)
ADAMS Lawrence
ADOLPHUS Allen
AGES BROOKSIDE Harlan
ALBANY Clinton
ALEXANDRIA Campbell
ALLEGRE Todd
ALLEN Floyd
ALLENSVILLE (42204) Todd(78), Logan(21)
ALLOCK Perry
ALMO Calloway
ALPHA (42603) Clinton(69), Wayne(30)
ALTRO Breathitt
ALVATON (42122) Warren(94), Allen(5)
AMBURGEY Knott
ANNVILLE (40402) Jackson(95), Clay(4)
ARGILLITE Greenup
ARJAY Bell
ARLINGTON (42021) Carlisle(92), Hickman(7)
ARTEMUS Knox
ARY Perry
ASHCAMP Pike
ASHER Leslie
ASHLAND (41102) Boyd(93), Greenup(6)
ASHLAND Boyd
ATHOL Breathitt
AUBURN (42206) Logan(92), Simpson(6), Warren(1)
AUGUSTA Bracken
AUSTIN Barren
AUXIER Floyd
AVAWAM Perry
AXTEL Breckinridge
BAGDAD (40003) Shelby(83), Franklin(16)
BAKERTON Cumberland
BANDANA Ballard
BANNER Floyd
BARBOURVILLE Knox
BARDSTOWN Nelson
BARDWELL Carlisle
BARLOW Ballard
BASKETT Henderson
BATTLETOWN Meade
BAXTER Harlan
BAYS Breathitt
BEAR BRANCH Leslie
BEATTYVILLE Lee
BEAUMONT Metcalfe
BEAUTY Martin
BEAVER Floyd
BEAVER DAM (42320) Ohio(98), Butler(1)
BEDFORD (40006) Trimble(97), Carroll(2)
BEE SPRING Edmonson
BEECH CREEK Muhlenberg
BEECH GROVE McLean
BEECHMONT Muhlenberg
BELCHER Pike
BELFRY Pike
BELLEVUE Campbell
BELTON Muhlenberg
BENHAM Harlan

BENTON (42025) Marshall(98), Calloway(1)
BEREA (40403) Madison(87), Garrard(10), Rockcastle(2)
BEREA Madison
BERRY (41003) Harrison(67), Grant(19), Pendleton(12)
BETHANY Wolfe
BETHEL Bath
BETHELRIDGE Casey
BETHLEHEM Henry
BETSY LAYNE (41605) Floyd(89), Pike(10)
BEULAH HEIGHTS McCreary
BEVERLY (40913) Bell(57), Clay(42)
BEVINSVILLE Floyd
BIG CLIFTY (42712) Grayson(60), Hardin(39)
BIG CREEK Clay
BIG LAUREL (40808) Harlan(50), Leslie(50)
BIG SPRING (40106) Breckinridge(80), Hardin(20)
BIGHILL Madison
BIMBLE Knox
BLACKEY Letcher
BLACKFORD Webster
BLAINE Lawrence
BLANDVILLE Ballard
BLEDSOE (40810) Harlan(87), Leslie(12)
BLOOMFIELD (40008) Nelson(89), Spencer(9)
BLUE RIVER Floyd
BLUEHOLE Clay
BOAZ (42027) Graves(80), McCracken(19)
BOND Jackson
BONNIEVILLE Hart
BONNYMAN Perry
BOONEVILLE (41314) Breathitt(56), Owsley(43)
BOONS CAMP Johnson
BOSTON Nelson
BOW (42714) Cumberland(92), Clinton(7)
BOWEN Powell
BOWLING GREEN (42101) Warren(96), Edmonson(2)
BOWLING GREEN Warren
BRADFORDSVILLE (40009) Marion(78), Taylor(16), Casey(5)
BRANDENBURG Meade
BREEDING (42715) Adair(94), Metcalfe(4), Cumberland(1)
BREMEN Muhlenberg
BRINKLEY Knott
BRODHEAD (40409) Rockcastle(90), Lincoln(9)
BRONSTON (42518) Pulaski(96), Wayne(3)
BROOKLYN Butler
BROOKS (40109) Bullitt(97), Jefferson(2)
BROOKSVILLE Bracken
BROWDER Muhlenberg
BROWNS FORK Perry
BROWNSVILLE Edmonson
BRUIN Elliott
BRYANTS STORE Knox
BRYANTSVILLE Garrard
BUCKHORN (41721) Perry(94), Breathitt(5)

BUCKNER Oldham
BUFFALO (42716) Larue(75), Green(20), Taylor(3)
BULAN (41722) Perry(65), Knott(34)
BURDINE Letcher
BURGIN Mercer
BURKESVILLE Cumberland
BURKHART Wolfe
BURLINGTON Boone
BURNA Livingston
BURNSIDE Pulaski
BURNWELL Pike
BUSH Laurel
BUSKIRK Morgan
BUSY (41723) Perry(76), Leslie(23)
BUTLER Pendleton
BYPRO Floyd
CADIZ Trigg
CALHOUN (42327) McLean(97), Daviess(2)
CALIFORNIA Campbell
CALVERT CITY Marshall
CALVIN Bell
CAMP DIX Lewis
CAMPBELLSBURG (40011) Henry(76), Trimble(18), Carroll(4)
CAMPBELLSVILLE (42718) Taylor(92), Marion(3), Green(2), Larue(1)
CAMPBELLSVILLE Taylor
CAMPTON (41301) Wolfe(93), Breathitt(3), Lee(2)
CANADA Pike
CANE VALLEY Adair
CANEY Morgan
CANEYVILLE (42721) Grayson(89), Butler(7), Edmonson(3)
CANMER Hart
CANNEL CITY Morgan
CANNON Knox
CANOE Breathitt
CANTON Trigg
CARLISLE (40311) Nicholas(90), Bourbon(8)
CARRIE Knott
CARTER Carter
CARVER Magoffin
CASEY CREEK (42723) Adair(61), Taylor(31), Casey(6)
CASEY CREEKG (42723) Adair(61), Taylor(31), Casey(6)
CATLETTSBURG (41129) Boyd(87), Lawrence(12)
CAVE CITY (42127) Barren(92), Hart(7)
CAWOOD Harlan
CECILIA Hardin
CENTER (42214) Metcalfe(70), Green(29)
CENTERTOWN Ohio
CENTRAL CITY Muhlenberg
CERULEAN (42215) Christian(52), Trigg(47)
CHAPLIN Nelson
CHAPPELL Leslie
CHAVIES Perry
CINDA Leslie
CISCO Magoffin
CLARKSON Grayson
CLAY (42404) Webster(90), Union(9)

CLAY CITY Powell
CLAYHOLE Breathitt
CLEARFIELD Rowan
CLEATON Muhlenberg
CLERMONT Bullitt
CLIFTY Todd
CLINTON Hickman
CLOSPLINT Harlan
CLOVERPORT Breckinridge
COALGOOD Harlan
COBHILL Estill
COLDIRON Harlan
COLUMBIA Adair
COLUMBUS Hickman
COMBS Perry
CONCORD Lewis
CONFLUENCE Leslie
CONLEY Magoffin
CONSTANCE Boone
CONSTANTINE Breckinridge
CONWAY Rockcastle
COOPERSVILLE Wayne
CORBIN (40701) Whitley(51), Knox(24), Laurel(24)
CORBIN Whitley
CORINTH (41010) Grant(59), Owen(30), Harrison(7), Scott(1)
CORNETTSVILLE (41731) Perry(68), Letcher(31)
CORYDON Henderson
COTTLE Morgan
COVINGTON Kenton
COXS CREEK (40013) Nelson(78), Spencer(13), Bullitt(7)
CRAB ORCHARD (40419) Lincoln(70), Garrard(17), Rockcastle(8), Pulaski(4)
CRANKS Harlan
CRAYNE Crittenden
CRAYNOR Floyd
CRESTWOOD Oldham
CRITTENDEN (41030) Grant(70), Boone(28), Kenton(1)
CROCKETT Morgan
CROFTON Christian
CROMONA Letcher
CROMWELL (42333) Ohio(87), Butler(12)
CROWN Letcher
CRYSTAL (40420) Lee(83), Estill(16)
CUB RUN (42729) Hart(70), Edmonson(29)
CULVER Elliott
CUMBERLAND (40823) Harlan(97), Letcher(2)
CUNDIFF Adair
CUNNINGHAM (42035) Carlisle(82), Graves(17)
CURDSVILLE Daviess
CUSTER Breckinridge
CUTSHIN Leslie
CYNTHIANA (41031) Harrison(97), Nicholas(1), Bourbon(1)
DABOLT Jackson
DAISY Perry
DANA Floyd
DANVILLE (40422) Boyle(98), Lincoln(1)
DANVILLE Boyle
DAVID Floyd

DAWSON SPRINGS (42408) Hopkins(86), Caldwell(10), Christian(3)
DAYHOIT Harlan
DAYTON Campbell
DE MOSSVILLE Pendleton
DEANE (41812) Letcher(81), Knott(18)
DEBORD Martin
DECOY (41321) Knott(80), Breathitt(20)
DEFOE Henry
DELPHIA Perry
DELTA Wayne
DEMA Knott
DENNISTON Menifee
DENTON (41132) Carter(75), Lawrence(22), Boyd(1)
DENVER Johnson
DEWITT Knox
DEXTER (42036) Calloway(98), Marshall(1)
DICE Perry
DINGUS Morgan
DIXON Webster
DIZNEY Harlan
DORTON Pike
DOVER (41034) Mason(97), Bracken(2)
DRAFFIN Pike
DRAKE Warren
DRAKESBORO Muhlenberg
DREYFUS Madison
DRIFT Floyd
DRY RIDGE Grant
DUBRE (42731) Cumberland(74), Metcalfe(25)
DUNBAR Butler
DUNDEE Ohio
DUNMOR (42339) Muhlenberg(92), Butler(7)
DUNNVILLE (42528) Casey(93), Russell(4), Adair(1)
DWALE Floyd
DWARF Perry
DYCUSBURG Crittenden
EARLINGTON Hopkins
EAST BERNSTADT Laurel
EAST POINT (41216) Floyd(52), Johnson(47)
EASTERN Floyd
EASTVIEW Hardin
EASTWOOD Jefferson
EDDYVILLE Lyon
EDMONTON (42129) Metcalfe(93), Adair(6)
EDNA Magoffin
EGYPT Jackson
EIGHTY EIGHT Barren
EKRON Meade
ELIZABETHTOWN Hardin
ELIZAVILLE Fleming
ELK HORN (42733) Taylor(79), Casey(17), Adair(3)
ELKFORK Morgan
ELKHORN CITY Pike
ELKTON (42220) Todd(97), Muhlenberg(1)
ELLIOTTVILLE Rowan
ELSIE Magoffin
EMERSON Lewis
EMINENCE (40019) Henry(97), Shelby(2)
EMLYN Whitley
EMMA Floyd
EMMALENA Knott
ENDICOTT Floyd
EOLIA Letcher
ERILINE Clay
ERLANGER Kenton
ERMINE Letcher
ESSIE Leslie
ESTILL Floyd
ETOILE Barren
EUBANK (42567) Pulaski(89), Lincoln(10)
EVARTS Harlan
EWING Fleming
EZEL Morgan

FAIRDALE Jefferson
FAIRFIELD Nelson
FAIRPLAY Adair
FAIRVIEW Christian
FALCON Magoffin
FALL ROCK Clay
FALLS OF ROUGH (40119) Grayson(61), Breckinridge(36), Ohio(2)
FALMOUTH Pendleton
FANCY FARM (42039) Graves(45), Carlisle(34), Hickman(20)
FARMERS Rowan
FARMINGTON (42040) Graves(76), Calloway(23)
FAUBUSH (42532) Pulaski(58), Russell(35), Wayne(6)
FEDSCREEK Pike
FERGUSON Pulaski
FILLMORE Lee
FINCHVILLE Shelby
FINLEY (42736) Taylor(56), Marion(43)
FIREBRICK Lewis
FISHERVILLE (40023) Spencer(51), Jefferson(47)
FISTY Knott
FLAT FORK Magoffin
FLAT LICK Knox
FLATGAP (41219) Johnson(98), Lawrence(1)
FLATWOODS Greenup
FLEMINGSBURG Fleming
FLORENCE Boone
FOGERTOWN Clay
FORD Clark
FORDS BRANCH Pike
FORDSVILLE (42343) Ohio(71), Hancock(28)
FOREST HILLS Pike
FORT CAMPBELL Christian
FORT KNOX (40121) Hardin(75), Meade(24)
FORT THOMAS Campbell
FOSTER Bracken
FOUNTAIN RUN (42133) Monroe(51), Barren(31), Allen(17)
FOURMILE (40939) Knox(71), Bell(28)
FRAKES (40940) Whitley(67), Bell(32)
FRANKFORT (40601) Franklin(96), Woodford(1), Shelby(1)
FRANKFORT Franklin
FRANKLIN (42134) Simpson(94), Allen(5)
FRANKLIN Simpson
FRAZER Wayne
FREDONIA (42411) Caldwell(60), Crittenden(34), Lyon(5)
FREDVILLE Magoffin
FREEBURN Pike
FRENCHBURG Menifee
FRITZ Magoffin
FT MITCHELL Kenton
FUGET Johnson
FULTON (42041) Fulton(71), Graves(16), Hickman(11)
GALVESTON Floyd
GAMALIEL Monroe
GAPVILLE Magoffin
GARFIELD (40140) Breckinridge(98), Hardin(1)
GARNER Knott
GARRARD Clay
GARRETT (41630) Floyd(52), Knott(47)
GARRISON (41141) Greenup(90), Lewis(5), Carter(3)
GAYS CREEK Perry
GEORGETOWN Scott
GERMANTOWN (41044) Mason(82), Bracken(17)
GHENT Carroll
GILBERTSVILLE Marshall
GILLMORE Wolfe
GIRDLER Knox
GLASGOW Barren

GLENCOE (41046) Grant(84), Gallatin(15)
GLENDALE Hardin
GLENS FORK (42741) Adair(94), Russell(5)
GLENVIEW Jefferson
GOODY Pike
GOOSE ROCK Clay
GORDON Letcher
GOSHEN Oldham
GRACEY (42232) Christian(71), Trigg(28)
GRADYVILLE Adair
GRAHAM Muhlenberg
GRAHN Carter
GRAND RIVERS Livingston
GRATZ Owen
GRAVEL SWITCH (40328) Boyle(40), Marion(38), Casey(19), Washington(1)
GRAY (40734) Knox(97), Laurel(2)
GRAY HAWK Jackson
GRAYS KNOB Harlan
GRAYSON (41143) Carter(90), Greenup(9)
GREEN HALL Owsley
GREEN ROAD Knox
GREENSBURG (42743) Green(98), Adair(1)
GREENUP Greenup
GREENVILLE Muhlenberg
GRETHEL Floyd
GULSTON Harlan
GUNLOCK Magoffin
GUSTON (40142) Meade(95), Breckinridge(4)
GUTHRIE Todd
GYPSY Magoffin
HADDIX Breathitt
HADLEY Warren
HAGERHILL Johnson
HALDEMAN Rowan
HALFWAY Allen
HALLIE Letcher
HALO Floyd
HAMLIN Calloway
HAMPTON Livingston
HANSON Hopkins
HAPPY Perry
HARDBURLY Perry
HARDIN (42048) Marshall(96), Calloway(3)
HARDINSBURG Breckinridge
HARDY Pike
HARDYVILLE (42746) Hart(78), Metcalfe(13), Green(7), Barren(1)
HARLAN Harlan
HARNED Breckinridge
HAROLD Floyd
HARRODS CREEK Jefferson
HARRODSBURG (40330) Mercer(95), Washington(4)
HARTFORD Ohio
HAWESVILLE (42348) Hancock(97), Daviess(2)
HAZARD (41701) Perry(90), Knott(9)
HAZARD Perry
HAZEL Calloway
HAZEL GREEN (41332) Morgan(62), Wolfe(37)
HEBRON Boone
HEIDELBERG Lee
HEIDRICK Knox
HELLIER Pike
HELTON (40840) Leslie(78), Harlan(21)
HENDERSON Henderson
HENDRICKS Magoffin
HERD Jackson
HERNDON (42236) Christian(87), Trigg(12)
HESTAND (42151) Monroe(91), Metcalfe(8)
HI HAT Floyd
HICKMAN Fulton
HICKORY Graves
HILLSBORO Fleming
HILLVIEW Bullitt
HIMA Clay

HINDMAN Knott
HINKLE Knox
HIPPO Floyd
HISEVILLE Barren
HITCHINS Carter
HODGENVILLE Larue
HOLLAND Allen
HOLLYBUSH Knott
HOLMES MILL Harlan
HONAKER Floyd
HOPE (40334) Bath(92), Montgomery(7)
HOPKINSVILLE Christian
HORSE BRANCH (42349) Ohio(82), Grayson(17)
HORSE CAVE (42749) Hart(90), Metcalfe(7), Barren(2)
HOSKINSTON Leslie
HOWARDSTOWN (40028) Nelson(84), Larue(16)
HUDDY Pike
HUDSON Breckinridge
HUEYSVILLE (41640) Knott(66), Floyd(33)
HUFF Edmonson
HULEN Bell
HUNTER Floyd
HUNTSVILLE Butler
HUSTONVILLE (40437) Lincoln(67), Casey(32)
HYDEN Leslie
INDEPENDENCE Kenton
INEZ Martin
INGLE Pulaski
INGRAM Bell
INSKO Morgan
IRVINE (40336) Estill(98), Lee(1)
IRVINGTON Breckinridge
ISLAND McLean
ISLAND CITY Owsley
ISOM Letcher
ISONVILLE Elliott
IVEL Floyd
IVYTON Magoffin
JACKHORN Letcher
JACKSON (41339) Breathitt(97), Knott(2)
JACOBS Carter
JAMBOREE Pike
JAMESTOWN Russell
JEFF Perry
JEFFERSONVILLE Montgomery
JENKINS (41537) Letcher(93), Pike(6)
JEREMIAH Letcher
JETSON Butler
JOB Martin
JOHNS RUN Carter
JONANCY Pike
JONESVILLE Grant
JUNCTION CITY (40440) Boyle(97), Lincoln(2)
KEATON Johnson
KEAVY Laurel
KEENE Jessamine
KEITH Harlan
KENTON Kenton
KENVIR Harlan
KERBY KNOB Jackson
KETTLE Cumberland
KETTLE ISLAND Bell
KEVIL (42053) McCracken(57), Ballard(42)
KIMPER Pike
KINGS MOUNTAIN (40442) Lincoln(50), Casey(49)
KIRKSEY (42054) Calloway(79), Marshall(14), Graves(5)
KITE Knott
KNIFLEY Adair
KNOB LICK (42154) Metcalfe(87), Barren(12)
KONA Letcher
KRYPTON (41754) Perry(97), Leslie(2)
KUTTAWA Lyon
LA CENTER Ballard
LA FAYETTE Christian

LA GRANGE (40031) Oldham(94),
Henry(5)
LA GRANGE Oldham
LACKEY (41643) Knott(88), Floyd(11)
LAMB (42155) Barren(60), Monroe(39)
LAMBRIC Breathitt
LAMERO Rockcastle
LANCASTER (40444) Garrard(98),
Lincoln(1)
LANCASTER Garrard
LANGLEY Floyd
LATONIA Kenton
LAWRENCEBURG Anderson
LEANDER Johnson
LEATHERWOOD Perry
LEBANON Marion
LEBANON JUNCTION (40150) Bullitt(97),
Hardin(2)
LEBURN Knott
LEDBETTER Livingston
LEE CITY Wolfe
LEECO Lee
LEITCHFIELD (42754) Grayson(91),
Breckinridge(8)
LEITCHFIELD Grayson
LEJUNIOR Harlan
LENOX Morgan
LEROSE Owsley
LETCHER Letcher
LEWISBURG (42256) Logan(74),
Butler(13), Todd(11)
LEWISPORT (42351) Hancock(90),
Daviess(9)
LEXINGTON (40509) Fayette(98), Clark(1)
LEXINGTON (40511) Fayette(97), Scott(1)
LEXINGTON (40515) Fayette(95),
Jessamine(3)
LEXINGTON (40516) Fayette(89),
Bourbon(10)
LEXINGTON Fayette
LIBERTY Casey
LICK CREEK Pike
LILY Laurel
LINDSEYVILLE Edmonson
LINEFORK Letcher
LITTCARR Knott
LITTLE Breathitt
LIVERMORE (42352) McLean(93), Ohio(6)
LIVINGSTON Rockcastle
LLOYD Greenup
LOCKPORT Henry
LOLA Livingston
LONDON Laurel
LONE Lee
LOOKOUT Pike
LORETTO (40037) Marion(75),
Washington(13), Nelson(10)
LOST CREEK (41348) Breathitt(91),
Perry(8)
LOUISA Lawrence
LOUISVILLE (40229) Jefferson(63),
Bullitt(36)
LOUISVILLE (40241) Jefferson(98),
Oldham(1)
LOUISVILLE (40245) Jefferson(90),
Shelby(8)
LOUISVILLE (40299) Jefferson(98),
Bullitt(1)
LOUISVILLE Jefferson
LOVELACEVILLE Ballard
LOVELY Martin
LOWES Graves
LOWMANSVILLE (41232) Lawrence(72),
Johnson(27)
LOYALL Harlan
LUCAS Barren
LYNCH Harlan
LYNNVILLE Graves
MACEDONIA Breathitt
MACEO Daviess
MACKVILLE Washington
MADISONVILLE Hopkins

MAGNOLIA (42757) Larue(48), Hart(45),
Green(6)
MAJESTIC Pike
MALLIE Knott
MALONE Morgan
MAMMOTH CAVE Edmonson
MANCHESTER Clay
MANITOU Hopkins
MANNSVILLE Taylor
MAPLE MOUNT Daviess
MARIBA Menifee
MARION (42064) Crittenden(98),
Caldwell(1)
MARROWBONE Cumberland
MARSHALLVILLE Magoffin
MARSHES SIDING McCreary
MARTHA (41159) Lawrence(97),
Johnson(2)
MARTIN Floyd
MARY ALICE Harlan
MARYDELL Laurel
MASON Grant
MASONIC HOME Jefferson
MAYFIELD Graves
MAYKING Letcher
MAYSLICK (41055) Mason(86),
Fleming(13)
MAYSVILLE Mason
MAZIE Lawrence
MC ANDREWS Pike
MC CARR Pike
MC COMBS (41545) Pike(90), Floyd(10)
MC DANIELS Breckinridge
MC DOWELL Floyd
MC HENRY Ohio
MC KEE (40447) Jackson(96),
Rockcastle(1), Estill(1)
MC KINNEY Lincoln
MC QUADY Breckinridge
MC ROBERTS Letcher
MC VEIGH Pike
MEALLY Johnson
MEANS (40346) Menifee(79), Bath(12),
Montgomery(8)
MELBER (42069) Graves(80),
McCracken(17), Carlisle(2)
MELBOURNE Campbell
MELVIN Floyd
MIDDLEBURG Casey
MIDDLESBORO Bell
MIDWAY (40347) Woodford(90),
Franklin(5), Scott(3)
MIGRATE Fayette
MILBURN Carlisle
MILFORD Bracken
MILL SPRINGS Wayne
MILLERSBURG Bourbon
MILLS Knox
MILLSTONE Letcher
MILLTOWN Adair
MILLWOOD Grayson
MILTON (40045) Trimble(85), Carroll(14)
MIMA Morgan
MINERVA Mason
MINNIE Floyd
MIRACLE Bell
MISTLETOE Owsley
MITCHELLSBURG Boyle
MIZE Morgan
MONTICELLO Wayne
MONTPELIER Adair
MOON Morgan
MOOREFIELD Nicholas
MOORMAN Muhlenberg
MOREHEAD (40351) Rowan(98), Elliott(1)
MORGANFIELD (42437) Union(97),
Webster(2)
MORGANTOWN Butler
MORNING VIEW Kenton
MORRILL Jackson
MORTONS GAP Hopkins

MOUNT EDEN (40046) Spencer(78),
Anderson(14), Shelby(7)
MOUNT HERMON Monroe
MOUNT OLIVET Robertson
MOUNT SHERMAN (42764) Green(57),
Larue(39), Hart(3)
MOUNT STERLING (40353)
Montgomery(97), Clark(1)
MOUNT VERNON Rockcastle
MOUNT WASHINGTON Bullitt
MOUSIE Knott
MOUTHCARD Pike
MOZELLE Leslie
MULDRAUGH Meade
MUNFORDVILLE Hart
MURRAY Calloway
MUSES MILLS Fleming
MYRA Pike
NANCY (42544) Pulaski(75), Wayne(17),
Russell(7)
NARROWS Ohio
NAZARETH Nelson
NEAFUS Grayson
NEBO (42441) Hopkins(96), Webster(3)
NELSE Pike
NEON Letcher
NERINX Marion
NEVISDALE Whitley
NEW CONCORD Calloway
NEW HAVEN (40051) Nelson(80),
Larue(19)
NEW HOPE (40052) Nelson(77),
Marion(17), Larue(5)
NEW LIBERTY Owen
NEWPORT Campbell
NICHOLASVILLE Jessamine
NOCTOR Breathitt
NORTH MIDDLETOWN Bourbon
NORTONVILLE (42442) Hopkins(96),
Christian(3)
OAK GROVE Christian
OAKLAND Warren
OAKVILLE Logan
OFFUTT Johnson
OIL SPRINGS Johnson
OLATON (42361) Ohio(89), Grayson(10)
OLD LANDING Lee
OLDTOWN Greenup
OLIVE HILL (41164) Carter(97), Elliott(1)
OLLIE Edmonson
OLMSTEAD (42265) Logan(88), Todd(11)
OLYMPIA Bath
ONEIDA Clay
OPHIR Morgan
ORLANDO Rockcastle
OVEN FORK Letcher
OWENSBORO Daviess
OWENTON Owen
OWINGSVILLE (40360) Bath(93),
Montgomery(6)
PADUCAH McCracken
PAINT LICK (40461) Garrard(61),
Madison(38)
PAINTSVILLE Johnson
PARIS Bourbon
PARK CITY (42160) Barren(74),
Edmonson(25)
PARKERS LAKE McCreary
PARKSVILLE (40464) Boyle(86),
Casey(13)
PARROT Jackson
PARTRIDGE Letcher
PATHFORK Harlan
PAW PAW Pike
PAYNEVILLE Meade
PELLVILLE Hancock
PEMBROKE (42266) Christian(92),
Todd(7)
PENDLETON (40055) Trimble(42),
Henry(37), Oldham(20)
PENROD Muhlenberg
PEOPLES Jackson

PERRY PARK Owen
PERRYVILLE (40468) Boyle(88),
Washington(6), Mercer(4)
PETERSBURG Boone
PEWEE VALLEY Oldham
PEYTONSBURG Cumberland
PHELPS Pike
PHILPOT (42366) Daviess(95),
Hancock(3), Ohio(1)
PHYLLIS Pike
PIKEVILLE Pike
PILGRIM Martin
PINE KNOT McCreary
PINE RIDGE (41360) Wolfe(92), Powell(7)
PINE TOP Knott
PINEVILLE Bell
PINSONFORK Pike
PIPPA PASSES Knott
PITTSBURG Laurel
PLANK Clay
PLEASUREVILLE (40057) Henry(72),
Shelby(27)
PLUMMERS LANDING Fleming
POMEROYTON Menifee
POOLE Webster
PORT ROYAL Henry
POWDERLY Muhlenberg
PREMIUM Letcher
PRESTON Bath
PRESTONSBURG Floyd
PRIMROSE Lee
PRINCETON (42445) Caldwell(93),
Lyon(2), Hopkins(2), Trigg(1)
PRINTER Floyd
PROSPECT (40059) Jefferson(56),
Oldham(43)
PROVIDENCE (42450) Webster(88),
Hopkins(7), Crittenden(4)
PROVO Butler
PRYSE Estill
PUTNEY Harlan
QUALITY (42268) Butler(72), Logan(27)
QUICKSAND Breathitt
QUINCY Lewis
RACCOON Pike
RADCLIFF Hardin
RANSOM Pike
RAVEN Knott
RAVENNA Estill
RAYWICK Marion
REDFOX Knott
REED Henderson
REGINA Pike
RENFRO VALLEY Rockcastle
REVELO McCreary
REYNOLDS STATION (42368)
Hancock(74), Ohio(25)
RHODELIA (40161) Meade(92),
Breckinridge(8)
RICETOWN Owsley
RICHARDSON Lawrence
RICHARDSVILLE Warren
RICHMOND Madison
RINEYVILLE Hardin
RIVER (41254) Johnson(88), Lawrence(11)
ROARK (40979) Leslie(82), Clay(17)
ROBARDS (42452) Henderson(88),
Webster(11)
ROBINSON CREEK Pike
ROCHESTER Butler
ROCKFIELD (42274) Warren(93), Logan(6)
ROCKHOLDS (40759) Whitley(85),
Knox(14)
ROCKHOUSE Pike
ROCKPORT Ohio
ROCKY HILL Edmonson
ROCKYBRANCH Wayne
ROGERS Wolfe
ROSINE Ohio
ROUNDHILL (42275) Butler(66),
Edmonson(33)
ROUSSEAU Breathitt

ROWDY Perry
ROWLETTS Hart
ROXANA Letcher
ROYALTON Magoffin
RUMSEY McLean
RUSH (41168) Boyd(64), Carter(34)
RUSSELL Greenup
RUSSELL SPRINGS (42642) Russell(93), Adair(5), Casey(1)
RUSSELLVILLE Logan
SACRAMENTO (42372) McLean(56), Muhlenberg(43)
SADIEVILLE (40370) Harrison(58), Scott(41)
SAINT CATHARINE Washington
SAINT CHARLES Hopkins
SAINT FRANCIS Marion
SAINT HELENS Lee
SAINT JOSEPH Daviess
SAINT MARY Marion
SAINT PAUL Lewis
SALDEE Breathitt
SALEM (42078) Livingston(64), Crittenden(35)
SALT LICK (40371) Bath(90), Menifee(9)
SALVISA (40372) Mercer(94), Anderson(5)
SALYERSVILLE Magoffin
SANDERS Carroll
SANDGAP Jackson
SANDY HOOK Elliott
SASSAFRAS Knott
SAUL Perry
SAWYER McCreary
SCALF Knox
SCIENCE HILL Pulaski
SCOTTSVILLE Allen
SCUDDY Perry
SE REE Breckinridge
SEBREE Webster
SECO Letcher
SEDALIA Graves
SEITZ Magoffin
SEXTONS CREEK (40983) Clay(91), Owsley(8)
SHARON GROVE Todd
SHARPSBURG (40374) Bath(86), Nicholas(11), Bourbon(2)
SHELBIANA Pike
SHELBY GAP Pike
SHEPHERDSVILLE Bullitt
SHOPVILLE Pulaski
SIDNEY Pike
SILER (40763) Whitley(84), Bell(15)
SILVER GROVE Campbell
SILVERHILL Morgan
SIMPSONVILLE Shelby
SITKA Johnson
SIZEROCK Leslie
SLADE Powell
SLAUGHTERS (42456) Webster(68), Hopkins(31)
SLEMP Perry
SLOANS VALLEY Pulaski
SMILAX Leslie
SMITH Harlan
SMITH MILLS Henderson
SMITHFIELD (40068) Henry(79), Shelby(10), Oldham(9)

SMITHLAND Livingston
SMITHS GROVE (42171) Warren(42), Edmonson(32), Barren(24)
SOLDIER Carter
SOMERSET Pulaski
SONORA (42776) Hardin(72), Larue(27)
SOUTH CARROLLTON Muhlenberg
SOUTH PORTSMOUTH (41174) Greenup(97), Lewis(2)
SOUTH SHORE Greenup
SOUTH UNION Logan
SOUTH WILLIAMSON Pike
SPARTA (41086) Owen(86), Gallatin(13)
SPEIGHT Pike
SPOTTSVILLE Henderson
SPRING LICK Grayson
SPRINGFIELD (40069) Washington(98), Marion(1)
STAB Pulaski
STAFFORDSVILLE Johnson
STAMBAUGH Johnson
STAMPING GROUND (40379) Scott(77), Owen(19), Franklin(3)
STANFORD (40484) Lincoln(94), Garrard(4)
STANLEY Daviess
STANTON (40380) Powell(95), Estill(4)
STANVILLE (41659) Floyd(93), Pike(6)
STEARNS McCreary
STEELE Pike
STEFF Grayson
STEPHENS Elliott
STEPHENSBURG Hardin
STEPHENSPORT Breckinridge
STEUBENVILLE Wayne
STINNETT Leslie
STONE Pike
STONEY FORK (40988) Harlan(53), Bell(46)
STOPOVER Pike
STRUNK McCreary
STURGIS (42459) Union(93), Crittenden(6)
SULLIVAN Union
SULPHUR Henry
SUMMER SHADE (42166) Metcalfe(67), Monroe(18), Barren(14)
SUMMERSVILLE (42782) Green(93), Hart(6)
SUMMIT Hardin
SUNFISH Edmonson
SWAMP BRANCH Johnson
SWEEDEN Edmonson
SYMSONIA (42082) Graves(72), Marshall(23), McCracken(4)
TALBERT Breathitt
TALCUM (41765) Knott(85), Perry(14)
TALLEGA Lee
TATEVILLE Pulaski
TAYLORSVILLE (40071) Spencer(90), Bullitt(8)
TEABERRY Floyd
THELMA Johnson
THORNTON Letcher
THOUSANDSTICKS Leslie
THREEFORKS Martin
TILINE Livingston
TOLER Pike
TOLLESBORO Lewis

TOLU Crittenden
TOMAHAWK Martin
TOMPKINSVILLE Monroe
TOPMOST Knott
TOTZ Harlan
TRAM Floyd
TRENTON (42286) Todd(96), Christian(3)
TROSPER Knox
TURKEY CREEK (41570) Pike(96), Martin(3)
TURNERS STATION (40075) Henry(77), Carroll(22)
TUTOR KEY Johnson
TYNER Jackson
TYPO Perry
ULYSSES Lawrence
UNION Boone
UNION STAR (40171) Meade(86), Breckinridge(13)
UNIONTOWN (42461) Union(95), Henderson(4)
UPTON (42784) Hardin(48), Larue(29), Hart(22)
UTICA (42376) Daviess(72), Ohio(20), McLean(7)
VAN LEAR Johnson
VANCEBURG (41179) Lewis(96), Carter(3)
VANCLEVE Breathitt
VARNEY Pike
VENTRESS Hardin
VERONA Boone
VERSAILLES (40383) Woodford(96), Jessamine(3)
VERSAILLES Woodford
VERTREES Hardin
VEST Knott
VICCO (41773) Perry(63), Knott(36)
VINCENT Owsley
VINE GROVE (40175) Hardin(53), Meade(45), Breckinridge(1)
VIPER Perry
VIRGIE Pike
VOLGA Johnson
WACO (40385) Madison(98), Estill(1)
WADDY (40076) Shelby(80), Franklin(12), Anderson(6)
WALKER Knox
WALLINGFORD (41093) Fleming(97), Lewis(2)
WALLINS CREEK Harlan
WALNUT GROVE Pulaski
WALTON Boone
WANETA Jackson
WARBRANCH (40874) Leslie(94), Clay(5)
WARFIELD Martin
WARSAW Gallatin
WASHINGTON Mason
WATER VALLEY (42085) Graves(68), Hickman(31)
WATERVIEW Cumberland
WAVERLY (42462) Union(90), Henderson(9)
WAX Grayson
WAYLAND Floyd
WAYNESBURG (40489) Lincoln(89), Casey(10)
WEBBVILLE (41180) Lawrence(90), Carter(9)

WEBSTER (40176) Breckinridge(95), Meade(4)
WEEKSBURY Floyd
WELCHS CREEK Butler
WELLINGTON (40387) Menifee(91), Morgan(7), Wolfe(1)
WENDOVER Leslie
WEST LIBERTY (41472) Morgan(98), Elliott(1)
WEST LOUISVILLE Daviess
WEST PADUCAH McCracken
WEST POINT (40177) Hardin(80), Bullitt(13), Jefferson(6)
WEST PRESTONSBURG Floyd
WEST SOMERSET Pulaski
WEST VAN LEAR Johnson
WESTPORT Oldham
WESTVIEW Breckinridge
WHEATCROFT Webster
WHEATLEY Owen
WHEELWRIGHT Floyd
WHICK Breathitt
WHITE MILLS Hardin
WHITE OAK Morgan
WHITE PLAINS (42464) Hopkins(72), Muhlenberg(15), Christian(11)
WHITEHOUSE Johnson
WHITESBURG Letcher
WHITESVILLE (42378) Daviess(55), Ohio(44)
WHITLEY CITY McCreary
WICKLIFFE Ballard
WIDECREEK Breathitt
WILDIE Rockcastle
WILLARD Carter
WILLIAMSBURG (40769) Whitley(98), McCreary(1)
WILLIAMSPORT Johnson
WILLIAMSTOWN Grant
WILLISBURG (40078) Washington(97), Mercer(1), Anderson(1)
WILLOW SHADE Metcalfe
WILMORE (40390) Jessamine(98), Woodford(1)
WINCHESTER Clark
WIND CAVE Jackson
WINDSOR Casey
WINDY Wayne
WINGO (42088) Graves(84), Hickman(15)
WINSTON Estill
WITTENSVILLE Johnson
WOODBINE (40771) Knox(86), Whitley(13)
WOODBURN (42170) Warren(62), Simpson(37)
WOODBURY Butler
WOODMAN Pike
WOOLLUM (40999) Knox(98), Clay(1)
WOOTON Leslie
WORTHINGTON Greenup
WORTHVILLE (41098) Owen(96), Carroll(3)
WRIGLEY Morgan
YEADDISS Leslie
YERKES Perry
YOSEMITE Casey
ZACHARIAH Lee
ZOE Lee

Kentucky ZIP/City Cross Reference

40003-40003	BAGDAD	40014-40014	CRESTWOOD	40028-40028	HOWARDSTOWN
40004-40004	BARDSTOWN	40017-40017	DEFOE	40031-40032	LA GRANGE
40006-40006	BEDFORD	40018-40018	EASTWOOD	40033-40033	LEBANON
40007-40007	BETHLEHEM	40019-40019	EMINENCE	40036-40036	LOCKPORT
40008-40008	BLOOMFIELD	40020-40020	FAIRFIELD	40037-40037	LORETTO
40009-40009	BRADFORDSVILLE	40022-40022	FINCHVILLE	40040-40040	MACKVILLE
40010-40010	BUCKNER	40023-40023	FISHERVILLE	40041-40041	MASONIC HOME
40011-40011	CAMPBELLSBURG	40025-40025	GLENVIEW	40045-40045	MILTON
40012-40012	CHAPLIN	40026-40026	GOSHEN	40046-40046	MOUNT EDEN
40013-40013	COXS CREEK	40027-40027	HARRODS CREEK	40047-40047	MOUNT WASHINGTON

40048-40048	NAZARETH
40049-40049	NERINX
40050-40050	NEW CASTLE
40051-40051	NEW HAVEN
40052-40052	NEW HOPE
40055-40055	PENDLETON
40056-40056	PEWEE VALLEY
40057-40057	PLEASUREVILLE
40058-40058	PORT ROYAL
40059-40059	PROSPECT

40060-40060 RAYWICK	40355-40355 NEW LIBERTY	40755-40755 PITTSBURG	40983-40983 SEXTONS CREEK
40061-40061 SAINT CATHARINE	40356-40356 NICHOLASVILLE	40759-40759 ROCKHOLDS	40988-40988 STONEY FORK
40062-40062 SAINT FRANCIS	40357-40357 NORTH MIDDLETOWN	40763-40763 SILER	40995-40995 TROSPER
40063-40063 SAINT MARY	40358-40358 OLYMPIA	40769-40769 WILLIAMSBURG	40997-40997 WALKER
40065-40066 SHELBYVILLE	40359-40359 OWENTON	40771-40771 WOODBINE	40999-40999 WOOLLUM
40067-40067 SIMPSONVILLE	40360-40360 OWINGSVILLE	40801-40801 AGES BROOKSIDE	41001-41001 ALEXANDRIA
40068-40068 SMITHFIELD	40361-40362 PARIS	40803-40803 ASHER	41002-41002 AUGUSTA
40069-40069 SPRINGFIELD	40363-40363 PERRY PARK	40806-40806 BAXTER	41003-41003 BERRY
40070-40070 SULPHUR	40365-40365 POMEROYTON	40807-40807 BENHAM	41004-41004 BROOKSVILLE
40071-40071 TAYLORSVILLE	40366-40366 PRESTON	40808-40808 BIG LAUREL	41005-41005 BURLINGTON
40075-40075 TURNERS STATION	40370-40370 SADIEVILLE	40810-40810 BLEDSOE	41006-41006 BUTLER
40076-40076 WADDY	40371-40371 SALT LICK	40813-40813 CALVIN	41007-41007 CALIFORNIA
40077-40077 WESTPORT	40372-40372 SALVISA	40815-40815 CAWOOD	41008-41008 CARROLLTON
40078-40078 WILLISBURG	40374-40374 SHARPSBURG	40816-40816 CHAPPELL	41009-41009 CONSTANCE
40103-40103 AXTEL	40376-40376 SLADE	40818-40818 COALGOOD	41010-41010 CORINTH
40104-40104 BATTLETOWN	40379-40379 STAMPING GROUND	40819-40819 COLDIRON	41011-41014 COVINGTON
40106-40106 BIG SPRING	40380-40380 STANTON	40820-40820 CRANKS	41015-41015 LATONIA
40107-40107 BOSTON	40383-40384 VERSAILLES	40823-40823 CUMBERLAND	41016-41016 COVINGTON
40108-40108 BRANDENBURG	40385-40385 WACO	40824-40824 DAYHOIT	41017-41017 FT MITCHELL
40109-40109 BROOKS	40386-40386 VERSAILLES	40825-40825 DIZNEY	41018-41018 ERLANGER
40110-40110 CLERMONT	40387-40387 WELLINGTON	40826-40826 EOLIA	41019-41019 COVINGTON
40111-40111 CLOVERPORT	40389-40389 WHEATLEY	40827-40827 ESSIE	41022-41022 FLORENCE
40114-40114 CONSTANTINE	40390-40390 WILMORE	40828-40828 EVARTS	41030-41030 CRITTENDEN
40115-40115 CUSTER	40391-40392 WINCHESTER	40829-40829 GRAYS KNOB	41031-41031 CYNTHIANA
40117-40117 EKRON	40402-40402 ANNVILLE	40830-40830 GULSTON	41033-41033 DE MOSSVILLE
40118-40118 FAIRDALE	40403-40404 BEREA	40831-40831 HARLAN	41034-41034 DOVER
40119-40119 FALLS OF ROUGH	40405-40405 BIGHILL	40840-40840 HELTON	41035-41035 DRY RIDGE
40121-40121 FORT KNOX	40407-40407 BOND	40843-40843 HOLMES MILL	41037-41037 ELIZAVILLE
40129-40129 HILLVIEW	40409-40409 BRODHEAD	40844-40844 HOSKINSTON	41039-41039 EWING
40140-40140 GARFIELD	40410-40410 BRYANTSVILLE	40845-40845 HULEN	41040-41040 FALMOUTH
40142-40142 GUSTON	40415-40415 COBHILL	40846-40846 KEITH	41041-41041 FLEMINGSBURG
40143-40143 HARDINSBURG	40417-40417 CONWAY	40847-40847 KENVIR	41042-41042 FLORENCE
40144-40144 HARNED	40419-40419 CRAB ORCHARD	40849-40849 LEJUNIOR	41043-41043 FOSTER
40145-40145 HUDSON	40420-40420 CRYSTAL	40854-40854 LOYALL	41044-41044 GERMANTOWN
40146-40146 IRVINGTON	40421-40421 DABOLT	40855-40855 LYNCH	41045-41045 GHENT
40150-40150 LEBANON JUNCTION	40422-40423 DANVILLE	40856-40856 MIRACLE	41046-41046 GLENCOE
40152-40152 MC DANIELS	40426-40426 DREYFUS	40858-40858 MOZELLE	41048-41048 HEBRON
40153-40153 MC QUADY	40430-40430 EGYPT	40861-40861 OVEN FORK	41049-41049 HILLSBORO
40155-40155 MULDRAUGH	40434-40434 GRAY HAWK	40862-40862 PARTRIDGE	41051-41051 INDEPENDENCE
40157-40157 PAYNEVILLE	40435-40435 HERD	40863-40863 PATHFORK	41052-41052 JONESVILLE
40159-40160 RADCLIFF	40437-40437 HUSTONVILLE	40865-40865 PUTNEY	41053-41053 KENTON
40161-40161 RHODELIA	40440-40440 JUNCTION CITY	40867-40867 SMITH	41054-41054 MASON
40162-40162 RINEYVILLE	40441-40441 KERBY KNOB	40868-40868 STINNETT	41055-41055 MAYSLICK
40164-40164 SE REE	40442-40442 KINGS MOUNTAIN	40870-40870 TOTZ	41056-41056 MAYSVILLE
40165-40165 SHEPHERDSVILLE	40444-40444 LANCASTER	40873-40873 WALLINS CREEK	41059-41059 MELBOURNE
40170-40170 STEPHENSPORT	40445-40445 LIVINGSTON	40874-40874 WARBRANCH	41061-41061 MILFORD
40171-40171 UNION STAR	40446-40446 LANCASTER	40902-40902 ARJAY	41062-41062 MINERVA
40175-40175 VINE GROVE	40447-40447 MC KEE	40903-40903 ARTEMUS	41063-41063 MORNING VIEW
40176-40176 WEBSTER	40448-40448 MC KINNEY	40906-40911 BARBOURVILLE	41064-41064 MOUNT OLIVET
40177-40177 WEST POINT	40452-40452 MITCHELLSBURG	40913-40913 BEVERLY	41065-41065 MUSES MILLS
40178-40178 WESTVIEW	40455-40455 MORRILL	40914-40914 BIG CREEK	41071-41072 NEWPORT
40200-40299 LOUISVILLE	40456-40456 MOUNT VERNON	40915-40915 BIMBLE	41073-41073 BELLEVUE
40306-40306 BETHEL	40460-40460 ORLANDO	40917-40917 BLUEHOLE	41074-41074 DAYTON
40309-40309 BOWEN	40461-40461 PAINT LICK	40921-40921 BRYANTS STORE	41075-41075 FORT THOMAS
40310-40310 BURGIN	40464-40464 PARKSVILLE	40923-40923 CANNON	41076-41076 NEWPORT
40311-40311 CARLISLE	40465-40465 PARROT	40927-40927 CLOSPLINT	41080-41080 PETERSBURG
40312-40312 CLAY CITY	40467-40467 PEOPLES	40930-40930 DEWITT	41081-41081 PLUMMERS LANDING
40313-40313 CLEARFIELD	40468-40468 PERRYVILLE	40931-40931 ERILINE	41083-41083 SANDERS
40316-40316 DENNISTON	40471-40471 PRYSE	40932-40932 FALL ROCK	41085-41085 SILVER GROVE
40317-40317 ELLIOTTVILLE	40472-40472 RAVENNA	40935-40935 FLAT LICK	41086-41086 SPARTA
40319-40319 FARMERS	40473-40473 RENFRO VALLEY	40936-40936 FOGERTOWN	41091-41091 UNION
40320-40320 FORD	40475-40476 RICHMOND	40939-40939 FOURMILE	41092-41092 VERONA
40322-40322 FRENCHBURG	40481-40481 SANDGAP	40940-40940 FRAKES	41093-41093 WALLINGFORD
40324-40324 GEORGETOWN	40484-40484 STANFORD	40941-40941 GARRARD	41094-41094 WALTON
40327-40327 GRATZ	40486-40486 TYNER	40943-40943 GIRDLER	41095-41095 WARSAW
40328-40328 GRAVEL SWITCH	40488-40488 WANETA	40944-40944 GOOSE ROCK	41096-41096 WASHINGTON
40329-40329 HALDEMAN	40489-40489 WAYNESBURG	40946-40946 GREEN ROAD	41097-41097 WILLIAMSTOWN
40330-40330 HARRODSBURG	40492-40492 WILDIE	40949-40949 HEIDRICK	41098-41098 WORTHVILLE
40334-40334 HOPE	40494-40494 WIND CAVE	40951-40951 HIMA	41099-41099 NEWPORT
40336-40336 IRVINE	40495-40495 WINSTON	40953-40953 HINKLE	41101-41114 ASHLAND
40337-40337 JEFFERSONVILLE	40500-40598 LEXINGTON	40955-40955 INGRAM	41121-41121 ARGILLITE
40339-40339 KEENE	40601-40622 FRANKFORT	40958-40958 KETTLE ISLAND	41124-41124 BLAINE
40340-40340 NICHOLASVILLE	40701-40702 CORBIN	40962-40962 MANCHESTER	41125-41125 BRUIN
40341-40341 LAMERO	40724-40724 BUSH	40964-40964 MARY ALICE	41127-41127 CAMP DIX
40342-40342 LAWRENCEBURG	40729-40729 EAST BERNSTADT	40965-40965 MIDDLESBORO	41128-41128 CARTER
40345-40345 MARIBA	40730-40730 EMLYN	40970-40970 MILLS	41129-41129 CATLETTSBURG
40346-40346 MEANS	40734-40734 GRAY	40972-40972 ONEIDA	41131-41131 CONCORD
40347-40347 MIDWAY	40737-40737 KEAVY	40977-40977 PINEVILLE	41132-41132 DENTON
40348-40348 MILLERSBURG	40740-40740 LILY	40978-40978 PLANK	41135-41135 EMERSON
40350-40350 MOOREFIELD	40741-40748 LONDON	40979-40979 ROARK	41137-41137 FIREBRICK
40351-40351 MOREHEAD	40751-40751 MARYDELL	40981-40981 SAUL	41139-41139 FLATWOODS
40353-40353 MOUNT STERLING	40754-40754 NEVISDALE	40982-40982 SCALF	41141-41141 GARRISON

ZIP	Name	ZIP	Name	ZIP	Name	ZIP	Name
41142-41142	GRAHN	41333-41333	HEIDELBERG	41529-41529	GOODY	41669-41669	WHEELWRIGHT
41143-41143	GRAYSON	41338-41338	ISLAND CITY	41531-41531	HARDY	41701-41702	HAZARD
41144-41144	GREENUP	41339-41339	JACKSON	41534-41534	HELLIER	41710-41710	ALLOCK
41146-41146	HITCHINS	41340-41340	LAMBRIC	41535-41535	HUDDY	41712-41712	ARY
41149-41149	ISONVILLE	41342-41342	LEE CITY	41536-41536	JAMBOREE	41713-41713	AVAWAM
41150-41150	JACOBS	41343-41343	LEECO	41537-41537	JENKINS	41714-41714	BEAR BRANCH
41152-41152	JOHNS RUN	41344-41344	LEROSE	41538-41538	JONANCY	41719-41719	BONNYMAN
41156-41156	LLOYD	41346-41346	LITTLE	41539-41539	KIMPER	41720-41720	BROWNS FORK
41159-41159	MARTHA	41347-41347	LONE	41540-41540	LICK CREEK	41721-41721	BUCKHORN
41160-41160	MAZIE	41348-41348	LOST CREEK	41542-41542	LOOKOUT	41722-41722	BULAN
41163-41163	OLDTOWN	41351-41351	MISTLETOE	41543-41543	MC ANDREWS	41723-41723	BUSY
41164-41164	OLIVE HILL	41352-41352	MIZE	41544-41544	MC CARR	41725-41725	CARRIE
41166-41166	QUINCY	41357-41357	NOCTOR	41545-41545	MC COMBS	41727-41727	CHAVIES
41168-41168	RUSH	41358-41358	OLD LANDING	41546-41546	MC VEIGH	41728-41728	CINDA
41169-41169	RUSSELL	41360-41360	PINE RIDGE	41547-41547	MAJESTIC	41729-41729	COMBS
41170-41170	SAINT PAUL	41362-41362	PRIMROSE	41548-41548	MOUTHCARD	41730-41730	CONFLUENCE
41171-41171	SANDY HOOK	41363-41363	QUICKSAND	41549-41549	MYRA	41731-41731	CORNETTSVILLE
41173-41173	SOLDIER	41364-41364	RICETOWN	41550-41550	NELSE	41732-41732	CUTSHIN
41174-41174	SOUTH PORTSMOUTH	41365-41365	ROGERS	41551-41551	PAW PAW	41733-41733	DAISY
41175-41175	SOUTH SHORE	41366-41366	ROUSSEAU	41553-41553	PHELPS	41735-41735	DELPHIA
41177-41177	STEPHENS	41367-41367	ROWDY	41554-41554	PHYLLIS	41736-41736	DICE
41179-41179	VANCEBURG	41368-41368	SAINT HELENS	41555-41555	PINSONFORK	41739-41739	DWARF
41180-41180	WEBBVILLE	41369-41369	SALDEE	41557-41557	RACCOON	41740-41740	EMMALENA
41181-41181	WILLARD	41370-41370	MACEDONIA	41558-41558	RANSOM	41743-41743	FISTY
41183-41183	WORTHINGTON	41377-41377	TALBERT	41559-41559	REGINA	41745-41745	GAYS CREEK
41189-41189	TOLLESBORO	41378-41378	TALLEGA	41560-41560	ROBINSON CREEK	41746-41746	HAPPY
41201-41201	ADAMS	41385-41385	VANCLEVE	41561-41561	ROCKHOUSE	41747-41747	HARDBURLY
41203-41203	BEAUTY	41386-41386	VINCENT	41562-41562	SHELBIANA	41749-41749	HYDEN
41204-41204	BOONS CAMP	41390-41390	WHICK	41563-41563	SHELBY GAP	41751-41751	JEFF
41211-41211	CULVER	41391-41391	WIDECREEK	41564-41564	SIDNEY	41754-41754	KRYPTON
41214-41214	DEBORD	41396-41396	ZACHARIAH	41565-41565	SPEIGHT	41756-41756	LEATHERWOOD
41215-41215	DENVER	41397-41397	ZOE	41566-41566	STEELE	41759-41759	SASSAFRAS
41216-41216	EAST POINT	41406-41406	BUSKIRK	41567-41567	STONE	41760-41760	SCUDDY
41219-41219	FLATGAP	41407-41407	CANEY	41568-41568	STOPOVER	41762-41762	SIZEROCK
41220-41220	FUGET	41408-41408	CANNEL CITY	41569-41569	TOLER	41763-41763	SLEMP
41222-41222	HAGERHILL	41409-41409	CARVER	41570-41570	TURKEY CREEK	41764-41764	SMILAX
41224-41224	INEZ	41410-41410	CISCO	41571-41571	VARNEY	41765-41765	TALCUM
41225-41225	JOB	41411-41411	CONLEY	41572-41572	VIRGIE	41766-41766	THOUSANDSTICKS
41226-41226	KEATON	41412-41412	COTTLE	41574-41574	WOODMAN	41771-41771	TYPO
41228-41228	LEANDER	41413-41413	CROCKETT	41601-41601	ALLEN	41772-41772	VEST
41230-41230	LOUISA	41417-41417	DINGUS	41602-41602	AUXIER	41773-41773	VICCO
41231-41231	LOVELY	41419-41419	EDNA	41603-41603	BANNER	41774-41774	VIPER
41232-41232	LOWMANSVILLE	41421-41421	ELKFORK	41604-41604	BEAVER	41775-41775	WENDOVER
41234-41234	MEALLY	41422-41422	ELSIE	41605-41605	BETSY LAYNE	41776-41776	WOOTON
41237-41237	OFFUTT	41425-41425	EZEL	41606-41606	BEVINSVILLE	41777-41777	YEADDISS
41238-41238	OIL SPRINGS	41426-41426	FALCON	41607-41607	BLUE RIVER	41778-41778	YERKES
41240-41240	PAINTSVILLE	41427-41427	FLAT FORK	41612-41612	BYPRO	41801-41801	AMBURGEY
41250-41250	PILGRIM	41430-41430	FREDVILLE	41614-41614	CRAYNOR	41804-41804	BLACKEY
41253-41253	RICHARDSON	41431-41431	FRITZ	41615-41615	DANA	41805-41805	BRINKLEY
41254-41254	RIVER	41433-41433	GAPVILLE	41616-41616	DAVID	41810-41810	CROMONA
41255-41255	SITKA	41438-41438	GYPSY	41619-41619	DRIFT	41811-41811	CROWN
41256-41256	STAFFORDSVILLE	41441-41441	HENDRICKS	41621-41621	DWALE	41812-41812	DEANE
41257-41257	STAMBAUGH	41443-41443	INSKO	41622-41622	EASTERN	41815-41815	ERMINE
41258-41258	SWAMP BRANCH	41444-41444	IVYTON	41625-41625	EMMA	41817-41817	GARNER
41260-41260	THELMA	41447-41447	LENOX	41626-41626	ENDICOTT	41819-41819	GORDON
41261-41261	THREEFORKS	41451-41451	MALONE	41627-41627	ESTILL	41821-41821	HALLIE
41262-41262	TOMAHAWK	41452-41452	MARSHALLVILLE	41629-41629	GALVESTON	41822-41822	HINDMAN
41263-41263	TUTOR KEY	41456-41456	MIMA	41630-41630	GARRETT	41823-41823	HOLLYBUSH
41264-41264	ULYSSES	41457-41457	MOON	41631-41631	GRETHEL	41824-41824	ISOM
41265-41265	VAN LEAR	41459-41459	OPHIR	41632-41632	GUNLOCK	41825-41825	JACKHORN
41266-41266	VOLGA	41464-41464	ROYALTON	41633-41633	HALO	41826-41826	JEREMIAH
41267-41267	WARFIELD	41465-41465	SALYERSVILLE	41635-41635	HAROLD	41828-41828	KITE
41268-41268	WEST VAN LEAR	41466-41466	SEITZ	41636-41636	HI HAT	41829-41829	KONA
41269-41269	WHITEHOUSE	41467-41467	SILVERHILL	41637-41637	HIPPO	41831-41831	LEBURN
41271-41271	WILLIAMSPORT	41472-41472	WEST LIBERTY	41639-41639	HONAKER	41832-41832	LETCHER
41274-41274	WITTENSVILLE	41474-41474	WHITE OAK	41640-41640	HUEYSVILLE	41833-41833	LINEFORK
41301-41301	CAMPTON	41477-41477	WRIGLEY	41641-41641	HUNTER	41834-41834	LITTCARR
41306-41306	ALTRO	41501-41502	PIKEVILLE	41642-41642	IVEL	41835-41835	MC ROBERTS
41307-41307	ATHOL	41503-41503	SOUTH WILLIAMSON	41643-41643	LACKEY	41836-41836	MALLIE
41310-41310	BAYS	41512-41512	ASHCAMP	41645-41645	LANGLEY	41837-41837	MAYKING
41311-41311	BEATTYVILLE	41513-41513	BELCHER	41647-41647	MC DOWELL	41838-41838	MILLSTONE
41313-41313	BETHANY	41514-41514	BELFRY	41649-41649	MARTIN	41839-41839	MOUSIE
41314-41314	BOONEVILLE	41517-41517	BURDINE	41650-41650	MELVIN	41840-41840	NEON
41315-41315	BURKHART	41518-41518	BURNWELL	41651-41651	MINNIE	41843-41843	PINE TOP
41316-41316	CANOE	41519-41519	CANADA	41653-41653	PRESTONSBURG	41844-41844	PIPPA PASSES
41317-41317	CLAYHOLE	41520-41520	DORTON	41655-41655	PRINTER	41845-41845	PREMIUM
41321-41321	DECOY	41521-41521	DRAFFIN	41659-41659	STANVILLE	41847-41847	REDFOX
41323-41323	FILLMORE	41522-41522	ELKHORN CITY	41660-41660	TEABERRY	41848-41848	ROXANA
41327-41327	GILLMORE	41524-41524	FEDSCREEK	41663-41663	TRAM	41849-41849	SECO
41328-41328	GREEN HALL	41526-41526	FORDS BRANCH	41666-41666	WAYLAND	41855-41855	THORNTON
41331-41331	HADDIX	41527-41527	FOREST HILLS	41667-41667	WEEKSBURY	41858-41858	WHITESBURG
41332-41332	HAZEL GREEN	41528-41528	FREEBURN	41668-41668	WEST PRESTONSBURG	41859-41859	DEMA

Range	Name
41861-41861	RAVEN
41862-41862	TOPMOST
41901-41906	MIGRATE
42001-42003	PADUCAH
42020-42020	ALMO
42021-42021	ARLINGTON
42022-42022	BANDANA
42023-42023	BARDWELL
42024-42024	BARLOW
42025-42025	BENTON
42026-42026	BLANDVILLE
42027-42027	BOAZ
42028-42028	BURNA
42029-42029	CALVERT CITY
42031-42031	CLINTON
42032-42032	COLUMBUS
42033-42033	CRAYNE
42035-42035	CUNNINGHAM
42036-42036	DEXTER
42037-42037	DYCUSBURG
42038-42038	EDDYVILLE
42039-42039	FANCY FARM
42040-42040	FARMINGTON
42041-42041	FULTON
42044-42044	GILBERTSVILLE
42045-42045	GRAND RIVERS
42046-42046	HAMLIN
42047-42047	HAMPTON
42048-42048	HARDIN
42049-42049	HAZEL
42050-42050	HICKMAN
42051-42051	HICKORY
42053-42053	KEVIL
42054-42054	KIRKSEY
42055-42055	KUTTAWA
42056-42056	LA CENTER
42058-42058	LEDBETTER
42059-42059	LOLA
42060-42060	LOVELACEVILLE
42061-42061	LOWES
42063-42063	LYNNVILLE
42064-42064	MARION
42066-42066	MAYFIELD
42069-42069	MELBER
42070-42070	MILBURN
42071-42071	MURRAY
42076-42076	NEW CONCORD
42078-42078	SALEM
42079-42079	SEDALIA
42081-42081	SMITHLAND
42082-42082	SYMSONIA
42083-42083	TILINE
42084-42084	TOLU
42085-42085	WATER VALLEY
42086-42086	WEST PADUCAH
42087-42087	WICKLIFFE
42088-42088	WINGO
42101-42104	BOWLING GREEN
42120-42120	ADOLPHUS
42122-42122	ALVATON
42123-42123	AUSTIN
42124-42124	BEAUMONT
42127-42127	CAVE CITY
42128-42128	DRAKE
42129-42129	EDMONTON
42130-42130	EIGHTY EIGHT
42131-42131	ETOILE
42133-42133	FOUNTAIN RUN
42134-42135	FRANKLIN
42140-42140	GAMALIEL
42141-42142	GLASGOW
42150-42150	HALFWAY
42151-42151	HESTAND
42152-42152	HISEVILLE
42153-42153	HOLLAND
42154-42154	KNOB LICK
42155-42155	LAMB
42156-42156	LUCAS
42157-42157	MOUNT HERMON
42159-42159	OAKLAND
42160-42160	PARK CITY
42163-42163	ROCKY HILL
42164-42164	SCOTTSVILLE
42166-42166	SUMMER SHADE
42167-42167	TOMPKINSVILLE
42169-42169	WILLOW SHADE
42170-42170	WOODBURN
42171-42171	SMITHS GROVE
42201-42201	ABERDEEN
42202-42202	ADAIRVILLE
42203-42203	ALLEGRE
42204-42204	ALLENSVILLE
42206-42206	AUBURN
42207-42207	BEE SPRING
42209-42209	BROOKLYN
42210-42210	BROWNSVILLE
42211-42211	CADIZ
42212-42212	CANTON
42214-42214	CENTER
42215-42215	CERULEAN
42216-42216	CLIFTY
42217-42217	CROFTON
42219-42219	DUNBAR
42220-42220	ELKTON
42221-42221	FAIRVIEW
42223-42223	FORT CAMPBELL
42232-42232	GRACEY
42234-42234	GUTHRIE
42235-42235	HADLEY
42236-42236	HERNDON
42240-42241	HOPKINSVILLE
42250-42250	HUFF
42251-42251	HUNTSVILLE
42252-42252	JETSON
42254-42254	LA FAYETTE
42256-42256	LEWISBURG
42257-42257	LINDSEYVILLE
42259-42259	MAMMOTH CAVE
42261-42261	MORGANTOWN
42262-42262	OAK GROVE
42263-42263	OAKVILLE
42264-42264	OLLIE
42265-42265	OLMSTEAD
42266-42266	PEMBROKE
42267-42267	PROVO
42268-42268	QUALITY
42270-42270	RICHARDSVILLE
42273-42273	ROCHESTER
42274-42274	ROCKFIELD
42275-42275	ROUNDHILL
42276-42276	RUSSELLVILLE
42280-42280	SHARON GROVE
42283-42283	SOUTH UNION
42284-42284	SUNFISH
42285-42285	SWEEDEN
42286-42286	TRENTON
42287-42287	WELCHS CREEK
42288-42288	WOODBURY
42301-42304	OWENSBORO
42320-42320	BEAVER DAM
42321-42321	BEECH CREEK
42322-42322	BEECH GROVE
42323-42323	BEECHMONT
42324-42324	BELTON
42325-42325	BREMEN
42326-42326	BROWDER
42327-42327	CALHOUN
42328-42328	CENTERTOWN
42330-42330	CENTRAL CITY
42332-42332	CLEATON
42333-42333	CROMWELL
42334-42334	CURDSVILLE
42337-42337	DRAKESBORO
42338-42338	DUNDEE
42339-42339	DUNMOR
42343-42343	FORDSVILLE
42344-42344	GRAHAM
42345-42345	GREENVILLE
42347-42347	HARTFORD
42348-42348	HAWESVILLE
42349-42349	HORSE BRANCH
42350-42350	ISLAND
42351-42351	LEWISPORT
42352-42352	LIVERMORE
42354-42354	MC HENRY
42355-42355	MACEO
42356-42356	MAPLE MOUNT
42357-42357	MOORMAN
42358-42358	NARROWS
42361-42361	OLATON
42364-42364	PELLVILLE
42365-42365	PENROD
42366-42366	PHILPOT
42367-42367	POWDERLY
42368-42368	REYNOLDS STATION
42369-42369	ROCKPORT
42370-42370	ROSINE
42371-42371	RUMSEY
42372-42372	SACRAMENTO
42373-42373	SAINT JOSEPH
42374-42374	SOUTH CARROLLTON
42375-42375	STANLEY
42376-42376	UTICA
42377-42377	WEST LOUISVILLE
42378-42378	WHITESVILLE
42402-42402	BASKETT
42403-42403	BLACKFORD
42404-42404	CLAY
42406-42406	CORYDON
42408-42408	DAWSON SPRINGS
42409-42409	DIXON
42410-42410	EARLINGTON
42411-42411	FREDONIA
42413-42413	HANSON
42419-42420	HENDERSON
42431-42431	MADISONVILLE
42436-42436	MANITOU
42437-42437	MORGANFIELD
42440-42440	MORTONS GAP
42441-42441	NEBO
42442-42442	NORTONVILLE
42444-42444	POOLE
42445-42445	PRINCETON
42450-42450	PROVIDENCE
42451-42451	REED
42452-42452	ROBARDS
42453-42453	SAINT CHARLES
42455-42455	SEBREE
42456-42456	SLAUGHTERS
42457-42457	SMITH MILLS
42458-42458	SPOTTSVILLE
42459-42459	STURGIS
42460-42460	SULLIVAN
42461-42461	UNIONTOWN
42462-42462	WAVERLY
42463-42463	WHEATCROFT
42464-42464	WHITE PLAINS
42501-42503	SOMERSET
42510-42510	ACORN
42516-42516	BETHELRIDGE
42518-42518	BRONSTON
42519-42519	BURNSIDE
42528-42528	DUNNVILLE
42532-42532	FAUBUSH
42533-42533	FERGUSON
42536-42536	INGLE
42539-42539	LIBERTY
42541-42541	MIDDLEBURG
42544-42544	NANCY
42553-42553	SCIENCE HILL
42554-42554	SHOPVILLE
42555-42555	SLOANS VALLEY
42557-42557	STAB
42558-42558	TATEVILLE
42563-42563	WALNUT GROVE
42564-42564	WEST SOMERSET
42565-42565	WINDSOR
42566-42566	YOSEMITE
42567-42567	EUBANK
42601-42601	AARON
42602-42602	ALBANY
42603-42603	ALPHA
42607-42607	BEULAH HEIGHTS
42611-42611	COOPERSVILLE
42613-42613	DELTA
42618-42618	FRAZER
42629-42629	JAMESTOWN
42631-42631	MARSHES SIDING
42632-42632	MILL SPRINGS
42633-42633	MONTICELLO
42634-42634	PARKERS LAKE
42635-42635	PINE KNOT
42638-42638	REVELO
42640-42640	ROCKYBRANCH
42642-42642	RUSSELL SPRINGS
42643-42643	SAWYER
42647-42647	STEARNS
42648-42648	STEUBENVILLE
42649-42649	STRUNK
42653-42653	WHITLEY CITY
42655-42655	WINDY
42701-42702	ELIZABETHTOWN
42711-42711	BAKERTON
42712-42712	BIG CLIFTY
42713-42713	BONNIEVILLE
42714-42714	BOW
42715-42715	BREEDING
42716-42716	BUFFALO
42717-42717	BURKESVILLE
42718-42719	CAMPBELLSVILLE
42720-42720	CANE VALLEY
42721-42721	CANEYVILLE
42722-42722	CANMER
42723-42723	CASEY CREEKG
42723-42723	CASEY CREEK
42724-42724	CECILIA
42726-42726	CLARKSON
42728-42728	COLUMBIA
42729-42729	CUB RUN
42730-42730	CUNDIFF
42731-42731	DUBRE
42732-42732	EASTVIEW
42733-42733	ELK HORN
42735-42735	FAIRPLAY
42736-42736	FINLEY
42740-42740	GLENDALE
42741-42741	GLENS FORK
42742-42742	GRADYVILLE
42743-42743	GREENSBURG
42746-42746	HARDYVILLE
42748-42748	HODGENVILLE
42749-42749	HORSE CAVE
42752-42752	KETTLE
42753-42753	KNIFLEY
42754-42755	LEITCHFIELD
42757-42757	MAGNOLIA
42758-42758	MANNSVILLE
42759-42759	MARROWBONE
42761-42761	MILLTOWN
42762-42762	MILLWOOD
42763-42763	MONTPELIER
42764-42764	MOUNT SHERMAN
42765-42765	MUNFORDVILLE
42766-42766	NEAFUS
42768-42768	PEYTONSBURG
42772-42772	ROWLETTS
42776-42776	SONORA
42779-42779	SPRING LICK
42780-42780	STEFF
42781-42781	STEPHENSBURG
42782-42782	SUMMERSVILLE
42783-42783	SUMMIT
42784-42784	UPTON
42785-42785	VENTRESS
42785-42785	VERTREES
42786-42786	WATERVIEW
42787-42787	WAX
42788-42788	WHITE MILLS

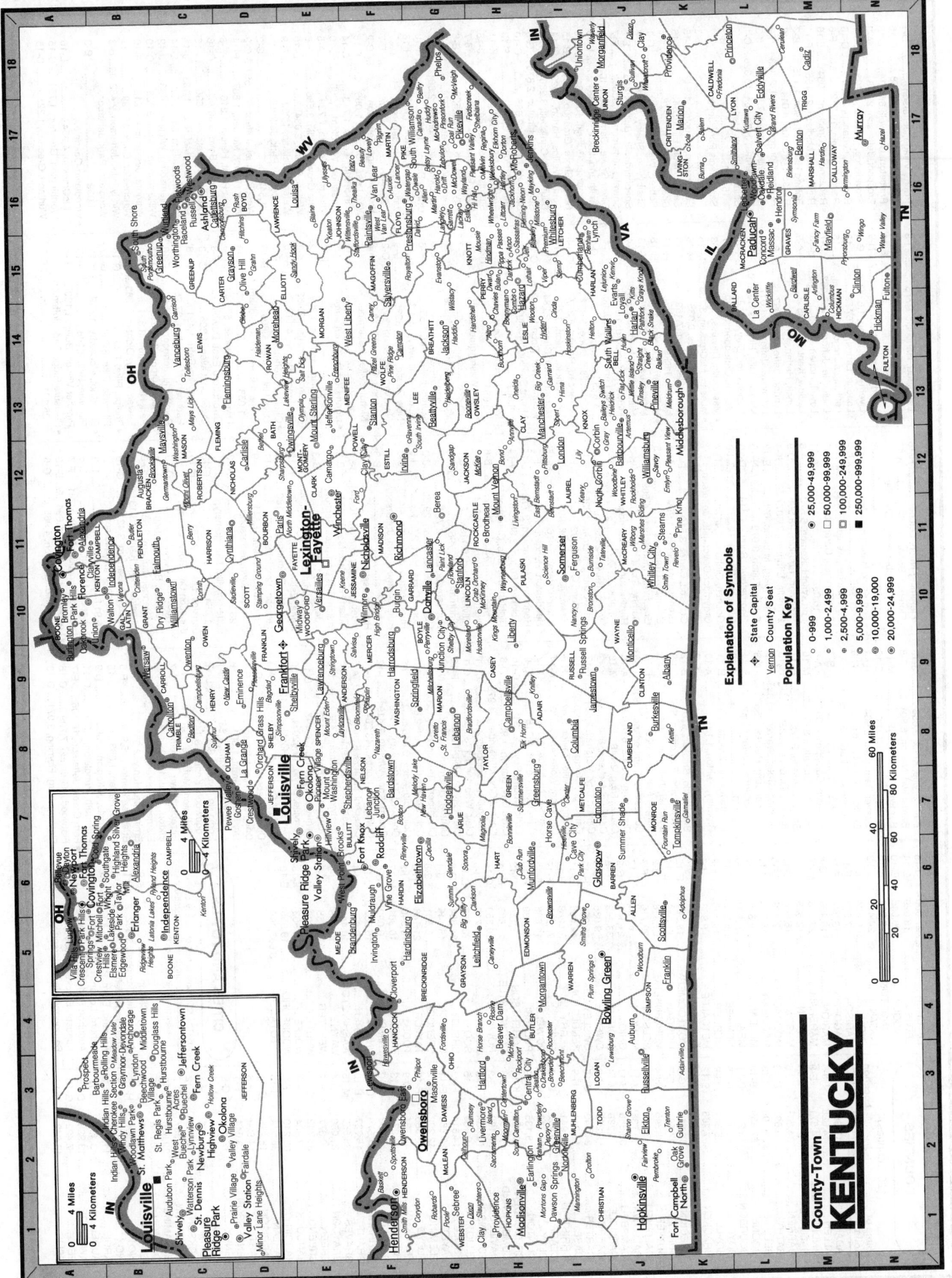

KENTUCKY
County-Town

Explanation of Symbols

✦ State Capital

Vernon ⊙ County Seat

Population Key

Symbol	Population
⊙	0-999
○	1,000-2,499
◉	2,500-4,999
⊙	5,000-9,999
◎	10,000-19,000
⊙	20,000-24,999
◉	25,000-49,999
□	50,000-99,999
▢	100,000-249,999
■	250,000-999,999

0   20   40   60 Miles

0 20 40 60 80 Kilometers

COUNTIES

(120 Counties)

Name of County	Population	Location on Map
ADAIR	15,360	I-8
ALLEN	14,628	J-5
ANDERSON	14,571	E-9
BALLARD	7,902	L-14
BARREN	34,001	J-6
BATH	9,692	D-13
BELL	31,506	J-13
BOONE	57,589	B-10
BOURBON	19,236	D-11
BOYD	51,150	D-16
BOYLE	25,641	G-9
BRACKEN	7,766	B-12
BREATHITT	15,703	G-14
BRECKINRIDGE	16,312	G-4
BULLITT	47,567	E-7
BUTLER	11,245	H-4
CALDWELL	13,232	K-17
CALLOWAY	30,735	M-16
CAMPBELL	83,866	B-11
CARLISLE	5,238	M-14
CARROLL	9,292	C-9
CARTER	24,340	D-15
CASEY	14,211	H-9
CHRISTIAN	68,941	I-1
CLARK	29,496	E-12
CLAY	21,746	H-13
CLINTON	9,135	J-9
CRITTENDEN	9,196	K-17
CUMBERLAND	6,784	J-8
DAVIESS	87,189	G-3
EDMONSON	10,357	H-5
ELLIOTT	6,455	E-15
ESTILL	14,614	F-12
FAYETTE	225,366	E-11
FLEMING	12,292	C-12
FLOYD	43,586	F-15
FRANKLIN	43,781	D-9
FULTON	8,271	N-13
GALLATIN	5,393	B-10
GARRARD	11,579	G-10
GRANT	15,737	B-10
GRAVES	33,550	M-15
GRAYSON	21,050	G-4
GREEN	10,371	H-7
GREENUP	36,742	C-15
HANCOCK	7,864	F-4
HARDIN	89,240	F-6
HARLAN	36,574	I-15
HARRISON	16,248	C-11
HART	14,890	H-6
HENDERSON	43,044	F-1
HENRY	12,823	C-9
HICKMAN	5,566	M-14
HOPKINS	46,126	H-1
JACKSON	11,955	G-12
JEFFERSON	664,937	D-7
JESSAMINE	30,508	F-10
JOHNSON	23,248	E-15
KENTON	142,031	B-10
KNOTT	17,906	H-15
KNOX	29,676	I-13
LARUE	11,679	G-7
LAUREL	43,438	I-12
LAWRENCE	13,998	D-16
LEE	7,422	G-13
LESLIE	13,642	H-14
LETCHER	27,000	I-15
LEWIS	13,029	C-14
LINCOLN	20,045	G-10
LIVINGSTON	9,062	K-16
LOGAN	24,416	I-3
LYON	6,624	L-17
MADISON	57,508	F-11
MAGOFFIN	13,077	F-15
MARION	16,499	G-8
MARSHALL	27,205	M-16
MARTIN	12,526	F-17
MASON	16,666	C-12
MCCRACKEN	62,879	L-15
MCCREARY	15,603	J-11
MCLEAN	9,628	G-2
MEADE	24,170	E-5
MENIFEE	5,092	F-13
MERCER	19,148	F-9
METCALFE	8,963	I-7
MONROE	11,401	J-7
MONTGOMERY	19,561	E-12
MORGAN	11,648	E-14
MUHLENBERG	31,318	I-2
NELSON	29,710	F-7
NICHOLAS	6,725	D-12
OHIO	21,105	G-3
OLDHAM	33,263	D-8
OWEN	9,035	C-9
OWSLEY	5,036	H-13
PENDLETON	12,036	B-11
PERRY	30,283	H-14
PIKE	72,583	F-17
POWELL	11,686	F-12
PULASKI	49,489	H-10
ROBERTSON	2,124	C-12
ROCKCASTLE	14,803	H-11
ROWAN	20,353	D-14
RUSSELL	14,716	I-9
SCOTT	23,867	D-10
SHELBY	24,824	D-8
SIMPSON	15,145	J-4
SPENCER	6,801	E-8
TAYLOR	21,146	H-8
TODD	10,940	I-2
TRIGG	10,361	M-17
TRIMBLE	6,090	C-8
UNION	16,557	J-17
WARREN	76,673	I-4
WASHINGTON	10,441	F-8
WAYNE	17,468	J-9
WEBSTER	13,955	G-1
WHITLEY	33,326	J-11
WOLFE	6,503	F-13
WOODFORD	19,955	E-10
TOTAL	3,685,296	

CITIES AND TOWNS

Note: The first name is that of the city or town, second, that of the county in which it is located, then the population and location on the map.

City, County, Population	Location
Albany, Clinton, 2,062	K-9
Alexandria, Campbell, 5,592	A-11
Anchorage, Jefferson, 2,082	B-4
Ashland, Boyd, 23,622	C-16
Auburn, Logan, 1,273	J-4
Audubon Park, Jefferson, 1,520	C-2
Augusta, Bracken, 1,336	B-12
Barbourmeade, Jefferson, 1,402	A-3
Barbourville, Knox, 3,658	J-13
Bardstown, Nelson, 6,801	F-8
Bardwell, Carlisle, 819	M-14
Beattyville, Lee, 1,131	G-13
Beaver Dam, Ohio, 2,904	H-3
Bedford, Trimble, 761	C-8
Beechwood Village, Jefferson, 1,263	B-3
Bellevue, Campbell, 6,997	A-6
Benton, Marshall, 3,899	M-16
Berea, Madison, 9,126	G-11
Booneville, Owsley, 232	G-13
Bowling Green, Warren, 40,641	I-5
Brandenburg, Meade, 1,857	A-6
• Breckinridge Center, Union, 2,375	J-18
Brodhead, Rockcastle, 1,140	H-11
Bromley, Kenton, 1,137	A-10
• Brooks, Bullitt, 2,464	E-7
Brooksville, Bracken, 670	B-12
Brownsville, Edmonson, 897	I-5
• Buechel, Jefferson, 7,081	C-3
Burgin, Mercer, 1,009	F-10
Burkesville, Cumberland, 1,815	J-8
• Burlington, Boone, 6,070	A-10
Cadiz, Trigg, 2,148	M-18
Calhoun, McLean, 854	G-2
Calvert City, Marshall, 2,531	L-17
Camargo, Montgomery, 1,022	E-12
Campbellsville, Taylor, 9,577	H-8
Campton, Wolfe, 484	F-14
Carlisle, Nicholas, 1,639	D-12
Carrollton, Carroll, 3,715	C-9
Catlettsburg, Boyd, 2,231	C-16
Cave City, Barren, 1,953	I-6
Central City, Muhlenberg, 4,979	H-3
• Claryville, Campbell, 2,038	B-11
Clay, Webster, 1,173	G-1
Clay City, Powell, 1,258	F-12
Clinton, Hickman, 1,547	N-14
Cloverport, Breckinridge, 1,207	F-4
Cold Spring, Campbell, 2,880	A-6
Columbia, Adair, 3,845	I-8
• Concord, McCracken, 1,560	L-15
Corbin, Knox/Whitley, 7,419	I-12
Covington, Kenton, 43,264	A-11
Crescent Springs, Kenton, 2,179	A-5
Crestview Hills, Kenton, 2,546	B-5
Crestwood, Oldham, 1,435	D-8
Cumberland, Harlan, 3,112	I-15
Cynthiana, Harrison, 6,497	D-11
Danville, Boyle, 12,420	D-10
Dawson Springs, Hopkins, 3,129	I-1
Dayton, Campbell, 6,576	A-6
Dixon, Webster, 552	G-1
Douglass Hills, Jefferson, 5,549	B-3
Dry Ridge, Grant, 1,601	B-10
Earlington, Hopkins, 1,833	H-1
Eddyville, Lyon, 1,889	L-17
Edgewood, Kenton, 8,143	B-5
Edmonton, Metcalfe, 1,477	I-7
Elizabethtown, Hardin, 18,167	G-7
Elkton, Todd, 1,789	J-3
Elsmere, Kenton, 6,847	B-5
Eminence, Henry, 2,055	D-9
Erlanger, Kenton, 15,979	B-5
Evarts, Harlan, 1,063	J-15
• Fairdale, Jefferson, 6,563	D-2
Falmouth, Pendleton, 2,378	C-11
• Fern Creek, Jefferson, 16,406	E-7
Flatwoods, Greenup, 7,799	C-16
Flemingsburg, Fleming, 3,071	D-13
Flemming-Neon, Letcher	H-16
Florence, Boone, 18,624	A-10
• Fort Campbell North, Christian, 18,861	K-2
• Fort Knox, Hardin/Meade, 21,495	F-6
Fort Mitchell, Kenton, 7,438	A-5
Fort Thomas, Campbell, 16,032	A-11
Fort Wright, Kenton, 6,570	A-6
Frankfort, Franklin, 25,968	D-9
Franklin, Simpson, 7,607	K-4
Frenchburg, Menifee, 625	E-13
Fulton, Fulton, 3,078	N-15
Georgetown, Scott, 11,414	D-10
Glasgow, Barren, 12,351	I-6
• Goshen, Oldham, 2,447	D-7
Graymoor-Devondale, Jefferson, 2,911	B-3
Grayson, Carter, 3,510	D-15
Greensburg, Green, 1,990	H-8
Greenup, Greenup, 1,158	C-15
Greenville, Muhlenberg, 4,689	I-3
Guthrie, Todd, 1,504	K-3
Hardinsburg, Breckinridge, 1,906	F-5
Harlan, Harlan, 2,686	J-14
Harrodsburg, Mercer, 7,335	F-10
Hartford, Ohio, 2,532	H-3
Hawesville, Hancock, 998	F-4
Hazard, Perry, 5,416	H-15
Henderson, Henderson, 25,945	F-2
• Hendron, McCracken, 3,712	L-15
Hickman, Fulton, 2,689	N-14
Highland Heights, Campbell, 4,223	B-6
• Highview, Jefferson, 14,814	C-3
Hillview, Bullitt, 6,119	E-7
Hindman, Knott, 798	H-15
Hodgenville, Larue, 2,721	G-7
Hopkinsville, Christian, 29,809	J-2
Horse Cave, Hart, 2,284	I-6
Hurstbourne, Jefferson, 4,420	B-3
Hurstbourne Acres, Jefferson, 1,072	B-3
Hyden, Leslie, 375	I-14
Independence, Kenton, 10,444	B-10
Indian Hills, Jefferson, 1,074	B-2
Indian Hills Cherokee Section, Jefferson, 1,005	B-3
Inez, Martin, 511	F-17
Irvine, Estill, 2,836	F-12
Irvington, Breckinridge, 1,180	F-5
Jackson, Breathitt, 2,466	G-14
Jamestown, Russell, 1,641	I-9
Jeffersontown, Jefferson, 23,221	C-3
Jeffersonville, Montgomery, 1,854	E-13
Jenkins, Letcher, 2,751	H-16
Junction City, Boyle/Lincoln, 1,983	D-10
La Center, Ballard, 1,040	L-14
La Grange, Oldham, 3,853	D-8
Lakeside Park, Kenton, 3,131	B-5
Lancaster, Garrard, 3,421	G-10
Lawrenceburg, Anderson, 5,911	E-9
Lebanon, Marion, 5,695	G-8
Lebanon Junction, Bullitt, 1,741	F-7
• Ledbetter, Livingston, 1,694	L-16
Leitchfield, Grayson, 4,965	G-5
Lewisport, Hancock, 1,778	I-3
Lexington-Fayette, Fayette, 225,366	E-11
Liberty, Casey, 1,937	H-9
Livermore, McLean, 1,534	G-3
London, Laurel, 5,757	I-12
Louisa, Lawrence, 1,990	E-16
Louisville, Jefferson, 269,063	D-7
Loyall, Harlan, 1,100	J-14
Ludlow, Kenton, 4,736	A-5
Lynch, Harlan, 1,166	I-16
Lyndon, Jefferson, 8,037	B-3
Lynnview, Jefferson, 1,017	C-2
Madisonville, Hopkins, 16,200	H-2
Manchester, Clay, 1,634	I-13
Marion, Crittenden, 3,320	K-17
• Masonville, Daviess, 1,119	G-3
• Massac, McCracken, 3,733	M-15
Mayfield, Graves, 9,935	M-16
Maysville, Mason, 7,169	C-13
McKee, Jackson, 870	H-12
• McRoberts, Letcher, 1,101	H-16
Middlesborough, Bell, 11,328	K-13
Middletown, Jefferson, 5,016	B-4
Midway, Woodford, 1,290	E-10
Minor Lane Heights, Jefferson, 1,675	D-1
Monticello, Wayne, 5,357	J-9
Morehead, Rowan, 8,357	D-14
Morganfield, Union, 3,776	J-18
Morgantown, Butler, 2,284	H-4
Mount Olivet, Robertson, 384	C-12
Mount Sterling, Montgomery, 5,362	E-12
Mount Vernon, Rockcastle, 2,654	H-11
Mount Washington, Bullitt, 5,226	E-7
Muldraugh, Hardin/Meade, 1,376	F-6
Munfordville, Hart, 1,556	H-6
Murray, Calloway, 14,439	N-17
New Castle, Henry, 893	D-9
• Newburg, Jefferson, 21,647	C-2
Newport, Campbell, 18,871	A-6
Nicholasville, Jessamine, 13,603	F-10
• North Corbin, Knox/Laurel, 1,601	I-12
Nortonville, Hopkins, 1,209	I-2
Oak Grove, Christian, 2,863	K-2
• Oakbrook, Boone, 4,113	A-10
• Okolona, Jefferson, 18,902	E-7
Olive Hill, Carter, 1,809	D-15
Orchard Grass Hills, Oldham, 1,058	D-8
Owensboro, Daviess, 53,549	F-3
Owensboro East, Daviess	F-3
Owenton, Owen, 1,306	C-10
Owingsville, Bath, 1,491	E-13
Paducah, McCracken, 27,256	L-16
Paintsville, Johnson, 4,354	F-16
Paris, Bourbon, 8,730	D-11
Park Hills, Kenton, 3,321	A-10
Pewee Valley, Oldham, 1,283	D-7
• Phelps, Pike, 1,298	G-18
Pikeville, Pike, 6,324	G-17
• Pine Knot, McCreary, 1,549	K-11
Pineville, Bell, 2,198	J-13
Pioneer Village, Bullitt, 1,130	E-7
• Pleasure Ridge Park, Jefferson, 25,131	E-7
Prairie Village, Jefferson	D-1
Prestonsburg, Floyd, 3,558	G-16
Princeton, Caldwell, 6,940	L-18
Prospect, Jefferson, 2,788	A-3
Providence, Webster, 4,123	J-1
Raceland, Greenup, 2,256	C-16
Radcliff, Hardin, 19,772	F-6
• Reidland, McCracken, 4,054	L-16
Richmond, Madison, 21,155	F-11
Rolling Hills, Jefferson, 1,135	B-3
Russell, Greenup, 4,014	C-16
Russell Springs, Russell, 2,363	I-9
Russellville, Logan, 7,454	J-3
• Saint Dennis, Jefferson, 10,326	C-1
Saint Matthews, Jefferson, 15,800	B-3
Saint Regis Park, Jefferson, 1,756	B-3
Salyersville, Magoffin, 1,917	F-15
Sandy Hook, Elliott, 548	E-15
Scottsville, Allen, 4,278	J-6
Sebree, Webster, 1,510	G-1
Shelbyville, Shelby, 6,238	E-8
Shepherdsville, Bullitt, 4,805	E-7
Shively, Jefferson, 15,535	E-7
Silver Grove, Campbell, 1,102	B-7
Smithland, Livingston, 384	L-16
Somerset, Pulaski, 10,733	I-10
South Shore, Greenup, 1,318	B-15
• South Wallins, Harlan, 1,022	J-14
Southgate, Campbell, 3,266	B-6
Springfield, Washington, 2,875	G-8
Stanford, Lincoln, 2,686	G-10
Stanton, Powell, 2,795	F-13
• Stearns, McCreary, 1,550	K-11
Sturgis, Union, 2,184	J-18
Summer Shade, Metcalfe	J-7
Taylor Mill, Kenton, 5,530	B-6
Taylorsville, Spencer, 774	E-8
Tompkinsville, Monroe, 2,861	K-7
Union, Boone, 1,001	B-10
Uniontown, Union, 1,008	I-18
• Valley Station, Jefferson, 22,840	E-7
Valley Village, Jefferson	C-2
• Van Lear, Johnson, 1,050	F-16
Vanceburg, Lewis, 1,713	C-14
Versailles, Woodford, 7,269	E-10
Villa Hills, Kenton, 7,739	A-5
Vine Grove, Hardin, 3,586	F-6
Walton, Boone, 2,034	B-10
Warsaw, Gallatin, 1,202	B-9
Watterson Park, Jefferson, 1,542	C-2
West Buechel, Jefferson, 1,587	C-2
West Liberty, Morgan, 1,887	F-14
West Point, Hardin, 1,216	E-6
• Westwood, Boyd, 5,300	C-16
Whitesburg, Letcher, 1,636	I-16
• Whitley City, McCreary, 1,133	J-11
Wickliffe, Ballard, 851	L-14
Williamsburg, Whitley, 5,493	J-12
Williamstown, Grant, 3,023	C-10
Wilmore, Jessamine, 4,215	F-10
Winchester, Clark, 15,799	E-12
Windy Hills, Jefferson, 2,452	B-3
Woodlawn Park, Jefferson, 1,099	B-3
• Woodlawn-Oakdale, McCracken, 4,954	L-16
Worthington, Greenup, 1,751	C-15
Wurtland, Greenup, 1,221	C-15

Explanation of symbols: • – Census Designated Place (CDP)

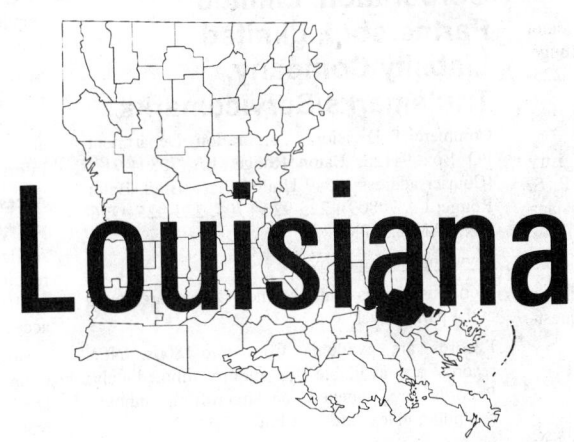

General Help Numbers:

Governor's Office
PO Box 94004
Baton Rouge, LA 70804-9004
www.gov.state.la.us

225-342-0991
Fax 225-342-7099
8AM-5PM

Attorney General's Office
LA Department of Justice
PO Box 94005
Baton Rouge, LA 70804-9005
www.ag.state.la.us

225-326-6705
Fax 225-326-6797
8:30AM-5PM

Legislative Records
State Capitol, 2nd Floor
PO Box 44486
Baton Rouge, LA 70804
www.legis.state.la.us

225-342-2456

8AM-5PM

State Archives
Records Mgt, & History
3851 Essen Lane
Baton Rouge, LA 70809-2137
www.sec.state.la.us/archives/
archives/archives-index.htm

225-922-1000
Fax 225-922-0433
8AM-4:30PM,
9-5 SA 1-5 SU

State Specifics:

Capital:	Baton Rouge East Baton Rouge Parish
Time Zone:	CST
Number of Parishes:	64
Population:	4,496,334
Web Site:	www.state.la.us

State Agencies

Criminal Records

Access to Records is Restricted.

State Police, Bureau of Criminal Identification, 7919 Independence Blvd, Baton Rouge, LA 70806; 225-925-6095, 225-925-7005-Fax; 8AM-4:30PM.

www.lsp.org

Records ARE RESTRICTED and are not available to the public in general. Records are available for employment or licensing purposes as state law dictates. Authorized forms are available from this department.

Statewide Court Records

Judicial Administrator, Judicial Council of the Supreme Court, 400 Royal Street, Suite 1190, New Orleans, LA 70130-8101; 504-310-2550, 504-310-2587-Fax; 9AM-5PM.

www.lasc.org

It takes 24 hours before new records are available for inquiry. Records are normally destroyed after no less than 3 years.

Searching: Include the following in your request- name; also helpful-specific information such as

DOB, years to search. Include your name and contact information.

Access by: mail, online.

Fee & Payment: There is no search fee

Mail search: Turnaround time: 72 hours. Appellate and Supreme Court records are available by mail.

Online search: Search opinions from the state Supreme Court at www.lasc.org/opinion_search.asp. Online records go back to 1995.

Sexual Offender Registry

State Police, Sex Offender and Child Predator Registry, PO Box 66614, Box A-6, Baton Rouge, LA 70896; 225-925-6100, 800-858-0551, 225-925-7005-Fax; 8AM-4:30PM.

www.lasocpr.lsp.org/socpr

The Sex Offender and Child Predator Registry program is statutorily provided through La. R. S. 15:542 & 15:542.1, et. seq., of the Louisiana Criminal Code.

Records are available from 6/18/92. It takes 1 to 3 days before new records are available for inquiry.

Searching: Include the following in your request-name or ZIP Code or parish.

Access by: mail, phone, fax, online.

Mail search: Turnaround time: 30 days.

Phone search: You must supply name, race, sex, DOB in a phone request. Request can be delayed due to limited staff.

Fax search: Same criteria as phone search.

Online search: Search by name, ZIP Code, or view the entire list at the website. Also search by city, school area or parish.

Expedited service: Will try to expedite request, if requested.

Incarceration Records

Department of Public Safety and Corrections, P.O. Box 94304, Attn: Office of Adult Services, Baton Rouge, LA 70804-9304; 225-342-6642, 225-342-9711 (Locator), 225-342-3349-Fax; 8AM-4:30PM.

www.corrections.state.la.us

Records are available on current and former inmates. It takes 1 to 3 days before new records are available for inquiry.

Searching: Under state law, the complete records of offenders, past, present, or future, in the custody of the Department of Public Safety and Corrections, Corrections Services, is confidential and cannot be disclosed, directly or indirectly, to anyone. Include the following in your request-full name; DOC number helpful. Only location, conviction and sentencing information are released. Records computerized since 1975.

Access by: mail, phone, fax, online.

Fee & Payment: There is no fee.

Mail search: Turnaround time: 30 days. No SASE is required.

Phone search: Limited name searching available.

Fax search: Location requests available by fax.

Online search: Access is limited to schedules for upcoming Parole Board hearings, as well as decisions from previous Parole Board hearings. Go to www.corrections.state.la.us/Offices/paroleboard/paroledockets.htm. Also, a private company offers free web access at www.inelink.com/index.jsp including state, DOC, and most county jail systems

Corporation, Limited Partnership, Limited Liability Company, Trademarks/Servicemarks

Commercial Division, Corporation Department, PO Box 94125, Baton Rouge, LA 70804-9125 (Courier address: 8549 United Plaza Blvd, Baton Rouge, LA 70809); 225-925-4704, 225-925-4726-Fax; 8AM-4:30PM.

www.sos.louisiana.gov

Fictitious Names and Assumed Names are found at the parish level.

Records are available from mid-1800s. New records are available for inquiry immediately. Records are indexed on microfilm, inhouse computer, index cards, on-line.

Searching: Include the following in your request-full name of business. In addition to the articles of incorporation, corporation records include the following information: Annual Reports, Officers, Directors, Prior (merged) names, Inactive names, and Reserved names.

Access by: mail, phone, fax, in person, online.

Fee & Payment: The search fee is $1.00. Copies cost $15.00 without amendments and $25.00 with amendments and $10.00 plus a fee of $.25 per page after 40 pages for specific query searches on computer. Fee payee: Secretary of State. Prepayment required. Personal checks accepted. Major credit cards accepted.

Mail search: Turnaround time: 5 to 10 working days. No SASE is required.

Phone search: You may call for information; however, only limited information is available.

Fax search: There is an additional $1.00 per page fee if returned by fax. Turnaround time is 5 to 10 working days.

In person search: There is a free public access terminal.

Online search: There are 2 ways to go: free on the Internet or pay. To view limited information on the website, go to "Commercial Division, Corporations Section," then "Search Corporations Database." The pay system is $360 per year for unlimited access. Almost any communications software will work. The system is open from 6:30 am to 11pm. For more information, call Carolyn Vogelaar at 225-925-4792.

Other access: This agency offers corporation, LLC, partnership, and trademark information on tape cartridges. For more info, call 225-925-4792.

Expedited service: Expedited service is available for mail and phone searches. Turnaround time: 1 day. Add $30.00 per business name.

Uniform Commercial Code

Secretary of State, UCC Records, PO Box 94125, Baton Rouge, LA 70804-9125; 800-256-3758, 225-342-7011-Fax; 8AM-4:30PM.

www.sos.louisiana.gov/comm/ucc/ucc-index.htm

The statewide index of UCC filings is available in each parish office. All tax liens and financial statements are filed at the parish level. IRS liens show up on UCC records. Records CANNOT be obtained from this office, except via the online system.

Records are available for all active listings. Records are indexed on computer since 1990. It takes 2 days before new records are available for inquiry. Records are normally destroyed after 1 year after lapse date.

Searching: All filing information including debtor names, property descriptions, and subsequent filings are available. Mail-in requests are sent to any parish, as all searches reflect statewide information.

Access by: online.

Fee & Payment: Fees are only for the online service. Fee payee: Secretary of State. Prepayment required. The payment information outlined here applies only to online access. Personal checks accepted. Credit cards accepted: MasterCard, Visa.

Online search: An annual $400 fee gives unlimited access to UCC filing informationon at Direct Access. This dial-up service is open from 6:30 AM to 11 PM daily. Most any software communications program can be configured to work. For further information, call Carolyn Vogelaar at 225-925-4792, or e-mail cvogelaar@sos.louisiana.gov or visit the website.

Federal and State Tax Liens

Records not maintained by a state level agency.

Records are filed with the Clerk of Court at the parish level.

Sales Tax Registrations

Access to Records is Restricted.

Revenue Department, Taxpayer Services Division, PO Box 201, Baton Rouge, LA 70821-0201 (Courier address: 617 N 3rd St, Baton Rouge, LA 70802); 225-219-7356, 225-219-2210-Fax; 8AM-4:30PM.

http://revenue.louisiana.gov

This agency will confirm is an entity has a sales tax permit. It will only provide registration information to the registrant itself.

Birth Certificates

Vital Records Registry, Office of Public Health, PO Box 60630, New Orleans, LA 70160 (Courier address: 325 Loyola Ave Room 102, New Orleans, LA 70112); 504-568-5152, 504-568-8353, 800-454-9570, 877-605-8562 (VitalChek), 866-761-1855-Fax; 8AM-4PM.

www.oph.dhh.state.la.us/recordsstatistics/vitalrecords

Some certificates (all types of vital records) contain information at the bottom of the document that is confidential and not released to anyone. This information is used for statistical purposes and varies depending on legislative action.

Records are available from 1915 on. Birth records for only the City of New Orleans are available for 100 years. Records older than 100 years should be ordered from the State Archives. New records are available for inquiry immediately. Records are indexed on microfiche, index cards, inhouse computer.

Searching: Birth certificates are considered confidential for 100 years. Requesters must be related to the person of record or have a signed release. Include the following in your request-full name, names of parents, mother's maiden name, date of birth, place of birth, relationship to person of record, reason for information request. Older records must be searched at the State Archives 225-922-1184.

Access by: mail, phone, fax, in person, online.

Fee & Payment: A "long form" birth certificate is $15.00, while a "birth card" is $9.00. Fee payee: Vital Records Registry. Prepayment required. Credit cards are not accepted for mail requests. Personal checks accepted. Credit cards accepted: MasterCard, Visa.

Mail search: Turnaround time: 4-6 weeks. No SASE is required.

Phone search: Use the VitalChek number above.

Fax search: Fax requests accepted, use of credit card required.

In person search: Photo ID required, turnaround time immediate.

Online search: Orders can be placed online at www.vitalchek.com, a state-appoved vendor.

Expedited service: If ordered from state, based on only an urgent need basis. You must provide documentation of the emergency with plane tickets, verifications of reservations, or official letters requesting documents by a specific date. A fee of $16.00 is charged for overnight delivery. Phone and online service from vitalchek includes a $12.95 fee for using a credit card. Turnaround time is 10 days via this agency, 2-3 days via www.vitalchek.com

Death Records

Vital Records Registry, Office of Public Health, PO Box 60630, New Orleans, LA 70160 (Courier address: 325 Loyola Ave Room 102, New Orleans, LA 70112); 504-568-5152, 504-568-8353, 800-454-9570, 877-605-8562 (VitalChek), 866-761-1855-Fax; 8AM-4PM.

www.oph.dhh.state.la.us/recordsstatistics/vitalrecords

This agency refers to expedited service as emergency service

Records are available from 1955 on. Records over 50 years old must be obtained from the State Archives. New records are available for inquiry immediately. Records are indexed on microfiche, index cards, inhouse computer.

Searching: Death records are considered confidential for 50 years. Must show how related or have a signed release from immediate family member if for investigative purposes. Include the following in your request-full name, date of death, place of death, relationship to person of record, reason for information request, photo ID. Records older than 50 years must be searched at the State Archives 225-922-1184.

Access by: mail, phone, fax, in person, online.

Fee & Payment: The search fee is $7.00. Fee payee: Department of Vital Records. Prepayment required. Credit cards accepted for fax and in person requests only. Personal checks accepted. Credit cards accepted: MasterCard, Visa.

Mail search: Turnaround time: 4-6 weeks. No SASE is required.

Phone search: Use the VitalChek number above.

Fax search: Fax requests accepted, use of credit card required.

In person search: In person search requires a photo ID. Turnaround time usually 45 minutes.

Online search: Orders can be placed online at www.vitalchek, a state-appoved vendor.

Expedited service: If ordered from state, based on only an urgent need basis. You must provide documentation of the emergency with plane tickets, verifications of reservations, or official letters requesting documents by a specific date. A fee of $16.00 is charged for overnight delivery. Phone and online service from vitalchek includes a $12.95 fee for using a credit card. Turnaround time is 10 days via this agency, 2-3 days via vitalchek.

Marriage Certificates, Divorce Records
Records not maintained by a state level agency.

Only Orleans Parish marriage records are available from 1948 on at the VR Registry for a $5.00 fee, same search criteria as others. Include bride name (maiden), groom and date of marriage. Other marriage & all divorce records are found at parish of event.

Marriage Records older than 50 years are open to the public. Use the VitalChek 877-605-8562 for marriage records in Orleans Parrish only.

Workers' Compensation Records

Department of Labor, Office of Workers' Compensation, PO Box 94040, Baton Rouge, LA 70804-9040 (Courier address: LA Department of Labor, Office of Workers' Compensation, Baton Rouge, LA 70802); 800-201-3457, 225-342-7582-Fax; 8AM-5PM.

www.laworks.net

For partial information, and to determine if a record exists, and if you have the name and SSN, see the Other Access section below.

Records are available from 1983 on an electronic format. Only cases on file are those where the employee lost 7 days or more of work and/or had disputed issues resolved or settlements approved. New records are available for inquiry immediately. Records are indexed on microfilm and an on electronic imaging system. Records are normally destroyed after 10 years.

Searching: Most records are considered confidential. Public records include decisions, awards, or orders in disputed cases. Include the following in your request-claimant name, Social Security Number, date of accident, reason for information request, specific records that you need copies of. Otherwise, signed release required. All record requests must be in writing. The following data is not released: pending records.

Access by: mail, phone, fax, in person.

Fee & Payment: Copies are $.25 per page, $1.00 to certify, there is no fee to search. Fee payee: Workers' Compensation Administrative Fund. Prepayment preferred Cash is not accepted. Personal checks accepted. No credit cards accepted.

Mail search: Turnaround time: 3 days.

Phone search: With a name and SSN (required), you may use the "Easy Call" Interactive Voice Response System at 225-342-8731 for partial public information, especially to determine if a record exists.

Fax search: Records can be requested by fax at no extra fee.

In person search: If you request in person, the turnaround time is shortened only by the mail time.

Other access: With a name and SSN (required), you may use the "Easy Call" Interactive Voice Response System at 225-342-8731 for partial public information, especially to determine if a record exists. Enter 1-4-1-2-2 after the phone answers.

Driver Records

Dept of Public Safety and Corrections, Office of Motor Vehicles, PO Box 64886, Baton Rouge, LA 70896 (Courier address: 109 S Foster Dr, Baton Rouge, LA 70806); 877-368-5463, 225-925-6388, 225-925-6915-Fax; 8AM-4:30PM.

www.expresslane.org

Copies of tickets may be obtained from the address listed above. The fee is $5.00 per document.

Records are available for 3 yrs for moving violations, 10 yrs from DWI conviction date, and 5 or 10 yrs for suspensions. Pre-8/15/01 accidents are displayed 3 yrs from accident date, no fault shown. Accidents after 8/01 shown only if license is suspended. It takes 2 to 3 weeks before new records are available for inquiry. Records are normally destroyed after 3, 5, or 10 years according to the type of violation.

Searching: Casual requesters can obtain driving records with proper release form signed by subject. Include the following in your request-driver's license number, full name, date of birth. It is sometimes helpful to include the race or sex when requesting a record.

Access by: mail, in person, online.

Fee & Payment: The fee for mail-in or walk-in requests is $15.00 per name, if accessed electronically then $6.00. The fee is $5.00 for basic driver license information. Fee payee: Office of Motor Vehicles. Prepayment required. Personal Checks not accepted. Credit cards accepted at web site only.

Mail search: Turnaround time: 10 working days. No SASE is required.

In person search: Walk-in requesters may "view" a record for no charge. Casual requesters must present signed form. The fee is for the hard copy. Records can be requested from the Motor Vehicle Offices in New Orleans, Lake Charles, Monroe, Baton Rouge, Shreveport, or Alexandria.

Online search: There are two methods. The commercial requester, interactive mode is available from 7 AM to 9:30 PM daily. There is a minimum order requirement of 2,000 requests per month. A bond or large deposit is required. Fee is $6.00 per record. For more information, call 225-925-6335. The 2nd method is for individuals to order their own record from the Internet site at www.expresslane.org. The fee is $17.00 and requires a credit card.

Other access: Tape ordering is available for batch delivery. Bulk database sales are available to permissible users.

Vehicle Ownership, Vehicle Identification

Department of Public Safety & Corrections, Office of Motor Vehicles, PO Box 64886, Baton Rouge, LA 70896 (Courier address: 7979 Independence Blvd, Baton Rouge, LA 70806); 225-925-7198, 877-368-5463, 225-925-4256-Fax; 8AM-4PM.

http://omv.dps.state.la.us

Records are available for 7 years. Records are normally destroyed after 7 years.

Searching: Casual requesters can obtain records, but personal information is not released without consent of subject. The agency requires a written request stating the nature of the inquiry. The following data is not released: Social Security Numbers.

Access by: mail.

Fee & Payment: The current fee for VIN, registration, and plate checks is $8.00 to search and $2.00 for certification. Fee payee: Office of Motor Vehicles. Prepayment required. Personal checks accepted. No credit cards accepted.

Mail search: Turnaround time: 2 - 4 weeks. Mail searches require license plate number or vehicle identification number (VIN).

Accident Reports

Louisiana State Police, Traffic Records Unit - A27, PO Box 66614, Baton Rouge, LA 70896 (Courier address: 7919 Independence Blvd, Baton Rouge, LA 70806); 225-925-6157, 225-925-4922-Fax; 8AM-4PM.

www.lsp.org/safety_crash.html

Send questions to ehardin@dps.state.la.us.

Records are available from 1990's to present. It takes 2 to 3 weeks before new records are available for inquiry. Records are normally destroyed after 8 years.

Searching: If photos needed, use same PO Box but attention Photo Lab D-3 or call 225-925-3518. The driver name(s), date of accident and parish are needed when ordering.

Access by: mail, phone, in person.

Fee & Payment: The fee is $7.50 per record. Fee payee: Louisiana State Police. Prepayment required. Personal checks are not accepted. No credit cards accepted.

Mail search: Turnaround time: 10 working days. A SASE is requested.

Phone search: Searching by telephone available for ongoing accounts.

In person search: Turnaround time is while you wait, if personnel not busy.

Vessel Ownership, Vessel Registration

Department of Wildlife & Fisheries, Vessel Records, PO Box 14796, Baton Rouge, LA 70898 (Courier address: 2000 Quail Dr, Baton Rouge, LA 70808); 225-765-2898, 225-763-5421-Fax; 8:15AM-4:15PM.

www.wlf.state.la.us/apps/netgear/page3.asp

Lien information is found at the parish level.

Records are available from 1960 to present. Record are indexed on computer from the 1970s to present. All motorized boats and sailboats over 12 ft must be registered. It takes seconds before new records are available for inquiry.

Searching: The hull ID # is not released. To search, one of the following is required: Louisiana #, name, or hull ID #, and from whom boat was acquired. Records are subject to DPPA and 14 permissible uses. Records not released to the public unless subject has given permission or by subpoena.

Access by: mail, fax.

Fee & Payment: There is no fee.

Mail search: Turnaround time: 7 to 10 days. No SASE is required.

Fax search: Records may be requested by fax.

Voter Registration

Access to Records is Restricted.

Louisiana Secretary of State, Elections Division, PO Box 94125, Baton Rouge, LA 70804-9125 (Courier address: 8549 United Plaza Boulevard, Baton Rouge, LA 70809); 225-922-0900, 225-922-0945-Fax; 8AM-5PM.

www.sos.louisiana.gov/elections/elections-index.htm

Although the information is public record, individual searching must be done at the parish level through the Parish Registrar of Voters. The agency will sell the database statewide or by parish. Media formats include email, labels, CD, and lists. There are no restrictions regarding purchasing for marketing purposes. Email questions to elections@sos.louisiana.gov.

GED Certificates

Div of Family, Career, and Technical Education, PO Box 94064, Baton Rouge, LA 70804-9064; 225-342-0444 (Main Number), 225-219-4439-Fax; 8AM - 4:30PM.

Searching: You may verify a GED. To search, you must use their form, which may be requested via phone, fax, or mail. Include the following in your request-name at time of test, DOB, SSN. If the request is for pre-employment screening purposes, there must be a signed release.

Access by: mail, phone, fax, in person.

Fee & Payment: There is no fee.

Mail search: Turnaround time 2 weeks. No SASE is required.

Phone search: The request must be in writing. The requester may call in for search results after sending.

Fax search: Results of a fax search will be mailed, same criteria as mail searches.

In person search: In person searchers must have a photo ID. Turnaround time: Immediate.

Hunting and Fishing License Information

Access to Records is Restricted.

Wildlife & Fisheries Department, License Division, PO Box 98000, Baton Rouge, LA 70898-9000 (Courier address: 2000 Quail Dr, Baton Rouge, LA 70808); 225-765-2881, 225-765-2887, 225-763-5466-Fax; 8:AM-4:30PM.

www.wlf.state.la.us

All license information is subject to the DPPA under US Code 18. At present, not all 14 permissible uses are readily available and use of a subpoena is suggested.

Louisiana State Licensing Agencies

For details about the agency responsible for licensing/certifying/registering an item below or in the Agency Quick Finder section, match an item's number with the number of the agency in the *Licensing Agency Information* section.

Louisiana Licenses Searchable Online

Acupuncturist #20	www.lsbme.org/verifications.htm
Architect/Architectural Firm #50	www.lastbdarchs.com/roster.htm
Athletic Trainer #20	www.lsbme.org/verifications.htm
Bank #32	www.ofi.state.la.us
Bond For Deed Agency #32	www.ofi.state.la.us
Check Casher #32	www.ofi.state.la.us
Chemical Engineer #40	www.lapels.com/indiv_search.asp
Child Residential Care #35	www.dss.state.la.us/departments/os/child_care_facilities_by_parish.html
Chiropractor #7	www.lachiropracticboard.com/lic-drs.htm
Clinical Lab Personnel #20	www.lsbme.org/verifications.htm
Collection Agency #32	www.ofi.state.la.us
Consumer Credit Grantor #32	www.ofi.state.la.us
Contractor, Commercial/Resident'l #30	www.lslbc.state.la.us/findcontractor.asp
Contractor, General/Subcontractor #41	www.lslbc.state.la.us/findcontractor.asp
Counselor, Professional (LPC) #46	www.lpcboard.org/lpc_alpha_list.htm
Credit Repair Agency #32	www.ofi.state.la.us
Credit Union #32	www.ofi.state.la.us
Day Care Facility #35	www.dss.state.la.us/departments/os/child_care_facilities_by_parish.html
Dental Hygienist #9	www.lsbd.org/DentistSearch.aspx
Dentist #9	www.lsbd.org/DentistSearch.aspx
Dietitian #13	www.lbedn.org/licensee_database.asp
Drug Distributor, Wholesale #64	www.lsbwdd.org
Electrical Engineer #40	www.lapels.com/indiv_search.asp
Emergency Shelter #35	www.dss.state.la.us/departments/os/child_care_facilities_by_parish.html
Engineer/Engineer Intern #40	www.lapels.com/indiv_search.asp
Engineering Firm #40	www.lapels.com/firm_search.asp
Environmental Engineer #40	www.lapels.com/indiv_search.asp
Exercise Physiologist, Clinical #20	www.lsbme.org/verifications.htm
Family Support #35	www.dss.state.la.us/departments/os/child_care_facilities_by_parish.html
Foster Care/Adoption Care #35	www.dss.state.la.us/departments/os/child_care_facilities_by_parish.html
Infant Intervention Service #35	www.dss.state.la.us/departments/os/child_care_facilities_by_parish.html
Insurance Agent, LHA/PC #33	www.ldi.state.la.us/search_forms/searchforms.htm
Insurance Agent/Broker/Producer #33	www.ldi.state.la.us/search_forms/searchforms.htm
Land Surveyor Firm #40	www.lapels.com/firm_search.asp
Land Surveyor/Surveyor Intern #40	www.lapels.com/indiv_search.asp
Lender #32	www.ofi.state.la.us
Lobbyist #31	www.ethics.state.la.us/lobs.htm
Medical Doctor #20	www.lsbme.org/verifications.htm
Midwife #20	www.lsbme.org/verifications.htm
Mortgage Lender/Broker, Resident'l #32	www.ofi.state.la.us/newrml.htm
Notary Public #54	www.sos.louisiana.gov/
Notification Filer #32	www.ofi.state.la.us/newnotif.htm
Nuclear Engineer #40	www.lapels.com/indiv_search.asp
Nutritionist #13	www.lbedn.org/licensee_database.asp
Occupational Therapist/Technolog't #20	www.lsbme.org/verifications.htm
Optometrist #22	www.arbo.org/index.php?action=findanoptometrist
Osteopathic Physician #20	www.lsbme.org/verifications.htm
Pawnbroker #32	www.ofi.state.la.us/newpawn.htm
Pharmacist/Pharmacy/Pharmacy Technican #23	www.labp.com/pbs.html
Pharmacy Interns (College) #23	www.labp.com/pbs.html
Pharmacy/Hospital #23	www.labp.com/pbs.html
Physician Assistant #20	www.lsbme.org/verifications.htm
Podiatrist #20	www.lsbme.org/verifications.htm

Psychologist #15	www.onesimuswebs.com/lsbep_db.asp
Radiologic Technologist, Private #20	www.lsbme.org/verifications.htm
Real Estate Agent/Broker/Sales #60	www.lrec.state.la.us/sblist/csblistmain.asp
Real Estate Appraiser #29	www.lreasbc.state.la.us/dbfiles/appraiserinfo.htm
Respiratory Therapist/Therapy Tech #20	www.lsbme.org/verifications.htm
Savings & Loan #32	www.ofi.state.la.us/newcus.htm
Solicitor #33	www.ldi.state.la.us/search_forms/searchforms.htm
Speech Pathologist/Audiologist #18	www.lbespa.org
Thrift & Loan Company #32	www.ofi.state.la.us/newthrift.htm
Vocational Rehabilitat'n Counselor #63	www.lrcboard.org/licensee_database.asp

Louisiana Licensing Quick Finder

Acupuncturist #20	504-568-6820
Adult Day Care #35	225-022-0015
Adult Education Instructor #42	225-342-3490
Adult Residential Care #35	225-022-0015
Agricultural Consultant #56	225-925-3787
Alarm/Security Company #26	225-272-2310
Alcoholic Beverage Vendor #3	225-925-4041
Amusement Ride/Attraction Inspector #55	225-925-7045
Amusement Ride/Attraction Owner/Operator #55	225-925-7045
Arborist/Utility Arborist #39	225-952-8100
Architect/Architectural Firm #50	225-925-4802
Art Therapist #42	225-342-3490
Athletic Trainer #20	504-568-6820
Attorney #49	800-421-5722
Auctioneer/Auction Company #44	225-922-2329
Bank #32	225-925-4660
Barber/Barber Shop/Instr/School #4	225-925-1701
Boiler Inspector/Installer #55	225-925-4344
Bond For Deed Agency #32	225-925-4660
Boxing/Wrestling Personnel #27	318-362-4529
Burglar Alarm Contractor #55	225-925-6766
Cemetery #2	504-838-5267
Check Casher #32	225-925-4660
Check Seller #32	225-925-4660
Chemical Engineer #40	225-925-6291
Child Nutrition Program Superv'r #42	225-342-3490
Child Residential Care #35	225-022-0015
Chiropractor #7	225-765-2322
Clinical Lab Personnel #20	504-568-6820
Collection Agency #32	225-925-4660
Compulsive Gambler Counselor #28	225-922-7700
Construction Projects, Comm.+50,000 #41	225-765-2301
Consumer Credit Grantor #32	225-925-4667
Contractor, Commercial/Resident'l #30.	504-736-7125
Contractor, General/Subcontr'r #41	225-765-2301
Cosmetologist/Cosmetology Instructor #8	225-756-3404
Counselor, Professional (LPC) #46	225-765-2515
Court Reporter #37	225-342-2668
Credit Repair Agency #32	225-925-4660
Credit Union #32	225-925-4660
Day Care Facility #35	225-922-0015
Dental Hygienist #9	504-568-8574
Dentist #9	504-568-8574
Dietitian #13	225-756-3490
Drug Distributor, Wholesale #64	225-295-8567
Electrical Engineer #40	225-925-6291
Electrologist #10	337-463-6180
Electronics Repairman #34	225-231-4710
Embalmer #12	504-838-5109
Emergency Medical Technician #20	504-568-6820
Emergency Shelter #35	225-922-0015
Engineer/Engineer Intern #40	225-925-6291
Engineering Firm #40	225-925-6291
Environmental Engineer #40	225-925-6291
Equine Dentist #45	225-342-2176
Esthetician #8	225-756-3404
Euthanasia Technician #45	225-342-2176
Exercise Physiologist, Clinical #20	504-568-6820
Explosives Dealer/Handler #38	225-925-6113
Family Support #35	225-022-0015
Fire Alarm Contractor #55	225-925-6766
Fire Extinguisher Contractor #55	225-925-6766
Fire Protection Sprinkler Contr #55	225-925-6766
Fire Suppression Contractor #55	225-925-6766
Florist, Retail/Wholesale #39	225-952-8100
Foster Care/Adoption Care #35	225-922-0015
Funeral Director/Establishment #12	504-838-5109
Funeral Home Internship/Worker #12	504-838-5109
Guidance Counselor #42	225-342-3490
Hearing Aid Dealer #19	318-362-3014
Horse Owner/Trainer #52	504-483-4000
Horse Racing #52	504-483-4000
Horse Racing-related Prof.(Groom, Plater, etc.) #52	504-483-4000
Horticulturist #39	225-952-8100
Infant Intervention Service #35	225-022-0015
Insurance Agent, LHA/PC #33	225-342-0860
Insurance Agent/Broker #33	225-342-0860
Insurance Producer #33	225-342-0860
Interior Designer #14	225-298-1283
Investment Advisor #53	225-925-4660
Jockey/Apprentice/Jockey Agent #52	504-483-4000
Juvenile Detention #35	225-022-0015
Land Surveyor Firm #40	225-925-6291
Land Surveyor/Surveyor Intern #40	225-925-6291
Landscape Architect #39	225-952-8100
Landscape Contractor #39	225-952-8100
Lender #32	225-925-4660
Livestock Branding #43	225-925-3962
Loan Broker #32	225-925-4660
Lobbyist #31	225-763-8777
Lottery #47	225-297-2000
Lottery Claims Center #48	504-889-0031
Manicurist #8	225-756-3404
Massage Therapist #62	225-771-4090
Maternity Home #35	225-922-0015
Medical Doctor #20	504-568-6820
Medical Gas Piping Installer #51	504-826-2382
Midwife #20	504-568-6820
Montessori Teacher #42	225-342-3490
Mortgage Lender/Broker, Residential #32	225-925-4662
Motor Vehicle Agent/Salesman #59	504-838-5207
Motor Vehicle Dealer; New/Used #59	504-838-5207
Motor Vehicle Inspector #1	225-667-1927
Motor Vehicle Leasing/Rental Company #59	504-838-5207
Motor Vehicle Sales Finance Company #59	504-838-5207
Music Therapist #42	225-342-3490
Notary Public #54	225-922-0507
Notification Filer #32	225-992-0634
Nuclear Engineer #40	225-925-6291
Nuclear Medicine Technologist #16	504-838-5231
Nurse (Practical) School #25	504-838-5791
Nurse, PRRN #21	504-838-5332
Nurse, Student #21	504-838-5332
Nurse- RN / LPN #25	504-838-5791
Nurses' Aide #36	225-295-8573
Nursing Home Administrator #36	225-295-8573
Nursing School #21	504-838-5332
Nutritionist #13	225-756-3490
Occupational Therapist/Tech. #20	504-568-6820
Optometrist #22	318-335-2989
Osteopathic Physician #20	504-568-6820
Pari-Mutuel Employee #52	504-483-4000
Pawnbroker #32	225-925-4660
Payday Lender #32	225-925-4660
Personal Care Attendant #35	225-922-0015
Pesticide Applicator #56	225-925-3796
Pesticide Dealer/Operator #56	225-925-3796
Pharmacist/Pharmacy #23	225-925-6496
Pharmacy Interns (College) #23	225-925-6496
Pharmacy Tech #23	225-925-6496
Pharmacy Tech Candidate #23	225-925-6496
Pharmacy/Hospital #23	225-925-6496
Physical Therapist/Therapist Asst #24	337-262-1043
Physician Assistant #20	504-568-6820
Plumber Journeyman/Master #51	504-826-2382
Podiatrist #20	504-568-6820
Polygraph Examiner #57	504-389-3836
Prevention Specialist (social work) #28	225-922-7700
Private Investigator/PI Company #58	225-763-3556
Private Security #26	225-272-2310
Psychologist #15	225-763-3935
Public Accountant-CPA #5	504-566-1244
Radiation Therapy Technologist #16	504-838-5231
Radiographer #16	504-838-5231
Radiologic Technologist #16	504-838-5231
Radiologic Technologist, Private #20	504-568-6820
Reading Specialist #42	225-342-3490
Real Estate Agent/Broker/Sales #60	225-765-0191
Real Estate Appraiser #29	225-765-0191
Real Estate School/Instructor/Educ. Vendor #60	225-765-0191
Respiratory Therapist/Therapy Tech. #20	504-568-6820
Respite Care #35	225-022-0015
Sanitarian #17	225-925-7204
Satellite Technician #34	225-231-4710
Savings & Loan #32	225-925-4660
School Counselor/Librarian/Nurse/Principal #42	225-342-3490
School Psychologist #42	225-342-3490
School Superintendent, Parish or City #42	225-342-3490
School Therapist #42	225-342-3490
Securities Salesperson/Dealer #53	225-925-4660
Security Guard #26	225-272-2310
Shorthand Reporter #37	225-342-2668
Social Worker #6	225-756-3470
Solicitor #33	225-342-0860
Speech Pathologist/Audiologist #18	225-763-5480
Speech/Language/Hearing Teacher #42	225-342-3490
Substance Abuse Counselor #28	225-922-7700
Supervised Independent Living #35	225-022-0015

Teacher, Temporary #42	225-342-3490	
Teacher/Teacher's Aide #11	225-342-5840	
Thrift & Loan Company #32	225-925-4660	
Timeshare Interest Salesperson #60	225-765-0191	
TV-Radio Technician #34	225-231-4710	

Used Vehicle Salesperson #61	225-925-3870
Veterinarian/Veterinary Tech #45	225-342-2176
Vocation Rehabilitation Counselor #63	225-922-1435
Water Supply Piping #51	504-826-2382

Veterinarian/Veterinary Technician #45	225-342-2176
Vocational Rehab. Counselor #63	225-922-1435
Water Supply Piping #51	504-826-2382

Louisiana Licensing Agency Information

1 State Police Safety & Enforcement, 527 Florida Blvd, Denham Springs, LA 70726; 225-667-1927, Fax: 225-667-3726.

2 Cemetery Board, 2901 Ridgelake Dr, #101, Metairie, LA 70002-4946; 504-838-5267, Fax: 504-838-5289.
www.lcb.state.la.us/

3 Board of Alcohol & Tobacco, 8549 United Plaza Blvd, Baton Rouge, LA 70809; 225-925-4041, Fax: 225-925-3975.
www.atc.rev.state.la.us/atcweb/home.htm
Email: info@atcla.com

4 Board of Barber Examiners, PO Box 14029, Baton Rouge, LA 70898-4029; 225-925-1701, Fax: 225-925-1703.

5 Board of Certified Public Accountants, 601 Poydras St, #1770, New Orleans, LA 70130; 504-566-1244, Fax: 504-566-1252.
www.cpaboard.state.la.us/
Email: sitemaster@cpaboard.state.la.us   Note: They do sell lists.

6 Board of Certified Social Work Examiners, 18550 Highland Rd Suite B, Baton Rouge, LA 70809; 225.756.3470, Fax: 225.756.3472.
www.labswe.org
Email: socialwork@labswe.org

7 Board of Chiropractic Examiners, 8621 Summa Ave, Baton Rouge, LA 70809; 225-765-2322, Fax: 225-765-2640.
www.lachiropracticboard.com/lic-drs.htm
Email: lsbce@eatel.net
Search Database at
www.lachiropracticboard.com/lic-drs.htm

8 Board of Cosmetology, 11622 Sunbelt Court, Baton Rouge, LA 70809; 225-756-3404, Fax: 225-756-3410/3109.

9 Board of Dentistry, 365 Canal Street, #2680, New Orleans, LA 70112; 504-568-8574, Fax: 504-568-8598.
www.lsbd.org
Email: carolyn@lsbd.org
Search Database at
http://www.lsbd.org/DentistSearch.aspx Note: Lists of all dentists is sold for $500.00; list of denatal hygienists is also available for $500.00.

10 Board of Electrolysis Examiners, PO Box 67, DeRidder, LA 70637-0067; 337-463-6180, Fax: 318-463-3991.
Email: istatebrdee@aol.com

11 Board of Elementary & Secondary Education, 1201 N 3rd St #5-190, Baton Rouge, LA 70802; 225-342-5840, Fax: 225-342-5843.
www.doe.state.la.us/lde/bese/home.html

12 Board of Embalmers & Funeral Directors, P.O. Box 8757, Metairie, LA 70011; 504-838-5109, Fax: 504-838-5112.
www.lsbefd.state.la.us
Email: labefd@bellsouth.net

13 Board of Examiners of Dietitics & Nutrition, 18550 Highland Rd, Baton Rouge, LA 70809; 225-756-3490, Fax: 225-756-3472.
www.lbedn.org
Email: admin@lbedn.org

14 Board of Examiners of Interior Designers, 2900 Westfork Dr #200, Baton Rouge, LA 70827-0004; 225-298-1283, Fax: 225-298-1284.

15 Board of Examiners of Psychologists, 8280 YMCA Plaza Dr, Bldg 8B, Baton Rouge, LA 70810; 225-763-3935, Fax: 225-763-3968.
www.lsbep.org
Email: lsbep@cmq.net
Search Database at
www.onesimuswebs.com/lsbep_db.asp

16 Board of Examiners of Radiologic Technologists, 3108 Cleary Ave, #207, Metairie, LA 70002; 504-838-5231, Fax: 504-780-1740.
Email: larabrd@bellsouth.net

17 Board of Examiners of Sanitarians, 1772 Wooddale Blvd, Baton Rouge, LA 70806; 225-925-7204, Fax: 225-925-7245.
www.lsbes.org
Email: dkuhns@dhh.state.la.us

18 Board of Examiners of Speech/Language Pathology & Audiology, 18550 Highland Rd Suite B, Baton Rouge, LA 70810; 225-763-3480, Fax: 225-763-3472.
www.lbespa.org/
Email: speech@ibespa.org
Search Database at www.lbespa.org

19 Board of Hearing Aid Dealers, 2200 Justice St, Monroe, LA 71201; 318-362-3014, Fax: 318-362-3019.

20 Executive Director, Board of Medical Examiners, 630 Camp St, New Orleans, LA 70130; 504-568-6820, auto response: dial 1, Fax: 504-568-8893.
www.lsbme.org
Email: lsbmever@lsbme.org
Search Database at
www.lsbme.org/verifications.htm

21 Board of Nursing, 3510 N Causeway Blvd, #601, Metairie, LA 70002; 504-838-5332, Fax: 504-838-5349.
www.lsbn.state.la.us
Email: lsbn@lsbn.state.la.us

22 Board of Optometry Examiners, 115 B N 13th St, Oakdale, LA 71463; 318-335-2989, Fax: 318-335-2989. Email: labor@yahoo.com
Search Database at
www.arbo.org/index.php?action=findanoptometrist

23 Board of Pharmacy, 5615 Corporate Blvd, #8E, Baton Rouge, LA 70808; 225-925-6496, Fax: 225-925-6499. www.labp.com
Email: labp@labp.com
Search Database at www.labp.com/pbs.html

24 Board of Physical Therapy Examiners, 104 Fairlane Dr, Lafayette, LA 70507-5307; 337-262-1043, Fax: 337-262-1054.

www.laptboard.org
Email: lsbpte@iamerica.net

25 Board of Practical Nurse Examiners, 3421 N Causeway Blvd #203, Metairie, LA 70002-3711; 504-838-5791, Fax: 504-838-5279.
www.lsbpne.com

26 Board of Private Security Examiners, 15703 Old Hammond Hwy, Baton Rouge, LA 70816; 225-272-2310, Fax: 225-272-5816.

27 Boxing & Wrestling Commission, PO Box 251, Franklin, LA 70538; 318-362-4529, Fax: 318-362-4628.

28 Board of Certification for Substance Abuse Counselors, 8738 Quarters Lake Rd, Baton Rouge, LA 70809; 225-922-7700, Fax: 225-922-7701.
www.lsbcsac.org
Email: admin@lsbcsac.org

29 Real Estate Commission, Real Estate Appraisers State Board of Certification, 5222 Summa Ct, Baton Rouge, LA 70809-3727; 225-765-0191 (in-state toll-free-800-821-4529, Fax: 225-765-0637.
www.lreasbc.state.la.us
Email: info@lreasbc.state.la.us
Search Database at
www.lreasbc.state.la.us/dbfiles/appraiserinfo.htm

30 Contractors Licensing Board (New Orleans), 1221 Elmwood Pk Blvd, New Orleans, LA 70141; 504-736-7125, Fax: 504-736-7125 *Key.
www.lslbc.state.la.us
Search Database at
www.lslbc.state.la.us/findcontractor.asp

31 Supervisory Committee on Campaign Finance Disclosure, Louisiana Board of Ethics, 2415 Quail Dr #314, Baton Rouge, LA 70808-0110; 225-763-8777; 800-842-6630, Fax: 225-763-8780.
www.ethics.state.la.us
Search Database at
www.ethics.state.la.us/lobs.htm

32 Office of Financial Institutions, 8660 United Plaza Blvd, 2nd Floor, Baton Rouge, LA 70809; 225-925-4660, Fax: 225-925-4548.
www.ofi.state.la.us
Email: ofila@ofi.state.la.us

33 Department of Insurance, Agent's License Division, 1702 N. 3rd Street, Baton Rouge, LA 70802; 225-342-0860, Fax: 225-219-9322.
www.ldi.state.la.us
Search Database at
www.ldi.state.la.us/search_forms/searchforms.htm

34 Radio And Television Technicians Board, 6554 Florida Boulevard #109, Baton Rouge, LA 70806; 225-231-4710, Fax: 225-231-4711.

35 Department of Social Services, Bureau of Licensing, PO Box 3078, Baton Rouge, LA 70821; 225-922-0015, Fax: 225-922-0014.
www.dss.state.la.us

36 Examiners of Nursing Facility Administrators, 5647 Superior Dr, Baton Rouge, LA 70816-6049; 225-295-8573, Fax: 225-295-8574.
Email: kempwright@compuserve.com

37 Examiners of Certified Shorthand Reporters, PO Box 3257, Baton Rouge, LA 70821-3257; 225-342-2668, Fax: 225-342-2698.
Email: courtreporter@lacourtreporterboard.com

38 Explosives Control Unit, PO Box 66614, Mail Stop 21, Baton Rouge, LA 70896; 225-925-6113, Fax: 225-925-4048.
www.lsp.org/tess.html#materials

39 Department of Agriculture, Horticulture Commission, PO Box 3596, Baton Rouge, LA 70821-3596; 225-952-8100, Fax: 225-952-3760.
www.ldaf.state.la.us

40 Professional Engineers & Land Surveying Board, 9643 Brookline Ave #121, Baton Rouge, LA 70809-1433; 225-925-6291, Fax: 225-925-6292.   www.lapels.com
Search Database at www.lapels.com/indiv_search.asp   Note: Will sell list of licensees.

41 Licensing Board for Contractors, PO Box 14419, Baton Rouge, LA 70898-4419; 225-765-2301, Fax: 225-765-2431.
www.lslbc.louisiana.gov
Email: info@lslbc.state.la.us
Search Database at www.lslbc.louisiana.gov

42 Department of Education, Licensing Bureau of Higher Education Certification, 626 N 4th St, Baton Rouge, LA 70804-9064; 225-342-3490, Fax: 225-342-3499.
www.doe.state.la.us

43 LA Dept of Agriculture & Forestry, Livestock Brand Commission, PO Box 1951 (5825 Florida Blvd, 70806), Baton Rouge, LA 70821; 225-925-3962, Fax: 225-925-4103.
www.ldaf.state.la.us
Email: linfo@ldaf.state.la.us

44 Auctioneers Licensing Board, 8017 Jefferson Hwy, #A-2, Baton Rouge, LA 70809; 225-922-2329, Fax: 225-925-1892.
www.lalb.org/
Email: auctionboard@eatel.net

45 Board of Veterinary Medicine, 263 3rd St, #104, Baton Rouge, LA 70801; 225-342-2176, Fax: 225-342-2142.
www.lsbvm.org
Email: lbvm@eatel.net   Note: They do sell lists.

46 Licensed Professional Counselors, Board of Examiners, 8631 Summa Ave, #A, Baton Rouge, LA 70809; 225-765-2515, Fax: 225-765-2514.
www.lpcboard.org
Email: lpcboard@eatel.net
Search Database at www.lpcboard.org/lpc_alpha_list.htm

47 Lottery Corporation, State Headquarters, 555 Laurel St., Baton Rouge, LA 70801; 225-297-2000, Fax: 225-297-2005.
www.lalottery.com

48 Lottery Corporation, 2222 Clearview Parkway, Metairie, LA 70001; 504-889-0031, Fax: 504-889-0490.
www.louisianalottery.com

49 State Bar Association, 601 St Charles Av, New Orleans, LA 70130; 800-421-5722, Fax: 504-566-0930.
www.lsba.org
Email: lsbainfo@lsba.org

50 Board of Architectural Examiners, 9625 Fenway Ave #B, Baton Rouge, LA 70809-1413; 225-925-4802, Fax: 225-925-4804.
www.lastbdarchs.com
Email: bd@lsbae.brcoxmail.com
Search Database at www.lastbdarchs.com/roster.htm

51 Plumbing Board, 2714 Canal St, #512, New Orleans, LA 70119; 504-826-2382, Fax: 504-826-2175.

52 Louisiana State Racing Commission, 320 N Carrollton Ave, #2B, New Orleans, LA 70119-5100; 504-483-4000, Fax: 504-483-4898.
http://horseracing.la.gov/
Email: webmaster@lre.state.la.us

53 Securities Division, Office of Financial Institutions, PO Box 94095 (8660 United Plaza Blvd, 2nd Fl), Baton Rouge, LA 70804; 225-925-4660, Fax: 225-925-4548.
www.ofi.state.la.us

54 Office of Secretary of State, PO Box 94125, Baton Rouge, LA 70804-9125; 225-922-0507, Fax: 225-922-0945.
www.sos.louisiana.gov/notary-pub/notary-index.htm
Email: notaries@sos.louisiana.gov
Search Database at www.sos.louisiana.gov/

55 Office of the State Fire Marshall, 8181 Independence Blvd, Baton Rouge, LA 70806; 225-925-4911; 800-256-5452, Fax: 225-925-3813.
www.dps.state.la.us/sfm

56 Agricultural & Environmental Sciences, Pest Control Commission, PO Box 3596 (5825 Florida Blvd), Baton Rouge, LA 70821; 225-925-3796, Fax: 225-925-3760.
www.ldaf.state.la.us/divisions/aes/default.asp
Email: info@ldaf.state.la.us

57 Baton Rouge Police Dept., Polygraph Board, PO Box 2406, Baton Rouge, LA 70821; 504-389-3836.

58 Board of Private Investigators Examiners, 2051 Silverside Dr. #190, Baton Rouge, LA 70808; 225-763-3556, Fax: 225-763-3536.
www.lsbpie.com/
Email: lsbpie@intersurf.com

59 Motor Vehicle Commission, 3519 12th Street, Metairie, LA 70002-3427; 504-838-5207.
www.lmvc.state.la.us/

60 Real Estate Commission, P.O. Box 14785 (5222 Summa Court), Baton Rouge, LA 70898-4785; 225-765-0191 (in-state toll-free 800-821-4529), Fax: 225-765-0637.
www.lrec.state.la.us
Email: mplunket@lrec.state.la.us
Search Database at www.lrec.state.la.us/sblist/csblistmain.asp

61 Used Motor Vehicle & Parts Commission, 3132 Valley Creek Drive, Baton Rouge, LA 70808; 225-925-3870, Fax: 225-925-3869.

62 Professional Licensing Boards, Board of Massage Therapy, 12022 Plank Road, Baton Rouge, LA 70811; 225-771-4090, Fax: 225-771-4021.
www.lsbmt.org
Email: lsbmt@eatel.net

63 Board of Examiners, Board of Vocational Rehabilitation Counselors, PO Box 41594, Baton Rouge, LA 70835; 225-922-1435, Fax: 225-922-1352.
www.lrcboard.org
Email: lrcboard@eatel.net

64 Board of Wholesale Drug Distributors, 12046 Justice Ave, #C, Baton Rouge, LA 70816; 225-295-8567, Fax: 225-295-8568.
www.lsbwdd.org
Email: lsbwdd@bellsouth.net
Search Database at www.lsbwdd.org

Louisiana Federal Courts

The following list indicates the district and division name for each Parish in the state. If the bankruptcy court location is different from the district court, then the location of the bankruptcy court appears in parentheses.

Louisiana Parish/Court Cross Reference

Parish	District	Division
Acadia Parish	Western	Lafayette (Lafayette-Opelousas)
Allen Parish	Western	Lake Charles
Ascension Parish	Middle	Baton Rouge
Assumption Parish	Eastern	New Orleans
Avoyelles Parish	Western	Alexandria
Beauregard Parish	Western	Lake Charles
Bienville Parish	Western	Shreveport
Bossier Parish	Western	Shreveport
Caddo Parish	Western	Shreveport
Calcasieu Parish	Western	Lake Charles
Caldwell Parish	Western	Monroe
Cameron Parish	Western	Lake Charles
Catahoula Parish	Western	Alexandria
Claiborne Parish	Western	Shreveport
Concordia Parish	Western	Alexandria
De Soto Parish	Western	Shreveport
East Baton Rouge Parish	Parish	Middle Baton Rouge
East Carroll Parish	Western	Monroe
East Feliciana Parish	Middle	Baton Rouge
Evangeline Parish	Western	Lafayette (Lafayette-Opelousas)
Franklin Parish	Western	Monroe
Grant Parish	Western	Alexandria
Iberia Parish	Western	Lafayette (Lafayette-Opelousas)
Iberville Parish	Middle	Baton Rouge
Jackson Parish	Western	Monroe
Jefferson Davis Parish	Western	Lake Charles
Jefferson Parish	Eastern	New Orleans
La Salle Parish	Western	Alexandria
Lafayette Parish	Western	Lafayette (Lafayette-Opelousas)
Lafourche Parish	Eastern	New Orleans
Lincoln Parish	Western	Monroe
Livingston Parish	Middle	Baton Rouge
Madison Parish	Western	Monroe
Morehouse Parish	Western	Monroe
Natchitoches Parish	Western	Alexandria
Orleans Parish	Eastern	New Orleans
Ouachita Parish	Western	Monroe
Plaquemines Parish	Eastern	New Orleans
Pointe Coupee Parish	Middle	Baton Rouge
Rapides Parish	Western	Alexandria
Red River Parish	Western	Shreveport
Richland Parish	Western	Monroe
Sabine Parish	Western	Shreveport
St. Bernard Parish	Eastern	New Orleans
St. Charles Parish	Eastern	New Orleans
St. Helena Parish	Middle	Baton Rouge
St. James Parish	Eastern	New Orleans
St. John the Baptist Parish	Parish	EasternNew Orleans
St. Landry Parish	Western	Lafayette (Lafayette-Opelousas)
St. Martin Parish	Western	Lafayette (Lafayette-Opelousas)
St. Mary Parish	Western	Lafayette (Lafayette-Opelousas)
St. Tammany Parish	Eastern	New Orleans
Tangipahoa Parish	Eastern	New Orleans
Tensas Parish	Western	Monroe
Terrebonne Parish	Eastern	New Orleans
Union Parish	Western	Monroe
Vermilion Parish	Western	Lafayette (Lafayette-Opelousas)
Vernon Parish	Western	Alexandria
Washington Parish	Eastern	New Orleans
Webster Parish	Western	Shreveport
West Baton Rouge Parish	Parish	Middle Baton Rouge
West Carroll Parish	Western	Monroe
West Feliciana Parish	Middle	Baton Rouge
Winn Parish	Western	Alexandria

Standards for Federal Courts: Search fee is $26.00 per item (one party name or case number). Copy fee is $.50 per page. Certification fee is $9.00 per document, double for exemplification, if available. All fees standard unless noted in profile. Mail Search: always enclose a stamped self addressed envelope unless otherwise noted. Most courts accept fax requests or will suggest a copying/search vendor. Before releasing records, all courts require prepayment, unless noted.

Open records are located at the court unless otherwise noted. District courts index by defendant and plaintiff as well as by case number. Bankruptcy courts usually index by debtor and case number. While most courts now have their indexes on computer, many may still maintain index card files as well.

Courts offering internet access via CM-ECF or older RACER, PACER, or Web-PACER systems charge $.08 per page fee unless noted as free. Where PACER is available, the universal sign-up number is 800-676-6856. Find PACER and the US Party/Case Index at http://pacer.psc.uscourts.gov.

US District Court

Eastern District of Louisiana

New Orleans Division Clerk of Court, 500 Poydras St, New Orleans, LA 70130 (also use mail address for courier delivery), 504-589-7600, records rm- 504-589-7671, Fax-504-589-7699. Hours- 8:30AM-5PM. www.laed.uscourts.gov

Parishes: Assumption Parish, Jefferson Parish, Lafourche Parish, Orleans Parish, Plaquemines Parish, St. Bernard Parish, St. Charles Parish, St. James Parish, St. John the Baptist Parish, St. Tammany Parish, Tangipahoa Parish, Terrebonne Parish, Washington Parish.

Searches & Indexing: Results do not include SSN or DOB. Both computer and card indexes maintained. New cases in the index 1-2 days after filing date. Records purged every 6 months.

Fee & Payment: Pay by money order, cashier's or personal check. Payee: Clerk, US District Court. Prepayment required.

Phone Search: Only docket information is available by phone.

Mail Search: search usually completed- 3-5 days. Include SASE for return.

In Person Search: Fee charged if court performs your search. No self-serve copier available.

E-Services: ECF replaces PACER. Document images available. PACER records go back to 1989. New records online after 1 day. ECF at https://ecf.laed.uscourts.gov

US Bankruptcy Court

Eastern District of Louisiana

New Orleans Division Clerk of Court, 500 Poydras St, B-601, New Orleans, LA 70130 (use mail address for courier delivery), 504-589-7878. Hours- 8:30AM-5PM. www.laeb.uscourts.gov

Parishes: Assumption Parish, Jefferson Parish, Lafourche Parish, Orleans Parish, Plaquemines Parish, St. Bernard Parish, St. Charles Parish, St. James Parish, St. John the Baptist Parish, St. Tammany Parish, Tangipahoa Parish, Terrebonne Parish, Washington Parish.

Searches & Indexing: Results do not include SSN or DOB. Both computer and card indexes maintained. Old records also indexed on microfiche. New cases in the index immediately after filing date. District-wide searches available here back to 11/1985 on computer and 1979 to 1985 on card index.

Fee & Payment: Pay by money order, cashier check, business check. No personal checks from debtors accepted. Payee: Clerk, US Bankruptcy Court. Prepayment required.

Phone Search: Information is available from 8:30AM-5PM via phone, without fee for case status information. Only docket data is released. Voice Case Information Service available, call VCIS at 504-589-7879.

Mail Search: search usually completed- same day if possible. Include SASE for return.

In Person Search: Fee charged if court performs your search. No self-serve copier available.

E-Services: ECF replaces PACER whose records did go back to 1985. ECF at https://ecf.laeb.uscourts.gov **Opinions Online:** www.laeb.uscourts.gov/Opinions/Opinions.htm.

US District Court

Middle District of Louisiana

Baton Rouge Division Court Clerk, PO Box 2630, Baton Rouge, LA 70821-2630 (courier address: 777 Florida St., #139, Baton Rouge, LA 70801), 225-389-3500, Fax-225-389-3501. Hours- 8AM-5PM. www.lamd.uscourts.gov

Parishes: Ascension Parish, East Baton Rouge Parish, East Feliciana Parish, Iberville Parish, Livingston Parish, Pointe Coupee Parish, St. Helena Parish, West Baton Rouge Parish, West Feliciana Parish.

Searches & Indexing: Results do not include SSN or DOB. Computer index back to 1998 maintained. Index prior to 1992 on microfiche and computer. New cases in the index immediately after filing date.

Fee & Payment: Pay by Visa/MC, money order, cashier check, business check. No personal checks. Payee: Clerk, US District Court. Prepayment required.

Phone Search: Only docket information is available by phone. If information is at the Federal Records Center, this court will give instructions.

Mail Search: search usually completed- 2-3 days. SASE not required.

In Person Search: Fee charged if court performs your search. Self-serve copier - $.25 per page.

E-Services: ECF replaces PACER. Document images available. PACER records go back to 10/1993. New records online after 1 day. ECF at https://ecf.lamd.uscourts.gov **Opinions Online:** www.lamd.uscourts.gov.

US Bankruptcy Court

Middle District of Louisiana

Baton Rouge Division Court Clerk, Rm 119, 707 Florida St, Baton Rouge, LA 70801 (also use mail address for courier delivery), 225-389-0211, Fax-229-389-0410. Hours- 8:30AM-4:30PM. www.lamb.uscourts.gov

Parishes: Ascension Parish, East Baton Rouge Parish, East Feliciana Parish, Iberville Parish, Livingston Parish, Pointe Coupee Parish, St. Helena Parish, West Baton Rouge Parish, West Feliciana Parish.

Searches & Indexing: Cases indexed by debtor, creditors, and case number. Results do not include SSN or DOB. Computer index maintained. New cases in the index immediately after filing date.

Fee & Payment: Pay by money order, cashier check, business check. No personal checks. Payee: Clerk, US Bankruptcy Court. Prepayment required.

Phone Search: Only docket information is available by phone. Voice Case Information Service available, call VCIS at 225-382-2175.

Mail Search: search usually completed- 1 week. Include SASE for return.

In Person Search: Fee charged if court performs your search. Self-serve copier - $.25 per page.

E-Services: ECF replaces PACER whose records did go back to 5/15/1992. New records online after 1 day. ECF at https://ecf.lamb.uscourts.gov **Opinions Online:** www.lamb.uscourts.gov/opinions.htm.

US District Court

Western District of Louisiana

Alexandria Division Court Clerk, PO Box 1269, Alexandria, LA 71309 (courier address: 515 Murray, Alexandria, LA 71301), 318-473-7415, records rm- 318-676-4273, crim dockets- 318-676-4272, civil dockets- 318-676-4273, Fax-318-473-7345. Hours- 8AM-12, 1-5PM. www.lawd.uscourts.gov

Parishes: Avoyelles Parish, Catahoula Parish, Concordia Parish, Grant Parish, La Salle Parish, Natchitoches Parish, Rapides Parish, Winn Parish.

Searches & Indexing: Results do not include SSN or DOB. Computer index maintained. New cases in the index 3 days after filing date. Records purged as deemed necessary.

Fee & Payment: Pay by money order, cashier's or personal check. Payee: Clerk, US District Court. Prepayment required.

Phone Search: Only docket information is available by phone.

Mail Search: search usually completed- 1-2 days. Include SASE for return.

In Person Search: Fee charged if court performs your search. No self-serve copier available.

E-Services: ECF replaces PACER. Document images available. PACER records go back to 10/1993. ECF at https://ecf.lawd.uscourts.gov

Lafayette Division Court Clerk, 800 Lafayette St #2100, Lafayette, LA 70501 (also use mail address for courier delivery), 337-593-5000. Hours- 8AM-4:30PM. www.lawd.uscourts.gov

Parishes: Acadia Parish, Evangeline Parish, Iberia Parish, Lafayette Parish, St. Landry Parish, St. Martin Parish, St. Mary Parish, Vermilion Parish.

Searches & Indexing: Results do not include SSN or DOB. Computer index maintained. New cases in the index 1 day after filing date. Records purged as deemed necessary.

Fee & Payment: Pay by money order, cashier's, business or personal check. Payee: Clerk, US District Court. Prepayment required.

Phone Search: Only docket information is available by phone.

Mail Search: Certified name searches only performed from the Shreveport office. SASE not required.

In Person Search: permitted. Certified name searches only available at Shreveport office. No self-serve copier available.

E-Services: ECF replaces PACER. Document images available. PACER records go back to 10/1993. ECF at https://ecf.lawd.uscourts.gov

Lake Charles Division Court Clerk, 611 Broad St, Suite 188, Lake Charles, LA 70601 (use mail address for courier delivery), 337-437-3870. Hours- 8AM-4:30PM. www.lawd.uscourts.gov

Parishes: Allen Parish, Beauregard Parish, Calcasieu Parish, Cameron Parish, Jefferson Davis Parish, Vernon Parish.

Searches & Indexing: Results do not include SSN or DOB. Computer index maintained. New cases in the index 3 days after filing date. Records purged as deemed necessary.

Fee & Payment: Pay by money order, cashier's, business or personal check. Payee: Clerk, US District Court. Prepayment required.

Phone Search: Only docket information is available by phone.

Mail Search: search usually completed- 1-2 days. Include SASE for return.

In Person Search: Fee charged if court performs your search. No self-serve copier available.

E-Services: ECF replaces PACER. Document images available. PACER records go back to 10/1993. ECF at https://ecf.lawd.uscourts.gov

Monroe Division Court Clerk, PO Drawer 3087, Monroe, LA 71210 (courier address: Rm 215, 201 Jackson St, Monroe, LA 71201), 318-322-6740. Hours- 8AM-12, 1-4:30PM. www.lawd.uscourts.gov

Parishes: Caldwell Parish, East Carroll Parish, Franklin Parish, Jackson Parish, Lincoln Parish, Madison Parish, Morehouse Parish, Ouachita Parish, Richland Parish, Tensas Parish, Union Parish, West Carroll Parish.

Searches & Indexing: Division without a judge since 1996 and may not get one - very few case records held here any longer; search at Shreveport Division. Shreveport computerized index used for searching. Results do not include SSN or DOB. Computer index maintained. New cases in the index 3 days after filing date. Records purged as deemed necessary.

Fee & Payment: Pay by money order, cashier's, business or personal check. Payee: Clerk, US District Court. Prepayment required.

Phone Search: Only docket information is available by phone.

Mail Search: search usually completed- 1-2 days. Include SASE for return.

In Person Search: Fee charged if court performs your search. No self-serve copier available.

E-Services: ECF replaces PACER. Document images available. PACER records go back to 10/1993. ECF at https://ecf.lawd.uscourts.gov

Shreveport Division
Court Clerk, US Courthouse, Suite 1167, 300 Fannin St, Shreveport, LA 71101-3083 (also use mail address for courier delivery), 318-676-4273. Hours- 8AM-5PM. www.lawd.uscourts.gov

Parishes: Bienville Parish, Bossier Parish, Caddo Parish, Claiborne Parish, De Soto Parish, Red River Parish, Sabine Parish, Webster Parish.

Searches & Indexing: Results do not include SSN or DOB. Computer index back to 1990 maintained. Computer index for cases filed back to 1977. Copies of closed records pre-1977 available on microfiche. New cases in the index immediately after filing date. Records purged as deemed necessary.

Fee & Payment: Pay by money order, cashier check, business check. No personal checks. Payee: Clerk, US District Court. Prepayment required.

Phone Search: Only docket information is available by phone. If information is at the Federal Records Center, this court will give instructions.

Mail Search: search usually completed- 1-2 days. SASE not required.

In Person Search: Fee charged if court performs your search. No self-serve copier available.

E-Services: ECF replaces PACER. Document images available. PACER records go back to 10/1993. ECF at https://ecf.lawd.uscourts.gov

US Bankruptcy Court
Western District of Louisiana

Alexandria Division
Court Clerk, 300 Jackson St, Suite 116, Hemenway Bldg, Alexandria, LA 71301-8357 (also use mail address for courier delivery), 318-445-1890, records rm- 318-445-1890. Hours- 8AM-5PM. www.lawb.uscourts.gov

Parishes: Avoyelles Parish, Catahoula Parish, Concordia Parish, Grant Parish, La Salle Parish, Natchitoches Parish, Rapides Parish, Vernon Parish, Winn Parish.

Searches & Indexing: Chapter 7 and 11 cases from the Monroe Division now at this court. Chapter 12 and Chapter 13 continue to be handled by Shreveport. Results include last 4 SSN digits only. Computer index maintained. New cases in the index 1 day after filing date.

Fee & Payment: Pay by money order, cashier's or personal check. Payee: Clerk, US Bankruptcy Court or copy service.

Phone Search: Only docket information is available by phone. Voice Case Information Service available, call VCIS at 800-326-4026 or 318-676-4234.

Mail Search: search usually completed- 5 days. SASE not required.

In Person Search: Fee charged if court performs your search. A copy service will also do search and make copies for fee plus cost of postage; copy service will bill law firms. No self-serve copier available.

E-Services: ECF replaces PACER. Document images available. PACER records go back to 1992. New records online after 1 day. ECF at https://ecf.lawb.uscourts.gov **Opinions Online:** www.lawb.uscourts.gov.

Lafayette-Opelousas Division
Court Clerk, 214 Jefferson St #100, Lafayette, LA 70501-7050 (also use mail address for courier delivery), 337-262-6800, Fax-337-262-6788. Hours- 8AM-5PM. www.lawb.uscourts.gov

Parishes: Acadia Parish, Evangeline Parish, Iberia Parish, Lafayette Parish, St. Landry Parish, St. Martin Parish, St. Mary Parish, Vermilion Parish.

Searches & Indexing: Office also handles case records for Lake Charles Division. Results include last 4 SSN digits only. Both computer and card indexes maintained. Pre-1987 files on index cards; records also on microfiche. New cases in the index 1 day after filing date. District-wide searches available here back to 1/1986.

Fee & Payment: Pay by money order, cashier check, business check. No personal checks. Payee: Clerk, US Bankruptcy Court. Prepayment required. Will fax back to toll-free numbers.

Phone Search: Only docket information is available by phone. Voice Case Information Service available, call VCIS at 800-326-4026 or 318-676-4234.

Mail Search: search usually completed- immediately. SASE not required.

In Person Search: Fee charged if court performs your search. Court personnel will assist searchers at no charge. No self-serve copier available.

E-Services: ECF replaces PACER whose records did go back to 1992. New records online after 1 day. ECF at https://ecf.lawb.uscourts.gov **Opinions Online:** www.lawb.uscourts.gov.

Lake Charles Division
Court Clerk, c/o Lafayette-Opelousas Division, 214 Jefferson St #100, Lafayette, LA 70501-7050 (also use mail address for courier delivery), 337-262-6800. Hours- 8AM-5PM. www.lawb.uscourts.gov

Parishes: Allen Parish, Beauregard Parish, Calcasieu Parish, Cameron Parish, Jefferson Davis Parish.

Searches & Indexing: Cases indexed by and case number. Results include last 4 SSN digits only.

Fee & Payment: Pay by money order or cashier's check.

Phone Search: No searching by telephone.

In Person Search: Fee charged if court performs your search.

E-Services: PACER online at http://pacer.lawb.uscourts.gov. Document images available. PACER records go back to 1992. New records online after 1 day. ECF at https://ecf.lawb.uscourts.gov **Opinions Online:** www.lawb.uscourts.gov.

Monroe Division
c/o Shreveport Division, Suite 2201, 300 Fannin St, Shreveport, LA 71101 (also use mail address for courier delivery), 318-676-4267, Fax-318-676-3699. Hours- 8AM-5PM. www.lawb.uscourts.gov

Parishes: Caldwell Parish, East Carroll Parish, Franklin Parish, Jackson Parish, Lincoln Parish, Madison Parish, Morehouse Parish, Ouachita Parish, Richland Parish, Tensas Parish, Union Parish, West Carroll Parish.

Searches & Indexing: Monroe court is unmanned; cases housed as follows: Chapter 7 and Chapter 11 cases to Alexandria; Chapter 12 and Chapter 13 cases to Shreveport. Results include last 4 SSN digits only. New cases in the index immediately after filing date. Open records located at Shreveport Division.

Fee & Payment: Pay by no business or personal checks accepted. Payee: Clerk, US Bankruptcy Court.

Phone Search: Voice Case Information Service available, call 800-326-4026 or 318-676-4234.

Mail Search: Include SASE for return.

In Person Search: permitted. No self-serve copier available.

E-Services: ECF replaces PACER whose records did go back to 1992. New records online after 1 day. ECF at https://ecf.lawb.uscourts.gov **Opinions Online:** www.lawb.uscourts.gov.

Shreveport Division
Court Clerk, Suite 2201, 300 Fannin St, Shreveport, LA 71101-3089 (also use mail address for courier delivery), 318-676-4267, Fax-318-676-3699. Hours- 8AM-5PM. www.lawb.uscourts.gov

Parishes: Bienville Parish, Bossier Parish, Caddo Parish, Claiborne Parish, De Soto Parish, Red River Parish, Sabine Parish, Webster Parish.

Searches & Indexing: Results include last 4 SSN digits only. Computer index maintained. New cases in the index immediately after filing date.

Fee & Payment: Pay by money order, business check. No personal or debtor's checks accepted. Payee: Clerk, US Bankruptcy Court. Prepayment required.

Phone Search: Voice Case Information Service available, call VCIS at 800-326-4026 or 318-676-4234.

Mail Search: search usually completed- 24 hours. Include SASE for return.

In Person Search: Fee charged if court performs your search. No self-serve copier available.

E-Services: ECF replaces PACER whose records did go back to 1992. New records online after 1 day. ECF at https://ecf.lawb.uscourts.gov **Opinions Online:** www.lawb.uscourts.gov.

Louisiana Parish Courts

Court	Jurisdiction	No. of Courts	How Organized
District Courts*	General	65	42 Districts
City Courts*	Limited	50	City Boundaries
Parish Courts	Limited	3	
Justice of the Peace Courts	Municipal	390	
Mayor's Courts	Municipal	250	
Family Court	Special	1	East Baton Rouge
Juvenile Courts	Special	5	

* Profiled in this Sourcebook.

Court	CIVIL								
	Tort	Contract	Real Estate	Min. Claim	Max. Claim	Small Claims	Estate	Eviction	Domestic Relations
District Courts*	X	X	X	$0	No Max		X		X
City Courts*	X	X	X	$0	$15,000	$3000			X
Parish Courts	X	X	X	$0	$10,000	$3000		X	X
Justice of the Peace Courts	X	X	X	$0	$3000	$3000		X	
Family Court									X
Juvenile Courts									X

Court	CRIMINAL				
	Felony	Misdemeanor	DWI/DUI	Preliminary Hearing	Juvenile
District Courts*	X	X	X		X
City Courts*		X	X	X	X
Parish Courts		X	X	X	X
Justice of the Peace Courts					
Mayor's Courts					
Family Court					X
Juvenile Courts					X

ADMINISTRATION   Judicial Administrator, Judicial Council of the Supreme Court, 400 Royal Street, Suite 1190, New Orleans, LA, 70130; 504-310-2550, Fax: 504-310-2587; www.lasc.org

COURT STRUCTURE   The trial court of general jurisdiction in Louisiana is the district court. A District Court Clerk in each Parish holds all the records for that Parish. Each Parish has its own clerk and courthouse. City courts are courts of record and generally exercise concurrent jurisdiction with the district court in civil cases where the amount in controversy does not exceed $15,000. In criminal matters, they generally have jurisdiction over ordinance violations and misdemeanor violations of state law. City judges also handle a large number of traffic cases. Parish courts exercise jurisdiction in civil cases worth up to $10,000 and criminal cases punishable by fines of $1,000 or less, or imprisonment of six months or less. Cases are appealable from the parish courts directly to the courts of appeal. A municipality may have a Mayor's Court; the mayor may hold trials, but nothing over $30.00, and there are no records.

ONLINE ACCESS   The online computer system, Case Management Information System (CMIS), is operating and development is continuing. It is for internal use only; there is no plan to permit online public access. However, Supreme Court and Appellate opinions are currently available.

There are a number of Parishes that offer a means of remote online access to the public.

Acadia Parish

15th District Court PO Box 922, Crowley, LA 70527; phone: 337-788-8881; fax: 337-788-1048; hours 8:30AM-4:30PM (CST). *Felony, Misdemeanor, Civil, Probate.*
www.acadiaparishclerk.com
Civil Records: Access: Phone, fax, mail, in person. Both court and visitors may perform in person searches. Search fee: $11.00 per name. Court makes copy: $1.00 per page. Required to search: name, years to search. Civil cases indexed by defendant, plaintiff; on computer from 1985, archived from 1800s. Mail turnaround time same day.
Criminal Records: Access: Phone, fax, mail, in person. Both court and visitors may perform in person searches. Search fee: $11.00 per name per year. Court makes copy: $1.00 per page. Required to search: name, years to search, DOB; also helpful: SSN. Criminal records on computer from 1979, archived from 1800s. Copy of check must be included in the fax request. Note: Copy of check must be faxed with request. Mail turnaround time 1-2 days.
General Information: Public use terminal available. No adoption or juvenile records released. Fee to fax documents is $6.00 1st page, $2.00 for any add'l pages; includes copies. If copies are to be returned by mail and you do not provide an SASE, add $1.00 per page mailing fee. Certification fee: $6.00 per document. Payee: Acadia Parish Clerk of Court. Personal checks accepted. Prepayment and SASE required.

Allen Parish

33rd District Court PO Box 248, Oberlin, LA 70655; phone: 337-639-4351; criminal fax: 337-639-2030; civil/probate fax is the same; hours 8AM-4:30PM (CST). *Felony, Misdemeanor, Civil, Probate.*
Note: Probate is in a separate index.
Civil Records: Access: Fax, mail, in person. Both court and visitors may perform in person searches. Search fee: $10.00 per name. Fee is for a 10 year search. Court makes copy: $1.00 per page. Required to search: name, years to search. Civil cases indexed by defendant, plaintiff. Civil records archived back to 1913; on computer back to 1985. Mail turnaround time 2 days.
Criminal Records: Access: Mail, in person. Both court and visitors may perform in person searches. Search fee: $10.00 per name. Fee is for a 10 year search. Court makes copy: $1.00 per page. Required to search: name, years to search, DOB, SSN. Criminal records archived back to 1913; on computer back to 7/94. Mail turnaround time 2 days.
General Information: Public terminal has criminal back to 1994 and civil back to 1985. No adoption or juvenile records released. Fee to fax documents is $5.00 and $2.00 each add'l page. Certification fee: $5.00 per certification. Payee: Allen Parish Clerk of Court. Personal checks accepted. Prepayment required. SASE requested.

Ascension Parish

23rd District Court PO Box 192, Donaldsonville, LA 70346; phone: 225-473-9866; criminal fax: 225-473-9287; civil fax: 225-473-8641; hours 8:30AM-4:30PM (CST). *Felony, Misdemeanor, Civil, Probate.*
www.eatel.net/~apcc/Clerk_of_Court/indexx.html
Civil Records: Access: Fax, mail, in person. Both court and visitors may perform in person searches. Search fee: $10.00 per name; add $5.00 on search fee if request made by fax. Court makes copy: $1.00 per page. Self serve copy fee: $.50 per page. Required to search: name, years to search. Civil cases indexed by defendant, plaintiff; on computer from 1987, index books back to 1800s, property tax since 1994, mortgage since 11/77. Mail turnaround time 2 days.
Criminal Records: Access: Fax, mail, in person. Both court and visitors may perform in person

searches. Search fee: $10.00 per name; add $5.00 on search fee if request made by fax. Court makes copy: $1.00 per page. Self serve copy fee: $.50 per page. Required to search: name, years to search, DOB; also helpful: SSN. Criminal Records go back to 1800s; computerized records since 11/86. Mail turnaround time 2 days.
General Information: Public terminal has only civil records back to 1987. No adoption or juvenile records released. Will fax documents $5.00 1st page, $1.00 each add'l. Certification fee: $3.00. Payee: Ascension Parish Clerk of Court. In state personal checks accepted. Prepayment required. SASE requested.

Assumption Parish

23rd District Court PO Box 249, Napoleonville, LA 70390; phone: 985-369-6653; criminal/ civil fax: 985-369-2032; hours 8:30AM-4:30PM (CST). *Felony, Misdemeanor, Civil, Probate.*
Civil Records: Access: Fax, mail, in person. Both court and visitors may perform in person searches. Search fee: $10.00 per name per 7 years; $15.00 for 10 years. Court makes copy: $1.00 per page. Self serve copy fee: $.75 per page. Required to search: name, years to search. Civil cases indexed by defendant, plaintiff. Civil records archived back to 1800s; on computer back to 1990. Mail turnaround time 1 day.
Criminal Records: Access: Fax, mail, in person. Both court and visitors may perform in person searches. Search fee: $10.00 per name per 7 years; $15.00 for 10 years. Court makes copy: $1.00 per page. Self serve copy fee: $.75 per page. Required to search: name, years to search, DOB. Criminal records archived back to 1800s; on computer back to 1994. Mail turnaround time 1 day.
General Information: Public terminal has criminal back to 1994 and civil back to 1990. No adoption or juvenile records released. Will fax documents $2.00 1st page, $1.00 each add'l. Certification fee: $5.00 per document. Payee: Assumption Parish Clerk of Court. Personal checks accepted. Prepayment required. SASE requested.

Avoyelles Parish

12th District Court PO Box 219, 300 N Main, Courthouse Bldg, Marksville, LA 71351; phone: 318-253-7523; probate phone: 318-253-7523; hours 8:30AM-4:30PM (CST). *Felony, Misdemeanor, Civil, Probate.*
Civil Records: Access: Mail, in person. Both court and visitors may perform in person searches. Search fee: $10.00 per name. Court makes copy: $1.00 per page. Self serve copy fee: $.50 per page. Required to search: name, years to search. Civil cases indexed by defendant, plaintiff; on computer from 1985, microfiche back to 1800s. Mail turnaround time 1 day.
Criminal Records: Access: Mail, in person. Both court and visitors may perform in person searches. Search fee: $10.00 per name. Court makes copy: $1.00 per page. Self serve copy fee: $.50 per page. Required to search: name, years to search, DOB; also helpful: SSN. Criminal records on computer from 1985, microfiche back to 1800s. Mail turnaround time 1 day.
General Information: Public terminal has criminal back to 1995 and civil back to 1985. No adoption or juvenile records released. Certification fee: $3.00 per page. Payee: Clerk of Court. Personal checks accepted. Prepayment required.

Beauregard Parish

36th District Court PO Box 100, DeRidder, LA 70634; phone: 337-463-8595; fax: 337-462-3916; hours 8AM-4:30PM (CST). *Felony, Misdemeanor, Civil, Probate.*
Civil Records: Access: Mail, in person. Both court and visitors may perform in person searches. Search fee: $15.00 per name. Fee is per 10 years searched. Court makes copy: $1.25 per page.

Required to search: name, years to search. Civil cases indexed by defendant, plaintiff; on computer since 1985, archived from 1913. Mail turnaround 1 week.
Criminal Records: Access: Access: in person. Both court and visitors may perform in person searches. Search fee: $15.00 per name. Fee is per 10 years searched. Court makes copy: $1.25 per page. Required to search: name, years to search, DOB; also helpful: SSN. Criminal record index in books. Mail turnaround time 1 week.
General Information: No public access terminal. No adoption or juvenile records released. Certification fee: $5.00 per doc. Payee: Clerk of Court. Personal checks accepted. Prepayment and SASE required.

Bienville Parish

2nd District Court 100 Courthouse Dr, Rm 100, Arcadia, LA 71001; phone: 318-263-2123; fax: 318-263-7426; hours 8:30AM-4:30PM (CST). *Felony, Misdemeanor, Civil, Probate.*
www.bienvilleparish.org/clerk
Note: Probate is a separate index at this same address.
Civil Records: Access: Fax, mail, in person. Both court and visitors may perform in person searches. Search fee: $10.00 per name. Court makes copy: $1.00 per page. Self serve copy fee: $.50 per page. Required to search: name, years to search. Civil cases indexed by defendant, plaintiff; on computer from 1991, index books prior. Mail turnaround time 2-3 days.
Criminal Records: Access: Fax, mail, in person. Both court and visitors may perform in person searches. Search fee: $10.00 per name. Court makes copy: $1.00 per page. Self serve copy fee: $.50 per page. Required to search: name, years to search, DOB; also helpful: SSN. Criminal records on computer from 1991, index books prior. Mail turnaround time 2-3 days.
General Information: Public terminal has only civil records back to 7/1989. No adoption or juvenile records released. Will fax documents $3.00 plus $1.00 per page. Certification fee: $5.00 per cert. Payee: Clerk of Court. Personal checks accepted. Prepayment and SASE required.

Bossier Parish

26th District Court PO Box 430, Benton, LA 71006; phone: 318-965-2336; fax: 318-965-2713; hours 8:30AM-4:30PM (CST). *Felony, Misdemeanor, Civil, Probate.*
www.bossierclerk.com
Civil Records: Access: Mail, online, in person. Both court and visitors may perform in person searches. Search fee: $15.00 per name. Court makes copy: $.50 per page; same fee for self serve. Required to search: name, years to search. Civil cases indexed by defendant, plaintiff; on computer from 1987, index books back to 1843. Access to the Parish Clerk of Court online records requires $50 setup fee and a $35 monthly flat fee. Civil, criminal, probate (1982 forward), traffic and domestic index information is by name or case number. Call 318-965-2336 for more information. Mail turnaround time same or next day.
Criminal Records: Access: Mail, online, in person. Both court and visitors may perform in person searches. Search fee: $15.00 per name. Court makes copy: $.50 per page; same fee for self serve. Required to search: name, years to search. Criminal records on computer since 1982. Online access to criminal records is the same as civil. Mail turnaround time same or next day.
General Information: Public terminal has criminal back to 1982 and civil back to 1987. No adoption or juvenile records released. Will fax documents for $5.00. Certification fee: $2.00. Payee: Clerk of Court. Business checks accepted. Prepayment required. SASE requested.

Caddo Parish

1st District Court 501 Texas St, Rm 103, Shreveport, LA 71101-5408; criminal phone: 318-226-6786; civil phone: 318-226-6776; probate phone: 318-226-6778; fax: 318-277-9080; hours 8:30AM-5PM (CST). *Felony, Misdemeanor, Civil, Probate.* www.caddoclerk.com

Civil Records: Access: Mail, in person, online. Both court and visitors may perform in person searches. Search fee: $10.00 per name. Court makes copy: $.50 per page in person; $1.25 per page if mail. Required to search: name, years to search. Civil cases indexed by defendant, plaintiff; on computer from 1984. Online access to civil records back to 1994 and name index back to 1984 is through county dial-up service. Registration and $50 set-up fee and $30 monthly usage fee is required. Marriage and recording information is also available. For information and sign-up, call 318-226-6523. Mail turnaround time 1-2 days.

Criminal Records: Access: Mail, in person, online. Both court and visitors may perform in person searches. Search fee: $10.00 per name. For criminal computer printouts, fee is $2.00 for first page and $1.00 each add'l. Court makes copy: $1.25 per page. Self serve copy fee: $.50 per page. Required to search: name, years to search, DOB; also helpful: SSN. Criminal records on computer from 1984. Online access to criminal records is the same as civil. Online criminal name index goes back to '80; minutes to '84. Current calendar is also available. Mail turnaround time 1-2 days.

General Information: Public use terminal available. No adoption or juvenile records released. Certification fee: $2.00. Payee: Clerk of Court. Personal checks accepted. Prepayment and SASE required.

Shreveport City Court 1244 Texas, Shreveport, LA 71101; phone: 318-673-5800; fax: 318-673-5813; hours 8AM-5PM (CST). *Civil Actions Under $25,000, Small Claims.*

Civil Records: Access: Mail, in person. Visitors must perform in person searches themselves. No search fee. Court makes copy: $.50 per page. Required to search: name, years to search. Civil cases indexed by defendant, plaintiff; on computer back to 1987. Must have case number for mail searches. Mail turnaround time 2-4 days.

General Information: Public terminal has only civil records back to 1987. No sealed records released. Certification fee: $2.00. Payee: Shreveport City Court. Personal checks accepted. Prepayment and SASE required.

Calcasieu Parish

14th District Court PO Box 1030, Lake Charles, LA 70602; phone: 337-437-3550; criminal fax: 337-437-3833; civil/probate fax is the same; hours 8:30AM-4:30PM (CST). *Felony, Misdemeanor, Civil, Probate.* www.calclerkofcourt.com

Civil Records: Access: Fax, mail, in person, online. Both court and visitors may perform in person searches. Search fee: $15.00 per name. Additional fee of $1.00 per year after 1st 10 years. Court makes copy: $1.00 per page; same fee for self serve. Required to search: name, years to search. Civil cases indexed by defendant, plaintiff; on computer since 1987. Online access to civil records is the same as criminal, see below. Mail turnaround time 24 hours.

Criminal Records: Access: Mail, in person, online. Both court and visitors may perform in person searches. Search fee: $15.00 per name. Additional fee of $2.00 per year after 1st 10 years. Court makes copy: $1.00 per page; same fee for self serve. Required to search: name, years to search, DOB; also helpful: SSN. Criminal records on computer since 1987. Online access to court record indices is free at www.calclerkofcourt.com/resolution/. Registration and password required. Full documents requires $100.00 per month subscription. Mail turnaround time 24 hours.

General Information: Public terminal goes back to 1987. No adoption or juvenile records released. Will fax documents $7.00 1st page, $2.00 each add'l. Fax available for civil division only. Certification fee: $10.00. Payee: Clerk of Court. Personal checks accepted. Prepayment and SASE required.

Lake Charles City Court PO Box 1664, Lake Charles, LA 70602; phone: 337-491-1564; hours 8AM-4:30PM (CST). *Civil Actions Under $25,000, Small Claims.* www.lakecharlescitycourt.com

Civil Records: Access: Mail, in person. Visitors must perform in person searches themselves. No search fee. Court makes copy: $1.00 per page; same fee for self serve. Required to search: name, years to search. Civil cases indexed by defendant, plaintiff. Civil records kept on paper for 10 years, older records archived on computer. Mail turnaround time 2-5 days.

General Information: Public terminal has only civil records back to 1989. No sealed records released. Will not fax documents. Certification fee: $1.00. Certification included in copy fee. Payee: Lake Charles City Court. Personal checks accepted. Prepayment required.

Caldwell Parish

37th District Court PO Box 1327, Columbia, LA 71418; phone: 318-649-2272; criminal fax: 318-649-2037; civil/probate fax is the same; hours 8AM-4:30PM (CST). *Felony, Misdemeanor, Civil, Probate.*

Note: All record requests must be in writing.

Civil Records: Access: Fax, mail, in person. Both court and visitors may perform in person searches. Search fee: $10.00 per name if court does search. Court makes copy: $1.00 per page; same fee for self serve. Required to search: name, years to search. Civil cases indexed by defendant, plaintiff; on books from 1838, computerized since 11/84. Mail turnaround time 1 week.

Criminal Records: Access: Mail, in person. Both court and visitors may perform in person searches. Search fee: $10.00 per name if court does search. Court makes copy: $1.00 per page; same fee for self serve. Required to search: name, years to search, DOB; also helpful: SSN. Note that some criminal records don't contain DOB or SSN. Criminal Records kept on books since 1970. Mail turnaround 1 week.

General Information: Public terminal has criminal back to 1/1999 and civil back to 11/1984. No adoption or juvenile records released. Will fax documents $3.00 1st page, $1.00 each add'l plus costs for the copies. Certification fee: $5.00 per document. Payee: Clerk of Court. Personal checks accepted. Prepayment required.

Cameron Parish

38th District Court PO Box 549, Cameron, LA 70631; phone: 337-775-5316; fax: 337-775-7172; hours 8:30AM-4:30PM (CST). *Felony, Misdemeanor, Civil, Probate.*

Civil Records: Access: Phone, mail, fax, in person. Both court and visitors may perform in person searches. Search fee: $10.00. Court makes copy: $1.00 per page. Self serve copy fee: $.75 per page. Required to search: name, years to search. Civil cases indexed by defendant, plaintiff. Civil records from 1874; on computer back to 7/1994. Mail turnaround time 2 days.

Criminal Records: Access: Fax, mail, in person. Both court and visitors may perform in person searches. Search fee: $10.00 per name. Court makes copy: $1.00 per page. Self serve copy fee: $.75 per page. Required to search: name, years to search, DOB. Criminal records from 1874; on computer back to 1980. Mail turnaround time 2 days.

General Information: Public use terminal available. No adoption, interdiction or juvenile records released. Fee to fax documents is $1.00 per page, plus cert fee. Certification fee: $5.00. Payee: Cameron Parish Clerk of Court. Personal checks accepted. Prepayment and SASE required.

Catahoula Parish

7th District Court PO Box 654, Harrisonburg, LA 71340; phone: 318-744-5497; fax: 318-744-5488; hours 8AM-4:30PM (CST). *Felony, Misdemeanor, Civil, Probate.*

Civil Records: Access: Mail, in person. Both court and visitors may perform in person searches. Search fee: $2.00 per name; $2.00 per year. Court makes copy: $1.00 per page; same fee for self serve. Required to search: name, years to search. Civil cases indexed by defendant, plaintiff. Civil records minute entries back to 1800s. Mail turnaround time 1-2 weeks.

Criminal Records: Access: Mail, in person. Both court and visitors may perform in person searches. Search fee: $2.00 per name; $2.00 per year. Court makes copy: $1.00 per page; same fee for self serve. Required to search: name, years to search, DOB. Criminal records minute entries back to 1800s. Mail turnaround time 1-2 weeks.

General Information: No public access terminal. No adoption or juvenile records released. Will fax documents for $5.00 plus $1.00 per page. Certification fee: $5.00. Payee: Clerk of Court. Personal checks accepted. Prepayment and SASE required.

Claiborne Parish

2nd District Court PO Box 330, Homer, LA 71040; phone: 318-927-9601; criminal fax: 318-927-2345; civil/probate fax is the same; hours 8:30AM-4:30PM (CST). *Felony, Misdemeanor, Civil, Probate.*

Note: Probate is a separate index at this same address.

Civil Records: Access: Mail, in person. Both court and visitors may perform in person searches. Search fee: $10.00 per name. Court makes copy: $1.00 per page. Required to search: name, years to search. Civil cases indexed by defendant, plaintiff; on index books back to early 1900s. Mail turnaround time 1-2 days.

Criminal Records: Access: Mail, in person. Both court and visitors may perform in person searches. Search fee: $10.00 per name. Court makes copy: $1.00 per page. Required to search: name, years to search, DOB; also helpful: SSN. Criminal records on computer 1993 forward. Mail turnaround 1-2 days.

General Information: No public access terminal. No adoption or juvenile records released. Fee to fax documents is $10.00 per document. Certification fee: $5.00 per document. Payee: Clerk of Court. Personal checks accepted. Prepayment and SASE required.

Concordia Parish

7th District Court PO Box 790, Vidalia, LA 71373; phone: 318-336-4204; fax: 318-336-8777; hours 8:30AM-4:30PM (CST). *Felony, Misdemeanor, Civil, Probate.* www.concordiaclerk.org

Civil Records: Access: Mail, in person. Visitors must perform in person searches themselves. Search fee: $25.00 per name. Court makes copy: $1.00 per page; same fee for self serve. Required to search: name, years to search. Civil cases indexed by defendant, plaintiff; on computer from 1983, index books back to 1800s. Mail turnaround time 3-4 days.

Criminal Records: Access: Mail, in person. Visitors must perform in person searches themselves. Search fee: $15.00 per name. Court makes copy: $1.00 per page; same fee for self serve. Required to search: name, years to search, DOB; also helpful: SSN. Criminal records on computer from 1983, index books back to 1800s. Mail turnaround 3-4 days.

General Information: Public terminal goes back to 1983. No adoption or juvenile records released. Will fax documents $5.00 per document plus $1.00 per page. Certification fee: $5.50. Payee: Clerk of Court. Personal checks accepted. Prepayment required.

De Soto Parish

11th District Court PO Box 1206, Mansfield, LA 71052; phone: 318-872-3110; criminal phone: 318-872-3181; fax: 318-872-4202; probate fax: 318-872-3788; hours 8AM-4:30PM (CST). *Felony, Misdemeanor, Civil, Probate.*

Civil Records: Access: Mail, in person. Both court and visitors may perform in person searches. Search fee: $10.00 per name. Court makes copy: $1.00 per page. Self serve copy fee: $.50 per page. Required to search: name, years to search. Civil cases indexed by defendant, plaintiff; on computer from 1991, index books back to 1843. Mail turnaround time 1-2 days.

Criminal Records: Access: Mail, in person. Both court and visitors may perform in person searches. Search fee: $10.00 per name. Court makes copy: $1.00 per page. Self serve copy fee: $.50 per page. Required to search: name, years to search, DOB. Criminal records on computer since 1991, archived or in books to 1950's. Mail turnaround time 1-2 days.

General Information: Public terminal goes back to 1991. No adoption or juvenile records released. Fee to fax documents is $5.00 plus $1.00 per page. Certification fee: $3.50. Payee: Clerk of Court. Prepayment and SASE required.

East Baton Rouge Parish

19th District Court PO Box 1991, Baton Rouge, LA 70821; phone: 225-389-3950; criminal phone: 225-389-3964; probate phone: 225-389-5118; fax: 225-389-3392; probate fax: 225-389-4612; hours 7:30AM-5:30PM (CST). *Felony, Misdemeanor, Civil, Probate.*
www.ebrclerkofcourt.org

Civil Records: Access: Fax, mail, online, in person. Both court and visitors may perform in person searches. Search fee: Search fee is determined by the years searched. Court makes copy: $.50 per page; same fee for self serve. Required to search: name, years to search. Civil cases indexed by defendant, plaintiff. Civil records in index books from 1942. Online access to the clerk's database is by subscription. Civil record indexes go back to '88; case tracking of civil and probate back to 1991. Setup fee is $100.00 plus $15.00 per month plus per-minute usage charges. Call MIS Dept at 225-389-5295 for info or visit the website. Mail turnaround time 3-5 days.

Criminal Records: Access: Mail, online, in person. Both court and visitors may perform in person searches. Search fee: $20.00 per name. Court makes copy: $.50 per page; same fee for self serve. Required to search: name, years to search, DOB; also helpful: SSN. Criminal records in index books from 1942; on computer back to 1990. Online access to criminal records is the same as civil. Criminal case tracking goes back to 8/1990. Mail turnaround time 3-5 days.

General Information: Public terminal has criminal back to 1990 and civil back to 1988. No adoption or juvenile records released. Fee to fax documents is $5.00 per document and $.50 per page. Certification fee: $1.00. Payee: East Baton Rouge Parish. Only cashiers checks, business checks, and money orders accepted. Prepayment required. SASE helpful.

Baton Rouge City Court 233 St Louis St, Baton Rouge, LA 70802; phone: 225-389-5279; criminal phone: 225-389-5294; civil phone: 225-389-3017; fax: 225-389-5260; hours 8AM-5PM (CST). *Misdemeanors, Civil Actions Under $20,000, Small Claims, Criminal Traffic.*
www.brgov.com/dept/citycourt

Civil Records: Access: Mail, in person, fax, online. Visitors must perform in person searches themselves. Search fee: $20.00 per name. Court makes copy: $.50 per page. Required to search: name, years to search. Civil cases indexed by defendant, plaintiff; on computer back to 1985, microfiche to 1980. Access city court's database including attorneys and warrants free at http://brcc.ci.baton-rouge.la.us/. Mail turnaround time 2-5 days.

Criminal Records: Access: In person, online. Court makes copy: $.50 per page. Required to search: name, years to search. Access city court's criminal dockets database and warrants free at http://brcc.ci.baton-rouge.la.us/. Note: Background checks for the City are performed in the Criminal Records Division at the Baton Rouge Police Dept located at 504 Mayflower or at Parish Prison.

General Information: Public terminal goes back to 1989. No sealed records released. Certification fee: $1.00 per page. Payee: Baton Rouge City Court. Personal checks accepted. Credit cards accepted: Visa, MC, with 5% surcharge. Prepayment required.

East Carroll Parish

6th District Court 400 1st St, Lake Providence, LA 71254; phone: 318-559-2399; hours 8:30AM-4:30PM (CST). *Felony, Misdemeanor, Civil, Probate.*

Civil Records: Access: Mail, in person. Both court and visitors may perform in person searches. Search fee: $20.00 per name per 10 years. Court makes copy: $2.00 per page. Required to search: name, years to search. Civil cases indexed by defendant, plaintiff; on index books back to 1832. Mail turnaround time same day.

Criminal Records: Access: Mail, in person. Both court and visitors may perform in person searches. Search fee: $20.00 for 10 yr check. Court makes copy: $2.00 per page. Required to search: name, years to search, DOB; also helpful: SSN. Criminal records on index books back to 1832. Mail turnaround time same day.

General Information: No public access terminal. No adoption or juvenile records released. Certification fee: $5.00 per cert.. Payee: Clerk of Court. Personal checks not accepted. Prepayment and SASE required.

East Feliciana Parish

20th District Court PO Box 599, Clinton, LA 70722; phone: 225-683-5145; criminal fax: 225-683-3556; civil/probate fax is the same; hours 8:30AM-4:30PM (CST). *Felony, Misdemeanor, Civil, Probate.*
www.eastfelicianaclerk.com/court.html

Civil Records: Access: Mail, in person, online. Both court and visitors may perform in person searches. Search fee: $10.00 per name per ten years. Court makes copy: $1.00 per page; same fee for self serve. Required to search: name, years to search; also helpful: address. Civil cases indexed by defendant, plaintiff; on computer from 1980, index books back to 1825. A web subscription service is available. $400.00 per quarter permits access to viewable documents; $250 per quarter permits access in indices. This database also includes recordings, conveyances, mortgages, and marriage records. Mail turnaround time 1-2 days.

Criminal Records: Access: Fax, mail, in person. Both court and visitors may perform in person searches. Search fee: $10.00 per name. Court makes copy: $1.00 per page; same fee for self serve. Required to search: name, years to search, DOB, SNN. Criminal records on computer from 1990, index books back to 1825. State which years to search. Mail turnaround time 1-2 days.

General Information: Public terminal has criminal back to 1990 and civil back to 1988. No adoption or juvenile records released. Will fax documents $5.00 1st page, $1.00 each add'l. Certification fee: $5.00 per page. Payee: Clerk of Court. Personal checks accepted. Prepayment and SASE required.

Evangeline Parish

13th District Court PO Drawer 347, Ville Platte, LA 70586; phone: 337-363-5671; criminal fax: 337-363-5780; civil/probate fax is the same; hours 8AM-4:30PM (CST). *Felony, Misdemeanor, Civil, Probate.*

Civil Records: Access: Fax, mail, in person. Both court and visitors may perform in person searches. Search fee: $15.00 per name. Fee is for first 7 years searched. Add $2.00 per add'l year. Court makes copy: $.75 per page; $5.00 minimum. Self serve copy fee: $.75 per page. Required to search: name, years to search. Civil cases indexed by defendant, plaintiff; on computer back to 1989; prior records archived from 1911. Mail turnaround time 1-2 days.

Criminal Records: Access: Fax, mail, in person. Both court and visitors may perform in person searches. Search fee: $15.00 per name. Fee is for first 7 years searched. Add $2.00 per add'l year. Court makes copy: $.75 per page; $5.00 minimum. Self serve copy fee: $.75 per page. Required to search: name, years to search; also helpful: DOB, SSN. Criminal records on computer back to 1989, prior archived from 1911. Mail turnaround 1-2 days.

General Information: Public terminal goes back to 1989. No adoption or juvenile records released. Will fax documents $5.00 1st page, $2.00 each add'l. Certification fee: $2.00 per page includes copy. Payee: Clerk of Court. Personal checks accepted. Prepayment required.

Franklin Parish

5th District Court PO Box 1564, Winnsboro, LA 71295; phone: 318-435-5133; criminal fax: 318-435-5134; civil/probate fax is the same; hours 8:30AM-4:30PM (CST). *Felony, Misdemeanor, Civil, Probate.*

Civil Records: Access: Mail, in person. Both court and visitors may perform in person searches. Search fee: $10.00 per name. Court makes copy: $1.00 per page. Required to search: name, years to search. Civil cases indexed by defendant, plaintiff; on computer from 1989, index books back to 1843. Mail turnaround time 1-2 days.

Criminal Records: Access: Mail, in person. Both court and visitors may perform in person searches. Search fee: $10.00 per name. Fee includes 10 year search. Court makes copy: $1.00 per page. Required to search: name, years to search, DOB; also helpful: SSN. Criminal records on computer since 1995. Mail turnaround time 1-2 days.

General Information: No public access terminal. No adoption or juvenile records released. Will fax documents $5.00 1st page, $1.00 each add'l. Certification fee: $5.00 per document. Payee: Clerk of Court. Business checks accepted. Prepayment and SASE required.

Grant Parish

35th District Court PO Box 263, Colfax, LA 71417; phone: 318-627-3246; fax: 318-627-3201; hours 8:30AM-4:30PM (CST). *Felony, Misdemeanor, Civil, Probate.*

Civil Records: Access: Phone, fax, mail, in person. Both court and visitors may perform in person searches. Search fee: $5.00 per name. Court makes copy: $1.00 per page. Self serve copy fee: $.50 per page. Required to search: name, years to search. Civil cases indexed by defendant, plaintiff; on computer back to 1990; index books back to 1878. Mail turnaround time 1-2 days.

Criminal Records: Access: Phone, fax, mail, in person. Both court and visitors may perform in person searches. Search fee: $5.00 per name. Court makes copy: $1.00 per page. Self serve copy fee: $.50 per page. Required to search: name, years to search, DOB; SSN helpful. Criminal index back to 1904; on computer to 1996. Mail turnaround 1-2 days.

General Information: No public access terminal. No adoption or juvenile records released without approval of a judge. Will fax documents for a prepaid fee of $5.00. Certification fee: $5.00. Payee: Grant Parish Clerk of Court. Personal checks accepted. Prepayment and SASE required.

Iberia Parish

16th District Court PO Drawer 12010, New Iberia, LA 70562-2010; phone: 337-365-7282; criminal fax: 337-365-0737; civil/probate fax is the same; hours 8:30AM-4:30PM (CST). *Felony, Misdemeanor, Civil, Probate.*

www.iberiaclerk.com

Civil Records: Access: In person only. Visitors must perform in person searches themselves. Court makes copy: $1.00 per page. Self serve copy fee: $.50 per page. Required to search: name, years to search; also helpful: address. Civil cases indexed by defendant, plaintiff; on computer back to 1974, index books back to 1868.

Criminal Records: Access: In person only. Visitors must perform in person searches themselves. Court makes copy: $1.00 per page. Self serve copy fee: $.50 per page. Required to search: name, years to search, DOB; also helpful: address, SSN. Criminal records on computer back to 1994, index books back to 1868.

General Information: Public terminal has criminal to 2 years and civil back to 4 years. No adoption or juvenile records released. Will fax specific case file data to local or toll-free number. Certification fee: $5.50 per document. Payee: Clerk of Court. Personal checks accepted. Prepayment required.

Iberville Parish

18th District Court PO Box 423, Plaquemine, LA 70764; phone: 225-687-5160; fax: 225-687-5260; hours 8:30AM-4:30PM (CST). *Felony, Misdemeanor, Civil, Probate.*

Civil Records: Access: Fax, mail, in person. Both court and visitors may perform in person searches. Search fee: $10.00 per name. Court makes copy: $1.00 per page; same fee for self serve. Required to search: name, years to search. Civil cases indexed by defendant, plaintiff; on books back to 1800s. Mail turnaround time 1-2 days.

Criminal Records: Access: Mail, in person. Both court and visitors may perform in person searches. Search fee: $10.00 per name. Court makes copy: $1.00 per page; same fee for self serve. Required to search: name, years to search, DOB; also helpful: SSN. Criminal records on books back to 1800s. Mail turnaround time 1-2 days.

General Information: Public use terminal available. No adoption or juvenile records released. Fee to fax documents is $5.00 1st page, $2.00 each add'l. Certification fee: $5.00. Payee: Clerk of Court. Personal checks accepted. Prepayment and SASE required.

Jackson Parish

2nd District Court PO Drawer 730, Jonesboro, LA 71251; phone: 318-259-2424; criminal fax: 318-395-0386; civil/probate fax is the same; hours 8:30AM-4:30PM (CST). *Felony, Misdemeanor, Civil, Probate.*

Civil Records: Access: Phone, mail, in person. Both court and visitors may perform in person searches. Search fee: $10.00 per name. Fee is per 10 years searched. Court makes copy: $1.00 per page; same fee for self serve. Required to search: name, years to search. Civil cases indexed by defendant, plaintiff; on index books from 1880 and on computer since 1988. Mail turnaround time immediate.

Criminal Records: Access: Phone, mail, in person. Both court and visitors may perform in person searches. Search fee: $10.00 per name. Fee is per 10 years searched. Court makes copy: $1.00 per page; same fee for self serve. Required to search: name, years to search, DOB; also helpful: SSN. Criminal records on computer since 1988. Mail turnaround time 1-2 days.

General Information: Public terminal goes back to 1988. No adoption or juvenile records released. Will fax documents for $5.00. Certification fee: $5.00 per certification. Payee: Clerk of Court. Personal checks accepted. Prepayment and SASE required.

Jefferson Davis Parish

31st District Court PO Box 799, Jennings, LA 70546; phone: 337-824-8340; fax: 337-824-1354; hours 8:30AM-4:30PM (CST). *Felony, Misdemeanor, Civil, Probate.*

Civil Records: Access: Mail, in person. Both court and visitors may perform in person searches.

Search fee: $10.00 per name for 10 years. Court makes copy: $1.00 per page. Self serve copy fee: $.50 per page. Required to search: name, years to search; also helpful: address. Civil cases indexed by defendant, plaintiff. Civil records archived from 1913, on computer back to 1991. Mail turnaround 2 days.

Criminal Records: Access: Mail, in person. Both court and visitors may perform in person searches. Search fee: $10.00 per name for 10 years. Court makes copy: $1.00 per page. Self serve copy fee: $.50 per page. Required to search: name, years to search; also helpful: DOB, SSN. Criminal records archived from 1913, on computer back to 1991. Include city of residence of subject in your search request. Mail turnaround time 2 days.

General Information: No public access terminal. No adoption or juvenile records released. Will fax documents for $1.00 per page plus a $10.00 fax fee. Certification fee: $5.00. Payee: Clerk of Court. Personal checks accepted. Prepayment required.

Jefferson Parish

24th District Court PO Box 10, Gretna, LA 70053; criminal phone: 504-364-2992; civil phone: 504-364-2611; fax: 504-364-3797; hours 8:30AM-4:30PM (CST). *Felony, Misdemeanor, Civil, Probate.*

www.jpclerkofcourt.us

Civil Records: Access: Fax, mail, online, in person. Both court and visitors may perform in person searches. Search fee: $20.00 per name per year. Court makes copy: $1.00 per page. Required to search: name, years to search. Civil cases indexed by defendant, plaintiff; on computer from 1986, in index books back to 1972, prior records archived. Online access is through dial-up service; initiation fee is $200, plus $85.00 monthly and $.25 per minute usage. Includes recordings, marriage index, and assessor rolls. For further information and sign-up, call 504-364-2908 or visit the website and click on "Jeffnet." Mail turnaround time 1-2 days.

Criminal Records: Access: Mail, online, in person. Both court and visitors may perform in person searches. Search fee: $10.00 per name. Court makes copy: $1.00 per page. Self serve copy fee: $.50 per page. Required to search: name, years to search, DOB; also helpful: SSN. Criminal records on computer from 1994 to present, active cases are in books from 1972. Online access is via a dial-up service, see civil. Mail turnaround time 1-2 days.

General Information: Public terminal has only criminal records back to 5/1994. No adoption, juvenile or grand jury records released. Will fax documents $5.00 1st page, $1.00 each add'l. Certification fee: $2.00 per page if copy machine, $1.50 if from computer. Payee: Clerk of Court. Only cashiers checks and money orders accepted. Prepayment and SASE required.

La Salle Parish

28th District Court PO Box 1316, Jena, LA 71342; phone: 318-992-2158; fax: 318-992-2157; hours 8:30AM-4:30PM (CST). *Felony, Misdemeanor, Civil, Probate.*

Civil Records: Access: Phone, fax, mail, in person. Both court and visitors may perform in person searches. Search fee: $20.00 1st name, $10.00 additional name. Fee is for 10 year search per name with certificate. Court makes copy: $1.00 per page. Required to search: name, years to search. Civil cases indexed by defendant, plaintiff. Civil records archived from 1916; on computer since 6/95. Mail turnaround time 1-2 weeks; will release results sooner by phone.

Criminal Records: Access: Phone, fax, mail, in person. Both court and visitors may perform in person searches. Search fee: $20.00 1st name, $10.00 additional name. Fee is for 10 year search per name with certificate. Court makes copy: $1.00 per page. Required to search: name, years to search, DOB; also helpful: SSN. Criminal records archived from 1936; on computer since 1999. Mail turnaround time 1-2 weeks; will release results sooner by phone.

General Information: No public access terminal. No adoption or juvenile records released. Fee to fax documents is $10.00 per document. Certification fee: $5.00 per cert. Payee: Clerk of Court. Personal checks accepted. Prepayment required.

Lafayette Parish

15th District Court PO Box 2009, c/o Clerk of Court, Lafayette, LA 70502; phone: 337-291-6400; criminal phone: 337-291-6329; civil phone: 337-291-6303; probate phone: 337-291-6303; criminal fax: 337-291-6475; civil fax: 337-291-6480; probate fax: 337-291-6480; hours 8:30AM-4:30PM (CST). *Felony, Misdemeanor, Civil, Probate.*

www.lafayetteparishclerk.com

Civil Records: Access: Phone, fax, mail, online, in person. Both court and visitors may perform in person searches. Search fee: $20.00 per name. Court makes copy: $1.00 per page. Required to search: name, years to search. Civil cases indexed by defendant, plaintiff. Civil records archived from 1923; on computer back to 1986. Access to the remote online system requires $100 setup fee plus $15 per month and $.50 per minute. Civil index goes back to 1986. For more information, call 337-291-6433. Mail turnaround time 1-2 days.

Criminal Records: Access: Phone, fax, mail, in person, online. Both court and visitors may perform in person searches. Search fee: $20.00 per name. Court makes copy: $1.00 per page. Required to search: name, years to search, DOB. Criminal records archived from 1966; on computer back to 1983. Online access to criminal records is the same as civil. Mail turnaround time 1-2 days.

General Information: Public terminal has criminal back to 1983 and civil back to 1986. No adoption or juvenile records released. Will fax documents to local or toll free line for $1.00 per page fee, 2 page minimum. Certification fee: $5.50 per certification. Payee: Clerk of Court. Personal checks accepted. Prepayment required.

Lafourche Parish

17th District Court PO Box 818, Thibodaux, LA 70302; phone: 985-447-4841; criminal: 985-448-0591; civil: 985-447-5550; probate: 985-447-5550; criminal fax: 985-447-5800; civil/probate fax is the same; hours 8:30AM-4:30PM (CST). *Felony, Misdemeanor, Civil, Probate.*

Note: Probate is separate index at this same address.

Civil Records: Access: Fax, mail, in person. Both court and visitors may perform in person searches. Search fee: $20.00 per name. Fee is for 10 year search. Court makes copy: $1.00 per page; same fee for self serve. Required to search: name, years to search. Civil cases indexed by defendant, plaintiff; on computer back to 7/1982, microfiche from 1968, index books back to 1800s. Mail turnaround time 7 days.

Criminal Records: Access: Fax, mail, in person. Both court and visitors may perform in person searches. Search fee: $20.00 per name. Fee is for 10 year search. Court makes copy: $1.00 per page; same fee for self serve. Required to search: name, years to search, DOB; also helpful: SSN, race, sex. Criminal records on computer back to 7/1982, microfiche from 1968, index books to 1800s. Mail turnaround 7 days.

General Information: Public terminal has criminal back to 1948 and civil back to 1813. No adoption or juvenile records released. Fee to fax documents is $2.00 per page. Certification fee: $5.00 per certification includes copies. Payee: Lafourche Parish Clerk of Court. Personal checks accepted. Prepayment required. SASE requested.

Lincoln Parish

3rd District Court PO Box 924, Ruston, LA 71273-0924; phone: 318-251-5130; fax: 318-255-6004; hours 8:30AM-4:30PM (CST). *Felony, Misdemeanor, Civil, Probate.*

Civil Records: Access: Mail, in person. Both court and visitors may perform in person searches.

Search fee: $10.00 per name. Fee is per 10 years searched. Court makes copy: $1.00 per page. Self serve copy fee: $.50 per page. Required to search: name, years to search. Civil cases indexed by defendant, plaintiff; on computer since 1985, index books back to 1800s. Mail turnaround 1-2 days.

Criminal Records: Access: Mail, in person. Both court and visitors may perform in person searches. Search fee: $10.00 per name. Fee is per 10 years searched. Court makes copy: $1.00 per page. Self serve copy fee: $.50 per page. Required to search: name, years to search, DOB; also helpful: SSN. Criminal records on computer since 1992. Mail turnaround time 1-2 days.

General Information: Public terminal goes back to 1984. No adoption or juvenile records released. Fee to fax documents is $5.00 for 1st page, $1.00 each add'l. Certification fee: $5.00 per doc. Payee: Clerk of Court. No personal checks accepted. Prepayment required.

Livingston Parish

21st District Court PO Box 1150, Livingston, LA 70754; phone: 225-686-2216; hours 8AM-4:30PM (CST). *Felony, Misdemeanor, Civil, Probate.*

Civil Records: Access: Mail, in person. Visitors must perform in person searches themselves. Search fee: $10.00 per name; add $3.00 if a mail search request. Court makes copy: $1.00 per page. Required to search: name, years to search. Civil cases indexed by defendant, plaintiff; on index books since 1800s; computerized records past 10 years. Mail turnaround time 1-2 days.

Criminal Records: Access: Mail, in person. Visitors must perform in person searches themselves. Search fee: $10.00 per name; add $3.00 if a mail search request. Court makes copy: $1.00 per page. Required to search: name, years to search, DOB; also helpful: SSN, race, sex. Criminal records on index books since 1800s; computerized records past 10 years. Mail turnaround time 1-2 days.

General Information: Public terminal goes back to 1989. No adoption or juvenile records released. Certification fee: $5.00 per doc. Payee: 21st District Court. Personal checks accepted. Prepayment required.

Madison Parish

6th District Court PO Box 1710, Tallulah, LA 71282; phone: 318-574-0655; fax: 318-574-3961; hours 8:30AM-4:30PM (CST). *Felony, Misdemeanor, Civil, Probate.*

Civil Records: Access: Phone, mail, in person. Both court and visitors may perform in person searches. Search fee: $10.00 per name. Court makes copy: $2.00 per page; same fee for self serve. Required to search: name, years to search. Civil cases indexed by defendant, plaintiff. Civil records kept on computer since 7/93. Mail turnaround time 1-2 days.

Criminal Records: Access: Phone, mail, in person, fax. Both court and visitors may perform in person searches. Search fee: $10.00 per name. Court makes copy: $2.00 per page; same fee for self serve. Required to search: name, years to search, DOB; also helpful: SSN. Criminal records on index, computerized since 1999. Mail turnaround 1-2 days.

General Information: Public terminal has criminal back to 1998 and civil back to 1993. No adoption or juvenile records released. Certification fee: $5.50. Payee: Clerk of Court. Personal checks accepted. Prepayment and SASE required.

Morehouse Parish

4th District Court PO Box 1543, Bastrop, LA 71221; phone: 318-281-3343; criminal fax: 318-281-3775; civil/probate fax is the same; hours 8:30AM-4:30PM (CST). *Felony, Misdemeanor, Civil, Probate.*

Civil Records: Access: Phone, fax, mail, in person. Both court and visitors may perform in person searches. Search fee: $15.00 per name. Fee is per 10

years searched. Court makes copy: $1.00 per page; same fee for self serve. Required to search: name, years to search; also helpful: address. Civil cases indexed by defendant, plaintiff; on computer since 1987, in books since 1898, some on microfilm. Mail turnaround time 2-3 days.

Criminal Records: Access: Phone, fax, mail, in person. Both court and visitors may perform in person searches. Search fee: $15.00 per name. Fee is per 10 years searched. Court makes copy: $1.00 per page; same fee for self serve. Required to search: name, years to search, DOB; also helpful: address, SSN. Criminal records in books since 1926 and on microfilm since 1974; computerized records go back to 1994. Mail turnaround time 2-3 days.

General Information: Public terminal has criminal to 1994 and civil to 1987. No adoption, juvenile or judicial commitment records released. Will fax documents $5.00 1st page, $1.00 each add'l. Certification fee: $5.00 per document. Payee: Clerk of Court. Personal checks accepted. Prepayment and SASE required.

Natchitoches Parish

10th District Court PO Box 476, Natchitoches, LA 71458; phone: 318-352-8152; fax: 318-352-9321; hours 8:30AM-4:30PM (CST). *Felony, Misdemeanor, Civil, Probate, Small Claims.*

Civil Records: Access: Phone, fax, mail, in person. Both court and visitors may perform in person searches. Search fee: $10.00 per name. Court makes copy: $1.00 per page; same fee for self serve. Required to search: name, years to search. Civil cases indexed by defendant, plaintiff; on computer back to 6/1991, archived from 1950, index books back to 1800s. Mail turnaround time 1 week.

Criminal Records: Access: Phone, mail, in person. Both court and visitors may perform in person searches. Search fee: $10.00 per name. Court makes copy: $1.00 per page; same fee for self serve. Required to search: name, years to search, DOB; also helpful: SSN. Criminal records on computer back to 6/1991, archived from 1950, index books back to 1800s. Mail turnaround time 1 week.

General Information: Public terminal has criminal back to 1991 and civil back to 1986. No adoption or juvenile records released. Will fax documents $5.00 1st page, $2.00 each add'l. Fax available for civil division only. Certification fee: $5.00 per document. Payee: Clerk of Court. Personal checks accepted. Prepayment and SASE required.

Orleans Parish

Civil District Court 421 Loyola Ave, Rm 402, Attn: Clerk of Civil Dist. Ct, New Orleans, LA 70112; phone: 504-592-9100; fax: 504-592-9128; hours 8AM-6PM (CST). *Civil, Probate, Domestic Relations.*
www.orleanscdc.gov
Civil Records: Access: Phone, mail, online, in person. Both court and visitors may perform in person searches. No search fee. Court makes copy: $1.00 per page. Required to search: name, years to search. Civil cases indexed by defendant, plaintiff; on computer since 1985, in books back to early 1800s. CDC Remote provides access to civil cases from 1985 and First City Court cases as well as parish mortgage and conveyance indexes. The fee is $250 or $300 per year. Call 504-592-9264 for more information. Mail turnaround time 1-2 days.

General Information: Public terminal has only civil records back to 1985. No adoptions or juvenile released. Will not fax documents. Certification fee: $2.00 per doc includes copies. Payee: Clerk of Court. Only attorneys' checks, cashiers checks and money orders accepted. Prepayment and SASE required.

Criminal District Court 2700 Tulane Ave, Rm 115, New Orleans, LA 70119; phone: 504-827-3546; fax: 504-827-3385; hours 8:15AM-3PM (CST). *Felony, Misdemeanor.*

Criminal Records: Access: Mail, fax, in person. Both court and visitors may perform in person

searches. Search fee: $10.00 per name. No copy fee. Required to search: name, DOB, SSN. SNN must be included. If you do not specify the years to search, then the search will include their complete records. Criminal records on computer past 8 years, books and files go back to early 1900s. Only government agencies and companies using their letterhead may fax in requests. Mail turnaround time 2 days.

General Information: No public access terminal. No adoption or juvenile records released. No certification fee. Payee: Clerk of Court. Business checks accepted. Prepayment and SASE required.

New Orleans City Court 421 Loyola Ave, Rm 201, New Orleans, LA 70112; phone: 504-592-9155; fax: 504-592-9281; hours 8:30AM-4PM (CST). *Civil Actions Under $25,000, Small Claims.*
www.orleanscdc.gov
Note: Small claims phone-504-592-9154.
Civil Records: Access: Mail, online, in person. Both court and visitors may perform in person searches. No search fee. Court makes copy: $1.00 per page. Required to search: name, years to search. Civil cases indexed by defendant, plaintiff; on computer back to 1989. CDC Remote provides access to First City Court cases from 1988 as well as civil cases, parish mortgage and conveyance indexes. The fee is $250 or $300 per year. Call 504-592-9264 for more information. Mail turnaround time 5-10 days.

General Information: Public terminal has only civil records back to 1988. (Terminal includes eviction and small claims records filed in FCC.) No sealed records released. Will fax documents for $5.00 1st two pages then $2.50 ea add'l. Certification fee: $3.00. Payee: New Orleans First City Court. Personal checks not accepted. Visa, MasterCard accepted. Checks not accepted for Small Claims. Prepayment required. SASE requested.

Ouachita Parish

4th District Court PO Box 1862, Monroe, LA 71210-1862; phone: 318-327-1444; fax: 318-327-1462; hours 8:30AM-5PM (CST). *Felony, Misdemeanor, Civil, Probate.*

Civil Records: Access: Fax, mail, in person. Both court and visitors may perform in person searches. Search fee: $10.00 per name. Court makes copy: $.25 per page; same fee for self serve. Required to search: name, years to search. Civil cases indexed by defendant, plaintiff; on computer from 1991, index books back to 1800s. Mail turnaround time 1-2 days.

Criminal Records: Access: Fax, mail, in person. Both court and visitors may perform in person searches. Search fee: $10.00 per name. Court makes copy: $.25 per page; same fee for self serve. Required to search: name, years to search, DOB; also helpful: SSN. Criminal records on computer from 1991, index books back to 1800s. Mail turnaround time 1-2 days.

General Information: Public terminal has criminal back to 1991 and civil back to 1989. No adoption or juvenile records released. Will fax documents $2.00 1st page, $1.00 each add'l. Certification fee: $.25 per page. Payee: Clerk of Court. Business checks accepted. Checks accepted up to $50.00. Prepayment required. SASE requested.

Plaquemines Parish

25th District Court PO Box 40 (301 Maine St), Belle Chasse, LA 70037; phone: 504-392-4969; criminal phone: 504-392-4969; civil phone: 504-297-5180; probate phone: 504-297-5180; probate fax: 504-297-5195; hours 8:30AM-4:30PM (CST). *Felony, Misdemeanor, Civil, Probate.*

Civil Records: Access: In person only. Visitors must perform in person searches themselves. Court makes copy: $1.00 per page. Self serve copy fee: $.50 per page. Required to search: name, years to search. Civil cases indexed by defendant, plaintiff; on index books back to 1800s; computerized since 1/91. Court will search probate records; fee is $10 per name.

Criminal Records: Access: In person only. Visitors must perform in person searches themselves. Court makes copy: $.50 per page. Required to search: name, years to search, DOB. Criminal records on index books back to 1966; computerized records go back to 1/91. The county sex offender database is free online at www.lasocpr.lsp.org/Static/Search.htm. Note: Contact the Plaquemines Sheriff's Office (18039 Hwy 15, Pointe-a-LaHache 70082) for a criminal search, 985-333-5002, fax-985-333-9238.
General Information: Public terminal has only civil records back to 1991. No adoption or juvenile records released. Certification fee: $5.00 per document. Payee: Clerk of Court. Personal checks accepted. Prepayment required.

Pointe Coupee Parish

18th District Court PO Box 86, New Roads, LA 70760; phone: 225-638-9596; fax: 225-638-9590; hours 8:30AM-4:30PM (CST). *Felony, Misdemeanor, Civil, Probate.*
Civil Records: Access: Mail, in person. Both court and visitors may perform in person searches. Search fee: $10.00 per name. Court makes copy: $1.25 per page. Required to search: name, years to search. Civil cases indexed by defendant, plaintiff; on index books back to 1800s.
Criminal Records: Access: In person only. Visitors must perform in person searches themselves. Court makes copy: $1.25 per page. Required to search: name, years to search, DOB; SSN helpful. Criminal records on index books back to 1800s.
General Information: Public terminal goes back to 2000. No adoption or juvenile records released. Will fax documents to local or toll free line. Certification fee: $5.00 per doc. Payee: Clerk of Court. Personal checks accepted. Prepayment required.

Rapides Parish

9th District Court PO Box 952, Alexandria, LA 71309; phone: 318-473-8153; criminal phone: 318-619-5845; civil phone: 318-619-5846; probate phone: 318-619-5847; criminal fax: 318-473-4667; civil/probate fax is the same; hours 8:30AM-4:30PM (CST). *Felony, Misdemeanor, Civil, Probate.*
www.rapidesclerk.org
Civil Records: Access: Mail, in person. Both court and visitors may perform in person searches. Search fee: $11.00 per name. Fee is per separate index. Court makes copy: $1.00 per page; same fee for self serve. Required to search: name, years to search. Civil cases indexed by defendant, plaintiff; on index books since 1864, civil in computer since 10/84. Mail turnaround time within 72 hours.
Criminal Records: Access: Mail, in person. Both court and visitors may perform in person searches. Search fee: $11.00 per name. Fee is per separate index. Court makes copy: $1.00 per page; same fee for self serve. Required to search: name, years to search, DOB; also helpful: SSN. Criminal records on computer since 1984; prior records in index books back to 1864. Mail turnaround time 2-4 days.
General Information: Public terminal goes back to 1984. No adoption, juvenile, or judicial commitment records released. Will fax documents to local or toll free line. Certification fee: $5.00 per cert. Payee: Rapides Parish Clerk of Court. Personal checks accepted. Prepayment required.

Red River Parish

39th District Court PO Box 485, Coushatta, LA 71019; phone: 318-932-6741; hours 8:30AM-4:30PM (CST). *Felony, Misdemeanor, Civil, Probate.*
Civil Records: Access: Mail, in person. Both court and visitors may perform in person searches. Search fee: $10.00 per name. Court makes copy: $1.00 per page; same fee for self serve. Required to search: name, years to search. Civil cases indexed by defendant, plaintiff; on index books. Mail turnaround time 1-2 days.

Criminal Records: Access: Mail, in person. Only the court performs in person searches; visitors may not. Search fee: $10.00 per name. Court makes copy: $1.00 per page; same fee for self serve. Required to search: name, years to search, DOB; also helpful: SSN. The index is kept in the DA's office. Mail turnaround time 1-2 days.
General Information: Public use terminal available. No adoption or juvenile records released. Will fax documents to local or toll free line. Certification fee: $5.00 per document. Payee: Clerk of Court. Personal checks accepted. Prepayment and SASE required.

Richland Parish

5th District Court PO Box 119, Rayville, LA 71269; phone: 318-728-4171; fax: 318-728-7020; hours 8:30AM-4:30PM (CST). *Felony, Misdemeanor, Civil, Probate.*
Civil Records: Access: Mail, in person. Both court and visitors may perform in person searches. Search fee: $10.00 per name. Court makes copy: $1.00 per page. Self serve copy fee: $.50 per page. Required to search: name, years to search. Civil cases indexed by defendant, plaintiff; on since 1/94, prior on books to 1800s. Mail turnaround time 1-2 days.
Criminal Records: Access: Mail, in person. Both court and visitors may perform in person searches. Search fee: $10.00 per name. Court makes copy: $1.00 per page. Self serve copy fee: $.50 per page. Required to search: name, years to search, DOB, SSN. Criminal records on since 1/94, prior on books to 1800s. Mail turnaround time 1-2 days.
General Information: No public access terminal. No adoption or juvenile records released. Will fax documents to local or toll free line. Certification fee: $5.00. Payee: Clerk of Court. Personal checks accepted. Prepayment and SASE required.

Sabine Parish

11th District Court Sabine Clerk of Court, PO Box 419, Many, LA 71449; phone: 318-256-6223; criminal fax: 318-256-9037; civil/probate fax is the same; hours 8AM-4:30PM (CST). *Felony, Misdemeanor, Civil, Probate.*
Civil Records: Access: Fax, mail, in person. Both court and visitors may perform in person searches. Search fee: $20.00 per name. Court makes copy: $1.25 per page. Self serve copy fee: $.75 per page. Required to search: name, years to search. Civil cases indexed by defendant, plaintiff; on index books back to 1843. Mail turnaround time 5-10 days.
Criminal Records: Access: Fax, mail, in person. Both court and visitors may perform in person searches. Search fee: $20.00 per name. Court makes copy: $1.25 per page. Self serve copy fee: $.75 per page. Required to search: name, years to search. Criminal records by name go back to 1843. Mail turnaround time 5-10 days.
General Information: Public terminal has only civil records back to 7/1990. No adoption or juvenile records released. Will fax documents $5.00 1st page, $2.00 each add'l. Certification fee: $5.00 per certification. Payee: Sabine Parish Clerk. Personal checks accepted. Prepayment and SASE required.

St. Bernard Parish

34th District Court PO Box 1746, Chalmette, LA 70044; phone: 504-271-3434; hours 8:30AM-4:30PM (CST). *Felony, Misdemeanor, Civil, Probate.*
Civil Records: Access: Mail, in person. Both court and visitors may perform in person searches. Search fee: $10.00 per name. Fee is per 10 years searched. Court makes copy: $1.00 per page; same fee for self serve. Required to search: name, years to search. Civil cases indexed by defendant, plaintiff; on index books back to 1800s, on computer since 1989. Mail turnaround time 2-3 days.
Criminal Records: Access: Mail, in person. Both court and visitors may perform in person searches. Search fee: $10.00 per name. Fee is per 10 years searched. Court makes copy: $1.00 per page; same fee

for self serve. Required to search: name, years to search, DOB; also helpful: SSN. Criminal records on index books back to 1800s, on computer since 1989. Mail turnaround time 2-3 days.
General Information: Public terminal goes back to 1989. No adoption or juvenile. Will not fax documents. Certification fee: $5.00. Payee: Clerk of Court. No personal checks accepted. Prepayment and SASE required.

St. Charles Parish

29th District Court PO Box 424, 15045 River Rd, Hahnville, LA 70057; phone: 985-783-6632; criminal fax: 985-783-2005; civil/probate fax is the same; hours 8:30AM-4:30PM (CST). *Felony, Misdemeanor, Civil, Probate.*
Note: Probate is a separate index at this same address.
Civil Records: Access: Mail, in person. Both court and visitors may perform in person searches. Search fee: $10.00 per name. Court makes copy: $.50 per page; same fee for self serve. Required to search: name, years to search. Civil cases indexed by defendant, plaintiff; on computer back to 1982, on index books back to 1890. Mail turnaround time 1 day.
Criminal Records: Access: Mail, in person. Both court and visitors may perform in person searches. Search fee: $10.00 per name. Court makes copy: $.50 per page; same fee for self serve. Required to search: name, years to search, DOB; also helpful: SSN, race, sex. Criminal records on computer back to 1981, on index books back to 1900s. Mail turnaround time 1 day.
General Information: Public terminal has criminal back to 5/1990 and civil back to 1982. No adoption or juvenile records released. Fee to fax documents is $4.00 per document. Certification fee: $2.00 per page includes copies. Payee: Clerk of Court. Personal checks accepted. Prepayment required.

St. Helena Parish

21st District Court PO Box 308, Greensburg, LA 70441; phone: 225-222-4514; criminal fax: 225-222-3443; civil fax: 225-222-3443; probate fax: same; hours 8:30AM-4:30PM (CST). *Felony, Misdemeanor, Civil, Probate.*
Civil Records: Access: Phone, mail, fax, in person. Both court and visitors may perform in person searches. Search fee: $10.00 per name. Court makes copy: $1.00 per page. Self serve copy fee: $.50 per page. Required to search: name, years to search. Civil cases indexed by defendant, plaintiff; on index books back to 1800s. Mail turnaround time 1-2 days.
Criminal Records: Access: Mail, in person. Both court and visitors may perform in person searches. Search fee: $10.00 per name. Court makes copy: $1.00 per page. Self serve copy fee: $.50 per page. Required to search: name, years to search, DOB; also helpful: SSN. Criminal records on index books back to 1800s. Mail turnaround time 1-2 days.
General Information: No public access terminal. No adoption or juvenile records released. Fee to fax documents is $2.00 per page. Certification fee: $5.00 per seal. Payee: Clerk of Court. Personal checks accepted. Prepayment and SASE required.

St. James Parish

23rd District Court PO Box 63, Convent, LA 70723; phone: 225-562-7496; criminal phone: 225-562-2271; civil phone: 225-562-2360; probate phone: 225-562-2360; criminal fax: 225-562-2383; civil/probate fax is the same; hours 8AM-4:30PM (CST). *Felony, Misdemeanor, Civil, Probate.*
Note: Probate is a separate index at this same address.
Civil Records: Access: Mail, in person. Both court and visitors may perform in person searches. Search fee: $15.00 per name. Court makes copy: $1.00 per page. Required to search: name, years to search. Civil cases indexed by defendant, plaintiff; on index books back to early 1900s; on computer back to 1988. Mail turnaround time 1-2 days.

Criminal Records: Access: Mail, in person. Both court and visitors may perform in person searches. Search fee: $15.00 per name. Court makes copy: $1.00 per page. Required to search: name, years to search, DOB. Criminal records on index books back to early 1900s; on computer back to 1988. Mail turnaround time 1-2 days.

General Information: Public terminal has criminal back to 1988 and civil back to 1987. No adoption or juvenile records released. Will fax documents for free. Certification fee: $5.00 per document. Payee: Clerk of Court. Only cashiers checks and money orders accepted. Prepayment and SASE required.

St. John the Baptist Parish

40th District Court PO Box 280, Edgard, LA 70049; phone: 985-497-3331; fax: 985-497-3972; hours 8:30AM-4:30PM (CST). *Felony, Misdemeanor, Civil, Probate.* www.stjohnclerk.org

Civil Records: Access: Mail, fax, in person. Both court and visitors may perform in person searches. Search fee: $15.00 per name. Fee is for first 15 years. Add $1.00 per add'l year. Court makes copy: $2.00 per page. Self serve copy fee: $1.00 per page. Required to search: name, years to search. Civil cases indexed by defendant, plaintiff; on computer since 1982. Mail turnaround time 3-4 days.

Criminal Records: Access: Mail, fax, in person. Both court and visitors may perform in person searches. Search fee: $15.00 per name. Fee is for first 15 years. Add $1.00 per add'l year. Court makes copy: $2.00 per page. Self serve copy fee: $1.00 per page. Required to search: name, years to search, DOB; also helpful: SSN. Felony records on computer since 1983, misdemeanors since 3/91. Mail turnaround time 3-4 days.

General Information: Public terminal goes back to 1988. No adoption or juvenile records released. Fee to fax documents is $5.00 per page. Certification fee: $5.00 per doc. Payee: Clerk of Court. Personal checks accepted. Prepayment and SASE required.

St. Landry Parish

27th District Court PO Box 750, Courthouse, Opelousas, LA 70570; phone: 337-942-5606; fax: 337-948-1653; hours 8AM-4:30PM (CST). *Felony, Misdemeanor, Civil, Probate.* www.stlandry.org

Civil Records: Access: Mail, fax, in person, online. Both court and visitors may perform in person searches. Search fee: $15.00 per name. Additional $1.00 fee per year after 1st 10 years. Court makes copy: $.75 per page. Required to search: name, years to search. Civil cases indexed by defendant, plaintiff; on index books back to 1800s, on computer back to 1992. A subscription access program to civil cases is available. The fee is $60.00 per month. Includes civil court records back to 1998, also land indexes and images. Contact the court or visit the web page for details. Mail turnaround time 1-2 days.

Criminal Records: Access: Mail, fax, in person. Both court and visitors may perform in person searches. Search fee: $15.00 per name. Additional $1.00 fee per year after 1st 10 years. Court makes copy: $.75 per page. Required to search: name, years to search, DOB; also helpful: SSN. Criminal records on index books back to 1800s, on computer back to 1992. Mail turnaround time 1-2 days.

General Information: Public terminal has only civil records. No adoption or juvenile records released. Fee to fax documents is $5.00 1st page, $1.00 each add'l. Certification fee: $5.50. Payee: Clerk of Court. Personal checks accepted. Prepayment and SASE required.

St. Martin Parish

16th District Court PO Box 308, St. Martinville, LA 70582; phone: 337-394-2210; fax: 337-394-7772; hours 8:30AM-4:30PM (CST). *Felony, Misdemeanor, Civil, Probate.*

Civil Records: Access: In person, online. Both court and visitors may perform in person searches. Search fee: $10.00 per name. Court makes copy: $.50 per page; same fee for self serve. Required to search: name, years to search; also helpful: address. Civil cases indexed by defendant, plaintiff. Civil records archived from 1760, on computer since 1990. Court indices to be available at the website.

Criminal Records: Access: In person. Both court and visitors may perform in person searches. Search fee: $10.00 per name. Court makes copy: $.50 per page; same fee for self serve. Required to search: name, years to search, DOB; also helpful: address, SSN. Criminal records archived from 1760, on computer since 1990.

General Information: Public terminal goes back to 1990. No adoption, sealed records, expunged or juvenile records released. Will fax documents $.75 per page. Certification fee: $6.00 per doc. Payee: Clerk of Court. Personal checks accepted. Prepayment required.

St. Mary Parish

16th Judicial District Court PO Box 1231, Franklin, LA 70538; phone: 337-828-4100 X200; fax: 337-828-2509; hours 8:30AM-4:30PM (CST). *Felony, Misdemeanor, Civil, Probate.*

Civil Records: Access: In person only. Visitors must perform in person searches. Court makes copy: $1.00 per page. Self serve copy fee: $.50 per page. Required to search: name, years to search. Civil cases indexed by defendant, plaintiff; on index books back to 1800s.

Criminal Records: Access: In person only. Visitors must perform in person searches themselves. Court makes copy: $1.00 per page. Self serve copy fee: $.50 per page. Required to search: name, years to search, DOB; SSN helpful. Criminal records on index books back to 1800s.

General Information: Public terminal has criminal back to 1983 and civil back to 1980. (Terminal is located in record room.) No adoption or juvenile records released. Certification fee: $5.00. Payee: St. Mary Parish Clerk of Court. Personal checks accepted. Prepayment required.

St. Tammany Parish

22nd District Court PO Box 1090, Covington, LA 70434; phone: 985-809-8700; criminal/civil fax: 985-809-8777; hours 8:30AM-4:30PM (CST). *Felony, Misdemeanor, Civil, Probate.* www.sttammanyclerk.org

Civil Records: Access: Mail, in person, online. Both court and visitors may perform in person searches. Search fee: $10.00 per name. Court makes copy: $.25 per page. Required to search: name, years to search. Civil cases indexed by defendant, plaintiff; on index books back to 1800s, on computer since 1967. Remote online access to civil records is from the Clerk of Court. $50 initial setup fee, $50.00 per month and $.20 to print a page. For information, call Kristie Howell at 985-809-8787. A dial-up service is also available; $100 setup and $.06 per minute. Civil index goes back to 1992; images to 1995. Search index free at https://www.sttammanyclerk.org/liveapp/default.asp. Mail turnaround time 2-3 days.

Criminal Records: Access: Mail, in person, online. Both court and visitors may perform in person searches. Search fee: $10.00 per name. Court makes copy: $.25 per page. Required to search: name, years to search, DOB; also helpful: SSN. Criminal records on computer since 10/87. Remote online access to criminal records is the same as civil. Dialup criminal indices go back to 1988. Mail turnaround time 2-3 days.

General Information: Public terminal has criminal back to 2987 and civil back to 1992. No adoption or juvenile records released. Certification fee: $2.00 per doc. Payee: Clerk of Court. Personal checks accepted. Prepayment and SASE required.

Tangipahoa Parish

21st District Court PO Box 667, Amite, LA 70422; phone: 985-748-4146; criminal fax: 985-747-3387; civil fax: 985-748-6746; hours 8:30AM-4:30PM (CST). *Felony, Misdemeanor, Civil, Probate.* www.tangiclerk.org

Civil Records: Access: Mail, in person, online. Both court and visitors may perform in person searches. Search fee: $10.00 per name per 10 years. Court makes copy: $1.00 per page; same fee for self serve. Required to search: name, years to search. Civil cases indexed by defendant, plaintiff. Civil records archived back to early 1900s; on computer back to 1980s. Online access to Parish notaries index records is by free subscription (subject to change); fee is $1.00 to print a document. Images go back to 1/1990; index to 1974. Visit www.tangiclerk.org/OnlineServices/onlineservices.asp for information or call Alison Theard: 985-748-4146. Mail turnaround time 3-4 days.

Criminal Records: Access: Mail, in person. Both court and visitors may perform in person searches. Search fee: $10.00 per name. Court makes copy: $1.00 per page; same fee for self serve. Required to search: name, years to search, DOB, SSN. Criminal records archived back to early 1900s; on computer back to 1993. Mail turnaround time 3-4 days.

General Information: Public terminal has only civil records back to 1980s. No adoption or juvenile records released. Fee to fax documents is $5.00 1st page, $1.00 each add'l. Certification fee: $5.50 per document. Payee: Clerk of Court. Personal checks accepted. Prepayment and SASE required.

Tensas Parish

6th District Court PO Box 78, 201 Courthouse Sq, St. Joseph, LA 71366; phone: 318-766-3921; hours 8:30AM-4:30PM (CST). *Felony, Misdemeanor, Civil, Probate.*

Civil Records: Access: In person only. Visitors must perform in person searches themselves. Court makes copy: $3.00 1st page, $2.00 ea add'l. Required to search: name, years to search. Civil cases indexed by defendant, plaintiff. Civil records archived back to 1800s, on computer since mid-1998.

Criminal Records: Access: In person only. Visitors must perform in person searches themselves. Court makes copy: $3.00 1st page, $2.00 ea add'l. Required to search: name, years to search; also helpful: DOB, SSN. Criminal records on computer since 1998; archived back to 1800s.

General Information: No public access terminal. No adoption or juvenile records released. Certification fee: $5.50. Payee: Clerk of Court. Personal checks accepted. Prepayment required.

Terrebonne Parish

32nd District Court PO Box 1569, 7856 Main St, Houma, LA 70361; phone: 985-868-5660; fax: 985-868-5143; hours 8:30AM-4:30PM (CST). *Felony, Misdemeanor, Civil, Probate, Traffic.* Note: Probate is separate index at this same address.

Civil Records: Access: Mail, in person. Both court and visitors may perform in person searches. Search fee: $20.00 per name. Court makes copy: $1.00 per page. Required to search: name, years to search. Civil cases indexed by defendant, plaintiff; on computer since 1986, in books to 1823. Mail turnaround time 1 week.

Criminal Records: Access: Mail, in person. Both court and visitors may perform in person searches. Search fee: $20.00 per name. Court makes copy: $1.00 per page. Required to search: name, years to search, DOB; also helpful: SSN, race, sex. Criminal records archived to 1800s. Mail turnaround time 1 week.

General Information: No public access terminal. No adoption or juvenile records released. Fee to fax documents is $2.00 per page. Certification fee: $5.00 per cert. Payee: Terrebonne Parish Clerk of Court. Personal checks accepted. Prepayment and SASE required.

Union Parish

3rd District Court Courthouse Bldg, 100 E Bayou #105, Farmerville, LA 71241; phone: 318-368-3055; criminal fax: 318-368-3861; civil/probate fax is the same; hours 8:30AM-4:30PM (CST). *Felony, Misdemeanor, Civil, Probate.*

Civil Records: Access: Mail, in person. Search fee: $5.00 per name. Court makes copy: $1.50 per page. Self serve copy fee: $1.00 per page. Required to search: name, years to search. Civil cases indexed by defendant, plaintiff; on index books back to 1839. Mail turnaround time 2-3 days.

Criminal Records: Access: Mail, fax, in person. Both court and visitors may perform in person searches. Search fee: $10.00 per name. Court makes copy: $1.50 per page. Self serve copy fee: $1.00 per page. Required to search: name, years to search, SSN. Criminal records on index books back to 1839; computerized records go back to 1982. Mail turnaround time 2-3 days.

General Information: No public access terminal. No adoption or juvenile records released. Will fax documents $5.00 per doc. Certification fee: $5.00 per instrument. Payee: Clerk of Court. Personal checks accepted. Prepayment and SASE required.

Vermilion Parish

15th District Court 100 N. State St, #101, Abbeville, LA 70511-0790; phone: 337-898-1992; fax: 337-898-9803; hours 8:30AM-4:30PM (CST). *Felony, Misdemeanor, Civil, Probate.*

Civil Records: Access: Phone, fax, mail, in person. Both court and visitors may perform in person searches. Search fee: $12.00 per name. Fee for second name on same search request is $6.50. Court makes copy: $.75 per page; same fee for self serve. Required to search: name, years to search. Civil cases indexed by defendant, plaintiff; on computer since 1982, in books since 1885, on microfilm since 1885. Mail turnaround time 1-2 days after payment.

Criminal Records: Access: Phone, fax, mail, in person. Both court and visitors may perform in person searches. Search fee: $12.00 per name. Fee for second name on same search request is $6.50. Court makes copy: $.75 per page; same fee for self serve. Required to search: name, years to search, DOB; also helpful: SSN, race, sex. Criminal records on computer since 1982, in books since 1885, on microfilm since 1885. Mail turnaround time 1-2 days after payment.

General Information: Public terminal has only criminal records back to 1980. No adoption or juvenile records released. Will fax documents $2.50 1st page, $1.50 each add'l. Certification fee: $5.00. Payee: Vermilion Parish Clerk of Court. Personal checks accepted. Prepayment and SASE required.

Vernon Parish

30th District Court PO Box 40, Leesville, LA 71496; phone: 337-238-1384; probate phone: 337-238-4345; fax: 337-238-9902; probate fax: same; hours 8AM-4:30PM (CST). *Felony, Misdemeanor, Civil, Probate.*

Civil Records: Access: Mail, fax, in person. Both court and visitors may perform in person searches. Search fee: $10.00 per name. Court makes copy: $1.25 per page. Required to search: name, years to search. Civil cases indexed by defendant, plaintiff; on computer from 11/1985, archived back to 1900. Mail turnaround time same day.

Criminal Records: Access: Mail, in person. Both court and visitors may perform in person searches. Search fee: $10.00 per name. Court makes copy: $1.25 per page. Required to search: name, years to search, DOB, SNN. Criminal records on computer from 11/1985, archived back to 1900. Mail turnaround time same day.

General Information: Public terminal has criminal back to 11/1985 and civil back to 1986. No adoption or juvenile records released. Will fax documents to local or toll free line. Certification fee: $5.00. Payee: Clerk of Court. Personal checks accepted. Prepayment and SASE required.

Washington Parish

22nd District Court PO Box 607, Franklinton, LA 70438; phone: 985-839-4663/7821; hours 8AM-4:30PM (CST). *Felony, Misdemeanor, Civil, Probate.*

Civil Records: Access: Mail, in person. Both court and visitors may perform in person searches. Search fee: $10.00 per name. Court makes copy: $1.00 per page. Self serve copy fee: $.50 per page. Required to search: name, years to search. Civil cases indexed by defendant, plaintiff; on computer from 1993, archived 4/1967, index books back to 1800s. Mail turnaround time 1-2 days.

Criminal Records: Access: Mail, in person. Both court and visitors may perform in person searches. Search fee: $10.00 per name. Court makes copy: $1.00 per page. Self serve copy fee: $.50 per page. Required to search: name, years to search, DOB, SSN. Criminal records on computer from 1993, archived 4/1967, index books back to 1800s. Mail turnaround time 1-2 days.

General Information: No adoption or juvenile records released. Certification fee: $5.00. Payee: Washington Parish Clerk of Court. Personal checks accepted. Prepayment required. SASE requested.

Webster Parish

26th District Court PO Box 370, Minden, LA 71058-0370; phone: 318-371-0366; fax: 318-371-0226; hours 8:30AM-4:30PM (CST). *Felony, Misdemeanor, Civil, Probate.*

Note: Probate is a separate index at this same address.

Civil Records: Access: Fax, mail, in person. Both court and visitors may perform in person searches. Search fee: $10.00 per name. Court makes copy: $1.00 per page. Self serve copy fee: $.50 per page. Required to search: name, years to search. Civil cases indexed by defendant, plaintiff. Civil records archived back to 1800s, on computer since 1986. Mail turnaround time 2-3 days.

Criminal Records: Access: Fax, mail, in person. Both court and visitors may perform in person searches. Search fee: $10.00 per name. Court makes copy: $1.00 per page. Self serve copy fee: $.50 per page. Required to search: name; also helpful: years to search. Criminal records not on computer, in books to 1800s. Mail turnaround time 2-3 days.

General Information: Public terminal has criminal back to 11/1992 and civil back to 4/1992. No adoption or juvenile records released. Will fax documents $5.00 per page. Certification fee: $5.00 per document. Payee: Clerk of Court. Personal checks accepted. Prepayment required.

West Baton Rouge Parish

18th District Court PO Box 107, Port Allen, LA 70767; phone: 225-383-0378; criminal fax: 225-383-3694; civil/probate fax is the same; hours 8:30AM-4:30PM (CST). *Felony, Misdemeanor, Civil, Probate.*

Civil Records: Access: Phone, mail, in person. Both court and visitors may perform in person searches. Search fee: $10.00 per name. Court makes copy: $1.00 per page. Self serve copy fee: $.50 per page. Required to search: name, years to search. Civil cases indexed by defendant, plaintiff; on computer from 1983. Mail turnaround time 1-2 days.

Criminal Records: Access: Phone, mail, in person. Both court and visitors may perform in person searches. Search fee: $10.00 per name. Court makes copy: $1.00 per page. Self serve copy fee: $.50 per page. Required to search: name, years to search, DOB; also helpful: SSN. Criminal records on computer from 1983. Mail turnaround 1-2 days.

General Information: Public terminal goes back to 1983. No adoption or juvenile records released. Will fax documents for $5.00 per document. Certification fee: $5.00 per doc. Payee: Clerk of Court. Personal checks accepted. Prepayment and SASE required.

West Carroll Parish

5th District Court PO Box 1078, Oak Grove, LA 71263; phone: 318-428-3281; fax: 318-428-9896; hours 8:30AM-4:30PM (CST). *Felony, Misdemeanor, Civil, Probate.*

Civil Records: Access: Mail, in person. Both court and visitors may perform in person searches. Search fee: $1.00 per name per year. Court makes copy: $1.00 per page. Required to search: name, years to search. Civil cases indexed by defendant, plaintiff; on index books back to 1800s. Mail turnaround time 1-2 days.

Criminal Records: Access: Mail, in person. Both court and visitors may perform in person searches. Search fee: $1.00 per name per year. Court makes copy: $1.00 per page. Required to search: name, years to search, DOB. Criminal records on index books back to 1800s. Mail turnaround time 1-2 days.

General Information: Public use terminal available. No adoption or juvenile records released. Will fax documents to local or toll free line. Certification fee: $5.00 per certification. Payee: Clerk of Court. Only cashiers checks and money orders accepted. Prepayment and SASE required.

West Feliciana Parish

20th District Court PO Box 1843, St Francisville, LA 70775; phone: 225-635-3794; fax: 225-635-3770; hours 8:30AM-4:30PM (CST). *Felony, Misdemeanor, Civil, Probate.*

Civil Records: Access: Mail, in person. Both court and visitors may perform in person searches. Search fee: $10.00 per name. Fee is per 10 years searched. Court makes copy: $1.00 per page; same fee for self serve. Required to search: name, years to search; also helpful: address. Civil cases indexed by defendant, plaintiff; on computer from 1984, index books back to 1800s. Mail turnaround time 3-5 days.

Criminal Records: Access: Mail, in person. Both court and visitors may perform in person searches. Search fee: $10.00 per name. Fee is per 10 years searched. Court makes copy: $1.00 per page; same fee for self serve. Required to search: name, years to search, DOB; also helpful: address. Criminal records on computer since 1992; prior on cards and dockets back to 1800s. Mail turnaround time 3-5 days.

General Information: Public use terminal available. No adoption, juvenile or juvenile records released. Certification fee: $5.00. Payee: Clerk of Court. Business checks accepted. Prepayment and SASE required.

Winn Parish

8th District Court 100 Main St, #103, Winnfield, LA 71483; phone: 318-628-3515; fax: 318-628-3527; hours 8AM-4:30PM (CST). *Felony, Misdemeanor, Civil, Probate.*

Civil Records: Access: Mail, in person. Both court and visitors may perform in person searches. Search fee: $20.00 per name; $10.00 for second name. Fee is for 10 year search. Court makes copy: $1.00 per page; same fee for self serve. Required to search: name, years to search, address. Civil cases indexed by defendant, plaintiff; on books from 1886 to present, on computer from 1988, mortgages since 1981, conveyances since 1993. Mail turnaround 2-3 days.

Criminal Records: Access: Mail, in person. Both court and visitors may perform in person searches. Search fee: $20.00 per name; $10.00 for second name. Fee is for 10 year search. Court makes copy: $1.00 per page; same fee for self serve. Required to search: name, years to search, address, DOB; also helpful: SSN. Criminal records in books since 1886, computerized since 1997. Mail turnaround 2-3 days.

General Information: No public access terminal. No adoption or juvenile records released. Fee to fax documents is $5.00 per document and $1.00 per page. Certification fee: $5.00. Payee: Winn Parish Clerk of Court. Personal checks accepted. Prepayment and SASE required.

Louisiana Recording Offices

ORGANIZATION: 64 parishes (not counties), 64 recording offices. One parish, St. Martin, has two non-contiguous segments. The recording officer is the Clerk of Court. Many parishes include tax and other non-UCC liens in their mortgage records. The entire state is in the Central Time Zone (CST).

REAL ESTATE RECORDS: Most parishes will perform a mortgage search. Some will provide a record owner search. Copy and certification fees vary widely.

UCC RECORDS: Financing statements are filed with the Clerk of Court in any parish in the state and are entered onto a statewide computerized database of UCC financing statements available for searching at any parish office. All parishes perform UCC searches for $30.00 per debtor name. Use search request form UCC-11. Copy fees are $1.00 to $1.25 per page.

TAX LIEN RECORDS: All federal and state tax liens are filed with the Clerk of Court. Parishes usually file tax liens on personal property in their UCC or mortgage records, and most will perform tax lien searches for varying fees. Some parishes will automatically include tax liens on personal property in a mortgage certificate search.

OTHER LIENS: Judgments, labor, material, hospital.

ONLINE ACCESS: A number of Parishes offer online access to recorded documents. Most are commercial fee systems.

Acadia Parish

Clerk of Court, PO Box 922, Crowley, LA 70526. RE & UCC recording phone-337-788-8881; fax-337-788-1048; hours: 8:30AM-4:30PM www.acadiaparishclerk.com
Separate indices to search include conveyances, mortgages, miscellaneous. Record index not computerized. Only the public may search. Search fee- mortgage: $20.00 1st, $10.00 each add'l. Will provide mortgage certificates. Copy fee $1.00 per page. Cert fee- $5.50 per cert plus copy fee. Payee- Acadia Parish Clerk of Court. **Other phones:** Treasurer- 337-788-8800; Elections- 337-788-8881; Vital Records- 337-788-8881. **Property tax/Assessor-** 337-788-8871.

Allen Parish

Clerk of Court, PO Box 248, Oberlin, LA 70655. RE & UCC recording phone-337-639-4351; fax-337-639-2030; hours: 8AM-4:30PM
Separate indices to search include mortgage, conveyance, misc. Office will perform a UCC search but public must search other records themselves. UCC search per debtor name- $30.00. Tax lien search fee- $20.00 1st name, $10.00 each add'l name. Copy fee $1.00 per page. Cert fee- $5.00 per cert plus copy fee. Payee- Allen Parish Clerk of Court. **Other phones:** Elections- 337-639-4351; Vital Records- 337-639-4351. **Property tax/Assessor-** 337-639-4391.

Ascension Parish

Clerk of Court, PO Box 192, Donaldsonville, LA 70346. RE & UCC recording phone-225-473-9866; fax-225-473-0758; hours: 8:30AM-4:30PM www.eatel.net/~apcc
Office personnel or visitors may perform searches. Search fee $6.00 per name. UCC search per debtor name- $15.00. Copy fee $1.00 per page. Cert fee- $5.00 per cert plus copy fee. Payee- Ascension Parish Clerk of Court. **Property tax/Assessor-** 225-473-9239.

Assumption Parish

Clerk of Court, PO Drawer 249, Napoleonville, LA 70390. 985-369-6653; fax-985-369-2032; hours: 8:30AM-4:30PM
Separate indices to search include conveyance and mortgage. Records indexed on a public use terminal back to 1990; back to 1981 for mortgages. Office personnel or visitors may perform searches. General index search fee $10.00 per name. Copy fee $1.00 per page. Cert fee- $5.00 per cert plus copy fee. Payee- Assumption Parish Clerk of Court. **Other phones:** ; Register of Voters- 985-369-7347. **Property tax/Assessor-** 985-369-6385.

Avoyelles Parish

Clerk of Court, PO Box 196, Marksville, LA 71351. RE & UCC recording phone-318-253-7523; fax-318-253-4614; hours: 8:30AM-4:30PM
Office personnel or visitors may perform searches. UCC search per debtor name- $30.00. Separate federal/state combined tax lien search- $21.00 per debtor. Copy fee $1.00 per page. Cert fee- $5.00 per cert plus copy fee. Payee- Avoyelles Parish Clerk of Court. **Other phones:** Treasurer- 318-253-9208. **Property tax/Assessor-** 318-253-4507.

Beauregard Parish

Clerk of Court, PO Box 100, De Ridder, LA 70634. 337-463-8595; fax-337-462-3916; hours: 8AM-4:30PM
Record index not computerized. Office personnel or visitors may perform searches. Search fee $30.00 UCCs, other searches vary. Copy fee $1.25 per page. Cert fee- $5.00 per cert plus copy fee. Payee- Beauregard Parish Clerk of Court. **Property tax/Assessor-** 337-463-8945.

Bienville Parish

Clerk of Court, 100 Courthouse Dr; Rm 100, Arcadia, LA 71001-3600. RE & UCC recording phone-318-263-2123; fax-318-263-7426; hours: 8:30AM-4:30PM www.bienvilleparish.org/clerk
Records indexed on a public use terminal back to 1986. Office will perform a UCC and Tax lien search but public must search other records themselves. General index search fee $20.00 1st name, $10.00 each add'l name. UCCs $30.00. Copy fee $2.00, if tax lien or real estate $1.00 per page. Cert fee- $5.00 per cert plus copy fee. Payee- Bienville Parish Clerk of Court. **Other phones:** Treasurer- 318-263-2019. **Property tax/Assessor-** 318-263-2214.

Bossier Parish

Clerk of Court, PO Box 430, Benton, LA 71006. 318-965-2336; fax-318-965-2713; hours: 8:30AM-4:30PM www.bossierclerk.com
Office personnel or visitors may perform searches. Search fee $15.00 per name. Copy fee $1.00 per page. RE or tax lien copy- $.50 per page. Cert fee- $2.00 per cert plus copy fee. Payee- Bossier Parish Clerk of Court. **Property tax/Assessor-** 318-965-2213.

Caddo Parish

Clerk of Court, 501 Texas St #103, Shreveport, LA 71101-5408. Main phone & R/E recording-318-226-6780, UCC recording phone-318-226-6783; fax-318-227-9080; hours: 8:30AM-5PM www.caddoclerk.com
Index: Many indexes. Records indexed on computer. Office will perform a UCC search but public must search other records themselves. Search fee $30.00; $10.00 each add'l name. Copy fee $.50 per page; $1.25 if mailed. Cert fee- $2.00 per doc plus copy fee. Payee- Caddo Parish Clerk of Court. **Online access to Real Estate, Lien, Marriage, Assessor, Property records:** Access to the Parish online records requires a $100 set up fee plus $30 monthly fee; $.25 per image. Mortgages and indirect conveyances date back to 1981; direct conveyances date back to 1914. Lending agency information available. Marriage licenses free back to 1937; use username "muser" and password "caddo." Signup and info at www.caddoclerk.com/remote.htm or call 318-226-6523. Also, search assessor property free at www.caddoassessor.org/cgi-bin/pub_search.pl; no name searching for free; Annual sub for full data-$1.00 per day. **Other phones:** Treasurer- 318-226-6900; Elections- 318-226-6788. **Property tax/Assessor-** same address as above. 318-226-6702.

Calcasieu Parish

Clerk of Court, PO Box 1030, Lake Charles, LA 70601-1030. 337-437-3550; fax-337-437-3350; hours: 8:30AM-4:30PM
Index: Several indexes. Only the public may search. Copy fee $1.00 per page. Cert fee- $5.00 per cert plus copy fee. Payee- Calcasieu Parish Clerk of Court. **Online access to Real Estate, Recording, Deed, Mortgage, Marriage, Court, UCC records:** Online access to court record indices is free at www.calclerkofcourt.com/resolution/. Registration and password required. Full documents requires $100.00 per month subscription. **Other phones:** Treasurer- 337-437-3680. **Property tax/Assessor-** 337-437-3461.

Caldwell Parish

Clerk of Court, PO Box 1327, Columbia, LA 71418. RE & UCC recording phone-318-649-2272; fax-318-649-2037; hours: 8AM-4:30PM
Separate indices to search include mortgage and conveyance indexes, civil and probate indexes, misc indexes, etc. Office personnel (simple searches) or visitors may perform searches. Search fee $20.00 per name. UCC search per debtor name- $30.00. Copy fee $1.00 per page. Cert fee- $5.00 per cert plus copy fee. Payee- Caldwell Parish Clerk of Court. **Other phones:** Treasurer- 318-649-2681. **Property tax/Assessor-** 318-649-2636.

Cameron Parish

Clerk of Court, PO Box 549, Cameron, LA 70631. RE & UCC recording phone-337-775-5316; fax-337-775-7172; hours: 8:30AM-4:30PM
Separate indices to search. Record index not computerized. Only the public may search. Copy

fee $1.00 per page. Cert fee- $5.00 per cert plus copy fee. Payee- Cameron Parish Clerk of Court. **Other phones:** Treasurer- 337-775-5718; Elections- 337-775-5316; Vital Records- 337-775-5316. **Property tax/Assessor-** 337-775-5416.

Catahoula Parish

Clerk of Court, PO Box 654, Harrisonburg, LA 71340. 318-744-5497; fax-318-744-5488; hours: 8:30AM-4:30PM
Separate indices to search include mortgage, conveyance, charter. Office will perform a UCC search but public must search other records themselves. Search fee $20.00 per name. UCC search per debtor name- $30.00. Copy fee $1.00 per page. Cert fee- $5.00 per cert plus copy fee. Payee- Catahoula Parish Clerk of Court. **Property tax/Assessor-** PO Box 570, Harrisonburg, LA 71340; 318-744-5291.

Claiborne Parish

Clerk of Court, PO Box 330, Homer, LA 71040. RE & UCC recording phone-318-927-9601; fax-318-927-2345; hours: 8:30AM-4:30PM
Office personnel or visitors may perform searches. General index search fee $20.00 for first name, $10.00 each add'l. UCC search per debtor name- $30.00. Separate federal tax lien search- $20.00 per debtor. Separate state tax lien search- $20.00 per debtor. Copy fee $1.00 per page. Cert fee- $5.00 per cert plus copy fee. Payee- Claiborne Parish Clerk of Court. **Other phones:** Treasurer- 318-927-2222; Elections- 318-927-9601; Vital Records- 318-927-9601. **Property tax/Assessor-** 508 E Main St, Homer, LA 71040; 318-927-3022.

Concordia Parish

Clerk of Court, PO Box 790, Vidalia, LA 71373. RE & UCC recording phone-318-336-4204; fax-318-336-8777;   hours: 8:30AM-4:30PM
www.concordiaclerk.org
Separate indices to search include conveyance, mtg. Records indexed on a public use terminal back to 1973. Office personnel or visitors may perform searches. Search fee $30.00. Copy fee $1.00 per page. Cert fee- $5.50 per cert plus copy fee. Payee- Concordia Parish Clerk of Court. **Other phones:** Treasurer- 318-336-2151; Appraiser/Auditor- 318-336-5122; Elections- 318-336-4204. **Property tax/Assessor-** 318-336-5122.

De Soto Parish

Clerk of Court, PO Box 1206, Mansfield, LA 71052. RE & UCC recording phone-318-872-3110; fax-318-872-4202;   hours: 8AM-4:30PM
www.desotoparishclerk.org
Separate indices to search include civil, criminal, conveyance, mtg, marriage. Records indexed on a public use terminal back to 1958. Office personnel or visitors may perform searches. Search fee $10.00. Copy fee $1.00 per page. Cert fee- $3.50 per cert plus copy fee. Payee- De Soto Parish Clerk of Court. **Online access to Real Estate, Recorder, Deed, Judgment, Lien, Mortgage records:** Access Clerk of Court records index by subscription at www.desotoparishclerk.org/online.html; set-up fee is $50.00 plus either $50 per month for index only searching or $100 per month for index, doc viewing, and images. **Other phones:** Elections- 318-872-3110; Criminal- 318-872-3181; Civil -318-872-3788. **Property tax/Assessor-** 318-872-3610.

East Baton Rouge Parish

Clerk of Court, PO Box 1991, Baton Rouge, LA 70821-1991. 225-389-3960, R/E recording phone-225-389-3975, UCC recording phone-225-389-3975; fax-225-389-3392;   hours: 7:30AM-5:30PM
www.ebrclerkofcourt.org
All records in one index. Records indexed on a public use terminal back to 1/1/1986. Office personnel or visitors may perform searches. General index search fee $23.10 per doc. Copy fee $.50 per page. Cert fee- $5.00 per cert plus copy

fee. Payee- East Baton Rouge Parish Clerk of Court. **Online access to Real Estate, Lien, Marriage, Probate, Court, Judgment, Map Data Index records:** Access to online records requires a $100 set up fee with a $5 monthly fee and $.33 per minute of use. Four years worth of data is kept active on the system. Lending agency information is available. For information, contact Wendy Gibbs at 225-398-5295. UCC information is located at the Secretary of State. **Other phones:** Elections- 225-389-4765. **Property tax/Assessor-** Assessor at same address, Rm 126 225-389-3920.

East Carroll Parish

Clerk of Court, 400 First St, Lake Providence, LA 71254. RE & UCC recording phone-318-559-2399; fax-318-559-1502; hours: 8:30AM-4:30PM
Office personnel or visitors may perform searches. Search fee $20.00 per debtor per 10 years. UCC search per debtor name- $30.00. Copy fee $2.00 per page. Cert fee- $5.00 per cert plus copy fee. Payee- East Carroll Parish Clerk of Court. **Other phones:** Treasurer- 318-559-2000. **Property tax/Assessor-** 318-559-2850.

East Feliciana Parish

Clerk of Court, PO Drawer 599, Clinton, LA 70722. RE & UCC recording phone-225-683-5145; fax-225-683-3556;   hours: 8:30AM-4:30PM
www.eastfelicianaclerk.com/
Separate indices to search include Conveyance, Mtg, Misc, and Marriage. Office will perform a UCC search but public must search other records themselves. Search fee $30.00. All Property searches done by name only. Copy fee $1.00 per page. Cert fee- $5.00 per page plus copy fee. Payee- East Feliciana Parish Clerk of Court. **Online access to Real Estate, Lien, Mortgage, Marriage, Civil Court records:** Access to online records requires a subscription, $100 set up fee with a $50 monthly usage fee for indices or $100.00 per month for indices plus images. Conveyances go back to 1962, mortgages to 1981. Marriages go back to 1987 and miscellaneous back to 1984. For information, contact clerk's office at 225-683-5145 or visit www.eastfelicianaclerk.com/. **Other phones:** Elections- 225-683-5145. **Property tax/Assessor-** PO Box 263, Clinton, LA 70722; 225-683-8945.

Evangeline Parish

Clerk of Court, PO Drawer 347, Ville Platte, LA 70586. RE & UCC recording phone-337-363-5671; fax-337-363-5780; hours: 8AM-4:30PM
Separate indices to search include civil, criminal, mortgage,   conveyance,   corporations, miscellaneous, etc. Office personnel or visitors may perform searches. Search fee $15.00 per name. Copy fee $1.00 per page, $5.00 minimum. Cert fee- $2.00 per page includes copy fee. Payee- Evangeline Parish Clerk of Court. **Other phones:** Treasurer- 337-363-5651; Elections- 337-363-5671. **Property tax/Assessor-** 337-363-4310.

Franklin Parish

Clerk of Court, PO Box 1564, Winnsboro, LA 71295. RE & UCC recording phone-318-435-5133; fax-318-435-5134; hours: 8:30AM-4:30PM
All records in one index. Records indexed on computer back to 1995. Office personnel or visitors may perform searches. General index search fee $20.00 per name. Mortgage searches available. Property description required. Will search UCC records, tax liens not included in UCC search. UCC search per debtor name- $30.00. Separate federal/state combined tax lien search- $30.00 per debtor. Copy fee $2.00, if tax lien or real estate $1.00 per page. Cert fee- $5.00 per cert plus copy fee. Payee- Franklin Parish Clerk of Court. **Property tax/Assessor-** 318-435-5390.

Grant Parish

Clerk of Court, PO Box 263, Colfax, LA 71417. RE & UCC recording phone-318-627-3246; fax-318-627-3201; hours: 8:30AM-4:30PM
Separate indices to search include mortgages, conveyances, civil suits, criminal suits, marriage records. Record index not computerized. Office personnel or visitors may perform searches. General index search fee $20.00 per search. Will not search real estate records. UCC search per debtor name- $30.00. Separate federal/state combined tax lien search- $20.00; $10.00 add'l name. Copy fee $1.00 per page. Cert fee- $5.00 per cert plus copy fee. Payee- Grant Parish Clerk of Court. **Other phones:** Treasurer- 318-627-3157; Elections- 318-627-3246. **Property tax/Assessor-** 318-627-5471.

Iberia Parish

Clerk of Court, PO Drawer 12010, New Iberia, LA 70562-2010. 337-365-7282; fax-337-365-0737; hours: 8:30AM-4:30PM
Separate indices to search include books conveyance to 1974, mtgs to 1959, marriage to 2000. Records indexed on computer. Office personnel or visitors may perform searches. Search fees- tax lien $20.00; UCCs $30.00. Copy fee $.75 per page. Cert fee- $5.50 per cert plus copy fee. Payee- Iberia Parish Clerk of Court. **Online access to Real Estate, Lien, Marriage, Divorce records:** Access to the Parish online records requires a $50 monthly usage fee. Records date back to 1959. Lending agency information is available. For information, contact Mike Thibodeaux at 337-365-7282. **Property tax/Assessor-** 337-369-4415.

Iberville Parish

Clerk of Court, PO Box 423, Plaquemine, LA 70765-0423. 225-687-5160; fax-225-687-5260; hours: 8:30AM-4:30PM
Mortgage searches available. UCC search per debtor name- $30.00. Copy fee $1.00 per page. Cert fee- $5.00 per cert plus copy fee. Payee- Iberville Parish Clerk of Court. **Property tax/Assessor-** 225-687-3568.

Jackson Parish

Clerk of Court, PO Box 370, Jonesboro, LA 71251. RE & UCC recording phone-318-259-2424; fax-318-395-0386; hours: 8:30AM-4:30PM
Separate indices to search include conveyances, mortgage, UCC, misc. Office personnel or visitors may perform searches. General index search fee $20.00 per name. Office will no do title searches, but will assist. UCC search per debtor name- $30.00. Tax liens show up on a mortgage certificate search. Separate federal/state combined tax lien search- $20.00 per debtor. Copy fee $1.00 per page. Cert fee- $5.00 per cert plus copy fee. Payee- Jackson Parish Clerk of Court. **Other phones:** Elections- 318-259-2424; Police Jury- 318-259-2361. **Property tax/Assessor-** 500 E Court Ave, Courthouse, Jonesboro, LA 71251; 318-259-2151.

Jefferson Davis Parish

Clerk of Court, PO Box 799, Jennings, LA 70546-0799. 337-824-1160/1161, R/E recording phone-337-824-1160, UCC recording phone-337-824-1160; fax-337-824-1354; hours: 8:30AM-4:30PM
Separate indices to search include mortgage, conveyance, sheriff sale, charger, partnership. Records indexed on a public use terminal back to 1978. Office personnel or visitors may perform searches. General index search fee $20.00 per 1st name, $10.00 each add'l name. UCC search per debtor name- $30.00. Copy fee $2.00, if tax lien or real estate $1.00 per page. Cert fee- $5.00 to $20.00 per cert plus copy fee. Payee- Jefferson Davis Parish Clerk of Court. **Other phones:** Treasurer- 337-824-4792; Elections- 337-824-1160; Vital Records- 337-824-1161; 337-824-8340- Civil Dept. **Property tax/Assessor-** 337-824-3451.

Jefferson Parish

Clerk of Court, PO Box 10, Gretna, LA 70054-0010. Main phone & R/E recording-504-364-2943/2944, UCC recording phone-504-364-2881; fax-504-364-2942; 7:30AM-4:30PM www.jpclerkofcourt.us

All records in one index. Records indexed on a public use terminal back to 1967. Office will perform a UCC search but public must search other records themselves. UCC search per debtor name- $30.00. Copy fee $1.00 per page. Cert fee-$2.00 per page includes copy fee. Payee- Jefferson Parish Clerk of Court. **Online access to Real Estate, Assessor, Marriage, Civil, Assessor, Property Tax records:** Access to the clerk's JeffNet database is by subscription; set-up fee is $200.00 plus $8.50 monthly and $.25 per minute. Mortgage and conveyance images go back to 1971 and changing; index to 1967. Marriage and assessor records go back to 1992. Visit https://ssl.jpclerkofcourt.us/JeffnetSetup/default.asp. Also, search the assessor property rolls free at www.jpassessor.com. Call Donna Richoux at 504-364-2900 for fees. **Other phones:** Elections- 504-364-2963.

La Salle Parish

Clerk of Court, PO Box 1316, Jena, LA 71342. RE & UCC recording phone-318-992-2158; fax-318-992-2157; hours: 8:30AM-4:30PM

Separate indices to search include mtgs, conveyances, civil, criminal. Records indexed on a public use terminal back to 1993. Office personnel or visitors may perform searches. General index search fee $20.00 first name; $10.00 each add'l name. Copy fee $1.00 per page. Cert fee- $5.00 per cert; $1.00 per page. Payee- La Salle Parish Clerk of Court. **Other phones:** Appraiser/Auditor-318-992-2211; Elections- 318-992-2158; Vital Records- 318-992-2158. **Property tax/Assessor-** 318-992-8256.

Lafayette Parish

Clerk of Court, PO Box 2009, Lafayette, LA 70502. 337-291-6400, R/E recording phone-337-291-6310, UCC recording phone-337-291-6310; fax-337-291-6392; hours: 8:30AM-4:30PM www.lafayetteparishclerk.com

All records in one index. Records indexed on computer. Office personnel or visitors may perform searches. Search fee $30.00 UCCs; tax lien $20.00. Copy fee $1.00 per page. Cert fee-$5.50 + copy fees. Payee- Lafayette Parish Clerk of Court. **Online access to Real Estate, Lien records:** Access to Parish online records requires a $100 set up fee plus $15 per month and $.50 per minute. Conveyances date back to 1936; mortgages to 1948; other records to 1986. Lending agency information is available. For information, contact Derek Comeaux at 337-291-6433. Tax and UCC lien information is for this parish only. Also, assessor property data is free at www.lafayetteassessor.com/search.html, but no name searching. **Other phones:** Elections- 337-291-6454; Vital Records- 337-262-5616 x139. **Property tax/Assessor-** 337-291-7080.

Lafourche Parish

Clerk of Court, PO Box 818, Thibodaux, LA 70302. RE & UCC recording phone-985-447-4841; fax-985-447-5800; hours: 8:30AM-4:30PM

Separate indices to search include conveyance, mortgage, misc., charter, wills, discharges, court orders, adoptions. Search fees- mortgage certificate $20.00 1st name, $10.00 2nd name. UCC search-$30.00 per name. Copy fee $1.00 per page. UCCs-$2.00 per page. Cert fee- $5.00 per cert plus copy fee. Payee- Lafourche Parish Clerk of Court. **Other phones:** Treasurer- 985-447-4841; Elections- 985-447-4841. **Property tax/Assessor-** 403 St Louis St, Thibodaux, LA 70301; 985-447-7242.

Lincoln Parish

Clerk of Court, PO Box 924, Ruston, LA 71273-0924. RE & UCC recording phone-318-251-5130; fax-318-255-6004; 8:30AM-4:30PM www.lincolnparish.org

Separate indices to search include Conveyance, Mtg, Charter, Oathes, and Bonds. Office will perform a UCC search but public must search other records themselves. Search fee $20.00. Copy fee $1.00 per page. Cert fee- $3.00 per cert plus copy fee. Payee- Lincoln Parish Clerk of Court. **Property tax/Assessor-** 318-251-5140.

Livingston Parish

Clerk of Court, PO Box 1150, Livingston, LA 70754. 225-686-2216; fax-225-686-1867; hours: 8AM-4:30PM

Office personnel or visitors may perform searches. General search fee $22.00 per name. Will not search real estate records. UCC search per debtor name-$15.00. Copy fee $1.00 per page. Cert fee- $5.00 per page. Payee- Livingston Parish Clerk of Court. **Property tax/Assessor-** 225-686-7278.

Madison Parish

Clerk of Court, PO Box 1710, Tallulah, LA 71282. RE & UCC recording phone-318-574-0655; fax-318-574-3961; hours: 8:30AM-4:30PM

Separate indices to search include conveyances, mortgages, partnerships, incorporations, bonds. Records indexed on a public use terminal back to 1981, 1983 for images. Office personnel or visitors may perform searches. UCC search per debtor name- $30.00. Copy fee $2.00 per page. Cert fee-$5.50 per cert plus copy fee. Payee- Madison Parish Clerk of Court. **Other phones:** Elections- 318-574-0655. **Property tax/Assessor-** 100 N. Cedar St, Courthouse, Tallulah, LA 71282; 318-574-0117.

Morehouse Parish

Clerk of Court, PO Box 1543, Bastrop, LA 71221-1543. RE & UCC recording phone-318-281-3343; fax-318-281-3775; hours: 8:30AM-4:30PM

Separate indices to search include mortgage, conveyance, marriage, UCC - direct and indirect. Records indexed on a public use terminal back to 1970. Office personnel or visitors may perform searches. General index search fee $15.00 per name. UCC search per debtor name- $30.00. Separate federal/state combined tax lien search-$20.00 per debtor. Copy fee $1.00 per page. Cert fee- $5.00 per cert plus copy fee. Payee- Morehouse Parish Clerk of Court. **Other phones:** Vital Records- 318-568-5050. **Property tax/Assessor-** 106 E Jefferson, Bastrop, LA 71220; 318-281-1802.

Natchitoches Parish

Clerk of Court, PO Box 476, Natchitoches, LA 71458-0476. 318-352-8152; fax-318-352-9321; hours: 8:30AM-4:30PM

Records indexed on a public use terminal back to 1986. Office personnel or visitors may perform searches. Search fee $10.00 per name, per year. Copy fee $1.00 per page. Cert fee- $5.00 per cert plus copy fee. Payee- Natchitoches Parish Clerk of Court. **Other phones:** Elections- 318-352-8152; Vital Records- 318-357-2243; Civil- 318-357-2293 or 2294. **Property tax/Assessor-** 318-352-2377.

Orleans Parish

Clerk of Court, 421 Loyola Ave; B-1, Rm 402, New Orleans, LA 70112. 504-592-9100, R/E recording phone-504-592-9176, UCC recording phone-504-592-9189; fax-504-592-9128; hours: 9AM-4PM www.orleanscdc.gov

Search fee $30.00 per name. Copy fee $2.00, if real estate $1.00 per page. Cert fee- $5.00 per page for UCC; $3.00 for real estate records. Payee-Orleans Parish Recorder of Mortgages. **Online access to Real Estate, Mortgage, Lien, Birth, Death records:** Access to the Parish online records requires a $300 yearly subscription fee. Records date back to 1989. Access includes real estate, liens, civil and 1st city court records. For information, contact at 504-592-9264. Also, unofficial birth records to 1900 and death records to 1950 are free at www.rootsweb.com/~usgenweb/la/orleans.htm. Also

includes limited marriage lists. **Other phones:** Vital Records- 504-568-5152. **Property tax/Assessor-** 504-592-7050.

Ouachita Parish

Clerk of Court, PO Box 1862, Monroe, LA 71210-1862. 318-327-1444; fax-318-327-1462; hours: 8:30AM-5PM

Office personnel or visitors may perform searches. Search fee $30.00 per name. Copy fee $1.00 per page. Cert fee- $3.50 per cert plus copy fee. Payee-Ouachita Parish Clerk of Court. **Property tax/Assessor-** 318-327-1300.

Plaquemines Parish

Clerk of Court, PO Box 40, Belle Chasse, LA 70037-0040. RE & UCC recording phone-504-297-5180; fax-504-297-5195; hours: 8:30AM-4:30PM

Separate indices to search include mortgage, conveyance, marriage, criminal, civil, UCC, other miscellaneous. Records indexed on a public use terminal. Office will perform a UCC search but public must search other records themselves. General index search fee $20.00 for 1st name, $10.00 each add'l name. Copy fee $.50 per page. Cert fee- $5.00 per cert plus copy fee. Payee-Plaquemines Parish Clerk of Court. **Other phones:** Elections- 504-297-5180. **Property tax/Assessor-** 504-297-5250.

Pointe Coupee Parish

Clerk of Court, PO Box 86, New Roads, LA 70760. RE & UCC recording phone-225-638-9596; fax-225-638-9590; hours: 8:30AM-4:30PM

Office personnel or visitors may perform searches. General index search fee $12.00 first name, $6.50 each add'l name. UCC search per debtor name-$30.00. Copy fee $1.00 per page. Cert fee- $5.00 per cert plus copy fee. Payee- Pointe Coupee Parish Clerk of Court. **Other phones:** Treasurer-504-638-9556. **Property tax/Assessor-** 225-638-7077.

Rapides Parish

Clerk of Court, PO Box 952, Alexandria, LA 71309. RE & UCC recording phone-318-473-8153; fax-318-473-4667; 8:30AM-4:30PM www.rapidesclerk.org

Separate indices to search include conveyance, UCC, chattel, mortgage, courts. Records indexed on a public use terminal back to 1984. Office will perform a UCC search but public must search other records themselves. Current owner searches available. UCC search per debtor name- $30.00. Separate federal/state combined tax lien- $20.00 per debtor. Copy fee $1.00 per page. Cert fee- $5.00 per cert plus copy fee. Payee- Rapides Parish Clerk of Court. **Other phones:** Elections- 318-473-6770. **Property tax/Assessor-** 701 Murray St., Alexandria, LA 71301; 318-448-8511.

Red River Parish

Clerk of Court, PO Box 485, Coushatta, LA 71019-0485. RE & UCC recording phone-318-932-6741; fax-318-932-3126; hours: 8:30AM-4:30PM

Separate indices to search include Conveyance and Mortgages. Office will perform a UCC and tax liens search but public must search other records themselves. Search fee $30.00 UCCs; tax liens $20.00. Copy fee $1.00 per page. Cert fee- $5.00 per cert plus copy fee. Payee- Red River Parish Clerk of Court. **Other phones:** Elections- 318-932-6741. **Property tax/Assessor-** PO Box 509, Coushatta, LA 71019; 318-932-4922.

Richland Parish

Clerk of Court, PO Box 119, Rayville, LA 71269. 318-728-4171; fax-318-728-7020; 8:30AM-4:30PM

Office personnel or visitors may perform searches. Search fee $20.00 per name. UCC search per debtor name- $30.00. Copy fee $1.00 per page. Cert fee- $5.00 per cert plus copy fee. Payee-Richland Parish Clerk of Court. **Property tax/Assessor-** 318-728-4491.

Sabine Parish

Clerk of Court, PO Box 419, Many, LA 71449. RE & UCC recording phone-318-256-6223; fax-318-256-9037; hours: 8AM-4:30PM
Separate indices to search include conveyance and mortgage. Office personnel or visitors may perform searches. Search fee $30.00 per name. Real estate owner, mortgage, and property transfer searches available. Copy fee $1.25 per page. Cert fee- $5.00 per cert plus copy fee. Payee- Sabine Parish Clerk of Court. **Other phones:** Treasurer- 318-256-5637; Sheriff- 318-256-9241. **Property tax/Assessor-** 318-256-3482.

St. Bernard Parish

Clerk of Court, PO Box 1746, Chalmette, LA 70044. RE & UCC recording phone-504-271-3434; hours: 8:30AM-4:30PM
All records in one index. Office personnel or visitors may perform searches. General index search fee $10.00 per name. Mortgage and property transfer searches available. Will search UCC records; search includes tax liens if requested. UCC search per debtor name- $15.00. Copy fee $1.00 per page. Cert fee- $5.00 per cert plus copy fee. Payee- St. Bernard Parish Clerk of Court. **Other phones:** Elections- 504-271-3434. **Property tax/Assessor-** 504-279-6379.

St. Charles Parish

Clerk of Court, PO Box 424, Hahnville, LA 70057. RE & UCC recording phone-985-783-6632; fax-985-783-2005; hours: 8:30AM-4:30PM
All records in one index. Records indexed on computer. Office will perform a UCC search but public must search other records themselves. Search fee $15.00. General copy fee $1.00 per page. RE or tax lien copy- $.50 per page. Cert fee- $20.00 1st name, $10.00 per add'l name. Payee- St. Charles Parish Clerk of Court. **Property tax/Assessor-** 985-783-6281.

St. Helena Parish

Clerk of Court, PO Box 308, Greensburg, LA 70441-0308. 225-222-4514, R/E recording phone-225-222-4521; fax-225-222-3443; hours: 8:30AM-4:30PM
All records in one index. Office personnel or visitors may perform searches. General index search fee $10.00 per name. Mortgage search- $10.00 per name. UCC search per debtor name- $15.00. Copy fee $1.00 per page. Cert fee- $5.00 per cert plus copy fee. Payee- St. Helena Parish Clerk of Court. **Other phones:** Appraiser/Auditor- 225-222-4553; Elections- 225-222-4440. **Property tax/Assessor-** 225-222-4540.

St. James Parish

Clerk of Court, PO Box 63, Convent, LA 70723. RE & UCC recording phone-225-562-7496; fax-225-562-2383; hours: 8AM-4:30PM
Separate indices to search include conveyances, mortgages, marriage, probate, oathes, bonds, UCC, minerals. Conveyances on computer back to 1973; mortgages to 1950. Office will perform a UCC search but public must search other records themselves. UCC certificate per debtor name- $30.00. Copy fee $1.00 per page. Cert fee- $5.00 per cert plus copy fee. Payee- St. James Parish Clerk of Court. **Other phones:** Treasurer- 504-562-2300; Elections- 225-562-7496. **Property tax/Assessor-** 225-562-2250.

St. John the Baptist Parish

Clerk of Court, PO Box 280, Edgard, LA 70049-0280. 985-497-3331, R/E recording phone-985-497-8836 x246, UCC recording phone-985-497-8836 x242; fax-985-497-3972; hours: 8:30AM-4:30PM
www.stjohnclerk.org
All records in one index. Records indexed on a public use terminal back to 1958. Office personnel or visitors may perform searches. Search fee $20.00. Copy fee $2.00 per page; fax back $3.00 per page. Cert fee- $5.00 per cert plus copy fee. Payee- St. John the Baptist Parish Clerk of Court. **Other phones:** Elections- 985-497-8836 x247. **Property tax/Assessor-** 985-497-8788.

St. Landry Parish

Clerk of Court, PO Box 750, Opelousas, LA 70571-0750. 337-942-5606, R/E recording phone-337-942-5606 x121, UCC recording phone-337-942-5606 x122; fax-337-948-7265; hours: 8AM-4:30PM
www.stlandry.org/index.htm
Office personnel or visitors may perform searches. General index search fee $20.00 first name, $10.00 each add'l name. UCC search per debtor name- $30.00. Copy fee $2.00, if tax or real estate $.75 per page. Cert fee- $1.00 per page. Payee- St. Landry Parish Clerk of Court. **Other phones:** Treasurer- 337-948-6516; Elections- 337-942-5606 x133; Vital Records- 337-942-5606 x122. **Property tax/Assessor-** 337-942-2316.

St. Martin Parish

Clerk of Court, PO Box 308, St. Martinville, LA 70582. 337-394-2210; fax-337-394-7772; hours: 8:30AM-4:30PM www.stmartinparishclerkofcourt.com
Office personnel or visitors may perform searches. UCC search per debtor name- $30.00. UCC copy fee $2.00 per page. RE record copy- $.75 per page. Cert fee- $5.00 per cert plus copy fee. Payee- St. Martin Parish Clerk of Court. **Other phones:** Treasurer- 337-394-2200; Elections- 337-394-2210; Vital Records- 337-394-2210. **Property tax/Assessor-** 337-394-2208.

St. Mary Parish

Clerk of Court, PO Drawer 1231, Franklin, LA 70538. 318-828-4100 x200, R/E recording phone-337-828-4100 x200, UCC recording phone-337-828-4100 x200; fax-318-828-2509; hours: 8:30AM-4:30PM
Separate indices to search include conveyance, mtgs, marriage, Incorp, Partnerships. Records indexed on computer. Office will perform a UCC and Tax lien search but public must search other records themselves. General index search fee $20.00 for 1st name, $10.00 each add'l name. Copy fee $2.00, if tax lien or real estate $1.00 per page. Cert fee- $5.00 per cert plus copy fee. Payee- St. Mary Parish Clerk of Court. **Property tax/Assessor-** 337-828-4100 x250.

St. Tammany Parish

Clerk of Court, PO Box 1090, Covington, LA 70434. Main phone & R/E recording-985-809-8740, UCC recording phone-985-809-8740 x27840; hours: 8:30AM-4:30PM www.sttammanyclerk.org
Separate indices to search include COB, MOB, misc. Records indexed on a public use terminal back to 1961. Office personnel or visitors may perform searches. Search fee $15.00 per hour. UCC search per debtor name- $30.00 fixed. Copy fee $.25 per page. Cert fee- $2.00 per cert plus copy fee. Payee- St. Tammany Parish Clerk of Court. **Online access to Recorder, Real Estate, Mortgage, Lien, Assessor, Property Tax records:** Access to online records requires a $50 per month plus $50.00 start-up fee, plus $.20 per printed page. Records date back to 1961; viewable images on conveyances back to 1980. For information, contact Eli Wilson or Kristie Howell at 985-809-8787. A dialup service is also available; $100 setup and $.06 per minute. Free public access is also at https://www.sttammanyclerk.org/liveapp/default.asp; includes marriages, land, and court cases. UCC lien information is with the Secretary of State. **Other phones:** Elections- 985-809-8743. **Property tax/Assessor-** 985-809-8180.

Tangipahoa Parish

Clerk of Court, PO Box 667, Amite, LA 70422. 985-748-4146, R/E recording phone-985-549-1612; fax-985-748-6746; hours: 8:30AM-4:30PM
www.tangiclerk.org

Office personnel or visitors may perform searches. General search fee $12.50 first name, $6.50 each add'l name. UCC search per debtor name- $15.00. Copy fee $1.00 per page. Cert fee- $5.50 per cert plus copy fee. Payee- Tangipahoa Parish Clerk of Court. **Online access to Real Estate, Lien, Recording, Civil, Marriage, Mortgage records:** Access to Parish online records requires registration and a trial membership. Print documents for $1.00 each. They may later charge a $55 monthly fee. Record dates vary though most indexes go back before 1990. Lending agency information is available. For information, contact Alison Carona at 504-549-1611. Also, a mapping feature is being developed that includes assessor basic information; access will be free.

Tensas Parish

Clerk of Court, PO Box 78, St. Joseph, LA 71366. 318-766-3921; fax-318-766-3926; hours: 8AM-4:30PM
Real estate owner, mortgage, and property transfer searches available. Will search UCC records, tax liens not included in UCC search. UCC search per debtor name- $15.00. General copy fee $3.00 for 1st page, $2.00 each add'l. RE record copy- $.75 per page. Cert fee- $5.50 per cert plus copy fee. Payee- Tensas Parish Clerk of Court. **Property tax/Assessor-** 225-766-3501.

Terrebonne Parish

Clerk of Court, PO Box 1569, Houma, LA 70361. 985-868-5660, UCC recording phone-985-868-5660 x15; fax-985-868-5143; hours: 8:30AM-4:30PM
Office personnel or visitors may perform searches. UCC search per debtor name- $30.00. Copy fee $1.00 per page. RE record copy- $.75 per page. Cert fee- $5.00 per cert plus copy fee. Payee- Terrebonne Parish Clerk of Court. **Property tax/Assessor-** 985-876-6620.

Union Parish

Clerk of Court, 100 E. Bayou St, #105; Courthouse, Farmerville, LA 71241. 318-368-3055; fax-318-368-3861; hours: 8:30AM-4:30PM
Records indexed on a public use terminal back to 9/1/1979. Office will perform a UCC search but public must search other records themselves. Search fee $30.00. Copy fee $1.00 per page. Cert fee- $3.00 per cert plus copy fee. Payee- Union Parish Clerk of Court. **Other phones:** Vital Records- 504-568-8385. **Property tax/Assessor-** same address as above. 318-368-3232.

Vermilion Parish

Clerk of Court, 100 N State St #101; Courthouse Bldg, Abbeville, LA 70510. RE & UCC recording phone-337-898-1992; fax-337-898-0404; hours: 8:30AM-4:30PM
Separate indices to search include conveyance, mortgage, UCC, chattel, marriage, licenses, civil, criminal. Records indexed on a public use terminal back to 1978 for conveyances, 1960 for mortgages. Office personnel or visitors may perform searches. General index search fee $12.00 per name, $6.50 each add'l name. Real estate owner, mortgage, and property transfer searches available. UCC search per debtor name- $30.00. Separate tax lien search fee- $12.00 per debtor, $6.50 each add'l. Copy fee $1.00 per page. Cert fee- $5.00 per cert plus copy fee. Payee- Vermilion Parish Clerk of Court. **Other phones:** Treasurer- 337-898-4300; Appraiser/Auditor- 337-898-2837; Elections- 337-898-1992; Vital Records- 337-898-1992. **Property tax/Assessor-** 100 N State St #110, Abberville, LA 70510; 337-893-2837.

Vernon Parish

Clerk of Court, PO Box 40, Leesville, LA 71496-0040. 337-238-1384, R/E recording phone-337-238-4824; fax-337-238-9902; hours: 8AM-4:30PM
Separate indices to search include Mtg to 1975 and Conveyance to 1980. Records indexed on a public use terminal back to 1975 and 1980. Office will perform a UCC search but public must search

other records themselves. Search fee $30.00. UCC copy fee $2.00 per page. Real estate or tax lien record copy- $1.25 per page. Cert fee- $5.00 per cert plus copy fee. Payee- Vernon Parish Clerk of Court. **Other phones:** Elections- 337-238-1384. **Property tax/Assessor-** 337-239-2167.

Washington Parish

Clerk of Court, PO Box 607, Franklinton, LA 70438. 985-839-7821; fax-985-839-7851; hours: 8AM-4:30PM

Separate indices to search include conveyance, mortgage, misc. Search fee $10.00 unless otherwise indicated. Real estate owner, mortgage, and property transfer searches available. Tax liens not included in UCC search. UCC search per debtor name- $30.00. Copy fee $1.00 per page. Cert fee- $5.00 per cert plus copy fee. Payee- Washington Parish Clerk of Court. **Property tax/Assessor-** 985-839-2280.

Webster Parish

Clerk of Court, PO Box 370, Minden, LA 71058-0370. RE & UCC recording phone-318-371-0366; fax-318-371-0226; hours: 8:30AM-4:30PM

Office personnel or visitors may perform searches. Search fee $30.00 per name. Copy fee $1.00 per page. Cert fee- $5.00 per cert plus copy fee. Payee- Webster Parish Clerk of Court. **Other phones:** Elections- 318-371-0366. **Property tax/Assessor-** 318-377-9311.

West Baton Rouge Parish

Clerk of Court, PO Box 107, Port Allen, LA 70767. RE & UCC recording phone-225-383-0378; fax-225-383-3694; hours: 8:30AM-4:30PM

Separate indices to search include conveyance, mortgage, marriage, misc. Records indexed on a public use terminal back to 1987. Office will perform a UCC search but public must search other records themselves. UCC search per debtor name- $30.00. Copy fee $1.00 per page by clerk; $.50 self serve. Cert fee- $5.00 per item plus $2.00 per page plus copy fee. Payee- West Baton Rouge Parish Clerk of Court. **Property tax/Assessor-** PO Box 76, Port Allen, LA 70767; 225-344-6777.

West Carroll Parish

Clerk of Court, PO Box 1078, Oak Grove, LA 71263. 318-428-2369, R/E recording phone-318-428-3281, UCC recording phone-318-428-3281; fax-318-428-9896; hours: 8:30AM-4:30PM

Separate indices to search include Mtg, Conveyance, lease, Charters, Bonds, Marriage, UCCs. Record index not computerized. Office personnel or visitors may perform searches. Search fee $30.00 UCCs; tax lien $20.00. Mortgage searches available only. Copy fee $1.00 per page. Cert fee- $5.00 per cert plus copy fee. Payee- West Carroll Parish Clerk of Court. **Other phones:** Elections- 318-428-3281. **Property tax/Assessor-** 318-428-2371.

West Feliciana Parish

Clerk of Court, PO Box 1843, St. Francisville, LA 70775. 225-635-3794; fax-225-635-3770; hours: 8:30AM-4:30PM

Separate indices to search include conveyance, mortgage, oil/gas/mineral leases. Records indexed on a public use terminal back to 1981. Earlier records are on paper. Search fee $10 per 10 years unless otherwise indicated. Will search UCC records, tax liens not included in UCC search. UCC search per debtor name- $30.00. Copy fee $1.00 per page. Cert fee- $5.00 per cert plus copy fee. Payee- West Feliciana Parish Clerk of Court. **Property tax/Assessor-** 225-635-3350.

Winn Parish

Clerk of Court, PO Box 137, Winnfield, LA 71483. RE & UCC recording phone-318-628-3515; fax-318-628-3527; hours: 8AM-4:30PM

Separate indices to search include conveyance, mortgage, oil & gas. Record index not computerized. Only the public may search. Copy fee $1.00 per page. Cert fee- $5.00 per cert plus copy fee. Payee- Winn Parish Clerk of Court. **Other phones:** Treasurer- 318-628-5824. **Property tax/Assessor-** 318-628-3267.

Louisiana County Locator

You will usually be able to find the city name in the City/Parish Cross Reference below. In that case, it is a simple matter to determine the county from the cross reference. However, only the official US Postal Service city names are included in this index. There are an additional 40,000 place names that people use in their addresses. Therefore, we have also included a ZIP/City Cross Reference immediately following the City/Parish Cross Reference.

If you know the ZIP Code but the city name does not appear in the City/Parish Cross Reference index, look up the ZIP Code in the ZIP/City Cross Reference, find the city name, then look up the city name in the City/Parish Cross Reference. For example, you want to know the county for an address of Menands, NY 12204. There is no "Menands" in the City/Parish Cross Reference. The ZIP/City Cross Reference shows that ZIP Codes 12201-12288 are for the city of Albany. Looking back in the City/Parish Cross Reference, Albany is in Albany Parish.

Louisiana City/Parish Cross Reference

ABBEVILLE Vermilion Parish
ABITA SPRINGS St. Tammany Parish
ACME Concordia Parish
ADDIS West Baton Rouge Parish
AIMWELL Catahoula Parish
AKERS Tangipahoa Parish
ALBANY Livingston Parish
ALEXANDRIA Rapides Parish
AMA St. Charles Parish
AMELIA St. Mary Parish
AMITE (70422) Tangipahoa Parish(71), St. Helena Parish(28)
ANACOCO (71403) Vernon Parish(97), Sabine Parish(2)
ANGIE Washington Parish
ANGOLA West Feliciana Parish
ARABI St. Bernard Parish
ARCADIA (71001) Bienville Parish(80), Lincoln Parish(9), Claiborne Parish(9)
ARCHIBALD Richland Parish
ARNAUDVILLE (70512) St. Landry Parish(59), St. Martin Parish(40)
ASHLAND Natchitoches Parish
ATHENS Claiborne Parish
ATLANTA (71404) Grant Parish(50), Winn Parish(49)
AVERY ISLAND Iberia Parish
BAKER East Baton Rouge Parish
BALDWIN St. Mary Parish
BALL Rapides Parish
BARATARIA Jefferson Parish
BARKSDALE AFB Bossier Parish
BASILE (70515) Acadia Parish(59), Evangeline Parish(40)
BASKIN Franklin Parish
BASTROP Morehouse Parish
BATCHELOR Pointe Coupee Parish
BATON ROUGE East Baton Rouge Parish
BAYOU GOULA Iberville Parish
BELCHER Caddo Parish
BELL CITY (70630) Calcasieu Parish(67), Cameron Parish(32)
BELLE CHASSE Plaquemines Parish
BELLE ROSE Assumption Parish
BELMONT Sabine Parish
BENTLEY Grant Parish
BENTON Bossier Parish
BERNICE (71222) Union Parish(81), Claiborne Parish(18)
BERWICK St. Mary Parish
BETHANY Caddo Parish
BIENVILLE Bienville Parish
BIG BEND Avoyelles Parish
BLANCHARD Caddo Parish
BLANKS Pointe Coupee Parish
BOGALUSA (70427) Washington Parish(97), St. Tammany Parish(2)
BOGALUSA Washington Parish
BONITA Morehouse Parish
BOOTHVILLE Plaquemines Parish
BORDELONVILLE Avoyelles Parish
BOSSIER CITY Bossier Parish
BOURG (70343) Terrebonne Parish(82), Lafourche Parish(17)

BOUTTE St. Charles Parish
BOYCE Rapides Parish
BRAITHWAITE Plaquemines Parish
BRANCH Acadia Parish
BREAUX BRIDGE St. Martin Parish
BRITTANY Ascension Parish
BROUSSARD (70518) Lafayette Parish(89), St. Martin Parish(6), Iberia Parish(3)
BRUSLY West Baton Rouge Parish
BRYCELAND Bienville Parish
BUCKEYE Rapides Parish
BUECHE West Baton Rouge Parish
BUNKIE (71322) Avoyelles Parish(86), St. Landry Parish(12), Rapides Parish(1)
BURAS Plaquemines Parish
BURNSIDE Ascension Parish
BUSH St. Tammany Parish
CADE St. Martin Parish
CALHOUN Ouachita Parish
CALVIN Winn Parish
CAMERON Cameron Parish
CAMPTI Natchitoches Parish
CARENCRO (70520) Lafayette Parish(98), St. Landry Parish(1)
CARLISLE Plaquemines Parish
CARVILLE Iberville Parish
CASTOR Bienville Parish
CECILIA St. Martin Parish
CENTER POINT (71323) Avoyelles Parish(98), Rapides Parish(1)
CENTERVILLE St. Mary Parish
CHALMETTE St. Bernard Parish
CHARENTON St. Mary Parish
CHASE Franklin Parish
CHATAIGNIER Evangeline Parish
CHATHAM Jackson Parish
CHAUVIN Terrebonne Parish
CHENEYVILLE (71325) Rapides Parish(67), Evangeline Parish(32)
CHOPIN Natchitoches Parish
CHOUDRANT (71227) Lincoln Parish(65), Jackson Parish(27), Ouachita Parish(6)
CHURCH POINT (70525) Acadia Parish(82), St. Landry Parish(17)
CLARENCE Natchitoches Parish
CLARKS Caldwell Parish
CLAYTON (71326) Catahoula Parish(65), Concordia Parish(33)
CLINTON (70722) East Feliciana Parish(96), East Baton Rouge Parish(3)
CLOUTIERVILLE Natchitoches Parish
COLFAX Grant Parish
COLLINSTON (71229) Morehouse Parish(82), Ouachita Parish(17)
COLUMBIA (71418) Caldwell Parish(86), Richland Parish(8), Ouachita Parish(3), Catahoula Parish(1)
CONVENT St. James Parish
CONVERSE (71419) Sabine Parish(85), De Soto Parish(14)
COTTON VALLEY (71018) Webster Parish(87), Bossier Parish(12)
COTTONPORT Avoyelles Parish

COUSHATTA (71019) Red River Parish(88), Natchitoches Parish(11)
COVINGTON St. Tammany Parish
CREOLE Cameron Parish
CRESTON Natchitoches Parish
CROWLEY Acadia Parish
CROWVILLE Franklin Parish
CULLEN Webster Parish
CUT OFF Lafourche Parish
CYPRESS Natchitoches Parish
DARROW Ascension Parish
DAVANT Plaquemines Parish
DELCAMBRE (70528) Vermilion Parish(77), Iberia Parish(22)
DELHI (71232) Richland Parish(61), Franklin Parish(19), Madison Parish(19)
DELTA Madison Parish
DENHAM SPRINGS (70706) Livingston Parish(89), St. Helena Parish(10)
DENHAM SPRINGS Livingston Parish
DEQUINCY Calcasieu Parish
DERIDDER (70634) Beauregard Parish(91), Vernon Parish(8)
DERRY Natchitoches Parish
DES ALLEMANDS (70030) St. Charles Parish(88), Lafourche Parish(11)
DESTREHAN St. Charles Parish
DEVILLE (71328) Rapides Parish(86), Avoyelles Parish(13)
DODSON Winn Parish
DONALDSONVILLE Ascension Parish
DONNER Terrebonne Parish
DOWNSVILLE (71234) Union Parish(80), Ouachita Parish(14), Lincoln Parish(5)
DOYLINE Webster Parish
DRY CREEK (70637) Beauregard Parish(72), Allen Parish(27)
DRY PRONG (71423) Grant Parish(96), Rapides Parish(3)
DUBACH (71235) Lincoln Parish(98), Claiborne Parish(1)
DUBBERLY (71024) Webster Parish(89), Bienville Parish(10)
DULAC Terrebonne Parish
DUPLESSIS Ascension Parish
DUPONT Avoyelles Parish
DUSON Lafayette Parish
EAST POINT Red River Parish
ECHO Rapides Parish
EDGARD St. John the Baptist Parish
EFFIE (71331) Avoyelles Parish(97), Catahoula Parish(2)
EGAN Acadia Parish
ELIZABETH Allen Parish
ELM GROVE Bossier Parish
ELMER Rapides Parish
ELTON (70532) Jefferson Davis Parish(79), Allen Parish(20)
EMPIRE Plaquemines Parish
ENTERPRISE (71425) Catahoula Parish(68), Rapides Parish(31)
EPPS (71237) West Carroll Parish(83), Madison Parish(13), East Carroll Parish(3)

ERATH Vermilion Parish
EROS (71238) Ouachita Parish(53), Jackson Parish(46)
ERWINVILLE (70729) West Baton Rouge Parish(97), Pointe Coupee Parish(2)
ESTHERWOOD Acadia Parish
ETHEL East Feliciana Parish
EUNICE (70535) St. Landry Parish(94), Acadia Parish(4), Evangeline Parish(1)
EVANGELINE Acadia Parish
EVANS Vernon Parish
EVERGREEN Avoyelles Parish
EXTENSION Franklin Parish
FAIRBANKS Ouachita Parish
FARMERVILLE Union Parish
FENTON Jefferson Davis Parish
FERRIDAY Concordia Parish
FISHER Sabine Parish
FLATWOODS (71427) Rapides Parish(75), Natchitoches Parish(24)
FLORA Natchitoches Parish
FLORIEN Sabine Parish
FLUKER (70436) Tangipahoa Parish(85), St. Helena Parish(14)
FOLSOM St. Tammany Parish
FORDOCHE Pointe Coupee Parish
FOREST West Carroll Parish
FOREST HILL Rapides Parish
FORT NECESSITY Franklin Parish
FRANKLIN St. Mary Parish
FRANKLINTON Washington Parish
FRENCH SETTLEMENT Livingston Parish
FRIERSON De Soto Parish
FROGMORE Concordia Parish
FULLERTON Vernon Parish
GALLIANO Lafourche Parish
GARDEN CITY St. Mary Parish
GARDNER Rapides Parish
GARYVILLE St. John the Baptist Parish
GEISMAR Ascension Parish
GEORGETOWN Grant Parish
GHEENS Lafourche Parish
GIBSLAND Bienville Parish
GIBSON Terrebonne Parish
GILBERT Franklin Parish
GILLIAM Caddo Parish
GLENMORA (71433) Rapides Parish(98), Allen Parish(1)
GLOSTER De Soto Parish
GLYNN (70736) Pointe Coupee Parish(98), West Baton Rouge Parish(1)
GOLDEN MEADOW Lafourche Parish
GOLDONNA (71031) Natchitoches Parish(53), Winn Parish(46)
GONZALES Ascension Parish
GORUM Natchitoches Parish
GOUDEAU Avoyelles Parish
GRAMBLING Lincoln Parish
GRAMERCY St. James Parish
GRAND CANE De Soto Parish
GRAND CHENIER Cameron Parish
GRAND COTEAU St. Landry Parish
GRAND ISLE Jefferson Parish
GRANT Allen Parish

GRAY Terrebonne Parish
GRAYSON (71435) Caldwell Parish(98), Catahoula Parish(1)
GREENSBURG St. Helena Parish
GREENWELL SPRINGS East Baton Rouge Parish
GREENWOOD Caddo Parish
GRETNA Jefferson Parish
GROSSE TETE Iberville Parish
GUEYDAN (70542) Vermilion Parish(95), Cameron Parish(4)
HACKBERRY Cameron Parish
HAHNVILLE St. Charles Parish
HALL SUMMIT Red River Parish
HAMBURG Avoyelles Parish
HAMMOND (70403) Tangipahoa Parish(95), Livingston Parish(4)
HAMMOND Tangipahoa Parish
HARMON Red River Parish
HARRISONBURG Catahoula Parish
HARVEY Jefferson Parish
HAUGHTON Bossier Parish
HAYES Calcasieu Parish
HAYNESVILLE Claiborne Parish
HEBERT Caldwell Parish
HEFLIN (71039) Webster Parish(80), Bienville Parish(19)
HESSMER Avoyelles Parish
HESTER St. James Parish
HICKS Vernon Parish
HINESTON (71438) Rapides Parish(82), Vernon Parish(17)
HODGE Jackson Parish
HOLDEN (70744) Livingston Parish(95), St. Helena Parish(4)
HOMER Claiborne Parish
HORNBECK (71439) Vernon Parish(78), Sabine Parish(21)
HOSSTON Caddo Parish
HOUMA (70364) Terrebonne Parish(81), Lafourche Parish(18)
HOUMA Terrebonne Parish
HUSSER Tangipahoa Parish
IDA Caddo Parish
INDEPENDENCE (70443) Tangipahoa Parish(52), Livingston Parish(29), St. Helena Parish(17)
INNIS Pointe Coupee Parish
IOTA Acadia Parish
IOWA Calcasieu Parish
JACKSON (70748) East Feliciana Parish(76), West Feliciana Parish(21), East Baton Rouge Parish(2)
JAMESTOWN Bienville Parish
JARREAU Pointe Coupee Parish
JEANERETTE (70544) Iberia Parish(84), St. Mary Parish(15)
JENA La Salle Parish
JENNINGS (70546) Jefferson Davis Parish(97), Acadia Parish(2)
JIGGER Franklin Parish
JONES Morehouse Parish
JONESBORO (71251) Jackson Parish(94), Bienville Parish(5)
JONESVILLE (71343) Catahoula Parish(88), Concordia Parish(11)
JOYCE Winn Parish
KAPLAN Vermilion Parish
KEATCHIE De Soto Parish
KEITHVILLE Caddo Parish
KELLY (71441) Caldwell Parish(82), La Salle Parish(17)
KENNER Jefferson Parish
KENTWOOD (70444) Tangipahoa Parish(82), St. Helena Parish(15), Washington Parish(1)
KILBOURNE West Carroll Parish
KILLONA St. Charles Parish
KINDER (70648) Allen Parish(98), Jefferson Davis Parish(1)
KRAEMER Lafourche Parish
KROTZ SPRINGS St. Landry Parish

KURTHWOOD Vernon Parish
LA PLACE (70068) St. John the Baptist Parish(95), St. Charles Parish(4)
LA PLACE St. John the Baptist Parish
LABADIEVILLE Assumption Parish
LABARRE Pointe Coupee Parish
LACAMP Vernon Parish
LACASSINE Jefferson Davis Parish
LACOMBE St. Tammany Parish
LAFAYETTE Lafayette Parish
LAFITTE Jefferson Parish
LAKE ARTHUR (70549) Jefferson Davis Parish(97), Cameron Parish(2)
LAKE CHARLES (70607) Calcasieu Parish(90), Cameron Parish(9)
LAKE CHARLES Calcasieu Parish
LAKE PROVIDENCE East Carroll Parish
LAKELAND Pointe Coupee Parish
LAROSE Lafourche Parish
LARTO Catahoula Parish
LAWTELL St. Landry Parish
LE MOYEN St. Landry Parish
LEANDER Vernon Parish
LEBEAU St. Landry Parish
LEBLANC Allen Parish
LECOMPTE Rapides Parish
LEESVILLE Vernon Parish
LENA (71447) Rapides Parish(54), Natchitoches Parish(45)
LEONVILLE St. Landry Parish
LETTSWORTH Pointe Coupee Parish
LIBUSE Rapides Parish
LILLIE (71256) Union Parish(94), Claiborne Parish(5)
LISBON Claiborne Parish
LIVINGSTON Livingston Parish
LIVONIA Pointe Coupee Parish
LOCKPORT Lafourche Parish
LOGANSPORT De Soto Parish
LONGLEAF Rapides Parish
LONGSTREET De Soto Parish
LONGVILLE Beauregard Parish
LORANGER Tangipahoa Parish
LOREAUVILLE Iberia Parish
LOTTIE Pointe Coupee Parish
LULING St. Charles Parish
LUTCHER St. James Parish
LYDIA Iberia Parish
MADISONVILLE St. Tammany Parish
MAMOU Evangeline Parish
MANDEVILLE St. Tammany Parish
MANGHAM Richland Parish
MANSFIELD De Soto Parish
MANSURA Avoyelles Parish
MANY Sabine Parish
MARINGOUIN Iberville Parish
MARION Union Parish
MARKSVILLE Avoyelles Parish
MARRERO Jefferson Parish
MARTHAVILLE (71450) Natchitoches Parish(68), Sabine Parish(31)
MATHEWS Lafourche Parish
MAUREPAS (70449) Livingston Parish(95), Ascension Parish(4)
MAURICE (70555) Vermilion Parish(96), Lafayette Parish(3)
MELDER Rapides Parish
MELROSE Natchitoches Parish
MELVILLE St. Landry Parish
MER ROUGE Morehouse Parish
MERAUX St. Bernard Parish
MERMENTAU Acadia Parish
MERRYVILLE Beauregard Parish
METAIRIE Jefferson Parish
MILTON Lafayette Parish
MINDEN (71055) Webster Parish(96), Claiborne Parish(2)
MINDEN Webster Parish
MIRA Caddo Parish
MITTIE Allen Parish
MODESTE Ascension Parish
MONROE Ouachita Parish

MONTEGUT (70377) Terrebonne Parish(89), Lafourche Parish(10)
MONTEREY Concordia Parish
MONTGOMERY (71454) Grant Parish(82), Winn Parish(17)
MOORINGSPORT Caddo Parish
MORA (71455) Rapides Parish(98), Natchitoches Parish(1)
MOREAUVILLE Avoyelles Parish
MORGAN CITY (70380) St. Mary Parish(91), Assumption Parish(8)
MORGAN CITY St. Mary Parish
MORGANZA Pointe Coupee Parish
MORROW (71356) St. Landry Parish(57), Avoyelles Parish(42)
MORSE Acadia Parish
MOUNT AIRY St. John the Baptist Parish
MOUNT HERMON Washington Parish
NAPOLEONVILLE Assumption Parish
NATALBANY Tangipahoa Parish
NATCHEZ Natchitoches Parish
NATCHITOCHES (71457) Natchitoches Parish(97), Winn Parish(2)
NATCHITOCHES Natchitoches Parish
NEGREET Sabine Parish
NEW IBERIA Iberia Parish
NEW ORLEANS (70146) Orleans Parish(91), Plaquemines Parish(8)
NEW ORLEANS Jefferson Parish
NEW ORLEANS Orleans Parish
NEW ROADS Pointe Coupee Parish
NEW SARPY St. Charles Parish
NEWELLTON Tensas Parish
NEWLLANO Vernon Parish
NOBLE Sabine Parish
NORCO St. Charles Parish
NORWOOD East Feliciana Parish
OAK GROVE West Carroll Parish
OAK RIDGE (71264) Morehouse Parish(77), Richland Parish(22)
OAKDALE (71463) Allen Parish(88), Evangeline Parish(6), Rapides Parish(4)
OBERLIN Allen Parish
OIL CITY Caddo Parish
OLLA (71465) La Salle Parish(87), Winn Parish(9), Caldwell Parish(2)
OPELOUSAS St. Landry Parish
OSCAR Pointe Coupee Parish
OTIS Rapides Parish
PAINCOURTVILLE Assumption Parish
PALMETTO St. Landry Parish
PARADIS St. Charles Parish
PATTERSON St. Mary Parish
PAULINA St. James Parish
PEARL RIVER St. Tammany Parish
PELICAN De Soto Parish
PERRY Vermilion Parish
PIERRE PART (70339) Assumption Parish(92), St. Martin Parish(7)
PILOTTOWN Plaquemines Parish
PINE GROVE (70453) St. Helena Parish(85), Livingston Parish(14)
PINE PRAIRIE Evangeline Parish
PINEVILLE (71360) Rapides Parish(96), Avoyelles Parish(2), Grant Parish(1)
PINEVILLE Rapides Parish
PIONEER West Carroll Parish
PITKIN (70656) Vernon Parish(62), Rapides Parish(18), Allen Parish(18)
PLAIN DEALING Bossier Parish
PLAQUEMINE Iberville Parish
PLATTENVILLE Assumption Parish
PLAUCHEVILLE Avoyelles Parish
PLEASANT HILL (71065) Sabine Parish(98), Natchitoches Parish(1)
POINTE A LA HACHE Plaquemines Parish
POLLOCK Grant Parish
PONCHATOULA Tangipahoa Parish
PORT ALLEN West Baton Rouge Parish
PORT BARRE St. Landry Parish
PORT SULPHUR Plaquemines Parish
POWHATAN Natchitoches Parish

PRAIRIEVILLE Ascension Parish
PRIDE East Baton Rouge Parish
PRINCETON Bossier Parish
PROVENCAL Natchitoches Parish
QUITMAN (71268) Jackson Parish(79), Bienville Parish(20)
RACELAND Lafourche Parish
RAGLEY (70657) Beauregard Parish(85), Allen Parish(14)
RAYNE (70578) Acadia Parish(90), Vermilion Parish(5), Lafayette Parish(4)
RAYVILLE Richland Parish
REDDELL Evangeline Parish
REEVES Allen Parish
RESERVE St. John the Baptist Parish
RHINEHART Catahoula Parish
RINGGOLD (71068) Bienville Parish(93), Red River Parish(6)
ROANOKE Jefferson Davis Parish
ROBELINE (71469) Natchitoches Parish(75), Sabine Parish(24)
ROBERT Tangipahoa Parish
RODESSA Caddo Parish
ROSA St. Landry Parish
ROSEDALE Iberville Parish
ROSELAND Tangipahoa Parish
ROSEPINE Vernon Parish
ROUGON Pointe Coupee Parish
RUBY Rapides Parish
RUSTON (71270) Lincoln Parish(94), Jackson Parish(5)
RUSTON Lincoln Parish
SAINT AMANT Ascension Parish
SAINT BENEDICT St. Tammany Parish
SAINT BERNARD St. Bernard Parish
SAINT FRANCISVILLE West Feliciana Parish
SAINT GABRIEL Iberville Parish
SAINT JAMES St. James Parish
SAINT JOSEPH Tensas Parish
SAINT LANDRY Evangeline Parish
SAINT MARTINVILLE St. Martin Parish
SAINT MAURICE Winn Parish
SAINT ROSE St. Charles Parish
SALINE (71070) Natchitoches Parish(59), Bienville Parish(40)
SAREPTA (71071) Webster Parish(95), Bossier Parish(4)
SCHRIEVER Terrebonne Parish
SCOTT (70583) Lafayette Parish(94), Acadia Parish(5)
SHONGALOO Webster Parish
SHREVEPORT (71107) Caddo Parish(98), Bossier Parish(1)
SHREVEPORT (71115) Caddo Parish(95), Red River Parish(4)
SHREVEPORT Caddo Parish
SIBLEY Webster Parish
SICILY ISLAND (71368) Catahoula Parish(98), Franklin Parish(1)
SIEPER Rapides Parish
SIKES Winn Parish
SIMMESPORT Avoyelles Parish
SIMPSON Vernon Parish
SIMSBORO (71275) Lincoln Parish(85), Bienville Parish(14)
SINGER Beauregard Parish
SLAGLE Vernon Parish
SLAUGHTER East Feliciana Parish
SLIDELL St. Tammany Parish
SONDHEIMER East Carroll Parish
SORRENTO Ascension Parish
SPEARSVILLE Union Parish
SPRINGFIELD (70462) Livingston Parish(97), Tangipahoa Parish(2)
SPRINGHILL (71075) Webster Parish(96), Bossier Parish(3)
STARKS Calcasieu Parish
START Richland Parish
STERLINGTON (71280) Ouachita Parish(55), Union Parish(44)
STONEWALL De Soto Parish

SUGARTOWN Beauregard Parish
SULPHUR Calcasieu Parish
SUMMERFIELD Claiborne Parish
SUN St. Tammany Parish
SUNSET St. Landry Parish
SUNSHINE Iberville Parish
SWARTZ Ouachita Parish
TALISHEEK St. Tammany Parish
TALLULAH Madison Parish
TANGIPAHOA Tangipahoa Parish
TAYLOR Bienville Parish
THERIOT Terrebonne Parish
THIBODAUX (70301) Lafourche Parish(95), Terrebonne Parish(3)
THIBODAUX Lafourche Parish

TICKFAW Tangipahoa Parish
TIOGA Rapides Parish
TORBERT Pointe Coupee Parish
TRANSYLVANIA East Carroll Parish
TROUT La Salle Parish
TULLOS (71479) Winn Parish(62), La Salle Parish(37)
TUNICA West Feliciana Parish
TURKEY CREEK Evangeline Parish
UNCLE SAM St. James Parish
URANIA La Salle Parish
VACHERIE (70090) St. James Parish(81), St. John the Baptist Parish(18)
VENICE Plaquemines Parish
VENTRESS Pointe Coupee Parish

VERDA Grant Parish
VICK Avoyelles Parish
VIDALIA Concordia Parish
VILLE PLATTE Evangeline Parish
VINTON Calcasieu Parish
VIOLET St. Bernard Parish
VIVIAN Caddo Parish
WAKEFIELD West Feliciana Parish
WALKER Livingston Parish
WASHINGTON (70589) St. Landry Parish(92), Evangeline Parish(7)
WATERPROOF Tensas Parish
WATSON Livingston Parish
WELSH Jefferson Davis Parish
WEST MONROE Ouachita Parish

WESTLAKE Calcasieu Parish
WESTWEGO Jefferson Parish
WEYANOKE West Feliciana Parish
WHITE CASTLE Iberville Parish
WILDSVILLE Concordia Parish
WILSON East Feliciana Parish
WINNFIELD Winn Parish
WINNSBORO Franklin Parish
WISNER Franklin Parish
WOODWORTH Rapides Parish
YOUNGSVILLE (70592) Lafayette Parish(81), Vermilion Parish(11), Iberia Parish(6)
ZACHARY East Baton Rouge Parish
ZWOLLE Sabine Parish

Louisiana ZIP/City Cross Reference

70001-70011	METAIRIE
70030-70030	DES ALLEMANDS
70031-70031	AMA
70032-70032	ARABI
70033-70033	METAIRIE
70036-70036	BARATARIA
70037-70037	BELLE CHASSE
70038-70038	BOOTHVILLE
70039-70039	BOUTTE
70040-70040	BRAITHWAITE
70041-70041	BURAS
70042-70042	CARLISLE
70043-70044	CHALMETTE
70046-70046	DAVANT
70047-70047	DESTREHAN
70049-70049	EDGARD
70050-70050	EMPIRE
70051-70051	GARYVILLE
70052-70052	GRAMERCY
70053-70054	GRETNA
70055-70055	METAIRIE
70056-70056	GRETNA
70057-70057	HAHNVILLE
70058-70059	HARVEY
70060-70060	METAIRIE
70062-70065	KENNER
70066-70066	KILLONA
70067-70067	LAFITTE
70068-70069	LA PLACE
70070-70070	LULING
70071-70071	LUTCHER
70072-70073	MARRERO
70075-70075	MERAUX
70076-70076	MOUNT AIRY
70078-70078	NEW SARPY
70079-70079	NORCO
70080-70080	PARADIS
70081-70081	PILOTTOWN
70082-70082	POINTE A LA HACHE
70083-70083	PORT SULPHUR
70084-70084	RESERVE
70085-70085	SAINT BERNARD
70086-70086	SAINT JAMES
70087-70087	SAINT ROSE
70090-70090	VACHERIE
70091-70091	VENICE
70092-70092	VIOLET
70094-70096	WESTWEGO
70100-70195	NEW ORLEANS
70301-70310	THIBODAUX
70339-70339	PIERRE PART
70340-70340	AMELIA
70341-70341	BELLE ROSE
70342-70342	BERWICK
70343-70343	BOURG
70344-70344	CHAUVIN
70345-70345	CUT OFF
70346-70346	DONALDSONVILLE
70352-70352	DONNER
70353-70353	DULAC
70354-70354	GALLIANO
70355-70355	GHEENS

70356-70356	GIBSON
70357-70357	GOLDEN MEADOW
70358-70358	GRAND ISLE
70359-70359	GRAY
70360-70364	HOUMA
70371-70371	KRAEMER
70372-70372	LABADIEVILLE
70373-70373	LAROSE
70374-70374	LOCKPORT
70375-70375	MATHEWS
70376-70376	MODESTE
70377-70377	MONTEGUT
70380-70381	MORGAN CITY
70390-70390	NAPOLEONVILLE
70391-70391	PAINCOURTVILLE
70392-70392	PATTERSON
70393-70393	PLATTENVILLE
70394-70394	RACELAND
70395-70395	SCHRIEVER
70397-70397	THERIOT
70401-70404	HAMMOND
70420-70420	ABITA SPRINGS
70421-70421	AKERS
70422-70422	AMITE
70426-70426	ANGIE
70427-70429	BOGALUSA
70431-70431	BUSH
70433-70435	COVINGTON
70436-70436	FLUKER
70437-70437	FOLSOM
70438-70438	FRANKLINTON
70441-70441	GREENSBURG
70442-70442	HUSSER
70443-70443	INDEPENDENCE
70444-70444	KENTWOOD
70445-70445	LACOMBE
70446-70446	LORANGER
70447-70447	MADISONVILLE
70448-70448	MANDEVILLE
70449-70449	MAUREPAS
70450-70450	MOUNT HERMON
70451-70451	NATALBANY
70452-70452	PEARL RIVER
70453-70453	PINE GROVE
70454-70454	PONCHATOULA
70455-70455	ROBERT
70456-70456	ROSELAND
70457-70457	SAINT BENEDICT
70458-70461	SLIDELL
70462-70462	SPRINGFIELD
70463-70463	SUN
70464-70464	TALISHEEK
70465-70465	TANGIPAHOA
70466-70466	TICKFAW
70467-70467	ANGIE
70469-70469	SLIDELL
70470-70471	MANDEVILLE
70501-70509	LAFAYETTE
70510-70511	ABBEVILLE
70512-70512	ARNAUDVILLE
70513-70513	AVERY ISLAND
70514-70514	BALDWIN

70515-70515	BASILE
70516-70516	BRANCH
70517-70517	BREAUX BRIDGE
70518-70518	BROUSSARD
70519-70519	CADE
70520-70520	CARENCRO
70521-70521	CECILIA
70522-70522	CENTERVILLE
70523-70523	CHARENTON
70524-70524	CHATAIGNIER
70525-70525	CHURCH POINT
70526-70527	CROWLEY
70528-70528	DELCAMBRE
70529-70529	DUSON
70531-70531	EGAN
70532-70532	ELTON
70533-70533	ERATH
70534-70534	ESTHERWOOD
70535-70535	EUNICE
70537-70537	EVANGELINE
70538-70538	FRANKLIN
70540-70540	GARDEN CITY
70541-70541	GRAND COTEAU
70542-70542	GUEYDAN
70543-70543	IOTA
70544-70544	JEANERETTE
70546-70546	JENNINGS
70548-70548	KAPLAN
70549-70549	LAKE ARTHUR
70550-70550	LAWTELL
70551-70551	LEONVILLE
70552-70552	LOREAUVILLE
70554-70554	MAMOU
70555-70555	MAURICE
70556-70556	MERMENTAU
70558-70558	MILTON
70559-70559	MORSE
70560-70563	NEW IBERIA
70569-70569	LYDIA
70570-70571	OPELOUSAS
70575-70575	PERRY
70576-70576	PINE PRAIRIE
70577-70577	PORT BARRE
70578-70578	RAYNE
70580-70580	REDDELL
70581-70581	ROANOKE
70582-70582	SAINT MARTINVILLE
70583-70583	SCOTT
70584-70584	SUNSET
70585-70585	TURKEY CREEK
70586-70586	VILLE PLATTE
70589-70589	WASHINGTON
70591-70591	WELSH
70592-70592	YOUNGSVILLE
70593-70598	LAFAYETTE
70601-70629	LAKE CHARLES
70630-70630	BELL CITY
70631-70631	CAMERON
70632-70632	CREOLE
70633-70633	DEQUINCY
70634-70634	DERIDDER
70637-70637	DRY CREEK

70638-70638	ELIZABETH
70639-70639	EVANS
70640-70640	FENTON
70642-70642	FULLERTON
70643-70643	GRAND CHENIER
70644-70644	GRANT
70645-70645	HACKBERRY
70646-70646	HAYES
70647-70647	IOWA
70648-70648	KINDER
70650-70650	LACASSINE
70651-70651	LEBLANC
70652-70652	LONGVILLE
70653-70653	MERRYVILLE
70654-70654	MITTIE
70655-70655	OBERLIN
70656-70656	PITKIN
70657-70657	RAGLEY
70658-70658	REEVES
70659-70659	ROSEPINE
70660-70660	SINGER
70661-70661	STARKS
70662-70662	SUGARTOWN
70663-70665	SULPHUR
70668-70668	VINTON
70669-70669	WESTLAKE
70704-70704	BAKER
70706-70706	DENHAM SPRINGS
70707-70707	GONZALES
70710-70710	ADDIS
70711-70711	ALBANY
70712-70712	ANGOLA
70714-70714	BAKER
70715-70715	BATCHELOR
70716-70716	BAYOU GOULA
70717-70717	BLANKS
70718-70718	BRITTANY
70719-70719	BRUSLY
70720-70720	BUECHE
70721-70721	CARVILLE
70722-70722	CLINTON
70723-70723	CONVENT
70725-70725	DARROW
70726-70727	DENHAM SPRINGS
70728-70728	DUPLESSIS
70729-70729	ERWINVILLE
70730-70730	ETHEL
70732-70732	FORDOCHE
70733-70733	FRENCH SETTLEMENT
70734-70734	GEISMAR
70736-70736	GLYNN
70737-70737	GONZALES
70738-70738	BURNSIDE
70739-70739	GREENWELL SPRINGS
70740-70740	GROSSE TETE
70743-70743	HESTER
70744-70744	HOLDEN
70747-70747	INNIS
70748-70748	JACKSON
70749-70749	JARREAU
70750-70750	KROTZ SPRINGS
70751-70751	LABARRE

70752-70752 LAKELAND	71066-71066 POWHATAN	71333-71333 EVERGREEN	71449-71449 MANY
70753-70753 LETTSWORTH	71067-71067 PRINCETON	71334-71334 FERRIDAY	71450-71450 MARTHAVILLE
70754-70754 LIVINGSTON	71068-71068 RINGGOLD	71335-71335 FROGMORE	71451-71451 MELDER
70755-70755 LIVONIA	71069-71069 RODESSA	71336-71336 GILBERT	71452-71452 MELROSE
70756-70756 LOTTIE	71070-71070 SALINE	71338-71338 GOUDEAU	71454-71454 MONTGOMERY
70757-70757 MARINGOUIN	71071-71071 SAREPTA	71339-71339 HAMBURG	71455-71455 MORA
70759-70759 MORGANZA	71072-71072 SHONGALOO	71340-71340 HARRISONBURG	71456-71456 NATCHEZ
70760-70760 NEW ROADS	71073-71073 SIBLEY	71341-71341 HESSMER	71457-71458 NATCHITOCHES
70761-70761 NORWOOD	71075-71075 SPRINGHILL	71342-71342 JENA	71459-71459 LEESVILLE
70762-70762 OSCAR	71078-71078 STONEWALL	71343-71343 JONESVILLE	71460-71460 NEGREET
70763-70763 PAULINA	71079-71079 SUMMERFIELD	71344-71344 LARTO	71461-71461 NEWLLANO
70764-70765 PLAQUEMINE	71080-71080 TAYLOR	71345-71345 LEBEAU	71462-71462 NOBLE
70767-70767 PORT ALLEN	71082-71082 VIVIAN	71346-71346 LECOMPTE	71463-71463 OAKDALE
70769-70769 PRAIRIEVILLE	71101-71109 SHREVEPORT	71347-71347 LE MOYEN	71465-71465 OLLA
70770-70770 PRIDE	71110-71110 BARKSDALE AFB	71348-71348 LIBUSE	71466-71466 OTIS
70772-70772 ROSEDALE	71111-71113 BOSSIER CITY	71350-71350 MANSURA	71467-71467 POLLOCK
70773-70773 ROUGON	71115-71166 SHREVEPORT	71351-71351 MARKSVILLE	71468-71468 PROVENCAL
70774-70774 SAINT AMANT	71171-71172 BOSSIER CITY	71353-71353 MELVILLE	71469-71469 ROBELINE
70775-70775 SAINT FRANCISVILLE	71201-71213 MONROE	71354-71354 MONTEREY	71471-71471 SAINT MAURICE
70776-70776 SAINT GABRIEL	71218-71218 ARCHIBALD	71355-71355 MOREAUVILLE	71472-71472 SIEPER
70777-70777 SLAUGHTER	71219-71219 BASKIN	71356-71356 MORROW	71473-71473 SIKES
70778-70778 SORRENTO	71220-71221 BASTROP	71357-71357 NEWELLTON	71474-71474 SIMPSON
70780-70780 SUNSHINE	71222-71222 BERNICE	71358-71358 PALMETTO	71475-71475 SLAGLE
70781-70781 TORBERT	71223-71223 BONITA	71359-71361 PINEVILLE	71477-71477 TIOGA
70782-70782 TUNICA	71225-71225 CALHOUN	71362-71362 PLAUCHEVILLE	71479-71479 TULLOS
70783-70783 VENTRESS	71226-71226 CHATHAM	71363-71363 RHINEHART	71480-71480 URANIA
70784-70784 WAKEFIELD	71227-71227 CHOUDRANT	71364-71364 ROSA	71481-71481 VERDA
70785-70785 WALKER	71229-71229 COLLINSTON	71365-71365 RUBY	71483-71483 WINNFIELD
70786-70786 WATSON	71230-71230 CROWVILLE	71366-71366 SAINT JOSEPH	71485-71485 WOODWORTH
70787-70787 WEYANOKE	71232-71232 DELHI	71367-71367 SAINT LANDRY	71486-71486 ZWOLLE
70788-70788 WHITE CASTLE	71233-71233 DELTA	71368-71368 SICILY ISLAND	71496-71496 LEESVILLE
70789-70789 WILSON	71234-71234 DOWNSVILLE	71369-71369 SIMMESPORT	71497-71497 NATCHITOCHES
70791-70791 ZACHARY	71235-71235 DUBACH	71371-71371 TROUT	
70792-70792 UNCLE SAM	71237-71237 EPPS	71372-71372 VICK	
70800-70898 BATON ROUGE	71238-71238 EROS	71373-71373 VIDALIA	
71001-71001 ARCADIA	71239-71239 EXTENSION	71375-71375 WATERPROOF	
71002-71002 ASHLAND	71240-71240 FAIRBANKS	71377-71377 WILDSVILLE	
71003-71003 ATHENS	71241-71241 FARMERVILLE	71378-71378 WISNER	
71004-71004 BELCHER	71242-71242 FOREST	71401-71401 AIMWELL	
71006-71006 BENTON	71243-71243 FORT NECESSITY	71403-71403 ANACOCO	
71007-71007 BETHANY	71245-71245 GRAMBLING	71404-71404 ATLANTA	
71008-71008 BIENVILLE	71247-71247 HODGE	71405-71405 BALL	
71009-71009 BLANCHARD	71249-71249 JIGGER	71406-71406 BELMONT	
71014-71014 BRYCELAND	71250-71250 JONES	71407-71407 BENTLEY	
71016-71016 CASTOR	71251-71251 JONESBORO	71409-71409 BOYCE	
71018-71018 COTTON VALLEY	71253-71253 KILBOURNE	71410-71410 CALVIN	
71019-71019 COUSHATTA	71254-71254 LAKE PROVIDENCE	71411-71411 CAMPTI	
71020-71020 CRESTON	71256-71256 LILLIE	71412-71412 CHOPIN	
71021-71021 CULLEN	71259-71259 MANGHAM	71414-71414 CLARENCE	
71023-71023 DOYLINE	71260-71260 MARION	71415-71415 CLARKS	
71024-71024 DUBBERLY	71261-71261 MER ROUGE	71416-71416 CLOUTIERVILLE	
71025-71025 EAST POINT	71263-71263 OAK GROVE	71417-71417 COLFAX	
71027-71027 FRIERSON	71264-71264 OAK RIDGE	71418-71418 COLUMBIA	
71028-71028 GIBSLAND	71266-71266 PIONEER	71419-71419 CONVERSE	
71029-71029 GILLIAM	71268-71268 QUITMAN	71420-71420 CYPRESS	
71030-71030 GLOSTER	71269-71269 RAYVILLE	71421-71421 DERRY	
71031-71031 GOLDONNA	71270-71273 RUSTON	71422-71422 DODSON	
71032-71032 GRAND CANE	71275-71275 SIMSBORO	71423-71423 DRY PRONG	
71033-71033 GREENWOOD	71276-71276 SONDHEIMER	71424-71424 ELMER	
71034-71034 HALL SUMMIT	71277-71277 SPEARSVILLE	71425-71425 ENTERPRISE	
71036-71036 HARMON	71279-71279 START	71426-71426 FISHER	
71037-71037 HAUGHTON	71280-71280 STERLINGTON	71427-71427 FLATWOODS	
71038-71038 HAYNESVILLE	71281-71281 SWARTZ	71428-71428 FLORA	
71039-71039 HEFLIN	71282-71284 TALLULAH	71429-71429 FLORIEN	
71040-71040 HOMER	71286-71286 TRANSYLVANIA	71430-71430 FOREST HILL	
71043-71043 HOSSTON	71291-71294 WEST MONROE	71431-71431 GARDNER	
71044-71044 IDA	71295-71295 WINNSBORO	71432-71432 GEORGETOWN	
71045-71045 JAMESTOWN	71301-71315 ALEXANDRIA	71433-71433 GLENMORA	
71046-71046 KEATCHIE	71316-71316 ACME	71434-71434 GORUM	
71047-71047 KEITHVILLE	71318-71318 BIG BEND	71435-71435 GRAYSON	
71048-71048 LISBON	71320-71320 BORDELONVILLE	71436-71436 HEBERT	
71049-71049 LOGANSPORT	71321-71321 BUCKEYE	71437-71437 HICKS	
71050-71050 LONGSTREET	71322-71322 BUNKIE	71438-71438 HINESTON	
71051-71051 ELM GROVE	71323-71323 CENTER POINT	71439-71439 HORNBECK	
71052-71052 MANSFIELD	71324-71324 CHASE	71440-71440 JOYCE	
71055-71058 MINDEN	71325-71325 CHENEYVILLE	71441-71441 KELLY	
71059-71059 MIRA	71326-71326 CLAYTON	71443-71443 KURTHWOOD	
71060-71060 MOORINGSPORT	71327-71327 COTTONPORT	71444-71444 LACAMP	
71061-71061 OIL CITY	71328-71328 DEVILLE	71445-71445 LEANDER	
71063-71063 PELICAN	71329-71329 DUPONT	71446-71446 LEESVILLE	
71064-71064 PLAIN DEALING	71330-71330 ECHO	71447-71447 LENA	
71065-71065 PLEASANT HILL	71331-71331 EFFIE	71448-71448 LONGLEAF	

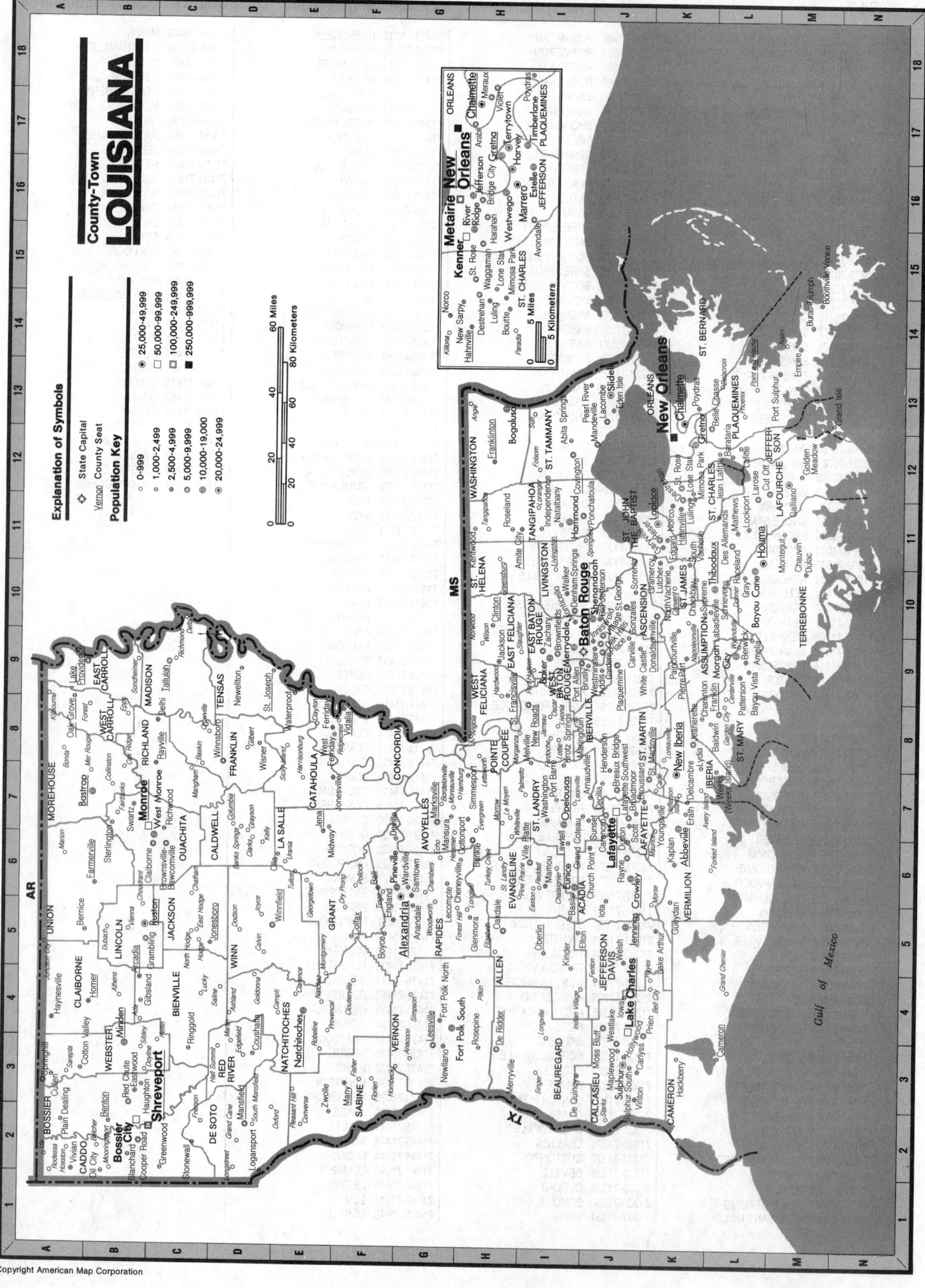

LOUISIANA

County-Town

CITIES AND TOWNS

Note: The first name is that of the city or town, second, that of the county in which it is located, then the population and location on the map.

Explanation of symbols: • – Census Designated Place (CDP)

General Help Numbers:

Governor's Office

1 State House Station, Room 236
Augusta, ME 04333-0001
www.state.me.us/governor

207-287-3531
Fax 207-287-1034
7:30AM-5:30PM

Attorney General's Office

6 State House Station
Augusta, ME 04333
www.state.me.us/ag

207-626-8800
Fax 207-626-8828
8AM-5PM

Legislative Records

Maine Legislature, 2 State House Station
Legislative Document Room
Augusta, ME 04333-0002
http://janus.state.me.us/legis

207-287-1692
Fax 207-287-1456
8AM-5PM

State Archives

84 State House Station
Augusta, ME 04333-0084
www.state.me.us/sos/arc

207-287-5795
Fax 207-287-5739
8:30AM-4PM

State Specifics:

Capital:	Augusta
	Kennebec County
Time Zone:	EST
Number of Counties:	16
Population:	1,305,728
Web Site:	www.state.me.us

State Agencies

Criminal Records

Maine State Police, State Bureau of Identification, 45 Commerce Dr #1, Augusta, ME 04333; 207-624-7240, 207-287-3421-Fax; 8AM-5PM.

www.informe.org/PCR

Records are available from 1937 on. It takes 1 to 2 days before new records are available for inquiry. Records are indexed on computer (43%) and court index cards. Records are normally destroyed after 99 years, if no activity within last five years. 90% of all arrests in database have final dispositions recorded, 90% for those arrests within last 5 years.

Searching: Requests must be in writing. Will only do FBI fingerprint checks as authorized by Maine Statutes. Records are updated as often as courts submit records to this agency. Include the following in your request-name, date of birth, any aliases. Fingerprints are optional. Include maiden name for females. Also include purpose of the inquiry and name and address of requester. 63% of the records are fingerprint-supported. Fingerprints generally are submitted with arrest information to this agency by the police. The following data is not released: juvenile records. All convictions and all pending cases less than 1 year old are reported, or if the case has not yet been adjudicated in court.

Access by: mail, fax, in person, online.

Fee & Payment: The search fee is $25.00 (unless requester is Maine resident ordering online), regardless if fingerprints are submitted. Fee payee: Treasurer, State of Maine. Personal checks accepted. Credit cards accepted at website.

Mail search: Turnaround time: 1 week.

Fax search: Records may be requested by fax, but only in approved emergency situations.

In person search: This only saves mail-in time; records are returned by mail.

Online search: One may request a record search at www.informe.org/PCR/. Results are usually returned via e-mail in 2 hours. Fee is $25.00, unless requester is an in-state subscriber to InforME, then fee is $15.00 per record. There is a $75.00 annual fee to be a subscriber.

Statewide Court Records

State Court Administrator, PO Box 4820, Portland, ME 04112; 207-822-0792, 207-822-0781-Fax; 8AM-4PM.

www.courts.state.me.us

Access to trial court records is not available from a central location. All trial court record access must be done at the local level. This web page, however, does offer a variety of resources and information.

Access by: online.

Online search: The website offers access to Maine Supreme Court opinions and administrative orders, but not all documents are available online. Also, the site offers online access to trial court schedules by region and case type.

Sexual Offender Registry

State Bureau of Investigation, 45 Commerce Drive, #1, Attn: SOR, Augusta, ME 04330; 207-624-7009, 207-624-7088-Fax; 8AM-5PM.

www.informe.org/sor

Records are available from 06/30/92 to present. It takes 1 to 2 days before new records are available for inquiry.

Searching: Include the following in your request-name, date of birth, any aliases (if requesting by mail, phone or fax). Once a request is made and a specific subject is brought up, the requester can ask this agency for more information, including personal information, the description of the offense, dates, and sentence imposed. The following data is not released: juvenile records, unless convicted as an adult.

Access by: mail, phone, fax, in person, online.

Fee & Payment: There is no fee.

Mail search: Turnaround time: 1-2 days. A SASE is requested.

Phone search: Will confirm by phone.

Fax search: Records are available by fax for ongoing requesters with lists.

In person search: Record information released for small request amounts.

Online search: Search at www.informe.org/sor/. Search by name, town or ZIP Code. Information is only provided for those individuals that are required to register pursuant to Title 34-A MRSA, Chapter 15. Records date to 06/30/92 and forward. The date of the last address verification is indicated next to the registrant's address.

Other access: The entire database is for sale.

Incarceration Records

Maine Department of Corrections, Inmate Records, 111 State House Station, Augusta, ME 04333; 207-287-2711, 207-287-4381 (Probation info), 800-968-6909 (Victim Services info), 207-287-4370-Fax; 8AM-4:30PM.

www.state.me.us/corrections

Records are available on current and former inmates. It takes 1 to 2 days before new records are available for inquiry. Records are normally

destroyed after never - archived seven years after release.

Searching: One may also do a search by sending an email to Corrections.Webdesk@maine.gov. Include your full name, address, and reasons for the search. Public information is provided. Include the following in your request-name, date of birth, any aliases. Fingerprints are optional.

Access by: mail, phone, fax, online.

Fee & Payment: There is no fee.

Mail search: Turnaround time: 1-2 weeks. A SASE is requested.

Phone search: Name searching available by phone, either through the agency main number or through Victim Services.

Fax search: Records are available by fax.

Online search: No direct online access available at this time (check website for updated information). Email requesting is available at Corrections.Webdesk@maine.gov.

Other access: Database sales/bulk records can be requested and will be reviewed.

Corporation, Limited Partnerships, Trademarks/Servicemarks, Assumed Name, Limited Liability Company Records, Limited Liability Partnerships

Secretary of State, Reports & Information Division, 101 State House Station, Augusta, ME 04333-0101; 207-624-7752, 207-624-7736 (Main Number), 207-287-5874-Fax; 8AM-5PM.

www.maine.gov/sos/cec/corp

Records are available from 1700's on. The older records are in law books. Records on the in-house computer are for all active and some inactive corporations. New records are available for inquiry immediately. Records are indexed on index cards, inhouse computer.

Searching: Include the following in your request-full name of business, specific records that you need copies of. In addition to the articles of incorporation, corporation records include the following information: Annual Reports (back to 1986), Officers, Directors, Prior (merged) names, Inactive and Reserved names.

Access by: mail, phone, fax, in person, online.

Fee & Payment: Copies are $2.00 per page, additional $5.00 if certified. A Certificate of Existence is $30.00 and $10.00 if not for profit. Fee payee: Secretary of State. They will invoice for copies. Personal checks and MasterCard/VISA accepted.

Mail search: Turnaround time: 1 week.

Phone search: They will provide names and addresses of officers and directors over the phone.

Fax search: Records are available by fax.

In person search: See expedited service.

Online search: Basic information about the entity including address, corp ID, agent, and status is found at www.informe.org/icrs/ICRS. A commercial subscriber account gives extensive information and ability to download files.

Other access: Lists of new entities filed with this office are available monthly.

Expedited service: Expedited service is available for mail and phone searches. Turnaround time: 24 hours. Add $50.00 per business name. For immediate service, the fee is $100.00 per business name.

Uniform Commercial Code, Federal and State Tax Liens

Secretary of State, UCC Records Section, 101 State House Station, Augusta, ME 04333-0101 (Courier address: Burton M. Cross State Office Bldg, 109 Sewell St, 4th Fl, Augusta, ME 04333); 207-624-7760, 207-287-5874-Fax; 8AM-5PM.

www.maine.gov/sos/cec/corp/ucc.htm

Records are available from 1964. Records are computerized since 1993. It takes 3 to 4 days before new records are available for inquiry. Records are indexed on inhouse computer. Records are normally destroyed after 5 years.

Searching: Use search request form UCC-11 when needed for certification. The search includes both federal and state tax liens. Searching is done by index number or debtor name only. Try to include a middle initial in your request. They will not search by address or collateral or secured party.

Access by: mail, phone, fax, in person, online.

Fee & Payment: Searches cost $20.00 per name, $12.00 if online. Certification is $5.00. Fee payee: Secretary of State Prepayment required. Ongoing requesters may make arrangements for invoicing. Personal checks accepted. VISA/MasterCard accepted.

Mail search: Turnaround time: a maximum of 5 days. If update or certain dates requested, state boldly.

Phone search: Limited information is available by phone. Usually this is limited to only those listed on the filing.

Fax search: Same criteria as mail requests. Up to 15 pages will be returned as long as request is in writing.

In person search: There are 2 public access terminals. If copies are needed, written request required and fees apply, see expedited services below.

Online search: Online access for official records is available at www.sosonline.org. Fees are involved. There is a free search of the index to find names or name variations at this site.

Other access: Farm products - buyers reports, secured party available in bulk.

Expedited service: Expedited service is available for mail searches. The Maine specific UCC-11 request form has a box to check if expedited service requested. Add $10.00 per name for overnight, $25.00 if immediate. If by mail, write and highlight the word "Expedite" on the search request.

Sales Tax Registrations

Maine Revenue Services, Sales, Fuel & Special Tax Division, 24 State House Station, Augusta, ME 04333; 207-624-9693, 207-287-6628-Fax; 8AM-5PM.

www.maine.gov/revenue

Records are available from 1993, on computer. It takes up to 2 months before new records are available for inquiry.

Searching: This agency will only confirm that a business is registered. They will provide no other information. Include the following in your request-business name. They will also search by tax permit number or federal ID.

Access by: mail, phone, fax, in person.

Mail search: Turnaround time: 7 to 10 days. A SASE is helpful. No fee for mail request.

Phone search: No fee for telephone request.

Fax search: Same criteria as mail searching.

In person search: No fee for request. Proper ID required.

Birth Certificates

Maine Department of Human Services, Vital Records, 244 Water St, Station 11, Augusta, ME 04333-0011; 207-287-3181, 877-523-2659 (VitalChek), 207-287-1093-Fax; 8AM-5PM.

www.state.me.us/dhs/vitalrecords.htm

The website has a link to VitalChek for online ordering.

Records are available from 1923 to present. Maine State Archives has records prior to 1923 (call 207-287-5795). Records are indexed on computer from 1975 to present, and on microfiche from 1892 to present. It takes up to one month before new records are available for inquiry. Records are indexed on books (volumes).

Searching: Must give relationship to person of record and reason for request. Confidential information will not be released except to the person listed on the birth certificate. Include the following in your request-full name, names of parents, mother's maiden name, date of birth, place of birth. Also include your daytime phone number with the request. The following data is not released: illegitimate births or adoption records.

Access by: mail, phone, in person.

Fee & Payment: $15.00 fee for certified copy, add $6.00 per name for additional copy of same record. Fee payee: Treasurer, State of Maine. Prepayment required. Personal checks accepted. Credit cards accepted: MasterCard, Visa.

Mail search: Turnaround time: 1 to 2 weeks. Specific dates are needed to search as well as names (if available). SASE requested.

Phone search: See expedited service.

In person search: Turnaround time is while you wait.

Other access: Physical birth lists are available for purchase, excluding restricted information.

Expedited service: Expedited service is available for mail, phone and fax searches. Turnaround time: 1-5 days. Use of credit card is required. Add fee of $29.95 for 1-3 days service or $22.95 for 3-5 days service.

Death Records

Maine Department of Human Services, Vital Records, 244 Water St, Station 11, Augusta, ME 04333-0011; 207-287-3181, 877-523-2659 (VitalChek), 207-287-1093-Fax; 8AM-5PM.

www.state.me.us/dhs/vitalrecords.htm

The website has a link to VitalChek for online ordering.

Records are available from 1923 to present. Maine State Archives has records prior to 1923 (call 207-287-5795). Records are indexed on computer from 1975 to present, and on microfiche from 1892 to present. It takes up to 1 month before new records are available for inquiry. Records are indexed on books (volumes).

Searching: Access to cause of death is restricted to those with a legitimate interest in the information. All information on certificate of death is confidential, except name, age, date of death, as well as city/town where death occurred. Include the following in your request-full name, date of death, place of death, relationship to person of record.

Access by: mail, phone, in person, online.

Fee & Payment: $15.00 fee for certified copy, add $6.00 per name for additional copy of same record. Fee payee: Treasurer, State of Maine. Prepayment required. Personal checks accepted. Credit cards accepted: MasterCard, Visa.

Mail search: Turnaround time: 1 to 2 weeks. When requesting a search, keep in mind that records are filed by the date of the death, and then by name. SASE required.

Phone search: See expedited service.

In person search: Turnaround time is while you wait.

Online search: Search death records 1960-1996 at www.state.me.us/sos/arc/geneology/homepage.html. Also, a free genealogy site at http://vitals.rootsweb.com/me/death/search.cgi has Death Indexes from 1960-1997. Search by surname, given name, place or year.

Other access: Bulk file purchases are available, with the exclusion of restricted data.

Expedited service: Expedited service is available for mail, phone and fax searches. Turnaround time: 1-5 days. Use of credit card is required. Add fee of $29.95 for 1-3 days service or $22.95 for 3-5 days service.

Marriage Certificates

Maine Department of Human Services, Vital Records, 244 Water St, Station 11, Augusta, ME 04333-0011; 207-287-3181, 877-523-2659 (VitalChek), 207-287-1093-Fax; 8AM-5PM.

www.state.me.us/dhs/vitalrecords.htm

The website has a link to VitalChek for online ordering.

Records are available from 1923 to present. Maine State Archives has records prior to 1923 (call 207-287-5795). Records are indexed on microfiche from 1892 to present. It takes up to one month before new records are available for inquiry. Records are indexed on books (volumes).

Searching: Must give relationship to persons of record and reason for request. Data recorded in the section of the certificate specified as confidential is not released (i.e. race, education, etc.). Include the following in your request-names of husband and wife, date of marriage, place or county of marriage.

Access by: mail, phone, in person, online.

Fee & Payment: $15.00 fee for certified copy, add $6.00 per name for additional copy of same record. Fee payee: Treasurer, State of Maine. Prepayment required. Personal checks accepted. Credit cards accepted: MasterCard, Visa.

Mail search: Turnaround time: 1 to 2 weeks. SASE requested.

Phone search: See expedited service.

In person search: Turnaround time is while you wait.

Online search: Records are available at www.state.me.us/sos/arc/geneology/homepage.html from 1892-1966 and 1976-1996. Marriage History records from the Maine State Archives are available at www.state.me.us/sos/arc/, click on marriage database.

Other access: Bulk file purchasing is available, with restricted data excluded.

Expedited service: Expedited service is available for mail, phone and fax searches. Turnaround time: 1-5 days. Use of credit card is required. Add fee of $29.95 for 1-3 days service or $22.95 for 3-5 days service.

Divorce Records

Maine Department of Human Services, Office of Vital Records, 244 Water St, Station 11, Augusta, ME 04333-0011; 207-287-3181, 877-523-2659 (VitalChek), 207-287-1093-Fax; 8AM-5PM.

www.state.me.us/dhs/vitalrecords.htm

The website has a link to VitalChek for online ordering.

Records are available from 1892 to present. Maine State Archives has records prior to 1923, call 207-287-5795. It takes up to 1 month before new records are available for inquiry. Records are indexed on books (volumes).

Searching: Must give relationship to persons of record and reason for request. Include the following in your request-names of husband and wife, date of divorce, place of divorce.

Access by: mail, phone, in person.

Fee & Payment: $15.00 fee for certified copy, add $6.00 per name for additional copy of same record. Fee payee: Treasurer, State of Maine. Prepayment required. Personal checks accepted. Credit cards accepted: MasterCard, Visa.

Mail search: Turnaround time: 1 to 2 weeks. SASE requested.

Phone search: See expedited service.

In person search: Turnaround time is while you wait for up to 2 requests.

Other access: Index information is available for bulk purchase.

Expedited service: Expedited service is available for phone requests. Turnaround time: 1-5 days. Use of credit card is required. Add fee of $29.95 for 1-3 days service or $22.95 for 3-5 days service.

Workers' Compensation Records

Workers Compensation Board, 27 State House Station, Augusta, ME 04333-0027; 207-287-7071, 207-287-5895-Fax; 7:30AM-5PM.

www.state.me.us

Both pre AND post employment checks are not permitted.

Records are available from 1984, indexed on computer. It takes 1 month before new records are available for inquiry. Records are normally destroyed after 6 years.

Searching: Records are considered confidential and are released "on a need-to-know basis." Include the following in your request-claimant name, Social Security Number, reason for information request. The following data is not released: personal information (height, weight, sex, eye color, etc.) or Social Security Numbers.

Access by: mail, in person.

Fee & Payment: The research fee is $5.00. Copies are $.50 per page. Fee payee: Trea. State of Maine, Workers' Compensation Board. When remitting payment, please include invoice number on your check. Personal checks accepted. No credit cards accepted.

Mail search: Turnaround time: 3 to 4 weeks. Requests should be addressed to: Linda Larrabee, Workers' Compensation Board, 27 State House Station, Augusta, ME 04333-0027. A SASE is requested.

In person search: Requests must still be in writing and prior approval is suggested.

Other access: Computer data is available, but requests are screened for purpose.

Driver Records

BMV - Driver License Services, 101 Hospital Street, 29 State House Station, Augusta, ME 04333-0029; 207-624-9000 x52116, 207-624-9090-Fax; 8AM-5PM.

www.state.me.us/sos/bmv

Records are available for 3 years for moving violations, DWIs and 3 years after the reinstatement of suspensions. Accidents are indicated on the record. It takes up to 30 days before new records are available for inquiry. Records are normally destroyed after filming.

Searching: Driving records and ticket information is released per DPPA guidelines. Personal information is not available to the general public unless the subject opts in, or a signed release is presented. The full name and DOB are required for a search. The driver's license number is optional. The following data is not released: medical information.

Access by: mail, fax, in person, online.

Fee & Payment: The fee is $5.00 for a non-certified record and $6.00 for a certified record, and $7.00 if accessed online. A "no record found" incurs a full charge, except for walk-in requesters. Fee payee: Secretary of State. Prepayment required. Personal checks accepted.

Mail search: Turnaround time: 3 days.

Fax search: Add $2.00 and results are returned by mail.

In person search: Up to 5 requests can be obtained in-person immediately; additional requests are available the next day.

Online search: Access is through InforME via the Internet. There are two access systems. Casual requesters can obtain records that have personal information cloaked. There is a subscription service for apporved requesters, records contain personal information. Records are released per DPPA. Records are $7.00 per request and go back three years. Visit www.informe.org/bmv/drc/ or call 207-621-2600. There is a $75.00 annual fee for the subscription service. A myriad of other state government records are available.

Other access: The state offers "Driver Cross Check" - a program for employers, to provide notification when activity occurs on a specific record.

Vehicle Ownership
Vehicle Identification

Department of Motor Vehicles, Registration Section, 29 State House Station, Augusta, ME 04333-0029; 207-624-9000 x52149 (Registration), 207-624-9000 x52138 (Titles), 207-624-9204-Fax; 8AM-5PM M-F.

www.state.me.us/sos/bmv

The above fax is for Registration, tax for Title is 207-624-9239.

Records are available from 1982, on microfilm. It takes up to 30 days before new records are available for inquiry. Records are normally destroyed after records converted to microfilm.

Searching: Casual requesters can obtain records, but personal information is not included unless the subject gives authorization. Opt-in is available. Include the following in your request-full name and DOB, or by VIN or by license plate number. It is suggested to become an account holder.

Access by: mail, phone, fax, in person, online.

Fee & Payment: Fees: $6.00 for certified Registration record, $23.00 for s certified Title record. Uncertified records are $5.00. Will also fax record back for an additional $2.00. Fee payee: Secretary of State. Prepayment required. Personal checks accepted. Credit cards accepted.

Mail search: Turnaround time: 5 days.

Phone search: Telephone searching is available for parties who establish an account. They are billed monthly.

Fax search: Established accounts may order by fax, and then have data returned by fax for an additional $2.00.

In person search: Immediate service limited to simple requests.

Online search: Maine offers online access to title and registration records via InfoME. Fee is $5.00 per record. Records are available as interactive online or FTP with a subscription account. Contact InfoME at info@informe.org.

Accident Reports

Maine State Police, Traffic Division, Station 20, Augusta, ME 04333-0020 (Courier address: 397 Water St, Gardiner, ME 04345); 207-624-8944, 207-624-8945-Fax; 8AM-5PM.

www.state.me.us/dps/msp/home.htm

Accidents must be reported involving death, injury, or property damage in excess of $1000.00.

Records are available from 1975. Most records are on microfilm. It takes up to 30 days before new records are available for inquiry.

Searching: Most accident records are public information. All requests must be in writing. If a fatality is involved, the fatality report is not released until the court case is concluded. Include the following in your request-full name, date of birth, date of accident, location of accident. Be sure to order by the operator's name, not by vehicle owner name.

Access by: mail, fax, in person, online.

Fee & Payment: The fee is $5.00 per copy for Police Traffic report, $10.00 for an Officer's Investigative Report (fatality involved), $10.00 for an Accident Reconstruction Report, and $10.00 for a Vehicle Autopsy Report. Fee payee: Maine State Police. Prepayment required. Personal checks accepted. No credit cards accepted.

Mail search: Turnaround time: 7 days.

Fax search: Records may be returned by fax, but email is preferred.

In person search: Turnaround time is usually immediate for walk-in requesters.

Online search: Records from 01/2003 forward may be ordered the web page. The fee is $5.00 per record. If you do not have a subscription to InforME, then a credit card must be used. Resulting reports is either returned by mail, or emailed in a PDF format. You can search by name, date of birth, crash location, crash date, or investigating agency (police department). These reports may include officer narratives, witness statements, photographs or other recordings.

Vessel Ownership
Vessel Registration

Dept of Inland Fisheries & Wildlife, Vessel Records, 41 State House Station, 284 State St, Augusta, ME 04333-0041; 207-287-5231, 207-287-8094-Fax; 8AM-5PM.

www.state.me.us/ifw

Liens are not recorded here and must be searched with UCCs.

Records are available from 1987 to present for registrations that have been continuously renewed. There are no titles, all motorized boats must be registered. It takes several months before new records are available for inquiry. Records are indexed on computer. Records are normally destroyed after 7 years and number is re-issued.

Searching: Include the following in your request-name or registration number.

Access by: mail, phone, fax, in person.

Fee & Payment: The search fee is $5.00 per record for a name search. A boat history fee is $25.00. Fee payee: Treasurer, State of Maine. Prepayment required. Personal checks and MasterCard, Visa, Discover accepted.

Mail search: Turnaround time: 1 to 2 weeks.

Phone search: Results will only be given verbally, if payment is arranged using a credit card.

Fax search: Turnaround time is within 72 hours. A credit card must be used for all fax searches.

In person search: Counter service available.

Other access: Bulk purchase available from InforME at 207-621-3800 x38

Voter Registration

Access to Records is Restricted.

Secretary of State, Department of Elections, 101 State House Station, 4th Fl, Augusta, ME 04333-0101; 207-624-7650, 207-287-5428-Fax; 8AM-5PM.

www.maine.gov/sos/cec/elec

The data is considered public record in Maine, but presently can only be accessed at the municipality level. The Federal Help America Vote Act of 2002 (HAVA) law requires implementation of a central, computerized, statewide voter registration system by 01/01/2006. At that time, this office will sell voter registration lists.

GED Certificates

Dept of Education, Attn: GED, 23 State House Station, Augusta, ME 04333; 207-624-6752, 207-624-6731-Fax; 8AM-5PM.

www.maine.gov/education/aded/hscompletion.htm

It takes 2 days before new records are available for inquiry.

Searching: Requests for transcripts must be in writing. To verify, all of the following is required: name, date of birth, and SSN. For transcripts, a signed release is required.

Access by: mail, phone, fax, in person, online.

Fee & Payment: There are no fees for verification or copy of transcript, but $13.00 for copy of the GED.

Mail search: Turnaround time 1-2 days.

Phone search: You can do a verification over the phone.

Fax search: Turnaround time 1-2 days.

In person search: Turnaround time: Immediate.

Online search: Email requests can be made by sending email to: lisa.perry@maine.gov

Hunting and Fishing License Information

Inland Fisheries & Wildlife Department, Licensing Division, 284 State St, Augusta, ME 04333; 207-287-8000, 207-287-8094-Fax; 8AM-5PM.

www.state.me.us/ifw

The state is in the process of computerizing license data. Licenses are issued online at the website. Also, licenses are issued by Town Clerks and approved businesses and forwarded monthly to this department.

Records are available from 1996 to present. It takes at least 3 months, if not online before new records are available for inquiry. Records are indexed on inhouse computer.

Searching: All information is considered open to the public. Include the following in your request- full name, date of birth, address.

Access by: mail, phone, fax, in person.

Fee & Payment: Individual searches are completed for $5.00 each. Fee payee: Treasurer, State of Maine. Prepayment required. Credit cards accepted: MasterCard, Visa.

Mail search: Turnaround time: 7 business days.

Phone search: Credit card required.

Fax search: Fax requests accepted with credit card.

In person search: Immediate service limited to simple requests.

Other access: Bulk data purchases are available at a cost of $.05 per name. Call InforME at 207-621-2600, x38.

Maine State Licensing Agencies

For details about the agency responsible for licensing/certifying/registering an item below or in the Agency Quick Finder section, match an item's number with the number of the agency in the *Licensing Agency Information* section.

Maine Licenses Searchable Online

Acupuncturist #13	http://pfr0.informe.org/almsquery/LicLookup.aspx
Adult Day Service #9	www.state.me.us/dhs/beas/facilities/fac_main.php
Advanced Practice Registered Nurse #8	www.maine.gov/boardofnursing
Aesthetician #13	http://pfr0.informe.org/almsquery/LicLookup.aspx
Alcohol/Drug Abuse Counselor #13	http://pfr0.informe.org/almsquery/LicLookup.aspx
Ambulatory Surgical Center #9	http://licert.dhs.state.me.us
Animal Medical Technician #13	http://pfr0.informe.org/almsquery/LicLookup.aspx
Appraiser, Residential Real Estate #13	http://pfr0.informe.org/almsquery/LicLookup.aspx
Architect #13	http://pfr0.informe.org/almsquery/LicLookup.aspx
Assisted Living Facility #9	www.state.me.us/dhs/beas/facilities/fac_main.php
Athletic Trainer #13	http://pfr0.informe.org/almsquery/LicLookup.aspx
Auctioneer #13	http://pfr0.informe.org/almsquery/LicLookup.aspx
Barber #13	http://pfr0.informe.org/almsquery/LicLookup.aspx
Body Piercer #19	www.state.me.us/dhs/eng/el/index.html
Boiler #13	http://pfr0.informe.org/almsquery/LicLookup.aspx
Boxer #13	http://pfr0.informe.org/almsquery/LicLookup.aspx
Charitable Solicitation #13	http://pfr0.informe.org/almsquery/LicLookup.aspx
Chiropractor #13	http://pfr0.informe.org/almsquery/LicLookup.aspx
Cosmetologist #13	http://pfr0.informe.org/almsquery/LicLookup.aspx
Counselor #13	http://pfr0.informe.org/almsquery/LicLookup.aspx
Dental Hygienist #16	www.mainedental.org/search.htm
Dental Radiographer #16	www.mainedental.org/search.htm
Dentist / Denturist #16	www.mainedental.org/search.htm
Dietitian #13	http://pfr0.informe.org/almsquery/LicLookup.aspx
Electrician #13	http://pfr0.informe.org/almsquery/LicLookup.aspx
Elevator/Tramway #13	http://pfr0.informe.org/almsquery/LicLookup.aspx
Employee Leasing Company #15	www.state.me.us/pfr/ins/emplease.htm
Engineer #17	https://www.maine.gov/professionalengineers/database.shtml
Forester #13	http://pfr0.informe.org/almsquery/LicLookup.aspx
Fund Raiser #13	http://pfr0.informe.org/almsquery/LicLookup.aspx
Funeral Service #13	http://pfr0.informe.org/almsquery/LicLookup.aspx
Geologist #13	http://pfr0.informe.org/almsquery/LicLookup.aspx
Hearing Aid Dealer/Fitter #13	http://pfr0.informe.org/almsquery/LicLookup.aspx
HMO #15	www.state.me.us/pfr/ins/inshmo.htm
Home Health Agency #9	http://licert.dhs.state.me.us
Home Health Care Svc Agency #9	http://licert.dhs.state.me.us
Hospice #9	http://licert.dhs.state.me.us
Hospital #9	http://licert.dhs.state.me.us
Insurance Adjuster #15	http://pfr0.informe.org/almsquery/LicLookup.aspx
Insurance Advisor #13	http://pfr0.informe.org/almsquery/LicLookup.aspx
Insurance Agency #15	http://pfr0.informe.org/almsquery/LicLookup.aspx
Insurance Agent/Company #13	http://pfr0.informe.org/almsquery/LicLookup.aspx
Insurance Company/Consultant #15	http://pfr0.informe.org/almsquery/LicLookup.aspx
Insurance Producer #15	http://pfr0.informe.org/almsquery/LicLookup.aspx
Interior Designer #13	http://pfr0.informe.org/almsquery/LicLookup.aspx
Interm. Care Facility (ment. retarded) #9	http://licert.dhs.state.me.us
Interpreter #13	http://pfr0.informe.org/almsquery/LicLookup.aspx
Investment Advisor #12	http://pfr.informe.org/almsquery/LicLookup.aspx
Kickboxer #13	http://pfr0.informe.org/almsquery/LicLookup.aspx
Landscape Architect #13	http://pfr0.informe.org/almsquery/LicLookup.aspx

Licensed Practical Nurse #8 .... www.maine.gov/boardofnursing
Lobbyist #1 .... www.mainecampaignfinance.com/public/entity_list.asp?TYPE=LOB
Manicurist #13 .... http://pfr0.informe.org/almsquery/LicLookup.aspx
Manufactured Housing #13 .... http://pfr0.informe.org/almsquery/LicLookup.aspx
Marriage & Family Therapist #13 .... http://pfr0.informe.org/almsquery/LicLookup.aspx
Massage Therapist #13 .... http://pfr0.informe.org/almsquery/LicLookup.aspx
Medical Doctor #23 .... www.docboard.org/me/df/mesearch.htm
Naturopathic Physician #13 .... http://pfr0.informe.org/almsquery/LicLookup.aspx
Notary Public #24 .... http://portalx.bisoex.state.me.us/pls/sos_bc/bcdev.notaries.search
Nurse #8 .... www.maine.gov/boardofnursing
Nursing Home #9 .... http://licert.dhs.state.me.us
Nursing Home Administrator #13 .... http://pfr0.informe.org/almsquery/LicLookup.aspx
Occupational Therapist #13 .... http://pfr0.informe.org/almsquery/LicLookup.aspx
Oil & Solid Fuel Prof./Company #13 .... http://pfr0.informe.org/almsquery/LicLookup.aspx
Optometrist #18 .... http://pfr.informe.org/almsquery/LicLookup.aspx
Osteopathic Physician/Phys. Assist. #26 .... www.docboard.org/me-osteo/df/index.htm
Osteopathic Resident/Intern #26 .... www.docboard.org/me-osteo/df/index.htm
Pastoral Counselor #13 .... http://pfr0.informe.org/almsquery/LicLookup.aspx
Pharmacist #13 .... http://pfr0.informe.org/almsquery/LicLookup.aspx
Physical Therapist #13 .... http://pfr0.informe.org/almsquery/LicLookup.aspx
Physician Assistant #23 .... www.docboard.org/me/df/mesearch.htm
Pilot #13 .... http://pfr0.informe.org/almsquery/LicLookup.aspx
Plumber #13 .... http://pfr0.informe.org/almsquery/LicLookup.aspx
Podiatrist #13 .... http://pfr0.informe.org/almsquery/LicLookup.aspx
Preferred Provider Organization #15 .... www.state.me.us/pfr/ins/insppo.htm
Psychologist #13 .... http://pfr0.informe.org/almsquery/LicLookup.aspx
Public Accountant-CPA #13 .... http://pfr0.informe.org/almsquery/LicLookup.aspx
Radiologic Technician #13 .... http://pfr0.informe.org/almsquery/LicLookup.aspx
Real Estate Appraiser, General #13 .... http://pfr0.informe.org/almsquery/LicLookup.aspx
Real Estate Appraiser/Trainee #13 .... http://pfr0.informe.org/almsquery/LicLookup.aspx
Real Estate Broker #13 .... http://pfr0.informe.org/almsquery/LicLookup.aspx
Registered Professional Nurse #8 .... www.maine.gov/boardofnursing
Reinsurance Intermediary #15 .... http://pfr0.informe.org/almsquery/LicLookup.aspx
Re-insurer, Approved #15 .... http://pfr0.informe.org/almsquery/LicLookup.aspx
Renal Disease (End Stage) Facility #9 .... http://licert.dhs.state.me.us
Respiratory Care Therapist #13 .... http://pfr0.informe.org/almsquery/LicLookup.aspx
Securities Agent/Broker #12 .... http://pfr.informe.org/almsquery/LicLookup.aspx
Social Worker #13 .... http://pfr0.informe.org/almsquery/LicLookup.aspx
Soil Scientist #13 .... http://pfr0.informe.org/almsquery/LicLookup.aspx
Speech Pathologist/Audiologist #13 .... http://pfr0.informe.org/almsquery/LicLookup.aspx
Substance Abuse Counselor #13 .... http://pfr0.informe.org/almsquery/LicLookup.aspx
Surplus Lines Company #15 .... http://pfr0.informe.org/almsquery/LicLookup.aspx
Surveyor, Land #13 .... http://pfr0.informe.org/almsquery/LicLookup.aspx
Third Party Administrator #15 .... http://pfr0.informe.org/almsquery/LicLookup.aspx
Utilization Review Entity #15 .... www.state.me.us/pfr/ins/insmedur.htm
Vendor, Itinerant/Transient #13 .... http://pfr0.informe.org/almsquery/LicLookup.aspx
Veterinarian/Veterinary Technician #13 .... http://pfr0.informe.org/almsquery/LicLookup.aspx
Wrestler #13 .... http://pfr0.informe.org/almsquery/LicLookup.aspx

Maine Licensing Quick Finder

Acupuncturist #13	207-624-8603
Adoption Agency #7	207-287-5060
Adult Day Service #9	207-287-9250
Adult/Child Homes, Inspection #20	207-626-3803
Aesthetician #13	207-624-8603
Air Quality Control Business #5	207-287-2437
Alcohol/Drug Abuse Counselor #13	207-624-8603
Ambulance Attendant #10	207-287-3953
Ambulatory Surgical Center #9	207-287-9300
Animal Medical Technician #13	207-624-8603
Appraiser, Residential Real Estate #13	207-624-8616
Architect #13	207-624-8522
Assisted Living Facility #9	207-287-9250
Athletic Trainer #13	207-624-8624
Attorney #22	207-623-1121
ATV-All-Terrain Vehicle #11	207-287-2043
Auctioneer #13	207-624-8521
Bank #14	207-624-8648
Barber #13	207-624-8579
Beekeeper #3	207-287-3117
Body Piercer #19	207-287-5671
Boiler #13	207-624-8606
Boxer #13	207-624-8603
Campground #19	207-287-5671
Charitable Solicitation #13	207-624-8624
Child Care Resource #7	207-287-5060
Children's Camp #19	207-287-5671
Chiropractor #13	207-624-8634
Circus/Carnival #20	207-626-3803
Commercial Shellfish #27	207-624-6550
Compressed Air Producer (Breathing) #19	207-287-5671
Construction Plan Review #20	207-626-3803
Cosmetologist #13	207-624-8620
Counselor #13	207-624-8626
Credit Union #14	207-624-8648
Dance Hall, Inspection #20	207-626-3803
Day Care #7	207-287-5060
Dental Hygienist #16	207-287-4746
Dental Radiographer #16	207-287-4746
Dentist #16	207-287-4746
Denturist #16	207-287-4746
Dietitian #13	207-624-8611
Eating Place #19	207-287-5671
Electrician #13	207-624-8611
Electrologist #19	207-287-5671
Elevator/Tramway #13	207-624-8672
Emergency Medical Technician #10	207-287-3953
Employee Leasing Company #15	207-624-8475
Engineer #17	207-287-3236
Explosive #20	207-626-3803
Firearm Permit (Concealed,Resident&Non Resi't) #25	207-624-7210
Fireworks #20	207-626-3803
First Responder #10	207-287-3953

Forester #13	207-624-8521
Foster Care #7	207-287-5060
Fund Raiser #13	207-624-8624
Funeral Service #13	207-624-8623
Games of Chance #25	207-624-7210
Geologist #13	207-624-8627
Hazardous Material/Solid Waste Op. #6	207-287-2651
Hearing Aid Dealer/Fitter #13	207-624-8674
HMO #15	207-624-8475
Home Health Agency #9	207-287-9300
Home Health Care Service Agency #9	207-287-9300
Hospice #9	207-287-9300
Hospital #9	207-287-9300
Insurance Adjuster #15	207-624-8475
Insurance Advisor #13	207-624-8545
Insurance Agency #15	207-624-8475
Insurance Agent/Company #13	207-624-8545
Insurance Company/Consultant #15	207-624-8475
Insurance Producer #15	207-624-8475
Interior Designer #13	207-624-8522
Intermediate Care Facility for the Mentally Retarded #9	207-287-9300
Interpreter #13	207-624-8624
Investment Advisor #12	207-624-8551
Kickboxer #13	207-624-8603
Landscape Architect #13	207-624-8522
Library Media Specialist #4	207-624-6603
Limited Purpose Bank #14	207-624-8648
Lobbyist #1	207-287-6221
Lobster Harvester #27	207-624-6550
Lottery Retailer #2	207-287-3721
Manicurist #13	207-624-8603
Manufactured Housing #13	207-624-8612
Marine Worm Digger #27	207-624-6550
Marriage & Family Therapist #13	207-624-8626
Massage Therapist #13	207-624-8613
Mechanical Ride, Inspection #20	207-626-3803
Medical Doctor #23	207-287-3601
Micropigmentation Practitioner #19	207-287-5671
Motor Vehicle Race #20	207-626-3803
Naturopathic Physician #13	207-624-8603
Notary Public #24	207-624-7650
Nursery School, Inspection #20	207-626-3803
Nursing Home #9	207-287-9300
Nursing Home Administrator #13	207-624-8623
Occupational Therapist #13	207-624-8626
Oil & Solid Fuel Prof./Company #13	207-624-8672
Optometrist #18	207-624-8691
Osteopathic Physician Extender #26	207-287-2480
Osteopathic Physician/Phys. Assist #26	207-287-2480
Osteopathic Resident/Intern #26	207-287-2480
Paramedic #10	207-287-3953
Pastoral Counselor #13	207-624-8626
Pesticide Applicator #3	207-287-2731
Pesticide Dealer #3	207-287-2731

Pharmacist #13	207-624-8620
Physical Therapist #13	207-624-8628
Physician Assistant #23	207-287-3601
Pilot #13	207-624-8620
Plumber #13	207-624-8628
Podiatrist #13	207-624-8626
Polygraph Examiner #20	207-626-3803
Preferred Provider Organization #15	207-624-8475
Private Investigator #25	207-624-7210
Propane/Loges Operator/Delivery #13	207-624-8610
Propane/LP Gas Technician #13	207-624-8610
Psychologist #13	207-624-8628
Public Accountant-CPA #13	207-582-8627
Radiologic Technician #13	207-624-8628
Real Estate Appraiser, General #13	207-624-8616
Real Estate Appraiser/Trainee #13	207-624-8616
Real Estate Broker #13	207-624-8603
Reinsurance Intermediary #15	207-624-8475
Re-insurer, Approved #15	207-624-8475
Renal Disease (End Stage) Facility #9	207-287-9300
Residential Child Care Provider #7	207-287-5060
Respiratory Care Therapist #13	207-624-8616
Risk Purchasing Group #15	207-624-8475
Risk Retention Group #15	207-624-8475
Savings & Loan #14	207-624-8648
School Guidance Counselor #4	207-624-6603
School Library Media Specialist #4	207-624-6603
School Principal/Superintendent #4	207-624-6603
Sea Urchin Harvester #27	207-624-6550
Seaweed Harvester #27	207-624-6550
Securities Agent/Broker #12	207-624-8551
Security Company, Guard/Alarm #25	207-624-7210
Self Insurance Company #15	207-624-8475
Snowmobile #11	207-287-2043
Social Worker #13	207-624-8631
Soil Scientist #13	207-624-8603
Speech Pathologist/Audiologist #13	207-624-8634
Storage Tanks, Above Ground #20	207-626-3803
Substance Abuse Counselor #13	207-624-8634
Surplus Lines Company #15	207-624-8475
Surveyor, Land #13	207-624-8611
Swimming Pool #19	207-287-5671
Tattoo Artist #19	207-287-5671
Taxidermist #11	207-287-2751
Teacher #4	207-624-6603
Theatre #20	207-626-3803
Third Party Administrator #15	207-624-8475
Tobacco Retailer #19	207-287-5671
Trust Company #14	207-624-8648
Utilization Review Entity #15	207-624-8475
Vendor, Itinerant/Transient #13	207-624-8624
Veterinarian/Veterinary Technician #13	207-624-8628
Viatical Settlements Provider #15	207-624-8475
Watercraft #11	207-287-2043
Wrestler #13	207-624-8603

Maine Licensing Agency Information

1 Registrar, Commission on Governmental Ethics & Elections, State House Station 135, Augusta, ME 04333; 207-287-6221, Fax: 207-287-6775. www.state.me.us/ethics Search Database at www.mainecampaignfinance.com/public/entity_list.asp?TYPE=LOB

2 Department of Administrative & Financial Services, Bureau of Alcoholic Beverages & Lottery Operations, 8 State House Station, Augusta, ME 04333-0008; 207-287-3721, Fax: 207-287-6769. www.mainelottery.com

3 Department of Agriculture, Food & Rural Resources, Board of Pesticides Control, 280 State House Station, Augusta, ME 04332-0028; 207-287-2731, Fax: 207-287-7548. www.state.me.us/agriculture/pesticides/ Email: gary.fish@maine.gov

4 Department of Education, Certification Office, 23 State House Station, Augusta Complex, Augusta, ME 04333-0023; 207-624-6603, Fax: 207-624-6604. www.state.me.us/education/homepage.htm Email: Pat.Julien@state.me.us Note: Make labels for school mailing lists at www.state.me.us/education/labels/labels.htm.

5 Department of Environmental Protection, Bureau of Air Quality Control, 17 State House Station, Augusta, ME 04333-0017; 207-287-2437, Fax: 207-287-7641. www.maine.gov/dep/air/

6 Department of Environmental Protection, Bureau/Hazardous Materials & Solid Waste Control, State House Station 17, Augusta, ME 04333; 207-287-2651, Fax: 207-287-7826. www.state.me.us/dep/staff.htm

7 Department of Human Services, Office of Child Care, 221 State St, 11 State House Station, Augusta, ME 04333-0011; 207-287-5060, Fax: 207-287-5282. www.maine.gov/dhhs/occhs/cclicensing.htm Email: childcare.info@state.me.us

8 Department of Professional & Financial Regulation, Maine State Board of Nursing, # 158 State House Station, Augusta, ME 04333-0158; 207-287-1133, Fax: 207-287-1149. www.maine.gov/boardofnursing Email: virginia.e.delormier@state.me.us

9 Department of Human Services, Division of Licensing and Certification, 11 State House Station, Augusta, ME 04333; 207-287-9300, Fax: 207-287-9304. www.state.me.us/bms/ Search Database at http://licert.dhs.state.me.us

10 Department of Public Safety, Main Emergency Medical Svcs, 152 State House Station, Augusta, ME 04333-0152; 207-626-3860, Fax: 207-287-6251. www.state.me.us/dps/ems Email: maine.ems@state.me.us

11 Department of Inland Fisheries & Wildlife, Licensing & Registration Division, 284 State St, 41 Statehouse Station, Augusta, ME 04333-0041; 207-287-8000, Fax: 207-287-8094. www.state.me.us/ifw/index.html Email: ifw@state.me.us

12 Department of Professional & Financial Regulation, Office of Securities, 121 State House Station, Augusta, ME 04333; 207-624-8551, Fax: 207-624-8590. www.state.me.us/pfr/sec/sec_index.htm Search Database at http://pfr.informe.org/almsquery/LicLookup.aspx

13 Department of Professional & Financial Regulation, Office of Licensing & Registration, 35 State House Station, Augusta, ME 04333-0035; 207-624-8603, Fax: 207-624-8637. www.maineprofessionalreg.org Search Database at http://pfr0.informe.org/almsquery/LicLookup.aspx

14 Department of Professional & Financial Regulation, Bureau of Financial Institutions, 36 State House Station, Augusta, ME 04333-0036; 207-624-8570, Fax: 207-624-8590. www.mainebankingreg.org

15 Department of Professional & Financial Regulation, Bureau of Insurance, State House Station 34, Augusta, ME 04333-0034; 207-624-8545, Fax: 207-624-8599. www.state.me.us/pfr/ins/ins_index.htm Email: webmaster_pfr@state.me.us Search Database at http://pfr0.informe.org/almsquery/LicLookup.aspx

16 Board of Dental Examiners, 143 Statehouse Station, 2 Bangor St, Augusta, ME 04333-0143; 207-287-3333/4746, Fax: 207-287-8140. www.mainedental.org Email: anita.c.merrow@maine.gov Search Database at www.mainedental.org/search.htm Note: To obtain lists of the above, contact Kim Haggan at 207-287-5459.

17 Professional Engineers Reg. Board, 92 State House Station, Augusta, ME 04333; 207-287-3236, Fax: 207-626-2309. http://www.maine.gov/professionalengineers/ Email: prexar.com Search Database at http://www.maine.gov/professionalengineers/database.shtml

18 Department of Professional & Financial Regulation, Board of Optometry, 113 State House Station, Augusta, ME 04333; 207-624-8691, Fax: 207-624-8691. www.state.me.us/pfr/auxboards/optometry/ Email: susan.a.giampetruzzi@maine.gov Search Database at http://pfr.informe.org/almsquery/LicLookup.aspx Note: The alternative search site is www.odfinder.org/LicSearch.asp.

19 Department of Human Services, Health Engineering, Eating & Lodging Program, 11 State House Station (161 Capitol St), Augusta, ME 04333-0011; 207-287-5671, Fax: 207-287-3165. www.state.me.us/dhs/eng/el/index.html Email: david.l.libby@maine.gov Note: Written requests may be mailed or faxed, only.

20 Department of Public Safety, Administrative Licensing & Permits, 45 Commerce Dr #1, 104 State House Station, Augusta, ME 04333-0042; 207-626-3803, Fax: 207-287-3042. www.state.me.us/dps

21 Department of Public Safety, Licensing & Inspection-Liquor, 104 State House Station, Augusta, ME 04333; 207-624-7220, Fax: 207-287-3424.

22 Board of Overseers of the Bar, PO Box 527 (97 Winthrop St), Augusta, ME 04332; 207-623-1121, Fax: 207-623-4175. www.mebaroverseers.org Email: board@mebaroverseers.org

23 Medical Doctor & Physician Assistant Licensing & Investigation, Board of Licensure in Medicine, 137 State House Station, 2 Bangor St, Augusta, ME 04333; 207-287-3601, Fax: 207-287-6590. www.docboard.org/me/me_home.htm Email: Tim.E.Terranova@state.me.us Search Database at www.docboard.org/me/df/mesearch.htm

24 Secretary of State, Div of Elections & Commissions, Notary Public Section, 101 State House Station, Augusta, ME 04333-0101; 207-624-7650, Fax: 207-287-6545. www.maine.gov/sos/cec/notary/notaries.html Search Database at http://portalx.bisoex.state.me.us/pls/sos_bc/bcdev.notaries.search

25 State Police Licensing Division, Department of Public Safety, 164 State House Station, Augusta, ME 04333; 207-624-7210, Fax: 207-287-3424.

26 State of Maine, Board of Osteopathic Licensure, 142 State House Station, Augusta, ME 04333-0142; 207-287-2480, Fax: 207-287-3015. www.docboard.org/me-osteo/ Email: susan.e.strout@maine.gov Search Database at www.docboard.org/me-osteo/df/index.htm

27 Department of Marine Resources, Bureau of Marine Patrol, Licensing Division, 21 State House Station, Hallowell Annex-Baker Bldg, Augusta, ME 04333-0021; 207-624-6550, Fax: 207-624-6024.

Maine Federal Courts

The following list indicates the district and division name for each county in the state. If the bankruptcy court location is different from the district court, then the location of the bankruptcy court appears in parentheses.

County/Court Cross Reference

Androscoggin	Portland	Oxford	Portland
Aroostook	Bangor	Penobscot	Bangor
Cumberland	Portland	Piscataquis	Bangor
Franklin	Bangor	Sagadahoc	Portland
Hancock	Bangor	Somerset	Bangor
Kennebec	Bangor	Waldo	Bangor
Knox	Portland (Bangor)	Washington	Bangor
Lincoln	Portland (Bangor)	York	Portland

Standards for Federal Courts: Search fee is $26.00 per item (one party name or case number). Copy fee is $.50 per page. Certification fee is $9.00 per document, double for exemplification, if available. All fees standard unless noted in profile. Mail Search: always enclose a stamped self addressed envelope unless otherwise noted. Most courts accept fax requests or will suggest a copying/search vendor. Before releasing records, all courts require prepayment, unless noted.

Open records are located at the court unless otherwise noted. District courts index by defendant and plaintiff as well as by case number. Bankruptcy courts usually index by debtor and case number. While most courts now have their indexes on computer, many may still maintain index card files as well.

Courts offering internet access via CM-ECF or older RACER, PACER, or Web-PACER systems charge $.08 per page fee unless noted as free. Where PACER is available, the universal sign-up number is 800-676-6856. Find PACER and the US Party/Case Index at http://pacer.psc.uscourts.gov.

US District Court

District of Maine

Bangor Division Court Clerk, PO Box 1007, Bangor, ME 04402-1007 (courier address: Rm 357, 202 Harlow St, Bangor, ME 04401), 207-945-0575, Fax-207-945-0362. Hours- 8AM-5PM. www.med.uscourts.gov

Counties: Aroostook, Franklin, Hancock, Kennebec, Penobscot, Piscataquis, Somerset, Waldo, Washington.

Searches & Indexing: Results include partial DOB; no SSN. Computer index maintained. Records indexed and stored by year, then docket number for case files and by name on electronic index system. New cases in the index immediately after filing date. Records purged every 6 months.

Fee & Payment: Pay by money order, cashier's or personal check. Payee: Clerk, US District Court. Prepayment required.

Phone Search: Any public record information is released via phone including accession number.

Mail Search: search usually completed- 1-2 days. SASE not required.

In Person Search: Fee charged if court performs your search. No self-serve copier available.

E-Services: ECF replaces PACER whose records did go back to 8/1991. New records online after 1 day. ECF at https://ecf.med.uscourts.gov **Opinions Online:** www.med.uscourts.gov/rulesandopinions.htm.

Portland Division Court Clerk, 156 Federal St, Portland, ME 04101 (also use mail address for courier delivery), 207-780-3356, Fax-207-780-3772. Hours- 8AM-4:30PM. www.med.uscourts.gov

Counties: Androscoggin, Cumberland, Knox, Lincoln, Oxford, Sagadahoc, York.

Searches & Indexing: Results do not include SSN or DOB. Computer index back to 1990 maintained. Records indexed and stored by year, then docket number for case files and by name on electronic index system. New cases in the index immediately after filing date. Records purged every 6 months.

Fee & Payment: Pay by money order, cashier's or personal check. Payee: Clerk, US District Court. Prepayment required.

Phone Search: Any public record information is released via phone including accession number.

Mail Search: search usually completed- 1-2 days. SASE not required.

In Person Search: Fee charged if court performs your search. No self-serve copier available.

E-Services: ECF replaces PACER whose records did go back to 8/1991. ECF at https://ecf.med.uscourts.gov **Opinions Online:** www.med.uscourts.gov/rulesandopinions.htm.

US Bankruptcy Court

District of Maine

Bangor Division Court Clerk, 202 Harlow St #31, Bangor, ME 04401 (also use mail address for courier delivery), 207-945-0348, Fax-207-945-0304. 8AM-4:30PM. www.meb.uscourts.gov

Counties: Aroostook, Franklin, Hancock, Kennebec, Knox, Lincoln, Penobscot, Piscataquis, Somerset, Waldo, Washington.

Searches & Indexing: Results include last 4 SSN digits only. Computer index maintained. New cases in the index immediately after filing date. Records purged every 2 years.

Fee & Payment: Pay by money order, cashier check, business check. No personal checks. Payee: United States Courts. Prepayment required.

Phone Search: Voice Case Information Service available, call VCIS at 800-650-7253 or 207-780-3755.

Mail Search: search usually completed- 1 week. SASE not required.

In Person Search: Fee charged if court performs your search. No charge for docket data. No self-serve copier available.

E-Services: ECF replaces PACER whose records did go back to 12/1988. New records online after 1 day. ECF at https://ecf.meb.uscourts.gov **Opinions Online:** www.meb.uscourts.gov/w_judges.html.

Portland Division Court Clerk, PO Box 17575, Portland, ME 04112 (courier address: 537 Congress St, Portland, ME 04101), 207-780-3482, Fax-207-780-3679. www.meb.uscourts.gov

Counties: Androscoggin, Cumberland, Oxford, Sagadahoc, York.

Searches & Indexing: Searches for cases filed pre-1988 require debtor's name. Computer index maintained. New cases in the index immediately after filing date. Records purged every 2 years. Information through VCIS and ECF available 24 hours after docketing.

Fee & Payment: Pay by money order, cashier check, business check. No personal checks. Payee: US Bankruptcy Court. Prepayment required for individual requesters.

Phone Search: Only docket information is available by phone. Voice Case Information Service available, call VCIS at 800-650-7253 or 207-780-3755.

Mail Search: search usually completed- 1 day. Include SASE for return.

In Person Search: Fee charged if court performs your search. No self-serve copier available.

E-Services: ECF replaces PACER whose records did go back to 12/1988. New records online after 1 day. ECF at https://ecf.meb.uscourts.gov **Opinions Online:** www.meb.uscourts.gov/w_judges.html.

Maine County Courts

Court	Jurisdiction	No. of Courts	How Organized
Superior Courts*	General	17	16 Counties
District Courts*	Limited	31	13 Districts
Probate Courts*	Special	16	

* Profiled in this Sourcebook.

Court	CIVIL								
	Tort	Contract	Real Estate	Min. Claim	Max. Claim	Small Claims	Estate	Eviction	Domestic Relations
Superior Courts*	X	X	X	No Min	No Max				X
District Courts*	X	X	X	No Min	No Max	$4500		X	X
Probate Courts*							X		X

Court	CRIMINAL				
	Felony	Misdemeanor	DWI/DUI	Preliminary Hearing	Juvenile
Superior Courts*	X	X	X	X	
District Courts*	X	X	X	X	X
Probate Courts*					

ADMINISTRATION   State Court Administrator, PO Box 4820, Portland, ME, 04112; 207-822-0792, Fax: 207-822-0781. www.state.me.us/courts

COURT STRUCTURE   One Superior Court, the court of general jurisdiction is located in each of Maine's sixteen counties, except for Aroostook County, which has two Superior Courts. Both Superior and District Courts handle misdemeanor and felony cases, with jury trials being held in Superior Court only. The District Court hears both civil and criminal and always sits without a jury.

Within the District Court is the Family Division, which hears all divorce and family matters, including child support and paternity cases. The District Court also hears child protection cases, and serves as Maine's juvenile court. Actions for protection from abuse or harassment, mental health, small claims cases and money judgments are filed in the District Court. Traffic violations are processed primarily through a centralized Violations Bureau, part of the District Court system. Prior to year 2001, District Courts accepted civil cases involving claims less than $30,000. Now, District Courts have jurisdiction concurrent with that of the Superior Court for all civil actions except cases vested in the Superior Court by statute.

ONLINE ACCESS   The website offers access to Maine Supreme Court opinions and administrative orders, but not all documents are available online. Also, the site offers online access to trial court schedules by region and case type. Some county level courts are online through a private vendor.

ADDITIONAL INFORMATION   Per administrative order, Maine Superior and District Court search fees are as follows: 1) $15.00 for a search; 2) Copy fee: 1st page is $2.00, $1.00 each additional; 3) If mail requests do not include a self-addressed stamped envelope, then add an additional $5.00.

Most mail requests of a name search for full criminal history record information are returned to the sender, referring them to the State Bureau of Investigation. Mail requests that make a specific inquiry related to an identified case are responded to in writing, with appropriate copy and attestation fees.

PROBATE COURTS   Probate Courts are part of the county court system, not the state system. Even though the Probate Court may be housed with other state courts, it is on a different phone system and calls may not be transferred.

Androscoggin County

Androscoggin Superior Court PO Box 3660, Auburn, ME 04212-3660; phone: 207-783-5450; hours 8AM-4PM (EST). *Felony, Misdemeanor, Civil Actions.*

Note: Now has records for old court 11 which is closed. Effective 9/1/03, the search fees and copy fees listed are mandatory per administrative rule. If a SASE is not supplied for mail searches, court may charge add'l $5.00.

Civil Records: Access: Phone, mail, in person. Only the court performs in person searches; visitors may not. Search fee: $15.00, includes both civil and criminal. Court makes copy: $2.00 1st page, $1.00 each add'l. Required to search: name, years to search; also helpful: address. Civil cases indexed by defendant, plaintiff. Civil records on index cards since 1977. Mail turnaround time 1 week.

Criminal Records: Access: Mail, in person. Only the court performs in person searches; visitors may not. Search fee: $15.00, includes both civil and criminal. Court makes copy: $2.00 1st page, $1.00 each add'l. Required to search: name, years to search; also helpful: DOB. Criminal records go back to 1920s; on computer back to 1997. Mail turnaround time 1 week.

General Information: No public access terminal. No adoption, juvenile, impounded by judge, certain domestic matters. Certification fee: $5.00 per doc. Payee: Androscoggin Superior Court. Personal checks accepted. Visa/MC accepted. Prepayment and SASE required.

Lewiston District Court - South 8 PO Box 1345, 71 Lisbon St, Lewiston, ME 04243-1345; criminal phone: 207-795-4800; civil phone: 207-795-4801; hours 8AM-4PM (EST). *Misdemeanor, Civil Actions, Eviction, Small Claims.*

Note: Effective 9/1/03, the search fees and copy fees listed are mandatory per administrative rule. If a SASE is not supplied for mail searches, court may charge add'l $5.00.

Civil Records: Access: Mail, in person. Both court and visitors may perform in person searches. Search fee: $15.00, includes both civil and criminal. Court makes copy: $2.00 1st page, $1.00 each add'l. Required to search: name, years to search; also helpful: address. Civil cases indexed by defendant. Civil records on docket books from 1956-1987; on computer back to 1987. Mail turnaround time 1-2 days.

Criminal Records: Access: Mail, in person. Both court and visitors may perform in person searches. Search fee: $15.00, includes both civil and criminal. Court makes copy: $2.00 1st page, $1.00 each add'l. Required to search: name, years to search, DOB; also helpful: address, SSN. Criminal records on computer back to 1987, docket books from 1956-1987. Mail turnaround time 1-2 days.

General Information: No public access terminal. No juvenile, protective custody records released. Certification fee: $5.00. Payee: Maine District Court. Personal checks accepted. Prepayment and SASE required.

Probate Court 2 Turner St, Auburn, ME 04210; phone: 207-782-0281; fax: 207-782-1135; hours 8:30AM-5PM (EST). *Probate.*

Aroostook County

Caribou Superior Court 144 Sweden St, #101, Caribou, ME 04736; phone: 207-498-8125; hours 8AM-4PM (EST). *Felony, Misdemeanor, Civil Actions.*

Note: Effective 9/1/03, the search fees and copy fees listed are mandatory per administrative rule. If a SASE is not supplied for mail searches, court may charge add'l $5.00.

Civil Records: Access: Mail, in person. Only the court performs in person searches; visitors may not. Search fee: One name no fee, two or more $15.00 each, includes both civil and criminal. Court makes copy: $2.00 1st page, $1.00 each add'l. Required to search: name, years to search. Civil cases indexed by defendant, plaintiff. Civil records on docket books since 1960. All cases 1990 forward stored in Caribou Court. Mail turnaround time 1 week.

Criminal Records: Access: Mail, in person. Only the court performs in person searches; visitors may not. Search fee: One name no fee, two or more $15.00 each, includes both civil and criminal. Court makes copy: $2.00 1st page, $1.00 each add'l. Required to search: name, years to search; also helpful: DOB. Criminal records on docket books since 1960. All cases 1990 forward stored in Caribou Court. Mail turnaround time 1 week.

General Information: No public access terminal. No juvenile, protective custody records released. Certification fee: $5.00. Payee: Treasurer, State of Maine or Superior Court. Personal checks accepted. Prepayment and SASE required.

Houlton Superior Court 144 Sweden St, Caribou, ME 04736; phone: 207-532-6563; hours 8AM-4PM (EST). *Felony, Misdemeanor, Civil Actions.*

Note: The Court only holds record prior to 1990. All cases are located at the Superior Court in Caribou, address Given here.

Caribou District Court - East 1 144 Sweden St, Caribou, ME 04736; phone: 207-493-3144; hours 8AM-4PM (EST). *Misdemeanor, Civil Actions, Eviction, Small Claims.*

Note: Effective 9/1/03, the search fees and copy fees listed are mandatory per administrative rule. If a SASE is not supplied for mail searches, court may charge add'l $5.00.

Civil Records: Access: Mail, in person. Only the court performs in person searches; visitors may not. Search fee: First name free, then $15.00, includes both civil and criminal. Court makes copy: $2.00 1st page, $1.00 each add'l. Required to search: name, years to search. Civil cases indexed by defendant. Civil records on docket books since 1963, on computer from 10/01. Mail turnaround time 1 week.

Criminal Records: Access: Mail, in person. Visitors must perform in person searches themselves. Search fee: First name free, then $15.00, includes both civil and criminal. Court makes copy: $2.00 1st page, $1.00 each add'l. Required to search: name, years to search; also helpful: DOB. Criminal records on computer since 1987 (includes traffic); docket books since 1963. Mail turnaround time 1 week.

General Information: Public terminal has only criminal records. No juvenile or child protective records released. Certification fee: $5.00 per page. Payee: Maine District Court. Personal checks accepted. Prepayment and SASE required.

District Court 2 PO Box 794, 27 Riverside Dr, Presque Isle, ME 04769; phone: 207-764-2055; hours 8AM-4PM (EST). *Misdemeanor, Civil Actions, Eviction, Small Claims.*

Note: Effective 9/1/03, the search fees and copy fees listed are mandatory per administrative rule. If a SASE is not supplied for mail searches, court may charge add'l $5.00.

Civil Records: Access: Mail, in person. Both court and visitors may perform in person searches. Search fee: $15.00, includes both civil and criminal. Court makes copy: $2.00 1st page, $1.00 each add'l. Required to search: name, years to search. Civil cases indexed by defendant. Civil records on computer since 1999, docket books since 1963. Mail turnaround time 1 week.

Criminal Records: Access: Mail, in person. Visitors must perform in person searches themselves. Search fee: $15.00, includes both civil and criminal. Court makes copy: $2.00 1st page, $1.00 each add'l. Required to search: name, years to search; also helpful: DOB. Criminal records on computer since 1987, docket books since 1963. Mail turnaround time 1 week.

General Information: Public terminal has only civil records back to 1999. No juvenile or child protective records released. Certification fee: $5.00.

Payee: Maine District Court. Personal checks accepted. Prepayment and SASE required.

Fort Kent District Court - District 1 Division of Western Aroostook, PO Box 473, Fort Kent, ME 04743; phone: 207-834-5003; hours 8AM-4PM (EST). *Misdemeanor, Civil Actions, Eviction, Small Claims.*

Note: If a SASE is not supplied for mail searches, court may charge add'l $5.00.

Civil Records: Access: Phone, mail, in person. Only the court performs in person searches; visitors may not. Search fee: $15.00, includes both civil and criminal. Court makes copy: $2.00 1st page, $1.00 each add'l. Required to search: name, years to search. Civil cases indexed by defendant, plaintiff. Civil records are computerized since 8/2001. Mail turnaround time within 5 days.

Criminal Records: Access: Phone, mail, in person. Only the court performs in person searches; visitors may not. Search fee: $15.00, includes both civil and criminal. Court makes copy: $2.00 1st page, $1.00 each add'l. Required to search: name, years to search. Criminal records on computer from 1988, on docket books from 1960-1988. Mail turnaround time 2-3 days.

General Information: No public access terminal. No juvenile, protective custody, impounded, mental health records released. Certification fee: $5.00 for attestation. Payee: Maine District Court. Personal checks accepted. Prepayment and SASE required.

Houlton District Court - South 2 PO Box 457, Houlton, ME 04730; phone: 207-532-2147; hours 8AM-4PM (EST). *Misdemeanor, Civil Actions, Eviction, Small Claims.*

Note: Effective 9/1/03, the search fees and copy fees listed are mandatory per administrative rule. If a SASE is not supplied for mail searches, court may charge add'l $5.00.

Civil Records: Access: Mail, in person. Both court and visitors may perform in person searches. Search fee: $15.00, includes both civil and criminal. Court makes copy: $1.00 per page. Required to search: name, years to search; also helpful: address. Civil cases indexed by defendant, plaintiff. Civil records on docket books since 1960. Mail turnaround time 2-3 days.

Criminal Records: Access: Mail, in person. Only the court performs in person searches; visitors may not. Search fee: $15.00, includes both civil and criminal. Court makes copy: $1.00 per page. Required to search: name, years to search; also helpful: address, DOB. Criminal records on computer since 6/1987, docket books since 1960. Mail turnaround time 2-3 days.

General Information: No public access terminal. No Juvenile or protective custody records released. Will not fax documents. Certification fee: $5.00. Payee: Maine District Court. Personal checks accepted. Prepayment and SASE required.

Madawaska District Court - West PO Box 127, 645 E Main St, Madawaska, ME 04756; phone: 207-728-4700; hours 8AM-4PM M,T,F (EST). *Misdemeanor, Civil Actions, Eviction, Small Claims.*

Note: Effective 9/1/03, the search fees and copy fees listed are mandatory per administrative rule. If a SASE is not supplied for mail searches, court may charge add'l $5.00.

Civil Records: Access: Phone, mail, in person. Only the court performs in person searches; visitors may not. Search fee: $15.00, includes both civil and criminal. Court makes copy: $2.00 1st page, $1.00 each add'l. Required to search: name, years to search. Civil cases indexed by defendant, plaintiff. Civil records on docket books from 1967; on computer back to 8/2001. Mail turnaround time 2-3 days.

Criminal Records: Access: Phone, mail, in person. Only the court performs in person searches; visitors may not. Search fee: $15.00, includes both civil and criminal. Court makes copy: $2.00 1st page, $1.00 each add'l. Required to search: name, years to search, DOB. Criminal records on computer back to

1988, docket books from 1965. Mail turnaround time 2-3 days.

General Information: No public access terminal. No juvenile, protected custody, impounded or mental health records released. Certification fee: $5.00. Payee: Maine District Court. Personal checks accepted. Prepayment and SASE required; if not provided, fee is $5.00 for postage.

Probate Court 26 Court St #103, Houlton, ME 04730; phone: 207-532-1502; hours 8AM-4:30PM (EST). *Probate.*

Cumberland County

Superior Court - Civil 142 Federal St, Portland, ME 04101; phone: 207-822-4105; criminal phone: 207-822-4113; civil phone: 207-822-4105; hours 8AM-4:30PM (EST). *Civil Actions.*
Note: Effective 9/1/03, the search fees and copy fees listed are mandatory per administrative rule. If a SASE not supplied for mail searches, court will charge an add'l $5.00.
Civil Records: Access: In person. Both court and visitors may perform in person searches. Search fee: $15.00 per name, but if only one name then free. Court makes copy: $2.00 1st page, $1.00 each add'l. Required to search: name, years to search. Civil cases indexed by defendant, plaintiff. Civil records on index cards since 1975, prior records archived. They will only answer general questions on filing and hearing dates by phone or mail. Mail turnaround time varies by number of requests presented.
General Information: No public access terminal. No juvenile, medical malpractice, impounded records released. Will not fax documents. Certification fee: $5.00. Payee: Superior Court. Personal checks accepted. Prepayment and SASE required.

Superior Court - Criminal 142 Federal St, Portland, ME 04101; phone: 207-822-4113; hours 8AM-4:30PM (EST). *Felony, Misdemeanor.*
Note: Effective 9/1/03, the search fees and copy fees listed are mandatory per administrative rule. If a SASE is not supplied for mail searches, court may charge add'l $5.00.
Criminal Records: Access: In person only. Both court and visitors may perform in person searches. Search fee: $15.00, includes both civil and criminal. Court makes copy: $2.00 1st page, $1.00 each add'l. Required to search: name, years to search, DOB. Criminal records on index cards since 1900s, some records from 8/98 to present are computerized. Mail turnaround time 2-3 days.
General Information: No public access terminal. No juvenile records released. Certification fee: $5.00. Payee: Clerk of Courts. Personal checks accepted. Prepayment and SASE required.

Portland District Court - South 9 Civil PO Box 412, 205 Newbury St, Portland, ME 04112; phone: 207-822-4200; hours 8AM-4:30PM (EST). *Civil Actions, Eviction, Small Claims.*
Note: Also see Sagadahoc District Court, which handles cases from eastern Cumberland County. Also see Brighton District Court which handles cases from western Cumberland County.
Civil Records: Access: In person. Both court and visitors may perform in person searches. Search fee: $15.00, includes both civil and criminal. Court makes copy: $2.00 1st page, $1.00 each add'l. Required to search: name, years to search. Civil cases indexed by defendant. Civil records go back ten years, small claims and eviction five years. Effective 09/01/03, the search fees and copy fees listed are mandatory per administrative rule. If a SASE not supplied for mail searches, court may charge add'l $5.00. Mail turnaround time 1 week.
General Information: No public access terminal. No child custody records released. Certification fee: $5.00 per doc. Payee: Maine District Court. Personal checks accepted. Prepayment and SASE required.

Portland District Court - South 9 Criminal PO Box 412, Portland, ME 04112; phone: 207-822-4204; hours 8AM-4:30PM (EST). *Misdemeanor.*
Note: Effective 9/1/03, the search fees and copy fees listed are mandatory per administrative rule. If a SASE is not supplied for mail searches, court may charge add'l $5.00.
Criminal Records: Access: Mail, in person. Only the court performs in person searches; visitors may not. Search fee: $15.00 per name. Court makes copy: $1.00 per page. Required to search: name, years to search, DOB, offense, date of offense. Criminal records on computer back to 9/86, prior records archived. Mail turnaround time 2 weeks.
General Information: No public access terminal. No impounded records released. Certification fee: $1.00 per cert. Payee: Maine District Court. Personal checks accepted. Prepayment and SASE required.

Bath District Court - East 6 147 New Meadows Rd, Bath, ME 04530; phone: 207-442-0200; hours 8AM-4PM. *Misdemeanor, Civil Actions, Eviction, Small Claims.*
Note: Combined with West Bath District Court 6 in Sagadahoc County.

Bridgton District Court - North 9 3 Chase St, #2, Bridgton, ME 04009; phone: 207-647-3535; hours 8AM-4PM (EST). *Misdemeanor, Civil Actions, Eviction, Small Claims.*
Note: Effective 9/1/03, the search fees and copy fees listed are mandatory per administrative rule. If a SASE is not supplied for mail searches, court may charge add'l $5.00.
Civil Records: Access: Phone, mail, in person. Visitors must perform in person searches themselves. Search fee: $15.00, includes both civil and criminal. Court makes copy: $2.00 1st page, $1.00 each add'l. Required to search: name, years to search. Civil cases indexed by defendant. Civil records go back to 1965; on computer back to 2001. Mail turnaround time 5 days.
Criminal Records: Access: Phone, mail, in person. Visitors must perform in person searches themselves. Search fee: $15.00, includes both civil and criminal. Court makes copy: $2.00 1st page, $1.00 each add'l. Required to search: name, years to search; also helpful: DOB. Criminal records on computer back to 1986, records go back to 1965. Mail turnaround time 5 days.
General Information: Public terminal has only criminal records back to 1988. No juvenile, protective custody, financial affidavits, impounded or domestic records released. Will not fax documents. Certification fee: $5.00 per page. Payee: Maine District Court. Personal checks accepted. Prepayment and SASE required.

Probate Court PO Box 15277, 142 Federal St, Portland, ME 04101-4196; phone: 207-871-8382; fax: 207-791-2658; hours 8:30AM-4:30PM (EST). *Probate.*
www.cumberlandcounty.org

Franklin County

Superior Court 140 Main St, Farmington, ME 04938; phone: 207-778-3346; hours 8AM-4PM (EST). *Felony, Misdemeanor, Civil Actions.*
Note: Effective 9/1/03, the search fees and copy fees listed are mandatory per administrative rule. If a SASE is not supplied for mail searches, court may charge add'l $5.00.
Civil Records: Access: Mail, in person. Both court and visitors may perform in person searches. Search fee: $15.00 per name, includes both civil and criminal. Court makes copy: $2.00 1st page, $1.00 each add'l. Required to search: name, years to search. Civil cases indexed by defendant, plaintiff. Civil records on docket books and index cards since 1900s. Mail turnaround time 1 week.
Criminal Records: Access: Mail, in person. Only the court performs in person searches; visitors may not. Search fee: $15.00 per name, includes both civil

and criminal. Court makes copy: $2.00 1st page, $1.00 each add'l. Required to search: name, years to search; also helpful: DOB, SSN. Criminal records on docket and index cards since 1900s. Mail turnaround time 1 week.
General Information: No public access terminal. No juvenile, impounded or medical malpractice records released. Certification fee: $5.00 per document. Payee: Superior Court. Personal checks accepted. Prepayment and SASE required.

Franklin District Court 12 129 Main St, Farmington, ME 04938; phone: 207-778-8200; hours 8AM-4PM (EST). *Misdemeanor, Civil Actions, Eviction, Small Claims.*
Note: Effective 9/1/03, the search fees and copy fees listed are mandatory per administrative rule.
Civil Records: Access: Mail, in person. Visitors must perform in person searches themselves. Search fee: $15.00 if request for more than one name. Court makes copy: $2.00 1st page, $1.00 each add'l. Required to search: name, years to search. Civil cases indexed by defendant. Civil records on docket books since 1965 (index cards in front). Mail turnaround time 1 week.
Criminal Records: Access: Mail, in person. Only the court performs in person searches; visitors may not. Search fee: $15.00 if request for more than one name. Court makes copy: $2.00 1st page, $1.00 each add'l. Required to search: name, years to search, DOB. Criminal records on computer since 1987, on docket books since 1965 (index cards in front). Mail turnaround time 1 week.
General Information: No public access terminal. No impounded records released. Will not fax documents. Certification fee: $5.00 per document. Add $1.00 per page copy fee on to cert fee. Payee: Maine District Court. Personal checks accepted. Prepayment.

Probate Court County Courthouse, 140 Main St, Farmington, ME 04938; phone: 207-778-5888; fax: 207-778-5899; hours 8:30AM-4PM (EST). *Probate.*

Hancock County

Superior Court 50 State St, Ellsworth, ME 04605-1926; phone: 207-667-7176; hours 8AM-4PM (EST). *Felony, Misdemeanor, Civil Actions.*
Note: Effective 9/1/03, the search fees and copy fees listed are mandatory per administrative rule.
Civil Records: Access: Mail, in person. Only the court performs in person searches; visitors may not. Search fee: $15.00 per name, if multiples. Court makes copy: $2.00 1st page, $1.00 each add'l. Required to search: name, years to search. Civil cases indexed by defendant, plaintiff. Civil records on card files since 1960.
Criminal Records: Access: Mail, person only. Only the court performs in person searches; visitors may not. Search fee: $15.00 per name, if multiples. Court makes copy: $2.00 1st page, $1.00 each add'l. Required to search: name, years to search, DOB. Criminal records on card files since 1960.
General Information: No public access terminal. No protective custody records released. Will not fax documents. They will bill you for copies, but search fee must be paid up front. Certification fee: $5.00 per cert. Payee: State of Maine. Personal checks accepted. Prepayment and SASE required.

Bar Harbor District Court - South 5 93 Cottage St, Bar Harbor, ME 04609; phone: 207-288-3082; hours 8AM-4PM (EST). *Misdemeanor, Civil Actions, Eviction, Small Claims.*
Note: Effective 9/1/03, the search fees and copy fees listed are mandatory per administrative rule.
Civil Records: Access: Mail, in person. Both court and visitors may perform in person searches. Search fee: $15.00, includes both civil and criminal. Court makes copy: $2.00 1st page, $1.00 each add'l. Required to search: name, years to search. Civil cases indexed by defendant, plaintiff. Civil records on docket books since 1970. Mail turnaround time 2-3 days.

Criminal Records: Access: Mail, in person. Only the court performs in person searches; visitors may not. Search fee: $15.00, includes both civil and criminal. Court makes copy: $2.00 1st page, $1.00 each add'l. Required to search: name, years to search, DOB. Criminal records on computer since 1987, on docket books since 1970. Mail turnaround time 2-3 days.

General Information: No public access terminal. No juvenile or impounded records released. Certification fee: $5.00 per certificate. Payee: Maine District Court. Personal checks accepted. Prepayment and SASE required.

Ellsworth District Court - Central 5 50 State St #2, Ellsworth, ME 04605; phone: 207-667-7141; hours 8AM-4PM (EST). *Misdemeanor, Civil Actions, Eviction, Small Claims.*

Civil Records: Access: Mail, in person. Both court and visitors may perform in person searches. Search fee: $15.00, includes both civil and criminal. Court makes copy: $2.00 1st page, $1.00 each add'l. Required to search: name, years to search. Civil cases indexed by defendant, plaintiff. Need to know names of both parties to search. Civil records on docket books since 1965; on computer back to 10/01. Mail turnaround time 1 week.

Criminal Records: Access: Mail, in person. Only the court performs in person searches; visitors may not. Search fee: $15.00, includes both civil and criminal. Court makes copy: $2.00 1st page, $1.00 each add'l. Required to search: name, years to search, DOB. Criminal records on computer back to 1987, docket books since 1965. Mail turnaround time 1 week.

General Information: Public use terminal available. No juvenile, child protection, adoption or mental health records released. Will not fax documents. Certification fee: $5.00 per document. Payee: Maine District Court. Personal checks accepted. Prepayment and SASE required.

Probate Court 50 State St, #6, Ellsworth, ME 04605; phone: 207-667-8434; probate phone: 207-667-9098; fax: 207-667-5316; hours 8:30AM-4PM (EST). *Probate.*

Kennebec County

Superior Court 95 State St, Clerk of Court, Augusta, ME 04330; phone: 207-624-5800; hours 8AM-4PM (EST). *Felony, Misdemeanor, Civil Actions.*

Civil Records: Access: In person only. Only the court performs in person searches; visitors may not. Search fee: First search free, then $15.00 per case. Court makes copy: $2.00 1st page, $1.00 each add'l. Required to search: name, years to search. Civil cases indexed by defendant, plaintiff. Civil records on index cards since 1977, docket books since 1970, on computer 2 years.

Criminal Records: Access: In person only. Only the court performs in person searches; visitors may not. Search fee: First search free, then $15.00 per case. Court makes copy: $2.00 1st page, $1.00 each add'l. Required to search: name, years to search; also helpful: DOB, docket number. Criminal records on index cards since 1977, docket books since 1978, on computer 5 years.

General Information: No public access terminal. No protective custody records released. Payee: Treasurer State of Maine. Personal checks and credit cards accepted. Prepayment required.

Maine District Court 7 Division of Southern Kennebec, 145 State St, Augusta, ME 04330-7495; phone: 207-287-8075; hours 8AM-4PM (EST). *Misdemeanor, Civil Actions, Eviction, Small Claims.*
Note: Effective 9/1/03, the search fees and copy fees listed are mandatory per administrative rule. If a SASE is not supplied for mail searches, court may charge add'l $5.00.

Civil Records: Access: Mail, in person. Both court and visitors may perform in person searches. Search fee: $15.00, includes both civil and criminal. Court makes copy: $2.00 1st page, $1.00 each add'l.

Required to search: name, years to search. Civil cases indexed by defendant. Civil records kept 10 years. Mail turnaround time 1 week.

Criminal Records: Access: Mail, in person. Only the court performs in person searches; visitors may not. Search fee: $15.00, includes both civil and criminal. Court makes copy: $2.00 1st page, $1.00 each add'l. Required to search: name, years to search, DOB; also helpful: SSN. Criminal records on computer back to 1987, docket books since 1963. Mail turnaround time 1 week.

General Information: No public access terminal. No juvenile, mental health, protective custody and closed proceeding case records released. Certification fee: $5.00 per doc. Payee: Maine District Court. Personal checks accepted. Prepayment and SASE required.

Waterville District Court - District 7 18 Colby St, PO Box 397, Waterville, ME 04903; phone: 207-873-2103; hours 8AM-4PM (EST). *Misdemeanor, Civil Actions, Eviction, Small Claims.*
Note: Effective 9/1/03, the search fees and copy fees listed are mandatory per administrative rule. If a SASE is not supplied for mail searches, court may charge add'l $5.00.

Civil Records: Access: Mail, in person. Both court and visitors may perform in person searches. Search fee: $15.00, includes both civil and criminal. Court makes copy: $2.00 1st page, $1.00 each add'l. Required to search: name, years to search; also helpful: address. Civil cases indexed by defendant. Civil records on docket books from 1979-1998; on computer since 2001. Mail turnaround time 1 week.

Criminal Records: Access: Mail, in person. Both court and visitors may perform in person searches. Search fee: $15.00, includes both civil and criminal. Court makes copy: $2.00 1st page, $1.00 each add'l. Required to search: name, years to search, DOB; also helpful: address, SSN. Criminal records on computer since 1999, docket books from 1979-1987. Mail turnaround time 2 weeks.

General Information: No public access terminal. No juvenile, protective custody records released. Court reserves the right to restrict the number of record requests. Certification fee: $5.00 per doc. Payee: Maine District Court. Personal checks accepted. Prepayment and SASE required.

Probate Court 95 State St, Augusta, ME 04330; phone: 207-622-7558 or 207-622-7559; fax: 207-621-1639; hours 8AM-4PM (EST). *Probate.*
www.datamaine.com/probate
Note: Search dockets back to 1995 online at www.datamaine.com/probate/docket.html.

Knox County

Superior Court 62 Union St, Rockland, ME 04841-2836; phone: 207-594-2576; hours 8AM-4PM (EST). *Felony, Misdemeanor, Civil Actions.*
Note: Effective 9/1/03, the search fees and copy fees listed are mandatory per administrative rule. If a SASE is not supplied for mail searches, court may charge add'l $5.00.

Civil Records: Access: Phone, mail, in person. Both court and visitors may perform in person searches. Search fee: $15.00, includes both civil and criminal. Court makes copy: $2.00 1st page, $1.00 each add'l. Required to search: name, years to search. Civil cases indexed by defendant, plaintiff. Civil records on docket books since 1930s, index cards (in office) since mid-1970s; on computer back to 1999. Mail turnaround time 1 week.

Criminal Records: Access: Mail, in person. Only the court performs in person searches; visitors may not. Search fee: $15.00, includes both civil and criminal. Court makes copy: $2.00 1st page, $1.00 each add'l. Required to search: name, years to search; also helpful: DOB. Criminal records on docket books since 1930s, index cards (in office) since mid-1970s; on computer back to 1999. Mail turnaround time 1 week.

General Information: No public access terminal. No Impounded or pre-sentence records released.

Certification fee: $5.00. Payee: State Treasurer. Personal checks or Visa/MC accepted. Prepayment and SASE required.

District Court 6 62 Union St, Rockland, ME 04841; phone: 207-596-2240; probate phone: 207-594-0427; hours 8AM-4PM (EST). *Misdemeanor, Civil Actions, Eviction, Small Claims.*
Note: Effective 9/1/03, the search fees and copy fees listed are mandatory per administrative rule. If a SASE is not supplied for mail searches, court may charge add'l $5.00.

Civil Records: Access: Mail, in person. Both court and visitors may perform in person searches. Search fee: $15.00 per name. Court makes copy: $2.00 1st page, $1.00 each add'l. Required to search: name, years to search. Civil cases indexed by defendant, plaintiff. Civil records on docket books. Mail turnaround time 2-3 weeks.

Criminal Records: Access: Mail, in person. Only the court performs in person searches; visitors may not. Search fee: $15.00 per name. Court makes copy: $2.00 1st page, $1.00 each add'l. Required to search: name, years to search, DOB. Criminal records on docket books. Mail turnaround time 2-3 weeks.

General Information: No public access terminal. No impounded records released. Certification fee: $5.00 per cert. Payee: Maine District Court. Personal checks accepted. Prepayment and SASE required.

Probate Court 62 Union St, Rockland, ME 04841; phone: 207-594-0427; fax: 207-594-0443; hours 8AM-4PM (EST). *Probate.*
http://knoxcounty.midcoast.com

Lincoln County

Lincoln County Superior Court High St, PO Box 249, Wiscasset, ME 04578; phone: 207-882-7517; fax: 207-882-7741; hours 8AM-4PM (EST). *Felony, Misdemeanor, Civil Actions.*
Note: Effective 9/1/03, the search fees and copy fees listed are mandatory per administrative rule. If a SASE is not supplied for mail searches, court may charge add'l $5.00.

Civil Records: Access: Mail, in person. Only the court performs in person searches; visitors may not. Search fee: No fee to search 1 case per day; each add'l search is $15.00, includes both civil and criminal. Court makes copy: $2.00 1st page, $1.00 each add'l. Required to search: name, years to search. Civil cases indexed by defendant, plaintiff. Civil records on docket books and index cards since 1960s. Mail turnaround time 1-2 days.

Criminal Records: Access: Mail, in person. Only the court performs in person searches; visitors may not. Search fee: No fee to search 1 case per day; each add'l search is $15.00, includes both civil and criminal. Court makes copy: $2.00 1st page, $1.00 each add'l. Required to search: name, years to search, DOB. Criminal records on docket books and index cards since 1960s. Mail turnaround time 1-2 days.

General Information: No public access terminal. No protective custody records released. Certification fee: $5.00. Payee: Lincoln County Superior Court. Personal checks accepted. Prepayment and SASE required.

District Court 6 32 High St, PO Box 249, Wiscasset, ME 04578; phone: 207-882-6363; criminal/civil fax: 207-882-5980; hours 8AM-4PM (EST). *Misdemeanor, Civil Actions, Eviction, Small Claims.*
www.co.lincoln.me.us
Note: Effective 9/1/03, the search fees and copy fees listed are mandatory per administrative rule. If a SASE is not supplied for mail searches, court may charge add'l $5.00.

Civil Records: Access: Phone, mail, in person. Both court and visitors may perform in person searches. Search fee: $15.00, includes both civil and criminal. Court makes copy: $1.00 per page. Required to search: name, years to search. Civil cases indexed by defendant, plaintiff. Civil records on docket books since 1965; on computer back to 1987. Mail turnaround time 1 week.

Criminal Records: Access: Mail, in person. Only the court performs in person searches; visitors may not. Search fee: $15.00, includes both civil and criminal. Court makes copy: $1.00 per page. Required to search: name, years to search, DOB or SSN. Criminal records on computer back to 1987, docket books since 1960. Mail turnaround time 1 week.

General Information: No public access terminal. No juvenile, child protective or impounded records released. Will fax documents to local or toll free line. Certification fee: $5.00 per page. Payee: Maine District Court. Personal checks accepted. Prepayment and SASE required.

Probate Court 32 High St, PO Box 249, Wiscasset, ME 04578; phone: 207-882-7392; fax: 207-882-4324; hours 8AM-4PM (EST). *Probate.* www.co.lincoln.me.us/dep.html

Oxford County

Superior Court Courthouse, 26 Western Ave, PO Box 179, South Paris, ME 04281-0179; phone: 207-743-8936; hours 8AM-4PM (EST). *Felony, Misdemeanor, Civil Actions.*

Note: Effective 9/1/03, the search fees and copy fees listed are mandatory per administrative rule. If a SASE is not supplied for mail searches, court may charge add'l $5.00.

Civil Records: Access: Mail, in person. Visitors must perform in person searches themselves. Search fee: $15.00, includes both civil and criminal. Court makes copy: $1.00 per page. Required to search: name, years to search, DOB. Civil cases indexed by defendant, plaintiff. Criminal records on computer back to 1998; on docket books since 1980. Mail turnaround time 3-4 days.

Criminal Records: Access: Mail, in person. Visitors must perform in person searches themselves. Search fee: $15.00, includes both civil and criminal. Court makes copy: $1.00 per page. Required to search: name, years to search, DOB. Criminal records on docket books since 1960. Mail turnaround time 3-4 days.

General Information: No public access terminal. No protective custody or protection from abuse records released. Will fax documents. Certification fee: $5.00 per document. Payee: Clerk of Superior Court. Personal checks accepted. Prepayment and SASE required.

Rumford District Court - Div. of North Oxford Municipal Bldg, 145 Congress St, Rumford, ME 04276; phone: 207-364-7171; hours 8AM-4PM (EST). *Misdemeanor, Civil Actions, Eviction, Small Claims.*

Note: Effective 9/1/03, the search fees and copy fees listed are mandatory per administrative rule. If a SASE is not supplied for mail searches, court may charge add'l $5.00.

Civil Records: Access: Mail, in person. Both court and visitors may perform in person searches. Search fee: $15.00 for two or more searches. Court makes copy: $2.00 1st page, $1.00 each add'l. Required to search: name, years to search. Civil cases indexed by defendant, plaintiff. Civil records on docket books since 1966. Mail turnaround time 1 week.

Criminal Records: Access: Mail, in person. Both court and visitors may perform in person searches. Search fee: $15.00 for two or more searches. Court makes copy: $2.00 1st page, $1.00 each add'l. Required to search: name, years to search, DOB. Criminal records on computer since 3/1988, docket books since 1966. Mail turnaround time 1 week.

General Information: No public access terminal. No impounded records released. Will not fax documents. Certification fee: $5.00 per stamp. Payee: Maine District Court. Personal checks accepted. Prepayment and SASE required.

South Paris District Court - South 11 26 Western Ave, South Paris, ME 04281; phone: 207-743-8942; hours 8AM-4PM (EST). *Misdemeanor, Civil Actions, Eviction, Small Claims.*

Note: Effective 9/1/03, the search fees and copy fees listed are mandatory per administrative rule. If a SASE is not supplied for mail searches, court may charge add'l $5.00.

Civil Records: Access: Mail, in person. Only the court performs in person searches; visitors may not. Search fee: $15.00, includes both civil and criminal. Court makes copy: $2.00 1st page, $1.00 each add'l. Required to search: name, years to search. Civil cases indexed by defendant. Civil records on docket books back 5 years. Mail turnaround time 1-2 days.

Criminal Records: Access: Mail, in person. Both court and visitors may perform in person searches. Search fee: $15.00, includes both civil and criminal. Court makes copy: $2.00 1st page, $1.00 each add'l. Required to search: name, years to search; also helpful: DOB. Criminal records on computer since 4/99, docket books back to 1966. Note: Records after 4/99 cannot be accessed on the public access computer; request a search in writing. Mail turnaround time 1-2 days.

General Information: Public terminal has only criminal records back to 3/1988. No juvenile or child protective records released. Will not fax documents. Certification fee: $5.00 per document. Payee: Maine District Court. Personal checks accepted. Prepayment and SASE required.

Probate Court PO Box 179, 26 Western Ave, South Paris, ME 04281; phone: 207-743-6616; fax: 207-743-4452; hours 8AM-4PM (EST). *Probate.* www.oxfordcounty.org/probate.htm

Penobscot County

Superior Court 97 Hammond St, Bangor, ME 04401; phone: 207-561-2300; hours 8AM-4PM (EST). *Felony, Misdemeanor, Civil Actions.*

Note: The search fees and copy fees listed are mandatory per administrative rule. If a SASE is not supplied for mail searches, court may charge add'l $5.00. There is no charge for a single search.

Civil Records: Access: Mail, in person. Only the court performs in person searches; visitors may not. Search fee: $15.00 per name multiple searches only (otherwise no fee for single case) includes both civil and criminal. Court makes copy: $2.00 1st page, $1.00 each add'l. Required to search: name, years to search. Civil cases indexed by defendant, plaintiff. Civil records on docket books since 1976; on computer back to 2002; archived back to 1927.

Criminal Records: Access: Mail, in person. Only the court performs in person searches; visitors may not. Search fee: $15.00 per name multiple searches only (otherwise no fee for single case) includes both civil and criminal. Court makes copy: $2.00 1st page, $1.00 each add'l. Required to search: name, years to search, DOB. Criminal records on docket books since 1976; on computer back to 1998; archived back to 1927.

General Information: No public access terminal. No impounded records released. Will not fax documents. Certification fee: $5.00 per doc. Payee: Treasurer, State of Maine. Personal checks accepted. Prepayment and SASE required.

Bangor District Court 73 Hammond St, Bangor, ME 04401; phone: 207-941-3040; hours 8AM-4PM (EST). *Misdemeanor, Civil Actions, Eviction, Small Claims.*

Note: Effective 9/1/03, the search fees and copy fees listed are mandatory per administrative rule. If a SASE is not supplied for mail searches, court may charge add'l $5.00.

Civil Records: Access: Mail, in person. Both court and visitors may perform in person searches. Search fee: $15.00, includes both civil and criminal. Court makes copy: $2.00 1st page, $1.00 each add'l. Required to search: name, years to search. Civil cases indexed by defendant. Civil records on docket books

since 1962. Court suggests using central state repository. Mail turnaround time 1 week.

Criminal Records: Access: Mail, in person. Both court and visitors may perform in person searches. Search fee: 1st name free, then $15.00 each add'l name; includes both civil and criminal. Court makes copy: $2.00 1st page, $1.00 each add'l. Required to search: name, years to search; also helpful: DOB. Criminal records on computer since late 1986, docket books since 1962. Mail turnaround time 1 week.

General Information: Public terminal has only criminal records back to 12/1986. No protective custody records released. Certification fee: $5.00 per seal. Payee: Maine District Court. Personal checks accepted. Prepayment and SASE required.

Central District Court - Central 13 52 Main St, Lincoln, ME 04457; phone: 207-794-8512; hours 8AM-4PM (EST). *Misdemeanor, Civil Actions, Eviction, Small Claims.*

Note: Effective 9/1/03, the search fees and copy fees listed are mandatory per administrative rule. If a SASE is not supplied for mail searches, court may charge add'l $5.00.

Civil Records: Access: In person only. Only the court performs in person searches; visitors may not. Search fee: $15.00. Court makes copy: $2.00 1st page, $1.00 each add'l. Required to search: name, years to search. Civil cases indexed by defendant. Civil records on docket books since 1964.

Criminal Records: Access: In person only. Only the court performs in person searches; visitors may not. Search fee: $15.00 per name. Court makes copy: $2.00 1st page, $1.00 each add'l. Required to search: name, years to search, DOB. Criminal records on computer since 1987, docket books since 1964.

General Information: No public access terminal. No juvenile or protective custody records released. Certification fee: $5.00 per piece. Payee: Maine District Court. Personal checks accepted. Prepayment required.

Millinocket District Court - North 13 207 Penobscot Ave, Millinocket, ME 04462; phone: 207-723-4786; hours 8AM-4PM (EST). *Misdemeanor, Civil Actions, Eviction, Small Claims.*

Note: Effective 9/1/03, the search fees and copy fees listed are mandatory per administrative rule. If a SASE is not supplied for mail searches, court may charge add'l $5.00.

Civil Records: Access: In person only. Both court and visitors may perform in person searches. Search fee: $15.00 per name. Court makes copy: $2.00 1st page, $1.00 each add'l. Required to search: name, years to search. Civil cases indexed by defendant, plaintiff. Civil records on docket books since 1964; computerized records since 1987.

Criminal Records: Access: Mail, in person. Both court and visitors may perform in person searches. Search fee: $15.00 per name. No charge if you provide docket numbers. Court makes copy: $2.00 1st page, $1.00 each add'l. Required to search: name, years to search, DOB. Criminal records on computer since 1987, docket books since 1964. Mail turnaround time 3-6 days.

General Information: No public access terminal. No juvenile or protective custody records released. Will not fax documents. Certification fee: $5.00 per doc. Payee: Maine District Court. Personal checks accepted. Prepayment required. SASE requested.

Newport District Court - West 3 12 Water St, Newport, ME 04953; phone: 207-368-5778; hours 8AM-4PM (EST). *Misdemeanor, Civil Actions, Eviction, Small Claims.*

Note: Effective 9/1/03, the search fees and copy fees listed are mandatory per administrative rule. If a SASE is not supplied for mail searches, court may charge add'l $5.00.

Civil Records: Access: Mail, in person. Both court and visitors may perform in person searches. Search fee: $15.00, includes both civil and criminal. Court makes copy: $2.00 1st page, $1.00 each add'l. Required to search: name, years to search. Civil cases indexed by defendant, plaintiff. Civil records on docket books back to 1965; computerized back to 2001. Mail turnaround time 1 week.

Criminal Records: Access: Mail, in person. Both court and visitors may perform in person searches. Search fee: $15.00, includes both civil and criminal. Court makes copy: $2.00 1st page, $1.00 each add'l. Required to search: name, years to search, DOB. Criminal records on computer for 5 years, on docket books since 1987. Mail turnaround time 1 week.

General Information: Public terminal has only criminal records back to 1987. No impounded records released. Will not fax documents. Certification fee: $5.00 per cert. Payee: Maine District Court. Personal checks accepted. Prepayment and SASE required.

Probate Court 97 Hammond St, Bangor, ME 04401-4996; phone: 207-942-8769; fax: 207-941-8499; hours 8AM-4:30PM (EST). *Probate.*

Piscataquis County

Superior Court 159 E Main St, Dover-Foxcroft, ME 04426; phone: 207-564-8419; fax: 207-564-3363; hours 8AM-4PM (EST). *Felony, Misdemeanor, Civil Actions.*
Note: Effective 9/1/03, the search fees and copy fees listed are mandatory per administrative rule. If a SASE is not supplied for mail searches, court may charge add'l $5.00.

Civil Records: Access: Mail, in person. Only the court performs in person searches; visitors may not. Search fee: $15.00 per name includes both civil and criminal. If only 1 name per day, will do free. Court makes copy: $2.00 1st page, $1.00 each add'l. Required to search: name, years to search. Civil cases indexed by defendant, plaintiff. Civil records on docket books since 1960; computerized records since 1998. Mail turnaround time 1 week.

Criminal Records: Access: Mail, in person. Only the court performs in person searches; visitors may not. Search fee: $15.00 per name includes both civil and criminal. If only 1 name per day, will do free. Court makes copy: $2.00 1st page, $1.00 each add'l. Required to search: name, years to search; also helpful: DOB. Criminal records on docket books since 1960; computerized records since 1998. Mail turnaround time 1 week.

General Information: No public access terminal. No pre-sentence report records released. Certification fee: $7.00 per page includes copy fee. Payee: State of Maine Superior Court. Personal checks or Visa/MC accepted. Prepayment and SASE required.

District Court 13 163 E Main St, Dover-Foxcroft, ME 04426; phone: 207-564-2240; hours 8AM-4PM (EST). *Misdemeanor, Civil Actions, Eviction, Small Claims.*
Note: Effective 9/1/03, the search fees and copy fees listed are mandatory per administrative rule. If a SASE is not supplied for mail searches, court may charge add'l $5.00.

Civil Records: Access: Mail, in person. Both court and visitors may perform in person searches. Search fee: $15.00 per name includes both civil and criminal. If only 1 name per day, will do free. Court makes copy: $2.00 1st page, $1.00 each add'l. Required to search: name, years to search. Civil cases indexed by defendant, plaintiff. Civil records on docket books since 1963. Mail turnaround time 1 week.

Criminal Records: Access: Mail, in person. Both court and visitors may perform in person searches. Search fee: $15.00 per name includes both civil and criminal. If only 1 name per day, will do free. Court makes copy: $2.00 1st page, $1.00 each add'l. Required to search: name, years to search; also helpful: DOB. Criminal records on computer since 1987, docket books since 1963. Mail turnaround time 1 week.

General Information: No public access terminal. No protective custody or juvenile records released. Certification fee: $7.00 per page include copy fee. Payee: Maine District Court. Personal checks or Visa/MC accepted. Prepayment and SASE required.

Probate Court 159 E Main St, Dover-Foxcroft, ME 04426; phone: 207-564-2431; fax: 207-564-2431; hours 8:30AM-4PM (EST). *Probate.*

Sagadahoc County

Superior Court 147 Mew Meadows Rd, West Bath, ME 04530; phone: 207-443-9733; hours 8AM-4:00PM (EST). *Felony, Misdemeanor, Civil Actions.*
Note: Effective 9/1/03, the search fees and copy fees listed are mandatory per administrative rule. If a SASE is not supplied for mail searches, court may charge add'l $5.00.

Civil Records: Access: Mail, in person. Both court and visitors may perform in person searches. Search fee: $15.00, includes both civil and criminal. Court makes copy: $2.00 1st page, $1.00 each add'l. Required to search: name, years to search. Civil cases indexed by defendant, plaintiff. Civil records on docket books since 1900s; on computer back to 1999. Mail turnaround time 2 days.

Criminal Records: Access: Mail, in person. Both court and visitors may perform in person searches. Search fee: $15.00, includes both civil and criminal. Court makes copy: $2.00 1st page, $1.00 each add'l. Required to search: name, years to search, DOB. Criminal records on docket books since 1900s; on computer back to 1999. Mail turnaround time 2 days.

General Information: No public access terminal. No impounded records released. Will not fax documents. Certification fee: $5.00 per document. Payee: Clerk of Superior Court. Cash, checks and money orders accepted. Prepayment and SASE required.

West Bath District Court 6 147 New Meadows Rd, West Bath, ME 04530; phone: 207-442-0200; hours 8AM-4PM (EST). *Misdemeanor, Civil Actions, Eviction, Small Claims.*
Note: This court handles the eastern part of Cumberland County and all of Sagadahoc County.

Civil Records: Access: In person only. Both court and visitors may perform in person searches. Search fee: $15.00, includes both civil and criminal. Court makes copy: $2.00 1st page, $1.00 each add'l. Required to search: name, years to search. Civil cases indexed by defendant, plaintiff. Civil records on docket books since 1980's; prior archived. Effective 09/01/03, the search fees and copy fees listed are mandatory per administrative rule. If a SASE not supplied for mail searches, court may charge add'l $5.00.

Criminal Records: Access: In person only. Both court and visitors may perform in person searches. Search fee: $15.00, includes both civil and criminal. Court makes copy: $2.00 1st page, $1.00 each add'l. Required to search: name, years to search; also helpful: DOB. Criminal records on computer since 1987, docket books back to 1975; prior archived. Effective 09/01/03, the search fees and copy fees listed are mandatory per administrative rule.

General Information: No public access terminal. No protective custody or juvenile records released. Certification fee: $5.00. Payee: Maine District Court. Personal checks accepted. Prepayment required.

Probate Court 752 High St, Bath, ME 04530; phone: 207-443-8218; fax: 207-443-8217; hours 8:30AM-4:30PM (EST). *Probate.*

Somerset County

Superior Court PO Box 725, Skowhegan, ME 04976; phone: 207-474-5161; probate phone: 207-474-3322; hours 8AM-4PM (EST). *Felony, Misdemeanor, Civil Actions.*
Civil Records: Access: Mail, in person. Only the court performs in person searches; visitors may not. Search fee: $15.00 per name; no fee for searching one name only. Court makes copy: $2.00 1st page, $1.00 each add'l. Required to search: name, years to search. Civil cases indexed by defendant, plaintiff. Civil records archived in Augusta back to 1800s, docket books and index cards back to 1900s.

Criminal Records: Access: Mail, in person. Only the court performs in person searches; visitors may not. Search fee: $15.00 per name; no fee for searching one name only. Court makes copy: $2.00 1st page, $1.00 each add'l. Required to search: name, years to search; also helpful: DOB. Criminal records archived in Augusta back to 1800s, docket books and index cards back to 1900s; on computer back to 1998.

General Information: No public access terminal. No impounded, present investigations, psychological evaluations or child support records released. Certification fee: $5.00 per doc. Payee: Clerk of Superior Court. Personal checks accepted. Prepayment required.

District Court 12 PO Box 525, 47 Court St, Skowhegan, ME 04976; phone: 207-474-9518; hours 8AM-4PM (EST). *Misdemeanor, Civil Actions, Eviction, Small Claims.*
Note: Effective 9/1/03, the search fees and copy fees listed are mandatory per administrative rule. If a SASE is not supplied for mail searches, court may charge add'l $5.00.

Civil Records: Access: Mail, in person. Both court and visitors may perform in person searches. Search fee: $15.00, includes both civil and criminal. Court makes copy: $2.00 1st page, $1.00 each add'l. Required to search: name, years to search. Civil cases indexed by defendant. Civil records on docket books since 1960s, divorces since 1970s. Mail turnaround time 2-4 weeks.

Criminal Records: Access: Mail, in person. Both court and visitors may perform in person searches. Search fee: $15.00, includes both civil and criminal. Court makes copy: $2.00 1st page, $1.00 each add'l. Required to search: name, years to search; also helpful: DOB. Criminal records on computer since 1987, docket books since 1960s. Mail turnaround time 2-4 weeks.

General Information: Public terminal has only criminal records back to 1987. No juvenile records released. Certification fee: $5.00 per doc. Payee: Maine District Court. Personal checks accepted. Prepayment and SASE required.

Probate Court 41 Court St, Skowhegan, ME 04976; phone: 207-474-3322; hours 8:30AM-4:30PM (EST). *Probate.*

Waldo County

Superior Court 137 Church St, Belfast, ME 04915; phone: 207-338-1940; hours 8AM-4PM (EST). *Felony, Misdemeanor, Civil Actions.*
Note: Effective 9/1/03, the search fees and copy fees listed are mandatory per administrative rule. If a SASE is not supplied for mail searches, court may charge add'l $5.00.

Civil Records: Access: Mail, in person. Only the court performs in person searches; visitors may not. Search fee: $15.00, includes both civil and criminal. Allows 1 name free search. Court makes copy: $2.00 1st page, $1.00 each add'l. Required to search: name, years to search. Civil cases indexed by defendant, plaintiff. Civil records archived back to 1980 (not in office), on docket books since 1980; on computer back to 1998. Mail turnaround time 1 week.

Criminal Records: Access: Mail, in person. Only the court performs in person searches; visitors may not. Search fee: $15.00, includes both civil and criminal. Allows 1 name free search. Court makes copy: $2.00 1st page, $1.00 each add'l. Required to search: name, years to search, DOB. Criminal records archived back to 1975 (not in office), on docket books since 1975; on computer back to 1998. Mail turnaround time 1 week.

General Information: No public access terminal. No protective custody records released. Will not fax documents. Certification fee: $5.00 per doc. Payee: State Treasurer. Personal checks accepted. Prepayment and SASE required.

District Court 5 PO Box 382, 103 Church St, Belfast, ME 04915; phone: 207-338-3107; hours 8AM-4PM (EST). *Misdemeanor, Civil Actions, Eviction, Small Claims.*
Note: Effective 9/1/03, the search fees and copy fees listed are mandatory per administrative rule. If a SASE is not supplied for mail searches, court may charge add'l $5.00.
Civil Records: Access: Mail, in person. Both court and visitors may perform in person searches. Search fee: $15.00, includes both civil and criminal. Court makes copy: $2.00 1st page, $1.00 each add'l. Required to search: name, years to search. Civil cases indexed by defendant, plaintiff. Civil records on docket books since 1966, computerized since 2001. Mail turnaround time 1 week.
Criminal Records: Access: Mail, in person. Both court and visitors may perform in person searches. Search fee: $15.00, includes both civil and criminal. Court makes copy: $2.00 1st page, $1.00 each add'l. Required to search: name, years to search, DOB. Criminal records on computer since 1987, docket books since 1966. Mail turnaround time 1 week.
General Information: No public access terminal. No juvenile or impounded records released. Will not fax documents. Certification fee: $5.00 per doc. Payee: Maine District Court. Personal checks accepted. Prepayment and SASE required.

Probate Court 39A Spring St, PO Box 323, Belfast, ME 04915-0323; phone: 207-338-2780/2963; fax: 207-338-2360; hours 8AM-4PM (EST). *Probate.*

Washington County

Superior Court Clerk of Court, PO Box 526, Machias, ME 04654; phone: 207-255-3326; hours 8AM-4PM (EST). *Felony, Misdemeanor, Civil.*
Note: Effective 9/1/03, the search fees and copy fees listed are mandatory per administrative rule. If a SASE is not supplied for mail searches, court may charge add'l $5.00.
Civil Records: Access: Mail, in person. Both court and visitors may perform in person searches. Search fee: $15.00, includes both civil and criminal. Court makes copy: $2.00 1st page, $1.00 each add'l. Required to search: name, years to search. Civil cases indexed by defendant, plaintiff. Civil records on docket books and index cards since 1930s. Mail turnaround time 1 week.
Criminal Records: Access: Mail, in person. Both court and visitors may perform in person searches. Search fee: $15.00, includes both civil and criminal. Court makes copy: $2.00 1st page, $1.00 each add'l. Required to search: name, years to search, DOB. Criminal records on docket books and index cards since 1930s. Mail turnaround time 1 week.
General Information: No public access terminal. No impounded records released. Will not fax documents. Certification fee: $5.00 per document. Payee: Treasurer, State of Maine. Personal checks accepted. Prepayment and SASE required.

Calais District Court - North 4 PO Box 929, Calais, ME 04619; phone: 207-454-2055; TTY# 207-454-0085; hours 8AM-4PM (EST). *Misdemeanor, Civil Actions, Eviction, Small Claims.*
Civil Records: Access: In person only. Both court and visitors may perform in person searches. Search fee: $15.00 per name, if more than 1 name. Court makes copy: $2.00 1st page, $1.00 each add'l. Required to search: name, years to search. Civil cases indexed by defendant, plaintiff. Civil records on docket books since 1964.
Criminal Records: Access: In person only. Both court and visitors may perform in person searches. Search fee: $15.00 per name, if more than 1 name. Court makes copy: $2.00 1st page, $1.00 each add'l. Required to search: name, years to search, DOB. Criminal records on computer since 1987, docket books since 07/79.
General Information: Public terminal has criminal back to 1987 and civil back to 1987; but ending in

1997. No juvenile or protective custody records released. Certification fee: $5.00 per doc. Payee: Maine District Court. Personal checks accepted. Prepayment required.

Maine District Court 4 47 Court St, PO Box 297, Machias, ME 04654; phone: 207-255-3044; hours 8AM-4PM (EST). *Misdemeanor, Civil Actions, Eviction, Small Claims.*
Note: Effective 9/1/03, the search fees and copy fees listed are mandatory per administrative rule. If a SASE is not supplied for mail searches, court may charge add'l $5.00.
Civil Records: Access: Mail, in person. Both court and visitors may perform in person searches. Search fee: 1st name free; add'l $15.00 per name. Court makes copy: $2.00 1st page, $1.00 each add'l. Required to search: name, years to search. Civil cases indexed by defendant, plaintiff. Civil records on docket books since 1964; on computer 1987-1999. Mail turnaround time 4 days.
Criminal Records: Access: Mail, in person. Both court and visitors may perform in person searches. Search fee: 1st name free add'l $15.00. Court makes copy: $2.00 1st page, $1.00 each add'l. Required to search: name, years to search, DOB. Criminal records on computer 1987-1999, docket books since 1964. Mail turnaround time 4 days.
General Information: No public access terminal. No protective custody or juvenile records released. Will not fax documents. Certification fee: $5.00 per document. Payee: Maine District Court. Personal checks accepted. Prepayment and SASE required.

Probate Court PO Box 297, 47 Court St, Machias, ME 04654; phone: 207-255-6591; hours 8AM-4PM (EST). *Probate.*

York County

Superior Court Clerk of Court, PO Box 160, Alfred, ME 04002; phone: 207-324-5122; probate phone: 207-324-5117; hours 8AM-4PM (EST). *Felony, Misdemeanor, Civil Actions.*
Note: Effective 9/1/03, the search fees and copy fees listed are mandatory per administrative rule. If a SASE is not supplied for mail searches, court may charge add'l $5.00.
Civil Records: Access: Mail, in person. Only the court performs in person searches; visitors may not. Search fee: $15.00, includes both civil and criminal. Court makes copy: $2.00 1st page, $1.00 each add'l. Required to search: name, years to search. Civil cases indexed by defendant, plaintiff. Civil records on docket books since 1960; computerized records go back to 2002. No faxes are accepted or sent. Mail turnaround time: 1-5 names is 5 days; 6-10 names 30 working days.
Criminal Records: Access: Mail, in person. Only the court performs in person searches; visitors may not. Search fee: $15.00, includes both civil and criminal. Court makes copy: $2.00 1st page, $1.00 each add'l. Required to search: name, years to search, DOB. Criminal records on docket books since 1966; computerized records go back to 1998. No faxes are accepted or sent. Mail turnaround time: 1-5 names is 5 days; 6-10 names 30 working days.
General Information: No public access terminal. No juvenile, or protective custody records released. Will not fax documents. Certification fee: $5.00 per attestation. Payee: Clerk of Courts. Only cashiers checks and money orders accepted. Prepayment and SASE required.

Biddeford District Court - East 10 25 Adams St, Biddeford, ME 04005; phone: 207-283-1147; hours 8AM-4PM (EST). *Misdemeanor, Civil Actions, Eviction, Small Claims.*
Note: Effective 9/1/03, the search fees and copy fees listed are mandatory per administrative rule. If a SASE is not supplied for mail searches, court may charge add'l $5.00.
Civil Records: Access: mail, in person. Visitors must perform in person searches themselves. Search fee: $15.00, includes both civil and criminal.

Court makes copy: $2.00 1st page, $1.00 each add'l. Required to search: name, years to search. Civil cases indexed on docket books since 1989. Court will do up to 3 searches.
Criminal Records: Access: Mail, in person. Visitors must perform in person searches themselves. Search fee: $15.00, includes both civil and criminal. Court makes copy: $2.00 1st page, $1.00 each add'l. Required to search: name, years to search; also helpful: DOB. Criminal records on computer since 1986. Court will do up to 3 searches.
General Information: No public access terminal. No child protection or juvenile records released. Will not fax documents. Certification fee: $5.00 per document. Payee: Maine District Court. Personal checks accepted. Prepayment and SASE required.

Springvale District Court - West 10 447 Main St, Springvale, ME 04083; phone: 207-459-1400; hours 8AM-4PM (EST). *Misdemeanor, Civil Actions, Eviction, Small Claims.*
Note: Effective 9/1/03, the search fees and copy fees listed are mandatory per administrative rule. If a SASE is not supplied for mail searches, court may charge add'l $5.00.
Civil Records: Access: Mail, in person. Both court and visitors may perform in person searches. Search fee: $15.00, includes both civil and criminal. Court makes copy: $2.00 1st page, $1.00 each add'l. Required to search: name, years to search. Civil cases indexed by defendant. Civil records on computer since 1985, docket books since 1985. Mail turnaround time 3-4 days.
Criminal Records: Access: Mail, in person. Both court and visitors may perform in person searches. Search fee: $15.00, includes both civil and criminal. Court makes copy: $2.00 1st page, $1.00 each add'l. Required to search: name, years to search, DOB. Criminal records on computer since 1997, dockets books since 1980. Mail turnaround time 3-4 days.
General Information: No public access terminal. No impounded, juvenile, mental health or protective custody records released. Certification fee: $5.00 per document includes copies. Payee: Maine District Court. Personal checks accepted. Prepayment and SASE required.

York District Court - South 10 PO Box 770, Chase's Pond Rd, York, ME 03909-0770; phone: 207-363-1230; hours 8AM-4PM (EST). *Misdemeanor, Civil Actions, Eviction, Small Claims.*
Note: Effective 9/1/03, the search fees and copy fees listed are mandatory per administrative rule. If a SASE is not supplied for mail searches, court may charge add'l $5.00.
Civil Records: Access: Mail, in person. Visitors must perform in person searches themselves. Search fee: $15.00, includes both civil and criminal. Allows 1 name free search. Court makes copy: $2.00 1st page, $1.00 each add'l. Required to search: name, years to search. Civil cases indexed by defendant, plaintiff. Civil records on docket books since 1975; on computer back to 1987. Mail turnaround time 2-4 days.
Criminal Records: Access: Mail, in person. Visitors must perform in person searches themselves. Search fee: $15.00, includes both civil and criminal. Allows 1 name free search. Court makes copy: $2.00 1st page, $1.00 each add'l. Required to search: name, years to search, DOB. Criminal records on computer back to 1987, docket books since 1975. Mail turnaround time 2-4 days.
General Information: No public access terminal. No impounded, juvenile and protective custody records released. Will not fax documents. Certification fee: $5.00 per doc. Payee: Maine District Court. Personal checks accepted. Prepayment and SASE required.

Probate Court PO Box 399, 45 Kennebunk Rd, Alfred, ME 04002; phone: 207-324-1577; fax: 207-324-0163; hours 8:30AM-4:30PM (EST). *Probate.*

Maine Recording Offices

ORGANIZATION: 16 counties, 17 recording offices. The recording officer is County Register of Deeds. Counties maintain a general index of all transactions recorded. Aroostock and Oxford Counties each have two recording offices. There are no county assessors; each town has its own. The entire state is in the Eastern Time Zone (EST).

REAL ESTATE RECORDS: Counties do not usually perform real estate name searches, but some will look up a name informally. Copy and certification fees vary widely. Assessor and tax records are located at the town/city level.

UCC RECORDS: Financing statements are filed at the state level, except for real estate related filings, which are filed only with the Register of Deeds. Counties do not perform UCC searches. Copy fees are usually $1.00 per page.

TAX LIEN RECORDS: All tax liens on personal property are filed with the Secretary of State. All tax liens on real property are filed with the Register of Deeds.

OTHER LIENS: Municipal, bail bond, mechanics.

ONLINE ACCESS: There is no statewide system. However, a private vendor has placed assessor records from a number of towns on the Internet. Visit http://www.visionappraisal.com/databases/maine/index.htm

Androscoggin County

County Register of Deeds, 2 Turner St; Courthouse, Auburn, ME 04210-5978. RE & UCC recording phone-207-782-0191; fax-207-784-3163; hours: 8AM-5PM http://androscoggindeeds.com
All records in one index. Only the public may search. Copy fee $1.00 per page. Cert fee- None. Payee- Androscoggin County Register of Deeds. **Online access to Real Estate, Deed, Tax Lien, Assessor records:** Access the Registry index by subscription for a $140.00 annual fee plus $1.00 per page/image printed. Indexes go back to 1976. For information and sign-up, contact Tina at 207-782-0191. Search for free at http://androscoggindeeds.com/ALIS/WW400R.PGM. Index goes back to 1976; images to 1/1980. Also, Town of Lisbon Assessor data is free at www.lisbonme.org/clerk/index.htm. No name searching. Also City of Auburn tax assessor data is free at www.auburnmaine.org/html/webgis.htm. **Other phones:** Treasurer- 207-784-7491.

Aroostook County (Northern District)

County Register of Deeds, PO Box 47, Fort Kent, ME 04743. RE & UCC recording phone-207-834-3925; fax-207-834-3138; hours: 8AM-4:30PM www.aroostook.me.us/deeds.html
All records in one index. Only the public may search. Copy fee $1.00 per page. Real estate copy- $.50 per page, $.25 if self serve. Cert fee- $2.00 per doc plus copy fee. Payee- Northern Aroostook County Register of Deeds. **Online access to Real Estate, Deed records:** Access via the commercial online system is $50.00 per year fee and $.25 per minute when online. Call for details. **Other phones:** Treasurer- 207-834-3090; Elections- 207-834-3090; Vital Records- 207-834-3090. **Property tax/Assessor-** 416 W Main St, Fort Kent, ME 04743; 207-834-3090.

Aroostook County (Southern District)

County Register of Deeds, 26 Court St, #102, Houlton, ME 04730. 207-532-1500, R/E recording phone-207-834-3925; fax-207-532-7319; hours: 8AM-4:30PM www.aroostook.me.us/indexhome.html
All locations from New Sweden south file in this office. Only the public may search. Copy fee $1.00 per page. RE record copy- $.25 per page, $.50 if register makes copy. Payee- Aroostook County Register of Deeds.

Cumberland County

County Register of Deeds, PO Box 7230, Portland, ME 04112. RE & UCC recording phone-207-871-8389; fax-207-772-4162; hours: 8:30AM-4:30PM www.cumberlandcounty.org/DEEDSmain.html
All records in one index. Records indexed on a public use terminal back to 1/1/1965. Only the public may search. Copy fee $1.50 per page. Cert fee- $2.00 per doc plus copy fee. Payee- Cumberland County Register of Deeds. **Online access to Assessor, Property Sale records:** Search Register of Deeds fee site at https://www.mainelandrecords.com/melr/controller. Cape Elizabeth Town assessor data free- www.capeelizabeth.com/taxdata.html. Gray Town assessor data- www.graymaine.org/vclerk/index.htm. Portland assessor- www.portlandassessor.com. Scarborough-www.scarborough.me.us/townhall/assessing/search.html. Cumberland, Raymond, Freeport, Gorham, Harpswell, Standish and S. Portland town assessors at www.visionappraisal.com/databases/maine/index.htm Falmouth 2002 data- www.town.falmouth.me.us/assessing/home.html. Yarmouth property info: www.yarmouth.me.us. **Other phones:** Treasurer- 207-871-8392. **Property tax/Assessor-** 207-874-8486.

Franklin County

County Register of Deeds, 140 Main St; Courthouse, Farmington, ME 04938-1818. 207-778-5889; fax-207-778-5899; hours: 8:30AM-4PM
Only the public may search. Copy fee $1.00 per financing statement. Cert fee- $.50 per cert plus copy fee. Payee- County Register of Deeds.

Hancock County

County Register of Deeds, 50 State St #9, Ellsworth, ME 04605. RE & UCC recording phone-207-667-8353; fax-207-667-1410; hours: 8:30AM-4PM www.co.hancock.me.us
Separate indices to search. Records indexed on a public use terminal back to 1972. Office personnel or visitors may perform searches. Copy fee $2.00 per page. Cert fee- $1.00 per doc plus copy fee. Payee- Hancock County Registry of Deeds. **Online access to Real Estate, Deed, Lien, UCC, Recording records:** Access to the county registry of deeds database at www.registryofdeeds.com requires registration. Viewing of records back to 1790 is free, but $2.00 per page to print. Register online. For info see website or call 888-833-3979. Also, City of Ellsworth real estate data is free at www.ci.ellsworth.me.us/realestatedb.html. Also, access to Bar Harbor property data is at http://data.visionappraisal.com/BarHarborME/. Free registration required.

Kennebec County

County Register of Deeds, PO Box 1053, Augusta, ME 04332-1053. 207-622-0431; fax-207-622-1598; hours: 8AM-4PM
Separate indices to search. Records indexed on a public use terminal back to 1935. Only the public may search. Copy fee $1.50 per financing statement. Cert fee- $.50 per cert plus copy fee. Payee- Kennebec County Register of Deeds. **Online access to Assessor, Property, Deed, Recording records:** Register free and search recorder index free at www.kennebec.me.us.landata.com. Fee for images by sub or pay-per-view. Also, records on the Winslow Town Property Records database are free at www.winslowmaine.org. Records on the Town of Waterville Assessor's database are free at http://data.visionappraisal.com/WatervilleME/. For full data, user ID is required; registration is free. Also, search the City of Augusta assessor database at http://data.visionappraisal.com/AugustaME/. Free registration for full data.

Knox County

County Register of Deeds, PO Box 943, Rockland, ME 04841. 207-594-0422; fax-207-594-0446; hours: 8AM-4PM www.knoxcounty.midcoast.com
Separate indices to search include grantor/grantee. Only the public may search. Copy fee $1.00 per financing statement. Cert fee- $1.00 per doc plus copy fee. Payee- Knox County Register of Deeds. **Online access to Property records:** Access to mainelandrecords.com. The indexes are available from 1966 to present. Document images are available from 1992 to present; fees for these records. Search Camden and Rockland town assessor data at www.visionappraisal.com/databases/maine/index.htm.

Lincoln County

County Register of Deeds, PO Box 249, Wiscasset, ME 04578-0249. 207-882-7515; fax-207-882-4061; hours: 8AM-4PM
All records in one index. Records indexed on a public use terminal back to 1954. Only the public may search. Copy fee $1.00 per page. Cert fee- $1.00 per doc plus copy fee. Payee- Lincoln County Register of Deeds. **Online access to Deed, Property, Recording records:** Search Register of Deeds index back to 1954 for free at www.lincolncomeregofdeeds.com. Click on Free Access at left. Images for a fee go back to 9/1999. Also Town of Boothbay property data is free at http://data.visionappraisal.com/BoothbayME/.

Oxford County

County Register of Deeds, PO Box 179, South Paris, ME 04281-0179. 207-743-6211; fax-207-743-2656; hours: 8AM-4PM

File in this office for all towns except the following: Brownfield, Denmark, Fryeburg, Hiram, Lovell, Porter, Stoneham, Stow, and Sweden. All records in one index. Only the public may search. Copy fee $1.00 per page. Cert fee- $1.00 per doc plus copy fee. Payee- Oxford County Register of Deeds. **Online access to Real Estate, Deed records:** Search the Eastern portion of the county at https://www.mainelandrecords.com/melr/MelrApp/index.jsp.

Penobscot County

County Register of Deeds, PO Box 2070, Bangor, ME 04402-2070. 207-942-8797; fax-207-945-4920; hours: 8AM-4:30PM www.penobscotdeeds.com

All records in one index. Records indexed on a public use terminal back to 1967. Only the public may search. Copy fee $1.00 per page. Cert fee- $1.00 per doc plus copy fee. Payee- Penobscot County Register of Deeds. **Online access to Real Estate, Deed, Recording, Assessor, Property records:** Search the Register of Deeds index back to 1967 and images back to 1/1985 for free at www.penobscotdeeds.com. A fee is charged for copies and you may not download with registering. Also, search the City of Old Town real estate database for free at www.old-town.me.us/assessor/rev.asp.

Piscataquis County

County Register of Deeds, 159 E. Main St, Dover-Foxcroft, ME 04426. 207-564-2411; fax-207-564-7708; hours: 8:30AM-4PM

All records in one index. Only the public may search. Copy fee $1.00 per page. Cert fee- $1.00 per page plus copy fee. Payee- Piscataquis County Register of Deeds. **Online access to Deed, Land, Judgment records:** In the process of developing a searchable website. Online searching expected in late 2005. **Property tax/Assessor-** 207-287-2011.

Sagadahoc County

County Register of Deeds, PO Box 246, Bath, ME 04530. 207-443-8214; fax-207-443-8216; hours: 8:30AM-4:30PM

Separate indices to search include plans. Only the public may search. Will check a name for recent recording. Copy fee $1.00 per financing statement; fax back- $2.00 per page. Cert fee- None but must pay copy fee. Payee- Sagadahoc County Register of Deeds. **Online access to Recording, Grantor/Grantee, Real Estate, Assessor records:** Register of Deeds records are online for a $50.00 per year fee plus $.25 per minute access fee. Records go back to 1964 on the index, Grantor/Grantee. For information and registration, call the Register of Deeds. Also, records on the City of Bath Assessor database are free at www.cityofbath.com/assessdb/search.asp.

Somerset County

County Register of Deeds, PO Box 248, Skowhegan, ME 04976-0248. 207-474-3421; fax-207-474-2793; hours: 8:30AM-4:30PM

All tax info and vital records are done at municipal level. All records in one index. Will not search real estate records. Will not search UCC records. Will make copies- provide book and page number. Will not search tax liens. Copy fee $1.00 per page; fax back- $2.00. Cert fee- $1.00 per document. Payee- Register of Deeds. **Online access to Real Estate, Deed records:** Access real estte records free at https://www.mainelandrecords.com/melr/MelrApp/index.jsp.

Waldo County

County Register of Deeds, PO Box D, Belfast, ME 04915. 207-338-1710; fax-207-338-6360; hours: 8AM-4PM

Separate indices to search include books, computer. Records indexed on a public use terminal back to 1985. Only the public may search. Copy fee $1.00 per page. Cert fee- $1.00 per cert plus copy fee. Payee- Waldo County Register of Deeds.

Washington County

County Register of Deeds, PO Box 297, Machias, ME 04654-0297. 207-255-6512; fax-207-255-3838; hours: 8AM-4PM

All records in one index. Records indexed on computer back to 1972; no public access to computer. Only the public may search. Copy fee $1.00 per page. Cert fee- $1.00 per doc plus copy fee. Payee- Washington County Register of Deeds. **Other phones:** Treasurer- 207-255-8354; County Clerk- 207-255-3127. **Property tax/Assessor-** 207-255-6621 (Machias area only).

York County

County Register of Deeds, PO Box 339, Alfred, ME 04002-0339. 207-324-1576; fax-207-324-2886; hours: 8:30AM-4:30PM www.york.me.us.landata.com/

Separate indices to search include grantor/grantee, plans. Records indexed on a public use terminal back to 1966. Only the public may search. Copy fee $1.25 per page. Plan copies- $5.00 per page. Cert fee- $1.00 per doc plus copy fee. Payee- York County Register of Deeds. **Online access to Real Estate, Deed, Recording, Assessor, Property records:** Search Register of Deeds records at www.york.me.us.landata.com. Register & search basic index free; fee for docs copies either by sub @ $1.25 per pg or non-sub @$2.00. Kennebunk Town data free at www.kennebunkmaine.org; click on Dept then Tax Assmt. Also, Berwick, Eliot, Kittery, Old Orchard Beach, Saco and York Town assessor data at www.visionappraisal.com/databases/maine/index.htm. Free registration required. **Other phones:** Treasurer- 207-324-1571.

Maine County Locator

You will usually be able to find the city name in the City/County Cross. Reference below. In that case, it is a simple matter to determine the county from the cross reference. However, only the official US Postal Service city names are included in this index. There are an additional 40,000 place names that people use in their addresses. Therefore, we have also included a ZIP/City Cross. Reference immediately following the City/County Cross. Reference.

If you know the ZIP Code but the city name does not appear in the City/County Cross. Reference index, look up the ZIP Code in the ZIP/City Cross. Reference, find the city name, then look up the city name in the City/County Cross. Reference. For example, you want to know the county for an address of Menands, NY 12204. There is no "Menands" in the City/County Cross. Reference. The ZIP/City Cross. Reference shows that ZIP Codes 12201-12288 are for the city of Albany. Looking back in the City/County Cross. Reference, Albany is in Albany County.

Maine City/County Cross Reference

ABBOT Piscataquis
ABBOT VILLAGE Piscataquis
ACTON York
ADDISON Washington
ALBION Kennebec
ALFRED York
ALNA Lincoln
ANDOVER Oxford
ANSON Somerset
ASHLAND Aroostook
ATHENS Somerset
ATLANTIC Hancock
AUBURN Androscoggin
AUGUSTA Kennebec
AURORA Hancock
BAILEY ISLAND Cumberland
BAILEYVILLE Washington
BANGOR Penobscot
BAR HARBOR Hancock
BAR MILLS York
BASS HARBOR Hancock
BATH Sagadahoc
BAYVILLE Lincoln
BEALS Washington
BELFAST Waldo
BELGRADE Kennebec
BELGRADE LAKES Kennebec
BENEDICTA Aroostook
BERNARD Hancock
BERWICK York
BETHEL Oxford
BIDDEFORD York
BIDDEFORD POOL York
BINGHAM Somerset
BIRCH HARBOR Hancock
BLAINE Aroostook
BLUE HILL Hancock
BLUE HILL FALLS Hancock
BOOTHBAY Lincoln
BOOTHBAY HARBOR Lincoln
BOWDOIN Sagadahoc
BOWDOINHAM Sagadahoc
BRADFORD Penobscot
BRADLEY Penobscot
BREMEN Lincoln
BREWER Penobscot
BRIDGEWATER Aroostook
BRIDGTON Cumberland
BRISTOL Lincoln
BROOKLIN Hancock
BROOKS Waldo
BROOKSVILLE Hancock
BROOKTON Washington
BROWNFIELD Oxford
BROWNVILLE Piscataquis
BROWNVILLE JUNCTION Piscataquis
BRUNSWICK Cumberland
BRYANT POND Oxford
BUCKFIELD Oxford
BUCKS HARBOR Washington
BUCKSPORT Hancock
BURLINGTON Penobscot
BURNHAM Waldo

BUSTINS ISLAND Cumberland
BUXTON York
CALAIS Washington
CAMBRIDGE Somerset
CAMDEN Knox
CANAAN Somerset
CANTON Oxford
CAPE ELIZABETH Cumberland
CAPE NEDDICK York
CAPE PORPOISE York
CARATUNK Somerset
CARDVILLE Penobscot
CARIBOU Aroostook
CARMEL Penobscot
CASCO Cumberland
CASTINE Hancock
CENTER LOVELL Oxford
CHAMBERLAIN Lincoln
CHARLESTON Penobscot
CHEBEAGUE ISLAND Cumberland
CHERRYFIELD Washington
CHINA Kennebec
CHINA VILLAGE Kennebec
CLAYTON LAKE Aroostook
CLIFF ISLAND Cumberland
CLINTON Kennebec
COLUMBIA FALLS Washington
COOPERS MILLS Lincoln
COREA Hancock
CORINNA Penobscot
CORINTH Penobscot
CORNISH York
COSTIGAN Penobscot
CRANBERRY ISLES Hancock
CROUSEVILLE Aroostook
CUMBERLAND CENTER Cumberland
CUMBERLAND FORESIDE Cumberland
CUSHING Knox
CUTLER Washington
DAMARISCOTTA Lincoln
DANFORTH Washington
DANVILLE Androscoggin
DEER ISLE Hancock
DENMARK Oxford
DENNYSVILLE Washington
DETROIT Somerset
DEXTER (04930) Penobscot(97),
   Somerset(2)
DIXFIELD Oxford
DIXMONT Penobscot
DOVER FOXCROFT Piscataquis
DRESDEN Lincoln
DRYDEN Franklin
DURHAM Androscoggin
EAGLE LAKE Aroostook
EAST ANDOVER Oxford
EAST BALDWIN Cumberland
EAST BLUE HILL Hancock
EAST BOOTHBAY Lincoln
EAST CORINTH Penobscot
EAST DIXFIELD Franklin
EAST LIVERMORE Androscoggin
EAST MACHIAS Washington

EAST MILLINOCKET Penobscot
EAST NEWPORT Penobscot
EAST ORLAND Hancock
EAST PARSONFIELD York
EAST POLAND Androscoggin
EAST STONEHAM Oxford
EAST VASSALBORO Kennebec
EAST WATERBORO York
EAST WATERFORD Oxford
EAST WILTON Franklin
EAST WINTHROP Kennebec
EASTON Aroostook
EASTPORT Washington
EDDINGTON Penobscot
EDGECOMB Lincoln
ELIOT York
ELLSWORTH Hancock
ENFIELD Penobscot
ESTCOURT STATION Aroostook
ETNA Penobscot
EUSTIS Franklin
EXETER Penobscot
FAIRFIELD (04937) Kennebec(97),
   Somerset(2)
FALMOUTH Cumberland
FARMINGDALE Kennebec
FARMINGTON Franklin
FARMINGTON FALLS Franklin
FORT FAIRFIELD Aroostook
FORT KENT Aroostook
FORT KENT MILLS Aroostook
FRANKFORT Waldo
FRANKLIN Hancock
FREEDOM Waldo
FREEPORT Cumberland
FRENCHBORO Hancock
FRENCHVILLE Aroostook
FRIENDSHIP Knox
FRYE Oxford
FRYEBURG Oxford
GARDINER Kennebec
GARLAND Penobscot
GEORGETOWN Sagadahoc
GLEN COVE Knox
GORHAM Cumberland
GOULDSBORO Hancock
GRAND ISLE Aroostook
GRAND LAKE STREAM Washington
GRAY Cumberland
GREENBUSH Penobscot
GREENE Androscoggin
GREENVILLE Piscataquis
GREENVILLE JUNCTION (04442)
   Piscataquis(86), Somerset(13)
GREENWOOD Oxford
GROVE Washington
GUILFORD Piscataquis
HALLOWELL Kennebec
HAMPDEN Penobscot
HANCOCK Hancock
HANOVER Oxford
HARBORSIDE Hancock
HARMONY Somerset

HARPSWELL Cumberland
HARRINGTON Washington
HARRISON Cumberland
HARTLAND Somerset
HAYNESVILLE Aroostook
HEBRON Oxford
HINCKLEY Somerset
HIRAM Oxford
HOLDEN (04429) Penobscot(98),
   Hancock(1)
HOLLIS CENTER York
HOPE Knox
HOULTON Aroostook
HOWLAND Penobscot
HUDSON Penobscot
HULLS COVE Hancock
ISLAND FALLS Aroostook
ISLE AU HAUT Knox
ISLE OF SPRINGS Lincoln
ISLESBORO Waldo
ISLESFORD Hancock
JACKMAN Somerset
JAY Franklin
JEFFERSON Lincoln
JONESBORO Washington
JONESPORT Washington
KENDUSKEAG Penobscot
KENNEBUNK York
KENNEBUNKPORT York
KENTS HILL Kennebec
KINGFIELD Franklin
KINGMAN Penobscot
KITTERY York
KITTERY POINT York
LAGRANGE (04453) Penobscot(98),
   Piscataquis(1)
LAMBERT LAKE Washington
LEBANON York
LEE Penobscot
LEEDS Androscoggin
LEVANT Penobscot
LEWISTON Androscoggin
LIBERTY Waldo
LILLE Aroostook
LIMERICK York
LIMESTONE Aroostook
LIMINGTON York
LINCOLN Penobscot
LINCOLN CENTER Penobscot
LINCOLNVILLE Waldo
LINCOLNVILLE CENTER Waldo
LISBON Androscoggin
LISBON CENTER Androscoggin
LISBON FALLS Androscoggin
LITCHFIELD Kennebec
LITTLE DEER ISLE Hancock
LIVERMORE Androscoggin
LIVERMORE FALLS Androscoggin
LOCKE MILLS Oxford
LONG ISLAND Cumberland
LOVELL Oxford
LUBEC Washington
MACHIAS Washington

MACHIASPORT Washington
MADAWASKA Aroostook
MADISON Somerset
MANCHESTER Kennebec
MANSET Hancock
MAPLETON Aroostook
MARS HILL Aroostook
MASARDIS Aroostook
MATINICUS Knox
MATTAWAMKEAG Penobscot
MECHANIC FALLS Androscoggin
MEDDYBEMPS Washington
MEDWAY Penobscot
MEREPOINT Cumberland
MEXICO Oxford
MILBRIDGE Washington
MILFORD Penobscot
MILLINOCKET Penobscot
MILO Piscataquis
MINOT Androscoggin
MINTURN Hancock
MONHEGAN Lincoln
MONMOUTH Kennebec
MONROE Waldo
MONSON Piscataquis
MONTICELLO Aroostook
MOODY York
MORRILL Waldo
MOUNT DESERT Hancock
MOUNT VERNON Kennebec
NAPLES Cumberland
NEW GLOUCESTER Cumberland
NEW HARBOR Lincoln
NEW LIMERICK Aroostook
NEW PORTLAND Somerset
NEW SHARON Franklin
NEW SWEDEN Aroostook
NEW VINEYARD Franklin
NEWAGEN Lincoln
NEWCASTLE Lincoln
NEWFIELD York
NEWPORT Penobscot
NEWRY Oxford
NOBLEBORO Lincoln
NORRIDGEWOCK Somerset
NORTH AMITY Aroostook
NORTH ANSON Somerset
NORTH BERWICK York
NORTH BRIDGTON Cumberland
NORTH BROOKLIN Hancock
NORTH FRYEBURG Oxford
NORTH HAVEN Knox
NORTH JAY Franklin
NORTH MONMOUTH Kennebec
NORTH NEW PORTLAND Somerset
NORTH SHAPLEIGH York
NORTH TURNER Androscoggin
NORTH VASSALBORO Kennebec
NORTH WATERBORO York
NORTH WATERFORD Oxford
NORTH YARMOUTH Cumberland
NORTHEAST HARBOR Hancock
NORWAY Oxford
OAKFIELD Aroostook
OAKLAND Kennebec
OCEAN PARK York
OGUNQUIT York
OLAMON Penobscot

OLD ORCHARD BEACH York
OLD TOWN Penobscot
OQUOSSOC Franklin
ORIENT Aroostook
ORLAND Hancock
ORONO Penobscot
ORRINGTON Penobscot
ORRS ISLAND Cumberland
OTTER CREEK Hancock
OWLS HEAD Knox
OXBOW Aroostook
OXFORD Oxford
PALERMO Waldo
PALMYRA Somerset
PARIS Oxford
PARSONSFIELD York
PASSADUMKEAG Penobscot
PATTEN Penobscot
PEAKS ISLAND Cumberland
PEJEPSCOT Sagadahoc
PEMAQUID Lincoln
PEMBROKE Washington
PENOBSCOT Hancock
PERHAM Aroostook
PERRY Washington
PERU Oxford
PHILLIPS Franklin
PHIPPSBURG Sagadahoc
PITTSFIELD Somerset
PLAISTED Aroostook
PLYMOUTH Penobscot
POLAND Androscoggin
PORT CLYDE Knox
PORTAGE Aroostook
PORTER Oxford
PORTLAND Cumberland
POWNAL Cumberland
PRESQUE ISLE Aroostook
PRINCETON Washington
PROSPECT HARBOR Hancock
QUIMBY Aroostook
RANDOLPH Kennebec
RANGELEY Franklin
RAYMOND Cumberland
READFIELD Kennebec
RICHMOND Sagadahoc
ROBBINSTON Washington
ROCKLAND Knox
ROCKPORT Knox
ROCKWOOD (04478) Somerset(86),
   Piscataquis(13)
ROUND POND Lincoln
ROXBURY Oxford
RUMFORD Oxford
RUMFORD CENTER Oxford
RUMFORD POINT Oxford
SABATTUS Androscoggin
SACO York
SAINT AGATHA Aroostook
SAINT ALBANS Somerset
SAINT DAVID Aroostook
SAINT FRANCIS Aroostook
SAINT GEORGE Knox
SALSBURY COVE Hancock
SANDY POINT Waldo
SANFORD York
SANGERVILLE Piscataquis
SARGENTVILLE Hancock

SCARBOROUGH Cumberland
SEAL COVE Hancock
SEAL HARBOR Hancock
SEARSMONT Waldo
SEARSPORT Waldo
SEBAGO Cumberland
SEBAGO LAKE Cumberland
SEBASCO ESTATES Sagadahoc
SEBEC Piscataquis
SEBEC LAKE Piscataquis
SEDGWICK Hancock
SHAPLEIGH York
SHAWMUT Somerset
SHERIDAN Aroostook
SHERMAN Aroostook
SHERMAN MILLS Aroostook
SHERMAN STATION (04777)
   Penobscot(90), Aroostook(9)
SHIRLEY MILLS Piscataquis
SINCLAIR Aroostook
SKOWHEGAN Somerset
SMALL POINT Sagadahoc
SMITHFIELD Somerset
SMYRNA MILLS Aroostook
SOLDIER POND Aroostook
SOLON Somerset
SORRENTO Hancock
SOUTH BERWICK York
SOUTH BRISTOL Lincoln
SOUTH CASCO Cumberland
SOUTH CHINA Kennebec
SOUTH FREEPORT Cumberland
SOUTH GARDINER Kennebec
SOUTH GOULDSBORO Hancock
SOUTH HIRAM Oxford
SOUTH PARIS Oxford
SOUTH PORTLAND Cumberland
SOUTH THOMASTON Knox
SOUTH WATERFORD Oxford
SOUTH WINDHAM Cumberland
SOUTHPORT Lincoln
SOUTHWEST HARBOR Hancock
SPRINGFIELD Penobscot
SPRINGVALE York
SPRUCE HEAD Knox
SQUIRREL ISLAND Lincoln
STACYVILLE (04777) Penobscot(90),
   Aroostook(9)
STACYVILLE Penobscot
STANDISH Cumberland
STEEP FALLS Cumberland
STETSON Penobscot
STEUBEN Washington
STILLWATER Penobscot
STOCKHOLM Aroostook
STOCKTON SPRINGS Waldo
STONEHAM Oxford
STONINGTON Hancock
STRATTON Franklin
STRONG Franklin
SULLIVAN Hancock
SUMNER Oxford
SUNSET Hancock
SURRY Hancock
SWANS ISLAND Hancock
TEMPLE Franklin
TENANTS HARBOR Knox
THOMASTON Knox

THORNDIKE Waldo
TOPSFIELD Washington
TOPSHAM Sagadahoc
TREVETT Lincoln
TROY Waldo
TURNER Androscoggin
TURNER CENTER Androscoggin
UNION Knox
UNITY Waldo
UPPER FRENCHVILLE Aroostook
VAN BUREN Aroostook
VANCEBORO Washington
VASSALBORO Kennebec
VIENNA Kennebec
VINALHAVEN Knox
WAITE Washington
WALDOBORO Lincoln
WALLAGRASS Aroostook
WALPOLE Lincoln
WARREN Knox
WASHBURN Aroostook
WASHINGTON Knox
WATERBORO York
WATERFORD Oxford
WATERVILLE Kennebec
WAYNE Kennebec
WEEKS MILLS Kennebec
WELD Franklin
WELLS York
WESLEY Washington
WEST BALDWIN Cumberland
WEST BETHEL Oxford
WEST BOOTHBAY HARBOR Lincoln
WEST BOWDOIN Sagadahoc
WEST BUXTON York
WEST ENFIELD Penobscot
WEST FARMINGTON Franklin
WEST FORKS Somerset
WEST KENNEBUNK York
WEST MINOT Androscoggin
WEST NEWFIELD York
WEST PARIS Oxford
WEST POLAND Androscoggin
WEST ROCKPORT Knox
WEST SOUTHPORT Lincoln
WEST TREMONT Hancock
WESTBROOK Cumberland
WESTFIELD Aroostook
WHITEFIELD Lincoln
WHITING Washington
WHITNEYVILLE Washington
WILEYS CORNER Knox
WILTON Franklin
WINDHAM Cumberland
WINDSOR Kennebec
WINN Penobscot
WINTER HARBOR Hancock
WINTERPORT Waldo
WINTERVILLE Aroostook
WINTHROP Kennebec
WISCASSET Lincoln
WOODLAND Washington
WOOLWICH Sagadahoc
WYTOPITLOCK Aroostook
YARMOUTH Cumberland
YORK York
YORK BEACH York
YORK HARBOR York

Maine ZIP/City Cross Reference

03901-03901 BERWICK	04085-04085 STEEP FALLS	04286-04286 WEST BETHEL	04461-04461 MILFORD
03902-03902 CAPE NEDDICK	04086-04086 TOPSHAM	04287-04287 WEST BOWDOIN	04462-04462 MILLINOCKET
03903-03903 ELIOT	04087-04087 WATERBORO	04287-04287 BOWDOIN	04463-04463 MILO
03904-03904 KITTERY	04088-04088 WATERFORD	04288-04288 WEST MINOT	04464-04464 MONSON
03905-03905 KITTERY POINT	04090-04090 WELLS	04289-04289 WEST PARIS	04465-04465 NORTH AMITY
03906-03906 NORTH BERWICK	04091-04091 WEST BALDWIN	04290-04290 PERU	04467-04467 OLAMON
03907-03907 OGUNQUIT	04092-04092 WESTBROOK	04291-04291 WEST POLAND	04468-04468 OLD TOWN
03908-03908 SOUTH BERWICK	04093-04093 WEST BUXTON	04292-04292 SUMNER	04469-04469 ORONO
03909-03909 YORK	04093-04093 BUXTON	04294-04294 WILTON	04471-04471 ORIENT
03910-03910 YORK BEACH	04094-04094 WEST KENNEBUNK	04330-04338 AUGUSTA	04472-04472 ORLAND
03911-03911 YORK HARBOR	04095-04095 WEST NEWFIELD	04341-04341 COOPERS MILLS	04473-04473 ORONO
04001-04001 ACTON	04096-04096 YARMOUTH	04342-04342 DRESDEN	04474-04474 ORRINGTON
04002-04002 ALFRED	04097-04097 NORTH YARMOUTH	04343-04343 EAST WINTHROP	04475-04475 PASSADUMKEAG
04003-04003 BAILEY ISLAND	04098-04098 WESTBROOK	04344-04344 FARMINGDALE	04476-04476 PENOBSCOT
04004-04004 BAR MILLS	04100-04104 PORTLAND	04345-04345 GARDINER	04478-04478 ROCKWOOD
04005-04005 BIDDEFORD	04105-04105 FALMOUTH	04346-04346 RANDOLPH	04479-04479 SANGERVILLE
04006-04006 BIDDEFORD POOL	04106-04106 SOUTH PORTLAND	04347-04347 HALLOWELL	04481-04481 SEBEC
04007-04007 BIDDEFORD	04107-04107 CAPE ELIZABETH	04348-04348 JEFFERSON	04482-04482 GUILFORD
04008-04008 BOWDOINHAM	04108-04108 PEAKS ISLAND	04349-04349 KENTS HILL	04482-04482 SEBEC LAKE
04009-04009 BRIDGTON	04109-04109 PORTLAND	04350-04350 LITCHFIELD	04485-04485 SHIRLEY MILLS
04010-04010 BROWNFIELD	04110-04110 CUMBERLAND FORESIDE	04351-04351 MANCHESTER	04487-04487 SPRINGFIELD
04011-04011 BRUNSWICK	04112-04112 PORTLAND	04352-04352 MOUNT VERNON	04488-04488 STETSON
04013-04013 BUSTINS ISLAND	04116-04116 SOUTH PORTLAND	04353-04353 WHITEFIELD	04489-04489 STILLWATER
04014-04014 CAPE PORPOISE	04122-04124 PORTLAND	04354-04354 PALERMO	04490-04490 TOPSFIELD
04015-04015 CASCO	04210-04212 AUBURN	04355-04355 READFIELD	04491-04491 VANCEBORO
04016-04016 CENTER LOVELL	04216-04216 ANDOVER	04357-04357 RICHMOND	04492-04492 WAITE
04017-04017 CHEBEAGUE ISLAND	04217-04217 BETHEL	04358-04358 SOUTH CHINA	04493-04493 WEST ENFIELD
04019-04019 CLIFF ISLAND	04219-04219 BRYANT POND	04359-04359 SOUTH GARDINER	04495-04495 WINN
04020-04020 CORNISH	04220-04220 BUCKFIELD	04360-04360 VIENNA	04496-04496 WINTERPORT
04021-04021 CUMBERLAND CENTER	04221-04221 CANTON	04361-04361 WEEKS MILLS	04497-04497 WYTOPITLOCK
04022-04022 DENMARK	04222-04222 DURHAM	04362-04362 WHITEFIELD	04530-04530 BATH
04024-04024 EAST BALDWIN	04223-04223 DANVILLE	04363-04363 WINDSOR	04535-04535 ALNA
04027-04027 LEBANON	04224-04224 DIXFIELD	04364-04364 WINTHROP	04536-04536 BAYVILLE
04028-04028 EAST PARSONFIELD	04225-04225 DRYDEN	04401-04402 BANGOR	04537-04537 BOOTHBAY
04029-04029 SEBAGO	04226-04226 EAST ANDOVER	04406-04406 ABBOT VILLAGE	04538-04538 BOOTHBAY HARBOR
04030-04030 EAST WATERBORO	04227-04227 EAST DIXFIELD	04406-04406 ABBOT	04539-04539 BRISTOL
04032-04034 FREEPORT	04228-04228 EAST LIVERMORE	04408-04408 AURORA	04541-04541 CHAMBERLAIN
04037-04037 FRYEBURG	04230-04230 EAST POLAND	04410-04410 BRADFORD	04543-04543 DAMARISCOTTA
04038-04038 GORHAM	04231-04231 EAST STONEHAM	04411-04411 BRADLEY	04544-04544 EAST BOOTHBAY
04039-04039 GRAY	04231-04231 STONEHAM	04412-04412 BREWER	04547-04547 FRIENDSHIP
04040-04040 HARRISON	04233-04233 EAST WATERFORD	04413-04413 BROOKTON	04548-04548 GEORGETOWN
04041-04041 HIRAM	04234-04234 EAST WILTON	04414-04414 BROWNVILLE	04549-04549 ISLE OF SPRINGS
04042-04042 HOLLIS CENTER	04235-04235 FRYE	04415-04415 BROWNVILLE JUNCTION	04551-04551 BREMEN
04043-04043 KENNEBUNK	04236-04236 GREENE	04416-04416 BUCKSPORT	04552-04552 NEWAGEN
04046-04046 KENNEBUNKPORT	04237-04237 HANOVER	04417-04417 BURLINGTON	04553-04553 NEWCASTLE
04047-04047 PARSONSFIELD	04238-04238 HEBRON	04418-04418 CARDVILLE	04554-04554 NEW HARBOR
04048-04048 LIMERICK	04239-04239 JAY	04418-04418 GREENBUSH	04555-04555 NOBLEBORO
04049-04049 LIMINGTON	04240-04243 LEWISTON	04419-04419 CARMEL	04556-04556 EDGECOMB
04050-04050 LONG ISLAND	04250-04250 LISBON	04420-04421 CASTINE	04558-04558 PEMAQUID
04051-04051 LOVELL	04251-04251 LISBON CENTER	04422-04422 CHARLESTON	04562-04562 PHIPPSBURG
04053-04053 MEREPOINT	04252-04252 LISBON FALLS	04423-04423 COSTIGAN	04563-04563 CUSHING
04054-04054 MOODY	04253-04253 LIVERMORE	04424-04424 DANFORTH	04564-04564 ROUND POND
04055-04055 NAPLES	04254-04254 LIVERMORE FALLS	04426-04426 DOVER FOXCROFT	04565-04565 SEBASCO ESTATES
04056-04056 NEWFIELD	04255-04255 LOCKE MILLS	04427-04427 EAST CORINTH	04567-04567 SMALL POINT
04057-04057 NORTH BRIDGTON	04255-04255 GREENWOOD	04427-04427 CORINTH	04568-04568 SOUTH BRISTOL
04058-04058 NORTH FRYEBURG	04256-04256 MECHANIC FALLS	04428-04428 EDDINGTON	04570-04570 SQUIRREL ISLAND
04060-04060 NORTH SHAPLEIGH	04257-04257 MEXICO	04429-04429 HOLDEN	04571-04571 TREVETT
04061-04061 NORTH WATERBORO	04258-04258 MINOT	04430-04430 EAST MILLINOCKET	04572-04572 WALDOBORO
04062-04062 WINDHAM	04259-04259 MONMOUTH	04431-04431 EAST ORLAND	04573-04573 WALPOLE
04063-04063 OCEAN PARK	04260-04260 NEW GLOUCESTER	04433-04433 ENFIELD	04574-04574 WASHINGTON
04064-04064 OLD ORCHARD BEACH	04261-04261 NEWRY	04434-04434 ETNA	04575-04575 WEST BOOTHBAY HARBOR
04066-04066 ORRS ISLAND	04262-04262 NORTH JAY	04435-04435 EXETER	04576-04576 WEST SOUTHPORT
04067-04067 PEJEPSCOT	04263-04263 LEEDS	04438-04438 FRANKFORT	04576-04576 SOUTHPORT
04068-04068 PORTER	04265-04265 NORTH MONMOUTH	04441-04441 GREENVILLE	04578-04578 WISCASSET
04069-04069 POWNAL	04266-04266 NORTH TURNER	04442-04442 GREENVILLE JUNCTION	04579-04579 WOOLWICH
04070-04070 SCARBOROUGH	04267-04267 NORTH WATERFORD	04443-04443 GUILFORD	04605-04605 ELLSWORTH
04071-04071 RAYMOND	04268-04268 NORWAY	04444-04444 HAMPDEN	04606-04606 ADDISON
04072-04072 SACO	04270-04270 OXFORD	04446-04446 HAYNESVILLE	04607-04607 GOULDSBORO
04073-04073 SANFORD	04271-04271 PARIS	04448-04448 HOWLAND	04608-04608 ATLANTIC
04074-04074 SCARBOROUGH	04273-04274 POLAND	04449-04449 HUDSON	04609-04609 BAR HARBOR
04075-04075 SEBAGO LAKE	04275-04275 ROXBURY	04450-04450 KENDUSKEAG	04611-04611 BEALS
04076-04076 SHAPLEIGH	04276-04276 RUMFORD	04451-04451 KINGMAN	04612-04612 BERNARD
04077-04077 SOUTH CASCO	04278-04278 RUMFORD CENTER	04453-04453 LAGRANGE	04613-04613 BIRCH HARBOR
04078-04078 SOUTH FREEPORT	04279-04279 RUMFORD POINT	04454-04454 LAMBERT LAKE	04614-04614 BLUE HILL
04079-04079 HARPSWELL	04280-04280 SABATTUS	04455-04455 LEE	04615-04615 BLUE HILL FALLS
04080-04080 SOUTH HIRAM	04281-04281 SOUTH PARIS	04456-04456 LEVANT	04616-04616 BROOKLIN
04081-04081 SOUTH WATERFORD	04282-04282 TURNER	04457-04457 LINCOLN	04617-04617 BROOKSVILLE
04082-04082 SOUTH WINDHAM	04283-04283 TURNER CENTER	04458-04458 LINCOLN CENTER	04618-04618 BUCKS HARBOR
04083-04083 SPRINGVALE	04284-04284 WAYNE	04459-04459 MATTAWAMKEAG	04619-04619 CALAIS
04084-04084 STANDISH	04285-04285 WELD	04460-04460 MEDWAY	04622-04622 CHERRYFIELD

04623-04623	COLUMBIA FALLS
04624-04624	COREA
04625-04625	CRANBERRY ISLES
04626-04626	CUTLER
04627-04627	DEER ISLE
04628-04628	DENNYSVILLE
04629-04629	EAST BLUE HILL
04630-04630	EAST MACHIAS
04631-04631	EASTPORT
04634-04634	FRANKLIN
04635-04635	FRENCHBORO
04637-04637	GRAND LAKE STREAM
04638-04638	GROVE
04640-04640	HANCOCK
04642-04642	HARBORSIDE
04643-04643	HARRINGTON
04644-04644	HULLS COVE
04645-04645	ISLE AU HAUT
04646-04646	ISLESFORD
04648-04648	JONESBORO
04649-04649	JONESPORT
04650-04650	LITTLE DEER ISLE
04652-04652	LUBEC
04653-04653	BASS HARBOR
04654-04654	MACHIAS
04655-04655	MACHIASPORT
04656-04656	MANSET
04657-04657	MEDDYBEMPS
04658-04658	MILBRIDGE
04659-04659	MINTURN
04660-04660	MOUNT DESERT
04661-04661	NORTH BROOKLIN
04662-04662	NORTHEAST HARBOR
04664-04664	SULLIVAN
04665-04665	OTTER CREEK
04666-04666	PEMBROKE
04667-04667	PERRY
04668-04668	PRINCETON
04669-04669	PROSPECT HARBOR
04671-04671	ROBBINSTON
04672-04672	SALSBURY COVE
04673-04673	SARGENTVILLE
04674-04674	SEAL COVE
04675-04675	SEAL HARBOR
04676-04676	SEDGWICK
04677-04677	SORRENTO
04678-04678	SOUTH GOULDSBORO
04679-04679	SOUTHWEST HARBOR
04680-04680	STEUBEN
04681-04681	STONINGTON
04683-04683	SUNSET
04684-04684	SURRY
04685-04685	SWANS ISLAND
04686-04686	WESLEY
04690-04690	WEST TREMONT
04691-04691	WHITING
04692-04692	WHITNEYVILLE
04693-04693	WINTER HARBOR
04694-04694	WOODLAND
04694-04694	BAILEYVILLE
04730-04730	HOULTON
04732-04732	ASHLAND
04733-04733	BENEDICTA
04734-04734	BLAINE
04735-04735	BRIDGEWATER
04736-04736	CARIBOU
04737-04737	CLAYTON LAKE
04738-04738	CROUSEVILLE
04739-04739	EAGLE LAKE
04740-04740	EASTON
04741-04741	ESTCOURT STATION
04742-04742	FORT FAIRFIELD
04743-04743	FORT KENT
04744-04744	FORT KENT MILLS
04745-04745	FRENCHVILLE
04746-04746	GRAND ISLE
04747-04747	ISLAND FALLS
04749-04749	LILLE
04750-04751	LIMESTONE
04756-04756	MADAWASKA
04757-04757	MAPLETON
04758-04758	MARS HILL
04759-04759	MASARDIS
04760-04760	MONTICELLO
04761-04761	NEW LIMERICK
04762-04762	NEW SWEDEN
04763-04763	OAKFIELD
04764-04764	OXBOW
04765-04765	PATTEN
04766-04766	PERHAM
04767-04767	PLAISTED
04768-04768	PORTAGE
04769-04769	PRESQUE ISLE
04770-04770	QUIMBY
04772-04772	SAINT AGATHA
04773-04773	SAINT DAVID
04774-04774	SAINT FRANCIS
04775-04775	SHERIDAN
04776-04776	SHERMAN MILLS
04776-04776	SHERMAN
04777-04777	SHERMAN STATION
04777-04777	STACYVILLE
04779-04779	SINCLAIR
04780-04780	SMYRNA MILLS
04781-04781	SOLDIER POND
04781-04781	WALLAGRASS
04782-04782	STACYVILLE
04783-04783	STOCKHOLM
04784-04784	UPPER FRENCHVILLE
04785-04785	VAN BUREN
04786-04786	WASHBURN
04787-04787	WESTFIELD
04788-04788	WINTERVILLE
04841-04841	ROCKLAND
04843-04843	CAMDEN
04846-04846	GLEN COVE
04847-04847	HOPE
04848-04848	ISLESBORO
04849-04849	LINCOLNVILLE
04850-04850	LINCOLNVILLE CENTER
04851-04851	MATINICUS
04852-04852	MONHEGAN
04853-04853	NORTH HAVEN
04854-04854	OWLS HEAD
04855-04855	PORT CLYDE
04856-04856	ROCKPORT
04857-04857	SAINT GEORGE
04857-04857	WILEYS CORNER
04858-04858	SOUTH THOMASTON
04859-04859	SPRUCE HEAD
04860-04860	TENANTS HARBOR
04861-04861	THOMASTON
04862-04862	UNION
04863-04863	VINALHAVEN
04864-04864	WARREN
04865-04865	WEST ROCKPORT
04901-04903	WATERVILLE
04910-04910	ALBION
04911-04911	ANSON
04912-04912	ATHENS
04915-04915	BELFAST
04917-04917	BELGRADE
04918-04918	BELGRADE LAKES
04920-04920	BINGHAM
04921-04921	BROOKS
04922-04922	BURNHAM
04923-04923	CAMBRIDGE
04924-04924	CANAAN
04925-04925	CARATUNK
04926-04926	CHINA
04926-04926	CHINA VILLAGE
04927-04927	CLINTON
04928-04928	CORINNA
04929-04929	DETROIT
04930-04930	DEXTER
04932-04932	DIXMONT
04933-04933	EAST NEWPORT
04935-04935	EAST VASSALBORO
04936-04936	EUSTIS
04937-04937	FAIRFIELD
04938-04938	FARMINGTON
04939-04939	GARLAND
04940-04940	FARMINGTON FALLS
04941-04941	FREEDOM
04942-04942	HARMONY
04943-04943	HARTLAND
04944-04944	HINCKLEY
04945-04945	JACKMAN
04947-04947	KINGFIELD
04949-04949	LIBERTY
04950-04950	MADISON
04951-04951	MONROE
04952-04952	MORRILL
04953-04953	NEWPORT
04954-04954	NEW PORTLAND
04955-04955	NEW SHARON
04956-04956	NEW VINEYARD
04957-04957	NORRIDGEWOCK
04958-04958	NORTH ANSON
04961-04961	NORTH NEW PORTLAND
04961-04961	NEW PORTLAND
04962-04962	NORTH VASSALBORO
04963-04963	OAKLAND
04964-04964	OQUOSSOC
04965-04965	PALMYRA
04966-04966	PHILLIPS
04967-04967	PITTSFIELD
04969-04969	PLYMOUTH
04970-04970	RANGELEY
04971-04971	SAINT ALBANS
04972-04972	SANDY POINT
04973-04973	SEARSMONT
04974-04974	SEARSPORT
04975-04975	SHAWMUT
04976-04976	SKOWHEGAN
04978-04978	SMITHFIELD
04979-04979	SOLON
04981-04981	STOCKTON SPRINGS
04982-04982	STRATTON
04983-04983	STRONG
04984-04984	TEMPLE
04985-04985	WEST FORKS
04986-04986	THORNDIKE
04987-04987	TROY
04988-04988	UNITY
04989-04989	VASSALBORO
04992-04992	WEST FARMINGTON

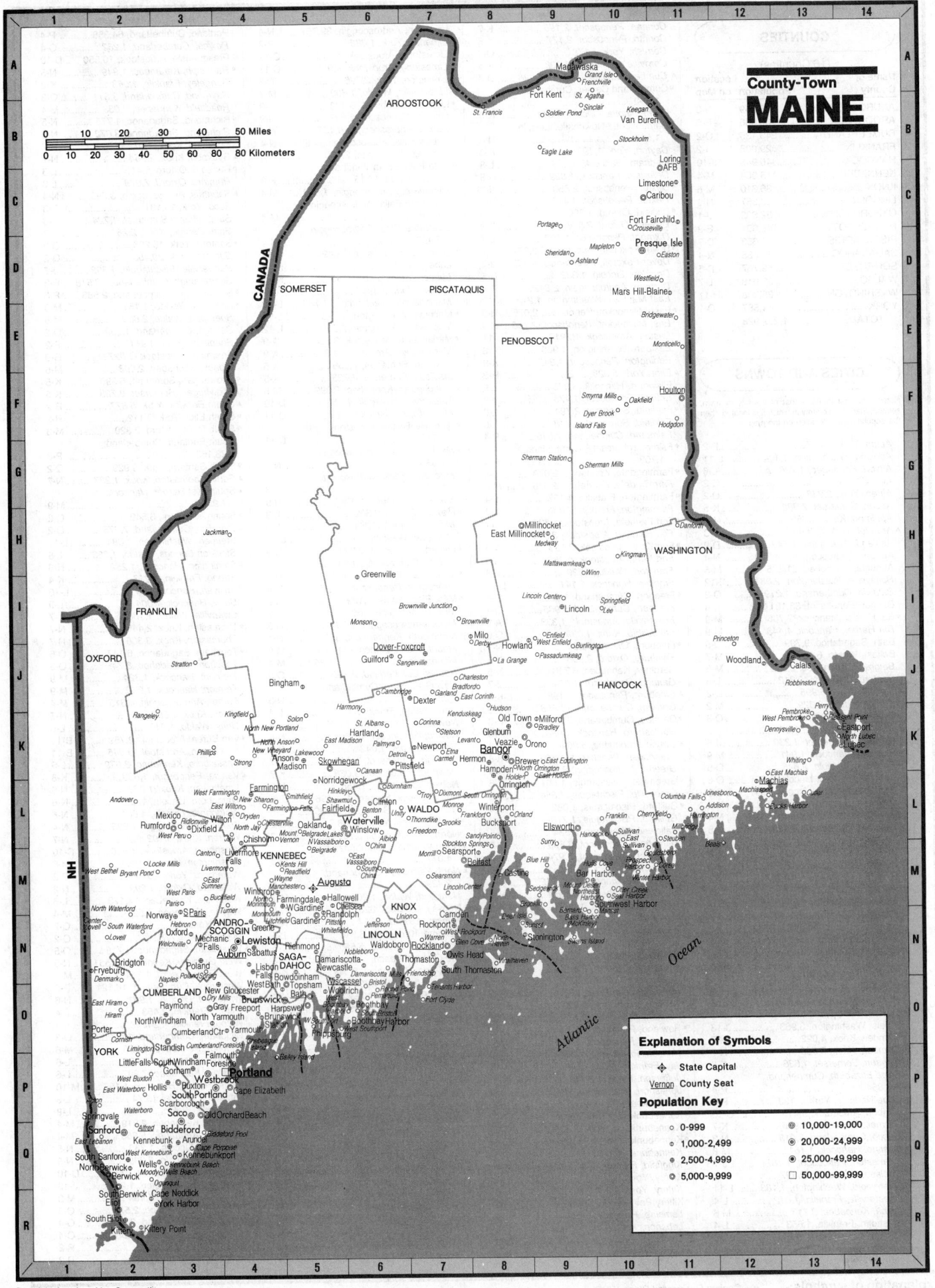

County-Town
MAINE

Explanation of Symbols

✪ State Capital
Vernon County Seat

Population Key

○ 0-999	⊛ 10,000-19,000
◉ 1,000-2,499	⊕ 20,000-24,999
⊕ 2,500-4,999	◉ 25,000-49,999
◉ 5,000-9,999	☐ 50,000-99,999

COUNTIES

(16 Counties)

Name of County	Population	Location on Map
ANDROSCOGGIN	105,259	N-3
AROOSTOOK	86,936	B-6
CUMBERLAND	243,135	O-2
FRANKLIN	29,008	I-2
HANCOCK	46,948	J-10
KENNEBEC	115,904	M-4
KNOX	36,310	M-6
LINCOLN	30,357	N-6
OXFORD	52,602	J-1
PENOBSCOT	146,601	E-8
PISCATAQUIS	18,653	D-7
SAGADAHOC	33,535	N-4
SOMERSET	49,767	D-5
WALDO	33,018	L-7
WASHINGTON	35,308	H-11
YORK	164,587	O-1
TOTAL	1,227,928	

CITIES AND TOWNS

Note: The first name is that of the city or town, second, that of the county in which it is located, then the population and location on the map.

Acton, York, 1,727	P-2
Addison, Washington, 1,114	L-11
Albion, Kennebec, 1,736	L-6
Alfred, York	Q-2
Alfred, York, 2,238	Q-2
Anson, Somerset, 2,382	K-5
Appleton, Knox, 1,069	M-7
▲ *Arundel, York, 2,669*	Q-3
Ashland, Aroostook, 1,542	D-9
Auburn, Androscoggin, 24,309	N-4
Augusta, Kennebec, 21,325	M-5
Baileyville, Washington, 2,031	J-12
Baldwin, Cumberland, 1,219	O-2
Bangor, Penobscot, 33,181	K-8
• Bar Harbor, Hancock, 2,768	M-9
Bar Harbor, Hancock, 4,443	M-9
Bath, Sagadahoc, 9,799	O-5
Belfast, Waldo, 6,355	M-7
Belgrade, Kennebec, 2,375	M-5
Benton, Kennebec, 2,312	L-6
▲ *Berwick, York, 5,995*	Q-2
Bethel, Oxford, 2,329	M-2
Biddeford, York, 20,710	Q-3
• Bingham, Somerset, 1,071	J-5
Bingham, Somerset, 1,230	J-5
Blue Hill, Hancock, 1,941	M-9
▲ *Boothbay, Lincoln, 2,648*	O-6
• Boothbay Harbor, Lincoln, 1,267	O-6
Boothbay Harbor, Lincoln, 2,347	O-6
Bowdoin, Sagadahoc, 2,207	N-4
Bowdoinham, Sagadahoc, 2,192	N-4
Bradford, Penobscot, 1,103	J-8
Bradley, Penobscot, 1,136	K-9
Brewer, Penobscot, 9,021	K-8
• Bridgton, Cumberland, 2,195	N-2
Bridgton, Cumberland, 4,307	N-2
Bristol, Lincoln, 2,326	O-6
Brownfield, Oxford, 1,034	O-1
Brownville, Piscataquis, 1,506	I-7
• Brunswick, Cumberland, 14,683	O-5
Brunswick, Cumberland, 20,906	O-5
• Brunswick Station, Cumberland, 1,829	O-5
Buckfield, Oxford, 1,566	M-3
• Bucksport, Hancock, 2,989	L-8
Bucksport, Hancock, 4,825	L-8
▲ *Buxton, York, 6,494*	P-3
Calais, Washington, 3,963	J-13
• Camden, Knox, 4,022	N-7
Camden, Knox, 5,060	N-7
Canaan, Somerset, 1,636	K-6
▲ *Cape Elizabeth, Cumberland, 8,854*	P-4
• Cape Neddick, York, 2,193	R-2
Caribou, Aroostook, 9,415	C-10
Carmel, Penobscot, 1,906	K-7
Casco, Cumberland, 3,018	N-3
▲ *Castine, Hancock, 1,161*	M-8
Charleston, Penobscot, 1,187	J-7
▲ *Chelsea, Kennebec, 2,497*	M-5
Cherryfield, Washington, 1,183	L-11
Chesterville, Franklin, 1,012	L-4
China, Kennebec, 3,713	M-6
• Chisholm, Franklin, 1,653	L-4
• Clinton, Kennebec, 1,485	L-6
Clinton, Kennebec, 3,332	L-6
Corinna, Penobscot, 2,196	K-7
Corinth, Penobscot, 2,177	K-8
Cornish, York, 1,178	O-2
Cornville, Somerset, 1,008	K-5
Cumberland, Cumberland, 5,836	O-3
• Cumberland Center, Cumberland, 1,890	O-4
Damariscotta, Lincoln, 1,811	N-6
• Damariscotta-Newcastle, Lincoln, 1,567	N-6
Dayton, York, 1,197	P-3
Dedham, Hancock, 1,229	L-8
Deer Isle, Hancock, 1,829	N-8
• Dexter, Penobscot, 2,650	J-7
Dexter, Penobscot, 4,419	J-7
• Dixfield, Oxford, 1,300	L-3
Dixfield, Oxford, 2,574	L-3
Dixmont, Penobscot, 1,007	L-7
• Dover-Foxcroft, Piscataquis, 3,077	J-7
Dover-Foxcroft, Piscataquis, 4,657	J-7
Dresden, Lincoln, 1,332	N-5
Durham, Androscoggin, 2,842	O-4
East Machias, Washington, 1,218	K-12
• East Millinocket, Penobscot, 2,075	H-9
East Millinocket, Penobscot, 2,166	H-9
Easton, Aroostook, 1,291	D-11
Eastport, Washington, 1,965	K-13
Eddington, Penobscot, 1,947	K-9
▲ *Eliot, York, 5,329*	R-2
Ellsworth, Hancock, 5,975	L-9
Enfield, Penobscot, 1,476	I-9
• Fairfield, Somerset, 2,794	L-6
Fairfield, Somerset, 6,718	L-6
Falmouth, Cumberland, 7,610	P-4
• Falmouth Foreside, Cumberland, 1,708	P-4
• Farmingdale, Kennebec, 2,070	M-5
Farmingdale, Kennebec, 2,918	M-5
• Farmington, Franklin, 4,197	L-4
Farmington, Franklin, 7,436	L-4
• Fort Fairfield, Aroostook, 1,729	C-11
Fort Fairfield, Aroostook, 3,998	C-11
• Fort Kent, Aroostook, 2,123	A-9
Fort Kent, Aroostook, 4,268	A-9
Frankfort, Waldo, 1,020	L-8
Franklin, Hancock, 1,141	L-10
• Freeport, Cumberland, 1,829	O-4
Freeport, Cumberland, 6,905	O-4
Frenchville, Aroostook, 1,338	A-9
Friendship, Knox, 1,099	O-6
• Fryeburg, Oxford, 1,580	N-1
Fryeburg, Oxford, 2,968	N-1
Gardiner, Kennebec, 6,746	N-5
Garland, Penobscot, 1,064	J-7
▲ *Glenburn, Penobscot, 3,198*	K-8
Gorham, Cumberland, 11,856	P-3
• Gorham, Cumberland, 3,618	P-3
Gouldsboro, Hancock, 1,986	M-10
▲ *Gray, Cumberland, 5,904*	O-3
Greenbush, Penobscot, 1,309	J-8
▲ *Greene, Androscoggin, 3,661*	N-4
• Greenville, Piscataquis, 1,601	I-6
Greenville, Piscataquis, 1,884	I-6
• Guilford, Piscataquis, 1,082	J-6
Guilford, Piscataquis, 1,710	J-6
Hallowell, Kennebec, 2,534	M-5
• Hampden, Penobscot, 3,895	L-8
Hampden, Penobscot, 5,974	L-8
Hancock, Hancock, 1,757	L-10
▲ *Harpswell, Cumberland, 5,012*	O-4
Harrison, Cumberland, 1,951	N-2
• Hartland, Somerset, 1,038	K-6
Hartland, Somerset, 1,806	K-6
▲ *Hermon, Penobscot, 3,755*	K-8
Hiram, Oxford, 1,260	O-2
Hodgdon, Aroostook, 1,257	F-11
Holden, Penobscot, 2,952	L-8
▲ *Hollis, York, 3,573*	P-2
Hope, Knox, 1,017	M-7
• Houlton, Aroostook, 5,627	F-11
Houlton, Aroostook, 6,613	F-11
• Howland, Penobscot, 1,304	J-8
Howland, Penobscot, 1,435	J-8
Hudson, Penobscot, 1,048	J-8
Jay, Franklin, 5,080	L-4
Jefferson, Lincoln, 2,111	N-6
Jonesport, Washington, 1,525	L-12
Kenduskeag, Penobscot, 1,234	K-8
• Kennebunkport, York, 1,100	Q-3
Kennebunkport, York, 3,356	Q-3
• Kennebunk, York, 4,206	Q-3
Kennebunk, York, 8,004	Q-3
Kingfield, Franklin, 1,114	K-4
• Kittery, York, 5,151	R-2
Kittery, York, 9,372	R-2
• Kittery Point, York, 1,093	R-2
Lamoine, Hancock, 1,311	L-10
Lebanon, York, 4,263	Q-2
Leeds, Androscoggin, 1,669	M-4
Levant, Penobscot, 1,627	K-8
Lewiston, Androscoggin, 39,757	N-4
Limerick, York, 1,688	P-2
• Limestone, Aroostook, 1,245	C-11
Limestone, Aroostook, 9,922	C-11
Limington, York, 2,796	P-2
Lincolnville, Waldo, 1,809	M-7
• Lincoln, Penobscot, 3,399	I-9
Lincoln, Penobscot, 5,587	I-9
Lisbon, Androscoggin, 9,457	N-4
• Lisbon Falls, Androscoggin, 4,674	N-4
Litchfield, Kennebec, 2,650	N-5
• Little Falls-South Windham, Cumberland, 1,715	P-3
Livermore, Androscoggin, 1,950	M-4
• Livermore Falls, Androscoggin, 1,935	M-4
Livermore Falls, Androscoggin, 3,455	M-4
• Loring AFB, Aroostook, 5,494	C-11
Lubec, Washington	K-13
Lubec, Washington, 1,853	K-13
Lyman, York, 3,390	Q-2
Machiasport, Washington, 1,166	L-12
• Machias, Washington, 1,773	L-12
Machias, Washington, 2,569	L-12
• Madawaska, Aroostook, 3,653	A-9
Madawaska, Aroostook, 4,803	A-9
• Madison, Somerset, 2,956	K-5
Madison, Somerset, 4,725	K-5
Manchester, Kennebec, 2,099	M-5
Mapleton, Aroostook, 1,853	D-10
Mars Hill, Aroostook, 1,760	D-11
• Mars Hill-Blaine, Aroostook, 1,717	D-11
• Mechanic Falls, Androscoggin, 2,388	N-3
Mechanic Falls, Androscoggin, 2,919	N-3
Medway, Penobscot, 1,922	H-9
• Mexico, Oxford, 2,302	L-3
Mexico, Oxford, 3,344	L-3
Milbridge, Washington, 1,305	L-11
• Milford, Penobscot, 2,228	K-9
Milford, Penobscot, 2,884	K-9
• Millinocket, Penobscot, 6,922	H-8
Millinocket, Penobscot, 6,956	H-8
• Milo, Piscataquis, 2,129	I-8
Milo, Piscataquis, 2,600	I-8
Minot, Androscoggin, 1,664	N-3
Monmouth, Kennebec, 3,353	N-4
Mount Desert, Hancock, 1,899	M-9
Mount Vernon, Kennebec, 1,362	M-4
Naples, Cumberland, 2,860	O-2
New Gloucester, Cumberland, 3,916	N-3
New Sharon, Franklin, 1,175	L-4
Newburgh, Penobscot, 1,317	L-7
Newcastle, Lincoln, 1,538	N-6
Newfield, York, 1,042	P-2
• Newport, Penobscot, 1,843	K-7
Newport, Penobscot, 3,036	K-7
Nobleboro, Lincoln, 1,455	N-6
• Norridgewock, Somerset, 1,496	L-5
Norridgewock, Somerset, 3,105	L-5
• North Berwick, York, 1,568	Q-2
North Berwick, York, 3,793	Q-2
• North Windham, Cumberland, 4,077	O-3
▲ *North Yarmouth, Cumberland, 2,429*	O-3
Northport, Waldo, 1,201	M-7
• Norway, Oxford, 3,023	N-3
Norway, Oxford, 4,754	N-3
• Oakland, Kennebec, 3,510	L-5
Oakland, Kennebec, 5,595	L-5
• *Old Orchard Beach, York, 7,789*	P-3
Old Town, Penobscot, 8,317	K-8
Orland, Hancock, 1,805	L-8
Orono, Penobscot, 10,573	K-8
• Orono, Penobscot, 9,789	K-8
▲ *Orrington, Penobscot, 3,309*	L-8
Otisfield, Oxford, 1,136	N-3
▲ *Owls Head, Knox, 1,574*	N-7
• Oxford, Oxford, 1,284	N-3
Oxford, Oxford, 3,705	N-3
Palermo, Waldo, 1,021	M-6
Palmyra, Somerset, 1,867	K-6
Paris, Oxford, 4,492	M-3
Parsonsfield, York, 1,472	P-2
Patten, Penobscot, 1,256	G-9
Penobscot, Hancock, 1,131	M-8
Peru, Oxford, 1,541	L-3
Phillips, Franklin, 1,148	K-3
Phippsburg, Sagadahoc, 1,815	O-5
• Pittsfield, Somerset, 3,222	K-6
Pittsfield, Somerset, 4,190	K-6
Pittston, Kennebec, 2,444	N-5
Plymouth, Penobscot, 1,152	K-7
▲ *Poland, Androscoggin, 4,342*	N-3
Porter, Oxford, 1,301	O-2
Portland, Cumberland, 64,358	P-4
Pownal, Cumberland, 1,262	O-4
Presque Isle, Aroostook, 10,550	D-10
• *Randolph, Kennebec, 1,949*	N-5
Rangeley, Franklin, 1,063	K-2
Raymond, Cumberland, 3,311	O-3
Readfield, Kennebec, 2,033	M-4
• Richmond, Sagadahoc, 1,775	N-5
Richmond, Sagadahoc, 3,072	N-5
Rockland, Knox, 7,972	N-7
▲ *Rockport, Knox, 2,854*	N-7
• Rumford, Oxford, 5,419	L-3
Rumford, Oxford, 7,078	L-3
▲ *Sabattus, Androscoggin, 3,696*	N-4
Saco, York, 15,181	P-3
Saint Albans, Somerset, 1,724	K-6
Saint George, Knox, 2,261	O-7
• Sanford, York, 10,296	Q-2
Sanford, York, 20,463	Q-2
Sangerville, Piscataquis, 1,398	J-7
Scarborough, Cumberland, 12,518	P-3
• Scarborough, Cumberland, 2,586	P-3
• Searsport, Waldo, 1,151	M-8
Searsport, Waldo, 2,603	M-8
Sebago, Cumberland, 1,259	O-2
Shapleigh, York, 1,911	P-2
Sherman, Aroostook, 1,027	G-9
Sidney, Kennebec, 2,593	M-5
• Skowhegan, Somerset, 6,990	K-5
Skowhegan, Somerset, 8,725	K-5
▲ *South Berwick, York, 5,877*	R-2
• South Eliot, York, 3,112	R-2
• South Paris, Oxford, 2,320	M-3
South Portland, Cumberland, 23,163	P-3
• South Sanford, York, 3,929	Q-2
▲ *South Thomaston, Knox, 1,227*	N-7
▲ *Southwest Harbor, Hancock, 1,952*	M-9
• Springvale, York, 3,542	Q-2
▲ *Standish, Cumberland, 7,678*	O-2
Steuben, Washington, 1,084	L-11
Stockton Springs, Waldo, 1,383	L-8
▲ *Stonington, Hancock, 1,252*	N-8
Strong, Franklin, 1,217	K-4
Sullivan, Hancock, 1,118	L-10
Surry, Hancock, 1,004	L-9
Swanville, Waldo, 1,130	L-7
• Thomaston, Knox, 2,445	N-7
Thomaston, Knox, 3,306	N-7
• Topsham, Sagadahoc, 6,147	O-5
Topsham, Sagadahoc, 8,746	O-5
Tremont, Hancock, 1,324	M-9
Trenton, Hancock, 1,060	M-9
Turner, Androscoggin, 4,315	M-4
Union, Knox, 1,989	N-7
Unity, Waldo, 1,817	L-6
• Van Buren, Aroostook, 2,759	B-11
Van Buren, Aroostook, 3,045	B-11
Vassalboro, Kennebec, 3,679	L-6
▲ *Veazie, Penobscot, 1,633*	K-8
Vinalhaven, Knox, 1,072	N-8
• Waldoboro, Lincoln, 1,420	N-6
Waldoboro, Lincoln, 4,601	N-6
Wales, Androscoggin, 1,223	N-4
Warren, Knox, 3,192	N-7
Washburn, Aroostook, 1,880	C-10
Washington, Knox, 1,185	M-6
Waterboro, York, 4,510	P-2
Waterford, Oxford, 1,299	N-2
Waterville, Kennebec, 17,173	L-6
Wayne, Kennebec, 1,029	M-4
Wells, York	Q-2
Wells, York, 7,778	Q-2
▲ *West Bath, Sagadahoc, 1,716*	O-5
▲ *West Gardiner, Kennebec, 2,531*	N-5
West Paris, Oxford, 1,514	M-3
Westbrook, Cumberland, 16,121	P-3
Whitefield, Lincoln, 1,931	N-6
• Wilton, Franklin, 2,453	L-4
Wilton, Franklin, 4,242	L-4
Windham, Cumberland, 13,020	O-3
Windsor, Kennebec, 1,895	M-6
• Winslow, Kennebec, 5,436	L-6
Winslow, Kennebec, 7,997	L-6
Winter Harbor, Hancock, 1,157	M-10
• Winterport, Waldo, 1,274	L-8
Winterport, Waldo, 3,175	L-8
• Winthrop, Kennebec, 2,819	M-4
Winthrop, Kennebec, 5,968	M-4
• Wiscasset, Lincoln, 1,233	N-5
Wiscasset, Lincoln, 3,339	N-5
Woodland, Aroostook, 1,402	D-10
• Woodland, Washington, 1,287	J-12
Woodstock, Oxford, 1,194	M-3
Woolwich, Sagadahoc, 2,570	O-5
• Yarmouth, Cumberland, 3,338	O-4
Yarmouth, Cumberland, 7,862	O-4
York, York, 9,818	R-2
• York Harbor, York, 2,555	R-2

Explanation of symbols:

• – Census Designated Place (CDP)

▲ *italics* – Townships (shown on the map)

• *italics* – Township shown which is also a CDP

italics – Townships (not shown on the map)

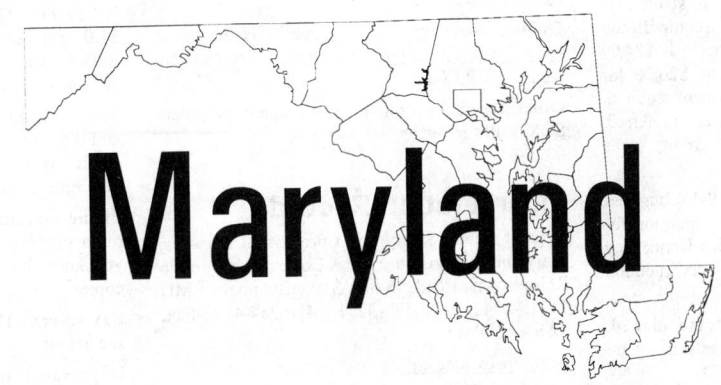

Maryland

General Help Numbers:

Governor's Office

State House, 100 State Circle
Annapolis, MD 21401
www.gov.state.md.us

410-974-3901
Fax 410-974-3275
9AM-5PM

Attorney General's Office

200 St Paul Place
Baltimore, MD 21202
www.oag.state.md.us

410-576-6300
Fax 410-576-6404
8AM-5PM

Legislative Records

Legislative Information Desk, Library & Information Srv
90 State Circle, Basement Level
Annapolis, MD 21401-1991
http://mlis.state.md.us

410-946-5400
Fax 410-946-5405
8AM-5PM

State Archives

Hall of Records
350 Rowe Blvd
Annapolis, MD 21401
www.mdarchives.state.md.us

410-260-6400
Fax 410-974-2525
8AM-4:30PM TU-FR;
8:30-4:30 SA

State Specifics:

Capital:	Annapolis
	Anne Arundel County
Time Zone:	EST
Number of Counties:	23
Population:	5,558,058
Web Site:	www.maryland.gov

State Agencies

Criminal Records

Criminal Justice Information System, Public Safety & Correctional Records, PO Box 32708, Pikeville, MD 21282-5743 (Courier address: 6776 Reisterstown Rd, Rm 102, Baltimore, MD 21215); 410-764-4501, 888-795-0011 , 410-653-6320-Fax; 8AM-5PM.

www.dpscs.state.md.us

Records are available from 1978. It takes 10 days if not submitted electronically. before new records are available for inquiry. Records are indexed on in-house computer. Records are normally destroyed after person reaches age 100. Approximately 80% of all arrests in database have final dispositions recorded.

Searching: Release of criminal records is restricted. All private parties must first write/fax/phone this office and request a "petition package," then apply for a petition number. Employers are eligible to request a petition number; 3rd parties may not, directly. Include the following in your request-set of fingerprints. A signed release is not necessary but is helpful. When applying for fingerprinting, a photo ID is required. 100% of records are fingerprint-supported. All searches require fingerprints and all require an authorization number including government. Investigators and all 3rd parties are considered as agents of employers and must use employer's authorization. All records are released to law enforcement; public receives records with conviction data only. Records with dispositions of acquittal are not released to private entities.

Access by: mail, in person.

Fee & Payment: The fee is $18.00 per request, add $1.00 for a "gold seal." If a statutorily-required FBI fingerprint check is required, add $24.00. Total fee, including FBI check, is $24.00 with a child care waiver stamp, or $26.00 for volunteers. Fee payee: CJIS. Prepayment required. Money orders and cashier's checks are preferred. Personal checks accepted. No credit cards accepted.

Mail search: Turnaround time: 10-15 business days. You may mail a request for a petition for authorization to the Customer Service Dept.; they can mail or fax you the necessary petition information.

In person search: In person requests are allowed, though signed release and fingerprints are required, and turnaround time is 5 days.

Other access: The State Court Administrator's Office has online access to criminal records from all state district courts, 3 circuit courts, and 1 city court. See that profile for more information.

Expedited service: Will rush expedite your request for no add'l charge, however a written request including a legitimate reason why must be submitted. An FBI check cannot be expedited. Will expedite the return if you provide a prepaid shipper envelope.

Statewide Court Records

Administrative Office of the Courts, 580 Taylor Ave, Annapolis, MD 21401; 410-260-1400, 8AM-5PM.

www.courts.state.md.us

For legal reference assistance email mdlaw.library@courts.state.md.us.

Access by: online.

Online search: Appellate opinions are available from www.courts.state.md.us/opinions.html. At www.courts.state.md.us/dialup.html, the Judicial Information System (JIS) or (SJIS) provides dial-up access to civil and criminal case information from certain courts. All District Courts provide civil and misdemeanors. All Circuit Courts provide civil records and three Circuit Courts (Anne Arundel, Carroll, and Baltimore City Court) provide criminal records on JIS. Fees are involved. All case information may be searched by party name or case number. For a registration packet, call 410-260-1031 or visit the website.

Sexual Offender Registry

Criminal Justice Information System, PO Box 5743, SOR Unit, Pikeville, MD 21282-5743 (Courier address: 6776 Reistertown Rd, Baltimore, MD); 410-585-3649, 866-368-8657 , 410-653-5690-Fax; 7:30AM-5:00PM.

www.dpscs.state.md.us/onlineservs/sor

Access to the Sexual Offender Registry can be requested by email at sor@dpscs.state.md.us.

Records are available from 10/01/95. It takes a week if not submitted electronically. before new records are available for inquiry. Records are indexed on in-house computer (90+%).

Searching: Copies of registration statements will include the registrant's photograph but will not include fingerprints, SSN, or the victim's date of birth.

Access by: mail, online.

Mail search: Turnaround time: 1 to 2 weeks. Include requester's full name, address, and reason for the request.

Online search: Online access is free at www.dpscs.state.md.us/sorSearch/. Search by name or ZIP Code.

Other access: A printout is available of complete SOR. Call for details.

Incarceration Records

Dept of Public Safety and Correctional Services, Maryland Division of Corrections, 6776 Reistertown Road, Suite 310, Baltimore, MD 21215-2342; 410-585-3351, 410-764-4182-Fax; 8AM-4:30PM.

www.dpscs.state.md.us

For an inmate's DOC # and location contact Data Processing via methods below or email to cwood@dpscs.state.md.us. To obtain any other information than DOC number you must contact individual institutions.

Records are available on current and former inmates. It takes 1 to 2 days before new records are available for inquiry.

Searching: Only location and DOC number are released from this agency. Include the following in your request-inmates race, sex, full name, DOB and the SSN if known. Records computerized since 1980. The following data is not released: medical and certain personal information

Access by: mail, phone, fax, online.

Fee & Payment: No fee for search.

Mail search: Turnaround time: 1-3 days.

Phone search: Name searching available by phone.

Fax search: Can request via the fax.

Online search: Search inmates online at http://www1.dpscs.state.md.us/inmate/. The Locator may not list some short sentenced inmates who, although committed to the Commissioner of Correction, are in fact housed at Division of Pretrial and Detention Services facilities. Also, a private company offers free web access at www.vinelink.com/index.jsp, including state, DOC, and a few county jails.

Corporation, Limited Partnerships, Trade Names, Limited Liability Company, Fictitious Name, Limited Liability Partnerships

Department of Assessments and Taxation, Corporations Division, 301 W Preston St, Room 801, Baltimore, MD 21201; 410-767-1340, 410-767-1330 (Charter Information), 410-333-7097-Fax; 8AM-4:30PM.

www.dat.state.md.us

Records are available from 1908 on. New records are available for inquiry immediately. Records are indexed on inhouse computer.

Searching: Officers and directors info is not immediately available. Include the following in your request-full name of business, corporation file number. The following is available; the Articles of Incorporation, Annual Reports, Officers, Directors, DBA's, Prior (merged) names, Inactive and Reserved names.

Access by: mail, phone, fax, in person, online.

Fee & Payment: An abstract of corporate records is $20.00, a Good Standing is $20.00. Copies are $1.00 per page plus $20.00 to certify. Fee payee: SDAT. Prepayment required. Personal checks accepted. Credit cards accepted: MasterCard, Visa.

Mail search: Turnaround time: 7 days. Officer and director information takes 2 weeks. Expedited service will improve turnaround time for mail or fax requests. No SASE is required.

Phone search: Charter information includes date of incorporation, agent, and status. They will let you know how many pages if you wish to order copies.

Fax search: This is considered expedited service, see below.

In person search: The office closes at 5 PM for searchers. Public access terminals are available.

Online search: Search for corporate name and trade name records for free at the main website (see above); also includes real estate statewide (cannot search by name) and UCC records. A Certificate of Good Standing is available online at http://sdatcert1.resiusa.org/certificate/.

Other access: This agency will release information in a bulk output format. Contact 410-561-9600 for details.

Expedited service: Expedited service is available for mail, phone and fax searches. Turnaround time: 3 days. There is an additional $20.00 fee to expedite a copy or expedite a certificate. A credit card must be used if requesting by fax.

Trademarks/Servicemarks

Secretary of State, Trademarks Division, State House, Annapolis, MD 21401; 410-974-5521, 410-974-5527-Fax; 9AM-5PM.

www.marylandsos.gov

Records are available for the past 10 years. New records are available for inquiry immediately. Records are indexed on inhouse computer.

Searching: Include the following in your request-trademark/servicemark name.

Access by: mail, phone, fax, in person, online.

Fee & Payment: There is no search fee. Certification is $5.00, copies are $.30 per page. Fee payee: Secretary of State. Prepayment required. Personal checks accepted. No credit cards accepted.

Mail search: Turnaround time: 1 week. No fee for mail request.

Phone search: No fee for telephone request. Only limited information is available.

Fax search: Will return information by mail in 1 week.

In person search: No fee for request. Call before visiting.

Online search: Online searching is available at the Internet site. Search can be by keyword in the description field, the service or product, the owner, the classification, or the mark name or keyword in the mark name. The site offers application forms to register, renew, or assign trade and service marks, and general information about registration. Click on "Trade & Service Marks."

Other access: A computer printout of all marks registered, renewed or assigned within a 3 month period is available for $.05 per trademark.

Uniform Commercial Code

UCC Division-Taxpayer's Services, Department of Assessments & Taxation, 301 West Preston St, Baltimore, MD 21201; 410-767-1340, 410-333-7097-Fax; 8:30AM-5PM.

http://sdatcert3.resiusa.org/ucc-charter

This agency will not do a general name or entity search. A searcher must come in person, hire a retriever, use the Internet, or buy the database.

Records are available for all active files.

Searching: Tax liens are not filed here, but are filed with the clerk of the circuit court of the debtor's jurisdiction. For help, email charterhelp@dat.state.md.us.

Access by: mail, in person, online.

Fee & Payment: There is no search fee. The copy fee is $1.00 per page. Fee payee: Department of Assessments & Taxation Prepayment required. Personal checks accepted. No credit cards accepted.

Mail search: Will not do name searching, but will make copies if exact number of pages paid in advance.

In person search: Records can be viewed at no charge on public access terminals.

Online search: The Internet site above offers free access to UCC index information. Also, there is a related site offering access to real property data for the whole state at www.dat.state.md.us/.

Other access: The agency has available for sale copies of public release master data files including corporation, real estate, and UCC. In addition, they can produce customized files on paper or disk. Visit the website for more information.

Federal and State Tax Liens

Records not maintained by a state level agency.

All tax liens are filed at the county level.

Sales Tax Registrations

Taxpayer Services, Revenue Administration Division, 301 W Preston St #206, Baltimore, MD 21201; 410-767-1313, 410-767-1300 , 410-767-1571-Fax; 8AM-5PM.

www.comp.state.md.us

Email questions to sut@comp.state.md.us.

Records are available on a computer index for the past 4 years of applicants. It takes 7 days before new records are available for inquiry.

Searching: This agency will only confirm that a business's number is valid and confirm the name and address of the business. They will provide no other information. The business name and federal ID# or SSN of owner is required to search.

Access by: mail, phone, fax, online.

Fee & Payment: There are no fees.

Mail search: Turnaround time: 7 working days. Records are not returned by mail, they will call you. No SASE is required.

Phone search: Call only if you have the permit number.

Fax search: Records are available by fax.

Online search: Using the web, one can determine if a MD sales tax account number is valid.

Birth Certificates

Department of Health, Division of Vital Records, PO Box 68760, Baltimore, MD 21215-0020 (Courier address: 6550 Reisterstown Plaza, Baltimore, MD 21215); 410-764-3038, 410-764-3170 (Order), 410-318-6119 (Recording), 410-358-7381-Fax; 8AM-4PM M-F; 3rd Saturday of each month.

www.dhmh.state.md.us

Records are available from 1898 to present for all counties and 1910 to present for City of Baltimore. For prior records, contact the State Archives or city of Baltimore. It takes 6-8 weeks before new records are available for inquiry. Records are indexed on index cards. Records are maintained indefinitely.

Searching: Must have a notarized signed release from person of record or mother or father, unless requester is parent or guardian or person listed. Include the following in your request-full name, names of parents, mother's maiden name, date of birth, place of birth, relationship to person of record.

Access by: mail, phone, fax, in person, online.

Fee & Payment: The search fee is $12.00. Only fax, phone and expedited requesters may use a credit card and there is an additional $7.00 fee. Fee payee: Division of Vital Records. Prepayment required. Cash is accepted for walk in requesters only. Personal checks accepted. Major credit cards accepted.

Mail search: Turnaround time: 2 to 3 weeks. A SASE is requested.

Phone search: Credit card prepayment required. Turnaround time is 3 to 5 days.

Fax search: See expedited service.

In person search: Turnaround time is same day (typically, 15 to 30 minutes). Walk in requesters may pay with cash or check; no credit cards. Presentation of original photo ID is required for walk in requesters.

Online search: Records may be ordered over the web at www.vitalchek.com. Use of credit card is required.

Expedited service: Expedited service is available with FedEx return of online, phone and fax searches. Turnaround time: 2 days. Add $13.50 per package plus charge for use of credit card.

Death Records

Department of Health, Division of Vital Records, PO Box 68760, Baltimore, MD 21215-0020 (Courier address: 6550 Reisterstown Plaza, Baltimore, MD 21215); 410-764-3038, 410-764-3170 (Order), 410-318-6119 (Recording), 410-358-7381-Fax; 8AM-4PM M-F; 3rd Saturday of each month.

www.dhmh.state.md.us

Records are available from 1969 to present. For records prior to 1969 contact Maryland State Archives, 410-260-6429. It takes 2-3 weeks (if filed at county) before new records are available for inquiry. Records are indexed on index cards.

Searching: Must have a signed release from immediate family member. A signature is required from the requester. Include the following in your request-full name, date of death, place of death, relationship to person of record, reason for information request. Request must be signed. Include copy of photo ID with request.

Access by: mail, phone, fax, in person, online.

Fee & Payment: The search fee is $12.00. Only phone, fax and expedited requesters may use a credit card for an extra $7.00 fee. Fee payee: Division of Vital Records. Prepayment required. Personal checks, M.O.s accepted. Major credit cards accepted.

Mail search: Turnaround time: 2 to 4 weeks. A SASE is requested.

Phone search: Credit card pre-payment required. Turnaround time is 2-3 days.

Fax search: See expedited service.

In person search: Turnaround time is same day.

Online search: Records may be ordered over the web at www.vitalchek.com. Use of credit card is required.

Expedited service: Expedited service is available with FedEx return of online, phone and fax searches. Turnaround time: 2 days. Add $13.50 per package for express delivery. Use of credit card and fee is required, also.

Marriage Certificates

Department of Health, Division of Vital Records, PO Box 68760, Baltimore, MD 21215-0020 (Courier address: 6550 Reisterstown Plaza, Baltimore, MD 21215); 410-764-3038, 410-764-3170 (Order), 410-318-6119 (Recording), 410-358-7381-Fax; 8AM-4PM M-F; 3rd Saturday of each month.

www.dhmh.state.md.us

Records are available from June 1951 to present. Prior records must be obtained from the court of record. Also, marriages from 1973, 1974, 1978, and 1979 are unavailable from this location and must be searched at local level. It takes 6 months before new records are available for inquiry. Records are indexed on computer. Records are normally destroyed after (records kept indefinitely).

Searching: Must have a notarized signed release from persons of record or authorized representative. Include the following in your request-names of husband and wife, date of marriage, place or county of marriage, besides permission letter. Include copy of photo ID with request.

Access by: mail, phone, fax, in person, online.

Fee & Payment: The search fee is $12.00. Only phone, fax and expedited requesters may use a credit card for an additional fee of $7.00. Fee payee: Division of Vital Records. Prepayment required. Personal checks & M.O.s accepted. Major credit cards accepted.

Mail search: Turnaround time: 2 to 3 weeks. A SASE is requested.

Phone search: Credit Card prepayment required. Turnaround time is 2-3 days.

Fax search: See expedited service.

In person search: Turnaround time same day.

Online search: Records may be ordered over the web at www.vitalchek.com. Use of credit card is required.

Expedited service: Expedited service is available with FedEx return of online, phone and fax searches. Turnaround time: 2 days. Add $13.50 per package for express delivery. Use of credit card and fee is required, also.

Divorce Records

Department of Health, Division of Vital Records, PO Box 68760, Baltimore, MD 21215-0020 (Courier address: 6550 Reisterstown Plaza, Baltimore, MD 21215); 410-764-3038, 410-318-6119 (Recording), 800-832-3277, 410-358-7381-Fax; 8AM-4PM M-F; 3rd Saturday of each month.

www.dhmh.state.md.us

This office does not issue a certificate of divorce, but can verify those names involved. The divorce decree must be obtained from the circuit court granting the divorce.

Records are available from July 1961 to present. It takes 6 months before new records are available for inquiry. Records are indexed on index cards. 1983-84 indexes are not available for searching. Paper indices from 1097-1991 are missing pages.

Searching: Must have a notarized release from persons of record or authorized agent. Include the following in your request-names of husband and wife (maiden name), date of divorce.

Access by: mail, fax, in person, online.

Fee & Payment: There is $12.00 fee to receive a Verification of Report of Divorce and Absolute Annulment. Add $7.00 for use of credit card. The clerk of the court issuing the decree holds the actual hard copy record. Fee payee: Division of Vital Records. Prepayment required. Personal checks accepted. Major credit cards accepted for expedited service.

Mail search: Turnaround time: 2 to 3 weeks. SASE is required.

Fax search: See expedited service.

In person search: Turnaround time same day.

Online search: Records may be ordered over the web at www.vitalchek.com. Use of credit card is required.

Expedited service: Expedited service is available with FedEx return of online, phone and fax searches. Turnaround time: 2 days. Add $13.50 per package for express delivery. Use of credit card and fee is required, also.

Workers' Compensation Records

Workers Compensation Commission, 10 E Baltimore St, Baltimore, MD 21202; 410-864-5100, 410-864-5120 (Information Technology), 8AM-4:30PM.

www.wcc.state.md.us

Records are available for past 10 years are on computer. New records are available for inquiry immediately. Records are indexed on microfilm, inhouse computer.

Searching: Include the following in your request-claimant name, Social Security Number, date of accident, place of employment at time of accident. The claim number helps. The following data is not released: medical records.

Access by: mail, phone, in person, online.

Fee & Payment: Fee for copies is $.50 per page. There is no search fee. Fee payee: Workers Compensation Commission. Prepayment required. Personal checks accepted. No credit cards accepted.

Mail search: Turnaround time: 1 week. For copies of documents, the claimant's authorization is needed for requesters not an involved party . A SASE is requested.

Phone search: Limited verification information is available by phone for three names only per call. You must have the 6 digit claim number or the name and SSN.

In person search: Turnaround time while you wait.

Online search: Request for online hook-up must be in writing on letterhead. There is no search fee, but there is a $7.00 set-up fee, $5.00 monthly fee and a $.01-03 per minute connect fee assessed by Verizon or other provider. The system is open 24 hours a day to only in-state accounts. Write to the Commission at address above, care of Information Technology Division, or at 410-864-5170.

Other access: This agency will sell its entire database depending on the use of the purchaser. Contact the commission for further information.

Driver Records

MVA, Driver Records Unit, 6601 Ritchie Hwy, NE, Glen Burnie, MD 21062; 410-787-7758, 410-424-3678-Fax; 8:15AM-4:30PM.

www.mva.state.md.us

Records are available for 3 years for moving violations, 10 years for DWIs, and 5 years for suspensions. Law requires a request from the driver to have violations purged from the driving record. Accidents are indicated. It takes 5 to 10 days before new records are available for inquiry.

Searching: Casual requesters cannot obtain records with personal information unless consent of subject is given. Records may not be resold or used for direct mail advertising or selling. Include the following in your request-driver's license number or the name and DOB, and necessary form. A business may request multiple records using Form DL-15. Requesters must submit form DR-057 if an account has not been established or if consent of subject is needed. The forms may be downloaded from the web.

Access by: mail, in person, online.

Fee & Payment: The fee for a driving record is $9.00. There is an additional $3.00 if you wish to have a non-electronic record certified. Fee payee: MVA. Prepayment required. Credit cards are not accepted for mail requests. Personal checks accepted. Credit cards accepted: MasterCard, Visa.

Mail search: Turnaround time: 2 to 3 days. MVA offices statewide will also accept mail-in requests for records. A SASE is requested.

In person search: Up to 5 requests will be processed in-person, additional requests are available the next day. In-person inquires may be processed at over 25 Motor Vehicle offices throughout the state.

Online search: Under the Direct Access Record System (DARS), participants access driver and vehicle record information via an Internet connection. The systems is open 24/6 to qualified and bonded individuals and businesses. Inquiries are processed interactive and may be accessed using either the driver's license number, name and date of birth, VIN or tag number. Fee is $9.00 per record. Call Ms. Barbara Bentley at 410-768-7234 for account information.

Other access: Drivers may order their own record online via the website. Records are not mailed out-of-state. Also, under the new License Monitoring System (LMS), transfers of record information to employers occur via an FTP server.

Vehicle Ownership
Vehicle Identification

Department of Motor Vehicles, Vehicle Registration Division, Room 204, 6601 Ritchie Hwy, NE, Glen Burnie, MD 21062; 410-768-7250, 410-768-7653-Fax; 8:15AM-4:30PM.

www.mva.state.md.us

Records are available from 1920. It takes 3 to 5 days before new records are available for inquiry. Records are normally destroyed after scanning to file.

Searching: All vehicle/ownership records are open to the public; however, personal information is not released to casual requesters without consent of subject. Include the following in your request-title, VIN, tag #, full name and DOB. The following data is not released: medical information.

Access by: mail, in person, online.

Fee & Payment: Fees are $9.00 for non-certified records and $12.00 for certified records. Fee payee: MVA. Prepayment required. Credit cards are only accepted for walk-in requesters. Personal checks accepted. Credit cards accepted: MasterCard, Visa.

Mail search: Turnaround time: 3 to 5 days. Requester can provide prepaid express mail package for faster service. Request on letterhead preferred. No SASE is required.

In person search: Turnaround time is generally in a few minutes.

Online search: The state offers vehicle and ownership data over the same online network (DARS) utilized for driving record searches. Fee is $9.00 per record. Access by VIN, tag # or full name. The network is available six days a week, twenty-four hours a day to qualified bonded accounts. Call 410-768-7234 for details.

Accident Reports

Maryland State Police, Central Records Division, 1711 Belmont Ave, Baltimore, MD 21244; 410-298-3390, 410-298-3198-Fax; 8AM-5PM.

This agency does not have reports for the City of Baltimore. Call 410-396-2359 for those reports.

Records are available for 5 years. Records are computer indexed from 1996 to present.

Searching: If a fatality was involved, please so state in the request. Copies of accident reports investigated by the state police and other police agencies may be requested by giving the date of incident and driver name(s).

Access by: mail, in person.

Fee & Payment: The search fee is $4.00 which includes all copies and is non-refundable. Fee payee: Maryland State Police. Prepayment required. Personal checks accepted. No credit cards accepted.

Mail search: Turnaround time: 3 to 4 weeks. A SASE is requested.

In person search: Immediate service limited to simple requests.

Vessel Ownership
Vessel Registration

Dept of Natural Resources, Licensing & Registration Service, 580 Taylor Ave C-1, Annapolis, MD 21401; 410-260-3220, 410-260-8214-Fax; 8:30AM-4:30PM.

www.dnr.state.md.us

Boat trailers, (only trailers) are registered through the Maryland Motor Vehicle Administration. They can be reached at 1-800-950-1682.

Records are available from the 1960s to the present. This is a title state: all motorized boats must be titled and registered. Records are on indexed on microfiche or CDs from the 1960s to the present, and on computer for the last 4 years. It takes 24 hours before new records are available for inquiry.

Searching: The agency follows the mandates of the DPPA. Only those with a legitimate business can obtain records with personal information. Casual requesters must have a signed release of subject. Include the following in your request-one of the following is required: Maryland boat #, tidal fish license #, or name and address of boat owner/license holder. There are five additional Regional Service Centers in the state that will process record requests.

Access by: mail, in person.

Fee & Payment: Certified true copies are $10.00 each. Microfiche history files are $5.00 each. Current computer file copies are $5.00 each. Fee payee: DNR. Prepayment required. Personal checks accepted. No credit cards accepted.

Mail search: Turnaround time: 2 weeks. No SASE is required.

In person search: Turnaround time is immediate, unless historical records needed.

Voter Registration

Access to Records is Restricted.

State Board of Elections, PO Box 6486, Annapolis, MD 21401-0486 (Courier address: 151 West Street, #200, Annapolis, MD 21401); 410-269-2840, 800-222-8683 , 410-974-2019-Fax; 8AM-5PM.

www.elections.state.md.us

Agency may sell voter registration lists in bulk media for all twenty-four jurisdictions to MD registered voters only. If voter history is requested, then list must be purchased from each local jurisdiction. Commercial use of list is banned. The website offers free access to the campaign finance database for checking campaign contributions and overall summaries and statistics. For questions, email sep@elections.state.md.us.

GED Certificates

State Department of Education, GED Office, 200 W Baltimore St, Baltimore, MD 21201 (Courier address: 4 N. Liberty St., Baltimore, MD 21201); 410-767-0538, 410-333-8435-Fax; 8:30AM-5PM.

www.umbc.edu/alrc/GED1.html

It takes 30 days before new records are available for inquiry.

Searching: Include the following in your request-name, date of birth, Social Security Number, signed release. The signed release is needed for either the verification or transcript copy.

Access by: mail, fax, in person.

Fee & Payment: The fee is $5.00 for a copy of a transcript. There is no fee for a verification. Fee payee: GED Office. Prepayment required. Personal checks accepted. No credit cards accepted.

Mail search: Turnaround time: 3 to 5 days. No SASE is required.

Fax search: For employment purposes requiring diploma verification, fax a release form with the social security number and full signature of the individual to the GED Office at 410-333-8435. Turnaround time is 2-3 days.

In person search: Counter service is available from 10AM-2PM at the N Liberty address.

Hunting and Fishing License Information

Department of Natural Resources, Licensing & Registration Service, 580 Taylor Ave, Annapolis, MD 21401; 410-260-3220, 410-260-8239-Fax; 8:30AM-4:30PM.

www.dnr.state.md.us

They have a central computer database. Licenses can be issued online at the webpage.

Records are available since 1999. It takes 1-2 days before new records are available for inquiry.

Searching: Requests are subject to DPPA. Requests must be in writing, submit as many identifiers as possible.

Access by: mail, in person.

Fee & Payment: There is a $5.00 fee per name. Fee payee: Department of Natural Resources. Personal checks accepted.

Mail search: Turnaround time: 7-10 days. Turnaround time is as time permits.

In person search: Records searched as time permits.

Maryland State Licensing Agencies

For details about the agency responsible for licensing/certifying/registering an item below or in the Agency Quick Finder section, match an item's number with the number of the agency in the *Licensing Agency Information* section.

Maryland Licenses Searchable Online

Architect #23	www.dllr.state.md.us/query/arch.html
Architectural Partnership/Corporation #12	www.dllr.state.md.us/license/occprof/
Attorney #3	www.courts.state.md.us/cpf/attylist.html
Barber #8	www.dllr.state.md.us/query/barber.html
Certification #16	www.sos.state.md.us/Certifications/certifications.htm
Charity #16	www.sos.state.md.us/charity/charityhome.htm
Condominium/Timeshare #16	www.sos.state.md.us/Registrations/condo_TS.htm
Contractor #10	www.dllr.state.md.us/query/home_imprv.html
Cosmetologist #8	www.dllr.state.md.us/query/cosmet.html
Election #16	www.sos.state.md.us/ElectionsInfo.htm
Electrician, Master #12	www.dllr.state.md.us/license/occprof/
Engineer, Examining #12	www.dllr.state.md.us/license/occprof/
Engineer, Professional #12	www.dllr.state.md.us/license/occprof/
Esthetician #8	www.dllr.state.md.us/query/cosmet.html
Extradition/Requisition #16	www.sos.state.md.us/Services/Extradit.htm
Forester #12	www.dllr.state.md.us/license/occprof/
Fund Raising Counsel #16	www.sos.state.md.us/charity/RegisterProfSol.htm
Grain Dealer #4	www.mda.state.md.us/pdf/grainbrochure2005.pdf
Home Improvement #12	www.dllr.state.md.us/license/occprof/
Home Improvement Salesperson #10	www.dllr.state.md.us/query/home_imprv.html
HVACR Contractor #12	www.dllr.state.md.us/license/occprof/
Interior Designer #12	www.dllr.state.md.us/license/occprof/
Land Surveyor #12	www.dllr.state.md.us/license/occprof/
Landscape Architect #12	www.dllr.state.md.us/license/occprof/
Limousine Driver #18	www.psc.state.md.us/psc/
Lobbyist #14	http://ethics.gov.state.md.us/listing.htm
Lobbyist Employer #14	http://ethics.gov.state.md.us/listing.htm
Makeup Artist #8	www.dllr.state.md.us/query/cosmet.html
MD Flag Protocol #16	www.sos.state.md.us/Services/flagprotocol.htm
Medical Doctor #22	www.mbp.state.md.us/
Military Monuments Commission #16	www.sos.state.md.us/MMMC/MMMChome.htm
Mortgage Broker #13	www.dllr.state.md.us/query/real_est.html
Nail Technician #8	www.dllr.state.md.us/query/cosmet.html
Notary Public #16	www.sos.state.md.us/notary/notary.htm
Nurse-RN/LPN #24	www.mbon.org/main.php
Nursery, Plant #4	www.mda.state.md.us/plants-pests/plant_protection_weed_mgmt/nurseries_plant_dealers/
Nursing Assistant #24	www.mbon.org/main.php
Optometrist #22	www.arbo.org/index.php?action=findanoptometrist
Pardon/Commutation #16	www.sos.state.md.us/Services/Pardons.htm
Pawnbroker #12	www.dllr.state.md.us/query/sec_hand_deal.html
Pesticide Applicator/Operator #4	www.mda.state.md.us/geninfo/genera10.htm
Pesticide Business/Dealer/Consultant #4	www.mda.state.md.us/geninfo/genera10.htm
Pesticide, Private Applicator #4	www.mda.state.md.us/geninfo/genera10.htm
Plant Broker/Dealer #4	www.mda.state.md.us/plants-pests/plant_protection_weed_mgmt/nurseries_plant_dealers/
Plumber #12	www.dllr.state.md.us/query/plumb.html
Polygraph Examiner #26	www.mpapolygraph.org/
Precious Metal/Gem Dealer/2nd-hand #12	www.dllr.state.md.us/query/sec_hand_deal.html
Public Accountant-CPA #12	www.dllr.state.md.us/query/cpa.html
Radiation Therapy Technician #22	www.mbp.state.md.us/
Real Estate Agent #15	www.dllr.state.md.us/query/real_est.html
Real Estate Appraiser #11	www.dllr.state.md.us/query/real_est_app.html
Respiratory Care Practitioner #22	www.mbp.state.md.us/
Solicitor, Professional #16	www.sos.state.md.us/charity/RegisterProfSol.htm#ps
Special Police/Railroad Police #16	www.sos.state.md.us/Services/Police.htm
Subcontractor #10	www.dllr.state.md.us/query/home_imprv.html
Taxi Driver #18	www.psc.state.md.us/psc/
Trademark/Service Mark #16	www.sos.state.md.us/Registrations/Trademarks/Trademarks.htm

Maryland Licensing Quick Finder

Acupuncturist #22 410-764-4766
Airport #19 410-859-7064
Airport License, Public/Priv. Regis. #19 410-859-7137
Alarm Technician #27 410-799-0191
Architect #23 410-230-6322
Architectural Partnership/Corp. #12 410-230-6261
Asbestos Abatement Company #6 410-537-3200
Athletic Agent #17 410-230-6223
Attorney #3 410-260-1950
Audiologist #22 410-764-4723
Bail Bondsman #21 410-468-2383
Barber #8 410-230-6320
Boxer/Boxing Professional #17 410-230-6223
Bus Driver #18 410-768-7232
Charity #16 410-974-5534
Chiropractor/Chiropractic Assistant #22 410-764-5902
Collection Agency #13 410-230-6230
Contractor #10 410-230-6231
Cosmetologist #8 410-230-6320
Counselor #22 410-764-4732
Day Care Provider #2 410-583-6214
Dental Assistant/ Hygienist #22 ..410-402-8500 opt. 4
Dental Teacher #22 .... 410-402-8500 opt. 4
Dentist #22 .... 410-402-8500 opt. 4
Dietitian/Nutritionist #22 410-764-4733
Electrician, Master #12 410-230-6231
Electrologist #7 410-585-1952
Embalmer #22 410-764-4792
Engineer, Examining #12 410-230-6231
Engineer, Professional #12 410-230-6322
Esthetician #8 410-230-6320
Forester #12 410-230-6231
Franchises, Bus. Opportunity, Multi-level Mktng
Programs #20 410-576-7785
Fund Raising Counsel #16 410-974-5534
Funeral Director #22 410-764-4792
Funeral Establishment #22 410-764-4792
Grain Dealer #4 410-841-5769
Guidance Counselor #5 410-767-0412
Handgun Permittee #27 410-799-0191
Harness Racing #9 410-230-6330
Hazardous Waste #6 410-537-3343

Hearing Aid Dispenser #22 410-764-4792
Home Improvement #12 410-230-6209
Home Improvement Salesperson #10 .. 410-230-6176
Horse Racing #9 410-230-6330
HVACR Contractor #12 410-230-6200
Insurance Agent #21 410-468-2383
Insurance Broker/Advisor #21 410-468-2383
Interior Designer #12 410-230-6322
Investment Adviser/Representative #20 410-576-7784
Land Surveyor #12 410-230-6322
Landscape Architect #12 410-230-6322
Lead Inspectors/Contractors #6 410-537-3863
Limousine Driver #18
.... 410-768-7232, PSC 410-767-8000
Lobbyist #14 410-974-2068
Lobbyist Employer #14 410-974-2068
Makeup Artist #8 410-230-6320
Massage Therapist #22 410-764-2431
Medical Doctor #22 410-764-4777
Mining Foreman/Fire Boss #6 410-537-3557
Mortgage Broker #13 410-230-6230
Mortician #22 410-764-4792
Nail Technician #8 410-230-6320
Notary Public #16 410-974-5520
Notice Filing #20 410-576-7050
Nurse-RN/LPN #24 410-585-1900
Nursery, Plant #4 410-841-5920
Nursing Assistant #24 410-585-1990
Nursing Home Administrator #22 410-764-4750
Occupational Therapist/Assistant #22 .. 410-402-8560
Optometrist #22 410-764-4710
Pawnbroker #12 410-230-4640
Pesticide Applicator/Operator #4 410-841-5710
Pesticide Business/Dealer #4 410-841-5710
Pesticide Consultant #4 410-841-5710
Pesticide, Private Applicator #4 410-841-5710
Pharmacist #22 410-764-4755
Physical Therapist #22 410-764-4752
Physical Therapist Assistant #22 410-764-4752
Pilot #12 410-230-6329
Plant Broker/Dealer #4 410-841-5920
Plumber #12 410-230-6231

Podiatrist #22 410-764-4785
Police Officer, Special #27 410-799-0191
Polygraph Examiner #26 .... 301 791-7039 x117
Precious Metals & Gem Dealer/2nd-hand #12
.... 410-230-4640
Private Investigator #27 410-799-0191
Psychologist #22 410-764-4787
Psychometrist (Education) #5 410-767-0412
Public Accountant-CPA #12 410-230-6258
Pump Installer #6 .... 410-537-3557 x3510
Pupil Personnel Worker #5 410-767-0412
Radiation Therapy Technician #22 410-764-4775
Reading Specialist #5 410-767-0412
Reading Teacher #5 410-767-0412
Real Estate Agent #15 410-230-6230
Real Estate Appraiser #11 410-230-6231
Referee #17 410-230-6223
Respiratory Care Practitioner #22 410-764-4775
Sanitarian #6 .... 410-537-3557 x3597
School Administrator/Superintend't #5 .. 410-767-0412
School Library Media Gen./Spec #5 410-767-0412
School Psychologist #5 410-767-0412
Securities Broker/Dealer #20 410-576-6494
Securities Sales Agent #20 410-576-6494
Security Guard #27 410-799-0191
Security Registration #20 410-576-7050
Sewage Treatment #6 410-537-3510
Social Worker #22 410-764-4788
Solicitor, Professional #16 410-974-5534
Speech Pathologist #22 410-764-4725
Subcontractor #10 410-230-6231
Taxi Driver #18 .... 410-768-7232, PSC 410-767-8000
Taxicab #25 410-767-8107
Teacher #5 410-767-0412
Truck Driver #18 410-768-7232
Veterinarian #1 410-841-5862
Veterinary Hospital #1 410-841-5862
Waste Water Treatment Plant Super. #6 410-537-3167
Water Conditioner Installer #6 410-537-3000
Well Driller #6 410-537-3597

Maryland Licensing Agency Information

1 Board of Veterinary Medical Examiners, 50 Harry S Truman Pky, Annapolis, MD 21401; 410-841-5862, Fax: 410-841-5999.

2 Child Care Administration, Region 3, 409 Washington Ave LL8, Towson, MD 21204; 410-583-6214, Fax: 410-321-2240.
www.dhr.state.md.us/cca-home.htm
Email: rhayes@dhr.state.md.us

3 Client Protection Fund of the Bar of Maryland, Robert F Sweeney Dist Ct Bldg, 251 Rowe Blvd 3rd Fl, Annapolis, MD 21401; 410-260-1950, Fax: 410-260-1954.
www.courts.state.md.us/cpf/index.html
Search Database at
www.courts.state.md.us/cpf/attylist.html Note: The state bar assoc. (MSBA) is a separate organization. MSBA phone number is 410-685-7878, fax 410-685-1016; 520 W Fayette St, Balt. MD 21201.

4 Department of Agriculture, Pesticide Regulation Section, 50 Harry S Truman Pky, Annapolis, MD 21401; 410-841-5710, Fax: 410-841-2765.
www.mda.state.md.us
Email: howarddw@mda.state.md.us

5 Department of Education, Division of Certification & Accreditation, 200 W Baltimore St, Baltimore, MD 21201-2595; 410-767-0412, Fax: 410-333-8963.

6 Department of Environment, 1800 Washington Blvd., Baltimore, MD 21230; 410-537-3000, Fax: separate at each unit.
www.mde.state.md.us

7 Department of Health & Mental Hygiene, Board of Nursing, Electrology Practice Committee, 4201 Patterson Ave, Baltimore, MD 21215; 410-585-1952, Fax: 410-358-3530.
www.bon.org

8 Department of Labor, Licensing & Regulation, Board of Barbers & Cosmetologists, 500 N Calvert St, 3rd Fl, Rm 307, Baltimore, MD 21202; 410-230-6320, Fax: 410-230-6314.
www.dllr.state.md.us/license/occprof/barber.html
Email: mbrown@dllr.state.md.us
Search Database at www.dllr.state.md.us/query/barber.html (or) cosmet.html

9 Department of Labor, Licensing & Regulation, Racing Commission, 500 N Calvert St #201, Baltimore, MD 21202; 410-230-6330, Fax: 410-333-8308.
www.dllr.state.md.us/racing/
Email: mhopkins@dllr.state.md.us

10 Department of Licensing & Regulation, Home Improvement Commission, 500 N Calvert St, #306, Baltimore, MD 21202-3651; 410-230-6176.
www.dllr.state.md.us/license/occprof/homeim.html
Email: krosenthal@dllr.state.md.us
Search Database at
www.dllr.state.md.us/query/home_imprv.html

11 Department of Labor, Licensing & Regulation, Board of Real Estate Appraisers, 500 N Calvert St, Baltimore, MD 21202; 410-230-6200, Fax: 410-333-1229.
www.dllr.state.md.us/license/occprof/reappr.html

Email: pschott@dllr.state.md.us   Search Database at www.dllr.state.md.us/query/real_est_app.html

12 Department of Licensing & Regulation, Occupational Boards, 500 N Calvert St, Baltimore, MD 21202; 410-230-6200, Fax: 410-333-1229.
www.dllr.state.md.us/license/occprof/
Email: twhite@dllr.state.md.us

13 Department of Licensing & Regulation, Office of Financial Regulations, 500 N Calvert St, #402, Baltimore, MD 21202; 1-888-218-5925 (toll free).
www.dllr.state.md.us/license/fin_reg/mortlend/md finreg.html

14 State Ethics Commission, 9 State Circle #200 (188 Main St), Annapolis, MD 21401; 877-669-6085, 410-974-2068, Fax: 410-974-2418.
http://ethics.gov.state.md.us
Search Database at http://ethics.gov.state.md.us/listing.htm Note: A paper copy of the lobbyist list can be purchased for $10.00.

15 Department of Licensing & Regulation, Real Estate Commission, 500 N Calvert St, 3rd Fl, Baltimore, MD 21202-3551; 410-230-6230, Fax: 410-230-0023.
www.dllr.state.md.us/license/occprof/recomm.html
Email: mrec@dllr.state.md.us
Search Database at
www.dllr.state.md.us/query/real_est.html

16 Office of Secretary of State, Statehouse, 16 Francis St, Annapolis, MD 21401; 410-974-5521, Fax: 410-974-5190.   www.sos.state.md.us
Email: mdsos@sos.state.md.us

17 Department of Licensing & Regulation, Athletic Commission, 500 N Calvert St, 2nd Fl, Baltimore, MD 21202; 410-230-6223, Fax: 410-230-6314.
www.dllr.state.md.us/license/occprof/athlet.html

18 Department of Transportation, Motor Vehicle Administration, 6601 Ritchie Hwy NE, Glen Burnie, MD 21062; 410-768-7232, Fax: 410-333-6088.   Note: Taxi and Limo drivers also have to have permits from the Public Service Commission.

19 Department of Transportation, Aviation Administration, PO Box 8766, BWI Airport, Baltimore, MD 21240; 410-859-7064, Fax: 410-859-7287.
Email: maaadmin@mdot.state.md.us

20 Securities Division, Attorney General's Office, 200 St. Paul Place, 25th Fl, Baltimore, MD 21202; 410-576-6360, Fax: 410-576-6532.
www.oag.state.md.us/Securities/index.htm
Email: securities@oag.state.md.us

21 Licensing & Regulation, Insurance Agent/Brokers Licensing & Investigation, 525 St Paul Pl, Baltimore, MD 21202; 410-468-2000, Fax: 410-468-2399.
www.mdinsurance.state.md.us

22 Licensing Boards, 4201 Patterson Ave, Baltimore, MD 21215-2299; 410-764-4700, Fax: 410-358-0128.
Email: jchull@dhmh.state.md.us

23 Board of Architects, 500 N Calvert St 3rd Fl, Baltimore, MD 21202-2272; 888-218-5925, 410-230-6322, Fax: 410-333-0021.
www.dllr.state.md.us
Email: architect@dllr.state.md.us
Search Database at
www.dllr.state.md.us/query/arch.html Note: Lists of currently licensed individual architect & firms can be purchased for a fee. Call 410-230-6352.

24 Board of Nursing, 4140 Patterson Ave, Baltimore, MD 21215; 888-202-9861, 410-585-1900, Fax: 410-358-3530.
www.mbon.org/main.php
Email: mbon@dhmh.state.md.us
Search Database at www.mbon.org/main.php Note: A telephone voice response system called IVR is available; 410-585-1978.

25 Public Service Commission, Transportation Division, 6 St. Paul St, 18th Fl, Baltimore, MD 21202; 410-767-8128, Fax: 410-333-6088.

26 Polygraph Association, PO Box 2224, Hagerstown, MD 21741; 301 791-7039 ex. 117.
www.mpapolygraph.org/

27 State Police, Licensing Division, 7751 Washington Blvd, Jessup, MD 20794; 410-799-0191, Fax: 410-799-5934.
www.mdsp.org/

Maryland Federal Courts

The following list indicates the district and division name for each county in the state. If the bankruptcy court location is different from the district court, then the location of the bankruptcy court appears in parentheses.

Maryland County/Court Cross Reference

Allegany ....Baltimore	Charles........................Greenbelt	Prince George's ....Greenbelt
Anne Arundel ....Baltimore	Dorchester..................Baltimore	Queen Anne's.............Baltimore
Baltimore...................Baltimore	Frederick ....Baltimore	Somerset ....Baltimore
Baltimore City City....Baltimore	Garrett.......................Baltimore	St. Mary's...................Greenbelt
Calvert ....Greenbelt	Harford ....Baltimore	Talbot ....Baltimore
Caroline ....Baltimore	Howard.......................Baltimore	Washington ....Baltimore
Carroll.......................Baltimore	Kent ....Baltimore	Wicomico ....Baltimore
Cecil..........................Baltimore	Montgomery..............Greenbelt	Worcester...................Baltimore

Standards for Federal Courts: See Maine or Massachusettts Federal Courts section for information on Federal Courts standards and fees.

US District Court

Northern District of Maryland

Baltimore Division Clerk of Court, 4th Fl, Rm 4415, 101 W Lombard St, Baltimore, MD 21201 (also use mail address for courier delivery), 410-962-2600. Hours- 9AM-4PM. www.mdd.uscourts.gov

Counties: Allegany, Anne Arundel, Baltimore, City of Baltimore, Caroline, Carroll, Cecil, Dorchester, Frederick, Garrett, Harford, Howard, Kent, Queen Anne's, Somerset, Talbot, Washington, Wicomico, Worcester.

Searches & Indexing: Results do not include SSN or DOB. Both computer and card indexes maintained; computer goes back to 1994. New cases in the index 1-2 days after filing date. Records purged every 6 months.

Fee & Payment: Pay by money order, cashier's or personal check. Payee: Clerk, USDC. Prepayment required.

Phone Search: Court will verify questions via phone, but will not read long dockets.

Mail Search: search usually completed- 3-4 working days. Include SASE for return.

In Person Search: Fee charged if court performs your search. No self-serve copier available.

E-Services: ECF replaces PACER whose records did go back to 10/1990. New records online after 1 day. ECF at https://ecf.mdd.uscourts.gov **Opinions Online:** www.mdd.uscourts.gov/Opinions152/SelectOpsMenu.asp. Selected opinions only. **Other Online Access:** Access calendars free at www.mdd.uscourts.gov/weeklycalnew/.

US Bankruptcy Court

Northern District of Maryland

Baltimore Division Court Clerk, US Courthouse, 101 W Lombard St, Ste 8308, Baltimore, MD 21201 (also use mail address for courier delivery), 410-962-2688, Fax-410-962-2110. Hours- 8AM-4PM. www.mdb.uscourts.gov

Counties: Anne Arundel, Baltimore, City of Baltimore, Caroline, Carroll, Cecil, Dorchester, Harford, Howard, Kent, Queen Anne's, Somerset, Talbot, Wicomico, Worcester.

Searches & Indexing: Debtor name and/or case number plus specific identification of the pleading involved are required to search. Results include last 4 SSN digits. Computer index maintained. New cases in the index 2 days after filing date. Records purged every 6 months. Closed files retained for the existing calendar year as well as the previous.

Fee & Payment: Pay by no business or personal checks accepted. Payee: Clerk, Bankruptcy Court.

Phone Search: Only docket information is available by phone. Voice Case Information Service available, call VCIS at 800-829-0145 or 410-962-0733.

Mail Search: search usually completed- 2-4 weeks. SASE not required.

In Person Search: Fee charged if court performs your search. Public can search automated records and paper dockets only. Non-certified copy work available from onsite vendor Document Technology, call 410-837-0409. No self-serve copier available.

E-Services: ECF replaces PACER whose records did go back to mid 1991. New records online after 1 day. ECF at https://ecf.mdb.uscourts.gov **Opinions Online:** http://207.41.17.84/QryOpinion.aspx?qTarget=Opinion. **Other Online Access:** Search judgments back through 2002 free at http://207.41.17.84/QryJudgment.aspx?qTarget=Judgment. Access calendars at https://ecf.mdb.uscourts.gov/cgi-bin/PublicCalendar4.pl.

US District Court

Southern District of Maryland

Greenbelt Division Clerk of Court, Rm 240, 6500 Cherrywood Lane, Greenbelt, MD 20770 (use mail address for courier delivery), 301-344-0660. 9AM-4PM. www.mdd.uscourts.gov

Counties: Calvert, Charles, Montgomery, Prince George's, St. Mary's.

Searches & Indexing: Results do not include SSN or DOB. Both computer and card indexes maintained; computer back to 1990. New cases in the index 1-2 days after filing date. Records purged every 6 months.

Fee & Payment: Pay by money order, cashier's or personal check. Payee: Clerk, USDC. Prepayment required.

Phone Search: Court will verify information via phone, but will not read long dockets.

Mail Search: search usually completed- 5 working days. Searches and copy requests must be made in writing to the clerks office.

In Person Search: Fee charged if court performs your search. Office Solutions, 301-982-4682, can do search/copies. No self-serve copier available.

E-Services: ECF replaces PACER whose records did go back to 10/1990. New records online immediately. ECF at https://ecf.mdd.uscourts.gov **Opinions Online:** www.mdd.uscourts.gov/Opinions152/SelectOpsMenu.asp. Selected opinions only. **Other Online Access:** Access calendars free at www.mdd.uscourts.gov/weeklycalnew/.

US Bankruptcy Court

Southern District of Maryland

Greenbelt Division Court Clerk, 6500 Cherrywood Ln, #300, Greenbelt, MD 20770 (also use mail address for courier delivery), 301-344-8018. Hours- 8AM-4PM. www.mdb.uscourts.gov

Counties: Allegany, Calvert, Charles, Frederick, Garrett, Montgomery, Prince George's, St. Mary's, Washington.

Searches & Indexing: Search requires debtor name and/or case number. Results include SSN. Computer index maintained. New cases in the index 2-3 days after filing date. Records purged every 6 months.

Fee & Payment: Pay by money order, cashier's or personal check. Payee: Clerk, US Bankruptcy Court. In house copy work - 4 pages or less and copies that need to be certified - done on an "as time permits" basis. Copy work of 5 pages or more is done off premises but the cost is less.

Phone Search: Only docket data is available by phone. Voice Case Information Service available, call VCIS at 800-829-0145 or 410-962-0733.

Mail Search: search usually completed- 5 days. Open cases are searched by IKON Office Solutions, 301-982-4682. SASE not required.

In Person Search: Fee charged if court performs your search. No self-serve copier available.

E-Services: ECF replaces PACER whose records did go back to mid 1991. New records online after 1 day. ECF at https://ecf.mdb.uscourts.gov **Opinions Online:** http://207.41.17.84/QryOpinion.aspx?qTarget=Opinion. **Other Online Access:** Search judgments back through 2002 free at http://207.41.17.84/QryJudgment.aspx?qTarget=Judgment. Access calendars at https://ecf.mdb.uscourts.gov/cgi-bin/PublicCalendar4.pl.

Maryland County Courts

Court	Jurisdiction	No. of Courts	How Organized
Circuit Courts*	General	25	8 Circuits
District Courts*	Limited	26	12 Districts
Orphan's Courts*	Probate	24	Register of Wills

* Profiled in this Sourcebook.

Court	CIVIL								
	Tort	Contract	Real Estate	Min. Claim	Max. Claim	Small Claims	Estate	Eviction	Domestic Relations
Circuit Courts*	X	X	X	$25000	No Max				X
District Courts*	X	X	X	$2500	$25000	$2500		X	X
Orphan's Court*							X		

Court	CRIMINAL				
	Felony	Misdemeanor	DWI/DUI	Preliminary Hearing	Juvenile
Circuit Courts*	X	X			X
District Courts*		X	X	X	X
Orphan's Court*					

ADMINISTRATION

Court Administrator, Administrative Office of the Courts, 580 Taylor Ave, Annapolis, MD, 21401; 410-260-1400, Fax: 410-974-2169.

www.courts.state.md.us

COURT STRUCTURE

The Circuit Court is the highest court of record. There is a Circuit Court with an elected clerk in each county of Maryland and Baltimore City.

The jurisdiction of the District Court includes all landlord-tenant cases, replevin actions, motor vehicle violations, misdemeanors and certain felonies. In civil cases the District Court has exclusive jurisdiction in claims for amounts up to $5,000, and concurrent jurisdiction with the circuit courts in claims for amounts above $5,000 but less than $25,000. The jurisdiction of the court in criminal cases is concurrent with the Circuit Court for offenses in which the penalty may be confinement for three years or more or a fine of $2,500 or more; or offenses which are felonies.

In most Circuit and District courts, copies are $.50 per page and certification is $5.00.

ONLINE ACCESS

At www.courts.state.md.us/dialup.html see the Judicial Information System (JIS) or (SJIS) for dial-up access to civil and criminal case information from the following:

      All District Courts - All civil and all misdemeanors

      All Circuit Courts Civil - All civil records are online through JIS.

      Circuit Courts Criminal - Three courts are on JIS - Anne Arundel, Carroll county, and Baltimore City Court

Inquiries may be made to: the District Court traffic system for case information data, calendar information data, court schedule data, or officer schedule data; the District Court criminal system for case information data or calendar caseload data; the District Court civil system for case information data, attorney name and address data; the land records system for land and plat records. There is an annual fee for JIS dial-up access of $50.00, which must be included with the application. For additional information or to receive a registration packet, write or call Judicial Information Systems, Security Administrator, 2661 Riva Rd., Suite 900, Annapolis, MD 21401, 410-260-1031, or visit the web site. Appellate opinions are available from www.courts.state.md.us/opinions.html.

PROBATE COURTS

The Circuit Court handles Probate in Montgomery and Harford counties. In other counties, probate is handled by the Register of Wills and is a county, not a court, function.

Allegany County

4th Judicial Circuit Court 30 Washington St, Cumberland, MD 21502; phone: 301-777-5922; fax: 301-777-2100; hours 8AM-4:30PM (EST). *Felony, Misdemeanor, Civil Actions Over $25,000.*

Civil Records: Access: In person, online. Visitors must perform in person searches themselves. Court makes copy: $.50 per page. Required to search: name, years to search. Civil cases indexed by defendant, plaintiff; on computer since 11/92, archived and indexed from 1790. Online access is through JIS. See state introduction or visit www.courts.state.md.us.

Criminal Records: Access: In person only. Visitors must perform in person searches themselves. Court makes copy: $.50 per page. Required to search: name, years to search; also helpful: DOB. Criminal records on computer since 9/99, archived and indexed from 1790.

General Information: Public terminal has criminal back to 6/1996 and civil back to 6/1997. No adoptions, juvenile, sealed, expunged or mental records released. Certification fee: $5.00 per instrument. Payee: Circuit Court. Personal checks accepted. Prepayment required.

District Court 3 Pershing St, 2nd Fl, Cumberland, MD 21502; phone: 301-723-3100; hours 8:30AM-4:30PM (EST). *Misdemeanor, Civil Actions Under $25,000, Eviction, Small Claims.*

Civil Records: Access: Mail, online, in person. Both court and visitors may perform in person searches. No search fee. Court makes copy: $.50 per page. Required to search: name, years to search. Civil cases indexed by defendant. Civil records on computer from 1990, on index books from 1970. Online access is through JIS. See state introduction or visit www.courts.state.md.us. Mail turnaround time 7 days.

Criminal Records: Access: Mail, online, in person. Visitors must perform in person searches themselves. No search fee. Court makes copy: $.50 per page. Required to search: name, years to search, signed release; also helpful: SSN. Criminal records on computer from 1980, index books. Online access through JIS. See state introduction or visit www.courts.state.md.us. Note: Court requires a case number for a search. Mail turnaround time 7 days.

General Information: No public access terminal. No adoptions, juvenile, sealed, expunged or mental records released. Certification fee: $5.00 per page. Payee: District Court of MD. Personal checks accepted. Prepayment and SASE required.

Register of Wills 59 Prospect Sq. 1st Fl, Cumberland, MD 21502; phone: 301-724-3760, 888-724-0148 in MD; fax: 301-724-1249; hours 8AM-4:30PM (EST). *Probate.*
www.registers.state.md.us/county/al/html/allegany.html

Anne Arundel County

5th Judicial Circuit Court PO Box 71, 7 Church St, Annapolis, MD 21401; phone: 410-222-1397; civil phone: 410-222-1431; hours 8:30AM-4:30PM; phone hours-11AM-3:30PM (EST). *Felony, Misdemeanor, Civil Actions Over $25,000.*

Civil Records: Access: Phone, mail, online, in person. Both court and visitors may perform in person searches. No search fee. Court makes copy: $.50 per page. Required to search: name, years to search. Civil cases indexed by defendant, plaintiff; on computer from 1991, on index from 1900. Online access is through JIS. See state introduction or visit www.courts.state.md.us.

Criminal Records: Access: Online, in person. Both court and visitors may perform in person searches. Court makes copy: $.50 per page. Required to search: name, years to search; also helpful: SSN. Criminal records on computer from 1988, indexed from 1960, archived from 1900. Online access through JIS. See state introduction or visit www.courts.state.md.us.

General Information: Public terminal has criminal back to 1988 and civil back to 1991. No adoptions, juvenile, sealed, expunged or mental records released. Certification fee: $5.00 per cert. Payee: Clerk of Circuit Court. Personal checks accepted. Prepayment and SASE required.

District Court 251 Rowe Blvd, #141, Annapolis, MD 21401; phone: 410-260-1370; hours 8:30AM-4:30PM (EST). *Misdemeanor, Civil Actions Under $25,000, Eviction, Small Claims.*

Civil Records: Access: Mail, online, in person. Both court and visitors may perform in person searches. No search fee. Court makes copy: $.50 per page. Required to search: name, years to search. Civil cases indexed by defendant. Civil records on computer from 1982, archived and indexed from 1900s. Online access is through JIS. See state introduction or visit www.courts.state.md.us. Mail turnaround time 5 days.

Criminal Records: Access: Mail, online, in person. Both court and visitors may perform in person searches. No search fee. Court makes copy: $.50 per page. Required to search: name, years to search. Criminal records on computer from 1982, archived and indexed from 1900s. Online access through JIS. See state introduction or visit www.courts.state.md.us. Mail turnaround time 5 days.

General Information: Public terminal has criminal back to 1982 and civil back to 1987. Certification fee: $5.00. Payee: District Court. Personal checks accepted. Prepayment and SASE required.

Register of Wills PO Box 2368, 7 1/2 Circuit Courthouse-Church Circle #403, Annapolis, MD 21404-2368; phone: 410-222-1430, 800-679-6665 in MD; fax: 410-222-1467; hours 8:30AM-3PM (EST). *Probate.*
www.registers.state.md.us/county/aa/html/annearundel.html
Note: Wills only; no genealogy searches

Baltimore County

3rd Judicial Circuit Court 401 Bosley Ave, 2nd Fl, Towson, MD 21204; phone: 410-887-2601; fax: 410-887-3062; hours 8:30AM-4:30PM (EST). *Felony, Civil Actions Over $25,000.*

Civil Records: Access: Online, in person. Visitors must perform in person searches themselves. Court makes copy: $.50 per page. Required to search: name, years to search; also helpful: address. Civil cases indexed by defendant, plaintiff. Civil records in books, file jackets. Online access is through JIS. See state introduction or visit www.courts.state.md.us.

Criminal Records: Access: In person only. Visitors must perform in person searches themselves. Court makes copy: $.50 per page. Required to search: name, years to search; also helpful: address, DOB, SSN. Criminal records on computer from 1984, prior on books.

General Information: Public terminal has only civil records. No adoptions, juvenile, sealed, expunged or mental records released. Will not fax documents. Certification fee: $5.00 per page. Payee: Suzanne Mensh, Clerk. Personal checks accepted. Out of state checks not accepted. Prepayment required.

District Court 120 E Chesapeake Ave, Towson, MD 21286-5307; phone: 410-512-2000; criminal phone: 410-512-2101; hours 8:30AM-4:30PM (EST). *Felonies assigned to District Court, Misdemeanor, Civil Actions Under $25,000, Eviction, Small Claims.*
Note: Court will not search but will provide case file information.

Civil Records: Access: Online, in person. Visitors must perform in person searches themselves. Court makes copy: $.50 per page. Required to search: name, years to search; also helpful: address. Civil cases indexed by defendant, plaintiff; on computer from 1985, on microfiche from 1971, archived from 1970, on card index from 1971. Online access is through JIS. See state introduction or visit www.courts.state.md.us.

Criminal Records: Access: Online, in person. Visitors must perform in person searches themselves. Court makes copy: $.50 per page. Required to search: name, years to search. Criminal records on computer since 1981. Online access through JIS. See state introduction or visit www.courts.state.md.us.

General Information: Public terminal has criminal back to 1981 and civil back to 1985. No adoptions, juvenile, sealed, expunged or medical records released. Certification fee: $5.00 per case. Payee: District Court of MD. Personal checks accepted. Prepayment required.

Register of Wills 401 Bosley Ave, Mail Stop 3507, Towson, MD 21204-4403; phone: 410-887-6685, 888-642-5387 in MD; fax: 410-583-2517; hours 8AM-3PM (EST). *Probate.*
www.registers.state.md.us/county/ba/html/baltimore.html

Baltimore City

8th Judicial Circuit Court - Civil Division 111 N Calvert, Rm 409, Baltimore, MD 21202; phone: 410-333-3722; civil phone: 410-369-3045; fax: 410-333-6986; hours 8:30AM-4:30PM (EST). *Civil Actions Over $25,000.*
www.baltocts.state.md.us

Civil Records: Access: Phone, mail, online, in person. Both court and visitors may perform in person searches. No search fee. Court makes copy: $.50 per page. Required to search: name, years to search; also helpful: address. Civil cases indexed by defendant. Civil records on computer from 1983. Online access is through JIS. See state introduction or visit www.courts.state.md.us. Note: Court conducts searches on a limited basis. Mail turnaround time 5 days.

General Information: Public terminal has only civil records. No adoptions, juvenile, sealed, expunged or mental records released. Certification fee: $5.00 per cert. Payee: Clerk of the Circuit Court. Business checks accepted. Prepayment required.

8th Judicial Circuit Court - Criminal Division 110 N Calvert Rm 200, Baltimore, MD 21202; phone: 410-333-3750; hours 8:30AM-4:30PM (EST). *Felony, Misdemeanor.*

Criminal Records: Access: Online, in person. Visitors must perform in person searches themselves. Court makes copy: $.50 per page; same fee for self serve. Required to search: name, years to search; also helpful: address, DOB. Criminal records on computer from 1994, on microfilm from 1973. Online access through SJIS; see www.courts.state.md.us.

General Information: Public terminal has only criminal records back to 1972. No adoptions, juvenile, sealed, expunged or mental records released. Certification fee: $5.00 per case. Payee: Clerk of Circuit Court. Business checks accepted.

District Court - Civil Division 501 E Fayette St, Baltimore, MD 21202; phone: 800-939-4523, 410-878-8900; hours 8:30AM-4:30PM (EST). *Civil Actions Under $25,000, Eviction, Small Claims.*

Civil Records: Access: Mail, online, in person. Both court and visitors may perform in person searches. No search fee. Court makes copy: $.25 per page. Required to search: name, years to search. Civil cases indexed by defendant. Civil records on computer from 1986, on card index from 1971. Online access is through JIS. See state introduction or visit www.courts.state.md.us. Mail turnaround time 1-2 days.

General Information: Public terminal has only civil records back to 1986. No medical or sealed records released. Certification fee: $5.00 per doc. Payee: District Court of MD. Personal checks accepted. Prepayment and SASE required.

District Court - Criminal Division 5800 Wabash Ave, Baltimore, MD 21215; phone: 800-939-4523, 410-878-8000; hours 8:30AM-4:30PM (EST). *Misdemeanor.*

Criminal Records: Access: Mail, online, in person. No search fee. Court makes copy: $.25 per page. Required to search: name, years to search; also helpful: SSN. Criminal records on computer from 1983, prior on index cards from 1970. Online access through JIS. See state introduction or visit www.courts.state.md.us. Mail turnaround time 1 week.

General Information: No public access terminal. No adoptions, juvenile, sealed, expunged, medical or mental records released. Certification fee: $5.00 per doc. Payee: District Court. Personal checks accepted. Prepayment and SASE required.

Register of Wills Courthouse East, 111 N Calvert St, Rm 352, Baltimore, MD 21202; phone: 410-752-5131, 888-876-0035 in MD; fax: 410-752-3494; hours 8AM-4:30PM (EST). *Probate.* www.registers.state.md.us/city/bc/html/baltimorecity.html

Calvert County

7th Judicial Circuit Court 175 Main St Courthouse, Prince Frederick, MD 20678; phone: 410-535-1660; criminal phone: x2266; civil phone: x2404; hours 8:30AM-4:30PM (EST). *Felony, Misdemeanor, Civil Actions Over $25,000.* www.courts.state.md.us/clerks/calvert

Civil Records: Access: Online, in person. Visitors must perform in person searches themselves. Court makes copy: $.25 per page; same fee for self serve. Required to search: name, years to search. Civil cases indexed by defendant, plaintiff; on computer back to 10/1997, prior on index books back to 1959. Online access is through JIS. See state introduction or visit www.courts.state.md.us.

Criminal Records: Access: In person only. Visitors must perform in person searches themselves. Court makes copy: $.25 per page; same fee for self serve. Required to search: name, years to search; SSN helpful. Criminal records on computer from 4/2000; prior in books back to 1967.

General Information: Public use terminal available. No adoptions, juvenile, sealed, expunged or mental records released. Will not fax documents. Certification fee: $5.00. Payee: Clerk of Circuit Court. Personal checks accepted. Prepayment required.

District Court 200 Duke St Rm 2200, Prince Frederick, MD 20678; phone: 443-550-6700; hours 8:30AM-4:30PM (EST). *Misdemeanor, Civil Actions Under $25,000, Eviction, Small Claims.*

Civil Records: Access: Mail, in person, online. Visitors must perform in person searches themselves. No search fee. Court makes copy: $.50 per page. Required to search: name; also helpful: address. Civil cases indexed by defendant. Civil records on computer from mid-80s, archived from 1971 to 1981, prior on Cott index. Online access is through JIS. See state introduction or visit www.courts.state.md.us. Mail turnaround time 1 week.

Criminal Records: Access: In person, online. Visitors must perform in person searches themselves. No search fee. Court makes copy: $.50 per page. Required to search: name; also helpful: address, DOB. Criminal records on computer from 1981, archived from 1971-1981, prior on cott index. Online access through JIS. See state introduction or visit www.courts.state.md.us. Mail turnaround time 1-3 days.

General Information: Public terminal goes back to 1991. No adoptions, juvenile, sealed, expunged or medical records released. Will not fax documents. Certification fee: $5.00 per cert includes copy fee. Payee: District Court of Maryland. Personal checks accepted. Prepayment and SASE required.

Register of Wills 175 Main St, Courthouse, Prince Frederick, MD 20678; phone: 410-535-0121, 888-374-0015 in MD; fax: 410-414-3952; hours 8:30AM-4:30PM (EST). *Probate.* www.registers.state.md.us/county/cv/html/calvert.html

Caroline County

2nd Judicial Circuit Court Box 458, Denton, MD 21629; phone: 410-479-1811; criminal/civil fax: 410-479-1142; hours 8:30AM-4:30PM (EST). *Felony, Misdemeanor, Civil Actions Over $25,000.* Note: Misdemeanor case records held at District Court until appealed, then stored at Circuit Court.

Civil Records: Access: Online, in person. Visitors must perform in person searches themselves. Court makes copy: $.50 per page. Self serve copy fee: $.25 per page. Required to search: name, years to search; also helpful: address. Civil cases indexed by defendant, plaintiff; on computer from 10/98, card index from 1774. Online access is through JIS. See state introduction or visit www.courts.state.md.us.

Criminal Records: Access: In person only. Visitors must perform in person searches themselves. Court makes copy: $.50 per page. Self serve copy fee: $.25 per page. Required to search: name, years to search; also helpful: address, DOB, SSN. Criminal records on computer from 2000, card index from 1774.

General Information: Public terminal goes back to 10/2000. No adoptions, juvenile, sealed, expunged or mental records released. Will not fax documents. Certification fee: $5.00 per cert. Payee: F Dale Minner, Clerk. Personal checks accepted. Prepayment required.

District Court 207 S 3rd St, Denton, MD 21629; phone: 410-819-4600; hours 8:30AM-4:30PM (EST). *Misdemeanor, Civil Actions Under $25,000, Eviction, Small Claims.*

Civil Records: Access: Online, in person. Visitors must perform in person searches themselves. Court makes copy: $.50. Required to search: name, years to search; also helpful: address. Civil cases indexed by defendant. Civil records on cards from 1971, computerized since 1981. Online access is through JIS. See state introduction or visit www.courts.state.md.us.

Criminal Records: Access: Online, in person. Visitors must perform in person searches themselves. Court makes copy: $.50. Required to search: name, years to search; also helpful: address, DOB. Criminal records on cards from 1971, computerized since 1981. Online access through JIS. See state introduction or visit www.courts.state.md.us.

General Information: No public access terminal. No adoptions, juvenile, sealed, expunged or mental records released. Certification fee: $5.00. Payee: District Court. Personal checks accepted. Prepayment required.

Register of Wills County Courthouse, 109 Market St, Rm 119, PO Box 416, Denton, MD 21629; phone: 410-479-0717, 888-786-0019 in MD; fax: 410-479-4983; hours 8AM-4:30PM (EST). *Probate.* www.registers.state.md.us/county/ca/html/caroline.html

Carroll County

5th Judicial Circuit Court 55 N Court St, Westminster, MD 21157; phone: 410-386-2985; criminal phone: 410-386-2025; civil phone: 410-386-2326; fax: 410-876-0822; hours 8:30AM-4:30PM (EST). *Felony, Misdemeanor, Civil Actions Over $25,000.*

Civil Records: Access: Online, in person. Visitors must perform in person searches themselves. Court makes copy: $.50 per page. Self serve copy fee: $.25 per page. Required to search: name; also helpful: years to search. Civil cases indexed by defendant, plaintiff; on computer from 1990, on card books from 1837 to 1990. Online access is through JIS. See state introduction or visit www.courts.state.md.us.

Criminal Records: Access: Online, in person. Visitors must perform in person searches themselves. Court makes copy: $.50 per page. Self

serve copy fee: $.25 per page. Required to search: name; also helpful: years to search. Criminal records on computer from 1990, on card books from 1837 to 1990. Online access through JIS. See state introduction or visit www.courts.state.md.us.

General Information: Public terminal goes back to 1990. No adoptions, juvenile, sealed, expunged or mental records released. Certification fee: $5.00 per document. Payee: Clerk of Court. Personal checks or Visa, MC accepted. Prepayment required.

District Court 101 N Court St, Westminster, MD 21157; phone: 410-871-3500; hours 8:30AM-4:30PM (EST). *Misdemeanor, Civil Actions Under $25,000, Eviction, Small Claims.*

Civil Records: Access: Online, in person. Visitors must perform in person searches themselves. Court makes copy: $.50 per page. Required to search: name, years to search. Civil cases indexed by defendant, plaintiff; on computer back to 1991; on card index from 1971. Online access is through JIS. See state introduction or visit www.courts.state.md.us.

Criminal Records: Access: Online, in person. Visitors must perform in person searches themselves. Court makes copy: $.50 per page. Required to search: name, years to search; also helpful: DOB. Criminal records on computer back to 1982; on card index from 1971. Online access through JIS. See state introduction or visit www.courts.state.md.us.

General Information: Public terminal has criminal back to 1982 and civil back to 1991. No adoptions, juvenile, sealed, shielded, expunged or mental records released. Will not fax documents. Certification fee: $5.00 per document. Payee: District Court. Personal checks accepted. Prepayment required.

Register of Wills 55 N Court St, Rm 124, Westminster, MD 21157; phone: 410-848-2586, 888-876-0034 in MD; fax: 410-876-0657; hours 8:30AM-4:30PM (EST). *Probate.* www.registers.state.md.us/county/cr/html/carroll.html

Cecil County

2nd Judicial Circuit Court 129 E Main St, Rm 108, Elkton, MD 21921; phone: 410-996-5325; civil phone: 410-996-5369; fax: 410-392-6032; hours 8:30AM-4:30PM (EST). *Felony, Misdemeanor, Civil Actions Over $25,000.*

Civil Records: Access: Online, in person. Visitors must perform in person searches themselves. Court makes copy: $1.00 per page. Self serve copy fee: $.50 per page. Required to search: name, years to search. Civil cases indexed by defendant. Civil records on card index from 1948. Online access is through JIS. See state introduction or visit www.courts.state.md.us.

Criminal Records: Access: in person only. Visitors must perform in person searches themselves. Court makes copy: $1.00 per page. Self serve copy fee: $.50 per page. Required to search: name, years to search; also helpful: DOB, SSN. Criminal records on card index from 1948; computerized since 1993.

General Information: Public terminal goes back to 1948. No adoptions, juvenile, sealed, expunged or mental records released. Certification fee: $5.00 per page. Payee: Clerk of Court. Personal checks accepted. Prepayment required.

District Court 170 E Main St, Elkton, MD 21921; phone: 410-996-2700; hours 8:30AM-4:30PM (EST). *Misdemeanor, Civil Actions Under $25,000, Eviction, Small Claims.*

Civil Records: Access: Online, in person. Visitors must perform in person searches themselves. Court makes copy: $.50 per page. Required to search: name, years to search. Civil cases indexed by defendant. Civil records on computer from 1987, on card index from 1971. Online access is through JIS. See state introduction or visit www.courts.state.md.us.

Criminal Records: Access: Online, in person. Visitors must perform in person searches themselves. Court makes copy: $.50 per page. Required to search: name, years to search. Criminal records on computer from 1981, on card index from

1971. Online access through JIS. See state introduction or visit www.courts.state.md.us.

General Information: Public terminal has criminal back to 1981 and civil back to 1987. No adoptions, juvenile, sealed, expunged or mental records released. Certification fee: $5.00. Payee: District Court. Personal checks accepted. Prepayment required.

Register of Wills County Courthouse, #101, PO Box 468, Elkton, MD 21922-0468; phone: 410-996-5330, 888-398-0301 in MD; fax: 410-996-1039; hours 8:30AM-4:30PM (EST). *Probate.*
www.registers.state.md.us/county/ce/html/cecil.html

Charles County

Circuit Court for Charles County PO Box 970, La Plata, MD 20646; phone: 301-932-3201 x223, 888-932-2072; fax: na/; hours 8:30AM-4:30PM (EST). *Felony, Misdemeanor, Civil Actions Over $2,500.*
www.courts.state.md.us/clerks/charles

Civil Records: Access: Online, in person. Visitors must perform in person searches themselves. Court makes copy: $.50 per page. Required to search: name, years to search. Civil cases indexed by defendant, plaintiff; on index books from 1950, on computer back to 1996. Online access is through JIS. See state introduction or visit www.courts.state.md.us.

Criminal Records: Access: In person only. Visitors must perform in person searches themselves. Court makes copy: $.50 per page. Required to search: name, years to search. Criminal records on index books from 1950, on computer back to 1996.

General Information: Public terminal goes back to 1996. No adoptions, juvenile, sealed, expunged or medical records released. Certification fee: $5.00 per cert. Payee: Clerk of the Circuit Court. Personal checks accepted. Prepayment required.

District Court PO Box 3070, La Plata, MD 20646; phone: 301-932-3300; criminal phone: 301-932-3295; civil phone: 301-932-3290; hours 8:30AM-4:30PM (EST). *Misdemeanor, Civil Actions Under $25,000, Eviction, Small Claims.*

Civil Records: Access: Online, in person. Visitors must perform in person searches themselves. Court makes copy: $.50 per page. Required to search: name, years to search. Civil cases indexed by defendant, plaintiff; on computer from 1987, on card index from 1980. Online access is through JIS. See state introduction or visit www.courts.state.md.us.

Criminal Records: Access: Online, in person. Visitors must perform in person searches themselves. Court makes copy: $.50 per page. Required to search: name, years to search. Criminal records on computer from 1984, on card index from 1980, from 9/98 on public access terminal. Online access through SJIS; see state introduction or visit www.courts.state.md.us.

General Information: Public terminal has criminal back to 1987 and civil back to 1981. No confidential info, unserved warrants, medical records released. Certification fee: $5.00 per doc; triple seal is $10.00. Payee: District Court. Personal checks accepted. Prepayment required.

Register of Wills Box 3080, Courthouse, 200 E Charles St, La Plata, MD 20646; phone: 301-932-3345, 888-256-0054 in MD; fax: 301-932-3349; hours 8:30AM-4:30PM (EST). *Probate.*
www.registers.state.md.us/county/ch/html/charles.html

Dorchester County

1st Judicial Circuit Court Box 150, Cambridge, MD 21613; phone: 410-228-0481; hours 8:30AM-4:30PM (EST). *Felony, Misdemeanor, Civil Actions Over $25,000.*

Civil Records: Access: Online, in person. Visitors must perform in person searches themselves. Court makes copy: $.25 per page; same fee for self serve. Required to search: name, years to search. Civil cases indexed by defendant, plaintiff; on computer from 1993. Online access is through JIS. See state introduction or visit www.courts.state.md.us.

Criminal Records: Access: In person only. Visitors must perform in person searches themselves. Court makes copy: $.25 per page; same fee for self serve. Required to search: name, years to search. Criminal records on computer from 1993.

General Information: Public use terminal available. No adoptions, juvenile, sealed, expunged or mental records released. Certification fee: $5.00. Payee: Clerk of Circuit Court.

District Court 310 Gay St, Cambridge, MD 21613; phone: 410-901-1420; hours 8:30AM-4:30PM (EST). *Misdemeanor, Civil Actions Under $25,000, Eviction, Small Claims.*

Civil Records: Access: Online, in person. Visitors must perform in person searches themselves. Court makes copy: $.50 per page. Required to search: name, years to search; also helpful: address. Civil cases indexed by defendant. Civil records archived and indexed from 1971; computerized records since 1985. Online access is through JIS. See state introduction or visit www.courts.state.md.us.

Criminal Records: Access: Online, in person. Visitors must perform in person searches themselves. Court makes copy: $.50 per page. Required to search: name, years to search; also helpful: address, DOB, SSN. Criminal records on card index from 1971; computerized records since 1985. Online access through JIS. See state introduction or visit www.courts.state.md.us.

General Information: Public terminal goes back to 1985. No adoptions, sealed, juvenile, expunged or mental records released. Certification fee: $5.00 per page. Payee: District Court. Personal checks accepted. Prepayment required.

Register of Wills 206 High St, Cambridge, MD 21613; phone: 410-228-4181, 888-242-6257 in MD; fax: 410-228-4988; hours 8AM-4:30PM; Public hours 8:30AM-4:30PM (EST). *Probate.*
www.registers.state.md.us/county/do/html/dorchester.html

Frederick County

6th Judicial Circuit Court 100 W Patrick St, Frederick, MD 21701; phone: 301-694-1970; hours 8:30AM-4:30PM (EST). *Felony, Misdemeanor, Civil Actions Over $25,000.*

Civil Records: Access: Online, in person. Visitors must perform in person searches themselves. Court makes copy: $.25 per page. Required to search: name, years to search. Civil cases indexed by defendant, plaintiff; on computer from 8/94, prior on card books. Online access is through JIS. See state introduction or visit www.courts.state.md.us.

Criminal Records: Access: In person only. Visitors must perform in person searches themselves. Court makes copy: $.25 per page. Required to search: name, years to search. Criminal records on computer from 12/81, prior on index books.

General Information: Public terminal goes back to 1987. No adoptions, juvenile, sealed, expunged or mental records released. Certification fee: $5.00 per doc. Payee: Clerk of Circuit Court. Personal checks accepted. Prepayment required.

District Court 100 W Patrick St, Frederick, MD 21701; phone: 301-694-2000; hours 8:30AM-4:30PM (EST). *Misdemeanor, Civil Actions Under $25,000, Eviction, Small Claims.*

Note: If the case number is known, the court will supply a copy of the disposition for $1.00 per page, turnaround time is 30 days.

Civil Records: Access: Online, in person. Visitors must perform in person searches themselves. Court makes copy: $.50 per page. Required to search: name; also helpful: years to search. Civil cases indexed by defendant, plaintiff; on computer and microfiche from 1986, archived and on card index from 1971. Online access is through JIS. See state introduction or visit www.courts.state.md.us.

Criminal Records: Access: Online, in person. Visitors must perform in person searches themselves. Court makes copy: $.50 per page. Required to search: name, DOB; also helpful: years to search. Criminal records on computer and microfiche

from 1982, archived and on card index from 1971. Online access through JIS. See state introduction or visit www.courts.state.md.us.

General Information: Public terminal has criminal back to 1982 and civil back to 1986. No adoptions, juvenile, sealed, expunged or mental records released. Certification fee: $5.00 per doc. Payee: District Court. Personal checks or Visa, MC, AmEx accepted. Prepayment required.

Register of Wills 100 W Patrick St, Frederick, MD 21701; phone: 301-663-3722, 888-258-0526; fax: 301-846-0744; hours 8AM-4:30PM (EST). *Probate.*
www.registers.state.md.us/county/fr/html/frederick.html

Garrett County

4th Judicial Circuit Court PO Box 447, Oakland, MD 21550; phone: 301-334-1937; criminal phone: 301-334-1943; civil phone: 301-334-1944; fax: 301-334-5017; hours 8:30AM-4:30PM (EST). *Felony, Misdemeanor, Civil Actions Over $25,000.*

Civil Records: Access: Mail, online, in person. No search fee. Court makes copy: $.50 per page. Required to search: name, years to search. Civil cases indexed by defendant, plaintiff; on computer since 11/97. Online access is through JIS. See state introduction or visit www.courts.state.md.us. Mail turnaround time 1 day.

Criminal Records: Access: Mail, in person. Both court and visitors may perform in person searches. No search fee. Court makes copy: $.50 per page. Required to search: name, years to search, DOB. Criminal records on computer since 11/97. Mail turnaround time 1 day.

General Information: Public use terminal available. No adoptions, juvenile, sealed, expunged or mental records released. Certification fee: $5.00 per page. Payee: David K Martin, Clerk. Personal checks accepted. Prepayment required.

District Court 205 S 3rd St, Oakland, MD 21550; phone: 301-334-8020; hours 8:30AM-4:30PM (EST). *Misdemeanor, Civil Actions Under $25,000, Eviction, Small Claims.*
www.courts.state.md.us/district

Civil Records: Access: Mail, online, in person. Visitors must perform in person searches themselves. Court makes copy: $.50 per page. Required to search: name, years to search. Civil cases indexed by defendant. Civil records on computer from 1990, on index books from 1971. Online access is through JIS. See state introduction or visit www.courts.state.md.us. Mail turnaround time 7 to 10 days.

Criminal Records: Access: Online, in person. Visitors must perform in person searches themselves. Court makes copy: $.50 per page. Required to search: name, years to search, DOB. Criminal records on computer from 1981. Online access through JIS. See state introduction or visit www.courts.state.md.us.

General Information: No public access terminal. No adoptions, juvenile, sealed, expunged or mental records released. Certification fee: $5.00 per page. Payee: District Court. Personal checks accepted. Prepayment and SASE required.

Register of Wills Courthouse, 313 E Alder St, Rm 103, Oakland, MD 21550; phone: 301-334-1999, 888-334-2203 in MD; fax: 301-334-1984; hours 8AM-4:30PM (EST). *Probate.*
www.registers.state.md.us/county/ga/html/garrett.html

Harford County

3rd Judicial Circuit 20 W Courtland St, Bel Air, MD 21014; criminal phone: 410-638-3042; civil phone: 410-638-3430; probate phone: 410-638-3275; hours 8:30AM-4:30PM (EST). *Felony, Misdemeanor, Civil Actions Over $25,000.*
www.courts.state.md.us/harford.html

Civil Records: Access: Online, in person. Visitors must perform in person searches themselves. Court

makes copy: $.50 per page. Self serve copy fee: $.25 per page. Required to search: name, years to search; also helpful: address. Civil cases indexed by defendant, plaintiff; on computer since 8/92 and books prior. Online access is through JIS. See state introduction or visit www.courts.state.md.us.
Criminal Records: Access: In person only. Visitors must perform in person searches themselves. Court makes copy: $.50 per page. Self serve copy fee: $.25 per page. Required to search: name, years to search; also helpful: DOB. Criminal records on computer since 8/92 and on books prior.
General Information: Public terminal goes back to 8/1992. No adoptions, presentence investigations, juvenile, sealed, expunged or mental records released. Certification fee: $5.00 per cert. Payee: Clerk of the Circuit Court. Only cashiers checks and money orders accepted. Prepayment required.

District Court 2 S Bond St, Bel Air, MD 21014; phone: 410-836-4545; hours 8:30AM-4:30PM (EST). *Misdemeanor, Civil Actions Under $25,000, Eviction, Small Claims.*
Civil Records: Access: Mail, online, in person. Visitors must perform in person searches themselves. No search fee. Court makes copy: $.50 per page. Required to search: name, years to search. Civil cases indexed by defendant. Civil records on computer from 1989, on microfiche from 1972, archived from 1900. Online access is through JIS. See state introduction or visit www.courts.state.md.us. Mail turnaround 4 days.
Criminal Records: Access: Mail, online, in person. Visitors must perform in person searches themselves. No search fee. Court makes copy: $.50 per page. Required to search: name, years to search; also helpful: address, DOB. Criminal records on computer from 1981, on microfiche from 1972, archived from 1900. Online access through JIS. See state introduction or visit www.courts.state.md.us. Mail turnaround time 3-4 days.
General Information: Public terminal goes back to 1981. No motor vehicle, sealed, expunged or mental records released. Certification fee: $5.00. Payee: District Court of MD. Personal checks or Visa, MC, AmEx accepted. Prepayment and SASE required.

Register of Wills 20 W Courtland St, Rm 304, Court House, Bel Air, MD 21014; phone: 410-638-3275, 888-258-0525 in MD; fax: 410-893-3177; hours 8:30AM-4:00PM (EST). *Probate.*
www.registers.state.md.us/county/ha/html/harford.html

Howard County

5th Judicial Circuit Court 8360 Court Ave, Ellicott City, MD 21043; phone: 410-313-2111; 888-313-0197; hours 8:30AM-4:30PM (EST). *Felony, Misdemeanor, Civil Actions Over $25,000.*
Civil Records: Access: Online, in person. Visitors must perform in person searches themselves. Court makes copy: $.50 per page. Required to search: name, years to search; also helpful: address. Civil cases indexed by defendant, plaintiff; on computer from 1984, archived from 1900, on card index from 1900. Online access is through JIS. See state introduction or visit www.courts.state.md.us.
Criminal Records: Access: In person only. Visitors must perform in person searches themselves. Court makes copy: $.50 per page. Required to search: name, years to search; also helpful: address, DOB, SSN. Criminal records on card index to 1840, on computer since 1984.
General Information: Public use terminal available. No adoptions, juvenile, sealed, expunged or mental records released. Certification fee: $5.00 per page. Payee: Office of Clerk. Personal checks accepted. Prepayment required.

District Court 3451 Courthouse Dr, Ellicott City, MD 21043; phone: 410-480-7700; hours 8:30AM-4:30PM (EST). *Misdemeanor, Civil Actions Under $25,000, Eviction, Small Claims.*
Civil Records: Access: Mail, online, in person. Both court and visitors may perform in person searches. No search fee. Court makes copy: $.50 per page; same

fee for self serve. Required to search: name, years to search. Civil cases indexed by defendant. Civil records on computer from 1992, on card index prior from 1971. Online access is through JIS. See state introduction or visit www.courts.state.md.us. Mail turnaround time before 1989 4-6 weeks, 1989-present 7 days.
Criminal Records: Access: Mail, online, in person. Both court and visitors may perform in person searches. No search fee. Court makes copy: $.50 per page; same fee for self serve. Required to search: name, years to search. Criminal records on computer from 1989, on card index prior from 1971. Online access through JIS. See state introduction or visit www.courts.state.md.us. Mail turnaround time before 1989- 4-6 weeks, 1989-present- 7 days.
General Information: Public terminal has criminal back to 1985 and civil back to 1990. No adoptions, juvenile, sealed, expunged or mental records released. Certification fee: $5.00. Payee: District Court of MD. Personal checks accepted. Credit cards accepted: Visa. Prepayment and SASE required if return receipt requested.

Register of Wills 8360 Court Ave, Ellicott City, MD 21043; phone: 410-313-2133, 888-848-0136 in MD; fax: 410-313-3409; hours 8:30AM-4:30PM (EST). *Probate.*
www.registers.state.md.us/county/ho/html/howard.html

Kent County

2nd Judicial Circuit Court 103 N Cross St Courthouse, Chestertown, MD 21620; phone: 410-778-7460; criminal phone: 410-778-7477; civil phone: 410-778-7461; criminal/civil fax: 410-778-7412; hours 8:30AM-4:30PM (EST). *Felony, Misdemeanor, Civil Actions Over $25,000.*
www.courts.state.md.us/clerks/kent/records.html
Civil Records: Access: Online, in person. Visitors must perform in person searches themselves. Court makes copy: $.50 per page. Self serve copy fee: $.25 per page. Required to search: name, years to search. Civil cases indexed by defendant, plaintiff; on computer from 1991, on card index from 1656. Online access is through JIS. See state introduction or visit www.courts.state.md.us.
Criminal Records: Access: In person only. Visitors must perform in person searches themselves. Court makes copy: $.50 per page. Self serve copy fee: $.25 per page. Required to search: name, years to search; also helpful: DOB, SSN. Criminal records on computer from 7/98, on card index from 1949, archived to 1656.
General Information: Public terminal goes back to 5/1998. No adoptions, juvenile, sealed, expunged or mental records released. Will not fax documents. Certification fee: $5.00 per cert. Payee: Mark L Mumford, Clerk. Personal checks accepted. Prepayment required.

District Court 103 N Cross St, Chestertown, MD 21620; phone: 410-810-3362; fax: 410-810-3361; hours 8:30AM-4:30PM (EST). *Misdemeanor, Civil Actions Under $25,000, Eviction, Small Claims.*
Civil Records: Access: Online, in person. Visitors must perform in person searches themselves. Court makes copy: $.50 per page. Required to search: name, years to search. Civil cases indexed by defendant. Civil records on computer from 1989; on card index from 1971. Online access is through JIS. See state introduction or visit www.courts.state.md.us.
Criminal Records: Access: Online, in person. Visitors must perform in person searches themselves. Court makes copy: $.50 per page. Required to search: name, years to search, DOB. Criminal records on computer from 1988, on card index from 1971. Online access through JIS. See state introduction or visit www.courts.state.md.us.
General Information: No public access terminal. No sealed, expunged, mental records or judge's notes released. Will not fax documents. Certification fee: $5.00 per document includes copies. Payee: District Court of MD. Personal checks accepted. Visa, AmEx accepted. Prepayment required.

Register of Wills 103 N Cross St, Chestertown, MD 21620; phone: 410-778-7466, 888-778-0179 in MD; fax: 410-778-2466; hours 8AM-4:30PM (EST). *Probate.*
www.registers.state.md.us/county/ke/html/kent.html

Montgomery County

6th Judicial Circuit Court 50 Maryland Ave, Rockville, MD 20850; phone: 240-777-9466; fax: 240-777-9468; hours 8:30AM-4:30PM (EST). *Felony, Misdemeanor, Civil Actions Over $25,000.*
www.montgomerycountymd.gov/mc/judicial
Civil Records: Access: Phone, mail, in person, online. Both court and visitors may perform in person searches. No search fee. Court makes copy: $.50 per page. Required to search: name, years to search; also helpful: case number. Civil cases indexed by defendant, plaintiff; on computer from 1977, archived from 1900, on card index from 1977. Online access is through JIS. See state introduction or v www.courts.state.md.us. The daily calendar free at www.montgomerycountymd.gov/mc/judicial/circu it/docket.html. Note: This court will not provide name searches, only copies of specific documents. Mail turnaround time 5-7 days.
Criminal Records: Access: Phone, mail, fax, in person. Both court and visitors may perform in person searches. No search fee. Court makes copy: $.50 per page. Required to search: name, years to search; also helpful: case number. Criminal records on computer from 1973, archived from 1900, on card index from 1977. Will not provide name searches, only copies of specific documents. Mail turnaround time 5-7 days.
General Information: Public terminal has criminal to 1973 and civil to 1977. No adoptions, juvenile, sealed, expunged or mental records released. Will not fax documents. Certification fee: $5.00 per document. Payee: Clerk of Circuit Court. Personal checks accepted. Prepayment required. SASE requested.

District Court 8552 Second Ave, Silver Spring, MD 20910; phone: 301-563-8500, 866-873-9785; hours 8:30AM-4:30PM (EST). *Misdemeanor, Civil Actions Under $25,000, Eviction, Small Claims.*
Civil Records: Access: Mail, online, in person. Both court and visitors may perform in person searches. No search fee. Court makes copy: $.50 per page. Required to search: name, years to search. Civil cases indexed by defendant, plaintiff; on computer from 1986, in book index and case folder. Online access is through JIS, visit www.courts.state.md.us. Mail turnaround 2-4 weeks.
Criminal Records: Access: Mail, online, in person. Both court and visitors may perform in person searches. No search fee. Court makes copy: $.50 per page. Required to search: name, years to search. Criminal records on computer, index book and case folder. Online access through JIS. See state introduction or visit www.courts.state.md.us. Mail turnaround time 2-4 weeks.
General Information: Public use terminal available. No juvenile, sealed, expunged or mental records or judge's notes released. Certification fee: $5.00 per cert. Payee: District Court. Personal checks accepted. Prepayment and SASE required.

Rockville District Court 27 Courthouse Square, Rockville, MD 20850; criminal phone: 301-279-1565; civil phone: 301-279-1500; hours 8:30AM-4:30PM (EST). *Misdemeanor, Civil Actions Under $25,000, Eviction, Small Claims.*
Civil Records: Access: Mail, online, in person. Both court and visitors may perform in person searches. No search fee. Court makes copy: $.50 per page. Required to search: name, years to search. Civil cases indexed by defendant. Civil records go back to 1971; on computer back to 1990, prior in case folder. Online access is through JIS. See state introduction or visit www.courts.state.md.us. Mail turnaround time 2-4 weeks.
Criminal Records: Access: Mail, online, in person. Both court and visitors may perform in person searches. No search fee. Court makes copy: $.50 per

page. Required to search: name, years to search; also helpful: DOB. Criminal records go back to 1971; on computer back to 1987. Online access to criminal records same as civil. Mail turnaround 2-4 weeks.
General Information: Public terminal has criminal back to 1987 and civil back to 1990. No juvenile, sealed, expunged, mental records or judge's notes released. Certification fee: $5.00 per page. Payee: District Court. Personal checks accepted. Prepayment and SASE required.

Register of Wills Judicial Ctr, 50 Maryland Ave, #322, Rockville, MD 20850; phone: 240-777-9600; fax: 240-777-9602; hours 8:30AM-4:30PM (EST). *Probate.* www.registers.state.md.us/county/mo/html/montgomery.html

Prince George's County

7th Judicial Circuit Court 14735 Main St, Upper Marlboro, MD 20772; criminal phone: 301-952-4828; civil phone: 301-952-3240; hours 8:30AM-4:30PM (EST). *Felony, Misdemeanor, Civil Actions Over $25,000.*
Note: Civil court physical address is Courthouse Annex Bldg, 14701 Gov Odenbilly Dr.
Civil Records: Access: In person, online. Visitors must perform in person searches themselves. Court makes copy: $.50 per page. Required to search: name, years to search. Civil cases indexed by defendant, plaintiff; on computer from 1981, on microfiche from 1979, on card index prior. Online access is through JIS. See state introduction or visit www.courts.state.md.us.
Criminal Records: Access: In person only. Visitors must perform in person searches themselves. Court makes copy: $.50 per page. Required to search: name, years to search, DOB; SSN helpful. Criminal records on computer from 1981, on microfiche from 1979, on card index prior. Court suggests criminal searches through law enforcement dept at 888-795-0011.
General Information: Public terminal has criminal back to 1980 and civil back to 1981. No adoptions, juvenile, sealed, expunged or mental records released. Certification fee: $5.00 per page. Payee: Clerk of Circuit Court. Personal checks accepted. Prepayment required.

District Court 14735 Main St, Rm 173B, Upper Marlboro, MD 20772; phone: 301-952-4080, 800-943-8853; hours 8:30AM-4:30PM (EST). *Misdemeanor, Civil Actions Under $25,000, Eviction, Small Claims.*
Civil Records: Access: Mail, online, in person. Both court and visitors may perform in person searches. No search fee. Court makes copy: $.50 per page. Required to search: name, years to search. Civil cases indexed by defendant. Civil records on computer from 1988, on card index from 1970. Online access is through JIS, visit www.courts.state.md.us. Mail turnaround 1-2 weeks.
Criminal Records: Access: Mail, online, in person. Visitors must perform in person searches themselves. Court makes copy: $.50 per page. Required to search: name, years to search. Criminal records on computer from 1984, on cards from 1970. Online access through JIS. See state introduction or visit www.courts.state.md.us. Mail turnaround time 1-2 weeks.
General Information: Public use terminal available. No adoptions, juvenile, sealed, expunged or mental records released. Certification fee: $5.00 per page. Payee: District Court of Maryland. Personal checks accepted. Prepayment and SASE required.

Register of Wills PO Box 1729, 5303 Chrysler Way #300, Upper Marlboro, MD 20773; phone: 301-952-3250, 888-464-4219 in MD; fax: 301-952-4489; hours 8:30AM-4:30PM (3:30 is paperwork cutoff time) (EST). *Probate.* www.registers.state.md.us/county/pg/html/princegeorges.html

Queen Anne's County

2nd Judicial Circuit Court Courthouse, 100 Courthouse Sq, Centreville, MD 21617; phone: 410-758-1773, 800-987-7591; hours 8:30AM-4:30PM (EST). *Felony, Misdemeanor, Civil Actions Over $25,000.*
Note: Misdemeanor case records held at District Court until appealed, then stored at Circuit Court.
Civil Records: Access: Online, in person. Visitors must perform in person searches themselves. Required to search: name, years to search. Civil cases indexed by defendant, plaintiff; on computer from 11/92; on index books from 1978. Online access is through JIS. See state introduction or visit www.courts.state.md.us.
Criminal Records: Access: In person only. Visitors must perform in person searches themselves. Required to search: name, years to search, SSN. Criminal records on computer from 11/92; on index books from 1978.
General Information: Public terminal goes back to 11/1992. No adoptions, juvenile, sealed, expunged or mental records released. Certification fee: $5.00 per cert. Payee: Clerk of Circuit Court. Personal checks accepted. Prepayment required.

District Court 120 Broadway, Centreville, MD 21617; phone: 410-819-4000; hours 8:30AM-4:30PM (EST). *Misdemeanor, Civil Actions Under $25,000, Eviction, Small Claims.*
Civil Records: Access: Online, in person. Visitors must perform in person searches themselves. Court makes copy: $.50. Required to search: name, years to search; also helpful: address. Civil cases indexed by defendant. Civil records on computer from 1988, archived from 1974, prior on index books. Online access is through JIS. See state introduction or visit www.courts.state.md.us.
Criminal Records: Access: Online, in person. Visitors must perform in person searches themselves. Court makes copy: $.50. Required to search: name, years to search; also helpful: address, DOB, SSN. Criminal records on computer from 1981, prior on index books. Online access through JIS. See state introduction or visit www.courts.state.md.us.
General Information: No public access terminal. No adoptions, juvenile, sealed, expunged or mental records released. Certification fee: $5.00. Payee: District Court of Maryland. Personal checks accepted. Visa, Discover accepted. Prepayment required.

Register of Wills Liberty Bldg, 107 N Liberty St #220, PO Box 59, Centreville, MD 21617; phone: 410-758-0585, 888-758-0010 in MD; fax: 410-758-4408; hours 8AM-4:30PM (EST). *Probate.* www.registers.state.md.us/county/qa/html/queenannes.html

Somerset County

1st Judicial Circuit Court PO Box 99, Princess Anne, MD 21853; criminal phone: 410-845-4850; civil phone: 410-845-4855; probate phone: 410-651-1630; fax: 410-845-4841; hours 8:30AM-4:30PM (EST). *Felony, Misdemeanor, Civil Actions Over $25,000.*
Civil Records: Access: Online, in person. Visitors must perform in person searches themselves. Court makes copy: $.50 per page. Required to search: name, years to search; also helpful: address. Civil cases indexed by defendant, plaintiff; on computer from 9/93; prior archived and on index books. Online access is through JIS. See state introduction or visit www.courts.state.md.us.
Criminal Records: Access: In person only. Visitors must perform in person searches themselves. Court makes copy: $.50 per page. Required to search: name, years to search; also helpful: address, DOB, SSN. Criminal records on computer from 9/93; prior archived and on index books.
General Information: Public terminal has criminal back to 1999 and civil back to 1997. No adoptions, juvenile, sealed, expunged or mental records released.

Will not fax documents. Certification fee: $5.00. Payee: Clerk of Circuit Court. Personal checks accepted. Prepayment required.

District Court 12155 Elm St #C, Princess Anne, MD 21853-1358; phone: 800-939-7306, 410-845-4700; fax: 410-845-4701; hours 8:30AM-4:30PM (EST). *Misdemeanor, Civil Actions Under $25,000, Eviction, Small Claims.*
Note: Misdemeanor cases go to Circuit Court if preliminary hearing waived. Records held at court where trial heard.
Civil Records: Access: Online, in person. Visitors must perform in person searches themselves. Court makes copy: $.25 per page. Required to search: name, years to search. Civil cases indexed by defendant, plaintiff; on computer from 1987, archived and on index books from 1971. Online access is through JIS. See state introduction or visit www.courts.state.md.us.
Criminal Records: Access: Online, in person. Visitors must perform in person searches themselves. Court makes copy: $.25 per page. Required to search: name, years to search; also helpful: SSN. Criminal records on computer from 1987, archived and on index books from 1971. Online access through JIS. See state introduction or visit www.courts.state.md.us.
General Information: Public terminal goes back to 1987. No adoptions, juvenile, sealed, expunged or mental records released. Certification fee: $5.00 per doc. Payee: District Court. Personal checks accepted. Prepayment required.

Register of Wills 30512 Prince William St, Princess Anne, MD 21853; phone: 410-651-1696, 888-758-0039 in MD; fax: 410-651-3873; hours 8:AM-4:30PM (EST). *Probate.* www.registers.state.md.us/county/so/html/somerset.html

St. Mary's County

7th Judicial Circuit Court PO Box 676, Leonardtown, MD 20650; phone: 301-475-4567; hours 8:30AM-4:30PM (EST). *Felony, Misdemeanor, Civil Actions Over $25,000.*
Civil Records: Access: Online, in person. Visitors must perform in person searches themselves. Court makes copy: $.50 per page. Required to search: name, years to search. Civil cases indexed by defendant, plaintiff; on computer from 1987, on card index from 1970. Online access is through JIS. See state introduction or visit www.courts.state.md.us.
Criminal Records: Access: In person only. Visitors must perform in person searches themselves. Court makes copy: $.50 per page. Required to search: name, years to search; SSN helpful. Criminal records on computer from 1987, on card index from 1970.
General Information: Public use terminal available. No adoptions, juvenile, sealed, expunged or mental records released. Certification fee: $5.00 per cert. Payee: Clerk of the Circuit Court. Personal checks accepted. Prepayment required.

District Court Carter State Office Bldg, 23110 Leonard Hall Dr, PO Box 653, Leonardtown, MD 20650; phone: 301-475-4530; hours 8:30AM-4:30PM (EST). *Misdemeanor, Civil Actions Under $25,000, Eviction, Small Claims.*
Civil Records: Access: Online, in person. Visitors must perform in person searches themselves. Court makes copy: $.50 per page; same fee for self serve. Required to search: name, years to search. Civil cases indexed by defendant. Civil records on computer from 1987, archived from 1971. Online access is through JIS. See state introduction or visit www.courts.state.md.us.
Criminal Records: Access: Online, in person. Visitors must perform in person searches themselves. Court makes copy: $.50 per page; same fee for self serve. Required to search: name, years to search; also helpful: DOB. Criminal records on computer from 1985, archived from 1971. Online access through JIS. See state introduction or visit www.courts.state.md.us.

General Information: Public use terminal available. No adoptions, juvenile, sealed, expunged or mental records released. Certification fee: $5.00, or triple seal for $10.00. Payee: District Court of Maryland. Personal checks accepted. Prepayment required.

Register of Wills 41605 Court House Drive, PO Box 602, Leonardtown, MD 20650; phone: 301-475-5566; fax: 301-475-4968; hours 8:30AM-4:30PM (EST). *Probate.*
www.registers.state.md.us/county/sm/html/stmarys.html

Talbot County

Circuit Court PO Box 723, Easton, MD 21601; phone: 410-822-2611; fax: 410-820-8168; hours 8:30AM-4:30PM (EST). *Felony, Misdemeanor, Civil Actions Over $25,000.*
www.courts.state.md.us/clerks/talbot/index.html
Civil Records: Access: Online, in person. Visitors must perform in person searches themselves. Court makes copy: $.50 per page. Self serve copy fee: $.25 per page. Required to search: name, years to search; also helpful: address. Civil cases indexed by defendant, plaintiff; on card index from 1993. Online access is through JIS. See state introduction or visit www.courts.state.md.us.
Criminal Records: Access: In person only. Visitors must perform in person searches themselves. Court makes copy: $.50 per page. Self serve copy fee: $.25 per page. Required to search: name, years to search; also helpful: address, DOB, SSN. Criminal records on card index from 1993.
General Information: Public terminal to 1997. No adoptions, juvenile, sealed, expunged or mental records released. Certification fee: $5.00. Payee: Mary Ann Shortall, Clerk of Court. Personal checks accepted. Prepayment required.

District Court 108 W Dover St, Easton, MD 21601; phone: 410-819-5850; hours 8:30AM-4:30PM (EST). *Misdemeanor, Civil Actions Under $25,000, Eviction, Small Claims.*
Civil Records: Access: Online, in person. Visitors must perform in person searches themselves. Court makes copy: $.50 per page. Required to search: name, years to search. Civil cases indexed by defendant. Civil records go back to 1971; on computer back to 1988. Online access is through JIS. See state introduction or visit www.courts.state.md.us.
Criminal Records: Access: Online, in person. Visitors must perform in person searches themselves. Court makes copy: $.50 per page. Required to search: name, years to search. Criminal records go back to 1971; on computer back to 1984. Online access through JIS. See state introduction or visit www.courts.state.md.us.
General Information: Public terminal has criminal back to 1984 and civil back to 1988. No adoptions, juvenile, sealed, expunged or mental records released. Will not fax documents. Certification fee: $5.00. Payee: District Court of MD. Personal checks accepted. Prepayment required.

Register of Wills Courthouse, 11 N Washington St, Easton, MD 21601; phone: 410-770-6700, 888-822-0039 in MD; fax: 410-822-5452; hours 8AM-4:30PM (EST). *Probate.*
www.registers.state.md.us/county/ta/html/talbot.html

Washington County

Washington County Circuit Court Box 229, Hagerstown, MD 21741; phone: 301-733-8660; criminal phone: 301-790-7941; civil phone: 301-790-4972; fax: 301-791-1151; hours 8:30AM-4:30PM (EST). *Felony, Misdemeanor, Civil Actions Over $25,000.*
Civil Records: Access: Online, in person. Visitors must perform in person searches themselves. Court makes copy: $.50 per page. Self serve copy fee: $.25 per page. Required to search: name, years to search. Civil cases indexed by defendant. Civil records on case files, docket books to 1900; on computer back to 1985. Online access is through JIS. See state introduction or visit www.courts.state.md.us.

Criminal Records: Access: In person only. Visitors must perform in person searches themselves. Court makes copy: $.50 per page. Self serve copy fee: $.25 per page. Required to search: name, years to search; also helpful: DOB. Criminal records on case files, docket books to 1900; on computer back to 1985.
General Information: Public use terminal available. No adoptions, juvenile, sealed, expunged or mental records released. Certification fee: $5.00. Payee: Clerk of Circuit Court. Personal checks accepted. Prepayment required.

District Court 36 W Antietam St, Hagerstown, MD 21740; phone: 800-945-1406, 240-420-4600; hours 8:30AM-4:30PM (EST). *Misdemeanor, Civil Actions Under $25,000, Eviction, Small Claims.*
Civil Records: Access: Phone, mail, online, in person. Both court and visitors may perform in person searches. No search fee. Court makes copy: $.25 per page. Required to search: name, years to search; also helpful: address. Civil cases indexed by defendant. Civil records on computer from 1986, archived and on index books from 1971. Online access is through JIS. See state introduction or visit www.courts.state.md.us.
Criminal Records: Access: Online, in person. Visitors must perform in person searches themselves. Required to search: name, years to search; also helpful: address, DOB, SSN, case number. Criminal records on computer from 1982, on index books from 1971. Online access through JIS. See state introduction or visit www.courts.state.md.us.
General Information: Public terminal has criminal back to 1982 and civil back to 1986. No adoptions, juvenile, sealed, expunged or mental records released. Certification fee: $5.00 per doc. Payee: District Court. Personal checks accepted. Visa, Discover accepted. Prepayment and SASE required.

Register of Wills 95 W Washington, Hagerstown, MD 21740; phone: 301-739-3612, 888-739-0013 in MD; fax: 301-733-8636; hours 8:00AM-4:30PM (EST). *Probate.*
www.registers.state.md.us/county/wa/html/washington.html

Wicomico County

1st Judicial Circuit Court PO Box 198, Salisbury, MD 21803-0198; phone: 410-543-6551; fax: 410-546-8590; hours 8:30AM-4:30PM (EST). *Felony, Misdemeanor, Civil Actions Over $25,000.*
Civil Records: Access: Phone, mail, online, in person. Both court and visitors may perform in person searches. Court makes copy: $.50 per page. Self serve copy fee: $.25 per page. Required to search: name, years to search. Civil cases indexed by defendant, plaintiff; on books since 1867, cases filed after 5/93 on computer. Online access through JIS; www.courts.state.md.us. All phone requests must include case number. Mail turnaround 1-2 days.
Criminal Records: Access: Phone, mail, in person. Both court and visitors may perform in person searches. No search fee. Court makes copy: $.50 per page. Self serve copy fee: $.25 per page. Required to search: name, years to search; also helpful: DOB, SSN. Criminal records on books since 1867, cases filed after 5/93 on computer. Phone requests must include case number. Mail turnaround 1-2 days.
General Information: Public terminal goes back to 1993. No adoptions, juvenile, sealed, expunged or mental records released. Certification fee: $5.00. Payee: Clerk of Circuit Court. Personal checks accepted. Out of state checks not accepted. Prepayment required.

District Court 201 Baptist St, Salisbury, MD 21801; phone: 410-543-6600; hours 8:30AM-4:30PM (EST). *Misdemeanor, Civil Actions Under $25,000, Eviction, Small Claims.*
Civil Records: Access: Online, in person. Visitors must perform in person searches themselves. Court makes copy: $.50 per page. Required to search: name, years to search; also helpful: address. Civil cases

indexed by defendant, plaintiff; on computer go back to 1985, archived from 1984, on card index from 1971. Online access is through JIS. See state introduction or visit www.courts.state.md.us.
Criminal Records: Access: Online, in person. Visitors must perform in person searches themselves. Court makes copy: $.50 per page. Required to search: name, years to search; also helpful: address, DOB. Criminal records go back to 1971; on computer back 1983. Online access through JIS. See state introduction or visit www.courts.state.md.us.
General Information: Public terminal has criminal back to 1985 and civil back to 1982. No adoptions, juvenile, sealed, expunged or mental records released. Certification fee: $5.00. Payee: District Court. Personal checks accepted. Prepayment required.

Register of Wills 101 N Division St, Rm 102, Salisbury, MD 21801; phone: 410-543-6635, 888-786-0018 in MD; fax: 410-334-3440; hours 8:30AM-4:30PM (EST). *Probate.*
www.registers.state.md.us/county/wi/html/wicomico.html

Worcester County

1st Judicial Circuit Court Clerk of Circuit Court, PO Box 40, Snow Hill, MD 21863; criminal phone: 410-632-5502; civil phone: 410-632-5501; hours 8:30AM-4:30PM (EST). *Felony, Misdemeanor, Civil Actions Over $25,000.*
Civil Records: Access: In person only. Visitors must perform in person searches themselves. Court makes copy: $.50 per page. Self serve copy fee: $.25 per page. Required to search: name, years to search. Civil cases indexed by defendant. Civil records indexed on computer since 7/93, on docket books prior.
Criminal Records: Access: In person only. Visitors must perform in person searches themselves. Court makes copy: $.50 per page. Self serve copy fee: $.25 per page. Required to search: name, years to search. Criminal records indexed on computer since 7/93, on docket books prior.
General Information: Public terminal goes back to 1993. No adoptions, juvenile, sealed or expunged records released. Will not fax specific case file. Certification fee: $5.00. Payee: Clerk of Circuit Court. Personal checks accepted. Prepayment required.

District Court 301 Commerce St, Snow Hill, MD 21863-1007; phone: 800-941-0282, 410-219-7830; fax: 410-219-7840; hours 8:30AM-4:30PM (EST). *Misdemeanor, Civil Actions Under $25,000, Eviction, Small Claims.*
Civil Records: Access: Online, in person. Visitors must perform in person searches themselves. Court makes copy: $.50 per page. Required to search: name, years to search; also helpful: address. Civil cases indexed by defendant. Civil records on computer since 1988. Online access is through JIS. See state intro or visit www.courts.state.md.us. Records can be researched via books in the lobby.
Criminal Records: Access: Online, in person. Visitors must perform in person searches themselves. Court makes copy: $.50 per page. Required to search: name, years to search; also helpful: address, DOB, SSN. Criminal records on computer since 1982. Online access through JIS. See state intro or visit www.courts.state.md.us. Records can be researched via books in the lobby.
General Information: Public terminal goes to 1993. No sealed or juvenile records released. Certification fee: $5.00 per page. Payee: District Court. Personal checks accepted. Prepayment required.

Register of Wills Courthouse, 1 W Market St, Rm 102, Snow Hill, MD 21863-1074; phone: 410-632-1529, 888-256-0047 in MD; fax: 410-632-5600; hours 8AM-4:30PM (EST). *Probate.*
www.registers.state.md.us/county/wo/html/worcester.html

Maryland Recording Offices

ORGANIZATION: 23 counties and one independent city, 24 recording offices. The recording officer is Clerk of the Circuit Court. Baltimore City has a recording office separate from the county of Baltimore. See the City/County Locator section at the end of this chapter for ZIP Codes that include both the city and the county. The entire state is in the Eastern Time Zone (EST).

REAL ESTATE RECORDS: Counties will not perform real estate searches. Copies usually cost $.50 per page, and certification fees $5.00 per document.

UCC RECORDS: This was a dual filing state until July 1995. As of July 1995, all new UCC filings except for consumer goods, farm related and real estate related filings were submitted only to the central filing office. Starting July 2001, only real estate related filing are submitted to the Clerk of Circuit Court.

TAX LIEN RECORDS: All tax liens are filed with the county Clerk of Circuit Court. Counties will not perform name searches.

OTHER LIENS: Judgment, mechanics, county, hospital, condominium.

ONLINE ACCESS: Search statewide property records data free at http://sdatcert3.resiusa.org/rp_rewrite/. There is no name searching. Also, the Maryland State Dept. of Planning offers MDPropertyview with property maps/parcels and assessments on the web or CD-Rom. Registration required; visit www.mdp.state.md.us or call 410-767-4614 or 410-767-4474. There is no name searching. Also, vendors provide online access in several places. County tax records are at www.taxrecords.com. Land survey, condominium and survey plats is available free by county at www.plats.net. Use username "Plato" and password "plato#". No name searching.

Allegany County

County Clerk of the Circuit Court, 30 Washington St, Cumberland, MD 21502-2948. 301-777-5922; fax-301-777-2100; hours: 8AM-4:30PM
Only the public may search. Copy fee $1.00 per page. RE or tax lien copy- $.50 per page. Cert fee- $5.00 per doc plus copy fee. Payee- Allegany County Clerk of Circuit Court. **Online access to Real Property, Land Survey/Plat records:** Search real property data free at http://sdatcert3.resiusa.org/rp_rewrite/. No name searching. Also, see state introduction for add'l land records online from www.plats.net (use username "Plato" and password "plato#") and MDPropertyview at www.mdp.state.md.us/data/mdview.htm. No name searching. **Other phones:** Treasurer- 301-777-5965. **Property tax/Assessor-** 301-777-2108.

Anne Arundel County

County Clerk of the Circuit Court, PO Box 71, Annapolis, MD 21404. 410-222-1425; fax-410-222-1087; hours: 8:30AM-4:30PM
Separate indices to search include mainframe, electronic, old books. Office will perform a UCC search but public must search other records themselves. Copy fee $.50 per page. Cert fee- $5.00 per copy plus copy fee. Payee- Clerk of Circuit Court. **Online access to Real Property, Land Survey/Plat records:** Search real property data free at http://sdatcert3.resiusa.org/rp_rewrite/. No name searching. Also, see state introduction for add'l land records online from www.plats.net (use username "Plato" and password "plato#") and MDPropertyview at www.mdp.state.md.us/data/mdview.htm. No name searching. **Other phones:** ; Tax Office- 410-222-1144. **Property tax/Assessor-** 45 Calvert, Annapoles, MD 21401; 410-974-5727.

Baltimore City

City Clerk, 100 N. Calvert St; Rm 610, Baltimore, MD 21202. 410-333-3760; hours: 8:30AM-4:30PM
www.courts.state.md.us
Separate indices to search include grantor/grantee, block index. Records indexed on computer back to 7/1/72. Only the public may search. Copy fee $.50 per page; $.25 self serve. Cert fee- $5.00 per cert plus copy fee. Payee- Circuit Court for Baltimore City. **Online to Real Property, Land Survey/Plat, Property Tax records:** Search real property data free at http://sdatcert3.resiusa.org/rp_rewrite/. No name searching. Search real property tax account data at http://cityservices.baltimorecity.gov/realproperty/default.aspx. Also, see state introduction for add'l land records online from MDPropertyview at www.mdp.state.md.us/data/mdview.htm. No name searching. **Property tax/Assessor-** 6 St. Paul St, 11th Fl, Baltimore, MD 21202; 410-767-8250.

Baltimore County

County Clerk of the Circuit Court, PO Box 6754, Baltimore, MD 21285. 410-887-2652; fax-410-887-2834; hours: 8:30AM-4:30PM
Separate indices to search include notices, Rd closings, judgments, plats, homeowner's assc. Records indexed on a public use terminal back to 1964. Only the public may search. Copy fee $.50 per page. Cert fee- $5.00 per cert + $.50 per page. Payee- Baltimore County Clerk of Circuit Court. **Online access to Real Property, Land Survey/Plat records:** Search real property data free at http://sdatcert3.resiusa.org/rp_rewrite/. No name searching. Also, see state introduction for add'l land records online from www.plats.net (use username "Plato" and password "plato#") and MDPropertyview at www.mdp.state.md.us/data/mdview.htm. No name searching. **Other phones:** Treasurer- 410-887-2416; Elections- 410-887-5700; Vital Records- 410-764-3038. **Property tax/Assessor-** 410-512-4906.

Calvert County

County Clerk of the Circuit Court, 175 Main St; Courthouse, Prince Frederick, MD 20678. 410-535-1660, R/E recording phone-410-535-1600 x269, UCC recording phone-410-535-1600 x269; hours: 8:30AM-4:30PM www.courts.state.md.us/clerks/calvert
Separate indices to search include plats, homeowner depository, miscellaneous. Records indexed on a public use terminal back to 1969. Only the public may search. Copy fee $1.00 per page. RE or tax lien copy- $.50 per page. Cert fee- $5.00 per instrument plus copy fee. Payee- Calvert County Clerk of Circuit Court. **Online access to Real Property, Land Survey/Plat records:** Search real property data free at http://sdatcert3.resiusa.org/rp_rewrite/. No name searching. Also, see state introduction for add'l land records online from www.plats.net (use username "Plato" and password "plato#") and MDPropertyview at www.mdp.state.md.us/data/mdview.htm or

www.dat.state.md.us. No name searching. **Other phones:** Treasurer- 410-535-1600 x272. **Property tax/Assessor-** 200 Duke St, Prince Frederick, MD 20678; 410-535-8850.

Caroline County

County Clerk of the Circuit Court, PO Box 458, Denton, MD 21629. RE & UCC recording phone-410-479-1811; fax-410-479-1142; hours: 8:30AM-4:30PM
Only the public may search. Copy fee $1.00 per page. Tax lien copy- $.50. Cert fee- $5.00 per cert plus copy fee. Payee- Caroline County Clerk of Circuit Court. **Online access to Real Property, Land Survey/Plat records:** Search real property data free at http://sdatcert3.resiusa.org/rp_rewrite/. No name searching. Also, see state introduction for add'l land records online from www.plats.net (use username "Plato" and password "plato#") and MDPropertyview at www.mdp.state.md.us/data/mdview.htm. No name searching. **Other phones:** Treasurer- 410-479-0410. **Property tax/Assessor-** 410-479-5950.

Carroll County

County Clerk of the Circuit Court, 55 N. Court St; Rm G8, Westminster, MD 21157. 410-386-2022; fax-410-876-0822; hours: 8:30AM-4:30PM
All records in one index. Records indexed on computer back to 1960. Only the public may search. Copy fee $.50 per page. Cert fee- $5.00 per cert plus copy fee. Payee- Carroll County Clerk of Circuit Court. **Online access to Real Property, Land Survey/Plat records:** Search real property data free at http://sdatcert3.resiusa.org/rp_rewrite/. No name searching. Access digital image land records at www.mdlandrec.net. Registration and password required. Also, see state introduction for add'l land records online from www.plats.net (use username "Plato" and password "plato#") and MDPropertyview at www.mdp.state.md.us/data/mdview.htm. No name searching. **Other phones:** Treasurer- 410-386-2971; Appraiser/Auditor- 410-857-0600. **Property tax/Assessor-** 410-857-0600.

Cecil County

County Clerk of the Circuit Court, 129 E. Main St.; Rm 108, Elkton, MD 21921-5971. 410-996-5375; hours: 8:30AM-4:30PM
Separate indices to search include liens, plat, financing statements, notices, notary public. Only

the public may search. Copy fee $.50 per page. Cert fee- $5.00 per doc plus copy fee. Payee- County Clerk of Circuit Court. **Online access to Real Property, Land Survey/Plat records:** Search real property data free at http://sdatcert3.resiusa.org/rp_rewrite/. No name searching. Also, see state introduction for add'l land records online from www.plats.net (use username "Plato" and password "plato#") and MDPropertyview at www.mdp.state.md.us/data/mdview.htm. No name searching. **Other phones:** Treasurer- 410-996-5394. **Property tax/Assessor-** 129 E Main St #177, Elkton, MD 21921; 410-996-0525.

Charles County

Clerk of the Circuit Court, PO Box 970, La Plata, MD 20646. 301-932-3201; hours: 8:30AM-4:30PM www.courts.state.md.us/clerks/charles
All records in one index. Records indexed on a public use terminal. Only the public may search. Copy fee $.50 per page. Cert fee- $5.00 per cert plus copy fee. Payee- Charles County Clerk of Circuit Court. **Online access to Real Property, Land Survey/Plat, Treasurer, Property Tax, Tax Sale records:** Search real property data free at http://sdatcert3.resiusa.org/rp_rewrite/. No name searching. Also, see state introduction for add'l land records online from www.plats.net (use username "Plato" and password "plato#") and MDPropertyview at www.mdp.state.md.us/data/mdview.htm. No name searching. Also, access to property tax data is free at www.charlescounty.org/treas/taxes/acctinquiry/selection.jsp. Tax sale list search free at www.charlescounty.org/treas/taxes/taxSale/selection.jsp . **Other phones:** Treasurer- 301-645-0685; Elections- 301-934-8962. **Property tax/Assessor-** 301-932-2440.

Dorchester County

County Clerk of the Circuit Court, PO Box 150, Cambridge, MD 21613. 410-228-0481, R/E recording phone-410-228-0480, UCC recording phone-410-228-0480; fax-410-228-1860; hours: 8:30AM-4:30PM
Records indexed on a public use terminal back to 1669. Only the public may search. Copy fee $.25 per page. Cert fee- $5.00 per cert plus copy fee. Payee- Dorchester County Clerk of Circuit Court. **Online access to Real Property, Land Survey/Plat records:** An online records system is planned for MDlandRec.net. Until then, search real property data free at http://sdatcert3.resiusa.org/rp_rewrite/. No name searching. Also, see state introduction for add'l land records online from www.plats.net (use username "Plato" and password "plato#") and MDPropertyview at www.mdp.state.md.us/data/mdview.htm. No name searching. **Other phones:** Treasurer- 410-228-4343 (County). **Property tax/Assessor-** 410-228-3380.

Frederick County

County Clerk of the Circuit Court, 100 W. Patrick St, Frederick, MD 21701. 301-694-1964; fax-301-846-2245; hours: 8:30AM-4:30PM
All records in one index. Records indexed on a public use terminal back to 1972. Office will perform a UCC search but public must search other records themselves. Copy fee $.50 per page. Cert fee- $5.00 per cert plus copy fee. Payee- Frederick County Clerk of Circuit Court. **Online access to Real Property, Land Survey/Plat records:** Search real property data free at http://sdatcert3.resiusa.org/rp_rewrite/. No name searching. Also, see state introduction for add'l land records online from www.plats.net (use username "Plato" and password "plato#") and MDPropertyview at www.mdp.state.md.us/data/mdview.htm. No name searching. **Other phones:** Treasurer- 301-694-1111. **Property tax/Assessor-** 12 E Church St, Frederick, MD 21701; 301-694-2040.

Garrett County

County Clerk of the Circuit Court, PO Box 447, Oakland, MD 21550-0447. 301-334-1937, R/E recording phone-301-334-1938, UCC recording phone-301-334-5016; fax-301-334-5017; 8:30AM-4:30PM
All records in one index. Only the public may search. Copy fee $1.00 per page. RE or tax lien copy- $.50 per page. Cert fee- $5.00 per cert plus copy fee. Payee- Garrett County Clerk of Circuit Court. **Online access to Real Property, Land Survey/Plat records:** Search real property data free at http://sdatcert3.resiusa.org/rp_rewrite/. No name searching. Also, see state introduction for add'l land records online from www.plats.net (use username "Plato" and password "plato#") and MDPropertyview at www.mdp.state.md.us/data/mdview.htm. No name searching. **Other phones:** Treasurer- 301-334-1965; Elections- 301-334-1962. **Property tax/Assessor-** 203 S Fourth St, Rm 106, Oakland, MD 21550; 301-334-1950.

Harford County

County Clerk of the Circuit Court, 20 W. Courtland St, Bel Air, MD 21014. 410-638-3244; 8:30AM-4PM
Only the public may search. Copy fee $.50, if real estate $.25 per page. Cert fee- $5.00 per cert plus copy fee. Payee- Harford County Clerk of Circuit Court. **Online access to Real Property, Land Survey/Plat records:** Search real property data free at http://sdatcert3.resiusa.org/rp_rewrite/. No name searching. Also, see state introduction for add'l land records online from www.plats.net (use username "Plato" and password "plato#") and MDPropertyview at www.mdp.state.md.us/data/mdview.htm. No name searching. **Other phones:** Treasurer- 410-638-3269. **Property tax/Assessor-** 410-838-4800.

Howard County

County Clerk of the Circuit Court, 9250 Bendix Rd, Columbia, MD 21045. 410-313-6117; hours: 8:30AM-4:30PM
All records in one index. Records indexed on computer back to 1700's. Only the public may search. Copy fee $.50 per page; self serve $.25. Cert fee- $5.00 per cert plus copy fee. Payee- Howard County Clerk of Circuit Court. **Online access to Real Property, Land Survey/Plat records:** Search real property data free at http://sdatcert3.resiusa.org/rp_rewrite/. No name searching. Also, see state introduction for add'l land records online from www.plats.net (use username "Plato" and password "plato#") and MDPropertyview at www.mdp.state.md.us/data/mdview.htm. No name searching. **Property tax/Assessor-** 410-480-7940.

Kent County

Clerk of the Circuit Court, 103 N. Cross St., Chestertown, MD 21620. 410-778-7460; hours: 8:30AM-4:30PM
Only the public may search. Copy fee $.50; plat copies-$1.00. Cert fee- $5.00 per cert plus copy fee. Payee- Kent County Clerk of Circuit Court. **Online access to Real Property, Land Survey/Plat records:** Search real property data free at http://sdatcert3.resiusa.org/rp_rewrite/. No name searching. Also, see state introduction for add'l land records online from www.plats.net (use username "Plato" and password "plato#") and MDPropertyview at www.mdp.state.md.us/data/mdview.htm. No name searching. **Other phones:** Treasurer- 410-778-7443; Elections- 410-778-0038. **Property tax/Assessor-** 410-778-7447.

Montgomery County

County Clerk of the Circuit Court, 50 Maryland Ave, Rm 122A; County Courthouse, Rockville, MD 20850. 240-777-9466, R/E recording phone-240-777-9470; fax-240-777-9486; hours: 8:30AM-4:30PM www.montgomerycountymd.gov/mc/judicial/
All records in one index. Records indexed on computer. Only the public may search. Copy fee $.50 per page. Cert fee- $5.00 per cert plus copy fee. Payee- Montgomery County Clerk of Circuit

Court. **Online access to Real Property, Land Survey/Plat, Property Tax, Assessor records:** Access to clerk records is via JIS Dialup Access; contact Mary Hutchins 410-260-1031. Also, search real property data for free at http://sdatcert3.resiusa.org/rp_rewrite. No name searching. Also, see state introduction for add'l land records online from www.plats.net (use username "Plato" and password "plato#") and MDPropertyview at www.mdp.state.md.us/data/mdview.htm. No name searching. Also, access to the assessor's property tax account database is free at https://www.montgomerycountymd.gov/apps/tax/index.asp. **Other phones:** Treasurer- 240-777-8995; Elections- 240-777-8500; Vital Records- 240-777-1755. **Property tax/Assessor-** 301-279-1701.

Prince George's County

County Clerk of the Circuit Court, 14735 Main St, Upper Marlboro, MD 20772. 301-952-3352; hours: 8:30AM-4:30PM www.co.pg.md.us
Record index not computerized. Only the public may search. Copy fee $1.00 per page. Cert fee- $5.00 per cert plus copy fee. Payee- Prince George's County Clerk of Circuit Court. **Online access to Real Property, Land Survey/Plat, Property Tax records:** Search real property data free at http://sdatcert3.resiusa.org/rp_rewrite. No name searching. Also, see state introduction for add'l land records online from www.plats.net (use username "Plato" and password "plato#") and MDPropertyview at www.mdp.state.md.us/data/mdview.htm. No name searching. Also, search the Treasurer's property tax inquiry system at http://tax-acct-info.co.pg.md.us/index1.html. No name searching. **Other phones:** Treasurer- 301-952-3946. **Property tax/Assessor-** 301-952-2500.

Queen Anne's County

County Clerk of the Circuit Court, 100 Court House Sq, Centreville, MD 21617. 410-758-1773; hours: 8:30AM-4:30PM
Only the public may search. Copy fee $.50 per page. Cert fee- $5.00 per cert plus copy fee. Payee- Queen Anne's County Clerk of Circuit Court. **Online access to Real Property, Land Survey/Plat records:** Search real property data free at http://sdatcert3.resiusa.org/rp_rewrite. No name searching. Also, see state introduction for add'l land records online from www.plats.net (use username "Plato" and password "plato#") and MDPropertyview at www.mdp.state.md.us/data/mdview.htm. No name searching. **Other phones:** Treasurer- 410-758-0414. **Property tax/Assessor-** 410-758-5030.

Somerset County

County Clerk of the Circuit Court, PO Box 99, Princess Anne, MD 21853. 410-651-1555, R/E recording phone-410-845-4840; fax-410-651-1048; hours: 8:30AM-4:30PM
All records in one index. Records indexed on computer. Only the public may search. Copy fee $.50 per page. Cert fee- $5.00 per page plus copy fee. Payee- Somerset County Clerk of Circuit Court. **Online access to Real Property, Land Survey/Plat records:** Search real property data free at http://sdatcert3.resiusa.org/rp_rewrite. No name searching. Also, see state introduction for add'l land records online from www.plats.net (use username "Plato" and password "plato#") and MDPropertyview at www.mdp.state.md.us/data/mdview.htm. No name searching. **Other phones:** Treasurer- 410-651-0440; Vital Records- 410-845-4840. **Property tax/Assessor-** 410-651-0868.

St. Mary's County

County Clerk of the Circuit Court, PO Box 676, Leonardtown, MD 20650. 301-475-4567, R/E recording phone-301-475-4554; hours: 8:30AM-4:30PM
Separate indices to search include land, plats, marriages, miscellaneous. Records indexed on a public use terminal back to 1968. Only the public

may search. Copy fee $.50 per page. Cert fee- $5.00 per cert plus copy fee. Payee- St. Mary's County Clerk of Circuit Court. **Online to Real Property, Land Survey/Plat records:** Rreal property data free at http://sdatcert3.resiusa.org/rp_rewrite. No name searching. Also, see state introduction for add'l land records online from www.plats.net (use username "Plato" and password "plato#") and MDPropertyview at www.mdp.state.md.us/data/mdview.htm. No name searching. **Other phones:** Treasurer- 301-475-4473. **Property tax/Assessor-** 301-475-4620.

Talbot County

County Clerk of the Circuit Court, PO Box 723, Easton, MD 21601. 410-822-2611; fax-410-820-8168; hours: 8:30AM-4:30PM www.courts.state.md.us
All records in one index. Records indexed on computer. Only the public may search. Copy fee $.50 per page. Cert fee- $5.00 per cert plus copy fee. Payee- Talbot County Clerk of Circuit Court. **Online access to Real Property, Land Survey/Plat records:** Search real property data free at http://sdatcert3.resiusa.org/rp_rewrite. No name searching. Also, see state introduction for add'l land records online from www.plats.net (use username "Plato" and password "plato#") and MDPropertyview at www.mdp.state.md.us/data/mdview.htm. No name searching. **Other phones:** Treasurer- 410-770-8020; Elections- 410-770-8099; Vital Records- 410-764-3038. **Property tax/Assessor-** 410-819-5920.

Washington County

Clerk of the Circuit Court, PO Box 229, Hagerstown, MD 21741-0229. RE & UCC recording phone-301-733-8660; fax-301-791-1151; 8:30AM-4:30PM www.courts.state.md.us/clerks/washington/index.html
All records in one index. Records indexed on computer back to 1963. Only the public may search. Copy fee $.50 per page. Cert fee- $5.00 per doc plus copy fee. Payee- Washington County Clerk of Circuit Court. **Online access to Real Property, Land Survey/Plat records:** Search real property data free at http://sdatcert3.resiusa.org/rp_rewrite. No name searching. Also, see state introduction for add'l land records online from www.plats.net (use username "Plato" and password "plato#") and MDPropertyview at www.mdp.state.md.us/data/mdview.htm. No name searching. **Other phones:** Treasurer- 240-313-2110; Elections- 240-313-2050; Vital Records- 301-733-8660. **Property tax/Assessor-** 3 Public Sq., Hagerstown, MD 21741; 301-791-3050.

Wicomico County

County Clerk of the Circuit Court, PO Box 198, Salisbury, MD 21803-0198. 410-543-6551; hours: 8:30AM-4:30PM
All records in one index. Only the public may search, except UCC. Copy fee $.50 per page. Cert fee- $5.00 per cert includes copies. Payee- Wicomico County Clerk of Circuit Court. **Online access to Real Property, Land Survey/Plat records:** Search real property data free at http://sdatcert3.resiusa.org/rp_rewrite. No name searching. Also, see state introduction for add'l land records online from www.plats.net (use username "Plato" and password "plato#") and MDPropertyview at www.mdp.state.md.us/data/mdview.htm. No name searching. **Property tax/Assessor-** 410-543-6623.

Worcester County

County Clerk of the Circuit Court, PO Box 40, Snow Hill, MD 21863-0040. 410-632-5500, UCC recording phone-410-632-1196; hours: 8:30AM-4:30PM

Only the public may search, except UCC. Will search UCC records, but not tax liens. Copy fee $.50 per page, $5.00 minimum. Cert fee- $5.00 per cert plus $.50 per page. Payee- Worcester County Clerk of Circuit Court. **Online access to Real Property, Land Survey/Plat records:** Search real property data free at http://sdatcert3.resiusa.org/rp_rewrite. No name searching. Also, see state introduction for add'l land records online from www.plats.net (use username "Plato" and password "plato#") and MDPropertyview at www.mdp.state.md.us/data/mdview.htm. No name searching. **Other phones:** Elections- 410-632-1320. **Property tax/Assessor-** 410-632-1194.

Maryland County Locator

You will usually be able to find the city name in the City/County Cross Reference below. In that case, it is a simple matter to determine the county from the cross reference. However, only the official US Postal Service city names are included in this index. There are an additional 40,000 place names that people use in their addresses. Therefore, we have also included a ZIP/City Cross Reference immediately following the City/County Cross Reference.

If you know the ZIP Code but the city name does not appear in the City/County Cross Reference index, look up the ZIP Code in the ZIP/City Cross Reference, find the city name, then look up the city name in the City/County Cross. Reference. For example, you want to know the county for an address of Menands, NY 12204. There is no "Menands" in the City/County Cross Reference. The ZIP/City Cross Reference shows that ZIP Codes 12201-12288 are for the city of Albany. Looking back in the City/County Cross Reference, Albany is in Albany County.

Maryland City/County Cross Reference

ABELL St. Mary's
ABERDEEN Harford
ABERDEEN PROVING GROUND Harford
ABINGDON Harford
ACCIDENT Garrett
ACCOKEEK Prince George's
ADAMSTOWN Frederick
ALESIA (21107) Carroll(59), Baltimore(40)
ALLEN Wicomico
ANDREWS AIR FORCE BASE Prince George's
ANNAPOLIS Anne Arundel
ANNAPOLIS JUNCTION (20701) Howard(77), Anne Arundel(22)
AQUASCO Prince George's
ARNOLD Anne Arundel
ASHTON Montgomery
AVENUE St. Mary's
BALDWIN (21013) Baltimore(70), Harford(29)
BALTIMORE (21209) Baltimore(52), Baltimore City(47)
BALTIMORE (21239) Baltimore City(80), Baltimore(19)
BALTIMORE Anne Arundel
BALTIMORE Baltimore
BALTIMORE Baltimore City
BARCLAY Queen Anne's
BARNESVILLE Montgomery
BARSTOW Calvert
BARTON (21521) Allegany(72), Garrett(27)
BEALLSVILLE Montgomery
BEL AIR Harford
BEL ALTON Charles
BELCAMP Harford
BELTSVILLE Prince George's
BENEDICT Charles
BENSON Harford
BETHESDA Montgomery
BETHLEHEM Caroline
BETTERTON Kent
BIG POOL Washington
BISHOPVILLE Worcester
BITTINGER Garrett
BIVALVE Wicomico
BLADENSBURG Prince George's
BLOOMINGTON Garrett
BOONSBORO Washington
BORING Baltimore
BOWIE Prince George's
BOYDS Montgomery
BOZMAN Talbot
BRADDOCK HEIGHTS Frederick
BRADSHAW Baltimore
BRANDYWINE (20613) Prince George's(88), Charles(11)
BRENTWOOD Prince George's
BRINKLOW Montgomery
BROOKEVILLE (20833) Montgomery(96), Howard(3)
BROOKLANDVILLE Baltimore
BROOKLYN (21225) Baltimore City(54), Anne Arundel(45)
BROOMES ISLAND Calvert

BROWNSVILLE Washington
BRUNSWICK Frederick
BRYANS ROAD Charles
BRYANTOWN Charles
BUCKEYSTOWN Frederick
BURKITTSVILLE Frederick
BURTONSVILLE Montgomery
BUSHWOOD St. Mary's
BUTLER Baltimore
CABIN JOHN Montgomery
CALIFORNIA St. Mary's
CALLAWAY St. Mary's
CAMBRIDGE Dorchester
CAPITOL HEIGHTS Prince George's
CARDIFF Harford
CASCADE (21719) Washington(98), Frederick(1)
CATONSVILLE Baltimore
CAVETOWN Washington
CECILTON Cecil
CENTREVILLE Queen Anne's
CHANCE Somerset
CHAPTICO St. Mary's
CHARLESTOWN Cecil
CHARLOTTE HALL (20622) Charles(64), St. Mary's(35)
CHASE Baltimore
CHELTENHAM Prince George's
CHESAPEAKE BEACH Calvert
CHESAPEAKE CITY Cecil
CHESTER Queen Anne's
CHESTERTOWN (21620) Kent(95), Queen Anne's(4)
CHESTERTOWN Queen Anne's
CHEVY CHASE Montgomery
CHEWSVILLE Washington
CHILDS Cecil
CHURCH CREEK Dorchester
CHURCH HILL Queen Anne's
CHURCHTON Anne Arundel
CHURCHVILLE Harford
CLAIBORNE Talbot
CLARKSBURG (20871) Montgomery(89), Frederick(10)
CLARKSVILLE Howard
CLEAR SPRING Washington
CLEMENTS St. Mary's
CLINTON Prince George's
COBB ISLAND Charles
COCKEYSVILLE Baltimore
COLLEGE PARK Prince George's
COLORA Cecil
COLTONS POINT St. Mary's
COLUMBIA Howard
COMPTON St. Mary's
CONOWINGO Cecil
COOKSVILLE (21723) Howard(85), Carroll(14)
CORDOVA Talbot
CORRIGANVILLE Allegany
CRAPO Dorchester
CRISFIELD Somerset
CROCHERON Dorchester
CROFTON Anne Arundel

CROWNSVILLE Anne Arundel
CRUMPTON Queen Anne's
CUMBERLAND Allegany
CURTIS BAY (21226) Baltimore City(56), Anne Arundel(43)
DAMASCUS Montgomery
DAMERON St. Mary's
DAMES QUARTER Somerset
DARLINGTON Harford
DAVIDSONVILLE Anne Arundel
DAYTON Howard
DEAL ISLAND Somerset
DEALE Anne Arundel
DELMAR Wicomico
DENTON Caroline
DERWOOD Montgomery
DETOUR Carroll
DICKERSON (20842) Montgomery(79), Frederick(20)
DISTRICT HEIGHTS Prince George's
DOWELL Calvert
DRAYDEN St. Mary's
DUNDALK (21222) Baltimore(97), Baltimore City(2)
DUNKIRK (20754) Calvert(90), Anne Arundel(10)
EARLEVILLE Cecil
EAST NEW MARKET Dorchester
EASTON Talbot
ECKHART MINES Allegany
EDEN (21822) Worcester(89), Somerset(10)
EDGEWATER Anne Arundel
EDGEWOOD Harford
ELK MILLS Cecil
ELKRIDGE Howard
ELKTON Cecil
ELLERSLIE Allegany
ELLICOTT CITY (21043) Howard(97), Baltimore(2)
ELLICOTT CITY Howard
EMMITSBURG Frederick
ESSEX Baltimore
EWELL Somerset
FAIRPLAY Washington
FALLSTON Harford
FAULKNER Charles
FEDERALSBURG Caroline
FINKSBURG Carroll
FISHING CREEK Dorchester
FLINTSTONE Allegany
FOREST HILL Harford
FORK Baltimore
FORT GEORGE G MEADE Anne Arundel
FORT HOWARD Baltimore
FORT WASHINGTON Prince George's
FREDERICK Frederick
FREELAND (21107) Carroll(59), Baltimore(40)
FREELAND Baltimore
FRIENDSHIP Anne Arundel
FRIENDSVILLE Garrett
FROSTBURG (21532) Allegany(84), Garrett(15)

FRUITLAND Wicomico
FULTON Howard
FUNKSTOWN Washington
GAITHER Carroll
GAITHERSBURG Montgomery
GALENA Kent
GALESVILLE Anne Arundel
GAMBRILLS Anne Arundel
GAPLAND Washington
GARRETT PARK Montgomery
GARRISON Baltimore
GEORGETOWN Cecil
GERMANTOWN Montgomery
GIBSON ISLAND Anne Arundel
GIRDLETREE Worcester
GLEN ARM Baltimore
GLEN BURNIE Anne Arundel
GLEN ECHO Montgomery
GLENELG Howard
GLENN DALE Prince George's
GLENWOOD Howard
GLYNDON Baltimore
GOLDSBORO Caroline
GRANTSVILLE Garrett
GRASONVILLE Queen Anne's
GREAT MILLS St. Mary's
GREENBELT Prince George's
GREENSBORO Caroline
GUNPOWDER Harford
GWYNN OAK (21207) Baltimore(67), Baltimore City(32)
GWYNN OAK Baltimore
HAGERSTOWN Washington
HALETHORPE (21227) Baltimore(98), Baltimore City(1)
HAMPSTEAD (21074) Carroll(88), Baltimore(11)
HANCOCK Washington
HANOVER (21076) Anne Arundel(91), Howard(8)
HANOVER Anne Arundel
HARMANS Anne Arundel
HARWOOD Anne Arundel
HAVRE DE GRACE Harford
HEBRON Wicomico
HELEN St. Mary's
HENDERSON Caroline
HENRYTON Carroll
HIGHLAND (20777) Howard(95), Montgomery(4)
HILLSBORO Caroline
HOLLYWOOD St. Mary's
HUGHESVILLE Charles
HUNT VALLEY Baltimore
HUNTINGTOWN Calvert
HURLOCK Dorchester
HYATTSVILLE Prince George's
HYDES (21082) Baltimore(96), Harford(3)
IJAMSVILLE Frederick
INDIAN HEAD Charles
INGLESIDE Queen Anne's
IRONSIDES Charles
ISSUE Charles
JARRETTSVILLE Harford

JEFFERSON Frederick
JESSUP (20794) Howard(80), Anne Arundel(19)
JOPPA Harford
KEEDYSVILLE Washington
KENNEDYVILLE Kent
KENSINGTON Montgomery
KEYMAR (21757) Frederick(50), Carroll(49)
KINGSVILLE (21087) Baltimore(79), Harford(20)
KITZMILLER Garrett
KNOXVILLE (21758) Frederick(50), Washington(49)
LA PLATA Charles
LADIESBURG Frederick
LANHAM Prince George's
LAUREL Anne Arundel
LAUREL Howard
LAUREL Prince George's
LEONARDTOWN St. Mary's
LEXINGTON PARK St. Mary's
LIBERTYTOWN Frederick
LINEBORO Carroll
LINEBORO CPO Carroll
LINKWOOD Dorchester
LINTHICUM HEIGHTS Anne Arundel
LINWOOD Carroll
LISBON Howard
LITTLE ORLEANS Allegany
LONACONING (21539) Allegany(67), Garrett(32)
LONG GREEN Baltimore
LOTHIAN Anne Arundel
LOVEVILLE St. Mary's
LUKE Allegany
LUSBY Calvert
LUTHERVILLE TIMONIUM Baltimore
LYNCH Kent
MADISON Dorchester
MAGNOLIA Harford
MANCHESTER (21102) Carroll(98), Baltimore(1)
MANOKIN Somerset
MARBURY Charles
MARDELA SPRINGS Wicomico
MARION STATION Somerset
MARRIOTTSVILLE (21104) Carroll(53), Howard(38), Baltimore(8)
MARYDEL Caroline
MARYLAND LINE Baltimore
MASSEY Kent
MAUGANSVILLE Washington
MAYO Anne Arundel
MC HENRY Garrett
MCDANIEL Talbot
MECHANICSVILLE (20659) St. Mary's(97), Charles(2)
MIDDLE RIVER Baltimore
MIDDLEBURG Carroll
MIDDLETOWN Frederick
MIDLAND Allegany
MIDLOTHIAN Allegany
MILLERS (21107) Carroll(59), Baltimore(40)
MILLERSVILLE Anne Arundel

MILLINGTON (21651) Queen Anne's(59), Kent(40)
MONKTON (21111) Baltimore(87), Harford(12)
MONROVIA Frederick
MONTGOMERY VILLAGE Montgomery
MORGANZA St. Mary's
MOUNT AIRY (21771) Frederick(47), Carroll(39), Howard(11), Montgomery(1)
MOUNT RAINIER Prince George's
MOUNT SAVAGE Allegany
MOUNT VICTORIA Charles
MYERSVILLE Frederick
NANJEMOY Charles
NANTICOKE Wicomico
NEAVITT Talbot
NEW MARKET Frederick
NEW MIDWAY Frederick
NEW WINDSOR (21776) Carroll(82), Frederick(17)
NEWARK Worcester
NEWBURG Charles
NEWCOMB Talbot
NIKEP Allegany
NORTH BEACH (20714) Calvert(87), Anne Arundel(12)
NORTH EAST Cecil
NOTTINGHAM Baltimore
OAKLAND Garrett
OCEAN CITY Worcester
ODENTON Anne Arundel
OLDTOWN Allegany
OLNEY Montgomery
OWINGS Calvert
OWINGS MILLS Baltimore
OXFORD Talbot
OXON HILL Prince George's
PARK HALL St. Mary's
PARKTON Baltimore
PARKVILLE (21234) Baltimore(89), Baltimore City(10)
PARSONSBURG Wicomico
PASADENA Anne Arundel
PATUXENT RIVER St. Mary's
PERRY HALL Baltimore
PERRY POINT Cecil
PERRYMAN Harford
PERRYVILLE Cecil
PHOENIX Baltimore
PIKESVILLE (21208) Baltimore(93), Baltimore City(6)
PINEY POINT St. Mary's
PINTO Allegany
PITTSVILLE Wicomico
POCOMOKE CITY (21851) Worcester(86), Somerset(13)
POINT OF ROCKS Frederick
POMFRET Charles
POOLESVILLE Montgomery
PORT DEPOSIT Cecil
PORT REPUBLIC Calvert
PORT TOBACCO Charles
POTOMAC Montgomery
POWELLVILLE Wicomico
PRESTON Caroline
PRINCE FREDERICK Calvert
PRINCESS ANNE Somerset

PYLESVILLE Harford
QUANTICO Wicomico
QUEEN ANNE Queen Anne's
QUEENSTOWN Queen Anne's
RANDALLSTOWN Baltimore
RAWLINGS Allegany
REHOBETH Somerset
REISTERSTOWN (21136) Baltimore(97), Carroll(2)
RHODES POINT Somerset
RHODESDALE Dorchester
RIDERWOOD Baltimore
RIDGE St. Mary's
RIDGELY Caroline
RISING SUN Cecil
RIVA Anne Arundel
RIVERDALE Prince George's
ROCK HALL Kent
ROCK POINT Charles
ROCKVILLE Montgomery
ROCKY RIDGE Frederick
ROHRERSVILLE Washington
ROSEDALE (21237) Baltimore(96), Baltimore City(3)
ROYAL OAK Talbot
SABILLASVILLE (21780) Frederick(94), Washington(5)
SAINT INIGOES St. Mary's
SAINT JAMES Washington
SAINT LEONARD Calvert
SAINT MARYS CITY St. Mary's
SAINT MICHAELS Talbot
SALISBURY Wicomico
SANDY SPRING Montgomery
SAVAGE Howard
SCOTLAND St. Mary's
SECRETARY Dorchester
SEVERN Anne Arundel
SEVERNA PARK Anne Arundel
SHADY SIDE Anne Arundel
SHARPSBURG Washington
SHARPTOWN Wicomico
SHERWOOD Talbot
SHOWELL Worcester
SILVER SPRING (20903) Montgomery(84), Prince George's(15)
SILVER SPRING Montgomery
SIMPSONVILLE Howard
SMITHSBURG (21783) Washington(79), Frederick(20)
SNOW HILL Worcester
SOLOMONS Calvert
SOUTHERN MD FACILITY Prince George's
SPARKS GLENCOE Baltimore
SPARROWS POINT Baltimore
SPENCERVILLE Montgomery
SPRING GAP Allegany
STEVENSON Baltimore
STEVENSVILLE Queen Anne's
STILL POND Kent
STOCKTON Worcester
STREET Harford
SUBURB MARYLAND FAC Montgomery
SUDLERSVILLE Queen Anne's
SUITLAND Prince George's
SUNDERLAND Calvert

SWANTON Garrett
SYKESVILLE (21784) Carroll(94), Howard(5)
TAKOMA PARK (20912) Montgomery(89), Prince George's(10)
TAKOMA PARK Prince George's
TALL TIMBERS St. Mary's
TANEYTOWN (21787) Carroll(93), Frederick(6)
TAYLORS ISLAND Dorchester
TEMPLE HILLS Prince George's
TEMPLEVILLE Caroline
THURMONT Frederick
TILGHMAN Talbot
TODDVILLE Dorchester
TOWSON Baltimore
TRACYS LANDING Anne Arundel
TRAPPE Talbot
TUSCARORA Frederick
TYASKIN Wicomico
TYLERTON Somerset
UNION BRIDGE (21791) Carroll(52), Frederick(47)
UNIONVILLE Frederick
UPPER FAIRMOUNT Somerset
UPPER FALLS Baltimore
UPPER HILL Somerset
UPPER MARLBORO Prince George's
UPPERCO (21155) Baltimore(90), Carroll(9)
VALLEY LEE St. Mary's
VIENNA Dorchester
WALDORF (20601) Charles(95), Prince George's(4)
WALDORF Charles
WALKERSVILLE Frederick
WARWICK Cecil
WASHINGTON Prince George's
WASHINGTON GROVE Montgomery
WELCOME Charles
WENONA Somerset
WEST FRIENDSHIP Howard
WEST RIVER Anne Arundel
WESTERNPORT Allegany
WESTMINSTER Carroll
WESTOVER Somerset
WHALEYVILLE Worcester
WHITE HALL (21161) Baltimore(57), Harford(42)
WHITE MARSH Baltimore
WHITE PLAINS Charles
WHITEFORD Harford
WILLARDS Wicomico
WILLIAMSPORT Washington
WINDSOR MILL Baltimore
WINGATE Dorchester
WITTMAN Talbot
WOODBINE (21797) Carroll(52), Howard(46)
WOODSBORO Frederick
WOODSTOCK (21163) Baltimore(51), Howard(48)
WOOLFORD Dorchester
WORTON Kent
WYE MILLS Talbot

Maryland ZIP/City Cross Reference

20331-20331 WASHINGTON	20732-20732 CHESAPEAKE BEACH	20892-20894 BETHESDA	21120-21120 PARKTON
20601-20604 WALDORF	20733-20733 CHURCHTON	20895-20895 KENSINGTON	21122-21123 PASADENA
20606-20606 ABELL	20735-20735 CLINTON	20896-20896 GARRETT PARK	21128-21128 PERRY HALL
20607-20607 ACCOKEEK	20736-20736 OWINGS	20897-20897 SUBURB MARYLAND FAC	21130-21130 PERRYMAN
20608-20608 AQUASCO	20737-20738 RIVERDALE	20898-20899 GAITHERSBURG	21131-21131 PHOENIX
20609-20609 AVENUE	20740-20742 COLLEGE PARK	20900-20911 SILVER SPRING	21132-21132 PYLESVILLE
20610-20610 BARSTOW	20743-20743 CAPITOL HEIGHTS	20912-20913 TAKOMA PARK	21133-21133 RANDALLSTOWN
20611-20611 BEL ALTON	20744-20744 FORT WASHINGTON	20914-20997 SILVER SPRING	21136-21136 REISTERSTOWN
20612-20612 BENEDICT	20745-20745 OXON HILL	21001-21001 ABERDEEN	21139-21139 RIDERWOOD
20613-20613 BRANDYWINE	20746-20746 SUITLAND	21005-21005 ABERDEEN PROVING	21140-21140 RIVA
20615-20615 BROOMES ISLAND	20747-20747 DISTRICT HEIGHTS	GROUND	21144-21144 SEVERN
20616-20616 BRYANS ROAD	20748-20748 TEMPLE HILLS	21009-21009 ABINGDON	21146-21146 SEVERNA PARK
20617-20617 BRYANTOWN	20749-20749 FORT WASHINGTON	21010-21010 GUNPOWDER	21150-21150 SIMPSONVILLE
20618-20618 BUSHWOOD	20750-20750 OXON HILL	21012-21012 ARNOLD	21152-21152 SPARKS GLENCOE
20619-20619 CALIFORNIA	20751-20751 DEALE	21013-21013 BALDWIN	21153-21153 STEVENSON
20620-20620 CALLAWAY	20752-20752 SUITLAND	21014-21015 BEL AIR	21154-21154 STREET
20621-20621 CHAPTICO	20753-20753 DISTRICT HEIGHTS	21017-21017 BELCAMP	21155-21155 UPPERCO
20622-20622 CHARLOTTE HALL	20754-20754 DUNKIRK	21018-21018 BENSON	21156-21156 UPPER FALLS
20623-20623 CHELTENHAM	20755-20755 FORT GEORGE G MEADE	21020-21020 BORING	21157-21158 WESTMINSTER
20624-20624 CLEMENTS	20757-20757 TEMPLE HILLS	21021-21021 BRADSHAW	21160-21160 WHITEFORD
20625-20625 COBB ISLAND	20758-20758 FRIENDSHIP	21022-21022 BROOKLANDVILLE	21161-21161 WHITE HALL
20626-20626 COLTONS POINT	20759-20759 FULTON	21023-21023 BUTLER	21162-21162 WHITE MARSH
20627-20627 COMPTON	20762-20762 ANDREWS AIR FORCE	21024-21024 CARDIFF	21163-21163 WOODSTOCK
20628-20628 DAMERON	BASE	21027-21027 CHASE	21200-21203 BALTIMORE
20629-20629 DOWELL	20763-20763 SAVAGE	21028-21028 CHURCHVILLE	21204-21204 TOWSON
20630-20630 DRAYDEN	20764-20764 SHADY SIDE	21029-21029 CLARKSVILLE	21205-21206 BALTIMORE
20632-20632 FAULKNER	20765-20765 GALESVILLE	21030-21030 COCKEYSVILLE	21207-21207 GWYNN OAK
20634-20634 GREAT MILLS	20768-20768 GREENBELT	21031-21031 HUNT VALLEY	21208-21208 PIKESVILLE
20635-20635 HELEN	20769-20769 GLENN DALE	21032-21032 CROWNSVILLE	21209-21218 BALTIMORE
20636-20636 HOLLYWOOD	20770-20771 GREENBELT	21034-21034 DARLINGTON	21219-21219 SPARROWS POINT
20637-20637 HUGHESVILLE	20772-20775 UPPER MARLBORO	21035-21035 DAVIDSONVILLE	21220-21220 MIDDLE RIVER
20639-20639 HUNTINGTOWN	20776-20776 HARWOOD	21036-21036 DAYTON	21221-21221 ESSEX
20640-20640 INDIAN HEAD	20777-20777 HIGHLAND	21037-21037 EDGEWATER	21222-21222 DUNDALK
20643-20643 IRONSIDES	20778-20778 WEST RIVER	21040-21040 EDGEWOOD	21223-21224 BALTIMORE
20645-20645 ISSUE	20779-20779 TRACYS LANDING	21041-21043 ELLICOTT CITY	21225-21225 BROOKLYN
20646-20646 LA PLATA	20780-20789 HYATTSVILLE	21044-21046 COLUMBIA	21226-21226 CURTIS BAY
20650-20650 LEONARDTOWN	20790-20791 CAPITOL HEIGHTS	21047-21047 FALLSTON	21227-21227 HALETHORPE
20653-20653 LEXINGTON PARK	20792-20792 UPPER MARLBORO	21048-21048 FINKSBURG	21228-21228 CATONSVILLE
20656-20656 LOVEVILLE	20794-20794 JESSUP	21050-21050 FOREST HILL	21229-21233 BALTIMORE
20657-20657 LUSBY	20797-20797 SOUTHERN MD FACILITY	21051-21051 FORK	21234-21234 PARKVILLE
20658-20658 MARBURY	20799-20799 CAPITOL HEIGHTS	21052-21052 FORT HOWARD	21235-21235 BALTIMORE
20659-20659 MECHANICSVILLE	20800-20800 SUBURB MARYLAND FAC	21053-21053 FREELAND	21236-21236 NOTTINGHAM
20660-20660 MORGANZA	20810-20811 BETHESDA	21054-21054 GAMBRILLS	21237-21237 ROSEDALE
20661-20661 MOUNT VICTORIA	20812-20812 GLEN ECHO	21055-21055 GARRISON	21239-21241 BALTIMORE
20662-20662 NANJEMOY	20813-20814 BETHESDA	21056-21056 GIBSON ISLAND	21244-21244 GWYNN OAK
20664-20664 NEWBURG	20815-20815 CHEVY CHASE	21057-21057 GLEN ARM	21244-21244 WINDSOR MILL
20667-20667 PARK HALL	20816-20817 BETHESDA	21060-21062 GLEN BURNIE	21250-21285 BALTIMORE
20670-20670 PATUXENT RIVER	20818-20818 CABIN JOHN	21065-21065 COCKEYSVILLE	21286-21286 TOWSON
20674-20674 PINEY POINT	20824-20824 BETHESDA	21065-21065 HUNT VALLEY	21287-21299 BALTIMORE
20675-20675 POMFRET	20825-20825 CHEVY CHASE	21071-21071 GLYNDON	21400-21412 ANNAPOLIS
20676-20676 PORT REPUBLIC	20827-20827 BETHESDA	21074-21074 HAMPSTEAD	21501-21505 CUMBERLAND
20677-20677 PORT TOBACCO	20830-20832 OLNEY	21075-21075 ELKRIDGE	21520-21520 ACCIDENT
20678-20678 PRINCE FREDERICK	20833-20833 BROOKEVILLE	21076-21076 HANOVER	21521-21521 BARTON
20680-20680 RIDGE	20837-20837 POOLESVILLE	21077-21077 HARMANS	21522-21522 BITTINGER
20682-20682 ROCK POINT	20838-20838 BARNESVILLE	21078-21078 HAVRE DE GRACE	21523-21523 BLOOMINGTON
20684-20684 SAINT INIGOES	20839-20839 BEALLSVILLE	21080-21080 HENRYTON	21524-21524 CORRIGANVILLE
20685-20685 SAINT LEONARD	20841-20841 BOYDS	21082-21082 HYDES	21528-21528 ECKHART MINES
20686-20686 SAINT MARYS CITY	20842-20842 DICKERSON	21084-21084 JARRETTSVILLE	21529-21529 ELLERSLIE
20687-20687 SCOTLAND	20847-20853 ROCKVILLE	21085-21085 JOPPA	21530-21530 FLINTSTONE
20688-20688 SOLOMONS	20854-20854 POTOMAC	21087-21087 KINGSVILLE	21531-21531 FRIENDSVILLE
20689-20689 SUNDERLAND	20855-20855 DERWOOD	21088-21088 LINEBORO	21532-21532 FROSTBURG
20690-20690 TALL TIMBERS	20856-20858 ROCKVILLE	21088-21088 LINEBORO CPO	21536-21536 GRANTSVILLE
20692-20692 VALLEY LEE	20858-20858 SILVER SPRING	21090-21090 LINTHICUM HEIGHTS	21538-21538 KITZMILLER
20693-20693 WELCOME	20859-20859 POTOMAC	21092-21092 LONG GREEN	21539-21539 LONACONING
20695-20695 WHITE PLAINS	20860-20860 SANDY SPRING	21093-21094 LUTHERVILLE TIMONIUM	21540-21540 LUKE
20697-20697 SOUTHERN MD FACILITY	20861-20861 ASHTON	21098-21098 HANOVER	21541-21541 MC HENRY
20701-20701 ANNAPOLIS JUNCTION	20862-20862 BRINKLOW	21101-21101 MAGNOLIA	21542-21542 MIDLAND
20703-20703 LANHAM	20866-20866 BURTONSVILLE	21102-21102 MANCHESTER	21543-21543 MIDLOTHIAN
20704-20705 BELTSVILLE	20868-20868 SPENCERVILLE	21104-21104 MARRIOTTSVILLE	21545-21545 MOUNT SAVAGE
20706-20706 LANHAM	20871-20871 CLARKSBURG	21105-21105 MARYLAND LINE	21546-21546 NIKEP
20707-20709 LAUREL	20872-20872 DAMASCUS	21106-21106 MAYO	21550-21550 OAKLAND
20710-20710 BLADENSBURG	20874-20876 GERMANTOWN	21107-21107 ALESIA	21555-21555 OLDTOWN
20711-20711 LOTHIAN	20877-20879 GAITHERSBURG	21107-21107 FREELAND	21556-21556 PINTO
20712-20712 MOUNT RAINIER	20880-20880 WASHINGTON GROVE	21107-21107 MILLERS	21557-21557 RAWLINGS
20714-20714 NORTH BEACH	20882-20885 GAITHERSBURG	21108-21108 MILLERSVILLE	21560-21560 SPRING GAP
20715-20721 BOWIE	20886-20886 MONTGOMERY VILLAGE	21111-21111 MONKTON	21561-21561 SWANTON
20722-20722 BRENTWOOD	20889-20889 BETHESDA	21113-21113 ODENTON	21562-21562 WESTERNPORT
20723-20726 LAUREL	20890-20890 SUBURB MARYLAND FAC	21114-21114 CROFTON	21601-21606 EASTON
20731-20731 CAPITOL HEIGHTS	20891-20891 KENSINGTON	21117-21117 OWINGS MILLS	21607-21607 BARCLAY

21609-21609 BETHLEHEM	21736-21736 GAPLAND	21872-21872 WHALEYVILLE
21610-21610 BETTERTON	21737-21737 GLENELG	21874-21874 WILLARDS
21612-21612 BOZMAN	21738-21738 GLENWOOD	21875-21875 DELMAR
21613-21613 CAMBRIDGE	21740-21749 HAGERSTOWN	21890-21890 WESTOVER
21617-21617 CENTREVILLE	21750-21750 HANCOCK	21901-21901 NORTH EAST
21619-21619 CHESTER	21754-21754 IJAMSVILLE	21902-21902 PERRY POINT
21620-21620 CHESTERTOWN	21755-21755 JEFFERSON	21903-21903 PERRYVILLE
21622-21622 CHURCH CREEK	21756-21756 KEEDYSVILLE	21904-21904 PORT DEPOSIT
21623-21623 CHURCH HILL	21757-21757 KEYMAR	21911-21911 RISING SUN
21624-21624 CLAIBORNE	21758-21758 KNOXVILLE	21912-21912 WARWICK
21625-21625 CORDOVA	21759-21759 LADIESBURG	21913-21913 CECILTON
21626-21626 CRAPO	21762-21762 LIBERTYTOWN	21914-21914 CHARLESTOWN
21627-21627 CROCHERON	21764-21764 LINWOOD	21915-21915 CHESAPEAKE CITY
21628-21628 CRUMPTON	21765-21765 LISBON	21916-21916 CHILDS
21629-21629 DENTON	21766-21766 LITTLE ORLEANS	21917-21917 COLORA
21631-21631 EAST NEW MARKET	21767-21767 MAUGANSVILLE	21918-21918 CONOWINGO
21632-21632 FEDERALSBURG	21768-21768 MIDDLEBURG	21919-21919 EARLEVILLE
21634-21634 FISHING CREEK	21769-21769 MIDDLETOWN	21920-21920 ELK MILLS
21635-21635 GALENA	21770-21770 MONROVIA	21921-21922 ELKTON
21636-21636 GOLDSBORO	21771-21771 MOUNT AIRY	21930-21930 GEORGETOWN
21637-21637 GALENA	21773-21773 MYERSVILLE	
21638-21638 GRASONVILLE	21774-21774 NEW MARKET	
21639-21639 GREENSBORO	21775-21775 NEW MIDWAY	
21640-21640 HENDERSON	21776-21776 NEW WINDSOR	
21641-21641 HILLSBORO	21777-21777 POINT OF ROCKS	
21643-21643 HURLOCK	21778-21778 ROCKY RIDGE	
21644-21644 INGLESIDE	21779-21779 ROHRERSVILLE	
21645-21645 KENNEDYVILLE	21780-21780 SABILLASVILLE	
21646-21646 LYNCH	21781-21781 SAINT JAMES	
21647-21647 MCDANIEL	21782-21782 SHARPSBURG	
21648-21648 MADISON	21783-21783 SMITHSBURG	
21649-21649 MARYDEL	21784-21784 SYKESVILLE	
21650-21650 MASSEY	21787-21787 TANEYTOWN	
21651-21651 MILLINGTON	21788-21788 THURMONT	
21652-21652 NEAVITT	21790-21790 TUSCARORA	
21653-21653 NEWCOMB	21791-21791 UNION BRIDGE	
21654-21654 OXFORD	21792-21792 UNIONVILLE	
21655-21655 PRESTON	21793-21793 WALKERSVILLE	
21656-21656 CHURCH HILL	21794-21794 WEST FRIENDSHIP	
21657-21657 QUEEN ANNE	21795-21795 WILLIAMSPORT	
21658-21658 QUEENSTOWN	21797-21797 WOODBINE	
21659-21659 RHODESDALE	21798-21798 WOODSBORO	
21660-21660 RIDGELY	21801-21804 SALISBURY	
21661-21661 ROCK HALL	21810-21810 ALLEN	
21662-21662 ROYAL OAK	21811-21811 BERLIN	
21663-21663 SAINT MICHAELS	21813-21813 BISHOPVILLE	
21664-21664 SECRETARY	21814-21814 BIVALVE	
21665-21665 SHERWOOD	21816-21816 CHANCE	
21666-21666 STEVENSVILLE	21817-21817 CRISFIELD	
21667-21667 STILL POND	21820-21820 DAMES QUARTER	
21668-21668 SUDLERSVILLE	21821-21821 DEAL ISLAND	
21669-21669 TAYLORS ISLAND	21822-21822 EDEN	
21670-21670 TEMPLEVILLE	21824-21824 EWELL	
21671-21671 TILGHMAN	21826-21826 FRUITLAND	
21672-21672 TODDVILLE	21829-21829 GIRDLETREE	
21673-21673 TRAPPE	21830-21830 HEBRON	
21675-21675 WINGATE	21835-21835 LINKWOOD	
21676-21676 WITTMAN	21836-21836 MANOKIN	
21677-21677 WOOLFORD	21837-21837 MARDELA SPRINGS	
21678-21678 WORTON	21838-21838 MARION STATION	
21679-21679 WYE MILLS	21840-21840 NANTICOKE	
21681-21688 RIDGELY	21841-21841 NEWARK	
21690-21690 CHESTERTOWN	21842-21843 OCEAN CITY	
21701-21709 FREDERICK	21849-21849 PARSONSBURG	
21710-21710 ADAMSTOWN	21850-21850 PITTSVILLE	
21711-21711 BIG POOL	21851-21851 POCOMOKE CITY	
21713-21713 BOONSBORO	21852-21852 POWELLVILLE	
21714-21714 BRADDOCK HEIGHTS	21853-21853 PRINCESS ANNE	
21715-21715 BROWNSVILLE	21856-21856 QUANTICO	
21716-21716 BRUNSWICK	21857-21857 REHOBETH	
21717-21717 BUCKEYSTOWN	21858-21858 RHODES POINT	
21718-21718 BURKITTSVILLE	21861-21861 SHARPTOWN	
21719-21719 CASCADE	21862-21862 SHOWELL	
21720-21720 CAVETOWN	21863-21863 SNOW HILL	
21721-21721 CHEWSVILLE	21864-21864 STOCKTON	
21722-21722 CLEAR SPRING	21865-21865 TYASKIN	
21723-21723 COOKSVILLE	21866-21866 TYLERTON	
21725-21725 DETOUR	21867-21867 UPPER FAIRMOUNT	
21727-21727 EMMITSBURG	21868-21868 UPPER HILL	
21733-21733 FAIRPLAY	21869-21869 VIENNA	
21734-21734 FUNKSTOWN	21870-21870 WENONA	
21735-21735 GAITHER	21871-21871 WESTOVER	

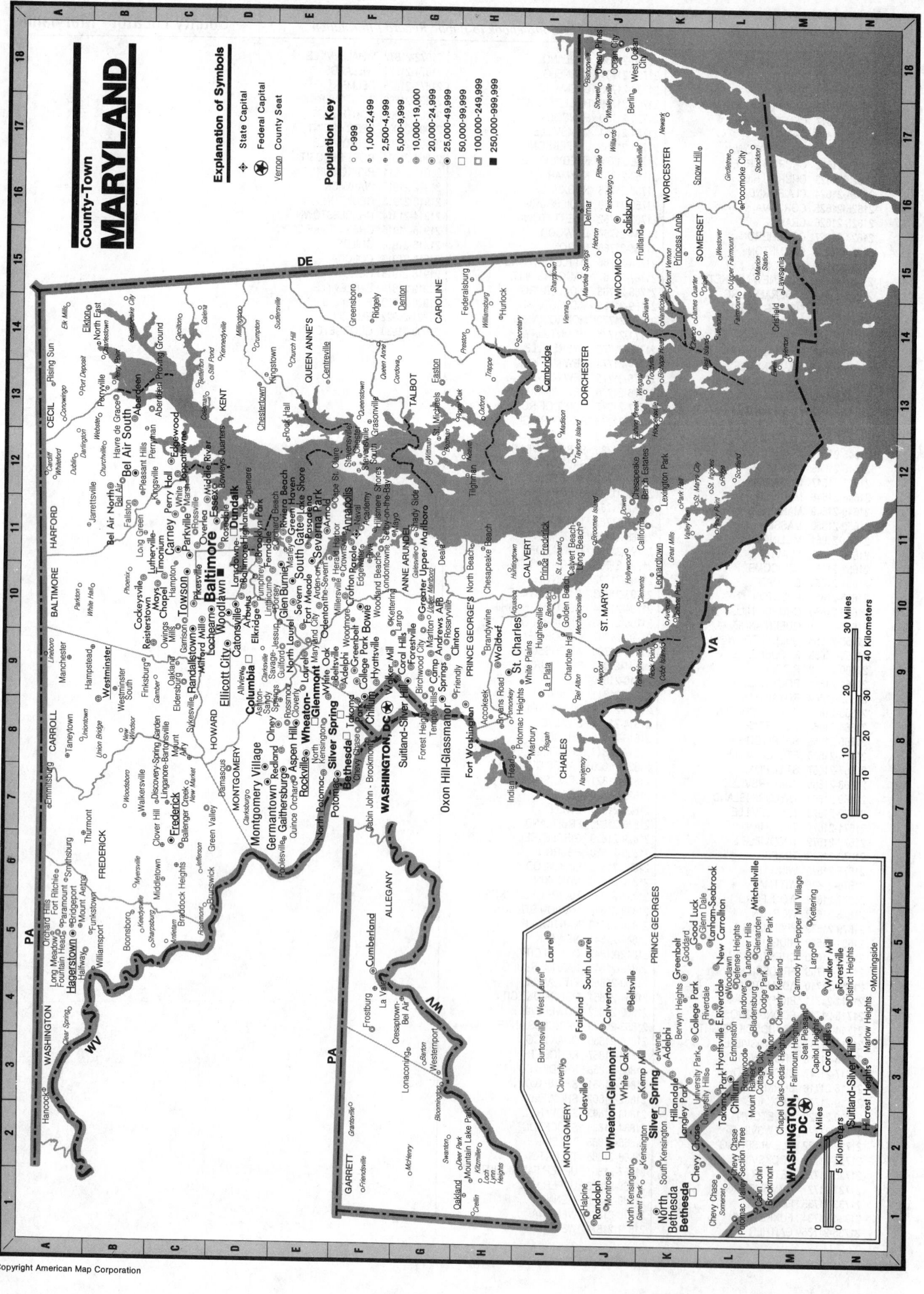

County-Town
MARYLAND

Explanation of Symbols

⊕ State Capital

✪ Federal Capital

Vernon ⊙ County Seat

Population Key

○ 0-999
⊕ 1,000-2,499
⊕ 2,500-4,999
⊕ 5,000-9,999
⊕ 10,000-19,000
⊕ 20,000-24,999
⊙ 25,000-49,999
□ 50,000-99,999
□ 100,000-249,999
■ 250,000-999,999

Explanation of symbols: • – Census Designated Place (CDP)

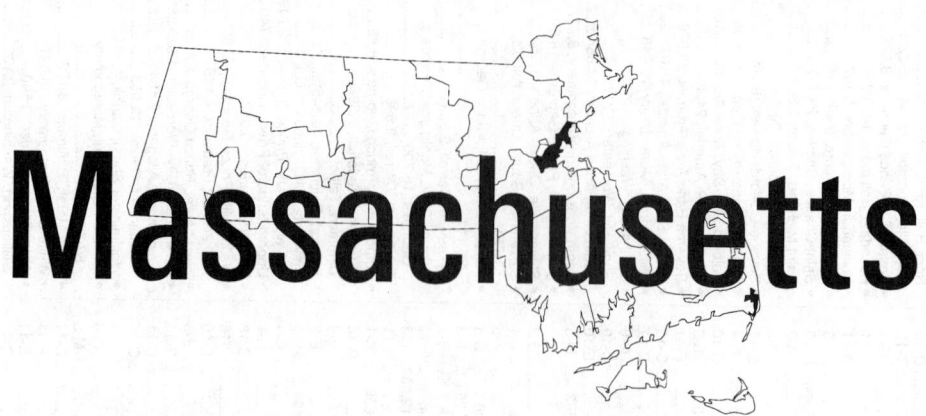

Massachusetts

General Help Numbers:

Governor's Office

State House, Room 360   617- 727-4000
Boston, MA 02133   Fax 617-727-9725
www.state.ma.us/gov   8AM-6PM

Attorney General's Office

One Ashburton Place, Room 2010   617-727-2200
Boston, MA 02108-1698   Fax 617-727-5768
www.ago.state.ma.us   9AM-5PM

Legislative Records

Massachusetts General Court, State House
Beacon St, Room 428 (Document Room)   617-722-2860
Boston, MA 02133
www.mass.gov/legis/   9AM-5PM

State Archives

Archives Division   617-727-2816
220 Morrissey Blvd   Fax 617-288-8429
Boston, MA 02125   9AM-5PM M-F; 9-3 SA
www.sec.state.ma.us/arc/

State Specifics:

Capital:	Boston
	Suffolk County
Time Zone:	EST
Number of Counties:	14
Population:	6,416,505
Website:	www.mass.gov/gov

State Agencies

Criminal Records

Criminal History Systems Board, 200 Arlington Street, #2200, Chelsea, MA 02150; 617-660-4600, 617-660-4613-Fax; 9AM-5PM.

www.mass.gov/chsb

These searches are offered: 1) Personal, 2) Certified Agency, 3) Publicly Accessible (PUBAC). Certified Agency requests are pre-approved via statute or the Board. PUBAC is open to the public; data is limited.

Records are available for at least 50 years. It takes 1 day before new records are available for inquiry. Records are indexed on inhouse computer, file folders. 100% of PUBAC records have final dispositions recorded.

Searching: PUBAC requesters are limited to adult records; the crime must include a sentence of 5 years or more OR sentenced and convicted for any term if, at the time of request, the subject is on probation or has been released within 2 years of felony conviction. Include the following in your

request-name, date of birth. The Personal request (on one's self) requires a notarized signature. A "certified agency" search may include youth organizations, child care providers, and others approved by CHSB. This agency does not conduct FBI fingerprint searches. A Certified Agency record includes all conviction and all open or pending actions. A PUBAC record contains only convictions.

Access by: mail.

Fee & Payment: The Personal request is $25.00. The Certified Agency request is $15.00. The PUBAC request is $30.00. No fingerprint requests are permitted, thus no fingerprint fees. In fact, 0% of the records are fingerprint-supported. Fee payee: The Commonwealth of Massachusetts. Prepayment required. Personal checks accepted. No credit cards accepted.

Mail search: Turnaround time: 2 weeks. A SASE is required.

Expedited service: Requests are expedited for an additional $10.00 per record.

Statewide Court Records

Chief Justice for Administration & Management, 2 Center Plaza, Room 540, Boston, MA 02108; 617-742-8575, 617-742-0968-Fax; 8:30AM-5PM.

www.mass.gov/courts/admin/index.html

Searching: Opinions to the Mass Supreme and Appellate courts can be found at http://massreports.com.

Access by: online.

Online search: Opinions to the Mass Supreme and Appellate courts can be found at http://massreports.com/. Online access to records on the statewide Trial Courts Information Center website is available to attorneys and law firms at www.ma-trialcourts.org/tcic/welcome.jsp. Contact Peter Nylin by email at nylin_p@jud.state.ma.us. Site is updated daily.

Sexual Offender Registry

Sex Offender Registry Board, PO Box 4547, Salem, MA 01970; 978-740-6400, 978-740-6464-Fax; 8:45AM-5PM.

www.mass.gov/sorb

The Sex Offender Registry Board estimates that there are nearly 18,000 sex offenders living and/or working in the Commonwealth of Massachusetts.

Records are available from 08/01/81.

Searching: Information about a sex offender is available to the public only if subject has been classified by the Board as a Level 2 or a Level 3 Offender. In person requests should be conducted at local law enforcement offices. Requests to this office must be in writing or online access is available from the Internet site.

Access by: mail, online.

Fee & Payment: There is no fee.

Mail search: Turnaround time: 1-2 weeks.

Online search: Search free at http://ma-sorb.gis.net/intro.htm. Pursuant to M.G.L. C. 6, §§ 178C - 178P, the individuals who appear on the web page have been designated a Level 3 Sex Offenders by the Sex Offender Registry Board.

Incarceration Records

Massachusetts Executive Office of Public Safety, Criminal History Systems Board, 200 Arlington #2200, Chelsea, MA 02150; 617-660-4600, 877-421-8463 (Locator), 617-660-4690 (Criminal Histories Systems Board), 8AM-5PM.

www.mass.gov/doc

Records are available on current and former inmates by mail. Current inmates only online from a vendor. It takes about 7 days before new records are available for inquiry.

Searching: Include the following in your request-full name; AIS number helpful.

Access by: mail, phone, online.

Fee & Payment: There is no fee.

Mail search: Turnaround time: 2-3 days. Requests in writing must be on letterhead paper

Phone search: Use the Locator phone number: 877-421-8463.

Online search: No searching online is offered by this agency, however a private company offers free web access to DOC offenders at www.vinelink.com/index.jsp.

Corporation, Trademarks/Servicemarks, Limited Liability Partnerships, Limited Partnerships, Limited Liability Companies

Secretary of the Commonwealth, Corporation Division, One Ashburton Pl, 17th Floor, Boston, MA 02108; 617-727-9640 (Corporations), 617-727-2850 (Records), 617-727-8329 (Trademarks), 617-727-9440 (Forms Requests), 617-742-4538-Fax; 8:45AM-5PM.

www.sec.state.ma.us/cor/coridx.htm

Records are available for corporations and business entities organized since 1978 on computer. Corporations and business entities organized prior to 1978 may or may not be available. Annual reports are maintained for 10 years. New records are available for inquiry immediately. Records are indexed on microfilm, inhouse computer. Images available August 2001 to present.

Searching: Include the following in your request-full name of business. In addition to the articles of incorporation, corporation records include the following information: Annual Reports, Officers and Directors names and addresses, Prior (merged) names, Inactive and Reserved names and US Tax ID numbers.

Access by: mail, phone, in person, online.

Fee & Payment: Uncertified copies cost $.30 per page. Certified copies cost $7.00 for the first page and $2.00 for each additional page. Certified copies of articles of incorporation are $12.00 per organization. Fee payee: Commonwealth of Massachusetts. Prepayment required. Personal checks accepted. Credit cards accepted for online orders only.

Mail search: Turnaround time: 3 to 5 days. A SASE is requested.

Phone search: No fee for telephone request. Telephone room hours are 8:45AM-5PM.

In person search: Turnaround time: while you wait.

Online search: There is a free Internet lookup from the website. This site also provides UCC information.

Other access: Bulk sale on CD is available.

Uniform Commercial Code, State Tax Liens

UCC Division, Secretary of the Commonwealth, One Ashburton Pl, Room 1711, Boston, MA

02108; 617-727-2860, 900-555-4500 (Computer Prints), 900-555-4600 (Copies), 8:45AM-5PM.

www.sec.state.ma.us/cor/corpweb/corucc/uccmain .html

Records are available from 09/01/81 on computer and 01/01/84 on microfiche. It takes 24 hours before new records are available for inquiry. Records are indexed on inhouse computer.

Searching: Use search request form UCC-11. Federal tax liens are filed at the US District Courts, PO & Courthouse Bldg, Boston, MA 02109 (617-233-9152). A list of state tax liens is available here, but must be searched in person separately from UCC filings. Include the following in your request-debtor name. Only active filings are available.

Access by: mail, fax, in person, online.

Fee & Payment: Information listing only is $10.00. Search with copies is $30.00 for first 15 pages, $1.00 per page of copies after 15. State tax liens cost $0.30 per copy made. The state does not certify any state tax lien. Fee payee: Commonwealth of Massachusetts. Prepayment required. VISA and MC cards accepted for fax and online searches. Personal checks accepted.

Mail search: Turnaround time: 2 days. Information requests are available.

Fax search: Requests accepted by fax if credit card given.

In person search: You may request information in person, but turnaround time for certified documents is 24 hours. You may search on an inhouse public terminal.

Online search: There is free access to record index from the website. Search by name, organization or file number. There is another site at www.state.me.us/sos/cec/corp/debtor_index.shtml.

Other access: Microfiche may be purchased.

Sales Tax Registrations

Revenue Department - Customer Srv. Bureau, Sales Tax Registrations, PO Box 7010, Boston, MA 02204 (Courier address: 200 Arlington Street, 4th Floor, Chelsea, MA 02150); 617-887-6367, 8AM-5PM.

www.dor.state.ma.us

There are actually 6 offices in the state that allow walk-in researchers. The office in Chelsea will not let you in the building.

Searching: This agency will only confirm that a business is registered. They will provide no other information. Include the following in your request-business name ot tax number.

Access by: mail, phone, fax, in person.

Mail search: Turnaround time: 5 to 10 days. A SASE is requested. No fee for mail request.

Phone search: No fee for telephone request.

Fax search: They ask that you call first to get the number, they do not wish to publish their fax number.

In person search: No fee for request. Call to find closest office.

Birth Certificates

Registry of Vital Records and Statistics, 150 Mt Vernon St, 1st FL, Dorchester, MA 02125; 617-

740-2600, 617-740-2606 , 617-825-7755-Fax; 8:45AM-4:45PM.

www.mass.gov/dph/bhsre/rvr/vrcopies.htm

Records are available from 1911 to present. Records from 1841 to 1905 are located at the Massachusetts Archives, 220 Morrissey Blvd., Boston, MA 02125. Records prior to 1841 are located at the town/city level. It takes 6 months before new records are available for inquiry.

Searching: Access to out-of-wedlock birth records and health information is strictly limited. A court order is required for adopted children's records. Otherwise, records are open. Include the following in your request-full name, names of parents, mother's maiden name, date of birth, place of birth. Must present a photo ID or provide a copy of a photo ID to search. Phone and fax searchers must give exact place and date of event.

Access by: mail, phone, fax, in person, online.

Fee & Payment: The fee is $18.00 per certified record if in person and $28.00 by mail. Fee payee: Commonwealth of Massachusetts. Personal checks accepted. Major credit cards accepted.

Mail search: Turnaround time: 3 to 4 weeks. A SASE is requested.

Phone search: See expedited service. Must use a credit card.

Fax search: See expedited service. Must use a credit card.

In person search: Turnaround time is immediate. You can also do your own searching of records. First 20 minutes is free, then there is a $9.00 fee. The research center is open 9AM-12PM and 2PM-4:30PM, M-F.

Online search: One may order online at www.uscerts.com, a state designated vendor.

Expedited service: Expedited service is available for phone, fax, and online orders. Turnaround time: 2 days. The fax number to use is 617-740-2713. Total fee is $42.50 plus cost of express delivery.

Death Records

Registry of Vital Records and Statistics, 150 Mt Vernon St, 1st FL, Dorchester, MA 02125; 617-740-2600, 617-740-2606 , 617-825-7755-Fax; 8:45AM-4:45PM.

www.mass.gov/dph/bhsre/rvr/vrcopies.htm

Records are available from 1906 to present. Prior records at State Archives to 1841. It takes 4 months before new records are available for inquiry.

Searching: Fetal death records are not available. A court order is required to access the originals of amended records. Include the following in your request-full name, date of death, place of death. Name of spouse and age at time of death will help facilitate the search. Phone and fax requesters must supply exact place and date of event.

Access by: mail, phone, fax, in person, online.

Fee & Payment: The fee is $18.00 per certified record if in person and $28.00 by mail. Fee payee: Commonwealth of Massachusetts. Personal checks accepted. Major credit cards accepted.

Mail search: Turnaround time: 3 to 4 weeks. A SASE is requested.

Phone search: See expedited service. You must use a credit card.

Fax search: See expedited service.

In person search: There is a research center open 9AM-12PM and 2PM-4:30PM M-F. Searching is free the first 20 minutes, then it is $9.00 per hour.

Online search: One may order online at www.uscerts.com, a state designated vendor.

Expedited service: Expedited service is available for phone, fax, and online orders. Turnaround time: 2 days. The fax number to use is 617-740-2713. Total fee is $42.50 plus cost of express delivery.

Marriage Certificates

Registry of Vital Records and Statistics, 150 Mt Vernon St, 1st FL, Dorchester, MA 02125; 617-740-2600, 617-740-2606 , 617-825-7755-Fax; 8:45AM-4:45PM.

www.mass.gov/dph/bhsre/rvr/vrcopies.htm

Records are available from 1906 to present. Prior records to 1841 are at State Archives. It takes 5 months before new records are available for inquiry.

Searching: A court order is required for originals of amended records. Include the following in your request-names of husband and wife, date of marriage, place or county of marriage. Phone or fax searchers must submit exact place and date of event. Also helpful are parents' names.

Access by: mail, phone, fax, in person, online.

Fee & Payment: The fee is $18.00 per certified record if in person and $28.00 by mail. Fee payee: Commonwealth of Massachusetts. Personal checks accepted. Major credit cards accepted.

Mail search: Turnaround time: 3 to 4 weeks. A SASE is requested. See expedited service.

Phone search: See expedited service. You must use a credit card.

Fax search: See expedited service.

In person search: There is a research center open from 9AM-12PM and 2PM-4:30PM, M-F. The first 20 minutes are free, then a $9.00 per hour fee is charged.

Online search: One may order online at www.uscerts.com, a state designated vendor.

Expedited service: Expedited service is available for phone, fax, and online orders. Turnaround time: 2 days. The fax number to use is 617-740-2713. Total fee is $42.50 plus cost of express delivery.

Divorce Records

Access to Records is Restricted.

Registry of Vital Records and Statistics, 150 Mt Vernon St, 1st FL, Dorchester, MA 02125; 617-740-2600, 617-740-2606 .

www.mass.gov/dph/bhsre/rvr/vrcopies.htm

Divorce records are found at county of issue. However, this agency maintains an index from 1952 to present. The state will do a search for free by mail only to determine the county.

Workers' Compensation Records

Keeper of Records, Department of Industrial Accidents, 600 Washington St, 7th Floor, Boston, MA 02111; 617-727-4900, 617-727-4440-Fax; 8AM-4PM.

www.mass.gov/dia

Records are under the jurisdiction of Sec of State, per the state public record law.

Records are available from 1995 on, and prior records located at State Archives. The index is computerized since 1982. Earlier records may be researched via microfiche for an index number. It takes 24 hours before new records are available for inquiry. Records are indexed on inhouse computer. Records are normally destroyed after 40 years.

Searching: You need a signed release from claimant to receive data regarding medical records, DOB, and SSN. Include the following in your request-claimant name, Social Security Number, date of injury, employer, insurance carrier, and other pertinent information. E-mail address is infodesk@dia.state.ma.us. The following data is not released: medical records, date of birth or Social Security Numbers.

Access by: mail, in person.

Fee & Payment: There is a standard fee of $5.00 prior to release of record(s). Add $.20 per page and $.50 per page if computer generated. They will invoice. Fee payee: Commonwealth of Massachusetts. Personal checks accepted. No credit cards accepted.

Mail search: Turnaround time: as much as 6 weeks. No SASE is required.

In person search: All requests must be in writing.

Driver Records-Registry

Registry of Motor Vehicles, Driver Control Unit, Box 199150, Boston, MA 02119-1950; 617-351-9213 (Registry), 617-351-9219-Fax; 8AM-4:30PM M-T-W-F; 8AM-7PM TH.

www.mass.gov/rmv

The driving records provided by the Registry are for employment or general business use. The Merit Rating Board oversees records for insurance use. Both the Registry and the Merit Rating Board use the same database of driving record histories.

Records are available for 6 years plus current year for moving violations. It takes 1 week before new records are available for inquiry.

Searching: Casual requesters can only obtain records without personal information. Include the following in your request-full name, driver's license number, date of birth. The address of the requester should also be included. Request form are found at www.mass.gov/rmv/forms/l21078.pdf and www.mass.gov/rmv/forms/21080.pdf. The following data is not released: bulk information or lists for commercial purposes.

Access by: mail, phone, in person, online.

Fee & Payment: The fee is $15.00 per record via the Registry, $6.00 if online. Fee payee: Registry of Motor Vehicles. Prepayment required. Personal checks accepted.

Mail search: Turnaround time: 8 working days. No SASE is required.

Phone search: For pre-approved accounts, the Registry offers a phone-in request line at 617-351-9213. Orders can be paid with a credit card, results are mailed.

In person search: Up to 10 requests will be processed immediately; the rest are available the next day. You may request a record from any field office.

Online search: Access is only available for the insurance industry. Fee is $6.00 per record. Call the above number for further details.

Driver Records-Insurance

Merit Rating Board, Attn: Driving Records, PO Box 199100, Boston, MA 02119-9100; 617-351-4400, 617-351-9660-Fax; 8:45AM-5:00PM.

www.mass.gov/rmv

The Merit Rating Board processes driving records for the insurance industry in accordance with state statutes.

Records are available for 6 years for moving violations and at fault accidents (process date). The license number and name are validated against the Registry license file. It takes 5 days before new records are available for inquiry.

Searching: These records do not show revocation or suspension action. Include the following in your request-driver's license number, full name, date of birth. All requests must be on the agency form.

Access by: mail, in person, online.

Fee & Payment: The fee is $15.00 per record. Fee payee: Commonwealth of Massachusetts. Prepayment required. Personal checks accepted. No credit cards accepted.

Mail search: Turnaround time: 2 days. No SASE is required.

In person search: Turnaround time is while you wait.

Online search: The Merit Rating Board provides both online and tape inquiry to the insurance industry for rating and issuance of new and renewal automobile insurance policies. Per statute, this method of retrieval is not open to the general public.

Vehicle Ownership
Vehicle Identification

Registry of Motor Vehicles, Document Control, PO Box 199100, Boston, MA 02119-9100; 617-351-9458, 617-351-9524-Fax; 8AM-4:30PM.

www.mass.gov/rmv

In general, license, ownership, and registration information is available to the public. Personal information is not available to casual requesters without consent.

Records are available from the 1940's for licenses, from 1963 for registrations and names. Records are computerized from 1986.

Searching: Requesters with a DPPA permissible use should use "A Request for Personal Information In RMV Records for Multiple Records." Casual requesters should use "A Request for Personal Information In RMV Records for Individual." The agency does not do VIN look-ups. Lien information is provided as part of the record.

Access by: mail, fax, in person, online.

Fee & Payment: The current fee is $5.00 for per record request if on computer, $10.00 if on microfiche. Fee payee: Commonwealth of Massachusetts. Prepayment required. Personal checks accepted. No credit cards accepted.

Mail search: Turnaround time: 7 to 10 days. A SASE is requested.

Fax search: Records are available by fax.

In person search: In person requesters may get computer records immediately, microfiche records take 3 days.

Online search: Searching is limited to Massachusetts based insurance companies and agents for the purpose of issuing or renewing insurance. This system is not open to the public. There is no fee, but line charges will be incurred.

Other access: This agency offers an extensive array of customized bulk record requests to authorized users. For further information, contact the Production Control Office.

Accident Reports

Crash Records, Registry of Motor Vehicles, PO Box 199100, Roxbury, MA 02119-9100; 617-351-9434, 617-351-9401-Fax; 8:45AM-5PM.

www.mass.gov/rmv/forms/accident.htm

Accident reports may also be obtained from the local police department in the investigating jurisdiction.

Records are available for 2 years to present. Records are indexed on computer. It takes 8 weeks before new records are available for inquiry. Records are normally destroyed after 2 years.

Searching: Criminal Offender Record Information (CORI) will not be released. Items required for search include; full name, date of accident, location of accident, and license or registration number.

Access by: mail.

Fee & Payment: The non-refundable charge is $10.00 per report. Fee payee: Registry of Motor Vehicles. Prepayment required. Personal checks accepted. No credit cards accepted.

Mail search: Turnaround time: 4 weeks.

Other access: Quarterly or yearly tapes are available for $2,500.

Vessel Ownership
Vessel Registration

Massachusetts Environmental Police, Registration and Titling Bureau, 251 Causeway Street, #101, Boston, MA 02114; 617-626-1610, 617-626-1630-Fax; 8:45AM-4:45PM.

www.mass.gov/dfwele/dle/dle_toc.htm

Lien information is kept by this agency and appears on the title record.

Records are available from 1988 to present. All motor powered boats and jet skis must be registered with this agency. All boats 4ft and over must be titled. Records are indexed on computer.

Searching: Include the following in your request-name or hull number. The following data is not released: Social Security Numbers or phone numbers.

Access by: mail, phone, fax, in person.

Fee & Payment: There is no search fee.

Mail search: Turnaround time: 1 week. No SASE is required.

Phone search: Records are available by phone.

Fax search: Turnaround time is usually 5 minutes, but up to 1 week in busy season.

In person search: Searching in person permitted.

Other access: To obtain printed lists or CD, contact the Bureau Chief at 617-626-1611. Generally, the fee is $50.00 for a CD. .

Voter Registration
Access to Records is Restricted.

Sec. of the Commonwealth - Elections Division, One Ashburton Place, McCormack Building, Room 1705, Boston, MA 02108; 617-727-2828, 617-742-3238-Fax; 9AM-5PM.

www.state.ma.us/sec/ele/eleidx.htm

The state has a database, but is not available to the public. Records are maintained at the local city and town level. In general, the records are open to the public locally. However, the Federal Help America Vote Act of 2002 (HAVA) law requires implementation of a central, computerized, statewide voter registration system by 01/01/2006. The state will comply.

GED Certificates

Massachusetts Dept of Education, GED Processing, 350 Main St, Malden, MA 02148; 781-338-6625, 781-338-6604 , 781-338-3394-Fax; 9AM-5PM.

www.doe.mass.edu/ged

It takes 1 month before new records are available for inquiry. Records are normally destroyed after 60 years.

Searching: Although this agency is able to verify a GED, they will not release copies of transcripts. You must go to one of the 32 test centers. They can tell you which center to request the copy. Include the following in your request-signed release, DOB, SSN, and name used at time of test. The year and the name of institution are also helpful.

Access by: mail, fax.

Fee & Payment: The fee is $2.00 per for a certified letter of verification. There is no fee for a simple eyes or no answer via fax. Fee payee: Commonwealth of Massachusetts. Prepayment required. Only money orders are accepted. Personal checks and credit cards not accepted.

Mail search: Turnaround time: 2 to 5 days. No SASE is required.

Fax search: Fax requesting is available to all requesters.

Hunting and Fishing License Information

Division of Fisheries & Wildlife, 251 Causeway St #400, Boston, MA 02114-2104; 617-626-1590, 617-626-1517-Fax; 9AM-5PM.

www.mass.gov/dfwele

Records are available for 1 year back only. Older records are maintained at one of several locations off premises and take longer to research.

Searching: All requests must be in writing and on their form. You may call to request the form. Need to know the store where license was purchased and month it was purchased. They are filed by license number only.

Access by: mail, in person.

Fee & Payment: There is no search fee.

Mail search: Turnaround time: same day if possible. No SASE is required.

In person search: You must complete their form.

Massachusetts State Licensing Agencies

For details about the agency responsible for licensing/certifying/registering an item below or in the Agency Quick Finder section, match an item's number with the number of the agency in the *Licensing Agency Information* section.

Massachusetts Licenses Searchable Online

Adjuster, Fire Loss #4 .... www.mass.gov/doi/Producer/Producer_list.html
Adoption Center #8 .... www.qualitychildcare.org/adoption_search_a.asp
Aesthetician #7 .... http://license.reg.state.ma.us/pubLic/licque.asp?color=red&Board=HD
Alarm Installer, Burglar/Fire #7 .... http://license.reg.state.ma.us/pubLic/licque.asp?color=red&Board=EL
Amusement Device Inspector #27 .... www.mass.gov/dps/LIC_SRCH.HTM
Appraiser, MVR Damage #4 .... www.mass.gov/doi/Producer/Producer_list.html
Architect #36 .... http://license.reg.state.ma.us/pubLic/licque.asp?color=red&Board=AR
Athletic Trainer #7 .... http://license.reg.state.ma.us/pubLic/licque.asp?color=red&Board=AH
Attorney #2 .... http://massbbo.org/
Auctioneer School #30   www.mass.gov/portal/index.jsp?pageID=ocaagencylanding&L=4&L0=Home&L1=Government&L2=Our+Agencies+an
              d+Divisions&L3=Division+of+Standards&sid=Eoca
Auto Repair Shop, Registered #4 .... www.aib.org/BDYSHOP/bdshind.htm
Automobile Dealer #11 .... www.mass.gov/dob/liclist.htm
Automobile Sales Finance Company #11 .... www.mass.gov/dob/liclist.htm
Bank & Savings Institution #35 .... http://db.state.ma.us/dob/in-choose.asp
Barber/Barber Shop #7 .... http://license.reg.state.ma.us/pubLic/licque.asp?color=red&Board=BR
Boilers/Pressure Vessels Inspector #27 .... www.mass.gov/dps/LIC_SRCH.HTM
Boxer #9 .... www.mass.gov/mbc/ranking.htm
Brokerage Firm #10 .... www.nasd.com/web/idcplg?IdcService=SS_GET_PAGE&nodeId=6
Building Inspector/Local Inspector #3 .... www.mass.gov/bbrs/bocert.PDF
Building Producer #3 .... www.mass.gov/bbrs/mfg98.pdf
Check Casher/Seller #35 .... www.mass.gov/dob/liclist.htm
Chiropractor #7 .... http://license.reg.state.ma.us/pubLic/licque.asp?color=red&Board=CH
Collection Agency #35 .... www.mass.gov/dob/liclist.htm
Concrete Technician #3 .... www.mass.gov/bbrs/programs.htm
Concrete Testing Laboratory #3 .... www.mass.gov/bbrs/programs.htm
Construction Supervisor #18 .... www.mass.gov/bbrs/cslsearch.htm
Construction Supervisor (Resid'l) #3 .... www.mass.gov/bbrs/programs.htm
Contractor, Home Improvement #3 .... www.mass.gov/bbrs/Hicsearch.htm
Cosmetologist/Manicurist/Aesthet'n #7 .... http://license.reg.state.ma.us/pubLic/licque.asp?color=red&Board=HD
Credit Union #35 .... http://db.state.ma.us/dob/in-choose.asp
Day Care Center #8 .... www.qualitychildcare.org/
Dental Hygienist #7 .... http://license.reg.state.ma.us/pubLic/licque.asp?color=red&Board=DN
Dentist #7 .... http://license.reg.state.ma.us/pubLic/licque.asp?color=red&Board=DN
Electrician #7 .... http://license.reg.state.ma.us/pubLic/licque.asp?color=red&Board=EL
Electrologist #7 .... http://license.reg.state.ma.us/pubLic/licque.asp?color=red&Board=ET
Embalmer #37 .... http://license.reg.state.ma.us/pubLic/licque.asp?color=red&Board=EM
Engineer #7 .... http://license.reg.state.ma.us/pubLic/licque.asp?color=red&Board=EN
Family Child Care Provider #8 .... www.qualitychildcare.org/
Finfishing, Commercial #34 .... www.mass.gov/dfwele/dmf/
Fire Sprinkler Contr./Fitter #27 .... www.mass.gov/dps/LIC_SRCH.HTM
Firemen / Engineer #27 .... www.mass.gov/dps/LIC_SRCH.HTM
Foreign Transmittal Agency #35 .... www.mass.gov/dob/liclist.htm
Foster Care Provider #8 .... www.qualitychildcare.org/adoption_search_fc.asp
Funeral Director #37 .... http://license.reg.state.ma.us/pubLic/licque.asp?color=red&Board=EM
Fur Buyer #34 .... www.mass.gov/dfwele/dfw/
Gas Fitter #7 .... http://license.reg.state.ma.us/pubLic/licque.asp?color=red&Board=PL
Health Insurer #4 .... www.mass.gov/doi/Companies/companies_lists.html
Health Officer, Certified #12 .... http://license.reg.state.ma.us/public/licque.asp?color=blue
Health Profession, Allied #7 .... http://license.reg.state.ma.us/pubLic/licque.asp?color=red&Board=AH
HMO #4 .... www.mass.gov/doi/Consumer/CSS_health_HMO_Licensed.HTML
Hoisting Machinery Operator #27 .... www.mass.gov/dps/LIC_SRCH.HTM
Home Improvement Contractor #3 .... www.mass.gov/bbrs/Hicsearch.htm
Home Improvement Supervisor #18 .... www.mass.gov/bbrs/Hicsearch.htm
Home Inspector #7 .... http://license.reg.state.ma.us/pubLic/v_list_hi.asp
Inspection Agency, 3rd Party #3 .... www.mass.gov/bbrs/MFB.htm
Insurance Advisor/Adjuster/Agent/Broker #4 .. www.mass.gov/doi/Producer/Producer_list.html
Insurance Premium Financer #35 .... www.mass.gov/dob/liclist.htm
Insurance, Domestic/Foreign Co. #4 .... www.mass.gov/doi/Companies/companies_lists.html
Investment Advisor #10 .... www.nasd.com/web/idcplg?IdcService=SS_GET_PAGE&nodeId=6

Land Surveyor #7	http://license.reg.state.ma.us/pubLic/licque.asp?color=red&Board=EN
Landscape Architect #36	http://license.reg.state.ma.us/pubLic/licque.asp?color=red&Board=LA
Loan Company, Small #11	www.mass.gov/dob/liclist.htm
Lobbyist/Lobbyist Employer #21	http://db.state.ma.us/SEC/PRE/search.asp
Lobstering #34	www.mass.gov/dfwele/dmf/
Lumber Producer, Native #3	www.mass.gov/bbrs/lumber.pdf
Manufactured Building Producer #3	www.mass.gov/bbrs/MFB.htm
Marriage & Family Therapist #7	http://license.reg.state.ma.us/pubLic/licque.asp?query=personal&color=red&board=MH
Medical Doctor #6	http://profiles.massmedboard.org/Profiles/MA-Physician-Profile-Find-Doctor.asp
Mental Health & Human Svcs Prof. #7	http://license.reg.state.ma.us/pubLic/licque.asp?query=personal&color=red&board=MH
Mental Health Counselor #7	http://license.reg.state.ma.us/pubLic/licque.asp?query=personal&color=red&board=MH
Mortgage Broker/Lender #11	www.mass.gov/dob/liclist.htm
Motor Vehicle Sales Financer #35	www.mass.gov/dob/liclist.htm
Nuclear Power Plant Eng./Operator #27	www.mass.gov/dps/LIC_SRCH.HTM
Nurse, LPN/RN/Midwife #7	http://license.reg.state.ma.us/pubLic/licque.asp?color=red&Board=RN
Nursing Home Administrator #12	http://license.reg.state.ma.us/public/licque.asp?color=blue
Nursing Home/Rest Home #28	www.medicare.gov/NHCompare/Home.asp
Occupational Therapist/Assistant #7	http://license.reg.state.ma.us/pubLic/licque.asp?color=red&Board=AH
Oil Burner Technician/Contr. #27	www.mass.gov/dps/LIC_SRCH.HTM
Optician #0	http://license.reg.state.ma.us/pubLic/licque.asp?query=personal&color=red&board=DO
Optician, Dispensing #7	http://license.reg.state.ma.us/pubLic/licque.asp?color=red&Board=DO
Optometrist #7	http://license.reg.state.ma.us/pubLic/licque.asp?color=red&Board=OP
P&C Insurance Agency #4	www.mass.gov/doi/Producer/Producer_list.html
Perfusionist #7	http://license.reg.state.ma.us/pubLic/licque.asp?color=red&Board=PF
Pharmacist #7	http://license.reg.state.ma.us/pubLic/licque.asp?color=red&Board=PH
Physical Therapist/Assistant #7	http://license.reg.state.ma.us/pubLic/licque.asp?color=red&Board=AH
Physician Assistant #13	http://license.reg.state.ma.us/pubLic/licque.asp?color=red&Board=AP
Pipefitter #27	www.mass.gov/dps/LIC_SRCH.HTM
Plumber #7	http://license.reg.state.ma.us/pubLic/licque.asp?color=red&Board=PL
Podiatrist #7	http://license.reg.state.ma.us/pubLic/licque.asp?color=red&Board=PD
Psychologist, Educational #7	http://license.reg.state.ma.us/pubLic/licque.asp?query=personal&color=red&board=MH
Psychologist/Provider #12	http://license.reg.state.ma.us/public/licque.asp?color=blue
Public Accountant-CPA #7	http://license.reg.state.ma.us/pubLic/licque.asp?color=red&Board=PA
Radio & TV Repair Technician #7	http://license.reg.state.ma.us/pubLic/licque.asp?color=red&Board=TV
Real Estate Agent/Broker/Sales #7	http://license.reg.state.ma.us/pubLic/licque.asp?color=red&Board=RE
Real Estate Appraiser #7	http://license.reg.state.ma.us/pubLic/licque.asp?color=red&Board=RA
Refrigeration Technician/Contr. #27	www.mass.gov/dps/LIC_SRCH.HTM
Rehabilitation Therapist #7	http://license.reg.state.ma.us/pubLic/licque.asp?query=personal&color=red&board=MH
Residential Care, Youth #8	www.qualitychildcare.org/residential_search.asp
Respiratory Care Therapist #7	http://license.reg.state.ma.us/pubLic/licque.asp?color=red&Board=RC
Retail Installment Financer #35	www.mass.gov/dob/liclist.htm
Sales Finance Company #11	www.mass.gov/dob/liclist.htm
Sanitarian #36	http://license.reg.state.ma.us/pubLic/licque.asp?color=red&Board=SA
Seafood Dealer #34	www.mass.gov/dfwele/dmf/
Securities Agent/Broker/Dealer #10	www.nasd.com/web/idcplg?IdcService=SS_GET_PAGE&nodeId=6
Shellfishing, Commercial #34	www.mass.gov/dfwele/dmf/
Social Worker #7	http://license.reg.state.ma.us/pubLic/licque.asp?color=red&Board=SW
Speech-Language Path'gist/Audiol't #7	http://license.reg.state.ma.us/pubLic/licque.asp?color=red&Board=SP
Surplus Lines Broker #4	www.mass.gov/doi/Producer/Producer_list.html
Taxidermist #34	www.mass.gov/dfwele/dfw/
Trapping #34	www.mass.gov/dfwele/dfw/
Veterinarian #7	http://license.reg.state.ma.us/pubLic/licque.asp?color=red&Board=VT
Water Supply Facility Operator #7	http://license.reg.state.ma.us/pubLic/licque.asp?color=red&Board=DW

Massachusetts Licensing Quick Finder

Acupuncturist #5	617-727-3086	Ambulance Service #14 617-753-7300	Automobile Sales Finance Company #11 617-956-1500 x501
Adjuster, Fire Loss #4	617-521-7794	Ambulatory Surgical Center #28 617-753-8000	Bank & Savings Institution #35 617-956-1500
Adoption Center #8	617-626-2069	Amusement Device Inspec'r #27 617-727-3200 x607	Bank, Cooperative #35 617-956-1500
Aerial Passenger Cable Car #27 617-727-3200 x662	Appraiser (MVD) #20 617-521-7453	Barber/Barber Shop #7 617-727-7367
Aesthetician #7 617-727-9940	Appraiser, MVR Damage #4 617-521-7447	Birthing Center #28 617-753-8000
Aircraft #23 617-973-8883	Architect #36 617-727-3072	Blood Bank #28 617-753-8000
Airport Manager #23 617-973-8883	Asbestos/Lead Abatement #24 617-727-7047	Boiler Engineer #27 617-727-3200
Alarm Installer, Burglar/Fire #7 617-727-9931	Athletic Trainer #7 617-727-3071	Boilers/Pressure Vessels Inspector #27 617-727-3200 x607
Alcoholic Bev./Wine Sales/Broker/Whlse #1 617-727-3040	Attorney #2 617-728-8800	Boxer #9 617-727-3200 x25257
Alcoholic Bev/Wine Transport Permit #1 617-727-3040	Auctioneer #30 617-727-3480	Boxing Judge/Referee/Trainer/2nd #9 617-727-3200 x25257
Alcoholism/Drug Facility #15 617-624-5111	Auctioneer School #30 617-727-3480	
Alcoholism/Drug Program #15 617-624-5111	Auto Repair Shop, Registered #4 617-727-3480	
	Automobile Dealer #11 617-956-1500 x501	

Boxing Physician #9 .... 617-727-3200 x25257
Boxing Professional #9 .... 617-727-3200 x25257
Boxing Timekeeper/Mgr/Promoter #9
.... 617-727-3200 x25257
Brewery/Pub/Sacramental Wine #1 617-727-3040
Brewery/Winery Storage/Farmer #1 617-727-3040
Brokerage Firm #10 617-727-3548
Building Inspector/Local Inspector #3 .. 617-727-7532
Building Producer #3 617-727-7532
Bus/Motor Coach Driver #31 617-305-3559
Cattle Dealer/Transporter #19 617-626-1700
Chair Lift #27 .... 617-727-3200 x662
Check Casher/Seller #35 617-956-1500
Chiropractor #7 617-727-3093
Cigarette Seller #32 617-887-5090
Clinic #28 617-753-8000
Collection Agency #35 617-956-1500
Concrete Technician #3 617-727-7532
Concrete Testing Laboratory #3 617-727-7532
Construction Supervisor #18 .. 617-727-7532 x25205
Construction Supervisor (Resid'l) #3 .. 617-727-7532
Consumer Credit Grantor #35 617-956-1500
Contractor,Home Improve'm't #3 .. 508-821-9375 x502
Cosmetologist/Manicurist/Aesthetician) #7
.... 617-727-9940
Credit Union #35 617-956-1500
Day Care Center #8 617-626-2069
Day Care Center Teacher/Director #8.. 617-626-2069
Dental Examiner #41 617-727-9928
Dental Hygienist #7 617-727-9928
Dentist #7 617-727-9928
Domestics Agency #22 617-727-3696
Electrician #7 617-727-9931
Electrologist #7 617-727-9957
Elevator Construction/Maintenance #27
.... 617-727-3200 x25238
Elevator Operator #27 .... 617-727-3200 x25238
Embalmer #37 617-727-1718
Emergency Medical Technician #14 .. 617-753-7300
Employment Agency, Placement/Temporary #22
.... 617-727-3696
Engineer #7 617-727-9957
Exterminator #19 617-626-1776
Family Child Care Assistant #8 617-626-2069
Family Child Care Provider #8............. 617-626-2069
Finfishing, Commercial #34 617-626-1520
Fire Protection Sprinkler Contr./Fitter #27
.... 617-727-3200 x607
Firemen / Engineer #27 .... 617-727-3200 x607
Foreign Transmittal Agency #35 617-956-1500
Foster Care Provider #8 617-626-2069
Funeral Director #37 617-727-1718
Fur Buyer #34 617-626-1590
Gas Fitter #7 617-727-9952
Gas Station Owner #30 617-727-3480
Guard Dog/Hearing Dog Business #19 . 617-626-1786
Hairdresser #7 617-727-9940
Health Care Plan, Managed #4 617-521-7372
Health Insurer #4 617-521-7794
Health Officer, Certified #12 617-727-3074
Health Profession, Allied #7 617-727-3071
HMO #4 617-521-7794
Hoisting Machinery (Forklift, Hydraulic, Crane) Operator
#27 .... 617-727-3200 x607

Home Health Care Provider #22 617-727-3696
Home Improvement Contrac'r #3 . 508-821-9375 x502
Home Improvement Supervisor #18
.... 617-727-7532 x25207
Home Inspector #7 617-727-4459
Horse (Equine) Dealer #19 617-626-1797
Horse/Greyhound #16 617-727-2581
Hospice #28 617-753-8000
Hospital #28 617-753-8000
Inspection Agency, 3rd Party #3 617-727-7532
Insurance Advisor/Adjuster #4 617-521-7794
Insurance Agent/Broker #4 617-521-7794
Insurance Premium Financer #35 617-956-1500
Insurance, Domestic/Foreign Company #4
.... 617-321-7391
Investment Advisor #10 617-727-3548
Jockey #16 617-727-2581
Justice of the Peace #29 .... 617-725-4016 x5
Laboratory, Medical-related #28 617-753-8000
Land Surveyor #7 617-727-9957
Landscape Architect #36 617-727-3072
Lead Inspector #24 617-727-7047
Library Media Specialist #17 ..... 781-338-3000 x6600
Loan Company, Small #11 .... 617-956-1500 x501
Lobbyist/Lobbyist Employer #21 617-878-3434
Lobstering #34 617-626-1520
Lumber Producer, Native #3 .. 617-727-3636 x561
Mammography Radiologic Tech. #26 . 617-427-2944
Manicurist #7 617-727-9940
Manufactured Building Producer #3..... 617-727-7532
Marriage & Family Therapist #7 617-727-3071
Medical Doctor #6........................... 617-654-9800
Mental Health & Human Svcs Prof., Allied #7
.... 617-727-3071
Mental Health Counselor #7 617-727-3071
Milk Plant #19 617-626-1811
Modeling Industry/Agency #22........... 617-727-3696
Mortgage Broker/Lender #11 ...... 617-956-1500 x501
Motion Picture Operator #27 ... 617-727-3200 x25223
Motor Vehicle Repair Shop (Auto Body/Glass/etc.) #30
.... 617-727-3480
Motor Vehicle Sales Financer #35 617-956-1500
Nanny Agency #22 617-727-3696
Notary Public #29 .... 617-725-4016 x1
Nuclear Medicine Technologists (Radiologists) #26
.... 617-427-2944
Nuclear Power Plant Engineer/Operator #27
.... 617-727-3200 x607
Nurse, LPN/RN/Midwife #7 617-727-9961
Nursery #19 617-626-1801
Nursery Agent #19.......................... 617-626-1801
Nurses' Aide in Long Term Care Facility #28
.... 617-753-8143
Nursing Home Administrator #12 617-727-3074
Nursing Home/Rest Home #28 617-753-8000
Occupational Therapist/Assistant #7.... 617-727-3071
Oil Burner Technician/Contr. #27 . 617-727-3200 x607
Optician, Dispensing #7 617-727-3093
Optometrist #7 617-727-3093
Out-Patient Rehabilitation Facility #28 . 617-753-8000
Owner/Trainer, Horse/Greyhound #16 . 617-727-2581
P&C Insurance Agency #4 617-521-7794
Pasteurization Plant #19 617-626-1811
Peddler/Hawker #30 617-727-3480

Perfusionist #7 617-727-4499
Personal Agent #27 .... 617-727-3200 x637
Pesticide Applicator/Dealer #19 617-626-1776
Pet Shop #19................................. 617-626-1795
Pharmacist #7 617-727-9953
Physical Therapist/Assistant #7 617-727-3071
Physician Assistant #13 617-973-0806
Pipefitter #27 .... 617-727-3200 x607
Plumber #7 617-727-9952
Podiatrist #7 617-727-1747
Private Detective #33 978-538-6128
Private Investigator #33 978-538-6128
Psychologist, Educational #7 617-727-3071
Psychologist/Provider #12................. 617-727-3074
Public Accountant-CPA #7................. 617-727-1806
Racetrack, Horse/Greyhound #16 617-727-2581
Radiation Therapy/Radiologic Technologist #26
.... 617-427-2944
Radio & TV Repair Technician #7......... 617-727-3074
Radiographer #26............................ 617-427-2944
Radiologic Technologist #26 617-427-2944
Radon Specialist #26 617-427-2944
Real Estate Agent/Broker/Sales #7 617-727-2373
Real Estate Appraiser #7 617-727-3055
Refrigeration Tech./Contr. #27.. 617-727-3200 x607
Rehabilitation Therapist #7 617-727-3071
Renal Dialysis (End Stage) #28 617-753-8000
Residential Care, Youth #8 617-626-2069
Respiratory Care Therapist #7 617-727-1747
Retail Installment Financer #35 617-956-1500
Riding Instructor #19 617-626-1797
Riding School #19 617-626-1797
Sales Finance Company #11 ...... 617-956-1500 x501
Sanitarian #36 617-727-3072
School Administrator #17 .... 781-338-3000 x6600
School Bus #31 617-305-3559
School Guidance Counselor #17 781-338-3000 x6600
Seafood Dealer #34 617-626-1520
Securities Agent #10 617-727-3548
Securities Broker/Dealer #10 617-727-3548
Security Guard Agency #33 978-538-6128
Shellfishing, Commercial #34 617-626-1520
Simulcast & Inter-Track Wagering #16 . 617-727-2581
Ski Tow #27................................... 617-727-3200 x662
Skimobile #27 .... 617-727-3200 x662
Social Worker #7 617-727-3073
Speech-Language Pathologist/Audiologist #7
.... 617-727-1747
Stable (Horse & Buggy Operator) #19 .. 617-626-1797
Surplus Lines Broker #4 617-521-7794
Swine Dealer #19 617-626-1700
Taxidermist #34 617-626-1590
Teacher #17 .... 781-338-3000 x6600
Theatrical Booking Agent #27 ..... 617-727-3200 x637
Ticket Reseller #27 .... 617-727-3200 x637
Tramway Inspector #27 .... 617-727-3200 x662
Trapping #34 617-626-1590
Trust Company #35.......................... 617-956-1500
Vending Machine #25 617-983-6712
Vendor, Transient #30...................... 617-727-3480
Veterinarian #7 617-727-3080
Water Supply Facility Operator #7 617-727-3074
Weights & Measures #30 617-727-3480
Wine & Malt Beverage Permit #1 617-727-3040

Massachusetts Licensing Agency Information

1 Alcoholic Beverages Control Commission, 239 Causeway St #200, Boston, MA 02114-2130; 617-727-3040, Fax: 617-727-1258.
Email: errol.flynn@state.ma.us

2 Board of Overseers Registry Dept, Board of Bar Examiners, 99 High Street, Boston, MA 02110; 617-728-8700, Fax: 617-482-8000.
http://massbbo.org/
Search Database at http://massbbo.org/

3 Board of Building Regulations & Standards, Construction-related Licensing Programs, 1 Ashburton Place, Rm 1301, Boston, MA 02108; 617-727-7532, Fax: 617-727-1754.
www.mass.gov/bbrs/
Email: david.bratton@eps.state.ma.us
Search Database at
www.mass.gov/bbrs/programs.htm

4 Division of Insurance, Agents & Brokers Licensing, One South Station, 5th Fl, Boston, MA 02110-2208; 617-521-7794, Fax: 617-521-7772.
www.state.ma.us/doi
Search Database at
www.mass.gov/doi/Consumer/CSS_health.html
Note: For searching, this agency provides lists which you can view or download.

5 Committee on Acupuncture, Board of Registration in Medicine, 560 Harrison Ave #G-4, Boston, MA 02118; 617-654-9800, Fax: 617-451-9568.
www.massmedboard.org/index.shtm
Email: nick@docboard.org

6 Board of Registration in Medicine, 560 Harrison Ave G4, Boston, MA 02118; 617-654-9800, 800-377-0550, Fax: 617-451-9568.
www.massmedboard.org
Email: webmaster@massmedboard.org
Search Database at
http://profiles.massmedboard.org/Profiles/MA-Physician-Profile-Find-Doctor.asp

7 Division of Registration, Boards of Registration & Examination, 239 Causeway St #400, Boston, MA 02114-2130; 617-727-3074, Fax: 617-727-2197.
www.state.ma.us/reg/home.htm
Email: REG.WebMaster@State.ma.us
Search Database at
http://license.reg.state.ma.us/pubLic/licque.asp

8 Executive Office of Human Svcs, Office for Children, Staff Qualifications, 1 Ashburton Pl Rm 1105, Boston, MA 02108-1518; 617-626-2069, Fax: 617-626-2027.
www.qualitychildcare.org
Search Database at
www.qualitychildcare.org/childcare_finding.asp

9 Boxing Commission, 1 Ashburton Pl Rm 1301, Boston, MA 02108; 617-727-3200 x25257, Fax: 617-727-5732.
www.mass.gov/dps/boxing.htm
Search Database at
www.mass.gov/mbc/ranking.htm

10 Securities Division, Licensing and Registration Section, 1 Ashburton Place, 17th Fl, Boston, MA 02108; 617-727-3548, Fax: 617-248-0177.
www.sec.state.ma.us/sct/
Email: securities@sec.state.ma.us
Search Database at
www.nasd.com/web/idcplg?IdcService=SS_GET_PAGE&nodeId=6

11 Consumer Compliance Unit, Division of Banks, 1 South Station, 3rd Fl, Boston, MA 02110; 617-956-1500 x501, Fax: 617-956-1599.
www.state.ma.us/dob
Search Database at www.mass.gov/dob/liclist.htm

12 Division of Registration, Boards of Registration of Nursing Home Admin., 239 Causeway St #400, Boston, MA 02114-2130; 617-727-3074, Fax: 617-727-2197.
www.mass.gov/dpl/home.htm
Search Database at
http://license.reg.state.ma.us/public/licque.asp?color=blue

13 Division of Professional Licensure, Boards of Registration of Physicians Assistants, 239 Causeway Street, Suite 500, Boston, MA 02114; 617-973-0806, Fax: 617-973-0982.
www.state.ma.us/reg/boards/ap/default.htm
Search Database at
http://license.reg.state.ma.us/pubLic/licque.asp

14 Office of Emergency Medical Services, 2 Boylston St 3rd Floor, Boston, MA 02116-4737; 617-753-7300, Fax: 617-753-7320.
www.state.ma.us/dph/oems

15 Department of Public Health, Bureau of Substance Abuse Services, 250 Washington St, 3rd Fl, Boston, MA 02108; 617-624-5111, Fax: 617-624-5185.
www.state.ma.us/dph/bsas/
Email: bsas.questions@state.ma.us

16 Consumer Department, Racing Commission, 1 Ashburton Place, 13th Fl, Rm 1313, Boston, MA 02108; 617-727-2581, Fax: 617-227-6062.
www.state.ma.us/src

17 Division of Educational Personnel, Department of Education & Arts, 350 Main St, Malven, MA 02148; 781-338-3000 x6600, Fax: 781-338-3391.
www.doe.mass.edu/cert

18 Home Improvement Contractor/Construction Supervisor Licensing, Board of Build Regulations and Standards, 1 Ashburton Pl, Rm 1301, Boston, MA 02108; 617-727-7532.
www.state.ma.us/bbrs/programs.htm
Search Database at
www.state.ma.us/bbrs/programs.htm

19 Department of Food & Agriculture, Pesticide Bureau, 251 Causeway St, Ste 500, Boston, MA 02114-2151; 617-626-1776, Fax: 617-626-1850.
www.mass.gov/agr/
Email: lee.corte-real@state.ma.us

20 Division of Insurance, Motor Vehicle Damage Appraisers Licensing Board, 1 South Station, 5th Fl, Boston, MA 02110; 617-521-7447, Fax: 617-521-7576.

21 Secretary of the Commonwealth, Lobbyist & Lobbyist Employer Directory, One Ashburton Place, Room 1719, Boston, MA 02108; 617-878-3434, Fax: 617-727-5914.
Email: lob@sec.state.ma.us
Search Database at
http://db.state.ma.us/SEC/PRE/search.asp

22 Division of Occupational Safety, Employment Agency Program, 399 Washington St, 5th Fl, Boston, MA 02108; 617-727-3696, Fax: 617-727-7568.
www.state.ma.us/dos/pages/employ.htm

23 Massachusetts Aeronautics Commission, 10 Park Plaza, Rm 6620, Boston, MA 02116-3966; 617-973-8881, Fax: 617-973-8889.
www.massaeronautics.org/default.htm

24 Department of Occupational Safety, Licensing Division, Labor & Workforce Development, 399 Washington St, 5th Fl, Boston, MA 02100-5212; 617-727-7047, Fax: 617-727-7568.
www.state.ma.us/dos

25 Department of Public Health, Divison of Food & Drugs, 305 South St, Jamaica Plain, MA 02130; 617-983-6712, Fax: 617-524-8062.
www.state.ma.us/dph
Email: mark.leccese@state.ma.us

26 Radiation Control Program, Department of Public Health, 90 Washington Street, Dorchester, MA 02121; 617-427-2944, Fax: 617-427-2925.
www.mass.gov/dph/rcp/

27 Department of Public Safety, 1 Ashburton Pl, 13th Fl, Rm 1301, Boston, MA 02108; 617-727-3200 x623, Fax: 617-727-5732.
www.state.ma.us/dps
Email: MailBox.DPS@state.ma.us

28 Department of Public Health, Health Care Quality, 10 West St, 5th Fl, Boston, MA 02111; 617-753-8000, Fax: 617-753-8095.
www.state.ma.us/dph/dhcq/hcqskel.htm

29 Governor's Council, Public Records Division, State House, Rm 184, Boston, MA 02133; 617-725-4016.
www.state.ma.us/sec/pre/preidx.htm

30 Division of Standards, 1 Ashburton Pl, Boston, MA 02108; 617-727-3480, Fax: 617-727-5705.
www.mass.gov/portal/index.jsp?pageID=ocaagencylanding&L=4&L0=Home&L1=Government&L2=Our+Agencies+and+Divisions&L3=Division+of+Standards&sid=Eoca
Email: charles.carroll@state.ma.us
Search Database at
www.mass.gov/portal/index.jsp?pageID=ocaagencylanding&L=4&L0=Home&L1=Government&L2=Our+Agencies+and+Divisions&L3=Division+of+Standards&sid=Eoca

31 Department of Telecommunications and Energy, Transportation Division, 1 South Sta #2, Boston, MA 02110-2208; 617-305-3559, Fax: 617-478-2598.
www.state.ma.us/dpu/transportation/transportation.htm

32 Department of Revenue, Excises Unit, PO Box 7012, Boston, MA 02204; 617-887-5090, Fax: 617-887-5039.
www.dor.state.ma.us/cigarette/cigarette.htm
Email: dortsd@shore.net

33 Department of State Police, Certification Unit, 485 Maple St, Danvers, MA 01923; 978-538-6128, Fax: 978-538-6021.
www.mass.gov/portal/index.jsp?pageID=eopsagencylanding&L=3&L0=Home&L1=Public+Safety+Agencies&L2=Massachusetts+State+Police&sid=Eeops
Email: webmaster@eps.state.ma.us

34 Department of Fisheries, Wildlife & Environmental Enforcement, Division of Fish & Wildlife, 251 Causeway St #S-400, Boston, MA 02114-2104; 617-626-1500, Fax: 617-626-1505.
www.state.ma.us/dfwele/dpt_toc.htm
Email: steve.mcrae@state.ma.us

35 Division of Banks & Loan Agencies, 1 South Station, 3rd FL, Boston, MA 02110; 617-956-1500, Fax: 617-956-1599.
www.state.ma.us/dob
Email: bernard.n.waxman@state.ma.us
Search Database at www.mass.gov/dob/liclist.htm

36 Division of Regulation of Architecture, 239 Causeway St #500, Boston, MA 02114; 617-727-3072, Fax: 617-727-2197.
www.state.ma.us/reg/boards/ar/default.htm
Email: REG.Webmaster@State.ma.us
Search Database at www.mass.gov/dpl/

37 Division of Registration, Board of Funeral Directors & Embalmers, 239 Causeway St #500, Boston, MA 02114-2130; 617-727-1718, Fax: 617-727-2197.
www.state.ma.us/reg/boards/em/default.htm
Search Database at
http://license.reg.state.ma.us/pubLic/licque.asp?color=red&Board=EM

Massachusetts Federal Courts

The following list indicates the district and division name for each county in the state. If the bankruptcy court location is different from the district court, then the location of the bankruptcy court appears in parentheses.

Massachusetts County/Court Cross Reference

Barnstable................Boston
Berkshire..................Springfield (Worcester)
Bristol......................Boston
Dukes.......................Boston
Essex........................Boston

Franklin....................Springfield (Worcester)
Hampden...................Springfield (Worcester)
Hampshire.................Springfield (Worcester)
Middlesex.................Boston
Nantucket.................Boston

Norfolk.....................Boston
Plymouth..................Boston
Suffolk.....................Boston
Worcester.................Worcester

Standards for Federal Courts: See Maine or Michigan Federal Courts section for information on Federal Courts standards and fees.

US District Court

Boston Division Court Clerk, US Courthouse, 1 Courthouse Way Ste 2300, Boston, MA 02210 (also use mail address for courier delivery), 617-748-9152, records rm- 617-748-9086, Fax-617-748-9096. www.mad.uscourts.gov **Counties:** Barnstable, Bristol, Dukes, Essex, Middlesex, Nantucket, Norfolk, Plymouth, Suffolk.

Searches & Indexing: Database dates from the early 1900's. Results do not include SSN or DOB. Computer index maintained. Records available when not in possession of judge or clerks. New cases in the index 1 day to 1 week after filing date. Records purged every 12 months.

Fee & Payment: Pay by money order, cashier's or personal check. Payee: Clerk, US District Court. Prepayment required.

Phone Search: No searching by telephone.

Mail Search: search usually completed- 2-4 weeks. SASE not required.

In Person Search: Fee charged if court performs your search. Self-serve copier - $.25 per page.

E-Services: PACER online at http://pacer.mad.uscourts.gov. Document images available. PACER records go back to 1/1990. New records online after 1 day. ECF at https://ecf.mad.uscourts.gov **Opinions Online:** http://pacer.mad.uscourts.gov/opinion.html. **Other Online Access:** Access calendars free at www.mad.uscourts.gov/Calendar/calendar.htm.

Springfield Division Court Clerk, 1550 Main St, Springfield, MA 01103 (also use mail address for courier delivery), 413-785-0015, crim dockets-413-785-0216, civil dockets- 413-785-0215, Fax-413-785-0204. Hours- 8:00AM-4:30PM. www.mad.uscourts.gov **Counties:** Berkshire, Franklin, Hampden, Hampshire.

Searches & Indexing: Results do not include SSN or DOB. Computer index maintained. New cases in the index immediately after filing date. Records purged every 12 months. Records not available when in possession of judge or judge's clerks.

Fee & Payment: Pay by money order, cashier's or personal check. Payee: Clerk, US District Court. Will fax documents $.50 per page.

Phone Search: Docket information available via phone if clerk has time.

Mail Search: search usually completed- 1-2 days. SASE not required.

In Person Search: Fee charged if court performs your search. No self-serve copier available.

E-Services: PACER online at http://pacer.mad.uscourts.gov. Document images available. PACER records go back to 1/1990. New records online after 1 day. ECF at https://ecf.mad.uscourts.gov **Opinions Online:** http://pacer.mad.uscourts.gov/opinion.html. **Other Online Access:** Access calendars free at www.mad.uscourts.gov/Calendar/calendar.htm.

Worcester Division Court Clerk, 595 Main St, Rm 502, Worcester, MA 01608 (also use mail address for courier delivery), 508-929-9900. Hours- 8:30AM-5PM. www.mad.uscourts.gov

Counties: Worcester.

Searches & Indexing: Indexes are on computer from 1988; on microfiche from 1981. Earlier indexes back to early 1900s in storage. Results do not include SSN or DOB. New cases in the index immediately after filing date. Records purged every 12 months. Records not available when in possession of judge or judge's clerks.

Fee & Payment: Pay by money order, cashier's or personal check. Payee: Clerk, US District Court.

Phone Search: Only docket information available by telephone.

Mail Search: search usually completed- 1-2 days. Include SASE for return.

In Person Search: Fee charged if court performs your search. No self-serve copier available.

E-Services: PACER online at http://pacer.mad.uscourts.gov. Document images available. PACER records go back to 1/1990. New records online after 1 day. ECF at https://ecf.mad.uscourts.gov **Opinions Online:** http://pacer.mad.uscourts.gov/opinion.html. **Other Online Access:** Access calendars free at www.mad.uscourts.gov/Calendar/calendar.htm.

US Bankruptcy Court

Boston Division Court Clerk, Rm 1101, 10 Causeway, Boston, MA 02222-1074 (also use mail address for courier delivery), 617-565-8950, Fax-617-565-6650 records rm fax- 617-565-6650; fax record requests to-617-565-6650. Hours- 8:30AM-5PM. www.mab.uscourts.gov

Counties: Barnstable, Bristol, Dukes, Essex (except towns assigned to Worcester Division), Nantucket, Norfolk (except towns assigned to Worcester Division), Plymouth, Suffolk, and the following towns in Middlesex: Arlington, Belmont, Burlington, Everett, Lexington, Malden, Medford, Melrose, Newton, North Reading, Reading, Stoneham, Wakefield, Waltham, Watertown, Wilmington, Winchester and Woburn.

Searches & Indexing: Results include SSN last 4 digits only. Computer index maintained. New cases in the index immediately after filing date. Records purged every 12 months.

Fee & Payment: Pay by money order, cashier's or personal check. No debtor's checks accepted. Payee: US Bankruptcy Court. Copy fees can be billed after search is completed.

Phone Search: Only general information released via phone. Voice Case Information Service available, call 888-201-3572 or 617-565-6025.

Mail Search: search usually completed- 7-10 days. Include SASE for return.

In Person Search: Fee charged if court performs your search. Self-serve copier - $.25 per page.

E-Services: ECF replaces PACER. Document images available. PACER records go back to 4/1987. New records online immediately. ECF at https://ecf.mab.uscourts.gov **Opinions Online:** www.mab.uscourts.gov/opinions.htm.

Worcester Division Court Clerk, 595 Main St, Rm 211, Worcester, MA 01608 (also use mail address for courier delivery), 508-770-8900, Fax-508-793-0189 records rm fax- 508-770-8958; fax record requests to-508-770-8958. Hours- 8:30AM-5PM. www.mab.uscourts.gov **Counties:** Berkshire, Franklin, Hampden, Hampshire, Middlesex (except the towns assigned to the Boston Division), Worcester and the following towns: in Essex-Andover, Haverhill, Lawrence, Methuen and North Andover; in Norfolk-Bellingham, Franklin, Medway, Millis and Norfolk.

Searches & Indexing: Results include SSN. Computer index maintained. New cases in the index immediately after filing date. Records purged every 12 months.

Fee & Payment: Pay by money order, cashier's or personal check. No debtor's checks accepted. Payee: Bankruptcy Court. Prepayment required.

Phone Search: Only docket data is available by phone. Voice Case Information Service available, call VCIS at 888-201-3572 or 617-565-6025.

Mail Search: search usually completed- 5 days. SASE not required.

In Person Search: Fee charged if court performs your search. Self-serve copier - $.25 per page.

E-Services: ECF replaces PACER. Document images available. PACER records go back to 4/1987. New records online after 1 day. ECF at https://ecf.mab.uscourts.gov **Opinions Online:** www.mab.uscourts.gov/opinions.htm.

Massachusetts County Courts

Court	Jurisdiction	No. of Courts	How Organized
Superior Courts*	General	19	14 Counties
District Courts*	General	68	62 Geographic Divisions
Boston Municipal Court*	General	1	
Housing Courts*	General	7	
Probate and Family Courts*	Probate	15	14 Counties
Juvenile Courts	Special	7	11 Divisions
Land Court	Special	1	

* Profiled in this Sourcebook.

CIVIL									
Court	Tort	Contract	Real Estate	Min. Claim	Max. Claim	Small Claims	Estate	Eviction	Domestic Relations
Superior Courts*	X	X	X	$25,000	No Max				
District Courts*	X	X	X	$0	No Max	$2000	X	X	X
Boston Municipal Court*	X	X	X	$0	No Max	$2000			X
Housing Courts*			X	$0	No Max	$2000			
Probate and Family Courts*							X		X
Juvenile Courts									
Land Court			X						

CRIMINAL					
Court	Felony	Misdemeanor	DWI/DUI	Preliminary Hearing	Juvenile
Superior Courts*	X				
District Courts*	X	X	X	X	X
Boston Municipal Court*		X	X		
Housing Courts*		X		X	
Probate and Family Courts*					
Juvenile Courts					X
Land Court					

ADMINISTRATION   Chief Justice for Administration and Management, 2 Center Plaza, Room 540, Boston, MA, 02108; 617-742-8575, Fax: 617-742-0968. www.mass.gov/courts/admin/index.html

COURT STRUCTURE   The various court sections are called "Departments." While Superior and District Courts have concurrent jurisdiction in civil cases, the practice is to assign cases less than $25,000 to the District Court and those over $25,000 to Superior Court. In addition to misdemeanors, District Courts and Boston Municipal Courts have jurisdiction over certain minor felonies. In Massachusetts courts, "attestation" is the term for what is known as certification in other states. In Mass., a "certificate" is a separate authentification page with a gold seal. In July 2003, the state mandated that the attestation fee be $2.50 per page (includes copy fee) and the copy fee be $1.00 per page for all Superior and District Courts.

Eviction cases may be filed at a county District Court or at the regional "Housing Court." A case may be moved from a District Court to a Housing Court, but never the reverse. They also hear misdemeanor "Code Violation" cases and prelims for these. There are five Housing Court Regions - Boston (Suffolk County), Worcester (County), Southeast (Plymouth and Bristol Counties), Northeast (Essex County), and Western (Berkshire, Franklin, Hampden and Hampshire Counties). The Southeast Housing Court has three branches - Brockton, Fall River, and New Bedford

ONLINE ACCESS   Opinions to the Mass Supreme and Appellate courts can be found at http://massreports.com/. An online access to records on the statewide Trial Courts Information Center web site is only available to attorneys and law firms. For more information, Contact Peter Nylin by email at nylin_p@jud.state.ma.us. Site updated daily.

PROBATE COURTS   There are more than 20 Probate and Family Court locations in MA - one per county plus two each in Bristol, plus a Middlesex satellite in Cambridge and Lawrence.

Barnstable County

Superior Court 3195 Main St, PO Box 425, Barnstable, MA 02630; phone: 508-375-6684; hours 8:30AM-4:30PM (EST). *Felony, Civil Actions Over $25,000.*
Note: Their public access terminal is connected to the statewide Superior Court system. Call court to recommend document retriever to search for you.
Civil Records: Access: In person only. Visitors must perform in person searches themselves. Court makes copy: $1.00 per page. Self serve copy fee: $.50 per page. Required to search: name, years to search; also helpful: address. Civil cases indexed by defendant, plaintiff; on computer back to 1/2001; on index cards from 1985 and books from 1830s.
Criminal Records: Access: In person only. Visitors must perform in person searches themselves. Court makes copy: $1.00 per page. Self serve copy fee: $.50 per page. Required to search: name, years to search, DOB; also helpful: address, SSN. Criminal records on computer back to 1/2001; on index cards from 1985 and books from 1830s.
General Information: Public use terminal available. No victims names released. Will not fax specific case file. Certification fee: $2.50. Payee: Barnstable Superior Court. Business checks not accepted. Prepayment required.

Barnstable District Court Route 6A, PO Box 427, Barnstable, MA 02630; phone: 508-375-6600; hours 8:30AM-4:30PM (EST). *Felony, Misdemeanor, Civil, Eviction, Small Claims.*
Note: Includes Barnstable, Yarmouth, and Sandwich.
Civil Records: Access: Phone, mail, in person. Only the court performs in person searches; visitors may not. No search fee. Court makes copy: $1.00 per page. Required to search: name, years to search. Civil cases indexed by defendant, plaintiff; on index cards and docket books. Mail turnaround time 1-2 weeks.
Criminal Records: Access: Phone, mail, in person. Only the court performs in person searches; visitors may not. No search fee. Court makes copy: $1.00 per page. Required to search: name, years to search; also helpful: DOB. Criminal records on computer since 1996; prior records on index cards and docket books. Mail turnaround time 1-2 weeks.
General Information: No public access terminal. No impounded records released. Will not fax documents. Certification fee: $2.50 includes copy fee. Payee: District Court. Only cashiers checks and money orders accepted. Prepayment required.

Falmouth District Court 161 Jones Rd, Falmouth, MA 02540; phone: 508-495-1500; fax: 508-495-0992; hours 8:30AM-4:30PM (EST). *Felony, Misdemeanor, Civil, Eviction, Small Claims.*
Note: Includes Falmouth, Mashpee, and Bourne.
Civil Records: Access: Phone, in person. Only the court performs in person searches; visitors may not. Court makes copy: $1.00 per page. Required to search: name, years to search. Civil cases indexed by defendant, plaintiff. Civil records computerized since 1996.
Criminal Records: Access: Phone, in person. Only the court performs in person searches; visitors may not. Court makes copy: $1.00 per page. Required to

search: name, years to search. Criminal records computerized since 1996.
General Information: No impounded records released. Certification fee: $2.50. Cert fee includes copies. Payee: Falmouth District Court. Personal checks accepted. Prepayment required.

Orleans District Court 237 Rock Harbor Rd, Orleans, MA 02653; phone: 508-255-4700; hours 8:30AM-4:30PM (EST). *Felony, Misdemeanor, Civil, Eviction, Small Claims.*
Note: Includes Brewster, Chatham, Dennis, Eastham, Orleans, Truro, Wellfleet, Harwich, and Provincetown.
Civil Records: Access: In person only. Visitors must perform in person searches themselves. Court makes copy: $1.00 per page. Required to search: name, years to search. Civil cases indexed by defendant, plaintiff. Civil records kept in storage from 1978. Some prior records destroyed.
Criminal Records: Access: In person only. Visitors must perform in person searches themselves. Court makes copy: $1.00 per page. Required to search: name, years to search. Criminal records kept in storage from 1978. Some prior records destroyed.
General Information: No public access terminal. No impounded records released. Certification fee: $2.50. Payee: Orleans District Court. Personal checks accepted. Prepayment required.

Probate & Family Court PO Box 346, 3195 Main St, Route 6A, Barnstable, MA 02630; 508-375-6600; probate phone: 508-375-6710; fax: 508-362-3662; hours 8AM-4PM (EST). *Probate.*

Berkshire County

Superior Court 76 East St, Pittsfield, MA 01201; phone: 413-499-7487; fax: 413-442-9190; hours 8:30AM-4:30PM (EST). *Felony, Civil Actions Over $25,000.*
Civil Records: Access: Mail, in person. Both court and visitors may perform in person searches. No search fee. Court makes copy: $1.00 per page. Required to search: name, years to search. Civil cases indexed by defendant, plaintiff; on index cards from 1900s, on computer back to 2000. Mail turnaround time 3-4 weeks.
Criminal Records: Access: Mail, in person. Both court and visitors may perform in person searches. No search fee. Court makes copy: $1.00 per page. Required to search: name, years to search. Criminal records on index cards from 1900s, on computer back to 2000. Because their index does not contain DOBs or SSNs, they cannot verify the subject, thus they recommend you contact the Criminal History Board in Boston, MA. Mail turnaround time 3-4 weeks.
General Information: Public terminal goes back to 2000. No impounded records released. Certification fee: $2.50 per document. Payee: Berkshire Superior Court. Personal checks accepted. Prepayment required.

North Berkshire District Court #28 111 Holden St, North Adams, MA 01247; phone: 413-663-5339; criminal/civil fax: 413-664-7209; hours 8AM-4:30PM (EST). *Felony, Misdemeanor, Civil, Eviction, Small Claims.*

Note: Handles cases for Adams, Chesire, Clarksburg, Florida, Hancock, New Ashford, North Adams, Savoy, Williamstown, and Windsor. Exercises concurrent jurisdiction over Hancock and Windsor with the Pittsfield Division. Includes cases from closed Court #30.
Civil Records: Access: Fax, mail, in person. Only the court performs in person searches; visitors may not. No search fee. Court makes copy: $1.00 per page. Required to search: name, years to search. Civil cases indexed by defendant, plaintiff; on index cards from 1983, docket books to 1900. Mail turnaround time 1-2 weeks.
Criminal Records: Access: Fax, mail, in person. Only the court performs in person searches; visitors may not. No search fee. Court makes copy: $1.00 per page. Required to search: name, years to search, DOB, SSN. Criminal records on index cards from 1983, docket books to 1900. Mail turnaround time 1-2 weeks.
General Information: No public access terminal. No impounded records released. Will fax documents to local or toll free line. Certification fee: $2.50. Payee: District Court. Business checks accepted. Prepayment required.

Pittsfield District Court #27 24 Wendell Ave, Pittsfield, MA 01201; criminal phone: 413-442-5468; civil phone: 413-499-0558; criminal fax: 413-499-7327; civil fax: 413-443-7090; hours 8:30AM-4:30PM (EST). *Felony, Misdemeanor, Civil, Eviction, Small Claims.*
Note: Includes Becket, Dalton, Hancock, Hinsdale, Lanesborough, Lenox, Peru, Pittsfield, Richmond, Washington and Windsor. This court exercises concurrent jurisdiction over Hancock and Windsor with the North Berkshire Divisions.
Civil Records: Access: Phone, mail, in person. Both court and visitors may perform in person searches. No search fee. Court makes copy: $1.00 per page; same fee for self serve. Required to search: name, years to search. Civil cases indexed by defendant, plaintiff; on docket books and in recent years in the computer. Mail turnaround time 1-2 weeks.
Criminal Records: Access: Phone, mail, in person. Both court and visitors may perform in person searches. No search fee. Court makes copy: $1.00 per page; same fee for self serve. Required to search: name, years to search; DOB. Criminal records on docket books and in recent years in the computer. Mail turnaround time 1-2 weeks.
General Information: Public terminal has criminal back to 1999 and civil back to 2001. No juvenile or sealed records released. Will fax documents for $1.00 per page. Certification fee: $2.50. Payee: Pittsfield District Court. Personal checks accepted. Prepayment and SASE required.

South Berkshire District Court 9 Gilmore Ave, Great Barrington, MA 01230; phone: 413-528-3520; criminal/civil fax: 413-528-0757; hours 8:30AM-4:30PM (EST). *Felony, Misdemeanor, Civil, Eviction, Small Claims.*
Note: Includes Alford, Becket, Egremont, Great Barrington, Lee, Lenox, Monterey, Mt. Washington, New Marlborough, Otis, Sandisfield, Sheffield, Stockbridge, Tyringham, and West Stockbridge. Shares jurisdiction of Becket and Lenox with Pittsfield Dist. Court.

Civil Records: Access: Fax, mail, in person. Both court and visitors may perform in person searches. No search fee. Court makes copy: $1.00 per page; same fee for self serve. Required to search: name, years to search. Civil cases indexed by defendant, plaintiff; on index cards from 1984, docket books to 1900. Court will only perform search if given the docket number. Mail turnaround time 1-2 weeks.

Criminal Records: Access: Fax, mail, in person. Both court and visitors may perform in person searches. No search fee. Court makes copy: $1.00 per page; same fee for self serve. Required to search: name, years to search, DOB. Criminal records on index cards from 1984, docket books to 1900. Court will only do search if given docket number. Mail turnaround time 1-2 weeks.

General Information: No public access terminal. No juvenile, impounded records released. Will not fax documents. Certification fee: $2.50 per cert. Payee: District Court. Personal checks accepted. Prepayment and SASE required.

Probate & Family Court 44 Bank Row, Pittsfield, MA 01201; phone: 413-442-6941; fax: 413-443-3430; hours 8:30AM-4PM (EST). *Probate.*

Western Housing Court, MA. *Eviction, Misdemeanor (Code Violations), Small Claims.*
Note: See Hampden County Western Housing Court for many housing code cases, real estate-related small claims and eviction cases for this county; also see district courts in this county.

Bristol County

Superior Court - Taunton 9 Court St, Taunton, MA 02780; phone: 508-823-6588 X1; hours 8AM-4:30PM (EST). *Felony, Civil Actions Over $25,000.*

Civil Records: Access: Mail, in person. Both court and visitors may perform in person searches. No search fee. Court makes copy: $1.00 per page. Self serve copy fee: $.40 per page. Required to search: name, years to search. Civil cases indexed by defendant, plaintiff; on computer link to Boston from 1985, index books from 1935. Mail turnaround time 2 weeks.

Criminal Records: Access: Mail, in person. Both court and visitors may perform in person searches. No search fee. Court makes copy: $1.00 per page. Self serve copy fee: $.40 per page. Required to search: name, years to search; also helpful: DOB. Criminal records on computer link to Boston from 1985, index books from 1935. Mail turnaround time 2 weeks.

General Information: Public terminal has criminal back to 2000 and civil back to 1980. No impounded records released. Certification fee: $2.50 per cert. Payee: Clerk of Superior Court of Bristol County. Personal checks accepted. Prepayment required.

Attleboro District Court 34 Courthouse, 88 N Main St, Attleboro, MA 02703; phone: 508-222-5900; criminal fax:; civil fax: 508-222-4869; hours 8AM-4:30PM (EST). *Felony, Misdemeanor, Civil, Eviction, Small Claims.*
Note: Includes Attleboro, Mansfield, North Attleboro, and Norton.

Civil Records: Access: Phone, mail, in person. Both court and visitors may perform in person searches. No search fee. Court makes copy: $1.00 per page. Required to search: name, years to search. Civil cases indexed by defendant, plaintiff; on computer since 1995; prior records on index cards from 1983, docket books from 1900. Mail turnaround time 1-2 weeks.

Criminal Records: Access: Phone, mail, in person. Only the court performs in person searches; visitors may not. No search fee. Court makes copy: $1.00 per page. Required to search: name, years to search, DOB, SSN. Criminal records on computer since 1995; prior records on index cards from 1983, docket books from 1900. Mail turnaround time 1-2 weeks.

General Information: Public terminal has only civil records back to 2001. No impounded records released. Certification fee: $2.50. Payee: District

Court, Attleboro District Court. Business checks accepted. Prepayment required.

Fall River District Court 45 Rock St, Fall River, MA 02720; phone: 508-679-8161; fax: 508-675-5477; hours 8AM-4:30PM (EST). *Felony, Misdemeanor, Civil, Eviction, Small Claims.*
Note: Includes Fall River, Freetown, Somerset, Swansea, and Westport.

Civil Records: Access: In person only. Both court and visitors may perform in person searches. Court makes copy: $1.00 per page. Required to search: name, years to search. Civil cases indexed by defendant, plaintiff; on index on computer from 1989, on docket books in vault from 1985. Office may do search; they are short-staffed and may not be able. Mail turnaround time 1-2 weeks.

Criminal Records: Access: In person only. Both court and visitors may perform in person searches. No search fee. Court makes copy: $1.00 per page. Required to search: name, years to search, DOB or SSN. Criminal records on index on computer from 1991, on docket books in vault from 1985. Office may do search; they are short-staffed and may not be able.

General Information: No public access terminal. No sealed, minor, confidential address records released. Fee to fax documents is $.50 per page. Certification fee: $2.50 per page. Payee: District Court. Only cashiers checks and money orders accepted. Prepayment required.

New Bedford District Court 33 75 N 6th St, New Bedford, MA 02740; phone: 508-999-9700; fax: 508-990-8094; hours 8AM-4:30 PM (EST). *Felony, Misdemeanor, Civil, Eviction, Small Claims.*
Note: Includes Acushnet, Dartmouth, Fairhaven, Freetown, New Bedford, and Westport.

Civil Records: Access: Mail, in person. Only the court performs in person searches; visitors may not. No search fee. Court makes copy: $1.00 per page. Required to search: name, years to search. Civil cases indexed by defendant, plaintiff. Civil records filed from 1989, prior on docket books; on computer back to 1995. Mail turnaround time 1-2 weeks.

Criminal Records: Access: Mail, in person, fax. Only the court performs in person searches; visitors may not. No search fee. Court makes copy: $1.00 per page. Required to search: name, years to search, DOB; also helpful: SSN. Criminal records filed from 1989, prior on docket books; on computer back to 1995. Searches are limited to pending charges, this agency recommends searching elsewhere for closed case files. Mail turnaround time 1-2 weeks.

General Information: No public access terminal. No impounded records released. Certification fee: $2.50 per cert. Payee: District Court. Business checks accepted. Prepayment and SASE required.

Taunton District Court 15 Court St, Taunton, MA 02780; phone: 508-824-4032; fax: 508-824-2282; hours 8:30AM-4:30PM (EST). *Felony, Misdemeanor, Civil, Eviction, Small Claims.*
Note: Includes Berkley, Dighton, Easton, Raynham, Rehoboth, Seekonk, and Taunton.

Civil Records: Access: Phone, mail, in person. Visitors must perform in person searches themselves. No search fee. Court makes copy: $1.00 per page. Required to search: name, years to search. Civil cases indexed by defendant, plaintiff; on index cards for 6 years. Mail turnaround time 1-2 days.

Criminal Records: Access: Phone, mail, in person. Visitors must perform in person searches themselves. No search fee. Court makes copy: $1.00 per page. Required to search: name, years to search, DOB. Criminal records on index cards for 6 year. Mail turnaround time 1-2 days.

General Information: No public access terminal. Certification fee: $2.50. Payee: District Court. Personal checks accepted. Prepayment required.

New Bedford Probate & Family Court 505 Pleasant St, New Bedford, MA 02740; phone: 508-999-5249; fax: 508-999-1269; hours 8AM-4:30PM (EST). *Probate.*

Southeast Housing Court - Fall River 289 Rock St, 2nd FL, Fall River, MA 02720; phone: 508-677-1505; hours 8AM-4PM (EST). *Eviction, Misdemeanor (Code Violations), Small Claims.*
Note: Also known as Fall River Trial Court. Includes housing code cases, real estate-related small claims, and many eviction cases for Bristol County except the New Bedford area; also see district courts.

Southeast Housing Court - New Bedford 139 Hathaway Rd, New Bedford, MA 02740; phone: 508-994-0156; hours 8;30AM-4;30PM Mon & Fri (EST). *Eviction, Misdemeanor (Code Violations), Small Claims.*
Note: Open Mondays and Fridays only. Includes many code, real estate-related small claims, and eviction cases for the New Bedford area only; also see area district court.

Taunton Probate & Family Court 11 Court St, Taunton, MA 02780; phone: 508-824-4004; fax: 508-821-4630; hours 9AM-4PM,M-Th, 8;30AM-4PM Fri (EST). *Probate.*

Dukes County

Superior Court PO Box 1267, Edgartown, MA 02539; phone: 508-627-4668; hours 8AM-4PM (EST). *Felony, Civil Actions Over $25,000.*

Civil Records: Access: Mail, in person. Both court and visitors may perform in person searches. No search fee. Court makes copy: $1.00 per page. Required to search: name, years to search. Civil cases indexed by defendant, plaintiff; on index cards from 1976 and books from 1695. Mail turnaround time 1-2 days.

Criminal Records: Access: Mail, in person. Both court and visitors may perform in person searches. No search fee. Court makes copy: $1.00 per page. Required to search: name, years to search. Criminal records on index cards from 1976 and books from 1695. Mail turnaround time 1-2 days.

General Information: Public use terminal available. No sealed records released. Certification fee: $2.50. Payee: Clerk of Superior Court. Personal checks accepted. Prepayment and SASE required.

Edgartown District Court PO Box 1284, Courthouse, 81 Main St, Edgartown, MA 02539-1284; phone: 508-627-3751/4622; fax: 508-627-7070; hours 8:30AM-4:30PM (EST). *Felony, Misdemeanor, Civil, Eviction, Small Claims.*
Note: Includes Edgartown, Oak Bluffs, Tisbury, West Tisbury, Aquinnah (formerly Gay Head), Gosnold, and Elizabeth Islands.

Civil Records: Access: In person only. Both court and visitors may perform in person searches. No search fee. Court makes copy: $1.00 per page. Required to search: name, years to search. Civil cases indexed by defendant, plaintiff; on index cards from 1983, docket books to 1900.

Criminal Records: Access: In person only. Both court and visitors may perform in person searches. No search fee. Court makes copy: $1.00 per page. Required to search: name, years to search, DOB; SSN helpful. Criminal records on index cards from 1983, docket books to 1900.

General Information: No public access terminal. No sealed records released. Will fax specific case file no add'l fee. Certification fee: $2.50 includes copy fee. Payee: District Court. Personal checks accepted. Prepayment required.

Probate & Family Court PO Box 237, Rm 104, 1st Fl, Edgartown, MA 02539; phone: 508-627-4703; fax: 508-627-7664; hours 10AM-3PM (EST). *Probate.*

Essex County

Superior Court - Lawrence
43 Appleton Way, Lawrence, MA 01840; phone: 978-687-7463 x4; fax: 978-687-7869; hours 8AM-4:30PM (EST). *Civil Actions Over $25,000.*
Note: Index cards - records prior to 1985 - are found in the Salem office; criminal records also in Salem Court.
Civil Records: Access: In person. Both court and visitors may perform in person searches. No search fee. Court makes copy: $1.00 per page. Required to search: name, years to search. Civil cases indexed by defendant, plaintiff; on computer since 1985; prior records on index cards in Salem office.
General Information: Public terminal has only civil records back to 1985. No impounded records released. Certification fee: $2.50 per cert. Payee: Clerk of Superior Court. Personal checks accepted. Prepayment required.

Superior Court - Newburyport
145 High St, Newburyport, MA 01950; phone: 978-462-4474; fax: 978-462-0432; hours 8AM-4:30PM (EST). *Felony, Civil Actions Over $25,000.*
Note: All finished criminal record files are in Salem and civil case records Session A in Salem, Session B in Newburyport and Session C & D in Lawrence.
Civil Records: Access: Mail, in person. Both court and visitors may perform in person searches. No search fee. Court makes copy: $1.00 per page. Required to search: name, years to search. Civil cases indexed by defendant, plaintiff; on computer back to 1988.
Criminal Records: Access: In person. Both court and visitors may perform in person searches. No search fee. Court makes copy: $1.00 per page. Required to search: name, years to search. Mail turnaround time 1-2 days.
General Information: No public access terminal. No impounded records released. Certification fee: $2.50 per cert. Payee: Clerk of Superior Court. Personal checks accepted. Prepayment required.

Superior Court - Salem
34 Federal St, Salem, MA 01970; phone: 978-744-5500; criminal phone: x2; civil phone: x1; criminal fax: 978-825-9989; civil fax: 978-741-0691; hours 8:00AM-4:30PM (EST). *Felony, Civil Actions Over $25,000.*
Civil Records: Access: Mail, in person. Visitors must perform in person searches themselves. Court makes copy: $1.00 per page. Required to search: name, years to search. Civil cases indexed by defendant, plaintiff. Civil records are entered on computer for civil actions from all three Superior courts in this county. Computer records go back to 1985.
Criminal Records: Access: In person only. Visitors must perform in person searches themselves. Court makes copy: $1.00 per page. Required to search: name, years to search. Criminal records are entered on computer for civil actions from all three Superior courts in this county. Computer records go back to 1985.
General Information: Public terminal has only civil records back to 1985. Impounded cases are not released. Fee to fax documents is $1.50 per page. Certification fee: $2.50 per cert. Payee: Clerk of Superior Court. Personal checks accepted. Prepayment required.

Gloucester District Court
197 Main St, Gloucester, MA 01930; phone: 978-283-2620; fax: 978-283-8784; hours 8:30AM-4:30PM (EST). *Felony, Misdemeanor, Civil, Eviction, Small Claims.*
Note: Includes Essex, Gloucester, and Rockport.
Civil Records: Access: Mail, in person. Visitors must perform in person searches themselves. Court makes copy: $1.00 per page. Required to search: name, years to search; also helpful: DOB. Civil cases indexed by defendant, plaintiff.
Criminal Records: Access: Mail, in person. Visitors must perform in person searches themselves. Court makes copy: $1.00 per page. Required to search: name, years to search; also helpful: DOB.

General Information: No public access terminal. No juvenile records released. Certification fee: $2.50 per page. Payee: Gloucester District Court. Personal checks accepted. Prepayment required.

Haverhill District Court
PO Box 1389, Haverhill, MA 01831; phone: 978-373-4151; fax: 978-521-6886; hours 8:30AM-4:30PM (EST). *Felony, Misdemeanor, Civil, Eviction, Small Claims.*
Note: Includes Boxford, Bradford, Georgetown, Groveland, and Haverhill.
Civil Records: Access: Phone, fax, mail, in person. Only the court performs in person searches; visitors may not. No search fee. Court makes copy: $1.00 per page. Required to search: name, years to search. Civil cases indexed by defendant, plaintiff; on index cards from 1983. Non-active in storage. Mail turnaround time 1-2 weeks.
Criminal Records: Access: Phone, fax, mail, in person. Only the court performs in person searches; visitors may not. No search fee. Court makes copy: $1.00 per page. Required to search: name, years to search; also helpful: DOB. Criminal records on index cards from 1992, computerized since 2000. Non-active in storage. Mail turnaround time 1-2 weeks.
General Information: No public access terminal. No juvenile, sealed cases, confidential records released. Certification fee: $2.50. Payee: District Court. Personal checks accepted. Prepayment and SASE required.

Ipswich District Court
100 State St, Ipswich, MA 01950; phone: 978-462-2652; fax: 978-462-5641; hours 8:30AM-4:30PM (EST). *Felony, Misdemeanor, Civil, Eviction, Small Claims.*
Note: Includes Hamilton, Ipswich, Topsfield, and Wenham.
Civil Records: Access: In person only. Visitors must perform in person searches themselves. Court makes copy: $1.00 per page. Required to search: name, years to search. Civil cases indexed by defendant, plaintiff; on index cards and computer, small claims from 1984, civil from 1964. Civil on docket books from 1970.
Criminal Records: Access: In person only. Visitors must perform in person searches themselves. Court makes copy: $1.00 per page. Required to search: name, years to search; also helpful: DOB. Criminal records on index cards from 1979.
General Information: Public terminal has only civil records. No juvenile records released. Certification fee: $2.50 per page. Payee: District Court. Personal checks accepted. Prepayment required.

Lawrence District Court
2 Appleton St, Lawrence, MA 01840; phone: 978-687-7184; hours 8AM-4:30PM (EST). *Felony, Misdemeanor, Civil, Eviction, Small Claims.*
Note: Includes Andover, Lawrence, Methuen, and North Andover.
Civil Records: Access: In person only. Visitors must perform in person searches themselves. Court makes copy: $1.00 per page. Required to search: name, years to search. Civil cases indexed by defendant, plaintiff; on index cards from 1983, docket books from 1900, on computer since 1990.
Criminal Records: Access: Mail, in person. Both court and visitors may perform in person searches. No search fee. Court makes copy: $1.00 per page. Required to search: name, years to search; DOB; also helpful: address, SSN. Criminal records on index cards from 1983, docket books from 1900, on computer since 1999. Mail turnaround time 1-2 weeks.
General Information: No public access terminal. No medical, police reports, impounded, juvenile records released. Will not fax documents. Certification fee: $2.50 per page includes copy fee. Payee: District Court. Personal checks accepted. Prepayment required. SASE requested.

Lynn District Court
580 Essex St, Lynn, MA 01901; phone: 781-598-5200; hours 8AM-4:30PM (EST). *Felony, Misdemeanor, Civil, Eviction, Small Claims.*
Note: Includes Lynn, Marblehead, Nahant, Saugus, and Swampscott.
Civil Records: Access: Mail, in person. Visitors must perform in person searches themselves. No search fee. Court makes copy: $1.00 per page. Required to search: name, years to search. Civil cases indexed by defendant, plaintiff; on index cards from 1983, docket books from approx 1900. Records older than 15 years are difficult to find and may take longer. Mail turnaround time 5 days.
Criminal Records: Access: Mail, in person. Visitors must perform in person searches themselves. No search fee. Court makes copy: $1.00 per page. Required to search: name, years to search; also helpful: DOB, SSN. Criminal records on index cards from 1983, docket books from approx 1900. Records older than 15 years are difficult to find and may take longer. Mail turnaround time 5 days.
General Information: Public terminal has only civil records. No juvenile, impounded or sealed records released. Certification fee: $2.50 per cert. Payee: Lynn District Court. Personal checks accepted. Prepayment required.

Newburyport District Court 22
188 State St, Newburyport, MA 01950; phone: 978-462-2652; fax: 978-463-0438; hours 8:30AM-4:30PM (EST). *Felony, Misdemeanor, Civil, Eviction, Small Claims.*
Note: Includes Amesbury, Merrimac, Newbury, Newburyport, Rowley, Salisbury, and West Newbury.
Civil Records: Access: Mail, in person. Only the court performs in person searches; visitors may not. No search fee. Court makes copy: $1.00 per page. Required to search: name, years to search. Civil cases indexed by defendant, plaintiff; on index cards from 1983, prior archived in Worcester. Mail turnaround time 1-2 weeks.
Criminal Records: Access: Mail, in person. Only the court performs in person searches; visitors may not. No search fee. Court makes copy: $1.00 per page. Required to search: name, years to search, DOB. Criminal records on index cards from 1983, prior archived in Worcester. Mail turnaround time 1-2 weeks.
General Information: No public access terminal. No juvenile or impounded records released. Certification fee: $2.50 per cert. Payee: District Court. Personal checks accepted. Prepayment required.

Peabody District Court 86
PO Box 666, One Lowell St, Peabody, MA 01960; phone: 978-532-3100; fax: 978-531-8524; hours 8:30AM-4:30PM (EST). *Felony, Misdemeanor, Civil, Eviction, Small Claims.*
Note: Includes Lynnfield and Peabody.
Civil Records: Access: In person only. Visitors must perform in person searches themselves. Court makes copy: $1.00 per page. Required to search: name, years to search. Civil cases indexed by defendant, plaintiff. Civil records stored in office for 10 years, prior stored in basement and are difficult to find.
Criminal Records: Access: Mail, in person. Visitors must perform in person searches themselves. No search fee. Court makes copy: $1.00 per page. Required to search: name, years to search, DOB. Criminal records stored in office for 10 years, prior stored in basement and are difficult to find. Note: Will do mail search for 1 name only.
General Information: Public terminal has only civil records. No juvenile or impounded records released. Certification fee: $2.50 per cert. Payee: District Court. Personal checks accepted. Prepayment required.

Salem District Court 36
65 Washington St, Salem, MA 01970; phone: 978-744-1167; fax: 978-744-3211; hours 8:30AM-4:30PM (EST). *Felony, Misdemeanor, Civil, Eviction, Small Claims.*
Note: Includes Beverly, Danvers, Manchester by the Sea, Middleton, and Salem.

Civil Records: Access: In person only. Visitors must perform in person searches themselves. Court makes copy: $1.00 per page. Required to search: name, years to search. Civil cases indexed by defendant, plaintiff; on index cards and docket books. Note: Visitors must perform in person searches Thursday or Friday 2-4:30PM

Criminal Records: Access: In person. Visitors must perform in person searches themselves. No search fee. Court makes copy: $1.00 per page. Required to search: name, years to search, DOB, SSN. Criminal records on index cards and docket books. Note: In person criminal searches on Thursday or Friday 2-4:30PM.

General Information: Public terminal goes back to 3 years. No juvenile or impounded records released. Certification fee: $2.50. Payee: District Court. Personal checks accepted. Prepayment required.

Northeast Housing Court 2 Appleton St, Fenton Judicial Ctr, Lawrence, MA 01840; phone: 978-689-7833; hours 8:30AM-4:30PM (EST). *Eviction, Misdemeanor (Code Violations), Small Claims.*
Note: Includes many housing code, real estate-related small claims and eviction cases for Essex County & Action, Ayer, Billerica, Chelmsford, Dracut, Dunstable, Groton, Lowell, Pepperell, Shirley, Stow, Tewksbury, Tyngsboro, Westford; also see district courts.

Probate & Family Court 36 Federal St, Salem, MA 01970; phone: 978-744-1020; fax: 978-741-2957; hours 8:00AM-4:30PM (EST). *Probate.*

Franklin County

Superior Court PO Box 1573, Greenfield, MA 01302; phone: 413-774-5535; criminal/civil fax: 413-774-4770; hours 8:30AM-4:30PM (EST). *Felony, Civil Actions Over $25,000.*
Civil Records: Access: Fax, in person. Both court and visitors may perform in person searches. No search fee. Court makes copy: $1.00 per page. Required to search: name, years to search. Civil cases indexed by defendant, plaintiff. Civil records in files; on computer back 25 years. Mail turnaround time-within 48 hours.
Criminal Records: Access: Fax, in person. Both court and visitors may perform in person searches. No search fee. Court makes copy: $1.00 per page. Required to search: name, years to search, DOB. Criminal records in files; on computer back 8 years.
General Information: Public terminal has criminal back to 8 years and civil back to 25 years. No impounded or juvenile records released. Will fax documents. Certification fee: $2.50 per page attested includes copy fee. What is known as a certified copy in most states is known as a attested copy in Mass. What Mass. calls a single page "Certificate" with gold seal is $20.00. Payee: Franklin County Superior Court. Personal checks accepted. Prepayment required.

Greenfield District Court 425 Main St, Greenfield, MA 01301; phone: 413-774-5533; probate phone: 413-774-7011; fax: 413-774-5328; hours 8:30AM-4:30PM (EST). *Felony, Misdemeanor, Civil, Eviction, Small Claims.*
Note: Includes Ashfield, Bernardston, Buckland, Charlemont, Colrain, Conway, Deerfield, Gill, Greenfield, Hawley, Heath, Leyden, Monroe, Montague, Northfield, Rowe, Shelburne, Sunderland, and Whately.
Civil Records: Access: In person only. Both court and visitors may perform in person searches. No search fee. Court makes copy: $1.00 per page. Required to search: name, years to search. Civil cases indexed by defendant, plaintiff; on docket books or index cards; on computer back to 1998.
Criminal Records: Access: In person only. Both court and visitors may perform in person searches. No search fee. Court makes copy: $1.00 per page. Required to search: name, years to search, DOB. Criminal records on docket books or index cards; on computer back to 1994.

General Information: Public use terminal available. No juvenile records released. Certification fee: $2.50. Payee: Greenfield District Court. Personal checks accepted. Prepayment required.

Orange District Court #42 One Court Square, Orange, MA 01364; phone: 978-544-8277; fax: 978-544-5204; hours 8:30AM-4:30PM (EST). *Felony, Misdemeanor, Civil, Eviction, Small Claims.*
Note: Includes Athol, Erving, New Salem, Orange, Warwick, and Wendell, Shutesbury, Leverett.
Civil Records: Access: Phone, mail, in person. Both court and visitors may perform in person searches. No search fee. Court makes copy: $1.00 per page. Required to search: name, years to search. Civil cases indexed by defendant, plaintiff; on docket books from 1975. Mail turnaround time 1-2 weeks.
Criminal Records: Access: Phone, mail, in person. Only the court performs in person searches; visitors may not. No search fee. Court makes copy: $1.00 per page. Required to search: name, years to search. Criminal records on docket books from 1975. Mail turnaround time 1-2 weeks.
General Information: No public access terminal. No juvenile records released. Certification fee: $2.50 per page. Payee: District Court. Personal checks accepted. Prepayment required.

Probate & Family Court PO Box 590, 450 Main St, Greenfield, MA 01302; phone: 413-774-7011; fax: 413-774-3829; hours 8AM-4:30PM (EST). *Probate.*

Western Housing Court, MA. *Eviction, Misdemeanor (Code Violations), Small Claims.*
Note: See Hampden County Western Housing Court for many housing code cases, real estate-related small claims and eviction cases for this county; also see district courts in this county.

Hampden County

Superior Court 50 State St, PO Box 559, Springfield, MA 01102-0559; criminal phone: 413-735-6017; civil phone: 413-735-6016; fax: 413-737-1611; hours 8:30AM-4:30PM (EST). *Felony, Civil Actions Over $25,000.*
Civil Records: Access: Phone, mail, in person. Both court and visitors may perform in person searches. No search fee. Court makes copy: $1.00 per page. Required to search: name, years to search. Civil cases indexed by defendant, plaintiff; on computer from 1989 to present; prior on index cards from 1930s, books from 1812.
Criminal Records: Access: In person only. Visitors must perform in person searches themselves. Court makes copy: $1.00 per page. Required to search: name, years to search. Criminal records on computer from 1992 to present; prior on index cards from 1930s.
General Information: Public use terminal available. No impounded case records released. Certification fee: $2.50. Payee: Clerk of Superior Court. Personal checks accepted. Prepayment required. SASE requested.

Chicopee District Court #20 30 Church St, Chicopee, MA 01020; phone: 413-598-0099; fax: 413-594-6187; hours 8:30AM-4:30PM (EST). *Felony, Misdemeanor, Civil, Eviction, Small Claims.*
Civil Records: Access: Phone, mail, in person. Visitors must perform in person searches themselves. No search fee. Court makes copy: $1.00 per page. Required to search: name, years to search. Civil cases indexed by defendant, plaintiff; on index cards from 1983, docket books to 1960; computerized since 2001.
Criminal Records: Access: In person. Both court and visitors may perform in person searches. No search fee. Court makes copy: $1.00 per page. Required to search: name, years to search, DOB. Criminal records on index cards from 1983, docket books to 1900. Mail turnaround time 1-2 weeks.
General Information: No public access terminal. No juvenile records released. Fee to fax documents is $.50 per page. Certification fee: $2.50 per cert. Payee:

District Court. Personal checks accepted. Prepayment and SASE required.

Holyoke District Court 20 Court Sq, Holyoke, MA 01041-5075; phone: 413-538-9710; fax: 413-533-7165; hours 9AM-3:00PM (EST). *Felony, Misdemeanor, Civil, Eviction, Small Claims.*
Civil Records: Access: Phone, mail, fax, in person. Both court and visitors may perform in person searches. No search fee. Court makes copy: $1.00 per page. Required to search: name, years to search. Civil cases indexed by defendant, plaintiff; on index cards and docket books back to 1989. Mail turnaround time 1-2 weeks.
Criminal Records: Access: Fax, mail, in person. Both court and visitors may perform in person searches. No search fee. Court makes copy: $1.00 per page. Required to search: name, years to search, DOB or SSN, signed release. Criminal records on index cards and docket books since 1976; on computer back to 1986. Mail turnaround time 1-2 weeks.
General Information: No public access terminal. No juvenile, sealed records released. Certification fee: $2.50. Payee: District Court. Only cashiers checks and money orders accepted. Prepayment required. SASE requested.

Palmer District Court 235 Sykes St, Palmer, MA 01069; phone: 413-283-8916; fax: 413-283-6775; hours 8:30AM-4:30PM (EST). *Felony, Misdemeanor, Civil, Eviction, Small Claims.*
Note: Includes Ludlow, Monson, Wilbraham, Palmer, Wales, Brimfield, Holland, and Hampden.
Civil Records: Access: In person only. Visitors must perform in person searches themselves. Court makes copy: $1.00 per page. Required to search: name, years to search. Civil cases indexed by defendant, plaintiff; on index cards back to 1982.
Criminal Records: Access: In person only. Visitors must perform in person searches themselves. Court makes copy: $1.00 per page. Required to search: name, years to search. Criminal records on index cards for 10 years; on computer back to 1995.
General Information: No public access terminal. No sealed or juvenile records released. Certification fee: $2.50 per cert. Payee: Palmer District Court. Personal checks accepted. Prepayment required.

Springfield District Court 50 State St, Springfield, MA 01103; phone: 413-748-7613; criminal phone: 413-748-7982; civil phone: 413-748-8659; criminal fax: 413-747-4842; civil fax: 413-747-4841; hours 8:00AM-4:30PM (EST). *Felony, Misdemeanor, Civil, Eviction, Small Claims.*
Note: Includes Agawam, East Longmeadow, Longmeadow, Springfield, and West Springfield.
Civil Records: Access: In person only. Visitors must perform in person searches themselves. Court makes copy: $1.00 per page. Required to search: name, years to search. Civil cases indexed by defendant, plaintiff; on index cards; computerized records since 7/03, small claims since 2001.
Criminal Records: Access: In person. Visitors must perform in person searches themselves. No search fee. Court makes copy: $1.00 per page. Required to search: name, years to search. Criminal records on index cards; computerized records since 1992.
General Information: No public access terminal. No sealed, expunged, or adoption records released. Certification fee: $2.50. Payee: District Court. Business checks accepted. Prepayment required.

Westfield District Court 224 Elm St, Westfield, MA 01085; phone: 413-568-8946; fax: 413-568-4863; hours 8AM-4PM (EST). *Felony, Misdemeanor, Civil, Eviction, Small Claims.*
Note: Includes Blandford, Chester, Granville, Montgomery, Russell, Southwick, Tolland, and Westfield.
Civil Records: Access: Mail, in person. Both court and visitors may perform in person searches. No search fee. Court makes copy: $1.00 per page. Required to search: name, years to search. Civil cases indexed by defendant, plaintiff; on index cards and in files.

Criminal Records: Access: In person only. Both court and visitors may perform in person searches. No search fee. Court makes copy: $1.00 per page. Required to search: name, years to search. Criminal records on index cards and in files. Mail turnaround time 1-2 weeks.

General Information: No public access terminal. No sealed or juvenile records released. Certification fee: $2.50 per cert. Payee: District Court. Only cashiers checks and money orders accepted. Prepayment required.

Probate & Family Court 50 State St, Springfield, MA 01103-0559; phone: 413-748-7746; fax: 413-781-5605; hours 7;30AM-4:25PM (EST). *Probate.*

Western Housing Court PO Box 559 (37 Elm St), Springfield, MA 01102; phone: 413-748-7838; fax: 413-732-4607; hours 8:30AM-4:30PM (EST). *Eviction, Misdemeanor (Code Violations), Small Claims.*
Note: Includes many housing code cases, real estate-related small claims and eviction cases for counties of Berkshire, Franklin, Hampden, and Hampshire; also see district courts.

Hampshire County

Superior Court PO Box 1119, Northampton, MA 01061; phone: 413-584-5810 x331; probate phone: 413-586-8500; fax: 413-586-8217; hours 9AM-4PM (EST). *Felony, Civil Actions Over $25,000.*
Civil Records: Access: Mail, fax, in person. Both court and visitors may perform in person searches. No search fee. Court makes copy: $1.00 per page. Required to search: name, years to search. Civil cases indexed by defendant, plaintiff. Civil records in files, index cards from 1800s; on computer back to 2000. Mail turnaround time 1 week.
Criminal Records: Access: Mail, fax, in person. Both court and visitors may perform in person searches. No search fee. Court makes copy: $1.00 per page. Required to search: name, years to search. Criminal records in files, index cards from 1800s; on computer back to 1983. Mail turnaround time 1 week.
General Information: Public terminal has criminal back to 1983 and civil back to 2000. No impounded case records released. Will fax documents to local or toll free line. Certification fee: $20.00. Payee: Clerk of Superior Court. Personal checks accepted. Prepayment required.

Hadley District Court PO Box 778, 116 Russell St, Hadley, MA 01035; phone: 413-587-3120; hours 8:30AM-4:30PM (EST). *Felony, Misdemeanor, Civil, Eviction, Small Claims.*
Note: Includes Amherst, Belchertown, Granby, Hadley, South Hadley, Pelham, Ware, all the MDC Quabbin Reservoir and Watershed Area. Includes cases formerly heard at the closed court in Ware.
Civil Records: Access: Fax, mail, in person. Only the court performs in person searches; visitors may not. No search fee. Court makes copy: $1.00 per page; same fee for self serve. Required to search: name, years to search. Civil cases indexed by defendant, plaintiff; on index cards or docket books back to 1960. Some records sent to archives in Worcester. Mail turnaround time 1-2 weeks.
Criminal Records: Access: Fax, mail, in person. Only the court performs in person searches; visitors may not. No search fee. Court makes copy: $1.00 per page; same fee for self serve. Required to search: name, years to search, DOB, SSN. Criminal records on index cards or docket books back to 1920; on computer back to 1996. Some records sent to archives in Worcester. Mail turnaround time 1-2 weeks.
General Information: No public access terminal. No sealed, impounded, confidential or juvenile records released. Certification fee: $2.50. Payee: Eastern Hampshire District Court. Personal checks accepted. Prepayment required. SASE helpful.

Northampton District Court Courthouse, 15 Gothic St, Northampton, MA 01060; phone: 413-584-7776; criminal phone: 413-584-7400; civil phone: 413-584-7400; criminal fax: 413-584-1980; civil fax: 413-584-9479; hours 8:30AM-4:30PM (EST). *Felony, Misdemeanor, Civil, Eviction, Small Claims.*
Note: Includes Chesterfield, Cummington, Easthampton, Goshen, Hatfield, Huntington, Middlefield, Northampton, Plainfield, Southampton, Westhampton, Williamsburg, and Worthington.
Civil Records: Access: Fax, mail, in person. Both court and visitors may perform in person searches. No search fee. Court makes copy: $1.00 per page; same fee for self serve. Required to search: name, years to search, address. Civil cases indexed by defendant, plaintiff; on index cards and docket books back to 1970, computerized since 5/02. Mail turnaround time 1-2 weeks.
Criminal Records: Access: Fax, mail, in person. Both court and visitors may perform in person searches. No search fee. Court makes copy: $1.00 per page; same fee for self serve. Required to search: name, years to search, DOB, SSN. Criminal records on docket books go back to 1970, on computer since 1997. Mail turnaround time 1-2 weeks.
General Information: No public access terminal. No CHINS-care & protection, show cause-mental health records released. No fee to fax documents. Certification fee: $2.50 per page. Payee: District Court. Personal checks not accepted. Prepayment required. SASE requested.

Probate & Family Court 33 King St #3, Northampton, MA 01060; phone: 413-586-8500; fax: 413-584-1132; hours 8:30AM-4:30PM (EST). *Probate.*

Western Housing Court, MA. *Eviction, Misdemeanor (Code Violations), Small Claims.*
Note: See Hampden County Western Housing Court for many housing code cases, real estate-related small claims and eviction cases for this county; also see district courts in this county.

Middlesex County

Superior Court - East Cambridge 40 Thorndike St, Edward J Sullivan Courthouse, East Cambridge, MA 02141; phone: 617-494-4010; hours 8:30AM-4:30PM (EST). *Felony, Civil Actions Over $25,000.*
Civil Records: Access: Mail, in person. Both court and visitors may perform in person searches. No search fee. Court makes copy: $1.00 per page. Required to search: name, years to search; also helpful: address. Civil cases indexed by defendant, plaintiff; on computer from 1986, rest on card indexes to 1986. The court is planning to have Internet access. Mail turnaround time 3-5 days for criminal records.
Criminal Records: Access: Mail, in person. Both court and visitors may perform in person searches. No search fee. Court makes copy: $1.00 per page. Required to search: name, years to search; also helpful: address. Criminal records on computer back to 1991, rest on card indexes to 1986. The court plans to have Internet access. Mail turnaround time 3-5 days for criminal records.
General Information: Public terminal goes back to 1991. No impounded or those restricted by statute records released. Certification fee: $2.50 per doc. Payee: Clerk of Superior Court. Personal checks accepted. Prepayment required.

Superior Court - Lowell 360 Gorham St, Lowell, MA 01852; phone: 978-453-0201; hours 8:30AM-4:30PM (EST). *Felony, Civil Actions Over $25,000.*
Civil Records: Access: Mail, in person. Both court and visitors may perform in person searches. No search fee. Court makes copy: $1.00 per page. Required to search: name, years to search. Civil cases indexed by defendant, plaintiff; on computer since 1990; prior records kept at East Cambridge Middlesex

Superior Court, 40 Thorndike, Cambridge, MA 02141. Mail turnaround time 1-2 days.
Criminal Records: Access: Mail, in person. Both court and visitors may perform in person searches. No search fee. Court makes copy: $1.00 per page. Required to search: name, years to search. Criminal records on computer since 1990; prior records kept at East Cambridge Middlesex Superior Court, 40 Thorndike, Cambridge, MA 02141. Mail turnaround time 1-2 days.
General Information: No public access terminal. Certification fee: $2.50 per cert. Payee: Clerk of Superior Court. Personal checks accepted. Prepayment required.

Ayer District Court 25 E Main St, Ayer, MA 01432; phone: 978-772-2100; fax: 978-772-5345; hours 8:30AM-4:30PM (EST). *Felony, Misdemeanor, Civil, Eviction, Small Claims.*
Note: Includes Ayer, Ashby, Boxborough, Dunstable, Groton, Littleton, Pepperell, Shirley, Townsend, Westford and Devens Regional Enterprise Zone.
Civil Records: Access: Mail, in person. No search fee. Court makes copy: $1.00 per page. Required to search: name, years to search. Civil cases indexed by defendant, plaintiff; on index cards from 1977 to present; only required to keep records 20 years. DOB required on subject. Mail turnaround time 1-2 weeks.
Criminal Records: Access: Mail, in person. Both court and visitors may perform in person searches. No search fee. Court makes copy: $1.00 per page. Required to search: name, years to search, DOB. Criminal records on index cards from 1977 to 1995, computerized 1996 forward; Only required to keep records 10 years. Mail turnaround time 1-2 weeks.
General Information: No public access terminal. Juvenile records not released. Certification fee: $1.50 per page. Payee: Ayer District Court. Personal checks accepted. Prepayment and SASE required.

Cambridge District Court 52 PO Box 338, 40 Thorndike St, East Cambridge, MA 02141; phone: 617-494-4095; criminal phone: 617-494-4095 X501; civil phone: 617-494-4095 X502; fax: 617-494-9129; hours 8:30AM-4:30PM (EST). *Felony, Misdemeanor, Civil, Eviction, Small Claims.*
Note: Includes Cambridge, Arlington, and Belmont.
Civil Records: Access: In person only. Visitors must perform in person searches themselves. Court makes copy: $1.00 per page. Required to search: name, years to search. Civil cases indexed by defendant, plaintiff; on index cards or docket books. State law requires records be retained for 10 years.
Criminal Records: Access: Mail, in person. Visitors must perform in person searches themselves. Court makes copy: $1.00 per page. Required to search: name, years to search, DOB. Criminal records on index cards or docket books; computerized records since 1997. State law requires records be retained for 10 years. Mail turnaround time 1-2 weeks.
General Information: No public access terminal. No sealed or juvenile records released. Will fax documents to local or toll free line. Certification fee: $2.50 per cert. Payee: District Court. Personal checks accepted. Prepayment and SASE required.

Concord District Court 47 305 Walden St, Concord, MA 01742; phone: 978-369-0500; fax: 978-371-2945; hours 8:30AM-4:30PM (EST). *Felony, Misdemeanor, Civil, Eviction, Small Claims.*
Note: Includes Concord, Carlisle, Lincoln, Lexington, Bedford, Acton, Maynard, and Stow.
Civil Records: Access: Mail, in person. Visitors must perform in person searches themselves. No search fee. Court makes copy: $1.00 per page. Required to search: name, years to search; also helpful: address. Civil cases indexed by defendant, plaintiff; on computer from 1991, index cards and books from 1950, archived from 1643. In person searches performed from 10AM-4PM only. Mail turnaround time 1-2 weeks.
Criminal Records: Access: Mail, in person. Visitors must perform in person searches themselves. No search fee. Court makes copy: $1.00 per page.

Required to search: name, years to search; also helpful: address, DOB, SSN. Criminal records index printed from computer from 1998, index cards and books from 1950, archived from 1643. In person searches performed from 10AM-4PM only. Mail turnaround time 1-2 weeks.

General Information: No public access terminal. No impounded files released. Certification fee: $2.50 per cert. Payee: Commonwealth of Massachusetts. Personal checks accepted. Prepayment required. SASE requested.

Framingham District Court PO Box 1669, 600 Concord St, Framingham, MA 01701; phone: 508-875-7461; fax: 508-626-2503; hours 8:30AM-4:30PM (EST). *Felony, Misdemeanor, Civil, Eviction, Small Claims.*

Note: Includes Ashland, Framingham, Holliston, Hopkinton, Sudbury, and Wayland.

Civil Records: Access: Mail, in person. Both court and visitors may perform in person searches. No search fee. Court makes copy: $1.00 per page. Required to search: name, years to search. Civil cases indexed by defendant, plaintiff; on index cards or docket books back to 1900; on computer back to 1986. Special form required for mail request. Mail turnaround time 7 days.

Criminal Records: Access: Mail, in person, fax. Both court and visitors may perform in person searches. No search fee. Court makes copy: $1.00 per page. Required to search: name, years to search. Criminal records on index cards or docket books back to 1900; on computer back to 1986. Special form required for mail request. Mail turnaround time 7 days.

General Information: Public terminal has criminal back to 2002 and civil back to 2002. No sealed, expunged or juvenile records released. Certification fee: $2.50 per page. Payee: District Court. Only cashiers checks and money orders accepted. Prepayment required. SASE requested.

Lowell District Court 41 Hurd St, Lowell, MA 01852; phone: 978-459-4101; criminal phone: X204; civil phone: x235; hours 8:30AM-4:30PM (EST). *Felony, Misdemeanor, Civil, Eviction, Small Claims.*

Note: Includes Billerica, Chelmsford, Dracut, Lowell, Tewksbury, and Tyngsboro.

Civil Records: Access: In person only. Visitors must perform in person searches themselves. Court makes copy: $1.00 per page. Required to search: name, years to search. Civil cases indexed by defendant, plaintiff; on index cards or docket books. Records retained for 10 years.

Criminal Records: Access: Mail, in person. Visitors must perform in person searches themselves. Court makes copy: $1.00 per page. Required to search: name, years to search, DOB. Criminal records on index cards or docket books. Records retained for 10 years.

General Information: No public access terminal. No impounded records released. Certification fee: $2.50. Payee: District Court, Lowell Division. Business checks accepted. Prepayment required.

Malden District Court 89 Summer St, Malden, MA 02148; phone: 781-322-7500; fax: 781-322-0169; hours 8:30AM-4:30PM (EST). *Felony, Misdemeanor, Civil, Eviction, Small Claims.*

Note: Includes Malden, Melrose, Everett, and Wakefield.

Civil Records: Access: Phone, mail, in person. Only the court performs in person searches; visitors may not. No search fee. Court makes copy: $1.00 per page. Required to search: name, years to search. Civil cases indexed by defendant, plaintiff; on index cards or docket books back to 1970; on computer back to 1992.

Criminal Records: Access: In person only. Both court and visitors may perform in person searches. No search fee. Court makes copy: $1.00 per page. Required to search: name, years to search, DOB. Criminal records on index cards or docket books back to 1970; on computer back to 1992.

General Information: No public access terminal. No juvenile records released. Certification fee: $2.50 per doc. Payee: District Court. Personal checks accepted. Prepayment required.

Marlborough District Court 21 45 Williams St, Marlborough, MA 01752; phone: 508-485-3700; fax: 508-485-1575; hours 8AM-4:30PM (EST). *Felony, Misdemeanor, Civil, Eviction, Small Claims.*

Note: Includes Marlborough and Hudson.

Civil Records: Access: Phone, mail, in person. Both court and visitors may perform in person searches. No search fee. Court makes copy: $1.00 per page. Required to search: name, years to search. Civil cases indexed by defendant, plaintiff; on index cards or docket books. State law requires records be retained for 10 years. Mail turnaround 1-2 weeks.

Criminal Records: Access: Phone, mail, in person. Both court and visitors may perform in person searches. No search fee. Court makes copy: $1.00 per page. Required to search: name, years to search, DOB. Criminal records on index cards or docket books. State law requires records be retained for 10 years. Mail turnaround time 1-2 weeks.

General Information: No public access terminal. No juvenile records released. Certification fee: $2.50 per cert. Payee: District Court. Personal checks accepted. Prepayment required.

Natick District Court 117 E Central, Natick, MA 01760; phone: 508-653-4332; fax: 508-655-8196; hours 8:30AM-4:30PM (EST). *Felony, Misdemeanor, Civil, Eviction, Small Claims.*

Note: Includes Natick and Sherborn.

Civil Records: Access: In person only. Visitors must perform in person searches themselves. Court makes copy: $1.00 per page. Required to search: name, years to search. Civil cases indexed by defendant, plaintiff; on index cards and docket books, back for 10 years. Note: Visitors must perform in person searches Friday 3-4:30PM.

Criminal Records: Access: In person only. Visitors must perform in person searches themselves. Court makes copy: $1.00 per page. Required to search: name, years to search, DOB. Criminal records on index cards and docket books, back for 10 years. Note: In person criminal searches on Friday 3-4:30PM.

General Information: No public access terminal. No juvenile records released. Certification fee: $2.50 per cert. Payee: District Court. Personal checks accepted. Prepayment required.

Newton District Court 1309 Washington, West Newton, MA 02141; phone: 617-244-3600; fax: 617-243-7291; hours 8:30AM-1PM; 2-4:30PM (EST). *Felony, Misdemeanor, Civil, Eviction, Small Claims.*

www.state.ma.us/courts/courtsandjudges/courts/newtondistrictmain.html

Civil Records: Access: Phone, mail, in person. Both court and visitors may perform in person searches. No search fee. Court makes copy: $1.00 per page. Required to search: name, years to search. Civil cases indexed by defendant, plaintiff; on index cards back to 1930. Mail turnaround time 1 week.

Criminal Records: Access: Phone, mail, in person. Both court and visitors may perform in person searches. No search fee. Court makes copy: $1.00 per page. Required to search: name, years to search. Criminal records on index books back to 1930. Mail turnaround time 1 week.

General Information: Public use terminal available. No juvenile, (some) 209-A cases or mental health records released. Will not fax documents. Certification fee: $2.50 per cert. Payee: District Court of Newton. Personal checks accepted.

Somerville District Court 175 Fellsway, Somerville, MA 02145; phone: 617-666-8000; fax: 617-776-2111; hours 8:30AM-4:30PM (EST). *Felony, Misdemeanor, Civil, Eviction, Small Claims.*

Note: Includes Medford and Somerville.

Civil Records: Access: In person only. Visitors must perform in person searches themselves. Court

makes copy: $1.00 per page. Required to search: name, years to search. Civil cases indexed by defendant, plaintiff; on index cards or docket books. State law requires records be retained for 20 years.

Criminal Records: Access: In person. Visitors must perform in person searches themselves. No search fee. Court makes copy: $1.00 per page. Required to search: name, years to search, DOB. Criminal records on computer since 1997; prior records on index cards or docket books. State law requires records be retained for 20 years.

General Information: No public access terminal. No juvenile or impounded records released. Certification fee: $2.50 per cert. Payee: District Court. Personal checks accepted. Prepayment required.

Waltham District Court 51 38 Linden St, Waltham, MA 02154; phone: 781-894-4500; hours 8:30AM-4:30PM (EST). *Felony, Misdemeanor, Civil, Eviction, Small Claims.*

Note: Includes Waltham, Watertown, and Weston.

Civil Records: Access: Mail, in person. Both court and visitors may perform in person searches. No search fee. Court makes copy: $1.00 per page. Required to search: name, years to search. Civil cases indexed by defendant, plaintiff; on index cards and docket books, back for 10 years. Mail turnaround time 1 week.

Criminal Records: Access: Mail, in person. Both court and visitors may perform in person searches. No search fee. Court makes copy: $1.00 per page. Required to search: name, years to search; also helpful: DOB. Criminal records on index cards and docket books, back for 10 years. Mail turnaround time 1 week.

General Information: Public use terminal available. No juvenile records released. Certification fee: $2.50. Payee: District Court. No personal checks. Prepayment and SASE required.

Woburn District Court 53 30 Pleasant St, Woburn, MA 01801; phone: 781-935-4000; fax: 781-933-4404; hours 8:30AM-4:30PM (EST). *Felony, Misdemeanor, Civil, Eviction, Small Claims.*

Note: Includes Burlington, North Reading, Reading, Stoneham, Wilmington, Winchester, and Woburn.

Civil Records: Access: Mail, in person. Both court and visitors may perform in person searches. No search fee. Court makes copy: $1.00 per page. Required to search: name, years to search. Civil cases indexed by defendant, plaintiff; on index cards, computer listing or docket books back 30 years. Mail turnaround time 1-2 weeks.

Criminal Records: Access: Mail, in person. Both court and visitors may perform in person searches. No search fee. Court makes copy: $1.00 per page. Required to search: name, years to search; also helpful: DOB. Criminal records on index cards, computer listing or docket books back 30 years. Mail turnaround time 1-2 weeks.

General Information: Public terminal goes back to 1996. No statutorily non-public records released. Certification fee: $2.50 per cert. Payee: District Court. Personal checks accepted. Prepayment required. SASE requested.

Probate & Family Court 208 Cambridge St, PO Box 410480, East Cambridge, MA 02141-0005; phone: 617-768-5800; fax: 617-225-0781; hours 8AM-4:30PM (EST). *Probate.*

Nantucket County

Superior Court PO Box 967, Nantucket, MA 02554; phone: 508-228-2559; fax: 508-228-3725; hours 8:30AM-4PM (EST). *Felony, Civil Actions Over $25,000.*

Civil Records: Access: Phone, fax, mail, in person. Both court and visitors may perform in person searches. No search fee. Court makes copy: $1.00 per page. Required to search: name, years to search. Civil cases indexed by defendant, plaintiff; on index books from 1762. Mail turnaround 1 week.

Criminal Records: Access: Phone, fax, mail, in person. Both court and visitors may perform in person searches. No search fee. Court makes copy: $1.00 per page. Required to search: name, years to search. Criminal records on index books from 1762. Mail turnaround time 1 week.

General Information: No public access terminal. No impounded records released. No fee to fax documents. In-state faxing only. Certification fee: $2.50 per cert. Payee: Nantucket Superior Court. Personal checks accepted. Prepayment and SASE required.

Nantucket District Court 16 Broad St, PO Box 1800, Nantucket, MA 02554; phone: 508-228-0460; fax: 508-325-5759; hours 8AM-4PM (EST). *Felony, Misdemeanor, Civil, Eviction, Small Claims.*
Civil Records: Access: In person only. Visitors must perform in person searches themselves. Court makes copy: $1.00 per page. Required to search: name, years to search. Civil cases indexed by defendant, plaintiff; on index cards or docket books. State law requires records be retained for 10 years.
Criminal Records: Access: In person only. Visitors must perform in person searches themselves. Court makes copy: $1.00 per page. Required to search: name, years to search. Criminal records on index cards or docket books back to 1917. State law requires records be retained for 10 years.
General Information: No public access terminal. Certification fee: $2.50 per cert. Payee: Nantucket District Court. Prepayment required.

Probate & Family Court PO Box 1116, 16 Broad St, Nantucket, MA 02554; phone: 508-228-2669; fax: 508-228-3662; hours 8AM-4PM (EST). *Probate.*

Norfolk County

Superior Court 650 High St, Dedham, MA 02026; phone: 781-326-1600; criminal phone: x2; civil phone: x1; criminal fax: 781-320-9726; civil fax: 781-326-3871; hours 8:30AM-4:30PM (EST). *Felony, Civil Actions Over $25,000.*
Civil Records: Access: Phone, mail, in person. Both court and visitors may perform in person searches. No search fee. Court makes copy: $1.00 per page. Required to search: name, years to search. Civil cases indexed by defendant, plaintiff; on index books from 1900, on computer back to 9/2000. Mail turnaround time 1 week; 1-2 days for criminal phone in requests.
Criminal Records: Access: Mail, in person. Visitors must perform in person searches themselves. No search fee. Court makes copy: $1.00 per page. Required to search: name, years to search; also helpful: address, DOB, SSN. Criminal records on index books from 1900; on computer back to 9/2000. Mail turnaround time 1 week; 1-2 days for criminal phone in requests.
General Information: Public use terminal available. No impounded records released. No one may view a file of a sex-related crime without authorization from a judge. Certification fee: $2.50 per cert. Payee: Clerk of Superior Court. Personal checks accepted for copies only. Prepayment required.

Brookline District Court 360 Washington St, Brookline, MA 02445; phone: 617-232-4660; fax: 617-739-0734; hours 8:30AM-4:30PM (EST). *Felony, Misdemeanor, Civil, Eviction, Small Claims.*
Civil Records: Access: Mail, in person. Both court and visitors may perform in person searches. No search fee. Court makes copy: $1.00 per page. Required to search: name, years to search. Civil cases indexed by defendant, plaintiff; on index cards and docket books back for 10 years. Mail turnaround time 1-2 weeks.
Criminal Records: Access: Mail, in person. Only the court performs in person searches; visitors may not. No search fee. Court makes copy: $1.00 per page. Required to search: name, years to search; also helpful: DOB. Criminal records on index cards and docket books back for 10 years. Mail turnaround time 1-2 weeks.
General Information: No public access terminal. No sealed case records released. Certification fee:

$2.50. Payee: Brookline District Court. Personal checks accepted. Prepayment required.

Dedham District Court 631 High St, Dedham, MA 02026; phone: 781-329-4777; fax: 781-329-8640; hours 8:15AM-4:30PM (EST). *Felony, Misdemeanor, Civil, Eviction, Small Claims.*
Note: Includes Dedham, Dover, Medfield, Needham, Norwood, Wellesley, and Westwood.
Civil Records: Access: In person only. Visitors must perform in person searches themselves. Court makes copy: $1.00 per page. Required to search: name, years to search. Civil cases indexed by defendant, plaintiff; on computer since 1997, and on index cards or docket books prior to that. State law requires records be retained for 10 years.
Criminal Records: Access: In person only. Visitors must perform in person searches themselves. Court makes copy: $1.00 per page. Required to search: name, years to search. Criminal records on computer since 1997, and on index cards or docket books prior to that. State law requires records be retained for 10 years. Access is available after 10AM.
General Information: No juvenile records released. Certification fee: $2.50 per cert. Payee: District Court. Personal checks accepted. Prepayment required.

Quincy District Court One Dennis Ryan Parkway, Quincy, MA 02169; phone: 617-471-1650; fax: 617-472-1924; hours 8:30AM-4:30PM (EST). *Felony, Misdemeanor, Civil, Eviction, Small Claims.*
Note: Includes Braintree, Cohasset, Holbrook, Quincy, Randolph, and Weymouth, Quincy.
Civil Records: Access: In person only. Visitors must perform in person searches themselves. Court makes copy: $1.00 per page. Required to search: name, years to search. Civil cases indexed by defendant, plaintiff; on index cards or docket books. State law requires records be retained for 10 years.
Criminal Records: Access: In person only. Visitors must perform in person searches themselves. Court makes copy: $1.00 per page. Required to search: name, years to search; also helpful: DOB. Criminal records on computer since 1996; prior records on index cards or docket books. State law requires records be retained for 10 years.
General Information: No public access terminal. Juvenile records current now with Norfolk Juv. Court; no juvenile records released. Certification fee: $2.50 per cert. Payee: District Court. Only cashiers checks and money orders accepted. Prepayment required.

Stoughton District Court 1288 Central St, Stoughton, MA 02072; phone: 781-344-2131; fax: 781-341-8744; hours 8:30AM-4:30PM (EST). *Felony, Misdemeanor, Civil, Eviction, Small Claims.*
Note: Includes Avon, Canton, Sharon, and Stoughton.
Civil Records: Access: Mail, in person. Both court and visitors may perform in person searches. No search fee. Court makes copy: $1.00 per page. Required to search: name, years to search. Civil cases indexed by defendant, plaintiff; on index cards or docket books for 10 years or more. Mail turnaround time 1 week; if in storage then 6 weeks.
Criminal Records: Access: Mail, in person. Only the court performs in person searches; visitors may not. No search fee. Court makes copy: $1.00 per page. Required to search: name, years to search; also helpful: DOB. Criminal records on computer since 1996; prior records on index cards or docket books for 10 years or more. Mail turnaround time 1 week; if in storage then 6 weeks.
General Information: Public terminal has only civil records back to 2005. No juvenile records released. Certification fee: $2.50. Payee: District Court. Personal checks accepted. Prepayment required.

Wrentham District Court 60 East St, Wrentham, MA 02093; phone: 508-384-3106; criminal fax: 508-384-5052; civil fax: 508-384-9454; hours 8:30AM-4:30PM (EST). *Felony, Misdemeanor, Civil, Eviction, Small Claims.*

Note: Includes Foxborough, Franklin, Medway, Millis, Norfolk, Plainville, Walpole, and Wrentham.
Civil Records: Access: In person only. Visitors must perform in person searches themselves. Court makes copy: $1.00 per page. Required to search: name, years to search. Civil cases indexed by defendant, plaintiff. Criminal records retained 20 years. Physical records go back to 1985; pre-1985 on docket books.
Criminal Records: Access: In person. Visitors must perform in person searches themselves. No search fee. Court makes copy: $1.00 per page. Required to search: name, years to search; also helpful: DOB. Criminal records retained 20 years. Physical records go back to 1985; on computer back to 1999; pre-1985 on docket books.
General Information: No public access terminal. No show cause hearing or juvenile records released. Will not fax documents. Certification fee: $2.50 per page. Payee: District Court. Personal checks accepted. Prepayment required.

Probate & Family Court 35 Shawmut Rd, Canton, MA 02021; phone: 781-830-1200; fax: 781-830-4310; hours 8:30AM-4:30PM (EST). *Probate.*
Note: Due to health concerns, Probate was moved from the old location on High St in Dedham in 2003. Should remain at this new Canton location until 2008. However, the Register of Deeds remains in Dedham at old address.

Plymouth County

Superior Court - Brockton 72 Belmont St, Brockton, MA 02401; phone: 508-583-8250; fax: 508-583-7701; hours 8:30AM-4:30PM (EST). *Felony, Civil Actions Over $25,000.*
Civil Records: Access: In person only. Visitors must perform in person searches themselves. Court makes copy: $1.00 per page. Required to search: name, years to search. Civil cases indexed by defendant, plaintiff. Civil records for current civil cases are here, closed case are in Plymouth, some pending; computerized records since 2000.
Criminal Records: Access: In person only. Visitors must perform in person searches themselves. Court makes copy: $1.00 per page. Required to search: name, years to search. Criminal records for current civil cases are here, closed case are in Plymouth, some pending; computerized records since 2000.
General Information: Public terminal goes back to 2000. No impounded records released. Certification fee: $2.50 per cert. Payee: Clerk of Superior Court. Personal checks accepted. Prepayment required.

Superior Court - Plymouth Plymouth Superior Court, Court St, Plymouth, MA 02360; phone: 508-747-6911; hours 8:30AM-4:30PM (EST). *Felony, Civil Actions Over $25,000.*
Civil Records: Access: Phone, mail, in person. Only the court performs in person searches; visitors may not. No search fee. Court makes copy: $1.00 per page. Required to search: name, years to search. Civil cases indexed by defendant, plaintiff. Civil records for all closed cases are kept here; computerized records since 1977.
Criminal Records: Access: In person only, with exception. Court makes copy: $1.00 per page. Required to search: name, years to search. Criminal records 10 years or older are here; for recent cases go to the Brockton Superior Court. This court's criminal records under ten years old can be searched in person only at Brockton Superior Court, 72 Belmont St, Brockton, 508-583-8250. Mail turnaround time 1 week; immediate four phone requests.
General Information: No public access terminal. No impounded records released. Certification fee: $2.50. Payee: Clerk of Superior Court. Personal checks accepted. Prepayment required.

Brockton District Court PO Box 7610, 215 Main St, Brockton, MA 02303-7610; phone: 508-587-8000; fax: 508-587-0034; hours 8:30AM-4:30PM (EST). *Felony, Misdemeanor, Civil, Eviction, Small Claims.*

Note: Includes Abington, Bridgewater, Brockton, East Bridgewater, West Bridgewater, and Whitman.

Civil Records: Access: Mail, in person. Both court and visitors may perform in person searches. No search fee. Court makes copy: $1.00 per page. Required to search: name, years to search. Civil cases indexed by defendant, plaintiff; on index cards or docket books, retained for 10 years; on computer back to 1994. Mail turnaround time 1-2 weeks.

Criminal Records: Access: Mail, in person. Both court and visitors may perform in person searches. No search fee. Court makes copy: $1.00 per page. Required to search: name, years to search; also helpful: DOB. Criminal records on index cards or docket books, retained for 10 years; on computer back to 1994. Mail turnaround time 1-2 weeks.

General Information: Public terminal has criminal back to 1994 and civil back to 1995. No juvenile or impounded records released. Certification fee: $2.50 per page. Payee: District Court. Personal checks accepted. Prepayment required.

Hingham District Court 28 George Washington Blvd, Hingham, MA 02043; phone: 781-749-7000; fax: 781-740-8390; hours 8:30AM-4:30PM (EST). *Felony, Misdemeanor, Civil, Eviction, Small Claims.*

Note: Includes Hanover, Hingham, Hull, Norwell, Rockland, and Scituate.

Civil Records: Access: Mail, in person. Only the court performs in person searches; visitors may not. No search fee. Court makes copy: $1.00 per page. Required to search: name, years to search. Civil cases indexed by defendant, plaintiff; on index cards or docket books, retained for 10 years or more. Mail turnaround time 1-2 weeks.

Criminal Records: Access: Mail, in person. Only the court performs in person searches; visitors may not. No search fee. Court makes copy: $1.00 per page. Required to search: name, years to search; also helpful: DOB. Criminal records on index cards or docket books, retained for 10 years or more. Mail turnaround time 1-2 weeks.

General Information: No public access terminal. No juvenile records released. Certification fee: $2.50 per cert. Payee: District Court. Personal checks accepted. Prepayment required.

Plymouth 3rd District Court Courthouse, S Russell St, Plymouth, MA 02360; phone: 508-747-0500; fax: 508-830-9303; hours 8:30AM-4:30PM (EST). *Felony, Misdemeanor, Civil, Eviction, Small Claims.*

Note: Includes Duxbury, Halifax, Hanson, Kingston, Marshfield, Pembroke, Plymouth, and Plympton.

Civil Records: Access: Mail, in person. Both court and visitors may perform in person searches. No search fee. Court makes copy: $1.00 per page. Required to search: name, years to search. Civil cases indexed by defendant, plaintiff; on index cards or docket books. State law requires records be retained for 10 years. Visitors can only access the index cards. Mail turnaround time 3-4 days.

Criminal Records: Access: Mail, in person. Both court and visitors may perform in person searches. No search fee. Court makes copy: $1.00 per page. Required to search: name, years to search; also helpful: DOB. Criminal records on index cards or docket books. State law requires records be retained for 10 years. Visitors can only access the index cards. Mail turnaround time 3-4 days.

General Information: No public access terminal. No juvenile or impounded records released. Certification fee: $2.50. Payee: Plymouth District Court. Personal checks accepted. Prepayment required.

Wareham District Court 2200 Cranberry Hwy, Junction Routes 28 & 58, West Wareham, MA 02576; phone: 508-295-8300; fax: 508-291-6376; hours 8AM-4:30PM (EST). *Felony, Misdemeanor, Civil, Eviction, Small Claims.*

Note: Includes Carver, Lakeville, Marion, Mattpoinsett, Middleboro, Rochester, and Wareham.

Civil Records: Access: Phone, mail, in person. Both court and visitors may perform in person searches. No search fee. Court makes copy: $1.00 per page; same fee for self serve. Required to search: name, years to search. Civil cases indexed by defendant, plaintiff. Criminal records back to 1960. Computerized records back to 1995. Mail turnaround time 1-2 weeks.

Criminal Records: Access: Phone, mail, in person. Only the court performs in person searches; visitors may not. No search fee. Court makes copy: $1.00 per page; same fee for self serve. Required to search: name, years to search; also helpful: DOB. Criminal records back to 1960. Computerized records back to 1995. Mail turnaround time 1-2 weeks.

General Information: No public access terminal. No juvenile records released. Certification fee: $2.50 per page includes copy fee. Payee: District Court. Personal checks accepted. Prepayment required. SASE requested.

Probate & Family Court 7 Russell, PO Box 3640, Plymouth, MA 02361; phone: 508-747-6204; fax: 508-746-6846; hours 8:30AM-4:30PM (EST). *Probate.*
www.pcpfc.com

Southeast Housing Court PO Box 7520 (215 Main St), Brockton, MA 02303; phone: 508-894-4170; fax: 508-894-4168; hours 8:30AM-4:30PM (EST). *Eviction, Misdemeanor (Code Violations), Small Claims.*

Note: Includes housing code cases, real estate-related small claims, and many eviction cases for Plymouth County; also see district courts.

Suffolk County

Superior Court - Civil 3 Pemberton Sq, Superior Court Clerk, Copy Dept, Boston, MA 02108; phone: 617-788-8175; hours 8:30AM-5PM (EST). *Civil.*

Civil Records: Access: Mail, in person. Both court and visitors may perform in person searches. No search fee. Court makes copy: $1.00 per page. Required to search: name, years to search. Civil cases indexed by defendant, plaintiff; on computer from 1991, index cards and books from 1860. Mail turnaround time 1 week.

General Information: Public terminal available. No impounded records released. Certification fee: $2.50. Payee: Clerk of Superior Court. Business checks accepted. Prepayment required.

Superior Court - Criminal Superior Court Clerk, Three Pemberton Sq, Boston, MA 02108; phone: 617-788-8160; fax: 617-788-7798; hours 8:30AM-5PM (EST). *Felony.*

Criminal Records: Access: Mail, in person. Both court and visitors may perform in person searches. No search fee. Court makes copy: $1.50 per page (attested). Required to search: name, years to search. Criminal records on computer back to 1991, index cards and books from 1950, archived from 1864. Mail turnaround time 1-2 weeks.

General Information: Public terminal has only criminal records back to 1991. Certification fee: $20.00. Payee: Superior Court. Personal checks accepted. Prepayment required.

Boston Municipal Court - Central Division Office of Clerk-Magistrate, Civil Business, 24 New Chardon St #1, Boston, MA 02114; phone: 617-788-8412; criminal phone: 617-788-8600; civil phone: 617-788-8400; criminal fax: 617-788-8465; civil fax: 617-788-8675; hours 8:30AM-4:30PM (EST). *Misdemeanor, Civil, Small Claims.*

Note: Misdemeanor records are located on the 6th floor in a separate index.

Civil Records: Access: Mail, in person. Both court and visitors may perform in person searches. No search fee. Court makes copy: $1.00 per page. Required to search: name, years to search. Civil cases indexed by defendant, plaintiff; on computer from 1995 to present, and only court searches those records. Public can search prior records on index cards and look-up. State law requires records be retained for 20 years. Mail turnaround time 1-2 weeks.

Criminal Records: Access: Mail, in person. Both court and visitors may perform in person searches. No search fee. Court makes copy: $1.00 per page. Required to search: name, years to search; also helpful: DOB. Criminal records on computer from 1995 to present, and only court searches those records. Public can search prior records on index cards and look-up. State law requires records be retained for 10 years. Mail turnaround time 1-2 weeks.

General Information: No public access terminal. No impounded records released. Will fax documents for $.00 per page fax fee. Certification fee: $2.50 per page includes copy fee. Payee: District Court. Personal checks accepted. Prepayment required.

Brighton District Court 52 Academy Hill Rd, Brighton, MA 02135; phone: 617-782-6521; fax: 617-254-2127; hours 8:30AM-4:30PM (EST). *Felony, Misdemeanor, Civil, Eviction, Small Claims.*

Note: Includes Allston and Brighton.

Civil Records: Access: In person only. Visitors must perform in person searches themselves. Court makes copy: $1.00 per page. Required to search: name, years to search. Civil cases indexed by defendant, plaintiff; on index cards or docket books back to 1980. State law requires records be retained for 10 years.

Criminal Records: Access: Phone, mail, in person. Visitors must perform in person searches themselves. No search fee. Court makes copy: $1.00 per page. Required to search: name, years to search, DOB. Computerized records from 1990, criminal records on index cards or docket books back to 1978. State law requires records be retained for 10 years. Mail turnaround time 1-2 weeks.

General Information: No public access terminal. No sealed or impounded records released. Certification fee: $2.50 per page. Payee: District Court. Personal checks accepted. Prepayment required.

Charlestown District Court 3 City Square, Charlestown, MA 02129; phone: 617-242-5400; fax: 617-242-1677; hours 8:30AM-4:30PM (EST). *Felony, Misdemeanor, Civil, Eviction, Small Claims.*

Civil Records: Access: Fax, mail, in person. Only the court performs in person searches; visitors may not. No search fee. Court makes copy: $1.00 per page. Required to search: name, years to search. Civil cases indexed by defendant, plaintiff; on index cards or docket books. State law requires records be retained for 10 years. Mail turnaround time 1-2 weeks.

Criminal Records: Access: Fax, mail, in person. Only the court performs in person searches; visitors may not. No search fee. Court makes copy: $1.00 per page. Required to search: name, years to search; also helpful: DOB. Criminal records on index cards or docket books. State law requires records be retained for 10 years. Mail turnaround time 1-2 weeks.

General Information: No public access terminal. No juvenile records released. Certification fee: $2.50 per cert. Payee: District Court. Personal checks accepted. Prepayment required.

Chelsea District Court 120 Broadway, Chelsea, MA 02150-2606; phone: 617-660-9200; hours 8:30AM-4:30PM (EST). *Felony, Misdemeanor, Civil, Eviction, Small Claims.*

Note: Includes Chelsea and Revere.

Civil Records: Access: Phone, mail, in person. Only the court performs in person searches; visitors may not. No search fee. Court makes copy: $1.00 per page. Required to search: name, years to search. Civil cases indexed by defendant, plaintiff; on index cards or docket books back to 1900; on computer back to 1990. Mail turnaround time 1-2 weeks.

Criminal Records: Access: Phone, mail, in person. Only the court performs in person searches; visitors may not. No search fee. Court makes copy: $1.00 per page. Required to search: name, years to search; also helpful: address, DOB. Criminal records on index cards or docket books back to 1900; on computer back to 1990. Mail turnaround 1-2 weeks.

General Information: No public access terminal. No closed cases, impounded, sealed, mental health commitment, alcoholic or victim of sexual offense records released. Certification fee: $2.50. Payee: District Court. Personal checks accepted. Prepayment and SASE required.

Dorchester District Court 510 Washington St, Dorchester, MA 02124; phone: 617-288-9500; criminal phone: x239; civil phone: x229; criminal/civil fax: 617-436-8250; hours 8:30AM-4:30PM (EST). *Felony, Misdemeanor, Civil, Eviction, Small Claims.*

Civil Records: Access: Mail, in person. Both court and visitors may perform in person searches. No search fee. Court makes copy: $1.00 per page. Required to search: name, years to search. Civil cases indexed by defendant, plaintiff; on index cards or docket books from 1970. State law requires records be retained for 20 years. Mail turnaround time 1-2 weeks.

Criminal Records: Access: Mail, in person. Only the court performs in person searches; visitors may not. No search fee. Court makes copy: $1.00 per page. Required to search: name, years to search, DOB. Criminal records on index cards or docket books to 1950's; on computer since 1998. State law requires records be retained for 20 years. Mail turnaround time 1-2 weeks.

General Information: No public access terminal. No juvenile records released. Will fax documents to local or toll free line. Certification fee: $2.50 per page. Payee: District Court. Personal checks accepted. Prepayment required.

East Boston District Court 37 Meridian St, East Boston, MA 02128; phone: 617-569-7550; criminal/civil fax: 617-561-4988; hours 8:30AM-4:30PM (EST). *Misdemeanor, Civil Actions Under $25,000, Eviction, Small Claims.*

Note: Includes East Boston and Winthrop.

Civil Records: Access: In person. Both court and visitors may perform in person searches. No search fee. Court makes copy: $1.00 per page. Required to search: name, years to search. Civil cases indexed by defendant, plaintiff; on index cards or docket books since 1965, computerized since 1988. State law requires records be retained for 20 years.

Criminal Records: Access: In person. Both court and visitors may perform in person searches. No search fee. Court makes copy: $1.00 per page. Required to search: name, years to search. Criminal records on index cards or docket books, computerized since 1988. State law requires records be retained for 20 years.

General Information: No public access terminal. No juvenile records released. Will fax documents. Certification fee: $1.50 per page. Payee: Boston Municipal Court/ East Boston Division. Personal checks accepted. Prepayment required.

Roxbury District Court 85 Warren St, Roxbury, MA 02119; phone: 617-427-7000 x1; fax: 617-541-0286; hours 8:30AM-4:30PM (EST). *Felony, Misdemeanor, Civil, Eviction, Small Claims.*

Civil Records: Access: Phone, fax, mail, in person. Both court and visitors may perform in person searches. No search fee. Court makes copy: $1.00 per page. Required to search: name, years to search. Civil cases indexed by defendant, plaintiff; on index cards or docket books since 1981; on computer back to 1999. State law requires records be retained for 10 years. Mail turnaround time 1-2 weeks.

Criminal Records: Access: Phone, fax, mail, in person. Both court and visitors may perform in person searches. No search fee. Court makes copy:

$1.00 per page. Required to search: name, years to search, DOB; also helpful: address. Criminal records on index cards or docket books since 1981; on computer back to 1999. State law requires records be retained for 10 years. Mail turnaround time 1-2 weeks.

General Information: Public terminal goes back to 1999. No juvenile records released. Fee to fax documents is $1.00 per page. Certification fee: $2.50 per cert. Payee: District Court. Prepayment required.

South Boston District Court 535 E Broadway, South Boston, MA 02127; phone: 617-268-9292/9293; fax: 617-268-7321; hours 8:30AM-4:30PM (EST). *Felony, Misdemeanor, Civil, Eviction, Small Claims.*

Civil Records: Access: In person only. Visitors must perform in person searches themselves. Court makes copy: $1.00 per page. Required to search: name, years to search, address. Civil cases indexed by defendant, plaintiff; on index cards or docket books. Records go back 20 years.

Criminal Records: Access: In person only. Visitors must perform in person searches themselves. Court makes copy: $1.00 per page. Required to search: name, years to search, address, DOB. Criminal records on index cards or docket books. Records go back 20 years; from 2000 on computer.

General Information: No public access terminal. No juvenile or medical records released. Certification fee: $2.50 per cert. Payee: District Court. Personal checks accepted. Prepayment required.

West Roxbury District Court 445 Arborway, Courthouse, Jamaica Plain, MA 02130; phone: 617-971-1200; hours 8:30AM-4:30PM (EST). *Felony, Misdemeanor, Civil, Eviction, Small Claims.*

Note: Includes West Roxbury, Jamaica Plain, Hyde Park, Roslindale, Parts of Mission Hill, and Mattapan sections of Boston.

Civil Records: Access: In person only. Visitors must perform in person searches themselves. Court makes copy: $1.00 per page. Required to search: name, years to search; also helpful: address. Civil cases indexed by defendant, plaintiff; on index cards or docket books. State law requires records be retained for 10 years. Include type of civil action to be searched.

Criminal Records: Access: In person. Visitors must perform in person searches themselves. No search fee. Court makes copy: $1.00 per page. Required to search: name, years to search; also helpful: DOB. Criminal records on index cards or docket books. State law requires records be retained for 10 years.

General Information: No public access terminal. No juvenile records released. Certification fee: $2.50. Payee: District Court. Personal checks accepted. Prepayment required.

Boston Housing Court 24 New Chardon St, 3rd Fl, Edward W Brooke Courthouse, Boston, MA 02114; phone: 617-788-8485; fax: 617-788-8981; hours 8:30AM-4:30PM (EST). *Eviction, Misdemeanor (Code Violations) for residential, commercial or industrial property.*

www.mass.gov/courts/

Note: Small claims phone is 617-788-8515. Includes many housing code cases, real estate-related small claims and eviction cases for Suffolk County, except Revere, Winthrop and Chelsea.

Probate & Family Court 24 New Chardon St, Edward W Brooke Courthouse, PO Box 9667, Boston, MA 02114-4703; phone: 617-788-8300; fax: 617-788-8962; hours 8AM-5PM (EST). *Probate.*

Worcester County

Superior Court 2 Main St Rm 21, Worcester, MA 01608; phone: 508-770-1899; fax: na/; hours 8AM-4:30PM (EST). *Felony, Civil Actions Over $25,000.*

Civil Records: Access: Mail, in person. Both court and visitors may perform in person searches. No search fee. Court makes copy: $1.00 per page.

Required to search: name, years to search. Civil cases indexed by defendant, plaintiff; on computer from 1990, index books from 1900. Mail turnaround time 1 week.

Criminal Records: Access: Mail, in person. Both court and visitors may perform in person searches. No search fee. Court makes copy: $1.00 per page. Required to search: name, years to search. Criminal records on computer from 1990, index books from 1900. Mail turnaround time 1 week.

General Information: Public terminal goes back to 1990. No impounded or juvenile records released. Certification fee: $2.50 per cert. Payee: Clerk of Superior Court. Personal checks accepted. Prepayment required.

Clinton District Court 300 Boylston St, Clinton, MA 01510; phone: 978-368-7811; criminal/civil fax: 978-368-7827; hours 8:30AM-4:30PM (EST). *Felony, Misdemeanor, Civil, Eviction, Small Claims.*

Note: Includes Berlin, Bolton, Boylston, Clinton, Harvard, Lancaster, Sterling, and West Boylston.

Civil Records: Access: Mail, in person. Only the court performs in person searches; visitors may not. No search fee. Court makes copy: $1.00 per page; same fee for self serve. Required to search: name, years to search; also helpful: DOB, SSN. Civil cases indexed by defendant, plaintiff; on index cards or docket books back to 1968. State law requires records be retained for 20 years. Mail turnaround time 1-2 weeks.

Criminal Records: Access: Mail, in person. Only the court performs in person searches; visitors may not. No search fee. Court makes copy: $1.00 per page; same fee for self serve. Required to search: name, years to search, address, DOB, SSN, signed release. Criminal records on index cards or docket books back to 1978. State law requires records be retained for 20 years. Mail turnaround time 1-2 weeks.

General Information: No public access terminal. No juvenile records released. Will not fax documents. Certification fee: $1.50 per page. Payee: District Court Clerk Magistrate. Prepayment and SASE required.

Dudley District Court 64 PO Box 100, Dudley, MA 01571; phone: 508-943-7123; fax: 508-949-0015; hours 8AM-4:30PM (EST). *Felony, Misdemeanor, Civil, Eviction, Small Claims.*

Note: Includes Charlton, Dudley, Oxford, Southbridge, Sturbridge, and Webster.

Civil Records: Access: Phone, fax, mail, in person. Both court and visitors may perform in person searches. No search fee. Court makes copy: $1.00 per page; same fee for self serve. Required to search: name, years to search. Civil cases indexed by defendant, plaintiff; on computer back to 2002; prior on index cards or docket books; records retained for 10 years. Mail turnaround time 1-2 weeks.

Criminal Records: Access: Phone, fax, mail, in person. Both court and visitors may perform in person searches. No search fee. Court makes copy: $1.00 per page; same fee for self serve. Required to search: name, years to search, DOB. Criminal records on computer back to 6/96; prior records on index cards or docket books; records retained for 10 years. Mail turnaround time 1-2 weeks.

General Information: Public terminal has only civil records back to 2002. No juvenile records released. Certification fee: $2.50. Payee: District Court. Business checks accepted. Prepayment required.

East Brookfield District Court 544 E Main St, East Brookfield, MA 01515-1701; phone: 508-885-6305 x109; fax: 508-885-7623; hours 8:30AM-4:30PM (EST). *Felony, Misdemeanor, Civil, Eviction, Small Claims.*

Note: Includes Brookfield, East Brookfield, Hardwick, Leicester, New Braintree, North Brookfield, Spencer, Warren, and West Brookfield.

Civil Records: Access: Mail, in person. Both court and visitors may perform in person searches. No search fee. Court makes copy: $1.00 per page.

Required to search: name, years to search. Civil cases indexed by defendant, plaintiff; on index cards or docket books. State law requires records be retained for 10 years. Mail turnaround time when possible; strongly suggest to use a retriever when possible.

Criminal Records: Access: Mail, in person. Both court and visitors may perform in person searches. No search fee. Court makes copy: $1.00 per page. Required to search: name, years to search; also helpful: DOB. Criminal records on index cards or docket books to 1945, computerized since 1999. Mail turnaround time 1-2 weeks; strongly suggest to use a retriever when possible.

General Information: Public terminal has only civil records back to 2004. (Terminal has civil and small claims only.) No juvenile, mental health records released. Certification fee: $2.50 per cert. Payee: District Court. Personal checks accepted. Prepayment required. SASE requested.

Fitchburg District Court 16 100 Elm St, Fitchburg, MA 01420; phone: 978-345-2111; fax: 978-342-2461; hours 8:30AM-4:30PM (EST). *Felony, Misdemeanor, Civil, Eviction, Small Claims.*
Note: Includes Fitchburg and Lunenburg.
Civil Records: Access: In person only. Visitors must perform in person searches themselves. Court makes copy: $1.00 per page. Required to search: name, years to search. Civil cases indexed by defendant, plaintiff; on index cards or docket books back 10 years.
Criminal Records: Access: In person only. Visitors must perform in person searches themselves. Court makes copy: $1.00 per page. Required to search: name, years to search. Criminal records on index cards or docket books back 10 years; on computer back to 1994.
General Information: Public use terminal available. No juvenile or mental health records released. Will not fax specific case file. Certification fee: $2.50. Payee: District Court. Personal checks accepted. Prepayment required.

Gardner District Court 108 Matthews St, Gardner, MA 01440-0040; phone: 978-632-2373; fax: 978-630-3902; hours 8:30AM-4:30PM (EST). *Felony, Misdemeanor, Civil, Small Claims.*
Note: Includes Gardner, Hubbardston, Petersham, and Westminster.
Civil Records: Access: Mail, in person. Both court and visitors may perform in person searches. No search fee. Court makes copy: $1.00 per page. Required to search: name, years to search, address. Civil cases indexed by defendant, plaintiff; on index cards or docket books. State law requires records be retained for 10 years. Mail turnaround time 1-2 weeks; quicker for phone and fax verifications.
Criminal Records: Access: Phone, fax, mail, in person. Both court and visitors may perform in person searches. No search fee. Court makes copy: $1.00 per page. Required to search: name, years to search, DOB. Criminal records on index cards or docket books. State law requires records be retained for 10 years. Mail turnaround time 1-2 weeks; quicker for phone and fax verifications.
General Information: No public access terminal. No juvenile records released. No fee to fax documents. Certification fee: $2.50 per cert. Payee: District Court. Personal checks accepted. Prepayment required.

Leominster District Court 25 School St, Leominster, MA 01453; phone: 978-537-3722; fax: 978-537-3970; hours 8:30AM-4:30PM (EST). *Felony, Misdemeanor, Civil, Eviction, Small Claims.*
Note: Includes Princeton and Leominster.
Civil Records: Access: Phone, mail, in person. Both court and visitors may perform in person searches. No search fee. Court makes copy: $1.00 per page. Required to search: name, years to search. Civil cases indexed by defendant, plaintiff; on index cards or

docket books. State law requires records be retained for 10 years. Mail turnaround time 1-2 weeks.
Criminal Records: Access: Phone, mail, in person. Both court and visitors may perform in person searches. No search fee. Court makes copy: $1.00 per page. Required to search: name, years to search; also helpful: DOB. Criminal records on computer since 1987; Prior records on index cards or docket books. State law requires records be retained for 10 years. Mail turnaround time 1-2 weeks.
General Information: No public access terminal. No juvenile or impounded records released. Certification fee: $2.50 per cert. Payee: District Court. Personal checks accepted. Prepayment required.

Milford District Court PO Box 370, Milford, MA 01757; phone: 508-473-1260; hours 8:30AM-4:30PM (EST). *Felony, Misdemeanor, Civil, Eviction, Small Claims.*
Note: Includes Mendon, Upton, Hopedale, and Milford in Worcester County; also includes Bellingham in Norfolk County.
Civil Records: Access: In person only. Both court and visitors may perform in person searches. No search fee. Court makes copy: $1.00 per page. Required to search: name, years to search. Civil cases indexed by defendant, plaintiff; on index cards or docket books.
Criminal Records: Access: In person only. Both court and visitors may perform in person searches. No search fee. Court makes copy: $1.00 per page. Required to search: name, years to search, DOB; also helpful: aliases. Criminal records on computer since 1998; prior records on index cards & docket books; computer indexes only searchable by court.
General Information: Public terminal has only civil records back to 2004. (Civil and small claims records only.) No mental health, impounded, alcohol, commitment, sexual abuse victim, waivers of fees or costs for indigents, delinquency, C & P, CHINS, 209A minor or 209A address records released. Certification fee: $2.50. Payee: District Court. Business checks accepted. Prepayment required.

Uxbridge District Court 261 S Main St, Uxbridge, MA 01569; phone: 508-278-2454; fax: 508-278-2929; hours 8:30AM-4:30PM (EST). *Felony, Misdemeanor, Civil, Eviction, Small Claims.*
Note: Includes Blackstone, Douglas, Millville, Northbridge, Sutton, and Uxbridge.
Civil Records: Access: Mail, in person. Only the court performs in person searches; visitors may not. No search fee. Court makes copy: $1.00 per page. Required to search: name, years to search. Civil cases indexed by defendant, plaintiff; on index cards or docket books. State law requires records be retained for 10 years. All requests must be in writing. Mail turnaround time 1-2 weeks.
Criminal Records: Access: Mail, in person. Only the court performs in person searches; visitors may not. No search fee. Court makes copy: $1.00 per page. Required to search: name, years to search; also helpful: DOB. Criminal records on index cards or docket books. State law requires records be retained for 10 years. All requests must be in writing. Mail turnaround time 1-2 weeks.
General Information: No public access terminal. Certification fee: $2.50. Payee: District Court. Personal checks accepted. Prepayment required.

Westborough District Court 175 Milk St, Westborough, MA 01581; phone: 508-366-8266; fax: 508-366-8268; hours 8AM-4:30PM (EST). *Felony, Misdemeanor, Civil, Eviction, Small Claims.*
Note: Includes Grafton, Northborough, Shrewsbury, Southborough, and Westborough.
Civil Records: Access: In person. Both court and visitors may perform in person searches. No search fee. Court makes copy: $1.00 per page. Required to search: name, years to search. Civil cases indexed by

defendant, plaintiff. Civil records go back to 1986, on books and cards.
Criminal Records: Access: Mail, in person. Both court and visitors may perform in person searches. No search fee. Court makes copy: $1.00 per page. Required to search: name, years to search; also helpful: DOB. Criminal records go back to 1986, on books and cards. Mail turnaround time 5 days.
General Information: No public access terminal. No impounded, juvenile records released. Certification fee: $2.50 per cert. Payee: District Court Westborough Division. Personal checks accepted. Prepayment and SASE required.

Winchendon District Court 80 Central St, Winchendon, MA 01475; phone: 978-297-0156; fax: 978-297-0161; hours 8:30AM-4:30PM (EST). *Felony, Misdemeanor, Civil, Eviction, Small Claims.*
Note: Includes Ashburnham, Winchendon, Phillipston, Royalston, and Templeton.
Civil Records: Access: Phone, mail, in person. Both court and visitors may perform in person searches. No search fee. Court makes copy: $1.00 per page. Required to search: name, years to search. Civil cases indexed by defendant, plaintiff; on index cards or docket books. State law requires records be retained for 10 years. Mail turnaround time 1-2 weeks.
Criminal Records: Access: Mail, in person. Both court and visitors may perform in person searches. No search fee. Court makes copy: $1.00 per page. Required to search: name, years to search; also helpful: DOB, docket number. Criminal records on index cards or docket books. State law requires records be retained for 10 years. Mail turnaround time 1-2 weeks.
General Information: Public terminal has criminal back to 1995 and civil back to 2004. (The further back, the less complete the case record database is.) Certification fee: $2.50 per page. Payee: District Court. Personal checks accepted. Prepayment required.

Worcester District Court 50 Harvard St, Worcester, MA 01608; phone: 508-757-8350; fax: 508-797-0716; hours 8AM-4:30PM (EST). *Felony, Misdemeanor, Civil, Eviction, Small Claims.*
Note: Includes Auburn, Millbury, and Worcester.
Civil Records: Access: Mail, in person. Both court and visitors may perform in person searches. No search fee. Court makes copy: $1.00 per page. Required to search: name, years to search. Civil cases indexed by defendant, plaintiff; on index cards or docket books since 1982. State law requires records be retained for 20 years. Mail turnaround time 1-2 weeks.
Criminal Records: Access: Mail, in person. Both court and visitors may perform in person searches. No search fee. Court makes copy: $1.00 per page. Required to search: name, years to search. Criminal records on computer since 1999; prior records on docket books since 1982. Mail turnaround time 1-2 weeks.
General Information: Public terminal has criminal back to 1999 and civil back to 2001. No sealed, expunged, adoption or sex offense records released. Will not fax documents. Certification fee: $2.50. Payee: District Court. Personal checks accepted. Prepayment required.

Probate & Family Court 2 Main St, Worcester, MA 01608; phone: 508-770-0825 x217; fax: 508-752-6138; hours 8:30AM-4:00PM (EST). *Probate.*

Worcester Housing Court 2 Main St, Rm #101, Worcester, MA 01608; phone: 508-792-0800; hours 8:30AM-4:30PM (EST). *Eviction, Misdemeanor (Code Violations), Small Claims.*
Note: Includes housing code cases, real estate-related small claims and many eviction cases for Worcester County; also see district courts.

Massachusetts Recording Offices

ORGANIZATION: 14 counties, 312 towns, and 39 cities; 21 recording offices and 365 UCC filing offices. Each town/city profile indicates the county in which the town/city is located. Filing locations vary depending upon the type of document, as noted below. Berkshire and Bristol counties each has three recording offices. Essex, Middlesex and Worcester counties each has two recording offices. Cities/towns bearing the same name as a county are Barnstable, Essex, Franklin, Hampden, Nantucket, Norfolk, Plymouth, and Worcester. Some UCC financing statements on personal property collateral are were submitted to cities/towns until June 30, 2001, while real estate recording is handled by the counties. Recording officers are Town/City Clerk (UCC), County Register of Deeds (real estate), and Clerk of US District Court (federal tax liens). The entire state is in the Eastern Time Zone (EST).

REAL ESTATE RECORDS: Real estate records are located at the county level. Each town/city profile indicates the county in which the town/city is located. Counties will not perform searches. Copy fee with certification is usually $.75 per page. Each town also has Assessor/Tax Collector/Treasurer offices from which real estate ownership and tax information is available.

UCC RECORDS: This was a dual filing state. Until July 1, 2001, financing statements were usually filed both with the Town/City clerk and at the state level, except for real estate related collateral, which is recorded at the county Register of Deeds. Now, all filing are at the state except for the real estate related collateral. Most all recording offices perform searches. Use search request form UCC-11. Search fees are usually $10.00 per debtor name. Copy fees vary widely.

TAX LIEN RECORDS: Federal tax liens on personal property were filed with the Town/City Clerks prior to 1970. Since that time, federal tax liens on personal property are filed with the US District Court in Boston as well as with the towns/cities. Following is how to search the central index for federal tax liens - Address:

> US District Court (617-748-9152)
> 1 Courthouse Way.
> Boston, MA 02110

The federal tax liens are indexed here on a computer system. Searches are available by mail or in person. Do not use the telephone. The court suggests including the Social Security number and/or address of individual names in your search request in order to narrow the results. A mail search costs $15.00 and will take about two weeks. Copies are included. Make your check payable to Clerk, US District Court. You can do the search yourself at no charge on their public computer terminal.

State tax liens on personal property are filed with the Town/City Clerk or Tax Collector. All tax liens against real estate are filed with the county Register of Deeds. Some towns file state tax liens on personal property with the UCC index and include tax liens on personal property automatically with a UCC search. Others will perform a separate state tax lien search, usually for a fee of $10.00 plus $1.00 per page of copies.

OTHER LIENS: Medical, town/city tax, child support.

ONLINE ACCESS: A large number of towns and several counties offer online access to assessor records via the Internet for no charge. Also, a private vendor has placed on the Internet the assessor records from a number of towns. Visit www.visionappraisal.com/databases/mass/index.htm

---

Abington Town

Town Clerk, 500 Gliniewicz Way, Abington, MA 02351. 781-982-2112, R/E recording phone-781-982-2107; fax-781-982-2138; hours: 8:30AM-4:30PM www.abingtonmass.com
Separate indices to search. Records indexed on computer back to 1999. Only the public may search. Real estate records located at Plymouth County. Copy fee $.50 per page. Cert fee- $5.00 per cert plus copy fee. Payee- Town of Abington. **Online access to Assessor records:** Search town assessor database at http://data.visionappraisal.com/AbingtonMA/. Does not require a username & password. Simply click on link. **Other phones:** Treasurer- 781-982-2131; Elections- 781-982-2112; Vital Records- 781-982-2112. **Property tax/Assessor-** same address. 781-982-2107.

Acton Town

Town Clerk, 472 Main St; Town Hall, Acton, MA 01720. 978-264-9615, R/E recording phone-978-264-9618; fax-978-264-9630; hours: 8AM-5PM www.acton-ma.gov
No real estate recordings. Only the public may search. Copy fee $1.00 per page. Cert fee- $5.00 per doc plus copy fee. Payee- Town of Acton.

Other phones: Treasurer- 978-264-9612; Elections-978-264-9615; Vital Records- 978-264-9615. **Property tax/Assessor-** 978-264-9622.

Acushnet Town

Town Clerk, 122 Main St; Town Hall, Acushnet, MA 02743. 508-998-0215; fax-508-998-0203; hours: 8AM-4PM
No real estate recordings. All records in one index. Office personnel or visitors may perform searches. Personnel search time is 7-10 days. Search fee $20.00 per name. Copy fee $.25 per page. Payee- Town of Acushnet. **Other phones:** Treasurer- 508-998-0212; Vital Records- 508-998-0215. **Property tax/Assessor-** 122 Main St, Acushnet, MA 02743; 508-998-0205.

Adams Town

Town Clerk, 8 Park St, Adams, MA 01220. 413-743-8320; fax-413-743-8316; hours: 8:30AM-4PM
No real estate recordings. Office personnel or visitors may perform searches. Search fee $10.00 per name. Real estate records located at Berkshire County. Copy fee $2.00 per page. Cert fee- $.25 per page. Payee- Town Clerk of Adams. **Property tax/Assessor-** 413-743-8350.

Agawam Town

Town Clerk, 36 Main St., Agawam, MA 01001-1837. 413-786-0400 x215; fax-413-786-9927; hours: 8:30AM-4:30PM www.agawam.ma.us
No real estate recordings. All records in one index. Record index not computerized. Office personnel or visitors may perform searches. Real estate records located at Hampden County. UCC search per debtor name- $10.00. Copy fee $.25 per page. Cert fee- $5.00 per page plus copy fee. Payee- Town of Agawam. **Online access to Property Assessor, Real Estate, Recording, Lien records:** Access Property Assessment Data free at http://agawam.patriotproperties.com/default.asp. See Hampden County for recording records searching. **Other phones:** Treasurer- 413-786-0400 x221; Elections- 413-786-0400 x215; Vital Records- 413-786-0400 x216. **Property tax/Assessor-** same address as above. 413-786-0400 x205.

Alford Town

Town Clerk, 5 Alford Center Rd; Town Hall, Alford, MA 01230-8914. 413-528-4536; fax-413-528-4581; hours: 4:30-7:30PM Th
No real estate recordings. Only the public may search. Payee- Town of Alford. **Online access to**

Property, Assessor records: Access property data free at http://csc-ma.us/AlfordPubAcc/jsp/Home.jsp. **Property tax/Assessor-** 413-528-4536 x2.

Amesbury Town

Town Clerk, 62 Friend St; Town Hall, Amesbury, MA 01913. 978-388-8100; fax-978-388-8150; hours: 8AM-4PM M-Th; 5PM-8PM Th; 8AM-N F www.amesburyma.gov
No real estate recordings. Only the office personnel may search. All unrestricted records are available. Search fee $10.00 per name. Real estate records located at Essex County. Copy fee $1.00 per page. Cert fee- No fee for cert, but copy fee charged. Payee- Town of Amesbury. **Online access to Assessor records:** Search the town assessor data at http://data.visionappraisal.com/AmesburyMA/. Free registration for full data. **Other phones:** Treasurer- 978-388-8105; Elections- 978-388-8100; Vital Records- 978-388-8100. **Property tax/Assessor-** same address as above. 978-388-8102.

Amherst Town

Town Clerk, 4 Boltwood Ave.; Town Hall, Amherst, MA 01002. RE & UCC recording phone-413-256-4035; fax-413-256-4007; hours: 8AM-4:30PM
No real estate recordings. Record index not computerized. Only the public may search, but clerk searches UCC. Real estate records located at Hampshire County. Tax lien searches conducted in Treasurer Office. UCC search per debtor name-$30.00. Copy fee $2.00 per page. Cert fee- $10.00 per cert plus copy fee. Payee- Town of Amherst. **Online access to Assessor records:** Search the town assessor data at http://data.visionappraisal.com/AmherstMA/. Free registration for full data. **Other phones:** Treasurer- 413-256-4020; Elections- 413-256-4035; Vital Records- 413-256-4035. **Property tax/Assessor-** 413-256-4024.

Andover Town

Town Clerk, 36 Bartlet St, Andover, MA 01810-3882. 978-623-8256, R/E recording phone-978-623-8200, UCC recording phone-978-623-8200; fax-978-623-8221; 8:30-4:30PM http://andoverma.gov/clerk/
No real estate recordings. All records in one index. Record index not computerized. Only the office personnel may search. Real estate records located at Essex County. Will search UCC records and tax liens. UCC search per debtor name- $10.00. Federal/state combined tax lien search- $10.00 per search. General copy fee $2.00 per copy/filing. Tax lien copy- $1.00 per copy/filing. Cert fee-$2.00 per cert plus copy fee. Payee- Town of Andover. **Online access to Assessor, Land, Grantor/Grantee, Recording records:** Property tax records on the Assessor's database are free at www.town.andover.ma.us/assess/values.htm. Also, search the recorder database for free at www.lawrencedeeds.com/dsSearch.asp. **Other phones:** Treasurer- 978-623-8200; Elections- 978-623-8200; Vital Records- 978-623-8200. **Property tax/Assessor-** 978-623-8200.

Arlington Town

Town Clerk, 730 Mass Ave; Town Hall, Arlington, MA 02476-9109. 781-316-3073, R/E recording phone-781-316-3051, UCC recording phone-781-316-3051; fax-781-316-3079; hours: 8AM-4PM, M-W, 8AM-7PM,Th, 8-N, Fri www.town.arlington.ma.us
No real estate recordings. Index: Card Index. Record index not computerized. Office personnel or visitors may perform searches. Search fee $15.00. Real estate records located at Middlesex County. Copy fee $2.00 per page. Cert fee- $10.00 per page plus copy fee. Payee- Town of Arlington. **Online access to Assessor records:** Search the town assessor database for free at http://arlserver.town.arlington.ma.us/property.html. There is also a website at http://arlingtonma.virtualtownhall.net/Search for searching for names on town public records. **Other phones:** Treasurer- 781-316-3030; Elections- 781-316-

3070; Vital Records- 781-316-3070. **Property tax/Assessor-** same address. 781-316-3051.

Ashburnham Town

Town Clerk, 32 Main St, Ashburnham, MA 01430. 978-827-4102; fax-978-827-4105; hours: 9AM-5PM (7-9PM 1st & 3rd Mon of month)
No real estate recordings. Record index not computerized. Office personnel or visitors may perform searches. Search fee $5.00 per name. Real estate records located at Worcester County. Copy fee $.50 per page. Payee- Town of Ashburnham. **Other phones:** Treasurer- 978-827-4102; Elections-978-827-4102; Vital Records- 978-827-4102. **Property tax/Assessor-** 978-827-4100.

Ashby Town

Town Clerk, 895 Main St., Ashby, MA 01431. 978-386-2424; fax-978-386-2490; hours: 9AM-2PM, 6-8PM W
No real estate recordings. All records in one index. Record index not computerized. Only the public may search. Real estate records located at Middlesex County. Copy fee $2.00 per page. Payee- Town of Ashby. **Online access to Property, Assessor records:** Access to property data is free at http://csc-ma.us/PropertyContent/jsp/Home.jsp?Page=1. Click on Ashby Town. **Other phones:** Treasurer- 978-386-2424; Elections- 978-386-2424; Vital Records- 978-386-2424. **Property tax/Assessor-** same address as above. 978-386-2427.

Ashfield Town

Town Clerk, PO Box 560, Ashfield, MA 01330-0595. RE & UCC recording phone-413-628-4441; fax-413-628-4588; hours: 9AM-12:30PM, 1:30-5PM M-W,F; 7-9PM F www.ashfield.org
No real estate recordings. Only the public may search. Copy fee $2.00, if tax lien $.25 per page. Payee- Town of Ashfield. **Other phones:** Treasurer-413-628-4441; Elections- 413-628-4441; Vital Records- 413-628-4441; Town Collector- 413-628-4428. **Property tax/Assessor-** 413-628-4439.

Ashland Town

Town Clerk, 101 Main St; Town Hall, Ashland, MA 01721. 508-881-0101; fax-508-881-0102; hours: 8:30AM-4:30PM www.ashlandmass.com
No real estate recordings. Separate indices to search include by year (5 volumes). Record index not computerized. Office personnel or visitors may perform searches. Search fee $10.00 per name. Real estate records located at Middlesex County. Copy fee $1.00 per page. Cert fee- $5.00 per seal plus copy fee. Payee- Town of Ashland. **Other phones:** Treasurer- 508-881-0107; Elections- 508-881-0101; Vital Records- 508-881-0101. **Property tax/Assessor-** same address as above. 508-881-0104.

Athol Town

Town Clerk, 584 Main St, Athol, MA 01331. 978-249-4551; fax-978-249-2491; hours: 8AM-5PM M,W,Th; 8AM-8PM T;Closed Fri.
No real estate recordings. All records in one index. Only the office personnel may search. Real estate records located at Worcester County. Will search UCC records, search includes tax liens. UCC search per debtor name- $10.00. Copy fee $2.00 for 1st 3 pages; $1.00 each add'l. Cert fee- $7.00 per page, includes copy fee. Payee- Town of Athol. **Other phones:** Treasurer- 978-249-3374; Elections- 978-249-4551; Vital Records- 978-249-4551. **Property tax/Assessor-** same address as above. 978-249-3880.

Attleboro City

City Clerk, 77 Park St; City Hall, Attleboro, MA 02703. 508-223-2222; fax-508-222-3046; hours: 8:30AM-4:30PM
No real estate recordings. Record index not computerized. Office personnel or visitors may perform searches. No search fee. Real estate records located at Bristol County. Separate state tax lien

search- $10.00 per debtor. Copy fee $2.00 per page. Payee- City of Attleboro. **Other phones:** Treasurer- 508-223-2222 x3214; Elections- 508-223-2222 x3271; Vital Records- 508-223-2222 x3111. **Property tax/Assessor-** same address as above. 508-223-2222 x3135.

Auburn Town

Town Clerk, 104 Central St, Auburn, MA 01501. 508-832-7701; fax-508-832-7702; hours: 8AM-4PM; extended hours 2nd & 4th Mon. 8AM-7PM www.auburnguide.com
No real estate recordings. Search fee $10.00 per debtor. Copy fee $2.00 per page. Cert fee- $5.00 per doc plus copy fee. Payee- Town of Auburn. **Other phones:** Treasurer- 508-832-7700; Elections-508-832-7701; Vital Records- 508-832-7701. **Property tax/Assessor-** 508-832-7708.

Avon Town

Town Clerk, Buckley Ctr, Avon, MA 02322. 508-588-0414; fax-508-559-0209; hours: 8:30AM-4:30PM
No real estate recordings. Record index not computerized. Office personnel or visitors may perform searches. Search fee $10.00 per name. Real estate records located at Norfolk County. Copy fee $.25 per page. Payee- Town of Avon. **Other phones:** Treasurer- 508-588-0414. **Property tax/Assessor-** 508-588-0414.

Ayer Town

Town Clerk, PO Box 308, Ayer, MA 01432. 978-772-8215; fax-978-772-8222; hours: 8:30AM-5PM www.ayer.ma.us/
No real estate recordings. Separate indices to search. Record index not computerized. Only the office personnel may search. Search fee $5.00 per name. Real estate records located at Middlesex County. Copy fee $.25 per page. Cert fee- $5.00 per cert plus copy fee. Payee- Town of Ayer. **Online access to Property, Assessor records:** Access to property data is free at http://csc-ma.us/PropertyContent/jsp/Home.jsp?Page=1. Click on Ayer Town. **Other phones:** Treasurer- 978-772-8216; Elections- 978-772-8215; Vital Records- 978-772-8215. **Property tax/Assessor-** PO Box 294, 1 Main St, Ayer, MA 01432; 978-772-8211.

Barnstable County

County Register of Deeds, PO Box 368, Barnstable, MA 02630. 508-362-7733; fax-508-362-5065; hours: 8AM-4PM www.bcrd.co.barnstable.ma.us
Only the public may search. Copy fee $1.00 per page. Cert fee- $10.00 per doc plus copy fee. Payee- Barnstable County Register of Deeds. **Online access to Real Estate, Lien, Deed records:** Access to County records is free at http://199.232.150.242/ALIS/WW400R.PGM. Search for free, but to print requires a $50 annual fee. Records date back to 1940. Lending agency information is available. **Other phones:** Treasurer- 508-362-4653. **Property tax/Assessor-** 508-362-4022.

Barnstable Town

Town Clerk, 367 Main St., Hyannis, MA 02601. 508-862-4044, R/E recording phone-508-362-7733, UCC recording phone-508-862-4094; fax-508-790-6326;: 8:30AM-4:30PM www.town.barnstable.ma.us/tob02/depts/default.asp
No real estate recordings. Hyannis, ZIP Code 02601, is located here, as well as the villages of Barnstable, West Barnstable, Centerville, Cotuit, Osterville and Marstons Mills. Separate indices to search too varied to name. Only the office personnel may search. Search fee $15.00 up to 15 pages, $1.00 each add'l page. Real estate records located at Barnstable County. Copy fee $.20 per page. Cert fee- $5.00 per doc plus copy fee. Payee- Town of Barnstable. **Online access to Assessor records:** Access town assessor records free at www.town.barnstable.ma.us/tob02/DNet/AssessingDNet/Disclaimer.aspx. Email questions or comments to webadm@town.barnstable.ma.us or call the Assessing Dept. at 508-862-4022. **Other**

phones: Treasurer- 508-862-4653; Elections- 508-862-4044; Vital Records- 508-862-4095. **Property tax/Assessor-** same address as above. 508-862-4022.

Barre Town

Town Clerk, PO Box 418, Barre, MA 01005. 978-355-5003, R/E recording phone-978-355-5001; fax-978-355-5025; hours: 7-9PM M,W; 9AM-N, 1-4PM T-F www.town.barre.ma.us/
No real estate recordings. Record index not computerized. Office will perform a UCC search but public must search other records themselves. Search fee $10.00. Real estate records located at Worcester County. Copy fee $1.00 per page. Cert fee- $5.00 per cert plus copy fee. **Other phones:** Treasurer- 978-355-5000; Elections- 978-355-5003; Vital Records- 978-355-5003. **Property tax/Assessor-** PO Box 724, Barre, MA 01005; 978-355-5010.

Becket Town

Town Clerk, 557 Main St.; Jeanne W Pryor, Becket, MA 01223. 413-623-8934; fax-413-623-6036; hours: 9AM-4:30PM M-Tu; Noon-8PM W
No real estate recordings. All records in one index. Record index not computerized. Only the office personnel may search. Real estate records located at Berkshire County. Will not search UCC records or tax liens. Copy fee $1.00 per page. Payee- Town of Becket. **Other phones:** Treasurer- 413-623-8934; Elections- 413-623-8934; Vital Records- 413-623-8934. **Property tax/Assessor-** same address as above. 413-623-8934.

Bedford Town

Town Clerk, 10 Mudge Way; Town Hall, Bedford, MA 01730-0083. 781-275-0083; fax-781-687-6157; hours: 8AM-4PM www.town.bedford.ma.us
No real estate recordings. Record index not computerized. Office personnel or visitors may perform searches. Search fee $10.00 per name. Real estate records located at Middlesex County. General copy fee $2.00 1st page; $1.00 each add'l. Tax lien copy- $.15 per page. Cert fee- $4.00 per cert plus copy fee. Payee- Town of Bedford. **Online access to Property, Assessor records:** Access to property data is free at http://csc-ma.com/PropertyContent/jsp/Home.jsp?Page=1. **Other phones:** Treasurer- 781-275-8996; Appraiser/Auditor- 781-275-0046; Elections- 781-275-0083; Vital Records- 781-275-0083. **Property tax/Assessor-** 781-275-0046.

Belchertown Town

Town Clerk, PO Box 629, Belchertown, MA 01007-0607. 413-323-0281, R/E recording phone-413-584-3637; fax-413-323-0107; hours: 8AM-5PM www.belchertown.org
No real estate recordings. UCC recordings from 7/1/2001 to date are at 617-727-4919. Office personnel or visitors may perform searches. Search fee $5.00 per name. Real estate records located at old county courthouse. UCC records up to 6/30/2001. Copy fee $2.00, if tax lien $.20 per page. Cert fee- $5.00 per page plus copy fee. Payee- Town of Belchertown. **Online access to Property, Assessor records:** Access property data free at http://belchertown.patriotproperties.com/default.asp. **Other phones:** Treasurer- 413-323-0400; Elections- 413-323-0281; Vital Records- 413-323-0281. **Property tax/Assessor-** PO Box 515, 2 Jabish St, Belchertown, MA 01007-0515; 413-323-0413.

Bellingham Town

Town Clerk, PO Box 367, Bellingham, MA 02019-0367. 508-966-5827, R/E recording phone-508-966-5826; fax-508-966-5804; hours: 8:30AM-4:30PM T,W,Th; 8:30AM-1PM F; 8:30AM-7PM M www.bellinghamma.org
No real estate recordings. Record index not computerized. Office will perform a UCC search but public must search other records themselves. Search fee $10.00. Real estate records located at

Norfolk County. Copy fee $2.00 per page. Cert fee- $2.00 per record. Payee- Town of Bellingham. **Online access to Assessor, Property records:** Access property data free at http://bellingham.patriotprop erties.com/default.asp. **Other phones:** Treasurer- 508-966-5828; Elections- 508-966-5827; Vital Records- 508-966-5827. **Property tax/Assessor-** 2 Mechanic St, Rm 4, Bellingham, MA 02019; 508-966-5825.

Belmont Town

Town Clerk, 455 Concord Ave; Town Hall, Belmont, MA 02178-2514. 617-993-2600; fax-617-993-2601; hours: 8AM-4PM www.town.belmont.ma.us
No real estate recordings. Record index not computerized. Only the office personnel may search. Search fee $5.00. Real estate records located at Middlesex County. Copy fee $1.00 per page. Cert fee- $3.00 per doc plus copy fee. Payee- Town of Belmont. **Online access to Assessor, Property records:** Access to the town assessor data is free at http://24.61.156.140/Belmont/. **Other phones:** Treasurer- 617-993-2770; Elections- 617-993-2600; Vital Records- 617-993-2600. **Property tax/Assessor-** 19 Moore St, Belmont, MA 02178; 617-993-2630.

Berkley Town

Town Clerk, 1 N. Main St, Berkley, MA 02779. 508-822-3348; fax-508-822-3511; hours: 9AM-3PM
No real estate recordings. Office personnel or visitors may perform searches. Search fee $5.00 per name. Real estate records located at Bristol County. UCC search per debtor name- $10.00. Copy fee $3.00 per page. Tax lien copy- $.20 per page. Payee- Town of Berkley. **Online access to Property, Assessor records:** Access to property data is free at http://csc-ma.us/PropertyContent/jsp/Home.jsp?Page=1. Click on Berkley Town. **Property tax/Assessor-** 508-822-7955.

Berkshire County (Middle District)

County Register of Deeds, 44 Bank Row, Pittsfield, MA 01201. 413-443-7438; fax-413-448-6025; hours: 8:30AM-4:30PM (No Recording after 3:59PM)
All records in one index. Records indexed on computer back to 1985. Only the public may search. Copy fee $1.00 per page. Cert fee- $1.00 per page plus copy fee. Payee- Commonwealth of Massachusetts. **Online access to Real Estate, Lien records:** Online search: see Berkshire County Middle District. **Property tax/Assessor-** 413-443-5502.

Berkshire County Northern District

Register of Deeds, 65 Park St, #1, Adams, MA 01220. RE & UCC recording phone-413-743-0035; fax-413-743-1003; hours: 8:30AM-4:30PM
Only the public may search. Copy fee $1.00 per page. Payee- Commonwealth of Massachusetts. **Online access to Real Estate, Lien records:** Online search: see Berkshire County Southern District. **Other phones:** Treasurer- 413-743-8390 (Town of Adams); Vital Records- 413-743-8320 (Town of Adams). **Property tax/Assessor-** 413-743-8350 (Town of Adams).

Berkshire County Southern District

County Register of Deeds, 334 Main St, Great Barrington, MA 01230. 413-528-0146; fax-413-528-6878; hours: 8:30AM-4:30PM; Recording hours 8:30AM-4PM
All records in one index. Records indexed on a public use terminal back to 1971. Only the public may search. Copy fee $1.00 per page. Cert fee- $1.00 per page. Payee- Berkshire County Register of Deeds. **Online access to Real Estate, Lien, Recording, Judgment, Deed, Will records:** Searching of Titlesearch records requires a one-time $100 signup and $.50 per minute of use. System provides access to all three District Recorder's records; records date back to 1985. Searchable indices: recorded land, plans, registered land. Lending agency

information available. For information, contact Sharon Henault at 413-443-7438. Also, search Register of Deeds Records for all Berkshire districts free at www.masslandrecords.com. Click on appropriate Division on map.

Berlin Town

Town Clerk, 23 Linden St, Box 8, Berlin, MA 01503. 978-838-2931; fax-978-838-0014; hours: 12-3PM T,Th; 7-9PM W www.townofberlin.com
No real estate recordings. Search fee $10.00. Real estate records located at Worcester County. Copy fee $.50 per page. Payee- Town of Berlin. **Other phones:** Treasurer- 978-838-0344; Elections- 978-838-2931; Vital Records- 978-838-2931; Tax Collector- 978-838-2765. **Property tax/Assessor-** same address as above. 978-838-2256.

Bernardston Town

Town Clerk, PO Box 504, Bernardston, MA 01337-0435. 413-648-5408, R/E recording phone-413-648-5407; fax-413-648-9381; hours: 9AM-2PM
No real estate recordings. Only the public may search. Real estate records located at Franklin County. Copy fee $1.00 per page. Cert fee- $10.00. Payee- Town of Bernardston. **Online access to Property Assessor records:** Access to property data is free at http://csc-ma.us/PropertyContent/jsp/Home.jsp?Page=1. Select Bernardston Town. **Other phones:** Treasurer- 413-648-5400; Elections- 413-648-5408; Vital Records- 413-648-5408; Tax Collector- 413-648-5401. **Property tax/Assessor-** 413-648-5407.

Beverly City

City Clerk, 191 Cabot St, Beverly, MA 01915-1031. 978-921-6000 x164; fax-978-921-8511; hours: 8:30AM-4:30PM M,T,W; 8:30AM-7:30PM Th; 8:30AM-1PM www.beverlyma.gov
Index: More than one index. Record index not computerized. General index search fee $10.00 per file. Copy fee $1.00 per page. Cert fee- $3.00. Payee- City of Beverly. **Online access to Assessor, Property records:** Access city property data free at http://beverly.patriotproperties.com/default.asp. **Other phones:** Treasurer- 978-921-6135; Elections- 978-921-6000 x163; Vital Records- 978-921-6000 x161-165. **Property tax/Assessor-** 978-921-6003, assessor fax- 978-921-6196.

Billerica Town

Town Clerk, 365 Boston Rd; Town Hall, Billerica, MA 01821-1885. 978-671-0924; fax-978-663-6510; hours: 8:30AM-4PM
No real estate recordings. Real estate records located at Middlesex County. Will search UCC records, but not tax liens. UCC search per debtor name- $10.00. Copy fee $2.00 per document. Cert fee- $3.00 per doc plus copy fee. Payee- Town of Billerica. **Online access to Assessor, Property records:** Access property data free at http://billerica.patriotprop erties.com/default.asp. No name searching. **Other phones:** Treasurer- 978-671-0928; Elections- 978-671-0926; Vital Records- 978-671-0924. **Property tax/Assessor-** 365 Boston Rd, Rm 109, Billerica, MA 01821; 978-671-0971.

Blackstone Town

Town Clerk, 15 St Paul St; Municipal Ctr, Blackstone, MA 01504-2295. 508-883-1500 x146; fax-508-883-7043; hours: 9AM-4:30PM M-F, 5:30-7:30PM Tues
No real estate recordings. Office will perform a UCC search but public must search other records themselves. Real estate records located at Worcester County. UCC search per debtor name- $10.00. Copy fee $5.00 per page, certified. Payee- Town of Blackstone. **Other phones:** Treasurer- 508-883-1500 x117; Elections- 508-883-1500 x116; Vital Records- 508-883-1500 x116. **Property tax/Assessor-** 508-883-1500 x122.

Blandford Town

Town Clerk, PO Box 101, Blandford, MA 01008. 413-848-2747, R/E recording phone-413-848-2804, UCC recording phone-413-848-0054; fax-413-848-0908; hours: 6-8PM Mon Evening

No real estate recordings. All records in one index. Record index not computerized. Office will perform a UCC search but public must search other records themselves. Search fee $10.00. Real estate records located at Hampden County. Copy fee $1.00 per page. Payee- Town of Blandford. **Online access to Real Estate, Recording, Lien records:** See Hampden County for recording records searching. **Other phones:** Treasurer- 413-848-2782; Elections- 413-848-0054; Vital Records- 413-848-0054. **Property tax/Assessor**- same address. 413-848-2791.

Bolton Town

Town Clerk, PO Box 278, Bolton, MA 01740. 978-779-2771; fax-978-779-5461; hours: 9AM-2;30PM M, W,Th; 9AM-4, 6-8PM T www.townofbolton.com

No real estate recordings available. Office will perform a UCC search but public must search other records themselves. Real estate records located at Worcester County. Tax liens not included in UCC search. Copy fee $.10 per page. Cert fee- $2.00 per seal. Payee- Town of Bolton. **Online access to Real Estate, Deed, Property, Assessor records:** See Worcester County Southern District for online information. Access to assessor property data free at http://csc-ma.us/PropertyContent/jsp/Home.jsp?Page=1. **Property tax/Assessor**- same address as above. 978-779-5556.

Boston City

City Clerk, 1 City Hall Plaza; City Hall, Rm 601, Boston, MA 02201. 617-635-4601, R/E recording phone-617-788-8575, UCC recording phone-617-727-2800; fax-617-635-4658; hours: 9AM-5PM www.cityofboston.gov/cityclerk/default.asp

No real estate recordings. Deeds for Suffolk County are on file with the Suffolk Co. Registry of Deeds or (617) 725-8575. All records in one index. The public may search for business certificates and UCC, this agency searches for all other documents. Search fee $10.00. Real estate records located at Suffolk County. Will not search UCC records. Copy fee $.50 per page; business certificates $10.00; domestic partnerships $12.00. Payee- City of Boston. **Online access to Assessor records:** Records on the City of Boston Assessor database are free at www.ci.boston.ma.us/assessing/search.asp. Also, property tax bill and payment is searchable by parcel number for free at www.cityofboston.gov/assessing/paysearch.asp. **Other phones:** Treasurer- 617-635-4138; Elections- 617-635-4634; Vital Records- 617-635-4175. **Property tax/Assessor**- 301 City Hall, Boston, MA 02201; 617-635-4287.

Bourne Town

Town Clerk, 24 Perry Ave; Town Hall, Buzzards Bay, MA 02532. 508-759-0613, UCC recording phone-508-759-0600; fax-508-759-8026; 8:30AM-4:30PM

No real estate recordings. All records in one index. Record index not computerized. Office will perform a UCC search but public must search other records themselves. Search fee $10.00. Real estate records located at Barnstable County. Copy fee $.20 per page. Cert fee- $2.00 per page plus copy fee. Payee- Town of Bourne. **Other phones:** Treasurer- 508-759-0600; Elections- 508-759-0600; Vital Records- 508-759-0600. **Property tax/Assessor**- 508-759-0600.

Boxborough Town

Town Clerk, 29 Middle Rd, Boxborough, MA 01719-1499. Main phone & R/E recording-978-263-1116, UCC recording phone-978-263-1116x117; fax-978-264-3127; hours: 10AM-2PM; Closed T; 7-9PM M; 10AM-1PM Th www.town.boxborough.ma.us

No real estate recordings. Separate indices to search include vitals, UCCs. Record index not

computerized. Office will perform a UCC search but public must search other records themselves. Search fee $10.00. Real estate records located at Middlesex County. Copy fee $1.00 per page. Cert fee- $2.00 per seal plus copies. Payee- Town of Boxborough. **Other phones:** Treasurer- 978-263-1116x104; Elections- 978-263-1116x117; Vital Records- 978-263-1116x117. **Property tax/Assessor**- same address as above. 978-263-1116x109.

Boxford Town

Town Clerk, 7A Spofford Rd, Boxford, MA 01921. 978-887-6000 x501; fax-978-887-3546; hours: 8AM-4:30PM M-Th

No real estate recordings. All records in one index. Record index not computerized. Office personnel or visitors may perform searches. Search fee $20.00 per name. Copy fee $1.00 per page. Payee- Town of Boxford. **Other phones:** Treasurer- 978-887-6000 x505; Elections- 978-887-6000 x501; Vital Records- 978-887-6000 x501. **Property tax/Assessor**- same address as above. 978-887-6000 x504.

Boylston Town

Town Clerk, 221 Main St, Boylston, MA 01505. 508-869-2234; fax-508-869-6210; hours: 8AM-2PM M,T; (til 1PM W,TH); 6-8PM M; 9AM-2PM T-Th

No real estate recordings. All records in one index. Record index not computerized. Only the public may search. Real estate records located at Worcester County. Copy fee $1.00 per page. Payee- Town of Boylston. **Other phones:** Treasurer- 508-869-2972; Elections- 508-869-2234; Tax Collector- 508-869-2972. **Property tax/Assessor**- same address as above. 508-869-6543.

Braintree Town

Town Clerk, 1 JFK Memorial Dr, Braintree, MA 02184-6498. 781-794-8000 x8241, UCC recording phone-781-794-8000; fax-781-794-8259; hours: 8:30AM-4:30PM

No real estate recordings. All records in one index. Record index not computerized. Only the office personnel may search. Search fee $10.00. Real estate records located at Norfolk County. Copy fee $2.00, if tax lien or real estate $1.00 1st 3 pages; $1.00 each add'l. Payee- Town of Braintree. **Online access to Assessor, Property records:** Access property data free at http://braintree.patriotproperties.com/default.asp. **Other phones:** Treasurer- 781-794-8060; Elections- 781-794-8241; Vital Records- 781-794-8241. **Property tax/Assessor**- same address as above. 781-794-8050, assessor fax- 781-794-8068.

Brewster Town

Town Clerk, 2198 Main St, Brewster, MA 02631. 508-896-4506; fax-508-896-8089; hours: 8:30AM-4PM www.town.brewster.ma.us

No real estate recordings. Separate indices to search include index cards, files and computer. Records indexed on computer back to 2000. Office personnel or visitors may perform searches. Search fee $16.42 hour. Real estate records located at Barnstable County. Copy fee $.20 per copy. Cert fee- $5.00 per cert plus copy fee. Payee- Town of Brewster. **Other phones:** Treasurer- 508-896-3701 x112; Elections- 508-896-4506; Vital Records- 508-896-4506. **Property tax/Assessor**- same address as above. 508-896-3701 x122.

Bridgewater Town

Town Clerk, 64 Central Sq; Town Hall, Bridgewater, MA 02324. RE & UCC recording phone-508-697-0921; fax-508-697-0941; hours: 8AM-4PM M-Th; 8AM-1PM F www.bridgewaterma.org

No real estate recordings. Record index not computerized. Only the office personnel may search. Real estate records located at Plymouth County. Will search UCC records, but not tax liens. UCC search per debtor name- $10.00. Copy fee $.20 per copy. Cert fee- $5.00 per doc, includes copy fee. Payee- Town of Bridgewater. **Other**

phones: Treasurer- 508-697-0923; Elections- 508-697-0921; Vital Records- 508-697-0921. **Property tax/Assessor**- 64 Central Sq, Town Hall, Bridgewater, MA 02324; 508-697-0928.

Brimfield Town

Town Clerk, PO Box 508, Brimfield, MA 01010. 413-245-4101; fax-413-245-4107; hours: 6:30PM-8PM T; 9-11AM Sat

No real estate recordings. Office personnel or visitors may perform searches. Search fee $10.00 per name. Real estate records located at Hampden County. Copy fee $1.00 per page. Payee- Town of Brimfield. **Online access to Real Estate, Recording, Lien records:** See Hampden County for recording records searching. **Property tax/Assessor**- 413-245-4100.

Bristol County (Fall River District)

County Register of Deeds, 441 N. Main St, Fall River, MA 02720. 508-673-1651, R/E recording phone-508-673-1651 or 2910, UCC recording phone-508-673-1651 or 2910; fax-508-673-7633; hours: 8AM-4:30PM www.fr-registry.com

All records in one index. Records indexed on a public use terminal back to 1986. Only the public may search. Copy fee $1.00 per page. Cert fee- None. Payee- Fall River Registry of Deeds. **Online access to Real Estate, Lien records:** Online search: see Bristol County Southern District. Indexes are 1982 to present. **Property tax/Assessor**- 508-324-2302.

Bristol County (Northern District)

County Register of Deeds, 11 Court St, Taunton, MA 02780-0248. 508-822-0502; fax-508-880-4975; hours: 8AM-4:00PM www.tauntondeeds.com

All records in one index. Records indexed on a public use terminal back to 1982. Only the public may search. Copy fee $1.00 per page. Cert fee- None. Payee- Bristol County Register of Deeds. **Online access to Real Estate, Lien records:** Online search: see Bristol County Southern District. **Other phones:** Treasurer- 508-824-4028.

Bristol County (Southern District)

County Register of Deeds, 25 N. 6th St, New Bedford, MA 02740. 508-993-2603; fax-508-997-4250; hours: 8:30AM-4:30PM www.newbedforddeeds.com

Separate indices to search include recorded land, registered land. Records indexed on a public use terminal back to 1978. Office will perform a UCC search but public must search other records themselves. Copy fee $1.00 per page; $.50 self serve. Cert fee- No extra fee. Payee- Bristol County Register of Deeds. **Online access to Real Estate, Lien records:** Access to County records requires a $100 set up fee and $.50 per minute of use. All three districts are on this system; the record dates vary by district. Lending agency information is available. For information, contact Sherrilynn at 508-993-2605 x17. Real Estate searches found at www.newbedforddeeds.com/mason/main/search/.

Brockton City

City Clerk, 45 School St, Brockton, MA 02401. RE & UCC recording phone-508-580-7114; fax-508-580-7104; 8:30AM-4:30PM www.ci.brockton.ma.us

No real estate recordings here. Only the public may search, but clerk searches real estate UCC. Real estate records located at Plymouth County. UCC search per debtor name- $10.00. Copy fee $1.00 per page. Payee- City of Brockton. **Other phones:** Treasurer- 508-580-7159; Elections- 508-580-7117; Vital Records- 508-580-7114. **Property tax/Assessor**- 508-580-7194.

Brookfield Town

Town Clerk, 6 Central St., Brookfield, MA 01506. 508-867-2930 X12, R/E recording phone-508-867-2930 x15; fax-508-867-5091; hours: 9AM-3PM M W Th, 9AM-2PM T; 9AM-N F www.brookfieldma.us

No real estate recordings. Separate indices to search include all records are in different volumes.

Record index not computerized. Office personnel or visitors may perform searches. General search fee $10.00 per name. Federal/state combined tax lien search- $25.00 per debtor. General copy fee $1.00 per page. Tax lien copy- $.20 per page. Cert fee- $5.00 per copy. Payee- Town of Brookfield. **Online access to Property, Assessor records:** Access to property data is free at http://csc-ma.us/PropertyContent/jsp/Home.jsp?Page=1. Select Brookfield Town. **Other phones:** Treasurer- 508-867-2930 x14; Elections- 508-867-2930 x12; Vital Records- 508-867-2930 x12. **Property tax/Assessor-** same address as above. 508-867-2930 x15.

Brookline Town

Town Clerk, 333 Washington St; Town Hall, Brookline, MA 02445. 617-730-2010, R/E recording phone-617-730-2020; fax-617-730-2043; hours: 8AM-5PM M-W, 8AM-8PM Th, 8AM-12:30PM F www.town.brookline.ma.us/Assessors
No real estate recordings. Office personnel or visitors may perform searches. State tax lien search is free. General copy fee $2.00 per page; $1.00 per page after 3rd. Tax lien copy-$.25 per page. Cert fee-$10.00. Payee- Town of Brookline. **Online access to Assessor, Property records:** Records on the Town of Brookline Assessors database are free at www.townofbrooklinemass.com/assessors/propertyloo kup.asp. **Other phones:** Treasurer- 617-730-2020; Elections- 617-730-2010; Vital Records- 617-730-2010. **Property tax/Assessor-** 617-730-2060.

Buckland Town

Town Clerk, PO Box 159, Buckland, MA 01338. 413-625-8572; fax-413-625-8570; 10AM-3PM M-Th
No real estate recordings. Postal designation "Shelburne Falls" is not a town. It refers either to Shelburne or Buckland. All records in one index. Record index not computerized. Office will perform a UCC search but public must search other records themselves. Search fee $10.00. Real estate records located at Franklin County. Copy fee $.35 per page. Cert fee- $5.00 per page plus copy fee. Payee- Town of Buckland. **Other phones:** Treasurer- 413-625-9474; Elections- 413-625-8572; Vital Records- 413-625-8572. **Property tax/Assessor-** Janice Purington, Town Clerk 413-625-2335.

Burlington Town

Town Clerk, 29 Center St; Town Hall, Burlington, MA 01803. 781-270-1660; fax-781-270-1608; hours: 8:30AM-4:30PM www.burlington.org/clerk
No real estate recordings. Records index not computerized. Only the office personnel may search. Real estate records located at Middlesex County. Will search UCC records; search includes tax liens if requested. UCC search per debtor name- $10.00. Copy fee $2.00 per page. Cert fee- $2.00 per filing. Payee- Town of Burlington. **Online to Property, Assessor records:** Property data free at http://burlington.patriotproperties.com/default.asp.
Other phones: Treasurer- 781-270-1624; Vital Records- 781-270-1660. **Property tax/Assessor-** same address as above. 781-270-1650.

Cambridge City

City Clerk, 795 Massachusetts Ave.; City Hall, Rm 103, Cambridge, MA 02139. 617-349-4260; fax-617-349-4269; 8:30AM-8PM M; 8:30AM-5PM T-TH; 8:30-noon F www.cambridgema.gov/CityClrk/
No real estate recordings. Record index not computerized. Only the office personnel may search. Search fee $10.00 per name. Real estate records located at Middlesex County. Copy fee $2.00 for 1st 3 pages, $1.00 each add'l. Cert fee- $10.00 per copy. Payee- City of Cambridge. **Online access to Assessor records:** Records on the City of Cambridge Assessor database are free at www.cambridgema.gov/fiscalaffairs/PropertySearch.cf m. No name searching. Also, search town assessor data at http://data.visionappraisal.com/CambridgeMA/. Does not require a username and password. Simply click on link. **Other phones:** Treasurer- 617-349-4220; Elections- 617-349-4361; Vital Records- 617-349-4260. **Property tax/Assessor-** 617-349-4343.

Canton Town

Town Clerk, 801 Washington St; Memorial Hall, Canton, MA 02021. 781-821-5013; fax-781-821-5016; hours: 9AM-5PM
No real estate recordings. Record index not computerized. Office will perform a UCC search but public must search other records themselves. Search fee $10.00. Real estate records located at Norfolk County. Copy fee $.50 per page. Cert fee- $10.00 per name plus copy fee. Payee- Town of Canton. **Other phones:** Treasurer- 781-821-5006; Elections- 781-821-5013; Vital Records- 781-821-5013. **Property tax/Assessor-** same address as above. 781-821-5008.

Carlisle Town

Town Clerk, 66 Westford St, Carlisle, MA 01741. 978-369-6155; fax-978-371-0594; hours: 9AM-3PM
No real estate recordings. Office will perform a UCC search but public must search other records themselves. Real estate records located at Middlesex County. UCC search per debtor name- $10.00. Payee- Town of Carlisle. **Other phones:** Treasurer- 978-369-5557; Elections- 978-369-6155; Vital Records- 978-369-6155. **Property tax/Assessor-** 978-369-0392.

Carver Town

Town Clerk, 108 Main St, Carver, MA 02330. 508-866-3403, UCC recording phone-508-86-3403; fax-508-866-3408; hours: 8AM-4PM M-Th; 8AM-N F, Tues. 8AM-4PM; 5-8PM
No real estate recordings. All records in one index. Record index not computerized. Only the public may search. Real estate records located at Plymouth County. Copy fee $1.00 per page. Cert fee- $5.00. Payee- Town of Carver. **Other phones:** Treasurer- 508-866-3435; Elections- 508-86-3403; Vital Records- 508-86-3403. **Property tax/Assessor-** same address as above. 508-86-3410.

Charlemont Town

Town Clerk, PO Box 605, Charlemont, MA 01339-0605. 413-625-6157; fax-413-625-6157; hours: by appointment www.charlemont-ma.us/Town/TownClerk.shtml
No real estate recordings. Record index not computerized. Only the office personnel may search. Real estate records located at Franklin County. Will search older UCC records but not tax liens. Copy fee $1.00 per page. Cert fee- $5.00 per doc plus copy fee. Payee- Town of Charlemont. **Online access to Assessor, Property Tax records:** Access is free at http://csc-ma.us/Charlemont. **Other phones:** Treasurer- 413-625-1097; Elections- 413-625-6157; Vital Records- 413-625-6157; Tax Lien/Tax Collector- 413-339-5707. **Property tax/Assessor-** PO Box 337, Charlemont, MA 01339; 413-339-8586.

Charlton Town

Town Clerk, 37 Main St, Charlton, MA 01507. 508-248-2249; fax-508-248-2073; hours: 10AM-3PM M-Th; 1st & 3rd Tues of month 6-8PM
No real estate recordings. All records in one index. Record index not computerized. Only the office personnel may search. Real estate records located at Worcester County. Will search UCC records, tax liens not included in UCC search. UCC search per debtor name- $5.00. Separate federal tax lien search- $5.00 per debtor. Separate state tax lien search- $5.00 per debtor. Separate federal/state combined tax lien search- $10.00 per debtor. Copy fee $2.00, if tax lien or estate $1.00 1st 3 pages; $1.00 each add'l. Payee- Town of Charlton. **Online access to Assessor, Property records:** Access property data free at http://charlton.patriotproperties.com/default.asp. **Other phones:** Treasurer- 508-248-2242; Elections- 508-248-2249; Vital Records- 508-248-2249. **Property tax/Assessor-** same address. 508-248-2203.

Chatham Town

Town Clerk, 549 Main St, Chatham, MA 02633. 508-945-5101; fax-508-945-3550; hours: 8AM-4PM www.town.chatham.ma.us
No real estate recordings. Records indexed on computer. Office will perform a UCC and Tax lien search but public must search other records themselves. Search fee $10.00. Real estate records located at Barnstable County. Copy fee $.20 per page. Cert fee- $5.00 per doc plus copy fee. Payee- Town of Chatham. **Other phones:** Treasurer- 508-945-5108; Elections- 508-945-5101; Vital Records- 508-945-5101. **Property tax/Assessor-** same address as above. 508-945-5103.

Chelmsford Town

Town Clerk, 50 Billerica Rd, Chelmsford, MA 01824. 978-250-5205; fax-978-840-5208; hours: 8:30AM-5PM www.townofchelmsford.us
No real estate recordings. All records in one index. Record index not computerized. Only the office personnel may search. Search fee $10.00 per name. Real estate records located at Middlesex County. Copy fee $2.00 per page. Cert fee- $1.00 per page plus copy fee. Payee- Town of Chelmsford. **Online access to Assessor records:** Search town assessor data at http://data.visionappraisal.com/ChelmsfordMA/. Free registration for full data. **Other phones:** Treasurer- 978-250-5210; Elections- 978-250-5205; Vital Records- 978-250-5205. **Property tax/Assessor-** same address as above. 978-250-5220.

Chelsea City

City Clerk, 500 Broadway; City Hall, Rm 209, Chelsea, MA 02150. 617-889-8227, R/E recording phone-617-889-8213, UCC recording phone-617-889-8226; fax-617-889-8367; hours: 8AM-4PM M,W,Th; 8AM-7PM F; 8AM-N F
No real estate recordings. Office personnel or visitors may perform searches. Search fee $10.00 per name. Real estate records located at Suffolk County. Copy fee $2.00 1st page; $1.00 each add'l. Payee- City of Chelsea. **Online access to Assessor records:** Search city assessor database at http://data.visionapp raisal.com/ChelseaMA/. Free registration for full data. **Other phones:** Treasurer- 617-889-8210; Elections- 617-889-8226; Vital Records- 617-889-8226. **Property tax/Assessor-** 617-889-8213.

Cheshire Town

Town Clerk, PO Box S, 80 Church St, Cheshire, MA 01225. 413-743-1690; fax-413-743-0389; hours: 9AM-3PM M,T,W; 9AM-N Th
No real estate recordings. All records in one index. Record index not computerized. Only the office personnel may search. Search fee $10.00. Real estate records located at Berkshire County. Copy fee $2.00 per page. Payee- Town of Cheshire. **Other phones:** Treasurer- 413-743-0403; Elections- 413-743-1690; Vital Records- 413-743-1690. **Property tax/Assessor-** same address. 413-743-1690.

Chester Town

Town Clerk, Town Hall, Chester, MA 01011. 413-354-6603; fax-413-354-2268; hours: 6-8PM M
No real estate recordings. All records in one index. Record index not computerized. Only the public may search. Copy fee $1.00 per page. Cert fee- $10.00 per cert includes copy fee. Payee- Town of Chester. **Online access to Property, Assessor, Real Estate, Recording, Lien records:** Access to property data is free at http://csc-ma.us/PropertyConten t/jsp/Home.jsp?Page=1. Select Chester Town. Also, see Hampden County for recording records searching. **Other phones:** Treasurer- 413-354-7761. **Property tax/Assessor-** 413-354-6357.

Chesterfield Town

Town Clerk, 422 Main St; Davenport Bldg, Chesterfield, MA 01012-0013. 413-296-4741, R/E recording phone-413-296-4051; fax-413-296-4394; hours: 7-9PM M or by Appointment

No real estate recordings. All records in one index. Record index not computerized. Only the office personnel may search. Search fee $10.00 per name. Real estate records located at Hampshire County. Copy fee $1.00 per page. Cert fee- $5.00 per record (Vitals Only) plus copy fee. Payee-Town of Chesterfield. **Other phones:** Treasurer-413-296-4771; Elections- 413-296-4741; Vital Records- 413-296-4741. **Property tax/Assessor**- same address as above. 413-296-4051.

Chicopee City

City Clerk, 17 Springfield St; City Hall, Chicopee, MA 01013. 413-594-1466; fax-413-594-1469; hours: 8AM-5PM
No real estate recordings. Record index not computerized. Office will perform a UCC search but public must search other records themselves. Real estate records located at Hampden County. UCC search per debtor name- $20.00. Copy fee $2.00 per copy. Payee- City of Chicopee. **Online access to Real Estate, Recording, Lien records:** See Hampden County for recording records searching. **Other phones:** Treasurer- 413-594-1560; Elections- 413-594-1550. **Property tax/Assessor**- 413-594-1430.

Chilmark Town

Town Clerk, PO Box 119, Chilmark, MA 02535-0119. 508-645-2107, R/E recording phone-508-645-2102; fax-508-645-2110; hours: 9AM-Noon www.ci.chilmark.ma.us
No real estate recordings; real estate records at courthouse in Edgartown, 508-627-3751. Office will perform a UCC and Tax lien search but public must search other records themselves. Search fee $10.00. Real estate records located at Dukes County. Copy fee $1.00 per page. Cert fee- $3.00 per page. Payee- Town of Chilmark. **Other phones:** Treasurer- 508-645-2106; Elections- 508-645-2107; Vital Records- 508-645-2107; Executive Secretary - Timothy R Carroll- 508-645-2101. **Property tax/Assessor**- 508-645-2102.

Clarksburg Town

Town Clerk, 111 River Rd; Town Hall, Clarksburg, MA 01247. 413-663-8247; fax-413-664-6575; hours: 9AM-2PM W-F
No real estate recordings. Record index not computerized. Only the public may search. Real estate records located at Berkshire County. Copy fee $1.00 per page. Payee- Town of Clarksburg. **Other phones:** Treasurer- 413-663-8247; Elections- 413-663-8247; Vital Records- 413-663-8247. **Property tax/Assessor**- 413-663-8255.

Clinton Town

Town Clerk, 242 Church St, Clinton, MA 01510. 978-365-4119; fax-978-895-4130; hours: 8AM-4PM
No real estate recordings. Separate indices to search include birth, death, marriage. Record index not computerized. Search fee $10.00 per name. Copy fee $2.00 per page. Payee- Town of Clinton. **Other phones:** Treasurer- 978-365-4129; Elections- 978-365-4119; Vital Records- 978-365-4119. **Property tax/Assessor**- same address. 978-365-4117.

Cohasset Town

Town Clerk, 41 Highland Ave, Cohasset, MA 02025-1814. 781-383-4100; fax-781-383-1561; hours: 8:30AM-4:30PM M,W,Th; 8:30AM-7PM Tu; 8:30AM-1PM F
No real estate recordings. Office will perform a UCC search but public must search other records themselves. Real estate records located at Norfolk County. UCC search per debtor name- $5.00. Copy fee $.20 per page. Payee- Town of Cohasset. **Other phones:** Treasurer- 781-383-4102; Elections- 781-383-4100; Vital Records- 781-383-4100. **Property tax/Assessor**- 781-383-4114.

Colrain Town

Town Clerk, 55 Main Rd., Colrain, MA 01340. 413-624-3454; fax-413-624-8852; hours: 9AM-4PM M-Th, 7PM-9PM M
No real estate recordings. All records in one index. Office personnel or visitors may perform searches. Real estate records located at Franklin County. Will search UCC records, tax liens included in UCC search. UCC search per debtor name- $10.00. Separate federal or state tax lien search- $10.00 per debtor. Separate federal/state combined tax lien search- $10.00 per debtor. Copy fee $.50 per page. Payee-Town of Colrain. **Other phones:** Treasurer- 413-624-3454; Elections- 413-624-3454; Vital Records- 413-624-3454. **Property tax/Assessor**- 55 Main Rd, Colrain, MA 01340-5500; 413-624-3356.

Concord Town

Town Clerk, PO Box 535, Concord, MA 01742. 978-318-3080, R/E recording phone-617-679-6300; fax-978-318-3093; hours: 8:30AM-4:30PM www.concordnet.org
No real estate recordings. UCC index not computerized; Birth on computer, 1987-present; Death & marriage on computer, 2001-present; DBA on computer, 1998-present; All others, manual index. Only the office personnel may search. Search fee $10.00 per name. Real estate records located at Middlesex County. Will search UCC records to 7/2001 only. Will search state tax liens. Copy fee $2.00 per page for 1st 3 pages, $1.00 each add'l. Cert fee- $2.00 per doc plus copy fee. Payee- Town of Concord. **Online access to Property Assessor records:** Alpha search residential and commercial assessments at www.concordnet.org/assessor/. **Other phones:** Treasurer- 978-318-3050; Elections- 978-318-3080; Vital Records- 978-318-3080. **Property tax/Assessor**- same address as above. 978-318-3070.

Conway Town

Town Clerk, PO Box 240, Conway, MA 01341. 413-369-4235; fax-413-369-4237; 9AM-Noon T,Th,F
No real estate recordings. All records in one index. Record index not computerized. Only the public may search. Real estate records located at Franklin County. Copy fee $.20 per page. Cert fee- $2.00 per page. Payee- Town of Conway. **Other phones:** Treasurer- 413-369-4235; Elections- 413-369-4235; Vital Records- 413-369-4235. **Property tax/Assessor**- 413-369-4773.

Cummington Town

Town Clerk, 585 Berkshire Trail, Cummington, MA 01026. 413-634-5458; fax-413-634-5568; 6-8PM W
No real estate recordings. Office will perform a tax lien search but public must search other records themselves. Federal/state combined tax lien search- $10.00 per debtor. Payee- Cummington Town Clerk. **Other phones:** Elections- 413-634-5458; Vital Records- 413-634-5457. **Property tax/Assessor**- 413-634-5354.

Dalton Town

Town Clerk, 462 Main St; Town Hall, Dalton, MA 01226. 413-684-6103 x14; fax-413-684-6129; hours: 8AM-4PM M-W; 8AM-6PM Th
No real estate recordings. Office personnel or visitors may perform searches. All filings now performed at state level. MA Town Clerks only do searches for those unexpired records they still hold. Search fee $10.00 per debtor. Office reserves right to charge more for an extended search. Real estate records located at Berkshire County. Copy fee $1.00 per page. Cert fee- $5.00 per page includes copy fee. Payee- Town of Dalton-Town Clerk. **Other phones:** Treasurer- 413-684-6111 x18; Elections- 413-684-6103 x15; Vital Records- 413-684-6103 x15. **Property tax/Assessor**- same address as above. 413-684-6105.

Danvers Town

Town Clerk, 1 Sylvan St; Town Hall, Danvers, MA 01923. RE & UCC recording phone-978-777-0001; fax-978-777-1025; hours: 8AM-5PM M-W; 8AM-7:30PM Th; 8AM-1:30PM F www.danvers.govoffice.com
No real estate recordings. Record index not computerized. Office will perform a UCC search but public must search other records themselves. Real estate records located at Essex County. UCC search per debtor name- $10.00. Copy fee $.25 per page. Cert fee- $6.00 per doc plus copy fee. Payee-Town of Danvers. **Online access to Assessor, Property records:** Access property data free at http://danvers.patriotproperties.com/default.asp. **Other phones:** Treasurer- 978-777-0001; Elections- 978-777-0001; Vital Records- 978-777-0001. **Property tax/Assessor**- same address as above. 978-777-0001 x3055, x3060.

Dartmouth Town

Town Clerk, PO Box 79399, Dartmouth, MA 02747. 508-910-1800, R/E recording phone-508-910-1809; fax-508-910-1894; hours: 8:30AM-4:30PM www.town.dartmouth.ma.us/town_hall.htm
No real estate recordings. Search fee- UCC $10.00. Real estate records located at Bristol County. Copy fee $.25 per page. Cert fee- $2.00 per page plus copy fee. Payee- Town of Dartmouth. **Online access to Assessor records:** Search the town assessor database at http://data.visionappraisal.com/DartmouthMA/. Free registration for full data. **Other phones:** Treasurer- 508-910-1802; Elections- 508-910-1800; Vital Records- 508-910-1800. **Property tax/Assessor**- same address as above. 508-910-1809.

Dedham Town

Town Clerk, PO Box 306, Dedham, MA 02027. 781-751-9200; fax-781-751-9109; 8:30AM-4:30PM
No real estate recordings. Record index not computerized. Office will perform a UCC search but public must search other records themselves. Search fee $10.00. Real estate records located at Norfolk County. Copy fee $2.00 per page. Cert fee-None. Payee- Town of Dedham. **Online access to Assessor records:** Property records on the Assessor's database are free at http://data.visionappraisal.com/dedhamma/. Does not require a username & password. Simply click on link. **Other phones:** Treasurer- 781-751-9170; Elections- 781-751-9200; Vital Records- 781-751-9200. **Property tax/Assessor**-same address. 781-751-9130.

Deerfield Town

Town Clerk, 8 Conway St., South Deerfield, MA 01373. RE & UCC recording phone-413-665-2130; fax-413-665-5512; hours: 9AM-4PM www.town.deerfield.ma.us
No real estate recordings. Record index not computerized. Only the public may search. Real estate records located at Franklin County. Copy fee $.25 per page. Cert fee- $.25 per page plus copy fee. Payee- Town of Deerfield. **Other phones:** Treasurer- 413-665-2130. **Property tax/Assessor**-same address as above. 413-665-7184.

Dennis Town

Town Clerk, PO Box 2060, South Dennis, MA 02660-1419. 508-760-6115; R/E recording phone-508-362-2511, UCC recording phone-508-760-6112; fax-508-394-8309; 8:30-4:30PM www.town.dennis.ma.us/
No real estate recordings. All records in one index. Real estate records located at Barnstable County. Will search UCC records, tax liens not included in UCC search. UCC search per debtor name- $10.00. Separate federal/state combined tax lien search- $10.00 per debtor. Copy fee $.25 per page. Cert fee- $1.00 per cert. Payee- Town of Dennis. **Online access to Assessor, Property records:** Access to assessor property records is free at http://townofdennis.bonsailogic.com/. **Other phones:** Treasurer- 508-760-6117; Elections- 508-760-6112;

Vital Records- 508-760-6112. **Property tax/Assessor**-same address as above. 508-760-6142.

Dighton Town

Town Clerk, 979 Somerset Ave, Dighton, MA 02715-0465. 508-669-5411; fax-508-669-5932; hours: 8AM-4PM M,T,Th; 8AM-5PM W; 8AM-N Fri. www.dighton-ma.gov/Home/
No real estate recordings. Office will perform a UCC search but public must search other records themselves. Search fee $5.00. Real estate records located at Bristol County. Copy fee $.25 per page. Cert fee- $5.00 per page plus copy fee. Payee- Town of Dighton. **Other phones:** Treasurer- 508-669-5411; Elections- 508-669-5411; Vital Records- 508-669-5411. **Property tax/Assessor-** same address as above. 508-669-5043.

Douglas Town

Town Clerk, 29 Depot St.; Municipal Ctr, Douglas, MA 01516. 508-476-4000 x355, R/E recording phone-508-476-4000 x354; fax-508-476-4012; hours: 9AM-1PM, 1:30-4PM M-Th; 6-8PM T www.douglasma.org
No real estate recordings. All records in one index. Record index not computerized. Only the office personnel may search. Search fee $5.00. Real estate records located at Worcester County. Copy fee $2.00 per page. Cert fee- $5.00 per page plus copy fee. Payee- Town of Douglas. **Other phones:** Treasurer- 508-476-4000 x356; Elections- 508-476-4000 x355; Vital Records- 508-476-4000 x355. **Property tax/Assessor-** same address as above. 508-476-4000 x353.

Dover Town

Town Clerk, PO Box 250, Dover, MA 02030-0250. 508-785-0032, R/E recording phone-508-785-0032 x241, UCC recording phone-508-785-0032 x226; fax-508-785-2341; hours: 9AM-1PM M,W,F; 9AM-4PM T,Th http://doverma.org/townclerk.php
No real estate recordings. Only the office personnel may search. Search fee $5.00. Real estate records located at Norfolk County. Copy fee $.20 per page. Cert fee- $5.00 per page plus copy fee. Payee- Town of Dover. **Online access to Property, Assessor records:** Access to the assessor's property values data is free at www.doverma.org/assessorsproposedvaluesnew.php. You must open individual tables to search by name. **Other phones:** Treasurer- 508-785-0032 x228; Elections- 508-785-0032 x226; Vital Records- 508-785-0032 x226. **Property tax/Assessor-** same address as above. 508-785-0032 x241.

Dracut Town

Town Clerk, 62 Arlington St; Rm 4, Dracut, MA 01826. 978-453-0951; fax-978-452-7924; hours: 8:30AM-4:30PM
No real estate recordings. Record index not computerized. Only the public may search. Real estate records located at Middlesex County. Copy fee $.20 per page. Cert fee- $2.00 per cert. Payee-Town of Dracut. **Online access to Assessor records:** Search the town assessor database at http://data.visionappraisal.com/DracutMA/. Free registration for full data. **Property tax/Assessor-** 978-453-2451.

Dudley Town

Town Clerk, 40 Schofield Ave, Town Hall #17, Dudley, MA 01571. 508-949-8004; fax-508-949-7115; hours: 8AM-noon, 12:30-4:30 PM M-Th; 6-8PM Th www.dudleyma.gov
No real estate recordings. All records in one index. Office personnel or visitors may perform searches. Search fee $10.00 per name. Real estate records located at Worcester County. Copy fee $2.00 per page. Payee- Town of Dudley. **Online access to Assessor records:** Search the town assessor database at http://data.visionappraisal.com/DudleyMA/. Free registration for full data. **Other phones:** Treasurer- 508-949-8002; Elections- 508-949-8004; Vital Records- 508-949-8004. **Property tax/Assessor-** same address as above. 508-949-8006.

Dukes County

County Register of Deeds, PO Box 5231, Edgartown, MA 02539. RE & UCC recording phone-508-627-4025; fax-508-627-7821; hours: 8:30AM-4:30PM http://dukescounty.org
This county is comprised of 7 towns; there is no County Assessor, Appraiser, Elections, etc. Records indexed on a public use terminal back to 1984. Only the public may search. Copy fee $1.00 per page. Cert fee- included in copy fee. Payee- Dukes County Register of Deeds.

Dunstable Town

Town Clerk, 511 Main St., Dunstable, MA 01827. 978-649-4514; fax-978-649-2205; hours: M 6PM-9PM; TWTH 9AM-2PM; F 9AM-N
No real estate recordings. Only the public may search. Copy fee $1.00 per page. Payee- Town of Dunstable. **Other phones:** Treasurer- 978-649-3257; Elections- 978-649-4514; Vital Records- 978-649-4514. **Property tax/Assessor-** 978-649-3257.

Duxbury Town

Town Treasurer, 878 Tremont St, Duxbury, MA 02332-4499. 781-934-1104; fax-781-934-9278; hours: 8AM-noon,1-4PM
No real estate recordings. Office will perform a tax lien search but public must search other records themselves. Search fee $25.00 per search. Real estate records located at Plymouth County. Copy fee $2.00 per financing statement. Payee- Town of Duxbury. **Online access to Property, Assessor records:** Search the town public documents free at http://duxburyma.virtualtownhall.net/Public_Documents/Search. Access to property data is free at http://csc-ma.us/PropertyContent/jsp/Home.jsp?Page=1. **Other phones:** Treasurer- 781-934-1102. **Property tax/Assessor-** 781-934-1109.

East Bridgewater Town

Town Clerk, PO Box 387, East Bridgewater, MA 02333. 508-378-1606, R/E recording phone-508-378-1602 (town collector); fax-508-378-1638; hours: 8:30AM-8PM M; 8:30AM-4:30PM T-TH; Closed of Fri.
No real estate recordings. Separate indices to search. Record index not computerized. Office will perform a UCC search but public must search other records themselves. Search fee $10.00 per name. Copy fee $1.00 per page. Payee- Town of East Bridgewater. **Other phones:** Treasurer- 508-378-1604; Elections- 508-378-1606; Vital Records- 508-378-1606. **Property tax/Assessor-** same address as above. 508-378-1609.

East Brookfield Town

Town Clerk, Town Hall, East Brookfield, MA 01515. Main phone & R/E recording-508-867-6769, UCC recording phone-508-867-6769 x301; fax-508-867-4190; hours: 9AM-12 Mon; 11AM-1PM Fri
No real estate recordings. All records in one index. Search fee $10.00 per name. Copy fee $1.00 per page. Cert fee- $10.00 per doc includes copies. Payee- Town of East Brookfield. **Online access to Assessor, Property records:** Access to property data is free at http://csc-ma.us/PropertyContent/jsp/Home.jsp?Page=1. Select East Brookfield Town. **Other phones:** Treasurer- 508-867-6769 x304; Elections- 508-867-6769 x301; Vital Records- 508-867-6769 x301. **Property tax/Assessor-** PO Box 395, East Brookfield, MA 01515; 508-867-6769 x302.

East Longmeadow Town

Town Clerk, 60 Center Sq, East Longmeadow, MA 01028-2446. RE & UCC recording phone-413-525-5400 x410; fax-413-525-0022; hours: 8AM-4PM www.eastlongmeadow.org
No real estate recordings. Record index not computerized. Office will perform a UCC search but public must search other records themselves. Real estate records located at Hampden County. UCC search per debtor name- $10.00 per name. Copy fee $1.00 per page. Cert fee- $1.00 per page. Payee- Town of East Longmeadow. **Online access to Real Estate, Recording, Lien records:** See Hampden County for recording records searching. **Other phones:** Treasurer- 413-525-5400 x410; Elections- 413-525-5400 x410; Vital Records- 413-525-5400 x410. **Property tax/Assessor-** same address as above. 413-525-5425 x450.

Eastham Town

Town Clerk, 2500 State Highway, Eastham, MA 02642. 508-240-5900 x223; hours: 8AM-4PM
Records are not available. Real estate records located at Barnstable County. Separate federal/state combined tax lien search- $6.00 per debtor. Cert fee- $5.00. Payee- Town of Eastham. **Property tax/Assessor-** 508-255-0333.

Easthampton City

City Clerk, 50 Payson Ave #100, Easthampton, MA 01027. 413-529-1460, R/E recording phone-413-529-1401; fax-413-529-1417; hours: 8AM-4PM M-F; 7-8PM W
No real estate recordings. All records in one index. Record index not computerized. Office will perform a UCC search but public must search other records themselves. Search fee $5.00. Real estate records located at Hampshire County. Copy fee $.30 per page. Payee- City of Easthampton. **Other phones:** Treasurer- 413-529-1416; Elections- 413-529-1460; Vital Records- 413-529-1460. **Property tax/Assessor-** 413-529-1401.

Easton Town

Town Clerk, 136 Elm St, North Easton, MA 02356. 508-230-0530, R/E recording phone-508-230-0520; fax-508-230-0539; hours: 8:30AM-8:30PM M; 7AM-4:30PM T Th; 8:30AM-12:30PM F www.easton.ma.us
No real estate recordings. Real estate records located at Bristol County. Will search UCC records, tax liens included if requested. UCC search per debtor name- $15.00. Separate federal/state combined tax lien search- $15.00 per debtor. Copy fee $8.00 for 1st 3 pages; $2.00 each add'l. Payee- Town of Easton. **Other phones:** Treasurer- 508-230-0610; Elections- 508-230-0530; Vital Records- 508-230-0530. **Assessor-** same address as above. 508-230-0520.

Edgartown Town

Town Clerk, PO Box 35, Edgartown, MA 02539-0035. 508-627-6110, R/E recording phone-508-627-4025 (county); fax-508-627-6123; hours: 8AM-4PM
No real estate recordings. All records in one index. Record index not computerized. Office will perform a UCC search but public must search other records themselves. Search fee $10.00 per name. Real Estate records located at Duke. Copy fee $2.00 per page. Cert fee- $1.00 per page plus copy fee. Payee- Town of Edgartown. **Online access to Real Estate, Property Tax records:** Search the Town assessor's database at http://data.visionappraisal.com/EdgartownMA. Free registration for full data. **Other phones:** Treasurer- 508-627-6130; Elections- 508-627-6110; Vital Records- 508-627-6110; Accountant (Kim Kane)- 508-627-6125. **Property tax/Assessor-** PO Box 886, Edgartown, MA 02539; 508-627-6140.

Egremont Town

Town Clerk, PO Box 368, North Egremont/ So. Egremont, MA 01258-0368. 413-528-0182, R/E recording phone-413-528-0182 x12; fax-413-528-5465; 7-9PM Tues. http://egremont-ma.gov/index.html
No real estate recordings. Office will perform a UCC search, includes tax liens if requested, but public must search other records themselves. Search fee $5.00 per name. Copy fee $1.00 per page. Payee- Town of Egremont. **Online access to Property, Assessor records:** Access to property data is free at http://csc-ma.us/PropertyContent/jsp/Home.jsp?Page=1. Select Egremont Town. **Other phones:** Elections- 413-528-0182; Vital Records- 413-528-0182. **Property tax/Assessor-** 413-528-0182.

Erving Town

Town Clerk, 12 E Main St; Town Hall, Erving, MA 01344. 413-422-2800, R/E recording phone-413-422-2800 x107, UCC recording phone-413-422-2800 x102; fax-413-422-2808; hours: 2-5PM, 6-9PM M

No real estate recordings. Record index not computerized. Only the office personnel may search. Search fee $10.00. Real estate records located at Franklin County. Copy fee $1.00 per page. Cert fee- $5.00 per page includes copy fee. Payee-Town of Erving. **Other phones:** Treasurer- 413-422-2800 x104; Elections- 413-422-2800 x102; Vital Records- 413-422-2800 x102. **Property tax/Assessor-** same address as above. 413-422-2800 x107.

Essex County (Northern District)

County Register of Deeds, 381 Common St, Lawrence, MA 01840. 978-683-2745; fax-978-681-5409; hours: 8AM-4:30PM (recording until 4PM). www.lawrencedeeds.com
Office will perform a UCC search but public must search other records themselves. Will not search real estate records. Only real estate related UCC filed here. Copy fee $1.00 per page. Cert fee- $1.00 per page. Payee- Essex County Register of Deeds. **Online access to Real Estate, Lien, Grantor/Grantee, Recording records:** Search the recorder database for free at www.lawrencedeeds.com/dsSearch.asp. Also see Andover Town and Essex County Southern District. **Other phones:** Treasurer- 978-683-2745. **Property tax/Assessor-** 978-683-2745.

Essex County (Southern District)

County Register of Deeds, 36 Federal St, Salem, MA 01970. 978-741-0201; fax-978-744-5865; hours: 8AM-4PM. www.salemdeeds.com
Records indexed on computer back to 1/3/1984. Only the public may search. Copy fee $1.00 per page; self serve $.50. Cert fee- $1.00 per page includes copy fee. Payee- Essex County Register of Deeds. **Online access to Real Estate, Lien, Deed records:** Records on the Essex County South Registry of Deeds database are free at www.salemdeeds.com. Click on "Deeds online". Images start 1/1992; records back to 1/1984. Search by grantee/grantor, town & date, street, or book & page. **Property tax/Assessor-** 978-741-0200.

Essex Town

Town Clerk, Martin St.; Town Hall, Essex, MA 01929. 978-768-7111; hours: 8:30AM-1PM, M,W; 1-4PM T & Th; Closed F. www.essexma.org/
No real estate recordings. Do not confuse Essex Town with Essex County. UCC records are filed with the Town/City Clerk, real estate records are at the county level with the Register of Deeds. Records indexed. Only the office personnel may search. Real estate records located at Essex County. Will search UCC records, but not tax liens. UCC search per debtor name- $10.00. Payee- Town of Essex. **Other phones:** Treasurer- 978-768-7111; Elections- 978-768-7111; Vital Records- 978-768-7111. **Property tax/Assessor-** 30 Martin St, Town of Essex, MA 01929; 978-768-7831.

Everett City

City Clerk, City Hall; Rm 10, Everett, MA 02149. 617-394-2225; fax-617-387-5770; hours: M 8AM-7:30PM; 8AM-4PM T-Th; 8-11:30AM Fri. www.ci.everett.ma.us
No real estate recordings. Record index not computerized. Office will perform a UCC and Tax lien search but public must search other records themselves. Search fee $10.00. Real estate records located at Middlesex County. Copy fee $2.00 1st page $1.00 each add'l. Cert fee- $3.00 per page plus copy fee. Payee- City of Everett. **Other phones:** Treasurer- 617-394-2315; Elections- 617-394-2229; Vital Records- 617-394-2225; Registrar of Voters- 617-394-2297. **Property tax/Assessor-** 484 Broadway, Everett, MA 02149; 617-394-2205.

Fairhaven Town

Town Clerk, 40 Center St, Fairhaven, MA 02719-2999. 508-979-4025; fax-508-979-4079; hours: 8:30AM-4:30PM.
No real estate recordings. All records in one index. Record index not computerized. Only the office personnel may search. Search fee $10.00. Real estate records located at Bristol County. Will search UCC records, tax liens not included in UCC search. Copy fee $.25 per page. Cert fee- $5.00 per copy. Payee- Town of Fairhaven. **Other phones:** Treasurer- 508-979-4026; Elections- 508-979-4025; Vital Records- 508-979-4025. **Property tax/Assessor-** 508-979-4018.

Fall River City

City Clerk, One Government Ctr, Fall River, MA 02722. 508-324-2220; fax-508-324-2211; hours: 9AM-5PM.
No real estate recordings. Office personnel or visitors may perform searches. Search fee $5.00 per name. Real estate records located at Bristol County. Copy fee $2.00, if tax lien or real estate $1.00 for 2st 3 pages; $1.00 each add'l. Cert fee- $1.00 per page. Payee- City of Fall River. **Online access to Assessor, Property records:** Access property data free at http://fallriver.patriotproperties.com/default.asp. **Other phones:** Treasurer- 508-324-2260; Elections- 508-324-2630; Vital Records- 508-324-2220. **Property tax/Assessor-** same address as above. 508-324-2300.

Falmouth Town

Town Clerk, PO Box 904, Falmouth, MA 02541. 508-548-7611, R/E recording phone-508-495-7675, UCC recording phone-508-495-7357; fax-508-457-2511; hours: 8AM-4:30PM. www.town.falmouth.ma.us
No real estate recordings. Office will perform a UCC search but public must search other records themselves. Search fee $10.00 per name. Real estate records located at Barnstable County. Cert fee- $5.00 per cert plus copy fee. Payee- Town of Falmouth. **Online access to Assessor, Property, Dog Tag records:** Access property data free at http://falmouth.patriotproperties.com/default.asp. Also, find lost dog owners at www.town.falmouth.ma.us/lostdog.php. **Other phones:** Treasurer- 508-495-7362; Elections- 508-495-7358; Vital Records- 508-495-7357; Switchboard- 508-548-7611. **Property tax/Assessor-** 508-495-7377.

Fitchburg City

City Clerk, 718 Main St, Fitchburg, MA 01420-3198. 978-345-9592; fax-978-345-9595; hours: 8:30AM-4:30PM.
No real estate recordings. All records in one index. Record index not computerized. Only the office personnel may search. Search fee $10.00. Real estate records located at Worcester County. Copy fee $2.00 per page. Cert fee- $7.00 per page. Payee- City of Fitchburg. **Other phones:** Treasurer- 978-345-9605; Elections- 978-345-9592; Vital Records- 978-345-9592. **Property tax/Assessor-** 978-345-9562.

Florida Town

Town Clerk, 20 South St; Town Hall, Drury, MA 01343. 413-664-6685; fax-413-664-8640; hours: by Appointment.
No real estate recordings. All records in one index. Office will perform a UCC search but public must search other records themselves. UCC search per debtor name- $10.00. Copy fee $1.00 per page. Payee- Town Clerk of Florida. **Other phones:** Treasurer- 413-663-9851. **Property tax/Assessor-** 379 Mohawk Trail, Drury, MA 01343; 413-662-2448.

Foxborough Town

Town Clerk, 40 South St, Foxborough, MA 02035-2397. 508-543-1208, R/E recording phone-508-543-1215, UCC recording phone-508-543-1208; fax-508-543-6278; hours: 8:30AM-4PM M,W,Th; 8:30AM-4PM, 5-8PM T; 8:30AM-12:.
No real estate recordings. All records in one index. Record index not computerized. Only the office personnel may search. Search fee $10.00 per name. Real estate records located at Norfolk County. Copy fee $2.00 for 3 pages; $1.00 each add'l. Cert fee- $2.00 per copy. Payee- Town of Foxborough. **Other phones:** Treasurer- 508-543-1216; Elections- 508-543-1208; Vital Records- 508-543-1208; Main Number- 508-543-1200. **Property tax/Assessor-** 508-543-1215.

Framingham Town

Town Clerk, 150 Concord St; Memorial Bldg. - Rm 105, Framingham, MA 01702-8374. 508-620-4863, R/E recording phone-508-628-1311, UCC recording phone-508-620-4863; fax-508-628-1358; hours: 8:30AM-5PM M; 8:30AM-5PM T-F. www.framinghamma.org
No real estate recordings. Record index not computerized. Office will perform a UCC search but public must search other records themselves. Real estate records located at Middlesex County. UCC search per debtor name- $10.00. Copy fee $1.00 per page. Cert fee- $6.00 per certified copy. Payee-Framingham Town Clerk. **Other phones:** Treasurer- 508-628-1311; Elections- 508-620-4863; Vital Records- 508-620-4863. **Property tax/Assessor-** 150 Concord St, Rm 101, Framingham, MA 01702; 508-620-4858.

Franklin County

County Register of Deeds, PO Box 1495, Greenfield, MA 01302-1495. 413-772-0239; fax-413-774-7150; hours: 8:30AM-4:30PM (Recording until 4PM). http://franklindeeds.com
All records in one index. Only the public may search. Copy fee $1.00 per page. Cert fee- No extra fee. Payee- Commonwealth of Massachusetts. **Online access to Real Property, Recording, Lien, Deed, Judgment, Will records:** Access to Registry of Deeds data is free at www.masslandrecords.com. Select Franklin County on map.

Franklin Town

Town Clerk, 355 E Central St.; Municipal Bldg, Franklin, MA 02038. 508-520-4900; fax-508-520-4903; hours: 8AM-4PM M,T,Th, 8AM-6PM W; 8AM -1PM F.
No real estate recordings. Record index not computerized. Office will perform a UCC search but public must search other records themselves. Search fee $5.00 per name. Real estate records located at Franklin County. Copy fee $1.00 per page. Cert fee- $3.00 per cert. Payee- Town of Franklin. **Online access to Assessor, Property records:** Access property data free at http://franklin.patriotproperties.com/default.asp. **Other phones:** Treasurer- 508-520-4950. **Property tax/Assessor-** 150 Emmons St, Franklin, MA 02038; 508-520-4920.

Freetown Town

Town Clerk, PO Box 438, Assonet, MA 02702. 508-644-2203, R/E recording phone-508-644-2205, UCC recording phone-508-644-2203; fax-508-644-9826; hours: 9AM-7PM M, 9AM-4PM T-F. http://town.freetown.ma.us
No real estate recordings. Only the office personnel may search. Real estate records located at Bristol County. Pre-2001 UCC search per debtor name- $15.00, includes up to 15 copies. Copy fee UCCs $1.00 per page. Tax lien copy- $.20 per copy. Cert fee- $2.00 per copy. Payee- Town of Freetown. **Other phones:** Treasurer- 508-644-2204; Elections- 508-644-2203; Vital Records- 508-644-2203; Tax Collector- 508-644-2206. **Property tax/Assessor-** same address as above. 508-644-2205.

Gardner City

City Clerk, 95 Pleasant St; City Hall, Rm 118, Gardner, MA 01440. 978-630-4008; fax-978-630-2520; hours: 8AM-4:30PM; F 8AM-4PM.
No real estate recordings. All records in one index. Record index not computerized. Only the office personnel may search. Search fee $10.00. Real estate records located at Worcester County. Copy fee $1.00 per page. Cert fee- $10.00. Payee- City of Gardner. **Online access to Property Assessor records:** Search the city assessor data at http://data.visionappraisal.com/GardnerMA/. Free registration for full data. **Other phones:** Treasurer- 978-630-4016; Elections- 978-630-4008; Vital Records- 978-630-4008. **Property tax/Assessor-** same address as above. 978-630-4004.

Georgetown Town

Town Clerk, 1 Library St, Georgetown, MA 01833. 978-352-5711, R/E recording phone-978-352-5708, UCC recording phone-978-352-5711; fax-978-352-5725; hours: M&W 9AM-N,T&Th 9AM-4PM; Closed Fri. www.georgetownma.gov
No real estate recordings. All records in one index. Record index not computerized. Only the office personnel may search. Search fee $5.00 per name. General copy fee $1.00 per page. Tax lien copy- $.20 per page. Payee- Town of Georgetown. **Other phones:** Treasurer- 978-352-5723; Elections- 978-352-5711; Vital Records- 978-352-5711. **Property tax/Assessor-** same address. 978-352-5708.

Gill Town

Town Clerk, 325 Main Rd; Town Clerk's Office, Gill, MA 01376. 413-863-8103, R/E recording phone-413-863-0138; fax-413-863-7775; hours: 6PM-7:30PM M T; Noon-5PM F; 9AM-Noon S.
No real estate recordings. Office will perform a UCC search but public must search other records themselves. Real estate records located at Franklin County. UCC search per debtor name- $20.00 per closure. Copy fee $1.00 per page. Cert fee- $5.00 per cert plus copy fee. Payee- Town of Gill. **Online access to Property, Assessor records:** Access to property data is free at http://csc-ma.us/PropertyContent/jsp/Home.jsp?Page=1. **Other phones:** Treasurer- 413-863-0138; Elections- 413-863-8103; Vital Records- 413-863-8103; Tax Collector- 413-863-8103. **Property tax/Assessor-** 413-863-0138.

Gloucester City

City Clerk, 9 Dale Ave, Gloucester, MA 01930-5998. 978-281-9720; fax-978-281-8472; hours: 8:30AM-4PM M-W,F Winter; 8:30AM-6:30PM Th. www.ci.gloucester.ma.us
No real estate recordings. Record index not computerized. Office will perform a UCC and Tax lien search but public must search other records themselves. Search fee $10.00. Real estate records located at Essex County. Copy fee $2.00 per page and $.25 per attachment. Payee- City of Gloucester. **Other phones:** Treasurer- 978-281-9707; Elections- 978-281-9720; Vital Records- 978-281-9720. **Property tax/Assessor-** same address as above. 978-281-9715.

Goshen Town

Town Clerk, PO Box 124, Goshen, MA 01032-0124. 413-268-8236; fax-413-268-8237; hours: 7-8:30PM Monday.
No real estate recordings. All records in one index. Record index not computerized. Only the public may search. Real estate records located at Hampshire County. Copy fee $1.00 per page. Cert fee- $3.00 per item. Payee- Town of Goshen. **Other phones:** Treasurer- 413-268-8236; Elections- 413-268-8236; Vital Records- 413-268-8236; Tax Collector- 413-268-8236. **Property tax/Assessor-** 413-268-7856.

Gosnold Town

Town Clerk, Town Hall, Gosnold, MA 02713. 508-990-7408; fax-508-990-7408; hours: by Appointment.
No real estate recordings. Office will perform a UCC search but public must search other records themselves. Real estate records located at Dukes County. UCC search per debtor name- $10.00. Copy fee $1.00 per page. Payee- Town of Gosnold. **Other phones:** Treasurer- 508-990-7408; Elections- 508-990-7408; Vital Records- 508-990-7408. **Property tax/Assessor-** 508-990-7408.

Grafton Town

Town Clerk, 30 Providence Rd; Municipal Ctr, Grafton, MA 01519-1186. 508-839-5335 x195; fax-508-839-4602; hours: 8:30AM-4:30PM; 8:30AM-7PM Tues. www.town.grafton.ma.us/Home/
No real estate recordings. Separate indices to search. Record index not computerized. Search fee $5.00 per name. Copy fee $1.00 per page. Cert fee- $1.00 per page. Payee- Town of Grafton. **Online access to Property, Assessor records:** Access to property data is free at http://csc-ma.us/GraftonPubAcc/jsp/Home.jsp?Page=1; also at http://csc-ma.us/PropertyContent/jsp/Home.jsp?Page=1. Select Grafton Town. **Other phones:** Treasurer- 508-839-5335 x170; Elections- 508-839-5335 x195; Vital Records- 508-839-5335 x195. **Property tax/Assessor-** 30 Providence Rd, Municipal Ctr, Grafton, MA 01519; 508-839-5335 x165, assessor fax- 508-839-4602.

Granby Town

Town Clerk, 250 State St.; Kellogg Hall, Granby, MA 01033. 413-467-7178, R/E recording phone-413-584-3637, UCC recording phone-413-467-7178; fax-413-467-2080; hours: 9AM-3PM M,T,W,Th; 9AM-N Fri; 7-9PM 1st & 3rd M.
No real estate recordings. Separate indices to search include alphabetic and numeric. Record index not computerized. Office personnel or visitors may perform searches. Search fee $10.00, but if over 15 minutes, add an add'l $10.00 per hour. Real estate records located at Hampshire County. Copy fee $1.00 per page. Cert fee- $6.00 per page plus copy fee. Payee- Town of Granby. **Other phones:** Treasurer- 413-467-7176; Elections- 413-467-7178; Vital Records- 413-467-7178. **Property tax/Assessor-** same address as above. 413-467-7196.

Granville Town

Town Clerk, PO Box 247, Granville, MA 01034-0247. 413-357-8585; fax-413-357-6002; hours: 9-11AM, 7-9PM M.
No real estate recordings. Record index not computerized. Office will perform a UCC or tax lien search but public must search other records themselves. Real estate records located at Hampden County. UCC or tax lien search per debtor name- $10.00. Copy fee $1.00 per page. Cert fee- $5.00 per page plus copy fee. Payee- Town of Granville. **Online access to Real Estate, Recording, Lien records:** See Hampden County for recording records searching. **Other phones:** Treasurer- 413-357-8585; Elections- 413-357-8585; Vital Records- 413-357-8585. **Property tax/Assessor-** 707 Main Rd, Granville, MA 01034; 413-357-8585.

Great Barrington Town

Town Clerk, 334 Main St, Great Barrington, MA 01230-1802. 413-528-3140, R/E recording phone-413-528-0146, UCC recording phone-413-528-3140; fax-413-528-2290; hours: 8:30AM-4PM.
No real estate recordings. Record index not computerized. Office will perform a UCC search but public must search other records themselves. Real estate records located at Southern Berkshire County. UCC search per debtor name- $10.00. Copy fee $2.00 per page. Payee- Town of Great Barrington. **Online access to Property, Assessor records:** Access to property data is free at http://csc-ma.us/PropertyContent/jsp/Home.jsp?Page=1. **Other**

phones: Treasurer- 413-528-1025; Elections- 413-528-3140; Vital Records- 413-528-3140; Selectman- 413-528-1619. **Property tax/Assessor-** 413-528-2220.

Greenfield Town

Town Clerk, 14 Court Sq; Town Hall, Greenfield, MA 01301. 413-772-1555 x112; fax-413-772-1542; hours: 8:30AM-5PM. www.cityofgreenfield.org
No real estate recordings. Office personnel or visitors may perform searches. No searches by phone. Search fee $20.00 per debtor. Real estate records located at Franklin County. Copy fee $2.00 for no more that 3 pages then $1.00 per page. Cert fee- $10.00 per cert includes copy fee. Payee- Town of Greenfield. **Other phones:** Treasurer- 413-772-1563. **Property tax/Assessor-** same address as above. 413-772-1506.

Groton Town

Town Clerk, 173 Main St.; Town Hall, Groton, MA 01450. 978-448-1100; fax-978-448-2030; hours: 8:30AM-7PM M; 8:30AM-4:30PM T-Th; 9-4 F; 9-1 Sat. http://townofgroton.org
No real estate recordings. Separate indices to search include various volumes. Record index not computerized. Office will perform a UCC search but public must search other records themselves. Search fee $5.00 per search. Real estate records located at Middlesex County. Copy fee $.25 per page. Payee- Town of Groton. **Online access to Map Browser, Property, records:** Access the free map browser at www.geozone.com/Groton/. Also, property search site for free to go http://host.appgeo.com/groton/Search.asp. **Other phones:** Treasurer- 978-448-1103; Elections- 978-448-1100; Vital Records- 978-448-1100. **Property tax/Assessor-** 978-448-1127.

Groveland Town

Town Clerk, Town Hall, Groveland, MA 01830. 978-469-6861, UCC recording phone-978-469-5005; fax-978-469-5006; hours: 9AM-1PM M,T,Th,F; 9AM-N Wed.
No real estate recordings. Index: More than one index. Record index not computerized. Only the office personnel may search. Real estate records located at Essex County. Will search UCC records, but not tax liens. UCC search per debtor name- $10.00. Copy fee $1.00 per page. Payee- Town of Groveland. **Other phones:** Treasurer- 978-372-6861; Elections- 978-469-5005; Vital Records- 978-469-5005. **Property tax/Assessor-** 183 Main St, Groveland, MA 01830; 978-372-8528.

Hadley Town

Town Clerk, 100 Middle St, Hadley, MA 01035-9517. 413-584-1590; fax-413-586-5661; hours: 9AM-4PM. www.hadleyma.org
No real estate recordings. All records in one index. Record index not computerized. Only the public may search. Real estate records located at Hampshire County. Copy fee $2.00 per page. Cert fee- $3.00 per page includes copy fee. Payee- Town of Hadley. **Other phones:** Treasurer- 413-586-3354; Elections- 413-584-1590; Vital Records- 413-584-1590. **Property tax/Assessor-** 413-586-6320.

Halifax Town

Town Clerk, 499 Plymouth St, Halifax, MA 02338-1395. 781-293-7970; fax-781-294-7684; hours: 7AM-4PM; 6:30-8:30PM Tues (closed Fri). http://town.halifax.ma.us
No real estate recordings. Office will perform a UCC search but public must search other records themselves. Real estate records located at Plymouth County. UCC search per debtor name- $10.00. Cert fee- $1.00 per cert plus copy fee. Payee- Town of Halifax. **Other phones:** Treasurer- 781-294-8348; Elections- 781-293-7970; Vital Records- 781-293-7970. **Property tax/Assessor-** 499 Plymouth St, Halifax, MA 02338; 781-293-5960.

Hamilton Town

Town Clerk, PO Box 429, Hamilton, MA 01936. 978-468-5570; fax-978-468-2682; hours: 8AM-4:30PM (Fri open until Noon); 4:30-7PM M Eve. www.town.hamilton.ma.us
No real estate recordings. Records indexed on computer. Office will perform a UCC search but public must search other records themselves. Search fee $5.00. Real estate records located at Essex County. Copy fee $1.00 per page. Cert fee- $5.00 per page plus copy fee. Payee- Town of Hamilton. **Other phones:** Treasurer- 978-468-5575; Elections- 978-468-5570; Vital Records- 978-468-5570; Selectmen- 978-468-5572. **Property tax/Assessor-** same address as above. 978-468-5574.

Hampden County

County Register of Deeds, 50 State St; Hall of Justice, Springfield, MA 01103. 413-755-1722; fax-413-731-8190; hours: 8:30AM-4:30PM; 9AM-4PM(Recording).
http://registryofdeeds.co.hampden.ma.us
Records indexed on computer back to 1964. Will not search real estate records. Will search UCC records, but only real estate related UCC filed here. Will not search tax liens. Copy fee $1.00 per page. Payee-Hampden County Register of Deeds. **Online access to Real Estate, Lien, Recording records:** Access to the county index of land records is free or via subscription at http://204.213.242.147/alis/ww400r.pgm. Images can be viewed free, but cannot be printed unless you subscribe. Access to images via dial-up or web requires a $100 annual fee and $.50 per minute of use. Records go back to 1962. Lending agency info is available. Searchable indexes are bankruptcy (from PACER), unregistered land site and registered land site. For information, contact Mary Caron at 413-755-1722 x121. **Property tax/Assessor-** 413-787-6160.

Hampden Town

Town Clerk, PO Box 215, Hampden, MA 01036. 413-566-3214, R/E recording phone-413-755-1722; fax-413-566-2010; hours: 9AM-3PM M-Th; Closed F. www.hampden.org
No real estate recordings. Office personnel or visitors may perform searches. Search fee $10.00 per name. Real estate records located at Hampden County. General copy fee $1.00 per page. Tax lien copy- $.15 per page. Cert fee- $25.00 per LMC. Payee- Town of Hampden. **Online access to Real Estate, Recording, Lien records:** See Hampden County for recording records searching. **Other phones:** Treasurer- 413-566-2401; Elections- 413-566-3214; Vital Records- 413-566-3214. **Property tax/Assessor-** 413-566-3223.

Hampshire County

County Register of Deeds, 33 King St; Hall of Records, Northampton, MA 01060. 413-584-3637; fax-413-584-4136; hours: 8:30AM-4:30PM.
All records in one index. Records indexed on a public use terminal back to 1/1/1985. Only the public may search. Copy fee $1.00 per page. Cert fee- No extra fee. Payee- Commonwealth of Massachusetts. **Online access to Real Estate, Lien, Recorder, Deed, Judgment, Will records:** Access to property records is available; records date back to 9/2/1986. Lending agency information is available. For information, contact MaryAnn Foster at 413-584-3637. Also, Registry of Deeds records are searchable at www.masslandrecords.com. Click on Hampshire on map.

Hancock Town

Town Clerk, 3650 Hancock Rd, Hancock, MA 01237-1097. 413-738-5225; fax-413-738-5310; hours: 7-9PM T; 9AM-N Th; 9-11AM 1st Sat of month.
No real estate recordings. Separate indices to search include birth, death, marriage. Record index not computerized. Real estate records located at Berkshire County. Will search UCC records, but not tax liens. UCC search per debtor name- $10.00. General

copy fee $1.00 per page. Tax lien copy- $.25 per page. Cert fee- $1.00 per page. Payee- Town of Hancock. **Other phones:** Treasurer- 413-738-5225; Elections- 413-738-5225; Vital Records- 413-738-5225. **Property tax/Assessor-** same address as above. 413-738-5225.

Hanover Town

Town Clerk, 550 Hanover St, Hanover, MA 02339-2217. 781-826-2691; fax-781-826-5950; hours: 8AM-4PM.
No real estate recordings. Separate indices to search include Birth, Death, and Marriage. Records indexed on computer back to 1992. Office personnel or visitors may perform searches. Search fee $10.00. Real estate records located at Plymouth County. Tax lien search fee- $5.00. Copy fee $.25 per page. Cert fee- $5.00 per page plus copy fee. Payee- Town of Hanover. **Other phones:** Treasurer- 781-826-3571; Elections- 781-826-8796; Vital Records- 781-826-2691. **Property tax/Assessor-** same address as above. 781-826-6401.

Hanson Town

Town Clerk, 542 Liberty St.; Town Hall, Hanson, MA 02341. 781-293-2772; fax-781-294-0884; hours: 8AM-5PM M,T,W,Th; 7-9PM Tue; closed Fri. www.hanson-ma.gov
No real estate recordings. Only the office personnel may search. Real estate records located at Plymouth County. Will search UCC records; State tax liens not included. UCC search per debtor name- $10.00. Separate state tax lien search- $15.00 per debtor. Copy fee $.20 per page. Payee- Town of Hanson. **Online access to Property, GIS-mapping records:** Access property records free at http://gis.virtualtownhall.net/hanson/index.htm; no name searching. **Other phones:** Treasurer- 781-293-2422; Elections- 781-293-2772; Vital Records- 781-293-2772. **Property tax/Assessor-** same address as above. 781-293-5259.

Hardwick Town

Town Clerk, PO Box 575, Gilbertville, MA 01031-0575. 413-477-6197; fax-413-477-6703; hours: 6:30-8:30PM M; 9AM-N Sat.
No real estate recordings. All records in one index. Search fee $10.00 per name. Copy fee $1.00 per page. Cert fee- $5.00 per page includes copy fee. Payee- Town of Hardwick. **Online access to Property, Assessor records:** Access to property data is free at http://csc-ma.us/PropertyContent/jsp/Home.jsp?Page=1. Select Harwick Town. **Other phones:** Treasurer- 413-477-6197 x105; Elections- 413-477-6700; Vital Records- 413-477-6700. **Property tax/Assessor-** same address as above. 413-477-6197 x102.

Harvard Town

Town Clerk, 13 Ayer Rd; Town Hall, Harvard, MA 01451-1458. 978-456-4100; fax-978-456-4113; 8:30-4PM M-Th. www.harvard.ma.us/townclerk.htm
No real estate recordings; real estate records are at the county level with the Register of Deeds. The Village of Still River is in the Town of Harvard. Separate indices to search include. Records indexed by year. Office personnel or visitors may perform searches. Search fee $10.00. Real estate records located at Worcester County. Copy fee $1.00 per page. Cert fee- $1.00 per doc plus copy fee. Payee- Town of Harvard. **Online access to Assessor records:** Search town assessor database at http://data.visionappraisal.com/HARVARDMA/. Free registration for full data. **Other phones:** Treasurer- 978-456-4100 x18; Elections- 978-456-4100 x16; Vital Records- 978-456-4100 x16. **Property tax/Assessor-** same address as above. 978-456-4100 x14.

Harwich Town

Town Clerk, 732 Main St, Harwich, MA 02645-2717. 508-430-7516, R/E recording phone-508-430-7503, UCC recording phone-508-430-7516; fax-508-432-5039; hours: 8:30AM-4PM.

No real estate recordings. Office will perform a UCC search but public must search other records themselves. Real estate records located at Barnstable County. UCC search per debtor name- $10.00. Copy fee $2.00 per page. Payee- Town of Harwich. **Other phones:** Treasurer- 508-430-7501; Elections- 508-430-7516; Vital Records- 508-430-7516; Board of Selectmen- 508-430-7513. **Property tax/Assessor-** 508-430-7503.

Hatfield Town

Town Clerk, 59 Main St, Hatfield, MA 01038-9702. 413-247-0492; fax-413-347-5029; hours: 8AM-Noon; 1PM-4:30PM.
No real estate recordings. Office personnel or visitors may perform searches. Search fee $10.00 per name. Real estate records located at Hampshire County. Copy fee $1.00 per page. Payee- Town of Hatfield. **Other phones:** Treasurer- 413-247-0492. **Property tax/Assessor-** 413-247-0322.

Haverhill City

City Clerk, 4 Summer St; City Hall, Rm 118, Haverhill, MA 01830-5880. 978-374-2312; fax-978-373-8490; hours: 8AM-4PM. www.ci.haverhill.ma.us
No real estate recordings. Office will perform a tax lien search but public must search other records themselves. Search fee $10.00 per name. Real estate records located at Essex County. Copy fee $2.00 1st page, $1.00 each add'l. Cert fee- $10.00 per cert plus copy fee. Payee- City of Haverhill. **Online access to Assessor, Property records:** Access property data free at http://haverhill.patriotproperties.com/default.asp. **Other phones:** Treasurer- 978-374-2320; Elections- 978-374-2312; Vital Records- 978-374-2312. **Property tax/Assessor-** 978-347-2316.

Hawley Town

Town Clerk, Town Hall, Hawley, MA 01339-9624. 413-339-5518; fax-413-339-4959; 3-5PM Wed.
Separate indices to search include separate books. Record index not computerized. Real estate records located at Franklin County. Will not search UCC records or tax liens. Copy fee $1.00 per page. Payee- Town of Hawley. **Other phones:** Treasurer- 413-339-4231; Elections- 413-339-5818; Vital Records- 413-339-5818. **Property tax/Assessor-** same address as above. 413-339-5518.

Heath Town

Town Clerk, 1 E Main St; Town Hall, Heath, MA 01346. 413-337-4934; fax-413-337-8542; hours: 9:30AM-1:30PM M-Th.
No real estate recordings. All records in one index. Office personnel or visitors may perform searches. Search fee $10.00 per debtor. Real estate records located at Franklin County. Will search UCC records, tax liens included if requested. Copy fee $1.00 per page. Cert fee- $5.00 per page included 1 copy. Payee- Town of Heath. **Online access to Property, Assessor records:** Access property data free http://csc-ma.us/PropertyContent/jsp/Home.jsp?Page=1. Select Heath Town. **Other phones:** Treasurer- 413-337-4934. **Property tax/Assessor-** 1 E Main St, Heath, MA 01346; 413-337-4934.

Hingham Town

Town Clerk, 210 Central St, Hingham, MA 02043. 781-741-1410, R/E recording phone-781-741-1408, UCC recording phone-781-741-1410; fax-781-740-0239; hours: 8:30AM-4:30PM.
No real estate recordings. All records in one index. Record index not computerized. Only the office personnel may search. Search fee $10.00. Real estate records located at Plymouth County. Copy fee $2.00 per page. Cert fee- $1.00 per copy. Payee- Town of Hingham. **Online access to Property, Assessor, Sale records:** Search the assessor rolls and property sales free at http://csc-ma.us/HinghamPubAcc/jsp/Home.jsp?. Click on "New Search" or "Sales.". **Other phones:** Treasurer- 781-741-1408; Elections- 781-741-1410; Vital Records-

781-741-1410. **Property tax/Assessor-** same address as above. 781-741-1455.

Hinsdale Town

Town Clerk, PO Box 803, Hinsdale, MA 01235. 413-655-2301, R/E recording phone-413-443-7438, UCC recording phone-413-655-2301; fax-413-655-8807; hours: 1-3PM, 6:30-8PM W; 12:45-3PM Th.
No real estate recordings. Office personnel or visitors may perform searches. Search fee $10.00 per name. Real estate records located at Berkshire County. Copy fee $1.00 per page. Payee- Town of Hinsdale. **Other phones:** Treasurer- 413-655-2306; Elections- 413-655-2301; Vital Records- 413-655-2301. **Property tax/Assessor-** 413-655-2300.

Holbrook Town

Town Clerk, Town Hall, Holbrook, MA 02343-1502. 781-767-4314; fax-781-767-9054; hours: 8AM-4PM.
No real estate recordings. Record index not computerized. Only the office personnel may search. Search fee $10.00. Real estate records located at Norfolk County. Copy fee $2.00 per page. Cert fee- $5.00 per doc plus copy fee. Payee- Town of Holbrook. **Online access to Assessor, Property records:** Access property data free at http://holbrook.patriotproperties.com/default.asp. **Other phones:** Treasurer- 781-767-4316; Elections- 781-767-4314; Vital Records- 781-767-4314. **Property tax/Assessor-** 50 N Franklin St, Holbrook, MA 02343; 781-767-4315.

Holden Town

Town Clerk, 1196 Main St; Town Hall, Holden, MA 01520-1092. 508-829-0265; fax-508-829-0281; hours: 8:30AM-4:30PM; Summer Hr 8AM-4Pm.
No real estate recordings. Office personnel or visitors may perform searches. Search fee $12.00 per name. Real estate records located at Worcester County. Copy fee $.25 per page. Cert fee- $1.00 per page. Payee- Town of Holden. **Online access to Real Estate, Property Tax records:** Search the Town assessor's database free at http://data.visionappraisal.com/HOLDENMA. Free registration for full data. **Other phones:** Treasurer- 508-829-0235. **Property tax/Assessor-** 508-829-0223.

Holland Town

Town Clerk, 27 Sturbridge Rd, Holland, MA 01521-9712. 413-245-7108; fax-413-245-7037; hours: 9AM-N, 1-4PM M-Th.
No real estate recordings. Only the public may search. Copy fee $1.00 per page. Payee- Town of Holland. **Online access to Real Estate, Recording, Deed, Lien records:** See Hampden County for recording records searching.

Holliston Town

Town Clerk, 703 Washington St, Holliston, MA 01746. 508-429-0601; fax-508-429-0684; hours: 8:30AM-4:30PM. www.townofholliston.us
No real estate recordings. Record index not computerized. Office will perform a UCC search but public must search other records themselves. Search fee $10.00. Real estate records located at Middlesex County. Copy fee $.25 per page. Payee- Town of Holliston. **Online access to Property, Assessor records:** Access to property data is free at http://csc-ma.us/PropertyContent/jsp/Home.jsp?Page=1. Select Holliston Town. **Other phones:** Treasurer- 508-429-0602; Elections- 508-429-0601; Vital Records- 508-429-0601. **Property tax/Assessor-** 723 Washington St, Holliston, MA 01746; 508-429-0604.

Holyoke City

City Clerk, 536 Dwight St; Rm 2, Holyoke, MA 01040. 413-322-5520; fax-413-322-5521; hours: 8:30AM-4:30PM. www.ci.holyoke.ma.us
No real estate recordings. All records in one index. Record index not computerized. Office personnel or visitors may perform searches. Search fee $10.00 per name. Real estate records located at

Hampden County. General copy fee $2.00 for 1st page; $1.00 per add'l. Tax lien copy- $1.00 per page. Payee- Holyoke City Clerk. **Online access to Assessor, Property, Real Estate, Recording, Lien records:** Access to property valuations on the tax assessor database are free at www.ci.holyoke.ma.us/legend.htm. No name searching, but you can search by property types. Also, see Hampden County for recording records searching. **Other phones:** Treasurer- 413-322-5560; Elections- 413-332-5520; Vital Records- 413-322-5520. **Property tax/Assessor-** 413-322-5550.

Hopedale Town

Town Clerk, PO Box 7, Hopedale, MA 01747. 508-634-2203 x15; fax-508-634-2200; hours: 9AM-7PM M; 9AM-2PM T-Th.
No real estate recordings. All search information should be called in first. Record index not computerized. Only the office personnel may search. Search fee $10.00 per name. Copy fee $1.00 per page; UCC copy $2.00 per page. Cert fee- $5.00 per cert plus copy fee. Payee- Town of Hopedale. **Other phones:** Treasurer- 508-634-2203 x18; Elections- 508-634-2203 x15. **Property tax/Assessor-** 508-634-2203 x14.

Hopkinton Town

Town Clerk, 18 Main St, Hopkinton, MA 01748-1260. 508-497-9710; fax-508-497-9702; hours: 8:30AM-4PM. www.hopkinton.org
No real estate recordings. All records in one index. Record index not computerized. Only the office personnel may search. Real estate records located at Middlesex County. Will search UCC records, but not tax liens. UCC search per debtor name- $10.00. Copy fee $2.00 per page. Payee- Town of Hopkinton. **Other phones:** Treasurer- 508-497-9715; Elections- 508-497-9710; Vital Records- 508-497-9710. **Property tax/Assessor-** same address as above. 508-497-9720.

Hubbardston Town

Town Clerk, PO Box H, Hubbardston, MA 01452. 978-928-5244; fax-978-928-1402; hours: 2-8PM M; 8AM-4PM T-Th.
No real estate recordings. All records in one index. Search fee $10.00 per name. Copy fee $2.00 per page. Cert fee- $5.00 per page plus copy fee. Payee- Town of Hubbardston. **Other phones:** Treasurer- 978-928-1401; Elections- 978-928-5244; Vital Records- 978-928-5244; Tax Collector- 978-928-5736. **Property tax/Assessor-** 7 Main St, Hubbardston, MA 01452; 978-928-1400.

Hudson Town

Town Clerk, 78 Main St; Town Hall, Hudson, MA 01749. 978-568-9615; fax-978-562-8508; hours: 8AM-4:30PM. www.townofhudson.org
No real estate recordings. Office will perform a older UCC record or tax lien search but public must search other records themselves. Real estate records located at Middlesex County. Separate state tax lien search- $10.00 per debtor. Copy fee $.20 per page; $.50 for computer page. Cert fee- $5.00 per page plus copy fee. Payee- Town of Hudson. **Online access to Property, Assessor records:** Access Town Assessor records free at http://beta.whatifnet.com/assess/hudsonma/. **Other phones:** Treasurer- 978-568-9605; Elections- 978-568-9615; Vital Records- 978-568-9615. **Property tax/Assessor-** same address as above. 978-568-9620.

Hull Town

Town Clerk, Town Hall; 253 Atlantic Ave, Hull, MA 02045. 781-925-2262; fax-781-925-0224; hours: 8AM-4PM M,W; 8:30AM-7:30PMT, Th.
No real estate recordings. Office personnel or visitors may perform searches. Search fee $10.00 per name. Real estate records located at Plymouth County. Copy fee $.20 per page. Cert fee- $5.00 per cert. Payee- Town of Hull. **Property tax/Assessor-** 781-925-2205.

Huntington Town

Town Clerk, PO Box 523; Office of Town Clerk, Huntington, MA 01050. 413-667-3186; fax-413-667-3507; hours: 9AM-Noon Mon; 6-8PM Wed.
No real estate recordings. Separate indices to search. Search fee $10.00 per name. Copy fee $1.00 per page. Cert fee- $5.00 per doc includes copies. Payee- Town of Huntington. **Other phones:** Treasurer- 413-667-3501; Vital Records- 413-667-3186. **Property tax/Assessor-** 413-667-3501.

Ipswich Town

Town Clerk, 25 Green St, Ipswich, MA 01938-2357. 978-356-6600; fax-978-356-6616; hours: 8AM-7PM M; 8AM-4PM T,W,Th; 8AM-N Fri. www.town.ipswich.ma.us/
No real estate recordings. Index: Indices by instrument type. Search fee $10.00 per name. Copy fee $2.00 per page. Cert fee- $5.00 per doc includes copies. Payee- Town of Ipswich. **Online access to Assessor, Property records:** Access property data free at http://ipswich.patriotproperties.com/default.asp. **Other phones:** Treasurer- 978-356-6610; Elections- 978-356-6600; Vital Records- 978-356-6600. **Property tax/Assessor-** same address as above. 978-356-6603.

Kingston Town

Town Clerk, 26 Evergreen St, Kingston, MA 02364. 781-585-0502; fax-781-585-0542; hours: 8:30AM-N, 1-4:30PM. www.kingstonmass.org
No real estate recordings. All records in one index. Only the office personnel may search. Search fee $5.00 per name. Copy fee $2.00 per page. Cert fee- $10.00 per doc, plus copy fee. Payee- Town of Kingston. **Other phones:** Treasurer- 781-585-0508; Elections- 781-585-0502; Vital Records- 781-585-0502. **Property tax/Assessor-** same address as above. 781-585-0509.

Lakeville Town

Town Clerk, 346 Bedford St, Lakeville, MA 02347. 508-946-8814; fax-508-946-3970; hours: 9AM-4PM.
No real estate recordings. All records in one index. Office personnel or visitors may perform searches. Search fee $2.00. Real estate records located at Plymouth County. Copy fee $1.00 per page. Cert fee- $5.00 per page plus copy fee. Payee- Town of Lakeville. **Other phones:** Treasurer- 508-946-8801; Elections- 508-946-8814; Vital Records- 508-946-8814. **Property tax/Assessor-** 239 Main St, Lakeville, MA 02347; 508-947-4428.

Lancaster Town

Town Clerk, Box 97; Town Hall, Lancaster, MA 01523-0097. 978-365-2542, R/E recording phone-978-365-9562, UCC recording phone-978-365-2542; fax-978-368-4005; hours: 9AM-6PM M; 9AM-4PM T-TH. www.ci.lancaster.ma.us
No real estate recordings. Only the public may search. Real estate records located at Worcester County. Copy fee $2.00 per page. Cert fee- $5.00 per cert plus copy fee. Payee- Town of Lancaster. **Online access to Property, Assessor records:** Access to property data is free at http://csc-ma.us/PropertyContent/jsp/Home.jsp?Page=1. Select Lancaster Town. **Other phones:** Treasurer- 978-365-6115; Elections- 978-365-2542; Vital Records- 978-365-2542. **Property tax/Assessor-** 695 Main St, PO Box 243, Lancaster, MA 01523; 978-365-9562.

Lanesborough Town

Town Clerk, PO Box 1492, Lanesborough, MA 01237. 413-442-1351, R/E recording phone-413-442-0813, UCC recording phone-413-442-1351; fax-413-443-5811; hours: 8AM-1PM.
No real estate recordings. Index: Indices to search include each year filed separate. Record index not computerized. Only the office personnel may search. Search fee $5.00 per hour. Real estate records located at Berkshire County. Copy fee $.30

per page. Cert fee- $5.00 per doc plus copy fee. Payee- Town of Lanesborough. **Other phones:** Treasurer- 413-442-1167 x23; Elections- 413-442-1351; Vital Records- 413-442-1351. **Property tax/Assessor-** PO Box 164, Lanesborough, MA 01237-0164; 413-442-8622.

Lawrence City

City Clerk, 200 Common St, Lawrence, MA 01840. 978-794-5803, R/E recording phone-978-683-2745, UCC recording phone-978-794-5803; fax-978-794-1354; hours: 8:30AM-4:30PM. www.cityoflawrence.com/Departments.asp
No real estate recordings. Office personnel or visitors may perform searches. Search fee $10.00 per name. Real estate records located at Essex County. Copy fee $2.00 per financing statement. Payee- City of Lawrence. **Online access to Land, Grantor/Grantee, Recording records:** Search the recorder database for free at www.lawrencedeeds.com/dsSearch.asp. **Other phones:** Treasurer- 978-794-5843; Elections- 978-794-5807; Vital Records- 978-794-5803. **Property tax/Assessor-** 978-794-5790.

Lee Town

Town Clerk, 32 Main St; Town Hall, Lee, MA 01238. 413-243-5505; fax-413-243-5507; hours: 8:30AM-4PM.
No real estate recordings. All records in one index. Record index not computerized. Office personnel or visitors may perform searches. Search fee $10.00 per name. Real estate records located at Berkshire County. Copy fee $.10 per page. Cert fee- $0.00 for UCC's. Payee- Town Clerk. **Online access to Property, Assessor records:** Access to property data is free at http://csc-ma.us/PropertyContent/jsp/Home.jsp?Page=1. **Other phones:** Treasurer- 413-243-5505; Vital Records- 413-243-5505; Tax Collector- 413-243-5515. **Property tax/Assessor-** same address as above. 413-243-5512.

Leicester Town

Town Clerk, 3 Washburn Sq, Leicester, MA 01524. 508-892-7011, R/E recording phone-508-892-7001, UCC recording phone-508-892-7011; fax-508-892-7070; hours: 8:30AM-4PM.
No real estate recordings. Record index not computerized. Only the public may search. Real estate records located at Worcester County. General copy fee $1.00 per page. Tax lien copy- $.50 per page. Cert fee- $5.00 per page plus copy fee. Payee- Town of Leicester. **Online access to Assessor, Property records:** Access property data free at http://leicester.patriotproperties.com/default.asp. **Other phones:** Treasurer- 508-892-7002; Elections- 508-892-7011; Vital Records- 508-892-7011. **Property tax/Assessor-** same address as above. 508-892-7001.

Lenox Town

Town Clerk, 6 Walker St; Town Hall, Lenox, MA 01240-2718. 413-637-5506, R/E recording phone-413-637-5505, UCC recording phone-413-637-5506; fax-413-637-5518; hours: 9AM-4PM. www.townoflenox.com
No real estate recordings. All records in one index. Will search UCC records or tax liens. Copy fee $.25 per page. Cert fee- $10.00 per doc includes copy fee. Payee- Town of Lenox. **Other phones:** Treasurer- 413-637-5506; Elections- 413-637-5506; Vital Records- 413-637-5506. **Property tax/Assessor-** same address as above. 413-637-5502, assessor fax- 413-637-5518.

Leominster City

City Clerk, 25 West St, Leominster, MA 01453. 978-534-7536; fax-978-534-7546; 8:30AM-4PM M-W & F; 8:30AM-5:30PM Th. www.ci.leominster.us
No real estate recordings. All records in one index. Office personnel or visitors may perform searches. Search fee $10.00. Real estate records located at

Worcester County. Federal/state combined tax lien search- $5.00 per copy. General copy fee $2.00 1st 3 pages; $1.00 each add'l. Tax lien copy- $5.00 per copy. Payee- City of Leominster. **Online access to Assessor records:** Search the assessor's database at http://data.visionappraisal.com/leominsterma. Free registration for full data. **Other phones:** Treasurer- 978-537-7509; Elections- 978-534-7536; Vital Records- 978-534-7536. **Property tax/Assessor-** same address as above. 978-534-7531.

Leverett Town

Town Clerk, PO Box 178, Leverett, MA 01054. 413-548-9150, R/E recording phone-413-548-9699; fax-413-548-9150; hours: 7PM-9PM M; 9AM-N W,Th. http://townhall.leverett.ma.us
No real estate recordings. All records in one index. Record index not computerized. Office will perform a UCC search but public must search other records themselves. Search fee $10.00. Real estate records located at Franklin County. Copy fee $1.00 per page. Cert fee- $5.00 per copy. Payee- Town of Leverett. **Assessor-** 413-548-4945.

Lexington Town

Town Clerk, 1625 Massachusetts Ave; Town Office Bldg, Lexington, MA 02420. 781-862-0500 x270; fax-781-861-2754; hours: 8:30AM-4:30PM. http://ci.lexington.ma.us
No real estate recordings. Separate indices to search. Office will perform a UCC search but public must search other records themselves. UCC search per debtor name- $5.00. Tax Department will do a separate state tax lien search, no charge. Copy fee $1.00 per page. Cert fee- $2.00 per page includes copies. Payee- Town of Lexington. **Online access to Assessor records:** Assessor information is at http://data.visionappraisal.com/LexingtonMA/. Does not require a username & password. Simply click on link. **Other phones:** Treasurer- 781-862-0500 x265; Elections- 781-862-0500 x270; Vital Records- 781-862-0500 x270. **Property tax/Assessor-** same address as above. 781-862-0500 x203.

Leyden Town

Town Clerk, Town Hall, Leyden, MA 01337. 413-774-7769; fax-413-772-0146; 8AM-1PM M; 1-5PM W.
No real estate recordings. All records in one index. Record index not computerized. Real estate records located at Franklin County. Copy fee $1.00 per page. Payee- Town of Leyden. **Other phones:** Treasurer- 413-774-4111; Elections- 413-774-7769; Vital Records- 413-774-7769. **Property tax/Assessor-** 413-774-4111.

Lincoln Town

Town Clerk, PO Box 6353, Lincoln Center, MA 01773-6353. 781-259-2607; fax-781-259-1677; hours: 8:30AM-4:30PM. www.mass.gov/cc/lincoln.html
No real estate recordings. All records in one index. Office personnel or visitors may perform searches. Real estate records located at Middlesex County. Will search UCC records and tax liens. UCC search per debtor name- $10.00. Copy fee $2.00 per page. Payee- Town of Lincoln. **Other phones:** Treasurer- 781-259-2606; Elections- 781-259-2607; Vital Records- 781-259-2607. **Property tax/Assessor-** 781-259-2611.

Littleton Town

Town Clerk, PO Box 1305, Littleton, MA 01460. 978-952-2314; fax-978-952-2321; hours: 9AM-3PM M,T,W,F; 9AM-9PM Th. www.littletonma.org
No real estate recordings. All records in one index. Record index not computerized. Only the office personnel may search. Search fee $10.00. Real estate records located at Middlesex County. Copy fee $.35 per page. Cert fee- $5.00. Payee- Town of Littleton. **Other phones:** Treasurer- 978-952-2306; Elections- 978-952-2314; Vital Records- 978-952-2314; Tax Collector- 978-952-2349. **Property tax/Assessor-** same address as above. 978-952-2309.

Longmeadow Town

Town Clerk, 20 Williams St; Town Hall, Longmeadow, MA 01106. 413-567-1066; fax-413-565-4112; hours: 8:15AM-4:30PM M-TH; 8:15AM-Noon F. www.longmeadow.org
No real estate recordings. All records in one index. Record index not computerized. Office will perform a UCC search but public must search other records themselves. Real estate records located at Hampden County. UCC search per debtor name- $14.00 per hour. Copy fee $.20 per page. Cert fee- $5.00 per copy plus copy fee. Payee- Town of Longmeadow. **Online access to Assessor, Real Estate, Recording, Lien records:** Access to tax records is at http://data.visionappraisal.com/LONGMEADOWMA/. Free registration for full data. Also, see Hampden County for recording records searching. **Other phones:** Treasurer- 413-567-1066; Elections- 413-567-1066; Vital Records- 413-567-1066. **Property tax/Assessor-** same address as above. 413-565-4115.

Lowell City

City Clerk, 375 Merrimack St; City Hall, Lowell, MA 01852. 978-970-4161, R/E recording phone-978-970-4224, UCC recording phone-978-970-4159; fax-978-970-4162; hours: 8AM-5PM. www.lowellma.gov/depts/clerk
No real estate recordings. Separate indices to search. Office personnel or visitors may perform searches. Search fee $10.00 per name. Real estate records located at Middlesex County. Copy fee $3.00 1st page, $2.00 each add'l. Tax lien copy- $1.00 per page. Cert fee- $5.00 per doc plus copy fee. Payee- City of Lowell. **Other phones:** Treasurer- 978-970-4224; Elections- 978-970-4046; Vital Records- 978-970-4161. **Property tax/Assessor-** 978-970-4200.

Ludlow Town

Town Clerk, 488 Chapin St, Ludlow, MA 01056. 413-583-5610, R/E recording phone-413-583-5608, UCC recording phone-413-583-5610; fax-413-583-5603; 8:30AM-4:30PM. www.ludlow.ma.us/clerk/
No real estate recordings. All records in one index. Record index not computerized. Only the office personnel may search. Real estate records located at Hampden County. Will search UCC records, tax liens included if requested. UCC search per debtor name- $10.00. Separate federal or state tax lien search- $2.00 per page. Copy fee $2.00, if tax lien or real estate $.50 per page. Cert fee- $1.00 per doc plus copy fee. Payee- Town of Ludlow. **Online access to Real Estate, Recording, Lien records:** See Hampden County for recording records searching. **Other phones:** Treasurer- 413-583-5616; Elections- 413-583-5610; Vital Records- 413-583-5610. **Property tax/Assessor-** same address as above. 413-583-5608.

Lunenburg Town

Town Clerk, PO Box 135, Lunenburg, MA 01462. 978-582-4131, R/E recording phone-978-582-4132 or 4130, UCC recording phone-978-582-4131; fax-978-582-4148; hours: 8AM-4PM M,W,Th; 8AM-6:30PM Tues; Closed Fri. www.lunenburgonline.com
No real estate recordings. All records in one index. Record index not computerized. Only the office personnel may search. Real estate records located at Worcester County. UCC search per debtor name- $10.00. Copy fee $1.00 per page. Cert fee- $10.00 per page plus copy fee. Payee- Town of Lunenburg. **Online access to Property, Assessor records:** Access to property data is free at http://csc-ma.us/PropertyContent/jsp/Home.jsp?Page=1. **Other phones:** Treasurer- 978-582-4130; Elections- 978-582-4132; Vital Records- 978-582-4131. **Property tax/Assessor-** same address as above. 978-582-4145.

Lynn City

City Clerk, 3 City Hall Sq, Lynn, MA 01901. 781-598-4000; fax-781-477-7032; hours: 8:30AM-4PM M,W,Th; 8:30AM-8PM T; 8:30AM-12:30PM F.

No real estate recordings. Office will perform a UCC search but public must search other records themselves. Search fee $10.00. Real estate records located at Essex County. Copy fee $1.00 per page. Payee- City of Lynn. **Online access to Assessor, Property records:** Access property data free at http://lynn.patriotproperties.com/default.asp. **Property tax/Assessor-** 3 City Hall Sq, Rm 202, Lynn, MA 01901; 781-598-4000.

Lynnfield Town

Town Clerk, 55 Summer St, Lynnfield, MA 01940-1823. 781-334-3128; fax-781-334-5829; 8AM-4:30PM (F 8am-1pm). www.town.lynnfield.ma.us No real estate recordings. Separate indices to search include card file (3 drawers). Record index not computerized. Search fee $10.00 per name. Copy fee $.20 per page. Cert fee- $5.00 per cert plus copy fee. Payee- Town of Lynnfield. **Online access to Assessor, Property records:** Access property data free at http://lynnfield.patriotproperties.com/default.asp. **Other phones:** Treasurer- 781-334-7663; Elections- 781-334-3128; Vital Records- 781-334-3128. **Property tax/Assessor-** same address as above. 781-334-2231.

Malden City

City Clerk, 200 Pleasant St; City Hall, Malden, MA 02148. 781-397-7116; fax-781-388-0610; hours: 8AM-4PM M,W,Th; 8AM-7PM T; 8AM-N Fri. No real estate recordings. Only the public may search. Payee- City of Malden. **Property tax/Assessor-** 781-397-7100.

Manchester-by-the-Sea Town

Town Clerk, 10 Central St; Town Hall, Manchester-by-the-Sea, MA 01944-1399. 978-526-2040; fax-978-526-2001; hours: 9AM-5PM M-W; 9AM-8PM Th. www.manchester.ma.us No real estate recordings. All records in one index. Office personnel or visitors may perform searches. Search fee $10.00 per name. Real estate records located at Essex County. Will search UCC records, tax liens not included in UCC search. Copy fee $1.00 per page. Cert fee- $5.00 per page plus copy fee. Payee- Town of Manchester-by-the-Sea. **Online access to Property Assessor records:** Search the property assessment data at http://manchester.patriotproperties.com/default.asp. **Other phones:** Treasurer- 978-526-2030; Elections- 978-526-2040; Vital Records- 978-526-2040. **Property tax/Assessor-** same address as above. 978-526-2010.

Mansfield Town

Town Clerk, 6 Park Row; Town Hall, Mansfield, MA 02048-2433. 508-261-7345; fax-508-261-1083; hours: 8AM-4PM M, T, Th; 8AM-8PM W; 8AM-N Fri. No real estate recordings. All records in one index. Record index not computerized. Only the office personnel may search. Search fee $10.00 per name. Real estate records located at Bristol County. Separate state tax lien search available. Payee- Town of Mansfield. **Online access to Assessor records:** Search town assessor database at http://data.visionappraisal.com/MansfieldMA/. Free registration for full data. **Other phones:** Treasurer- 508-261-7340; Elections- 508-261-7345; Vital Records- 508-261-7345. **Property tax/Assessor-** 508-261-7350.

Marblehead Town

Town Clerk, Abbot Hall, Marblehead, MA 01945. 781-631-0528; fax-781-631-8571; hours: 8AM-5PM, M, T, Th; 7:30AM-7:30PM, W; 8AM-1PM F. www.marblehead.org No real estate recordings. Index: There are separate indices to search. Record index not computerized. Only the office personnel may search. Real estate records located at Essex County. Will search UCC records, but not tax liens. UCC search per debtor name- $10.00. Copy fee $.10 per page. Payee- Town of Marblehead. **Online access to Assessor, Property records:** Access property data free at http://marblehead.patriotproperties.com/default.asp. **Other phones:** Treasurer- 781-631-1033; Elections- 781-631-0528; Vital Records- 781-631-0528. **Property tax/Assessor-** 7 Widger Rd, Marblehead, MA 01945; 781-631-0236.

Marion Town

Town Clerk, 2 Spring St, Marion, MA 02738. 508-748-3502; fax-508-748-2845; hours: 8AM-4:30PM M-Th; 8AM-3:30PM F. www.townofmarion.org No real estate recordings. Office personnel or visitors may perform searches. Real estate records located at Plymouth County. UCC search per debtor name- $10.00. Federal/state combined tax lien search- $25.00 per debtor. Copy fee $1.00 per page. Payee- Town of Marion. **Online access to Assessor records:** Search town assessor data at http://data.visionappraisal.com/MarionMA/. Free registration for full data. **Other phones:** Treasurer- 508-748-3505. **Property tax/Assessor-** 508-748-3510.

Marlborough City

City Clerk, 140 Main St, Marlborough, MA 01752-3812. 508-460-3775; fax-508-624-6504; hours: 8:30AM-5PM. No real estate recordings. All records in one index; UCC is not indexed. Record index not computerized. Office will perform a Tax search but public must search other records themselves. Search fee $10.00. Real estate records located at Middlesex County. Copy fee $2.00 per page. Payee- City of Marlborough. **Online access to Property Assessor records:** Search the city assessor data at http://data.visionappraisal.com/MarlboroughMA/. Free registration for full data. **Other phones:** Treasurer- 508-460-3730; Elections- 508-460-3775; Vital Records- 508-460-3775. **Property tax/Assessor-** same address as above. 508-460-3779.

Marshfield Town

Town Clerk, Town Hall, Marshfield, MA 02050. 781-834-5540; fax-781-837-7163; hours: 8:30AM-4:30PM. No real estate recordings. All records in one index. Record index not computerized. Only the office personnel may search. Search fee $10.00. Real estate records located at Plymouth County. Copy fee $1.00 per copy. Payee- Town of Marshfield. **Online access to Assessor records:** Search town assessor database at http://data.visionappraisal.com/MarshfieldMA/. Does not require a username & password. Simply click on link. **Other phones:** Treasurer- 781-834-5545; Elections- 781-834-5540; Vital Records- 781-834-5540. **Property tax/Assessor-** Town Hall, 870 Moraine St, Marshfield, MA 02050; 781-834-5585.

Mashpee Town

Town Clerk, 16 Great Neck Rd. N.; Town Hall, Mashpee, MA 02649. 508-539-1400 x561, R/E recording phone-508-539-1400 x537, UCC recording phone-508-539-1400 x561; fax-508-539-1403; hours: 9AM-4PM. www.ci.mashpee.ma.us No real estate recordings. Office personnel or visitors may perform searches. Search fee $5.00 per name. Real estate records located at Barnstable County. Copy fee $.20 per page. Cert fee- $5.00 per cert. Payee- Town of Mashpee. **Online access to Assessor records:** Records on the Town of Mashpee Assessor database are free at www.capecode.com/mashpee/search.asp. **Other phones:** Treasurer- 508-539-1400 x537; Elections- 508-539-1400 x561; Vital Records- 508-539-1400 x529. **Property tax/Assessor-** 508-539-1400 x529.

Mattapoisett Town

Town Clerk, PO Box 89, Mattapoisett, MA 02739-0089. 508-758-4103, R/E recording phone-508-758-4106, UCC recording phone-508-758-4103; fax-508-758-3030; hours: 8AM-4PM. www.mattapoisett.net No real estate recordings. All records in one index. Office personnel or visitors may perform searches.

Search fee $10.00 per name. Real estate records located at Plymouth County. General copy fee $1.00 per page. Tax lien copy- $2.00 per page. Cert fee- $1.00 per page plus copy fee. Payee- Town of Mattapoisett. **Online access to Property, Assessor records:** Access to property data is free at http://csc-ma.us/PropertyContent/jsp/Home.jsp?Page=1. Select Mattapoisett Town. **Other phones:** Treasurer- 508-758-4108; Elections- 508-758-4103; Vital Records- 508-758-4103. **Property tax/Assessor-** PO Box 435, Mattapoisett, MA 02739; 508-758-4106.

Maynard Town

Town Clerk, 195 Main St; Town Hall, Maynard, MA 01754-2575. 978-897-1000, R/E recording phone-978-897-1005, UCC recording phone-978-897-1000; fax-978-897-8457; 8-4. http://web.maynard.ma.us No real estate recordings. All records in one index. Record index not computerized. Only the office personnel may search. Search fee $5.00 per name. Copy fee $1.00 per page. Cert fee- $10.00 per page plus copy fee. Payee- Town of Maynard. **Other phones:** Treasurer- 978-897-1005; Elections- 978-897-1000; Vital Records- 978-897-1000. **Assessor-** same address as above. 978-897-1004.

Medfield Town

Town Clerk, 459 Main St; Town Hall, Medfield, MA 02052. 508-359-8505, R/E recording phone-508-359-8505 x625, UCC recording phone-508-359-8505x630; fax-508-359-6182; hours: 8:30AM-4:30PM M-W; 8:30AM-7:30PM Th; 8:30AM-1PM F. www.town.medfield.net No real estate recordings. Office personnel or visitors may perform searches. Search fee $10.00. Real estate records located at Norfolk County. Copy fee $1.00 per page. Payee- Town of Medfield. **Other phones:** Treasurer- 508-359-8505 X625.

Medford City

City Clerk, 85 George P. Hassett Drive; City Clerk, Medford, MA 02155. 781-393-2425; fax-781-391-1895; hours: 8:30AM-4:30PM M,T,Th; 8:30AM-7:30PM W; 8:30AM-12:3. www.medford.org No real estate recordings. Record index not computerized. Office will perform a UCC search but public must search other records themselves. Real estate records located at Middlesex County. UCC search per debtor name- $10.00. Payee- City of Medford. **Online access to Assessor records:** Search the city assessor database at http://data.visionappraisal.com/MedfordMA/. Free registration for full data. **Other phones:** Treasurer- 781-393-2550; Elections- 781-393-2491; Vital Records- 781-393-2425. **Property tax/Assessor-** 781-393-2435.

Medway Town

Town Clerk, 155 Village St, Medway, MA 02053. 508-533-3204; fax-508-533-3287; hours: 8AM-7:30PM M; 8AM-4PM Tu-Th; 8AM-1PM F. http://townofmedway.org No real estate recordings. Office will perform a UCC search but public must search other records themselves. Real estate records located at Norfolk County. Copy fee $2.00 per page. Payee- Town of Medway. **Other phones:** Treasurer- 508-533-3205. **Property tax/Assessor-** 508-533-3203.

Melrose City

City Clerk, 562 Main St, Melrose, MA 02176. 781-979-4114; fax-781-665-6877; hours: 8AM-4:30PM (July-August:8AM-4:30PM M-Th; 8AM-1PM F. www.cityofmelrose.org No real estate recordings. Office personnel or visitors may perform searches. Search fee $15.00 per name. Real estate records located at Middlesex County. Copy fee $.25 per page. Payee- City of Melrose. **Online access to Assessor, Property records:** Access property data free at http://melrose.patriotproperties.com/default.asp. **Other phones:** Treasurer- 781-979-4160; Elections- 781-979-4125; Vital Records- 781-979-4114. **Property tax/Assessor-** 781-979-4104.

Mendon Town

Town Clerk, PO Box 54, Mendon, MA 01756-0054. 508-473-1085; fax-508-478-8241; 8-6PM Mon; 8AM-2:30PM Tu.Th; 8AM-5PM W; Closed F. No real estate recordings. All records in one index. Only the office personnel may search. Real estate records located at Worcester County. UCC search per debtor name- $5.00. This agency will do a state tax lien search. Copy fee $2.00 per page. Cert fee- $10.00 per doc plus copy fee. Payee- Town of Mendon. **Other phones:** Treasurer- 508-473-6410; Elections- 508-473-1085; Vital Records- 508-473-1085; Tax Collector- 508-473-6410. **Property tax/Assessor-** 20 Main St, Mendon, MA 01756; 508-473-2738.

Merrimac Town

Town Clerk, 2 School St, Merrimac, MA 01860. 978-346-8013; fax-978-346-7832; hours: 9AM-4PM, M,T, W,Th. No real estate recordings. Record index not computerized. Only the office personnel may search. Search fee $5.00. Real estate records located at Essex County. Copy fee $2.00 per page. Cert fee- $2.00 per page includes copy fee. Payee- Town of Merrimac. **Other phones:** Treasurer- 978-346-0524; Elections- 978-346-8013; Vital Records- 978-346-8013. **Property tax/Assessor-** 978-346-9022.

Methuen City

City Clerk, 41 Pleasant St, Rm 112, Methuen, MA 01844. 978-794-3213, R/E recording phone-978-794-3219, UCC recording phone-978-794-3213; fax-978-794-3215; hours: 8:30AM-5:30PM M-TH; 8:30AM-N Fri. www.ci.methuen.ma.us No real estate recordings. All records in one index. Record index not computerized. Office will perform a UCC search but public must search other records themselves. Real estate records located at Essex County at Northern Essex Register of Deeds, Lawrence, MA. UCC search per debtor name- $10.00 minimum. Copy fee $2.00 per page. Payee- City of Methuen. **Online access to Property Assessor, Land, Grantor/Grantee, Recording records:** Search the property assessment data free at http://host229.ci.methuen.ma.us. Also, search the recorder database for free at www.lawrencedeeds.com/dsSearch.asp. **Other phones:** Treasurer- 978-794-3205; Elections- 978-794-3213; Vital Records- 978-794-3213. **Property tax/Assessor-** 978-794-3220.

Middleborough Town

Town Clerk, 20 Centre St, 1st Fl, Middleborough, MA 02346. 508-946-2415, R/E recording phone-508-946-2410, UCC recording phone-508-946-2415; fax-508-946-2308; hours: 8:45AM-5PM. No real estate recordings. All records in one index. Record index not computerized. Office will perform a UCC search but public must search other records themselves. Search fee $15.00. Real estate records located at Plymouth County. Copy fee $5.00 per page. Cert fee- $5.00 per doc, plus copy fee. Payee- Town of Middleborough. **Online access to Assessor records:** Search town assessor database at http://data.visionappraisal.com/MiddleboroMA/. Does not require a username & password. Simply click on link. **Other phones:** Treasurer- 508-946-2420; Elections- 508-946-2415; Vital Records- 508-946-2415. **Property tax/Assessor-** 508-946-2410.

Middlefield Town

Town Clerk, PO Box 265, Middlefield, MA 01243. 413-623-8966; fax-413-623-6108; hours: 7PM-9PM; 9AM-N Sat. No real estate recordings. Record index not computerized. Only the public may search. Real estate records located at Hampshire County. General copy fee $1.00 per page. Tax lien copy- $10.00 per document. Payee- Town of Middlefield. **Other phones:** Treasurer- 413-623-5182; Elections- 413-623-8966; Town Clerk- 413-623-2079. **Property**

tax/Assessor- 188 Skyline Trail, Middlefield, MA 01243; 413-623-8966.

Middlesex County Northern District

County Register of Deeds, 360 Gorham St, Lowell, MA 01852. 978-322-9000; fax-978-322-9001; hours: 8:30AM-4:15PM. www.lowelldeeds.com Separate indices to search include recorded land, registered land, plans. Records indexed on a public use terminal back to 1/2/1976. Only the public may search. Copy fee $1.00 per page. Cert fee- $1.00 per page plus copy fee. Payee- Commonwealth of Massachusetts. **Online access to Recorder, Deed, Lien, Judgment, UCC, Will records:** Access Register of Deeds data free at www.masslandrecords.com. Click on North Middlesex on map. **Property tax/Assessor-** 978-970-4200.

Middlesex County Southern District

County Registry of Deeds, 208 Cambridge St, Cambridge, MA 02141. 617-679-6300; 8AM-4PM. Will not search real estate records. Will not search UCC records or tax liens. Copy fee $1.00 per page. Cert fee- $1.00 per page. Payee- Commonwealth of Massachusetts. **Online access to Real Estate, Lien, Recording, Deed, Judgment, Will records:** Access to Register of Deeds data is free www.masslandrecords.com. Click on South Middlesex on map.

Middleton Town

Town Clerk, Memorial Hall; 48 South Main St, Middleton, MA 01949. 978-774-6927; fax-978-774-6167; hours: 9AM-4PM M-W-Th; 9AM-1PM F; 6-8PM T. www.townofmiddleton.org No real estate recordings. Separate indices to search. Search fee $5.00 per name. Copy fee $.20 per page. Cert fee- $5.00 per page plus copy fee. Payee- Town of Middleton. **Other phones:** Treasurer- 978-774-8327; Elections- 978-774-6927; Vital Records- 978-774-6927. **Property tax/Assessor-** same address as above. 978-774-2099.

Milford Town

Town Clerk, 52 Main St, Milford, MA 01757. 508-634-2307; fax-508-634-2324; hours: 8:30AM-4:30PM. No real estate recordings. Office will perform a tax lien search but public must search other records themselves. Search fee $10.00 per name. Copy fee $1.00 per page. Cert fee- $6.00,$5.00 in person. Payee- Town of Milford. **Online access to Assessor, Property records:** Access property data free at http://milford.patriotproperties.com/default.asp. **Property tax/Assessor-** same address as above. 508-634-2306.

Millbury Town

Town Clerk, 127 Elm St; Municipal Office Bldg, Millbury, MA 01527. 508-865-9110, R/E recording phone-508-865-9121, UCC recording phone-508-865-9110; fax-508-865-0857; hours: 9AM-4PM. No real estate recordings. Separate indices to search. Office personnel or visitors may perform searches. Real estate records located at Worcester County. UCC search per debtor name- $10.00. Payee- Town of Millbury. **Online access to Assessor records:** Access to the town tax assessor info is free at http://data.visionappraisal.com/MillburyMA/. **Other phones:** Treasurer- 508-865-8040; Elections- 508-865-9110; Vital Records- 508-865-9110. **Property tax/Assessor-** 127 Elm Street, Millbury, MA 01527; 508-865-4732.

Millis Town

Town Clerk, 900 Main St, Millis, MA 02054-1512. 508-376-7046; fax-508-376-7053; 8:30AM-4:30PM. No real estate recordings. All records in one index. Record index not computerized. Only the office personnel may search. UCC search per debtor name- $10.00. Copy fee $1.00 per page. Payee-

Town of Millis. **Other phones:** Treasurer- 508-376-7048; Elections- 508-376-7046; Vital Records- 508-376-7046; Tax Collector- 508-376-7048. **Property tax/Assessor-** 900 Main St, Millis, MA 02054; 508-376-7049.

Millville Town

Town Clerk, PO Box 703, Millville, MA 01529-0703. 508-883-5849; fax-508-883-2994; hours: M-Th 8:30-1PM; 6-8PM W. http://millvillema.org No real estate recordings here. See Worcester County Register of Deeds searchable website for Town recordings. Only the public may search. Copy fee $1.00 per page. Cert fee- $5.00 per doc plus copy fee. Payee- Town of Millville. **Online access to Real Estate, Deed, Tax Lien records:** Access the index at www.worcesterdeeds.com/worcester/dsbppagelist.asp. **Other phones:** Treasurer- 508-883-7449; Elections- 508-883-5849; Vital Records- 508-883-5849. **Property tax/Assessor-** same address as above. 508-883-5031.

Milton Town

Town Clerk, 525 Canton Ave; Town Hall, Milton, MA 02186. 617-696-5414; hours: 8:30AM-5PM. No real estate recordings. All records in one index. Office personnel or visitors may perform searches. Search fee $10.00 per name. Real estate records located at Norfolk County. Will search UCC records, tax liens included if requested. Copy fee $2.00 per page. Cert fee- $2.00 per page. Payee- Town of Milton. **Other phones:** Treasurer- 617-696-5409. **Property tax/Assessor-** same address as above. 617-696-5703.

Monroe Town

Town Clerk, PO Box 6, Monroe, MA 01350. 413-424-5272; fax-413-424-7580; hours: 8AM-N, M-W. No real estate recordings. Record index not computerized. Only the public may search. Real estate records located at Franklin County. General copy fee $1.00 per page. Tax lien copy- $2.00 per page. Payee- Town of Monroe. **Other phones:** Treasurer- 413-424-5272. **Property tax/Assessor-** same address as above. 413-424-5272.

Monson Town

Town Clerk, 110 Main St. #4, Monson, MA 01057-1332. 413-267-4115; fax-413-267-3726; hours: 9AM-12:30 PM, 1:30-4PM (3:30 on Tu). www.monson-ma.gov No real estate recordings. All records in one index. Real estate records located at Hampden County. Will search UCC records. UCC search per debtor name- $14.72 per hour. Separate state tax lien search- $14.72 per hour. General copy fee $7.00 each filing regardless of page number. Tax lien copy- $.20 per page. Cert fee- No extra fee. Payee- Town of Monson. **Online access to Real Estate, Recording, Lien records:** See Hampden County for recording records searching. **Other phones:** Treasurer- 413-267-4125; Elections- 413-267-4115; Vital Records- 413-267-4115. **Property tax/Assessor-** 110 Main St, Monson, MA 01057; 413-267-4120.

Montague Town

Town Clerk, 1 Avenue A, Turners Falls, MA 01376-1128. 413-863-3211; fax-413-863-3224; hours: 8:30AM-4:30PM. No real estate recordings. Only the public may search. Copy fee $1.00 per page. Payee- Town of Montague. **Other phones:** Treasurer- 413-863-3207; Elections- 413-863-3211; Vital Records- 413-863-3211. **Property tax/Assessor-** 413-863-4654.

Monterey Town

Town Clerk, Town Hall, Monterey, MA 01245. 413-528-5175; fax-413-528-9452; hours: 9:30AM-12:30PM Sat, or by appointment. No real estate recordings. Office personnel or visitors may perform searches. Search fee $10.00 per name. Real estate records located at Berkshire County Registers Office. General copy fee $1.00 per page.

Tax lien copy- $.50 per page. Cert fee- $5.00 per page. Payee- Town of Monterey. **Other phones:** Treasurer- 413-528-1443; Elections- 413-528-5175; Vital Records- 413-528-5175. **Property tax/Assessor-** 413-528-6481.

Montgomery Town

Town Clerk, Town Hall; 161 Main Rd, Montgomery, MA 01085. 413-862-3386; fax-413-862-3204; hours: by appointment.
No real estate recordings. Record index not computerized. Office will perform a UCC search or tax lien search but public must search other records themselves. Search fee $5.00 per name. Copy fee $1.00 per page. Cert fee- $1.00 per page plus copy fee. Payee- Town of Montgomery. **Online access to Real Estate, Recording, Lien records:** See Hampden County for recording records searching. **Other phones:** Treasurer- 413-862-3386. **Assessor-** same address as above. 413-862-3386.

Mt. Washington Town

Town Clerk, 118 East St, Mt. Washington, MA 01258. 413-528-2839; fax-413-528-2839; hours: 9AM-3PM M-W; 9AM-1PM Sat.
No real estate recordings. Records indexed. Office will perform a UCC search but public must search other records themselves. Real estate records located at Berkshire County. UCC search per debtor name- $10.00. Copy fee $1.00 per page. Payee- Town of Mt. Washington. **Other phones:** Treasurer- 413-528-2839; Elections- 413-528-2839; Vital Records- 413-528-2839. **Property tax/Assessor-** 413-528-2839.

Nahant Town

Town Clerk, Town Hall, Nahant, MA 01908-0075. 781-581-0018; fax-781-593-0340; hours: 9AM-Noon. www.nahant.org/townhall/clerk.shtml
No real estate recordings. All records in one index. Record index not computerized. Only the office personnel may search. Real estate records located at Essex County. Payee- Town of Nahant. **Online access to Assessor, Property records:** Access property data free at http://nahant.patriotprope rties.com/default.asp. **Other phones:** Treasurer- 781-581-0018; Elections- 781-581-0018; Vital Records- 781-581-0018; Town Accountant- 781-581-0099; Town Adminstrator -781-581-9927. **Property tax/Assessor-** 334 Nahant Rd, Basement Level, Nahant, MA 01908; 781-581-0212.

Nantucket County

County Register of Deeds, 16 Broad St, Nantucket, MA 02554. 508-228-7250; fax-508-325-5331; hours: 8AM-4PM; Recording Hours: 8AM-N, 1-3:45PM. Only the public may search. Copy fee $1.00 per page. **Online access to Real estate, Deed, Recording, Lien records:.** **Other phones:** Treasurer- 508-228-7265; Elections- 508-228-7217; Vital Records- 508-228-7217. **Property tax/Assessor-** 508-228-7211.

Nantucket Town

Town Clerk, 16 Broad St; Town & County Bldg, Nantucket, MA 02554. 508-228-7217, R/E recording phone-508-228-7250, UCC recording phone-508-228-7217; fax-508-325-5313; hours: 8AM-4PM. www.nantucket-ma.gov
No real estate recordings. Record index not computerized. Office will perform a UCC and Tax lien search but public must search other records themselves. Search fee $20.00. Real estate records located at Nantucket County. Copy fee $.50 per page. Cert fee- $5.00 per page plus copy fee. Payee- Nantucket Town Clerk. **Other phones:** Treasurer- 508-325-5314; Elections- 508-228-7217; Vital Records- 508-228-7217; 508-228-7255. **Assessor-** same address as above. 508-228-7211.

Natick Town

Town Clerk, 13 E. Central St, Natick, MA 01760. 508-647-6430; fax-508-655-6715; hours: 8AM-5PM. www.natickma.org

No real estate recordings. All records in one index. Record index not computerized. Only the office personnel may search. Search fee $5.00 per name. Real estate records located at Middlesex County. Copy fee $1.00 per page. Payee- Town of Natick. **Online access to Assessor, Property records:** Search town assessments free at www.natickma.org/assess/a ssessinfo.asp. Includes name searches. **Other phones:** Treasurer- 508-647-6425; Elections- 508-647-6430; Vital Records- 508-647-6430. **Property tax/Assessor-** same address as above. 508-647-6420.

Needham Town

Town Clerk, PO Box 920663, Needham, MA 02492. 781-455-7510; fax-781-449-4569; hours: 8:30AM-5PM. www.town.needham.ma.us
No real estate recordings. All records in one index. Record index not computerized. Office personnel or visitors may perform searches. Search fee $10.00 per hour. Real estate records located at Norfolk County. Copy fee $1.00 per page. Cert fee- $1.00 per item plus copy fee. Payee- Town of Needham. **Online access to Property, Assessor records:** Access to property data is free at http://csc-ma.us/PropertyContent/jsp/Home.jsp?Page=1. Select Needham Town. **Other phones:** Treasurer- 781-455-7504; Elections- 781-455-7510; Vital Records- 781-455-7510. **Property tax/Assessor-** same address as above. 781-455-7507.

New Ashford Town

Town Clerk, 142 Beach Hill Rd, New Ashford, MA 01237. 413-458-5491; fax-413-458-5461; hours: by appointment.
No real estate recordings. Office personnel or visitors may perform searches. Search fee $10.00 per name. Real estate records located at Berkshire County. Copy fee $2.00 per page. Payee- Town of New Ashford. **Property tax/Assessor-** 413-743-9154.

New Bedford City

City Clerk, 133 William St, New Bedford, MA 02740. 508-979-1450; fax-508-991-6225; hours: 8AM-4PM. www.ci.new-bedford.ma.us/Nav3.htm
No real estate recordings. Office personnel or visitors may perform searches. Search fee $10.00 per name. Real estate records located at Bristol County. Copy fee $2.00, if tax lien $.20 per page. Cert fee- $5.00 per page base rate. Payee- City of New Bedford. **Online access to Property, Assessor records:** Access to the assessor's property database is free at www.ci.new-bedford.ma.us/Assessors/RealPro pertyLookup.htm. **Other phones:** Treasurer- 508-979-1430; Elections- 508-979-1420; Vital Records- 508-979-1450. **Property tax/Assessor-** 508-979-1440.

New Braintree Town

Town Clerk, 20 Memorial Dr Rm 5, New Braintree, MA 01531. 508-867-4952; fax-508-867-6316; hours: 7PM-9PM M. www.newbraintree.net
No real estate recordings. All records in one index. Office will perform a Tax lien search but public must search other records themselves. Search fee $5.00. Real estate records located at Worcester County. Copy fee $.25 per page. Cert fee- $5.00 per page plus copy fee. Payee- Town of New Braintree. **Other phones:** Treasurer- 508-867-2581; Elections- 508-867-4952; Vital Records- 508-867-4952. **Property tax/Assessor-** 508-867-4467.

New Marlborough Town

Town Clerk, PO Box 99, Mill River, MA 01244. 413-229-8116; fax-413-229-6674; hours: 9AM-2PM. www.new-marlborough.ma.us
No real estate recordings. Record index not computerized. Office will perform a UCC search but public must search other records themselves. Search fee $10.00. Real estate records located at Berkshire County. Copy fee $1.00 per page. Cert fee- $5.00 per page. Payee- New Marlborough Town CLerk. **Other phones:** Treasurer- 413-229-8963; Elections- 413-229-8278; Vital Records- 413-229-8278. **Property tax/Assessor-** 413-229-8926.

New Salem Town

Town Clerk, 15 S Main St; Town Hall, New Salem, MA 01355. 978-544-2731; fax-978-544-5775; hours: 7-9PM T; 9-11AM W.
No real estate recordings. All records in one index. Office personnel or visitors may perform searches. Search fee $10.00 per hour. Real estate records located at Franklin County. Copy fee $1.00 per page. Payee- Town of New Salem.

Newbury Town

Town Clerk, 25 High Rd, Newbury, MA 01951-4799. 978-462-2332; fax-978-465-3064; hours: 8AM-3:30PM M,T,W,Th; 8AM-1PM F. www.townofnewbury.org
No real estate recordings. Separate indices to search include vitals (birth, marriage, death), minutes by year. Record index not computerized. Office personnel or visitors may perform searches. Search fee $10.00 per name. Real estate records located at Essex County. Copy fee $1.00 per page. Cert fee- $5.00 per page plus copy fee. Payee- Town of Newbury. **Online access to Assessor, Property Tax records:** Access property tax data free at http://newbury.patriotproperties.com/default.asp. **Other phones:** Treasurer- 978-465-0862; Elections- 978-462-2332; Vital Records- 978-462-2332. **Property tax/Assessor-** same address as above. 978-465-0211.

Newburyport City

City Clerk, PO Box 550, Newburyport, MA 01950. 978-465-4407; hours: 8AM-4PM M,T,W; 8AM-8PM Th; 8AM-N Fri.
No real estate recordings. All records in one index. Record index not computerized. Only the public may search. Real estate records located at Essex County. Copy fee $1.00 per page. Cert fee- $7.00 per cert. Payee- City of Newburyport. **Online access to Assessor records:** Search the city assessor database at http://data.visionappraisal.com/NewBU RYPORTMA/. Free registration for full data. **Other phones:** Treasurer- 978-465-4415; Elections- 978-465-4407; Vital Records- 978-465-4407. **Property tax/Assessor-** 978-465-4403.

Newton City

City Clerk, 1000 Commonwealth Ave, Newton Center, MA 02159. 617-796-1200; fax-617-796-1214; hours: 8:30AM-5PM M; 8:30AM-8PM T 8:30AM-5PM W. www.ci.newton.ma.us
No real estate recordings. Record index not computerized. Office will perform a UCC search but public must search other records themselves. Search fee $10.00. Real estate records located at Middlesex County. Copy fee $.20 per page. Payee- City of Newton. **Online access to Assessor records:** Records on the City of Newton Fiscal 1998 Assessment database are free at www.ci.newton.ma.us/asses sors2003/Search.asp. Data represents market value as of January of current year. **Other phones:** Treasurer- 615-796-7080; Elections- 617-796-1350; Vital Records- 617-796-1200. **Property tax/Assessor-** same address as above. 617-796-7065.

Norfolk County

County Register of Deeds, PO Box 69, Dedham, MA 02027-0069. 781-461-6122; fax-781-326-4742; hours: 8:30AM-4:45PM. www.norfolkdeeds.org
All records in one index. Records indexed on a public use terminal back to 1974. Only the public may search. Copy fee $1.00 per page. Cert fee- No extra fee. Payee- Norfolk County Register of Deeds. **Online access to Real Estate, Lien, Deed, Judgment records:** Access to county online records is on two levels, both accessible via www.norfolkdeeds.org/Search/. You may search images and indices free, however, to print requires a subscription; $100 per year plus $1.00 per page. Land records go back to 1974; images to 1974. Land court records go back to 9/1984, with images back to 1901. This replaces the old subscription system. **Other phones:** ; Customer Service- 781-461-6101.

Norfolk Town

Town Clerk, 1 Liberty Lane, Norfolk, MA 02056. 508-528-1400, R/E recording phone-781-461-6100, UCC recording phone-617-727-9180; fax-508-541-3363; hours: 9AM-4PM. www.virtualnorfolk.org
No real estate recordings. Office will perform a UCC search but public must search other records themselves. Real estate records located at Norfolk County. UCC search per debtor name- $10.00. Copy fee $2.00, if tax lien $.25 per page. Payee-Town of Norfolk. **Other phones:** Treasurer- 508-528-0058; Vital Records- 508-528-1400. **Property tax/Assessor-** 508-528-1120.

North Adams City

City Clerk, 10 Main St, North Adams, MA 01247. 413-662-3015, R/E recording phone-413-743-0035 North; 443-7438 Cent.; 528-0146 South; hours: 8AM-4:30PM.
No real estate recordings. All records in one index. Record index not computerized. Office personnel or visitors may perform searches. Real estate records located at Berkshire County. Copy fee $2.00 per page. Cert fee- $5.00 each plus copy fee. Payee-City of North Adams. **Other phones:** Treasurer- 413-662-3044; Elections- 413-662-3015; Vital Records-413-662-3015. **Property tax/Assessor-** same address as above. 413-662-3012.

North Andover Town

Town Clerk, 120 Main St, North Andover, MA 01845. 978-688-9502; fax-978-688-9556; 8:30AM-4:30PM.
No real estate recordings. Record index not computerized. Office will perform a UCC search but public must search other records themselves. Real estate records located at Essex County. UCC search per debtor name- $10.00. Copy fee $2.00 per page. Payee- Town of North Andover. **Online access to Land, Grantor/Grantee, Recording, Property, Assessor records:** Search the recorder database for free at www.lawrencedeeds.com/dsSearch.asp. Also, access property data free at http://csc-ma.us/PropertyContent/jsp/Home.jsp?Page=1. **Other phones:** Treasurer- 978-688-9550; Elections- 978-688-9501; Vital Records- 978-688-9501. **Property tax/Assessor-** 978-688-9566.

North Attleborough Town

Town Clerk, 43 S. Washington St, North Attleborough, MA 02761-0871. 508-699-0142, R/E recording phone-508-822-3081, UCC recording phone-508-699-0108; fax-508-699-2354; hours: 8AM-4PM (Th 8AM-7PM).
No real estate recordings. All records in one index. Record index not computerized. Office will perform a UCC search but public must search other records themselves. Search fee $5.00. Real estate records located at Bristol County. Copy fee $1.00 per page. Payee- Town of North Attleborough. **Online access to Assessor records:** Search the town assessor database at http://data.visionappraisal.com/NorthAttleboroMA/. Free registration for full data. **Other phones:** Treasurer- 508-699-0114; Elections- 508-699-0106; Vital Records- 508-699-0142; Tax Office:- 508-699-0108. **Property tax/Assessor-** 508-699-0117.

North Brookfield Town

Town Clerk, 185 N Main St, North Brookfield, MA 01535. 508-867-0203; fax-508-867-0249; hours: Noon-2:30PM 6PM-8PM T; Noon-2:30PM Th; 9AM-N Fri.
No real estate recordings. Office personnel or visitors may perform searches. Search fee $10.00 per name. Real estate records located at Worcester County. Copy fee $1.00 per page. Tax lien copy- $.50 per page. Payee- Town of North Brookfield. **Online access to Property, Assessor records:** Access to property data is free at http://csc-ma.us/PropertyContent/jsp/Home.jsp?Page=1. Select North Brookfield Town. **Other phones:** Treasurer- 508-867-0204; Elections- 508-867-0203; Vital

Records- 508-867-0203. **Property tax/Assessor-** 508-867-0209.

North Reading Town

Town Clerk, 235 N. St, North Reading, MA 01864-1294. 978-664-6030, R/E recording phone-978-664-6021, UCC recording phone-978-664-6030; fax-978-664-6048; hours: 8AM-4PM M-Th; 8AM-1PM F.
No real estate recordings. Index: Indices arranged by years. Record index not computerized. Office personnel or visitors may perform searches. Search fee $10.00 per name. Real estate records located at Middlesex County. Will search UCC records up to 6/30/2001. Copy fee $1.00 per page. Cert fee- $10.00 per doc plus copy fee. Payee- Town of North Reading. **Other phones:** Treasurer- 978-664-6019; Elections- 978-664-6030; Vital Records- 978-664-6030. **Property tax/Assessor-** same address as above. 978-664-6021.

Northampton City

City Clerk, 210 Main St, Northampton, MA 01060. 413-587-1224; fax-413-587-1220; 8:30AM-4:30PM.
No real estate recordings. Record index not computerized. Only the office personnel may search. Search fee $10.00. Real estate records located at Hampshire County. Copy fee $1.00 per page. Payee- City of Northampton. **Other phones:** Treasurer- 413-587-1297; Elections- 413-587-1224; Vital Records- 413-587-1224. **Property tax/Assessor-** 413-587-1200.

Northborough Town

Town Clerk, 63 Main St, Northborough, MA 01532-1994. 508-393-5001; fax-508-393-6996; hours: 8AM-4PM M,W,Th; 8AM-7PM T; 7AM-N Fri. www.town.northborough.ma.us
No real estate recordings. Office personnel or visitors may perform searches. Search fee $10.00 per name. Real estate records located at Worcester County. General copy fee $2.00 per page. Tax lien copy-$.20 per page. Cert fee- $5.00 per doc plus copy fee. Payee- Town of Northborough. **Online access to Property, Assessor records:** Access to property data is free at http://csc-ma.us/PropertyContent/jsp/Home.jsp?Page=1. **Other phones:** Treasurer- 508-393-5045; Elections- 508-393-5001; Vital Records- 508-393-5001; 508-393-5002-. **Property tax/Assessor-** 508-393-5005.

Northbridge Town

Town Clerk, 7 Main St, Town Hall, Whitinsville, MA 01588. 508-234-2001, R/E recording phone-508-234-5432, UCC recording phone-508-234-2001; fax-508-234-2001; hours: 8:30AM-7PM M; 8:30AM-4:30PM T-Th; 8:30AM-1PM F. www.northbridgemass.org
No real estate recordings. All records in one index. Record index not computerized. Only the office personnel may search. Search fee $10.00. Real estate records located at Worcester County. Copy fee $10.00 per name. Payee- Town of Northbridge. **Other phones:** Treasurer- 508-234-5432; Elections- 508-234-2001; Vital Records- 508-234-2001. **Assessor-** same address as above. 508-234-2740.

Northfield Town

Town Clerk, Town Hall; 69 Main St, Northfield, MA 01360. 413-498-2901; fax-413-498-5103; hours: 9AM-3PM M-T; 9-N, 12-8PM Wed.
No real estate recordings. All records in one index. Record index not computerized. Only the office personnel may search. Search fee $10.00. Real estate records located at Franklin County. Copy fee $.10 per page. Payee- Town of Northfield. **Other phones:** Treasurer- 413-498-2901; Elections- 413-498-2901; Vital Records- 413-498-2901. **Assessor-** same address as above. 413-498-2901.

Norton Town

Town Clerk, 70 E. Main St; Town Hall, Norton, MA 02766. 508-285-0231, R/E recording phone-508-285-0270, UCC recording phone-508-285-0230; fax-508-

285-0297; hours: 8:30AM-4:30PM M,T,W,F; 8:30AM-8PM Th. www.nortonma.org
No real estate recordings. Separate indices to search. Record index not computerized. Office personnel or visitors may perform searches. Search fee $10.00 per name. Real estate records located at Bristol County. Copy fee $2.00, if tax lien $.20 per page. Payee- Town of Norton. **Other phones:** Treasurer- 508-285-0223; Elections- 508-285-0230; Vital Records- 508-285-0230. **Property tax/Assessor-** same address as above. 508-285-0270.

Norwell Town

Town Clerk, PO Box 295, Norwell, MA 02061-0295. 781-659-8072, R/E recording phone-781-659-8014, UCC recording phone-781-659-8072; fax-781-659-7795; hours: 8AM-4PM. www.townofnorwell.net
No real estate recordings. Index: Vital records have cross files as well as bound copies. Record index not computerized. Only the office personnel may search. Real estate records located at Plymouth County. UCC search per debtor name- $10.00 (includes tax liens if requested). Separate federal/state combined tax lien search- $10.00 per debtor. Copy fee $1.00 per page. Cert fee- $10.00 per certification. Payee- Town of Norwell. **Other phones:** Treasurer- 781-659-8070; Elections- 781-659-8072; Vital Records- 781-659-8072. **Property tax/Assessor-** same address as above. 781-659-8014.

Norwood Town

Town Clerk, PO Box 40, Norwood, MA 02062. 781-762-1240 x193; fax-781-762-0954; hours: 8:15AM-4:30PM.
No real estate recordings. Office personnel or visitors may perform searches. Search fee $10.00 per name. Real estate records located at Norfolk County. Copy fee $2.00 per UCC; $1.00 per attachment. Payee- Town of Norwood. **Other phones:** Treasurer- 781-762-1240; Elections- 781-762-1240; Vital Records- 781-762-1240. **Property tax/Assessor-** 781-762-1240.

Oak Bluffs Town

Town Clerk, PO Box 2490, Oak Bluffs, MA 02557-2490. 508-693-5515; fax-508-693-5124; hours: 8:30AM-4PM. www.ci.oak-bluffs.ma.us
No real estate recordings. Separate indices to search by year include vital records, MA tax liens, personal property bills. Record index not computerized. Search fee $20.00 per name. No UCC records; real estate records located at Dukes County. Copy fee $1.00 per page. Tax lien copy-$5.00. Cert fee- $5.00 per copy. Payee- Town of Oak Bluffs. **Online access to Assessor records:** Search the town assessor database at http://data.visionappraisal.com/OakBluffsMA/. Free registration for full data. **Other phones:** Treasurer- 508-693-5514; Elections- 508-693-5515; Vital Records- 508-693-5515. **Property tax/Assessor-** PO Box 1327, 56 School St, Oak Bluffs, MA 02557; 508-693-5519.

Oakham Town

Town Clerk, PO Box 222, Oakham, MA 01068-0222. 508-882-5549; fax-508-882-3060; hours: 9-11:30AM T; 6-7:30PM Wed.
No real estate recordings. All records in one index. Records indexed not computerized. Only the public may search. Clerk indicates that if she does do a search, the fee is $10.00 per name. Real estate records located at Worcester County. Copy fee $1.00 per page. Payee- Town of Oakham. **Online access to Property, Assessor records:** Access to property data is free at http://csc-ma.us/PropertyContent/jsp/Home.jsp?Page=1. Select Oakham Town. **Other phones:** Treasurer- 508-882-5549; Elections- 508-882-5549; Vital Records- 508-882-5549. **Property tax/Assessor-** 2 Coldbrook Rd, Oakham, MA 01068; 508-882-5549.

Orange Town

Town Clerk, 6 Prospect St, Orange, MA 01364. 978-544-1100 x101; fax-978-544-1134; hours: 8AM-4PM M-Th; 8AM-1PM F.
No real estate recordings. All records in one index. Record index not computerized. Only the public may search. Real estate records located at Franklin County. Cert fee- $2.00 per page. Payee- Town of Orange. **Other phones:** Treasurer- 978-544-1100 x103; Elections- 978-544-1100 x101; Vital Records- 978-544-1100 x101. **Property tax/Assessor-** same address as above. 978-544-1100 x108.

Orleans Town

Town Clerk, 19 School Rd, Orleans, MA 02653-3699. 508-240-3700; fax-508-240-3388; hours: 8:30AM-4:30PM. www.town.orleans.ma.us
No real estate recordings. Records indexed on computer. Office will perform a UCC and Tax lien search but public must search other records themselves. Search fee $5.00. Real estate records located at Barnstable County. Copy fee $2.00 per page. Cert fee- $5.00 per page includes copy fee. Payee- Town of Orleans. **Other phones:** Treasurer- 508-240-3700 x323. **Property tax/Assessor-** 508-240-3700 x331.

Otis Town

Town Clerk, PO Box 237, Otis, MA 01253. 413-269-0101; fax-413-269-0111; hours: 9AM-4PM Tu-F; 9AM-N Sat.
No real estate or UCC recordings. Index: Indices in books. Real estate records located at Berkshire County. Separate state tax lien search- $5.00 per debtor. Copy fee $2.00 per page. Cert fee- $5.00 per page plus copy fee. Payee- Town of Otis. **Other phones:** Treasurer- 413-269-0108; Elections- 413-269-0101; Vital Records- 413-269-0101. **Property tax/Assessor-** 413-269-0102.

Oxford Town

Town Clerk, 325 Main St, Oxford, MA 01540. 508-987-6032; fax-508-987-6048; hours: 9AM-4:30PM. www.town.oxford.ma.us
No real estate recordings. All records in one index. Record index not computerized. Only the office personnel may search. Search fee $10.00. Real estate records located at Worcester County. Copy fee $2.00 per page. Cert fee- $5.00 per page plus copy fee. Payee- Town of Oxford. **Online access to Property Assessor records:** Search the property assessments by street name for free at www.town.oxford.ma.us/Assessor/Assessor.htm. **Other phones:** Treasurer- 508-987-6038; Elections- 508-987-6032; Vital Records- 508-987-6032. **Property tax/Assessor-** same address as above. 508-987-6036.

Palmer Town

Town Clerk, 4417 Main St.; Palmer Town Bldg, Palmer, MA 01069. 413-283-2608, R/E recording phone-413-283-2607, UCC recording phone-413-283-2608; fax-413-283-2637; hours: 9AM-4:30PM.
No real estate recordings. Record index not computerized. Only the public may search. Real estate records located at Hampden County. Copy fee $2.00 per page. Payee- Town of Palmer. **Online access to Real Estate, Recording, Lien records:** See Hampden County for recording records searching. **Other phones:** Treasurer- 413-283-2600; Elections- 413-283-2608; Vital Records- 413-283-2608. **Property tax/Assessor-** same address as above. 413-283-2607.

Paxton Town

Town Clerk, 697 Pleasant St, Paxton, MA 01612. 508-799-7347 x13; fax-508-797-0966; 8AM-2PM M-Th.
No real estate recordings. Only the office personnel may search. Search fee $10.00. Real estate records located at Worcester County. Copy fee $1.00 per page. Cert fee- $1.00 per page plus copy fee. Payee- Town of Paxton. **Online access to Assessor**

records: Search town assessor database at http://data.visionappraisal.com/PaxtonMA/. Does not require a username & password. Simply click on link. **Other phones:** Treasurer- 508-799-7347 x15; Elections- 508-799-7347 x13; Vital Records- 508-799-7347 x13. **Property tax/Assessor-** same address as above. 508-799-7231 x16.

Peabody City

City Clerk, 24 Lowell St; City Hall, Peabody, MA 01960. 978-538-5900; fax-978-538-5985; hours: 8:30AM-4PM M-W; 8:30AM-7PM Th; 8:30AM-12:30PM F. www.peabody-ma.gov
No real estate recordings. All records in one index. Search fee $10.00 per name. Copy fee $.25 per copy. Cert fee- $1.00 per page includes copy fee. Payee- City of Peabody. **Online access to Assessor, Property records:** Access property data free at http://207.234.185.50/assessorasp/. **Other phones:** Treasurer- 978-538-5764; Elections- 978-538-5750; Vital Records- 978-538-5752 or 5751. **Property tax/Assessor-** same address as above. 978-538-5729.

Pelham Town

Town Clerk, 351 Amherst Rd.; Rhodes Bldg, Pelham, MA 01002-9753. 413-253-7129; fax-413-256-1061; 8:30AM-4:30PM M-Th. www.townofpelham.org
No real estate recordings. Separate indices to search. Office personnel or visitors may perform searches. Search fee $10.00 per name. Real estate records located at Hampshire County. Will search UCC records and tax lien searches. Copy fee $2.00, if tax lien $.25 per copy. Cert fee- $5.00 per cert plus copy fee. Payee- Town of Pelham. **Other phones:** Treasurer- 413-253-2267; Elections- 413-253-7129; Vital Records- 413-253-7129. **Property tax/Assessor-** same address as above. 413-253-0734.

Pembroke Town

Town Clerk, 100 Center St, Pembroke, MA 02359. 781-293-7211; fax-781-293-4650; hours: 8:30AM-4:30PM.
No real estate recordings. Index: More than one index. Record index not computerized. Only the office personnel may search. Search fee $10.00. Real estate records located at Plymouth County. Will search UCC records, but not tax liens. Copy fee $1.00 per page. Cert fee- $1.00 per page plus copy fee. Payee- Town of Pembroke. **Other phones:** Treasurer- 781-293-3893; Elections- 781-293-7211; Vital Records- 781-293-7211; Town Administrator- 781-293-3844. **Property tax/Assessor-** same address as above. 781-293-2393.

Pepperell Town

Town Clerk, 1 Main St; Town Hall, Pepperell, MA 01463-1644. 978-433-0339; fax-978-433-0338; hours: 8AM-4:30PM. www.town.pepperell.ma.us
No real estate recordings. Only the public may search. Real estate records located at Middlesex County. Payee- Town of Pepperell. **Other phones:** Treasurer- 978-433-0337; Elections- 978-433-0339; Vital Records- 978-433-0339. **Property tax/Assessor-** 978-433-0322.

Peru Town

Town Clerk, PO Box 1175, Peru, MA 01235. 413-655-8312; fax-413-655-8312; hours: 6-8PM Mondays.
No real estate recordings. Only the public may search. Real estate records located at Berkshire County. Copy fee $1.00 per page. Cert fee- $25.00 per Municipal Lien Certificate plus copies. Payee- Town of Peru. **Other phones:** Treasurer- 413-655-8312; Elections- 413-655-8312; Vital Records- 413-655-8326; Tax Collector- 413-655-0072. **Property tax/Assessor-** 413-655-8312.

Petersham Town

Town Clerk, PO Box 486, Petersham, MA 01366. 978-724-6649; fax-978-724-3501; hours: 6-8PM Monday.
Real estate records searches and tax lien searches are performed by the tax collector. All records in one

index. Record index not computerized. Office personnel or visitors may perform searches. Real estate records located at Worcester County. Will not search UCC records or tax liens. Copy fee $1.00 per page. Payee- Town of Petersham. **Other phones:** Treasurer- 978-724-6699; Elections- 978-724-6649; Vital Records- 978-724-6649; Tax Collector- 978-724-6620. **Property tax/Assessor-** same address as above. 978-724-6658.

Phillipston Town

Town Clerk, 50 The Common, Phillipston, MA 01331. 978-249-1733, R/E recording phone-978-249-1732, UCC recording phone-978-249-1733; fax-978-249-1733; hours: 12-2PM, 6-8PM M; 5-7PM W; 8:30AM-10AM SAT.
No real estate recordings. All records in one index. Record index not computerized. Only the office personnel may search. Search fee $10.00 per name. Real estate records located at Worcester County. Will not search tax liens. See Tax Collector's Office. Copy fee $1.00 per page. Cert fee- $5.00 per cert plus copy fee. Payee- Town of Phillipston. **Other phones:** Treasurer- 978-249-3415; Elections- 978-249-1733; Vital Records- 978-249-1733; General Town Hall- 978-249-6828; Tax Collector -978-249-1731. **Property tax/Assessor-** same address as above. 978-249-1732.

Pittsfield City

City Clerk, 70 Allen St; City Hall, Rm 103, Pittsfield, MA 01201. 413-499-9361; fax-413-499-9363; hours: 8:30AM-4PM. www.pittsfield-ma.org
No real estate recordings. Office personnel or visitors may perform searches. Search fee $5.00 per name. Real estate records located at Berkshire County. Copy fee $1.00 per page. Cert fee- $5.00 per copy. Payee- City of Pittsfield. **Other phones:** Treasurer- 413-499-9466; Elections- 413-499-9460; Vital Records- 413-499-9361. **Property tax/Assessor-** 413-395-0102.

Plainfield Town

Town Clerk, 12 Broom St, Plainfield, MA 01070. 413-634-5582; fax-413-634-5785; 10AM-Noon Sat.
No real estate recordings. Office will perform a UCC search but public must search other records themselves. Search fee $5.00 per name. Copy fee $1.00 per page. Payee- Town of Plainfield. **Other phones:** Treasurer- 413-634-5420; Elections- 413-634-5417; Vital Records- 413-634-5417. **Property tax/Assessor-** 304 Main St, Plainfield, MA 01070; 413-634-5420.

Plainville Town

Town Clerk, PO Box 1717, Plainville, MA 02762. 508-695-3142 x20, R/E recording phone-508-695-3142 x14, UCC recording phone-508-695-3142 x20; fax-508-695-1857; hours: 8AM-4PM.
No real estate recordings. Office personnel or visitors may perform searches. Search fee $10.00 per name. Real estate records located at Norfolk County. Copy fee $2.00 per page. Cert fee- $5.00 per cert plus copy fee. Payee- Town of Plainville. **Other phones:** Treasurer- 508-695-3142 x17,18; Elections- 508-695-3142 x19; Vital Records- 508-695-3142 x20. **Property tax/Assessor-** 508-695-3142 x14.

Plymouth County

Registry of Deeds, 50 Obery St, Plymouth, MA 02361. 508-830-9200, R/E recording phone-508-830-9261; fax-508-830-9280; 8:15AM-4:30PM (Recording 8:30AM-4PM). www.regdeeds.co.plymouth.ma.us
Separate indices to search include grantor/grantee by year. Records indexed on a public use terminal back to 1971. Only the public may search. Copy fee $1.00 per page. Payee- Plymouth County Register of Deeds. **Online access to Real Estate, Lien, Judgment records:** Access to Online Titleview for Plymouth County records requires a usage charge of $.60 per minute of use. Indices date back to 1971. Lending agency information is available. Unlimited viewing and printing of documents available for $30.00

per month. A fax back service is $3 plus $1 per page in county, $5. plus $1 per page, outside. For info, call 508-830-9287.

Plymouth Town

Town Clerk, 11 Lincoln St, Plymouth, MA 02360-3386. 508-747-1620X189; fax-508-830-4062; hours: 8AM-4:30PM. www.townofplymouth.org
No real estate recordings. All records in one index. Records indexed on computer back to 2000. Office will perform a UCC search but public must search other records themselves. Search fee $3.00 per UCC. Real estate records located at Plymouth County. Copy fee $3.00 per UCC plus $.20 per page. Tax lien copy- $.20 per page. Cert fee- $2.00 per item. Payee- Town of Plymouth. **Online access to Assessor, Property records:** Access property data free at http://plymouth.patriotproperties.com/default.asp. **Other phones:** Treasurer- 508-747-1620 X167; Elections- 508-747-1620 x161; Vital Records- 508-747-1620 X170. **Property tax/Assessor-** same address as above. 508-830-4020, 508-747-1620 x152.

Plympton Town

Town Clerk, PO Box 153, Plympton, MA 02367-0153. 781-585-3220; fax-781-582-1505; hours: 9AM-2PM, 7-9PM M; 9AM-2PM T-Th. http://town.plympton.ma.us
No real estate recordings. Record index not computerized. Only the office personnel may search. Real estate records located at Plymouth County. Will search UCC records, but not tax liens. UCC search per debtor name- $10.00. Copy fee $1.00 per page. Payee- Town of Plympton. **Other phones:** Treasurer- 781-585-0409; Elections- 781-585-3220; Vital Records- 781-585-3220. **Property tax/Assessor-** PO Box 176, Plympton, MA 02367; 781-585-3227.

Princeton Town

Town Clerk, 6 Town Hall Drive, Princeton, MA 01541-1137. 978-464-2103; fax-978-464-2106; hours: 8:30AM-3:30PM. http://town.princeton.ma.us
No real estate recordings. Separate indices. Records indexed on computer back to 2000. Only the public may search. Search fee $10.00. Real estate records located at Worcester County. Copy fee $2.00 per page. Cert fee- $10.00 per record. Payee- Town of Princeton. **Other phones:** Treasurer- 978-464-2105; Elections- 978-464-2103; Vital Records- 978-464-2103; Switchboard- 978-464-2100. **Property tax/Assessor-** 978-464-2104.

Provincetown Town

Town Clerk, 260 Commercial St, Provincetown, MA 02657. 508-487-7013 x528; fax-508-487-9560; hours: 8AM-5PM. www.provincetowngov.org
No real estate recordings. Record index not computerized. Office personnel or visitors may perform searches. Search fee $5.00 per name. Real estate records located at Barnstable County. UCC search per debtor name- $10.00. Copy fee $.25 per page. Payee- Town of Provincetown. **Online access to Assessor, Property Sale records:** Records on the Provincetown Assessor database are free at www.provincetowngov.org/assessor.html. **Other phones:** Treasurer- 508-487-7015; Elections- 508-487-7013; Vital Records- 508-487-7013. **Property tax/Assessor-** 508-487-7017.

Quincy City

City Clerk, 1305 Hancock St; City Hall, Quincy, MA 02169. 617-376-1136; fax-617-376-1139; hours: 8:30AM-4:30PM. www.ci.quincy.ma.us
No real estate recordings. Separate indices to search include computer, index books, but birth, death, marriages, UCCs only on card file. Records indexed on computer back to 1989. Search fee $10.00 per name. Real estate records located at Norfolk County. UCC search includes tax liens. Copy fee $1.00 per page. Cert fee- $8.00 per page includes copy fee. Payee- City of Quincy. **Online**

access to **Assessor, Property records:** Access assessor property data free at http://data.visionappraisal.com/QuincyMA/search.asp. No name searching. Also a sales look-up. **Other phones:** Elections- 617-376-1141; Vital Records- 617-376-1135, 1136, 1137. **Property tax/Assessor-** 617-376-1178.

Randolph Town

Town Clerk, 41 S. Main St, Randolph, MA 02368. 781-961-0900; fax-781-961-0919; 8:30AM-4:30PM.
No real estate recordings. Office will perform a UCC search but public must search other records themselves. Real estate records located at Norfolk County. UCC search per debtor name- $10.00. Copy fee $2.00, if tax lien $.25 per page. Payee- Town of Randolph. **Other phones:** Treasurer- 781-961-0934. **Property tax/Assessor-** 781-961-0906.

Raynham Town

Town Clerk, 53 Orchard St, Raynham, MA 02767-1320. 508-824-2700, R/E recording phone-508-824-2709, UCC recording phone-508-824-2700; fax-508-823-1812; hours: 8:30AM-4:30PM M-Th; 8:30AM-N Fri. www.town.raynham.ma.us
No real estate recordings. Record index not computerized. Only the office personnel may search. Search fee $10.00 per name. Real estate records located at Bristol County. Copy fee $2.00 per page. Cert fee- $10.00 per name plus copy fee. Payee- Town of Raynham. **Other phones:** Treasurer- 508-824-2702; Elections- 508-824-2700; Vital Records- 508-824-2700; Tax Collector Office- 508-824-2709. **Property tax/Assessor-** same address as above. 508-824-2704.

Reading Town

Town Clerk, 16 Lowell St, Reading, MA 01867. 781-942-9050; fax-781-942-9070; hours: 8:30AM-5PM. www.ci.reading.ma.us
No real estate recordings. Separate indices to search. Only the public may search. Real estate records located at Middlesex County. UCC search per debtor name- $10.00. Copy fee $2.00 1st page; $1.00 each add'l. Cert fee- $5.00 per doc, $10.00 per vital record plus copy fee. Payee- Town of Reading. **Online access to Assessor records:** Records on the Town of Reading Assessor database are free at www.ziplink.net/~reading1/assessor.htm. **Other phones:** Treasurer- 781-942-9032; Elections- 781-942-9050; Vital Records- 781-942-9048. **Property tax/Assessor-** 781-942-9027.

Rehoboth Town

Town Clerk, 148 Peck St, Rehoboth, MA 02769-3099. 508-252-6502; fax-508-252-5342; hours: 9AM-4PM.
No real estate recordings. All records in one index. Record index not computerized. Only the office personnel may search. Search fee $5.00. Real estate records located at Bristol County. General copy fee $2.00 per page. Tax lien copy- $2.00 1st 3 pages; $1.00 each add'l page. Cert fee- $5.00. Payee- Town of Rehoboth. **Other phones:** Treasurer- 508-252-3571; Elections- 508-252-6502; Vital Records- 508-252-6502. **Property tax/Assessor-** same address as above. 508-252-3352.

Revere City

City Clerk, 281 Broadway; City Hall, Revere, MA 02151-5087. 781-286-8160; fax-781-286-8135; hours: 8:15AM-5PM M-Th; 8:15AM-N Fri. www.revere.org/greeting.htm
No real estate recordings. Only the public may search. Copy fee $1.00 per page. Cert fee- $10.00. Payee- City of Revere. **Online access to Assessor, Property records:** Access property data free at http://revere.patriotproperties.com/default.asp. Free registration for full data. **Other phones:** Treasurer- 781-286-8136. **Property tax/Assessor-** 781-286-8169.

Richmond Town

Town Clerk, PO Box 81, Richmond, MA 01254. 413-698-3315; fax-413-698-3272; hours: 9AM-Noon M T Th F.
No real estate recordings. Only the public may search. Real estate records located at Berkshire County. Copy fee $.20 per page. Cert fee- $5.00 per unit plus copy fee. Payee- Town of Richmond. **Online access to Property, Assessor records:** Access property data is free at http://csc-ma.us/PropertyContent/jsp/Home.jsp?Page=1. **Other phones:** Treasurer- 413-698-3315; Elections- 413-698-3315. **Property tax/Assessor-** 1529 State Rd, PO Box 124, Richmond, MO 01254; 413-698-2525.

Rochester Town

Town Clerk, 1 Constitution Way; Town Hall, Rochester, MA 02770. 508-763-3866; fax-508-763-4892; hours: 7-9PM M.
No real estate recordings. Office personnel or visitors may perform searches. Search fee $10.00 per name. Real estate records located at Plymouth County. Payee- Town of Rochester.

Rockland Town

Town Clerk, 242 Union St, Rockland, MA 02370. 781-871-1892, R/E recording phone-781-871-0137, UCC recording phone-781-871-1892; 8:30AM-4:30PM.
No real estate recordings. All records in one index. Office will perform a UCC search but public must search other records themselves. Real estate records located at Plymouth County. UCC search per debtor name- $10.00. Copy fee $2.00 per page. Cert fee- $5.00 per cert. Payee- Town of Rockland. **Other phones:** Treasurer- 781-871-1895; Elections- 781-871-1892; Vital Records- 781-871-1892. **Property tax/Assessor-** same address as above. 781-871-0137.

Rockport Town

Town Clerk, PO Box 429, Rockport, MA 01966. 978-546-6894, R/E recording phone-978-546-2011; fax-978-546-3562; hours: 8AM-4PM. www.town.rockport.ma.us
No real estate recordings. All records in one index. Record index not computerized. Office personnel or visitors may perform searches. Search fee $10.00. Real estate records located at Essex County. Copy fee $1.00 per copy. Payee- Town of Rockport. **Other phones:** Treasurer- 978-546-6648; Elections- 978-546-6894; Vital Records- 978-546-6894. **Property tax/Assessor-** 978-546-2011.

Rowe Town

Town Clerk, Town Hall, Rowe, MA 01367. 413-339-5520; fax-413-339-5316; hours: 8-11AM W.
No real estate recordings. Record index not computerized. Office will perform a UCC search but public must search other records themselves. Real estate records located at Berkshire County. UCC search per debtor name- $10.00. Copy fee $1.00 per page. Payee- Town of Rowe. **Other phones:** Treasurer- 413-339-5520; Vital Records- 413-339-5520. **Property tax/Assessor-** 413-339-5520.

Rowley Town

Town Clerk, PO Box 351, Rowley, MA 01969-0351. 978-948-2081; fax-978-948-2162; hours: 1-8PM M, 8AM-4;30PM W, 8AM-N T, Th, F.
No real estate recordings. Records indexed on computer. Only the public may search. Copy fee $.20 per page. Cert fee- $5.00 per page includes copy fee. Payee- Town of Rowley. **Online access to Assessor records:** Search the town assessor data at http://data.visionappraisal.com/RowleyMA/. Free registration for full data. **Other phones:** Treasurer- 978-948-2631; Elections- 978-948-2081; Vital Records- 978-948-2081. **Property tax/Assessor-** 978-948-2021.

Royalston Town

Town Clerk, 94 Athol Rd, Royalston, MA 01368-0118. 978-249-0493; fax-978-575-0493; hours: 9:30AM-2:30PM Tuesdays.

No real estate recordings. Office will perform a UCC search but public must search other records themselves. Real estate records located at Worcester County. UCC search per debtor name- $10.00. Copy fee $1.00 per page. Payee- Town of Royalston. **Online access to Assessor, Property records:** Access to property data is free at http://csc-ma.us/PropertyContent/jsp/Home.jsp?Page=1. Select Royalston Town. **Other phones:** Treasurer- 978-249-0493; Elections- 978-249-0493; Vital Records- 978-249-0493; Tax Collector- 978-249-2927. **Property tax/Assessor-** 978-249-0337.

Russell Town

Town Clerk, 65 Main St; Town Hall, Russell, MA 01071. 413-862-3265; fax-413-862-3103; hours: 4:30-6:30PM T; 4-6PM F.

No real estate recordings. All records in one index. Office personnel or visitors may perform searches. Real estate records located at Hampden County. Will search UCC records, but not tax liens. UCC search per debtor name- $10.00. Copy fee $1.00 per page. Payee- Town of Russell. **Online access to Real Estate, Recording, Lien records:** See Hampden County for recording records searching. **Other phones:** Treasurer- 413-862-3265; Elections- 413-862-3265; Vital Records- 413-862-3265. **Property tax/Assessor-** 65 Main St, Russell, MA 01071; 413-862-3103.

Rutland Town

Town Clerk, 250 Main St, Rutland, MA 01543. 508-886-4104; fax-508-886-2929; hours: 7:30AM-4PM M,W,Th; 7:30AM-7PM T.

No real estate recordings. Separate indices to search include birth, death, marriage. Only the office personnel may search. Search fee $6.00 per name. Real estate records located at Worcester County. Copy fee $2.00 per page. Cert fee- $5.00 per cert. Payee- Town of Rutland. **Online access to Assessor, Property records:** Access to Rutland town assessor records is free at http://data.visionappraisal.com/RutlandMA/. **Other phones:** Treasurer- 508-886-4103; Elections- 508-886-4104; Vital Records- 508-886-4104. **Property tax/Assessor-** same address as above. 508-886-4101.

Salem City

City Clerk, 93 Washington; City Hall, Salem, MA 01970-3593. 978-745-9595; fax-978-740-9209; hours: 8AM-4PM M-W; 8AM-7PM Th; 8AM-N Fri.

No real estate recordings. All records in one index prior to June, 2003. Record index not computerized. Only the public may search. Copy fee $.20 per page. Cert fee- $3.00 per doc plus copy fee. Payee- City of Salem. **Online access to Assessor, Property records:** Access property data free at http://salem.patriotproperties.com/default.asp. No name searching. **Property tax/Assessor-** same address as above. 978-745-9595 x261.

Salisbury Town

Town Clerk, 5 Beach Rd, Salisbury, MA 01952. 978-462-7591; fax-978-462-4176; hours: 8:30AM-4PM, 7-9PM M; 8:30AM-4PM T-Th; 8:30AM-1PM F. www.salisburyma.gov

No real estate recordings. Separate indices to search. Record index not computerized. Search fee $10.00 per name. Real estate records located at Essex County. Copy fee $2.00 per page. Cert fee- $1.00 per page plus copy fee. Payee- Town of Salisbury. **Online access to Property, Assessor records:** Access town property data free online at http://salisbury.patriotproperties.com/default.asp. **Other phones:** Treasurer- 978-465-0331; Vital Records- 978-462-7591. **Property tax/Assessor-** same address as above. 978-462-7591.

Sandisfield Town

Town Clerk, PO Box 163, Sandisfield, MA 01255. 413-258-4711, R/E recording phone-413-258-4701, UCC recording phone-413-258-4075; fax-413-258-4225; hours: 10AM-2PM, 6-8PM M; 10AM-2PM Th or by Appointment.

No real estate recordings. Record index not computerized. Office will perform a UCC search but public must search other records themselves. Search fee $10.00. Real estate records located at Berkshire County. Copy fee $1.00 per page. Payee- Sandisfield Town Clerk. **Other phones:** Treasurer- 413-258-4712; Elections- 413-258-4075; Vital Records- 413-258-4075; Selectmen- 413-258-4711. **Property tax/Assessor-** PO Box 45, Sandisfield, MA 01255; 413-258-4701.

Sandwich Town

Town Clerk, 145 Main St, Sandwich, MA 02563. 508-888-0340; fax-508-888-2497; hours: 8:30AM-4:30PM. www.sandwichmass.org

No real estate recordings. Office personnel or visitors may perform searches. Search fee $10.00 per name. Real estate records located at Barnstable County. Copy fee $.20 per page. Cert fee- $2.00 per page. Payee- Town of Sandwich. **Other phones:** Treasurer- 508-888-6508; Elections- 508-888-0340; Vital Records- 508-888-0340. **Property tax/Assessor-** 508-888-0157.

Saugus Town

Town Clerk, 298 Central St; Town Hall, Saugus, MA 01906. 781-231-4101; fax-781-231-4109; hours: 8:30AM-7PM M; 8:30AM-5PM T,W,Th; 8:30AM-12:30PM F. www.saugus.net

This office observes Summer hours June 1-Sept 1 and closes at 4PM. No real estate recordings here. All records in one index. Record index not computerized. Office personnel or visitors may perform searches. Search fee $15.00. Real estate records located at Essex County. Will not search UCC records or tax liens. Copy fee $2.00 per page. Cert fee- $5.00 per page plus copy fee. Payee- Town of Saugus. **Online access to Property, Assessor records:** Access property data free at http://csc-ma.us/SaugusPubAcc/jsp/Home.jsp. **Other phones:** Treasurer- 781-231-4135; Elections- 781-231-4101; Vital Records- 781-231-4101. **Property tax/Assessor-** same address as above. 781-231-4130.

Savoy Town

Town Clerk, 720 Main Rd.; Town Office, Savoy, MA 01256. 413-743-3759; fax-413-743-4292; hours: 1-4PM Tu,Th; 10AM-N Sat; and by app't only. http://townofsavoy.org

No real estate recordings. All records in one index. Office will perform a UCC search but public must search other records themselves. UCC search per debtor name- $10.00. Copy fee $1.00 per page. Cert fee- $5.00 per page plus copy fee. Payee- Town of Savoy. **Other phones:** Treasurer- 413-743-4290; Elections- 413-743-3759; Vital Records- 413-743-3759; Main Town Office- 413-743-4290. **Property tax/Assessor-** same address as above. 413-743-4290.

Scituate Town

Town Clerk, 600 C. J. Cushing Way; Town Hall, Scituate, MA 02066. 781-545-8744; fax-781-545-8704; hours: 8:30AM-4:45PM M,W,Th; 8:30-7:30 Tu, 8:30-11:45AM F. www.town.scituate.ma.us

No real estate recordings. Office personnel or visitors may perform searches. Search fee $10.00 per name. Real estate records located at Plymouth County. Copy fee $2.00 per page. Cert fee- $2.00 per page. Payee- Town of Scituate. **Other phones:** Treasurer- 781-545-8719; Elections- 781-545-8744; Vital Records- 781-545-8744. **Property tax/Assessor-** 781-545-8713.

Seekonk Town

Town Clerk, 100 Peck St, Seekonk, MA 02771. 508-336-2920; fax-508-336-0764; hours: 8:30AM-4:30PM M,T,Th; 8:30AM-7PM Wed; 8:30AM-N Fri. www.ci.seekonk.ma.us

No real estate recordings. Separate indices to search include births, deaths, marriages, UCCs. Real estate records located at Bristol County. Will search UCC records, tax liens included in UCC search. UCC search per debtor name- $10.00. Copy fee $1.00 per page. Cert fee- $3.00 per page plus copy fee. Payee- Town of Seekonk. **Other phones:** Treasurer- 508-336-2930; Elections- 508-336-2920; Vital Records- 508-336-2920. **Property tax/Assessor-** 508-336-2980.

Sharon Town

Town Clerk, 90 S. Main St; Town Hall, Sharon, MA 02067. 781-784-1505; fax-781-784-1503; hours: 8:30AM-5PM M-W; 8:30AM-8PM Th; 8:30AM-12:30PM F. www.townofsharon.net

No real estate recordings. All records in one index. Records indexed on computer. Only the public may search. Real estate records located at Norfolk County. Copy fee $.20 per page. Cert fee- $5.20 per doc, plus copy fee. Payee- Town of Sharon. **Other phones:** Treasurer- 781-784-1500; Elections- 781-784-1505; Vital Records- 781-784-1505. **Property tax/Assessor-** same address as above. 781-784-1507.

Sheffield Town

Town Clerk, PO Box 175, Sheffield, MA 01257. 413-229-8752; fax-413-229-7010; hours: 9AM-4PM.

No real estate recordings. Office will perform a UCC search but public must search other records themselves. Real estate records located at Berkshire County. UCC search per debtor name- $15.00. Copy fee $.20 per page. Payee- Town of Sheffield. **Other phones:** Treasurer- 413-229-7007; Elections- 413-229-8752; Vital Records- 413-229-8752. **Property tax/Assessor-** 413-229-7001.

Shelburne Town

Town Clerk, 51 Bridge St; Town Hall, Shelburne, MA 01370. 413-625-0301; fax-413-625-0312; hours: 9AM-5PM M T; 5-8PM Th.

No real estate recordings. All records in one index. Record index not computerized. Only the office personnel may search. Search fee $10.00 per name. Real estate records located at Franklin County. Copy fee $1.00 per page. Tax lien copy- $.25 per page. Payee- Town of Shelburne. **Other phones:** Treasurer- 413-625-0312. **Property tax/Assessor-** 413-625-0302.

Sherborn Town

Town Clerk, 19 Washington St, Sherborn, MA 01770. 508-651-7853; fax-508-651-7854; hours: 9AM-1PM M-Th & Tues eves 6-8PM. www.sherbornma.org

No real estate recordings. All records in one index. Record index not computerized. Only the office personnel may search. Search fee $10.00. Real estate records located at Middlesex County. Copy fee $3.00 per page. Tax lien copy- $.25 per page. Cert fee- $5.00 per copy. Payee- Town of Sherborn. **Other phones:** Treasurer- 508-651-7859; Elections- 508-651-7853; Vital Records- 508-651-7853. **Property tax/Assessor-** 508-651-7857.

Shirley Town

Town Clerk, 7 Keady Way, Shirley, MA 01464. 978-425-2600 x205; fax-978-425-2602; hours: 8:30AM-1PM-3PM M-F; 6PM-8:30PM M. www.shirley-ma.gov/controller.action?mod=10&submod=15

No real estate recordings. Record index not computerized. Office personnel or visitors may perform searches. Search fee $6.00 per name. Real estate records located at Middlesex County. UCC search per debtor name- $10.00. Copy fee $1.00 per page. Payee- Town of Shirley. **Online access to Assessor, Property records:** Access property data free at http://shirley.patriotproperties.com/default.asp. **Other phones:** Treasurer- 978-425-2600 x215; Vital Records- 978-425-2610. **Property tax/Assessor-** 978-425-2600 x220.

Shrewsbury Town

Town Clerk, 100 Maple Ave; Town Hall, Shrewsbury, MA 01545. 508-841-8507; fax-508-842-0587; hours: 8AM-4:30PM.
No real estate recordings. Office personnel or visitors may perform searches. Search fee $10.00 per name. Real estate records located at Worcester County. Copy fee $2.00 per page. Payee- Town of Shrewsbury. **Other phones:** Treasurer- 508-841-8509; Elections- 508-841-8507; Vital Records- 508-841-8507. **Property tax/Assessor-** 508-841-8501.

Shutesbury Town

Town Clerk, PO Box 264, Shutesbury, MA 01072-0264. 413-259-1204, R/E recording phone-413-259-3790, UCC recording phone-413-259-1204; fax-413-259-1107; hours: 9AM-1PM M-Th. www.shutesbury.org
No real estate recordings. All records in one index. Record index not computerized. Only the office personnel may search. Search fee $10.00 (UCCs 7yrs only). Real estate records located at Franklin County. Copy fee $1.00 per page. Cert fee- $5.00 per page. Payee- Town of Shutesbury. **Other phones:** Treasurer- 413-259-1801; Elections- 413-259-1204; Vital Records- 413-259-1204; Local Tax Collector for local liens- 413-259-1615. **Property tax/Assessor-** same address as above. 413-259-3790.

Somerset Town

Town Clerk, 140 Wood St, Somerset, MA 02726. 508-646-2818; fax-508-646-2802; hours: 8:30AM-4PM.
No real estate recordings. Office will perform a UCC search but public must search other records themselves. Real estate records located at Bristol County. UCC search per debtor name- $10.00. Copy fee $2.00 per page. Payee- Town of Somerset. **Online access to Property, Assessor records:** Access to property data is free at http://csc-ma.us/PropertyContent/jsp/Home.jsp?Page=1. Select Somerset Town. **Other phones:** Treasurer- 508-646-2822; Vital Records- 508-646-2818. **Property tax/Assessor-** 508-646-2824.

Somerville City

City Clerk, 93 Highland Ave, Somerville, MA 02143. 617-625-6600 x4100; fax-617-625-4239; hours: 8:30AM-4:30PM M-W; 8:30-7:30PM Th; 8:30-12:30PM F. www.ci.somerville.ma.us
No real estate recordings. All records in one index. Will search UCC records and tax liens. UCC search per debtor name- $10.00. Tax lien search fee- $10.00 per search. Copy fee $1.00 per page. Payee- City of Somerville. **Online access to Assessor records:** Search the city assessor database at http://data.visionappraisal.com/SomervilleMA/. Free registration for full data. **Other phones:** Treasurer- 617-625-6600 x3500; Elections- 617-625-6600 x4200; Vital Records- 617-625-6600 x4100. **Property tax/Assessor-** 93 Highland Ave, Somerville, MA 02143; 617-625-6600 x3100.

South Hadley Town

Town Clerk, 116 Main St, South Hadley, MA 01075-2833. 413-538-5023; fax-413-538-7565; hours: 8:30AM-4:30PM. www.southhadley.org
No real estate recordings. Separate indices. Record index not computerized. Office will perform a UCC search but public must search other records themselves. Search fee $5.00. Real estate records located at Hampshire County. Copy fee $1.00 per page. Cert fee- $5.00 per page. Payee- Town of South Hadley. **Other phones:** Treasurer- 413-538-5023; Elections- 413-538-5023; Vital Records- 413-538-5023. **Property tax/Assessor-** 413-538-5027.

Southampton Town

Town Clerk, PO Box 276, Southampton, MA 01073. 413-527-8392; fax-413-529-1006; hours: 8:30AM-4PM M-Th. www.town.southampton.ma.us
No real estate recordings. Record index not computerized. Office will perform a UCC search but public must search other records themselves. Search fee $5.00. Real estate records located at Hampshire County. Copy fee $.25 per page. Cert fee- $3.00 per page includes copy fee. Payee- Town of Southampton. **Other phones:** Treasurer- 413-527-4920; Elections- 413-527-8392; Vital Records- 413-527-8392; Selectman- 413-529-0106. **Property tax/Assessor-** PO Box 188, Southampton, MA 01073; 413-527-4741.

Southborough Town

Town Clerk, 17 Common St, Town Hall, Southborough, MA 01772-9109. 508-485-0710; fax-508-480-0161; hours: 9AM-5PM.
No real estate recordings. All records in one index. Search fee $10.00 per name. Copy fee $2.00 per page. Cert fee- $2.00 per page includes copy fee. Payee- Town Clerk. **Online access to Assessor, Property records:** Access property tax data free at http://csc-ma.us/SouthboroughPubAcc/jsp/Home.jsp?Page=1. No name searching. **Other phones:** Treasurer- 508-485-0710; Elections- 508-485-0710; Vital Records- 508-485-0710. **Property tax/Assessor-** same address as above. 508-485-0710.

Southbridge Town

Town Clerk, 41 Elm St, Southbridge, MA 01550. 508-764-5408; fax-508-764-5425; hours: 8AM-4PM M-W; 8AM-8PM Th; 8AM-N Fri. www.ci.southbridge.ma.us
No real estate recordings. All records in one index. Record index not computerized. Office personnel or visitors may perform searches. Search fee $10.00 per name. Real estate records located at Worcester County. Copy fee $2.00 per page. Payee- Town of Southbridge. **Other phones:** Treasurer- 508-764-5401; Elections- 508-764-5408; Vital Records- 508-764-5408. **Property tax/Assessor-** same address as above. 508-764-5404.

Southwick Town

Town Clerk, 454 College Hwy, Southwick, MA 01077. 413-569-5504; fax-413-569-0667; hours: 8:30AM-4:30PM. www.southwickma.org
No real estate recordings. All records in one index. Record index not computerized. Only the office personnel may search. Search fee $15.00 per hour plus $1.00 per page. Real estate records located at Hampden County. Copy fee $.75 per page. Cert fee- $25.00 per doc plus copy fee. Payee- Town of Southwick. **Online access to Assessor, Real Estate, Recording, Lien records:** Search the town assessor database at http://data.visionappraisal.com/SouthwickMA/. Free registration for full data. Also, see Hampden County for recording records searching. **Other phones:** Treasurer- 413-569-5504; Elections- 413-569-5504; Vital Records- 413-569-5504. **Property tax/Assessor-** 413-569-0565.

Spencer Town

Town Clerk, 157 Main St; Town Hall, Spencer, MA 01562-2197. 508-885-7500; fax-508-885-7528; hours: 8-4, 6-8PM M; 8-4 TTh; 8-N, 1-4 W; 8-N F.
No real estate recordings. Separate indices to search include UCC, vital records, tax liens. Record index not computerized. Office personnel or visitors may perform searches. Search fee $10.00 per name. Real estate records located at Worcester County. Copy fee $2.00, if tax lien $.20 per page. Cert fee- $3.00 per cert plus copy fee. Payee- Town of Spencer. **Other phones:** Treasurer- 508-885-7500 x175; Elections- 508-885-7500 x150; Vital Records- 508-885-7500 x150. **Property tax/Assessor-** 508-885-7500 x160.

Springfield City

City Clerk, 36 Court St, Springfield, MA 01103. 413-787-6094; hours: 9AM-4PM (Th open until 6PM).
No real estate recordings. Office personnel or visitors may perform searches. Search fee $20.00 per name. Real estate records located at Hampden County. Copy fee $2.00 for 3 pages; $1.00 each add'l. Cert fee- $15.00 per page plus copy fee. Payee- City of Springfield. **Online access to Real Estate, Recording, Lien records:** See Hampden County for recording records searching. **Other phones:** Treasurer- 413-787-6130. **Property tax/Assessor-** same address as above. 413-787-6160.

Sterling Town

Town Clerk, 1 Park St; Mary Ellen Butterick Muni. Bldg, Sterling, MA 01564. 978-422-8111; fax-978-422-0289; hours: 8AM-4:30PM.
No real estate recordings. Office will perform a UCC search but public must search other records themselves. Real estate records located at Worcester County. UCC search per debtor name- $10.00. Copy fee $1.00 per page. Payee- Town of Sterling. SASE required. **Other phones:** Treasurer- 978-422-3028; Elections- 978-422-8111; Vital Records- 978-422-8111. **Property tax/Assessor-** 978-422-8113.

Stockbridge Town

Town Clerk, PO Box 417, Stockbridge, MA 01262-0417. 413-298-4568; fax-413-298-4485; hours: 9AM-Noon; 1PM-4PM. www.townofstockbridge.com
No real estate recordings. All records in one index. Only the office personnel may search. Search fee $10.00 per name. Real estate records located at Berkshire County. Will search UCC records; search includes tax liens if requested. Copy fee $1.00 per page. Cert fee- $5.00 per signature includes copy fee. Payee- Town of Stockbridge. **Other phones:** Treasurer- 413-298-4534; Elections- 413-298-4568; Vital Records- 413-298-4568; Central Switchboard- 413-298-4714. **Property tax/Assessor-** PO Box 417, Stockbridge, MA 01262-0417; 413-298-3509.

Stoneham Town

Town Clerk, 35 Central St, Stoneham, MA 02180. 781-279-2650; fax-781-279-2653; hours: 8AM-4PM M,W-Th; 8AM-7PM T; 8AM-N Fri.
No real estate recordings. Office personnel or visitors may perform searches. Search fee $10.00 per name. Real estate records located at Middlesex County. Will search UCC records prior to 7/2001. Copy fee $2.00, if tax lien or real estate $1.00 per page. Cert fee- $10.00 per cert. Payee- Town of Stoneham. **Property tax/Assessor-** 781-279-2640.

Stoughton Town

Town Clerk, 10 Pearl St; Town Hall, Stoughton, MA 02072. 781-341-1300; fax-781-341-1032; hours: 8:30AM-4:30PM M-W; 8:30AM-7PM Th; 8:30AM-1PM F. www.stoughton.org
No real estate recordings. All records in one index. Record index not computerized. Only the public may search. Real estate records located at Norfolk County. Copy fee $2.00 per page. Payee- Town of Stoughton. **Other phones:** Treasurer- 781-341-1300. **Property tax/Assessor-** same address as above. 781-341-1300.

Stow Town

Town Clerk, 380 Great Rd; Town Bldg, Stow, MA 01775. 978-897-4514; fax-978-897-4534; hours: 8AM-7PM M; 8AM-12:30PM T; 8AM-4PM W-F.
No real estate recordings. Records indexed for vital records and UCC prior to 7/2001. Office will perform a UCC search prior to 7/2001, but public must search other records themselves. Search fee $10.00 per name. Real estate records located at Middlesex County. Copy fee $.20 per page. Cert fee- $5.00 per doc plus copy fee. Payee- Town of Stow. **Other phones:** Treasurer- 978-897-2834; Elections- 978-897-4514 x1; Vital Records- 978-897-

4514 x1. **Property tax/Assessor**- same address as above. 978-897-4597.

Sturbridge Town

Town Clerk, 308 Main, Sturbridge, MA 01566. 508-347-2510, R/E recording phone-508-347-2503, UCC recording phone-508-347-2510; fax-508-347-5886; hours: 8AM-N, 1-4PM, 6-8PM M; 8AM-N, 1-4PM T-F. www.town.sturbridge.ma.us
No real estate recordings. All records in one index. Record index not computerized. Only the office personnel may search. Real estate records located at Worcester County. Will search UCC records; search includes tax liens if requested. UCC search per debtor name- $10.00. Separate state/federal tax lien search fee-$10.00 per name. Copy fee $2.00 per page. Cert fee- $1.00 per page. Payee- Town of Sturbridge. **Online access to Real Estate, Deed records:** See Worcester County Southern District for online information. **Other phones:** Treasurer- 508-347-2509; Elections- 508-347-2510; Vital Records- 508-347-2510. **Property tax/Assessor**- 508-347-2503.

Sudbury Town

Town Clerk, 322 Concord Rd, Sudbury, MA 01776-1800. 978-443-8891 x351; fax-978-443-0264; hours: 9AM-5PM. www.town.sudbury.ma.us/services
No real estate recordings. Index: UCCs and Fed tax liens here; municipal liens at tax collector's office. Record index not computerized. Office will perform a pre-2001 UCC search but public must search other records themselves. Real estate records located at Middlesex County. UCC search per debtor name- $5.00. Federal/state combined tax lien search- $5.00. Copy fee $2.00 per page. Cert fee- $2.00 per cert plus copy fee. Payee- Town of Sudbury. **Online access to Assessor, Property records:** Access to the property valuations list for current year is free at www.town.sudbury.ma.us/services/department_home.asp?dept=Assessors. No name searching on this address index list. **Other phones:** Treasurer- 978-443-8891 x375; Elections-978-443-8891 x351; Vital Records- 978-443-8891 x351. **Property tax/Assessor**- 278 Old Sudbury Rd, Sudbury, MA 01776; 978-443-8891 x393.

Suffolk County

County Register of Deeds, PO Box 9660, Boston, MA 02114-9660. 617-788-8575; fax-617-720-4163; hours: 8AM-4:30PM. www.suffolkdeeds.com
Only the public may search. Copy fee $1.00 per page. Cert fee- No extra fee. Payee- Suffolk County Register of Deeds. **Online access to Real Estate, Lien, Deed, Judgment, Property Assessor records:** Searches on Registry of Deeds site are free; real estate/liens on the county online system is not. Access to the County online system requires a written request submitted to Register of Deeds, POB 9660, Boston. Online charges are $.50 per minute. Also, Records on the County Registry of Deeds database are free at www.suffolkdeeds.com/search/default.asp. Search by name, corporation, and grantor/grantee. Recorded land records begin 1979; Registered land, 1983. Also, Registry of Deeds data is free at www.masslandrecords.com; click on Suffolk on the map. Also, search Boston assessor property records free at www.cityofboston.gov/assessing/search.asp. City property taxes also available, but no name searching. **Other phones:** Treasurer- 617-788-8575; Elections-617-788-8575; Vital Records- 617-788-8575. **Property tax/Assessor**- 617-788-8575.

Sunderland Town

Town Clerk, 12 School St, Sunderland, MA 01375-9503. 413-665-1442, R/E recording phone-413-665-1445, UCC recording phone-413-665-1442; fax-413-665-1446; hours: 8AM-4PM M-Th. www.townofsunderland.us
No real estate recordings. All records in one index. Office personnel or visitors may perform searches. General search fee $10.00 per name. Real estate records located at Franklin County. State tax lien search fee-$25.00 per debtor. Copy fee $1.00 per

page. Payee- Town of Sunderland. **Other phones:** Treasurer- 413-665-1444; Elections- 413-665-1442; Vital Records- 413-665-1442. **Property tax/Assessor**- same address as above. 413-665-1445.

Sutton Town

Town Clerk, 4 Uxbridge Rd.; Town Hall, Sutton, MA 01590. 508-865-8725; fax-508-865-8721; hours: 9AM-4PM M,T,W,Th; 7-9PM T; 9AM-N Fri. http://town.sutton.ma.us/
No real estate recordings. Office personnel or visitors may perform searches. Search fee $10.00 per name. Real estate records located at Worcester County. Copy fee $1.00 per page. Tax lien copy- $.20 per page. Payee- Town of Sutton.

Swampscott Town

Town Clerk, 22 Monument Ave; Town Hall, Swampscott, MA 01907. 781-596-4167; fax-781-596-8870; hours: 8:30AM-4:30PM M-Th; 8AM-Noon F. www.town.swampscott.ma.us
No real estate recordings. All records in one index. Only the public may search. Real estate records located at Essex County. Copy fee $2.00 per page. Cert fee- $2.00 per doc plus copy fee. Payee- Town of Swampscott. **Online access to Assessor, Property records:** Access property data free at http://swampscott.patriotproperties.com/default.asp. **Other phones:** Elections- 781-596-8855; Vital Records- 781-596-8856. **Property tax/Assessor**- 781-596-8858.

Swansea Town

Town Clerk, 81 Main St; Town Hall, Swansea, MA 02777. 508-678-9389; hours: 9AM-4PM M,T,Th,F; 9AM-5PM W.
No real estate recordings, no UCC here. Separate indices to search. Real estate records located at Bristol County, Fall River Registry of Deeds. Copy fee $1.00 per page. Cert fee- $10.00 per page. Payee- Town of Swansea. **Online access to Property, Assessor records:** Access to property data is free at http://csc-ma.us/PropertyContent/jsp/Home.jsp?Page=1. Select Swansea Town. **Other phones:** Treasurer- 508-679-6489; Elections- 508-678-9389; Vital Records- 508-678-9389; Selectman's Office- 508-678-2981. **Property tax/Assessor**- 81 Main St, Swansea, MA 02777; 508-324-6702.

Taunton City

City Clerk, 15 Summer St; City Hall, Taunton, MA 02780. 508-821-1024, R/E recording phone-508-822-0502, UCC recording phone-508-821-1024; fax-508-821-1098; 9AM-5PM. www.ci.taunton.ma.us
No real estate recordings. Office personnel or visitors may perform searches. Search fee $10.00 per name. Real estate records located at Bristol County. Copy fee $2.00 per copy. Payee- City of Taunton. **Online access to Assessor records:** Access assessor data at http://data.visionappraisal.com/TauntonMA/. Does not require a username & password. Simply click on link. **Other phones:** Treasurer- 508-821-1057; Elections- 508-821-1044; Vital Records- 508-821-1024. **Property tax/Assessor**- 508-821-1011.

Templeton Town

Town Clerk, 4 Elm St.; Town Office Bldg, Baldwinville, MA 01436. 978-939-8466; fax-978-939-8327; hours: 8AM-5PM M; 8AM-3PM T,TH; 8AM-1PM F (Closed W).
No real estate recordings. Real estate records located at Worcester County. Will not search UCC records. Copy fee $1.00 per page plus postage. Payee- Town of Templeton. **Online access to Assessor records:** Access assessor data at http://data.visionappraisal.com/TempletonMA/. Free registration for full data. **Other phones:** Treasurer- 978-939-4475; Elections- 978-939-8466; Vital Records- 978-939-8466; Tax Collector- 978-939-2216. **Property tax/Assessor**- 978-939-2793.

Tewksbury Town

Town Clerk, 1009 Main St; Town Hall, Tewksbury, MA 01876-2796. 978-640-4355; fax-978-851-8610; hours: 8:30AM-4:30PM. www.tewksbury.info
No real estate recordings. All records in one index. Record index not computerized. Only the office personnel may search. Search fee $10.00 per name. Copy fee $.20 per page. Cert fee- $1.00 per page plus copy fee. Payee- Town of Tewksbury. **Other phones:** Treasurer- 978-640-4355; Vital Records- 978-640-4355. **Property tax/Assessor**- 11 Town Hall Ave, Tewksbury, MA 01876; 978-640-4330.

Tisbury Town

Town Clerk, PO Box 606, Tisbury, MA 02568-0606. 508-696-4215; fax-508-693-5876; hours: 8:30AM-4:30PM. www.ci.tisbury.ma.us
No real estate recordings. Separate indices to search. Record index not computerized. Office will perform a UCC search but public must search other records themselves. Real estate records located at Dukes County. UCC search per debtor name- $10.00. Copy fee $2.00 per page. Cert fee- $10.00 per name. Payee- Town of Tisbury. **Online access to Assessor records:** Search the town assessor database at http://data.visionappraisal.com/TisburyMA/. Free registration for full data. **Other phones:** Treasurer- 508-696-4250; Elections- 508-696-4215; Vital Records- 508-696-4215. **Property tax/Assessor**- 508-696-4206.

Tolland Town

Town Clerk, 241 W. Granville Rd, Tolland, MA 01034. 413-259-4794; fax-413-258-4048; 2-7PM Mondays.
No real estate recordings. Record index not computerized. Office will perform a Tax lien search but public must search other records themselves. Search fee $5.00 min, $15.00 hr. Real estate records located at Hampden County. Copy fee $5.00 each. Cert fee- $5.00 per page plus copy fee. Payee- Town of Tolland. **Online access to Real Estate, Recording, Lien, Property, Assessor records:** See Hampden County for recording records searching. Also, access property data free at http://csc-ma.us/PropertyContent/jsp/Home.jsp?Page=1. **Other phones:** Treasurer- 413-259-4794; Elections- 413-259-4794; Vital Records- 413-259-4794. **Property tax/Assessor**- 413-259-4794.

Topsfield Town

Town Clerk, 8 W. Common St; Town Hall, Topsfield, MA 01983. 978-887-1505; fax-978-887-1502; hours: 8:30AM-4PM M-Th (Summer Hours: 8AM-N). www.topsfield-ma.gov/clerk/townclerk.shtml
Real estate records located at Essex County. Separate indices to search include vital, election, archival records, older UCCs. Records index not computerized. Only the office personnel may search. Search fee- hourly rate of lowest paid office employee. Copy fee $1.00 per page. Cert fee- $10.00 per sheet includes copy fee. Payee- Town of Topsfield. **Other phones:** Treasurer- 978-887-1511; Elections- 978-887-1505; Vital Records- 978-887-1505. **Property tax/Assessor**- same address as above. 978-887-1514.

Town of Aquinnah

Town Clerk, 65 State Rd, Aquinnah, MA 02535. 508-645-2306; fax-508-645-2310; hours: by Appointment.
No real estate recordings. The Town of Aquinnah was formerly known as Gay Head. Only the public may search. Copy fee $1.00 per page. Payee- Clerk of Aquinnah. **Other phones:** 508-645-2300.

Townsend Town

Town Clerk, 272 Main St; Memorial Hall, Townsend, MA 01469. 978-597-1704; fax-978-597-8135; hours: 9AM-4PM; 9AM-8PM Tu; 9AM-N 1st & 3rd Sat.
No real estate recordings. Only the public may search. Real estate records located at Middlesex

County. Copy fee $2.00 per page. Payee- Town of Townsend. **Other phones:** Treasurer- 978-597-1708; Elections- 978-597-1704; Vital Records- 978-597-1704. **Property tax/Assessor-** 978-597-6612.

Truro Town

Town Clerk, PO Box 2012, Truro, MA 02666-2012. 508-349-7004 ext 14; fax-508-349-7720; hours: 8AM-4PM.

No real estate recordings. Records indexed on a public use terminal. Office personnel or visitors may perform searches. Search fee $10.00 per name. Real estate records located at Barnstable County. Copy fee $1.00 per page. Tax lien copy- $.20 per page. Cert fee- $1.00 per cert. Payee- Town of Truro. **Other phones:** Treasurer- 508-349-3860. **Property tax/Assessor-** 508-349-9248.

Tyngsborough Town

Town Clerk, 25 Bryants Lane, Tyngsborough, MA 01879. 978-649-2300 x129; fax-978-649-2301; hours: 8AM-7PM M; 8AM-4PM Tu-Th; 8AM-12:30PM F. www.tyngsboroughmass.com

No real estate recordings. Office personnel or visitors may perform searches. Search fee $10.00 per name. Real estate records located at Middlesex County. Copy fee $1.00 per page. Cert fee- $4.00 per page. Payee- Town of Tyngsborough. **Other phones:** Treasurer- 978-649-2300 x125; Elections- 978-649-2300 x129; Vital Records- 978-649-2300 x129. **Property tax/Assessor-** 978-649-2300 x121.

Tyringham Town

Town Clerk, Main Rd, Tyringham, MA 01264. 413-243-1749; R/E recording phone-413-234-1749; fax-413-243-4942; 9AM-1PM or by appointment. www.tyngsboroughmass.com/clerk.htm

No real estate recordings. Record index not computerized. Office will perform a UCC search but public must search other records themselves. Search fee $15.00. Real estate records located at Berkshire County. Copy fee $4.00 per page. Cert fee- $5.00 per page plus copy fee. Payee- Town Clerk. **Other phones:** Treasurer- 413-234-1749; Elections- 413-234-1749; Vital Records- 413-234-1749. **Property tax/Assessor-** 413-234-1749.

Upton Town

Town Clerk, Box 969, Upton, MA 01568. 508-529-3565; fax-508-529-1010; hours: M&W 9AM-3PM; T&Th 9AM-1 & 6-8PM; Fri 9AM - 1PM. www.upton.ma.us

No real estate recordings. Office will perform a UCC search but public must search other records themselves. Real estate records located at Worcester County. UCC search per debtor name- $10.00. Copy fee $5.00 per page. Payee- Town of Upton. **Other phones:** Treasurer- 508-529-3737; Elections- 508-529-3565; Vital Records- 508-529-3565. **Property tax/Assessor-** 508-529-1002.

Uxbridge Town

Town Clerk, 21 S. Main St, Uxbridge, MA 01569. 508-278-3156; fax-508-278-3154; hours: 9AM-4PM.

No real estate recordings. Separate indices to search. Record index not computerized. Office personnel or visitors may perform searches. Search fee $5.00 per debtor, or $2.00 per statement. Real estate records located at Worcester County. Copy fee $.25 per page. Cert fee- $5.00 per cert plus copy fee. Payee- Town of Uxbridge. **Other phones:** Treasurer- 508-278-8606; Elections- 508-278-3156; Vital Records- 508-278-3156; Switchboard- 508-278-8600. **Property tax/Assessor-** 508-278-8602.

Wakefield Town

Town Clerk, 1 Lafayette St; Town Hall, Wakefield, MA 01880-2383. 781-246-6383, R/E recording phone-781-246-6380, UCC recording phone-781-246-6383; fax-781-246-4155; hours: 8:30AM-5PM.

No real estate recordings. Record index not computerized. Office personnel or visitors may perform searches. Search fee $10.00 per name.

Real estate records located at Middlesex County. Copy fee $2.00 per page. Cert fee- $3.00 per cert. Payee- Town of Wakefield. **Online access to Assessor, Property records:** Access property data free at http://wakefield.patriotproperties.com/default.asp. **Other phones:** Treasurer- 781-246-6340; Elections- 781-246-6384; Vital Records- 781-246-6383; Town Adm./Selectmen- 781-246-6390. **Property tax/Assessor-** same address as above. 781-246-5159.

Wales Town

Town Clerk, PO Box 834, Wales, MA 01081-0834. 413-245-7571; fax-413-245-3261; hours: 9AM-3PM M-Tu.

No real estate recordings. All records in one index. Only the office personnel may search. Search fee $25.00 per name. Real estate records located at Hampden County. Copy fee $1.00 per page. Payee- Town of Wales. **Online access to Real Estate, Recording, Lien records:** See Hampden County for recording records searching. **Other phones:** Treasurer- 413-245-3260 x102; Vital Records- 413-245-7571 x101. **Property tax/Assessor-** same address as above. 413-245-3260 x103.

Walpole Town

Town Clerk, 135 School St; Town Hall, Walpole, MA 02081-2898. 508-660-7297, R/E recording phone-508-660-7315, UCC recording phone-508-660-7296; fax-508-660-7303; hours: 8AM-4PM M W TH; 8AM-8PM T; 8AM-Noon F. www.walpole-ma.gov

No real estate recordings. Separate indices to search. Record index not computerized. Office will perform a UCC search but public must search other records themselves. Real estate records located at Norfolk County. UCC search per debtor name- $10.00. Copy fee $2.00 per page. Cert fee- $.50 per page plus copy fee. Payee- Town of Walpole. **Online access to Property Assessor records:** Search the town assessor database at http://data.visionappraisal.com/WalpoleMA/. Free registration for full data. **Other phones:** Treasurer- 508-660-7311; Elections- 508-660-7296; Vital Records- 508-660-7296. **Property tax/Assessor-** same address as above. 508-660-7314.

Waltham City

City Clerk, 610 Main St; 2nd Fl, Waltham, MA 02452. 781-314-3120; fax-781-314-3130; hours: 8:30AM-4:30PM. www.city.waltham.ma.us

No real estate recordings. Record index not computerized. Office personnel or visitors may perform searches. Search fee $5.00 per name. Real estate records located at Middlesex County. Copy fee $5.00 for 1st 3 pages; $1.00 each add'l. Payee- City of Waltham. **Online access to Assessor, Property records:** Access property data free at http://waltham.patriotproperties.com/default.asp. **Other phones:** Treasurer- 781-314-3250; Elections- 781-314-3120; Vital Records- 781-314-3120. **Property tax/Assessor-** same address as above. 781-314-3200, 781-893-4040.

Ware Town

Town Clerk, 126 Main St, Ware, MA 01082. 413-967-4471; fax-413-967-9600; hours: 8:30AM-4:30PM.

No real estate recordings. Record index not computerized. Office will perform a UCC search but public must search other records themselves. Search fee $10.00. Real estate records located at Hampshire County. Copy fee $2.00 per page. Payee- Town of Ware. **Other phones:** Treasurer- 413-967-4471; Vital Records- 413-967-4471 x103. **Property tax/Assessor-** 413-967-9610.

Wareham Town

Town Clerk, 54 Marion Rd, Wareham, MA 02571. 508-291-3140, R/E recording phone-508-830-9200, UCC recording phone-508-291-3140; fax-508-291-3116; hours: 8:30AM-4:30PM.

No real estate recordings. Separate indices for certain records. Record index not computerized. Office

personnel or visitors may perform searches. Search fee- hourly rate of the lowest paid clerk. Real estate records located at Plymouth County. Will search UCC records, tax liens included if requested. UCC search per debtor name- $10.00 fixed. Copy fee $1.00 per page. Tax lien copy- $.20 per page. Payee- Town of Wareham. **Online access to Assessor records:** Search town assessor database at http://data.visionappraisal.com/WarehamMA/. Free registration for full data. **Other phones:** Treasurer- 508-291-3100 x3146; Elections- 508-291-3140; Vital Records- 508-291-3140. **Property tax/Assessor-** same address as above. 508-291-3160.

Warren Town

Town Clerk, PO Box 603, Warren, MA 01083-0603. 413-436-5701; fax-413-436-9754; hours: 9AM-3:30PM M-W,F; 5-8PM Th.

No real estate recordings. All records in one index. Record index not computerized. Office will perform a UCC search but public must search other records themselves. Search fee $10.00 per name. Real estate records located at Worcester County at Assessor's Office. Copy fee $2.00 per page. **Other phones:** Treasurer- 413-436-5701; Elections- 413-436-5701; Vital Records- 413-436-5701; Tax Collector- 413-436-5701. **Property tax/Assessor-** 413-436-5703.

Warwick Town

Town Clerk, 12 Athol Rd; Town Hall, Warwick, MA 01378. 978-544-8304; fax-978-544-6499; hours: 8AM-2PM, M.

No real estate recordings. All records in one index. Record index not computerized. Real estate records located at Franklin County. Will not search UCC records or tax liens. Copy fee $1.00 per page. Cert fee- $10.00 per cert plus copy fee. Payee- Town Clerk. **Other phones:** Treasurer- 978-544-3845; Vital Records- 978-544-8304. **Property tax/Assessor-** same address as above. 978-544-8304.

Washington Town

Town Clerk, 8 Summit Hill Rd.; GA094, Washington, MA 01223. 413-623-8878; fax-413-623-2116; hours: 7PM-9PM M or by appointment.

No real estate recordings. All records in one index. Record index not computerized. Office personnel or visitors may perform searches. Search fee $10.00. Real estate records located at Berkshire County. Copy fee $.50 per page. Payee- Town of Washington. **Other phones:** Treasurer- 413-623-8878; Elections- 413-623-2185; Vital Records- 413-623-2185. **Property tax/Assessor-** same address as above. 413-623-8878.

Watertown Town

Town Clerk, 149 Main St; Admin. Bldg, Watertown, MA 02472. 617-972-6486; fax-617-972-6595; hours: 8:30AM-5PM. www.ci.watertown.ma.us

No real estate recordings. All records in one index. Office will perform a UCC search but public must search other records themselves. UCC search per debtor name- $10.00. Copy fee $.20 per page. Tax lien copy- $.25 per residential unit, $1.25 per commercial unit. Cert fee- $10.00 per page. Payee- Town of Watertown. **Online access to Assessor, Property records:** Access property data free at http://watertown.patriotproperties.com/default.asp. **Other phones:** Treasurer- 617-972-6450; Elections- 617-972-6488; Vital Records- 617-972-6486. **Property tax/Assessor-** same address as above. 617-972-6410.

Wayland Town

Town Clerk, 41 Cochituate Rd, Wayland, MA 01778-2697. 508-358-3630 or 3631; fax-508-358-3627; hours: 8:30AM-4:30PM. www.wayland.ma.us

No real estate recordings. Separate indices to search. Record index not computerized. Only the public may search. Real estate records located at Middlesex County. Copy fee $.20 per page. Cert fee- $2.00 per page plus copy fee. Payee- Town of Wayland.

Online access to Assessor records: Assessment records on the Assessor's database are free at www.wayland.ma.us/assessors/index.htm. No name searching; street name required. **Other phones:** Treasurer- 508-358-3635; Elections- 508-358-3631; Vital Records- 508-358-3630. **Property tax/Assessor-** same address as above. 508-358-3658.

Webster Town

Town Clerk, 350 Main St, Webster, MA 01570. 508-949-3850, R/E recording phone-508-949-3810, UCC recording phone-508-949-3850; fax-508-949-3888; hours: 8AM-4PM, Closed F.
No real estate recordings. Separate indices to search include deaths, marriages. Record index not computerized. Will search UCC records; search includes tax liens if requested. Real estate records located at Worcester County. UCC search per debtor name- $10.00. Copy fee $2.00 per page. Cert fee- $5.00. Payee- Town of Webster. **Other phones:** Treasurer- 508-949-3820; Elections- 508-949-3850; Vital Records- 508-949-3850. **Property tax/Assessor-** same address as above. 508-949-3810.

Wellesley Town

Town Clerk, 525 Washington St, Wellesley, MA 02482. 781-431-1019 x250; fax-781-239-1043; hours: 8AM-5PM.
www.ci.wellesley.ma.us/town/index.html
Real estate records located at Norfolk County. Will search UCC records, search includes tax liens. UCC search per debtor name- $5.00. Separate tax lien search-no fee. Copy fee $2.00, if tax lien $.25 for 1st page 3 pages, $1.00 each add'l. Cert fee- $10.00 per record. Payee- Town of Wellesley. **Online access to Assessor, Town By-Law, Zoning By-Law, Election results records:** Property tax records on the Assessor's database are free at www.ci.wellesley.ma.us/asr/index.html. **Other phones:** Elections- 781-431-1019 x253; Vital Records- 781-431-1019 x252. **Assessor-** 781-431-1019.

Wellfleet Town

Town Clerk, 300 Main St, Wellfleet, MA 02667. 508-349-0301, R/E recording phone-508-349-0304; fax-508-349-0317; hours: 8AM-4PM.
No real estate recordings. Only the public may search. Real estate records located at Barnstable County. General copy fee $1.00 per page. Tax lien copy- $.25 per page. Payee- Town of Wellfleet. **Other phones:** Treasurer- 508-349-0301; Elections- 508-349-0301; Vital Records- 508-349-0301. **Property tax/Assessor-** same address. 508-349-0304.

Wendell Town

Town Clerk, 270 Wendell Depot Rd, Wendell Depot, MA 01380. 978-544-6682; fax-978-544-6052; hours: by appointment.
No real estate recordings. All records in one index. Record index not computerized. Only the public may search. Real estate records located at Franklin County. Copy fee $1.00 per page. Cert fee- $2.00 per page includes copy fee. Payee- Town of Wendell. **Property tax/Assessor-** 978-544-3395.

Wenham Town

Town Clerk, 138 Main St.; Town Hall, Wenham, MA 01984. 978-468-5520; fax-978-468-6164; 9AM-4:30PM M,W,Th; 9AM-7PM T; 9AM-1PM F.
No real estate recordings. Office will perform a UCC search but public must search other records themselves. Real estate records located at Essex County. UCC search per debtor name- $10.00. Copy fee $.20 per page. Cert fee- $5.00 per copy. Payee- Town of Wenham. **Other phones:** Treasurer- 978-468-5525; Elections- 978-468-5520; Vital Records- 978-468-5520. **Property tax/Assessor-** 978-468-5524.

West Boylston Town

Town Clerk, 120 Prescott St, West Boylston, MA 01583. 508-835-6240, R/E recording phone-508-835-6093, UCC recording phone-508-835-6240; fax-508-835-4102; hours: 9AM-3:30PM M,T,Th,F; 5-9PM W. www.westboylston.com
Separate indices to search include BK format. Records indexed to 1850. Only the office personnel may search. Search fee $10.00 per hour. Real estate records located at Worcester County. Copy fee $.50 per page. Cert fee- $2.00 per page. Payee- Town of West Boylston. **Other phones:** Treasurer- 508-835-6092; Elections- 508-835-6240; Vital Records- 508-835-6240. **Property tax/Assessor-** 508-835-6093.

West Bridgewater Town

Town Clerk, 65 N. Main St; Town Hall, West Bridgewater, MA 02379-1734. 508-894-1200; 508-894-1210; hours: 8AM-4PM; 1st & 3rd W 7PM-9PM. www.town.west-bridgewater.ma.us
No real estate recordings. Bridgewater, East Bridgewater and West Bridgewater are separate towns. Real estate records are at the county level with the Register of Deeds. Record index not computerized. Only the office personnel may search. Search fee $10.00 per search. Real estate records located at Plymouth County. Copy fee $.20 per page. Cert fee- $10.00 per cert includes copy fee. Payee- Town of West Bridgewater. **Other phones:** Treasurer- 508-894-1203; Elections- 508-894-1200; Vital Records- 508-894-1200. **Property tax/Assessor-** same address as above. 508-894-1212.

West Brookfield Town

Town Clerk, PO Box 766, West Brookfield, MA 01585. 508-867-1421; fax-508-867-1401; 9AM-N.
No real estate recordings. Only the public may search. Real estate records located at Worcester County. Copy fee $1.00 per page. Payee- Town of West Brookfield. **Online access to Property, Assessor records:** Access property data free at http://csc-ma.us/PropertyContent/jsp/Home.jsp?Page=1 **Other phones:** Treasurer- 508-867-1418; Elections- 508-867-1415; Vital Records- 508-867-1415. **Property tax/Assessor-** 508-867-1402.

West Newbury Town

Town Clerk, 381 Main St.; Town Office Bldg, West Newbury, MA 01985-1499. 978-363-1100 x110; fax-978-363-1117; hours: 8AM-4:30PM M-Th. www.town.west-newbury.ma.us
No real estate recordings. Record index not computerized. Office will perform a UCC search but public must search other records themselves. Search fee $10.00. Copy fee $1.00 per page. Cert fee- $10.00 per page plus copy fee. Payee- Town of West Newbury. **Other phones:** Treasurer- 978-363-1100 x114; Elections- 978-363-1100 x110; Vital Records- 978-363-1100 x110. **Property tax/Assessor-** same address as above. 978-363-1100 x119.

West Springfield Town

Town Clerk, 26 Central St; Town Hall, West Springfield, MA 01089-2779. 413-263-3012, R/E recording phone-413-263-3055, UCC recording phone-413-263-3012; fax-413-263-3046; hours: 8AM-4:30PM. www.west-springfield.ma.us
No real estate recordings. All records in one index. Office personnel or visitors may perform searches. Search fee $10.00 per record. Real estate records located at Hampden County. Copy fee $3.50 for 1st page; $.25 each add'l. Cert fee- $5.00 per record plus $3.00 1st page, $1.00 each add'l page. Payee- Town of West Springfield. **Online access to Assessor, Real Estate, Recording, Lien records:** Search the town assessor database at http://data.visionappraisal.com/WestSpringfieldMA/. Free registration for full data. Also, see Hampden County for recording records searching. **Other phones:** Treasurer- 413-263-3004; Elections- 413-263-3012; Vital Records- 413-263-3012. **Property tax/Assessor-** same address as above. 413-263-3055.

West Stockbridge Town

Town Clerk, PO Box 163, West Stockbridge, MA 01266. 413-232-0300, R/E recording phone-413-528-0146, UCC recording phone-413-232-0300; fax-413-232-0318; hours: 4PM-8PM M; 8AM-3PM T TH F. www.weststockbridgetown.com
No real estate recordings. All records in one index. Office personnel or visitors may perform searches. Will search UCC records, tax liens not included in UCC search. UCC search per debtor name- $10.00. Separate state tax lien search- $25.00 per debtor. Copy fee $1.00 per page. Cert fee- $5.00 per sheet plus copy fee. Payee- Town of West Stockbridge. **Other phones:** Treasurer- 413-232-0316; Elections- 413-232-0300; Vital Records- 413-232-0300. **Property tax/Assessor-** 9 Main St, PO Box 365, West Stockbridge, MA 01266; 413-232-0303.

West Tisbury Town

Town Clerk, Box 278, West Tisbury, MA 02575-0278. 508-696-0148; fax-508-696-0103; hours: 8:30AM-1:30PM. www.town.west-tisbury.ma.us/
No real estate recordings. Separate indices to search. Record index not computerized. Office will perform a UCC search but public must search other records themselves. Real estate records located at Dukes County. Copy fee $.20 per page. Cert fee- $2.00 per page includes copy fee. Payee- Town of West Tisbury. **Online access to Assessor records:** Access assessor data at http://data.visionappraisal.com/WestTisburyMA/. Free registration for full data. **Other phones:** Treasurer- 508-696-0108; Elections- 508-696-0148; Vital Records- 508-696-0148. **Property tax/Assessor-** same address as above. 508-693-0101.

Westborough Town

Town Clerk, 34 W. Main St; Town Hall, Westborough, MA 01581-1998. 508-366-3020; fax-508-366-3012; hours: 8AM-5PM M W TH; 8AM-8PM T; 7:30AM-N Fri.
No real estate recordings. Record index not computerized. Office personnel or visitors may perform searches. Search fee $10.00. Real estate records located at Worcester County. Copy fee $.20 per page. Payee- Town of Westborough. **Online access to Assessor, Property records:** Access property data free at http://westborough.patriotproperties.com/default.asp. **Other phones:** Treasurer- 508-366-3025; Elections- 508-366-3020; Vital Records- 508-366-3020. **Property tax/Assessor-** same address as above. 508-366-3010.

Westfield City

City Clerk, 59 Court St, Westfield, MA 01085-3574. 413-572-6235; fax-413-564-3114; hours: 9AM-5PM. www.cityofwestfield.org
No real estate recordings. Separate indices to search. Record index not computerized. Only the office personnel may search. Real estate records located at Hampden County. UCC search per debtor name- $10.00. Copy fee $1.00 per page. Cert fee- $5.00 per page plus copy fee. Payee- City of Westfield. **Online access to Real Estate, Recording, Lien, Assessor records:** Assessor records can be found online for Westfield City at http://data.visionappraisal.com/WestfieldMA/. Does not require a username & password. Simply click on link. Also see the Hampden County Register of Deeds for online recorded property data. **Other phones:** Treasurer- 413-572-6230; Elections- 413-572-6266; Vital Records- 413-572-6236. **Property tax/Assessor-** 413-572-6222.

Westford Town

Town Clerk, 55 Main St; Town Hall, Westford, MA 01886. 978-692-5515; fax-978-399-2555; hours: 8AM-4PM. www.westford-ma.gov
No real estate recordings. Separate indices to search. Record index not computerized. Only the office personnel may search. Search fee $5.00 per name. Real estate records located at Middlesex County. Copy fee $1.00 per page. Cert fee- $2.00 per page plus

copy fee. Payee- Town of Westford. **Other phones:** Treasurer- 978-692-5518; Elections- 978-692-5515; Vital Records- 978-692-5515; Tax Collector- 978-692-5506. **Property tax/Assessor-** same address as above. 978-692-5504.

Westhampton Town

Town Clerk, Town Hall, Westhampton, MA 01027. 413-527-0463; fax-413-527-8655; hours: 7PM-8:30PM M.
No real estate recordings. All records in one index. Record index not computerized. Only the office personnel may search. Real estate records located at Hampshire County. Will search UCC records, but not tax liens. UCC search per debtor name- $10.00. Copy fee $1.00 per page. Cert fee- $1.00 per page. Payee- Town of Westhampton. **Property tax/Assessor-** 1 South Rd, Westhampton, MA 01027; 413-527-0463.

Westminster Town

Town Clerk, PO Box 456, Westminster, MA 01473. 978-874-7406; fax-978-874-7411; hours: 8AM-1PM, 2-4:30PM M-Th; 8AM-1PM F. www.westminster-ma.org
No real estate recordings. All records in one index. Office personnel or visitors may perform searches. Real estate records located at Worcester County. Will search UCC records, tax liens included in UCC search. UCC search per debtor name- $10.00. Separate federal/state combined tax lien search- $10.00 per debtor. Copy fee $2.00 per page. Payee- Town of Westminster. **Other phones:** Treasurer- 978-874-7403; Elections- 978-874-7406; Vital Records- 978-874-7406. **Property tax/Assessor-** 3 Bacon St, Westminster, MA 01473; 978-874-7401.

Weston Town

Town Clerk, PO Box 378, Weston, MA 02493. 781-893-7320; fax-781-891-3697; hours: 8:30AM-5PM. www.weston.org
No real estate recordings. Only the public may search. Real estate records located at Registry of Deeds; Southern Middlesex District located in Cambridge. Copy fee $.20 per page. Cert fee- $1.00 per page. Payee- Town of Weston. **Other phones:** Treasurer- 781-893-7320 x316; Elections- 781-893-7320 x303; Vital Records- 781-893-7320 x303. **Property tax/Assessor-** 781-893-7320 x313.

Westport Town

Town Clerk, 816 Main Rd.; Town Hall, Westport, MA 02790. 508-636-1000, R/E recording phone-508-993-2605 (Registry of Deeds in New Bedford), UCC recording phone-508-636-1000; fax-508-636-1147; hours: 8:30AM-N, 12:30-4PM.
No real estate recordings. All records in one index. Record index not computerized. Only the public may search. Real estate records located at Bristol County. Copy fee $2.00 per page. Cert fee- $2.00 per page. Payee- Town of Westport. **Other phones:** Treasurer- 508-636-1007; Elections- 508-636-1001; Vital Records- 508-636-1000; Selectmen- 508-636-1003. **Property tax/Assessor-** same address as above. 508-636-1012.

Westwood Town

Town Clerk, 580 High St, Westwood, MA 02090. 781-326-3964; fax-781-329-8030; 8:30AM-4:30PM M,W,Th; 8:30AM-7PM T; 8:30AM-1PM F.
No real estate recordings. Office personnel or visitors may perform searches. Search fee $10.00 per name. State tax lien search-$25.00 per debtor. Real estate records located at Norfolk County. Payee- Town of Westwood. **Property/Assessor-** 781-326-6450.

Weymouth Town

Town Clerk, 75 Middle St; Town Hall, East Weymouth, MA 02189. 781-335-2000, R/E recording phone-781-340-2401, UCC recording phone-781-340-5017; fax-781-335-3283; hours: 8:30AM-4:30PM. www.weymouth.ma.us

No real estate recordings. Record index not computerized. Office personnel or visitors may perform searches. Search fee $10.00. Real estate records located at Norfolk County. Will search UCC records. Copy fee $.25 per page. Cert fee- $2.00. Payee- Town of Weymouth. **Online access to Property, Assessor records:** Property data is free at http://weymouth.appgeo.com/PropertySearch.asp.
Other phones: Treasurer- 781-335-2000; Elections- 781-340-5017; Vital Records- 781-340-5017. **Property tax/Assessor-** same address. 781-335-2000.

Whately Town

Town Clerk, PO Box 89, Whately, MA 01093-0089. 413-665-0054; fax-413-665-9560; Noon-7PM M; 9AM-1PM Th. www.whately.org/towngov.html
No real estate recordings. Index: Indices by document type. Office personnel or visitors may perform searches. UCC search per debtor name-$10.00 per hour. Copy fee $.20 per page. Cert fee-$3.00 per cert plus copy fee. Payee- Town of Whately. **Other phones:** Treasurer- 413-665-2595; Elections- 413-665-0054; Vital Records- 413-665-0054. **Property tax/Assessor-** PO Box 156, Whately, MA 01093-0156; 413-665-3470.

Whitman Town

Town Clerk, PO Box 426, Whitman, MA 02382. 781-618-9710; fax-781-618-9791; hours: 8AM-4PM M,W,Th-F; 8AM-7:30PM T.
No real estate recordings. Separate indices to search include vitals, minutes of mortgages, voters. Record index not computerized. Only the office personnel may search. Search fee- no fee if under 10 minutes to search, then $10.00. Real estate records located at Plymouth County. Copy fee $2.00 per page. Cert fee- $5.00 per document plus copy fee. Payee- Town of Whitman. **Other phones:** Treasurer- 781-618-9730; Elections- 781-618-9710; Vital Records- 781-618-9710; Tax Collector- 781-618-9720. **Property tax/Assessor-** same address as above. 781-618-9760.

Wilbraham Town

Town Clerk, 240 Springfield St, Wilbraham, MA 01095. 413-596-2809; fax-413-596-2830; hours: 8:30AM-4:30PM.
No real estate recordings. All records in one index. Record index not computerized. Office personnel or visitors may perform searches. Search fee $15.00. Real estate records located at Hampden County. Copy fee $1.00 for cover; $.25 each add'l page. Cert fee- $8.00 per page plus copy fee. Payee- Town of Wilbraham. **Online access to Real Estate, Recording, Lien records:** See Hampden County for recording records searching. **Other phones:** Treasurer- 413-596-2811; Elections- 413-596-2809; Vital Records- 413-596-2809; Collector- 413-596-2813. **Property tax/Assessor-** same address as above. 413-596-2818.

Williamsburg Town

Town Clerk, PO Box 447, Haydenville, MA 01039-0447. 413-268-8402; fax-413-268-8409; hours: 9:15-3PM M-Th; 5:30-7PM Tu; Summer- 9:15-3 M,W. www.burgy.org
No real estate recordings. Separate indices to search. Record index not computerized. Only the office personnel may search. Search fee $15.00 per name. Real estate records located at Hampshire County. Will search UCC records, but not tax liens. General copy fee $5.00 per page. Tax lien copy-$.20 per page. Cert fee- $3.00 per page includes copy fee. Payee- Town of Williamsburg. **Other phones:** Treasurer- 413-268-8415; Elections- 413-268-8402; Vital Records- 413-268-8402. **Property tax/Assessor-** 141 Main St, Haydenville, MA 01039; 413-268-8403.

Williamstown Town

Town Clerk, 31 North St, Williamstown, MA 01267. 413-458-9341, R/E recording phone-413-743-0035, UCC recording phone-413-458-9341; fax-413-458-4839; 8:30AM-5PM. www.williamstown.net
No real estate recordings. All records in one index. Office personnel or visitors may perform searches. Real estate records located at Berkshire County. UCC search per debtor name- $5.00. Tax lien search fee- $25.00 per search. Copy fee $1.00 per page. Cert fee- $10.00. Payee- Town of Williamstown. **Other phones:** Treasurer- 413-458-9342; Elections- 413-458-9341; Vital Records- 413-458-9341. **Property tax/Assessor-** same address. 413-458-9342.

Wilmington Town

Town Clerk, 121 Glen Rd; Town Hall, Wilmington, MA 01887. 978-658-2030, R/E recording phone-978-658-3531, UCC recording phone-978-658-2030; fax-978-658-3334; hours: 8:30AM-4:30PM. www.town.wilmington.ma.us
No real estate recordings. All records in one index. Search fee $10.00. Real estate records located at Middlesex County. Copy fee $1.00 per page. Cert fee- $1.00 per page. Payee- Town of Wilmington. **Other phones:** Treasurer- 978-658-3531; Elections- 978-658-2030; Vital Records- 978-658-2030. **Property tax/Assessor-** same address. 978-658-3675.

Winchendon Town

Town Clerk, 109 Front St, Winchendon, MA 01475. 978-297-2766; fax-978-297-1616; hours: 8:30AM-6PM M; 8:30AM-4:30PM T-Th; 8:30AM-N Fri.
No real estate recordings. Office personnel or visitors may perform searches. Search fee $10.00 per name. Real estate records located at Worcester County. Copy fee $2.00, if tax lien $.20 per page. Payee- Town of Winchendon. **Other phones:** Treasurer- 978-297-0152; Elections- 978-297-2766; Vital Records- 978-297-2766. **Property tax/Assessor-** 978-297-0155.

Winchester Town

Town Clerk, 71 Mount Vernon St; Town Hall, Winchester, MA 01890. 781-721-7130; fax-781-721-1153; hours: 8AM-4PM.
No real estate recordings. Records indexed on computer back to 1990. Only the office personnel may search. Search fee $10.00. Real estate records located at Middlesex County. Copy fee $.20 per page. Cert fee- $3.00 per doc plus copy fee. Payee- Town of Winchester. **Online access to Assessor, Property records:** Access property data free at http://winchester.patriotproperties.com/default.asp.
Other phones: Treasurer- 781-721-7123; Elections- 781-721-7130; Vital Records- 781-721-7130. **Property tax/Assessor-** same address as above. 781-721-7111.

Windsor Town

Town Clerk, PO Box 277, Windsor, MA 01270. 413-684-3977; fax-413-684-1585; hours: 5-7PM Monday or by appointment.
No real estate recordings. All records in one index. Record index not computerized. Office will perform a UCC search but public must search other records themselves. Search fee $10.00. Real estate records located at Berkshire County. Copy fee $1.00 per page. Cert fee- $1.00 per page plus copy fee. Payee- Town of Windsor-Clerk. **Other phones:** Treasurer- 413-684-3811; Elections- 413-684-3977; Vital Records- 413-684-3977. **Property tax/Assessor-** 413-684-3811.

Winthrop Town

Town Clerk, Town Hall, Winthrop, MA 02152-3156. 617-846-1742; fax-617-539-5814; hours: 8AM-7PM M; 8AM-4PM T-Th; 8AM-N Fri.
No real estate recordings. Office personnel or visitors may perform searches. General search fee $10.00 per name. Real estate records located at Suffolk County. Federal/state combined tax lien search-

$25.00 per debtor. Copy fee $1.00 per page. Payee- Town of Winthrop. **Other phones:** Treasurer- 617-846-3226; Elections- 617-846-1742; Vital Records- 617-846-1742; Municipal Tax Liens- 617-846-1750. **Property tax/Assessor-** 617-846-2716.

Woburn City

City Clerk, 10 Common St, Woburn, MA 01801-4197. 781-932-4450; fax-781-932-4455; hours: 9AM-4:30PM M-W; 9AM-7PM Th; 9AM-1PM Fri. www.cityofwoburn.com
No real estate recordings or UCC recordings. Record index not computerized. Only the office personnel may search. Real estate records located at Middlesex County. Copy fee $.20 per page. Cert fee- $3.00 for vital records, $2.00 for Old UCC records plus $1.00 per page plus copy fee. Payee- City of Woburn. **Online access to Assessor records:** Search the city assessor data at http://data.visionappraisal.com/WoburnMA/. Free registration for full data. **Other phones:** Treasurer- 781-932-4470; Elections- 781-932-4450; Vital Records- 781-932-4450. **Property tax/Assessor-** same address as above. 781-932-4430, assessor fax- 781-932-4489.

Worcester City

City Clerk, 455 Main St; City Hall, Rm 206, Worcester, MA 01608. 508-799-1126; fax-508-799-1194; hours: 8:45AM-4:15PM T,W,Th,F; 8:45AM-5PM M.
No real estate recordings. Office personnel or visitors may perform searches. Search fee $10.00 per name. Real estate records located at Worcester County. Copy fee $.50 per page. Cert fee- $4.00 for 1st 3 pages; $2.00 each add'l page. **Online access to Real Estate, Lien, Assessor records:** Data is online in 2 ways. Online access to the City Assessor Valuation Search database is free at www.ci.worcester.ma.us/aso/value_search.htm. And, access to the "Landtrack System" for Worcester District records requires a $50 annual fee plus $.25 per minute of use. Index records date back to 1966. Images are viewable from 1974 onward. Lending agency info is available. Fax back service: $.50 per page. For information, contact Joe Ursoleo at 508-798-7713 X233. **Other phones:** Treasurer- 508-799-1077. **Property tax/Assessor-** 508-799-1112.

Worcester County Northern District

County Register of Deeds, 166 Boulder Dr #202, Fitchburg, MA 01420. 978-342-2132; fax-978-345-2865; hours: 8:30AM-4:30PM; Recording Hours 8:30AM-4PM. www.fitchburgdeeds.com
Will not search real estate records. Will not search UCC records or tax liens. Copy fee $1.00 per page. Cert fee- $1.00 per page. Payee- Worcester North Register of Deeds. **Online access to Real Estate, Lien, Recording, Land Court, Assessor records:** Access to Registry of Deeds is now free at http://151.203.96.11/alis/ww400r.pgm. Small fee to copy or certify documents. Land index back to 1982; images to 1983. Also, county recorded land images from 1731 to 1974 are free at www.worcesterdeeds.com/worcester/dsbppagelist.asp; book and page number required. **Other phones:** ; http://151.203.96.11/alis/ww400r.pgm-. **Property tax/Assessor-** 508-799-1098.

Worcester County Worcester District

County Register of Deeds, 2 Main St; Courthouse, Worcester, MA 01608. 508-798-7717; fax-508-753-1338; hours: 8:15AM-4:30PM (recording: 9AM-N, 1-4PM). www.worcesterdeeds.com
Only the public may search. Copy fee $1.00 per page. Cert fee- $1.00 per cert plus copy fee. Payee- Worcester County Register of Deeds. **Online access to Real Estate, Deed, Lien, Grantor/Grantee, Judgment, Will, Property Tax records:** Access to the Register of Deeds database is free at www.masslandrecords.com. Click on South Worcester on map. Also, county recorded land images from 1731 to 1974 are free at www.worcesterdeeds.com/worcester/dsbppagelist.asp. **Other phones:** Treasurer- 508-798-2441. **Property tax/Assessor-** 508-799-1000.

Worthington Town

Town Clerk, Town Hall, Worthington, MA 01098-0247. 413-238-5578; fax-413-238-5579; hours: 10AM-Noon Sat.
No real estate recordings. Office will perform a UCC search but public must search other records themselves. Real estate records located at Hampshire County. UCC search per debtor name- $10.00. Copy fee $1.00 per page. Cert fee- $5.00 per page. Payee- Town of Worthington. **Other phones:** Treasurer- 413-238-5577. **Property tax/Assessor-** 413-238-5578.

Wrentham Town

Town Clerk, 79 South St, Wrentham, MA 02093. 508-384-5415; fax-508-384-5434; hours: 8AM-4PM M-Th; 8AM-1:30PM F. http://wrentham.ma.us
No real estate recordings. All records in one index. Search fee $10.00. Real estate records located at Norfolk County. Copy fee $2.00 per page. Cert fee- $3.00 per page. Payee- Town of Wrentham. **Other phones:** Treasurer- 508-384-5413; Elections- 508-384-5415; Vital Records- 508-384-5415. **Property tax/Assessor-** 508-384-5408.

Yarmouth Town

Town Clerk, 1146 Route 28; Town Hall, South Yarmouth, MA 02664. 508-398-2231, R/E recording phone-508-362-7733 x106, UCC recording phone-508-398-2231 x216; fax-508-760-4842; hours: 8:30AM-4:30PM. http://yarmouth.ma.us
No real estate recordings. Record index not computerized. Office will perform a UCC search but public must search other records themselves. Search fee $10.00. Real estate records located at Barnstable County. Copy fee $.20 per page. Cert fee- $1.00 per page plus copy fee. Payee- Town of Yarmouth. **Online access to Assessor records:** Records on the Assessor's database are free at http://data.visionappraisal.com/yarmouthma. Free registration for full data. Non-registered users can access a limited set of data. **Other phones:** Treasurer- 508-398-2231 x219; Elections- 508-398-2231 x216; Vital Records- 508-398-2231 x216. **Property tax/Assessor-** same address as above. 508-398-2231 x221.

Massachusetts County Locator

You will usually be able to find the city name in the City/County Cross Reference below. In that case, it is a simple matter to determine the county from the cross reference. However, only the official US Postal Service city names are included in this index. There are an additional 40,000 place names that people use in their addresses. Therefore, we have also included a ZIP/City Cross Reference immediately following the City/County Cross Reference.

If you know the ZIP Code but the city name does not appear in the City/County Cross Reference index, look up the ZIP Code in the ZIP/City Cross Reference, find the city name, then look up the city name in the City/County Cross Reference. For example, you want to know the county for an address of Menands, NY 12204. There is no "Menands" in the City/County Cross Reference. The ZIP/City Cross Reference shows that ZIP Codes 12201-12288 are for the city of Albany. Looking back in the City/County Cross Reference, Albany is in Albany County.

Massachusetts City/County Cross Reference

ABINGTON Plymouth
ACCORD Plymouth
ACTON Middlesex
ACUSHNET Bristol
ADAMS Berkshire
AGAWAM Hampden
ALLSTON Suffolk
AMESBURY Essex
AMHERST Hampshire
ANDOVER Essex
ARLINGTON Middlesex
ARLINGTON HEIGHTS Middlesex
ASHBURNHAM Worcester
ASHBY Middlesex
ASHFIELD Franklin
ASHLAND Middlesex
ASHLEY FALLS Berkshire
ASSONET Bristol
ATHOL Worcester
ATTLEBORO Bristol
ATTLEBORO FALLS Bristol
AUBURN Worcester
AUBURNDALE Middlesex
AVON Norfolk
AYER Middlesex
BABSON PARK Norfolk
BALDWINVILLE Worcester
BAR CODE MCCORMACK Suffolk
BARNSTABLE Barnstable
BARRE Worcester
BECKET Berkshire
BEDFORD Middlesex
BELCHERTOWN Hampshire
BELLINGHAM Norfolk
BELMONT Middlesex
BERKLEY Bristol
BERKSHIRE Berkshire
BERLIN Worcester
BERNARDSTON Franklin
BEVERLY Essex
BILLERICA Middlesex
BLACKSTONE Worcester
BLANDFORD Hampden
BOLTON Worcester
BONDSVILLE Hampden
BOSTON Middlesex
BOSTON Suffolk
BOXBOROUGH Middlesex
BOXFORD Essex
BOYLSTON Worcester
BRAINTREE Norfolk
BRANT ROCK Plymouth
BREWSTER Barnstable
BRIDGEWATER Plymouth
BRIGHTON Suffolk
BRIMFIELD Hampden
BROCKTON Plymouth
BROOKFIELD Worcester
BROOKLINE Norfolk
BROOKLINE VILLAGE Norfolk
BRYANTVILLE Plymouth
BUCKLAND Franklin
BURLINGTON Middlesex

BUZZARDS BAY (02532) Barnstable(74), Plymouth(25)
BUZZARDS BAY Barnstable
BYFIELD Essex
CAMBRIDGE Middlesex
CANTON Norfolk
CARLISLE Middlesex
CARVER Plymouth
CATAUMET Barnstable
CENTERVILLE Barnstable
CHARLEMONT Franklin
CHARLESTOWN Suffolk
CHARLTON Worcester
CHARLTON CITY Worcester
CHARLTON DEPOT Worcester
CHARTLEY Bristol
CHATHAM Barnstable
CHELMSFORD Middlesex
CHELSEA Suffolk
CHERRY VALLEY Worcester
CHESHIRE Berkshire
CHESTER (01011) Hampden(89), Hampshire(5), Berkshire(5)
CHESTERFIELD Hampshire
CHESTNUT HILL Middlesex
CHICOPEE Hampden
CHILMARK Dukes
CLINTON Worcester
COHASSET Norfolk
COLRAIN Franklin
CONCORD Middlesex
CONWAY Franklin
COTUIT Barnstable
CUMMAQUID Barnstable
CUMMINGTON Hampshire
CUTTYHUNK Dukes
DALTON Berkshire
DANVERS Essex
DARTMOUTH Bristol
DEDHAM Norfolk
DEERFIELD Franklin
DENNIS Barnstable
DENNIS PORT Barnstable
DEVENS (01434) Worcester(54), Middlesex(45)
DIGHTON Bristol
DOUGLAS Worcester
DOVER Norfolk
DRACUT Middlesex
DRURY Berkshire
DUDLEY Worcester
DUNSTABLE Middlesex
DUXBURY Plymouth
EAST BOSTON Suffolk
EAST BRIDGEWATER Plymouth
EAST BROOKFIELD Worcester
EAST DENNIS Barnstable
EAST FALMOUTH Barnstable
EAST FREETOWN Bristol
EAST LONGMEADOW Hampden
EAST MANSFIELD Bristol
EAST ORLEANS Barnstable
EAST OTIS Berkshire

EAST PRINCETON Worcester
EAST SANDWICH Barnstable
EAST TAUNTON Bristol
EAST TEMPLETON Worcester
EAST WALPOLE Norfolk
EAST WAREHAM Plymouth
EASTHAM Barnstable
EASTHAMPTON Hampshire
EASTON Bristol
EDGARTOWN Dukes
ELMWOOD Plymouth
ERVING Franklin
ESSEX Essex
EVERETT Middlesex
FAIRHAVEN Bristol
FALL RIVER Bristol
FALMOUTH Barnstable
FAYVILLE Worcester
FEEDING HILLS Hampden
FISKDALE Worcester
FITCHBURG Worcester
FLORENCE Hampshire
FORESTDALE Barnstable
FORT DEVENS (01433) Worcester(53), Middlesex(46)
FOXBORO Norfolk
FRAMINGHAM Middlesex
FRANKLIN Norfolk
GARDNER Worcester
GEORGETOWN Essex
GILBERTVILLE Worcester
GLENDALE Berkshire
GLOUCESTER Essex
GOSHEN Hampshire
GRAFTON Worcester
GRANBY Hampshire
GRANVILLE Hampden
GREAT BARRINGTON Berkshire
GREEN HARBOR Plymouth
GREENBUSH Plymouth
GREENFIELD Franklin
GROTON Middlesex
GROVELAND Essex
HADLEY Hampshire
HALIFAX Plymouth
HAMILTON Essex
HAMPDEN Hampden
HANOVER (02339) Plymouth(98), Norfolk(1)
HANOVER Plymouth
HANSCOM AFB Middlesex
HANSON Plymouth
HARDWICK Worcester
HARVARD Worcester
HARWICH Barnstable
HARWICH PORT Barnstable
HATFIELD Hampshire
HATHORNE Essex
HAVERHILL Essex
HAYDENVILLE Hampshire
HEATH Franklin
HINGHAM Plymouth
HINSDALE Berkshire

HOLBROOK Norfolk
HOLDEN Worcester
HOLLAND Hampden
HOLLISTON Middlesex
HOLYOKE Hampden
HOPEDALE Worcester
HOPKINTON Middlesex
HOUSATONIC Berkshire
HUBBARDSTON Worcester
HUDSON Middlesex
HULL Plymouth
HUMAROCK Plymouth
HUNTINGTON (01050) Hampshire(98), Hampden(1)
HYANNIS Barnstable
HYANNIS PORT Barnstable
HYDE PARK Suffolk
INDIAN ORCHARD Hampden
IPSWICH Essex
JAMAICA PLAIN Suffolk
JEFFERSON Worcester
KINGSTON Plymouth
LAKE PLEASANT Franklin
LAKEVILLE Plymouth
LANCASTER Worcester
LANESBORO Berkshire
LAWRENCE Essex
LEE Berkshire
LEEDS Hampshire
LEICESTER Worcester
LENOX Berkshire
LENOX DALE Berkshire
LEOMINSTER Worcester
LEVERETT (01054) Franklin(77), Hampshire(22)
LEXINGTON Middlesex
LINCOLN Middlesex
LINWOOD Worcester
LITTLETON Middlesex
LONGMEADOW Hampden
LOWELL Middlesex
LUDLOW Hampden
LUNENBURG Worcester
LYNN Essex
LYNNFIELD Essex
MALDEN Middlesex
MANCHAUG Worcester
MANCHESTER Essex
MANOMET Plymouth
MANSFIELD Bristol
MARBLEHEAD Essex
MARION Plymouth
MARLBOROUGH Middlesex
MARSHFIELD Plymouth
MARSHFIELD HILLS Plymouth
MARSTONS MILLS Barnstable
MASHPEE Barnstable
MATTAPAN Suffolk
MATTAPOISETT Plymouth
MAYNARD Middlesex
MEDFIELD Norfolk
MEDFORD Middlesex
MEDWAY Norfolk

MELROSE Middlesex
MENDON Worcester
MENEMSHA Dukes
MERRIMAC Essex
METHUEN Essex
MIDDLEBORO Plymouth
MIDDLEFIELD Hampshire
MIDDLETON Essex
MILFORD Worcester
MILL RIVER Berkshire
MILLBURY Worcester
MILLIS Norfolk
MILLVILLE Worcester
MILTON Norfolk
MILTON VILLAGE Norfolk
MINOT Plymouth
MONPONSETT Plymouth
MONROE BRIDGE Franklin
MONSON Hampden
MONTAGUE Franklin
MONTEREY Berkshire
MONUMENT BEACH Barnstable
NAHANT Essex
NANTUCKET Nantucket
NATICK Middlesex
NEEDHAM Norfolk
NEW BEDFORD Bristol
NEW BRAINTREE Worcester
NEW SALEM Franklin
NEW TOWN Middlesex
NEWBURY Essex
NEWBURYPORT Essex
NEWTON Middlesex
NEWTON CENTER Middlesex
NEWTON HIGHLANDS Middlesex
NEWTON LOWER FALLS Middlesex
NEWTON UPPER FALLS Middlesex
NEWTONVILLE Middlesex
NONANTUM Middlesex
NORFOLK Norfolk
NORTH ADAMS Berkshire
NORTH AMHERST Hampshire
NORTH ANDOVER Essex
NORTH ATTLEBORO Bristol
NORTH BILLERICA Middlesex
NORTH BROOKFIELD Worcester
NORTH CARVER Plymouth
NORTH CHATHAM Barnstable
NORTH CHELMSFORD Middlesex
NORTH DARTMOUTH Bristol
NORTH DIGHTON Bristol
NORTH EASTHAM Barnstable
NORTH EASTON Bristol
NORTH EGREMONT Berkshire
NORTH FALMOUTH Barnstable
NORTH GRAFTON Worcester
NORTH HATFIELD Hampshire
NORTH MARSHFIELD Plymouth
NORTH OXFORD Worcester
NORTH PEMBROKE Plymouth
NORTH READING Middlesex
NORTH SCITUATE Plymouth
NORTH TRURO Barnstable
NORTH UXBRIDGE Worcester
NORTH WALTHAM Middlesex
NORTHAMPTON Hampshire
NORTHBOROUGH Worcester
NORTHBRIDGE Worcester
NORTHFIELD Franklin

NORTON Bristol
NORWELL Plymouth
NORWOOD Norfolk
NUTTING LAKE Middlesex
OAK BLUFFS Dukes
OAKDALE Worcester
OAKHAM Worcester
OCEAN BLUFF Plymouth
ONSET Plymouth
ORANGE Franklin
ORLEANS Barnstable
OSTERVILLE Barnstable
OTIS Berkshire
OXFORD Worcester
PALMER Hampden
PAXTON Worcester
PEABODY Essex
PEMBROKE Plymouth
PEPPERELL Middlesex
PETERSHAM (01366) Franklin(51),
    Worcester(48)
PINEHURST Middlesex
PITTSFIELD Berkshire
PLAINFIELD Hampshire
PLAINVILLE (02762) Norfolk(98), Bristol(1)
PLYMOUTH Plymouth
PLYMPTON Plymouth
POCASSET Barnstable
PRIDES CROSSING Essex
PRINCETON Worcester
PROVINCETOWN Barnstable
QUINCY Norfolk
RANDOLPH Norfolk
RAYNHAM Bristol
RAYNHAM CENTER Bristol
READING Middlesex
READVILLE Suffolk
REHOBOTH Bristol
REVERE Suffolk
RICHMOND Berkshire
ROCHDALE Worcester
ROCHESTER Plymouth
ROCKLAND Plymouth
ROCKPORT Essex
ROSLINDALE Suffolk
ROWE Franklin
ROWLEY Essex
ROYALSTON Worcester
RUSSELL Hampden
RUTLAND Worcester
SAGAMORE Barnstable
SAGAMORE BEACH (02562)
    Barnstable(98), Plymouth(1)
SALEM Essex
SALISBURY Essex
SANDISFIELD Berkshire
SANDWICH Barnstable
SAUGUS Essex
SAVOY Berkshire
SCITUATE Plymouth
SEARS ROEBUCK Suffolk
SEEKONK Bristol
SHARON Norfolk
SHATTUCKVILLE Franklin
SHEFFIELD Berkshire
SHELBURNE FALLS Franklin
SHELDONVILLE Norfolk
SHERBORN Middlesex
SHIRLEY Middlesex

SHREWSBURY Worcester
SHUTESBURY Franklin
SIASCONSET Nantucket
SILVER BEACH Barnstable
SOMERSET Bristol
SOMERVILLE Middlesex
SOUTH BARRE Worcester
SOUTH CARVER Plymouth
SOUTH CHATHAM Barnstable
SOUTH DARTMOUTH Bristol
SOUTH DEERFIELD Franklin
SOUTH DENNIS Barnstable
SOUTH EASTON Bristol
SOUTH EGREMONT Berkshire
SOUTH GRAFTON Worcester
SOUTH HADLEY Hampshire
SOUTH HAMILTON Essex
SOUTH HARWICH Barnstable
SOUTH LANCASTER Worcester
SOUTH LEE Berkshire
SOUTH ORLEANS Barnstable
SOUTH WALPOLE Norfolk
SOUTH WELLFLEET Barnstable
SOUTH YARMOUTH Barnstable
SOUTHAMPTON Hampshire
SOUTHBOROUGH Worcester
SOUTHBRIDGE Worcester
SOUTHFIELD Berkshire
SOUTHWICK Hampden
SPENCER Worcester
SPRINGFIELD Hampden
STERLING Worcester
STILL RIVER Worcester
STOCKBRIDGE Berkshire
STONEHAM Middlesex
STOUGHTON Norfolk
STOW Middlesex
STURBRIDGE Worcester
SUDBURY Middlesex
SUNDERLAND Franklin
SUTTON Worcester
SWAMPSCOTT Essex
SWANSEA Bristol
TAUNTON Bristol
TEMPLETON Worcester
TEWKSBURY Middlesex
THORNDIKE Hampden
THREE RIVERS Hampden
TOPSFIELD Essex
TOWNSEND Middlesex
TRURO Barnstable
TURNERS FALLS Franklin
TYNGSBORO Middlesex
TYRINGHAM Berkshire
UPTON Worcester
UXBRIDGE Worcester
VILLAGE OF NAGOG WOODS Middlesex
VINEYARD HAVEN Dukes
WABAN Middlesex
WAKEFIELD Middlesex
WALES Hampden
WALPOLE Norfolk
WALTHAM Middlesex
WARE Hampshire
WAREHAM Plymouth
WARREN Worcester
WARWICK Franklin
WATERTOWN Middlesex
WAVERLEY Middlesex

WAYLAND Middlesex
WEBSTER Worcester
WELLESLEY Norfolk
WELLESLEY HILLS Norfolk
WELLFLEET Barnstable
WENDELL Franklin
WENDELL DEPOT Franklin
WENHAM Essex
WEST BARNSTABLE Barnstable
WEST BOXFORD Essex
WEST BOYLSTON Worcester
WEST BRIDGEWATER Plymouth
WEST BROOKFIELD Worcester
WEST CHATHAM Barnstable
WEST CHESTERFIELD Hampshire
WEST DENNIS Barnstable
WEST FALMOUTH Barnstable
WEST GROTON Middlesex
WEST HARWICH Barnstable
WEST HATFIELD (01088) Worcester(98),
    Hampshire(1)
WEST HYANNISPORT Barnstable
WEST MEDFORD Middlesex
WEST MILLBURY Worcester
WEST NEWBURY Essex
WEST NEWTON Middlesex
WEST ROXBURY Suffolk
WEST SPRINGFIELD Hampden
WEST STOCKBRIDGE Berkshire
WEST TISBURY Dukes
WEST TOWNSEND Middlesex
WEST WAREHAM Plymouth
WEST WARREN Worcester
WEST YARMOUTH Barnstable
WESTBOROUGH Worcester
WESTFIELD Hampden
WESTFORD Middlesex
WESTMINSTER Worcester
WESTON Middlesex
WESTPORT Bristol
WESTPORT POINT Bristol
WESTWOOD Norfolk
WEYMOUTH Norfolk
WHATELY Franklin
WHEELWRIGHT Worcester
WHITE HORSE BEACH Plymouth
WHITINSVILLE Worcester
WHITMAN Plymouth
WILBRAHAM Hampden
WILLIAMSBURG Hampshire
WILLIAMSTOWN Berkshire
WILMINGTON Middlesex
WINCHENDON Worcester
WINCHENDON SPRINGS Worcester
WINCHESTER Middlesex
WINDSOR (01270) Franklin(95),
    Berkshire(4)
WINTHROP Suffolk
WOBURN Middlesex
WOODS HOLE Barnstable
WOODVILLE Middlesex
WORCESTER Worcester
WORONOCO Hampden
WORTHINGTON Hampshire
WRENTHAM Norfolk
YARMOUTH PORT Barnstable

Massachusetts ZIP/City Cross Reference

01001-01001	AGAWAM
01002-01004	AMHERST
01005-01005	BARRE
01007-01007	BELCHERTOWN
01008-01008	BLANDFORD
01009-01009	BONDSVILLE
01010-01010	BRIMFIELD
01011-01011	CHESTER
01012-01012	CHESTERFIELD
01013-01022	CHICOPEE
01026-01026	CUMMINGTON
01027-01027	EASTHAMPTON
01028-01028	EAST LONGMEADOW
01029-01029	EAST OTIS
01030-01030	FEEDING HILLS
01031-01031	GILBERTVILLE
01032-01032	GOSHEN
01033-01033	GRANBY
01034-01034	GRANVILLE
01035-01035	HADLEY
01036-01036	HAMPDEN
01037-01037	HARDWICK
01038-01038	HATFIELD
01039-01039	HAYDENVILLE
01040-01041	HOLYOKE
01050-01050	HUNTINGTON
01053-01053	LEEDS
01054-01054	LEVERETT
01056-01056	LUDLOW
01057-01057	MONSON
01059-01059	NORTH AMHERST
01060-01061	NORTHAMPTON
01062-01062	FLORENCE
01063-01063	NORTHAMPTON
01066-01066	NORTH HATFIELD
01068-01068	OAKHAM
01069-01069	PALMER
01070-01070	PLAINFIELD
01071-01071	RUSSELL
01072-01072	SHUTESBURY
01073-01073	SOUTHAMPTON
01074-01074	SOUTH BARRE
01075-01075	SOUTH HADLEY
01077-01077	SOUTHWICK
01079-01079	THORNDIKE
01080-01080	THREE RIVERS
01081-01081	WALES
01082-01082	WARE
01083-01083	WARREN
01084-01084	WEST CHESTERFIELD
01085-01086	WESTFIELD
01088-01088	WEST HATFIELD
01089-01090	WEST SPRINGFIELD
01092-01092	WEST WARREN
01093-01093	WHATELY
01094-01094	WHEELWRIGHT
01095-01095	WILBRAHAM
01096-01096	WILLIAMSBURG
01097-01097	WORONOCO
01098-01098	WORTHINGTON
01101-01105	SPRINGFIELD
01106-01106	LONGMEADOW
01107-01115	SPRINGFIELD
01116-01116	LONGMEADOW
01118-01144	SPRINGFIELD
01151-01151	INDIAN ORCHARD
01152-01199	SPRINGFIELD
01201-01203	PITTSFIELD
01220-01220	ADAMS
01222-01222	ASHLEY FALLS
01223-01223	BECKET
01224-01224	BERKSHIRE
01225-01225	CHESHIRE
01226-01227	DALTON
01229-01229	GLENDALE
01230-01230	GREAT BARRINGTON
01235-01235	HINSDALE
01236-01236	HOUSATONIC
01237-01237	LANESBORO
01238-01238	LEE
01240-01240	LENOX
01242-01242	LENOX DALE
01243-01243	MIDDLEFIELD
01244-01244	MILL RIVER
01245-01245	MONTEREY
01247-01247	NORTH ADAMS
01252-01252	NORTH EGREMONT
01253-01253	OTIS
01254-01254	RICHMOND
01255-01255	SANDISFIELD
01256-01256	SAVOY
01257-01257	SHEFFIELD
01258-01258	SOUTH EGREMONT
01259-01259	SOUTHFIELD
01260-01260	SOUTH LEE
01262-01263	STOCKBRIDGE
01264-01264	TYRINGHAM
01266-01266	WEST STOCKBRIDGE
01267-01267	WILLIAMSTOWN
01270-01270	WINDSOR
01301-01302	GREENFIELD
01330-01330	ASHFIELD
01331-01331	ATHOL
01337-01337	BERNARDSTON
01338-01338	BUCKLAND
01339-01339	CHARLEMONT
01340-01340	COLRAIN
01341-01341	CONWAY
01342-01342	DEERFIELD
01343-01343	DRURY
01344-01344	ERVING
01346-01346	HEATH
01347-01347	LAKE PLEASANT
01349-01349	TURNERS FALLS
01350-01350	MONROE BRIDGE
01351-01351	MONTAGUE
01354-01354	NORTHFIELD
01355-01355	NEW SALEM
01360-01360	NORTHFIELD
01364-01364	ORANGE
01366-01366	PETERSHAM
01367-01367	ROWE
01368-01368	ROYALSTON
01369-01369	SHATTUCKVILLE
01370-01370	SHELBURNE FALLS
01373-01373	SOUTH DEERFIELD
01375-01375	SUNDERLAND
01376-01376	TURNERS FALLS
01378-01378	WARWICK
01379-01379	WENDELL
01380-01380	WENDELL DEPOT
01420-01420	FITCHBURG
01430-01430	ASHBURNHAM
01431-01431	ASHBY
01432-01432	AYER
01433-01433	FORT DEVENS
01434-01434	DEVENS
01436-01436	BALDWINVILLE
01438-01438	EAST TEMPLETON
01440-01441	GARDNER
01441-01441	WESTMINSTER
01450-01450	GROTON
01451-01451	HARVARD
01452-01452	HUBBARDSTON
01453-01453	LEOMINSTER
01460-01460	LITTLETON
01462-01462	LUNENBURG
01463-01463	PEPPERELL
01464-01464	SHIRLEY
01466-01466	ASHBURNHAM
01467-01467	STILL RIVER
01468-01468	TEMPLETON
01469-01469	TOWNSEND
01470-01471	GROTON
01472-01472	WEST GROTON
01473-01473	WESTMINSTER
01474-01474	WEST TOWNSEND
01475-01475	WINCHENDON
01477-01477	WINCHENDON SPRINGS
01501-01501	AUBURN
01503-01503	BERLIN
01504-01504	BLACKSTONE
01505-01505	BOYLSTON
01506-01506	BROOKFIELD
01507-01507	CHARLTON
01508-01508	CHARLTON CITY
01509-01509	CHARLTON DEPOT
01510-01510	CLINTON
01515-01515	EAST BROOKFIELD
01516-01516	DOUGLAS
01517-01517	EAST PRINCETON
01518-01518	FISKDALE
01519-01519	GRAFTON
01520-01520	HOLDEN
01521-01521	HOLLAND
01522-01522	JEFFERSON
01523-01523	LANCASTER
01524-01524	LEICESTER
01525-01525	LINWOOD
01526-01526	MANCHAUG
01527-01527	MILLBURY
01529-01529	MILLVILLE
01531-01531	NEW BRAINTREE
01532-01532	NORTHBOROUGH
01534-01534	NORTHBRIDGE
01535-01535	NORTH BROOKFIELD
01536-01536	NORTH GRAFTON
01537-01537	NORTH OXFORD
01538-01538	NORTH UXBRIDGE
01539-01539	OAKDALE
01540-01540	OXFORD
01541-01541	PRINCETON
01542-01542	ROCHDALE
01543-01543	RUTLAND
01545-01546	SHREWSBURY
01549-01549	BERLIN
01550-01550	SOUTHBRIDGE
01560-01560	SOUTH GRAFTON
01561-01561	SOUTH LANCASTER
01562-01562	SPENCER
01564-01564	STERLING
01566-01566	STURBRIDGE
01568-01568	UPTON
01569-01569	UXBRIDGE
01570-01570	WEBSTER
01571-01571	DUDLEY
01580-01582	WESTBOROUGH
01583-01583	WEST BOYLSTON
01585-01585	WEST BROOKFIELD
01586-01586	WEST MILLBURY
01587-01587	UPTON
01588-01588	WHITINSVILLE
01590-01590	SUTTON
01600-01610	WORCESTER
01611-01611	CHERRY VALLEY
01612-01612	PAXTON
01613-01655	WORCESTER
01701-01705	FRAMINGHAM
01718-01718	VILLAGE OF NAGOG WOODS
01719-01719	BOXBOROUGH
01720-01720	ACTON
01721-01721	ASHLAND
01730-01730	BEDFORD
01731-01731	HANSCOM AFB
01740-01740	BOLTON
01741-01741	CARLISLE
01742-01742	CONCORD
01745-01745	FAYVILLE
01746-01746	HOLLISTON
01747-01747	HOPEDALE
01748-01748	HOPKINTON
01749-01749	HUDSON
01752-01752	MARLBOROUGH
01754-01754	MAYNARD
01756-01756	MENDON
01757-01757	MILFORD
01760-01760	NATICK
01770-01770	SHERBORN
01772-01772	SOUTHBOROUGH
01773-01773	LINCOLN
01775-01775	STOW
01776-01776	SUDBURY
01778-01778	WAYLAND
01784-01784	WOODVILLE
01801-01801	WOBURN
01803-01805	BURLINGTON
01806-01808	WOBURN
01810-01812	ANDOVER
01813-01815	WOBURN
01821-01822	BILLERICA
01824-01824	CHELMSFORD
01826-01826	DRACUT
01827-01827	DUNSTABLE
01830-01832	HAVERHILL
01833-01833	GEORGETOWN
01834-01834	GROVELAND
01835-01835	HAVERHILL
01840-01843	LAWRENCE
01844-01844	METHUEN
01845-01845	NORTH ANDOVER
01850-01854	LOWELL
01860-01860	MERRIMAC
01862-01862	NORTH BILLERICA
01863-01863	NORTH CHELMSFORD
01864-01864	NORTH READING
01865-01865	NUTTING LAKE
01866-01866	PINEHURST
01867-01867	READING
01876-01876	TEWKSBURY
01879-01879	TYNGSBORO
01880-01880	WAKEFIELD
01885-01885	WEST BOXFORD
01886-01886	WESTFORD
01887-01887	WILMINGTON
01888-01888	WOBURN
01889-01889	NORTH READING
01890-01890	WINCHESTER
01899-01899	ANDOVER
01901-01905	LYNN
01906-01906	SAUGUS
01907-01907	SWAMPSCOTT
01908-01908	NAHANT
01910-01910	LYNN
01913-01913	AMESBURY
01915-01915	BEVERLY
01921-01921	BOXFORD
01922-01922	BYFIELD
01923-01923	DANVERS
01929-01929	ESSEX
01930-01931	GLOUCESTER
01936-01936	HAMILTON
01937-01937	HATHORNE
01938-01938	IPSWICH
01940-01940	LYNNFIELD
01944-01944	MANCHESTER
01945-01945	MARBLEHEAD
01947-01947	SALEM
01949-01949	MIDDLETON
01950-01950	NEWBURYPORT
01951-01951	NEWBURY
01952-01952	SALISBURY
01960-01964	PEABODY
01965-01965	PRIDES CROSSING
01966-01966	ROCKPORT
01969-01969	ROWLEY
01970-01971	SALEM
01982-01982	SOUTH HAMILTON
01983-01983	TOPSFIELD
01984-01984	WENHAM
01985-01985	WEST NEWBURY
02018-02018	ACCORD
02019-02019	BELLINGHAM
02020-02020	BRANT ROCK
02021-02021	CANTON
02025-02025	COHASSET
02026-02027	DEDHAM
02030-02030	DOVER
02031-02031	EAST MANSFIELD
02032-02032	EAST WALPOLE

02035-02035 FOXBORO	02254-02254 WALTHAM	02540-02541 FALMOUTH	02760-02761 NORTH ATTLEBORO
02038-02038 FRANKLIN	02258-02258 NEWTON	02542-02542 BUZZARDS BAY	02762-02762 PLAINVILLE
02040-02040 GREENBUSH	02266-02266 BOSTON	02543-02543 WOODS HOLE	02763-02763 ATTLEBORO FALLS
02041-02041 GREEN HARBOR	02269-02269 QUINCY	02552-02552 MENEMSHA	02764-02764 NORTH DIGHTON
02043-02044 HINGHAM	02272-02277 WATERTOWN	02553-02553 MONUMENT BEACH	02766-02766 NORTON
02045-02045 HULL	02283-02293 BOSTON	02554-02554 NANTUCKET	02767-02767 RAYNHAM
02047-02047 HUMAROCK	02294-02294 SEARS ROEBUCK	02556-02556 NORTH FALMOUTH	02768-02768 RAYNHAM CENTER
02048-02048 MANSFIELD	02295-02297 BOSTON	02557-02557 OAK BLUFFS	02769-02769 REHOBOTH
02050-02050 MARSHFIELD	02299-02299 BAR CODE MCCORMACK	02558-02558 ONSET	02770-02770 ROCHESTER
02051-02051 MARSHFIELD HILLS	02301-02305 BROCKTON	02559-02559 POCASSET	02771-02771 SEEKONK
02052-02052 MEDFIELD	02322-02322 AVON	02561-02561 SAGAMORE	02777-02777 SWANSEA
02053-02053 MEDWAY	02324-02325 BRIDGEWATER	02562-02562 SAGAMORE BEACH	02779-02779 BERKLEY
02054-02054 MILLIS	02327-02327 BRYANTVILLE	02563-02563 SANDWICH	02780-02783 TAUNTON
02055-02055 MINOT	02330-02330 CARVER	02564-02564 SIASCONSET	02790-02790 WESTPORT
02056-02056 NORFOLK	02331-02332 DUXBURY	02565-02565 SILVER BEACH	02791-02791 WESTPORT POINT
02059-02059 NORTH MARSHFIELD	02333-02333 EAST BRIDGEWATER	02568-02568 VINEYARD HAVEN	05501-05544 ANDOVER
02060-02060 NORTH SCITUATE	02334-02334 EASTON	02571-02571 WAREHAM	
02061-02061 NORWELL	02337-02337 ELMWOOD	02573-02573 VINEYARD HAVEN	
02062-02062 NORWOOD	02338-02338 HALIFAX	02574-02574 WEST FALMOUTH	
02065-02065 OCEAN BLUFF	02339-02340 HANOVER	02575-02575 WEST TISBURY	
02066-02066 SCITUATE	02341-02341 HANSON	02576-02576 WEST WAREHAM	
02067-02067 SHARON	02343-02343 HOLBROOK	02584-02584 NANTUCKET	
02070-02070 SHELDONVILLE	02344-02344 MIDDLEBORO	02601-02601 HYANNIS	
02071-02071 SOUTH WALPOLE	02345-02345 MANOMET	02630-02630 BARNSTABLE	
02072-02072 STOUGHTON	02346-02346 MIDDLEBORO	02631-02631 BREWSTER	
02081-02081 WALPOLE	02347-02347 LAKEVILLE	02632-02632 CENTERVILLE	
02090-02090 WESTWOOD	02348-02349 MIDDLEBORO	02633-02633 CHATHAM	
02093-02093 WRENTHAM	02350-02350 MONPONSETT	02634-02634 CENTERVILLE	
02100-02125 BOSTON	02351-02351 ABINGTON	02635-02635 COTUIT	
02126-02126 MATTAPAN	02355-02355 NORTH CARVER	02636-02636 CENTERVILLE	
02127-02128 BOSTON	02356-02357 NORTH EASTON	02637-02637 CUMMAQUID	
02129-02129 CHARLESTOWN	02358-02358 NORTH PEMBROKE	02638-02638 DENNIS	
02130-02130 JAMAICA PLAIN	02359-02359 PEMBROKE	02639-02639 DENNIS PORT	
02131-02131 ROSLINDALE	02360-02363 PLYMOUTH	02641-02641 EAST DENNIS	
02132-02132 WEST ROXBURY	02364-02364 KINGSTON	02642-02642 EASTHAM	
02133-02133 BOSTON	02366-02366 SOUTH CARVER	02643-02643 EAST ORLEANS	
02134-02134 ALLSTON	02367-02367 PLYMPTON	02644-02644 FORESTDALE	
02135-02135 BRIGHTON	02368-02368 RANDOLPH	02645-02645 HARWICH	
02136-02136 HYDE PARK	02370-02371 ROCKLAND	02646-02646 HARWICH PORT	
02137-02137 READVILLE	02375-02375 SOUTH EASTON	02647-02647 HYANNIS PORT	
02138-02142 CAMBRIDGE	02379-02379 WEST BRIDGEWATER	02648-02648 MARSTONS MILLS	
02143-02145 SOMERVILLE	02381-02381 WHITE HORSE BEACH	02649-02649 MASHPEE	
02146-02146 BROOKLINE	02382-02382 WHITMAN	02650-02650 NORTH CHATHAM	
02147-02147 BROOKLINE VILLAGE	02401-02411 BROCKTON	02651-02651 NORTH EASTHAM	
02148-02148 MALDEN	02420-02421 LEXINGTON	02652-02652 NORTH TRURO	
02149-02149 EVERETT	02445-02446 BROOKLINE	02653-02653 ORLEANS	
02150-02150 CHELSEA	02447-02447 BROOKLINE VILLAGE	02655-02655 OSTERVILLE	
02151-02151 REVERE	02451-02454 WALTHAM	02657-02657 PROVINCETOWN	
02152-02152 WINTHROP	02455-02455 NORTH WALTHAM	02659-02659 SOUTH CHATHAM	
02153-02153 MEDFORD	02456-02456 NEW TOWN	02660-02660 SOUTH DENNIS	
02154-02154 WALTHAM	02457-02457 BABSON PARK	02661-02661 SOUTH HARWICH	
02155-02155 MEDFORD	02458-02458 NEWTON	02662-02662 SOUTH ORLEANS	
02156-02156 WEST MEDFORD	02459-02459 NEWTON CENTER	02663-02663 SOUTH WELLFLEET	
02157-02157 BABSON PARK	02460-02460 NEWTONVILLE	02664-02664 SOUTH YARMOUTH	
02158-02162 NEWTON	02461-02461 NEWTON HIGHLANDS	02666-02666 TRURO	
02163-02163 BOSTON	02462-02462 NEWTON LOWER FALLS	02667-02667 WELLFLEET	
02164-02165 NEWTON	02464-02464 NEWTON UPPER FALLS	02668-02668 WEST BARNSTABLE	
02166-02166 AUBURNDALE	02465-02465 WEST NEWTON	02669-02669 WEST CHATHAM	
02167-02167 CHESTNUT HILL	02466-02466 AUBURNDALE	02670-02670 WEST DENNIS	
02168-02168 WABAN	02467-02467 CHESTNUT HILL	02671-02671 WEST HARWICH	
02169-02171 QUINCY	02468-02468 WABAN	02672-02672 WEST HYANNISPORT	
02172-02172 WATERTOWN	02471-02472 WATERTOWN	02673-02673 WEST YARMOUTH	
02173-02173 LEXINGTON	02474-02474 ARLINGTON	02675-02675 YARMOUTH PORT	
02174-02174 ARLINGTON	02475-02475 ARLINGTON HEIGHTS	02702-02702 ASSONET	
02175-02175 ARLINGTON HEIGHTS	02476-02476 ARLINGTON	02703-02703 ATTLEBORO	
02176-02177 MELROSE	02477-02477 WATERTOWN	02712-02712 CHARTLEY	
02178-02178 BELMONT	02478-02478 BELMONT	02713-02713 CUTTYHUNK	
02179-02179 WAVERLEY	02479-02479 WAVERLEY	02714-02714 DARTMOUTH	
02180-02180 STONEHAM	02481-02481 WELLESLEY HILLS	02715-02715 DIGHTON	
02181-02181 WELLESLEY	02482-02482 WELLESLEY	02717-02717 EAST FREETOWN	
02184-02185 BRAINTREE	02492-02492 NEEDHAM	02718-02718 EAST TAUNTON	
02186-02186 MILTON	02493-02493 WESTON	02719-02719 FAIRHAVEN	
02187-02187 MILTON VILLAGE	02494-02494 NEEDHAM	02720-02724 FALL RIVER	
02188-02191 WEYMOUTH	02495-02495 NONANTUM	02725-02726 SOMERSET	
02192-02192 NEEDHAM	02499-02499 BROCKTON	02738-02738 MARION	
02193-02193 WESTON	02532-02532 BUZZARDS BAY	02739-02739 MATTAPOISETT	
02194-02194 NEEDHAM	02534-02534 CATAUMET	02740-02742 NEW BEDFORD	
02195-02195 NEWTON	02535-02535 CHILMARK	02743-02743 ACUSHNET	
02196-02222 BOSTON	02536-02536 EAST FALMOUTH	02744-02746 NEW BEDFORD	
02228-02228 EAST BOSTON	02537-02537 EAST SANDWICH	02747-02747 NORTH DARTMOUTH	
02238-02239 CAMBRIDGE	02538-02538 EAST WAREHAM	02748-02748 SOUTH DARTMOUTH	
02241-02241 BOSTON	02539-02539 EDGARTOWN	02754-02754 NORTH DIGHTON	

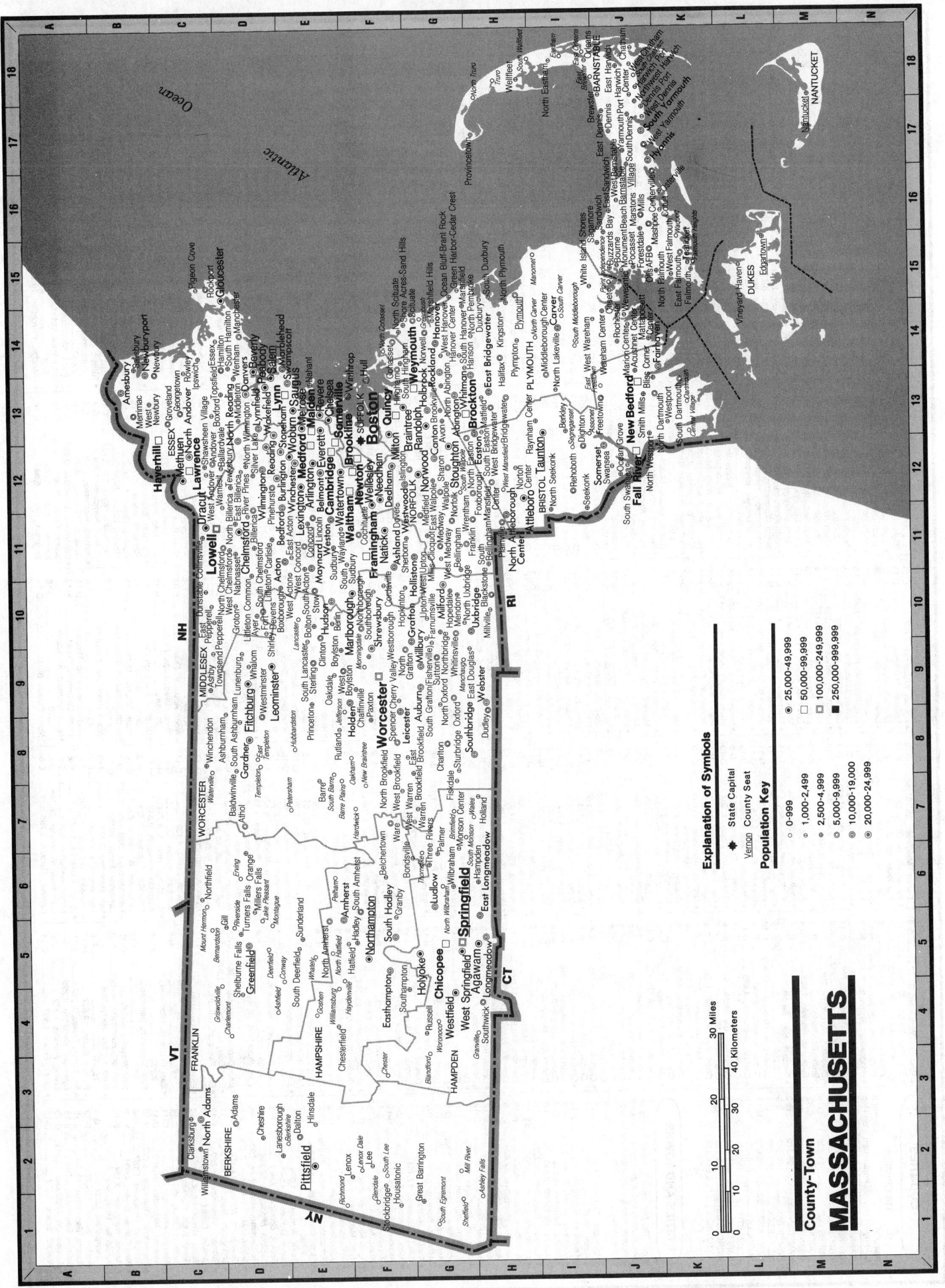

MASSACHUSETTS

County-Town

Explanation of Symbols

✦ State Capital

Vernon ⊙ County Seat

Population Key

○ 0-999	⊙ 25,000-49,999
⊙ 1,000-2,499	⊙ 50,000-99,999
⊙ 2,500-4,999	▫ 100,000-249,999
⊙ 5,000-9,999	■ 250,000-999,999
⊙ 10,000-19,000	
⊙ 20,000-24,999	

30 Miles
40 Kilometers

COUNTIES

(14 Counties)

Name of County	Population	Location on Map
BARNSTABLE	186,605	J-15
BERKSHIRE	139,352	D-2
BRISTOL	506,325	I-12
DUKES	11,639	L-15
ESSEX	670,080	C-12
FRANKLIN	70,092	C-3
HAMPDEN	456,310	G-3
HAMPSHIRE	146,568	E-3
MIDDLESEX	1,398,468	C-9
NANTUCKET	6,012	M-17
NORFOLK	616,087	G-11
PLYMOUTH	435,276	I-13
SUFFOLK	663,906	F-13
WORCESTER	709,705	C-7
TOTAL	6,016,425	

CITIES AND TOWNS

Note: The first name is that of the city or town, second, that of the county in which it is located, then the population and location on the map.

• *Abington, Plymouth, 13,817* ... G-13
▲ *Acton, Middlesex, 17,872* ... E-11
Acushnet, Bristol, 9,554 ... J-13
• Acushnet Center, Bristol, 3,170 ... J-14
• Adams, Berkshire, 6,356 ... D-3
Adams, Berkshire, 9,445 ... D-3
▲ *Agawam, Hampden, 27,323* ... H-5
• Amesbury, Essex, 12,109 ... B-13
Amesbury, Essex, 14,997 ... B-13
• Amherst, Hampshire, 17,824 ... E-5
Amherst, Hampshire, 35,228 ... E-5
Andover, Essex, 29,151 ... C-12
• Andover, Essex, 8,242 ... C-12
• *Arlington, Middlesex, 44,630* ... E-12
Ashburnham, Worcester ... D-8
Ashburnham, Worcester, 5,433 ... D-8
▲ *Ashby, Middlesex, 2,717* ... C-9
Ashfield, Franklin, 1,715 ... D-4
▲ *Ashland, Middlesex, 12,066* ... F-11
Athol, Worcester, 11,451 ... D-7
• Athol, Worcester, 8,732 ... D-7
Attleboro, Bristol, 38,383 ... H-12
▲ *Auburn, Worcester, 15,005* ... G-9
▲ *Avon, Norfolk, 4,558* ... G-13
• Ayer, Middlesex, 2,889 ... D-10
Ayer, Middlesex, 6,871 ... D-10
• Baldwinville, Worcester, 1,795 ... D-8
Ballardvale, Essex ... D-12
Barnstable, Barnstable, 40,949 ... J-17
• Barnstable Village, Barnstable, 2,790 ... J-17
• Barre, Worcester, 1,094 ... E-7
Barre, Worcester, 4,546 ... E-7
Becket, Berkshire, 1,481 ... F-3
▲ *Bedford, Middlesex, 12,996* ... E-12
Belchertown, Hampshire, 10,579 .. F-6
• Belchertown, Hampshire, 2,339 ... F-6
Bellingham, Norfolk, 14,877 ... G-11
• Bellingham, Norfolk, 4,535 ... G-11
• *Belmont, Middlesex, 24,720* ... E-12
▲ *Berkley, Bristol, 4,237* ... I-13
▲ *Berlin, Worcester, 2,293* ... E-10
Bernardston, Franklin, 2,048 ... C-5
Beverly, Essex, 38,195 ... D-14
Billerica, Middlesex ... D-11
Billerica, Middlesex, 37,609 ... D-11
▲ *Blackstone, Worcester, 8,023* ... H-10
Blandford, Hampden, 1,187 ... G-3
• Bliss Corner, Bristol, 4,908 ... K-13
▲ *Bolton, Worcester, 3,134* ... E-10
• Bondsville, Hampden/ Hampshire, 1,992 ... G-6
Boston, Suffolk, 574,283 ... F-13
Bourne, Barnstable, 16,064 ... J-15
• Bourne, Barnstable, 1,284 ... J-15
▲ *Boxborough, Middlesex, 3,343* ... D-10
• Boxford, Essex, 2,072 ... C-13
Boxford, Essex, 6,266 ... C-13
▲ *Boylston, Worcester, 3,517* ... E-9
• *Braintree, Norfolk, 33,836* ... F-13
• Brewster, Barnstable, 1,818 ... J-18
Brewster, Barnstable, 8,440 ... J-18
Bridgewater, Plymouth, 21,249 ... H-13
• Bridgewater, Plymouth, 7,242 ... H-13
Brimfield, Hampden, 3,001 ... G-7
Brockton, Plymouth, 92,788 ... G-13
▲ *Brookfield, Worcester, 2,968* ... G-8
• *Brookline, Norfolk, 54,718* ... F-12
Brookville, Norfolk ... G-13
Buckland, Franklin, 1,928 ... D-4
• *Burlington, Middlesex, 23,302* ... D-12
• Buzzards Bay, Barnstable, 3,250 ... J-15
Cambridge, Middlesex, 95,802 ... E-12
Canton, Norfolk, 18,530 ... F-12
▲ *Carlisle, Middlesex, 4,333* ... D-11
▲ *Carver, Plymouth, 10,590* ... I-14
• Centerville, Barnstable, 9,190 ... K-16
Chaffinville, Worcester ... F-9
Charlemont, Franklin, 1,249 ... D-4
▲ *Charlton, Worcester, 9,576* ... G-8
• Chatham, Barnstable, 1,916 ... J-18
Chatham, Barnstable, 6,579 ... J-18
Chelmsford, Middlesex, 32,383 ... D-11
• Chelmsford, Middlesex, 32,388 ... D-11
Chelsea, Suffolk, 28,710 ... E-13
Cherry Valley, Worcester ... F-9
▲ *Cheshire, Berkshire, 3,479* ... D-2
Chester, Hampden, 1,280 ... F-3
Chesterfield, Hampshire, 1,048 ... E-4
Chicopee, Hampden, 56,632 ... G-5
▲ *Clarksburg, Berkshire, 1,745* ... C-2
Clinton, Worcester, 13,222 ... E-10
• Clinton, Worcester, 7,943 ... E-10
• Cochituate, Middlesex, 6,046 ... F-11
▲ *Cohasset, Norfolk, 7,075* ... F-14
Collinsville, Middlesex ... C-11
Colrain, Franklin, 1,757 ... C-5
Concord, Middlesex ... E-11
Concord, Middlesex, 17,076 ... E-11
Conway, Franklin, 1,529 ... D-5
• Cordaville, Worcester, 1,530 ... F-10
• Cotuit, Barnstable, 2,364 ... K-16
▲ *Dalton, Berkshire, 7,155* ... E-2
• *Danvers, Essex, 24,174* ... D-13
Dartmouth, Bristol, 27,244 ... K-13
• *Dedham, Norfolk, 23,782* ... F-12
Deerfield, Franklin, 5,018 ... D-5
• Dennis, Barnstable, 2,633 ... J-17
Dennis, Barnstable, 13,864 ... J-17
• Dennis Port, Barnstable, 2,775 ... J-17
▲ *Dighton, Bristol, 5,631* ... I-12
Douglas, Worcester, 5,438 ... H-9
• Dover, Norfolk, 2,163 ... F-12
Dover, Norfolk, 4,915 ... F-12
▲ *Dracut, Middlesex, 25,594* ... C-11
▲ *Dudley, Worcester, 9,540* ... H-8
▲ *Dunstable, Middlesex, 2,236* ... C-10
Duxbury, Plymouth, 13,895 ... H-15
• Duxbury, Plymouth, 1,637 ... H-15
East Acton, Middlesex ... E-11
East Billerica, Middlesex ... D-12
▲ *East Bridgewater, Plymouth, 11,104* ... H-13
• East Brookfield, Worcester, 1,396 ... F-8
East Brookfield, Worcester, 2,033 ... F-8
• East Dennis, Barnstable, 2,584 ... J-17
• East Douglas, Worcester, 1,945 ... G-9
• East Falmouth, Barnstable, 5,577 ... K-15
• East Harwich, Barnstable, 3,828 . J-18
▲ *East Longmeadow, Hampden, 13,367* ... H-5
• East Pepperell, Middlesex, 2,296 ... C-10
• East Sandwich, Barnstable, 3,171 ... J-15
East Walpole, Norfolk ... G-12
Eastham, Barnstable, 4,462 ... I-18
▲ *Easthampton, Hampshire, 15,537* ... F-5
▲ *Easton, Bristol, 19,807* ... H-13
▲ *Edgartown, Dukes, 3,062* ... L-15
Egremont, Berkshire, 1,229 ... G-1
Erving, Franklin, 1,372 ... D-6
• Essex, Essex, 1,507 ... C-14
Essex, Essex, 3,260 ... C-14
Everett, Middlesex, 35,701 ... E-13
▲ *Fairhaven, Bristol, 16,132* ... K-14
Fall River, Bristol, 92,703 ... J-12
Falmouth, Barnstable, 27,960 ... K-15
• Falmouth, Barnstable, 4,047 ... K-15
Farnumsville, Worcester ... G-10
• Fiskdale, Worcester, 2,189 ... G-7
Fitchburg, Worcester, 41,194 ... D-9
• Forestdale, Barnstable, 2,833 ... J-15
• Fort Devens, Middlesex/ Worcester, 8,973 ... D-10
Foxborough, Norfolk, 14,637 ... H-12
• Foxborough, Norfolk, 5,706 ... H-12
Framingham, Middlesex, 64,989 .. F-11
• Framingham, Middlesex, 64,994 .. F-11
Franklin, Norfolk, 22,095 ... G-11
• Franklin, Norfolk, 9,965 ... G-11
▲ *Freetown, Bristol, 8,522* ... J-13
Gardner, Worcester, 20,125 ... D-8
▲ *Georgetown, Essex, 6,384* ... C-13
▲ *Gill, Franklin, 1,583* ... D-7
Gloucester, Essex, 28,716 ... D-15
▲ *Grafton, Worcester, 13,035* ... G-10
• Granby, Hampshire, 1,327 ... F-5
Granby, Hampshire, 5,565 ... F-5
Granville, Hampden, 1,403 ... H-4
• Great Barrington, Berkshire, 2,810 ... G-1
Great Barrington, Berkshire, 7,725 ... G-1
• Green Harbor-Cedar Crest, Plymouth, 2,205 ... G-15
• Greenfield, Franklin, 14,016 ... D-5
Greenfield, Franklin, 18,666 ... D-5
• Groton, Middlesex, 1,044 ... D-10
Groton, Middlesex, 7,511 ... D-10
▲ *Groveland, Essex, 5,214* ... C-13
▲ *Hadley, Hampshire, 4,231* ... F-5
▲ *Halifax, Plymouth, 6,526* ... H-14
▲ *Hamilton, Essex, 7,280* ... D-14
▲ *Hampden, Hampden, 4,709* ... H-6
▲ *Hanover, Plymouth, 11,912* ... G-14
• Hanson, Plymouth, 2,188 ... G-14
Hanson, Plymouth, 9,028 ... G-14
Hardwick, Worcester, 2,385 ... F-7
Harvard, Worcester, 12,329 ... D-10
Harwich, Barnstable, 10,275 ... J-18
• Harwich Center, Barnstable, 1,668 ... J-17
• Harwich Port, Barnstable, 1,742 .. J-18
• Hatfield, Hampshire, 1,234 ... E-5
Hatfield, Hampshire, 3,184 ... E-5
Haverhill, Essex, 51,418 ... C-13
Hingham, Plymouth, 19,821 ... F-14
• Hingham, Plymouth, 5,454 ... F-14
Hinsdale, Berkshire ... E-2
Hinsdale, Berkshire, 1,959 ... E-2
• *Holbrook, Norfolk, 11,041* ... G-13
▲ *Holden, Worcester, 14,628* ... F-9
• Holland, Hampden, 1,331 ... H-7
Holland, Hampden, 2,185 ... H-7
▲ *Holliston, Middlesex, 12,926* ... G-11
Holyoke, Hampden, 43,704 ... G-5
• Hopedale, Worcester, 3,961 ... G-10
Hopedale, Worcester, 5,666 ... G-10
• Hopkinton, Middlesex, 2,305 ... F-10
Hopkinton, Middlesex, 9,191 ... F-10
• Housatonic, Berkshire, 1,184 ... F-1
Hubbardston, Worcester, 2,797 ... E-8
• Hudson, Middlesex, 14,267 ... E-10
Hudson, Middlesex, 17,233 ... E-10
• *Hull, Plymouth, 10,466* ... F-13
Huntington, Hampshire, 1,987 ... F-4
• Hyannis, Barnstable, 14,120 ... J-17
Ipswich, Essex, 11,873 ... C-14
• Ipswich, Essex, 4,132 ... C-14
Islington, Norfolk ... G-12
• Kingston, Plymouth, 4,774 ... H-14
Kingston, Plymouth, 9,045 ... H-14
Lakeville, Plymouth, 7,785 ... I-13
Lancaster, Worcester, 6,661 ... E-10
▲ *Lanesborough, Berkshire, 3,032* ... D-2
Lawrence, Essex, 70,207 ... C-12
• Lee, Berkshire, 2,020 ... F-2
Lee, Berkshire, 5,849 ... F-2
▲ *Leicester, Worcester, 10,191* ... F-8
• Lenox, Berkshire, 1,687 ... E-2
Lenox, Berkshire, 5,069 ... E-2
Leominster, Worcester, 38,145 ... D-9
Leverett, Franklin, 1,785 ... E-6
• *Lexington, Middlesex, 28,974* ... E-12
▲ *Lincoln, Middlesex, 7,666* ... E-11
Littleton, Middlesex ... D-11
Littleton, Middlesex, 7,051 ... D-11
• Littleton Common, Middlesex, 2,867 ... D-11
• *Longmeadow, Hampden, 15,467* .. H-5
Lowell, Middlesex, 103,439 ... C-11
▲ *Ludlow, Hampden, 18,820* ... G-6
• Lunenburg, Worcester, 1,694 ... D-9
Lunenburg, Worcester, 9,117 ... D-9
Lynn, Essex, 81,245 ... E-13
• *Lynnfield, Essex, 11,274* ... D-13
Malden, Middlesex, 53,884 ... E-13
▲ *Manchester, Essex, 5,286* ... D-14
Mansfield, Bristol, 16,568 ... H-12
• Mansfield Center, Bristol, 7,170 .. H-12
• *Marblehead, Essex, 19,971* ... E-14
Marion, Plymouth, 4,496 ... J-14
• Marion Center, Plymouth, 1,426 ... J-14
Marlborough, Middlesex, 31,813 . F-10
• Marshfield, Plymouth, 4,002 ... G-14
Marshfield, Plymouth, 21,531 ... G-14
• Marshfield Hills, Plymouth, 2,201 ... G-14
• Marstons Mills, Barnstable, 8,017 ... J-16
▲ *Mashpee, Barnstable, 7,884* ... J-16
Matfield, Plymouth ... H-13
Mattapoisett, Plymouth, 5,850 ... J-14
• Mattapoisett Center, Plymouth, 2,949 ... J-14
• *Maynard, Middlesex, 10,325* ... E-11
Medfield, Norfolk, 10,531 ... G-11
• Medfield, Norfolk, 5,985 ... G-11
Medford, Middlesex, 57,407 ... E-12
▲ *Medway, Norfolk, 9,931* ... G-11
Melrose, Middlesex, 28,150 ... E-13
▲ *Mendon, Worcester, 4,010* ... G-10
▲ *Merrimac, Essex, 5,166* ... B-13
▲ *Methuen, Essex, 39,990* ... C-12
Middleborough, Plymouth, 17,867 ... I-13
• Middleborough Center, Plymouth, 6,837 ... I-13
▲ *Middleton, Essex, 4,921* ... D-13
• Milford, Worcester, 23,339 ... G-10
Milford, Worcester, 25,355 ... G-10
▲ *Millbury, Worcester, 12,228* ... G-9
• Millers Falls, Franklin, 1,084 ... D-6
Millis, Norfolk, 7,613 ... G-11
• Millis-Clicquot, Norfolk, 4,081 ... G-11
▲ *Millville, Worcester, 2,236* ... H-10
• *Milton, Norfolk, 25,725* ... F-13
Monson, Hampden, 7,776 ... G-6
• Monson Center, Hampden, 2,101 . G-6
Montague, Franklin, 8,316 ... D-5
• Monument Beach, Barnstable, 1,842 ... J-15
Nabnasset, Middlesex ... D-11
• *Nahant, Essex, 3,828* ... E-13
• Nantucket, Nantucket, 3,069 ... M-18
Nantucket, Nantucket, 6,012 ... M-18
Natick, Middlesex, 30,510 ... F-11
• *Needham, Norfolk, 27,557* ... F-12
New Bedford, Bristol, 99,922 ... J-13
New Marlborough, Berkshire, 1,240 ... G-2
▲ *Newbury, Essex, 5,623* ... C-14
Newburyport, Essex, 16,317 ... B-14
Newton, Middlesex, 82,585 ... F-12
▲ *Norfolk, Norfolk, 9,270* ... G-11
North Abington, Plymouth ... G-13
North Adams, Berkshire, 16,797 ... C-3
• North Amherst, Hampshire, 6,239 ... E-5
▲ *North Andover, Essex, 22,792* ... C-12
North Attleborough, Bristol, 25,038 ... H-11
• North Attleborough Center, Bristol, 16,178 ... H-11
North Billerica, Middlesex ... D-11
• North Brookfield, Worcester, 2,635 ... F-8
North Brookfield, Worcester, 4,708 ... F-8
North Chelmsford, Middlesex ... D-11
North Dartmouth, Bristol ... K-13
• North Eastham, Barnstable, 1,570 ... I-18
North Easton, Bristol ... G-13
• North Falmouth, Barnstable, 2,625 ... K-15
North Grafton, Worcester ... F-9
• North Lakeville, Plymouth, 2,048 .. I-13
North Oxford, Worcester ... G-9
• North Pembroke, Plymouth, 2,485 ... H-14
• North Plymouth, Plymouth, 3,450 ... H-14
▲ *North Reading, Middlesex, 12,002* ... D-13
• North Scituate, Plymouth, 4,891 .. F-14
• North Seekonk, Bristol, 2,635 ... I-11
• North Uxbridge, Worcester ... H-10
• North Westport, Bristol, 4,697 ... J-13
• North Wilmington, Middlesex ... D-12
Northampton, Hampshire, 29,289 . F-5
Northborough, Worcester, 11,929 ... F-10
• Northborough, Worcester, 5,761 . F-10
Northbridge, Worcester ... G-10
Northbridge, Worcester, 13,371 .. G-10
• Northfield, Franklin, 1,322 ... C-6
Northfield, Franklin, 2,838 ... C-6
• Northwest Harwich, Barnstable, 3,037 ... J-17
Norton, Bristol, 14,265 ... H-12
• Norton Center, Bristol, 1,899 ... H-12
▲ *Norwell, Plymouth, 9,279* ... G-14
• *Norwood, Norfolk, 28,700* ... G-12
▲ *Oak Bluffs, Dukes, 2,804* ... L-15
Oakdale, Worcester ... E-9
Oakham, Worcester, 1,503 ... E-8
• Ocean Bluff-Brant Rock, Plymouth, 4,541 ... G-15
• Ocean Grove, Bristol, 3,169 ... J-12
• Onset, Plymouth, 1,461 ... J-15
• Orange, Franklin, 3,791 ... D-6
Orange, Franklin, 7,312 ... D-6
• Orleans, Barnstable, 1,699 ... I-18
Orleans, Barnstable, 5,838 ... I-18
• Osterville, Barnstable, 2,911 ... K-16
Otis, Barnstable ... J-15
Oxford, Worcester, 12,588 ... G-9
• Oxford, Worcester, 5,969 ... G-9
Palmer, Hampden, 12,054 ... G-6
• Palmer, Hampden, 4,069 ... G-6
▲ *Paxton, Worcester, 4,047* ... F-8
Peabody, Essex, 47,039 ... D-14
Pelham, Hampshire, 1,373 ... E-6
Pembroke, Plymouth, 14,544 ... H-14
Pepperell, Middlesex, 10,098 ... C-10
• Pepperell, Middlesex, 2,350 ... C-10
Petersham, Worcester, 1,131 ... E-7
Phillipston, Worcester, 1,485 ... D-7
Pigeon Cove, Essex ... C-15
• Pinehurst, Middlesex, 6,614 ... D-12
Pittsfield, Berkshire, 48,622 ... E-2
▲ *Plainville, Norfolk, 6,871* ... H-11
Plymouth, Plymouth, 45,608 ... H-15
• Plymouth, Plymouth, 7,258 ... H-15
▲ *Plympton, Plymouth, 2,384* ... H-14
• Pocasset, Barnstable, 2,756 ... J-15
Princeton, Worcester, 3,189 ... E-9
• Provincetown, Barnstable, 3,374 ... H-17
Provincetown, Barnstable, 3,561 ... H-17
Quincy, Norfolk, 84,985 ... F-13
• *Randolph, Norfolk, 30,093* ... G-13
Raynham, Bristol, 9,867 ... H-13
• Raynham Center, Bristol, 3,709 ... I-13
• *Reading, Middlesex, 22,539* ... D-12
▲ *Rehoboth, Bristol, 8,656* ... I-12
Revere, Suffolk, 42,786 ... E-13
Richmond, Berkshire, 1,677 ... E-1
River Pines, Middlesex ... D-11
▲ *Rochester, Plymouth, 3,921* ... J-14
▲ *Rockland, Plymouth, 16,123* ... G-14
• Rockport, Essex, 5,448 ... C-15
Rockport, Essex, 7,482 ... C-15
• Rowley, Essex, 1,144 ... C-14
Rowley, Essex, 4,452 ... C-14
Royalston, Worcester, 1,147 ... C-7
Russell, Hampden, 1,594 ... G-4
• Rutland, Worcester, 2,145 ... E-8
Rutland, Worcester, 4,936 ... E-8
• Sagamore, Barnstable, 2,589 ... J-15
Salem, Essex, 38,091 ... D-13
• Salisbury, Essex, 3,729 ... B-14
Salisbury, Essex, 6,882 ... B-14
Sandwich, Barnstable, 15,489 ... J-16
• Sandwich, Barnstable, 2,998 ... J-16
• *Saugus, Essex, 25,549* ... E-13
Scituate, Plymouth, 16,786 ... G-14
• Scituate, Plymouth, 5,180 ... G-14
Seekonk, Bristol ... I-11
Seekonk, Bristol, 13,046 ... I-11
Sharon, Norfolk, 15,517 ... G-12
• Sharon, Norfolk, 5,893 ... G-12
Shawsheen Village, Essex ... C-12
Sheffield, Berkshire, 2,910 ... G-1
Shelburne, Franklin, 2,012 ... D-5
• Shelburne Falls, Franklin, 1,996 ... D-4
▲ *Sherborn, Middlesex, 3,989* ... F-11
• Shirley, Middlesex, 1,559 ... D-10
Shirley, Middlesex, 6,118 ... D-10
Shore Acres-Sand Hills, Plymouth ... F-14
▲ *Shrewsbury, Worcester, 24,146* ... F-9
Shutesbury, Franklin, 1,561 ... E-6
Silver Lake, Middlesex ... D-12
• Smith Mills, Bristol, 4,593 ... J-13
• *Somerset, Bristol, 17,655* ... J-12
Somerville, Middlesex, 76,210 ... E-13
South Acton, Middlesex ... E-11
• South Amherst, Hampshire, 5,053 ... F-6
• South Ashburnham, Worcester, 1,110 ... D-8
South Bellingham, Norfolk ... H-11
South Chelmsford, Middlesex ... D-11
South Dartmouth, Bristol ... K-13
• South Deerfield, Franklin, 1,906 ... E-5
• South Dennis, Barnstable, 3,559 . J-17
• South Duxbury, Plymouth, 3,017 . H-15
South Easton, Bristol ... H-13
South Grafton (Fisherville), Worcester ... G-9
▲ *South Hadley, Hampshire, 16,685* . F-5
South Hamilton, Essex ... D-14
South Hanover, Plymouth ... G-14
South Hingham, Plymouth ... F-14
• South Lancaster, Worcester, 1,772 ... E-10
South Sudbury, Middlesex ... F-11
South Swansea, Bristol ... J-12
• South Yarmouth, Barnstable, 10,358 ... J-17
▲ *Southampton, Hampshire, 4,478* ... F-4
Southborough, Worcester ... F-10
Southborough, Worcester, 6,628 ... F-10
• Southbridge, Worcester, 13,631 ... H-8
Southbridge, Worcester, 17,816 ... H-8
▲ *Southwick, Hampden, 7,667* ... H-4
Spencer, Worcester, 11,645 ... F-8
• Spencer, Worcester, 6,306 ... F-8
Springfield, Hampden, 156,983 ... G-5
▲ *Sterling, Worcester, 6,481* ... E-9
▲ *Stockbridge, Berkshire, 2,408* ... F-2
• *Stoneham, Middlesex, 22,203* ... E-12
▲ *Stoughton, Norfolk, 26,777* ... G-12
▲ *Stow, Middlesex, 5,328* ... E-10
• Sturbridge, Worcester, 2,093 ... G-8
Sturbridge, Worcester, 7,775 ... G-8
Sudbury, Middlesex ... E-11
Sudbury, Middlesex, 14,358 ... E-11
▲ *Sunderland, Franklin, 3,399* ... E-5
▲ *Sutton, Worcester, 6,824* ... G-9
• *Swampscott, Essex, 13,650* ... E-13
Swansea, Bristol ... J-12
Swansea, Bristol, 15,411 ... J-12
Taunton, Bristol, 49,832 ... I-13
• Teaticket, Barnstable, 1,856 ... K-15
Templeton, Worcester, 6,438 ... D-8
Tewksbury, Middlesex ... D-12
Tewksbury, Middlesex, 27,266 ... D-12
• Three Rivers, Hampden, 3,006 ... G-6
Tisbury, Dukes, 3,120 ... L-15
• Topsfield, Essex, 2,711 ... D-13
Topsfield, Essex, 5,754 ... D-13
• Townsend, Middlesex, 1,164 ... C-9
Townsend, Middlesex, 8,496 ... C-9
Truro, Barnstable, 1,573 ... H-18
• Turners Falls, Franklin, 4,731 ... D-5
Tyngsborough, Middlesex, 8,642 ... C-11
Upton, Worcester, 4,677 ... G-10
• Upton-West Upton, Worcester, 2,347 ... G-10
▲ *Uxbridge, Worcester, 10,415* ... H-10
• Vineyard Haven, Dukes, 1,762 ... L-15
• *Wakefield, Middlesex, 24,825* ... D-13
Wales, Hampden, 1,566 ... H-7
Walpole, Norfolk, 20,212 ... G-12
• Walpole, Norfolk, 5,495 ... G-12
Waltham, Middlesex, 57,878 ... F-12
Wamesit, Middlesex ... D-12
• Ware, Hampshire, 6,533 ... F-7
Ware, Hampshire, 9,808 ... F-7
Wareham, Plymouth, 19,232 ... J-14
• Wareham Center, Plymouth, 2,607 ... J-14
• Warren, Worcester, 1,516 ... G-7
Warren, Worcester, 4,437 ... G-7
• *Watertown, Middlesex, 33,284* ... E-12
Wayland, Middlesex ... E-11
Wayland, Middlesex, 11,874 ... E-11
• Webster, Worcester, 11,849 ... H-9
Webster, Worcester, 16,196 ... H-9
• *Wellesley, Norfolk, 26,615* ... F-12
▲ *Wellfleet, Barnstable, 2,493* ... H-18
▲ *Wenham, Essex, 4,212* ... D-13
West Acton, Middlesex ... E-11
West Andover, Essex ... C-12
• West Barnstable, Barnstable, 1,508 ... J-16
▲ *West Boylston, Worcester, 6,611* .. E-9
▲ *West Bridgewater, Plymouth, 6,389* ... H-13
• West Brookfield, Worcester, 1,419 ... F-7
West Brookfield, Worcester, 3,532 ... F-7
• West Chatham, Barnstable, 1,504 ... J-18
West Chelmsford, Middlesex ... D-11
• West Concord, Middlesex, 5,761 ... E-11
• West Dennis, Barnstable, 2,307 .. J-17
• West Falmouth, Barnstable, 1,752 ... K-15
West Hanover, Plymouth ... G-14
West Medway, Norfolk ... G-11
▲ *West Newbury, Essex, 3,421* ... B-13
▲ *West Springfield, Hampden, 27,537* ... G-5
West Stockbridge, Berkshire, 1,483 ... F-1
West Tisbury, Dukes, 1,704 ... L-15
• West Wareham, Plymouth, 2,059 ... I-14
West Warren, Worcester ... G-7
• West Yarmouth, Barnstable, 5,409 ... J-17
Westborough, Worcester, 14,133 ... F-10
• Westborough, Worcester, 3,917 .. F-10
Westfield, Hampden, 38,372 ... G-4
Westford, Middlesex, 16,392 ... D-11
Westhampton, Hampshire, 1,327 ... F-4
▲ *Westminster, Worcester, 6,191* ... D-8
▲ *Weston, Middlesex, 10,200* ... E-11
Westport, Bristol ... K-13
Westport, Bristol, 13,852 ... K-13
▲ *Westwood, Norfolk, 12,557* ... F-12
• Weweantic, Plymouth, 1,812 ... J-14
• *Weymouth, Norfolk, 54,063* ... G-13
Whalom, Worcester ... D-9
Whately, Franklin, 1,375 ... E-5
• White Island Shores, Plymouth, 1,827 ... I-15
• Whitinsville, Worcester, 5,639 ... G-10
▲ *Whitman, Plymouth, 13,240* ... G-13
Wilbraham, Hampden, 12,635 ... G-6
• Wilbraham, Hampden, 3,352 ... G-6
▲ *Williamsburg, Hampshire, 2,515* ... E-4
Williamstown, Berkshire, 4,791 ... C-2
Williamstown, Berkshire, 8,220 ... C-2
• *Wilmington, Middlesex, 17,651* ... D-12
• Winchendon, Worcester, 4,316 ... C-8
Winchendon, Worcester, 8,805 ... C-8
• *Winchester, Middlesex, 20,267* ... E-12
• *Winthrop, Suffolk, 18,127* ... E-13
Woburn, Middlesex, 35,943 ... E-12
Worcester, Worcester, 169,759 ... F-9
Worthington, Hampshire, 1,156 ... E-4
▲ *Wrentham, Norfolk, 9,006* ... H-11
Yarmouth, Barnstable, 21,174 ... J-17
• Yarmouth Port, Barnstable, 4,271 ... J-17

Explanation of symbols:
• – Census Designated Place (CDP)
▲ *italics* – Township (shown on the map)
• *italics* – Township shown which is also a CDP
italics – Township (not shown on the map)

Michigan

General Help Numbers:

Governor's Office
PO Box 30013
Lansing, MI 48909
www.michigan.gov/gov

517-373-3400
Fax 517-335-6863
8AM-5PM

Attorney General's Office
PO Box 30212
Lansing, MI 48909
http://www.michigan.gov/ag/

517-373-1110
Fax 517-373-3042
8AM-5PM

Legislative Records
Michigan Legislature Document Room
State Capitol, PO Box 30036
Lansing, MI 48909
www.michiganlegislature.org

517-373-0169

8:30AM-5PM

State Archives
Michigan Historical Center
702 W. Kalamazoo
Lansing, MI 48809
www.sos.state.mi.us/history/archive

517-373-1408
Fax 517-241-1658
10AM-4PM

State Specifics:

Capital:

Lansing
Ingham County

Time Zone:

EST*

* Four north-western Michigan counties are CST:
They are: Dickinson, Gogebic, Iron, Menominee.

Number of Counties:

83

Population:

10,112,620

Web Site:

www.michigan.gov

State Agencies

Criminal Records

Michigan State Police, Criminal History Section, Criminal Justice Information Center, 7150 Harris Dr, Lansing, MI 48913; 517-322-1956, 517-322-0635-Fax; 8AM-5PM.

www.michigan.gov/msp

Non-profit and charitable organizations may submit a copy of Federal Form 501C3 in lieu of payment for a name search.

Records are available until the subject's DOB indicates 99 years or a death is reported. It takes up to 30 days before new records are available for inquiry. Records are indexed on inhouse computer. 100% of arrest records are fingerprint supported. Records are normally destroyed after death. 80% of all arrests in database have final dispositions recorded.

Searching: Search state police lists of missing persons/children, most wanted, and fugitives at www.michigan.gov/msp/0,1607,7-123-1589_1878---,00.html. Include the following in your request-full name, sex, race, date of birth. A SSN or maiden name/previous name is very helpful. Records can be searched with or without a fingerprint card. The following data is not released: non-conviction information. This search includes only Michigan felony or misdemeanor arrests where a person has been convicted in a court and the conviction has been added to that person's criminal history record. It does not include arrests without a conviction, outstanding warrants, federal arrests or arrests from other states.

Access by: mail, online.

Fee & Payment: The non-fingerprint search fee is $10.00 per name, $30.00 with a fingerprint card, and $54.00 with state and FBI fingerprint cards. Registered users may be eligible for a fee waiver on name searches. Fee payee: State of Michigan. Prepayment required. Payment required in advance unless a prepaid account has been arranged with Division cashier. Personal checks accepted. Credit cards accepted for online access.

Mail search: Turnaround time: 4 to 6 weeks. Limited searches with fingerprints available by mail; should be in person.

Online search: Online access is available at www.michigan.gov/ichat. Results are available in seconds; fee is $10.00 per name. Call 517-322-1377. This is a non-fingerprint search. You are also allowed up to three variations on one name search.

Statewide Court Records

State Court Administrative Officer, PO Box 30048, Lansing, MI 48909 (Courier address: 925 W Ottawa St, Lansing, MI 48909); 517-373-0130, 517-373-9831-Fax; 8:30AM-5PM.

http://courts.michigan.gov/scao

No trial court records are available from this agency.

Access by: online.

Online search: Subscribe to email updates of appellate opinions at http://courtofappeals.mijud.net/resources/subscribe.htm. There is no fee. There is a wide range of online computerization of the judicial system from "none" to "fairly complete," but there is no statewide court records network.

Other access: Zip files are provided for recent Supreme Court and Court of Appeals releases.

Sexual Offender Registry

Michigan State Police, SOR Unit, 7150 Harris Dr, Lansing, MI 48913; 517-322-5098, 517-322-4957-Fax; 8AM-5PM.

www.mipsor.state.mi.us

Records may be searched at the local law enforcement level. There are over 36,000 registered sex offenders living in Michigan.

Records are available since 1995. It takes up to 24 hours before new records are available for inquiry.

Searching: The agency recommends in person searchers to visit local law enforcement offices. Include the following in your request-name and DOB. Only those offenders who have been convicted of a listed offense on or after October 1, 1995 or convicted prior to that date who were still incarcerated, on parole or probation for a listed offense on October 1, 1995 are listed.

Access by: online.

Fee & Payment: There is no search fee.

Online search: One may search the registry at the website, there is no charge.

Incarceration Records

Michigan Department of Corrections, Central Records Office, PO Box 30003, Lansing, MI 48909 (Courier address: 206 E. Michigan Ave., Lansing, MI 48909); 517-373-0284, 517-373-2628-Fax; 8AM-4:30PM.

www.michigan.gov/corrections

For physical copies of records, contact Freedom of Information Act Coordinator, FOIA Coordinator: Michigan Department of Corrections, 206 E. Michigan Ave, Grandview Plaza, PO Box 30003, Lansing, MI 48909.

Records are available on current and former inmates. It takes 2-3 weeks before new records are available for inquiry. Records are normally destroyed after 7 years from discharge.

Searching: Almost complete computer records go back to 1981. Computer records prior to that year become less complete the further back you search. Include the following in your request-full name or MDOC number. The DOB and SSN are helpful. Location, MDOC number, conviction and sentencing information, physical identifiers, and release dates are provided.

Access by: mail, phone, fax, online.

Fee & Payment: There is a fee for copies; usually these are FOIA requests.

Mail search: Turnaround time: 5 to 7 days. A mail search can also be directed through the Attorney General's office (phone 510-682-2007).

Phone search: Name searches are available by phone.

Fax search: Requests may be faxed.

Online search: The online access through the main website and at www.state.mi.us/mdoc/asp/otis2.html has many search criteria capabilites. There is also a DOC Most Wanted list at www.state.mi.us/mdoc/MostWanted/MostWanted.asp.

Other access: Bulk sales of database information is available.

Corporation, Limited Liability Company, Limited Partnership, Assumed Name

Department of Labor & Economic Growth, Bureau of Commercial Services, PO Box 30054, Lansing, MI 48909-7554 (Courier address: 7150 Harris Dr, Lansing, MI 48909); 517-241-6470, 517-241-0538-Fax; 8AM-noon, 1-5PM.

http://michigan.gov/cis/0,1607,7-154-10557_12901---,00.html

The Harris address above represents the delivery address for shipping. The actual physical location is on 2501 Woodlake Circle in Okemos MI.

Records are available from the first corporation in Michigan. Older records were indexed on cards. The index to records for active entities are maintained on computer. It takes 24 hours or less before new records are available for inquiry.

Searching: Forms, policies, and procedures may be viewed at their website. The fax listed above is for record requests. The fax for copies or certificates is 517-241-0537. Include the following in your request-full name of business, corporation file number. The directors are only listed on the annual report.

Access by: mail, phone, fax, in person, online.

Fee & Payment: There is no search fee. The minimum charge for copies is $6.00 per record and $1.00 per page if over 6 pages. The minimum charge for a certificate is $10.00. Fee payee: State of Michigan. Credit cards are accepted for in person requests only. Personal checks accepted. Credit cards accepted: MasterCard, Visa.

Mail search: Turnaround time: 5 to 7 days. There is no fee unless copies or certificates are needed, then there is a minimum $6.00 fee. No SASE is required. Copies cost $1.00 per page.

Phone search: You can order copies or certificates.

Fax search: Same criteria as mail searches.

In person search: The agency has a public access terminal for viewing records.

Online search: A the website, search by company name or file number for records of domestic corporations, limited liability companies, and limited partnerships and of foreign corporations, and limited partnerships qualified to transact business in the state.

Other access: The database is for sale by contract.

Expedited service: The fee for expedited service is 25% of the invoice.

Trademarks/Servicemarks

Corporation Division, Trademarks & Service Marks, PO Box 30054, Lansing, MI 48909-7554 (Courier address: 7150 Harris Dr, Lansing, MI 48909); 517-241-6470, 8AM-5PM (closed at noon for 1 hr).

www.michigan.gov/cis/0,1607,7-154-10557_21107---,00.html

The Harris address above represents the delivery address for shipping. The actual physical location is on 2501 Woodlake Circle in Okemos MI.

Records are available for current records. The index is available since 1990.

Access by: mail, phone, fax, in person, online.

Fee & Payment: The fee is $5.00 if this agency does the search.

Mail search: They suggest to use the web instead.

Phone search: No fee for telephone request. Search is limited, they will let you know if a wording exists.

Fax search: Requests are accepted by fax.

In person search: No fee for request. There is a public access terminal.

Online search: Free searching is available at www.cis.state.mi.us/bcsc/forms/corp/mark/markcom.pdf. This is a search of a PDF file of their system. It is very tricky to get to on the web.

Uniform Commercial Code, Federal and State Tax Liens

MI Department of State, UCC Section, PO Box 30197, Lansing, MI 48909-7697 (Courier address: 7064 Crowner Dr, Dimondale, MI 48821); 517-322-1144, 517-322-5434-Fax; 8AM-5PM.

www.michigan.gov/sos

To find information at the website on UCC, click on the Services to Businesses tab.

Records are available from 1964. Records are computerized since 1990. It takes 2 to 3 days, only hours if online, before new records are available for inquiry.

Searching: Use search request form UCC-11. The search includes federal and state tax liens on businesses and individuals except collateral specified per UCC Revised Article 9. Include the following in your request-debtor name.

Access by: mail, phone, fax, in person, online.

Fee & Payment: The search fee is $6.00. The copy fee is $2.00. Certification (official seal) is an additional $6.00. Fee payee: State of Michigan. Prepayment required. Personal checks accepted. Credit cards accepted for online access only.

Mail search: Turnaround time: 1 week.

Phone search: Phone searching is available on a prepaid account basis, results are returned by mail.

Fax search: See expedited services.

In person search: Requests are serviced in person, but the agency would prefer that requesters use the online access. See expedited services.

Online search: From the website, click on UCC Online Service. Conducting a Debtor Name Quick Search is free. No login is needed. Documents may be ordered for a fee. Registration and credit card are required.

Other access: A monthly subscription service is available for the bulk purchase of UCC filings on microfilm. The fee is $50 or actual cost, whichever is greater. Call 517-322-1144 for additional information.

Expedited service: Expedited service is available for an additional $25.00 fee. Expedited searches are provided on a prepaid account basis at $25.00 + $6.00 per debtor name. If request is received by 11 AM, search is mailed that same day.

Sales Tax Registrations

Access to Records is Restricted.

Michigan Dept of Treasury, Sales, Use, Withholding Tax Division, Registration, Lansing, MI 48922; 517-636-4660, 517-636-4491-Fax; 8AM-4:45PM.

www.michigan.gov/treasury

The agency will only verify or confirm data, no searches provided.

Birth Certificates

Department of Health, Vital Records Requests, PO Box 30721, Lansing, MI 48909 (Courier address: 3423 N Martin Luther King, Jr Blvd, Lansing, MI 48906); 517-335-8656 (Instructions), 517-335-8666 (Request Unit), 517-321-5884-Fax; 8AM-5PM.

www.michigan.gov/mdch

Any Michigan vital record can be "verified" for a fee of $5.00. Verification is only for names, date and place of filing. Application for records can be downloaded from the website.

Records are available from 1867 on. Records over 100 yrs old are open to the public. It takes 90 to 120 days after birth before new records are available for inquiry. Records are indexed on microfiche, inhouse computer.

Searching: Certified copies of birth records are only issued to the individual to whom the record pertains, the parent(s) named on the record, an heir, legal guardian or legal rep. of an eligible person, or through court order. Include the following in your request-full name, names of parents, mother's maiden name, date of birth, place of birth, relationship to person of record. The signature and relationship to the subject are required items on the request form. Also include copy of photo ID. The following data is not released: sealed records.

Access by: mail, in person, online.

Fee & Payment: The fee for a certified copy is $26.00 which includes 3 years searched. Each additional year searched is another $12.00. Use of credit card is an additional $8.00. An "Authenticated Copy" is available for $29.00. Fee payee: State of Michigan. Prepayment required. Personal checks accepted. Major credit cards accepted online.

Mail search: Turnaround time: 2 to 5 days. No SASE is required.

In person search: Turnaround time up to 3 hours. Counter open 9AM to 4:30PM, same day requests must be submitted by 3PM.

Online search: Records may be ordered from the web site. Step-by-step instructions given, use of credit card required.

Expedited service: Expedited service is available for mail and online searches. Turnaround time: 1 to 2 days. Add credit card fee and express mail fee. Add $10.00 for same day service.

Death Records

Department of Health, Vital Records Requests, PO Box 30721, Lansing, MI 48909 (Courier address: 3423 N Martin Luther King, Jr Blvd, Lansing, MI 48906); 517-335-8656 (Instructions), 517-335-8666 (Request Unit), 517-321-5884-Fax; 8AM-5PM.

www.michigan.gov/mdch

Application for records can be downloaded from the website.

Records are available from 1867 to present. New records are available for inquiry immediately. Records are indexed on microfiche, inhouse computer.

Searching: Records are open to the public. Include the following in your request-full name, date of death, place of death, relationship to person of record. The following data is not released: sealed records.

Access by: mail, in person, online.

Fee & Payment: The fee for a certified copy is $26.00 which includes 3 years searched. Each additional year searched is another $12.00. Use of credit card is an additional $8.00. An "Authenticated Copy" is available for $29.00. Fee payee: State of Michigan. Prepayment required. Personal checks, money orders accepted. Major credit cards accepted online.

Mail search: Turnaround time: 2 to 5 days. No SASE is required.

In person search: Turnaround time up to 3 hours. Counter open 9AM to 4:30PM, same day requests must be submitted by 3PM.

Online search: Records may be ordered from the web. Use of a credit card is required. Records are returned by mail or express delivery. If problems, call 800-255-2414.

Expedited service: Expedited service is available for mail and online searches. Turnaround time: 1 to 2 days. Add credit card fee and express mail fee. Add $10.00 for same day service.

Marriage Certificates

Department of Health, Vital Records Requests, PO Box 30721, Lansing, MI 48909 (Courier address: 3423 N Martin Luther King, Jr Blvd, Lansing, MI 48906); 517-335-8656 (Instructions), 517-335-8666 (Requests Unit), 517-321-5884-Fax; 8AM-5PM.

www.michigan.gov/mdch

Application for records can be downloaded from the website.

Records are available from 1867 to present. New records are available for inquiry immediately. Records are indexed on microfiche, inhouse computer.

Searching: Records are open to the public. There is no bride index for the years 1950 thru 1975. Include the following in your request-names of husband and wife, date of marriage, place or county of marriage.

Access by: mail, in person, online.

Fee & Payment: The fee for a certified copy is $26.00 which includes 3 years searched. Each additional year searched is another $12.00. Use of credit card is an additional $8.00. An "Authenticated Copy" is available for $29.00. Fee payee: State of Michigan. Prepayment required. Personal checks accepted. Major credit cards accepted online.

Mail search: Turnaround time: 2 to 5 days. No SASE is required.

In person search: Turnaround time up to 3 hours. Counter open 9AM to 4:30PM, same day requests must be submitted by 3PM.

Online search: Records can be ordered from the web site, credit card is required.

Expedited service: Expedited service is available for mail and online searches. Turnaround time: 1 to 2 business days. Add credit card fee and express mail fee. Add $10.00 for same day service.

Divorce Records

Department of Health, Vital Records Requests, PO Box 30721, Lansing, MI 48909 (Courier address: 3423 N Martin Luther King, Jr Blvd, Lansing, MI 48906); 517-335-8656 (Instructions), 517-335-8666 (Requests Unit), 517-321-5884-Fax; 8AM-5PM.

www.michigan.gov/mdch

Application for records can be downloaded from the website.

Records are available from 1897 to present. It takes 6-10 months before new records are available for inquiry. Records are indexed on microfiche, inhouse computer.

Searching: Records are not restricted. There are no divorce records for Detroit for 1973 and 1974. There is no "wife index" available prior to 1978. Include the following in your request-names of husband and wife, date of divorce, county where divorce granted.

Access by: mail, in person, online.

Fee & Payment: The fee for a certified copy is $26.00 which includes 3 years searched. Each additional year searched is another $12.00. Use of credit card is an additional $8.00. An "Authenticated Copy" is available for $29.00. Fee payee: State of Michigan. Prepayment required. Personal checks accepted. Major credit cards accepted online.

Mail search: Turnaround time: 2 to 5 days. No SASE is required.

In person search: Turnaround time up to 3 hours. Counter open 9AM to 4:30PM, same day requests must be submitted by 3PM.

Online search: Records can be ordered from the web site, credit card is required.

Expedited service: Expedited service is available for mail and online searches. Turnaround time: 1 to 2 days. Add credit card fee and express mail fee. Add $10.00 for same day service.

Workers' Compensation Records

Department of Labor & Economic Dev., Workers' Compensation Agency, 7150 Harris Dr, Lansing, MI 48909; 888-396-5041, 517-322-1808-Fax; 8AM-5PM.

www.michigan.gov/wca

In person requests are discouraged due to confidentiality of records and records may not be on site. Injured employee may review their own records, but should call first and make arrangements.

Records are available from 1981 on computer and from 1976 to 1981 records on microfilm. You can request by fax, but results are mailed. It takes 1 week before new records are available for inquiry. Records are normally destroyed after 20 years from date of file closure.

Searching: Request must be in writing and cannot be for pre-employment screening. Only litigated cases are released. Include the following in your request-claimant name, Social Security Number, and date of injury.

Access by: mail, fax, online.

Fee & Payment: Fee is $.25 per page plus postage and research labor cost if over 30 pages. Fee payee: Labor & Economic Growth Personal checks accepted. No credit cards accepted.

Mail search: Turnaround time: 1 to 2 weeks. Turnaround time may be longer if records must be searched at archives. No SASE is required.

Fax search: Fax requests accepted.

Online search: Go to the website and follow the links to see if an employer has coverage. The site does not allow searching by employee name.

Driver Records

Department of State, Record Lookup Unit, 7064 Crowner Dr, Lansing, MI 48918; 517-322-1624 (Look-up Unit), 517-322-1181-Fax; 8AM-4:45PM.

www.michigan.gov/sos

Copies of court abstracts of convictions may be purchased at the same address for a fee of $7.00 per copy. Copies of tickets must be obtained from the courts involved.

Records are available for 7 years from conviction date; unless there is an alcohol or controlled substance conviction which will remain on record for 10 years. Accidents are reported on the record only if the driver is cited. It takes 8 days before new records are available for inquiry.

Searching: Casual requesters must submit form BDVR-154, with written consent of subject or show a permissible DPPA purpose, to receive records with personal information. Otherwise, records without personal information are released. Include the following in your request-name and either DOB or DL number.

Access by: mail, phone, fax, in person, online.

Fee & Payment: The fee for obtaining a record is $7.00 per search. If certification is needed, there is an additional $1.00 fee. Fee payee: State of Michigan. The fee may accompany the request for mail-in, or a bill can be sent with the records. There is a full charge for a "no record found." Credit cards are accepted for fax and phone requests only. Personal checks and MasterCard, Visa, Discover accepted.

Mail search: Turnaround time: 15 working days. No SASE is required.

Phone search: Phone requesting is available for pre-approved accounts and government agencies or with a credit card.

Fax search: Established accounts can order by fax, results are returned by mail.

In person search: Turnaround time is 24 hours unless you are the actual driver, then the record is immediately available.

Online search: Online ordering is available on an interactive basis. The system is open 7 days a week. Ordering is by DL or name and DOB. An account must be established and billing is monthly. Access is also available from the Internet. Fee is $7.00 per record. A $25,000 surety bond is required. For more information, call 517-322-6281.

Other access: Magnetic tape inquiry is available. Also, the state offers the license file for bulk purchase. Customized runs are $64.00 per thousand records; complete database can be purchased for $16.00 per thousand. A $10,000 surety bond is required. Call 322-1042.

Vehiclel Ownership Vehicle Identification, Vessel Ownership Vessel Registration

Department of State, Record Lookup Unit, 7064 Crowner Dr, Lansing, MI 48918; 517-322-1624, 517-322-1181-Fax; 8AM-4:45PM.

www.michigan.gov/sos

Records are available for 10 years to present for title information and 4 years to present for registration information. Vessel titles are on computer since 1974. All motorized boats must be registered, if 20 ft or over they must also be titled. It takes 8 days before new records are available for inquiry.

Searching: Requests for vehicle and ownership records must be submitted on Form BDVR154 or in writing with a statement of intended use. Large volume users or fax requesters must be pre-approved. The request form is available online. Normally, a search requires the plate or VIN number. Records to be accessed include mobile homes and boats.

Access by: mail, phone, fax, in person, online.

Fee & Payment: The fee is $7.00 per transaction. Certification is $1.00 per record. Fee payee: State of Michigan. The fee may accompany the request for mail-in, or a bill can be sent with the records. Requests made by fax will be sent a bill with the records. There is a full charge for a "no record found." Personal checks and MasterCard, Visa, Discover accepted.

Mail search: Turnaround time: 15 days. A SASE is requested.

Phone search: Call-in requests are for established, approved accounts only. Records may be mailed or faxed back. Credit cards accepted.

Fax search: Established accounts may order by fax and receive results by fax.

In person search: You can make your request in person, but they will mail back the records in 4 or 5 days. Requests must be in writing or on form mentioned above.

Online search: Online searching via the Internet is single inquiry and requires a VIN or plate number. (no name searches). A $25,000 surety bond is required. Fee is $7.00 per record. For more information, call 517-322-6281.

Other access: Michigan offers bulk retrieval from the VIN and plate database. A written request letter, stating purpose, must be submitted and approved. A $10,000 surety bond is required upon approval. Please call 517-322-1042.

Accident Reports

Department of State Police, Criminal Justice Information Center, 7150 Harris Dr, Lansing, MI 48913; 517-322-5509 (FOIA), 517-322-1150 (Online Questions), 517-323-5350-Fax; 8AM-5PM.

www.michigan.gov/msp/0,1607,7-123--28578--.00.html

Requests must be in writing or through the web page.

Records are available from 1983 to present for state police records. UD10's for all law enforcement agencies in Michigan are available for the current year plus 2 years back, first page only. It takes 3 to 4 weeks before new records are available for inquiry.

Searching: Include the following in your request-full name, date of accident, location of accident.

Access by: mail, fax, in person, online.

Fee & Payment: Accident reports are $10.00 per report and more if extensive searching required. Fee payee: State of Michigan. Prepayment required. Personal checks accepted. Credit cards accepted only at web page.

Mail search: Turnaround time: 10 days. A SASE is requested.

Fax search: Records are available by fax. Turnaround time is 5 days.

In person search: You may request information in person; turnaround time for return is 5 days.

Online search: Records may be requested from the Traffic Crash Purchasing System at https://mdotwas1.mdot.state.mi.us/TCPS/login/welcome.jsp. There is a fee and credit cards are accpted. For specific questions email CrashPurchaseTCPS@michigan.gov.

Voter Registration

Bureau of Elections, Election Liaison Division, 430 W Allegan St, 1st Fl, Lansing, MI 48918; 517-373-2540, 517-241-1591-Fax; 8AM-5PM.

www.michigan.gov/sos/1,1607,7-127-1633---.00.html

In general, the records are open to the public.

Records are available from 08/98 forward. It takes 1 to 2 days before new records are available for inquiry.

Searching: Include the following in your request-name, DOB. The record includes name, address, and the birth year.

Access by: mail, fax.

Fee & Payment: The fee is $6.55 per name. If an identifier (such as a DOB) is not given, each common name is $6.55. Fee payee: State of Michigan Prepayment required.

Mail search: Turnaround time: 2 to 3 days. Records are available by mail.

Fax search: Records are available by fax, if request is prepaid.

Other access: The agency will sell district, statewide or customized subsets of the database on CD. Fees are usually $100 to $170, depending on data requested.

Expedited service: If shipping label and account information provided, the agency will expedite.

GED Certificates

MI Department of Labor & Econ Growth, Adult Education - GED Testing, 201 N Washington Square, 3rd Fl, Lansing, MI 48913; 517-373-1692, 517-335-3461-Fax; 7AM-5PM.

www.michigan.gov/adulteducation

Records are available 3/1969 to present. It takes up to 1 week before new records are available for inquiry.

Searching: To search, include the SSN, DOB and date and location of test. For a copy of a transcript, also include a signed release.

Access by: mail, phone, fax, in person, online.

Fee & Payment: There are no fees.

Mail search: Turnaround time is 1 week; 3 weeks if record is prior to 1979. No SASE is required.

Phone search: You request a verification by leaving a message and fax a signed release. The agency will call back with the information.

Fax search: Same criteria as mail searching.

In person search: The building is also known as the Victor Building.

Online search: Will accept e-mail requests with a scanned signature.

Hunting and Fishing License Information

Access to Records is Restricted.

Dept of Natural Resources, Customer Systems, PO Box 30033, Lansing, MI 48909 (Courier address: 530 W Allegan St, Lansing, MI 48933); 517-241-1919, 517-241-4278-Fax; 8AM-5PM.

www.michigan.gov/dnr

Hunting and fishing license information is no longer released. All FOIA requests are now being denied because it is personal information.

Michigan State Licensing Agencies

For details about the agency responsible for licensing/certifying/registering an item below or in the Agency Quick Finder section, match an item's number with the number of the agency in the *Licensing Agency Information* section.

Michigan Licenses Searchable Online

License	Agency #	URL
Abstractor	#23	https://www.egov.state.mn.us/Commerce/license_lookup.do?action=lookupForm
Acupuncturist	#9	www.docboard.org/mn/df/mndf.htm
Adjuster	#23	https://www.egov.state.mn.us/Commerce/license_lookup.do?action=lookupForm
Alarm & Com. System Contr./Installer	#6	www.electricity.state.mn.us/Elec_lic/index.html
Alcohol/Drug Counselor	#29	www.health.state.mn.us/divs/hpsc/hop/adc/index.html
Ambulance Service/Personnel	#28	www.emsrb.state.mn.us/cert.asp?p=s
Appraiser	#23	https://www.egov.state.mn.us/Commerce/license_lookup.do?action=lookupForm
Architect	#37	www.aelslagid.state.mn.us/roster.html
Athletic Trainer	#9	www.docboard.org/mn/df/mndf.htm
Attorney	#40	www.courts.state.mn.us/mars/default.aspx
Attorney Specialist	#31	http://mail.statebar.gen.mn.us/search/search.asp
Auditor	#39	www.boa.state.mn.us/Licensees/LicenseeList.aspx
Bingo Operation	#35	www.gcb.state.mn.us/
Campground Membership Agent	#23	https://www.egov.state.mn.us/Commerce/license_lookup.do?action=lookupForm
Chiropractor	#4	https://www.hlb.state.mn.us/chi/publicaccess/search.asp
Collection Agency	#23	https://www.egov.state.mn.us/Commerce/license_lookup.do?action=lookupForm
Consumer Credit/Payday Lender	#24	www.state.mn.us/ebranch/commerce/pages/FinService/FSLicensees/sl.html
Contract'r/Remodeler, Residential	#23	https://www.egov.state.mn.us/Commerce/license_lookup.do?action=lookupForm
Cosmetologist / Cosmo School/Shop	#23	https://www.egov.state.mn.us/Commerce/license_lookup.do?action=lookupForm
CPA Firm	#39	www.boa.state.mn.us/Licensees/FirmList.aspx
Credit Union	#24	www.state.mn.us/ebranch/commerce/pages/FinService/FSLicensees/cu.html
Crematory	#27	www.health.state.mn.us/divs/hpsc/mortsci/mortsciselect.cfm
Currency Exchange	#23	https://www.egov.state.mn.us/Commerce/license_lookup.do?action=lookupForm
Debt Collector	#23	https://www.egov.state.mn.us/Commerce/license_lookup.do?action=lookupForm
Debt Prorate Company	#24	www.state.mn.us/ebranch/commerce/pages/FinService/FSLicensees/dp.html
Dentist / Dental Assistant / Hygienist	#5	https://www.hlb.state.mn.us/mnbod/glsuiteweb/homeframe.aspx
Electrician	#6	www.electricity.state.mn.us/Elec_lic/index.html
Emergency Medical Technician	#28	www.emsrb.state.mn.us/cert.asp?p=s
EMS Examiner	#28	www.emsrb.state.mn.us/examiner.asp?p=s
Engineer	#37	www.aelslagid.state.mn.us/roster.html
Esthetician	#23	https://www.egov.state.mn.us/Commerce/license_lookup.do?action=lookupForm
Funeral Director	#27	www.health.state.mn.us/divs/hpsc/mortsci/mortsciselect.cfm
Funeral Establishment	#27	www.health.state.mn.us/divs/hpsc/mortsci/mortsciselect.cfm
Gambling Equipment Dist./Mfg.	#35	www.gcb.state.mn.us/
Gambling, Lawful Organization	#35	www.gcb.state.mn.us/
Geologist	#37	www.aelslagid.state.mn.us/roster.html
Grain Licensing	#21	http://www2.mda.state.mn.us/webapp/lis/default.jsp
Insurance Agency/Agent/Salesman	#23	https://www.egov.state.mn.us/Commerce/license_lookup.do?action=lookupForm
Interior Designer	#37	www.aelslagid.state.mn.us/roster.html
Landscape Architect	#37	www.aelslagid.state.mn.us/roster.html
Lender, Small	#24	www.state.mn.us/ebranch/commerce/pages/FinService/FSLicensees/sl.html
Liquor Store/On-sale Retail	#34	www.dps.state.mn.us/alcgamb/alcenf/liquorlic/liquorlic.html
Livestock Dealer/Market	#21	http://www2.mda.state.mn.us/webapp/lis/default.jsp
Livestock Weigher	#21	http://www2.mda.state.mn.us/webapp/lis/default.jsp
Loan Company	#24	www.state.mn.us/ebranch/commerce/pages/FinService/FSLicensees/rl.html
Lobbyist	#19	www.cfboard.state.mn.us/Lobby.htm
LPA	#39	www.boa.state.mn.us/Licensees/LicenseeList.aspx
Managing General Agent	#23	https://www.egov.state.mn.us/Commerce/license_lookup.do?action=lookupForm
Manicurist	#23	https://www.egov.state.mn.us/Commerce/license_lookup.do?action=lookupForm
Medical Doctor	#9	www.docboard.org/mn/df/mndf.htm
Midwife	#9	www.docboard.org/mn/df/mndf.htm
Money Transmitter	#24	www.commerce.state.mn.us/pages/FinService/FSLicensees/MoneyTransmitList.pdf
Mortgage Originator/Servicer, Resid'l	#24	https://www.egov.state.mn.us/Commerce/license_lookup.do?action=lookupForm
Mortician	#27	www.health.state.mn.us/divs/hpsc/mortsci/mortsciselect.cfm
Motor Vehicle Financer	#24	www.state.mn.us/ebranch/commerce/pages/FinService/FSLicensees/mv.html
Notary Public	#23	https://www.egov.state.mn.us/Commerce/license_lookup.do?action=lookupForm
Nurse-LPN / RN	#10	www.nursingboard.state.mn.us

Occupational Therapist/Assistant #29 ....www.health.state.mn.us/divs/hpsc/hop/otp/licprac.html
Optometrist #11 ....www.optometryboard.state.mn.us/Default.aspx?tabid=799
Pesticide Applicator Company #22................................http://www2.mda.state.mn.us/webapp/lis/pestappdefault.jsp
Pesticide Applicator, Private #22.................................http://www2.mda.state.mn.us/webapp/PrivApp/default.jsp
Physical Therapist #9 ....www.docboard.org/mn/df/mndf.htm
Physician Assistant #9...www.docboard.org/mn/df/mndf.htm
Political Action Committee #19 ....www.cfboard.state.mn.us/campfin/pcfatoz.html
Political Candidate #19 ....www.cfboard.state.mn.us/cand_lists.html
Professional Firm, Medical #9 ....www.docboard.org/mn/df/mndf.htm
Public Accountant Firm #39 ....www.boa.state.mn.us/Licensees/FirmList.aspx
Public Accountant-CPA #39 ....www.boa.state.mn.us/Licensees/LicenseeList.aspx
Real Estate Agent/Broker/Dealer #23.........................https://www.egov.state.mn.us/Commerce/license_lookup.do?action=lookupForm
Re-Insurance Intermediary #23 ....https://www.egov.state.mn.us/Commerce/license_lookup.do?action=lookupForm
Respiratory Care Practitioner #9 ....www.docboard.org/mn/df/mndf.htm
Soil Scientist #37 ....www.aelslagid.state.mn.us/roster.html
Surgeon #9 ....www.docboard.org/mn/df/mndf.htm
Surveyor, Land #37 ....www.aelslagid.state.mn.us/roster.html
Teacher #17..(search site being reconstructed)
Telemedicine #9 ....www.docboard.org/mn/df/mndf.htm
Thrift/Industrial Loan Company #24............................www.state.mn.us/ebranch/commerce/pages/FinService/FSLicensees/il.html
Underg'd Storage Tank Contr./Spvr. #43 ....www.pca.state.mn.us/cleanup/ust.html#certification
Weather Modifier #21 ....http://www2.mda.state.mn.us/webapp/lis/default.jsp

Michigan Licensing Quick Finder

Adoption Service #13 517-373-3513
Aircraft/Aeronautics #24 517-335-9283
Airport Manager #24 517-335-9283
Airport/ Heliport #24......................517-335-9283
Alarm System Service #23 517-241-5645
Ambulance Attendant #10 517-241-0179
Amusement Ride #8 517-241-9265
Animal (Dead) Renderer #2..................800-292-3939
Animal Control Officer #2 800-292-3939
Animal Feed (Commercial) #2..............800-292-3939
Animal Shelter #2 800-292-3939
Appraiser, Real Estate/General/Residential #8
......................517-241-9201
Aquaculture Facility #2 800-292-3939
Architect #8......................517-241-9253
Asbestos Accreditation, Individual #11..517-322-1320
Asbestos License #11 517-322-1320
Assessor #25......................517-373-8320
Athletic-related Event, Boxing, etc. #8 ..517-241-9246
Attorney, State Bar #27 800-968-1442
Auto Dealer/Mechanic/Repair Facility #28
......................517-636-6400
Bank & Trust Company #14 517-373-0220
Barber #8......................517-241-9201
Barber Shop/School #8 517-241-9258
BIDCO #14......................517-373-0220
Bingo Operation, Special or Weekly #1517-335-5756
Boiler Repairer #7......................517-241-9334
Boilermaker (Installer) #7 517-241-9334
Boxing/Wrestling Occupation #8 517-241-9246
Builder, Residential #8......................517-241-9427
Camp, Children/Adult Foster Care #13 .517-335-6124
Carnival #8......................517-241-9265
Casino Interest Personnel/Company#29517-373-2540
Cemetery #8......................517-241-9244
Charitable Gaming (Supplier) #1 517-335-5756
Check Seller #3 517-373-0220
Child Care Institution #26 517-373-8383
Child Day Care #13 517-335-6124
Child Facility, Court Operated #26 517-373-8383
Child Welfare/Child Placing Agency#26 517-373-8383
Chiropractor #15......................517-241-9427
Collection Manager #8......................517-241-9258
Community Planner #8......................517-241-9253
Community Planner (Mfg. Home) #16..517-241-6300
Consumer Financial Service #3 517-373-0220
Contractor, Residential #8..................517-241-9427
Corrections Officer #18......................517-335-1426

Cosmetologist #8......................517-241-9201
Cosmetology Shop/School #8 517-241-9258
Counselor #15......................517-241-9427
Counselor, School Guidance #19 517-373-6505
Credit Card Issuer #3 517-373-0220
Credit Union #14......................517-373-0220
Debt Management Firm #12..............877-999-6442
Dental Hygienist #15......................517-241-9427
Dentist/Dental Assistant #15 517-241-9427
Election Campaign Finance Committee #29
......................517-373-2540
Election Candidate Committee #29......517-373-2540
Electrician (various types) #7 517-241-9320
Elevator Service #7......................517-241-9337
Emergency Medical Personnel #15 517-241-9427
Employment Agency, fee only #8.........517-241-9258
EMT Advanced/Specialist/Instr. #10 ...517-241-0179
Engineer #9......................517-241-9253
Family/Group Day Care #13..............517-335-6124
Fieldperson (Dairy/Farm related) #2 ..800-292-3939
Flight School #24......................517-335-9283
Forester #8 517-241-9288
Foster Care Facility/Adult Camp #13 ...517-335-6124
Foster Care Program #21....................517-335-6124
Foster Care, Child #13 517-335-6124
Foster Family Home #21......................517-335-6124
Funeral Home / Salesperson #8 517-241-9252
Funeral, Prepaid Funeral Contract Regis. #8
......................517-241-9252
Gasoline Seller (Retail) #2 800-292-3939
Grain Dealer #2......................800-292-3939
Grain Trucker #2......................800-292-3939
Health Facilities/Laboratory #15...........517-241-2648
Hearing Aid Dealer #8 517-241-9234
HMO #5......................877-999-6442
Insurance Adjuster #5 877-999-6442
Insurance Agent/Counselor/Solicitor/Admin. #5
......................877-999-6442
Insurance Counselor / Solicitor #5 877-999-6442
Insurance-related Entity #5 877-999-6442
Investment Adviser #12......................877-999-6442
Landscape Architect #8 517-241-8364
Liquor Dist./Whlse./Mfg. #6 517-322-1415
Liquor Finance Division #6..................517-322-1071
Liquor Hearings & Appeals #6 517-322-1390
Liquor License #6......................517-322-1408
Liquor Licensing Director #6................517-322-1408
Livestock Dealer #2......................800-292-3939

Living Care Facility #12......................877-999-6442
Lobbyable Public Official #29.............517-373-2540
Lobbyist/Lobbyist Agent #29 517-373-2540
Long Term Care Company #5 877-999-6442
Lottery Retailer #1 517-335-5756
Mammography Facility #15.................517-241-1989
Manufactured Home Community #16 ..517-241-6300
Manufactured Home Installer/Svcs./Retailer #16
......................517-241-6300
Marriage & Family Therapist #15.........517-241-9427
Mechanical Construction #7................517-241-9325
Medical Doctor #15......................517-241-9427
Medical First Responder #10 517-241-0179
Milk Distributor #2......................800-292-3939
Milk Facility/Hauler #2......................800-292-3939
Millionaire Party/Vegas Night Gaming#1517-335-5756
Mortgage Licensee #3.......................517-373-0220
Mortuary Science #8......................517-241-9252
Motor Vehicle Installment Seller/Financer #3
......................517-373-0220
Notary Public #22......................517-373-2531
Nurse #15......................517-241-9427
Nursery Dealer/Grower #2 800-292-3939
Nurses' Aide #15......................517-241-9427
Nursing Home #15......................517-334-8408
Nursing Home Administrator #15.........517-241-9427
Ocularist #8......................517-241-9258
Optometrist #15......................517-241-9427
Osteopathic Physician #15..................517-241-9427
Paramedic #10......................517-241-0179
Personnel Agency #17......................517-241-5645
Pesticide Applicator Company #2........800-292-3939
Pesticide Applicator/Technician #2......800-292-3939
Pet Shop #2......................800-292-3939
Pharmacist #15......................517-241-9427
Physical Therapist #15......................517-241-9427
Physician Assistant #15......................517-241-9427
Plumber #7......................517-241-9330
Podiatrist #15......................517-241-9427
Political Action Committee #29 517-373-2540
Polygraph Examiner #8......................517-241-9234
Potato Dealer #2......................800-292-3939
Private Detective #23......................517-241-5645
Private Investigator #17......................517-241-5645
Private Security/Security Arrest Authority #23
......................517-241-5645
Psychologist #15......................517-241-9427
Public Accountant-CPA #8..................517-241-9427

Pump Installer #20	517-241-1389
Race Track Employee #4	734-462-2400
Racing Professional #4	734-462-2400
Raffle #1	517-335-5756
Railroad Commission #23	517-241-5645
Real Estate Agent/Broker/Sales #9	517-241-9288
Regulatory Loan Licensee #3	517-373-0220
Riding Stable #2	800-292-3939

Sanitarian #15	517-241-9427
Savings Bank #14	517-373-0220
School Librarian #19	517-373-6505
Securities Agent #12	877-999-6442
Securities Broker/Dealer #12	877-999-6442
Security Agency #17	517-241-5645
Security Alarm Installer #17	517-241-5645
Security Guard, Private #17	517-241-5645

Social Worker #15	517-241-9427
Surety Company #5	877-999-6442
Surplus Line Broker #5	877-999-6442
Surveyor, Professional #9	517-241-9253
Teacher #19	517-373-6505
Third-Party Administrator #5	877-999-6442
Veterinarian/Veterinary Technician #15	517-241-9427
Well Contractor #20	517-241-1389

Michigan Licensing Agency Information

1 Bureau of State Lottery, PO Box 30023 (101 E Hillsdale), Lansing, MI 48909; 517-335-5756, Fax: 517-373-5644. www.michigan.gov/lottery

2 Department of Agriculture, Licensing, Certification & Registration, PO Box 30017 (525 W Alegan, 4th Fl), Lansing, MI 48909; 800-292-3939. www.michigan.gov/mda Email: mdainfo@state.mi.us Note: Food establishment licensing is at the local/county level.

3 Department of Consumer & Industry Services, Consumer Finance Division, PO Box 30220 (611 Ottawa, 2nd Fl), Lansing, MI 48909; 517-373-0220. www.michigan.gov/cis/ Email: ofis-fin-info@michigan.gov Search Database at www.michigan.gov/cis/0,1607,7-154-10555_13251_13257---,00.html

4 Department of Agriculture, Office of Racing Commissioner, 37650 Professional Center Dr, Livonia, MI 48154-1100; 734-462-2400, Fax: 734-462-2429. www.michigan.gov/mda
5 Department of Commerce, Financial and Insurance Services, PO Box 30220 (611 W Ottawa, 2nd Fl), Lansing, MI 48909; 877-999-6442, Fax: 517-335-4978. www.michigan.gov/ofis Email: ofis-ins-info@michigan.gov Search Database at www.michigan.gov/cis/0,1607,7-154-10555_13251_13262---,00.html

6 Department of Labor & Economic Growth, Liquor Control Commission, PO Box 30005 (7150 Harris Dr), Lansing, MI 48909-7505; 517-322-1345, Fax: 517-322-5188. www.michigan.gov/dleg Email: lccinfo@cis.state.mi.us Search Database at http://cis.state.mi.us/bcs_free/default.asp Note: They do sell/provide lists or offer other means of verification.

7 Department of Consumer & Industry Services, Bureau of Construction Codes, PO Box 30254, Lansing, MI 48909; 517-241-9313, Fax: 517-241-9308. www.michigan.gov/bccfs

8 Department of Consumer & Industry Services, Commercial Services/Licensing Division, PO Box 30018, Lansing, MI 48909; 517-241-9288, Fax: 517-241-9280. www.michigan.gov/cis/ Search Database at http://cis.state.mi.us/verify.htm Note: Also, search licensees lists at http://cis.state.mi.us/bcs_free/default.asp.

9 Department of Consumer & Industry Services, Bureau of Commercial Services/Licensing Division, PO Box 30018, Lansing, MI 48909; 517-241-9254, Fax: 517-373-2162. www.michigan.gov/cis/ Search Database at http://cis.state.mi.us/verify.htm

10 Department of Community Health, Division of Emergency Medical Services, 320 S Walnut, Lansing, MI 48909; 517-241-0179, Fax: 517-241-9458. www.michigan.gov/healthlicense

Search Database at www.michigan.gov/cis/0,1607,7-154-10557---,00.html

11 Department of Consumer & Industry Services, Occupational Health Division, PO Box 30671, Lansing, MI 48909-8171; 517-322-1320, Fax: 517-322-1713. www.michigan.gov/cis/0,1607,7-154-11407---,00.html

12 Department of Consumer & Industry Services, Securities Division, OFIS, PO Box 30220 (611 Ottawa, 2nd Fl), Lansing, MI 48909; 517-373-0220, Fax: 517-335-4978. www.michigan.gov/cis/ Email: ofis-sec-info@michigan.gov

13 Department Human Services, Health and Human Services, 7109 W. Saginaw 2nd Floor, Lansing, MI 48909; 517-335-6124, Fax: 517-335-6121. www.michigan.gov/dhs

14 Department of Consumer & Industry Services, Office of Financial & Insurance Services, PO Box 30220 (333 S. Capitol Ave, #A) (611 W Ottawa St), Lansing, MI 48933; 517-373-0220, Fax: 517-335-4978. www.michigan.gov/cis/ Email: ofis-fin-info@michigan.gov Search Database at www.cis.state.mi.us/fis/ind_srch/cht_bank/state_charter_bank_criteria.asp

15 Department of Consumer & Industry Services, Health Services Licensing Division, 611 W Ottawa, 1st Fl, Lansing, MI 48909-8170; 517-335-0918, Fax: 517-373-2179. www.michigan.gov/healthlicense Search Database at www.michigan.gov/healthlicense

16 Department of Consumer & Industry Services, Manufactured Home & Land Development Division, PO Box 30703, Lansing, MI 48909; 517-241-6300, Fax: 517-241-6301. www.michigan.gov/cis Search Database at www.cis.state.mi.us/bcs_free/

17 Bureau of Commercial Services, Commercial Services/Licensing Division/Security, P.O. Box 30018, Lansing, MI 48909; 517-241-9288, Fax: 517-241-9280. www.michigan.gov/cis Search Database at http://cis.state.mi.us/verify.htm

18 Department of Corrections, 206 E Michigan Ave, Lansing, MI 48909; 517-335-1426. www.michigan.gov/corrections

19 Department of Education, Office of Professional Preparation & Certification, Hannah Bldg, 2nd Fl, Lansing, MI 48909; 517-373-3310, Fax: 517-373-0542. www.michigan.gov/mde Search Database at https://mdoe.state.mi.us/teachercert/

20 Department of Environmental Quality, Ground Water Supply Sec., Well Construction, PO Box 30273 (525 W Allegan, 2nd Fl North), Lansing, MI 48909-7773; 517-241-1389, Fax: 517-241-1328. www.michigan.gov/deq

Email: crigieri@state.mi.us Search Database at www.deq.state.mi.us/documents/deq-dwrpd-gws-wcu-Reg-Contractors-By-County.pdf

21 Department of Consumer & Industry Services, Office of Child and Adult Licensing-Div of Child Welfare Licensing/Child Foster Home Licensing, 7109 W Saginaw, 2nd Floor, Lansing, MI 48909-8150; 517-335-6108, Fax: 517-335-6121. www.michigan.gov/cis/ Search Database at www.dleg.state.mi.us/verify.htm

22 Department of State, Office of the Great Seal, 110 W Michigan Ave, Lansing, MI 48918; 517-373-2531, Fax: 517-373-3706. www.michigan.gov/sos Email: www.sos.state.mi.us/greatse/index.html

23 Department of Consumer and Industry Services, Private Security & Investigator Unit, P.O. Box 30018, Lansing, MI 48909; 517-241-5645, Fax: 517-373-2162. www.michigan.gov/commerciallicensing Email: besinfo@michigan.gov Search Database at http://cis.state.mi.us/bcs_free/default.asp

24 Department of Transportation, Bureau of Aeronautics, 2700 E Airport Service Dr, Lansing, MI 48906; 517-335-9283, Fax: 517-321-6422. www.mdot.state.mi.us/aero Email: krashent@state.mi.us

25 Department of Treasury, Treasury Bldg, Lansing, MI 48922; 517-373-3200, Fax: 517-241-3583. www.michigan.gov/treasury/0,1607,7-121-1751_2220---,00.html Search Database at www.michigan.gov/documents/CertificationLevel_3022_7.pdf

26 Department of labor & Economic Growth, Family Independence Agency, 7109 W Saginaw, 2nd Fl, Lansing, MI 48909-8150; 517-373-8383, Fax: 517-335-6121. www.michigan.gov/cis/ Search Database at www.dleg.state.mi.us/brs_cwl/sr_cwl.asp

27 State Bar, 306 Townsend, Lansing, MI 48933; 800-968-1442, Fax: 517-482-6248. www.michbar.org Search Database at www.michbar.org/memberdirectory/

28 Business Licensing Section, Bureau of Automobile Regulation, 208 N Capitol Ave, Lansing, MI 48918; 517-636-6400, Fax: 517-335-2810. www.michigan.gov/sos

29 Bureau of Elections, Campaign Finance & Elections Reporting, PO Box 20126 (430 W Allegan St, Treasury Bldg, 1st Fl, 48913), Lansing, MI 48901-0726; 517-373-2540. http://miboecfr.nicusa.com Search Database at http://miboecfr.nicusa.com Search Database at http://miboecfr.nicusa.com

Michigan Federal Courts

The following list indicates the district and division name for each county in the state. If the bankruptcy court location is different from the district court, then the location of the bankruptcy court appears in parentheses.

County/Court Cross Reference

County	District	Division
Alcona	Eastern	Bay City
Alger	Western	Marquette-Northern (Marquette)
Allegan	Western	Kalamazoo (Grand Rapids)
Alpena	Eastern	Bay City
Antrim	Western	Grand Rapids
Arenac	Eastern	Bay City
Baraga	Western	Marquette-Northern (Marquette)
Barry	Western	Grand Rapids
Bay	Eastern	Bay City
Benzie	Western	Grand Rapids
Berrien	Western	Kalamazoo (Grand Rapids)
Branch	Western	Lansing (Grand Rapids)
Calhoun	Western	Kalamazoo (Grand Rapids)
Cass	Western	Kalamazoo (Grand Rapids)
Charlevoix	Western	Grand Rapids
Cheboygan	Eastern	Bay City
Chippewa	Western	Marquette-Northern (Marquette)
Clare	Eastern	Bay City
Clinton	Western	Lansing (Grand Rapids)
Crawford	Eastern	Bay City
Delta	Western	Marquette-Northern (Marquette)
Dickinson	Western	Marquette-Northern (Marquette)
Eaton	Western	Lansing (Grand Rapids)
Emmet	Western	Grand Rapids
Genesee	Eastern	Flint
Gladwin	Eastern	Bay City
Gogebic	Western	Marquette-Northern (Marquette)
Grand Traverse	Western	Grand Rapids
Gratiot	Eastern	Bay City
Hillsdale	Western	Lansing (Grand Rapids)
Houghton	Western	Marquette-Northern (Marquette)
Huron	Eastern	Bay City
Ingham	Western	Lansing (Grand Rapids)
Ionia	Western	Grand Rapids
Iosco	Eastern	Bay City
Iron	Western	Marquette-Northern (Marquette)
Isabella	Eastern	Bay City
Jackson	Eastern	Ann Arbor (Detroit)
Kalamazoo	Western	Kalamazoo (Grand Rapids)
Kalkaska	Western	Grand Rapids
Kent	Western	Grand Rapids
Keweenaw	Western	Marquette-Northern (Marquette)
Lake	Western	Grand Rapids
Lapeer	Eastern	Flint
Leelanau	Western	Grand Rapids
Lenawee	Eastern	Ann Arbor (Detroit)
Livingston	Eastern	Flint
Luce	Western	Marquette-Northern (Marquette)
Mackinac	Western	Marquette-Northern (Marquette)
Macomb	Eastern	Detroit
Manistee	Western	Grand Rapids
Marquette	Western	Marquette-Northern (Marquette)
Mason	Western	Grand Rapids
Mecosta	Western	Grand Rapids
Menominee	Western	Marquette-Northern (Marquette)
Midland	Eastern	Bay City
Missaukee	Western	Grand Rapids
Monroe	Eastern	Ann Arbor (Detroit)
Montcalm	Western	Grand Rapids
Montmorency	Eastern	Bay City
Muskegon	Western	Grand Rapids
Newaygo	Western	Grand Rapids
Oakland	Eastern	Ann Arbor (Detroit)
Oceana	Western	Grand Rapids
Ogemaw	Eastern	Bay City
Ontonagon	Western	Marquette-Northern (Marquette)
Osceola	Western	Grand Rapids
Oscoda	Eastern	Bay City
Otsego	Eastern	Bay City
Ottawa	Western	Grand Rapids
Presque Isle	Eastern	Bay City
Roscommon	Eastern	Bay City
Saginaw	Eastern	Bay City
Sanilac	Eastern	Detroit
Schoolcraft	Western	Marquette-Northern (Marquette)
Shiawassee	Eastern	Flint
St. Clair	Eastern	Detroit
St. Joseph	Western	Kalamazoo (Grand Rapids)
Tuscola	Eastern	Bay City
Van Buren	Western	Kalamazoo (Grand Rapids)
Washtenaw	Eastern	Ann Arbor (Detroit)
Wayne	Eastern	Detroit
Wexford	Western	Grand Rapids

Standards for Federal Courts: Search fee is $26.00 per item (one party name or case number). Copy fee is $.50 per page. Certification fee is $9.00 per document, double for exemplification, if available. All fees standard unless noted in profile. Mail Search: always enclose a stamped self addressed envelope unless otherwise noted. Most courts accept fax requests or will suggest a copying/search vendor. Before releasing records, all courts require prepayment, unless noted.

Open records are located at the court unless otherwise noted. District courts index by defendant and plaintiff as well as by case number. Bankruptcy courts usually index by debtor and case number. While most courts now have their indexes on computer, many may still maintain index card files as well.

Courts offering internet access via CM-ECF or older RACER, PACER, or Web-PACER systems charge $.08 per page fee unless noted as free. Where PACER is available, the universal sign-up number is 800-676-6856. Find PACER and the US Party/Case Index at http://pacer.psc.uscourts.gov.

US District Court

Eastern District of Michigan

Ann Arbor Division Court Clerk, PO Box 8199, Ann Arbor, MI 48107 (courier address: 200 E Liberty St, Rm 120, Ann Arbor, MI 48104), 734-741-2380, Fax-734-741-2065. Hours-8:30AM-5PM. www.mied.uscourts.gov

Counties: Jackson, Lenawee, Monroe, Oakland, Washtenaw. Many Oakland cases are heard in the Detroit Division. Civil cases in these counties are assigned randomly to Detroit, Flint, Ann Arbor, or Port Huron Divisions. Case files maintained where case is assigned. However, all cases can be accessed electronically in the District-wide index.

Searches & Indexing: Computer index maintained. New cases in the index immediately after filing date.

Fee & Payment: Pay by money order, cashier's or personal check. Payee: Clerk, US District Court. Prepayment required.

Phone Search: Only docket information is available by phone. **Mail Search:** search usually completed- 3 days. Include SASE for return.

In Person Search: Fee charged if court performs your search. Self-serve copier - $.10 per page.

E-Services: ECF replaces PACER whose records did go back to 1988. New records online after 1 day. ECF at https://ecf.mied.uscourts.gov **Opinions Online:** www.mied.uscourts.gov/_opinions/opinion.htm.

Bay City Division Court Clerk, 1000 Washington Ave Rm 304, PO Box 913, Bay City, MI 48707 (also use mail address for courier delivery), 989-894-8800, Fax-989-894-8804. Hours- 8:30AM-5PM. www.mied.uscourts.gov

Counties: Alcona, Alpena, Arenac, Bay, Cheboygan, Clare, Crawford, Gladwin, Gratiot, Huron, Iosco, Isabella, Midland, Montmorency, Ogemaw, Oscoda, Otsego, Presque Isle, Roscommon, Saginaw, Tuscola.

Searches & Indexing: Results do not include SSN or DOB. Computer, microfiche and card indexes maintained. New cases in the index 24 hours after filing date. District-wide searches available back to 1985.

Fee & Payment: Pay by money order, cashier's or personal check. Payee: Clerk, US District Court. Prepayment required.

Phone Search: Only docket information is available by phone. **Mail Search:** search usually completed- 1-2 days. Include SASE for return.

In Person Search: Fee charged if court performs your search. No self-serve copier available.

E-Services: ECF replaces PACER whose records did go back to 1988. New records online after 1 day. ECF at https://ecf.mied.uscourts.gov **Opinions Online:** www.mied.uscourts.gov/_opinions/opinion.htm.

Detroit Division Court Clerk, 231 W Lafayette Blvd, Detroit, MI 48226 (also use mail address for courier delivery), 313-234-5005, records rm- 313-234-5010, Fax-313-234-5393. Hours- 8:30AM-5PM. www.mied.uscourts.gov

Counties: Macomb, St. Clair, Sanilac, Wayne (and Oakland County). Civil cases for these counties are assigned randomly among the Flint, Ann Arbor and Detroit divisions. Port Huron cases may also be assigned here. Case files are kept where the case is assigned. However, all cases can be accessed electronically in the District index.

Searches & Indexing: Results do not include SSN or DOB. Both computer and card indexes maintained; computer goes back to 1990. New cases in the index 2 days after filing date.

Fee & Payment: Pay by Visa/MC (in person only), money order, cashier's or personal check. Payee: Clerk, District Court. Prepayment required for all copying. Make checks out for exact amount.

Phone Search: Only docket information on active cases is released via phone. **Mail Search:** search usually completed- 3 days. SASE not required.

In Person Search: Fee charged if court performs your search. No self-serve copier available.

E-Services: ECF replaces PACER whose records did go back to 1988. New records online after 1 day. ECF at https://ecf.mied.uscourts.gov **Opinions Online:** www.mied.uscourts.gov/_opinions/opinion.htm.

Flint Division Court Clerk, Clerk, Federal Bldg, Rm 140, 600 Church St, Flint, MI 48502 (also use mail address for courier delivery), 810-341-7840. 8:30AM-5PM. www.mied.uscourts.gov

Counties: Genesee, Lapeer, Livingston, Shiawassee. This office handles all criminal cases for these counties. Civil cases are assigned randomly among the Detroit, Ann Arbor and Flint divisions. However, all cases can be accessed electronically in the District index.

Searches & Indexing: As of 7/1995, cases from Genesee, Lapeer, Livingston, or Shiawassee counties may also be assigned to Detroit, Ann Arbor or Port Huron. Case files maintained where case is handled. Results do not include SSN or DOB. Both computer, microfiche and card indexes maintained; computer goes back to 1996. Only old Flint cases records are indexed on cards. New cases in index 2-5 days after filing date. District-wide searches available here; record dates vary.

Fee & Payment: Pay by money order, cashier's or personal check. Payee: Clerk, US District Court. Prepayment required.

Phone Search: Only general information released via phone. Only a reasonable number of requests per call. All docket data will not be released.

Mail Search: search usually completed- within 2 days. SASE not required.

In Person Search: permitted. A reasonable number of free searches can be requested in person. Search microfiched cases in person free. Court personnel can also conduct free searches for cases on computer. No self-serve copier available.

E-Services: ECF replaces PACER whose records did go back to 1988. New records online after 1 day. ECF at https://ecf.mied.uscourts.gov **Opinions Online:** www.mied.uscourts.gov/_opinions/opinion.htm.

US Bankruptcy Court

Eastern District of Michigan

Bay City Division Court Clerk, PO Box 911, Bay City, MI 48707 (courier address: 111 1st St, Bay City, MI 48708), 989-894-8840. Hours-8:30AM-4PM. www.mieb.uscourts.gov

Counties: Alcona, Alpena, Arenac, Bay, Cheboygan, Clare, Crawford, Gladwin, Gratiot, Huron, Iosco, Isabella, Midland, Montmorency, Ogemaw, Oscoda, Otsego, Presque Isle, Roscommon, Saginaw, Tuscola.

Searches & Indexing: Results include SSN. Both computer and card indexes maintained; computer back to 8/2005. New cases in the index immediately after filing date. District-wide searches available back to 10/1992.

Fee & Payment: Pay by money order, cashier's or personal check. Payee: US Bankruptcy Court. Prepayment required.

Phone Search: Use VCIS to obtain docket information. Voice Case Information Service available, call 877-422-3066 or 313-961-4940.

Mail Search: search usually completed- 2 days. Include SASE for return. **In Person Search:** permitted. No self-serve copier available.

E-Services: ECF replaces PACER whose records did go back to 10/1992. New records online after 1 day. ECF at https://ecf.mieb.uscourts.gov **Opinions Online:** www.mieb.uscourts.gov/courtOpinions/index.html. **Other Online Access:** PDF versions of daily dockets free at www.mieb.uscourts.gov/courtDocket/index.html.

Detroit Division Clerk of Court, 21st Fl, 211 W Fort St, Detroit, MI 48226 (also use mail address for courier delivery), 313-234-0065, records rm- 313-234-0051. Hours- 8:30AM-4:00PM. www.mieb.uscourts.gov

Counties: Jackson, Lenawee, Macomb, Monroe, Oakland, Sanilac, St. Clair, Washtenaw, Wayne.

Searches & Indexing: Computer index maintained. New cases in the index immediately after filing date. District-wide searches available back to 10/1992.

Fee & Payment: Pay by money order, cashier check, business check. No personal checks. Payee: US Bankruptcy Court. Prepayment required.

Phone Search: Only case number, case name, filing date, chapter, 341 date, attorney and trustee names released. Voice Case Information Service available, call 877-422-3066 or 313-961-4940.

Mail Search: search usually completed- 2 days. Include SASE for return. **In Person Search:** Fee charged if court performs your search. No self-serve copier available.

E-Services: ECF replaces PACER whose records did go back to 10/1992. New records online after 1 day. ECF at https://ecf.mieb.uscourts.gov **Opinions Online:** www.mieb.uscourts.gov/courtOpinions/index.html. **Other Online Access:** PDF versions of daily dockets free at www.mieb.uscourts.gov/courtDocket/index.html.

Flint Division Court Clerk, 226 W 2nd St, Flint, MI 48502 (also use mail address for courier delivery), 810-235-4126. Hours- 9AM-4PM. www.mieb.uscourts.gov

Counties: Genesee, Lapeer, Livingston, Shiawassee. **Searches & Indexing:** Results include last 4 SSN digits. Both computer and card indexes maintained. New cases in the index immediately after filing date. District-wide searches available back to 10/1992.

Fee & Payment: Pay by money order, cashier check, business check. No personal checks. Payee: Clerk, Bankruptcy Court. Prepayment required.

Phone Search: Only case number, case name, filing date, chapter, 341 date, attorney and trustee names released. Voice Case Information Service available, call 877-422-3066 or 313-961-4940.

Mail Search: search usually completed- 2 days. Include SASE for return.

In Person Search: Fee charged if court performs your search. No self-serve copier available.

E-Services: ECF replaces PACER whose records did go back to 10/1992. New records online after 1 day. ECF at https://ecf.mieb.uscourts.gov **Opinions Online:** www.mieb.uscourts.gov/courtOpinions/index.html. **Other Online Access:** PDF versions of daily dockets free at www.mieb.uscourts.gov/courtDocket/index.html.

US District Court

Western District of Michigan

Grand Rapids Division Court Clerk, PO Box 3310, Grand Rapids, MI 49501 (courier address: Gerald Ford Federal Building, 110 Michigan St NW, Rm 399, Grand Rapids, MI 49503), 616-456-2381. Hours- 8:30AM-4:30PM. www.miwd.uscourts.gov

Counties: Antrim, Barry, Benzie, Charlevoix, Emmet, Grand Traverse, Ionia, Kalkaska, Kent, Lake, Leelanau, Manistee, Mason, Mecosta, Missaukee, Montcalm, Muskegon, Newaygo, Oceana, Osceola, Ottawa, Wexford. The Lansing and Kalamazoo Divisions also handle cases from these counties. Cases in these counties may also be tried in the Kalamazoo or Lansing courts.

Searches & Indexing: Results do not include SSN or DOB. Both computer and card indexes maintained; computer goes back to 1988. New cases in the index 24-48 hours after filing date. Records purged never.

Fee & Payment: Pay by Visa/MC, money order, cashier's or personal check. Payee: Clerk, US District Court. Will bill businesses and law firms for search and copy fees only, otherwise prepayment required.

Phone Search: Only docket information is available by phone. **Mail Search:** search usually completed- 1-2 days.

In Person Search: Fee charged if court performs your search. No self-serve copier available.

E-Services: ECF replaces PACER whose records did go back to 9/1989. ECF at https://ecf.miwd.uscourts.gov

Kalamazoo Division Court Clerk, 410 W Michigan, Rm B-35, Kalamazoo, MI 49007 (also use mail address for courier delivery), 269-337-5706, Fax-269-337-5703. Hours- 8:30AM-4:30PM. www.miwd.uscourts.gov

Counties: Allegan, Berrien, Calhoun, Cass, Kalamazoo, St. Joseph, Van Buren. Also handles cases from counties in the Grand Rapids Division.

Searches & Indexing: Results do not include SSN or DOB. Both computer and card indexes maintained; computer goes back to 1992. New cases in the index 24-48 hours after filing date. Records purged never.

Fee & Payment: Pay by Visa/MC, money order, cashier's or personal check. Payee: Clerk, US District Court. Prepayment required, except for law firms.

Phone Search: Only docket information is available by phone. **Mail Search:** search usually completed- 1-2 days. Include SASE for return.

In Person Search: Fee charged if court performs your search. No self-serve copier available.

E-Services: ECF replaces PACER whose records did go back to 9/1989. ECF at https://ecf.miwd.uscourts.gov

Lansing Division Court Clerk, 113 Federal Building, 315 W Allegan, Rm 113, Lansing, MI 48933 (also use mail address for courier delivery), 517-377-1559. Hours- 8:30AM-4:30PM. www.miwd.uscourts.gov

Counties: Branch, Clinton, Eaton, Hillsdale, Ingham. Also handle cases from the counties in the Grand Rapids Division.

Searches & Indexing: Results do not include SSN or DOB. Both computer and card indexes maintained. New cases in the index 24-48 hours after filing date. Records purged never.

Fee & Payment: Pay by Visa/MC, money order, cashier's or personal check. Payee: Clerk, US District Court. Prepayment required except from businesses and law firms.

Phone Search: Only docket information is available by phone. **Mail Search:** search usually completed- 1-2 days. Include SASE for return.

In Person Search: Fee charged if court performs your search. No self-serve copier available.

E-Services: ECF replaces PACER whose records did go back to 9/1989. ECF at https://ecf.miwd.uscourts.gov

Marquette-Northern Division Court Clerk, PO Box 698, Marquette, MI 49855 (courier address: 202 W Washington, Rm 229, Marquette, MI 49855), 906-226-2117, Fax-906-226-6735. Hours- 8AM-4:30PM. www.miwd.uscourts.gov

Counties: Alger, Baraga, Chippewa, Delta, Dickinson, Gogebic, Houghton, Iron, Keweenaw, Luce, Mackinac, Marquette, Menominee, Ontonagon, Schoolcraft.

Searches & Indexing: Results do not include SSN or DOB. Both computer and card indexes maintained; computer goes back to 1999. New cases in the index 24-48 hours after filing date. Records purged never.

Fee & Payment: Pay by Visa/MC, money order, cashier's or personal check. Payee: Clerk, US District Court. Prepayment required except from businesses and law firms.

Phone Search: Use a credit card for telephone searching; copies will be mailed.

Mail Search: search usually completed- 1-2 days. SASE not required.

In Person Search: Fee charged if court performs your search. No self-serve copier available.

E-Services: ECF replaces PACER whose records did go back to 9/1989. ECF at https://ecf.miwd.uscourts.gov

US Bankruptcy Court

Western District of Michigan

Grand Rapids Division Court Clerk, PO Box 3310, Grand Rapids, MI 49501 (courier address: 1 Division NW, Grand Rapids, MI 49503), 616-456-2693, Fax-616-456-2919. Hours- 8AM-4PM. www.miwb.uscourts.gov

Counties: Allegan, Antrim, Barry, Benzie, Berrien, Branch, Calhoun, Cass, Charlevoix, Clinton, Eaton, Emmet, Grand Traverse, Hillsdale, Ingham, Ionia, Kalamazoo, Kalkaska, Kent, Lake, Leelanau, Manistee, Mason, Mecosta, Missaukee, Montcalm, Muskegon, Newaygo, Oceana, Osceola, Ottawa, St. Joseph, Van Buren, Wexford. Marquette cases also available electronically on the Grand Rapids Division public access terminal.

Searches & Indexing: Cases indexed by debtor, creditors, and case number. Results include last 4 SSN digits. Computer index back to 1990 maintained. New cases in the index immediately after filing date. Records purged 6 months after case closed.

Fee & Payment: Pay by Visa/MC, money order, cashier's or personal check. No debtor's checks accepted. Payee: US Bankruptcy Court. Will fax back results.

Phone Search: Court will only verify by phone whether a case was filed. Voice Case Information Service available, call VCIS at 866-729-9098 or 616-456-2075.

Mail Search: search usually completed- 1 week. Include SASE for return.

In Person Search: Fee charged if court performs your search. No self-serve copier available.

E-Services: ECF replaces PACER whose records did go back to 9/1989. New records online after 1 day. ECF at https://ecf.miwb.uscourts.gov **Opinions Online:** www.miwb.uscourts.gov/content/opinions/query_all.asp. Opinions can also be mailed to annual subscribers, $30.00 per year. **Other Online Access:** Active motional calendars free- www.miwb.uscourts.gov/content/calendars/.

Marquette Division Court Clerk, PO Box 909, Marquette, MI 49855 (courier address: 202 W Washington, Rm 314, Marquette, MI 49855), 906-226-2117, Fax-906-226-7388. Hours- 8AM-4PM. www.miwb.uscourts.gov

Counties: Alger, Baraga, Chippewa, Delta, Dickinson, Gogebic, Houghton, Iron, Keweenaw, Luce, Mackinac, Marquette, Menominee, Ontonagon, Schoolcraft. Marquette cases are also available electronically on the Grand Rapids Division public access terminal, but Grand Rapids cases are not available on Marquette's pub access computer as yet.

Searches & Indexing: Results include SSN. Computer index back to 1990 maintained. New cases in the index immediately after filing date. Records purged 6 months after case closed.

Fee & Payment: Pay by Visa/MC, money order, cashier's or personal check. No debtor's checks accepted. Payee: US Bankruptcy Court. Will fax documents $.50 per page.

Phone Search: Court will only verify by phone if a case is filed. Voice Case Information Service available, call VCIS at 616-456-2075.

Mail Search: search usually completed- 1 day. For the fee, the following items are sent: case number, list of creditors, first scheduled meeting of creditors. SASE not required.

In Person Search: Fee charged if court performs your search. No self-serve copier available.

E-Services: ECF replaces PACER whose records did go back to 9/1989. New records online after 1 day. ECF at https://ecf.miwb.uscourts.gov **Opinions Online:** www.miwb.uscourts.gov/content/opinions/query_all.asp. **Other Online Access:** Active motional calendars free at www.miwb.uscourts.gov/content/calendars/.

Michigan County Courts

Court	Jurisdiction	No. of Courts	How Organized
Circuit Courts*	General	83	57 Circuits
District Courts*	Limited	104	98 Districts
Municipal Courts	Municipal	5	
Probate Courts*	Probate	78	83 Counties

* Profiled in this Sourcebook.

Court	CIVIL								
	Tort	Contract	Real Estate	Min. Claim	Max. Claim	Small Claims	Estate	Eviction	Domestic Relations
Circuit Courts*	X	X	X	$25,000	No Max				X
District Courts*	X	X	X	$0	$25,000	$3000		X	
Municipal Courts	X	X	X	$0	$3000				
Probate Courts*							X		

Court	CRIMINAL				
	Felony	Misdemeanor	DWI/DUI	Preliminary Hearing	Juvenile
Circuit Courts*	X				X
District Courts*		X	X	X	
Municipal Courts		X	X	X	
Probate Courts*					

ADMINISTRATION

State Court Administrator, 309 N. Washington Sq, PO Box 30048, Lansing, MI, 48909; 517-373-0130, Fax: 517-373-9831. http://courts.michigan.gov/scao/

COURT STRUCTURE

The Circuit Court is the court of general jurisdiction. District Courts and Municipal Courts have jurisdiction over certain minor felonies and handle all preliminary hearings.

There is a Court of Claims in Lansing that is a function of the 30th Circuit Court with jurisdiction over claims against the state of Michigan. A Recorder's Court in Detroit was abolished as of October 1, 1997.

As of January 1, 1998, the Family Division of the Circuit Court was created. Domestic relations actions and juvenile cases, including criminal and abuse/neglect, formerly adjudicated in the Probate Court, were transferred to the Family Division of the Circuit Court. Mental health and estate cases continue to be handled by the Probate Courts.

Several counties (Barry, Berrien, Iron, Isabella, Lake, and Washtenaw) and the 46th Circuit Court are participating in a "Demonstration" pilot project designed to streamline court services and consolidate case management. These courts may refer to themselves as County Trial Courts.

ONLINE ACCESS

There is a wide range of online computerization of the judicial system from "none" to "fairly complete," but there is no statewide court records network. Some Michigan courts provide public access terminals in clerk's offices, and some courts are developing off-site electronic filing and searching capability. A few offer remote online to the public. The Criminal Justice Information Center (CJIC), the repository for MI criminal record info, offers online access. Results are available in seconds; fee is $10.00 per name. Go to www.michigan.gov/ichat or call 517-322-5546. Subscribe to email updates of appellate opinions at http://courtofappeals.mijud.net/resources/subscribe.htm. There is no fee.

ADDITIONAL INFORMATION

Court records are considered public except for specific categories: controlled substances, spousal abuse, Holmes youthful trainee, parental kidnapping, set aside convictions and probation, and sealed records. Courts will, however, affirm that cases exist and provide case numbers. Some courts will not perform criminal searches. Rather, they refer requests to the State Police. Note that costs, search requirements, and procedures vary widely because each jurisdiction may create its own administrative orders.

Alcona County

23rd Circuit Court PO Box 308, Harrisville, MI 48740; phone: 989-724-9410; fax: 989-724-9419; hours 8:30AM-N, 1-4:30PM (EST). *Felony, Civil Actions Over $25,000.*
Civil Records: Access: Phone, mail, in person. Only the court performs in person searches. No search fee. Court makes copy: $1.00 per page. Required to search: name, years to search. Civil cases indexed by defendant, plaintiff; on computer since 1990, pleading headings in books since 1869. Mail turnaround time 1-2 days.
Criminal Records: Access: Phone, mail, in person. Only the court performs in person searches. Search fee: $5.00 per name. Court makes copy: $1.00 per page. Required to search: name, years to search, DOB. Criminal records on computer since 1990, pleading headings in books since 1869. Mail turnaround time 1-2 days.
General Information: No public access terminal. No suppressed, juvenile, sex offenders, mental health, or adoption records released. Will fax documents for no fee if search fee is paid. Certification fee: $10.00 plus $1.00 per page copy fee after first page. Payee: Alcona County Clerk. Personal checks accepted. Prepayment and SASE required.

81st District Court PO Box 385, Harrisville, MI 48740; phone: 989-724-9500; hours 8:30AM-4:30PM (EST). *Misdemeanor, Civil Actions Under $25,000, Eviction, Small Claims.*
Civil Records: Access: Phone, fax, mail, in person. Both court and visitors may perform in person searches. Search fee: $5.00. Court makes copy: $1.00 per page. Required to search: name, years to search. Civil cases indexed by defendant, plaintiff; on books since 1980; on computer back to 1997. Mail turnaround time 1 week.
Criminal Records: Access: Fax, mail, in person. Both court and visitors may perform in person searches. Search fee: $5.00. Court makes copy: $1.00 per page. Required to search: name, years to search, DOB; also helpful: SSN. Criminal records on books since 1980; on computer back to 1997. Mail turnaround time 1 week.
General Information: No public access terminal. No suppressed, juvenile, sex offenders, mental health, or adoption records released. Fee to fax documents is $10.00 1st page, $1.00 each add'l. Certification fee: $15.00. Payee: 81st District Court. Personal checks accepted. Prepayment and SASE required.

Probate Court PO Box 328, 106 Fifth St, Harrisville, MI 48740; phone: 989-724-9490; fax: 989-724-9499; hours 8:30AM-4:30PM (EST). *Probate.*

Alger County

11th Circuit Court 101 Court St, PO Box 538, Munising, MI 49862; phone: 906-387-2076; criminal/civil fax: 906-387-2156; hours 8AM-4PM (EST). *Felony, Civil Actions Over $25,000.*
Civil Records: Access: Phone, mail, in person. Both court and visitors may perform in person searches. No search fee. Court makes copy: $1.00 per page. Required to search: name, years to search. Civil cases indexed by defendant, plaintiff; on index books back to 1884; on computer back to 2000. Mail turnaround time 1 week.
Criminal Records: Access: Phone, mail, in person. Both court and visitors may perform in person searches. No search fee. Court makes copy: $1.00 per page. Required to search: name, years to search. Criminal records on index books back to 1884; on computer back to 2000. Mail turnaround time 1 week.
General Information: No public access terminal. No juvenile, sex offenders, mental health, or adoption records released. Will fax documents to toll-free number. Certification fee: $10.00 per document. Payee: Alger County Clerk. Personal checks accepted. Prepayment required.

93rd District Court PO Box 186, Munising, MI 49862; phone: 906-387-3879; criminal/civil fax: 906-387-2688; hours 8AM-4PM (EST). *Misdemeanor, Civil Actions Under $25,000, Eviction, Small Claims.*
Civil Records: Access: Mail, in person. Only the court performs in person searches. Court makes copy: $.25 per page. Required to search: name, years to search. Civil cases indexed by defendant, plaintiff; on index books from 1993; on computer back to 2000. Mail turnaround time 5-7 days.
Criminal Records: Access: Fax, mail, in person. Only the court performs in person searches. Search fee: $10.00 per name. Court makes copy: $.25 per page. Required to search: name, years to search, DOB. Criminal records on index books from 1994; on computer back to 2000. Mail turnaround time 5-7 days.
General Information: No public access terminal. No suppressed records released. Will fax documents to local or toll free line. Certification fee: $10.00 per document for any add'l pages. Payee: District Court. Business checks accepted. Prepayment and SASE required.

Probate Court 101 Court St, Munising, MI 49862; phone: 906-387-2080; fax: 906-387-4134; hours 8AM-N, 1-4PM (EST). *Probate.*

Allegan County

48th Circuit Court 113 Chestnut St, Allegan, MI 49010; phone: 269-673-0300; probate phone: 269-673-0250; criminal/civil fax: 269-673-0298; hours 8AM-5PM (EST). *Felony, Civil Actions Over $25,000.*
Civil Records: Access: Mail, fax, in person. Only the court performs in person searches. Search fee: $5.00 per name. Court makes copy: $1.00 per page. Required to search: name, years to search. Civil cases indexed by defendant, plaintiff; on computer since 1985. Mail turnaround time 1-7 days.
Criminal Records: Access: Mail, fax, in person. Only the court performs in person searches. Search fee: $5.00 per name. Court makes copy: $1.00 per page. Required to search: name, years to search, DOB; also helpful: SSN. Criminal records on computer since 1985. Mail turnaround time 1-7 days.
General Information: No public access terminal. No suppressed, juvenile, sex offenders, mental health, or adoption records released. Will fax documents to local or toll free line. Certification fee: $10.00 per page. Payee: Allegan County Clerk. Personal checks accepted. Visa, MC accepted for fax filings only. Prepayment and SASE required.

57th District Court 113 Chestnut St, Allegan, MI 49010; phone: 269-673-0400; criminal phone: 269-673-0400; civil phone: 269-673-0355; fax: 269-673-0490; hours 8:30AM-4:30PM (EST). *Misdemeanor, Civil Actions Under $25,000, Eviction, Small Claims.*
Civil Records: Access: Mail, in person. Both court and visitors may perform in person searches. No search fee. Court makes copy: $1.00 per page. Required to search: name, years to search. Civil cases indexed by defendant, plaintiff; on index books. Mail turnaround time 1 week.
Criminal Records: Access: Mail, in person. Both court and visitors may perform in person searches. No search fee. Court makes copy: $1.00 per page. Required to search: name, years to search, DOB. Criminal records on index books. Mail turnaround time 1 week.
General Information: Public use terminal available. No non-public records released. Will fax documents to local or toll free line. Certification fee: $10.00. Payee: 57th District Court. Prepayment required.

Probate Court 2243 33rd St, Allegan, MI 49010; phone: 269-673-0250; fax: 269-673-5875; hours 8AM-5PM (EST). *Probate.*

Alpena County

26th Circuit Court 720 W Chisholm #2, Alpena, MI 49707; phone: 989-354-9520; fax: 989-354-9643; hours 8:30AM-4:30PM (EST). *Felony, Civil Actions Over $25,000.*
Civil Records: Access: Fax, mail, in person. Only the court performs in person searches. Search fee: $5.00 per name. Court makes copy: $2.00 per page. Required to search: name, years to search. Civil cases indexed by defendant, plaintiff; on computer since 1988, prior on docket books. Mail turnaround time 3 days or less.
Criminal Records: Access: Fax, mail, in person. Only the court performs in person searches. Search fee: $5.00 per name. Court makes copy: $2.00 per page. Required to search: name, years to search. Criminal records on computer since 1988; prior on docket books. Mail turnaround time 2-3 days.
General Information: No public access terminal. No suppressed, juvenile, sex offenders, mental health, or adoption records released. Will fax documents for $5.00 per document plus $1.00 per page. Certification fee: $10.00. Payee: County Clerk. Personal checks accepted. Prepayment and SASE required.

88th District Court 719 W Chisholm #3, Alpena, MI 49707; phone: 989-354-9678; criminal phone: 989-354-9686; civil phone: 989-354-9685; criminal/civil fax: 989-354-9785; hours 8:30AM-4:30PM (EST). *Misdemeanor, Civil Actions Under $25,000, Eviction, Small Claims.*
Civil Records: Access: Fax, mail, in person. Only the court performs in person searches. Search fee: $5.00 per name. Court makes copy: $1.00 per page. Required to search: name, years to search. Civil cases indexed by defendant, plaintiff; on computer back to 1989, prior on cards back to 1970s. Mail turnaround time 1-2 days.
Criminal Records: Access: Fax, mail, in person. Only the court performs in person searches. Search fee: $5.00 per name. Court makes copy: $1.00 per page. Required to search: name, years to search, DOB; also helpful: SSN. Criminal records on computer back to 1989, prior on cards back to 1970s. Mail turnaround time 1-2 days.
General Information: No public access terminal. No suppressed, juvenile, sex offenders, mental health, or adoption records released. Will fax documents to local or toll free line. Certification fee: $5.00. Payee: 88th District Court. Only cashiers checks and money orders accepted. Prepayment and SASE required.

Probate Court 719 W Chisholm St, Alpena, MI 49707; phone: 989-354-9650; fax: 989-354-9782; hours 8:30AM-4:30PM (EST). *Probate.*

Antrim County

13th Circuit Court PO Box 520, Bellaire, MI 49615; phone: 231-533-6353; probate phone: 231-533-6681; fax: 231-533-6935; hours 8:30AM-5PM (EST). *Felony, Civil Actions Over $25,000.*
Civil Records: Access: Fax, mail, in person. Both court and visitors may perform in person searches. Search fee: $5.00 per name. Court makes copy: $.25 per page. Required to search: name, years to search. Civil cases indexed by defendant, plaintiff; on computer since 1977, prior on books. Only court can search on computer, in person searchers may look at old records on docket books. Mail turnaround time 1 week.
Criminal Records: Access: Fax, mail, in person. Both court and visitors may perform in person searches. Search fee: $5.00 per name. Court makes copy: $.25 per page. Required to search: name, years to search; also helpful: SSN, DOB. Criminal records on books from 1800s, on computer since 1997. Only court can search on computer, in person searchers may review old docket books. Mail turnaround time 1 week.
General Information: No public access terminal. No suppressed, juvenile, sex offenders, mental health, or adoption records released. Will fax documents $5.00 per doc. Certification fee: $10.00 plus $1.00 per

page. Payee: Antrim County Clerk. Prepayment and SASE required.

86th District Court PO Box 597, Bellaire, MI 49615; phone: 231-533-6441; criminal/civil fax: 231-533-6322; hours 8AM-4:30PM (EST). *Misdemeanor, Civil Actions Under $25,000, Eviction, Small Claims.*

Civil Records: Access: Fax, mail, in person. Only the court performs in person searches. Search fee: $10.00. Court makes copy: $1.00 per page. Required to search: name, years to search. Civil cases indexed by defendant, plaintiff; on computer since 1986, prior on cards. Mail turnaround time usually same day.

Criminal Records: Access: Fax, mail, in person. Only the court performs in person searches. Search fee: $10.00 per name. Court makes copy: $1.00 per page. Required to search: name, years to search, DOB; also helpful: SSN. Criminal records on computer since 1986, prior on cards. Mail turnaround time usually same day.

General Information: No public access terminal. No suppressed, sex offenders records released. Will fax documents. Certification fee: $10.00 per doc. Payee: District Court. Business checks accepted. Prepayment and SASE required.

Probate Court 205 Cayuga St, PO Box 130, Bellaire, MI 49615; phone: 231-533-6681; fax: 231-533-6600; hours 8:30AM-12;00, 12;30-4:30PM (EST). *Probate.*

Arenac County

23rd Circuit Court 120 N Grove St, PO Box 747, Standish, MI 48658; phone: 989-846-9186; criminal/civil fax: 989-846-9199; hours 8:30AM-5PM (EST). *Felony, Civil Actions Over $25,000.*

Civil Records: Access: Mail, in person. Both court and visitors may perform in person searches. Search fee: $5.00 per name. Court makes copy: $1.00 per page. Required to search: name, years to search. Civil cases indexed by defendant, plaintiff. Civil records go back to 1883, civil records on computer back to 1991, prior on index books. Mail turnaround time 1-5 days.

Criminal Records: Access: Mail, in person. Both court and visitors may perform in person searches. Search fee: $5.00 per name. Court makes copy: $1.00 per page. Required to search: name, years to search, DOB; also helpful: SSN. Criminal records go back to 1883, criminal records on computer back to 1991, prior on index books. Mail turnaround time 1-5 days.

General Information: Public terminal goes back to 1991. No suppressed, juvenile, mental health, or adoption records released. Will not fax documents. Certification fee: $10.00 per doc. Payee: Arenac County Clerk. Personal checks accepted. Prepayment and SASE required.

81st District Court PO Box 129, Standish, MI 48658; phone: 989-846-9538; fax: 989-846-2008; hours 8:30AM-4:30PM (EST). *Misdemeanor, Civil Actions Under $25,000, Eviction, Small Claims.*

Civil Records: Access: Phone, fax, mail, in person. Only the court performs in person searches. Search fee: $5.00. Court makes copy: $1.00 1st page, $.25 ea add'l. Required to search: name, years to search. Civil cases indexed by defendant, plaintiff; on computer since 1990, prior on docket books. Mail turnaround time 5 days.

Criminal Records: Access: Phone, fax, mail, in person. Only the court performs in person searches. Search fee: $5.00. Court makes copy: $1.00 1st page, $.25 ea add'l. Required to search: name, years to search, DOB; also helpful: SSN. Criminal records on computer since 1990, prior on cards by name. Mail turnaround time 5 days.

General Information: No public access terminal. No suppressed, juvenile, sex offenders, mental health, or adoption records released. Will fax documents $2.00 1st page, $.50 each add'l. No charge for fax cover sheet. No certification fee. Payee: 81st District Court. Personal checks accepted. Prepayment and SASE required.

Probate Court 120 N Grove, PO Box 666, Standish, MI 48658; phone: 989-846-6941; fax: 989-846-6757; hours 8:30AM-5PM (EST). *Probate.*
Note: Alternate fax number is 989-846-9199.

Baraga County

12th Circuit Court 16 N 3rd St, L'Anse, MI 49946; phone: 906-524-6183; fax: 906-524-6186; hours 8:30AM-4:30PM (EST). *Felony, Civil Actions Over $25,000.*

Civil Records: Access: Phone, mail, in person. Both court and visitors may perform in person searches. Search fee: $5.00. Court makes copy: $1.00 per page; same fee for self serve. Required to search: name, years to search. Civil cases indexed by defendant, plaintiff; on docket books, are computerized since 1998. Mail turnaround time same day.

Criminal Records: Access: Phone, mail, in person. Both court and visitors may perform in person searches. Search fee: $5.00 per name. Court makes copy: $1.00 per page; same fee for self serve. Required to search: name, years to search, DOB; also helpful: SSN. Criminal records on docket books, are computerized since 1998. Mail turnaround time same day.

General Information: Public terminal goes back to 6/1998. No suppressed records released. Will fax documents. Certification fee: $10.00 per doc; add copy fee for add'l pages. Payee: County Clerk. Personal checks accepted. Prepayment and SASE required.

97th District Court 16 N 3rd St, L'Anse, MI 49946; phone: 906-524-6109; fax: 906-524-7017; hours 8:30AM-N,1-4:30PM (EST). *Misdemeanor, Civil Actions Under $25,000, Eviction, Small Claims.*

Civil Records: Access: Mail, in person. Only the court performs in person searches. Search fee: $10.00 per name. Court makes copy: $1.00 per page. Required to search: name, years to search. Civil cases indexed by defendant, plaintiff. Civil records listed on docket books since 1968. Mail turnaround time 2-3 days.

Criminal Records: Access: Mail, in person. Only the court performs in person searches. Search fee: $10.00 per name. Court makes copy: $1.00 per page. Required to search: name, years to search, DOB; also helpful: SSN. Criminal records listed on docket books since 1968. Mail turnaround time 2-3 days.

General Information: No public access terminal. No suppressed, sex offenders records released. Certification fee: $10.00 plus $1.00 per page after first. Payee: 97th District Court. Personal checks accepted. Prepayment required. SASE requested.

Probate Court County Courthouse, 16 N 3rd St, L'Anse, MI 49946; phone: 906-524-6390; fax: 906-524-6186; hours 8:30AM-N, 1-4:30PM (EST). *Probate.*

Barry County

5th Circuit Court 220 W State St, Hastings, MI 49058; phone: 269-945-1285; criminal/civil fax: 269-945-0209; hours 8AM-5PM (EST). *Felony, Civil Actions Over $25,000.*
www.barrycounty.org

Civil Records: Access: Fax, mail, in person. Both court and visitors may perform in person searches. Search fee: $5.00 per name; $10.00 per name if prior to 1992. Court makes copy: $.25 per page; same fee for self serve. Required to search: name, years to search. Civil cases indexed by defendant, plaintiff; on computer since 1992, card index back to 1977, prior on books. Mail turnaround time 2 days.

Criminal Records: Access: Fax, mail, in person. Both court and visitors may perform in person searches. Search fee: $5.00 per name; $10.00 per name if prior to 1992. Court makes copy: $.25 per page; same fee for self serve. Required to search: name, years to search, DOB; also helpful: SSN. Criminal records on computer since 1992, card index back to 1977, prior on books. Mail turnaround time 2 days.

General Information: No public access terminal. No suppressed, juvenile, sex offenders, mental health, or adoption records released. Will fax documents $1.00 per page. Certification fee: $10.00 for 1st page, $1.00 each add'l includes copy fee. Payee: County Clerk. Personal checks accepted. Prepayment and SASE required.

56B District Court 206 W Court St #202, Hastings, MI 49058; phone: 269-945-1404; fax: 269-948-3314; hours 8AM-5PM (EST). *Misdemeanor, Civil Actions Under $25,000, Eviction, Small Claims.*

Civil Records: Access: Phone, fax, mail, in person. Only the court performs in person searches. Search fee: $5.00 per name. Court makes copy: $.25 per page. Required to search: name, years to search. Civil cases indexed by defendant, plaintiff; on computer since 1990, prior on index books. Mail turnaround time 2 days.

Criminal Records: Access: Phone, fax, mail, in person. Only the court performs in person searches. Search fee: $5.00 per name. Court makes copy: $.25 per page. Required to search: name, years to search, DOB; also helpful: SSN. Criminal records on computer since 1990, prior on index books. Mail turnaround time 2 days.

General Information: No public access terminal. No suppressed, sex offenders, or mental health records released. Will fax documents $1.00 per page. Certification fee: $10.00 plus $1.00 per page after first. Payee: 56B District Court. Personal checks accepted. Prepayment and SASE required.

Probate Court 206 W Court St, #302, Hastings, MI 49058; phone: 269-945-1390; fax: 269-948-3322; hours 8AM-5PM (EST). *Probate.*
www.barrycounty.org/Departments/Probate.htm
Note: Also handles name changes, adoptions, emancipations.

Bay County

18th Circuit Court 1230 Washington Ave #725, Bay City, MI 48708-5737; phone: 989-895-4265; fax: 989-895-4099; hours 8AM-5PM (EST). *Felony, Civil Actions Over $25,000.*
http://baycountycourt.com

Civil Records: Access: Phone, fax, mail, in person. Both court and visitors may perform in person searches. No search fee. Court makes copy: $1.00 per page. Required to search: name, years to search. Civil cases indexed by defendant, plaintiff; on computer for the last since 1986. Access the county courts' calendar of scheduled cases for free at www.baycountycourts.com/bcc/home.nsf/public/court_calendar.htm. Mail turnaround time same day.

Criminal Records: Access: Phone, fax, mail, in person. Both court and visitors may perform in person searches. No search fee. Court makes copy: $1.00 per page. Required to search: name, years to search, DOB. Criminal records on computer for the last since 1986. Access the county courts' calendar of scheduled cases for free at www.baycountycourts.com/bcc/home.nsf/public/court_calendar.htm. Mail turnaround time same day.

General Information: Public terminal goes back to 1986. No suppressed records released. Certification fee: $10.00, $1.00 each add'l. Payee: County Clerk. Personal checks accepted. Prepayment required. SASE requested.

74th District Court 1230 Washington Ave, Bay City, MI 48708; phone: 989-895-4232; criminal phone: 989-895-4229; civil phone: 989-895-4203; fax: 989-895-4233; hours 8AM-5PM (EST). *Misdemeanor, Civil Actions Under $25,000, Eviction, Small Claims.*
www.baycountycourts.com
Note: Current docket data is available on the website; in the future, case information will also be available.

Civil Records: Access: In person only. Visitors must perform in person searches themselves. Court makes copy: $1.00 per page. Self serve copy fee: $.25

per page. Required to search: name, years to search. Civil cases indexed by defendant, plaintiff; on computer since 1992, listed on index cards prior.

Criminal Records: Access: In person only. Visitors must perform in person searches themselves. Court makes copy: $1.00 per page. Self serve copy fee: $.25 per page. Required to search: name, years to search, DOB; SSN helpful. Criminal records on computer since 1992, listed on index cards prior.

General Information: Public terminal has criminal back to 1992 and civil back to 1994. No suppressed, juvenile, sex offenders, mental health, or adoption records released. Certification fee: $10.00. Payee: 74th District Court. Personal checks accepted. Prepayment required.

Probate Court 1230 Washington, #715, Bay City, MI 48708; phone: 989-895-4205; fax: 989-895-4194; hours 8AM-5PM (EST). *Probate.*
Note: Access the county courts' calendar free at www.baycountycourts.com/bcc/home.nsf/public/court_calendar.htm.

Benzie County

19th Circuit Court PO Box 377, Beulah, MI 49617; phone: 231-882-9671 & 800-315-3593; fax: 231-882-5941; hours 8AM-5PM (EST). *Felony, Civil Actions Over $25,000.*

Civil Records: Access: Phone, fax, mail, in person. Both court and visitors may perform in person searches. No search fee. Court makes copy: $.50 per page. Required to search: name, years to search. Civil cases indexed by defendant, plaintiff; on computer since 1980, records go back to 1869. Mail turnaround time 1-2 days.

Criminal Records: Access: Phone, fax, mail, in person. Both court and visitors may perform in person searches. No search fee. Court makes copy: $.50 per page. Required to search: name, years to search. Criminal records on computer since 1980, records go back to 1869. Mail turnaround time 1-2 days.

General Information: No public access terminal. No suppressed or home-youthful training case records released. Will fax documents $3.00 1st page, $1.00 each add'l. Certification fee: $10.00 beyond 1st page. Payee: Benzie County Clerk. Personal checks accepted. Prepayment and SASE required.

85th District Court PO Box 377, Beulah, MI 49617; phone: 231-882-0019; fax: 231-882-0022; hours 9AM-5PM (EST). *Misdemeanor, Civil Actions Under $25,000, Eviction, Small Claims.*

Civil Records: Access: Fax, mail, in person. Both court and visitors may perform in person searches. Search fee: $3.00 per name. Court makes copy: $.50 per page. Required to search: name, years to search. Civil cases indexed by defendant, plaintiff; on computer back to 1990, prior on cards to 1965. Visitors may use the law library to do their own searches at no charge. Mail turnaround time 1 week.

Criminal Records: Access: Fax, mail, in person. Both court and visitors may perform in person searches. Search fee: $3.00 per name. Court makes copy: $.50 per page. Required to search: name, years to search, DOB; also helpful: SSN. Criminal records on computer back to 1990, prior on cards to 1965. Mail turnaround time 1 week.

General Information: Public terminal goes back to 1990. (The public access terminal can be used to look up by case number.) No suppressed, juvenile, sex offenders, mental health, or adoption records released. Will fax documents for $3.00 for 1st page, $1.00 each add'l. Certification fee: $10.00 per page includes copies. Payee: 85th District Court. Personal checks accepted. Out of state checks not accepted. Prepayment and SASE required.

Probate Court 448 Court Pl, County Gov't Ctr, PO Box 377, Beulah, MI 49617; phone: 231-882-9675; fax: 231-882-5987; hours 8:30AM-N, 1-5PM (EST). *Probate.*

Berrien County

2nd Circuit Court 811 Port St, St Joseph, MI 49085; phone: 269-983-7111 x8368; criminal phone: x8368; civil phone: x8382; criminal fax: 269-982-8642; civil fax: 269-983-3604; hours 8:30AM-5PM (EST). *Felony, Civil Actions Over $25,000.*
www.berriencounty.org

Civil Records: Access: Mail, in person. Only the court performs in person searches. Search fee: $10.00 per name. Court makes copy: $1.00 per page. Required to search: name, years to search. Civil cases indexed by defendant, plaintiff; on computer since 1981, prior on books (domestic) back to 1835, (civil & criminal) back to 1837. Mail turnaround time same or next day.

Criminal Records: Access: Mail, in person. Only the court performs in person searches. Search fee: $10.00 per name. Court makes copy: $1.00 per page. Required to search: name, years to search, DOB; also helpful: SSN. Criminal records on computer since 1981, prior on books (domestic) back to 1835, (civil & criminal) back to 1837. Mail turnaround time 2-3 days.

General Information: No public access terminal. No suppressed, juvenile, sex offenders, mental health, or adoption records released. Will fax documents to local or toll free line. Certification fee: $14.00. Payee: Berrien County Clerk. Personal checks accepted. Prepayment and SASE required.

5th District Court - Trial Court Criminal Division Attn: Records, 811 Port St, St Joseph, MI 49085; phone: 269-983-7111; fax: 269-982-8643; hours 8:30AM-5PM (EST). *Misdemeanor, Civil Actions Under $25,000, Eviction, Small Claims.*
www.berriencounty.org

Civil Records: Access: Mail, in person. Both court and visitors may perform in person searches. Search fee: $10.00 per name. Court makes copy: $1.00 per page; microfilm copies are $2.00 per page. Required to search: name, years to search; also helpful: address. Civil cases indexed by defendant, plaintiff; on computer since 1988, on logs from 1976-87, on index cards from 1969-75. Will do civil record check searches for only seven years. Note: In person requesters must call ahead five days in advance; records held for 3 add'l days. Searching is limited and must be supervised. Mail turnaround time 5 days.

Criminal Records: Access: Mail, in person. Only the court performs in person searches. Search fee: $10.00 per name. Court makes copy: $1.00 per page; microfilm copies are $2.00 per page. Required to search: name, years to search, DOB or SSN; also helpful: signed release, address. Criminal records on computer back ten years, on microfiche back to 1970. Note: In person requesters must call ahead five days in advance; records held for 3 add'l days. Mail turnaround time 5 days.

General Information: No public access terminal. No suppressed or mental health records released. Will fax documents if prepaid. Certification fee: Included in search fee. $10.00 plus $1.00 per page after 1st. Payee: 5th District Court. Personal checks accepted. Prepayment required.

Probate Court 811 Port St, St Joseph, MI 49085; phone: 269-983-7111 X8365; fax: 269-982-8644; hours 8:30AM-5PM (EST). *Probate.*
www.berriencounty.org/?dept=8&pid=239

Branch County

15th Circuit Court 31 Division St, Coldwater, MI 49036; phone: 517-279-4306; fax: 517-278-5627; hours 8AM-5PM (EST). *Felony, Civil Actions Over $25,000.*
www.co.branch.mi.us

Civil Records: Access: Mail, in person. Both court and visitors may perform in person searches. Search fee: $10.00 for 10 year search; $1.00 per name per each add'l year. Court makes copy: $1.00 per page. Required to search: name, years to search. Civil cases indexed by defendant, plaintiff; on computer since 1988, prior in books back to 1830s. Mail turnaround time 1-5 days.

Criminal Records: Access: Mail, in person. Both court and visitors may perform in person searches. Search fee: $10.00 for 10 year search; $1.00 per name per each add'l year. Court makes copy: $1.00 per page. Required to search: name, years to search, DOB. Criminal records on computer since 1988, prior in books back to 1830s. Mail turnaround time 1-5 days.

General Information: Public terminal goes back to 1988. No suppressed records released. Will fax documents if all other fees paid. Certification fee: $10.00 per document. Payee: Branch County Clerk. Business checks accepted. Prepayment and SASE required.

3A District Court 31 Division St, Coldwater, MI 49036; phone: 517-279-4308; criminal phone: 517-279-4329; civil phone: 517-279-4331; fax: 517-279-4333; hours 8AM-5PM (EST). *Misdemeanor, Civil Actions Under $25,000, Eviction, Small Claims.*
www.branchcountycourts.com
Note: Small Claims is 279-4330 and Traffic is 279-4328.

Civil Records: Access: Mail, in person. Only the court performs in person searches. Search fee: $10.00 per name. Court makes copy: $1.00 per page. Required to search: name, years to search. Civil cases indexed by defendant, plaintiff; on computer since 6/1991, prior on index books. Mail turnaround time immediate if possible, otherwise 2-3 days.

Criminal Records: Access: Mail, in person. Only the court performs in person searches. Search fee: $10.00 per name. Court makes copy: $1.00 per page. Required to search: name, years to search, DOB; also helpful: SSN. Criminal records on computer since 10/1988. Mail turnaround time: immediate if possible, otherwise 2-3 days.

General Information: No public access terminal. No suppressed or non-public records released. Will fax documents if search fee paid. Certification fee: $10.00. Payee: 3A District Court. Personal checks accepted. Credit cards accepted. Prepayment required.

Probate Court 31 Division St, Coldwater, MI 49036; phone: 517-279-4318; fax: 517-279-6444; hours 8AM-N, 1-5PM (EST). *Probate.*

Calhoun County

37th Circuit Court 161 E Michigan Ave, Battle Creek, MI 49014-4066; phone: 269-969-6530; hours 8AM-N, 1-5PM (EST). *Felony, Civil Actions Over $25,000.*
www.calhouncountymi.gov
Note: Expect some delays on phone calls to this jurisdiction.

Civil Records: Access: Mail, in person. Both court and visitors may perform in person searches. Search fee: $5.00 per name. Court makes copy: $1.00 per page. Required to search: name, years to search. Civil cases indexed by defendant, plaintiff; on computer since 1984, prior on microfilm. Court will provide case number, filed date, case title, case status, and date of final judgment for the search fee.

Criminal Records: Access: In person only. Both court and visitors may perform in person searches. Search fee: $5.00 per name if in person and court does search. Court makes copy: $1.00 per page. Required to search: name, years to search, DOB; SSN helpful. Criminal records on computer since 1984, prior on microfilm. Court prefers requests go to State Police (517-322-5531). Searcher may view public court file if case number known. Mail turnaround time 1 week; 2-3 weeks for microfilm records.

General Information: No public access terminal. No suppressed, juvenile, sex offenders, mental health, or adoption records released. Will fax documents for $3.00 plus $1.00 per copy. Certification fee: $10.00 per doc. Payee: 37th Circuit Court Clerk. Personal checks accepted. Prepayment and SASE required.

10th District Court 161 E Michigan Ave, Battle Creek, MI 49014; phone: 269-969-6666; criminal phone: 269-969-6678; civil phone: 269-969-6683; probate phone: 269-969-6794; fax: 269-969-6647; hours 8:00AM-4PM (EST). *Misdemeanor, Civil Actions Under $25,000, Eviction, Small Claims.*
www.calhouncountymi.gov/Departments/DistrictCourt/OverviewDistrictCourt.htm
Note: The 10th District Court Marshall Branch's records and administration is now housed here.
Civil Records: Access: Mail, fax, in person. Visitors must perform in person searches themselves. Search fee: None unless case is in archives, then $10.00. Court makes copy: $1.00 per page. Required to search: name, years to search. Civil cases indexed by defendant, plaintiff; on computer back to 1986, prior on docket books. Public access terminal searches back to 10/1997. Note: Fax requests must be signed. Mail turnaround time 5 days.
Criminal Records: Access: Fax, mail, in person. Visitors must perform in person searches themselves. Search fee: $0.00 unless case is in archives, then $10.00. Court makes copy: $1.00 per page. Required to search: name, DOB; also helpful-case number. Criminal records on computer back to 1986, prior on docket books. Public access terminal searches back to 10/1997. Note: One to five requests per day are accepted. Fax requests must be signed. Mail turnaround time 5 days.
General Information: Public terminal goes back to 1997. No suppressed or non-public records released. Will fax documents to an toll-free number only. Certification fee: $10.00 plus $1.00 per page after first. Payee: 10th District Court. Personal checks or Visa, MC credit cards accepted. Prepayment and SASE required.

Probate Court Justice Ctr, 161 E Michigan Ave, Battle Creek, MI 49014; phone: 269-969-6794; fax: 269-969-6797; hours 8AM-5PM, F 9-5PM (EST). *Probate.*
www.calhouncountymi.gov/Departments/ProbateCourt/OverviewProbateCourt.htm

Cass County

43rd Circuit Court 120 N Broadway, File Room; 60296 M-62, #10, Cassopolis, MI 49031; criminal phone: 269-445-4416; civil phone: 269-445-4453; fax: 269-445-4453; hours 8AM-5PM (EST). *Felony, Civil Actions Over $25,000.*
Civil Records: Access: Phone, fax, mail, in person. Both court and visitors may perform in person searches. Search fee: $1.00 per name. Court makes copy: $1.00 per page. Required to search: name, years to search. Civil cases indexed by defendant, plaintiff; on computer back to 1988; books since 1963. Mail turnaround time 2 weeks by mail.
Criminal Records: Access: Fax, mail, in person. Only the court performs in person searches. Search fee: $1.00 per name. Court makes copy: $1.00 per page. Required to search: name, years to search, DOB; also helpful: SSN. Criminal records on computer back to 1988; books since 1963. Mail turnaround time 2 weeks by mail.
General Information: No public access terminal. No suppressed, juvenile, sex offenders, mental health, or adoption records released. No fee to fax to a toll-free number. Certification fee: $10.00. Payee: Cass County Clerk. Business checks accepted. Prepayment and SASE required.

4th District Court 60296 M 62 #10, Cassopolis, MI 49031-8716; phone: 269-445-4424; fax: 269-445-4486; hours 8AM-5PM (EST). *Misdemeanor, Civil Actions Under $25,000, Eviction, Small Claims, Traffic.*
Civil Records: Access: Phone, mail, fax, in person. Only the court performs in person searches. Search fee: $10.00 per name. Court makes copy: $1.00 for first page, $.10 each add'l. Required to search: name, years to search; also helpful: address. Civil cases indexed by defendant, plaintiff; on computer since 1988, indexed on cards prior back to 1969. Note:

You can fax requests, but results will not be returned by fax. Mail turnaround time 2 weeks.
Criminal Records: Access: Phone, mail, fax, in person. Only the court performs in person searches. Search fee: $10.00 per name. Court makes copy: $1.00 for first page, $.10 each add'l. Required to search: name, years to search, DOB; also helpful: address. Criminal records on computer since 1988, indexed on cards prior back to 1969. Mail turnaround time 2 weeks.
General Information: No public access terminal. No suppressed, juvenile, sex offenders, mental health, or adoption records released. Will fax documents for $10.00 per name. Certification fee: $10.00 plus $1.00 per page after first. Payee: 4th District Court. Personal checks accepted. Prepayment required.

Probate Court 60296 - M62, Cassopolis, MI 49031; phone: 269-445-4454; fax: 269-445-4453; hours 8AM-N, 1-5PM (EST). *Probate.*

Charlevoix County

33rd Circuit Court 203 Antrim St, Charlevoix, MI 49720; phone: 231-547-7200; criminal phone: 231-547-7200 x11; civil phone: 231-547-7200 x14; fax: 231-547-7217; hours 9AM-5PM (EST). *Felony, Civil Actions Over $25,000.*
www.charlevoixcounty.org/clerk.asp
Civil Records: Access: Mail, by fax, in person. Only the court performs in person searches. No search fee. Court makes copy: $1.00 per page. Required to search: name, years to search. Civil cases indexed by defendant, plaintiff; on computer from 1991, microfiche and archives from 1868. Mail turnaround time 1 week.
Criminal Records: Access: Mail, by fax, in person. Only the court performs in person searches. No search fee. Court makes copy: $1.00 per page. Required to search: name, years to search, DOB; also helpful: SSN. Criminal records on computer from 1991, microfiche and archives from 1868. Mail turnaround time 1 week.
General Information: No public access terminal. No suppressed, juvenile, adoption records released. Will fax documents, usually same day. Certification fee: $10.00 first page plus $1.00 each add'l. Payee: Charlevoix County Clerk. Personal checks accepted. Prepayment required. SASE requested.

90th District Court 301 State St, Court Bldg, Charlevoix, MI 49720; phone: 231-547-7227; civil phone: 231-547-7254; fax: 231-547-7253; hours 9AM-5PM (EST). *Misdemeanor, Civil Actions Under $25,000, Eviction, Small Claims.*
Civil Records: Access: Phone, mail, fax, in person. Both court and visitors may perform in person searches. No search fee. Court makes copy: $1.00 per page. Required to search: name, years to search. Civil cases indexed by defendant, plaintiff; on computer back to 1987, listed on index cards to 1963. Mail turnaround time 1-2 days.
Criminal Records: Access: Mail, fax, in person. Both court and visitors may perform in person searches. No search fee. Court makes copy: $1.00 per page. Required to search: name, years to search, DOB. Criminal records on computer back to 1987, listed on index cards to 1963. Mail turnaround time 1-2 days.
General Information: Public use terminal available. No suppressed records released. Payee: 90th District Court. Personal checks accepted. Prepayment required. SASE helpful.

Probate Court 301 State St, County Bldg, Charlevoix, MI 49720; phone: 231-547-7214; 547-7215; fax: 231-547-7256; hours 9AM-5PM (EST). *Probate.*
Note: Shares the same judge with Emmet County Probate Court.

Cheboygan County

53rd Circuit Court PO Box 70, Cheboygan, MI 49721; phone: 231-627-8846; fax: 231-627-8453; hours 8:30AM-5PM (EST). *Felony, Civil Actions Over $25,000.*
Civil Records: Access: Phone, mail, in person. Both court and visitors may perform in person searches. No search fee. Court makes copy: $1.00 per page. Required to search: name, years to search. Civil cases indexed by defendant, plaintiff; on computer from 1987, index cards from 1886. Mail turnaround time 3-4 days.
Criminal Records: Access: Phone, mail, in person. Both court and visitors may perform in person searches. No search fee. Court makes copy: $1.00 per page. Required to search: name, years to search, DOB. Criminal records on computer from 1987, index cards from 1886. Mail turnaround time 3-4 days.
General Information: Public terminal goes back to 1987. No suppressed records released. Will fax documents for $1.00 per page payable in advance. Certification fee: $10.00 plus $1.00 each add'l page. Cert fee includes copies. Payee: County Clerk. Personal checks accepted. Prepayment required. SASE requested.

89th District Court PO Box 70, Cheboygan, MI 49721; phone: 231-627-8809; fax: 231-627-8444; hours 8:30AM-4PM (EST). *Misdemeanor, Civil Actions Under $25,000, Eviction, Small Claims.*
www.89thdistrictcourt.org
Civil Records: Access: Phone, fax, mail, in person. Both court and visitors may perform in person searches. No search fee. Court makes copy: $1.00 per page, $.20 ea add'l. Required to search: name, years to search. Civil cases indexed by defendant, plaintiff; on computer back to 1988, microfilmed prior. Mail turnaround time 3-4 days.
Criminal Records: Access: Phone, fax, mail, in person. Both court and visitors may perform in person searches. No search fee. Court makes copy: $1.00 per page, $.20 ea add'l. Required to search: name, years to search, DOB. Criminal records on computer back to 1986. Mail turnaround time 3-4 days.
General Information: Public terminal has criminal back to 1986 and civil back to 1988. No suppressed, juvenile, sex offenders, mental health, or adoption records released. No fee to fax documents. Certification fee: $10.00 plus $1.00 per page after first. Payee: 89th District Court. Personal checks accepted. Prepayment and SASE required.

Probate Court 870 S Main St, PO Box 70, Cheboygan, MI 49721; phone: 231-627-8823; fax: 231-627-8868; hours 8:30AM-4:30PM (EST). *Probate.*

Chippewa County

50th Circuit Court 319 Court St, Sault Ste Marie, MI 49783; phone: 906-635-6300; fax: 906-635-6851; hours 8AM-5PM (EST). *Felony, Civil Actions Over $25,000.*
Civil Records: Access: Mail, in person. Only the court performs in person searches. Search fee: $5.00 per name. Fee is for 10 year search. Court makes copy: $1.00 per page. Required to search: name, years to search. Civil cases indexed by defendant, plaintiff; on computer since 1990, prior on index books to late 1800s. Mail turnaround time 1-2 days.
Criminal Records: Access: Mail, in person. Only the court performs in person searches. Search fee: $5.00 per name. Fee is for 10 year search. Court makes copy: $1.00 per page. Required to search: name, years to search, DOB; also helpful: SSN. Criminal records on computer since 1990, prior on index books to late 1800s. Mail turnaround time 1-2 days.
General Information: No public access terminal. No suppressed, juvenile, sex offenders, mental health, or adoption records released. Will fax documents to local or toll free line. Certification fee: $10.00 plus

$1.00 per page after first. Payee: County Clerk. Personal checks accepted. Prepayment required.

91st District Court 325 Court St, Sault Ste Marie, MI 49783; phone: 906-635-6320; criminal phone: 906-635-6322; civil phone: 906-635-7614; fax: 906-635-7605; hours 9AM-4:30PM (EST). *Misdemeanor, Civil Actions Under $25,000, Eviction, Small Claims.*
Note: Call before faxing for instructions.
Civil Records: Access: Mail, fax, in person. Both court and visitors may perform in person searches. Search fee: $5.00 per name. Court makes copy: $1.00 per page. Required to search: name, years to search. Civil cases indexed by defendant, plaintiff; on computer since 1989, prior on index books to 1969. Mail turnaround time 10 days.
Criminal Records: Access: Mail, fax, in person. Both court and visitors may perform in person searches. Search fee: $5.00 per name. Court makes copy: $1.00 per page. Required to search: name, years to search, DOB; also helpful: SSN. Criminal records on computer since 1989, prior on index books to 1969. Mail turnaround time 10 days.
General Information: Public terminal has criminal back to 1989 and civil back to 1989. No suppressed records released. Will fax documents to toll-free number. Certification fee: $10.00 after 1st page. Payee: 91st District Court. Only cashiers checks and money orders accepted. Prepayment and SASE required.

Probate Court 319 Court St, Sault Ste Marie, MI 49783; phone: 906-635-6314; fax: 906-635-6852; hours 9AM-5PM (EST). *Probate.*

Clare County

55th Circuit Court 225 W Main St, PO Box 438, Harrison, MI 48625; phone: 989-539-7131; fax: 989-539-6616; hours 8AM-4:30PM (EST). *Felony, Civil Actions Over $25,000.*
Civil Records: Access: Mail, in person. Only the court performs in person searches. Search fee: $6.00 per name. Add $1.00 per year if more than five. Court makes copy: $1.00 per page. Required to search: name, years to search DOB. Civil cases indexed by defendant, plaintiff; on computer since 1992, on books from 1925. Mail turnaround time 1-5 days.
Criminal Records: Access: Mail, in person. Only the court performs in person searches. Search fee: $6.00 per name. Add $1.00 per year if more than five. Court makes copy: $1.00 per page. Required to search: name, years to search, DOB; also helpful: SSN. Criminal records on computer since 1992, on books from 1925. Mail turnaround time 1-5 days.
General Information: No public access terminal. No suppressed, juvenile, sex offenders, mental health, or adoption records released. Fax documents will be sent to 800 fax numbers only. Certification fee: $10.00 per document. Payee: Clare County Clerk. Personal checks accepted. Prepayment and SASE required.

80th District Court 225 W. Main St, Harrison, MI 48625; phone: 989-539-7173; fax: 989-539-4036; hours 8AM-4:30PM (EST). *Misdemeanor, Civil Actions Under $25,000, Eviction, Small Claims.*
Civil Records: Access: Mail, fax, in person. Only the court performs in person searches. Search fee: $6.00 per name; $1.00 per yr over 5 years. Court makes copy: $1.00 per page. Required to search: name, years to search. Civil cases indexed by defendant, plaintiff. Civil records go back to 1969; on computer back to 1988. Mail turnaround time 5 days.
Criminal Records: Access: Mail, fax, in person. Only the court performs in person searches. Search fee: $6.00 per name; $1.00 per yr over 5 years. Court makes copy: $1.00 per page. Required to search: name, years to search, DOB, SSN. Criminal records go back to 1969; on computer back to 1988. Mail turnaround time 5 days.
General Information: No public access terminal. No suppressed, juvenile, sex offenders, mental health, or adoption records released. Will fax documents.

Certification fee: $10.00 per doc includes copy fee. Payee: 80th District Court. Personal checks accepted. Prepayment and SASE required.

Probate Court 225 W. Main St, PO Box 96, Harrison, MI 48625; phone: 989-539-7109; hours 8AM-4:30PM (EST). *Probate.*
Note: This is combined with Gladwin County Probate Court.

Clinton County

29th Circuit Court PO Box 69, St Johns, MI 48879-0069; phone: 989-224-5140; fax: 989-227-6421; hours 8AM-5PM (EST). *Felony, Civil Actions Over $25,000.*
www.clinton-county.org
Civil Records: Access: Mail, in person. Both court and visitors may perform in person searches. Search fee: $10.00 per name. Fee is for 10 year search. Court makes copy: $1.00 per page 1st 10, then $.50 each add'l. Required to search: name, years to search. Civil cases indexed by defendant, plaintiff. Civil records in calendar books since 1800s, some on microfiche; on computer since 1996. Mail turnaround time 24 hours.
Criminal Records: Access: Mail, in person. Both court and visitors may perform in person searches. Search fee: $10.00 per name. Fee is for 10 year search. Court makes copy: $1.00 per page 1st 10, then $.50 each add'l. Required to search: name, years to search; also helpful: DOB. Criminal records in calendar books since 1800s, some on microfiche; on computer since 1996. Mail turnaround time 24 hrs.
General Information: No public access terminal. No suppressed or non public records released. Will fax documents for $3.00 plus normal copy fee up to 20 pages. Certification fee: $10.00 per document. Payee: Clinton County Clerk. Personal checks accepted. Prepayment and SASE required.

65th District Court 100 E State St, #3400, St Johns, MI 48879-1571; phone: 989-224-5150; criminal phone: 989-224-5153; civil phone: 989-224-5152; fax: 989-224-5154; hours 8AM-5PM (EST). *Misdemeanor, Civil Actions Under $25,000, Eviction, Small Claims.*
Civil Records: Access: In person only. Visitors must perform in person searches themselves. Court makes copy: $1.00 per page. Required to search: name, years to search. Civil cases indexed by defendant, plaintiff; on computer since 1989-90.
Criminal Records: Access: In person only. Visitors must perform in person searches themselves. Court makes copy: $1.00 per page. Required to search: name, years to search, DOB, SSN. Criminal records on computer since 1986.
General Information: Public use terminal available. No suppressed, juvenile, sex offenders, mental health, or adoption records released. Will not fax specific case file. Certification fee: $10.00 per document. Payee: 65th District Court. Personal checks accepted. Prepayment required.

Probate Court 100 E State St #4300, St Johns, MI 48879; phone: 989-224-5190; fax: 989-224-5102; hours 8AM-5PM (EST). *Probate.*
www.clinton-county.org

Crawford County

46th Circuit Court 200 W Michigan Ave, Grayling, MI 49738; phone: 989-348-2841; fax: 989-344-3223; hours 8:30AM-3:30PM (EST). *Felony, Civil Actions Over $25,000.*
www.Circuit46.org
Civil Records: Access: Mail, in person, online. Only the court performs in person searches. Search fee: $5.00 per name. Court makes copy: $1.00 per page. Required to search: name, years to search. Civil cases indexed by defendant, plaintiff; on computer since 1990, prior on books to 1930s. Online access to court case records (closed cases for 90 days only) is free at www.circuit46.org/Cases/cases.html. Mail turnaround time 2-3 days.

Criminal Records: Access: Mail, in person, online, phone,fax. Only the court performs in person searches. Search fee: $5.00 per name. Court makes copy: $1.00 per page. Required to search: name, years to search, DOB. Criminal records on computer since 1990, prior on books to 1960. Online access to criminal records is the same as civil. Mail turnaround time 2-3 days.
General Information: No public access terminal. No suppressed records released. Certification fee: $10.00. Payee: Crawford County. Personal checks accepted. Prepayment and SASE required.

46th Circuit Trial Court - District Division 200 W Michigan Ave, Grayling, MI 49738; phone: 989-348-2841 X242; fax: 989-344-3290; hours 8AM-4:30PM (EST). *Misdemeanor, Civil Actions Under $25,000, Eviction, Small Claims.*
www.Circuit46.org
Civil Records: Access: Phone, mail, fax, in person, online. Only the court performs in person searches. No search fee. Court makes copy: $.25 per page; same fee for self serve. Required to search: name, years to search. Civil cases indexed by defendant, plaintiff; on computer since 1990, books from 1969. Online access to court case records (open or closed cases for 90 days only) is free at www.circuit46.org/Cases/cases.html. Mail turnaround time 1-4 days.
Criminal Records: Access: Phone, mail, fax, in person, online. Only the court performs in person searches. No search fee. Court makes copy: $.25 per page; same fee for self serve. Required to search: name, years to search, DOB. Criminal records on computer since 1989. Online access to criminal records is the same as civil. Mail turnaround time 1-4 days.
General Information: No public access terminal. No suppressed, juvenile, sex offenders, mental health, or adoption records released. Certification fee: $10.00 plus $1.00 each add'l page. Payee: District Division Court. Personal checks or Visa, MC accepted. Prepayment required.

Probate Court 200 W Michigan Ave, Grayling, MI 49738; phone: 989-344-3237; fax: 989-344-3277; hours 8:00AM-4:30PM (EST). *Probate.*
www.Circuit46.org
Note: Search cases by name free at www.circuit46.org/Cases/cases.html.

Delta County

47th Circuit Court 310 Ludington St, Escanaba, MI 49829; phone: 906-789-5105; fax: 906-789-5196; hours 8AM-4PM (EST). *Felony, Civil Actions Over $25,000.*
Civil Records: Access: Mail, in person. Both court and visitors may perform in person searches. Search fee: $5.00 per name. Court makes copy: $1.00 per page. Required to search: name; also helpful: years to search, address. Civil cases indexed by defendant, plaintiff; on computer from 1986, archived into 1800s. Mail turnaround time same day.
Criminal Records: Access: Mail, in person. Both court and visitors may perform in person searches. Search fee: $5.00 per name. Court makes copy: $1.00 per page. Required to search: name; also helpful: years to search, DOB, SSN. Criminal records on computer from 1989, archived into 1800s. Mail turnaround time same day.
General Information: No public access terminal. No suppressed, juvenile, sex offenders, mental health, or adoption records released. Will fax documents no add'l fee. Certification fee: $10.00 plus $1.00 per page after first. Payee: Delta County. Personal checks accepted. Prepayment and SASE required.

94th District Court 310 Ludington St, Escanaba, MI 49829; criminal phone: 906-789-5108; civil phone: 906-789-5106; fax: 906-789-5198; hours 8AM-4PM (EST). *Misdemeanor, Civil Actions Under $25,000, Eviction, Small Claims.*
Civil Records: Access: Mail, in person. Only the court performs in person searches. Search fee:

$5.00. Court makes copy: $.25 per page. Required to search: name, years to search; also helpful: address. Civil cases indexed by defendant, plaintiff; on computer back to 1988, prior on books to 1968. Mail turnaround time 3 days.

Criminal Records: Access: Mail, in person. Only the court performs in person searches. Search fee: $5.00 per name. Court makes copy: $.25 per page. Required to search: name, years to search, DOB; also helpful: address, SSN. Criminal records on computer back to 1988, prior on books to 1968. Mail turnaround time 3 days.

General Information: No public access terminal. No suppressed, juvenile, sex offenders, mental health, or adoption records released. Will fax documents to toll-free number. Certification fee: $10.00 per document. Payee: 94th District Court. Personal checks accepted. Prepayment and SASE required.

Probate Court 310 Ludington St, Escanaba, MI 49829; phone: 906-789-5112; fax: 906-789-5140; hours 8AM-N, 1-4PM (EST). *Probate.*

Dickinson County

41st Circuit Court PO Box 609, Iron Mountain, MI 49801; phone: 906-774-0988; fax: 906-774-4660; hours 8AM-4:30PM (CST). *Felony, Civil Actions Over $25,000.*

Civil Records: Access: Mail, in person. Both court and visitors may perform in person searches. Search fee: $15.00 per name. Fee is for 10 year search. Court makes copy: $1.00 per page; same fee for self serve. Required to search: name, years to search. Civil cases indexed by defendant, plaintiff; on docket books since 1891; on computer since 5/95. Mail turnaround time 1-2 days.

Criminal Records: Access: Mail, in person. Both court and visitors may perform in person searches. Search fee: $5.00 per name. Fee is for 10 year search. Court makes copy: $1.00 per page; same fee for self serve. Required to search: name, years to search, DOB; also helpful: SSN. Criminal records on docket books since 1891; on computer since 5/95. Mail turnaround time 1-2 days.

General Information: No public access terminal. No suppressed, juvenile, sex offenders, mental health, or adoption records released. Fee to fax documents is $1.50 per page. Certification fee: $10.00 per doc. Payee: County Clerk. Business checks accepted. Prepayment and SASE required.

95 B District Court County Courthouse, PO Box 609, Iron Mountain, MI 49801; phone: 906-774-0506; fax: 906-774-8560; hours 8AM-4:30PM (CST). *Misdemeanor, Civil Actions Under $25,000, Eviction, Small Claims.*

Note: May require a signed release for certain records.

Civil Records: Access: Phone, mail, fax. Only the court performs in person searches. Search fee: $5.00 per name if pre-2/1995. Court makes copy: $1.00 1st page; $.50 each add'l page. Required to search: name, years to search; also helpful: address. Civil cases indexed by defendant, plaintiff; on index cards from 1981; on computer back to 2/1995. Mail turnaround time 1 week.

Criminal Records: Access: Mail, fax, in person. Only the court performs in person searches. Search fee: $5.00 per name if pre-2/1995. Court makes copy: $1.00 1st page; $.50 each add'l page. Required to search: name, years to search, DOB; also helpful: address, SSN. Criminal records on index cards from 1981; on computer back to 2/1995. Mail turnaround time 1 week.

General Information: No public access terminal. No suppressed, juvenile, sex offenders, mental health, or adoption records released. Will fax documents for no fee. Certification fee: $10.00 per document. Payee: 95-B District Court. Only cashiers checks and money orders accepted. Prepayment required.

Probate Court PO Box 609, 705 S Stephenson, Iron Mountain, MI 49801; phone: 906-774-1555; fax: 906-774-1561; hours 8AM-4:30PM (CST). *Probate.*

Eaton County

56th Circuit Court 1045 Independence Blvd, Charlotte, MI 48813; phone: 517-543-7500 X396; fax: 517-543-4475; hours 8AM-5PM (EST). *Felony, Civil Actions Over $25,000.*

www.eatoncountycourts.org/courts.html

Civil Records: Access: Phone, fax, mail, in person. Both court and visitors may perform in person searches. Search fee: $8.00 per name. Court makes copy: $1.00 for first page, $.50 each add'l. Required to search: name, years to search. Civil cases indexed by defendant, plaintiff; on computer back to 1988, microfilm since 1930s, books from 1848. Mail turnaround time 1-3 days.

Criminal Records: Access: Fax, mail, in person. Both court and visitors may perform in person searches. Search fee: $8.00 per name. Court makes copy: $1.00 for first page, $.50 each add'l. Required to search: name, years to search, DOB; also helpful: SSN. Criminal records on computer back to 1985, microfilm since 1930s, books from 1860s. Mail turnaround time 1-3 days.

General Information: No public access terminal. No suppressed, juvenile, sex offenders, mental health, or adoption records released. Will fax documents. Certification fee: $10.00. Payee: Eaton County Circuit Court Clerk. Personal checks accepted. Prepayment and SASE required.

56A District Court 1045 Independence Blvd, Charlotte, MI 48813; phone: 517-543-7500; criminal phone: x283; civil phone: x281; fax: 517-543-1469; hours 8AM-5PM (EST). *Misdemeanor, Civil Actions Under $25,000, Eviction, Small Claims.*

www.eatoncountycourts.org/courts.html

Civil Records: Access: Mail, fax, in person. Visitors must perform in person searches themselves. No search fee. Court makes copy: $.30 per page. Required to search: name, years to search. Civil records on computer back to 1990; prior in books.

Criminal Records: Access: In person only. Visitors must perform in person searches themselves. Court makes copy: $.30 per page. Required to search: name, years to search, DOB; SSN helpful. Criminal records on computer back to 1990.

General Information: Public terminal goes back to 1989. No suppressed, sex offenders, mental health, or adoption records released. Certification fee: $10.00 per doc. Payee: 56A District Court. Personal checks accepted. Prepayment and SASE required.

Probate Court 1045 Independence Blvd, Probate Court, Charlotte, MI 48813; phone: 517-543-7500 X234; fax: 517-543-8439; hours 8AM-5PM (EST). *Probate.*

www.eatoncountycourts.org/courts.html

Emmet County

57th Circuit Court 200 Division St, Petoskey, MI 49770; phone: 231-348-1744; fax: 231-348-0602; hours 8AM-5PM (EST). *Felony, Civil Actions Over $25,000.*

www.co.emmet.mi.us

Civil Records: Access: Mail, in person. Only the court performs in person searches. Search fee: $5.00 per name. Court makes copy: $.50 per page. Required to search: name, years to search. Civil cases indexed by defendant, plaintiff; on computer from 1867 to present. Mail turnaround time 5 days.

Criminal Records: Access: Mail, in person. Only the court performs in person searches. Search fee: $5.00 per name. Court makes copy: $.50 per page. Required to search: name, years to search, DOB. Criminal records on computer from 1867 to present. Mail turnaround time 5 days.

General Information: No public access terminal. No suppressed records released. Certification fee: $10.00 per doc. Payee: Emmet County Clerk. Personal checks or Visa, MC accepted. Prepayment and SASE required.

90th District Court 200 Division St, Petoskey, MI 49770; phone: 231-348-1750; criminal phone: 231-348-1752; civil phone: 231-348-1753; fax: 231-348-0616; hours 8AM-5PM (EST). *Misdemeanor, Civil Actions Under $25,000, Eviction, Small Claims.*

Civil Records: Access: Fax, mail, in person. Only the court performs in person searches. Search fee: $5.00 per name. Court makes copy: $.50 per page. Required to search: name, years to search. Civil cases indexed by defendant, plaintiff; on computer since 1981; prior listed in books. Mail turnaround time on all Division searches is 24 hours.

Criminal Records: Access: Fax, mail, in person. Only the court performs in person searches. Search fee: $5.00 per name. Court makes copy: $.50 per page. Required to search: name, years to search, DOB; also helpful: SSN. Criminal records on computer since 1981, prior listed on microfiche. Mail turnaround time on all Division searches is 24 hours.

General Information: No public access terminal. No suppressed, juvenile, sex offenders, mental health, or adoption records released. Will fax documents $6.00 1st page, $1.00 each add'l. Certification fee: $10.00. Payee: 90th District Court. Business checks accepted. Prepayment required.

Probate Court 200 Division St, Petoskey, MI 49770; phone: 231-348-1764; fax: 231-348-0672; hours 8AM-5PM (EST). *Probate.*

Note: Shares the same judge with Charlevoix County Probate Court.

Genesee County

7th Circuit Court 900 S Saginaw, Flint, MI 48502; phone: 810-257-3220; hours 8AM-5PM (EST). *Felony, Civil Actions Over $25,000, Family.*

www.co.genesee.mi.us

Note: Cases files could be located at one of seven lower courts in the county. Probate court is located in a separate office at the same address.

Civil Records: Access: Mail, in person, online. Both court and visitors may perform in person searches. Search fee: $5.00 per name. Court makes copy: $1.00 per page. Required to search: name, years to search. Civil cases indexed by defendant, plaintiff; on computer since 1979, prior on index cards. Online access to court records is free at www.co.genesee.mi.us/clerk/#; click on "Circuit Court Records." Mail turnaround time 1-2 weeks.

Criminal Records: Access: Mail, in person, online. Both court and visitors may perform in person searches. Search fee: $5.00 per name. Court makes copy: $1.00 per page. Required to search: name, years to search, DOB; also helpful: race, sex. Criminal records on computer since 1979, prior on index cards. Online access to criminal records is the same as civil. Mail turnaround time 1-2 weeks.

General Information: Public terminal goes back to 1979. No suppressed, juvenile, adoption, or mental health records released. Will not fax documents. Certification fee: $10.00 per doc. Payee: Genesee County Clerk. Business checks and money orders accepted. Prepayment and SASE required.

67th District Court 630 S Saginaw, Flint, MI 48502; phone: 810-257-3170; hours 8AM-4PM (EST). *Misdemeanor, Civil Actions Under $25,000, Eviction, Small Claims.*

www.co.genesee.mi.us

Note: Cases files can be located at any one of 7 lower courts in the county. The Clerk's index will indicate the exact location.

Civil Records: Access: Mail, in person. Only the court performs in person searches. Search fee: $15.00 per name, $2.00 for a computer printout. Court makes copy: $1.00 per page. Required to search: name, years to search; also helpful: address. Civil cases indexed by defendant, plaintiff; on computer since 1983, on microfilm since 1969, prior archived. Mail turnaround time 1 week.

Criminal Records: Access: Mail, in person. Only the court performs in person searches. Search fee:

$15.00 per name, $2.00 for a computer printout. Court makes copy: $1.00 per page. Required to search: name, years to search, DOB, offense; also helpful: address, SSN. Criminal records on computer since 1983, on microfilm since 1969, prior archived. Mail turnaround time 1 week.

General Information: No public access terminal. No drug related case records released. Certification fee: $10.00. Payee: 67th District Court. Only cashiers checks, business checks, and money orders accepted. Prepayment required. SASE helpful.

Probate Court 900 S Saginaw St #502, Flint, MI 48502; phone: 810-257-3528; fax: 810-257-2713; hours 8AM-4PM (EST). *Probate.*

Gladwin County

55th Circuit Court 401 W Cedar, Gladwin, MI 48624; phone: 989-426-7351; fax: 989-426-6917; hours 8:30AM-4:30PM (EST). *Felony, Civil Actions Over $25,000.*

Civil Records: Access: Fax, mail, in person. Both court and visitors may perform in person searches. Search fee: None, but if search requirements are not met, fee is $5.00. Court makes copy: $1.00 per page. Required to search: name, years to search. Civil cases indexed by defendant, plaintiff; on computer since 1994, prior on books. Mail turnaround 2-3 days.

Criminal Records: Access: Fax, mail, in person. Both court and visitors may perform in person searches. Search fee: None, but if search requirements are not met, fee is $5.00. Court makes copy: $1.00 per page. Required to search: name, years to search, DOB; also helpful: SSN. Criminal records on computer since 1994, prior on books. Mail turnaround time 2-3 days.

General Information: No public access terminal. No suppressed, juvenile, sex offenders, mental health, or adoption records released. Will fax documents. Certification fee: $10.00 per doc. Payee: Gladwin County Clerk. Personal checks accepted. Prepayment and SASE required.

80th District Court 401 W Cedar, Gladwin, MI 48624; phone: 989-426-9207; fax: 989-246-0894; hours 8:30AM-4:30PM (EST). *Misdemeanor, Civil Actions Under $25,000, Eviction, Small Claims.*

Civil Records: Access: Mail, fax, in person. Only the court performs in person searches. No search fee. Court makes copy: $1.00 per page. Required to search: name, years to search. Civil cases indexed by defendant, plaintiff; on computer since 1988, prior on index cards and docket books, archived to late 1968. Mail turnaround time same day when possible.

Criminal Records: Access: Mail, fax, in person. Only the court performs in person searches. Search fee: $1.00 per summery; $5.00 per case documents. Court makes copy: $1.00 per page. Required to search: name, years to search, DOB; also helpful: SSN. Criminal records on computer since 1988, prior on index cards and docket books, archived to late 1968. Mail turnaround time same day when possible.

General Information: No public access terminal. No suppressed, juvenile, sex offenders, mental health, or adoption records released. Certification fee: $10.00 per doc for add'l pages. Payee: 80th District Court. Personal checks accepted. Prepayment and SASE required.

Probate Court 401 W Cedar, Gladwin, MI 48624; phone: 989-426-7451; fax: 989-426-6936; hours 8:30AM-4:30PM (EST). *Probate.*
This is combined with Clare County Probate Court.

Gogebic County

32nd Circuit Court 200 N Moore St, Bessemer, MI 49911; phone: 906-663-4518; probate phone: 906-667-0421; fax: 906-663-4660; probate fax: same; hours 8:30AM-4:30PM (CST). *Felony, Civil Actions Over $25,000.*
www.gogebic.org/circuit.htm
Civil Records: Access: Fax, mail, in person. Only the court performs in person searches. Search fee:

$5.00 per name. Court makes copy: $1.00 per page. Required to search: name, years to search. Civil cases indexed by defendant, plaintiff. Civil records in books since 1887, computerized since 1996. Mail turnaround time 1-2 days.

Criminal Records: Access: Fax, mail, in person. Only the court performs in person searches. Search fee: $25.00 per name. Court makes copy: $1.00 per page. Required to search: name, years to search, DOB; also helpful: SSN. Criminal records in books since 1887, computerized since 1996. Mail turnaround time 1-2 days.

General Information: No public access terminal. No suppressed, juvenile, sex offenders, mental health, or adoption records released. Will fax documents for $1.50 per page. Certification fee: $10.00 per doc. Payee: Gogebic County Clerk's Office. Personal checks accepted. Prepayment required. SASE requested.

98th District Court 200 N Moore St, Bessemer, MI 49911; phone: 906-663-4611; fax: 906-667-1102; 8:30AM-4:30PM (CST). *Misdemeanor, Civil Actions Under $25,000, Eviction, Small Claims.*
www.gogebic.org/district.htm
Civil Records: Access: Mail, in person. Only the court performs in person searches. Search fee: $25.00 per name. Court makes copy: $1.00 per page. Required to search: name, years to search. Civil cases indexed by defendant, plaintiff; on computer since 6/88. Mail turnaround time 10 days.

Criminal Records: Access: Mail, in person. Only the court performs in person searches. Search fee: $25.00 per name. Court makes copy: $1.00 per page. Required to search: name, years to search, DOB, SSN. Criminal records on computer since 6/88. Mail turnaround time 10 days.

General Information: No public access terminal. No suppressed, juvenile, sex offenders, mental health, or adoption records released. Certification fee: $10.00 per doc. Payee: District Court. Business checks accepted. Prepayment required.

Probate Court 200 N Moore St, Bessemer, MI 49911; phone: 906-667-0421; fax: 906-663-4660; hours 8:30AM-N, 1-4:30PM (CST). *Probate.*
www.gogebic.org/probate.htm

Grand Traverse County

13th Circuit Court 328 Washington St, Traverse City, MI 49684; phone: 231-922-4710; hours 8AM-5PM (EST). *Felony, Civil Actions Over $25,000.*
www.co.grand-traverse.mi.us
Civil Records: Access: Phone, mail, in person, online. Only the court performs in person searches. Search fee: $10.00 per name. Court makes copy: $1.00 for first page, $.25 each add'l. Required to search: name, years to search. Civil cases indexed by defendant, plaintiff; on computer since 1971, prior on books since 1859. Search civil records free at www.co.grand-traverse.mi.us; 1981 through 1985 contain only index information.1986 to present include case information and register of actions. Database updated nightly. Mail turnaround time 1 week.

Criminal Records: Access: Phone, mail, in person, online. Only the court performs in person searches. Search fee: $10.00 per name. Court makes copy: $1.00 for first page, $.25 each add'l. Required to search: name, years to search; also helpful: DOB, SSN. Criminal records on computer since 1981. Search civil records free at www.co.grand-traverse.mi.us; 1967 through 1985 contain only index information. 1986 to present include case information and register of actions. Database updated nightly. Mail turnaround time 1 week.

General Information: No public access terminal. No suppressed records released. Certification fee: $10.00 plus $1.00 per page after first. Payee: 13th Circuit Court. Personal checks accepted. Prepayment and SASE required.

86th District Court 328 Washington St, Traverse City, MI 49684; phone: 231-922-4580; fax: 231-922-4454; hours 8AM-5PM (EST). *Misdemeanor, Civil Actions Under $25,000, Eviction, Small Claims.*

Civil Records: Access: Phone, mail, in person. Only the court performs in person searches. No search fee. Court makes copy: $.25 per page. Required to search: name, years to search. Civil cases indexed by defendant, plaintiff; on computer since 1988, prior on books. Mail turnaround time 2-3 days.

Criminal Records: Access: Phone, mail, in person. Only the court performs in person searches. No search fee. Court makes copy: $.25 per page. Required to search: name, years to search, DOB; also helpful: SSN. Most criminal records on computer. Mail turnaround time 2-3 days.

General Information: No public access terminal. No suppressed, juvenile, sex offenders, mental health, or adoption records released. Certification fee: $10.00 per doc. Payee: 86th District Court. Business checks accepted. Prepayment and SASE required.

Probate Court 400 Boardman Av, Traverse City, MI 49684; phone: 231-922-6862; fax: 231-922-4458; hours 8AM-5PM (EST). *Probate.*

Gratiot County

29th Circuit Court 214 E Center St, Ithaca, MI 48847; phone: 989-875-5215; fax: 989-875-5254; hours 8:00AM-N, 1:00PM-4:30PM (EST). *Felony, Civil Actions Over $25,000.*

Civil Records: Access: Mail, in person. Only the court performs in person searches. Search fee: $10.00 per name. Fee is for 5 years, $1.00 each additional year. Court makes copy: $1.00 per page. Required to search: name, years to search. Civil cases indexed by defendant, plaintiff. Records computerized back 7 years. Mail turnaround time 1-3 days.

Criminal Records: Access: Mail, in person. Only the court performs in person searches. Search fee: $10.00 per name. Fee is for 5 years, $1.00 each additional year. Court makes copy: $1.00 per page. Required to search: name, years to search. Records computerized back 7 years. Mail turnaround time 1-3 days.

General Information: No public access terminal. No suppressed, juvenile, sex offenders, mental health, or adoption records released. Will fax documents to local or toll free line. Certification fee: $10.00 per doc. Payee: Gratiot County Clerk. Personal checks accepted. Prepayment and SASE required.

65-B District Court 245 E Newark St, Ithaca, MI 48847; phone: 989-875-5240; fax: 989-875-5290; hours 8AM-4:30PM (EST). *Misdemeanor, Civil Actions Under $25,000, Eviction, Small Claims.*

Civil Records: Access: In person only. Visitors must perform in person searches themselves. Court makes copy: $1.00 per page. Required to search: name, years to search. Civil cases indexed by defendant, plaintiff; on index books from 1969 to present, computerized since 1996.

Criminal Records: Access: In person only. Visitors must perform in person searches themselves. Court makes copy: $1.00 per page. Required to search: name, years to search, DOB; SSN helpful. Criminal records on computer since 2/20/96, in books since 1969.

General Information: Public terminal goes back to 1996. No non-public records released. Will not fax specific case file. Certification fee: $10.00 plus $1.00 per page after first. Payee: 65B District Court. Personal checks accepted. Prepayment required.

Probate Court 214 E Center St, PO Box 217, Ithaca, MI 48847; phone: 989-875-5231; fax: 989-875-5331; hours 8AM-12;00,1PM-4:30PM (EST). *Probate.*

Hillsdale County

1st Circuit Court 29 N Howell, Hillsdale, MI 49242; phone: 517-437-3391; fax: 517-437-3392; hours 8:30AM-5PM (EST). *Felony, Civil Actions Over $25,000.*

Civil Records: Access: Mail, in person. Only the court performs in person searches. Search fee: $1.00 per name per year. Court makes copy: $1.00 per page. Required to search: name, years to search. Civil cases indexed by defendant, plaintiff; on computer back to 1985, prior on docket books, archived to 1844. Mail turnaround time 1-2 days.

Criminal Records: Access: Mail, in person. Only the court performs in person searches. Search fee: $1.00 per name per year. Court makes copy: $1.00 per page. Required to search: name, years to search, DOB; also helpful: SSN. Criminal records on computer back to 1985, prior on docket books, archived to 1844. Mail turnaround time 1-2 days.

General Information: No public access terminal. No suppressed, juvenile, sex offenders, mental health, or adoption records released. Will fax documents to local or toll free line. Certification fee: $10.00 per doc plus $1 each add'l page. Payee: Hillsdale County Clerk. Personal checks accepted; out-of-state personal checks not accepted. Prepayment and SASE required.

2nd District Court 49 N Howell, Hillsdale, MI 49242; phone: 517-437-7329; fax: 517-437-2908; hours 8AM-4:30PM; 8AM-5PM Traffic (EST). *Misdemeanor, Civil Actions Under $25,000, Eviction, Small Claims.*

Civil Records: Access: Phone, mail, in person. Both court and visitors may perform in person searches. Search fee: $10.00. Court makes copy: $.15 per page. Required to search: name, years to search. Civil cases indexed by defendant, plaintiff. Civil records kept in docket books back to 1969; on computer back to 2001. A request in writing may be required. Mail turnaround time 1 week.

Criminal Records: Access: Phone, mail, in person. Only the court performs in person searches. Search fee: $10.00. Court makes copy: $.15 per page. Required to search: name, years to search, DOB; also helpful: SSN. Criminal records kept in docket books back to 1964; on computer back to 2001. Mail turnaround time 1 week.

General Information: No public access terminal. No suppressed records released. Will fax documents to local or toll free line. Certification fee: $10.00 plus $1.00 each add'l page. Payee: Hillsdale District Court. Personal checks accepted. Prepayment required.

Probate Court 29 N Howell, Hillsdale, MI 49242; phone: 517-437-4643; fax: 517-437-4148; hours 8:30AM-N, 1-5PM (EST). *Probate.*

Houghton County

12th Circuit Court 401 E Houghton Ave, Houghton, MI 49931; phone: 906-482-5420; fax: 906-483-0364; hours 8AM-4:30PM (EST). *Felony, Civil Actions Over $25,000.*

Civil Records: Access: Mail, in person. Only the court performs in person searches. Search fee: $20.00 per name. Court makes copy: $1.00 per page. Required by search: name, years to search. Civil cases indexed by defendant, plaintiff. Civil records kept on docket books, cards since 6/76; are computerized as of 1997. Mail turnaround time 1-2 days.

Criminal Records: Access: Mail, in person. Only the court performs in person searches. Search fee: $20.00 per name. Court makes copy: $1.00 per page. Required to search: name, years to search, DOB; also helpful: SSN. Criminal records kept on docket books, cards since 11/63; are computerized as of 1997. Mail turnaround time 1-2 days.

General Information: No public access terminal. No suppressed, juvenile, sex offenders, mental health, or adoption records released. Will fax documents to local or toll free line. Certification fee: $10.00. Payee: Clerk of Circuit Court. Personal checks accepted. Prepayment and SASE required.

97th District Court 401 E Houghton Ave, Houghton, MI 49931; phone: 906-482-4980; fax: 906-482-5270; hours 8AM-4:30PM (EST). *Misdemeanor, Civil Actions Under $25,000, Eviction, Small Claims.*

Civil Records: Access: Mail, fax, in person. Only the court performs in person searches. Search fee: $10.00 per name. Court makes copy: $1.00 for first page, $.25 each add'l. Required to search: name, years to search; also helpful: address. Civil cases indexed by defendant, plaintiff. Civil records listed in "Registers of Actions." Records on computer back to 1998; others back to 1969. Mail turnaround time up to 1 week.

Criminal Records: Access: Mail, fax, in person. Only the court performs in person searches. Search fee: $10.00 per name. Court makes copy: $1.00 for first page, $.25 each add'l. Required to search: name, years to search, DOB, SSN; also helpful: address, signed release. Criminal records listed in "Registers of Actions." Records on computer back to 1998; others back to 1969. Mail turnaround time up to 1 week.

General Information: No public access terminal. Will not fax documents. Certification fee: $10.00. Payee: 97th District Court. Business checks accepted. Prepayment and SASE required.

Probate Court 401 E. Houghton Ave, Houghton, MI 49931; phone: 906-482-3120; fax: 906-487-5964; hours 8AM-4:30PM (EST). *Probate.*

Huron County

52nd Circuit Court 250 E Huron Ave, Bad Axe, MI 48413; phone: 989-269-9942; probate phone: 989-269-9944; fax: 989-269-6160; hours 8:30AM-5PM (EST). *Felony, Civil Actions Over $25,000.*

Civil Records: Access: Mail, in person. Both court and visitors may perform in person searches. Search fee: $5.00 per name. Court makes copy: $1.00 per page. Required to search: name, years to search. Civil cases indexed by defendant, plaintiff; on computer since 1992, prior on books to 1867. Mail turnaround time 2-3 days.

Criminal Records: Access: Phone, mail, in person. Both court and visitors may perform in person searches. Search fee: $5.00 per name. Court makes copy: $1.00 per page. Required to search: name, years to search, DOB; also helpful: SSN. Criminal records on computer since 1992, prior on books to 1867. Mail turnaround time 2-3 days.

General Information: No public access terminal. No suppressed, juvenile, sex offenders, mental health, or adoption records released. Will fax documents to local or toll free line. Certification fee: $10.00 plus $1.00 per page after first. Payee: Huron County Clerk. Personal checks accepted. Prepayment and SASE required.

73B District Court 250 E Huron Ave, Bad Axe, MI 48413; phone: 989-269-9987; fax: 989-269-6167; hours 8:30AM-5PM (EST). *Misdemeanor, Civil Actions Under $25,000, Eviction, Small Claims.*

Civil Records: Access: Phone, fax, mail, in person. Only the court performs in person searches. Search fee: $5.00 per name. Court makes copy: $1.00 per page. Required to search: name, years to search. Civil cases indexed by defendant, plaintiff; on computer since 6/1992, prior on books since 1969. Mail turnaround time 1-5 days.

Criminal Records: Access: Phone, fax, mail, in person. Only the court performs in person searches. Search fee: $5.00 per name. Court makes copy: $1.00 per page. Required to search: name, years to search, DOB; also helpful: SSN. Criminal records on computer since 6/1992, prior on books since 1969. Mail turnaround time 1-5 days.

General Information: No public access terminal. No suppressed, juvenile, sex offenders, mental health, or adoption records released. No fee to fax documents. Certification fee: $10.00. Payee: 73B District Court. Business checks accepted. Prepayment and SASE required.

Probate Court 250 E. Huron Ave, Bad Axe, MI 48413; phone: 989-269-9944; fax: 989-269-0004; hours 8:30AM-N, 1-5PM (EST). *Probate.*

Ingham County

30th Circuit Court PO Box 40771, 313 W. Kalamazoo, Lansing, MI 48933; phone: 517-483-6500; fax: 517-483-6501; hours 9:00AM-5:00PM M-F (EST). *Felony, Civil Actions Over $25,000.* www.ingham.org/cc/circuit.htm

Civil Records: Access: Phone, mail, in person. Both court and visitors may perform in person searches. No search fee. Court makes copy: $5.00 for 1st 5 pages $.50 thereafter. Required to search: name, years to search. Civil cases indexed by defendant, plaintiff; on computer since 1986. Mail turnaround time 1-2 days; if file is in storage, then 1 week.

Criminal Records: Access: Mail, in person. Both court and visitors may perform in person searches. Search fee: $8.00 per name. Court makes copy: $5.00 for 1st 5 pages $.50 each add'l. Required to search: name, years to search; also helpful: DOB. Criminal records on computer since 1986. Mail turnaround time 1-2 days; if file is in storage, then 1 week.

General Information: Public use terminal available. All circuit court files are public record unless specifically suppressed by Law. Certification fee: $10.00 plus $1.00 per page after first. Payee: Ingham County Circuit Court. Personal checks accepted. Prepayment and SASE required.

54 A District Court 124 W Michigan Ave, Lansing, MI 48933; phone: 517-483-4433; criminal phone: 517-483-4445; civil phone: 517-483-4426; fax: 517-483-4108; hours 8AM-4:30PM (EST). *Misdemeanor, Civil Actions Under $25,000, Eviction, Small Claims.*

Note: This court covers the City of Lansing.

Civil Records: Access: In person only. Visitors must perform in person searches themselves. Court makes copy: $.50 per page. Required to search: name, years to search. Civil cases indexed by defendant, plaintiff; on computer since 1990, microfiche from 1985, prior archived.

Criminal Records: Access: In person only. Visitors must perform in person searches themselves. Court makes copy: $.50 per page. Required to search: name, years to search, DOB, offense, date of offense. Criminal records on computer since 1990, microfiche from 1985, prior not archived may be available on microfiche before 1969.

General Information: Public use terminal available. No suppressed, juvenile, sex offenders, mental health, or adoption, non-public records released. Will not fax specific case file. Certification fee: $10.00 plus $1.00 per page after first. Payee: 54A District Court. No personal checks accepted. Visa, MC accepted. Prepayment required.

54 B District Court 101 Linden, East Lansing, MI 48823; phone: 517-351-7000; criminal phone: 517-336-8630; civil phone: 517-351-1730; fax: 517-351-3371; hours 8AM-4:30PM (EST). *Misdemeanor, Civil Actions Under $25,000, Eviction, Small Claims.* http://cityofeastlansing.com

Note: This court covers the City of East Lansing.

Civil Records: Access: Mail, in person. Both court and visitors may perform in person searches. No search fee. Court makes copy: $.25 per page. Required to search: name, years to search. Civil cases indexed by defendant, plaintiff; on computer since 1991, ROA's are kept indefinitely. Note: Older records must be searched by court personnel and can take 1-3 days. Mail turnaround time 1 hour to 1 week; depends on availability.

Criminal Records: Access: Mail, in person. Both court and visitors may perform in person searches. No search fee. Court makes copy: $.25 per page. Required to search: name, DOB; if prior to 1989 give years needed. Criminal records on computer since 1989, files stored prior, ROAs keep indefinitely. Mail turnaround time 1 hour to 1 week; depends on availability.

General Information: Public terminal has criminal back to 1989 and civil back to 1991. No suppressed, juvenile, sex offenders, mental health, or adoption records released. Certification fee: $10.00 plus $1.00 per page after first. Payee: 54-B District Court. Two party or payroll checks not allowed. Visa, MC accepted. Debit card. Prepayment required.

55th District Court 700 Buhl St, Mason, MI 48854; phone: 517-676-8400; hours 8:30AM-5PM (EST). *Misdemeanor, Civil Actions Under $25,000, Eviction, Small Claims.*
Note: This court covers all of Ingham County except for Lansing and East Lansing.
Civil Records: Access: Mail, in person. Both court and visitors may perform in person searches. No search fee. Court makes copy: $1.00 per page. Required to search: name, years to search. Civil records on computer since 11/91, prior listed in index books. Mail turnaround time varies.
Criminal Records: Access: Mail, in person. Both court and visitors may perform in person searches. No search fee. Court makes copy: $1.00 per page. Required to search: name, years to search, DOB; case number; also helpful: SSN. Criminal records on computer since 1994, prior on books. Mail turnaround time varies.
General Information: Public terminal has criminal back to 1994 and civil back to 11/91. No suppressed, juvenile, sex offenders, mental health, or adoption records released. Certification fee: $10.00 plus $1.00 each add'l page. Payee: 55th District Court. Personal checks accepted. Prepayment required. SASE helpful.

Lansing Probate Court 313 W Kalamazoo, Lansing, MI 48933; phone: 517-483-6300; fax: 517-483-6150; hours 8AM-N, 1-5PM (EST). *Probate.*
Note: The probate court located in Mason was closed; all of their records reside here.

Ionia County

8th Circuit Court 100 Main, Ionia, MI 48846; phone: 616-527-5322; probate phone: 616-527-5326; criminal fax: 616-527-8201; civil/probate fax is the same; hours 8:30AM-5PM (EST). *Felony, Civil Actions Over $25,000.*
www.ioniacounty.org/Circuit/Circuit-Home.asp
Civil Records: Access: Phone, fax, mail, in person. Only the court performs in person searches. No search fee. Court makes copy: $1.00 per page. Required to search: name, years to search. Civil cases indexed by defendant, plaintiff; on computer since 1990; prior records kept in books and files, archived to 1800s. Mail turnaround time 1 week.
Criminal Records: Access: Phone, fax, mail, in person. Only the court performs in person searches. No search fee. Court makes copy: $1.00 per page. Required to search: name, years to search; also helpful: DOB, SSN. Criminal records on computer since 6/84; in books and files prior. Mail turnaround time 1 week.
General Information: No public access terminal. No suppressed records released. Will fax documents. Certification fee: $10.00 plus $1.00 per page copy fee after first. Payee: Ionia County Clerk. Personal checks accepted. Prepayment required.

64 A District Court 101 W Main, Ionia, MI 48846; phone: 616-527-5343; hours 7:45AM-5:30PM (EST). *Misdemeanor, Civil Actions Under $25,000, Eviction, Small Claims.*
www.ioniacounty.org/district/home1.asp
Civil Records: Access: Fax, mail, in person. Only the court performs in person searches. Search fee: $3.00 per name. Court makes copy: $.50 per page. Required to search: name, years to search. Civil cases indexed by defendant, plaintiff. Civil records in files and books available since 1969. Fax request must be followed up by originals. Mail turnaround time 10 days.
Criminal Records: Access: Fax, mail, in person. Only the court performs in person searches. Search fee: $3.00 per name. Court makes copy: $.50 per

page. Required to search: name, years to search, DOB; also helpful: address. Criminal records in files and books available since 1969. Fax must be followed up by originals. Mail turnaround time 10 days.
General Information: No public access terminal. No suppressed, juvenile, sex offenders, mental health, or adoption records released. Certification fee: $10.00 plus $1.00 per page after first. Payee: 64-A District Court. Personal checks accepted. Prepayment required. SASE requested.

Probate Court 100 Main, Ionia, MI 48846; phone: 616-527-5326; fax: 616-527-5321; hours 8:30AM-5PM (EST). *Probate.*
www.ioniacounty.org/Probate/Probate_home.asp

Iosco County

23rd Circuit Court PO Box 838, Tawas City, MI 48764; phone: 989-362-3497; fax: 989-984-1012; hours 9AM-5PM (EST). *Felony, Civil Actions Over $25,000.*
www.iosco.net
Civil Records: Access: Phone, mail, in person. Only the court performs in person searches. Search fee: $5.00 per name. Court makes copy: $1.00 per page. Required to search: name, years to search. Civil records on computer since 1987, prior on books. Mail turnaround time 1 week.
Criminal Records: Access: Phone, mail, in person. Only the court performs in person searches. Search fee: $5.00 per name. Court makes copy: $1.00 per page. Required to search: name, years to search, DOB; also helpful: SSN. Criminal records on computer since 1983. Mail turnaround time 1 week.
General Information: No public access terminal. No suppressed, parental waivers, mental health, or adoption records released. Will not fax documents. Certification fee: $10.00 plus $1.00 per page after first. Payee: Iosco County Clerk. Cashiers checks and money orders. Credit cards accepted through GPS, 888-604-7888. Prepayment required.

81st District Court PO Box 388, Tawas City, MI 48764; phone: 989-362-4441; fax: 989-984-1021; hours 8:30AM-5PM (EST). *Misdemeanor, Civil Actions Under $25,000, Eviction, Small Claims.*
Civil Records: Access: Mail, in person. Only the court performs in person searches. Search fee: $5.00. Court makes copy: $2.00 for first page, $.50 each add'l. Required to search: name, years to search. Civil cases indexed by defendant, plaintiff; on computer since 1987, prior on books. Mail turnaround time 2-3 days.
Criminal Records: Access: Mail, in person. Only the court performs in person searches. Search fee: $5.00. Court makes copy: $2.00 for first page, $.50 each add'l. Required to search: name, years to search, DOB; also helpful: SSN. Criminal records on computer since 1987, prior on books. Mail turnaround time 2-3 days.
General Information: No public access terminal. No suppressed, juvenile, sex offenders, mental health, or adoption records released. Will fax documents to local or toll free line. Certification fee: $10.00 plus $1.00 per page after first. Payee: 81st District Court. Personal checks not accepted. Prepayment and SASE required.

Probate Court PO Box 421, 422 Lake St, Tawas City, MI 48764; phone: 989-984-1037; fax: 989-984-1035; hours 8AM-5PM (EST). *Probate.*

Iron County

41st Circuit Court 2 South 6th St #9, Crystal Falls, MI 49920; phone: 906-875-3221; fax: 906-875-6675; hours 8AM-Noon; 12:30-4PM (CST). *Felony, Civil Actions Over $25,000.*
www.iron.org
Civil Records: Access: Fax, mail, in person. Only the court performs in person searches. Search fee: $10.00 per name. Court makes copy: $.25 per page. Required to search: name, years to search. Civil cases

indexed by defendant, plaintiff. Most records on books, on microfiche 1958-67. Mail turnaround time 2-3 days.
Criminal Records: Access: Fax, mail, in person. Only the court performs in person searches. Search fee: $10.00 per name. Court makes copy: $.25 per page. Required to search: name, years to search, DOB. Most records on books, on microfiche 1958-67. Mail turnaround time 2-3 days.
General Information: No public access terminal. No suppressed, juvenile, sex offenders, mental health, or adoption records released. Will fax documents $1.50 per page. Certification fee: $10.00 plus $5.00 per page after first. Payee: Iron County Clerk. Personal checks accepted. Prepayment required. SASE requested.

95 B District Court 2 S 6th St, Crystal Falls, MI 49920; phone: 906-875-0619; fax: 906-875-0656; hours 8AM-4PM (CST). *Misdemeanor, Civil Actions Under $25,000, Eviction, Small Claims.*
www.iron.org
Civil Records: Access: Mail, in person. Only the court performs in person searches. Search fee: $5.00. Court makes copy: $.25 per page. Required to search: name, years to search. Civil cases indexed by defendant, plaintiff. Civil records computerized since 1999, earlier records index kept on cards, accessible from 1970. There is no search fee if a name and DOB are submitted for a Yes or No answer. The fee kick in for accessing details of the case. Mail turnaround time 1 week.
Criminal Records: Access: Mail, in person. Only the court performs in person searches. Search fee: $5.00. Court makes copy: $.25 per page. Required to search: name, years to search, DOB; also helpful: SSN. Criminal records computerized since 1999, earlier records index kept on cards, accessible from 1970. There is no search fee if a name and DOB are submitted for a Yes or No answer. The fee kick in for accessing details of the case. Mail turnaround time 1 week.
General Information: No public access terminal. No suppressed, juvenile, sex offenders, mental health, or adoption records released. Certification fee: $10.00 plus $1.00 per page after first. Payee: 95-B District Court. Personal checks accepted. Prepayment and SASE required.

Probate Court 2 S 6th St, #10, Crystal Falls, MI 49920; phone: 906-875-0659; fax: 906-875-0656; hours 8AM-N, 12:30-4PM (CST). *Probate.*
www.iron.org

Isabella County

21st Circuit Court 200 N Main St, Mount Pleasant, MI 48858; phone: 989-772-0911 X259; hours 8AM-4:30PM (EST). *Felony, Civil Actions Over $25,000.*
Civil Records: Access: Mail, in person. Both court and visitors may perform in person searches. Search fee: $5.00 from 1980 to present. Prior years $1.00 per year. Court makes copy: $1.00 per page. Required to search: name, years to search. Civil cases indexed by defendant, plaintiff; on computer since 1980, archived from 1900. Mail turnaround time 1-2 weeks.
Criminal Records: Access: Mail, in person. Only the court performs in person searches. Search fee: $5.00 from 1980 to present. Prior years $1.00 per year. Court makes copy: $1.00 per page. Required to search: name, years to search, DOB; also helpful: SSN. Criminal records on computer since 1980, archived from 1900. Mail turnaround time 1-2 weeks.
General Information: No public access terminal. No suppressed, juvenile, sex offenders, mental health, or adoption records released. Will fax documents to local or toll free line. Certification fee: $10.00 plus $1.00 per page after first. Payee: Isabella County Court. Personal checks accepted. Prepayment and SASE required.

76th District Court 300 N Main St, Mount Pleasant, MI 48858; phone: 989-772-0911 X490; probate phone: x316; fax: 989-779-8022; hours 8AM-4:30PM (EST). *Misdemeanor, Civil Actions Under $25,000, Eviction, Small Claims.*
www.isabellacounty.org/trial.html
Civil Records: Access: Mail, in person. Both court and visitors may perform in person searches. Search fee: $5.00 per name. Court makes copy: $1.00 per page. Required to search: name, years to search. Civil cases indexed by defendant, plaintiff; on computer since 1988, on books since 1969. Mail turnaround time 5-7 days.
Criminal Records: Access: Mail, in person. Both court and visitors may perform in person searches. Search fee: $5.00 per name. Court makes copy: $1.00 per page. Required to search: name, years to search, DOB; also helpful: SSN. Criminal records on computer since 1988, on books since 1969. Mail turnaround time 5-7 days.
General Information: No public access terminal. No suppressed, juvenile, sex offenders, or adoption records released. Will fax documents. Certification fee: $10.00 1st page; $1.00 each add'l. Payee: Isabella County Trial Court. Business checks accepted. Prepayment and SASE required.

Probate Court 300 N Main St, Mount Pleasant, MI 48858; phone: 989-772-0911 x316 (or x276); fax: 989-779-8022; hours 8AM-4:30PM (EST). *Probate.*
www.isabellacounty.org

Jackson County

4th Circuit Court 312 S Jackson St, Jackson, MI 49201; phone: 517-788-4268; fax: 517-788-4601; hours 8AM-5PM (EST). *Felony, Civil Actions Over $25,000.*
www.co.jackson.mi.us
Civil Records: Access: Phone, mail, in person. Only the court performs in person searches. Search fee: $10.50 per hour. Court makes copy: $.50 per page; same for self serve. Required to search: name, years to search. Civil cases indexed by defendant, plaintiff; on computer since 1982, prior on index cards and docket books since 1800s. Mail turnaround time 1 week.
Criminal Records: Access: Phone, mail, in person. Only the court performs in person searches. Search fee: $10.00 per hour. Court makes copy: $.50 per page; same fee for self serve. Required to search: name, years to search; also helpful: DOB, SSN. Criminal records on computer since 1982, prior on index cards and docket books since 1800s. Mail turnaround time 1 week.
General Information: No public access terminal. No adoption or juvenile records released. Will fax documents for $3.00 per page. Certification fee: $10.00 plus $2.00 per page after first;. Payee: Jackson County Clerk. Only cashiers checks and money orders accepted. Visa, MC accepted. Prepayment required. Prepayment of fax and mail service required. Fees billed to Attorneys.

12th District Court 312 S Jackson St, Jackson, MI 49201; phone: 517-788-4260; fax: 517-788-4262; hours 7AM-6PM (EST). *Misdemeanor, Civil Actions Under $25,000, Eviction, Small Claims.*
www.d12.com
Civil Records: Access: Fax, mail, in person. Only the court performs in person searches. No search fee. Court makes copy: $.30 per page (first 10 free to county resident). Required to search: name, years to search. Civil cases indexed by defendant, plaintiff; on computer since 1986; microfilm to 1969. Mail turnaround time 5 days.
Criminal Records: Access: Fax, mail, in person. Only the court performs in person searches. No search fee. Court makes copy: $.30 per page (first 10 free to county resident). Required to search: name, years to search, DOB; also helpful: SSN. Criminal records on computer since 1986; microfilm from 1969. Mail turnaround time 5 days.

General Information: Public terminal has only civil records back to 1986. No suppressed, juvenile, sex offenders, mental health, or probation records released. Will fax documents $5.00 1st page, $1.00 each add'l. Certification fee: $10.00 plus $1.00 per page after first. Payee: 12th District Court. Personal checks accepted. Prepayment required. SASE helpful.

Probate Court 312 S Jackson St, 1st Fl, Jackson, MI 49201; phone: 517-788-4290; fax: 517-788-4291; hours 8AM-5PM (EST). *Probate.*

Kalamazoo County

9th Circuit Court 227 W Michigan Ave, Kalamazoo, MI 49007; phone: 269-383-8837; hours 8AM-5PM (EST). *Felony, Civil Actions Over $25,000.*
www.kalcounty.com/courts/index.htm
Civil Records: Access: Mail, in person. Visitors must perform in person searches themselves. Search fee: $1.00 per name. Court makes copy: $1.00 per page. Required to search: name, years to search. Civil cases indexed by defendant, plaintiff. Civil records stored as hard copies, some records kept off-site; computerized records go back to 1984. Mail turnaround time 2 days.
Criminal Records: Access: Mail, in person. Visitors must perform in person searches themselves. Search fee: $1.00 per name. Court makes copy: $1.00 per page. Required to search: name, years to search, DOB. Criminal records stored as hard copies, some records kept off-site; computerized records go back to 1984. Mail turnaround time 2 days.
General Information: Public terminal has criminal back to 1984 and civil back to 1970s. (Terminal has index of case numbers only.) No suppressed or non-public records released. Will not fax documents. Certification fee: $1.00 per page for criminal includes copy fee. $13.00 per doc for gold seal, civil only. Payee: Circuit Court Clerk. Personal checks accepted. Prepayment and SASE required.

8th District Court - North 227 W Michigan St, Kalamazoo, MI 49007; phone: 269-384-8171; fax: 269-384-8047; hours 8AM-5PM (EST). *Misdemeanor.*
Note: This court covers Kalamazoo County.
Criminal Records: Access: Fax, mail, in person. Both court and visitors may perform in person searches. No search fee. Court makes copy: $1.00 per page. Required to search: name, years to search, DOB; also helpful: SSN. Some criminal records on computer back to 1991, prior on books to 1969. This court will not do general name searches; a specific case number must be given. All requests to review files or obtain document copies must be made on the File/Copy Request Form. Each requester may only request 5 case files per day. Mail turnaround time 2 days, 5 days if files in storage.
General Information: Public terminal has only criminal records. No suppressed or non-public records released. No fee to fax documents. Certification fee: $10.00 1st page, $1.00 ea add'l. Cert fee includes copies. Payee: 8th District Court. Personal checks or Visa, MC, Discover accepted. Prepayment required. SASE requested.

8th District Court - South 7810 Shaver Rd, Portage, MI 49002; phone: 269-383-6460; fax: 269-321-3645; hours 8AM-5PM (EST). *Misdemeanor, Civil Actions Under $25,000, Eviction, Small Claims.*
Note: This court covers Kalamazoo County South of N Ave. (Kilgore Rd).
Civil Records: Access: Mail, in person. Both court and visitors may perform in person searches. Search fee: $20.00 per name if prior to 1992. Court makes copy: $1.00 per page. Required to search: name, years to search. Civil cases indexed by defendant, plaintiff; on computer back to 1991, prior on index books to 1969. Up to 5 case files may be reviewed in person immediately, otherwise subject to availability of court staff. Mail turnaround time 5 days.

Criminal Records: Access: Mail, in person. Both court and visitors may perform in person searches. Search fee: $20.00 per name if prior to 1992. Court makes copy: $1.00 per page. Required to search: name, years to search, DOB; also helpful: SSN. Criminal records on computer back to 1991, prior on index books to 1969. Up to 5 case files may be reviewed in person immediately, otherwise subject to availability of court staff. Mail turnaround time 5 days.
General Information: Public terminal goes back to 1991. No suppressed, juvenile, sex offenders, mental health, or adoption records released. Fee to fax documents is $1.00 per page. Certification fee: $10.00. Payee: 8th District Court. Personal checks accepted. Prepayment and SASE required.

8th District Court - Crosstown 150 E Crosstown Parkway, Kalamazoo, MI 49001; phone: 269-384-8171; fax: 269-383-8899; hours 8AM-5PM (EST). *Civil Actions Under $25,000, Eviction, Small Claims.*
Note: This court covers City of Kalamazoo.
Civil Records: Access: Fax, mail, in person. Visitors must perform in person searches themselves. No search fee. Court makes copy: $1.00 per page. Required to search: name, years to search. Civil cases indexed by defendant, plaintiff; on computer back to 1998, prior on index books to 1969. In person case record reviewing is subject to availability of court staff and court files. Mail turnaround time 1-3 days.
General Information: Public terminal has only civil records. Certification fee: $10.00. Payee: 8th District Court. Personal checks or Visa, MC, Discover accepted. Prepayment required.

Probate Court 150 E Crosstown Parkway, Kalamazoo, MI 49001; phone: 269-383-8666; fax: 269-383-8685; hours 9AM-N, 1-5PM (EST). *Probate.*

Kalkaska County

46th Circuit Court PO Box 10, Kalkaska, MI 49646; phone: 231-258-3300; probate phone: 231-258-3314; fax: 231-258-3337; hours 9AM-5PM (EST). *Felony, Civil Actions Over $25,000.*
www.Circuit46.org
Note: Probate records located at 605 N Birch St.
Civil Records: Access: Mail, in person, online. Only the court performs in person searches. Search fee: $5.00 per name. Court makes copy: $1.00 per page. Required to search: name, years to search. Civil cases indexed by defendant, plaintiff; on computer since 1989, prior on books, indexed to 1800s. Online access to court case records (open or closed cases for 90 days only) is free at www.circuit46.org/Cases/cases.html. Mail turnaround time 2-3 days.
Criminal Records: Access: Mail, in person, online. Only the court performs in person searches. Search fee: $5.00 per name. Court makes copy: $1.00 per page. Required to search: name, years to search, DOB; also helpful: SSN. Criminal records on computer since 1989, prior on books, indexed to 1800s. Online access to criminal records is the same as civil. Mail turnaround time 2-3 days.
General Information: No public access terminal. No suppressed records released. Will fax documents for $3.00 plus $1.00 per page (on certain records some we are unable to fax). Certification fee: $10.00 per document. Payee: Kalkaska County Clerk. Personal checks accepted. Prepayment and SASE required.

46th Circuit Trial Court - District Court 605 N Birch St, Kalkaska, MI 49646; phone: 231-258-9031; fax: 231-258-2424; hours 8AM-4:30PM (EST). *Misdemeanor, Civil Actions Under $25,000, Eviction, Small Claims.*
www.Circuit46.org
Civil Records: Access: Phone, mail, in person, online. Both court and visitors may perform in person searches. No search fee. Court makes copy: $1.00 per page. Required to search: name, years to search. Civil cases indexed by defendant, plaintiff; on

computer since 1989, prior on books. Online access to court case records (open or closed cases for 90 days only) is free at www.circuit46.org/Cases/cases.html. Mail turnaround time 4 days plus mailing time.

Criminal Records: Access: Phone, mail, in person, online. Both court and visitors may perform in person searches. No search fee. Court makes copy: $1.00 per page. Required to search: name, years to search, DOB. Criminal records on computer since 1989, prior on books. Online access to criminal records is the same as civil. Mail turnaround time 4 days plus mailing time.

General Information: Public terminal goes back to 1989. (Terminal is in a secured area, available by approved appointment only.) No suppressed records released. Will fax documents to local or toll free line. Certification fee: $10.00 plus $1.00 per page after first. Payee: 46th Circuit Trial Court. Only cashiers checks and money orders accepted. Prepayment and SASE required.

Circuit Trial Court - Probate Division 605
N Birch, Kalkaska, MI 49646; phone: 231-258-3330 x2; fax: 231-258-3329; hours 8AM-4:30PM (EST). *Probate.*
www.Circuit46.org
Note: Search cases by name free at www.circuit46.org/Cases/cases.html.

Kent County

17th Circuit Court 180 Ottawa Ave NW, #2400,
Grand Rapids, MI 49503; phone: 616-632-5480; fax: 616-632-5458; hours 8AM-5PM (EST). *Felony, Civil Actions Over $25,000.*
www.accesskent.com/CourtsAndLawEnforcement
Civil Records: Access: Mail, in person, online. Only the court performs in person searches. Search fee: $5.00 per name. Court makes copy: $1.00 per page. Required to search: name, years to search. Civil cases indexed by defendant, plaintiff; on computer since 1986, prior on books. Search for $6.00 per name at https://www.accesskent.com/CourtNameSearch/. DOB not required but credit card is for record found. Also, search hearings schedule free at https://www.accesskent.com/CCHearing/ Mail turnaround time 2-3 days.
Criminal Records: Access: Mail, in person, online. Only the court performs in person searches. Search fee: $5.00 per name. Court makes copy: $1.00 per page. Required to search: name, years to search, DOB. Criminal records on computer since 1986, prior on books. Search for $6.00 per name at https://www.accesskent.com/CourtNameSearch/. DOB and credit card required for results. Also, search for accident reports at $3.00 per name at https://www.accesskent.com/AccidentReports/ Mail turnaround time 2-3 days.
General Information: No public access terminal. No suppressed records released. Will fax documents to local or toll free line. Certification fee: $10.00 after 1st page. Payee: Kent County Clerk. Personal checks accepted. Prepayment required.

59th District Court - Walker 4343
Remembrance Rd NW, Walker, MI 49544; phone: 616-453-5765; fax: 616-791-6851; hours 8AM--5PM (EST). *Misdemeanor, Civil Actions Under $25,000, Eviction, Small Claims.*
Civil Records: Access: Mail, in person. Only the court performs in person searches. Search fee: $1.00 per name. Add $.50 per year requested. Court makes copy: $1.00 per page. Required to search: name, years to search; also helpful: address. Civil cases indexed by defendant, plaintiff; on computer from 1989, docket books and cards prior. Mail turnaround time varies.
Criminal Records: Access: Mail, in person. Only the court performs in person searches. Search fee: $1.00 per name. Add $.50 per year requested. Court makes copy: $1.00 per page. Required to search: name, years to search, DOB; also helpful: address, SSN. Criminal records on computer from 1989, docket books and cards prior. Mail turnaround time varies.

General Information: No public access terminal. No suppressed, juvenile, sex offenders, mental health, or adoption records released. Will fax documents for $1.00 per name. Certification fee: $10.00 plus $1.00 per page after first. Payee: 59th District Court. Personal checks accepted. Prepayment and SASE required.

59th District Court - Grandville 3161
Wilson Ave SW, Grandville, MI 49418; phone: 616-538-9660; fax: 616-538-5144; hours 8:30AM--5PM (EST). *Misdemeanor, Civil Actions Under $25,000, Eviction, Small Claims.*
www.cityofgrandville.com/Services/Courts/Overview
Courts.htm
Civil Records: Access: Mail, in person. Both court and visitors may perform in person searches. Search fee: $8.00. Court makes copy: $1.00 per page. Required to search: name, years to search; also helpful: address. Civil cases indexed by defendant, plaintiff; on computer from 1986, docket books and cards prior. Mail turnaround time 1-2 days.
Criminal Records: Access: Mail, in person. Both court and visitors may perform in person searches. Search fee: $8.00. Court makes copy: $1.00 per page. Required to search: name, years to search, DOB; also helpful: address, SSN. Criminal records on computer from 1986, docket books and cards prior. Mail turnaround time 1-2 days.
General Information: Public terminal goes back to 1986. No suppressed, juvenile, sex offenders, mental health, or adoption records released. Certification fee: $10.00 plus $1.00 per page after first. Payee: 59th District Court. Personal checks accepted. Prepayment and SASE required.

61st District Court - Grand Rapids 180
Ottawa Ave NW #1400, Kent County Courthouse, Grand Rapids, MI 49503; phone: 616-632-5700; fax: 616-632-5592; hours 7:45AM-4:45PM (EST). *Misdemeanor, Civil Actions Under $25,000, Eviction, Small Claims.*
www.ci.grand-rapids.mi.us/197
Civil Records: Access: Mail, in person, online. Both court and visitors may perform in person searches. No search fee. Court makes copy: $1.00 for first page, $.50 each add'l. Required to search: name, years to search. Civil cases indexed by defendant, plaintiff. Civil records kept in files and books, computerized since 1999. Search online at www.ci.grand-rapids.mi.us/index.pl?page_id=645. Mail turnaround time 7-10 days.
Criminal Records: Access: Mail, in person, online. Both court and visitors may perform in person searches. Search fee: $1.00 per name per year. Court makes copy: $1.00 for first page, $.50 each add'l. Required to search: name, years to search, DOB; also helpful: SSN. Criminal records are automated from 1999, images on microfiche from 1980. Search online at www.ci.grand-rapids.mi.us/index.pl?page_id=645. Mail turnaround time 7-10 days.
General Information: Public terminal goes back to 10/1999. No suppressed, juvenile, sex offenders, mental health, or adoption records released. Certification fee: $10.00 plus $1.00 per page after first. Payee: 61st District Court. Personal checks accepted. Prepayment required. Prepayment of mail service required.

62 A District Court - Wyoming 2650 De
Hoop Ave SW, Wyoming, MI 49509; phone: 616-530-7385; criminal phone: 616-257-9814; civil phone: 616-530-7386; fax: 616-249-3419; hours 8AM-5PM (EST). *Misdemeanor, Civil Actions Under $25,000, Eviction, Small Claims.*
www.ci.wyoming.mi.us/courts.htm
Civil Records: Access: Mail, fax, in person. Both court and visitors may perform in person searches. Search fee: $1.00 per name & $.50 per year. Court makes copy: $1.00 per page. Required to search: name, years to search. Civil cases indexed by defendant, plaintiff. Civil records kept on docket books since 1980; on computer back to 1997. The

judge must approve all requests from collection agencies. Mail turnaround time 2-3 days.
Criminal Records: Access: Mail, fax, in person. Both court and visitors may perform in person searches. Search fee: $1.00 per name & $.50 per year. Court makes copy: $1.00 per page. Required to search: name, years to search; also helpful: Case #. Criminal records kept on docket books since 1980; on computer back to 1997. The court suggests mail requests be sent to the state police. Mail turnaround time 2-3 days.
General Information: Public terminal goes back to 1997. No suppressed, juvenile, sex offenders, mental health, or adoption records released. Certification fee: $10.00 plus $1.00 per page after first. Payee: 62 A District Court. Personal checks accepted. Credit cards accepted: Visa. Accepted in person only. Prepayment and SASE required.

62 B District Court - Kentwood 4740
Walma Ave SW, Kentwood, MI 49512; phone: 616-698-9310; fax: 616-698-8199; hours 8AM-5PM (EST). *Misdemeanor, Civil Actions Under $25,000, Eviction, Small Claims.*
Civil Records: Access: Mail, in person. Both court and visitors may perform in person searches. Search fee: $5.00 per name. Court makes copy: $2.00 for first page, $.25 each add'l. Required to search: name, years to search. Civil cases indexed by defendant, plaintiff; on computer since 11/88, prior on books. Mail turnaround time 1-2 days.
Criminal Records: Access: Mail, in person. Both court and visitors may perform in person searches. Search fee: $5.00 per name. Court makes copy: $2.00 for first page, $.25 each add'l. Required to search: name, years to search, DOB. Criminal records on computer since 11/88, prior on books. Mail turnaround time 1-2 days.
General Information: Public terminal goes back to 11/1988. No suppressed, juvenile, sex offenders, mental health, or adoption records released. Certification fee: $10.00. Payee: 62 B District Court. Personal checks accepted. Prepayment and SASE required.

63rd District Court - 1st Division 105
Maple St, Rockford, MI 49341; phone: 616-866-1576; fax: 616-866-3080; hours 8AM-5PM (EST). *Misdemeanor, Civil Actions Under $25,000, Eviction, Small Claims.*
Civil Records: Access: In person only. Visitors must perform in person searches themselves. Court makes copy: $1.00 per page. Required to search: name, years to search. Civil cases indexed by defendant, plaintiff; on computer since 8/94, prior on books. Mail turnaround time 1 week.
Criminal Records: Access: In person, fax. Visitors must perform in person searches themselves. No search fee. Court makes copy: $1.00 per page. Required to search: name, years to search, DOB; also helpful: SSN. Criminal records on computer since 8/94, prior on books.
General Information: Public use terminal available. No suppressed, juvenile, sex offenders, mental health, or adoption records released. Certification fee: $10.00. Payee: 63rd District Court. Personal checks accepted. Prepayment required.

Probate Court 180 Ottawa Ave NW #2500,
Grand Rapids, MI 49503; phone: 616-632-5440; fax: 616-632-5430; hours 8:30AM-4:30PM (EST). *Probate.*

Keweenaw County

12th Circuit Court 5095 4th St, Eagle River, MI
49950-9744; phone: 906-337-2229; fax: 906-337-2795; hours 9AM-4PM (EST). *Felony, Civil Actions Over $25,000.*
Civil Records: Access: Mail, in person. Only the court performs in person searches. No search fee. Court makes copy: $1.00 per page; same fee for self serve. Required to search: name, years to search. Civil cases indexed by defendant, plaintiff. Civil records kept on index books since 1963. Mail turnaround time 1-2 days.

Criminal Records: Access: Mail, in person. Only the court performs in person searches. Search fee: $10.00. Court makes copy: $1.00 per page; same fee for self serve. Required to search: name, years to search, DOB. Criminal records kept on index books since 1964. Mail turnaround 1-2 days.

General Information: No public access terminal. No suppressed, juvenile, sex offenders, mental health, or adoption records released. Will fax documents. Certification fee: $10.00 per document. Payee: Keweenaw County. Personal checks accepted. Prepayment required. SASE requested.

97th District Court 5095 4th St, Eagle River, MI 49950; phone: 906-337-2229; fax: 906-337-2795; hours 9AM-4PM (EST). *Misdemeanor, Civil Actions Under $25,000, Eviction, Small Claims.*

Civil Records: Access: Fax, mail, in person. Only the court performs in person searches. Search fee: $10.00 per name. Court makes copy: $1.00 per page; same fee for self serve. Required to search: name, years to search. Civil cases indexed by defendant, plaintiff. Civil records kept on books to 1970's. Results cannot be faxed. Mail turnaround time 1-2 days.

Criminal Records: Access: Fax, mail, in person. Only the court performs in person searches. Search fee: $10.00 per name. Court makes copy: $1.00 per page; same fee for self serve. Required to search: name, years to search, DOB; also helpful: SSN. Criminal records on books to 1970's. Results cannot be faxed. Mail turnaround 1-2 days.

General Information: No suppressed, juvenile, sex offenders, mental health, or adoption records released. Will fax documents. Certification fee: $10.00 per document. Payee: Keweenaw County. Personal checks accepted. Prepayment and SASE required.

Probate Court 5095 4th St, Eagle River, MI 49950; phone: 906-337-1927; fax: 906-337-2795; hours 9AM-4PM (EST). *Probate.*

Lake County

Lake County Trial Court 800 10th St, #300, Baldwin, MI 49304; phone: 231-745-4614; criminal phone: same; hours 8AM-N, 1-5PM (EST). *Felony, Misdemeanor, Civil Actions, Eviction, Small Claims, Probate.*

Civil Records: Access: Mail, in person. Only the court performs in person searches. Search fee: $5.00 per name per year. Court makes copy: $1.00 per page. Required to search: name, years to search. Civil cases indexed by defendant, plaintiff; on computer since 7/89, prior on books to 1876. Mail turnaround time 1-2 days.

Criminal Records: Access: Mail, in person. Only the court performs in person searches. Search fee: $5.00 per name per year. Court makes copy: $1.00 per page. Required to search: name, years to search, DOB; also helpful: SSN. Criminal records on computer since 7/89, prior on books to 1876. Mail turnaround time 1-2 days.

General Information: No public access terminal. No suppressed, sex offenders, mental health, or adoption records released. Fee to fax documents is $1.00 per document. Certification fee: $10.00. Payee: Lake County Trial Court. Personal checks accepted. Prepayment required.

Lapeer County

40th Circuit Court 255 Clay St, Lapeer, MI 48446; phone: 810-667-0358; hours 8AM-5PM (EST). *Felony, Civil Actions Over $25,000.*

Civil Records: Access: Mail, in person. Visitors must perform in person searches themselves. Search fee: $5.00 search fee covers 10 year span. Court makes copy: $1.00 per page. Required to search: name, years to search. Civil cases indexed by defendant, plaintiff; on computer since 1994, prior on index cards. Mail turnaround time 48 hours.

Criminal Records: Access: Mail, in person. Visitors must perform in person searches themselves. Search fee: $5.00 search fee covers 10 year span. Court makes copy: $1.00 per page. Required to

search: name, years to search; DOB, sex helpful. Criminal records on computer since 1996, prior on index cards. Mail turnaround time 48 hours.

General Information: Public terminal has criminal back to 1996 and civil back to 1994. No suppressed records released. Certification fee: $10.00 plus $1.00 per page after first. Cert fee includes copies. Payee: 40th Circuit Court. Personal checks accepted. Prepayment and SASE required.

71 A District Court 255 Clay St, Lapeer, MI 48446; phone: 810-667-0314; hours 8AM-5PM (EST). *Misdemeanor, Civil Actions Under $25,000, Eviction, Small Claims.*

Civil Records: Access: Mail, in person. Only the court performs in person searches. Search fee: $5.00 per name. Court makes copy: $1.00 per page. Required to search: name, years to search. Civil cases indexed by defendant, plaintiff; on computer since 1992, cards and dockets from 1969. Mail turnaround time 10 days.

Criminal Records: Access: Mail, in person. Only the court performs in person searches. Search fee: $5.00 per name. Court makes copy: $1.00 per page. Required to search: name, years to search, DOB; also helpful: SSN. Criminal records on computer since 1992, cards and dockets from 1969. Mail turnaround time 10 days.

General Information: No public access terminal. No suppressed, juvenile, sex offenders, mental health, or adoption records released. Certification fee: $10.00 plus $1.00 per page after first. Payee: 71 A District Court. Third party checks not accepted. Prepayment and SASE required.

Probate Court 255 Clay St, Lapeer, MI 48446; phone: 810-667-0261; fax: 810-667-0271; hours 8AM-5PM (EST). *Probate.*

Leelanau County

13th Circuit Court PO Box 467, Leland, MI 49654; phone: 231-256-9824; fax: 231-256-8295; hours 9AM-5PM (EST). *Felony, Civil Actions Over $25,000.*

Civil Records: Access: Mail, fax, in person. Both court and visitors may perform in person searches. Search fee: $3.00 per name. Court makes copy: $.50 per page. Required to search: name, years to search. Civil cases indexed by defendant, plaintiff; on computer since 1/93, prior on docket books. Mail turnaround time 2-3 days.

Criminal Records: Access: Mail, fax, in person. Both court and visitors may perform in person searches. Search fee: $3.00 per name. Court makes copy: $.50 per page. Required to search: name, years to search. Criminal records on computer since 1/97; prior records on books. Mail turnaround time 2-3 days.

General Information: No public access terminal. No suppressed, juvenile, sex offenders, mental health, or adoption records released. Will fax documents to local or toll free line. Certification fee: $10.00 plus $1.00 per page after first copy fee. Payee: County Clerk. Personal checks accepted. Prepayment and SASE required.

86th District Court PO Box 486, 301 E Cedar St, Leland, MI 49654; phone: 231-256-8250; fax: 231-256-8275; hours 8AM-4PM (EST). *Misdemeanor, Civil Actions Under $25,000, Eviction, Small Claims.*

www.co.leelanau.mi.us/government0254.asp

Civil Records: Access: Fax, mail, in person. Only the court performs in person searches. No search fee. Court makes copy: $1.00 per page. Required to search: name, years to search. Civil cases indexed by defendant, plaintiff; on computer since 1991, prior on books to 1969. Mail turnaround time 3 days.

Criminal Records: Access: Phone, fax, mail, in person. Only the court performs in person searches. No search fee. Court makes copy: $1.00 per page. Required to search: name, years to search, DOB; also helpful: SSN. Criminal records on computer since 1991, prior on books to 1969. Mail turnaround time 3 days.

General Information: No public access terminal. No suppressed, sex offenders records released. Fee to fax documents is $.25 per page. Certification fee: $10.00 per document. Payee: 86th District Court. Business checks accepted. Prepayment required. SASE requested.

Family Court PO Box 595, 301 E Cedar St, Leland, MI 49654; phone: 231-256-9803; fax: 231-256-9845; hours 9AM-5PM (EST). *Probate.*

Lenawee County

39th Circuit Court 425 N Main St, Adrian, MI 49221; phone: 517-264-4597; fax: 517-264-4790; hours 8AM-4:30PM (EST). *Felony, Civil Actions Over $25,000.*

Civil Records: Access: Mail, in person. Both court and visitors may perform in person searches. Search fee: $10.00 per name. Fee is for ten years. Court makes copy: $1.00 per page. Required to search: name, years to search. Civil records on computer back to 1/89, prior on books. Mail turnaround time 1-2 days.

Criminal Records: Access: Mail, in person. Both court and visitors may perform in person searches. Search fee: $10.00 per name. Fee is for 10 years. Court makes copy: $1.00 per page. Required to search: name, years to search. Criminal records on computer back to 1/89, prior on books. Mail turnaround time 1-2 days.

General Information: Public terminal goes back to 1989. No suppressed, juvenile, sex offenders, mental health, or adoption records released. Will fax documents. Certification fee: $13.00 per doc includes copy fee. Payee: Lenawee County Clerk or 39th Circuit Court. Personal checks accepted. Prepayment required. SASE helpful.

2A District Court 425 N Main St, Adrian, MI 49221; phone: 517-264-4673 & 264-4668; fax: 517-264-4665; hours 8AM-4:30PM (EST). *Misdemeanor, Civil Actions Under $25,000, Eviction, Small Claims.*

Note: Fax Probation at 517-264-4665.

Civil Records: Access: Fax, mail, in person. Both court and visitors may perform in person searches. Search fee: $10.00 per name. Court makes copy: $.25 per page. Required to search: name, years to search. Civil cases indexed by defendant, plaintiff; on computer since 1988, prior on index books, cards and microfilm back to 1968.

Criminal Records: Access: In person only. Both court and visitors may perform in person searches. Search fee: $10.00 per name. Court makes copy: $.25 per page. Required to search: name, years to search, DOB. Criminal records on computer since 1988, prior on index books, cards and microfilm back to 1969. Mail turnaround time 1 week.

General Information: No public access terminal. No suppressed, juvenile, sex offenders, mental health, or adoption records released. Will fax documents to local or toll free line. Certification fee: $10.00. Payee: 2A District Court. Personal checks accepted. Prepayment and SASE required.

Probate Court 425 N Main St, Adrian, MI 49221; phone: 517-264-4614; fax: 517-264-4616; hours 8AM-4:30PM (EST). *Probate.*

Livingston County

44th Circuit Court 204 S Highlander Way #4, Howell, MI 48843; phone: 517-546-9816; probate phone: 517-346-3750; fax: 517-548-4219; probate fax: 517-552-2510; hours 8AM-5PM (EST). *Felony, Civil Actions Over $25,000.*

www.co.livingston.mi.us/

Note: Juvenile Unit records are at 517-546-1500. Probate in a separate index at this same address.

Civil Records: Access: Mail, in person. Both court and visitors may perform in person searches. No search fee. Court makes copy: $1.00 per page. Required to search: name, years to search. Civil cases indexed by defendant, plaintiff. Civil records computerized from 1987, on microfiche and archived from 1900s. Mail turnaround time 5 days.

Criminal Records: Access: Mail, in person. Both court and visitors may perform in person searches. No search fee. Court makes copy: $1.00 per page. Required to search: name, years to search. Criminal records computerized from 1987, microfiche and archived from 1900s. Mail turnaround time 5 days.

General Information: Public terminal goes back to 1987. All records released, none are restricted. Will fax documents to local or toll free line. Certification fee: $10.00 per document. Payee: Livingston County Clerk. Personal checks accepted. Out of state checks not accepted. Prepayment and SASE required.

53 A District Court 204 S Highlander Way #1, Howell, MI 48843; phone: 517-548-1000; criminal phone: 517-548-1000 x7642; civil phone: 517-548-1000 x7648; fax: 517-548-9445; hours 8AM-5PM (EST). *Misdemeanor, Civil Actions Under $25,000, Eviction, Small Claims.*

http://co.livingston.mi.us/DistrictCourt

Civil Records: Access: Mail, in person. Visitors must perform in person searches themselves. No search fee. Court makes copy: $1.00 per page. Required to search: name, years to search; also helpful: address. Civil cases indexed by defendant, plaintiff; on computer since 1982.

Criminal Records: Access: In person only. Visitors must perform in person searches themselves. Court makes copy: $1.00 per page. Required to search: name, years to search, DOB; also helpful: address, SSN. Criminal records on computer since 1982.

General Information: Public terminal goes back to 10 years. No suppressed, juvenile, sex offenders, mental health, or adoption records released. Certification fee: $10.00. Payee: 53 District Court. Personal checks accepted. Prepayment required.

53 B District Court 224 N1st St, Brighton, MI 48116; phone: 810-229-6615; fax: 810-229-1770; hours 8AM-5PM (EST). *Misdemeanor, Civil Actions Under $25,000, Eviction, Small Claims.*

http://co.livingston.mi.us/DistrictCourt/brighton.htm

Civil Records: Access: Mail, in person. Only the court performs in person searches. No search fee. Court makes copy: $1.00 per page. Required to search: name, years to search. Civil cases indexed by defendant, plaintiff; on computer since 1985, prior on index books. Mail turnaround time 1 week.

Criminal Records: Access: Mail, in person, fax. Only the court performs in person searches. No search fee. Court makes copy: $1.00 per page. Required to search: name, years to search, DOB; also helpful: SSN. Criminal records on computer since 1985, prior on index books. Mail turnaround time 1 week.

General Information: No public access terminal. No suppressed, juvenile, sex offenders, mental health, or adoption records released. Certification fee: $10.00. Payee: 53rd District Court. Personal checks accepted. Prepayment and SASE required.

Probate Court 204 Highlander Way #2, Howell, MI 48843; phone: 517-546-3750; fax: 517-552-2510; hours 8AM-5PM (EST). *Probate.*

www.co.livingston.mi.us/probatecourt

Luce County

11th Circuit Court 407 W Harrie, Newberry, MI 49868; phone: 906-293-5521; probate phone: 906-293-5601; fax: 906-293-5553; hours 8AM-4PM (EST). *Felony, Civil Actions Over $25,000.*

Civil Records: Access: Mail, in person. Only the court performs in person searches. No search fee. Court makes copy: $1.00 per page. Required to search: name, years to search. Civil cases indexed by defendant, plaintiff. Civil records listed on cards since 1876. Mail turnaround time 4-5 days.

Criminal Records: Access: Mail, in person. Only the court performs in person searches. No search fee. Court makes copy: $1.00 per page. Required to search: name, years to search, DOB. Criminal records listed on cards since 1876. Mail turnaround time 4-5 days.

General Information: No public access terminal. No suppressed, juvenile, sex offenders, mental health, or adoption records released. Will fax documents for $1.00 per page plus $1.00 fax fee. Certification fee: $10.00. Payee: 11th Circuit Court. Personal checks accepted. Prepayment and SASE required.

92nd District Court 407 W Harrie, Newberry, MI 49868; phone: 906-293-5531; fax: 906-293-5773; hours 8AM-4PM (EST). *Misdemeanor, Civil Actions Under $25,000, Eviction, Small Claims.*

Civil Records: Access: Phone, fax, mail, in person. Only the court performs in person searches. No search fee. Court makes copy: $1.00 per page. Required to search: name, years to search. Civil records indexed by defendant, plaintiff. Civil records to 1969, some on computer. Mail turnaround time 1 week.

Criminal Records: Access: Phone, fax, mail, in person. Only the court performs in person searches. No search fee. Court makes copy: $1.00 per page. Required to search: name, years to search, DOB; also helpful: SSN. Criminal records to 1969, some on computer. Mail turnaround time 1 week.

General Information: No public access terminal. Will fax documents $1.00 per page. No certification fee. Payee: 92nd District Court. In state personal checks accepted. Prepayment required. SASE preferred.

Probate Court 407 W. Harrie, Newberry, MI 49868; phone: 906-293-5601; fax: 906-293-3581; hours 8AM-N, 1-4PM (EST). *Probate.*

Note: This is a combined court with Mackinac County Probate Court.

Mackinac County

11th Circuit Court 100 S Marley St, Rm 10, St Ignace, MI 49781; phone: 906-643-7300; fax: 906-643-7302; hours 8:30AM-4:30PM (EST). *Felony, Civil Actions Over $25,000.*

Civil Records: Access: Mail, in person. Both court and visitors may perform in person searches. Search fee: $10.00. Court makes copy: $1.00 per page. Required to search: name, years to search. Civil cases indexed by defendant, plaintiff; on docket book; on computer back to 1998. Mail turnaround time 10 days.

Criminal Records: Access: Mail, in person. Only the court performs in person searches. Search fee: $10.00. Court makes copy: $1.00 per page. Required to search: name, years to search, DOB. Criminal records on docket book; on computer back to 1998. Mail turnaround time 10 days.

General Information: No public access terminal. No suppressed, juvenile, sex offenders, mental health, or adoption records released. Will fax documents. Certification fee: $10.00 per cert. Payee: County Clerk. Personal checks accepted. Prepayment and SASE required.

92nd District Court 100 S Marley, Rm 55, St Ignace, MI 49781; phone: 906-643-7321; fax: 906-643-7302; hours 8:30AM-4:30PM (EST). *Misdemeanor, Civil Actions Under $25,000, Eviction, Small Claims.*

Civil Records: Access: Mail, in person, fax, phone. Both court and visitors may perform in person searches. Search fee: $10.00 per name. Court makes copy: $1.00 per page. Required to search: name, years to search. Civil cases indexed by defendant. Civil records on computer since 11/92, prior in files to 1980. Mail turnaround time 1 week.

Criminal Records: Access: Fax, mail, in person. Both court and visitors may perform in person searches. Search fee: $10.00 per name. Court makes copy: $1.00 per page. Required to search: name, years to search, DOB. Criminal records on computer since 11/92, prior in files to 1970. Mail turnaround time 1 week.

General Information: No public access terminal. No suppressed, juvenile, sex offenders, mental health, or adoption records released. Will fax documents for $10.00 per name. No certification fee. Prepayment and SASE required.

Probate Court 100 S Marley St Rm. 15, St Ignace, MI 49781; phone: 906-643-7303; fax: 906-643-8861; hours 8:30AM-N, 1-4:30PM (EST). *Probate.*

Note: This is a combined court with Luce County Probate Court.

Macomb County

16th Circuit Court 40 N Main St, Mount Clemens, MI 48043; phone: 586-469-5120; fax: 586-783-8184; hours 8AM-4:30PM (EST). *Felony, Civil Actions Over $25,000.*

www.macombcountymi.gov/circuitcourt

Civil Records: Access: Mail, fax, in person, online. Both court and visitors may perform in person searches. Search fee: $1.00 per name per year. Court makes copy: $.40 per page. Required to search: name, years to search. Civil cases indexed by defendant, plaintiff; on computer since 1977, on microfiche to 1969, prior to 1800s archived. Civil online access is the same as criminal, see below. Online includes divorces. Mail turnaround time 1 week.

Criminal Records: Access: Mail, fax, in person, online. Both court and visitors may perform in person searches. Search fee: $1.00 per name. Court makes copy: $.40 per page. Required to search: name, years to search; also helpful: DOB. Criminal records on computer since 1970, on microfiche to 1969, prior to 1800s archived. Access Circuit Court index for free at http://209.131.29.171/pa/pa.urd/pamw6500.display. Fee to copy and view documents. Mail turnaround time 1 week.

General Information: Public use terminal available. No suppressed, juvenile, sex offenders, mental health, or adoption records released. Will fax documents for $10.00 plus $1.00 per page fax fee. Certification fee: $10.00 per doc. Payee: Macomb County Clerk. Personal checks accepted. Most credit cards accepted. Prepayment and SASE required.

37th District Court - Warren & Center Line 8300 Common Rd, Warren, MI 48093; phone: 586-574-4900; fax: 586-574-4932; hours 8:30AM-4:30PM (EST). *Misdemeanor, Civil Actions Under $25,000, Eviction, Small Claims.*

Civil Records: Access: Mail, in person. Only the court performs in person searches. Search fee: $10.00 per name. Court makes copy: $.50 per page. Required to search: name, years to search. Civil cases indexed by defendant, plaintiff; on computer since 1992, prior on index cards. Mail turnaround time 2 weeks.

Criminal Records: Access: Mail, in person, fax. Only the court performs in person searches. Search fee: $10.00 per name. Court makes copy: $.25 per page. Required to search: name, years to search, DOB; also helpful: SSN. Criminal records on computer since 1992, prior on index cards. Mail turnaround time 2 weeks.

General Information: No public access terminal. No suppressed, juvenile, sex offenders, mental health, or adoption records released. Certification fee: $10.00. Payee: 37th District Court. Personal checks accepted. Prepayment required.

39th District Court - Roseville & Fraser 29733 Gratiot Ave, Roseville, MI 48066; phone: 586-773-2010; criminal phone: 586-447-4430; civil phone: 586-447-4420; fax: 586-445-5070; hours 8AM-4:30PM (EST). *Misdemeanor, Civil Actions Under $25,000, Eviction, Small Claims.*

Civil Records: Access: Mail, in person. Only the court performs in person searches. No search fee. Court makes copy: $1.00 per page, $2.00 if on microfilm. Required to search: name, years to search. Civil cases indexed by defendant, plaintiff; on computer since 1985, prior on microfilm. Mail turnaround time 1-2 days.

Criminal Records: Access: Mail, in person. Only the court performs in person searches. No search fee. Court makes copy: $1.00 per page, $2.00 if on microfilm. Required to search: name, years to search, DOB; also helpful: SSN. Criminal records on computer since 1985, prior on microfilm. Mail turnaround time 1-2 days.

General Information: No public access terminal. No suppressed, juvenile, sex offenders, mental health, or adoption records released. Will fax documents to local or toll-free number. No certification fee. Payee: 39th District Court. Personal checks accepted. Prepayment required.

40th District Court - St. Clair Shores

27701 Jefferson, St. Clair Shores, MI 48081; phone: 586-445-5281; criminal phone: 586-445-5281; civil phone: 586-445-5282; fax: 586-445-4003; hours 8:30AM-4:30PM (EST). *Misdemeanor, Civil Actions Under $25,000, Eviction, Small Claims.*

Civil Records: Access: Mail, in person. Visitors must perform in person searches themselves. Search fee: $10.00 per name. Court makes copy: $1.00 per page. Required to search: name, years to search. Civil cases indexed by defendant, plaintiff; on computer since 1991; prior records on index books. The court has a request form that must be used with all searches. Mail turnaround time 2 weeks.

Criminal Records: Access: Mail, in person, fax. Only the court performs in person searches. Search fee: $10.00 per name. Court makes copy: $1.00 per page. Required to search: name, years to search, DOB; also helpful: SSN. Criminal records on computer since 1991; prior records on index books. Mail requests must have case number. The court has a request form that must be used with all searches. Mail turnaround time 2 weeks.

General Information: No public access terminal. No suppressed, juvenile, sex offenders, mental health, or adoption records released. Certification fee: $10.00 per certification. Payee: 40th District Court. Personal checks accepted. Prepayment of mail search required. SASE required.

41 A District Court - Shelby

51660 Van Dyke, Shelby Township, MI 48316; phone: 586-739-7325; fax: 586-726-4555; hours 8AM-Noon; 1-4PM (EST). *Misdemeanor, Civil Actions Under $25,000, Eviction, Small Claims.*

Civil Records: Access: Mail, in person. Both court and visitors may perform in person searches. No search fee. Court makes copy: $1.00 per page. Required to search: name, years to search. Civil cases indexed by defendant, plaintiff; on computer since 1992, prior on index cards. Mail turnaround time 10 days.

Criminal Records: Access: Mail, in person. Both court and visitors may perform in person searches. No search fee. Court makes copy: $1.00 per page. Required to search: name, years to search, DOB. Criminal records on computer since 1992, prior on index cards. Mail turnaround time 10 days.

General Information: Public terminal goes back to 1997. (Available Friday afternoons by appointment only.) No suppressed, sex offenders, mental health records released. Certification fee: $10.00. Payee: 41A District Court. Personal checks accepted. Credit cards accepted. Prepayment and SASE required.

41 A District Court - Sterling Heights

40111 Dodge Park, Sterling Heights, MI 48313; phone: 586-446-2500; criminal phone: 586-446-2550; civil phone: 586-446-2535; hours 8:30AM-4:30PM (EST). *Misdemeanor, Civil Actions Under $25,000, Eviction, Small Claims.*

Civil Records: Access: Mail, in person. Only the court performs in person searches. No search fee. Court makes copy: $.50 per page. Required to search: name, years to search. Civil cases indexed by defendant, plaintiff; on computer since 1986; prior records on books. Mail turnaround time 1 week.

Criminal Records: Access: Mail, in person. Only the court performs in person searches. No search fee. Court makes copy: $.50 per page. Required to search: name, years to search, DOB; also helpful: SSN. Criminal records on computer since 1986; prior records on books. Mail turnaround time 1 week.

General Information: No public access terminal. No suppressed, juvenile, sex offenders, mental health, or adoption records released. Certification fee: $10.00.

Payee: Clerk of Court. Personal checks accepted. Prepayment and SASE required.

41 B District Court - Clinton TWP

40700 Romeo Plank Rd, Clinton Township, MI 48038-2951; phone: 586-286-8010; fax: 586-228-2555; hours 8:30AM-4:30PM (EST). *Misdemeanor, Civil Actions Under $25,000, Eviction, Small Claims.*

Civil Records: Access: Mail, in person. Only the court performs in person searches. No search fee. Court makes copy: $.50 per page. Required to search: name, years to search. Civil cases indexed by defendant, plaintiff; on computer back to 1993, prior on microfilm to 1970s.

Criminal Records: Access: Mail, in person. Only the court performs in person searches. No search fee. Court makes copy: $.50 per page. Required to search: name, years to search, DOB. Criminal records on computer back to 1993, prior on microfilm to 1970s.

General Information: No public access terminal. No suppressed, juvenile, sex offenders, mental health, or adoption records released. Certification fee: $10.00. Payee: 41 B District Court. Personal, cashiers checks and money orders accepted. Visa, MasterCard accepted. Prepayment and SASE required.

42nd District Court Division 1

14713 Thirty-three Mile Rd, PO Box 6, Romeo, MI 48065; phone: 586-752-9679; fax: 586-469-5515; hours 8:30AM-4:45PM (EST). *Misdemeanor, Civil Actions Under $25,000, Eviction, Small Claims.* www.macombcountymi.gov

Civil Records: Access: Mail, in person. Only the court performs in person searches. Search fee: $10.00 per name. Court makes copy: $.35 per page. Required to search: name, years to search. Civil cases indexed by defendant, plaintiff; on computer since 1990, prior on index books. Mail turnaround time 2-3 days.

Criminal Records: Access: Mail, in person. Only the court performs in person searches. Search fee: $10.00 per name. Court makes copy: $.35 per page. Required to search: name, years to search, DOB; also helpful: SSN, sex, signed release. Criminal records on computer since 1990, prior on index books. Mail turnaround time 2-3 days.

General Information: No public access terminal. Certification fee: $10.00. Payee: 42-1 District Court. Personal checks accepted. Prepayment required. SASE requested.

42nd District Court Division 2

43565 Elizabeth St, Mount Clemens, MI 48043; phone: 586-725-9500; criminal phone: 586-469-5046; civil phone: 586-493-0567; fax: 586-469-5516; hours 8:30AM-5PM (EST). *Misdemeanor, Civil Actions Under $25,000, Eviction, Small Claims.* www.macombcountymi.gov

Note: Includes City of New Baltimore, Village of New Haven, and townships of Lenox and Chesterfield. This court was formerly located in New Baltimore.

Civil Records: Access: Mail, in person. Only the court performs in person searches. No search fee. Court makes copy: $1.00 per page. Required to search: name, years to search. Civil cases indexed by defendant, plaintiff; on computer back to 1990. Mail turnaround time 1 week.

Criminal Records: Access: Mail, in person. Only the court performs in person searches. No search fee. Court makes copy: $1.00 per page. Required to search: name, years to search, DOB; also helpful: SSN. Criminal records on computer back to 1990. Mail turnaround time 1 week.

General Information: No public access terminal. Will fax case file for $.50 per page. Certification fee: $10.00 per doc includes copies. Payee: 42nd District Court. Personal checks accepted. Prepayment required. Prepayment of mail search required. SASE required.

41 B District Court - Mt Clemens

1 Crocker Blvd, Mount Clemens, MI 48043; phone: 586-469-6870; fax: 586-469-5037; hours 8AM-4:30PM (EST). *Civil Actions Under $25,000, Eviction, Small Claims.*

Note: Small claims fax is 586-469-5710.

Civil Records: Access: Mail, fax, in person. Only the court performs in person searches. No search fee. Court makes copy: $.50 per page. Required to search: name, years to search; also helpful-DOB, case number. Civil cases indexed by defendant, plaintiff; on computer back to 1996; prior on books back to 1930's. Mail turnaround time 3 days.

General Information: No public access terminal. No suppressed, juvenile, sex offenders, mental health, or adoption records released. Will not fax documents. Certification fee: $10.00 per certification. Payee: 41 B District Court. Business checks or Visa, MC accepted. Prepayment and SASE required.

Probate Court 21850 Dumham, Mount Clemens, MI 48043-1075; phone: 586-469-5290; fax: 586-783-0971; hours 8:30AM-4;30PM (EST). *Probate.* www.macombcountymi.gov

Manistee County

19th Circuit Court 415 3rd St, Manistee, MI 49660; phone: 231-723-3331; fax: 231-723-1492; hours 8:30AM-5PM (EST). *Felony, Civil Actions Over $25,000.*

Civil Records: Access: Mail, in person. Only the court performs in person searches. Search fee: $5.00 per name. Court makes copy: $.50 per page. Required to search: name, years to search. Civil cases indexed by defendant, plaintiff; on computer since 7/90, index books from 1867. Mail turnaround time 2-3 days.

Criminal Records: Access: Mail, in person. Only the court performs in person searches. Search fee: $5.00 per name. Court makes copy: $.50 per page. Required to search: name, years to search, DOB. Criminal records on computer since 7/90, index books from 1867. Mail turnaround time 2-3 days.

General Information: No public access terminal. No suppressed, juvenile, sex offenders, mental health, or adoption records released. Will fax documents for $2.00 per page. Certification fee: $13.00 1st page, includes copy fee. Add $2.00 each add'l page. Payee: Manistee County Clerk. Personal checks accepted. Prepayment and SASE required.

85th District Court 415 3rd St, Manistee, MI 49660; phone: 231-723-5010; fax: 231-723-1491; hours 8:30AM-5PM (EST). *Misdemeanor, Civil Actions Under $25,000, Eviction, Small Claims.*

Civil Records: Access: Fax, mail, in person. Both court and visitors may perform in person searches. Search fee: $5.00 per name plus $1.00 per page. Court makes copy: $1.00 per page. Required to search: name, years to search. Civil cases indexed by defendant, plaintiff; on computer since 4/89, prior on index books. Mail turnaround time 21 days maximum.

Criminal Records: Access: Fax, mail, in person. Both court and visitors may perform in person searches. Search fee: $5.00 per name plus $1.00 per page. Court makes copy: $1.00 per page. Required to search: name, years to search, DOB. Criminal records on computer since 4/89, prior on index books. Mail turnaround time 5-7 days; 21 days max.

General Information: Public use terminal available. No suppressed, juvenile, sex offenders, mental health, or adoption records released. Will fax documents no fee. Certification fee: $10.00 per document. Payee: 85th District Court. Personal checks accepted. Prepayment and SASE required.

Probate Court 415 3rd St, Manistee, MI 49660; phone: 231-723-3261; fax: 231-398-3558; hours 8:30AM-N, 1-5PM (EST). *Probate.* http://manisteecounty.net/Probate/index.html

Marquette County

25th Circuit Court 234 W Baraga, Marquette, MI 49855; phone: 906-225-8330; fax: 906-228-1572; hours 8AM-5PM (EST). *Felony, Civil Actions Over $25,000.*
Civil Records: Access: Mail, in person. Only the court performs in person searches. Search fee: $5.00 per name. Court makes copy: $1.00 per page. Required to search: name, years to search. Civil cases indexed by defendant, plaintiff; on books since 1852, on computer from 4/95. Mail turnaround time 1-2 days.
Criminal Records: Access: Mail, in person. Only the court performs in person searches. Search fee: $5.00 per name. Court makes copy: $1.00 per page. Required to search: name, years to search, DOB. Criminal records on books since 1852, on computer from 4/95. Mail turnaround time 1-2 days.
General Information: No public access terminal. No suppressed, juvenile, sex offenders, mental health, or adoption records released. Will fax documents to local or toll free line. Certification fee: $10.00 plus $1.00 per page. Payee: County Clerk. Personal checks accepted. Prepayment required.

96th District Court County Courthouse, Marquette, MI 49855; phone: 906-225-8235; fax: 906-225-8255; hours 8:00AM-5PM (EST). *Misdemeanor, Civil Actions Under $25,000, Eviction, Small Claims.*
Civil Records: Access: Fax, mail, in person. Only the court performs in person searches. Search fee: $5.00 per name. Court makes copy: $1.00 per page. Required to search: name, years to search; also helpful: address. Civil cases indexed by defendant, plaintiff; on computer since 1995, prior on docket books and microfiche. Mail turnaround time 1-2 weeks.
Criminal Records: Access: Fax, mail, in person. Only the court performs in person searches. Search fee: $5.00 per name. Court makes copy: $1.00 per page. Required to search: name, years to search, DOB. Criminal records on computer since 1995, prior on docket books and microfiche. Mail turnaround time 1-2 weeks.
General Information: No public access terminal. No suppressed records released. No fee to fax documents. Certification fee: $10.00 plus $1.00 per page after first. Payee: 96th District Court. Business checks accepted. Prepayment and SASE required.

Probate Court 234 W Baraga, Marquette, MI 49855; phone: 906-225-8300; fax: 906-228-1533; hours 8AM-5PM (EST). *Probate.*
Note: Copy fee is $1.00 per page.

Mason County

51st Circuit Court 304 E Ludington Ave, Ludington, MI 49431; phone: 231-845-1445; fax: 231-843-1972; hours 8AM-5PM (EST). *Felony, Civil Actions Over $25,000.*
Civil Records: Access: Phone, fax, mail, in person. Only the court performs in person searches. No search fee. Court makes copy: $1.00 per page. Self serve copy fee: $1.00 per page. Required to search: name, years to search. Civil cases indexed by defendant, plaintiff; on file since 1867. Mail turnaround time 1 week.
Criminal Records: Access: Phone, fax, mail, in person. Only the court performs in person searches. No search fee. Court makes copy: $1.00 per page. Self serve copy fee: $1.00 per page. Required to search: name, years to search, DOB; also helpful: SSN. Criminal records on file since 1867. Mail turnaround time 1 week.
General Information: No public access terminal. No suppressed, juvenile, sex offenders, mental health, or adoption records released. Certification fee: $10.00 per doc. Payee: Mason County Clerk. Personal checks accepted. Prepayment required. Prepayment of mail service required. SASE required.

79th District Court County Court, 304 E.Ludington Ave, Ludington, MI 49431; phone: 231-843-4130; fax: 231-845-9076; hours 9AM-5PM (EST). *Misdemeanor, Civil Actions Under $25,000, Eviction, Small Claims.*
Civil Records: Access: Fax, mail, in person. Only the court performs in person searches. No search fee. Court makes copy: $1.00 per page. Required to search: name, years to search. Civil cases indexed by defendant, plaintiff; on Register of Action Docket Cards since 1969, computerized since 10/96.
Criminal Records: Access: In person only. Only the court performs in person searches. No search fee. Court makes copy: $1.00 per page. Required to search: name, years to search, DOB. Criminal records on Register of Action Docket Cards since 1969, computerized since 10/96.
General Information: No public access terminal. No suppressed, juvenile, sex offenders, mental health, or adoption records released. No fee to fax documents. Local faxing only. Certification fee: $10.00 plus $1.00 per page after first. Payee: 79th District Court. Only cashiers checks and money orders accepted. Prepayment required.

Probate Court 304 E Ludington Ave, Ludington, MI 49431; phone: 231-843-8666; fax: 231-843-1972; hours 9AM-N, 1-5PM (EST). *Probate.*

Mecosta County

49th Circuit Court 400 Elm, Big Rapids, MI 49307; phone: 231-592-0783; fax: 231-592-0193; hours 8:30AM-5PM (EST). *Felony, Civil Actions Over $25,000.*
www.co.mecosta.mi.us/circuit.asp
Civil Records: Access: Fax, mail, in person. Only the court performs in person searches. Search fee: $5.00 per name. Court makes copy: $1.00 per page. Required to search: name, years to search. Civil cases indexed by defendant, plaintiff; on computer since 10/70, archived and microfiche since 1900s. Mail turnaround time 1 week.
Criminal Records: Access: Fax, mail, in person. Only the court performs in person searches. Search fee: $5.00 per name. Court makes copy: $1.00 per page. Required to search: name, years to search. Criminal records on computer since 10/70, archived and microfiche since 1900s. Mail turnaround time 1 week.
General Information: No public access terminal. No suppressed, juvenile, mental health, or adoption records released. Will fax documents to local or toll free line. Certification fee: $10.00 per page includes copy fee. Payee: Mecosta County Clerk. Personal checks not accepted; money orders and cashiers checks preferred. Prepayment required. SASE requested.

77th District Court 400 Elm, Big Rapids, MI 49307; phone: 231-592-0799; civil phone: 231-592-0796; probate phone: 231-592-0135; fax: 231-796-2180; hours 8:30AM-4:30PM (EST). *Misdemeanor, Civil Actions Under $25,000, Eviction, Small Claims.*
Civil Records: Access: Mail, fax, in person. Only the court performs in person searches. Search fee: $10.00 per name. Court makes copy: $1.00 per page. Required to search: name, years to search. Civil cases indexed by defendant, plaintiff; on computer to 1995. Mail turnaround time 7 days.
Criminal Records: Access: Mail, in person. Only the court performs in person searches. Search fee: $5.00 per name. Court makes copy: $1.00 per page. Required to search: name, years to search, DOB. Criminal records on computer for 10 years, archived and microfiche prior. Signed release required for employment screening. Mail turnaround time 7 days.
General Information: No public access terminal. No suppressed, juvenile, sex offenders, mental health, or adoption records released. Will fax documents to local or toll free line. Certification fee: $10.00. Payee: 77th District Court. Business checks accepted. Prepayment required.

Probate Court PO Box 820, 400 Elm St, Big Rapids, MI 49307; phone: 231-592-0135; fax: 231-592-0191; hours 8:30AM-5PM Tu,Th,F (EST). *Probate.*
www.co.mecosta.mi.us/probate.asp
Note: Shares the same judge with Osceola County Probate Court.

Menominee County

41st Circuit Court 839 10th Ave, Menominee, MI 49858; phone: 906-863-9968; fax: 906-863-8839; hours 8AM-4:30PM (CST). *Felony, Civil Actions Over $25,000.*
Civil Records: Access: Mail, in person. Only the court performs in person searches. Search fee: $1.00 per name per year. Court makes copy: $1.00 per page. Required to search: name, years to search. Civil cases indexed by defendant, plaintiff. Civil records kept by docket entry in file folders, archived to 1900, computerized since 1998. Mail turnaround time 2-3 days.
Criminal Records: Access: Mail, in person. Only the court performs in person searches. Search fee: $7.00 per name for first 7 years, then $1.00 each additional year. Court makes copy: $1.00 per page. Required to search: name, years to search, DOB; also helpful: SSN. Criminal records kept by docket entry in file folders to 1900; on computer back to 1998. Mail turnaround time 2-3 days.
General Information: No public access terminal. No suppressed, juvenile, sex offenders, mental health, or adoption records released. Will fax documents for no fee. Certification fee: $10.00 per document. Payee: 41st Circuit Court. Personal checks accepted. Prepayment required.

95 A District Court 839 10th Ave, Menominee, MI 49858; phone: 906-863-8532; fax: 906-863-2023; hours 8AM-4:30PM (CST). *Misdemeanor, Civil Actions Under $25,000, Eviction, Small Claims.*
Civil Records: Access: Fax, mail, in person. Only the court performs in person searches. Search fee: $5.00 per name. Court makes copy: $.20 per page. Required to search: name, years to search. Civil cases indexed by defendant, plaintiff; on index books since 1969. Mail turnaround time 1 week.
Criminal Records: Access: Fax, mail, in person. Only the court performs in person searches. Search fee: $5.00 per name. Court makes copy: $.20 per page. Required to search: name, years to search, DOB. Criminal records on index books since 1969. Mail turnaround time 1 week.
General Information: No public access terminal. No suppressed, juvenile, sex offenders, mental health, or adoption records released. Will fax documents $.20 per page. Certification fee: $10.00. Payee: District Court 95A. Personal checks accepted. Prepayment and SASE required.

Probate Court 839 10th Ave, Menominee, MI 49858; phone: 906-863-2634; fax: 906-863-9904; hours 8AM-4:30PM (CST). *Probate, Juvenile.*

Midland County

42nd Circuit Court Courthouse, 301 W Main St, Midland, MI 48640; phone: 989-832-6735; fax: 989-832-6610; hours 8AM-5PM (EST). *Felony, Civil Actions Over $25,000.*
www.midlandcounty.org/circuitcourt/index.htm
Civil Records: Access: Phone, mail, in person. Only the court performs in person searches. No search fee. Court makes copy: $1.00 per page. Required to search: name, years to search. Civil cases indexed by defendant, plaintiff; on computer from 1985, prior on books since 1800s. Mail turnaround time same day.
Criminal Records: Access: Phone, mail, in person. Only the court performs in person searches. No search fee. Court makes copy: $1.00 per page. Required to search: name, years to search, DOB. Criminal records on computer from 1985, prior on books since 1800s. Mail turnaround time same day.
General Information: No public access terminal. No suppressed records released. Certification fee:

$15.00. Payee: Clerk of Circuit Court. Personal checks accepted. Prepayment and SASE required.

75th District Court - Criminal Division
301 W Main St, Midland, MI 48640-5183; phone: 989-832-6702 (6714-traffic); criminal phone: 989-832-6718; fax: 989-832-6601; hours 8:30AM-5PM (EST). *Misdemeanor.*

Criminal Records: Access: Mail, in person. Only the court performs in person searches. Search fee: $1.00 per name per year. Court makes copy: $1.00 per page. Required to search: name, years to search, DOB. Criminal records on computer since 1991, prior on docket books and paper index. Mail turnaround time 1 week.

General Information: No public access terminal. No suppressed, sex offenders or mental health records released. Will fax documents. Certification fee: $1.00 per document. Payee: 75th District Court. Personal checks accepted. Prepayment required.

75th District Court - Civil Division
301 W Main St, Midland, MI 48640; phone: 989-832-6701; hours 8:30AM-4:30PM (EST). *Civil Actions Under $25,000, Eviction, Small Claims.*

Note: Small Claims can be reached at 989-832-6717.

Civil Records: Access: Mail, in person. Both court and visitors may perform in person searches. Search fee: $1.00 per name per year. Court makes copy: $1.00 per page. Required to search: name, years to search; also helpful: address. Civil cases indexed by defendant, plaintiff; on computer since 6/89; on index books until 6/89. Mail turnaround time 5-7 days.

General Information: No public access terminal. No suppressed, juvenile, sex offenders, mental health, or adoption records released. Certification fee: $10.00 1st page, $1.00 each add'l. Payee: 75th District Court. Personal checks accepted. Prepayment required.

Probate Court
301 W Main St, Midland, MI 48640; phone: 989-832-6880; fax: 989-832-6607; hours 8AM-5PM (EST). *Probate.*
www.midlandcounty.org

Missaukee County

28th Circuit Court
PO Box 800, Lake City, MI 49651; phone: 231-839-4967; fax: 231-839-3684; hours 9AM-5PM (EST). *Felony, Civil Actions Over $25,000.*
www.missaukee.org/court.htm?

Civil Records: Access: Phone, fax, mail, in person. Both court and visitors may perform in person searches. Search fee: $5.00 per name. Court makes copy: $1.00 per page. Required to search: name, years to search. Civil cases indexed by defendant, plaintiff; on computer since 1990, prior on books. Mail turnaround time 2 days.

Criminal Records: Access: Phone, fax, mail, in person. Both court and visitors may perform in person searches. Search fee: $5.00 per name. Court makes copy: $1.00 per page. Required to search: name, years to search; also helpful: DOB, SSN. Criminal records on computer since 1990, prior on books. Mail turnaround time 2 days.

General Information: Public terminal goes back to 1990. No suppressed, juvenile, sex offenders, mental health, or adoption records released. Will fax documents $5.00 1st page, $1.00 each add'l. Certification fee: $10.00 per document. Payee: Missaukee County Clerk. Personal checks accepted. Prepayment required.

84th District Court
PO Box 800, Lake City, MI 49651; phone: 231-839-4590; fax: 231-839-8821; hours 9AM-5PM (EST). *Misdemeanor, Civil Actions Under $25,000, Eviction, Small Claims.*

Civil Records: Access: Fax, mail, in person. Both court and visitors may perform in person searches. Search fee: $5.00 per name. Court makes copy: $1.00 per page. Required to search: name, years to search. Civil cases indexed by defendant, plaintiff; on computer since 1989. Mail turnaround time 1 week.

Criminal Records: Access: Fax, mail, in person. Both court and visitors may perform in person searches. No search fee. Court makes copy: $1.00 per

page. Required to search: name, years to search, DOB, SSN. Criminal records on computer since 1988. Mail turnaround time 1 week.

General Information: No public access terminal. No suppressed, juvenile, sex offenders, mental health, or adoption records released. Will fax documents to local or toll free line. Certification fee: $10.00 plus $1.00 per page after first. Payee: District Court. Personal checks accepted. Prepayment and SASE required.

Probate Court
PO Box 800, 111 S canal, Lake City, MI 49651; phone: 231-839-2266; fax: 231-839-5856; hours 9AM-N, 1-5PM (EST). *Probate.*
Note: Will accept email search requests.

Monroe County

38th Circuit Court
106 E 1st St, Monroe, MI 48161; phone: 734-240-7020; fax: 734-240-7045; hours 8:30AM-5PM (EST). *Felony, Civil Actions Over $25,000.*
www.co.monroe.mi.us

Civil Records: Access: Mail, fax, in person. Both court and visitors may perform in person searches. Search fee: $8.00 per name. Fee is per name per 5 years. Court makes copy: $1.00 per page; same fee for self serve. Required to search: name, years to search. Civil cases indexed by defendant, plaintiff; on computer back to 1990; prior on docket books. Mail turnaround time same day.

Criminal Records: Access: Mail, in person. Both court and visitors may perform in person searches. Search fee: $8.00 per name. Fee is per name per 5 years. Court makes copy: $1.00 per page; same fee for self serve. Required to search: name, years to search, DOB. Criminal records on computer back to 1990; prior on docket books. Mail turnaround time same day.

General Information: Public terminal goes back to 1990. No suppressed records released. Certification fee: $3.00. Payee: 38th Circuit Court. Personal checks accepted and SASE required.

1st District Court
106 E 1st St, Monroe, MI 48161; phone: 734-240-7075; criminal phone: 734-240-7080; civil phone: 734-240-7090; criminal/civil fax: 734-240-7098; hours 8AM-4:45 PM (EST). *Misdemeanor, Civil Actions Under $25,000, Eviction, Small Claims.*
www.co.monroe.mi.us

Civil Records: Access: Mail, in person. Both court and visitors may perform in person searches. No search fee. Court makes copy: $1.00 per page. Required to search: name, years to search, address. Civil cases indexed by defendant, plaintiff; on computer since 1993; prior records to 1969 on microfiche. Mail turnaround time 1 week.

Criminal Records: Access: Mail, in person. Both court and visitors may perform in person searches. No search fee. Court makes copy: $1.00 per page. Required to search: name, years to search, DOB; also helpful: address, SSN. Criminal records on computer since 1993; prior records to 1969 on microfiche. Mail turnaround time 1 week.

General Information: Public use terminal available. No suppressed, juvenile, sex offenders, mental health, or adoption records released. Will not fax documents. Certification fee: $10.00 per page. Payee: 1st District Court. Business checks accepted. Prepayment required.

Probate Court
106 E 1st St, Monroe, MI 48161; phone: 734-240-7346; fax: 734-240-7354; hours 9AM-N, 1-5PM (EST). *Probate.*

Montcalm County

8th Circuit Court
639 N.State St, Stanton, MI 48888; phone: 989-831-3520; fax: 989-831-3525; hours 8AM-5PM (EST). *Felony, Civil Actions Over $25,000.*
www.montcalm.org
Note: The office closes for lunch hour at noon.

Civil Records: Access: Mail, in person. Only the court performs in person searches. Search fee:

$10.00 for 1st. yr. $1.00 each yr after. Court makes copy: $1.00 per page. Required to search: name, years to search. Civil cases indexed by defendant, plaintiff; on docket books to 1867, computerized since 1990. Mail turnaround time 1-3 days.

Criminal Records: Access: Mail, in person, fax. Only the court performs in person searches. Search fee: $10.00 for 1st. yr. $1.00 each yr after. Court makes copy: $1.00 per page. Required to search: name, years to search, DOB. Criminal records on docket books to 1867, computerized since 1990. Mail turnaround time 1-3 days.

General Information: No public access terminal. No suppressed, juvenile, sex offenders, mental health, adoption, birth or DD214 records released. Certification fee: $10.00 plus $1.00 per page after first. Payee: Montcalm County Clerk. Personal checks accepted. Prepayment and SASE required.

64 B District Court
617 N State Rd #D, Stanton, MI 48888; phone: 989-831-7450; fax: 989-831-7453; hours 8AM-5PM (EST). *Misdemeanor, Civil Actions Under $25,000, Eviction, Small Claims.*

Civil Records: Access: Mail, in person. Only the court performs in person searches. No search fee. Court makes copy: $.25 per page; same fee for self serve. Required to search: name, years to search. Civil cases indexed by defendant, plaintiff; on computer since 1989, prior on books and microfiche. Mail turnaround time 7 days.

Criminal Records: Access: Mail, in person, fax. Only the court performs in person searches. No search fee. Court makes copy: $.25 per page; same fee for self serve. Required to search: name, years to search, DOB; also helpful: SSN. Criminal records on computer since 1989, prior on books and microfiche. Mail turnaround time 7 days.

General Information: No public access terminal. No suppressed records released. Certification fee: $10.00 plus $1.00 each add'l page. Payee: 64 B District Court. Personal checks accepted. Prepayment and SASE required.

Probate Court
625 N State St, PO Box 309, Stanton, MI 48888; phone: 989-831-7316; fax: 989-831-7314; hours 8AM-5PM (EST). *Probate.*

Montmorency County

26th Circuit Court
PO Box 789, Atlanta, MI 49709; phone: 989-785-8022; probate phone: 989-785-8064; criminal/civil: 989-785-8023; hours 8:30AM-N, 1-4:30PM (EST). *Felony, Civil Actions Over $25,000.*

Civil Records: Access: Mail, in person. Both court and visitors may perform in person searches. Search fee: $5.00 per name. Court makes copy: $1.00 per page. Required to search: name, years to search. Civil cases indexed by defendant, plaintiff; on computer since 1990, prior on books since 1940s, microfiche to 1970. Note: For in person searches, call ahead two days in advance. Mail turnaround time 3-5 days.

Criminal Records: Access: Mail, in person. Both court and visitors may perform in person searches. Search fee: $5.00 per name. Court makes copy: $1.00 per page. Required to search: name, years to search; also helpful: DOB. Criminal records on computer since 1990, prior on books since 1940s. Note: For in person searches, call ahead two days in advance. Mail turnaround time 3-5 days.

General Information: No public access terminal. No suppressed, birth certificate (except to heir or parent) adoption records released. Fee to fax documents is $1.00 per page. Certification fee: $10.00 plus $1.00 each add'l page. Payee: County Clerk. Personal checks accepted. Prepayment required.

88th District Court
County Courthouse, PO Box 789, Atlanta, MI 49709; phone: 989-785-8035; criminal phone: 989-785-8038; civil phone: 989-785-8040; criminal/civil fax: 989-785-8036; hours 8:30AM-N, 1-4:30PM (EST). *Misdemeanor, Civil Actions Under $25,000, Eviction, Small Claims.*

Civil Records: Access: Mail, fax, in person. Only the court performs in person searches. Search fee: $5.00

per name. Court makes copy: $1.00 per page; same fee for self serve. Required to search: name, years to search; also helpful: address. Civil cases indexed by defendant, plaintiff; on computer back to 1990, prior on books and card file since 1969. Mail turnaround time 1-3 days.

Criminal Records: Access: Mail, fax, in person. Only the court performs in person searches. Search fee: $5.00 per name. Court makes copy: $1.00 per page; same fee for self serve. Required to search: name, years to search, DOB; also helpful: address, SSN, signed release. Criminal records on computer back to 1990, prior on books and card file since 1969. Mail turnaround time 1-3 days.

General Information: No public access terminal. No suppressed, juvenile, sex offenders, mental health, or adoption records released. Fee to fax documents is $1.00 per document. Certification fee: $10.00 per page. Payee: 88th District Court-Montmorency County. Personal checks accepted; credit cards accepted. Prepayment and SASE required.

Probate Court PO Box 789, Atlanta, MI 49709-0789; phone: 989-785-8064; fax: 989-785-8065; hours 8:30AM-N, 1-4:30PM (EST). *Probate.*

Muskegon County

14th Circuit Court County Bldg, 6th Fl, 990 Terrace St, Muskegon, MI 49442; criminal phone: 231-724-1124; civil phone: 231-724-6251; fax: 231-724-6695; hours 8AM-5PM (EST). *Felony, Civil Actions Over $25,000.*

Civil Records: Access: Phone, mail, fax, in person. Both court and visitors may perform in person searches. Search fee: $10.00 per name. Court makes copy: $1.00 per page. Required to search: name, years to search. Civil cases indexed by defendant, plaintiff; on computer back to 1984, prior on books since 1853. Mail turnaround time 2-3 days.

Criminal Records: Access: Phone, mail, fax, in person. Both court and visitors may perform in person searches. Search fee: $10.00 per name. Court makes copy: $1.00 per page. Required to search: name, years to search, DOB; also helpful: SSN. Criminal records on computer back to 1984, prior on books since 1853. Mail turnaround time 2-3 days.

General Information: Public terminal goes back to 1984. No suppressed, juvenile, sex offenders, mental health, or adoption records released. Fee to fax documents is $1.00 per page. Certification fee: $10.00 plus $1.00 per page after first. Payee: Circuit Court Records. Personal checks not accepted. Prepayment and SASE required.

60th District Court 990 Terrace, 1st Fl, Muskegon, MI 49442; phone: 231-724-6250; fax: 231-724-3489; hours 8:30AM-4:45PM (EST). *Misdemeanor, Civil Actions Under $25,000, Eviction, Small Claims.*

www.co.muskegon.mi.us/60thdistrict

Civil Records: Access: Mail, in person. Both court and visitors may perform in person searches. No search fee. Court makes copy: $1.00 per page. Required to search: name, years to search. Civil cases indexed by defendant, plaintiff; on computer since 5/93, prior on hard copy. Online access to the court weekly docket is free at www.co.muskegon.mi.us/60thdistrict/docket.htm. Mail turnaround time 3 days.

Criminal Records: Access: Mail, in person. Both court and visitors may perform in person searches. No search fee. Court makes copy: $1.00 per page. Required to search: name, years to search, DOB. Criminal records on computer since 5/93, prior on hard copy. Online access to the court weekly docket is free at www.co.muskegon.mi.us/60thdistrict/docket.htm. Mail turnaround time 3 days.

General Information: Public terminal goes back to 5/1993. No suppressed, juvenile, sex offenders, mental health, or adoption records released. Certification fee: $10.00. Payee: 60th District Court. Personal checks accepted. Prepayment and SASE required.

Probate Court 990 Terrace St, 5th Fl, Muskegon, MI 49442; phone: 231-724-6241; fax: 231-724-6232; hours 8AM-N, 1-5PM (EST). *Probate.*

Newaygo County

27th Circuit Court PO Box 885, Attn: Court Clerk, White Cloud, MI 49349-0885; phone: 231-689-7269; fax: 231-689-7007; hours 8AM-N; 1-5PM (EST). *Felony, Civil Actions Over $25,000.*

www.countyofnewaygo.com/Clerk/court_services.htm

Civil Records: Access: Mail, fax, in person. Only the court performs in person searches. No search fee. Court makes copy: $1.00 per page. Required to search: name, years to search. Civil cases indexed by defendant, plaintiff. Civil records archived since 1880s; on computer since 7/1994. Mail turnaround time 2-5 days.

Criminal Records: Access: Mail, fax, in person. Only the court performs in person searches. No search fee. Court makes copy: $1.00 per page. Required to search: name, years to search; also helpful: DOB. Criminal records archived since 1880s; on computer since 7/1994. Mail turnaround time 2-5 days.

General Information: No public access terminal. No suppressed records released. Will fax documents to toll-free number only. Certification fee: $10.00 plus $1.00 per page for copy after first. Payee: Newaygo County Circuit Court. Personal checks accepted. Prepayment required. SASE requested.

78th District Court 1092 Newell St, White Cloud, MI 49349; phone: 231-689-7257; fax: 231-689-7258; hours 8AM-N, 1-5PM (EST). *Misdemeanor, Civil Actions Under $25,000, Eviction, Small Claims.*

www.countyofnewaygo.com/Courts/courtshomepg.htm

Civil Records: Access: Fax, mail, in person. Both court and visitors may perform in person searches. No search fee. Court makes copy: $1.00 per page; same fee for self serve. Required to search: name, years to search; also helpful: address. Civil cases indexed by defendant, plaintiff; on computer since 7/27/89, prior in folders. Mail turnaround time 7-10 days.

Criminal Records: Access: Fax, mail, in person. Both court and visitors may perform in person searches. No search fee. Court makes copy: $1.00 per page; same fee for self serve. Required to search: name, years to search, DOB; also helpful: address, SSN. Criminal records on computer since 7/27/89, prior in folders. Mail turnaround time 7-10 days.

General Information: Public terminal goes back to 1989. No suppressed records released. No fee to fax documents. Certification fee: $10.00 plus $1.00 per page after first. Payee: 78th District Court. Personal checks accepted. Prepayment and SASE required.

Probate Court PO Box 885, 1092 Newell St, White Cloud, MI 49349; phone: 231-689-7270; fax: 231-689-7276; hours 8AM-N, 1-5PM (EST). *Probate.*

www.countyofnewaygo.com/Courts/Probate%20Court/ProbateHomePg.htm

Oakland County

6th Circuit Court 1200 N Telegraph Rd, Pontiac, MI 48341; phone: 248-858-0582; fax: 248-452-9221; hours 8:30AM-4:30PM (EST). *Felony, Civil Actions Over $25,000.*

www.co.oakland.mi.us

Civil Records: Access: Mail, in person. Both court and visitors may perform in person searches. Search fee: $1.00 per name. Court makes copy: $1.00 per page. Self serve copy fee: $1.00 per page. Required to search: name, years to search. Civil cases indexed by defendant, plaintiff; on computer since 1963, prior on microfilm & books. Mail turnaround time 7 days.

Criminal Records: Access: Mail, in person. Both court and visitors may perform in person searches. Search fee: $1.00 per name. Court makes copy: $1.00

per page. Self serve copy fee: $1.00 per page. Required to search: name; also helpful: years to search, DOB, SSN. Criminal records on computer since 1963, prior on microfilm & books. Mail turnaround time 7 days.

General Information: Public terminal goes back to 1963. No suppressed, non-public, sex offenders or mental health records released. Will fax documents to local or toll free line. Certification fee: $10.00 plus $1.00 per page after first. Payee: Circuit Court. Personal checks not accepted, but most credit cards are. Prepayment and SASE required.

43rd District Court 43 E Nine Mile Rd, Hazel Park, MI 48030; phone: 248-547-3034; hours 8:30AM-4:30PM (EST). *Misdemeanor, Civil Actions Under $25,000, Eviction, Small Claims.*

Civil Records: Access: In person only. Both court and visitors may perform in person searches. No search fee. Court makes copy: $1.00 per page. Required to search: name, years to search. Civil cases indexed by defendant, plaintiff; on computer since 1989, prior on books since 1970. Mail turnaround time 3-7 days.

Criminal Records: Access: Mail, in person. Both court and visitors may perform in person searches. No search fee. Court makes copy: $1.00 per page. Required to search: name, years to search, DOB. Criminal records on computer since 1989, prior on books since 1970. Mail turnaround time 3-7 days.

General Information: No public access terminal. No suppressed, juvenile, sex offenders, mental health, or adoption records released. Certification fee: $10.00 per doc includes copy fee. Payee: 43rd District Court. Only cashiers checks, cash or money orders accepted. Prepayment required.

44th District Court - Royal Oak 400 E Eleven Mile Rd, Box 20, Royal Oak, MI 48068; phone: 248-246-3600; fax: 248-246-3601; hours 8AM-4:30PM (EST). *Misdemeanor, Civil Actions Under $25,000, Eviction, Small Claims.*

www.ci.royal-oak.mi.us

Civil Records: Access: Mail, in person. Both court and visitors may perform in person searches. Search fee: $10.00 per name. Court makes copy: $1.00 per page. Required to search: name, years to search. Civil cases indexed by defendant, plaintiff; on computer since 1983s, prior on docket books and index cards. Mail turnaround time 5 days.

Criminal Records: Access: Mail, in person. Both court and visitors may perform in person searches. Search fee: $10.00 per name. Court makes copy: $1.00 per page. Required to search: name, years to search, DOB, signed release, offense; also helpful: address. Criminal records on computer since 1983s, prior on docket books and index cards. Mail turnaround time 5 days.

General Information: No public access terminal. No suppressed, juvenile, sex offenders, mental health, or adoption records released. Will not fax documents. Certification fee: $10.00 per page, includes copy fee. Payee: 44th District Court. Personal checks accepted. Prepayment and SASE required.

45 A District Court - Berkley 3338 Coolidge, Berkley, MI 48072; phone: 248-544-3300; criminal phone: 248-544-3300; civil phone: 248-544-3301; criminal/civil fax: 248-546-2416; hours 8:30AM-4:45PM (EST). *Misdemeanor, Civil Actions Under $25,000, Eviction, Small Claims.*

www.45adistrictcourt.com

Civil Records: Access: Mail, in person. Only the court performs in person searches. Search fee: $1.00 per name. Court makes copy: $1.00 per page. Required to search: name, years to search. Civil cases indexed by defendant, plaintiff; on computer since 1989 prior on books. Mail turnaround time 1 week.

Criminal Records: Access: Mail, in person. Only the court performs in person searches. No search fee. Court makes copy: $1.00 per page. Required to search: name, years to search, DOB; also helpful: SSN. Criminal records on computer since 1989, prior on books. Mail turnaround time 1 week.

General Information: No public access terminal. No suppressed records released. Will fax documents. Certification fee: $10.00 per request. Payee: 45 A District Court. Personal checks accepted. Prepayment and SASE required.

45 B District Court 13600 Oak Park Blvd, Oak Park, MI 48237; phone: 248-691-7440; fax: 248-691-7158; hours 9AM-5PM (EST). *Misdemeanor, Civil Actions Under $25,000, Eviction, Small Claims.*
Note: Court covers Huntington Woods, Oak Park, Pleasant Ridge, and Royal Oak Township.
Civil Records: Access: Mail, in person. Both court and visitors may perform in person searches. No search fee. Court makes copy: $1.00 per page. Required to search: name, years to search. Civil cases indexed by defendant, plaintiff; on computer back to 1988. Docket books and index cards back to 1987. Mail turnaround time varies.
Criminal Records: Access: Mail, in person. Both court and visitors may perform in person searches. No search fee. Court makes copy: $1.00 per page. Required to search: name, years to search, DOB; also helpful: SSN. Criminal records on computer back to 1993. Docket books and index cards go back to 1988. Mail turnaround time varies.
General Information: Public use terminal available. No suppressed records released. Certification fee: $10.00. Payee: 45 B District Court. Business checks accepted. Prepayment required.

46th District Court 26000 Evergreen Rd, Southfield, MI 48076; phone: 248-796-5800; criminal phone: 248-796-5880; civil phone: 248-796-5870; criminal/civil fax: 248-796-5875; hours 8AM-4:30PM (counter) (EST). *Misdemeanor, Civil Actions Under $25,000, Eviction, Small Claims.*
www.cityofsouthfield.com/46court
Civil Records: Access: Mail, in person. Both court and visitors may perform in person searches. No search fee. Court makes copy: $.50 per page. Required to search: name or case number. Civil cases indexed by defendant, plaintiff. Civil records prior to 1992 are on microfilm; most recent records are computerized. Mail turnaround time varies.
Criminal Records: Access: Mail, in person. Both court and visitors may perform in person searches. No search fee. Court makes copy: $.50 per page. Required to search: name, years to search, DOB. Criminal records on computer since 1992, prior on microfiche. Note: Court will criminal search only 1990 to present with case # provided. Mail turnaround time varies.
General Information: No public access terminal. No suppressed or "non-public" records released, such as juvenile, sex offenders, mental health, or adoption records. Will not fax documents. If copies are made from microfilm, the copy fee is $1.00 per page. Certification fee: $10.00 per document. Payee: 46th District Court. Personal checks or Visa, MC accepted. Prepayment required. SASE not requested.

47th District Court - Farmington, Farmington Hills 31605 W 11 Mile Rd, Farmington Hills, MI 48336; phone: 248-871-2900; hours 8:30AM-4:30PM; 'til 6:30PM 3rd Tues each month (EST). *Misdemeanor, Civil Actions Under $25,000, Eviction, Small Claims.*
Civil Records: Access: In person only. Visitors must perform in person searches themselves. Court makes copy: $1.00 per page. Required to search: name, years to search, case number. Civil cases indexed by defendant, plaintiff; on computer since 7/19/93; prior on microfiche since 1975.
Criminal Records: Access: In person only. Visitors must perform in person searches themselves. Court makes copy: $1.00 per page. Required to search: name, years to search, case number DOB; also helpful: offense. Criminal records on computer since 7/19/93; prior on microfiche since 1975.
General Information: Public terminal goes back to 7/19/93. No suppressed, sex offenders or mental health records released. Certification fee: $10.00 plus $1.00 per page after first. Payee: 47th District Court.

Personal checks or Visa, MC accepted. Prepayment required.

48th District Court 4280 Telegraph Rd, Bloomfield Hills, MI 48302; phone: 248-647-1141; fax: 248-647-8955; hours 8:30AM-4:30PM (EST). *Misdemeanor, Civil Actions Under $25,000, Eviction, Small Claims.*
Civil Records: Access: Phone, mail, in person. Both court and visitors may perform in person searches. No search fee. Court makes copy: $.50 per page; may be increased to $1.00. Required to search: name, years to search, address. Civil cases indexed by defendant, plaintiff; on computer since 1980, prior on index cards. Mail turnaround time varies.
Criminal Records: Access: Phone, mail, in person. Both court and visitors may perform in person searches. No search fee. Court makes copy: $.50 per page. Required to search: name, years to search, address, DOB; also helpful: SSN. Criminal records on computer since 1980, prior on index cards. Mail turnaround time varies.
General Information: Public terminal goes back to 1980. No suppressed, juvenile, sex offenders, mental health, victim or adoption records released. Certification fee: $10.00 plus $1.00 per page after first - this applies to civil, eviction and small claims cases only. No fee to certify a criminal record. Payee: 48th District Court. Personal checks or Visa, MC, AmEx accepted. Debit Card accepted. Prepayment required.

50th District Court - Pontiac Criminal Division 70 N Saganaw, Pontiac, MI 48342; phone: 248-758-3820; fax: 248-758-3888; hours 8:30AM-4:30PM (EST). *Misdemeanor.*
Criminal Records: Access: Mail, fax, in person. Both court and visitors may perform in person searches. No search fee. Court makes copy: $1.00 first page, $.25 each add'l; same fee for self serve. Required to search: name, years to search, DOB; also helpful: SSN. Criminal records on computer since 1984, prior on index cards since 1975. Mail turnaround time 2-3 days.
General Information: Public terminal has only criminal records back to 4/2004. No suppressed, juvenile, sex offenders, mental health, or adoption records released. Will fax documents to local or toll free line. Certification fee: $10.00 per doc. Payee: 50th District Court. Business checks accepted. Prepayment required.

51st District Court - Waterford 5100 Civic Center Dr, Waterford, MI 48329; phone: 248-674-4655; hours 8:30AM-4:45PM (EST). *Misdemeanor, Civil Actions Under $25,000, Eviction, Small Claims.*
Civil Records: Access: Mail, in person. Only the court performs in person searches. No search fee. Will perform in person searches 10-11AM and 2-4PM. Court makes copy: $.25 per page. Required to search: name, years to search. Civil cases indexed by defendant, plaintiff; on computer since 1980s, prior on docket books and index cards to 1969. Mail turnaround time 10 days.
Criminal Records: Access: Mail, in person. Only the court performs in person searches. No search fee. Will perform in person searches 10-11AM and 2-4PM only. Court makes copy: $.25 per page. Required to search: name, years to search, DOB; also helpful: SSN. Criminal records on computer since 1980s, prior on docket books and index cards to 1969. Mail turnaround time 10 days.
General Information: No public access terminal. No suppressed, juvenile, sex offenders, mental health, or adoption records released. Certification fee: $10.00 per doc. Payee: 51st District Court. Personal checks or Visa, MC accepted. Prepayment required.

52nd District Court - Division 1 48150 Grand River, Novi, MI 48374; criminal phone: 248-305-6460; civil phone: 248-305-6080; hours 8:30AM-4:30PM (EST). *Misdemeanor, Civil Actions Under $25,000, Eviction, Small Claims.*
www.52-1districtcourt.com

Civil Records: Access: Phone, mail, in person. Only the court performs in person searches. No search fee. Prefers to do large name lists on Tuesday & Friday. Court makes copy: $1.00 per page. Required to search: name, years to search. Civil cases indexed by defendant, plaintiff; on computer since 1984, prior on books. Mail turnaround time 1 month.
Criminal Records: Access: Phone, mail, in person. Only the court performs in person searches. No search fee. Best to do large name lists on Thursday & Friday. Court makes copy: $1.00 per page. Required to search: name, years to search; also helpful: DOB. Criminal records on computer since 1984, prior on books. Mail turnaround time 1 month.
General Information: No public access terminal. No suppressed, juvenile, sex offenders or mental health records released. Certification fee: $10.00. Payee: 52-1 District Court. Personal checks or Visa, MC accepted. Prepayment and SASE required.

52nd District Court - Division 2 5850 Lorac, Clarkston, MI 48346; criminal phone: 248-625-4888; civil phone: 248-625-4994; fax: 248-625-5602; hours 8:30AM-4:30PM (EST). *Misdemeanor, Civil Actions Under $25,000, Eviction, Small Claims.*
Note: Court covers Springfield, Holly, Groveland, Brandon, Independence, Clarkston & Ortonville and townships of Whie Lake and Rose.
Civil Records: Access: Phone, fax, mail, in person. Only the court performs in person searches. No search fee. Court makes copy: $1.00 per page. Required to search: name, years to search. Civil cases indexed by defendant, plaintiff; on computer since 1982, prior on microfiche since 1976. Mail turnaround time 3-5 days.
Criminal Records: Access: Phone, fax, mail, in person. Only the court performs in person searches. No search fee. Court makes copy: $1.00 per page. Required to search: name, years to search, DOB; also helpful: SSN. Criminal records on computer since 1982, prior on microfiche since 1976. Mail turnaround time 3-5 days.
General Information: No public access terminal. No suppressed, juvenile or sex offender records released. Fax service and fee is under consideration. Certification fee: $10.00. Payee: 52-2 District Court. No personal checks accepted. Visa, MC accepted in person only. Prepayment required.

52nd District Court - Division 3 700 Barclay Circle, Rochester Hills, MI 48307; phone: 248-853-5553; fax: 248-853-3277; hours 8AM-4:30PM (EST). *Misdemeanor, Civil Actions Under $25,000, Eviction, Small Claims.*
www.co.oakland.mi.us/courts
Civil Records: Access: Phone, fax, mail, in person. Only the court performs in person searches. No search fee. Court makes copy: $1.00 per page. Required to search: name; also helpful: years to search. Civil cases indexed by defendant, plaintiff; on computer for 10 years, prior on docket books and index cards. Mail turnaround time varies.
Criminal Records: Access: Phone, fax, mail, in person. Only the court performs in person searches. No search fee. Court makes copy: $1.00 per page. Required to search: name, DOB; also helpful: years to search. Criminal records on computer for 10 years, prior on docket books and index cards. Mail turnaround time varies.
General Information: No suppressed records released. Certification fee: $10.00. Payee: 52-3 District Court. Personal checks or Visa, MC accepted in person only. Prepayment required.

52nd District Court - Division 4 (Troy, Clawson) 520 W Big Beaver Rd, Troy, MI 48084; phone: 248-528-0400; fax: 248-528-3588; hours 8:15AM-4:15PM (EST). *Misdemeanor, Civil Actions Under $25,000, Eviction, Small Claims.*
Civil Records: Access: Mail, fax, in person. Only the court performs in person searches. No search fee. Court makes copy: $1.00 per page. Required to search: name, years to search. Civil cases indexed by defendant, plaintiff. Mail turnaround time 1 week.

Criminal Records: Access: Fax, mail, in person. Only the court performs in person searches. No search fee. Court makes copy: $1.00 per page. Required to search: name; also helpful: years to search, DOB, SSN. Criminal records. Mail turnaround time 1 week.

General Information: No suppressed, juvenile, sex offenders, mental health, or adoption records released. No fee to fax documents. Fax for criminal records and local calls only. Certification fee: $10.00 per doc. Payee: 52-4 District Court. Personal checks or Visa, MC accepted. Prepayment and SASE required.

50th District Court - Pontiac Civil Division 70 N Saganaw, Pontiac, MI 48342; phone: 248-758-3820; criminal phone: 248-758-3820; fax: 248-758-3888; hours 8:30AM-4:30PM (EST). *Civil Actions Under $25,000, Eviction, Small Claims.*

Civil Records: Access: Fax, mail, in person, best results via Fax. Both court and visitors may perform in person searches. No search fee. Court makes copy: $1.00 1st page, $.25 each add'l. Required to search: name, years to search. Civil cases indexed by defendant, plaintiff; on computer since 1985. Mail turnaround time 3-4 days.

General Information: Public terminal has only civil records back to 2004. No suppressed, juvenile, sex offenders, mental health, or adoption records released. Certification fee: $10.00 per doc includes copies. Payee: 50th District Court. Personal checks accepted. Prepayment required.

Probate Court 1200 N Telegraph Rd, 1st Fl, Oakland County Complex, East Wing, Pontiac, MI 48341; phone: 248-858-0260; fax: 248-452-2016; hours 8AM-5PM (EST). *Probate.*

Oceana County

27th Circuit Court 100 State St, #M-34, Hart, MI 49420; phone: 231-873-3977; hours 9AM-5PM (EST). *Felony, Civil Actions Over $25,000.*

Civil Records: Access: Mail, in person. Only the court performs in person searches. Search fee: $5.00 per name. Court makes copy: $1.00 per page. Required to search: name, years to search. Civil cases indexed by defendant, plaintiff; on computer since 1994, paper records to 1800s. Mail turnaround time same day.

Criminal Records: Access: Mail, in person. Only the court performs in person searches. Search fee: $5.00 per name. Court makes copy: $1.00 per page. Required to search: name, years to search; also helpful: DOB. Criminal records on computer since 1994, paper records to 1800s. Mail turnaround time same day.

General Information: No public access terminal. No suppressed, juvenile, sex offenders, mental health, or adoption records released. Certification fee: $10.00 plus $1.00 per page after first. Payee: Oceana County Circuit Court. Personal checks accepted. Prepayment required. SASE requested.

78th District Court PO Box 471, Hart, MI 49420; phone: 231-873-4530; fax: 231-873-1861; hours 8AM-5PM (EST). *Misdemeanor, Civil Actions Under $25,000, Eviction, Small Claims.*

Civil Records: Access: Fax, mail, in person. Only the court performs in person searches. Search fee: $5.00 per name. Court makes copy: $1.00 per page. Required to search: name, years to search. Civil cases indexed by plaintiff. Civil records on file cards and in file folders since 1967; on computer back to 1999. Mail turnaround time same day.

Criminal Records: Access: Fax, mail, in person. Only the court performs in person searches. Search fee: $5.00 per name. Court makes copy: $5.00 for 1st page; $1.00 per add'l. Required to search: name, years to search, DOB. Criminal records on file cards and in file folders since 1967; on computer back to 1999. Mail turnaround time same day.

General Information: No public access terminal. No suppressed records released. Certification fee: $10.00 per doc includes copy fee. Payee: 79th District

Court. No personal checks accepted. Prepayment required.

Probate Court County Bldg, 100 S State St, #M-10, Hart, MI 49420; phone: 231-873-3666; fax: 231-873-1943; hours 9AM-5PM (EST). *Probate.*

Ogemaw County

34th Circuit Court 806 W Houghton, West Branch, MI 48661; phone: 989-345-0215; fax: 989-345-7223; hours 8:30AM-4:30PM (EST). *Felony, Civil Actions Over $25,000.*

Civil Records: Access: Phone, fax, mail, in person. Only the court performs in person searches. Search fee: $10.00 per name. Fee is for search prior to 1993. Court makes copy: $.50 per page. Required to search: name, years to search. Civil cases indexed by defendant, plaintiff; on index cards since 1970, library books in vault since 1960; on computer back to 1993. Mail turnaround time 1-3 weeks.

Criminal Records: Access: Phone, fax, mail, in person. Only the court performs in person searches. Search fee: $10.00 per name. Fee is for search prior to 1993. Court makes copy: $.50 per page. Required to search: name, years to search, DOB; also helpful: SSN. Criminal records on index cards since 1970, library books in vault since 1960; on computer back to 1993. Mail turnaround time 1-3 weeks.

General Information: No public access terminal. No suppressed, juvenile, sex offenders, mental health, or adoption records released. Will fax documents $2.00 1st page, $1.00 each add'l. Certification fee: $10.00 plus $1.00 per page. Payee: 34th Circuit Court. Personal checks accepted. Prepayment and SASE required.

82nd District Court PO Box 365, West Branch, MI 48661; phone: 989-345-5040; fax: 989-345-5910; hours 8:30AM-4:30PM (EST). *Misdemeanor, Civil Actions Under $25,000, Eviction, Small Claims.*

Civil Records: Access: Fax, mail, in person. Only the court performs in person searches. Search fee: $2.00 per name. Court makes copy: $.50 per page. Required to search: name, years to search. Civil cases indexed by defendant, plaintiff; on computer since 1990, prior on books since 1969. Mail turnaround time 2-3 days.

Criminal Records: Access: Fax, mail, in person. Only the court performs in person searches. Search fee: $2.00 per name. Court makes copy: $.50 per page. Required to search: name, years to search, DOB. Criminal records on computer since 1990, prior on books since 1969. Mail turnaround time 2-3 days.

General Information: No public access terminal. No suppressed records released. No fee to fax documents. Certification fee: $10.00 per case includes copy fee. Payee: 82nd District Court. Personal checks accepted. Prepayment required. Prepayment of mail search required. SASE requested.

Probate Court County Courthouse, Rm 203, 806 W Houghton Ave, West Branch, MI 48661; phone: 989-345-0145; fax: 989-345-5901; hours 8:30AM-N, 1-4:30PM (EST). *Probate.*

Ontonagon County

32nd Circuit Court 725 Greenland Rd, Ontonagon, MI 49953; phone: 906-884-2806; fax: 906-884-6796; hours 8:30AM-4:30PM (EST). *Felony, Civil Actions Over $25,000.*

Civil Records: Access: Mail, fax, in person. Both court and visitors may perform in person searches. Search fee: $5.00 per name. Court makes copy: $1.00 per page; same fee for self serve. Required to search: name, years to search. Civil cases indexed by defendant, plaintiff; on index cards and in folders. Mail turnaround time 2-3 days.

Criminal Records: Access: Mail, fax, in person. Both court and visitors may perform in person searches. Search fee: $5.00 per name. Court makes copy: $1.00 per page; same fee for self serve.

Required to search: name, years to search. Criminal records in folders. Mail turnaround time 2-3 days.

General Information: No public access terminal. No suppressed records released. Will fax documents for $2.00 fax fee. Certification fee: $10.00. Payee: County Clerk. Personal checks accepted. Prepayment required.

98th District Court 725 Greenland Rd, Ontonagon, MI 49953; criminal phone: 906-884-2865; civil phone: 906-884-2857; criminal/civil fax: 906-884-2916; hours 8:30AM-4:30PM (EST). *Misdemeanor, Civil Actions Under $25,000, Eviction, Small Claims.*

Civil Records: Access: Mail, in person. Only the court performs in person searches. Search fee: $5.00 each name. Court makes copy: $1.00 per page. Required to search: name, years to search. Civil cases indexed by defendant, plaintiff. Civil records kept for 10 years then destroyed. Small claims kept 6 years only. Mail turnaround time 1 week.

Criminal Records: Access: Mail, in person. Only the court performs in person searches. Search fee: $5.00 each name. Court makes copy: $1.00 per page. Required to search: name, years to search, DOB. Criminal records kept for 10 years then destroyed. Mail turnaround time 1 week.

General Information: No public access terminal. No suppressed records released. Will fax documents. Certification fee: $10.00. Payee: 98th District Court. Business checks accepted. Prepayment and SASE required.

Probate Court 725 Greenland Rd, Ontonagon, MI 49953; phone: 906-884-4117; fax: 906-884-2916; hours 8:30AM-N, 1-4:30PM (EST). *Probate.*

Osceola County

49th Circuit Court 301 W Upton, Reed City, MI 49677; phone: 231-832-6103; fax: 231-832-6149; hours 9AM-5PM (EST). *Felony, Civil Actions Over $25,000.*

Civil Records: Access: Phone, fax, mail, in person. Both court and visitors may perform in person searches. No search fee. Court makes copy: $1.00 per page if filed, otherwise $.50 per page. Required to search: name, years to search. Civil cases indexed by defendant, plaintiff; on computer since 1992, prior on docket books. Mail turnaround time 1-2 days.

Criminal Records: Access: Phone, fax, mail, in person. Both court and visitors may perform in person searches. No search fee. Court makes copy: $1.00 per page if filed, otherwise $.50 per page. Required to search: name, years to search, DOB. Criminal records on computer since 1992, prior on docket books back to 1967. Mail turnaround time 1-2 days.

General Information: No public access terminal. No suppressed or adoption records released. Will fax documents for $1.00 1st 5 pages, $.50 each add'l. Certification fee: $10.00 plus $1.00 per page after first. Payee: 49th Circuit Court. Personal checks accepted. Prepayment and SASE required.

77th District Court 410 W Upton, Reed City, MI 49677; phone: 231-832-6155; fax: 231-832-9190; hours 8:30AM-4:30PM (EST). *Misdemeanor, Civil Actions Under $25,000, Eviction, Small Claims.*

Civil Records: Access: Phone, mail, fax, in person. Only the court performs in person searches. No search fee. Court makes copy: $1.00 per page. Required to search: name, years to search. Civil cases indexed by defendant, plaintiff; on computer since 6/91. Mail turnaround time 2 days.

Criminal Records: Access: Phone, mail, fax, in person. Only the court performs in person searches. No search fee. Court makes copy: $1.00 per page. Required to search: name, years to search, DOB. Criminal records on computer since 6/91. Mail turnaround time 2 days.

General Information: No public access terminal. No suppressed records released. Will fax documents for no fee. Certification fee: $10.00 per doc includes copy fee. Payee: 77th District Court. Only cashiers checks and money orders accepted. Prepayment and SASE required.

Probate Court 410 W Upton, Reed City, MI 49677; phone: 231-832-6124; fax: 231-832-6181; hours 8:30AM-N, 1-4:30PM (EST). *Probate.*

Note: Shares the same judge with Mecosta County Probate Court.

Oscoda County

23rd Circuit Court PO Box 399, 311 Morenci Ave, Mio, MI 48647; phone: 989-826-1110; probate phone: 989-826-1107; criminal/civil fax: 989-826-1136; probate fax: 989-826-1158; hours 8:30AM-4:30PM (EST). *Felony, Civil Actions Over $25,000.*
Civil Records: Access: Mail, in person. Only the court performs in person searches. Search fee: $15.00 per name per year. Court makes copy: $1.00 per page. Required to search: name, years to search. Civil cases indexed by defendant, plaintiff; on computer since 1989, prior on docket books to 1880s. Mail turnaround time 2-3 weeks.
Criminal Records: Access: Mail, in person. Only the court performs in person searches. Search fee: $15.00 per name per year. Court makes copy: $1.00 per page. Required to search: name, years to search, DOB. Criminal records on computer since 1989, prior on docket books to 1880s. Mail turnaround time 2-3 weeks.
General Information: No public access terminal. No suppressed records released. Certification fee: $10.00 plus $1.00 per page copy fee after first. Payee: Oscoda County Clerk. Personal checks accepted. Prepayment and SASE required.

81st District Court PO Box 625, Mio, MI 48647; phone: 989-826-1106; fax: 989-826-1188; hours 8:30AM-4:30PM (EST). *Misdemeanor, Civil Actions Under $25,000, Eviction, Small Claims.*
Civil Records: Access: Mail, in person. Only the court performs in person searches. Search fee: $2.00 per name. Court makes copy: $.50 per page. Required to search: name, years to search. Civil cases indexed by defendant, plaintiff; on computer back to 1990, prior on index cards. Mail turnaround time 1-2 days.
Criminal Records: Access: Mail, in person. Only the court performs in person searches. Search fee: $2.00 per name. Court makes copy: $.50 per page. Required to search: name, years to search, DOB; also helpful: SSN. Criminal records on computer back to 1990, prior on index cards. Mail turnaround time 1-2 days.
General Information: No public access terminal. No suppressed records released. Will fax documents to local or toll free line. Certification fee: $10.00 plus $1.00 per page after first. Payee: 81st District Court. Personal checks not accepted. Prepayment and SASE required.

Probate Court PO Box 399, 105 S Court St, Mio, MI 48647; phone: 989-826-1107; fax: 989-826-1158; hours 8:30AM-N, 1-4:30PM (EST). *Probate.*

Otsego County

46th Circuit Court 225 Main St, Gaylord, MI 49735; phone: 989-731-7500(Clerk); fax: 989-731-7519; hours 8AM-4:30PM (EST). *Felony, Civil Actions Over $25,000.*
www.Circuit46.org
Civil Records: Access: Mail, in person, online. Both court and visitors may perform in person searches. Search fee: $1.00 per name. Court makes copy: $1.00 per page. Required to search: name, years to search. Civil records on computer since 1988, prior on indexes since 1800s. Online access to court case records (closed cases for 90 days only) is free at www.circuit46.org/Cases/cases.html. Mail turnaround time varies.
Criminal Records: Access: Mail, in person, online. Both court and visitors may perform in person searches. Search fee: $1.00 per name. Court makes copy: $1.00 per page. Required to search: name, years to search, DOB. Criminal records on computer since 1988, prior on indexes since 1800s. Online access to

criminal records is the same as civil. Mail turnaround time varies.
General Information: No public access terminal. No suppressed, juvenile, mental health, or adoption records released. Will fax documents to local or toll-free number; all others for fee of $5.00 per page. Certification fee: $10.00 per document. Payee: Otsego County Clerk. Personal checks accepted. Prepayment and SASE required.

46th Circuit Trial Court - District Court 800 Livingston Blvd, #1C, Gaylord, MI 49735; phone: 989-731-0201; fax: 989-732-5130; hours 8AM-4:30PM (EST). *Misdemeanor, Civil Actions Under $25,000, Eviction, Small Claims.*
www.circuit46.org
Civil Records: Access: Mail, in person, online. Both court and visitors may perform in person searches. No search fee. Court makes copy: $1.00 per page. Required to search: name, years to search. Civil cases indexed by defendant, plaintiff; on computer since 1985, prior index cards. Online access to court case records (closed cases for 90 days only) is free at www.circuit46.org/Cases/cases.html. Mail turnaround time 4 days.
Criminal Records: Access: Mail, in person, online. Both court and visitors may perform in person searches. No search fee. Court makes copy: $1.00 per page. Required to search: name, years to search, DOB. Criminal records on computer since 1985, prior index cards to 1969. Access to online criminal records is the same as civil, but records go back 6 months. Mail turnaround time 4 days.
General Information: Public terminal goes back to 1985. No suppressed records released. Certification fee: $10.00 plus $1.00 per page after first. Payee: 46th Circuit Trial Court. Personal checks accepted. Prepayment and SASE required.

Probate Court 800 Livingston Blvd, #1C, Gaylord, MI 49735; phone: 989-731-0204, 989-731-0201; fax: 989-732-5130; hours 8AM-4:30PM (EST). *Probate.*
www.Circuit46.org
Note: Search cases by name free at www.circuit46.org/Cases/cases.html.

Ottawa County

20th Circuit Court 414 Washington Ave, Grand Haven, MI 49417; phone: 616-846-8315; fax: 616-846-8138; hours 8AM-5PM (EST). *Felony, Civil Actions Over $25,000.*
www.co.ottawa.mi.us/Courts/courts.htm
Civil Records: Access: Mail, fax, in person. Visitors must perform in person searches themselves. Search fee: $10.00 per name per decade. Court makes copy: $.50 per page; same fee for self serve. Required to search: name, years to search. Civil cases indexed by defendant, plaintiff, number. Civil records on computer since 1989. Mail turnaround time 2-3 days; phone search - 24 hours.
Criminal Records: Access: Mail, fax, in person. Visitors must perform in person searches themselves. Search fee: $10.00 per name per decade. Court makes copy: $.50 per page; same fee for self serve. Required to search: name, years to search, DOB; also helpful: SSN. Criminal records on computer since 1990. Mail turnaround time 2-3 days; phone search - 24 hours.
General Information: Public terminal goes back to 1990. No suppressed, juvenile, sex offenders, mental health, or adoption records released. Certification fee: $10.00 plus $1.00 per page. Payee: Ottawa County Clerk. Personal checks accepted. Prepayment required. SASE requested.

58th District Court - Grand Haven 414 Washington Ave, Grand Haven, MI 49417; phone: 616-846-8280; criminal phone: 616-846-8127; civil phone: 616-846-8289; criminal fax: 616-846-8291; civil fax: 616-846-8035; hours 8AM-5PM (EST). *Misdemeanor, Civil Actions Under $25,000, Eviction, Small Claims.*
www.co.ottawa.mi.us/Courts/courts.htm

Civil Records: Access: Mail, fax, in person. Both court and visitors may perform in person searches. Search fee: $3.00. Court makes copy: $1.00 per page; same fee for self serve. Required to search: name, years to search. Civil cases indexed by defendant, plaintiff; on computer back to 1993, prior on index cards since 1969. Mail turnaround time 4 days.
Criminal Records: Access: Mail, fax, in person. Both court and visitors may perform in person searches. Search fee: $3.00. Court makes copy: $1.00 per page; same fee for self serve. Required to search: name, years to search, DOB. Criminal records on computer back to 1990, prior on index cards since 1969. Mail turnaround time 4 days.
General Information: Public terminal has criminal back to 1990 and civil back to 1993. No suppressed records released. Will fax documents for $3.00 per page. Certification fee: $10.00 plus $1.00 per page after first. Payee: 58th District Court. Personal checks accepted. Out of state checks not accepted. Prepayment and SASE required.

58th District Court - Holland 57 W 8th St, Holland, MI 49423; phone: 616-392-6991; fax: 616-392-5013; hours 8AM-5PM (EST). *Misdemeanor, Civil Actions Under $25,000, Eviction, Small Claims.*
www.co.ottawa.mi.us/Courts/courts.htm
Civil Records: Access: Fax, mail, in person. Only the court performs in person searches. Search fee: $3.00 per name. Court makes copy: $1.00 per page. Required to search: name, years to search. Civil cases indexed by defendant, plaintiff; on computer since 1988, prior on books since 1969. Mail turnaround time varies.
Criminal Records: Access: Fax, mail, in person. Only the court performs in person searches. Search fee: $3.00 per name. Court makes copy: $1.00 per page. Required to search: name, years to search, DOB; also helpful: SSN. Criminal records on computer since 1988, prior on books since 1969. Mail turnaround time varies.
General Information: No public access terminal. No suppressed records released. Certification fee: $10.00 per doc includes copies. Payee: 58th District Court. Personal checks accepted. Out of state checks not accepted. Prepayment and SASE required.

58th District Court - Hudsonville 3100 Port Sheldon, Hudsonville, MI 49426; phone: 616-662-3100 x2; fax: 616-669-2950; hours 8AM-Noon; 1-5PM (EST). *Misdemeanor, Civil Actions Under $25,000, Eviction, Small Claims.*
www.co.ottawa.mi.us/Courts/courts.htm
Civil Records: Access: Mail, in person. Only the court performs in person searches. Search fee: $3.00 per name. Court makes copy: $1.00 per page. Required to search: name, years to search; also helpful: address. Civil cases indexed by defendant, plaintiff; on computer since 7/1993, prior on index file. Mail turnaround time 2 days.
Criminal Records: Access: Mail, in person. Only the court performs in person searches. Search fee: $3.00 per name. Court makes copy: $1.00 per page. Required to search: name, years to search, DOB; also helpful: address. Criminal records on computer since 1990. Mail turnaround time 2 days.
General Information: No public access terminal. No suppressed records released. Will fax documents for $3.00 per name; $1.00 per copied page. Certification fee: $10.00. Payee: 58th District Court. Personal checks accepted. Prepayment required.

Probate Court 12120 Fillmore St, West Olive, MI 49460; phone: 616-786-4110; fax: 616-738-4624; hours 8AM-5PM (EST). *Probate.*
www.co.ottawa.mi.us/Courts/Probate/probate.htm

Presque Isle County

53rd Circuit Court PO Box 110, Rogers City, MI 49779; phone: 989-734-3288; probate phone: 989-734-3268; fax: 989-734-7635; hours 8:30AM-4:30PM (EST). *Felony, Civil Actions Over $25,000.*
Civil Records: Access: Phone, fax, mail, in person. Only the court performs in person searches. No

search fee. Court makes copy: $1.00 per page. Required to search: name, years to search. Civil cases indexed by defendant, plaintiff; on docket books since 1800s. Mail turnaround time 1 week.

Criminal Records: Access: Phone, fax, mail, in person. Only the court performs in person searches. No search fee. Court makes copy: $1.00 per page. Required to search: name, years to search, DOB. Criminal records on docket books since 1800s. Mail turnaround time 1 week.

General Information: No public access terminal. No suppressed, juvenile, sex offenders, mental health, or adoption records released. Will fax documents for $1.00 per page. Certification fee: $10.00. Cert fee includes copies. Payee: Presque Isle County Clerk. Personal checks accepted. Prepayment and SASE required.

89th District Court PO Box 110, Rogers City, MI 49779; phone: 989-734-2411; fax: 989-734-3400; hours 8AM-4PM (EST). *Misdemeanor, Civil Actions Under $25,000, Eviction, Small Claims.*

Civil Records: Access: Mail, in person. Only the court performs in person searches. No search fee. Court makes copy: $1.00 for first page, $.25 each add'l; same fee for self serve. Required to search: name, years to search. Civil cases indexed by defendant, plaintiff; on computer since 6/94, prior on index books. Mail turnaround time 2 weeks.

Criminal Records: Access: Mail, in person. Only the court performs in person searches. No search fee. Court makes copy: $1.00 for first page, $.25 each add'l; same fee for self serve. Required to search: name, years to search, DOB. Criminal records on computer since 6/94, prior on index books. Mail turnaround time 2 weeks or less.

General Information: No public access terminal. No suppressed records released. Certification fee: $10.00 plus $1.00 per page after first. Payee: 89th District Court. Personal checks accepted. Prepayment and SASE required.

Probate Court 151 Huron Ave, PO Box 110, Rogers City, MI 49779; phone: 989-734-3268; fax: 989-734-4420; hours 8:30AM-N, 1-4:30PM (EST). *Probate.*

Roscommon County

34th Circuit Court 500 Lake St #1, Attn: County Clerk Reg of Deeds, Roscommon, MI 48653; phone: 989-275-1902; fax: 989-275-0602; hours 8:30AM-4:30PM (EST). *Felony, Civil Actions Over $25,000.*

Civil Records: Access: Fax, mail, in person. Both court and visitors may perform in person searches. Search fee: $5.00 per name. Court makes copy: $.50 per page. Required to search: name, years to search. Civil records on computer since 3/94, prior on docket books and cards. Mail turnaround time 24 hours.

Criminal Records: Access: Fax, mail, in person. Both court and visitors may perform in person searches. Search fee: $5.00 per name. Court makes copy: $.50 per page. Required to search: name, years to search, DOB. Criminal records on computer since 3/94, prior on docket books and cards. Mail turnaround time 24 hours.

General Information: No public access terminal. No suppressed, sex offenders or mental health records released. Fee to fax documents is $3.00 1st page, $1.00 each add'l. Certification fee: $10.00 plus $1.00 per page after first. Payee: 34th Circuit Court. Personal checks accepted. Prepayment and SASE required.

83rd District Court 500 Lake St, Roscommon, MI 48653; phone: 989-275-5312; fax: 989-275-6033; hours 8:30AM-4:30PM (EST). *Misdemeanor, Civil Actions Under $25,000, Eviction, Small Claims.*

Civil Records: Access: Phone, fax, mail, in person. Only the court performs in person searches. No search fee. Court makes copy: $.50 per page. Required to search: name, years to search. Civil cases indexed by defendant, plaintiff; on computer since 1988, prior on index cards since 1969. Mail turnaround time same day.

Criminal Records: Access: Phone, fax, mail, in person. Only the court performs in person searches. No search fee. Court makes copy: $.50 per page. Required to search: name, years to search, DOB; also helpful: SSN. Criminal records on computer since 1988, prior on index cards since 1969. Mail turnaround time same day.

General Information: No public access terminal. No suppressed, juvenile, sex offenders, mental health, or adoption records released. No fee to fax documents. No certification fee. Payee: 83rd District Court. Personal checks accepted. Prepayment required.

Probate Court 500 Lake St. Rm. 132, Roscommon, MI 48653; phone: 989-275-5221; fax: 989-275-8537; hours 8:30AM-4:30PM (EST). *Probate.*

Saginaw County

10th Circuit Court 111 S Michigan Ave, Saginaw, MI 48602; phone: 989-790-5541; probate phone: 989-790-5233; fax: 989-790-5248; hours 8AM-5:00PM (EST). *Felony, Civil Actions Over $25,000.*
www.saginawcounty.com/clerk/court/index.html

Civil Records: Access: Mail, in person. Both court and visitors may perform in person searches. Search fee: None at this time. Court makes copy: $1.00 per page. Required to search: name, years to search. Civil cases indexed by defendant, plaintiff; on computer since 1985, prior on index books, microfilm. Calendars may be searched at www.saginawcounty.com/clerk/docket/index.html. Mail turnaround time 2 days.

Criminal Records: Access: Mail, in person. Both court and visitors may perform in person searches. Search fee: None at this time. Court makes copy: $1.00 per page. Required to search: name, years to search, DOB. Criminal records on computer since 1986, prior on index books. Mail turnaround time 2 days.

General Information: Public terminal goes back to 1986. No suppressed, sex offenders, mental health or guardianship records released. Will fax documents. Certification fee: $10.00 plus $.25 per docket page. Payee: Saginaw County Clerk. No personal checks accepted. Prepayment and SASE required.

70th District Court - Criminal Division 111 S Michigan Ave, Saginaw, MI 48602; phone: 989-790-5385; fax: 989-790-5589; hours 8AM-4:45PM (EST). *Misdemeanor.*
www.saginawcounty.com/DistrictCourt

Criminal Records: Access: Fax, mail, in person. Only the court performs in person searches. Search fee: $10.00 per name. Court makes copy: $1.00 per page. Required to search: name, years to search, DOB, signed release; also helpful: address. Criminal records on computer back to 1987, prior on microfiche since 1972. Fax information received only if pre-paid. They must receive $5.00 fee before they fax out information. Mail turnaround time 1 week.

General Information: No public access terminal. No suppressed, juvenile, sex offenders, mental health, or adoption records released. Will fax documents to local or toll free line. Certification fee: $10.00 per document includes copy fee. Payee: 70th District Court. Business checks or Visa, MC accepted. Prepayment and SASE required.

70th District Court - Civil Division 111 S Michigan Ave, Saginaw, MI 48602; phone: 989-790-5380; fax: 989-790-5562; hours 8AM-4:45PM (EST). *Civil Actions Under $25,000, Eviction, Small Claims.*

Civil Records: Access: Mail, in person. Only the court performs in person searches. Search fee: $10.00 per name. Court makes copy: $1.00 per page. Required to search: name, years to search. Civil cases indexed by defendant, plaintiff; on computer since 1982, prior on docket books. Mail turnaround time 1 week.

General Information: Public terminal has only civil records back to 1988. No suppressed records released. Will fax documents to local or toll free line. Certification fee: $10.00. Payee: 70th District court. Personal checks accepted. Prepayment and SASE required.

Probate/Family Court 111 S Michigan St, Saginaw, MI 48602; phone: 989-790-5320; fax: 989-790-5328; hours 8AM-5PM (EST). *Probate.*

Sanilac County

24th Circuit Court 60 W Sanilac, Rm 203, Sandusky, MI 48471; phone: 810-648-3212 x8227; fax: 810-648-5466; hours 8AM-4:30PM (EST). *Felony, Civil Actions Over $25,000.*
www.sanilaccounty.net

Civil Records: Access: Mail, in person. Both court and visitors may perform in person searches. Search fee: $10.00 per name. Court makes copy: $1.00 per page; same fee for self serve. Required to search: name, years to search. Civil cases indexed by defendant, plaintiff; on computer since 1993. Mail turnaround time 2-3 days.

Criminal Records: Access: Mail, in person. Both court and visitors may perform in person searches. Search fee: $10.00 per name. Court makes copy: $1.00 per page; same fee for self serve. Required to search: name, years to search. Criminal records on computer since 1993. Mail turnaround time 2-3 days.

General Information: Public terminal goes back to 1993. No suppressed, juvenile, sex offenders, mental health, or adoption records released. Will fax documents to local or toll free line. Certification fee: $10.00. Payee: Sanilac County Clerk. Personal checks accepted. Prepayment and SASE required.

73A District Court 60 W Sanilac, Sandusky, MI 48471; phone: 810-648-3250; criminal phone: 810-648-3424; civil phone: 810-648-3424; hours 8AM-4:30PM (EST). *Misdemeanor, Civil Actions Under $25,000, Eviction, Small Claims.*

Civil Records: Access: Mail, in person. Only the court performs in person searches. Search fee: $1.00 per name per year. Court makes copy: $1.00 per page. Required to search: name, years to search; also helpful: address. Civil cases indexed by defendant, plaintiff; on computer back to 1989, prior on docket books to 1969. Mail turnaround time 1 week.

Criminal Records: Access: Mail, in person. Only the court performs in person searches. Search fee: $1.00 per name per year. Court makes copy: $1.00 per page. Required to search: name, years to search, DOB; also helpful: address. Criminal records on computer back to 1989, prior on docket books to 1969. Mail turnaround time 1 week.

General Information: No public access terminal. No suppressed records released. Will fax documents to local or toll free line. Fax fee included in search. Certification fee: $10.00 plus $1.00 per page after first. Payee: 73A District Court. Personal checks accepted. Prepayment and SASE required.

Probate Court 60 W Sanilac Ave, Rm 106, Sandusky, MI 48471-1096; phone: 810-648-3221; fax: 810-648-2900; hours 8AM-N, 1-4:30PM (EST). *Probate.*

Schoolcraft County

11th Circuit Court 300 Walnut St, Rm 164, Manistique, MI 49854; phone: 906-341-3618; probate phone: 906-341-3644; criminal/civil fax: 906-341-5680; probate fax: 906-341-3627; hours 8AM-4PM (EST). *Felony, Civil Actions Over $25,000.*

Note: Probate is a separate index in Rm 129.

Civil Records: Access: Phone, fax, mail, in person. Both court and visitors may perform in person searches. No search fee. Court makes copy: $1.00 per page. Required to search: name, years to search. Civil cases indexed by defendant, plaintiff; on docket books and index since 1881. Mail turnaround time 2-3 days.

Criminal Records: Access: Phone, fax, mail, in person. Only the court performs in person searches. No search fee. Court makes copy: $1.00 per page. Required to search: name, years to search. Criminal records on docket books and index since 1881. Mail turnaround time 2-3 days.

General Information: No public access terminal. No suppressed, juvenile, sex offenders, mental health, or adoption records released. Will fax documents to local or toll free line. Certification fee: $10.00 per document. Payee: Schoolcraft County Clerk. Personal checks accepted. Prepayment required. SASE requested.

93rd District Court 300 Walnut St, Rm 135, Manistique, MI 49854; phone: 906-341-3630; fax: 906-341-8006; hours 8AM-4PM (EST). *Misdemeanor, Civil Actions Under $25,000, Eviction, Small Claims.*

Civil Records: Access: Mail, in person. Both court and visitors may perform in person searches. Search fee: $10.00. Court makes copy: $1.00 per page; same fee for self serve. Required to search: name, years to search. Civil cases indexed by defendant, plaintiff. Civil records kept on index cards. Mail turnaround time 2-3 days.

Criminal Records: Access: Mail, in person. Only the court performs in person searches. Search fee: $10.00. Court makes copy: $1.00 per page; same fee for self serve. Required to search: name, years to search, DOB; also helpful: SSN. Criminal records kept on index cards. Mail turnaround time 2-3 days.

General Information: No public access terminal. No suppressed, sex offenders or mental health records released. Will fax documents. Certification fee: $10.00 if more than 1 page. Payee: 93rd District Court. Business checks accepted. Prepayment and SASE required.

Probate Court 300 Walnut St, Rm 129, Manistique, MI 49854; phone: 906-341-3641; fax: 906-341-3627; hours 8AM-N, 1-4PM (EST). *Probate.*

Shiawassee County

35th Circuit Court 208 N Shiawassee St, Corunna, MI 48817; phone: 989-743-2262; fax: 989-743-2241; hours 8AM-5PM, may close for lunch hour (EST). *Felony, Civil Actions Over $25,000.*

Civil Records: Access: Phone, fax, mail, in person. Both court and visitors may perform in person searches. Search fee: $1.00 per name per 10 years. Court makes copy: $1.00 per page 1st 5 pages; $.15 per page each add'l. Required to search: name, years to search. Civil cases indexed by defendant, plaintiff; on computer since 9/87, prior on docket books and cards. Mail turnaround time 1 week.

Criminal Records: Access: Phone, fax, mail, in person. Both court and visitors may perform in person searches. Search fee: $10.00 for up to 10 years. Court makes copy: $1.00 per page 1st 5 pages; $.15 per page each add'l. Required to search: name, years to search, DOB. Criminal records on computer since 10/93; prior on docket books. Mail turnaround time 1 week.

General Information: No public access terminal. No suppressed records released. Certification fee: $10.00 per document. A Register of Action fee is $10.00. Payee: 35th Circuit Court. Personal checks accepted. Prepayment and SASE required.

66th District Court 110 E Mack St, Corunna, MI 48817; phone: 989-743-2395; fax: 989-743-2469; hours 8AM-5PM (EST). *Misdemeanor, Civil Actions Under $25,000, Eviction, Small Claims.*

Civil Records: Access: Phone, fax, mail, in person. Both court and visitors may perform in person searches. No search fee. Court makes copy: $1.00 per page. Required to search: name, years to search; also helpful: DOB, SSN. Civil cases indexed by defendant, plaintiff; on computer back to 1995, prior on microfiche. Mail turnaround time 1 week.

Criminal Records: Access: Phone, fax, mail, in person. Both court and visitors may perform in

person searches. No search fee. Court makes copy: $1.00 per page. Required to search: name, years to search, DOB. Case number required for pre-1995 research. Criminal records on computer back to 1995, prior on microfiche to 1969. Mail turnaround time 1 week.

General Information: Public terminal goes back to 1995. No suppressed records released. Friday is their day to fax documents. Certification fee: $10.00 includes copy fee. Payee: 66th District Court. Personal checks accepted. Prepayment and SASE required.

Probate Court 110 E Mack St, Corunna, MI 48817; phone: 989-743-2211; fax: 989-743-2349; hours 8AM-5PM (EST). *Probate.*

St. Clair County

31st Circuit Court 201 McMorran Blvd, Port Huron, MI 48060; phone: 810-985-2200; fax: 810-985-4796; hours 8AM-4:30PM (EST). *Felony, Civil Actions Over $25,000.*

www.stclaircounty.org/Offices/courts

Civil Records: Access: Mail, fax, in person. Both court and visitors may perform in person searches. No search fee. Court makes copy: $1.00 per page. Required to search: name, years to search; also helpful: address. Civil cases indexed by defendant, plaintiff; on computer back to 1987, non computerized records back to 1936. Mail turnaround time 24 hours.

Criminal Records: Access: Mail, fax, in person. Both court and visitors may perform in person searches. No search fee. Court makes copy: $1.00 per page. Required to search: name, years to search, DOB; also helpful: address. Criminal records on computer back to 1987, non computerized records back to 1936. Mail turnaround time 24 hours.

General Information: No public access terminal. No suppressed, juvenile, mental health, or adoption records released. Will fax documents for $10.00 per searched name. Certification fee: $10.00. Payee: St. Clair Clerk of Court. Will accept In state checks. Prepayment and SASE required.

72nd District Court 201 McMorran Blvd, Rm 2900, Port Huron, MI 48060; criminal phone: 810-985-2072; civil phone: 810-985-2077; fax: 810-982-1260; hours 8AM-4:30PM M-Thl; 9AM-4:30PM (EST). *Misdemeanor, Civil Actions Under $25,000, Eviction, Small Claims.*

Civil Records: Access: In person only. Visitors must perform in person searches themselves. Court makes copy: $1.00 per page. Required to search: name, years to search. Civil cases indexed by defendant, plaintiff; on computer since 1987, prior on docket books back to 1969.

Criminal Records: Access: in person only. Visitors must perform in person searches themselves. Court makes copy: $1.00 per page. Required to search: name, years to search, DOB; SSN helpful. Criminal records on computer since 1987, prior on docket books back to 1969.

General Information: Public terminal goes back to 1989. No suppressed records released. Certification fee: $10.00 per doc includes copy fee. Payee: 72nd District Court. Personal checks accepted. Prepayment required.

Probate Court 201 McMorran Blvd Rm 2600, Port Huron, MI 48060; phone: 810-985-2066; fax: 810-985-2179; hours 8AM-4:30PM (EST). *Probate.*

St. Joseph County

45th Circuit Court PO Box 189, Centreville, MI 49032; phone: 269-467-5531; fax: 269-467-5628; hours 9AM-5PM (EST). *Felony, Civil Actions Over $25,000.*

www.stjosephcountymi.org/ccircuit.htm

Civil Records: Access: Mail, in person. Both court and visitors may perform in person searches. Search fee: $1.00 per name. For records prior to 1988, fee is $1.00 per year searched. Court makes copy: $1.00 per page. Required to search: name, years to

search. Civil cases indexed by defendant, plaintiff; on computer since 1988, prior on books from 1900, earlier in archives. Mail turnaround time 1 day.

Criminal Records: Access: Mail, in person. Both court and visitors may perform in person searches. Search fee: $1.00 per name. For records prior to 1988, fee is $1.00 per year searched. Court makes copy: $1.00 per page. Required to search: name, years to search. Criminal records on computer since 1988, prior on books from 1900, earlier in archives. Mail turnaround time same day.

General Information: Public terminal goes back to 1988. No suppressed records released. Will fax documents for $2.00 1st page, $1.00 each add'l. Certification fee: $10.00 per certification includes copies. Payee: St. Joseph County Clerk. Business checks accepted. Prepayment required.

3-B District Court PO Box 67, Centreville, MI 49032; phone: 269-467-5627; criminal phone: 269-467-5627; civil phone: 269-467-5623; hours 8AM-5PM (EST). *Misdemeanor, Civil Actions Under $25,000, Eviction, Small Claims.*

Civil Records: Access: Phone, mail, in person. Both court and visitors may perform in person searches. No search fee. Court makes copy: $.15 per page. Required to search: name, years to search; also helpful: address. Civil cases indexed by defendant, plaintiff; on computer since 1987, prior in archives. Phone search access limited. Note: Both court and visitors may perform in person computer searches. Mail turnaround time 2 weeks.

Criminal Records: Access: Fax, mail, in person. Both court and visitors may perform in person searches. No search fee. Court makes copy: $.15 per page. Required to search: name, years to search, DOB, date of offense. Criminal records on computer since 1987, prior in archives. Signed release required for some searches. Mail turnaround time 2 weeks.

General Information: Public terminal goes back to 9/1987. No suppressed records released. Certification fee: $10.00 per doc. Payee: 3-B District Court. Business checks accepted. Prepayment required.

Probate Court PO Box 190, 125 W Main, Centreville, MI 49032; phone: 269-467-5538; fax: 269-467-5560; hours 8AM-5PM (EST). *Probate.*

www.stjosephcountymi.org/cprobate.htm

Tuscola County

54th Circuit Court 440 N State St, Caro, MI 48723; phone: 989-672-3780; criminal phone: 989-672-3776; civil phone: 989-672-3775; probate phone: 989-672-3850; fax: 989-672-4266; hours 8AM-N, 1-4:30PM (EST). *Felony, Civil Actions Over $25,000.*

www.tuscolacounty.org

Civil Records: Access: Mail, in person. Only the court performs in person searches. Search fee: $5.00 per name. Fee is $1.00 for each year prior to 1989. Court makes copy: $1.00 per page. Required to search: name, years to search. Civil cases indexed by defendant, plaintiff; on computer since 1989, prior on books since beginning. Mail turnaround time 3-4 days.

Criminal Records: Access: Mail, in person. Only the court performs in person searches. Search fee: $5.00 per name. Fee is $1.00 for each year prior to 1989. Court makes copy: $1.00 per page. Required to search: name, years to search, DOB; also helpful: SSN. Criminal records on computer since 1989, prior on books since beginning. Mail turnaround time 3-4 days.

General Information: No public access terminal. No suppressed, juvenile, sex offenders, mental health, or adoption records released. Will not fax documents. Certification fee: $10.00 plus $1.00 per page after first. Payee: County Clerk. Personal checks not accepted. Prepayment and SASE required.

71 B District Court 440 N State St, Caro, MI 48723; phone: 989-672-3800; criminal phone: 989-672-3790; civil phone: 989-672-3800; criminal fax: 989-672-4526; civil fax: 989-673-0451; hours 8AM-4:30PM (EST). *Misdemeanor, Civil Actions Under $25,000, Eviction, Small Claims.*

Civil Records: Access: Phone, mail, in person. Both court and visitors may perform in person searches. No search fee. Court makes copy: $.50 per page. Required to search: name, years to search. Civil cases indexed by defendant, plaintiff; on computer since 1991, prior on cards.

Criminal Records: Access: Phone, mail, in person. Both court and visitors may perform in person searches. No search fee. Court makes copy: $.50 per page. Required to search: name, years to search, DOB; also helpful: SSN. Criminal records on computer since 1991; others back to 1969.

General Information: No public access terminal. No suppressed records released. Will not fax documents. Certification fee: $10.00 plus $1.00 per page after first. Payee: 71 B District Court. Personal checks accepted. Prepayment and SASE required.

Probate Court 440 N State St, Caro, MI 48723; phone: 989-672-3850; fax: 989-672-2057; hours 8AM-N, 1-4:30PM (EST). *Probate.*

Van Buren County

36th Circuit Court 212 Paw Paw St #101, Paw Paw, MI 49079; phone: 269-657-8218; criminal phone: 269-657-8218; civil phone: 269-657-8222; criminal fax: 269-657-8298; civil fax: 269-657-0719; hours 8:30AM-5PM (EST). *Felony, Civil Actions Over $25,000.*

Civil Records: Access: Mail, in person. Only the court performs in person searches. Search fee: $1.00 per name per year. Fee includes combined civil and criminal search. Court makes copy: $1.00 per page. Required to search: name, years to search. Civil cases indexed by defendant, plaintiff; on computer back to 1990, prior on docket books since 1800s. Mail turnaround time 1 day.

Criminal Records: Access: Mail, in person. Only the court performs in person searches. Search fee: $1.00 per name per year. Court makes copy: $1.00 per page. Required to search: name, years to search, DOB, signed release. Criminal records on computer back to 1990, prior on docket books since 1800s. Mail turnaround time 1 day.

General Information: No public access terminal. No suppressed, sex offender records released. Will phone with documents if a toll-free number is provided. Certification fee: $10.00 plus $1.00 per page after first. Payee: Van Buren County Clerk. Personal checks accepted. Prepayment and SASE required.

7th District Court 212 Paw Paw St, Paw Paw, MI 49079; phone: 269-657-8222; fax: 269-657-0719; hours 9AM-4:30PM (EST). *Misdemeanor, Civil Actions Under $25,000, Eviction, Small Claims.*

Civil Records: Access: Mail, fax, in person. Both court and visitors may perform in person searches. No search fee. Court makes copy: $1.00 per page. Required to search: name, years to search. Civil cases indexed by defendant, plaintiff. Civil records kept in file folder; computerized records since 1999. Mail turnaround time 1-2 days.

Criminal Records: Access: Mail, fax, in person. Both court and visitors may perform in person searches. No search fee. Court makes copy: $1.00 per page. Required to search: name, years to search, DOB, SSN. Criminal records kept in file folder; computerized since 1999. Mail turnaround time 1-2 days.

General Information: No public access terminal. No suppressed records released. Certification fee: $10.00 per doc. Payee: 7th District Court. No personal checks accepted. Prepayment and SASE required.

7th District Court - West Division 1007 E Wells, PO Box 311, South Haven, MI 49090; phone: 269-637-5258; fax: 269-639-4517; hours 8:30AM-4:30PM (EST). *Misdemeanor, Civil Actions Under $25,000, Eviction, Small Claims.*

Civil Records: Access: Mail, in person. Only the court performs in person searches. Search fee: $1.00 per name. Court makes copy: $1.00 per page. Self serve copy fee: $.25 per page. Required to search:

name, years to search. Civil cases indexed by defendant, plaintiff; on computer since 1991, prior on index cards since 1982. Mail turnaround 3 days.

Criminal Records: Access: Mail, in person. Only the court performs in person searches. Search fee: $1.00 per name. Court makes copy: $1.00 per page. Self serve copy fee: $.25 per page. Required to search: name, years to search, DOB; also helpful: SSN. Criminal records on computer since 1991, prior on index cards since 1982. Mail turnaround time 3 days. **General Information:** No public access terminal. No suppressed, juvenile, sex offenders, mental health, or adoption records released. Certification fee: $10.00 plus $1.00 per page after first. Payee: 7th District Court. Personal checks accepted. Prepayment required.

Probate Court 212 Paw Paw St, #220, Paw Paw, MI 49079; phone: 269-657-8225; fax: 269-657-7573; hours 8:30AM-5PM (EST). *Probate.*

Washtenaw County

22nd Circuit Court PO Box 8645, Ann Arbor, MI 48107-8645; phone: 734-222-3001; hours 8:30AM-4:30PM (EST). *Felony, Civil Actions Over $25,000.* http://courts.ewashtenaw.org

Weekly court dockets listed by judge are available online at http://courts.ewashtenaw.org/docket.htm.

Civil Records: Access: Mail, in person. Both court and visitors may perform in person searches. Search fee: $5.00 per name from 1979 to present; $1.00 per name per year prior to 1979. Court makes copy: $1.00 per page. Required to search: name, years to search. Civil cases indexed by defendant, plaintiff. Civil records kept as originals in file folders, records go back to 1900; computerized since 1979. Mail turnaround time 3-7 days.

Criminal Records: Access: Mail, in person. Both court and visitors may perform in person searches. Search fee: Same fees as civil. Court makes copy: $1.00 per page. Required to search: name, years to search, DOB. Criminal records kept as originals in file folders, records go back to 1900; computerized since 1979. Mail turnaround time 2-3 days.

General Information: Public terminal goes back to 1979. No suppressed records released. Will not fax documents. Certification fee: $10.00 per document. Payee: Washtenaw County Clerk. Personal checks accepted. Prepayment and SASE required.

14A-1 District Court 4133 Washtenaw, Ann Arbor, MI 48107-8645; phone: 734-973-4545; fax: 734-973-4693; hours 8AM-4:30PM (EST). *Misdemeanor, Civil Actions Under $25,000, Eviction, Small Claims.* www.co.washtenaw.mi.us/depts/courts/index.htm

Civil Records: Access: Mail, in person. Both court and visitors may perform in person searches. No search fee. Court makes copy: $1.00 per page. Required to search: name, years to search. Civil cases indexed by defendant, plaintiff; on computer since 1985, prior on index cards. Mail turnaround time 1-2 weeks.

Criminal Records: Access: Mail, in person. Both court and visitors may perform in person searches. No search fee. Court makes copy: $1.00 per page. Required to search: name, years to search, DOB, SSN. Criminal records on computer since 1985, prior on index cards. Mail turnaround time 1-2 weeks.

General Information: Public terminal goes back to 1985. No suppressed records released. Will fax documents to local number. Certification fee: $10.00 per page. Payee: 14 A-1 District Court. Personal checks accepted. Prepayment and SASE required.

14th District Court A-2 415 W Michigan Ave, Ypsilanti, MI 48197; phone: 734-484-6690; fax: 734-484-6697; hours 8AM-4:30PM (EST). *Misdemeanor, Civil Actions Under $25,000, Eviction, Small Claims.*

Civil Records: Access: Mail, in person. Only the court performs in person searches. No search fee. Court makes copy: $.25 per page. Required to search: name, years to search. Civil cases indexed by defendant, plaintiff; on computer since 1985, prior on

file cards since 1969. Specific docket information must be given, the court will not do name searches. Mail turnaround time 1 week; phone turnaround is immediate up to 2 days.

Criminal Records: Access: Mail, in person. Only the court performs in person searches. No search fee. Court makes copy: $.25 per page. Required to search: name, years to search, DOB; also helpful: SSN. Criminal records on computer since 1985, prior on file cards since 1969. The court will not do name searches. Mail turnaround time 1 week; phone turnaround is immediate up to 2 days.

General Information: No public access terminal. No suppressed, juvenile, sex offenders, mental health, or adoption records released. Certification fee: $11.00 per doc plus $1.00 per page. Payee: 14 A-2 District Court. Personal checks accepted. Prepayment and SASE requested.

14th District Court A-3 122 S Main St, Chelsea, MI 48118; phone: 734-475-8606; fax: 734-475-0460; hours 8AM-4:30PM (EST). *Misdemeanor, Civil Actions Under $25,000, Eviction, Small Claims.*

Civil Records: Access: Mail, fax, in person. No search fee. Court makes copy: $.25 per page. Required to search: name, years to search. Civil cases indexed by defendant, plaintiff; on computer since 1986; prior on index cards. Note: Court will perform search time permitting.

Criminal Records: Access: In person only. Only the court performs in person searches. No search fee. Court makes copy: $.25 per page. Required to search: name, years to search, DOB; SSN helpful. Criminal records on computer since 1986; prior on index cards. Note: Court performs in person searches time permitting.

General Information: No public access terminal. No suppressed records released. Certification fee: $10.00. Payee: 14th District Court. Personal checks accepted. Prepayment and SASE required.

14th District Court B - Criminal Division 7200 S Huron River Dr, Ypsilanti, MI 48197; phone: 734-483-1333; fax: 734-483-3630; hours 8AM-5PM (EST). *Misdemeanor.*

Criminal Records: Access: Fax, mail, in person. Only the court performs in person searches. No search fee. Court makes copy: $.50 per page. Required to search: name, years to search, DOB; also helpful: SSN. Criminal records on computer since 1990, prior records kept by name. Mail turnaround time 1 week; phone turnaround is 1 day.

General Information: No public access terminal. No suppressed, probation, juvenile, sex offenders, probation, mental health, or adoption records released. Certification fee: $10.00 per doc includes copies. Payee: 14-B District Court. Personal checks accepted. Credit cards accepted. Prepayment required.

15th District Court - Civil Division 101 E Huron, Box 8650, Ann Arbor, MI 48107; phone: 734-222-3389; criminal phone: 734-222-3380 (crim traffic); fax: 734-222-3335; 8:30AM-4:30PM (EST). *Civil Actions Under $25,000, Eviction, Small Claims.* www.co.washtenaw.mi.us/depts/courts/index.htm

Civil Records: Access: Phone, fax, mail, in person. Both court and visitors may perform in person searches. No search fee. Court makes copy: $.25 per page. Required to search: name, years to search. Civil cases indexed by defendant, plaintiff; on computer since 1990, prior on docket books. Mail turnaround time 2-3 days.

General Information: No public access terminal. No suppressed records released. Will not fax documents. Certification fee: $10.00 per doc. Payee: 15th District Court. Personal checks or Visa, MC, Discover accepted. Prepayment and SASE required.

15th District Court - Criminal Division 101 E Huron, Box 8650, Ann Arbor, MI 48107-8650; phone: 734-222-3380; civil phone: 734-222-3389; fax: 734-222-3335; hours 8AM-4:30PM (EST). *Misdemeanor, Traffic.*

www.co.washtenaw.mi.us/depts/courts/index.htm
Criminal Records: Access: Mail, fax, in person. Both court and visitors may perform in person searches. No search fee. Court makes copy: $.25 per page. Required to search: name, years to search, DOB; also helpful: offense. Criminal records on computer since 1996; prior on docket cards since 1969. The court will not do a name search. Either a case number or charge and incident date is required. Mail turnaround time 2-3 days.
General Information: Public terminal has only criminal records. No suppressed, juvenile, sex offenders, mental health, or adoption records released. Certification fee: $10.00 per doc. Payee: 15th District Court. Checks or Visa, MC, Discover accepted. Prepayment required.

14th District Court B - Civil Division 7200 S Huron River Dr, Ypsilanti, MI 48197; phone: 734-483-5300; fax: 734-483-3630; hours 8AM-5PM (EST). *Civil Actions Under $25,000, Eviction, Small Claims.*
Civil Records: Access: Mail, in person. Only the court performs in person searches. No search fee. Court makes copy: $.50 per page. Required to search: name, years to search. Civil cases indexed by defendant, plaintiff; on computer since 1990, prior on card files from 1985-1989. Mail turnaround time 1 week, phone turnaround is 1 day.
General Information: No public access terminal. No suppressed, juvenile, sex offenders, probation, mental health, or adoption records released. Certification fee: $10.00. Payee: 14-B District Court. Business checks or credit cards accepted. Prepayment required.

Probate Court PO Box 8645, Ann Arbor, MI 48107; phone: 734-994-2474 x2; fax: 734-222-3019; hours 8:30AM-4:30PM (EST). *Probate.*
www.co.washtenaw.mi.us/depts/courts/index.htm

Wayne County

Frank Murphy Hall of Justice 1441 St Antoine, Rm 904, Detroit, MI 48226; phone: 313-224-2500; criminal phone: 313-224-2502/2503; fax: 313-224-2786; hours 8AM-4:30PM (EST). *Felony.*
Criminal Records: Access: Mail, in person. Both court and visitors may perform in person searches. Search fee: $5.00 per name. Court makes copy: $1.00 per page. Required to search: name, years to search, DOB; also helpful: city where crime occurred, aliases. Criminal records on computer since mid 1974, prior on microfiche through 1976, archives off-site 1800s to 2000. Mail turnaround time 3-4 days.
General Information: Public terminal has only criminal records back to mid-1974. No suppressed, juvenile, sex offenders, mental health, or adoption records released. Will not fax documents. Certification fee: $10.00 per doc. Payee: Wayne County Clerk. Prepayment and SASE required.

36th District Court 421 Madison, Detroit, MI 48226; criminal phone: 313-965-5029; civil phone: 313-965-6098; hours 8AM-4:30PM (EST). *Felony, Misdemeanor, Civil Actions Under $25,000, Eviction, Small Claims Under $3000.*
www.36thdistrictcourt.org/criminal-faq.html
Note: Small Claims phone number is 313-965-5972.
Civil Records: Access: In person only. Visitors must perform in person searches themselves. Court makes copy: $1.00 per page. Required to search: name, years to search, address. Civil cases indexed by name, case number. Civil records on computer since 1985, prior kept in file folders. Note: If a case number is provided, then court will retrieve records.
Criminal Records: Access: In person only. Both court and visitors may perform in person searches. No search fee. Court makes copy: $1.00 per page. Required to search: name, DOB; SSN helpful. Note: Will do a single name search over the phone to let you know index numbers, if any.
General Information: Public terminal goes back to 1981. (Civil records terminal is on 2nd Fl; Criminal records on 1st Fl.) No suppressed records released.

Certification fee: $10.00 plus $1.00 per page after first. Payee: 36th District Court. Personal checks or Visa, MC accepted. Prepayment required.

16th District Court 15140 Farmington Rd, Livonia, MI 48154-5498; phone: 734-466-2500; 466-2550 Probation; criminal phone: X3452; civil phone: X3541; hours 8:30AM-4:30PM (EST). *Misdemeanor, Civil Actions Under $25,000, Eviction, Small Claims.*
Civil Records: Access: Mail, in person. Both court and visitors may perform in person searches. No search fee. Court makes copy: $1.00 per page. Required to search: name, years to search. Civil cases indexed by defendant, plaintiff; on computer since 1990, prior on microfiche. Mail turnaround time 1 week.
Criminal Records: Access: In person only. Visitors must perform in person searches themselves. Court makes copy: $1.00 per page. Required to search: name, years to search, DOB; also helpful: offense, date of offense, case number. Criminal records on computer since 1991, prior on microfiche. General searches are not performed.
General Information: Public terminal has criminal back to 1991 and civil back to 1990. No suppressed records released. Will fax documents to local or toll free line. Certification fee: $10.00 per cert. Payee: 16th District Court. Personal checks accepted. Prepayment and SASE required.

17th District Court 15111 Beech-Daly Rd, Redford, MI 48239; phone: 313-387-2790; fax: 313-387-2712; hours 8:30AM-4:15PM (EST). *Misdemeanor, Civil Actions Under $25,000, Eviction, Small Claims.*
Civil Records: Access: Mail, in person. Only the court performs in person searches. No search fee. Court makes copy: $1.00 per page. Required to search: name, years to search. Civil cases indexed by defendant, plaintiff; on computer since 1990, prior on index cards. Mail turnaround time 2 days.
Criminal Records: Access: Fax, mail, in person. Only the court performs in person searches. No search fee. Court makes copy: $1.00 per page. Required to search: name, years to search, DOB, SSN. Criminal records on computer since 1990, prior on index cards. Mail turnaround time 2 days.
General Information: No public access terminal. No suppressed, child and spousal abuse records released. Certification fee: $10.00 per doc. Payee: 17th District Court. Personal checks or Visa, MC accepted. ATM cards accepted. Prepayment and SASE required.

18th District Court 36675 Ford Rd, Westland, MI 48185; phone: 734-595-8720; fax: 734-595-0160; hours 8:30AM-4PM M,F; 8:30AM-5:30PM T,W; 8:30AM-5:30PM Th (EST). *Misdemeanor, Civil Actions Under $25,000, Eviction, Small Claims.*
www.18thdistrictcourt.com
Civil Records: Access: Phone, mail, fax, in person. Only the court performs in person searches. No search fee. Court makes copy: $1.00 per page. Required to search: name, years to search; also helpful: case number or title. Civil cases indexed by defendant, plaintiff; on computer since 1987, prior on microfilm back to 1969. Will name search free, but cert fee applied to copy. Mail turnaround time 1-2 weeks.
Criminal Records: Access: Phone, mail, in person. Only the court performs in person searches. Search fee: None. Court makes copy: $1.00 per page. Required to search: name, years to search, DOB; also helpful: case number. Criminal records on computer since 1992, prior on microfilm back to 1969. Will name search free, but cert fee applied to copy. Mail turnaround time 1-2 weeks.
General Information: No public access terminal. No suppressed records released. Will fax documents to local or toll free line. Certification fee: $10.00 per doc includes copies. Payee: 18th District Court. Personal checks accepted. Prepayment and SASE required.

19th District Court 16077 Michigan Ave, Dearborn, MI 48126; phone: 313-943-2060; fax: 313-943-3071; hours 8AM-4:30PM (EST). *Misdemeanor, Civil Actions Under $25,000, Eviction, Small Claims.*
www.cityofdearborn.org
Civil Records: Access: Fax, mail, in person. Only the court performs in person searches. No search fee. Court makes copy: $1.00 per page. Required to search: name, years to search. Civil cases indexed by defendant, plaintiff; on computer since 1986.
Criminal Records: Access: Fax, mail, in person. Only the court performs in person searches. No search fee. Court makes copy: $1.00 per page. Required to search: name, years to search, DOB, offense, date of offense. Criminal records on computer since 1987, prior on docket books.
General Information: No public access terminal. No suppressed records released. Certification fee: $10.00. Payee: 19th District Court. Only cashiers checks and money orders accepted. Visa, MC accepted. Prepayment required. SASE helpful.

20th District Court 25637 Michigan Ave, Dearborn Heights, MI 48125; phone: 313-277-7480; fax: 313-277-7141; hours 9AM-5PM (EST). *Misdemeanor, Civil Actions Under $25,000, Eviction, Small Claims.*
Civil Records: Access: Mail, in person. Only the court performs in person searches. No search fee. Court makes copy: $1.00 per page; same fee for self serve. Required to search: name, years to search; also helpful: address. Civil cases indexed by defendant, plaintiff; on computer since 4/1991, prior records on microfiche or books. Mail turnaround time 1 week-10 days.
Criminal Records: Access: Mail, in person. Only the court performs in person searches. No search fee. Court makes copy: $1.00 per page; same fee for self serve. Required to search: name, years to search, DOB; also helpful: SSN. Criminal records on computer since 4/1991, prior records on microfiche or books. Mail turnaround time 1 week-10 days.
General Information: No public access terminal. No suppressed, juvenile, sex offenders, mental health, or adoption records released. Certification fee: $10.00. Payee: 20th District Court. Business checks or Visa, MC accepted. Prepayment and SASE required.

21st District Court 6000 Middlebelt Rd, Garden City, MI 48135; phone: 734-793-1680; criminal phone: x1; civil phone: x2; criminal/civil fax: 734-793-1681; hours 8:30AM-4:30PM (EST). *Misdemeanor, Civil Actions Under $25,000, Eviction, Small Claims.*
Civil Records: Access: Mail, in person. Only the court performs in person searches. No search fee. Court makes copy: $1.00 per page. Required to search: name, years to search. Civil cases indexed by defendant, plaintiff; on computer back to 1989, prior on books, microfilm, and cards. In person searchers must fill out a "File/copy Request Form." Note: Visitors can search the printed case index to locate a case number. Mail turnaround time 1-2 days.
Criminal Records: Access: Mail, in person. Only the court performs in person searches. No search fee. Court makes copy: $1.00 per page. Required to search: name, years to search, DOB. Criminal records on computer back to 1989, prior on books, microfilm, and cards. In person searchers must fill out a "File/copy Request Form." Note: Visitors can first search the printed case index to locate a criminal case number. Mail turnaround time 1-2 days.
General Information: No public access terminal. No suppressed records released. Will not fax documents. Certification fee: $10.00 per cert includes copies. Payee: 21st District Court. Personal checks accepted. Prepayment and SASE required.

22nd District Court 27331 S River Park Dr, Inkster, MI 48141; phone: 313-277-8200; fax: 313-277-8221; hours 8:30AM-4:30PM (EST). *Misdemeanor, Civil Actions Under $25,000, Eviction, Small Claims.*

Civil Records: Access: Mail, in person. Only the court performs in person searches. No search fee. Court makes copy: $1.00 per page. Required to search: name, years to search. Civil cases indexed by defendant, plaintiff; on computer since 1985, prior on docket books. Mail turnaround time 2 weeks.

Criminal Records: Access: Mail, in person. Only the court performs in person searches. No search fee. Court makes copy: $1.00 per page. Required to search: name, years to search, DOB; also helpful: SSN. Criminal records on computer since 1985, prior on books. Mail turnaround time 2 weeks.

General Information: No public access terminal. No suppressed records released. Certification fee: $10.00 per doc. Payee: 22nd District Court. Personal checks accepted. Prepayment and SASE required.

23rd District Court

23511 Goddard Rd, Taylor, MI 48180; criminal phone: 734-374-1334; civil phone: 734-374-1328; fax: 734-374-1303; hours 8:15AM-4:45PM (EST). *Misdemeanor, Civil Actions Under $25,000, Eviction, Small Claims.*

Civil Records: Access: Mail, in person. Only the court performs in person searches. No search fee. Court makes copy: $1.00 per page. Required to search: name, years to search. Civil cases indexed by defendant, plaintiff; on computer since 1993, prior on books. Mail turnaround time 1-2 days.

Criminal Records: Access: Mail, in person. Only the court performs in person searches. No search fee. Court makes copy: $1.00 per page. Required to search: name, years to search, DOB; also helpful: SSN. Criminal records on computer since 1993, prior on index cards. Mail turnaround time 1-2 days.

General Information: No public access terminal. No suppressed, sexual abuse or drug abuse records released. Will fax or documents for $1.00 per page if call long distance. Certification fee: $10.00. Payee: 23rd District Court. Personal checks accepted. Prepayment required.

24th District Court - Allen Park & Melvindale

6515 Roosevelt, Allen Park, MI 48101-2524; phone: 313-928-0535; criminal phone: x225 or x226; civil phone: 313-928-1899; criminal/civil fax: 313-928-1860; hours 8:30AM-4:30PM (EST). *Misdemeanor, Civil Actions Under $25,000, Eviction, Small Claims.*
www.24thdiscourt.org

Civil Records: Access: Phone, mail, fax, in person. Only the court performs in person searches. No search fee. Court makes copy: $.50 per page. Self serve copy fee: $.50 per page. Required to search: name, years to search, case number. Civil cases indexed by defendant, plaintiff; on computer since 1992, prior records stored as hard-copies. Mail turnaround time 1 week.

Criminal Records: Access: Fax, mail, in person. Only the court performs in person searches. No search fee. Court makes copy: $.50 per page. Self serve copy fee: $.50 per page. Required to search: name, years to search, DOB; also helpful: SSN. Criminal records on computer since 1993, prior records stored as hard-copies. Mail turnaround time 1 week.

General Information: No public access terminal. No non-public records, including driving and probation records, released. Will fax documents to local or toll free line. Certification fee: $10.00. Payee: 24th District Court. Personal checks accepted. Prepayment and SASE required if return mail requested.

25th District Court

1475 Cleophus, Lincoln Park, MI 48146; phone: 313-382-8603; criminal phone: 313-382-8600; civil phone: 313-382-9317; fax: 313-382-9361; hours 9AM-4:30PM (EST). *Misdemeanor, Civil Actions Under $25,000, Eviction, Small Claims.*

Civil Records: Access: Mail, phone, in person. Only the court performs in person searches. No search fee. Court makes copy: $1.00 per page. Required to search: name, years to search. Civil cases indexed by defendant, plaintiff; on computer since 1988, prior

records stored as hard-copies. Mail turnaround time 1 week.

Criminal Records: Access: Mail, phone, in person. Only the court performs in person searches. No search fee. Court makes copy: $1.00 per page. Required to search: name, years to search, DOB. Criminal records on computer since 1987, prior on docket books and cards. Mail turnaround time 1 week.

General Information: No public access terminal. No suppressed or expunged records released. Certification fee: $11.00. Payee: 25th District Court. Personal checks or Visa, MC accepted. Prepayment and SASE required.

26-1 District Court

10600 W Jefferson, River Rouge, MI 48218; phone: 313-842-7819; fax: 313-842-5923; hours 8:30AM-4:30PM (EST). *Misdemeanor, Civil Actions Under $25,000, Eviction, Small Claims.*

Civil Records: Access: Fax, mail, in person. Only the court performs in person searches. No search fee. Court makes copy: $1.00 per page; same fee for self serve. Required to search: name, years to search. Civil cases indexed by defendant, plaintiff; on computer since 11/93; prior records on cards. Mail turnaround time 1 week.

Criminal Records: Access: Fax, mail, in person. Only the court performs in person searches. No search fee. Court makes copy: $1.00 per page; same fee for self serve. Required to search: name, years to search, DOB. Criminal records on computer since 1993, prior on index cards. Mail turnaround time 1 week.

General Information: No public access terminal. No suppressed records released. Will fax documents for $2.00. Certification fee: $10.00 per doc. Payee: 26-1 District Court. No personal checks accepted. Prepayment and SASE required.

26-2 District Court

3869 W Jefferson, Ecorse, MI 48229; phone: 313-386-7900; fax: 313-928-5956; hours 9AM-4PM (EST). *Misdemeanor, Civil Actions Under $25,000, Eviction, Small Claims.*

Civil Records: Access: Mail, in person. Only the court performs in person searches. Search fee: $25.00. Court makes copy: $1.00 per page. Required to search: name, years to search. Civil cases indexed by defendant, plaintiff; on computer back to 1992, prior on index cards. Mail turnaround time 1 week.

Criminal Records: Access: Mail, in person. Only the court performs in person searches. Search fee: $25.00. Court makes copy: $1.00 per page. Required to search: name, years to search, DOB; also helpful: SSN. Criminal records on computer back to 1992, prior on index cards. Mail turnaround time 1 week.

General Information: No public access terminal. No suppressed records released. Will fax documents for a fee of $.25 per name. Certification fee: $10.00 per doc. Payee: 26-2 District Court. Business checks accepted. Prepayment required.

27th District Court

2015 Biddle Ave, Wyandotte, MI 48192; phone: 734-324-4475; criminal phone: 734-324-4477; civil phone: 734-324-4491; criminal/civil fax: 734-324-4472; hours 8:30AM-4:30PM (EST). *Misdemeanor, Civil Actions Under $25,000, Eviction, Small Claims.*

Note: The 27-2 District Court in Riverview was closed as of 12/31/03. All of their records are now at this court.

Civil Records: Access: Mail, in person. Only the court performs in person searches. Search fee: $1.00. Court makes copy: $1.00 per page. Required to search: name, years to search. Civil cases indexed by defendant, plaintiff; on computer since 1988, prior on index cards. Mail turnaround time varies.

Criminal Records: Access: Mail, in person. Only the court performs in person searches. Search fee: $1.00. Court makes copy: $1.00 per page. Required to search: name, years to search, DOB. Criminal records on computer since 1988, prior on index cards. Mail turnaround time varies.

General Information: No public access terminal. No suppressed records released. Will fax documents

to local or toll free line. Certification fee: $10.00 for add'l pages. Payee: 27th District Court. Money order or in person cash accepted. Prepayment and SASE required.

28th District Court

14720 Reaume Parkway, Southgate, MI 48195; phone: 734-258-3068; criminal phone: 734-258-3068; civil phone: 734-258-3068; fax: 734-246-1405; hours 8:30AM-4:30PM (EST). *Misdemeanor, Civil Actions Under $25,000, Eviction, Small Claims.*
www.28thdistrictcourt.com

Civil Records: Access: In person only. Both court and visitors may perform in person searches. No search fee. Court makes copy: $1.00 per page. Required to search: name, years to search; also helpful: address. Civil cases indexed by defendant, plaintiff; on computer back to 1987, prior on card files by party back to 1979.

Criminal Records: Access: In person only. Only the court performs in person searches. No search fee. Court makes copy: $1.00 per page. Required to search: name, years to search, DOB; also helpful: address, SSN, case number. Criminal records go back to 1979; on computer back to 1986.

General Information: No public access terminal. No suppressed, probation, sex offenders, or mental health records released. Will not fax specific case file. Certification fee: $10.00 per document includes copies. Payee: 28th District Court. Cash, cashiers check, money order, Visa, MC or Discover accepted in person only. Prepayment required.

29th District Court

34808 Sims Ave, Wayne, MI 48184; phone: 734-722-5220; fax: 734-722-7003; hours 8AM-4:30PM (EST). *Misdemeanor, Civil Actions Under $25,000, Eviction, Small Claims.*

Civil Records: Access: Phone, mail, in person. Only the court performs in person searches. No search fee. Court makes copy: $.50 per page. Required to search: name, years to search. Civil cases indexed by defendant, plaintiff; on computer since 1990. Will name search free, but a copy fee applies. Mail turnaround time 1 week.

Criminal Records: Access: Phone, mail, in person. Only the court performs in person searches. No search fee. Court makes copy: $.50 per page. Required to search: name, years to search, DOB; also helpful: address, SSN. Criminal records on computer since 1990. Will name search free, but a copy fee applies. Mail turnaround time 1 week, phone turnaround time 1 day.

General Information: No public access terminal. No suppressed, juvenile, sex offenders, mental health, or adoption records released. Will fax documents to local or toll free line. Certification fee: $10.00. Payee: 29th District Court. Personal checks or Visa/MC accepted. Prepayment and SASE required.

30th District Court

12050 Wood Ward Ave, Highland Park, MI 48203; phone: 313-252-0300; fax: 313-865-1115; hours 8AM-4:30PM (EST). *Misdemeanor, Civil Actions Under $25,000, Eviction, Small Claims.*

Civil Records: Access: Mail, in person. Both court and visitors may perform in person searches. Search fee: $5.00 per name. Court makes copy: $1.00 per page. Required to search: name, years to search. Civil cases indexed by defendant, plaintiff; on computer since 1989, prior on index cards or docket books. Mail turnaround time 1-2 weeks.

Criminal Records: Access: Mail, in person. Both court and visitors may perform in person searches. Search fee: $5.00 per name. Court makes copy: $1.00 per page. Required to search: name, years to search, DOB. Criminal records on computer since 1989, prior on index cards or docket books. Mail turnaround time 1-2 weeks.

General Information: No public access terminal. No suppressed records released. Will fax documents. Certification fee: $5.00. Payee: 30th District Court. Prepayment and SASE required.

31st District Court 3401 Evaline Ave, Hamtramck, MI 48212; phone: 313-876-7710; fax: 313-876-7724; hours 8AM-4PM (EST). *Misdemeanor, Civil Actions Under $25,000, Eviction, Small Claims.*

Civil Records: Access: Mail, in person. Only the court performs in person searches. No search fee. Court makes copy: $1.00 per page; same fee for self serve. Required to search: name, years to search. Civil cases indexed by defendant, plaintiff; on computer since 1989, prior on index cards. Mail turnaround time 1-2 days.

Criminal Records: Access: Mail, in person. Only the court performs in person searches. No search fee. Court makes copy: $1.00 per page; same fee for self serve. Required to search: name, years to search, DOB. Criminal records on computer since 1989, prior on index cards. Mail turnaround time 1-2 days.

General Information: No public access terminal. No suppressed records released. Will fax documents for $1.00 per page. Certification fee: $10.00 after first page. Payee: 31st District Court. Personal checks accepted. Prepayment and SASE required.

32 A District Court 19617 Harper Ave, Harper Woods, MI 48225; phone: 313-343-2590; civil phone: 313-343-2592; fax: 313-343-2594; hours 8:30AM-4:30PM (EST). *Misdemeanor, Civil Actions Under $25,000, Small Claims.*

Civil Records: Access: Phone, fax, mail, in person. Only the court performs in person searches. No search fee. Court makes copy: $.50 per page. Required to search: name, years to search. Civil cases indexed by defendant, plaintiff. Civil records indexed by name and case number on computer, microfiche, and paper. Mail turnaround time same day.

Criminal Records: Access: Phone, fax, mail, in person. Only the court performs in person searches. No search fee. Court makes copy: $.50 per page. Required to search: name, years to search. Criminal records indexed by name and case number on computer, microfiche, and paper. Mail turnaround time same day.

General Information: No public access terminal. No suppressed records released. Will fax documents, no fee. Certification fee: $10.00 per page. Payee: 32A District Court. Personal checks or Visa, MC accepted. Prepayment required. SASE requested.

33rd District Court 19000 Van Horn Rd, Woodhaven, MI 48183; phone: 734-671-0201; criminal phone: 734-671-0201; civil phone: 734-671-0225; fax: 734-671-0307; hours 8:30AM-4:30PM (EST). *Misdemeanor, Civil Actions Under $25,000, Eviction, Small Claims.*

Civil Records: Access: In person only. Both court and visitors may perform in person searches. No search fee. Court makes copy: $.25 per page. Required to search: name, years to search; also helpful: address. Civil cases indexed by defendant, plaintiff; on computer since 1995, prior on microfilm and microfiche.

Criminal Records: Access: In person only. Both court and visitors may perform in person searches. No search fee. Court makes copy: $.25 per page. Required to search: name, years to search, DOB; also helpful: address. Criminal records on computer since 1995, prior on microfilm and microfiche.

General Information: Public terminal goes back to 1999. No suppressed records released. Certification

fee: $10.00 plus $1.00 per page after first. Payee: 33rd District Court. Business checks or Visa, MC accepted. Prepayment required.

34th District Court 11131 S Wayne Rd, Romulus, MI 48174; phone: 734-941-4462; fax: 734-941-7530; hours 8:30AM-4PM (EST). *Misdemeanor, Civil Actions Under $25,000, Eviction, Small Claims.*

Civil Records: Access: Fax, mail, in person. Only the court performs in person searches. No search fee. Court makes copy: $1.00 per page. Required to search: name, years to search. Civil cases indexed by defendant, plaintiff; on computer since 1984, prior on index cards and docket books. Mail turnaround time 1 week.

Criminal Records: Access: Fax, mail, in person. Only the court performs in person searches. No search fee. Court makes copy: $1.00 per page. Required to search: name, years to search, DOB; also helpful: SSN. Criminal records on computer since 1984, prior on index cards and docket books. Mail turnaround time 1 week.

General Information: No public access terminal. No suppressed records released. Certification fee: $10.00 per page includes copy fee. Payee: 34th District Court. Personal checks accepted. Prepayment and SASE required.

35th District Court 660 Plymouth Rd, Plymouth, MI 48170; phone: 734-459-4740; fax: 734-454-9303; hours 8:30AM-4:25PM (EST). *Misdemeanor, Civil Infractions, Civil Actions Under $25,000, Eviction, Small Claims.* www.35thdistrictcourt.org

Civil Records: Access: Fax, mail, in person. Both court and visitors may perform in person searches. No search fee. Court makes copy: $1.00 per page. Required to search: name, years to search. Civil cases indexed by defendant, plaintiff; on computer since 1990. Mail turnaround time 1 week.

Criminal Records: Access: Fax, mail, in person. Both court and visitors may perform in person searches. No search fee. Court makes copy: $1.00 per page. Required to search: name, years to search, DOB; also helpful: SSN, sex, signed release. Criminal records on computer since 1990. Mail turnaround time 1 week.

General Information: Public terminal goes back to 1998. No suppressed, juvenile, sex offenders, mental health, or adoption records released. Fee to fax documents is $1.00 per document. Certification fee: $10.00 per cert includes copies. Payee: 35th District Court. Third party checks not accepted. Debit cards accepted. Prepayment required.

3rd Circuit Court 201 Coleman A Young Municipal Ctr, Detroit, MI 48226; phone: 313-224-5530; hours 8AM-4:30PM (EST). *Civil Actions Over $25,000.* www.3rdcc.org

Civil Records: Access: Mail, in person. Both court and visitors may perform in person searches. Search fee: $1.00 per name. Court makes copy: $2.25 per page. Required to search: name, years to search. Civil cases indexed by defendant, plaintiff; on computer since 1984, prior on index cards. Mail turnaround time 1 week.

General Information: Public terminal has only civil records back to 1985. No suppressed records released. Certification fee: $10.00 plus $1.00 per page.

Payee: 3rd Circuit Court. Business checks accepted. Prepayment required.

Probate Court 1307 Coleman A Young Muni. Ctr, 13th Fl, 2 Woodland Ave, Detroit, MI 48226; phone: 313-224-5706; hours 8AM-4:30PM (EST). *Probate.* www.probatewayneco.org

Note: Search probate records at http://public.wcpc.us/pa/pa.urd/pamw6500.display. Summary, party, event, docket, disposition, costs available. Records go back into 1980s.

Wexford County

28th Circuit Court PO Box 490, Cadillac, MI 49601; phone: 231-779-9450; fax: 231-779-0447; hours 8:30AM-5PM (EST). *Felony, Civil Actions Over $25,000.*

Civil Records: Access: Mail, in person. Only the court performs in person searches. Search fee: $1.00 per name. Court makes copy: $1.00 per page. Required to search: name, years to search. Civil cases indexed by defendant, plaintiff. Civil records go back to 1868, civil records on computer since 1977. Mail turnaround time same day if possible.

Criminal Records: Access: Mail, in person. Only the court performs in person searches. Search fee: $1.00 per name. Court makes copy: $1.00 per page. Required to search: name, years to search. Criminal records go back to 1868, criminal records on computer since 1977. Mail turnaround time same day.

General Information: No public access terminal. No suppressed, YTA files, juvenile, sex offenders, mental health, or adoption records released. Certification fee: $10.00, plus $1.00 each add'l page. Payee: Wexford County Clerk. Only cashiers checks and money orders accepted. Prepayment and SASE required.

84th District Court 437 E Division St, Cadillac, MI 49601; phone: 231-779-9515; fax: 231-779-5396; hours 8:30AM-5PM (EST). *Misdemeanor, Civil Actions Under $25,000, Eviction, Small Claims.*

Civil Records: Access: Phone, fax, mail, in person. Both court and visitors may perform in person searches. Search fee: $1.00 per page found. Court makes copy: $1.00 per page. Required to search: name, years to search. Civil cases indexed by defendant, plaintiff; on computer since 1984; on index from 1969 to 1984. Mail turnaround time 1 week.

Criminal Records: Access: Mail, fax, in person. Both court and visitors may perform in person searches. Search fee: $1.00 per name found. Court makes copy: $1.00 per page. Required to search: name, years to search, DOB; also helpful: SSN. Criminal records on computer since 1984; prior records on blue cards. Mail turnaround time 1 week.

General Information: No public access terminal. No suppressed, juvenile, sex offenders, mental health, or adoption records released. Certification fee: $10.00 per doc. Payee: 84th District Court. Personal checks accepted. Prepayment and SASE required.

Probate Court 437 E Division, Cadillac, MI 49601; phone: 231-779-9510; probate phone: 231-779-9511; fax: 231-779-9485; hours 8:30AM-5PM (EST). *Probate.*

Michigan Recording Offices

ORGANIZATION: 83 counties, 83 recording offices. The recording officer is County Register of Deeds. 79 counties are in the Eastern Time Zone (EST) and 4 counties that border on Wisconsin (Gogebic, Iron, Dickinson, and Menominee) are in the Central Time Zone (CST).

REAL ESTATE RECORDS: Some counties will perform real estate searches. Copies usually cost $1.00 per page. and certification fees vary. Ownership records are located at the Equalization Office, designated "Assessor" in this section. Tax records are located at the Treasurer's Office.

UCC RECORDS: Financing statements are filed at the state level, except for real estate related collateral, which are filed with the County Register. However, prior to 07/2001, consumer goods and farm collateral were also filed at the County Register and these older records can be searched there. All counties will perform UCC searches. Use search request form UCC-11. Search fees are usually $3.00 to $6.00 per debtor name if federal tax identification number or Social Security Number are given, or $6.00 to $12.00 without a number. Copies usually cost $1.00 per page.

TAX LIEN RECORDS: Federal and state tax liens on personal property of businesses are filed with the Secretary of State. Other federal and state tax liens are filed with the Register of Deeds. Most counties search each tax lien index separately. Some charge one fee to search both, while others charge a separate fee for each one. When combining a UCC and tax lien search, total fee is usually $9.00 for all three searches. Some counties require tax identification number as well as name to do a search. Copy fees are usually $1.00 per page.

OTHER LIENS: Construction, lis pendens.

ONLINE ACCESS: There is no statewide online access, but a number of counties, including Wayne, offer free access to assessor and register of deeds records.

Alcona County

County Register of Deeds, PO Box 269, Harrisville, MI 48740-0269. 989-724-9450, R/E recording phone-989-724-6802; fax-989-724-5684; hours: 8:30AM-4:30PM.
Records indexed on a public use terminal back to 1985. Office personnel or visitors may perform searches. Search fee $10.00 per name. Copy fee $1.00 per page. Cert fee- $2.00 per cert plus copy fee. Payee- Alcona County Register of Deeds. **Other phones:** Treasurer- 989-724-5140; Elections- 989-724-6807; Vital Records- 989-724-6807. **Property tax/Assessor-** 989-724-6223.

Alger County

County Register of Deeds, PO Box 538, Munising, MI 49862. 906-387-2076; fax-906-387-2156; hours: 8AM-4PM.
Separate indices to search include deeds, mortgages. Records indexed on computer back to 1/2005. Search fee $6.00 per name. Will not search real estate records. Copy fee $1.00 per page. Cert fee- $1.00 per cert plus copy fee. Payee- Alger County Register of Deeds. **Other phones:** Treasurer- 906-387-4535; Elections- 906-387-2076; Vital Records- 906-387-2076. **Property tax/Assessor-** 101 Court St, Munising, MI 49862; 906-387-2567.

Allegan County

County Register of Deeds, 113 Chestnut St; County Court House, Allegan, MI 49010-1360. 269-673-0390; fax-269-673-0289; hours: 8AM-5PM. www.allegancounty.org/
Records indexed on computer from 1978 to present, from 1978-1958 on index cards, from 1958-1935 in books. Office personnel or visitors may perform searches. General index search fee $6.00 per search. Copy fee $2.00, if tax lien or real estate $1.00 per page. Cert fee- $1.00 per page plus copy fee. Payee- Allegan County Register of Deeds. **Online access to Real Estate records:** Search by name or address at www.allegancounty.org/prdwebeq/. **Other phones:** Treasurer- 269-673-0260; Elections- 269-673-0450; Vital Records- 269-673-0450. **Property tax/Assessor-** 269-673-0230.

Alpena County

County Register of Deeds, 720 W. Chisholm St; Courthouse, Alpena, MI 49707-2487. 989-354-9547, R/E recording phone-989-356-3887; fax-989-354-9646; hours: 8:30AM-4:30PM.
Separate indices to search. Records indexed on a public use terminal back to 1993. Only the office personnel may search. Search fee $12.00 per name. Copy fee $1.00 per page. Cert fee- $1.00 per cert plus copy fee. Payee- Alpena County Register of Deeds. **Other phones:** Treasurer- 989-356-1751. **Property tax/Assessor-** 989-356-2015.

Antrim County

County Register of Deeds, PO Box 376, Bellaire, MI 49615. 231-533-6683; fax-231-533-8317; hours: 8:30AM-5PM. www.antrimcounty.org
Separate indices to search. Records indexed on a public use terminal back to 1993. Only the office personnel may search. General index search fee $5.00 minimum + $.50 per year. Copy fee $2.00, if tax lien or real estate $1.00 per page. Cert fee- $1.00 per cert plus copy fee. Payee- Antrim County Register of Deeds. **Online access to Most Wanted records:** Access to the sheriff's most wanted list is free at www.torchlake.com/acsd/. **Other phones:** Treasurer- 231-533-6720. **Property tax/Assessor-** 231-533-6320.

Arenac County

County Register of Deeds, PO Box 296, Standish, MI 48658. 989-846-9201, R/E recording phone-517-846-9201; hours: 8:30AM-5PM.
Records indexed on a public use terminal back to 1992. Only the public may search. Copy fee $1.00 per page. Cert fee- $1.00 per cert plus copy fee. Payee- Arenac County Register of Deeds. **Other phones:** Treasurer- 517-846-4106; Elections- 517-846-4626; Vital Records- 517-846-4626. **Property tax/Assessor-** 517-846-6246.

Baraga County

County Register of Deeds, 16 N. 3rd St.; Courthouse, L'Anse, MI 49946-1085. 906-524-6183; fax-906-524-6186; 8:30AM-4:30PM. www.baragacounty.org
All records in one index as of 2005, Prior to that is indexed by Mtg, deeds, Misc, and Survey's. Records indexed on a public use terminal back to 2000. Office will perform a UCC search but public must search other records themselves. Search fee $5.00. Copy fee $2.00 per page. Cert fee- $7.00 per cert plus copy fee. Payee- Baraga County Register of Deeds. **Other phones:** Treasurer- 906-524-7773; Elections- 906-524-6183; Vital Records- 906-524-6183. **Property tax/Assessor-** 906-524-7331.

Barry County

County Register of Deeds, PO Box 7, Hastings, MI 49058-0007. 269-948-4824, R/E recording phone-269-945-1289; fax-269-948-1298; hours: 8AM-5PM. www.barrycounty.org
Separate indices to search. Records indexed on a public use terminal back to 1997. Only the office personnel may search. Search fee $6.00 per name. Will not search real estate records. Copy fee $1.00 per page. Cert fee- $1.00 per cert plus copy fee. Payee- Barry County Register of Deeds. **Online access to Property, Assessor, Delinquent Tax records:** Access to county parcel data is free at www.barrycounty.org/ParcelData.htm. County property Index is from 12/95 to 1/04. **Other phones:** Treasurer- 269-945-1287; Elections- 269-945-1285; Vital Records- 269-945-1285. **Assessor-** 269-945-1288.

Bay County

County Register of Deeds, 515 Center Ave #2, Bay City, MI 48708-5994. 989-895-4228; fax-989-895-4296; hours: 8AM-5PM (June-Sept. 7:30AM-4PM). www.co.bay.mi.us
Index: Index complete on computer back to 1985; index on card file 1984-1958; before 1958 on old books. Records indexed on a public use terminal back to 1985. Office will perform a UCC search but public must search other records themselves. UCC search or combined tax lien search per debtor name- $6.00. Separate federal tax lien search, or separate state lien search- $3.00 per debtor. General copy fee $2.00 per page; $1.00 if tax lien or real estate. Cert fee- $3.00 per cert plus copy fee. Payee- Bay County Register of Deeds. **Online access to Property Tax records:** Access county property tax data for free at www.co.bay.mi.us/bay/ptq.nsf. **Other phones:** Treasurer- 989-895-4285; Vital Records- 989-895-4280. **Property tax/Assessor-** same address as above. 989-895-4075.

Benzie County

County Register of Deeds, PO Box 377, Beulah, MI 49617. 231-882-0016; fax-231-882-0167; hours: 8AM-N, 1-5PM.

Separate indices prior to 2004 to search include grantor/grantee, mortgage, discharge mortgage, tax liens. General index search fee $5.00 minimum. Will not search real estate records unless document specified. Tax liens not included in UCC search. UCC search per debtor name-$6.00. Copy fee $1.00 per page; $2.00 per page for UCC. Cert fee- $1.00 per seal plus copy fee. Payee- Benzie County Register of Deeds. **Online access to Recording, Real Estate, Deed, Lien records:** Recorder office data by subscription on either the Laredo system using subscription and fees or the Tapestry System using credit card, https://tapestry.fidlar.com/tapsearch.aspx; $3.99 search; $.50 per image. **Other phones:** Treasurer- 231-882-0011; Elections- 231-882-0001; Vital Records- 231-882-0001. **Property tax/Assessor-** 231-882-0015.

Berrien County

County Register of Deeds, 701 Main St.; Berrien County Admin. Ctr, St. Joseph, MI 49085. 616-983-7111 x8562, R/E recording phone-269-983-7111 x8562; fax-616-982-8659; hours: 8:30AM-5PM. www.berriencounty.org/

Records indexed on a public use terminal back to 1982. Office personnel or visitors may perform searches. Search fee $.50 per name per year, $5.00 minimum. UCC search per debtor name-$6.00 per name.32. UCC copy fee $2.00 per page. R/E record copy- $1.00 per page. Cert fee- $1.00 per doc, plus copy fee. Payee- Berrien County Register of Deeds. **Other phones:** Treasurer- 269-983-7111 x8208; Vital Records- 269-983-7111 x8233. **Property tax/Assessor-** 269-983-7111 x8215.

Branch County

County Register of Deeds, 570 Marshall Rd, #C, Coldwater, MI 49036. 517-279-4320; 8AM-5PM.

Index: 2001-present records on computer; grantor/grantee index and cards back to 1974; before 1974 in books. Records indexed on a public use terminal back to 2001. Only the public may search. Search fee $6.00 unless otherwise indicated. Copy fee $2.00 for UCC; if tax lien or real estate $1.00 per page. Cert fee- $1.00 per cert plus copy fee. Payee- Branch County Register of Deeds. **Online access to Vital Statistic, Business Name, DBA records:** Search the county vital records free at www.co.branch.mi.us/vital/vital.html#dba. Search business names and DBAs at www.co.branch.mi.us/dbasearch.taf. **Other phones:** Treasurer- 517-279-4321. **Property tax/Assessor-** 517-279-4312.

Calhoun County

County Register of Deeds, 315 W. Green St, Marshall, MI 49068. 269-781-0718; fax-269-781-0721; hours: 8AM-5PM. http://co.calhoun.mi.us

Separate indices to search include books, card files. Records indexed on computer back to 1982. Office will perform a UCC and Tax lien search but public must search other records themselves. Search fee $3.00. Copy fee $1.00 per page. Cert fee- $1.00 per page. Payee- Calhoun County Register of Deeds. **Other phones:** Treasurer- 269-969-6910/616-781-0807; Elections- 269-781-0988; Vital Records- 269-781-0718. **Property tax/Assessor-** 269-781-0745.

Cass County

Register of Deeds, PO Box 355, Cassopolis, MI 49031-0355. 269-445-4464; fax-269-445-4406; hours: 8AM-5PM. www.casscountymi.org

All records in one index. Office personnel or visitors may perform searches. Search fee $6.00 per name. Copy fee $2.00, if tax lien or real estate $1.00 per page. Cert fee- $1.00 per cert plus copy fee. Payee- Cass County Clerk/Register. **Other** phones: Treasurer- 269-445-4468; Elections- 269-445-4464; Vital Records- 269-445-4464.

Charlevoix County

County Register of Deeds, 301 State St; County Bldg, Charlevoix, MI 49720. 231-547-7204; fax-231-237-0106; hours: 9AM-5PM.

Separate indices to search. Records indexed on a public use terminal back to 1989. Only the office personnel may search. Search fee $3.00 per name. Will not search real estate records. UCC search request with SS/TIN, per name- $6.00. Copy fee $1.00 per page. Cert fee- $1.00 per cert plus copy fee. Payee- Charlevoix County Register of Deeds. **Online access to Birth, Marriage, Obituary, Cemetery, Birth records:** Access to these unofficial records is courtesy of genealogical researcher at www.rootsweb.com/~micharle/charlevx.htm. **Other phones:** Treasurer- 231-547-7202. **Property tax/Assessor-** 231-547-7230.

Cheboygan County

County Register of Deeds, PO Box 70, Cheboygan, MI 49721. 231-627-8866; fax-231-627-8453; hours: 8:30AM-5PM. www.cheboygancounty.net

All records in one index. Records indexed on computer back to 1985. Office personnel or visitors may perform searches. Will not guarantee searches. Search fee $5.00 per name. State tax lien search- $3.00 per debtor. UCC copy fee $2.00 per page. R/E record copy- $1.00 per page plus $1.00 for fax. Cert fee- $1.00 per cert plus copy fee. Payee- Cheboygan County Register of Deeds. **Other phones:** Treasurer- 231-627-8821; Elections- 231-627-8808; Vital Records- 231-627-8808. **Property tax/Assessor-** 231-627-8845.

Chippewa County

County Register of Deeds, 319 Court St; Courthouse, Sault Ste. Marie, MI 49783. 906-635-6312; fax-906-635-6855; hours: 8AM-5PM. www.chippewacountymi.gov

All records in one index. Office personnel (depending on time involved and available manpower) or visitors may perform searches. Search fee $1.00-$10.00 depending on years. Copy fee $1.00 per page. Cert fee- $1.00 per cert plus copy fee. Payee- Chippewa County Register of Deeds. **Other phones:** Treasurer- 906-635-6308; Elections- 906-635-6300; Vital Records- 906-635-6300. **Property tax/Assessor-** same address as above. 906-635-6304.

Clare County

County Register of Deeds, PO Box 586, Harrison, MI 48625. 989-539-7131; fax-989-539-6616; hours: 8AM-4:30PM.

Separate indices to search. Records indexed on a public use terminal back to 1986. Only the office personnel may search. Search fee $50.00 initial fee, $10.00 per entry if real estate. UCC search per debtor name- $6.00. Separate federal/state tax lien search- $3.00 per debtor. Copy fee $2.00, if tax lien or real estate $1.00 per page. Cert fee- $1.00 per cert plus copy fee. Payee- Clare County Register of Deeds. **Other phones:** Treasurer- 989-539-7801; Elections- 989-539-7131; Vital Records- 989-539-7131. **Property tax/Assessor-** 989-539-3867.

Clinton County

County Register of Deeds, PO Box 435, St. Johns, MI 48879-0435. 989-224-5270; fax-989-227-6473; hours: 8AM-5PM. www.clinton-county.org/rod/register_of_deeds.htm

Records indexed on a public use terminal back to 1994. Office personnel or visitors may perform searches. Office personnel will only search for out-of-state requesters, as a general rule. Search fee $.50 per year, $5.00 minimum. Will not search real estate records. Will search UCC records prior to 7/2001 and current fixture (land) files. UCC search per debtor name- $6.00. Separate federal or state tax lien search- $3.00 per debtor. Separate combined federal and state combined tax lien search- $6.00 per debtor. Copy fee $2.00 per UCC page; if tax lien or real estate $1.00 per page. per page. Cert fee- $1.00 per cert plus copy fee. Payee- Clinton County Register of Deeds. **Online access to Property Tax, Assessor, Recording, Deed, Judgment, Lien, Fictitious Business Name records:** Register to search free on the recorders database at www.clinton-county.org/rod/index_search.htm. Username and password is required. Also, search fictitious business names free at www.clinton-county.org/clerk/dba_search.asp. Also, the assessor's property tax data is available online by subscription; visit www.clinton-county.org/treasurer/delq_tax_search.htm. A $20 processing fee is charged, plus $.25 for each parcel retrieved. Also, search for property info free on the gis-mapping site at http://maps.clinton-county.org/ClintonCountyCX/Disclaimer.htm; does not appear to have name searching. **Other phones:** Treasurer- 989-224-5280. **Property tax/Assessor-** 100 E State St, #1200, St Johns, MI 48879; 989-224-5170, assessor fax- 989-224-5127.

Crawford County

County Register of Deeds, 200 W. Michigan, Grayling, MI 49738. 989-348-2841, R/E recording phone-989-344-3203; fax-989-344-3223; hours: 8:30AM-4:30PM. www.crawfordco.org/deeds/deeds.htm

Separate indices to search. Records indexed on a public use terminal back to 1/2004. Only the office personnel may search. Search fee $3.00 per name. Will not search real estate records. UCC search per debtor name- $6.00. Copy fee $2.00, if tax lien or real estate $1.00 per page. Cert fee- $1.00 per doc plus copy fee. Payee- Crawford County Register of Deeds. **Online access to Most Wanted records:** Access to the sheriff's most wanted list is at www.crawfordsheriff.org/Misc/wanted/wanted.htm. **Other phones:** Treasurer- 989-344-3229; Appraiser/Auditor- 989-344-3234; Elections- 989-344-3200; Vital Records- 989-344-3207. **Property tax/Assessor-** 989-344-3235.

Delta County

County Register of Deeds, 310 Ludington St, #104, Escanaba, MI 49829-4039. 906-789-5116; fax-906-789-5196; hours: 8AM-4PM.

All records in one index. Records indexed on a public use terminal back to 2/1990. Office personnel or visitors may perform searches. Search fee $6.00. UCC copy fee $2.00 per page. R/E record copy- $.50 per year, $5.00 minimum. Cert fee- $2.00 per cert plus copy fee. Payee- Register of Deeds. **Other phones:** Treasurer- 906-789-5117; Appraiser/Auditor- 906-789-5109; Elections- 906-789-5105; Vital Records- 906-789-5105. **Property tax/Assessor-** 906-789-5109.

Dickinson County

County Register of Deeds, PO Box 609, Iron Mountain, MI 49801. 906-774-0955; fax-906-774-4660; hours: 8AM-4:30PM.

Records indexed on a public use terminal back to 1994. Office personnel or visitors may perform searches. Search fee $5.00 per name. UCC copy fee $2.00 per page. R/E record copy- $1.00 per page. Cert fee- $1.00 per doc plus copy fee. Payee- Dickinson County Register of Deeds. **Other phones:** Treasurer- 906-774-8130. **Property tax/Assessor-** 906-774-2515.

Eaton County

County Register of Deeds, 1045 Independence Blvd.; Rm 104, Charlotte, MI 48813-1095. 517-543-7500 x232, UCC recording phone-517-543-7500 x231; fax-517-543-7377; hours: 8AM-5PM. www.eatoncounty.org/County_Clerk/CountyClerk.htm

Records indexed on computer, cards and books back to 1836. Only the public may search. General index search fee $.50 per name/per year - $5.00 minimum fee. Copy fee $2.00, if UCC or real estate $1.00 per page. Cert fee- $1.00 per cert plus copy fee. Payee- Eaton County Register of Deeds. **Online access to Assessor, Tax, Recorder, Marriage, Divorce records:** Two levels of service are on the County Online Data Service site at www.eatoncounty.org/County_Services/Online.htm. Here is a free service and a subscription service. Marriages and Divorces back to 5/2004 are also here. The direct link to the tax assessor records is www.eatoncounty.org/tax/PublicParcelselect.aspx Also, search the Delta Charter Township assessments free at https://is.bsasoftware.com/bsa.is/default.aspx. **Other phones:** Treasurer- 517-543-7500 x210; Appraiser/Auditor- 517-543-7500 x219; Elections- 517-543-7500 x225; Vital Records- 517-543-7500 x225; Information Systems- 517-543-7500 x207. **Property tax/Assessor-** same address as above. 517-543-7500 x236.

Emmet County

County Register of Deeds, 200 Division St, Petoskey, MI 49770. 231-348-1761; fax-231-348-1773; hours: 8:30AM-5PM. www.co.emmet.mi.us/deeds/
All records in one index. Records indexed on a public use terminal back to 1/1984. Only the office personnel may search. Search fee $6.00 per name. Will not search real estate records. UCC copy fee $2.00 per page. R/E record copy- $1.00 per page. Cert fee- $1.00 per cert plus copy fee. Payee- Emmet County Register of Deeds. **Online access to Real Estate, Recorder, Deed, Lien, Property Tax, Assessor, Marriage, Death, Fictitious Name records:** Access the recorder land records at www.co.emmet.mi.us:8080/icris/Login.jsp; registration, logon and password required to view full data; full access to all images back to 1994 is $1,000.00 per month. Also, access assessor property records free at www.co.emmet.mi.us/equalization/propsrcheq.htm. Use username "general" and password "general." Also, search marriages, deaths, and assumed names free at www.co.emmet.mi.us/clerk/. **Other phones:** Treasurer- 231-348-1715. **Property tax/Assessor-** 200 Division St, Petoskey, MI 49770; 231-348-1708, assessor fax- 231-348-1768.

Genesee County

County Register of Deeds, 1101 Beach St; Admin. Bldg, Flint, MI 48502. 810-257-3060; fax-810-768-7965; hours: 8AM-5PM. www.co.genesee.mi.us
All records in one index. Records indexed on a public use terminal back to 1990. Only the office personnel may search. Search fee $4.00 per name. Will not search real estate records. UCC search per debtor name- $3.00. Copy fee $2.00, if real estate $1.00 per page. Cert fee- $1.00 per cert plus copy fee. Payee- Genesee County Register of Deeds. **Online access to Recording, Property, Deed, Marriage, Death records:** Access to Register of Deeds database is free at www.co.genesee.mi.us/rod/. But to view documents back to 10/2000, there is a fee, and user ID and password required. Also, online access to the county clerk's marriage (back to 1963) and death (back to 1930) indexes are free at www.co.genesee.mi.us/vitalrec. Search property index at www.co.genesee.mi.us/cgi-bin/gweb.exe?mode=7800&sessionname=gentax&command=connect. **Other phones:** Treasurer- 810-257-3059; Elections- 810-257-3283; Vital Records- 810-257-3225. **Property tax/Assessor-** 810-257-3017.

Gladwin County

County Register of Deeds, 401 W. Cedar Ave, #7, Gladwin, MI 48624-2093. 989-426-7551; fax-989-426-6902; 8:30AM-4:30PM. www.gladwinco.com/
Will fax back results for add'l $1.00 per page, prepaid. Separate indices to search include books, computer. Records indexed on computer being added to. General index search fee $.50 per year per name; $5.00 minimum. Will only search real estate records on computer since 3/14/1991. UCC search includes tax liens if requested. UCC or tax lien search per debtor name- $10.00. Copy fee $1.00 per page. UCC copy $2.00 per page. Cert fee-

$1.00 per cert plus copy fee. Payee- Gladwin County Register of Deeds. **Other phones:** Treasurer- 989-426-7351; Elections- 989-426-7351; Vital Records- 989-426-7351. **Assessor-** 989-426-9327.

Gogebic County

County Register of Deeds, 200 N. Moore St; Courthouse, Bessemer, MI 49911. 906-667-0381; fax-906-663-4660; hours: 8:30AM-4:30PM.
All records in one index. Records indexed on a public use terminal back to 1991. Only the public may search. Copy fee $1.00 per page. Cert fee- $5.00 per cert plus copy fee. Payee- Gogebic County Register of Deeds. **Other phones:** Treasurer- 906-667-4517; Elections- 906-667-4518; Vital Records- 906-667-4518. **Property tax/Assessor-** 906-663-4414, assessor fax- 906-663-4105.

Grand Traverse County

County Register of Deeds, 400 Boardman Ave, Traverse City, MI 49684-2577. 231-922-4753, R/E recording phone-231-922-4750; fax-231-922-2770; hours: 8AM-5PM (Vault closes at 4:30PM). www.co.grand-traverse.mi.us
Separate indices to search. Records indexed on a public use terminal back to 1986. Only the office personnel may search. Search fee $6.00 per name. Will not search real estate records. UCC search per debtor name- $15.00. Copy fee $1.00 per page. Cert fee- $1.00 per cert plus copy fee. Payee- Grand Traverse County Register of Deeds. **Online access to Recording, Deed, Real Estate, Tax Lien, Judgment, Assumed Name, Construction Permit, Marriage, Death records:** Except for document images, all searches are free at www.co.grand-traverse.mi.us; click on "Online Records." Recorder's document index search is free but images require fee; pay by credit card. Recording records go back to 1986. Deaths go back to 1867; marriages to 1853; permits and assumed names are all current; District civil court judgments go back to 1966; images from mid-1980s. Criminal records also available. Also, access to death and marriage indices are free at www.tcnet.org/gtcounty/index.html. **Other phones:** Treasurer- 231-922-4735. **Property tax/Assessor-** 231-922-4772.

Gratiot County

County Register of Deeds, PO Box 5, Ithaca, MI 48847. 989-875-5217; hours: 8AM-N, 1PM-4:30PM.
All records in one index. Office will perform a UCC search but public must search other records themselves. UCC search per debtor name- $6.00. $25.00 add'l for fee for expedited service. Copy fee $1.00 per page. Cert fee- $1.00 per cert plus copy fee. Payee- Gratiot County Register of Deeds. **Other phones:** Treasurer- 989-875-5220. **Property tax/Assessor-** 989-875-5203.

Hillsdale County

County Register of Deeds, 29 N Howell, Rm 3; Courthouse, Hillsdale, MI 49242. 517-437-2231; fax-517-437-3139; hours: 8:30AM-5PM.
All records in one index. Only the public may search, but office personnel can assist. UCC copy fee $2.00 per page. R/E record copy- $1.00 per page. Cert fee- $1.00 per cert plus copy fee. Payee- Hillsdale County Register of Deeds. **Online access to Recording, Deed, Judgment, Lien, UCC, Tax Sale, Property Tax records:** The recorder's index and images are available online by subscription. Records go back to 9/1984 and more are being added. Fee is $300.00 for recorder, or $50.00 for just the assessor's equalization records. Copy fees are included. Call the recorder office for signup and add'l info. Also, the treasurer's tax sale lists are online at www.co.hillsdale.mi.us/hc-treasurer.htm. **Other phones:** Treasurer- 517-437-4700; Elections- 517-437-3391; Vital Records- 517-437-3391. **Property tax/Assessor-** 29 N Howell, Rm 12, Hillsdale, MI 49242; 517-439-9166.

Houghton County

County Register of Deeds, 401 E. Houghton Ave, Houghton, MI 49931. 906-482-1311; fax-906-483-0364; hours: 8AM-4:30PM.
Separate indices to search. Records indexed on a public use terminal back to 1997. Only the office personnel may search. Search fee $3.00 per name. Will not search real estate records. UCC search per debtor name- $6.00. Copy fee $2.00, if real estate $1.00 per page. Cert fee- $8.00 per doc plus copy fees. Payee- Houghton County Register of Deeds. **Other phones:** Treasurer- 906-482-0560. **Property tax/Assessor-** 906-482-0250.

Huron County

County Register of Deeds, 250 E Huron Ave, Bad Axe, MI 48413. 989-269-9941; fax-989-269-8786; hours: 8:30AM-5PM.
Records indexed on computer back to 1984. Search fee $6.00 per name. Will not search real estate records. UCC search includes tax liens if requested. Federal or state tax lien search- $3.00 per debtor. Copy fee $2.00, if tax lien or real estate $1.00 per page. Cert fee- $1.00 per cert plus copy fee. Payee- Huron County Register of Deeds. **Other phones:** Treasurer- 989-269-9238; Elections- 989-269-9942; Vital Records- 989-269-9942. **Property tax/Assessor-** 989-269-6497.

Ingham County

County Register of Deeds, PO Box 195, Mason, MI 48854-0195. 517-676-7216; fax-517-676-7287; hours: 8AM-5PM. www.ingham.org/rd/rodindex.htm
All records in one index. Records indexed on a public use terminal back to 1982. Office personnel or visitors may perform searches. Will not search real estate records. UCC search per debtor name- $6.00. Separate federal tax lien search- $3.00 per debtor. Separate state tax lien search- $3.00 per debtor. Separate federal & state combined tax lien search including MSE-$13.00 per debtor. Copy fee $1.00 per page. Cert fee- $1.00 per cert plus copy fee. Payee- Ingham County Register of Deeds. **Online access to Assumed Business Name, Recording, Deed, Grantor/Grantee, Assessor, Property, Delinquent Tax, Marriage Applicant records:** Access to the Register of Deeds database is free at www.ingham.org/icors/deeds.asp. Also, county DBA and co-partnership listings are free at www.ingham.org/CL/dbalists.htm. Also, marriage applicants can be searched by the week for free at www.ingham.org/CL/marrind.htm. **Other phones:** Treasurer- 517-676-7220; Elections- 517-676-7205; Vital Records- 517-676-7201. **Property tax/Assessor-** 517-676-7212.

Ionia County

County Register of Deeds, PO Box 35, Ionia, MI 48846. 616-527-5320; fax-616-527-8234; hours: 8:30AM-N, 1-5PM. www.ioniacounty.org
All records in one index. Records indexed on a public use terminal back to 1994. Office personnel or visitors may perform searches. Search fee $60.00 unless otherwise indicated. Copy fee $1.00 per page. Cert fee- $1.00 per cert plus copy fee. Payee- Ionia County Register of Deeds. **Online access to Recorder, Deed, Judgment, Lien, Will, Death, Property, Assessor records:** Access recorder records free at http://66.39.252.38/cland2/landweb.dll. Also, access county property data free at www.ioniacounty.org/taxweb/viewparcels.asp. **Other phones:** Treasurer- 616-527-5329; Elections- 616-527-5322; Vital Records- 616-527-5322. **Property tax/Assessor-** 100 Main St, Ionia, MI 48846; 616-527-5376.

Iosco County

County Register of Deeds, PO Box 367, Tawas City, MI 48764. 989-362-2021; fax-989-984-1101; hours: 9AM-5PM. www.iosco.net
Index: Pre-1986 records indexed by grantor/grantee and mortgage. Records indexed on a public use terminal back to 1987. Office

personnel or visitors may perform searches. Real estate owner, mortgage, and property transfer searches available only over phone or in person UCC search includes tax liens if requested. UCC search request with SS/TIN (per name)- $3.00. UCC search request without SS/TIN (per name)- $6.00. Separate state or federal tax lien search- $3.00 per debtor. Copy fee $1.25 per page. Cert fee- $1.00 per cert plus copy fee. Payee- Iosco County Register of Deeds. **Other phones:** Treasurer- 989-362-4409; Elections- 989-362-3497; Vital Records- 989-362-3497. **Property tax/Assessor-** 989-984-1111.

Iron County

County Register of Deeds, 2 S. Sixth St, #11; Courthouse Annex, #11, Crystal Falls, MI 49920-1413. 906-875-3321; fax-906-875-0658; hours: 8AM-N, 12:30-4PM.
Separate indices to search include Grantee/Grantor, Mortgagor/Mortgagee, and Books. Records indexed on computer back to 1995. General index search fee $.50 per year with $5.00 minimum. Will do limited searches of real estate records. Copy fee $1.00 per page, UCC record copy $2.00 per page. Cert fee- $1.00 per cert plus copy fee. Payee- Iron County Register of Deeds. **Other phones:** Treasurer- 906-875-3362; Vital Records- 906-875-3221. **Property tax/Assessor-** 906-875-6502.

Isabella County

County Register of Deeds, 200 N. Main St, Mt. Pleasant, MI 48858. 989-772-0911 x253; fax-989-953-7219; hours: 8AM-4:30PM. www.isabellacounty.org
Faxed search request- they will name search for $5.00 for 10 years. Need exact name as you want it searched, approx. date of document & type of document, need name of person requesting search, name of company, and how to return. Add'l $5.00 if faxed. Office personnel or visitors may perform searches. Search fee $5.00 for 10 yrs. Will not search real estate records. UCC copy fee $2.00 per page. R/E record copy- $1.00 per page. Cert fee- $1.00 per cert plus copy fee. Payee- Isabella County Register of Deeds. **Other phones:** Treasurer- 989-772-0911 x258; Elections- 989-772-0911 x259; Vital Records- 989-772-0911 x259. **Property tax/Assessor-** 989-772-0911 x242.

Jackson County

County Register of Deeds, 120 W. Michigan Ave; 11th Fl, Jackson, MI 49201. 517-788-4350; fax-517-788-4686; 8AM-5PM. www.co.jackson.mi.us/rod/
Separate indices to search. Records indexed on a public use terminal back to 1985. Only the office personnel may search. Search fee $6.00 per name. Will not search real estate records. Copy fee $2.00, if real estate $1.00 per page. Cert fee- $1.00 per page plus copy fee. Payee- Jackson County Register of Deeds. **Online access to Real Estate, Lien, Deed, Grantor/Grantee, Foreclosed Property Sale records:** Search recorded documents at http://68.23.73.16/icris/splash.jsp. Search foreclosed property sales lists at www.jacksoncountytaxsale.com/local_units.htm. No name searching. **Other phones:** Treasurer- 517-788-4418. **Property tax/Assessor-** 517-788-4378.

Kalamazoo County

County Register of Deeds, 201 W. Kalamazoo Ave, #102, Kalamazoo, MI 49007. 269-383-8970; hours: 8AM-4:30PM. www.kalcounty.com
Records indexed on computer back to 1985. Office will perform a UCC search but public must search other records themselves. UCC search per debtor name- $6.00. Copy fee $1.00 per page. Cert fee- $1.00 per cert plus copy fee. Payee- Kalamazoo County Register of Deeds. **Online access to Assessor, Property records:** Access property assessor data free at www.kalcounty.com/equalization/parcel_search.php.

Other phones: Treasurer- 269-383-8124. **Property tax/Assessor-** 201 W. Kalamazoo Ave, #101, Kalamazoo, MI 49007; 269-383-8960, assessor fax- 269-383-8962.

Kalkaska County

County Register of Deeds, 605 N. Birch St, Kalkaska, MI 49646. 231-258-3315; fax-231-258-3345; hours: 9AM-5PM.
Separate indices to search. Records indexed on a public use terminal back to 5/20/1996. Office personnel or visitors may perform searches. Search fee $6.00 per name. Will not search real estate records. Copy fee $2.00, if tax lien or real estate $1.00 per page. Cert fee- $1.00 per page plus copy fee. Payee- Kalkaska County Register of Deeds. **Other phones:** Treasurer- 231-258-3310; Vital Records- 231-258-3300. **Property tax/Assessor-** 231-258-3340.

Kent County

County Register of Deeds, 300 Monroe Ave NW, Grand Rapids, MI 49503-2286. 616-336-3558; fax-616-336-8938; hours: 8AM-5PM. www.accesskent.com/YourGovernment/Registerof Deeds/deeds_index.htm
Separate indices to search. Records indexed on a public use terminal back to 1980. Office will perform a UCC search but public must search other records themselves. UCC search per debtor name- $6.00. Copy fee $1.00 per page. Cert fee- $1.00 per cert plus copy fee. Payee- Kent County Register of Deeds. **Online access to Recording, Deed, Lien, Assessor, Property, Accident Report, Vital Statistic, Treasurer, Inmate records:** Search county parcel data free at https://www.accesskent.com/Property/. With username, password & credit card, view records for $1. or subscribe for $75. per year at 616-632-6516. Accident reports $3.00 at https://www.accesskent.com/Acci dentReports/. Kent deeds index free at https://www.accesskent.com/deeds/. Walker City assessor- https://is.bsasoftware.com/bsa.is/default.aspx. Search assessment- Ada, Bowne, Caledonia, G.R, Lowell, Vergennes at www.addorio.com/assessmen ttax.htm. Also, Alpine Assessments at http://alpine.data-web.net. No name search. Order vital statistic records $7 at https://www.accesskent.com/servlet/VitalRec. Access Grand Rapids property at www.ci.grand-rapids.mi.us/22. Search for county Inmates at www.accesskent.com/InmateLookup/. **Other phones:** Treasurer- 616-336-0762. **Property tax/Assessor-** 616-336-3527.

Keweenaw County

County Register of Deeds, 5095 4th St, Eagle River, MI 49950-9744. 906-337-2229; fax-906-337-2795; hours: 9AM-4PM.
Record index not computerized. Office personnel or visitors may perform searches. Search fee $3.00 per name. Will not search real estate records. Will search UCC records; search includes tax liens if requested. Copy fee $1.00 per page. Cert fee- $10.00 per cert plus copy fee. Payee- Keweenaw County Register of Deeds. **Other phones:** Treasurer- 906-337-1625. **Property tax/Assessor-** 906-337-3471.

Lake County

County Register of Deeds, 800 Tenth St. #200, Baldwin, MI 49304. 231-745-4641; fax-231-745-2241; hours: 8:30AM-N, 1-5PM. www.michigan.gov
All records in one index. Records indexed on a public use terminal back to 1990. Office personnel or visitors may perform searches. Search fee $.50 per name $5.00 Minimum. Will search real estate records prior to 1990, if request is in writing. Will search UCC records prior to 7/2001 and current fixture (land) files. UCC search includes tax liens if requested. UCC search request with SS/TIN (per name)- $3.00. Tax lien search- $3.00 per debtor. Copy fee $1.00 per page. Cert fee- $1.00 per cert plus copy fee. Payee- Lake County Register of Deeds. **Other**

phones: Treasurer- 231-745-4622; Appraiser/Auditor- 231-745-4641; Elections- 231-745-4641; Vital Records- 231-745-2725. **Property tax/Assessor-** same address as above. 231-745-2723.

Lapeer County

County Register of Deeds, 279 N. Court St, Lapeer, MI 48446. 810-667-0211; fax-810-667-0293; hours: 8AM-5PM. www.county.lapeer.org/deeds
Separate indices to search include General, surveys, plats, and land records. Only the public may search. Copy fee $2.00, if tax lien or real estate $1.00 per page. Cert fee- $1.00 per cert plus copy fee. Payee- Lapeer County Register of Deeds. **Other phones:** Treasurer- 810-667-0239; Elections- 810-667-0356; Vital Records- 810-667-0356. **Property tax/Assessor-** 810-667-0228.

Leelanau County

County Register of Deeds, PO Box 595, Leland, MI 49654. 231-256-9682; fax-231-256-8149; hours: 9AM-5PM. www.leelanau.cc/default.asp
Records indexed on computer back to 1991. Office will perform a UCC search but public must search other records themselves. Search fee $5.00 min. Copy fee $1.00 per page. Cert fee- $1.00 per cert plus copy fee. Payee- Leelanau County Register of Deeds. **Other phones:** Treasurer- 231-256-9838; Appraiser/Auditor- 231-256-9823; Elections- 231-256-9824; Vital Records- 231-256-9824. **Property tax/Assessor-** 231-256-9823.

Lenawee County

County Register of Deeds, 301 N. Main St, Adrian, MI 49221. 517-264-4538, UCC recording phone-517-264-4541; fax-517-264-4543; hours: 8AM-4:30PM. www.lenawee.mi.us/regdeeds.html
Office will perform a UCC search but public must search other records themselves. UCC search per debtor name- $6.00. Copy fee for plats & UCCs- $2.00 per page. Cert fee- $1.00 per cert plus copy fee. Payee- Lenawee County Register of Deeds. **Online access to Real Estate, Recording, Deed, Will, Probate Order, Lien, Personal Property, Assessor, Property Tax records:** Recording records available by subscription, call 517-264-4539 (Register of Deeds) for info and fees. Also, search assessing/property data free at http://lenawee.zenacomp.com. **Other phones:** Treasurer- 517-264-4554; Vital Records- 517-264-4595. **Property tax/Assessor-** same address as above. 517-264-4522.

Livingston County

County Register of Deeds, PO Box 197, Howell, MI 48844. 517-546-0270; fax-517-546-5966; hours: 8AM-5PM. www.co.livingston.mi.us/RegisterofDeeds/
Separate indices to search include tract, grantor/grantee. Records indexed on a public use terminal back to 10/1984. Office personnel or visitors may perform searches. Search fee $5.00 unless otherwise indicated. UCC search per debtor name- $6.00. Separate federal/state combined tax lien search- $6.00 per debtor. Copy fee $2.00 per page; tax lien or real estate $1.00 per page. Cert fee- $1.00 per cert plus copy fee. Payee- Livingston County Register of Deeds. **Online access to Real Estate, Lien, Tax Assessor, Death records:** Access to county online records is available for occasional users, and a dedicated line is available for $1200 for professional users. Annual fee for occasional use is $400, plus $.000043 per second. Records date back to 1984. Lending agency information is available. For information, contact IT Dept at 517-548-3230. Also, search the county death indices to 1948 for free at www.livgenmi.com/deathlisting.htm. **Other phones:** Treasurer- 517-546-7010; Elections- 517-546-0500; Vital Records- 517-546-0500. **Property tax/Assessor-** 304 E Grand River, Howell, MI 48843; 517-546-4182.

Luce County

County Register of Deeds, County Gov't Bldg, Newberry, MI 49868. 906-293-5521; fax-906-293-0050; hours: 8AM-4PM.

Office personnel or visitors may perform searches. General index search fee $5.00 per name searched. Copy fee $2.00, if tax lien or real estate $1.00 per page. Cert fee- $10.00 per cert plus copy fee. Payee- Luce County Register of Deeds. **Other phones:** Treasurer- 906-293-8171; Elections- 906-293-5521; Vital Records- 906-293-5521. **Property tax/Assessor-** 906-293-5611.

Mackinac County

County Register of Deeds, 100 Marley St, Saint Ignace, MI 49781. 906-643-7306; fax-906-643-7302; hours: 8:30AM-4:30PM.

Separate indices to search. Records indexed on a public use terminal back to 1990. Office personnel or visitors may perform searches. Search fee $3.00 per name. Copy fee $1.00 per page. Cert fee- $1.00 per cert plus copy fee. Payee- Mackinac County Register of Deeds. **Other phones:** Treasurer- 906-643-7317; Vital Records- 906-643-7300. **Property tax/Assessor-** 906-643-7310.

Macomb County

County Register of Deeds, 10 N. Main, Mt. Clemens, MI 48043. 586-469-7953, R/E recording phone-586-469-5309, UCC recording phone-586-469-5342; fax-586-469-5130; hours: 8:30AM-5PM. http://macombcountymi.gov/clerksoffice/index.asp Records indexed on computer from 10/1/81 to present, card file from 4/1/65 to 9/30/81, old books divided by blocks or years all prior to 4/1/65. Office personnel or visitors may perform searches. General index search fee $5.00 minimum (10 years). Real estate record owner and mortgage searches available. Will search UCC records prior to 7/2001 and current fixture (land) files. Will search tax liens. UCC search per debtor name- $12.00. Separate federal tax lien search- $3.00 per debtor. Separate state tax lien search- $3.00 per debtor. Federal/state combined tax lien search- $6.00 per debtor name. Copy fee $2.00, if tax lien or real estate $1.00 per page. Cert fee- $1.00 per page plus copy fee. Payee- Macomb County Register of Deeds. **Online access to Recorder, Deed, Business Registration, Death, Campaign Committee/Candidate, Most Wanted, Sex Offender records:** Business registration information is free online at http://macomb.mcntv.com/businessnames. Search by full or partial company name. County death records are at http://macomb.mcntv.com/deathrecords. Search by name or apx. date. Also, county recorder images are from a private source at www.courthousedirect.com/pac-info/Main.asp; Fees/registration required. Search sex offender and most wanted lists at sheriff site at www.macombsheriff.com. Also, Land records from the assessor database found at www.landaccess.com/index.jsp?content=register. Free registration for password and user name. **Other phones:** Treasurer- 586-469-5190; Elections- 586-469-5209; Vital Records- 586-469-5120; Search- 586-469-7953. **Property tax/Assessor-** 586-469-5190.

Manistee County

County Register of Deeds, 415 Third St; Courthouse, Manistee, MI 49660-1606. 231-723-2146; fax-231-398-3544; hours: 8:30AM-N, 1-5PM.

Separate indices to search. Records indexed on a public use terminal back to 8/19/1991. Office personnel or visitors may perform searches. Search fee $6.00 per name. Will not search real estate records. UCC copy fee $2.00 per page. R/E record copy- $1.00 per page. Cert fee- $2.00 per cert plus copy fee. Payee- Manistee County Register of Deeds.

Marquette County

County Register of Deeds, 234 W. Baraga Ave; C-105, Marquette, MI 49855. 906-225-8415; fax-906-225-8420; hours: 8AM-5PM. www.co.marquette.mi.us/register.htm Records indexed on a public use terminal back to 1988. Search fee $5.00 unless otherwise indicated. UCC search includes tax liens if requested. UCC search per debtor name- $6.00. Separate federal/state combined tax lien search- $6.00 per debtor. General copy fee $1.00 per page. UCC copy $2.00 per page. Cert fee- $1.00 per cert plus copy fee. Payee- Marquette County Register of Deeds. **Other phones:** Treasurer- 906-225-8425; Appraiser/Auditor- 906-225-8405; Elections- 906-225-8330; Vital Records- 906-225-8330. **Property tax/Assessor-** Equalization Department, County Courthouse, Marquette, MI 49855; 906-225-8405.

Mason County

County Register of Deeds, 304 E. Ludington Ave, Ludington, MI 49431. 231-843-4466; fax-231-845-7977; hours: 9AM-5PM.

Separate indices to search. Records indexed on a public use terminal back to 1995. Office personnel or visitors may perform searches. Search fee $3.00 per name. Copy fee $1.00 per page. Cert fee- $1.00 per cert plus copy fee. Payee- Mason County Register of Deeds.

Mecosta County

County Register of Deeds, PO Box 718, Big Rapids, MI 49307. 231-592-0148; hours: 8:30AM-5PM. Only the public may search. Copy fee $2.00, if tax lien or real estate $1.00 per page. Cert fee- $1.00 per cert plus copy fee. Payee- Mecosta County Register of Deeds. **Online access to Assessor, Property, Animal License records:** Search the City of Big Rapids assessing and tax page for free at https://is.bsasoftware.com/bsa.is/default.aspx. Includes special assignments and animal license search . **Other phones:** Treasurer- 231-592-0169. **Property tax/Assessor-** 231-592-0108.

Menominee County

Register of Deeds, 839 10th Ave; Courthouse, Menominee, MI 49858. 906-863-2822; fax-906-863-8839; hours: 8AM-4:30PM. www.menomineecounty.com/rod/rgstr1.html All records in one index back to 1/2000; prior indices were deeds and mortgages. Records indexed on a public use terminal back to 6/1996. Office personnel or visitors may perform searches. Office searches are minimal. General index search fee minimum of $5.00. Property transfer searches available. Will search UCC records prior to 7/2001 and current fixture (land) files. Tax liens not included in UCC search. UCC search request per name- $6.00. Tax lien search fee- $3.00 per debtor. Copy fee $1.00 per page. Cert fee- $1.00 per page plus copy fee. Payee- Register of Deeds. **Online access to Land, Deed, Recording records:** Access to land records is free at http://66.84.189.211/landweb.dll. Search is free - use "guest" - but document images may be ordered by fax for $1.50 each or mail for $1.00 each; contact the Register of Deeds, 906-863-2822, for ID and password. **Other phones:** Treasurer- 906-863-5548; Elections- 906-863-9968; Vital Records- 906-863-9968; Equalization- 906-863-2683. **Property tax/Assessor-** same address as above. 906-863-2683, assessor fax- 906-863-8839.

Midland County

County Register of Deeds, 220 W. Ellsworth St; County Services Bldg, Midland, MI 48640-5194. 989-832-6820; fax-932-832-6842; hours: 8AM-5PM. www.co.midland.mi.us All records in one index. Records indexed on a public use terminal. Office will perform a UCC search but public must search other records themselves. UCC search per debtor name- $10.00. Copy fee $1.00 per page. Cert fee- $1.00 per page plus copy fee. Payee- Midland County Register of Deeds. **Other phones:** Treasurer- 989-832-6850; Elections- 989-832-6739; Vital Records- 989-832-6739. **Property tax/Assessor-** 989-837-3334.

Missaukee County

County Register of Deeds, PO Box 800, Lake City, MI 49651. 231-839-4967; fax-231-839-3684; hours: 9AM-5PM. www.missaukee.org All records in one index. Records indexed on a public use terminal back to 1989. Office personnel or visitors may perform searches. General index search fee $.50 per year per document with a minimum of $5.00. Copy fee $2.00, if tax lien or real estate $1.00 per page. Cert fee- $8.00 per cert plus copy fee. Payee- Missaukee County Register of Deeds. **Other phones:** Treasurer- 231-839-2169; Elections- 231-839-4967; Vital Records- 231-839-4967. **Property tax/Assessor-** 231-839-2702.

Monroe County

County Register of Deeds, 51 S Macomb St, Monroe, MI 48161. 734-240-7390; hours: 8:30AM-5PM. www.co.monroe.mi.us All records in one index. Office will perform a UCC or tax lien search but public must search other records themselves. UCC or tax lien search per debtor name- $6.00. Copy fee $1.00 per page. Cert fee- None. Payee- Monroe County Register of Deeds. **Online access to Real Estate, Recorder, Deed, Fictitious Name, Voter Registration records:** Access recorder land index free at https://www.co.monroe.mi.us/egov/landrecords/. Access to images requires credit card payment. Access fictitious business names free at https://www.co.monroe.mi.us/egov/searchdbanames.aspx. Also, order voter registration lists at https://www.co.monroe.mi.us/egov/ordervoterlist.aspx; fee is $20 per copy on CD-rom. **Other phones:** Treasurer- 734-240-7365; County Clerk- 734-240-7020. **Property tax/Assessor-** same address as above. 734-240-7235.

Montcalm County

County Register of Deeds, PO Box 188, Stanton, MI 48888. 989-831-7337; fax-989-831-7320; hours: 8AM-N, 1-5PM.

All records in one index. Records indexed on a public use terminal back to approximately 1970. Office personnel or visitors may perform searches. General index search fee $10.00. UCC copy fee $2.00 per page. R/E record copy- $1.00 per page. Cert fee- $1.00 per doc plus copy fee. Payee- Montcalm County Register of Deeds. **Online access to Real Estate, Recorder, Deed, Lien, Judgment, Assessor, Treasurer, Tax Roll, Tax Sale, Inmate records:** No fee to view the index at http://65.118.226.83/landweb.dll, but a $50 monthly fee for details. Unlimited access is $300 monthly. Access plus printable document images is $700 monthly. Records date back to 1/1/1988. Lending agency information is available. For information, call the Register of Deeds office. Also, assessor property tax data is free at www.montcalm.org/taxweb/viewparcels.asp. Also, search tax roll, tax sale online free at www.co.whatcom.wa.us/treasurer/index.jsp. Search jail roster- www.co.whatcom.wa.us/sheriff/jail/roster.jsp. **Other phones:** Treasurer- 989-831-7334; Elections- 989-831-7339; Vital Records- 989-831-7339. **Property tax/Assessor-** 989-831-5226 x203.

Montmorency County

County Register of Deeds, PO Box 789, Atlanta, MI 49709. 989-785-8079; fax-989-785-8080; hours: 8:30AM-N, 1-4:30PM.

Separate indices to search include deeds, mortgages, liens, judgments/lps, surveys, land corners, deaths, remon, oil & gas. Records indexed on a public use terminal back to 8/1987. Office will perform a UCC search but public must search other records themselves. Will search UCC records prior to 7/2001 and current fixture (land) files. UCC search includes tax liens if requested. UCC search per debtor name- $6.00. Separate federal or state tax lien search- $5.00 per debtor. Copy fee $2.00, if tax lien or real estate $1.00 per page. Cert fee- $3.00 per cert plus copy fee. Payee- Montmorency

County Register of Deeds. **Other phones:** Treasurer- 989-785-8086; Elections- 989-785-8022; Vital Records- 989-785-8022. **Property tax/Assessor-** same address as above. 989-785-8046.

Muskegon County

County Register of Deeds, 990 Terrace St.; 2nd Fl, Muskegon, MI 49442. 231-724-6271; fax-231-724-6842; hours: 8AM-5PM; Recording hours: 8AM-4:30PM. www.co.muskegon.mi.us/deeds/

Separate indices to search. Records indexed on a public use terminal back to 1985. Office personnel or visitors may perform searches. Search fee $6.00 per name. Copy fee $2.00, if tax lien or real estate $1.00 per page. Cert fee- $1.00 per page plus copy fee. Payee- Muskegon County Register of Deeds. **Online access to Death records:** Access the county genealogical death index system for free at www.co.muskegon.mi.us/clerk/websearch.cfm. Records 1867-1965. **Property tax/Assessor-** 231-724-6386.

Newaygo County

County Register of Deeds, PO Box 885, White Cloud, MI 49349. 231-689-7246; fax-231-689-7271; hours: 8:30AM-N, 1-4:30PM.

Records indexed on a public use terminal back to 1989. Only the public may search. Copy fee $2.00 for UCC, if tax lien or real estate $1.00 per page. Cert fee- $1.00 per page. Payee- Newaygo County Register of Deeds. **Other phones:** Treasurer- 231-689-7230; Elections- 231-689-7235; Vital Records- 231-689-7235; Sheriff- 231-689-6623. **Property tax/Assessor-** 231-689-7240.

Oakland County

County Register of Deeds, 1200 N. Telegraph Rd; Bldg 12 East, Pontiac, MI 48341-0480. 248-858-0605, R/E recording phone-248-858-0597, UCC recording phone-248-858-0600; hours: 8AM-4:30PM. www.co.oakland.mi.us/clerkrod/

Separate indices to search include land and UCC records. Office will perform a UCC search but public must search other records themselves. Search fee $5.00, UCC search $9.00. Copy fee $1.00 per page. Cert fee- $1.00 per copy. Payee- Oakland County Register of Deeds. **Online access to Real Estate, Property Tax, Tax Lien, Most Wanted, Foreclosure records:** Access to Access Oakland property information is by subscription. Available monthly or per use. For information or sign-up, visit www.oakland.mi.us (click on "Access Oakland") or call Information Services at 248-858-0861. Search foreclosure property lists for free at www.co.oakland.mi.us/fcloser/fmain?cmd=fcvt. Also, search the county sheriff's most wanted list at www.co.oakland.mi.us/sheriff/most_wanted/. Search the tax assessor database at www.rochesterhills.org/. Click on "online tax and assessing inquiry.". **Other phones:** Treasurer- 248-858-0611; Elections- 248-858-0564; Vital Records- 248-858-0571. **Property tax/Assessor-** 248-858-0740.

Oceana County

County Register of Deeds, PO Box 111, Hart, MI 49420. 231-873-4158; fax-231-873-9218; hours: 9AM-5PM.

Separate indices to search include from 2002 to present on computer, 1961 - 2002 index cards, before 1961-books. Only the public may search. Copy fee $2.00, if real estate $1.00 per page. Cert fee- $1.00 per cert plus copy fee. Payee- Oceana County Register of Deeds. **Other phones:** Treasurer- 231-873-3980; Elections- 231-873-4328; Vital Records- 231-873-1748. **Property tax/Assessor-** same address as above. 231-873-4609.

Ogemaw County

County Register of Deeds, 806 W. Houghton Ave; Rm 104, West Branch, MI 48661. 989-345-0728; fax-989-345-6221; hours: 8:30AM-4:30PM.

All records in one index. Office will perform a UCC search but public must search other records

themselves. Only UCC records are prior to 7/2001. Tax liens not included in UCC search. UCC search per debtor name- $6.00. Copy fee $2.00, if tax lien or real estate $1.00 per page; $1.50 if mailed. Cert fee- $1.00 per cert plus copy fee. Payee- Ogemaw County Register of Deeds. **Other phones:** Treasurer- 989-345-0084; Elections- 989-345-0215; Vital Records- 989-345-0215. **Property tax/Assessor-** Equalization Dept, 806 W Houghton Ave, Rm 105, West Branch, MI 48661; 989-345-0328.

Ontonagon County

County Register of Deeds, 725 Greenland Rd, Ontonagon, MI 49953-1492. 906-884-4255; fax-906-884-6796; hours: 8:30AM-4:30PM.

Separate indices to search include deeds, mortgage, misc. General index search fee $5.00 per name. UCC search per debtor name- $6.00. Separate federal/state combined tax lien search-$3.00 per debtor. Copy fee $1.00 per page. Cert fee- $1.00 per cert plus copy fee. Payee- Ontonagon County Register of Deeds. **Other phones:** Treasurer- 906-884-4665; Appraiser/Auditor- 906-884-2765; Elections- 906-884-4255; Vital Records- 906-884-2806. **Property tax/Assessor-** same address as above. 906-884-2765.

Osceola County

County Register of Deeds, 301 W Upton Ave, Reed City, MI 49677-0208. 231-832-6113; hours: 9AM-5PM.

Separate indices to search include Grantor/Grantee, mtgor/mtgee, 1856-2002. Records indexed on a public use terminal back to 2003. Only the public may search. Copy fee $2.00, if real estate $1.00 per page. Cert fee- $2.00 per page. Payee- Osceola County Register of Deeds. **Other phones:** Treasurer- 231-832-6110. **Property tax/Assessor-** 231-832-6119.

Oscoda County

County Register of Deeds, PO Box 399, Mio, MI 48647. 989-826-1116; fax-989-826-1136; hours: 8:30AM-12PM, 1PM-4.30PM.

All records in one index. Will not search real estate records. Will search UCC records prior to 7/2001 and current fixture (land) files. Tax liens not included in UCC search. UCC search per debtor name- $6.00. Separate federal tax lien search- $3.00 per debtor. Separate federal/state combined tax lien search-$3.00 per debtor. Copy fee $1.00 per page. Cert fee- $1.00 per cert plus copy fee. Payee- Oscoda County Register of Deeds. **Other phones:** Treasurer- 989-826-1112. **Property tax/Assessor-** 989-826-1116.

Otsego County

County Register of Deeds, 225 W. Main St, Rm 110; Rm 108, Gaylord, MI 49735. 989-731-7550, R/E recording phone-989-989-731-7550; fax-989-731-7519; hours: 8AM-N, 1-4:30PM.

Requests must be in writing along with money up front. All records in one index. Records indexed on a public use terminal back to 1984. Office personnel or visitors may perform searches. Search fee $5.00 in writing or prepaid, back to 1984; prior $.50 per year. Will not search UCC records. Copy fee $2.00, if real estate $1.00 per page. Cert fee- $1.00 per doc plus copy fee. Payee- Otsego County Register of Deeds. **Other phones:** Treasurer- 989-731-7560; Elections- 989-731-7501; Vital Records- 989-731-7500. **Property tax/Assessor-** 1066 Cross St, Gaylord, MI 49735; 989-731-7410.

Ottawa County

County Register of Deeds, PO Box 265, Grand Haven, MI 49417-0265. 616-846-8240; fax-616-846-8131; hours: 8AM-5PM. www.co.ottawa.mi.us

All records in one index. Records indexed on a public use terminal back to 9/1/1973. Only the public may search. Copy fee $2.00, if tax lien or real estate $1.00 per page. Cert fee- $1.00 per cert plus copy fee. Payee- Ottawa County Register of

Deeds. **Online access to Property, Mapping, Deed, UCC, Judgment records:** The county offers a free online mapping service with parcel identification at www.gis.co.ottawa.mi.us/ottawa/. No name searching. Also, access to recorder records by subscription is at www.landaccess.com/ottawa/sub.jsp?county=miottawa. Yearly sub fee is $200.00 per year plus $.50 per search and $.25 per document. Credit cards searching accepted. **Other phones:** Treasurer- 616-846-8230; Elections- 616-846-8310; Vital Records- 616-846-8310.

Presque Isle County

County Register of Deeds, PO Box 110, Rogers City, MI 49779-0110. 989-734-2676; fax-989-734-0506; hours: 8:30AM-4:30PM.

All records in one index. Records indexed on a public use terminal back to 1989. Only the public may search. Copy fee $1.00 per page. Cert fee- $1.00 per cert plus copy fee. Payee- Presque Isle County Register of Deeds. **Other phones:** Treasurer- 989-734-4075; Elections- 989-734-3288; Vital Records- 989-734-3288. **Property tax/Assessor-** same address as above. 989-734-3810.

Roscommon County

County Register of Deeds, 500 Lake St, Roscommon, MI 48653. 989-275-5931, R/E recording phone-517-275-5931; fax-989-275-8640; hours: 8:30AM-4:30PM.

Separate indices to search include computer and various pre-1985 indices. Records indexed on computer back to 1985. Will not search real estate records. UCC search request with SS/TIN (per name)- $6.00. UCC search request without SS/TIN (per name)- $12.00. Separate federal or state tax lien search- $3.00 per debtor. Copy fee $1.00 per page. UCC copy $2.00 per page. Cert fee- $1.00 per cert plus copy fee. Payee- Roscommon County Register of Deeds. **Other phones:** Treasurer- 989-275-5823; Elections- 989-275-5923; Vital Records- 989-275-5923. **Property tax/Assessor-** 989-275-8121 x5754.

Saginaw County

County Register of Deeds, 111 S. Michigan Ave, Saginaw, MI 48602. 989-790-5270; fax-989-790-5278; hours: 8AM-5PM. www.saginawcounty.com

All records in one index. Records indexed on a public use terminal back to 1982. Office personnel or visitors may perform searches. General index search fee $5.00 per name (no phone searches). Copy fee $1.00, if UCC $2.00 per page. Cert fee- $1.00 per cert plus copy fee. Payee- Saginaw County Register of Deeds. **Online access to Assessor, Assumed Business Name, Marriage, Death, Election, Notary, Grantor/Grantee, Recording, Obituary records:** Access to the county clerks database is free at www.saginawcounty.com/clerk/search/index.html. Vital statistic records go back to 1995. Search obituaries at www.tricitynet.com/pls/obit.nsf Also, search Register of Deeds data (except tax liens) back to 1982 for free at www.saginawtownship.org/property/search.cfm. Also, search equalization board tax records at www.saginawcounty.com/equ/prop_info.htm. **Other phones:** Treasurer- 989-790-5225; Elections- 989-790-5251; Vital Records- 989-790-5251. **Property tax/Assessor-** 989-790-5260.

Sanilac County

County Register of Deeds, Box 168, Sandusky, MI 48471-0168. 810-648-2313; fax-810-648-5461; hours: 8AM-N, 1-4:30PM.

Records indexed on computer from 1991 to present, anything before 1991 is indexed in grantor/grantee indexes. Are currently working on entering recordings before 1991 into the computer. Office personnel or visitors may perform searches. General index search fee $.50 per name per year. Real estate record owner and property searches available. Will search UCC records prior to 7/2001. UCC search includes tax liens if requested. UCC search per debtor name- $6.00. Separate federal tax lien search- $6.00 per debtor. Separate state tax lien search- $3.00 per debtor. Separate federal/state combined tax lien search- $12.00 per debtor. UCC copy fee $2.00 per copy. R/E record copy- $1.00 per copy. Cert fee- $1.00 per cert plus copy fee. Payee- Sanilac County Register of Deeds. **Other phones:** Treasurer- 810-648-2127; Elections- 810-648-3212; Vital Records- 810-648-3212. **Property tax/Assessor-** 60 W Sanilac Ave, Sandusky, MI 48471; 810-648-2955.

Schoolcraft County

County Register of Deeds, 300 Walnut St; Rm 164, Manistique, MI 49854. 906-341-3618; fax-906-341-5680; hours: 8AM-4PM.

All records in one index. Only the public may search. Copy fee $1.00 per page. Cert fee- $1.00 per cert plus copy fee. Payee- Schoolcraft County Register of Deeds. **Other phones:** Treasurer- 906-341-3622; Vital Records- 906-341-3618. **Property tax/Assessor-** 300 Walnut St, Rm 207, Manistique, MI 49854; 906-341-3677.

Shiawassee County

County Register of Deeds, PO Box 103, Corunna, MI 48817. 989-743-2216; fax-989-743-2459; 8AM-5PM. Separate indices to search. Records indexed on a public use terminal back to 1980. Office personnel or visitors may perform searches. Search fee $3.00 per name. Will not search real estate records. UCC search per debtor name- $6.00. Copy fee $2.00, if tax lien or real estate $1.00 per page. Cert fee- $1.00 per cert plus copy fee. Payee- Shiawassee County Register of Deeds.

St. Clair County

County Register of Deeds, 200 Grand River Blvd; Rm 105, Port Huron, MI 48060. 810-989-6930, R/E recording phone-810-985-2275; fax-810-985-4297; 8AM-4:30PM.
www.stclaircounty.org/Offices/register_of_deeds/
Office will perform a UCC or tax lien search but public must search other records themselves. UCC or tax lien search per debtor name- $6.00. Copy fee $1.00 per page; UCC copy $2.00 per page. Cert fee- $1.00 per cert plus copy fee. Payee- St. Clair County Register of Deeds. **Online access to Real Estate, Recorder, Deed, Lien, Marriage, Death, Property, Assessor, GIS-map records:** Access register of deeds database free at http://publicdeeds.stclaircounty.org. Click on OPR. Online records go back to 10/1993. Search tax equalization data free at www.stclaircounty.org/offices/equalization/search.asp. Also, data may be available at http://gis.stclaircounty.org/landmanagement on the map site. Access to unofficial death records up to 1974 is free at www.rootsweb.com/~mistcla2/. 19th century marriages are also available. **Other phones:** Treasurer- 810-985-2295. **Property tax/Assessor-** 810-985-6925, assessor fax- 810-989-6328.

St. Joseph County

County Register of Deeds, PO Box 388, Centreville, MI 49032-0388. 269-467-5552 x552; fax-269-467-5593; hours: 9AM-5PM. www.stjosephcountymi.org
Separate indices to search. Records indexed on a public use terminal back to 1993. Office personnel or visitors may perform searches. Search fee $5.00 minimum for real estate records. UCC search per debtor name- $6.00. Copy fee $2.00, if tax lien or real estate $1.00 per page. Cert fee- $1.00 per cert plus copy fee. Payee- St. Joseph County Register of Deeds. **Online access to Assessor records:** Search assessor records at www.stjosephcountymi.org/taxsearch/default.asp. Can do a name search.

Tuscola County

Register of Deeds, 440 N. State St, Caro, MI 48723. 989-672-3840, UCC recording phone-989-672-3780; fax-989-672-4266; hours: 8AM-N, 1-4:30PM. www.tuscolacounty.org/
All records in one index. Records indexed on a public use terminal back to 1992. Office will perform a UCC and Tax lien search but public must search other records themselves. Search fee $6.00. General copy fee $2.00 per page. R/E record copy- $1.00 per page. Cert fee- $1.00 per cert plus copy fee. Payee- Tuscola County Register of Deeds. **Online access to Land Tract Index records:** Access to the county land tract index is free at www.landaccess.com/sites/mi/tuscola/index.php?mituscola. **Other phones:** Treasurer- 989-672-3890; Elections- 989-672-3780; Vital Records- 989-672-3780.

Van Buren County

County Register of Deeds, 219 Paw Paw St, #102, Paw Paw, MI 49079. 269-657-8242, R/E recording phone-269-657-8200; fax-269-657-7573; hours: 8:30AM-5PM. www.vbco.org/government0104.asp
All records in one index. Records indexed on a public use terminal. Office personnel or visitors may perform searches. Search fee- as state law allows. Will search real estate records only if on UCC side. Copy fee $1.00 per page. Cert fee- $1.00 per cert plus copy fee. Payee- Van Buren County Register of Deeds. **Online access to Real Estate records:** Search ownership of real property at www.vbco.org/mapsearch.asp. **Other phones:** Treasurer- 269-657-8228; Elections- 269-657-8218; Vital Records- 269-657-8218. **Property tax/Assessor-** 269-657-8234.

Washtenaw County

County Register of Deeds, PO Box 8645, Ann Arbor, MI 48107. 734-222-6710; fax-734-222-6819; hours: 8:30AM-5PM.
www.ewashtenaw.org/government/clerk_register
All records in one index. Records indexed on a public use terminal back to 1986. Office will perform a UCC search but public must search other records themselves. Search fee $6.00. Copy fee $2.00; if UCC or real estate $1.00 per page.

Cert fee- $1.00 per cert plus copy fee. Payee- Washtenaw County Register of Deeds. **Online access to Property, Vital Statistic, Business Name, Deed records:** Go to www.ewashtenaw.org/online/ for a menu of searchable databases. **Other phones:** Treasurer- 734-222-6600; Elections- 734-222-6730; Vital Records- 734-222-6700. **Property tax/Assessor-** 734-994-2511.

Wayne County

County Register of Deeds, 400 Monroe; Rm 620, Detroit, MI 48226. 313-224-5860/5860; fax-313-224-5884; 8AM-4:30PM.

www.waynecounty.com/register/
Separate indices to search. Records indexed on a public use terminal back to 1986. Office personnel or visitors may perform searches. Search fee for index of last owner search by property location- $5.00 in person; by mail-$15.00. Will not search real estate records. General copy fee $1.00. Plat copy- $5.00 per page. Plat copies and large volume search requests by special request; call 224-5868 for information. Cert fee- $10.00 per cert plus copy fee. Payee- Wayne County Register of Deeds. **Online access to Assessor, Recording, Deed, Judgment, Lien, Assumed Name, Delinquent Property records:** Search the recorders land records database for free at www.waynecountylandrecords.com/. A full data on-demand or business service is also available; call 313-967-6857 for info or sign-up or visit www.waynecountylandrecords.com/RODC/Default.asp. Search the county assumed names at www.waynecounty.com/clerk/AssumedNames/search.asp. Search the treasurers delinquent tax list free at www.waynecounty.com/pta/Default.asp. Records on the City of Dearborn Residential Property Assessment Database are free online at www.dearbornfordcenter.com/dbnassessor/. No name searching.

Wexford County

County Register of Deeds, 437 E. Division St; PO Box 303, Cadillac, MI 49601. 231-779-9455; fax-231-779-0292; hours: 8:30AM-5PM (vault 8:30AM-4PM). www.wexfordcounty.org/services_deeds.php
All records in one index. Search fee $5.00 min. Will not search real estate records. UCC search per debtor name- $6.00. Separate federal/state combined tax lien search- $6.00 per debtor. Copy fee $1.00 per page. UCC copy fee $2.00 per page. Cert fee- $1.00 per cert plus copy fee. Payee- County Register of Deeds. **Online access to Real Estate records:** Search treasurer's record at www.wexfordcounty.org/treas/search.htm. **Other phones:** Treasurer- 231-779-9475. **Property tax/Assessor-** 231-779-9531.

Michigan County Locator

You will usually be able to find the city name in the City/County Cross Reference below. In that case, it is a simple matter to determine the county from the cross reference. However, only the official US Postal Service city names are included in this index. There are an additional 40,000 place names that people use in their addresses. Therefore, we have also included a ZIP/City Cross Reference immediately following the City/County Cross Reference.

If you know the ZIP Code but the city name does not appear in the City/County Cross Reference index, look up the ZIP Code in the ZIP/City Cross Reference, find the city name, then look up the city name in the City/County Cross Reference. For example, you want to know the county for an address of Menands, NY 12204. There is no "Menands" in the City/County Cross Reference. The ZIP/City Cross Reference shows that ZIP Codes 12201-12288 are for the city of Albany. Looking back in the City/County Cross Reference, Albany is in Albany County.

Michigan City/County Cross Reference

ACME Grand Traverse
ADA Kent
ADDISON Lenawee
ADRIAN Lenawee
AFTON Cheboygan
AHMEEK Keweenaw
AKRON Tuscola
ALANSON (49706) Emmet(82), Cheboygan(17)
ALBA Antrim
ALBION Calhoun
ALDEN (49612) Antrim(69), Kalkaska(30)
ALGER (48610) Arenac(34), Ogemaw(33), Gladwin(32)
ALGONAC St. Clair
ALLEGAN Allegan
ALLEN Hillsdale
ALLEN PARK Wayne
ALLENDALE Ottawa
ALLENTON St. Clair
ALLOUEZ Keweenaw
ALMA Gratiot
ALMONT Lapeer
ALPENA (49707) Alpena(97), Presque Isle(2)
ALPHA Iron
ALTO Kent
AMASA Iron
ANCHORVILLE St. Clair
ANN ARBOR Washtenaw
APPLEGATE Sanilac
ARCADIA (49613) Manistee(79), Benzie(20)
ARGYLE Sanilac
ARMADA (48005) Macomb(96), St. Clair(3)
ARNOLD Marquette
ASHLEY Gratiot
ATHENS (49011) Calhoun(96), St. Joseph(1), Branch(1)
ATLANTA Montmorency
ATLANTIC MINE Houghton
ATLAS Genesee
ATTICA Lapeer
AU GRES Arenac
AU TRAIN Alger
AUBURN Bay
AUBURN HILLS Oakland
AUGUSTA Kalamazoo
AVOCA St. Clair
AZALIA Monroe
BAD AXE Huron
BAILEY (49303) Muskegon(86), Newaygo(12)
BALDWIN Lake
BANCROFT Shiawassee
BANGOR Van Buren
BANNISTER (48807) Gratiot(63), Saginaw(34), Clinton(1)
BARAGA Baraga
BARBEAU Chippewa
BARK RIVER (49807) Delta(47), Dickinson(33), Menominee(19)
BARODA Berrien
BARRYTON (49305) Mecosta(93), Isabella(6)

BARTON CITY Alcona
BATH Clinton
BATTLE CREEK Calhoun
BAY CITY Bay
BAY PORT Huron
BAY SHORE Charlevoix
BEAR LAKE Manistee
BEAVER ISLAND Charlevoix
BEAVERTON (48612) Gladwin(96), Clare(2), Midland(1)
BEDFORD Calhoun
BELDING (48809) Ionia(90), Kent(9)
BELLAIRE Antrim
BELLEVILLE Wayne
BELLEVUE (49021) Eaton(63), Barry(27), Calhoun(9)
BELMONT Kent
BENTLEY (48613) Bay(88), Gladwin(9), Arenac(1)
BENTON HARBOR (49022) Berrien(98), Van Buren(1)
BENTON HARBOR Berrien
BENZONIA Benzie
BERGLAND Ontonagon
BERKLEY Oakland
BERRIEN CENTER (49102) Berrien(98), Cass(1)
BERRIEN SPRINGS Berrien
BESSEMER Gogebic
BEULAH Benzie
BIG BAY Marquette
BIG RAPIDS (49307) Mecosta(97), Newaygo(2)
BIRCH RUN (48415) Saginaw(97), Tuscola(1), Genesee(1)
BIRMINGHAM Oakland
BITELY (49309) Newaygo(90), Lake(9)
BLACK RIVER Alcona
BLANCHARD (49310) Isabella(63), Mecosta(33), Montcalm(3)
BLISSFIELD Lenawee
BLOOMFIELD HILLS Oakland
BLOOMINGDALE (49026) Van Buren(89), Allegan(10)
BOON Wexford
BOYNE CITY (49712) Charlevoix(97), Antrim(2)
BOYNE FALLS (49713) Charlevoix(92), Emmet(7)
BRADLEY Allegan
BRANCH (49402) Mason(51), Lake(45), Oceana(3)
BRANT Saginaw
BRECKENRIDGE (48615) Gratiot(73), Midland(26)
BREEDSVILLE Van Buren
BRETHREN Manistee
BRIDGEPORT Saginaw
BRIDGEWATER Washtenaw
BRIDGMAN Berrien
BRIGHTON Livingston
BRIMLEY Chippewa
BRITTON (49229) Lenawee(89), Monroe(8), Washtenaw(1)
BROHMAN Newaygo

BRONSON Branch
BROOKLYN Jackson
BROWN CITY (48416) Sanilac(57), Lapeer(36), St. Clair(5)
BRUCE CROSSING Ontonagon
BRUNSWICK (49313) Muskegon(77), Newaygo(22)
BRUTUS (49716) Emmet(56), Cheboygan(43)
BUCHANAN Berrien
BUCKLEY (49620) Wexford(56), Grand Traverse(43)
BURLINGTON Calhoun
BURNIPS Allegan
BURR OAK (49030) St. Joseph(90), Branch(9)
BURT Saginaw
BURT LAKE Cheboygan
BURTON Genesee
BYRON (48418) Shiawassee(67), Genesee(23), Livingston(9)
BYRON CENTER (49315) Kent(94), Ottawa(3), Allegan(1)
CADILLAC (49601) Wexford(98), Missaukee(1)
CADMUS Lenawee
CALEDONIA (49316) Kent(88), Allegan(8), Barry(3)
CALUMET Houghton
CAMDEN Hillsdale
CANNONSBURG Kent
CANTON Wayne
CAPAC (48014) St. Clair(98), Lapeer(1)
CARLETON Monroe
CARNEY Menominee
CARO Tuscola
CARP LAKE (49718) Emmet(70), Cheboygan(29)
CARROLLTON Saginaw
CARSON CITY (48811) Montcalm(75), Gratiot(24)
CARSONVILLE Sanilac
CASCO St. Clair
CASEVILLE Huron
CASNOVIA (49318) Muskegon(66), Newaygo(22), Kent(10)
CASPIAN Iron
CASS CITY (48726) Tuscola(84), Sanilac(12), Huron(3)
CASSOPOLIS Cass
CEDAR Leelanau
CEDAR LAKE Montcalm
CEDAR RIVER Menominee
CEDAR SPRINGS Kent
CEDARVILLE Mackinac
CEMENT CITY (49233) Lenawee(77), Jackson(22)
CENTER LINE Macomb
CENTRAL LAKE Antrim
CENTREVILLE St. Joseph
CERESCO Calhoun
CHAMPION Marquette
CHANNING Dickinson
CHARLEVOIX (49720) Charlevoix(98), Antrim(1)

CHARLOTTE Eaton
CHASE Lake
CHASSELL Houghton
CHATHAM Alger
CHEBOYGAN Cheboygan
CHELSEA Washtenaw
CHESANING Saginaw
CHIPPEWA LAKE Mecosta
CLARE (48617) Clare(79), Isabella(20)
CLARKLAKE Jackson
CLARKSTON Oakland
CLARKSVILLE (48815) Ionia(97), Kent(2)
CLAWSON Oakland
CLAYTON Lenawee
CLIFFORD (48727) Lapeer(50), Tuscola(49)
CLIMAX Kalamazoo
CLINTON (49236) Lenawee(83), Washtenaw(16)
CLINTON TOWNSHIP Macomb
CLIO (48420) Genesee(97), Tuscola(1)
CLOVERDALE Barry
COHOCTAH Livingston
COLDWATER Branch
COLEMAN (48618) Midland(83), Isabella(13), Gladwin(2)
COLOMA (49038) Berrien(94), Van Buren(5)
COLON (49040) St. Joseph(89), Branch(10)
COLUMBIAVILLE (48421) Lapeer(95), Genesee(4)
COLUMBUS St. Clair
COMINS (48619) Oscoda(78), Montmorency(21)
COMMERCE TOWNSHIP Oakland
COMSTOCK Kalamazoo
COMSTOCK PARK Kent
CONCORD Jackson
CONKLIN (49403) Ottawa(91), Muskegon(4), Kent(3)
CONSTANTINE (49042) St. Joseph(98), Cass(1)
CONWAY Emmet
COOKS (49817) Delta(56), Schoolcraft(43)
COOPERSVILLE (49404) Ottawa(96), Muskegon(3)
COPEMISH (49625) Manistee(92), Wexford(7)
COPPER CITY Houghton
COPPER HARBOR Keweenaw
CORAL Montcalm
CORNELL (49818) Delta(86), Marquette(13)
CORUNNA Shiawassee
COVERT Van Buren
COVINGTON Baraga
CROSS VILLAGE Emmet
CROSWELL Sanilac
CRYSTAL Montcalm
CRYSTAL FALLS Iron
CURRAN (48728) Alcona(87), Oscoda(12)
CURTIS Mackinac
CUSTER Mason
DAFTER Chippewa

DAGGETT Menominee
DANSVILLE Ingham
DAVISBURG Oakland
DAVISON Genesee
DE TOUR VILLAGE Chippewa
DEARBORN Wayne
DEARBORN HEIGHTS Wayne
DECATUR (49045) Van Buren(90), Cass(8)
DECKER (48426) Sanilac(91), Tuscola(8)
DECKERVILLE Sanilac
DEERFIELD Lenawee
DEERTON (49822) Alger(96), Marquette(3)
DEFORD (48729) Tuscola(98), Sanilac(1)
DELTON Barry
DETROIT Wayne
DEWITT Clinton
DEXTER Washtenaw
DIMONDALE (48821) Eaton(95), Ingham(4)
DODGEVILLE Houghton
DOLLAR BAY Houghton
DORR (49323) Allegan(98), Ottawa(1)
DOUGLAS Allegan
DOWAGIAC (49047) Cass(93), Van Buren(6)
DOWLING Barry
DRAYTON PLAINS Oakland
DRUMMOND ISLAND Chippewa
DRYDEN (48428) Lapeer(97), Oakland(2)
DUNDEE Monroe
DURAND (48429) Shiawassee(97), Genesee(2)
EAGLE Clinton
EAGLE RIVER Keweenaw
EAST CHINA St. Clair
EAST JORDAN (49727) Charlevoix(68), Antrim(31)
EAST LANSING (48823) Ingham(84), Clinton(15)
EAST LANSING Ingham
EAST LEROY Calhoun
EAST TAWAS Iosco
EASTLAKE Manistee
EASTPOINTE Macomb
EASTPORT Antrim
EATON RAPIDS (48827) Eaton(93), Ingham(6)
EAU CLAIRE (49111) Berrien(90), Cass(9)
EBEN JUNCTION Alger
ECKERMAN Chippewa
ECORSE Wayne
EDENVILLE Midland
EDMORE (48829) Montcalm(98), Isabella(1)
EDWARDSBURG Cass
ELBERTA Benzie
ELK RAPIDS Antrim
ELKTON Huron
ELLSWORTH (49729) Antrim(88), Charlevoix(11)
ELM HALL Gratiot
ELMIRA (49730) Antrim(70), Otsego(22), Charlevoix(6)
ELSIE (48831) Clinton(58), Shiawassee(20), Saginaw(17), Gratiot(3)
ELWELL Gratiot
EMMETT St. Clair
EMPIRE (49630) Leelanau(98), Benzie(1)
ENGADINE Mackinac
ERIE Monroe
ESCANABA Delta
ESSEXVILLE Bay
EUREKA Clinton
EVART (49631) Osceola(92), Mecosta(7)
EWEN Ontonagon
FAIR HAVEN St. Clair
FAIRGROVE Tuscola
FAIRVIEW Oscoda
FALMOUTH Missaukee
FARMINGTON Oakland
FARWELL (48622) Clare(82), Isabella(17)

FELCH (49831) Dickinson(82), Marquette(17)
FENNVILLE Allegan
FENTON (48430) Genesee(65), Livingston(30), Oakland(4)
FENWICK (48834) Montcalm(64), Ionia(35)
FERNDALE Oakland
FERRYSBURG Ottawa
FIFE LAKE (49633) Kalkaska(60), Grand Traverse(32), Wexford(4), Missaukee(2)
FILER CITY Manistee
FILION Huron
FLAT ROCK Wayne
FLINT Genesee
FLUSHING Genesee
FORESTVILLE Sanilac
FORT GRATIOT St. Clair
FOSTER CITY Dickinson
FOSTORIA (48435) Tuscola(56), Lapeer(43)
FOUNTAIN Mason
FOWLER (48835) Clinton(98), Gratiot(1)
FOWLERVILLE Livingston
FRANKENMUTH (48734) Saginaw(97), Tuscola(2)
FRANKENMUTH Saginaw
FRANKFORT Benzie
FRANKLIN Oakland
FRASER Macomb
FREDERIC (49733) Crawford(78), Otsego(21)
FREE SOIL (49411) Mason(97), Manistee(2)
FREELAND (48623) Saginaw(81), Midland(10), Bay(8)
FREEPORT (49325) Barry(77), Ionia(13), Kent(9)
FREMONT (49412) Newaygo(96), Oceana(2)
FREMONT Newaygo
FRONTIER Hillsdale
FRUITPORT (49415) Muskegon(89), Ottawa(10)
FULTON (49052) Kalamazoo(78), Calhoun(17), St. Joseph(4)
GAASTRA Iron
GAGETOWN (48735) Tuscola(60), Huron(39)
GAINES (48436) Genesee(90), Shiawassee(9)
GALESBURG Kalamazoo
GALIEN Berrien
GARDEN Delta
GARDEN CITY Wayne
GAYLORD Otsego
GENESEE Genesee
GERMFASK (49836) Schoolcraft(57), Mackinac(42)
GILFORD Tuscola
GLADSTONE Delta
GLADWIN (48624) Gladwin(91), Clare(5), Roscommon(1)
GLEN ARBOR Leelanau
GLENN Allegan
GLENNIE (48737) Alcona(91), Iosco(8)
GOBLES (49055) Van Buren(92), Allegan(7)
GOETZVILLE Chippewa
GOOD HART Emmet
GOODELLS St. Clair
GOODRICH (48438) Genesee(81), Lapeer(18)
GOULD CITY Mackinac
GOWEN (49326) Kent(71), Montcalm(28)
GRAND BLANC (48439) Genesee(98), Oakland(1)
GRAND BLANC Genesee
GRAND HAVEN Ottawa
GRAND JUNCTION (49056) Van Buren(75), Allegan(24)
GRAND LEDGE (48837) Eaton(89), Clinton(9)

GRAND MARAIS Alger
GRAND RAPIDS (49544) Kent(72), Ottawa(27)
GRAND RAPIDS Kent
GRANDVILLE (49418) Kent(84), Ottawa(15)
GRANDVILLE Kent
GRANT Newaygo
GRASS LAKE (49240) Jackson(91), Washtenaw(8)
GRAWN Grand Traverse
GRAYLING (49738) Crawford(95), Kalkaska(3)
GRAYLING Crawford
GREENBUSH (48738) Alcona(90), Iosco(9)
GREENLAND Ontonagon
GREENVILLE (48838) Montcalm(89), Kent(10)
GREGORY (48137) Livingston(98), Washtenaw(1)
GROSSE ILE Wayne
GROSSE POINTE Wayne
GULLIVER Schoolcraft
GWINN Marquette
HADLEY Lapeer
HAGAR SHORES Berrien
HALE (48739) Iosco(75), Ogemaw(24)
HAMBURG Livingston
HAMILTON Allegan
HAMTRAMCK Wayne
HANCOCK Houghton
HANOVER Jackson
HARBERT Berrien
HARBOR BEACH Huron
HARBOR SPRINGS Emmet
HARPER WOODS Wayne
HARRIETTA (49638) Wexford(91), Manistee(8)
HARRIS Menominee
HARRISON Clare
HARRISON TOWNSHIP Macomb
HARRISVILLE Alcona
HARSENS ISLAND St. Clair
HART Oceana
HARTFORD Van Buren
HARTLAND Livingston
HASLETT (48840) Ingham(94), Clinton(5)
HASTINGS Barry
HAWKS Presque Isle
HAZEL PARK Oakland
HEMLOCK (48626) Saginaw(95), Midland(4)
HENDERSON (48841) Shiawassee(82), Saginaw(17)
HERMANSVILLE Menominee
HERRON Alpena
HERSEY (49639) Osceola(78), Mecosta(21)
HESPERIA (49421) Oceana(70), Newaygo(29)
HESSEL Mackinac
HICKORY CORNERS (49060) Barry(66), Kalamazoo(33)
HIGGINS LAKE Roscommon
HIGHLAND Oakland
HIGHLAND PARK Wayne
HILLMAN (49746) Montmorency(88), Alpena(11)
HILLSDALE Hillsdale
HOLLAND (49423) Ottawa(66), Allegan(33)
HOLLAND Ottawa
HOLLY (48442) Oakland(93), Genesee(5), Livingston(1)
HOLT Ingham
HOLTON (49425) Muskegon(83), Oceana(10), Newaygo(6)
HOMER Calhoun
HONOR Benzie
HOPE (48628) Midland(82), Gladwin(17)
HOPKINS Allegan
HORTON (49246) Jackson(96), Hillsdale(3)
HOUGHTON Houghton

HOUGHTON LAKE Roscommon
HOUGHTON LAKE HEIGHTS Roscommon
HOWARD CITY (49329) Montcalm(84), Newaygo(15)
HOWELL Livingston
HUBBARD LAKE (49747) Alpena(50), Alcona(49)
HUBBARDSTON (48845) Ionia(59), Clinton(20), Montcalm(14), Gratiot(6)
HUBBELL Houghton
HUDSON (49247) Lenawee(72), Hillsdale(27)
HUDSONVILLE Ottawa
HULBERT Chippewa
HUNTINGTON WOODS Oakland
IDA Monroe
IDLEWILD Lake
IMLAY CITY (48444) Lapeer(97), St. Clair(2)
INDIAN RIVER Cheboygan
INGALLS Menominee
INKSTER Wayne
INTERLOCHEN (49643) Grand Traverse(67), Benzie(32)
IONIA Ionia
IRON MOUNTAIN Dickinson
IRON RIVER Iron
IRONS (49644) Lake(79), Manistee(19)
IRONWOOD Gogebic
ISHPEMING Marquette
ITHACA Gratiot
JACKSON Jackson
JAMESTOWN Ottawa
JASPER Lenawee
JEDDO (48032) St. Clair(81), Sanilac(18)
JENISON Ottawa
JEROME (49249) Hillsdale(95), Jackson(4)
JOHANNESBURG (49751) Otsego(93), Montmorency(6)
JONES Cass
JONESVILLE Hillsdale
KALAMAZOO Kalamazoo
KALEVA Manistee
KALKASKA Kalkaska
KARLIN Grand Traverse
KAWKAWLIN Bay
KEARSARGE Houghton
KEEGO HARBOR Oakland
KENDALL Van Buren
KENT CITY (49330) Kent(91), Newaygo(5), Ottawa(1), Muskegon(1)
KENTON Houghton
KEWADIN Antrim
KINCHELOE Chippewa
KINDE Huron
KINGSFORD Dickinson
KINGSLEY (49649) Grand Traverse(96), Wexford(3)
KINGSTON (48741) Tuscola(93), Sanilac(6)
KINROSS Chippewa
LA SALLE Monroe
LACHINE Alpena
LACOTA Van Buren
LAINGSBURG (48848) Shiawassee(67), Clinton(32)
LAKE (48632) Clare(76), Isabella(22), Osceola(1)
LAKE ANN Benzie
LAKE CITY Missaukee
LAKE GEORGE Clare
LAKE LEELANAU Leelanau
LAKE LINDEN (49945) Houghton(97), Keweenaw(2)
LAKE ODESSA (48849) Ionia(81), Barry(14), Eaton(3)
LAKE ORION Oakland
LAKELAND Livingston
LAKESIDE Berrien
LAKEVIEW (48850) Montcalm(81), Mecosta(18)
LAKEVILLE Oakland

LAMBERTVILLE Monroe
LAMONT Ottawa
LANSE Baraga
LANSING (48917) Eaton(81), Ingham(18)
LANSING (48906) Ingham(60), Clinton(37), Eaton(2)
LANSING (48911) Ingham(87), Eaton(12)
LANSING Eaton
LANSING Ingham
LAPEER Lapeer
LAWRENCE Van Buren
LAWTON Van Buren
LELAND Leelanau
LENNON (48449) Shiawassee(57), Genesee(42)
LEONARD Oakland
LEONIDAS St. Joseph
LEROY (49655) Osceola(93), Lake(6)
LESLIE Ingham
LEVERING (49755) Emmet(64), Cheboygan(35)
LEWISTON (49756) Montmorency(50), Oscoda(47), Otsego(1)
LEXINGTON Sanilac
LINCOLN Alcona
LINCOLN PARK Wayne
LINDEN (48451) Genesee(90), Livingston(9)
LINWOOD Bay
LITCHFIELD (49252) Hillsdale(91), Jackson(3), Branch(2), Calhoun(2)
LITTLE LAKE Marquette
LIVONIA Wayne
LONG LAKE (48743) Iosco(92), Ogemaw(8)
LORETTO Dickinson
LOWELL (49331) Kent(89), Ionia(10)
LUDINGTON Mason
LUNA PIER Monroe
LUPTON Ogemaw
LUTHER Lake
LUZERNE Oscoda
LYONS Ionia
MACATAWA Ottawa
MACKINAC ISLAND Mackinac
MACKINAW CITY (49701) Emmet(63), Cheboygan(36)
MACOMB Macomb
MADISON HEIGHTS Oakland
MANCELONA (49659) Antrim(78), Kalkaska(21)
MANCHESTER Washtenaw
MANISTEE (49660) Manistee(96), Mason(3)
MANISTIQUE (49854) Schoolcraft(98), Delta(1)
MANITOU BEACH Lenawee
MANTON (49663) Wexford(79), Missaukee(20)
MAPLE CITY Leelanau
MAPLE RAPIDS Clinton
MARCELLUS (49067) Cass(63), St. Joseph(24), Van Buren(11)
MARENISCO (49947) Gogebic(66), Ontonagon(33)
MARINE CITY St. Clair
MARION (49665) Osceola(83), Clare(11), Missaukee(4)
MARLETTE (48453) Sanilac(88), Lapeer(7), Tuscola(4)
MARNE (49435) Ottawa(96), Kent(3)
MARQUETTE Marquette
MARSHALL Calhoun
MARTIN Allegan
MARYSVILLE St. Clair
MASON Ingham
MASS CITY Ontonagon
MATTAWAN (49071) Van Buren(83), Kalamazoo(16)
MAYBEE Monroe
MAYFIELD Grand Traverse

MAYVILLE (48744) Tuscola(89), Lapeer(10)
MC BAIN Missaukee
MC MILLAN Luce
MCBRIDES Montcalm
MEARS Oceana
MECOSTA Mecosta
MELVIN Sanilac
MELVINDALE Wayne
MEMPHIS (48041) St. Clair(74), Macomb(25)
MENDON St. Joseph
MENOMINEE Menominee
MERRILL (48637) Saginaw(73), Midland(14), Gratiot(12)
MERRITT Missaukee
MESICK (49668) Wexford(98), Manistee(1)
METAMORA (48455) Lapeer(98), Oakland(1)
MICHIGAMME (49861) Baraga(59), Marquette(40)
MICHIGAN CENTER Jackson
MIDDLETON Gratiot
MIDDLEVILLE (49333) Barry(97), Kent(1)
MIDLAND (48642) Midland(96), Bay(3)
MIDLAND Midland
MIKADO (48745) Alcona(94), Iosco(5)
MILAN (48160) Washtenaw(70), Monroe(29)
MILFORD (48380) Oakland(73), Livingston(26)
MILFORD Oakland
MILLBROOK Mecosta
MILLERSBURG Presque Isle
MILLINGTON (48746) Tuscola(89), Genesee(10)
MINDEN CITY (48456) Sanilac(79), Huron(20)
MIO Oscoda
MOHAWK Keweenaw
MOLINE Allegan
MONTAGUE (49437) Muskegon(84), Oceana(15)
MONTGOMERY (49255) Branch(96), Hillsdale(3)
MONTROSE (48457) Genesee(78), Saginaw(21)
MORAN Mackinac
MORENCI Lenawee
MORLEY (49336) Mecosta(92), Montcalm(7)
MORRICE Shiawassee
MOSCOW Hillsdale
MOSHERVILLE Hillsdale
MOUNT CLEMENS Macomb
MOUNT MORRIS Genesee
MOUNT PLEASANT Isabella
MUIR Ionia
MULLETT LAKE Cheboygan
MULLIKEN (48861) Eaton(89), Ionia(10)
MUNGER (48747) Bay(96), Saginaw(3)
MUNISING Alger
MUNITH Jackson
MUSKEGON Muskegon
NADEAU Menominee
NAHMA Delta
NAPOLEON Jackson
NASHVILLE (49073) Barry(90), Eaton(9)
NATIONAL CITY Iosco
NATIONAL MINE Marquette
NAUBINWAY Mackinac
NAZARETH Kalamazoo
NEGAUNEE Marquette
NEW BALTIMORE Macomb
NEW BOSTON Wayne
NEW BUFFALO Berrien
NEW ERA Oceana
NEW HAVEN Macomb
NEW HUDSON Oakland
NEW LOTHROP (48460) Shiawassee(60), Saginaw(34), Genesee(5)
NEW RICHMOND Allegan

NEW TROY Berrien
NEWAYGO (49337) Newaygo(96), Montcalm(2), Mecosta(1)
NEWBERRY Luce
NEWPORT Monroe
NILES (49120) Berrien(82), Cass(17)
NILES Berrien
NISULA Houghton
NORTH ADAMS Hillsdale
NORTH BRANCH Lapeer
NORTH STAR Gratiot
NORTH STREET St. Clair
NORTHLAND Marquette
NORTHPORT Leelanau
NORTHVILLE (48167) Wayne(61), Oakland(31), Washtenaw(6)
NORVELL Jackson
NORWAY Dickinson
NOTTAWA St. Joseph
NOVI Oakland
NUNICA (49448) Ottawa(86), Muskegon(13)
OAK GROVE Livingston
OAK PARK Oakland
OAKLAND Oakland
OAKLEY (48649) Saginaw(95), Shiawassee(4)
ODEN Emmet
OKEMOS Ingham
OLD MISSION Grand Traverse
OLIVET (49076) Eaton(71), Calhoun(28)
OMENA Leelanau
OMER Arenac
ONAWAY (49765) Presque Isle(66), Cheboygan(33)
ONEKAMA Manistee
ONONDAGA (49264) Ingham(65), Jackson(30), Eaton(4)
ONSTED Lenawee
ONTONAGON Ontonagon
ORLEANS Ionia
ORTONVILLE (48462) Oakland(95), Lapeer(3)
OSCODA Iosco
OSHTEMO Kalamazoo
OSSEO Hillsdale
OSSINEKE Alpena
OTISVILLE (48463) Genesee(98), Lapeer(1)
OTSEGO (49078) Allegan(92), Kalamazoo(5), Van Buren(2)
OTTAWA LAKE (49267) Monroe(83), Lenawee(16)
OTTER LAKE (48464) Lapeer(82), Genesee(9), Tuscola(8)
OVID (48866) Clinton(64), Shiawassee(35)
OWENDALE Huron
OWOSSO Shiawassee
OXFORD (48371) Oakland(94), Lapeer(5)
OXFORD Oakland
PAINESDALE Houghton
PALMER Marquette
PALMS Sanilac
PALMYRA Lenawee
PALO Ionia
PARADISE Chippewa
PARIS (49338) Mecosta(63), Newaygo(29), Osceola(6)
PARMA Jackson
PAW PAW Van Buren
PECK Sanilac
PELKIE (49958) Houghton(80), Baraga(20)
PELLSTON (49769) Emmet(86), Cheboygan(13)
PENTWATER (49449) Oceana(80), Mason(19)
PERKINS Delta
PERRINTON Gratiot
PERRONVILLE (49873) Menominee(87), Dickinson(12)
PERRY (48872) Shiawassee(92), Ingham(6)

PETERSBURG Monroe
PETOSKEY Emmet
PEWAMO (48873) Ionia(72), Clinton(27)
PICKFORD (49774) Chippewa(91), Mackinac(8)
PIERSON Montcalm
PIGEON Huron
PINCKNEY Livingston
PINCONNING (48650) Bay(95), Arenac(4)
PITTSFORD Hillsdale
PLAINWELL (49080) Allegan(69), Barry(20), Kalamazoo(9)
PLEASANT LAKE Jackson
PLEASANT RIDGE Oakland
PLYMOUTH (48170) Wayne(95), Washtenaw(4)
POINTE AUX PINS Mackinac
POMPEII Gratiot
PONTIAC Oakland
PORT AUSTIN Huron
PORT HOPE Huron
PORT HURON St. Clair
PORT SANILAC Sanilac
PORTAGE Kalamazoo
PORTLAND (48875) Ionia(93), Clinton(6)
POSEN (49776) Presque Isle(74), Alpena(25)
POTTERVILLE Eaton
POWERS Menominee
PRATTVILLE Hillsdale
PRESCOTT Ogemaw
PRESQUE ISLE Presque Isle
PRUDENVILLE Roscommon
PULLMAN Allegan
QUINCY (49082) Branch(91), Hillsdale(8)
QUINNESEC Dickinson
RALPH Dickinson
RAMSAY Gogebic
RAPID CITY (49676) Kalkaska(61), Antrim(38)
RAPID RIVER (49878) Delta(91), Alger(8)
RAVENNA (49451) Muskegon(96), Ottawa(3)
RAY Macomb
READING Hillsdale
REDFORD Wayne
REED CITY (49677) Osceola(82), Lake(14), Newaygo(2)
REESE (48757) Tuscola(68), Saginaw(28), Bay(3)
REMUS (49340) Mecosta(66), Isabella(33)
REPUBLIC Marquette
RHODES (48652) Gladwin(58), Bay(26), Midland(15)
RICHLAND Kalamazoo
RICHMOND Macomb
RICHVILLE Tuscola
RIDGEWAY Lenawee
RIGA (49276) Lenawee(70), Monroe(29)
RIVER ROUGE Wayne
RIVERDALE (48877) Gratiot(57), Montcalm(31), Isabella(11)
RIVERSIDE Berrien
RIVES JUNCTION Jackson
ROCHESTER (48306) Oakland(97), Macomb(2)
ROCHESTER Oakland
ROCK (49880) Delta(68), Marquette(31)
ROCKFORD Kent
ROCKLAND Ontonagon
ROCKWOOD Wayne
RODNEY Mecosta
ROGERS CITY Presque Isle
ROLLIN Lenawee
ROMEO Macomb
ROMULUS Wayne
ROSCOMMON (48653) Roscommon(80), Crawford(19)
ROSE CITY (48654) Ogemaw(81), Oscoda(18)
ROSEBUSH Isabella
ROSEVILLE Macomb

ROTHBURY Oceana
ROYAL OAK Oakland
RUDYARD (49780) Chippewa(95), Mackinac(4)
RUMELY Alger
RUTH (48470) Huron(98), Sanilac(1)
SAGINAW Saginaw
SAGOLA Dickinson
SAINT CHARLES Saginaw
SAINT CLAIR St. Clair
SAINT CLAIR SHORES Macomb
SAINT HELEN Roscommon
SAINT IGNACE Mackinac
SAINT JOHNS Clinton
SAINT JOSEPH Berrien
SAINT LOUIS (48880) Gratiot(91), Midland(8)
SALEM Washtenaw
SALINE Washtenaw
SAMARIA Monroe
SAND CREEK Lenawee
SAND LAKE (49343) Kent(60), Newaygo(22), Montcalm(16)
SANDUSKY Sanilac
SANFORD Midland
SARANAC Ionia
SAUGATUCK Allegan
SAULT SAINTE MARIE Chippewa
SAWYER Berrien
SCHOOLCRAFT (49087) Kalamazoo(96), Van Buren(2)
SCOTTS Kalamazoo
SCOTTVILLE Mason
SEARS Osceola
SEBEWAING (48759) Huron(98), Tuscola(1)
SENECA Lenawee
SENEY (49883) Alger(60), Schoolcraft(39)
SHAFTSBURG Shiawassee
SHELBY Oceana
SHELBYVILLE (49344) Barry(51), Allegan(48)
SHEPHERD (48883) Isabella(75), Midland(23), Gratiot(1)
SHERIDAN Montcalm
SHERWOOD Branch
SHINGLETON (49884) Alger(97), Schoolcraft(2)
SIDNAW Houghton
SIDNEY Montcalm
SILVERWOOD (48760) Tuscola(59), Lapeer(40)
SIX LAKES (48886) Montcalm(98), Mecosta(1)

SKANDIA (49885) Marquette(78), Alger(21)
SKANEE Baraga
SMITHS CREEK St. Clair
SMYRNA Ionia
SNOVER Sanilac
SODUS Berrien
SOMERSET Hillsdale
SOMERSET CENTER Hillsdale
SOUTH BOARDMAN Kalkaska
SOUTH BRANCH (48761) Iosco(41), Ogemaw(28), Alcona(27), Oscoda(2)
SOUTH HAVEN (49090) Van Buren(95), Allegan(4)
SOUTH LYON (48178) Oakland(65), Livingston(23), Washtenaw(10)
SOUTH RANGE Houghton
SOUTH ROCKWOOD Monroe
SOUTHFIELD Oakland
SOUTHGATE Wayne
SPALDING Menominee
SPARTA Kent
SPRING ARBOR Jackson
SPRING LAKE (49456) Ottawa(95), Muskegon(4)
SPRINGPORT (49284) Jackson(60), Calhoun(30), Eaton(9)
SPRUCE (48762) Alcona(89), Alpena(10)
STALWART Chippewa
STAMBAUGH Iron
STANDISH (48658) Arenac(95), Bay(4)
STANTON Montcalm
STANWOOD Mecosta
STEPHENSON Menominee
STERLING (48659) Arenac(95), Bay(4)
STERLING HEIGHTS Macomb
STEVENSVILLE Berrien
STOCKBRIDGE (49285) Ingham(87), Jackson(4), Livingston(4), Washtenaw(3)
STRONGS Chippewa
STURGIS St. Joseph
SUMNER (48889) Gratiot(98), Montcalm(1)
SUNFIELD (48890) Eaton(61), Ionia(38)
SUTTONS BAY Leelanau
SWARTZ CREEK Genesee
TAWAS CITY (48763) Iosco(94), Arenac(5)
TAWAS CITY Iosco
TAYLOR Wayne
TECUMSEH Lenawee
TEKONSHA (49092) Calhoun(83), Branch(16)
TEMPERANCE Monroe
THOMPSONVILLE (49683) Benzie(61), Manistee(31), Grand Traverse(6)
THREE OAKS Berrien

THREE RIVERS St. Joseph
TIPTON Lenawee
TOIVOLA (49965) Houghton(94), Ontonagon(5)
TOPINABEE Cheboygan
TOWER Cheboygan
TRAUNIK Alger
TRAVERSE CITY (49684) Grand Traverse(79), Leelanau(20)
TRAVERSE CITY Grand Traverse
TRENARY Alger
TRENTON Wayne
TROUT CREEK (49967) Ontonagon(58), Houghton(34), Iron(7)
TROUT LAKE Chippewa
TROY Oakland
TRUFANT (49347) Montcalm(94), Kent(5)
TURNER (48765) Arenac(65), Iosco(34)
TUSCOLA Tuscola
TUSTIN (49688) Osceola(91), Lake(5), Wexford(2)
TWIN LAKE Muskegon
TWINING (48766) Arenac(96), Iosco(3)
UBLY (48475) Huron(64), Sanilac(35)
UNION Cass
UNION CITY (49094) Branch(97), Calhoun(2)
UNION LAKE Oakland
UNION PIER Berrien
UNIONVILLE (48767) Tuscola(97), Huron(2)
UNIVERSITY CENTER Bay
UTICA Macomb
VANDALIA Cass
VANDERBILT (49795) Otsego(81), Cheboygan(15), Charlevoix(3)
VASSAR Tuscola
VERMONTVILLE Eaton
VERNON Shiawassee
VESTABURG Montcalm
VICKSBURG (49097) Kalamazoo(97), St. Joseph(2)
VULCAN (49892) Dickinson(76), Menominee(23)
WABANINGO Muskegon
WAKEFIELD Gogebic
WALDRON Hillsdale
WALHALLA Mason
WALKERVILLE (49459) Oceana(90), Newaygo(9)
WALLACE Menominee
WALLED LAKE Oakland
WALLOON LAKE Charlevoix
WARREN Macomb

WASHINGTON Macomb
WATERFORD Oakland
WATERS Otsego
WATERSMEET Gogebic
WATERVLIET (49098) Berrien(91), Van Buren(8)
WATTON Baraga
WAYLAND (49348) Allegan(78), Barry(21)
WAYNE Wayne
WEBBERVILLE (48892) Ingham(78), Livingston(21)
WEIDMAN Isabella
WELLS Delta
WELLSTON (49689) Manistee(86), Wexford(13)
WEST BLOOMFIELD Oakland
WEST BRANCH Ogemaw
WEST OLIVE Ottawa
WESTLAND Wayne
WESTON Lenawee
WESTPHALIA Clinton
WETMORE (49895) Alger(65), Delta(29), Schoolcraft(4)
WHEELER (48662) Gratiot(85), Midland(14)
WHITE CLOUD Newaygo
WHITE LAKE Oakland
WHITE PIGEON (49099) St. Joseph(87), Cass(12)
WHITE PINE Ontonagon
WHITEHALL Muskegon
WHITMORE LAKE (48189) Washtenaw(54), Livingston(45)
WHITTAKER Washtenaw
WHITTEMORE (48770) Iosco(96), Ogemaw(2), Arenac(1)
WILLIAMSBURG (49690) Grand Traverse(87), Antrim(7), Kalkaska(5)
WILLIAMSTON Ingham
WILLIS Washtenaw
WILSON Menominee
WINN Isabella
WIXOM Oakland
WOLVERINE Cheboygan
WOODLAND Barry
WYANDOTTE Wayne
WYOMING Kent
YALE (48097) St. Clair(82), Sanilac(17)
YPSILANTI Washtenaw
ZEELAND Ottawa

Michigan ZIP/City Cross Reference

48001-48001	ALGONAC
48002-48002	ALLENTON
48003-48003	ALMONT
48004-48004	ANCHORVILLE
48005-48005	ARMADA
48006-48006	AVOCA
48007-48007	TROY
48009-48012	BIRMINGHAM
48014-48014	CAPAC
48015-48015	CENTER LINE
48017-48017	CLAWSON
48021-48021	EASTPOINTE
48022-48022	EMMETT
48023-48023	FAIR HAVEN
48025-48025	FRANKLIN
48026-48026	FRASER
48027-48027	GOODELLS
48028-48028	HARSENS ISLAND
48030-48030	HAZEL PARK
48032-48032	JEDDO
48034-48034	SOUTHFIELD
48035-48036	CLINTON TOWNSHIP
48037-48037	SOUTHFIELD

48038-48038	CLINTON TOWNSHIP
48039-48039	MARINE CITY
48040-48040	MARYSVILLE
48041-48041	MEMPHIS
48042-48042	MACOMB
48043-48043	MOUNT CLEMENS
48044-48044	MACOMB
48045-48045	HARRISON TOWNSHIP
48046-48046	MOUNT CLEMENS
48047-48047	NEW BALTIMORE
48048-48048	NEW HAVEN
48049-48049	NORTH STREET
48050-48050	NEW HAVEN
48051-48051	NEW BALTIMORE
48052-48052	ALGONAC
48054-48054	EAST CHINA
48059-48059	FORT GRATIOT
48060-48061	PORT HURON
48062-48062	RICHMOND
48063-48063	COLUMBUS
48064-48064	CASCO
48065-48065	ROMEO
48066-48066	ROSEVILLE

48067-48068	ROYAL OAK
48069-48069	PLEASANT RIDGE
48070-48070	HUNTINGTON WOODS
48071-48071	MADISON HEIGHTS
48072-48072	BERKLEY
48073-48073	ROYAL OAK
48074-48074	SMITHS CREEK
48075-48076	SOUTHFIELD
48079-48079	SAINT CLAIR
48080-48082	SAINT CLAIR SHORES
48083-48085	TROY
48086-48086	SOUTHFIELD
48088-48093	WARREN
48094-48095	WASHINGTON
48096-48096	RAY
48097-48097	YALE
48098-48099	TROY
48101-48102	ALLEN PARK
48103-48109	ANN ARBOR
48110-48110	AZALIA
48111-48112	BELLEVILLE
48113-48113	ANN ARBOR
48114-48114	BRIGHTON

48115-48115	BRIDGEWATER
48116-48116	BRIGHTON
48117-48117	CARLETON
48118-48118	CHELSEA
48120-48121	DEARBORN
48122-48122	MELVINDALE
48123-48124	DEARBORN
48125-48125	DEARBORN HEIGHTS
48126-48126	DEARBORN
48127-48127	DEARBORN HEIGHTS
48128-48128	DEARBORN
48130-48130	DEXTER
48131-48131	DUNDEE
48133-48133	ERIE
48134-48134	FLAT ROCK
48135-48136	GARDEN CITY
48137-48137	GREGORY
48138-48138	GROSSE ILE
48139-48139	HAMBURG
48140-48140	IDA
48141-48141	INKSTER
48143-48143	LAKELAND
48144-48144	LAMBERTVILLE

48145-48145	LA SALLE
48146-48146	LINCOLN PARK
48150-48154	LIVONIA
48157-48157	LUNA PIER
48158-48158	MANCHESTER
48159-48159	MAYBEE
48160-48160	MILAN
48161-48162	MONROE
48164-48164	NEW BOSTON
48165-48165	NEW HUDSON
48166-48166	NEWPORT
48167-48168	NORTHVILLE
48169-48169	PINCKNEY
48170-48170	PLYMOUTH
48173-48173	ROCKWOOD
48174-48174	ROMULUS
48175-48175	SALEM
48176-48176	SALINE
48177-48177	SAMARIA
48178-48178	SOUTH LYON
48179-48179	SOUTH ROCKWOOD
48180-48180	TAYLOR
48182-48182	TEMPERANCE
48183-48183	TRENTON
48184-48184	WAYNE
48185-48186	WESTLAND
48187-48188	CANTON
48189-48189	WHITMORE LAKE
48190-48190	WHITTAKER
48191-48191	WILLIS
48192-48193	WYANDOTTE
48195-48195	SOUTHGATE
48197-48198	YPSILANTI
48200-48202	DETROIT
48203-48203	HIGHLAND PARK
48204-48211	DETROIT
48212-48212	HAMTRAMCK
48213-48217	DETROIT
48218-48218	RIVER ROUGE
48219-48219	DETROIT
48220-48220	FERNDALE
48221-48224	DETROIT
48225-48225	HARPER WOODS
48226-48228	DETROIT
48229-48229	ECORSE
48230-48230	GROSSE POINTE
48231-48235	DETROIT
48236-48236	GROSSE POINTE
48237-48237	OAK PARK
48238-48238	DETROIT
48239-48240	REDFORD
48242-48299	DETROIT
48301-48304	BLOOMFIELD HILLS
48306-48309	ROCHESTER
48310-48314	STERLING HEIGHTS
48315-48318	UTICA
48320-48320	KEEGO HARBOR
48321-48321	AUBURN HILLS
48322-48325	WEST BLOOMFIELD
48326-48326	AUBURN HILLS
48327-48329	WATERFORD
48330-48330	DRAYTON PLAINS
48331-48336	FARMINGTON
48340-48343	PONTIAC
48346-48348	CLARKSTON
48350-48350	DAVISBURG
48353-48353	HARTLAND
48356-48357	HIGHLAND
48359-48362	LAKE ORION
48363-48363	OAKLAND
48366-48366	LAKEVILLE
48367-48367	LEONARD
48370-48371	OXFORD
48374-48377	NOVI
48380-48381	MILFORD
48382-48382	COMMERCE TOWNSHIP
48383-48386	WHITE LAKE
48387-48387	UNION LAKE
48390-48391	WALLED LAKE
48393-48393	WIXOM
48397-48397	WARREN
48398-48398	CLAWSON
48401-48401	APPLEGATE
48410-48410	ARGYLE
48411-48411	ATLAS
48412-48412	ATTICA
48413-48413	BAD AXE
48414-48414	BANCROFT
48415-48415	BIRCH RUN
48416-48416	BROWN CITY
48417-48417	BURT
48418-48418	BYRON
48419-48419	CARSONVILLE
48420-48420	CLIO
48421-48421	COLUMBIAVILLE
48422-48422	CROSWELL
48423-48423	DAVISON
48426-48426	DECKER
48427-48427	DECKERVILLE
48428-48428	DRYDEN
48429-48429	DURAND
48430-48430	FENTON
48432-48432	FILION
48433-48433	FLUSHING
48434-48434	FORESTVILLE
48435-48435	FOSTORIA
48436-48436	GAINES
48437-48437	GENESEE
48438-48438	GOODRICH
48439-48439	GRAND BLANC
48440-48440	HADLEY
48441-48441	HARBOR BEACH
48442-48442	HOLLY
48444-48444	IMLAY CITY
48445-48445	KINDE
48446-48446	LAPEER
48449-48449	LENNON
48450-48450	LEXINGTON
48451-48451	LINDEN
48452-48452	ATTICA
48453-48453	MARLETTE
48454-48454	MELVIN
48455-48455	METAMORA
48456-48456	MINDEN CITY
48457-48457	MONTROSE
48458-48458	MOUNT MORRIS
48460-48460	NEW LOTHROP
48461-48461	NORTH BRANCH
48462-48462	ORTONVILLE
48463-48463	OTISVILLE
48464-48464	OTTER LAKE
48465-48465	PALMS
48466-48466	PECK
48467-48467	PORT AUSTIN
48468-48468	PORT HOPE
48469-48469	PORT SANILAC
48470-48470	RUTH
48471-48471	SANDUSKY
48472-48472	SNOVER
48473-48473	SWARTZ CREEK
48475-48475	UBLY
48476-48476	VERNON
48480-48480	GRAND BLANC
48500-48507	FLINT
48509-48529	BURTON
48531-48559	FLINT
48601-48609	SAGINAW
48610-48610	ALGER
48611-48611	AUBURN
48612-48612	BEAVERTON
48613-48613	BENTLEY
48614-48614	BRANT
48615-48615	BRECKENRIDGE
48616-48616	CHESANING
48617-48617	CLARE
48618-48618	COLEMAN
48619-48619	COMINS
48620-48620	EDENVILLE
48621-48621	FAIRVIEW
48622-48622	FARWELL
48623-48623	FREELAND
48624-48624	GLADWIN
48625-48625	HARRISON
48626-48626	HEMLOCK
48627-48627	HIGGINS LAKE
48628-48628	HOPE
48629-48629	HOUGHTON LAKE
48630-48630	HOUGHTON LAKE HEIGHTS
48631-48631	KAWKAWLIN
48632-48632	LAKE
48633-48633	LAKE GEORGE
48634-48634	LINWOOD
48635-48635	LUPTON
48636-48636	LUZERNE
48637-48637	MERRILL
48638-48638	SAGINAW
48640-48642	MIDLAND
48647-48647	MIO
48649-48649	OAKLEY
48650-48650	PINCONNING
48651-48651	PRUDENVILLE
48652-48652	RHODES
48653-48653	ROSCOMMON
48654-48654	ROSE CITY
48655-48655	SAINT CHARLES
48656-48656	SAINT HELEN
48657-48657	SANFORD
48658-48658	STANDISH
48659-48659	STERLING
48661-48661	WEST BRANCH
48662-48662	WHEELER
48663-48663	SAGINAW
48667-48686	MIDLAND
48701-48701	AKRON
48703-48703	AU GRES
48705-48705	BARTON CITY
48706-48707	BAY CITY
48710-48710	UNIVERSITY CENTER
48720-48720	BAY PORT
48721-48721	BLACK RIVER
48722-48722	BRIDGEPORT
48723-48723	CARO
48724-48724	CARROLLTON
48725-48725	CASEVILLE
48726-48726	CASS CITY
48727-48727	CLIFFORD
48728-48728	CURRAN
48729-48729	DEFORD
48730-48730	EAST TAWAS
48731-48731	ELKTON
48732-48732	ESSEXVILLE
48733-48733	FAIRGROVE
48734-48734	FRANKENMUTH
48735-48735	GAGETOWN
48736-48736	GILFORD
48737-48737	GLENNIE
48738-48738	GREENBUSH
48739-48739	HALE
48740-48740	HARRISVILLE
48741-48741	KINGSTON
48742-48742	LINCOLN
48743-48743	LONG LAKE
48744-48744	MAYVILLE
48745-48745	MIKADO
48746-48746	MILLINGTON
48747-48747	MUNGER
48748-48748	NATIONAL CITY
48749-48749	OMER
48750-48753	OSCODA
48754-48754	OWENDALE
48755-48755	PIGEON
48756-48756	PRESCOTT
48757-48757	REESE
48758-48758	RICHVILLE
48759-48759	SEBEWAING
48760-48760	SILVERWOOD
48761-48761	SOUTH BRANCH
48762-48762	SPRUCE
48763-48764	TAWAS CITY
48765-48765	TURNER
48766-48766	TWINING
48767-48767	UNIONVILLE
48768-48768	VASSAR
48769-48769	TUSCOLA
48770-48770	WHITTEMORE
48787-48787	FRANKENMUTH
48801-48802	ALMA
48804-48804	MOUNT PLEASANT
48805-48805	OKEMOS
48806-48806	ASHLEY
48807-48807	BANNISTER
48808-48808	BATH
48809-48809	BELDING
48811-48811	CARSON CITY
48812-48812	CEDAR LAKE
48813-48813	CHARLOTTE
48815-48815	CLARKSVILLE
48816-48816	COHOCTAH
48817-48817	CORUNNA
48818-48818	CRYSTAL
48819-48819	DANSVILLE
48820-48820	DEWITT
48821-48821	DIMONDALE
48822-48822	EAGLE
48823-48826	EAST LANSING
48827-48827	EATON RAPIDS
48829-48829	EDMORE
48830-48830	ELM HALL
48831-48831	ELSIE
48832-48832	ELWELL
48833-48833	EUREKA
48834-48834	FENWICK
48835-48835	FOWLER
48836-48836	FOWLERVILLE
48837-48837	GRAND LEDGE
48838-48838	GREENVILLE
48840-48840	HASLETT
48841-48841	HENDERSON
48842-48842	HOLT
48843-48844	HOWELL
48845-48845	HUBBARDSTON
48846-48846	IONIA
48847-48847	ITHACA
48848-48848	LAINGSBURG
48849-48849	LAKE ODESSA
48850-48850	LAKEVIEW
48851-48851	LYONS
48852-48852	MCBRIDES
48853-48853	MAPLE RAPIDS
48854-48854	MASON
48855-48855	HOWELL
48856-48856	MIDDLETON
48857-48857	MORRICE
48858-48859	MOUNT PLEASANT
48860-48860	MUIR
48861-48861	MULLIKEN
48862-48862	NORTH STAR
48863-48863	OAK GROVE
48864-48864	OKEMOS
48865-48865	ORLEANS
48866-48866	OVID
48867-48867	OWOSSO
48870-48870	PALO
48871-48871	PERRINTON
48872-48872	PERRY
48873-48873	PEWAMO
48874-48874	POMPEII
48875-48875	PORTLAND
48876-48876	POTTERVILLE
48877-48877	RIVERDALE
48878-48878	ROSEBUSH
48879-48879	SAINT JOHNS
48880-48880	SAINT LOUIS
48881-48881	SARANAC
48882-48882	SHAFTSBURG
48883-48883	SHEPHERD
48884-48884	SHERIDAN
48885-48885	SIDNEY
48886-48886	SIX LAKES
48887-48887	SMYRNA
48888-48888	STANTON
48889-48889	SUMNER
48890-48890	SUNFIELD
48891-48891	VESTABURG
48892-48892	WEBBERVILLE
48893-48893	WEIDMAN
48894-48894	WESTPHALIA
48895-48895	WILLIAMSTON

48896-48896 WINN
48897-48897 WOODLAND
48900-48980 LANSING
49001-49001 KALAMAZOO
49002-49002 PORTAGE
49003-49009 KALAMAZOO
49010-49010 ALLEGAN
49011-49011 ATHENS
49012-49012 AUGUSTA
49013-49013 BANGOR
49014-49018 BATTLE CREEK
49019-49019 KALAMAZOO
49020-49020 BEDFORD
49021-49021 BELLEVUE
49022-49023 BENTON HARBOR
49024-49024 PORTAGE
49026-49026 BLOOMINGDALE
49027-49027 BREEDSVILLE
49028-49028 BRONSON
49029-49029 BURLINGTON
49030-49030 BURR OAK
49031-49031 CASSOPOLIS
49032-49032 CENTREVILLE
49033-49033 CERESCO
49034-49034 CLIMAX
49035-49035 CLOVERDALE
49036-49036 COLDWATER
49038-49038 COLOMA
49039-49039 HAGAR SHORES
49040-49040 COLON
49041-49041 COMSTOCK
49042-49042 CONSTANTINE
49043-49043 COVERT
49045-49045 DECATUR
49046-49046 DELTON
49047-49047 DOWAGIAC
49048-49048 KALAMAZOO
49050-49050 DOWLING
49051-49051 EAST LEROY
49052-49052 FULTON
49053-49053 GALESBURG
49055-49055 GOBLES
49056-49056 GRAND JUNCTION
49057-49057 HARTFORD
49058-49058 HASTINGS
49060-49060 HICKORY CORNERS
49061-49061 JONES
49062-49062 KENDALL
49063-49063 LACOTA
49064-49064 LAWRENCE
49065-49065 LAWTON
49066-49066 LEONIDAS
49067-49067 MARCELLUS
49068-49069 MARSHALL
49070-49070 MARTIN
49071-49071 MATTAWAN
49072-49072 MENDON
49073-49073 NASHVILLE
49074-49074 NAZARETH
49075-49075 NOTTAWA
49076-49076 OLIVET
49077-49077 OSHTEMO
49078-49078 OTSEGO
49079-49079 PAW PAW
49080-49080 PLAINWELL
49081-49081 PORTAGE
49082-49082 QUINCY
49083-49083 RICHLAND
49084-49084 RIVERSIDE
49085-49085 SAINT JOSEPH
49087-49087 SCHOOLCRAFT
49088-49088 SCOTTS
49089-49089 SHERWOOD
49090-49090 SOUTH HAVEN
49091-49091 STURGIS
49092-49092 TEKONSHA
49093-49093 THREE RIVERS
49094-49094 UNION CITY
49095-49095 VANDALIA
49096-49096 VERMONTVILLE
49097-49097 VICKSBURG
49098-49098 WATERVLIET

49099-49099 WHITE PIGEON
49101-49101 BARODA
49102-49102 BERRIEN CENTER
49103-49104 BERRIEN SPRINGS
49106-49106 BRIDGMAN
49107-49107 BUCHANAN
49111-49111 EAU CLAIRE
49112-49112 EDWARDSBURG
49113-49113 GALIEN
49115-49115 HARBERT
49116-49116 LAKESIDE
49117-49117 NEW BUFFALO
49119-49119 NEW TROY
49120-49121 NILES
49125-49125 SAWYER
49126-49126 SODUS
49127-49127 STEVENSVILLE
49128-49128 THREE OAKS
49129-49129 UNION PIER
49130-49130 UNION
49201-49204 JACKSON
49220-49220 ADDISON
49221-49221 ADRIAN
49224-49224 ALBION
49227-49227 ALLEN
49228-49228 BLISSFIELD
49229-49229 BRITTON
49230-49230 BROOKLYN
49231-49231 CADMUS
49232-49232 CAMDEN
49233-49233 CEMENT CITY
49234-49234 CLARKLAKE
49235-49235 CLAYTON
49236-49236 CLINTON
49237-49237 CONCORD
49238-49238 DEERFIELD
49239-49239 FRONTIER
49240-49240 GRASS LAKE
49241-49241 HANOVER
49242-49242 HILLSDALE
49245-49245 HOMER
49246-49246 HORTON
49247-49247 HUDSON
49248-49248 JASPER
49249-49249 JEROME
49250-49250 JONESVILLE
49251-49251 LESLIE
49252-49252 LITCHFIELD
49253-49253 MANITOU BEACH
49254-49254 MICHIGAN CENTER
49255-49255 MONTGOMERY
49256-49256 MORENCI
49257-49257 MOSCOW
49258-49258 MOSHERVILLE
49259-49259 MUNITH
49261-49261 NAPOLEON
49262-49262 NORTH ADAMS
49263-49263 NORVELL
49264-49264 ONONDAGA
49265-49265 ONSTED
49266-49266 OSSEO
49267-49267 OTTAWA LAKE
49268-49268 PALMYRA
49269-49269 PARMA
49270-49270 PETERSBURG
49271-49271 PITTSFORD
49272-49272 PLEASANT LAKE
49273-49273 PRATTVILLE
49274-49274 READING
49275-49275 RIDGEWAY
49276-49276 RIGA
49277-49277 RIVES JUNCTION
49278-49278 ROLLIN
49279-49279 SAND CREEK
49280-49280 SENECA
49281-49281 SOMERSET
49282-49282 SOMERSET CENTER
49283-49283 SPRING ARBOR
49284-49284 SPRINGPORT
49285-49285 STOCKBRIDGE
49286-49286 TECUMSEH
49287-49287 TIPTON

49288-49288 WALDRON
49289-49289 WESTON
49301-49301 ADA
49302-49302 ALTO
49303-49303 BAILEY
49304-49304 BALDWIN
49305-49305 BARRYTON
49306-49306 BELMONT
49307-49307 BIG RAPIDS
49309-49309 BITELY
49310-49310 BLANCHARD
49311-49311 BRADLEY
49312-49312 BROHMAN
49313-49313 BRUNSWICK
49314-49314 BURNIPS
49315-49315 BYRON CENTER
49316-49316 CALEDONIA
49317-49317 CANNONSBURG
49318-49318 CASNOVIA
49319-49319 CEDAR SPRINGS
49320-49320 CHIPPEWA LAKE
49321-49321 COMSTOCK PARK
49322-49322 CORAL
49323-49323 DORR
49325-49325 FREEPORT
49326-49326 GOWEN
49327-49327 GRANT
49328-49328 HOPKINS
49329-49329 HOWARD CITY
49330-49330 KENT CITY
49331-49331 LOWELL
49332-49332 MECOSTA
49333-49333 MIDDLEVILLE
49334-49334 MILLBROOK
49335-49335 MOLINE
49336-49336 MORLEY
49337-49337 NEWAYGO
49338-49338 PARIS
49339-49339 PIERSON
49340-49340 REMUS
49341-49341 ROCKFORD
49342-49342 RODNEY
49343-49343 SAND LAKE
49344-49344 SHELBYVILLE
49345-49345 SPARTA
49346-49346 STANWOOD
49347-49347 TRUFANT
49348-49348 WAYLAND
49349-49349 WHITE CLOUD
49351-49351 ROCKFORD
49355-49357 ADA
49401-49401 ALLENDALE
49402-49402 BRANCH
49403-49403 CONKLIN
49404-49404 COOPERSVILLE
49405-49405 CUSTER
49406-49406 DOUGLAS
49408-49408 FENNVILLE
49409-49409 FERRYSBURG
49410-49410 FOUNTAIN
49411-49411 FREE SOIL
49412-49413 FREMONT
49415-49415 FRUITPORT
49416-49416 GLENN
49417-49417 GRAND HAVEN
49418-49418 GRANDVILLE
49419-49419 HAMILTON
49420-49420 HART
49421-49421 HESPERIA
49422-49424 HOLLAND
49425-49425 HOLTON
49426-49426 HUDSONVILLE
49427-49427 JAMESTOWN
49428-49429 JENISON
49430-49430 LAMONT
49431-49431 LUDINGTON
49434-49434 MACATAWA
49435-49435 MARNE
49436-49436 MEARS
49437-49437 MONTAGUE
49440-49445 MUSKEGON
49446-49446 NEW ERA

49447-49447 NEW RICHMOND
49448-49448 NUNICA
49449-49449 PENTWATER
49450-49450 PULLMAN
49451-49451 RAVENNA
49452-49452 ROTHBURY
49453-49453 SAUGATUCK
49454-49454 SCOTTVILLE
49455-49455 SHELBY
49456-49456 SPRING LAKE
49457-49457 TWIN LAKE
49458-49458 WALHALLA
49459-49459 WALKERVILLE
49460-49460 WEST OLIVE
49461-49461 WHITEHALL
49463-49463 WABANINGO
49464-49464 ZEELAND
49468-49468 GRANDVILLE
49500-49518 GRAND RAPIDS
49519-49519 WYOMING
49523-49599 GRAND RAPIDS
49601-49601 CADILLAC
49610-49610 ACME
49611-49611 ALBA
49612-49612 ALDEN
49613-49613 ARCADIA
49614-49614 BEAR LAKE
49615-49615 BELLAIRE
49616-49616 BENZONIA
49617-49617 BEULAH
49618-49618 BOON
49619-49619 BRETHREN
49620-49620 BUCKLEY
49621-49621 CEDAR
49622-49622 CENTRAL LAKE
49623-49623 CHASE
49625-49625 COPEMISH
49626-49626 EASTLAKE
49627-49627 EASTPORT
49628-49628 ELBERTA
49629-49629 ELK RAPIDS
49630-49630 EMPIRE
49631-49631 EVART
49632-49632 FALMOUTH
49633-49633 FIFE LAKE
49634-49634 FILER CITY
49635-49635 FRANKFORT
49636-49636 GLEN ARBOR
49637-49637 GRAWN
49638-49638 HARRIETTA
49639-49639 HERSEY
49640-49640 HONOR
49642-49642 IDLEWILD
49643-49643 INTERLOCHEN
49644-49644 IRONS
49645-49645 KALEVA
49646-49646 KALKASKA
49647-49647 KARLIN
49648-49648 KEWADIN
49649-49649 KINGSLEY
49650-49650 LAKE ANN
49651-49651 LAKE CITY
49653-49653 LAKE LEELANAU
49654-49654 LELAND
49655-49655 LEROY
49656-49656 LUTHER
49657-49657 MC BAIN
49659-49659 MANCELONA
49660-49660 MANISTEE
49663-49663 MANTON
49664-49664 MAPLE CITY
49665-49665 MARION
49666-49666 MAYFIELD
49667-49667 MERRITT
49668-49668 MESICK
49670-49670 NORTHPORT
49673-49673 OLD MISSION
49674-49674 OMENA
49675-49675 ONEKAMA
49676-49676 RAPID CITY
49677-49677 REED CITY
49679-49679 SEARS

49680-49680 SOUTH BOARDMAN	49689-49689 WELLSTON	49706-49706 ALANSON	49712-49712 BOYNE CITY
49682-49682 SUTTONS BAY	49690-49690 WILLIAMSBURG	49707-49707 ALPENA	49713-49713 BOYNE FALLS
49683-49683 THOMPSONVILLE	49696-49696 TRAVERSE CITY	49709-49709 ATLANTA	49715-49715 BRIMLEY
49684-49686 TRAVERSE CITY	49701-49701 MACKINAW CITY	49710-49710 BARBEAU	49716-49716 BRUTUS
49688-49688 TUSTIN	49705-49705 AFTON	49711-49711 BAY SHORE	49717-49717
BURT LAKE	49777-49777 PRESQUE ISLE	49840-49840 GULLIVER	49908-49908 BARAGA
49718-49718 CARP LAKE	49778-49778 BRIMLEY	49841-49843 GWINN	49909-49909 IRON RIVER
49719-49719 CEDARVILLE	49779-49779 ROGERS CITY	49845-49845 HARRIS	49910-49910 BERGLAND
49720-49720 CHARLEVOIX	49780-49780 RUDYARD	49847-49847 HERMANSVILLE	49911-49911 BESSEMER
49721-49721 CHEBOYGAN	49781-49781 SAINT IGNACE	49848-49848 INGALLS	49912-49912 BRUCE CROSSING
49722-49722 CONWAY	49782-49782 BEAVER ISLAND	49849-49849 ISHPEMING	49913-49913 CALUMET
49723-49723 CROSS VILLAGE	49783-49783 SAULT SAINTE MARIE	49852-49852 LORETTO	49915-49915 CASPIAN
49724-49724 DAFTER	49784-49788 KINCHELOE	49853-49853 MC MILLAN	49916-49916 CHASSELL
49725-49725 DE TOUR VILLAGE	49789-49789 STALWART	49854-49854 MANISTIQUE	49917-49917 COPPER CITY
49726-49726 DRUMMOND ISLAND	49790-49790 STRONGS	49855-49855 MARQUETTE	49918-49918 COPPER HARBOR
49727-49727 EAST JORDAN	49791-49791 TOPINABEE	49858-49858 MENOMINEE	49919-49919 COVINGTON
49728-49728 ECKERMAN	49792-49792 TOWER	49861-49861 MICHIGAMME	49920-49920 CRYSTAL FALLS
49729-49729 ELLSWORTH	49793-49793 TROUT LAKE	49862-49862 MUNISING	49921-49921 DODGEVILLE
49730-49730 ELMIRA	49795-49795 VANDERBILT	49863-49863 NADEAU	49922-49922 DOLLAR BAY
49733-49733 FREDERIC	49796-49796 WALLOON LAKE	49864-49864 NAHMA	49924-49924 EAGLE RIVER
49734-49735 GAYLORD	49797-49797 WATERS	49865-49865 NATIONAL MINE	49925-49925 EWEN
49736-49736 GOETZVILLE	49799-49799 WOLVERINE	49866-49866 NEGAUNEE	49927-49927 GAASTRA
49737-49737 GOOD HART	49801-49801 IRON MOUNTAIN	49868-49868 NEWBERRY	49929-49929 GREENLAND
49738-49739 GRAYLING	49802-49802 KINGSFORD	49869-49869 NORTHLAND	49930-49930 HANCOCK
49740-49740 HARBOR SPRINGS	49805-49805 ALLOUEZ	49870-49870 NORWAY	49931-49931 HOUGHTON
49743-49743 HAWKS	49806-49806 AU TRAIN	49871-49871 PALMER	49934-49934 HUBBELL
49744-49744 HERRON	49807-49807 BARK RIVER	49872-49872 PERKINS	49935-49935 IRON RIVER
49745-49745 HESSEL	49808-49808 BIG BAY	49873-49873 PERRONVILLE	49938-49938 IRONWOOD
49746-49746 HILLMAN	49812-49812 CARNEY	49874-49874 POWERS	49942-49942 KEARSARGE
49747-49747 HUBBARD LAKE	49813-49813 CEDAR RIVER	49876-49876 QUINNESEC	49943-49943 KENTON
49748-49748 HULBERT	49814-49814 CHAMPION	49877-49877 RALPH	49945-49945 LAKE LINDEN
49749-49749 INDIAN RIVER	49815-49815 CHANNING	49878-49878 RAPID RIVER	49946-49946 LANSE
49751-49751 JOHANNESBURG	49816-49816 CHATHAM	49879-49879 REPUBLIC	49947-49947 MARENISCO
49752-49752 KINROSS	49817-49817 COOKS	49880-49880 ROCK	49948-49948 MASS CITY
49753-49753 LACHINE	49818-49818 CORNELL	49881-49881 SAGOLA	49950-49950 MOHAWK
49755-49755 LEVERING	49819-49819 ARNOLD	49883-49883 SENEY	49952-49952 NISULA
49756-49756 LEWISTON	49820-49820 CURTIS	49884-49884 SHINGLETON	49953-49953 ONTONAGON
49757-49757 MACKINAC ISLAND	49821-49821 DAGGETT	49885-49885 SKANDIA	49955-49955 PAINESDALE
49759-49759 MILLERSBURG	49822-49822 DEERTON	49886-49886 SPALDING	49958-49958 PELKIE
49760-49760 MORAN	49825-49825 EBEN JUNCTION	49887-49887 STEPHENSON	49959-49959 RAMSAY
49761-49761 MULLETT LAKE	49826-49826 RUMELY	49890-49890 TRAUNIK	49960-49960 ROCKLAND
49762-49762 NAUBINWAY	49827-49827 ENGADINE	49891-49891 TRENARY	49961-49961 SIDNAW
49764-49764 ODEN	49829-49829 ESCANABA	49892-49892 VULCAN	49962-49962 SKANEE
49765-49765 ONAWAY	49831-49831 FELCH	49893-49893 WALLACE	49963-49963 SOUTH RANGE
49766-49766 OSSINEKE	49833-49833 LITTLE LAKE	49894-49894 WELLS	49964-49964 STAMBAUGH
49768-49768 PARADISE	49834-49834 FOSTER CITY	49895-49895 WETMORE	49965-49965 TOIVOLA
49769-49769 PELLSTON	49835-49835 GARDEN	49896-49896 WILSON	49967-49967 TROUT CREEK
49770-49770 PETOSKEY	49836-49836 GERMFASK	49901-49901 AHMEEK	49968-49968 WAKEFIELD
49774-49774 PICKFORD	49837-49837 GLADSTONE	49902-49902 ALPHA	49969-49969 WATERSMEET
49775-49775 POINTE AUX PINS	49838-49838 GOULD CITY	49903-49903 AMASA	49970-49970 WATTON
49776-49776 POSEN	49839-49839 GRAND MARAIS	49905-49905 ATLANTIC MINE	49971-49971 WHITE PINE

Explanation of Symbols

State Capital
Vernon County Seat

Population Key

0-999
1,000-2,499
2,500-4,999
5,000-9,999
10,000-19,000
20,000-24,999
25,000-49,999
50,000-99,999
100,000-249,999
250,000-999,999
1,000,000+

County-Town
MICHIGAN

CITIES AND TOWNS

Note: The first name is that of the city or town, second, that of the county in which it is located, then the population and location on the map.

Explanation of symbols: • – Census Designated Place (CDP)

Minnesota

General Help Numbers:

Governor's Office
130 State Capitol Bldg, 75 Constitution Ave 651-296-3391
St Paul, MN 55155   Fax 651-296-2089
www.governor.state.mn.us   7:30AM-5PM

Attorney General's Office
1400 Bremer Tower   651-296-3353
445 Minnesota St   Fax 651-297-4193
St Paul, MN 55101   8AM-5PM
www.ag.state.mn.us

Legislative Records
Minnesota Legislature, State Capitol
House-Room 211, Senate-Room 231   651-296-2887
St Paul, MN 55155   Fax 651-651-296-1563
www.leg.state.mn.us   8AM-5PM

State Archives
Division of Library & Archives   651-296-1906
345 Kellogg Blvd West   Fax 651-297-9961
St Paul, MN 55102-1906   9AM-5PM M-SA;
www.mnhs.org   till 9PM TU

State Specifics:

Capital:	St. Paul
	Ramsey County
Time Zone:	CST
Number of Counties:	87
Population:	5,100,958
Web Site:	www.state.mn.us

State Agencies

Criminal Records

Bureau of Criminal Apprehension, Criminal Justice Information Systems, 1430 Maryland Ave E, St Paul, MN 55106; 651-793-2400, 651-793-2401-Fax; 8:15AM-4PM.

www.bca.state.mn.us

Records are available from 1924. It takes 1 day before new records are available for inquiry. Records are indexed on inhouse computer, microfilm and digital disc. Records are normally destroyed after subject reaches 100 years of age or death. 72% of all arrests in database have final dispositions recorded, 63% for those arrests within last 5 years.

Searching: For most requesters, to obtain the entire adult history, including all arrests, you must have a notarized release form signed by person of record. To get a 15-year record of convictions only, a consent form is not required. Include the following in your request-name, date of birth, and sex. Fingerprint searches are not permitted. However, 100% of records are fingerprint-supported. The following data is not released: juvenile records. With consent, all records, including those without dispositions, are released. If no consent then only conviction records released. Targeted misdemeanors (violent, DV, DUI, etc, where a jail sentence may be imposed) are released; other misdemeanors are if received.

Access by: mail, in person, online.

Fee & Payment: The fee for the full adult history is $15.00, for non-profits the fee is $8.00. The fee for the 15-year public record is $4.00. Non-profits have a reduced fee, call first. Fee payee: BCA. Prepayment required. Business checks, personal checks, money orders and certified funds are accepted. Credit cards accepted only for online access.

Mail search: Turnaround time: 1 to 2 weeks. A SASE is requested.

In person search: Using a public access terminal, a copy of a public record is available for $4.00 per name. For the full adult history the turnaround time is 2 days, unless you are the person of record, then it is immediate.

Online search: Acess to the public criminal history system is available from the web. The fee is $5.00 per name searched, use of a credit card is required.

Other access: A public database is available on CD-ROM. Monthly updates can be purchased. Data is in ASCII format and is raw data. Fee is $40.00

Statewide Court Records

State Court Administrator, 135 Minnesota Judicial Center, 25 Rev ML King Blvd, St Paul, MN 55155; 651-296-2474, 651-297-5636-Fax; 8AM-4:30PM.

www.courts.state.mn.us/home

Except for certain online research capabilities, all court record access must be done at the local level.

Access by: online.

Online search: Appellate and Supreme Court opinions are available from the website. There is an online system in place that allows internal and external access for government personnel only.

Sexual Offender Registry

Bureau of Criminal Apprehension, Minnesota Predatory Offender Program, 1430 Maryland Ave E, St Paul, MN 55106; 651-793-7070, 888-234-1248 , 651-793-7071-Fax; 8AM-4:30PM.

www.dps.state.mn.us/bca

This is not a notification state. The state does not permit public access to this information beyond the Level 3 names found on the web page. This means local law enforcement offices cannot give the public access to all names.

It takes 48 hours before new records are available for inquiry.

Access by: online.

Fee & Payment: There is no fee.

Online search: Level 3 offenders may be searched at www.doc.state.mn.us/level3/Search.asp. Also, you can bring up lists by city, county, or ZIP Code.

Incarceration Records

Minnesota Department of Corrections, Records Management Unit, 450 Energy Park Drive, Suite 200, St. Paul, MN 55108; 651-642-0200, 651-643-3588-Fax; 8AM-5PM.

www.corr.state.mn.us

The main fax number for the DOC is 651-642-0223.

Records are available on current and former inmates; however, the online search is limited to those either still in prison or under probation. It

takes about 7 days before new records are available for inquiry. Records are normally destroyed after ninety-nine years.

Searching: Records are computerized since 1978. Include the following in your request-name and DOB. Location, OID number, physical identifiers, conviction and sentencing information, and release dates are provided.

Access by: mail, phone, fax, online.

Fee & Payment: There is a $10.00 retrieval fee and a copy fee of $.25 per page. Personal checks accepted.

Mail search: Turnaround time: 2-4 days.

Phone search: Searching is available via telephone.

Fax search: Fax requires full name and DOB.

Online search: Search at the web to retrieve public information about adult offenders who have been committed to the Commissioner of Corrections, and who are still under our jurisdiction (i.e. in prison, or released from prison and still under supervision). Search by name, with or without DOB, or by OID number. Also, there is a separate search for Level 3 offender/predatory information. Also, a private company offers free web access at www.vinelink.com/index.jsp, including state, DOC, and most county jail systems.

Corporation, Limited Liability Company Assumed Name, Trademarks/Servicemarks, Limited Partnerships

Business Records Services, Secretary of State, 180 State Office Bldg, 100 Martin Luther King Blvd, St Paul, MN 55155-1299; 651-296-2803 (Information), 651-297-7067-Fax; 8AM-4:30PM.

www.sos.state.mn.us

Records are also held for non-profits.

Records are available from 1850's on. All records are indexed together. It takes one day before new records are available for inquiry. Records are indexed on computer and microfilm.

Searching: Part II of foreign corporation annual reports are not released. Include the following in your request-full name of business, corporation file number. In addition to articles of incorporation, corporation records include the following information: Annual Reports, Prior (merged) names, Inactive and Reserved names.

Access by: mail, phone, in person, online.

Fee & Payment: Copies of most documents are $3.00 per page, $6.00 if original document plus amendments requested. Add $5.00 for certification. Fee payee: Secretary of State. Prepayment required. Personal checks accepted. No credit cards accepted.

Mail search: Turnaround time: 10 business days. No SASE is required.

Phone search: Phone hours are 9AM to 4PM. Limited verification information is given over the phone.

In person search: The counter closes at 3PM. There is no fee to view the database or microfilm. However, if you walk-in and wish copies immediately, there is an additional $20.00 fee.

Online search: The Internet site permits free look-ups of "business" names. Also, a commercial program called Direct Access is available 24 hours. There is an annual subscription fee of $75.00. Record copies or certificates may be ordered for an additional fee. Visit www.online.sos.state.mn.us/ for more information.

Other access: Information can be purchased in bulk format. Call for more information.

Expedited service: Add $20.00 per transaction. Turnaround time: immediate.

Uniform Commercial Code, Federal and State Tax Liens

UCC Division, Secretary of State, 60 Empire Dr, St Paul, MN 55103; 651-296-2803, 651-215-1009-Fax; 8AM-4:30PM.

www.sos.state.mn.us

Records are available from 1966 on computer. Tax liens are on microfilm. Records are indexed on inhouse computer. Records are normally destroyed after imaging completed.

Searching: Use search request form UCC-11 for UCC filings. Use a separate UCC-12 request form to obtain federal and state tax liens on businesses. All tax liens on individuals are filed at the county level. Include the following in your request-debtor name, type of debtor, organization or individual.

Access by: mail, fax, in person, online.

Fee & Payment: Search fee is $20.00 per name. The search fee includes all copies. Fee payee: Secretary of State. Prepayment required. Personal checks accepted.

Mail search: Turnaround time: 2 days.

Fax search: Same criteria as mail searches.

In person search: A free public access terminal is available. In person service is usually one hour or less, no need for expedited fees.

Online search: There is a free look-up by filing number available from the website. A comprehensive commercial program called Direct Access is available 24 hours. There is an annual subscription fee of $75.00 per year, plus $5.00 per debtor name. Call 651-296-2803 for more information.

Other access: This agency will provide information in bulk form on paper, CD or disk. Call 651-296-2803 or 877-551-6767 for more information.

Sales Tax Registrations

Minnesota Revenue Dept, Sale and Use Tax, 600 N Robert Street MS:6330, St Paul, MN 55146-6330; 651-282-5225, 651-556-3124-Fax; 9AM-4PM.

www.taxes.state.mn.us

Records are available from 1967 on computer. It takes 3 days before new records are available for inquiry.

Searching: This agency will only confirm that a business is registered, business name, tax number, and date permit was issued. They can't provide any other information. Include the following in your request-business name and MN business identification number.

Access by: mail, phone, fax, in person, online.

Fee & Payment: There is no fee. No credit cards accepted.

Mail search: Turnaround time: 7 days. No SASE is required.

Phone search: Record information will be given over the phone within 3 minutes.

Fax search: Fax searching available.

In person search: In many instances, walk-in requesters must come back the next day for results.

Online search: Email requests are accepted at sales.use@state.mn.us@state.mn.us.

Birth Certificates

Minnesota Department of Health, Vital Records, PO Box 9441, Minneapolis, MN 55440-9441 (Courier address: 717 Delaware St SE, Minneapolis, MN 55414); 612-676-5120, 612-331-5776-Fax; 8AM-4:30PM.

www.health.state.mn.us

For information pertaining to adoption records, call 612-676-5129. If other questions, email osr1@health.state.mn.us.

Records are available from 1900 on. Prior records must be obtained from the county level. It takes 3 months before new records are available for inquiry. Records are indexed on microfiche, inhouse computer, depending on years.

Searching: Only those with a "tangible interest" may request a certified record. Anyone may order a non-certified record. Births to unmarried parents require a notarized from parent or child if 16 years or older. Include the following in your request-full name, date of birth, place of birth, names of parents, mother's maiden name. Also, requester's signature must be notarized.

Access by: mail, fax, in person.

Fee & Payment: Fees are $10.00 for a non-certified copy, $13.00 for a certified copy and $7.00 for an additional certified copy of the same name. Fee payee: Minnesota Department of Health. Prepayment required. Credit cards may be used for fax requesters. Personal checks accepted. Major credit cards accepted.

Mail search: Turnaround time: 3 to 6 weeks. No SASE is required.

Fax search: See expedited services.

In person search: Since MDH no longer handles in-person requests, you must go to a local registrar office to obtain a birth or death certificate or non-certified copy of a birth or death record in person. One may go to a registrar's office in any county in Minnesota for births that took place during or after 1900.

Other access: Bulk lists and files of information, if public record, are available on paper and in electronic format. Call Linda Salkowicz at 612-676-5120 for details.

Expedited service: Fax search requests are considered expedited. Turnaround time: 4 weeks. Add $7.00 to go to front of line, add $6.00 for use of credit card and $16.00 for overnight delivery.

Death Records

Minnesota Department of Health, Section of Vital Records, PO Box 9441, Minneapolis, MN 55440-9441 (Courier address: 717 Delaware St SE, Minneapolis, MN 55414); 612-676-5120, 612-331-5776-Fax; 8AM-4:30PM.

www.health.state.mn.us

If questions, email osr1@health.state.mn.us.

Records are available from 1908 on. Prior records must be obtained at the county level. It takes 3 months before new records are available for inquiry.

Searching: Only those with a "tangible interest" may request a certified record. Those without such interest made receive non-certified. Include the following in your request-full name, date of death, place of death. Also, requester's signature must be notarized. If date or place not known, include last year known to be alive.

Access by: mail, fax, in person, online.

Fee & Payment: The search fees are $13.00 for a certified record or $1.00 for a non-certified, and $5.00 for additional identical copy of same name. Fee payee: Minnesota Department of Health. Prepayment required. Credit cards may be used for ordering by fax only. Personal checks accepted. Major credit cards accepted.

Mail search: Turnaround time: 3 to 6 weeks. No SASE is required.

Fax search: See expedited services.

In person search: Since MDH no longer handles in-person requests, you must go to a local registrar office to obtain a birth or death certificate or non-certified copy of a birth or death record in person. One may go to a registrar's office in any county in Minnesota for deaths that took place during or after 1997.

Online search: No official online access available however the State Historical Society offers a free Death Certificate Search at http://people.mnhs.org/dci/Search.cfm. Records are from 1906 to 1996.

Other access: The State Health agency offers bulk lists and files of information, if public record, are available on paper and in electronic format. Call Linda Salkowicz at 612-676-5120 for details.

Expedited service: Expedited service is available for fax searches. Turnaround time: 4 weeks. Add $7.00 to go to front of line, add $6.00 for use of credit card and $16.00 for overnight delivery.

Marriage Certificates, Divorce Records

Records not maintained by a state level agency.

Marriage and divorce records are found at the county level. The Section of Vital Records has an index and they will direct you to the proper county (Marriage since 1958, Divorce since 1970). Call the Section of Vital Records at 612-676-5120.

Workers' Compensation Records

Labor & Industry Department, Workers Compensation Division - File Review, 443 Lafayette Rd, St Paul, MN 55155; 651-284-5435, 651-284-5731-Fax; 8AM-4:30PM.

www.doli.state.mn.us/workcomp.html

Records are available on microfilm or image and paper for 18 years after file closure. New records are available for inquiry immediately. Records are indexed on microfilm, microfiche, inhouse computer. Records are normally destroyed after 18 years old or more.

Searching: Must have a signed release from claimant to obtain all files. Include the following in your request-claimant name, Social Security Number. Include any and all dates of injury in your authorized request.

Access by: mail, phone, fax, in person.

Fee & Payment: There is no search fee. Copies are $.65 each. Add 6.5% tax and postage. Fee payee: Department of Labor & Industry. Prepayment required. Personal checks accepted. No credit cards accepted.

Mail search: Turnaround time: 2 to 4 weeks. No SASE is required.

Phone search: Phone searching is limited to employees involved within a case.

Fax search: This office will accept fax search requests.

In person search: If you request in person, they will mail requested copies.

Driver Records

Driver & Vehicle Services, Records Section, 445 Minnesota St, #161, St Paul, MN 55101; 651-215-1335, 8AM-4:30PM.

www.mndriveinfo.org

Copies of tickets can be requested from the same address. The fee is $4.00 per record, $5.00 if certified.

Records are available for 5 years minimum for moving violations and suspensions; 10 years for open revocation; retained indefinitely for DWIs for 2 or more convictions. Accidents and up to 10 mph over in a 55 zone on interstate roads are not shown. It takes no more than 15 days before new records are available for inquiry.

Searching: A casual requester can only receive a record without personal information, unless the consent of the driver is given. The driver's license number or full name and DOB is required for a search. Surrendered licenses will be purged after one year if clear; after five years if the record has convictions. The following data is not released: medical information.

Access by: mail, in person, online.

Fee & Payment: The fee is $4.50 per non-certified record or $4.00 if requester is obtaining own record. Add $1.00 for certification. Fee payee: Department of Public Safety. Prepayment required. Personal checks accepted. No credit cards accepted.

Mail search: Turnaround time: 1 week or more. No SASE is required.

In person search: Up to 3 requests will be processed for walk-in requesters, the rest are available the next day.

Online search: Online access costs $2.50 per record. Online inquiries can be processed either as interactive or as batch files (overnight) 24 hours a day, 7 days a week. Requesters operate from a "bank." Records are accessed by either DL number or full name and DOB. Call Data Services at 651-297-5352 for more information. Also, at www.mndriveinfo.org one may view a Status Report of a driver; the DL# is needed.

Other access: Minnesota will sell its entire database of driving record information with monthly updates. Customized request sorts are available. Fees vary by type with programming and computer time and are quite reasonable.

Vehicle Ownership
Vehicle Identification

Driver & Vehicle Services, Vehicle Record Requests, 445 Minnesota St, #161, St Paul, MN 55101; 651-215-1335, 8AM-4:30PM.

www.dps.state.mn.us/dvs/index.html

Their "Record Request Form" can be downloaded from the website.

Records are available for past 7 years. It takes 5 days before new records are available for inquiry.

Searching: The agency adopted the 14 permissible uses of DPPA. Casual requesters can obtain records without personal information. If consent is given, then personal information is released.

Access by: mail, in person, online.

Fee & Payment: The fee is $4.50 per "display record" (print screen), and for a copy of a $1.50 for a vehicle title document or vehicle registration document. Certification is an additional $1.00. Fee payee: Department of Public Safety. Prepayment required. Personal checks accepted. No credit cards accepted.

Mail search: Turnaround time: 1 week. A SASE is requested.

In person search: Turnaround time is immediate for walk-in requesters.

Online search: Online access costs $2.50 per record. There is an additional monthly charge for dial-in access. The system is the same as described for driving record requests. It is open 24 hours a day, 7 days a week. Lien holder information is included. Users, who must qualify per DPPA, will receive address information. Call Data Services 651-297-5352 for more information.

Accident Reports

Driver & Vehicle Services, Accident Records, 445 Minnesota St, Suite 161, St Paul, MN 55101-5181; 651-296-2060, 651-282-2360-Fax; 8AM-4:30PM.

www.mndriveinfo.org

Records are available from 1994 to 1997 on microfilm, and from 1998 to present records are electronically imaged. It takes 3 weeks from date of accident before new records are available for inquiry. Records are normally destroyed after 10 years.

Searching: Police reports may be obtained with the written and signed authorization from the person involved in the accident. Include the following in your request-date of accident, full name, date of birth, driver's license number, license plate number. Records are indexed by driver names.

Access by: mail, fax, in person.

Fee & Payment: The fee is $4.00 per police report. Fee payee: DVS. Prepayment required.

Personal checks accepted. No credit cards accepted.

Mail search: Turnaround time: 1 week. A SASE is requested.

Fax search: Fax requests require an account with the agency. Turnaround time 3 days if the request is received after the file has become available.

In person search: Walk-in requesters may obtain copies of accident reports with the authorization of the individual(s) involved in the accident. Turnaround time: while you wait (typically, 5 to 10 minutes).

Vessel Ownership
Vessel Registration

Department of Natural Resources, License Bureau, 500 Lafayette Rd, St Paul, MN 55155-4026; 651-296-2316, 800-285-2000 , 651-297-8851-Fax; 8AM-4:30PM.

www.dnr.state.mn.us

Lien information shows on title records obtained at this agency.

Records are available for the last 15 yrs. Records maintained for watercraft, snowmobiles, off-highway vehicles (all terrain) and off-highway motorcycles. A watercraft must be titled if over 16 ft and 1980 model or newer; registered if over 9 ft. It takes 1 month before new records are available for inquiry.

Searching: The name and hull number or registration number is required to complete a search.

Access by: mail, phone, fax, in person.

Fee & Payment: There is no search fee.

Mail search: Turnaround time: 1 week.

Phone search: Up to 2 names may be searched over the phone.

Fax search: Same criteria as mail searching.

In person search: Turnaround time is usually immediate.

Other access: Bulk requests are offered in several media types. Call 651-297-8023 for more information.

Voter Registration

Access to Records is Restricted.

Secretary of State-Election Division, 180 State Office Bldg, 100 Dr Martin L King Blvd, St Paul, MN 55155; 651-215-1440, 877-600-8683 , 651-296-9073-Fax; 8AM-4:30PM.

www.sos.state.mn.us/home/index.asp?page=4

Records are sold by the state only for political, election, or law enforcement purposes and only to MN registered voters. Some counties will honor record requests.

GED Certificates

Department of Education, GED Testing, 1500 Highway 36 West, Roseville, MN 55113-4266; 651-582-8446, 651-582-8445 (Instructions), 651-582-8458-Fax; 8AM-4:30PM.

http://education.state.mn.us/html/intro_adult_ged.htm

It takes 3 weeks before new records are available for inquiry.

Searching: Include the following in your request-name when test taken, DOB, last four digits of SSN, and signed release. The year of the test is helpful. A signed release is needed for a either a copy of a transcript or a verification.

Access by: mail, fax.

Fee & Payment: There is no fee.

Mail search: Turnaround time: 1 to 2 days. No SASE is required.

Fax search: Same criteria as mail searching.

Hunting and Fishing License Information

ELS Licensing, DNR License Bureau, 500 Lafayette Rd, St Paul, MN 55155-4026; 651-297-1230, 888-646-6367 , 651-297-8851-Fax; 8AM-4:30PM.

www.dnr.state.mn.us

Records are available on computer for 4 years for doe, turkey; Spring permits for moose; for bear and turkey Fall permits, as well as other hunting and fishing licenses. It takes 30 days before new records are available for inquiry.

Searching: Records are open to public; all information is released. Include the following in your request-full name, date of birth. The driver's license is also helpful.

Access by: mail, phone, fax, in person.

Fee & Payment: There is no search fee. Fee payee: DNR. Prepayment required. Personal checks accepted. No credit cards accepted.

Mail search: Turnaround time: 1 to 3 days. No SASE is required.

Phone search: They will confirm information over the phone.

Fax search: They will confirm information, turnaround time is 1 week.

In person search: Simple requests are processed, time permitting.

Other access: They have mailing lists available for purchase. Call 651-296-0930 for details.

Minnesota State Licensing Agencies

For details about the agency responsible for licensing/certifying/registering an item below or in the Agency Quick Finder section, match an item's number with the number of the agency in the *Licensing Agency Information* section.

Minnesota Licenses Searchable Online

Abstractor #23	https://www.egov.state.mn.us/Commerce/license_lookup.do?action=lookupForm
Acupuncturist #9	www.docboard.org/mn/df/mndf.htm
Adjuster #23	https://www.egov.state.mn.us/Commerce/license_lookup.do?action=lookupForm
Alarm & Com. System Contr./Installer #6	www.electricity.state.mn.us/Elec_lic/index.html
Alcohol/Drug Counselor #29	www.health.state.mn.us/divs/hpsc/hop/adc/index.html
Ambulance Service/Personnel #28	www.emsrb.state.mn.us/cert.asp?p=s
Appraiser #23	https://www.egov.state.mn.us/Commerce/license_lookup.do?action=lookupForm
Architect #37	www.aelslagid.state.mn.us/roster.html
Athletic Trainer #9	www.docboard.org/mn/df/mndf.htm
Attorney #40	www.courts.state.mn.us/mars/default.aspx
Attorney Specialist #31	http://mail.statebar.gen.mn.us/search/search.asp
Auditor #39	www.boa.state.mn.us/Licensees/LicenseeList.aspx
Bingo Operation #35	www.gcb.state.mn.us/
Campground Membership Agent #23	https://www.egov.state.mn.us/Commerce/license_lookup.do?action=lookupForm
Chiropractor #4	https://www.hlb.state.mn.us/chi/publicaccess/search.asp
Collection Agency #23	https://www.egov.state.mn.us/Commerce/license_lookup.do?action=lookupForm
Consumer Credit/Payday Lender #24	www.state.mn.us/ebranch/commerce/pages/FinService/FSLicensees/sl.html
Contract'r/Remodeler, Residential #23	https://www.egov.state.mn.us/Commerce/license_lookup.do?action=lookupForm
Cosmetologist #23	https://www.egov.state.mn.us/Commerce/license_lookup.do?action=lookupForm
Cosmetology School/Shop #23	https://www.egov.state.mn.us/Commerce/license_lookup.do?action=lookupForm
CPA Firm #39	www.boa.state.mn.us/Licensees/FirmList.aspx
Credit Union #24	www.state.mn.us/ebranch/commerce/pages/FinService/FSLicensees/cu.html
Crematory #27	www.health.state.mn.us/divs/hpsc/mortsci/mortsciselect.cfm
Currency Exchange #23	https://www.egov.state.mn.us/Commerce/license_lookup.do?action=lookupForm
Debt Collector #23	https://www.egov.state.mn.us/Commerce/license_lookup.do?action=lookupForm
Debt Prorate Company #24	www.state.mn.us/ebranch/commerce/pages/FinService/FSLicensees/dp.html
Dental Assistant #5	https://www.hlb.state.mn.us/mnbod/glsuiteweb/homeframe.aspx
Dental Hygienist #5	https://www.hlb.state.mn.us/mnbod/glsuiteweb/homeframe.aspx
Dentist #5	https://www.hlb.state.mn.us/mnbod/glsuiteweb/homeframe.aspx
Electrician #6	www.electricity.state.mn.us/Elec_lic/index.html
Emergency Medical Technician #28	www.emsrb.state.mn.us/cert.asp?p=s
EMS Examiner #28	www.emsrb.state.mn.us/examiner.asp?p=s
Engineer #37	www.aelslagid.state.mn.us/roster.html
Esthetician #23	https://www.egov.state.mn.us/Commerce/license_lookup.do?action=lookupForm
Funeral Director #27	www.health.state.mn.us/divs/hpsc/mortsci/mortsciselect.cfm
Funeral Establishment #27	www.health.state.mn.us/divs/hpsc/mortsci/mortsciselect.cfm
Gambling Equipment Dist./Mfg. #35	www.gcb.state.mn.us/
Gambling, Lawful Organization #35	www.gcb.state.mn.us/
Geologist #37	www.aelslagid.state.mn.us/roster.html
Grain Licensing #21	http://www2.mda.state.mn.us/webapp/lis/default.jsp
Insurance Agency #23	https://www.egov.state.mn.us/Commerce/license_lookup.do?action=lookupForm
Insurance Agent/Salesman #23	https://www.egov.state.mn.us/Commerce/license_lookup.do?action=lookupForm
Interior Designer #37	www.aelslagid.state.mn.us/roster.html
Landscape Architect #37	www.aelslagid.state.mn.us/roster.html
Lender, Small #24	www.state.mn.us/ebranch/commerce/pages/FinService/FSLicensees/sl.html
Liquor On-sale Retail #34	www.dps.state.mn.us/alcgamb/alcenf/liquorlic/liquorlic.html
Liquor Store, On-sale Retail/Muni'l #34	www.dps.state.mn.us/alcgamb/alcenf/liquorlic/liquorlic.html
Livestock Dealer/Market #21	http://www2.mda.state.mn.us/webapp/lis/default.jsp
Livestock Weigher #21	http://www2.mda.state.mn.us/webapp/lis/default.jsp
Loan Company #24	www.state.mn.us/ebranch/commerce/pages/FinService/FSLicensees/rl.html
Lobbyist #19	www.cfboard.state.mn.us/Lobby.htm
LPA #39	www.boa.state.mn.us/Licensees/LicenseeList.aspx
Managing General Agent #23	https://www.egov.state.mn.us/Commerce/license_lookup.do?action=lookupForm

Manicurist #23	https://www.egov.state.mn.us/Commerce/license_lookup.do?action=lookupForm
Medical Doctor #9	www.docboard.org/mn/df/mndf.htm
Midwife #9	www.docboard.org/mn/df/mndf.htm
Money Transmitter #24	www.commerce.state.mn.us/pages/FinService/FSLicensees/MoneyTransmitList.pdf
Mortgage Originator/Servicer, Resid'l #24	https://www.egov.state.mn.us/Commerce/license_lookup.do?action=lookupForm
Mortician #27	www.health.state.mn.us/divs/hpsc/mortsci/mortsciselect.cfm
Motor Vehicle Financer #24	www.state.mn.us/ebranch/commerce/pages/FinService/FSLicensees/mv.html
Notary Public #23	https://www.egov.state.mn.us/Commerce/license_lookup.do?action=lookupForm
Nurse-LPN #10	www.nursingboard.state.mn.us
Nurse-RN #10	www.nursingboard.state.mn.us
Occupational Therapist/Assistant #29	www.health.state.mn.us/divs/hpsc/hop/otp/licprac.html
Optometrist #11	www.optometryboard.state.mn.us/Default.aspx?tabid=799
Pesticide Applicator Company #22	http://www2.mda.state.mn.us/webapp/lis/pestappdefault.jsp
Pesticide Applicator, Private #22	http://www2.mda.state.mn.us/webapp/PrivApp/default.jsp
Physical Therapist #9	www.docboard.org/mn/df/mndf.htm
Physician Assistant #9	www.docboard.org/mn/df/mndf.htm
Political Action Committee #19	www.cfboard.state.mn.us/campfin/pcfatoz.html
Political Candidate #19	www.cfboard.state.mn.us/cand_lists.html
Professional Firm #9	www.docboard.org/mn/df/mndf.htm
Public Accountant Firm #39	www.boa.state.mn.us/Licensees/FirmList.aspx
Public Accountant-CPA #39	www.boa.state.mn.us/Licensees/LicenseeList.aspx
Real Estate Agent/Broker/Dealer #23	https://www.egov.state.mn.us/Commerce/license_lookup.do?action=lookupForm
Re-Insurance Intermediary #23	https://www.egov.state.mn.us/Commerce/license_lookup.do?action=lookupForm
Respiratory Care Practitioner #9	www.docboard.org/mn/df/mndf.htm
Soil Scientist #37	www.aelslagid.state.mn.us/roster.html
Surgeon #9	www.docboard.org/mn/df/mndf.htm
Surveyor, Land #37	www.aelslagid.state.mn.us/roster.html
Teacher #17	(search site being reconstructed)
Telemedicine #9	www.docboard.org/mn/df/mndf.htm
Thrift/Industrial Loan Company #24	www.state.mn.us/ebranch/commerce/pages/FinService/FSLicensees/il.html
Underg'd Storage Tank Contr./Spvr. #43	www.pca.state.mn.us/cleanup/ust.html#certification
Weather Modifier #21	http://www2.mda.state.mn.us/webapp/lis/default.jsp

Minnesota Licensing Quick Finder

Abstractor #23	651-296-6319
Abstractor/Abstractor Company #25	800-657-3978
Acupuncturist #9	612-617-2130
Adjuster #23	651-296-6319
Adoption/Guardianship Agency #30	651-296-0584
Alarm & Com. System Contr./Install #6	651-642-0800
Alcohol/Drug Counselor #29	651-282-5619
All-Terrain Vehicle Registration #32	651-296-2316
Ambulance Service/Personnel #28	612-627-6000
Applicant Backgr'nd Study&Invest#30	651-296-3971
Appraiser #23	651-296-6319
Architect #37	651-297-2208
Asbestos Abatement Contr/Worker #26	651-215-0900
Assessor, Accredited #1	651-296-0209
Assessor/Assessor Specialist #1	651-296-0209
Athletic Trainer #9	612-617-2130
Attorney #40	651-296-2254
Attorney Specialist #31	651-297-1857
Audiologist #29	651-282-5629
Auditor #39	651-296-7937
Bank #24	651-297-3779
Barber #2	651-642-0489
Bingo Operation #35	651-639-4000
Boat & Canoe Registration #32	651-296-2316
Boat Title #32	651-296-2316
Boats for Hire #36	651-284-5080
Boiler Inspector #36	651-284-5080
Bondsman (Insurance) #23	651-296-6319
Building Contractor, Residential #23	651-296-6319
Campground Membership Agent #23	651-296-6319
Chemical Dependency Profess'l #30	651-582-1832
Child Care Facility #30	651-296-3971
Children's Service #30	651-297-3840
Chiropractor #4	612-617-2222
Collection Agency #23	651-296-6319
Consumer Credit/Payday Lender #24	651-296-2297
Contract'r/Remodeler, Residential #23	651-296-6319
Controlled substance #13	612-617-2201
Cosmetologist #23	651-296-6319
Cosmetology School/Shop #23	651-296-6319
County Fair #41	952-496-7950
Credit Union #24	651-296-2297
Crematory #27	651-282-3829
Currency Exchange #23	651-296-6319
Debt Collector #23	651-296-6319
Debt Prorate Company #24	651-296-2297
Dental Assistant #5	888-240-4762, 612-617-2250
Dental Hygienist #5	888-240-4762, 612-617-2250
Dentist #5	888-240-4762, 612-617-2250
Developmental Disabilities License#30	651-582-1998
Dietitian #33	612-617-2175
Electrician #6	651-642-0800
Emergency Medical Technician #28	612-627-6000
EMS Examiner #28	612-627-6000
Engineer #37	651-296-2388
Esthetician #23	651-296-6319
Food Manager #26	651-215-0870
Foster Care Program #30	651-296-3971
Funeral Director #27	651-282-3829
Funeral Establishment #27	651-282-3829
Gambling Equipment Dist./Mfg. #35	651-639-4000
Gambling, Lawful Organization #35	651-639-4000
Geologist #37	651-296-2388
Grain Licensing #21	651-296-2980
Hearing Aid Dispenser #29	651-282-5620
High Pressure Inspector #36	651-284-5080
Insurance Agency #23	651-296-6319
Insurance Agent/Salesman #23	651-296-6319
Interior Designer #37	651-296-2388
Landscape Architect #37	651-296-2388
Lender, Small #24	651-296-2297
Liquor and Wine Offsale Retail #34	651-296-9519
Liquor Consumption & Display Info #34	651-296-6439
Liquor On-sale Retail #34	651-296-6939
Liquor Store-Retail/Municipal #34	651-215-6209
Liquor Whlse/Mfg./Labeler/Import'r #34	651-296-6939
Livestock Dealer/Market/Weigher #21	651-296-2292
Loan Company #24	651-296-2297
Lobbyist #19	651-296-5148
Lottery Retailer #42	651-635-8119
LPA #39	651-296-7937
Managing General Agent #23	651-296-6319
Manicurist #23	800-657-3978
Manufactured Home Installer #38	651-296-4639
Manufactured Home Mfg./Dealer #38	651-296-4639
Manufactured Structures Section #38	651-296-4639
Marriage & Family Therapist #8	612-617-2220
Med Gas Dist #13	612-617-2201
Medical Doctor #9	612-617-2130
Medical Professional Firm #9	612-617-2130
Mental Health Practitioner, Unlicensed #29	651-282-5621
Mental Health, Chemical Dependency Professional #30	651-582-1990
Midwife #9	612-617-2130
Money Transmitter #24	651-296-2297
Mortgage Originator/Servicer, Residential #24	651-282-9855
Mortician #27	651-282-3829

Motor Vehicle Financer #24	651-296-2297
Notary Public #23	651-296-6319
Nurse-LPN #10	612-617-2270
Nurse-RN #10	612-617-2270
Nursing Home Administrator #7	612-617-2117
Nutritionist #33	612-617-2175
Occupational Therapist/Assistant #29	651-282-5624
Off-Highway Motorcycle #32	651-296-2316
Off-Road Vehicle #32	651-296-2316
Optometrist #11	612-617-2173
Pesticide Applicator Company #22	651-297-2200
Pesticide Applicator, Private #22	651-297-2200
Pharmaceutical Mfg./Whlse #13	612-617-2201
Pharmaceutical Technician #13	612-617-2201
Pharmacist #13	612-617-2201
Pharmacy #13	612-617-2201
Physical Therapist #9	612-627-5406
Physician Assistant #9	612-617-2130
Plumber #26	651-215-0836

Podiatrist #14	612-617-2200
Police (Peace) Officer #12	651-643-3060
Political Candidate #19	651-296-5148
Private Detective #44	651-793-2666
Private Investigator #44	651-793-2666
Psychological Practitioner #15	651-617-2230
Psychologist #15	651-617-2230
Public Accountant-CPA #39	651-296-7937
Racetrack/Card Club Operator #41	952-496-7950
Racing (Class "A"Track Owners)#41	952-496-7950
Racing/Card Club Occupation #41	952-496-7950
Real Estate Agent/Broker/Dealer #23	651-296-6319
Re-Insurance Intermediary #23	651-296-6319
Respiratory Care Practitioner #9	612-617-2130
Sanitarian #26	651-215-0870
Securities Sales/Invest. Advisor #23	651-296-2283
Security Agent/Protective Agent #44	651-793-2666
Snowmobile Registration #32	651-296-2316
Social Worker #16	612-617-2100

Soil Scientist #37	651-296-2388
Speech-Language Pathologist #29	651-282-5629
Surgeon #9	612-617-2130
Surveyor, Land #37	651-296-2388
Teacher #17	651-582-8691
Telemedicine #9	612-617-2130
Thrift/Industrial Loan Company #24	651-296-2297
Underground Storage Tank Contr./Supervisor #43	651-297-8616
Veterinarian #18	612-617-2170
Waste Disposal Facility Inspector #43	651-296-6300
Waste Water Disposal Facility Op #43	651-296-6300
Water Conditioning Installer/Cont #26	651-215-0836
Water Supply Operator #26	651-215-0770
Water Well Contractor #26	651-215-0811
Watercraft #32	651-296-2316
Weather Modifier #21	651-296-0591
X-ray Operator #20	651-643-2151

Minnesota Licensing Agency Information

1 Board of Assessors, Mail Station 3340, St Paul, MN 55146-3340; 651-556-6086, Fax: 651-556-3128. www.taxes.state.mn.us/ Email: pam.e.lundgrn@state.mn.us

2 Board of Barber Examiners, 1885 University Ave W, #335, St Paul, MN 55104-3403; 651-642-0489, Fax: 651-649-5997.

3 Department of Commerce, Board of Boxing (Abolished in 2001), , St Paul, MN 55101-.

4 Board of Chiropractic Examiners, 2829 University Ave SE, ste 300, Minneapolis, MN 55414-3220; 612-617-2222, Fax: 612-617-2224. www.mn-chiroboard.state.mn.us Email: chiropractic.board@state.mn.us Search Database at https://www.hlb.state.mn.us/chi/publicaccess/search.asp

5 Board of Dentistry, 2829 University Ave SE, #450, Minneapolis, MN 55414; 888-240-4762, 612-617-2250, Fax: 612-617-2260. www.dentalboard.state.mn.us Email: julie.jeppesen@state.mn.us Search Database at https://www.hlb.state.mn.us/mnbod/glsuiteweb/homeframe.aspx

6 Board of Electricity, 1821 University - RM S-128, St Paul, MN 55104; 651-642-0800, Fax: 651-642-0441. www.electricity.state.mn.us Search Database at c

7 Board of Examiners for Nursing Home Administrators, 2829 University Ave SE #440, Minneapolis, MN 55414; 612-617-2117, Fax: 612-617-2119. www.benha.state.mn.us Email: benha@state.mn.us

8 Board of Marriage & Family Therapy, 2829 University Ave SE #330, Minneapolis, MN 55414-3222; 612-617-2220, Fax: 612-617-2221. www.bmft.state.mn.us Email: robert.butler@state.mn.us

9 Board of Medical Practice, 2829 University Ave SE, #400, Minneapolis, MN 55414-3246; 612-617-2130, Fax: 612-617-2166. www.bmp.state.mn.us Email: medical.board@state.mn.us Search Database at www.docboard.org/mn/df/mndf.htm

10 Board of Nursing, 2829 University Ave SE, #500, Minneapolis, MN 55414; 612-617-2270, Fax: 612-617-2190. www.nursingboard.state.mn.us Email: nursing.board@state.mn.us Search Database at www.nursingboard.state.mn.us

11 Board of Optometry, 2829 University Av SE #550, Minneapolis, MN 55414; 612-617-2173, Fax: 612-617-2174. www.optometryboard.state.mn.us/ Email: optometry.board@state.mn.us Search Database at www.optometryboard.state.mn.us/Default.aspx?tabid=799

12 Board of Peace Officers Standards & Training, 1600 University Av #200, St Paul, MN 55104-3825; 651-643-3060, Fax: 651-643-3072. www.dps.state.mn.us/newpost/ Email: neil.melton@state.mn.us

13 Board of Pharmacy, 2829 University Ave SE, #530, Minneapolis, MN 55414-3251; 612-617-2201, Fax: 651-617-2212. www.phcybrd.state.mn.us Email: pharmacy.board@state.mn.us

14 Board of Podiatric Medicine, 2829 University Av SE #430, Minneapolis, MN 55414; 612-617-2200, Fax: 612-617-2698. www.podiatry.state.mn.us Email: benesh.pod@state.mn.us

15 Board of Psychology, 2829 University Ave. SE, #320, Minneapolis, MN 55414-3237; 612-612-2230, Fax: 612-617-2240. www.psychologyboard.state.mn.us Email: psychology.board@state.mn.us Note: Written requests only. There may be a $20 per name verification fee.

16 Board of Social Work, 2829 University Ave SE, #340, Minneapolis, MN 55414-3239; 612-617-2100, Fax: 612-617-2103. www.socialwork.state.mn.us Email: social.work@state.mn.us

17 Licensing Unit, Department of Education, Board of Teaching, 1500 Highway 36 W, Roseville, MN 55113-4266; 651-582-8691, Fax: 651-582-8809. Email: personnellicensing@state.mn.us

18 Board of Veterinary Medicine, 2829 University Ave SE, Minneapolis, MN 55414; 612-617-2170, Fax: 612-617-2172. www.vetmed.state.mn.us Email: vet.med@state.mn.us

19 Division of Plant Health, Campaign Finance Board, 658 Cedar St, Centennial Bld, 1st Fl, St Paul, MN 55155; 651-296-5148, Fax: 651-296-1722. www.cfboard.state.mn.us Email: cf.board@state.mn.us Search Database at www.cfboard.state.mn.us/

20 Department of Health, Radiation Control, 1645 Energy Park Dr #300, St Paul, MN 55108; 651-643-2151, Fax: 651-613-2152. www.health.state.mn.us/divs/eh/radiation/

21 Department of Agriculture, Livestock Weighing & Licensing, 90 W Plato Blvd, St Paul, MN 55107; 651-297-2980, Fax: 651-297-2504. www.mda.state.mn.us Search Database at http://www2.mda.state.mn.us/webapp/lis/default.jsp

22 Department of Agriculture, Pesticide Registration, 90 W Plato Blvd, St Paul, MN 55107; 651-297-2200, Fax: 651-297-2271. www.mda.state.mn.us Search Database at www.mda.state.mn.us/lis/default.htm

23 Department of Commerce, Licenses, Registration, Certification Division, 85 7th Pl E #500, St Paul, MN 55101-2198; 800-657-3978, Fax: 651-284-4107. www.commerce.state.mn.us Email: licensing.commerce@state.mn.us Note: For securities registration requests, you may email securities.commerce@state.mn.us.

24 Department of Commerce, Division of Financial Examinations, 85 7th Place E #500, St Paul, MN 55101; 651-296-4026, Fax: 651-284-4107. www.commerce.state.mn.us Email: commerce@state.mn.us Search Database at https://www.egov.state.mn.us/Commerce/license_lookup.do?action=lookupForm

25 Department of Commerce, Licensing Unit for Abstractors, 85 7th Pl E #600, St Paul, MN 55101-2198; 800-657-3978, Fax: 651-284-4107. www.state.mn.us/cgi-bin/portal/mn/jsp/home.do?agency=Commerce

26 Department of Health, Environmental Health Division, 121 E 7th Pl #230, St Paul, MN 55164-0975; 651-215-0700, Fax: 651-215-0979. www.health.state.mn.us/divs/eh/

27 Department of Health, Mortuary Science Section, PO Box 64882, St Paul, MN 55164-0882; 651-282-3829, Fax: 651-282-3839. www.health.state.mn.us/divs/hpsc/mortsci/mortsci.htm
Email: mortsci@health.state.mn.us
Search Database at www.health.state.mn.us/divs/hpsc/mortsci/finda.htm

28 Emergency Medical Services, Regulatory Board, 2829 University Av SE #310, Minneapolis, MN 55414-3222;
612-627-6000, Fax: 612-627-5442.
www.emsrb.state.mn.us
Search Database at www.emsrb.state.mn.us

29 Health Occupation Programs, Health Policy & Systems Compliance, 85 E 7th Pl # 300, St Paul, MN 55164-0882; 651-282-6366, Fax: 651-282-5628. Online searching is under construction at the website.

30 Department of Human Services, 444 Lafayette Rd, St Paul, MN 55155; 651-296-6117, Fax: 651-297-1490. www.dhs.state.mn.us

31 State Board of Law Examiners, Board of Legal Certification, St. Galtier Plaza, #201, 380 Jackson St, St Paul, MN 55101; 651-297-1857, Fax: 651-296-5866.
www.blc.state.mn.us/Specialty_Fields/specialty_fields.html　Search Database at
http://mail.statebar.gen.mn.us/search/search.asp
Note: The web search features only Bar Association members.

32 Department of Natural Resources, License Bureau, 500 Lafayette Rd, St Paul, MN 55155; 651-296-2316, Fax: 651-297-8851.
www.dnr.state.mn.us
Email: info@dnr.state.mn.us

33 Board of Dietetics & Nutrition Practice, 2829 University Ave SE #555, Minneapolis, MN 55414-3250; 612-617-2175, Fax: 612- 617-2174.
www.dieteticsnutritionboard.state.mn.us/
Email: board.dietetics-nutrition@state.mn.us

34 Department of Public Safety, Alcohol & Gambling Enforcement, 444 Cedar St #133, St Paul, MN 55101-5133;
651-296-6159, Fax: 651-297-5259.　*more*

www.dps.state.mn.us/alcgamb/alcenf/alcenf.html
Email: dps.webmaster@state.mn.us
Search Database at
www.dps.state.mn.us/alcgamb/alcenf/liquorlic/liquorlic.html　Note: Also, search the liquor license database at www.dps.state.mn.us/alcgamb/New_Folder/search1.asp.

35 Gambling Control Board, 1711 W County B, #300 South, Roseville, MN 55113; 651-639-4000.
www.gcb.state.mn.us
Search Database at www.gcb.state.mn.us

36 Labor & Industry, Code Administration & Inspection Services, 443 Lafayette Rd, St Paul, MN 55155-4304; 651-284-5080, Fax: 651-284-5737.
www.doli.state.mn.us/code.html
Email: dli.code@state.mn.us

37 Board of AELSLAGID, Licensing Boards, 85 E 7th Pl #160, St Paul, MN 55101; 651-296-2388, Fax: 651-297-5310.
Search Database at
www.aelslagid.state.mn.us/roster.html

38 Building Codes & Standards Division, Manufactured Structures Section, 408 Metro Square Bldg, 121 7th Pl E, St Paul, MN 55101-2181; 651-296-4639, Fax: 651-297-1973.
www.admin.state.mn.us/buildingcodes

39 Board of Accountancy, 85 E. 7th Pl #125, St Paul, MN 55101; 651-296-7937, Fax: 651-282-2644.
www.boa.state.mn.us

40 Supreme Court, Attorney Registration, 25 Rev. Martin Luther King Jr. Blvd. #305, St Paul, MN 55155; 651-296-2254, Fax: 651-297-4149.
www.courts.state.mn.us
Email: attorneyregistration@courts.state.mn.us
Search Database at
www.courts.state.mn.us/mars/default.aspx　Note: Lists are also available to download for free at the search page.

41 Racing Commission, PO Box 630, Shakopee, MN 55379; 952-496-7950, Fax: 952-496-7954.
www.mnrace.commission.state.mn.us/
Email: colleen.hurlbert@state.mn.us

42 State Lottery, 2645 Long Lake Rd, Roseville, MN 55113; 651-635-8119, Fax: 651-297-7498.
www.lottery.state.mn.us
Email: drewv@msl.state.mn.us

43 Pollution Control Agency, 520 Lafayette Rd N, St Paul, MN 55155-4194; 651-296-6300, Fax: 651-297-8676.
www.pca.state.mn.us/index.cfm
Email: webmaster@pca.state.mn.us

44 Private Detective & Protective Agent Services Board, 1430 E Maryland Ave, St Paul, MN 55106; 651-793-2666, Fax: 651-793-7065.
www.dps.state.mn.us/pdb/
Email: mn.pdb@state.mn.us

39 Board of Accountancy, 85 E. 7th Pl #125, St Paul, MN 55101;
651-296-7938, Fax: 651-282-2644.
www.boa.state.mn.us/Contact/contact_us.html

40 Supreme Court, Attorney Registration, 25 Rev. Martin Luther King Jr. Blvd. #305, St Paul, MN 55155; 651-296-2254, Fax: 651-297-4149.
www.courts.state.mn.us
Email: attorneyregistration@courts.state.mn.us
Search Database at www.courts.state.mn.us/mars/default.aspx Note: Lists are also available to download for free at the search page.

41 Racing Commission, PO Box 630, Shakopee, MN 55379; 952-496-7950, Fax: 952-496-7954.
www.mnrace.commission.state.mn.us/
Email: colleen.hurlbert@state.mn.us

42 State Lottery, 2645 Long Lake Rd, Roseville, MN 55113; 651-635-8100, Fax: 651-297-7498.
www.lottery.state.mn.us
Email: drewv@msl.state.mn.us　Search Database at www.lottery.state.mn.us/retailer/lookup.html

43 Pollution Control Agency, 520 Lafayette Rd N, St Paul, MN 55155-4194;
651-297-8367, Fax: 651-282-6247.
www.pca.state.mn.us/index.cfm
Email: webmaster@pca.state.mn.us

44 Private Detective & Protective Agent Services Board, 1430 E Maryland Ave, St Paul, MN 55106; 651-793-2666, Fax: 651-793-7065.
www.dps.state.mn.us/pdb/
Email: mn.pdb@state.mn.us

46 Board of Dietetics & Nutrition Practice, 2829 University Ave SE #555, Minneapolis, MN 55414-3250; 612-617-2175, Fax: 612- 617-2174.
www.dieteticsnutritionboard.state.mn.us/
Email: board.dietetics-nutrition@state.mn.us

Minnesota Federal Courts

The following list indicates the district and division name for each county in the state. If the bankruptcy court location is different from the district court, then the location of the bankruptcy court appears in parentheses.

County/Court Cross Reference

County	Court
Aitkin	Duluth
Anoka	Minneapolis
Becker	Minneapolis (Fergus Falls)
Beltrami	Minneapolis (Fergus Falls)
Benton	Duluth
Big Stone	Minneapolis (Fergus Falls)
Blue Earth	Minneapolis (St Paul)
Brown	Minneapolis (St Paul)
Carlton	Duluth
Carver	Minneapolis
Cass	Duluth
Chippewa	Minneapolis
Chisago	Minneapolis (St Paul)
Clay	Minneapolis (Fergus Falls)
Clearwater	Minneapolis (Fergus Falls)
Cook	Duluth
Cottonwood	Minneapolis (St Paul)
Crow Wing	Duluth
Dakota	Minneapolis (St Paul)
Dodge	Minneapolis (St Paul)
Douglas	Minneapolis (Fergus Falls)
Faribault	Minneapolis (St Paul)
Fillmore	Minneapolis (St Paul)
Freeborn	Minneapolis (St Paul)
Goodhue	Minneapolis (St Paul)
Grant	Minneapolis (Fergus Falls)
Hennepin	Minneapolis
Houston	Minneapolis (St Paul)
Hubbard	Minneapolis (Fergus Falls)
Isanti	Minneapolis
Itasca	Duluth
Jackson	Minneapolis (St Paul)
Kanabec	Duluth
Kandiyohi	Minneapolis
Kittson	Minneapolis (Fergus Falls)
Koochiching	Duluth
Lac qui Parle	Minneapolis (St Paul)
Lake	Duluth
Lake of the Woods	Minneapolis (Fergus Falls)
Le Sueur	Minneapolis (St Paul)
Lincoln	Minneapolis (St Paul)
Lyon	Minneapolis (St Paul)
Mahnomen	Minneapolis (Fergus Falls)
Marshall	Minneapolis (Fergus Falls)
Martin	Minneapolis (St Paul)
McLeod	Minneapolis
Meeker	Minneapolis
Mille Lacs	Duluth
Morrison	Duluth
Mower	Minneapolis (St Paul)
Murray	Minneapolis (St Paul)
Nicollet	Minneapolis (St Paul)
Nobles	Minneapolis (St Paul)
Norman	Minneapolis (Fergus Falls)
Olmsted	Minneapolis (St Paul)
Otter Tail	Minneapolis (Fergus Falls)
Pennington	Minneapolis (Fergus Falls)
Pine	Duluth
Pipestone	Minneapolis (St Paul)
Polk	Minneapolis (Fergus Falls)
Pope	Minneapolis (Fergus Falls)
Ramsey	St Paul
Red Lake	Minneapolis (Fergus Falls)
Redwood	Minneapolis (St Paul)
Renville	Minneapolis
Rice	Minneapolis (St Paul)
Rock	Minneapolis (St Paul)
Roseau	Minneapolis (Fergus Falls)
Scott	Minneapolis (St Paul)
Sherburne	Minneapolis
Sibley	Minneapolis (St Paul)
St. Louis	Duluth
Stearns	Minneapolis (Fergus Falls)
Steele	Minneapolis (St Paul)
Stevens	Minneapolis (Fergus Falls)
Swift	Minneapolis
Todd	Minneapolis (Fergus Falls)
Traverse	Minneapolis (Fergus Falls)
Wabasha	Minneapolis (St Paul)
Wadena	Minneapolis (Fergus Falls)
Waseca	Minneapolis (St Paul)
Washington	Minneapolis (St Paul)
Watonwan	Minneapolis (St Paul)
Wilkin	Minneapolis (Fergus Falls)
Winona	Minneapolis (St Paul)
Wright	Minneapolis
Yellow Medicine	Minneapolis (St Paul)

Standards for Federal Courts: Search fee is $26.00 per item (one party name or case number). Copy fee is $.50 per page. Certification fee is $9.00 per document, double for exemplification, if available. All fees standard unless noted in profile. Mail Search: always enclose a stamped self addressed envelope unless otherwise noted. Most courts accept fax requests or will suggest a copying/search vendor. Before releasing records, all courts require prepayment, unless noted. Open records are located at the court unless otherwise noted. District courts index by defendant and plaintiff as well as by case number. Bankruptcy courts usually index by debtor and case number. While most courts now have their indexes on computer, many may still maintain index card files as well. Courts offering internet access via CM-ECF or older RACER, PACER, or Web-PACER systems charge $.08 per page fee unless noted as free. Where PACER is available, the universal sign-up number is 800-676-6856. Find PACER and the US Party/Case Index at http://pacer.psc.uscourts.gov.

US District Court

Duluth Division Court Clerk, Clerk's Office, 417 Federal Bldg, 515 W 1st St, Duluth, MN 55802-1397 (also use mail address for courier delivery), 218-529-3500, Fax-218-529-3505. Hours- 8AM-5PM. www.mnd.uscourts.gov

Counties: Aitkin, Becker*, Beltrami*, Benton, Big Stone*, Carlton, Cass, Clay*, Clearwater*, Cook, Crow Wing, Douglas*, Grant*, Hubbard*, Itasca, Kanabec, Kittson*, Koochiching, Lake, Lake of the Woods*, Mahnomen*, Marshall*, Mille Lacs, Morrison, Norman*, Otter, Tail,* Pennington*, Pine, Polk*, Pope*, Red Lake*, Roseau*, Stearns*, Stevens*, St. Louis, Todd*, Traverse*, Wadena*, Wilkin*. From 3/1995, to 1998, cases from the counties marked with an asterisk (*) were heard here. Before and after that period, cases were and are allocated between St. Paul and Minneapolis.

Searches & Indexing: Results do not include SSN or DOB. Computer index maintained back to 1990. New cases in the index immediately after filing date.

Fee & Payment: Pay by Visa/MC, money order, cashier's or personal check. Payee: Clerk, US District Court. Prepayment required.

Phone Search: Only docket information is available by phone. **Mail Search:** search usually completed- 24 hours. SASE not required. **In Person Search:** Fee charged if court performs your search. No self-serve copier available.

E-Services: PACER online at http://pacer.mnd.uscourts.gov. PACER records go back to 2/1990. New records online after 1 day. ECF at https://ecf.mnd.uscourts.gov **Opinions Online:** www.nysd.uscourts.gov/courtweb/PubMain.htm. **Other Online Access:** Search recent filings at www.mnd.uscourts.gov/ncs/caselist.html.

Minneapolis Division Court Clerk, Court Clerk, Rm 202, 300 S 4th St, Minneapolis, MN 55415 (also use mail address for courier delivery),

612-664-5000, Fax-612-664-5033. Hours- 8AM-5PM. www.mnd.uscourts.gov

Counties: Cases are allocated between Minneapolis and St Paul.

Searches & Indexing: Results do not include SSN or DOB. Computer, microfiche and card indexes maintained. New cases in the index immediately after filing date.

Fee & Payment: Pay by money order, cashier's or personal check. Payee: Clerk, US District Court. Prepayment required.

Phone Search: Case number and parties involved is released via phone. **Mail Search:** search usually completed- 1-2 days. SASE not required.

In Person Search: Fee charged if court performs your search. No self-serve copier available.

E-Services: PACER online at http://pacer.mnd.uscourts.gov. PACER records go back to 2/1990. New records online after 1 day. ECF at https://ecf.mnd.uscourts.gov **Opinions Online:** www.nysd.uscourts.gov/courtweb/PubMain.htm. **Other Online Access:** Search recent filings at www.mnd.uscourts.gov/ncs/caselist.html.

St Paul Division
Court Clerk, 700 Federal Bldg, 316 N Robert, St Paul, MN 55101 (also use mail address for courier delivery), 651-848-1100, Fax-651-848-1109. Hours- 8AM-5PM. www.mnd.uscourts.gov

Counties: All counties not covered by the Duluth Division. Cases are allocated between Minneapolis and St Paul.

Searches & Indexing: Results do not include SSN or DOB. Computer, microfiche and card indexes maintained. New cases in the index immediately after filing date.

Fee & Payment: Pay by money order, cashier's or personal check. Payee: Clerk, US District Court. Prepayment required.

Phone Search: Only case number and parties involved released via phone.

Mail Search: search usually completed- 24 hours. SASE not required.

In Person Search: Fee charged if court performs your search. No self-serve copier available.

E-Services: PACER online at http://pacer.mnd.uscourts.gov. PACER records go back to 2/1990. New records online after 1 day. ECF at https://ecf.mnd.uscourts.gov **Opinions Online:** www.nysd.uscourts.gov/courtweb/PubMain.htm. **Other Online Access:** Search recent filings at www.mnd.uscourts.gov/ncs/caselist.html.

US Bankruptcy Court

Duluth Division
Court Clerk, 416 US Courthouse, 515 W 1st St, Duluth, MN 55802 (also use mail address for courier delivery), 218-529-3600. 8AM-4:30PM. www.mnb.uscourts.gov

Counties: Aitkin, Benton, Carlton, Cass, Cook, Crow Wing, Itasca, Kanabec, Koochiching, Lake, Mille Lacs, Morrison, Pine, St. Louis. A petition commencing Chapter 11 or 12 proceedings may initially be filed in any of the 4 divisions, but may be assigned to another division.

Searches & Indexing: Chapter 7 and 13 cases in Benton, Kanabec, Mille Lacs, Morrison and Pine may also be filed in St. Paul. Results include last 4 SSN digits. Computer index maintained. New cases in the index 1-2 days after filing date.

Fee & Payment: Pay by money order, personal check. Payee: Clerk, US Bankruptcy Court. Prepayment required.

Phone Search: Only basic information is released via phone. Voice Case Information Service available, call 800-959-9002 or 612-664-5302.

Mail Search: search usually completed- 3 days. SASE not required.

In Person Search: Fee charged if court performs your search. Self-serve copier - $.15 per page.

E-Services: PACER online not available. PACER records go back to 1/1993. New records online after 1 day. ECF at https://ecf.mnb.uscourts.gov. May still be in testing stage; if so, do not use. **Opinions Online:** www.mnb.uscourts.gov/WebDir/Html/judge_opinions.html. **Other Online Access:** Search records free at www.mnb.uscourts.gov/ers-bin/mnb-651-main.pl. Images go back to 1997. Judges calendars at www.mnb.uscourts.gov/Calendar/CalSelect2.html.

Fergus Falls Division
Court Clerk, 204 US Courthouse, 118 S Mill St, Fergus Falls, MN 56537 (also use mail address for courier delivery), 218-739-4671. Hours- 8AM-5PM. www.mnb.uscourts.gov

Counties: Becker, Beltrami, Big Stone, Clay, Clearwater, Douglas, Grant, Hubbard, Kittson, Lake of the Woods, Mahnomen, Marshall, Norman, Otter Tail, Pennington, Polk, Pope, Red Lake, Roseau, Stearns, Stevens, Todd, Traverse, Wadena, Wilkin. A petition commencing Chapter 11 or 12 proceedings may be filed initially in any of the four divisions, but may then be assigned to another division.

Searches & Indexing: Results include last 4 SSN digits. Computer index maintained. New cases in the index immediately after filing date.

Fee & Payment: Pay by money order, cashier's or personal check. Payee: US Bankruptcy Court. Prepayment required.

Phone Search: Only docket information is available by phone. Voice Case Information Service available, call VCIS at 800-959-9002 or 612-664-5302.

Mail Search: search usually completed- 1-7 days. SASE not required.

In Person Search: Fee charged if court performs your search. No self-serve copier available.

E-Services: PACER online not available. PACER records go back to 1/1993. New records online after 1 day. ECF at https://ecf.mnb.uscourts.gov. May still be in testing stage; if so, do not use. **Opinions Online:** www.mnb.uscourts.gov/WebDir/Html/judge_opinions.html. **Other Online Access:** Search records free at www.mnb.uscourts.gov/ers-bin/mnb-651-main.pl. Images go back to 1997. Judges calendars at www.mnb.uscourts.gov/Calendar/CalSelect2.html.

Minneapolis Division
Court Clerk, 301 US Courthouse, 300 S 4th St, Minneapolis, MN 55415 (also use mail address for courier delivery), 612-664-5200, records rm- 612-664-5209. Hours- 8AM-5PM. www.mnb.uscourts.gov

Counties: Anoka, Carver, Chippewa, Hennepin, Isanti, Kandiyohi, McLeod, Meeker, Renville, Sherburne, Swift, Wright. Initial petitions for Chapter 11 or 12 may be filed initially at any of the 4 divisions, but may then be assigned to a judge in another division.

Searches & Indexing: Results include last 4 SSN digits. Computer and microfiche indexes maintained. New cases in the index immediately after filing date. District-wide searches available back to 1/1992 from Minneapolis; holds closed cases from St. Paul for 4 years but no indexing available at this office.

Fee & Payment: Pay by money order, cashier's or personal check. Payee: Clerk, US Bankruptcy Court. Prepayment required.

Phone Search: Only basic information is released via phone. Voice Case Information Service available, call 800-959-9002 or 612-664-5302.

Mail Search: search usually completed- same day if possible. SASE not required.

In Person Search: Fee charged if court performs your search. Self-serve copier - $.15 per page.

E-Services: PACER online not available. PACER records go back to 1/1993. New records online after 1 day. ECF at https://ecf.mnb.uscourts.gov. May still be in testing stage; if so, do not use. **Opinions Online:** www.mnb.uscourts.gov/WebDir/Html/judge_opinions.html. **Other Online Access:** Search records free at www.mnb.uscourts.gov/ers-bin/mnb-651-main.pl. Images go back to 1997. Judges calendars at www.mnb.uscourts.gov/Calendar/CalSelect2.html.

St Paul Division
Court Clerk, 301 US Courthouse, Minneapolis, 300 S 4th St, Minneapolis, MN 55415 (also use mail address for courier delivery), 612-664-5200, records rm- 612-664-5209. 8AM-5PM. www.mnb.uscourts.gov

Counties: St Paul court re-located to Minneapolis courthouse 7/15/2005. Blue Earth, Brown, Chisago, Cottonwood, Dakota, Dodge, Faribault, Fillmore, Freeborn, Goodhue, Houston, Jackson, Lac qui Parle, Le Sueur, Lincoln, Lyon, Martin, Mower, Murray, Nicollet, Nobles, Olmsted, Pipestone, Ramsey, Redwood, Rice, Rock, Scott, Sibley, Steele, Wabasha, Waseca, Washington, Watonwan, Winona, Yellow Medicine. Cases from Benton, Kanabec, Mille Lacs, Morrison and Pine may also be heard here. A petition commencing Chapter 11 or 12 proceedings may be filed initially with any of the four divisions, but may then be assigned to another division.

Searches & Indexing: Results include last 4 SSN digits. Computer index maintained. Open records located here.

Fee & Payment: Pay by Visa/MC, money order, cashier's or personal check. Payee: Clerk, US Bankruptcy Court.

Phone Search: Only docket information is available by phone. Voice Case Information Service available, call VCIS at 800-959-9002 or 612-664-5302.

Mail Search: search usually completed- 2-3 days. SASE not required.

In Person Search: Fee charged if court performs your search. No self-serve copier available.

E-Services: PACER online not available. PACER records go back to 1/1993. New records online after 1 day. ECF at https://ecf.mnb.uscourts.gov. May still be in testing stage; if so, do not use. **Opinions Online:** www.mnb.uscourts.gov/WebDir/Html/judge_opinions.html. **Other Online Access:** Search records free at www.mnb.uscourts.gov/ers-bin/mnb-651-main.pl. Images go back to 1997. Judges calendars at www.mnb.uscourts.gov/Calendar/CalSelect2.html

Minnesota County Courts

Court	Jurisdiction	No. of Courts	How Organized
District Courts*	General	97	10 Districts

* Profiled in this Sourcebook.

Court	Tort	Contract	Real Estate	Min. Claim	Max. Claim	Small Claims	Estate	Eviction	Domestic Relations
					CIVIL				
District Courts*	X	X	X	$0	No Max	$7500	X	X	X

Court	Felony	Misdemeanor	DWI/DUI	Preliminary Hearing	Juvenile
			CRIMINAL		
District Courts*	X	X	X		X

ADMINISTRATION
State Court Adminstrator, 135 Minn. Judicial Center, 25 Constitution Ave, St Paul, MN, 55155; 651-296-2474, Fax: 651-297-5636. www.courts.state.mn.us

COURT STRUCTURE
There are 97 District Courts (some counties gave divisional courts) comprising 10 judicial districts. Effective July 1, 1994, the limit for small claims was raised from $5000 to $7500. The limit is $4,000 if it involves a consumer credit transaction.

ONLINE ACCESS
Appellate and Supreme Court opinions are available from the web site. There is an online system in place that allows internal and external access for government personnel only.

ADDITIONAL INFORMATION
In general, the search, copy and certification fees are each $5.00. Some courts charge an addition $10.00 plus the copy free. Most Judicial Districts no longer perform criminal record name searches for the public, but may do civil name searches.

An exact name is required to search, e.g., a request for "Robert Smith" will not result in finding "Bob Smith." The requester must request both names and pay two search and copy fees.

When a search is permitted by "plaintiff or defendant," most jurisdictions state that a case is indexed by only the 1st plaintiff or defendant and a 2nd or 3rd party would not be sufficient information for a search.

Most courts take personal checks. Exceptions are noted.

Aitkin County

9th Judicial District Court 209 Second St NW, Aitkin, MN 56431; phone: 218-927-7350; fax: 218-927-4535; hours 8AM-4:30PM (CST). *Felony, Misdemeanor, Civil, Eviction, Small Claims, Probate.*
Civil Records: Access: Mail, in person. Both court and visitors may perform in person searches. Search fee: $5.00 per name. Court makes copy: $5.00 per document. Required to search: name, years to search. Civil cases indexed by defendant, plaintiff; on computer from 2/90, cards to 1982, index books prior. Mail turnaround time 1 week.
Criminal Records: Access: Mail, in person. Both court and visitors may perform in person searches. Search fee: $5.00 per name. Court makes copy: $5.00 per document. Required to search: name, years to search, DOB. Criminal records on computer from 2/90, cards to 1982, index books prior. Mail turnaround time 1 week.
General Information: Public use terminal available. No adoption, juvenile, sex offender or sealed records released. Certification fee: $5.00 per doc. Payee: Aitkin District Court. Personal checks accepted. Prepayment and SASE required.

Anoka County

10th Judicial District Court Attn: File Room, 325 E Main St, Anoka, MN 55303; phone: 763-422-7350; criminal phone: 763-422-7385; probate phone: 763-422-7471; criminal fax: 763-323-6013; civil fax: 763-422-6919; hours 8AM-4:30PM (CST). *Felony, Misdemeanor, Civil, Eviction, Small Claims, Probate.*
www.co.anoka.mn.us/departments/courts/index.htm
Civil Records: Access: Mail, in person. Both court and visitors may perform in person searches. No search fee. Court makes copy: $5.00 per document. Required to search: name, years to search. Civil cases indexed by defendant, plaintiff; on computer from 1985, prior on microfiche.
Criminal Records: Access: In person only. Visitors must perform in person searches themselves. Court makes copy: $5.00 per document. Required to search: name, years to search, DOB; SSN helpful. Criminal records on computer from 1985, prior on microfiche.
General Information: Public use terminal available. No adoption, juvenile, sex offender or sealed records released. Certification fee: $5.00 per doc. Cert fee includes copies. Payee: Court Administrator. Personal checks or Visa, MC accepted. Prepayment required.

Becker County

7th Judicial District Court PO Box 787, Detroit Lakes, MN 56502; phone: 218-846-7305; fax: 218-847-7620; hours 8AM-4:30PM (CST). *Felony, Misdemeanor, Civil, Eviction, Small Claims, Probate.*
Civil Records: Access: Phone, fax, mail, in person. Both court and visitors may perform in person searches. No search fee. Court makes copy: $5.00 per document. Required to search: name; also helpful: years to search. Civil cases indexed by defendant, plaintiff; on computer from 8/86, prior on books from 1891.
Criminal Records: Access: In person only. Visitors must perform in person searches themselves. Court makes copy: $5.00 per document. Required to search: name, years to search. Criminal records on computer from 8/86, prior on books from 1891.
General Information: Public use terminal available. No adoption, juvenile, sex offender or sealed records released. Will fax documents $5.00 per doc. Certification fee: $5.00 per doc. Payee: Becker County. Personal checks accepted. Prepayment and SASE required.

Beltrami County

District Court 619 Beltrami Ave NW, #10, Bemidji, MN 56601-3068; phone: 218-333-4531; criminal phone: 281-333-4125; civil phone: 218-333-4128; probate phone: 218-333-4211; criminal fax: 218-333-4209; civil/probate fax is the same; hours 8AM-4:30PM (CST). *Felony, Misdemeanor, Civil, Eviction, Small Claims, Probate.*
Civil Records: Access: Mail, in person. Both court and visitors may perform in person searches. Search fee: $5.00 per name. Court makes copy: $5.00 per document. Required to search: name, years to search. Civil cases indexed by defendant, plaintiff; on computer back to 1983, Mail turnaround -5 days.
Criminal Records: Access: In person only. Visitors must perform in person searches themselves. Court makes copy: $5.00 per document. Required to search: name, years to search, DOB. Criminal records on computer back to 1983.
General Information: Public terminal back to 1983. No adoption, juvenile, sex offender or sealed records released. Will fax documents to local or toll free line. Certification fee: $5.00 per doc. Payee: Court Administrator. Personal checks accepted. Prepayment required.

Benton County

7th Judicial District Court 615 Highway 23, PO Box 189, Foley, MN 56329-0189; phone: 320-968-5205; fax: 320-968-5353; hours 8AM-4:30PM (CST). *Felony, Misdemeanor, Civil, Eviction, Small Claims, Probate, Family.*
Civil Records: Access: In person only. Visitors must perform in person searches themselves. Court makes copy: $5.00 per document. Self serve copy fee: no charge if off computer. Required to search: name, years to search. Civil cases indexed by defendant, plaintiff; on computer from 1986.
Criminal Records: Access: In person only. Visitors must perform in person searches themselves. Court makes copy: $5.00 per document. Self serve copy fee: no charge if off computer. Required to search: name, years to search, DOB. Criminal records on computer from 1986.
General Information: Public terminal back to 1986. No adoption, juvenile records released. Will not fax specific case file. Certification fee: $5.00 per doc. Payee: Court Administrator. Personal checks accepted. Prepayment required.

Big Stone County

Big Stone District Court 20 SE 2nd St, Ortonville, MN 56278; phone: 320-839-2536; probate phone: 320-839-2536; fax: 320-839-2537; probate fax: same; hours 8AM-4:30PM (CST). *Felony, Misdemeanor, Civil, Eviction, Small Claims, Probate.*
Civil Records: Access: Mail, in person. Both court and visitors may perform in person searches. Search fee: $5.00. Court makes copy: $5.00 per document. Required to search: name, years to search. Civil cases indexed by defendant, plaintiff; on computer from 1989, prior on cards and in books.
Criminal Records: Access: In person only. Visitors must perform in person searches themselves. Court makes copy: $5.00 per document. Required to search: name, years to search, DOB; SSN helpful. Criminal records on computer from 1989, prior on cards and in books.
General Information: Public terminal back to 1990. No adoption, juvenile, sex offender or sealed records released. Will not fax documents. Certification fee: $5.00 per doc. Payee: Court Administrator. Personal checks accepted. Prepayment and SASE required.

Blue Earth County

5th Judicial District Court 204 S 5th St, Mankato, MN 56001; phone: 507-389-8841; fax: 507-389-8437; hours 8AM-4:30PM (CST). *Felony, Misdemeanor, Civil, Eviction, Small Claims, Probate.*

www.co.blue-earth.mn.us/dept/courts.php3
Civil Records: Access: Mail, in person. Both court and visitors may perform in person searches. Search fee: $10.00 per hour. Court makes copy: $5.00 per document. Required to search: name, years to search. Civil cases indexed by defendant, plaintiff; on computer from 8/85, prior in books and cards. Mail turnaround time 7-10 days.
Criminal Records: Access: In person only. Visitors must perform in person searches themselves. Court makes copy: $5.00 per document. Required to search: name, years to search; also helpful: DOB. Criminal records on computer from 8/85, prior in books and cards. The county forwards mail requests to the state Bureau of Criminal Apprehension.
General Information: Public terminal back to 1985. No juvenile, adoption, sealed records released. Will fax documents for $5.00 per doc. Certification fee: $5.00 per doc. Payee: Court Administrator. Personal checks accepted. MC/Visa accepted. Prepayment required.

Brown County

5th Judicial District Court PO Box 248, 14 S State St, New Ulm, MN 56073-0248; phone: 507-233-6670; fax: 507-359-9562; hours 8AM-5PM (CST). *Felony, Misdemeanor, Civil, Eviction, Small Claims, Probate.*
Civil Records: Access: Mail, in person. Both court and visitors may perform in person searches. Search fee: $5.00 per name. Court makes copy: $5.00 per document. Required to search: name, years to search. Civil cases indexed by defendant, plaintiff; on computer from 1988, microfiche 1981-1988, prior on books.
Criminal Records: Access: In person only. Visitors must perform in person searches themselves. Court makes copy: $5.00 per document. Required to search: name, years to search. Criminal records on computer from 1988, microfiche 1981-1988, prior on books. Make written requests to the state Bureau of Criminal Apprehension.
General Information: Public terminal back to 1988. No adoption, juvenile, sex offender or sealed records released. Fee to fax back is $5.00 per doc. Certification fee: $5.00 per doc. Payee: Court Administrator. Personal checks or Visa, MC accepted. Prepayment and SASE required.

Carlton County

6th Judicial District Court PO Box 190 (301 Walnut St), Carlton, MN 55718; phone: 218-384-4281; criminal phone: 218-384-9109; civil phone: 218-384-9139; probate phone: 218-384-9113; fax: 218-384-9182; hours 8AM-4PM (CST). *Felony, Misdemeanor, Civil, Eviction, Small Claims, Probate.*
www.courts.state.mn.us/districts/sixth/index.html
Civil Records: Access: Mail, fax, in person. Both court and visitors may perform in person searches. Search fee: $5.00 per name. Court makes copy: $5.00 per document. Required to search: name, years to search; also helpful: address. Civil cases indexed by defendant, plaintiff; on computer from 1985, in books from 1982.
Criminal Records: Access: In person only. Visitors must perform in person searches themselves. Court makes copy: $5.00 per document. Required to search: name, years to search; also helpful: address, DOB. Criminal records on computer from 1985, in books from 1972. If you cannot come to the courthouse, the court recommends using a retriever or contact the state Bureau of Criminal Apprehension.
General Information: Public terminal back to 1986. No adoption, juvenile, sex offender or sealed records released. Will fax documents for $5.00. Certification fee: $5.00 per doc. Payee: Court Administrator. Personal checks accepted. Prepayment and SASE required.

Carver County

1st Judicial District Court 604 E 4th St, Box 4, Chaska, MN 55318-2183; phone: 952-361-1420; fax: 952-361-1491; hours 8AM-4:30PM (CST). *Felony, Misdemeanor, Civil, Eviction, Small Claims, Probate.*
Civil Records: Access: Mail, in person. Both court and visitors may perform in person searches. Search fee: $5.00 per name. Court makes copy: $5.00 per document. Required to search: name, years to search. Civil cases indexed by defendant, plaintiff; on computer from 2/92, prior on books. Mail turnaround time up to 7 days.
Criminal Records: Access: Mail, in person. Both court and visitors may perform in person searches. Search fee: $5.00 per name. Court makes copy: $5.00 per document. Required to search: name, years to search, DOB. Criminal records on computer from 2/92, prior on books. Mail turnaround time 7 days.
General Information: Public use terminal available. No adoption, juvenile, sex offender or sealed records released. Certification fee: $5.00 per doc. Payee: Court Administrator. Personal checks accepted. Prepayment required.

Cass County

9th Judicial District Court PO Box 3000, 300 Minnesota Ave, Walker, MN 56484; phone: 218-547-7200; fax: 218-547-1904; hours 8AM-4:30PM (CST). *Felony, Misdemeanor, Civil, Eviction, Small Claims, Probate.*
Civil Records: Access: Mail, in person. Both court and visitors may perform in person searches. Search fee: $5.00 per name. Court makes copy: $5.00 per document. Required to search: name, years to search; also helpful: address. Civil cases indexed by defendant, plaintiff; on computer from mid-1990, on index cards from 1983-1990, on books to 1983, cards to 1900.
Criminal Records: Access: In person only. Visitors must perform in person searches themselves. Court makes copy: $5.00 per document. Required to search: name, years to search, DOB; also helpful: address. Criminal records on computer from mid-1990, on index cards from 1983-1990, on books to 1983; cards to 1900.
General Information: Public terminal back to mid-1990. No adoption, juvenile records released. Fee to fax is $5.00 per document. Certification fee: $5.00. Payee: District Court. Personal checks accepted. Prepayment, SASE required.

Chippewa County

8th Judicial District Court Chippewa County Court Administor, 629 N 11th St, Montevideo, MN 56265; phone: 320-269-7774; fax: 320-269-7733; hours 8AM-4:30PM (CST). *Felony, Misdemeanor, Civil, Eviction, Small Claims, Probate.*
Civil Records: Access: Mail, in person. Visitors must perform in person searches themselves. No search fee. Court makes copy: $5.00 per document. Required to search: name, years to search. Civil cases indexed by defendant, plaintiff; on computer from 1988, in books from 1870.
Criminal Records: Access: In person only. Visitors must perform in person searches themselves. Court makes copy: $5.00 per document. Required to search: name, years to search, DOB. Criminal records on computer from 1988, in books from 1870.
General Information: Public terminal back to 1988. No adoption, juvenile, sex offender or sealed records released. Certification fee: $5.00 per doc. Payee: Court Administrator. Personal checks accepted. Prepayment and SASE required.

Chisago County

10th Judicial District Court 313 N Main St, Rm 358, Center City, MN 55012; phone: 651-213-0485; fax: 651-213-0359; hours 8AM-4:30PM (CST). *Felony, Misdemeanor, Civil, Eviction, Small Claims, Probate.*
www.courts.state.mn.us/districts/tenth

Civil Records: Access: Mail, in person. Both court and visitors may perform in person searches. Search fee: $5.00. Court makes copy: $.25 per page. Required to search: name, years to search. Civil cases indexed by defendant, plaintiff; on computer from 1984, prior on index cards.

Criminal Records: Access: In person only. Visitors must perform in person searches themselves. Court makes copy: $.25 per page. Required to search: name, years to search; also helpful: DOB. Criminal records on computer from 1984, prior on index cards.

General Information: Public terminal back to late 1980s. No adoption, juvenile, sex offender or sealed records released. Certification fee: $5.00 per doc. Payee: Court Administrator. Personal checks accepted. Prepayment and SASE required.

Clay County

7th Judicial District Court PO Box 280, c/o County Court Admin, 807 11th St N, Moorhead, MN 56561; phone: 218-299-5065; fax: 218-299-7307; hours 8AM-4:30PM (CST). *Felony, Misdemeanor, Civil, Eviction, Small Claims, Probate.*
www.co.clay.mn.us/Depts/CourtAdm/CourtAdm.htm
Civil Records: Access: Mail, in person. Both court and visitors may perform in person searches. Search fee: $5.00. Court makes copy: $5.00 per document; same fee for self serve. Required to search: name; also helpful: years to search. Civil cases indexed by defendant, plaintiff; on computer back to 1982; prior on microfiche and microfilm.

Criminal Records: Access: In person only. Visitors must perform in person searches themselves. Court makes copy: $5.00 per document; same fee for self serve. Required to search: name, years to search, DOB. Criminal records on computer back to 1982; prior on microfiche and microfilm.

General Information: Public terminal back to 1981. No adoption or sealed records released. Will fax documents for $5.00. Certification fee: $5.00 per doc. Payee: Court Administrator. Personal checks accepted. No credit cards accepted. Prepayment and SASE required.

Clearwater County

9th Judicial District Court 213 Main Ave North, Dept 303, Bagley, MN 56621; phone: 218-694-6177; fax: 218-694-6213; hours 8AM-4:30PM (CST). *Felony, Misdemeanor, Civil, Eviction, Small Claims, Probate.*
Civil Records: Access: Mail, in person. Both court and visitors may perform in person searches. Search fee: $5.00 per name, by court. Court makes copy: $5.00 per document. Required to search: name, years to search. Civil cases indexed by defendant, plaintiff; on computer from 1990, on cards and books prior back to 1903.

Criminal Records: Access: In person only. Visitors must perform in person searches themselves. Court makes copy: $5.00 per document. Required to search: name, years to search; also helpful: DOB. Criminal records on computer from 1990, on cards and books prior back to 1903. Court personnel will not perform name searches. Requests are referred to the state criminal agency.

General Information: Public terminal back to 1990. No adoption, juvenile or sealed records released. Certification fee: $5.00 per document. Payee: Court Administrator. Personal checks accepted. Prepayment required.

Cook County

6th Judicial District Court 411 W 2nd St, Grand Marais, MN 55604-2307; phone: 218-387-3610; fax: 218-387-3007; hours 8AM-4PM (CST). *Felony, Misdemeanor, Civil, Eviction, Small Claims, Probate, Juvenile, Traffic.*
Civil Records: Access: In person only. Visitors must perform in person searches themselves. Court makes copy: $5.00 per document. Required to search: name, years to search. Civil cases indexed by

defendant, plaintiff; on computer back to 2/91, prior on card files.

Criminal Records: Access: In person only. Visitors must perform in person searches themselves. Court makes copy: $5.00 per document. Required to search: name, years to search, DOB. Criminal records on computer back to 2/91, prior on card files.

General Information: Public terminal back to 1991. No adoption, juvenile, sex offender or sealed records released. Certification fee: $5.00 per doc. Payee: Court Administrator. Business checks accepted. Prepayment required.

Cottonwood County

5th Judicial District Court PO Box 97, Windom, MN 56101; phone: 507-831-4551; fax: 507-831-1425; hours 8AM-4:30PM (CST). *Felony, Misdemeanor, Civil, Eviction, Small Claims, Probate.*
Civil Records: Access: Mail, fax, in person. Only the court performs in person searches. Search fee: $10.00 per name. Court makes copy: $5.00 per document. Required to search: name; also helpful: years to search. Civil cases indexed by defendant, plaintiff; on computer back to 1989; probate on microfilm. There is a $5.00 fee to certify a judgment search done on computer. Mail turnaround time 2-3 days.

Criminal Records: Access: Mail, fax, in person. Both court and visitors may perform in person searches. Search fee: $10.00 per name. Court makes copy: $5.00 per document. Required to search: name, years to search, DOB. Criminal records on computer back to 1989; prior records on card file. Court will only do searches if caseload permits. Mail turnaround time 2-3 days.

General Information: Public terminal has only criminal records. No adoption, juvenile, sex offender or sealed records released. Will fax documents to local or toll free line. Certification fee: $5.00 per doc. Payee: Court Administrator. Personal checks accepted. Prepayment and SASE required.

Crow Wing County

District Court 326 Laurel St, Brainerd, MN 56401; phone: 218-824-1310; fax: 218-824-1311; hours 8AM-5PM (CST). *Felony, Misdemeanor, Civil, Eviction, Small Claims, Probate.*
Civil Records: Access: Mail, in person. Both court and visitors may perform in person searches. Search fee: $5.00 per name. Court makes copy: $5.00 per document. Required to search: name, years to search. Civil cases indexed by defendant, plaintiff; on computer from 1989, prior in books from 1873.

Criminal Records: Access: In person only. Both court and visitors may perform in person searches. Search fee: $5.00 per name. Court makes copy: $5.00 per document. Required to search: name, years to search; also helpful: DOB. Criminal records on computer from 1989, prior in books from 1873. Mail turnaround time 7-14 days.

General Information: Public terminal back to 1989. No adoption, juvenile, sex offender or sealed records released. Certification fee: $5.00 per doc. Payee: Court Administrator. Personal checks accepted. Prepayment and SASE required.

Dakota County

1st Judicial District Court - Apple Valley 14955 Galaxie Ave, Apple Valley, MN 55124; phone: 952-891-7256; criminal phone: 952-891-7239; civil phone: 952-891-7244; criminal fax: 952-891-7312; civil fax: 952-891-7285; hours 8AM-4:30PM (CST). *Misdemeanor, Civil, Eviction, Small Claims, Traffic.*
www.co.dakota.mn.us/courts
Note: Send criminal record faxes to attention Cindy.
Civil Records: Access: In person only. Visitors must perform in person searches themselves. Court makes copy: $5.00 per document. Required to search: name, years to search. Civil cases indexed by

defendant, plaintiff; on computer back to 1988, prior in files in index books back to 1969.

Criminal Records: Access: Main, fax, in person. Visitors must perform in person searches themselves. Search fee: $5.00 per name. Court makes copy: $5.00 per file. Required to search: name, years to search, DOB. Criminal records on computer back to 1988, prior in files to 1987 if not destroyed.

General Information: Public terminal back to 1988. No adoption, juvenile, sex offender or sealed records released. Certification fee: $5.00 per doc. Payee: District Court. Personal checks accepted. Prepayment required.

1st Judicial District Court - Division 3 1 Mendota Rd West, #140, West St Paul, MN 55118-4767; phone: 651-554-6200; fax: 651-554-6226; hours 8AM-4:30PM (CST). *Felony, Misdemeanor, Civil, Eviction, Small Claims.*
www.co.dakota.mn.us/courts
Note: Formerly located at 125 3rd Ave North, S. St. Paul.
Civil Records: Access: In person only. Visitors must perform in person searches themselves. Court makes copy: $5.00 per document. Required to search: name, years to search. Civil records on computer from 12/87, prior on ledgers.

Criminal Records: Access: In person only. Visitors must perform in person searches themselves. Court makes copy: $5.00 per document. Required to search: name, years to search. Criminal records on computer from 12/87, prior on ledgers.

General Information: Public terminal has criminal back to 12/1987 and civil back to 1/1988. No adoption, juvenile, sex offender or sealed records released. Will not fax specific case file. Certification fee: $5.00 per doc. Payee: Court Administrator. Personal checks accepted. Prepayment required.

District Court Judicial Center, 1560 Hwy 55, Hastings, MN 55033; phone: 651-438-8100; criminal fax: 651-438-8160; civil fax: 651-438-8162; probate fax: 651-438-8161; hours 8AM-4:30PM (CST). *Felony, Misdemeanor, Civil, Eviction, Small Claims, Probate.*
www.co.dakota.mn.us/courts
Civil Records: Access: In person only. Visitors must perform in person searches themselves. Court makes copy: $5.00 per document. Required to search: name, years to search. Civil cases indexed by defendant, plaintiff; on computer from 1/88, on ledgers prior.

Criminal Records: Access: In person only. Visitors must perform in person searches themselves. Court makes copy: $5.00 per document. Required to search: name, years to search. Criminal records on computer from 1/88, on ledgers prior.

General Information: Public terminal back to 1/1988. No adoption, juvenile, sealed records released. Will not fax specific case file. Certification fee: $5.00 per doc. Payee: District Court. Personal checks accepted. Prepayment required.

Dodge County

3rd Judicial District Court 22 Sixth St E, Dept. 12, Mantorville, MN 55955; phone: 507-635-6260; fax: 507-635-6271; hours 8AM-4:30PM (CST). *Felony, Misdemeanor, Civil, Eviction, Small Claims, Probate.*
www.courts.state.mn.us/districts/third/counties/dodge.htm
Civil Records: Access: Fax, mail, in person. Both court and visitors may perform in person searches. No search fee. Court makes copy: $5.00 per document. Required to search: name, years to search. Civil cases indexed by defendant, plaintiff; on computer back to 1989, on cards from 1984, on books from 1972. Daily Court calendar is posted at www.courts.state.mn.us/districts/third/counties/dodge.htm.

Criminal Records: Access: In person only. Visitors must perform in person searches themselves. Court makes copy: $5.00 per document. Required to search: name, years to search, DOB. Criminal records on computer back to 1984, on cards from 1984, on books from 1972. Daily court calendar is posted at the website.

General Information: Public terminal back to 1989. No adoption, juvenile, sex offender or sealed records released. Fee to fax documents is $5.00 per document. Certification fee: $5.00 per doc. Payee: Court Administrator. Personal checks accepted. Prepayment and SASE required.

Douglas County

7th Judicial District Court 305 8th Ave West, Alexandria, MN 56308; phone: 320-762-3882; criminal fax: 320-762-8863; civil/probate fax is the same; hours 8AM-4:30PM (CST). *Felony, Misdemeanor, Civil, Eviction, Small Claims, Probate.*

Civil Records: Access: Mail, in person. Both court and visitors may perform in person searches. Search fee: $5.00 per name. Court makes copy: $5.00 per document. Required to search: name, years to search. Civil cases indexed by defendant, plaintiff; on computer from 1987, on microfiche from 1951, books prior. The books are grouped by letter, but not alphabetized.

Criminal Records: Access: In person only. Visitors must perform in person searches themselves. Court makes copy: $5.00 per document. Required to search: name. Criminal records on computer from 1987, on microfiche from 1951, books prior. The books are grouped by letter, but not alphabetized. Court recommends search through BCA.

General Information: Public terminal back to 1987. No adoption, juvenile or sealed records released. Will not fax documents. Certification fee: $5.00 per doc. Payee: Court Administrator. Personal checks accepted. Prepayment and SASE required.

Faribault County

5th Judicial District Court PO Box 130, Blue Earth, MN 56013; phone: 507-526-6273; fax: 507-526-3054; hours 8AM-4:30PM (CST). *Felony, Misdemeanor, Civil, Eviction, Small Claims, Probate.*

Civil Records: Access: Mail, in person. Visitors must perform in person searches themselves. Court makes copy: $5.00 per document. Required to search: name, years to search. Civil cases indexed by defendant, plaintiff; on computer from 1989, in books from 1870.

Criminal Records: Access: In person only. Visitors must perform in person searches themselves. Court makes copy: $5.00 per document. Required to search: name, years to search; also helpful: DOB. Criminal records on computer from 1989, in books from 1870. The county suggests sending requests to the state Bureau of Criminal Apprehension.

General Information: Public terminal back to 1989. No adoption, juvenile, sex offender or sealed records released. Will fax documents for $5.00. Certification fee: $5.00 per doc. Payee: Court Administrator. Personal checks accepted. Prepayment and SASE required.

Fillmore County

3rd Judicial District Court 101 Fillmore St, PO Box 436, Preston, MN 55965; phone: 507-765-4483; criminal fax: 507-765-4571; civil/probate fax is the same; hours 8AM-4:30PM (CST). *Felony, Misdemeanor, Civil, Eviction, Small Claims, Probate.*

www.courts.state.mn.us/districts/third

Civil Records: Access: Mail, in person. Both court and visitors may perform in person searches. Search fee: $5.00 per name. Court makes copy: $5.00 per document. Required to search: name, years to search. Civil cases indexed by defendant, plaintiff; on computer from 1990, books from 1860s. Mail turnaround time 1-2 days.

Criminal Records: Access: In person only. Visitors must perform in person searches themselves. Court makes copy: $5.00 per document. Required to search:

name, years to search, DOB. Criminal records on computer from 1990, books from 1860s.

General Information: Public terminal back to 1990. No adoption, juvenile or sealed records released. Will fax documents for $2.00 per page. Certification fee: $5.00 per doc. Payee: Court Administrator. Personal checks accepted. Prepayment required.

Freeborn County

3rd Judicial District Court 411 S Broadway, Albert Lea, MN 56007; phone: 507-377-5153; fax: 507-377-5260; hours 8AM-5PM (CST). *Felony, Misdemeanor, Civil, Eviction, Small Claims, Probate.*

www.courts.state.mn.us/districts/third

Civil Records: Access: Mail, in person. Both court and visitors may perform in person searches. Search fee: $5.00. Court makes copy: $5.00 per document. Required to search: name, years to search. Civil cases indexed by defendant, plaintiff; on computer from 11/89.

Criminal Records: Access: In person only. Visitors must perform in person searches themselves. Court makes copy: $5.00 per document. Required to search: name, years to search, DOB. Criminal records on computer from 11/89.

General Information: Public terminal back to 11/1989. No adoption, juvenile, sex offender or sealed records released. Certification fee: $5.00 per doc. Payee: Court Administrator. Personal checks or Visa/MC accepted. Prepayment and SASE required.

Goodhue County

1st Judicial District Court 454 W 6th St, Red Wing, MN 55066; phone: 651-267-4800; probate phone: 651-267-4806; criminal fax: 651-267-4989; civil/probate fax is the same; hours 8AM-4:30PM (CST). *Felony, Misdemeanor, Civil, Eviction, Small Claims, Probate.*

Civil Records: Access: Mail, in person. Both court and visitors may perform in person searches. No search fee. Court makes copy: $5.00 per filed document. Required to search: name, years to search. Civil cases indexed by defendant, plaintiff; on computer from 3/92, prior records on docket books.

Criminal Records: Access: In person only. Visitors must perform in person searches themselves. Court makes copy: $5.00 per filed document. Required to search: name. Criminal records on computer from 3/92, prior records on docket books.

General Information: Public terminal back to 1992. No adoption, juvenile, sex offender or sealed records released. Will fax documents if prepaid and not-certified. Certification fee: $5.00 per doc. Payee: Court Administrator. Personal checks accepted. Prepayment and SASE required.

Grant County

8th Judicial District Court PO Box 1007 (10 2nd St NE), Elbow Lake, MN 56531; phone: 218-685-4825; 8AM-4PM (CST). *Felony, Misdemeanor, Civil, Eviction, Small Claims, Probate.*

Civil Records: Access: Mail, in person. Visitors must perform in person searches themselves. Search fee: $5.00 per name. Court makes copy: $5.00 per document. Required to search: name, years to search. Civil cases indexed by defendant, plaintiff; on computer from 6/89, on cards from 1930, prior at Historical Society.

Criminal Records: Access: In person only. Visitors must perform in person searches themselves. Court makes copy: $5.00 per document. Required to search: name, years to search; also helpful: DOB. Criminal records on computer from 6/89, on cards from 1930, prior at Historical Society.

General Information: Public terminal back to 1989. No adoption, juvenile, sex offender or sealed records released. Fee to fax documents is add'l $5.00 per document. Certification fee: $5.00 per doc. Payee: Court Administrator. Personal checks accepted. Prepayment and SASE required.

Hennepin County

4th Judicial District Court - Division 1 Civil 1251 C Government Ctr, 300 S 6th St, Minneapolis, MN 55487; phone: 612-348-3170; fax: 612-348-2131; hours 8AM-4:30PM (CST). *Civil.*

www.courts.state.mn.us/districts/fourth

Civil Records: Access: Fax, mail, in person. Both court and visitors may perform in person searches. Search fee: $5.00 per name by mail, no fee for in person. Court makes copy: $.50 per document. Required to search: name, years to search. Civil cases indexed by defendant, plaintiff; on computer from 1978, prior on microfilm. Mail turnaround time 7-10 days.

General Information: Public terminal has only civil records. No sex offender or sealed records released, domestic abuse and paternity cases are limited. Certification fee: $5.00 per doc. Payee: Court Administrator. Personal checks accepted. Prepayment and SASE required.

4th Judicial District Court - Division 1 Criminal 300 S 6th St, Minneapolis, MN 55487; phone: 612-348-2612; fax: 612-348-6099; hours 8AM-4:30PM (CST). *Felony, Misdemeanor.*

www.courts.state.mn.us/districts/fourth/

Note: Online access to court records is under development.

Criminal Records: Access: Fax, mail, in person. Both court and visitors may perform in person searches. Search fee: $5.00 per name if no record found; otherwise $10.00 per name. Court makes copy: $.50 per page. Required to search: name, years to search, DOB. Felony records go back to 1886. Computerized records back to 1978. Online information about criminal searching is at www.courts.state.mn.us/districts/fourth/Criminal/crfaq.htm Mail turnaround time 14-21 days.

General Information: Public terminal has only criminal records back to 1989. No adoption, juvenile, sex offender or sealed records released. Will fax documents. Certification fee: $10.00 per document. Payee: Court Administrator. Personal checks accepted. Prepayment and SASE required.

4th Judicial District Court - Division 2 Brookdale 6125 Shingle Creek Parkway, Brooklyn Center, MN 55430; phone: 763-569-2799; fax: 763-569-3697; hours 8AM-4:30PM (CST). *Misdemeanor.*

www.courts.state.mn.us/districts/fourth

Criminal Records: Access: Mail, in person. Both court and visitors may perform in person searches. Search fee: $5.00 per name. Court makes copy: $5.00 per document. Required to search: name, years to search, DOB. Criminal records on computer since 1987. Mail turnaround time 1-7 days.

General Information: No public access terminal. No juvenile court, conciliation court, unlawful detainers or sealed records released. Certification fee: $5.00 per doc. Payee: Hennepin County District Court. Personal checks accepted. Prepayment and SASE required.

4th Judicial District Court - Division 3 Ridgedale 12601 Ridgedale Dr, Minnetonka, MN 55305; phone: 952-541-7000; fax: 952-541-6297; hours 8AM-4:30PM (CST). *Misdemeanor, Eviction, Small Claims.*

www.courts.state.mn.us/districts/fourth

Civil Records: Access: Mail, in person, online. Both court and visitors may perform in person searches. Search fee: $5.00 per name. Court makes copy: $.50 per page. Required to search: name, years to search. Civil cases indexed by defendant and plaintiff. Civil records on computer. A plaintiff, defendant search of small claims is free at www2.co.hennepin.mn.us/ccourt/ccsrch.jsp. Mail turnaround time 3-4 weeks.

Criminal Records: Access: Mail, in person. Both court and visitors may perform in person searches. Search fee: $5.00 per name. Court makes copy: $.50 per page. Required to search: name, years to search;

also helpful: DOB. Criminal records on computer since 1989; prior records on microfiche. Mail turnaround time 3-4 weeks.

General Information: Public terminal has only criminal records back to 1986. (Limited data available.) No police reports, juvenile or sealed records released. Certification fee: $5.00 per doc. Payee: Hennepin County District Court. Personal checks accepted. Prepayment and SASE required.

4th Judicial District Court - Division 4 Southdale
7009 York Ave South, Edina, MN 55435; phone: 952-830-4877; fax: 952-830-4993; hours 8AM-4:30PM (CST). *Misdemeanor.*
www.courts.state.mn.us/districts/fourth
Criminal Records: Access: Mail, in person. Visitors must perform in person searches themselves. Search fee: $5.00 per name. Court makes copy: $.50 per page. Required to search: name, years to search, DOB; also helpful: offense, date of offense. Criminal records on computer since late 1970s, felonies on computer earlier. In person search with court assistance $10.00. Mail turnaround time 1 week.
General Information: No public access terminal. No juvenile or sealed records released. Certification fee: $10.00 per doc. Payee: Hennepin County District Court. Personal checks accepted. Prepayment and SASE required.

4th Judicial District Court - Division 1
C400 Government Ctr, 300 S 6th St, Minneapolis, MN 55487; phone: 612-348-3244; fax: 612-348-2130; hours 8:30AM-4:30PM (CST). *Probate.*
www.courts.state.mn.us/districts/fourth

Houston County

3rd Judicial District Court
304 S Marshall, Rm 204, Caledonia, MN 55921; phone: 507-725-5806; criminal phone: 507-725-5828; fax: 507-725-5550; 8AM-4:30PM (CST). *Felony, Misdemeanor, Civil, Eviction, Small Claims, Probate.*
www.courts.state.mn.us/districts/third
Civil Records: Access: Mail, in person. Visitors must perform in person searches themselves. No search fee. Court makes copy: $5.00 per document. Required to search: name, years to search, DOB. Civil cases indexed by defendant, plaintiff; on computer back to 8/89, prior on cards and books. Probate on microfilm to 1990. Mail turnaround time 2 days.
Criminal Records: Access: In person only. Visitors must perform in person searches themselves. Court makes copy: $5.00 per document. Required to search: name, years to search; also helpful: DOB. Criminal records on computer back to 8/89, prior on cards and books.
General Information: Public use terminal available. No adoption, juvenile, sex offender or sealed records released. Fee to fax documents is $5.00 per document. Certification fee: $5.00 per doc. Payee: Court Administrator. Personal checks accepted. Prepayment and SASE required.

Hubbard County

9th Judicial District Court
301 Court St, Park Rapids, MN 56470; phone: 218-732-3573; fax: 218-732-0137; hours 8AM-4:30PM (CST). *Felony, Misdemeanor, Civil, Eviction, Small Claims, Probate.*
Civil Records: Access: Mail, in person. Visitors must perform in person searches themselves. Search fee: $5.00 per name. Court makes copy: $5.00 per document. Required to search: name, years to search. Civil cases indexed by defendant, plaintiff; on computer since 1990, prior on index cards. Mail turnaround time 1 week.
Criminal Records: Access: Mail, in person. Visitors must perform in person searches themselves. Search fee: $5.00 per name. Court makes copy: $5.00 per document. Required to search: name, DOB. Criminal records on computer since 1990, prior on index cards. Mail turnaround time 1 week.
General Information: Public terminal back to 1990. No adoption, juvenile, sex offender or sealed records released. Certification fee: $5.00 per doc.

Payee: Court Administrator. Personal checks accepted. Prepayment and SASE required.

Isanti County

10th Judicial District Court
555 18th Ave SW, Cambridge, MN 55008-9386; phone: 763-689-2292; criminal fax: 763-689-8340; civil/probate fax is the same; hours 8AM-4:30PM (CST). *Felony, Misdemeanor, Civil, Eviction, Small Claims, Probate.*
Civil Records: Access: Mail, in person. Visitors must perform in person searches themselves. No search fee. Court makes copy: $5.00 per document. Required to search: name, years to search. Civil cases indexed by defendant, plaintiff; on computer from 12/84, prior on microfiche.
Criminal Records: Access: In person only. Visitors must perform in person searches themselves. Court makes copy: $5.00 per document. Required to search: name, years to search. Criminal records on computer from 12/84, prior on microfiche.
General Information: Public terminal back to 1985. No adoption, juvenile, sex offender or sealed records released. Will fax free to local or toll-free numbers. Certification fee: $5.00 per doc. Payee: Court Administrator. Personal checks accepted. Prepayment and SASE required.

Itasca County

9th Judicial District Court
123 4th St NE, Grand Rapids, MN 55744-2600; phone: 218-327-2870; fax: 218-327-2897; hours 8AM-4PM (CST). *Felony, Misdemeanor, Civil, Eviction, Small Claims, Probate.*
www.co.itasca.mn.us/Court/Gov_cou.htm
Civil Records: Access: Mail, in person. Both court and visitors may perform in person searches. Search fee: $5.00 per name. Court makes copy: $5.00 per document. Required to search: name, years to search, DOB. Civil cases indexed by defendant, plaintiff; on computer from 4-87, on microfiche to 1982, on books prior. Mail turnaround time 20 days, 24 hours required to pull from off-site storage.
Criminal Records: Access: Mail, in person. Visitors must perform in person searches themselves. Court makes copy: $5.00 per document. Required to search: name, years to search, DOB. Criminal records on computer from 4-87, on microfiche to 1982, on books prior. Record checks are made through the Bureau of Criminal Apprehension; see state section on criminal records. Mail turnaround time 7-14 days, 24 hours required to pull from off-site storage.
General Information: Public terminal back to 4/87. No adoption, juvenile or sealed records released. Fee to fax documents is add'l $5.00 per document. Certification fee: $5.00 per doc. Payee: Court Administrator. Personal checks accepted. Prepayment required.

Jackson County

5th Judicial District Court
PO Box 177, Jackson, MN 56143; phone: 507-847-4400; fax: 507-847-5433; hours 8AM-4:30PM (CST). *Felony, Misdemeanor, Civil, Eviction, Small Claims, Probate.*
Note: Probate is a separate index at this same address.
Civil Records: Access: Fax, mail, in person. Both court and visitors may perform in person searches. Search fee: $10.00 per name. Court makes copy: $5.00 per document. Required to search: name, years to search, address. Civil cases indexed by defendant, plaintiff; on computer from 5/89. Probate on microfiche from 1870. Mail turnaround time 2-3 days.
Criminal Records: Access: Fax, mail, in person. Visitors must perform in person searches themselves. Search fee: $10.00 per name if referred to BCA state agency. Court makes copy: $5.00 per document. Required to search: name, years to search, DOB. Criminal records on computer from 5/89. Probate on microfiche from 1870. Mail turnaround time 2-3 days.

General Information: Public terminal back to 5/1989. No adoption, juvenile, sex offender or sealed records released. Will fax documents for $5.00 up to 5 pages, each add'l page $1.00. Certification fee: $5.00 per doc. Payee: Court Administrator. Personal checks accepted. Prepayment and SASE required.

Kanabec County

10th Judicial District Court
18 N Vine, #318, Mora, MN 55051-1385; phone: 320-679-6400; fax: 320-679-6411; hours 8AM-4:30PM (CST). *Felony, Misdemeanor, Civil, Eviction, Small Claims, Probate.*
Civil Records: Access: In person only. Visitors must perform in person searches themselves. Court makes copy: $5.00 per document. Required to search: name, years to search. Civil cases indexed by defendant, plaintiff; on computer from 1986, prior on books and microfiche.
Criminal Records: Access: In person only. Visitors must perform in person searches themselves. Court makes copy: $5.00 per document. Required to search: name, years to search; also helpful: DOB. Criminal records on computer from 1986, prior on books and microfiche.
General Information: Public terminal back to 1986. No adoption, juvenile or sealed records released. Certification fee: $5.00 per doc. Payee: Court Administrator. Personal checks accepted. Prepayment required.

Kandiyohi County

8th Judicial District Court
505 Becker Ave SW, Willmar, MN 56201; phone: 320-231-6206; fax: 320-231-6276; hours 8:30AM-4:30PM (CST). *Felony, Misdemeanor, Civil, Eviction, Small Claims, Probate.*
Civil Records: Access: Mail, in person. Both court and visitors may perform in person searches. Search fee: $5.00 per name. Court makes copy: $5.00 per document. Required to search: name, years to search. Civil cases indexed by defendant, plaintiff; on computer from 1986, prior on microfilm. Mail turnaround time 48 hours.
Criminal Records: Access: In person only. Visitors must perform in person searches themselves. Court makes copy: $5.00 per document. Required to search: name, years to search, DOB; SSN helpful. Criminal records on computer from 1986, prior on microfilm.
General Information: Public terminal back to 1986. No adoption, juvenile, sex offender or sealed records released. Will fax specific document for $10.00; emergency requests only. Certification fee: $5.00 per doc. Payee: Court Administrator. Personal checks accepted. Prepayment required.

Kittson County

9th Judicial District Court
410 Fifth St S, #204, Hallock, MN 56728; phone: 218-843-3632; hours 8:00AM-4:30PM (CST). *Felony, Misdemeanor, Civil, Eviction, Small Claims, Probate.*
Civil Records: Access: In person. Both court and visitors may perform in person searches. Search fee: $5.00 per name. Will charge $20.00 per hour for extensive searches. Court makes copy: $5.00 per document. Required to search: name, years to search. Civil cases indexed by defendant, plaintiff; on computer from 9/90, prior on books and index cards. Visitors may look at judgment docket.
Criminal Records: Access: In person. Visitors must perform in person searches themselves. Court makes copy: $5.00 per document. Required to search: name, years to search, DOB, offense. Criminal records on computer from 9/90, prior on books and index cards.
General Information: Public use terminal available. No adoption, juvenile, sex offender or sealed records released. No fee to fax documents. Certification fee: $5.00 per doc. Payee: Court Administrator. Personal checks accepted. Prepayment required.

Koochiching County

9th Judicial District Court Court House, 715 4th St, International Falls, MN 56649; phone: 218-283-1160; fax: 218-283-1162; probate fax: same; hours 8AM-4PM (CST). *Felony, Misdemeanor, Civil, Eviction, Small Claims, Probate.*

www.courts.state.mn.us/districts/ninth

Civil Records: Access: Mail, in person. Both court and visitors may perform in person searches. Search fee: $5.00 per name. Court makes copy: $5.00 per document. Required to search: name, years to search. Civil cases indexed by defendant, plaintiff; on computer from 5/90, on TCIS cards from 1984, on books from 1906. The weekly court calendar is at the website.

Criminal Records: Access: In person only. Visitors must perform in person searches themselves. Court makes copy: $5.00 per document. Required to search: name, years to search, DOB. Criminal records on computer from 5/90, on TCIS cards from 1984, on books from 1906. Weekly court calendar is at the website. Note: Criminal record checks can be done via BCA.

General Information: Public terminal back to 8/1990. No adoption, juvenile, sex offender or sealed records released. Fee to fax back is $5.00 per document. Certification fee: $5.00 per doc. Payee: Court Administrator. Personal checks accepted. Prepayment and SASE required.

Lac qui Parle County

8th Judicial District Court PO Box 36, 600 6th St, Madison, MN 56256; phone: 320-598-3536; fax: 320-598-3915; hours 8:30AM-4:30PM (CST). *Felony, Misdemeanor, Civil, Eviction, Small Claims, Probate.*

www.courts.state.mn.us/districts/eighth/dist08.htm

Civil Records: Access: Fax, phone, mail, in person. Both court and visitors may perform in person searches. Search fee: $5.00 per name. Court makes copy: $5.00 per document. Required to search: name, years to search. Civil cases indexed by defendant, plaintiff; on computer from 1988, prior on index cards.

Criminal Records: Access: In person only. Both court and visitors may perform in person searches. Court makes copy: $5.00 per document. Required to search: name, years to search, DOB; SSN helpful. Criminal records on computer from 1988, prior on index cards. Court may refer criminal searches requests to the sheriff's office, 320-598-3720. Sheriff address is 600 6th St. Mail turnaround time 1-3 days.

General Information: Public terminal back to 1988. No adoption, juvenile, sex offender or sealed records released. Will fax documents $5.00 per doc. Certification fee: $5.00 per doc. Payee: Court Administrator. Personal checks accepted. Prepayment and SASE required.

Lake County

6th Judicial District Court 601 3rd Ave, Two Harbors, MN 55616; phone: 218-834-8330; probate phone: 218-834-8329; criminal fax: 218-834-8397; civil/probate fax is the same; hours 8AM-4:30PM (CST). *Felony, Misdemeanor, Civil, Eviction, Small Claims, Probate.*

www.6courts.com

Civil Records: Access: Fax, mail, in person. Both court and visitors may perform in person searches. Search fee: $5.00 per name. Court makes copy: $5.00 per document. Required to search: name, years to search. Civil cases indexed by defendant, plaintiff; on computer back to 1991, prior on index cards.

Criminal Records: Access: In person only. Visitors must perform in person searches themselves. Court makes copy: $5.00 per document. Required to search: name, years to search, DOB. Criminal records on computer back to 1991, prior on index cards.

General Information: Public terminal back to 1991. No adoption, juvenile, sex offender or sealed records released. Fee to fax documents is $5.00 per document. Certification fee: $5.00 per doc. Payee: Court Administrator. Personal checks or Visa, MC accepted. Prepayment and SASE required.

Lake of the Woods County

9th Judicial District Court PO Box 808, Baudette, MN 56623; phone: 218-634-1451/1388; fax: 218-634-9444; hours 7:30AM-4PM (CST). *Felony, Misdemeanor, Civil, Eviction, Small Claims, Probate.*

Civil Records: Access: Fax, mail, in person. Both court and visitors may perform in person searches. Search fee: $10.00 per name. Court makes copy: $5.00 per document. Required to search: name, years to search. Civil records on computer back to 1990; on microfilm to 1923. Mail turnaround time 2 days.

Criminal Records: Access: In person only. Both court and visitors may perform in person searches. Search fee: $10.00 per name. Court makes copy: $5.00 per document. Required to search: name, years to search, DOB. Criminal records on computer back to 1990; on microfilm back to 1923.

General Information: Public terminal back to 1991. No adoption, juvenile, sex offender or sealed records released. No fee to fax documents. Certification fee: $5.00 per doc. Payee: Court Administrator. Personal checks accepted. Prepayment required.

Le Sueur County

1st Judicial District Court 88 S Park Ave, Le Center, MN 56057; phone: 507-357-2251; fax: 507-357-6433; hours 8AM-4:30PM (CST). *Felony, Misdemeanor, Civil, Eviction, Small Claims, Probate.*

Civil Records: Access: In person only. Visitors must perform in person searches themselves. Court makes copy: $5.00 per document. Required to search: name, years to search. Civil cases indexed by defendant, plaintiff; on computer from 1992, prior on books.

Criminal Records: Access: In person only. Visitors must perform in person searches themselves. Court makes copy: $5.00 per document. Required to search: name, years to search, DOB. Criminal records on computer from 1992, prior on books.

General Information: Public terminal back to 1994. No adoption, juvenile, sex offender or sealed records released. Certification fee: $5.00 per doc. Payee: Court Administrator. Personal checks accepted. Prepayment required.

Lincoln County

5th Judicial District Court PO Box 15, Ivanhoe, MN 56142-0015; phone: 507-694-1355 or 1505; probate 507-694-1355; fax: 507-694-1717; hours 8AM-4:30PM (CST). *Felony, Misdemeanor, Civil, Eviction, Small Claims, Probate.*

Civil Records: Access: Mail, in person. Both court and visitors may perform in person searches. Court makes copy: $5.00 per document. Required to search: name, years to search. Civil cases indexed by defendant(s), plaintiff(s). The TCIS public terminal is available to access cases from 1/1989, on TCIS index cards from 12/82, on books from late 1800.

Criminal Records: Access: In person only. Both court and visitors may perform in person searches. Court makes copy: $5.00 per document. Required to search: name, years to search, DOB. Criminal records on computer from 1989, on TCIS from 12/82, on books from late 1800. All written requests for criminal records are referred to statewide BCA; call for form, 650-793-2420.

General Information: Public terminal back to 1989. No adoption, juvenile, sex offender or sealed records released. Will fax court files for fee of $5.00 per transmission. Certification fee: $5.00 per doc. Payee: Court Administrator. Personal checks accepted. Prepayment and SASE required.

Lyon County

5th Judicial District Court 607 W Main, Marshall, MN 56258; phone: 507-537-6734; fax: 507-537-6150; hours 8:30AM-4:30PM (CST). *Felony, Misdemeanor, Civil, Eviction, Small Claims, Probate.*

Civil Records: Access: Mail, in person. Both court and visitors may perform in person searches. Search fee: $5.00. Court makes copy: $5.00 per document. Required to search: name, years to search. Civil cases indexed by defendant, plaintiff; on computer from 1987, prior on index cards.

Criminal Records: Access: In person only. Visitors must perform in person searches themselves. Court makes copy: $5.00 per document. The court requires sending requests to the state Bureau of Criminal Apprehension.

General Information: Public terminal back to 1997. No adoption, juvenile, sex offender or sealed records released. Certification fee: $5.00 per doc. Payee: Court Administrator. Personal checks or Visa, MC accepted. Prepayment and SASE required.

Mahnomen County

9th Judicial District Court PO Box 459, Mahnomen, MN 56557; phone: 218-935-2251; fax: 218-935-2851; hours 8AM-4:30PM (CST). *Felony, Misdemeanor, Civil, Eviction, Small Claims, Probate.*

Civil Records: Access: In person only. Both court and visitors may perform in person searches. Search fee: $5.00 per name. Court makes copy: $5.00 per document. Required to search: name, years to search. Civil cases indexed by defendant, plaintiff; on computer from 8/90, prior on books from 1907.

Criminal Records: Access: In person only. Both court and visitors may perform in person searches. Search fee: $5.00 per name. Court makes copy: $5.00 per document. Required to search: name, years to search. Criminal records on computer from 8/90, prior on books from 1907.

General Information: Public terminal back to 1991. No adoption, juvenile, sex offender or sealed records released. Certification fee: $5.00 per doc. Payee: Court Administrator. Personal checks accepted. Prepayment required.

Marshall County

9th Judicial District Court Court Administrator - Records, 208 E Colvin, Warren, MN 56762; phone: 218-745-4921; fax: 218-745-4343; hours 8AM-4:30PM (CST). *Felony, Misdemeanor, Civil, Eviction, Small Claims, Probate.*

Civil Records: Access: Mail, in person. Both court and visitors may perform in person searches. Search fee: $5.00 per name. Court makes copy: $5.00 per document. Required to search: name, years to search; also helpful: address. Civil cases indexed by defendant, plaintiff; on computer from 5/90, on cards from 1982, on books from 1885. Mail turnaround time same day.

Criminal Records: Access: Mail, in person. Visitors must perform in person searches themselves. Search fee: $5.00 per name. Court makes copy: $5.00 per document. Required to search: name, years to search; also helpful: address, DOB. Criminal records on computer from 5/90, on cards from 1982, on books from 1885. Most name searchers with written requests are asked to contact the BCA State repository. Mail turnaround time same day.

General Information: Public terminal back to 1990. No adoption, juvenile, sex offender or sealed records released. Certification fee: $5.00 per doc. Payee: Court Administrator. Personal checks accepted. Prepayment and SASE required.

Martin County

5th Judicial District Court 201 Lake Ave, Rm 304, Martin County Court Admin, Fairmont, MN 56031; phone: 507-238-3205; fax: 507-238-1913; hours 8AM-5PM (CST). *Felony, Misdemeanor, Civil, Eviction, Small Claims, Probate.*

Civil Records: Access: Mail, in person. Both court and visitors may perform in person searches. Search fee: $10.00 per name. Court makes copy: $5.00 per document. Required to search: name, years to search; also helpful: address. Civil cases indexed by defendant, plaintiff; on computer from 7/89, on cards from 1986, on books from 1800s.

Criminal Records: Access: In person only. Visitors must perform in person searches themselves. Court makes copy: $5.00 per document. Required to search: name, years to search, DOB; also helpful: address, SSN. Criminal records on computer from 7/89, on cards from 1986, on books from 1800s. Court suggests sending requests to State Bureau of Criminal Apprehension.

General Information: Public terminal back to 7/1989. No adoption, most juvenile, or sealed records released. Will fax civil search documents or specific case files for $5.00 per fax if prepaid. Certification fee: $5.00 per doc. Payee: Court Administrator. Personal checks or Visa, MC accepted. Prepayment and SASE required.

McLeod County

1st Judicial District Court 830 E 11th, Glencoe, MN 55336; phone: 320-864-1281; fax: 320-864-5905; hours 8AM-4:30PM (CST). *Felony, Misdemeanor, Civil, Eviction, Small Claims, Probate.*
www.co.mcleod.mn.us/mcleodco.cfm?pageID=14&sub=yes
Civil Records: Access: Mail, in person. Both court and visitors may perform in person searches. No search fee. Court makes copy: $5.00 per document. Required to search: name, years to search. Civil records on computer from 4/92, prior on books.
Criminal Records: Access: In person only. Visitors must perform in person searches themselves. Court makes copy: $5.00 per document. Required to search: name, years to search. Criminal records on computer from 4/92, prior on books.
General Information: Public terminal back to 1989. No adoption, juvenile, sex offender or sealed records released. Certification fee: $5.00 per doc. Payee: Court Administrator. Personal checks accepted. Prepayment and SASE required.

Meeker County

8th Judicial District Court 325 N Sibley, Litchfield, MN 55355; phone: 320-693-5230; fax: 320-693-5254; hours 8AM-4:30PM (CST). *Felony, Misdemeanor, Civil, Eviction, Small Claims, Probate.*
Civil Records: Access: Mail, in person. Both court and visitors may perform in person searches. Search fee: $5.00 per name. Court makes copy: $5.00 per document. Required to search: name; also helpful: years to search, address. Civil cases indexed by defendant, plaintiff; on computer from 11/88, prior on index cards. Mail turnaround time 2-3 days.
Criminal Records: Access: In person only. Visitors must perform in person searches themselves. Court makes copy: $5.00 per document. Required to search: name; also helpful: years to search, DOB. Criminal records on computer from 11/88, prior on index cards back to 1880s.
General Information: Public terminal back to 11/1988. No adoption, juvenile, sex offender or sealed records released. Will fax documents $5.00 per doc. Certification fee: $5.00 per doc. Payee: Court Administrator. Personal checks accepted. Prepayment and SASE required.

Mille Lacs County

7th Judicial District Court Courthouse, 635 2nd St SE, Milaca, MN 56353; phone: 320-983-8313; fax: 320-983-8384; hours 8AM-4:30PM (CST). *Felony, Misdemeanor, Civil, Eviction, Small Claims, Probate.*
Civil Records: Access: Mail, in person. Both court and visitors may perform in person searches. Search fee: $5.00. Court makes copy: $5.00 per

document. Required to search: name, years to search. Civil records on computer from 4/86, cards from 1981, books prior. Mail turnaround time 2 weeks.
Criminal Records: Access: In person only. Visitors must perform in person searches themselves. Court makes copy: $5.00 per document. Required to search: name, years to search. Criminal records on computer from 4/86, cards from 1981, books prior. Mail turnaround time 1 week.
General Information: Public terminal back to 1986. No adoption, juvenile, sex offender or sealed records released. Will fax documents $5.00 per doc. Certification fee: $5.00 per doc. Payee: District Court. Personal checks accepted. Prepayment and SASE required.

Morrison County

7th Judicial District Court 213 SE 1st Ave, Little Falls, MN 56345; phone: 320-632-0325; probate phone: 320-632-0327; fax: 320-632-0340; hours 8AM-4:30PM (CST). *Felony, Misdemeanor, Civil, Eviction, Small Claims, Probate.*
Civil Records: Access: Fax, mail, in person. Both court and visitors may perform in person searches. Search fee: $5.00. Court makes copy: $5.00 per document. Required to search: name, years to search. Civil cases indexed by defendant, plaintiff; on computer from 5/86, prior on cards and books.
Criminal Records: Access: In person only. Visitors must perform in person searches themselves. Court makes copy: $5.00 per document. Required to search: name, years to search, DOB. Criminal records on computer from 5/86, prior on cards and books.
General Information: Public use terminal available. No adoption, juvenile, sex offender or sealed records released. Will fax documents $5.00 per doc. Certification fee: $5.00 per doc. Payee: Court Administrator. Personal checks accepted. Prepayment and SASE required.

Mower County

Mower County District Court 201 1st St NE, Austin, MN 55912; phone: 507-437-9465; fax: 507-434-2702; hours 8AM-5PM (CST). *Felony, Misdemeanor, Civil, Eviction, Small Claims, Probate.*
www.co.mower.mn.us
Civil Records: Access: Mail, in person. Both court and visitors may perform in person searches. Search fee: $5.00. Court makes copy: $5.00 per document. Required to search: name, years to search. Civil cases indexed by defendant, plaintiff; on computer from 1989.
Criminal Records: Access: In person only. Visitors must perform in person searches themselves. Court makes copy: $5.00 per document. Required to search: name, years to search, DOB. Criminal records on computer from 1989.
General Information: Public terminal back to 1989. No adoption, juvenile, paternity or sealed records released. Will fax documents for $5.00 fee. Certification fee: $5.00 per doc. Payee: Court Administrator. Personal checks accepted. Prepayment and SASE required.

Murray County

5th Judicial District Court PO Box 57, Slayton, MN 56172-0057; phone: 507-836-6163; fax: 507-836-6019; hours 8AM-5PM (CST). *Felony, Misdemeanor, Civil, Eviction, Small Claims, Probate.*
Civil Records: Access: Fax, mail, in person. Both court and visitors may perform in person searches. Search fee: $5.00 per name. Court makes copy: $5.00 per document. Required to search: name, years to search. Civil cases indexed by defendant, plaintiff; on computer from 7/88.
Criminal Records: Access: In person only. Visitors must perform in person searches themselves. Court makes copy: $5.00 per document. Required to search: name, years to search; SSN helpful. Criminal records

on computer from 7/88. The court suggests sending requests to Bureau of Criminal Apprehension.
General Information: No public access terminal. No adoption, juvenile, or sealed records released. Will fax documents $5.00 per doc. Certification fee: $5.00 per doc. Payee: Court Administrator. Personal checks accepted. Prepayment required.

Nicollet County

5th Judicial District Court PO Box 496, St Peter, MN 56082; phone: 507-931-6800; criminal phone: 507-934-0388; civil phone: 507-934-0386; probate phone: 507-934-0380; fax: 507-931-4278; hours 8AM-5PM (CST). *Felony, Misdemeanor, Civil, Eviction, Small Claims, Probate.*
Note: Fine Inquiry telephone is 507-934-7503.
Civil Records: Access: Mail, in person. Both court and visitors may perform in person searches. No search fee. Court makes copy: $5.00 per document. Required to search: name, years to search. Civil cases indexed by defendant, plaintiff; on computer from 9/25/88, on books from 1890. The civil records prior to 9/25/88 for the entire county are located here. The court in North Mankato is closed. All records from that District Court branch are located here.
Criminal Records: Access: In person only. Visitors must perform in person searches themselves. Court makes copy: $5.00 per document. Required to search: name, years to search, DOB. Criminal records on computer since 9/25/88. Prior records for this court only are located here on books and cards. The court will not do criminal searches.
General Information: Public terminal back to 1988. No adoption, juvenile, sex offender or sealed records released. Will not fax documents. Certification fee: $5.00 per doc. Cert fee includes copies. Payee: Court Administrator. Personal checks accepted. Prepayment and SASE required.

Nobles County

5th Judicial District Court PO Box 547, Worthington, MN 56187; phone: 507-372-8263; fax: 507-372-4994; hours 8AM-4:30PM (CST). *Felony, Misdemeanor, Civil, Eviction, Small Claims, Probate.*
Civil Records: Access: Mail, in person. Both court and visitors may perform in person searches. Search fee: $5.00 per name. Court makes copy: $5.00 per document. Self serve copy fee: $1.00 per page. Required to search: name, years to search. Civil cases indexed by defendant, plaintiff; on computer from 7/88, on books and index cards prior.
Criminal Records: Access: In person only. Visitors must perform in person searches themselves. Court makes copy: $5.00 per document. Required to search: name, years to search; SSN helpful. Criminal records on computer from 7/88, on books and index cards prior. The court suggests sending requests to the state Bureau of Criminal Apprehension.
General Information: Public terminal back to 7/88. No adoption, juvenile, sex offender or sealed records released. Certification fee: $5.00 per doc. Payee: Court Administrator. Personal checks or Visa, MC accepted. In person only. Prepayment and SASE required.

Norman County

9th Judicial District Court 16 3rd Ave E, Ada, MN 56510-0146; phone: 218-784-5458; criminal fax: 218-784-3110; civil/probate fax is the same; hours 8AM-4:30PM (CST). *Felony, Misdemeanor, Civil, Eviction, Small Claims, Probate.*
Civil Records: Access: Mail, in person. Both court and visitors may perform in person searches. Search fee: $5.00 per name. Court makes copy: $5.00 per document. Required to search: name, years to search. Civil records on computer since 5/90, prior on index cards.
Criminal Records: Access: In person only. Visitors must perform in person searches themselves. Court makes copy: $5.00 per document. Required to search:

name, years to search, DOB. Criminal records on computer since 5/90, prior on index cards. Note: Criminal searches directed to BCA- 1-800-832-6446, Fax 218-935-9999.
General Information: No public access terminal. No adoption, juvenile, sex offender or sealed records released. Will fax documents for $5.00 add'l fee. Certification fee: $5.00 per doc. Payee: Court Administrator. Business checks accepted. Prepayment required.

Olmsted County

Olmsted County District Court 151 4th St SE, Rochester, MN 55904; criminal phone: 507-285-8201; civil phone: 507-285-8108; probate phone: 507-285-8484; fax: 507-285-8996; hours 8AM-5PM (CST). *Felony, Misdemeanor, Civil, Eviction, Small Claims, Probate, Juvenile.* www.courts.state.mn.us/districts/third/counties/olmsted.htm
Civil Records: Access: Mail, in person, online. Both court and visitors may perform in person searches. Search fee: $5.00 for each name found. Court makes copy: $5.00 per document. Required to search: name, years to search. Civil cases indexed by defendant, plaintiff; on computer from mid-1989, prior to 1856 on index cards. Online access is to probate records only, and these are from a private library source at www.selco.lib.mn.us/apps/ochs/probate.cfm. Files vary greatly, but most contain date and place of death, list of heirs, copy of will (if one was written), inventory of personal property, and final disposition of the estate
Criminal Records: Access: In person only. Visitors must perform in person searches themselves. Court makes copy: $5.00 per document. Required to search: name, DOB. Criminal records on computer from mid-1989, prior to 1856 on index cards. Note: Access the daily court calendar at the website.
General Information: Public terminal back to 1983. No adoption, juvenile, sex offender or sealed records released. Certification fee: $5.00 per doc. Payee: Court Administrator. Personal checks or Visa, MC accepted. Prepayment and SASE required.

Otter Tail County

Otter Tail County District Court 121 W Junius Ave #310, Fergus Falls, MN 56538-0417; phone: 218-998-8420; fax: 218-998-8438; hours 8AM-5PM (CST). *Felony, Misdemeanor, Civil, Eviction, Small Claims, Probate, Traffic.* www.co.otter-tail.mn.us
Civil Records: Access: Mail, in person. Both court and visitors may perform in person searches. Search fee: $5.00 per name. Court makes copy: $5.00 per document. Required to search: name; also helpful: years to search. Civil cases indexed by defendant, plaintiff; on computer from 1987, prior on index books.
Criminal Records: Access: In person only. Visitors must perform in person searches themselves. Court makes copy: $5.00 per document. Required to search: name, years to search, DOB; also helpful: address. Criminal records on computer from 1987, prior on index books.
General Information: Public terminal back to 1987. No adoption, juvenile or sealed records released. Certification fee: $5.00 per doc. Payee: Court Administrator. Personal checks accepted. Prepayment and SASE required.

Pennington County

9th Judicial District Court Court Admin Offcie, PO Box 619, Thief River Falls, MN 56701; phone: 218-681-7023; fax: 218-681-0907; hours 8AM-4:30PM (CST). *Felony, Misdemeanor, Civil, Eviction, Small Claims, Probate.*
Civil Records: Access: In person only. Both court and visitors may perform in person searches. Search fee: $5.00 per name. Court makes copy: $5.00 per document. Required to search: name, years to search. Civil cases indexed by defendant, plaintiff; on

computer back to 1990, prior on TCIS cards and books to 1911.
Criminal Records: Access: In person only. Visitors must perform in person searches themselves. Court makes copy: $5.00 per document. Required to search: name, years to search, DOB. Criminal records on computer back to 1990, prior on TCIS cards and books to 1911.
General Information: Public terminal back to 1990. No adoption, juvenile, sex offender or sealed records released. Certification fee: $5.00 per doc. Payee: Court Administrator. Personal checks accepted. Prepayment required.

Pine County

10th Judicial District Court 315 Main St S, Pine City, MN 55063; phone: 320-629-5634; fax: 320-629-5762; hours 8AM-4:30PM (CST). *Felony, Misdemeanor, Civil, Eviction, Small Claims, Probate.*
Civil Records: Access: In person only. Visitors must perform in person searches themselves. Court makes copy: $10.00 per document. Required to search: name, years to search. Civil records on computer from 2/85.
Criminal Records: Access: In person only. Visitors must perform in person searches themselves. Court makes copy: $10.00 per document. Required to search: name, years to search. Criminal records on computer from 2/85.
General Information: Public terminal back to 2/1985. No adoption, juvenile, or sealed records released. Certification fee: $5.00 per doc. Cert fee includes copies. Payee: Court Administrator. Personal checks accepted. Prepayment required.

Pipestone County

5th Judicial District Court PO Box 337, 416 S Hiawatha Ave, Pipestone, MN 56164; phone: 507-825-6730; fax: 507-825-6733; hours 8:30AM-4:30PM (CST). *Felony, Misdemeanor, Civil, Eviction, Small Claims, Probate.*
Civil Records: Access: Mail, in person. Both court and visitors may perform in person searches. Search fee: $5.00 per name. Court makes copy: $5.00 per document. Required to search: name, years to search. Civil cases indexed by defendant, plaintiff; on computer from 1989, prior on books.
Criminal Records: Access: In person only. Visitors must perform in person searches themselves. Court makes copy: $5.00 per document. Required to search: name, years to search. Criminal records on computer from 1989, prior on books. The court suggests sending requests to the state Bureau of Criminal Apprehension.
General Information: Public terminal back to 1989. No adoption, juvenile, sex offender victims or sealed records released. Certification fee: $5.00 per doc. Payee: Court Administrator. Personal checks accepted. Prepayment and SASE required.

Polk County

9th Judicial District Court Court Administrator, 612 N Broadway #301, Crookston, MN 56716; phone: 218-281-2332; fax: 218-281-2204; 8AM-4:30PM (CST). *Felony, Misdemeanor, Civil, Eviction, Small Claims, Probate.*
Note: Child protection and child service cases are available as of 7/1/2002.
Civil Records: Access: Mail, in person. Visitors must perform in person searches themselves. Search fee: $5.00 per name. Court makes copy: $5.00 per document. Required to search: name, years to search. Civil cases indexed by defendant, plaintiff; on computer from 1990, prior on index cards or books. Mail turnaround time 3-5 days.
Criminal Records: Access: Mail, in person. Visitors must perform in person searches themselves. Search fee: $5.00 per name. Court makes copy: $5.00 per document. Required to search: name, years to search, DOB. Criminal records on computer from

1990, prior on index cards or books. Mail turnaround time 3-5 days.
General Information: Public use terminal available. No adoption, non-felony under age 16 juvenile or sealed records released. Will fax documents for $5.00. Certification fee: $5.00 per doc. Payee: Court Administrator. Personal checks accepted. Credit cards accepted. Prepayment and SASE required.

Pope County

8th Judicial District Court 130 E Minnesota Ave, Glenwood, MN 56334; phone: 320-634-5222; fax: 320-634-5527; hours 8AM-4:30PM (CST). *Felony, Misdemeanor, Civil, Eviction, Small Claims, Probate.*
www.courts.state.mn.us/districts/eighth/default.htm
Civil Records: Access: Mail, in person. Court makes copy: $10.00 per document. Required to search: name, years to search. Civil cases indexed by defendant, plaintiff; on computer from 2/89, prior on TCIS cards ad books.
Criminal Records: Access: In person only. Visitors must perform in person searches themselves. Court makes copy: $10.00 per document. Required to search: name, years to search. Criminal records on computer from 2/89, prior on TCIS cards ad books.
General Information: Public use terminal available. No adoption, juvenile, sex offender or sealed records released. Certification fee: $5.00 per doc. Payee: Court Administrator. Personal checks accepted. Prepayment and SASE required.

Ramsey County

2nd Judicial District Court 15 W Kellogg, Rm 1700, St Paul, MN 55102; criminal 651-266-8180; civil 651-266-8253; criminal fax: 651-266-8172; civil fax: 651-266-8263; hours 8AM-4:30PM (CST). *Felony, Misdemeanor, Civil, Probate.*
www.ramsey.courts.state.mn.us
Civil Records: Access: Mail, in person. Both court and visitors may perform in person searches. Search fee: $10.00 per name. Court makes copy: $5.00 per document. Required to search: name, years to search. Civil cases indexed by defendant or plaintiff, on computer from 5/88, prior on books.
Criminal Records: Access: In person only. Visitors must perform in person searches themselves. Court makes copy: $5.00 per document; name printouts-$.50 each. Required to search: name, years to search, DOB. Felony records on computer go back to 1987; misdemeanors go back to 1985, prior on books to 1953 felonies only.
General Information: Public terminal has criminal back to 1987 and civil back to 1988. No adoption, juvenile, sex offender or sealed records released. Certification fee: $5.00 per doc. Payee: Court Administrator. Personal checks accepted. Prepayment and SASE required.

2nd Judicial District Court - Maplewood Area 2050 White Bear Ave, Maplewood, MN 55109; phone: 651-266-1999; fax: 651-266-1978; hours 8AM-4:30PM (CST). *Misdemeanor.*
www.ramsey.courts.state.mn.us
This court holds the records for the closed New Brighton Court.
Criminal Records: Access: In person only. Visitors must perform in person searches themselves. Court makes copy: $5.00 per document. Required to search: name; also helpful: address, DOB, offense, date of offense. Criminal records on computer from 11/90.
General Information: Public terminal has only criminal records back to 11/1990. No adoption, juvenile, sex offender victim, sealed or medical records released. Certification fee: $5.00 per doc. Payee: Ramsey County District Court. Personal checks or Visa, MC, Discover accepted. Not accepted over the phone. Prepayment required.

Red Lake County

9th Judicial District Court PO Box 339, Red Lake Falls, MN 56750; phone: 218-253-4281; criminal fax: 218-253-4287; civil/probate fax is

the same; hours 8AM-4:30PM (CST). *Felony, Misdemeanor, Civil, Eviction, Small Claims, Probate.*
Civil Records: Access: Mail, in person. Both court and visitors may perform in person searches. Search fee: $5.00 per name. Court makes copy: $5.00 per document. Required to search: name, years to search. Civil cases indexed by defendant, plaintiff; on computer and microfiche from 1990, on books from 1897.
Criminal Records: Access: In person only. Visitors must perform in person searches themselves. Court makes copy: $5.00 per document. Required to search: name, years to search, DOB. Criminal records on computer and microfiche from 1990, on books from 1897. Note: Court suggest you perform criminal search through BCA.
General Information: Public terminal back to 1990. No adoption, juvenile, sex offender or sealed records released. Will not fax documents. Certification fee: $5.00 per doc. Payee: Court Administrator. Personal checks accepted. Prepayment and SASE required.

Redwood County

5th Judicial District Court PO Box 130, Redwood Falls, MN 56283; phone: 507-637-4020; probate phone: 507-637-4018; fax: 507-637-4021; probate fax: same; hours 8AM-4:30PM (CST). *Felony, Misdemeanor, Civil, Eviction, Small Claims, Probate.*
Civil Records: Access: Mail, in person. Both court and visitors may perform in person searches. Search fee: $5.00 per name. Court makes copy: $5.00 per document. Required to search: name, years to search. Civil cases indexed by defendant, plaintiff; on computer from 11/88, prior on card and books.
Criminal Records: Access: In person only. Visitors must perform in person searches themselves. Court makes copy: $5.00 per document. Required to search: name, years to search. Criminal records on computer from 11/88, prior on card and books. No felony or gross misdemeanor searches will be performed.
General Information: Public terminal back to 1988. No adoption, juvenile, sex offender or sealed records released. Certification fee: $5.00 per doc. Payee: Court Administrator. Personal checks accepted. Prepayment and SASE required.

Renville County

8th Judicial District Court 500 E DePue Ave, 3rd level, Olivia, MN 56277; phone: 320-523-3680; fax: 320-523-3689; hours 8AM-4:30PM (CST). *Felony, Misdemeanor, Civil, Eviction, Small Claims, Probate.*
Civil Records: Access: Mail, in person. Visitors must perform in person searches themselves. Court makes copy: $5.00 per document. Required to search: name, years to search. Civil cases indexed by defendant, plaintiff; on computer from 1988, prior on index cards.
Criminal Records: Access: In person only. Visitors must perform in person searches themselves. Court makes copy: $5.00 per document. Required to search: name. Criminal records on computer from 1988, prior on index cards. Court recommends that written requests be submitted to the MN Bureau of Criminal Apprehension.
General Information: Public use terminal available. No adoption, juvenile, sex offender, criminal or sealed records released. Certification fee: $5.00 per doc. Payee: Court Administrator. Personal checks accepted. Prepayment and SASE required.

Rice County

3rd Judicial District Court 218 NW 3rd St, Faribault, MN 55021; phone: 507-332-6107; fax: 507-332-6199; hours 8AM-4:30PM (CST). *Felony, Misdemeanor, Civil, Eviction, Small Claims, Probate.*
www.courts.state.mn.us/districts/third

Civil, Eviction, Small Claims, Probate.
Civil Records: Access: Mail, in person. Both court and visitors may perform in person searches. Search fee: $5.00. Court makes copy: $5.00 per document. Required to search: name, years to search. Civil cases indexed by defendant, plaintiff; on computer from 1990, prior on index cards.
Criminal Records: Access: In person only. Visitors must perform in person searches themselves. Court makes copy: $5.00 per document. Required to search: name, years to search; SSN helpful. Criminal records on computer from 1990, prior on index cards.
General Information: Public use terminal available. No adoption, juvenile, sex offender or sealed records released. Certification fee: $5.00 per doc. Payee: Court Administrator. Personal checks accepted. Prepayment and SASE required.

Rock County

5th Judicial District Court PO Box 745, Luverne, MN 56156; phone: 507-283-5020; fax: 507-283-5017; hours 8AM-5PM (CST). *Felony, Misdemeanor, Civil, Eviction, Small Claims, Probate.*
Civil Records: Access: Mail, in person. Both court and visitors may perform in person searches. Search fee: $10.00 per name. Court makes copy: $5.00 per document. Required to search: name, years to search. Civil cases indexed by defendant, plaintiff; on computer from 1989, prior on books. Note: Visitors may search in books for records prior to 1985. Mail turnaround time same day if possible.
Criminal Records: Access: Mail, in person. Both court and visitors may perform in person searches. Search fee: $10.00 per name. Court makes copy: $5.00 per document. Required to search: name, years to search; also helpful: SSN. Criminal records on computer from 1989, prior on books. The court will provide address for the state Bureau of Criminal Apprehension for complete record searches. Note: Visitors may search in books for records prior to 1985. Mail turnaround time same day if possible.
General Information: Public use terminal available. No adoption, juvenile, sex offender or sealed records released. Will fax documents for $5.00 if search fee has been received. Certification fee: $5.00 per doc. Payee: Court Administrator. Personal checks accepted. Prepayment and SASE required.

Roseau County

9th Judicial District Court 606 5th Ave SW Rm 20, Roseau, MN 56751; phone: 218-463-2541; fax: 218-463-1889; hours 8AM-4:30PM (CST). *Felony, Misdemeanor, Civil, Eviction, Small Claims, Probate.*
Civil Records: Access: Mail, in person. Both court and visitors may perform in person searches. Search fee: $5.00 per name. Court makes copy: $5.00 per document. Required to search: name, years to search. Civil cases indexed by defendant, plaintiff; on computer back to 1990, prior on index cards to 1895. Mail turnaround time same day if possible.
Criminal Records: Access: In person only. Visitors must perform in person searches themselves. Court makes copy: $5.00 per document. Required to search: name, years to search; also helpful: DOB. Criminal records on computer back to 1990, prior on index cards to 1895. Note: Court will perform only statutorily required criminal searches. Mail turnaround time same day if possible.
General Information: Public terminal back to 1991. (The terminal is made available to ongoing, experienced requesters.) No adoption, juvenile, paternity or sealed records released. Will fax documents to toll-free number only. Certification fee: $5.00 per doc. Payee: Court Administrator. Personal checks accepted. Prepayment and SASE required.

Scott County

1st Judicial District Court Scott County Justice Ctr, 200 Fourth Ave W, Shakopee, MN 55379; phone: 952-496-8200; fax: 952-496-8211; hours 8AM-4:30PM (CST). *Felony, Misdemeanor,*

Civil, Eviction, Small Claims, Probate.
Civil Records: Access: Mail, in person. Both court and visitors may perform in person searches. Search fee: $5.00 per name. Court makes copy: $5.00 per doc. Required to search: name, years to search. Civil cases indexed by defendant, plaintiff; on computer from 1981, prior on books.
Criminal Records: Access: In person only. Visitors must perform in person searches themselves. Court makes copy: $5.00 per doc. Required to search: name, years to search, DOB. Criminal records on computer from 1981, prior on books.
General Information: Public terminal back to 1996. (Terminal located in Library.) No adoption, juvenile or sealed records released. Will fax documents $5.00. Certification fee: $10.00 per doc. Payee: Scott County. Personal checks accepted. Prepayment and SASE required.

Sherburne County

10th Judicial District Court Sherburne County Government Ctr, 13880 Hwy #10, Elk River, MN 55330-4608; phone: 763-241-2800; fax: 763-241-2816; hours 8AM-5PM (CST). *Felony, Misdemeanor, Civil, Eviction, Small Claims, Probate.*
Civil Records: Access: Mail, in person. Both court and visitors may perform in person searches. Search fee: $5.00 per name. Court makes copy: $5.00 per document. Required to search: name, years to search. Civil cases indexed by defendant, plaintiff; on computer from 2/85, prior on books.
Criminal Records: Access: In person only. Both court and visitors may perform in person searches themselves. Search fee: $5.00 per name. Court makes copy: $5.00 per document. Required to search: name, years to search, DOB. Criminal records on computer from 2/85, prior on books back to 1930s. Mail turnaround time 5 days.
General Information: Public terminal back to 1985. No adoption, juvenile, confidential or sealed records released. Certification fee: $5.00 per doc. Payee: Court Administrator. Personal checks accepted. Prepayment and SASE required.

Sibley County

1st Judicial District Court PO Box 867, Gaylord, MN 55334; phone: 507-237-4051; criminal fax: 507-237-4062; civil/probate fax is the same; hours 8AM-4:30PM (CST). *Felony, Misdemeanor, Civil, Eviction, Small Claims, Probate.*
Civil Records: Access: Mail, in person. Both court and visitors may perform in person searches. Search fee: $5.00 per name. Court makes copy: $5.00 per document. Required to search: name, years to search. Civil cases indexed by defendant, plaintiff; on computer from 5/92, prior on books to 1800s. Mail turnaround time 2-3 weeks.
Criminal Records: Access: Mail, in person. Both court and visitors may perform in person searches. Search fee: $5.00 per name. Court makes copy: $5.00 per document. Required to search: name, years to search, DOB. Criminal records on computer from 5/92, prior on books to 1800s. Mail turnaround time 2-3 weeks.
General Information: Public terminal back to 1992. No adoption, juvenile or sealed records released. Fee to fax documents is $5.00 per document. Certification fee: $5.00 per doc. Payee: Court Administrator. Personal checks accepted. Prepayment and SASE required.

St. Louis County

6th Judicial District Court 100 N 5th Ave W, Rm 320, Duluth, MN 55802-1294; phone: 218-726-2460; criminal phone: 218-726-2460; civil phone: 218-726-2430; probate phone: 218-726-2521; fax: 218-726-2473; probate fax: same; hours 8AM-4:30PM (CST). *Felony, Misdemeanor, Civil, Eviction, Small Claims, Probate.*
www.courts.state.mn.us/districts/sixth/index.html

Note: All three St Louis County courts can access computer records for the county and direct you to the appropriate court to get the physical file.

Civil Records: Access: Mail, in person. Both court and visitors may perform in person searches. Search fee: $5.00 per name. Court makes copy: $5.00 per document. Required to search: name, years to search. Civil records on computer from 1976. Mail turnaround time 1 week.

Criminal Records: Access: In person only. Visitors must perform in person searches themselves. Court makes copy: $5.00 per document. Required to search: name. Criminal records on computer from 1976.

General Information: Public terminal back to 1976. No adoption, juvenile, juvenile victim of sex offense, sealed records released. Will not fax documents. Certification fee: $5.00 per doc. Payee: Court Administrator. Personal checks accepted. Prepayment required.

6th Judicial District Court - Hibbing Branch
1810 12th Ave East, Hibbing, MN 55746; phone: 218-262-0105; probate phone: 218-726-2400; criminal fax: 218-262-0219; civil/probate fax is the same; hours 8AM-4:30PM (CST). *Felony, Misdemeanor, Civil, Eviction, Small Claims, Probate.*

www.courts.state.mn.us/districts/sixth/index.html

Note: All three St Louis County courts can access county computer records and direct you to the appropriate court for the physical file.

Civil Records: Access: Mail, in person. Both court and visitors may perform in person searches. Search fee: $5.00 per name/per judgment. Court makes copy: $5.00 per document. Required to search: name, years to search. Civil cases indexed by defendant, plaintiff; on computer from 1985, prior on card or books.

Criminal Records: Access: In person only. Visitors must perform in person searches themselves. Court makes copy: $5.00 per document. Required to search: name, years to search. Criminal records on computer from 1985, prior on card or books. Note: Mail requests are forwarded to MN BCA for processing.

General Information: Public terminal back to 1991. No adoption, juvenile, sex offender or sealed records released. Will fax documents for a $10.00 fee. Certification fee: $5.00 per doc. Payee: Court Administrator. Personal checks accepted. Prepayment and SASE required.

6th Judicial District Court - Virginia Branch
300 S 5th Ave, Virginia, MN 55792; phone: 218-749-7106; fax: 218-749-7109; hours 8AM-4:30PM (CST). *Felony, Misdemeanor, Civil, Eviction, Small Claims, Probate.*

www.6courts.com

Note: All three St Louis County courts can access computer records for the county and direct you to the appropriate court for the physical files.

Civil Records: Access: Mail, in person. Both court and visitors may perform in person searches. Search fee: $5.00 per name. Court makes copy: $5.00 per document. Required to search: name, years to search. Civil cases indexed by defendant, plaintiff; on computer back to 1991, prior on books.

Criminal Records: Access: In person only. Visitors must perform in person searches themselves. Court makes copy: $5.00 per document. Required to search: name, years to search, DOB. Criminal records on computer back to 1991, prior on books.

General Information: Public terminal back to 1990. No adoption, juvenile, sex offender or sealed records released. Certification fee: $5.00 per doc. Payee: Court Administrator. Personal checks accepted. Prepayment and SASE required.

Stearns County

Stearns County District Court 725 Courthouse Square, St Cloud, MN 56303; phone: 320-656-3620; fax: 320-656-6335; hours 8AM-4:30PM (CST). *Felony, Misdemeanor, Civil, Small Claims, Eviction, Probate, Traffic.*

www.co.stearns.mn.us/departments/other/court/index.htm

Note: Court calendars free at website.

Civil Records: Access: Mail, in person. Both court and visitors may perform in person searches. Search fee: $5.00 per name. Court makes copy: $5.00 per document. Required to search: name, years to search. Civil cases indexed by defendant, plaintiff; on computer back to 1984, on books from the 1920s.

Criminal Records: Access: In person only. Both court and visitors may perform in person searches. Search fee: $5.00 per name. Court makes copy: $5.00 per document. Required to search: name. Criminal records on computer back to 1984, on books from the 1920s. Mail turnaround time 1-2 days.

General Information: Public terminal back to 1984. No adoption or other sealed records released without court petition. Will fax documents for $5.00 fee. Certification fee: $5.00 per doc. Payee: District Court. Personal checks or Visa, MC, Discover accepted. Prepayment required.

Steele County

3rd Judicial District Court PO Box 487 (111 E Main St), Owatonna, MN 55060; phone: 507-444-7700; probate phone: 507-444-7707; fax: 507-444-7491; hours 8AM-4:30PM (CST). *Felony, Misdemeanor, Civil, Eviction, Small Claims, Probate.*

www.courts.state.mn.us/districts/third

Civil Records: Access: Mail, in person. Both court and visitors may perform in person searches. Search fee: $5.00. Court makes copy: $5.00 per document. Required to search: name, years to search. Civil cases indexed by defendant, plaintiff; on computer from 1990, on books from 1870.

Criminal Records: Access: In person only. Visitors must perform in person searches themselves. Court makes copy: $5.00 per document. Required to search: name, years to search; SSN helpful. Criminal records on computer from 1990, on books from 1870.

General Information: Public terminal back to 1990. No adoption, juvenile, sex offender or sealed records released. Certification fee: $5.00 per doc. Payee: Court Administrator. Personal checks accepted. Will accept VISA and MasterCard. Prepayment and SASE required.

Stevens County

8th Judicial District Court PO Box 530, Morris, MN 56267; phone: 320-589-7287; fax: 320-589-7288; hours 8AM-4:30PM (8AM-4PM Summer hours) (CST). *Felony, Misdemeanor, Civil, Eviction, Small Claims, Probate.*

Civil Records: Access: Mail, in person. Both court and visitors may perform in person searches. Search fee: $5.00 per name. Court makes copy: $5.00 per document. Required to search: name, years to search. Civil cases indexed by defendant, plaintiff; on computer from 2/89, on cards from 5/86, on books from 1900.

Criminal Records: Access: In person only. Both court and visitors may perform in person searches. Court makes copy: $5.00 per document. Required to search: name, years to search. Criminal records on computer from 2/89, on cards from 5/86, on books from 1900. Note: For access to criminal history information, the court recommends the BCA at 651-642-0610. Mail turnaround time 1-2 days.

General Information: Public terminal back to 2/89. No adoption, juvenile, sex offender or sealed records released. Will fax documents to local or toll free line. Certification fee: $5.00 per doc. Payee: Court Administrator. Personal checks accepted. Prepayment and SASE required.

Swift County

8th Judicial District Court PO Box 110, Benson, MN 56215; phone: 320-843-2744; criminal fax: 320-843-4124; civil/probate fax is the same; hours 8AM-4:30PM (CST). *Felony, Misdemeanor, Civil, Eviction, Small Claims, Probate.*

Note: Probate records prior to 1983 are in a separate index.

Civil Records: Access: Phone, fax, mail, in person. Both court and visitors may perform in person searches. No search fee. Court makes copy: $5.00 per document. Required to search: name, years to search. Civil cases indexed by defendant, plaintiff; on computer back to 8/1988, prior in files and books from 1800s.

Criminal Records: Access: In person only. Visitors must perform in person searches themselves. Court makes copy: $5.00 per document. Required to search: name, years to search; also helpful: DOB. Criminal records on computer back to 1988, prior in files and books from 1800s except those destroyed per retention schedule.

General Information: Public use terminal available. No adoption, juvenile, minor victim of sex offense, sealed records released. Will fax documents for $5.00 fee. Certification fee: $5.00 per doc. Payee: Court Administrator. Personal checks accepted. Prepayment and SASE required.

Todd County

7th Judicial District Court 221 1st Ave South, Long Prairie, MN 56347; phone: 320-732-7800; criminal fax: 320-732-2506; civil/probate fax is the same; hours 8AM-4:30PM (CST). *Felony, Misdemeanor, Civil, Eviction, Small Claims, Probate.*

Civil Records: Access: Mail, in person. Both court and visitors may perform in person searches. Search fee: $5.00 per name. Court makes copy: $5.00 per document. Required to search: name, years to search, address. Civil cases indexed by defendant, plaintiff; on computer 7/86, prior on index cards and books. Mail turnaround time 3-4 days.

Criminal Records: Access: Mail, in person. Both court and visitors may perform in person searches. Search fee: $5.00 per name. Court makes copy: $5.00 per document. Required to search: name, years to search, address, DOB; also helpful: SSN. Criminal records on computer 7/86, prior on index cards and books. Mail turnaround time 3-4 days.

General Information: Public terminal back to 1986. No adoption, juvenile or sealed records released. Fee to fax documents is $5.00 per document. Certification fee: $5.00 per doc. Payee: Court Administrator. Personal checks accepted. Prepayment and SASE required.

Traverse County

8th Judicial District Court 702 2nd Ave N, PO Box 867, Wheaton, MN 56296; phone: 320-563-4343; criminal fax: 320-563-4311; civil/probate fax is the same; hours 8AM-N, 12:30-4:30PM (CST). *Felony, Misdemeanor, Civil, Eviction, Small Claims, Probate.*

Civil Records: Access: Mail, in person. Both court and visitors may perform in person searches. Search fee: $5.00 per name. Court makes copy: $5.00 per document. Required to search: name, years to search. Civil cases indexed by defendant, plaintiff; on computer from 6/89, prior on index cards and books. Only judgment searches accepted by mail.

Criminal Records: Access: In person only. Visitors must perform in person searches themselves. Court makes copy: $5.00 per document. Required to search: name, years to search. Criminal records on computer from 6/89, prior on index cards and books.

General Information: Public use terminal available. No adoption, juvenile, sex offender or sealed records released. Will fax documents for $5.00 per document. Certification fee: $5.00 per doc. Payee: Court Administrator. Personal checks accepted. Prepayment and SASE required.

Wabasha County

3rd Judicial District Court 625 Jefferson Ave, Wabasha, MN 55981; phone: 651-565-3012; criminal phone: 651-565-3010/3524/3097; civil phone: 651-565-3579/3087/3051; probate phone: 651-565-3051/3579/3087; criminal fax: 651-565-8214; civil/probate fax is the same; hours 8AM-4PM (CST). *Felony, Misdemeanor, Civil, Eviction, Small Claims, Probate.* www.courts.state.mn.us/districts/third/counties/wabasha.htm

Civil Records: Access: Phone, fax, mail, in person. Both court and visitors may perform in person searches. Search fee: $5.00 for judgment searches. Court makes copy: $5.00 per document. Required to search: name, years to search. Civil cases indexed by defendant, plaintiff; on computer from 6/89, prior on index cards and books. Search daily court calendar at the website.

Criminal Records: Access: In person only. Visitors must perform in person searches themselves. Court makes copy: $5.00 per document. Required to search: name, years to search; also helpful: DOB. Criminal records on computer from 6/89, prior on index cards and books. Daily court calendar is at the website.

General Information: No adoption, juvenile, sex offender or sealed records released. Fee to fax documents is $5.00 1st page; $1.00 each add'l. Certification fee: $5.00 per doc. Payee: Wabasha District Court. Personal checks accepted. Prepayment and SASE required.

Wadena County

7th Judicial District Court County Courthouse, 415 S Jefferson St, Wadena, MN 56482; phone: 218-631-7634; fax: 218-631-7635; hours 8AM-4:30PM (CST). *Felony, Misdemeanor, Civil, Eviction, Small Claims, Probate.*

Note: Note that the search fee is $5.00 and the copy fee is an additional $5.00.

Civil Records: Access: Mail, in person. Both court and visitors may perform in person searches. Search fee: $5.00 per name. Court makes copy: $5.00 per document. Required to search: name, years to search. Civil cases indexed by defendant, plaintiff; on computer from 7/86; prior on books, cards and microfiche. Mail turnaround time 7 to 10 days.

Criminal Records: Access: Mail, in person. Both court and visitors may perform in person searches. Search fee: $5.00 per name. Court makes copy: $5.00 per document. Required to search: name, years to search, DOB; also helpful: address. Criminal records on computer from 7/86; prior on books, cards and microfiche. Mail turnaround time 7 to 10 days.

General Information: Public terminal back to 7/1986. No adoption, juvenile, or sealed records released. Will fax documents for additional $5.00. Certification fee: $5.00 per doc. Payee: Court Administrator. Personal checks accepted. Prepayment required.

Waseca County

3rd Judicial District Court 307 N State St, Waseca, MN 56093; phone: 507-835-0540; fax: 507-837-5317; hours 8AM-4:30PM (CST). *Felony, Misdemeanor, Civil, Eviction, Small Claims, Probate.* www.courts.state.mn.us/districts/third

Civil Records: Access: Mail, in person. Both court and visitors may perform in person searches. Search fee: $5.00 per name. Court makes copy: $5.00 per document. Required to search: name, years to search. Civil cases indexed by defendant, plaintiff; on computer from 1990, prior on TCIS cards and books. Mail turnaround time 5 days.

Criminal Records: Access: In person only. Visitors must perform in person searches themselves. Court makes copy: $5.00 per document. Required to search: name, years to search, DOB. Criminal records on computer from 1990, prior on TCIS cards and books.

General Information: Public terminal back to 1990. No adoption, juvenile, sex offender victim or sealed records released. Will fax documents for $5.00 per document. Certification fee: $5.00 per doc. Payee:

Court Administrator. Personal checks accepted. Prepayment and SASE required.

Washington County

10th Judicial District Court 14949 62nd St North, PO Box 3802, Stillwater, MN 55082-3802; phone: 651-430-6263; fax: 651-430-6300; hours 7:30AM-5PM (CST). *Felony, Misdemeanor, Civil, Eviction, Small Claims, Probate.* www.co.washington.mn.us

Civil Records: Access: Mail, in person. Both court and visitors may perform in person searches. Search fee: $5.00 per name. Court makes copy: $5.00 per document. Required to search: name, years to search. Civil cases indexed by defendant, plaintiff; on computer back to 12/83, prior on books.

Criminal Records: Access: In person only. Visitors must perform in person searches themselves. Court makes copy: $5.00 per document. Required to search: name, years to search, DOB. Criminal records on computer back to 12/83, prior on books. Fax & mail access limited to statute requirements.

General Information: Public terminal back to 1991. No adoption, juvenile, sex offender or sealed records released. Will not fax documents. Certification fee: $5.00 per doc. Payee: Court Administrator. Personal checks or Visa, MC accepted. Prepayment and SASE required.

Watonwan County

5th Judicial District Court PO Box 518, 710 2nd Ave.South, St James, MN 56081; phone: 507-375-1236; criminal phone: 507-375-1237; civil phone: 507-375-1235; probate phone: 507-375-1234; fax: 507-375-5010; hours 8AM-5PM (CST). *Felony, Misdemeanor, Civil, Eviction, Small Claims, Probate.*

Note: The Jury Office can be reached at 507-375-1230.

Civil Records: Access: Fax, mail, in person. Both court and visitors may perform in person searches. Search fee: $5.00 per name. Court makes copy: $5.00 per document. Required to search: name, years to search. Civil cases indexed by defendant, plaintiff; on computer from 5/89, prior on index cards. Mail turnaround time 5 business days.

Criminal Records: Access: In person only. Visitors must perform in person searches themselves. Court makes copy: $5.00 per document. Required to search: name, years to search; also helpful: DOB. Criminal records on computer from 5/89, prior on index cards. Mail turnaround time 5 business days.

General Information: Public terminal back to 4/1988. No adoption, juvenile, sex offender or sealed records released. Fee to fax documents is $5.00 per page. Certification fee: $5.00 per doc. Payee: Court Administrator. Personal checks accepted. Prepayment and SASE required.

Wilkin County

8th Judicial District Court PO Box 219, Breckenridge, MN 56520; phone: 218-643-7172; fax: 218-643-7167; hours 8AM-4:30PM (CST). *Felony, Misdemeanor, Civil, Eviction, Small Claims, Probate.*

Civil Records: Access: Phone, mail, in person. Both court and visitors may perform in person searches. No search fee. Court makes copy: $5.00 per document. Required to search: name; also helpful: years to search. Civil cases indexed by defendant, plaintiff; on computer from 1989, prior on books. Mail turnaround time 1-2 days.

Criminal Records: Access: In person only. Both court and visitors may perform in person searches. Court makes copy: $5.00 per document. Required to search: name; also helpful: years to search. Criminal records on computer from 1989, prior on books.

General Information: Public terminal back to 1989. No adoption, juvenile, sex offender or sealed records released. Certification fee: $5.00 per doc. Payee: Court Administrator. Personal checks accepted. Prepayment and SASE required.

Winona County

3rd Judicial District Court 171 W 3rd St, Winona, MN 55987; phone: 507-457-6385; fax: 507-457-6392; hours 8AM-4:30PM (CST). *Felony, Misdemeanor, Civil, Eviction, Small Claims, Probate.* www.courts.state.mn.us/districts/third/counties/winona.htm

Civil Records: Access: Mail, in person. Both court and visitors may perform in person searches. Search fee: $10.00 per hour. Court makes copy: $5.00 per document. Required to search: name, years to search. Civil cases indexed by defendant, plaintiff; on computer from 1986, on books from 1888. Mail turnaround time 5-10 working days.

Criminal Records: Access: In person only. Visitors must perform in person searches themselves. Court makes copy: $5.00 per document. Required to search: name, years to search, DOB. Criminal records on computer from 1986, on books from 1888. Criminal searchers are usually referred to the MN State BCA.

General Information: Public terminal back to 1986. No adoption, juvenile or sealed records released. Will not fax documents. Certification fee: $5.00 per doc. Payee: Court Administrator. Personal checks accepted. Prepayment required.

Wright County

10th Judicial District Court 10 NW 2nd St, Rm 201, Buffalo, MN 55313-1192; phone: 763-682-7549; fax: 763-682-7300; hours 8AM-4:30PM (CST). *Felony, Misdemeanor, Civil, Eviction, Small Claims, Probate.* www.courts.state.mn.us/home

Civil Records: Access: In person only. Visitors must perform in person searches themselves. Court makes copy: $5.00 per document. Required to search: name, years to search, approx. date. Civil cases indexed by defendant, plaintiff; on computer from 8/84, prior on books, cards & microfiche. Certificates for outstanding docketed money judgments may be requested by mail. Each name variation requires $5.00 fee.

Criminal Records: Access: In person only. Visitors must perform in person searches themselves. Court makes copy: $5.00 per document. Required to search: name, years to search; also helpful: DOB, approx. date. Criminal records on computer from 8/84, prior on books, cards & microfiche.

General Information: Public terminal back to 1990. No adoption, juvenile, confidential or sealed records released. Certification fee: $5.00 per doc. Payee: Court Administrator. Personal checks or Visa, MC accepted. Prepayment required.

Yellow Medicine County

8th Judicial District Court 415 9th Ave, Granite Falls, MN 56241; phone: 320-564-3325; fax: 320-564-4435; hours 8AM-4PM (CST). *Felony, Misdemeanor, Civil, Eviction, Small Claims, Probate.*

Civil Records: Access: Mail, in person. Both court and visitors may perform in person searches. Search fee: $10.00 for certified search. Court makes copy: $5.00 per document. Required to search: name, years to search; also helpful: address. Civil cases indexed by defendant, plaintiff; on computer from 1988.

Criminal Records: Access: In person only. Visitors must perform in person searches themselves. Court makes copy: $5.00 per document. Required to search: name, years to search. Criminal records on computer from 1988.

General Information: Public terminal back to 1988. No adoption, juvenile or sealed records released. Will not fax documents. Certification fee: $5.00 per doc. Payee: Court Administrator. Personal checks accepted. Prepayment and SASE required.

Minnesota Recording Offices

ORGANIZATION:	87 counties, 87 recording offices. The recording officer is County Recorder. The entire state is in the Central Time Zone (CST).
REAL ESTATE RECORDS:	Many Minnesota counties will perform real estate searches, especially short questions over the telephone. Copy fees vary, but do not apply to certified copies. Certification fees are usually $1.00 per page with a minimum of $5.00.
UCC RECORDS:	Until July 2001, Minnesota maintained a centralized database of financing statements filed at the state level and all counties entered all non-real estate filings into the central statewide database which was accessible from any county office. Now, the only filings recorded by the County Recorder are real estate related collateral. All counties will perform UCC searches. Use search request form UCC-11. Search fees are usually $20.00 per debtor name. A UCC search can include tax liens. Copies usually cost $1.00 per page.
TAX LIEN RECORDS:	Federal and state tax liens on personal property of businesses are filed with the Secretary of State. Other federal and state tax liens are filed with the County Recorder. A special search form UCC-12 is used for separate tax lien searches. Some counties search each tax lien index separately. Some charge one $15.00 or $20.00 fee to search both indexes, but others charge a separate fee for each index searched. Search and copy fees vary widely.
OTHER LIENS:	Mechanics, hospital, judgment, attorneys.
ONLINE ACCESS:	There is no statewide system, but a number of counties offer web access to assessor data and recorded deeds.

Aitkin County

County Recorder, 209 Second St NW; Rm 205, Aitkin, MN 56431. 218-927-7336; fax-218-927-7324; hours: 8AM-4:30PM.
Separate indices to search. Records indexed on a public use terminal back to 1985. Office personnel or visitors may perform searches. Search fee $20.00 per name. General copy fee $1.00 per page after 10 pages. R/E or tax lien copy- $.25 per page. Cert fee- $1.00 per page, $5.00 minimum. Payee- Aitkin County Recorder. **Other phones:** Treasurer- 218-927-7325; Appraiser/Auditor- 218-927-7327; Elections- 218-927-7354; Vital Records- 218-927-7336; Marriage Records- 218-927-7325. **Property tax/Assessor-** 218-927-7327.

Anoka County

County Recorder, 2100 3rd Ave, Anoka, MN 55303-2265. 763-323-5416, R/E recording phone-763-323-5413; fax-763-323-5421; hours: 8AM-4:30PM. www.co.anoka.mn.us
Office personnel or visitors may perform searches. Search fee $15.00 per name. General copy fee $1.00 per page after 10 pages. R/E record copy- $.55 per page uncertified. Cert fee- $1.00 per page, $5.00 minimum. Payee- Anoka County Recorder. **Online access to Real Estate, Tax Assessor records:** Access to the County online records requires an annual fee of $35 and a $25 monthly fee and $.25 per transaction. Records date back to 1995. Lending agency information is available. For information, contact Pam LeBlanc at 763-323-5424. There is also a dial-up property information system at 763-323-5400. Also, you may access property information at https://prtinfo.co.anoka.mn.us/(2sqvv055oxsegqmkh22u4nvx)/search.aspx. No name searching. **Other phones:** Treasurer- 763-323-5400. **Property tax/Assessor-** 763-323-5400.

Becker County

County Recorder, PO Box 787, Detroit Lakes, MN 56502. 218-846-7304; fax-218-846-7323; hours: 8AM-4:30PM. www.beckercounty.com
Office personnel or visitors may perform searches. Search fee $10.00 per name. General copy fee $1.00 per page after 5 pages. R/E record copy- $1.00 per page. Fax back- 5.00 per doc. Cert fee- $5.00 up to 10 pages. Payee- Becker County Recorder. **Online access to Property Tax, Assessor records:** Access to the assessor property data is free at www.co.becker.mn.us/. **Other phones:** Treasurer- 218-846-7311; Appraiser/Auditor- 218-846-7301; Elections- 218-846-7301; Vital Records- 218-846-7304. **Property tax/Assessor-** 218-846-7300.

Beltrami County

County Recorder, 619 Beltrami Ave NW; Courthouse, Bemidji, MN 56601. 218-333-4170; fax-218-333-4527; hours: 8AM-4:30PM.
Separate indices to search include books and computer. Records indexed on a public use terminal back to 1987. Office personnel or visitors may perform searches. Search fee $30.00 per hour. Copy fee $1.00 per page. Cert fee- $10.00 per cert includes copy fee. Payee- Beltrami County Recorder. **Online access to Recording, Real Estate, Lien, Deed records:** Recorder office data by subscription on either the Nazca using subscription and fees or the Tapestry System using credit card, https://tapestry.fidlar.com/tapsearch.aspx; $3.99 search; $.50 per image. **Other phones:** Treasurer- 218-333-4175. **Property tax/Assessor-** 218-333-4114.

Benton County

County Recorder, PO Box 129, Foley, MN 56329. 320-968-5037; fax-320-968-5329; hours: 8AM-4:30PM. www.co.benton.mn.us/departments/recorder/
Office personnel or visitors may perform searches. Search fee $20.00 per name. General copy fee $1.00 per page. Tax lien copy- $.50 per page, $1.00 minimum. Cert fee- $1.00 per page, $5.00 minimum. Payee- Benton County Recorder. **Other phones:** Treasurer- 320-968-5006; Elections- 320-968-5027; Vital Records- 320-968-5037. **Property tax/Assessor-** 320-968-5019.

Big Stone County

County Recorder, PO Box 218, Ortonville, MN 56278. 320-839-2308; fax-320-839-2308; hours: 8AM-4:30PM.
Office personnel or visitors may perform searches. Search fee $15.00 per name. Will not search real estate records. UCC search per debtor name- $20.00. Copy fee $1.00 per page. Real estate copy- $2.00 minimum per document. Cert fee- $1.00 per page, $5.00 minimum. Payee- Big Stone County Recorder. **Other phones:** Treasurer- 320-839-3445; Vital Records- 320-839-2308. **Property tax/Assessor-** 320-839-3272.

Blue Earth County

County Recorder, PO Box 3567, Mankato, MN 56002-3567. 507-304-4251, UCC recording phone-507-304-4469; fax-507-304-4079; hours: 8AM-5PM. www.co.blue-earth.mn.us
All records in one index. Records indexed on computer back 1 year. Real estate owner, mortgage, and property transfer searches available. Legal description required. Will search UCC records, tax liens not included in UCC search. UCC search per debtor name- $20.00. Separate federal/state combined tax lien search- $15.00 per debtor. Copy fee $3.00 per page; self serve- $1.00. Cert fee- $1.00 per page, $5.00 minimum plus copy fee. Payee- Blue Earth County Recorder. **Online access to Property, Assessor records:** Access to the property information search database is free at www.co.blue-earth.mn.us/tax/. Also, you may search at www.blueearth.minnesotaassessors.com. No name searching at either site, but a subscription service is available at the latter. **Other phones:** Treasurer- 507-304-4251; Elections- 507-304-4341; Vital Records- 507-304-4343. **Property tax/Assessor-** same address as above. 507-304-4251.

Brown County

County Recorder, PO Box 248, New Ulm, MN 56073-0248. 507-233-6653, UCC recording phone-507-233-6657; fax-507-233-6668; hours: 8AM-5PM. www.co.brown.mn.us
All records in one index. Records indexed on a public use terminal back to 1987. Office personnel or visitors may perform searches. Real estate owner, mortgage, and property transfer searches available. Will search UCC records, tax liens not included in UCC search. UCC search per debtor, including 10 copies/listings- $20.00. Tax lien search- $2.00 per debtor. Copy fee $1.00 per page. Cert fee- $5.00 per doc plus copy fee. Payee- Brown County Recorder. **Other phones:** Treasurer- 507-233-6617; Appraiser/Auditor- 507-233-6609; Elections- 507-233-6617; Vital Records- 507-233-6657. **Property tax/Assessor-** same address as above. 507-233-6609.

Carlton County

County Recorder, Box 70, Carlton, MN 55718. 218-384-9122, UCC recording phone-218-384-9156; fax-218-384-9157; hours: 8AM-4PM.
General index search fee $20.00 for two hour search, and $10.00 per add'l hour up to four. Real estate owner, mortgage, and property transfer searches available. Legal description required. Will search UCC records, but not tax liens. UCC search per debtor, including 10 copies/listings- $20.00. Copy fee $1.00 per page after 1st 10 pages free. Cert fee- $1.00 per page, $5.00 minimum. Payee- Carlton County Treasurer. **Other phones:** Treasurer- 218-384-9594; Vital Records- 218-384-9156. **Property tax/Assessor-** 218-384-9144.

Carver County

County Recorder, 600 E Fourth St; Carver County Govt Ctr, Admin Bldg, Chaska, MN 55318-2158. 952-361-1930; fax-952-361-1931; hours: 8AM-4:30PM. www.co.carver.mn.us
Office personnel or visitors may perform searches. Search fee $15.00 per name. Will not search real estate records. UCC search per debtor, including 10 copies/listings- $20.00. Copy fee $1.00 per page after 10 pages. Cert fee- $1.00 per page, $5.00 minimum. Payee- Carver County Treasurer. **Online access to Real Estate, Grantor/Grantee, Lien, Property Tax records:** Access to recorder land records and property tax records is free at www.co.carver.mn.us/egov.html. Select Land Title Information or Property Tax Information. **Other phones:** Treasurer- 952-361-1980; Vital Records- 952-361-1930. **Property tax/Assessor-** 952-361-1960.

Cass County

County Recorder, PO Box 3000, Walker, MN 56484. 218-547-7381, R/E recording phone-218-547-7381/7249, UCC recording phone-218-547-7233; fax-218-547-7292; hours: 8AM-4:30PM. www.co.cass.mn.us
Separate indices to search include abstract and torrens. Records indexed on computer back to 4/1/87. Office personnel or visitors may perform searches. Search fee $20.00 per name. Copy fee $1.00 per page. Cert fee- $10.00 per page, $5.00 minimum includes copy fee. Payee- Cass County Recorder. **Online access to Property, GIS, Recording, Real Estate, Deed records:** Access to parcel, tax, and limited real estate data is free at the GID-mapping site at www.co.cass.mn.us/maps/map_parcel_info.html. No name searching.. Also, recorder office data by subscription on either the Laredo system using subscription and fees or the Tapestry System using credit card, https://tapestry.fidlar.com/tapsearch.aspx; $3.99 search; $.50 per image. From 4-1-87 to present. **Other phones:** Treasurer- 218-547-7247; Elections- 218-547-7281; Vital Records- 218-547-7293; Auditor- 218-547-7260. **Property tax/Assessor-** same address as above. 218-547-7298.

Chippewa County

County Recorder, 629 No. 11th St, Montevideo, MN 56265. 320-269-9431; fax-320-269-7168; hours: 8AM-4:30PM.
Separate indices to search include tract index by descriptions, images are in books or computer. General index search fee $20.00 per hour. Will search real estate records. Will search UCC records, tax liens not included in UCC search. UCC search fee- $20.00 per hour. Tax lien search fee- $20.00 per debtor. Separate federal tax lien search- $8.00 per debtor. Federal/state combined tax lien search- $20.00 per debtor. Copy fee $.50 per page. Cert fee- $1.00 per page, $5.00 minimum plus copy fee. Payee- Chippewa County Recorder. **Online access to Recorder, Real Estate, Deed, Lien records:** Recorder office data by subscription on either the Laredo system using subscription and fees or the Tapestry System using credit card, https://tapestry.fidlar.com/tapsearch.aspx; $3.99 search; $.50 per image. **Other phones:** Treasurer- 320-269-7347; Elections- 320-269-7447; Vital Records- 320-269-9431. **Property tax/Assessor-** 629 N 11th St,, Montevideo, MN 56265; 320-269-7696.

Chisago County

County Recorder, 313 N Main St.; Government Ctr, Rm/Box 277, Center City, MN 55012-9663. 651-213-0438, R/E recording phone-651-257-1300; fax-651-213-0454; hours: 8AM-4:30PM.
Only the public may search. Copy fee $1.00 per page after 10 pages. Cert fee- $5.00 per doc plus copy fee. Payee- Chisago County Recorder. **Property tax/Assessor-** 651-213-0401.

Clay County

County Recorder, PO Box 280, Moorhead, MN 56561-0280. 218-299-5031; fax-218-299-7500; hours: 8AM-4:30PM. www.co.clay.mn.us
Separate indices to search include torrens and abstract, UCC/CNS, marriage, birth, death and others separate. Records indexed on a public use terminal back to 1987 (grantor/grantee). Office personnel or visitors may perform searches. Search fee $20.00 per name. Will not search real estate records. Copy fee $1.00 per page. Cert fee- $1.00 per page, $10.00 minimum. Payee- Clay County Recorder. **Online access to Real Estate, Deed, Recording, Lien records:** The county online GIS mapping service at www.gis.co.clay.mn.us/map/Clay/disclaimer.htm provides property record searching, but by parcel number only. Recorder records may be searched at the website in the near future. Plats and corner certificates online free at www.co.clay.mn.us/depts/recorder/laredo/rerrol.htm. Also, recorder office data by subscription on either the Laredo system using subscription and fees or the Tapestry System using credit card, https://tapestry.fidlar.com/tapsearch.aspx; $3.99 search; $.50 per image. **Other phones:** Treasurer- 218-299-5011; Elections- 218-299-5006; Vital Records- 218-299-5031. **Property tax/Assessor-** same address as above. 218-299-5017.

Clearwater County

County Recorder, 213 Main Ave North, Dept. 207, Bagley, MN 56621. 218-694-6129; fax-218-694-6179; hours: 8AM-4:30PM.
All records in one index. Records indexed on computer. Office personnel or visitors may perform searches. Search fee $20.00. Copy fee $1.00 per page after 10 pages. Cert fee- $5.00 per doc plus copy fee. Payee- Clearwater County Recorder. **Other phones:** Treasurer- 218-694-6130; Vital Records- 218-694-6129. **Property tax/Assessor-** 218-694-6260.

Cook County

County Recorder, 411 W. 2nd St, Grand Marais, MN 55604-2307. 218-387-3660; fax-218-387-3043; hours: 8AM-4PM.
Separate indices to search include Grantee/Grantor, Tract. Records indexed on a public use terminal back to 1988. Office personnel or visitors may perform searches. Search fee $20.00 UCCs, $5.00 tax liens. Copy fee $1.00 per page after 10 pages. Cert fee- $10.00 minimum. Payee- Cook County Recorder. **Online access to Recording, Real Estate, Deed, Lien records:** Recorder office data by subscription on either the Laredo system using subscription and fees or the Tapestry System using credit card, https://tapestry.fidlar.com/tapsearch.aspx; $3.99 search; $.50 per image. **Other phones:** Treasurer- 218-387-3640; Elections- 218-387-3640; Vital Records- 218-387-3660. **Property tax/Assessor-** 218-387-3650.

Cottonwood County

County Recorder, PO Box 326, Windom, MN 56101. 507-831-1458; fax-507-831-3675; hours: 8AM-4:30PM. www.co.cottonwood.mn.us
All records in one index. Records indexed on a public use terminal back to 9/2000; computer index is not complete. Office personnel or visitors may perform searches. Search fee $20.00 unless otherwise indicated. Federal and/or state tax lien search- $15.00 per debtor. Copy fee $1.00 per page. Cert fee- $1.00 per page, $5.00 minimum. Payee- Cottonwood County Recorder. **Other phones:** Treasurer- 507-831-1342; Elections- 507-831-1905; Vital Records- 507-831-1458. **Property tax/Assessor-** 900 Third Ave, Windom, MN 56101; 507-831-2458.

Crow Wing County

County Recorder, PO Box 383, Brainerd, MN 56401. 218-824-1280; fax-218-824-1281; hours: 8AM-5PM.
Office personnel or visitors may perform searches. Search fee $20.00 per name. Will not search real estate records. Copy fee $.25 per page. Cert fee- $1.00 per page, $5.00 minimum. Payee- Crow Wing County Recorder. **Property tax/Assessor-** 218-824-1010.

Dakota County

County Recorder, 1590 Highway 55, Hastings, MN 55033. 651-438-4355; fax-651-438-8176; hours: 8AM-4:30PM. www.co.dakota.mn.us
Office personnel or visitors may perform searches. Search fee $15.00 per name. Will not search real estate records. UCC search per debtor, including 10 copies/listings- $20.00. Copy fee $1.00 per page after 10 pages. Cert fee- $1.00 per page, $5.00 minimum. Payee- Dakota County Recorder. **Online access to Real Estate, Assessor records:** Records on the County Real Estate Inquiry database are free at www.co.dakota.mn.us/assessor/real_estate_inquiry.htm. Information includes items such as address, estimated value, taxes, last sale price, building details. **Other phones:** Treasurer- 651-438-4576 **Property tax/Assessor-** 651-438-4200.

Dodge County

County Recorder, 22 6th St. East; Dept. 101, Mantorville, MN 55955. 507-635-6250; fax-507-635-6265; hours: 8AM-4:30PM. www.co.dodge.mn.us
Separate indices to search include books, computer. Search fee $11.00 per name unless otherwise indicated. UCC search per debtor, including 10 copies/listings- $20.00. Separate federal or state tax lien search- $2.00 per debtor. Copy fee $1.00 per page. Cert fee- $5.00 per doc plus copy fee. Payee- Dodge County Recorder. **Other phones:** Treasurer- 507-635-6240; Elections- 507-635-6239; Vital Records- 507-635-6250. **Property tax/Assessor-** 507-635-6245.

Douglas County

County Recorder, 305 8th Ave West; Courthouse, Alexandria, MN 56308. 320-762-3877; fax-320-762-2389; hours: 8AM-4:30PM. www.co.douglas.mn.us
Office personnel or visitors may perform searches. Search fee $20.00 per name. Copy fee $1.00 per page after 10 pages. Mailing and faxing fee extra. Cert fee- $5.00 per cert up to 5 pages; $1.00 each add'l page. Payee- Douglas County Recorder. **Online access to Assessor records:** Look-up assessor property tax data free at http://morris.state.mn.us/tax/. **Other phones:** Treasurer- 320-762-3077; Vital Records- 320-762-3877. **Property tax/Assessor-** 320-762-3854.

Faribault County

County Recorder, PO Box 130, Blue Earth, MN 56013. 507-526-6252; fax-507-526-6227; hours: 8AM-4:30PM.
Office personnel or visitors may perform searches. Search fee $20.00 per name. Copy fee $1.00 per page. Cert fee- $1.00 per page, $5.00 minimum. Payee- Faribault County Recorder. **Online access to Recording, Real Estate, Lien, Deed records:** Recorder office data by subscription on either the Laredo system using subscription and fees or the Tapestry System using credit card, https://tapestry.fidlar.com/tapsearch.aspx; $3.99 search;

\$.50 per image. Index back to 1995; images to 9/2003. **Other phones:** Treasurer- 507-526-6260; Appraiser/Auditor- 507-526-6201; Elections- 507-526-6212; Vital Records- 507-526-6252. **Property tax/Assessor-** 507-526-6201.

Fillmore County

County Recorder, Box 465, Preston, MN 55965-0465. 507-765-3852; fax-507-765-2802; hours: 8AM-4:30PM.

Search fee \$5.00 unless otherwise indicated. UCC search per debtor, including 10 copies/listings- \$20.00. Copy fee \$1.00 per page after 10 pages. Cert fee- \$5.00 per cert plus copy fee. Payee- Fillmore County Recorder. **Other phones:** Treasurer- 507-765-3811; Elections- 507-765-4701; Vital Records- 507-765-5339. **Property tax/Assessor-** PO Box 67, Preston, MN 55965-0067; 507-765-3868.

Freeborn County

County Recorder, 411 S. Broadway; Court House, Albert Lea, MN 56007-4506. 507-377-5130; fax-507-377-5265; hours: 8AM-5PM. www.co.freeborn.mn.us/recorder.html

Separate indices to search include tract and grantor/grantee. Records indexed on a public use terminal back to 11/95. Only the public may search. Copies included in search fee. R/E or tax lien copy- \$1.00 per page uncertified. Cert fee- \$1.00 per page, \$5.00 minimum includes copy fee. Payee- Freeborn County Recorder. **Other phones:** Treasurer- 507-377-5117; Elections- 507-377-5116; Vital Records- 507-377-5130. **Property tax/Assessor-** same address as above. 507-377-5176.

Goodhue County

County Recorder, Box 408, Red Wing, MN 55066. 651-385-3149; fax-651-385-3119; hours: 8AM-4:30PM.

Will accept faxed search requests for add'l \$5.00 fee. All records in one index. Records indexed on a public use terminal back to 1987. Office personnel or visitors may perform searches. Search fee \$20.00 per name. Will not search real estate records. Copy fee \$1.00 per page. Cert fee- \$1.00 per page, \$6.00 minimum plus copy fee. Payee- Goodhue County Recorder. **Other phones:** Treasurer- 651-385-3032. **Property tax/Assessor-** 651-385-3006.

Grant County

County Recorder, PO Box 1007, Elbow Lake, MN 56531-4300. 218-685-4133; fax-218-685-4521; hours: 8AM-4PM.

Office personnel or visitors may perform searches. General search fee \$2.00 per name. UCC search per debtor name- \$20.00. Copies included in search fee. Tax lien copy- \$1.00 per page. Cert fee- \$5.00 per cert plus copy fee. Payee- Grant County Recorder. **Property tax/Assessor-** 218-685-4644.

Hennepin County

County Recorder, 300 S. 6th St; A-500 Gov't Ctr, Minneapolis, MN 55487. 612-348-5139, R/E recording phone-612-348-3139; fax-612-348-4948; hours: 8AM-4:30PM. www.co.hennepin.mn.us

Separate indices to search include torrens, abstract. Records indexed on a public use terminal back to 1988. Only the public may search. Will do a tax lien search for \$20.00. Copy fee \$1.00 per page. Cert fee- \$0.00 per document plus copy fee. Payee- Hennepin County Recorder. **Online access to Real Estate, Lien, Most Wanted records:** Three sources available. Access to Hennepin County online records requires a \$35 annual fee with a charge of \$5 per hour from 7AM-7PM, or \$4.15 per hour at other times. Records date back to 1988. Only lending agency information is available. Property tax info is at Treasurer office; call 612-348-3011. Also, search records on county Property Information Search database free at http://www2.co.hennepin.mn.us/pins/. Or, search at www.co.hennepin.mn.us/ Click on

Property Info Search. Search by Property ID #, address, or addition name. An Automated phone system is also available; 612-348-3011. **Other phones:** Treasurer- 612-348-3011; Elections- 612-348-5151; Vital Records- 612-348-8240. **Property tax/Assessor-** 2100 Gov't Ctr, 300 S 6th St, Minneapolis, MN 55487; 612-348-3046, assessor fax- 612-348-8751.

Houston County

County Recorder, PO Box 29, Caledonia, MN 55921-0029. 507-725-5813; fax-507-725-2647; hours: 8AM-4:30PM. www.houstoncounty.govoffice2.com

Separate indices to search include legal description, grantor/grantee, document number, date of recording. Records indexed on a public use terminal back to 1996. Office personnel or visitors may perform searches. General index search fee \$35.00 per hour, minimum is \$10.00. Copy fee \$1.00 per number. Cert fee- \$1.00 per page, \$5.00 minimum. Payee- Houston County Recorder. **Other phones:** Treasurer- 507-725-5815; Appraiser/Auditor- 507-725-5801; Elections- 507-725-5803; Vital Records- 507-725-5813. **Property tax/Assessor-** 304 S. Marshall St, Rm 109,, Caledonia, MN 55921; 507-725-5801.

Hubbard County

County Recorder, 301 Court Ave, Park Rapids, MN 56470. 218-732-3552; fax-218-732-3645; hours: 8AM-4:30PM. www.co.hubbard.mn.us/Recorder.htm

Separate indices to search include grantor/grantee, abstract, torrens, tract, etc. Records indexed on a public use terminal for abstract 5/1994; for torrens 3/2004. Office will perform a real estate search but public must search other records themselves. General index search fee \$15.00 per name. Copy fee \$10.00 for 1st page, \$.50 each add'l page per doc. Cert fee- \$1.00 per page, \$5.00 minimum plus copy fee. Payee- Hubbard County Recorder. **Online access to Property, GIS, Real Estate, Recording, Deed, Lien records:** Access to parcel data is free at www.co.hubbard.mn.us/website/hubbard/disclaimer.htm. Also, recorder office data by subscription on either the Laredo system using subscription and fees or the Tapestry System using credit card, https://tapestry.fidlar.com/tapsearch.aspx; \$3.99 search; \$.50 per image. **Other phones:** Treasurer- 218-732-4348; Vital Records- 218-732-3552; Auditor- 218-732-3196. **Property tax/Assessor-** same address as above. 218-732-3452.

Isanti County

County Recorder, 555 18th Ave SW, Courthouse, Cambridge, MN 55008. 763-689-1191, R/E recording phone-612-689-1191, UCC recording phone-763-689-1191; fax-none; hours: 8AM-4:30PM. www.co.isanti.mn.us

Records indexed on computer from 1996 to present, books prior to 1996. Only the public may search. Copies included in search fee. R/E record copy- \$1.00 per page. Tax lien copy- \$3.00 per doc. Cert fee- \$10.00 per doc plus \$1.00 per page over 5. Payee- Isanti County Recorder. **Other phones:** Treasurer- 763-689-1781; Appraiser/Auditor- 763-689-2752; Elections- 763-689-1644; Vital Records- 763-689-1191. **Property tax/Assessor-** same address as above. 763-689-2752.

Itasca County

County Recorder, 123 NE 4th St, Grand Rapids, MN 55744-2600. 218-327-2856; fax-218-327-0689; hours: 8AM-4:30PM. www.co.itasca.mn.us

Separate indices to search include computer, microfilm. General index search fee \$10.00 per search. Add'l \$12.00 fee if search is over an hour. UCC search per debtor, including 10 copies/listings- \$20.00. Separate federal/state combined tax lien search- \$20.00 per debtor. Copy fee \$1.00 per page. Cert fee- \$5.00 per cert plus copy fee. Payee- Itasca County Recorder. **Online access to Property, Auditor, Real Estate, Recorder,**

Deed, Lien records: Access to property and parcel data is from a private company at www.parcelinfo.com/main.php. Also, recorder office data by subscription on either the Laredo system using subscription and fees or the Tapestry System using credit card, https://tapestry.fidlar.com/tapsearch.aspx; \$3.99 search; \$.50 per image. **Other phones:** Treasurer- 218-327-2859; Appraiser/Auditor- 218-327-2860; Elections- 218-327-2849; Vital Records- 218-327-7327. **Property tax/Assessor-** same address as above. 218-327-2861.

Jackson County

County Recorder, PO Box 209; Jackson County Recorder, Jackson, MN 56143. 507-847-2580; fax-507-847-6824; hours: 8AM-4:30PM. www.co.jackson.mn.us

All records in one index. Records indexed on a public use terminal back to 1/1999. Office personnel or visitors may perform searches. Search fee \$20.00. Copy fee \$.50 per page. Cert fee- \$10.00 per doc plus copy fee. Payee- Jackson County Recorder. **Other phones:** Treasurer- 507-847-2763; Elections- 507-847-2763; Vital Records- 507-847-2580. **Property tax/Assessor-** same address as above. 507-847-4033.

Kanabec County

County Recorder, 18 N. Vine St, Mora, MN 55051. 320-679-6466; fax-320-679-6431; hours: 8AM-4:30PM.

Separate indices to search include 10 separate indexes and public cubicles. Only the public may search. Copy fee \$1.00 per page. Fax back- \$5.00 per page. Cert fee- \$5.00 per cert up to 5 pages, \$1.00 per page over plus copy fee. Payee- Kanabec County Recorder. **Other phones:** Treasurer- 320-679-6430. **Property tax/Assessor-** same address as above. 320-679-6420.

Kandiyohi County

County Recorder, PO Box 736, Willmar, MN 56201-0736. 320-231-6223; fax-320-231-6284; hours: 8AM-4:30PM. www.co.kandiyohi.mn.us

Office personnel or visitors may perform searches. Search fee \$20.00 per name. General copy fee \$1.00 per page after 10 pages; no charge if tax lien. R/E record copy- \$1.00 per page. Cert fee- \$5.00 per cert, plus \$1.00 per page over 5 pages. Payee- Kandiyohi County Recorder. **Online access to Property, Assessor, Recording, Real Estate, Deed, Lien records:** Access to county property tax data is free at http://morris.state.mn.us/tax/. Also, recorder office data by subscription on either the Laredo system using subscription w/ fees or the Tapestry System using credit card, https://tapestry.fidlar.com/tapsearch.aspx; \$3.99 search; \$.50 per image. Index back to 3/1987; images to 3/1988. **Other phones:** Treasurer- 320-231-6202; Appraiser/Auditor- 320-231-6202; Elections- 320-231-6202 x6338; Vital Records- 320-231-6532. **Property tax/Assessor-** 320-231-6200.

Kittson County

County Recorder, 410 Fifth St #202, Hallock, MN 56728. 218-843-2842; fax-218-843-2538; hours: 8:30AM-4:30PM.

All records in one index. Record index not computerized. Office personnel or visitors may perform searches. Search fee \$20.00. Copy fee \$1.00 per page after 10 pages. Cert fee- \$10.00 per cert plus copy fee. Payee- Kittson County Recorder. **Other phones:** Treasurer- 218-843-3432; Vital Records- 218-843-2842. **Property tax/Assessor-** 218-843-3615.

Koochiching County

County Recorder, 715 4th St.; Courthouse, International Falls, MN 56649. 218-283-1193; fax-218-283-1194; hours: 8AM-5PM. www.co.koochiching.mn.us

All records in one index. Records indexed on a public use terminal back to 1990. Office personnel or visitors may perform searches. Will not search real estate records. Copy fee \$10.00 per name. Cert fee- $5.00 per doc plus copy fee. Payee-Koochiching County Treasurer. **Online access to Property, Auditor, Recording, Real Estate, Deed, Lien records:** Access to property and parcel data is from a private company at www.parcelinfo.com. Subscriptions are as low as $15 per month - $50 if you require weekly updates. A limited free guest account is available. Also recorder office data by subscription on either the Laredo system using subscription and fees or the Tapestry System using credit card, https://tapestry.fidlar.com/tapsearch.aspx; $.50 per image. **Other phones:** Treasurer- 218-283-1112; Elections- 218-283-1101; Vital Records- 218-283-1193. **Property tax/Assessor**- same address as above. 218-283-1121.

Lac qui Parle County

County Recorder, PO Box 132, Madison, MN 56256-0132. 320-598-3724; fax-320-598-7555; hours: 8:30AM-4:30PM.
Office personnel or visitors may perform searches. Real estate owner, mortgage, and property transfer searches available. UCC search per debtor, including 10 copies/listings- $20.00. Copy fee $1.00 per page after 10 pages. Cert fee- $5.00 per cert plus copy fee. Payee- Lac qui Parle County Recorder. **Other phones:** Treasurer- 320-598-3648. **Property tax/Assessor**- 320-598-3187.

Lake County

County Recorder, 601 Third Ave, Two Harbors, MN 55616. 218-834-8347; fax-218-834-8493; hours: 8AM-4:30PM. www.co.lake.mn.us
Separate indices to search include abstract, torrens, state & federal tax liens. Records indexed on a public use terminal back to 1996. Office will perform a UCC search but public must search other records themselves. UCC search per debtor, including 10 copies/listings- $20.00, with appropriate request forms and fees. Copy fee $1.00 per page. Cert fee- $1.00 per page, $5.00 minimum includes copy fee. Payee- Lake County Recorder. **Online access to Assessor, Property, Recording, Real Estate, Deed, Lien records:** Recorder office data by subscription on either the Laredo system using subscription and fees or the Tapestry System using credit card, https://tapestry.fidlar.com/tapsearch.aspx; $3.99 search; $.50 per image. Also, access property data free at www.parcelinfo.com/parcels/. **Other phones:** Treasurer- 218-834-8344; Elections- 218-834-8318; Vital Records- 218-834-8301. **Property tax/Assessor**-same address as above. 218-834-8313.

Lake of the Woods County

County Recorder, PO Box 808, Baudette, MN 56623. 218-634-1902; fax-218-634-2509; hours: 7:30AM-4PM.
Office personnel or visitors may perform searches. Search fee $15.00 per name. Will not search real estate records. UCC search per debtor, including 10 copies/listings- $20.00. Copy fee $1.00 per page after 10 pages. Cert fee- $5.00 per doc plus copy fee. Payee- Lake of the Woods County Recorder. **Other phones:** Treasurer- 218-634-2361. **Property tax/Assessor**- 218-634-2536.

Le Sueur County

County Recorder, 88 S. Park Ave; Courthouse, Le Center, MN 56057-1620. 507-357-8235, R/E recording phone-507-357-2251; fax-507-357-6375; hours: 8AM-4:30PM.
Office personnel or visitors may perform searches. Search fee $6.00 per name. UCC search per debtor, including 10 copies/listings- $20.00. Copy fee $1.00 per page after 10 pages. Cert fee- $5.00 per cert. Payee- Le Sueur County Recorder. **Property tax/Assessor**- 507-357-2257.

Lincoln County

County Recorder, PO Box 119, Ivanhoe, MN 56142. 507-694-1360; fax-507-694-1198; hours: 8:30AM-4:30PM.

Office personnel or visitors may perform searches. Search fee $15.00 per name. UCC search per debtor name- $20.00. Copies included in search fee. Cert fee- $5.00 per doc plus copy fee. Payee-Lincoln County Recorder. **Online access to Recording, Real estate, Deed, Lien records:** Recorder office data by subscription on either the Laredo system using subscription and fees or the Tapestry System using credit card, https://tapestry.fidlar.com/tapsearch.aspx; $3.99 search; $.50 per image. **Other phones:** Treasurer- 507-694-1550. **Property tax/Assessor**- 507-694-1522.

Lyon County

County Recorder, 607 W. Main St, Marshall, MN 56258. 507-537-6722; fax-507-537-7988; hours: 8:30AM-4:30PM.
Office personnel or visitors may perform searches. Search fee $15.00 per name. Only telephone searches performed for real estate records. UCC search per debtor name- $20.00. Copies included in search fee. Tax lien copy- $1.00. Cert fee- $1.00 per page, $5.00 minimum. For certified copies by mail include $2.50 postage. Payee- Lyon County Recorder. **Online access to Recording, Real Estate, Deed, Lien records:** Recorder office data by subscription on either the Laredo system using subscription and fees or the Tapestry System using credit card, https://tapestry.fidlar.com/tapsearch.aspx; $3.99 search; $.50 per image. Index back to 1987; images to 1988. **Property tax/Assessor**- 507-537-6731.

Mahnomen County

County Recorder, PO Box 380, Mahnomen, MN 56557. 218-935-5528; fax-218-935-5946; hours: 8AM-4:30PM M-T.
Office personnel or visitors may perform searches. Search fee $15.00 per name. UCC search per debtor name- $20.00. General copy fee $1.00 per page after 10 pages. R/E record copy- $2.00 per page. Cert fee- $5.00 per doc plus copy fee. Payee-Mahnomen County Recorder. **Property tax/Assessor**- 218-935-2417.

Marshall County

County Recorder, 208 E Colvin #7, Warren, MN 56762. 218-745-4801; fax-218-745-5013; hours: 8AM-4:30PM.
All records in one index. Office personnel or visitors may perform searches. Search fee $13.00 per name. Will search real estate records for $30.00 per hour minimum real estate research fee. UCC search per debtor $20.00. Copy fee $1.00 per page. Cert fee- $5.00 per doc up to 5 pages, $1.00 per page after plus copy fee. Payee- Marshall County Recorder. **Other phones:** Treasurer- 218-745-4831; Vital Records- 218-745-4801. **Property tax/Assessor**- 208 E Colvin Ave, #13, Warren, MN 56762; 218-745-5331.

Martin County

County Recorder, PO Box 785, Fairmont, MN 56031-0785. 507-238-3213; fax-507-235-8537; hours: 8AM-5PM. www.co.martin.mn.us
Separate indices to search include books before 1987, after on computer. Records indexed on a public use terminal back to 1987. Office personnel or visitors may perform searches. Search fee $15.00 per hour. Will not search UCC records. Copy fee $1.00 per page. Cert fee- $10.00 per cert includes copy fee. Payee- Martin County Recorder. **Online access to Recording, Real Estate, Deed, Lien records:** Recorder office data by subscription on either the Laredo system using subscription and fees or the Tapestry System using credit card, https://tapestry.fidlar.com/tapsearch.aspx; $3.99 search; $.50 per image. Index back to 1987; images to 1992. **Other phones:** Treasurer- 507-238-3211; Elections- 507-238-3211; Vital Records- 507-238-3213. **Property tax/Assessor**- same address as above. 507-238-3210.

McLeod County

County Recorder, 2389 Hennepin Ave N, Glencoe, MN 55336. 320-864-1327; fax-320-864-1295; hours: 8AM-4:30PM. www.co.mcleod.mn.us
Separate indices to search include paper and computer. Records indexed on a public use terminal back to 4/1993. Only the public may search. Federal/state separate or combined tax lien search- $6.00 per debtor. Copy fee $1.00 per page. Cert fee- $5.00 per name plus copy fee. Payee-McLeod County Recorder. **Online access to Real Estate, Recording, Deed records:** Access recorder data by subscription at http://landshark.co.mcleod.mn.us/eddie/. Set-up $50 plus $50.00 per month, plus $2.00 per image. **Other phones:** Treasurer- 320-864-1203; Vital Records- 320-864-1234. **Property tax/Assessor**- 320-864-1254.

Meeker County

County Recorder, 325 N. Sibley Ave; Courthouse, Litchfield, MN 55355. 320-693-5440; fax-320-693-5444; hours: 8AM-4:30PM.
Office personnel or visitors may perform searches. Search fee $15.00 per name. UCC search per debtor name- $20.00. General copy fee $1.00 per page. R/E record copy- $.50 per page. Cert fee- $5.00 per cert plus copy fee. Payee- Meeker County Recorder. **Other phones:** Treasurer- 320-693-5345; Elections- 320-693-5212; Vital Records- 320-693-5345. **Property tax/Assessor**- 320-693-5205.

Mille Lacs County

County Recorder, 635 2nd St S.E, Milaca, MN 56353. 320-983-8308, UCC recording phone-320-983-8309; fax-320-983-8388; hours: 8AM-4:30PM.
Office personnel or visitors may perform searches. Search fee $20.00 per name. Will not search real estate records. Copy fee $1.00 per page after 10 pages. Cert fee- $1.00 per page, $5.00 minimum. Payee- Mille Lacs County Recorder. **Other phones:** Treasurer- 320-983-8310; Appraiser/Auditor- 320-983-8281; Elections- 320-983-8301; Vital Records- 320-983-8236. **Property tax/Assessor**- 320-983-8311.

Morrison County

County Recorder, 213 SE 1st Ave.; Admin. Bldg, Little Falls, MN 56345. 320-632-0145, R/E recording phone-320-632-0145,0142, 0146, 0143, 0144 or 0147, UCC recording phone-320-632-0142; fax-320-632-0141; hours: 8AM-4:30PM. www.co.morrison.mn.us/wsite/index.htm
Files UCC's in their office. Index: Books, computer, microfilm. Records indexed on a public use terminal back to 1/1987. Office personnel or visitors may perform searches. Charge only for lengthy searches; fee $30.00. Copy fee $1.00 per page. Cert fee- $10.00 per page plus copy fee. Payee- Morrison County Recorder. **Other phones:** Treasurer- 320-632-0150; Appraiser/Auditor- 320-632-0101; Elections- 320-632-0132; Vital Records- 320-632-0146. **Property tax/Assessor**- same address as above. 320-632-0100.

Mower County

County Recorder, 201 First St NE, Austin, MN 55912-3475. 507-437-9446; fax-507-437-9471; hours: 8AM-5PM. www.co.mower.mn.us/Recorder01.htm
Payments must be paid in advance or an account set up with a security deposit for copies mailed or faxed. Separate indices to search include document number, date, grantor/grantee, reception book. Records indexed on a public use terminal back to January 15, 1988. Office will perform a UCC search and tax lien search, but public must search other records themselves. Search fee $20.00 per name. Copy fee $1.00 per page. Cert fee- $5.00 per cert plus copy fee. Payee- Mower County Recorder. **Online access to Property, Assessor, Recording, Grantor/Grantee, Deed, Lien records:** Search property assessor data free at www.mower.minnesotaassessors.com. No name searching for free, but a sub service is also available.

Also, recorder office data by subscription on either the Laredo system using subscription and fees or the Tapestry System using credit card, https://tapestry.fidlar.com/tapsearch.aspx; $3.99 search; $.50 per image. Index back to 1988; images to 8/1999. **Other phones:** Treasurer- 507-437-9456; Appraiser/Auditor- 507-437-9440; Elections- 507-437-9536; Vital Records- 507-437-9456; Information- 507-437-9493; Auditor -507-437-9535. **Property tax/Assessor-** same address as above. 507-437-9440.

Murray County

County Recorder, PO Box 57, Slayton, MN 56172-0057. 507-836-6148 x144, R/E recording phone-507-836-6148 x143, UCC recording phone-507-836-6148 x144; fax-507-836-8904; hours: 8:30AM-N, 1-5PM. www.murray-countymn.com
Separate indices to search include print out indexes for computer, index books before the computer. Records indexed on a public use terminal back to 11/1/2002. Office will perform a UCC search with proper forms and fees, but public must search other records themselves. UCC search per debtor name- $20.00. Copy fee $1.00 per page. Cert fee- $10.00 per cert includes up to 5 pages, then copy fees apply. Payee- Murray County Recorder. **Other phones:** Treasurer- 507-836-6148 x150; Elections- 507-836-6148 x147; Vital Records- 507-836-6148 x150. **Property tax/Assessor-** same address as above. 507-836-6148 x151.

Nicollet County

County Recorder, PO Box 493, St. Peter, MN 56082-0493. 507-934-0320; fax-507-934-4487; hours: 8AM-5PM. www.co.nicollet.mn.us/dept.php3?id=16
All records in one index. Office personnel or visitors may perform searches. UCC search per debtor name- $20.00. Separate federal/state combined tax lien search- $2.00 per debtor. General copy fee $1.00 per page. R/E record copy- $3.00 per large page. Cert fee- $5.00 includes copy fee. Payee- Nicollet County Recorder. **Other phones:** Treasurer- 507-934-0335; Elections- 507-935-0348; Vital Records- 507-934-0325. **Property tax/Assessor-** 501 S Minnesota Ave, St. Peter, MN 56082; 507-934-0241.

Nobles County

County Recorder, PO Box 757, Worthington, MN 56187. 507-372-8236; fax-507-372-8236; hours: 8AM-4:30PM.
Office personnel or visitors may perform searches. Search fee $20.00 per name. Will not search real estate records. Cert fee- $5.00 per doc plus copy fee. Payee- Nobles County Recorder. **Other phones:** Treasurer- 507-372-8231. **Property tax/Assessor-** 507-372-8234.

Norman County

County Recorder, PO Box 146, Ada, MN 56510. 218-784-5481; fax-218-784-2399; hours: 8:30AM-4:30PM.
Office personnel or visitors may perform searches. Search fee $20.00 per name. Will not search UCC records. R/E or tax lien copy- $2.00 per document. Cert fee- $5.00 per cert plus copy fee. Payee- Norman County Recorder. **Online access to Assessor records:** Look-up assessor property tax data free at http://morris.state.mn.us/tax/. **Other phones:** Treasurer- 218-784-5473; Elections- 218-784-5481; Vital Records- 218-784-5481. **Property tax/Assessor-** 218-784-5487.

Olmsted County

Property Records & Licensing, 151 4th St. SE, Rochester, MN 55904. 507-285-8194, R/E recording phone-507-285-8195, UCC recording phone-507-285-8204; fax-507-287-7186; hours: 8AM-5PM. www.olmstedcounty.com
Separate indices to search include computer, books by legal description, and miscellaneous. Records indexed on a public use terminal back to

11/12/1993. Search fee $4.00; $5.00 minimum. Will not search UCC records. Copy fee $1.00 per page. Cert fee- $10.00 per cert plus copy fee. Payee- Olmsted County Property Records & Licensing. **Online access to Probate, Property records:** Access to county probate records is free at www.selco.lib.mn.us/apps/ochs/probate.cfm. Files vary greatly, but most contain date and place of death, list of heirs, copy of will (if one was written), inventory of personal property, and final disposition of the estate. Also, a Tract Index of recorded documents is available from a contract vendor; call for details. **Other phones:** Treasurer- 507-285-8197; Appraiser/Auditor- 507-285-8124; Elections- 507-287-2118; Vital Records- 507-287-1444. **Property tax/Assessor-** same address as above. 507-285-8124.

Otter Tail County

County Recorder, PO Box 867, Fergus Falls, MN 56538. 218-998-8140; hours: 8AM-5PM. www.co.otter-tail.mn.us
Office personnel or visitors may perform searches. Real estate owner, mortgage, and property transfer searches available. UCC search per debtor name- $20.00. Tax lien search fee- $20.00 per debtor. UCC copy fee $1.00 per page. R/E record copy- $2.00 per page. Cert fee- $1.00 per page, $5.00 minimum. Payee- Otter Tail County Recorder. **Online access to Property Tax, Assessor, Real Estate, Recorder records:** Access recorder office real estate data by a LandShark subscription at www.co.otter-tail.mn.us/eddie/login.jsp. User name and login required. Call recorder office for details and sign-up Also, search property tax data at www.co.otter-tail.mn.us/taxes/. Parcel searching or map searching only. **Other phones:** Treasurer- 218-998-8295. **Property tax/Assessor-** 505 Fir Ave W, Fergus Falls, MN 56537; 218-998-8010.

Pennington County

County Recorder, PO Box 616, Thief River Falls, MN 56701. 218-683-7027, R/E recording phone-218-683-7027218-683-7027; fax-218-683-7026; hours: 8AM-4:30PM.
Separate indices to search. Records indexed on a public use terminal back to 1989. Office personnel or visitors may perform searches. Search fee $20.00 per name. Office will give recent real estate documents related to a property location. Copy fee $.50 per page. Cert fee- $1.00 per page, $5.00 minimum includes copy fee. Payee- Pennington County Recorder. **Other phones:** Treasurer- 218-683-7022; Elections- 218-683-7000; Vital Records- 218-683-7027. **Property tax/Assessor-** same address as above. 218-683-7029.

Pine County

County Recorder, 315 Main St S. #3, Pine City, MN 55063. 320-629-5665, R/E recording phone-320-629-6781; fax-320-629-5765; hours: 8AM-4:30PM.
Office personnel or visitors may perform searches. Search fee $5.00 per name. Will not search real estate records. UCC search per debtor, including 10 copies/listings- $20.00. Copy fee $1.00 per page after 10 pages. Cert fee- $5.00 per doc plus copy fee. Payee- Pine County Recorder. **Other phones:** Treasurer- 320-629-6781 x138. **Property tax/Assessor-** 320-629-6781 x150.

Pipestone County

County Recorder, 416 Hiawatha Ave. S, Pipestone, MN 56164. 507-825-6755; fax-507-825-6767; hours: 8AM-4:30PM.
All records in one index. Records indexed on a public use terminal back to 1986. Office personnel or visitors may perform searches. Search fee $20.00. Copy fee $1.00 per page. Cert fee- $10.00 per page includes copy fee. Payee- Pipestone County Recorder. **Other phones:** Treasurer- 507-825-6745; Elections- 507-825-6740; Vital Records- 507-825-6755. **Property tax/Assessor-** 507-825-6750.

Polk County

County Recorder, PO Box 397, Crookston, MN 56716. 218-281-3464; fax-218-281-1636; hours: 8AM-4:30PM.
All records in one index. Records indexed on computer back to 1974. Office personnel or visitors may perform searches. Search fee $20.00 per name. Tax liens not included in UCC search. Copy fee $1.00 per page after 10 pages. Cert fee- $5.00 per page plus copy fee. Payee- Polk County Recorder. **Other phones:** Treasurer- 218-281-2554; Elections- 218-281-2554; Vital Records- 218-281-3464. **Property tax/Assessor-** 218-281-4186.

Pope County

County Recorder, 130 E. Minnesota Ave, Glenwood, MN 56334. 320-634-5723; fax-320-634-5717; hours: 8AM-4:30PM. www.mncounties3.org/pope/
Office personnel or visitors may perform searches. Search fee $15.00 per name. UCC search per debtor name- $20.00. Copy fee $.50 per page. Cert fee- $5.00 per page. Payee- Pope County Recorder. **Online access to Property, Assessor, Recording, Real Estate, Lien, Deed records:** Recorder office data by subscription on either the Laredo system using subscription and fees or the Tapestry System using credit card, https://tapestry.fidlar.com/tapsearch.aspx; $3.99 search; $.50 per image. Index and images goes back to 11/1996. Also, for records search go to www.mncounties3.org/pope/. Look-up assessor property tax data free at http://morris.state.mn.us/tax/. **Other phones:** Treasurer- 320-634-5705; Appraiser/Auditor- 320-634-5728; Elections- 320-634-5705; Vital Records- 320-634-5723. **Property tax/Assessor-** 320-634-5728.

Ramsey County

County Recorder, 50 W. Kellogg Blvd.; #860 RCGC-W, St. Paul, MN 55102-1693. 651-266-2060; fax-651-266-2066; hours: 8AM-4:30PM. www.rrinfo.co.ramsey.mn.us
Separate indices. Records indexed on a public use terminal back to 1993. Office personnel or visitors may perform searches. Search fee $55.00. Copy fee $1.00 per page. Cert fee- $10.00 per cert minimum; add $1 per pg over 5. Payee- Ramsey County Recorder. **Online to Property Assessor records:** Search the property assessment rolls free at www.co.ramsey.mn.us/prr/propertytax/index.asp. No name searching. **Other phones:** Treasurer- 651-266-2000; Elections- 651-266-2171; Vital Records- 651-266-1333. **Property tax/Assessor-** 651-266-2000.

Red Lake County

County Recorder, Box 3, Red Lake Falls, MN 56750-0003. 218-253-2997; fax-218-253-2052; hours: 9AM-5PM.
Office personnel or visitors may perform searches. Search fee $15.00 per name. UCC search per debtor name- $20.00. Copy fee $1.00 per document. Cert fee- $5.00 per cert plus copy fee. Payee- Red Lake County Recorder. **Other phones:** Treasurer- 218-253-2797; Vital Records- 218-253-2997. **Property tax/Assessor-** 218-253-2596.

Redwood County

County Recorder, PO Box 130, Redwood Falls, MN 56283. 507-637-4032; fax-507-637-4064; hours: 8AM-4:30PM.
All records in one index. Records indexed on a public use terminal back to 6/1/1995. Office personnel or visitors may perform searches. Will not search real estate records. Will search UCC records; search includes tax liens if requested. UCC search per debtor, including 10 copies/listings- $20.00. Separate federal/state combined tax lien search- $5.00 per debtor. Copy fee $1.00 per page after 10 pages. Cert fee- $1.00 per page, $5.00 minimum. Payee- Redwood County Recorder. **Other phones:** Treasurer- 507-637-4013; Elections- 507-637-4069; Vital Records- 507-637-4032. **Property tax/Assessor-** same address as above. 507-637-4008.

Renville County

County Recorder, 500 E. DePue, 2nd Fl, Olivia, MN 56277. 320-523-3669; fax-320-523-3679; hours: 8AM-4:30PM. www.co.renville.mn.us
Office personnel or visitors may perform searches. Search fee $15.00 per name. Will not search real estate records. UCC search per debtor name- $20.00. General copy fee $1.00 per page. R/E record copy- $.50 per page, minimum $1.00. Cert fee- $7.00 per doc, $1.00 each page. Payee- Renville County Recorder. **Online access to Assessor records:** Look-up assessor property tax data free at http://morris.state.mn.us/tax/. **Other phones:** Treasurer- 320-523-3676; Appraiser/Auditor- 320-523-3645; Elections- 320-523-2071; Vital Records- 320-523-3669. **Property tax/Assessor-** 320-523-3645.

Rice County

County Recorder, 320 NW 3rd St, #10, Faribault, MN 55021-6146. 507-332-6114; fax-507-333-3754; hours: 8AM-4:30PM. www.co.rice.mn.us
All records in one index. Records indexed on a public use terminal back to March, 1992. Only the public may search. General copy fee $1.00 per page. R/E record copy- $.50 per page. Cert fee- $1.00 per page with a $5.00 minimum. Payee- Rice County Recorder. **Online access to Property Assessor, Property Sale records:** Search parcel information and residential/commercial sales data free at www.rice.minnesotaassessors.com. No name searching for free but a sub service is also available. **Other phones:** Treasurer- 507-332-6104; Appraiser/Auditor- 507-332-6102; Elections- 507-332-6104; Vital Records- 507-332-6114. **Property tax/Assessor-** same address as above. 507-332-6102.

Rock County

County Recorder, PO Box 509, Luverne, MN 56156. 507-283-5014; fax-507-283-1343; hours: 8AM-5PM. www.co.rock.mn.us
Separate indices to search include Torrens, State tax liens, federal tax liens. Records indexed on a public use terminal back to 1992. Office personnel or visitors may perform searches. General search fee $25.00 per hour; $10.00 minimum. UCC search includes tax liens if requested. UCC search per debtor, including 10 copies/listings- $20.00 fixed. Tax lien search fee-$20.00 per debtor. Copy fee $1.00 per page. Cert fee- $5.00 minimum or $1.00 per page, plus copy fee. Payee- Rock County Recorder. **Online access to Assessor, Property, Warrants records:** Look-up assessor property tax data free at http://morris.state.mn.us/tax/. Also, sheriff's warrant list is online at www.sheriff.co.rock.mn.us. **Other phones:** Treasurer- 507-283-5055; Elections- 507-283-5060; Vital Records- 507-283-5060. **Property tax/Assessor-** same address as above. 507-283-5022.

Roseau County

County Recorder, 606 5th Ave. SW, Rm 170, Roseau, MN 56751-1477. 218-463-2061; fax-218-463-4294; hours: 8AM-4:30PM.
Office personnel or visitors may perform searches. Search fee $15.00 per name. Will not search real estate records. UCC search per debtor, including 10 copies/listings- $20.00. Copy fee $1.00 per page after 10 pages. Cert fee- $1.00 per page, $5.00 minimum. Payee- Roseau County Recorder. **Other phones:** Treasurer- 218-463-1215; Elections- 218-463-1282; Vital Records- 218-463-1215. **Property tax/Assessor-** 218-463-1861.

Scott County

County Recorder, 200 Fourth Ave West, Shakopee, MN 55379. 952-496-8150; fax-952-496-8138; hours: 8AM-4:30PM. www.co.scott.mn.us
All records in one index. Records indexed on a public use terminal back to 1985. Office personnel or visitors may perform searches. Copy fee $1.00 per page. Cert fee- $10.00 per page. Payee- Scott County Recorder. **Online access to Real Estate,**

Recorder, Property Tax, Assessor, GIS records: Search the county property databases free at www.co.scott.mn.us/xpedio/groups/public/documents/web_files/scottcountywebframe.hcsp. There is also a free online document subscription service and GIS mapping. At left hand side, click on land records for recordings, or property tax for assessor records. **Other phones:** Treasurer- 952-496-8150; Appraiser/Auditor- 952-496-8150; Elections- 952-496-8161; Vital Records- 952-496-8150. **Property tax/Assessor-** 952-496-8150.

Sherburne County

County Recorder, 13880 Highway 10, Elk River, MN 55330. 763-241-2915, R/E recording phone-800-719-2826; fax-763-241-2995; hours: 8AM-4:30PM. www.co.sherburne.mn.us
Office personnel or visitors may perform searches. Search fee $20.00 per name. General copy fee $1.00 per page after 10 pages. R/E or tax lien copy- $2.00 1st page, $.50 each add'l page. Cert fee- $1.00 per page, minimum $5.00. Payee- Sherburne County Recorder. **Online access to Real Estate, Tax Assessor, Most Wanted records:** Property records from the county tax assessor database are free at www.sherburne.mn.promap.com. However, to perform a name search, you must subscribe; fee is $25.00 setup and $300.00 per year. A free 30-day trial is offered. Call 763-241-2880 for information on how to subscribe, or visit website. Also, search the sheriff's most wanted list at www.co.sherburne.mn.us/sheriff/mostwanted.htm. **Other phones:** Treasurer- 800-438-0575; Vital Records- 800-719-2826. **Property tax/Assessor-** 800-438-0577.

Sibley County

County Recorder, PO Box 44, Gaylord, MN 55334-0044. 507-237-4080; fax-507-237-4306; hours: 8AM-4:30PM. http://co.sibley.mn.us/Dept_Frame.htm
All records in one index. Records indexed on a public use terminal back to 8/1994. Office personnel or visitors may perform searches. Search fee $40.00 for deed forward; $4.00 for each add'l RE entry. UCC search per debtor, including 10 copies/listings- $20.00. Tax liens not included in UCC search; tax lien search fee- $5.00 per debtor. Copy fee $1.00 per page; $3.00 per page if found in books. Cert fee- $1.00 per page, $5.00 minimum. Payee- Sibley County Recorder. **Other phones:** Treasurer- 507-237-4084; Elections- 507-237-4070; Vital Records- 507-237-4080. **Property tax/Assessor-** PO Box 532, Gaylord, MN 55334-0532; 507-237-4078.

St. Louis County

County Recorder, PO Box 157, Duluth, MN 55801-0157. 218-726-2677; fax-218-725-5052; hours: 8AM-4:30PM. www.co.st-louis.mn.us/
Separate indices to search include abstract and torrens title. Records indexed on a public use terminal back to 1987 for abstracts, all for torrens. Office personnel or visitors may perform searches. Search fee $20.00 per debtor. Will not search real estate records. Copy fee $1.00 per page. Cert fee- $1.00 per page, $5.00 minimum plus copy fee. Payee- St. Louis County Recorder. **Online access to Real Estate, Property Tax, Auditor records:** Access to the auditor and recorder's tax records for tax professionals database is by subscription. Fee is $100 monthly; password provided. For info or sign-up, contact Pam Palen at 218-726-2380 or email to palenp@co.st-louis.mn.us or visit www.co.st-louis.mn.us/auditorsoffice/subscription.pdf. Also, search auditor info for free at www.co.st-louis.mn.us/parcelinfo/st-louis/start.asp. Also, search the City of Duluth property assessor data free at www.ci.duluth.mn.us/city/assessor/index.htm. **Other phones:** Treasurer- 218-726-2380; Appraiser/Auditor- 218-726-2304; Elections- 218-726-2385; Vital Records- 218-726-2559; Torrens Division- 218-726-2680. **Property tax/Assessor-** 218-726-2304.

Stearns County

County Recorder, 705 Courthouse Sq; Admin. Ctr, Rm 131, St. Cloud, MN 56303. 320-656-3855, R/E recording phone-320-259-3855; fax-320-656-3916; hours: 8AM-4:30PM. www.co.stearns.mn.us
Office personnel or visitors may perform searches. Search fee $15.00 per name. Will not search real estate records. UCC search per debtor name- $20.00. Copy fee $1.00 per page. Cert fee- $1.00 per page, $5.00 minimum. Payee- Stearns County Recorder. **Online access to Real Estate, Tax Assessor records:** Records from the county tax assessor database are free at http://secure.co.stearns.mn.us/. No name searching. **Other phones:** Treasurer- 320-656-3870; Elections- 320-656-3920. **Property tax/Assessor-** 320-656-3680.

Steele County

County Recorder, PO Box 890, Owatonna, MN 55060. 507-444-7450; fax-507-444-7470; hours: 8AM-5PM. www.co.steele.mn.us
Records indexed on a public use terminal from 1991 to present. Office will perform a UCC search but public must search other records themselves. Search fee $20.00 per name. Copy fee $1.00 per page. A SASE is required. Cert fee- $10.00 per doc includes copy fee. Payee- Steele County Recorder. **Online access to Property Tax, Recording, Real Estate, Deed, Lien records:** Search using parcel data at www.co.steele.mn.us/auditor/auditor.html. Also, recorder office data by subscription on either the Laredo system using subscription and fees or the Tapestry System using credit card, https://tapestry.fidlar.com/tapsearch.aspx; $3.99 search; $.50 per image. **Other phones:** Treasurer- 507-444-7420; Elections- 507-444-7410; Vital Records- 507-444-7490. **Property tax/Assessor-** same address as above. 507-444-7435.

Stevens County

County Recorder, PO Box 530, Morris, MN 56267. 320-589-7414; fax-320-589-7112; hours: 8:30AM-4:30PM (Summer Hours 8AM-4PM).
All records in one index. Records indexed on computer back to 1996. Office personnel or visitors may perform searches. Search fee $20.00 per hour. Copy fee $1.00 per page. Cert fee- $10.00 per doc plus copy fee. Payee- Stevens County Recorder. **Online access to Assessor records:** Look-up assessor property tax data free at http://morris.state.mn.us/tax/. **Other phones:** Treasurer- 320-589-7418; Elections- 320-589-7409; Vital Records- 320-589-7414. **Property tax/Assessor-** same address as above. 320-589-7407.

Swift County

County Recorder, PO Box 246, Benson, MN 56215. 320-843-3377; fax-320-843-2275; hours: 8AM-4:30PM. www.swiftcounty.com
Separate indices to search include Torrens, abstract, State & Fed tax liens. Records indexed on a public use terminal back to 1987. Office personnel or visitors may perform searches. Search fee- varies. General copy fee $1.00 per page after 10 pages. R/E record copy- $2.00 per document. Cert fee- $10.00 up to 15 pages. Payee- Swift County Recorder. **Other phones:** Treasurer- 320-843-3544; Elections- 320-843-4069; Vital Records- 320-843-3544. **Property tax/Assessor-** same address as above. 320-842-5891.

Todd County

County Recorder, 221 First Ave South, #300, Long Prairie, MN 56347-1391. 320-732-4428; fax-320-732-4001; hours: 8AM-4:30PM. www.co.todd.mn.us/Recorder/recorder.htm
All records in one index. Records indexed on a public use terminal back to 1993. Office personnel or visitors may perform searches. Search fee $35.00 per hour. Copy fee $1.00 per page. Cert fee- $10.00 per doc plus copy fee. Payee- Todd

County Recorder. **Online access to Property, GIS-Mapping records:** Access to property information on the GIS-mapping site is free at www.co.todd.mn.us/toddcounty/propertyinfo0009.asp, although search options are limited; no name or address searching. **Other phones:** Treasurer- 320-732-4471; Appraiser/Auditor- 320-732-4430; Elections- 320-732-4471; Vital Records- 320-732-4428. **Property tax/Assessor-** 221 First Ave South, #400, Long Prairie, MN 56347; 320-732-4430.

Traverse County

County Recorder, PO Box 487, Wheaton, MN 56296-0487. 320-563-4622, R/E recording phone-320-563-4242; fax-320-563-4424; hours: 8AM-4:30PM. Office personnel or visitors may perform searches. Search of general index performed by phone is free. General search fee-$20.00 per name. Copy fee $1.00 per page after 10 pages. Cert fee- $10.00 per doc plus copy fee. Payee- Traverse County Recorder. **Other phones:** Treasurer- 320-563-4616. **Property tax/Assessor-** 320-563-4113.

Wabasha County

County Recorder, 625 Jefferson Ave, Wabasha, MN 55981. 651-565-3623, R/E recording phone-612-565-3623; fax-651-565-2774; hours: 8AM-4PM. Office personnel or visitors may perform searches. General search fee $1.00 per name. UCC search per debtor, copies included $20.00. Cert fee- $5.00 per doc for 1st 5 pages; $1.00 each add'l page. Payee- Wabasha County Recorder. **Other phones:** Treasurer- 651-565-3669. **Property tax/Assessor-** 651-565-3669.

Wadena County

County Recorder, 415 Jefferson St S, Wadena, MN 56482. 218-631-7622; fax-218-631-5709; hours: 8AM-4:30PM. www.co.wadena.mn.us Separate indices to search. Records indexed on computer back to 1995. Office personnel or visitors may perform searches. Search fee $10.00 per name. Copy fee $1.00 per page. Cert fee- $5.00 per doc plus copy fee. Payee- Wadena County Recorder. **Other phones:** Treasurer- 218-631-7621; Appraiser/Auditor- 218-631-7628; Elections- 218-631-7650; Vital Records- 218-631-7788; Auditor- 218-631-7785. **Property tax/Assessor-** same address as above. 218-631-7628.

Waseca County

County Recorder, 307 N. State St, Waseca, MN 56093. 507-835-0670; fax-507-835-0633; hours: 8AM-4:30PM. All records in one index. Office will perform a UCC search but public must search other records

themselves. UCC search per debtor name- $20.00. Copy fee $1.00 per page. Cert fee- $5.00 minimum. Payee- Waseca County Recorder. **Property tax/Assessor-** same address as above. 507-835-0640.

Washington County

County Recorder, 14900 N. 61st St; PO Box 6, Stillwater, MN 55082. 651-430-6755, UCC recording phone-651-275-7061; fax-651-275-7060; hours: 7:30AM-5PM. www.co.washington.mn.us All records in one index. Records indexed on a public use terminal back to 1984. Office personnel or visitors may perform searches. Search fee $20.00 per name. Will not search real estate records. Copy fee $1.00 per page. Cert fee- $10.00 per cert includes copy fee. Payee- Washington County Recorder. **Online access to Real Estate Tract records:** Access to county online records requires a monthly set up fee; UCC information is on a state system. Online access to property tax records is free at http://www2.co.washington.mn.us/opip/; no name searching - property ID or address required. **Other phones:** Treasurer- 651-430-6175; Vital Records- 651-275-7062; Torren Division- 651-430-6756. **Property tax/Assessor-** 651-430-6175.

Watonwan County

County Recorder, PO Box 518, St. James, MN 56081. 507-375-1216; hours: 8:30AM-N, 1-5PM. All records in one index. Office will perform a UCC or tax lien search but public must search other records themselves. UCC search per debtor, including 10 copies/listings- $20.00. Tax lien search fee- $15.00 per debtor. Copy fee $1.00 per page. Cert fee- $5.00 per doc plus copy fee. Payee- Watonwan County Recorder. **Other phones:** Treasurer- 507-375-1213; Vital Records- 507-375-1216. **Property tax/Assessor-** 507-375-1205.

Wilkin County

County Recorder, PO Box 29, Breckenridge, MN 56520. 218-643-7164; fax-218-643-7170; hours: 8AM-4:30PM. www.co.wilkin.mn.us/recorder.asp All records in one index. Records indexed on a public use terminal back to 1994. Office personnel or visitors may perform searches. General index search fee $20.00 per hour. Copy fee $1.00 per page. R/E record copy- $3.00 1st 2 pages; $.50 each add'l page. Cert fee- $10.00 per cert includes copy fee. Payee- Wilkin County Recorder. **Other phones:** Treasurer- 218-643-7112; Elections- 218 643-7165; Vital Records- 218-643-7112. **Property tax/Assessor-** PO Box 167,, Breckenridge, MN 56520; 218-643-7162.

Winona County

County Recorder, 177 Main St, Winona, MN 55987. 507-457-6340, UCC recording phone-507-457-6396; fax-507-454-9371; hours: 8AM-4:30PM. www.co.winona.mn.us All records in one index. Records indexed on a public use terminal back to 1987. Office personnel or visitors may perform searches. Search fee $20.00. Copy fee $2.00 per doc. Cert fee- $10.00 per doc includes copy fee. Payee- Winona County Recorder. **Other phones:** Treasurer- 507-457-6450; Elections- 507-457-6420; Vital Records- 507-457-6395. **Property tax/Assessor-** same address as above. 507-457-6300.

Wright County

County Recorder, 10 2nd St NW, Rm 210, Buffalo, MN 55313-1196. 763-682-7357, UCC recording phone-763-684-4551; fax-763-684-4558; hours: 8AM-4:30PM. www.co.wright.mn.us Separate indices to search include microfilm, tract books, computer. Office personnel or visitors may perform searches, but office will only search back 2 months. Search fee $5.00 per name unless otherwise indicated. UCC search per debtor, including 10 copies/listings- $20.00. Tax lien search fee- $15.00 per debtor. Copy fee $1.00 per page. Cert fee- $1.00 per page, $5.00 minimum. Payee- Wright County Recorder. **Online access to Recorder, Land, Lien, Grantor/Grantee, Property Tax records:** Access to Land Title database is free at www.co.wright.mn.us/department/recorder/landtitle/index.htm. Also, search the property tax database for free at www.co.wright.mn.us/department/audtreas/proptax/default.asp. **Other phones:** Treasurer- 763-682-7578; Elections- 763-682-7578; Vital Records- 763-682-7594. **Property tax/Assessor-** same address as above. 763-682-7367.

Yellow Medicine County

County Recorder, 415 9th Ave; Courthouse, Granite Falls, MN 56241. 320-564-2529; fax-320-564-3670; hours: 8AM-4PM. http://yellowmedicine.govoffice.com Index: Book, computer. Records indexed on a public use terminal back to 11/1989. Office will perform a UCC and Tax lien search but public must search other records themselves. Search fee $20.00. Copy fee $1.00 per page after 10 pages. Cert fee- $10.00 per page. Payee- Yellow Medicine County Recorder. **Other phones:** Treasurer- 320-564-3231. **Property tax/Assessor-** same address as above. 320-564-3678.

Minnesota County Locator

You will usually be able to find the city name in the City/County Cross Reference below. In that case, it is a simple matter to determine the county from the cross reference. However, only the official US Postal Service city names are included in this index. There are an additional 40,000 place names that people use in their addresses. Therefore, we have also included a ZIP/City Cross Reference immediately following the City/County Cross Reference.

If you know the ZIP Code but the city name does not appear in the City/County Cross Reference index, look up the ZIP Code in the ZIP/City Cross Reference, find the city name, then look up the city name in the City/County Cross Reference. For example, you want to know the county for an address of Menands, NY 12204. There is no "Menands" in the City/County Cross Reference. The ZIP/City Cross Reference shows that ZIP Codes 12201-12288 are for the city of Albany. Looking back in the City/County Cross Reference, Albany is in Albany County.

Minnesota City/County Cross Reference

ADA Norman
ADAMS Mower
ADOLPH St. Louis
ADRIAN Nobles
AFTON Washington
AH GWAH CHING Cass
AITKIN (56431) Aitkin(69), Crow Wing(30)
AKELEY (56433) Hubbard(84), Cass(15)
ALBANY Stearns
ALBERT LEA Freeborn
ALBERTA (56207) Stevens(98), Swift(1)
ALBERTVILLE Wright
ALBORN St. Louis
ALDEN Freeborn
ALDRICH (56434) Todd(67), Wadena(32)
ALEXANDRIA Douglas
ALMELUND Chisago
ALPHA (56111) Martin(60), Jackson(39)
ALTURA (55910) Winona(86), Wabasha(14)
ALVARADO (56710) Marshall(85), Polk(14)
AMBOY (56010) Blue Earth(97), Faribault(1)
AMIRET Lyon
ANGLE INLET Lake of the Woods
ANGORA St. Louis
ANGUS Polk
ANNANDALE Wright
ANOKA Anoka
APPLETON (56208) Swift(91), Lac qui Parle(5), Big Stone(2)
ARCO (56113) Lincoln(81), Lyon(18)
ARGYLE Marshall
ARLINGTON Sibley
ASHBY (56309) Grant(64), Otter Tail(29), Douglas(6)
ASKOV Pine
ATWATER (56209) Kandiyohi(83), Meeker(16)
AUDUBON Becker
AURORA St. Louis
AUSTIN (55912) Mower(94), Freeborn(5)
AVOCA Murray
AVON Stearns
BABBITT St. Louis
BACKUS (56435) Cass(96), Crow Wing(3)
BADGER Roseau
BAGLEY (56621) Clearwater(94), Polk(5)
BAKER Clay
BALATON (56115) Lyon(56), Murray(43)
BANGOR Pope
BARNESVILLE (56514) Clay(90), Wilkin(8)
BARNUM Carlton
BARRETT Grant
BARRY Big Stone
BATTLE LAKE Otter Tail
BAUDETTE (56623) Lake of the Woods(84), Koochiching(15)
BAXTER Crow Wing
BAYPORT Washington
BEARDSLEY (56211) Big Stone(72), Traverse(27)
BEAVER BAY Lake

BEAVER CREEK Rock
BECIDA Hubbard
BECKER Sherburne
BEJOU (56516) Mahnomen(77), Norman(22)
BELGRADE (56312) Stearns(67), Kandiyohi(32)
BELLE PLAINE (56011) Scott(78), Sibley(13), Le Sueur(4), Carver(2)
BELLINGHAM Lac qui Parle
BELTRAMI (56517) Polk(98), Norman(1)
BELVIEW (56214) Redwood(90), Yellow Medicine(9)
BEMIDJI (56601) Beltrami(93), Hubbard(6)
BEMIDJI Beltrami
BENA Cass
BENEDICT Hubbard
BENSON (56215) Swift(95), Pope(4)
BEROUN Pine
BERTHA (56437) Todd(85), Otter Tail(14)
BETHEL (55005) Anoka(97), Isanti(2)
BIG FALLS Koochiching
BIG LAKE Sherburne
BIGELOW Nobles
BIGFORK Itasca
BINGHAM LAKE (56118) Cottonwood(92), Jackson(7)
BIRCHDALE Koochiching
BIRD ISLAND Renville
BIWABIK St. Louis
BLACKDUCK (56630) Itasca(42), Aitkin(41), Beltrami(16)
BLOMKEST Kandiyohi
BLOOMING PRAIRIE (55917) Steele(65), Dodge(19), Mower(8), Freeborn(6)
BLUE EARTH (56013) Faribault(97), Martin(2)
BLUFFTON Otter Tail
BOCK Mille Lacs
BORUP (56519) Norman(58), Clay(42)
BOVEY Itasca
BOWLUS (56314) Morrison(95), Stearns(4)
BOWSTRING Itasca
BOY RIVER Cass
BOYD (56218) Lac qui Parle(61), Yellow Medicine(38)
BRAHAM (55006) Isanti(35), Washington(31), Pine(13), Kanabec(11)
BRAINERD (56401) Crow Wing(94), Cass(5)
BRANDON (56315) Douglas(96), Otter Tail(3)
BRECKENRIDGE Wilkin
BREWSTER (56119) Nobles(68), Jackson(31)
BRICELYN Faribault
BRIMSON (55602) St. Louis(93), Lake(6)
BRITT St. Louis
BROOK PARK (55007) Pine(98), Kanabec(1)
BROOKS (56715) Red Lake(97), Polk(2)
BROOKSTON St. Louis

BROOTEN (56316) Stearns(88), Kandiyohi(10)
BROWERVILLE Todd
BROWNS VALLEY (56219) Traverse(95), Big Stone(4)
BROWNSDALE Mower
BROWNSVILLE Houston
BROWNTON McLeod
BRUNO Pine
BUCKMAN Morrison
BUFFALO Wright
BUFFALO LAKE (55314) Renville(81), Sibley(18)
BUHL St. Louis
BURNSVILLE Dakota
BURTRUM (56318) Todd(71), Morrison(28)
BUTTERFIELD (56120) Watonwan(59), Cottonwood(40)
BYRON (55920) Olmsted(98), Dodge(1)
CALEDONIA Houston
CALLAWAY Becker
CALUMET Itasca
CAMBRIDGE Isanti
CAMPBELL (56522) Wilkin(88), Otter Tail(9), Grant(2)
CANBY (56220) Yellow Medicine(80), Lac qui Parle(11), Lincoln(7)
CANNON FALLS (55009) Goodhue(92), Dakota(7)
CANTON Fillmore
CANYON St. Louis
CARLOS Douglas
CARLTON Carlton
CARVER Carver
CASS LAKE (56633) Cass(69), Beltrami(26), Hubbard(3)
CASTLE ROCK Dakota
CEDAR Anoka
CENTER CITY Chisago
CEYLON Martin
CHAMPLIN Hennepin
CHANDLER Murray
CHANHASSEN Carver
CHASKA Carver
CHATFIELD (55923) Fillmore(53), Olmsted(46)
CHISAGO CITY Chisago
CHISHOLM St. Louis
CHOKIO (56221) Stevens(90), Big Stone(8), Traverse(1)
CIRCLE PINES Anoka
CLARA CITY Chippewa
CLAREMONT (55924) Dodge(72), Steele(27)
CLARISSA Todd
CLARKFIELD (56223) Yellow Medicine(98), Lac qui Parle(1)
CLARKS GROVE Freeborn
CLEAR LAKE Sherburne
CLEARBROOK (56634) Clearwater(55), Polk(44)
CLEARWATER (55320) Wright(61), Stearns(38)

CLEMENTS Redwood
CLEVELAND Le Sueur
CLIMAX Polk
CLINTON Big Stone
CLITHERALL Otter Tail
CLONTARF (56226) Swift(85), Pope(14)
CLOQUET (55720) Carlton(90), St. Louis(9)
COHASSET Itasca
COKATO Wright
COLD SPRING Stearns
COLERAINE Itasca
COLLEGEVILLE Stearns
COLOGNE Carver
COMFREY (56019) Brown(64), Cottonwood(27), Watonwan(7)
COMSTOCK Clay
CONGER Freeborn
COOK (55788) Itasca(77), St. Louis(22)
COOK (55723) St. Louis(78), Itasca(21)
CORRELL Big Stone
COSMOS (56228) Meeker(94), Renville(5)
COTTAGE GROVE Washington
COTTON St. Louis
COTTONWOOD (56229) Lyon(78), Yellow Medicine(20)
COURTLAND Nicollet
CRANE LAKE St. Louis
CROMWELL Carlton
CROOKSTON Polk
CROSBY Crow Wing
CROSSLAKE Crow Wing
CRYSTAL BAY Hennepin
CULVER St. Louis
CURRIE Murray
CUSHING (56443) Morrison(77), Todd(22)
CYRUS (56323) Pope(86), Stevens(13)
DAKOTA Winona
DALBO Isanti
DALTON (56324) Otter Tail(97), Grant(2)
DANUBE Renville
DANVERS Swift
DARFUR Watonwan
DARWIN Meeker
DASSEL Meeker
DAWSON Lac qui Parle
DAYTON Hennepin
DE GRAFF (56233) Swift(82), Chippewa(17)
DEBS Beltrami
DEER CREEK Otter Tail
DEER RIVER (56636) Itasca(92), Cass(7)
DEERWOOD Crow Wing
DELANO (55328) Wright(97), Carver(2)
DELAVAN Faribault
DELFT Cottonwood
DENHAM Pine
DENHAM St. Louis
DENNISON (55018) Goodhue(86), Rice(12)
DENT Otter Tail
DETROIT LAKES (56501) Becker(97), Otter Tail(2)

DETROIT LAKES Becker
DEXTER Mower
DILWORTH Clay
DODGE CENTER Dodge
DONALDSON Kittson
DONNELLY (56235) Grant(53), Stevens(46)
DOVER Olmsted
DOVRAY Murray
DULUTH (55810) St. Louis(97), Carlton(2)
DULUTH St. Louis
DUMONT (56236) Traverse(70), Big Stone(29)
DUNDAS Rice
DUNDEE (56126) Nobles(65), Cottonwood(18), Murray(12), Jackson(3)
DUNNELL Martin
DUQUETTE Pine
EAGLE BEND (56446) Todd(93), Douglas(6)
EAGLE LAKE Blue Earth
EAST GRAND FORKS Polk
EASTON Faribault
ECHO Yellow Medicine
EDEN PRAIRIE Hennepin
EDEN VALLEY (55329) Stearns(50), Meeker(49)
EDGERTON (56128) Pipestone(76), Nobles(16), Rock(6)
EFFIE (56639) Itasca(93), Koochiching(6)
EITZEN Houston
ELBOW LAKE Grant
ELGIN (55932) Wabasha(55), Olmsted(44)
ELIZABETH Otter Tail
ELK RIVER (55330) Sherburne(76), Wright(17), Anoka(5)
ELKO Scott
ELKTON Mower
ELLENDALE (56026) Steele(57), Freeborn(41), Waseca(1)
ELLSWORTH (56129) Nobles(84), Rock(14), Lyon(1)
ELMORE (56027) Faribault(96), Martin(3)
ELROSA Stearns
ELY (55731) St. Louis(88), Lake(11)
ELYSIAN (56028) Le Sueur(92), Waseca(7)
EMBARRASS St. Louis
EMILY Crow Wing
EMMONS Freeborn
ERHARD Otter Tail
ERSKINE (56535) Polk(96), Red Lake(3)
ESKO (55733) Carlton(96), St. Louis(3)
ESSIG Brown
EUCLID Polk
EVAN (56238) Redwood(75), Brown(25)
EVANSVILLE (56326) Douglas(85), Otter Tail(11), Grant(3)
EVELETH St. Louis
EXCELSIOR (55331) Hennepin(98), Carver(1)
EYOTA Olmsted
FAIRFAX (55332) Renville(85), Nicollet(13), Sibley(1)
FAIRMONT Martin
FARIBAULT Rice
FARMINGTON Dakota
FARWELL (56327) Douglas(56), Pope(43)
FEDERAL DAM Cass
FELTON Clay
FERGUS FALLS Otter Tail
FERTILE (56540) Polk(93), Norman(6)
FIFTY LAKES Crow Wing
FINLAND Lake
FINLAYSON (55735) Pine(75), Aitkin(24)
FISHER Polk
FLENSBURG Morrison
FLOM Norman
FLOODWOOD (55736) St. Louis(93), Itasca(6)
FOLEY (56329) Benton(94), Morrison(5)
FORBES St. Louis

FOREST LAKE (55025) Washington(78), Anoka(12), Chisago(9)
FORESTON (56330) Mille Lacs(77), Benton(22)
FORT RIPLEY (56449) Crow Wing(84), Morrison(15)
FOSSTON (56542) Polk(95), Mahnomen(4)
FOUNTAIN Fillmore
FOXHOME Wilkin
FRANKLIN (55333) Renville(92), Redwood(4), Brown(3)
FRAZEE (56544) Becker(83), Otter Tail(16)
FREEBORN Freeborn
FREEPORT (56331) Stearns(98), Todd(1)
FRONTENAC Goodhue
FROST Faribault
FULDA (56131) Murray(84), Nobles(10), Cottonwood(5)
GARDEN CITY Blue Earth
GARFIELD Douglas
GARRISON (56450) Crow Wing(60), Mille Lacs(39)
GARVIN Lyon
GARY Norman
GATZKE (56724) Marshall(98), Roseau(1)
GAYLORD (55334) Sibley(93), Nicollet(6)
GENEVA Freeborn
GEORGETOWN Clay
GHENT Lyon
GIBBON (55335) Sibley(78), Nicollet(21)
GILBERT St. Louis
GILMAN Benton
GLENCOE (55336) McLeod(93), Sibley(6)
GLENVILLE Freeborn
GLENWOOD Pope
GLYNDON Clay
GONVICK (56644) Clearwater(84), Polk(15)
GOOD THUNDER Blue Earth
GOODHUE (55027) Goodhue(97), Wabasha(2)
GOODLAND Itasca
GOODRIDGE (56725) Pennington(71), Marshall(27)
GRACEVILLE (56240) Big Stone(75), Traverse(24)
GRANADA (56039) Martin(97), Faribault(2)
GRAND MARAIS Cook
GRAND MEADOW Mower
GRAND PORTAGE Cook
GRAND RAPIDS Itasca
GRANDY Isanti
GRANGER Fillmore
GRANITE FALLS (56241) Yellow Medicine(83), Chippewa(11), Renville(4)
GRASSTON (55030) Pine(91), Kanabec(8)
GREEN ISLE (55338) Sibley(96), Carver(3)
GREENBUSH Roseau
GREENWALD Stearns
GREY EAGLE Todd
GROVE CITY Meeker
GRYGLA (56727) Beltrami(59), Marshall(40)
GULLY (56646) Polk(95), Clearwater(4)
HACKENSACK Cass
HADLEY Murray
HALLOCK Kittson
HALMA Kittson
HALSTAD Norman
HAMBURG (55339) Carver(69), Sibley(26), McLeod(4)
HAMEL Hennepin
HAMMOND Wabasha
HAMPTON Dakota
HANCOCK (56244) Stevens(68), Pope(29), Swift(2)
HANLEY FALLS Yellow Medicine
HANOVER (55341) Wright(76), Hennepin(23)
HANSKA (56041) Brown(98), Watonwan(1)
HARDWICK Rock
HARMONY Fillmore

HARRIS Chisago
HARTLAND (56042) Freeborn(95), Waseca(4)
HASTINGS (55033) Dakota(91), Washington(8)
HAWICK Kandiyohi
HAWLEY Clay
HAYFIELD (55940) Dodge(81), Olmsted(17), Mower(1)
HAYWARD Freeborn
HAZEL RUN Yellow Medicine
HECTOR (55342) Renville(95), Sibley(3)
HENDERSON (56044) Sibley(88), Le Sueur(10)
HENDRICKS (56136) Lincoln(97), Dodge(2)
HENDRUM Norman
HENNING Otter Tail
HENRIETTE Pine
HERMAN (56248) Grant(87), Traverse(6), Stevens(5)
HERON LAKE (56137) Jackson(74), Cottonwood(19), Nobles(5)
HEWITT (56453) Todd(79), Otter Tail(20)
HIBBING (55746) St. Louis(98), Itasca(1)
HIBBING St. Louis
HILL CITY (55748) Aitkin(68), Itasca(31)
HILLMAN (56338) Morrison(95), Crow Wing(4)
HILLS Rock
HINCKLEY (55037) Pine(97), Kanabec(2)
HINES Beltrami
HITTERDAL (56552) Clay(79), Becker(20)
HOFFMAN (56339) Grant(88), Douglas(11)
HOKAH Houston
HOLDINGFORD Stearns
HOLLAND Pipestone
HOLLANDALE Freeborn
HOLLOWAY Swift
HOLMES CITY Douglas
HOLYOKE (55749) Carlton(71), Pine(28)
HOMER Winona
HOPE Steele
HOPKINS Hennepin
HOUSTON (55943) Houston(84), Winona(15)
HOVLAND Cook
HOWARD LAKE Hennepin
HOWARD LAKE Wright
HOYT LAKES St. Louis
HUGO (55038) Washington(67), Anoka(32)
HUMBOLDT Kittson
HUNTLEY Faribault
HUTCHINSON (55350) McLeod(91), Renville(5), Meeker(3)
IHLEN Pipestone
INTERNATIONAL FALLS Koochiching
INVER GROVE HEIGHTS Dakota
IONA (56141) Murray(90), Nobles(10)
IRON St. Louis
IRONTON Crow Wing
ISABELLA Lake
ISANTI Isanti
ISLE (56342) Mille Lacs(74), Kanabec(18), Aitkin(6)
IVANHOE Lincoln
JACOBSON (55752) Itasca(82), Aitkin(17)
JANESVILLE (56048) Waseca(98), Blue Earth(1)
JASPER (56144) Rock(77), Pipestone(18), Murray(3), Mower(1)
JEFFERS Cottonwood
JENKINS Crow Wing
JOHNSON (56250) Big Stone(70), Traverse(29)
JORDAN Scott
KABETOGAMA (56669) Koochiching(60), St. Louis(39)
KANARANZI (56146) Nobles(96), Rock(3)
KANDIYOHI Kandiyohi
KARLSTAD (56732) Kittson(89), Marshall(6), Roseau(4)

KASOTA (56050) Le Sueur(97), Blue Earth(2)
KASSON (55944) Dodge(94), Olmsted(5)
KEEWATIN Itasca
KELLIHER Beltrami
KELLOGG Wabasha
KELSEY St. Louis
KENNEDY Kittson
KENNETH (56147) Rock(72), Nobles(27)
KENSINGTON (56343) Douglas(69), Pope(15), Stevens(7), Grant(6)
KENT Wilkin
KENYON (55946) Goodhue(83), Rice(12), Dodge(3), Steele(1)
KERKHOVEN (56252) Kandiyohi(58), Swift(32), Chippewa(9)
KERRICK (55756) Pine(92), Carlton(7)
KETTLE RIVER Carlton
KIESTER (56051) Faribault(97), Freeborn(2)
KILKENNY (56052) Rice(66), Le Sueur(33)
KIMBALL (55353) Stearns(76), Meeker(23)
KINNEY St. Louis
KLOSSNER Nicollet
KNIFE RIVER Lake
LA CRESCENT (55947) Houston(88), Winona(11)
LA SALLE Watonwan
LAFAYETTE (56054) Nicollet(90), Sibley(9)
LAKE BENTON (56149) Lincoln(97), Pipestone(2)
LAKE BRONSON Kittson
LAKE CITY (55041) Wabasha(84), Goodhue(15)
LAKE CRYSTAL Blue Earth
LAKE ELMO Washington
LAKE GEORGE Hubbard
LAKE HUBERT Crow Wing
LAKE ITASCA Clearwater
LAKE LILLIAN Kandiyohi
LAKE PARK (56554) Becker(95), Clay(4)
LAKE WILSON Murray
LAKEFIELD Jackson
LAKELAND Washington
LAKEVILLE (55044) Dakota(86), Scott(13)
LAMBERTON (56152) Redwood(81), Cottonwood(18)
LANCASTER (56735) Kittson(97), Roseau(2)
LANESBORO Fillmore
LANSING Mower
LAPORTE (56461) Hubbard(94), Cass(5)
LASTRUP Morrison
LE CENTER Le Sueur
LE ROY (55951) Rice(60), Fillmore(40)
LE SUEUR (56058) Le Sueur(84), Sibley(11), Nicollet(3)
LENGBY (56651) Mahnomen(61), Polk(38)
LEONARD (56652) Clearwater(97), Beltrami(2)
LEOTA Nobles
LESTER PRAIRIE McLeod
LEWISTON Winona
LEWISVILLE (56060) Watonwan(87), Blue Earth(12)
LINDSTROM Chisago
LISMORE Nobles
LITCHFIELD Meeker
LITTLE FALLS Morrison
LITTLEFORK Koochiching
LOMAN Koochiching
LONDON Freeborn
LONG LAKE Hennepin
LONG PRAIRIE (56347) Todd(98), Morrison(1)
LONG PRAIRIE Todd
LONGVILLE Cass
LONSDALE Rice
LORETTO Hennepin
LOUISBURG Lac qui Parle
LOWRY (56349) Pope(84), Douglas(15)
LUCAN Redwood

LUTSEN Cook
LUVERNE Rock
LYLE (55953) Mower(80), Rice(14), Freeborn(4)
LYND Lyon
MABEL (55954) Fillmore(89), Houston(10)
MADELIA (56062) Watonwan(91), Brown(8)
MADISON Lac qui Parle
MADISON LAKE (56063) Blue Earth(59), Waseca(28), Le Sueur(11)
MAGNOLIA (56158) Rock(75), Nobles(25)
MAHNOMEN (56557) Mahnomen(95), Clearwater(2), Norman(2)
MAHTOWA Carlton
MAKINEN St. Louis
MANCHESTER Freeborn
MANHATTAN BEACH Crow Wing
MANKATO Blue Earth
MANKATO Nicollet
MANTORVILLE Dodge
MAPLE LAKE Wright
MAPLE PLAIN Hennepin
MAPLE PLAIN Wright
MAPLETON (56065) Blue Earth(56), Faribault(32), Waseca(11)
MARBLE Itasca
MARCELL Itasca
MARGIE Koochiching
MARIETTA (56257) Lac qui Parle(98), Grant(1)
MARINE ON SAINT CROIX Washington
MARSHALL Lyon
MAX Itasca
MAYER Carver
MAYNARD (56260) Chippewa(70), Renville(29)
MAZEPPA (55956) Wabasha(74), Goodhue(24), Olmsted(1)
MC GRATH Aitkin
MC KINLEY St. Louis
MCGREGOR Aitkin
MCINTOSH Polk
MEADOWLANDS St. Louis
MEDFORD (55049) Steele(89), Rice(10)
MELROSE Stearns
MELRUDE St. Louis
MENAHGA (56464) Wadena(52), Becker(29), Hubbard(15), Otter Tail(2)
MENDOTA Dakota
MENTOR (56736) Polk(88), Red Lake(11)
MERIDEN (56067) Waseca(69), Steele(30)
MERRIFIELD Crow Wing
MIDDLE RIVER Marshall
MILACA (56353) Mille Lacs(97), Isanti(2)
MILAN (56262) Chippewa(83), Swift(16)
MILLVILLE Wabasha
MILROY (56263) Redwood(83), Lyon(16)
MILTONA Douglas
MINNEAPOLIS Anoka
MINNEAPOLIS Carver
MINNEAPOLIS Hennepin
MINNEOTA (56264) Lyon(87), Yellow Medicine(11), Lincoln(1)
MINNESOTA CITY Winona
MINNESOTA LAKE (56068) Waseca(44), Faribault(43), Blue Earth(11)
MINNETONKA Hennepin
MINNETONKA BEACH Hennepin
MIZPAH Koochiching
MONTEVIDEO (56265) Chippewa(88), Lac qui Parle(8), Yellow Medicine(3)
MONTGOMERY (56069) Le Sueur(61), Rice(38)
MONTICELLO Carver
MONTICELLO Wright
MONTROSE (55363) Wright(98), Carver(1)
MOORHEAD Clay
MOOSE LAKE (55767) Carlton(80), Pine(19)
MORA Kanabec

MORGAN (56266) Redwood(75), Brown(24)
MORRIS Stevens
MORRISTOWN (55052) Rice(94), Waseca(5)
MORTON (56270) Renville(52), Redwood(47)
MOTLEY (56466) Morrison(48), Cass(40), Todd(11)
MOUND Hennepin
MOUNTAIN IRON St. Louis
MOUNTAIN LAKE (56159) Cottonwood(95), Jackson(3)
MURDOCK (56271) Swift(84), Chippewa(15)
MYRTLE Freeborn
NASHUA (56565) Wilkin(80), Grant(19)
NASHWAUK Itasca
NASSAU Lac qui Parle
NAVARRE Hennepin
NAYTAHWAUSH Mahnomen
NELSON Douglas
NERSTRAND (55053) Rice(80), Goodhue(19)
NETT LAKE St. Louis
NEVIS Hubbard
NEW AUBURN Sibley
NEW GERMANY Carver
NEW LONDON Kandiyohi
NEW MARKET Scott
NEW MUNICH Stearns
NEW PRAGUE (56071) Scott(55), Le Sueur(41), Rice(3)
NEW RICHLAND (56072) Waseca(90), Freeborn(9)
NEW ULM (56073) Brown(86), Nicollet(12), Blue Earth(1)
NEW YORK MILLS Otter Tail
NEWFOLDEN Marshall
NEWPORT Washington
NICOLLET Nicollet
NIELSVILLE (56568) Polk(92), Norman(7)
NIMROD Wadena
NISSWA (56468) Crow Wing(69), Cass(30)
NORCROSS (56274) Grant(68), Traverse(31)
NORTH BRANCH (55056) Chisago(79), Isanti(20)
NORTHFIELD (55057) Rice(81), Dakota(18)
NORTHHOME (56661) Itasca(51), Koochiching(36), Beltrami(12)
NORTHROP Martin
NORWOOD (55368) Carver(97), McLeod(2)
NORWOOD Carver
NOYES Kittson
OAK ISLAND Lake of the Woods
OAK PARK Benton
OAKLAND Freeborn
ODESSA (56276) Big Stone(74), Lac qui Parle(25)
ODIN (56160) Watonwan(41), Martin(36), Jackson(21)
OGEMA Becker
OGILVIE (56358) Kanabec(88), Mille Lacs(11)
OKABENA Jackson
OKLEE (56742) Red Lake(79), Pennington(16), Polk(3)
OLIVIA Renville
ONAMIA Mille Lacs
ORMSBY (56162) Martin(55), Watonwan(44)
ORONOCO Olmsted
ORR (55771) St. Louis(91), Koochiching(8)
ORTONVILLE (56278) Big Stone(98), Lac qui Parle(1)
OSAGE Becker
OSAKIS (56360) Todd(57), Douglas(42)
OSLO (56744) Marshall(57), Polk(24), Mower(15), Crow Wing(3)

OSSEO Hennepin
OSTRANDER (55961) Mower(66), Fillmore(33)
OTISCO Waseca
OTTERTAIL Otter Tail
OUTING Cass
OWATONNA Steele
PALISADE Aitkin
PARK RAPIDS (56470) Hubbard(88), Becker(11)
PARKERS PRAIRIE (56361) Otter Tail(63), Douglas(36)
PARKVILLE St. Louis
PAYNESVILLE (56362) Stearns(89), Meeker(6), Kandiyohi(3)
PEASE Mille Lacs
PELICAN RAPIDS (56572) Otter Tail(95), Becker(2), Clay(1)
PEMBERTON (56078) Waseca(73), Blue Earth(26)
PENGILLY Itasca
PENNINGTON Beltrami
PENNOCK Kandiyohi
PEQUOT LAKES (56472) Crow Wing(76), Cass(23)
PERHAM Otter Tail
PERLEY (56574) Norman(95), Clay(4)
PETERSON (55962) Fillmore(94), Winona(5)
PIERZ (56364) Morrison(97), Crow Wing(2)
PILLAGER Cass
PINE CITY Pine
PINE ISLAND (55963) Goodhue(51), Olmsted(31), Dodge(17)
PINE RIVER (56474) Cass(95), Crow Wing(4)
PIPESTONE (56164) Pipestone(97), Lincoln(2)
PITT Lake of the Woods
PLAINVIEW (55964) Wabasha(96), Olmsted(2), Winona(1)
PLATO McLeod
PLUMMER (56748) Red Lake(90), Pennington(9)
PONEMAH Beltrami
PONSFORD Becker
PORTER (56280) Yellow Medicine(63), Lincoln(36)
PRESTON Fillmore
PRINCETON (55371) Mille Lacs(59), Sherburne(23), Isanti(15), Benton(1)
PRINSBURG Kandiyohi
PRIOR LAKE Scott
PUPOSKY Beltrami
RACINE Mower
RANDALL Morrison
RANDOLPH Dakota
RANIER Koochiching
RAY (56669) Koochiching(60), St. Louis(39)
RAYMOND (56282) Kandiyohi(81), Chippewa(18)
READING Nobles
READS LANDING Wabasha
RED LAKE FALLS (56750) Red Lake(94), Polk(3), Pennington(2)
RED WING Goodhue
REDBY Beltrami
REDLAKE Beltrami
REDWOOD FALLS (56283) Redwood(95), Renville(4)
REMER Cass
RENVILLE (56284) Renville(86), Kandiyohi(10), Redwood(2)
REVERE (56166) Redwood(74), Cottonwood(25)
RICE (56367) Benton(82), Stearns(16)
RICHMOND Stearns
RICHVILLE Otter Tail
RICHWOOD Becker
ROCHERT Becker
ROCHESTER Olmsted

ROCK CREEK Pine
ROCKFORD (55373) Wright(65), Hennepin(34)
ROCKFORD Hennepin
ROCKVILLE Stearns
ROGERS (55374) Hennepin(94), Wright(5)
ROLLINGSTONE Winona
ROOSEVELT (56673) Roseau(83), Lake of the Woods(16)
ROSCOE Stearns
ROSE CREEK Mower
ROSEAU Roseau
ROSEMOUNT Dakota
ROTHSAY (56579) Wilkin(63), Otter Tail(36)
ROUND LAKE (56167) Nobles(54), Jackson(45)
ROYALTON (56373) Morrison(89), Benton(10)
RUSH CITY (55069) Chisago(95), Pine(4)
RUSHFORD (55971) Fillmore(82), Houston(10), Winona(6)
RUSHMORE Nobles
RUSSELL Lyon
RUTHTON (56170) Pipestone(73), Lyon(13), Murray(10), Lincoln(2)
RUTLEDGE Pine
SABIN Clay
SACRED HEART Renville
SAGINAW St. Louis
SAINT BONIFACIUS (55375) Hennepin(98), Carver(1)
SAINT CHARLES (55972) Winona(85), Olmsted(14)
SAINT CLAIR Blue Earth
SAINT CLOUD (56304) Sherburne(50), Benton(49)
SAINT CLOUD Stearns
SAINT FRANCIS (55070) Anoka(90), Isanti(9)
SAINT HILAIRE (56754) Pennington(87), Red Lake(12)
SAINT JAMES (56081) Watonwan(98), Brown(1)
SAINT JOSEPH Stearns
SAINT LEO Yellow Medicine
SAINT MARTIN Stearns
SAINT MICHAEL Wright
SAINT PAUL (55118) Dakota(98), Ramsey(1)
SAINT PAUL (55110) Ramsey(85), Washington(13), Anoka(1)
SAINT PAUL (55126) Ramsey(98), Anoka(1)
SAINT PAUL Dakota
SAINT PAUL Hennepin
SAINT PAUL Ramsey
SAINT PAUL Washington
SAINT PAUL PARK Washington
SAINT PETER (56082) Nicollet(89), Le Sueur(10)
SAINT STEPHEN Stearns
SAINT VINCENT Kittson
SALOL Roseau
SANBORN (56083) Redwood(54), Cottonwood(29), Brown(15)
SANDSTONE (55072) Pine(83), Kanabec(16)
SANTIAGO Sherburne
SARGEANT (55973) Mower(96), Dodge(3)
SARTELL (56377) Stearns(79), Benton(20)
SAUK CENTRE (56378) Stearns(80), Todd(19)
SAUK RAPIDS (56379) Benton(98), Stearns(1)
SAUM Beltrami
SAVAGE Scott
SAWYER Carlton
SCANDIA (55073) Washington(62), Chisago(37)
SCHROEDER Cook
SEAFORTH Redwood

SEARLES Brown
SEBEKA (56477) Wadena(80), Otter Tail(19)
SEDAN Pope
SHAFER Chisago
SHAKOPEE Scott
SHELLY Norman
SHERBURN Martin
SHEVLIN (56676) Beltrami(54), Clearwater(45)
SIDE LAKE St. Louis
SILVER BAY Lake
SILVER CREEK Wright
SILVER LAKE McLeod
SLAYTON Murray
SLEEPY EYE (56085) Brown(97), Redwood(2)
SOLWAY (56678) Hubbard(74), Beltrami(24)
SOUDAN St. Louis
SOUTH HAVEN (55382) Stearns(46), Wright(45), Meeker(7)
SOUTH INTERNATIONAL FALLS Koochiching
SOUTH SAINT PAUL Dakota
SPICER Kandiyohi
SPRING GROVE (55974) Houston(98), Fillmore(1)
SPRING LAKE Itasca
SPRING PARK Hennepin
SPRING VALLEY (55975) Fillmore(87), Mower(12)
SPRINGFIELD (56087) Brown(90), Redwood(9)
SQUAW LAKE Itasca
STACY (55079) Chisago(48), Anoka(31), Isanti(20)
STACY (55078) Washington(80), Chisago(20)
STANCHFIELD (55080) Isanti(63), Chisago(36)
STAPLES (56479) Todd(67), Wadena(32)
STARBUCK Pope
STEEN (56173) Rock(71), Polk(28)
STEPHEN (56757) Marshall(98), Kittson(1)
STEWART (55385) McLeod(53), Renville(33), Sibley(12)
STEWARTVILLE (55976) Olmsted(96), Mower(2), Fillmore(1)
STILLWATER Washington

STOCKTON Winona
STORDEN Cottonwood
STRANDQUIST Marshall
STRATHCONA (56759) Roseau(73), Marshall(26)
STURGEON LAKE (55783) Pine(97), Carlton(2)
SUNBURG (56289) Kandiyohi(75), Swift(22), Pope(1)
SWAN RIVER Itasca
SWANVILLE (56382) Morrison(58), Todd(41)
SWATARA (55785) Cass(53), Aitkin(46)
SWIFT Roseau
TACONITE Itasca
TALMOON Itasca
TAMARACK (55787) Aitkin(79), Carlton(20)
TAOPI Mower
TAUNTON (56291) Lyon(46), Yellow Medicine(34), Lincoln(18)
TAYLORS FALLS Chisago
TENSTRIKE Beltrami
THEILMAN Wabasha
THIEF RIVER FALLS (56701) Pennington(95), Marshall(4)
TINTAH (56583) Wilkin(86), Traverse(13)
TOFTE Cook
TOWER St. Louis
TRACY (56175) Lyon(92), Redwood(7)
TRAIL (56684) Pennington(57), Polk(28), Red Lake(13)
TRIMONT Martin
TROSKY Pipestone
TRUMAN (56088) Martin(71), Watonwan(24), Blue Earth(4)
TWIG St. Louis
TWIN LAKES Freeborn
TWIN VALLEY Norman
TWO HARBORS Lake
TYLER (56178) Lincoln(89), Lyon(10)
ULEN (56585) Clay(76), Becker(21), Norman(1)
UNDERWOOD Otter Tail
UPSALA Morrison
UTICA (55979) Winona(98), Fillmore(1)
VERDI (56179) Lincoln(92), Pipestone(7)
VERGAS Otter Tail
VERMILLION Dakota
VERNDALE (56481) Wadena(78), Todd(18), Cass(2)

VERNON CENTER Blue Earth
VESTA (56292) Redwood(97), Yellow Medicine(2)
VICTORIA Carver
VIKING (56760) Marshall(98), Pennington(1)
VILLARD (56385) Pope(57), Stearns(37), Douglas(5)
VINING Otter Tail
VIRGINIA St. Louis
WABASHA Wabasha
WABASSO Redwood
WACONIA (55387) Carver(98), Hennepin(1)
WADENA (56482) Wadena(81), Otter Tail(17)
WAHKON Mille Lacs
WAITE PARK Stearns
WALDORF Waseca
WALKER Cass
WALNUT GROVE (56180) Redwood(81), Cottonwood(12), Murray(6)
WALTERS (56092) Faribault(92), Freeborn(7)
WALTHAM (55982) Mower(98), Dodge(1)
WANAMINGO Goodhue
WANDA Redwood
WANNASKA (56761) Roseau(95), Marshall(3)
WARBA Itasca
WARREN (56762) Marshall(70), Polk(29)
WARROAD Roseau
WARSAW Rice
WASECA (56093) Waseca(96), Steele(3)
WASKISH Beltrami
WATERTOWN (55388) Carver(85), Wright(12), Hennepin(2)
WATERVILLE (56096) Le Sueur(84), Rice(7), Waseca(7)
WATKINS (55389) Meeker(80), Stearns(20)
WATSON Chippewa
WAUBUN (56589) Becker(98), Mahnomen(1)
WAVERLY Wright
WAWINA Itasca
WAYZATA Hennepin
WEBSTER (55088) Rice(68), Scott(30)
WELCH (55089) Goodhue(88), Dakota(11)
WELCOME Martin

WELLS (56097) Faribault(86), Freeborn(11), Waseca(2)
WENDELL (56590) Grant(98), Otter Tail(1)
WEST CONCORD Dodge
WEST UNION Todd
WESTBROOK (56183) Cottonwood(92), Murray(7)
WHALAN Fillmore
WHEATON Traverse
WHIPHOLT Cass
WHITE EARTH Becker
WILLERNIE Washington
WILLIAMS Lake of the Woods
WILLMAR Kandiyohi
WILLOW RIVER Pine
WILMONT Nobles
WILTON Beltrami
WINDOM (56101) Cottonwood(84), Jackson(15)
WINGER (56592) Polk(97), Mahnomen(2)
WINNEBAGO (56098) Faribault(89), Martin(10)
WINONA Winona
WINSTED (55395) McLeod(91), Carver(8)
WINTHROP Sibley
WINTON St. Louis
WIRT Itasca
WOLF LAKE Becker
WOLVERTON Wilkin
WOOD LAKE (56297) Yellow Medicine(94), Redwood(3), Lyon(1)
WOODSTOCK (56186) Murray(79), Pipestone(20)
WORTHINGTON (56187) Nobles(98), Jackson(1)
WRENSHALL (55797) Carlton(94), Pine(5)
WRIGHT Carlton
WYKOFF Fillmore
WYOMING (55092) Chisago(60), Anoka(40)
YOUNG AMERICA Carver
YOUNG AMERICA Hennepin
ZIM St. Louis
ZIMMERMAN (55398) Sherburne(90), Isanti(9)
ZUMBRO FALLS (55991) Wabasha(90), Olmsted(9)
ZUMBROTA Goodhue

Minnesota ZIP/City Cross Reference

55001-55001	AFTON
55002-55002	ALMELUND
55003-55003	BAYPORT
55004-55004	BEROUN
55005-55005	BETHEL
55006-55006	BRAHAM
55007-55007	BROOK PARK
55008-55008	CAMBRIDGE
55009-55009	CANNON FALLS
55010-55010	CASTLE ROCK
55011-55011	CEDAR
55012-55012	CENTER CITY
55013-55013	CHISAGO CITY
55014-55014	CIRCLE PINES
55016-55016	COTTAGE GROVE
55017-55017	DALBO
55018-55018	DENNISON
55019-55019	DUNDAS
55020-55020	ELKO
55021-55021	FARIBAULT
55024-55024	FARMINGTON
55025-55025	FOREST LAKE
55026-55026	FRONTENAC
55027-55027	GOODHUE
55029-55029	GRANDY
55030-55030	GRASSTON
55031-55031	HAMPTON

55032-55032	HARRIS
55033-55033	HASTINGS
55036-55036	HENRIETTE
55037-55037	HINCKLEY
55038-55038	HUGO
55040-55040	ISANTI
55041-55041	LAKE CITY
55042-55042	LAKE ELMO
55043-55043	LAKELAND
55044-55044	LAKEVILLE
55045-55045	LINDSTROM
55046-55046	LONSDALE
55047-55047	MARINE ON SAINT CROIX
55049-55049	MEDFORD
55051-55051	MORA
55052-55052	MORRISTOWN
55053-55053	NERSTRAND
55054-55054	NEW MARKET
55055-55055	NEWPORT
55056-55056	NORTH BRANCH
55057-55057	NORTHFIELD
55060-55060	OWATONNA
55063-55063	PINE CITY
55065-55065	RANDOLPH
55066-55066	RED WING
55067-55067	ROCK CREEK
55068-55068	ROSEMOUNT

55069-55069	RUSH CITY
55070-55070	SAINT FRANCIS
55071-55071	SAINT PAUL PARK
55072-55072	SANDSTONE
55073-55073	SCANDIA
55074-55074	SHAFER
55075-55075	SOUTH SAINT PAUL
55076-55077	INVER GROVE HEIGHTS
55078-55079	STACY
55080-55080	STANCHFIELD
55082-55083	STILLWATER
55084-55084	TAYLORS FALLS
55085-55085	VERMILLION
55087-55087	WARSAW
55088-55088	WEBSTER
55089-55089	WELCH
55090-55090	WILLERNIE
55092-55092	WYOMING
55100-55146	SAINT PAUL
55150-55150	MENDOTA
55155-55199	SAINT PAUL
55301-55301	ALBERTVILLE
55302-55302	ANNANDALE
55303-55303	ANOKA
55305-55305	HOPKINS
55306-55306	BURNSVILLE
55307-55307	ARLINGTON

55308-55308	BECKER
55309-55309	BIG LAKE
55310-55310	BIRD ISLAND
55311-55311	OSSEO
55312-55312	BROWNTON
55313-55313	BUFFALO
55314-55314	BUFFALO LAKE
55315-55315	CARVER
55316-55316	CHAMPLIN
55317-55317	CHANHASSEN
55318-55318	CHASKA
55319-55319	CLEAR LAKE
55320-55320	CLEARWATER
55321-55321	COKATO
55322-55322	COLOGNE
55323-55323	CRYSTAL BAY
55324-55324	DARWIN
55325-55325	DASSEL
55327-55327	DAYTON
55328-55328	DELANO
55329-55329	EDEN VALLEY
55330-55330	ELK RIVER
55331-55331	EXCELSIOR
55332-55332	FAIRFAX
55333-55333	FRANKLIN
55334-55334	GAYLORD
55335-55335	GIBBON

Zip Range	City	Zip Range	City	Zip Range	City	Zip Range	City
55336-55336	GLENCOE	55580-55582	MONTICELLO	55773-55773	PARKVILLE	55974-55974	SPRING GROVE
55337-55337	BURNSVILLE	55583-55583	NORWOOD	55775-55775	PENGILLY	55975-55975	SPRING VALLEY
55338-55338	GREEN ISLE	55584-55591	MONTICELLO	55777-55777	VIRGINIA	55976-55976	STEWARTVILLE
55339-55339	HAMBURG	55592-55593	MAPLE PLAIN	55778-55778	RUTLEDGE	55977-55977	TAOPI
55340-55340	HAMEL	55594-55594	YOUNG AMERICA	55779-55779	SAGINAW	55978-55978	THEILMAN
55341-55341	HANOVER	55595-55599	LORETTO	55780-55780	SAWYER	55979-55979	UTICA
55342-55342	HECTOR	55601-55601	BEAVER BAY	55781-55781	SIDE LAKE	55981-55981	WABASHA
55343-55343	HOPKINS	55602-55602	BRIMSON	55782-55782	SOUDAN	55982-55982	WALTHAM
55344-55344	EDEN PRAIRIE	55603-55603	FINLAND	55783-55783	STURGEON LAKE	55983-55983	WANAMINGO
55345-55345	MINNETONKA	55604-55604	GRAND MARAIS	55784-55784	SWAN RIVER	55985-55985	WEST CONCORD
55346-55347	EDEN PRAIRIE	55605-55605	GRAND PORTAGE	55785-55785	SWATARA	55986-55986	WHALAN
55348-55348	MAPLE PLAIN	55606-55606	HOVLAND	55786-55786	TACONITE	55987-55987	WINONA
55349-55349	HOWARD LAKE	55607-55607	ISABELLA	55787-55787	TAMARACK	55988-55988	STOCKTON
55350-55350	HUTCHINSON	55609-55609	KNIFE RIVER	55788-55788	COOK	55990-55990	WYKOFF
55351-55351	YOUNG AMERICA	55612-55612	LUTSEN	55789-55789	MEADOWLANDS	55991-55991	ZUMBRO FALLS
55352-55352	JORDAN	55613-55613	SCHROEDER	55790-55790	TOWER	55992-55992	ZUMBROTA
55353-55353	KIMBALL	55614-55614	SILVER BAY	55791-55791	TWIG	56001-56006	MANKATO
55354-55354	LESTER PRAIRIE	55615-55615	TOFTE	55792-55792	VIRGINIA	56007-56007	ALBERT LEA
55355-55355	LITCHFIELD	55616-55616	TWO HARBORS	55793-55793	WARBA	56009-56009	ALDEN
55356-55356	LONG LAKE	55701-55701	ADOLPH	55794-55794	WAWINA	56010-56010	AMBOY
55357-55357	LORETTO	55702-55702	ALBORN	55795-55795	WILLOW RIVER	56011-56011	BELLE PLAINE
55358-55358	MAPLE LAKE	55703-55703	ANGORA	55796-55796	WINTON	56013-56013	BLUE EARTH
55359-55359	MAPLE PLAIN	55704-55704	ASKOV	55797-55797	WRENSHALL	56014-56014	BRICELYN
55360-55360	MAYER	55705-55705	AURORA	55798-55798	WRIGHT	56016-56016	CLARKS GROVE
55361-55361	MINNETONKA BEACH	55706-55706	BABBITT	55799-55799	ZIM	56017-56017	CLEVELAND
55362-55362	MONTICELLO	55707-55707	BARNUM	55800-55816	DULUTH	56019-56019	COMFREY
55363-55363	MONTROSE	55708-55708	BIWABIK	55901-55906	ROCHESTER	56020-56020	CONGER
55364-55364	MOUND	55709-55709	BOVEY	55909-55909	ADAMS	56021-56021	COURTLAND
55365-55365	MONTICELLO	55710-55710	BRITT	55910-55910	ALTURA	56022-56022	DARFUR
55366-55366	NEW AUBURN	55711-55711	BROOKSTON	55912-55912	AUSTIN	56023-56023	DELAVAN
55367-55367	NEW GERMANY	55712-55712	BRUNO	55917-55917	BLOOMING PRAIRIE	56024-56024	EAGLE LAKE
55368-55368	NORWOOD	55713-55713	BUHL	55918-55918	BROWNSDALE	56025-56025	EASTON
55369-55369	OSSEO	55716-55716	CALUMET	55919-55919	BROWNSVILLE	56026-56026	ELLENDALE
55370-55370	PLATO	55717-55717	CANYON	55920-55920	BYRON	56027-56027	ELMORE
55371-55371	PRINCETON	55718-55718	CARLTON	55921-55921	CALEDONIA	56028-56028	ELYSIAN
55372-55372	PRIOR LAKE	55719-55719	CHISHOLM	55922-55922	CANTON	56029-56029	EMMONS
55373-55373	ROCKFORD	55720-55720	CLOQUET	55923-55923	CHATFIELD	56030-56030	ESSIG
55374-55374	ROGERS	55721-55721	COHASSET	55924-55924	CLAREMONT	56031-56031	FAIRMONT
55375-55375	SAINT BONIFACIUS	55722-55722	COLERAINE	55925-55925	DAKOTA	56032-56032	FREEBORN
55376-55376	SAINT MICHAEL	55723-55723	COOK	55926-55926	DEXTER	56033-56033	FROST
55377-55377	SANTIAGO	55724-55724	COTTON	55927-55927	DODGE CENTER	56034-56034	GARDEN CITY
55378-55378	SAVAGE	55725-55725	CRANE LAKE	55929-55929	DOVER	56035-56035	GENEVA
55379-55379	SHAKOPEE	55726-55726	CROMWELL	55931-55931	EITZEN	56036-56036	GLENVILLE
55380-55380	SILVER CREEK	55727-55727	CULVER	55932-55932	ELGIN	56037-56037	GOOD THUNDER
55381-55381	SILVER LAKE	55728-55728	DENHAM	55933-55933	ELKTON	56039-56039	GRANADA
55382-55382	SOUTH HAVEN	55729-55729	DUQUETTE	55934-55934	EYOTA	56041-56041	HANSKA
55383-55383	NORWOOD	55730-55730	GRAND RAPIDS	55935-55935	FOUNTAIN	56042-56042	HARTLAND
55384-55384	SPRING PARK	55731-55731	ELY	55936-55936	GRAND MEADOW	56043-56043	HAYWARD
55385-55385	STEWART	55732-55732	EMBARRASS	55937-55937	GRANGER	56044-56044	HENDERSON
55386-55386	VICTORIA	55733-55733	ESKO	55938-55938	HAMMOND	56045-56045	HOLLANDALE
55387-55387	WACONIA	55734-55734	EVELETH	55939-55939	HARMONY	56046-56046	HOPE
55388-55388	WATERTOWN	55735-55735	FINLAYSON	55940-55940	HAYFIELD	56047-56047	HUNTLEY
55389-55389	WATKINS	55736-55736	FLOODWOOD	55941-55941	HOKAH	56048-56048	JANESVILLE
55390-55390	WAVERLY	55738-55738	FORBES	55942-55942	HOMER	56050-56050	KASOTA
55391-55391	WAYZATA	55740-55740	DENHAM	55943-55943	HOUSTON	56051-56051	KIESTER
55392-55392	NAVARRE	55741-55741	GILBERT	55944-55944	KASSON	56052-56052	KILKENNY
55393-55393	MAPLE PLAIN	55742-55742	GOODLAND	55945-55945	KELLOGG	56053-56053	KLOSSNER
55394-55394	YOUNG AMERICA	55744-55745	GRAND RAPIDS	55946-55946	KENYON	56054-56054	LAFAYETTE
55395-55395	WINSTED	55746-55747	HIBBING	55947-55947	LA CRESCENT	56055-56055	LAKE CRYSTAL
55396-55396	WINTHROP	55748-55748	HILL CITY	55949-55949	LANESBORO	56056-56056	LA SALLE
55397-55397	YOUNG AMERICA	55749-55749	HOLYOKE	55950-55950	LANSING	56057-56057	LE CENTER
55398-55398	ZIMMERMAN	55750-55750	HOYT LAKES	55951-55951	LE ROY	56058-56058	LE SUEUR
55399-55399	YOUNG AMERICA	55751-55751	IRON	55952-55952	LEWISTON	56060-56060	LEWISVILLE
55400-55488	MINNEAPOLIS	55752-55752	JACOBSON	55953-55953	LYLE	56061-56061	LONDON
55550-55554	YOUNG AMERICA	55753-55753	KEEWATIN	55954-55954	MABEL	56062-56062	MADELIA
55554-55554	NORWOOD	55754-55754	HIBBING	55955-55955	MANTORVILLE	56063-56063	MADISON LAKE
55555-55560	YOUNG AMERICA	55755-55755	KELSEY	55956-55956	MAZEPPA	56064-56064	MANCHESTER
55561-55561	MONTICELLO	55756-55756	KERRICK	55957-55957	MILLVILLE	56065-56065	MAPLETON
55562-55562	YOUNG AMERICA	55757-55757	KETTLE RIVER	55959-55959	MINNESOTA CITY	56067-56067	MERIDEN
55563-55563	MONTICELLO	55758-55758	KINNEY	55960-55960	ORONOCO	56068-56068	MINNESOTA LAKE
55564-55564	YOUNG AMERICA	55760-55760	MCGREGOR	55961-55961	OSTRANDER	56069-56069	MONTGOMERY
55565-55565	MONTICELLO	55761-55761	MC KINLEY	55962-55962	PETERSON	56070-56070	MYRTLE
55566-55568	YOUNG AMERICA	55762-55762	MAHTOWA	55963-55963	PINE ISLAND	56071-56071	NEW PRAGUE
55569-55569	OSSEO	55763-55763	MAKINEN	55964-55964	PLAINVIEW	56072-56072	NEW RICHLAND
55570-55572	MAPLE PLAIN	55764-55764	MARBLE	55965-55965	PRESTON	56073-56073	NEW ULM
55572-55572	ROCKFORD	55765-55765	MEADOWLANDS	55967-55967	RACINE	56074-56074	NICOLLET
55573-55573	YOUNG AMERICA	55766-55766	MELRUDE	55968-55968	READS LANDING	56075-56075	NORTHROP
55574-55574	MAPLE PLAIN	55767-55767	MOOSE LAKE	55969-55969	ROLLINGSTONE	56076-56076	OAKLAND
55575-55575	HOWARD LAKE	55768-55768	MOUNTAIN IRON	55970-55970	ROSE CREEK	56077-56077	OTISCO
55576-55577	MAPLE PLAIN	55769-55769	NASHWAUK	55971-55971	RUSHFORD	56078-56078	PEMBERTON
55577-55577	ROCKFORD	55771-55771	ORR	55972-55972	SAINT CHARLES	56080-56080	SAINT CLAIR
55578-55579	MAPLE PLAIN	55772-55772	NETT LAKE	55973-55973	SARGEANT	56081-56081	SAINT JAMES

Zip Range	Place	Zip Range	Place	Zip Range	Place	Zip Range	Place
56082-56082	SAINT PETER	56183-56183	WESTBROOK	56294-56294	WANDA	56430-56430	AH GWAH CHING
56083-56083	SANBORN	56185-56185	WILMONT	56295-56295	WATSON	56431-56431	AITKIN
56084-56084	SEARLES	56186-56186	WOODSTOCK	56296-56296	WHEATON	56433-56433	AKELEY
56085-56085	SLEEPY EYE	56187-56187	WORTHINGTON	56297-56297	WOOD LAKE	56434-56434	ALDRICH
56087-56087	SPRINGFIELD	56201-56201	WILLMAR	56301-56304	SAINT CLOUD	56435-56435	BACKUS
56088-56088	TRUMAN	56207-56207	ALBERTA	56307-56307	ALBANY	56436-56436	BENEDICT
56089-56089	TWIN LAKES	56208-56208	APPLETON	56308-56308	ALEXANDRIA	56437-56437	BERTHA
56090-56090	VERNON CENTER	56209-56209	ATWATER	56309-56309	ASHBY	56438-56438	BROWERVILLE
56091-56091	WALDORF	56210-56210	BARRY	56310-56310	AVON	56440-56440	CLARISSA
56092-56092	WALTERS	56211-56211	BEARDSLEY	56311-56311	BARRETT	56441-56441	CROSBY
56093-56093	WASECA	56212-56212	BELLINGHAM	56312-56312	BELGRADE	56442-56442	CROSSLAKE
56096-56096	WATERVILLE	56214-56214	BELVIEW	56313-56313	BOCK	56443-56443	CUSHING
56097-56097	WELLS	56215-56215	BENSON	56314-56314	BOWLUS	56444-56444	DEERWOOD
56098-56098	WINNEBAGO	56216-56216	BLOMKEST	56315-56315	BRANDON	56446-56446	EAGLE BEND
56101-56101	WINDOM	56218-56218	BOYD	56316-56316	BROOTEN	56447-56447	EMILY
56110-56110	ADRIAN	56219-56219	BROWNS VALLEY	56317-56317	BUCKMAN	56448-56448	FIFTY LAKES
56111-56111	ALPHA	56220-56220	CANBY	56318-56318	BURTRUM	56449-56449	FORT RIPLEY
56112-56112	AMIRET	56221-56221	CHOKIO	56319-56319	CARLOS	56450-56450	GARRISON
56113-56113	ARCO	56222-56222	CLARA CITY	56320-56320	COLD SPRING	56452-56452	HACKENSACK
56114-56114	AVOCA	56223-56223	CLARKFIELD	56321-56321	COLLEGEVILLE	56453-56453	HEWITT
56115-56115	BALATON	56224-56224	CLEMENTS	56323-56323	CYRUS	56455-56455	IRONTON
56116-56116	BEAVER CREEK	56225-56225	CLINTON	56324-56324	DALTON	56456-56456	JENKINS
56117-56117	BIGELOW	56226-56226	CLONTARF	56325-56325	ELROSA	56458-56458	LAKE GEORGE
56118-56118	BINGHAM LAKE	56227-56227	CORRELL	56326-56326	EVANSVILLE	56459-56459	LAKE HUBERT
56119-56119	BREWSTER	56228-56228	COSMOS	56327-56327	FARWELL	56460-56460	LAKE ITASCA
56120-56120	BUTTERFIELD	56229-56229	COTTONWOOD	56328-56328	FLENSBURG	56461-56461	LAPORTE
56121-56121	CEYLON	56230-56230	DANUBE	56329-56329	FOLEY	56463-56463	MANHATTAN BEACH
56122-56122	CHANDLER	56231-56231	DANVERS	56330-56330	FORESTON	56464-56464	MENAHGA
56123-56123	CURRIE	56232-56232	DAWSON	56331-56331	FREEPORT	56465-56465	MERRIFIELD
56124-56124	DELFT	56233-56233	DE GRAFF	56332-56332	GARFIELD	56466-56466	MOTLEY
56125-56125	DOVRAY	56235-56235	DONNELLY	56333-56333	GILMAN	56467-56467	NEVIS
56126-56126	DUNDEE	56236-56236	DUMONT	56334-56334	GLENWOOD	56468-56468	NISSWA
56127-56127	DUNNELL	56237-56237	ECHO	56335-56335	GREENWALD	56469-56469	PALISADE
56128-56128	EDGERTON	56238-56238	EVAN	56336-56336	GREY EAGLE	56470-56470	PARK RAPIDS
56129-56129	ELLSWORTH	56239-56239	GHENT	56338-56338	HILLMAN	56472-56472	PEQUOT LAKES
56131-56131	FULDA	56240-56240	GRACEVILLE	56339-56339	HOFFMAN	56473-56473	PILLAGER
56132-56132	GARVIN	56241-56241	GRANITE FALLS	56340-56340	HOLDINGFORD	56474-56474	PINE RIVER
56133-56133	HADLEY	56243-56243	GROVE CITY	56341-56341	HOLMES CITY	56475-56475	RANDALL
56134-56134	HARDWICK	56244-56244	HANCOCK	56342-56342	ISLE	56477-56477	SEBEKA
56136-56136	HENDRICKS	56245-56245	HANLEY FALLS	56343-56343	KENSINGTON	56478-56478	NIMROD
56137-56137	HERON LAKE	56246-56246	HAWICK	56344-56344	LASTRUP	56479-56479	STAPLES
56138-56138	HILLS	56247-56247	HAZEL RUN	56345-56345	LITTLE FALLS	56481-56481	VERNDALE
56139-56139	HOLLAND	56248-56248	HERMAN	56346-56347	LONG PRAIRIE	56482-56482	WADENA
56140-56140	IHLEN	56249-56249	HOLLOWAY	56349-56349	LOWRY	56484-56484	WALKER
56141-56141	IONA	56250-56250	JOHNSON	56350-56350	MC GRATH	56485-56485	WHIPHOLT
56142-56142	IVANHOE	56251-56251	KANDIYOHI	56352-56352	MELROSE	56501-56502	DETROIT LAKES
56143-56143	JACKSON	56252-56252	KERKHOVEN	56353-56353	MILACA	56510-56510	ADA
56144-56144	JASPER	56253-56253	LAKE LILLIAN	56354-56354	MILTONA	56511-56511	AUDUBON
56145-56145	JEFFERS	56254-56254	LOUISBURG	56355-56355	NELSON	56513-56513	BAKER
56146-56146	KANARANZI	56255-56255	LUCAN	56356-56356	NEW MUNICH	56514-56514	BARNESVILLE
56147-56147	KENNETH	56256-56256	MADISON	56357-56357	OAK PARK	56515-56515	BATTLE LAKE
56149-56149	LAKE BENTON	56257-56257	MARIETTA	56358-56358	OGILVIE	56516-56516	BEJOU
56150-56150	LAKEFIELD	56258-56258	MARSHALL	56359-56359	ONAMIA	56517-56517	BELTRAMI
56151-56151	LAKE WILSON	56260-56260	MAYNARD	56360-56360	OSAKIS	56518-56518	BLUFFTON
56152-56152	LAMBERTON	56262-56262	MILAN	56361-56361	PARKERS PRAIRIE	56519-56519	BORUP
56153-56153	LEOTA	56263-56263	MILROY	56362-56362	PAYNESVILLE	56520-56520	BRECKENRIDGE
56155-56155	LISMORE	56264-56264	MINNEOTA	56363-56363	PEASE	56521-56521	CALLAWAY
56156-56156	LUVERNE	56265-56265	MONTEVIDEO	56364-56364	PIERZ	56522-56522	CAMPBELL
56157-56157	LYND	56266-56266	MORGAN	56367-56367	RICE	56523-56523	CLIMAX
56158-56158	MAGNOLIA	56267-56267	MORRIS	56368-56368	RICHMOND	56524-56524	CLITHERALL
56159-56159	MOUNTAIN LAKE	56270-56270	MORTON	56369-56369	ROCKVILLE	56525-56525	COMSTOCK
56160-56160	ODIN	56271-56271	MURDOCK	56371-56371	ROSCOE	56527-56527	DEER CREEK
56161-56161	OKABENA	56272-56272	NASSAU	56372-56372	SAINT CLOUD	56528-56528	DENT
56162-56162	ORMSBY	56273-56273	NEW LONDON	56373-56373	ROYALTON	56529-56529	DILWORTH
56164-56164	PIPESTONE	56274-56274	NORCROSS	56374-56374	SAINT JOSEPH	56531-56531	ELBOW LAKE
56165-56165	READING	56276-56276	ODESSA	56375-56375	SAINT STEPHEN	56533-56533	ELIZABETH
56166-56166	REVERE	56277-56277	OLIVIA	56376-56376	SAINT MARTIN	56534-56534	ERHARD
56167-56167	ROUND LAKE	56278-56278	ORTONVILLE	56377-56377	SARTELL	56535-56535	ERSKINE
56168-56168	RUSHMORE	56279-56279	PENNOCK	56378-56378	SAUK CENTRE	56536-56536	FELTON
56169-56169	RUSSELL	56280-56280	PORTER	56379-56379	SAUK RAPIDS	56537-56538	FERGUS FALLS
56170-56170	RUTHTON	56281-56281	PRINSBURG	56380-56380	BANGOR	56540-56540	FERTILE
56171-56171	SHERBURN	56282-56282	RAYMOND	56380-56380	SEDAN	56541-56541	FLOM
56172-56172	SLAYTON	56283-56283	REDWOOD FALLS	56381-56381	STARBUCK	56542-56542	FOSSTON
56173-56173	STEEN	56284-56284	RENVILLE	56382-56382	SWANVILLE	56543-56543	FOXHOME
56174-56174	STORDEN	56285-56285	SACRED HEART	56384-56384	UPSALA	56544-56544	FRAZEE
56175-56175	TRACY	56286-56286	SAINT LEO	56385-56385	VILLARD	56545-56545	GARY
56176-56176	TRIMONT	56287-56287	SEAFORTH	56386-56386	WAHKON	56546-56546	GEORGETOWN
56177-56177	TROSKY	56288-56288	SPICER	56387-56388	WAITE PARK	56547-56547	GLYNDON
56178-56178	TYLER	56289-56289	SUNBURG	56389-56389	WEST UNION	56548-56548	HALSTAD
56179-56179	VERDI	56291-56291	TAUNTON	56393-56399	SAINT CLOUD	56549-56549	HAWLEY
56180-56180	WALNUT GROVE	56292-56292	VESTA	56401-56401	BRAINERD	56550-56550	HENDRUM
56181-56181	WELCOME	56293-56293	WABASSO	56425-56425	BAXTER	56551-56551	HENNING

56552-56552 HITTERDAL	56566-56566 NAYTAHWAUSH	56573-56573 PERHAM	56580-56580 SABIN
56553-56553 KENT	56567-56567 NEW YORK MILLS	56574-56574 PERLEY	56581-56581 SHELLY
56554-56554 LAKE PARK	56568-56568 NIELSVILLE	56575-56575 PONSFORD	56583-56583 TINTAH
56556-56556 MCINTOSH	56569-56569 OGEMA	56576-56576 RICHVILLE	56584-56584 TWIN VALLEY
56557-56557 MAHNOMEN	56570-56570 OSAGE	56577-56577 RICHWOOD	56585-56585 ULEN
56560-56563 MOORHEAD	56571-56571 OTTERTAIL	56578-56578 ROCHERT	56586-56586 UNDERWOOD
56565-56565 NASHUA	56572-56572 PELICAN RAPIDS	56579-56579 ROTHSAY	56587-56587 VERGAS
56588-56588 VINING	56650-56650 KELLIHER	56679-56679 SOUTH INTERNATIONAL	56729-56729 HALMA
56589-56589 WAUBUN	56651-56651 LENGBY	FALLS	56731-56731 HUMBOLDT
56590-56590 WENDELL	56652-56652 LEONARD	56680-56680 SPRING LAKE	56732-56732 KARLSTAD
56591-56591 WHITE EARTH	56653-56653 LITTLEFORK	56681-56681 SQUAW LAKE	56733-56733 KENNEDY
56592-56592 WINGER	56654-56654 LOMAN	56682-56682 SWIFT	56734-56734 LAKE BRONSON
56593-56593 WOLF LAKE	56655-56655 LONGVILLE	56683-56683 TENSTRIKE	56735-56735 LANCASTER
56594-56594 WOLVERTON	56657-56657 MARCELL	56684-56684 TRAIL	56736-56736 MENTOR
56601-56619 BEMIDJI	56658-56658 MARGIE	56685-56685 WASKISH	56737-56737 MIDDLE RIVER
56621-56621 BAGLEY	56659-56659 MAX	56686-56686 WILLIAMS	56738-56738 NEWFOLDEN
56623-56623 BAUDETTE	56660-56660 MIZPAH	56687-56687 WILTON	56740-56740 NOYES
56625-56625 BECIDA	56661-56661 NORTHOME	56688-56688 WIRT	56741-56741 OAK ISLAND
56626-56626 BENA	56662-56662 OUTING	56701-56701 THIEF RIVER FALLS	56742-56742 OKLEE
56627-56627 BIG FALLS	56663-56663 PENNINGTON	56710-56710 ALVARADO	56744-56744 OSLO
56628-56628 BIGFORK	56664-56664 DEBS	56711-56711 ANGLE INLET	56748-56748 PLUMMER
56629-56629 BIRCHDALE	56665-56665 PITT	56712-56712 ANGUS	56750-56750 RED LAKE FALLS
56630-56630 BLACKDUCK	56666-56666 PONEMAH	56713-56713 ARGYLE	56751-56751 ROSEAU
56631-56631 BOWSTRING	56667-56667 PUPOSKY	56714-56714 BADGER	56754-56754 SAINT HILAIRE
56632-56632 BOY RIVER	56668-56668 RANIER	56715-56715 BROOKS	56755-56755 SAINT VINCENT
56633-56633 CASS LAKE	56669-56669 RAY	56716-56716 CROOKSTON	56756-56756 SALOL
56634-56634 CLEARBROOK	56669-56669 KABETOGAMA	56720-56720 DONALDSON	56757-56757 STEPHEN
56636-56636 DEER RIVER	56670-56670 REDBY	56721-56721 EAST GRAND FORKS	56758-56758 STRANDQUIST
56637-56637 TALMOON	56671-56671 REDLAKE	56722-56722 EUCLID	56759-56759 STRATHCONA
56639-56639 EFFIE	56672-56672 REMER	56723-56723 FISHER	56760-56760 VIKING
56641-56641 FEDERAL DAM	56673-56673 ROOSEVELT	56724-56724 GATZKE	56761-56761 WANNASKA
56644-56644 GONVICK	56674-56674 SAUM	56725-56725 GOODRIDGE	56762-56762 WARREN
56646-56646 GULLY	56676-56676 SHEVLIN	56726-56726 GREENBUSH	56763-56763 WARROAD
56647-56647 HINES	56678-56678 SOLWAY	56727-56727 GRYGLA	
56649-56649 INTERNATIONAL FALLS		56728-56728 HALLOCK	

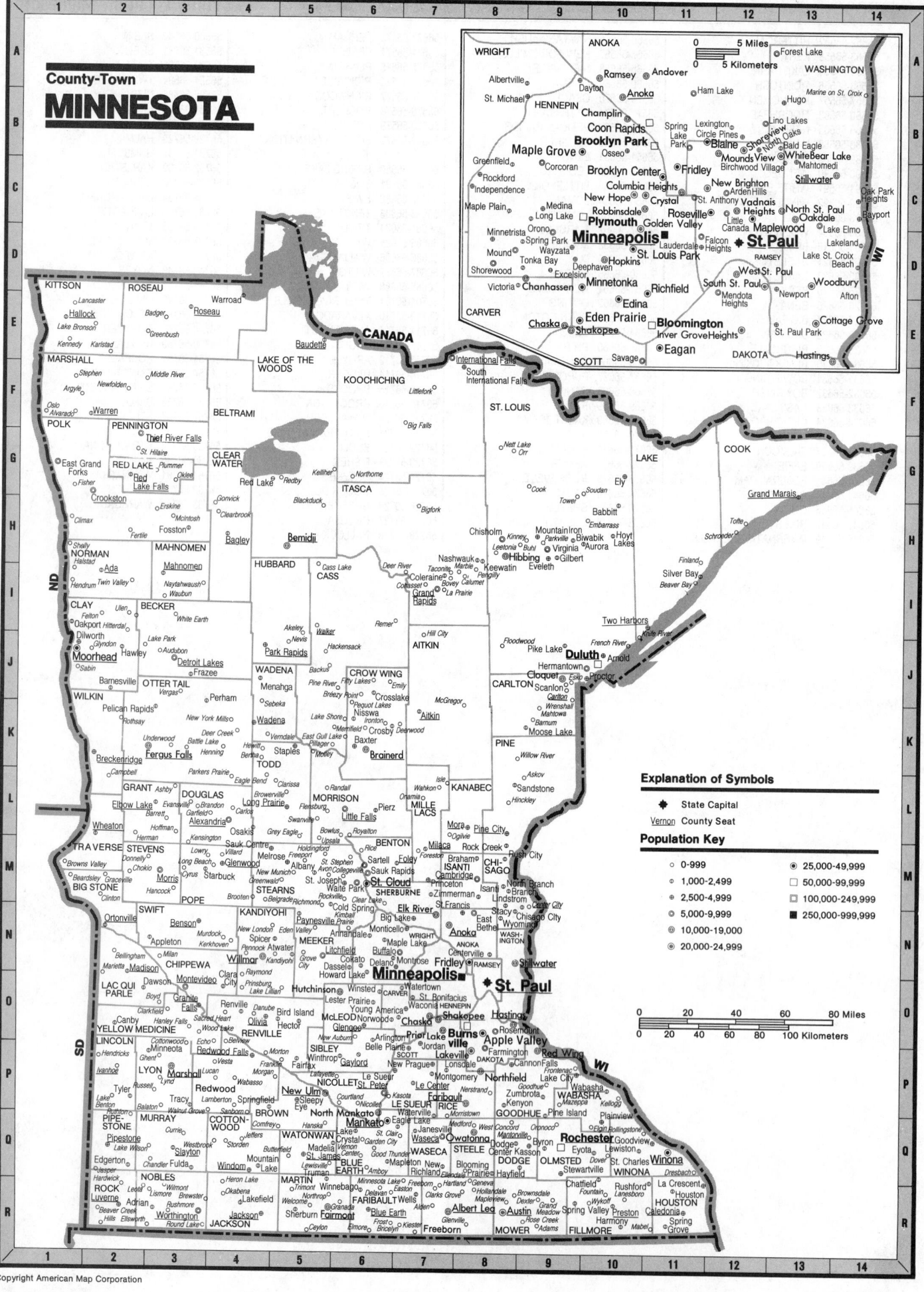

County-Town
MINNESOTA

CITIES AND TOWNS

Note: The first name is that of the city or town, second, that of the county in which it is located, then the population and location on the map.

Explanation of symbols: ● – Census Designated Place (CDP)

Mississippi

General Help Numbers:

Governor's Office

PO Box 139
Jackson, MS 39201
www.governor.state.ms.us

601-359-3150
Fax 601-359-3741
8AM-5PM

Attorney General's Office

PO Box 220
Jackson, MS 39205
www.ago.state.ms.us

601-359-3680
Fax 601-359-3796
8AM-5PM

Legislative Records

PO Box 1018
Jackson, MS 39215
www.ls.state.ms.us

601-359-3229

8:30AM-5PM

State Archives

Archives & Library Division
PO Box 571
Jackson, MS 39205-0571
www.mdah.state.ms.us

601-576-6850
Fax 601-576-6975

8AM-5PM TU-F;
8AM-1PM SAT

State Specifics:

Capital:	Jackson
	Hinds County
Time Zone:	CST
Number of Counties:	82
Population:	2,902,966
Web Site:	www.ms.gov

State Agencies

Criminal Records

Access to Records is Restricted.

Criminal Information Center, Dept. of Public Safety, PO Box 958, Jackson, MS 39205; 601-933-2600, 601-933-2677 (Fax) .

Mississippi does not permit the public to access their central state repository of criminal records, except for pre-approved entities with purposes provided for by state statute such as health care, banking/finance, military, childcare and schools. Approved requestors must submit fingerprint cards. The agency suggests that the employers and general public obtain information at the county level. The records on file are 100% fingerprint supported. 40% of the records contain dispositions.

Statewide Court Records

Administrative Office of Courts, PO Box 117, Jackson, MS 39205 (Courier address: 450 High St, Jackson, MS 39205); 601-354-7406, 601-354-7459-Fax; 8AM-5PM.

www.mssc.state.ms.us

It takes 30 days or so before new records are available for inquiry.

Access by: fax, online.

Fee & Payment: For fax requests, there is a $25.00 start-up fee and a $5.00 per name search fee.

Fax search: The Administrative Office of Courts offers a statewide search via fax requesting with a

24 hour turnaround time. Call 601-354-7449 or fax 601-354-7459 for details.

Online search: The website offers searching of the MS Supreme Court and Court of Appeals Decisions, and dockets of the trial courts. It is difficult to do a name search in the trial courts because the sequence number of the docket must be included in request.

Sexual Offender Registry

Dept. of Public Safety, Sexual Offender Registry, PO Box 958, Jackson, MS 39205; 601-368-1740, 8AM-5PM.

www.sor.mdps.state.ms.us

SOR questions may be directed to msor@mdps.state.ms.us.

Records are available from 07/01/95.

Searching: Searches may also be directed to the local sheriff's office.

Access by: mail, phone, online.

Mail search: Turnaround time: 1 to 2 weeks.

Phone search: Time permitting.

Online search: The state Sex Offender Registry can be accesed at the website. Search by last name, city, county, or ZIP Code.

Incarceration Records

Mississippi Department of Corrections, Records Department, 723 N President Street, Jackson, MS 39202;, 601-359-5600, 8AM-5PM.

www.mdoc.state.ms.us

Records are available on current and former inmates. It takes less than 72 hours before new records are available for inquiry.

Searching: Computer records go back to 1978. Include the following in your request-provide full name. The inmate #, county of crime and DOB are helpful.

Access by: mail, phone, online.

Fee & Payment: There is no fee.

Mail search: Turnaround time: 1-2 weeks.

Phone search: Name searching available via phone.

Online search: Search online by name only from the website. Click on Inmate Search. Also, search the Parole Board records (click on Parole Board and follow instructions).

Corporation, Limited Partnership, Limited Liability Company, Trademarks/Servicemarks

Secretary of State, Business Services, PO Box 136, Jackson, MS 39205-0136; 601-359-1633, 800-256-3494, 601-359-1607-Fax; 8AM-5PM.

www.sos.state.ms.us

Records are available from the 1800's, computerized since 1995. New records are available for inquiry immediately. Records are indexed on microfilm, inhouse computer.

Searching: Include the following in your request-full name of business. In addition to the articles of incorporation, corporation records include the following information: Annual Reports, Officers, Directors, Prior (merged) names, Inactive and Reserved names. The following data is not released: phone numbers.

Access by: mail, phone, fax, in person, online.

Fee & Payment: There is no search fee. The certification fee is $10.00 per document. Copies are $1.00 per page. A Good Standing is $25.00, and $27.00 if ordered online. Fee payee: Secretary of State. Prepayment required. You must prepay if the invoice amount is over $50.00. If under $50.00 they will invoice. Personal checks accepted. Credit cards accepted: MasterCard, Visa.

Mail search: Turnaround time: 1 to 2 days.

Phone search: Will only verify if record exists.

Fax search: Requests only are accepted, will return to toll-free fax numbers.

In person search: Computer screen prints are free.

Online search: A variety of online search services are available at www.sos.state.ms.us/busserv/corp/soskb/csearch.asp. There is no fee to view records, including officers and registered agents. A Good Standing can be ordered. You can download images for no charge.

Other access: The Data Division offers bulk release of information on paper or disk. Monthly subscription to list of new corporations and new qualifications is $25.00.

Uniform Commercial Code, Federal and State Tax Liens

Secretary of State, Business Services - UCC, PO Box 136, Jackson, MS 39205-0136 (Courier address: 700 N Jackson St, Jackson, MS 39202); 601-359-1633, 800-256-3494, 601-359-1607-Fax; 8AM-5PM.

www.sos.state.ms.us/busserv/ucc/ucc.asp

Records are available from 1968. Records are computerized since 1987. It takes 24-48 hours before new records are available for inquiry. Records are indexed on inhouse computer. Records are normally destroyed after lapsing, per a retention schedule (not disclosed).

Searching: Use search request form UCC-11. The search includes tax liens. Include the following in your request-debtor name.

Access by: mail, phone, in person, online.

Fee & Payment: The search fee is $5.00, copies are $2.00 each, financing statements are $2.00 each. Fee payee: Secretary of State. Prepayment required. The state offers ACH accounts for regular requesters. Personal checks accepted. Credit cards accepted: MasterCard, Visa.

Mail search: Turnaround time: 1 to 2 days.

Phone search: Limited information is released over the phone.

In person search: Simple requests are processed, time permitting.

Online search: Two systems available. Free searching for UCC debtors is at www.sos.state.ms.us/busserv/ucc/soskb/SearchStandardRA9.asp.

Other access: A monthly list of farm liens is available for purchase.

Sales Tax Registrations

Office of Revenue, Sales and Use Tax Bureau, PO Box 1033, Jackson, MS 39215-1033 (Courier address: 1577 Springridge Rd, Raymond, MS 39154); 601-923-7000, 601-923-7034-Fax; 8AM-5PM.

www.mstc.state.ms.us

Records are available for the most current 3 years and are computerized. It takes minutes after set-up before new records are available for inquiry.

Searching: The agency will only verify if a business is registered and will not release ownership data. Include the following in your request-business name. They will also search by tax permit number.

Access by: mail, phone, fax, in person, online.

Fee & Payment: Prepayment required. Fee payee: Revenue Bureau. Personal checks accepted. No credit cards accepted.

Mail search: Turnaround time: 5 to 10 working days. No fee for mail request. Copies cost $2.00 per page.

Phone search: No fee for telephone request.

Fax search: Same criteria as phone or mail searches.

In person search: No fee for request. Copies cost $2.00 per page.

Online search: Requests may be emailed to sales@mstc.state.ms.us.

Birth Certificates

State Department of Health, Vital Statistics & Records, PO Box 1700, Jackson, MS 39215-1700 (Courier address: 571 Stadium Dr, Jackson, MS 39216); 601-576-7960, 601-576-7988, 601-576-7505-Fax; 8AM-5PM.

www.msdh.state.ms.us/phs/index.htm

Records are available from November 1, 1912 to present. New records are available for inquiry immediately. Records are indexed on microfiche, inhouse computer.

Searching: Employers need written release from person of record. Records are not public access documents, they are only available to persons with legitimate and tangible interest. Include the following in your request-full name, names of parents, mother's maiden name, date of birth, place of birth, relationship to person of record, reason for information request. Records may be ordered online via a vendor at www.vitalchek.com. The following data is not released: original records of adoption.

Access by: mail, phone, fax, in person, online.

Fee & Payment: The $7.00 fee is for the short form. The fee for the long form certified is $12.00, plus is a $3.00 per for each additional copy. There is a $7.00 charge for no record found. Fee payee: Mississippi Vital Records Prepayment required. Use credit card for phone and/or expedited service only. Personal checks accepted only if in-state. Major credit cards accepted.

Mail search: Turnaround time: 7 to 10 days.

Phone search: Must use a credit card for an additional $5.50 fee. Turnaround time is 2 to 3 days.

Fax search: Same criteria as phone searching. Use 601-351-0013 for VitalChek, an approved vendor.

In person search: Turnaround time for Short Form-while you wait, Long Form-next day mail.

Online search: Records may be ordered online via a designateed vendor - www.uscerts.com.

Expedited service: Expedited service is available for mail, phone and fax searches, via www.vitalchek.com. Turnaround time: overnight delivery. Add a $5.50 credit card fee and $$ for overnight shipping if desired.

Death Records

State Department of Health, Vital Statistics & Records, PO Box 1700, Jackson, MS 39215-1700 (Courier address: 571 Stadium Dr, Jackson, MS 39216); 601-576-7960, 601-576-7988, 601-576-7505-Fax; 8AM-5PM.

www.msdh.state.ms.us/phs/index.htm

Records are available from November 1, 1912 to present. New records are available for inquiry immediately. Records are indexed on microfiche, inhouse computer.

Searching: Employers need written release from immediate family member. Records are not considered public access documents. They are only available to persons with legitimate and tangible interest. Include the following in your request-full name, date of death, place of death, Social Security Number, relationship to person of record, reason for information request. Records may be ordered online via a vendor at www.vitalchek.com.

Access by: mail, phone, fax, in person, online.

Fee & Payment: Fee is $10.00 if you want a certified copy, and an additional $2.00 for each additional copy ordered at same time. If no record is found, the fee is $6.00. Fee payee: Mississippi Vital Records Prepayment required. Use credit cards for phone, fax and/or expedited service only. Major credit cards accepted.

Mail search: Turnaround time: 7 to 10 days.

Phone search: Must use a credit card for an additional $5.50 fee. Turnaround time is 2 to 3 days.

Fax search: Same criteria as phone searching. Use 601-351-0013 for VitalChek, an approved vendor.

In person search: Turnaround time next day mail.

Online search: Records may be ordered online via a designateed vendor - www.uscerts.com.

Expedited service: Expedited service is available for mail, phone and fax searches, via www.vitalchek.com. Turnaround time: 1 day. Add a $5.50 credit card fee and $$ for overnight shipping if desired.

Marriage Certificates

State Department of Health, Vital Statistics & Records, PO Box 1700, Jackson, MS 39215-1700 (Courier address: 571 Stadium Dr, Jackson, MS 39216); 601-576-7960, 601-576-7988, 601-576-7505-Fax; 8AM-5PM.

www.msdh.state.ms.us/phs/index.htm

Records are also available at the county level, including those records from 1938 to 1942.

Records are available from January 1926 to June 1938 and January 1942 to present. New records are available for inquiry immediately. Records are indexed on microfiche, inhouse computer.

Searching: Employers need written release from persons of record. Records are not considered public access documents. They are only available to persons with legitimate and tangible interest. Include the following in your request-names of husband and wife, date of marriage, place or county of marriage, relationship to person of record, reason for information request, wife's maiden name. Records may be ordered online via a vendor at www.vitalchek.com.

Access by: mail, phone, fax, in person, online.

Fee & Payment: The fee is $10.00 and $2.00 for each additional copy ordered at same time. If record not found fee is $6.00. Fee payee: Mississippi Vital Records Prepayment required. Use credit cards for phone, fax and/or expedited service only. Personal checks accepted only if in-state. Major credit cards accepted.

Mail search: Turnaround time: 4 to 7 days.

Phone search: Must use a credit card for an additional $5.50 fee. Turnaround time is 2 to 3 days.

Fax search: Same criteria as phone searching. Use 601-351-0013 for VitalChek, an approved vendor.

In person search: Search costs $10.00 per request. Turnaround time next day mail.

Online search: Records may be ordered online via a designateed vendor - www.uscerts.com.

Expedited service: Expedited service is available for mail, phone and fax searches, via www.vitalchek.com. Turnaround time: 1 day. Add a $5.50 credit card fee and $$ for overnight shipping if desired.

Divorce Records

State Department of Health, Vital Statistics & Records, PO Box 1700, Jackson, MS 39215-1700 (Courier address: 571 Stadium Dr, Jackson, MS 39216); 601-576-7960, 601-576-7988, 601-576-7505-Fax; 8AM-5PM.

www.msdh.state.ms.us/phs/index.htm

The state maintains a state-wide index and can refer to book and page number in county records. Requests for copies must be made to the county of record.

Records are available from 1930 to present in county of record. This office will only confirm that a record exists and where. New records are available for inquiry immediately. Records are indexed on microfiche, inhouse computer.

Searching: Employers need written release from person of record. Records are not public access documents and are available only to persons with legitimate and tangible interest. Include the following in your request-names of husband and wife, date of divorce, year divorce case began, case number (if known), relationship to person of record, reason for information request. Records may be ordered online via a vendor at www.vitalchek.com.

Access by: mail, phone, fax, in person, online.

Fee & Payment: The fee to do an index search is $6.00. Copies are not released from this agency. Fee payee: Mississippi Vital Records Prepayment required. Personal checks accepted if in-state. Major credit cards accepted.

Mail search: Turnaround time: 1 to 3 days.

Phone search: Must use a credit card for an additional $5.50 fee. Turnaround time is 2 to 3 days.

Fax search: Same criteria as phone searching. Use 601-351-0013 for VitalChek, an approved vendor.

In person search: Turnaround time next day mail.

Online search: Records may be ordered online via a designateed vendor - www.uscerts.com.

Expedited service: Expedited service is available for mail, phone and fax searches, via www.vitalchek.com. Turnaround time: 1 day. Add a $5.50 credit card fee and $$ for overnight shipping if desired.

Workers' Compensation Records

Workers Compensation Commission, PO Box 5300, Jackson, MS 39296-5300 (Courier address: 1428 Lakeland Dr, Jackson, MS 39216); 601-987-4200, 8AM-5PM.

www.mwcc.state.ms.us

Records are available for 10 years back to present. New records are available for inquiry immediately. Records are indexed on inhouse computer.

Searching: All requests must be in writing. Claimant's attorney must have contract or medical

authorization. Employer/carrier must be party to action to obtain records. They do not conduct searches for pre-employment screening. Include the following in your request-claimant name, SSN, docket number, place of employment at time of accident.

Access by: mail, in person, online.

Fee & Payment: Copy fee is $.50 with a $5.00 minimum, there is no search fee. Fee payee: Mississippi Workers' Compensation Commission. They will invoice. Personal checks accepted. No credit cards accepted.

Mail search: Turnaround time: 3 to 4 working days.

In person search: Anyone can come in to view. Medical information is not made available and copies cannot be made unless there is written authorization by party of record.

Online search: The First Report of Injury and other documents are available via the web. There is no fee, but users must register.

Other access: A first report of injury database is available on CD-ROM for $500.00.

Driver Records

Department of Public Safety, Driver Services, PO Box 958, Jackson, MS 39205 (Courier address: 1900 E Woodrow Wilson, Jackson, MS 39216); 601-987-1274, 8AM-5PM.

www.dps.state.ms.us

Copies of tickets may be obtained from the same address for a fee of $5.00 per record and notarized signature. A pre-addressed, stamped envelope is advised.

Records are available for 3 years for moving violations, DUIs and suspensions. Accidents and non-moving violations do not appear on MVRs. The driver's address is provided on the record. It takes 45 days or more before new records are available for inquiry.

Searching: Casual requesters can obtain personal information only with notarized consent of subject. The state adopted the provisions of the DPPA. The request form is available at the web page. The driver's full name, license number, and/or DOB are needed when ordering. Surrendered license records can only be obtained by a manual search.

Access by: mail, in person, online.

Fee & Payment: The fee is $11.00 per request. Fee payee: Department of Public Safety. Prepayment required. Personal checks accepted. No credit cards accepted.

Mail search: Turnaround time: 2 days. A SASE is requested.

In person search: Walk-in requesters may submit up to 10 requests for immediate delivery; the rest are available the next day.

Online search: Both interactive and batch delivery is offer for high volume users only. Billing is monthly. Hook-up is through the Advantis System, fees apply. Lookup is by name only; not by driver license number. Fee is $11.00 per record. For more information, call the Director's office. Another service is available. Drivers may view their own record online at https://www.ms.gov/hp/drivers/license/mvr_review.jsp. The MVR shows the current status of the license and the moving violations on record.

Other access: Overnight batch delivery by tape is available.

Vehicle Ownership
Vehicle Identification

Mississippi State Tax Commission, Registration Department, PO Box 1140, Jackson, MS 39215 (Courier address: 1577 Springridge Rd, Raymond, MS 39154); 601-923-7100 (Registration), 601-923-7200 (Titles), 601-923-7134-Fax; 8AM-5PM.

www.mstc.state.ms.us/mvl/main.htm

Please note that title information (liens, histories) requests are processed by a different section than registration information. For mail requests, use PO Box 1033 for the Title Department.

Records are available from July 1, 1969 to present. Title records are computer indexed from July 1, 1969 to present, and on microfiche from July 1, 1969 to present. It takes 6 to 8 weeks before new records are available for inquiry.

Searching: Personal information is not released to casual requesters without consent from the subject. State suggests to use their disclosure form found at www.mstc.state.ms.us/title/forms/77-969-04-1.pdf. The turnaround time will be one week longer if the request requires a search farther back than 5 years.

Access by: mail, fax, in person, online.

Fee & Payment: Fees are $8.00 per search for title, $3.00 per search for VIN or registration, and $5.00 for lien history. Fee payee: Mississippi State Tax Commission. Prepayment required. No cash will be accepted for mail requests. Personal checks accepted. No credit cards accepted.

Mail search: Turnaround time: 2 days.

Fax search: Fax requests are accepted by account holders.

In person search: Turnaround time is immediate.

Online search: Interent access to vehicle records is available to approved, DPPA compliant entities. Accounts must pay an initial $25.00 registration fee, record search fees are the same as listed above.

Other access: Mississippi offers some standardized files as well as some customization for bulk requesters of VIN and registration information. For more information, contact MLVB at the address listed above.

Accident Reports

Safety Responsibility, Accident Records, PO Box 958, Jackson, MS 39205 (Courier address: 1900 E Woodrow Wilson, Jackson, MS 39216); 601-987-1254, 8AM-5PM.

www.dps.state.ms.us

The above address is for Highway Patrol accident investigations only. Reports require authorization from person involved. You must go to the agency that did the investigation for reports not found with the Highway Patrol.

Records are available for 3 years to present on computer. Records are on microfiche from 1990 to present. Records are normally destroyed after 5 years.

Searching: Must have authorization from individuals involved in the accident. Accident reports are only available to persons involved, their legal counsel and their insurance representative. Include the following in your request-date of accident, location of accident, full name, written authorization. SSN is helpful. Requests must be in writing. In person requests are returned by mail.

Access by: mail.

Fee & Payment: The fee is $10.00 per record. Fee payee: Department of Public Safety. Prepayment required. Personal checks accepted. No credit cards accepted.

Mail search: Turnaround time: 5 days. A SASE is requested.

Vessel Ownership
Vessel Registration

Dept of Wildlife, Fisheries, & Parks, Boating Registration, PO Box 451, Jackson, MS 39205; 601-432-2067, 601-432-2066, 601-432-2071-Fax; 8AM-5PM.

www.mdwfp.com

All motorized vessels and all sailboats have to be registered. Liens are recorded if the vessel has been titled. Starting July 1998, boats are titled at the option of the owner/lender.

Records are available from 1981 to present. Records are indexed on computer from 1985 to present. It takes 2 weeks or so before new records are available for inquiry.

Searching: This agency follows the mandates of the DPPA, allowing access to record information for those with a legitimate business interest. Casual requesters must present a signed release before information is released. Include the following in your request-the name or DL number or MS number or hull number.

Access by: mail, phone, fax, in person.

Fee & Payment: There is no search fee.

Mail search: Turnaround time is the same day, except during the summer, which can take 3-4 weeks. A SASE is requested.

Phone search: Records are available by phone.

Fax search: Results will be mailed back usually the same day.

In person search: Turnaround time is usually immediate.

Other access: This agency makes records available on printed lists and magnetic tapes. Fees vary.

Voter Registration
Access to Records is Restricted.

Secretary of State, Elections Division, PO Box 136, Jackson, MS 39205-0136 (Courier address: 401 Mississippi Street, 1st Floor, Jackson, MS 39201); 800-829-6786, 601-576-2550, 601-359-5019-Fax; 8AM-5PM.

www.sos.state.ms.us/elections/elections.asp

Records are open to the public, but currently name searches must be done at the county level. Also lists may be purchased at the county level. The Federal Help America Vote Act of 2002 (HAVA) law requires implementation of a central, computerized, statewide voter registration system by 01/01/2006. The state will comply.

GED Certificates

State Board for Community & Jr Colleges, GED Office, 3825 Ridgewood Rd, Jackson, MS 39211; 601-432-6338, 601-432-6890-Fax; 8AM-5PM.

www.colin.edu/gedonline

Searching: Verifications and transcripts are only available by written request. A request form may be downloaded from the web. Include the following in your request-a signed release, name, date of birth, SSN, date of text. If known, the diploma number is helpful.

Access by: mail, in person.

Fee & Payment: The fee is $5.00 for either a verification or a transcript.

Mail search: Turnaround time: 3 days. Turnaround time is longer in July and August.

In person search: The agency will only release information to the test taker, not to a third party or employer.

Hunting and Fishing License Information

Department of Wildlife, Fisheries & Parks, PO Box 451, Jackson, MS 39205; 601-432-2055 (License Division), 601-432-2041 (Data Processing Div), 601-432-2071-Fax; 8AM-5PM.

www.mdwfp.com

Records are available for present data only.

Searching: Records are open to the public. They hold records on "sportsman" license holders which is a combination of hunting and fishing. Temporary license information is not maintained. You can search using the name or driver's license number.

Access by: mail, phone, fax, in person.

Fee & Payment: There is no search fee.

Mail search: Turnaround time: 10 days.

Phone search: Records are available by phone.

Fax search: Same criteria as mail searches.

In person search: You can make the request in person but they will mail back your response. **Other access:** They offer bulk sale of various license groups in a variety of media methods. Visit the website for more information.

Mississippi State Licensing Agencies

For details about the agency responsible for licensing/certifying/registering an item below or in the Agency Quick Finder section, match an item's number with the number of the agency in the *Licensing Agency Information* section.

Mississippi Licenses Searchable Online

Architect #3 .... www.archbd.state.ms.us/roster.html

Attorney/Attorney Firm #27 .... www.msbar.org/lawyerdirectory.htm

Camp, Youth #38 .... www.msdh.state.ms.us/msdhsite/index.cfm/30,332,183,html

Charity #32 .... www.sos.state.ms.us/regenf/charities/charannrpt/index.asp

Child Care Facility #38 .... www.msdh.state.ms.us/msdhsite/index.cfm/30,332,183,html

Chiropractor #35 .... www.msbce.ms.gov/msbce/msbce.nsf/Search?OpenForm

Contractor, General #6 .... www.msboc.state.ms.us/Search.cfm

CPA-Certified Public Accountant #19 .... www.msbpa.state.ms.us/licsearch.html

Dental Hygienist #8 .... www.msbde.state.ms.us

Dental Radiologist #8 .... www.msbde.state.ms.us

Dentist #8 .... www.msbde.state.ms.us

Engineer #9 .... http://dsitspe01.its.state.ms.us/pepls/EngSurveyors.nsf

Fund Raiser #32 .... www.sos.state.ms.us/regenf/charities/charannrpt/index.asp

Funeral Pre-Need Contractor #32 .... www.sos.state.ms.us

Geologist #23 .... www.msbrpg.state.ms.us/rpg.htm

HMO #25 .... www.doi.state.ms.us/hmolist.pdf

Home Inspector #34 .... www.mrec.state.ms.us/asp/findrealtor.asp

Insurance Agent/Solicitor/Advisor #25 .... www.doi.state.ms.us/licapp/

Insurance Company #25 .... www.doi.state.ms.us/licapp/

Investment Advisor #32 .... www.sos.state.ms.us

Landscape Architect #3 .... www.archbd.state.ms.us/roster.html

Lobbyist #31 .... www.sos.state.ms.us/elections/Lobbying/Lobbyist_Dir.asp

Long-term Care Insurance Company #25 .... www.doi.state.ms.us/ltclist.html

Medical Doctor #12 .... www.msbml.state.ms.us

Notary Public #31 .... www.sos.state.ms.us/busserv/notaries/notaries.asp

Optometrist #15 .... www.arbo.org/index.php?action=findanoptometrist

Osteopathic Physician #12 .... www.msbml.state.ms.us

Pharmacist #16 .... www.mbp.state.ms.us

Pharmacy #16 .... www.mbp.state.ms.us

Pharmacy Intern/Technician #16 .... www.mbp.state.ms.us

Podiatrist #12 .... www.msbml.state.ms.us

Psychologist #18 .... www.psychologyboard.state.ms.us/msbp/msbp.nsf/Search?OpenForm

Real Estate Agent/Sales #34 .... www.mrec.state.ms.us/asp/findrealtor.asp

Real Estate Appraiser #30 .... www.mrec.state.ms.us/asp/findappraiser.asp

Real Estate Broker #34 .... www.mrec.state.ms.us/asp/findrealtor.asp

Securities Agent #32 .... www.sos.state.ms.us

Securities Broker/Dealer #32 .... www.sos.state.ms.us

Security Offering #32 .... www.sos.state.ms.us

Surveyor, Land #9 .... http://dsitspe01.its.state.ms.us/pepls/EngSurveyors.nsf

Youth Home, Residential #38 .... www.msdh.state.ms.us/msdhsite/index.cfm/30,332,183,html

Mississippi Licensing Quick Finder

Air Monitor #22	601-961-5100	Engineer #9	601-359-6160	Optometrist #15	601-853-4338
Alcohol Beverage Employee #26	601-856-1330	Esthetician #7	601-987-6837	Osteopathic Physician #12	601-987-3079
Alcoholic Beverage Retailer #2	601-856-1320	Eye Enucleator #37	601-576-7260	Pawn Shop #4	601-359-1031
Animal/Veterinary Technician #29	662-324-9380	Finance Company #4	601-359-1031	Pharmacist #16	601-354-6750
Architect #3	601-899-9071	Fishing, Commercial #24	601-432-2400	Pharmacy #16	601-354-6750
Asbestos Contr./Insp/Supv #22	601-961-5100	Fund Raiser #32	601-359-6371	Pharmacy Intern/Technician #16	601-354-6750
Asbestos Project Designer/Mgmt. Planner #22		Funeral Director #11	601-932-1973	Physical Therapist/Assistant #33	601-576-7260
	601-961-5100	Funeral Pre-Need Contractor #32	601-359-6371	Podiatrist #12	601-987-3079
Asbestos Worker #22	601-961-5100	Funeral Service Practitioner #11	601-932-1973	Polygraph Examiner #17	601-987-1212
Athletic Trainer #37	601-576-7260	Gaming #26	601-351-2800	Psychologist #18	662-716-3934
Attorney/Attorney Firm #27	601-948-4471	Geologist #23	601-54-6370	Radiation Technician #37	601-576-7260
Bank #4	601-359-1031	Health Facility #1	601-576-7400	Real Estate Agent/Sales #34	601-932-9191
Barber Instructor/School #5	601-359-1015	Hearing Aid Dealer (Specialist) #37	601-576-7260	Real Estate Appraiser #30	601-932-6770
Barber/Barber Shop #5	601-359-1015	HMO #25	601-359-3582	Real Estate Broker #34	601-932-9191
Beauty Shop/Salon #7	601-987-6837	Home Inspector #34	601-932-9191	Savings Institution #4	601-359-1031
Boiler & Pressure Vessel Insp. #37	601-576-7917	Insurance Agent/Solicitor/Advisor #25	601-359-3582	School Administrator #36	601-359-3483
Camp, Youth #38	601-576-7613	Insurance Company #25	601-359-3582	Securities Agent #32	601-359-6363
Charity #32	601-359-1371	Investment Advisor #32	601-359-6363	Securities Broker/Dealer #32	601-359-6363
Child Care Facility #38	601-576-7613	Landscape Architect #3	601-899-9071	Security Offering #32	601-359-6369
Chiropractor #35	662-773-4433	Liquor Control #2	601-856-1310	Septic Tank Installer #37	601-576-7260
Contractor, General #6	601-354-6161	Lobbyist #31	601-359-6353	Shorthand Reporter #20	601-354-6056
Cosmetologist #7	601-987-6837	Long Term Care Insurance Company #25		Social Worker #28	601-987-6806
Cosmetology Instructor #7	601-987-6837		601-359-3582	Speech-Language Pathologist/Audiologist #21	
Counselor, Professional #10	662-716-3932	Manicurist #7	601-987-6837		601-576-7260
CPA-Certified Public Accountant #19	601-354-7320	Marriage & Family Therapist #28	601-987-6806	Surveyor, Land #9	601-359-6160
Dental Hygienist #8	601-944-9622	Medical Doctor #12	601-987-3079	Tattoo Artist #37	601-576-7260
Dental Radiologist #8	601-944-9622	Mortgage Lender/Company #4	601-359-1031	Teacher #36	601-359-3483
Dentist #8	601-944-9622	Notary Public #31	601-359-1633	Title & Loan Company #4	601-359-1031
Dietitian #37	601-576-7260	Nurse #13	601-987-6858	Veterinarian #29	662-324-9380
Educator, Citizen/Emergency/Non-Licensed #36		Nurse-LPN #13	601-987-6858	Veterinary Facility #29	662-324-9380
	601-359-3483	Nursing Home Administrator #14	601-932-1442	Youth Home, Residential #38	601-576-7613
Emergency Medical Technician #37	601-576-7681	Occupational Therapist/Assistant #33	601-576-7260		

Mississippi Licensing Agency Information

1 Department of Health, Health Facilities Licensure & Certification, PO Box 1700 (570 E Woodrow Wilson Blvd), Jackson, MS 39216; 601-576-7400, Fax: 601-576-7350.
www.msdh.state.ms.us

2 Office of Alcoholic Beverage Control, PO Box 540, Madison, MS 39110-0540; 601-856-1330, Fax: 601-856-1390.
www.mstc.state.ms.us
Email: bsmith@mstc.state.ms.us

3 Board of Architecture, 400 Legacy Park Dr #B, Ridgeland, MS 39157; 601-899-9071, Fax: 601-899-9171.
www.archbd.state.ms.us
Email: msboa@archbd.state.ms.us
Search Database at
www.archbd.state.ms.us/roster.html Note: Includes the Landscape Architecture Advisory Committee.

4 Department of Banking & Consumer Finance, Board of Banking Review, 501 NW St, 901 Woolfolk Bldg, Ste. A, Jackson, MS 39202; 601-359-1031, Fax: 601-359-3557.
www.dbcf.state.ms.us/review.htm

5 Board of Barber Examiners, 510 George St, Rm 240, Jackson, MS 39205; 601-359-1015, Fax: 601-359-1050. Email: msbbe@bellsouth.net

6 Board of Contractors, 215 Woodline Dr #B, Jackson, MS 39208; 601-354-6161, Fax: 601-354-6715. www.msboc.state.ms.us/index.cfm
Search Database at
www.msboc.state.ms.us/Search.cfm

7 Board of Cosmetology, PO Box 55689, Jackson, MS 39296-5689; 601-987-6837, Fax: 601-987-6840.
www.msbc.state.ms.us/msbc/Cosmetology.nsf

8 Mississippi State Board of Dental Examiners, 600 E Amite #100, Jackson, MS 39201-2801; 601-944-9622, Fax: 601-924-9624.
www.msbde.state.ms.us
Email: dental@msbde.state.ms.us
Search Database at www.msbde.state.ms.us Note: There is a $125.00 fee for list or labels; $150.00 fee for diskette.

9 Board of Engineers & Land Surveyors, PO Box 3 (239 N. Lamar St #501), Jackson, MS 39205-0003; 601-359-6160, Fax: 601-359-6159.
www.pepls.state.ms.us
Email: information@pepls.state.ms.us
Search Database at http://dsitspe01.its.state.ms.us/pepls/EngSurveyors.nsf

10 Board of Examiners for Licensed Professional Counselors, 419 E Broadway St, Yazoo City, MS 39194-4530; 662-716-3932, Fax: 662-751-4628.
www.lpc.state.ms.us
Email: acox@maminc.net

11 Board of Funeral Service, 3010 Lakeland Cove, Suite W, Flowood, MS 39232; 601-932-1973, Fax: 601-932-1901.
www.msfuneralboard.com
Email: msfuneralboard@msfuneralboard.com Note: The website will soon list funeral homes.

12 Board of Medical Licensure, 1867 Crane Ridge Drive, Ste 200-B, Jackson, MS 39216; 601-987-3079, Fax: 601-987-4159.
www.msbml.state.ms.us
Email: mboard@msbml.state.ms.us Note: A fee based online verification system is available.

13 Board of Nursing, 1935 Lakeland Dr #B, Jackson, MS 39216; 601-987-4188, Fax: 601-364-2352.
www.msbn.state.ms.us/index.html
Search Database at
https://www.ms.gov/msbn/inquiry_disclaimer.do

14 Board of Nursing Home Administrators, 644 Lakeland East Dr. Ste C, Flowood, MS 39232; 601-932-1442, Fax: 601-932-1544.
www.bnha.state.ms.us/

15 Board of Optometry, PO Box 12370, Jackson, MS 39236; 601-853-4338, Fax: 601-853-0336.
www.msoptometry.org
Email: office@msoptometry.org
Search Database at www.arbo.org/index.php?action=findanoptometrist

16 Board of Pharmacy, 204 Key Dr #D, Madison, MS 39110-7361; 601-605-5388, Fax: 601-605-9546. www.mbp.state.ms.us
Email: sstovall@mbp.state.ms.us
Search Database at www.mbp.state.ms.us Note: Click on "Licensing>".

17 Board of Polygraph Examiners, PO Box 958, Jackson, MS 39205; 601-987-1212.

18 Board of Psychology, 419 E Broadway St, Yazoo City, MS 39194-4530; 662-716-3934, Fax: 662-751-4628.
www.psychologyboard.state.ms.us/msbp/msbp.nsf
Search Database at
www.psychologyboard.state.ms.us/msbp/msbp.nsf
/Search?OpenForm

19 Board of Public Accountancy, 5 Old River Place Ste 104, Jackson, MS 39202; 601-354-7320, Fax: 601-354-7290.
www.msbpa.state.ms.us
Search Database at
www.msbpa.state.ms.us/licsearch.html

20 Board of Certified Court Reporters, PO Box 369 (656 N State St, Jackson, MS 39205; 601-354-6056, Fax: 601-354-6058.
www.mssc.state.ms.us/cle/
Email: tgraves@mssc.state.ms.us

21 Department of Health, Council of Advisors in Speech Pathology/Audiology, PO Box 1700 (570 Woodrow Wilson, 39216), Jackson, MS 39215-1700; 601-576-7260, Fax: 601-576-7267.
www.msdh.state.ms.us
Email: stephanie.boyette@ohr.ms.gov

22 Department of Environmental Quality, Pollution Control, PO Box 10385, Jackson, MS 39289-0385; 601-961-5171, Fax: 601-354-6612.
www.deq.state.ms.us/MDEQ.nsf

23 Board of Registered Professional Geologists, PO Box 22742 (931 Hwy. 80 West), Jackson, MS 39225-2742; 601-54-6370, Fax: 601-354-6032.
www.msbrpg.state.ms.us
Email: geology@msbrpg.state.ms.us
Search Database at
www.msbrpg.state.ms.us/rpg.htm

24 Department of Wildlife, Fisheries & Parks, 1505 Eastover Dr, Jackson, MS 39211-6322; 601-432-2400, Fax: 601-432-2024.
www.mdwfp.com

25 Insurance Department, Licensing Division, PO Box 79, Jackson, MS 39205; 601-359-3582, Fax: 601-359-1951.
www.doi.state.ms.us/agents.html
Email: licensing@mid.state.ms.us
Search Database at www.doi.state.ms.us/licapp/
Note: Also find a pdf version insurance company list at www.doi.state.ms.us/compdir.html.
Company lists also available on diskette.

26 Gaming Commission, 620 North St., Jackson, MS 39205; 601-576-3800, Fax: 601-576-3817.
www.mgc.state.ms.us/

27 Board of Bar Admissions, PO Box 2168, Jackson, MS 39225; 601-948-4471, Fax: 601-355-8635. www.msbar.org
Search Database at
www.msbar.org/lawyerdirectory.htm

28 Marriage & Family Therapists, Board of Examiners for Social Workers, PO Box 4508, Jackson, MS 39296-4508; 601-987-6806, Fax: 601-987-6808.
www.msboeswmft.com
Email: mboe@swmft.state.ms.us

29 Board of Veterinary Medicine, 209 S Lafayette, Starkville, MS 39759; 662-324-9380, Fax: 662-324-9380.   Note: Lists of Veterinarians are available in paper form only. Resuests must be approved, and they are charged by the minute.

30 Real Estate Appraiser, Licensing & Certification Board, 2506 Lakeland Dr. Ste 300 PO Box 12685, Jackson, MS 39236-2685; 601-932-9191, Fax: 601-932-3880.
www.mrec.state.ms.us/default.asp
Search Database at
www.mrec.state.ms.us/asp/findappraiser.asp

31 Office of Secretary of State, Regulation & Enforcement, PO Box 136, Jackson, MS 39205-0136; 601-359-1350, Fax: 601-359-1499.
www.sos.state.ms.us
Search Database at www.sos.state.ms.us

32 Office of Secretary of State, Business Regulation & Enforcement Division, PO Box 136

(700 North St, 39202), Jackson, MS 39205-0136; 601-359-1350, Fax: 601-359-1499.
www.sos.state.ms.us
Email: administrator@sos.state.ms.us Note: They provid lists. Contact for price.

33 Professional Licensure Division, MSDH, PO Box 1700, Jackson, MS 39215-1700; 601-576-7260, Fax: 601-576-7267.
www.msdh.state.ms.us
Email: stephanie.boyette@ohr.doh.ms.gov

34 Real Estate Commission, Licensing & Certification Board, PO Box 12685 (2506 Lakeland Dr, #300), Jackson, MS 39236; 601-932-9191, Fax: 601-932-2990.
www.mrec.state.ms.us/
Search Database at
www.mrec.state.ms.us/asp/findrealtor.asp

35 Board of Chiropractic Examiners, PO Box 775, Louisville, MS 39339; 662-773-4478, Fax: 662-773-4433.
www.msbce.ms.gov/msbce/msbce.nsf/webpages/1?OpenDocument
Email: msbce@bellsouth.net   Search Database at www.msbce.ms.gov/msbce/msbce.nsf/Search?OpenForm

36 Department of Education, Teacher Licensure/Certification, PO Box 771 (359 N West Street), Jackson, MS 39205; 601-359-3483, Fax: 601-359-2778.
www.mde.k12.ms.us
Email: cchester@mde.k12.ms.us

37 Department of Health, Licensing Division, 570 E Woodrow Wilson, Jackson, MS 39215; 601-576-7917, Fax: 601-576-7923.
www.msdh.state.ms.us

38 Department of Health, Childcare Facilities Licensure, 570 E Woodrow Wilson, Jackson, MS 39215; 601-576-7613, Fax: 601-576-7813.
Search Database at
www.msdh.state.ms.us/msdhsite/index.cfm/30,332,183,html

Mississippi Federal Courts

The following list indicates the district and division name for each county in the state. If the bankruptcy court location is different from the district court, then the location of the bankruptcy court appears in parentheses.

County/Court Cross Reference

County	District	Division
Adams	Southern	Vicksburg (Jackson)
Alcorn	Northern	Aberdeen-Eastern (Aberdeen)
Amite	Southern	Jackson
Attala	Northern	Aberdeen-Eastern (Aberdeen)
Benton	Northern	Oxford-Northern (Aberdeen)
Bolivar	Northern	Clarksdale/Delta (Aberdeen)
Calhoun	Northern	Oxford-Northern (Aberdeen)
Carroll	Northern	Greenville (Aberdeen)
Chickasaw	Northern	Aberdeen-Eastern (Aberdeen)
Choctaw	Northern	Aberdeen-Eastern (Aberdeen)
Claiborne	Southern	Vicksburg (Jackson)
Clarke	Southern	Meridian (Biloxi)
Clay	Northern	Aberdeen-Eastern (Aberdeen)
Coahoma	Northern	Clarksdale/Delta (Aberdeen)
Copiah	Southern	Jackson
Covington	Southern	Hattiesburg (Biloxi)
De Soto	Northern	Clarksdale/Delta (Aberdeen)
Forrest	Southern	Hattiesburg (Biloxi)
Franklin	Southern	Jackson
George	Southern	Biloxi-Southern (Biloxi)
Greene	Southern	Hattiesburg (Biloxi)
Grenada	Northern	Oxford-Northern (Aberdeen)
Hancock	Southern	Biloxi-Southern (Biloxi)
Harrison	Southern	Biloxi-Southern (Biloxi)
Hinds	Southern	Jackson
Holmes	Southern	Jackson
Humphreys	Northern	Greenville (Aberdeen)
Issaquena	Southern	Vicksburg (Jackson)
Itawamba	Northern	Aberdeen-Eastern (Aberdeen)
Jackson	Southern	Biloxi-Southern (Biloxi)
Jasper	Southern	Meridian (Biloxi)
Jefferson	Southern	Vicksburg (Jackson)
Jefferson Davis	Southern	Hattiesburg (Biloxi)
Jones	Southern	Hattiesburg (Biloxi)
Kemper	Southern	Meridian (Biloxi)
Lafayette	Northern	Oxford-Northern (Aberdeen)
Lamar	Southern	Hattiesburg (Biloxi)
Lauderdale	Southern	Meridian (Biloxi)
Lawrence	Southern	Hattiesburg (Biloxi)
Leake	Southern	Jackson
Lee	Northern	Aberdeen-Eastern (Aberdeen)
Leflore	Northern	Greenville (Aberdeen)
Lincoln	Southern	Jackson
Lowndes	Northern	Aberdeen-Eastern (Aberdeen)
Madison	Southern	Jackson
Marion	Southern	Hattiesburg (Jackson)
Marshall	Northern	Oxford-Northern (Aberdeen)
Monroe	Northern	Aberdeen-Eastern (Aberdeen)
Montgomery	Northern	Oxford-Northern (Aberdeen)
Neshoba	Southern	Meridian (Biloxi)
Newton	Southern	Meridian (Biloxi)
Noxubee	Southern	Meridian (Biloxi)
Oktibbeha	Northern	Aberdeen-Eastern (Aberdeen)
Panola	Northern	Clarksdale/Delta (Aberdeen)
Pearl River	Southern	Biloxi-Southern (Biloxi)
Perry	Southern	Hattiesburg (Biloxi)
Pike	Southern	Jackson
Pontotoc	Northern	Oxford-Northern (Aberdeen)
Prentiss	Northern	Aberdeen-Eastern (Aberdeen)
Quitman	Northern	Clarksdale/Delta (Aberdeen)
Rankin	Southern	Jackson
Scott	Southern	Jackson
Sharkey	Southern	Vicksburg (Jackson)
Simpson	Southern	Jackson
Smith	Southern	Jackson
Stone	Southern	Biloxi-Southern (Biloxi)
Sunflower	Northern	Greenville (Aberdeen)
Tallahatchie	Northern	Clarksdale/Delta (Aberdeen)
Tate	Northern	Clarksdale/Delta (Aberdeen)
Tippah	Northern	Oxford-Northern (Aberdeen)
Tishomingo	Northern	Aberdeen-Eastern (Aberdeen)
Tunica	Northern	Clarksdale/Delta (Aberdeen)
Union	Northern	Oxford-Northern (Aberdeen)
Walthall	Southern	Hattiesburg (Biloxi)
Warren	Southern	Vicksburg (Jackson)
Washington	Northern	Greenville (Aberdeen)
Wayne	Southern	Meridian (Biloxi)
Webster	Northern	Oxford-Northern (Aberdeen)
Wilkinson	Southern	Vicksburg (Jackson)
Winston	Northern	Aberdeen-Eastern (Aberdeen)
Yalobusha	Northern	Oxford-Northern (Aberdeen)
Yazoo	Southern	Vicksburg (Jackson)

Standards for Federal Courts: Search fee is $26.00 per item (one party name or case number). Copy fee is $.50 per page. Certification fee is $9.00 per document, double for exemplification, if available. All fees standard unless noted in profile. Mail Search: always enclose a stamped self addressed envelope unless otherwise noted. Most courts accept fax requests or will suggest a copying/search vendor. Before releasing records, all courts require prepayment, unless noted.

Open records are located at the court unless otherwise noted. District courts index by defendant and plaintiff as well as by case number. Bankruptcy courts usually index by debtor and case number. While most courts now have their indexes on computer, many may still maintain index card files as well.

Courts offering internet access via CM-ECF or older RACER, PACER, or Web-PACER systems charge $.08 per page fee unless noted as free. Where PACER is available, the universal sign-up number is 800-676-6856. Find PACER and the US Party/Case Index at http://pacer.psc.uscourts.gov.

US District Court

Northern District of Mississippi

Aberdeen-Eastern Division Court Clerk, PO Box 704, Aberdeen, MS 39730 (courier address: 301 W Commerce, Rm 310, Aberdeen, MS 39730), 662-369-4952. Hours- 8AM-12, 1-5PM. www.msnd.uscourts.gov

Counties: Alcorn, Attala, Chickasaw, Choctaw, Clay, Itawamba, Lee, Lowndes, Monroe, Oktibbeha, Prentiss, Tishomingo, Winston.

Searches & Indexing: Results do not include SSN or DOB. Both computer and card indexes maintained; computer goes back to 1992. New cases in the index 48 hours after filing date. Records purged every 6 months.

Fee & Payment: Pay by Visa/MC, money order, cashier check. No personal checks. Payee: Clerk, US District Court. Prepayment required.

Phone Search: No searching by telephone. If case number is provided via phone, this court will verify that case number.

Mail Search: search usually completed- 1-2 days. Include SASE for return.

In Person Search: Fee charged if court performs your search. Self-serve copier available - $.25 per page.

E-Services: ECF replaces PACER whose records did go back to 1990. New records online after 1 day. ECF at https://ecf.msnd.uscourts.gov **Opinions Online:** www.msnd.uscourts.gov/opinions/index.htm. Also, search opinions by year back to 1994 at http://home.olemiss.edu/~llibcoll/ndms/#OPINIONS.

Clarksdale/Delta Division c/o Oxford-Northern Division, 911 Jackson Ave, Rm 359, Oxford, MS 38655 (also use mail address for courier delivery), 662-234-1971, records rm- 662-234-1351. www.msnd.uscourts.gov

Counties: Bolivar, Coahoma, De Soto, Panola, Quitman, Tallahatchie, Tate, Tunica.

Searches & Indexing: Cases indexed by and case number. Results do not include SSN or DOB. Records purged every 6 months. Open records located at Oxford-Northern Division.

Fee & Payment: Pay by no business or personal checks accepted.

Phone Search: No searching by telephone.

Mail Search: Include SASE for return.

In Person Search: permitted. No self-serve copier available.

E-Services: ECF replaces PACER whose records did go back to 1990. New records online after 1 day. ECF at https://ecf.msnd.uscourts.gov **Opinions Online:** www.msnd.uscourts.gov/opinions/index.htm. Also, search opinions by year back to 1994 at http://home.olemiss.edu/~llibcoll/ndms/#OPINIONS.

Greenville Division Court Clerk, PO Box 190, Greenville, MS 38702-0190 (courier address: US Post Office & Federal Bldg, 305 Main, Greenville, MS 38701), 662-335-1651, Fax-662-332-4292. Hours- 8AM-12, 1-5PM. www.msnd.uscourts.gov

Counties: Carroll, Humphreys, Leflore, Sunflower, Washington.

Searches & Indexing: Results do not include SSN or DOB. Computer index maintained back to 11/04. New cases in the index immediately after filing date. Records purged every 6 months.

Fee & Payment: Pay by money order, cashier check. No personal checks. Payee: Clerk, US District Court. Prepayment required.

Phone Search: Only docket information based on case number is available by phone.

Mail Search: search usually completed- 1-2 days. Include SASE for return.

In Person Search: Fee charged if court performs your search. Self-serve copier available - $.25 per page.

E-Services: ECF replaces PACER whose records did go back to 1990. New records online after 1 day. ECF at https://ecf.msnd.uscourts.gov **Opinions Online:** www.msnd.uscourts.gov/opinions/index.htm. Also, search opinions by year back to 1994 at http://home.olemiss.edu/~llibcoll/ndms/#OPINIONS.

Oxford-Northern Division Court Clerk, 911 Jackson Ave, Rm 359, Oxford, MS 38655 (also use mail address for courier delivery), 662-234-1971, records rm- 662-234-1351. Hours- 8AM-5PM. www.msnd.uscourts.gov

Counties: Benton, Calhoun, Grenada, Lafayette, Marshall, Montgomery, Pontotoc, Tippah, Union, Webster, Yalobusha.

Searches & Indexing: All criminal records for Delta Division also maintained here. Results do not include SSN or DOB. Computer, microfiche and card indexes maintained. New cases in the index 48 hours after filing date. Civil records sent to the Atlanta Records Center 5 years after closing; criminal records 10 years after closing.

Fee & Payment: Pay by money order, cashier's or personal check. Payee: Clerk, US District Court. Prepayment required.

Phone Search: No searching by telephone. If case number is provided via phone, this court will verify that case number.

Mail Search: search usually completed- 2 days. Include SASE for return.

In Person Search: Fee charged if court performs your search. Self-serve copier available - $.25 per page.

E-Services: ECF replaces PACER. All records after 11/1/2004 available on ECF. New records online after 1 day. ECF at https://ecf.msnd.uscourts.gov **Opinions Online:** www.msnd.uscourts.gov/opinions/index.htm. Also, search opinions by year back to 1994 at http://home.olemiss.edu/~llibcoll/ndms/#OPINIONS.

US Bankruptcy Court

Northern District of Mississippi

Aberdeen Division Court Clerk, 703 Hwy 145 N, Rm 178, Aberdeen, MS 39730 (also use mail address for courier delivery), 662-369-2596, records rm- 662-369-2596. Hours- 8AM-12, 1-5PM. www.msnb.uscourts.gov

Counties: Alcorn, Attala, Benton, Bolivar, Calhoun, Carroll, Chickasaw, Choctaw, Clay, Coahoma, De Soto, Grenada, Humphreys, Itawamba, Lafayette, Lee, Leflore, Lowndes, Marshall, Monroe, Montgomery, Oktibbeha, Panola, Pontotoc, Prentiss, Quitman, Sunflower, Tallahatchie, Tate, Tippah, Tishomingo, Tunica, Union, Washington, Webster, Winston, Yalobusha.

Searches & Indexing: Results include last 4 SSN digits. Computer index maintained. New cases in the index 1-2 days after filing date. Records purged every 6 months.

Fee & Payment: Pay by money order, cashier's or personal check. Payee: Clerk, US Bankruptcy Court, Northern District. Prepayment required.

Phone Search: Only docket information is available by phone. Voice Case Information Service available, call VCIS at 800-392-8653 or 662-369-8147.

Mail Search: search usually completed- soon as work load permits. Include SASE for return.

In Person Search: Fee charged if court performs your search. You may not take case files from the court for copies. Self-serve copier available - $.50 per page.

E-Services: ECF replaces PACER whose records did go back to 4/1987. New records online after 1 day. ECF at https://ecf.msnb.uscourts.gov

US District Court

Southern District of Mississippi

Biloxi-Southern Division Court Clerk, Rm 403, 2012 15th S, 228-563-1700 (also use mail address for courier delivery), 228-563-1700. www.mssd.uscourts.gov

Counties: George, Hancock, Harrison, Jackson, Pearl River, Stone.

Searches & Indexing: Results do not include SSN or DOB. Both computer and card indexes maintained. New cases in the index 48 hours after filing date.

Fee & Payment: Pay by money order, cashier's or personal check. Payee: Clerk, US District Court. Prepayment required.

Phone Search: Only docket information is available by phone.

Mail Search: search usually completed- 1-2 days. Include SASE for return.

In Person Search: Fee charged if court performs your search. Self-serve copier - $.25 per page.

E-Services: ECF replaces PACER whose records did go back to 1992. ECF at https://ecf.mssd.uscourts.gov

Eastern Division Court Clerk, c/o Jackson Division, PO Box 23552, Jackson, MS 39225-3552 (courier address: c/o Jackson Division, 245 E Capitol St, #316, Jackson, MS 39201), 601-965-4439. Hours- 8AM-5PM. www.mssd.uscourts.gov

Counties: Clarke, Jasper, Kemper, Lauderdale, Neshoba, Newton, Noxubee, Wayne.

Searches & Indexing: Results do not include SSN or DOB. New cases in the index 2-3 days after filing date. Open records located at Jackson Division.

Fee & Payment: Pay by money order, cashier's, business or personal check. Payee: Clerk, U.S. District Court. Prepayment required.

Phone Search: No searching by telephone.

Mail Search: Include SASE for return.

In Person Search: permitted. No self-serve copier available.

E-Services: ECF replaces PACER whose records did go back to 1992. ECF at https://ecf.mssd.uscourts.gov

Hattiesburg Division Court Clerk, Suite 200, 701 Main St, Hattiesburg, MS 39401 (also use mail address for courier delivery), 601-583-2433, Fax-601-544-8335. Hours- 8AM-5PM. www.mssd.uscourts.gov

Counties: Covington, Forrest, Greene, Jefferson Davis, Jones, Lamar, Lawrence, Marion, Perry, Walthall.

Searches & Indexing: Results do not include SSN or DOB. Both computer and card indexes maintained; computer goes back to 1993. New cases in the index 48 hours after filing date.

Fee & Payment: Pay by money order, cashier's or personal check. Payee: Clerk, US District Court. Prepayment required.

Phone Search: Only docket information is available by case number via phone.

Mail Search: search usually completed- 3-4 working days. Include SASE for return.

In Person Search: Fee charged if court performs your search. Self-serve copier available - $.25 per page.

E-Services: ECF replaces PACER whose records did go back to 1992. ECF at https://ecf.mssd.uscourts.gov

Jackson Division Court Clerk, PO Box 23552, Jackson, MS 39225-3552 (courier address: Suite 316, 245 E Capitol St, Jackson, MS 39201), 601-965-4439. Hours- 8AM-5PM. www.mssd.uscourts.gov

Counties: Amite, Copiah, Franklin, Hinds, Holmes, Leake, Lincoln, Madison, Pike, Rankin, Scott, Simpson, Smith.

Searches & Indexing: Results do not include SSN or DOB. Computer, microfiche and card indexes maintained. New cases in the index 48 hours after filing date.

Fee & Payment: Pay by money order, cashier check, personal or business check. Payee: Clerk, US District Court. Prepayment required. Documents faxed back only with clerk's special permission; $1.00 per page.

Phone Search: No searching by telephone.

Mail Search: search usually completed- 1-2 days. Include SASE for return.

In Person Search: Fee charged if court performs your search. Self-serve copier available - $.25 per page.

E-Services: ECF replaces PACER whose records did go back to 1992. ECF at https://ecf.mssd.uscourts.gov

Western Division Court Clerk, PO Box 23552, Jackson, MS 39225-3552 (courier address: Jackson Division, 245 E Capitol St, Suite 316, Jackson, MS 39201), 601-965-4439. Hours- 8AM-5PM. www.mssd.uscourts.gov

Counties: Adams, Claiborne, Issaquena, Jefferson, Sharkey, Warren, Wilkinson, Yazoo.

Searches & Indexing: Results do not include SSN or DOB. New cases in the index 2-3 days after filing date. Open records located at Jackson Division.

Fee & Payment: Pay by money order, cashier's, business or personal check. Payee: Clerk, U.S. District Court. Prepayment required.

Phone Search: No searching by telephone.

Mail Search: Include SASE for return.

In Person Search: permitted. No self-serve copier available.

E-Services: ECF replaces PACER whose records did go back to 1992. ECF at https://ecf.mssd.uscourts.gov

US Bankruptcy Court

Southern District of Mississippi

Biloxi Division Court Clerk, Dan M Russell, Jr U S Courthouse, 2012 15th St, #244, Gulfport, MS 39501 (also use mail address for courier delivery), 228-563-1790. Hours- 8AM-4:30PM. www.mssb.uscourts.gov

Counties: Formerly located in Biloxi. Clarke, Covington, Forrest, George, Greene, Hancock, Harrison, Jackson, Jasper, Jefferson Davis, Jones, Kemper, Lamar, Lauderdale, Lawrence, Marion, Neshoba, Newton, Noxubee, Pearl River, Perry, Stone, Walthall, Wayne.

Searches & Indexing: Results include last 4 SSN digits only. Both computer and card indexes maintained. New cases in the index a few hours after filing date.

Fee & Payment: Pay by money order, cashier's or personal check. Payee: Clerk, US Bankruptcy Court. Prepayment required.

Phone Search: Voice Case Information Service available, call VCIS at 800-601-8859 or 601-965-6106.

Mail Search: search usually completed- within 1 day. Include SASE for return.

In Person Search: Fee charged if court performs your search. No self-serve copier available.

E-Services: PACER online at https://pacer.login.uscourts.gov/cgi-bin/login.pl?court_id=mssbk. PACER records go back to 1986. New records online after 1 day. ECF at http://ecf.mssb.uscourts.gov **Opinions Online:** www.mssb.uscourts.gov/Opinions/OpinionsList.htm. **Other Online Access:** Judges calendars free at www.mssb.uscourts.gov/Calendars.htm.

Jackson Division Court Clerk, PO Box 2448, Jackson, MS 39225-2448 (courier address: 100 E Capitol St #100, Jackson, MS 39201), 601-965-5301. 8AM-4:30PM. www.mssb.uscourts.gov

Counties: Adams, Amite, Claiborne, Copiah, Franklin, Hinds, Holmes, Issaquena, Jefferson, Leake, Lincoln, Madison, Pike, Rankin, Scott, Sharkey, Simpson, Smith, Warren, Wilkinson, Yazoo.

Searches & Indexing: Results include last 4 SSN digits only. Both computer and card indexes maintained. New cases in the index a few hours after filing date.

Fee & Payment: Pay by money order, cashier's or personal check. Payee: Clerk, US Bankruptcy Court. Prepayment required.

Phone Search: Voice Case Information Service available, call VCIS at 800-601-8859 or 601-965-6106.

Mail Search: search usually completed- 5 days. Include SASE for return.

In Person Search: Fee charged if court performs your search. No self-serve copier available.

E-Services: PACER online at https://pacer.login.uscourts.gov/cgi-bin/login.pl?court_id=mssbk. ECF at http://ecf.mssb.uscourts.gov **Opinions Online:** www.mssb.uscourts.gov/Opinions/OpinionsList.htm. **Other Online Access:** Judges calendars free at www.mssb.uscourts.gov/Calendars.htm.

Mississippi County Courts

Court	Jurisdiction	No. of Courts	How Organized
Circuit Courts*	General	70	22 Districts
County Courts*	Limited	3	19 Counties
Combined Courts*		20	
Chancery Courts*	General	91	20 Districts
Justice Courts	Limited	88	
Municipal Courts	Municipal	154	
Family Court	Special	1	

* Profiled in this Sourcebook.

Court	CIVIL								
	Tort	Contract	Real Estate	Min. Claim	Max. Claim	Small Claims	Estate	Eviction	Domestic Relations
Circuit Courts*	X	X	X	$2500	No Max			X	X
County Courts*	X	X	X	$0	$75,000			X	X
Combined Courts*									
Chancery Court*	X	X	X	$0	No Max		X		X
Justice Courts*	X	X	X	$0	$2500	$2500		X	
Municipal Courts								X	
Family Court									X

Court	CRIMINAL				
	Felony	Misdemeanor	DWI/DUI	Preliminary Hearing	Juvenile
Circuit Courts*	X				
County Courts*		X	X	X	X
Combined Courts*					
Chancery Court*					X
Justice Courts*		X	X	X	
Municipal Courts		X	X	X	
Family Court					X

ADMINISTRATION
Court Administrator, Supreme Court, Box 117, Jackson, MS, 39205; 601-354-7406, Fax: 601-354-7459. www.mssc.state.ms.us

COURT STRUCTURE
The court of general jurisdiction is the Circuit Court with 70 courts in 22 districts. Justice Courts were first created in 1984, replacing the Justice of the Peace. Prior to 1984, records were kept separately by each Justice of the Peace, so the location of such records today is often unknown. Probate is handled by the Chancery Courts, as are property matters.

ONLINE ACCESS
A statewide online computer system is in use internally for court personnel. There are plans underway to make this system available to the public, however this has been put on hold. The web site offers searching of the MS Supreme Court and Court of Appeals Decisions, including dockets of the trial courts. It is difficult to do a name search in the trial courts because the sequence number of the docket must be included in request.

ADDITIONAL INFORMATION
A number of Mississippi counties have two Circuit Court Districts. A search of either court in such a county will include the index from the other court.

Full Name is a search requirement for all courts. DOB and SSN are very helpful for differentiating between like-named individuals.

CRIMINAL RECORDS

The Administrative Office of Courts offers a statewide search via fax requesting with a 24 hour turnaround time. There is a $25.00 start-up fee and a $5.00 per name search fee. Call 601-354-7449 or fax 601-354-7459 for details.

Adams County

Circuit & County Court PO Box 1224, 115 S Wall, Natchez, MS 39121; phone: 601-446-6326; hours 8AM-5PM (CST). *Felony, Misdemeanor, Civil Actions Over $2,500.*
Civil Records: Access: Mail, in person. Both court and visitors may perform in person searches. Search fee: $10.00 per name. Court makes copy: $1.00 per page. Required to search: name, years to search. Civil cases indexed by defendant, plaintiff, on computer; docket books to 1950s; records stored in basement to 1799. Mail turnaround time 1-2 days if on computer.
Criminal Records: Access: Mail, in person. Both court and visitors may perform in person searches. Search fee: $10.00 per name. Court makes copy: $1.00 per page. Required to search: name, years to search; also helpful: SSN. Criminal records on computer; docket books to 1950s; records stored in basement to 1799. Mail turnaround time 1-2 days if on computer.
General Information: Public terminal goes back to 1997. No sealed, adoptions, mental health, juvenile, sex, or expunged records released. Certification fee: $2.00 per cert. Payee: Circuit Clerk. Personal checks accepted. Prepayment required.

Justice Court 115 S Wall, Natchez, MS 39121; phone: 601-446-6326; fax: 601-445-7955; hours 8AM-5PM (CST). *Misdemeanor, Civil Actions Under $2,500, Eviction, Small Claims.*

Chancery Court PO Box 1006, 1 Courthouse Sq, Natchez, MS 39121; phone: 601-446-6684; fax: 601-445-7913; hours 8AM-5PM (CST). *Probate.*

Alcorn County

Circuit Court PO Box 430 Attn: Circuit Clerk, Corinth, MS 38835; phone: 662-286-7740; fax: 662-286-7767; hours 8AM-5PM (CST). *Felony, Civil Actions Over $2,500.*
Civil Records: Access: Mail, fax, in person. Both court and visitors may perform in person searches. Search fee: $10.00 per name. Court makes copy: $1.50 per page. Self serve copy fee: $1.00 per page. Required to search: name, years to search. Civil cases indexed by defendant, plaintiff, on docket books from the 1930s. Mail turnaround time varies.
Criminal Records: Access: Mail, fax, in person. Both court and visitors may perform in person searches. Search fee: $10.00 per name. Court makes copy: $1.50 per page. Self serve copy fee: $1.00 per page. Required to search: name, years to search, DOB; also helpful: SSN, sex. Criminal records on docket books from the 1930s. Mail turnaround time varies.
General Information: Public terminal goes back to 2/03. No sealed, adoptions, mental health, juvenile, sex, or expunged records released. Fee to fax documents is $10.00 per document. No certification fee . Payee: Circuit Clerk. Personal checks accepted. Prepayment and SASE required.

Justice Court PO Box 226, 600 E Waldron St, Corinth, MS 38834; phone: 662-286-7776; fax: 662-286-2157; hours 8AM-5PM (CST). *Misdemeanor, Civil Actions Under $2,500, Eviction, Small Claims.*

Chancery Court PO Box 69, 501 Waldron St, Corinth, MS 38835-0069; phone: 662-286-7702; fax: 662-286-7706; hours 8AM-5PM (CST). *Probate.*

Amite County

Circuit Court PO Box 312, Liberty, MS 39645; phone: 601-657-8932; fax: 601-657-1082; hours 8AM-5PM (CST). *Felony, Civil Actions Over $2,500.*
Civil Records: Access: Phone, fax, mail, in person. Both court and visitors may perform in person searches. Search fee: $10.00 per name. Court makes copy: $.50 per page. Self serve copy fee: $.25 per page. Required to search: name, years to search. Civil cases indexed by defendant, plaintiff, on docket books since 1976; judgments on computer back to 1990. Mail turnaround time same day.
Criminal Records: Access: Fax, mail, in person. Both court and visitors may perform in person searches. Search fee: $10.00 per name. Court makes copy: $.50 per page. Self serve copy fee: $.25 per page. Required to search: name, years to search, DOB; also helpful: SSN. Criminal records on docket books since 1976. Mail turnaround time same day.
General Information: No public access terminal. Marriage records from 1809 - present. Will fax documents for $3.00. Certification fee: $10.00 per document. Payee: Circuit Clerk. Personal checks accepted.

Justice Court PO Box 362, 243 Broad St, Liberty, MS 39645; phone: 601-657-4527; fax: 601-657-8604; hours 8AM-4;30PM (CST). *Misdemeanor, Civil Actions Under $2,500, Eviction, Small Claims.*

Chancery Court PO Box 680, 243 W Main, Liberty, MS 39645; phone: 601-657-8022; fax: 601-657-8288; hours 8AM-5PM (CST). *Probate.*

Attala County

Circuit Court Courthouse, Kosciusko, MS 39090; phone: 662-289-1471; fax: 662-289-7666; hours 8AM-5PM (CST). *Felony, Civil Actions Over $2,500.*
Civil Records: Access: Fax, mail, in person. Both court and visitors may perform in person searches. Search fee: $10.00 per name. Court makes copy: $.50 per page; same fee for self serve. Required to search: name, years to search. Civil cases indexed by defendant, plaintiff. Civil records kept on docket books since 1915. Mail turnaround time same day.
Criminal Records: Access: Fax, mail, in person. Both court and visitors may perform in person searches. Search fee: $10.00 per name. Court makes copy: $.50 per page; same fee for self serve. Required to search: name, years to search, DOB; also helpful: SSN. Criminal records kept on docket books since 1915. Mail turnaround time same day.
General Information: No public access terminal. Will fax documents. Certification fee: $1.00 per document. Payee: Circuit Clerk. Business checks accepted. Prepayment and SASE required.

Justice Court 100 Courthouse, #4, Kosciusko, MS 39090; phone: 662-289-7272; fax: 662-289-0105; hours 8AM-5PM (CST). *Misdemeanor, Civil Actions Under $2,500, Eviction, Small Claims.*

Chancery Court 230 W. Washington, Kosciusko, MS 39090; phone: 662-289-2921; fax: 662-289-7662; hours 8AM-5PM (CST). *Probate.*

Benton County

Circuit Court PO Box 262, Ashland, MS 38603; phone: 662-224-6310; fax: 662-224-6312; hours 8AM-5PM (CST). *Felony, Civil Actions Over $2,500.*
Civil Records: Access: Mail, in person. Both court and visitors may perform in person searches. Search fee: $10.00 per name. Court makes copy: $1.00 per page. Self serve copy fee: $.25 per page.

Required to search: name, years to search, address. Civil cases indexed by defendant, plaintiff. Civil records kept on index books since 1871. Mail turnaround time same day.
Criminal Records: Access: Mail, in person. Both court and visitors may perform in person searches. Search fee: $10.00 per name. Court makes copy: $1.00 per page. Self serve copy fee: $.25 per page. Required to search: name, years to search, DOB; also helpful: SSN. Criminal records kept on index books since 1871. Mail turnaround time same day.
General Information: Public terminal goes back to 1999. No sealed, adoptions, mental health, juvenile, sex, or expunged records released. Will fax documents for fee. Certification fee: $1.00. Payee: Circuit Court. Only cashiers checks and money orders accepted. Prepayment required.

Justice Court PO Box 152, 190 Ripley Ave, Ashland, MS 38603; phone: 662-224-6320; fax: 662-224-6313; hours 8AM-5PM (CST). *Misdemeanor, Civil Actions Under $2,500, Eviction, Small Claims.*

Chancery Court PO Box 218, 190 Ripley Ave, Ashland, MS 38603; phone: 662-224-6300; fax: 662-224-6303; hours 8AM-5PM (CST). *Probate.*

Bolivar County

Circuit & County Court - 1st District PO Box 205, Rosedale, MS 38769; phone: 662-759-6521; fax: 662-759-3717; hours 8AM-5PM (CST). *Felony, Misdemeanor, Civil.*
Civil Records: Access: In person only. Visitors must perform in person searches themselves. Court makes copy: $.50 per page. Self serve copy fee: $.25 per page. Required to search: name, years to search. Civil cases indexed by defendant, plaintiff, on docket books since 1900s.
Criminal Records: Access: Mail, in person. Both court and visitors may perform in person searches. Search fee: $10.00 per name. Fee is for 7 year search. Court makes copy: $.50 per page. Self serve copy fee: $.25 per page. Required to search: name, years to search. Criminal records on docket books since 1900s. Mail turnaround time 2-3 days.
General Information: Public use terminal available. No sealed, juvenile, sex, or expunged records released. Certification fee: $1.50. Payee: Circuit Clerk. Personal checks accepted. Prepayment and SASE required.

Circuit & County Court - 2nd District PO Box 670, Cleveland, MS 38732; phone: 662-843-2061; fax: 662-846-2943; hours 8AM-5PM (CST). *Felony, Misdemeanor, Civil.*
Civil Records: Access: In person only. Visitors must perform in person searches themselves. Court makes copy: $.50 per page. Required to search: name, years to search. Civil cases indexed by defendant, plaintiff, on docket books since 1940.
Criminal Records: Access: Mail, in person. Both court and visitors may perform in person searches. Search fee: $10.00 per name. Fee is for 7 year search. Court makes copy: $.50 per page. Required to search: name, years to search. Criminal records on docket books since 1940. Mail turnaround time 2-3 days.
General Information: Public terminal has criminal back to 1992 and civil back to 1998. No sealed, juvenile or expunged records released. Certification fee: $1.50 per cert. Payee: Circuit Clerk. Personal checks accepted. Prepayment and SASE required.

Justice Court PO Box 1507, 404 MLK Dr, Cleveland, MS 38732; phone: 662-843-4008; fax: 662-846-6783; hours 8:00AM-5:00PM (CST). *Misdemeanor, Civil Actions Under $2,500, Eviction, Small Claims.*

Cleveland Chancery Court PO Box 789, 200 Court St, Cleveland, MS 38732; phone: 662-843-2071; fax: 662-846-2940; hours 8AM-5PM (CST). *Probate.*

Rosedale Chancery Court PO Box 238, 801 Main St, Rosedale, MS 38769; phone: 662-759-3762; fax: 662-759-3467; hours 8AM-N, 1-5PM (CST). *Probate.*

Calhoun County

Circuit Court PO Box 25, Pittsboro, MS 38951; phone: 662-412-3101; fax: 662-412-3103; hours 8AM-5PM (CST). *Felony, Civil Actions Over $2,500.*

Civil Records: Access: Mail, in person. Both court and visitors may perform in person searches. Search fee: $10.00 per name. Court makes copy: $1.00 per page. Self serve copy fee: $.25 per page. Required to search: name, years to search, DOB or SSN. Civil cases indexed by defendant, plaintiff, on docket books since 1922; computerized records go back to 1922. Mail turnaround time 1 day.

Criminal Records: Access: Mail, in person. Both court and visitors may perform in person searches. Search fee: $10.00 per name. Court makes copy: $1.00 per page. Self serve copy fee: $.25 per page. Required to search: name, years to search, DOB; also helpful: SSN. Criminal records on docket books since 1922; computerized records go back to 1922. Mail turnaround time 1 day; phone search info released when payment is received.

General Information: Public terminal goes back to 12 years. No sealed, mental health, juvenile, sex, or expunged records released. Fee to fax documents is $2.00 per page. Certification fee: $1.50. Payee: Circuit Clerk. Personal checks accepted. Prepayment and SASE required.

Justice Court PO Box 7, Hwy 9 Courthouse Sq, Pittsboro, MS 38951; phone: 662-412-3134; fax: 662-412-3136; hours 8AM-5PM (CST). *Misdemeanor, Civil Actions Under $2,500, Eviction, Small Claims.*

Chancery Court PO Box 8, 103 W Main, Pittsboro, MS 38951; phone: 662-412-3117; fax: 662-412-3128; hours 8AM-5PM (CST). *Probate.*

Carroll County

Circuit Court PO Box 6, Vaiden, MS 39176; phone: 662-464-5476; fax: 662-464-5407; hours 8AM-5PM (CST). *Felony, Civil Actions Over $2,500.*

Civil Records: Access: Mail, in person. Both court and visitors may perform in person searches. Search fee: $10.00 per name. Court makes copy: $.50 per page. Self serve copy fee: $.25 per page. Required to search: name, years to search. Civil cases indexed by defendant, plaintiff, on books since 1900s. Mail turnaround time 2 days.

Criminal Records: Access: Mail, in person. Both court and visitors may perform in person searches. Search fee: $10.00 per name. Court makes copy: $.50 per page. Self serve copy fee: $.25 per page. Required to search: name, years to search; also helpful: SSN. Criminal records on books since 1900s. Mail turnaround time 2 days.

General Information: No public access terminal. No adoptions, mental health or juvenile records released. Will fax documents to local or toll free line. Certification fee: $2.00. Payee: Circuit Court. Personal checks accepted. Prepayment required.

Justice Court PO Box 10, Courthouse, Lexington St, Carrollton, MS 38917; phone: 662-237-9285; fax: 662-237-6833; hours 8AM-5PM (CST). *Misdemeanor, Civil Actions Under $2,500, Eviction, Small Claims.*

Chancery Court PO Box 60, Lexington St, Carrollton, MS 38917; phone: 662-237-9274; fax: 662-237-9642; hours 8AM-12; 1-5PM (CST). *Probate.*

Chickasaw County

Circuit Court - 1st District 1 Pinson Sq, Rm 2, Houston, MS 38851; phone: 662-456-2331; fax: 662-456-4831; hours 8AM-5PM (CST). *Felony, Civil Actions Over $2,500.*

Civil Records: Access: Fax, mail, in person. Both court and visitors may perform in person searches. Search fee: $10.00 per name. There is no fee if the visitor performs the search. Court makes copy: $1.00 per page. Self serve copy fee: $.25 per page. Required to search: name, years to search; also helpful: address. Civil cases indexed by defendant, plaintiff, on docket books since mid-1800s. Mail turnaround time 2-3 days.

Criminal Records: Access: Fax, mail, in person. Both court and visitors may perform in person searches. Search fee: $10.00 per name. Court makes copy: $1.00 per page. Self serve copy fee: $.25 per page. Required to search: name, years to search, DOB; also helpful: address, SSN. Criminal records on docket books since mid-1800s. Mail turnaround time 2-3 days.

General Information: Public terminal goes back to 2004. No sealed, adoptions, mental health, juvenile, sex, or expunged records released. Will fax documents $1.00 plus $.50 per page after first. Payee: Circuit Clerk. Business checks accepted. Prepayment and SASE required.

Circuit Court - 2nd District Courthouse, 234 W Main St Rm #203, Okolona, MS 38860; phone: 662-447-2838; fax: 662-447-5024; hours 8AM-5PM (CST). *Felony, Civil Actions Over $2,500.*

Civil Records: Access: Fax, mail, in person. Both court and visitors may perform in person searches. Search fee: $10.00 per name. Court makes copy: $1.00 per page. Self serve copy fee: $.50 per page. Required to search: name, years to search; also helpful: address. Civil cases indexed by defendant, plaintiff, on docket books. Mail turnaround time 2-3 days.

Criminal Records: Access: Fax, mail, in person. Both court and visitors may perform in person searches. Search fee: $10.00 per name. Court makes copy: $1.00 per page. Self serve copy fee: $.50 per page. Required to search: name, years to search, DOB; also helpful: SSN. Criminal records on docket books. Mail turnaround time 2-3 days.

General Information: Public use terminal available. No sealed, adoptions, mental health, juvenile, sex, or expunged records released. Will fax documents to local or toll free line. Certification fee: $1.00 plus $.50 per page after first. Payee: Circuit Clerk. Business checks accepted. Prepayment and SASE required.

Justice Court Courthouse, 1 Pinson Sq, Houston, MS 38851; phone: 662-456-3941; fax: 662-448-8122; hours 8AM-5PM (CST). *Misdemeanor, Civil Actions Under $2,500, Eviction, Small Claims.*

Justice Court District 2 236 W Main, Okolona, MS 38860; phone: 662-447-3402; fax: 662-447-5020; hours 8AM-N; 1-5PM (CST). *Misdemeanor, Civil Actions Under $2,500, Eviction, Small Claims.*

Note: Research fee is $10.00 per name.

Chancery Court Courthouse Bldg, 1 Pinson Square, Houston, MS 38851; phone: 662-456-2513; fax: 662-456-5295; hours 8AM-5PM (CST). *Probate.*

Chancery Court 234 W Main, Rm 201, Okolona, MS 38860-1438; phone: 662-447-2092; fax: 662-447-5024; hours 8AM-N;1-5PM (CST). *Probate.*

Choctaw County

Circuit Court PO Box 34, Ackerman, MS 39735; phone: 662-285-6245; fax: 662-285-2196; hours 8AM-5PM (CST). *Felony, Civil Actions Over $2,500.*

Civil Records: Access: Mail, in person. Both court and visitors may perform in person searches.

Search fee: $10.00 per name. Court makes copy: $1.00 per page. Self serve copy fee: $.50 per page. Required to search: name, years to search. Civil cases indexed by defendant, plaintiff. Civil records in books back to 1926. Mail turnaround time 14 days legal maximum.

Criminal Records: Access: Mail, in person. Both court and visitors may perform in person searches. Search fee: $10.00 per name. Same fee for in person search. Court makes copy: $1.00 per page. Self serve copy fee: $.50 per page. Required to search: name, years to search; also helpful: DOB, SSN. Criminal records in books back to 1926. Mail turnaround time 14 days legal maximum.

General Information: No public access terminal. No sealed, adoptions, mental health, juvenile, sex, or expunged records released. Will fax documents to local or toll free line. Certification fee: $1.00 per page. Payee: Choctaw County Circuit Clerk. Personal checks accepted. Prepayment and SASE required.

Justice Court 140 Jailhouse Rd, Ackerman, MS 39735; phone: 662-285-3599; fax: 662-285-9039; hours 8AM-5PM (CST). *Misdemeanor, Civil Actions Under $2,500, Eviction, Small Claims.*

Chancery Court PO Box 250, 22 Quinn St, Ackerman, MS 39735; phone: 662-285-6329; fax: 662-285-3444; hours 8AM-5PM (CST). *Probate.*

Claiborne County

Circuit Court PO Box 549, Port Gibson, MS 39150; phone: 601-437-5841; fax: 601-437-4543; hours 8AM-5PM (CST). *Felony, Civil Actions Over $2,500.*

Civil Records: Access: Mail, in person. Both court and visitors may perform in person searches. Search fee: $10.00 per name. Court makes copy: $1.00 per page; docket sheets $2.00 per page. Required to search: name, years to search, address. Civil cases indexed by defendant, plaintiff, on docket books since 1820. Mail turnaround time varies.

Criminal Records: Access: Mail, in person. Both court and visitors may perform in person searches. Search fee: $10.00 per name. Court makes copy: $1.00 per page; docket sheets $2.00 per page. Required to search: name, years to search, address, DOB, signed release. Criminal records on docket books since 1820. Mail turnaround time varies.

General Information: No public access terminal. No sealed, adoptions, mental health, juvenile, sex, or expunged records released. Will fax documents for $2.00 per page, if not extensive. Certification fee: $1.50 per case. Payee: Sammie L Good, Circuit Clerk. Personal checks accepted. Prepayment required.

Justice Court PO Box 497, 510 Market St, Port Gibson, MS 39150; phone: 601-437-4478; fax: 601-437-3833; hours 8AM-5PM (CST). *Misdemeanor, Civil Actions Under $2,500, Eviction, Small Claims.*

Chancery Court PO Box 449, 410 Market St, Port Gibson, MS 39150; phone: 601-437-4992; fax: 601-437-3137; hours 8AM-5PM (CST). *Probate, Small Claims.*

Clarke County

Circuit Court PO Box 216, Quitman, MS 39355; phone: 601-776-3111; fax: 601-776-1001; hours 8AM-5PM (CST). *Felony, Civil Actions.*

Civil Records: Access: Fax, mail, in person. Both court and visitors may perform in person searches. Search fee: $10.00 per name. Court makes copy: $.50 per page. Self serve copy fee: $.25 per page. Required to search: name, years to search; also helpful: address. Civil cases indexed by defendant, plaintiff. Civil records kept on docket books since 1950s. Mail turnaround time 1 day.

Criminal Records: Access: Fax, mail, in person. Both court and visitors may perform in person searches. Search fee: $10.00 per name. Court makes copy: $.50 per page. Self serve copy fee: $.25 per page. Required to search: name, years to search; also helpful: address, DOB, SSN, sex. Criminal records kept on docket books since 1950s. Mail turnaround time 1 day.

General Information: Public terminal has only civil records back to 1995. No sealed, adoptions, mental health, juvenile, sex, or expunged records released. No fee to fax documents. Certification fee: $1.50. Payee: Circuit Clerk. Personal checks accepted. Prepayment required.

Justice Court PO Box 4, 100 E Church St, Quitman, MS 39355; phone: 601-776-5371; fax: 601-776-1014; hours 8AM-5PM (CST). *Misdemeanor, Civil Actions Under $2,500, Eviction, Small Claims.*

Chancery Court PO Box 689, 101 S Archusa, Quitman, MS 39355; phone: 601-776-2126; fax: 601-776-2756; hours 8AM-5PM (CST). *Probate.*

Clay County

Circuit Court PO Box 364, West Point, MS 39773; phone: 662-494-3384; fax: 662-495-2057; hours 8AM-5PM (CST). *Felony, Civil Actions Over $2,500.*

Civil Records: Access: Phone, mail, in person. Both court and visitors may perform in person searches. Search fee: $10.00 per name. Court makes copy: $1.00 per page. Self serve copy fee: $.25 per page. Required to search: name, years to search. Civil cases indexed by defendant, plaintiff, on docket books back to 1962; archived since mid-1800s. Mail turnaround time same day.

Criminal Records: Access: Mail, in person. Both court and visitors may perform in person searches. Search fee: $10.00 per name. Court makes copy: $1.00 per page. Self serve copy fee: $.25 per page. Required to search: name, years to search, address, DOB; also helpful: SSN. Criminal records on docket books back to 1962; archived since mid-1800s. Mail turnaround time same day.

General Information: No public access terminal. No sealed, adoptions, mental health, juvenile, sex, or expunged records released. Will fax documents. Certification fee: $1.00 per page. Payee: Clay County Circuit Clerk. Personal checks accepted. Prepayment and SASE required.

Justice Court PO Box 674, West Point, MS 39773; phone: 662-494-6141; fax: 662-494-6141; hours 8AM-5PM (CST). *Misdemeanor, Civil Actions Under $2,500, Eviction, Small Claims.*

Chancery Court PO Box 815, 205 Court St, West Point, MS 39773; phone: 662-494-3124; fax: 662-492-4059; hours 8AM-5PM (CST). *Probate, Small Claims, Divorce.*

Note: Send faxes to Attention Chancery Court.

Coahoma County

Circuit & County Court PO Box 849, Clarksdale, MS 38614-0849; phone: 662-624-3014; fax: 662-624-3075; hours 8AM-5PM (CST). *Felony, Civil.*

Civil Records: Access: Fax, mail, in person. Both court and visitors may perform in person searches. Search fee: $10.00 per name. Court makes copy: $1.00 per page. Self serve copy fee: $.50 per page. Required to search: name, years to search, address. Civil cases indexed by defendant, plaintiff, on dockets since 1950, archived since 1836. Note: Will also search judgment rolls. Mail turnaround time 2 days.

Criminal Records: Access: Fax, mail, in person. Both court and visitors may perform in person searches. Search fee: $10.00 per name. Court makes copy: $1.00 per page. Self serve copy fee: $.50 per page. Required to search: name, years to search, DOB, signed release; also helpful: address, SSN. Criminal records on dockets since 1910, archived since 1836. Mail turnaround time 2 days.

General Information: No public access terminal. No sealed, adoptions, mental health, juvenile, sex, or expunged records released. No fee to fax documents. Certification fee: $1.00. Payee: Circuit Clerk. Personal checks accepted. Prepayment required.

Justice Court 144 Ritch St, Clarksdale, MS 38614; phone: 662-624-3060; fax: 662-624-5528; hours 8AM-5PM (CST). *Misdemeanor, Civil Actions Under $2,500, Eviction, Small Claims.*

Chancery Court PO Box 98, 115 1st St, Clarksdale, MS 38614; phone: 662-624-3000; fax: 662-624-3040; hours 8AM-5PM (CST). *Probate.*

Copiah County

Circuit Court PO Box 467, Hazlehurst, MS 39083; phone: 601-894-1241; fax: 601-894-3026; hours 8AM-5PM (CST). *Felony, Civil Actions Over $2,500.*: Also, use 601-894-3301 for the 22nd Circuit Court District.

Civil Records: Access: Fax, mail, in person. Both court and visitors may perform in person searches. No search fee. Court makes copy: $.50 per page. Self serve copy fee: $.25 per page. Required to search: name, years to search. Civil cases indexed by defendant. Civil records on docket books since late 1800s. Mail turnaround time 1-2 days.

Criminal Records: Access: Fax, mail, in person. Both court and visitors may perform in person searches. Search fee: $10.00 per name. Court makes copy: $.50 per page. Self serve copy fee: $.25 per page. Required to search: name, years to search; also helpful: DOB, SSN. Criminal records on docket books since late 1800s. Mail turnaround 1-2 days.

General Information: No public access terminal. No sealed, adoptions, mental health, juvenile, sex, or expunged records released. No fee to fax documents. Certification fee: $1.50. Payee: Circuit Clerk. Business checks accepted. Prepayment required.

Justice Court PO Box 798, 121 W Frost St, Hazlehurst, MS 39083; phone: 601-894-3218; fax: 601-894-6038; hours 8:00AM-5:00PM (CST). *Misdemeanor, Civil Actions Under $2,500, Eviction, Small Claims.*

Chancery Court 122 S Lowe St, Hazlehurst, MS 39083; phone: 601-894-3021; fax: 601-894-4081; hours 8AM-5PM (CST). *Probate.*

Covington County

Circuit Court PO Box 667, Collins, MS 39428; phone: 601-765-6506; fax: 601-765-5012; hours 8AM-5PM (CST). *Felony, Civil Actions Over $2,500.*

Civil Records: Access: Fax, mail, in person. Both court and visitors may perform in person searches. Search fee: $10.00 per name. Court makes copy: $.50 per page. Self serve copy fee: $.25 per page. Required to search: name, years to search. Civil cases indexed by defendant, plaintiff, on docket books since 1915. Mail turnaround time 2-3 days.

Criminal Records: Access: Fax, mail, in person. Both court and visitors may perform in person searches. Search fee: $10.00 per name. Court makes copy: $.50 per page. Self serve copy fee: $.25 per page. Required to search: name, years to search, DOB; also helpful: SSN. Criminal records on docket books since 1915. Mail turnaround time 2-3 days.

General Information: No public access terminal. No sealed, adoptions, mental health, juvenile, sex, or expunged records released. No fee to fax documents. Certification fee: $3.00. Payee: Circuit Clerk. Personal checks accepted. Prepayment required.

Justice Court PO Box 665, 101 Dogwood St, Collins, MS 39428; phone: 601-765-6581; fax: 601-765-5014; hours 8AM-5PM (CST). *Misdemeanor, Civil Actions Under $2,500, Eviction, Small Claims.*

Chancery Court PO Box 1679, 101 S Elm St, Collins, MS 39428; phone: 601-765-4242; fax: 601-765-5016; hours 8AM-5PM (CST). *Probate.*

De Soto County

Circuit & County Court 2535 Hwy 51 South, Hernando, MS 38632; phone: 662-429-1325; criminal phone: 662-429-1325; civil phone: 662-429-1326; criminal fax: 662-449-1416; civil fax: 662-449-1415; hours 8AM-5PM (CST). *Felony, Misdemeanor, Civil.*

www.desotoms.com

Civil Records: Access: Mail, in person. Both court and visitors may perform in person searches. Search fee: $10.00 per name. Court makes copy: $.50 per page. Self serve copy fee: $.25 per page. Required to search: name, years to search; also helpful: address. Civil cases indexed by defendant, plaintiff, on docket books since 1972. Mail turnaround time 3 days.

Criminal Records: Access: Mail, in person. Both court and visitors may perform in person searches. Search fee: $10.00 per name. Court makes copy: $.50 per page. Self serve copy fee: $.25 per page. Required to search: name, years to search, DOB; also helpful: SSN. Criminal records on docket books since 1972. Mail turnaround time 3 days.

General Information: Public use terminal available. No sealed, juvenile, sex, or expunged records released. Will not fax documents. Certification fee: $2.50 per document. Payee: Circuit Clerk. No personal checks accepted. Prepayment required.

Justice Court 8525 Highway 51 North, Southaven, MS 38671; phone: 662-393-5810; fax: 662-393-5859; hours 8AM-5PM (CST). *Misdemeanor, Civil Actions Under $2,500, Eviction, Small Claims.*

Note: Records maintained since 1984, search fee is $5.00.

Chancery Court, Rm 100 PO Box 949, 2535 Hwy 51 South, Hernando, MS 38632; phone: 662-429-1320; fax: 662-449-1420; hours 8AM-5PM (CST). *Probate, Civil, Divorce.*

Forrest County

Circuit & County Court PO Box 992, Hattiesburg, MS 39403; phone: 601-582-3213; fax: 601-545-6065; hours 8AM-5PM (CST). *Felony, Misdemeanor, Civil.*

Civil Records: Access: Phone, mail, in person. Both court and visitors may perform in person searches. Search fee: $10.00 per name. Court makes copy: $.50 per page. Required to search: name, years to search; also helpful: address. Civil cases indexed by defendant, plaintiff, on docket books since 1900s. Limited phone access. Mail turnaround 10 days.

Criminal Records: Access: Mail, in person. Both court and visitors may perform in person searches. Search fee: $10.00 per name. Court makes copy: $.50 per page. Required to search: name, years to search, DOB, SSN; also helpful: address. Criminal records on docket books since 1900s; on computer since 1995. Mail turnaround time 10 days.

General Information: Public terminal goes back to 2000. No juvenile or expunged records released. Will fax documents. Certification fee: $1.50 per cert. Payee: Circuit Clerk. Business checks or attorney checks accepted. Prepayment required.

Justice Court 316 Forrest St, Hattiesburg, MS 39401; phone: 601-544-3136 x500; fax: 601-545-6114; hours 8AM-5PM (CST). *Misdemeanor, Civil Actions Under $2,500, Eviction, Small Claims.*

Note: Searches performed by the court only on Thursdays, or after 2PM rest of week.

Chancery Court PO Box 951, 641 Main St, Hattiesburg, MS 39403; phone: 601-545-6040; fax: 601-545-6043; hours 8AM-5PM (CST). *Probate.*

Franklin County

Circuit Court PO Box 267, Meadville, MS 39653; phone: 601-384-2320; fax: 601-384-8244; hours 8AM-5PM (CST). *Felony, Civil Actions Over $2,500.*

Civil Records: Access: Phone, fax, mail, in person. Both court and visitors may perform in person searches. Search fee: $10.00 per name. Court makes copy: $1.00 per page. Self serve copy fee: $.50 per page. Required to search: name, years to search. Civil cases indexed by defendant, plaintiff, on books since 1944. Mail turnaround time 2-3 days.

Criminal Records: Access: Fax, mail, in person. Both court and visitors may perform in person searches. Search fee: $10.00 per name. Court makes copy: $1.00 per page. Self serve copy fee: $.50 per page. Required to search: name, years to search, DOB or SSN; also helpful: address. Criminal records on books since 1944. Mail turnaround time 2-3 days.

General Information: Public terminal has only civil records back to 1993. (Judgments only on terminal.) No sealed, adoptions, mental health, juvenile, sex, or expunged records released. Will fax documents to a local or toll free line. Certification fee: $.50 per page. Payee: Circuit Clerk. Personal checks accepted. Prepayment required.

Justice Court PO Box 365, Courthouse Sq/Main, Meadville, MS 39653; phone: 601-384-2002; fax: 601-384-2253; hours 8AM-5PM (CST). *Misdemeanor, Civil Actions Under $2,500, Eviction, Small Claims.*

Chancery Court PO Box 297, Meadville, MS 39653; phone: 601-384-2330; fax: 601-384-5864; hours 8AM-5PM (CST). *Probate.*

George County

Circuit Court 355 Cox St, #C, Lucedale, MS 39452; phone: 601-947-4881; fax: 601-947-8804; hours 8AM-5PM M-F, 9AM-N Sat (CST). *Felony, Civil Actions Over $2,500.*

Civil Records: Access: Fax, mail, in person. Both court and visitors may perform in person searches. Search fee: $10.00 per name. Court makes copy: $1.00 per page. Required to search: name, years to search. Civil cases indexed by defendant, plaintiff, on docket books since 1910. Mail turnaround time 1-2 days.

Criminal Records: Access: Fax, mail, in person. Both court and visitors may perform in person searches. Search fee: $10.00 per name. Court makes copy: $1.00 per page. Required to search: name, years to search; also helpful: SSN. Criminal records on docket books since 1910. Mail turnaround time 1-2 days.

General Information: No public access terminal. No sealed, adoptions, mental health, juvenile, sex, or expunged records released. Will fax documents for no add'l fee. Certification fee: $2.00 per cert. Payee: Circuit Clerk. Personal checks accepted. Prepayment required. SASE requested.

Justice Court 356 Cox St, Lucedale, MS 39452; phone: 601-947-4834; fax: 601-947-1911; hours 8AM-5PM (CST). *Misdemeanor, Civil Actions Under $2,500, Eviction, Small Claims.*
Note: Records on computer (5/92 forward) are $4.00 per name. Prior to 5/92, searches are $20 for first 1/2 hour then $5.00 each 1/4 hour.

Chancery Court 355 Cox St, #A, Lucedale, MS 39452; phone: 601-947-4801; fax: 601-947-1300; hours 8AM-5PM (CST). *Probate.*

Greene County

Circuit Court PO Box 310, Leakesville, MS 39451; phone: 601-394-2379; fax: 601-394-2334; hours 8AM-5PM M-F (CST). *Felony, Civil Actions Over $2,500.*

Civil Records: Access: Phone, fax, mail, in person. Both court and visitors may perform in person searches. Search fee: $10.00 per name. Court makes copy: $.50 per page. Self serve copy fee: $.25 per page. Required to search: name, years to search; also helpful: address. Civil cases indexed by defendant, plaintiff, on docket books since early 1900s. Mail turnaround time 1-2 days.

Criminal Records: Access: Phone, fax, mail, in person. Both court and visitors may perform in person searches. Search fee: $10.00 per name. Court makes copy: $.50 per page. Self serve copy fee: $.25 per page. Required to search: name, years to search; also helpful: SSN. Criminal records on docket books since early 1900s. Note: Misdemeanor records are kept in Greene County Justice Court, 601-394-2347. Mail turnaround time 1-2 days.

General Information: No public access terminal. No sealed, adoptions, mental health, juvenile, sex, or

expunged records released. No fee to fax documents. Certification fee: $1.00. Payee: Circuit Clerk. Personal checks accepted. Prepayment required. SASE requested.

Justice Court PO Box 547, 407 Green St, Leakesville, MS 39451; phone: 601-394-2347; fax: 601-394-2114; hours 8AM-5PM (CST). *Misdemeanor, Civil Actions Under $2,500, Eviction, Small Claims.*

Chancery Court PO Box 610, 400 Main St, Leakesville, MS 39451; phone: 601-394-2377; fax: 601-394-4445; hours 8AM-5PM (CST). *Probate.*

Grenada County

Circuit Court PO Box 1517, Grenada, MS 38902-1517; phone: 662-226-1941; fax: 662-227-2865; hours 8AM-5PM (CST). *Felony, Civil Actions Over $2,500.*

Civil Records: Access: In person only. Visitors must perform in person searches themselves. Court makes copy: $.50 per page. Self serve copy fee: $.25 per page. Required to search: name, years to search. Civil cases indexed by defendant, plaintiff, on docket books since mid-1970s.

Criminal Records: Access: In person only. Visitors must perform in person searches themselves. Court makes copy: $.50 per page. Self serve copy fee: $.25 per page. Required to search: name, years to search. Criminal records on docket books since mid-1970s.

General Information: No public access terminal. No sealed, juvenile, or expunged records released. Certification fee: $1.50. Payee: Circuit Clerk. No personal checks accepted. Prepayment required.

Justice Court 16 First St, Grenada, MS 38901; phone: 662-226-3331; fax: 662-227-5513; hours 8AM-5PM (CST). *Misdemeanor, Civil Actions Under $2,500, Eviction, Small Claims.*

Chancery Court PO Box 1208, Grenada, MS 38902; phone: 662-226-1821; fax: 662-227-2860; hours 8AM-5PM (CST). *Probate.*

Hancock County

Circuit Court PO Box 249, 152 Main St, Bay St. Louis, MS 39520; phone: 228-467-5265; probate phone: 228-467-5404; fax: 228-467-2779; hours 8AM-5PM (CST). *Felony, Civil Actions Over $2,500.*

Civil Records: Access: Mail, in person. Both court and visitors may perform in person searches. Search fee: $10.00 per name. Court makes copy: $.50 per page; same fee for self serve. Required to search: name, years to search. Civil cases indexed by defendant, plaintiff, on docket books since 1975. Mail turnaround time 1 week.

Criminal Records: Access: Mail, in person. Both court and visitors may perform in person searches. Search fee: $10.00 per name. Court makes copy: $.50 per page; same fee for self serve. Required to search: name, years to search, DOB; also helpful: SSN. Criminal records on docket books since 1970. Mail turnaround time 1 week.

General Information: Public terminal goes back to 1970. No sealed, adoptions, mental health, juvenile, sex, or expunged records released. Certification fee: $1.50 per page. Payee: Circuit Clerk. Personal checks accepted. Prepayment required.

Justice Court 306 Hwy 90, Bay St. Louis, MS 39520; phone: 228-467-5573; fax: 228-467-3126; hours 8AM-5PM (CST). *Misdemeanor, Civil Actions Under $2,500, Eviction, Small Claims.*

Chancery Court PO Box 550, 152 Main St, Bay St. Louis, MS 39520; phone: 228-467-5404; fax: 228-467-3159; hours 8AM-5PM (CST). *Probate.*

Harrison County

Circuit Court - 1st District PO Box 998, Gulfport, MS 39502; phone: 228-865-4147; fax: 228-865-4009; hours 8AM-5PM (CST). *Felony, Civil Actions Over $75,000.*

Civil Records: Access: Fax, mail, in person, online. Both court and visitors may perform in person searches. Search fee: $10.00 per name. Court makes copy: $.50 per page. Self serve copy fee: $.25 per page. Required to search: name, years to search. Civil cases indexed by defendant, plaintiff, on computer back to 7/1991, prior on docket books, older records are archived. Access to Judicial District judgments are free at http://co.harrison.ms.us/departments/circlerk/rolls/. Search current court dockets free at http://co.harrison.ms.us/dockets/. Mail turnaround time 1-2 days.

Criminal Records: Access: Fax, mail, in person. Both court and visitors may perform in person searches. Search fee: $10.00 per name. Court makes copy: $.50 per page. Self serve copy fee: $.25 per page. Required to search: name, years to search, DOB; also helpful: SSN. Criminal records on computer back to 7/1991, prior on docket books, older records are archived. Search current court dockets free at http://co.harrison.ms.us/dockets/. Mail turnaround time 1-2 days.

General Information: Public terminal goes back to 10 years. No sealed, adoptions, mental health, juvenile, sex, or expunged records released. Certification fee: $1.00 per cert. Payee: Circuit Clerk. Business checks accepted. Prepayment required. SASE requested.

Circuit Court - 2nd District PO Box 235, Biloxi, MS 39533; phone: 228-435-8258; fax: 228-435-8277; hours 8AM-5PM (CST). *Felony, Civil Actions Over $75,000.*

Civil Records: Access: Fax, mail, in person, online. Both court and visitors may perform in person searches. Search fee: $10.00 per name. Court makes copy: $.50 per page. Self serve copy fee: $.25 per page. Required to search: name, years to search. Civil cases indexed by defendant, plaintiff, on computer since 7/1991. Access to Judicial District judgments are free at http://co.harrison.ms.us/departments/circlerk/rolls/. Search current court dockets free at http://co.harrison.ms.us/dockets/. Mail turnaround time 3 days.

Criminal Records: Access: Fax, mail, in person. Both court and visitors may perform in person searches. Search fee: $10.00 per name. Court makes copy: $.50 per page. Self serve copy fee: $.25 per page. Required to search: name, years to search, DOB; also helpful: SSN. Criminal records on computer since 7/1991. Search current court dockets free at http://co.harrison.ms.us/dockets/. Mail turnaround time 3 days.

General Information: Public terminal goes back to 1995. No sealed or expunged records released. Will fax documents $.50 per page. Certification fee: $1.00 per cert. Payee: Circuit Clerk. Business checks or attorney checks accepted. Prepayment and SASE required.

County Court - 1st District PO Box 998, Gulfport, MS 39502; phone: 228-865-4097; criminal phone: 228-865-4145; fax: 228-865-4099; hours 8AM-5PM (CST). *Misdemeanor, Civil Actions Under $200,000.*

Civil Records: Access: Mail, in person. Both court and visitors may perform in person searches. Search fee: $10.00 per name. Court makes copy: $.50 per page. Self serve copy fee: $.25 per page. Required to search: name, years to search. Civil cases indexed by defendant, plaintiff, on computer since 1991, prior on docket books since early 1900s. Search current court dockets free at http://co.harrison.ms.us/dockets/. Mail turnaround time 1-2 days.

Criminal Records: Access: Mail, in person. Both court and visitors may perform in person searches. Search fee: $10.00 per name. Court makes copy: $.50 per page. Self serve copy fee: $.25 per page. Required to search: name, years to search; also helpful: DOB. Criminal records on computer since 1991, prior on docket books since early 1900s. Search current court dockets free at http://co.harrison.ms.us/dockets/. Mail turnaround time 1-2 days.

General Information: Public terminal goes back to 9/1991. No sealed, adoptions, mental health, juvenile, sex, or expunged records released. Certification fee: $1.00 per cert. Payee: County Clerk. Business checks accepted. Prepayment required. SASE helpful.

County Court - 2nd District PO Box 235, 730 MLK Blvd, Biloxi, MS 39533; phone: 228-435-8294/8232; fax: 228-435-8277; hours 8AM-5PM (CST). *Misdemeanor, Civil Actions Under $200,000.*
Civil Records: Access: Fax, mail, in person. Both court and visitors may perform in person searches. Search fee: $10.00 per name. Court makes copy: $.50 per page. Self serve copy fee: $.25 per page. Required to search: name, years to search. Civil cases indexed by defendant, plaintiff, on computer since 7/1991, prior on books. Search current court dockets free at http://co.harrison.ms.us/dockets/. Mail turnaround time 3 days.
Criminal Records: Access: Fax, mail, in person. Both court and visitors may perform in person searches. Search fee: $10.00 per name. Court makes copy: $.50 per page. Self serve copy fee: $.25 per page. Required to search: name, years to search, DOB; also helpful: SSN, aliases. Criminal records on computer since 7/1991, prior on books. Search current court dockets free at http://co.harrison.ms.us/dockets/. Mail turnaround time 3 days.
General Information: Public terminal goes back to 2005. No sealed or expunged records released. No fee to fax documents. Certification fee: $1.00 per doc. Payee: Circuit Clerk. Business checks or attorney checks accepted. Prepayment and SASE required.

Justice Court District 1 PO Box 1754, 1620 23rd Ave, Gulfport, MS 39502; criminal phone: 228-865-4214; civil phone: 228-865-4193; fax: 228-865-4216; hours 8AM-5PM (CST). *Misdemeanor, Civil Actions Under $2,500, Eviction, Small Claims.*

http://co.harrison.ms.us/departments/justice/cntdst1.asp
Note: Search Justice court tickets free at http://co.harrison.ms.us/departments/justice/tickets/index.asp.

Justice Court District 2 PO Box 1141, 190 Lameuse St, Biloxi, MS 39533; criminal phone: 228-435-8251; civil phone: 228-435-8250; fax: 228-435-8279; hours 8AM-5PM (CST). *Misdemeanor, Civil Actions Under $2,500, Eviction, Small Claims.*

http://co.harrison.ms.us/departments/justice/cntdst2.asp
Note: Search Justice court tickets free at http://co.harrison.ms.us/departments/justice/tickets/index.asp.

Biloxi Chancery Court PO Box 544, 730 Martin Luther King Jr Blvd, Biloxi, MS 39533; phone: 228-435-8228; fax: 228-435-8281; hours 8AM-5PM (CST). *Probate.*

http://co.harrison.ms.us/departments/chanclerk/court.asp
Note: Search Chancery Court dockets for free at http://co.harrison.ms.us/dockets/.

Gulfport Chancery Court PO Drawer CC, 1801 23rd Ave, Gulfport, MS 39502; phone: 228-865-4092; fax: 228-865-4054; hours 8AM-5PM (CST). *Probate.*

http://co.harrison.ms.us/departments/chanclerk/court.asp
Note: Search Chancery Court dockets for free at http://co.harrison.ms.us/dockets/.

Hinds County

Circuit & County Court - 1st District PO Box 327, Jackson, MS 39205; phone: 601-968-6628; fax: 601-973-5547; hours 8AM-5PM (CST). *Felony, Misdemeanor, Civil.*
www.co.hinds.ms.us/pgs/index.asp
Civil Records: Access: Mail, in person. Both court and visitors may perform in person searches. Search fee: $9.00 per name. Court makes copy: $1.00

per page. Self serve copy fee: $.50 per page. Required to search: name, years to search. Civil cases indexed by defendant, plaintiff, on docket books back to 1900s. Mail turnaround time 14 days.
Criminal Records: Access: Mail, in person. Both court and visitors may perform in person searches. Search fee: $9.00 per name. Court makes copy: $1.00 per page. Self serve copy fee: $.50 per page. Required to search: name, years to search, DOB; also helpful: SSN. Criminal records on docket books back to 1900s. Mail turnaround time 14 days.
General Information: Public terminal goes back to 1990. No sealed, adoptions, mental health, juvenile, sex, or expunged records released. Certification fee: $1.00. Payee: Circuit Clerk. Personal checks accepted. Prepayment required.

Circuit & County Court - 2nd District PO Box 999, Raymond, MS 39154; phone: 601-857-8038; hours 8AM-N, 1-5PM (CST). *Felony, Misdemeanor, Civil.*
Civil Records: Access: Mail, in person. Both court and visitors may perform in person searches. Search fee: $9.00 per name. Court makes copy: $1.00 per page. Self serve copy fee: $.50 per page. Required to search: name, years to search. Civil cases indexed by defendant, plaintiff, on computer since 1994, prior on docket books since late 1800s. Mail turnaround time 1 week.
Criminal Records: Access: Mail, in person. Both court and visitors may perform in person searches. Search fee: $9.00 per name. Court makes copy: $1.00 per page. Self serve copy fee: $.50 per page. Required to search: name, years to search; also helpful: DOB, SSN. Criminal records on computer since 1994, prior on docket books since late 1800s. Mail turnaround time 1 week.
General Information: No public access terminal. No sealed, adoptions, mental health, juvenile, sex, expunged or some preliminary criminal records released. Certification fee: $1.50 per cert. Payee: Circuit Clerk. Personal checks accepted. Prepayment required. SASE requested.

Justice Court 407 E Pascagoula, 3rd Fl, PO Box 3490, Jackson, MS 39207; phone: 601-965-8800; hours 8AM-5PM (CST). *Misdemeanor, Civil Actions Under $2,500, Eviction, Small Claims.*

Chancery Court - Jackson PO Box 686, 316 S President St, Jackson, MS 39205; phone: 601-968-6540; fax: 601-973-5554; hours 8AM-5PM (CST). *Probate, Divorce.*

Chancery Court - Raymond PO Box 88, 127 W Main, Raymond, MS 39154; phone: 601-857-8055; fax: 601-857-4953; hours 8AM-5PM (CST). *Probate.*

Holmes County

Circuit Court PO Box 718, Lexington, MS 39095; phone: 662-834-2476; fax: 662-834-3870; hours 8AM-5PM (CST). *Felony, Civil Actions Over $2,500.*
Civil Records: Access: Fax, mail, in person. Both court and visitors may perform in person searches. Search fee: $10.00 per name. Court makes copy: $1.00 per page. Self serve copy fee: $.50 per page. Required to search: name, years to search. Civil cases indexed by defendant, plaintiff, on docket books since 1940s. Mail turnaround time 1-2 days.
Criminal Records: Access: Fax, mail, in person. Both court and visitors may perform in person searches. Search fee: $10.00 per name. Court makes copy: $1.00 per page. Self serve copy fee: $.50 per page. Required to search: name, years to search; also helpful: DOB, SSN. Criminal records on docket books since 1940s. Mail turnaround time 1-2 days.
General Information: No public access terminal. No sealed or expunged records released. No fee to fax documents. Certification fee: $1.50. Payee: Holmes County Circuit Clerk. Business checks accepted. Prepayment required.

Justice Court PO Box 99, 200 Court St, Lexington, MS 39095; phone: 662-834-4565; fax: 662-834-1402; hours 8AM-5PM (CST). *Misdemeanor, Civil Actions Under $2,500, Eviction, Small Claims.*

Chancery Court PO Box 239, 2 Court Sq, Lexington, MS 39095; phone: 662-834-2508; fax: 662-834-1872; hours 8AM-5PM (CST). *Probate.*

Humphreys County

Circuit Court PO Box 696, Belzoni, MS 39038; phone: 662-247-3065; fax: 662-247-3906; hours 8AM-5PM (CST). *Felony, Civil Actions Over $2,500.*
Civil Records: Access: Fax, mail, in person. Both court and visitors may perform in person searches. Search fee: $10.00 per name. Court makes copy: $1.00 per page. Self serve copy fee: $.50 per page. Required to search: name, years to search. Civil cases indexed by defendant, plaintiff, on books since 1918. Mail turnaround time 1 day.
Criminal Records: Access: Fax, mail, in person. Both court and visitors may perform in person searches. Search fee: $10.00 per name. Court makes copy: $1.00 per page. Self serve copy fee: $.50 per page. Required to search: name, years to search; also helpful: DOB, SSN. Criminal records on books since 1918. Mail turnaround time 1 day; phone turnaround 30 minutes.
General Information: No public access terminal. No sealed, adoptions, mental health, juvenile, sex, or expunged records released. Will fax documents for $1.00. Certification fee: $1.00 per page if you perform search. No cert fee if court performs search. Payee: Circuit Clerk. Personal checks accepted. Prepayment required.

Justice Court 102 Castleman St, Belzoni, MS 39038; phone: 662-247-4337; fax: 662-247-1095; hours 8AM-5PM (CST). *Misdemeanor, Civil Actions Under $2,500, Eviction, Small Claims.*

Chancery Court PO Box 547, 102 Castleman St, Belzoni, MS 39038; phone: 662-247-1740; fax: 662-247-0101; hours 8AM-N, 1-5PM (CST). *Probate.*

Issaquena County

Circuit Court PO Box 27, Mayersville, MS 39113; phone: 662-873-2761; fax: 662-873-2061; hours 8AM-Noon; 1-5PM (CST). *Felony, Civil Actions Over $2,500.*
Civil Records: Access: Fax, mail, in person. Both court and visitors may perform in person searches. Search fee: $20.00 per name. Court makes copy: $.50 per page. Self serve copy fee: $.25 per page. Required to search: name, years to search. Civil cases indexed by defendant, plaintiff, on docket books since 1846. Mail turnaround time 1 week.
Criminal Records: Access: Fax, mail, in person. Both court and visitors may perform in person searches. Search fee: $20.00 per name. Court makes copy: $.50 per page. Self serve copy fee: $.25 per page. Required to search: name, years to search; also helpful: DOB, SSN. Criminal records on docket books since 1846. Mail turnaround time 1 week.
General Information: No public access terminal. No sealed, adoptions, mental health, juvenile, sex, or expunged records released. Will fax documents to local or toll free line. Certification fee: $1.00 per cert. Payee: Circuit Clerk. Personal checks accepted. Prepayment required. SASE requested.

Justice Court PO Box 58, 129 Court St, Mayersville, MS 39113; phone: 662-873-6287; fax: 662-873-2061; hours 8AM-N, 1-5PM (CST). *Misdemeanor, Civil Actions Under $2,500, Eviction, Small Claims.*

Chancery Court PO Box 27, 129 Court St, Mayersville, MS 39113; phone: 662-873-2761; fax: 662-873-2061; hours 8AM-N, 1-5PM (CST). *Probate.*

Itawamba County

Circuit Court 201 W Main, Fulton, MS 38843; phone: 662-862-3511; fax: 662-862-4006; hours 8AM-5PM (CST). *Felony, Civil Actions Over $2,500.*

Civil Records: Access: Phone, fax, mail, in person. Both court and visitors may perform in person searches. Search fee: $10.00 with a written request. Court makes copy: $.25 per page. Required to search: name, years to search. Civil cases indexed by defendant, plaintiff, on books since 1940s. Mail turnaround time 1 week.

Criminal Records: Access: Phone, fax, mail, in person. Both court and visitors may perform in person searches. Search fee: $10.00 with a written request. Court makes copy: $.25 per page. Required to search: name, years to search, DOB; also helpful: SSN. Criminal records on books since 1940s. Mail turnaround time 1 week.

General Information: Public use terminal available. Will fax documents to local or toll free line. No certification fee . SASE required.

Justice Court 304 D W Wiygul St, Fulton, MS 38843; phone: 662-862-4315; fax: 662-862-5805; hours 8am-5PM (CST). *Misdemeanor, Civil Actions Under $2,500, Eviction, Small Claims.*

Chancery Court 201 W Main, Fulton, MS 38843; phone: 662-862-3421; fax: 662-862-3421; hours 8AM-5PM M-F; 8AM-N Sat (CST). *Probate.*

Jackson County

Circuit Court PO Box 998, Pascagoula, MS 39568-0998; phone: 228-769-3025; fax: 228-769-3180; hours 8AM-5PM (CST). *Felony, Civil.*
www.co.jackson.ms.us
Civil Records: Access: Mail, in person, online. Both court and visitors may perform in person searches. Search fee: $10.00 per name per 10 years searched. Court makes copy: $1.00 per page. Self serve copy fee: $.25 per page. Required to search: name, years to search. Civil cases indexed by defendant, plaintiff, on computer back to 1993, prior on docket books since 1920s. Access to Circuit Court monthly dockets is free   at www.co.jackson.ms.us/DS/CircuitDockets.html. Mail turnaround time varies.

Criminal Records: Access: Mail, in person, online. Both court and visitors may perform in person searches. Search fee: $10.00 per name, per 10 years searched. Court makes copy: $1.00 per page. Self serve copy fee: $.25 per page. Required to search: name, years to search, DOB; also helpful: SSN. Criminal records on computer back to 1992, prior on docket books since 1920s. Online access to criminal dockets is the same as civil. Mail turnaround time varies.

General Information: Public terminal goes back to 1992. No sealed or expunged records released. Fee to fax documents is $2.00 per page. Certification fee: $2.00 per page. Payee: Circuit Clerk. Business checks accepted. Prepayment and SASE required.

County Court PO Box 998 (3104 Magnolia St), Pascagoula, MS 39568; phone: 228-769-3181; fax: 228-769-3180; hours 8AM-5PM (CST). *Misdemeanor, Civil Actions over $25,000.*
www.co.jackson.ms.us
Civil Records: Access: Mail, in person. Both court and visitors may perform in person searches. Search fee: $10.00 per name per 10 years. Court makes copy: $1.00 per page. Required to search: name, years to search. Civil cases indexed by defendant, plaintiff. Civil records files go back 20 years; on computer back to 1992. Mail turnaround time 1 week.

Criminal Records: Access: Mail, in person. Both court and visitors may perform in person searches. Search fee: $10.00 per name per 10 years. Court makes copy: $1.00 per page. Required to search: name, years to search, DOB. Criminal records go back 12 years; on computer back to 1992. Mail turnaround time 1 week.

General Information: Public terminal goes back to 1992. No sealed, adoptions, mental health, juvenile, sex, or expunged records released. Will fax documents. Certification fee: $2.00. Payee: Clerk of County Court. Only cashiers checks and money orders accepted. Prepayment required.

Justice Court 5343 Jefferson St, Moss Point, MS 39563; phone: 228-769-3096; criminal phone: 228-769-3080; civil phone: 228-769-3087; fax: 228-769-3364; hours 8AM-5PM (CST). *Misdemeanor, Civil Actions Under $2,500, Eviction, Small Claims.*
www.co.jackson.ms.us

Chancery Court PO Box 998, Pascagoula, MS 39568; phone: 228-769-3124, 769-3124; fax: 228-769-3397; hours 8AM-5PM (CST). *Probate.*

www.co.jackson.ms.us/
Note: Access to Chancery Court monthly dockets are available   free   at www.co.jackson.ms.us/DS/ChanceryDockets.html.

Jasper County

Circuit Court - 1st District PO Box 58, Paulding, MS 39348; phone: 601-727-4941; fax: 601-727-4475; hours 8AM-5PM (CST). *Felony, Civil Actions Over $2,500.*

Civil Records: Access: Fax, mail, in person. Both court and visitors may perform in person searches. Search fee: $10.00 per name. Fee includes a search of both districts in the county. Court makes copy: $.50 per page. Self serve copy fee: $.25 per page. Required to search: name, years to search. Civil cases indexed by defendant, plaintiff, on docket books since 1932. Mail turnaround time 1 week.

Criminal Records: Access: Fax, mail, in person. Both court and visitors may perform in person searches. Search fee: $10.00 per name. Fee includes a search of both districts in the county. Court makes copy: $.50 per page. Self serve copy fee: $.25 per page. Required to search: name, years to search; also helpful: DOB, SSN. Criminal records on docket books since 1932. Mail turnaround time 1 week.

General Information: No public access terminal. No sealed or expunged records released. Will fax documents $5.00 per doc. Certification fee: $1.50. Payee: Circuit Clerk. Personal checks accepted. Prepayment required.

Circuit Court - 2nd District PO Box 447, Bay Springs, MS 39422; phone: 601-764-2245; fax: 601-764-3078; hours 8AM-5PM (CST). *Felony, Civil Actions Over $2,500.*

Civil Records: Access: Mail, in person. Both court and visitors may perform in person searches. Search fee: $10.00 per name. Fee includes a search of both districts in the county. Court makes copy: $.50 per page. Self serve copy fee: $.25 per page. Required to search: name, years to search. Civil cases indexed by defendant, plaintiff, on docket books since 1932. Mail turnaround time 1-2 days.

Criminal Records: Access: Mail, in person, fax. Both court and visitors may perform in person searches. Search fee: $10.00 per name. Fee includes a search of both districts in the county. Court makes copy: $.50 per page. Self serve copy fee: $.25 per page. Required to search: name, years to search; also helpful: SSN. Criminal records on docket books since 1932. Mail turnaround time 1-2 days.

General Information: No public access terminal. No sealed, adoptions, mental health, juvenile, sex, or expunged records released. Will fax documents to local or toll free line. Certification fee: $1.50 per page. Payee: Circuit Clerk. Personal checks accepted. Prepayment required. SASE requested.

Justice Court PO Box 1054, 27 W 8th Ave, Bay Springs, MS 39422; phone: 601-764-2065; fax: 601-764-3402; hours 8AM-5PM (CST). *Misdemeanor, Civil Actions Under $2,500, Eviction, Small Claims.*
Note: This Justice Court houses all the Justices for Jasper County.

Bay Springs Chancery Court PO Box 1047, 27 W 8th Ave, Bay Springs, MS 39422; phone: 601-764-3368; fax: 601-764-3999; hours 8AM-5PM (CST). *Probate.*

Paulding Chancery Court PO Box 38, 1782 Highway 503, Paulding, MS 39348; phone: 601-727-4941; fax: 601-727-4475; hours 8AM-5PM (CST). *Probate.*

Jefferson County

Circuit Court PO Box 305, Fayette, MS 39069; phone: 601-786-3422; fax: 601-786-9676; hours 8AM-5PM (CST). *Felony, Civil Actions Over $2,500.*

Civil Records: Access: Phone, mail, in person. Both court and visitors may perform in person searches. Search fee: $10.00 per name. Court makes copy: $.50 per page. Required to search: name, years to search, DOB; also helpful: SSN, sex, signed release. Civil cases indexed by defendant, plaintiff, on docket books since 1966, prior archived. Mail turnaround time same day.

Criminal Records: Access: Phone, mail, in person. Both court and visitors may perform in person searches. Search fee: $10.00 per name. Court makes copy: $.50 per page. Required to search: name, years to search, DOB; also helpful: SSN. Criminal records on docket books since 1971, prior archived. Mail turnaround time same day.

General Information: No public access terminal. No sealed, adoptions, mental health, juvenile, sex, or expunged records released. Will fax documents to local or toll free line. Certification fee: $1.50. Payee: Jefferson County Circuit Court. Business checks accepted. Prepayment and SASE required.

Justice Court PO Box 1047, 307 S Main St, Fayette, MS 39069; phone: 601-786-8594; criminal phone: 601-786-3423; civil phone: 601-786-3423; fax: 601-786-6017; hours 8AM-5PM (CST). *Misdemeanor, Civil Actions Under $2,500, Eviction, Small Claims.*

Chancery Court PO Box 145, 307 Main St, Fayette, MS 39069; phone: 601-786-3021; fax: 601-786-6009; hours 8AM-5PM (CST). *Probate.*

Jefferson Davis County

Circuit Court PO Box 1082, Prentiss, MS 39474; phone: 601-792-4231; fax: 601-792-4957; hours 8AM-5PM (CST). *Felony, Civil Actions Over $2,500.*

Civil Records: Access: Phone, fax, mail, in person. Both court and visitors may perform in person searches. Search fee: $10.00 per name. Court makes copy: $1.00 per page. Self serve copy fee: $.50 per page. Required to search: name, years to search. Civil cases indexed by defendant, plaintiff, on docket books since 1906. Mail turnaround time 1-2 days.

Criminal Records: Access: Phone, fax, mail, in person. Both court and visitors may perform in person searches. Search fee: $10.00 per name. Court makes copy: $1.00 per page. Self serve copy fee: $.50 per page. Required to search: name, years to search; also helpful: SSN. Criminal records on docket books since 1906. Mail turnaround time 1-2 days.

General Information: No public access terminal. No sealed, adoptions, mental health, juvenile, sex, or expunged records released. Fee to fax documents is $1.00 per page. Certification fee: $2.00. Payee: Circuit Clerk. Personal checks accepted. Prepayment required.

Justice Court PO Box 1407, Prentiss, MS 39474; phone: 601-792-5129; fax: 601-792-5128; hours 8AM-N, 1-5PM (CST). *Misdemeanor, Civil Actions Under $2,500, Eviction, Small Claims.*

Chancery Court PO Box 1137, Prentiss, MS 39474; phone: 601-792-4204; fax: 601-792-2894; hours 8AM-5PM (CST). *Probate.*

Jones County

Circuit & County Court - 1st District 101 N. Court St, #B, Ellisville, MS 39437; phone: 601-477-8538; fax: 601-477-8539; hours 8AM-5PM (CST). *Felony, Misdemeanor, Civil.*
Civil Records: Access: Mail, fax, in person. Visitors must perform in person searches themselves. Search fee: $10.00. Court makes copy: $.50 per page. Self serve copy fee: $.25 per page. Required to search: name, years to search. Civil cases indexed by defendant, plaintiff, on docket books since 1960s. Mail turnaround time 1-2 days.
Criminal Records: Access: Mail, fax, in person. Both court and visitors may perform in person searches. Search fee: $10.00 per name. Court makes copy: $.50 per page. Self serve copy fee: $.25 per page. Required to search: name, years to search. Criminal records on docket books since 1960s. Mail turnaround time 1-2 days.
General Information: No public access terminal. No sealed, adoptions, mental health, juvenile, sex, or expunged records released. Will fax documents to local or toll free line. Certification fee: $1.50. Payee: Circuit Clerk. Personal checks accepted. Prepayment required.

Circuit & County Court - 2nd District PO Box 1336, Laurel, MS 39441; phone: 601-425-2556; fax: 601-399-4774; hours 8AM-5PM (CST). *Felony, Misdemeanor, Civil.*
Civil Records: Access: In person only. Visitors must perform in person searches themselves. Court makes copy: $.50 per page. Self serve copy fee: $.25 per page. Required to search: name, years to search. Civil cases indexed by defendant, plaintiff, on docket books since 1960s.
Criminal Records: Access: Mail, in person. Both court and visitors may perform in person searches. Search fee: $10.00 per name. Fee is per district. Court makes copy: $.50 per page. Self serve copy fee: $.25 per page. Required to search: name, years to search; also helpful: SSN. Criminal records on docket books since 1960s. Mail turnaround time 2 days.
General Information: No public access terminal. No sealed or Juvenile Youth Court records released. Will fax documents to local or toll free line. Certification fee: $1.50. Payee: Jones County Circuit Clerk. Personal checks accepted. Prepayment and SASE required.

Justice Court PO Box 1997, 402 Central Ave, Laurel, MS 39441; phone: 601-428-3137; fax: 601-428-0526; hours 8AM-5PM (CST). *Misdemeanor, Civil Actions Under $2,500, Eviction, Small Claims.*
Note: This Justice Court houses all the Justices for Jones County.

Ellisville Chancery Court 101 N Court St. #D, PO Box 248, Ellisville, MS 39437; phone: 601-477-3307; fax: 601-477-1240; hours 8AM-N, 1-5PM (CST). *Probate.*

Laurel Chancery Court PO Box 1468, 415 N 5th Ave, Laurel, MS 39441; phone: 601-428-3182, 601-428-0527; probate phone: 602-428-3182; fax: 601-428-3610; hours 8AM-5PM (CST). *Probate.*

Kemper County

Circuit Court PO Box 130, De Kalb, MS 39328; phone: 601-743-2224; fax: 601-743-4173; hours 8AM-5PM (CST). *Felony, Civil Actions Over $2,500.*
Civil Records: Access: Phone, fax, mail, in person. Both court and visitors may perform in person searches. Search fee: $10.00 per name. Court makes copy: $.50 per page. Self serve copy fee: $.25 per page. Required to search: name, years to search, address. Civil cases indexed by defendant, plaintiff, on docket books since 1960s, archived since 1912. Mail turnaround time 1 week.
Criminal Records: Access: Fax, mail, in person. Both court and visitors may perform in person searches. Search fee: $10.00 per name. Court makes copy: $.50 per page. Self serve copy fee: $.25 per

page. Required to search: name, years to search, address, DOB; also helpful: SSN. Criminal records on docket books since 1960s, archived since 1912. Mail turnaround time 1 week.
General Information: No public access terminal. No sealed, adoptions, mental health, juvenile, sex, or expunged records released. Will fax documents $.25 per page. Certification fee: $1.00 per page. Payee: Circuit Clerk. Business checks accepted. Prepayment required. SASE requested.

Justice Court PO Box 661, De Kalb, MS 39328; phone: 601-743-2793; criminal phone: 601-743-2793; civil phone: 601-743-9933; fax: 601-743-4893; hours 8AM-5PM (CST). *Misdemeanor, Civil Actions Under $2,500, Eviction, Small Claims.*

Chancery Court PO Box 188, Main St, De Kalb, MS 39328; phone: 601-743-2460; fax: 601-743-2789; hours 8AM-5PM (CST). *Probate.*

Lafayette County

Circuit Court LaFayette County Courthouse, One Couerthouse Sq, #201, Oxford, MS 38655; phone: 662-234-4951; fax: 662-236-0238; hours 8AM-5PM (CST). *Felony, Civil Actions Over $2,500.*
Civil Records: Access: Mail, in person. Both court and visitors may perform in person searches. Search fee: $10.00 per name. Fee is per 10 years searched. Court makes copy: $1.00 per page. Required to search: name, years to search; also helpful: address. Civil cases indexed by defendant, plaintiff, on docket books from 1900; on computer back to 1997. Mail turnaround time next day.
Criminal Records: Access: Mail, in person. Both court and visitors may perform in person searches. Search fee: $10.00 per name. Fee is per 10 years searched. Court makes copy: $1.00 per page. Required to search: name, years to search, DOB; also helpful: address, SSN. Criminal records on docket books from 1900, on computer back to 1995. Mail turnaround time 1-2 days.
General Information: Public use terminal available. No sealed, adoptions, mental health, juvenile, or expunged records released. Will fax documents to local or toll free line. Certification fee: $1.50. Payee: Circuit Clerk. Business checks accepted. Prepayment required.

Justice Court 713 Jackson Ave E, Oxford, MS 38655; phone: 662-234-1545; fax: 662-238-7990; hours 8AM-5PM (CST). *Misdemeanor, Civil Actions Under $2,500, Eviction, Small Claims.*

Chancery Court PO Box 1240, 300 N Lamar Blvd, Oxford, MS 38655; phone: 662-234-2131; fax: 662-234-5038; hours 8AM-5PM (CST). *Probate.*

Lamar County

Circuit Court PO Box 369, Purvis, MS 39475; phone: 601-794-8504; fax: 601-794-3905; hours 8AM-5PM (CST). *Felony, Civil Actions Over $2,500.*
Civil Records: Access: Mail, in person. Both court and visitors may perform in person searches. Search fee: $10.00 per name. Court makes copy: $1.00 per page. Self serve copy fee: $.25 per page. Required to search: name, years to search. Civil cases indexed by defendant, plaintiff, on docket books since 1904. Mail turnaround time 1-2 days.
Criminal Records: Access: Mail, in person. Both court and visitors may perform in person searches. Search fee: $10.00 per name. Court makes copy: $1.00 per page. Self serve copy fee: $.25 per page. Required to search: name, years to search; also helpful: SSN. Criminal records on docket books since 1904. Mail turnaround time 1-2 days.
General Information: No public access terminal. No sealed, adoptions, mental health, juvenile, sex, or expunged records released. Will not fax documents. No certification fee . Payee: Circuit Clerk. Business checks accepted. Prepayment required. SASE requested.

Justice Court PO Box 1010, 205 Main St, #A, Purvis, MS 39475; phone: 601-794-2950; fax: 601-794-1076; hours 8AM-5PM (CST). *Misdemeanor, Civil Actions Under $2,500, Eviction, Small Claims.*

Chancery Court PO Box 247, 403 Main St, Purvis, MS 39475; phone: 601-794-8504; fax: 601-794-3903; hours 8AM-5PM (CST). *Probate, Domestic Relations.*

Lauderdale County

Circuit & County Court PO Box 1005, Meridian, MS 39302-1005; phone: 601-482-9738; fax: 601-484-3970; hours 8AM-5PM (CST). *Felony, Civil Actions Over $2,500.*
Note: County Court can be reached at 601-482-9715.
Civil Records: Access: Phone, mail, fax, in person. Both court and visitors may perform in person searches. Search fee: $10.00 per name. Court makes copy: $.50 per page. Self serve copy fee: $.25 per page. Required to search: name, years to search, SSN. Civil cases indexed by defendant, plaintiff, on docket books back to 1950s, on computer back to 1992. Court will only search computer records. Mail turnaround time 1 week.
Criminal Records: Access: Mail, fax, in person. Both court and visitors may perform in person searches. Search fee: $10.00 per name. Court makes copy: $.50 per page. Self serve copy fee: $.25 per page. Required to search: name, years to search, DOB; also helpful: SSN. Criminal records on computer (Felony) back to 1965. Mail turnaround time 1 week, phone turnaround is 1 week.
General Information: Public terminal has criminal back to 1965 and civil back to 1992. No sealed, adoptions, mental health, juvenile, sex, or expunged records released. Will fax documents to local or toll-free number. No certification fee . Payee: Circuit Clerk. Business checks accepted. Prepayment required. Will bill complete files to attorneys. SASE requested.

Justice Court PO Box 5126, Meridian, MS 39302; phone: 601-482-9879; fax: 601-482-9813; hours 8AM-5PM (CST). *Misdemeanor, Civil Actions Under $2,500, Eviction, Small Claims.*

Chancery Court PO Box 1587, 500 Constitution Ave, Meridian, MS 39302; phone: 601-482-9701; fax: 601-486-4921; hours 8AM-5PM (CST). *Probate.*

Lawrence County

Circuit Court PO Box 1249, Monticello, MS 39654; phone: 601-587-4791; fax: 601-587-0750; hours 8AM-5PM (CST). *Felony, Civil Actions Over $2,500.*
Civil Records: Access: Phone, fax, mail, in person. Both court and visitors may perform in person searches. Search fee: $10.00 per name. Court makes copy: $.25 per page. Self serve copy fee: none. Required to search: name, years to search; also helpful: address. Civil cases indexed by defendant, plaintiff, on docket books since 1977. For fax request send copy of check for fee. Mail turnaround time 1 week.
Criminal Records: Access: Phone, fax, mail, in person. Both court and visitors may perform in person searches. Search fee: $10.00 per name. Court makes copy: $.25 per page. Self serve copy fee: none. Required to search: name, years to search, DOB; also helpful: address, SSN. Criminal records on docket books since 1977. For fax request send copy of check for fee. Mail turnaround time 1 week, phone turnaround is 1-2 days.
General Information: No public access terminal. No sealed, adoptions, mental health, juvenile, sex, or expunged records released. Will fax documents $10.00 per doc. Certification fee: $1.50. Payee: Circuit Clerk. Personal checks accepted. Prepayment required. SASE requested.

Justice Court PO Box 903, 435 Brimson St, Monticello, MS 39654; phone: 601-587-7183, 587-4854; civil phone: 601-587-4854; fax: 601-587-0755; hours 8AM-5PM (CST). *Misdemeanor, Civil Actions Under $2,500, Eviction, Small Claims.*

Chancery Court PO Box 821, 517 E Broad St, Courthouse Sq, Monticello, MS 39654; phone: 601-587-7162; fax: 601-587-0767; hours 8AM-5PM (CST). *Probate.*

Leake County

Circuit Court PO Box 67, Carthage, MS 39051; phone: 601-267-8357; fax: 601-267-8889; hours 8AM-5PM (CST). *Felony, Civil Actions Over $2,500.*
Civil Records: Access: In person only. Visitors must perform in person searches themselves. Court makes copy: $.50 per page. Required to search: name, years to search. Civil cases indexed by defendant, plaintiff, on docket books since 1970s.
Criminal Records: Access: Mail, in person. Both court and visitors may perform in person searches. Search fee: $10.00 per name. Court makes copy: $.50 per page. Required to search: name, years to search, DOB; also helpful: SSN. Criminal records on docket books since 1977. Mail turnaround time 1-2 days.
General Information: Public terminal has only civil records. (Voting and Judgments only.) No sealed, adoptions, mental health, juvenile, sex, or expunged records released. Certification fee: $1.50. Payee: Circuit Clerk. Prepayment and SASE required.

Justice Court PO Box 69, 121 W Main St, Carthage, MS 39051; phone: 601-267-5677; fax: 601-267-6134; hours 8:00AM-5:00PM (CST). *Misdemeanor, Civil Actions Under $2,500, Eviction, Small Claims.*

Chancery Court PO Box 72, Carthage, MS 39051; phone: 601-267-7371/72; fax: 601-267-6137; hours 8AM-5PM (CST). *Probate.*

www.co.leake.ms.us/
Note: Records also include divorce, custody, land disputes, mental and drug commitments.

Lee County

Circuit & County Court Circuit Court - PO Box 762, County Court - PO Box 736, Tupelo, MS 38802; phone: 662-841-9022/9023(Circuit) 9730 (County); fax: 662-680-6079; hours 8AM-5PM (CST). *Felony, Civil Actions Over $2,500.*
Civil Records: Access: Mail, in person. Both court and visitors may perform in person searches. Search fee: $10.00 per name. Court makes copy: $.25 per page; same fee for self serve. Required to search: name, years to search. Civil cases indexed by defendant, plaintiff. Circuit records on computer since 1990, others on docket books since 1987. County records not on computer. Mail turnaround time 1-2 days.
Criminal Records: Access: Mail, in person. Both court and visitors may perform in person searches. Search fee: $10.00 per name. Court makes copy: $.25 per page; same fee for self serve. Required to search: name, years to search; also helpful: DOB, SSN. Circuit records on computer since 1990, others on docket books since 1987. County records not on computer. Mail turnaround time 1-2 days.
General Information: Public terminal goes back to 2003. No sealed or expunged records released. Certification fee: $1.50. Payee: Lee County & Circuit Court. Business checks accepted. Prepayment and SASE required.

Justice Court PO Box 108, 331 N Broadway St, Tupelo, MS 38802; phone: 662-841-9014; fax: 662-841-2960; hours 8AM-11;30, 12;30-5PM (CST). *Misdemeanor, Civil Actions Under $2,500, Eviction, Small Claims.*

Chancery Court PO Box 7127, 200 W Jefferson, Tupelo, MS 38802; phone: 662-841-9100; fax: 662-680-6091; hours 8AM-5PM (CST). *Probate.*

Leflore County

Circuit & County Court PO Box 1953, Greenwood, MS 38935-1953; phone: 662-453-1435; fax: 662-455-1278; hours 8AM-5PM (CST). *Felony, Civil Actions Over $2,500.*
Civil Records: Access: Phone, fax, mail, in person. Both court and visitors may perform in person searches. Search fee: $10.00 per name. Court makes copy: $1.00 per page. Self serve copy fee: $.50 per page. Required to search: name, years to search. Civil cases indexed by defendant, plaintiff, on computer index goes back 10 years; prior records on docket books since mid-1800s. There is a private company that permits online access to civil records. Go to www.recordsusa.com. User ID and password are both demo. Mail turnaround time 1-2 days.
Criminal Records: Access: Fax, mail, in person. Both court and visitors may perform in person searches. Search fee: $10.00 per name. Court makes copy: $1.00 per page. Self serve copy fee: $.50 per page. Required to search: name, years to search; also helpful: DOB, SSN. Criminal records on computer index goes back 10 years; prior records on docket books since mid-1800s. Mail turnaround time 1-2 days.
General Information: Public terminal goes back to 10 years. No sealed or expunged records released. Call for fax fee. Certification fee: $1.50. Payee: Circuit Clerk. Personal checks accepted. Prepayment required.

Justice Court PO Box 8056, 310 W Market St, Greenwood, MS 38935; phone: 662-453-1605; fax: 662-453-8759; hours 8AM-5PM (CST). *Misdemeanor, Civil Actions Under $2,500, Eviction, Small Claims.*

Chancery Court PO Box 1579, 310 W Market St, County Courthouse, Greenwood, MS 38935-1579; phone: 662-455-7910; fax: 662-455-7959; hours 8AM-5PM (CST). *Probate, Divorce.*

Lincoln County

Circuit Court PO Box 357, Brookhaven, MS 39602; phone: 601-835-3435; fax: 601-835-3482; hours 8AM-5PM (CST). *Felony, Civil Actions Over $2,500.*
Civil Records: Access: Fax, mail, in person. Both court and visitors may perform in person searches. Search fee: $10.00 per name. Court makes copy: $1.00 per page. Self serve copy fee: $.50 per page. Required to search: name, years to search. Civil cases indexed by defendant, plaintiff, on computer since 1986, prior on docket books. Mail turnaround time 1-2 days.
Criminal Records: Access: Fax, mail, in person. Both court and visitors may perform in person searches. Search fee: $10.00 per name. Court makes copy: $1.00 per page. Self serve copy fee: $.50 per page. Required to search: name, years to search; also helpful: DOB, SSN. Criminal records on computer since 1982, prior on docket books. Mail turnaround time 1-2 days.
General Information: Public terminal goes back to 1982. No sealed or expunged records released. Will fax documents $10.00 per doc. Certification fee: $1.00 per page includes copy. Payee: Circuit Clerk. Personal checks accepted. Out of state checks not accepted. Prepayment required.

Justice Court PO Box 767, Brookhaven, MS 39602; phone: 601-835-3474; fax: 601-835-3494; hours 8:00AM-5:00PM (CST). *Misdemeanor, Civil Actions Under $2,500, Eviction, Small Claims.*

Chancery Court PO Box 555, 300 S First St, Brookhaven, MS 39602; phone: 601-835-3412; fax: 601-835-3423; hours 8AM-5PM (CST). *Probate.*
www.15thchancerydistrictms.org

Lowndes County

Circuit & County Court PO Box 31, Columbus, MS 39703; phone: 662-329-5900; hours 8AM-5PM (CST). *Felony, Civil.*
Civil Records: Access: Mail, in person. Both court and visitors may perform in person searches. Search fee: $10.00 per name. Court makes copy: $1.00 per page. Required to search: name, years to search. Civil cases indexed by defendant, plaintiff, on computer from 2/94, on docket books from 1900s. Mail turnaround time 7 to 14 days.
Criminal Records: Access: Mail, in person. Both court and visitors may perform in person searches. Search fee: $10.00 per name. Court makes copy: $1.00 per page. Required to search: name, years to search, DOB; also helpful: SSN. Criminal records on computer since 11/93; prior on docket books. Mail turnaround time 14 days.
General Information: Public use terminal available. No sealed, adoption, mental health, juvenile, sex or expunged cases released. Will fax documents to local or toll free line. Certification fee: $1.00. Payee: Clerk of Court. Personal checks accepted. Prepayment and SASE required.

Justice Court 11 Airline Rd, Columbus, MS 39702; phone: 662-329-5929; fax: 662-245-4619; hours 8AM-5PM (CST). *Misdemeanor, Civil Actions Under $2,500, Eviction, Small Claims.*

Chancery Court PO Box 684, 515 2nd Ave North, Columbus, MS 39703; phone: 662-329-5800; hours 8AM-5PM (CST). *Probate.*

Madison County

Circuit & County Court PO Box 1626, Canton, MS 39046; phone: 601-859-4365; fax: 601-859-8555; hours 8AM-5PM (CST). *Felony, Civil.*
Civil Records: Access: Phone, fax, mail, in person. Both court and visitors may perform in person searches. No search fee. Court makes copy: $.50 per page. Self serve copy fee: $.25 per page. Required to search: name, years to search. Civil cases indexed by defendant, plaintiff, on computer since 1987, prior on docket books since 1950. Mail turnaround time 1 week.
Criminal Records: Access: Mail, in person. Both court and visitors may perform in person searches. Search fee: $10.00 per name. Court makes copy: $.50 per page. Self serve copy fee: $.25 per page. Required to search: name, years to search. Criminal records on computer since 1992, prior on docket books since 1945. Mail turnaround time 1 week.
General Information: Public terminal has criminal back to 1984 and civil back to 1989. No sealed, adoptions, mental health, juvenile, sex, or expunged records released. Will fax documents to local or toll free line. Certification fee: $1.50. Payee: Circuit Clerk. Personal checks accepted. Prepayment required. SASE requested.

Justice Court 175 N Union, Canton, MS 39046; phone: 601-859-6337; fax: 601-859-5878; hours 8AM-5PM (CST). *Misdemeanor, Civil Actions Under $2,500, Eviction, Small Claims.*
Note: Request for history must be in writing with a $6.00 fee made out to Madison County Justice Court.

Chancery Court PO Box 404, 146 W Center St, Canton, MS 39046; phone: 601-859-1177; fax: 601-855-5759; hours 8AM-5PM (CST). *Probate.*

Marion County

Circuit Court 250 Broad St, #1, Columbia, MS 39429; phone: 601-736-8246; hours 8AM-5PM (CST). *Felony, Civil Actions Over $2,500.*
Civil Records: Access: Mail, in person. Both court and visitors may perform in person searches. Search fee: $10.00 per name. Court makes copy: $.50 per page. Self serve copy fee: $.25 per page. Required to search: name, years to search. Civil cases indexed by defendant, plaintiff, on docket books since 1800s. Mail turnaround time 3 days.

Criminal Records: Access: Mail, in person, fax. Both court and visitors may perform in person searches. Search fee: $10.00 per name. Court makes copy: $.50 per page. Self serve copy fee: $.25 per page. Required to search: name, years to search; also helpful: SSN. Criminal records on docket books since 1800s. Mail turnaround time 1-2 days.
General Information: No public access terminal. No sealed, adoptions, mental health, juvenile, sex, or expunged records released. Will fax documents to local or toll free line. No certification fee . Payee: Circuit Clerk. Personal checks accepted. Prepayment and SASE required.

Justice Court 500 Courthouse Square #2, Columbia, MS 39429; phone: 601-736-2572; fax: 601-731-3781; hours 8AM-5PM (CST). *Misdemeanor, Civil Actions Under $2,500, Eviction, Small Claims.*

Chancery Court 250 Broad St, #2, Columbia, MS 39429; phone: 601-444-0205; civil phone: 601-736-2691; fax: 601-444-0206; hours 8AM-5PM (CST). *Probate.*
Note: Court records and calendars online at www.deltacomputersystems.com/MS/MS46/INDEX.html.

Marshall County

Circuit Court PO Box 459, Holly Springs, MS 38635; phone: 662-252-3434; fax: 662-252-5951; hours 8AM-5PM (CST). *Felony, Civil Actions Over $2,500.*
Note: Fax requests- include copy of payment check.
Civil Records: Access: Fax, mail, in person. Both court and visitors may perform in person searches. Search fee: $10.00 per name. Court makes copy: $1.00 per page. Self serve copy fee: $.50 per page. Required to search: name, years to search. Civil cases indexed by defendant, plaintiff, on docket books since 1960s; computerized records go back to 1999. Mail turnaround time 1-2 days.
Criminal Records: Access: Fax, mail, in person, fax. Both court and visitors may perform in person searches. Search fee: $10.00 per name. Court makes copy: $1.00 per page. Self serve copy fee: $.50 per page. Required to search: name, years to search; also helpful: DOB, SSN. Criminal records on docket books since 1960s; computerized records go back to 1999. Mail turnaround time 1-2 days.
General Information: Public terminal goes back to 1999. No sealed or expunged records released. No fee to fax documents. Fax copy of your search fee check. Certification fee: $3.50 per cert. Payee: Circuit Court Clerk. Personal checks accepted. Prepayment required. SASE requested.

Justice Court - North & South Districts PO Box 729, 819 West St, Holly Springs, MS 38635; phone: 662-252-3585; fax: 662-252-0028; hours 8AM-5PM (CST). *Misdemeanor, Civil Actions Under $2,500, Eviction, Small Claims.*

Chancery Court PO Box 219, Court Sq, Holly Springs, MS 38635; phone: 662-252-4431; fax: 662-252-3306; hours 8AM-5PM (CST). *Probate.*

Monroe County

Circuit Court PO Box 843, Aberdeen, MS 39730; phone: 662-369-2732; fax: 662-319-5993; hours 8AM-5PM (CST). *Felony, Civil Actions Over $2,500.*
Civil Records: Access: In person only. Visitors must perform in person searches themselves. Court makes copy: $1.00 per page. Self serve copy fee: $.25 per page. Required to search: name, years to search; also helpful: address. Civil cases indexed by defendant, plaintiff, on docket books since 1821.
Criminal Records: Access: In person only. Visitors must perform in person searches themselves. Court makes copy: $1.00 per page. Self serve copy fee: $.25 per page. Required to search: name, years to search, DOB; also helpful: address, SSN. Criminal records on docket books since 1821.

General Information: No public access terminal. No sealed, adoptions, mental health, juvenile, sex, or expunged records released. Will not fax specific case file. Certification fee: $3.00. Payee: Monroe County Circuit Clerk. Only cashiers checks and money orders accepted. Prepayment required.

Justice Court - District 2 PO Box 518, 1619 Hwy 25 N, Amory, MS 38821; phone: 662-256-8493; fax: 662-256-7876; hours 8AM-5PM (CST). *Misdemeanor, Civil Actions Under $2,500, Eviction, Small Claims.*
Note: Aberdeen Justice Court Dist. 2 is closed; records here.

Chancery Court PO Box 578, 201 W Commerce St, Aberdeen, MS 39730; phone: 662-369-8143; fax: 662-369-7928; hours 8AM-5PM (CST). *Probate.*

Montgomery County

Circuit Court PO Box 765, Winona, MS 38967; phone: 662-283-4161; fax: 662-283-3363; hours 8AM-5PM (CST). *Felony, Civil Actions Over $2,500.*
Civil Records: Access: Mail, in person. Both court and visitors may perform in person searches. Search fee: $10.00 per name. Court makes copy: $1.00 per page. Self serve copy fee: $.25 per page. Required to search: name, years to search. Civil cases indexed by defendant, plaintiff, on docket books since early 1900s. Mail turnaround time 1-2 days.
Criminal Records: Access: Mail, in person. Both court and visitors may perform in person searches. Search fee: $10.00 per name. Court makes copy: $1.00 per page. Self serve copy fee: $.25 per page. Required to search: name, years to search. Criminal records on docket books since early 1900s. Mail turnaround time 1-2 days.
General Information: No public access terminal. No sealed or expunged records released. Will fax documents to local or toll free line. Certification fee: $2.00. Payee: Circuit Clerk. Personal checks accepted. Prepayment and SASE required.

Justice Court PO Box 229, 614 Summit St, Winona, MS 38967; phone: 662-283-2290; fax: 662-283-2233; hours 8AM-5PM (CST). *Misdemeanor, Civil Actions Under $2,500, Eviction, Small Claims.*

Chancery Court PO Box 71, 614 Summit St, Winona, MS 38967; phone: 662-283-2333; fax: 662-283-2233; hours 8AM-5PM (CST). *Probate.*

Neshoba County

Circuit Court 401 E Beacon St #110, Philadelphia, MS 39350; phone: 601-656-4781; fax: 601-650-3997; hours 8AM-5PM (CST). *Felony, Civil Actions Over $2,500.*
Civil Records: Access: Mail, in person. Both court and visitors may perform in person searches. Search fee: $10.00 per name. Court makes copy: $.50 per page. Required to search: name, years to search. Civil cases indexed by defendant. Civil records in-house back 10 years; indexed back 50 years. Mail turnaround time 1-2 days.
Criminal Records: Access: Mail, in person. Both court and visitors may perform in person searches. Search fee: $10.00 per name. Court makes copy: $.50 per page. Required to search: name, years to search, DOB; also helpful: SSN. Criminal records in-house back 20 years; on docket books back 50 years. Mail turnaround time 1-2 days.
General Information: No public access terminal. No sealed, adoptions, mental health, juvenile, sex, or expunged records released. Will fax documents. Certification fee: $2.00. Payee: Circuit Clerk. Business checks accepted. Prepayment required. SASE requested.

Justice Court 200 Byrd Ave, Philadelphia, MS 39350; phone: 601-656-5361/1101; fax: 601-656-6482; hours 8AM-5PM (CST). *Misdemeanor, Civil Actions Under $2,500, Eviction, Small Claims.*

Chancery Court 401 Beacon St #107, Philadelphia, MS 39350; phone: 601-656-3581; fax: 601-656-5915; hours 8AM-5PM (CST). *Probate.*

Newton County

Circuit Court PO Box 447, Decatur, MS 39327; phone: 601-635-2368; fax: 601-635-3210; hours 8AM-5PM (CST). *Felony, Civil Actions Over $2,500.*
Civil Records: Access: Mail, in person. Both court and visitors may perform in person searches. Search fee: $10.00 per name. Court makes copy: $.50 per page. Self serve copy fee: $.25 per page. Required to search: name, years to search. Civil cases indexed by defendant, plaintiff, on docket books since 1968. Mail turnaround time same day.
Criminal Records: Access: Mail, in person. Both court and visitors may perform in person searches. Search fee: $10.00 per name. Court makes copy: $.50 per page. Self serve copy fee: $.25 per page. Required to search: name, years to search, DOB; also helpful: SSN. Criminal records on docket books since 1968. Mail turnaround time same day.
General Information: Public terminal goes back to 2003. No sealed, adoptions, mental health, juvenile, sex, or expunged records released. Will fax documents to local or toll free line. Certification fee: $1.50 per cert. Payee: Circuit Court. Personal checks accepted. Prepayment and SASE required.

Justice Court PO Box 69, 11 4th Ave, Decatur, MS 39327; phone: 601-635-2740; fax: 601-635-4047; hours 8AM-5PM (CST). *Misdemeanor, Civil Actions Under $2,500, Eviction, Small Claims.*

Chancery Clerk Office PO Box 68, 92 W Broad St, Decatur, MS 39327; phone: 601-635-2367; civil phone: 601-635-3370; fax: 601-635-3479; hours 8AM-5PM (CST). *Probate.*

Noxubee County

Circuit Court PO Box 431, Macon, MS 39341; phone: 662-726-5737; fax: 662-726-4166; hours 8AM-5PM (CST). *Felony, Civil Actions Over $2,500.*
Civil Records: Access: Mail, fax, in person. Both court and visitors may perform in person searches. Search fee: $10.00 per name. Court makes copy: $.50 per page. Self serve copy fee: $.25 per page. Required to search: name, years to search. Civil cases indexed by defendant. Civil records on docket books since 1800s. Mail turnaround time 1 week.
Criminal Records: Access: Mail, fax, in person. Both court and visitors may perform in person searches. Search fee: $10.00 per name. Court makes copy: $.50 per page. Self serve copy fee: $.25 per page. Required to search: name, years to search; also helpful: SSN. Criminal records on docket books since 1800s. Mail turnaround time 1 week.
General Information: Public terminal has criminal back to 1965 and civil back to 1970. No sealed, adoptions, mental health, juvenile, sex, or expunged records released. Certification fee: $5.00. Payee: Circuit Clerk. Business checks accepted. Prepayment and SASE required.

Justice Court - North & South Districts 507 S Jefferson, PO Box 550, Macon, MS 39341; phone: 662-726-5834; fax: 662-726-2944; hours 8AM-5PM (CST). *Misdemeanor, Civil Actions Under $2,500, Eviction, Small Claims.*

Chancery Court PO Box 147, Macon, MS 39341; phone: 662-726-4243; fax: 662-726-2272; hours 8AM-5PM (CST). *Probate.*

Oktibbeha County

Circuit Court Courthouse, 101 E Main, Starkville, MS 39759; phone: 662-323-1356; fax: 662-323-1400; hours 8AM-5PM (CST). *Felony, Civil Actions Over $2,500.*
Civil Records: Access: Mail, fax, in person. Both court and visitors may perform in person searches. Search fee: $10.00 per name. Court makes copy: $1.00 per page. Self serve copy fee: $.50 per page.

Required to search: name, years to search; also helpful: address. Civil cases indexed by defendant, plaintiff, on docket books since 1938. Mail turnaround time 1 week.

Criminal Records: Access: Mail, fax, in person. Both court and visitors may perform in person searches. Search fee: $10.00 per name. Court makes copy: $1.00 per page. Self serve copy fee: $.50 per page. Required to search: name, years to search; also helpful: DOB, SSN. Criminal records on docket since 1950. Mail turnaround time 1 week.

General Information: Public terminal has criminal back to 1997 and civil back to 1990. No sealed, adoptions, mental health, juvenile, sex, or expunged records released. Certification fee: $1.50. Payee: Circuit Clerk. Personal checks accepted. Prepayment and SASE required.

Justice Court - Districts 1-3 104 Felix Long Dr, Starkville, MS 39759; phone: 662-324-3032; criminal phone: 662-324-3040; fax: 662-338-1078; hours 8AM-5PM (CST). *Misdemeanor, Civil Actions Under $2,500, Eviction, Small Claims.*

Chancery Court Courthouse, 101 E Main, Starkville, MS 39759; phone: 662-323-5834; fax: 662-338-1064; hours 8AM-5PM (CST). *Probate.*

Panola County

Circuit Court - 1st District PO Box 130, 215 S Pocahontas St, Sardis, MS 38666; phone: 662-487-2073; fax: 662-487-3595; hours 8AM-5PM (CST). *Felony, Civil Actions Over $2,500.*

Civil Records: Access: Fax, mail, in person. Both court and visitors may perform in person searches. Search fee: $10.00 per name. Fee is for each district searched. Court makes copy: $.50 per page. Required to search: name, years to search. Civil cases indexed by defendant, plaintiff, on docket books since 1970s, archived since 1925. Mail turnaround time 1-2 days.

Criminal Records: Access: Fax, mail, in person. Both court and visitors may perform in person searches. Search fee: $10.00 per name. Fee is for each district searched. Court makes copy: $.50 per page. Required to search: name, years to search, DOB; also helpful: SSN. Criminal records on docket books since 1970, archived since 1925, records are not computerized. Mail turnaround time 1-2 days.

General Information: No public access terminal. No sealed, adoptions, mental health, juvenile, sex, or expunged records released. No fee to fax documents. Fax copy of your search fee check. Certification fee: $1.50. Payee: Circuit Clerk. Business checks accepted. Prepayment and SASE required.

Circuit Court - 2nd District PO Box 346, Batesville, MS 38606; phone: 662-563-6210; fax: 662-563-8233; hours 8AM-5PM (CST). *Felony, Civil Actions Over $2,500.*

Civil Records: Access: Phone, fax, mail, in person. Both court and visitors may perform in person searches. Search fee: $10.00 per name. Fee is per district. Court makes copy: $.50 per page. Self serve copy fee: $.25 per page. Required to search: name, years to search. Civil cases indexed by defendant, plaintiff, on docket books since 1900. Mail turnaround time same day.

Criminal Records: Access: Fax, mail, in person. Both court and visitors may perform in person searches. Search fee: $10.00 per name. Fee is per district. Court makes copy: $1.00 per page. Self serve copy fee: $.25 per page. Required to search: name, years to search, address, DOB; also helpful: SSN. Criminal records on docket books since 1900. Mail turnaround time same day.

General Information: Public terminal goes back to 2004. No sealed, adoptions, mental health, juvenile, sex, or expunged records released. Will fax documents $1.00 per page. Certification fee: $10.00. Payee: Circuit Clerk's Office. Personal checks accepted. Prepayment and SASE required.

Justice Court PO Box 249, 2155 Pocohontas, Sardis, MS 38666; phone: 662-487-2080; criminal phone: 662-487-2080; civil phone: 662-487-2082; fax: 662-487-2008; hours 8AM-5PM (CST). *Misdemeanor, Civil Actions Under $2,500, Eviction, Small Claims.*

Note: This Justice Court houses all the Justices for Panola County.

Panola County Chancery Clerk 151 Public Square, Batesville, MS 38606; phone: 662-563-6205; fax: 662-563-6277; hours 8AM-5PM (CST). *Probate.*

Sardis Chancery Court 215 S Pocahontas St, Sardis, MS 38666; phone: 662-487-2070; fax: 662-487-3559; hours 8AM-N, 1-5PM (CST). *Probate.*

Pearl River County

Circuit Court Courthouse, Poplarville, MS 39470; phone: 601-403-2300; criminal phone: x323; civil phone: Ext 324; fax: 601-403-2327; hours 8AM-5PM (CST). *Felony, All Civil Actions.*

Civil Records: Access: Mail, fax, in person. Both court and visitors may perform in person searches. Search fee: $10.00 per name. Court makes copy: $1.00 per page. Self serve copy fee: $.50 per page. Required to search: name, years to search, DOB, SSN. Civil cases indexed by defendant, plaintiff, on docket books since 1890. Mail turnaround time 1-2 days.

Criminal Records: Access: Mail, fax, in person. Both court and visitors may perform in person searches. Search fee: $10.00 per name. Court makes copy: $1.00 per page. Self serve copy fee: $.50 per page. Required to search: name, years to search. Criminal records on computer since late 1960s, prior on docket books since 1890. Mail turnaround time 1-2 days.

General Information: Public terminal goes back to 2003. No sealed, adoptions, mental health, juvenile, sex, or expunged records released. Will fax documents to local or toll free line. Certification fee: $2.50. Payee: Circuit Clerk. Personal checks accepted. Prepayment required.

Justice Court - Northern, Southeastern & Southwestern Districts 204 Julia St, Poplarville, MS 39470; phone: 601-403-2300; fax: 601-403-2364; hours 8AM-5PM (CST). *Misdemeanor, Civil Actions Under $2,500, Eviction, Small Claims.*

Chancery Court PO Box 431, Poplarville, MS 39470; phone: 601-403-2300 X316; fax: 601-403-2317; hours 8AM-5PM (CST). *Probate.*

Perry County

Circuit Court PO Box 198, New Augusta, MS 39462; phone: 601-964-8663; fax: 601-964-8740; hours 8AM-5PM (CST). *Felony, Civil Actions Over $2,500.*

Civil Records: Access: Mail, fax, in person. Both court and visitors may perform in person searches. Search fee: $10.00 per name. Fee is per 10 years searched. Court makes copy: $.50 per page. Self serve copy fee: $.25 per page. Required to search: name, years to search. Civil cases indexed by defendant, plaintiff, on docket books since 1980. Mail turnaround time 1-2 days.

Criminal Records: Access: Mail, fax, in person. Both court and visitors may perform in person searches. Search fee: $10.00 per name. Fee is per 10 years searched. Court makes copy: $.50 per page. Self serve copy fee: $.25 per page. Required to search: name, years to search, DOB; also helpful: SSN, sex, signed release. Criminal records on docket books since 1971; on computer since. Mail turnaround time 1-2 days.

General Information: No public access terminal. No sealed, adoptions, mental health, juvenile, sex, or expunged records released. Will fax documents to local or toll free line. Certification fee: $2.50 per document. Payee: Circuit Clerk. Personal checks accepted. Prepayment required.

Justice Court PO Box 455, 103 1st St W, New Augusta, MS 39462; phone: 601-964-8366; fax: 601-964-8368; hours 8AM-5PM (CST). *Misdemeanor, Civil Actions Under $2,500, Eviction, Small Claims.*

Chancery Court PO Box 198, 103 Main St, New Augusta, MS 39462; phone: 601-964-8398; fax: 601-964-8746; hours 8AM-5PM (CST). *Probate.*

Pike County

Circuit & County Court PO Drawer 31, Magnolia, MS 39652; phone: 601-783-2581; fax: 601-783-6322; hours 8AM-5PM (CST). *Felony, Civil.*

Civil Records: Access: Fax, mail, in person. Both court and visitors may perform in person searches. Search fee: $6.00 per name. Court makes copy: $1.00 per page. Required to search: name, years to search. Civil cases indexed by defendant, plaintiff, on docket books since 1950s; on computer from 2000 to present. Mail turnaround time 1-2 days.

Criminal Records: Access: Fax, mail, in person. Both court and visitors may perform in person searches. Search fee: $6.00 per name. Court makes copy: $1.00 per page. Required to search: name, years to search, DOB; also helpful: SSN. Criminal records on docket books and computerized since 1960s. Mail turnaround time 1-2 days.

General Information: Public terminal goes back to 1971. No sealed, adoptions, mental health, juvenile, sex, or expunged records released. Certification fee: $1.50 per cert. Payee: Circuit Clerk. Personal checks accepted. Prepayment and SASE required.

Justice Court - Divisions 1-3 PO Box 509, 2109 Jesse Hall Memorial Dr, Magnolia, MS 39652; phone: 601-783-5333; fax: 601-783-4181; hours 8AM-5PM (CST). *Misdemeanor, Civil Actions Under $2,500, Eviction, Small Claims.*

Chancery Court PO Box 309, 175 S Cherry St, Magnolia, MS 39652; phone: 601-783-3362; fax: 601-783-5982; hours 8AM-5PM (CST). *Probate, Civil, Divorce.*

Pontotoc County

Circuit Court PO Box 428, Pontotoc, MS 38863; phone: 662-489-3908; hours 8AM-5PM (CST). *Felony, Civil Actions Over $2,500.*

Civil Records: Access: Mail, in person. Both court and visitors may perform in person searches. Search fee: $5.00 per name. Court makes copy: $.50 per page; same fee for self serve. Required to search: name, years to search. Civil cases indexed by defendant, plaintiff, on books from 1849. Mail turnaround time 1 week.

Criminal Records: Access: Mail, in person. Both court and visitors may perform in person searches. Search fee: $5.00 per name. Court makes copy: $.50 per page; same fee for self serve. Required to search: name, years to search, DOB; also helpful: SSN. Criminal records on books from 1849. Records are not computerized. Mail turnaround time 1 week.

General Information: Public terminal goes back to 2003. No sealed, adoptions, mental health, juvenile, sex, or expunged records released. Will fax documents to local or toll free line. No certification fee . Payee: Circuit Clerk. Prepayment and SASE required.

Justice Court - East & West Districts 29 E Washington St, Pontotoc, MS 38863-2923; phone: 662-489-3920; fax: 662-488-2986; hours 8AM-5PM (CST). *Misdemeanor, Civil Actions Under $2,500, Eviction, Small Claims.*

Chancery Court PO Box 209, 34 S Liberty, Pontotoc, MS 38863; phone: 662-489-3900; fax: 662-489-3940; hours 8AM-5PM (CST). *Probate.*

Prentiss County

Circuit Court PO Box 727, 101 N Main St, Booneville, MS 38829; phone: 662-728-4611; fax: 662-728-2006; hours 8AM-5PM (CST). *Felony, Civil Actions Over $2,500.*
Civil Records: Access: Mail, in person. Both court and visitors may perform in person searches. Search fee: $10.00 per name. Court makes copy: $.50 per page. Self serve copy fee: $.25 per page. Required to search: name, years to search. Civil cases indexed by defendant, plaintiff, on docket books; judgments only on computer since 1985. Mail turnaround time varies.
Criminal Records: Access: Fax, mail, in person. Both court and visitors may perform in person searches. Search fee: $10.00 per name. Court makes copy: $.50 per page. Self serve copy fee: $.25 per page. Required to search: name, years to search; also helpful: DOB, SSN. Criminal records on docket books. Prepaid account is required for fax access. Mail turnaround time varies.
General Information: No public access terminal. No sealed, adoptions, mental health, juvenile, sex, or expunged records released. Will fax documents. Certification fee: $2.00. Payee: Circuit Clerk. Personal checks accepted. Billing accounts available. SASE required.

Justice Court 1901C E Chambers Dr, Booneville, MS 38829; phone: 662-728-8696; civil phone: 662-728-2011; fax: 662-728-2009; hours 8AM-5PM (CST). *Misdemeanor, Civil Actions Under $2,500, Eviction, Small Claims.*

Chancery Court PO Box 477, 100 N Main, Booneville, MS 38829; phone: 662-728-8151; fax: 662-728-2007; hours 8AM-5PM (CST). *Probate.*

Quitman County

Circuit Court Courthouse, 230 Chestnut St, Marks, MS 38646; phone: 662-326-8003; fax: 662-326-8004; hours 8AM-5PM (CST). *Felony, Civil Actions Over $2,500.*
Civil Records: Access: Fax, mail, in person. Both court and visitors may perform in person searches. Search fee: $10.00 per name. Court makes copy: $.50 per page. Self serve copy fee: $.25 per page. Required to search: name, years to search. Civil cases indexed by defendant, plaintiff, on books and files since 1890. Mail turnaround time 2 days; phone results 10 minutes.
Criminal Records: Access: Fax, mail, in person. Both court and visitors may perform in person searches. Search fee: $10.00 per name. Court makes copy: $.50 per page. Self serve copy fee: $.25 per page. Required to search: name, years to search; DOB; also helpful: SSN. Criminal records on books and files since 1890. Mail turnaround time 2 days; phone results 10 minutes.
General Information: No public access terminal. No sealed, adoptions, mental health, juvenile, sex, or expunged records released. No fax fee when $10.00 has been paid. Certification fee: $1.50 per document. Payee: Circuit Clerk. Business checks accepted. Prepayment required.

Justice Court - Districts 1 & 2 PO Box 100, 275 E Main St, Marks, MS 38646; phone: 662-326-2104/7906; fax: 662-326-2330; hours 8AM-5PM (CST). *Misdemeanor, Civil Actions Under $2,500, Eviction, Small Claims.*

Chancery Court 230 Chestnut St, Marks, MS 38646; phone: 662-326-2661; fax: 662-326-8004; hours 8AM-N, 1-5PM (CST). *Probate.*

Rankin County

Circuit & County Court PO Drawer 1599, Brandon, MS 39043; criminal phone: 601-825-2401; civil phone: 601-825-1466; criminal fax: 601-825-2582; civil fax: 601-825-1465; hours 8AM-5PM (CST). *Felony, Misdemeanor, Civil.*
www.rankincounty.org

Civil Records: Access: Mail, in person. Both court and visitors may perform in person searches. Search fee: $10.00 per name. Court makes copy: $1.00 per page. Self serve copy fee: $.25 per page. Required to search: name, years to search. Civil cases indexed by defendant, plaintiff, on computer since 1990, prior on docket books. Mail turnaround time 1-2 days.
Criminal Records: Access: Mail, in person. Both court and visitors may perform in person searches. Search fee: $10.00 per name. Court makes copy: $1.00 per page. Self serve copy fee: $.25 per page. Required to search: name, years to search; also helpful: DOB, SSN. Criminal records on computer since 1990, prior on docket books. Mail turnaround time 1-2 days.
General Information: Public terminal goes back to 1990. No sealed or expunged records released. Will fax documents to local or toll free line. Certification fee: $1.50. Payee: Circuit Clerk. Personal checks accepted. Prepayment required.

Justice Court - Districts 1-4 117 N. Timber, Brandon, MS 39042; phone: 601-824-2665; fax: 601-824-2668; hours 8AM-5PM (CST). *Misdemeanor, Civil Actions Under $2,500, Eviction, Small Claims.*
www.rankincounty.org

Chancery Court 203 Town Sq, PO Box 700, Brandon, MS 39042; phone: 601-825-1649; fax: 601-824-2450; hours 8AM-5PM (CST). *Probate, Civil.*
www.rankincounty.org

Scott County

Circuit Court PO Box 371, Forest, MS 39074; phone: 601-469-3601; hours 8AM-5PM (CST). *Felony, Civil Actions Over $2,500.*
Note: The court began computerization of records in 2002.
Civil Records: Access: Mail, in person. Both court and visitors may perform in person searches. Search fee: $10.00 per name. Fee is for 7 year search. Court makes copy: $.50 per page. Self serve copy fee: $.25 per page. Required to search: name, years to search. Civil cases indexed by defendant, plaintiff, on docket books since 1865. Mail turnaround time 1 week.
Criminal Records: Access: Mail, in person. Both court and visitors may perform in person searches. Search fee: $10.00 per name. Fee is for 7 year search. Court makes copy: $.50 per page. Self serve copy fee: $.25 per page. Required to search: name, years to search, DOB; also helpful: SSN. Criminal records on docket books since 1865. Mail turnaround time 1 week.
General Information: Public use terminal available. No sealed, adoptions, mental health, juvenile, sex, or expunged records released. Will fax documents to local or toll free line. Certification fee: $1.50 per page. Payee: Circuit Clerk. Personal checks accepted. Prepayment and SASE required.

Justice Court PO Box 371, 100 Main St, Forest, MS 39074; phone: 601-469-4555; fax: 601-469-5193; hours 8AM-5PM (CST). *Misdemeanor, Civil Actions Under $2,500, Eviction, Small Claims.*

Chancery Court 100 Main St, PO Box 630, Forest, MS 39074; phone: 601-469-1922, 601-469-1927; fax: 601-469-5180; hours 8AM-5PM (CST). *Probate.*

Sharkey County

Circuit Court PO Box 218 (400 Locust St), Rolling Fork, MS 39159; phone: 662-873-2766; criminal phone: 662-873-2755; civil phone: 662-873-2755; fax: 662-873-6045; hours 8AM-N, 1-5PM (CST). *Felony, Civil Actions Over $2,500.*
Civil Records: Access: Fax, mail, in person. Both court and visitors may perform in person searches. Search fee: $10.00 per name. Court makes copy: $.50 per page. Self serve copy fee: $.25 per page. Required to search: name, years to search. Civil cases indexed

by defendant, plaintiff, on docket books since 1893. Mail turnaround time 1 week.
Criminal Records: Access: Fax, mail, in person. Both court and visitors may perform in person searches. Search fee: $10.00 per name. Court makes copy: $.50 per page. Self serve copy fee: $.25 per page. Required to search: name, years to search, DOB; also helpful: SSN. Criminal records on docket books since 1893. Mail turnaround time 1 week.
General Information: No public access terminal. No sealed, adoptions, mental health, juvenile, sex, or expunged records released. Fee to fax documents is $1.00 per page. Certification fee: $2.00 per document. Payee: Circuit Clerk. Business checks accepted. Prepayment required.

Justice Court PO Box 235, 110 Locust St, Rolling Fork, MS 39159; phone: 662-873-6140; fax: 662-873-0154; hours 8AM-N, 1-5PM (CST). *Misdemeanor, Civil Actions Under $2,500, Eviction, Small Claims.*

Chancery Court 120 Locust St, PO Box 218, Rolling Fork, MS 39159; phone: 662-873-2755; fax: 662-873-6045; hours 8AM-N,1-5PM (CST). *Probate.*

Simpson County

Circuit Court PO Box 307, Mendenhall, MS 39114; phone: 601-847-2474; fax: 601-847-4011; hours 8AM-5PM (CST). *Felony, Civil Actions Over $2,500.*
Civil Records: Access: Fax, mail, in person. Both court and visitors may perform in person searches. Search fee: $10.00 per name. Court makes copy: $.50 per page. Self serve copy fee: $.25 per page. Required to search: name, years to search. Civil cases indexed by defendant, plaintiff, on docket books since 1978. Mail turnaround time 1-2 days.
Criminal Records: Access: Fax, mail, in person. Both court and visitors may perform in person searches. Search fee: $10.00 per name. Court makes copy: $.50 per page. Self serve copy fee: $.25 per page. Required to search: name, years to search; also helpful: DOB, SSN. Criminal records on docket books since 1978. Mail turnaround time 1-2 days.
General Information: No public access terminal. No sealed or expunged records released. No fee to fax documents. Certification fee: $1.50 per page. Payee: Circuit Clerk. Business checks accepted. Prepayment required.

Justice Court 1498 Simpson Highway, 149, Mendenhall, MS 39114; phone: 601-847-5848; fax: 601-847-5856; hours 8AM-4;45PM (CST). *Misdemeanor, Civil Actions Under $2,500, Eviction, Small Claims.*

Chancery Court PO Box 367, 111 W Pine, Mendenhall, MS 39114; phone: 601-847-2626; fax: 601-847-7016; hours 8AM-5PM (CST). *Probate.*

Smith County

Circuit Court PO Box 517, Raleigh, MS 39153; phone: 601-782-4751; fax: 601-782-4007; hours 8AM-5PM (CST). *Felony, Civil Actions Over $2,500.*
Civil Records: Access: Mail, in person. Both court and visitors may perform in person searches. Search fee: $10.00 per name. Court makes copy: $1.00 per page. Self serve copy fee: $.25 per page. Required to search: name, years to search. Civil cases indexed by defendant, plaintiff, on docket books since 1912. Mail turnaround time 2 days.
Criminal Records: Access: Mail, in person. Both court and visitors may perform in person searches. Search fee: $10.00 per name. Court makes copy: $1.00 per page. Self serve copy fee: $.25 per page. Required to search: name, years to search, DOB; also helpful: SSN. Criminal records on docket books since 1912. Mail turnaround time 2 days.
General Information: No public access terminal. No sealed or expunged records released. Fee to fax documents is $3.00 1st page, $.50 each add'l. Certification fee: $5.00 per document. Payee: Circuit

Clerk. Personal checks accepted. Prepayment and SASE required.

Justice Court PO Box 171, 212 Sylverena Ave #4, Raleigh, MS 39153; phone: 601-782-4334; fax: 601-782-4005; hours 8AM-5PM (CST). *Misdemeanor, Civil Actions Under $2,500, Eviction, Small Claims.*

Chancery Court 123 Main St, PO Box 39, Raleigh, MS 39153; phone: 601-782-9811; fax: 601-782-4690; hours 8AM-5PM (CST). *Probate.*

Stone County

Circuit Court Courthouse, 323 Cavers Ave, Wiggins, MS 39577; phone: 601-928-5246; fax: 601-928-5248; hours 8AM-5PM (CST). *Felony, Civil Actions Over $2,500.*
Civil Records: Access: Fax, mail, in person. Both court and visitors may perform in person searches. Search fee: $10.00 per name. Court makes copy: $.50 per page. Required to search: name, years to search. Civil cases indexed by defendant, plaintiff, on docket books since 1945. Mail turnaround time same day.
Criminal Records: Access: Fax, mail, in person. Both court and visitors may perform in person searches. Search fee: $10.00 per name. Court makes copy: $.50 per page. Required to search: name, years to search, DOB, notarized release; also helpful: SSN. Criminal records on docket books since 1945. Mail turnaround time same day.
General Information: No public access terminal. No sealed, adoptions, mental health, juvenile, sex, or expunged records released. Will fax documents $3.00 1st page, $.50 each add'l. Certification fee: $1.50. Payee: Circuit Clerk. Business checks accepted. Prepayment required.

Justice Court - West District 231 3rd St South, Wiggins, MS 39577-2808; phone: 601-928-4415; fax: 601-928-2114; hours 8AM-5PM (CST). *Misdemeanor, Civil Actions Under $2,500, Eviction, Small Claims.*

Chancery Court 323 E Cavers, PO Drawer 7, Wiggins, MS 39577; phone: 601-928-5266; fax: 601-928-6464; hours 8AM-5PM (CST). *Probate.*

Sunflower County

Circuit Court PO Box 569, Indianola, MS 38751; phone: 662-887-1252; fax: 662-887-7077; hours 8AM-5PM (CST). *Felony, Civil Actions Over $2,500.*
Civil Records: Access: Mail, in person. Both court and visitors may perform in person searches. Search fee: $10.00 per name. Fee is for 7 year search. Court makes copy: $.50 per page. Self serve copy fee: $.25 per page. Required to search: name, years to search. Civil cases indexed by defendant, plaintiff, on docket books since 1881; on computer since 2000. Mail turnaround time 2 days.
Criminal Records: Access: Mail, in person. Both court and visitors may perform in person searches. Search fee: $10.00 per name. Fee is for 7 year search. Court makes copy: $.50 per page. Self serve copy fee: $.25 per page. Required to search: name, years to search, DOB; also helpful: SSN. Criminal records on docket books since 1913; on computer since 2000. Mail turnaround time 1-3 days.
General Information: Public terminal has criminal back to 10/1999 and civil back to 2000. (Has partial civil and criminal records back to 1996.) No sealed, adoptions, mental health, juvenile, sex, or expunged records released. Fee to fax documents is $1.00 per page. Certification fee: $1.50 per document. Payee: Circuit Clerk. Personal checks accepted. Prepayment required.

Justice Court - Northern District PO Box 52, Ruleville, MS 38771; phone: 662-756-2835; fax: 662-756-4175; hours 8AM-N, 1-5PM (CST). *Misdemeanor, Civil Actions Under $2,500, Eviction, Small Claims.*

Justice Court - Southern District PO Box 487, 202 Main St, Indianola, MS 38751; phone: 662-887-6921; fax: 662-887-2798; hours 8AM-N, 1-5PM (CST). *Misdemeanor, Civil Actions Under $2,500, Eviction, Small Claims.*

Chancery Court 200 Main St, PO Box 988, Indianola, MS 38751; phone: 662-887-4703; fax: 662-887-7054; hours 8AM-5PM (CST). *Probate.*

Tallahatchie County

Charleston Circuit Court PO Box 86, Charleston, MS 38921; phone: 662-647-8758; probate phone: 662-647-5551; fax: 662-647-8490; hours 8AM-5PM (CST). *Felony, Civil Actions Over $2,500.*
Civil Records: Access: Fax, mail, in person. Both court and visitors may perform in person searches. Search fee: $10.00 per name. Court makes copy: $.25 per page. Required to search: name, years to search. Civil cases indexed by defendant, plaintiff, on books since 1920s. Mail turnaround time 3 days.
Criminal Records: Access: Fax, mail, in person. Both court and visitors may perform in person searches. Search fee: $10.00 per name. Court makes copy: $.25 per page. Required to search: name, years to search, DOB; also helpful: SSN. Criminal records on books since 1920s. Mail turnaround time 3 days.
General Information: No public access terminal. No sealed, adoptions, mental health, juvenile, sex, or expunged records released. Will fax documents for fee. Certification fee: $3.00 per cert. Payee: Circuit Clerk. Personal checks accepted. Prepayment required. SASE requested.

Charleston Justice Court PO Box 440, Main St, 2nd Fl, Charleston, MS 38921; phone: 662-647-3477; fax: 662-647-3478; hours 8AM-5PM (CST). *Misdemeanor, Civil Actions Under $2,500, Eviction, Small Claims.*
Note: Court is located upstairs of the Charleston Circuit Court; records are not co-mingled.

Sumner Justice Court PO Box 155, Sumner, MS 38957; phone: 662-375-9452; fax: 662-375-8200; hours 8AM-N; 1-5PM (CST). *Misdemeanor, Civil Actions Under $2,500, Eviction, Small Claims.*

Chancery Court #1 Main St, #1 Court Sq, PO Box 350, Charleston, MS 38921; phone: 662-647-5551; fax: 662-647-3702; hours 8AM-5PM (CST). *Probate.*

Chancery Court PO Box 180, Sumner, MS 38957; phone: 662-375-8731; fax: 662-375-7252; hours 8AM-N, 1-5PM (CST). *Probate.*

Tate County

Circuit Court 201 Ward St, Senatobia, MS 38668; phone: 662-562-5211; fax: 662-562-7486; hours 8AM-5PM (CST). *Felony, Civil Actions Over $2,500.*
Civil Records: Access: Mail, in person. Both court and visitors may perform in person searches. Search fee: $10.00 per name. Court makes copy: $.50 for 1st page, $.25 each add'l. Self serve copy fee: $.25 per page. Required to search: name, years to search. Civil cases indexed by defendant, plaintiff, on books since 1872. Mail turnaround time same day.
Criminal Records: Access: Mail, in person. Both court and visitors may perform in person searches. Search fee: $10.00 per name. Court makes copy: $.50 for first page, $.25 each add'l. Self serve copy fee: $.25 per page. Required to search: name, years to search; also helpful: SSN. Criminal records on books since 1872. Mail turnaround time same day.
General Information: Public terminal goes back to 1990. No sealed, adoptions, mental health, juvenile, sex, or expunged records released. Will not fax documents. Certification fee: $1.00 per page. Payee: Circuit Clerk. Personal checks accepted. Prepayment required. SASE requested.

Justice Court 103 Preston Mccay Dr, Senatobia, MS 38668; phone: 662-562-7626; fax: 662-562-7663; hours 8AM-N,1-5PM (CST). *Misdemeanor,*

Civil Actions Under $2,500, Eviction, Small Claims.

Chancery Court 201 Ward St, Senatobia, MS 38668; phone: 662-562-5661; fax: 662-560-6205; hours 8AM-5PM (CST). *Probate.*

Tippah County

Circuit Court Courthouse, Ripley, MS 38663; phone: 662-837-7370; criminal fax: 662-837-1030; same fax for civil/probate; hours 8AM-5PM (CST). *Felony, Civil Actions Over $2,500.*
Civil Records: Access: Phone, fax, mail, in person. Both court and visitors may perform in person searches. Search fee: $5.00 per name. Court makes copy: $.50 per page. Self serve copy fee: $.25 per page. Required to search: name, years to search. Civil cases indexed by defendant. Civil records on docket books since 1800s. Mail turnaround time 1 week; phone turnaround is 30 minutes.
Criminal Records: Access: Phone, fax, mail, in person. Both court and visitors may perform in person searches. Search fee: $5.00 per name. Court makes copy: $.50 per page. Self serve copy fee: $.25 per page. Required to search: name, years to search, DOB; also helpful: SSN. Criminal records on docket books since 1800s. Mail turnaround time 1 week; phone turnaround is 30 minutes.
General Information: No public access terminal. No sealed, adoptions, mental health, juvenile, sex or expunged records released. Will fax documents $1.00 per page. No certification fee . Payee: Circuit Clerk. Personal checks accepted. Prepayment and SASE required.

Justice Court Justice Court, 205-B Spring Ave, Ripley, MS 38663; phone: 662-837-8842; fax: 662-837-1398; hours 8AM-5PM (CST). *Misdemeanor, Civil Actions Under $2,500, Eviction, Small Claims.*

Chancery Court 101 Spring St, Ripley, MS 38663; phone: 662-837-7374; probate phone: 662-837-3607; fax: 662-837-7148; hours 8AM-5PM (CST). *Probate.*

Tishomingo County

Circuit Court 1008 Battleground Dr, Iuka, MS 38852; phone: 662-423-7026; fax: 662-423-1667; hours 8AM-5PM (CST). *Felony, Civil Actions Over $2,500.*
Civil Records: Access: Mail, in person. Both court and visitors may perform in person searches. Search fee: $10.00 per name. Court makes copy: $1.00 per page. Self serve copy fee: $.25 per page. Required to search: name, years to search. Civil cases indexed by defendant, plaintiff, on computer back to 2000, in docket books since 1950s, others in storage. Mail turnaround time 1-2 days.
Criminal Records: Access: Mail, in person. Both court and visitors may perform in person searches. Search fee: $10.00 per name. Court makes copy: $1.00 per page. Self serve copy fee: $.25 per page. Required to search: name, years to search, DOB; also helpful: SSN, signed release. Criminal records on computer back to 2000, in docket books since 1950s, others in storage. Mail turnaround time 1-2 days.
General Information: Public terminal goes back to 2000. No sealed, adoptions, mental health, juvenile, sex, or expunged records released. Will fax documents for $10.00 per name. Certification fee: $1.00 per page. Payee: Circuit Clerk. Business checks accepted. Prepayment required. SASE requested.

Justice Court - Northern & Southern Districts 1008 Battleground Drive, Rm 212, Iuka, MS 38852; phone: 662-423-7033; fax: 662-423-7094; hours 8AM-5PM (CST). *Misdemeanor, Civil Actions Under $2,500, Eviction, Small Claims.*

Chancery Court 1008 Battleground Dr, Iuka, MS 38852; phone: 662-423-7010; fax: 662-423-7005; hours 8AM-5PM (CST). *Probate.*

Tunica County

Circuit Court PO Box 184, Tunica, MS 38676; phone: 662-363-2842; fax: 662-363-2413; hours 8AM-5PM (CST). *Felony, Civil Actions Over $2,500.*
Civil Records: Access: Mail, in person. Both court and visitors may perform in person searches. Search fee: $10.00 per name. Court makes copy: $.50 per page. Add'l fee for postage. Self serve copy fee: $.25 per page. Required to search: name, years to search. Civil cases indexed by defendant, plaintiff, on docket books for 10 years; archived prior. Mail turnaround time 1 week.
Criminal Records: Access: Mail, in person. Both court and visitors may perform in person searches. Search fee: $10.00 per name. Court makes copy: $.50 per page. Add'l for postage. Self serve copy fee: $.25 per page. Required to search: name, years to search, DOB; also helpful: SSN. Criminal records on docket books for 10 years. Mail turnaround time 1 week.
General Information: No public access terminal. No sealed, adoptions, mental health, juvenile, sex, or expunged records released. Will fax documents to local or toll free line. Certification fee: $1.50. Payee: Circuit Clerk. Personal checks accepted. Prepayment required. SASE requested.

Justice Court 5130 Old Moon Landing Rd, Tunica, MS 38676; phone: 662-363-2178; fax: 662-363-4234; hours 8AM-5PM (CST). *Misdemeanor, Civil Actions Under $2,500, Eviction, Small Claims.*

Chancery Court PO Box 217, 1300 School St, Rm 104, Tunica, MS 38676; phone: 662-363-2451; fax: 662-357-5934; hours 8AM-N, 1-5PM (CST). *Probate.*

Union County

Circuit Court PO Box 298, New Albany, MS 38652; phone: 662-534-1910; fax: 662-534-2059; hours 8AM-5PM (CST). *Felony, Civil Actions Over $2,500.*
Civil Records: Access: Fax, mail, in person. Both court and visitors may perform in person searches. Search fee: $10.00 per name. Includes certification fee. Court makes copy: $.50 per page. Self serve copy fee: $.25 per page. Required to search: name, years to search, address. Civil cases indexed by defendant, plaintiff, on docket books since early 1900s. Mail turnaround time 1 week.
Criminal Records: Access: Fax, mail, in person. Both court and visitors may perform in person searches. Search fee: $10.00 per name. Fee includes certification. Court makes copy: $.50 per page. Self serve copy fee: $.25 per page. Required to search: name, years to search, DOB; also helpful: SSN. Criminal records on docket books since early 1900s. Mail turnaround time 1 week.
General Information: No public access terminal. No adoptions, mental health or juvenile records released. No fee to fax documents. Certification fee: $5.00 per doc. Payee: Union County Circuit Clerk. Personal checks accepted. Prepayment required. SASE requested.

Justice Court - East & West Posts PO Box 27, New Albany, MS 38652; phone: 662-534-1951; fax: 662-534-1935; hours 8AM-5PM (CST). *Misdemeanor, Civil Actions Under $2,500, Eviction, Small Claims.*

Chancery Court PO Box 847, New Albany, MS 38652; phone: 662-534-1900; fax: 662-534-1907; hours 8AM-5PM (CST). *Probate.*
Note: Misdemeanor records phone is 662-534-1951.

Walthall County

Circuit Court 200 Ball Ave, Tylertown, MS 39667; phone: 601-876-5677; fax: 601-876-4077; hours 8AM-N; 1-5PM (CST). *Felony, Civil Actions Over $2,500.*
Civil Records: Access: Mail, in person. Both court and visitors may perform in person searches. Search fee: $10.00 per name includes copies. Court

makes copy: $.50 per page. Self serve copy fee: $.25 per page. Required to search: name, years to search. Civil cases indexed by defendant, plaintiff, on docket books since 1914. Mail turnaround time 1-2 days.
Criminal Records: Access: Mail, in person. Both court and visitors may perform in person searches. Search fee: $10.00 per name includes copies. Court makes copy: $.50 per page. Self serve copy fee: $.25 per page. Required to search: name, years to search; also helpful: SSN. Criminal records on docket books since 1914. Mail turnaround time 1-2 days.
General Information: No public access terminal. No sealed, adoptions, mental health, juvenile, sex, or expunged records released. Will fax documents. Certification fee: $1.50 per document. Payee: Circuit Clerk. Personal checks accepted. Prepayment required.

Justice Court - Districts 1 & 2 PO Box 507, 807 Magnolia Ave, Tylertown, MS 39667; phone: 601-876-2311; fax: 601-876-6866; hours 8AM-N, 1-5PM (CST). *Misdemeanor, Civil Actions Under $2,500, Eviction, Small Claims.*

Chancery Court PO Box 351, 200 Ball Ave, Tylertown, MS 39667; phone: 601-876-3553; fax: 601-876-6026; hours 8AM-5PM (CST). *Probate.*

Warren County

Circuit & County Court PO Box 351, Vicksburg, MS 39181; phone: 601-636-3961; hours 8AM-5PM (CST). *Felony, Misdemeanor, Civil.*
Civil Records: Access: Mail, in person. Both court and visitors may perform in person searches. Search fee: $10.00 per name. Court makes copy: $1.00 per page. Self serve copy fee: $.25 per page. Required to search: name, years to search. Civil cases indexed by defendant, plaintiff, on books since 1970s. Mail turnaround time 1 day.
Criminal Records: Access: Mail, in person. Both court and visitors may perform in person searches. Search fee: $10.00 per name. Court makes copy: $1.00 per page. Self serve copy fee: $.25 per page. Required to search: name, years to search; also helpful: DOB, SSN. Criminal records on books since 1970s. Mail turnaround time 1 day.
General Information: Public terminal goes back to 2002. No sealed or expunged records released. Certification fee: $5.00 per page. Payee: Circuit Clerk. No personal checks accepted. Prepayment and SASE required.

Justice Court - Northern, Central & Southern Districts PO Box 1598, Vicksburg, MS 39181; phone: 601-634-6402; fax: 601-630-8015; hours 8AM-5PM (CST). *Misdemeanor, Civil Actions Under $2,500, Eviction, Small Claims.*

Chancery Court PO Box 351, 1009 Cherry St, Vicksburg, MS 39181; phone: 601-636-4415; fax: 601-630-8016; hours 8AM-5PM (CST). *Probate.*
Note: Also handles adoption, divorce, lunacy, Uresa, and minor settlements

Washington County

Circuit & County Court PO Box 1276, Greenville, MS 38702; phone: 662-378-2747; fax: 662-334-2698; hours 8AM-5PM (CST). *Felony, Misdemeanor, Civil.*
Civil Records: Access: Fax, mail, in person. Both court and visitors may perform in person searches. Search fee: $10.00 per name. Court makes copy: $1.00 per page. Self serve copy fee: $.25 per page. Required to search: name, years to search. Civil cases indexed by defendant, plaintiff, on books since 1964. Mail turnaround time 5-10 days.
Criminal Records: Access: Fax, mail, in person. Both court and visitors may perform in person searches. Search fee: $10.00 per name for 7 years, $1.00 each add'l year. Court makes copy: $1.00 per page. Self serve copy fee: $.25 per page. Required to search: name, years to search; also helpful: DOB, SSN. Criminal records on books since 1964. Mail turnaround time 5-10 days.

General Information: No public access terminal. No sealed or expunged records released. No fee to fax documents. Certification fee: $1.50. Payee: Circuit Clerk. Business checks accepted. Prepayment and SASE required.

Justice Court - Districts 1-3 905 W Alexander, Greenville, MS 38701; phone: 662-332-0633; fax: 662-390-4760; hours 8AM-5PM (CST). *Misdemeanor, Civil Actions Under $2,500, Eviction, Small Claims.*

Chancery Court PO Box 309, 900 Washington Ave, Greenville, MS 38702-0309; phone: 662-332-1595; fax: 662-334-2725; hours 8AM-5PM (CST). *Probate.*

Wayne County

Circuit Court PO Box 428, Waynesboro, MS 39367; phone: 601-735-1171; fax: 601-735-6261; hours 8AM-5PM (CST). *Felony, Civil Actions Over $2,500.*
Note: This court is in process of computerizing their records.
Civil Records: Access: Phone, fax, mail, in person. Both court and visitors may perform in person searches. Search fee: $10.00 per name. Court makes copy: $.50 per page. Required to search: name, years to search. Civil cases indexed by defendant, plaintiff, on docket books since 1980, others in storage. Mail turnaround time 1-2 days.
Criminal Records: Access: Fax, mail, in person. Both court and visitors may perform in person searches. Search fee: $10.00 per name. Court makes copy: $.50 per page. Required to search: name, years to search; also helpful: DOB, SSN, signed release. Criminal records on docket books since 1980, others in storage. Mail turnaround time 1-2 days.
General Information: Public use terminal available. No sealed or expunged records released. Fee to fax documents is $1.00 per page. Certification fee: $1.50. Payee: Circuit Clerk. Business checks accepted. Prepayment required.

Justice Court - Posts 1 & 2 810 Chickasawhay St, #C, Waynesboro, MS 39367; phone: 601-735-3118; fax: 601-735-6266; hours 8AM-5PM (CST). *Misdemeanor, Civil Actions Under $2,500, Eviction, Small Claims.*

Chancery Court Courthouse, 609 Azalea Dr, Waynesboro, MS 39367; phone: 601-735-2873; fax: 601-735-6224; hours 8AM-5PM (CST). *Probate.*

Webster County

Circuit Court PO Box 308, Walthall, MS 39771; phone: 662-258-6287; fax: 662-258-7686; hours 8AM-5PM *elony, Civil Actions Over $2,500.*
Civil Records: Access: Phone, fax, mail, in person. Both court and visitors may perform in person searches. Search fee: $10.00 per name. Court makes copy: $.50 per page. Required to search: name, years to search. Civil cases indexed by defendant, plaintiff, on docket books since 1874. Mail turnaround time 1-2 days.
Criminal Records: Access: Fax, mail, in person. Both court and visitors may perform in person searches. Search fee: $10.00 per name. Court makes copy: $.50 per page. Required to search: name, years to search, DOB; also helpful: SSN. Criminal records on docket books since 1874. Mail turnaround time 1-2 days.
General Information: Public use terminal available. No sealed, adoptions, mental health, juvenile, sex, or expunged records released. No fee to fax documents. Certification fee: $1.00. Payee: Circuit Clerk. Business checks accepted. Prepayment required.

Justice Court - Districts 1 & 2 114 Hwy 9 N, Eupora, MS 39744; phone: 662-258-2590; fax: 662-258-3093; hours 8AM-5PM (CST). *Misdemeanor, Civil Actions Under $2,500, Eviction, Small Claims.*

Chancery Court PO Box 398, 101 Main St, Walthall, MS 39771; phone: 662-258-4131; fax: 662-258-6657; hours 8AM-5PM (CST). *Probate.*

Wilkinson County

Circuit Court PO Box 327, Woodville, MS 39669; phone: 601-888-6697; fax: 601-888-6984; hours 8:00AM-5:00PM (CST). *Felony, Civil Actions Over $2,500.*
Civil Records: Access: Mail, in person. Both court and visitors may perform in person searches. Search fee: $10.00 per name. Court makes copy: $.50 per page. Self serve copy fee: $.25 per page. Required to search: name, years to search. Civil cases indexed by defendant, plaintiff, on docket books since 1940s. Mail turnaround time 1-2 days.
Criminal Records: Access: Mail, in person. Both court and visitors may perform in person searches. Search fee: $10.00 per name. Court makes copy: $.50 per page. Self serve copy fee: $.25 per page. Required to search: name, years to search; also helpful: DOB, SSN. Criminal records on docket books since 1940s. Mail turnaround time 1-2 days.
General Information: No public access terminal. No sealed or expunged records released. Certification fee: $10.00 per doc. Payee: Circuit Clerk. Personal checks accepted. Prepayment required.

Justice Court PO Box 40, 1389 Highway 6 South, Woodville, MS 39669; phone: 601-888-3538, 601-888-3972; fax: 601-888-7591; hours 8AM-5PM (CST). *Misdemeanor, Civil Actions Under $2,500, Eviction, Small Claims.*

Chancery Court PO Box 516, Woodville, MS 39669; phone: 601-888-4381; fax: 601-888-6776; hours 8AM-5PM (CST). *Probate.*

Winston County

Circuit Court PO Drawer 785, Louisville, MS 39339; phone: 662-773-3581; fax: 662-773-7192; hours 8AM-5PM (CST). *Felony, Civil Actions Over $2,500.*
Note: You may email requests to kim@winstoncounty.org.
Civil Records: Access: Phone, fax, mail, in person. Both court and visitors may perform in person searches. Search fee: $10.00 per name. Court makes copy: $1.00 per page. Self serve copy fee: $.25 per page. Required to search: name, years to search. Civil cases indexed by defendant, plaintiff, on docket books since early 1950s; some on computer back to 1994; all since 2000. Mail turnaround time 14 day maximum.
Criminal Records: Access: Fax, mail, in person. Both court and visitors may perform in person searches. Search fee: $10.00 per name. Court makes copy: $1.00 per page. Self serve copy fee: $.25 per page. Required to search: name, years to search, DOB; also helpful: SSN. Criminal records on docket books since early 1800s; on computer back to 2000. Mail turnaround time 14 day maximum
General Information: Public use terminal available. No sealed, adoptions, mental health, juvenile or expunged records released. Will fax documents $5.00 1st page, $1.00 each add'l. Certification fee: $2.00. Payee: Circuit Clerk. Personal checks accepted. Prepayment required. SASE requested.

Justice Court PO Box 327, 115 S Court St, Louisville, MS 39339; phone: 662-773-6016; fax: 662-773-8817; hours 8AM-5PM (CST). *Misdemeanor, Civil Actions Under $2,500, Eviction, Small Claims.*

Chancery Court PO Drawer 69, 115 S Court St, Louisville, MS 39339; phone: 662-773-3631; fax: 662-773-8814; hours 8AM-5PM (CST). *Probate.*

Yalobusha County

Coffeeville Circuit Court PO Box 260, Coffeeville, MS 38922; phone: 662-675-8187; fax: 662-675-8004; hours 8AM-5PM (CST). *Felony, Civil Actions Over $2,500.*
Note: Records to be Internet accessible in late 2005 or early 2006. Call for details.
Civil Records: Access: Phone, fax, mail, in person. Both court and visitors may perform in person searches. Search fee: $10.00 per name. May mail request with check or fax request with copy of check to be mailed. Court makes copy: $.50 per page. Self serve copy fee: $.25 per page. Required to search: name, years to search. Civil cases indexed by defendant, plaintiff, on docket books since 1930s. Mail turnaround time 1-2 days.
Criminal Records: Access: Phone, fax, mail, in person. Both court and visitors may perform in person searches. Search fee: $10.00 per name. May mail request with check or fax request with copy of check to be mailed. Court makes copy: $.50 per page. Self serve copy fee: $.25 per page. Required to search: name, years to search; also helpful: DOB. Criminal records on docket books since 1930s. Mail turnaround time 1-2 days.
General Information: No public access terminal. No sealed, adoptions, mental health, juvenile, sex, or expunged records released. Will fax documents to local or toll free line. Certification fee: $10.00. Payee: Circuit Clerk. Personal checks accepted. Prepayment required. SASE requested.

Water Valley Circuit Court PO Box 1431, Water Valley, MS 38965; phone: 662-473-1341; fax: 662-473-5020; hours 8AM-5PM (CST). *Felony, Civil Actions Over $2,500.*
Note: Records to be Internet accessible in late 2005 or early 2006. Call for details.
Civil Records: Access: Fax, mail, in person. Both court and visitors may perform in person searches. Search fee: $10.00 per name. Includes certification fee. Court makes copy: $.50 per page. Self serve copy fee: $.25 per page. Required to search: name, years to search. Civil cases indexed by defendant, plaintiff, on docket books since 1930s. Mail turnaround time 1 week.
Criminal Records: Access: Fax, mail, in person. Both court and visitors may perform in person searches. Search fee: $10.00 per name. Fee includes certification. Court makes copy: $.50 per page. Self serve copy fee: $.25 per page. Required to search: name, years to search, DOB; also helpful: SSN. Criminal records on docket books since 1930s. Mail turnaround time 1 week.
General Information: No public access terminal. No sealed, adoptions, mental health, juvenile, sex, or expunged records released. No fee to fax documents. Certification fee: $10.00 per docket. Payee: Circuit Clerk. Personal checks accepted. Prepayment required.

Justice Court - District 1 PO Box 218, 14400 Main Street, Coffeeville, MS 38922; phone: 662-675-8115; fax: 662-675-8452; hours 8AM-5PM (CST). *Misdemeanor, Civil Actions Under $2,500, Eviction, Small Claims.*

Justice Court - Division 2 PO Box 918, Water Valley, MS 38965; phone: 662-473-4502; hours 8AM-5PM, T,W, only (CST). *Misdemeanor, Civil Actions Under $2,500, Eviction, Small Claims.*

Chancery Court PO Box 260, Coffeeville, MS 38922; phone: 662-675-2716; fax: 662-675-8004; hours 8AM-N, 1-5PM (CST). *Probate.*

Chancery Court PO Box 664, Water Valley, MS 38965; phone: 662-473-2091; fax: 662-473-3622; hours 8AM-5PM (CST). *Probate.*

Yazoo County

Circuit & County Court PO Box 108, Yazoo City, MS 39194; phone: 662-746-1872; hours 8AM-5PM (CST). *Felony, Misdemeanor, Civil.*
Note: Probate is also located in this office.
Civil Records: Access: Mail, in person. Both court and visitors may perform in person searches. Search fee: $10.00 per name. Court makes copy: $.50 per page. Self serve copy fee: $.25 per page. Required to search: name, years to search. Civil cases indexed by defendant, plaintiff. Civil records for Civil Circuit on docket books since 1973; for Civil County on docket books since 1977. Mail turnaround time 1 day.
Criminal Records: Access: Mail, in person. Both court and visitors may perform in person searches. Search fee: $10.00 per name. Court makes copy: $.50 per page. Self serve copy fee: $.25 per page. Required to search: name, years to search, DOB; also helpful: SSN. Criminal records for Criminal Circuit from 1975; Criminal County on docket books since 1975. Mail turnaround time 1 day.
General Information: No public access terminal. No sealed, adoptions, mental health, juvenile, sex, or expunged records released. Will fax documents. Certification fee: $1.00 per page. Payee: Circuit Clerk. Business checks accepted. Prepayment and SASE required.

Justice Court - Northern & Southern Districts PO Box 798, 211 E Broadway, Yazoo City, MS 39194; phone: 662-746-8181; fax: 662-746-2186; hours 8AM-5PM (CST). *Misdemeanor, Civil Actions Under $2,500, Eviction, Small Claims.*

Chancery Court PO Box 68, 211 E Broadway, Yazoo City, MS 39194; phone: 662-746-2661; fax: 662-746-3893; hours 8AM-5PM (CST). *Probate.*

Mississippi Recording Offices

ORGANIZATION: 82 counties, 92 recording offices. The recording officers are Chancery Clerk and Clerk of Circuit Court (state tax liens). Ten counties have two separate recording offices - Bolivar, Carroll, Chickasaw, Craighead, Harrison, Hinds, Jasper, Jones, Panola, Tallahatchie, and Yalobusha. See the notes under each county for how to determine which office is appropriate to search. The entire state is in the Central Time Zone (CST).

REAL ESTATE RECORDS: A few counties will perform real estate searches. Copies usually cost $.50 per page and certification fees $1.00 per document. The Assessor maintains tax records.

UCC RECORDS: This was a dual filing state. Until 07/2001, financing statements were filed both at the state level and with the Chancery Clerk, except for consumer goods, farm related and real estate related filings, which were filed only with the Chancery Clerk. Now, only real estate related filings are filed at the county level. Nearly all counties will perform UCC searches. Use search request form UCC-11. Search fees are usually $5.00 per debtor name. Copy fees vary from $.25 to $2.00 per page.

TAX LIEN RECORDS: Federal tax liens on personal property of businesses are filed with the Secretary of State. Federal tax liens on personal property of individuals are filed with the county Chancery Clerk. State tax liens on personal property are filed with the county Clerk of Circuit Court. Refer to the County Court section for information about Mississippi Circuit Courts. State tax liens on real property are filed with the Chancery Clerk. Most Chancery Clerk offices will perform a federal tax lien search for a fee of $5.00 per name. Copy fees vary.

OTHER LIENS: Mechanics, lis pendens, judgment (Circuit Court), construction.

ONLINE ACCESS: A limited number of counties offer online access to records, there is no statewide system except for the Secretary of State's UCC access – see State Agencies section.

Adams County

Chancery Clerk, PO Box 1006, Natchez, MS 39121. 601-446-6684; fax-601-445-7913; hours: 8AM-5PM. Office personnel or visitors may perform searches. Search fee $10.00 per name. Will not search real estate records. Copy fee $2.00 per page. R/E or tax lien copy- $.50 per page. Cert fee- $1.00 per cert plus copy fee. Payee- Chancery Clerk. **Online access to Judgment, Circuit Court, Voter Registration records:** Access judgments, voter registration, circuit courts (go back to 1997, scanned 12/02 to present) for a fee go to www.deltacomputersystems.com/search.html. **Other phones:** Elections- 601-446-6326. **Property tax/Assessor-** 601-442-6732.

Alcorn County

Chancery Clerk, PO Box 69, Corinth, MS 38835-0069. 662-286-7700; fax-662-286-7706; hours: 8AM-5PM. Separate indices to search include computer (with canned images), mortgages, warranty deeds. Records indexed on a public use terminal back to 2/2005. Only the public may search. Copy fee $2.00 per page; $.25 self serve. Cert fee- $1.00 per cert plus copy fee. Payee- Chancery Clerk. **Online to Property Tax, Appraisal records:** Access is free at www.deltacomputersystems.com/MS/MS02/index.html. **Other phones:** Elections- 662-286-7740. **Property tax/Assessor-** 662-286-7733.

Amite County

Chancery Clerk, PO Box 680, Liberty, MS 39645-0680. 601-657-8022; fax-601-657-8288; hours: 8AM-5PM. Office personnel or visitors may perform searches. Search fee $10.00 per name. Will not search real estate records. Copy fee $.50 per page. Cert fee- $3.00 per cert. Payee- Amite County Chancery Clerk. **Other phones:** Treasurer- 601-657-8932; Elections- 601-657-8932. **Property tax/Assessor-** 601-657-8973.

Attala County

Chancery Clerk, 230 W. Washington St.; Chancery Court Bldg, Kosciusko, MS 39090. 662-289-2921; fax-662-289-7662; hours: 8AM-5PM. Office personnel or visitors may perform searches. Search fee $5.00 per name. Will not search real estate records. Copy fee $1.00 per page. Cert fee- $1.00 per cert plus copy fee. Payee- Attala County Chancery Clerk. **Other phones:** Elections- 662-289-1471. **Property tax/Assessor-** 662-289-5731.

Benton County

Chancery Clerk, PO Box 218, Ashland, MS 38603. 662-224-6300; fax-662-224-6303; hours: 8AM-5PM. Office will perform a UCC search but public must search other records themselves. UCC search per debtor name- $5.00. General copy fee $2.00 per page. Tax lien copy- $.25. Cert fee- $1.50 per cert. Payee- Benton County Chancery Clerk. **Other phones:** Elections- 662-224-6310. **Property tax/Assessor-** 662-224-6315.

Bolivar County (1st District)

Chancery Clerk, PO Box 238, Rosedale, MS 38769-0238. 662-759-3762; fax-662-759-3467; hours: 8AM-N, 1-5PM. All records in one index. Records indexed on computer back to 1985. Office will perform a UCC search but public must search other records themselves. Search fee $10.00. Copy fee $2.00 per page. Cert fee- $1.00 per cert plus copy fee. Payee- Bolivar County Chancery Clerk. **Other phones:** Treasurer- 662-843-2531; Elections- 662-843-2061. **Property tax/Assessor-** 662-843-3826.

Bolivar County (2nd District)

Chancery Clerk, PO Box 789, Cleveland, MS 38732. 662-843-2071; fax-662-846-2940; hours: 8-5. Office personnel or visitors may perform searches. Search fee $5.00 per name. Will not search real estate records. Copy fee $.50 per page self serve. Cert fee- $1.00 per record. Payee- Jeanne Walker-Chancery Clerk. **Other phones:** Treasurer- 662-843-2071; Elections- 662-843-2061. **Property tax/Assessor-** 662-843-3926.

Calhoun County

Chancery Clerk, PO Box 8, Pittsboro, MS 38951. 662-412-3117, UCC recording phone-662-412-3121; fax-662-412-3128; hours: 8AM-5PM. Separate indices to search include deed, deed tract. Records indexed on a public use terminal. Office will perform a UCC search but public must search other records themselves. UCC search per debtor name- $5.00. Copy fee $.50 per page; UCC copy $2.00. Cert fee- $5.00 per page. Payee- Calhoun County Clerk of the Chancery Court. **Other phones:** Treasurer- 662-412-3117; Appraiser/Auditor- 662-412-3146; Elections- 662-412-3101; Vital Records- 662-412-3101. **Property tax/Assessor-** PO Box 6, Pittsboro, MS 38951; 662-412-3140.

Carroll County (1st District)

Chancery Clerk, PO Box 60, Carrollton, MS 38917. 662-237-9274; fax-662-237-9642; 8AM-N, 1-5PM. Separate indices to search include deeds in books, deeds of trust in books. Records indexed on a public use terminal back to 11/03. Only the public may search. Copy fee $.50 per page. Cert fee- $5.00 per instrument plus copy fee. Payee- Carroll County Chancery Clerk. **Other phones:** Elections- 662-464-5476. **Property tax/Assessor-** 662-237-9217.

Carroll County (2nd District)

Chancery Clerk, PO Box 6, Vaiden, MS 39176. 662-464-5476; fax-662-464-5407; hours: 8AM-5PM. The 2nd district is split by section, township and range. All records in one index. Record index not computerized. Only the public may search. Copy fee $2.00, if tax lien or real estate $1.00 per page. Cert fee- $2.00 per doc plus copy fee. Payee- Carroll County Clerk of the Chancery Court. **Other phones:** Elections- 662-464-5476. **Property tax/Assessor-** 662-464-8852.

Chickasaw County (1st District)

Chancery Clerk, 1 Pinson Sq, Houston, MS 38851. 662-456-2513; fax-662-456-5295; hours: 8AM-N, 1-5PM.

Records indexed on a public use terminal back to 1997. Office personnel or visitors may perform searches. Search fee $5.00 per name. Will not search real estate records. Copy fee $2.00 per page. Cert fee- $1.00 per cert. Payee- Chancery Clerk. **Other phones:** Treasurer- 662-456-3941; Elections- 662-456-2331. **Property tax/Assessor-** 662-456-3327.

Chickasaw County (2nd District)

Chancery Clerk, 234 Main St; Rm 201, Okolona, MS 38860-1438. 662-447-2092; fax-662-447-5024; hours: 8AM-N.1-5PM.

Records indexed on a public use terminal back to 1990. Office will perform a UCC search but public must search other records themselves. Search fee $5.00. Copy fee $.50 per page. Cert fee- $1.00 per page plus copy fee. Payee- Chancery Clerk. **Other phones:** Treasurer- 662-456-2513; Elections- 662-456-2331. **Property tax/Assessor-** 662-447-2242.

Choctaw County

Chancery Clerk, PO Box 250, Ackerman, MS 39735-0250. 662-285-6329; fax-662-285-3444; hours: 8AM-5PM.

Office personnel or visitors may perform searches. Search fee $10.00 per name. Will not search real estate records. Copy fee $1.00 per page. Cert fee- $2.00 per cert. Payee- Choctaw County Chancery Clerk. **Other phones:** Elections- 662-285-6245. **Property tax/Assessor-** 662-285-6320.

Claiborne County

Chancery Clerk, PO Box 449, Port Gibson, MS 39150. 601-437-4992; fax-601-437-3731; hours: 8AM-5PM.

Separate indices to search include mortgages, land deeds, chancery court. Records indexed on computer back to 1981 for deeds and mortgages. Office will perform a UCC search but public must search other records themselves. UCC search per debtor name- $5.00. Copy fee $.50 per page. Tax lien copy- $5.00. Cert fee- $1.00 per cert plus copy fee. Payee- Claiborne County Clerk of the Chancery Court. **Other phones:** Treasurer- 601-437-4992; Appraiser/Auditor- 601-437-5591; Elections- 601-437-5841. **Property tax/Assessor-** PO Box 469, Port Gibson, MS 39150; 601-437-5591.

Clarke County

Chancery Clerk, PO Box 689, Quitman, MS 39355. 601-776-2126; fax-601-776-2756; hours: 8AM-5PM.

All records in one index. Record index not computerized. Only the public may search. UCC copy fee $2.00 per page. R/E record copy- $.50 per page. Cert fee- $1.00 per cert plus copy fee. Payee- Clarke County Clerk of the Chancery Court. **Other phones:** Treasurer- 601-776-2126; Appraiser/Auditor- 601-776-1021; Elections- 601-776-3111. **Property tax/Assessor-** 601-776-6931.

Clay County

Chancery Clerk, PO Box 815, West Point, MS 39773. 662-494-3124; hours: 8AM-5PM.

Separate indices to search include general deed index, general land mortgage index. Record index not computerized. Only the public may search. Copy fee $2.00, if tax lien or real estate $.50 per page. Cert fee- $1.00 per page plus copy fee. Payee- Clay County Clerk of the Chancery Court. **Other phones:** Appraiser/Auditor- 662-494-3432; Elections- 662-494-3384. **Property tax/Assessor-** 662-494-3432.

Coahoma County

Chancery Clerk, PO Box 98, Clarksdale, MS 38614. 662-624-3000; fax-662-624-3040; hours: 8AM-5PM.
Index: General index for both land deeds and Mtgs. Only the public may search. Copy fee $.50 per page. Cert fee- $1.00 per instrument. Payee- Coahoma County Chancery Clerk. **Other phones:** Treasurer- 662-624-3000; Elections- 662-624-3014; Vital Records- 601-576-7988. **Property/Assessor-** PO Box 219, Clarksdale, MS 38614; 662-624-3006.

Copiah County

Chancery Clerk, PO Box 507, Hazlehurst, MS 39083-0507. 601-894-3021; fax-601-894-4081; www.copiahcounty.org
All records in one index. Records indexed on computer back to 1995. Office will perform a UCC search but public must search other records themselves. UCC search per debtor name- $10.00. Separate federal tax lien search fee-$10.00 per debtor. Copy fee $2.00 per page. R/E or tax lien copy- $.50 per page. Cert fee- $1.00 per cert plus copy fee. Payee- Chancery Clerk. **Other phones:** Elections- 601-894-1241. **Property tax/Assessor-** 601-894-2721.

Covington County

Chancery Clerk, PO Box 1679, Collins, MS 39428. 601-765-4242; fax-601-765-5016; hours: 8AM-5PM.
Only the public may search. R/E record copy-$1.00 per page. Tax lien copy- $.50. Cert fee-$1.00 per cert plus copy fee. Payee- Covington County Clerk of the Chancery Court. **Other phones:** Elections- 601-765-6506. **Property tax/Assessor-** 601-756-6402.

De Soto County

Chancery Clerk, PO Box 949, Hernando, MS 38632. 662-429-1318; fax-662-449-1420; hours: 8AM-5PM. www.desotoms.info
Separate indices to search include Liens, Bankruptcies, Incorporations, Substitutions, Lis Pendens, Miscellaneous, Warranty Deeds, Trust Deeds, Subdivisions, Military Discharges. Records indexed on a public use terminal back to mid-1995. Office will perform a UCC search but public must search other records themselves. UCC search per debtor name- $5.00. Separate federal tax lien search- $5.00 per debtor. Copy fee $2.00, if tax lien or real estate $.50 per page. Cert fee- $1.00 per cert + $.50 per page. Payee- De Soto County Clerk of the Chancery Court. **Online access to Property Tax, Assessor, Grantor/Grantee, Deed, Recording, Voter Registration records:** Access to assessor property data is free at www.desotoms.info. Click on "Tax Assessor." GIS-mapping site is also available. Also, access to Chancery Clerk grantor/grantee index is also available; click on "Chancery Clerk." For voter registration data, click on Circuit Clerk and then Voter Registration tab. GIS mapping site is also available, also county board and planning commission minutes. **Other phones:** Treasurer- 662-429-1340; Elections- 662-429-1325. **Property tax/Assessor-** 365 Losher St #100, Hernando, MS 38632; 662-429-1335.

Forrest County

Chancery Clerk, PO Box 951, Hattiesburg, MS 39403. 601-545-6014; fax-601-545-6095; hours: 8AM-5PM.
All records in one index. Records indexed on a public use terminal back to 1994. Office will perform a UCC search but public must search other records themselves. UCC search per debtor name- $5.00. Separate federal tax lien search fee-$5.00 per name. Copy fee $.50 per page. UUC copy $2.00 per page. Cert fee- $1.00 per instrument plus copy fee. Payee- Chancery Clerk. **Online access to Property Tax, Appraisal records:** Access property tax or appraisal records free at www.deltacomputersystems.com/search.html. **Other phones:** Treasurer- 601-582-8228; Elections- 601-582-3213; Vital Records- 601-576-7960. **Property tax/Assessor-** PO Box 1626, Hattiesburg, MS 39403; 601-545-6130.

Franklin County

Chancery Clerk, PO Box 297, Meadville, MS 39653-0297. 601-384-2330; fax-601-384-5864; 8AM-5PM.
Office will perform a UCC search but public must search other records themselves. Will not search real estate records. UCC search per debtor name- $5.00. UCC search must be pre-paid. Copy fee $2.00 per page. Cert fee- $1.00 per cert. Payee- Franklin County Chancery Clerk. **Other phones:** Elections-

601-384-2320; Tax Collector- 601-384-2359. **Property tax/Assessor-** 601-384-2359.

George County

Chancery Clerk, 355 Cox St, Lucedale, MS 39452. 601-947-4801; fax-601-947-1300; hours: 8AM-5PM; 9AM-N Sat.
Records indexed on a public use terminal back to 1993. Office will perform a UCC search but public must search other records themselves. Search fee $5.00. Copy fee $2.00, if tax lien or real estate $.50 per page. Cert fee- $1.00 per cert plus copy fee. Payee- George County Clerk of the Chancery Court. **Online access to Assessor, Property records:** Access to the property tax records is free at www.deltacomputersystems.com/MS/MS20/plinkquerym.html. **Other phones:** Treasurer- 601-947-3766; Appraiser/Auditor- 601-947-7541; Elections- 601-947-4881. **Property tax/Assessor-** 601-947-7541.

Greene County

Chancery Clerk, PO Box 610, Leakesville, MS 39451. 601-394-2377; fax-601-394-2334; hours: 8AM-5PM.
Office personnel or visitors may perform searches. Search fee $5.00 per name. Copy fee $1.00 per page. R/E record copy- $.50 per copy. Cert fee-$1.00 per cert plus copy fee. Payee- Greene County Chancery Clerk. **Other phones:** Treasurer- 601-394-2377; Elections- 601-394-2379. **Property tax/Assessor-** 601-394-2377.

Grenada County

Chancery Clerk, PO Drawer 1208, Grenada, MS 38902-1208. 662-226-1821; fax-662-227-2860; hours: 8AM-5PM.
Office will perform a UCC search but public must search other records themselves. Search fee $5.00. Will not search real estate records. UCC copy fee $2.00 per page. R/E record copy- $.50 per page. Cert fee- $1.00 per cert plus copy fee. Payee- Grenada County Clerk of the Chancery Court. **Other phones:** Treasurer- 662-226-1821; Elections- 662-226-1941; Tax Collector- 662-226-1741. **Property tax/Assessor-** PO Box 1488, Grenada, MS 38902; not known.

Hancock County

Chancery Clerk, PO Box 429, Bay Saint Louis, MS 39520. 228-467-5404, R/E recording phone-228-467-0455; fax-228-467-3159; hours: 8AM-5PM.
Office personnel or visitors may perform searches. Search fee $5.00 per name. Will not search real estate records. Copy fee $.50 per page. Cert fee- $1.00 per cert plus copy fee. Payee- Chancery Clerk. **Other phones:** Treasurer- 228-467-4425; Appraiser/Auditor- 228-467-0130; Elections- 228-467-5265; Tax Collector- 228-467-4425; Delinquent Taxes -228-467-2252. **Property tax/Assessor-** 228-467-5727.

Harrison County (1st District)

Chancery Clerk, PO Drawer CC, Gulfport, MS 39502. 228-865-4036, UCC recording phone-228-865-4235; fax-228-214-1513; hours: 8AM-5PM. http://co.harrison.ms.us
Separate indices to search include deeds/mortgages, liens, and UCCs. Records indexed on a public use terminal back to 1985. Office personnel or visitors may perform searches. Will not search real estate records. Will search UCC and federal tax lien records. UCC or tax lien search per debtor name- $5.00. Copy fee $2.00 per page for UCC or tax lien; $.50 for other records. Cert fee- $1.00 per doc plus copy fee. Payee- Chancery Clerk. **Online access to Property, Deed, Recording, UCC, Voter Registration, Deed, Grantor/Grantee, Marriage, Inmate, Court, Property Tax records:** Access all records through the county portal at http://co.harrison.ms.us. Also, access to property tax data is free online at www.deltacomputersystems.com/MS/MS24DELTA/DATALINK.html or http://co.harrison.ms.us/departments/chanclerk/proplink.asp. Also, search chancery clerk Deed & Record index back 20 years. Also, search voter registration and

marriage licenses. Also, the delinquent tax sales list no longer appears on the web. Access to the jail docket is free at www.harrisoncountysheriff.com/docket/. Also, search circuit court judgment rolls at http://co.harrison.ms.us/departments/circlerk/rolls/ and chancery court dockets at http://co.harrison.ms.us/dockets/. **Other phones:** Appraiser/Auditor- 228-865-4044; Elections- 228-865-4049; Vital Records- 228-960-7981; Tax Collector- 228-865-4040. **Property tax/Assessor**- PO Box 462, Gulfport, MS 39305; 228-865-4043.

Harrison County (2nd District)

Chancery Clerk, PO Box 544, Biloxi, MS 39533. 228-435-8220; fax-228-435-8292; hours: 8AM-5PM. http://co.harrison.ms.us
Office will perform a UCC search but public must search other records themselves. UCC search per debtor name- $5.00. Copy fee $2.00 per page. **Online access to Property, Deed, Recording, UCC, Voter Registration, Deed, Grantor/Grantee, Marriage, Inmate, Court records:** Access to property tax data is free at www.deltacomputersystems.com/MS/MS24DELTA/DATALINK.html or http://co.harrison.ms.us. You may also choose to search chancery clerk Deed & Record index back 15 years. Also search voter registration and marriage licenses. Also, the delinquent tax sales list no longer appears on the web. Access to the jail docket is free at www.harrisoncountysheriff.com/docket/. Also, search circuit court judgment rolls at http://co.harrison.ms.us/departments/circlerk/rolls/ and chancery court dockets at http://co.harrison.ms.us/dockets/. **Other phones:** Elections- 228-865-4167. **Property tax/Assessor**- 228-435-8265.

Hinds County (1st District)

Chancery Clerk, PO Box 686, Jackson, MS 39205-0686. 601-968-6508, UCC recording phone-601-968-6516; fax-601-973-5535; hours: 8AM-5PM. www.co.hinds.ms.us/pgs/elected/chanceryclerk.asp
Office personnel or visitors may perform searches. Search fee $5.00 per name. Will not search real estate records. Copy fee $.50 per page. Cert fee- $1.00 per doc plus copy fee. Payee- Hinds County Chancery. **Online access to Real Estate, Grantor/Grantee, Judgment, Lien, Assessor, Condominium, Acreage records:** Access to the county records databases are free at www.co.hinds.ms.us/pgs/apps/gindex.asp. Also, search the assessor landrolls for free at www.co.hinds.ms.us/pgs/apps/landroll_query.asp. **Other phones:** Treasurer- 601-968-6588; Elections- 601-968-6628; Tax Collector- 601-968-6588. **Property tax/Assessor**- 601-968-6616.

Hinds County (2nd District)

Chancery Clerk, PO Box 88, Raymond, MS 39154. 601-857-8055; fax-601-857-4953; hours: 8AM-5PM. www.co.hinds.ms.us
The 2nd District consists of all towns/cities outside the limits of Jackson, including Bolton, part of Clinton, Edwards, Learned, Raymond, part of Terry, and Utica. Records indexed on computer from 11/87 to present, prior to 11/87 in index books. Only the public may search. UCC copy fee $2.00 per page. R/E record copy- $.50 per page. Cert fee- $1.00 per cert plus copy fee. Payee- Hinds County Clerk of the Chancery Court. **Online access to Real Estate, Assessor, Grantor/Grantee, Judgment records:** Access to the county clerk database is free at www.co.hinds.ms.us/pgs/apps/gindex.asp. Chose to search general index, landroll, judgments, acreage, subdivision, condominiums. **Other phones:** Treasurer- 601-857-5574; Elections- 601-968-6628; Tax Collector- 601-857-5574. **Property tax/Assessor**- 601-857-8787.

Holmes County

Chancery Clerk, PO Box 239, Lexington, MS 39095. 662-834-2508, R/E recording phone-662-834-0005; fax-662-834-3020; hours: 8AM-5PM.
All records in one index. Records indexed on computer back to 4/1/2004. Office will perform a

UCC and Tax lien search but public must search other records themselves. Search fee $5.00. Copy fee $.50 per page. Cert fee- $1.00 per page plus copy fee. **Other phones:** Treasurer- 662-834-0005; Appraiser/Auditor- 662-834-3737; Elections- 662-834-2476; Vital Records- 662-834-2476. **Property tax/Assessor**- 662-834-2865.

Humphreys County

Chancery Clerk, PO Box 547, Belzoni, MS 39038. 662-247-1740; fax-662-247-0101; hours: 8AM-N, 1-5PM.
Office personnel or visitors may perform searches. Search fee $5.00 per name. UCC copy fee $2.00 per page. R/E record copy- $.50 per page. Cert fee- $1.00 per cert plus copy fee. Payee- Humphreys County Clerk of the Chancery Court. **Other phones:** Treasurer- 662-247-2552; Appraiser/Auditor- 662-247-0106; Elections- 662-247-3065; Tax Collector- 662-247-2552. **Property tax/Assessor**- 662-247-3174.

Issaquena County

Chancery Clerk, PO Box 27, Mayersville, MS 39113-0027. 662-873-2761; fax-662-873-2061; hours: 8AM-N; 1-5PM.
Separate indices to search include alphabetical and sectionals. Office will perform a UCC search but public must search other records themselves. UCC search per debtor name- $5.00. Copy fee $2.00 per page. Cert fee- $1.00 per instrument plus copy fee. Payee- Chancery Clerk. **Other phones:** Treasurer- 662-873-2761; Elections- 662-873-2761; Marriages/Divorces- 662-873-2761. **Property tax/Assessor**- PO Box 67, Mayersville, MS 39113; 662-873-4665.

Itawamba County

Chancery Clerk, PO Box 776, Fulton, MS 38843. 662-862-3421; fax-662-862-3421; hours: 8AM-5PM M-F; 8AM-N Sat.
Records indexed on a public use terminal back to about 2000. Only the public may search. Copy fee $2.00 per page. Cert fee- $1.00 per cert. **Other phones:** Appraiser/Auditor- 662-862-7598; Elections- 662-862-3511; Vital Records- 662-862-3511. **Property tax/Assessor**- 662-862-7598.

Jackson County

Chancery Clerk, PO Box 998, Pascagoula, MS 39568. 228-769-3131; fax-228-769-3135; hours: 8-5PM.
Office personnel or visitors may perform searches. Search fee $5.00 per name. Will not search real estate records. Copy fee $2.00 per page. Cert fee- $1.00 per cert. Payee- Jackson County Chancery Clerk. **Other phones:** Treasurer- 228-769-3131; Elections- 228-769-3040. **Property tax/Assessor**- 228-769-3070.

Jasper County (1st District)

Chancery Clerk, PO Box 38, Paulding, MS 39348-0038. 601-727-4941, R/E recording phone-601-764-3368; fax-601-727-4475; hours: 8AM-5PM.
Office will perform a UCC search but public must search other records themselves. UCC search per debtor name- $5.00. Copy fee $2.00, if tax lien or real estate $.50 per page. Cert fee- $1.00 per page. Payee- Jasper County Clerk of the Chancery Court. **Other phones:** Elections- 601-764-2245. **Property tax/Assessor**- 601-764-2813.

Jasper County (2nd District)

Chancery Clerk, PO Box 1047, Bay Springs, MS 39422. 601-764-3026; fax-601-764-3999; hours: 8AM-5PM.
All records in one index. Record index not computerized. Only the public may search. Copy fee $.50 per copy. Cert fee- $1.00 per page plus copy fee. **Other phones:** Treasurer- 601-764-3469; Elections- 601-764-2245. **Property tax/Assessor**- 601764-2813.

Jefferson County

Chancery Clerk, PO Box 145, Fayette, MS 39069. 601-786-3021, UCC recording phone-601-359-1350; fax-601-786-6009; hours: 8AM-5PM.
Separate indices to search include deeds, oil & gas, POA, affidavits, judgments, deeds of trust, cancellations, assignments. Record index not computerized. Office will perform a UCC search but public must search other records themselves. UCC search per debtor name- $10.00. Copy fee $2.00 per each. R/E or tax lien copy- $.50 per page. Cert fee- $1.00 per doc plus copy fee. Payee- Chancery Clerk. **Other phones:** Appraiser/Auditor- 601-786-3781; Elections- 601-786-3422; Tax Collector- 601-786-3781. **Assessor**- 601-786-3781.

Jefferson Davis County

Chancery Clerk, PO Box 1137, Prentiss, MS 39474. 601-792-4204; fax-601-792-2894;
Office will perform a UCC search but public must search other records themselves. Search fee $5.00. General copy fee $.50 per page. Tax lien copy- $1.00 per page. Cert fee- $1.00 per page. Payee- Chancery Clerk. **Other phones:** Treasurer- 601-792-4204; Elections- 601-792-4231. **Property tax/Assessor**- 601-792-4291.

Jones County (1st District)

Chancery Clerk, 101 N. Court St; Jones County Courthouse, Ellisville, MS 39437. 601-477-3307; fax-601-477-1240; hours: 8AM-N, 1-5PM.
Record index not computerized. Office will perform a UCC search but public must search other records themselves. UCC search per debtor name- $5.00. Copy fee $.50 per page. Cert fee- $1.00 per page. Payee- Jones County Chancery Clerk. **Other phones:** Elections- 601-425-2556. **Property tax/Assessor**- 601-477-3250.

Jones County (2nd District)

Chancery Clerk, PO Box 1468, Laurel, MS 39441. 601-428-0527, UCC recording phone-601-428-3131; fax-601-428-3602; hours: 8AM-5PM.
Separate indices to search include deeds, deeds of trust. Record index not computerized. Office will perform a UCC search but public must search other records themselves. Search fee $5.00. Copy fee $2.00 per page. R/E record copy- $5.00 per request. Cert fee- $1.00 per page plus copy fee. Payee- Chancery Clerk. **Other phones:** Treasurer- 501-428-3128; Appraiser/Auditor- 601-649-1896; Elections- 601-425-2556; Vital Records- 601-576-7981. **Property tax/Assessor**- same address as above. 601-428-3248.

Kemper County

Chancery Clerk, PO Box 188, De Kalb, MS 39328. 601-743-2560, R/E recording phone-601-743-2460; fax-601-743-2789; hours: 8AM-5PM. http://co.kemper.ms.us/
Office will perform a UCC search but public must search other records themselves. UCC search per debtor name- $5.00. Copy fee $.50 per page. Tax lien copy- $1.00 per page. Cert fee- $1.00 per page. Payee- Chancery Clerk. **Other phones:** Treasurer- 601-743-4290; Appraiser/Auditor- 601-743-2693; Elections- 601-743-2224; Vital Records- 601-743-2224. **Property tax/Assessor**- 601-743-2693.

Lafayette County

Chancery Clerk, PO Box 1240, Oxford, MS 38655. 662-234-2131; fax-662-234-5038; hours: 8AM-5PM.
Records indexed on a public use terminal back to 7/2004. Only the public may search. Copy fee $2.00, if tax lien or real estate $.50 per page. Cert fee- $3.50 per page plus copy fee. Payee- Lafayette County Clerk of the Chancery Court. **Online access to Property Tax, Appraisal records:** Access to property data is free at www.deltacomputersystems.com/ms/ms36/plinkquerym.html . **Other phones:** Appraiser/Auditor- 662-234-

5562; Elections- 662-234-4951. **Property tax/Assessor**- 662-234-6006.

Lamar County

Chancery Clerk, PO Box 247, Purvis, MS 39475. 601-794-8504; fax-601-794-3903; hours: 8AM-5PM. Office personnel or visitors may perform searches. Search fee $5.00 per name. Will not search real estate records. Copy fee $2.00 per page. Cert fee- $1.00 per cert. Payee- Lamar County Chancery Clerk. **Online access to Property Tax, Appraisal records:** Access to property data is free at www.deltacomputersystems.com/MS/MS37/INDEX.html . Other phones: Elections- 601-794-8504.

Lauderdale County

Chancery Clerk, PO Box 1587, Meridian, MS 39302-1587. 601-482-9701, UCC recording phone-601-482-9710; fax-601-486-4943; hours: 8AM-5PM. www.lauderdalecounty.org Separate indices to search include deeds, mortgages. Records indexed on a public use terminal back to 2000. Only the public may search. General copy fee $1.00 per page. UCC copy fee $2.00 per page. Tax lien copy- $2.50 per page. Cert fee- $7.00 per cert plus copy fee. Payee- Lauderdale County Clerk of the Chancery Court. **Online access to Property Tax, Appraisal records:** Access property data free online at www.deltacomputersystems.com/MS/MS38/INDEX.html. **Other phones:** Treasurer- 601-482-4701; Elections- 601-482-9731. **Property tax/Assessor**- 601-482-9779.

Lawrence County

Chancery Clerk, PO Box 821, Monticello, MS 39654. 601-587-7162; fax-601-587-0767; hours: 8AM-5PM. Record index not computerized. Office will perform a UCC search but public must search other records themselves. Search fee $10.00. Copy fee $.50 per copy. Cert fee- $2.00 per copy. Payee- Lawrence County Chancery Clerk. **Other phones:** Treasurer- 601-587-2211; Elections- 601-587-4791; Tax Collector- 601-587-2211. **Property tax/Assessor**- PO Box 812, Monticello, MS 39654; not known.

Leake County

Chancery Clerk, PO Box 72, Carthage, MS 39051. 601-267-7371; fax-601-267-6137; hours: 8AM-5PM. Office personnel or visitors may perform searches. Search fee $5.00 per name. Will not search real estate records. UCC search per debtor name- $10.00. Copy fee $1.00 per page. Cert fee- $1.00 per cert. Payee- Leake County Leake County. **Other phones:** Treasurer- 601-267-7371; Elections- 601-267-8357. **Property tax/Assessor**- 601-267-3021.

Lee County

Chancery Clerk, PO Box 7127, Tupelo, MS 38802. 662-841-9100; fax-662-680-6091; Office personnel or visitors may perform searches. Search fee $5.00 per name. Will not search real estate records. Copy fee $2.00 per page. Cert fee- $1.00 per doc plus copy fee. **Online access to Property Tax, Appraisal records:** Access is to property records is free at www.deltacomputersystems.com/MS/MS41/INDEX.html. **Other phones:** Treasurer- 662-841-9100; Elections- 662-841-9024. **Property tax/Assessor**- 662-841-9030.

Leflore County

Chancery Clerk, PO Box 250, Greenwood, MS 38935-0250. 662-455-7913; fax-662-455-7965; Office personnel or visitors may perform searches. Search fee $5.00 per name. Will not search real estate records. General copy fee $2.00 per page. Tax lien copy- $.50 per page. Cert fee- $1.50 per page. **Other phones:** Elections- 662-453-1435. **Property tax/Assessor**- 662-453-1041.

Lincoln County

Chancery Clerk, PO Box 555, Brookhaven, MS 39602. 601-835-3411; fax-601-835-3423; hours: 8AM-5PM. Office personnel or visitors may perform searches. Search fee $5.00 per name. Will not search real estate records. UCC copy fee $2.00 per page. R/E record copy- $.50 per page. Cert fee- $1.00 per page. Payee- Lincoln County Clerk of the Chancery Court. **Online access to Real Estate, Grantor/Grantee, Deed records:** Access to county deed records is free online at www.deltacomputersystems.com/MS/MS43/drlinkquerym.html. **Other phones:** Treasurer- 601-835-3412; Elections- 601-835-3435. **Property tax/Assessor**- 601-835-3428.

Lowndes County

Chancery Clerk, PO Box 684, Columbus, MS 39703. 662-329-5800, UCC recording phone-662-329-5807; hours: 8AM-5PM. All records in one index. Only the public may search. Copy fee $.50 per page; UCC copy $2.00 per page. Cert fee- $1.00 per cert plus copy fee. Payee- Lowndes County Chancery Clerk. **Other phones:** Treasurer- 662-329-5700; Appraiser/Auditor- 662-329-5701; Elections- 662-329-5900; Vital Records- 601-576-7960. **Property tax/Assessor**- PO Box 1077, Columbus, MS 39703; 662-329-5700.

Madison County

Chancery Clerk, PO Box 404, Canton, MS 39046. 800 428-0584, 601-859-1177; fax-601-859-0337; 8AM-5PM. www.madison-co.com/L2ChanClerk.asp Office personnel or visitors may perform searches. Search fee $5.00 per name. Will not search real estate records. UCC copy fee $2.00 per page. R/E record copy- $.50 per page. Cert fee- $1.00 per cert plus copy fee. Payee- Madison County Clerk. **Other phones:** Elections- 601-352-2049. **Property tax/Assessor**- 601-859-1921.

Marion County

Chancery Clerk, 250 Broad St; #2, Columbia, MS 39429. 601-736-2691; fax-601-444-0206; 8AM-5PM. All records in one index. Records indexed on a public use terminal back to 8/1997. Office personnel or visitors may perform searches. Search fee $5.00 per name. Copy fee $2.00 per page; $.50 self serve. Cert fee- $1.00 per instrument plus copy fee. Payee- Chancery Clerk. **Online access to Real Estate, Recorder, Property Tax, Probate, Judgment, Redemption, Landroll records:** Access county records free at www.deltacomputersystems.com/MS/MS46/INDEX.HTML. Says it is a subscription service, but searching is free. **Other phones:** Elections- 601-736-8246; Vital Records- 601-736-2691. **Property tax/Assessor**- 250 Broad St #3, Columbia, MS 39429; 601-736-8256.

Marshall County

Chancery Clerk, PO Box 219, Holly Springs, MS 38635. 662-252-4431; fax-662-252-0004; Records indexed on a public use terminal. Office personnel or visitors may perform searches. Search fee $5.00 per name. Copy fee $.25 per page. **Online access to Property Tax, Appraisal records:** Access to property tax records is free at www.deltacomputersystems.com/MS/MS47/INDEX.html. **Other phones:** Elections- 662-252-3434. **Property tax/Assessor**- 662-252-3661.

Monroe County

Chancery Clerk, PO Box 578, Aberdeen, MS 39730. 662-369-8143; fax-662-369-7928; hours: 8AM-5PM. Records indexed on a public use terminal back to 1998. Office will perform a UCC and Tax lien search but public must search other records themselves. Search fee $5.00. Copy fee $2.00 per copy. R/E or tax lien copy- $.50 per page. Cert fee- $1.00 per cert plus copy fee. Payee- Chancery Clerk. **Other phones:** Treasurer- 662-369-8143;

Elections- 662-369-8695. **Property tax/Assessor**- 662-369-2033.

Montgomery County

Chancery Clerk, PO Box 71, Winona, MS 38967. 662-283-2333; fax-662-283-2233; hours: 8AM-5PM. Office will perform a UCC search but public must search other records themselves. UCC search per debtor name- $5.00. Copy fee $2.00 per page. Cert fee- $1.00 per cert. Payee- Montgomery County Chancery Clerk. **Other phones:** Elections- 662-283-4161. **Property tax/Assessor**- 662-283-2112.

Neshoba County

Chancery Clerk, 401 Beacon St; #107, Philadelphia, MS 39350. 601-656-3581; hours: 8AM-5PM. Office will perform a UCC search but public must search other records themselves. UCC search per debtor name- $5.00. Copy fee $2.00 per page. Cert fee- $1.00 per page. Payee- Neshoba County Clerk of the Chancery Court. **Online access to Property Tax, Appraisal records:** Property data is free at http://deltacomputersystems.com/MS/MS50/plinkquerym.html. **Other phones:** Elections- 601-656-4781.

Newton County

Chancery Clerk, PO Box 68, Decatur, MS 39327. 601-635-2367; fax-601-635-3210; Office will perform a UCC search but public must search other records themselves. UCC search per debtor name- $5.00. Copy fee $2.00 per sheet. R/E or tax lien copy- $.50 per sheet. Cert fee- $1.00 per cert plus copy fee. Payee- Newton County Chancery Clerk. **Other phones:** Elections- 601-635-2368. **Property tax/Assessor**- 601-635-2367.

Noxubee County

Chancery Clerk, PO Box 147, Macon, MS 39341. 662-726-4243; fax-662-726-2272; hours: 8AM-5PM. Office personnel or visitors may perform searches. Search fee $5.00 per name. Will not search real estate records. Copy fee $2.00 per page. Cert fee- $.50 per page. Payee- Noxubee County Clerk of the Chancery Court. **Other phones:** Treasurer- 662-726-4243; Appraiser/Auditor- 662-726-2772; Elections- 662-726-5737; Vital Records- 601-576-7981. **Property tax/Assessor**- 662-726-4744.

Oktibbeha County

Chancery Clerk, 101 E. Main; Courthouse, Starkville, MS 39759. 662-323-5834; fax-662-338-1064; hours: 8AM-5PM. Separate indices to search include computer and books. Office will perform a UCC search but public must search other records themselves. Tax liens not included in UCC search. UCC search per debtor name- $5.00. Copy fee $1.00, if real estate $.25 per page. Cert fee- $1.00 per cert plus copy fee. Payee- Oktibbeha County Clerk of the Chancery Court. **Other phones:** Appraiser/Auditor- 662-323-1273; Elections- 662-323-1356. **Property tax/Assessor**- 662-323-1273.

Panola County (1st District)

Chancery Clerk, PO Box 130, Sardis, MS 38666. 662-487-2070; fax-662-487-3595; hours: 8AM-N, 1-5PM. Records indexed on a public use terminal back to 2004. Office will perform a UCC search but public must search other records themselves. Search fee $10.00. Copy fee $2.00 per page. Cert fee- $1.00 per cert plus copy fee. Payee- Panola County Clerk. **Other phones:** Treasurer- 662-487-6215; Elections- 662-563-6210; Tax Collector- 662-487-6215. **Property tax/Assessor**- 662-487-2093.

Panola County (2nd District)

Chancery Clerk, 151 Public Sq, Batesville, MS 38606. 662-563-6205; fax-662-563-8233; hours: 8AM-5PM. Office personnel or visitors may perform searches. Search fee $5.00 per name. Will not search real estate records. UCC search per debtor name- $10.00. General copy fee $2.00 per page. Tax lien copy-

$.25. Cert fee- $1.50 per cert. Payee- Panola County Chancery Clerk. **Other phones:** Treasurer- 662-563-6215; Elections- 662-563-6210. **Property tax/Assessor-** 662-563-6270.

Pearl River County

Chancery Clerk, PO Box 431, Poplarville, MS 39470. 601-403-2316; fax-601-403-2317; hours: 8AM-5PM. All records in one index. Record index not computerized. Only the public may search. UCC copy fee $2.00 per page. R/E record copy- $.50 per page. Cert fee- $1.00 per cert plus copy fee. Payee- Pearl River County Clerk of the Chancery Court. **Online access to Property Tax, Appraisal records:** Access to property data is free at www.deltacomputersystems.com/MS/MS55/INDEX.html . **Other phones:** Elections- 601-795-4911. **Property tax/Assessor-** 601-403-2215.

Perry County

Chancery Clerk, PO Box 198, New Augusta, MS 39462. 601-964-8398; fax-601-964-8265; Office will perform a UCC search but public must search other records themselves. UCC search per debtor name- $5.00. Copy fee $.50 per page. Cert fee- $1.00 per doc plus copy fee. Payee- Vickie Walters-Clerk. **Other phones:** Appraiser/Auditor- 601-964-3400; Elections- 601-964-8663. **Property tax/Assessor-** 601-964-3398.

Pike County

Chancery Clerk, PO Box 309, Magnolia, MS 39652. 601-783-3362; fax-601-783-2001; hours: 8AM-5PM. www.co.pike.ms.us
Separate indices to search include Grantor/Grantee, sectional indexes. Records indexed on a public use terminal back to 10/1985. Office will perform a UCC and Tax lien search but public must search other records themselves. Search fee $5.00. Copy fee $.50 per page. Cert fee- $1.00 per page plus copy fee. Payee- Pike County Chancery Clerk. **Online access to Real Estate, Grantor/Grantee, Deed records:** Access to the county Deeds & Records Link is free at www.co.pike.ms.us/drlinkquery.html. Also property assessor records may soon be at www.co.pike.ms.us/tax.html. **Other phones:** Treasurer- 601-783-5289; Elections- 601-783-2581. **Property tax/Assessor-** PO Box 111, Magnolia, MS 39652; 601-783-5511.

Pontotoc County

Chancery Clerk, PO Box 209, Pontotoc, MS 38863. 662-489-3900; fax-662-489-3940; hours: 8AM-5PM. Separate indices to search include deeds, deed of trust, federal tax lien, power of attorneys, UCC's. Records indexed on a public use terminal. Office personnel or visitors may perform searches. Search fee $10.00 per name. Copy fee $4.00 per page. Cert fee- $1.00 per page includes copy fee. Payee- Pontotoc County Clerk of the Chancery Court. **Other phones:** Treasurer- 662-489-3904; Appraiser/Auditor- 662-489-3903; Elections- 662-489-3908; Tax Collector- 662-489-3904. **Property tax/Assessor-** 11 E Washington St, Pontotoc, MS 38863; 662-489-3903.

Prentiss County

Chancery Clerk, PO Box 477, Booneville, MS 38829. 662-728-8151; fax-662-728-2007; hours: 8AM-5PM. Separate indices to search include warranty deeds, trust deeds. Record index not computerized. Office personnel or visitors may perform searches. Search fee $5.00 per name. Will not search real estate records. Copy fee $1.00 per page. Cert fee- $1.00 per doc plus copy fee. Payee- Chancery Clerk. **Other phones:** Treasurer- 662-728-8151; Appraiser/Auditor- 662-728-4349; Elections- 662-728-4611. **Property tax/Assessor-** 662-728-5044.

Quitman County

Chancery Clerk, Chestnut St; Courthouse, Marks, MS 38646. 662-326-2661; fax-662-326-8004; hours: 8AM-N, 1PM-5PM.
Separate indices to search include computer and some hand written. Construction liens, tax liens, judgments. Records indexed on computer back to 1996. Office personnel or visitors may perform searches. Search fee $5.00 per name. Copy fee $.50 per page. Cert fee- $1.00 per cert plus copy fee. Payee- Chancery Clerk. **Other phones:** Treasurer- 662-326-2661; Appraiser/Auditor- 662-326-8928; Elections- 662-326-8003. **Property tax/Assessor-** same address as above. 662-326-8928.

Rankin County

Chancery Clerk, PO Box 1437, Brandon, MS 39043. 601-825-1477; fax-601-824-2450; www.rankincounty.org
Office personnel or visitors may perform searches. Search fee $5.00 per name. Will not search real estate records. **Online access to Real Estate, Tax Assessor, Voter Registration records:** Records on the county Land Roll database are free at www.rankincounty.org/ta/interact.html. Also, voter registration files can be downloaded at www.rankincounty.org/ci. **Other phones:** Treasurer- 601-825-1366; Elections- 601-825-1466. **Property tax/Assessor-** 601-825-1470.

Scott County

Chancery Clerk, PO Box 630, Forest, MS 39074. 601-469-1922; fax-601-469-5180; hours: 8AM-5PM. Records indexed on a public use terminal back to 12/2000. Office will perform a UCC search but public must search other records themselves. Search fee $5.00 base, $2.00 finding. Copy fee $2.00 per page. R/E record copy- $.50 per page. Cert fee- $1.00 per doc plus copy fee. **Other phones:** Elections- 601-469-3601; Tax Collector- 601-469-4051.

Sharkey County

Chancery Clerk, PO Box 218, Rolling Fork, MS 39159. 662-873-2755; fax-662-873-6045; hours: 8AM-5PM. Search fee $10.00 per name. Will not search real estate records. Copy fee $.50 per page. Cert fee- $2.00 per doc plus copy fee. Payee- Sharkey County Clerk. **Other phones:** Elections- 662-873-2755; Tax Collector- 662-873-4317.

Simpson County

Chancery Clerk, PO Box 367, Mendenhall, MS 39114. 601-847-2626, R/E recording phone-601-847-2624, UCC recording phone-601-847-2626; fax-601-847-7016; hours: 8AM-5PM.
Records indexed on a public use terminal back to 1994. Only the public may search. Copy fee $.50 per page. Cert fee- $1.00 per page plus copy fee. Payee- Simpson County Chancery Clerk. **Other phones:** Elections- 601-847-2474. **Property tax/Assessor-** 601-847-1744.

Smith County

Chancery Clerk, PO Box 39, Raleigh, MS 39153. 601-782-9811; fax-601-782-4690; hours: 8AM-5PM. Record index not computerized. Only the public may search. Copy fee $2.00, if tax lien or real estate $.50 per listing. Cert fee- $1.00 per page plus copy fee. Payee- Chancery Clerk. **Other phones:** Treasurer- 601-782-9811; Elections- 601-782-4751. **Property tax/Assessor-** 601-782-9803.

Stone County

Chancery Clerk, PO Drawer 7, Wiggins, MS 39577. 601-928-5266; fax-601-928-6464; hours: 8-5PM. Separate indices to search include land records, power of attorney, construction liens, LIS, deed of trust records, chattel deeds, charter records, pendens, federal judgments. Office will perform a UCC search and federal tax liens, but public must search other records themselves. Search fee $5.00 per name. Copy fee $.50 per page; self serve $.25 per page. Cert fee- $1.00 per doc, plus copy fee. Payee- Stone County Chancery Clerk. **Online access to Property Tax, Appraisal records:** Access property tax records free online at www.deltacomputersystems.com/search.html. **Other phones:** Treasurer- 601-928-5266; Elections- 601-928-5246. **Property tax/Assessor-** 601-928-3121.

Sunflower County

Chancery Clerk, PO Box 988, Indianola, MS 38751-0988. 662-887-4703; fax-662-887-7054; Office personnel or visitors may perform searches. Search fee $5.00 per name. Will not search real estate records. **Other phones:** Treasurer- 662-887-4703; Appraiser/Auditor- 662-887-1454; Elections- 662-887-1252; Vital Records- 662-887-1252. **Property tax/Assessor-** 662-887-1454.

Tallahatchie County (1st District)

Chancery Clerk, PO Box 350, Charleston, MS 38921. 662-647-5551; fax-662-647-3702; 8AM-N,1-5PM. Separate indices to search include land deed records, deeds of trust and Mtgs. Only the public may search. Copy fee $2.00 per page. Cert fee- $2.00 per page. Payee- Tallahatchie County Clerk of the Chancery Court. **Other phones:** Elections- 662-647-8758. **Property tax/Assessor-** PO Box 507, Charleston, MS 38921; 662-647-8922.

Tallahatchie County (2nd District)

Chancery Clerk, PO Box 180, Sumner, MS 38957. 662-375-8731; fax-662-375-7252; hours: 8AM-5PM. All records in one index. Office personnel or visitors may perform searches. Search fee $5.00. Copy fee $2.00, if tax lien or real estate $.50 per page. Cert fee- $1.00 per cert plus copy fee. Payee- Tallahatchie County Clerk of the Chancery Court. **Other phones:** Elections- 662-375-8515. **Property tax/Assessor-** 662-375-8386.

Tate County

Chancery Clerk, 201 Ward St; PO Box 309, Senatobia, MS 38668. 662-562-5661; fax-662-560-6205; hours: 8AM-5PM.
Index: More than one index. Deed records indexed on a public use terminal back to 1986; D/Ts back to 2001. Office will perform a UCC search but public must search other records themselves. UCC search or Fed tax lien search per debtor name- $5.00. Copy fee $.50 per page. R/E record copy- $1.00 per page. Will fax back- $1.00 per page. Cert fee- $1.00 per doc plus copy fee. Payee- Tate Co Chancery Clerk. **Other phones:** Elections- 662-562-5211; Tax Collector- 662-562-4404; Vital Records (Jackson, MS) -601-576-7960. **Property tax/Assessor-** 662-562-6011.

Tippah County

Chancery Clerk, PO Box 99, Ripley, MS 38663. 662-837-7374; fax-662-837-7148; hours: 8AM-5PM. Separate index books to search include deed, trust deed. Records indexed on a public use terminal. Only the public may search. General copy fee $.25 per page. UCC or tax lien copy $2.00 per page. Cert fee- $1.00 per page plus copy fee. Payee- Tippah Chancery Clerk. **Other phones:** Elections- 662-837-7370. **Property tax/Assessor-** 662-837-9410.

Tishomingo County

Chancery Clerk, 1008 Battleground Dr.; Courthouse, Iuka, MS 38852. 662-423-7010; fax-662-423-7005; hours: 8-5PM.
Office personnel or visitors may perform searches. Search fee $7.00 per name. Will not search real estate records. Copy fee $.25 per page. Cert fee- $1.00 per cert. Payee- Chancery Clerk. **Other phones:** Treasurer- 662-423-7032; Elections- 662-423-7026. **Property tax/Assessor-** 662-423-7048.

Tunica County

Chancery Clerk, PO Box 217, Tunica, MS 38676. 662-363-2451; fax-662-357-5934; 8AM-N, 1-5PM. Separate indices to search include land deeds, mtgs. Record index not computerized. Office will perform a UCC and Tax lien search but public must search other records themselves. Search fee $5.00. Copy fee $2.00, if tax lien or real estate $.50 per page. Cert fee- $1.00 per page plus copy fee. Payee- Tunica County Clerk of the Chancery Court. **Other phones:** Treasurer- 662-363-1465; Elections- 662-363-2842. **Property tax/Assessor-** 662-363-1266.

Union County

Chancery Clerk, PO Box 847, New Albany, MS 38652. 662-534-1900; fax-662-534-1907; hours: 8AM-5PM. All records in one index. Records indexed on a public use terminal back to 1999. Only the public may search. Copy fee $.50 per copy. Cert fee- $1.00 per doc includes copy fee. **Other phones:** Treasurer- 662-534-1900; Elections- 662-534-1910; Tax Collector- 662-534-1973. **Property tax/Assessor-** 662-534-1972.

Walthall County

Chancery Clerk, PO Box 351, Tylertown, MS 39667. 601-876-3553; fax-601-876-6026; www.walthallcountychamber.org/ Office personnel or visitors may perform searches. Search fee $10.00 per name. Will not search real estate records. Copy fee $2.00 per page. Cert fee- $1.00 per instrument. Payee- Chancery Clerk. **Other phones:** Appraiser/Auditor- 601-876-4349; Elections- 601-876-5677. **Property tax/Assessor-** 601-876-4349.

Warren County

Chancery Clerk, PO Box 351, Vicksburg, MS 39181. 601-636-4415; fax-601-634-4815; www.co.warren.ms.us Separate indices to search include Land documents and Chancery Court. Records indexed on a public use terminal back to 1984. Office will perform a UCC search but public must search other records themselves. Search fee $5.00. Copy fee $.50 per document. Cert fee- $1.00 per page plus copy fee. Payee- Warren County. **Online access to Property Tax, Appraisal records:** Access is free at www.deltacomputersystems.com/MS/MS75/INDEX.html. **Other phones:** Treasurer- 601-638-6181; Appraiser/Auditor- 601-638-6161; Elections- 601-636-3961; Tax Collector- 601-638-6181. **Property tax/Assessor-** same address. 601-638-6161.

Washington County

Chancery Clerk, PO Box 309, Greenville, MS 38702-0309. 662-332-1595; fax-662-334-2725; 8AM-5PM. Office personnel or visitors may perform searches. Search fee $5.00 per name. Will not search real estate records. UCC copy fee $2.00 per page. R/E record copy- $.50 per page. Cert fee- $1.00 per page. Payee- Washington County Clerk of the Chancery Court. **Online access to Property Tax, Appraisal records:** Access is free at www.deltacomputersystems.com/MS/MS76/INDEX.html. **Other phones:** Treasurer- 662-332-2922; Appraiser/Auditor- 662-332-2651; Elections- 662-378-2747. **Property tax/Assessor-** 662-332-2651.

Wayne County

Chancery Clerk, 609 Azalea Dr.; Wayne County Courthouse, Waynesboro, MS 39367. 601-735-2873; fax-601-735-6224; hours: 8AM-5PM. All records in one index. Records indexed on computer. Only the public may search. Copy fee $2.00 per copy. Cert fee- $1.00. Payee- Wayne County Chancery Clerk. **Other phones:** Treasurer- 601-735-2588; Appraiser/Auditor- 601-735-3381; Elections- 601-735-1171. **Property tax/Assessor-** 601-735-3381.

Webster County

Chancery Clerk, PO Box 398, Walthall, MS 39771. 662-258-4131; fax-662-258-6657; hours: 8-5PM. Separate indices to search include deeds of trust. Office personnel or visitors may perform searches. Search fee $5.00 per name. Will not search real estate records. Copy fee $.50 per page. Cert fee- $1.00 per cert plus copy fee. Payee- Webster County Clerk. **Other phones:** Elections- 662-258-6287. **Property tax/Assessor-** 662-258-6446.

Wilkinson County

Chancery Clerk, PO Box 516, Woodville, MS 39669. 601-888-4381; fax-601-888-6776; hours: 8AM-5PM. Office personnel or visitors may perform searches. Search fee $5.00 per name. Will not search real estate records. Copy fee $2.00 per page. **Other phones:** Treasurer- 601-888-4381; Appraiser/Auditor- 601-888-6146; Elections- 601-888-6697; Vital Records- 601-960-7960. **Property tax/Assessor-** 601-888-4562.

Winston County

Chancery Clerk, PO Drawer 69, Louisville, MS 39339. 662-773-3631; fax-662-773-8814; hours: 8AM-5PM. Office will perform a UCC search but public must search other records themselves. UCC search per debtor name- $5.00. Copy fee $1.00 per page. Tax lien copy- $.50 per page. Cert fee- None. Payee- Winston County Chancery Clerk. **Other phones:** Treasurer- 662-773-3631; Elections- 662-773-3581. **Property tax/Assessor-** 662-773-3694.

Yalobusha County (1st District)

Chancery Clerk, PO Box 260, Coffeeville, MS 38922. 662-675-2716, R/E recording phone-662-675-2091; fax-662-675-8004; hours: 8AM-Noon; 1PM-5PM. Separate indices to search include Deeds, Deeds of Trust, Power of Attorneys. Only the public may search. Copy fee $.50 per page. Cert fee- $1.00 per cert + $.50 per page plus copy fee. Payee- Amy F McMinn, Chancery Clerk. **Other phones:** Treasurer- 662-675-2091; Appraiser/Auditor- 662-675-1235; Elections- 662-675-1341. **Property tax/Assessor-** PO Box 260, Coffeeville, MS 38922 OR PO Box 1552, Water Valley, MS 38965 662-473-1235.

Yalobusha County (2nd District)

Chancery Clerk, PO Box 664, Water Valley, MS 38965. 662-473-2091; fax-662-473-3622; hours: 8AM-5PM. Separate indices to search include deed, trust, reverse, direct. Will not search real estate records. UCC search per debtor name- $5.00. Tax lien search fee- $10.00 per debtor. Copy fee $.50 per page. UCC copy $2.00 per page. Cert fee- $1.00 per doc plus copy fee. Payee- Chancery Clerk. **Other phones:** Treasurer- 662-473-2092; Appraiser/Auditor- 662-473-1235; Elections- 662-473-1341; Vital Records- 601-576-7960. **Property tax/Assessor-** PO Box 1552, Water Valley, MS 38965; 662-473-1235.

Yazoo County

Chancery Clerk, PO Box 68, Yazoo City, MS 39194. 662-746-2661; fax-662-746-3893; hours: 8AM-5PM. Records indexed on a public use terminal back to 1984. Office will perform a UCC search but public must search other records themselves. Search fee $5.00. UCC copy fee $2.00 per page. R/E record copy- $.50 per page. Cert fee- $1.00 per cert plus copy fee. Payee- Yazoo County Clerk of the Chancery Court. **Other phones:** Treasurer- 662-746-2661; Appraiser/Auditor- 662-746-1583; Elections- 662-746-1872. **Property tax/Assessor-** PO Box 108, Yazoo City, MS 39194; 662-746-1583.

Mississippi County Locator

You will usually be able to find the city name in the City/County Cross Reference below. In that case, it is a simple matter to determine the county from the cross reference. However, only the official US Postal Service city names are included in this index. We have also included a ZIP/City Cross Reference immediately following the City/County Cross Reference. If you know the ZIP Code but the city name does not appear in the City/County Cross Reference index, look up the ZIP Code in the ZIP/City Cross Reference, find the city name, then look up the city name in the City/County Cross Reference.

Mississippi City/County Cross Reference

ABBEVILLE Lafayette
ABERDEEN Monroe
ACKERMAN Choctaw
ALGOMA Pontotoc
ALLIGATOR (38720) Bolivar(67), Coahoma(32)
AMORY Monroe
ANGUILLA Sharkey
ARCOLA Washington
ARKABUTLA Tate
ARTESIA Lowndes
ASHLAND (38603) Benton(97), Tippah(2)
AVALON Carroll
AVON Washington
BAILEY (39320) Lauderdale(81), Kemper(18)
BALDWYN (38824) Prentiss(47), Lee(31), Itawamba(14), Union(4)
BANNER (38913) Calhoun(91), Lafayette(8)
BASSFIELD (39421) Jefferson Davis(77), Marion(22)
BATESVILLE Panola
BAY SAINT LOUIS Hancock
BAY SPRINGS (39422) Jasper(72), Smith(27)
BEAUMONT Perry
BECKER Monroe
BELDEN (38826) Lee(55), Pontotoc(44)
BELEN Quitman
BELLEFONTAINE Webster
BELMONT Tishomingo
BELZONI (39038) Humphreys(90), Holmes(7), Leflore(1)
BENOIT Bolivar
BENTON Yazoo
BENTONIA Yazoo
BEULAH Bolivar
BIG CREEK Calhoun
BIGBEE VALLEY Noxubee
BILOXI (39532) Harrison(71), Jackson(28)
BILOXI Harrison
BLUE MOUNTAIN (38610) Tippah(85), Benton(7), Union(6)
BLUE SPRINGS Union
BOGUE CHITTO Lincoln
BOLTON Hinds
BOONEVILLE (38829) Prentiss(94), Tippah(5)
BOYLE Bolivar
BRANDON Rankin
BRAXTON (39044) Simpson(77), Rankin(22)
BROOKHAVEN (39601) Lincoln(97), Franklin(2)
BROOKHAVEN Lincoln
BROOKLYN (39425) Forrest(55), Perry(44)
BROOKSVILLE Noxubee
BRUCE Calhoun
BUCKATUNNA Wayne
BUDE Franklin
BURNSVILLE (38833) Tishomingo(89), Prentiss(5), Alcorn(4)
BYHALIA (38611) Marshall(81), De Soto(18)
BYRAM Hinds
CALEDONIA (39740) Lowndes(90), Monroe(9)
CALHOUN CITY (38916) Calhoun(97), Webster(2)

CAMDEN Madison
CANTON Madison
CARLISLE Claiborne
CARRIERE Pearl River
CARSON Jefferson Davis
CARTHAGE (39051) Leake(94), Neshoba(3), Attala(1)
CARY Sharkey
CASCILLA (38920) Grenada(82), Tallahatchie(17)
CEDARBLUFF Clay
CENTREVILLE (39631) Wilkinson(77), Amite(22)
CHARLESTON Tallahatchie
CHATAWA Pike
CHATHAM Washington
CHUNKY (39323) Newton(79), Lauderdale(20)
CHURCH HILL Jefferson
CLARA Wayne
CLARKSDALE Coahoma
CLEVELAND (38732) Bolivar(96), Sunflower(3)
CLEVELAND Bolivar
CLINTON Hinds
COAHOMA (38617) Coahoma(91), Quitman(8)
COFFEEVILLE (38922) Yalobusha(86), Grenada(13)
COILA Carroll
COLDWATER Tate
COLLINS Covington
COLLINSVILLE (39325) Lauderdale(68), Neshoba(13), Kemper(9), Newton(8)
COLUMBUS Lowndes
COMO (38619) Panola(81), Lafayette(12), Tate(6)
CONEHATTA (39057) Newton(87), Scott(12)
CORINTH Alcorn
COURTLAND Panola
CRAWFORD (39743) Lowndes(74), Oktibbeha(21), Noxubee(4)
CRENSHAW (38621) Panola(75), Quitman(24)
CROSBY (39633) Wilkinson(75), Amite(24)
CROWDER Quitman
CRUGER (38924) Holmes(81), Leflore(11), Carroll(7)
CRYSTAL SPRINGS (39059) Copiah(96), Hinds(3)
D LO Simpson
DALEVILLE (39326) Lauderdale(71), Kemper(28)
DARLING Quitman
DE KALB (39328) Kemper(52), Neshoba(31), Noxubee(15)
DECATUR Newton
DELTA CITY Sharkey
DENNIS Tishomingo
DERMA Calhoun
DIAMONDHEAD Hancock
DIBERVILLE Harrison
DODDSVILLE (38736) Sunflower(57), Leflore(42)
DREW (38737) Sunflower(98), Tallahatchie(1)
DUBLIN Coahoma
DUCK HILL (38925) Montgomery(69), Grenada(30)

DUMAS (38625) Tippah(83), Union(16)
DUNCAN Bolivar
DUNDEE (38626) Tunica(73), Coahoma(26)
DURANT Holmes
EASTABUCHIE Jones
EBENEZER Holmes
ECRU (38841) Pontotoc(97), Union(2)
EDWARDS Hinds
ELLIOTT Grenada
ELLISVILLE Jones
ENID (38927) Tallahatchie(82), Panola(16)
ENTERPRISE (39330) Clarke(85), Lauderdale(8), Jasper(3), Newton(2)
ESCATAWPA Jackson
ETHEL Attala
ETTA Union
EUPORA (39744) Webster(91), Choctaw(6), Calhoun(2)
FALCON Quitman
FALKNER (38629) Tippah(77), Benton(22)
FARRELL Coahoma
FAYETTE Jefferson
FERNWOOD Pike
FITLER Issaquena
FLORA (39071) Madison(96), Hinds(3)
FLORENCE Rankin
FLOWOOD Rankin
FOREST (39074) Scott(90), Smith(9)
FORKVILLE Scott
FOXWORTH (39483) Marion(97), Walthall(2)
FRENCH CAMP (39745) Choctaw(46), Montgomery(38), Attala(15)
FRIARS POINT Coahoma
FULTON Itawamba
GALLMAN Copiah
GATTMAN Monroe
GAUTIER Jackson
GEORGETOWN Copiah
GLEN (38846) Alcorn(84), Tishomingo(15)
GLEN ALLAN Washington
GLENDORA Tallahatchie
GLOSTER Amite
GOLDEN (38847) Itawamba(88), Tishomingo(11)
GOODMAN (39079) Holmes(92), Attala(4), Madison(3)
GORE SPRINGS (38929) Grenada(89), Webster(5), Calhoun(5)
GRACE Issaquena
GREENVILLE Bolivar
GREENVILLE Washington
GREENWOOD Leflore
GREENWOOD SPRINGS (38848) Monroe(98), Itawamba(1)
GRENADA Grenada
GULFPORT Harrison
GUNNISON Bolivar
GUNTOWN (38849) Lee(89), Union(8), Itawamba(1)
HAMILTON Monroe
HARPERVILLE Scott
HARRISTON Jefferson
HARRISVILLE Simpson
HATTIESBURG (39402) Lamar(66), Forrest(33)
HATTIESBURG Forrest
HAZLEHURST Copiah

HEIDELBERG (39439) Jasper(66), Jones(21), Clarke(9), Wayne(3)
HERMANVILLE (39086) Claiborne(78), Copiah(21)
HERNANDO De Soto
HICKORY (39332) Newton(89), Jasper(10)
HICKORY FLAT (38633) Benton(90), Union(9)
HILLSBORO Scott
HOLCOMB (38940) Grenada(93), Carroll(3), Tallahatchie(2)
HOLLANDALE (38748) Washington(90), Sharkey(9)
HOLLY BLUFF Yazoo
HOLLY RIDGE Sunflower
HOLLY SPRINGS (38635) Marshall(89), Benton(6), Tate(3)
HOLLY SPRINGS Marshall
HORN LAKE De Soto
HOULKA (38850) Chickasaw(56), Pontotoc(29), Calhoun(13)
HOUSTON Chickasaw
HURLEY Jackson
INDEPENDENCE Tate
INDIANOLA Sunflower
INVERNESS (38753) Sunflower(93), Humphreys(6)
ISOLA (38754) Humphreys(85), Sunflower(14)
ITTA BENA Leflore
IUKA Tishomingo
JACKSON (39213) Hinds(98), Madison(1)
JACKSON Hinds
JACKSON Rankin
JAYESS (39641) Lawrence(52), Walthall(37), Pike(7), Lincoln(1)
JONESTOWN Coahoma
KILMICHAEL (39747) Montgomery(97), Attala(2)
KILN Hancock
KOKOMO (39643) Marion(85), Walthall(14)
KOSCIUSKO (39090) Attala(84), Leake(15)
LAKE (39092) Scott(71), Newton(25), Smith(3)
LAKE CORMORANT De Soto
LAKESHORE Hancock
LAMAR (38642) Benton(58), Marshall(41)
LAMBERT (38643) Quitman(97), Tallahatchie(2)
LAUDERDALE (39335) Lauderdale(93), Kemper(6)
LAUREL (39443) Jones(86), Jasper(8), Wayne(4)
LAUREL Jones
LAWRENCE Newton
LEAKESVILLE Greene
LELAND Washington
LENA (39094) Leake(53), Scott(38), Rankin(7)
LEXINGTON (39095) Holmes(98), Yazoo(1)
LIBERTY Amite
LITTLE ROCK (39337) Newton(95), Neshoba(4)
LONG BEACH Harrison
LORMAN (39096) Jefferson(64), Claiborne(35)
LOUIN (39338) Jasper(51), Smith(48)
LOUISE Humphreys
LOUISVILLE Winston

LUCEDALE (39452) George(83), Jackson(16)
LUDLOW Scott
LULA Coahoma
LUMBERTON (39455) Lamar(44), Pearl River(42), Stone(11)
LYON Coahoma
MABEN (39750) Webster(77), Oktibbeha(15), Clay(6)
MACON (39341) Noxubee(88), Winston(11)
MADDEN Leake
MAGEE Simpson
MAGNOLIA (39652) Pike(87), Amite(12)
MANTACHIE (38855) Itawamba(98), Lee(1)
MANTEE (39751) Clay(63), Webster(25), Chickasaw(9), Calhoun(2)
MARIETTA (38856) Itawamba(70), Prentiss(29)
MARION Lauderdale
MARKS (38646) Quitman(98), Panola(1)
MATHISTON (39752) Webster(95), Choctaw(4)
MATTSON Coahoma
MAYERSVILLE Issaquena
MAYHEW Lowndes
MC ADAMS Attala
MC CALL CREEK (39647) Franklin(96), Lincoln(2), Wilkinson(1)
MC CARLEY Carroll
MC COMB Pike
MC CONDY Chickasaw
MC COOL (39108) Winston(40), Attala(37), Choctaw(21)
MC HENRY Stone
MC LAIN (39456) Greene(68), Perry(30)
MC NEILL Pearl River
MEADVILLE (39653) Franklin(97), Jefferson(1)
MENDENHALL (39114) Simpson(93), Rankin(6)
MERIDIAN (39301) Lauderdale(89), Clarke(10)
MERIDIAN Lauderdale
MERIGOLD (38759) Sunflower(85), Bolivar(14)
METCALFE Washington
MICHIGAN CITY Benton
MIDNIGHT Humphreys
MINERAL WELLS De Soto
MINTER CITY Leflore
MISSISSIPPI STATE Oktibbeha
MIZE Smith
MONEY Leflore
MONTICELLO (39654) Lawrence(98), Lincoln(1)
MONTPELIER Clay
MOOREVILLE Lee
MOORHEAD Sunflower
MORGAN CITY Leflore
MORGANTOWN Marion
MORTON (39117) Scott(77), Smith(19), Rankin(2)
MOSELLE Jones
MOSS Jasper
MOSS POINT Jackson
MOUND BAYOU Bolivar
MOUNT OLIVE (39119) Covington(50), Simpson(25), Smith(14), Jefferson Davis(8)
MOUNT PLEASANT Marshall
MYRTLE (38650) Union(91), Benton(7)
NATCHEZ (39120) Adams(90), Jefferson(9)
NATCHEZ Adams
NEELY Greene
NESBIT De Soto
NETTLETON (38858) Itawamba(42), Monroe(31), Lee(26)
NEW ALBANY Union
NEW AUGUSTA Perry

NEW SITE Prentiss
NEWHEBRON (39140) Lawrence(91), Jefferson Davis(8)
NEWTON Newton
NICHOLSON Pearl River
NITTA YUMA Sharkey
NORTH CARROLLTON Carroll
NOXAPATER Winston
OAK VALE (39656) Jefferson Davis(80), Lawrence(19)
OAKLAND (38948) Yalobusha(89), Tallahatchie(10)
OCEAN SPRINGS Jackson
OKOLONA (38860) Chickasaw(82), Monroe(8), Lee(7), Pontotoc(1)
OLIVE BRANCH De Soto
OSYKA (39657) Pike(70), Amite(26), Walthall(3)
OVETT (39464) Jones(91), Perry(8)
OXFORD Lafayette
PACE Bolivar
PACHUTA (39347) Jasper(68), Clarke(31)
PANTHER BURN Sharkey
PARCHMAN Sunflower
PARIS Lafayette
PASCAGOULA Jackson
PASS CHRISTIAN (39571) Harrison(97), Hancock(2)
PATTISON (39144) Claiborne(80), Jefferson(14), Copiah(5)
PAULDING Jasper
PEARL Rankin
PEARLINGTON Hancock
PELAHATCHIE (39145) Rankin(95), Scott(4)
PERKINSTON (39573) Stone(59), Hancock(28), George(5), Pearl River(3)
PETAL (39465) Forrest(89), Perry(10)
PHEBA (39755) Clay(91), Oktibbeha(8)
PHILADELPHIA Neshoba
PHILIPP (38950) Tallahatchie(71), Leflore(28)
PICAYUNE Pearl River
PICKENS (39146) Yazoo(66), Madison(31), Holmes(2)
PINEY WOODS Rankin
PINOLA Simpson
PITTSBORO Calhoun
PLANTERSVILLE Lee
PLEASANT GROVE Panola
POCAHONTAS Hinds
PONTOTOC Pontotoc
POPE Panola
POPLARVILLE (39470) Pearl River(98), Hancock(1)
PORT GIBSON Claiborne
PORTERVILLE Kemper
POTTS CAMP (38659) Marshall(82), Benton(17)
PRAIRIE (39756) Clay(75), Monroe(20), Chickasaw(4)
PRAIRIE POINT Noxubee
PRENTISS Jefferson Davis
PRESTON (39354) Kemper(61), Winston(32), Neshoba(4), Noxubee(1)
PUCKETT Rankin
PULASKI (39152) Smith(66), Scott(33)
PURVIS Lamar
QUITMAN Clarke
RALEIGH Smith
RANDOLPH (38864) Pontotoc(95), Calhoun(4)
RAYMOND Hinds
RED BANKS Marshall
REDWOOD Warren
REFORM Choctaw
RENA LARA Coahoma
RICH Coahoma
RICHTON (39476) Perry(94), Wayne(5)
RIDGELAND Madison
RIENZI Alcorn
RIPLEY Tippah

ROBINSONVILLE Tunica
ROLLING FORK Sharkey
ROME Sunflower
ROSE HILL Jasper
ROSEDALE Bolivar
ROXIE (39661) Franklin(89), Adams(8), Jefferson(1)
RULEVILLE Sunflower
RUTH (39662) Lincoln(63), Pike(29), Lawrence(7)
SALLIS Attala
SALTILLO Lee
SANATORIUM Simpson
SANDERSVILLE Jones
SANDHILL Rankin
SANDY HOOK (39478) Marion(56), Walthall(43)
SARAH (38665) Tate(79), Panola(19), Tunica(1)
SARDIS Panola
SATARTIA (39162) Warren(95), Yazoo(4)
SAUCIER Harrison
SCHLATER Leflore
SCOBEY (38953) Yalobusha(52), Grenada(32), Tallahatchie(14)
SCOOBA Kemper
SCOTT Bolivar
SEBASTOPOL Scott
SEMINARY Covington
SENATOBIA Tate
SHANNON (38868) Lee(84), Pontotoc(10), Monroe(3), Chickasaw(1)
SHARON Madison
SHAW (38773) Bolivar(75), Sunflower(24)
SHELBY Bolivar
SHERARD Coahoma
SHERMAN Pontotoc
SHUBUTA (39360) Clarke(78), Wayne(21)
SHUQUALAK Noxubee
SIBLEY Adams
SIDON (38954) Leflore(93), Carroll(5), Holmes(1)
SILVER CITY Humphreys
SILVER CREEK (39663) Lawrence(97), Jefferson Davis(2)
SKENE Bolivar
SLATE SPRING Calhoun
SLEDGE (38670) Quitman(79), Tunica(19)
SMITHDALE (39664) Franklin(59), Amite(33), Lincoln(7)
SMITHVILLE (38870) Monroe(90), Itawamba(9)
SONTAG (39665) Lawrence(80), Lincoln(19)
SOSO (39480) Jones(97), Smith(2)
SOUTHAVEN De Soto
STAR Rankin
STARKVILLE Oktibbeha
STATE LINE (39362) Greene(64), Wayne(35)
STEENS Lowndes
STENNIS SPACE CENTER Hancock
STEWART (39767) Montgomery(41), Webster(37), Choctaw(21)
STONEVILLE Washington
STONEWALL Clarke
STRINGER Jasper
STURGIS (39769) Oktibbeha(79), Winston(19), Choctaw(1)
SUMMIT (39666) Pike(72), Amite(17), Lincoln(9)
SUMNER Tallahatchie
SUMRALL (39482) Lamar(94), Jefferson Davis(3), Marion(2)
SUNFLOWER Sunflower
SWAN LAKE Tallahatchie
SWIFTOWN Leflore
TAYLOR Lafayette
TAYLORSVILLE (39168) Smith(83), Jones(14), Covington(2)
TCHULA Holmes
TERRY Hinds

THAXTON (38871) Pontotoc(87), Lafayette(10), Union(1)
THOMASTOWN Leake
THORNTON Holmes
TIE PLANT Grenada
TILLATOBA (38961) Yalobusha(83), Tallahatchie(15), Grenada(1)
TINSLEY Yazoo
TIPLERSVILLE Tippah
TIPPO Tallahatchie
TISHOMINGO (38873) Tishomingo(91), Prentiss(8)
TOCCOPOLA Lafayette
TOOMSUBA Lauderdale
TOUGALOO (39174) Hinds(91), Madison(8)
TREBLOC Chickasaw
TREMONT Itawamba
TRIBBETT Washington
TULA Lafayette
TUNICA Tunica
TUPELO (38801) Lee(93), Pontotoc(6)
TUPELO (38804) Lee(98), Itawamba(1)
TUPELO Lee
TUTWILER (38963) Coahoma(79), Tallahatchie(18), Sunflower(2)
TYLERTOWN (39667) Walthall(91), Pike(5), Marion(2)
UNION (39365) Neshoba(70), Newton(28), Leake(1)
UNION CHURCH (39668) Jefferson(81), Lincoln(10), Copiah(4), Franklin(3)
UNIVERSITY Lafayette
UTICA (39175) Hinds(82), Copiah(8), Claiborne(8)
VAIDEN (39176) Carroll(65), Attala(29), Montgomery(4)
VALLEY PARK Issaquena
VAN VLEET Chickasaw
VANCE (38964) Quitman(87), Tallahatchie(12)
VARDAMAN (38878) Calhoun(95), Chickasaw(4)
VAUGHAN Yazoo
VERONA Lee
VICKSBURG Warren
VICTORIA Marshall
VOSSBURG (39366) Clarke(63), Jasper(36)
WALLS De Soto
WALNUT (38683) Tippah(79), Alcorn(15), Benton(5)
WALNUT GROVE (39189) Leake(76), Scott(23)
WALTHALL Webster
WASHINGTON Adams
WATER VALLEY (38965) Yalobusha(92), Panola(4), Lafayette(2)
WATERFORD (38685) Marshall(92), Lafayette(7)
WAVELAND Hancock
WAYNESBORO (39367) Wayne(97), Clarke(2)
WAYSIDE Washington
WEBB Tallahatchie
WEIR Choctaw
WESSON (39191) Copiah(58), Lincoln(40)
WEST (39192) Holmes(81), Attala(17), Carroll(1)
WEST POINT (39773) Clay(97), Monroe(2)
WHEELER Prentiss
WHITFIELD Rankin
WIGGINS (39577) Stone(84), Forrest(8), Perry(6)
WINONA (38967) Montgomery(95), Carroll(4)
WINSTONVILLE Bolivar
WINTERVILLE Washington
WOODLAND (39776) Chickasaw(77), Clay(22)
WOODVILLE Wilkinson
YAZOO CITY Yazoo

Mississippi ZIP/City Cross Reference

38601-38601	ABBEVILLE
38602-38602	ARKABUTLA
38603-38603	ASHLAND
38606-38606	BATESVILLE
38609-38609	BELEN
38610-38610	BLUE MOUNTAIN
38611-38611	BYHALIA
38614-38614	CLARKSDALE
38617-38617	COAHOMA
38618-38618	COLDWATER
38619-38619	COMO
38620-38620	COURTLAND
38621-38621	CRENSHAW
38622-38622	CROWDER
38623-38623	DARLING
38625-38625	DUMAS
38626-38626	DUNDEE
38627-38627	ETTA
38628-38628	FALCON
38629-38629	FALKNER
38630-38630	FARRELL
38631-38631	FRIARS POINT
38632-38632	HERNANDO
38633-38633	HICKORY FLAT
38634-38634	HOLLY SPRINGS
38637-38637	HORN LAKE
38638-38638	INDEPENDENCE
38639-38639	JONESTOWN
38641-38641	LAKE CORMORANT
38642-38642	LAMAR
38643-38643	LAMBERT
38644-38644	LULA
38645-38645	LYON
38646-38646	MARKS
38647-38647	MICHIGAN CITY
38648-38648	MINERAL WELLS
38649-38649	MOUNT PLEASANT
38650-38650	MYRTLE
38651-38651	NESBIT
38652-38652	NEW ALBANY
38654-38654	OLIVE BRANCH
38655-38655	OXFORD
38657-38657	PLEASANT GROVE
38658-38658	POPE
38659-38659	POTTS CAMP
38661-38661	RED BANKS
38662-38662	RICH
38663-38663	RIPLEY
38664-38664	ROBINSONVILLE
38665-38665	SARAH
38666-38666	SARDIS
38668-38668	SENATOBIA
38669-38669	SHERARD
38670-38670	SLEDGE
38671-38672	SOUTHAVEN
38673-38673	TAYLOR
38674-38674	TIPLERSVILLE
38675-38675	TULA
38676-38676	TUNICA
38677-38677	UNIVERSITY
38679-38679	VICTORIA
38680-38680	WALLS
38683-38683	WALNUT
38685-38685	WATERFORD
38686-38686	WALLS
38701-38704	GREENVILLE
38720-38720	ALLIGATOR
38721-38721	ANGUILLA
38722-38722	ARCOLA
38723-38723	AVON
38725-38725	BENOIT
38726-38726	BEULAH
38730-38730	BOYLE
38731-38731	CHATHAM
38732-38733	CLEVELAND
38736-38736	DODDSVILLE
38737-38737	DREW
38738-38738	PARCHMAN
38739-38739	DUBLIN
38740-38740	DUNCAN
38744-38744	GLEN ALLAN
38745-38745	GRACE
38746-38746	GUNNISON
38748-38748	HOLLANDALE
38749-38749	HOLLY RIDGE
38751-38751	INDIANOLA
38753-38753	INVERNESS
38754-38754	ISOLA
38755-38755	GREENVILLE
38756-38756	LELAND
38758-38758	MATTSON
38759-38759	MERIGOLD
38760-38760	METCALFE
38761-38761	MOORHEAD
38762-38762	MOUND BAYOU
38763-38763	NITTA YUMA
38764-38764	PACE
38765-38765	PANTHER BURN
38767-38767	RENA LARA
38768-38768	ROME
38769-38769	ROSEDALE
38771-38771	RULEVILLE
38772-38772	SCOTT
38773-38773	SHAW
38774-38774	SHELBY
38775-38775	SKENE
38776-38776	STONEVILLE
38778-38778	SUNFLOWER
38779-38779	TRIBBETT
38780-38780	WAYSIDE
38781-38781	WINSTONVILLE
38782-38782	WINTERVILLE
38801-38804	TUPELO
38820-38820	ALGOMA
38821-38821	AMORY
38824-38824	BALDWYN
38825-38825	BECKER
38826-38826	BELDEN
38827-38827	BELMONT
38828-38828	BLUE SPRINGS
38829-38829	BOONEVILLE
38833-38833	BURNSVILLE
38834-38835	CORINTH
38838-38838	DENNIS
38839-38839	DERMA
38841-38841	ECRU
38843-38843	FULTON
38844-38844	GATTMAN
38846-38846	GLEN
38847-38847	GOLDEN
38848-38848	GREENWOOD SPRINGS
38849-38849	GUNTOWN
38850-38850	HOULKA
38851-38851	HOUSTON
38852-38852	IUKA
38854-38854	MC CONDY
38855-38855	MANTACHIE
38856-38856	MARIETTA
38857-38857	MOOREVILLE
38858-38858	NETTLETON
38859-38859	NEW SITE
38860-38860	OKOLONA
38862-38862	PLANTERSVILLE
38863-38863	PONTOTOC
38864-38864	RANDOLPH
38865-38865	RIENZI
38866-38866	SALTILLO
38868-38868	SHANNON
38869-38869	SHERMAN
38870-38870	SMITHVILLE
38871-38871	THAXTON
38873-38873	TISHOMINGO
38874-38874	TOCCOPOLA
38875-38875	TREBLOC
38876-38876	TREMONT
38877-38877	VAN VLEET
38878-38878	VARDAMAN
38879-38879	VERONA
38880-38880	WHEELER
38901-38902	GRENADA
38912-38912	AVALON
38913-38913	BANNER
38914-38914	BIG CREEK
38915-38915	BRUCE
38916-38916	CALHOUN CITY
38917-38917	CARROLLTON
38920-38920	CASCILLA
38921-38921	CHARLESTON
38922-38922	COFFEEVILLE
38923-38923	COILA
38924-38924	CRUGER
38925-38925	DUCK HILL
38926-38926	ELLIOTT
38927-38927	ENID
38928-38928	GLENDORA
38929-38929	GORE SPRINGS
38930-38935	GREENWOOD
38940-38940	HOLCOMB
38941-38941	ITTA BENA
38943-38943	MC CARLEY
38944-38944	MINTER CITY
38945-38945	MONEY
38946-38946	MORGAN CITY
38947-38947	NORTH CARROLLTON
38948-38948	OAKLAND
38949-38949	PARIS
38950-38950	PHILIPP
38951-38951	PITTSBORO
38952-38952	SCHLATER
38953-38953	SCOBEY
38954-38954	SIDON
38955-38955	SLATE SPRING
38957-38957	SUMNER
38958-38958	SWAN LAKE
38959-38959	SWIFTOWN
38960-38960	TIE PLANT
38961-38961	TILLATOBA
38962-38962	TIPPO
38963-38963	TUTWILER
38964-38964	VANCE
38965-38965	WATER VALLEY
38966-38966	WEBB
38967-38967	WINONA
39038-39038	BELZONI
39039-39039	BENTON
39040-39040	BENTONIA
39041-39041	BOLTON
39042-39043	BRANDON
39044-39044	BRAXTON
39045-39045	CAMDEN
39046-39046	CANTON
39047-39047	BRANDON
39049-39049	CARLISLE
39051-39051	CARTHAGE
39054-39054	CARY
39055-39055	CHURCH HILL
39056-39056	CLINTON
39057-39057	CONEHATTA
39058-39058	CLINTON
39059-39059	CRYSTAL SPRINGS
39060-39060	CLINTON
39061-39061	DELTA CITY
39062-39062	D LO
39063-39063	DURANT
39064-39064	EBENEZER
39066-39066	EDWARDS
39067-39067	ETHEL
39069-39069	FAYETTE
39070-39070	FITLER
39071-39071	FLORA
39072-39072	POCAHONTAS
39073-39073	FLORENCE
39074-39074	FOREST
39076-39076	FORKVILLE
39077-39077	GALLMAN
39078-39078	GEORGETOWN
39079-39079	GOODMAN
39080-39080	HARPERVILLE
39081-39081	HARRISTON
39082-39082	HARRISVILLE
39083-39083	HAZLEHURST
39086-39086	HERMANVILLE
39087-39087	HILLSBORO
39088-39088	HOLLY BLUFF
39090-39090	KOSCIUSKO
39092-39092	LAKE
39094-39094	LENA
39095-39095	LEXINGTON
39096-39096	LORMAN
39097-39097	LOUISE
39098-39098	LUDLOW
39107-39107	MC ADAMS
39108-39108	MC COOL
39109-39109	MADDEN
39110-39110	MADISON
39111-39111	MAGEE
39112-39112	SANATORIUM
39113-39113	MAYERSVILLE
39114-39114	MENDENHALL
39115-39115	MIDNIGHT
39116-39116	MIZE
39117-39117	MORTON
39119-39119	MOUNT OLIVE
39120-39122	NATCHEZ
39130-39130	MADISON
39140-39140	NEWHEBRON
39144-39144	PATTISON
39145-39145	PELAHATCHIE
39146-39146	PICKENS
39148-39148	PINEY WOODS
39149-39149	PINOLA
39150-39150	PORT GIBSON
39151-39151	PUCKETT
39152-39152	PULASKI
39153-39153	RALEIGH
39154-39154	RAYMOND
39156-39156	REDWOOD
39157-39158	RIDGELAND
39159-39159	ROLLING FORK
39160-39160	SALLIS
39161-39161	SANDHILL
39162-39162	SATARTIA
39163-39163	SHARON
39165-39165	SIBLEY
39166-39166	SILVER CITY
39167-39167	STAR
39168-39168	TAYLORSVILLE
39169-39169	TCHULA
39170-39170	TERRY
39171-39171	THOMASTOWN
39172-39172	THORNTON
39173-39173	TINSLEY
39174-39174	TOUGALOO
39175-39175	UTICA
39176-39176	VAIDEN
39177-39177	VALLEY PARK
39179-39179	VAUGHAN
39180-39183	VICKSBURG
39189-39189	WALNUT GROVE
39190-39190	WASHINGTON
39191-39191	WESSON
39192-39192	WEST
39193-39193	WHITFIELD
39194-39194	YAZOO CITY
39200-39208	JACKSON
39208-39208	PEARL
39209-39232	JACKSON
39232-39232	FLOWOOD
39235-39272	JACKSON
39272-39272	BYRAM
39282-39298	JACKSON
39301-39309	MERIDIAN
39320-39320	BAILEY
39322-39322	BUCKATUNNA
39323-39323	CHUNKY
39324-39324	CLARA

39325-39325	COLLINSVILLE	
39326-39326	DALEVILLE	
39327-39327	DECATUR	
39328-39328	DE KALB	
39330-39330	ENTERPRISE	
39332-39332	HICKORY	
39335-39335	LAUDERDALE	
39336-39336	LAWRENCE	
39337-39337	LITTLE ROCK	
39338-39338	LOUIN	
39339-39339	LOUISVILLE	
39341-39341	MACON	
39342-39342	MARION	
39345-39345	NEWTON	
39346-39346	NOXAPATER	
39347-39347	PACHUTA	
39348-39348	PAULDING	
39350-39350	PHILADELPHIA	
39352-39352	PORTERVILLE	
39353-39353	PRAIRIE POINT	
39354-39354	PRESTON	
39355-39355	QUITMAN	
39356-39356	ROSE HILL	
39358-39358	SCOOBA	
39359-39359	SEBASTOPOL	
39360-39360	SHUBUTA	
39361-39361	SHUQUALAK	
39362-39362	STATE LINE	
39363-39363	STONEWALL	
39364-39364	TOOMSUBA	
39365-39365	UNION	
39366-39366	VOSSBURG	
39367-39367	WAYNESBORO	
39400-39407	HATTIESBURG	
39421-39421	BASSFIELD	
39422-39422	BAY SPRINGS	
39423-39423	BEAUMONT	
39425-39425	BROOKLYN	
39426-39426	CARRIERE	

39427-39427	CARSON
39428-39428	COLLINS
39429-39429	COLUMBIA
39436-39436	EASTABUCHIE
39437-39437	ELLISVILLE
39439-39439	HEIDELBERG
39440-39443	LAUREL
39451-39451	LEAKESVILLE
39452-39452	LUCEDALE
39455-39455	LUMBERTON
39456-39456	MC LAIN
39457-39457	MC NEILL
39459-39459	MOSELLE
39460-39460	MOSS
39461-39461	NEELY
39462-39462	NEW AUGUSTA
39463-39463	NICHOLSON
39464-39464	OVETT
39465-39465	PETAL
39466-39466	PICAYUNE
39470-39470	POPLARVILLE
39474-39474	PRENTISS
39475-39475	PURVIS
39476-39476	RICHTON
39477-39477	SANDERSVILLE
39478-39478	SANDY HOOK
39479-39479	SEMINARY
39480-39480	SOSO
39481-39481	STRINGER
39482-39482	SUMRALL
39483-39483	FOXWORTH
39484-39484	MORGANTOWN
39500-39507	GULFPORT
39520-39522	BAY SAINT LOUIS
39522-39522	STENNIS SPACE CENTER
39525-39525	DIAMONDHEAD
39529-39529	BAY SAINT LOUIS
39530-39535	BILOXI
39540-39540	DIBERVILLE

39552-39552	ESCATAWPA
39553-39553	GAUTIER
39555-39555	HURLEY
39556-39556	KILN
39558-39558	LAKESHORE
39560-39560	LONG BEACH
39561-39561	MC HENRY
39562-39563	MOSS POINT
39564-39566	OCEAN SPRINGS
39567-39569	PASCAGOULA
39571-39571	PASS CHRISTIAN
39572-39572	PEARLINGTON
39573-39573	PERKINSTON
39574-39574	SAUCIER
39576-39576	WAVELAND
39577-39577	WIGGINS
39581-39595	PASCAGOULA
39601-39603	BROOKHAVEN
39629-39629	BOGUE CHITTO
39630-39630	BUDE
39631-39631	CENTREVILLE
39632-39632	CHATAWA
39633-39633	CROSBY
39635-39635	FERNWOOD
39638-39638	GLOSTER
39641-39641	JAYESS
39643-39643	KOKOMO
39645-39645	LIBERTY
39647-39647	MC CALL CREEK
39648-39649	MC COMB
39652-39652	MAGNOLIA
39653-39653	MEADVILLE
39654-39654	MONTICELLO
39656-39656	OAK VALE
39657-39657	OSYKA
39661-39661	ROXIE
39662-39662	RUTH
39663-39663	SILVER CREEK
39664-39664	SMITHDALE

39665-39665	SONTAG
39666-39666	SUMMIT
39667-39667	TYLERTOWN
39668-39668	UNION CHURCH
39669-39669	WOODVILLE
39701-39710	COLUMBUS
39730-39730	ABERDEEN
39735-39735	ACKERMAN
39736-39736	ARTESIA
39737-39737	BELLEFONTAINE
39738-39738	BIGBEE VALLEY
39739-39739	BROOKSVILLE
39740-39740	CALEDONIA
39741-39741	CEDARBLUFF
39743-39743	CRAWFORD
39744-39744	EUPORA
39745-39745	FRENCH CAMP
39746-39746	HAMILTON
39747-39747	KILMICHAEL
39750-39750	MABEN
39751-39751	MANTEE
39752-39752	MATHISTON
39753-39753	MAYHEW
39754-39754	MONTPELIER
39755-39755	PHEBA
39756-39756	PRAIRIE
39757-39757	REFORM
39759-39760	STARKVILLE
39762-39762	MISSISSIPPI STATE
39766-39766	STEENS
39767-39767	STEWART
39769-39769	STURGIS
39771-39771	WALTHALL
39772-39772	WEIR
39773-39773	WEST POINT
39776-39776	WOODLAND

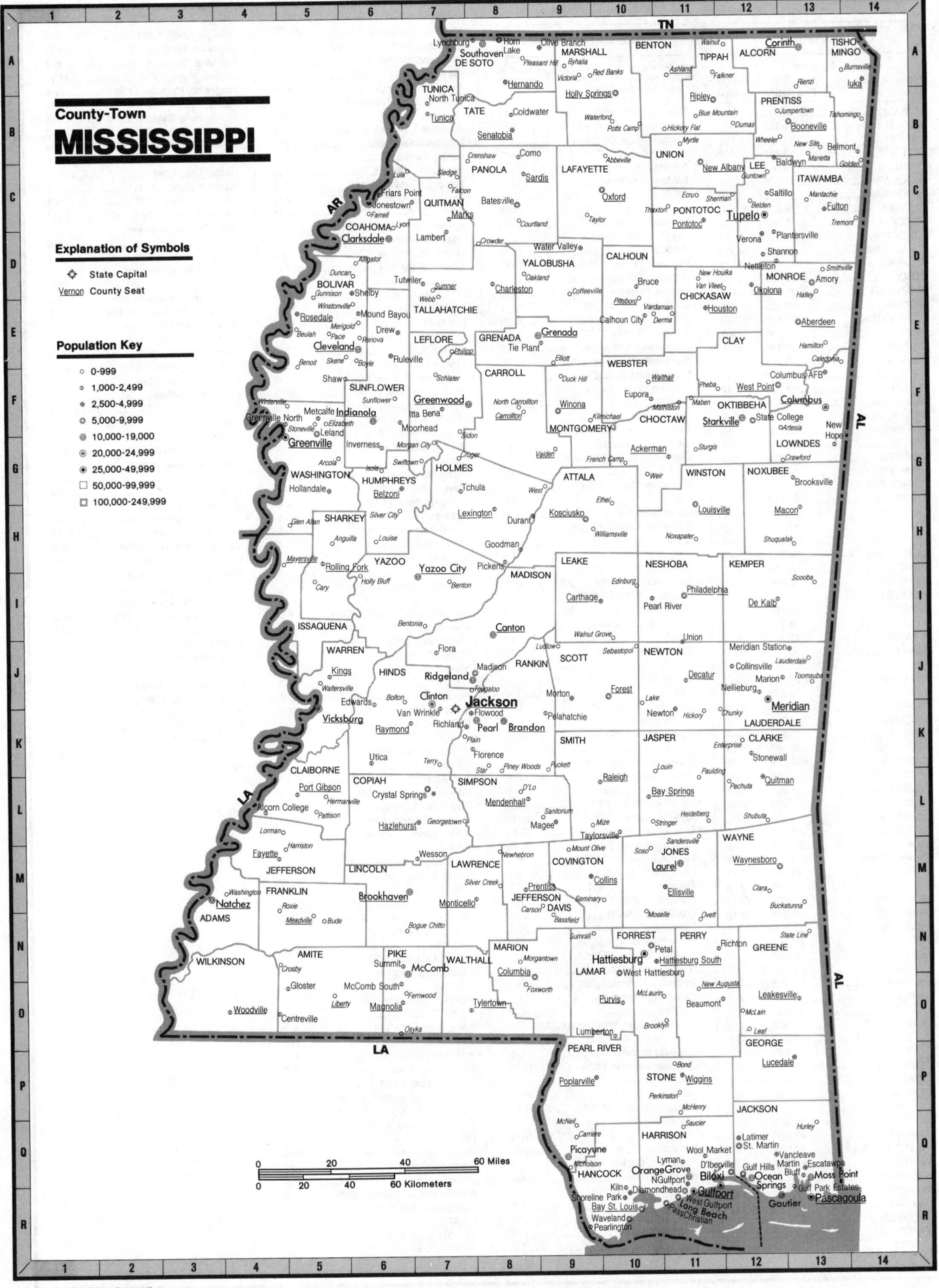

County-Town

MISSISSIPPI

Explanation of Symbols

✧ State Capital

Vernon County Seat

Population Key

○ 0-999
⊕ 1,000-2,499
⊕ 2,500-4,999
⊙ 5,000-9,999
◉ 10,000-19,000
◉ 20,000-24,999
◉ 25,000-49,999
☐ 50,000-99,999
☐ 100,000-249,999

COUNTIES

(82 Counties)

Name of County	Population	Location on Map
ADAMS	35,356	N-3
ALCORN	31,722	A-12
AMITE	13,328	N-5
ATTALA	18,481	G-9
BENTON	8,046	A-10
BOLIVAR	41,875	D-5
CALHOUN	14,908	D-10
CARROLL	9,237	F-8
CHICKASAW	18,085	E-11
CHOCTAW	9,071	F-10
CLAIBORNE	11,370	K-5
CLARKE	17,313	K-12
CLAY	21,120	E-12
COAHOMA	31,665	C-6
COPIAH	27,592	L-6
COVINGTON	16,527	M-9
DESOTO	67,910	A-7
FORREST	68,314	N-10
FRANKLIN	8,377	M-4
GEORGE	16,673	O-12
GREENE	10,220	N-12
GRENADA	21,555	E-8
HANCOCK	31,760	Q-9
HARRISON	165,365	Q-10
HINDS	254,441	J-6
HOLMES	21,604	G-7
HUMPHREYS	12,134	G-6
ISSAQUENA	1,909	I-5
ITAWAMBA	20,017	C-13
JACKSON	115,243	P-12
JASPER	17,114	K-10
JEFFERSON	8,653	M-4
JEFFERSON DAVIS	14,051	M-8
JONES	62,031	M-11
KEMPER	10,356	H-12
LAFAYETTE	31,826	C-9
LAMAR	30,424	N-9
LAUDERDALE	75,555	K-12
LAWRENCE	12,458	M-7
LEAKE	18,436	H-9
LEE	65,581	C-12
LEFLORE	37,341	E-7
LINCOLN	30,278	M-6
LOWNDES	59,308	G-12
MADISON	53,794	I-8
MARION	25,544	N-8
MARSHALL	30,361	A-9
MONROE	36,582	D-12
MONTGOMERY	12,388	F-9
NESHOBA	24,800	H-10
NEWTON	20,291	J-10
NOXUBEE	12,604	G-12
OKTIBBEHA	38,375	F-12
PANOLA	29,996	C-8
PEARL RIVER	38,714	P-9
PERRY	10,865	N-11
PIKE	36,882	N-6
PONTOTOC	22,237	C-11
PRENTISS	23,278	B-12
QUITMAN	10,490	C-7
RANKIN	87,161	J-8
SCOTT	24,137	J-9
SHARKEY	7,066	H-5
SIMPSON	23,953	L-8
SMITH	14,798	K-9
STONE	10,750	P-10
SUNFLOWER	32,867	F-6
TALLAHATCHIE	15,210	E-7
TATE	21,432	B-8
TIPPAH	19,523	A-11
TISHOMINGO	17,683	A-13
TUNICA	8,164	A-7
UNION	22,085	B-11
WALTHALL	14,352	N-7
WARREN	47,880	J-5
WASHINGTON	67,935	G-5
WAYNE	19,517	L-12
WEBSTER	10,222	E-10
WILKINSON	9,678	N-3
WINSTON	19,433	G-11
YALOBUSHA	12,033	D-8
YAZOO	25,506	H-6
TOTAL	**2,573,216**	

CITIES AND TOWNS

Note: The first name is that of the city or town, second, that of the county in which it is located, then the population and location on the map.

Aberdeen, Monroe, 6,837 .... E-13
Ackerman, Choctaw, 1,573 .... G-11
Alcorn College, Claiborne L-4
Amory, Monroe, 7,093 .... D-13
Ashland, Benton, 490 .... A-11
Baldwyn, Lee/Prentiss, 3,204 ...... C-12
Batesville, Panola, 6,403 .... C-8
Bay Springs, Jasper, 1,729 .... L-10
Bay St. Louis, Hancock, 8,063 ..... R-10
Beaumont, Perry, 1,054 .... O-11
Belmont, Tishomingo, 1,554 .... B-14
Belzoni, Humphreys, 2,536 .... G-6
Biloxi, Harrison, 46,319 .... R-11
Booneville, Prentiss, 7,955 .... B-13
Brandon, Rankin, 11,077 .... K-8
Brookhaven, Lincoln, 10,243 .... M-6
Brooksville, Noxubee, 1,098 .... G-13
Bruce, Calhoun, 2,127 .... D-10
Calhoun City, Calhoun, 1,838 ...... E-10
Canton, Madison, 10,062 .... I-8
Carrollton, Carroll, 221 .... F-8
Carthage, Leake, 3,819 .... I-10
Centreville, Amite/Wilkinson, 1,771 .... O-4
Charleston, Tallahatchie, 2,328 .... D-8
Clarksdale, Coahoma, 19,717 ...... D-6
Cleveland, Bolivar, 15,384 .... E-6
Clinton, Hinds, 21,847 .... J-7
Coldwater, Tate, 1,502 .... B-8
Collins, Covington, 2,541 .... M-9
• Collinsville, Lauderdale, 1,364 ... J-10
Columbia, Marion, 6,815 .... N-8
Columbus, Lowndes, 23,799 .... F-13
• Columbus AFB, Lowndes, 2,890 .... F-13
Como, Panola, 1,387 .... B-8
Corinth, Alcorn, 11,820 .... A-13
Crystal Springs, Copiah, 5,643 ..... L-7
De Kalb, Kemper, 1,073 .... I-12
Decatur, Newton, 1,248 .... J-11
• Diamondhead, Hancock, 2,661 .... R-10
D'Iberville, Harrison, 6,566 .... Q-12
Drew, Sunflower, 2,349 .... E-6
Durant, Holmes, 2,838 .... H-8
Edwards, Hinds, 1,279 .... J-6
Ellisville, Jones, 3,634 .... M-11
• Escatawpa, Jackson, 3,902 .... Q-13
Eupora, Webster, 2,145 .... F-10
Fayette, Jefferson, 1,853 .... M-4
Flora, Madison, 1,482 .... J-7
Florence, Rankin, 1,831 .... K-8
Flowood, Rankin, 2,860 .... K-6
Forest, Scott, 5,060 .... J-10
Friars Point, Coahoma, 1,334 ...... C-6
Fulton, Itawamba, 3,387 .... C-13
Gautier, Jackson, 10,088 .... R-11
Gloster, Amite, 1,323 .... O-5
Goodman, Holmes, 1,256 .... H-8
Greenville, Washington, 45,226 ... G-5
Greenville North, Washington F-5
Greenwood, Leflore, 18,906 .... F-7
Grenada, Grenada, 10,864 .... E-9
• Gulf Hills, Jackson, 5,004 .... Q-12
• Gulf Park Estates, Jackson, 2,314 .... R-11
Gulfport, Harrison, 40,775 .... R-11
Hattiesburg, Forrest/Lamar, 41,882 .... N-10
Hattiesburg South, Forrest N-10
Hazlehurst, Copiah, 4,221 .... L-7
Hernando, DeSoto, 3,125 .... A-8
Hollandale, Washington, 3,576 ..... G-5
Holly Springs, Marshall, 7,261 ..... A-8
Horn Lake, DeSoto, 9,069 .... A-7

Houston, Chickasaw, 3,903 .... E-11
Indianola, Sunflower, 11,809 .... F-6
Inverness, Sunflower, 1,174 .... G-6
Itta Bena, Leflore, 2,377 .... F-6
Iuka, Tishomingo, 3,122 .... A-14
Jackson, Hinds/Madison/ Rankin, 196,637 .... J-7
Jonestown, Coahoma, 1,467 .... C-7
• Kiln, Hancock, 1,262 .... R-8
Kings, Warren J-5
Kosciusko, Attala, 6,986 .... H-9
Lambert, Quitman, 1,131 .... D-7
Latimer, Jackson, 3,222 .... Q-10
Laurel, Jones, 18,827 .... M-11
Leakesville, Greene, 1,129 .... O-13
Leland, Washington, 6,366 .... F-5
Lexington, Holmes, 2,227 .... H-8
Liberty, Amite, 624 .... O-5
Long Beach, Harrison, 15,804 ..... R-9
Louisville, Winston, 7,169 .... H-11
Lucedale, George, 2,592 .... P-13
Lumberton, Lamar/Pearl River, 2,121 .... O-10
• Lyman, Harrison, 1,117 .... Q-9
• Lynchburg, DeSoto, 2,071 .... A-6
Macon, Noxubee, 2,256 .... H-13
Madison, Madison, 7,471 .... J-8
Magee, Simpson, 3,607 .... L-9
Magnolia, Pike, 2,245 .... O-6
Marion, Lauderdale, 1,359 .... J-11
Marks, Quitman, 1,758 .... C-7
• Martin Bluff, Jackson, 1,928 ...... R-11
Mayersville, Issaquena, 329 .... H-5
McComb, Pike, 11,591 .... N-6
McComb South, Pike O-6
Meadville, Franklin, 453 .... N-5
Mendenhall, Simpson, 2,463 .... L-8
Meridian, Lauderdale, 41,036 ...... J-12
• Meridian Station, Lauderdale, 2,503 .... J-13
Metcalfe, Washington, 1,092 .... F-3
Monticello, Lawrence, 1,755 .... M-8
Moorhead, Sunflower, 2,417 .... F-6
Morton, Scott, 3,212 .... J-9
Moss Point, Jackson, 17,837 .... Q-13
Mound Bayou, Bolivar, 2,222 ...... E-6
Natchez, Adams, 19,460 .... M-3
• Nellieburg, Lauderdale, 1,208 .... J-12
Nettleton, Lee/Monroe, 2,462 ...... D-12
New Albany, Union, 6,775 .... C-11
New Augusta, Perry, 668 .... O-11
• New Hope, Lowndes, 1,663 .... G-12
Newton, Newton, 3,701 .... K-11
• North Gulfport, Harrison, 4,966 .... Q-11
• North Tunica, Tunica, 1,314 .... B-7
Ocean Springs, Jackson, 14,658 .... Q-12
Okolona, Chickasaw, 3,267 .... D-12
Olive Branch, DeSoto, 3,567 .... A-9
• Orange Grove, Harrison, 15,676 .... Q-11
Oxford, Lafayette, 9,984 .... C-10
Pascagoula, Jackson, 25,899 ...... R-13
Pass Christian, Harrison, 5,557 ... R-11
Pearl, Rankin, 19,588 .... K-8
• Pearl River, Neshoba, 2,136 ...... I-9
• Pearlington, Hancock, 1,603 ...... R-8
Pelahatchie, Rankin, 1,553 .... K-9
Petal, Forrest, 7,883 .... N-10
Philadelphia, Neshoba, 6,758 ...... I-11
Picayune, Pearl River, 10,633 ..... Q-9
Pickens, Holmes, 1,285 .... H-8
Pittsboro, Calhoun, 277 .... E-10
Plantersville, Lee, 1,046 .... D-11
Pontotoc, Pontotoc, 4,570 .... C-11
Poplarville, Pearl River, 2,561 ..... P-9
Port Gibson, Claiborne, 1,810 ..... L-5
Prentiss, Jefferson Davis, 1,487 .... M-8
Purvis, Lamar, 2,140 .... O-10
Quitman, Clarke, 2,736 .... L-12

Raleigh, Smith, 1,291 .... L-8
Raymond, Hinds, 2,275 .... K-7
Richland, Rankin, 4,014 .... K-7
Richton, Perry, 1,034 .... N-11
Ridgeland, Madison, 11,714 .... J-6
Ripley, Tippah, 5,371 .... B-11
Rolling Fork, Sharkey, 2,444 .... H-5
Rosedale, Bolivar, 2,595 .... E-5
Ruleville, Sunflower, 3,245 .... E-6
• Saint Martin, Jackson, 6,349 ..... Q-10
Saltillo, Lee, 1,782 .... C-12
Sardis, Panola, 2,128 .... C-8
Senatobia, Tate, 4,772 .... B-8
Shannon, Lee, 1,419 .... D-11
Shaw, Bolivar/Sunflower, 2,349 .... F-6
• Shelby, Bolivar, 2,806 .... D-6
• Shoreline Park, Hancock, 2,775 .... R-8
Southaven, DeSoto, 17,949 .... A-8
Starkville, Oktibbeha, 18,458 ...... F-12
State College, Oktibbeha, 1,148 .. F-12
Stonewall, Clarke, 1,148 .... K-12
Summit, Pike, 1,566 .... N-6
Taylorsville, Smith, 1,412 .... L-10
Tchula, Holmes, 2,186 .... G-7
Tie Plant, Grenada E-9
Tunica, Tunica, 1,175 .... B-7
Tupelo, Lee, 30,685 .... C-12
Tutwiler, Tallahatchie, 1,391 .... D-7
Tylertown, Walthall, 1,938 .... O-7
Union, Neshoba/Newton, 1,875 .... J-11
Utica, Hinds, 1,033 .... K-4
Van Wrinkle, Hinds K-7
• Vancleave, Jackson, 3,214 .... Q-12
Verona, Lee, 2,893 .... D-12
Vicksburg, Warren, 20,908 .... K-4
Walthall, Webster, 167 .... F-10
Water Valley, Yalobusha, 3,610 .... D-9
Waveland, Hancock, 5,369 .... R-10
Waynesboro, Wayne, 5,143 .... M-12
Wesson, Copiah, 1,510 .... M-7
West Gulfport, Harrison R-11
• West Hattiesburg, Lamar, 5,450 .... O-8
West Point, Clay, 8,489 .... F-12
Wiggins, Stone, 3,185 .... P-11
Winona, Montgomery, 5,705 .... F-9
Woodville, Wilkinson, 1,393 .... O-4
• Wool Market, Harrison, 1,166 .... Q-10
Yazoo City, Yazoo, 12,427 .... I-7

Explanation of symbols: ● – Census Designated Place (CDP)

Missouri

General Help Numbers:

Governor's Office
PO Box 720
Jefferson City, MO 65102-0720
www.gov.state.mo.us

573-751-3222
Fax 573-751-1495
8AM-5PM

Attorney General's Office
PO Box 899
Jefferson City, MO 65102
www.ago.state.mo.us

573-751-3321
Fax 573-751-0774
8AM-5PM

Legislative Records
Legislative Library
117A State Capitol
Jefferson City, MO 65101
www.moga.state.mo.us

573-751-4633

8:30AM-4:30PM

State Archives
Archives Division
PO Box 1747
Jefferson City, MO 65101
www.sos.mo.gov/archives/

573-751-3280
Fax 573-526-7333
8-5 M-F
(till 9PM on Th);
8:30-3:30 SA

State Specifics:

Capital:	Jefferson City
	Cole County
Time Zone:	CST
Number of Counties:	114
Population:	5,754,618
Web Site:	www.state.mo.us

State Agencies

Criminal Records

Missouri State Highway Patrol, Criminal Record & Identification Division, 1510 E Elm St, Jefferson City, MO 65102; 573-526-6153, 573-751-9382-Fax; 8AM-5PM.

www.mshp.dps.missouri.gov

Records are available from 1970 on. It takes 5 weeks before new records are available for inquiry. Records are indexed on inhouse computer (84%) including images. Records are maintained indefinitely. 64% of all arrests in database have final dispositions recorded, 62% for those arrests within last 5 years.

Searching: Youth service providers must have signature of the subject. Include the following in your request-full name, date of birth, sex, race, Social Security Number. Fingerprints are an option. A request form can be downloaded from the website. Records are 100% fingerprint-supported. Open records are accessible by the public. These are convictions, or arrests less than 30 days old unless charges are sought, or suspended imposition of sentence during probation period. Certain entities may access closed record files in accordance with state statute, with the submission of fingerprints and required fee.

Access by: mail, in person.

Fee & Payment: The search fee is $5.00 per individual for a name search. Searches by fingerprint cost $14.00 each. Add $24.00 if the fingerprint search to include an FBI fingerprint check. Fee payee: State of Missouri Criminal

Record System Fund Prepayment required. Personal checks accepted. No credit cards accepted.

Mail search: Turnaround time: 4-6 weeks. No SASE is required.

In person search: Turnaround time is while you wait for one search only.

Other access: Bulk/multiple requests can be submitted on diskette; prior arrangement and agency approval required. Responses are printed out, checked for accuracy and returned; however they cannot be returned on diskette. Alias or maiden names require separate search.

Statewide Court Records

Court Administrator, 2112 Industrial Drive - PO Box 104480, Jefferson City, MO 65110; 573-751-4377, 573-751-5540-Fax; 8AM-5PM.

www.osca.state.mo.us

Access by: online.

Online search: Casenet, a limited but growing online system, is available at www.courts.mo.gov/casenet/base/welcome.do. One may inquire on case records including docket entries, parties, judgments, and charges in public court. The system includes over 70 counties (with more projected) as well as the Eastern, Western, and Southern Appellate Courts, the Supreme Court, and Fine Collection Center. Cases can be searched by case number, filing date, or litigant name from 6AM-1AM M-F. New records entered into the system in real time. One may search supreme and appellate court opinions at the home page.

Sexual Offender Registry

Missouri State Highway Patrol, Sexual Offender Registry, PO Box 9500, Jefferson City, MO 65102-0568 (Courier address: 1510 E Elm St, Jefferson City, MO 65102); 573-526-6153, 573-751-9382-Fax; 8AM-5PM.

www.mshp.dps.missouri.gov

The Revised Statutes of Missouri, Sections 589.400 to 589.425 and 43.650, RSMo., mandate that the Missouri State Highway Patrol shall maintain a sex offender database and a web site on the Internet that is accessible to the public.

Records are available 07/01/79 to date. It takes t to 7 days before new records are available for inquiry.

Searching: Registry information is available from the sheriff (or CLEO) in the county where the offender resides. The county list may be released to any person upon request. The only information released is the name, address and offense.

Access by: online.

Online search: The name index can be searched at the website, by name, county or ZIP Code. The web page also gives links lists to the county sheriffs that have online access.

Incarceration Records

Missouri Department of Corrections, Probation and Parole, 1511 Christy Dr., Jefferson City, MO 65101; 573-751-8488, 573-751-8501-Fax; 8AM-5PM.

www.corrections.state.mo.us

Records are available on current and former inmates. Will release limited information on former inmates. It takes about 30 days before new records are available for inquiry.

Searching: Include the following in your request-full name, DOB; SSN helpful. Location, conviction and sentencing information are released.

Access by: mail, phone, fax, online.

Fee & Payment: There is no fee.

Mail search: Turnaround time: 4-6 days. Record requests must include reason for request.

Phone search: Searching available by phone.

Fax search: Same criteria as mail search.

Online search: No internet searching is available from this agency. However, you may email a single request to probation&parole@doc.mo.gov. Spell the full name correctly. An email response will be provided to you, usually within 24 hours of receipt during regular business hours. This only provides general search information and policy information. Department does not provide search information to companies conducting employee background checks. Although this agency provides no direct internet access, a private company offers free web access at www.vinelink.com/index.jsp.

Corporation, Fictitious Name, Limited Partnership, Assumed Name, Trademarks/Servicemarks, Limited Liability Company Records

Secretary of State, Corporation Services, PO Box 778, Jefferson City, MO 65102 (Courier address: 600 W Main, Jefferson City, MO 65101); 573-751-4153, 866-223-6535, 573-751-5841-Fax; 8AM-5PM.

www.sos.mo.gov

Trademarks and servicemarks are handled by the Commissions Division within Sec. of State and can be reached at the same phone number.

Records are available from the 1800s. New records are available for inquiry immediately. Records are indexed on microfilm, inhouse computer, hard copy.

Searching: Include the following in your request-full name of business, specific records that you need copies of. In addition to the articles of incorporation, corporation records include the following information: Annual Reports, Officers, Directors, DBAs, Prior (merged) names, Inactive and Reserved names.

Access by: mail, phone, fax, in person, online.

Fee & Payment: The fee for an abstract is $10.00, including a Good Standing. An uncertified copy of a record is $.50 per page, a certified copy of a record is $10.00 certification fee plus $.50 per page. A trademark or servicemark search is $5.00. Fee payee: Secretary of State. Prepayment

required. They will invoice. Personal checks accepted. Major credit cards accepted.

Mail search: Turnaround time: 2 to 3 days. No SASE is required.

Phone search: Status, registered agent, type of entity, and historical information is given over the phone at no charge.

Fax search: Same criteria as mail searching. Records are returned by mail.

In person search: Results are returned by mail, if numerous searches involved.

Online search: Search free online at https://www.sos.mo.gov/BusinessEntity/soskb/csearch.asp. The corporate name, the agent name or the charter number is required to search. The site will indicate the currency of the data. Many business entity type searches are available.

Uniform Commercial Code

UCC Division, Attn: Records, PO Box 1159, Jefferson City, MO 65102 (Courier address: 600 W Main St, Rm 302, Jefferson City, MO 65101); 866-223-6565, 8AM-5PM.

www.sos.state.mo.us/ucc

Records are available from 1965. Records are on microfiche from 7-1-80 to present.

Searching: Use search request form UCC-11. Please note that all tax liens are filed at the county level. Include the following in your request-debtor name.

Access by: mail, phone, in person, online.

Fee & Payment: A UCC-11 search is $27.00 plus $1.00 per page for copies. UCC-3's are not listed on the summary; order copies to review them. Fee payee: Secretary of State. Prepayment required. Personal checks accepted. Credit cards accepted: MasterCard, Visa.

Mail search: Turnaround time: 2 weeks.

Phone search: General information is available without charge.

In person search: You may request information in person.

Online search: Free searching for debtor names is available on the Internet at www.sos.state.mo.us/ucc/soskb/SearchStandardRA9.asp. Search by name or file number. Images are available for a fee.

Other access: The agency will release information for bulk purchase, call for procedures and pricing.

Federal and State Tax Liens

Records not maintained by a state level agency.

All tax liens are filed at the county level.

Sales Tax Registrations

Access to Records is Restricted.

Department of Revenue, Business Tax, PO Box 3300, Jefferson City, MO 65105-3300; 573-751-5860, 573-751-2836, 573-522-1722-Fax; 7:30AM-5:30PM. www.dor.mo.gov/tax

This agency will neither confirm nor supply any information. Confidential information is only released to owners or corporate officers registered with the Department. They suggest requesters to check at the city level.

Birth Certificates

Department of Health & Senior Srvs, Bureau of Vital Records, PO Box 570, Jefferson City, MO 65102-0570 (Courier address: 930 Wildwood, Jefferson City, MO 65109); 573-751-6387, 573-751-6400 (Message Number), 877-817-7363 (Orders), 573-526-3846-Fax; 8AM-5PM.

www.dhss.mo.gov

Records are available from 1910 on. Older records archived or see online below. New records are available for inquiry immediately. Records are indexed on microfiche, inhouse computer.

Searching: Records are only released to person of record or legal representative of immediate family member. Must have a signed release from person of record or immediate family member for investigative purposes. Include the following in your request-full name, names of parents, mother's maiden name, date of birth, place of birth, relationship to person of record, reason for information request.

Access by: mail, phone, in person, online.

Fee & Payment: Search fee is $15.00 per 5 years searched. Fee is charged regardless if record is found. Emergency requests using a credit card pay an additional $9.95 fee. Fee payee: Missouri Department of Health. Prepayment required. Personal checks accepted. Major credit cards accepted.

Mail search: Turnaround time: 2 to 3 weeks. A SASE is required.

Phone search: See expedited service.

In person search: Turnaround time is usually 10 minutes.

Online search: Orders may be placed online at www.vitalchek.com. Records prior to 1910 are available by county at www.sos.mo.gov/archives/resources/birthdeath/.

Expedited service: Expedited service is available for online and phone searches via www.vitalchek.com. Turnaround time: 1-3 days. Add $9.95 fee for use of credit and additional fee for express delivery.

Death Records

Department of Health & Senior Srvs, Bureau of Vital Records, PO Box 570, Jefferson City, MO 65102-0570 (Courier address: 930 Wildwood, Jefferson City, MO 65109); 573-751-6370, 573-751-6400 (Message Number), 877-817-7363 (Orders), 573-526-3846-Fax; 8AM-5PM.

www.dhss.mo.gov

Records are available from 1910 on. Older records archived or see online below. New records are available for inquiry immediately. Records are indexed on microfiche, inhouse computer.

Searching: Records are only released to legal representative of person of record or immediate family member. Must have a signed release from immediate family member for investigative purposes. Include the following in your request-full name, date of death, place of death, relationship to person of record, reason for information request.

Access by: mail, phone, in person, online.

Fee & Payment: The $13.00 search fee is for 5 years searched. Use of credit card is additional $9.95. Fee payee: Missouri Department of Health. Prepayment required. Personal checks accepted.

Mail search: Turnaround time: 2 to 3 weeks. A SASE is required.

Phone search: See expedited service.

In person search: Turnaround time is usually 10 minutes.

Online search: Orders accepted online only at www.vitalchek.com. Records prior to 1910 at www.sos.mo.gov/archives/resources/birthdeath/.

Expedited service: Expedited service is available for online and phone searches via www.vitalchek.com. Turnaround time: 1-3 days. Add $9.95 fee for use of credit and additional fee for express delivery.

Marriage Certificates, Divorce Records

Records not maintained by a state level agency.

Actual marriage and divorce records are found at county of issue. For marriage, contact the Record of Deeds in the county where license was issued. For divorce decrees, visit the Clerk of the county where issued.

Workers' Compensation Records

Labor & Industrial Relations Department, Workers Compensation Division, PO Box 58, Jefferson City, MO 65102-0058 (Courier address: 3315 W Truman Blvd, Jefferson City, MO 65101); 573-751-4231 x5, 573-751-2012-Fax; 8AM-4:30PM.

www.dolir.mo.gov

Records are available from 1945. Records are computerized since 1994. It takes 1 day before new records are available for inquiry. Records are indexed on inhouse computer.

Searching: Report of injury and medical records released only with a release form. All other records are open. Include the following in your request-claimant name, Social Security Number, date of accident.

Access by: mail, fax, in person.

Fee & Payment: The search fee is $5.00. Fee payee: Workers Compensation Division. Personal checks accepted. No credit cards accepted.

Mail search: Turnaround time: 1 to 2 days. No SASE is required.

Fax search: The initial fax must include a written request for the search. Turnaround time is 1 to 2 days.

In person search: To search in person, you must be party to the case in question or possess written authorization.

Driver Records

Department of Revenue, Driver and Vehicle Services Bureau, PO Box 200, Jefferson City, MO 65105-0200 (Courier address: Harry S Truman Bldg, 301 W High St, Room 470, Jefferson City, MO 65105); 573-751-4300, 573-526-7367-Fax; 7:30AM-5PM.

http://dor.mo.gov/mvdl/drivers

Copies of tickets are available from the same address. Requests must be in writing, include the name, DOB, license number, and specific violation information. The cost is $3.75 per ticket.

Records are available for 3 yrs for moving violations, 5 yrs for suspensions, permanent for alcohol-related, disq's and mand. ins. 0-point violations are not shown on non-CDL record. Accidents are not shown on driving record unless suspension/revocation action taken.

Searching: The agency complies with DPPA. Frequent requesters should establish an account for electronic access. Casual requesters receive records without personal information; if written consent of subject is provided then personal info provided. Include the following in your request-full name, DOB and DL or SSN.

Access by: mail, fax, in person, online.

Fee & Payment: The fee is $1.25 per record for walk-in or mail-in requests, $4.00 if certified. The fee for online retrieval is $1.25 per record plus network line charges. Fee payee: Department of Revenue. Prepayment required. Cashier's check and money orders preferred. Personal checks accepted. No credit cards accepted.

Mail search: Turnaround time: 2 days. A SASE is requested.

Fax search: Pre-approved accounts may order records and receive by fax for an additional $.50 per record.

In person search: You may request information in person.

Online search: Online access of Information Exchange costs $1.25 per record. Online inquiries can be put in Missouri's "mailbox" any time of the day. These inquiries are then picked up at 2 AM the following morning, and the resulting MVR's are sent back to each customer's "mailbox" approx. 2 hours later.

Other access: The tape-to-tape process has been replaced by the online system. The entire license file can be purchased, with updates. Call 573-751-5579 for more information.

Vehicle Ownership Vehicle Identification, Vessel Ownership Vessel Registration

Department of Revenue, Motor Vehicle Bureau, PO Box 100, Jefferson City, MO 65105-0100 (Courier address: Harry S Truman Bldg, 301 W High St, Jefferson City, MO 65105); 573-526-3669, 573-751-4509, 573-751-7060-Fax; 7:30AM-5:30PM.

www.dor.mo.gov

Lien information shows on the title records.

Records are available from 1968 to present. Records are indexed on microfiche from 1968 to present, and microfilm from 1981 to present. Records include boats and mobile homes. All motorized boats 12 ft or longer must be titled and registered. It takes 24-48 for vehicle and 2 weeks for marine before new records are available for inquiry. Records are normally destroyed after microfilmed.

Searching: Ownership and vehicle information is available with no restrictions to access, if request complies with DPPA. Casual requesters must have consent of subject to obtain records with personal information, otherwise this data is blocked. Include the following in your request-year, make, VIN. Current registration/title records are on computer. Records are purged from the computer files after 2 years of no activity. However, the records will remain on microfiche.

Access by: mail, in person, online.

Fee & Payment: The fee for a walk-in search is $1.25, by mail is $4.50. A complete title history walk-in is $6.00, by mail $8.00. There is an additional $3.00 for certification. If a mail in wants to be billed, add $2.50 per record. Fee payee: Department of Revenue. Prepayment required. Pre-approved accounts may be billed. Personal checks accepted. No credit cards accepted.

Mail search: Turnaround time: 2 to 4 weeks.

In person search: You may request records in person.

Online search: Online record searches are available to registered entities who have a DPPA security access code issued by the Department. The fee is $1.25 per record and is automatically withdrawn through the requestor's ACH account. Access is via the Internet. Visit www.dor.mo.gov for more information.

Other access: Missouri has an extensive range of records and information available on magnetic tape, labels or paper. Besides offering license, vehicle, title, dealer, and marine records, specific public report data is also available.

Expedited service: The cost is the same as stated above. Depending on the type of request, turnaround time could be the same or next day.

Accident Reports

Missouri State Highway Patrol, Traffic Division, PO Box 568, Jefferson City, MO 65102-0568 (Courier address: 1510 E Elm St, Jefferson City, MO 65101); 573-526-6113, 573-751-9921-Fax; 8AM-5PM.

www.mshp.dps.mo.gov

Records are available from 1997 to present on computer. Records are indexed on an in-house computer. Records are on a document imaging system or microfilm from 1941. It takes 14 to 30 days before new records are available for inquiry. Records are normally destroyed after being microfilmed.

Searching: Record requests must be in writing. Generally, these records are open to the public. Include the following in your request-full name, date of accident, location of accident, relationship of requester to the subject. There is no telephone

searching, but you can call to determine if an accident is on file.

Access by: mail, fax, in person.

Fee & Payment: There is a $4.00 fee for a standard 4-page report on record. Fee payee: DPS - Missouri State Highway Patrol Prepayment required. Personal checks are accepted. Credit cards not accepted.

Mail search: Turnaround time: 3 to 4 working days. A SASE is requested.

Fax search: Fax requests are accepted from ongoing requesters, if prepaid.

In person search: Turnaround time is immediate.

Voter Registration

Secretary of State, Division of Elections, PO Box 1767, Jefferson City, MO 65102; 573-751-2301, 573-526-3242-Fax; 8AM-5PM.

www.sos.mo.gov/section4.asp

For individual look-ups, the agency recommends searching at the county level by the County Clerks.

Records are available as counties release record information to the state.

Searching: Include the following in your request-name and county. There is no fee for an individual look-up, but fees are involved for media sales. The following data is not released: SSNs.

Access by: mail, in person.

Mail search: Turnaround time: 2-3 days. Individual name requests are available.

In person search: Response is as time permits.

Other access: Records are sold in various media formats for political purposes, but not for commercial marketing purposes.

GED Certificates

GED Office, PO Box 480, Jefferson City, MO 65102; 573-751-3504, 8AM-4:30PM.

http://dese.mo.gov/divcareered

Records are available from 1960 to present. It takes 2 to 3 weeks before new records are available for inquiry.

Searching: Include the following in your request-signed release, date of birth, Social Security Number. The year and location of the test are very helpful and should also be included in the request.

Access by: mail, in person.

Fee & Payment: The fee is $2.00 for either a verification or a transcript. Fee payee: Treasurer, State of Missouri. Prepayment required. Personal checks accepted.

Mail search: Turnaround time: same day. No SASE is required.

In person search: $2.00 fee per request.

Hunting and Fishing License Information

Conservation Department, Licenses, PO Box 180, Jefferson City, MO 65102-0180 (Courier address: 2901 W Truman Blvd, Jefferson City, MO 65109); 573-751-4115, 573-751-4467-Fax; 8AM-5PM.

www.mdc.mo.gov

Hunting and fishing permits issued and records of recorded deer and turkey kills are public records and available upon written request. SSNs are redacted prior to release.

Records are available from 1/1/99 to present. It takes hours before new records are available for inquiry. Records are indexed on inhouse computer, hard copy. Records are normally destroyed after 5 years.

Searching: Records are only released to the permitee. Otherwise, they are not released until the reason for the request is reviewed by the Department's General Counsel. Names and addresses may be released, if request is approved. Include the following in your request-full name, DOB; SSN helpful. For older records, you will need the permittee's name, date of birth, and type of permit.

Access by: mail, fax.

Fee & Payment: Search fee is $10.00, copy fee is $.10. Certification is $5.00. Fee payee: Missouri Conservation Department. Price is based upon type of service provided. Personal checks accepted.

Mail search: Turnaround time: 5 days. No SASE is required.

Fax search: Record requests may be faxed.

Other access: Mailing lists of the hunting and fishing permit vendors are available. The cost is about $100.

Missouri State Licensing Agencies

For details about the agency responsible for licensing/certifying/registering an item below or in the Agency Quick Finder section, match an item's number with the number of the agency in the *Licensing Agency Information* section.

Missouri Licenses Searchable Online

Acupuncturist #45 ....http://pr.mo.gov/licensee-search.asp
Anesthesia Permit, Dental #17 ....http://pr.mo.gov/licensee-search.asp
Animal Technician #31.....................................http://pr.mo.gov/licensee-search.asp
Ankle Specialist #10..http://pr.mo.gov/licensee-search.asp
Announcer, Ring #44 ....http://pr.mo.gov/licensee-search.asp
Architect #2...http://pr.mo.gov/licensee-search.asp
Athletic Trainer #11..http://pr.mo.gov/licensee-search.asp
Attorney #40..www.mobar.org/directory/index.htm
Audiologist #11 ....http://pr.mo.gov/licensee-search.asp
Audiologist, Clinical #16...................................http://pr.mo.gov/licensee-search.asp
Audiologist/Speech Path'gist, Clinical #16.....http://pr.mo.gov/licensee-search.asp
Barber Instructor/School #3 ....http://pr.mo.gov/licensee-search.asp
Barber/Barber Shop #3 ....http://pr.mo.gov/licensee-search.asp
Beauty Shop #5 ....http://pr.mo.gov/licensee-search.asp
Body Piercer #13 ....http://pr.mo.gov/licensee-search.asp
Body Piercing/Branding Establ. #13 ....http://pr.mo.gov/licensee-search.asp
Boxer/Boxing Professional #44.....................http://pr.mo.gov/licensee-search.asp
Brander, Cosmetic #13 ....http://pr.mo.gov/licensee-search.asp
Cemetery #25 ....http://pr.mo.gov/licensee-search.asp
Chiropractor #4 ....http://pr.mo.gov/licensee-search.asp
Cosmetologist #5 ....http://pr.mo.gov/licensee-search.asp
Cosmetology School/Instrut'r/Shop #5..........http://pr.mo.gov/licensee-search.asp
Counselor, Professional/Trainee #23.............http://pr.mo.gov/licensee-search.asp
Dental Hygienist #17...http://pr.mo.gov/licensee-search.asp
Dental Specialist #17 ....http://pr.mo.gov/licensee-search.asp
Dentist #17...http://pr.mo.gov/licensee-search.asp
Drug Distributor #9..http://pr.mo.gov/licensee-search.asp
Embalmer #6..http://pr.mo.gov/licensee-search.asp
Engineer #2..http://pr.mo.gov/licensee-search.asp
Esthetician #5 ....http://pr.mo.gov/licensee-search.asp
Funeral Director #6 ....http://pr.mo.gov/licensee-search.asp
Funeral Establishment #6 ....http://pr.mo.gov/licensee-search.asp
Funeral Pre-Need Provider/Seller #6..............http://pr.mo.gov/licensee-search.asp
Geologist #26...http://pr.mo.gov/licensee-search.asp
Geologist Registrant in Training #26...............http://pr.mo.gov/licensee-search.asp
Hairdresser #5 ....http://pr.mo.gov/licensee-search.asp
Hearing Instrument Specialist #27 ....http://pr.mo.gov/licensee-search.asp
Insurance Agent/Broker #20 ....www.insurance.mo.gov/industry/producer/agtstatus.htm
Insurance Consultant, Chiropractic #4...........http://pr.mo.gov/licensee-search.asp
Interior Designer #22 ....http://pr.mo.gov/licensee-search.asp
Interpreter for the Deaf #12.............................http://pr.mo.gov/licensee-search.asp
Landfill #37...www.dnr.state.mo.us/alpd/swmp/forms/form_permit.htm
Landfill Operator #37 ....www.dnr.state.mo.us/alpd/swmp/forms/form_permit.htm
Landscape Architect #2 ....http://pr.mo.gov/licensee-search.asp
Manicurist #5...http://pr.mo.gov/licensee-search.asp
Marital & Family Therapist #43 ....http://pr.mo.gov/licensee-search.asp
Martial Artist/Martial Arts Occupation #44......http://pr.mo.gov/licensee-search.asp
Massage Therapist #28 ....http://pr.mo.gov/licensee-search.asp
Massage Therapy Business #28.....................http://pr.mo.gov/licensee-search.asp
Medical Doctor #11 ....http://pr.mo.gov/licensee-search.asp
Nurse Midwife #7 ....http://pr.mo.gov/licensee-search.asp
Nurse, Advanced Practical #7.........................http://pr.mo.gov/licensee-search.asp
Nurse, Registered #7..http://pr.mo.gov/licensee-search.asp

Nurse, Specialist #7 .... http://pr.mo.gov/licensee-search.asp
Nurse-LPN #7 .... http://pr.mo.gov/licensee-search.asp
Nursing School #7 .... http://pr.mo.gov/licensee-search.asp
Occ. Therapist/Therapist Assist #41 .... http://pr.mo.gov/licensee-search.asp
Optometrist #8 .... http://pr.mo.gov/licensee-search.asp
Osteopathic Physician #11 .... http://pr.mo.gov/licensee-search.asp
Perfusionist #11 .... http://pr.mo.gov/licensee-search.asp
Pesticide Applicator/Technician #18 .... www.kellysolutions.com/MO/
Pesticide Dealer #18 .... www.kellysolutions.com/MO/
Pesticide Technician #18 .... www.kellysolutions.com/MO/
Pharmacist/Pharmacy Intern/Tech #9 .... http://pr.mo.gov/licensee-search.asp
Pharmacy #9 .... http://pr.mo.gov/licensee-search.asp
Physical Therapist #11 .... http://pr.mo.gov/licensee-search.asp
Physical Therapist Assistant #11 .... http://pr.mo.gov/licensee-search.asp
Physician Assistant #11 .... http://pr.mo.gov/licensee-search.asp
Physician, Athletic Event #44 .... http://pr.mo.gov/licensee-search.asp
Podiatrist #10 .... http://pr.mo.gov/licensee-search.asp
Pre-Need Provider/Seller, Funeral #6 .... http://pr.mo.gov/licensee-search.asp
Psychologist #36 .... http://pr.mo.gov/licensee-search.asp
Public Accountant Partnership #1 .... http://pr.mo.gov/licensee-search.asp
Public Accountant-CPA #1 .... http://pr.mo.gov/licensee-search.asp
Real Estate Agent/Seller #35 .... http://pr.mo.gov/licensee-search.asp
Real Estate Appraiser #14 .... http://pr.mo.gov/licensee-search.asp
Real Estate Broker/Partner/Assoc. #35 .... http://pr.mo.gov/licensee-search.asp
Real Estate Instructor/School #35 .... http://pr.mo.gov/licensee-search.asp
Real Estate Officer/Corp/Assoc. #35 .... http://pr.mo.gov/licensee-search.asp
Respiratory Care Practitioner #42 .... http://pr.mo.gov/licensee-search.asp
School Nurse #7 .... http://pr.mo.gov/licensee-search.asp
Social Worker, Clinical #15 .... http://pr.mo.gov/licensee-search.asp
Speech Language Pathologist #11 .... http://pr.mo.gov/licensee-search.asp
Speech-Language Path'gist/Audio'gist #16 ... http://pr.mo.gov/licensee-search.asp
Surveyor, Land #2 .... http://pr.mo.gov/licensee-search.asp
Tattoo Artist #13 .... http://pr.mo.gov/licensee-search.asp
Teacher #24 .... http://k12apps.dese.mo.gov/webapps/tcertsearch/tc_search1.asp
Timekeeper, Athletic Event #44 .... http://pr.mo.gov/licensee-search.asp
Transfer Station #37 .... www.dnr.state.mo.us/alpd/swmp/facilities/tranlist.htm
Veterinarian/Veterinary Technician #31 .... http://pr.mo.gov/licensee-search.asp
Veterinary Facility #31 .... http://pr.mo.gov/licensee-search.asp
Waste Tire Processor/Hauler #37 .... www.dnr.state.mo.us/alpd/swmp/tires/tirehaul.htm
Wrestler/Wrestling Professional #44 .... http://pr.mo.gov/licensee-search.asp

Missouri Licensing Quick Finder

Acupuncturist #45 573-526-1555
Alcohol & Tobacco Control #21 573-751-2333
Anesthesia Permit, Dental #17 573-751-0040
Animal Technician #31 573-751-0031
Ankle Specialist #10 573-751-0873
Announcer, Ring #44 573-751-0243
Architect #2 573-751-0047
Athletic Trainer #11 573-751-0098
Attorney #40 573-635-4128
Audiologist #11 573-751-0171
Audiologist, Clinical #16 573-751-0098
Audiologist/Speech Pathologist, Clinical #16
.... 573-751-0098
Barber Instructor/School #3 573-751-0805
Barber/Barber Shop #3 573-751-0805
Beauty Shop #5 573-751-1052
Bingo Worker/Officer/Operation #30 573-526-5370
Body Piercer #13 573-526-8288
Body Piercing/Branding Establishment #13
.... 573-526-8288
Boxer/Boxing Professional #44 573-751-0243
Brander, Cosmetic #13 573-526-8288

Cemetery #25 573-751-0849
Child Care Facility #29 573-751-2450
Chiropractor #4 573-751-2104
Cosmetologist #5 573-751-1052
Cosmetology School/Instruc'r/Shop #5 . 573-751-1052
Counselor, Professional/Trainee #23 ... 573-751-0018
Counselor, Substance Abuse #39 573-751-9211
Court Reporter #12 573-751-4144
Dental Hygienist #17 573-751-0040
Dental Specialist #17 573-751-0040
Dentist #17 573-751-0040
Drug Distributor #9 573-751-0091
Embalmer #6 573-751-0813
Emergency Medical Tech. Basic #19 573-751-6356
Engineer #2 573-751-0047
Esthetician #5 573-751-1052
Funeral Director #6 573-751-0813
Funeral Establishment #6 573-751-0813
Funeral Pre-Need Provider/Seller #6 ... 573-751-0813
Gaming Occupation #30 573-526-4092
Gaming Property, Boat #30 573-526-4092
Gaming Supply #30 573-526-4092

Geologist #26 573-526-7625
Geologist Registrant in Training #26.... 573-526-7625
Hairdresser #5 573-751-1052
Hearing Instrument Specialist #27 573-751-0240
Horse Racing Occupation #30 573-526-4083
Insurance Agent/Broker #20 573-751-3518
Insurance Consultant, Chiropractic #4. 573-751-2104
Interior Designer #22 573-522-4683
Interpreter for the Deaf #12 573-526-7787
Investment Advisor #34 573-751-2061
Landfill #37 573-751-5401
Landfill Operator #37 573-751-5401
Landscape Architect #2 573-751-0047
Manicurist #5 573-751-1052
Marital & Family Therapist #43 573-751-0870
Martial Artist/Martial Arts Occup.#44 ... 573-751-0243
Massage Therapist #28 573-522-6277
Massage Therapy Business #28 573-522-6277
Medical Doctor #11 573-751-0108
Notary Public #33 573-751-2783
Nurse Midwife #7 573-751-0681
Nurse, Advanced Practical #7 573-751-0681

Nurse, Registered #7	573-751-0681
Nurse, Specialist #7	573-751-0681
Nurse-LPN #7	573-751-0681
Nursing Home Administrator #32	573-751-3511
Nursing School #7	573-751-0681
Occupational Therapist/Therapist Assistant #41	573-751-0877
Optometrist #8	573-751-0814
Osteopathic Physician #11	573-751-0108
Perfusionist #11	573-751-0108
Pesticide Applicator/Technician #18	573-751-5504
Pesticide Dealer #18	573-751-5504
Pesticide Technician #18	573-751-5504
Pharmacist/Pharmacy Intern/Technician #9	573-751-0091
Pharmacy #9	573-751-0091
Physical Therapist #11	573-751-0171
Physical Therapist Assistant #11	573-751-0171
Physician Assistant #11	573-751-0171

Physician, Athletic Event #44	573-751-0243
Podiatrist #10	573-751-0873
Pre-Need Provider/Seller, Funeral #6	573-751-0813
Prevention Specialist (social work) #39	573-751-9211
Psychologist #36	573-751-0099
Public Accountant Partnership #1	573-751-0012
Public Accountant-CPA #1	573-751-0012
Real Estate Agent/Seller #35	573-751-2628
Real Estate Appraiser #14	573-751-2628
Real Estate Broker/Partner/Assoc. #35	573-751-2628
Real Estate Instructor/School #35	573-751-2628
Real Estate Officer/Corp/Assoc. #35	573-751-2628
Respiratory Care Practitioner #42	573-522-2864
School Commissioner Assistant #24	573-751-4369
School Librarian #24	573-751-4369
School Nurse #7	573-751-0681
Securities Agent #34	573-751-2061
Securities Broker/Dealer #34	573-751-2061
Social Worker, Clinical #15	573-751-0885

Speech Language Pathologist #11	573-751-0171
Speech-Language Pathologist/Audiologist #16	573-751-0098
Substance Abuse Assoc-in-training #39	573-751-9211
Substance Abuse Counselor #39	573-751-9211
Surveyor, Land #2	573-751-0047
Tattoo Artist #13	573-526-8288
Teacher #24	573-751-0051, 751-4369
Timekeeper, Athletic Event #44	573-751-0243
Transfer Station #37	573-751-5401
Veterinarian/Veterinary Technician #31	573-751-0031
Veterinary Facility #31	573-751-0031
Waste Tire End User/Site #37	573-751-5401
Waste Tire Processor/Hauler #37	573-751-5401
Waste Water System Operator #38	573-751-3443
Water Supply Operator #38	573-751-3443
Wrestler/Wrestling Professional #44	573-751-0243

Missouri Licensing Agency Information

1 Board of Accountancy, 3605 Missouri Blvd (PO Box 613), Jefferson City, MO 65102-0613; 573-751-0012, Fax: 573-751-0890.
Email: boa@mail.state.mo.us
Search Database at http://pr.mo.gov/licensee-search.asp Note: Lists are available at

2 Engineers, Land Survey & Landscape Architects, Board of Architects, 3605 Missouri Blvd, #380, Jefferson City, MO 65102; 573-751-0047, Fax: 573-751-8046.
http://pr.mo.gov/apelsla.asp
Email: moapels@pr.mo.gov
Search Database at http://pr.mo.gov/licensee-search.asp Note: Lists are available at www.ecodev.state.mo.us/pr/ftp4.htm.

3 Board of Barber Examiners, 3605 Missouri Blvd (PO Box 1335), Jefferson City, MO 65102-1335; 573-751-0805, Fax: 573-751-8167.
www.pr.mo.gov/barbers.asp
Email: barber.board@pr.mo.gov
Search Database at http://pr.mo.gov/licensee-search.asp Note: Lists are available at www.ecodev.state.mo.us/pr/ftp4.htm.

4 Board of Chiropractic Examiners, 3605 Missouri Blvd (PO Box 672), Jefferson City, MO 65102-0672; 573-751-2104, Fax: 573-751-0735.
http://pr.mo.gov
Email: chiropractic@pr.mo.gov
Search Database at http://pr.mo.gov/licensee-search.asp Note: Lists are available at http://pr.mo.gov.

5 Board of Cosmetology, 3605 Missouri Blvd (PO Box 1062), Jefferson City, MO 65102; 573-751-1052, Fax: 573-751-8167.
www.pr.mo.gov/cosmetology.asp
Email: cosmo@pr.mo.gov
Search Database at http://pr.mo.gov/licensee-search.asp Note: Lists are available through cosmo@pr.mo.gov.

6 Board of Embalmers & Funeral Directors, 3605 Missouri Blvd (PO Box 423), Jefferson City, MO 65102-0625; 573-751-0813, Fax: 573-751-1155.
www.pr.mo.gov/embalmers.asp
Email: emblamer@mail.state.mo.us
Search Database at http://pr.mo.gov/licensee-search.asp Note: Lists are available at www.ecodev.state.mo.us/pr/ftp4.htm.

7 Board of Nursing, PO Box 656, Jefferson City, MO 65102; 573-751-0681, Fax: 573-751-0075.
www.pr.mo.gov/nursing.asp
Email: nursing@mail.state.mo.us
Search Database at http://pr.mo.gov/licensee-search.asp Note: Nursing lists are available at www.ecodev.state.mo.us/pr/nursingdown.html.

8 Board of Optometry, PO Box 1335 (3605 Missouri Blvd), Jefferson City, MO 65102-0423; 573-751-0814, Fax: 573-751-8216.
http://pr.mo.gov/optometrists.asp
Email: optom@mail.state.mo.us
Search Database at http://pr.mo.gov/licensee-search.asp Note: Lists are available at www.ecodev.state.mo.us/pr/ftp4.htm.

9 Board of Pharmacy, 3605 Missouri Blvd (PO Box 625), Jefferson City, MO 65102; 573-751-0091, Fax: 573-526-3464.
www.pr.mo.gov/pharmacists.asp
Email: pharmacy@mail.state.mo.us
Search Database at http://pr.mo.gov/licensee-search.asp Note: Lists are available at www.ecodev.state.mo.us/pr/ftp4.htm.

10 Board of Podiatric Medicine, 3605 Missouri Blvd (PO Box 423), Jefferson City, MO 65102; 573-751-0873, Fax: 573-751-1155.
http://pr.mo.gov/podiatrists.asp
Email: podiatry@mail.state.mo.us
Search Database at http://pr.mo.gov/licensee-search.asp Note: Lists are available at www.ecodev.state.mo.us/pr/ftp4.htm.

11 Board of Registration for Healing Arts, 3605 Missouri Blvd (PO Box 4), Jefferson City, MO 65102; 573-751-0098, Fax: 573-751-3166.
www.pr.mo.gov/healingarts.asp
Email: healarts@mail.state.mo.us
Search Database at http://pr.mo.gov/licensee-search.asp Note: Lists are available at www.ecodev.state.mo.us/pr/healingdown.html.

12 Committee of Interpreters, PO Box 1335 (3605 Missouri Blvd), Jefferson City, MO 65102-1335; 573-526-7787, Fax: 573-526-0661.
http://pr.mo.gov/interpreters.asp
Email: interp@mail.state.mo.us
Search Database at http://pr.mo.gov/licensee-search.asp Note: Lists are available at www.ecodev.state.mo.us/pr/ftp4.htm.

13 Office of Tattooing, Body Piercing and Branding, PO Box 1335, Jefferson City, MO 65102-1335; 573-526-8288, Fax: 573.526.3489.
http://pr.mo.gov/tattooing.asp
Search Database at http://pr.mo.gov/licensee-search.asp

14 Commission of Real Estate Appraisers, 3605 Missouri Blvd (PO Box 1339), Jefferson City, MO 65109; 573-751-2628, Fax: 573-751-2777.
Email: reacom@mail.state.mo.us
Search Database at http://pr.mo.gov/licensee-search.asp .

15 Division of Professional Registration, Committee for Licensed Clinical Social Workers, 3605 Missouri Blvd (PO Box 1335), Jefferson City, MO 65102; 573-751-0885, Fax: 573-526-3489.
http://pr.mo.gov/socialworkers.asp
Email: lcsw@pr.mo.gov
Search Database at http://pr.mo.gov/licensee-search.asp Note: Lists are available at www.ecodev.state.mo.us/pr/ftp4.htm.

16 Committee of Speech Pathology & Audiology, 3605 Missouri Blvd, PO Box 4, Jefferson City, MO 65102; 573-751-0098, Fax: 573-751-3166.
http://pr.mo.gov/speech.asp
Email: healarts@mail.state.mo.us
Search Database at http://pr.mo.gov/licensee-search.asp Note: Lists are available at www.ecodev.state.mo.us/pr/healingdown.html.

17 Dental Board, 3605 Missouri Blvd, PO Box 1367, Jefferson City, MO 65102; 573-751-0040, Fax: 573-751-8216.
http://pr.mo.gov/dental.asp Email: dental@pr.mo.gov
Search Database at http://pr.mo.gov/licensee-search.asp Note: Lists are available at www.ecodev.state.mo.us/pr/ftp4.htm.

18 Department of Agriculture, Division of Plant Industries, Bureau of Pesticide, PO Box 630 (1616 Missouri Blvd), Jefferson City, MO 65102; 573-751-5504, Fax: 573-751-0005.
www.mda.mo.gov
Email: paul_bailey@mda.mo.gov
Search Database at www.kellysolutions.com/MO/

19 Department of Health, Emergency Medical Services, PO Box 570 (912 Wildwood Dr), Jefferson City, MO 65102-0570; 573-751-6356, Fax: 573-751-6348.
www.health.state.mo.us/EMS/

20 Department of Insurance, Licensing Section, PO Box 690 (301 W High St), Jefferson City, MO 65102-0690; 573-751-4126, Fax: 573-526-3416. www.insurance.mo.gov
Email: mdimedia@mail.state.mo.us
Search Database at www.insurance.mo.gov/indus try/producer/agtstatus.htm

21 Department of Public Safety, Division of Alcohol & Tobacco Control, Truman Bldg, Rm 860 (PO Box 837), Jefferson City, MO 65102-0837; 573-751-2333, Fax: 573-526-4540.
www.mdlc.state.mo.us
Email: liquor@mail.state.mo.us

22 Interior Design Council, PO Box 1335 (3605 Missouri Blvd), Jefferson City, MO 65109; 573-522-4683, Fax: 573-526-3489.
http://pr.mo.gov/interior.asp
Email: intdesn@pr.mo.gov
Search Database at http://pr.mo.gov/licensee-search.asp

23 Division of Professional Regulation, Committee for Professional Counselors, PO Box 1335 (3605 Missouri Blvd), Jefferson City, MO 65102-1335; 573-751-0018, Fax: 573-751-0735.
Email: couns@mail.state.ma.us
Search Database at http://pr.mo.gov/licensee-search.asp.

24 Department of Elementary & Secondary Education, Division of Teacher Quality & Urban Education, PO Box 480 (205 Jefferson St), Jefferson City, MO 65102-0480; 573-751-0051, 751-4212, Fax: 573-751-8613.
www.dese.state.mo.us

25 Endowed Care Cemeteries Registration, Missouri Division of Professional Registration, 3605 Missouri Blvd (PO Box 1335, 65102), Jefferson City, MO 65102-1335; 573-751-0849, Fax: 573-526-3489.
Email: endocare@mail.state.mo.us
Search Database at http://pr.mo.gov/licensee-search.asp

26 Board of Geologist Registration, 3605 Missouri Blvd, PO Box 1335, Jefferson City, MO 65102; 573-526-0661, Fax: 573-526-3489.
http://pr.mo.gov/geologists.asp
Email: geo@mail.state.mo.us
Search Database at http://pr.mo.gov/licensee-search.asp   Note: Lists are available at www.ecodev.state.mo.us/pr/ftp4.htm.

27 Board of Hearing Instrument Specialists, PO Box 1335 (3605 Missouri Blvd), Jefferson City, MO 65102-1335; 573-751-0240, Fax: 573-526-3856.
www.pr.mo.gov/hearing.asp
Email: behis@mail.state.mo.us
Search Database at http://pr.mo.gov/licensee-search.asp

28 State Board of Therapeutic Massage, PO Box 1335 (3605 Missouri Blvd), Jefferson City, MO 65102-1335; 573-522-6277, Fax: 573-751-0735.
http://pr.mo.gov/massage.asp
Email: massagether@pr.mo.gov
Search Database at http://pr.mo.gov/licensee-search.asp

29 Department of Health, Bureau of Child Care Safety & Licensure, 1715 South Ridge, Jefferson City, MO 65109; 573-751-2450,
Fax: 573-526-5345.   www.health.state.mo.us/

30 Gaming Commission, 3417 Knipp Dr, Jefferson City, MO 65102; 573-526-4080, Fax: 573-526-1999.   www.mgc.state.mo.us/
Email: hbailey@mail.state.mo.us

31 Veterinary Medical Board, 3605 Missouri Blvd, Jefferson City, MO 65102-0633; 573-751-0031, Fax: 573-751-3856.
http://pr.mo.gov/veterinarian.asp
Email: vets@mail.state.mo.us
Search Database at http://pr.mo.gov/licensee-search.asp   Note: Lists are available at www.ecodev.state.mo.us/pr/ftp4.htm.

32 Board of Nursing Home Administrators, PO Box 570 (912 Wildwood Dr), Jefferson City, MO 65102-0570; 573-751-3511, Fax: 573-526-4314.
www.dhss.mo.gov/BNHA/index.html
Email: loved2@dhhs.mo.gov

33 Office of Secretary of State, State Capitol Rm 208, Jefferson City, MO 65101; 573-751-4936, Fax: 573-526-3489.   www.sos.mo.gov
Email: trish.vincent@sos.mo.gov

34 Secretary of State, Securities Division, 600 W Main St #229, Jefferson City, MO 65101; 573-751-4136, Fax: 573-526-3124.
www.sos.mo.gov/securities/

35 Real Estate Commission, PO Box 1339 (3605 Missouri Blvd), Jefferson City, MO 65102-1339; 573-751-2628, Fax: 573-751-2777.
http://pr.mo.gov/realestate.asp
Email: realesta@mail.state.mo.us
Search Database at http://pr.mo.gov/licensee-search.asp   Note: Lists are available at www.ded.state.mo.us/regulatorylicensing/professi onalregistration/.

36 Committee of Psychology, 3605 Missouri Blvd, Jefferson City, MO 65102-1335; 573-751-0099, Fax: 573-526-0661.
http://pr.mo.gov/psychologists.asp
Email: scop@mail.state.mo.us
Search Database at http://pr.mo.gov/licensee-search.asp   Note: Lists are available at www.ecodev.state.mo.us/pr/ftp4.htm.

37 Department of Natural Resources, Div of Environmental Quality, Solid Waste Mgmt, PO Box 176 (1738 E Elm), Jefferson City, MO 65102-0176; 573-751-5401, Fax: 573-526-3902.

www.dnr.mo.gov   Email: beth.marsala@dnr.mo.gov
Search Database at www.dnr.state.mo.us/alpd/sw mp/forms/form_permit.htm

38 Department of Natural Resources, Environmental Assistance Program, PO Box 176 (1659 Elm St), Jefferson City, MO 65102; 573-751-3443, Fax: 573-526-5808.
www.dnr.state.mo.us/oac/oprtrain.htm

39 Substance Abuse Counselors Certification Board, PO Box 1250, Jefferson City, MO 65102; 573-751-9211, Fax: 573-522-2073.
http://pr.mo.gov/
Email: msaccb@mail.dmh.state.mo.us

40 The Missouri Bar, PO Box 119 (326 Monroe St), Jefferson City, MO 65102-0119; 573-635-4128, Fax: 573-635-2811.
www.mobar.org   Search Database at www.mobar.org/directory/index.htm

41 Division of Professional Registration, Board of Occupational Therapy, PO Box 1335 (3605 Missouri Blvd, 65109), Jefferson City, MO 65102-1335; 573-751-0877, Fax: 573-526-3489.
Email: ot@mail.state.mo.us
Search Database at http://pr.mo.gov/licensee-search.asp   Note: Lists are available at

42 Board for Respiratory Care, 3605 Missouri Blvd, Jefferson City, MO 65102-1335; 573-522-5864, Fax: 573-526-3464.
www.pr.mo.gov/respiratorycare.asp
Email: rcp@mail.state.mo.us
Search Database at http://pr.mo.gov/licensee-search.asp   Note: Lists are available at www.ecodev.state.mo.us/pr/ftp4.htm.

43 Committee of Marital & Family Therapists, 3605 Missouri Blvd, Jefferson City, MO 65102-1335; 573-751-0870, Fax: 573-526-3489.
http://pr.mo.gov
Email: maritalfam@pr.mo.gov
Search Database at http://pr.mo.gov/licensee-search.asp   Note: Lists are available at http://pr.mo.gov.

44 Office of Athletics, 3605 Missouri Blvd, Jefferson City, MO 65102-1335; 573-751-0243, Fax: 573-751-5649.
http://pr.mo.gov/athletics.asp
Email: athletic@mail.state.mo.us
Search Database at http://pr.mo.gov/licensee-search.asp

45 Acupuncturist Advisory Committee, P.O. Box 1335 (3605 Missouri Blvd), Jefferson City, MO 65102-0672; 573-526-1555, Fax: 573-751-0735.
http://pr.mo.gov/acupuncturist.asp
Email: acupuncture@pr.mo.gov
Search Database at http://pr.mo.gov/licensee-search.asp

Missouri Federal Courts

The following list indicates the district and division name for each county in the state. If the bankruptcy court location is different from the district court, then the location of the bankruptcy court appears in parentheses.

Missouri County/Court Cross Reference

County	District	Division
Adair	Eastern	Hannibal (St Louis)
Andrew	Western	St Joseph (Kansas City - Western)
Atchison	Western	St Joseph (Kansas City - Western)
Audrain	Eastern	Hannibal (St Louis)
Barry	Western	Joplin-Southwestern (Kansas City)
Barton	Western	Joplin-Southwestern (Kansas City)
Bates	Western	Kansas City - Western
Benton	Western	Jefferson City-Central (Kansas City)
Bollinger	Eastern	Cape Girardeau (St Louis)
Boone	Western	Jefferson City-Central (Kansas City)
Buchanan	Western	St Joseph (Kansas City - Western)
Butler	Eastern	Cape Girardeau (St Louis)
Caldwell	Western	St Joseph (Kansas City - Western)
Callaway	Western	Jefferson City-Central (Kansas City)
Camden	Western	Jefferson City-Central (Kansas City)
Cape Girardeau	Eastern	Cape Girardeau (St Louis)
Carroll	Western	Kansas City - Western
Carter	Eastern	Cape Girardeau (St Louis)
Cass	Western	Kansas City - Western
Cedar	Western	Springfield-Southern (Kansas City)
Chariton	Eastern	Hannibal (St Louis)
Christian	Western	Springfield-Southern (Kansas City)
Clark	Eastern	Hannibal (St Louis)
Clay	Western	Kansas City - Western
Clinton	Western	St Joseph (Kansas City - Western)
Cole	Western	Jefferson City-Central (Kansas City)
Cooper	Western	Jefferson City-Central (Kansas City)
Crawford	Eastern	St Louis
Dade	Western	Springfield-Southern (Kansas City)
Dallas	Western	Springfield-Southern (Kansas City)
Daviess	Western	St Joseph (Kansas City - Western)
De Kalb	Western	St Joseph (Kansas City - Western)
Dent	Eastern	St Louis
Douglas	Western	Springfield-Southern ((Kansas City)
Dunklin	Eastern	Cape Girardeau (St Louis)
Franklin	Eastern	St Louis
Gasconade	Eastern	St Louis
Gentry	Western	St Joseph (Kansas City - Western)
Greene	Western	Springfield-Southern (Kansas City)
Grundy	Western	St Joseph (Kansas City - Western)
Harrison	Western	St Joseph (Kansas City - Western)
Henry	Western	Kansas City - Western
Hickory	Western	Jefferson City-Central (Kansas City)
Holt	Western	St Joseph (Kansas City - Western)
Howard	Western	Jefferson City-Central (Kansas City)
Howell	Western	Springfield-Southern (Kansas City)
Iron	Eastern	St Louis
Jackson	Western	Kansas City – Western
Jasper	Western	Joplin-Southwestern (Kansas City)
Jefferson	Eastern	St Louis
Johnson	Western	Kansas City - Western
Knox	Eastern	Hannibal (St Louis)
Laclede	Western	Springfield-Southern (Kansas City
Lafayette	Western	Kansas City - Western
Lawrence	Western	Joplin-Southwestern (Kansas City)
Lewis	Eastern	Hannibal (St Louis)
Lincoln	Eastern	St Louis
Linn	Eastern	Hannibal (St Louis)
Livingston	Western	St Joseph (Kansas City - Western)
Macon	Eastern	Hannibal (St Louis)
Madison	Eastern	Cape Girardeau (St Louis)
Maries	Eastern	St Louis
Marion	Eastern	Hannibal (St Louis)
McDonald	Western	Joplin-Southwestern (Kansas City)
Mercer	Western	St Joseph (Kansas City - Western)
Miller	Western	Jefferson City-Central (Kansas City)
Mississippi	Eastern	Cape Girardeau (St Louis)
Moniteau	Western	Jefferson City-Central (Kansas City)
Monroe	Eastern	Hannibal (St Louis)
Montgomery	Eastern	Hannibal (St Louis)
Morgan	Western	Jefferson City-Central (Kansas City)
New Madrid	Eastern	Cape Girardeau (St Louis)
Newton	Western	Joplin-Southwestern (Kansas City)
Nodaway	Western	St Joseph (Kansas City - Western)
Oregon	Western	Springfield-Southern (Kansas City)
Osage	Western	Jefferson City-Central (Kansas City)
Ozark	Western	Springfield-Southern (Kansas City)
Pemiscot	Eastern	Cape Girardeau (St Louis)
Perry	Eastern	Cape Girardeau (St Louis)
Pettis	Western	Jefferson City-Central (Kansas City)
Phelps	Eastern	St Louis
Pike	Eastern	Hannibal (St Louis)
Platte	Western	St Joseph (Kansas City - Western)
Polk	Western	Springfield-Southern (Kansas City)
Pulaski	Western	Springfield-Southern (Kansas City)
Putnam	Western	St Joseph (Kansas City - Western)
Ralls	Eastern	Hannibal (St Louis)
Randolph	Eastern	Hannibal (St Louis)
Ray	Western	Kansas City - Western)
Reynolds	Eastern	Cape Girardeau (St Louis)
Ripley	Eastern	Cape Girardeau (St Louis)
Saline	Western	Kansas City - Western
Schuyler	Eastern	Hannibal (St Louis)
Scotland	Eastern	Hannibal (St Louis)
Scott	Eastern	Cape Girardeau (St Louis)
Shannon	Eastern	Cape Girardeau (St Louis)
Shelby	Eastern	Hannibal (St Louis)
St. Charles	Eastern	St Louis
St. Clair	Western	Kansas City - Western
St. Francois	Eastern	St Louis

St. Louis	Eastern	St Louis
St. Louis City City	Eastern	St Louis
Ste. Genevieve	Eastern	St Louis
Stoddard	Eastern	Cape Girardeau (St Louis)
Stone	Western	Joplin-Southwestern (Kansas City)
Sullivan	Western	St Joseph (Kansas City - Western)
Taney	Western	Springfield-Southern (Kansas City)
Texas	Western	Springfield-Southern (Kansas City)

Vernon	Western	Joplin-Southwestern (Kansas City)
Warren	Eastern	St Louis
Washington	Eastern	St Louis
Wayne	Eastern	Cape Girardeau (St Louis)
Webster	Western	Springfield-Southern (Kansas City)
Worth	Western	St Joseph (Kansas City - Western)
Wright	Western	Springfield-Southern (Kansas City)

Standards for Federal Courts: Search fee is $26.00 per item (one party name or case number). Copy fee is $.50 per page. Certification fee is $9.00 per document, double for exemplification, if available. All fees standard unless noted in profile. Mail Search: always enclose a stamped self addressed envelope unless otherwise noted. Most courts accept fax requests or will suggest a copying/search vendor. Before releasing records, all courts require prepayment, unless noted.

Open records are located at the court unless otherwise noted. District courts index by defendant and plaintiff as well as by case number. Bankruptcy courts usually index by debtor and case number. While most courts now have their indexes on computer, many may still maintain index card files as well.

Courts offering internet access via CM-ECF or older RACER, PACER, or Web-PACER systems charge $.08 per page fee unless noted as free. Where PACER is available, the universal sign-up number is 800-676-6856. Find PACER and the US Party/Case Index at http://pacer.psc.uscourts.gov.

US District Court

Eastern District of Missouri

Cape Girardeau Division Court Clerk, 339 Broadway, Rm 240, Cape Girardeau, MO 63701 (also use mail address for courier delivery), 573-335-8538, Fax-573-335-0379. Hours- 8:30AM-5PM. www.moed.uscourts.gov

Counties: Bollinger, Butler, Cape Girardeau, Carter, Dunklin, Madison, Mississippi, New Madrid, Pemiscot, Perry, Reynolds, Ripley, Scott, Shannon, Stoddard, Wayne.

Searches & Indexing: Results do not include SSN or DOB. Both computer and card indexes maintained; computer goes back to 1995. New cases in the index 1-2 days after filing date. Records purged never.

Fee & Payment: Pay by money order, cashier's or personal check. Payee: Clerk, US District Court. Prepayment required.

Phone Search: Only docket information is available by phone.

Mail Search: search usually completed- 1-2 days. SASE not required.

In Person Search: Fee charged if court performs your search. No self-serve copier available.

E-Services: ECF replaces PACER whose records did go back to 1992. New records online after 1 day. ECF at https://ecf.moed.uscourts.gov **Opinions Online:** https://ecf.moed.uscourts.gov/cgi-bin/briefs.cgi.

St Louis Division Court Clerk, 111 S 10th St, Ste 3-300, St Louis, MO 63102 (also use mail address for courier delivery), 314-244-7900, Fax-314-244-7909. Hours- 8:30AM-4:30PM. www.moed.uscourts.gov

Counties: Adair, Audrain, Chariton, Clark, Crawford, Dent, Franklin, Gasconade, Iron, Jefferson, Knox, Lewis, Lincoln, Linn, Macon, Maries, Marion, Monroe, Montgomery, Phelps, Pike, Ralls, Randolph, Schuyler, Scotland, Shelby, St. Charles, St. Francois, St. Louis, St. Louis City, Ste. Genevieve, Warren, Washington, This court also holds records for the Hannibal Division.

Searches & Indexing: Results do not include SSN or DOB. Computer index maintained. New cases in the index immediately after filing date. Records purged never.

Fee & Payment: Pay by money order, cashier's or personal check. Payee: Clerk, US District Court. Prepayment required.

Phone Search: Only docket information is available by phone.

Mail Search: search usually completed- 1-2 days. SASE not required.

In Person Search: Fee charged if court performs your search. No self-serve copier available.

E-Services: ECF replaces PACER whose records did go back to 1992. New records online after 1 day. ECF at https://ecf.moed.uscourts.gov **Opinions Online:** https://ecf.moed.uscourts.gov/cgi-bin/briefs.cgi.

US Bankruptcy Court

Eastern District of Missouri

St Louis Division Court Clerk, 4th Fl, 111 S 10th St, St Louis, MO 63102-2734 (also use mail address for courier delivery), 314-244-4500, Fax-314-244-4990. Hours- 8:30AM-4:30PM. www.moeb.uscourts.gov

Counties: Adair, Audrain, Bollinger, Butler, Cape Girardeau, Carter, Chariton, Clark, Crawford, Dent, Dunklin, Franklin, Gasconade, Iron, Jefferson, Knox, Lewis, Lincoln, Linn, Macon, Madison, Maries, Marion, Mississippi, Monroe, Montgomery, New Madrid, Pemiscot, Perry, Phelps, Pike, Ralls, Randolph, Reynolds, Ripley, Schuyler, Scotland, Scott, Shannon, Shelby, St. Charles, St. Francois, St. Louis, St.Louis City, Ste. Genevieve, Stoddard, Warren, Washington, Wayne.

Searches & Indexing: Results do not include SSN or DOB; court will verify what is on a record if asked. Computer index maintained. New cases in the index 24 hours after filing date. Records purged every 6 months.

Fee & Payment: Pay by money order, cashier's or personal check. Payee: Clerk, US Bankruptcy Court. Prepayment required.

Phone Search: Docket information available by phone. Voice Case Information Service available, call VCIS at 888-223-6431 or 314-244-4999.

Mail Search: search usually completed- 1-2 days. SASE not required.

In Person Search: Fee charged if court performs your search. No self-serve copier available.

E-Services: ECF replaces PACER. Document images available. PACER records go back to 1/1991. New records online after 1 day. ECF at https://ecf.moeb.uscourts.gov **Opinions Online:** www.moeb.uscourts.gov/opin_search/opin_search.html. **Other Online Access:** Search records on the Internet using RACER at http://racer.moeb.uscourts.gov/perl/bkplog.html. Access fee is $.08 per page. Also, access calendars free at www.moeb.uscourts.gov/calendar.htm.

US District Court

Western District of Missouri

Jefferson City-Central Division Court Clerk, 131 W High St, Jefferson City, MO 65101 (also use mail address for courier delivery), 573-636-4015, Fax-573-636-3456. Hours- 9AM-4:30PM. www.mow.uscourts.gov

Counties: Benton, Boone, Callaway, Camden, Cole, Cooper, Hickory, Howard, Miller, Moniteau, Morgan, Osage, Pettis.

Searches & Indexing: Results do not include SSN or DOB. Computer index maintained back to 1988. New cases in the index 1-2 days after filing date. Records purged as deemed necessary.

Fee & Payment: Pay by Visa/MC, money order, cashier's or personal check. Payee: Clerk, US District Court. Prepayment required.

Phone Search: Only docket information is available by phone.

Mail Search: search usually completed- 1-2 days. Include SASE for return.

In Person Search: Fee charged if court performs your search. No self-serve copier available.

E-Services: ECF replaces PACER whose records did go back to 5/1989. ECF at https://ecf.mowd.uscourts.gov **Opinions Online:** www.mow.uscourts.gov/New_Opinions.html.

Joplin-Southwestern Division c/o Kansas City Division, Charles Evans Whittaker Courthouse, 400 E 9th St, Kansas City, MO 64106 (also use mail address for courier delivery), 816-512-5000, Fax-816-512-5078. Hours- 9AM-4:30PM. www.mow.uscourts.gov

Counties: Barry, Barton, Jasper, Lawrence, McDonald, Newton, Stone, Vernon.

Searches & Indexing: Results do not include SSN or DOB. Computer index maintained back to 1990. New cases in the index 2 days after filing date. Records purged as deemed necessary. Open records located at Kansas City Division.

Fee & Payment: Pay by Visa/MC, money order, cashier's or personal check. No business checks accepted. Payee: Clerk of Court.

Phone Search: No searching by telephone. Searching is not available by phone.

Mail Search: search usually completed- 7 days. SASE not required.

In Person Search: permitted. No self-serve copier available.

E-Services: ECF replaces PACER whose records did go back to 5/1989. ECF at https://ecf.mowd.uscourts.gov **Opinions Online:** www.mow.uscourts.gov/New_Opinions.html.

Kansas City - Western Division Court Clerk, Clerk of Court, Rm 1510, 400 E 9th St, Kansas City, MO 64106 (also use mail address for courier delivery), 816-512-5000, records rm- 816-512-5068, Fax-816-512-5078. Hours- 9AM-4:30PM. www.mow.uscourts.gov

Counties: Bates, Carroll, Cass, Clay, Henry, Jackson, Johnson, Lafayette, Ray, St. Clair, Saline.

Searches & Indexing: Results include last 4 SSN digits, also birth year. Records indexed on computer and microfiche. New cases in the index 1-2 days after filing date. Records purged as deemed necessary.

Fee & Payment: Pay by money order, cashier's or personal check. Payee: US District Court Clerk. Prepayment required.

Phone Search: Only docket information is available by phone.

Mail Search: search usually completed- 1 week. SASE not required.

In Person Search: Fee charged if court performs your search. No self-serve copier available.

E-Services: ECF replaces PACER whose records did go back to 5/1989. ECF at https://ecf.mowd.uscourts.gov **Opinions Online:** www.mow.uscourts.gov/New_Opinions.html.

Springfield-Southern Division Court Clerk, 222 N John Q Hammons Pkwy, Suite 1400, Springfield, MO 65806 (use mail address for courier delivery), 417-865-3869, Fax-417-865-7719. 9AM-4:30PM. www.mow.uscourts.gov

Counties: Cedar, Christian, Dade, Dallas, Douglas, Greene, Howell, Laclede, Oregon, Ozark, Polk, Pulaski, Taney, Texas, Webster, Wright.

Searches & Indexing: Results do not include SSN or DOB. Computer index maintained; criminal goes back to 1991, civil to 1988. New cases in the index immediately after filing date. Records purged as deemed necessary.

Fee & Payment: Pay by Visa/MC, money order, cashier's or personal check. Payee: Clerk, US District Court. Prepayment required.

Phone Search: Only docket information is available by phone.

Mail Search: search usually completed- 1 week. Include SASE for return.

In Person Search: Fee charged if court performs your search. No self-serve copier available.

E-Services: ECF replaces PACER whose records did go back to 5/1989. ECF at https://ecf.mowb.uscourts.gov **Opinions Online:** www.mow.uscourts.gov/New_Opinions.html.

St Joseph Division c/o Kansas City Division, Clerk of Court, 201 US Courthouse,, 400 E 9th St, Kansas City, MO 64106 (also use mail address for courier delivery), 816-512-5000, Fax-816-512-5078. www.mow.uscourts.gov

Counties: Andrew, Atchison, Buchanan, Caldwell, Clinton, Daviess, De Kalb, Gentry, Grundy, Harrison, Holt, Livingston, Mercer, Nodaway, Platte, Putnam, Sullivan, Worth.

Searches & Indexing: Computer index maintained. New cases in the index immediately after filing date. Records purged as deemed necessary. Open records located at this Kansas City court.

Fee & Payment: Pay by money order, cashier's or personal check. Payee: Clerk, US District Court. Prepayment required. Will fax documents $.50 per page, prepaid.

Phone Search: Only docket information is available by phone.

Mail Search: search usually completed- 1-2 days. SASE not required.

In Person Search: Fee charged if court performs your search. No self-serve copier available.

E-Services: ECF replaces PACER whose records did go back to 5/1989. ECF at https://ecf.mowd.uscourts.gov **Opinions Online:** www.mow.uscourts.gov/New_Opinions.html.

US Bankruptcy Court

Western District of Missouri

Kansas City - Western Division Court Clerk, Rm 1510, 400 E 9th St, Kansas City, MO 64106 (also use mail address for courier delivery), 816-512-1800. Hours- 9AM-4:30PM. www.mow.uscourt.gov

Counties: Andrew, Atchison, Barry, Barton, Bates, Benton, Boone, Buchanan, Caldwell, Callaway, Camden, Carroll, Cass, Cedar, Christian, Clay, Clinton, Cole, Cooper, Dade, Dallas, Daviess, De Kalb, Douglas, Gentry, Greene, Grundy, Harrison, Henry, Hickory, Holt, Howard, Howell, Jackson, Jasper, Johnson, Laclede, Lafayette, Lawrence, Livingston, McDonald, Mercer, Miller, Moniteau, Morgan, Newton, Nodaway, Oregon, Osage, Ozark, Pettis, Platte, Polk, Pulaski, Putnam, Ray, Saline, St. Clair, Stone, Sullivan, Taney, Texas, Vernon, Webster, Worth, Wright.

Searches & Indexing: Cases indexed by debtor, creditors, and case number. Results include last 4 SSN digits. Computer index maintained. Older records indexed on microfiche. New cases in the index immediately after filing date. District-wide searches available here back to 6/1989

Fee & Payment: Pay by money order, cashier's or personal check. Payee: Clerk, US Bankruptcy Court. Prepayment required.

Phone Search: Use VCIS for docket information. In addition to numbers given, call 816-426-2913 for data on cases closed prior to 10/1995. Voice Case Information Service available, call VCIS at 888-205-2527 or 816-512-5110.

Mail Search: search usually completed- 24 hours. Include SASE for return.

In Person Search: permitted. Self-serve copier available - $.10 per page.

E-Services: ECF replaces PACER. ECF at https://ecf.mowb.uscourts.gov **Opinions Online:** www.mow.uscourts.gov/New_Opinions.html.

Missouri County Courts

Court	Jurisdiction	No. of Courts	How Organized
Circuit Courts*	General	115	45 Circuits
Associate Circuit Courts*	Limited	114	45 Circuits
Combined Courts*		23	
Probate Courts*	Probate	5	
Municipal Courts	Municipal	406	
Family Courts	Special	8	

* Profiled in this Sourcebook.

	CIVIL								
Court	Tort	Contract	Real Estate	Min. Claim	Max. Claim	Small Claims	Estate	Eviction	Domestic Relations
Circuit Courts*	X	X	X	$25,000	No Max				X
Associate Circuit Courts*	X	X	X	$0	$25,000	$3000		X	
Municipal Courts									
Probate Courts*							X		
Family Courts									X

	CRIMINAL				
Court	Felony	Misdemeanor	DWI/DUI	Preliminary Hearing	Juvenile
Circuit Courts*	X				X
Associate Circuit Courts*		X	X	X	
Probate Courts*					
Family Courts					X

ADMINISTRATION　State Court Administrator, 2112 Industrial Dr., PO Box 104480, Jefferson City, MO, 65109; 573-751-4377, Fax: 573-751-5540. www.osca.state.mo.us

COURT STRUCTURE　The Circuit Court is the court of general jurisdiction. There are 45 circuits comprised of 114 county circuit courts and one independent city court. There are also Associate Circuit Courts with limited jurisdiction and some counties have Combined Courts, a growing trend. Municipal Courts only have jurisdiction over traffic and ordinance violations.

ONLINE ACCESS　Available at www.courts.mo.gov/casenet/base/welcome.do is Casenet, a limited but growing online system. The system includes over 70 counties (with more projected) as well as the Eastern, Western, and Southern Appellate Courts, the Supreme Court, and Fine Collection Center. Cases can be searched case number, filing date, or litigant name. One may search supreme and appellate court opinions at the home page.

ADDITIONAL INFORMATION　Starting in 2004, many circuit and associate courts no longer accept mail or fax requests to perform criminal record searches. Instead, the courts instruct requesters to mail criminal search request to the MO State Highway Patrol Criminal Records Division, 1510 E Elm St, Jefferson City, MO 65102. 573-526-6288 (instructions) or 573-526-6153 (voice); Fax 573-751-9382. $5.00 check or money order required for search. Note that most courts participate in the MO CaseNet online system where record searches can be perfomed for free on the Internet.

While the MO State Statutes set the Civil Case limit at $25,000 for the Associate Courts, and over $25,000 for the Circuit Courts, a great many MO County Courts have adopted their own Local Court Rules regarding civil cases and the monetary limits. Presumably, Local Court's Rules are setup to allow the county to choose which court - Circuit or Associate - to send a case. This may depend on the court's case load, but generally, the cases are assigned more by "the nature of the case" and less by the monetary amount involved. Often, Local Court Rules are found where both the Circuit and the Associate Court are located in the same building, or share the same offices and even the same phones. A solution for court record searches is to call the County's Court Clerk, and call to determine the court location of the case.

Adair County

Circuit Court PO Box 690, Kirksville, MO 63501; phone: 660-665-2552; fax: 660-665-3420; hours 8AM-5PM (CST). *Felony, Misdemeanor, Civil Actions Over $25,000.*
Civil Records: Access: In person only. Only the court performs in person searches. Court makes copy: $.10 per page. Required to search: name, years to search. Civil cases indexed by defendant, plaintiff. Prior on index cards.
Criminal Records: Access: In person only. Visitors must perform in person searches themselves. Court makes copy: $.10 per page. Required to search: name, years to search. Criminal records on computer since 1991, prior on index cards. Court recommends searching MO State Hwy Patrol, 573-526-6288.
General Information: No public access terminal. No juvenile, mental, expunged, sealed, dismissed or suspended records released. Certification fee: $1.00 per cert. Payee: Circuit Clerk. Personal checks accepted. Prepayment required.

Associate Circuit Court Courthouse, Kirksville, MO 63501; phone: 660-665-3877; fax: 660-785-3222; hours 8AM-5PM (CST). *Misdemeanor, Civil Actions Under $25,000, Small Claims, Probate.*
Civil Records: Access: Phone, fax, mail, in person. Visitors must perform in person searches themselves. No search fee. Court makes copy: $.25 per page. Required to search: name, years to search. Civil cases indexed by defendant, plaintiff; oncomputer back to 1990; probate records on microfilm since 1840.
Criminal Records: Access: In person. Visitors must perform in person searches themselves. Court makes copy: $.25 per page. Criminal records on computer back to 1990; prior records in files. Note: Court personnel will not perform a name search. They refer requesters to the state criminal record agency.
General Information: Public terminal goes back to 1990. No juvenile, mental, expunged, sealed, dismissed or suspended imposition of case records released. No certification fee. Payee: Associate Circuit Court. Personal checks accepted. Prepayment and SASE required.

Andrew County

Circuit Court PO Box 208 Division I, Savannah, MO 64485; phone: 816-324-4221; fax: 816-324-5667; hours 8AM-5PM (CST). *Felony, Civil Actions Over $45,000.*
Civil Records: Access: In person, online. Both court and visitors may perform in person searches. Court makes copy: $.25 per page. Required to search: name, years to search. Civil cases indexed by defendant, plaintiff; onindex cards since 1976, archived since 1850, computerized since 6/00. Participates in the free court record system at www.courts.mo.gov/casenet/base/welcome.do. Online records go back to 1993.
Criminal Records: Access: In person, online. Visitors must perform in person searches themselves. No search fee. Court makes copy: $.25 per page. Required to search: name, years to search; also helpful: DOB. Criminal records on computer since 6/00, archived from 1841. Online access to criminal records is the same as civil. Note: Court recommends criminal searches at MO State Hwy Patrol, 573-526-6288.
General Information: Public terminal goes back to 2001. No juvenile, mental, expunged, sealed, dismissed or suspended imposition of sentence records released. Certification fee: $2.50 per cert. Payee: Andrew County Circuit Clerk. Personal checks accepted. Prepayment required.

Associate Circuit Court PO Box 49, Savannah, MO 64485; phone: 816-324-3921; fax: 816-324-3191; hours 8AM-5PM (CST). *Misdemeanor, Civil Actions Under $45,000, Eviction, Small Claims, Probate.*

Civil Records: Access: Mail, in person, online. Both court and visitors may perform in person searches. No search fee. Court makes copy: $.25 per page. Required to search: name, years to search. Civil cases indexed by defendant, plaintiff; oncard file, archived from 1950. Participates in the free court record system at www.courts.mo.gov/casenet/cases/searchCases.do. Online records go back to 1993. Mail turnaround time varies.
Criminal Records: Access: Mail, in person, online. Both court and visitors may perform in person searches. No search fee. Court makes copy: $.25 per page. Required to search: name, years to search. Criminal records on computer since mid-1993. Online access to criminal records is the same as civil. Mail turnaround time varies.
General Information: No juvenile, mental, expunged, sealed, dismissed or suspended imposition of sentence records released. Certification fee: $1.50 plus $.25 each add'l page. Payee: Associate Circuit Court. Personal checks accepted. Prepayment and SASE required.

Atchison County

Circuit Court PO Box 280, Rock Port, MO 64482; phone: 660-744-2707; fax: 660-744-5705; hours 8:30AM-4:30PM (CST). *Felony, Misdemeanor, Civil Actions Over $25,000.*
Civil Records: Access: Mail, in person. Visitors must perform in person searches themselves. Court makes copy: $1.00 per page. Required to search: name, years to search. Civil cases indexed by defendant, plaintiff; onindex books, and archived from 1845.
Criminal Records: Access: In person only. Visitors must perform in person searches themselves. Court makes copy: $1.00 per page. Required to search: name, years to search. Criminal records on index books, and archived from 1845. Note: Court recommends criminal searches at MO State Hwy Patrol, 573-526-6153 or www.mshp.dps.mo.gov.
General Information: No public access terminal. No juvenile, mental, expunged, sealed, dismissed or suspended imposition of sentence records released. Will fax documents to local or toll free line. Certification fee: $1.00. Payee: Circuit Clerk. Personal checks accepted. Prepayment required.

Associate Division PO Box 187, Rock Port, MO 64482; phone: 660-744-2700; criminal fax: 660-744-6100; civil/probate fax is the same; hours 8AM-4:30PM (CST). *Misdemeanor, Civil Actions Under $25,000, Eviction, Small Claims, Probate, Traffic.*
Note: Probate is a separate index at this same address.
Civil Records: Access: In person only. Only the court performs in person searches. No search fee. Court makes copy: $1.00 per page. Required to search: name, years to search; also helpful: address. Civil cases indexed by defendant, plaintiff; onbooks and cardex system, archived since 1845.
Criminal Records: Access: In person only. Visitors must perform in person searches themselves. Court makes copy: $1.00 per page. Required to search: name, years to search; also helpful: address, DOB, SSN, offense. Criminal records on computer since mid 1980s; prior on books and cardex system. Traffic cases disposed through the Fine Collection Center may appear free on the state online court record system at www.courts.mo.gov/casenet/base/welcome.do. Note: Court recommends criminal searches at MO State Hwy Patrol, 573-526-6288.
General Information: No public access terminal. No juvenile, mental, expunged, sealed, dismissed or suspended imposition of sentence records released. Will not fax specific case file. Certification fee: $1.50 per page. Payee: Circuit Court Division II. Personal checks not accepted. Prepayment required.

Audrain County

Circuit Court Courthouse, 101 N Jefferson, Mexico, MO 65265; criminal phone: 573-473-5840; civil phone: 573-473-5842; fax: 573-581-3237; hours 8AM-5PM (CST). *Felony, Misdemeanor, Civil Actions Over $25,000.*
Civil Records: Access: In person, online. Visitors must perform in person searches themselves. Court makes copy: $.25 per page. Required to search: name, years to search. Civil cases indexed by defendant, plaintiff; oncomputer since 8/92, prior on index cards, older records archived at Genealogy Club in Mexico, MO. Participates in the free court record system at www.courts.mo.gov/casenet/base/welcome.do.
Criminal Records: Access: In person, online. Visitors must perform in person searches themselves. No search fee. Court makes copy: $.25 per page. Required to search: name, years to search; also SSN, case number. Criminal records on computer since 8/92, stored for 25 years on site then archived (back to 1800s). Participates in the free court record system at www.courts.mo.gov/casenet/base/welcome.do. Note: Court recommends criminal searches at MO State Hwy Patrol, 573-526-6288.
General Information: Public terminal goes back to 1992. No juvenile, mental, expunged, sealed, dismissed or suspended imposition of sentence records released. Certification fee: $1.50 for first 2 pages; $.25 each add'l. Payee: Circuit Clerk. Prepayment required.

Associate Circuit Court Div II Courthouse, 101 N Jefferson, Rm 205, Mexico, MO 65265; phone: 573-473-5850; probate phone: 573-473-5854; fax: 573-581-3364; hours 8AM-5PM (CST). *Misdemeanor, Civil Actions Under $25,000, Eviction, Small Claims, Probate.*
Civil Records: Access: Mail, in person, online. Both court and visitors may perform in person searches. No search fee. Court makes copy: $.15 per page. Required to search: name, years to search. Civil cases indexed by defendant, plaintiff; oncomputer since 9/93, prior on cards, archived to 1800s. Participates in the free court record system at www.courts.mo.gov/casenet/base/welcome.do. Mail turnaround time 1 week.
Criminal Records: Access: Mail, in person, online. Both court and visitors may perform in person searches. No search fee. Court makes copy: $.15 per page. Required to search: name, years to search, DOB, SSN, signed release. Criminal records on computer since 9/93, prior on cards, archived to 1800s. Participates in the free court record system at www.courts.mo.gov/casenet/base/welcome.do. Mail turnaround time 1 week.
General Information: Public terminal goes back to 2003. No juvenile, mental, expunged, sealed, dismissed or suspended imposition of sentence records released. Will fax documents to toll-free numbers. Certification fee: $1.50 first page, $1.00 each add'l. Payee: Circuit Court Division II. Only cashiers checks and money orders accepted. Prepayment required.

Barry County

Circuit Court 102 West St #1, Barry County Courthouse, Cassville, MO 65625; phone: 417-847-2361; hours 8AM-4PM (CST). *Felony, Misdemeanor, Civil Actions Over $25,000.*
Civil Records: Access: Mail, in person. Both court and visitors may perform in person searches. Search fee: $4.00 per name. Court makes copy: $.25 per page. Required to search: name, years to search. Civil cases indexed by defendant, plaintiff; onindex cards, archived since mid-1800s.
Criminal Records: Access: None, unless case number known. Court makes copy: $.25 per page. Required to search: case number. Criminal records on index cards, archived since mid-1800s. Note: Court recommends criminal searches at MO State Hwy Patrol, 573-526-6288.

General Information: No public access terminal. No juvenile, mental expunged, sealed, dismissed or suspended imposition of sentence records released. Certification fee: $1.00. Payee: Circuit Clerk. Personal checks not accepted. Prepayment and SASE required.

Associate Circuit Court 102 West St #2, Judicial Center, Cassville, MO 65625; criminal phone: 417-847-6557; civil phone: 417-847-2146; probate phone: 417-847-2127; fax: 417-847-0182; hours 7:30AM-4PM (CST). *Misdemeanor, Civil Actions Under $25,000, Eviction, Small Claims, Probate.*
Civil Records: Access: Mail, in person. Both court and visitors may perform in person searches. No search fee. Court makes copy: $1.00 per page. Required to search: name, years to search. Civil cases indexed by defendant, plaintiff; on index cards since 1982; prior records on index books to mid 1800s. Mail turnaround time 1-3 days.
Criminal Records: Access: Mail, in person. Both court and visitors may perform in person searches. No search fee. Court makes copy: $1.00 per page. Required to search: name, years to search. Criminal records on computer since 1996; prior records on index books to mid 1800s. Mail turnaround time 1-3 days.
General Information: No public access terminal. No juvenile, mental, expunged, sealed, dismissed or suspended imposition of sentence records released. No certification fee. Payee: Barry County. Personal checks accepted. Prepayment required.

Barton County

Circuit & Associate Court Courthouse, 1007 Broadway, Lamar, MO 64759; phone: 417-682-2444; fax: 417-682-2960; hours 8AM-4:30PM (CST). *Felony, Misdemeanor, Civil, Eviction, Small Claims, Probate.*
Civil Records: Access: Mail, online, in person. Both court and visitors may perform in person searches. No search fee. Court makes copy: $1.00 per page. Required to search: name, years to search; also helpful: address. Civil cases indexed by defendant, plaintiff; on computer since 1999; prior from 1880 on books or archived. Participates in the free court record system at www.courts.mo.gov/casenet/base/welcome.do. Online records go back to 4/1/1999. Mail turnaround time 3 weeks.
Criminal Records: Access: Mail, online, in person. Both court and visitors may perform in person searches. No search fee. Court makes copy: $1.00 per page. Required to search: name, years to search; also helpful: address, DOB, SSN. Criminal records on computer since 1993; prior from 1880 on books or archived. Online access to criminal records is the same as civil. Mail turnaround time 3 weeks.
General Information: Public use terminal available. No juvenile, mental, expunged, dismissed, or suspended imposition of sentence records released. Fee to fax documents is $2.00 per document. Certification fee: $1.50. Payee: Circuit Court. Personal checks accepted. Prepayment and SASE required.

Bates County

Circuit Court 1 N Delaware St, Bates County Courthouse, Butler, MO 64730; phone: 660-679-5171; fax: 660-679-4446; hours 8AM-4:30PM (CST). *Felony, Misdemeanor, Civil Actions Over $25,000.*
http://tacnet.missouri.org/~court27
Civil Records: Access: Fax, mail, in person, online. Both court and visitors may perform in person searches. No search fee. Court makes copy: $.25 per page; same fee for self serve. Required to search: name, years to search. Civil cases indexed by defendant, plaintiff; on computer since 9/1/92, prior on books since 1858. Participates in the free court record system at www.courts.mo.gov/casenet/base/welcome.do. Mail Turnarund time-within 48 hours.

Criminal Records: Access: Fax, mail, in person, online. Both court and visitors may perform in person searches. No search fee. Court makes copy: $.25 per page; same fee for self serve. Required to search: name, years to search. Criminal records on computer since 9/1/92, prior on books since 1858. Participates in the free court record system at www.courts.mo.gov/casenet/base/welcome.do. Mail turnaround time-within 48 hours.
General Information: Public terminal goes back to 8/13/2003. No juvenile, mental, expunged, dismissed, or suspended imposition of sentence records released. No fee to fax documents. Certification fee: $1.50 per certification. Payee: Circuit Court. Only cashiers checks and money orders accepted. Prepayment and SASE required.

Associate Circuit Court Courthouse, Butler, MO 64730; phone: 660-679-3311; fax: n/s; hours 8:30AM-4PM (CST). *Misdemeanor, Civil Actions Under $25,000, Eviction, Small Claims, Probate.*
Civil Records: Access: Mail, in person, online. Both court and visitors may perform in person searches. No search fee. Court makes copy: $.50 per page. Required to search: name, years to search. Civil cases indexed by defendant, plaintiff; on index cards (unsure of starting date). Participates in the free court record system at www.courts.mo.gov/casenet/base/welcome.do. Note: There are limits on what in person searches can search. Mail turnaround time 1 week.
Criminal Records: Access: Mail, in person, online. Both court and visitors may perform in person searches. No search fee. Court makes copy: $.50 per page. Required to search: name, years to search, DOB; also helpful: SSN. Criminal records on computer since 1992, prior on index cards. Participates in the free court record system at www.courts.mo.gov/casenet/base/welcome.do. Mail turnaround time 1 week.
General Information: Public terminal goes back to 2002. No juvenile, mental, expunged, dismissed, or suspended imposition of sentence records released. Certification fee: $1.50 per cert. Payee: Associate Circuit Court. Only cashiers checks and money orders accepted. Prepayment and SASE required.

Benton County

Circuit & Associate Court PO Box 37, Warsaw, MO 65355; phone: 660-438-7712; fax: 660-438-5755; hours 8AM-4:30PM (CST). *Felony, Misdemeanor, Civil Actions, Eviction, Small Claims, Probate.*
www.positech.net/~dcourt
Note: Associate court clerk phone is 660-438-6231.
Civil Records: Access: Mail, in person, online. Visitors must perform in person searches themselves. No search fee. Court makes copy: $.10 per page; same fee for self serve. Required to search: name, years to search. Civil cases indexed by defendant, plaintiff; on computer since 1993, prior on index cards since 1800. Participates in the statewide Casenet system at www.courts.mo.gov/casenet/base/welcome.do.
Criminal Records: Access: In person, online. Visitors must perform in person searches themselves. No search fee. Court makes copy: $.10 per page. Required to search: name, years to search, DOB; also helpful: SSN. Criminal records on computer since 1993, prior on index cards since 1800. Participates in the statewide Casenet system at www.courts.mo.gov/casenet/base/welcome.do/. Note: Court may perform search if time permits. Court will only indicate if subject is on probation or has open case. Court recommends criminal searches at MO State Hwy Patrol, 573-526-6288.
General Information: Public terminal goes back to 11/2001. No juvenile, mental, expunged, dismissed, or suspended imposition of sentence records released. Certification fee: $2.50 per cert. Payee: Clerk of Circuit Court. Personal checks accepted. Prepayment required.

Bollinger County

Circuit Court PO Box 949, Marble Hill, MO 63764; phone: 573-238-1900 x6; fax: 573-238-2773; hours 8AM-4PM (CST). *Felony, Misdemeanor, Civil Actions Over $25,000.*
Civil Records: Access: Mail, in person, online. Both court and visitors may perform in person searches. No search fee. Court makes copy: $.15 per page. Required to search: name, years to search. Civil cases indexed by defendant, plaintiff; on computer since 1990, prior on index cards 1976-1990. Access to civil records is free at www.courts.mo.gov/casenet/base/welcome.do. Search by litigant name, case # or date. Online records go back to 7/1/2001.
Criminal Records: Access: In person, online. Both court and visitors may perform in person searches. No search fee. Court makes copy: $.15 per page; same fee for self serve. Required to search: name, years to search. Criminal records on computer since 1990, prior on index cards 1976-1990. Online access to criminal records is the same as civil. Online public case records go back to 7/1/2001; judgments to 8/23/1993. Mail turnaround time 1 day to 1 week.
General Information: Public terminal has criminal back to 1994 and civil back to 2001. No juvenile, mental, expunged, dismissed, or suspended imposition of sentence records released. Certification fee: $1.00 per cert. Payee: Circuit Clerk. Personal checks accepted. Prepayment and SASE required.

Associate Circuit Court PO Box 1040, Marble Hill, MO 63764-1040; phone: 573-238-1900 x4; criminal fax: 573-238-4511; civil/probate fax is the same; hours 8AM-4PM (CST). *Misdemeanor, Civil Actions Under $25,000, Eviction, Small Claims, Probate.*
Civil Records: Access: In person, online. Visitors must perform in person searches themselves. Court makes copy: $1.00 per page. Required to search: name, years to search. Civil cases indexed by defendant, plaintiff; on computer back to 1995, prior on books, archived to 1890. Participates in the free state online Banner court record system at www.courts.mo.gov/casenet/base/welcome.do. Online records go back to 7/1/2001.
Criminal Records: Access: In person, online. Visitors must perform in person searches themselves. No search fee. Court makes copy: $1.00 per page. Required to search: name, years to search. Criminal records on computer back to 1995, prior on books, archived to 1890. Online access to criminal records is the same as civil. Online public case records go back to 7/1/2001; judgments to 8/23/1993. Note: Court recommends criminal searches at MO State Hwy Patrol, 573-526-6288.
General Information: Public terminal has criminal back to 6/1994 and civil back to 7/2001. No juvenile, mental, expunged, dismissed, or suspended imposition of sentence records released. Will not fax documents. Certification fee: $1.00 per certification. Payee: Circuit Court Division V. Personal checks accepted. Prepayment required.

Boone County

Circuit and Associate Court 705 E Walnut, Columbia, MO 65201; phone: 573-886-4000; probate phone: 573-886-4090; fax: 573-886-4044; hours 8AM-5PM (CST). *Felony, Misdemeanor, Civil, Eviction, Small Claims, Probate.*
Civil Records: Access: Phone, mail, online, in person. Visitors must perform in person searches themselves. Court makes copy: $1.00 for 1st page; $.10 each add'l. Required to search: name, years to search. Civil cases indexed by defendant, plaintiff; on computer for recent cases, others on books. Participates in the free court record system at www.courts.mo.gov/casenet/base/welcome.do. Online civil records go back to 1986. Probate records back to 1986 are also online.
Criminal Records: Access: Online, in person. Visitors must perform in person searches themselves. Court makes copy: $1.00 for 1st page;

$.10 each add'l. Required to search: name, years to search, DOB. Criminal records on computer for recent cases, others on books. Online access to criminal records is the same as civil. Online criminal records go back to 1983. Note: Court recommends criminal searches at MO State Hwy Patrol, 573-526-6288.

General Information: No juvenile, mental, paternity, expunged, dismissed, or suspended imposition of sentence records released. Will not fax documents. Certification fee: $1.00 per cert. Payee: Boone County Circuit Clerk. Business checks accepted. Prepayment and SASE required.

Buchanan County

Circuit & Associate Court 411 Jules St, Rm 331, St Joseph, MO 64501; phone: 816-271-1462; fax: 816-271-1538; hours 8AM-5PM (CST). *Felony, Misdemeanor, Civil, Eviction, Small Claims.*
www.5thcircuit.org
Civil Records: Access: In person, online. Visitors must perform in person searches themselves. Court makes copy: $.25 per page; same fee for self serve. Required to search: name, years to search. Civil cases indexed by defendant, plaintiff; oncomputer since 2/92, on index cards since 1976, prior archived. Participates in the free court record system at www.courts.mo.gov/casenet/base/welcome.do. Online records go back to 2000.
Criminal Records: Access: In person, online. Visitors must perform in person searches themselves. Search fee: None. Court makes copy: $.25 per page; same fee for self serve. Required to search: name, years to search. Criminal records on computer since 2/92, on index cards since 1976, prior archived. Online access to criminal records is the same as civil. County Case.net records go back to 1992. Note: Court recommends criminal searches at MO State Hwy Patrol, 573-526-6288.
General Information: Public terminal goes back to 1992. No juvenile, mental, expunged, dismissed, or suspended imposition of sentence records released. Certification fee: $2.50. Payee: Buchanan Circuit Clerk. Personal checks accepted. Prepayment required.

Probate Court Buchanan County Courthouse, 411 Jules St, Rm 333, St Joseph, MO 64501; phone: 816-271-1477; fax: 816-271-1538; hours 8AM-5PM (CST). *Probate.*
www.5thcircuit.org

Butler County

Circuit Court Courthouse, Poplar Bluff, MO 63901; criminal phone: 573-686-8087; civil phone: 573-686-8082; criminal fax: 573-686-8093; civil fax: 573-686-8094; hours 7:30AM-4PM (CST). *Felony, Misdemeanor, Civil Actions Over $25,000.*
Civil Records: Access: Fax, mail, in person. Visitors must perform in person searches themselves. Search fee: $1.00 per name per year. Court makes copy: $.25 per page; same fee for self serve. Required to search: name, years to search. Civil cases indexed by defendant, plaintiff; oncomputer since 9/91, prior on cards and books since 1865.
Criminal Records: Access: In person only. Visitors must perform in person searches themselves. Court makes copy: $.25 per page; same fee for self serve. Required to search: name, years to search. Criminal records on computer since 9/91, prior on cards and books since 1865. Note: Court personnel will not do name searches. Court recommends criminal searches at MO State Hwy Patrol, 573-526-6288.
General Information: Public terminal goes back to 1992. No juvenile, mental, expunged, dismissed, or suspended imposition of sentence records released. Will fax documents $1.00 per page. Certification fee: $2.50. Payee: Clerk of Circuit Court. Business checks accepted. Prepayment required.

Associate Circuit Court Courthouse, Poplar Bluff, MO 63901; criminal phone: 573-686-8087; civil phone: 573-686-8082; probate phone: 573-686-8073; criminal fax: 573-686-8093; civil fax: 573-686-8094; probate fax: 573-686-0056; hours 7:30AM-4PM (CST). *Misdemeanor, Civil Actions Under $25,000, Eviction, Small Claims, Probate.*
Civil Records: Access: Phone, fax, mail, in person. Both court and visitors may perform in person searches. Search fee: $1.00 per name per year. Court makes copy: $.25 per page; same fee for self serve. Required to search: name, years to search. Civil cases indexed by defendant, plaintiff; oncards since 1976, and index books since 1900s. Mail turnaround time varies.
Criminal Records: Access: Fax, mail, in person. Only the court performs in person searches. Search fee: $1.00 per name per year. Court makes copy: $.25 per page; same fee for self serve. Required to search: name, years to search, signed release. Criminal records on cards since 1976, and index books since early 1990s, computer back to 1991. Mail turnaround time varies.
General Information: No public access terminal. No juvenile, mental, expunged, dismissed, or suspended imposition of sentence records released. Fee to fax documents is $1.00 per page. Certification fee: $2.50. Payee: Circuit Court Division II. Business checks accepted. Prepayment and SASE required.

Caldwell County

Circuit and Associate Court PO Box 68, Kingston, MO 64650; phone: 816-586-2581; fax: 816-586-2333; hours 7:30AM-4:30PM (CST). *Felony, Misdemeanor, Civil, Eviction, Small Claims, Probate.*
Civil Records: Access: Phone, mail, in person. Both court and visitors may perform in person searches. No search fee. Court makes copy: $1.00 per page. Required to search: name, years to search. Civil cases indexed by defendant, plaintiff. Civil records archived since 1860; on computer back to 1995. Mail turnaround time 3 days; phone turnaround time 1 day.
Criminal Records: Access: Phone, mail, in person. Both court and visitors may perform in person searches. No search fee. Court makes copy: $1.00 per page. Required to search: name, years to search. Criminal records archived since 1860; on computer back to 1995. Mail turnaround time 3 days; phone turnaround time 1 day.
General Information: Public use terminal available. No juvenile, mental, expunged, dismissed, or suspended imposition of sentence records released. Certification fee: $1.50 per page. Payee: Circuit Clerk. Personal checks accepted. Prepayment and SASE required.

Callaway County

Circuit & Associate Court 10 E 5th St, Fulton, MO 65251; phone: 573-642-0780; probate phone: 573-642-7080; fax: 573-642-0700; hours 8AM-5PM (CST). *Felony, Misdemeanor, Civil Actions, Eviction, Small Claims, Probate.*
Civil Records: Access: Fax, mail, in person, online. Both court and visitors may perform in person searches. Search fee: $1.00. Court makes copy: $.10 per page, $1.00 minimum. Self serve copy fee: $.10 per page. Required to search: name, years to search. Civil cases indexed by defendant, plaintiff; onindex books and cards since 1821. Participates in the free court record online system at www.courts.mo.gov/casenet/base/welcome.do. Online public cases go back to 2000; online probate to 1977. Note: Court will only perform searches as time permits
Criminal Records: Access: In person, online. Visitors must perform in person searches themselves. No search fee. Court makes copy: $.10 per page, $1.00 minimum. Self serve copy fee: $.10 per page. Required to search: name, years to search; also helpful: DOB, SSN. Criminal records on computer since 1993, prior on index books and cards since 1821. Online access to criminal records is the same as civil. Mail turnaround time 3 days.
General Information: Public terminal goes back to 2000. No juvenile, mental, expunged, dismissed, or suspended imposition of sentence records released. Will fax documents $.10 per page to local phone. Certification fee: $1.50. Payee: Circuit Clerk. Business checks accepted. Attorney/law firm checks accepted. Prepayment required.

Camden County

Circuit Court 1 Court Circle, #8, Camdenton, MO 65020; phone: 573-346-4440; fax: 573-346-5422; hours 8:30AM-4:30PM (CST). *Felony, Misdemeanor, Civil Actions Over $25,000.*
www.camdenmo.org
Civil Records: Access: Mail, in person. Both court and visitors may perform in person searches. No search fee. Court makes copy: $.25 per page. Required to search: name, years to search. Civil cases indexed by defendant, plaintiff; oncomputer since 1989, on index cards from 1965 to 1989, prior on index books since 1903.
Criminal Records: Access: In person only. Both court and visitors may perform in person searches. No search fee. Court makes copy: $.25 per page. Required to search: name, years to search; also helpful: DOB, SSN. Criminal records on computer since 1989, on index cards from 1965 to 1989, prior on index books since 1903. Note: Court recommends criminal searches at MO State Hwy Patrol, 573-526-6288.
General Information: No juvenile, mental, expunged, dismissed, or suspended imposition of sentence records released. Certification fee: $1.50 per cert. Payee: Circuit Clerk. Only cashiers checks and money orders accepted.

Associate Circuit Court 1 Court Circle #8, Camdenton, MO 65020; phone: 573-346-4440; criminal phone: X305; civil phone: X261; probate phone: X303; fax: 573-346-5422; hours 8:00AM-5:00PM (CST). *Misdemeanor, Civil Actions Under $25,000, Eviction, Small Claims, Probate.*
www.camdenmo.org
Civil Records: Access: In person only. Visitors must perform in person searches themselves. Court makes copy: $.25 per page. Required to search: name, years to search. Civil cases indexed by defendant, plaintiff; onindex cards since 1976; on computer back to 1989.
Criminal Records: Access: In person only. Both court and visitors may perform in person searches. No search fee. Court makes copy: $.25 per page. Required to search: name, years to search, DOB; SSN helpful. Criminal records on computer back to 1989, prior on index cards since 1980. Note: Court recommends criminal searches at MO State Hwy Patrol, 573-526-6288.
General Information: Public terminal goes back to 1989. No juvenile, mental, expunged, dismissed, or suspended imposition of sentence records released. Will fax specific case file for $1.00 per page. Certification fee: $1.50. Payee: Circuit Clerk. Personal checks accepted.

Cape Girardeau County

Circuit & Associate Circuit Court - Civil Division 44 N Lorimier, PO Box 2047, Cape Girardeau, MO 63702; phone: 573-335-8253; fax: 573-331-2565; hours 8AM-4:30PM (CST). *Civil.*
Civil Records: Access: Mail, in person, online. Both court and visitors may perform in person searches. No search fee. Court makes copy: $1.00 per page. Required to search: name, years to search. Civil cases indexed by defendant, plaintiff; oncomputer since 1994, prior on index cards since 10/75. Access to civil records is free online at www.courts.mo.gov/casenet/base/welcome.do. Search by litigant name, case # or date. Online records go back to 7/1/2001. Mail turnaround time 1 week.
General Information: Public terminal has only civil records back to 1994. No juvenile, mental, expunged, dismissed, or suspended imposition of sentence, paternity, cases where one party on AFDC records released. Will fax documents to local or toll

free line. Certification fee: $1.00 per cert. Payee: Circuit Clerk. Personal checks accepted. Prepayment and SASE required.

Circuit Court - Criminal Division I & II 100
Court St, Jackson, MO 63755; phone: 573-243-8446 (misdemeanors); criminal phone: 573-243-1755 (felo.); fax: 573-204-2405; hours 8AM-4:30PM (CST). *Felony, Misdemeanor.*
Criminal Records: Access: Mail, in person, online. Both court and visitors may perform in person searches. Search fee: $10.00 per name. Court makes copy: $1.00 for first page, $.50 each add'l. Required to search: name, years to search. Criminal records on computer since 1991, prior on books. Access to criminal records is free at www.courts.mo.gov/casenet/base/welcome.do/. Online public case records go back to 7/1/01; Circuit court judgments to 8/23/1993. Mail turnaround time 1 week.
General Information: Public terminal has only criminal records. No juvenile, mental, expunged, dismissed, or suspended imposition of sentence records released. Will fax documents to local or toll free line. Certification fee: $1.00 per cert seal. Payee: Circuit Clerk. Personal checks accepted. Prepayment and SASE required.

Carroll County

Circuit Court PO Box 245, Carrollton, MO
64633; phone: 660-542-1466; fax: 660-542-1444; hours 8:30AM-4:30PM (CST). *Felony, Misdemeanor, Civil Actions Over $25,000.*
Civil Records: Access: Fax, mail, in person, online. Both court and visitors may perform in person searches. No search fee. Court makes copy: $.35 per page; same fee for self serve. Required to search: name, years to search. Civil cases indexed by defendant, plaintiff; onbooks since 1833. Participates in the free court record system at www.courts.mo.gov/casenet/base/welcome.do. Records from 09/19/01 forward. Mail turnaround time varies.
Criminal Records: Access: Fax, mail, in person, online. Both court and visitors may perform in person searches. No search fee. Court makes copy: $.35 per page; same fee for self serve. Required to search: name, years to search. Criminal records on books since 1833. Participates in the free court record system at www.courts.mo.gov/casenet/base/welcome.do. Records go back to 9/19/01 forward. Mail turnaround time varies.
General Information: No public access terminal. No juvenile, mental, expunged, dismissed, or suspended imposition of sentence records released. No fee to fax documents. Certification fee: $2.00 per document includes copy fee. Payee: Circuit Clerk. Personal checks accepted. Prepayment required.

Associate Circuit Court Courthouse, 8 S
Main, #1, Carrollton, MO 64633; phone: 660-542-1818; criminal phone: 660-542-2494; civil phone: 660-542-1818; probate phone: 660-542-1818; criminal fax: 660-542-1877; civil/probate fax is the same; hours 8:30AM-4:30PM (CST). *Misdemeanor, Civil Actions Under $25,000, Eviction, Small Claims, Probate.*
Civil Records: Access: Mail, in person, online. Visitors must perform in person searches themselves. No search fee. Court makes copy: $.35 per page. Required to search: name, years to search, address. Civil cases indexed by defendant, plaintiff. Civil records go back to 1990; on computer back to 12/2001. Participates in the free statewide Casenet court record online system at www.courts.mo.gov/casenet/base/welcome.do. Online records go back to 09/19/01.
Criminal Records: Access: In person, online. Visitors must perform in person searches themselves. No search fee. Court makes copy: $.35 per page. Required to search: name, years to search, address, DOB. Criminal records go back to 1990; on computer back to 12/2001. Participates in the free statewide Casenet court record system at

www.courts.mo.gov/casenet/base/welcome.do. Online records go back to 09/19/01. Note: Court recommends criminal searches at MO State Hwy Patrol, 573-526-6288.
General Information: Public terminal goes back to 12/2001. No juvenile, mental, expunged, dismissed, or suspended imposition of sentence records released. Will fax documents for no fee. Certification fee: $1.50 per document. Payee: Associate Circuit Court. Only cashiers checks and money orders accepted. Prepayment required.

Carter County

Circuit Court PO Box 578, Van Buren, MO
63965; phone: 573-323-4513; fax: 573-323-4885; hours 8AM-4PM (CST). *Felony, Misdemeanor, Civil Actions Over $20,000.*
Civil Records: Access: In person, online. Both court and visitors may perform in person searches. Court makes copy: $.25 per page. Required to search: name, years to search. Civil cases indexed by defendant, plaintiff; oncomputer since 1979, on index cards since 1988, archived since late-1800s. Participates in the free court record system at www.courts.mo.gov/casenet/base/welcome.do. Online records go back to 4/17/2000.
Criminal Records: Access: In person, online. Visitors must perform in person searches themselves. Court makes copy: $.25 per page. Required to search: name, years to search. Criminal records on computer since 1979, on index cards since 1988, archived since late-1800s. Online access to criminal records is the same as civil. Note: Court recommends criminal searches at MO State Hwy Patrol, 573-526-6288.
General Information: No public access terminal. No juvenile, mental, paternity, expunged, dismissed, or suspended imposition of sentence records released. Will fax documents for fee. Certification fee: $1.00 per cert. Payee: Circuit Clerk. Personal checks accepted. Prepayment required.

Associate Circuit Court PO Box 328, Van
Buren, MO 63965; phone: 573-323-4344; fax: 573-323-8914; hours 8AM-4PM (CST). *Misdemeanor, Civil Actions Under $20,000, Eviction, Small Claims, Probate.*
Civil Records: Access: In person, online. Only the court performs in person searches. Court makes copy: $.25 per page. Required to search: name, years to search. Civil cases indexed by defendant, plaintiff; onindex since 1994, prior on docket sheets. Participates in the free court record system at www.courts.mo.gov/casenet/base/welcome.do. Online records go back to 4/17/2000.
Criminal Records: Access: In person, online. Only the court performs in person searches. Court makes copy: $.25 per page. Required to search: name, years to search. Criminal records on index since 1999, prior on docket sheets. Online access to criminal records is the same as civil.
General Information: No public access terminal. No juvenile, mental, expunged, dismissed, or suspended imposition of sentence records released. No certification fee. Payee: Circuit Court Division II. Personal checks accepted. Prepayment required.

Cass County

Circuit Court 2501 W Wall, Harrisonville, MO
64701; phone: 816-380-8226; probate phone: 816-380-8218; criminal/civil fax: 816-380-8225; hours 8AM-5:00PM (CST). *Felony, Misdemeanor, Civil Actions Over $25,000.*
Civil Records: Access: Phone, mail, in person. Both court and visitors may perform in person searches. No search fee. Court makes copy: $.25 per page. Required to search: name, years to search. Civil cases indexed by defendant, plaintiff; oncomputer since 1992, on index cards since 1976, prior on judgment books since 1800s. Mail turnaround time 1 week.
Criminal Records: Access: Phone, mail, in person. Both court and visitors may perform in person searches. No search fee. Court makes copy: $.25 per

page. Required to search: name, years to search. Criminal records on computer since 1992, on index cards since 1976, prior on judgment books since 1800s. Mail turnaround time 1 week.
General Information: Public terminal goes back to 1992. No juvenile, mental, expunged, dismissed, or suspended imposition of sentence records released. Will fax documents for $.25 per page. Certification fee: $1.50 per page includes copy fee. Payee: Cass County Circuit Clerk. Personal checks not accepted. Prepayment and SASE required.

Associate Circuit Court 2501 W Wall St,
Harrisonville, MO 64701; phone: 816-380-8200; fax: 816-380-8195; hours 8AM-4:30PM (CST). *Misdemeanor, Civil Actions Under $25,000, Eviction, Small Claims, Felony.*
Civil Records: Access: Mail, in person. Visitors must perform in person searches themselves. No search fee. Court makes copy: $.35 per page. Required to search: name, years to search. Civil cases indexed by defendant, plaintiff. Civil records go back to 1960s; on index cards since 1983. Mail turnaround time varies.
Criminal Records: Access: Mail, in person. Visitors must perform in person searches themselves. No search fee. Court makes copy: $.35 per page. Required to search: name, years to search, signed release. Criminal records go back to 1960s; on index cards since 1983; on computer back to 1995. Mail turnaround time varies.
General Information: Public use terminal available. No juvenile, mental, expunged, dismissed, or suspended imposition of sentence records released. No certification fee. Payee: Division III. Business checks accepted. Prepayment and SASE required.

Probate Court 2501 W. Wall St, Harrisonville,
MO 64701; phone: 816-380-8217; fax: 816-380-8215; hours 8AM-N, 1-4:30PM (CST). *Probate.*

Cedar County

Circuit & Associate Court PO Box 665,
Stockton, MO 65785; phone: 417-276-6700; fax: 417-276-5001; hours 8AM-4:30PM (CST). *Felony, Misdemeanor, Civil Actions, Eviction, Small Claims, Probate.*
Civil Records: Access: Fax, mail, in person, online. Visitors must perform in person searches themselves. No search fee. Court makes copy: $.25 per page; Probate $1.00 per page. Self serve copy fee: $.25 per page. Required to search: name, years to search. Civil cases indexed by defendant, plaintiff; onindex cards since 1979, prior on docket books to 1830. Participates in the free court record system at www.courts.mo.gov/casenet/base/welcome.do. online records go back to 9/11/2000. Online records include Probate Court.
Criminal Records: Access: In person, online. Visitors must perform in person searches themselves. Court makes copy: $.25 per page. Self serve copy fee: $.25 per page. Required to search: name, years to search. Criminal records on index cards since 1979, prior on docket books. Online access to criminal records is the same as civil.
General Information: Public terminal goes back to 9/11/2000. No juvenile, mental, expunged, or suspended imposition of sentence records released. Will fax documents for $1.00 per page. Certification fee: $1.50. Payee: Cedar County Circuit Court. Personal checks accepted. Prepayment required.

Chariton County

Circuit Court PO Box 112, Keytesville, MO
65261; phone: 660-288-3602; fax: 660-288-3763; hours 8:30AM-4:30PM (CST). *Felony, Misdemeanor, Civil Actions Over $25,000.*
Civil Records: Access: Fax, mail, in person, online. Both court and visitors may perform in person searches. Search fee: $4.00 per name. Court makes copy: $1.00 per page; same fee for self serve. Required to search: name, years to search. Civil cases indexed by defendant, plaintiff; onindex books since 1975, prior on docket books to 1827. Access at

www.courts.mo.gov/casenet/base/welcome.do, fees involved. Mail turnaround time same day.

Criminal Records: Access: Fax, mail, in person, online. Both court and visitors may perform in person searches. Search fee: $4.00 per name. Court makes copy: $1.00 per page; same for self serve. Required to search: name, years to search; also helpful: DOB, SSN. Criminal records on index books since 1975, prior on docket books to 1827. Participates in the free court record system at www.courts.mo.gov/casenet/base/welcome.do. Mail turnaround time same day.

General Information: Public terminal goes back to 2002. No juvenile, mental, expunged, dismissed, or suspended imposition of sentence records released. Fee to fax documents is $1.00 per page. Certification fee: $1.50 per page. Payee: Chariton County Circuit Clerk. Personal checks accepted. Prepayment and SASE required.

Associate Circuit Court 306 S Cherry, Keytesville, MO 65261; phone: 660-288-3271; fax: 660-288-1511; hours 8AM-4:30PM (CST). *Misdemeanor, Civil Actions Under $25,000, Eviction, Small Claims, Probate.*

Civil Records: Access: Phone, fax, mail, in person, online. Both court and visitors may perform in person searches. No search fee. Court makes copy: $.25 per page ($1.00 if for probate). Required to search: name, years to search. Civil cases indexed by defendant, plaintiff. Civil from records indexed on cards by year 1977 thru 2002, and on computer from 5/13/2002. Participates in the free court record system at www.courts.mo.gov/casenet/cases/searchCases.do. Mail turnaround time 1 week; phone turnaround is 2 days.

Criminal Records: Access: Phone, fax, mail, in person, online. Both court and visitors may perform in person searches. No search fee. Court makes copy: $.25 per page. Required to search: name, years to search; also helpful: DOB, SSN. Criminal from records indexed on cards by year 1977 thru 2002, and on computer from 5/13/2002. Participates in the free court record system at www.courts.mo.gov/casenet/base/welcome.do/. Mail turnaround time 1 week; phone turnaround is 2 days.

General Information: Public terminal goes back to 5/13/2002. (The terminal is in the Circuit Court room, not in the Associate Court room.) No juvenile, mental, expunged, dismissed, or suspended imposition of sentence records released. Certification fee: $1.50. Payee: Associate Circuit Court or Probate Court (depending on search). Personal checks accepted. Prepayment and SASE required.

Christian County

Circuit Court PO Box 278, Ozark, MO 65721; phone: 417-581-6372; probate phone: 417-581-4523; fax: 417-581-0391; hours 8AM-4:30PM (CST). *Felony, Misdemeanor, Civil Actions Over $45,000.*

www.geocities.com/circuit38

Civil Records: Access: Mail, in person, online. Both court and visitors may perform in person searches. Search fee: $6.00 per name. Court makes copy: $.50 per page; same fee for self serve. Required to search: name, years to search. Civil cases indexed by defendant, plaintiff; oncomputer since 9/97, pending cases indexed in card files. Old case card files back to 1979. Participates in the free court record system at www.courts.mo.gov/casenet/base/welcome.do. Online records are from 6/13/03 forward only. Mail turnaround time 1 week.

Criminal Records: Access: Mail, in person, online. Both court and visitors may perform in person searches. Search fee: $6.00 per name. Court makes copy: $.50 per page; same fee for self serve. Required to search: name, years to search. Criminal records on computer since 9/97, pending cases indexed in card files. Old case card files back to 1979. Participates in the free court record system at www.courts.mo.gov/casenet/base/welcome.do.

Online records are from 6/13/03 forward only. Mail turnaround time 1 week.

General Information: Public terminal goes back to 1991. No juvenile, mental, expunged, dismissed, or suspended imposition of sentence records released. Will fax documents for $.50 per page. Certification fee: $1.00. Payee: Christian County Circuit Clerk. Personal checks accepted. Prepayment and SASE required.

Associate Circuit Court - Civil Division 1 110 W Elm St, Rm 203, Ozark, MO 65721; phone: 417-581-2425; fax: 417-581-0391; hours 8AM-4:30PM (CST). *Civil Actions Under $45,000, Eviction, Small Claims.*

Civil Records: Access: Phone, mail, in person, online. Both court and visitors may perform in person searches. No search fee. Court makes copy: $.50 per page. Self serve copy fee: none. Required to search: name, years to search. Civil cases indexed by defendant. Civil records on computer since 7/91. Participates in the free state court record system at www.courts.mo.gov/casenet/base/welcome.do. Mail turnaround time 5 days, phone turnaround is immediate.

General Information: Public terminal has only civil records back to 7/1991. No juvenile, mental, expunged or dismissed records released. No certification fee. Payee: Associate Division I. Personal checks accepted. Prepayment and SASE required.

Associate Circuit Court - Criminal Division 2 110 W Elm St, Rm 105, Ozark, MO 65721; phone: 417-581-4523; fax: 417-581-1443; hours 8AM-4:30PM (CST). *Misdemeanor, Probate.*

Note: This court will not perform name searches and asks searchers to contact MSHP at 573-526-6288.

Criminal Records: Access: In person, online. Visitors must perform in person searches themselves. No search fee. Court makes copy: $.50 per page. Self serve copy fee: $.30 per page. Required to search: name, years to search. Criminal records on computer since 1989; some prior on index cards. Participates in the free state court record system at www.courts.mo.gov/casenet/base/welcome.do. Note: Will accept phone requests from attorneys and law enforcement officials. Court recommends criminal searches at MO State Hwy Patrol, 573-526-6288.

General Information: Public terminal has only criminal records back to 1989. (probate records on terminal back to 1991.) No juvenile, mental, expunged or dismissed records released. Certification fee: $1.50. Payee: Associate Division 2. Prepayment required.

Clark County

Circuit Court 111 E Court, #2, Kahoka, MO 63445; phone: 660-727-3292; fax: 660-727-1051; hours 8AM-4PM (CST). *Felony, Misdemeanor, Civil Actions Over $45,000.*

Civil Records: Access: Phone, fax, mail, in person, online. Both court and visitors may perform in person searches. No search fee. Court makes copy: $.50 per page; same for self serve. Required to search: name, years to search. Civil cases indexed by defendant, plaintiff; onbooks since 1991, prior archived since 1836. Participates in the free statewide Casenet court record system at www.courts.mo.gov/casenet/base/welcome.do. Online records go back to 09/19/01. Mail turnaround time 4 days.

Criminal Records: Access: Phone, fax, mail, in person, online. Both court and visitors may perform in person searches. No search fee. Court makes copy: $.50 per page; same fee for self serve. Required to search: name, years to search. Criminal records on books since 1991, prior archived since 1836. Participates in the free statewide Casenet court record system at www.courts.mo.gov/casenet/base/welcome.do. Online records go back to 09/19/01. Mail turnaround time 4 days.

General Information: Public terminal goes back to 9/19/2001. No juvenile, mental, expunged, dismissed, or suspended imposition of sentence records released. Fee to fax documents is $1.00 per page. Certification fee: $3.00 per document. Payee: Clerk of Circuit Court. Personal checks accepted. Prepayment and SASE required.

Associate Circuit Court 113 W Court, Kahoka, MO 63445; phone: 660-727-3628; fax: 660-727-2600; hours 8AM-4PM (CST). *Misdemeanor, Civil Actions Under $45,000, Eviction, Small Claims, Probate.*

Civil Records: Access: Mail, fax, in person, online. Both court and visitors may perform in person searches. No search fee. Court makes copy: $.25 per page. Required to search: name, years to search. Civil cases indexed by defendant, plaintiff; onindex cards, archived since 1836. Participates in the free statewide Casenet court record system at www.courts.mo.gov/casenet/base/welcome.do. Online records go back to 09/19/01. Mail turnaround time 1-10 days.

Criminal Records: Access: Mail, fax, in person, online. Both court and visitors may perform in person searches. No search fee. Court makes copy: $.25 per page. Required to search: name, years to search. Criminal records on computer since 1988, prior archived since 1836. Participates in the free statewide Casenet court record system at www.courts.mo.gov/casenet/base/welcome.do. Online records go back to 09/19/01. Mail turnaround time 1-10 days.

General Information: Public terminal has only criminal records back to 1988. No juvenile, mental, expunged, dismissed, or suspended imposition of sentence records released. Certification fee: $1.50 plus $1.00 per add'l page. Payee: Associate Circuit Court. Personal checks accepted. Prepayment and SASE required.

Clay County

Circuit Court 11 S Water St, Liberty, MO 64068; phone: 816-792-7706; fax: 816-792-7778; hours 8AM-5PM (CST). *Felony, Misdemeanor, Civil Actions Over $25,000.*

www.circuit7.net

Civil Records: Access: Mail, in person, online. Both court and visitors may perform in person searches. Court makes copy: $.25 per page. Required to search: name, years to search. Civil cases indexed by defendant, plaintiff; oncomputer since 1988; prior records on index. Access civil records on circuit database free at www.circuit7.net/pages/publicaccess/publicaccess.htm. Includes traffic.

Criminal Records: Access: In person, online. Visitors must perform in person searches themselves. Court makes copy: $.25 per page. Required to search: name, years to search, DOB. Criminal records on computer since 1994, prior on index cards. Online access to Circuit criminal records is free at www.circuit7.net/pages/publicaccess/publicaccess.htm. Note: Court recommends criminal searches at MO State Hwy Patrol, 573-526-6288. Mail turnaround time 1-2 days.

General Information: Public terminal goes back to 1987. No juvenile, mental, expunged, dismissed, or suspended imposition of sentence records released. Certification fee: $5.00 per cert. Payee: Clay County Circuit Clerk. Personal checks accepted, but no credit cards. Prepayment and SASE required.

Associate Circuit Court 11 S Water St, Liberty, MO 64068; phone: 816-792-7706; probate phone: 816-792-7722; fax: 816-792-7778; hours 8AM-5PM (CST). *Misdemeanor, Civil Actions Under $25,000, Eviction, Small Claims, Probate.*

www.circuit7.net

Civil Records: Access: Mail, in person, online. Both court and visitors may perform in person searches. No search fee. Court makes copy: $.25 per page. Required to search: name, years to search. Civil cases indexed by defendant, plaintiff; oncomputer since 6/86, prior on microfilm. Online access to Circuit records is free online at www.circuit7.net/pages/publicaccess/publicaccess. htm. Mail turnaround time 7-10 days.

Criminal Records: Access: Mail, in person, online. Both court and visitors may perform in person searches. No search fee. Court makes copy: $.25 per page. Required to search: name, years to search. Criminal records on computer since 1/99, prior on microfilm. Access to Circuit 7 records free at www.circuit7.net/pages/publicaccess/publicaccess. htm. Mail turnaround time 7-10 days.

General Information: Public use terminal available. No juvenile, mental, expunged, dismissed, or suspended imposition of sentence records if record closed released. Certification fee: $5.00. Payee: Clay County Circuit Court. Personal checks accepted. Prepayment and SASE required.

Clinton County

Circuit Court PO Box 275, Plattsburg, MO 64477; phone: 816-539-3731; fax: 816-539-3893; hours 8AM-5PM (CST). *Felony, Misdemeanor, Civil Actions Over $25,000.*

Civil Records: Access: In person only. Visitors must perform in person searches themselves. Court makes copy: $1.00 per page. Required to search: name, years to search. Civil cases indexed by defendant, plaintiff. Civil records (Judgments) on computer from 1976, archived since 1833.

Criminal Records: Access: In person only. Visitors must perform in person searches themselves. Court makes copy: $1.00 per page. Required to search: name, years to search. Criminal records (Judgments) on computer from 1976, archived since 1833. Note: Court recommends criminal searches at MO State Hwy Patrol, 573-526-6288.

General Information: Public terminal goes back to 1976. No juvenile, mental, expunged, dismissed, or suspended imposition of sentence records released. Certification fee: $1.50. Payee: Circuit Clerk. Personal checks not accepted. Prepayment required.

Associate Circuit Court PO Box 383, Plattsburg, MO 64477; phone: 816-539-3755; probate phone: 816-539-3298; criminal fax: 816-539-3439; civil/probate fax is the same; hours 8AM-4:30PM (CST). *Misdemeanor, Civil Actions Under $45,000, Eviction, Small Claims, Probate.*

Note: Probate records are in a separate index.

Civil Records: Access: Fax, mail, in person. Only the court performs in person searches. No search fee. No copy fee. Required to search: name, years to search. Civil cases indexed by defendant, plaintiff; oncomputer since 1992, prior on index cards since 1940s. Note: Letterhead required for mail searches. Mail turnaround time 1 week.

Criminal Records: Access: Fax, mail, in person. Only the court performs in person searches. No search fee. Court makes copy: no fee. Required to search: name, years to search, DOB; also helpful - SSN. Criminal records on computer since 1992, prior on index cards since 1940s. Note: Letterhead required for mail searches. Mail turnaround time 1 week.

General Information: No public access terminal. No juvenile, mental, expunged, dismissed, or suspended imposition of sentence records released. Will fax documents, no fee. No certification fee. SASE required.

Cole County

Circuit & Associate Court PO Box 1870, Jefferson City, MO 65102-1870; criminal phone: 573-634-9171; civil phone: 573-634-9151; fax: 573-635-0796; hours 7:30AM-4:30PM (CST). *Felony, Misdemeanor, Civil Actions, Eviction, Small Claims, Probate.*

Note: The Circuit and Associate Courts consolidated on 01/01.

Civil Records: Access: Fax, mail, in person, online. Both court and visitors may perform in person searches. Court makes copy: $.40 per page. Required to search: name, years to search. Civil cases indexed by defendant, plaintiff. Civil records (pending) on

computer, on books since 1820. Participates in the free court record system at www.courts.mo.gov/casenet/base/welcome.do. Online records go back to 1/1980; probate to 6/2/72. Mail turnaround time 2-5 days.

Criminal Records: Access: In person, online. Both court and visitors may perform in person searches. Court makes copy: $.40 per page. Required to search: name, years to search; also helpful: DOB, SSN. Criminal records on computer since 1989, prior on book since 1820. Participates in the free court record system at www.courts.mo.gov/casenet/base/welcome.do. Online records go back to 1/1980. Note: Court recommends criminal searches at MO State Hwy Patrol, 573-526-6288.

General Information: Public terminal goes back to 2000. No juvenile, mental, expunged, dismissed, or suspended imposition of sentence records released. Other access to criminal records: the court prefers that requesters go to the state highway patrol. Certification fee: $1.50 per page. Payee: Cole County Circuit Clerk. Personal checks accepted. Prepayment required. SASE requested.

Cooper County

Circuit Court 200 Main St, Rm 26, Boonville, MO 65233; phone: 660-882-2232; fax: 660-882-2043; hours 8:30AM-5:00PM (CST). *Felony, Misdemeanor, Civil Actions Over $25,000.*

Civil Records: Access: Phone, fax, mail, in person, online. Both court and visitors may perform in person searches. No search fee. Court makes copy: $1.00 per page. Required to search: name, years to search. Civil cases indexed by defendant, plaintiff; oncards since 1975, case files from 1819 forward; on computer back to 2001. Access to civil records is free at www.courts.mo.gov/casenet/cases/searchCases.do. Search by litigant name, case # or date. Online records go back to 4/2001. Mail turnaround time 1-2 days. Can tell you if record is available and cost over phone.

Criminal Records: Access: In person, online. Both court and visitors may perform in person searches. Court makes copy: $1.00 per page. Required to search: name, years to search, DOB; also helpful: SSN. Criminal records on cards since 1975, case files from 1819 forward; on computer back to 2001. Online access to criminal records is the same as civil. Note: Court can say if record is available and cost over phone.

General Information: Public terminal goes back to 4/2001. No juvenile, mental, expunged, dismissed, or suspended imposition of sentence records released. Certification fee: $1.50 per cert. Payee: Circuit Clerk or Recorder of Deeds. Personal checks accepted. Prepayment and SASE required.

Associate Circuit Court 200 Main, Rm 31, Boonville, MO 65233; phone: 660-882-5604; fax: 660-882-8747; hours 8:30AM-5PM (CST). *Misdemeanor, Civil Actions Under $25,000, Eviction, Small Claims, Probate.*

Civil Records: Access: Mail, in person, online. Only the court performs in person searches. No search fee. Court makes copy: $1.00 per page. Required to search: name, years to search. Civil cases indexed by defendant, plaintiff; onindex cards since 1990, computerized since 2000. Access to civil records is free at www.courts.mo.gov/casenet/cases/searchCases.do. Search by litigant name, case # or date. Online records go back to 4/2001. Mail turnaround time 10 days.

Criminal Records: Access: Mail, in person, online. Both court and visitors may perform in person searches. No search fee. Court makes copy: $1.00 per page. Required to search: name, years to search, DOB; also helpful: SSN. Criminal records on computer since mid-1990s, on index cards from 1980-1990. Online access to criminal records is the same as civil. Online criminal records go back 1/1990. Mail turnaround time 10 days.

General Information: Public terminal goes back to 1990. No juvenile, mental, expunged, dismissed, or suspended imposition of sentence records released.

Will fax documents for $1.00 per page, prepaid, if time available. Certification fee: $1.00 per page. Payee: Cooper County Associate Circuit Court. Prepayment and SASE required.

Crawford County

Circuit Court PO Box 177, Steelville, MO 65565; phone: 573-775-2866; fax: 573-775-2452; hours 8AM-4:30PM (CST). *Felony, Misdemeanor, Civil Actions Over $25,000.*

Civil Records: Access: Mail, in person, online. Both court and visitors may perform in person searches. No search fee. Court makes copy: $.30 per page. Required to search: name, years to search. Civil cases indexed by defendant, plaintiff; oncomputer from 3/02/92 for judgments only, archived from 1800s, some records on index cards and books. Participates in the free state online JIS Banner court record system at www.courts.mo.gov/casenet/base/welcome.do. Mail turnaround time as time permits.

Criminal Records: Access: Mail, in person, online. Both court and visitors may perform in person searches. No search fee. Court makes copy: $.30 per page. Required to search: name, years to search, offense, date of offense. Criminal records on computer since 3/02/92, prior on cards. Online access to criminal court records is the same as civil. Mail turnaround time as time permits.

General Information: Public terminal goes back to 3/1992. No juvenile, mental, expunged, dismissed, or suspended imposition of sentence records released. Will fax documents for $1.00 per page. Certification fee: $1.00 per seal. Payee: Crawford County Circuit Clerk. Personal checks not accepted. Prepayment and SASE required.

Associate Circuit Court PO Box B.C, 111 Third St, Steelville, MO 65565; phone: 573-775-2149; criminal fax: 573-775-4010; civil/probate fax is the same; hours 8AM-5PM (CST). *Misdemeanor, Civil Actions Under $25,000, Eviction, Small Claims, Probate.*

The court will not do record searches, however will look up specific case file is case number given.

Civil Records: Access: In person, online. Visitors must perform in person searches themselves. Court makes copy: $.30 per page; same fee for self serve. Required to search: name, years to search. Civil cases indexed by defendant, plaintiff. Civil records kept since 1989 on paper, prior destroyed. Access to records is free online at www.courts.mo.gov/casenet/cases/searchCases.do.

Criminal Records: Access: Online. Visitors must perform in person searches themselves. No search fee. Court makes copy: $.30 per page; same fee for self serve. Criminal records kept since 1996, prior destroyed. Access to records is free at www.courts.mo.gov/casenet/base/welcome.do/.

Note: Per judge's orders, court will not accept search requests or perform criminal record searches. Court recommends criminal searches at State Hwy Patrol, 573-526-6288.

General Information: Public terminal goes back to 4/2001. No sealed records released. Will fax specific case file requests. Certification fee: $2.50 per page. Payee: Associate Circuit Court. Personal checks accepted. Prepayment required.

Dade County

Circuit & Associate Court Courthouse, Greenfield, MO 65661; phone: 417-637-2271; fax: 417-637-5055; hours 8AM-4PM (CST). *Felony, Misdemeanor, Civil Actions, Eviction, Small Claims, Probate.*

Civil Records: Access: Mail, in person, online. Both court and visitors may perform in person searches. Search fee: $5.00. Court makes copy: $.10 per page; same fee for self serve. Required to search: name, years to search. Civil cases indexed by defendant, plaintiff. Civil records in index cards since 1982, prior on books to 1800s; on computer back to 2000. Participates in the free court record system at www.courts.mo.gov/casenet/base/welcome.do.

Online records go back to 9/20/1999. Online records include Probate Court. Mail turnaround time 2-3 days.

Criminal Records: Access: Mail, in person, online. Both court and visitors may perform in person searches. Search fee: $5.00. Court makes copy: $.10 per page; same fee for self serve. Required to search: name, years to search; also helpful-DOB, SSN, signed release. Criminal records in index cards since 1982, prior on book to 1800s; on computer back to 2000. Online access to criminal records is the same as civil. Mail turnaround time 2-3 days.

General Information: Public terminal goes back to 2000. No juvenile, mental, expunged, dismissed, or suspended imposition of sentence records released. Will fax documents. Certification fee: $2.50. Payee: Dade County Circuit Clerk. Personal checks accepted. Prepayment and SASE required.

Dallas County

Circuit Court PO Box 373, 108 S Maple St, Buffalo, MO 65622; phone: 417-345-2243; fax: 417-345-5539; hours 7:30AM-4PM (CST). *Felony, Misdemeanor, Civil Actions Over $25,000.* www.positech.net/~dcourt

Civil Records: Access: Phone, fax, mail, in person, online. Both court and visitors may perform in person searches. No search fee. Court makes copy: $.25 per page; same fee for self serve. Required to search: name, years to search. Civil cases indexed by defendant, plaintiff; oncomputer since 1991, prior on book since 1951. Participates in the free court record system at www.courts.mo.gov/casenet/base/welcome.do.

Criminal Records: Access: In person, online. Visitors must perform in person searches themselves. No search fee. Court makes copy: $.25 per page; same fee for self serve. Required to search: name, years to search; also helpful: DOB. Criminal records on computer since 1992, prior on book since 1951. Online access to criminal records is the same as civil. Note: Court recommends criminal searches at MO State Hwy Patrol, 573-526-6288. Mail turnaround time 1-2 days.

General Information: Public terminal goes back to 11/13/01. No juvenile, mental, expunged, dismissed, or suspended imposition of sentence records released. Fee to fax documents is $1.00 per page. Certification fee: $1.00 per document. Payee: Circuit Clerk. Personal checks accepted. Prepayment and SASE required.

Associate Circuit Court PO Box 1150, Buffalo, MO 65622; phone: 417-345-7641; fax: 417-345-5358; hours 8AM-N, 1-4PM (CST). *Misdemeanor, Civil Actions Under $45,000, Eviction, Small Claims, Probate.*

Civil Records: Access: In person, online. Both court and visitors may perform in person searches. No search fee. Court makes copy: $.25 per page. Required to search: name, years to search. Civil cases indexed by defendant, plaintiff; onindex cards since 1800s; computerized since 1990. Participates in the free statewide Casenet court record system at www.courts.mo.gov/casenet/base/welcome.do. Records go back to 1992.

Criminal Records: Access: In person, online. Visitors must perform in person searches themselves. No search fee. Court makes copy: $.25 per page. Required to search: name, years to search. Criminal records on computer since 1990, on index cards since 1800s. Participates in the free statewide Casenet court record system at www.courts.mo.gov/casenet/base/welcome.do. Records go back to 1992. Note: Court recommends criminal searches at MO State Hwy Patrol, 573-526-6288. Court will do a single name search only, maybe.

General Information: Public terminal has criminal back to 1991 and civil back to 11/2000. (Public terminal located in main Circuit Court Clerk office.) No juvenile, mental, expunged, dismissed, or suspended imposition of sentence records released. Certification fee: $1.00 per page. Payee: Associate

Circuit Court. Only cashiers checks and money orders accepted. Prepayment required.

Daviess County

Circuit Court PO Box 337, Gallatin, MO 64640; phone: 660-663-2932; fax: 660-663-3876; hours 8AM-4:30PM (CST). *Felony, Misdemeanor, Civil Actions Over $30,000.*

Civil Records: Access: Phone, fax, mail, in person. Both court and visitors may perform in person searches. Search fee: $10.00 per name. Court makes copy: $1.00 per page. Required to search: name, years to search. Civil cases indexed by defendant, plaintiff; onrecords books since 1839. Mail turnaround time 1 day; phone turnaround is immediate.

Criminal Records: Access: Phone, fax, mail, in person. Both court and visitors may perform in person searches. Search fee: $10.00 per name. Court makes copy: $1.00 per page. Required to search: name, years to search, DOB. Criminal records on records books since 1839. Mail turnaround time 1 day; phone turnaround is immediate.

General Information: No public access terminal. No juvenile, mental, expunged, dismissed, or suspended imposition of sentence records released. Will fax documents $2.00 per page. Certification fee: $2.00. Payee: Daviess County Circuit Clerk. Business checks accepted. Prepayment and SASE required.

Associate Division Circuit Court PO Box 233, 102 N Main St, Courthouse #6, Gallatin, MO 64640; phone: 660-663-2532; probate phone: 660-663-2532; fax: 660-663-2646; hours 8AM-4:30PM (CST). *Misdemeanor, Civil Actions Under $45,000, Eviction, Small Claims, Probate.*

Note: Probate records are unavailable before 1890 due to Courthouse fire.

Civil Records: Access: Fax, phone, in person. Only the court performs in person searches. No search fee. Court makes copy: $1.00 per page. Required to search: name, years to search. Civil cases indexed by defendant, plaintiff. Civil records index cards since 9/84, prior on judgment books. Mail turnaround time 1-2 days.

Criminal Records: Access: Mail, in person. Only the court performs in person searches. No search fee. Court makes copy: $1.00 per page. Required to search: name, years to search. Criminal records on index cards since 1979, prior on judgment books. Mail turnaround time 1-2 days.

General Information: No public access terminal. No juvenile, mental, expunged, dismissed, or suspended imposition of sentence records released. Will fax documents for $2.00. Certification fee: $1.50. Payee: Associate Division Court. Only cashiers checks and money orders accepted. Prepayment and SASE required.

De Kalb County

Circuit Court PO Box 248, Maysville, MO 64469; phone: 816-449-2602; probate phone: 816-449-5400; hours 8:30AM-4:30PM (CST). *Felony, Civil Actions Over $45,000.*

Civil Records: Access: In person only. Visitors must perform in person searches themselves. Court makes copy: $1.00 per page; same fee for self serve. Required to search: name, years to search. Civil cases indexed by defendant, plaintiff; onindex cards since 1970, computerized since 2003.

Criminal Records: Access: In person only. Visitors must perform in person searches themselves. Court makes copy: $1.00 per page; same fee for self serve. Required to search: name, years to search. Criminal records on index cards since 1970, computerized since 2003. Note: Court recommends criminal searches at MO State Hwy Patrol, 573-526-6288.

General Information: No public access terminal. No juvenile or suspended imposition of sentence records released. Will fax specific case file for $1.00 per document. Certification fee: $1.00. Payee: Clifton DeShon, Circuit Clerk. Personal checks accepted. Prepayment required.

Associate Circuit Court PO Box 248, Maysville, MO 64469; phone: 816-449-5400; probate phone: 816-449-5400; criminal fax: 816-449-2440; civil/probate fax is the same; hours 8:30AM-N, 1-4:30PM (CST). *Misdemeanor, Civil Actions Under $45,000, Eviction, Small Claims, Probate.*

Note: Court personnel will not do name searches. Probate index is separate index at this same address.

Civil Records: Access: In person only. Visitors must perform in person searches themselves. Court makes copy: $1.00 per page; same fee for self serve. Required to search: name, years to search. Civil cases indexed by defendant, plaintiff; onindex cards since 1960s.

Criminal Records: Access: In person only. Visitors must perform in person searches themselves. Court makes copy: $1.00 per page; same fee for self serve. Required to search: name, years to search; DOB; also helpful-SSN, case number. Criminal records on index cards since 1980s. Note: Court recommends criminal searches at MO State Hwy Patrol, 573-526-6288.

General Information: No public access terminal. No juvenile, mental, expunged, dismissed, or suspended imposition of sentence records released. Will fax specific case file, but not certified. Certification fee: $1.50 per cert. Payee: Associate Circuit Court. Only cashiers checks and money orders accepted. Prepayment required.

Dent County

Circuit Court 112 E 5th St, Salem, MO 65560; phone: 573-729-3931; fax: 573-729-9414; hours 8AM-4:30PM (CST). *Felony, Misdemeanor, Civil Actions Over $25,000.*

Civil Records: Access: Mail, fax, in person, online. Both court and visitors may perform in person searches. No search fee. Court makes copy: $.25 per page. Required to search: name, years to search. Civil cases indexed by defendant, plaintiff; oncomputer since 1993, on index cards since 1978. Participates in the free statewide Casenet court record system at www.courts.mo.gov/casenet/base/welcome.do.

Criminal Records: Access: In person, online. Visitors must perform in person searches themselves. Court makes copy: $.25 per page. Required to search: name, years to search. Criminal records on computer since 1993, on index cards since 1978. Participates in the free statewide Casenet court record system at www.courts.mo.gov/casenet/base/welcome.do.

General Information: Public terminal goes back to 1996. No juvenile, mental, expunged, dismissed, or suspended imposition of sentence records released. Certification fee: $2.00 per cert. Payee: Dent County Circuit Clerk. Only cashiers checks and money orders accepted. Prepayment and SASE required.

Associate Circuit Court 112 E 5th St, Salem, MO 65560; phone: 573-729-3134; probate phone: 573-729-3134; fax: 573-729-5172; hours 8AM-4:30PM (CST). *Misdemeanor, Civil Actions Under $25,000, Eviction, Small Claims, Probate.*

Note: Small Claims and Probate fax is 573-729-5172.

Civil Records: Access: Mail, fax, in person, online. Both court and visitors may perform in person searches. No search fee. Court makes copy: $.25 per page. Required to search: name, years to search. Civil cases indexed by defendant, plaintiff; oncomputer since 1985, prior on index cards. Participates in the free statewide Casenet court record system at www.courts.mo.gov/casenet/base/welcome.do. Mail turnaround time 2-3 days.

Criminal Records: Access: Mail, fax, in person, online. Both court and visitors may perform in person searches. No search fee. Court makes copy: $.25 per page. Required to search: name, years to search, DOB, signed release. Criminal records on computer since 1985, prior on index cards. Participates in the free statewide Casenet court record system at www.courts.mo.gov/casenet/base/welcome.do. Mail turnaround time 2-3 days.

General Information: Public use terminal available. No juvenile, mental, expunged, dismissed, or suspended imposition of sentence records released. Will not fax documents. Certification fee: $2.00. Payee: Associate Circuit Court or Probate Court. Business checks accepted. Prepayment and SASE required.

Douglas County

Circuit Court PO Box 249, Ava, MO 65608; phone: 417-683-4713; fax: 417-683-2794; hours 8AM-4:30PM (CST). *Felony, Misdemeanor, Civil Actions Over $25,000.*
Note: This court expects to be online on the Missouri Casenet.com system near 2/2006.
Civil Records: Access: Phone, mail, in person. Visitors must perform in person searches themselves. Search fee: $10.00 per hour. Court makes copy: $.25 per page. Required to search: name, years to search. Civil cases indexed by defendant, plaintiff; on alpha cards since 1977. Mail turnaround time 1 week.
Criminal Records: Access: Phone, mail, in person. Visitors must perform in person searches themselves. Search fee: $10.00 per hour. Court makes copy: $.25 per page. Required to search: name, years to search; also helpful: DOB, SSN. Criminal records on alpha cards since 1977. Mail turnaround time 1 week.
General Information: Public terminal has only civil records. (Judgments only on terminal in 2005.) No juvenile, mental, expunged, dismissed, or suspended imposition of sentence records released. Will fax documents to local or toll free line. Certification fee: $2.50. Payee: Circuit Clerk. Personal checks accepted. Prepayment and SASE required.

Associate Circuit Court PO Box 276, 203 SE 2nd St, Ava, MO 65608; phone: 417-683-2114; fax: 417-683-3121; hours 8AM-4:30PM (CST). *Misdemeanor, Civil Actions Under $25,000, Eviction, Small Claims, Probate.*
Civil Records: Access: Mail, in person. Only the court performs in person searches. No search fee. Court makes copy: $.30 per page. Required to search: name, years to search. Civil cases indexed by defendant, plaintiff; on index cards and computer.
Criminal Records: Access: In person only. Only the court performs in person searches. No search fee. Court makes copy: $.30 per page. Required to search: name, years to search; SSN helpful. Criminal records on computer back to 1991. Note: Court rarely allows for mail requests. Mail turnaround time 2-3 days.
General Information: No public access terminal. No juvenile, mental, expunged, dismissed, or suspended imposition of sentence records released. Certification fee: $1.50 per cert. Payee: Associate Circuit Court. Personal checks accepted. Prepayment and SASE required.

Dunklin County

Circuit Court Division I PO Box 567, Kennett, MO 63857; phone: 573-888-2456; fax: 573-888-0319; hours 8:30AM-4:30PM (CST). *Felony, Misdemeanor, Civil Actions Over $25,000.*
Civil Records: Access: In person, online. Visitors must perform in person searches themselves. Court makes copy: $.50 per page. Required to search: name, years to search. Civil cases indexed by defendant, plaintiff; on index cards back to 1900; on computer back to 1990. Access to civil records is free at www.courts.mo.gov/casenet/cases/searchCases.do. Search by litigant name, case number or date. Online records go back to 7/1/2001.
Criminal Records: Access: In person, online. Visitors must perform in person searches themselves. Court makes copy: $.50 per page. Required to search: name, years to search, DOB, SSN. Criminal records on computer back to 8/94. Online access to criminal records is the same as civil. Note: Court recommends criminal searches at MO State Hwy Patrol, 573-526-6288.

General Information: Public terminal has criminal back to 8/1994 and civil back to 1990. No juvenile, mental, expunged or dismissed records released. Certification fee: $2.00 per document. Payee: Circuit Clerk. Personal checks accepted. Prepayment required. Will bill attorneys, courts and abstract companies.

Associate Circuit Court Courthouse Rm 103, Kennett, MO 63857; phone: 573-888-3378; probate phone: 573-888-3272; fax: 573-888-0754; hours 8AM-4:30PM (CST). *Felony, Misdemeanor, Civil Actions Under $25,000, Eviction, Small Claims, Probate.*
Note: Probate address is Rm #202.
Civil Records: Access: In person, online. Visitors must perform in person searches themselves. Court makes copy: $.50 per page; same fee for self serve. Required to search: name, years to search. Civil cases indexed by defendant, plaintiff; on index cards; on computer back to 2001. Access to civil records is free at www.courts.mo.gov/casenet/cases/searchCases.do. Search by litigant name, case number or date. Online records go back to 7/1/2001.
Criminal Records: Access: In person, online. Visitors must perform in person searches themselves. Court makes copy: $.50 per page; same fee for self serve. Required to search: name, years to search, DOB. Criminal records on index cards back to 1979; on computer back to 1990. Online access to criminal records is the same as civil. Note: Court recommends criminal searches at MO State Hwy Patrol, 573-526-6288.
General Information: Public use terminal available. (Terminal is located in Division 1.) No juvenile, mental, expunged, dismissed, or suspended imposition of sentence records released. Certification fee: $2.50. Payee: Circuit Court Div 2. Business checks accepted. Prepayment required.

Franklin County

Circuit Court 300 E Main St, Rm 301, Union, MO 63084; phone: 636-583-6303; hours 8AM-4:30PM (CST). *Felony, Civil Actions Over $25,000.*
Civil Records: Access: Mail, online, in person. Both court and visitors may perform in person searches. Search fee: $2.00 per name. Court makes copy: $.25 per page. Self serve copy fee: $.25 per page. Required to search: name, years to search. Civil cases indexed by defendant, plaintiff; on computer back to 1995; others filed as originals to 1821. Participates in the free court record system at www.courts.mo.gov/casenet/base/welcome.do. Online records go back to 1/1995. Mail turnaround time 1-5 days.
Criminal Records: Access: Mail, online, in person. Both court and visitors may perform in person searches. Search fee: $2.00 per name. Court makes copy: $.25 per page. Self serve copy fee: $.25 per page. Required to search: name, years to search, DOB. Criminal records on computer back to 1995; others filed as originals to 1940. Participates in the free court record system at www.courts.mo.gov/casenet/base/welcome.do. Online records go back to 1/1995. Mail turnaround time 1-5 days.
General Information: Public terminal goes back to 1995. No juvenile, mental, expunged, dismissed, or suspended imposition of sentence records released. Certification fee: $1.00. Payee: Circuit Clerk. Personal checks accepted. Prepayment and SASE required.

Associate Circuit Court 120 S Church St, #B, Union, MO 63084; phone: 636-583-6326; probate phone: 636-583-6312; probate fax: 636-583-7368; hours 8AM-4:30PM (CST). *Misdemeanor, Civil Actions Under $25,000, Eviction, Small Claims, Probate.*
Note: Probate court located at 491 E Springfield St.
Civil Records: Access: Online, in person. Both court and visitors may perform in person searches. No search fee. Court makes copy: $.25. Required to search: name, years to search. Civil cases indexed by

defendant, plaintiff; on computer (limited), on index cards since 1983. Participates in the free court record system at www.courts.mo.gov/casenet/base/welcome.do. Online records go back to 1/1995. Online probate court records go back to 10/14/1967.
Criminal Records: Access: Online, in person. Both court and visitors may perform in person searches. Court makes copy: $.25. Required to search: name, years to search. Criminal records on index cards since 1979. Participates in the free court record system at www.courts.mo.gov/casenet/base/welcome.do. Online records go back to 1/1995. Note: Court recommends criminal searches at MO State Hwy Patrol, 573-526-6288.
General Information: No public access terminal. No juvenile, mental, expunged, dismissed, or suspended imposition of sentence records released. Will not fax documents. No certification fee. Prepayment required.

Gasconade County

Circuit Court 119 E 1st St, Rm 6, Hermann, MO 65041-1182; phone: 573-486-2632; fax: 573-486-5812; hours 8AM-4:30PM (CST). *Felony, Misdemeanor, Civil Actions Over $25,000.*
Civil Records: Access: Mail, in person, online. Both court and visitors may perform in person searches. No search fee. Court makes copy: $1.00 per page. Self serve copy fee: $.10 per page. Required to search: name, years to search. Civil cases indexed by defendant, plaintiff; on index cards since 1976, prior on books stored in vault; online since 9/2001. Participates in the free court record system at www.courts.mo.gov/casenet/base/welcome.do.
Criminal Records: Access: In person, online. Visitors must perform in person searches themselves. No search fee. Court makes copy: $1.00 per page. Self serve copy fee: $.10 per page. Required to search: name, years to search. Criminal records on index cards since 1976, prior on books stored in vault; online since 9/2001. Participates in the free court record system at www.courts.mo.gov/casenet/base/welcome.do. Note: Court recommends criminal searches at MO State Hwy Patrol, 573-526-6288.
General Information: Public terminal goes back to 1990. No juvenile, mental, expunged, dismissed, or suspended imposition of sentence records released. Will fax documents for $2.00 1st page, $1.00 each add'l. Certification fee: $1.00 per cert seal. Payee: Gasconade Circuit Court. Prepayment required.

Associate Circuit Court 119 E. 1st St. Rm 3, Hermann, MO 65041; phone: 573-486-2632; fax: 573-486-5812; hours 8AM-4:30PM (CST). *Misdemeanor, Civil Actions Under $25,000, Eviction, Small Claims, Probate.*
Civil Records: Access: In person, online. Both court and visitors may perform in person searches. No search fee. Court makes copy: $.10 per page. Required to search: name, years to search. Civil cases indexed by defendant, plaintiff; on computer since 9/00, prior on index cards since 1979. Participates in the free court record system at www.courts.mo.gov/casenet/base/welcome.do. Online records go back to 7/31/2000. Note: Only the court performs in person searches for records prior to 09/00.
Criminal Records: Access: Online, in person. Both court and visitors may perform in person searches. Court makes copy: $.10 per page. Required to search: name, years to search. Criminal records on computer since 1988, prior on index cards since 1979. Participates in the free court record system at www.courts.mo.gov/casenet/base/welcome.do. Online records go back to 7/31/2000. Note: Both court and visitors may perform in person searches of records before 9/2000. Court recommends criminal searches at State Hwy Patrol, 573-526-6288.
General Information: Public terminal goes back to 2000. (Terminal is in Circuit Court office.) No juvenile, mental, expunged, dismissed, or suspended

imposition of sentence records released. Certification fee: $2.50 per cert. Payee: Associate Circuit Court. Personal checks accepted. Prepayment required. Will bill probate fees.

Gentry County

Circuit Court PO Box 27, Albany, MO 64402; phone: 660-726-3618; fax: 660-726-4102; hours 8AM-4:30PM (CST). *Felony, Misdemeanor, Civil Actions Over $25,000.*
Civil Records: Access: Mail, fax, in person. Both court and visitors may perform in person searches. No search fee. Court makes copy: $.30 per page. Self serve copy fee: $.10 per page. Required to search: name, years to search. Civil cases indexed by defendant, plaintiff. Civil records archived since 1885. Mail turnaround time 5 working days.
Criminal Records: Access: Mail, in person. Both court and visitors may perform in person searches. No search fee. Court makes copy: $.30 per page. Self serve copy fee: $.10 per page. Required to search: name, years to search; also helpful: DOB, SSN. Criminal records archived since 1885. Mail turnaround time 5 working days.
General Information: No public access terminal. No juvenile, mental, expunged, dismissed, or suspended imposition of sentence records released. Fee to fax documents is $1.00 per page. Certification fee: $1.00 per page. Payee: Circuit Clerk. Personal checks accepted. Prepayment and SASE required.

Associate Circuit Court 200 W Clay St, Albany, MO 64402; phone: 660-726-3411; fax: 660-726-4102; hours 8AM-4:30PM (CST). *Misdemeanor, Civil Actions Under $25,000, Eviction, Small Claims, Probate.*
Civil Records: Access: In person only. Visitors must perform in person searches themselves. Court makes copy: $1.00 per page; not-open file- $.25 per page. Required to search: name, years to search. Civil cases indexed by defendant, plaintiff; on index cards.
Criminal Records: Access: Fax, mail, in person. Visitors must perform in person searches themselves. Search fee: $5.00 per name. Court makes copy: $1.00 per page; not-open file- $.25 per page. Required to search: name, years to search. Criminal records on index cards. Note: Court recommends criminal searches at MO State Hwy Patrol, 573-526-6288. Mail turnaround time 7 days.
General Information: No public access terminal. No juvenile, mental, expunged, dismissed, or suspended imposition of sentence records released. Certification fee: $1.50 per cert. Payee: Associate Circuit Court. Personal checks accepted, no credit cards. Prepayment and SASE required.

Greene County

Circuit Court 1010 Booneville, Springfield, MO 65802; phone: 417-868-4074; hours 8AM-5AM (CST). *Felony, Civil Actions Over $25,000.*
www.greenecountymo.org
Civil Records: Access: Mail, in person, online. Both court and visitors may perform in person searches. Search fee: $5.00 per name. Court makes copy: $.20 per page; same fee for self serve. Required to search: name, years to search. Civil cases indexed by defendant, plaintiff; on computer back to 7/89, prior on index cards. Access to records at the court's website is free at www.greenecountymo.org/ccourt31/search.htm. Mail turnaround time 1 week.
Criminal Records: Access: Mail, in person, online. Both court and visitors may perform in person searches. Search fee: $5.00 per name. Court makes copy: $.20 per page; same fee for self serve. Required to search: name, years to search; also helpful: address, DOB, SSN. Criminal records on computer back to 7/89, prior on index cards. Access to records at the court's website is free at www.greenecountymo.org/ccourt31/search.htm. Mail turnaround time 1 week.
General Information: Public terminal goes back to 1989. No juvenile, mental, expunged, sealed,

dismissed or suspended imposition of sentence records released. Certification fee: $5.00. Payee: Circuit Clerk. Personal checks accepted. Prepayment and SASE required.

Associate Circuit Court 1010 N Boonville, Springfield, MO 65802; phone: 417-868-4110; probate phone: 417-868-4027; hours 8AM-5PM (CST). *Misdemeanor, Civil Actions Under $25,000, Eviction, Small Claims, Probate.*
www.greenecountymo.org
Note: Probate is a separate court at the same address.
Civil Records: Access: Phone, mail, in person, online. Both court and visitors may perform in person searches. Search fee: $5.00 per name. Court makes copy: $.10 per page. Required to search: name, years to search. Civil cases indexed by defendant, plaintiff; oncomputer since mid-1989, prior on index cards. Access records at the court's website free at www.greenecountymo.org/ccourt31/search.htm. Mail turnaround time 2 days; if certified, 1 week.
Criminal Records: Access: Mail, in person, online. Both court and visitors may perform in person searches. Search fee: $5.00 per name. Court makes copy: $.10 per page. Required to search: name, years to search; also helpful: SSN. Criminal records on computer since mid-1989, prior on index cards. Access records at the court's website free at www.greenecountymo.org/ccourt31/search.htm. Mail turnaround time 2 days; if certified, 1 week.
General Information: Public terminal goes back to 1989. (Terminal records limited.) No juvenile, mental, expunged, sealed, dismissed or suspended imposition of sentence records released. No certification fee. Payee: Associate Circuit Clerk. Business checks accepted. Prepayment and SASE required.

Grundy County

Circuit Court Courthouse, 700 Main St, PO Box 196, Trenton, MO 64683; phone: 660-359-6605; fax: 660-359-6604; hours 8:30AM-4:30PM (CST). *Felony, Misdemeanor, Civil Actions Over $25,000.*
Civil Records: Access: In person, online. Visitors must perform in person searches themselves. Court makes copy: $.25 per page. Required to search: name, years to search. Civil cases indexed by defendant, plaintiff. Civil records archived since 1841; on computer back to 2000. Participates in the free court record system at www.courts.mo.gov/casenet/base/welcome.do. Online records go back to 3/2000.
Criminal Records: Access: In person, online. Visitors must perform in person searches themselves. No search fee. Court makes copy: $.25 per page. Required to search: name, years to search. Criminal records archived since 1841; on computer back to 2000. Online access to criminal records is the same as civil. Online records go back to 3/2000. Note: Court recommends criminal searches at MO State Hwy Patrol, 573-526-6288.
General Information: Public terminal goes back to 3/2000. No juvenile, Title 4D, child support, mental, expunged, dismissed, or suspended imposition of sentence cases. Will fax specific file data for $2.00 fee per document. Certification fee: $2.50 per cert. Payee: Circuit Clerk. Personal checks accepted. Prepayment required.

Associate Circuit Court PO Box 26, 7th and Main Sts, Trenton, MO 64683; phone: 660-359-6606/6909; hours 8AM-4:30PM (CST). *Misdemeanor, Civil Actions Under $25,000, Eviction, Small Claims, Probate.*
Civil Records: Access: Mail, in person, online. Visitors must perform in person searches themselves. No search fee. Court makes copy: $1.00 per page. Required to search: name, years to search. Civil cases indexed by defendant, plaintiff; onindex cards, probate records archived. Participates in the free court record system at www.courts.mo.gov/casenet/base/welcome.do.
Online records go back to 3/29/2000

Criminal Records: Access: In person, online. Visitors must perform in person searches themselves. No search fee. Court makes copy: $1.00 per page. Required to search: name, years to search. Criminal records on index cards, probate records archived. Online access to criminal records is the same as civil. Mail turnaround time 1-2 days.
General Information: Public terminal goes back to 2000. No juvenile, mental, expunged, dismissed, or suspended imposition of sentence records released. Certification fee: $2.50 per doc includes copy fee. Payee: Grundy County Circuit Court Division II. Business checks accepted. Prepayment and SASE required.

Harrison County

Circuit & Associate Court PO Box 189, Bethany, MO 64424; phone: 660-425-6425/6432; fax: 660-425-6390; hours 8AM-4:30PM (CST). *Felony, Misdemeanor, Civil Actions, Eviction, Small Claims, Probate.*
Civil Records: Access: Mail, in person, online. Visitors must perform in person searches themselves. No search fee. Court makes copy: $.25 per page. Required to search: name, years to search. Civil cases indexed by defendant, plaintiff; onindex cards since 1979, prior on index books. Participates in the free court record system at www.courts.mo.gov/casenet/base/welcome.do.
Online records go back to 3/29/2000.
Criminal Records: Access: In person, online. Visitors must perform in person searches themselves. Court makes copy: $.25 per page. Required to search: name, years to search. Criminal records on index cards since 1979, prior on index books. Online access to criminal records is the same as civil. Note: Court recommends criminal searches at MO State Hwy Patrol, 573-526-6288.
General Information: Public terminal goes back to 2000. No juvenile, mental, expunged, dismissed, or suspended imposition of sentence records released. Certification fee: $1.00 per page. Payee: Harrison County Circuit Court. Personal checks accepted. Prepayment and SASE required.

Henry County

Circuit & Associate Court PO Box 487, Clinton, MO 64735; phone: 660-885-7232; fax: 660-885-8247; hours 8AM-4:30PM (CST). *Felony, Misdemeanor, Civil, Small Claims.*
http://tacnet.missouri.org/~court27
Note: The Circuit and Associate Courts merged into a consolidated court as of 01/03.
Civil Records: Access: Mail, in person, online. Both court and visitors may perform in person searches. No search fee. Court makes copy: $.25 per page. There is a $2.50 fee for records copied from big books. Required to search: name, years to search. Civil cases indexed by defendant, plaintiff; oncomputer since 8/92, on index cards since 1979, archived since 1877. Participates in the free court record system at www.courts.mo.gov/casenet/base/welcome.do.
Criminal Records: Access: In person, online. Only the court performs in person searches. No search fee. Court makes copy: $.25 per page. There is a $2.50 fee for records copied from big books. Required to search: name, years to search. Criminal records on computer since 8/92, on index cards since 1979, archived since 1877. Participates in the free court record system at www.courts.mo.gov/casenet/base/welcome.do.
Note: Court recommends criminal searches at MO State Hwy Patrol, 573-526-6288. Mail turnaround time 2 days.
General Information: Public terminal has only civil records. No juvenile, mental, expunged, dismissed, or suspended imposition of sentence records released. Will not fax documents. Certification fee: $1.50. Payee: Henry County Circuit Clerk. Personal checks accepted. Prepayment required. Copy fees may be billed. SASE required.

Hickory County

Circuit Court PO Box 101, Hermitage, MO 65668; phone: 417-745-6421; fax: 417-745-6670; hours 8AM-4:30PM (CST). *Felony, Misdemeanor, Civil Actions Over $45,000.*
www.courts.net/~dcourt
Civil Records: Access: In person, online. Both court and visitors may perform in person searches. Court makes copy: $.25 per page. Required to search: name, years to search. Civil cases indexed by defendant, plaintiff; oncomputer since 1992, prior on index books since 1976. Participates in the free court record system at www.courts.mo.gov/casenet/base/welcome.do.
Criminal Records: Access: In person, online. Both court and visitors may perform in person searches. Court makes copy: $1.00 per page microfilm; $.25 per page paper. Required to search: name, years to search, signed release. Criminal records on computer since 1992, prior on index books since 1976. Online access to criminal records is the same as civil.
General Information: Public terminal goes back to 2001. No juvenile, mental, expunged, dismissed, or suspended imposition of sentence records released. Fee to fax documents is $1.00 per page. Certification fee: $1.00 per page. Payee: Hickory County Circuit Clerk. Personal checks accepted. Prepayment required.

Associate Circuit Court PO Box 75, Courthouse Sq, Hermitage, MO 65668; phone: 417-745-6822; fax: 417-745-6670; hours 8AM-N; 12:30PM-4:30PM (CST). *Misdemeanor, Civil Actions Under $45,000, Eviction, Small Claims, Probate.*
www.positech.net/~dcourt
Civil Records: Access: In person, online. Both court and visitors may perform in person searches. Court makes copy: $.25 per page; same fee for self serve. Required to search: name, years to search. Civil cases indexed by defendant, plaintiff; onindex cards since 1980. Participates in the free statewide Casenet court record system at www.courts.mo.gov/casenet/base/welcome.do.
Criminal Records: Access: In person, online. Both court and visitors may perform in person searches. Court makes copy: $.25 per page; same fee for self serve. Required to search: name, years to search, DOB. Criminal records on index cards since 1980. Participates in the free statewide Casenet court record system at www.courts.mo.gov/casenet/base/welcome.do.
General Information: Public terminal goes back to 2001. No juvenile, mental, expunged, dismissed, or suspended imposition of sentence records released. Will fax documents no fee. Certification fee: $1.00 per cert.

Holt County

Circuit Court PO Box 318, Oregon, MO 64473; phone: 660-446-3301; fax: 660-446-3328; hours 8AM-4:30PM (CST). *Felony, Misdemeanor, Civil Actions Over $25,000.*
Civil Records: Access: Fax, mail, in person. Only the court performs in person searches. Search fee: $4.00. Court makes copy: $1.00 per page. Required to search: name, years to search. Civil cases indexed by defendant, plaintiff; onbooks. Mail turnaround time varies.
Criminal Records: Access: In person only. Only the court performs in person searches. Court makes copy: $1.00 per page. Required to search: name, years to search. Criminal records on books.
General Information: No public access terminal. No juvenile, mental, expunged, dismissed, or suspended imposition of sentence records released. Will fax documents $2.00 per doc. Certification fee: $1.00 per page. Payee: Recorder. Personal checks accepted. Prepayment and SASE required.

Associate Circuit Court PO Box 173, Oregon, MO 64473; phone: 660-446-3380; hours 8:30AM-4:30PM (CST). *Misdemeanor, Civil Actions Under $25,000, Eviction, Small Claims, Probate.*
Civil Records: Access: Mail, fax, in person. Both court and visitors may perform in person searches. No search fee. Court makes copy: $.25 per page. Required to search: name, years to search. Civil cases indexed by defendant, plaintiff; onindex cards since 1979.
Criminal Records: Access: In person only. Visitors must perform in person searches themselves. Court makes copy: $.25 per page. Required to search: name, years to search. Criminal records on computer since 1991, prior on index cards since 1979. Note: Court recommends criminal searches at MO State Hwy Patrol, 573-526-6288.
General Information: No public access terminal. No juvenile, mental, expunged, dismissed, or suspended imposition of sentence records released. Certification fee: $1.50 per page. Payee: Associate Circuit Court. Personal checks accepted. Prepayment and SASE required.

Howard County

Circuit Court 1 Courthouse Square, Fayette, MO 65248; phone: 660-248-2194; fax: 660-248-5009; hours 8:30AM-4:30PM (CST). *Felony, Civil Actions Over $30,000.*
Civil Records: Access: In person, online. Visitors must perform in person searches themselves. Court makes copy: $.25 per page. Required to search: name, years to search. Civil cases indexed by defendant, plaintiff; onindex cards; computer records go back to the 1970's. Participates in the free court record system at www.courts.mo.gov/casenet/base/welcome.do. Cases include those filed from 10/01 to present.
Criminal Records: Access: In person, online. Visitors must perform in person searches themselves. Court makes copy: $.25 per page. Required to search: name, years to search. Criminal records on index cards; computer records go back to the 1970's. Online access to criminal records is the same as civil. Note: Court recommends criminal searches at MO State Hwy Patrol, 573-526-6288.
General Information: Public terminal goes back to 1970s. No juvenile, mental, expunged, dismissed, or suspended imposition of sentence records released. Will fax specific case file requests for $2.00 per document. Certification fee: $2.00. Payee: Circuit Clerk. Personal checks accepted. Prepayment required.

Associate Circuit Court PO Box 370, Fayette, MO 65248; phone: 660-248-3326; probate phone: 660-248-3326.; fax: 660-248-1075; hours 8:30AM-4:30PM (CST). *Misdemeanor, Civil Actions Under $45,000, Eviction, Small Claims, Probate.*
Civil Records: Access: In person, online. Visitors must perform in person searches themselves. Court makes copy: $.25 per page. Required to search: name, years to search. Civil cases indexed by defendant, plaintiff. Civil records go back to 1975. Participates in the free court record system at www.courts.mo.gov/casenet/base/welcome.do. Includes Probate and Traffic records.
Criminal Records: Access: In person, online. Visitors must perform in person searches themselves. Court makes copy: $.25 per page. Required to search: name, years to search, DOB. Criminal records go back to 1975. Online access to criminal records is the same as civil, see above. Note: Court recommends criminal searches at MO State Hwy Patrol, 573-526-6288.
General Information: Public terminal goes back to 2001. No juvenile, mental, expunged, dismissed, or suspended imposition of sentence records released. Certification fee: $1.50 per cert. Payee: Associate Circuit Court. Personal checks accepted. Prepayment required.

Howell County

Circuit Court PO Box 967, West Plains, MO 65775; phone: 417-256-3741; fax: 417-256-4650; hours 8AM-4:30PM (CST). *Felony, Misdemeanor, Civil Actions Over $25,000.*
Civil Records: Access: Phone, fax, mail, in person, online. Both court and visitors may perform in person searches. Court makes copy: $.10 per page. Required to search: name, years to search. Civil cases indexed by defendant, plaintiff; onindex cards since 1977. Participates in the free court record system at www.courts.mo.gov/casenet/base/welcome.do. Online records go back to 8/2000; pending cases back to 1990.
Criminal Records: Access: In person, online. Visitors must perform in person searches themselves. Court makes copy: $.10 per page. Required to search: name, years to search. Criminal records on index cards since 1977. Online access to criminal records is the same as civil. Note: Court recommends criminal searches at MO State Hwy Patrol, 573-526-6288. Mail turnaround time varies.
General Information: Public terminal goes back to 8/1991. No juvenile, mental, expunged, dismissed, or suspended imposition of sentence records released. Will fax documents $1.00 per page. Certification fee: $1.50. Payee: Howell County Circuit Clerk. Personal checks accepted. Prepayment required. Will bill to attorneys. SASE required.

Associate Circuit Court 222 Courthouse, West Plains, MO 65775; phone: 417-256-4050; criminal fax: 417-256-5826; civil/probate fax is the same; hours 8AM-4:30PM (CST). *Misdemeanor, Civil Actions Under $25,000, Eviction, Small Claims, Probate.*
Civil Records: Access: Mail, in person, online. Both court and visitors may perform in person searches. No search fee. Court makes copy: $.10 per page; same fee for self serve. Required to search: name, years to search. Civil cases indexed by defendant, plaintiff; onindex cards since 1/1/79, computerized since 4/2000. Participates in the free court record system at www.courts.mo.gov/casenet/base/welcome.do. Online records go back to 1990. Mail turnaround time ASAP.
Criminal Records: Access: Mail, in person, online. Both court and visitors may perform in person searches. No search fee. Court makes copy: $.10 per page; same fee for self serve. Required to search: name, years to search, DOB; also helpful: SSN. Criminal records on computer since early 1991, on index cards since 1/1/79, prior on books. Online access to criminal records is the same as civil. Mail turnaround time ASAP.
General Information: No public access terminal. No juvenile, mental, expunged, dismissed, or suspended imposition of sentence records released. Will not fax documents. Certification fee: $1.50 per document. Payee: Associate/Probate Court. Only cashiers checks and money orders accepted. Prepayment and SASE required.

Iron County

Circuit Court PO Box 24, Ironton, MO 63650; phone: 573-546-2811; fax: 573-546-2166; hours 8AM-4PM (CST). *Felony, Civil Actions Over $25,000.*
Civil Records: Access: In person, online. Visitors must perform in person searches themselves. Court makes copy: $1.00 per page. Required to search: name, years to search. Civil cases indexed by defendant, plaintiff; onindex cards since 1976, prior on books. Participates in the free statewide Casenet court record system at www.courts.mo.gov/casenet/base/welcome.do. Files requested by case number take 10 days.
Criminal Records: Access: In person, online. Visitors must perform in person searches themselves. Court makes copy: $1.00 per page. Required to search: name, years to search. Criminal records on index cards since 1976, prior on books to 1856. Participates in the free statewide Casenet

court record system at www.courts.mo.gov/casenet/base/welcome.do. Files requested by case number take 10 days. Note: Court recommends criminal searches at MO State Hwy Patrol, 573-526-6288.

General Information: Public use terminal available. No juvenile, mental, expunged, dismissed, or suspended imposition of sentence records released. Certification fee: $2.00. Payee: Iron County Circuit Clerk. Personal checks not accepted. Prepayment required.

Associate Circuit Court PO Box 325, Ironton, MO 63650; phone: 573-546-2511; criminal fax: 573-546-6006; civil/probate fax is the same; hours 8:30AM-4PM (CST). *Misdemeanor, Civil Actions Under $25,000, Eviction, Small Claims, Probate.*

Civil Records: Access: Mail, in person, online. Both court and visitors may perform in person searches. No search fee. Court makes copy: $.30 per page; same fee for self serve. Required to search: name, years to search; also helpful: address. Civil cases indexed by defendant, plaintiff; onindex cards since 1979, computerized from 4/01. Participates in the free statewide Casenet court record system at www.courts.mo.gov/casenet/base/welcome.do. Mail turnaround time 5 days.

Criminal Records: Access: Fax, mail, in person, online. Both court and visitors may perform in person searches. No search fee. Court makes copy: $.30 per page; same fee for self serve. Required to search: name, years to search, DOB; also helpful: address, signed release. Criminal records computerized from 4/01. Participates in the free statewide Casenet court record system at www.courts.mo.gov/casenet/base/welcome.do. Mail turnaround time 5 days.

General Information: Public terminal goes back to 4/2001. No juvenile, mental, expunged, dismissed, or suspended imposition of sentence records released. Will fax documents. Certification fee: $1.50 plus $1.00 per page includes copies. Payee: Associate Circuit Court. Personal checks accepted. Prepayment and SASE required.

Jackson County

Circuit Court - Civil Division 415 E 12th, 3rd Fl, Kansas City, MO 64106; phone: 816-881-3926; 881-3522; probate phone: 816-881-3755; fax: 816-881-4327; hours 8AM-5PM (CST). *Civil, Eviction, Small Claims, Probate.*
www.16thcircuit.org
Note: There is a combined computer system with the Independence civil court.

Civil Records: Access: Online, in person. Visitors must perform in person searches themselves. Court makes copy: $.50 per page. Required to search: name, years to search. Civil cases indexed by defendant, plaintiff; oncomputer since 1973, some records on microfiche and books, older records archived off-site. Participates in the free court record system at www.courts.mo.gov/casenet/base/welcome.do. Jackson Casenet records go back to 1/89. The Probate Court also participates in the Casenet system; also, probate records are at www.16thcircuit.org/publicaccess.asp,

General Information: Public terminal has only civil records back to 1989. No juvenile, mental, expunged, dismissed, or suspended imposition of sentence records released. Certification fee: $2.50 per cert. Payee: Court Administrator's Office. Business checks accepted. Prepayment required.

Independence Circuit Court - Civil Annex 308 W Kansas #310, Independence, MO 64050; phone: 816-881-3943; probate phone: 816-881-4552; fax: 816-881-3681; hours 8AM-5PM (CST). *Civil, Eviction, Small Claims, Probate.*
Note: Direct mail criminal record searches to Rm 310; civil to Rm 204. This court on the same computer system as Kansas City for civil cases, but files maintained separately.

Civil Records: Access: In person, online. Visitors must perform in person searches themselves. Court makes copy: $.50 per page. Required to search: name, years to search. Civil cases indexed by defendant, plaintiff; oncomputer since 1989. Participates in the free court record system at www.courts.mo.gov/casenet/base/welcome.do. Online records go back to 1/89. Online access to probate records is free at www.16thcircuit.org/publicaccess.asp. This includes private process servers, jury verdicts, criminal traffic, and criminal sureties. Note: The court will not do background checks, except for attorneys. You must have case number if the court is to pull a record. Mail turnaround time 1 day.

General Information: Public terminal has only civil records back to 1989. No sealed records released. Certification fee: $2.50 per cert. Payee: District Court Clerk. Only cashiers checks and money orders accepted. Prepayment required.

Circuit Court - Criminal Division 1315 Locust, 2nd Fl, Kansas City, MO 64106; phone: 816-881-4350; fax: 816-881-3420; hours 8AM-5PM (CST). *Felony, Misdemeanor.*
www.16thcircuit.org
Note: All background checks are sent to the Missouri Highway Patrol in Jefferson City. Court will only pull file copies if a case number is given.

Criminal Records: Access: Online, in person. Visitors must perform in person searches themselves. Court makes copy: $.50 per page. Required to search: name, years to search, DOB, signed release; also helpful: SSN. Criminal records on computer since 1968 for felonies, 1980 for misdemeanors. Participates in the free court record system at www.courts.mo.gov/casenet/base/welcome.do. Jackson Casenet records go back to 1/89. Also, online access to criminal traffic dockets is at www.16thcircuit.org/trafficdockets.asp. Also, search surety bonding agents at www.16thcircuit.org/suretyqualifications.asp Note: Court recommends criminal searches at MO State Hwy Patrol, 573-526-6288.

General Information: Public terminal has criminal back to 1970 and civil back to 1970. No juvenile, mental, expunged, dismissed, or suspended imposition of sentence records released. Certification fee: $1.50. Payee: Dept. of Civil or Criminal Records. Only cashiers checks and money orders accepted. Prepayment required.

Jasper County

Carthage Circuit Court Courthouse, Rm 303, 302 S. Main St, Carthage, MO 64836; phone: 417-358-0441; fax: 417-358-0461; hours 8:00AM-5:00PM (CST). *Felony, Misdemeanor, Civil Actions, Eviction, Small Claims, Probate.*
www.osca.state.mo.us/circuits/index.nsf
Note: Although the Carthage Circuit and Associate Circuit courts merged, the records are only co-mingled from 7/2000 forward. Each of the 4 courts in the county must be searched for an accurate overall search. Probate is separate index, separate address.

Civil Records: Access: Mail, in person, online. Both court and visitors may perform in person searches. No search fee. Court makes copy: $.25 per page; same fee for self serve. Required to search: name, years to search. Civil cases indexed by defendant, plaintiff; oncomputer since 7/1/91, prior on cards since 1975. Participates in the free statewide Casenet court record system at www.courts.mo.gov/casenet/base/welcome.do. Online records go back to 6/26/2000. Mail turnaround time 1 week.

Criminal Records: Access: Mail, in person, online. Both court and visitors may perform in person searches. No search fee. Court makes copy: $.25 per page; same fee for self serve. Required to search: name, years to search. Criminal records on computer since 7/1/91, prior on cards since 1975. Online access to criminal records is the same as civil. Mail turnaround time 1 week.

General Information: Public terminal goes back to 1991. No juvenile, mental, expunged, dismissed, or suspended imposition of sentence records released. Will fax documents to local number only. Certification fee: $1.25 per page. Payee: Jasper County Circuit Clerk. Business checks accepted. Prepayment and SASE required.

Joplin Circuit Court Courthouse, 3rd Fl, 601 S Pearl, Joplin, MO 64801; phone: 417-625-4310; fax: 417-781-7172; hours 8:00AM-N, 1-5PM (CST). *Felony, Civil Actions Over $45,000.*
Note: Although the Joplin Circuit and Associate Circuit courts merged, the records are only co-mingled from 07/00 forward. Each of the 4 courts in the county must be searched for an accurate overall search.

Civil Records: Access: In person, online. Visitors must perform in person searches themselves. Court makes copy: $.25 per page. Required to search: name, years to search. Civil cases indexed by defendant, plaintiff; oncomputer since 7/1/91, prior on cards since 1975. Participates in the free statewide Casenet court record system at www.courts.mo.gov/casenet/base/welcome.do. Online records go back to 6/26/2000.

Criminal Records: Access: In person, online. Visitors must perform in person searches themselves. No search fee. Court makes copy: $.25 per page. Required to search: name, years to search. Criminal records on computer back to 1993, prior on cards back to 1975. Online access to criminal records is the same as civil. Note: Court recommends criminal searches at MO State Hwy Patrol, 573-526-6288.

General Information: Public terminal goes back to 1991. No juvenile, mental, expunged, dismissed, or suspended imposition of sentence records released. Will fax specific case file requests. Certification fee: $1.50 per page. Payee: Jasper County Circuit Clerk. No personal checks accepted. Prepayment required.

Carthage Associate Circuit Court Courthouse, Rm 304, 302 S. Main St, Carthage, MO 64836; phone: 417-358-0450; fax: 417-358-0460; hours 8:30AM-N, 1-4:30PM (CST). *Misdemeanor, Civil Actions Under $45,000, Eviction, Small Claims, Probate.*
Note: Although Carthage Circuit and Associate Circuit courts merged, the records are co-mingled from 7/2000 forward only. Each of the 4 courts in the county must be searched for an accurate overall search.

Civil Records: Access: Fax, in person, online. Visitors must perform in person searches themselves. Search fee: Court does not perform civil searches. Court makes copy: $.25 per page. Required to search: name, years to search. Civil cases indexed by defendant, plaintiff; oncomputer back to 2000, prior on cards back to 1979. Participates in the free statewide Casenet record system at www.courts.mo.gov/casenet/base/welcome.do. Online records go back to 6/26/2000. Note: For mail or fax searches, court recommends Amer. Research at 417-358-6494.

Criminal Records: Access: In person, online. Visitors must perform in person searches themselves. Search fee: Court does not perform criminal searches. Court makes copy: $.25 per page. Required to search: name, years to search. Criminal records on computer back to 2000, prior on cards back to 1979. Online access to criminal records is the same as civil. Note: For mail or fax searches, court recommends Amer. Research at 417-358-6494. Court recommends criminal searches at MO State Hwy Patrol, 573-526-6288.

General Information: Public terminal goes back to 1999. No juvenile, mental, expunged, dismissed, or suspended imposition of sentence records released. Certification fee: $1.50 per cert includes copy fee. Prepayment required.

Joplin Associate Circuit Court Courthouse, 2nd Fl, 601 S Pearl, Joplin, MO 64801; phone: 417-625-4316; fax: 417-625-4340; probate fax: 417-358-0404; hours 8AM-N, 1-5PM (CST). *Misdemeanor, Civil Actions Under $45,000, Eviction, Small Claims, Probate.*

Note: Although the Joplin Circuit and Associate Circuit courts merged, the records are only co-mingled from 07/00 forward. Each of the 4 courts in the county must be searched for an accurate overall search.

Civil Records: Access: Mail, fax, in person, online. Both court and visitors may perform in person searches. No search fee. Court makes copy: $.25 per page. Required to search: name, years to search. Civil cases indexed by defendant, plaintiff; oncomputer back to 1993, prior on cards back to mid-1970s. Participates in the free statewide Casenet court record system at www.courts.mo.gov/casenet/base/welcome.do. Online records go back to 6/26/2000. Mail turnaround time 1-3 days.

Criminal Records: Access: Mail, fax, in person, online. Both court and visitors may perform in person searches. No search fee. Court makes copy: $.25 per page. Required to search: name, years to search. Criminal records on computer back to 1993, prior on cards back to mid-1970s. Online access to criminal records is the same as civil. Online records only go back to 6/26/2000. Mail turnaround time 1-3 days.

General Information: Public terminal goes back to 2000. No juvenile, mental, expunged, dismissed, or suspended imposition of sentence records released. Will fax documents, no fee. Certification fee: $1.50 per cert. Personal checks accepted. Prepayment and SASE required.

Jefferson County

Circuit & Associate Court - Civil Division PO Box 100, Hillsboro, MO 63050; phone: 636-797-5443; fax: 636-797-5073; hours 8AM-5PM (CST). *Civil Actions, Eviction, Small Claims, Probate.*

Civil Records: Access: Phone, fax, mail, in person. Both court and visitors may perform in person searches. Search fee: $1.00 per name. Court makes copy: $1.00 per page. Required to search: name, years to search. Civil cases indexed by defendant, plaintiff; oncomputer since 10/90, prior on books since 1966.

General Information: Public terminal goes back to 1985. No juvenile, mental, expunged, dismissed, or suspended imposition of sentence records released. Certification fee: $.50 per page. Payee: Circuit Clerk. Business checks accepted. Prepayment and SASE required.

Circuit & Associate Court - Criminal Division PO Box 100, Hillsboro, MO 63050; phone: 636-797-5370; fax: 636-797-5073; hours 8AM-4:30PM (CST). *Felony, Misdemeanor.*

Criminal Records: Access: In person only. Visitors must perform in person searches themselves. Court makes copy: $1.00 per page. Required to search: name, years to search, signed release, DOB or SSN. Criminal records on computer since 1989, on index cards 1976 to 1988, prior on books or microfilm.

General Information: Public terminal has only criminal records back to 1989. No juvenile, mental, expunged, dismissed, or suspended imposition of sentence records released. Certification fee: $.50 per file. Payee: Circuit Clerk. Business checks accepted. Prepayment and SASE required.

Johnson County

Circuit Court Johnson County Justice Ctr, 101 W Market, Warrensburg, MO 64093; phone: 660-422-7413; fax: 660-422-7417; hours 8AM-4:30PM (CST). *Felony, Civil Actions Over $25,000.*

Civil Records: Access: Mail, in person. Visitors must perform in person searches themselves. Search fee: $10.00. Court makes copy: $.50 per page. Self serve copy fee: $.25 per page. Required to search:

name, years to search. Civil cases indexed by defendant, plaintiff; onfile since 1800s, microfilmed from 1950s to 1988. Note: Only the court can pull records prior to 1976. Mail turnaround time 1 week.

Criminal Records: Access: Mail, in person. Visitors must perform in person searches themselves. Search fee: $10.00. Court makes copy: $.50 per page. Self serve copy fee: $.25 per page. Required to search: name, years to search, DOB, SSN. Criminal records on file since 1800s, microfilmed through 1988. Note: Court will perform search if prior to 1976. Mail turnaround time 1 week.

General Information: Public terminal goes back to 1994. No juvenile, adoptions, mental, expunged, dismissed, or suspended imposition of sentence records released. Will fax documents for $3.00 1st.page + $1.00 add'l pages. Certification fee: $1.50. Payee: Circuit Clerk. Personal checks accepted. Prepayment required.

Associate Circuit Court Johnson County Courthouse, 300 N Holden #304, Warrensburg, MO 64093; phone: 660-422-7410; hours 8AM-4:30PM (CST). *Misdemeanor, Civil Actions Under $45,000, Eviction, Small Claims.*

Civil Records: Access: In person only. Visitors must perform in person searches themselves. Court makes copy: $.25 per page. Required to search: name, years to search. Civil cases indexed by defendant, plaintiff; oncomputer since 1994, prior on index since 1979.

Criminal Records: Access: In person only. Visitors must perform in person searches themselves. No search fee. Court makes copy: $.25 per page. Required to search: name, years to search. Criminal records on computer since 1994, prior on index since 1979.

General Information: Public terminal goes back to 1992. No juvenile, mental, expunged, dismissed, or suspended imposition of sentence records released. Certification fee: $1.50 per cert. Payee: Associate Circuit Court. Personal checks accepted; no credit cards. Prepayment required.

Knox County

Circuit Court PO Box 116, Edina, MO 63537; phone: 660-397-2305; fax: 660-397-3331; hours 8:30AM-N, 1-4PM (CST). *Felony, Misdemeanor, Civil Actions Over $25,000.*

Civil Records: Access: Mail, in person. Both court and visitors may perform in person searches. No search fee. Court makes copy: $1.00 per page; same fee for self serve. Required to search: name, years to search. Civil cases indexed by defendant, plaintiff; onmicrofiche since 3/83, archived since 1845, no computerization. Mail turnaround time same day.

Criminal Records: Access: Mail, in person. Both court and visitors may perform in person searches. No search fee. Court makes copy: $1.00 per page; same fee for self serve. Required to search: name, years to search. Criminal records archived since 1845, no computerization. Mail turnaround time same day.

General Information: No public access terminal. No juvenile, mental, expunged, dismissed, or suspended imposition of sentence records released. Will fax documents; fee varies but usually $3.50 per doc. Certification fee: $2.00. Payee: Circuit Court. Personal checks accepted. Prepayment required.

Associate Circuit Court PO Box 126, Edina, MO 63537; phone: 660-397-3146; fax: 660-397-3331; hours 8:30AM-4PM (CST). *Misdemeanor, Civil Actions Under $25,000, Eviction, Small Claims, Probate.*

Civil Records: Access: In person only. Both court and visitors may perform in person searches. No search fee. Court makes copy: $.25 per page. Required to search: name, years to search. Civil cases indexed by defendant, plaintiff; oncomputer since 1993, prior on index cards to 1850. Mail turnaround time 2-3 days.

Criminal Records: Access: In person only. Only the court performs in person searches. No search fee. Court makes copy: $.25 per page. Required to search: name, years to search; also helpful: DOB, SSN. Criminal records on computer since 1993, prior on index cards.

General Information: No public access terminal. No juvenile, mental, expunged, dismissed, or suspended imposition of sentence records released. Certification fee: $2.00 per cert. Payee: Associate Circuit Court. Personal checks accepted. Prepayment required.

Laclede County

Circuit & Associate Court 200 N Adams St, Lebanon, MO 65536; phone: 417-532-2471, 532-9196; criminal phone: 417-532-2471; criminal fax: 417-532-3683; civil/probate fax is the same; hours 8AM-4PM (CST). *Felony, Misdemeanor, Civil. Eviction, Small Claims, Probate.*

Note: Probate is a separate index at this same address.

Civil Records: Access: Phone, fax, mail, in person. Both court and visitors may perform in person searches. No search fee. Court makes copy: $.25 per page; same fee for self serve. Required to search: name, years to search. Civil cases indexed by defendant, plaintiff; oncards since 1976, prior on books. Mail turnaround time varies.

Criminal Records: Access: Phone, fax, mail, in person. Both court and visitors may perform in person searches. No search fee. Court makes copy: $.25 per page; same fee for self serve. Required to search: name, years to search; also helpful: SSN. Criminal records on cards since 1976, prior on books. Mail turnaround time varies.

General Information: Public terminal has only civil records back to 1995; Judgment index only. No juvenile, mental, expunged, dismissed, or suspended imposition of sentence records released. Will fax documents $3.00 1st page, $1.00 each add'l. Certification fee: $1.50 per document. Payee: Laclede County Circuit Clerk. Personal checks accepted. Prepayment required. Copy fees may be billed. SASE required.

Lafayette County

Circuit & Associate Court PO Box 10, Lexington, MO 64067; phone: 660-259-6101; probate phone: 660-259-2324; criminal/civil fax: 660-259-6148; probate fax: 660-259-4997; hours 8AM-4:30PM (CST). *Felony, Misdemeanor, Civil Actions, Eviction, Small Claims, Probate.*

Note: Circuit and Associate courts are combined as of 9/2004.

Civil Records: Access: Mail, fax, in person, online. Visitors must perform in person searches themselves. No search fee. Court makes copy: $.25 per page; same fee for self serve. Required to search: name, years to search. Civil cases indexed by defendant, plaintiff, case number. Civil records on books, archived since 1821; on computer back to 1987. Participates in the free statewide Casenet court record system at www.courts.mo.gov/casenet/base/welcome.do. Online records go back to 04/01/02. Note: All search requests to clerk must be in writing.

Criminal Records: Access: In person, online. Visitors must perform in person searches themselves. No search fee. Court makes copy: $.25 per page; same fee for self serve. Required to search: name, years to search; also helpful-case number. Criminal records on books, archived since 1823; on computer back to 1987. Participates in the free statewide Casenet court record system at www.courts.mo.gov/casenet/base/welcome.do. Online records go back to 04/01/02. Mail turnaround time up to 5 days.

General Information: Public terminal goes back to 1994. No juvenile, mental, expunged, dismissed, or suspended imposition of sentence records released. Fee to fax documents is $1.00 per page. Certification fee: $2.50 per document. Payee: Circuit Clerk. No personal checks accepted; money orders only.

Attorney of record and copy fees may be billed. SASE required.

Lawrence County

Circuit Court One Courthouse Square #201, Mt Vernon, MO 65712; phone: 417-466-2471; hours 8AM-4:30PM (CST). *Felony, Civil Actions Over $25,000.*

Civil Records: Access: Mail, in person. Both court and visitors may perform in person searches. Search fee: $5.00 per name. Court makes copy: $.25 per page. Required to search: name, years to search. Civil cases indexed by defendant, plaintiff; oncomputer back to 1991, prior archived since 1890. Mail turnaround time 1 week.

Criminal Records: Access: Mail, in person. Both court and visitors may perform in person searches. Search fee: $5.00 per name. Court makes copy: $.25 per page. Required to search: name, years to search, DOB; also helpful: SSN. Criminal records on computer back to 1991, prior archived since 1890. Mail turnaround time 1 week.

General Information: Public terminal goes back to 1991. No juvenile, mental, expunged, dismissed, or suspended imposition of sentence records released. Certification fee: $2.00 per cert. Payee: Circuit Court. Business checks accepted. Prepayment and SASE required.

Associate Circuit Court 1 Courthouse Sq, #102, Mt Vernon, MO 65712; phone: 417-466-2463; probate phone: 417-466-2105; hours 8:30AM-5PM (CST). *Misdemeanor, Civil Actions Under $45,000, Eviction, Small Claims, Probate.*

Civil Records: Access: Mail, in person. Both court and visitors may perform in person searches. No search fee. Court makes copy: $.35 per page; same fee for self serve. Required to search: name, years to search. Civil cases indexed by defendant, plaintiff; onindex cards since 1979, prior on books. Mail turnaround time 2-3 days.

Criminal Records: Access: Mail, in person. Both court and visitors may perform in person searches. No search fee. Court makes copy: $.35 per page; same fee for self serve. Required to search: name, years to search; also helpful: DOB, SSN. Criminal records on index cards since 1979, prior on books. Mail turnaround time 2-3 days.

General Information: No public access terminal. No juvenile, mental, expunged, dismissed, or suspended imposition of sentence records released. No certification fee. Payee: Associate Circuit Court. Personal checks accepted. Prepayment and SASE required.

Lewis County

Circuit & Associate Court PO Box 8, Monticello, MO 63457; phone: 573-767-5232; fax: 573-767-5342; hours 8AM-N,1-4:30PM (CST). *Felony, Misdemeanor, Civil Actions, Eviction, Small Claims, Probate.*

Note: Consolidated court on 4-1-03.

Civil Records: Access: Mail, in person. Visitors must perform in person searches themselves. No search fee. Court makes copy: $.10 per page plus $.20 per minute. Self serve copy fee: $.10 per page. Required to search: name, years to search. Civil cases indexed by defendant, plaintiff; oncomputer back to 1976 (judgments) and index books, archived since 1830s. Mail turnaround time 3 days.

Criminal Records: Access: In person only. Visitors must perform in person searches themselves. Court makes copy: $.10 per page plus $.20 per minute. Self serve copy fee: $.10 per page. Required to search: name, years to search. Criminal records on computer and index books, archived since 1830s. Note: Court recommends criminal searches at MO State Hwy Patrol, 573-526-6288.

General Information: Public use terminal available. (Terminal became operational 9/1/2005.) No juvenile, mental, expunged, dismissed, or suspended imposition of sentence records released. Certification fee: $2.50. Prepayment required.

Lincoln County

Circuit & Associate Court Lincoln County Justice Ctr, 45 Business park Dr, Troy, MO 63379; phone: 636-528-6300; fax: 636-528-9168; hours 8:00AM-4:30PM (CST). *Felony, Misdemeanor, Civil Actions, Eviction, Small Claims, Probate.*

Civil Records: Access: In person, online. Visitors must perform in person searches themselves. Court makes copy: $.25 per page; same fee for self serve. Required to search: name, years to search. Civil cases indexed by defendant, plaintiff; oncomputer since 8/92, prior on index cards since 1978. Record access fee at www.courts.mo.gov/casenet/cases/searchCases.do. Records from 04/03/02 forward.

Criminal Records: Access: In person, online. Visitors must perform in person searches themselves. Court makes copy: $.25 per page; same fee for self serve. Required to search: name, years to search. Criminal records on computer since 8/92, prior on index cards since 1978. Participates in the free court record system at www.courts.mo.gov/casenet/base/welcome.do. Records go back to 4/03/02 forward. Note: Court recommends criminal searches at MO State Hwy Patrol, 573-526-6288.

General Information: Public terminal goes back to 4/2002. No juvenile, mental, expunged, dismissed, or suspended imposition of sentence records released. Will fax specific case file information only, not search documents. Certification fee: $.50 per page. Cert fee includes copies. Payee: Lincoln County Circuit Clerk. Personal checks accepted. Prepayment required.

Linn County

Circuit & Associate Court PO Box 84, 108 S High St, Linneus, MO 64653-0084; phone: 660-895-5212; fax: 660-895-5277; hours 8AM-N, 1-4:30PM (CST). *Felony, Misdemeanor, Civil Actions, Eviction, Small Claims, Probate.*

Civil Records: Access: Fax, mail, in person, online. Both court and visitors may perform in person searches. No search fee. Court makes copy: $1.00 per page. Required to search: name, years to search. Civil cases indexed by defendant, plaintiff; onbooks. Participates in the free statewide Casenet court record system at www.courts.mo.gov/casenet/base/welcome.do. Mail turnaround time 1 week.

Criminal Records: Access: Fax, mail, in person, online. Both court and visitors may perform in person searches. No search fee. Court makes copy: $1.00 per page. Required to search: name, years to search. Criminal records on books. Participates in the free statewide Casenet court record system at www.courts.mo.gov/casenet/base/welcome.do. Mail turnaround time 1 week, phone turnaround is 1-2 days.

General Information: Public terminal goes back to 5/2001. No juvenile, mental, expunged, dismissed, or suspended imposition of sentence records released. No fee to fax documents. Certification fee: $1.50 per page includes copies. Payee: Linn County Circuit Court. Only cashiers checks and money orders accepted. Prepayment and SASE required.

Consolidated Circuit Court Box 84, Linneus, MO 64653; phone: 660-895-5212; fax: 660-895-5277; hours 8AM-4:30PM (CST). *Misdemeanor, Civil Actions Under $25,000, Eviction, Small Claims, Probate.*

Civil Records: Access: Phone, mail, in person, online. Both court and visitors may perform in person searches. No search fee. Court makes copy: $1.00 per page. Required to search: name, years to search. Civil cases indexed by defendant, plaintiff; onindex cards since 1979. Participates in the free statewide Casenet court record system at www.courts.mo.gov/casenet/base/welcome.do.

Criminal Records: Access: Phone, mail, in person, online. Both court and visitors may perform in person searches. No search fee. Court makes copy: $1.00 per page. Required to search: name, years to

search. Criminal records on index cards since 1979. Participates in the free statewide Casenet court record system at www.courts.mo.gov/casenet/base/welcome.do.

General Information: Public terminal goes back to 5/2001. No juvenile, mental, expunged, dismissed, or suspended imposition of sentence records released. Certification fee: $1.50 per cert. Payee: Associate Circuit Court. Personal checks accepted. Prepayment and SASE required.

Livingston County

Circuit Court 700 Webster St, Chillicothe, MO 64601; phone: 660-646-1718; fax: 660-646-2734; hours 8:00AM-5:00PM (CST). *Felony, Civil Actions Over $25,000.*

Civil Records: Access: Mail, fax, in person. Visitors must perform in person searches. No search fee. Court makes copy: $1.00 per page; same fee for self serve. Required to search: name, years to search. Civil cases indexed by defendant, plaintiff; onindex cards since 1974, prior on record books.

Criminal Records: Access: In person only. Visitors must perform in person searches themselves. Court makes copy: $1.00 per page; same fee for self serve. Required to search: name, years to search. Criminal records on index cards since 1974, prior on record books.

General Information: Public use terminal available. No juvenile, mental, expunged, dismissed, or suspended imposition of sentence records released. Will fax documents to local or toll free line. No certification fee. Payee: Livingston County Circuit Clerk. Personal checks accepted. Prepayment required. Attorneys may be billed for copy fees.

Associate Circuit Court Livingston County Courthouse, #8, Chillicothe, MO 64601; phone: 660-646-3103; probate phone: 660-646-2055; fax: 660-646-8014; hours Public hours: 8:30AM-4:30PM; Office hours: 8AM-5PM (CST). *Misdemeanor, Civil Actions Under $25,000, Eviction, Small Claims, Probate.*

Civil Records: Access: Phone, fax, mail, in person. Both court and visitors may perform in person searches. No search fee. Court makes copy: $1.00 per page. Required to search: name, years to search; also helpful: address; Signed release required for closed records. Civil cases indexed by defendant, plaintiff; onindex cards and record books since 1975, prior on record books. Mail turnaround time 5 days.

Criminal Records: Access: Phone, fax, mail, in person. Both court and visitors may perform in person searches. No search fee. Court makes copy: $1.00 per page. Required to search: name, years to search, DOB; Signed release required for closed records. Criminal records on index cards and record books since 1975, prior on record books. Mail turnaround time 5 days.

General Information: No public access terminal. No juvenile, mental, expunged, dismissed, or suspended imposition of sentence records released. Call for fax fee. Certification fee: $1.50. Payee: Associate Circuit Court. Personal checks accepted. Prepayment and SASE required.

Macon County

Circuit Court PO Box 382, Macon, MO 63552; phone: 660-385-4631; criminal phone: 660-385-4631; civil phone: 660-385-4631; fax: 660-385-4235; hours 8:AM-5PM (CST). *Felony, Misdemeanor, Civil Actions Over $25,000.*

Civil Records: Access: Fax, mail, in person, online. Both court and visitors may perform in person searches. No search fee. Court makes copy: $.25 per page; same fee for self serve. Required to search: name, years to search. Civil cases indexed by defendant, plaintiff; oncomputer since 1/1/91, on index cards from 1976-1990, prior on books. Participates in the free court record system at www.courts.mo.gov/casenet/base/welcome.do. Online records go back to 4/17/2000. Mail turnaround time 2-5 days.

Criminal Records: Access: Fax, mail, in person, online. Both court and visitors may perform in person searches. Search fee: $1.00 per name. Court makes copy: $.25 per page; same fee for self serve. Required to search: name, years to search. Criminal records on computer since 1/1/91, on index cards from 1976-1990, prior on books. Online access same as civil. Mail turnaround time 2-5 days.

General Information: Public terminal goes back to 1991. No juvenile, mental, expunged, dismissed, or suspended imposition of sentence records released. Will fax documents $1.00 1st page, $.25 each add'l. Certification fee: $3.00. Payee: Clerk of Circuit Court. Personal checks accepted. Prepayment and SASE required.

Associate Circuit Court PO Box 491, Macon, MO 63552; phone: 660-385-3531; probate phone: 660-385-3531; criminal fax: 660-385-3132; civil/probate fax is the same; hours 8AM-4:30PM (CST). *Misdemeanor, Civil Actions Under $25,000, Eviction, Small Claims, Probate.*

Civil Records: Access: Fax, mail, in person, online. Both court and visitors may perform in person searches. Court makes copy: $1.00 per page. Required to search: name, years to search. Civil cases indexed by defendant, plaintiff; onindex cards and books; on computer back to 1992. Participates in the free court record system at www.courts.mo.gov/casenet/base/welcome.do. Online records go back to 4/17/2000.

Criminal Records: Access: In person, online. Visitors must perform in person searches themselves. Court makes copy: $1.00 per page. Required to search: name, years to search, DOB. Criminal records on computer since 1992, prior on index cards back to 1989. Online access is the same as civil. Note: Court recommends criminal searches at MO State Hwy Patrol, 573-526-6288. Mail turnaround time 2 weeks.

General Information: Public terminal has criminal back to 1992 and civil back to 1976. (Older civil records are incomplete.) No juvenile, mental, expunged, dismissed, or suspended imposition of sentence records released. Will fax documents for fee. Certification fee: $1.50. Payee: Circuit Court Division II or Probate Court. Prepayment and SASE required.

Madison County

Circuit Court PO Box 470, Fredericktown, MO 63645-0470; phone: 573-783-2102; fax: 573-783-2715; hours 8AM-5PM (CST). *Felony, Misdemeanor, Civil Actions Over $25,000.*

Civil Records: Access: In person, online. Visitors must perform in person searches themselves. No search fee. Court makes copy: $1.00 per page. Required to search: name, years to search. Civil cases indexed by defendant, plaintiff; oncomputer back to 1993, prior on index cards from 1979-1992. Participates in the free court record system at www.courts.mo.gov/casenet/base/welcome.do. Records from 11/01/00 forward.

Criminal Records: Access: In person, online. Visitors must perform in person searches themselves. No search fee. Court makes copy: $1.00 per page. Required to search: name, years to search. Criminal records on computer back to 1993, prior on index cards from 1979-1993. Participates in the free court record system at www.courts.mo.gov/casenet/base/welcome.do. Records go back to 11/01/00 forward. Note: Court recommends criminal searches at MO State Hwy Patrol, 573-526-6288.

General Information: Public terminal goes back to 1993. No juvenile, mental, expunged, dismissed, or suspended imposition of sentence records released. Will not fax documents. Certification fee: $2.00 per page includes copy. Payee: Madison County Circuit Clerk. Personal checks accepted. Prepayment required.

Associate Circuit Court PO Box 521, Fredericktown, MO 63645; phone: 573-783-3105; criminal fax: 573-783-5920; civil/probate fax is the same; hours 8AM-5PM (CST). *Misdemeanor, Civil Actions Under $25,000, Small Claims, Probate, Traffic.*

Note: Probate records are a separate index.

Civil Records: Access: Phone, fax, mail, in person, online. Both court and visitors may perform in person searches. No search fee. Court makes copy: $.50 per page; same fee for self serve. Required to search: name, years to search. Civil cases indexed by defendant, plaintiff; onindex cards since 1979, prior on judgment books to 1960s; on computer back to 11/2000. Participates in the free statewide Casenet court record system at www.courts.mo.gov/casenet/base/welcome.do. Online records go back to 11/00. Mail turnaround time 1 week.

Criminal Records: Access: Phone, fax, mail, in person, online. Both court and visitors may perform in person searches. No search fee. Court makes copy: $.50 per page; same fee for self serve. Required to search: name, years to search; also helpful: DOB, SSN. Criminal records on index cards since 1979, prior on judgment books; on computer back to 11/2000. Participates in the free statewide Casenet court record system at www.courts.mo.gov/casenet/base/welcome.do. Online records go back to 11/00. Mail turnaround time 1 week.

General Information: Public terminal goes back to 11/2000. No juvenile, mental, expunged, dismissed, or suspended imposition of sentence records released. Will fax documents. Certification fee: $1.50 per instrument. Payee: Associate Circuit Court. Only cashiers checks and money orders accepted. Prepayment and SASE required.

Maries County

Circuit Court PO Box 213, Vienna, MO 65582; phone: 573-422-3338; fax: 573-422-3976; hours 8AM-4PM (CST). *Felony, Misdemeanor, Civil Actions Over $25,000.*

Civil Records: Access: Fax, mail, in person. Both court and visitors may perform in person searches. No search fee. Court makes copy: $.25 per page; same fee for self serve. Required to search: name, years to search. Civil cases indexed by defendant, plaintiff. Civil records go back to 1940. Mail turnaround time 1-3 days.

Criminal Records: Access: Fax, mail, in person. Both court and visitors may perform in person searches. No search fee. Court makes copy: $.25 per page; same fee for self serve. Required to search: name, years to search. Criminal records go back 10 1940. Mail turnaround time 1-3 days.

General Information: No public access terminal. No juvenile, mental, expunged, dismissed, or suspended imposition of sentence records released. Will fax documents $.25 per page. Certification fee: $1.50 per cert. Payee: Maries County Circuit Clerk. Personal checks accepted. Prepayment required.

Associate Circuit Court PO Box 490, Vienna, MO 65582; phone: 573-422-3303; fax: 573-422-9917; hours 8AM-4PM (CST). *Misdemeanor, Civil Actions Under $25,000, Eviction, Small Claims, Probate.*

Note: Most civil cases are directed to the Circuit Court regardless of limit.

Civil Records: Access: Mail, fax, in person. Both court and visitors may perform in person searches. No search fee. Court makes copy: $.25 per page. Required to search: name, years to search. Civil cases indexed by defendant, plaintiff; onindex cards since 1985, archived since 1868.

Criminal Records: Access: in person only. Only the court performs in person searches. No search fee. Court makes copy: $.25 per page. Required to search: name, years to search, DOB, signed release; also helpful-SSN. Criminal records on index cards since 1985, archived since 1868. Note: Court recommends

criminal searches at MO State Hwy Patrol, 573-526-6288. Mail turnaround time 5 days.

General Information: No public access terminal. No juvenile, mental, expunged, dismissed, or suspended imposition of sentence records released. Will not fax documents. Certification fee: $1.50 per cert. Payee: Sheriff of Maries County. Only cashiers checks and money orders accepted. Prepayment and SASE required.

Marion County

Circuit Court District 1 PO Box 392, 100 S Main St, Palmyra, MO 63461; phone: 573-769-2550; fax: 573-769-6012; hours 8:30AM-5PM (CST). *Felony, Civil Actions Over $25,000.*

Civil Records: Access: In person only. Visitors must perform in person searches themselves. Court makes copy: $.25 per page. Required to search: name, years to search. Civil cases indexed by defendant, plaintiff; onindex cards since 1977, prior on judgment books.

Criminal Records: Access: In person only. Visitors must perform in person searches themselves. Court makes copy: $.25 per page. Required to search: name, years to search, DOB. Criminal records on index cards since 1977, prior on judgment books. Note: Court recommends criminal searches at MO State Hwy Patrol, 573-526-6288.

General Information: Public terminal goes back to 1987. No juvenile, mental, expunged, dismissed, or suspended imposition of sentence records released. Certification fee: $2.00 per cert. Payee: Marion County Circuit Clerk of Division I. Business checks accepted.

Circuit Court District 2 906 Broadway, Rm 105, Hannibal, MO 63401; phone: 573-221-0198; fax: 573-221-9328; hours 8:30AM-N, 1-5PM (CST). *Felony, Misdemeanor, Civil Actions Over $45,000.*

Note: Jurisdiction is Twps of Miller and Mason only.

Civil Records: Access: Fax, mail, in person. Both court and visitors may perform in person searches. No search fee. Court makes copy: $.50 per page. Required to search: name, years to search. Civil cases indexed by defendant, plaintiff; oncomputer since 1991, prior on index cards.

Criminal Records: Access: In person only. Visitors must perform in person searches themselves. Court makes copy: $.50 per page. Required to search: name, years to search. Criminal records on computer. Note: Court recommends criminal searches at MO State Hwy Patrol, 573-526-6288.

General Information: Public terminal goes back to 1976. No juvenile, mental, expunged, dismissed, or suspended imposition of sentence records released. Will fax civil documents only. Certification fee: $5.00 per document. Payee: Circuit Clerk District II. Personal checks accepted.

Hannibal Associate Circuit Court 906 Broadway, Hannibal, MO 63401; phone: 573-221-0288; fax: 573-221-0945; hours 8AM-5PM (CST). *Misdemeanor, Civil Actions Under $45,000, Eviction, Small Claims, Probate.*

Civil Records: Access: Mail, in person. Visitors must perform in person searches themselves. No search fee. Court makes copy: $.25 per page. Required to search: name, years to search. Civil cases indexed by defendant, plaintiff; onindex cards since 1979, prior on judgment books.

Criminal Records: Access: in person only. Visitors must perform in person searches themselves. Court makes copy: $.25 per page. Required to search: name, years to search. Criminal records on computer since 3/93, on index cards since 1979, prior on judgment books. Note: Court recommends criminal searches at MO State Hwy Patrol, 573-526-6288.

General Information: Public terminal goes back to 1993. No juvenile, mental, expunged, dismissed, or suspended imposition of sentence records released. No certification fee. Payee: Hannibal Assoc Circuit Clerk. Prepayment required.

Palmyra Associate Circuit Court PO Box 449, 100 S. Main St, Palmyra, MO 63461; phone: 573-769-2318; fax: 573-769-4558; hours 8AM-N, 1-5PM (CST). *Misdemeanor, Civil Actions Under $45,000, Eviction, Small Claims, Probate.*

Civil Records: Access: Mail, in person. Only the court performs in person searches. No search fee. Court makes copy: $.50 per page. Required to search: name, years to search. Civil cases indexed by defendant, plaintiff; onindex cards since 1979, prior on judgment books.

Criminal Records: Access: In person only. Only the court performs in person searches. No search fee. Court makes copy: $.50 per page. Required to search: name, years to search; also helpful: DOB. Criminal records on computer since 1994, on index cards from 1979-1994, prior on judgment books. Note: Court recommends criminal searches at MO State Hwy Patrol, 573-526-6288. Mail turnaround time varies.

General Information: Public terminal has only civil records back to 2005. No juvenile, mental, expunged, dismissed, or suspended imposition of sentence records released. Will fax documents. No certification fee. Payee: Circuit Court. Personal checks accepted. Prepayment and SASE required.

McDonald County

Circuit & Associate Court PO Box 157, Pineville, MO 64856; phone: 417-223-7515; fax: 417-223-4125; hours 8AM-4:30PM (CST). *Felony, Misdemeanor, Civil, Small Claims, Probate.*

Civil Records: Access: Fax, mail, in person, online. Visitors must perform in person searches themselves. No search fee. Court makes copy: $.25 per page. Required to search: name, years to search. Civil cases indexed by defendant, plaintiff; oncomputer since 1991, on index cards since 1979, prior on index cards. Participates in the free court record system at www.courts.mo.gov/casenet/base/welcome.do. Mail turnaround time less than 10 days.

Criminal Records: Access: Fax, mail, in person, online. Visitors must perform in person searches themselves. No search fee. Court makes copy: $.25 per page. Required to search: name, years to search; also helpful-charge. Criminal records on computer since 1991, on index cards since 1979, prior on index cards. Participates in the free court record system at www.courts.mo.gov/casenet/base/welcome.do. Note: Court recommends criminal searches at MO State Hwy Patrol, 573-526-6288. Mail turnaround time less than 10 days.

General Information: Public use terminal available. No juvenile, mental, expunged, dismissed, paternity or suspended imposition of sentence records released. Fee to fax documents is $.25 per page, $1.00 if for probate. Certification fee: $2.00; Probate $1.00 per page. Payee: McDonald County Circuit Clerk. Business checks accepted. Prepayment and SASE required.

Mercer County

Circuit Court Courthouse, 802 E Main, Princeton, MO 64673; phone: 660-748-4335; fax: 660-748-4339; hours 8:30AM-N, 1-4:30PM (CST). *Felony, Misdemeanor, Civil Actions Over $45,000.*

Civil Records: Access: In person, online. Visitors must perform in person searches themselves. Court makes copy: $.25 per page. Required to search: name, years to search. Civil cases indexed by defendant, plaintiff; oncomputer since 1991, on index cards since 1977, prior on books. Participates in the free court record system at www.courts.mo.gov/casenet/base/welcome.do. Online records go back to 3/29/2000.

Criminal Records: Access: In person, online. Visitors must perform in person searches themselves. No search fee. Court makes copy: $.25 per page. Required to search: name, years to search, DOB. Criminal records on computer since 1991, on index cards since 1977, prior on books. Online access to criminal records is the same as civil.

Note: Court recommends criminal searches at MO State Hwy Patrol, 573-526-6288.

General Information: Public terminal goes back to 1999. No juvenile, mental, expunged, dismissed, or suspended imposition of sentence records released. Certification fee: $1.00 per page. Payee: Mercer County Circuit Clerk. Personal checks not accepted if out of state; money orders preferred. Prepayment required.

Associate Circuit Court Mercer County Courthouse, 802 E Main St, Princeton, MO 64673; phone: 660-748-4232; criminal fax: 660-748-4292; civil/probate fax is the same; hours 8:30AM-4:30PM (CST). *Misdemeanor, Civil Actions Under $45,000, Eviction, Small Claims, Probate.*

Civil Records: Access: In person, online. Visitors must perform in person searches themselves. Court makes copy: $.25 per page. Required to search: name, years to search. Civil cases indexed by defendant. Civil records on index. Participates in the free court record system at www.courts.mo.gov/casenet/base/welcome.do. Online records go back to 3/2000.

Criminal Records: Access: In person, online. Visitors must perform in person searches themselves. No search fee. Court makes copy: $.25 per page. Required to search: name, years to search; also helpful: DOB, SSN. Criminal records on index. Online access to criminal records is the same as civil. Note: Court recommends criminal searches at MO State Hwy Patrol, 573-526-6288.

General Information: Public terminal goes back to 3/2000. (Terminal located in Circuit Clerk's office.) No juvenile, mental, expunged, dismissed, or suspended imposition of sentence records released. Certification fee: $1.50 plus $1.00 per page. Payee: Circuit Court Division II. Personal checks accepted. Prepayment required.

Associate Circuit Court Courthouse Rm 304, 302 S Main St, Carthage, MO 64836; phone: 417-358-0450; fax: 417-358-0460; hours 8:30AM-4:30PM (CST). *Misdemeanor, Civil Actions Under $45,000, Eviction, Small Claims, Probate.*

Civil Records: Access: In person, online. Visitors must perform in person searches themselves. Court makes copy: $.25 per page. Required to search: name, years to search. Civil cases indexed by defendant, plaintiff; oncomputer since 2000, prior on index cards since 1979. Free access to court record system at www.courts.mo.gov/casenet/base/welcome.do. Online records go back to 3/29/2000.

Criminal Records: Access: In person, online. Visitors must perform in person searches themselves. Search fee: None. Court makes copy: $.25 per page. Required to search: name, years to search. Criminal records on computer since 2000, prior on index cards since 1979. Online access to criminal records is the same as civil. Note: Court recommends criminal searches at MO State Hwy Patrol, 573-526-6288.

General Information: Public terminal goes back to 1999. No juvenile, mental, expunged, dismissed, or suspended imposition of sentence records released. No certification fee.

Miller County

Circuit Court PO Box 11, Tuscumbia, MO 65082; phone: 573-369-1980; hours 8AM-4:30PM (CST). *Felony, Misdemeanor, Civil Actions Over $25,000.*

Civil Records: Access: Phone, fax, mail, in person. Both court and visitors may perform in person searches. Search fee: $4.00 per name. Court makes copy: $.50 per page; same fee for self serve. Required to search: name, years to search. Civil cases indexed by defendant, plaintiff; onindex cards since 1976, prior on books.

Criminal Records: Access: In person only. Both court and visitors may perform in person searches. Court makes copy: $.50 per page; same fee for self serve. Required to search: name, years to search. Criminal records on index cards since 1976, prior on

books. All criminal record name searches referred to MO State Hwy Patrol at 573-526-6153. Mail turnaround time 1 week.

General Information: Public terminal goes back to 1991. No juvenile, mental, expunged, dismissed, or suspended imposition of sentence records released. No fee to fax documents; other fees must be prepaid. Will fax to local and toll-free numbers only. Certification fee: $2.00. Payee: Miller County Circuit Court. Personal checks accepted. Prepayment and SASE required.

Associate Circuit Court Miller County Courthouse Annex, 2001 Hwy 52, Tuscumbia, MO 65082; phone: 573-369-1970; hours 8AM-4PM (CST). *Misdemeanor, Civil Actions Under $25,000, Eviction, Small Claims, Probate.*

Civil Records: Access: Mail, in person. Only the court performs in person searches. No search fee. Court makes copy: $1.00 per page. Required to search: name, years to search. Civil cases indexed by defendant, plaintiff; oncomputer since 1/92, on microfiche since 1980, on cards since 1979, prior archived. Mail turnaround time 1 week.

Criminal Records: Access: Mail, in person. Only the court performs in person searches. No search fee. Court makes copy: $1.00 per page. Required to search: name, years to search. Criminal records on computer since 1979, on microfiche since 1980, prior archived. Mail turnaround time 1 week.

General Information: No public access terminal. No juvenile, mental, expunged, dismissed, or suspended imposition of sentence records released. Certification fee: $1.50. Payee: Associate Circuit Court. Only cashiers checks and money orders accepted. Prepayment and SASE required.

Mississippi County

Circuit & Associate Court PO Box 369, Charleston, MO 63834; phone: 573-683-2146 x1; fax: 573-683-7696; hours 8AM-5PM (CST). *Felony, Misdemeanor, Civil, Small Claims, Eviction, Probate.*

Civil Records: Access: In person, online. Visitors must perform in person searches themselves. Court makes copy: $.25 per page. Required to search: name, years to search. Civil cases indexed by defendant, plaintiff. Civil records in case files since 1976. Access to civil records is free at www.courts.mo.gov/casenet/cases/searchCases.do. Search by litigant name, case # or date. Online records go back to 6/15/2001.

Criminal Records: Access: in person, online. Visitors must perform in person searches themselves. No search fee. Court makes copy: $.25 per page. Required to search: name, years to search, DOB. Criminal records in case files since 1951. Online access to criminal records is the same as civil.

General Information: Public terminal goes back to 1979. No juvenile, mental, expunged, dismissed, or suspended imposition of sentence records released. Will fax specific case file requests. Certification fee: $.50 per cert. Payee: Circuit Clerk. Personal checks accepted. Prepayment required.

Moniteau County

Circuit Court 200 E Main, California, MO 65018; phone: 573-796-2071; hours 8AM-4:30PM (CST). *Felony, Misdemeanor, Civil Actions Over $25,000, Small Claims.*

Civil Records: Access: In person only. Both court and visitors may perform in person searches. No search fee. Court makes copy: $.50 per page; same fee for self serve. Required to search: name, years to search; also helpful: case number. Civil cases indexed by defendant, plaintiff; oncomputer since 1992, prior on index cards and books.

Criminal Records: Access: In person only. Both court and visitors may perform in person searches. No search fee. Court makes copy: $.50 per page; same fee for self serve. Required to search: name, years to search; also helpful: case number. Criminal records on

computer since 1980, prior on index cards and books to 1845. Note: Court recommends criminal searches at MO State Hwy Patrol, 573-526-6288.
General Information: No public access terminal. No juvenile, mental, expunged, dismissed, or suspended imposition of sentence records released. Will not fax specific case file. Certification fee: $1.00 per page. Payee: Moniteau County Circuit Court. Personal checks accepted. Prepayment required.

Associate Circuit Court 200 E Main, California, MO 65018; phone: 573-796-4671; probate phone: 573-796-2814; hours 8AM-4:30PM (CST). *Misdemeanor, Civil Actions Under $25,000, Eviction, Small Claims, Probate.*
Note: The court will not do probate record searches.
Civil Records: Access: Phone, in person. Visitors must perform in person searches themselves. No search fee. Court makes copy: $.25 per page; same fee for self serve. Required to search: name, years to search. Civil cases indexed by defendant, plaintiff; onindex cards since 1979, prior on index books from 1948 to 1979, archived before.
Criminal Records: Access: In person only. Visitors must perform in person searches themselves. Court makes copy: $.25 per page; same fee for self serve. Required to search: name, years to search. Criminal records on index cards since 1979, prior on index books from 1948 to 1979, archived before. Note: Court recommends criminal searches at MO State Hwy Patrol, 573-526-6288.
General Information: No public access terminal. No juvenile, mental, expunged, dismissed, or suspended imposition of sentence records released. Certification fee: $2.50 for 1st page, $1.00 each add'l. Personal checks accepted. Prepayment required.

Monroe County

Circuit Court PO Box 227, Paris, MO 65275; phone: 660-327-5204; fax: 660-327-5781; hours 8AM-4:30PM (CST). *Felony, Misdemeanor, Civil Actions Over $45,000.*
Civil Records: Access: Mail, in person. Both court and visitors may perform in person searches. Search fee: $14.00 per name. Court makes copy: $1.00 per page. Self serve copy fee: $.50 per page. Required to search: name, years to search. Civil cases indexed by defendant, plaintiff; oncomputer since 1996; index cards since 1979, prior on index books. Mail turnaround time 1 week.
Criminal Records: Access: Mail, in person. Both court and visitors may perform in person searches. Search fee: $14.00 per name. Court makes copy: $1.00 per page. Self serve copy fee: $.50 per page. Required to search: name, years to search, SSN, signed release. Criminal records on computer since 1996, on index cards from 1979 to 1990. Mail turnaround time 1 week.
General Information: No public access terminal. No juvenile, mental, expunged, dismissed, or suspended imposition of sentence records released. Fee to fax documents is $1.00 per page. Certification fee: $2.00. Payee: Monroe County Circuit Court. Personal checks accepted. Prepayment and SASE required.

Associate Circuit Court 300 N Main, Courthouse, Paris, MO 65275; phone: 660-327-5220; fax: 660-327-5651; hours 8AM-N, 1-4:30PM (CST). *Misdemeanor, Civil Actions Under $45,000, Eviction, Small Claims, Probate.*
Civil Records: Access: Mail, in person. Both court and visitors may perform in person searches. No search fee. Court makes copy: $.25 per page. Required to search: name, years to search. Civil cases indexed by defendant, plaintiff; onindex cards since 1979, prior on books. Mail turnaround 2 weeks.
Criminal Records: Access: Mail, in person. Both court and visitors may perform in person searches. Search fee: None. Court makes copy: $.25 per page. Required to search: name, years to search. Criminal records on index cards since 1979, prior on books. Mail turnaround time 2 weeks.

General Information: No public access terminal. No juvenile, mental, expunged, dismissed, or suspended imposition of sentence records released. Certification fee: $1.50 first page, $1.00 each add'l. Payee: Associate Circuit Court. Personal checks accepted. Prepayment and SASE required.

Montgomery County

Circuit Court 211 E 3rd, Montgomery City, MO 63361; phone: 573-564-3341; fax: 573-564-3914; hours 8AM-4:30PM (CST). *Felony, Misdemeanor, Civil Actions Over $25,000.*
Civil Records: Access: Online, in person. Visitors must perform in person searches themselves. Court makes copy: $.25 per page; same fee for self serve. Required to search: name, years to search. Civil cases indexed by defendant, plaintiff; oncomputer since 1987 for judgments, on index cards since 1979, prior on books to 1864. Participates in the free court record system at www.courts.mo.gov/casenet/base/welcome.do. Online records go back to 6/25/1997.
Criminal Records: Access: Online, in person. Visitors must perform in person searches themselves. Court makes copy: $.25 per page; same fee for self serve. Required to search: name, years to search. Criminal records on computer since 1987 for judgments, on index cards since 1979, prior on books. Online access to criminal records is the same as civil. Online criminal records go back to 12/10/1996. Note: Court recommends criminal searches at MO State Hwy Patrol, 573-526-6288.
General Information: Public terminal goes back to 1996. No juvenile, mental, expunged, dismissed, or suspended imposition of sentence records released. Certification fee: $1.50 plus $.25 per page. Payee: Montgomery County Circuit Court. Personal checks accepted. Prepayment required.

Associate Circuit Court 211 E 3rd St, Montgomery City, MO 63361; phone: 573-564-3348; fax: 573-564-8081; hours 8:00AM-4:30PM (CST). *Misdemeanor, Civil Actions Under $25,000, Eviction, Small Claims, Probate.*
Civil Records: Access: Online, in person. Visitors must perform in person searches themselves. Court makes copy: $.25 per page. Required to search: name, years to search. Civil cases indexed by defendant, plaintiff; oncomputer back to 1976, prior on index cards. Participates in the free court record system at www.courts.mo.gov/casenet/base/welcome.do. Online civil records go back to 6/25/1997.
Criminal Records: Access: Online, in person. Visitors must perform in person searches themselves. Court makes copy: $.25 per page. Required to search: name, years to search, DOB. Criminal records on computer back to 1976, prior on index cards. Online access to criminal records is the same as civil. Online criminal records go back to 8/29/1950. Note: Court recommends criminal searches at MO State Hwy Patrol, 573-526-6288.
General Information: Public terminal has only civil records. No juvenile, mental, expunged, dismissed, or suspended imposition of sentence records released. Certification fee: $1.50 per page. Payee: Montgomery Circuit Clerk's Office. Personal checks accepted. Prepayment required.

Morgan County

Circuit Court 211 E Newton, Versailles, MO 65084; phone: 573-378-4413; fax: 573-378-5356; hours 8AM-5PM (CST). *Felony, Civil Actions Over $25,000.*
Civil Records: Access: Phone, mail, in person. Both court and visitors may perform in person searches. No search fee. Court makes copy: $.50 per page. Self serve copy fee: $.25 per page. Required to search: name, years to search. Civil cases indexed by defendant, plaintiff; oncomputer since 1992, on index cards since 1979, prior archived since mid-1800s. Mail turnaround time 1 week; phone turnaround is immediate.

Criminal Records: Access: Phone, mail, in person. Both court and visitors may perform in person searches. No search fee. Court makes copy: $.50 per page. Self serve copy fee: $.25 per page. Required to search: name, years to search. Criminal records on computer since 1992, on index cards since 1979, prior archived since mid-1800s. Mail turnaround time 1 week; phone turnaround is immediate.
General Information: Public terminal goes back to 1984. No juvenile, mental, expunged, dismissed, or suspended imposition of sentence records released. Certification fee: $1.50. Payee: Circuit Court. Personal checks accepted. Prepayment required. Copy fees may be billed. SASE required.

Associate Circuit Court 211 E Newton St, Versailles, MO 65084; phone: 573-378-4235; criminal phone: 573-378-4060; civil phone: 573-378-4235; probate phone: 573-378-4235; criminal fax: 573-378-5356; civil fax: 573-378-6847; probate fax: 573-378-6847; hours 8AM-5PM (CST). *Misdemeanor, Civil Actions Under $25,000, Eviction, Small Claims, Probate.*
Note: Probate has a separate index. Traffic is with the criminal division.
Civil Records: Access: Phone, mail, in person. Both court and visitors may perform in person searches. No search fee. Court makes copy: $1.00 per page. Self serve copy fee: $.50 per page. Required to search: name, years to search. Civil cases indexed by defendant, plaintiff; oncomputer since 1991, prior on index to 1970. Mail turnaround time 2-3 days.
Criminal Records: Access: Phone, mail, in person. Only the court performs in person searches. No search fee. Court makes copy: $1.00 per page. Self serve copy fee: $.50 per page. Required to search: name, years to search; also helpful: address, DOB, SSN, singed release. Criminal records on computer since 1989, prior on index to 1970. Note: Signed release required for some searches. Mail turnaround time 2-3 days.
General Information: No public access terminal. No juvenile, mental, expunged, dismissed, or suspended imposition of sentence records released. Will fax documents. Certification fee: $1.50 per page. Payee: Associate Circuit Court or Probate Court. Only cashiers checks and money orders accepted. Prepayment and SASE required.

New Madrid County

Circuit and Associate Court County Courthouse, 450 Main St, New Madrid, MO 63869; phone: 573-748-2228; fax: 573-748-5409; hours 8AM-4:30PM (CST). *Felony, Misdemeanor, Civil Actions Over $25,000.*
Civil Records: Access: In person, online. Visitors must perform in person searches themselves. Court makes copy: $1.00 per page. Required to search: name, years to search. Civil cases indexed by defendant, plaintiff; onCott index since 1979, prior on books. Access to civil records is free at www.courts.mo.gov/casenet/cases/searchCases.do. Search by litigant name, case # or date. Online records go back to 2/7/2001.
Criminal Records: Access: In person, online. Visitors must perform in person searches themselves. No search fee. Court makes copy: $1.00 per page. Required to search: name, years to search. Criminal records on Cott index since 1979, prior on books. Online access to criminal records is the same as civil.
General Information: Public terminal goes back to 2/2001. No juvenile, mental, expunged, dismissed, or suspended imposition of sentence records released. Will fax specific case file requests. Certification fee: $5.00 per doc. Payee: Circuit Clerk. Personal checks not accepted. Prepayment required.

Newton County

Circuit and Associate Court PO Box 130, 101 S Wood St, Courthouse, Neosho, MO 64850; phone: 417-451-8257; criminal phone: 417-451-8210 x108; civil phone: 417-451-8210 x174; probate phone: 417-451-8210 x116; criminal fax: 417-451-8272; civil fax: 417-451-8282; probate fax: 417-451-8265; hours 8AM-5PM (CST). *Felony, Misdemeanor, Civil Actions, Eviction, Small Claims, Probate.*
Note: Probate is a separate division; probate address is 101 S Wood, #204.
Civil Records: Access: Mail, in person, online. Visitors must perform in person searches themselves. No search fee. Court makes copy: $.25 per page. Required to search: name, years to search. Civil cases indexed by defendant, plaintiff; oncomputer since 1991, microfilm since 2000, prior on index cards and books. Participates in the free court record system at www.courts.mo.gov/casenet/base/welcome.do.
Criminal Records: Access: In person, online. Visitors must perform in person searches themselves. No search fee. Court makes copy: $.25 per page. Required to search: name, years to search. Criminal records on computer since 1991, microfilm since 2000, prior on index cards and books. Online access to criminal records is the same as civil.
General Information: Public terminal goes back to 1991. No juvenile, mental, expunged, dismissed, or suspended imposition of sentence records released. Certification fee: $1.00 per document. Payee: Newton County Circuit Clerk. Business checks accepted. Prepayment and SASE required.

Nodaway County

Circuit Court 305 N Main St #206, Maryville, MO 64468; phone: 660-582-5431; fax: 660-582-5499; hours 8AM-4:30PM (CST). *Felony, Misdemeanor, Civil Actions Over $25,000.*
Civil Records: Access: Phone, mail, in person. Visitors must perform in person searches themselves. No search fee. Court makes copy: $.25 per page. Required to search: name, years to search. Civil cases indexed by defendant, plaintiff; oncomputer back to 5/91, archived since 1845.
Criminal Records: Access: In person only. Visitors must perform in person searches themselves. Court makes copy: $.25 per page. Required to search: name, years to search, DOB. Criminal records on computer back to 5/91, archived since 1845. Note: Court recommends criminal searches at MO State Hwy Patrol, 573-526-6288.
General Information: Public terminal goes back to 5/1991. No juvenile, mental, expunged, dismissed, or suspended imposition of sentence records released. Fee to fax documents is $1.00 per page. Certification fee: $1.00. Payee: Circuit Clerk. Personal checks accepted. Prepayment required.

Associate Circuit Court 303 N Market, Courthouse Annex, Maryville, MO 64468; phone: 660-582-2531; probate phone: 660-582-4221; fax: 660-582-2047; probate fax: same; hours 8AM-Noon; 1-4:30PM (CST). *Misdemeanor, Civil Actions Under $45,000, Eviction, Small Claims, Probate.*
Civil Records: Access: In person only. Only the court performs in person searches. No search fee. Court makes copy: $.50 per page. Required to search: name, years to search. Civil cases indexed by defendant, plaintiff; oncomputer since 1981, archived since 1845. Note: Court will look up name for you.
Criminal Records: Access: In person only. Only the court performs in person searches. Search fee: None. Court makes copy: $.50 per page. Required to search: name, years to search. Criminal records on computer since 1981, archived since 1845. Note: Court recommends criminal searches at State Hwy Patrol, 573-526-6288.
General Information: No public access terminal. No juvenile, mental, expunged, dismissed, or suspended imposition of sentence records released. Certification fee: $1.50. Payee: Circuit Court

Associate Division. Business checks accepted. Prepayment required.

Oregon County

Circuit Court PO Box 406, Alton, MO 65606; phone: 417-778-7460; fax: 417-778-7206; hours 8AM-4PM (CST). *Felony, Misdemeanor, Civil Actions Over $45,000.*
Civil Records: Access: In person, online. Both court and visitors may perform in person searches. Court makes copy: $1.00 per page. Required to search: name, years to search. Civil cases indexed by defendant, plaintiff; onbooks. Participates in the free court record system at www.courts.mo.gov/casenet/base/welcome.do. Online records go back to 1991.
Criminal Records: Access: In person, online. Both court and visitors may perform in person searches. Court makes copy: $1.00 per page. Required to search: name, years to search. Criminal records on books. Online access to criminal records is the same as civil. Note: Court will only search if not busy, and may refer you to State Hiway Patrol.
General Information: Public terminal goes back to 2000. No juvenile, mental, expunged, dismissed, or suspended imposition of sentence records released. Will fax documents $1.00 1st page, $.50 each add'l. Certification fee: $2.00 per cert. Payee: Circuit Court. Personal checks accepted. Prepayment required.

Associate Circuit Court PO Box 211, Alton, MO 65606; phone: 417-778-7461; fax: 417-778-6209; hours 8:00AM-4:00PM (CST). *Misdemeanor, Civil Actions Under $45,000, Eviction, Small Claims, Probate.*
Civil Records: Access: In person, online. Both court and visitors may perform in person searches. Court makes copy: $1.00 per page. Self serve copy fee: $.10 per page. Required to search: name, years to search. Civil cases indexed by defendant, plaintiff; onindex cards, archived since 1850. Participates in the free court record system at www.courts.mo.gov/casenet/base/welcome.do. Online records go back to 1991.
Criminal Records: Access: In person, online. Both court and visitors may perform in person searches. No search fee. Court makes copy: $1.00 per page. Self serve copy fee: $.10 per page. Required to search: name, years to search. Criminal records on computer since 3/11/92, prior on files. Online access to criminal records is the same as civil.
General Information: Public terminal goes back to 2000. No juvenile, mental, expunged, or dismissed records released. (Suspended Imposition of Sentence only available during probationary period.). Certification fee: $2.00 per cert. Payee: Associate Circuit Court. Business checks accepted. Prepayment required.

Osage County

Circuit Court PO Box 825, Linn, MO 65051; phone: 573-897-3114; fax: 573-897-4075; hours 8AM-4:30PM (CST). *Felony, Misdemeanor, Civil Actions Over $25,000.*
Civil Records: Access: Phone, mail, in person, online. Both court and visitors may perform in person searches. No search fee. Court makes copy: $.25 per page. Required to search: name, years to search. Civil cases indexed by defendant, plaintiff; onindex cards and books. Participates in the free court record system at www.courts.mo.gov/casenet/base/welcome.do. Online civil records go back to 9/01/2000. Mail turnaround time ASAP.
Criminal Records: Access: Phone, mail, fax, in person, online. Both court and visitors may perform in person searches. No search fee. Court makes copy: $.25 per page. Required to search: name, years to search, DOB; also helpful: SSN. Criminal records on index cards and books, computerized since 1992. Participates in the free court record system at www.courts.mo.gov/casenet/base/welcome.do.

Online criminal records go back to 8/28/1992. Mail turnaround time ASAP.
General Information: Public terminal goes back to 1992. No juvenile, mental, expunged, dismissed, or suspended imposition of sentence records released. Fee to fax documents is $1.00 per page. Certification fee: $2.00 per cert. Payee: Circuit Clerk. Personal checks accepted. Prepayment and SASE required.

Associate Circuit Court PO Box 470, Linn, MO 65051; phone: 573-897-2136; fax: 573-897-0458; hours 8AM-4:30PM (CST). *Misdemeanor, Civil Actions Under $25,000, Eviction, Small Claims, Probate.*
Civil Records: Access: Mail, in person, online. Both court and visitors may perform in person searches. No search fee. Court makes copy: $.25 per page; same fee for self serve. Required to search: name, years to search. Civil cases indexed by defendant, plaintiff; oncomputer back to 2000, prior on index cards. Participates in the free court record system at www.courts.mo.gov/casenet/base/welcome.do. Online civil records go back to 9/5/00. Online probate records go back to 9/05/2000. Mail turnaround time 2 weeks.
Criminal Records: Access: Mail, in person, online. Both court and visitors may perform in person searches. No search fee. Court makes copy: $.25 per page; same fee for self serve. Required to search: name, years to search; also helpful: DOB, SSN. Criminal records on computer back to 1995, prior on index cards. Participates in the free court record system at www.courts.mo.gov/casenet/base/welcome.do. Online criminal records go back to 1995. Also, traffic records go back to 9/5/00. Mail turnaround time 2 weeks.
General Information: Public terminal has criminal back to 1995 and civil back to 2000. (Traffic and probate go back to 2000.) No juvenile, mental, expunged, dismissed, or suspended imposition of sentence records released. Certification fee: $2.00 per cert. Payee: Osage County Circuit Court-Associate Division. Personal checks accepted. Prepayment required.

Ozark County

Circuit Court PO Box 36, Gainesville, MO 65655; phone: 417-679-4232; fax: 417-679-4554; hours 8AM-N, 12:30-4:30PM (CST). *Felony, Misdemeanor, Civil Actions Over $25,000.*
Civil Records: Access: Mail, in person. Only the court performs in person searches. No search fee. Court makes copy: $.25 per page. Required to search: name, years to search. Civil cases indexed by defendant, plaintiff; onindex cards since 1979, archived since 1933.
Criminal Records: Access: In person only. Only the court performs in person searches. No search fee. Court makes copy: $.25 per page. Required to search: name, years to search, DOB. Criminal records on index cards since 1979, archived since 1933. Note: Court recommends criminal searches at MO State Hwy Patrol, 573-526-6288.
General Information: No public access terminal. No juvenile, mental, expunged, dismissed, or suspended imposition of sentence records released. Certification fee: $1.50. Payee: Ozark County Circuit Court. Personal checks accepted. Prepayment required.

Associate Circuit Court PO Box 278, Gainesville, MO 65655; phone: 417-679-4611; fax: 417-679-2099; hours 8AM-4:30PM (CST). *Misdemeanor, Civil Actions Under $25,000, Eviction, Small Claims, Probate.*
Civil Records: Access: Fax, mail, in person. Only the court performs in person searches. No search fee. Court makes copy: $1.00 per page. Required to search: name, years to search. Civil cases indexed by defendant, plaintiff; oncase files.
Criminal Records: Access: In person only. Only the court performs in person searches. No search fee. Court makes copy: $1.00 per page. Required to

search: name, years to search, DOB, signed release; SSN helpful. Criminal records on computer since 1990. Note: Court recommends criminal searches at MO State Hwy Patrol, 573-526-6288. Mail turnaround time 2 weeks.

General Information: No public access terminal. No juvenile, mental, expunged, dismissed, or suspended imposition of sentence records released. Will fax documents for $1.00 per page. Certification fee: $1.50 per cert. Payee: Associate Circuit Court. Personal checks accepted. Prepayment and SASE required.

Pemiscot County

Circuit Court, Division I County Courthouse, PO Box 34, Caruthersville, MO 63830; phone: 573-333-0182; fax: 573-333-1272; hours 8:00AM-4:30PM (CST). *Felony, Misdemeanor, Civil Actions Over $45,000.*
Civil Records: Access: In person, online. Visitors must perform in person searches themselves. Court makes copy: $.50 per page. Required to search: name, years to search. Civil cases indexed by defendant, plaintiff; onindex cards since 1979, prior on books. Participates in the free court record system at www.courts.mo.gov/casenet/base/welcome.do. Online records go back to 2/7/2001.
Criminal Records: Access: In person, online. Visitors must perform in person searches themselves. Court makes copy: $.50 per page. Required to search: name, years to search. Criminal records on index cards since 1979, prior on books. Online access to criminal records is the same as civil. Note: Court recommends criminal searches at MO State Hwy Patrol, 573-526-6288.
General Information: Public terminal goes back to 1/7/2001. No juvenile, mental, expunged, dismissed, or suspended imposition of sentence records released. No certification fee . Payee: Pemiscot County Treasurer. No personal checks accepted.

Associate Circuit Court County Courthouse, PO Drawer 228, Caruthersville, MO 63830; phone: 573-333-2784; hours 7:30AM-4:30PM (CST). *Misdemeanor, Civil Actions Under $45,000, Eviction, Small Claims, Probate.*
Civil Records: Access: In person, online. Both court and visitors may perform in person searches. Court makes copy: $1.00 per page. Required to search: name, years to search. Civil cases indexed by defendant, plaintiff; oncomputer back to 2001, index cards since 1979, prior on books. Participates in the free court record system at www.courts.mo.gov/casenet/base/welcome.do. Online records go back to 2/14/2001. Mail turnaround time varies.
Criminal Records: Access: In person, online. Both court and visitors may perform in person searches. Court makes copy: $1.00 per page. Required to search: name, years to search. Criminal records on computer since 5/90, on index cards from 1979-1990, prior on books. Online access to criminal records is the same as civil.
General Information: Public terminal goes back to 1999. No juvenile, mental, expunged, dismissed, or suspended imposition of sentence records released. No certification fee . Payee: Pemiscot County Clerk. Only cashiers checks and money orders accepted. Prepayment required.

Perry County

Circuit Court 15 W Saint Maries St #2, Perryville, MO 63775-1399; phone: 573-547-6581; fax: 573-547-9323; hours 8AM-5PM (CST). *Felony, Misdemeanor, Civil Actions Over $25,000.*
Civil Records: Access: In person, online. Visitors must perform in person searches themselves. Court makes copy: $1.00 per page. Required to search: name, years to search. Civil cases indexed by defendant, plaintiff; oncomputer since 1994, prior on index cards. Access to civil records is free at www.courts.mo.gov/casenet/cases/searchCases.do.

Search by litigant name, case # or date. Online records go back to 7/1/2001.
Criminal Records: Access: In person, online. Both court and visitors may perform in person searches. Court makes copy: $1.00 per page. Required to search: name, years to search. Criminal records on computer since 1993, prior on index cards. Online access to criminal records is the same as civil. Online public case records go back to 7/1/2001; judgments to 8/23/1993.
General Information: Public terminal goes back to 1994. No juvenile, mental, paternity (except final judgment), expunged, dismissed, or suspended imposition of sentence records released. Will fax documents for $1.00 per page. Certification fee: $1.00 per cert. Payee: Perry County Circuit Clerk. Personal checks accepted. Prepayment required.

Associate Circuit Court 15 W Ste Marie, #2, Perryville, MO 63775-1399; phone: 573-547-7861; fax: 573-547-9323; hours 8AM-5PM (CST). *Misdemeanor, Civil Actions Under $25,000, Eviction, Small Claims, Probate.*
Civil Records: Access: In person, online. Visitors must perform in person searches themselves. Court makes copy: $1.00 per page. Required to search: name, years to search; also helpful: address. Civil cases indexed by defendant, plaintiff; oncomputer since 1994, prior on index cards. Access to civil records is free at www.courts.mo.gov/casenet/cases/searchCases.do. Search by litigant name, case # or date. Online records go back to 7/1/2001.
Criminal Records: Access: In person, online. Visitors must perform in person searches themselves. Court makes copy: $1.00 per page. Required to search: name, years to search, DOB; also helpful: address, SSN. Criminal records on computer since 1994, prior on index cards. Online access to criminal records is the same as civil. Online public case records go back to 7/1/2001.
General Information: Public terminal goes back to 1994. No juvenile, mental, expunged, dismissed, or suspended imposition of sentence records released. Will fax documents for $1.00 per page. Certification fee: $1.00 per page. Payee: Circuit Court Division 6. Only cashiers checks and money orders accepted. Prepayment required.

Pettis County

Circuit Court PO Box 804, Sedalia, MO 65302-0804; phone: 660-826-0617; fax: 660-826-4520; hours 8AM-5PM (CST). *Felony, Misdemeanor, Civil Actions Over $45,000.*
Note: Also see Associate Circuit Court for add'l civil actions over $45,000.
Civil Records: Access: Phone, fax, mail, in person, online. Both court and visitors may perform in person searches. No search fee. Court makes copy: $1.00 1st page, $.50 ea add'l. Required to search: name, years to search. Civil cases indexed by defendant, plaintiff; onindex books since 9/75, prior on judgment books. Access to civil records is free at www.courts.mo.gov/casenet/cases/searchCases.do. Search by litigant name, case # or date. Online records go back to 4/2001. Mail turnaround time 1-2 days.
Criminal Records: Access: Phone, fax, mail, in person, online. Both court and visitors may perform in person searches. No search fee. Court makes copy: $1.00 1st page, $.50 ea add'l. Required to search: name, years to search, DOB. Criminal records on computer since 1993, prior on index cards since 9/75. Online access to criminal records is the same as civil. Online criminal records go back to 1/1992. Mail turnaround time 1-2 days.
General Information: Public terminal has criminal back to 1992 and civil back to 4/2001; judgments back to 1991. No juvenile, mental, expunged, dismissed, or suspended imposition of sentence records released. Will fax documents $2.50 1st page, $1.50 each add'l. Certification fee: $1.50. Payee:

Pettis County Circuit Clerk. Personal checks accepted. Prepayment and SASE required.

Associate Circuit Court 415 S Ohio, Sedalia, MO 65301; phone: 660-826-4699; probate phone: 660-826-0368; fax: 660-827-8613; hours 8:30AM-5PM (CST). *Misdemeanor, Civil Actions Under $45,000, Eviction, Small Claims, Probate.*
Note: Civil actions over $45,000 may also be filed here.
Civil Records: Access: Phone, fax, mail, in person, online. Both court and visitors may perform in person searches. No search fee. Court makes copy: $1.00 for 1st page; $.50 each add'l. Required to search: name, years to search. Civil cases indexed by defendant, plaintiff; onindex cards since 1975, prior on judgment books; on computer back to 4/2001. Access to civil records is free at www.courts.mo.gov/casenet/cases/searchCases.do. Search by litigant name, case # or date. Online records go back to 4/2001. Mail turnaround time 1-2 weeks.
Criminal Records: Access: Phone, fax, mail, in person, online. Both court and visitors may perform in person searches. No search fee. Court makes copy: $1.00 for 1st page; $.50 each add'l. Required to search: name, years to search, DOB, SSN; on some cases: signed release. Criminal records on computer back to 1993, on index cards from 1975-1993, prior on judgment books. Online access to criminal records is the same as civil. Online criminal records go back to 1/1993. Mail turnaround time 1-2 weeks.
General Information: Public terminal goes back to 1995. No juvenile, mental, expunged, dismissed, or suspended imposition of sentence records released. Will fax documents for free. Certification fee: $1.50 per page. Payee: Circuit Court Division 6. Only cashiers checks and money orders accepted. Prepayment and SASE required.

Probate Court 415 S. Ohio, Sedalia, MO 65301; phone: 660-826-0368; fax: 660-827-8620; hours 8:30AM-5PM (CST). *Probate.*
Note: Access to probate records is available free at http://casenet.osca.state.mo.us/casenet/. At the website, select the judicial district, then search by name, case # or date.

Phelps County

Circuit & Associate Court 200 N Main St, Rolla, MO 65401; phone: 573-458-6210; probate phone: 573-458-6245; probate fax: 573-458-6235; hours 8AM-5PM (CST). *Felony, Misdemeanor, Civil, Small Claims, Eviction, Probate.*
Civil Records: Access: Fax, mail, in person. Visitors must perform in person searches themselves. No search fee. Court makes copy: $.25 per page; same fee for self serve. Required to search: name, years to search. Civil cases indexed by defendant, plaintiff; oncomputer since 1992; prior on books to 1957.
Criminal Records: Access: In person only. Visitors must perform in person searches themselves. Court makes copy: $.25 per page; same fee for self serve. Required to search: names, years to search. Criminal records computerized since 1991, prior indexed on books to 1957. Note: Court recommends criminal searches at MO State Hwy Patrol, 573-526-6288.
General Information: Public terminal goes back to 1992. No juvenile, mental, expunged or dismissed records released. Will fax documents for $1.00 per page. Certification fee: $1.00 per page does include copies. Payee: Circuit Clerk. No out-of-state checks accepted. Prepayment required. Copy fees may be billed. SASE required.

Pike County

Circuit Court 115 W Main, Bowling Green, MO 63334; phone: 573-324-3112; fax: 573-324-3150; hours 8AM-4:30PM (CST). *Felony, Misdemeanor, Civil Actions Over $25,000.*
Civil Records: Access: Mail, in person, online. Both court and visitors may perform in person searches. Court makes copy: $.50 per page; same fee for self

serve. Required to search: name, years to search; also helpful: address. Civil cases indexed by defendant, plaintiff; onindex cards since 1977, prior on books. Participates in the free court record system at www.courts.mo.gov/casenet/base/welcome.do.
Online records go back 4/2002.
Criminal Records: Access: In person, online. Visitors must perform in person searches themselves. Court makes copy: $.50 per page; same fee for self serve. Required to search: name, years to search; also helpful: DOB. Criminal records on index cards since 1977, prior on books. Participates in the free court record system at www.courts.mo.gov/casenet/base/welcome.do.
Online records go back 4/2002. Note: Court recommends criminal searches at MO State Hwy Patrol, 573-526-6288. Mail turnaround time 1-2 days.
General Information: Public terminal goes back to 1992. No juvenile, mental, expunged, dismissed, or suspended imposition of sentence records released. Certification fee: $1.00 per page and $1.00 per doc. Payee: Pike County Circuit Clerk. Personal checks accepted. Prepayment and SASE required.

Associate Circuit Court 115 W Main, Bowling Green, MO 63334; phone: 573-324-5582; fax: 573-324-6297; hours 8AM-4:30PM (CST). *Misdemeanor, Civil Actions Under $25,000, Eviction, Small Claims, Probate.*
Civil Records: Access: Phone, mail, fax, in person, online. Both court and visitors may perform in person searches. No search fee. Court makes copy: $.25 per page. Required to search: name, years to search. Civil cases indexed by defendant, plaintiff; onindex cards since 1979, archived since 1819. Record access fee at www.courts.mo.gov/casenet/cases/searchCases.do. Records go back to 04/03/02.
Criminal Records: Access: In person, online. Visitors must perform in person searches themselves. Court makes copy: $.25 per page. Required to search: name, years to search; also helpful: DOB. Criminal records on index cards since 1979, archived since 1819. Participates in the free statewide Casenet court record system at www.courts.mo.gov/casenet/base/welcome.do.
Online records go back to 04/03/02. Note: Court recommends criminal searches at MO State Hwy Patrol, 573-526-6288. Mail turnaround time 3-7 days.
General Information: Public terminal goes back to 8/2002. No juvenile, mental, expunged, dismissed records released. Certification fee: $1.50 per cert. Payee: Associate Circuit or Probate Court. Business checks accepted. Prepayment and SASE required.

Platte County

Circuit Court 415 Third St #5, Platte City, MO 64079; phone: 816-858-2232; fax: 816-858-3392; hours 8AM-5PM (CST). *Felony, Misdemeanor, Civil Actions Over $25,000.*
Civil Records: Access: Online, in person. Visitors must perform in person searches themselves. Court makes copy: $.25 per page. Required to search: name, years to search. Civil cases indexed by defendant, plaintiff; oncomputer since 10/91. Participates in the free court record system at www.courts.mo.gov/casenet/base/welcome.do.
Criminal Records: Access: Online, in person. Visitors must perform in person searches themselves. Court makes copy: $.25 per page. Required to search: name, years to search, DOB; also helpful: SSN. Criminal records on computer since 10/91. Online access to criminal records is the same as civil.
General Information: Public terminal has criminal back to 10/1991 and civil back to 10/91. The public access terminal provides the same screen as Casenet (the online system). No juvenile, mental, expunged, dismissed, or suspended imposition of sentence records released. Certification fee: $1.00. Payee: Platte County Circuit Clerk. Only cashiers checks and money orders accepted. Prepayment required.

Associate Circuit Court 415 Third St #5, Platte City, MO 64079; phone: 816-858-2232; fax: 816-858-3392; hours 8AM-5PM (CST). *Misdemeanor, Civil Actions Under $25,000, Eviction, Small Claims.*
Civil Records: Access: Online, in person. Visitors must perform in person searches themselves. Court makes copy: $.25 per page. Required to search: name, years to search. Civil cases indexed by defendant, plaintiff; oncomputer since 11/91, prior on index cards. Participates in the free court record system at www.courts.mo.gov/casenet/base/welcome.do.
Criminal Records: Access: Online, in person. Visitors must perform in person searches themselves. Court makes copy: $.25 per page. Required to search: name, years to search, DOB; also helpful: SSN. Criminal records on computer since 11/91, prior on index cards. Online access to criminal records is the same as civil.
General Information: Public use terminal available. No juvenile, mental, expunged, dismissed, or suspended imposition of sentence records released. Certification fee: $1.00. Payee: Circuit Clerk. Only cashiers checks and money orders accepted. Prepayment required.

Probate Court 415 Third St, #95, Platte City, MO 64079; phone: 816-858-3438; probate phone: 816-858-3440; fax: 816-858-3392; hours 8AM-5PM (CST). *Probate.*
Note: Can search by name or case number at http://casenet.osca.state.mo.us/casenet/.

Polk County

Circuit & Associate Court 102 E Broadway, Rm 14, Bolivar, MO 65613; phone: 417-326-4912; fax: 417-326-4194; hours 8AM-5PM (CST). *Felony, Misdemeanor, Civil Actions, Eviction, Small Claims, Probate.*
www.positech.net/~dcourt
The Circuit and Associate courts consolidated 01/03.
Civil Records: Access: In person, online. Visitors must perform in person searches themselves. Court makes copy: $.25 per page. Self serve copy fee: $.10 per page. Required to search: name, years to search. Civil cases indexed by defendant, plaintiff; oncomputer since 1991, prior on card index since 1979. Participates in the free court record system at www.courts.mo.gov/casenet/base/welcome.do.
Criminal Records: Access: In person, online. Visitors must perform in person searches themselves. No search fee. Court makes copy: $.25 per page. Self serve copy fee: $.10 per page. Required to search: name, years to search. Criminal records on computer since 1991, prior on card index since 1979. Online access to criminal records is the same as civil. Note: Court recommends criminal searches at MO State Hwy Patrol, 573-526-6288.
General Information: Public terminal goes back to 2001. No juvenile, mental, expunged, dismissed, or suspended imposition of sentence records released. Certification fee: $2.00 per cert. Payee: Circuit Clerk. Personal checks accepted. Prepayment required.

Pulaski County

Circuit & Associate Circuit Courts 301 Historic Rt 66 E, #202, Waynesville, MO 65583; phone: 573-774-4755; probate phone: 573-774-4784; fax: 573-774-6967; hours 8AM-4:30PM (CST). *Felony, Misdemeanor, Civil, Eviction, Small Claims.*
Civil Records: Access: In person only. Visitors must perform in person searches themselves. Court makes copy: $.25 per page. Required to search: name, years to search; also helpful: address. Civil cases indexed by defendant, plaintiff; oncomputer since 1990, prior on books since 1903.
Criminal Records: Access: In person only. Visitors must perform in person searches themselves. Court makes copy: $.25 per page. Required to search: name, years to search; also helpful: DOB, SSN. Criminal records on computer since 1990, prior on books since 1903. Note: Court recommends criminal searches at MO State Hwy Patrol, 573-526-6288.
General Information: Public terminal goes back to 1991. No juvenile, mental, paternity, expunged, dismissed, or suspended imposition of sentence records released. Will fax specific case files for $2.00 per 5 pages. Certification fee: $2.00 per cert. Payee: Circuit Clerk. Business checks accepted. Prepayment required.

Probate Court 301 Historic 66 East, #316, Waynesville, MO 65583; phone: 573-774-4784; fax: 573-774-6673; hours 8:00AM-4:30PM (CST). *Probate.*

Putnam County

Circuit Court Courthouse Rm 202, Unionville, MO 63565; phone: 660-947-2071; fax: 660-947-2320; hours 8AM-12; 1PM-5PM (CST). *Felony, Misdemeanor, Civil Actions Over $45,000.*
Civil Records: Access: Mail, in person, online. Both court and visitors may perform in person searches. No search fee. Court makes copy: $.25 per page; same fee for self serve. Required to search: name, years to search. Civil cases indexed by defendant, plaintiff; onindex cards since 1848; on computer since 3/00. Participates in the free court record system at www.courts.mo.gov/casenet/base/welcome.do.
Online records go back to 3/29/2000. Mail turnaround time same day.
Criminal Records: Access: In person, online. Visitors must perform in person searches themselves. Court makes copy: $.25 per page; same fee for self serve. Required to search: name, years to search. Criminal records on index cards since 1848; on computer since 3/00. Online access to criminal records is the same as civil. No criminal histories are researched by court staff. The refer requesters to the State Hwy Patrol.
General Information: Public terminal goes back to 1990. No juvenile, mental, expunged, dismissed, or suspended imposition of sentence records released. Will fax documents for $1.00 for 1st page; $50 each add'l; plus copy fee of $.25 per page. Certification fee: $1.00. Payee: Circuit Clerk. Business checks accepted. Prepayment and SASE required.

Associate Circuit Court Courthouse Rm 101, 1601 W Main, Unionville, MO 63565; phone: 660-947-2117; fax: 660-947-7348; hours 9AM-5PM (CST). *Misdemeanor, Civil Actions Under $45,000, Eviction, Small Claims, Probate.*
Civil Records: Access: Mail, in person, online. Both court and visitors may perform in person searches. No search fee. Court makes copy: $1.00 per page; same fee for self serve. Required to search: name, years to search. Civil cases indexed by defendant, plaintiff; oncomputer since 1994, prior on books. Participates in the free court record system at www.courts.mo.gov/casenet/base/welcome.do.
Online records go back to 3/29/2000. Mail turnaround time as long as 30-60 days.
Criminal Records: Access: Mail, in person, online. Both court and visitors may perform in person searches. No search fee. Court makes copy: $1.00 per page; same fee for self serve. Required to search: name, years to search, DOB, SSN. Criminal records on computer since 1994, prior on books. Online access to criminal records is the same as civil. Mail turnaround time as long as 30-60 days.
General Information: Public use terminal available. No mental, expunged, dismissed, or suspended imposition of sentence records released. Will fax documents. Certification fee: $1.50. Payee: Associate Circuit Court. Only cashiers checks and money orders accepted. Prepayment and SASE required.

Ralls County

Circuit Court PO Box 444, New London, MO 63459; phone: 573-985-5633; fax: 573-985-5630; hours 8:30AM-4:30PM (CST). *Felony, Misdemeanor, Civil Actions Over $25,000.*
Civil Records: Access: Mail, in person. Both court and visitors may perform in person searches. No

search fee. Court makes copy: $.25 per page; same fee for self serve. Required to search: name, years to search, DOB, SSN and signed release. Civil cases indexed by defendant, plaintiff; onindex cards since 1976, prior on books. Mail turnaround time varies.

Criminal Records: Access: Mail, in person. Only the court performs in person searches. No search fee. Court makes copy: $.25 per page; same fee for self serve. Required to search: name, years to search, signed release and SSN. Criminal records on index cards since 1976, prior on books. Mail turnaround time varies.

General Information: Public terminal has only civil records back to 1990. No juvenile, mental, expunged, dismissed, or suspended imposition of sentence records released. Certification fee: $1.00. Payee: Ralls County Circuit Clerk. Personal checks accepted. Prepayment and SASE required.

Associate Circuit Court PO Box 466, 311 S Main, New London, MO 63459; phone: 573-985-5641; fax: 573-985-3446; hours 8:00AM-4:30PM (CST). *Misdemeanor, Civil Actions Under $25,000, Eviction, Small Claims, Probate.*

Civil Records: Access: Phone, mail, fax, in person. Both court and visitors may perform in person searches. No search fee. Court makes copy: $.25 per page (subject to change). Required to search: name, years to search. Civil cases indexed by defendant, plaintiff; onindex cards since 1979, prior on record books. Mail turnaround time 1-2 weeks; genealogy turnaround time varies.

Criminal Records: Access: Phone, mail, fax, in person. Both court and visitors may perform in person searches. No search fee. Court makes copy: $.25 per page, subject to change. Required to search: name, years to search, signed release. Criminal records on index cards since 1979, prior on record books. Note: Court will search only if not busy and will only search back 7 years for criminal records. Mail turnaround time 1-2 weeks; genealogy turnaround time varies.

General Information: Public terminal has only civil records. No juvenile, mental, expunged, dismissed, or suspended imposition of sentence records released. Certification fee: $1.50. Payee: Associate Circuit Court. Personal checks accepted. Prepayment and SASE required.

Randolph County

Circuit & Associate Court 223 N Williams, Moberly, MO 65270; phone: 660-263-4474; criminal fax: 660-263-5966; civil fax: 660-263-1007; hours 8AM-4:30PM (CST). *Felony, Misdemeanor, Civil Actions, Eviction, Small Claims, Probate.*

Civil Records: Access: Fax, mail, in person, online. Both court and visitors may perform in person searches. No search fee. Court makes copy: $.25 per page. Required to search: name, years to search, address. Civil cases indexed by defendant, plaintiff; onindex cards since 1975, prior on record books. Participates in the free court record system at www.courts.mo.gov/casenet/base/welcome.do. Mail turnaround time 1 week.

Criminal Records: Access: Fax, mail, in person, online. Both court and visitors may perform in person searches. No search fee. Court makes copy: $.25 per page. Required to search: name, years to search, address, DOB; also helpful: SSN. Criminal records on computer since 1994, prior on index books. Online access to criminal records is the same as civil. Mail turnaround time 1 week.

General Information: Public use terminal available. No juvenile, mental, expunged, dismissed, or suspended imposition of sentence records released. Will fax documents for $4.00 per page. Advanced payment required. Certification fee: $1.50. Payee: Randolph County Circuit Clerk. No personal checks accepted. Prepayment and SASE required.

Ray County

Circuit Court PO Box 594, Richmond, MO 64085; phone: 816-776-3377; fax: 816-776-6016; hours 8AM-4PM (CST). *Felony, Misdemeanor, Civil Actions Over $25,000.*

www.osca.state.mo.us/circuits/index.nsf/County+/+Ray

Civil Records: Access: Phone, fax, mail, in person, online. Both court and visitors may perform in person searches. No search fee. Court makes copy: $.25 per page. Required to search: name, years to search. Civil cases indexed by defendant, plaintiff; onindex cards since 1977, prior on judgment books. Participates in the free court record system at www.courts.mo.gov/casenet/base/welcome.do. Online records only go back to 2001.

Criminal Records: Access: In person, online. Both court and visitors may perform in person searches. No search fee. Court makes copy: $.25 per page. Required to search: name, years to search; also helpful: DOB, SSN. Criminal records on index cards since 1977, prior on judgment books. Online access to criminal records is the same as civil. Note: Court recommends criminal searches at MO State Hwy Patrol, 573-526-6288. Mail turnaround time varies.

General Information: Public terminal goes back to 12/2001. No juvenile, mental, expunged, dismissed, or suspended imposition of sentence records released. Fee to fax documents is $1.00 per page. Certification fee: $1.50 per cert. Payee: Ray County Circuit Clerk. Business checks accepted. Prepayment and SASE required.

Associate Circuit Court Ray County Courthouse, 100 W Main St, Richmond, MO 64085-1710; phone: 816-776-2335; criminal fax: 816-776-2185; same fax for civil/probate; hours 8AM-4PM (CST). *Misdemeanor, Civil Actions Under $25,000, Eviction, Small Claims, Probate.*

Note: Probate records are in a separate index.

Civil Records: Access: Fax, mail, in person, online. Both court and visitors may perform in person searches. No search fee. Court makes copy: $.20 per page; same fee for self serve. Required to search: name; also helpful: years to search. Civil cases indexed by defendant, plaintiff; onindex cards since 1979, prior on books. Participates in the free court record system at www.courts.mo.gov/casenet/base/welcome.do.

Criminal Records: Access: Fax, mail, in person, online. Both court and visitors may perform in person searches. No search fee. Court makes copy: $.20 per page; same fee for self serve. Required to search: name, DOB; also helpful: years to search. Criminal records on index cards since 1979, prior on books. Online access to criminal records is the same as civil.

General Information: Public terminal goes back to 2001. (Public terminal located in main Circuit Court Clerk office.) No juvenile, mental, expunged, dismissed, or suspended imposition of sentence records released. No fee to fax documents. Certification fee: $1.50 to certify and $1.00 per page. Payee: Associate Circuit Court. Business checks accepted. Prepayment required.

Reynolds County

Circuit Court PO Box 76, Centerville, MO 63633; phone: 573-648-2494 x34; fax: 573-648-2503; hours 8AM-4PM (CST). *Felony, Civil Actions Over $45,000.*

Civil Records: Access: Phone, mail, in person, online. Both court and visitors may perform in person searches. No search fee. Court makes copy: $1.00 per page. Self serve copy fee: $.50 per page. Required to search: name, years to search. Civil cases indexed by defendant, plaintiff; oncards and books, archived since 1872. Access to civil records is free at www.courts.mo.gov/casenet/cases/searchCases.do. Search by litigant name, case number or date. Mail turnaround time 2 days.

Criminal Records: Access: Phone, mail, in person, online. Both court and visitors may perform in person searches. No search fee. Court makes copy: $1.00 per page. Self serve copy fee: $.50 per page. Required to search: name, years to search, DOB; also helpful: SSN, sex, signed release. Criminal records on cards and books, archived since 1872. Online access to criminal records is the same as civil. Mail turnaround time 2 days.

General Information: Public terminal goes back to 2001. No juvenile, mental, expunged, dismissed, or suspended imposition of sentence records released. Fee to fax documents is $2.00 per document plus $1.00 per page. Certification fee: $2.00 per document. Payee: Randy L Cowin. Personal checks accepted. Prepayment and SASE required.

Associate Circuit Court PO Box 39, Centerville, MO 63633; phone: 573-648-2494 X31; probate phone: x35; criminal fax: 573-648-2503; same fax for civil/probate; hours 8AM-4PM (CST). *Misdemeanor, Civil Actions Under $45,000, Eviction, Small Claims, Probate.*

Civil Records: Access: Phone, mail, in person, online. Both court and visitors may perform in person searches. No search fee. Court makes copy: $1.00 per page. Required to search: name, years to search. Civil cases indexed by defendant, plaintiff; onindex cards and files (probate in books); on computer back to 2000. Participates in the free court record system at www.courts.mo.gov/casenet/base/welcome.do.

Criminal Records: Access: In person, online. Both court and visitors may perform in person searches. No search fee. Court makes copy: $1.00 per page. Required to search: name, years to search. Criminal records on index cards and files back to early 1970's; on computer back to 2000. Online access to criminal records is the same as civil. Note: Court recommends criminal searches at MO State Hwy Patrol, 573-526-6288. Mail turnaround time 1 day; phone turnaround is same day.

General Information: Public terminal goes back to 2001. No juvenile, mental, expunged, dismissed, or suspended imposition of sentence records released. Certification fee: $2.00. Payee: Associate Circuit Court. Personal checks accepted. Prepayment required.

Ripley County

Circuit and Associate Court 100 Courthouse Sq, Doniphan, MO 63935; phone: 573-996-2818, 573-996-2013; probate phone: 573-996-2013; fax: 573-996-7826; hours 7:30AM-4PM (CST). *Felony, Misdemeanor, Civil Actions, Eviction, Small Claims, Probate.*

Note: This court combined in 2004. 2nd fax number is 573-996-5014. Probate is a separate index at this same address.

Civil Records: Access: Phone, fax, mail, in person. Both court and visitors may perform in person searches. Search fee: $5.00 per name. Court makes copy: $1.00 per page. Self serve copy fee: $.25 per page. Required to search: name, years to search. Civil cases indexed by defendant, plaintiff; oncards and books since 1976, archived since 1850s. Mail turnaround time same day.

Criminal Records: Access: Fax, mail, in person. Both court and visitors may perform in person searches. Search fee: $5.00 per name. Court makes copy: $1.00 per page. Self serve copy fee: $.25 per page. Required to search: name, years to search, DOB. Criminal records on cards and books since 1976, archived since 1850s. Mail turnaround time same day.

General Information: Public terminal has criminal back to 2003 and civil back to 1993. No juvenile, mental, expunged, dismissed, or suspended imposition of sentence records released. Will fax documents for $5.00 per name. Certification fee: $2.00 if done by in-person searcher. Cert fee included in search fee. Payee: Circuit Clerk. Personal checks accepted. Prepayment and SASE required.

Associate Circuit Court 100 Court Sq, Courthouse, Doniphan, MO 63935; phone: 573-996-2013; fax: 573-996-5014; hours 8AM-4PM (CST). *Misdemeanor, Civil Actions Under $25,000, Eviction, Small Claims, Probate.*
Note: This court combined with the Circuit Court in 2004. See Circuit Court for more information.

Saline County

Circuit Court PO Box 597, 101 E Main St #205, Marshall, MO 65340; phone: 660-886-2300; fax: 660-831-5360; hours 8:00AM-4:30PM (CST). *Felony, Misdemeanor, Civil Actions Over $25,000.*
Civil Records: Access: Mail, in person, online. Visitors must perform in person searches themselves. Court makes copy: $.25 per page; same fee for self serve. Required to search: name, years to search. Civil cases indexed by defendant, plaintiff; onindex cards since 1974, prior on books since 1820. Records free on state online court record system at www.courts.mo.gov/casenet/base/welcome.do. Records only go back to 4/2002.
Criminal Records: Access: In person, online. Visitors must perform in person searches themselves. No search fee. Court makes copy: $.25 per page; same fee for self serve. Required to search: name, years to search. Criminal records on index cards since 1974, prior on books since 1820. Records free on state online court record system at www.courts.mo.gov/casenet/base/welcome.do. Records only go back to 4/2002. Note: Court recommends criminal searches at MO State Hwy Patrol, 573-526-6288.
General Information: Public terminal goes back to 1985. No juvenile, mental, expunged, dismissed, or suspended imposition of sentence records released. Certification fee: $1.50 per cert. Payee: Saline County Circuit Court. Personal checks accepted. Prepayment required.

Associate Circuit Court PO Box 751, Marshall, MO 65340; phone: 660-886-6988; probate phone: 660-886-8808; fax: 660-886-2919; hours 8AM-4:30PM (CST). *Misdemeanor, Civil Actions Under $25,000, Eviction, Small Claims.*
Civil Records: Access: Phone, mail, in person, online. Only the court performs in person searches. No search fee. No copy fee. Required to search: name, years to search. Civil cases indexed by defendant, plaintiff; onindex cards since 1979, prior on books. Participates in the free statewide Casenet court record system at www.courts.mo.gov/casenet/base/welcome.do. Mail turnaround time 1-2 days.
Criminal Records: Access: Phone, mail, in person, online. Only the court performs in person searches. No search fee. No copy fee. Required to search: name, years to search. Criminal records on computer since 1993, prior on cards and books. Participates in the free statewide Casenet court record system at www.courts.mo.gov/casenet/base/welcome.do. Mail turnaround time 1-2 days.
General Information: No public access terminal. No juvenile, mental, expunged, dismissed, or suspended imposition of sentence records released. Will fax documents, no fax fee. No certification fee . SASE required.

Schuyler County

Circuit Court PO Box 186, Lancaster, MO 63548; phone: 660-457-3784; fax: 660-457-3016; hours 8AM-4PM (CST). *Felony, Misdemeanor, Civil Actions Over $45,000.*
Note: Misdemeanor and probate phone is 660-457-3755.
Civil Records: Access: Mail, in person, online. Both court and visitors may perform in person searches. Search fee: $14.00 per name. Court makes copy: $1.00 per page; same fee for self serve. Required to search: name, years to search. Civil cases indexed by defendant, plaintiff; onindex cards & books. Participates in the free court record system at www.courts.mo.gov/casenet/base/welcome.do.

Records from 9/19/01 forward. Mail turnaround time 1-2 days.
Criminal Records: Access: Mail, in person, online. Both court and visitors may perform in person searches. Search fee: $14.00 per name, Court makes copy: $1.00 per page; same fee for self serve. Required to search: name, years to search. Criminal records on index cards & books. Participates in the free court record system at www.courts.mo.gov/casenet/base/welcome.do. Records go back to 9/19/01. Mail turnaround time 1-2 days.
General Information: Public terminal goes back to 9/19/01. No juvenile, mental, expunged, dismissed, or suspended imposition of sentence records released. Will fax documents for $2.00 plus $1.00 each page. Certification fee: $1.00. Payee: Schuyler County Circuit Clerk. Personal checks accepted. Prepayment and SASE required.

Associate Circuit Court Box 158, Lancaster, MO 63548; phone: 660-457-3755; fax: 660-457-3016; hours 8:00AM-4PM (CST). *Misdemeanor, Civil Actions Under $45,000, Eviction, Small Claims, Probate.*
Civil Records: Access: Mail, fax, in person, online. Both court and visitors may perform in person searches. Search fee: $5.00 per name. Court makes copy: $1.00 per page. Required to search: name, years to search. Civil cases indexed by defendant, plaintiff; onindex cards since 1976; computerized records go back to 1992. Participates in the free statewide Casenet court record system at www.courts.mo.gov/casenet/base/welcome.do. Online records go back to 09/19/01. Mail turnaround time 4 days.
Criminal Records: Access: Mail, fax, in person, online. Both court and visitors may perform in person searches. Search fee: $5.00 per name. Court makes copy: $1.00 per page. Required to search: name, years to search, SSN, DOB. Criminal records on computer since 5/92, prior on index cards. Free access to statewide Casenet court record system at www.courts.mo.gov/casenet/base/welcome.do. Online records go back to 09/19/01. Mail turnaround time 4 days.
General Information: Public use terminal available. No juvenile, mental, expunged, dismissed, or suspended imposition of sentence records released. Certification fee: $1.50. Payee: Associate Circuit Court. Business checks accepted. Prepayment and SASE required.

Scotland County

Circuit Court 117 S Market St #106, Memphis, MO 63555; phone: 660-465-8605; fax: 660-465-8673; hours 8AM-4PM (CST). *Felony, Civil Actions Over $25,000.*
Civil Records: Access: Mail, in person, online. Both court and visitors may perform in person searches. No search fee. Court makes copy: $.25 per page. Required to search: name, years to search. Civil cases indexed by defendant, plaintiff; onindex cards since 1979, prior on books. Computerized records go back to 2001. Participates in the free court record system at www.courts.mo.gov/casenet/base/welcome.do. Records from 9/19/01 forward. Mail turnaround time same day.
Criminal Records: Access: Mail, in person, online. Both court and visitors may perform in person searches. No search fee. Court makes copy: $.25 per page. Required to search: name, years to search, DOB, signed release; also helpful: address. Criminal records on index cards since 1979, prior on books. Computerized records go back to 9/2001. Participates in the free court record system at www.courts.mo.gov/casenet/base/welcome.do. Records go back to 9/19/01 forward. Mail turnaround time same day.
General Information: Public terminal goes back to 9/19/2001. No juvenile, mental, expunged, dismissed, or suspended imposition of sentence records released. Will fax documents for $1.00 per page. Certification fee: $1.50 per certification. Payee: Scotland County

Circuit Clerk. Personal checks accepted. Prepayment and SASE required.

Associate Circuit Court Courthouse, Rm 102, 117 S Market, Memphis, MO 63555; phone: 660-465-2404; fax: 660-465-8673; hours 8AM-4:30PM (CST). *Misdemeanor, Civil Actions Under $25,000, Eviction, Small Claims, Probate.*
Civil Records: Access: Phone, mail, fax, in person, online. Both court and visitors may perform in person searches. No search fee. Court makes copy: $.10 per page. Required to search: name, years to search. Civil cases indexed by defendant, plaintiff; oncomputer since 1993, prior on cards and books to 1841. Participates in the free statewide Casenet court record system at www.courts.mo.gov/casenet/base/welcome.do. Online records go back to 09/19/01. Mail turnaround time 7 days.
Criminal Records: Access: Phone, mail, in person, online. Both court and visitors may perform in person searches. No search fee. Court makes copy: $.10 per page. Required to search: name, years to search. Criminal records on computer since 1993, prior on cards and books to 1841. Participates in the free statewide Casenet court record system at www.courts.mo.gov/casenet/base/welcome.do. Online records go back to 09/19/01. Mail turnaround time ASAP.
General Information: Public terminal goes back to 1993. (Public terminal located in main Circuit Court Clerk office.) No juvenile, mental, expunged, dismissed, or suspended imposition of sentence records released. Fee to fax documents is 1.00 per page. Certification fee: $1.50 plus $1.00 per page. Payee: Info provided on bill. Personal checks accepted. Prepayment and SASE required.

Scott County

Circuit Court PO Box 277, Benton, MO 63736; phone: 573-545-3596; fax: 573-545-3597; hours 8:00AM-5PM (CST). *Felony, Misdemeanor, Civil Actions Over $25,000.*
Civil Records: Access: In person, online. Visitors must perform in person searches themselves. Court makes copy: $1.00 for first page, $.25 each add'l. Required to search: name, years to search. Civil cases indexed by defendant, plaintiff; oncomputer since 1991, prior on index cards and books. Access to civil records is free at www.courts.mo.gov/casenet/cases/searchCases.do. Search by litigant name, case # or date. Online records go back to 6/15/2001.
Criminal Records: Access: In person, online. Visitors must perform in person searches themselves. No search fee. Court makes copy: $1.00 for first page, $.25 each add'l. Required to search: name, years to search, DOB. Criminal records on computer since 1991, prior on index cards and books. Online access to criminal records is the same as civil. Note: Court recommends criminal searches at MO State Hwy Patrol, 573-526-6288.
General Information: Public use terminal available. No juvenile, mental, expunged, dismissed, or suspended imposition of sentence records released. Certification fee: $3.00. Payee: Pam Glastetter, Circuit Clerk. Personal checks accepted. Prepayment required.

Associate Circuit Court PO Box 249, Benton, MO 63736; phone: 573-545-3576; fax: 573-545-4231; hours 8AM-N, 1-5PM (CST). *Misdemeanor, Civil Actions Under $45,000, Eviction, Small Claims, Probate.*
Civil Records: Access: Phone, mail, in person, online. Visitors must perform in person searches themselves. No search fee. Court makes copy: $1.00 plus $.25 per page. Required to search: name, years to search. Civil cases indexed by defendant, plaintiff; onindex cards and books. Access to civil records is free at www.courts.mo.gov/casenet/cases/searchCases.do. Search by litigant name, case # or date. Online

records go back to 6/15/2001. Mail turnaround time varies.

Criminal Records: Access: In person, online. Visitors must perform in person searches themselves. Court makes copy: $1.00 plus $.25 per page. Required to search: name, years to search. Criminal records on index cards and books. Online access to criminal records is the same as civil. Mail turnaround time varies.

General Information: Public terminal goes back to 1975. (Call 573-545-3596 for a public terminal lookup.) No juvenile, mental, expunged, dismissed, or suspended imposition of sentence records released. No certification fee . SASE required.

Shannon County

Circuit Court PO Box 148, Courthouse, South Side Entrance, Eminence, MO 65466; phone: 573-226-3315; fax: 573-226-5321; hours 8AM-4:30PM (CST). *Felony, Misdemeanor, Civil Actions Over $45,000.*

Note: Associate court records will soon be co-located with this Circuit Court.

Civil Records: Access: Mail, in person, online. Both court and visitors may perform in person searches. No search fee. Court makes copy: $.25 per page. Required to search: name, years to search. Civil cases indexed by defendant, plaintiff; onindex cards and books. Record index on computer back to 1980. Participates in the free court record system at www.courts.mo.gov/casenet/base/welcome.do. Online records go back to 1992. Mail turnaround time 1 week.

Criminal Records: Access: Mail, in person, online. Both court and visitors may perform in person searches. No search fee. Court makes copy: $.25 per page. Required to search: name, years to search, offense. Criminal records on index cards and books. Record index on computer back to 1980. Online access to criminal records is the same as civil. Mail turnaround time 1 week.

General Information: Public terminal goes back to 4/2000. No juvenile, mental, expunged, dismissed, or suspended imposition of sentence records released. Fee to fax documents is $2.00 per page. Certification fee: $2.00 per cert. Payee: Shannon County Circuit Clerk. Personal checks accepted. Prepayment and SASE required.

Associate Circuit Court PO Box 845, Eminence, MO 65466-0845; phone: 573-226-5515; fax: 573-226-3239; probate fax: same; hours 8AM-4:30PM (CST). *Misdemeanor, Civil Actions Under $45,000, Eviction, Small Claims, Probate.*

Note: Associate court records will soon be co-located with the Circuit Court.

Civil Records: Access: Mail, fax, in person, online. Only the court performs in person searches. Search fee: $10.00 per name. Court makes copy: $.25 per page; same fee for self serve. Required to search: name, years to search. Civil cases indexed by defendant, plaintiff; onindex cards since 1979, archived since 1881, on computer back to 2000. Participates in the free court record system at www.courts.mo.gov/casenet/base/welcome.do. Online records go back to 1992. Mail turnaround time 1 week.

Criminal Records: Access: Mail, fax, in person, online. Only the court performs in person searches. Search fee: $10.00 per name. Court makes copy: $.25 per page; same fee for self serve. Required to search: name, years to search, DOB; also helpful: SSN. Criminal records on computer since 1992; prior on index cards to 1979. Online access to criminal records is the same as civil. Mail turnaround time 1 week.

General Information: No public access terminal. No juvenile, mental, expunged, dismissed, or suspended imposition of sentence records released. Fee to fax documents is $3.00 per page. Certification fee: $3.00. Payee: Associate Circuit Court. Personal checks accepted. Prepayment and SASE required.

Shelby County

Circuit Court PO Box 176, Shelbyville, MO 63469; phone: 573-633-2151; fax: 573-633-1004; hours 8AM-4:30PM (CST). *Felony, Misdemeanor, Civil Actions Over $45,000.*

Civil Records: Access: Mail, fax, in person, online. Only the court performs in person searches. No search fee. Court makes copy: $.25 per page. Self serve copy fee: $.10 per page. Required to search: name, years to search. Civil cases indexed by defendant, plaintiff; onindex cards since 1975, prior on books since 1835. Participates in the free court record system at www.courts.mo.gov/casenet/base/welcome.do. Online civil records go back to 4/17/2000. Mail turnaround time 1 day.

Criminal Records: Access: Mail, fax, in person, online. Only the court performs in person searches. No search fee. Court makes copy: $.25 per page. Self serve copy fee: $.10 per page. Required to search: name, years to search. Criminal records on index cards since 1975, prior on books since 1835. Online access to criminal records is the same as civil. Online criminal records go back to 4/17/2000. Mail turnaround time 1 day.

General Information: No public access terminal. No juvenile, mental, expunged, dismissed, or suspended imposition of sentence records released. Fee to fax documents is $3.00 per document. Certification fee: $2.00. Payee: Shelby County Circuit Clerk. Personal checks accepted. Prepayment and SASE required.

Associate Circuit Court PO Box 206, Shelbyville, MO 63469; phone: 573-633-2151, 573-633-2251; fax: 573-633-2142; hours 8AM-4:30PM (CST). *Misdemeanor, Civil Actions Under $25,000, Eviction, Small Claims, Probate.*

Civil Records: Access: Phone, fax, mail, in person, online. Both court and visitors may perform in person searches. No search fee. Court makes copy: $.25 per page. Required to search: name, years to search. Civil cases indexed by defendant, plaintiff; onindex cards to 1990, archived from 1845. Participates in the free court record system at www.courts.mo.gov/casenet/base/welcome.do. Online civil records go back to 4/17/2000. Mail turnaround time 2 weeks.

Criminal Records: Access: Phone, fax, mail, in person, online. Both court and visitors may perform in person searches. No search fee. Court makes copy: $.25 per page. Required to search: name, years to search, DOB. Criminal records on index cards to 1980, archived from 1845. Online access to criminal records is the same as civil. Online criminal records go back to 4/17/2000. Mail turnaround time 2 weeks.

General Information: Public terminal goes back to 2003. No juvenile, mental, expunged, dismissed, or suspended imposition of sentence records released. No fee to fax documents. Certification fee: $1.50 per cert. Payee: Probate Court or Associate Circuit Court. Personal checks accepted. Prepayment required.

St. Charles County

Circuit & Associate Court 300 N 2nd St, St. Charles, MO 63301; phone: 636-949-7900 x3098; criminal phone: 636-949-7380; probate phone: 636-949-7900 x3086; fax: 636-949-7390; probate fax: 636-949-3070; hours 8:30AM-5PM (CST). *Felony, Misdemeanor, Civil Actions, Eviction, Small Claims, Probate.*

Note: The Circuit and Associate courts consolidated as of 01/03. Traffic Court is reached at 636-949-7385.

Civil Records: Access: Mail, online, in person. Both court and visitors may perform in person searches. Court makes copy: $.10 per page. Required to search: name, years to search. Civil cases indexed by defendant, plaintiff; onindex cards since 1971, prior on books; judgment records (A-M) on computer since 1987. Participates in the free court record system at www.courts.mo.gov/casenet/base/welcome.do. Online civil records go back to 1982.

Criminal Records: Access: Online, in person. Visitors must perform in person searches themselves. Court makes copy: $.10 per page. Required to search: name, years to search; also helpful: DOB. Criminal records on index cards since 1971, prior on books; judgment records (A-M) on computer since 1987. Online access to criminal records is the same as civil. Online criminal records go back to 10/1992. The court will not perform a criminal record check and recommends criminal searches at MO State Hwy Patrol, 573-526-6288.

General Information: Public use terminal available. No juvenile, mental, expunged, dismissed, or suspended imposition of sentence records released. Certification fee: $1.00. Payee: St. Charles Circuit Clerk. Personal checks accepted. Prepayment and SASE required.

St. Clair County

Circuit & Associate Circuit Courts PO Box 493, Osceola, MO 64776; phone: 417-646-2226; fax: 417-646-2401; hours 8AM-4:30PM (CST). *Felony, Misdemeanor, Civil, Eviction, Small Claims, Probate.*

Civil Records: Access: Mail, in person, online. Both court and visitors may perform in person searches. Search fee: $2.00 per name. Court makes copy: $1.00 per page. Required to search: name, years to search. Civil cases indexed by defendant, plaintiff. Civil judgment records on computer since 1991, on index cards since 1980, prior records on index books. Participates in the free court record system at www.courts.mo.gov/casenet/base/welcome.do. Mail turnaround time 1-2 days.

Criminal Records: Access: Mail, in person, online. Both court and visitors may perform in person searches. Search fee: $2.00 per name. Court makes copy: $1.00 per page. Required to search: name, years to search, DOB. Criminal records on computer since 1991, on index cards since 1980, prior records on index books. Free free court record access at www.courts.mo.gov/casenet/base/welcome.do. Mail turnaround time 1-2 days.

General Information: Public terminal goes back to 8/2003; Casenet from 1991. No juvenile, mental, expunged, dismissed, or suspended imposition of sentence records released. Will fax documents. Certification fee: $.50 per document. Payee: St Clair County Circuit Clerk. Personal checks accepted. Prepayment and SASE required.

St. Francois County

Circuit Court - Division I & II 1 N Washington, Rm 303, Farmington, MO 63640; phone: 573-756-4551; fax: 573-756-3733; hours 8AM-5PM (CST). *Felony, Civil Actions Over $25,000.*

www.sfcgov.org

Civil Records: Access: Fax, mail, in person, online. Both court and visitors may perform in person searches. No search fee. Court makes copy: $.25 per page. Self serve copy fee: $.25 per page. Required to search: name, years to search. Civil cases indexed by defendant, plaintiff; oncomputer since 6/90, on microfiche since 1970, archived since 1821. Participates in the free court record system at www.courts.mo.gov/casenet/base/welcome.do. Records from 11/01/00 forward.

Criminal Records: Access: In person, online. Both court and visitors may perform in person searches. No search fee. Court makes copy: $.25 per page. Self serve copy fee: $.25 per page. Required to search: name, years to search; also helpful: DOB, SSN. Criminal records on computer since 3/1/93. Participates in the free court record system at www.courts.mo.gov/casenet/base/welcome.do. Records go back to 11/01/00 forward. Note: Court recommends criminal searches at MO State Hwy Patrol, 573-526-6288. Mail turnaround time 1-2 weeks.

General Information: Public terminal has criminal back to 3/1993 and civil back to 6/1990. No juvenile, mental, expunged, dismissed, or suspended imposition of sentence records released. Will not fax documents. Attorney copy fee is $1.00 per page. Certification fee: $1.50 per document. Payee: Clerk of Circuit Court. Business checks accepted. Prepayment and SASE required.

Associate Circuit Court County Courthouse, 2nd Fl, 1 N Washington, Rm 202, Farmington, MO 63640; phone: 573-756-5755; probate phone: x42; civil/criminal fax: 573-756-8173; probate fax: 573-756-6602; hours 8AM-5PM (CST). *Misdemeanor, Civil Actions Under $25,000, Eviction, Small Claims, Probate.*
Note: Probate is located in Rm 201.
Civil Records: Access: Phone, in person, online. Only the court performs in person searches. No search fee. Court makes copy: $.30 per page. Required to search: name, years to search. Civil cases indexed by defendant, plaintiff; onindex cards since 1979; on computer back to 1990. Participates in the free statewide Casenet court record system at www.courts.mo.gov/casenet/base/welcome.do.
Online records go back to 1992, probate records to 11/06/00.
Criminal Records: Access: In person, online. Visitors must perform in person searches themselves. No search fee. Court makes copy: $.30 per page. Required to search: name, years to search. Criminal records on computer back to 1990; other records go back to 1980. Participates in the free statewide Casenet court record system at www.courts.mo.gov/casenet/base/welcome.do.
Online records go back to 1992. Note: Court recommends criminal searches at MO State Hwy Patrol, 573-526-6288.
General Information: No public access terminal. No juvenile, mental, expunged, dismissed, or suspended imposition of sentence records released. No certification fee . Business checks accepted.

St. Louis County

Circuit Court of St. Louis County 7900 Carondelet, Clayton, MO 63105-1766; phone: 314-615-8029; fax: 314-615-8739; hours 8AM-5PM (CST). *Felony, Misdemeanor, Civil.*
www.stlouisco.com/circuitcourt
Civil Records: Access: Phone, fax, mail, in person. Both court and visitors may perform in person searches. No search fee. Court makes copy: $.30 per page. Required to search: name, years to search; also helpful: address. Civil cases indexed by defendant, plaintiff; oncomputer back to 1978, prior on index cards. Case files archived for 25 years. Mail turnaround time up to 3 days.
Criminal Records: Access: Phone, fax, mail, in person. Both court and visitors may perform in person searches. No search fee. Court makes copy: $.30 per page. Required to search: name, years to search, DOB; also helpful: address, SSN. Criminal records on computer back to 1990; prior on index cards. Case files archived for 25 years. Mail turnaround time up to 3 days.
General Information: Public use terminal available. No juvenile, paternity, mental, expunged, dismissed, or suspended imposition of sentence records released. Will not fax documents. Certification fee: $1.50. Payee: Circuit Clerk. Personal checks accepted. Prepayment required.

Associate Circuit - Civil Division 7900 Carondolet, Clayton, MO 63105; phone: 314-615-8090; probate phone: 314-615-2629; fax: 314-615-2689; hours 8AM-5PM (CST). *Civil Actions Under $25,000, Eviction, Small Claims, Probate.*
Note: The small claims court can be reached at 314-615-8091.
Civil Records: Access: Phone, mail, in person, online. Both court and visitors may perform in person searches. No search fee. Court makes copy: $.30 per page. Required to search: name, years to search. Civil cases indexed by defendant, plaintiff; oncomputer since 1986, prior on cards. Probate records are free on the state online court record

system at www.courts.mo.gov/casenet/base/welcome.do. Mail turnaround time 1 week.
 Mail turnaround time 1 week.
General Information: Public terminal has only civil records back to 1986. No juvenile, mental, expunged, dismissed, paternity, suspended imposition of sentence records released. Certification fee: $1.50 per cert includes copies. Payee: Circuit Clerk-Civil Division. Personal checks accepted. Prepayment and SASE required.

Associate Circuit Court - Criminal Division 7900 Carondolet Av, Clayton, MO 63105; phone: 314-615-2675; fax: 314-615-2689; hours 8AM-5PM (CST). *Misdemeanor.*
www.stlouisco.com/circuitcourt
Criminal Records: Access: Phone, mail, fax, in person. Both court and visitors may perform in person searches. No search fee. Court makes copy: $.30 per page. Required to search: name, years to search, DOB, offense, date of offense. Criminal records on computer back to 1990, prior on index cards. Permanent records on microfiche since 1978, earlier in books. Case files archived for 25 years. Mail turnaround time varies.
General Information: Public terminal has only criminal records back to 1986. No juvenile, mental, expunged, dismissed, or suspended imposition of sentence records released. Will not fax documents. Certification fee: $1.50. Payee: Circuit Clerk. Personal checks accepted. Prepayment and SASE required.

St. Louis City

Circuit & Associate Circuit Courts - Civil 10 N Tucker, Civil Courts Bldg, St Louis, MO 63101; phone: 314-622-4405; probate phone: 314-622-4300; fax: 314-622-4537; hours 8:00AM-5:00PM (CST). *Civil, Eviction, Small Claims, Probate.*
www.stlcitycircuitcourt.com
Note: Small Claims telephone number is 314-622-3788. Probate is located on the 10th Fl.
Civil Records: Access: Mail, online, in person. Both court and visitors may perform in person searches. No search fee. Court makes copy: $.30 per page. Required to search: name, years to search. Civil cases indexed by defendant, plaintiff; oncomputer since 1/80, on index cards since early 1800s. Online access to civil records is free at https://www.stlcitycircuitcourt.com/SSL/getCivil.cfm. Remote access is also through MoBar Net and is open only to attorneys. Call 314-535-1950 for information. Also, probate records are free online at www.courts.mo.gov/casenet/base/welcome.do. Online probate records go back to 5/31/2000. Mail turnaround time usually 1 week.
 Mail turnaround time usually 1 week.
General Information: Public terminal has only civil records back to 1980. No sealed or confidential records released. Will not fax documents. Certification fee: $3.50 for 1st page; $.50 each add'l. Payee: City of St. Louis Circuit Clerk. Only cashiers checks and money orders accepted. SASE required.

City of St Louis Circuit Court - Criminal 1114 Market St, 2nd Fl, Carnahan Courthouse, Attn: Case Records/File Section, St Louis, MO 63101; phone: 314-622-4773 (gen info); criminal phone: 314-622-4485 or 4486 (felony), 314-622-4548 (misd.); fax: 314-613-7486; hours 9AM-4PM (CST). *Felony, Misdemeanor.*
www.stlcitycircuitcourt.com/PDF/TelephoneList/TeleDirectory.pdf
Criminal Records: Access: In person, mail, fax, online. Both court and visitors may perform in person searches. No search fee. Court makes copy: $.50 per page. Required to search: name, years to search, DOB, signed release; also helpful: address, SSN. Criminal records on computer since 1990 for misdemeanor; since 1992 for felony. Access to criminal records is free at https://www.stlcitycircuitcourt.com/SSL/getCriminal.cfm. Note: Courts criminal case records/copy section telephone is 714-613-4156 or 4408 (fax given above). Criminal searches may also be

conducted through MO State Hwy Patrol, 573-526-6288.
General Information: Public terminal has only criminal records. (There is a public access terminal on the 3rd fl with limited case information.) No juvenile, mental, expunged, or suspended imposition of sentence records released. Certification fee: $3.50. Payee: City of St. Louis Circuit Clerk. Business checks accepted. Prepayment and SASE required.

Ste. Genevieve County

Circuit Court 55 S 3rd, Rm 23, Ste Genevieve, MO 63670; phone: 573-883-2705; fax: 573-883-9351; hours 8AM-5PM (CST). *Felony, Misdemeanor, Civil Actions Over $25,000.*
Civil Records: Access: In person, online. Visitors must perform in person searches themselves. Court makes copy: $1.00 per page. Self serve copy fee: $.25 per page. Required to search: name, years to search. Civil cases indexed by defendant, plaintiff; onbooks since early 1800s, recent civil records (1995) computerized. Participates in the free court record system at www.courts.mo.gov/casenet/base/welcome.do. Records from 11/06/00 forward.
Criminal Records: Access: In person, online. Visitors must perform in person searches themselves. Court makes copy: $1.00 per page. Self serve copy fee: $.25 per page. Required to search: name, years to search. Criminal Record indexes on books, not computerized. Participates in the free court record system at www.courts.mo.gov/casenet/base/welcome.do. Records go back to 11/06/00 forward. Note: Court recommends criminal searches at MO State Hwy Patrol, 573-526-6288.
General Information: Public terminal goes back to 1993. No juvenile, mental, expunged, paternity, dismissed, or suspended imposition of sentence records released. Certification fee: $1.50 per cert. Payee: St Genevieve County Circuit Clerk. Business checks accepted. Prepayment required.

Associate Circuit Court 55 S 3rd St, Ste Genevieve, MO 63670; phone: 573-883-2265; fax: 573-883-9351; hours 8AM-5PM (CST). *Misdemeanor, Civil Actions Under $45,000, Eviction, Small Claims, Probate.*
Note: The court will not make copies of documents for the public.
Civil Records: Access: In person, online. Visitors must perform in person searches themselves. Self serve copy fee: $.25 per page. Required to search: name, years to search. Civil cases indexed by defendant, plaintiff; onbooks. Participates in the free statewide Casenet court record system at www.courts.mo.gov/casenet/base/welcome.do. Online records go back to 11/06/00.
Criminal Records: Access: In person, online. Visitors must perform in person searches themselves. Self serve copy fee: $.25 per page. Required to search: name, years to search. Criminal records on books. Participates in the free statewide Casenet court record system at www.courts.mo.gov/casenet/base/welcome.do. Online records go back to 11/06/00. Note: Court recommends criminal searches at MO State Hwy Patrol, 573-526-6288.
General Information: Public terminal has criminal back to 1994 and civil back to 1997. No juvenile, mental, expunged, dismissed, or suspended imposition of sentence records released. Certification fee: $2.50. Only cashiers checks and money orders accepted.

Stoddard County

Circuit Court PO Box 30, Bloomfield, MO 63825; phone: 573-568-4640; fax: 573-568-2271; hours 8:30AM-4:30PM (CST). *Felony, Misdemeanor, Civil Actions Over $25,000.*
Civil Records: Access: Fax, mail, in person, online. Both court and visitors may perform in person searches. No search fee. Court makes copy: $.10 per

page. Required to search: name, years to search. Civil cases indexed by defendant, plaintiff; oncomputer since 1991, prior on cards and books. Access to civil records is free at www.courts.mo.gov/casenet/cases/searchCases.do. Search by litigant name, case # or date. Online records go back to 7/1/2001. Mail turnaround time 1-3 days.

Criminal Records: Access: Mail, in person, online. Both court and visitors may perform in person searches. No search fee. Court makes copy: $.10 per page. Required to search: name, years to search; also helpful: DOB, SSN. Criminal records on computer since 1991, prior on cards and books. Online access to criminal records is the same as civil. Mail turnaround time 1-3 days.

General Information: Public use terminal available. No juvenile, mental, expunged, dismissed, or suspended imposition of sentence records released. Certification fee: $1.50. Payee: Stoddard County Circuit Clerk. Personal checks accepted. Prepayment and SASE required.

Associate Division III & Probate PO Box 518, Bloomfield, MO 63825; phone: 573-568-4640 x3; fax: 573-568-3229; hours 7:30AM-4PM (CST). *Civil Actions Under $25,000, Eviction, Small Claims, Probate.*

Civil Records: Access: Phone, fax, mail, in person, online. Both court and visitors may perform in person searches. No search fee. Court makes copy: $.50 per page. Required to search: name; also helpful: years to search. Civil cases indexed by defendant, plaintiff. Civil judgment records on computer since 1/93; prior records on index cards. Access to civil records is free at www.courts.mo.gov/casenet/cases/searchCases.do. Search by litigant name, case # or date. Online records go back to 7/1/2001. Mail turnaround time 2-3 days.

General Information: Public terminal has only civil records back to 1993. No mental health records released. Certification fee: $1.50. Payee: Clerk of Court. Personal checks accepted. Prepayment required.

Associate Circuit Court - Criminal Division II PO Box 218, Bloomfield, MO 63825; phone: 573-568-4640 x2; fax: 573-568-2299; hours 8:30AM-4:30PM (CST). *Misdemeanor.*

Criminal Records: Access: Mail, in person, online. Visitors must perform in person searches themselves. No search fee. Court makes copy: $.10 per page. Required to search: name, years to search, DOB, SSN, signed release. Criminal records on index cards, traffic on computer since 1996. Access to records is free at www.courts.mo.gov/casenet/base/welcome.do/. Search by litigant name, case # or date. Online records go back to 7/1/2001. Note: Court recommends criminal searches at MO State Hwy Patrol, 573-526-6288.

General Information: Public terminal has only criminal records back to 1996. No juvenile, mental, expunged, dismissed, or suspended imposition of sentence records released. Certification fee: $1.50 per cert. Payee: Stoddard County. Personal checks accepted. Prepayment required.

Stone County

Circuit Court PO Box 18, 100 S Maple, Judicial Ctr, 2nd Fl, Galena, MO 65656; phone: 417-357-6114; fax: 417-357-6163; hours 7:30AM-N; 12:30PM-4:00PM (CST). *Felony, Misdemeanor, Civil Actions Over $25,000.*

Civil Records: Access: Phone, fax, mail, in person. Both court and visitors may perform in person searches. No search fee. Court makes copy: $.25 per page. Required to search: name, years to search. Civil cases indexed by defendant, plaintiff; oncards and books, archived since 1852; computerized records since 1992. Mail turnaround time 1 week.

Criminal Records: Access: Phone, fax, mail, in person. Both court and visitors may perform in person searches. No search fee. Court makes copy: $.25 per page. Required to search: name, years to

search; also helpful: DOB, SSN. Criminal records on cards and books, archived since 1852; computerized records since 1992. Mail turnaround time 1 week.

General Information: Public terminal goes back to 1992. No juvenile, mental, expunged, dismissed, or suspended imposition of sentence records released. Will fax documents for $3.00 per page. Certification fee: $1.50 per cert. Payee: Circuit Court. Personal checks accepted. Prepayment and SASE required.

Circuit Court - Division II & III PO Box 18, 110 S Maple St, Galena, MO 65656; phone: 417-357-6511; probate phone: 417-357-3085; fax: 417-357-6163; hours 7:30AM-4PM (CST). *Misdemeanor, Civil Actions, Eviction, Small Claims, Probate.*

www.stoneco-mo.us

Note: No collar limit on civil actions; prior to 2001, the civil action maximum limit was $25,000.

Civil Records: Access: Mail, in person, online. Both court and visitors may perform in person searches. No search fee. Court makes copy: $.25 per page; same fee for self serve. Required to search: name, years to search; also helpful: address. Civil cases indexed by defendant, plaintiff. Civil records go back to 1970. Sept. 2005, began participation in the free state online court record system at www.courts.mo.gov/casenet/base/welcome.do. Mail turnaround time 2-3 weeks.

Criminal Records: Access: Fax, mail, in person, online. Both court and visitors may perform in person searches. No search fee. Court makes copy: $.25 per page; same fee for self serve. Required to search: name, years to search, DOB, SSN, signed release. Criminal records on computer back to 1990 and on microfiche. Sept. 2005, began participation in the free state online court record system at www.courts.mo.gov/casenet/base/welcome.do. Mail turnaround time 2-3 weeks.

General Information: Public terminal has only civil records back to 2001. No juvenile, mental, expunged, dismissed, or suspended imposition of sentence records released. May fax documents $3.00 per page. Certification fee: $2.50 first page, $.50 each add'l page, includes copies. Payee: Circuit Court Division II. Only cashiers checks and money orders accepted. Prepayment and SASE required.

Sullivan County

Circuit & Associate Court Courthouse, 109 N Main, Milan, MO 63556-1358; phone: 660-265-4717 (Circ,); 660-265-3303 (Assoc. Circ); fax: 660-265-5071; hours 9:00AM-4:30PM (CST). *Felony, Misdemeanor, Civil Actions, Eviction, Small Claims, Probate.*

Civil Records: Access: In person, online. Visitors must perform in person searches themselves. Court makes copy: $1.00 per page. Self serve copy fee: $.25 per page. Required to search: name, years to search. Civil cases indexed by defendant, plaintiff; onindex cards since 1979, prior on books. Participates in the free statewide Casenet court record system at www.courts.mo.gov/casenet/base/welcome.do.

Criminal Records: Access: In person, online. Visitors must perform in person searches themselves. Court makes copy: $1.00 per page. Self serve copy fee: $.25 per page. Required to search: name, years to search; also helpful: DOB, SSN. Criminal records on index cards since 1979, prior on books. Participates in the free statewide Casenet court record system at www.courts.mo.gov/casenet/base/welcome.do. Note: Court recommends criminal searches at MO State Hwy Patrol, 573-526-6288.

General Information: Public use terminal available. No juvenile, mental, expunged, dismissed, or suspended imposition of sentence records released. Certification fee: $1.50. Payee: Consolidated Circuit Court of Sullivan County. Personal checks accepted. Prepayment required.

Taney County

Circuit Court PO Box 335, Forsyth, MO 65653; phone: 417-546-7230; fax: 417-546-6133; hours 8AM-5PM (CST). *Felony, Civil Actions Over $25,000.*

Civil Records: Access: Mail, in person, online. Both court and visitors may perform in person searches. Search fee: $4.00 per name. Court makes copy: $.25 per page. Required to search: name, years to search. Civil cases indexed by defendant, plaintiff; oncomputer since 1/95, prior on index cards and books since 1885. Participates in the free court record system at www.courts.mo.gov/casenet/base/welcome.do. Online records include probate court. Mail turnaround time 2 days.

Criminal Records: Access: In person, online. Both court and visitors may perform in person searches. Court makes copy: $.25 per page. Required to search: name, years to search, DOB. Criminal records on computer since 1/95, prior on index cards and books since 1885. Online access to criminal records is the same as civil.

General Information: Public terminal goes back to 1995. No juvenile, mental, expunged, dismissed, or suspended imposition of sentence records released. Will fax documents. Certification fee: $1.50 per cert. Payee: Circuit Clerk. Personal checks accepted. Prepayment required. SASE helpful.

Associate Circuit Court - Division I PO Box 129, Forsyth, MO 65653; phone: 417-546-7212; fax: 417-546-4513; hours 8AM-5PM (CST). *Felony, Misdemeanor, Probate.*

Note: Probate Division is at PO Box 789.

Criminal Records: Access: Mail, in person, online. Only the court performs in person searches. Search fee: $4.00 per name. Court makes copy: $.25 per page, $1.00 if probate; same fee for self serve. Required to search: name, years to search, DOB, SSN. Criminal records on computer since 1984, prior on cards and books. Participates in the free statewide Casenet court record system at www.courts.mo.gov/casenet/base/welcome.do. Mail turnaround time 10 days, more if busy.

General Information: No public access terminal. No juvenile, mental, expunged, dismissed, or suspended imposition of sentence records released. Certification fee: $1.50; Probate is $1.00 per page. Payee: Associate Circuit Court. Personal checks not accepted. Prepayment and SASE required.

Associate Circuit Court - Division II PO Box 1030, Forsyth, MO 65653; phone: 417-546-7206; fax: 417-546-5821; hours 8AM-5PM (CST). *Civil Actions Under $25,000, Eviction, Small Claims.*

Civil Records: Access: Mail, in person, online. Only the court performs in person searches. Search fee: $4.00 per name. Court makes copy: $.25 per page; same fee for self serve. Required to search: name, years to search. Civil cases indexed by defendant, plaintiff; oncomputer since 1984, prior on cards and books. This court participates in the free statewide Casenet court record system at www.courts.mo.gov/casenet/base/welcome.do. Mail turnaround time 2 days, more if busy.

General Information: No public access terminal. No juvenile, mental, expunged, dismissed, or suspended imposition of sentence records released. Will fax documents to local or toll-free number if less than 5 pages. Certification fee: $1.50. Payee: Associate Circuit Court. Personal checks accepted. Prepayment and SASE required.

Texas County

Circuit Court 210 N Grand, Houston, MO 65483; phone: 417-967-3742; fax: 417-967-4220; hours 8:30-N; 12:30PM-4:30PM (CST). *Felony, Misdemeanor, Civil Actions Over $25,000.*

Civil Records: Access: In person only. Visitors must perform in person searches themselves. Court makes copy: $1.00 per page. Required to search:

name, years to search. Civil cases indexed by defendant, plaintiff; onindex books since 1900s.

Criminal Records: Access: In person only. Visitors must perform in person searches themselves. Court makes copy: $1.00 per page. Required to search: name, years to search. Criminal records on index books since 1900s. Note: Court recommends criminal searches at MO State Hwy Patrol, 573-526-6288.

General Information: No juvenile, mental, expunged, dismissed, or suspended imposition of sentence records released. Certification fee: $2.00. Payee: Texas County Circuit Clerk. Personal checks accepted. Prepayment required.

Associate Circuit Court County Courthouse, 210 N Grand, #302, Houston, MO 65483; phone: 417-967-3663; probate phone: 417-967-2100; criminal fax: 417-967-4128; same fax for civil/probate; hours 8AM-N; 1-5PM (CST). *Misdemeanor, Civil Actions Under $25,000, Eviction, Small Claims, Probate.*

Note: Probate is a separate index at this address.

Civil Records: Access: Phone, fax, mail, in person. Only the court performs in person searches. No search fee. Court makes copy: $1.00 per page. Required to search: name, years to search. Civil cases indexed by defendant, plaintiff; onindex cards since 1979, prior on cards and books. Mail turnaround time 7-10 days; phone turnaround is immediate.

Criminal Records: Access: Phone, fax, mail, in person. Only the court performs in person searches. No search fee. Court makes copy: $1.00 per page. Required to search: name, years to search, SSN. Criminal records on index cards since 1979, prior on cards and books. Mail turnaround time 7-10 days; phone turnaround is immediate.

General Information: No public access terminal. No juvenile, mental, expunged, dismissed, or suspended imposition of sentence records released. Will fax documents $2.00 1st page, $.50 each add'l. Certification fee: $2.00. Payee: Associate Circuit Court. Business checks accepted. Prepayment and SASE required.

Vernon County

Circuit & Associate Court Courthouse, 3rd Fl, 100 W Cherry St, Nevada, MO 64772; phone: 417-448-2525/2550; criminal fax: 417-448-2512; same fax for civil/probate; hours 8AM-4:30PM (CST). *Felony, Misdemeanor, Civil Actions, Eviction, Small Claims, Probate.*

Civil Records: Access: In person, online, email. Visitors must perform in person searches themselves. No search fee. Court makes copy: $.20 per page; microfilmed records copies are $1.00 per page. Self serve copy fee: $.20 per page. Required to search: name, years to search. Civil cases indexed by defendant, plaintiff. Civil records go back to 1863; on computer back to 2000. Judgments on index cards up until 1992. Participates in the free court record system at www.courts.mo.gov/casenet/base/welcome.do. Online records go back to 9/11/2001. Online records include probate court.

Criminal Records: Access: In person, online. Visitors must perform in person searches themselves. Search fee: $5.00 per name. Court makes copy: $.20 per page; microfilmed records copies are $1.00 per page. Self serve copy fee: $.20 per page. Required to search: name, years to search, DOB. Criminal records go back to 1863; on computer back to 1990 for Assoc. Court records, back to 2001 for Circuit Court records. Online access to criminal records is the same as civil. Note: Court recommends criminal searches at MO State Hwy Patrol, 573-526-6288.

General Information: Public terminal goes back to 1990. No juvenile, mental, expunged, dismissed, or suspended imposition of sentence records released. Will fax documents. Certification fee: $1.50. Payee: Vernon County Circuit Clerk. Personal checks accepted. Prepayment required.

Warren County

Circuit Court 104 W Main, Warrenton, MO 63383; phone: 636-456-3363; fax: 636-456-8573; hours 8AM-4:30PM (CST). *Felony, Misdemeanor, Civil Actions Over $25,000.*

Civil Records: Access: Online, in person. Visitors must perform in person searches themselves. Court makes copy: $.25 per page. Required to search: name, years to search. Civil cases indexed by defendant, plaintiff; onindex cards since 1976, prior on books. Participates in the free court record system at www.courts.mo.gov/casenet/base/welcome.do. Online records go back to 9/20/1999.

Criminal Records: Access: Online, in person. Visitors must perform in person searches themselves. Court makes copy: $.25 per page. Required to search: name, years to search. Criminal records on index cards since 1976, prior on books. Online access to criminal records is the same as civil. Note: Court recommends criminal searches at MO State Hwy Patrol, 573-526-6288.

General Information: Public use terminal available. No juvenile, mental, expunged, dismissed, or suspended imposition of sentence records released. Certification fee: $1.00 per certification. Payee: Warren County Circuit Clerk. Business checks accepted. Prepayment required.

Associate Circuit Court Warren County Courthouse, 104 W Main, Warrenton, MO 63383; phone: 636-456-3375; criminal fax: 636-456-2422; same fax for civil/probate; hours 8:30AM-4:30PM (CST). *Misdemeanor, Civil Actions Under $25,000, Eviction, Small Claims, Probate.*

Civil Records: Access: Phone, fax, online, mail, in person. Both court and visitors may perform in person searches. No search fee. Court makes copy: $.50 per page; same fee for self serve. Required to search: name, years to search. Civil cases indexed by defendant, plaintiff; onindex cards since 1979, prior on books. Records may be free on state online court record system at www.courts.mo.gov/casenet/base/welcome.do. Mail turnaround time 1 week.

Criminal Records: Access: Phone, fax, mail, online, in person. Only the court performs in person searches. No search fee. Court makes copy: $.50 per page; same fee for self serve. Required to search: name, years to search; also helpful: DOB, SSN. Criminal records on computer since 2/92, on cards since 1979, prior on books. Online access to criminal records is the same as civil. Mail turnaround time 1 week.

General Information: Public terminal has only civil records back to 5/19/2003. No juvenile, mental, expunged, dismissed, or suspended imposition of sentence records released. Will fax documents for $1.00 per page; limit on number of pages. Certification fee: $2.50 per cert. Payee: Associate Circuit Clerk. No personal checks accepted. Prepayment required.

Washington County

Circuit Court PO Box 216, Potosi, MO 63664; phone: 573-438-4171; fax: 573-438-7900; hours 8AM-5PM (CST). *Felony, Misdemeanor, Civil Actions Over $45,000.*

Civil Records: Access: Mail, online, in person. Both court and visitors may perform in person searches. No search fee. Court makes copy: $.50 per page. Required to search: name, years to search. Civil cases indexed by defendant, plaintiff; onindex cards since 1976, prior on books. Participates in the free court record system at www.courts.mo.gov/casenet/base/welcome.do. Records from 11/09/00 forward. Mail turnaround time 5-10 days.

Criminal Records: Access: Mail, in person, online. Both court and visitors may perform in person searches. No search fee. Court makes copy: $.50 per page. Required to search: name, years to search. Criminal records on index cards since 1976, prior on books. Participates in the free court record system at www.courts.mo.gov/casenet/base/welcome.do.

Records go back to 11/09/00 forward. Mail turnaround time 5-10 days.

General Information: Public terminal has criminal back to 11/2000 and civil back to 1988. (A card file open to the public to view older criminal records.) No juvenile, mental, expunged, dismissed, or suspended imposition of sentence records released. Certification fee: $2.00. Payee: Washington County Circuit Clerk. Personal checks accepted. Prepayment and SASE required.

Associate Circuit Court 102 N Missouri St, Potosi, MO 63664; phone: 573-438-3691; criminal phone: 573-438-4171; civil phone: 573-438-4171; probate phone: 573-438-3691; criminal fax: 573-438-7900; same fax for civil/probate; hours 8AM-5PM (CST). *Misdemeanor, Civil Actions Under $45,000, Eviction, Small Claims, Probate.*

Note: Probate is a separate index as this same address.

Civil Records: Access: Phone, fax, mail, in person, online. Only the court performs in person searches. No search fee. Court makes copy: $.50 per page. Required to search: name, years to search. Civil cases indexed by defendant, plaintiff; onindex cards for 12 years, computerized since 1996, older records archived. Participates in the free statewide Casenet court record system at www.courts.mo.gov/casenet/base/welcome.do. Online records go back to 11/00. Mail turnaround time 1 week.

Criminal Records: Access: Phone, fax, mail, in person, online. Only the court performs in person searches. No search fee. Court makes copy: $.50 per page. Required to search: name, years to search; also helpful: DOB, SSN. Criminal records on index cards for 12 years, computerized since 1996, older records archived. Participates in the free statewide Casenet court record system at www.courts.mo.gov/casenet/base/welcome.do. Online records go back to 11/00. Mail turnaround time 1 week.

General Information: No public access terminal. No juvenile, mental, expunged, dismissed, or suspended imposition of sentence records released. Will not fax documents. Certification fee: $2.50 per cert. Payee: Associate Circuit Clerk. Personal checks accepted. Prepayment and SASE required.

Wayne County

Circuit Court PO Box 78, Greenville, MO 63944; phone: 573-224-3014; fax: 573-224-3015; hours 8:30AM-4:30PM (CST). *Felony, Misdemeanor, Civil Actions Over $45,000.*

Civil Records: Access: Mail, in person, online. Both court and visitors may perform in person searches. Search fee: $14.00 per name. Court makes copy: $.50 per page. Required to search: name, years to search. Civil cases indexed by defendant, plaintiff; onindex cards since 1978, prior on books. Participates in the free statewide Casenet court record system at www.courts.mo.gov/casenet/base/welcome.do. Mail turnaround time 1 week.

Criminal Records: Access: In person, online. Both court and visitors may perform in person searches. Court makes copy: $.50 per page. Required to search: name, years to search; also helpful: DOB. Criminal records on index cards since 1978, prior on books. Participates in the free statewide Casenet court record system at www.courts.mo.gov/casenet/base/welcome.do. Online records go back to 09/19/01. Mail turnaround time 1 week.

General Information: Public terminal has criminal back to 2000 and civil back to 2001. No juvenile, mental, expunged, dismissed, or suspended imposition of sentence records released. Certification fee: $2.00 per cert. Payee: Wayne County Circuit Clerk. Personal checks accepted. Prepayment and SASE required.

Div. III Circuit Court PO Box 47, Greenville, MO 63944; phone: 573-224-3052; fax: 573-224-3225; hours 8:30AM-4:30PM (CST). *Misdemeanor, Civil Actions Under $45,000, Eviction, Small Claims, Probate.*

Note: Divisions will consolidate late 2005 or early 2006.

Civil Records: Access: Phone, fax, mail, in person, online. Both court and visitors may perform in person searches. No search fee. Court makes copy: $.25 per page. Required to search: name, years to search. Civil cases indexed by defendant, plaintiff; onindex cards since 1979; on computer back to 4/2001. Participates in the free statewide Casenet court record system at www.courts.mo.gov/casenet/base/welcome.do. Mail turnaround time 1 day.

Criminal Records: Access: Phone, fax, mail, in person, online. Both court and visitors may perform in person searches. No search fee. Court makes copy: $.25 per page. Required to search: name, years to search, DOB; also helpful: SSN. Criminal records on computer since 1992, prior on index cards. Participates in the free statewide Casenet court record system at www.courts.mo.gov/casenet/base/welcome.do. Mail turnaround time 1 day.

General Information: Public use terminal available. (Public terminal in Circuit Court office.) No juvenile, mental, expunged, dismissed, or suspended imposition of sentence records released. Will fax documents $.50 per page. Certification fee: $1.50 per page. Payee: Div. III Circuit Court. Personal checks accepted. Prepayment and SASE required.

Webster County

Circuit Court PO Box 529, Marshfield, MO 65706; phone: 417-859-2006; fax: 417-468-3786; hours 8AM-5PM (CST). *Felony, Civil Actions Over $25,000.*

Civil Records: Access: Fax, mail, in person, online. Both court and visitors may perform in person searches. No search fee. Court makes copy: $.15 per page; same fee for self serve. Required to search: name, years to search. Civil cases indexed by defendant, plaintiff; oncomputer since 1976 (judgment index). Participates in the free court record system at www.courts.mo.gov/casenet/base/welcome.do.

Criminal Records: Access: In person, online. Only the court performs in person searches. No search fee. Court makes copy: $.15 per page; same fee for self serve. Required to search: name, years to search, DOB. Criminal records on computer since 1976 (judgment index). Online access to criminal records is the same as civil. Note: Court recommends criminal searches at MO State Hwy Patrol, 573-526-6288. Mail turnaround time 1 day.

General Information: Public terminal has only civil records back to 1976 - judgments only. No juvenile, mental, expunged, dismissed, or suspended imposition of sentence records released. Will fax documents $2.00 per page. Certification fee: $2.00. Payee: Webster County Circuit Clerk. Personal checks accepted. Prepayment and SASE required.

Associate Circuit Court

PO Box 7, Courthouse, Marshfield, MO 65706; phone: 417-859-2041; probate phone: 417-859-2041; fax: 417-859-6265; hours 8AM-5PM (CST). *Misdemeanor, Civil Actions Under $25,000, Eviction, Small Claims, Probate.*

Civil Records: Access: Phone, fax, mail, in person, online. Only the court performs in person searches.

No search fee. Court makes copy: $1.00 per page. Required to search: name, years to search. Civil cases indexed by defendant, plaintiff; oncomputer since 1992; prior records on index cards since 1980 & on books. Access to civil records is free at www.courts.mo.gov/casenet/cases/searchCases.do. Search by litigant name, case # or date. Mail turnaround time varies.

Criminal Records: Access: Mail, in person, online. Only the court performs in person searches. No search fee. Court makes copy: $1.00 per page. Required to search: name, years to search; also helpful: DOB, SSN. Criminal records on computer since 1992. Online access to criminal records is the same as civil. Mail turnaround time varies.

General Information: No public access terminal. No juvenile, mental, expunged, dismissed, or suspended imposition of sentence records released. Certification fee: $1.50. Payee: Associate Circuit Court. Only cashiers checks and money orders accepted. Prepayment and SASE required.

Worth County

Circuit Court PO Box 340, Grant City, MO 64456; phone: 660-564-2210; fax: 660-564-2432; hours 8:30AM-4:30PM (CST). *Felony, Misdemeanor, Civil Actions Over $45,000.*

Civil Records: Access: Fax, mail, in person. Both court and visitors may perform in person searches. Search fee: $5.00 per name. Court makes copy: $.20 per page. Required to search: name, years to search. Civil cases indexed by defendant, plaintiff; oncomputer since 1990, prior on index cards. Mail turnaround time same day.

Criminal Records: Access: Fax, mail, in person. Both court and visitors may perform in person searches. Search fee: $5.00 per name. Court makes copy: $.20 per page. Required to search: name, years to search. Criminal records on computer since 1990, prior on index cards. Mail turnaround time same day.

General Information: Public terminal goes back to 1996. No juvenile, mental, expunged, dismissed, or suspended imposition of sentence records released. Certification fee: $2.50. Payee: Worth County Circuit Clerk. Personal checks accepted. Prepayment and SASE required.

Associate Circuit Court

PO Box 428, Grant City, MO 64456; phone: 660-564-2152; fax: 660-564-2432; hours 9AM-4:30PM (CST). *Misdemeanor, Civil Actions Under $45,000, Eviction, Small Claims, Probate.*

Civil Records: Access: In person only. Visitors must perform in person searches themselves. Court makes copy: $1.00 per page. Required to search: name, years to search. Civil cases indexed by defendant, plaintiff; onindex cards since 1979, prior on index books.

Criminal Records: Access: In person only. Both court and visitors may perform in person searches. No search fee. Court makes copy: $1.00 per page. Required to search: name, years to search. Criminal records on index cards since 1979, prior on index books.

General Information: No public access terminal. No juvenile, mental, expunged, dismissed, or suspended imposition of sentence records released. Certification fee: $2.50 per cert. Payee: Associate Circuit Court. Personal checks accepted. Prepayment required.

Wright County

Circuit Court PO Box 39, Hartville, MO 65667; phone: 417-741-7121; fax: 417-741-7504; hours 8AM-4:30PM (CST). *Felony, Misdemeanor, Civil Actions Over $25,000.*

Civil Records: Access: Mail, in person. Both court and visitors may perform in person searches. No search fee. Court makes copy: $.25 per page; same fee for self serve. Required to search: name, years to search. Civil cases indexed by defendant, plaintiff; onindex cards since 1979, prior on books to 1900s. Mail turnaround time 1 day.

Criminal Records: Access: Mail, in person. Both court and visitors may perform in person searches. No search fee. Court makes copy: $.25 per page; same fee for self serve. Required to search: name, years to search. Criminal records on index cards since 1979, prior on books to 1900s. Mail turnaround time 1 day.

General Information: No public access terminal. No juvenile, mental, expunged, dismissed, or suspended imposition of sentence records released. Will fax documents for $3.00. Certification fee: $2.00. Payee: Wright County Circuit Clerk. Personal checks accepted. Prepayment required.

Associate Circuit Court

PO Box 58, Hartville, MO 65667; phone: 417-741-6450; criminal fax: 417-741-7120; same fax for civil/probate; hours 8AM-4:30PM (CST). *Misdemeanor, Civil Actions Under $25,000, Eviction, Small Claims, Probate.*

Civil Records: Access: Phone, fax, mail, in person. Only the court performs in person searches. No search fee. Court makes copy: $.25 per page; same fee for self serve. Required to search: name, years to search. Civil cases indexed by defendant, plaintiff; onindex cards since 1979, prior on books. Mail turnaround time appox. 1 week.

Criminal Records: Access: Phone, fax, mail, in person. Only the court performs in person searches. No search fee. Court makes copy: $.25 per page; same fee for self serve. Required to search: name, years to search; also helpful: DOB, SSN. Criminal records on computer since 1990, prior on cards and books; on computer back to 1990. Mail turnaround time 1 week.

General Information: No public access terminal. No juvenile, mental, expunged, or dismissed records released. Fee to fax documents is $1.00 per page. Certification fee: $1.00 per page includes copy fee. Payee: Associate Circuit Court. Only cashiers checks and money orders accepted. Prepayment and SASE required.

Missouri Recording Offices

ORGANIZATION: 114 counties and one independent city, 115 recording offices. The recording officer is. Recorder of Deeds. The City of St. Louis has its own recording office. See the City/County Locator section at the end of this chapter for ZIP Codes that cover both the city and county of St. Louis. The entire state is in the Central Time Zone (CST).

REAL ESTATE RECORDS: A few counties will perform real estate searches. Copy and certification fees vary.

UCC RECORDS: Missouri was a dual filing state. Until 07/2001, financing statements were filed both at the state level and with the Recorder of Deeds, except for consumer goods, farm related and real estate related filings, which were filed only with the Recorder. Now only real estate relating filings are filed at the county level. Most all counties will perform UCC searches. Use search request form UCC-11. Search fees are usually $14.00 per debtor name without copies and $28.00 with copies. Copies usually cost $.50 per page.

TAX LIEN RECORDS: All federal and state tax liens are filed with the county Recorder of Deeds. They are usually indexed together. Some counties will perform tax lien searches. Search and copy fees vary widely.

OTHER LIENS: Mechanics, judgment, child support.

ONLINE ACCESS: A handful of counties offer online access. UCCs are available from the Secretary of State.

Adair County

Recorder of Deeds, 106 W. Washington St.; Courthouse, Kirksville, MO 63501. 660-665-3890; fax-660-785-3212; hours: 8:30AM-N, 1-4:30PM.
Separate indices to search include documents prior to April, 1985. In one index from April, 1985 to current. Records indexed on a public use terminal back to April, 1985. Office will perform a UCC search but public must search other records themselves. UCC search per debtor name- $14.00. UCC search & copy request (including 10 pages of copies)- $28.00. Copy fee $1.00 per page after 10 pages. Cert fee- $2.00 per cert plus copy fee. Payee- Adair County Recorder of Deeds. **Other phones:** Treasurer- 660-665-6755; Appraiser/Auditor-660-665-4423; Elections- 660-665-3350; Vital Records- 660-665-8491. **Property tax/Assessor-** same address as above. 660-665-4423.

Andrew County

Recorder of Deeds, PO Box 208, Savannah, MO 64485. 816-324-4221; fax-816-324-5667; 8AM-5PM.
All records in one index. Records indexed on a public use terminal back to 2003. Only the public may search. Copy fee $1.00 per page after 10 pages. Payee- Andrew County Recorder of Deeds. **Other phones:** Treasurer- 816-324-3614; Elections-816-324-3624. **Assessor-** 816-324-3023.

Atchison County

Recorder of Deeds, Box 280, Rock Port, MO 64482. 660-744-2707, R/E recording phone-660-744-2707/2705; fax-660-744-5705; hours: 8:30AM-N, 1-4:30PM. www.morecorders.com
Separate indices must be searched, land records up to present have been indexed separately. Will not search real estate records. Will search UCC records, but not tax liens. UCC search per debtor name- $14.00. UCC search & copy request (including 10 pages of copies)- $14.00. Copy fee $.50 per page after 10 pages. R/E or tax lien copy- $1.00 per page. Cert fee- $1.00 per cert, does not include copy fee. Payee- Atchison County Recorder of Deeds. **Other phones:** Treasurer- 660-744-2800; Elections- 660-744-6214. **Property tax/Assessor-** same address as above. 660-744-2948.

Audrain County

Recorder of Deeds, 101 N Jefferson; Rm 105, Audrain County Courthouse, Mexico, MO 65265. 573-473-5830; fax-573-581-8087; hours: 8AM-5PM.

Separate indices to search include deed trust, UCC. Records indexed on a public use terminal back to 6/1988. Office will perform a UCC search but public must search other records themselves. Will not search real estate records. UCC search per debtor name- $14.00. UCC search & copy request (including 10 pages of copies)- $28.00. Copy fee $1.00 per page. Cert fee- $1.00 per cert plus copy fee. Payee- Audrain County Recorder of Deeds. **Property tax/Assessor-** 573-473-5827.

Barry County

Recorder of Deeds, PO Box 340, Cassville, MO 65625. 417-847-2914; fax-417-847-8740; hours: 8AM-4PM.
All records in one index. Records indexed on a public use terminal back to 1992. Office will perform a UCC search but public must search other records themselves. UCC search per debtor name- $14.00. UCC search & copy request (including 10 pages of copies)- $28.00. Tax lien search fee- $4.00 per debtor. Copy fee $.50 per page after 10 pages. R/E or tax lien copy- $2.00 per document. Cert fee- $1.00 per doc plus copy fee. Payee- Barry County Recorder of Deeds. **Property tax/Assessor-** 417-847-4589.

Barton County

Recorder of Deeds, 1004 Gulf; Courthouse, Rm 107, Lamar, MO 64759. 417-682-2110; fax-417-682-4102; hours: 8:30AM-N, 12:30-4:30PM.
Separate indices to search include land, UCC's, tax liens. Records indexed on computer back to 9/1/2004. Only the public may search. Copy fee $1.00 per page after 10 pages. Cert fee- $1.00 per cert plus copy fee. Payee- Barton County Recorder of Deeds. **Other phones:** Treasurer- 417-682-5881; Elections- 417-682-3529; Circuit Court- 417-682-2444. **Property tax/Assessor-** 417-682-3553.

Bates County

Recorder of Deeds, Box 186, Butler, MO 64730. 660-679-3611; hours: 8:30AM-N, 1-4:30PM.
All records in one index. Only the public may search. Copy fee $1.00 per page. Cert fee- $1.00 per page plus copy fee. Payee- Bates County Recorder of Deeds. **Other phones:** Treasurer- 660-679-3341; Elections- 660-679-3371. **Property tax/Assessor-** same address as above. 660-679-3157.

Benton County

Recorder of Deeds, PO Box 37, Warsaw, MO 65355. 660-438-5732; fax-660-438-3652; hours: 8AM-N, 1-4:30PM.
Office will perform a UCC search but public must search other records themselves. UCC search per debtor name- $14.00. UCC search & copy request (including 10 pages of copies)- $28.00. Copy fee $1.00 per page after 10 pages. Cert fee- $2.00 per cert plus copy fee. Payee- Benton County Recorder of Deeds. **Other phones:** Treasurer- 660-438-6313; Elections- 660-438-7326. **Property tax/Assessor-** 660-438-5323.

Bollinger County

Recorder of Deeds, Box 49, Marble Hill, MO 63764. 573-238-1900 x301, R/E recording phone-573-238-1900 x7; fax-573-238-2674; hours: 8AM-4PM.
All records in one index. Records indexed on a public use terminal back to 1993. Only the public may search. Copy fee $2.00 for 1st page; $1.00 each add'l. Cert fee- $2.00 plus copy fee; Marriage record certified-$9.00. Payee- Bollinger County Recorder of Deeds. **Property tax/Assessor-** PO Box 6164, 204 High St, Marble Hill, MO 63764; 573-238-1900 x1.

Boone County

Recorder of Deeds, 801 E. Walnut, Rm 132; Boone County Gov't Ctr, Columbia, MO 65201-7728. 573-886-4345, UCC recording phone-573-886-4355; fax-573-886-4359; hours: 8AM-5PM. www.showmeboone.com/RECORDER/
All records in one index. Will not search real estate records. Will search UCC records, but not tax liens. UCC search per debtor name- $14.00. UCC search & copy request (including 10 pages of copies)- $28.00. Copy fee $1.00 per page. Cert fee- $1.00 per cert plus copy fee. Payee- Boone County Recorder of Deeds. **Online access to Real Estate, Lien, Marriage, UCC, Real Property, Personal Property records:** Access to the recorder database is free at www.showmeboone.com/recorder. Also, the assessor data is free at www.showmeboone.com/assessor/. Free registration and password are required for access. **Other phones:** Treasurer- 573-886-4365; Appraiser/Auditor- 573-886-4270; Elections- 573-886-4295; Marriage License- 573-886-4350. **Property tax/Assessor-** 801 E. Walnut, Rm 143, Columbia, MO 65201; 573-886-4270.

Buchanan County

Recorder of Deeds, 411 Jules Sts, Rm 103; Courthouse, St. Joseph, MO 64501-1789. 816-271-1437; fax-816-271-1582; 8AM-4:30PM. www.co.buchanan.mo.us All records in one index. Records indexed on a public use terminal back to 1990. Only the public may search. Copy fee $.50 per page. R/E record copy- $2.00 1st page, $1.00 per page thereafter. Cert fee- $1.00 per doc plus copy fee. Payee- Buchanan County Recorder of Deeds. **Other phones:** Treasurer- 816-271-1432. **Property tax/Assessor-** 816-271-1469.

Butler County

Recorder of Deeds, 100 N. Main St; Courthouse, Poplar Bluff, MO 63901. 573-686-8086; hours: 8AM-4PM. Only the public may search. Copy fee $.50 per page after 10 pages. R/E or tax lien copy- $2.00 1st page, $1.00 per page thereafter. Cert fee- $1.00 per cert plus copy fee. Payee- Butler County Recorder of Deeds. **Online access to Death Index records:** Search the county death index at www.rootsweb.com/~mobutle2/dndx/bc-death.htm?. **Other phones:** Treasurer- 573-686-8083; Appraiser/Auditor- 573-686-8084; Elections- 573-686-8050; Vital Records- 573-686-8086. **Property tax/Assessor-** 573-686-8084.

Caldwell County

Recorder of Deeds, PO Box 65, Kingston, MO 64650. 816-586-3080; hours: 8AM-4:30PM. Separate indices to search include transfers of real estate, deed of trust, miscellaneous, et al. Only the public may search. Copy fee $.50 per page after 10 pages. R/E record copy- $2.00 1st page; $1.00 each add'l. Payee- Caldwell County Recorder of Deeds. **Other phones:** Treasurer- 816-586-2781; Elections- 816-586-2571. **Property tax/Assessor-** 816-586-5261.

Callaway County

Recorder of Deeds, PO Box 406, Fulton, MO 65251. 573-642-0787; fax-573-642-7929; hours: 8AM-5PM. Separate indices to search include deeds, and deeds of trust. Records indexed on a public use terminal back to 1996. Office will perform a UCC search but public must search other records themselves. UCC search per debtor name- $14.00. Copy fee $1.00 per page. Cert fee- $1.00 per cert plus copy fee. Payee- Callaway County Recorder of Deeds. **Online access to Death records:** Access to unofficial death records up to 1926 are free from a private company at www.ancestry.com/ancestry/search/3074.htm. **Other phones:** Treasurer- 573-642-0770; Elections- 573-642-0730. **Property tax/Assessor-** 10 E 5th St, Fulton, MO 65251; 573-642-0766.

Camden County

Recorder of Deeds, 1 Court Circle, #5, Camdenton, MO 65020. 573-346-4440, R/E recording phone-573-346-4440 x234, UCC recording phone-573-346-4440 x235; fax-573-346-8367; hours: 8:30AM-4:30PM. Separate indices to search. Records indexed on a public use terminal back to 1972. Office will perform a UCC search but public must search other records themselves. UCC search (using the request form only) per debtor name- $14.00. Copy fee $1.00 per page. Cert fee- $1.00 per page plus copy fee. Payee- Camden County Recorder of Deeds. **Other phones:** Treasurer- 573-346-4440 x215-6. **Property tax/Assessor-** 1 Court Circle, Camdenton, MO 65020; 573-346-4440 x224-6.

Cape Girardeau County

Recorder of Deeds, PO Box 248, Jackson, MO 63755. 573-243-8123; fax-573-204-2477; 8AM-4:30PM. All records in one index. Office will perform a UCC search but public must search other records themselves. UCC search per debtor name- $14.00. UCC search & copy request (including 10 pages of copies)- $28.00. General copy fee $1.00 per page after 10 pages. R/E record copy- $2.00 for 1st page; $1.00 each add'l. Cert fee- $1.00 per cert plus copy fee. Payee- Cape Girardeau County Recorder of Deeds. **Online access to Recording, Real Estate, Deed, Lien records:** Recorder office data by subscription on either the Laredo system using subscription and fees or the Tapestry System using credit card, https://tapestry.fidlar.com/tapsearch.aspx; $3.99 search; $.50 per image. **Other phones:** Treasurer- 573-243-3720. **Property tax/Assessor-** same address as above. 573-243-2468.

Carroll County

Recorder of Deeds, PO Box 245, Carrollton, MO 64633. 660-542-1466; fax-660-542-1444; hours: 8:30AM-4:30PM. All records in one index. Record index not computerized. Only the public may search. Copy fee $1.00 per page after 10 pages. Tax lien copy- $.35. Cert fee- $2.00 per page plus copy fee. Payee- Carroll County Recorder of Deeds. **Other phones:** Treasurer- 660-542-1977. **Property tax/Assessor-** 660-542-2184.

Carter County

Recorder of Deeds, PO Box 1107, Van Buren, MO 63965. 573-323-9656; fax-573-323-4885; hours: 8AM-N, 1-4PM. All records in one index. Record index not computerized. Office will perform a UCC search but public must search other records themselves. Search fee $14.00. Copy fee $1.00 per page after 10 pages. Cert fee- $1.00 per page. Payee- Carter County Recorder of Deeds. **Other phones:** Treasurer- 573-323-8271; Elections- 573-323-4527. **Property tax/Assessor-** 573-323-4709.

Cass County

Recorder of Deeds, 102 E. Wall St; Cass County Court House, Harrisonville, MO 64701. 816-380-8117, UCC recording phone-816-380-8119; fax-816-380-8165; 8AM-4:30PM. www.casscounty.com/cassfr.htm Computer records date back to 1990. Prepaid fax accounts available. For information, contact Sandy Gregory at 816-380-8117. Office will perform a UCC search but public must search other records themselves. Search fee $14.00. Copy fee $1.00 per page. Cert fee- $1.00 per seal plus $1 per page. Payee- Cass County Recorder of Deeds. **Property tax/Assessor-** 816-380-8165 (FAX).

Cedar County

Recorder of Deeds, PO Box 607, Stockton, MO 65785. 417-276-6700 x246; fax-417-276-5499; hours: 8AM-N, 1-4PM. Separate indices to search include records from 1999 to present by name on the computer, prior to 1999 on film. Office will perform a UCC search but public must search other records themselves. UCC search per debtor name- $14.00. UCC search & copy request (including 10 pages of copies)- $28.00. Copy fee $1.00 per page after 10 pages. Cert fee- $1.00 per cert plus copy fee. Payee- Cedar County Recorder of Deeds. **Other phones:** Treasurer- 417-276-6700 X245; Elections- 417-276-6700 X221. **Property tax/Assessor-** 417-276-6700 X248.

Chariton County

Recorder of Deeds, PO Box 112, Keytesville, MO 65261. 660-288-3602; fax-660-288-3763; hours: 8:30AM-N, 1-4:30PM. Separate indices to search. Land records indexed on computer back to 1988; marriages back to 1827. Search fee $4.00 per name. Will not search real estate records. Will search UCC records, but not tax liens. UCC search per debtor name- $14.00. Copy fee $1.00 per page. Cert fee- $1.50 per cert plus copy fee. Payee- Chariton County Recorder of Deeds. **Other phones:** Treasurer- 660-288-3789; Elections- 660-288-3273; Vital Records- 660-288-3602. **Property tax/Assessor-** 306 S Cherry St, Keytesville, MO 65261; 660-288-3873.

Christian County

Recorder of Deeds, PO Box 358, Ozark, MO 65721. 417-581-9941; fax-417-581-9943; hours: 8AM-4:30PM. All records in one index. Only the public may search, except UCC. Will search UCC records, but not tax liens. UCC search per debtor name- $14.00. UCC search & copy request (including 10 pages of copies)- $28.00. Copy fee $1.00 per page. Cert fee- $1.00 per doc, does not include copy fee. Payee- Christian County Recorder of Deeds. **Property tax/Assessor-** same address as above. 417-581-2440.

Clark County

Recorder of Deeds, 111 E. Court #2; Courthouse, Kahoka, MO 63445. 660-727-3292; fax-660-727-1051; hours: 8AM-N,1-4PM. Office will perform a UCC search but public must search other records themselves. Search fee $14.00. Will not search real estate records. Copy fee $1.00 per page after 10 pages. Cert fee- $3.00 per doc, plus copy fee. Payee- Clark County Recorder of Deeds. **Other phones:** Treasurer- 660-727-3272; Elections- 660-727-3283. **Property tax/Assessor-** 660-727-3023.

Clay County

Recorder of Deeds, PO Box 238, Liberty, MO 64069. 816-407-3550; fax-816-407-3601; hours: 8AM-4PM. http://recorder.claycogov.com/pages/index.asp Database from July 1, 1986 is on website. All records in one index. Records indexed on a public use terminal back to 7/1/1986. Office will perform a UCC search but public must search other records themselves. Search fee $14.00. Copy fee $.50 per page. Tax lien copy- $2.00 per page, $1.00 add'l page. Cert fee- $1.00 per cert plus copy fee. Payee- Clay County Recorder of Deeds. **Online access to Real Estate, Marriage, Military Discharge, UCC, Recording records:** Access to the recorder's database is free at http://recorder.claycogov.com/pages/index.asp. Overall index goes back to 1986; images back to 1998. UCCs are 1986-91 real estate only. Access to real estate records from Collector's Office is at www.claycogov.com/county/offices/collector/realprop.php. **Other phones:** Treasurer- 816-792-7649 x284. **Property tax/Assessor-** 816-792-7664.

Clinton County

Recorder of Deeds, PO Box 275, Plattsburg, MO 64477. 816-539-3719; fax-816-539-3893; hours: 8AM-N, 1-5PM. Records indexed on a public use terminal back to 1993. Office will perform a UCC search but public must search other records themselves. Search fee $14.00. UCC copy fee $2.00 per page after 10 pages. R/E or tax lien copy- $2.00; $1.00 add'l. Cert fee- $3.00 per cert plus copy fee. Payee- Clinton County Recorder of Deeds. **Other phones:** Treasurer- 816-539-3724; Elections- 816-539-3713. **Property tax/Assessor-** 816-539-3716.

Cole County

Recorder of Deeds, PO Box 353, Jefferson City, MO 65102. 573-634-9115; hours: 8AM-4:30PM. Office personnel or visitors may perform searches. Search fee $14.00 per name. Copy fee $1.00 per page after 1st 10 pages. Cert fee- $1.00 per cert plus copy fee. Payee- Cole County Recorder of Deeds. **Online access to Death records:** Access to unofficial death records up to 1907 are free from a private company at www.ancestry.com/ancestry/search/3074.htm. **Other phones:** Treasurer- 573-634-9121. **Property tax/Assessor-** 573-634-9135.

Cooper County

Recorder of Deeds, 200 Main St; Courthouse - Rm 26, Boonville, MO 65233-1276. 660-882-2232; fax-660-882-2043; hours: 8:30AM-5PM. All records in one index. Records indexed on a public use terminal back to 1994. Office will perform a UCC search but public must search other records themselves. Search fee $14.00. Copy fee $1.00 per page. Cert fee- $1.50 per cert plus copy fee. Payee- Cooper County Recorder of Deeds. **Other phones:** Elections- 660-882-2114; Vital Records- 660-882-2626. **Property tax/Assessor-** 660-882-2646.

Crawford County

Recorder of Deeds, PO Box 177, Steelville, MO 65565. 573-775-5048; fax-573-775-3365; 8AM-4:30PM. Index: Books and Computer. Records indexed on a public use terminal back to WD-1987, TD-1970. Office will perform a UCC search but public must search other records themselves. Search fee $14.00. Copy fee $.50 per page after 10 pages. Cert fee- $2.00 per cert plus copy fee. Payee- Crawford County Recorder of Deeds. **Other phones:** Treasurer- 573-775-2897. **Property tax/Assessor-** 573-775-2065.

Dade County

Recorder of Deeds, Courthouse, Greenfield, MO 65661. 417-637-5373; fax-417-637-5055; hours: 8AM-4PM. All records in one index. Records indexed on computer back to 1997. Only the public may search. Copy fee $1.00 per page. Cert fee- $1.00 per doc includes copy fee. Payee- Dade County Recorder of Deeds. **Other phones:** Treasurer- 417-637-2732. **Property tax/Assessor-** 417-637-2224.

Dallas County

Recorder of Deeds, PO Box 406, Buffalo, MO 65622. 417-345-2242; fax-417-345-2230; 8AM-N,1-4PM. All records in one index. Land records indexed on computer back to 1992; marriage records back to 1867. Office will perform a UCC search but public must search other records themselves. UCC search per debtor name- $14.00. UCC search & copy request (including 10 pages of copies)- $28.00. Copy fee $1.00 per page. Cert fee- $1.00 per cert plus copy fee. Payee- Dallas County Recorder of Deeds. **Other phones:** Treasurer- 417-345-2020; Elections- 417-345-2632. **Property tax/Assessor-** 417-345-8774.

Daviess County

Recorder of Deeds, PO Box 132, Gallatin, MO 64640. 660-663-3183; fax-660-663-3376 8AM-N,1-4:30PM. Separate indices to search include mortgage trust deeds, general & miscellaneous deeds, tax liens and request for notice. Office will perform a UCC search but public must search other records themselves. UCC search includes tax liens if requested. UCC search per debtor name- $14.00. UCC search & copy request (including 10 pages of copies)- $28.00. Copy fee $1.00 per page after 10 pages. Cert fee- $4.00 per doc plus copy fee. Payee- Daviess County Recorder of Deeds. **Other phones:** Treasurer- 660-663-2432. **Property tax/Assessor-** 660-663-3300.

De Kalb County

Recorder of Deeds, PO Box 248, Maysville, MO 64469-0248. 816-449-2602; fax-816-449-2440; hours: 8:30AM-N, 1-4:30PM. All records in one index. Records indexed on a public use terminal back to 1992. Only the public may search. Copy fee $1.00 per page per page. Cert fee- $1.00 per cert plus copy fee. Payee- De Kalb County Recorder of Deeds. **Other phones:** Treasurer- 816-449-5810. **Property tax/Assessor-** 816-449-2212.

Dent County

Recorder of Deeds, 112 E. 5th St, Salem, MO 65560-1444. 573-729-3931; fax-573-729-9414; 8am-4:30pm. Separate indices to search include computer. Records indexed on a public use terminal back to 1955. Office personnel or visitors may perform searches. Separate federal/state combined tax lien search- $8.00 per debtor. General copy fee $1.00 per page. R/E record copy- $.25 per page. Cert fee- $1.00 per cert plus copy fee. Payee- Dent County Recorder of Deeds. **Other phones:** Treasurer- 573-729-8260. **Property tax/Assessor-** 573-729-6010.

Douglas County

Recorder of Deeds, PO Box 249, Ava, MO 65608. 417-683-4713; fax-417-683-2794; hours: 8AM-4:30PM. Office personnel or visitors may perform searches. UCC search per debtor name- $14.00. UCC search & copy request (including 10 pages of copies)- $28.00. General copy fee $1.00 per page after 10 pages. Tax lien copy- $.25 per page. Cert fee- $2.50 per page. Payee- Douglas County Recorder of Deeds. **Other phones:** Treasurer- 417-683-2183; Elections- 417-683-4714. **Property tax/Assessor-** 417-683-2829.

Dunklin County

Recorder of Deeds, PO Box 389, Kennett, MO 63857. 573-888-3468; hours: 8:30AM-N, 1-4:30PM. Office will perform a UCC search but public must search other records themselves. UCC search per debtor name- $14.00. UCC search & copy request (including 10 pages of copies)- $28.00. Copy fee $.50 per page after 10 pages. Tax lien copy- $1.00. Cert fee- $1.00 per cert. Payee- Dunklin County Recorder of Deeds. **Property tax/Assessor-** 573-888-1409.

Franklin County

Recorder of Deeds, 300 E Main St #101, Union, MO 63084. 636-583-6367; fax-636-583-7330; hours: 8AM-4:30PM. www.franklinmo.org. All records in one index. Records indexed on a public use terminal back to 1984. Office will perform a UCC search but public must search other records themselves. UCC search per debtor name- $14.00. Copy fee $1.00 per page after 10 pages; if real estate- $2.00 first page. Cert fee- $1.00 per cert plus copy fee. Payee- Franklin County Recorder of Deeds. **Other phones:** Treasurer- 636-583-6392; Elections- 636-583-7382; Vital Records- 636-583-7300. **Assessor-** 8A N Church St, Union, MO 63084; 636-583-6346.

Gasconade County

Recorder of Deeds, 119 E.1st St, Rm 6, Hermann, MO 65041-1182. 573-486-2632; fax-573-486-5812; hours: 8AM-4:30PM. All records in one index. Records indexed on computer back to January, 1989. Office will perform a UCC search but public must search other records themselves. UCC search per debtor name- $14.00. UCC search & copy request (including 10 pages of copies)- $28.00. Copy fee $2.00 1st page, $1.00 each add'l. Cert fee- $1.00 per page plus copy fee. Payee- Gasconade County Recorder of Deeds. **Other phones:** Treasurer- 573-486-2411; Appraiser/Auditor- 573-486-3100; Elections- 573-486-5427. **Assessor-** 119 E 1st St, Rm 23, Hermann, MO 65041; 573-486-3100.

Gentry County

Recorder of Deeds, PO Box 27, Albany, MO 64402. 660-726-3618; fax-660-726-4102; 8AM-4:30PM. All records in one index. Records indexed on computer back to 4/5/2005. Office will perform a UCC search but public must search other records themselves. Search fee $14.00. Copy fee $1.00 per page after 10 pages. R/E record copy- $1.00 per page if book and page number is provided. Cert fee- $1.00 per doc, plus copy fee. Payee- Gentry County Recorder of Deeds. **Property tax/Assessor-** 660-726-5289.

Greene County

Recorder of Deeds, 940 Boonville, Rm 100, Springfield, MO 65802. 417-868-4068; fax-417-868-4807; 8AM-4:30PM. www.greenecountymo.org All records in one index. Records indexed on a public use terminal back to 1988. Office will perform a UCC search and tax liens, but public must search other records themselves. UCC info request only per debtor name- $14.00. UCC search & copy request (including 10 pages of copies) - $28.00. Separate federal tax lien search- $1.00 per page. Separate state tax lien search- $1.00 per page. Federal/state combined tax lien search- $1.00 per page. Copy fee $1.00 per page after 10 pages. Cert fee- $1.00 per cert plus copy fee. Payee- Recorder of Deeds. **Online access to Assessor, Property, Deed, Lien, UCC, Recording, Death, Divorce records:** The recorder database for free at www.greenecountymo.org/Recorder/search.php. Search UCCs & tax liens at www.greenecountymo.org/Recorder/ucctaxsearch.php. Records for divorces that occurred 1837 to 1920 in Greene County are free at http://userdb.rootsweb.com/divorces. **Other phones:** Treasurer- 417-868-4051; Elections- 417-868-4055. **Property tax/Assessor-** same address as above. 417-868-4101.

Grundy County

Recorder of Deeds, PO Box 196, Trenton, MO 64683. 660-359-5409; fax-660-359-6604; 8:30AM-4:30PM. All records in one index. Records indexed on computer back to 2004. Office will perform a UCC search but public must search other records themselves. UCC search per debtor name- $14.00. General copy fee $1.00 per page after 10 pages. R/E record copy- $.25 per page. Cert fee- $2.00 per doc includes copy fee. Payee- Grundy County Recorder of Deeds. **Other phones:** Treasurer- 660-359-2171; Elections- 660-359-6305. **Property tax/Assessor-** 700 Main St, Trenton,MO 64683; 660-359-2413.

Harrison County

Recorder of Deeds, PO Box 189, Bethany, MO 64424. 660-425-6425; fax-660-425-3772; hours: 8AM-N, 1-4:30PM. Only the public may search. Copy fee $1.00 per page after 10 pages. Cert fee- $1.00 per cert plus copy fee. Payee- Harrison County Recorder of Deeds. **Other phones:** Treasurer- 660-425-6442. **Property tax/Assessor-** 660-425-2313.

Henry County

Recorder of Deeds, 100 W. Franklin #4; Courthouse, Clinton, MO 64735. 660-885-6963 x7209; fax-660-885-2264; hours: 8:30AM-4:30PM. All records in one index. Records indexed on a public use terminal back to July, 1989. Only the public may search. Copy fee $1.00 per page after 10 pages. Cert fee- $1.00 per page plus copy fee. Payee- Henry County Recorder of Deeds. **Other phones:** Treasurer- 660-885-6963 x7208; Elections- 660-885-6963 x7206. **Property tax/Assessor-** 660-885-6963 x7213.

Hickory County

Recorder of Deeds, PO Box 101, Hermitage, MO 65668. 417-745-6421; fax-417-745-6670; hours: 8AM-N, 12:30-4:30PM. Office will perform a UCC search but public must search other records themselves. UCC search per debtor name- $14.00. UCC search & copy request (including 10 pages of copies)- $28.00. Copy fee $1.00 per page after 10 pages. Cert fee- $1.00 per page. Payee- Hickory County Recorder of Deeds. **Other phones:** Treasurer- 417-745-6310; Appraiser/Auditor- 417-745-6957; Elections- 417-745-6450. **Property tax/Assessor-** 417-745-6346.

Holt County

Recorder of Deeds, PO Box 318, Oregon, MO 64473. 660-446-3301; hours: 8:30AM-N, 1-4:30PM. All records in one index. Only the public may search. Copy fee $1.00 per pages. Cert fee- $1.00 per cert plus copy fee. Payee- Holt County Recorder of Deeds. **Other phones:** Treasurer- 660-446-3397; Elections- 660-446-3303. **Property tax/Assessor-** 102 W Nodaway, Oregon, MO 64473; 660-446-3329.

Howard County

Recorder of Deeds, 1 Courthouse Sq, Fayette, MO 65248. 660-248-2194; fax-660-248-1075; hours: 8:30AM-4:30PM. Office personnel or visitors may perform searches. Search fee $15.00 per name. Will not search tax liens. General copy fee $1.00 per page after 10 pages. R/E or tax lien copy- $.25 per page. Cert fee- $3.00 per cert plus copy fee. Payee- Howard County Recorder of Deeds. **Other phones:** Treasurer- 660-248-2196. **Property tax/Assessor-** 660-248-3400.

Howell County

Recorder of Deeds, PO Box 967, West Plains, MO 65775. 417-256-3750; hours: 8AM-4:30PM. All records in one index. Records indexed on a public use terminal back to 1/1/1991. Only the public may search. Copy fee $1.00 per page after 10 copies. Cert fee- $1.50 per cert plus copy fee. Payee- Howell County Recorder of Deeds. **Other phones:** Treasurer- 417-256-4261. **Property tax/Assessor-** 417-256-8284.

Iron County

Recorder of Deeds, PO Box 24, Ironton, MO 63650. 573-546-2811; fax-573-546-2166; 8AM-4:30PM. Office will perform a UCC search but public must search other records themselves. UCC search per debtor name- $14.00. UCC search & copy request (including 10 pages of copies)- $28.00. Copy fee $1.00 per page after 10 pages. Cert fee- $2.00 per cert plus copy fee. Payee- Iron County Recorder of Deeds. **Other phones:** Treasurer- 573-546-7611; Elections- 573-546-2912; Vital Records- 573-546-2811. **Property tax/Assessor-** 573-546-7319.

Jackson County (Kansas City)

Recorder of Deeds, 415 E. 12th St; Rm 104, Kansas City, MO 64106. 816-881-3192, R/E recording phone-816-881-3048; fax-816-881-3719; hours: 8AM-5PM. www.jackson.gov.org
There is another office in Independence, which covers the eastern part of the county. It is not necessary to file proper documents in that office for the eastern section of the county. Call for more details. All records in one index. Office personnel or visitors may perform searches. Search fee $8.00 per name. UCC search & copy request (including 10 pages of copies)- $16.00. General copy fee $1.00 per page after 10 pages. R/E record copy- $2.00 per page for the 1st page, $1.00 each add'l page. Cert fee- $1.00 per cert plus copy fee. Payee- Jackson County Recorder of Deeds. **Online access to Property, Tax Assessor, Recording, Marriages, Grantor/Grantee, Deed, Lien, Judgment, UCC records:** Search the recorder Grantor/Grantee database for free at http://records.co.jackson.mo.us/search.asp?cabinet=opr. Search property tax data free at www.jacksongov.org/ser_os_ta_SrchIntro.asp. Also, access recording office land data at www.etitlesearch.com; registration required, fee based on usage. Also, search Kansas City land data free at http://kivaweb.kcmo.org/kivanet/2/land/lookup/index.cfm?fa=dslladdr. Search the marriage records free at http://records.co.jackson.mo.us/search.asp?cabinet=marriage. Search the UCC database at http://records.co.jackson.mo.us/search.asp?cabinet=ucc. **Other phones:** Treasurer- 816-881-3232; Appraiser/Auditor- 816-881-3091; Elections- 816-881-4820. **Property tax/Assessor-** 816-881-3530.

Jasper County

Recorder of Deeds, PO Box 387, Carthage, MO 64836-0387. 417-358-0432; fax-417-359-1200; hours: 8:30AM-4:30PM. www.jaspercounty.org/recorder/ Office will perform a UCC search but public must search other records themselves. UCC search per debtor name- $14.00. UCC search & copy request (including 10 pages of copies)- $28.00. Copy fee $1.00 per page. Cert fee- $1.00 per cert plus copy fee. Payee- Jasper County Recorder of Deeds. **Other phones:** Treasurer- 417-358-0448. **Property tax/Assessor-** 417-358-0437.

Jefferson County

Recorder of Deeds, PO Box 100, Hillsboro, MO 63050. 636-797-5414, UCC recording phone-636-797-5499; fax-636-797-6310; 8AM-5PM. www.jeffcomo.org All records in one index. Records indexed on a public use terminal back to 1985. Office will perform a UCC search but public must search other records themselves. UCC search per debtor name- $14.00. Copy fee $2.00 1st page, $1.00 each add'l. Cert fee- $1.00 per doc plus copy fee. Payee- Jefferson County Recorder of Deeds. **Online access to Real Estate Recording, Deed, Judgment, Assessor, Property Tax records:** Access recording office land data at www.etitlesearch.com; registration required, fee based on usage; call 870-856-3055 for info. Also, search the assessor property data for free at www.jcao.org/myinfo.htm. **Other phones:** Treasurer- 636-797-5368; Appraiser/Auditor- 636-797-5474; Elections- 636-797-5486; Birth & Death Records- 636-789-3372. **Assessor-** 636-797-5466.

Johnson County

Recorder of Deeds, PO Box 32, Warrensburg, MO 64093. 660-747-6811; fax-660-747-0062; hours: 8:30AM-4:30PM. All records in one index. Only the public may search. Copy fee $1.00 1st pg $.25 add'l per page. Cert fee- $1.00 per page plus copy fee. Payee- Johnson County Recorder of Deeds. **Other phones:** Treasurer- 660-747-7411. **Property tax/Assessor-** 660-747-9822.

Knox County

Recorder of Deeds, PO Box 116, Edina, MO 63537. 660-397-2305; fax-660-397-3331; 8:30am-N, 1-4PM. All records in one index. Record index not computerized. Office will perform a UCC search but public must search other records themselves. UCC search per debtor name- $14.00. UCC search & copy request (including 10 pages of copies)- $28.00. Copy fee $1.00 per page. Cert fee- $1.50 per cert plus copy fee. Payee- Knox County Recorder of Deeds. **Other phones:** Treasurer- 660-397-3364. **Property tax/Assessor-** 660-397-4002.

Laclede County

Recorder of Deeds, 200 N Adams, Lebanon, MO 65536-3046. 417-532-4011; fax-417-532-3852; 8AM-4PM. http://lacledecountymissouri.org/recorder/ Office will perform a UCC search but public must search other records themselves. UCC search per debtor name- $14.00. UCC search & copy request (including 10 pages of copies)- $28.00. Copy fee $1.00 per page. Cert fee- $.50 per cert plus copy fee. Payee- Laclede County Recorder of Deeds. **Other phones:** Treasurer- 417-532-4741; Appraiser/Auditor- 417-532-7163; Elections- 417-532-5471; Vital Records- 417-532-2134 (Birth); 4011 (Marriage); Collector- 417-532-4301. **Property tax/Assessor-** same address. 417-532-7163.

Lafayette County

Recorder of Deeds, PO Box 416, Lexington, MO 64067. 660-259-6178; fax-660-259-2918; hours: 8:30AM-4:30PM. Records indexed on a public use terminal back to 1991. Office will perform a UCC search but public must search other records themselves. UCC search per debtor name- $14.00. UCC search & copy request (including 10 pages of copies)- $28.00. Copy fee $1.00 per page after 10 pages. Cert fee- $1.00 per cert plus copy fee. Payee- Lafayette County Recorder of Deeds. **Other phones:** Treasurer- 660-259-3711. **Property tax/Assessor-** 660-259-6158.

Lawrence County

Recorder of Deeds, PO Box 449, Mount Vernon, MO 65712. 417-466-2670; fax-417-466-4995; hours: 9AM-N, 1-5PM. All records in one index. Records indexed on a public use terminal back to 1992. Only the public may search. Copy fee $1.00 per page after 10 pages. Cert fee- $2.00 per doc plus copy fee.

Payee- Lawrence County Recorder of Deeds. **Other phones:** Treasurer- 417-466-2662. **Property tax/Assessor-** 417-466-2831.

Lewis County

Recorder of Deeds, PO Box 97, Monticello, MO 63457-0097. 573-767-5440; fax-573-767-5378; hours: 8AM-N,1-4PM. All records in one index. Will not search real estate records. Will search UCC records, but not tax liens. UCC search per debtor name- $14.00. Copy fee $1.00 per page after 10 pages. Cert fee- $1.00 per document. Payee- Lewis County Recorder of Deeds. **Other phones:** Treasurer- 573-767-5446; Elections- 573-767-5205. **Property tax/Assessor-** 573-767-5209.

Lincoln County

Recorder of Deeds, 201 Main St, Troy, MO 63379. 636-528-6300, R/E recording phone-636-528-6300 or 528-0325; fax-636-528-2665; hours: 8AM-4:30PM. All records in one index. Will not search real estate records. Will search UCC records, but not tax liens. UCC search per debtor name- $15.00 per name. Copy fee $.50 per page. Cert fee- $1.00 per cert plus copy fee. Payee- Lincoln County Recorder of Deeds. **Online access to Recording, Real Estate, Tax Lien records:** Access recording records with subscription; details not yet available; call Recorder. **Assessor-** same address as above. 636-528-0320.

Linn County

Recorder of Deeds, PO Box 151, Linneus, MO 64653. 660-895-5216, R/E recording phone-660-895-5216/Real Estate Records; fax-660-895-5379; hours: 9AM-N, 1-4:30PM. All records in one index. Office will perform a UCC search but public must search other records themselves. UCC search per debtor name- $14.00. UCC search & copy request (including 10 pages of copies)- $28.00. Copy fee $1.00 per page. Cert fee- $1.00 per doc, plus copy fee. Payee- Linn County Recorder of Deeds. **Other phones:** Treasurer- 660-895-5410; County Clerk- 660-895-5417; Circuit Clerk -660-895-5212. **Property tax/Assessor-** 660-895-5387.

Livingston County

Recorder of Deeds, 700 Webster St; Courthouse, #6, Chillicothe, MO 64601. 660-646-0166; fax-660-646-6139; hours: 8:30AM-N, 1-4:30PM. Office will perform a UCC search but public must search other records themselves. UCC search per debtor name- $14.00. Copy fee $1.00 per page after 10 pages. Cert fee- $2.00 per cert plus copy fee. Payee- Livingston County Recorder of Deeds. **Other phones:** Treasurer- 660-646-3076; Elections- 660-646-2293. **Property tax/Assessor-** 660-646-2027.

Macon County

Recorder of Deeds, PO Box 382, Macon, MO 63552. 660-385-2732; fax-660-385-4235; 8:30AM-4PM. Will not search real estate records. Will search UCC records, but not tax liens. UCC search per debtor name- $14.00. Copy fee $.25 per page. Cert fee- $1.00 per cert plus copy fee. Marriage license copy, $3.00, certified, $9.00. Payee- Macon County Recorder of Deeds. **Other phones:** Treasurer- 660-385-2713; Elections- 660-385-2913. **Property tax/Assessor-** 660-385-2416.

Madison County

Recorder of Deeds, PO Box 470, Fredericktown, MO 63645-0470. 573-783-2102; fax-573-783-2715; hours: 8AM-5PM. Office will perform a UCC search but public must search other records themselves. UCC search per debtor name- $14.00. Copy fee $.50 per page after 10 pages. Cert fee- $2.00 per cert plus copy fee. Payee- Madison County Recorder of Deeds. **Other phones:** Treasurer- 573-783-3325. **Property tax/Assessor-** 573-783-3325.

Maries County

Recorder of Deeds, PO Box 213, Vienna, MO 65582. 573-422-3338; fax-573-422-3976; hours: 8AM-4PM. All records in one index. Office will perform a UCC search but public must search other records themselves. UCC search per debtor name- $14.00. UCC search & copy request (including 10 pages of copies)- $28.00. Separate federal/state combined tax lien search- $14.00 per debtor. Copy fee $.25 per page. Cert fee- $1.50 per cert plus copy fee. Payee- Maries County Recorder of Deeds. **Other phones:** Treasurer- 573-422-3311; Elections- 573-422-3388; Vital Records- 573-422-3338; Collector- 573-422-3343; Sheriff -573-422-3381. **Property tax/Assessor-** 573-422-3540.

Marion County

Recorder of Deeds, PO Box 392, Palmyra, MO 63461. 573-769-2550; fax-573-769-6012; 8:30AM-5PM. All records in one index. Records indexed on a public use terminal back to 1997. Office will perform a UCC search but public must search other records themselves. Search fee $14.00. Copy fee $.50 per page after 10 pages. Cert fee- $2.00 per cert plus copy fee. Payee- Marion County Recorder of Deeds. **Other phones:** Treasurer- 573-769-2552; Elections- 573-729-2549. **Property tax/Assessor-** 573-248-1514.

McDonald County

Recorder of Deeds, PO Box 157, Pineville, MO 64856. 417-223-7523; fax-417-223-4125; hours: 8AM-4PM. All records in one index. Records indexed on computer from 2001 to present. Only the public may search. Will look up deeds if you have date. Will not search real estate records. Will not search UCC records or tax liens. Copy fee $1.00 per page. Cert fee- $2.00 per doc includes copy fee. Payee- McDonald County Recorder of Deeds. **Other phones:** Treasurer- 417-223-4462. **Property tax/Assessor-** PO Box 606, Pineville, MO 64856 417-223-4361.

Mercer County

Recorder of Deeds, 802 E Main St, Princeton, MO 64673. 660-748-4335; fax-660-748-4339; hours: 8:30AM-N, 1-4:30PM. Office personnel or visitors may perform searches. Search fee $14.00 per name. Will not search real estate records. Copy fee $1.00 per page after 10 pages. Cert fee- $1.50 per cert. Payee- Mercer County Recorder of Deeds. **Other phones:** Treasurer- 660-748-3435. **Property tax/Assessor-** 660-748-3511.

Miller County

Recorder of Deeds, PO Box 11, Tuscumbia, MO 65082. 573-369-1935; fax-573-369-1939; hours: 8:30AM-4:30PM. Records indexed on a public use terminal back to 11/1/1993. Only the public may search. Copy fee $.50 per page. Cert fee- $2.00 per cert plus copy fee. **Other phones:** Treasurer- 573-369-1920; Vital Records- 573-751-6387. **Property tax/Assessor-** 573-369-1960.

Mississippi County

County Recorder, PO Box 369, Charleston, MO 63834. 573-683-2146, R/E recording phone-573-683-2146 x226; fax-573-683-7696; hours: 8AM-5PM. All records in one index. Records indexed on a public use terminal back to 1992. Office will perform a UCC search but public must search other records themselves. Search fee $14.00. Copy fee $.50 per page. Cert fee- $3.00 1st page $1.00 add'l. Payee- Recorder of Deeds. **Online access to Real Estate Recording records:** Access land records at http://etitlesearch.com. You can do a name search; choose from $200.00 monthly subscription or per click account. **Other phones:** Treasurer- 573-683-2146 x235; Elections- 573-683-2146 x222. **Property tax/Assessor-** 573-683-2146 x238.

Moniteau County

Circuit Clerk and Recorder, 200 E. Main St, California, MO 65018. 573-796-2071, R/E recording phone-573-796-4822; fax-573-796-2591; hours: 8AM-4:30PM. All records in one index. Records indexed on a public use terminal back to 1996. Only the public may search. Copy fee $.50 per page. Cert fee- $1.00 per doc plus copy fee. Payee- Recorder of Deeds. **Other phones:** Treasurer- 573-796-4608; Elections- 573-796-4661; Vital Records- 573-796-4671. **Property tax/Assessor-** same address as above. 573-796-4637.

Monroe County

Recorder of Deeds, PO Box 246, Paris, MO 65275. 660-327-1131; fax-660-327-1130; hours: 8AM-4:30PM. Records indexed on a public use terminal back to 1996. Office personnel or visitors may perform searches. Search fee $14.00 per name. Copy fee $.50 per page after 10 pages. Tax lien copy- $1.00 per page. Cert fee- $2.00 per doc plus copy fee. Payee- Monroe County Recorder. **Other phones:** Treasurer- 660-327-4711; Elections- 660-327-5106. **Property tax/Assessor-** 660-327-5607.

Montgomery County

Recorder of Deeds, 211 E. 3rd St, Montgomery City, MO 63361. 573-564-3157; hours: 8AM-4:30PM. Records indexed on a public use terminal back to 1996. Only the public may search. Copy fee $1.00 per page. Cert fee- $1.50 per page plus copy fee. Payee- Montgomery County Recorder. **Online access to Death records:** Access to unofficial death records up to 1994 are free from a private company at www.ancestry.com/ancestry/search/3074.htm. **Other phones:** Treasurer- 573-564-2319; Elections- 573-564-3357. **Property tax/Assessor-** 573-564-2445.

Morgan County

County Recorder, 100 E. Newton St; Courthouse, Versailles, MO 65084. 573-378-4029; fax-573-378-6431; hours: 8AM-4:30PM. All records in one index. Only the public may search. Copy fee $.50 per page. Cert fee- $.50 per page. Payee- Morgan County Recorder. **Other phones:** Treasurer- 573-378-4404; Elections- 573-378-5436. **Property tax/Assessor-** 573-378-5459.

New Madrid County

Recorder of Deeds, PO Box 217, New Madrid, MO 63869. 573-748-5146; hours: 8:30AM-N, 1-4:30PM. Records indexed from 1804 to present in many books. Records indexed on computer back 3 years. Only the public may search. R/E record copy- $2.00 1st page, $1.00 each add'l page. Tax lien copy- $1.00 per lien. Cert fee- $1.00 per cert plus copy fee. Payee- New Madrid County Recorder of Deeds. **Online access to Real Estate Recording records:** Land records may be available at http://etitlesearch.com. You can do a name search; choose from $200.00 monthly subscription or per click account. **Property tax/Assessor-** 573-748-2387.

Newton County

Recorder of Deeds, PO Box 604, Neosho, MO 64850-0130. 417-451-8224, R/E recording phone-417-451-8224 or 8225, UCC recording phone-417-451-8225; fax-417-451-8273; hours: 8:30AM-5PM. Separate indices to search include grantor, grantee, WD books. Records indexed on a public use terminal back to 1994. Office will perform a UCC search but public must search other records themselves. UCC search per debtor name- $14.00. Copy fee $1.00 per page. Cert fee- $2.00 1st page, plus copy fee. Payee- Recorder of Deeds. **Online access to Deed, Mortgage, UCC, Lien, Vital Statistic records:** Access to the Recorder's database requires a $200 sign-up fee; images go back to 1999; index to 1994. System may be temporarily down. **Other phones:** Treasurer- 417-451-8226; Appraiser/Auditor- 417-451-8379; Elections- 417-451-8220; Vital Records- 573-751-6387; Health Dept (Birth & Death)-

417-451-3743; Mapping -417-451-8229. **Assessor-** 101 S Wood St #205, Neosho, MO 64850; 417-451-8228 or 8218, assessor fax- 417-451-8259.

Nodaway County

Recorder of Deeds, 305 N. Main, Rm 104, Maryville, MO 64468. 660-582-5711; fax-660-582-5282; hours: 8:30AM-4:30PM. Office personnel or visitors may perform searches. Search fee $15.00 per name. Will not search real estate records. Copy fee $1.00 per page. Cert fee- $5.00 per cert. Payee- Recorder of Deeds. **Property tax/Assessor-** 660-582-3372.

Oregon County

Recorder of Deeds, PO Box 406, Alton, MO 65606. 417-778-7460; fax-417-778-7206; hours: 8AM-4PM. Separate indices to search include warranty deed, misc and deed of trust. Record index not computerized. Only the public may search. Copy fee $.25 per page. Cert fee- $1.00 per instrument includes copy fee. Payee- Recorder of Deeds. **Other phones:** Treasurer- 417-778-6303; Elections- 417-778-7475. **Property tax/Assessor-** PO Box 361, Alton, MO 65606; 417-778-7471.

Osage County

Recorder of Deeds, PO Box 825, Linn, MO 65051-0825. 573-897-3114; fax-573-897-4075; hours: 8AM-4:30PM. All records in one index. Records indexed on computer back to 11/1993. Only the public may search. Copy fee $.50 per page. Cert fee- $2.00 per cert plus copy fee. Payee- Osage County Recorder of Deeds. **Other phones:** Treasurer- 573-897-3095; Elections- 573-897-2139; Vital Records-573-751-6001. **assessor-**573-897-2217.

Ozark County

Circuit Clerk & Recorder, PO Box 36, Gainesville, MO 65655. 417-679-4232; fax-417-679-4554; hours: 8AM-N, 12:30-4:30PM. Office personnel or visitors may perform searches. Will not search real estate records. UCC search per debtor name- $14.00. UCC search & copy request (including 10 pages of copies)- $28.00. Copy fee $.50 per page after 10 pages. Tax lien copy- $.25 per page. **Other phones:** Treasurer- 417-679-3553; Elections- 417-679-3516. **Assessor-** 417-679-4705.

Pemiscot County

Recorder of Deeds, 610 Ward Ave, Ste. 1A; Pemiscot County Courthouse, Caruthersville, MO 63830. 573-333-2204; hours: 8:30AM-4:30PM. Separate indices to search include deed of trust, warranty & miscellaneous. Only the public may search. 1st 10 copies fee, then copy fee $.50 per page. R/E record copy- $1.00 per page. Cert fee- $1.00 per doc, plus copy fee. Payee- Pemiscot County Recorder of Deeds. **Online access to Real Estate Recording, Deed records:** Access land records at http://etitlesearch.com. You can do a name search; choose from $200.00 monthly subscription or per click account. **Other phones:** Treasurer- 573-333-4171. **Property tax/Assessor-** 573-333-1390.

Perry County

Recorder of Deeds, 15 W. Ste. Marie St; #1, Perryville, MO 63775. 573-547-1611; fax-573-547-3879; hours: 8AM-5PM. All records in one index. Records indexed on a public use terminal back to 1993. Only the public may search. Copy fee after 1st 10 pages is $.50 per page. R/E or tax lien copy- $2.00 1st page; $1.00 each add'l page. Cert fee- $1.00 per doc plus copy fee. Payee- Perry County recorder. **Other phones:** Treasurer- 573-547-4502; Elections- 573-547-4242. **Assessor-** 573-547-5211.

Pettis County

Recorder of Deeds, 415 S. Ohio, Sedalia, MO 65301. 660-826-1136; fax-660-829-4479; hours: 8AM-5PM. Office personnel or visitors may perform searches. Will not search real estate records. UCC search per debtor name- $14.00. Copy fee $1.00 per page.

Cert fee- $1.00 per doc plus copy fee. Payee-Recorder of Deeds. **Other phones:** Treasurer- 660-827-0486; Elections- 660-826-5395; Vital Records- 660-826-1136. **Assessor**- 660-827-0023.

Phelps County

Recorder of Deeds, 200 N Main #133; Courthouse, Rolla, MO 65401. 573-458-6095; fax-573-458-6098; 8AM-5PM. www.phelpscounty.org/cthouse.html
All records in one index. Records indexed on a public use terminal back to 5/1991. Office will perform a UCC search but public must search other records themselves. Search fee $14.00. Copy fee $1.00 per page. Cert fee- $2.00 per page plus copy fee. Payee- Phelps County Recorder. **Other phones:** Treasurer- 573-458-6130; Elections- 573-458-6100; Vital Records- 573-458-6123. **Property tax/Assessor**- address above. 573-458-6140.

Pike County

Recorder of Deeds, 115 W. Main St, Bowling Green, MO 63334. 573-324-5567; hours: 8AM-4:30PM.
All records in one index. Only the office personnel may search. Copy fee $1.00 per page after 10 pages. Cert fee- $1.00 per cert plus copy fee. Payee- Pike County Recorder of Deeds. **Other phones:** Treasurer- 573-324-2102; Appraiser/Auditor- 573-406-5483; Elections- 573-324-2412. **Property tax/Assessor**- 573-324-3261.

Platte County

Chief Deputy, 415 3rd St, #70, Platte City, MO 64079. 816-858-3323, R/E recording phone-816-858-3320, UCC recording phone-816-858-1832; fax-816-858-2379; hours: 8AM-5PM. www.co.platte.mo.us/county_off_rec.html
Separate indices to search include deeds, durable power of attorney, request for notice. Records indexed on a public use terminal back to November, 1990, prior in index books. Office will perform a UCC search only if you have proper request document, but public must search other records themselves. UCC search per debtor name- $14.00. Copy fee $1.00 per page after 10 pages for UCC's only. Cert fee- $1.00 per doc plus copy fee. Payee- Recorder of Deeds. **Other phones:** Treasurer- 816-858-3318; Elections- 816-858-4400. **Property tax/Assessor**- 415 3rd St #20, Platte City, MO 64079; 816-858-3301.

Polk County

Recorder of Deeds, 102 E. Broadway; Courthouse, Bolivar, MO 65613-1502. 417-326-4924; fax-417-326-6898; hours: 8AM-5PM.
Separate indices to search include grantor/grantee. Office will perform a UCC search but public must search other records themselves. Tax liens not included in UCC search. UCC search per debtor name- $14.00 per search. Copy fee $1.00 per page. Cert fee- $2.00 per doc plus copy fee. Payee-Recorder. **Other phones:** Treasurer- 417-326-4913; Appraiser/Auditor- 417-326-4346; Elections- 417-326-4031; Vital Records- 417-326-4031. **Property tax/Assessor**- 102 E Broadway, Courthouse, Rm 9, Bolivar, MO 65613; 417-326-4643.

Pulaski County

Recorder of Deeds, 301 Historic Route 66 E.; Courthouse #202, Waynesville, MO 65583. 573-774-4760; fax-573-774-6967; hours: 8AM-4:30PM.
Office will perform a UCC search but public must search other records themselves. UCC search per debtor name- $14.00. UCC search & copy request (including 10 pages of copies)- $28.00. Copy fee $1.00 per page after 10 pages. Cert fee- $5.00 per cert. Payee- Pulaski County Recorder of Deeds. **Other phones:** Treasurer- 573-774-6609 x124. **Property tax/Assessor**- 573-774-6609 x117.

Putnam County

Recorder of Deeds, Courthouse, Rm 202, Unionville, MO 63565-1659. 660-947-2071; fax-660-947-2320; hours: 8AM-N, 1-5PM. None.

If you contact them with a book and page they can make a copy of that document for $1.00 per page. Must be prepaid. All records in one index. Records indexed on a public use terminal back to 1996. Only the public may search. Copy fee $14.00 for copy request/info filed. Cert fee- $1.00 per doc, plus copy fee. Payee- Putnam County Recorder. **Other phones:** Treasurer- 660-947-2095; Elections- 660-947-2674. **Property tax/Assessor**- same address as above. 660-947-3900.

Ralls County

Recorder of Deeds, PO Box 444, New London, MO 63459-0444. 573-985-5631; 8:30AM-N, 1-4:30PM. Separate indices to search include computer and books. Records indexed on a public use terminal back to 1989. Office will perform a UCC search but public must search other records themselves. UCC search per debtor name- $14.00. UCC search & copy request (including 10 pages of copies)- $28.00. Copy fee $1.00 per page after 10 pages. Cert fee- $1.00 per cert plus copy fee. Payee- Ralls County Recorder of Deeds. **Other phones:** Treasurer- 573-985-7151. **Property tax/Assessor**- 573-985-5671.

Randolph County

Recorder of Deeds, 110 S. Main St.; Courthouse, Huntsville, MO 65259. 660-277-4718; fax-660-277-3246; hours: 8AM-4PM.
Index: Indices by year. Records indexed on a public use terminal back to 1996. Only the public may search. Copy fee $2.00 1st page, $1.00 each add'l. Cert fee- $1.00 per page plus copy fee. Payee- Recorder of Deeds. **Other phones:** Treasurer- 660-277-4714; Elections- 660-277-4717. **Property tax/Assessor**- 660-277-4716.

Ray County

Recorder of Deeds, PO Box 167, Richmond, MO 64085. 816-776-4500; hours: 8AM-N, 1-4PM.
Office will perform a UCC search but public must search other records themselves. UCC search per debtor name- $14.00. UCC search & copy request (including 10 pages of copies)- $28.00. Copy fee $1.00 per page after 10 pages. Cert fee- $1.00 per page. Payee- Ray County Recorder of Deeds. **Other phones:** Treasurer- 660-776-6140. **Property tax/Assessor**- 660-776-2676.

Reynolds County

Recorder of Deeds, PO Box 76, Centerville, MO 63633-0076. 573-648-2494; fax-573-648-2503; hours: 8AM-4PM. Index: Books in Alpha order up to 2/2003. Records indexed on a public use terminal back to 2/2003. Office personnel or visitors may perform searches. Search fee $14.00 UCCs. Copy fee $2.00 per document. Cert fee- $4.00 per doc, plus copy fee. Payee- Reynolds County Recorder. **Other phones:** Treasurer- 573-648-2494 x37; Elections- 573-648-2494 x12; Vital Records- 573-648-2494 x12. **Assessor**- 573-648-2494 x18.

Ripley County

Recorder of Deeds, 100 Courthouse Sq; #3, Doniphan, MO 63935. 573-996-7941; fax-573-966-9706; Office personnel or visitors may perform searches. Search fee $14.00 per name. **Property tax/Assessor**- 573-996-7113.

Saline County

Recorder of Deeds, Courthouse; Rm 206, Marshall, MO 65340. 660-886-2677; fax-660-886-2603; hours: 8AM-4:30PM.
Separate indices to search include land, UCC, marriage. Records indexed on a public use terminal back to 1992. Office will perform a UCC search but public must search other records themselves. UCC search per debtor name- $14.00. UCC search & copy request (including 10 pages of copies)- $28.00. Copy fee $.50 per page after 10 pages. Cert fee- $1.00 per page plus copy fee. Payee- Saline County Recorder of Deeds. **Other**

phones: Treasurer- 660-886-3636; Elections- 660-886-3331; Vital Records- 660-886-3434. **Property tax/Assessor**- 660-335-3111.

Schuyler County

Recorder of Deeds, PO Box 186, Lancaster, MO 63548. 660-457-3784; fax-660-457-3016; hours: 8AM-4PM.
Separate indices to search include land transfers, financials. Record index not computerized. Only the public may search. Copy fee $1.00 per copy/page. Cert fee- $1.00 per doc plus copy fee. Payee- Recorder of Deeds. **Other phones:** Treasurer- 660-457-3825; Elections- 660-457-3842. **Property tax/Assessor**- 660-457-3211.

Scotland County

Recorder of Deeds, 117 S. Market St, #106, Memphis, MO 63555-1449. 660-465-8605; fax-660-465-8673; hours: 8AM-4PM.
Office personnel or visitors may perform searches. Search fee $14.00 per name. Will not search real estate records. Copy fee $.50 per page after 10 pages. R/E record copy- $1.00 per page. Cert fee- $1.50 per cert plus copy fee. Payee- Scotland County Recorder of Deeds. **Other phones:** Treasurer- 660-465-2529. **Property tax/Assessor**- 660-465-2269.

Scott County

Recorder of Deeds, PO Box 78, Benton, MO 63736. 573-545-3551; fax-573-545-3551; 8:30AM-5PM. Office will perform a UCC search but public must search other records themselves. UCC search per debtor name- $14.00. UCC search & copy request (including 10 pages of copies)- $28.00. General copy fee $1.00 per page after 10 pages. Real estate copy- $2.00 1st page, $1.00 each add'l. Cert fee- $2.00 per cert 1st. $1.00 each add'l page. Payee- Scott County Recorder of Deeds. **Online access to Real Estate Recording, Deed records:** Access recording office land data at www.etitlesearch.com; registration required, fee based on usage. **Other phones:** Treasurer- 573-545-3543. **Property tax/Assessor**- 573-545-3535.

Shannon County

Recorder of Deeds, PO Box 148, Eminence, MO 65466. 573-226-3315; fax-573-226-5321; hours: 8AM-N, 12:30-4:30PM.
Records indexed on a public use terminal back to 5/95. Office will perform a UCC search but public must search other records themselves. UCC search per debtor name- $14.00. UCC search & copy request (including 10 pages of copies)- $28.00. Copy fee $.25 per page. Cert fee- $2.25 per cert plus copy fee. Payee- Shannon County Recorder of Deeds. **Other phones:** Treasurer- 573-226-3051. **Property tax/Assessor**- 573-226-5539.

Shelby County

Recorder of Deeds, PO Box 176, Shelbyville, MO 63469. 573-633-2151; fax-573-633-1004; hours: 8AM-4:30PM.
Separate indices to search include Deeds, UCC's, Marriage, Surveys, Tax Liens. Only the public may search. Copy fee $1.00 per UCC. Cert fee- $3.00 per page includes copy fee. Payee- Shelby Co. Recorder. **Other phones:** Treasurer- 573-633-2574; Elections- 573-633-2187. **Property tax/Assessor**- PO Box 165, Shelbyville, MO 63469; 573-633-2521.

St. Charles County

Recorder of Deeds, PO Box 99, St. Charles, MO 63302-0099. 636-949-7505, UCC recording phone-636-949-7508; fax-636-949-7512; hours: 8AM-5PM. www.saintcharlescounty.org
All records in one index. Office will perform a UCC search but public must search other records themselves. UCC search per debtor name- $8.00. UCC search & copy request (including 10 pages of copies)- $16.00. Copy fee $2.00 1st page, $1.00

each add'l; $.50 self serve. Cert fee- $1.00 per cert plus copy fee. Payee- St. Charles County Recorder of Deeds. **Online access to Assessor, Property records:** Access recorder records free at http://65.125.29.166/scweb/. Search index free; images -$1.00 per page. Also, search Property Assessment data free at www.win.org/library/library_office/assessment. No name searching; search by address, street or map ID. **Other phones:** Appraiser/Auditor- 636-949-7431; Elections- 636-949-7550; Vital Records- 636-949-7558. **Property tax/Assessor-** 201 N Second, Rm 212, St. Charles, MO 63301; 636-949-7425.

St. Clair County

Recorder of Deeds, PO Box 323, Osceola, MO 64776. 417-646-2950; fax-417-646-2951 8AM-4:30PM. Only the public may search. Copy fee $1.00 per page. Cert fee- $1.00 per cert plus copy fee. Payee- St. Clair Recorder. **Other phones:** Treasurer- 417-646-8068. **Property tax/Assessor-** 417-646-2449.

St. Francois County

Recorder of Deeds, 1 N Washington, Courthouse Rm 105, Farmington, MO 63640. 573-756-2323; hours: 8AM-4PM.
All records in one index. Records indexed on a public use terminal back to 1994. Real estate record owner searches available. Will search UCC records, but not tax liens. UCC search per debtor name- $14.00. UCC search & copy request (including 10 pages of copies)- $28.00. Copy fee $.50 per page after 10 pages. Real estate record or tax lien copy- $1.00 per page. Cert fee- $1.00 per cert plus copy fee. Payee- St. Francois County Recorder of Deeds. **Online access to Assessor, Property records:** Access property assessor data free at www.sfcassessor.org/parcel_search.html. **Other phones:** Treasurer- 573-756-3349. **Property tax/Assessor-** 1 N Washington, Courthouse Rm 101, Farmington, MO 63640; 573-756-2509 x1.

St. Genevieve County

Recorder of Deeds, 55 S.3rd St. RM 3; Court House, Ste. Genevieve, MO 63670. 573-883-2706; fax-573-883-5312; hours: 8AM-4:30PM.
Office will perform a UCC search but public must search other records themselves. UCC search per debtor name- $14.00. UCC search & copy request (including 10 pages of copies)- $28.00. Copy fee $.50 per page. Tax lien copy- $.25. Cert fee- $2.00 per cert. Payee- Recorder of Deeds. **Property tax/Assessor-** 573-883-2333.

St. Louis City

Recorder of Deeds, 1200 Market St; Rm 126, St. Louis, MO 63103. 314-622-4328; fax-314-622-4175;
Office personnel or visitors may perform searches. Search fee $8.00 per name. Will not search real estate records. Copy fee $3.00 1st page; $2.00 each add'l. Cert fee- $2.00 per cert plus copy fee. **Online access to Recording, Real Estate, Deed, Lien records:** Recorder office data by subscription on either the Laredo system using subscription and fees or the Tapestry System using credit card, https://tapestry.fidlar.com/tapsearch.aspx; $3.99 search; $.50 per image. **Other phones:** Treasurer- 314-622-2062. **Property tax/Assessor-** 314-615-5124.

St. Louis County

Recorder of Deeds, 41 S. Central Ave, 4th Fl, Clayton, MO 63105. 314-615-2500; fax-314-615-4964; hours: 8AM-5PM.
www.stlouiscounty.org/RecordersOffice
All records in one index. Records indexed on a public use terminal back to 6/1992. Office will perform a UCC search but public must search other records themselves. UCC search per debtor name- $8.00. UCC search & copy request (including 10 pages of copies)- $16.00. UCC copy fee $.50 per page after 10 pages. Cert fee- $1.00 per cert plus copy fee. Payee- St. Louis County Recorder of Deeds. **Online access to Assessor, Property, Recorder, Deed records:** Access property

data free at www.stlouiscounty.org/auditor/parcelinfo/. For full, professional information, $100 per month subscription and registration required. **Other phones:** Vital Records- 314-615-1684. **Property tax/Assessor-** 41 S. Central Ave, 3rd Fl, Admin. Bldg, Clayton, MO 63105; 314-615-4225.

Stoddard County

Recorder of Deeds, PO Box 217, Bloomfield, MO 63825-0217. 573-568-3444; fax-573-568-2545;
Separate indices to search include Computer and Books by year. Records indexed on computer back to 4/26/2004. Office will perform a UCC search but public must search other records themselves. Search fee $14.00. Copy fee $.50 per pages. Cert fee- $1.00 per doc, plus copy fee. Payee- Recorder of Deeds. **Other phones:** Treasurer- 573-568-3327. **Property tax/Assessor-** 573-568-3163.

Stone County

Recorder of Deeds, PO Box 18, Galena, MO 65656. 417-357-6362; fax-417-357-8131; hours: 8AM-4PM.
All records in one index. Only the public may search. Copy fee $.25; if real estate $2.00 per page. Cert fee- $1.00 per doc, plus copy fee. Payee- Stone County Recorder. **Online access to Property, Assessor records:** Access property data from the GIS interactive map at www.stoneco-mo.us/disclaim.htm. Download the MapGuide viewer first. **Other phones:** Treasurer- 417-357-6131; Elections- 417-357-6127. **Property tax/Assessor-** PO Box 135, Galena, MO 65656; 417-357-6141.

Sullivan County

Recorder of Deeds, Courthouse, Milan, MO 63556. 660-265-3630; fax-660-265-5071; hours: 9AM-N; 1PM-4:30PM.
Office personnel or visitors may perform searches. Search fee $14.00 per search. Will not search real estate records. Copy fee $1.00 per page. Cert fee- $1.00 per doc plus copy fee. Payee- Recorder of Deeds. **Other phones:** Treasurer- 660-265-4514. **Property tax/Assessor-** 660-265-4474.

Taney County

Recorder of Deeds, PO Box 428, Forsyth, MO 65653. 417-546-7234; fax-417-546-9021; hours: 8AM-5PM.
www.co.taney.mo.us
All records in one index. Office will perform a UCC search but public must search other records themselves. UCC searches do not include tax lien searches. UCC search per debtor name- $14.00. UCC search & copy request (including 10 pages of copies)- $28.00. Separate federal/state combined tax lien search- $4.00 per debtor. Copy fee $.50 per page after 10 pages. R/E or tax lien copy- $1.00 per page. Cert fee- $1.50 per cert plus copy fee. Payee- Taney County Recorder of Deeds. **Other phones:** Treasurer- 417-546-7207. **Property tax/Assessor-** 417-546-7240.

Texas County

Recorder of Deeds, PO Box 287, Houston, MO 65483. 417-967-3742; fax-417-967-4220;
Only the public may search. Copy fee $1.00 per page. Cert fee- $3.00. Payee- Recorder of Deeds. **Other phones:** Treasurer- 417-967-2589. **Property tax/Assessor-** 417-967-4709.

Vernon County

Recorder of Deeds, 100 W. Cherry, Courthouse, Nevada, MO 64772. 417-448-2520; fax-417-448-2524; hours: 8:30AM-N, 1-4:30PM.
Office will perform a UCC search but public must search other records themselves. UCC search per debtor name- $14.00. UCC search & copy request (including 10 pages of copies)- $28.00. Copy fee $1.00 per page after 10 pages. Cert fee- $1.00 per cert plus copy fee. Payee- Vernon County Recorder of Deeds. **Other phones:** Treasurer- 417-448-2510; Elections- 417-448-2500. **Property tax/Assessor-** 417-448-2530.

Warren County

Recorder of Deeds, 104 W Boone's Lick Rd, Warrenton, MO 63383. 636-456-9800; 8AM-4:30PM.
Office will perform a UCC search but public must search other records themselves. UCC search per debtor name- $14.00. UCC search & copy request (including 10 pages of copies)- $28.00. Copy fee $1.00 per page. Cert fee- $1.00 per doc plus copy fee. Payee- Warren County Recorder of Deeds. **Other phones:** Treasurer- 636-456-3389. **Property tax/Assessor-** 105 S Market, Warrenton, MO 63383; 636-456-8885.

Washington County

Recorder of Deeds, 102 N. Missouri St, Potosi, MO 63664. 573-438-6111; fax-573-438-7900; hours: 8AM-4:30PM.
Separate indices to search. Office will perform a UCC search but public must search other records themselves. UCC search per debtor name- $14.00. UCC search & copy request (including 10 pages of copies)- $28.00. Copy fee $1.00 per page. R/E record copy- $.50 per page. Cert fee- $2.00 for cert. & $.50 per page plus copy fee. Payee- Recorder of Deeds. **Other phones:** Treasurer- 573-438-6111; Elections- 573-438-6111. **Property tax/Assessor-** 573-438-4992.

Wayne County

Recorder of Deeds, PO Box 78, Greenville, MO 63944. 573-224-3041; fax-573-224-3015; hours: 8:30AM-N; 1PM-4:30PM.
Index: Books. Records indexed on computer back to 1/27/2003. Office will perform a UCC search but public must search other records themselves. Search fee $14.00. Copy fee $.50 per page. Cert fee- $2.00 per page. Payee- Recorder of Deeds. **Other phones:** Treasurer- 573-224-3011. **Property tax/Assessor-** PO Box 54, Greenville, MO 63944; 573-224-3006.

Webster County

Recorder of Deeds, PO Box 546, Marshfield, MO 65706. 417-859-5882; fax-417-468-3843; hours: 8AM-5PM.
Separate indices to search include land, UCCs, State & Fed tax liens, marriage. Records indexed on a public use terminal back to 1985. Office will perform a UCC search but public must search other records themselves. Search fee $14.00. Copy fee $1.00 per page. Cert fee- $1.00 per doc plus copy fee. **Other phones:** Treasurer- 417-468-2108; Elections- 417-859-8683. **Property tax/Assessor-** 417-859-2169.

Worth County

Recorder of Deeds, PO Box 14, Grant City, MO 64456. 660-564-2484; fax-660-564-2432; hours: 8AM-4PM.
Office personnel or visitors may perform searches. General search fee $4.00 per name. UCC search per debtor name- $14.00. UCC search & copy request (including 10 pages of copies)- $28.00. Copy fee $1.00 per page. Cert fee- None. Payee- Worth County Recorder of Deeds. **Other phones:** Treasurer- 660-564-2154. **Property tax/Assessor-** 660-564-2153.

Wright County

County Recorder, PO Box 39, Hartville, MO 65667. 417-741-7322; fax-417-741-7504; hours: 8AM-4:30PM.
Separate indices to search include computer and books. Records indexed on a public use terminal back to 1993, books up to 1993. Only the public may search. Copy fee $1.00 per page. Cert fee- $2.00 per doc plus copy fee. Payee- Wright County Recorder. **Other phones:** Treasurer- 417-741-7225; Elections- 417-741-6661; Vital Records- 573-751-6400. **Property tax/Assessor-** 417-741-6400.

Missouri County Locator

You will usually be able to find the city name in the City/County Cross Reference below. In that case, it is a simple matter to determine the county from the cross reference. However, only the official US Postal Service city names are included in this index. There are an additional 40,000 place names that people use in their addresses. Therefore, we have also included a ZIP/City Cross Reference immediately following the City/County Cross Reference.

Missouri City/County Cross Reference

ADRIAN Bates
ADVANCE (63730) Stoddard(78), Cape Girardeau(16), Bollinger(5)
AGENCY Buchanan
ALBA Jasper
ALBANY Gentry
ALDRICH (65601) Polk(70), Dade(28), Cedar(1)
ALEXANDRIA Clark
ALLENDALE Worth
ALLENTON St. Louis
ALMA Lafayette
ALTAMONT Daviess
ALTENBURG (63732) Cape Girardeau(95), Perry(4)
ALTON Oregon
AMAZONIA Andrew
AMITY De Kalb
AMORET Bates
AMSTERDAM Bates
ANABEL Macon
ANDERSON McDonald
ANNADA Pike
ANNAPOLIS (63620) Iron(56), Madison(32), Reynolds(10)
ANNISTON Mississippi
APPLETON CITY (64724) St. Clair(93), Bates(6)
ARBELA (63432) Scotland(88), Clark(11)
ARBYRD Dunklin
ARCADIA (63621) Iron(79), Madison(20)
ARCHIE Cass
ARCOLA (65603) Dade(97), Cedar(2)
ARGYLE (65001) Osage(61), Maries(38)
ARMSTRONG (65230) Howard(86), Randolph(13)
ARNOLD Jefferson
ARROW ROCK Saline
ASBURY (64832) Barton(83), Jasper(16)
ASH GROVE (65604) Greene(65), Lawrence(32), Dade(1)
ASHBURN Pike
ASHLAND Boone
ATLANTA Macon
AUGUSTA St. Charles
AURORA (65605) Lawrence(90), Barry(9)
AUXVASSE (65231) Callaway(98), Audrain(1)
AVA (65608) Douglas(90), Taney(9)
AVALON Livingston
AVILLA Jasper
BAKERSFIELD (65609) Ozark(77), Howell(22)
BALLWIN St. Louis
BARING (63531) Knox(59), Scotland(40)
BARNARD Nodaway
BARNETT (65011) Morgan(94), Moniteau(5)
BARNHART Jefferson
BATES CITY (64011) Lafayette(92), Johnson(7)
BEAUFORT Franklin
BELGRADE Washington
BELL CITY (63735) Stoddard(91), Scott(8)
BELLE (65013) Maries(68), Osage(31)
BELLEVIEW (63623) Iron(97), Reynolds(2)
BELLFLOWER (63333) Montgomery(96), Lincoln(3)
BELTON Cass
BENDAVIS Texas

BENTON Scott
BENTON CITY Audrain
BERGER Franklin
BERNIE (63822) Stoddard(95), Dunklin(4)
BERTRAND (63823) Mississippi(90), Scott(9)
BETHANY Harrison
BETHEL Shelby
BEULAH (65436) Phelps(87), Texas(8), Pulaski(3)
BEVIER Macon
BILLINGS (65610) Christian(95), Lawrence(3)
BIRCH TREE (65438) Shannon(74), Oregon(25)
BISMARCK (63624) St. Francois(70), Washington(25), Iron(4)
BIXBY Iron
BLACK (63625) Reynolds(89), Iron(10)
BLACKBURN (65321) Saline(61), Lafayette(38)
BLACKWATER Cooper
BLACKWELL (63626) Washington(80), St. Francois(19)
BLAIRSTOWN Henry
BLAND (65014) Gasconade(68), Osage(25), Maries(6)
BLODGETT Scott
BLOOMFIELD Stoddard
BLOOMSDALE (63627) Ste. Genevieve(90), Jefferson(9)
BLUE EYE (65611) Stone(95), Taney(4)
BLUE SPRINGS Jackson
BLYTHEDALE Harrison
BOGARD Carroll
BOIS D ARC (65612) Greene(93), Lawrence(6)
BOLCKOW (64427) Andrew(83), Nodaway(16)
BOLIVAR Polk
BONNE TERRE (63628) St. Francois(94), Ste. Genevieve(2), Washington(2)
BONNOTS MILL Osage
BOONVILLE Cooper
BOSS (65440) Dent(59), Reynolds(31), Iron(9)
BOSWORTH Carroll
BOURBON (65441) Crawford(95), Washington(3)
BOWLING GREEN (63334) Pike(98), Lincoln(1)
BRADLEYVILLE (65614) Taney(90), Christian(9)
BRAGG CITY Pemiscot
BRAGGADOCIO Pemiscot
BRANDSVILLE Howell
BRANSON (65616) Taney(93), Stone(6)
BRANSON Taney
BRASHEAR Adair
BRAYMER (64624) Caldwell(69), Carroll(14), Ray(12), Livingston(3)
BRAZEAU Perry
BRECKENRIDGE (64625) Caldwell(82), Livingston(8), Daviess(8)
BRIAR Ripley
BRIDGETON St. Louis
BRIGHTON Polk
BRINKTOWN Maries
BRIXEY Ozark

BRONAUGH (64728) Vernon(73), Barton(26)
BROOKFIELD (64628) Linn(96), Chariton(3)
BROOKLINE STATION Greene
BROSELEY Butler
BROWNING (64630) Linn(64), Sullivan(35)
BROWNWOOD Stoddard
BRUMLEY Miller
BRUNER (65620) Christian(98), Douglas(1)
BRUNSWICK Chariton
BUCKLIN (64631) Linn(79), Macon(20)
BUCKNER Jackson
BUCYRUS Texas
BUFFALO (65622) Dallas(97), Polk(2)
BUNCETON Cooper
BUNKER (63629) Reynolds(66), Dent(25), Shannon(7)
BURFORDVILLE Cape Girardeau
BURLINGTON JUNCTION Nodaway
BUTLER Bates
BUTTERFIELD Barry
CABOOL (65689) Howell(72), Texas(25), Douglas(2)
CADET Washington
CAINSVILLE (64632) Harrison(70), Mercer(29)
CAIRO Randolph
CALEDONIA Washington
CALHOUN Henry
CALIFORNIA (65018) Moniteau(96), Cooper(3)
CALLAO Macon
CAMDEN Ray
CAMDEN POINT Platte
CAMDENTON Camden
CAMERON (64429) Clinton(68), De Kalb(29), Daviess(1)
CAMPBELL Dunklin
CANALOU New Madrid
CANTON (63435) Lewis(94), Clark(5)
CAPE FAIR (65624) Stone(95), Barry(3)
CAPE GIRARDEAU Cape Girardeau
CAPLINGER MILLS Cedar
CARDWELL Dunklin
CARL JUNCTION Jasper
CARTERVILLE Jasper
CARTHAGE Jasper
CARUTHERSVILLE Pemiscot
CASCADE Wayne
CASSVILLE Barry
CATAWISSA (63015) Franklin(75), Jefferson(24)
CATRON New Madrid
CAULFIELD (65626) Howell(66), Ozark(33)
CEDAR CITY Callaway
CEDAR HILL Jefferson
CEDARCREEK Taney
CENSUS BUREAU Boone
CENTER Ralls
CENTERTOWN (65023) Cole(83), Moniteau(16)
CENTERVIEW Johnson
CENTERVILLE Reynolds
CENTRALIA (65240) Boone(72), Audrain(25), Callaway(1)
CHADWICK (65629) Christian(98), Douglas(1)
CHAFFEE Scott
CHAMOIS Osage

CHARLESTON (63834) Mississippi(94), Scott(5)
CHERRYVILLE Crawford
CHESTERFIELD St. Louis
CHESTNUTRIDGE Christian
CHILHOWEE (64733) Johnson(70), Henry(24), Jackson(4)
CHILLICOTHE (64601) Livingston(98), Sullivan(1)
CHULA (64635) Livingston(79), Linn(11), Grundy(9)
CLARENCE (63437) Shelby(88), Macon(6), Monroe(4)
CLARK (65243) Randolph(40), Boone(29), Audrain(22), Howard(5)
CLARKSBURG (65025) Moniteau(57), Cooper(42)
CLARKSDALE De Kalb
CLARKSVILLE Pike
CLARKTON Dunklin
CLEARMONT Nodaway
CLEVELAND Cass
CLEVER Christian
CLIFTON HILL (65244) Randolph(96), Chariton(3)
CLIMAX SPRINGS Camden
CLINTON (64735) Henry(95), Benton(4)
CLUBB Wayne
CLYDE Nodaway
COATSVILLE (63535) Schuyler(56), Putnam(43)
COFFEY (64636) Daviess(93), Harrison(6)
COLE CAMP (65325) Benton(90), Morgan(6), Pettis(3)
COLLINS St. Clair
COLUMBIA Boone
COMMERCE Scott
CONCEPTION Nodaway
CONCEPTION JUNCTION Nodaway
CONCORDIA (64020) Lafayette(90), Johnson(8), Saline(1)
CONRAN New Madrid
CONTEL CORPORATION St. Charles
CONWAY (65632) Laclede(54), Webster(27), Dallas(18)
COOK STATION (65449) Crawford(97), Phelps(2)
COOTER Pemiscot
CORDER Lafayette
CORNING Holt
COSBY Andrew
COTTLEVILLE St. Charles
COUCH Oregon
COWGILL (64637) Caldwell(78), Ray(21)
CRAIG Holt
CRANE (65633) Stone(93), Barry(6)
CREIGHTON (64739) Henry(77), Cass(22)
CROCKER (65452) Pulaski(95), Miller(4)
CROSS TIMBERS (65634) Hickory(89), Benton(9), Camden(1)
CRYSTAL CITY Jefferson
CUBA Crawford
CURRYVILLE Pike
DADEVILLE Dade
DAISY Cape Girardeau
DALTON Chariton
DARDENNE St. Charles
DARLINGTON Gentry
DAVISVILLE (65456) Crawford(98), Iron(2)
DAWN (64638) Livingston(72), Carroll(27)

DE KALB Buchanan
DE SOTO Jefferson
DE WITT Carroll
DEARBORN Platte
DEEPWATER (64740) Henry(71), St. Clair(28)
DEERFIELD Vernon
DEERING Pemiscot
DEFIANCE St. Charles
DELTA Cape Girardeau
DENVER (64441) Worth(50), Gentry(49)
DES ARC (63636) Iron(66), Madison(29), Wayne(3)
DEVILS ELBOW (65457) Pulaski(95), Phelps(4)
DEXTER Stoddard
DIAMOND (64840) Newton(98), Jasper(1)
DIGGINS Webster
DITTMER Jefferson
DIXON (65459) Pulaski(74), Maries(23), Miller(2)
DOE RUN St. Francois
DONIPHAN (63935) Ripley(96), Carter(1), Oregon(1)
DORA (65637) Ozark(63), Howell(22), Douglas(14)
DOVER Lafayette
DOWNING (63536) Schuyler(73), Scotland(26)
DREXEL (64742) Cass(87), Bates(12)
DRURY (65638) Douglas(89), Ozark(10)
DUDLEY Stoddard
DUENWEG Jasper
DUKE (65461) Phelps(95), Pulaski(4)
DUNNEGAN (65640) Polk(92), Cedar(7)
DURHAM (63438) Lewis(66), Marion(33)
DUTCHTOWN Cape Girardeau
DUTZOW Warren
EAGLE ROCK Barry
EAGLEVILLE Harrison
EARTH CITY St. Louis
EAST LYNNE Cass
EAST PRAIRIE Mississippi
EASTON Buchanan
EDGAR SPRINGS (65462) Phelps(97), Dent(2)
EDGERTON (64444) Platte(93), Buchanan(6)
EDINA Knox
EDWARDS (65326) Benton(58), Camden(40)
EL DORADO SPRINGS (64744) Cedar(90), Vernon(5), St. Clair(3)
ELDON (65026) Miller(95), Morgan(4)
ELDRIDGE Laclede
ELK CREEK Texas
ELKLAND (65644) Webster(56), Dallas(43)
ELLINGTON (63638) Reynolds(94), Shannon(3), Carter(1)
ELLSINORE (63937) Carter(84), Butler(15)
ELMER Macon
ELMO Nodaway
ELSBERRY (63343) Lincoln(96), Pike(3)
EMDEN (63439) Shelby(65), Marion(34)
EMINENCE Shannon
EMMA Lafayette
EOLIA (63344) Pike(62), Lincoln(37)
ESSEX Stoddard
ETHEL Macon
ETTERVILLE Miller
EUDORA Polk
EUGENE (65032) Cole(66), Miller(33)
EUNICE Texas
EUREKA (63025) St. Louis(66), Jefferson(33)
EVERTON (65646) Dade(61), Lawrence(38)
EWING (63440) Lewis(70), Marion(25), Shelby(4)
EXCELLO Macon
EXCELSIOR SPRINGS (64024) Clay(73), Ray(26)

EXETER (65647) Barry(78), Newton(19), McDonald(1)
FAGUS Butler
FAIR GROVE (65648) Greene(77), Dallas(12), Webster(9)
FAIR PLAY (65649) Polk(95), Cedar(4)
FAIRDEALING Ripley
FAIRFAX (64446) Atchison(94), Holt(5)
FAIRPORT De Kalb
FAIRVIEW (64842) Newton(97), Barry(1)
FALCON (65470) Laclede(82), Wright(16)
FARBER Audrain
FARLEY Platte
FARMINGTON (63640) St. Francois(98), Ste. Genevieve(1)
FARRAR Perry
FAUCETT Buchanan
FAYETTE Howard
FENTON (63026) St. Louis(51), Jefferson(48)
FENTON St. Louis
FESTUS (63028) Jefferson(93), Ste. Genevieve(6)
FILLMORE Andrew
FISK Butler
FLEMINGTON (65650) Polk(51), Hickory(48)
FLETCHER (63030) Washington(57), Jefferson(42)
FLINTHILL St. Charles
FLORENCE Morgan
FLORISSANT St. Louis
FOLEY Lincoln
FORDLAND (65652) Webster(91), Christian(7), Douglas(1)
FOREST CITY Holt
FORISTELL (63348) St. Charles(66), Warren(30), Lincoln(3)
FORSYTH (65653) Taney(98), Christian(2)
FORT LEONARD WOOD Pulaski
FORTESCUE Holt
FORTUNA (65034) Morgan(63), Moniteau(36)
FOSTER Bates
FRANKFORD (63441) Pike(97), Ralls(2)
FRANKLIN Howard
FREDERICKTOWN (63645) Madison(97), Ste. Genevieve(1)
FREEBURG Osage
FREEMAN Cass
FREISTATT Lawrence
FREMONT (63941) Carter(62), Oregon(25), Ripley(11)
FRENCH VILLAGE (63036) St. Francois(74), Ste. Genevieve(25)
FRIEDHEIM Cape Girardeau
FROHNA Perry
FULTON Callaway
GAINESVILLE Ozark
GALENA (65656) Stone(77), Christian(22)
GALLATIN Daviess
GALT (64641) Grundy(79), Sullivan(20)
GARDEN CITY Cass
GARRISON (65657) Christian(98), Taney(1)
GASCONADE Gasconade
GATEWOOD Ripley
GENTRY Gentry
GERALD Franklin
GIBBS Adair
GIBSON Dunklin
GIDEON (63848) New Madrid(62), Pemiscot(37)
GILLIAM Saline
GILMAN CITY (64642) Harrison(76), Daviess(15), Grundy(8)
GIPSY Bollinger
GLASGOW (65254) Howard(95), Chariton(4)
GLENALLEN Bollinger
GLENCOE St. Louis
GLENWOOD Schuyler

GLOVER Iron
GOBLER (63849) Dunklin(63), Pemiscot(36)
GOLDEN Barry
GOLDEN CITY (64748) Barton(63), Jasper(21), Dade(15)
GOODMAN (64843) McDonald(73), Newton(26)
GOODSON Polk
GORDONVILLE Cape Girardeau
GORIN (63543) Scotland(96), Knox(2)
GOWER (64454) Buchanan(53), Clinton(46)
GRAFF Wright
GRAHAM (64455) Nodaway(95), Andrew(4)
GRAIN VALLEY Jackson
GRANBY Newton
GRANDIN (63943) Carter(79), Ripley(20)
GRANDVIEW Jackson
GRANGER Scotland
GRANT CITY (64456) Worth(98), Harrison(1)
GRASSY Bollinger
GRAVOIS MILLS (65037) Morgan(78), Camden(21)
GRAY SUMMIT Franklin
GRAYRIDGE Stoddard
GREEN CASTLE (63544) Sullivan(48), Adair(44), Putnam(6)
GREEN CITY Sullivan
GREEN RIDGE Pettis
GREENFIELD Dade
GREENTOP (63546) Adair(83), Schuyler(14), Scotland(1)
GREENVILLE Wayne
GREENWOOD (64034) Jackson(91), Cass(8)
GROVER St. Louis
GROVESPRING (65662) Wright(79), Laclede(19)
GRUBVILLE (63041) Franklin(85), Jefferson(14)
GUILFORD Nodaway
HALE (64643) Carroll(56), Livingston(43)
HALF WAY Polk
HALLSVILLE Boone
HALLTOWN Lawrence
HAMILTON (64644) Caldwell(84), Daviess(15)
HANNIBAL (63401) Marion(83), Ralls(16)
HARDENVILLE Ozark
HARDIN (64035) Ray(95), Carroll(4)
HARRIS (64645) Sullivan(85), Mercer(14)
HARRISBURG (65256) Boone(87), Howard(12)
HARRISONVILLE Cass
HARTSBURG (65039) Boone(93), Callaway(6)
HARTSHORN (65479) Texas(92), Shannon(7)
HARTVILLE Wright
HARVIELL (63945) Butler(97), Ripley(2)
HARWOOD Vernon
HATFIELD (64458) Harrison(96), Worth(3)
HAWK POINT (63349) Lincoln(98), Warren(1)
HAYTI Pemiscot
HAZELWOOD St. Louis
HELENA Andrew
HEMATITE Jefferson
HENLEY (65040) Cole(91), Miller(8)
HENRIETTA Ray
HERCULANEUM Jefferson
HERMANN (65041) Gasconade(84), Montgomery(13), Warren(1)
HERMANN Montgomery
HERMITAGE Hickory
HIGBEE (65257) Randolph(72), Howard(27)
HIGGINSVILLE Lafayette
HIGH HILL Montgomery

HIGH POINT Moniteau
HIGH RIDGE (63049) Jefferson(96), St. Louis(3)
HIGHLANDVILLE (65669) Christian(87), Stone(12)
HILLSBORO Jefferson
HIRAM Wayne
HOLCOMB (63852) Dunklin(98), Pemiscot(1)
HOLDEN Johnson
HOLLAND (63853) Pemiscot(92), Dunklin(7)
HOLLIDAY Monroe
HOLLISTER Taney
HOLT Clay
HOLTS SUMMIT Callaway
HOPKINS Nodaway
HORNERSVILLE Dunklin
HORTON Vernon
HOUSE SPRINGS Jefferson
HOUSTON Texas
HOUSTONIA (65333) Pettis(97), Saline(2)
HUGGINS Texas
HUGHESVILLE Pettis
HUMANSVILLE (65674) Polk(81), Cedar(13), Hickory(2), St. Clair(2)
HUME (64752) Bates(72), Vernon(27)
HUMPHREYS (64646) Sullivan(88), Linn(11)
HUNNEWELL (63443) Shelby(38), Monroe(31), Marion(29)
HUNTSVILLE Randolph
HURDLAND (63547) Knox(95), Adair(4)
HURLEY Stone
IBERIA Miller
IMPERIAL Jefferson
INDEPENDENCE Jackson
IONIA (65335) Pettis(66), Benton(33)
IRONDALE (63648) St. Francois(60), Washington(39)
IRONTON (63650) Iron(82), St. Francois(15), Madison(2)
ISABELLA Ozark
JACKSON Cape Girardeau
JACKSONVILLE (65260) Macon(62), Randolph(27), Monroe(9)
JADWIN Dent
JAMESON Daviess
JAMESPORT (64648) Daviess(97), Livingston(2)
JAMESTOWN (65046) Moniteau(92), Cooper(7)
JASPER (64755) Jasper(91), Barton(8)
JEFFERSON CITY Cole
JERICO SPRINGS (64756) Cedar(91), Dade(8)
JEROME Phelps
JONESBURG (63351) Montgomery(56), Warren(43)
JOPLIN Jasper
KAHOKA Clark
KAISER (65047) Miller(97), Camden(2)
KANSAS CITY (64188) Clay(92), Jackson(7)
KANSAS CITY (64147) Jackson(74), Cass(25)
KANSAS CITY (64164) Platte(98), Clay(1)
KANSAS CITY Clay
KANSAS CITY Jackson
KANSAS CITY Platte
KEARNEY Clay
KELSO Scott
KENNETT Dunklin
KEWANEE New Madrid
KEYTESVILLE Chariton
KIDDER (64649) Caldwell(73), Daviess(26)
KIMBERLING CITY Stone
KIMMSWICK Jefferson
KING CITY (64463) Gentry(94), De Kalb(3), Andrew(1)
KINGDOM CITY Callaway
KINGSTON Caldwell

KINGSVILLE (64061) Johnson(98), Jackson(1)
KIRBYVILLE Taney
KIRKSVILLE Adair
KISSEE MILLS Taney
KNOB LICK St. Francois
KNOB NOSTER (65336) Johnson(91), Pettis(8)
KNOX CITY (63446) Knox(90), Lewis(9)
KOELTZTOWN Osage
KOSHKONONG (65692) Oregon(53), Howell(46)
LA BELLE (63447) Lewis(97), Knox(2)
LA GRANGE Lewis
LA MONTE Pettis
LA PLATA (63549) Macon(95), Adair(3)
LA RUSSELL (64848) Lawrence(93), Jasper(6)
LABADIE Franklin
LACLEDE Linn
LADDONIA (63352) Audrain(93), Ralls(6)
LAKE OZARK (65049) Camden(72), Miller(27)
LAKE SAINT LOUIS St. Charles
LAKE SPRING Dent
LAMAR Barton
LAMPE Stone
LANAGAN McDonald
LANCASTER Schuyler
LAQUEY (65534) Pulaski(84), Laclede(15)
LAREDO (64652) Grundy(97), Sullivan(1)
LATHAM Moniteau
LATHROP (64465) Clinton(90), Caldwell(9)
LATOUR (64760) Johnson(50), Cass(49)
LAURIE Morgan
LAWSON (64062) Ray(66), Clay(17), Clinton(16)
LEADWOOD St. Francois
LEASBURG Crawford
LEBANON (65536) Laclede(98), Dallas(1)
LECOMA (65540) Dent(70), Phelps(29)
LEES SUMMIT (64082) Jackson(89), Cass(10)
LEES SUMMIT Jackson
LEETON (64761) Johnson(92), Henry(7)
LENOX Dent
LENTNER (63450) Shelby(70), Monroe(29)
LEONARD (63451) Shelby(95), Knox(2), Macon(2)
LEOPOLD Bollinger
LESLIE Franklin
LESTERVILLE (63654) Reynolds(89), Iron(10)
LEVASY Jackson
LEWISTOWN Lewis
LEXINGTON Lafayette
LIBERAL Barton
LIBERTY Clay
LICKING Texas
LIGUORI Jefferson
LILBOURN (63862) Bollinger(77), New Madrid(22)
LINCOLN Benton
LINN Osage
LINN CREEK Camden
LINNEUS Linn
LIVONIA Putnam
LOCK SPRINGS Daviess
LOCKWOOD (65682) Dade(83), Lawrence(10), Barton(5)
LODI Wayne
LOHMAN Cole
LONE JACK (64070) Jackson(96), Johnson(3)
LONEDELL Franklin
LONG LANE Dallas
LOOSE CREEK Osage
LOUISBURG (65685) Dallas(97), Polk(2)
LOUISIANA Pike
LOWNDES Wayne
LOWRY CITY St. Clair
LUCERNE (64655) Putnam(98), Sullivan(1)

LUDLOW Livingston
LUEBBERING Franklin
LURAY Clark
LYNCHBURG Laclede
MACKS CREEK (65786) Camden(98), Dallas(1)
MACOMB (65702) Wright(72), Douglas(27)
MADISON (65263) Monroe(95), Randolph(3)
MAITLAND Holt
MALDEN (63863) Dunklin(98), New Madrid(1)
MALTA BEND Saline
MANSFIELD (65704) Wright(95), Douglas(4)
MAPAVILLE Jefferson
MARBLE HILL (63764) Bollinger(91), Cape Girardeau(8)
MARCELINE (64658) Linn(68), Chariton(31)
MARIONVILLE (65705) Lawrence(81), Stone(18)
MARQUAND (63655) Madison(74), Bollinger(24), Wayne(1)
MARSHALL (65340) Saline(96), Pettis(3)
MARSHFIELD Webster
MARSTON New Madrid
MARTHASVILLE (63357) Warren(93), St. Charles(6)
MARTINSBURG (65264) Audrain(75), Callaway(21), Montgomery(3)
MARTINSVILLE Harrison
MARYLAND HEIGHTS St. Louis
MARYVILLE Nodaway
MATTHEWS New Madrid
MAYSVILLE De Kalb
MAYVIEW Lafayette
MAYWOOD (63454) Marion(68), Lewis(31)
MC BRIDE Perry
MC CLURG (65701) Taney(71), Douglas(28)
MC FALL (64657) Gentry(65), Harrison(25), Daviess(8)
MC GEE Wayne
MC GIRK Moniteau
MEADVILLE Linn
MEMPHIS Scotland
MENDON Chariton
MENFRO Perry
MERCER Mercer
META (65058) Maries(51), Osage(29), Miller(12), Cole(5)
METZ Vernon
MEXICO (65265) Audrain(98), Monroe(1)
MIAMI Saline
MID MISSOURI Boone
MIDDLE BROOK (63656) Iron(85), Reynolds(14)
MIDDLETOWN (63359) Pike(57), Montgomery(31), Lincoln(6), Audrain(4)
MILAN Sullivan
MILFORD Barton
MILL SPRING Wayne
MILLER Lawrence
MILLERSVILLE (63766) Cape Girardeau(88), Bollinger(11)
MILO Vernon
MINDENMINES Barton
MINERAL POINT Washington
MISSOURI CITY Clay
MISSOURI STATE LOTTERY COMM Cole
MOBERLY Randolph
MOKANE Callaway
MONETT (65708) Barry(58), Lawrence(41)
MONROE CITY (63456) Monroe(46), Marion(33), Ralls(19)
MONTGOMERY CITY (63361) Montgomery(82), Callaway(17)
MONTICELLO Lewis
MONTIER Shannon
MONTREAL Camden
MONTROSE (64770) Henry(90), Bates(8)

MOODY Howell
MOORESVILLE (64664) Livingston(98), Sullivan(1)
MORA (65345) Pettis(64), Benton(23), Morgan(11)
MOREHOUSE New Madrid
MORLEY Scott
MORRISON (65061) Gasconade(86), Osage(13)
MORRISVILLE Polk
MORSE MILL Jefferson
MOSBY Clay
MOSCOW MILLS Lincoln
MOUND CITY Holt
MOUNDVILLE Vernon
MOUNT MORIAH Harrison
MOUNT STERLING (65062) Gasconade(69), Ozark(21), Osage(9)
MOUNT VERNON Lawrence
MOUNTAIN GROVE (65711) Wright(94), Douglas(4)
MOUNTAIN VIEW (65548) Howell(95), Shannon(4)
MYRTLE Oregon
NAPOLEON Lafayette
NAYLOR (63953) Ripley(96), Butler(3)
NECK CITY Jasper
NEELYVILLE (63954) Butler(96), Ripley(3)
NELSON (65347) Pettis(46), Saline(31), Cooper(22)
NEOSHO Newton
NEVADA Vernon
NEW BLOOMFIELD Callaway
NEW BOSTON (63557) Linn(67), Macon(29), Sullivan(1)
NEW CAMBRIA (63558) Macon(83), Chariton(16)
NEW FLORENCE (63363) Montgomery(88), Warren(11)
NEW FRANKLIN Howard
NEW HAMPTON (64471) Harrison(93), Gentry(6)
NEW HARTFORD Pike
NEW HAVEN (63068) Franklin(98), Gasconade(1)
NEW LONDON (63459) Ralls(93), Pike(6)
NEW MADRID New Madrid
NEW MELLE St. Charles
NEW OFFENBURG Ste. Genevieve
NEWARK Knox
NEWBURG Phelps
NEWTONIA Newton
NEWTOWN (64667) Sullivan(77), Mercer(15), Putnam(7)
NIANGUA (65713) Webster(89), Wright(10)
NIXA (65714) Christian(94), Stone(5)
NOBLE Ozark
NOEL McDonald
NORBORNE (64668) Carroll(78), Ray(21)
NORWOOD (65717) Wright(86), Douglas(13)
NOVELTY Knox
NOVINGER (63559) Adair(51), Putnam(48)
O FALLON St. Charles
OAK GROVE (64075) Jackson(89), Lafayette(10)
OAK RIDGE Cape Girardeau
ODESSA (64076) Lafayette(98), Johnson(1)
OLD APPLETON (63770) Cape Girardeau(63), Perry(36)
OLD MONROE Lincoln
OLDFIELD (65720) Christian(78), Douglas(21)
OLEAN Miller
OLNEY Lincoln
ORAN (63771) Scott(82), Stoddard(16)
OREGON Holt
ORONOGO (64855) Jasper(95), Barton(4)
ORRICK (64077) Ray(74), Clay(25)
OSAGE BEACH Camden
OSBORN (64474) De Kalb(97), Clinton(2)

OSCEOLA (64776) St. Clair(97), Benton(2)
OTTERVILLE (65348) Cooper(85), Morgan(11), Pettis(3)
OWENSVILLE (65066) Gasconade(92), Crawford(7)
OXLY Ripley
OZARK (65721) Christian(98), Greene(1)
PACIFIC (63069) Franklin(67), Jefferson(16), St. Louis(15)
PAINTON Stoddard
PALMYRA Marion
PARIS Monroe
PARK HILLS St. Francois
PARMA (63870) Stoddard(83), New Madrid(16)
PARNELL (64475) Nodaway(88), Worth(9), Gentry(2)
PASCOLA Pemiscot
PASSAIC Bates
PATTERSON Wayne
PATTON Bollinger
PATTONSBURG (64670) Daviess(79), De Kalb(13), Harrison(4), Gentry(2)
PAYNESVILLE Pike
PEACE VALLEY (65788) Howell(95), Oregon(4)
PECULIAR Cass
PERKINS Scott
PERRY (63462) Ralls(79), Monroe(20)
PERRYVILLE Perry
PEVELY Jefferson
PHILADELPHIA (63463) Marion(97), Shelby(2)
PHILLIPSBURG (65722) Laclede(87), Dallas(12)
PICKERING Nodaway
PIEDMONT Wayne
PIERCE CITY (65723) Lawrence(90), Newton(6), Barry(3)
PILOT GROVE Cooper
PILOT KNOB Iron
PINEVILLE McDonald
PITTSBURG Hickory
PLATO (65552) Texas(98), Laclede(1)
PLATTE CITY Platte
PLATTSBURG Clinton
PLEASANT HILL (64080) Cass(96), Jackson(3)
PLEASANT HOPE (65725) Greene(89), Polk(10)
PLEVNA (63464) Knox(76), Marion(23)
POCAHONTAS Cape Girardeau
POINT LOOKOUT Taney
POLK (65727) Polk(87), Hickory(12)
POLLOCK (63560) Sullivan(92), Putnam(7)
POLO (64671) Caldwell(70), Ray(29)
POMONA Howell
PONCE DE LEON (65728) Christian(75), Stone(24)
PONTIAC Ozark
POPLAR BLUFF Butler
PORTAGE DES SIOUX St. Charles
PORTAGEVILLE (63873) New Madrid(84), Pemiscot(15)
PORTLAND Callaway
POTOSI Washington
POTTERSVILLE (65790) Howell(88), Ozark(11)
POWELL McDonald
POWERSITE Taney
POWERSVILLE (64672) Putnam(97), Mercer(2)
PRAIRIE HOME Cooper
PRESTON (65732) Hickory(94), Dallas(5)
PRINCETON Mercer
PROTEM Taney
PURCELL Jasper
PURDIN Linn
PURDY Barry
PUXICO (63960) Stoddard(96), Bollinger(3)
QUEEN CITY Schuyler

QUINCY (65735) Hickory(68), Benton(24), St. Clair(6)
QUITMAN Nodaway
QULIN Butler
RACINE Newton
RAVENWOOD (64479) Nodaway(95), Gentry(4)
RAYMONDVILLE Texas
RAYMORE Cass
RAYVILLE Ray
REA Andrew
REDFORD Reynolds
REEDS Jasper
REEDS SPRING (65737) Stone(98), Taney(1)
RENICK Randolph
REPUBLIC (65738) Greene(85), Christian(14)
REVERE Clark
REYNOLDS Reynolds
RHINELAND (65069) Montgomery(86), Callaway(13)
RICH HILL (64779) Bates(93), Vernon(6)
RICHARDS Vernon
RICHLAND (65556) Pulaski(61), Laclede(20), Camden(18)
RICHMOND Ray
RICHWOODS (63071) Washington(88), Jefferson(11)
RIDGEDALE Taney
RIDGEWAY Harrison
RISCO New Madrid
RIVES Dunklin
ROACH Camden
ROBERTSVILLE (63072) Franklin(96), Jefferson(3)
ROBY Texas
ROCHEPORT (65279) Boone(86), Howard(13)
ROCK PORT Atchison
ROCKAWAY BEACH Taney
ROCKBRIDGE Ozark
ROCKVILLE (64780) St. Clair(62), Bates(37)
ROCKY COMFORT (64861) McDonald(92), Newton(5), Barry(1)
ROCKY MOUNT (65072) Morgan(85), Miller(14)
ROGERSVILLE (65742) Webster(53), Greene(46)
ROLLA Phelps
ROMBAUER Butler
ROSCOE St. Clair
ROSEBUD (63091) Gasconade(73), Franklin(26)
ROSENDALE Andrew
ROTHVILLE Chariton
RUETER Taney
RUSH HILL Audrain
RUSHVILLE (64484) Buchanan(74), Platte(25)
RUSSELLVILLE (65074) Cole(68), Moniteau(29), Miller(1)
RUTLEDGE (63563) Scotland(56), Knox(43)
SAGINAW Newton
SAINT ALBANS Franklin
SAINT ANN St. Louis
SAINT CATHARINE Linn
SAINT CATHERINE Linn
SAINT CHARLES St. Charles
SAINT CLAIR Franklin
SAINT ELIZABETH Miller
SAINT JAMES (65559) Phelps(98), Maries(1)
SAINT JOSEPH (64506) Buchanan(97), Andrew(2)
SAINT JOSEPH Buchanan
SAINT LOUIS (63143) St. Louis(88), St. Louis City(11)

SAINT LOUIS (63120) St. Louis City(89), St. Louis(10)
SAINT LOUIS St. Louis
SAINT LOUIS St. Louis City
SAINT MARY Ste. Genevieve
SAINT PATRICK Clark
SAINT PETERS St. Charles
SAINT ROBERT Pulaski
SAINT THOMAS (65076) Cole(83), Osage(16)
SAINTE GENEVIEVE Ste. Genevieve
SALEM (65560) Dent(98), Shannon(1)
SALISBURY (65281) Chariton(98), Howard(1)
SANTA FE Monroe
SARCOXIE (64862) Jasper(87), Lawrence(8), Newton(4)
SAVANNAH Andrew
SAVERTON Ralls
SCHELL CITY (64783) Vernon(58), St. Clair(41)
SCOTT CITY Scott
SEDALIA Pettis
SEDGEWICKVILLE (63781) Bollinger(77), Perry(20), Cape Girardeau(2)
SELIGMAN Barry
SENATH Dunklin
SENECA (64865) Newton(89), McDonald(10)
SEYMOUR (65746) Webster(98), Douglas(1)
SHELBINA (63468) Shelby(80), Monroe(19)
SHELBYVILLE (63469) Shelby(98), Knox(1)
SHELDON (64784) Vernon(74), Barton(16), Cedar(7)
SHELL KNOB (65747) Stone(56), Barry(43)
SHERIDAN (64486) Worth(54), Nodaway(45)
SHOOK Wayne
SIBLEY Jackson
SIKESTON (63801) Scott(94), New Madrid(4)
SILEX Lincoln
SILVA (63964) Wayne(88), Madison(11)
SKIDMORE (64487) Nodaway(93), Holt(6)
SLATER Saline
SMITHTON (65350) Pettis(93), Morgan(5)
SMITHVILLE (64089) Clay(98), Platte(1)
SOLO Texas
SOUTH FORK Howell
SOUTH GREENFIELD (65752) Dade(67), Lawrence(32)
SOUTH WEST CITY McDonald
SPARTA (65753) Christian(98), Douglas(1)
SPICKARD (64679) Grundy(89), Mercer(10)
SPOKANE (65754) Christian(84), Stone(15)
SPRINGFIELD Greene
SQUIRES (65755) Douglas(53), Ozark(46)
ST CATHARINE Linn
ST JOSEPH Buchanan
STANBERRY (64489) Gentry(98), Nodaway(1)
STANTON Franklin
STARK CITY Newton
STEEDMAN Callaway
STEELE (63877) Pemiscot(97), Dunklin(2)
STEELVILLE (65565) Crawford(96), Washington(2)
STEFFENVILLE (63470) Lewis(93), Shelby(6)
STELLA (64867) Newton(90), McDonald(9)
STET Carroll
STEWARTSVILLE (64490) De Kalb(56), Clinton(38), Buchanan(4)
STOCKTON (65785) Cedar(98), St. Clair(1)
STOTTS CITY Lawrence

STOUTLAND (65567) Laclede(62), Camden(37)
STOUTSVILLE Monroe
STOVER (65078) Morgan(98), Benton(1)
STRAFFORD (65757) Greene(77), Webster(22)
STRASBURG Cass
STURDIVANT Bollinger
STURGEON (65284) Boone(95), Audrain(4)
SUCCESS Texas
SULLIVAN (63080) Franklin(82), Crawford(12), Washington(4)
SULPHUR SPRINGS Jefferson
SUMMERSVILLE (65571) Texas(83), Shannon(16)
SUMNER (64681) Linn(51), Chariton(48)
SUNRISE BEACH (65079) Camden(87), Morgan(12)
SWEDEBORG Pulaski
SWEET SPRINGS (65351) Saline(76), Pettis(22), Johnson(1)
SYRACUSE (65354) Morgan(89), Cooper(10)
TALLAPOOSA New Madrid
TANEYVILLE Taney
TARKIO Atchison
TAYLOR (63471) Marion(93), Lewis(6)
TEBBETTS Callaway
TECUMSEH Ozark
TERESITA Shannon
THAYER Oregon
THEODOSIA (65761) Ozark(75), Taney(25)
THOMPSON (65285) Audrain(98), Monroe(1)
THORNFIELD Ozark
TIFF Washington
TIFF CITY McDonald
TINA Carroll
TIPTON (65081) Moniteau(89), Cooper(9), Morgan(1)
TRELOAR Warren
TRENTON Grundy
TRIMBLE Clinton
TRIPLETT Chariton
TROY Lincoln
TRUXTON (63381) Lincoln(45), Warren(40), Montgomery(13)
TUNAS Dallas
TURNERS Greene
TURNEY Clinton
TUSCUMBIA Miller
UDALL Ozark
ULMAN Miller
UNION Franklin
UNION STAR De Kalb
UNIONTOWN Perry
UNIONVILLE (63565) Putnam(89), Sullivan(10)
URBANA (65767) Dallas(83), Hickory(15)
URICH (64788) Henry(82), Bates(17)
UTICA Livingston
VALLES MINES (63087) St. Francois(90), Jefferson(9)
VALLEY PARK St. Louis
VAN BUREN (63965) Carter(93), Reynolds(6)
VANDALIA (63382) Audrain(80), Ralls(10), Pike(8)
VANDUSER Scott
VANZANT Douglas
VERONA (65769) Lawrence(78), Barry(21)
VERSAILLES Morgan
VIBURNUM Iron
VICHY Maries
VIENNA Maries
VILLA RIDGE Franklin
VISTA St. Clair
VULCAN (63675) Iron(92), Washington(4), Reynolds(2)

WACO Jasper
WAKENDA Carroll
WALDRON Platte
WALKER Vernon
WALNUT GROVE Greene
WALNUT SHADE Taney
WAPPAPELLO (63966) Butler(67), Wayne(32)
WARDELL (63879) Pemiscot(98), New Madrid(1)
WARRENSBURG Johnson
WARRENTON (63383) Warren(97), Lincoln(2)
WARSAW Benton
WASHBURN (65772) Barry(93), McDonald(6)
WASHINGTON Franklin
WASOLA Ozark
WATSON Atchison
WAVERLY (64096) Lafayette(98), Saline(1)
WAYLAND Clark
WAYNESVILLE Pulaski
WEATHERBY (64497) De Kalb(69), Daviess(30)
WEAUBLEAU (65774) Hickory(90), St. Clair(9)
WEBB CITY Jasper
WELDON SPRING St. Charles
WELLINGTON Lafayette
WELLSVILLE (63384) Montgomery(88), Audrain(9), Callaway(1)
WENTWORTH (64873) Lawrence(66), Newton(33)
WENTZVILLE St. Charles
WESCO Crawford
WEST ALTON St. Charles
WEST PLAINS Howell
WESTBORO Atchison
WESTON Platte
WESTPHALIA Osage
WHEATLAND (65779) Hickory(85), Benton(14)
WHEATON Barry
WHEELING (64688) Livingston(77), Linn(22)
WHITEMAN AIR FORCE BASE Johnson
WHITEOAK Dunklin
WHITESIDE Lincoln
WHITEWATER Cape Girardeau
WILLARD Greene
WILLIAMSBURG Callaway
WILLIAMSTOWN (63473) Lewis(76), Clark(23)
WILLIAMSVILLE (63967) Butler(58), Wayne(41)
WILLOW SPRINGS (65793) Howell(95), Texas(4)
WINDSOR (65360) Henry(51), Pettis(25), Benton(12), Johnson(9)
WINDYVILLE Dallas
WINFIELD Lincoln
WINIGAN (63566) Linn(80), Sullivan(19)
WINONA (65588) Shannon(93), Oregon(6)
WINSTON Daviess
WITTENBERG Perry
WOLF ISLAND Mississippi
WOOLDRIDGE (65287) Cooper(79), Moniteau(20)
WORTH (64499) Worth(75), Gentry(24)
WORTHINGTON Putnam
WRIGHT CITY (63390) Warren(90), Lincoln(9)
WYACONDA (63474) Clark(91), Scotland(5), Lewis(3)
WYATT Mississippi
YUKON Texas
ZALMA (63787) Bollinger(94), Wayne(5)
ZALMA Bollinger
ZANONI Ozark

Missouri ZIP/City Cross Reference

63001-63001 ALLENTON	63361-63361 MONTGOMERY CITY	63546-63546 GREENTOP	63769-63769 OAK RIDGE
63005-63006 CHESTERFIELD	63362-63362 MOSCOW MILLS	63547-63547 HURDLAND	63770-63770 OLD APPLETON
63010-63010 ARNOLD	63363-63363 NEW FLORENCE	63548-63548 LANCASTER	63771-63771 ORAN
63011-63011 BALLWIN	63364-63364 NEW HARTFORD	63549-63549 LA PLATA	63772-63772 PAINTON
63012-63012 BARNHART	63365-63365 NEW MELLE	63551-63551 LIVONIA	63774-63774 PERKINS
63013-63013 BEAUFORT	63366-63366 O FALLON	63552-63552 MACON	63775-63775 PERRYVILLE
63014-63014 BERGER	63367-63367 LAKE SAINT LOUIS	63555-63555 MEMPHIS	63776-63776 MC BRIDE
63015-63015 CATAWISSA	63368-63368 DARDENNE	63556-63556 MILAN	63779-63779 POCAHONTAS
63016-63016 CEDAR HILL	63369-63369 OLD MONROE	63557-63557 NEW BOSTON	63780-63780 SCOTT CITY
63017-63017 CHESTERFIELD	63370-63370 OLNEY	63558-63558 NEW CAMBRIA	63781-63781 SEDGEWICKVILLE
63019-63019 CRYSTAL CITY	63371-63371 PAYNESVILLE	63559-63559 NOVINGER	63782-63782 STURDIVANT
63020-63020 DE SOTO	63373-63373 PORTAGE DES SIOUX	63560-63560 POLLOCK	63783-63783 UNIONTOWN
63021-63022 BALLWIN	63376-63376 SAINT PETERS	63561-63561 QUEEN CITY	63784-63784 VANDUSER
63023-63023 DITTMER	63377-63377 SILEX	63563-63563 RUTLEDGE	63785-63785 WHITEWATER
63024-63024 BALLWIN	63378-63378 TRELOAR	63565-63565 UNIONVILLE	63786-63786 WITTENBERG
63025-63025 EUREKA	63379-63379 TROY	63566-63566 WINIGAN	63787-63787 ZALMA
63026-63026 FENTON	63381-63381 TRUXTON	63567-63567 WORTHINGTON	63801-63801 SIKESTON
63028-63028 FESTUS	63382-63382 VANDALIA	63601-63601 PARK HILLS	63820-63820 ANNISTON
63030-63030 FLETCHER	63383-63383 WARRENTON	63620-63620 ANNAPOLIS	63821-63821 ARBYRD
63031-63034 FLORISSANT	63384-63384 WELLSVILLE	63621-63621 ARCADIA	63822-63822 BERNIE
63036-63036 FRENCH VILLAGE	63385-63385 WENTZVILLE	63622-63622 BELGRADE	63823-63823 BERTRAND
63037-63037 GERALD	63386-63386 WEST ALTON	63623-63623 BELLEVIEW	63824-63824 BLODGETT
63038-63038 GLENCOE	63387-63387 WHITESIDE	63624-63624 BISMARCK	63825-63825 BLOOMFIELD
63039-63039 GRAY SUMMIT	63388-63388 WILLIAMSBURG	63625-63625 BLACK	63826-63826 BRAGGADOCIO
63040-63040 GROVER	63389-63389 WINFIELD	63626-63626 BLACKWELL	63827-63827 BRAGG CITY
63041-63041 GRUBVILLE	63390-63390 WRIGHT CITY	63627-63627 BLOOMSDALE	63828-63828 CANALOU
63042-63042 HAZELWOOD	63394-63394 CONTEL CORPORATION	63628-63628 BONNE TERRE	63829-63829 CARDWELL
63043-63043 MARYLAND HEIGHTS	63401-63401 HANNIBAL	63629-63629 BUNKER	63830-63830 CARUTHERSVILLE
63044-63044 BRIDGETON	63430-63430 ALEXANDRIA	63630-63630 CADET	63833-63833 CATRON
63045-63045 EARTH CITY	63431-63431 ANABEL	63631-63631 CALEDONIA	63834-63834 CHARLESTON
63047-63047 HEMATITE	63432-63432 ARBELA	63632-63632 CASCADE	63837-63837 CLARKTON
63048-63048 HERCULANEUM	63433-63433 ASHBURN	63633-63633 CENTERVILLE	63838-63838 CONRAN
63049-63049 HIGH RIDGE	63434-63434 BETHEL	63636-63636 DES ARC	63839-63839 COOTER
63050-63050 HILLSBORO	63435-63435 CANTON	63637-63637 DOE RUN	63840-63840 DEERING
63051-63051 HOUSE SPRINGS	63436-63436 CENTER	63638-63638 ELLINGTON	63841-63841 DEXTER
63052-63052 IMPERIAL	63437-63437 CLARENCE	63640-63640 FARMINGTON	63845-63845 EAST PRAIRIE
63053-63053 KIMMSWICK	63438-63438 DURHAM	63644-63644 PARK HILLS	63846-63846 ESSEX
63055-63055 LABADIE	63439-63439 EMDEN	63645-63645 FREDERICKTOWN	63847-63847 GIBSON
63056-63056 LESLIE	63440-63440 EWING	63646-63646 GLOVER	63848-63848 GIDEON
63057-63057 LIGUORI	63441-63441 FRANKFORD	63648-63648 IRONDALE	63849-63849 GOBLER
63060-63060 LONEDELL	63442-63442 GRANGER	63650-63650 IRONTON	63850-63850 GRAYRIDGE
63061-63061 LUEBBERING	63443-63443 HUNNEWELL	63651-63651 KNOB LICK	63851-63851 HAYTI
63065-63065 MAPAVILLE	63445-63445 KAHOKA	63653-63653 LEADWOOD	63852-63852 HOLCOMB
63066-63066 MORSE MILL	63446-63446 KNOX CITY	63654-63654 LESTERVILLE	63853-63853 HOLLAND
63068-63068 NEW HAVEN	63447-63447 LA BELLE	63655-63655 MARQUAND	63855-63855 HORNERSVILLE
63069-63069 PACIFIC	63448-63448 LA GRANGE	63656-63656 MIDDLE BROOK	63857-63857 KENNETT
63070-63070 PEVELY	63450-63450 LENTNER	63660-63660 MINERAL POINT	63860-63860 KEWANEE
63071-63071 RICHWOODS	63451-63451 LEONARD	63661-63661 NEW OFFENBURG	63862-63862 LILBOURN
63072-63072 ROBERTSVILLE	63452-63452 LEWISTOWN	63662-63662 PATTON	63863-63863 MALDEN
63073-63073 SAINT ALBANS	63453-63453 LURAY	63663-63663 PILOT KNOB	63866-63866 MARSTON
63074-63074 SAINT ANN	63454-63454 MAYWOOD	63664-63664 POTOSI	63867-63867 MATTHEWS
63077-63077 SAINT CLAIR	63456-63456 MONROE CITY	63665-63665 REDFORD	63868-63868 MOREHOUSE
63079-63079 STANTON	63457-63457 MONTICELLO	63666-63666 REYNOLDS	63869-63869 NEW MADRID
63080-63080 SULLIVAN	63458-63458 NEWARK	63670-63670 SAINTE GENEVIEVE	63870-63870 PARMA
63083-63083 SULPHUR SPRINGS	63459-63459 NEW LONDON	63673-63673 SAINT MARY	63871-63871 PASCOLA
63084-63084 UNION	63460-63460 NOVELTY	63674-63674 TIFF	63873-63873 PORTAGEVILLE
63087-63087 VALLES MINES	63461-63461 PALMYRA	63675-63675 VULCAN	63874-63874 RISCO
63088-63088 VALLEY PARK	63462-63462 PERRY	63701-63705 CAPE GIRARDEAU	63875-63875 RIVES
63089-63089 VILLA RIDGE	63463-63463 PHILADELPHIA	63730-63730 ADVANCE	63876-63876 SENATH
63090-63090 WASHINGTON	63464-63464 PLEVNA	63732-63732 ALTENBURG	63877-63877 STEELE
63091-63091 ROSEBUD	63465-63465 REVERE	63733-63733 ZALMA	63878-63878 TALLAPOOSA
63099-63099 FENTON	63466-63466 SAINT PATRICK	63735-63735 BELL CITY	63879-63879 WARDELL
63100-63199 SAINT LOUIS	63467-63467 SAVERTON	63736-63736 BENTON	63880-63880 WHITEOAK
63301-63304 SAINT CHARLES	63468-63468 SHELBINA	63737-63737 BRAZEAU	63881-63881 WOLF ISLAND
63330-63330 ANNADA	63469-63469 SHELBYVILLE	63738-63738 BROWNWOOD	63882-63882 WYATT
63332-63332 AUGUSTA	63470-63470 STEFFENVILLE	63739-63739 BURFORDVILLE	63901-63902 POPLAR BLUFF
63333-63333 BELLFLOWER	63471-63471 TAYLOR	63740-63740 CHAFFEE	63931-63931 BRIAR
63334-63334 BOWLING GREEN	63472-63472 WAYLAND	63742-63742 COMMERCE	63932-63932 BROSELEY
63336-63336 CLARKSVILLE	63473-63473 WILLIAMSTOWN	63743-63743 DAISY	63933-63933 CAMPBELL
63338-63338 COTTLEVILLE	63474-63474 WYACONDA	63744-63744 DELTA	63934-63934 CLUBB
63339-63339 CURRYVILLE	63501-63501 KIRKSVILLE	63745-63745 DUTCHTOWN	63935-63935 DONIPHAN
63341-63341 DEFIANCE	63530-63530 ATLANTA	63746-63746 FARRAR	63936-63936 DUDLEY
63342-63342 DUTZOW	63531-63531 BARING	63747-63747 FRIEDHEIM	63937-63937 ELLSINORE
63343-63343 ELSBERRY	63532-63532 BEVIER	63748-63748 FROHNA	63938-63938 FAGUS
63344-63344 EOLIA	63533-63533 BRASHEAR	63750-63750 GIPSY	63939-63939 FAIRDEALING
63345-63345 FARBER	63534-63534 CALLAO	63751-63751 GLENALLEN	63940-63940 FISK
63346-63346 FLINTHILL	63535-63535 COATSVILLE	63752-63752 GORDONVILLE	63941-63941 FREMONT
63347-63347 FOLEY	63536-63536 DOWNING	63753-63753 GRASSY	63942-63942 GATEWOOD
63348-63348 FORISTELL	63537-63537 EDINA	63755-63755 JACKSON	63943-63943 GRANDIN
63349-63349 HAWK POINT	63538-63538 ELMER	63758-63758 KELSO	63944-63944 GREENVILLE
63350-63350 HIGH HILL	63539-63539 ETHEL	63760-63760 LEOPOLD	63945-63945 HARVIELL
63351-63351 JONESBURG	63540-63540 GIBBS	63763-63763 MC GEE	63947-63947 HIRAM
63352-63352 LADDONIA	63541-63541 GLENWOOD	63764-63764 MARBLE HILL	63950-63950 LODI
63353-63353 LOUISIANA	63543-63543 GORIN	63765-63765 MENFRO	63951-63951 LOWNDES
63357-63357 MARTHASVILLE	63544-63544 GREEN CASTLE	63766-63766 MILLERSVILLE	63952-63952 MILL SPRING
63359-63359 MIDDLETOWN	63545-63545 GREEN CITY	63767-63767 MORLEY	63953-63953 NAYLOR

63954-63954 NEELYVILLE	64441-64441 DENVER	64657-64657 MC FALL	64843-64843 GOODMAN
63955-63955 OXLY	64442-64442 EAGLEVILLE	64658-64658 MARCELINE	64844-64844 GRANBY
63956-63956 PATTERSON	64443-64443 EASTON	64659-64659 MEADVILLE	64847-64847 LANAGAN
63957-63957 PIEDMONT	64444-64444 EDGERTON	64660-64660 MENDON	64848-64848 LA RUSSELL
63960-63960 PUXICO	64445-64445 ELMO	64661-64661 MERCER	64849-64849 NECK CITY
63961-63961 QULIN	64446-64446 FAIRFAX	64664-64664 MOORESVILLE	64850-64850 NEOSHO
63962-63962 ROMBAUER	64447-64447 FAIRPORT	64665-64665 MOUNT MORIAH	64853-64853 NEWTONIA
63963-63963 SHOOK	64448-64448 FAUCETT	64667-64667 NEWTOWN	64854-64854 NOEL
63964-63964 SILVA	64449-64449 FILLMORE	64668-64668 NORBORNE	64855-64855 ORONOGO
63965-63965 VAN BUREN	64451-64451 FOREST CITY	64670-64670 PATTONSBURG	64856-64856 PINEVILLE
63966-63966 WAPPAPELLO	64452-64452 FORTESCUE	64671-64671 POLO	64857-64857 PURCELL
63967-63967 WILLIAMSVILLE	64453-64453 GENTRY	64672-64672 POWERSVILLE	64858-64858 RACINE
64001-64001 ALMA	64454-64454 GOWER	64673-64673 PRINCETON	64859-64859 REEDS
64011-64011 BATES CITY	64455-64455 GRAHAM	64674-64674 PURDIN	64861-64861 ROCKY COMFORT
64012-64012 BELTON	64456-64456 GRANT CITY	64676-64676 ROTHVILLE	64862-64862 SARCOXIE
64013-64015 BLUE SPRINGS	64457-64457 GUILFORD	64677-64677 SAINT CATHERINE	64863-64863 SOUTH WEST CITY
64016-64016 BUCKNER	64458-64458 HATFIELD	64677-64677 SAINT CATHARINE	64864-64864 SAGINAW
64017-64017 CAMDEN	64459-64459 HELENA	64677-64677 ST CATHARINE	64865-64865 SENECA
64018-64018 CAMDEN POINT	64461-64461 HOPKINS	64679-64679 SPICKARD	64866-64866 STARK CITY
64019-64019 CENTERVIEW	64463-64463 KING CITY	64680-64680 STET	64867-64867 STELLA
64020-64020 CONCORDIA	64465-64465 LATHROP	64681-64681 SUMNER	64868-64868 TIFF CITY
64021-64021 CORDER	64466-64466 MAITLAND	64682-64682 TINA	64869-64869 WACO
64022-64022 DOVER	64467-64467 MARTINSVILLE	64683-64683 TRENTON	64870-64870 WEBB CITY
64024-64024 EXCELSIOR SPRINGS	64468-64468 MARYVILLE	64686-64686 UTICA	64873-64873 WENTWORTH
64028-64028 FARLEY	64469-64469 MAYSVILLE	64687-64687 WAKENDA	64874-64874 WHEATON
64029-64029 GRAIN VALLEY	64470-64470 MOUND CITY	64688-64688 WHEELING	64944-64999 KANSAS CITY
64030-64030 GRANDVIEW	64471-64471 NEW HAMPTON	64689-64689 WINSTON	65001-65001 ARGYLE
64034-64034 GREENWOOD	64473-64473 OREGON	64701-64701 HARRISONVILLE	65010-65010 ASHLAND
64035-64035 HARDIN	64474-64474 OSBORN	64720-64720 ADRIAN	65011-65011 BARNETT
64036-64036 HENRIETTA	64475-64475 PARNELL	64722-64722 AMORET	65013-65013 BELLE
64037-64037 HIGGINSVILLE	64476-64476 PICKERING	64723-64723 AMSTERDAM	65014-65014 BLAND
64040-64040 HOLDEN	64477-64477 PLATTSBURG	64724-64724 APPLETON CITY	65016-65016 BONNOTS MILL
64048-64048 HOLT	64478-64478 QUITMAN	64725-64725 ARCHIE	65017-65017 BRUMLEY
64050-64058 INDEPENDENCE	64479-64479 RAVENWOOD	64726-64726 BLAIRSTOWN	65018-65018 CALIFORNIA
64060-64060 KEARNEY	64480-64480 REA	64728-64728 BRONAUGH	65020-65020 CAMDENTON
64061-64061 KINGSVILLE	64481-64481 RIDGEWAY	64730-64730 BUTLER	65022-65022 CEDAR CITY
64062-64062 LAWSON	64482-64482 ROCK PORT	64733-64733 CHILHOWEE	65023-65023 CENTERTOWN
64063-64065 LEES SUMMIT	64483-64483 ROSENDALE	64734-64734 CLEVELAND	65024-65024 CHAMOIS
64066-64066 LEVASY	64484-64484 RUSHVILLE	64735-64735 CLINTON	65025-65025 CLARKSBURG
64067-64067 LEXINGTON	64485-64485 SAVANNAH	64738-64738 COLLINS	65026-65026 ELDON
64068-64069 LIBERTY	64486-64486 SHERIDAN	64739-64739 CREIGHTON	65031-65031 ETTERVILLE
64070-64070 LONE JACK	64487-64487 SKIDMORE	64740-64740 DEEPWATER	65032-65032 EUGENE
64071-64071 MAYVIEW	64489-64489 STANBERRY	64741-64741 DEERFIELD	65034-65034 FORTUNA
64072-64072 MISSOURI CITY	64490-64490 STEWARTSVILLE	64742-64742 DREXEL	65035-65035 FREEBURG
64073-64073 MOSBY	64491-64491 TARKIO	64743-64743 EAST LYNNE	65036-65036 GASCONADE
64074-64074 NAPOLEON	64492-64492 TRIMBLE	64744-64744 EL DORADO SPRINGS	65037-65037 GRAVOIS MILLS
64075-64075 OAK GROVE	64493-64493 TURNEY	64745-64745 FOSTER	65038-65038 LAURIE
64076-64076 ODESSA	64494-64494 UNION STAR	64746-64746 FREEMAN	65039-65039 HARTSBURG
64077-64077 ORRICK	64496-64496 WATSON	64747-64747 GARDEN CITY	65040-65040 HENLEY
64078-64078 PECULIAR	64497-64497 WEATHERBY	64748-64748 GOLDEN CITY	65041-65041 HERMANN
64079-64079 PLATTE CITY	64498-64498 WESTBORO	64750-64750 HARWOOD	65042-65042 HIGH POINT
64080-64080 PLEASANT HILL	64499-64499 WORTH	64751-64751 HORTON	65043-65043 HOLTS SUMMIT
64081-64082 LEES SUMMIT	64500-64500 SAINT JOSEPH	64752-64752 HUME	65046-65046 JAMESTOWN
64083-64083 RAYMORE	64500-64500 ST JOSEPH	64755-64755 JASPER	65047-65047 KAISER
64084-64084 RAYVILLE	64501-64508 SAINT JOSEPH	64756-64756 JERICO SPRINGS	65048-65048 KOELTZTOWN
64085-64085 RICHMOND	64601-64601 CHILLICOTHE	64759-64759 LAMAR	65049-65049 LAKE OZARK
64086-64086 LEES SUMMIT	64620-64620 ALTAMONT	64760-64760 LATOUR	65050-65050 LATHAM
64087-64087 LIBERTY	64621-64621 AVALON	64761-64761 LEETON	65051-65051 LINN
64088-64088 SIBLEY	64622-64622 BOGARD	64762-64762 LIBERAL	65052-65052 LINN CREEK
64089-64089 SMITHVILLE	64623-64623 BOSWORTH	64763-64763 LOWRY CITY	65053-65053 LOHMAN
64090-64090 STRASBURG	64624-64624 BRAYMER	64765-64765 METZ	65054-65054 LOOSE CREEK
64092-64092 WALDRON	64625-64625 BRECKENRIDGE	64766-64766 MILFORD	65055-65055 MC GIRK
64093-64093 WARRENSBURG	64628-64628 BROOKFIELD	64767-64767 MILO	65056-65056 HERMANN
64096-64096 WAVERLY	64630-64630 BROWNING	64769-64769 MINDENMINES	65058-65058 META
64097-64097 WELLINGTON	64631-64631 BUCKLIN	64770-64770 MONTROSE	65059-65059 MOKANE
64098-64098 WESTON	64632-64632 CAINSVILLE	64771-64771 MOUNDVILLE	65061-65061 MORRISON
64100-64199 KANSAS CITY	64633-64633 CARROLLTON	64772-64772 NEVADA	65062-65062 MOUNT STERLING
64401-64401 AGENCY	64635-64635 CHULA	64776-64776 OSCEOLA	65063-65063 NEW BLOOMFIELD
64402-64402 ALBANY	64636-64636 COFFEY	64777-64777 PASSAIC	65064-65064 OLEAN
64420-64420 ALLENDALE	64637-64637 COWGILL	64778-64778 RICHARDS	65065-65065 OSAGE BEACH
64421-64421 AMAZONIA	64638-64638 DAWN	64779-64779 RICH HILL	65066-65066 OWENSVILLE
64422-64422 AMITY	64639-64639 DE WITT	64780-64780 ROCKVILLE	65067-65067 PORTLAND
64423-64423 BARNARD	64640-64640 GALLATIN	64781-64781 ROSCOE	65068-65068 PRAIRIE HOME
64424-64424 BETHANY	64641-64641 GALT	64783-64783 SCHELL CITY	65069-65069 RHINELAND
64426-64426 BLYTHEDALE	64642-64642 GILMAN CITY	64784-64784 SHELDON	65072-65072 ROCKY MOUNT
64427-64427 BOLCKOW	64643-64643 HALE	64788-64788 URICH	65074-65074 RUSSELLVILLE
64428-64428 BURLINGTON JUNCTION	64644-64644 HAMILTON	64789-64789 VISTA	65075-65075 SAINT ELIZABETH
64429-64429 CAMERON	64645-64645 HARRIS	64790-64790 WALKER	65076-65076 SAINT THOMAS
64430-64430 CLARKSDALE	64646-64646 HUMPHREYS	64801-64804 JOPLIN	65077-65077 STEEDMAN
64431-64431 CLEARMONT	64647-64647 JAMESON	64830-64830 ALBA	65078-65078 STOVER
64432-64432 CLYDE	64648-64648 JAMESPORT	64831-64831 ANDERSON	65079-65079 SUNRISE BEACH
64433-64433 CONCEPTION	64649-64649 KIDDER	64832-64832 ASBURY	65080-65080 TEBBETTS
64434-64434 CONCEPTION JUNCTION	64650-64650 KINGSTON	64833-64833 AVILLA	65081-65081 TIPTON
64435-64435 CORNING	64651-64651 LACLEDE	64834-64834 CARL JUNCTION	65082-65082 TUSCUMBIA
64436-64436 COSBY	64652-64652 LAREDO	64835-64835 CARTERVILLE	65083-65083 ULMAN
64437-64437 CRAIG	64653-64653 LINNEUS	64836-64836 CARTHAGE	65084-65084 VERSAILLES
64438-64438 DARLINGTON	64654-64654 LOCK SPRINGS	64840-64840 DIAMOND	65085-65085 WESTPHALIA
64439-64439 DEARBORN	64655-64655 LUCERNE	64841-64841 DUENWEG	65101-65111 JEFFERSON CITY
64440-64440 DE KALB	64656-64656 LUDLOW	64842-64842 FAIRVIEW	

Zip Range	Location
65199-65199	MISSOURI STATE LOTTERY COMM
65201-65218	COLUMBIA
65230-65230	ARMSTRONG
65231-65231	AUXVASSE
65232-65232	BENTON CITY
65233-65233	BOONVILLE
65236-65236	BRUNSWICK
65237-65237	BUNCETON
65239-65239	CAIRO
65240-65240	CENTRALIA
65243-65243	CLARK
65244-65244	CLIFTON HILL
65246-65246	DALTON
65247-65247	EXCELLO
65248-65248	FAYETTE
65250-65250	FRANKLIN
65251-65251	FULTON
65254-65254	GLASGOW
65255-65255	HALLSVILLE
65256-65256	HARRISBURG
65257-65257	HIGBEE
65258-65258	HOLLIDAY
65259-65259	HUNTSVILLE
65260-65260	JACKSONVILLE
65261-65261	KEYTESVILLE
65262-65262	KINGDOM CITY
65263-65263	MADISON
65264-65264	MARTINSBURG
65265-65265	MEXICO
65270-65270	MOBERLY
65274-65274	NEW FRANKLIN
65275-65275	PARIS
65276-65276	PILOT GROVE
65278-65278	RENICK
65279-65279	ROCHEPORT
65280-65280	RUSH HILL
65281-65281	SALISBURY
65282-65282	SANTA FE
65283-65283	STOUTSVILLE
65284-65284	STURGEON
65285-65285	THOMPSON
65286-65286	TRIPLETT
65287-65287	WOOLDRIDGE
65291-65291	CENSUS BUREAU
65299-65299	MID MISSOURI
65299-65299	COLUMBIA
65301-65302	SEDALIA
65305-65305	WHITEMAN AIR FORCE BASE
65320-65320	ARROW ROCK
65321-65321	BLACKBURN
65322-65322	BLACKWATER
65323-65323	CALHOUN
65324-65324	CLIMAX SPRINGS
65325-65325	COLE CAMP
65326-65326	EDWARDS
65327-65327	EMMA
65329-65329	FLORENCE
65330-65330	GILLIAM
65332-65332	GREEN RIDGE
65333-65333	HOUSTONIA
65334-65334	HUGHESVILLE
65335-65335	IONIA
65336-65336	KNOB NOSTER
65337-65337	LA MONTE
65338-65338	LINCOLN
65339-65339	MALTA BEND
65340-65340	MARSHALL
65344-65344	MIAMI
65345-65345	MORA
65347-65347	NELSON
65348-65348	OTTERVILLE
65349-65349	SLATER
65350-65350	SMITHTON
65351-65351	SWEET SPRINGS
65354-65354	SYRACUSE
65355-65355	WARSAW
65360-65360	WINDSOR
65401-65409	ROLLA
65433-65433	BENDAVIS
65436-65436	BEULAH
65438-65438	BIRCH TREE
65439-65439	BIXBY
65440-65440	BOSS
65441-65441	BOURBON
65443-65443	BRINKTOWN
65444-65444	BUCYRUS
65446-65446	CHERRYVILLE
65449-65449	COOK STATION
65452-65452	CROCKER
65453-65453	CUBA
65456-65456	DAVISVILLE
65457-65457	DEVILS ELBOW
65459-65459	DIXON
65461-65461	DUKE
65462-65462	EDGAR SPRINGS
65463-65463	ELDRIDGE
65464-65464	ELK CREEK
65466-65466	EMINENCE
65468-65468	EUNICE
65470-65470	FALCON
65473-65473	FORT LEONARD WOOD
65479-65479	HARTSHORN
65483-65483	HOUSTON
65484-65484	HUGGINS
65486-65486	IBERIA
65501-65501	JADWIN
65529-65529	JEROME
65532-65532	LAKE SPRING
65534-65534	LAQUEY
65535-65535	LEASBURG
65536-65536	LEBANON
65540-65540	LECOMA
65541-65541	LENOX
65542-65542	LICKING
65543-65543	LYNCHBURG
65546-65546	MONTIER
65548-65548	MOUNTAIN VIEW
65550-65550	NEWBURG
65552-65552	PLATO
65555-65555	RAYMONDVILLE
65556-65556	RICHLAND
65557-65557	ROBY
65559-65559	SAINT JAMES
65560-65560	SALEM
65564-65564	SOLO
65565-65565	STEELVILLE
65566-65566	VIBURNUM
65567-65567	STOUTLAND
65570-65570	SUCCESS
65571-65571	SUMMERSVILLE
65572-65572	SWEDEBORG
65573-65573	TERESITA
65580-65580	VICHY
65582-65582	VIENNA
65583-65583	WAYNESVILLE
65584-65584	SAINT ROBERT
65586-65586	WESCO
65588-65588	WINONA
65589-65589	YUKON
65590-65590	LONG LANE
65591-65591	MONTREAL
65601-65601	ALDRICH
65603-65603	ARCOLA
65604-65604	ASH GROVE
65605-65605	AURORA
65606-65606	ALTON
65607-65607	CAPLINGER MILLS
65608-65608	AVA
65609-65609	BAKERSFIELD
65610-65610	BILLINGS
65611-65611	BLUE EYE
65612-65612	BOIS D ARC
65613-65613	BOLIVAR
65614-65614	BRADLEYVILLE
65615-65616	BRANSON
65617-65617	BRIGHTON
65618-65618	BRIXEY
65619-65619	BROOKLINE STATION
65620-65620	BRUNER
65622-65622	BUFFALO
65623-65623	BUTTERFIELD
65624-65624	CAPE FAIR
65625-65625	CASSVILLE
65626-65626	CAULFIELD
65627-65627	CEDARCREEK
65629-65629	CHADWICK
65630-65630	CHESTNUTRIDGE
65631-65631	CLEVER
65632-65632	CONWAY
65633-65633	CRANE
65634-65634	CROSS TIMBERS
65635-65635	DADEVILLE
65636-65636	DIGGINS
65637-65637	DORA
65638-65638	DRURY
65640-65640	DUNNEGAN
65641-65641	EAGLE ROCK
65644-65644	ELKLAND
65645-65645	EUDORA
65646-65646	EVERTON
65647-65647	EXETER
65648-65648	FAIR GROVE
65649-65649	FAIR PLAY
65650-65650	FLEMINGTON
65652-65652	FORDLAND
65653-65653	FORSYTH
65654-65654	FREISTATT
65655-65655	GAINESVILLE
65656-65656	GALENA
65657-65657	GARRISON
65658-65658	GOLDEN
65659-65659	GOODSON
65660-65660	GRAFF
65661-65661	GREENFIELD
65662-65662	GROVESPRING
65663-65663	HALF WAY
65664-65664	HALLTOWN
65666-65666	HARDENVILLE
65667-65667	HARTVILLE
65668-65668	HERMITAGE
65669-65669	HIGHLANDVILLE
65672-65673	HOLLISTER
65674-65674	HUMANSVILLE
65675-65675	HURLEY
65676-65676	ISABELLA
65679-65679	KIRBYVILLE
65680-65680	KISSEE MILLS
65681-65681	LAMPE
65682-65682	LOCKWOOD
65685-65685	LOUISBURG
65686-65686	KIMBERLING CITY
65688-65688	BRANDSVILLE
65689-65689	CABOOL
65690-65690	COUCH
65692-65692	KOSHKONONG
65701-65701	MC CLURG
65702-65702	MACOMB
65704-65704	MANSFIELD
65705-65705	MARIONVILLE
65706-65706	MARSHFIELD
65707-65707	MILLER
65708-65708	MONETT
65710-65710	MORRISVILLE
65711-65711	MOUNTAIN GROVE
65712-65712	MOUNT VERNON
65713-65713	NIANGUA
65714-65714	NIXA
65715-65715	NOBLE
65717-65717	NORWOOD
65720-65720	OLDFIELD
65721-65721	OZARK
65722-65722	PHILLIPSBURG
65723-65723	PIERCE CITY
65724-65724	PITTSBURG
65725-65725	PLEASANT HOPE
65726-65726	POINT LOOKOUT
65727-65727	POLK
65728-65728	PONCE DE LEON
65729-65729	PONTIAC
65730-65730	POWELL
65731-65731	POWERSITE
65732-65732	PRESTON
65733-65733	PROTEM
65734-65734	PURDY
65735-65735	QUINCY
65737-65737	REEDS SPRING
65738-65738	REPUBLIC
65739-65739	RIDGEDALE
65740-65740	ROCKAWAY BEACH
65741-65741	ROCKBRIDGE
65742-65742	ROGERSVILLE
65744-65744	RUETER
65745-65745	SELIGMAN
65746-65746	SEYMOUR
65747-65747	SHELL KNOB
65752-65752	SOUTH GREENFIELD
65753-65753	SPARTA
65754-65754	SPOKANE
65755-65755	SQUIRES
65756-65756	STOTTS CITY
65757-65757	STRAFFORD
65758-65758	GAINESVILLE
65759-65759	TANEYVILLE
65760-65760	TECUMSEH
65761-65761	THEODOSIA
65762-65762	THORNFIELD
65764-65764	TUNAS
65765-65765	TURNERS
65766-65766	UDALL
65767-65767	URBANA
65768-65768	VANZANT
65769-65769	VERONA
65770-65770	WALNUT GROVE
65771-65771	WALNUT SHADE
65772-65772	WASHBURN
65773-65773	WASOLA
65774-65774	WEAUBLEAU
65775-65775	WEST PLAINS
65776-65776	SOUTH FORK
65777-65777	MOODY
65778-65778	MYRTLE
65779-65779	WHEATLAND
65781-65781	WILLARD
65783-65783	WINDYVILLE
65784-65784	ZANONI
65785-65785	STOCKTON
65786-65786	MACKS CREEK
65787-65787	ROACH
65788-65788	PEACE VALLEY
65789-65789	POMONA
65790-65790	POTTERSVILLE
65791-65791	THAYER
65793-65793	WILLOW SPRINGS
65800-65899	SPRINGFIELD

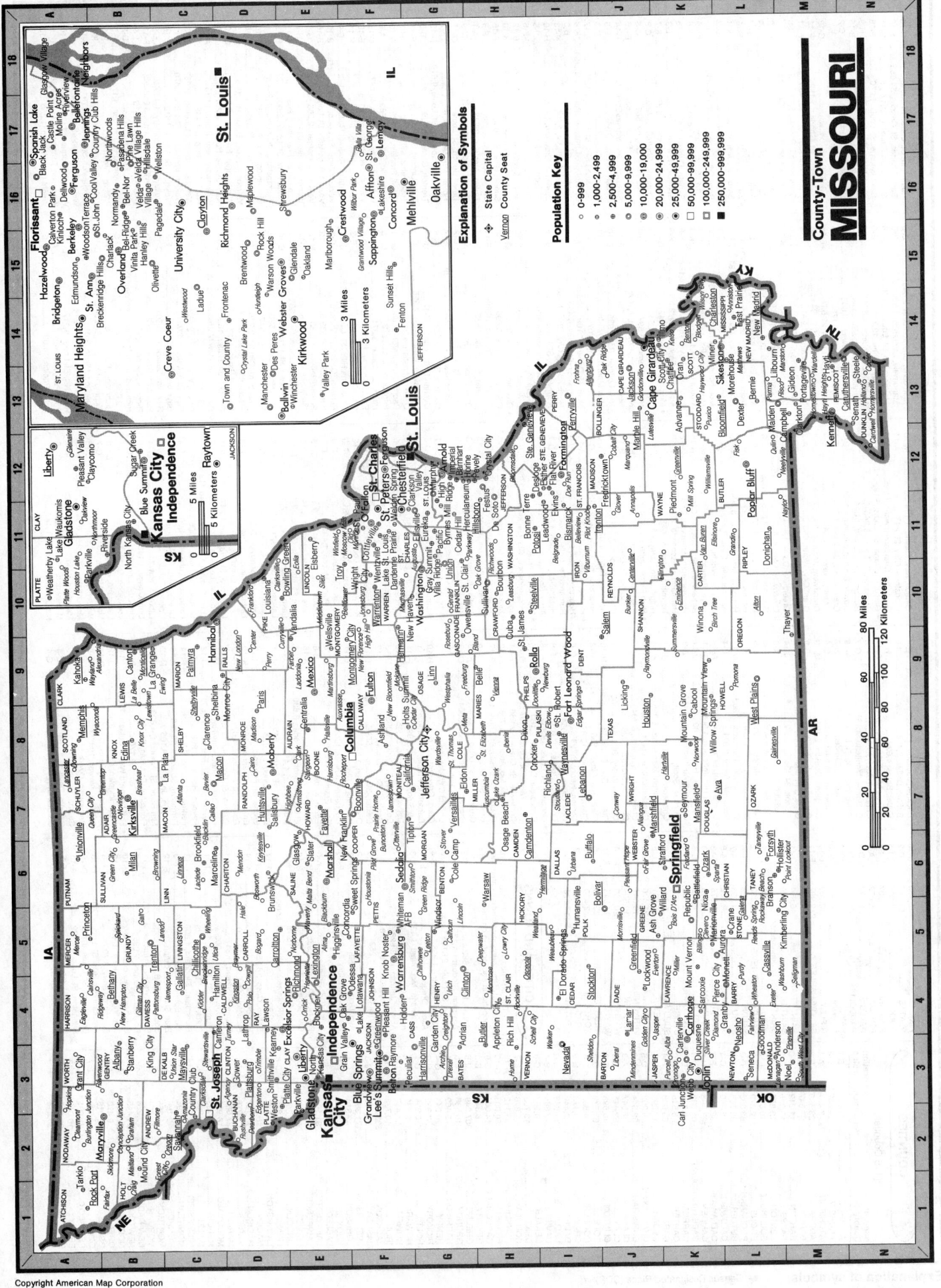

County-Town
MISSOURI

Explanation of Symbols

⟡ State Capital

Vernon County Seat

Population Key

- ∘ 0-999
- ⊙ 1,000-2,499
- ⊕ 2,500-4,999
- ⊛ 5,000-9,999
- ⊙ 10,000-19,000
- ⊚ 20,000-24,999
- ⊚ 25,000-49,999
- ▫ 50,000-99,999
- ◻ 100,000-249,999
- ■ 250,000-999,999

Explanation of symbols: ●– Census Designated Place (CDP)

General Help Numbers:

Governor's Office
PO Box 200801, State Capitol
Helena, MT 59620-0801
www.discoveringmontana.com/
gov2/css/default.asp

406-444-3111
Fax 406-444-5529
8AM-5PM

Attorney General's Office
PO Box 201401
Helena, MT 59620
www.doj.mt.gov/department/attorneygeneral.asp

406-444-2026
Fax 406-444-3549

8AM-5PM

Legislative Records
State Capitol, Rm 10
PO Box 201706
Helena, MT 59620-1706
www.leg.state.mt.us

406-444-3064
406-444-3660 (Research)
Fax 406-444-2588
8AM-5PM

State Archives
Library/Archives Division
PO Box 201201, 225 N Roberts St
Helena, MT 59620-1201
www.his.state.mt.us

406-444-2681
Fax 406-444*5297
8AM-5PM M-F;
9AM-4:30PM
1st SA of each month

State Specifics:

Capital:	Helena
	Lewis and Clark County
Time Zone:	MST
Number of Counties:	56
Population:	926,865
Web Site:	www.discoveringmontana.com/default.asp

State Agencies

Criminal Records

Department of Justice, Criminal Records, PO Box 201403, Helena, MT 59620-1403 (Courier address: 303 N Roberts, 4th Floor, Helena, MT 59620); 406-444-3625, 406-444-0689-Fax; 8AM-5PM.

www.doj.state.mt.us/department/criminalinvestigationdivision.asp

Records are available from 1950's on and are 100% computerized. It takes 1 week to 1 month before new records are available for inquiry. Records are normally destroyed after court order. 85% of all arrests in database have final dispositions recorded.

Searching: Include the following in your request-name, alias, date of birth. The Social Security

Number and any aliases are helpful. Place written requests on letterhead. Fingerprint searches are optional. 100% of records are fingerprint-supported. The following data is not released: traffic offenses, unless felony driving under the influence of alcohol. All felonies and misdemeanors (except traffic violations) are released. Records without dispositions are released; the agency attempts to locate the disposition prior to public release. Deferred impositions that have been dismissed are not released.

Access by: mail, in person.

Fee & Payment: The fee is $10.00 per individual for a name check or $8.00 per individual for a fingerprint check; $32.00 for a fingerprint check plus FBI fingerprint check, when required by statute for child care or schools. Account status to approved screening firms. Fee payee: Montana Criminal Records Prepayment required. Personal checks accepted. No credit cards accepted.

Mail search: Turnaround time: 5-10 days. A SASE is requested.

In person search: This agency will create the individual's fingerprint card needed for a fingerprint check for a $5.00 fee plus the search fee of $8.00. Turnaround time is usually immediate, unless there is a record or "hit."

Statewide Court Records

Court Administrator, PO Box 203002, Helena, MT 59620-3002 (Courier address: 215 N Sanders, Justice Bldg Rm 315, Helena, MT 59620); 406-444-2621, 406-444-0834-Fax; 8AM-5PM.

www.lawlibrary.state.mt.us

All trial court record access must be done at the local level.

Access by: online.

Online search: Montana Supreme Court opinions and orders are found at the website.

Sexual Offender Registry

Department of Justice, Sexual and Violent Offender Registry, PO Box 201417, Helena, MT 59620; 406-444-2497, 406-444-2759-Fax; 8AM-5PM.

http://doj.state.mt.us/svor/search.asp

There are over 2,500 registered offenders in the database. There are three Tier Levels of offenders, 1 being the lowest and 3 being the highest. Level 3 also indicates the offender is a sexually violent predator.

Records are available from 1989 forward. Tier Levels were instituted in 1997. It takes 1 week to 1 month before new records are available for inquiry.

Searching: Include the following in your request-city, county, ZIP or name.

Access by: online.

Fee & Payment: There is no fee to search.

Online search: The state sexual offender list is available at the website. You can search for this information by name, by city or county, or by the type of offense committed.

Incarceration Records

Montana Department of Corrections, Directors Office, PO Box 201301, Helena, MT 59620-1301 (Courier address: 1539 11th Ave, Helena, MT 59620); 406-444-3930, 406-444-7461 (Information Officer), 406-444-4920-Fax; 8:30AM-4:30PM.

www.cor.state.mt.us

Records are available on current and former inmates, except for the website which is current only. Computerized records go back to 1980.

Older records sent to Historical Society. It takes about 30 days before new records are available for inquiry.

Searching: Location, physical identifiers, conviction and sentencing information, and release dates are provided. Include the following in your request-name; and DOB. Computer records go back to 1978. The following data is not released: SSN and medical information.

Access by: mail, phone, fax, online.

Fee & Payment: There is no fee.

Mail search: Turnaround time: 10 to 40 days.

Phone search: Name searching is permitted by phone.

Fax search: Fax requests are accepted, depending on complexity of search.

Online search: Search current or former inmates on the ConWeb system at http://app.discoveringmontana.com/conweb/index.html. Search by ID# or name. Also, a private company offers free web access to DOC records at www.vinelink.com/index.jsp.

Other access: Entire offender database is available for purchase for $100.00; call Discovering Montana, 406-449-3468. Academic or social researchers can acquire the same database for no charge.

Corporation, Limited Liability Company, Fictitious Name, Limited Partnerships, Assumed Name, Trademarks/Servicemarks

Business Services Bureau, Secretary of State, PO Box 202801, Helena, MT 59620-2801 (Courier address: 1236 East 6th Ave, Helena, MT 59620); 406-444-3665, 406-444-3976-Fax; 8AM-5PM.

http://sos.state.mt.us/css/index.asp

Records are available from the 1860s. New records are available for inquiry immediately. Records are indexed on inhouse computer.

Searching: Include the following in your request-full name of business, specific records that you need copies of. In addition to the articles of incorporation, corporation records include the following information: Annual Reports, Officers, Directors, DBAs, Prior (merged) names, Inactive and Reserved names.

Access by: mail, phone, fax, in person, online.

Fee & Payment: There is no search fee, but there is a flat fee of $10.00 for all copies of file, records are certified for this price. Fee payee: Secretary of State. Prepayment required. Prepaid accounts may be established. Personal checks accepted. No credit cards accepted.

Mail search: Turnaround time: 2 weeks. A SASE is requested.

Phone search: Limit of three requests per call.

Fax search: Fax requests are accepted for prepaid accounts at a cost of $3.00 for up to 10 pages and $.25 per additional page to fax back. Turnaround time is up to 10 business days.

In person search: Counter service is available.

Online search: Fee searches of business entities at http://app.discoveringmontana.com/bes/ There is a commercial service for finding registered principles, the fee is $4.00 per search. Go to

http://app.discoveringmontana.com/walkthrough/rps/.

Other access: Lists of the new corporations per month are available.

Expedited service: Expedited service is available for mail, phone and in person searches. Turnaround time: 1 day. Add $20.00 per search.

Uniform Commercial Code, Federal Tax Liens

Business Services Bureau, Secretary of State, Rm 260, PO Box 202801, Helena, MT 59620-2801 (Courier address: 1236 East 6th Ave, Helena, MT 59620); 406-444-1212, 406-444-3976-Fax; 8AM-5PM.

www.sos.mt.gov/css/index.asp

Records are available from 1965, indexed on computer and on microfiche. Terminated or expired financing statements are not available prior to 6/30/01, with the exception of notices of federal tax liens. It takes one day before new records are available for inquiry.

Searching: Use search request form UCC-11. The search includes notice of federal tax liens on businesses and individuals. All state tax liens are filed at the county level. Include the following in your request-debtor exact name and any fictitious names.

Access by: mail, fax, in person, online.

Fee & Payment: The search fee is $7.00 per debtor name, copies are $.50 per page. Fee payee: Secretary of State. The state will accept prepaid accounts. Personal checks accepted. No credit cards accepted.

Mail search: Turnaround time: 1 to 3 days.

Fax search: Same fees and turnaround time apply.

In person search: Counter service is 1 to 3 days unless expedite fee is paid.

Online search: This web-based subscription service provides information about all active liens filed with the office. To use the service, you need to establish an with Discovering Montana for a fee of $25 per month. Contact Discovering Montana at 101 N Rodney #3, Helena MT 59601, or call 406-449-3468, or visit their web site at www.discoveringmontana.com.

Other access: The agency offers farm bill filings lists on a monthly basis for $5.00 per category on paper or microfiche. A CD-Rom for all Farm Products is available for $20.00.

State Tax Liens

Records not maintained by a state level agency.

Records are at the county level.

Sales Tax Registrations

State does not impose sales tax.

Birth Certificates

Montana Department of Health, Vital Records, PO Box 4210, Helena, MT 59604 (Courier address: 111 N Sanders, Rm 209, Helena, MT 59601); 406-444-4228 (Recording), 406-444-2685, 406-444-1803-Fax; 8AM-5PM.

http://vhsp.dphhs.state.mt.us/dph_12.htm

Records are available from 1907 on. It takes 3 months before new records are available for inquiry.

Searching: Must be able to show direct and tangible interest of records. The decision if you can get copies of records will be up to the staff of the Vital Records department. Include the following in your request-full name, names of parents, mother's maiden name, date of birth, place of birth, relationship to person of record, reason for information request. Must include copy of guardianship papers, if you are guardian. All requesters must include photo ID and phone number.

Access by: mail, fax, in person, online.

Fee & Payment: A certified copy is $12.00. If you don't know the year add a search fee of $10.00 for first 5 years search, and $1.00 each add'l year. Add $6.00 for using a credit card. The search fee is per 5 years searched. Fee payee: Montana Vital Records. Prepayment required. Personal checks accepted. Major credit cards accepted.

Mail search: Turnaround time: 10 days. No SASE is required.

Fax search: Must use credit card for additional $6.00. Turnaround time is 2-3 days.

In person search: Search costs $10.00 for each name in request. Turnaround time same day.

Online search: The state agency offers an online ordering system of approved vendors via the webpage. Order records via state designated vendor at www.vitalchek.com.

Expedited service: Expedited service is available for fax and online orders. Turnaround time: overnight delivery. Add $16.00 per package for FedEx return plus the $6.00 credit card fee, and the $10.00 search fee.

Death Records

Montana Department of Health, Vital Records, PO Box 4210, Helena, MT 59604 (Courier address: 111 N Sanders, Rm 209, Helena, MT 59601); 406-444-4228 (Recording), 406-444-2685, 406-444-1803-Fax; 8AM-5PM.

http://vhsp.dphhs.state.mt.us/dph_12.htm

Records are available from 1908 on. It takes 3 months before new records are available for inquiry.

Searching: Records are open. Include the following in your request-full name, date of death, place of death, relationship to person of record, reason for information request. Requesters should include a copy of picture ID and phone number.

Access by: mail, fax, in person, online.

Fee & Payment: A certified copy is $12.00. If year not known, then add a search fee of $10.00 for 5 years searched and $1.00 each add'l year. Add $6.00for using a credit card. Fee payee: Montana Vital Records. Prepayment required. Personal checks accepted. Major credit cards accepted.

Mail search: Turnaround time: 10 days.

Fax search: Must use credit card for additional $6.00. Turnaround time is 2-3 days.

In person search: Turnaround time same day.

Online search: Order records via state designated vendor at www.vitalchek.com.

Expedited service: Expedited service is available for fax and online orders. Turnaround time: overnight delivery. Add $16.00 per package for

FedEx return plus the $6.00 credit card fee, and the $10.00 search fee.

Marriage Certificates, Divorce Records

Records not maintained by a state level agency.

Marriage and divorce records are found at county of issue. This agency is required by law to maintain an index of these records. The index is from 1943 to present. The State can direct you to the correct county for a fee of $10.00 per 5 years searched.

Workers' Compensation Records

Montana State Fund, General Legal Inquiries, PO Box 4759, Helena, MT 59604-4759 (Courier address: 5 S. Last Chance Gulch, Helena, MT 59601); 406-444-6500, 406-444-5963-Fax; 8AM-5PM.

www.montanastatefund.com/wps/portal

Records are available from mid 1980's to 1995 on microfiche. Records 1996 forward are computerized. It takes 30 days before new records are available for inquiry.

Searching: Put request in writing, including reason for the request. They will determine whether the request is legitimate, unless you include a signed release form. Include the following in your request-claimant name, Social Security Number, date of accident, employer.

Access by: mail, fax.

Fee & Payment: Copy fees are $.35 per page if from computer, $.50 per page if from microfiche. There is no search fee. Fee payee: Montana State Fund. Prepayment required. Personal checks accepted. No credit cards accepted.

Mail search: Turnaround time: 7 days. No SASE is required.

Fax search: Same criteria as mail searches.

Driver Records

Motor Vehicle Division, Driver's Services, PO Box 201430, Helena, MT 59620-1430 (Courier address: Records Unit, 303 N Roberts, Room 260, Helena, MT 59620); 406-444-3292, 406-444-7623-Fax; 8AM-5PM.

www.doj.state.mt.us/driving/default.asp

Records are available for lifetime. It takes up to 45 days before new records are available for inquiry. Records are normally destroyed after scanned and indexed.

Searching: Anyone may order a driving record; however, personal information including address, SSN, photo, and medical information is not released. Opt out is not necessary. Use of the State Form is required. The form can be downloaded at the website. Include the following in your request-driver's full name, DOB, and/or license number. Requester must present copy of state issued ID or have request notarized.

Access by: mail, in person, online.

Fee & Payment: The fee is $4.00 per three year record history and $10.00 for a certified history. Fee payee: Motor Vehicle Division. Prepayment required. Billing or draw accounts available.

Personal checks accepted. No credit cards accepted.

Mail search: Turnaround time: 3 days. Requests must be in writing, stating purpose and on letterhead. A SASE is requested.

In person search: Simple requests processed immediately. Up to 5 records may be requested in person for immediate delivery at this location. Use of forms are required.

Online search: A Restricted Use Agreement and a Requestor Services Agreement must be completed and approved in advance. Both interactive and batch delivery is offered ($6.50 per record) to users who sign up in advance and pay a $50.00 annual registration fee. Online services also include a License Status Conviction Activity batch search, at a reduced price. This is a monitoring service, for a small fee users may submit a monthly query. For more information, visit http://app.discoveringmontana.com/dojdrs/ or call 406-449-3468.

Expedited service: Fax return service is available for an additional $3.00 per page.

Vehicle Ownership Vehicle Identification, Vessel Ownership Vessel Registration

Department of Justice, Title and Registration Bureau, 1003 Buckskin Drive, Deer Lodge, MT 59722; 406-846-6000, 406-846-6039-Fax; 8AM-5PM.

www.doj.state.mt.us/driving/vehicletitleregistration.asp

Lien information appears on the title record.

Records are available from 1976 to present on microfiche. Watercraft data is available from 1988. It takes 5 to 10 days before new records are available for inquiry. Records are normally destroyed after 4 years.

Searching: Casual requesters may not obtain records without written consent of the subject. DPPA requirements enforced. MV210 Form - Release of Motor Vehicle Records - can be downloaded from the website. Requires notarization of the requester or copy of DL. Items required for search could include full name, VIN, plate number, or title number.

Access by: mail, in person, online.

Fee & Payment: The fee is $6.00 per vehicle/vessel or name search; $25.00 for title or odometer history. Fee payee: State of Montana Prepayment required. Personal checks accepted. No credit cards accepted.

Mail search: Turnaround time: 5 to 7 days. Requests must be in writing, signed and notarized. Use of the state form is required. No SASE is required.

In person search: Simple requests may be processed while you wait, if staffing available.

Online search: Online access to vehicle records is available   at https://app.discoveringmontana.com/dojvs/. Requesters must pay an annual $50.00 registration fee, and the purpose of the requests must pass DPPA muster. The following is available (authority level determined by DOJ): Vehicle Information, License Plate Information, Vehicle Owner Information, Lien History, Title History and Registration Information. Call 866-449-3468 for more information.

Other access: Bulk or batch ordering of registration information is available on tape, disk, or paper. The user must fill out a specific form, which gives the user the capability of customization. For further information, contact the Registrar at address above.

Accident Reports

Montana Highway Patrol, Crash Records, 2550 Prospect Ave, Helena, MT 59620-1419; 406-444-3278, 406-444-4169-Fax; 8AM-5PM.

www.doj.state.mt.us/department/highwaypatroldivision.asp

Digital images are available with previous year's data.

Records are available for 10 years to present. Computer indexing since 1996. Digital images are available starting with the year 1995. It takes 10 to 14 days after the accident before new records are available for inquiry. Records are normally destroyed after 10 years.

Searching: Records are only released to persons involved in crash, owner, attorney or insurance representing someone involved in the case. Witness statements are released. An Accident Release Form available on web. Include the following in your request-location of accident, date of accident, full name(s) of drivers, signature of requester.

Access by: mail, phone, in person.

Fee & Payment: The search fee is $2.00 per report, non-fundable. Fee payee: Montana Highway Patrol. Prepayment required. Personal checks accepted. No credit cards accepted.

Mail search: Turnaround time: 3 to 4 working days. Requests must be submitted in writing following guidelines mentioned above. No SASE is required.

Phone search: The agency will only release names over the phone of people involved in crash.

In person search: Records will be released if proper authorization is shown.

Other access: Statistics, but not reports, are available.

Voter Registration

Secretary of State, Elections Bureau, PO Box 202801, Helena, MT 59620-2801; 406-444-5376, 406-444-2023-Fax; 8AM-5PM.

http://sos.state.mt.us/css/ELB/Contents.asp

Searching by state personnel depends on the voter file system workload.

Records are available from 2004 (new centralized system). Counties will update the state database periodically. Therefore, it is suggested to also search at the county level. Records are normally destroyed after 2 years (archived).

Searching: The following data is not released: Social Security Numbers.

Access by: mail, phone, fax, in person, online.

Fee & Payment: There are no fees for searches unless large lists or bulk records needed.

Mail search: Turnaround time: 2 to 4 days. No SASE is required.

Phone search: Records are available by phone.

Fax search: Fax searching available.

In person search: Simple requests may be processed immediately.

Online search: Access records at http://app.mt.gov/voterfile/select_criteria.html. Customized lists are available for $.04 per record. Records can be purchased for non-commercial use only.

Other access: This agency database can be purchased on disk or CD-ROM, or downloaded from the web site mentioned above. Fee of $.012 per record will be assessed. For more information, contact Elaine Graveley.

GED Certificates

Office of Public Instruction, GED Program, PO Box 202501, Helena, MT 59620-2501; 406-444-4438, 406-444-1373-Fax; 7AM-4PM.

www.opi.state.mt.us/GED/Index.html

It takes three weeks before new records are available for inquiry.

Searching: The agency will not issue duplicate diplomas. Include the following in your request-name, SSN, DOB, approximate year of test, SASE. If the information is going to a third party (employer or screening company) include a signed release from the subject and indicate where to send the documentation.

Access by: mail, in person.

Fee & Payment: There is no search fee for either a verification or transcript. The fee is the cost of the stamped envelope.

Mail search: Turnaround time 1 week. A SASE is required.

In person search: No fee for request. Turnaround time same day.

Hunting and Fishing License Information

Fish, Wildlife & Parks Department, Licensing, PO Box 200701, Helena, MT 59620-0701 (Courier address: 1420 E 6th Ave, Helena, MT 59620); 406-444-2950, 406-444-9733-Fax; 8AM-5PM.

http://fwp.state.mt.us/default.html

Records are available from 1976 for the special resident and non-resident permits and the general permits go back for 5 years. Records are computerized for the current year, prior on microfiche. Records are indexed on inhouse computer, microfiche.

Searching: The agency will verify if a person has purchased a license. Include the following in your request-full name, date of birth, Social Security Number. The following data is not released: phone number and SSN.

Access by: mail, phone, in person.

Fee & Payment: There is no search fee.

Mail search: Turnaround time: 1 week. A SASE is requested.

Phone search: Records are available by phone.

In person search: Simple requests may be processed immediately.

Other access: A master list showing names, address, and types of licenses purchased can be ordered from this agency. The cost is $100.00. Starting in 2005, licensees have the choice of opting in/out to have their names distributed, thus the master list is shrinking.

Montana State Licensing Agencies

For details about the agency responsible for licensing/certifying/registering an item below or in the Agency Quick Finder section, match an item's number with the number of the agency in the *Licensing Agency Information* section.

Montana Licenses Searchable Online

Acupuncturist #33	http://app.discoveringmontana.com/bsdinq/index.html
Architect #34	http://app.discoveringmontana.com/bsdinq/index.html
Athletic Event/Event Timekeeper #3	http://app.discoveringmontana.com/bsdinq/index.html
Audiologist #21	http://app.discoveringmontana.com/bsdinq/index.html
Barber/Barber Instructor #2	http://app.discoveringmontana.com/bsdinq/index.html
Boxer/Boxing Professional/Manager/Promoter/Judge #3	http://app.discoveringmontana.com/bsdinq/index.html
Cemetery, Privately Owned #3	http://app.discoveringmontana.com/bsdinq/index.html
Chemical Dependency Counselor #19	http://app.discoveringmontana.com/bsdinq/index.html
Child Care Provider #26	http://vhsp.dphhs.state.mt.us/dph_r2.htm
Chiropractor #3	http://app.discoveringmontana.com/bsdinq/index.html
Clinical Nurse Specialist #32	http://app.discoveringmontana.com/lookup/
Clinical Social Worker #17	http://app.discoveringmontana.com/bsdinq/index.html
Construction Blaster #18	http://app.discoveringmontana.com/bsdinq/index.html
Contractor, Public #36	http://erd.dli.state.mt.us/wcregs/mtcontractor.asp
Cosmetologist/Cosmo. Instr./School #2	http://app.discoveringmontana.com/bsdinq/index.html
Crematory/Crematory Operator/Tech #3	http://app.discoveringmontana.com/bsdinq/index.html
Day Care Center #26	http://vhsp.dphhs.state.mt.us/dph_r2.htm
Dentist/Dental Hygienist/Dental Assis't/Denturist #5	http://discoveringmontana.com/dli/bsd/index.asp
Drug Registration, Dangerous #7	http://app.discoveringmontana.com/bsdinq/index.html
Drug Wholesaler #7	http://app.discoveringmontana.com/bsdinq/index.html
Electrician #8	http://app.discoveringmontana.com/bsdinq/index.html
Electrologist #2	http://app.discoveringmontana.com/bsdinq/index.html
Emergency Medical Technician #33	http://app.discoveringmontana.com/bsdinq/index.html
Engineer #10	http://app.discoveringmontana.com/bsdinq/index.html
Esthetician #2	http://app.discoveringmontana.com/bsdinq/index.html
Firearms Instructor #9	http://app.discoveringmontana.com/bsdinq/index.html
Funeral Director #3	http://app.discoveringmontana.com/bsdinq/index.html
Guide #6	http://app.mt.gov/lookup/
Hairstylist #21	http://app.discoveringmontana.com/bsdinq/index.html
Hearing Aid Dispenser #3	http://app.discoveringmontana.com/bsdinq/index.html
Insurance Adjuster/Producer #37	www.discoveringmontana.com/sao/insurance/findagent.html
Land Surveyor #10	http://app.discoveringmontana.com/bsdinq/index.html
Landscape Architect #3	http://app.discoveringmontana.com/bsdinq/index.html
Manicurist #2	http://app.discoveringmontana.com/bsdinq/index.html
Medical Doctor #33	http://app.discoveringmontana.com/bsdinq/index.html
Midwife Nurse #32	http://app.discoveringmontana.com/lookup/
Midwife, Direct Entry/Apprentice #1	http://app.discoveringmontana.com/bsdinq/index.html
Mortuary/Mortician #3	http://app.discoveringmontana.com/bsdinq/index.html
Naturopathic Physician #1	http://app.discoveringmontana.com/bsdinq/index.html
Nurse Anesthetist #32	http://app.discoveringmontana.com/lookup/
Nurse RN/LPN/Practitioner #32	http://app.discoveringmontana.com/lookup/
Nutritionist #33	http://app.discoveringmontana.com/bsdinq/index.html
Occupational Therapist #21	http://app.discoveringmontana.com/bsdinq/index.html
Optometrist #7	http://discoveringmontana.com/dli/opt
Osteopathic Physician #33	http://app.discoveringmontana.com/bsdinq/index.html
Outfitter, Hunting/Fishing #6	http://app.mt.gov/lookup/
Pharmacist #7	http://app.discoveringmontana.com/bsdinq/index.html
Physical Therapist #17	http://app.discoveringmontana.com/bsdinq/index.html
Physician Assistant #33	http://app.discoveringmontana.com/bsdinq/index.html
Plumber #8	http://app.discoveringmontana.com/bsdinq/index.html
Podiatrist #33	http://app.discoveringmontana.com/bsdinq/index.html
Private Investigator/Private Security Guard #9	http://app.discoveringmontana.com/bsdinq/index.html
Process Server #9	http://app.discoveringmontana.com/bsdinq/index.html
Property Manager #15	http://app.discoveringmontana.com/bsdinq/index.html
Psychologist #11	http://app.discoveringmontana.com/bsdinq/index.html
Public Accountant #12	http://app.discoveringmontana.com/bsdinq/
Radiologic Technologist #21	http://app.discoveringmontana.com/bsdinq/index.html
Real Estate Agent/Broker/Sales #15	http://app.discoveringmontana.com/bsdinq/index.html
Real Estate Appraiser #14	http://app.discoveringmontana.com/bsdinq/index.html
Referee #3	http://app.discoveringmontana.com/bsdinq/index.html

Respiratory Care Practitioner #21 .... http://app.discoveringmontana.com/bsdinq/index.html
Sanitarian #21 .... http://app.discoveringmontana.com/bsdinq/index.html
Security Alarm Installer #9 .... http://app.discoveringmontana.com/bsdinq/index.html
Security Company/Organization/Security Guard #21 .... http://app.discoveringmontana.com/bsdinq/index.html
Social Worker, LSW #17 .... http://app.discoveringmontana.com/bsdinq/index.html
Speech Pathologist #21 .... http://app.discoveringmontana.com/bsdinq/index.html
Surveyor, Land #10 .... http://app.discoveringmontana.com/bsdinq/index.html
Teacher #35 .... http://data.opi.state.mt.us/certification/
Timeshare Broker/Salesperson #15 .... http://app.discoveringmontana.com/bsdinq/index.html
Veterinarian #11 .... http://app.discoveringmontana.com/bsdinq/index.html
Wrestler #3 .... http://app.discoveringmontana.com/bsdinq/index.html
X-ray Technician #21 .... http://app.discoveringmontana.com/bsdinq/index.html

Montana Licensing Quick Finder

Acupuncturist #33 406-841-2364	Funeral Director #3 406-841-2393	Plumber #8 406-841-2328
Adoption Agency #4 406-444-5916	Fur/Hide Dealer #27 406-444-4558	Podiatrist #33 406-841-2364
Apiary #20 406-444-5400	Gambling Machine,Video/Electr'c #28 .. 406-444-1971	Private Investigator #9 406-841-2387
Architect #34 406-841-2367	Gambling Operator/Mfg./Dist. #28 406-444-1971	Private Placement Offering #38 406-444-2040
Asbestos related Occupation #25 406-444-3490	Grain Elevator #20 406-444-5400	Private Security Guard #9 406-841-2387
Athletic Event/Event Timekeeper #3 406-841-2393	Group Home, Youth #30 406-444-6587	Process Server #9 406-841-2387
Attorney #16 406-442-7660	Guide #6 406-444-2373	Property Manager #15 406-444-2961
Audiologist #21 406-444-3091	Hairstylist #21 406-444-4288	Psychologist #11 406-841-2394
Barber/Barber Instructor #2 406-841-2300	Hearing Aid Dispenser #3 406-841-2395	Public Accountant #12 406-841-2388
Boxer/Boxing Professional #3 406-841-2393	Horse Racing Occupation #22 406-444-4287	Radiologic Technologist #21 406-444-3091
Brand (Livestock)/Brand Inspector #29. 406-444-2045	Insurance Adjuster #37 406-444-2040	Real Estate Agent/Broker/Sales #15 ... 406-444-2961
Card Dealer /Card Gaming, Live #28 ... 406-444-1971	Insurance Producer #37 406-444-2040	Real Estate Appraiser #14 406-444-2386
Casino Night #28 406-444-1971	Jockey #22 406-444-4287	Referee #3 406-841-2393
Cemetery, Privately Owned #3 406-841-2393	Land Surveyor #10 406-841-2367	Respiratory Care Practitioner #21 406-444-3091
Chemical Dependency Counselor #19. 406-444-2827	Landscape Architect #3 406-841-2395	Sanitarian #21 406-444-3091
Child Care Agency #4 406-444-1675	Livestock Dealer #29 406-444-2045	School Guidance Counselor/ School Psychologist #35
Child Care Provider #26 406-444-2012	Living Trust Seller #38 406-444-2040	 406-444-3150
Chiropractor #3 406-841-2393	Lobbyist #24 406-444-2942	School Superintend't/Principal #35 406-444-3150
Clinical Nurse Specialist #32 406-841-2340	Lottery Retailer #23 406-444-5825	Securities Broker/Salesperson #38 406-444-2040
Clinical Social Worker #17 406-841-2369	Manicurist #2 406-841-2300	Security Alarm Installer #9 406-841-2387
Commodity Dealer #20 406-444-5400	Meat and Poultry #29 406-444-5202	Security Company/Organization #9 406-841-2387
Construction Blaster #18 406-841-2351	Medical Doctor #33 406-841-2364	Security Guard #21 406-444-4288
Contractor, Public #36 406-444-7734	Midwife Nurse #32 406-841-2340	Seed Dealer #20 406-444-5400
Cosmetologist/Cosmetology Instr./School #2	Midwife, Direct Entry/Apprentice #1 406-841-2394	Septic Tank Cleaner #25 406-444-5294
.... 406-841-2300	Milk/Cream Weigher/Grader/Sampler/Tester #29	Social Worker, LSW #17 406-841-2369
Crematory/Crematory Operator/Technician #3	 406-444-2875	Speech Pathologist #21 406-444-3091
.... 406-841-2393	Mint Oil Producer #20 406-444-5400	Surveyor, Land #10 406-841-2367
Dam Safety Operation Permit #39 406-444-6601	Mortuary/Mortician #3 406-841-2393	Taxidermist #27 406-444-4558
Day Care Center #26 406-444-2012	Multi-level Marketing Company #38 406-444-2040	Teacher #35 406-444-3150
Dental Hygienist #5 406-841-2390	Naturopathic Physician #1 406-841-2394	Telephone, Customer-Owned, Coin-Operated #38
Dentist/Dental Assistant #5 406-841-2390	Notary Public #13 406-444-5379	 406-444-2040
Denturist #5 406-841-2390	Nurse Anesthetist #32 406-841-2340	Timeshare Broker/Salesperson #15 406-444-2961
Dietitian #33 406-841-2364	Nurse RN / LPN / Practitioner #32 406-841-2340	Underground Storage Tank Inspector #31
Drug Registration, Dangerous #7 406-841-2356	Nurseryman #20 406-444-5400	 406-444-5300
Drug Wholesaler #7 406-841-2356	Nutritionist #33 406-841-2364	Underground Storage Tank Installer/Remover #31
Electrician #8 406-841-2328	Occupational Therapist #21 406-444-3091	 406-444-5300
Electrologist #2 406-841-2300	Optometrist #7 406-841-2390	Variable Annuities Seller #38 406-444-2040
Emergency Medical Technician #33 406-841-2380	Osteopathic Physician #33 406-841-2364	Veterinarian #11 406-841-2394
Engineer #10 406-841-2367	Outfitter, Hunting/Fishing #6 406-444-2373	Water & Sewage Plant Operator #25. 406-444-5294
Esthetician #2 406-841-2300	Pesticide Applicator/Dealer #20 406-444-5400	Weather Modifier #39 406-444-6601
Fertilizer Dealer #20 406-444-5400	Pharmacist #7 406-841-2356	Well Driller #39 406-444-6601
Firearms Instructor #9 406-841-2387	Physical Therapist #17 406-841-2369	Wrestler #3 406-841-2393
Foster Care Home/Program #4 406-444-1675	Physician Assistant #33 406-841-2361	X-ray Technician #21 406-444-3091

Montana Licensing Agency Information

1 Board of Alternative Health Care, Health Care License Bureau, PO Box 200513 (301 S Park, 4th Fl), Helena, MT 59620-0513; 406-841-2365, Fax: 406-841-2305. www.discoveringmontana.com/dli/ahc Email: dlibsdahc@state.mt.us Search data at http://app.discoveringmontana.com/bsdinq/index.html

2 Board of Barbers & Cosmetologists, Division of Professional & Occupational Licensing, PO Box 200513 (301 S Park, 4th Fl), Helena, MT 59620-0513; 406-444-2961, Fax: 406-841-2325. www.discoveringmontana.com/dli/cos Email: dlibsdcos@state.mt.us Search data at http://app.discoveringmontana.com/bsdinq/index.html

3 Boards: Chiropractor, Funerary, Hearing, Landscape Architect, Athletic Events, Division of Professional & Occupational Licensing, PO Box 200513 (301 S Park, 4th Fl, #428), Helena, MT 59620-0513; 406-841-2393, Fax: 406-841-2343. www.discoveringmontana.com/dli/bsd Email: cheryls@state.mt.us Search data at http://app.discoveringmontana.com/bsdinq/index.html

4 Department of Public Health Human Services, Child & Family Services Division, PO Box 8005 (1400 Boadway), Helena, MT 59604; 406-444-5900, Fax: 406-444-5956. www.dphhs.state.mt.us

5 Board of Dentistry, Division of Health Care Licensing, PO Box 200513 (301 S Park), 4th Floor, Helena, MT 59620-0513; 406-841-2390, Fax: 406-841-2305. www.discoveringmontana.com/dli/den Email: compolden@state.mt.us Search Database at http://discoveringmontana.com/dli/bsd/index.asp Note: Records availabe online from July 1996.

6 Board of Outfitters, Division of Professional & Occupational Licensing, PO Box 200513 (301 S Park, 4th Fl), Helena, MT 59620-0513; 406-444-2373, Fax: 406-841-2305. Email: compolout@state.mt.us Search Database at http://app.mt.gov/lookup/

7 Board of Optometry, Division of Professional & Occupational Licensing, PO Box 200513 (301 S Park, 4th Fl), Helena, MT 59620-0513; 406-841-2390, Fax: 406-841-2305.
http://discoveringmontana.com/dli/opt
Email: dlibsdopt@state.mt.us Search Database at http://discoveringmontana.com/dli/bsd/index.asp

8 Plumbing and Electrical Board, Division of Professional & Occupational Licensing, PO Box 200513 (301 S Park, 4th Fl), Helena, MT 59620-0513; 406-841-2328, Fax: 406-841-2309.
Email: dlibsdele@state.mt.us Search data at http://app.discoveringmontana.com/bsdinq/index.html

9 Board of Private Security Patrol Officers & Invest., Division of Professional & Occupational Licensing, PO Box 200513 (301 S Park, 4th Fl), Helena, MT 59620-0513; 406-841-2387, 841-2304, Fax: 406-841-2305.
www.discoveringmontana.com/dli/bsd/license/bsd_boards/psp_board/board_page.asp
Email: tersmith@state.mt.us
Search Database at http://app.discoveringmontana.com/bsdinq/index.html Note: Physical Therapy Board (406-841-2369) is separate, but at the same address. Physical Therapy Board email is dlibsdptp@state.mt.us.

10 Board of Professional Engineers & Land Surveyors, Division of Professional & Occupational Licensing, PO Box 200513 (301 S Park, 4th Fl), Helena, MT 59620-0513; 406-841-2367, Fax: 406-841-2309.
www.discoveringmontana.com/dli/bsd/contact.asp
Email: compolpel@state.mt.us Search data at http://app.discoveringmontana.com/bsdinq/index.html

11 Veterinary Board, Board of Psychologists, PO Box 200513 (301 S Park, 4th Fl), Helena, MT 59620-0513; 406-841-2394, Fax: 406-841-2305.
www.discoveringmontana.com/dli/bsd/contact.asp#bolb Email: compolpsy@state.mt.us
Search Database at http://app.discoveringmontana.com/bsdinq/index.html

12 Board of Public Accountants, PO Box 200513 (301 South Park), Helena, MT 59620-0513; 406-841-2389, Fax: 406-841-2323.
www.discoveringmontana.com/dli/pac
Email: dlibsdpac@state.mt.us Search Database at http://app.discoveringmontana.com/bsdinq/

13 Notary Division, Secretary of State, PO Box 202801 (Rm 260), Helena, MT 59620; 406-444-5379, Fax: 406-444-3976.
www.sos.state.mt.us/css/Notary/Contents.asp
Email: sosnotary@state.mt.us

14 Board of Real Estate Appraisers, PO Box 200513 (301 S Park Ave), Helena, MT 59620-0513; 406-841-2320, Fax: 406-841-2323.
http://mt.gov/dli/bsd/license/bsd_boards/rea_board/board_page.asp Email: dlibsdrea@state.mt.us
Search Database at http://app.discoveringmontana.com/bsdinq/index.html

15 Board of Realty Regulation, Division of Professional & Occupational Licensing, PO Box 200513 (301 S. Park, 4th Fl), Helena, MT 59620-0513; 406-444-2961, Fax: 406-841-2323.
http://mt.gov/dli/bsd/license/bsd_boards/rre_board/board_page.asp Email: compolre@state.mt.us
Search Database at http://app.discoveringmontana.com/bsdinq/index.html

16 State Bar of Montana, PO Box 577 (7 W 6th Ave, #2B), Helena, MT 59624; 406-442-7660, Fax: 406-442-7763. www.montanabar.org

Email: cwood@montanabar.org Note: Use email cwood@montanabar.org to request to confirm an attorney's membership.

17 Physical Therapy Board, Division of Professional & Occupational Licensing, PO Box 200513 (301 S Park), Helena, MT 59620-0513; 406-841-2369, Fax: 406-841-2305.
Search Database at http://app.discoveringmontana.com/bsdinq/index.html

18 Construction Blasters, Division of Professional & Occupational Licensing, PO Box 200513 (301 S Park), Helena, MT 59620-0513; 406-841-2352, Fax: 406-841-2309.
www.discoveringmontana.com/dli/bsd/license/bsd_boards/bla_prg/board_page.asp
Email: dlibsdbbc@state.mt.us Search data at http://app.discoveringmontana.com/bsdinq/index.html

19 Chemical Dependency Counselors Board, Division of Prof & Occupational Licensing, PO Box 200513 (301 S Park), Helena, MT 59620-0513; 406-444-2827, Fax: 406-841-2305.
www.discoveringmontana.com/dli/bsd/license/bsd_boards/swp_board/board_page.asp
Search Database at http://app.discoveringmontana.com/bsdinq/index.html

20 Department of Agriculture, Licensing and Registration, PO Box 200201, Helena, MT 59620; 406-444-5400, Fax: 406-444-7336.
www.agr.mt.gov/

21 Department of Commerce, Licensing Boards, PO Box 200513 (301 S Park, 4th Fl), Helena, MT 59620-0513; 406-841-2300, Fax: 406-841-2305.
Email: jokershisnik@state.mt.us
Search Database at http://app.discoveringmontana.com/bsdinq/index.html

22 Department of Livestock, Board of Horse Racing, PO Box 200512 (301 S.Park Rm 468), Helena, MT 59620-0512; 406-444-4287, Fax: 406-444-4305. www.discoveringmontana.com/liv/
Email: mstark@state.mt.us

23 Department of Commerce, Montana Lottery, 2525 N Montana Ave, Helena, MT 59601; 406-444-5825, Fax: 406-444-5830.
www.montanalottery.com
Email: montanalottery@mail.com

24 Commissioner of Political Practices, Lobbyist Licensing, PO Box 202401 (1205 8th Ave), Helena, MT 59620; 406-444-2942, Fax: 406-444-1643. www.state.mt.us/cpp/
Email: lvaughey@state.mt.us

25 Department of Environmental Quality, Permitting & Compliance Division, 1520 E 6th Ave, PO Box 200901, Helena, MT 59620-0901; 406-444-2544, Fax: 406-444-1374.
www.deq.state.mt.us Email: ebenedict@state.mt.us

26 Department of Health & Human Services, Quality Assurance Division, PO Box 202953 (1400 Broadway, Helena), Helena, MT 59620; 406-444-2012, Fax: 406-444-1742.
www.dphhs.mt.gov/index.shtml
Email: bfleming@state.mt.us Search data at http://vhsp.dphhs.state.mt.us/dph_r2.htm

27 Department of Fish, Wildlife & Parks, Licensing/Data Bureau, 1420 E 6th Ave, Helena, MT 59620-0701; 406-444-2535, Fax: 406-444-4952. www.fwp.state.mt.us/insidefwp/regoffice.asp Email: bbeukelman@state.mt.us

28 Department of Justice, Gambling Control Division, 2550 Prospect Ave, Helena, MT 59620-1424; 406-444-1971, Fax: 406-444-9157.
www.doj.state.mt.us/department/gamblingcontroldivision.asp

29 Department of Livestock, Brand Enforcement, Milk Control, PO Box 202001, Helena, MT 59620; 406-444-2045, Fax: 406-444-2877.
www.discoveringmontana.com/liv/

30 Department of Public Health Human Services, Research & Planning Bureau, 48 N Last Chance Gulch, Helena, MT 59620-4001; 406-444-6587, Fax: 406-444-5956.

31 Department of Environmental Quality, Waste and Underground Tanks Division, PO Box 200901, Helena, MT 59620-0901; 406-444-5300, Fax: 406-444-1374.
www.deq.state.mt.us/ust/index.asp
Email: ustprogram@state.mt.us

32 Board of Nursing, Division of Professional & Occupational Licensing, PO Box 200513 (301 S Park), Helena, MT 59620-0513; 406-841-2340, Fax: 406-841-2343. http://mt.gov/dli/bsd/license/bsd_boards/nur_board/board_page.asp
Email: dlibsdnur@state.mt.us Search Database at http://app.discoveringmontana.com/lookup/

33 Board of Medical Examiners, PO Box 200513, Helena, MT 59620-0513; 406-841-2364, Fax: 406-841-2305. www.discoveringmontana.com/dli/med Email: dlibsdmed@state.mt.us Search Database at http://app.discoveringmontana.com/bsdinq/index.html Note: Lists are provided for a fee if offering continuing educational credits.

34 Board of Architects, Division of Professional & Occupational Licensing, PO Box 200513 (301 S Park), Helena, MT 59620-0513; 406-841-2367, Fax: 406-841-2301.
www.discoveringmontana.com/dli/arc
Search Database at http://app.discoveringmontana.com/bsdinq/index.html

35 Certification Division, Office of Public Instruction, PO Box 202501, Helena, MT 59620; 406-444-3150, Fax: 406-444-3924.
www.opi.state.mt.us Search Database at http://data.opi.state.mt.us/certification/

36 Public Contractors Licensing, Department of Labor, PO Box 8011, Helena, MT 59604; 406-444-7734, Fax: 406-444-3465.
http://erd.dli.state.mt.us/wcregs/mtcontractor.asp
Search Database at http://erd.dli.state.mt.us/wcregs/mtcontractor.asp

37 Insurance Division, State Auditor's Office, 840 Helena Ave, Helena, MT 59601; 406-444-2040.
www.discoveringmontana.com/sao/
Search Database at www.discoveringmontana.com/sao/insurance/findagent.html

38 Securities Division, State Auditor's Office, 840 Helena Ave, Helena, MT 59601; 406-444-2040, Fax: 406-444-3497. www.sao.state.mt.us/

39 Department of Natural Resources & Conservation, Water Resources Division, PO Box 201601 (1424 N. 0th Ave.), Helena, MT 59620-1601; 406-444-6601, Fax: 406-444-0533.
www.dnrc.state.mt.us They do not provide lists.

Montana Federal Courts

The following list indicates the district and division name for each county in the state. If the bankruptcy court location is different from the district court, then the location of the bankruptcy court appears in parentheses.

County/Court Cross Reference

County	Court	County	Court
Beaverhead	Butte	Meagher	Helena (Butte)
Big Horn	Billings (Butte)	Mineral	Missoula (Butte)
Blaine	Great Falls (Butte)	Missoula	Missoula (Butte)
Broadwater	Helena (Butte)	Musselshell	Billings (Butte)
Carbon	Billings (Butte)	Park	Billings (Butte)
Carter	Billings (Butte)	Petroleum	Billings (Butte)
Cascade	Great Falls (Butte)	Phillips	Billings (Butte)
Chouteau	Great Falls (Butte)	Pondera	Great Falls (Butte)
Custer	Billings (Butte)	Powder River	Billings (Butte)
Daniels	Billings (Butte)	Powell	Helena (Butte)
Dawson	Billings (Butte)	Prairie	Billings (Butte)
Deer Lodge	Butte	Ravalli	Missoula (Butte)
Fallon	Billings (Butte)	Richland	Billings (Butte)
Fergus	Great Falls (Butte)	Roosevelt	Billings (Butte)
Flathead	Missoula (Butte)	Rosebud	Billings (Butte)
Gallatin	Butte	Sanders	Missoula (Butte)
Garfield	Billings (Butte)	Sheridan	Billings (Butte)
Glacier	Great Falls (Butte)	Silver Bow	Butte
Golden Valley	Billings (Butte)	Stillwater	Billings (Butte)
Granite	Missoula (Butte)	Sweet Grass	Billings (Butte)
Hill	Great Falls (Butte)	Teton	Great Falls (Butte)
Jefferson	Helena (Butte)	Toole	Great Falls (Butte)
Judith Basin	Great Falls (Butte)	Treasure	Billings (Butte)
Lake	Missoula (Butte)	Valley	Billings (Butte)
Lewis and Clark	Helena (Butte)	Wheatland	Billings (Butte)
Liberty	Great Falls (Butte)	Wibaux	Billings (Butte)
Lincoln	Missoula (Butte)	Yellowstone	Billings (Butte)
Madison	Butte	Yellowstone Nat. Park (part)	Billings (Butte)
McCone	Billings (Butte)		

Standards for Federal Courts: Search fee is $26.00 per item (one party name or case number). Copy fee is $.50 per page. Certification fee is $9.00 per document, double for exemplification, if available. All fees standard unless noted in profile. Mail Search: always enclose a stamped self addressed envelope unless otherwise noted. Most courts accept fax requests or will suggest a copying/search vendor. Before releasing records, all courts require prepayment, unless noted.

Open records are located at the court unless otherwise noted. District courts index by defendant and plaintiff as well as by case number. Bankruptcy courts usually index by debtor and case number. While most courts now have their indexes on computer, many may still maintain index card files as well.

Courts offering internet access via CM-ECF or older RACER, PACER, or Web-PACER systems charge $.08 per page fee unless noted as free. Where PACER is available, the universal sign-up number is 800-676-6856. Find PACER and the US Party/Case Index at http://pacer.psc.uscourts.gov.

US District Court

District of Montana

Billings Division Court Clerk, Clerk, Rm 5405, Federal Bldg, 316 N 26th St, Billings, MT 59101 (also use mail address for courier delivery), 406-247-7000, Fax-406-247-7008. Hours- 8:30AM-5PM. www.mtd.uscourts.gov

Counties: Big Horn, Carbon, Carter, Custer, Daniels, Dawson, Fallon, Garfield, Golden Valley, McCone, Musselshell, Park, Petroleum, Powder River, Prairie, Richland, Rosebud, Sheridan, Stillwater, Sweet Grass, Treasure, Wheatland, Wibaux, Yellowstone, Yellowstone National Park.

Searches & Indexing: Results do not include SSN or DOB. Computer index maintained. New cases in the index 1 week after filing date. Records purged never.

Fee & Payment: Pay by money order, cashier's or personal check. Payee: Clerk, US District Court. Prepayment required.

Phone Search: Only docket information is available by phone.

Mail Search: search usually completed- 1 week. SASE not required.

In Person Search: Fee charged if court performs your search. Self-serve copier - $.10 per page.

E-Services: PACER online at http://pacer.mtd.uscourts.gov. PACER records go back to 1992. New records online after 1 day. ECF at https://ecf.mtd.uscourts.gov **Other Online Access:** Access calendars at www.mtd.uscourts.gov.

Butte Division Court Clerk, US District Court, 400 N Main, Butte, MT 59701 (also use mail address for courier delivery), 406-782-0432, records rm- 406-782-3354, Fax-406-782-0537 records rm fax- 406-782-9045; fax record requests to-406-782-9045. Hours- 8:30AM-5PM. www.mtd.uscourts.gov

Counties: Beaverhead, Deer Lodge, Gallatin, Madison, Silver Bow.

Searches & Indexing: Results do not include SSN or DOB. Computer index maintained. New cases in the index 1 week after filing date. Records purged never.

Fee & Payment: Pay by money order, cashier's or personal check. Payee: Clerk, US District Court. Prepayment required.

Phone Search: No searching by telephone.

Mail Search: search usually completed- 1-2 days. SASE not required.

In Person Search: Fee charged if court performs your search. Self-serve copier - $.10 per page.

E-Services: PACER online at http://pacer.mtd.uscourts.gov. PACER records go back to 1992. New records online after 1 day. ECF at https://ecf.mtd.uscourts.gov **Other Online Access:** Access calendars at www.mtd.uscourts.gov.

Great Falls Division Clerk of Court, PO Box 2186, Great Falls, MT 59403 (courier address: 215 1st Ave N, Great Falls, MT 59401), 406-727-1922, Fax-406-727-7648. Hours- 8:30AM-5PM. www.mtd.uscourts.gov

Counties: Blaine, Cascade, Chouteau, Daniels, Fergus, Glacier, Hill, Judith Basin, Liberty, Phillips, Pondera, Roosevelt, Sheridan, Teton, Toole, Valley.

Searches & Indexing: Results do not include SSN or DOB. Computer index maintained. New cases in the index immediately after filing date. Records purged never. District-wide searches available here.

Fee & Payment: Pay by money order, cashier's or personal check. No out of state attorney checks accepted. Payee: Clerk, US District Court. Prepayment required.

Phone Search: Only docket information available by case number.

Mail Search: search usually completed- 1 day. Include SASE for return.

In Person Search: Fee charged if court performs your search. No self-serve copier available.

E-Services: PACER online at http://pacer.mtd.uscourts.gov. PACER records go back to 1992. New records online after 1 day. ECF at https://ecf.mtd.uscourts.gov **Other Online Access:** Access calendars at www.mtd.uscourts.gov.

Helena Division Court Clerk, Paul G Hatfield Courthouse, 901 Front St, Helena, MT 59626 (also use mail address for courier delivery), 406-441-1355, Fax-406-441-1357. Hours- 8:30AM-5PM. www.mtd.uscourts.gov

Counties: Broadwater, Jefferson, Lewis and Clark, Meagher, Powell.

Searches & Indexing: After 1/1997, cases filed in the Missoula division also held here. Results do not include SSN or DOB. Both computer and card indexes maintained. New cases in the index same day if possible after filing date. Records purged never.

Fee & Payment: Pay by money order, cashier's or personal check. Payee: Clerk, US District Court. Prepayment required. Will fax documents for add'l $5.00 fee, prepaid.

Phone Search: No searching by telephone.

Mail Search: search usually completed- soon as work load permits. Include SASE for return.

In Person Search: Fee charged if court performs your search. No self-serve copier available.

E-Services: PACER online at http://pacer.mtd.uscourts.gov. PACER records go back to 1992. New records online after 1 day. ECF at https://ecf.mtd.uscourts.gov **Other Online Access:** Access calendars at www.mtd.uscourts.gov.

Missoula Division Court Clerk, 201 E Broadway, Russell Smith Courthouse, Missoula, MT 59801 (also use mail address for courier delivery), 406-542-7260, Fax-406-542-7272. Hours- 8:30AM-5PM. www.mtd.uscourts.gov

Counties: Flathead, Granite, Lake, Lincoln, Mineral, Missoula, Ravalli, Sanders.

Searches & Indexing: Results do not include SSN or DOB. Computer index maintained back to 1996. New cases in the index 1-2 days after filing date. Records purged never. Cases in this district originate here; after closing, cases held here rather than being sent to Federal Records Center.

Fee & Payment: Pay by money order, cashier's or personal check. Payee: Clerk, US District Court. Prepayment required except for attorneys. Will fax documents $5.00 plus $.50 per page.

Phone Search: Docket information available by phone.

Mail Search: search usually completed- 1-2 days. SASE not required.

In Person Search: Fee charged if court performs your search. No self-serve copier available.

E-Services: PACER online at http://ecf.mtd.uscourts.gov. PACER records go back to 1992. New records online after 1 day. ECF at https://ecf.mtd.uscourts.gov **Other Online Access:** Access calendars at www.mtd.uscourts.gov.

US Bankruptcy Court

District of Montana

Butte Division Court Clerk, PO Box 689, Butte, MT 59703 (courier address: 303 Federal Bldg, 400 N Main St, Butte, MT 59703), 406-782-3354, Fax-406-782-0537. Hours- 8AM-4:30PM. www.mtb.uscourts.gov

Counties: All counties in Montana.

Searches & Indexing: Results include last 4 SSN digits. Computer index maintained. New cases in the index immediately after filing date.

Fee & Payment: Pay by money order, cashier's or personal check. No debtor's checks accepted. Payee: Clerk, US Bankruptcy Court. Will fax documents $1.00 per page.

Phone Search: Only docket information is available by phone. Voice Case Information Service available, call VCIS at 888-879-0071 or 406-782-1060.

Mail Search: search usually completed- 2-3 days. SASE not required.

In Person Search: Fee charged if court performs your search. No self-serve copier available.

E-Services: ECF replaces PACER whose records did go back to 1986. New records online after 1 day. ECF at https://ecf.mtb.uscourts.gov. Calendars on ECF. **Opinions Online:** www.mtb.uscourts.gov/mtb_opinions.asp. Judge's Decisions posted here are selected by the judges to inform the public. **Other Online Access:** Court now participates in the US party case index.

Montana County Courts

Court	Jurisdiction	No. of Courts	How Organized
District Courts*	General	56	22 Districts
Limited Jurisdiction Courts*	Limited	70	56 Counties
City Courts	Limited	83	
Municipal Court	Municipal	5	
Water Courts	Special		4 Divisions
Workers' Compensation Court	Special	1	

* Profiled in this Sourcebook.

Court	CIVIL								
	Tort	Contract	Real Estate	Min. Claim	Max. Claim	Small Claims	Estate	Eviction	Domestic Relations
District Courts*	X	X	X	$5000-7000	No Max		X		X
Limited Jurisdiction Courts*	X	X	X	$0	$5000-7000	$3000		X	
City Courts	X	X	X	$0	$5000				
Municipal Court	X	X	X	$0	$5000	$3000			
Water Courts			X						
Workers' Comp. Court									

Court	CRIMINAL				
	Felony	Misdemeanor	DWI/DUI	Preliminary Hearing	Juvenile
District Courts*	X			X	X
Limited Jurisdiction Courts*		X	X	X	
City Courts		X	X	X	
Municipal Court		X	X	X	
Water Courts					
Workers' Comp. Court					

ADMINISTRATION   Court Administrator, Justice Building, 215 N Sanders, Room 315 (PO Box 203002), Helena, MT, 59620; 406-444-2621, Fax: 406-444-0834. http://www.lawlibrary.state.mt.us

COURT STRUCTURE   The District Courts have no maximum amount for civil judgment cases. Most District Courts handle civil over $7,000; there are exceptions that handle a civil minimum as low as $5,000. Limited Jurisdiction Courts, which are also known as Justice Courts, may handle civil actions up to $7,000. The Small Claims limit is $3000.

Many Montana Justices of the Peace maintain case record indexes on their personal PCs, which does speed the retrieval process.

ONLINE ACCESS   Supreme Courts Opinions, Orders, and recently Filed Briefs may be found at www.lawlibrary.state.mt.us/dscgi/ds.py/View/Collection-36. Federal District court records are also available here. A few individual county courts offer online access.

Beaverhead County

District Court Beaverhead County Courthouse, 2 S Pacific St, Dillon, MT 59725; phone: 406-683-3725; criminal fax: 406-683-3728; same fax for civil/probate; hours 8AM-5PM (MST). *Felony, Civil Actions Over $7,000, Eviction, Probate.*
Civil Records: Access: Fax, mail, in person. Both court and visitors may perform in person searches. Search fee: $2.00 per name per year, first 7 years, then $1.00 per year. Court makes copy: $1.00 per page first 10 pages, then $.50 per page after; same fee for self serve. Required to search: name, years to search. Civil cases indexed by defendant, plaintiff. Civil records in books back to 1870s; on computer since 1997. For fax, send fax copy of check for fee. Mail turnaround time 1-2 days.
Criminal Records: Access: Fax, mail, in person. Both court and visitors may perform in person searches. Search fee: $2.00 per name per year, first 7 years, then $1.00 per year. Court makes copy: $1.00 per page first 10 pages, then $.50 per page after; same fee for self serve. Required to search: name, years to search. Criminal records in books back to 1870s; on computer since 1997. For fax, send fax copy of check for fee. Mail turnaround time 1-2 days.
General Information: Public terminal goes back to 7/1997. No adoption, juvenile, sanity, paternity or dismissed criminal records released. Will fax documents $1.00 per page. Certification fee: $2.00. Payee: Clerk of Court. Personal checks not accepted. Prepayment and SASE required.

Beaverhead Justice Court 2 S Pacific, Cluster #16, Dillon, MT 59725; phone: 406-683-3755; fax: 406-683-3736; hours 8AM-3PM (MST). *Misdemeanor, Civil Actions Under $7,000, Eviction, Small Claims.*

Big Horn County

District Court 121 W 3rd St, Rm 221, PO Box 908, Hardin, MT 59034; phone: 406-665-9750; fax: 406-665-9755; hours 8AM-5PM (MST). *Felony, Civil Actions Over $7,000, Probate.*
Civil Records: Access: Fax, mail, in person. Both court and visitors may perform in person searches. Search fee: $2.00 per name per year, first 7 years, then $1.00 per year. Court makes copy: $1.00 per page first 10 pages, then $.50 per page after; same fee for self serve. Required to search: name, years to search. Civil cases indexed by defendant, plaintiff. Civil records in books , microfilm, and computer back to 1913. Mail turnaround time same day.
Criminal Records: Access: Fax, mail, in person. Both court and visitors may perform in person searches. Search fee: $2.00 per name per year, first 7 years, then $1.00 per year. Court makes copy: $1.00 per page first 10 pages, then $.50 per page after; same fee for self serve. Required to search: name, years to search, DOB; also helpful, SSN. Criminal records in books and on microfilm back to 1913; on computer back to 1913. Court order required for confidential information. Mail turnaround time same day.
General Information: Public terminal goes back to 1913. No adoption, sanity, pre-sentence, psychiatric evaluation, dependent & neglected, or confidential criminal justice records released. Fee to fax documents is $1.00 per page. Certification fee: $2.00. Payee: Clerk of Court. No personal checks accepted. Prepayment required. Will bill government agencies. SASE required.

Limited Jurisdiction Court PO Box 908, 121 W 3rd, Hardin, MT 59034; phone: 406-665-9760; fax: 406-665-9764; hours 8AM-5PM (MST). *Misdemeanor, Civil Actions Under $7,000, Eviction, Small Claims.*

Blaine County

District Court PO Box 969, Chinook, MT 59523; phone: 406-357-3230; criminal fax: 406-357-3109; same fax for civil/probate; hours 8AM-5PM (MST). *Felony, Civil Actions Over $5,000, Eviction, Probate.*
Civil Records: Access: Fax, mail, in person. Both court and visitors may perform in person searches. Search fee: $2.00 per name per year, first 7 years, then $1.00 per year. Court makes copy: $1.00 per page first 10 pages, then $.50 per page after. Required to search: name, years to search. Civil records indexed by defendant, plaintiff. Civil records in books from 1912; on computer back to 1995. Mail turnaround time same day.
Criminal Records: Access: Fax, mail, in person. Both court and visitors may perform in person searches. Search fee: $2.00 per name per year, first 7 years, then $1.00 per year. Court makes copy: $1.00 per page first 10 pages, then $.50 per page after. Required to search: name, years to search, signed release. Criminal records in books from 1912; on computer back to 1995. Mail turnaround time same day.
General Information: Public terminal goes back to 1995. No adoption, juvenile or sanity records released. Fee to fax documents is $1.00 per page. Certification fee: $2.00 per certification. Payee: Clerk of Court. Personal checks accepted. Prepayment and SASE required.

Chinook Justice Court PO Box 1266, 400 Ohio St, Chinook, MT 59523; phone: 406-357-2335; fax: 406-357-2361; hours 8AM-5PM M-F (MST). *Misdemeanor, Civil Actions Under $7,000, Eviction, Small Claims.*

Broadwater County

District Court 515 Broadway, Townsend, MT 59644; phone: 406-266-9236; fax: 406-266-4720; hours 8AM-N, 1-5PM (MST). *Felony, Civil Actions Over $7,000, Probate.*
Civil Records: Access: Fax, mail, in person. Both court and visitors may perform in person searches. Search fee: $2.00 per name per year, first 7 years, then $1.00 per year. Court makes copy: $1.00 per page first 10 pages, then $.50 per page after. Self serve copy fee: $1.00 per page. Required to search: name, years to search, DOB. Civil records on microfiche and archives back to 1897; on computer back to 1997. Mail turnaround time same day.
Criminal Records: Access: Fax, mail, in person. Both court and visitors may perform in person searches. Search fee: $2.00 per name per year, first 7 years, then $1.00 per year. Court makes copy: $1.00 per page first 10 pages, then $.50 per page after. Self serve copy fee: $1.00 per page. Required to search: name, years to search, DOB. Criminal records on microfiche and archives back to 1897; on computer back to 1997. Mail turnaround time same day.
General Information: Public terminal goes back to 1997. No adoption, juvenile or sanity records released. Will fax documents. Certification fee: $2.00. Payee: Clerk of Court. Personal checks accepted. Prepayment and SASE required.

Limited Jurisdiction Court 515 Broadway, Townsend, MT 59644; phone: 406-266-9231; fax: 406-266-4720; hours 8AM-5PM (MST). *Misdemeanor, Civil Actions Under $7,000, Eviction, Small Claims.*

Carbon County

District Court PO Box 948, Red Lodge, MT 59068; phone: 406-446-1225; fax: 406-446-1911; hours 8AM-5PM (MST). *Felony, Civil Actions, Probate.*
Civil Records: Access: Phone, fax, mail, in person. Both court and visitors may perform in person searches. Search fee: $2.00 per name per year, first 7 years, then $1.00 per year. Court makes copy: $1.00 per page first 10 pages, then $.50 per page after. Required to search: name, years to search. Civil cases indexed by defendant, plaintiff, on docket books from 1895; on computer back to 1997. Mail turnaround time 1-2 days.
Criminal Records: Access: Fax, mail, in person. Only the court performs in person searches; visitors may not. Search fee: $2.00 per name per year, first 7 years, then $1.00 per year. Court makes copy: $1.00 per page first 10 pages, then $.50 per page after. Required to search: name, years to search. Criminal records on docket books from 1895; on computer back to 1997. Mail turnaround time 1-2 days.
General Information: No public access terminal. No adoption, juvenile or sanity records released. Will fax documents $1.00 per page; no charge to toll free number. Certification fee: $2.00. Payee: Clerk of Court. Personal checks accepted. Prepayment and SASE required.

Carbon County Justice Court PO Box 2, Red Lodge, MT 59068; phone: 406-446-1440; fax: 406-446-9175; hours 8AM-5PM (MST). *Misdemeanor, Civil Actions Under $7,000, Eviction, Small Claims.*

Joliet City Court PO Box 210, Joliet, MT 59041; phone: 406-962-3567; hours 8AM-12;00PM, Wed only (MST). *Misdemeanor, Civil Actions Under $7,000.*

Carter County

District Court PO Box 322, Ekalaka, MT 59324; phone: 406-775-8714; fax: 406-775-8703; hours 8AM-5PM (MST). *Felony, Civil Actions Over $5,000, Eviction, Probate.*
Note: Probate is separate index at this same address.
Civil Records: Access: Phone, fax, mail, in person. Both court and visitors may perform in person searches. Search fee: $2.00 per name per year, first 7 years, then $1.00 per year. Court makes copy: $1.00 per page first 10 pages, then $.50 per page after; same fee for self serve. Required to search: name, years to search. Civil cases indexed by defendant, plaintiff. Civil records in books from 1917; computerized back to 1996. Mail turnaround time same or next day.
Criminal Records: Access: Phone, fax, mail, in person. Only the court performs in person searches; visitors may not. Search fee: $2.00 per name per year, first 7 years, then $1.00 per year. Court makes copy: $1.00 per page first 10 pages, then $.50 per page after; same fee for self serve. Required to search: name, years to search, signed release; also helpful: SSN. Criminal records in books from 1917; computerized back to 1996. Mail turnaround time 1-2 days; same to next day for phone requests.
General Information: No public access terminal. No adoption, juvenile or sanity records released. Will fax documents $1.00 per page. Certification fee: $2.00 per instrument. Payee: Clerk of Court. Personal checks accepted. Prepayment and SASE required.

Limited Jurisdiction Court PO Box 72, Ekalaka, MT 59324-0072; phone: 406-775-8754, 406-775-8838; hours 8AM-5PM 1st,2nd,3rd Wed of the month; 10AM-3:PM every 4th Wed of the month (MST). *Misdemeanor, Civil Actions Under $7,000, Eviction, Small Claims.*

Cascade County

District Court County Courthouse, 415 2nd Ave North, Great Falls, MT 59401; phone: 406-454-6780 x4; fax: 406-454-6907; hours 8AM-5PM (MST). *Felony, Civil Actions Over $7,000, Probate.*
Civil Records: Access: Fax, mail, in person. Both court and visitors may perform in person searches. Search fee: $2.00 per name per year, first 7 years, then $1.00 per year. Court makes copy: $1.00 per page, then $.50 per page after first 10. Required to search: name, years to search. Civil cases indexed by defendant, plaintiff, on computer from 1987; on docket books to 1889. Mail turnaround time 1-2 days.
Criminal Records: Access: Fax, mail, in person. Both court and visitors may perform in person searches. Search fee: $2.00 per name per year, first 7 years, then $1.00 per year. Court makes copy: $1.00 per page; $.50 per page after first 10. Required to search: name, years to search. Criminal records on computer from 1987; on docket books to 1889. Mail turnaround time 1-2 days.

General Information: Public terminal goes back to 1987. No adoption or sanity records released. Will not fax documents. Certification fee: $2.00 per cert. Payee: Clerk of Court. Business checks accepted. Prepayment and SASE required.

Cascade Justice Court Cascade County Courthouse, 415 2nd Ave N, Great Falls, MT 59401; phone: 406-454-6870; fax: 406-454-6877; hours 8AM-5PM (MST). *Misdemeanor, Civil Actions Under $7,000, Eviction, Small Claims.*

Chouteau County

District Court PO Box 459, Ft Benton, MT 59442; phone: 406-622-5024; fax: 406-622-3028; hours 8AM-5PM (MST). *Felony, Civil Actions Over $5,000, Eviction, Probate.*

Civil Records: Access: Fax, mail, in person. Both court and visitors may perform in person searches. Search fee: $2.00 per name per year, first 7 years, then $1.00 per year. Court makes copy: $1.00 per page first 10 pages, then $.50 per page after. Required to search: name, years to search. Civil cases indexed by defendant, plaintiff, on books from 1886; on computer back for 10 years. Mail turnaround time 1 day.

Criminal Records: Access: Fax, mail, in person. Both court and visitors may perform in person searches. Search fee: $2.00 per name per year, first 7 years, then $1.00 per year. Court makes copy: $1.00 per page first 10 pages, then $.50 per page after. Required to search: name, years to search. Criminal records on books from 1886; on computer back for 10 years. Mail turnaround time 1 day.

General Information: Public terminal back to 1997. No adoption, paternity, juvenile or sanity records released. Will fax documents $2.00 1st page, $1.00 each add'l. Certification fee: $2.00. Payee: Clerk of Court. Business and personal checks accepted; no credit cards. Prepayment and SASE required.

Chouteau County Justice Court PO Box 459, Ft Benton, MT 59442; phone: 406-622-5502; fax: 406-622-3815; hours 9AM-4PM M-F (MST). *Misdemeanor, Civil Actions Under $7,000, Eviction, Small Claims.* As of 12/02, the records from the former Justice Court in Big Sandy are housed at this location.

Custer County

District Court 1010 Main, Miles City, MT 59301-3419; phone: 406-874-3326; criminal fax: 406-874-3451; same fax for civil/probate; hours 8AM-5PM (MST). *Felony, Civil Actions Over $5,000, Eviction, Probate.*

Civil Records: Access: Phone, fax, mail, in person. Both court and visitors may perform in person searches. Search fee: $2.00 per name per year, first 7 years, then $1.00 per name per year. Court makes copy: $1.00 per page first 10 pages, then $.50 per page after. Required to search: name, years to search. Civil cases indexed by defendant, plaintiff, on computer back to 1990; also in books. Mail turnaround time 1-2 days.

Criminal Records: Access: Mail, in person. Both court and visitors may perform in person searches. Search fee: $2.00 per name per year, first 7 years, then $1.00 per name per year. Court makes copy: $1.00 per page first 10 pages, then $.50 per page after. Required to search: name, years to search. Criminal records on computer back to 1990; also in books. Mail turnaround time 1-2 days.

General Information: Public terminal goes back to 1990. No dependent & neglected, juvenile or sanity records released. Will fax documents for $1.00 per page. Certification fee: $2.00 per document. Payee: Clerk of District Court. Personal checks accepted. Prepayment and SASE required.

Limited Jurisdiction Court 1010 Main St, Miles City, MT 59301; phone: 406-874-3408; fax: 406-874-3452; hours 8AM-5PM (MST). *Misdemeanor, Civil Actions Under $7,000, Eviction, Small Claims, Traffic.*

www.co.custer.mt.us/
Note: Record search request must be in writing, fee is $25.00 per search.

Daniels County

District Court PO Box 67, Scobey, MT 59263; phone: 406-487-2651; criminal fax: 406-487-5432; same fax for civil/probate; hours 8AM-5PM (MST). *Felony, Civil Actions Over $5,000, Probate.*

Civil Records: Access: Phone, mail, in person. Both court and visitors may perform in person searches. Search fee: $2.00 per name per year, first 7 years, then $1.00 per year. Court makes copy: $1.00 per page first 10 pages, then $.50 per page after. Required to search: name, years to search. Civil cases indexed by defendant, plaintiff, on books since 1920; on computer back to 1997. Mail turnaround same day.

Criminal Records: Access: Mail, in person, fax. Only the court performs in person searches; visitors may not. Search fee: $2.00 per name per year, first 7 years, then $1.00 per year. Court makes copy: $1.00 per page first 10 pages, then $.50 per page after. Required to search: name, years to search. Criminal records on books since 1920; on computer back to 1986. Mail turnaround time 1-2 days.

General Information: No public access terminal. No adoption, juvenile or sanity records released. Fee to fax documents is $.50 per page. Certification fee: $2.00 per document. Payee: Clerk of Court. Personal checks accepted. Prepayment and SASE required.

Limited Jurisdiction Court PO Box 838, Daniels County Courthouse, Upstairs, Scobey, MT 59263; phone: 406-487-5432; fax: 406-487-5432; hours 8AM-10AM (MST). *Misdemeanor, Civil Actions Under $7,000, Eviction, Small Claims.*

Dawson County

District Court 207 W Bell, Glendive, MT 59330; phone: 406-377-3967; fax: 406-377-7280; hours 8AM-5PM (MST). *Felony, Civil Actions Over $3,000, Probate.*

www.dawsoncountymontana.com/clerk_of_court.htm
Civil Records: Access: Mail, in person. Both court and visitors may perform in person searches. Search fee: $2.00 per name per year, first 7 years, then $1.00 per year. Court makes copy: $1.00 per page first 10 pages, then $.50 per page after; same fee for self serve. Required to search: name, years to search. Civil cases indexed by defendant, plaintiff, on computer from 1997, on card index prior. Mail turnaround time usually same or next day.

Criminal Records: Access: Mail, in person. Both court and visitors may perform in person searches. Search fee: $2.00 per name per year, first 7 years, then $1.00 per year. Court makes copy: $1.00 per page first 10 pages, then $.50 per page after; same fee for self serve. Required to search: name, years to search, DOB, SSN. Criminal records on computer from 1997, on card index prior. Mail turnaround time usually same or next day.

General Information: Public terminal goes back to 1997. No adoption, juvenile, sanity or expunged records released. Will fax documents to local or toll free line. Marriage license copy-$5.00 plus cert fee; divorce decree copy-$10.00 plus cert fee. Certification fee: $2.00 per document. Payee: Clerk of District Court. Only cashiers checks and money orders accepted. Prepayment and SASE required.

Limited Jurisdiction Court 207 W Bell, Glendive, MT 59330; phone: 406-377-5425; fax: 406-377-1869; hours 8AM-5PM (MST). *Misdemeanor, Civil Actions Under $7,000, Eviction, Small Claims.*

Deer Lodge County

District Court 800 S Main, Anaconda, MT 59711; phone: 406-563-4041; fax: 406-563-4077; hours 8AM-5PM (MST). *Felony, Civil Actions Over $5,000, Eviction, Probate.*

Civil Records: Access: Phone, mail, in person. Both court and visitors may perform in person searches.

Search fee: $2.00 per name per year, first 7 years, then $1.00 per year. Court makes copy: $1.00 per page first 10 pages, then $.50 per page after. Required to search: name, years to search. Civil cases indexed by defendant, plaintiff. Civil records in archives and index books; on computer back to 1992. Mail turnaround time 2-3 days.

Criminal Records: Access: Mail, in person. Both court and visitors may perform in person searches. Search fee: $2.00 per name per year, first 7 years, then $1.00 per year. Court makes copy: $1.00 per page first 10 pages, then $.50 per page after. Required to search: name, years to search. Criminal records in archives and index books; on computer back to 1992. Mail turnaround time 2-3 days.

General Information: Public terminal goes back to 1992. No adoption, juvenile or sanity records released. Fee to fax documents is $4.00 per document. Certification fee: $2.00. Payee: Clerk of Court. Personal checks accepted. Prepayment and SASE required.

Limited Jurisdiction Court 800 S Main, Anaconda, MT 59711; phone: 406-563-4025; fax: 406-563-4028; hours 8AM-N, 1-5PM (MST). *Misdemeanor, Civil Actions Under $7,000, Eviction, Small Claims.*

Fallon County

District Court PO Box 1521, Baker, MT 59313; phone: 406-778-7114; criminal fax: 406-778-2815; same fax for civil/probate; hours 8AM-5PM (MST). *Felony, Civil Actions Over $5,000, Eviction, Probate.*

Civil Records: Access: Mail, in person. Both court and visitors may perform in person searches. Search fee: $2.00 per name per year, first 7 years, then $1.00 per year. Court makes copy: $1.00 per page first 10 pages, then $.50 per page after. Required to search: name, years to search, address. Civil cases indexed by defendant, plaintiff. Civil records in books. Mail turnaround time same day.

Criminal Records: Access: Mail, in person. Both court and visitors may perform in person searches. Search fee: $2.00 per name per year, first 7 years, then $1.00 per year. Court makes copy: $1.00 per page first 10 pages, then $.50 per page after. Required to search: name, years to search. Criminal records in books. Mail turnaround time same day.

General Information: Public terminal has criminal back to 1914 and civil back to 1913. No confidential records released. Fee to fax documents is $1.00 per page. Certification fee: $2.00. Payee: Clerk of Court. Personal checks accepted. Prepayment and SASE required.

Justice Court Box 846, Baker, MT 59313; phone: 406-778-7128; fax: 406-778-2815; hours 11:00AM-4:00PM T,W,Th (MST). *Misdemeanor, Civil Actions Under $7,000, Eviction, Small Claims.*

Fergus County

District Court PO Box 1074 (712 W Main), Lewistown, MT 59457; phone: 406-538-5026; criminal fax: 406-538-6076; same fax for civil/probate; hours 8AM-5PM (MST). *Felony, Civil Actions Over $7,000, Eviction, Probate.*

www.co.fergus.mt.us
Civil Records: Access: Phone, fax, mail, in person. Both court and visitors may perform in person searches. Search fee: $2.00 per name per year, first 7 years, then $1.00 per year. Court makes copy: $1.00 per page first 10 pages, then $.50 per page after; same fee for self serve. Required to search: name, years to search. Civil cases indexed by defendant, plaintiff, on computer back to 1997; prior on docket books, microfiche. Mail turnaround time 1 day.

Criminal Records: Access: Phone, fax, mail, in person. Both court and visitors may perform in person searches. Search fee: $2.00 per name per year, first 7 years, then $1.00 per year. Court makes copy: $1.00 per page first 10 pages, then $.50 per page after; same fee for self serve. Required to search: name, years to search. Criminal records on computer back to 1997; prior on docket books, microfiche. Mail turnaround time 1 day.

General Information: Public terminal goes back to 1999. No adoption, juvenile, sanity or expunged records released. Fee to fax documents is $1.00 per page. Certification fee: $2.00 per document. Payee: Clerk of Court. Personal checks accepted. Prepayment and SASE required.

Limited Jurisdiction Court 121 8th Ave South, Lewistown, MT 59457; phone: 406-538-5418; fax: 406-538-3860; hours 9AM-4PM (MST). *Misdemeanor, Civil Actions Under $7,000, Eviction, Small Claims.*

Note: You may email requests to jpcourt@co.fergus.mt.us

Flathead County

District Court 800 S Main, Kalispell, MT 59901; phone: 406-758-5660; hours 8AM-5PM (MST). *Felony, Civil Actions Over $5,000, Probate.*

www.co.flathead.mt.us/clkcrt/index.html
Note: Court clerk location is 920 S. Main, 3rd Fl.
Civil Records: Access: Mail, in person. Both court and visitors may perform in person searches. Search fee: $2.00 per name per year, first 7 years, then $1.00 per year. Court makes copy: $1.00. Required to search: name, years to search. Civil cases indexed by defendant, plaintiff, on computer since 1990; records go back to 1893. Mail turnaround time 24-48 hours.
Criminal Records: Access: Mail, in person. Both court and visitors may perform in person searches. Search fee: $2.00 per name per year, first 7 years, then $1.00 per year. Court makes copy: $1.00. Required to search: name, years to search. Criminal records on computer since 1990; records go back to 1893. Mail turnaround time 3 days.
General Information: Public terminal goes back to 1990. No adoption, dependent/neglected children or sanity records released. Fee to fax documents is $1.00 per page. Certification fee: $2.00 per document. Payee: Clerk of Court. Personal checks accepted. Prepayment and SASE required.

Limited Jurisdiction Court 920 S Main St, Kalispell, MT 59901; phone: 406-758-5643; fax: 406-758-5842; hours 8AM-5PM (MST). *Misdemeanor, Civil Actions Under $7,000, Eviction, Small Claims.*
www.co.flathead.mt.us/justice/index.html

Gallatin County

Clerk of District Court 615 S 16th, Rm 302, Bozeman, MT 59715; phone: 406-582-2165; fax: 406-582-2176; hours 8AM-5PM (MST). *Felony, Civil Actions Over $7,000, Probate.*
Civil Records: Access: Phone, mail, fax, in person. Both court and visitors may perform in person searches. Search fee: $2.00 per name per year, first 7 years, then $1.00 per year. Court makes copy: $1.00 per page. $.50 per page after first 10 pages. Required to search: name, years to search. Civil cases indexed by defendant, plaintiff, on computer back to 1985; docket books back to 1860. Mail turnaround time 1-3 days.
Criminal Records: Access: Mail, in person. Both court and visitors may perform in person searches. Search fee: $2.00 per name per year, first 7 years, then $1.00 per year. Court makes copy: $1.00 per page; $.50 per page after first 10 pages. Required to search: name, years to search. Criminal records on computer back to 1985; docket books back to 1860. Mail turnaround time 1-3 days.
General Information: Public terminal goes back to 1985. No adoption or sanity records released. Fee to fax documents is $2.00 per page for the 1st page, $1.00 per page thereafter. Certification fee: $2.00. Payee: Clerk of Court. Personal checks accepted. Prepayment and SASE required.

Belgrade City Court 91 E Central, Belgrade, MT 59714; phone: 406-388-3774; fax: 406-388-3779; hours 8AM-N; 1PM-5PM M-F (MST). *Misdemeanor, Civil Actions Under $7,000, Eviction.*
Note: Formerly Belgrade Justice and City Court.

Bozeman Justice Court 615 S 16th St, Bozeman, MT 59715; phone: 406-582-2191; fax: 406-582-2041; hours 8AM-5PM (MST). *Misdemeanor, Civil Actions Under $7,000, Eviction, Small Claims.*

Garfield County

District Court PO Box 8, Jordan, MT 59337; phone: 406-557-6254; fax: 406-557-2625; hours 8AM-5PM (MST). *Felony, Civil Actions Over $5,000, Eviction, Probate.*
Civil Records: Access: Phone, mail, in person. Both court and visitors may perform in person searches. Search fee: $2.00 per name per year, first 7 years, then $1.00 per year. Court makes copy: $1.00 per page first 10 pages, then $.50 per page after. Required to search: name, years to search. Civil cases indexed by plaintiff. Civil records in books from early 1900s; computerized records go back to 1998. Some records lost due to fire in December, 1997. Mail turnaround time 1 week.
Criminal Records: Access: Phone, mail, in person. Both court and visitors may perform in person searches. Search fee: $2.00 per name per year, first 7 years, then $1.00 per year. Court makes copy: $1.00 per page first 10 pages, then $.50 per page after. Required to search: name, years to search; also helpful: DOB. Criminal records in books from early 1900s, computerized records go back to 1998. Note: Some records lost due to fire in December, 1997. Mail turnaround time 1 week.
General Information: No public access terminal. No adoption, juvenile or sanity records released. Will fax documents to local or toll free line. Certification fee: $2.00 per cert. Payee: Clerk of Court. Personal checks accepted. Prepayment and SASE required.

Limited Jurisdiction Court PO Box 482, 352 Leavitt St, Jordan, MT 59337; phone: 406-557-2733; fax: 406-557-2735; hours 8AM-5PM Wed (MST). *Misdemeanor, Civil Actions Under $7,000, Eviction, Small Claims.*

Glacier County

District Court 512 E Main St, Cut Bank, MT 59427; phone: 406-873-5063 X36; criminal fax: 406-873-5627; same fax for civil/probate; hours 8AM-5PM (MST). *Felony, Civil Actions, Probate.*
Civil Records: Access: Phone, fax, mail, in person, email. Both court and visitors may perform in person searches. Search fee: $2.00 per name per year, first 7 years, then $1.00 per year. Court makes copy: $1.00 per page first 10 pages, then $.50 per page after. Self serve copy fee: $1.00 per page. Required to search: name, years to search. Civil cases indexed by defendant, plaintiff. Civil records in books from 1919; on computer since 1992. Note: Email requests to dianderson@state.mt.us. Mail turnaround time usually same day, 2-3 hours for phone requests depending on workload.
Criminal Records: Access: Fax, mail, in person. Both court and visitors may perform in person searches. Search fee: $2.00 per name per year, first 7 years, then $1.00 per year. Court makes copy: $1.00 per page first 10 pages, then $.50 per page after. Self serve copy fee: $1.00 per page. Required to search: name, years to search, DOB, SSN. Criminal records in books from 1919; on computer since 1992. Written request required. Mail turnaround time usually same day, 2-3 hours for phone requests depending on workload.
General Information: No public access terminal. No adoption, juvenile, sanity or paternity records released without court order. Fee to fax documents is $1.00 per page. Certification fee: $2.00 per cert. Payee: Clerk of District Court. Personal checks accepted. Prepayment and SASE required.

Limited Jurisdiction Court 512 E Main St, Cut Bank, MT 59427; phone: 406-873-5063 X39; fax: 406-873-4218; hours 8AM-N, 1-5PM (MST). *Misdemeanor, Civil Actions Under $7,000, Eviction, Small Claims.*

Golden Valley County

District Court PO Box 10, Ryegate, MT 59074; phone: 406-568-2231; fax: 406-568-2231; hours 8AM-5PM (MST). *Felony, Civil Actions Over $5,000, Eviction, Probate.*
Civil Records: Access: Fax, mail, in person. Only the court performs in person searches; visitors may not. Search fee: $2.00 per name per year, first 7 years, then $1.00 per year. Court makes copy: $1.00 per page first 10 pages, then $.50 per page after; same fee for self serve. Required to search: name, years to search, signed release. Civil cases indexed by defendant, plaintiff, on books back to 1923. Computerized records back to 1997. Mail turnaround time 2-3 days.
Criminal Records: Access: Fax, mail, in person. Only the court performs in person searches; visitors may not. Search fee: $2.00 per name per year, first 7 years, then $1.00 per year. Court makes copy: $1.00 per page first 10 pages, then $.50 per page after; same fee for self serve. Required to search: name, years to search, signed release. Criminal records on books to 1923. Computerized records go back to 1997. Mail turnaround time 2-3 days.
General Information: No public access terminal. No adoption, juvenile or sanity records released. Will fax documents for $1.00 per page. Same fee applies to send them a fax. Certification fee: $2.00. Payee: Clerk of Court. Personal checks accepted. Prepayment and SASE required.

Limited Jurisdiction Court PO Box 10, 104 Kemp, Ryegate, MT 59074; phone: 406-568-2102; fax: 406-568-2231; hours 10AM-2PM Tues (MST). *Misdemeanor, Civil Actions Under $7,000, Eviction, Small Claims.*

Granite County

District Court PO Box 399, Philipsburg, MT 59858-0399; phone: 406-859-3712; fax: 406-859-3817; hours 8AM-N, 1-5PM (MST). *Felony, Civil Actions Over $7,000, Eviction, Probate.*
Civil Records: Access: Phone, fax, mail, in person. Both court and visitors may perform in person searches. Search fee: $2.00 per name per year, first 7 years, then $1.00 per year. Court makes copy: $1.00 per page first 10 pages, then $.50 per page after; same fee for self serve. Required to search: name, years to search. Civil cases indexed by defendant, plaintiff, on docket books since 1893. Mail turnaround time 1-4 days.
Criminal Records: Access: Phone, fax, mail, in person. Both court and visitors may perform in person searches. Search fee: $2.00 per name per year, first 7 years, then $1.00 per year. Court makes copy: $1.00 per page first 10 pages, then $.50 per page after; same fee for self serve. Required to search: name, years to search. Criminal records on docket books since 1893. Mail turnaround time 1-4 days.
General Information: Public terminal goes back to 1990. No adoption, juvenile or sanity records released. Certification fee: $2.00. Payee: Clerk of Court. Personal checks accepted. Prepayment and SASE required.

Drummond Justice Court #2 PO Box 159, Drummond, MT 59832; phone: 406-288-3446; fax: 406-288-3050; hours 9AM-N, 1-4PM M,W,F (MST). *Misdemeanor, Civil Actions Under $7,000, Eviction, Small Claims.*

Philipsburg Justice Court PO Box 356, Philipsburg, MT 59858; phone: 406-859-3006; fax: 406-859-3817; hours 11AM-N, 1-5PM M,W,F (MST). *Misdemeanor, Civil Actions Under $7,000, Eviction, Small Claims.*

Hill County

District Court Hill County Courthouse, Havre, MT 59501; phone: 406-265-5481 X224; fax: 406-265-3693; hours 8AM-5PM (MST). *Felony, Civil Actions Over $5,000, Eviction, Probate.*
http://co.hill.mt.us
Civil Records: Access: Phone, fax, mail, in person. Both court and visitors may perform in person searches. Search fee: $2.00 per name per year, first 7 years, then $1.00 per year. Court makes copy: $1.00 per page first 10 pages, then $.50 per page after. Required to search: name, years to search. Civil cases indexed by defendant, plaintiff, on computer since 1985; prior records on docket books to 1912. Maiden name helpful in searching. Mail turnaround time same day.
Criminal Records: Access: Fax, mail, in person. Both court and visitors may perform in person searches. Search fee: $2.00 per name per year, first 7 years, then $1.00 per year. Court makes copy: $1.00 per page first 10 pages, then $.50 per page after. Required to search: name, years to search; also helpful: maiden name. Criminal records on computer since 1988; prior records on docket books to 1912. Absolutely no criminal record checks by phone. Mail turnaround time same day.
General Information: Public terminal has criminal back to 1988 and civil back to 1985. No adoption, juvenile, paternity, sanity records released. Will fax documents $1.00 per page. Certification fee: $2.00. Payee: Clerk of Court. Business checks accepted. Prepayment and SASE required.

Justice Court Hill County Courthouse, 315 4th St, Havre, MT 59501; phone: 406-265-5481 X240; fax: 406-262-9441; hours 8AM-5PM (MST). *Misdemeanor, Civil Actions Under $7,000, Eviction, Small Claims.*
http://co.hill.mt.us
Note: Also known as a Limited Jurisdiction Court.

Jefferson County

District Court PO Box H, Boulder, MT 59632; phone: 406-225-4041 & 4042; fax: 406-225-4044; hours 8AM-N, 1-5PM (MST). *Felony, Civil Actions Over $7,000, Eviction, Probate.*
Civil Records: Access: Mail, fax, in person. Both court and visitors may perform in person searches. Search fee: $2.00 per name per year, first 7 years, then $1.00 per year. Court makes copy: $1.00 per page first 10 pages, then $.50 per page. Required to search: name, years to search. Civil cases indexed by defendant, plaintiff, on computer since 1993, on microfilm since 1925. Mail turnaround time same day.
Criminal Records: Access: Mail, fax, in person. Both court and visitors may perform in person searches. Search fee: $2.00 per name per year, first 7 years, then $1.00 per year. Court makes copy: $1.00 per page first 10 pages, then $.50 per page. Required to search: name, years to search. Criminal records on computer since 1992, on microfilm since 1925. Mail turnaround time same day.
General Information: Public use terminal available. Juvenile, sanity or adoption records not released. Fee to fax documents is $1.00 per page. Certification fee: $2.00. Payee: Clerk of Court. Personal checks accepted. Prepayment and SASE required.

Limited Jurisdiction Court PO Box H, 108 S Washington, Boulder, MT 59632; phone: 406-225-4055; fax: 406-225-4088; hours 8AM-N, 1-5PM (MST). *Misdemeanor, Civil Actions Under $7,000, Eviction, Small Claims.*

Judith Basin County

District Court PO Box 307, Stanford, MT 59479; phone: 406-566-2277 X113; criminal fax: 406-566-2211; same fax for civil/probate; hours 8AM-5PM (MST). *Felony, Civil Actions Over $5,000, Probate.*
Note: Probate is a separate index at this same address.

Civil Records: Access: Phone, fax, mail, in person. Both court and visitors may perform in person searches. Search fee: $2.00 per name per year, first 7 years, then $1.00 per year. Court makes copy: $1.00 per page first 10 pages, then $.50 per page after. Required to search: name, years to search. Civil cases indexed by defendant, plaintiff, on books back to 1920; on computer back to 1996. Mail turnaround time 10 days.
Criminal Records: Access: Phone, mail, in person. Both court and visitors may perform in person searches. Search fee: $2.00 per name per year, first 7 years, then $1.00 per year. Court makes copy: $1.00 per page first 10 pages, then $.50 per page after. Required to search: name, years to search, signed release. Criminal records on books back to 1920; on computer back to 1996. Mail turnaround time 10 days.
General Information: No public access terminal. No adoption, sanity records released. Will fax documents. Certification fee: $2.00 per document. Payee: Clerk of Court. Business checks accepted. Prepayment and SASE required.

Justice Court PO Box 339, 39 Third St NW, Stanford, MT 59479; phone: 406-566-2277 X117; fax: 406-566-2211; hours 8:00AM-5:00PM (MST). *Misdemeanor, Civil Actions Under $7,000, Eviction, Small Claims.*

Lake County

District Court Clerk of District Court Office, 106 4th Ave E, Polson, MT 59860; phone: 406-883-7254; fax: 406-883-7343; hours 8AM-5PM (MST). *Felony, Civil Actions Over $7,000, Probate.*
Civil Records: Access: Phone, fax, mail, in person. Both court and visitors may perform in person searches. Search fee: $2.00 per name per year, first 7 years, then $1.00 per year. Court makes copy: $1.00 per page first 10 pages, then $.50 per page after. Required to search: name, years to search. Civil cases indexed by defendant, plaintiff, on books since 1923; on computer since 1990. Mail turnaround time 3 days; 2 hours for phone requests.
Criminal Records: Access: Phone, fax, mail, in person. Both court and visitors may perform in person searches. Search fee: $2.00 per name per year, first 7 years, then $1.00 per year. Court makes copy: $1.00 per page first 10 pages, then $.50 per page after. Required to search: name, years to search, DOB, SSN. Criminal records on books since 1923; on computer since 1990. Mail turnaround time 3 days; 2 hours for phone requests.
General Information: Public use terminal available. No adoption, juvenile, sanity or expunged records released. Will fax documents $1.00 per page. Certification fee: $2.00. Payee: Clerk of Court. Business checks accepted. No credit cards. Prepayment and SASE required.

Limited Jurisdiction Court 106 4th Ave E, Polson, MT 59860; phone: 406-883-7258; fax: 406-883-7343; hours 8AM-5PM (MST). *Misdemeanor, Civil Actions Under $7,000, Eviction, Small Claims.*

Lewis and Clark County

District Court 228 Broadway, PO Box 158, Helena, MT 59624; phone: 406-447-8216; fax: 406-447-8275; hours 8AM-5PM (MST). *Felony, Civil Actions Over $5,000, Eviction, Probate, Small Claims.*
www.co.lewis-clark.mt.us
Civil Records: Access: Fax, mail, online, in person, email. Both court and visitors may perform in person searches. Search fee: $2.00 per name per year, first 7 years, then $1.00 per year. Court makes copy: $1.00 per page first 10 pages, then $.50 per page after; same fee for self serve. Required to search: name, years to search. Civil cases indexed by defendant, plaintiff, on computer since 1990, microfilm prior to 1/90. Will accept email record requests to kallio@co.lewis-clark.mt.us. Mail turnaround time 2 days.

Criminal Records: Access: Fax, mail, online, in person, email. Both court and visitors may perform in person searches. Search fee: $2.00 per name per year, first 7 years, then $1.00 per year. Court makes copy: $1.00 per page first 10 pages, then $.50 per page after; same fee for self serve. Required to search: name, years to search. Criminal records on computer since 1990, microfilm prior to 1/90. Will accept email record requests to ikallio@co.lewis-clark.mt.us. Mail turnaround time 2 days.
General Information: Public terminal goes back to 1992. No adoption or sanity records released. Fee to fax documents is $1.00 per page. Certification fee: $2.00. Payee: Clerk of Court. Personal checks accepted. Prepayment and SASE required.

Justice Court 228 Broadway, Helena, MT 59623; phone: 406-447-8202; criminal phone: 406-447-8202; civil phone: 406-447-8201; fax: 406-447-8269; hours 8AM-N; 1PM-4PM (MST). *Misdemeanor, Civil Actions Under $7,000, Eviction, Small Claims.*
Note: Formerly a Limited Jurisdiction Court.

Liberty County

District Court PO Box 549, Chester, MT 59522; phone: 406-759-5615; fax: 406-759-5996; hours 8AM-5PM (MST). *Felony, Civil Actions Over $5,000, Eviction, Probate.*
Note: With fax requests, include copy of your check.
Civil Records: Access: Fax, mail, in person. Only the court performs in person searches; visitors may not. Search fee: $2.00 per name per year, first 7 years, then $1.00 per year. Court makes copy: $1.00 per page first 10 pages, then $.50 per page after. Required to search: name, years to search, address. Civil cases indexed by defendant, plaintiff, on books since 1920. Mail turnaround time 2-3 days.
Criminal Records: Access: Fax, mail, in person, fax. Both court and visitors may perform in person searches. Search fee: $2.00 per name per year, first 7 years, then $1.00 per year. Court makes copy: $1.00 per page first 10 pages, then $.50 per page after. Required to search: name, years to search, signed release. Criminal records on books since 1920. Mail turnaround time 2-3 days.
General Information: No public access terminal. No adoption, juvenile or sanity records released. Will fax documents to local or toll free line. Certification fee: $2.00 per cert. Payee: Clerk of Court. Personal checks accepted. Prepayment and SASE required.

Limited Jurisdiction Court PO Box 170, Courthouse, 1st E, Chester, MT 59522; phone: 406-759-5172; fax: 406-759-5395; hours 9AM-N, 1-5PM Tues (MST). *Misdemeanor, Civil Actions Under $7,000, Eviction, Small Claims.*

Lincoln County

District Court 512 California Ave, Libby, MT 59923; phone: 406-293-7781; probate phone: x224; fax: 406-293-9816; hours 8AM-5PM (MST). *Felony, Civil Actions Over $7,000, Probate.*
Civil Records: Access: Mail, in person. Both court and visitors may perform in person searches. Search fee: $2.00 per name per year, first 7 years, then $1.00 per year. Court makes copy: $1.00 per page first 10 pages, then $.50 per page after. Required to search: name, years to search. Civil cases indexed by defendant, plaintiff, on computer from 1991, prior on docket books. Mail turnaround time 1 week.
Criminal Records: Access: Mail, in person. Both court and visitors may perform in person searches. Search fee: $2.00 per name per year, first 7 years, then $1.00 per year. Court makes copy: $1.00 per page first 10 pages, then $.50 per page after. Required to search: name, years to search, DOB. Criminal records on computer from 1996, prior on docket books. Mail turnaround time 1 week.
General Information: Public terminal goes back to 1996. No adoption, juvenile or sanity records released. Will fax documents, no extra fee. Certification fee: $2.00. Payee: Clerk of Court.

Personal checks accepted. Prepayment and SASE required.

Eureka Justice Court #2 PO Box 403, 152 Hwy 37, Eureka, MT 59917; phone: 406-297-2622; fax: 406-297-3829; hours 8AM-N, 1-5PM (MST). *Misdemeanor, Civil Actions Under $7,000, Eviction, Small Claims.*

Libby Justice Court #1 418 Mineral Ave, Libby, MT 59923; phone: 406-293-7781 x236, x235; criminal phone: x259; civil phone: x235; fax: 406-293-5948; hours 8AM-5PM (MST). *Misdemeanor, Civil Actions Under $7,000, Eviction, Small Claims.*

Madison County

District Court PO Box 185, Virginia City, MT 59755; phone: 406-843-4230; fax: 406-843-5207; hours 8AM-5PM (MST). *Felony, Civil Actions Over $5,000, Eviction, Probate.*
Civil Records: Access: Phone, fax, mail, in person. Both court and visitors may perform in person searches. Search fee: $2.00 per name per year, first 7 years, then $1.00 per year. Court makes copy: $1.00 per page first 10 pages, then $.50 per page after. Required to search: name, years to search. Civil cases indexed by defendant, plaintiff, on books since 1864; on computer back to 1990. Mail turnaround time 1 week.
Criminal Records: Access: Fax, mail, in person. Both court and visitors may perform in person searches. Search fee: $2.00 per name per year, first 7 years, then $1.00 per year. Court makes copy: $1.00 per page first 10 pages, then $.50 per page after. Required to search: name, years to search. Criminal records on books since 1864; on computer back to 1990. Mail turnaround time 1 week.
General Information: Public terminal goes back to 1990. No adoption, juvenile or sanity records released. Fee to fax documents is $4.00 1st page, $1.00 each add'l. Certification fee: $2.00. Payee: Clerk of Court. Personal checks accepted. Prepayment and SASE required.

Madison Couny Justice Court PO Box 277, Virginia City, MT 59755; phone: 406-843-4237; fax: 406-843-4219; hours 8AM-5PM (MST). *Misdemeanor, Civil Actions Under $7,000, Eviction, Small Claims.*

McCone County

District Court PO Box 199, Circle, MT 59215; phone: 406-485-3410; fax: 406-485-3410; hours 8AM-5PM (MST). *Felony, Civil Actions Over $5,000, Eviction, Probate.*
Civil Records: Access: Mail, in person. Only the court performs in person searches; visitors may not. Search fee: $2.00 per name per year, first 7 years, then $1.00 per year. Court makes copy: $1.00 per page first 10 pages, then $.50 per page after. Required to search: name, years to search. Civil cases indexed by defendant, plaintiff. Civil records in books from 1919, computerized since 1996. Mail turnaround time 1-2 days.
Criminal Records: Access: Mail, in person. Only the court performs in person searches; visitors may not. Search fee: $2.00 per name per year, first 7 years, then $1.00 per year. Court makes copy: $1.00 per page first 10 pages, then $.50 per page after. Required to search: name, years to search. Criminal records in books and microfilm since 1919, computerized since 1996. Mail turnaround time 1-2 days.
General Information: No public access terminal. No adoption, juvenile, sanity or mental health records released. Will fax documents to local or toll free line. Certification fee: $2.00 per cert. Payee: Clerk of Court. Personal checks accepted. Prepayment and SASE required.

Limited Jurisdiction Court PO Box 192, 1004 Circle Ave, Circle, MT 59215; phone: 406-485-3548; fax: 406-485-2689; hours 9AM-N Tu & W (MST). *Misdemeanor, Civil Actions Under $7,000, Eviction, Small Claims.*

Meagher County

District Court PO Box 443, White Sulphur Springs, MT 59645; phone: 406-547-3612 x110; hours &;30AM-4PM (MST). *Felony, Civil Actions Over $5,000, Eviction, Probate.*
Civil Records: Access: Phone, mail, fax, in person. Both court and visitors may perform in person searches. Search fee: $2.00 per name per year, first 7 years, then $1.00 per year. Court makes copy: $1.00 per page first 10 pages, then $.50 per page after. Required to search: name, years to search. Civil cases indexed by defendant, plaintiff, on docket books or microfiche to 1900; on computer back to 1996. Mail turnaround time 1 day or same day.
Criminal Records: Access: Phone, mail, fax, in person. Both court and visitors may perform in person searches. Search fee: $2.00 per name per year, first 7 years, then $1.00 per year. Court makes copy: $1.00 per page first 10 pages, then $.50 per page after. Required to search: name, years to search, DOB. Criminal records on docket books or microfiche to 1900; on computer back to 1996. Mail turnaround time 3 days.
General Information: No public access terminal. No adoption, juvenile or sanity records released. Will fax documents to local or toll-free number. Certification fee: $2.00. Payee: Clerk of Court. Personal checks accepted. Prepayment and SASE required.

Limited Jurisdiction Court PO Box 698, Justice Court, 15 W Main St, White Sulphur Springs, MT 59645; phone: 406-547-3954 X115; fax: 406-547-3336; hours 8AM-12 M-F (MST). *Misdemeanor, Civil Actions Under $7,000, Eviction, Small Claims.*
Note: 2nd fax number is 406-547-3836.

Mineral County

District Court PO Box 129, Superior, MT 59872; phone: 406-822-3538; fax: 406-822-3579; hours 8AM-N,1-5PM (MST). *Felony, Civil Actions Over $5,000, Probate.*
Note: Probate is a separate index at this same address.
Civil Records: Access: Fax, mail, in person. Both court and visitors may perform in person searches. Search fee: $2.00 per name per year, first 7 years, then $1.00 per year. Court makes copy: $1.00 per page first 10 pages, then $.50 per page after. Required to search: name, years to search. Civil cases indexed by defendant, plaintiff, on docket books from 1914, on computer back to 1990. Mail turnaround time same day after payment received.
Criminal Records: Access: Fax, mail, in person. Both court and visitors may perform in person searches. Search fee: $2.00 per name per year, first 7 years, then $1.00 per year. Court makes copy: $1.00 per page first 10 pages, then $.50 per page after. Required to search: name, years to search. Criminal records on docket books from 1914, on computer back to 1990. Mail turnaround time same day after payment received.
General Information: No public access terminal. No adoption, sanity records released. Fee to fax documents is $5.00 per document. You must fax request with copy of payment check. Certification fee: $2.00 per document. Payee: Clerk of Court. Personal checks accepted. Prepayment and SASE required.

Limited Jurisdiction Court PO Box 658, 300 River St, Superior, MT 59872; phone: 406-822-3550; fax: 406-822-3579; hours 8AM-N, 1-5PM (MST). *Misdemeanor, Civil Actions Under $7,000, Eviction, Small Claims.*

Missoula County

District Court 200 W Broadway, Missoula, MT 59802; phone: 406-258-4780; fax: 406-258-4899; hours 8AM-5PM (MST). *Felony, Civil Actions Over $7,000, Probate.*
www.co.missoula.mt.us/coc/
Civil Records: Access: Fax, mail, in person. Both court and visitors may perform in person searches.

Search fee: $2.00 per name per year, first 7 years, then $1.00 per year. Court makes copy: $1.00 per page first 10 pages, then $.50 per page after. Required to search: name, years to search. Civil cases indexed by defendant, plaintiff, on computer from 10/89, microfilm from 1970s, archived to late 1800s. Mail turnaround time up to 2 weeks.
Criminal Records: Access: Fax, mail, in person. Both court and visitors may perform in person searches. Search fee: $2.00 per name per year, first 7 years, then $1.00 per year. Court makes copy: $1.00 per page first 10 pages, then $.50 per page after. Required to search: name, years to search. Criminal records on computer from 10/89, microfilm from 1970s, archived to late 1800s. Mail turnaround time up to 2 weeks.
General Information: Public terminal goes back to 1989. No adoption, juvenile, sealed, expunged or pre-sentence psychiatric records released. Will fax documents $2.00 per doc. No fee if returning on toll free line. Certification fee: $2.00. Payee: Clerk of Court. Personal checks or Visa, MC accepted. Prepayment required. SASE requested.

Limited Jurisdiction Court - Dept 1 200 W Broadway, Missoula County Courthouse, Missoula, MT 59802; phone: 406-523-4871; fax: 406-258-3935; hours 8AM-5PM (MST). *Misdemeanor, Civil Actions Under $7,000, Eviction, Small Claims.*
www.co.missoula.mt.us/jp1

Musselshell County

District Court 506 Main St, Roundup, MT 59072; phone: 406-323-1413; criminal fax: 406-323-1710; same fax for civil/probate; hours 8AM-5PM (MST). *Felony, Civil Actions Over $5,000, Eviction, Probate.*
Note: Include copy of the fees check with fax requests.
Civil Records: Access: Mail, fax, in person. Both court and visitors may perform in person searches. Search fee: $2.00 per name per year, first 7 years, then $1.00 per year. Court makes copy: $1.00 per page first 10 pages, then $.50 per page after; same fee for self serve. Required to search: name, years to search. Civil cases indexed by defendant, plaintiff. Computerized records from 7/96, civil records on docket books from 1911. Mail turnaround time 2-3 days.
Criminal Records: Access: Mail, fax, in person. Both court and visitors may perform in person searches. Search fee: $2.00 per name per year, first 7 years, then $1.00 per year. Court makes copy: $1.00 per page first 10 pages, then $.50 per page after; same fee for self serve. Required to search: name, years to search. Criminal records on docket books from 1911. Mail turnaround time 2-3 days.
General Information: No public access terminal. No adoption, (some) juvenile or sanity records released. Will fax documents to local or toll free line. Certification fee: $2.00 per document. Payee: Clerk of Court. Personal checks accepted. Prepayment and SASE required.

Limited Jurisdiction Court PO Box 660, Roundup, MT 59072; phone: 406-323-1078; fax: 406-323-3452; hours 9AM-4PM (MST). *Misdemeanor, Civil Actions Under $7,000, Eviction, Small Claims.*

Park County

District Court PO Box 437, Livingston, MT 59047; phone: 406-222-4125; fax: 406-222-4128; hours 8AM-5PM (MST). *Felony, Civil Actions Over $7,000, Eviction, Probate.*
Civil Records: Access: Fax, mail, in person. Both court and visitors may perform in person searches. Search fee: $2.00 per name per year, first 7 years, then $1.00 per year. Court makes copy: $1.00 per page first 10 pages, then $.50 per page after. Required to search: name, years to search. Civil cases indexed by defendant, plaintiff, on computer, microfiche, and docket books from 1889 to present. Mail turnaround time 1-2 days for all requests.

Criminal Records: Access: Fax, mail, in person. Both court and visitors may perform in person searches. Search fee: $2.00 per name per year, first 7 years, then $1.00 per year. Court makes copy: $2.00 per page first 10 pages, then $1.00 per page after. Required to search: name, years to search. Criminal records on computer, microfiche, and docket books from 1889 to present. Mail turnaround time 1-2 days for all requests.
General Information: Public terminal has criminal back to 1996 and civil back to 1980. No adoption, juvenile or sanity records released. Certification fee: $2.00. Payee: Clerk of Court. Personal checks accepted. Prepayment required.

Limited Jurisdiction Court 414 E Callender, Livingston, MT 59047; phone: 406-222-4169/4170; civil phone: 406-222-4171; fax: 406-222-4103; hours 8AM-N, 1-5:00PM (MST). *Misdemeanor, Civil Actions Under $7,000, Eviction, Small Claims.*

Petroleum County

District Court PO Box 226, Winnett, MT 59087; phone: 406-429-5311; fax: 406-429-6328; hours 8AM-5PM (MST). *Felony, Civil Actions Over $5,000, Eviction, Probate.*
Civil Records: Access: Phone, mail, in person. Both court and visitors may perform in person searches. Search fee: $2.00 per name per year, first 7 years, then $1.00 per year. Court makes copy: $1.00 per page first 10 pages, then $.50 per page after; same fee for self serve. Required to search: name, years to search. Civil cases indexed by defendant, plaintiff, on docket books from 1924. Mail turnaround time 1 day.
Criminal Records: Access: Phone, mail, in person. Only the court performs in person searches; visitors may not. Search fee: $2.00 per name per year, first 7 years, then $1.00 per year. Court makes copy: $1.00 per page first 10 pages, then $.50 per page after; same fee for self serve. Required to search: name, years to search. Criminal records on docket books from 1924. Mail turnaround time 1 day.
General Information: No public access terminal. No adoption, juvenile or sanity records released. Will fax documents to local or toll free line. Certification fee: $2.00. Payee: Clerk of Court. Personal checks accepted. Prepayment and SASE required.

Limited Jurisdiction Court PO Box 226, Winnett, MT 59087; phone: 406-429-5311; fax: 406-429-6328; hours 9AM-Noon Th (MST). *Misdemeanor, Civil Actions Under $7,000, Eviction, Small Claims.*

Phillips County

District Court PO Box 530, Malta, MT 59538; phone: 406-654-1023; criminal fax: 406-654-1023; same fax for civil/probate; hours 8AM-5PM (MST). *Felony, Civil Actions Over $5,000, Eviction, Probate.*
Civil Records: Access: Mail, in person. Only the court performs in person searches; visitors may not. Search fee: $2.00 per name per year, first 7 years, then $1.00 per year. Court makes copy: $1.00 per page first 10 pages, then $.50 per page after. Required to search: name, years to search; also helpful: address. Civil cases indexed by defendant, plaintiff, on computer back to 1997; books, microfilm back to 1915. Mail turnaround time 1-2 days.
Criminal Records: Access: Mail, in person. Only the court performs in person searches; visitors may not. Search fee: $2.00 per name per year, first 7 years, then $1.00 per year. Court makes copy: $1.00 per page first 10 pages, then $.50 per page after. Required to search: name, years to search, signed release, DOB or SSN; also helpful: address. Criminal records on computer back to 1997; books, microfilm back to 1915. Mail turnaround time 1-2 days.
General Information: No public access terminal. No adoption, juvenile or sanity records released. Will fax documents for $5.00; no charge to toll free number. Certification fee: $2.00 per document. Payee: Clerk of Court. Personal checks accepted. Prepayment and SASE required.

Limited Jurisdiction Court PO Box 1396, Malta, MT 59538; phone: 406-654-1118; fax: 406-654-1213; hours 9AM-3PM M-Th (MST). *Misdemeanor, Civil Actions Under $7,000, Eviction, Small Claims.*

Pondera County

District Court 20 Fourth Ave SW, Conrad, MT 59425; phone: 406-271-4026; criminal fax: 406-271-4081; same fax for civil/probate; hours 8AM-5PM (MST). *Felony, Civil Actions Over $5,000, Eviction, Probate.*
Civil Records: Access: Fax, mail, in person. Both court and visitors may perform in person searches. Search fee: $2.00 per name per year, first 7 years, then $1.00 per year. Court makes copy: $1.00 per page first 10 pages, then $.50 per page after. Required to search: name, years to search. Civil cases indexed by defendant, plaintiff, on docket books from 1919; on computer back to 1995. Mail turnaround time 2-3 days.
Criminal Records: Access: Fax, mail, in person. Both court and visitors may perform in person searches. Search fee: $2.00 per name per year, first 7 years, then $1.00 per year. Court makes copy: $1.00 per page first 10 pages, then $.50 per page after. Required to search: name, years to search. Criminal records on docket books from 1919; on computer back to 1995. Mail turnaround time 2-3 days.
General Information: No public access terminal. No adoption or sanity records released. Will fax documents to toll-free number or apply copy fee as fax-back fee. Certification fee: $2.00 per document. Payee: Clerk of Court. Personal checks accepted. Prepayment and SASE required.

Limited Jurisdiction Court 20 Fourth Ave SW, Conrad, MT 59425; phone: 406-271-4030; fax: 406-271-4031; hours 9AM-4PM (MST). *Misdemeanor, Civil Actions Under $7,000, Eviction, Small Claims.*

Powder River County

District Court PO Box 239, Broadus, MT 59317; phone: 406-436-2320; criminal fax: 406-436-2325; same fax for civil/probate; hours 8AM-N, 1-5PM (MST). *Felony, Civil Actions Over $5,000, Probate.*
Note: Probate is a separate index at this same address.
Civil Records: Access: Fax, mail, in person. Both court and visitors may perform in person searches. Search fee: $2.00 per name per year, first 7 years, then $1.00 per year. Court makes copy: $1.00 per page first 10 pages, then $.50 per page after. Self serve copy fee: $1.00 per page. Required to search: name, years to search. Civil cases indexed by defendant, plaintiff, on computer since 1993, microfiche since 1974, and books since 1919. Mail turnaround time same day.
Criminal Records: Access: Fax, mail, in person. Both court and visitors may perform in person searches. Search fee: $2.00 per name per year, first 7 years, then $1.00 per year. Court makes copy: $1.00 per page first 10 pages, then $.50 per page after. Self serve copy fee: $1.00 per page. Required to search: name, years to search. Criminal records on computer since 1993, microfiche since 1974, and books since 1919. Mail turnaround time same day if prepaid.
General Information: Public terminal goes back to 1993. No adoption, juvenile, sanity, dismissed criminal records released. Fee to fax documents is $1.00 per page. Certification fee: $2.00 per cert. Payee: Clerk of Court. Only cashiers checks and money orders accepted. Prepayment and SASE required.

Justice Court PO Box 488, Courthouse Sq, Broadus, MT 59317; phone: 406-436-2503; fax: 406-436-2866; hours 9AM-3:30PM M-Th (MST). *Misdemeanor, Civil Actions Under $7,000, Eviction, Small Claims.*

Powell County

District Court 409 Missouri Ave, Deer Lodge, MT 59722; phone: 406-846-3680 X234/235; fax: 406-846-2784; hours 8AM-5PM (MST). *Felony, Civil Actions Over $5,000, Eviction, Probate.*
Civil Records: Access: Mail, in person. Both court and visitors may perform in person searches. Search fee: $2.00 per name per year, first 7 years, then $1.00 per year. Court makes copy: $1.00 per page first 10 pages, then $.50 per page after. Required to search: name, years to search. Civil cases indexed by defendant, plaintiff, on docket books since turn of century, on computer since 1996. Mail turnaround time 2-3 days.
Criminal Records: Access: Mail, in person. Both court and visitors may perform in person searches. Search fee: $2.00 per name per year, first 7 years, then $1.00 per year. Court makes copy: $1.00 per page first 10 pages, then $.50 per page after. Required to search: name, years to search, DOB, SSN. Criminal records on docket books since turn of century, on computer since 1996. Mail turnaround time 2-3 days.
General Information: Public terminal goes back to 1996. No adoption, juvenile or sanity records released. Will fax documents for $1.00 per page. Certification fee: $2.00. Payee: Clerk of Court. Personal checks accepted. Prepayment and SASE required.

Limited Jurisdiction Court 409 Missouri, Powell County Courthouse, Deer Lodge, MT 59722; phone: 406-846-3680; fax: 406-846-2784; hours 8AM-5PM (MST). *Misdemeanor, Civil Actions Under $7,000, Eviction, Small Claims.*

Prairie County

District Court PO Box 125, Terry, MT 59349; phone: 406-635-5575; fax: 406-635-5576; hours 8AM-N; 1PM-5PM (MST). *Felony, Civil Actions Over $5,000, Eviction, Probate.*
Civil Records: Access: Fax, mail, in person. Both court and visitors may perform in person searches. Search fee: $2.00 per name per year, first 7 years, then $1.00 per year. Court makes copy: $.25 per page. Required to search: name, years to search. Civil cases indexed by defendant, plaintiff, on books since 1915; computerized records go back to 1997. Mail turnaround time 5 days.
Criminal Records: Access: Fax, mail, in person. Both court and visitors may perform in person searches. Search fee: $2.00 per name per year, first 7 years, then $1.00 per year. Court makes copy: $.25 per page. Required to search: name, years to search, DOB, SSN. Criminal records on books since 1915; computerized records go back to 1997. Mail turnaround time 5 days.
General Information: No public access terminal. No adoption, juvenile or sanity records released. Will fax documents to local or toll free line. Certification fee: $2.00 per cert. Payee: Clerk of Court. Personal checks accepted. Prepayment and SASE required.

Limited Jurisdiction Court PO Box 40, 217 Park, Terry, MT 59349; phone: 406-635-4466; fax: 406-635-4126; hours 12:30-3PM (MST). *Misdemeanor, Civil Actions Under $7,000, Eviction, Small Claims.*

Ravalli County

District Court Ravalli County Courthouse, 205 Bedford #D, Hamilton, MT 59840; phone: 406-375-6214; criminal fax: 406-375-6327; same fax for civil/probate; hours 8AM-5PM (MST). *Felony, Civil Actions Over $7,000, Probate.*
http://co.ravalli.mt.us
Civil Records: Access: Mail, in person. Both court and visitors may perform in person searches. Search fee: $2.00 per name per year, first 7 years, then $1.00 per year. Court makes copy: $1.00 per page first 10 pages, then $.50 per page after; same fee for self serve. Required to search: name, years to search. Civil cases indexed by defendant, plaintiff, on microfiche

(1989), docket books (1914). Mail turnaround time 4-5 days.

Criminal Records: Access: Mail, in person. Both court and visitors may perform in person searches. Search fee: $2.00 per name per year, first 7 years, then $1.00 per year. Court makes copy: $1.00 per page first 10 pages, then $.50 per page after; same fee for self serve. Required to search: name, years to search. Criminal records on microfiche (1989), docket books (1914). Mail turnaround time 4-5 days.

General Information: Public terminal goes back to 1996. No adoption, juvenile, psychological, medical or expunged records released. Will fax documents $1.00 per page. Certification fee: $2.00 per cert. Payee: Clerk of Court. Personal checks accepted. Prepayment and SASE required.

Justice Court 205 Bedford St. #F, Hamilton, MT 59840; phone: 406-375-6252; fax: 406-375-6383; hours 9AM-5PM (MST). *Misdemeanor, Civil Actions Under $7,000, Eviction, Small Claims.*
Note: Dept #2, Judge Jim Bailey; Dept #1, Judge Rubin Clue.

Richland County

District Court 201 W Main, Sidney, MT 59270; phone: 406-433-1709; criminal fax: 406-433-6945; same fax for civil/probate; hours 8AM-5PM (MST). *Felony, Civil Actions Over $5,000, Eviction, Probate.*
Civil Records: Access: Phone, fax, mail, in person. Both court and visitors may perform in person searches. Search fee: $2.00 per name per year, first 7 years, then $1.00 per year. Court makes copy: $1.00 per page first 10 pages, then $.50 per page after; same fee for self serve. Required to search: name, years to search. Civil cases indexed by defendant, plaintiff. Civil records in books since 1914; on computer back to 1997. Mail turnaround time 1-3 days.
Criminal Records: Access: Phone, fax, mail, in person. Both court and visitors may perform in person searches. Search fee: $2.00 per name per year, first 7 years, then $1.00 per year. Court makes copy: $1.00 per page first 10 pages, then $.50 per page after; same fee for self serve. Required to search: name, years to search. Criminal records in books since 1914; on computer back to 1997. Mail turnaround time 1-3 days.
General Information: No public access terminal. No adoption, juvenile, paternity, sanity, dismissed or expunged records released. Will fax documents $1.00 per page. Certification fee: $2.00 per seal. Payee: Clerk of Court. Personal checks accepted. Prepayment and SASE required.

Limited Jurisdiction Court 123 W Main, Sidney, MT 59270; phone: 406-433-2815; fax: 406-433-6885; hours 8AM-5PM (MST). *Misdemeanor, Civil Actions Under $7,000, Eviction, Small Claims.*

Roosevelt County

District Court County Courthouse, 400 2nd Ave S, Wolf Point, MT 59201; phone: 406-653-6266; fax: 406-653-6203; hours 8AM-5PM (MST). *Felony, Civil Actions Over $5,000, Eviction, Probate.*
Note: Probate Court located at 212 Broadway Ave.
Civil Records: Access: Phone, fax, mail, in person. Only the court performs in person searches; visitors may not. Search fee: $2.00 per name per year, first 7 years, then $1.00 per year. Court makes copy: $1.00 per page first 10 pages, then $.50 per page after. Required to search: name, years to search. Civil cases indexed by defendant, plaintiff, on books and microfiche back to 1919, computerized back to 1996. Mail turnaround time 2-3 days after payment receipt.
Criminal Records: Access: Fax, mail, in person. Only the court performs in person searches; visitors may not. Search fee: $2.00 per name per year, first 7 years, then $1.00 per year. Court makes copy: $1.00 per page first 10 pages, then $.50 per page after. Required to search: name, years to search; also helpful: DOB. Criminal records on books and microfiche back to 1919, computerized back to 1996. Mail turnaround time 2-3 days after payment receipt.

General Information: No public access terminal. No adoption, juvenile or sanity records released. Will fax documents for $3.00 per document. Certification fee: $2.00. Payee: Clerk of Court. Personal checks accepted. Prepayment and SASE required.

Culbertson Justice Court Post #2 PO Box 421, Culbertson, MT 59218; phone: 406-787-6607; fax: 406-787-6608; hours 9AM-3PM M-Th (MST). *Misdemeanor, Civil Actions Under $7,000, Eviction, Small Claims.*

Wolf Point Justice Court Post #1 County Courthouse, 400 Second Ave. S, Wolf Point, MT 59201; phone: 406-653-6261, 406-653-6258; fax: 406-653-6203; hours 8AM-N M-F (MST). *Misdemeanor, Civil Actions Under $7,000, Eviction, Small Claims.*

Rosebud County

District Court PO Box 48, Forsyth, MT 59327; phone: 406-356-7322; hours 8AM-5PM (MST). *Felony, Civil Actions Over $5,000, Eviction, Probate.*
Civil Records: Access: Fax, mail, in person. Only the court performs in person searches; visitors may not. Search fee: $2.00 per name per year, first 7 years, then $1.00 per year. Written requests only. Court makes copy: $1.00 per page first 10 pages, then $.50 per page after; same fee for self serve. Required to search: name, years to search. Civil cases indexed by defendant, plaintiff. Civil records in books, on microfiche back to 1901; on computer back to 1996. Mail turnaround time 2 days.
Criminal Records: Access: Mail, in person. Both court and visitors may perform in person searches. Search fee: $2.00 per name per year, first 7 years, then $1.00 per year. Written requests only. Court makes copy: $1.00 per page first 10 pages, then $.50 per page after; same fee for self serve. Required to search: name, years to search, signed release. Criminal records in books, on microfiche back to 1901; on computer back to 1996. Mail turnaround time 2 days.
General Information: Public terminal has only criminal records. No adoption, juvenile, sanity or sealed records released. Certification fee: $2.50. Payee: Clerk of Court. Personal checks accepted. Prepayment and SASE required.

Limited Jurisdiction Court #1 PO Box 504, 1200 Main St, County Courthouse, Forsyth, MT 59327; phone: 406-346-2638; fax: 406-346-7551; hours 8AM-5PM (MST). *Misdemeanor, Civil Actions Under $7,000, Eviction, Small Claims.*

Limited Jurisdiction Court #2 PO Box 575, 303 Willow Ave, Colstrip, MT 59323; phone: 406-748-2934; fax: 406-748-3212; hours 8AM-5PM; Ashland 2nd & 4th Wed 1PM (MST). *Misdemeanor, Civil Actions Under $10,000, Eviction, Small Claims.*

Sanders County

District Court PO Box 519, Thompson Falls, MT 59873; phone: 406-827-6962; fax: 406-827-0094; hours 8AM-5PM (MST). *Felony, Civil Actions Over $7,000, Eviction, Probate.*
Civil Records: Access: Mail, in person. Both court and visitors may perform in person searches. Search fee: $2.00 per name per year, first 7 years, then $1.00 per year. Court makes copy: $1.00 per page first 10 pages, then $.50 per page after. Required to search: name, years to search. Civil cases indexed by defendant, plaintiff, on docket books since 1906, on computer since 1999. Mail turnaround time 1-4 days.
Criminal Records: Access: Mail, in person. Both court and visitors may perform in person searches. Search fee: $2.00 per name per year, first 7 years, then $1.00 per year. Court makes copy: $1.00 per page first 10 pages, then $.50 per page after. Required to search:

name, years to search, DOB, SSN, signed release. Criminal records on docket books since 1906, on computer since 1999. Mail turnaround time 1-4 days.
General Information: Public use terminal available. No adoption, juvenile, sanity or pre-sentence investigation records released. Will fax documents to local or toll free line. Certification fee: $2.00. Payee: Clerk of Court. Personal checks accepted. Prepayment and SASE required.

Limited Jurisdiction Court PO Box 519, Thompson Falls, MT 59873; phone: 406-827-6941; fax: 406-827-0094; hours 8AM-12;00, 1-5PM (MST). *Misdemeanor, Civil Actions Under $7,000, Eviction, Small Claims.*

Sheridan County

District Court 100 W Laurel, Plentywood, MT 59254; phone: 406-765-3404; fax: 406-765-2602; hours 8AM-N, 1-5PM (MST). *Felony, Civil Actions Over $5,000, Eviction, Probate.*
www.co.sheridan.mt.us
Civil Records: Access: Phone, mail, in person. Both court and visitors may perform in person searches. Search fee: $2.00 per name per year, first 7 years, then $1.00 per year. Court makes copy: $1.00 per page first 10 pages, then $.50 per page after. Required to search: name, years to search. Civil cases indexed by defendant, plaintiff, on docket books since 1913. Mail turnaround time 1-2 days.
Criminal Records: Access: Phone, mail, in person. Both court and visitors may perform in person searches. Search fee: $2.00 per name per year, first 7 years, then $1.00 per year. Court makes copy: $1.00 per page first 10 pages, then $.50 per page after. Required to search: name, years to search. Criminal records on docket books since 1913. Mail turnaround time 1-2 days.
General Information: No public access terminal. No adoption, juvenile or sanity records released. Will fax documents to toll free line, must be prepaid. Certification fee: $2.00. Payee: Clerk of District Court. Personal checks accepted. Prepayment and SASE required.

Justice Court 100 W Laurel, Plentywood, MT 59254; phone: 406-765-2310; fax: 406-765-3489; hours 8AM-5PM (MST). *Misdemeanor, Civil Actions Under $7,000, Eviction, Small Claims.*

Silver Bow County

District Court 155 W Granite St, Butte, MT 59701; phone: 406-497-6350; fax: 406-497-6358; hours 8AM-5PM (MST). *Felony, Civil Actions Over $7,000, Probate.*
Civil Records: Access: Fax, mail, in person. Both court and visitors may perform in person searches. Search fee: $2.00 per name per year, first 7 years, then $1.00 per year. Court makes copy: $1.00 per page first 10 pages, then $.50 per page after. Required to search: name, years to search. Civil cases indexed by defendant, plaintiff. Civil records in original files since 1970, on microfilm back to 1887; on computer back to 1996. Mail turnaround time 3 days.
Criminal Records: Access: Fax, mail, in person. Both court and visitors may perform in person searches. Search fee: $2.00 per name per year, first 7 years, then $1.00 per year. Court makes copy: $1.00 per page first 10 pages, then $.50 per page after. Required to search: name, years to search. Criminal records in original files since 1970, on microfilm back to 1887; on computer back to 1995. Mail turnaround time 1-3 days; will not do phone searches.
General Information: Public use terminal available. No adoption, juvenile or sanity records released. Fee to fax documents is $1.00 per page. Certification fee: $2.00. Payee: Clerk of Court. Personal checks accepted. Prepayment and SASE required.

Limited Jurisdiction Court #1 & #2 155 W Granite St, Rm 305, Silver Bow County Courthouse, Butte, MT 59701; phone: 406-497-6391/6392; criminal phone: 406-497-6390; civil phone: 406-497-

6390; fax: 406-497-6468; hours 8AM-5PM (MST). *Misdemeanor, Civil Actions Under $7,000, Eviction, Small Claims.*

Note: There are two Justice Courts at this location. Both courts must be searched for records

Stillwater County

District Court PO Box 367, Columbus, MT 59019; phone: 406-322-8030; fax: 406-322-8048; hours 8AM-5PM (MST). *Felony, Civil Actions Over $5,000, Eviction, Probate.*

Civil Records: Access: Phone, mail, in person. Both court and visitors may perform in person searches. Search fee: $2.00 per name per year, first 7 years, then $1.00 per year. Court makes copy: $1.00 per page first 10 pages, then $.50 per page after. Required to search: name, years to search. Civil cases indexed by defendant, plaintiff, on docket books since 1913; on computer back to 1994. Mail turnaround time 1-2 days.

Criminal Records: Access: Phone, mail, in person. Both court and visitors may perform in person searches. Search fee: $2.00 per name per year, first 7 years, then $1.00 per year. Court makes copy: $1.00 per page first 10 pages, then $.50 per page after. Required to search: name, years to search. Criminal records on docket books since 1913; on computer back to 1994. Mail turnaround time 1-2 days.

General Information: No public access terminal. No adoption, juvenile or sanity records released. Will fax documents for $1.00 per page. Certification fee: $2.00. Payee: Clerk of Court. Personal checks accepted. Prepayment and SASE required.

Limited Jurisdiction Court PO Box 77, 400 E 3rd Ave N, Columbus, MT 59019; phone: 406-322-8040; fax: 406-322-8048; hours 9AM-5PM M-Th (MST). *Misdemeanor, Civil Actions Under $7,000, Eviction, Small Claims.*

Sweet Grass County

District Court PO Box 698, Big Timber, MT 59011; phone: 406-932-5154; criminal fax: 406-932-5433; same fax for civil/probate; hours 8AM-N, 1-5PM (MST). *Felony, Civil Actions Over $5,000, Eviction, Probate.*

Note: Probate records in a separate index at same address.

Civil Records: Access: Phone, mail, in person. Only the court performs in person searches; visitors may not. Search fee: $2.00 per name per year, first 7 years, then $1.00 per year. Court makes copy: $1.00 per page first 10 pages, then $.50 per page after. Required to search: name, years to search. Civil cases indexed by defendant, plaintiff. Civil records in books since 1895, on microfiche since 1972, computerized since 1996. Mail turnaround time 1 day.

Criminal Records: Access: Phone, mail, in person. Only the court performs in person searches; visitors may not. Search fee: $2.00 per name per year, first 7 years, then $1.00 per year. Court makes copy: $1.00 per page first 10 pages, then $.50 per page after. Required to search: name, years to search. Criminal records in books since 1895, on microfiche since 1972, computerized since 1996. Mail turnaround time 1 day.

General Information: No public access terminal. No adoption, juvenile or sanity records released. Will fax documents for $1.50 if not a toll free fax return. Certification fee: $2.00 per document. Payee: Clerk of Court. Personal checks accepted. Prepayment and SASE required.

Limited Jurisdiction Court PO Box 1432, 200 West 1st, Big Timber, MT 59011; phone: 406-932-5150; fax: 406-932-5433; hours 8AM-5PM (MST). *Misdemeanor, Civil Actions Under $7,000, Eviction, Small Claims.*

Teton County

District Court PO Box 487, Choteau, MT 59422; phone: 406-466-2909; fax: 406-466-2910; hours 8AM-5PM (MST). *Felony, Civil Actions Over $5,000, Eviction, Probate.*

Civil Records: Access: Phone, fax, mail, in person. Only the court performs in person searches; visitors may not. Search fee: $2.00 per name per year, first 7 years, then $1.00 per year. Court makes copy: $1.00 per page 1st 10 pages, then $.50 per page after. Required to search: name, years to search. Civil cases indexed by defendant, plaintiff, on books from 1893; on computer back to 1995. Mail turnaround time 1 day.

Criminal Records: Access: Phone, mail, in person. Only the court performs in person searches; visitors may not. Search fee: $2.00 per name per year, first 7 years, then $1.00 per year. Court makes copy: $1.00 per page 1st 10 pages, $.50 each add'l. Required to search: name, years to search. Criminal records on books from 1893; on computer back to 1995. Mail turnaround time 1 day.

General Information: No public access terminal. No adoption, juvenile or sanity records released. Fee to fax documents is $1.00 per page. Certification fee: $2.00 per document. Payee: Clerk of Court. Personal checks accepted. Prepayment and SASE required.

Limited Jurisdiction Court PO Box 337, 1 Main Ave S, Choteau, MT 59422; phone: 406-466-5611; fax: 406-466-2138; hours 8AM-N, 1-5PM (MST). *Misdemeanor, Civil Actions Under $7,000, Eviction, Small Claims.*

Toole County

District Court PO Box 850, Shelby, MT 59474; phone: 406-424-8330; criminal fax: 406-424-8331; same fax for civil/probate; hours 8AM-5PM (MST). *Felony, Civil Actions Over $5,000, Eviction, Probate.*

Civil Records: Access: Phone, fax, mail, in person. Both court and visitors may perform in person searches. Search fee: $2.00 per name per year, first 7 years, then $1.00 per year. Court makes copy: $1.00 per page first 10 pages, then $.50 per page after. Self serve copy fee: $1.00 per page. Required to search: name, years to search. Civil cases indexed by defendant, plaintiff. Civil records in books from 1914; on computer since 1997. Mail turnaround time same day as request received.

Criminal Records: Access: Phone, fax, mail, in person. Both court and visitors may perform in person searches. Search fee: $2.00 per name per year, first 7 years, then $1.00 per year. Court makes copy: $1.00 per page first 10 pages, then $.50 per page after. Self serve copy fee: $1.00 per page. Required to search: name, years to search, DOB, SSN. Criminal records in books from 1914; on computer since 1997. Mail turnaround time same day as request received.

General Information: No public access terminal. No adoption, juvenile or sanity records released. Will fax documents $.50 per page. Certification fee: $2.00 per document. Payee: Clerk of Court. Personal checks accepted. Prepayment and SASE required.

Limited Jurisdiction Court PO Box 738, Shelby, MT 59474; phone: 406-924-8315; fax: 406-424-8316; hours 9AM-5PM M-F (MST). *Misdemeanor, Civil Actions Under $7,000, Eviction, Small Claims.*

Treasure County

District Court PO Box 392, Hysham, MT 59038; phone: 406-342-5547; fax: 406-342-5445; hours 8AM-5PM (MST). *Felony, Civil Actions Over $5,000, Eviction, Probate.*

Civil Records: Access: Fax, mail, in person. Both court and visitors may perform in person searches. Search fee: $2.00 per name per year, first 7 years, then $1.00 per year. Court makes copy: $1.00 per page first 10 pages, then $.50 per page after. Required to search: name, years to search. Civil cases indexed by

defendant, plaintiff, on books since 1919, on microfilm from 1985 to present; on computer back to 1996. Mail turnaround time usually 1 day.

Criminal Records: Access: Fax, mail, in person. Both court and visitors may perform in person searches. Search fee: $2.00 per name per year, first 7 years, then $1.00 per year. Court makes copy: $1.00 per page first 10 pages, then $.50 per page after. Required to search: name, years to search, DOB. Criminal records on books since 1919, on microfilm from 1985 to present; on computer back to 1996. Mail turnaround time 1 week.

General Information: No public access terminal. No adoption or sanity records released. Fee to fax documents to $1.50 per page. Certification fee: $2.00. Payee: Clerk of Court. Personal checks accepted. Prepayment and SASE required.

Limited Jurisdiction Court PO Box 297, 307 Rapelje Ave, Hysham, MT 59038-0297; phone: 406-342-5532; fax: 406-342-5532; hours 9AM-N (MST). *Misdemeanor, Civil Actions Under $7,000, Eviction, Small Claims.*

Valley County

Clerk of District Court 501 Court Sq #6, Glasgow, MT 59230; phone: 406-228-6268; criminal fax: 406-228-6212; same fax for civil/probate; hours 8AM-5PM (MST). *Felony, Civil Actions Over $5,000, Eviction, Probate.*

Civil Records: Access: Phone, fax, mail, in person. Only the court performs in person searches; visitors may not. Search fee: $2.00 per name per year, first 7 years, then $1.00 per year. Court makes copy: $1.00 per page first 10 pages, then $.50 per page after. Required to search: name, years to search. Civil cases indexed by defendant, plaintiff. Civil records in books since 1893; on computer back to 1996. Mail turnaround time same day.

Criminal Records: Access: Fax, mail, in person. Only the court performs in person searches; visitors may not. Search fee: $2.00 per name per year, first 7 years, then $1.00 per year. Court makes copy: $1.00 per page first 10 pages, then $.50 per page after. Required to search: name, years to search, signed release. Criminal records in books since 1893; on computer back to 1996. Mail turnaround time same day.

General Information: No public access terminal. No adoption, juvenile or sanity records released. Fee to fax documents is $1.00 per page. Certification fee: $2.00 per document. Payee: Clerk of Court. Business checks accepted. Prepayment and SASE required.

Limited Jurisdiction Court 501 Court Sq #10, Glasgow, MT 59230; phone: 406-228-6271; fax: 406-228-4601; hours 8AM-N (MST). *Misdemeanor, Civil Actions Under $7,000, Eviction, Small Claims.*

Wheatland County

District Court Box 227, Harlowton, MT 59036; phone: 406-632-4893; fax: 406-632-4873; probate fax: same; hours 8AM-N, 1-5PM (MST). *Felony, Civil Actions Over $5,000, Eviction, Probate.*

Civil Records: Access: Fax, mail, in person. Both court and visitors may perform in person searches. Search fee: $2.00 per name per year, first 7 years, then $1.00 per year. Court makes copy: $1.00 per page first 10 pages, then $.50 per page after. Required to search: name, years to search. Civil cases indexed by defendant, plaintiff. Computerized records back to 1996, civil records on docket books since 1917, probate on microfiche from 1984. Mail turnaround time next day.

Criminal Records: Access: Mail, in person. Both court and visitors may perform in person searches. Search fee: $2.00 per name per year, first 7 years, then $1.00 per year. Court makes copy: $1.00 per page first 10 pages, then $.50 per page after. Required to search: name, years to search. Computerized records back to 1996, criminal records on docket books since 1917, probate on microfiche from 1984. Mail turnaround time next day.

General Information: No public access terminal. No adoption, juvenile or sanity records released. Will fax documents to local or toll free line. Certification fee: $2.00. Payee: Clerk of Court. Personal checks accepted. Prepayment and SASE required.

Limited Jurisdiction Court PO Box 524, 201 A Ave NW, Harlowton, MT 59036; phone: 406-632-4821; fax: 406-632-4880; hours 10AM-1PM T,Th (MST). *Misdemeanor, Civil Actions Under $7,000, Eviction, Small Claims.*

Wibaux County

District Court PO Box 292, Wibaux, MT 59353; phone: 406-796-2484; hours 8AM-5PM, Closed 12-1 (MST). *Felony, Civil Actions Over $5,000, Eviction, Probate.*

Civil Records: Access: Phone, fax, mail, in person. Both court and visitors may perform in person searches. Search fee: $2.00 per name per year, first 7 years, then $1.00 per year. Court makes copy: $1.00 per page first 10 pages, then $.50 per page after. Self serve copy fee: $.10 per page. Required to search: name, years to search. Civil records on docket books since 1914, on computer since 1/97. Mail turnaround time 1 week.

Criminal Records: Access: Phone, fax, mail, in person. Only the court performs in person searches; visitors may not. Search fee: $2.00 per name per year, first 7 years, then $1.00 per year. Court makes copy: $1.00 per page first 10 pages, then $.50 per page after. Required to search: name, years to search. Criminal records on docket books since 1914, on computer since 1/97. Mail turnaround time 1 week.

General Information: No public access terminal. No adoption, juvenile or sanity records released. Will fax documents $2.00 1st page, $.50 each add'l, turnaround time is 2-3 days. Certification fee: $2.00. Payee: Clerk of Court. Personal checks accepted. Prepayment and SASE required.

Limited Jurisdiction Court PO Box 445, Wibaux, MT 59353; phone: 406-796-2484; fax: 406-796-2484; hours 1-5PM M&W, 8AM-N Fri (MST). *Misdemeanor, Civil Actions Under $7,000, Eviction, Small Claims.*

Yellowstone County

District Court PO Box 35030, 217 N 27 St, Billings, MT 59107; phone: 406-256-2862; criminal phone: 406-256-2860; civil phone: 406-256-2851; probate phone: 406-256-2865; fax: 406-256-2995; hours 8AM-5PM (MST). *Felony, Civil Actions Over $7,000, Probate.*
www.co.yellowstone.mt.us/clerk_court

Civil Records: Access: Mail, in person. Both court and visitors may perform in person searches. Search fee: $2.00 per name per year, first 7 years, then $1.00 per year. Court makes copy: $1.00 per page first 10 pages, then $.50 per page after. Required to search: name, years to search. Civil cases indexed by defendant, plaintiff. Civil records in books, on microfilm back to 1800s; on computer back to 1992. Mail turnaround time 1 day if record less than 10 years old.

Criminal Records: Access: Mail, in person. Both court and visitors may perform in person searches. Search fee: $2.00 per name per year, first 7 years, then $1.00 per year. Court makes copy: $1.00 per page first 10 pages, then $.50 per page after. Required to search: name, years to search. Criminal records in books, on microfilm back to 1800s; on computer back to 1990. Mail turnaround time 1 day if record less than 10 years old.

General Information: Public terminal goes back to 1990. No adoption, juvenile or sanity records released. Certification fee: $2.00 per cert. Payee: Clerk of Court. Personal checks not accepted. Prepayment and SASE required.

Limited Jurisdiction Court PO Box 35032, Billings, MT 59107; phone: 406-256-2895; fax: 406-256-2898; hours 9AM-5PM (MST). *Misdemeanor, Civil Actions Under $7,000, Eviction, Small Claims.*
www.co.yellowstone.mt.us

Montana Recording Offices

ORGANIZATION: 57 counties, 56 recording offices. The recording officer is County Clerk and Recorder (Clerk of District Court for state tax liens). Yellowstone National Park is considered a county, but is not included as a filing location. The entire state is in the Mountain Time Zone (MST).

REAL ESTATE RECORDS: Many Montana counties will perform real estate searches. Search and copy fees vary. Certification usually costs $2.00 per document.

UCC RECORDS: Financing statements are filed at the state level, except for real estate related collateral, which are filed with the Clerk and Recorder. However, prior to 07/2001, consumer goods collateral were also filed at the county and these older records can be searched there. All counties will perform UCC searches. Use search request form UCC-11. Search fees are usually $7.00 per debtor name. Copy fees vary.

TAX LIEN RECORDS: Federal tax liens on personal property of businesses are filed with the Secretary of State. Other federal tax liens are filed with the county Clerk and Recorder. State tax liens are filed with the Clerk of District Court. Usually tax liens on personal property filed with the Clerk and Recorder are in the same index with UCC financing statements. Most counties will perform tax lien searches, some as part of a UCC search and others for a separate fee, usually $7.00 per name. Copy fees vary.

OTHER LIENS: Mechanics, thresherman, judgment, lis pendens, construction, logger.

ONLINE ACCESS: Search for a for a Montana property owner by name and county on the Montana Cadastral Mapping Project GIS mapping database at http://gis.doa.state.mt.us

Beaverhead County

Clerk and Recorder, 2 South Pacific, Dillon, MT 59725-2799. 406-683-3720; fax-406-683-3769; hours: 8AM-5PM.
Separate indices to search include deeds, mortgages, POA, cert of survey & plats, mining claim locations, mining claim work. Records indexed on a public use terminal back to 2003. Office will perform a UCC search but public must search other records themselves. UCC search per debtor name- $7.00. Copy fee $1.00 per page. R/E record copy- $.50 1st page, $.25 each add'l page. Cert fee- $2.00 per cert plus copy fee. Payee-Beaverhead County Clerk and Recorder. **Online access to Property records:** Name searching on the statewide Cadastral database is free at http://gis.doa.state.mt.us/searchOwner.htm. **Other phones:** Treasurer- 406-683-5821; Appraiser/Auditor-406-683-4000; Elections- 406-683-3720; Vital Records- 406-683-3720.

Big Horn County

Clerk and Recorder, PO Box 908, Hardin, MT 59034. 406-665-9730, UCC recording phone-406-665-9732; fax-406-665-9738; hours: 8AM-5PM.
All records in one index, since 07/01/01. Office personnel or visitors may perform searches. Search fee $7.00. Copy fee $.50 1st page, $.25 each add'l. Cert fee- $2.00 per doc, copies not included. Payee- Clerk - Recorder. **Other phones:** Treasurer-406-665-9830; Appraiser/Auditor- 406-665-9710; Elections- 406-665-9730; Vital Records- 406-665-9730. **Property tax/Assessor-** 406-665-9710.

Blaine County

Clerk and Recorder, PO Box 278, Chinook, MT 59523-0278. 406-357-3240; fax-406-357-2199; hours: 8AM-5PM.
Records indexed on a public use terminal back to 2004. Only the public may search. Copy fee $.25 per copy. Cert fee- $2.00 per doc plus copy fee. Payee- Blaine County Clerk. **Online access to Property records:** Name searching on the statewide Cadastral database is free at http://gis.doa.state.mt.us/searchOwner.htm. **Other phones:** Treasurer- 406-357-3280; Appraiser/Auditor-406-357-3210; Elections- 406-357-3240; Vital Records- 406-357-3240. **Property tax/Assessor-** 406-357-3210.

Broadwater County

Clerk and Recorder, 515 Broadway, Townsend, MT 59644. 406-266-3443; fax-406-266-3674; hours: 8AM-5PM.
All records in one index. Records indexed on a public use terminal back to 1995. Office will perform a UCC search but public must search other records themselves. UCC search per debtor name- $7.00. Copy fee $.50 for 1st page, $.25 each add'l. Cert fee- $2.00 per doc plus copy fee. Payee- Broadwater County Clerk. **Online access to Property records:** Name searching on the statewide Cadastral database is free at http://gis.doa.state.mt.us/searchOwner.htm. **Other phones:** Treasurer- 406-266-3445; Appraiser/Auditor-406-266-3430; Elections- 406-266-3443; Vital Records- 406-266-3443. **Property tax/Assessor-** same address as above. 406-266-3430.

Carbon County

Clerk and Recorder, PO Box 887, Red Lodge, MT 59068. 406-446-1220; fax-406-446-2640; hours: 7AM-5:30PM. www.co.carbon.mt.us
All records in one index. Records indexed back to May, 1995. Will not search real estate records. Will search UCC records. UCC search per debtor name- $7.00. Separate federal tax lien search- $7.00 per debtor. Copy fee $.25 per page, $1.00 minimum if real estate. Cert fee- $2.00 per doc includes copy fee. Payee- Clerk and Recorder. **Online access to Property records:** Name searching on the statewide Cadastral database is free at http://gis.doa.state.mt.us/searchOwner.htm. **Other phones:** Treasurer- 406-446-1221; Appraiser/Auditor-406-446-1224; Elections- 406-446-1595; Vital Records- 406-446-1220. **Property tax/Assessor-** PO Box 647, Red Lodge, MT 59068; 406-466-1223.

Carter County

Clerk and Recorder, PO Box 315, Ekalaka, MT 59324-0315. 406-775-8749; fax-406-775-8750; hours: 8AM-N, 1-5PM. www.cartercountymt.com
Separate indices to search include deed, mortgage, misc. Records indexed on a public use terminal back to 2/2002. General index search fee $7.00 per name. Copy fee $.50 1st page; $.25 each add'l. Cert fee- $2.00 per doc plus copy fee. Payee- Carter County Clerk. **Online access to Property records:** Name searching on the statewide Cadastral

database is free at http://gis.doa.state.mt.us/searchOwner.htm. **Other phones:** Treasurer- 406-775-8735; Elections- 406-775-8749; Vital Records- 406-775-8749. **Property tax/Assessor-** 406-775-8717.

Cascade County

Clerk and Recorder, PO Box 2867, Great Falls, MT 59403-2867. 406-454-6800, R/E recording phone-406-454-6801; fax-406-454-6802; hours: 8AM-5PM. www.co.cascade.mt.us
All records in one index. Records indexed on a public use terminal back to 1988. Office personnel or visitors may perform searches. Search fee $37.00 for lien searches. Copy fee $.50 per page. R/E record copy- $.50 1st page, $.25 each add'l page. Tax lien copy- $7.00 per name. Cert fee- $2.00 per doc plus copy fee. Payee- Clerk & Recorder. **Online access to Property, Real Estate Recording, Deed records:** Name searching on the statewide Cadastral database is free at http://gis.doa.state.mt.us/searchOwner.htm. Also, access recording office land data at www.etitlesearch.com; registration required, fee based on usage. **Other phones:** Treasurer- 406-454-6850; Appraiser/Auditor-406-454-7460; Elections- 406-454-6803; Vital Records- 406-454-6718. **Property tax/Assessor-** 406-454-6744.

Chouteau County

Clerk and Recorder, PO Box 459, Fort Benton, MT 59442-0459. 406-622-5151; fax-406-622-3012; hours: 8AM-5PM.
Records indexed on a public use terminal back to 4/95. Office personnel or visitors may perform searches. General index search fee $5.00 per name. UCC search per debtor name- $7.00. Separate federal tax lien search- $7.00 per debtor. Separate federal/state combined tax lien search- $7.00 per debtor. Copy fee $.50 per page. Cert fee- $2.00 per cert plus copy fee. Payee- Chouteau County Clerk and Recorder. **Online access to Property records:** Name searching on the statewide Cadastral database is free at http://gis.doa.state.mt.us/searchOwner.htm. **Other phones:** Treasurer- 406-622-5032; Elections-406-622-5151; Vital Records- 406-622-5151. **Property tax/Assessor-** 406-622-5261.

Custer County

Clerk and Recorder, 1010 Main St, Miles City, MT 59301-1010. 406-874-3343; fax-406-874-3452; hours: 8AM-5PM.

Records indexed on a public use terminal back to June, 1994. Office personnel or visitors may perform searches. Search fee $7.00 per book. Copy fee $.50 per page. R/E or tax lien copy- $7.00 per 10 years per book. Cert fee- $2.00 per cert plus copy fee. Payee- Custer County Clerk and Recorder. **Online access to Property records:** Name searching on the statewide Cadastral database is free at http://gis.doa.state.mt.us/searchOwner.htm. **Other phones:** Treasurer- 406-874-3427; Appraiser/Auditor-406-232-6437; Elections- 406-874-3343; Vital Records- 406-444-4228. **Property tax/Assessor-** same address as above. 406-232-1295.

Daniels County

Clerk and Recorder, PO Box 247, Scobey, MT 59263. 406-487-5561; hours: 8AM-5PM.

Separate indices to search include deeds, mortgages, misc. Only the office personnel may search. Search fee $.50 per year unless otherwise indicated. UCC search per debtor name- $7.00. Separate federal tax lien search- $7.00 per debtor. Copy fee $.50 1st page, $.25 each add'l. Cert fee- $2.00 per cert plus copy fee. Payee- Daniels County Clerk and Recorder. **Online access to Property records:** Name searching on the statewide Cadastral database is free at http://gis.doa.state.mt.us/searchOwner.htm. **Other phones:** Treasurer- 406-487-2671; Appraiser/Auditor-406-487-2791; Elections- 406-487-5561; Vital Records- 406-487-5561. **Property tax/Assessor-** PO Box 397, Scobey, MT 59263; 406-487-2791.

Dawson County

Clerk and Recorder, 207 W. Bell, Glendive, MT 59330. 406-377-3058; fax-406-377-1717; hours: 8AM-5PM. www.dawsoncountymontana.org

All records in one index. Records indexed on computer by document number. Office personnel or visitors may perform searches. Will not search real estate records. Will search UCC records, but not tax liens. UCC search per debtor name- $7.00. Copy fee $.50 1st page; $.25 each add'l. Cert fee- $2.00 per doc plus $.50 1st page, $.25 each add'l page plus copy fee. Payee- Clerk and Recorder. **Online access to Property records:** Name searching on the statewide Cadastral database is free at http://gis.doa.state.mt.us/searchOwner.htm. **Other phones:** Treasurer- 406-377-3026; Appraiser/Auditor-406-377-4500; Elections- 406-377-3058; Vital Records- 406-377-3058. **Property tax/Assessor-** 207 W Bell, Glendive, MT 59330; 406-377-4256.

Deer Lodge County

Clerk and Recorder, 800 Main St.; Courthouse, Anaconda, MT 59711-2999. 406-563-4060, R/E recording phone-406-563-4061; fax-406-563-4001; hours: 8AM-5PM.

Records indexed on a public use terminal back to 1987. Only the public may search. General index search fee $6.00 per page. Copy fee $.50 per page. Cert fee- $2.00 per doc plus copy fee. **Online access to Property, Real Estate Recording, Deed records:** Name searching on the statewide Cadastral database is free at http://gis.doa.state.mt.us/searchOwner.htm. Also, access recording office land data at www.etitlesearch.com; registration required, fee based on usage. **Other phones:** Treasurer- 406-563-4051; Appraiser/Auditor-406-563-4045; Elections- 406-563-4060; Vital Records- 406-563-4062. **Property tax/Assessor-** same address as above. 406-563-4045.

Fallon County

Clerk and Recorder, PO Box 846, Baker, MT 59313-0846. 406-778-7106; fax-406-778-2048; hours: 8AM-5PM.

Separate indices in books to search include deeds, misc, mortgages, assignments. Newer records

indexed on computer. General index search fee $7.00 per debtor. Copy fee $.50 per page; $.25 each add'l. Cert fee- $2.00 per doc plus copy fee. Payee- Clerk and Recorder. **Online access to Property records:** Name searching on the statewide Cadastral database is free at http://gis.doa.state.mt.us/searchOwner.htm. **Other phones:** Treasurer- 406-778-7109; Appraiser/Auditor-406-778-7172; Elections- 406-778-7105; Vital Records- 406-778-7106. **Property tax/Assessor-** 406-778-7109.

Fergus County

Clerk and Recorder, 712 W. Main, Lewistown, MT 59457. 406-538-5242; fax-406-538-9023; hours: 8AM-5PM.

Records indexed on computer since 1989, otherwise indexed by document type in separate book indexes. Search fee $7.00 per name. Will not search real estate records. Will search UCC records; search includes tax liens if requested. Copy fee $.50 per page. Cert fee- $2.00 per doc plus copy fee. Payee- Clerk Recorder. **Online access to Property, Real estate Recording, Deed records:** Name searching on the statewide Cadastral database is free at http://gis.doa.state.mt.us/searchOwner.htm. Also, access recording office land data at www.etitlesearch.com; registration required, fee based on usage. **Other phones:** Treasurer- 406-538-9220; Appraiser/Auditor-406-538-5723; Elections- 406-538-5242; Vital Records- 406-538-5242. **Property tax/Assessor-** same address as above. 406-538-5723.

Flathead County

Clerk and Recorder, 800 S. Main, 2nd Fl; Courthouse, Kalispell, MT 59901-5400. 406-758-5534, R/E recording phone-406-758-5526; fax-406-758-5865; hours: 8AM-5PM. www.co.flathead.mt.us

All records in one index. Records indexed on a public use terminal back to 1/1/1984. Office personnel or visitors may perform searches. Search fee $7.00 per name. Copy fee $1.00 per page. R/E or tax lien copy- $.50 1st copy, $.25 each add'l page. Cert fee- $2.00 per doc plus copy fee. Payee- Flathead County Clerk and Recorder. **Online access to Property records:** Name searching on the statewide Cadastral database is free at http://gis.doa.state.mt.us/searchOwner.htm. **Other phones:** Treasurer- 406-758-5688; Elections- 406-758-5535; Vital Records- 406-758-5527. **Property tax/Assessor-** 100 Financial Dr #210, Kallspell, MT 59901; 406-758-5700.

Gallatin County

Clerk and Recorder, 311 W. Main, Rm 204; Rm 204, Bozeman, MT 59715. 406-582-3050; fax-406-582-3037; hours: 8AM-5PM. www.co.gallatin.mt.us/webtax/default.asp

All records in one index. Records indexed on a public use terminal back to 1/1/1990. Office personnel or visitors may perform searches. Search fee $.50 per year/per name/per index. Copy fee $1.00 per page. R/E or tax lien copy- $.50 1st page; $.25 each add'l page. Cert fee- $2.00 per doc plus copy fee. Payee- Gallatin County Clerk and Recorder. **Online access to Property, Tax, Treasurer, Real Estate, Deed records:** Name searching on the statewide Cadastral database is free at http://gis.doa.state.mt.us/searchOwner.htm. Also, access to the treasurer's property tax data is free at www.co.gallatin.mt.us/webtax/default.asp. Also, access recording office land data at www.etitlesearch.com; registration required, fee based on usage. **Other phones:** Treasurer- 406-582-3030; Appraiser/Auditor-406-582 3400; Elections- 406-582-3060; Vital Records- 406-582-3050; State tax liens/district court- 406-582-2165. **Property tax/Assessor-** 2273 Boothill Ct #100, Bozeman, MT 59715; 406-582-3400.

Garfield County

Clerk and Recorder, PO Box 7, Jordan, MT 59337-0007. 406-557-2760; fax-406-557-2625; hours: 8AM-5PM.

Separate indices to search include Deeds, mtgs, misc. Record index not computerized. Office personnel or visitors may perform searches. Search fee $7.00. Copy fee $.50 1st page, $.25 each add'l. Cert fee- $2.00 per doc plus copy fee. **Online access to Property records:** Name searching on the statewide Cadastral database is free at http://gis.doa.state.mt.us/searchOwner.htm. **Other phones:** Treasurer- 406-557-2233; Appraiser/Auditor-406-557-2772; Elections- 406-557-2760; Vital Records- 406-557-2760. **Property tax/Assessor-** 406-557-6164.

Glacier County

County Clerk and Recorder, 512 E. Main, Cut Bank, MT 59427. 406-873-5063 x22; fax-406-873-2125; hours: 8AM-5PM.

Separate indices to search include Deed, Mortgage (various), Liens, UCC, Misc, O/G (various). Records indexed on a public use terminal. Office will perform a UCC search but public must search other records themselves. UCC search includes tax liens if requested. UCC search per debtor name- $7.00. Separate federal tax lien search- $7.00 per debtor. Copy fee $.50 per page. Tax lien copy- $.25 per page. Cert fee- $2.00 per doc plus copy fee. **Online access to Property records:** Name searching on the statewide Cadastral database is free at http://gis.doa.state.mt.us/searchOwner.htm. **Other phones:** Treasurer- 406-873-5063 x31; Appraiser/Auditor- 406-873-5063 x45; Elections- 406-873-5063 x19; Vital Records- 406-873-5063 x22. **Property tax/Assessor-** 406-873-5063 x43.

Golden Valley County

Clerk and Recorder, PO Box 10, Ryegate, MT 59074. 406-568-2231; fax-406-568-2231; hours: 8AM-5PM.

Separate indices to search. Record index not computerized. Office will perform a UCC and Lis Pendens search but public must search other records themselves. UCC search per debtor name- $7.00 per year. Copy fee $.50 per page. Cert fee- $2.00 per doc plus copy fee. Payee- Clerk/ Recorder/ Clerk of Court. **Online access to Property records:** Name searching on the statewide Cadastral database is free at http://gis.doa.state.mt.us/searchOwner.htm. **Other phones:** Treasurer- 406-586-2342; Elections- 406-568-2231; Vital Records- 406-568-2231. **Property tax/Assessor-** 107 Kemp, Ryegate, MT 59074; 406-586-2371.

Granite County

Clerk and Recorder, PO Box 925, Philipsburg, MT 59858. 406-859-3771; fax-406-859-3817; hours: 8AM-5PM.

Records indexed on a public use terminal back to 11/2000. Office will perform a UCC and Tax lien search but public must search other records themselves. Search fee $7.00. Copy fee $.50 1st page; $.25 each add'l. Cert fee- $2.00 per doc plus copy fee. Payee- Clerk & Recorder. **Online access to Property, Real Estate Recording, Deed records:** Name searching on the statewide Cadastral database is free at http://gis.doa.state.mt.us/searchOwner.htm. Also, access recording office land data at www.etitlesearch.com; registration required, fee based on usage. **Other phones:** Treasurer- 406-859-3831; Elections- 406-859-3771; Vital Records- 406-859-3771. **Property tax/Assessor-** 406-859-3521.

Hill County

Clerk and Recorder, 315 4th St; Courthouse, Havre, MT 59501. 406-265-5481; fax-406-265-2445; hours: 8AM-5PM. http://co.hill.mt.us

Separate indices to search include Deed, Mortgage, Miscellaneous, Leases, Satisfactions, UCC's, Liens. Records indexed on computer since 10/1/2001. Above records in alphabetical order in prior main indexes. Only the public may search. Copy fee $.50 1st page, $.25 each add'l. Cert fee- $2.00 per doc plus copy fee. Payee- Hill County Clerk and Recorder. **Online access to Property**

records: Name searching on the statewide Cadastral database is free at http://gis.doa.state.mt.us/searchOwner.htm. (These are Revenue Tax Records and do not include most current ownership and legal description. Are incomplete. **Other phones:** Treasurer- 406-265-5481 x257; Elections- 406-265-5481 x221, 222, 223; Vital Records- 406-265-5481 x221, 222, 223. **Property tax/Assessor-** 315 4th St, Courthouse, Havre, MT 59501; 406-265-5481 x210.

Jefferson County

Clerk and Recorder, PO Box H, Boulder, MT 59632. 406-225-4020; fax-406-225-4149; hours: 8AM-N, 1-5PM. http://co.jefferson.mt.us
Separate indices to search. Records indexed on a public use terminal back to 1990. Only the public may search. Copy fee $.50 1st page, $.25 each add'l. Cert fee- $2.00 per doc plus copy fee. **Online access to Property records:** Name searching on the statewide Cadastral database is free at http://gis.doa.state.mt.us/searchOwner.htm. **Other phones:** Treasurer- 406-225-4103; Appraiser/Auditor- 406-225-4001; Elections- 406-225-4018; Vital Records- 406-225-4020. **Property tax/Assessor-** 406-225-4001.

Judith Basin County

Clerk and Recorder, PO Box 427, Stanford, MT 59479. 406-566-2277; fax-406-566-2211; hours: 8AM-5PM. Separate indices are too numerous to list here. Records indexed on a public use terminal back to 1/1/2002. Search fee $7.00 per name. Real estate searches are subject to limitations. Copy fee $.50 1st page; $.25 each add'l. Cert fee- $2.00 per page plus copy fee. Payee- Clerk & Recorder. **Online access to Property, Real Estate Recording, Deed records:** Name searching on the statewide Cadastral database is free at http://gis.doa.state.mt.us/searchOwner.htm. Also, access recording office land data at www.etitlesearch.com; registration required, fee based on usage. **Other phones:** Treasurer- 406-566-2277; Appraiser/Auditor- 406-566-2291; Elections- 406-566-2277; Vital Records- 406-566-2277. **Property tax/Assessor-** 406-566-2291.

Lake County

Clerk and Recorder, 106 4th Ave East, Polson, MT 59860. 406-883-7210, R/E recording phone-406-883-7208, UCC recording phone-406-883-7210; fax-406-883-7283; hours: 8AM-5PM. www.lakecounty-mt.org
All records in one index. Records indexed on a public use terminal back to January 1, 1989. Office personnel or visitors may perform searches. General index search fee $7.00 per name. Limited Real Estate searches available. Mortgage searches available. Copy fee $.50 per 1st page; $.25 each add'l page. Cert fee- $2.00 per cert plus copy fee. Payee- Lake County Clerk and Recorder. **Online access to Property, Real Estate Recording, Deed records:** Name searching on the statewide Cadastral database is free at http://gis.doa.state.mt.us/searchOwner.htm. Also, access recording office land data at www.etitlesearch.com; registration required, fee based on usage. **Other phones:** Treasurer- 406-883-7224; Appraiser/Auditor- 406-883-7232; Elections- 406-883-7268; Vital Records- 406-883-7208; Clerk of Court (tax liens)- 406-883-7254; Commissioners- 406-883-7204. **Property tax/Assessor-** same address as above. 406-883-7232.

Lewis and Clark County

Clerk and Recorder, PO Box 1721, Helena, MT 59624. 406-447-8337; fax-406-457-8598; hours: 8AM-5PM. www.co.lewis-clark.mt.us
Records indexed on a public use terminal back to 2001. Office personnel or visitors may perform searches. Search fee $7.00 per name. Copy fee $1.00 per page. R/E record copy- $.50 1st page, $.25 each add'l page. Cert fee- $2.00 per cert plus

copy fee. Payee- Lewis and Clark County Clerk and Recorder. **Online access to Grantor/Grantee, Real Estate, Lien, Recording, Property records:** The Grantor/Grantee index and recorder records are free at http://records.co.lewis-clark.mt.us/splash.jsp. Registration, logon and password required. This new automation includes document imaging via subscription online service. Records go back to 4/2001. Also, name searching on the statewide Cadastral database is free at http://gis.doa.state.mt.us/searchOwner.htm. **Other phones:** Treasurer- 406-447-8329; Elections- 406-447-8338; Vital Records- 406-447-8335. **Property tax/Assessor-** 406-444-4000.

Liberty County

Clerk and Recorder, PO Box 459, Chester, MT 59522-0459. 406-759-5365; fax-406-759-5395; hours: 8AM-5PM. www.co.liberty.mt.us
Separate indices to search include Deeds, Assets, Oil and Gas leases, mtgs, misc. Records indexed on a public use terminal back to 2000. Office will perform a UCC and Tax lien search but public must search other records themselves. Search fee $7.00. Copy fee $.50, if real estate $.25 per page. Cert fee- $2.00 per doc, plus $.50 per page. Payee- Clerk & Recorder. **Online access to Property records:** Name searching on the statewide Cadastral database is free at http://gis.doa.state.mt.us/searchOwner.htm. **Other phones:** Treasurer- 406-759-5455; Appraiser/Auditor- 406-759-5126; Elections- 406-759-5365; Vital Records- 406-759-5365.

Lincoln County

Recorder, 512 California Ave, Libby, MT 59923. 406-293-7781, R/E recording phone-406-293-7781 x205; fax-406-293-8577; hours: 8AM-5PM.
Office personnel or visitors may perform searches. Search fee $7.00 per name. Will not search real estate records. Copy fee $.50 per page. Cert fee- $2.00 per page. Payee- Clerk/Recorder. **Online access to Property, Real Estate Recording, Deed records:** Name searching on the statewide Cadastral database is free at http://gis.doa.state.mt.us/searchOwner.htm. Also, access recording office land data at www.etitlesearch.com; registration required, fee based on usage. **Other phones:** Treasurer- 406-293-7781 x253; Appraiser/Auditor- 406-293-7781 x219; Elections- 406-293-7781 x283; Vital Records- 406-293-7781 x205; Clerk of Court- 406-293-7781 x243. **Property tax/Assessor-** 406-293-7781 x213.

Madison County

Clerk and Recorder, PO Box 366, Virginia City, MT 59755. 406-843-4270; hours: 8AM-N,1-5PM.
Search fee $7.00 per name. Copy fee $1.00 per page. R/E or tax lien copy- $.50 per page. Cert fee- $2.00 per doc plus $.50 per copy. Payee- Madison County Clerk and Recorder. **Online access to Property, Real Estate Recording, Deed records:** Name searching on the statewide Cadastral database is free at http://gis.doa.state.mt.us/searchOwner.htm. Also, access recording office land data at www.etitlesearch.com; registration required, fee based on usage. **Other phones:** Treasurer- 406-843-4212. **Property tax/Assessor-** 406-843-5392.

McCone County

Clerk and Recorder, PO Box 199, Circle, MT 59215-0199. 406-485-3505; fax-406-485-2689; hours: 8AM-5PM.
Separate indices to search include deed, miscellaneous, mortgages, satisfaction of mortgages, liens, UCC's, tract books. Record index not computerized. Office personnel or visitors may perform searches. Search fee $7.00 per name. Copy fee $.25 per page. Cert fee- $2.00 per cert plus copy fee. Payee- McCone County Clerk and Recorder. **Online access to Property records:** Name searching on the statewide Cadastral database is free at http://gis.doa.state.mt.us/searchOwner.htm. **Other phones:** Treasurer- 406-485-3590; Appraiser/Auditor-

406-485-3432; Elections- 406-485-3505; Vital Records- 406-485-3505. **Property tax/Assessor-** 406-485-3565.

Meagher County

Deputy Clerk & Recording, PO Box 309, White Sulphur Springs, MT 59645. 406-547-3612; fax-406-547-3388; hours: 9AM-4PM.
Separate indices to search include Deeds, Mortgages, Miscellaneous. Records indexed on computer back to 1995. Office will perform a UCC search but public must search other records themselves. UCC search per debtor name- $7.00. Copy fee $.50 1st page; $.25 each add'l. R/E record copy- $.50 per page, with book and page info given. Cert fee- $2.00 per cert plus copy fee. Payee- Meagher County Clerk & Recorder. **Online access to Property records:** Name searching on the statewide Cadastral database is free at http://gis.doa.state.mt.us/searchOwner.htm. **Other phones:** Treasurer- 406-547-3641; Appraiser/Auditor- 406-547-3653; Elections- 406-547-3612; Vital Records- 406-547-3612. **Property tax/Assessor-** 406-547-3653.

Mineral County

Clerk and Recorder, PO Box 550, Superior, MT 59872-0550. 406-822-3520; fax-406-822-3579; hours: 8AM-5PM.
All records in one index. Records indexed on a public use terminal back to 1998. Office will perform a UCC search but public must search other records themselves. UCC search per debtor name- $7.00. Copy fee $.50 1st page; $.25 each add'l. Cert fee- $2.00 per doc plus copy fee. Payee- Clerk & Recorder. **Online access to Property, Real Estate Recording, Deed records:** Name searching on the statewide Cadastral database is free at http://gis.doa.state.mt.us/searchOwner.htm. Also, access recording office land data at www.etitlesearch.com; registration required, fee based on usage. **Other phones:** Treasurer- 406-822-3530; Appraiser/Auditor- 406-822-3540; Elections- 406-822-3520; Vital Records- 406-822-3520. **Property tax/Assessor-** PO Box 669, Superior, MT 59872; 406-822-3540.

Missoula County

Clerk and Recorder, 200 W. Broadway, Missoula, MT 59802-4292. 406-258-4752; fax-406-523-2812; hours: 8AM-5PM. www.co.missoula.mt.us
All records in one index. Search fee $7.00 per name. Will not search real estate records. Copy fee $.50 per page. Tax lien copy- $.50 1st page, $.25 each add'l. Cert fee- $2.00 per doc plus copy fee. Payee- Missoula Clerk & Recorder. **Online access to Property, Assessor, Real Estate Recording, Deed records:** Access to the county property information system is free at www.co.missoula.mt.us/owner/. No name searching at this time. Also, name searching on the statewide Cadastral database is free at http://gis.doa.state.mt.us/searchOwner.htm. Also, access recording office land data at www.etitlesearch.com; registration required, fee based on usage. **Other phones:** Treasurer- 406-258-4847; Appraiser/Auditor- 406-329-1400; Elections- 406-258-4751; Vital Records- 406-258-4752. **Property tax/Assessor-** 2681 Palmer St #2, Missoula, MT 59808; 406-329-1400.

Musselshell County

Clerk and Recorder, 506 Main St; Courthouse, Roundup, MT 59072. 406-323-1104; fax-406-323-3303; hours: 8AM-5PM.
Office will perform a UCC or tax lien search but public must search other records themselves. Search per debtor name- $7.00. Copy fee $.50 per page. Cert fee- $2.00 per doc plus copy fee. Payee- Musselshell County. **Online access to Property records:** Name searching on the statewide Cadastral database is free at http://gis.doa.state.mt.us/searchOwner.htm. **Other phones:** Treasurer- 406-323-2504; Appraiser/Auditor-

406-323-1513; Elections- 406-323-1104; Vital Records- 406-323-1104. **Property tax/Assessor**- same address as above. 406-323-1513.

Park County

Clerk and Recorder, 414 E. Callendar, Livingston, MT 59047. 406-222-4110; hours: 8AM-5PM.
All records in one index. Will not search real estate records. Will search UCC records, UCC search does not include tax liens. UCC search per debtor name- $7.00. Separate federal tax lien search- $7.00 per debtor. R/E record copy- $.50 1st page. Cert fee- $2.00 per cert plus copy fee. Payee- Park County Clerk and Recorder. **Online access to State Property records:** Name searching on the statewide Cadastral database is free at http://gis.doa.state.mt.us/searchOwner.htm. **Other phones:** Treasurer- 406-222-4119; Vital Records- 406-222-4111. **Property tax/Assessor-** 406-222-4113.

Petroleum County

Clerk and Recorder, PO Box 226, Winnett, MT 59087. 406-429-5311; fax-406-429-6328; hours: 8AM-5PM.
Separate indices to search include deeds, mortgages, leases, conveys, liens, assignments, water logs. Search fee $7.00 per name. Mortgage searches available, but will not search other real estate. Copy fee $.50 per page. Cert fee- $2.00 per doc plus copy fee. Payee- Petroleum County Clerk and Recorder. **Online access to Property records:** Name searching on the statewide Cadastral database is free at http://gis.doa.state.mt.us/searchOwner.htm. **Other phones:** Treasurer- 406-429-5551; Appraiser/Auditor- 406-429-5231; Elections- 406-429-5311. **Property tax/Assessor-** same address as above. 406-429-5531.

Phillips County

Recorder, PO Box 360, Malta, MT 59538. 406-654-2423; fax-406-654-2429; hours: 8AM-5PM.
All records in one index. Search fee $7.00. UCC search includes tax liens if requested. Copy fee $.50 per page. Cert fee- $2.00 per doc plus copy fee. Payee- Clerk & Recorder. **Online access to Property records:** Name searching on the statewide Cadastral database is free at http://gis.doa.state.mt.us/searchOwner.htm. **Other phones:** Treasurer- 406-654-1742; Marriage Records- 406-654-1023. **Property tax/Assessor-** 406-654-2123.

Pondera County

Clerk and Recorder, 20 4th Ave S.W, Conrad, MT 59425. 406-271-4000, R/E recording phone-406-271-4001; fax-406-271-4070; hours: 8AM-5PM. http://ponderacountymontana.org
Records indexed on a public use terminal back to 1997. Office personnel or visitors may perform searches. Search fee $7.00 per name. Copy fee $.50 per page. R/E or tax lien copy- $.25 per page plus postage. Cert fee- $2.00 per doc plus copy fee. Payee- Clerk & Recorder. **Other phones:** Treasurer- 406-271-4015; Appraiser/Auditor- 406-271-4012; Elections- 406-271-4000; Vital Records- 406-271-4000. **Property tax/Assessor-** 406-271-4015.

Powder River County

Clerk and Recorder, PO Box 270, Broadus, MT 59317-0270. 406-436-2361; fax-406-436-2151; hours: 8AM-5PM.
Separate indices to search include Deeds, Mortgages,)&G, Assignments, Miscellaneous & Filed, but these are now all consolidated on computer as of 1999. Records indexed on a public use terminal. Office personnel or visitors may perform searches. Search fee $.50 per name per each index. Limited mortgage and property transfer searches available, also UCC and tax liens. Copy fee $.50 $.50 1st page, $.25 each add'l. Cert fee- $2.00 per cert plus copy fee. Payee- Powder River County Clerk and Recorder. **Online access to Property records:** Name searching on the statewide Cadastral database is free at

http://gis.doa.state.mt.us/searchOwner.htm. **Other phones:** Treasurer- 406-436-2444; Elections- 406-436-2361; Vital Records- 406-436-2361. **Property tax/Assessor-** Powder River County Courthouse, Broadus, MT 59317; 406-436-2407.

Powell County

Clerk and Recorder, 409 Missouri Ave, Deer Lodge, MT 59722. 406-846-3680 x222; fax-406-846-3891; hours: 8AM-5PM.
All records in one index. Search fee $7.00 per name. Will not search real estate records. Will search UCC records and tax liens. Copy fee $.50 per page. R/E or tax lien copy- $.50 1st page, $.25 each add'l. Cert fee- $2.00 per cert 1st page, $.25 ea add'l. Payee- Powell County Clerk and Recorder. **Online access to Property records:** Name searching on the statewide Cadastral database is free at http://gis.doa.state.mt.us/searchOwner.htm. **Other phones:** Treasurer- 406-846-3680 x226; Appraiser/Auditor- 406-846-3680 x211; Elections- 406-846-3680 x223; Vital Records- 406-846-3680 x222. **Property tax/Assessor-** same address as above. 406-846-3680 x230.

Prairie County

Clerk and Recorder, PO Box 125, Terry, MT 59349. 406-635-5575; fax-406-635-5576; hours: 8AM-N; 1PM-5PM.
Separate indices to search include all documents, i.e.: deeds, mortgages, etc. Office personnel or visitors may perform searches. Search fee $2.00 per name per year. Will search UCC records. Copy fee $.50 per page. Cert fee- $2.00 per doc plus copy fee. Payee- Clerk and Recorder. **Online access to Property records:** Name searching on the statewide Cadastral database is free at http://gis.doa.state.mt.us/searchOwner.htm. **Other phones:** Treasurer- 406-635-5577; Assessor-. **Property tax/Assessor-** PO Box 566, Terry, MT 59349; 406-635-5560.

Ravalli County

Clerk and Recorder, 215 S Fourth St #C, Hamilton, MT 59840. 406-375-6212; fax-406-375-6326; hours: 9AM-5PM.
www.ravallicounty.mt.gov/county/clerk&recorder.htm
All records in one index. Office personnel or visitors may perform searches. Search fee $7.00 per name. Copy fee $.50 per page. Cert fee- $2.00 per doc includes copy fees. **Online access to Property, Real Estate, Recording, Deed records:** Name searching on the statewide Cadastral database is free at http://gis.doa.state.mt.us/searchOwner.htm. Also, access property tax and recorder real estate and recording data by subscription at www.ravallicounty.mt.gov/county/clerk_services.htm; fee is $400 yearly plus $125 user fee. Also, access recording office land data at www.etitlesearch.com; registration required, fee based on usage. **Other phones:** Treasurer- 406-375-6300; Appraiser/Auditor- 406-375-6312; Elections- 406-375-6213; Vital Records- 406-375-6212. **Property tax/Assessor-** 406-375-6311.

Richland County

Clerk and Recorder, 201 W. Main St, Sidney, MT 59270. 406-433-1708; fax-406-433-3731; hours: 8AM-5PM. www.richland.org
Separate indices to search include deeds, mortgages, misc, tracking indices, town. Will search real estate records. Will search UCC records, but not tax liens. UCC search per debtor name- $7.00. Copy fee $1.00 per page; $.50 self serve, or $.25 if the lucky copy machine used. Cert fee- $2.00 per doc plus copy fee. Payee- Richland County Clerk and Recorder. **Online access to Property records:** Name searching on the statewide Cadastral database is free at http://gis.doa.state.mt.us/searchOwner.htm. **Other phones:** Treasurer- 406-433-1707; Appraiser/Auditor- 406-433-2850; Elections- 406-433-1708; Vital Records- 406-433-1708. **Property**

tax/Assessor- same address as above. 406-433-1203.

Roosevelt County

Clerk and Recorder, 400 2nd Ave South, Wolf Point, MT 59201. 406-653-6250; fax-406-653-6289; hours: 8AM-5PM.
Separate indices to search include tract, ownership. Records indexed on computer back to 1995. Office will perform a UCC search but public must search other records themselves. UCC or tax lien search per debtor name- $7.00. Copy fee $.50 per page. Cert fee- $2.00 per doc plus copy fee. Payee- Clerk & Recorder. **Online access to Property records:** Name searching on the statewide Cadastral database is free at http://gis.doa.state.mt.us/searchOwner.htm. **Other phones:** Treasurer- 406-653-6239; Appraiser/Auditor- 406-653-6257; Elections- 406-653-6229; Vital Records- 406-653-6252; 406-653-6233. **Property tax/Assessor-** same address as above. 406-653-6256.

Rosebud County

Clerk and Recorder, PO Box 47, Forsyth, MT 59327. 406-346-2251; fax-406-346-7551; hours: 8AM-5PM.
Records indexed on a public use terminal back to 11/1993. Office will perform a UCC and Tax lien search but public must search other records themselves. Search fee $7.00. Copy fee $.50 1st page, $.25 each add'l. Cert fee- $2.00 per doc plus copy fee. **Online access to Property records:** Name searching on the statewide Cadastral database is free at http://gis.doa.state.mt.us/searchOwner.htm. **Other phones:** Vital Records- 406-444-4228. **Property tax/Assessor-** 406-346-2516.

Sanders County

Clerk and Recorder, PO Box 519, Thompson Falls, MT 59873. 406-827-6922; fax-406-827-4388; hours: 8AM-5PM.
All records in one index. Records indexed on a public use terminal back to 1991. Office will perform a UCC search but public must search other records themselves. Search fee $7.00. Copy fee $.25 per page. Cert fee- $2.00 per doc plus copy fee. Payee- Sanders County Clerk. **Online access to Property records:** Name searching on the statewide Cadastral database is free at http://gis.doa.state.mt.us/searchOwner.htm. **Other phones:** Treasurer- 406-827-6924; Appraiser/Auditor- 406-827-6932; Elections- 406-827-6922; Vital Records- 406-827-6922. **Property tax/Assessor-** PO Box 267, Thompson Falls, MT 59873; 406-827-6932.

Sheridan County

Clerk and Recorder, 100 W. Laurel Ave, Plentywood, MT 59254. 406-765-3403; fax-406-765-2609; hours: 8AM-5PM. www.co.sheridan.mt.us
All records in one index. Records indexed on computer back to 1993. Office will perform a UCC search but public must search other records themselves. UCC search per debtor name- $7.00. Copy fee $.50 1st page, $.25 each add'l. Cert fee- $2.00 per doc plus copy fee. **Online access to Property records:** Name searching on the statewide Cadastral database is free at http://gis.doa.state.mt.us/searchOwner.htm. Also, the sexual & violent offender registry is found at http://svor.doj.state.mt.us Also, parcel look-ups go to http://gis.doa.state.mt.us/index.htm. **Other phones:** Treasurer- 406-765-3414; Appraiser/Auditor- 406-765-2291; Elections- 406-765-3403; Vital Records- 406-765-3403. **Property tax/Assessor-** 406-765-2291.

Silver Bow County

Clerk and Recorder, 155 W Granite St #208, Butte, MT 59701. 406-497-6335, R/E recording phone-406-497-6338, UCC recording phone-406-497-6339; fax-406-497-6328; hours: 8AM-5PM. www.co.silverbow.mt.us/clerk_and_recorder.htm

Index: Tax Liens, UCC, Notice of attachments, Mining Claim, Misc. Leases. Records indexed on a public use terminal back to 1996. Only the public may search. Copy fee $.50 per page 1st page, $.25 each add'l. Cert fee- $2.00 per doc copy fee. Payee- Clerk and Recorder. **Online access to Property records:** Name searching on the statewide Cadastral database is free at http://gis.doa.state.mt.us/searchOwner.htm. **Other phones:** Treasurer- 406-497-6300; Elections- 406-497-6344; Vital Records- 406-497-6340. **Property tax/Assessor-** same address. 406-497-6290.

Stillwater County

Clerk and Recorder, PO Box 149, Columbus, MT 59019. 406-322-8000; fax-406-322-8007; hours: 8AM-5PM. http://co.stillwater.mt.us
Only the public may search. Copy fee $.50 per page. R/E record copy- $.25 per page. Cert fee- $2.00 per cert, $.50 per page for copy. Payee- Stillwater County Clerk and Recorder. **Online access to Property records:** Name searching on the statewide Cadastral database is free at http://gis.doa.state.mt.us/searchOwner.htm. **Other phones:** Treasurer- 406-322-8020; Appraiser/Auditor- 406-322-8015; Elections- 406-322-8000; Vital Records- 406-322-8000. **Property tax/Assessor-** 406-322-8015.

Sweet Grass County

Clerk and Recorder, PO Box 888, Big Timber, MT 59011. 406-932-5152; fax-406-932-5177; hours: 8AM-5PM.
Separate indices to search include deeds, mortgages, satisfactions, misc. Records indexed on computer back to 9/00. Only the public may search. Copy fee $.25 per page. Cert fee- $2.50 1st page; $.25 each add'l plus copy fee. Payee- Sweet Grass County. **Online access to Property records:** Name searching on the statewide Cadastral database is free at http://gis.doa.state.mt.us/searchOwner.htm. **Other phones:** Treasurer- 406-932-5151; Appraiser/Auditor- 406-932-5149; Elections- 406-932-5152; Vital Records- 406-932-5152. **Property tax/Assessor-** same address. 406-932-5149.

Teton County

Clerk and Recorder, PO Box 610, Choteau, MT 59422. 406-466-2693; fax-406-466-2138; hours: 8AM-5PM. www.tetoncomt.org
All records in one index. Records indexed on a public use terminal back to 2000. Office will perform a UCC search but public must search other records themselves. Search fee $7.00. Copy fee $.50 for 1st page; $.25 each add'l. Cert fee- $2.00 per doc plus copy fee. **Online access to Property records:** Name searching on the statewide Cadastral database is free at

http://gis.doa.state.mt.us/searchOwner.htm. **Other phones:** Treasurer- 406-466-2694; Appraiser/Auditor- 406-466-2908; Elections- 406-466-2693; Vital Records- 406-466-2693. **Property tax/Assessor-** 406-466-2908.

Toole County

Clerk and Recorder, 226 1st St South, Shelby, MT 59474. 406-424-8300; fax-406-424-8301; hours: 8AM-5PM.
All records in one index. Records indexed on a public use terminal back to 1995. Only the public may search. Copy fee $.50 per page. Cert fee- $2.00 per doc plus copy fee. **Online access to Property records:** Name searching on the statewide Cadastral database is free at http://gis.doa.state.mt.us/searchOwner.htm. **Other phones:** Treasurer- 406-424-8320; Appraiser/Auditor- 406-424-8370; Elections- 406-424-8300; Vital Records- 406-424-8300. **Property tax/Assessor-** same address as above. 406-424-8370.

Treasure County

Clerk and Recorder, PO Box 392, Hysham, MT 59038. 406-342-5547; fax-406-342-5445; hours: 8AM-N,1-5PM.
Separate indices to search include grantor/grantee, misc book, deed book, tract index. Record index not computerized. Office personnel or visitors may perform searches. Search fee $7.00 per name. Copy fee $.50 per 1st page; $.25 each add'l. Cert fee- $2.00 per doc plus copy fee. Payee- Treasure County Clerk and Recorder. **Online access to Property records:** Name searching on the statewide Cadastral database is free at http://gis.doa.state.mt.us/searchOwner.htm. **Other phones:** Treasurer- 406-342-5545; Appraiser/Auditor- 406-342-5540; Elections- 406-342-5547; Vital Records- 406-342-5547. **Property tax/Assessor-** 406-342-5540.

Valley County

Clerk and Recorder, Box 2, 501 Court Sq, Glasgow, MT 59230. 406-228-6220; fax-406-228-9027; hours: 8AM-5PM.
Separate indices to search include as of 5/1/2005 by document number & refer to kind of instrument, before 5/1/2005-deeds, mortgages, real estate, misc, liens, misc numbers, misc records. Office will perform a UCC search but public must search other records themselves. UCC search per debtor name- $7.00. Copy fee $.50 per page. Cert fee- $2.00 per doc plus copy fee. **Online access to Property records:** Name searching on the statewide Cadastral database is free at http://gis.doa.state.mt.us/searchOwner.htm. **Other phones:** Treasurer- 406-228-6231; Appraiser/Auditor- 406-228-6250; Elections- 406-228-6220; Vital

Records- 406-228-6268; Dept of Revenue- 406-228-6233.

Wheatland County

Clerk and Recorder, PO Box 1903, Harlowton, MT 59036. 406-632-4891; fax-406-632-4880; 8-12; 1-5.
Separate indices to search include deed, mortgage, assignments, lease, contract, military, misc. Record index not computerized. Only the public may search. Copy fee $.50 1st page; $.25 each add'l. Cert fee- $2.00 per doc. **Online access to Property records:** Name searching on the statewide Cadastral database is free at http://gis.doa.state.mt.us/searchOwner.htm. **Other phones:** Treasurer- 406-632-4892; Elections- 406-632-4891; Vital Records- 406-632-4891. **Property tax/Assessor-** 406-632-4894.

Wibaux County

Clerk and Recorder, PO Box 199, Wibaux, MT 59353-0199. 406-796-2481; fax-406-796-2625; hours: 8AM-5PM.
Record index not computerized. Only the public may search. General index search fee $7.00 per name. Copy fee $.10 per page. Cert fee- $2.00 per doc and $.25 each add'l page plus copy fee. Payee- Clerk & Recorder. **Online access to Property records:** Name searching on the statewide Cadastral database is free at http://gis.doa.state.mt.us/searchOwner.htm. **Other phones:** Treasurer- 406-795-2482; Elections- 406-796-2481; Vital Records- 406-796-2481. **Property tax/Assessor-** 406-795-2483.

Yellowstone County

Clerk and Recorder, PO Box 35001, Billings, MT 59107. 406-256-2785; fax-406-256-2736; hours: 8AM-5PM. www.co.yellowstone.mt.us/clerk
Records indexed on a public use terminal back to 1998. Office personnel or visitors may perform searches. Search fee $.50 per year per debtor. UCC search per debtor name- $7.00. Copy fee $.50 per page. R/E or tax lien copy- $.50 1st page, $.25 each add'l. Cert fee- $2.00 per cert plus copy fee. Payee- Yellowstone County Clerk and Recorder. **Online access to Assessor, Tax, Grantor/Grantee, Property records:** Access to the county clerk & recorder document searches are free at https://secure.co.yellowstone.mt.us/clerk/secure_search.asp. Also, access to the tax assessor records is free at www.co.yellowstone.mt.us/gis. Also, name searching on the statewide Cadastral database is free at http://gis.doa.state.mt.us/searchOwner.htm. **Other phones:** Treasurer- 406-256-2785; Elections- 406-256-2743; Vital Records- 406-256-2788. **Property tax/Assessor-** 406-896-4000.

Montana County Locator

You will usually be able to find the city name in the City/County Cross Reference below. In that case, it is a simple matter to determine the county from the cross reference. However, only the official US Postal Service city names are included in this index. There are an additional 40,000 place names that people use in their addresses. Therefore, we have also included a ZIP/City Cross Reference immediately following the City/County Cross Reference.

If you know the ZIP Code but the city name does not appear in the City/County Cross Reference index, look up the ZIP Code in the ZIP/City Cross Reference, find the city name, then look up the city name in the City/County Cross Reference. For example, you want to know the county for an address of Menands, NY 12204. There is no "Menands" in the City/County Cross Reference. The ZIP/City Cross Reference shows that ZIP Codes 12201-12288 are for the city of Albany. Looking back in the City/County Cross Reference, Albany is in Albany County.

Montana City/County Cross Reference

ABSAROKEE Stillwater
ACTON Yellowstone
ALBERTON (59820) Missoula(58), Mineral(41)
ALDER Madison
ALZADA Carter
ANACONDA (59711) Deer Lodge(87), Granite(9), Silver Bow(2)
ANGELA (59312) Garfield(66), Rosebud(33)
ANTELOPE Sheridan
ARLEE (59821) Lake(69), Missoula(28), Sanders(2)
ASHLAND Rosebud
AUGUSTA Lewis and Clark
AVON Powell
BABB Glacier
BAINVILLE Roosevelt
BAKER Fallon
BALLANTINE Yellowstone
BASIN Jefferson
BEARCREEK Carbon
BELFRY Carbon
BELGRADE Gallatin
BELT Cascade
BIDDLE Powder River
BIG ARM Lake
BIG SANDY Chouteau
BIG SKY Gallatin
BIG TIMBER Sweet Grass
BIGFORK (59911) Flathead(57), Lake(42)
BIGHORN Treasure
BILLINGS Yellowstone
BIRNEY Rosebud
BLACK EAGLE Cascade
BLOOMFIELD Dawson
BONNER Missoula
BOULDER Jefferson
BOX ELDER Hill
BOYD Carbon
BOYES Carter
BOZEMAN Gallatin
BRADY (59416) Pondera(55), Chouteau(39), Teton(4), Liberty(1)
BRIDGER Carbon
BROADUS Powder River
BROADVIEW (59015) Yellowstone(67), Musselshell(20), Stillwater(11)
BROCKTON Roosevelt
BROCKWAY (59214) McCone(86), Prairie(13)
BROWNING Glacier
BRUSETT Garfield
BUFFALO Fergus
BUSBY Big Horn
BUTTE Silver Bow
BYNUM Teton
CAMERON Madison
CANYON CREEK Lewis and Clark
CAPITOL Carter
CARDWELL (59721) Madison(53), Jefferson(46)
CARTER Chouteau

CASCADE Cascade
CAT CREEK Petroleum
CHARLO Lake
CHESTER Liberty
CHINOOK (59523) Blaine(91), Hill(8)
CHOTEAU Teton
CIRCLE (59215) McCone(93), Dawson(6)
CLANCY Jefferson
CLINTON (59825) Missoula(84), Granite(15)
CLYDE PARK Park
COFFEE CREEK Fergus
COHAGEN Garfield
COLSTRIP Rosebud
COLUMBIA FALLS Flathead
COLUMBUS Stillwater
CONDON Missoula
CONNER Ravalli
CONRAD (59425) Pondera(98), Teton(1)
COOKE CITY Park
CORAM Flathead
CORVALLIS Ravalli
CORWIN SPRINGS Park
CRANE Richland
CROW AGENCY Big Horn
CULBERTSON Roosevelt
CUSTER Yellowstone
CUT BANK Glacier
DAGMAR Sheridan
DARBY Ravalli
DAYTON (59914) Flathead(69), Lake(30)
DE BORGIA Mineral
DECKER Big Horn
DEER LODGE (59722) Powell(92), Deer Lodge(7)
DELL Beaverhead
DENTON Fergus
DILLON Beaverhead
DIVIDE Silver Bow
DIXON Sanders
DODSON (59524) Phillips(88), Blaine(11)
DRUMMOND Granite
DUPUYER Pondera
DUTTON Teton
EAST GLACIER PARK Glacier
EAST HELENA (59635) Lewis and Clark(93), Jefferson(3), Broadwater(3)
EDGAR Carbon
EKALAKA Carter
ELLISTON Powell
ELMO Lake
EMIGRANT Park
ENNIS Madison
ESSEX Flathead
ETHRIDGE Toole
EUREKA Lincoln
FAIRFIELD Teton
FAIRVIEW Richland
FALLON Prairie
FISHTAIL Stillwater
FLAXVILLE Daniels
FLORENCE (59833) Ravalli(64), Missoula(35)

FLOWEREE (59440) Chouteau(73), Cascade(26)
FORESTGROVE Fergus
FORSYTH Rosebud
FORT BENTON Chouteau
FORT HARRISON Lewis and Clark
FORT PECK Valley
FORT SHAW (59443) Cascade(92), Teton(7)
FORTINE Lincoln
FOUR BUTTES Daniels
FRAZER Valley
FRENCHTOWN Missoula
FROID (59226) Roosevelt(78), Sheridan(21)
FROMBERG Carbon
GALATA (59444) Toole(76), Liberty(23)
GALLATIN GATEWAY Gallatin
GARDINER Park
GARNEILL Fergus
GARRISON Powell
GARRYOWEN Big Horn
GERALDINE Chouteau
GEYSER (59447) Judith Basin(96), Chouteau(4)
GILDFORD Hill
GLASGOW Valley
GLEN Beaverhead
GLENDIVE Dawson
GLENTANA Valley
GOLD CREEK Powell
GRANTSDALE Ravalli
GRASS RANGE Fergus
GREAT FALLS Cascade
GREENOUGH Missoula
GREYCLIFF Sweet Grass
HALL Granite
HAMILTON Ravalli
HAMMOND Carter
HARDIN Big Horn
HARLEM Blaine
HARLOWTON Wheatland
HARRISON Madison
HATHAWAY Rosebud
HAUGAN Mineral
HAVRE Hill
HAYS Blaine
HEART BUTTE Pondera
HELENA Lewis and Clark
HELMVILLE Powell
HERON Sanders
HIGHWOOD Chouteau
HILGER Fergus
HINGHAM Hill
HINSDALE Valley
HOBSON Judith Basin
HOGELAND Blaine
HOMESTEAD (59242) Sheridan(83), Roosevelt(16)
HOT SPRINGS (59845) Sanders(86), Lake(9), Flathead(4)
HUNGRY HORSE Flathead

HUNTLEY (59037) Yellowstone(98), Big Horn(1)
HUSON Missoula
HYSHAM Treasure
INGOMAR Rosebud
INVERNESS (59530) Hill(97), Liberty(2)
ISMAY (59336) Custer(42), Fallon(40), Prairie(11), Carter(5)
JACKSON Beaverhead
JEFFERSON CITY Jefferson
JOLIET Carbon
JOPLIN (59531) Liberty(84), Hill(15)
JORDAN Garfield
JUDITH GAP (59453) Fergus(55), Wheatland(44)
KALISPELL Flathead
KEVIN Toole
KILA Flathead
KINSEY Custer
KREMLIN Hill
LAKE MC DONALD Flathead
LAKESIDE (59922) Flathead(73), Lake(26)
LAMBERT Richland
LAME DEER Rosebud
LARSLAN Valley
LAUREL (59044) Yellowstone(97), Carbon(2)
LAVINA Golden Valley
LEDGER (59456) Pondera(52), Liberty(31), Toole(15)
LEWISTOWN Fergus
LIBBY Lincoln
LIMA Beaverhead
LINCOLN (59639) Powell(73), Lewis and Clark(26)
LINDSAY (59339) Dawson(92), Prairie(7)
LIVINGSTON Park
LLOYD Blaine
LODGE GRASS Big Horn
LOLO Missoula
LOMA Chouteau
LONEPINE Sanders
LORING Phillips
LOTHAIR Liberty
LUTHER Carbon
MALMSTROM A F B Cascade
MALTA Phillips
MANHATTAN Gallatin
MARION Flathead
MARTIN CITY Flathead
MARTINSDALE Meagher
MARYSVILLE Lewis and Clark
MC ALLISTER Madison
MC CABE Roosevelt
MC LEOD (59052) Sweet Grass(80), Park(19)
MEDICINE LAKE Sheridan
MELROSE Silver Bow
MELSTONE Musselshell
MELVILLE Sweet Grass
MILDRED Prairie
MILES CITY Custer
MILL IRON Carter

MILLTOWN Missoula
MISSOULA Missoula
MOCCASIN Judith Basin
MOLT (59057) Yellowstone(72), Stillwater(27)
MONARCH Cascade
MOORE Fergus
MOSBY Garfield
MUSSELSHELL Musselshell
NASHUA Valley
NEIHART Cascade
NIARADA (59852) Sanders(85), Flathead(14)
NORRIS Madison
NOXON Sanders
NYE Stillwater
OILMONT Toole
OLIVE Powder River
OLNEY Flathead
OPHEIM Valley
OTTER (59062) Powder River(86), Rosebud(13)
OUTLOOK Sheridan
OVANDO Powell
PABLO Lake
PARADISE Sanders
PARK CITY Stillwater
PEERLESS Daniels
PENDROY Teton
PHILIPSBURG Granite
PINESDALE Ravalli
PLAINS Sanders
PLENTYWOOD Sheridan
PLEVNA Fallon
POLARIS Beaverhead
POLEBRIDGE Flathead
POLSON Lake
POMPEYS PILLAR Yellowstone
PONY Madison
POPLAR Roosevelt
POWDERVILLE Powder River

POWER (59468) Teton(83), Cascade(15)
PRAY Park
PROCTOR Lake
PRYOR Big Horn
RADERSBURG Broadwater
RAMSAY Silver Bow
RAPELJE Stillwater
RAVALLI Lake
RAYMOND Sheridan
RAYNESFORD Judith Basin
RED LODGE Carbon
REDSTONE Sheridan
REED POINT (59069) Stillwater(71), Sweet Grass(28)
REEDPOINT (59069) Stillwater(71), Sweet Grass(28)
RESERVE (59258) Sheridan(88), Roosevelt(11)
REXFORD Lincoln
RICHEY Dawson
RICHLAND Valley
RINGLING Meagher
ROBERTS Carbon
ROLLINS (59931) Flathead(89), Lake(10)
RONAN Lake
ROSCOE Carbon
ROSEBUD (59347) Rosebud(97), Custer(2)
ROUNDUP Musselshell
ROY Fergus
RUDYARD (59540) Hill(86), Chouteau(13)
RYEGATE (59074) Golden Valley(96), Stillwater(3)
SACO Phillips
SAINT IGNATIUS Lake
SAINT MARIE Valley
SAINT REGIS Mineral
SAINT XAVIER Big Horn
SALTESE Mineral
SAND COULEE Cascade
SAND SPRINGS Garfield

SANDERS Treasure
SANTA RITA Glacier
SAVAGE (59262) Richland(60), Dawson(39)
SCOBEY Daniels
SEELEY LAKE Missoula
SHAWMUT Wheatland
SHELBY Toole
SHEPHERD Yellowstone
SHERIDAN Madison
SIDNEY Richland
SILVER GATE Park
SILVER STAR Madison
SIMMS Cascade
SOMERS Flathead
SONNETTE Powder River
SPRINGDALE Park
STANFORD Judith Basin
STEVENSVILLE Ravalli
STOCKETT Cascade
STRYKER Lincoln
SULA Ravalli
SUMATRA Rosebud
SUN RIVER Cascade
SUNBURST Toole
SUPERIOR Mineral
SWEET GRASS Toole
SWEETGRASS Toole
TEIGEN (59084) Petroleum(80), Fergus(20)
TERRY (59349) Prairie(86), Custer(13)
THOMPSON FALLS Sanders
THREE FORKS (59752) Gallatin(88), Broadwater(10)
TOSTON Broadwater
TOWNSEND Broadwater
TREGO Lincoln
TROUT CREEK Sanders
TURNER Blaine
TWIN BRIDGES Madison
TWO DOT Wheatland

TWODOT Wheatland
ULM Cascade
VALIER Pondera
VANDALIA Valley
VAUGHN (59487) Cascade(93), Teton(6)
VICTOR Ravalli
VIDA McCone
VIRGINIA CITY Madison
VOLBORG Custer
WARM SPRINGS Deer Lodge
WARMSPRINGS Deer Lodge
WEST GLACIER Flathead
WEST YELLOWSTONE Gallatin
WESTBY Sheridan
WHITE SULPHUR SPRINGS Meagher
WHITEFISH Flathead
WHITEHALL (59759) Jefferson(84), Madison(15)
WHITETAIL Daniels
WHITEWATER Phillips
WHITLASH Liberty
WIBAUX Wibaux
WILLARD Fallon
WILLOW CREEK Gallatin
WILSALL (59086) Park(79), Gallatin(19), Meagher(1)
WINIFRED Fergus
WINNETT Petroleum
WINSTON Broadwater
WISDOM Beaverhead
WISE RIVER (59762) Beaverhead(53), Deer Lodge(46)
WOLF CREEK Lewis and Clark
WOLF POINT Roosevelt
WORDEN Yellowstone
WYOLA Big Horn
YELLOWTAIL Big Horn
ZORTMAN Phillips
ZURICH Blaine

Montana ZIP/City Cross Reference

59001-59001	ABSAROKEE
59002-59002	ACTON
59003-59004	ASHLAND
59006-59006	BALLANTINE
59007-59007	BEARCREEK
59008-59008	BELFRY
59010-59010	BIGHORN
59011-59011	BIG TIMBER
59012-59012	BIRNEY
59013-59013	BOYD
59014-59014	BRIDGER
59015-59015	BROADVIEW
59016-59016	BUSBY
59017-59017	CAT CREEK
59018-59018	CLYDE PARK
59019-59019	COLUMBUS
59020-59020	COOKE CITY
59021-59021	CORWIN SPRINGS
59022-59022	CROW AGENCY
59024-59024	CUSTER
59025-59025	DECKER
59026-59026	EDGAR
59027-59027	EMIGRANT
59028-59028	FISHTAIL
59029-59029	FROMBERG
59030-59030	GARDINER
59031-59031	GARRYOWEN
59032-59032	GRASS RANGE
59033-59033	GREYCLIFF
59034-59034	HARDIN
59035-59035	YELLOWTAIL
59036-59036	HARLOWTON
59037-59037	HUNTLEY
59038-59038	HYSHAM
59039-59039	INGOMAR
59041-59041	JOLIET
59043-59043	LAME DEER
59044-59044	LAUREL
59046-59046	LAVINA
59047-59047	LIVINGSTON
59050-59050	LODGE GRASS
59051-59051	LUTHER
59052-59052	MC LEOD
59053-59053	MARTINSDALE
59054-59054	MELSTONE
59055-59055	MELVILLE
59057-59057	MOLT
59058-59058	MOSBY
59059-59059	MUSSELSHELL
59061-59061	NYE
59062-59062	OTTER
59063-59063	PARK CITY
59064-59064	POMPEYS PILLAR
59065-59065	PRAY
59066-59066	PRYOR
59067-59067	RAPELJE
59068-59068	RED LODGE
59069-59069	REEDPOINT
59069-59069	REED POINT
59070-59070	ROBERTS
59071-59071	ROSCOE
59072-59073	ROUNDUP
59074-59074	RYEGATE
59075-59075	SAINT XAVIER
59076-59076	SANDERS
59077-59077	SAND SPRINGS
59078-59078	SHAWMUT
59079-59079	SHEPHERD
59080-59080	JOLIET
59081-59081	SILVER GATE
59082-59082	SPRINGDALE
59083-59083	SUMATRA
59084-59084	TEIGEN
59085-59085	TWODOT
59085-59085	TWO DOT
59086-59086	WILSALL
59087-59087	WINNETT
59088-59088	WORDEN
59089-59089	WYOLA
59100-59117	BILLINGS
59201-59201	WOLF POINT
59211-59211	ANTELOPE
59212-59212	BAINVILLE
59213-59213	BROCKTON
59214-59214	BROCKWAY
59215-59215	CIRCLE
59217-59217	CRANE
59218-59218	CULBERTSON
59219-59219	DAGMAR
59221-59221	FAIRVIEW
59222-59222	FLAXVILLE
59223-59223	FORT PECK
59224-59224	FOUR BUTTES
59225-59225	FRAZER
59226-59226	FROID
59230-59230	GLASGOW
59231-59231	SAINT MARIE
59240-59240	GLENTANA
59241-59241	HINSDALE
59242-59242	HOMESTEAD
59243-59243	LAMBERT
59244-59244	LARSLAN
59245-59245	MC CABE
59247-59247	MEDICINE LAKE
59248-59248	NASHUA
59250-59250	OPHEIM
59252-59252	OUTLOOK
59253-59253	PEERLESS
59254-59254	PLENTYWOOD
59255-59255	POPLAR
59256-59256	RAYMOND
59257-59257	REDSTONE
59258-59258	RESERVE
59259-59259	RICHEY
59260-59260	RICHLAND
59261-59261	SACO
59262-59262	SAVAGE
59263-59263	SCOBEY
59270-59270	SIDNEY
59273-59273	VANDALIA
59274-59274	VIDA
59275-59275	WESTBY
59276-59276	WHITETAIL
59301-59301	MILES CITY
59311-59311	ALZADA
59312-59312	ANGELA
59313-59313	BAKER
59314-59314	BIDDLE
59315-59315	BLOOMFIELD
59316-59316	BOYES
59317-59317	BROADUS
59318-59318	BRUSETT
59319-59319	CAPITOL
59322-59322	COHAGEN
59323-59323	COLSTRIP
59324-59324	EKALAKA
59326-59326	FALLON
59327-59327	FORSYTH
59330-59330	GLENDIVE
59332-59332	HAMMOND
59333-59333	HATHAWAY
59336-59336	ISMAY
59337-59337	JORDAN
59338-59338	KINSEY

59339-59339 LINDSAY	59342-59342 MILL IRON	59344-59344 PLEVNA	59347-59347 ROSEBUD
59341-59341 MILDRED	59343-59343 OLIVE	59345-59345 POWDERVILLE	59348-59348 SONNETTE
59349-59349 TERRY	59477-59477 SIMMS	59716-59716 BIG SKY	59841-59841 PINESDALE
59351-59351 VOLBORG	59479-59479 STANFORD	59717-59719 BOZEMAN	59842-59842 HAUGAN
59353-59353 WIBAUX	59480-59480 STOCKETT	59720-59720 CAMERON	59843-59843 HELMVILLE
59354-59354 WILLARD	59482-59482 SUNBURST	59721-59721 CARDWELL	59844-59844 HERON
59401-59401 GREAT FALLS	59483-59483 SUN RIVER	59722-59722 DEER LODGE	59845-59845 HOT SPRINGS
59402-59402 MALMSTROM A F B	59484-59484 SWEETGRASS	59724-59724 DELL	59846-59846 HUSON
59403-59406 GREAT FALLS	59484-59484 SWEET GRASS	59725-59725 DILLON	59847-59847 LOLO
59410-59410 AUGUSTA	59485-59485 ULM	59727-59727 DIVIDE	59848-59848 LONEPINE
59411-59411 BABB	59486-59486 VALIER	59728-59728 ELLISTON	59851-59851 MILLTOWN
59412-59412 BELT	59487-59487 VAUGHN	59729-59729 ENNIS	59852-59852 NIARADA
59414-59414 BLACK EAGLE	59489-59489 WINIFRED	59730-59730 GALLATIN GATEWAY	59853-59853 NOXON
59416-59416 BRADY	59501-59501 HAVRE	59731-59731 GARRISON	59854-59854 OVANDO
59417-59417 BROWNING	59520-59520 BIG SANDY	59732-59732 GLEN	59855-59855 PABLO
59418-59418 BUFFALO	59521-59521 BOX ELDER	59733-59733 GOLD CREEK	59856-59856 PARADISE
59419-59419 BYNUM	59522-59522 CHESTER	59735-59735 HARRISON	59858-59858 PHILIPSBURG
59420-59420 CARTER	59523-59523 CHINOOK	59736-59736 JACKSON	59859-59859 PLAINS
59421-59421 CASCADE	59524-59524 DODSON	59739-59739 LIMA	59860-59860 POLSON
59422-59422 CHOTEAU	59525-59525 GILDFORD	59740-59740 MC ALLISTER	59863-59863 RAVALLI
59424-59424 COFFEE CREEK	59526-59526 HARLEM	59741-59741 MANHATTAN	59864-59864 RONAN
59425-59425 CONRAD	59527-59527 HAYS	59743-59743 MELROSE	59865-59865 SAINT IGNATIUS
59427-59427 CUT BANK	59528-59528 HINGHAM	59745-59745 NORRIS	59866-59866 SAINT REGIS
59430-59430 DENTON	59529-59529 HOGELAND	59746-59746 POLARIS	59867-59867 SALTESE
59432-59432 DUPUYER	59530-59530 INVERNESS	59747-59747 PONY	59868-59868 SEELEY LAKE
59433-59433 DUTTON	59531-59531 JOPLIN	59748-59748 RAMSAY	59870-59870 STEVENSVILLE
59434-59434 EAST GLACIER PARK	59532-59532 KREMLIN	59749-59749 SHERIDAN	59871-59871 SULA
59435-59435 ETHRIDGE	59535-59535 LLOYD	59750-59750 BUTTE	59872-59872 SUPERIOR
59436-59436 FAIRFIELD	59537-59537 LORING	59751-59751 SILVER STAR	59873-59873 THOMPSON FALLS
59440-59440 FLOWEREE	59538-59538 MALTA	59752-59752 THREE FORKS	59874-59874 TROUT CREEK
59441-59441 FORESTGROVE	59540-59540 RUDYARD	59754-59754 TWIN BRIDGES	59875-59875 VICTOR
59442-59442 FORT BENTON	59542-59542 TURNER	59755-59755 VIRGINIA CITY	59901-59904 KALISPELL
59443-59443 FORT SHAW	59544-59544 WHITEWATER	59756-59756 WARMSPRINGS	59910-59910 BIG ARM
59444-59444 GALATA	59545-59545 WHITLASH	59756-59756 WARM SPRINGS	59911-59911 BIGFORK
59445-59445 GARNEILL	59546-59546 ZORTMAN	59758-59758 WEST YELLOWSTONE	59912-59912 COLUMBIA FALLS
59446-59446 GERALDINE	59547-59547 ZURICH	59759-59759 WHITEHALL	59913-59913 CORAM
59447-59447 GEYSER	59601-59626 HELENA	59760-59760 WILLOW CREEK	59914-59914 DAYTON
59448-59448 HEART BUTTE	59631-59631 BASIN	59761-59761 WISDOM	59915-59915 ELMO
59450-59450 HIGHWOOD	59632-59632 BOULDER	59762-59762 WISE RIVER	59916-59916 ESSEX
59451-59451 HILGER	59633-59633 CANYON CREEK	59771-59773 BOZEMAN	59917-59917 EUREKA
59452-59452 HOBSON	59634-59634 CLANCY	59801-59812 MISSOULA	59918-59918 FORTINE
59453-59453 JUDITH GAP	59635-59635 EAST HELENA	59820-59820 ALBERTON	59919-59919 HUNGRY HORSE
59454-59454 KEVIN	59636-59636 FORT HARRISON	59821-59821 ARLEE	59920-59920 KILA
59456-59456 LEDGER	59638-59638 JEFFERSON CITY	59823-59823 BONNER	59921-59921 LAKE MC DONALD
59457-59457 LEWISTOWN	59639-59639 LINCOLN	59824-59824 CHARLO	59922-59922 LAKESIDE
59460-59460 LOMA	59640-59640 MARYSVILLE	59825-59825 CLINTON	59923-59923 LIBBY
59461-59461 LOTHAIR	59641-59641 RADERSBURG	59826-59826 CONDON	59925-59925 MARION
59462-59462 MOCCASIN	59642-59642 RINGLING	59827-59827 CONNER	59926-59926 MARTIN CITY
59463-59463 MONARCH	59643-59643 TOSTON	59828-59828 CORVALLIS	59927-59927 OLNEY
59464-59464 MOORE	59644-59644 TOWNSEND	59829-59829 DARBY	59928-59928 POLEBRIDGE
59465-59465 NEIHART	59645-59645 WHITE SULPHUR SPRINGS	59830-59830 DE BORGIA	59929-59929 PROCTOR
59466-59466 OILMONT	59647-59647 WINSTON	59831-59831 DIXON	59930-59930 REXFORD
59467-59467 PENDROY	59648-59648 WOLF CREEK	59832-59832 DRUMMOND	59931-59931 ROLLINS
59468-59468 POWER	59701-59707 BUTTE	59833-59833 FLORENCE	59932-59932 SOMERS
59469-59469 RAYNESFORD	59710-59710 ALDER	59834-59834 FRENCHTOWN	59933-59933 STRYKER
59471-59471 ROY	59711-59711 ANACONDA	59835-59835 GRANTSDALE	59934-59934 TREGO
59472-59472 SAND COULEE	59713-59713 AVON	59836-59836 GREENOUGH	59935-59935 TROY
59473-59473 SANTA RITA	59714-59714 BELGRADE	59837-59837 HALL	59936-59936 WEST GLACIER
59474-59474 SHELBY	59715-59715 BOZEMAN	59840-59840 HAMILTON	59937-59937 WHITEFISH

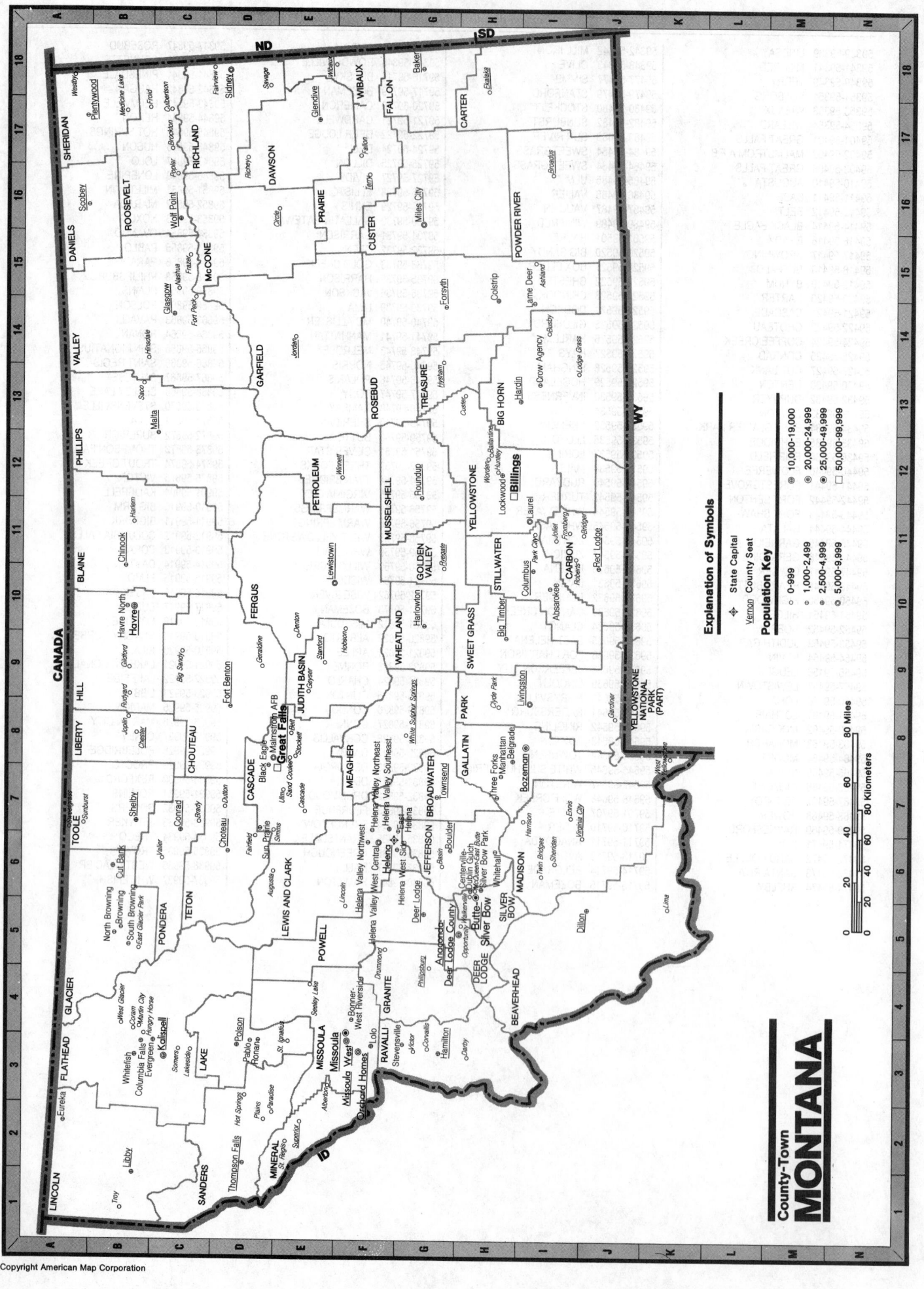

MONTANA
County-Town

Explanation of Symbols

◆ State Capital

Vernon County Seat

Population Key

○ 0-999
◉ 1,000-2,499
⊕ 2,500-4,999
⊗ 5,000-9,999
⊛ 10,000-19,000
⊕ 20,000-24,999
⊕ 25,000-49,999
□ 50,000-99,999

COUNTIES

(56 Counties)

Name of County	Population	Location on Map
BEAVERHEAD	8,424	H-4
BIG HORN	11,337	H-13
BLAINE	6,728	A-10
BROADWATER	3,318	G-7
CARBON	8,080	I-10
CARTER	1,503	H-17
CASCADE	77,691	D-7
CHOUTEAU	5,452	C-7
CUSTER	11,697	F-15
DANIELS	2,266	A-15
DAWSON	9,505	D-16
DEER LODGE	10,278	H-4
FALLON	3,103	F-17
FERGUS	12,083	D-10
FLATHEAD	59,218	A-3
GALLATIN	50,463	H-7
GARFIELD	1,589	D-13
GLACIER	12,121	A-4
GOLDEN VALLEY	912	G-10
GRANITE	2,548	F-4
HILL	17,654	A-8
JEFFERSON	7,939	G-6
JUDITH BASIN	2,282	C-3
LAKE	21,041	E-5
LEWIS AND CLARK	47,495	A-8
LIBERTY	2,295	A-1
LINCOLN	17,481	I-6
MADISON	5,989	C-15
McCONE	2,276	F-7
MEAGHER	1,819	E-1
MINERAL	3,315	E-3
MISSOULA	78,687	F-11
MUSSELSHELL	4,106	H-8
PARK	14,562	E-11
PETROLEUM	519	A-12
PHILLIPS	5,163	C-5
PONDERA	6,433	H-15
POWDER RIVER	2,090	C-1
POWELL	6,620	E-5
PRAIRIE	1,383	E-16
RAVALLI	25,010	F-3
RICHLAND	10,716	C-16
ROOSEVELT	10,999	B-16
ROSEBUD	10,505	F-13
SANDERS	8,669	C-1
SHERIDAN	4,732	A-17
SILVER BOW	33,941	H-5
STILLWATER	6,536	H-10
SWEET GRASS	3,154	H-9
TETON	6,271	C-5
TOOLE	5,056	A-6
TREASURE	874	G-13
VALLEY	8,239	A-14
WHEATLAND	2,246	G-9
WIBAUX	1,191	F-18
YELLOWSTONE	113,419	H-11
TOTAL	799,023	

CITIES AND TOWNS

Note: The first name is that of the city or town, second, that of the county in which it is located, then the population and location on the map.

- Absarokee, Stillwater, 1,067 ... I-10
- Anaconda-Deer Lodge County, Deer Lodge, 10,278 ... H-5
- Baker, Fallon, 1,818 ... G-18
- Belgrade, Gallatin, 3,411 ... H-8
- Big Timber, Sweet Grass, 1,557 ... H-9
- Billings, Yellowstone, 81,151 ... H-12
- Black Eagle, Cascade ... D-8
- Bonner-West Riverside, Missoula, 1,669 ... F-4
- Boulder, Jefferson, 1,316 ... G-6
- Bozeman, Gallatin, 22,660 ... I-8
- Broadus, Powder River, 572 ... I-16
- Browning, Glacier, 1,170 ... B-5
- Butte-Silver Bow, Silver Bow, 33,336 ... H-6
- Centerville-Dublin Gulch, Silver Bow ... B-8
- Chester, Liberty, 942 ... B-10
- Chinook, Blaine, 1,512 ... D-6
- Choteau, Teton, 1,741 ... E-16
- Circle, McCone, 805 ... H-14
- Colstrip, Rosebud, 3,035 ... B-3
- Columbia Falls, Flathead, 2,942 ... I-10
- Columbus, Stillwater, 1,573 ... C-7
- Conrad, Pondera, 2,891 ... I-13
- Crow Agency, Big Horn, 1,446 ... B-6
- Cut Bank, Glacier, 3,329 ... G-5
- Deer Lodge, Powell, 3,378 ... J-5
- Dillon, Beaverhead, 3,991 ... G-7
- East Helena, Lewis and Clark, 1,538 ... H-18
- Ekalaka, Carter, 439 ... A-2
- Eureka, Lincoln, 1,043 ... B-3
- Evergreen, Flathead, 4,109 ... G-14
- Forsyth, Rosebud, 2,178 ... D-8
- Fort Benton, Chouteau, 1,660 ... C-14
- Glasgow, Valley, 3,572 ... E-17
- Glendive, Dawson, 4,802 ... E-7
- Great Falls, Cascade, 55,097 ... G-3
- Hamilton, Ravalli, 2,737 ... I-13
- Hardin, Big Horn, 2,940 ... G-10
- Harlowton, Wheatland, 1,049 ... B-10
- Havre, Hill, 10,201 ... B-10
- Havre North, Hill, 1,110 ... F-6
- Helena, Lewis and Clark, 24,569 ...

- Helena Valley Northeast, Lewis and Clark, 1,585 ... F-6
- Helena Valley Northwest, Lewis and Clark, 1,215 ... F-6
- Helena Valley Southeast, Lewis and Clark, 4,601 ... F-6
- Helena Valley West Central, Lewis and Clark, 6,327 ... F-6
- Helena West Side, Lewis and Clark, 1,847 ... F-6
- Hysham, Treasure, 361 ... G-14
- Jordan, Garfield, 494 ... E-14
- Kalispell, Flathead, 11,917 ... C-3
- Lame Deer, Rosebud, 1,918 ... I-14
- Laurel, Yellowstone, 5,686 ... I-11
- Lewistown, Fergus, 6,051 ... E-10
- Libby, Lincoln, 2,532 ... B-1
- Livingston, Park, 6,701 ... I-8
- Lockwood, Yellowstone, 3,967 ... H-12
- Lolo, Missoula, 2,746 ... F-3
- Malmstrom AFB, Cascade, 5,938 ... D-8
- Matta, Phillips, 2,340 ... C-12
- Manhattan, Gallatin, 1,034 ... H-7
- Miles City, Custer, 8,461 ... G-16
- Missoula, Missoula, 42,918 ... F-3
- Missoula West, Missoula ... F-3
- North Browning, Glacier, 1,630 ... B-5
- Orchard Homes, Missoula, 10,317 ... F-3
- Pablo, Lake, 1,298 ... D-3
- Philipsburg, Granite, 925 ... G-4
- Plentywood, Sheridan, 2,136 ... A-17
- Polson, Lake, 3,283 ... D-3
- Red Lodge, Carbon, 1,958 ... J-10
- Ronan, Lake, 1,547 ... D-3
- Roundup, Musselshell, 1,808 ... G-12
- Ryegate, Golden Valley, 260 ... G-11
- Scobey, Daniels, 1,154 ... A-16
- Shelby, Toole, 2,763 ... B-7
- Sidney, Richland, 5,217 ... D-18
- Silver Bow Park, Silver Bow ... H-6
- South Browning, Glacier, 1,748 ... B-5
- Stanford, Judith Basin, 529 ... E-9
- Stevensville, Ravalli, 1,221 ... G-3
- Sun Prairie, Cascade, 1,424 ... D-7
- Superior, Mineral, 881 ... E-2
- Terry, Prairie, 659 ... F-16
- Thompson Falls, Sanders, 1,319 ... D-2
- Three Forks, Gallatin, 1,203 ... H-7
- Townsend, Broadwater, 1,635 ... G-7
- Virginia City, Madison, 142 ... J-6
- White Sulphur Springs, Meagher, 963 ... G-8
- Whitefish, Flathead, 4,368 ... B-3
- Whitehall, Jefferson, 1,067 ... H-6
- Wibaux, Wibaux, 628 ... E-18
- Winnett, Petroleum, 188 ... F-12
- Wolf Point, Roosevelt, 2,880 ... C-16

Explanation of symbols: ● – Census Designated Place (CDP)

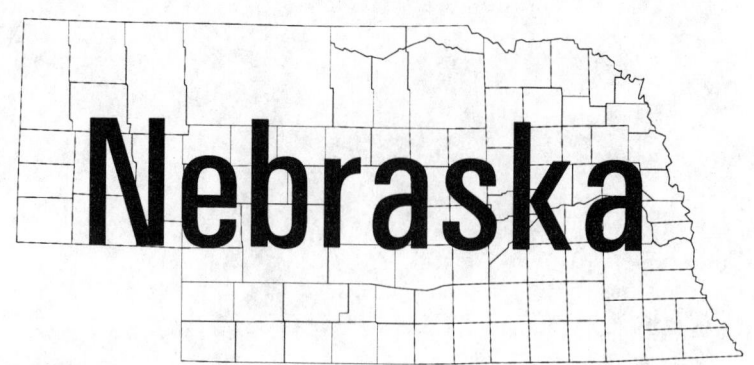

General Help Numbers:

Governor's Office

PO Box 94848
Lincoln, NE 68509-4848
http://gov.nol.org

402-471-2244
Fax 402-471-6031
8AM-5PM

Attorney General's Office

2115 State Capitol
Lincoln, NE 68509
www.ago.state.ne.us/

402-471-2682
Fax 402-471-3297
8AM-5PM

Legislative Records

Clerk of Legislature Office
PO Box 94604
Lincoln, NE 68509-4604
http://court.nol.org/AOC

402-471-2271
Fax 402-471-2126
8AM-5PM

State Archives

Archives
PO Box 82554
Lincoln, NE 68501-2554

402-471-4771
Fax 402-471-8922
9:30AM-4:30PM M-F;
8-5 SA; 1:30PM-5PM SU

www.nebraskahistory.org

State Specifics:

Capital:

Lincoln
Lancaster County

Time Zone: CST*

* Nebraska's nineteen western-most counties are MST:

They are: Arthur, Banner, Box Butte, Chase, Cherry, Cheyenne, Dawes, Deuel, Dundy, Garden, Grant, Hooker, Keith, Kimball, Morrill, Perkins, Scotts. Bluff, Sheridan, Sioux.

Number of Counties: 93

Population: 1,747,214

Web Site: www.state.ne.us

State Agencies

Criminal Records

Nebraska State Patrol, CID, PO Box 94907, Lincoln, NE 68509-4907 (Courier address: 233 S 10th St, Lincoln, NE 68508); 402-479-4924, 402-471-4545, 402-479-4002-Fax; 8AM-5PM.

www.nsp.state.ne.us

Records are available from 1937 to present. It takes 15 to 60 days before new records are available for inquiry. Records are indexed on inhouse computer, fingerprint cards. 64% of all arrests in database have final dispositions recorded.

Searching: Include the following in your request-full name, disposition, date of birth, Social Security Number, sex, race. Fingerprints required for certain state occupation checks; this includes an FBI fingerprint search. State keeps record of requesters and will inform the person of record if asked. 100% of records are fingerprint-supported. Felonies are required to be submitted this agency, though not all misdemeanors are. Agency will refer you to the proper county. The following data is not released: juvenile records. Records without dispositions are not released, except if an arrest without disposition is less than one year old.

Access by: mail, fax, in person.

Fee & Payment: The search fee is $10.00 per name. Fee payee: Nebraska State Patrol. Prepayment required. Personal checks accepted. No credit cards accepted.

Mail search: Turnaround time: 2 to 15 days.

Fax search: Requests by fax are accepted, if prepaid.

In person search: They accept requests in person and turnaround is 15 minutes, but they will mail back the report if it is lengthy or incomplete (unless it is the requester's own report). Fingerprint rolling service is offered from 8AM to 4PM daily, at no charge.

Statewide Court Records

Court Administrator, PO Box 98910, Lincoln, NE 68509-8910 (Courier address: 1213 State Capitol Building, Lincoln, NE 68509); 402-471-3730, 402-471-2197-Fax; 8AM-4:30PM.

http://court.nol.org/AOC/index.html

Appellate and Supreme Court opinions are available from the website.

Records are available available as courts enter data. It takes 24 hours before new records are available for inquiry.

Access by: online.

Online search: An online access subscription service is available for NE District and County courts, except Douglas County District Court. Case details, all party listings, payments and actions taken for criminal, civil, probate, juvenile, and traffic is available. Users must be registered with Nebrask@ Online, there is a start-up fee. The fee is $.60 per record or a flat rate of $300.00 per month. Go to www.nebraska.gov/faqs/justice for more info and how far back records go per county. Supreme Court opinions are available from http://court.nol.org/opinions/.

Sexual Offender Registry

Nebraska State Patrol, Sexual Offender Registry, PO Box 94907, Lincoln, NE 68509-4907 (Courier address: 1500 Nebraska Highway 2, Lincoln, NE 68502); 402-471-8647, 402-471-8496-Fax; 8AM-5PM.

www.nsp.state.ne.us/sor

The public is only granted access to sex offenders who are classified as high risk/Level 3 sex offenders. As of April 2005, there were over 2045 active registered sex offenders in the state of Nebraska.

Records are available from 1997 to present. It takes 24 hours or less before new records are available for inquiry.

Access by: mail, phone, online.

Mail search: Turnaround time: 15 days. No SASE is requested

Phone search: Limited searching by telephone.

Online search: A Level 3 sexual offender registry search is available at the website. The records may be searched by either ZIP Code, last name, city, or county. Search or review the entire list of names.

Incarceration Records

Nebraska Department of Correctional Services, Central Records Office, PO Box 94661, Lincoln, NE 68509-4661; 402-479-5765, 402-479-5913-Fax; 8AM-5PM.

www.corrections.state.ne.us

Records are available on current and former inmates back to 1977. It takes 1 day before new records are available for inquiry. Records are indexed on microfilm and books. Records are normally destroyed after 3 years.

Searching: Include the following in your request-full name or DOC inmate #. The DOB and SSN number are helpful. To search online, only the name is needed. Location, DOC number, physical identifiers, conviction and sentencing information, and release dates are provided.

Access by: mail, phone, fax, online.

Mail search: Turnaround time: 2 to 4 weeks.

Phone search: Limited searching permitted.

Fax search: Records may be requested by fax.

Online search: Click on Inmate Records at the website for a search of inmates incarcerated after 1977. Also, a private company offers free web access at www.vinelink.com/index.jsp; includes state, DOC, and county jails.

Corporation, Limited Liability Company, Limited Partnerships, Trade Names, Trademarks/Servicemarks

Secretary of State, Corporation Commission, 1301 State Capitol Bldg, Lincoln, NE 68509; 402-471-4079, 402-471-3666-Fax; 8AM-5PM.

www.sos.state.ne.us/business/corp_serv

Records are available from the beginning of state corporation filings. It takes less than a day, one week to view online. before new records are available for inquiry. Records are indexed on microfilm, index cards. Records are normally destroyed after 5 years if biannual report, otherwise not destroyed.

Searching: Include the following in your request-full name of business. In addition to the articles of incorporation, corporation records include the following information: Reports, Officers, Directors, Prior (merged) names, Inactive and Reserved names and Occupation Tax records for the last 5 years.

Access by: mail, phone, fax, in person, online.

Fee & Payment: No search fee, copies are $1.00 per page, $.45 for copies ordered online. Fee payee: Secretary of State. Prepayment required. Personal checks accepted. No credit cards accepted.

Mail search: Turnaround time: 2 days.

Phone search: Records are available by phone.

Fax search: Fax searching available.

In person search: Simple requests may be processed immediately.

Online search: There are two levels of service. The free lookup at https://www.nebraska.gov/sos/corp/corpsearch.cgi?nav=search provides general information to obtain information on the status of corporations and other business entities registered in this state. The state has designated Nebrask@ Online (800-747-8177) to facilitate online retrieval of records. This access to records requires fees and the lookup can be accessed from the same webpage.

Other access: Nebrask@ Online has the capability of offering database purchases.

Uniform Commercial Code, Federal and State Tax Liens

UCC Division, Secretary of State, Rm 1301, PO Box 95104, Lincoln, NE 68509-5104 (Courier address: 1301 State Capitol Bldg, 1445 "K" Street,

Lincoln, NE 68509); 402-471-4080, 402-471-4429-Fax; 7:30AM-5PM.

www.sos.state.ne.us/business/ucc

Effective July 1, 1999, all federal and state tax liens are filed at this agency. Previously tax liens were filed at the county level.

Records are available from 1981 to present, on both computer and microfiche. It takes only minutes before new records are available for inquiry.

Searching: Use search request Nebraska version of the UCC-11 form.

Access by: mail, fax, in person, online.

Fee & Payment: The search fee is $4.50 per debtor name. Copies are $.50 per page. Certification is an additional $10.00. Fee payee: Secretary of State. They will invoice established accounts. Personal checks accepted. No credit cards accepted.

Mail search: Turnaround time: 1 day. A SASE is requested.

Fax search: The fee is $4.50 per debtor. Use the Nebraska Search Form (UCC-11). Turnaround time is 4 hours or less.

In person search: Records are generally available with a short wait.

Online search: Access is outsourced to Nebrask@ Online To set an account, go to www.nol.org. The system is available 24 hours daily. There is an annual $50.00 fee in addition to charges to view records. Call 800-747-8177 for more information.

Other access: Check with Nebrask@ Online for bulk purchase programs.

Sales Tax Registrations

Revenue Department, Taxpayer Assistance, PO Box 94818, Lincoln, NE 68509-4818 (Courier address: 301 Centennial Mall South, Lincoln, NE 68509); 402-471-5729, 402-471-5990-Fax; 8AM-5PM.

www.revenue.state.ne.us/salestax.htm

Records are available from 1967. Records are indexed on computer.

Searching: This office will confirm that a business is registered and supply requester with name, address and date of license. Include the following in your request-business name. They will also search by tax permit number or by federal tax ID.

Access by: mail, phone, in person.

Mail search: A SASE is requested. No fee for mail request.

Phone search: No fee for telephone request.

In person search: Simple requests may be processed immediately.

Birth Certificates

Health & Human Services System, Vital Statistics Section, PO Box 95065, Lincoln, NE 68509-5065 (Courier address: 301 Centennial Mall S, 3rd Floor, Lincoln, NE 68509); 402-471-2871, 402-471-6440, 402-471-8230-Fax; 8AM-5PM.

www.hhs.state.ne.us/ced/nevrinfo.htm

Records may also be ordered at regional offices in Omaha, Kearney, North Platte, Norfolk, and Gering.

Records are available from 1904 to present. Records are indexed by Soundex code, year and county. Records are indexed by computer since 1912, and can be found on microfiche from 1912 to 1977. It takes 30 days before new records are available for inquiry.

Searching: Non-family members must have a notarized, signed release from person of record or immediate family member for investigative purposes. If the birth certificate is more than 50 years old, a release form is not required. Closed records are not released. Include the following in your request-full name, DOB, place of birth, names of parents, mother's maiden name, relationship to person of record, reason for information request. If adopted, indicate so. Also, all requesters must include copy of photo ID. The following data is not released: original records of adoption or sealed records.

Access by: mail, phone, fax, in person, online.

Fee & Payment: The fee is $8.00 per record. Fee payee: Vital Records. Prepayment required. Credit cards may only be used for expedited searches by walk in or calling in. The file search fee is non-refundable if no records are found. Personal checks accepted. Major credit cards accepted.

Mail search: Turnaround time: 2 to 3 weeks. If the agency receives the request by overnight mail, they will mail it back within 2 to 3 days. A SASE is requested.

Phone search: See expedited service.

Fax search: The fax number above is for this agency; VitalChek's fax is 402-471-8238.

In person search: Turnaround time is 20 to 30 minutes.

Online search: Records may be ordered online from the Internet site or from www.vitalchek.com (see expedited services).

Expedited service: Expedited service is available from www.vitalchek.com via online or fax. Fee is $30.00 and includes overnight delivery and fee for required use of credit card. Turnaround time: overnight delivery. Expedited service is available between 9AM and 3PM Central Time.

Death Records

Health and Human Services System, Vital Statistics Section, PO Box 95065, Lincoln, NE 68509-5065 (Courier address: 301 Centennial Mall S, 3rd Floor, Lincoln, NE 68509); 402-471-2871, 402-471-6440, 402-471-8230-Fax; 8AM-5PM.

www.hhs.state.ne.us/ced/nevrinfo.htm

If a certificate is more than 50 years in the past, release form is not required.

Records are available from 1904 to present. It takes 30 days before new records are available for inquiry.

Searching: Must have a notarized, signed release from immediate family member for investigative purposes. Include the following in your request-full name, date of death, place of death, relationship to person of record, reason for information request. Also, all requesters must include copy of photo ID.

Access by: mail, phone, fax, in person, online.

Fee & Payment: The fee is $7.00 per record. Fee payee: Vital Records. Prepayment required. Credit cards may only be used for phone or walk-in expedited service. The file search fee is non-refundable if no records are found. Personal checks accepted. Major credit cards accepted.

Mail search: Turnaround time: 2 to 3 weeks. If the agency receives a search request by overnight mail, they will mail the response within 2 to 3 days. A SASE is requested.

Phone search: See expedited service.

Fax search: The fax number above is for this agency; VitalChek's fax is 402-471-8238.

In person search: Turnaround time is 20 to 30 minutes.

Online search: Records may be ordered online from www.vitalchek.com (see expedited services).

Expedited service: Expedited service is available from www.vitalchek.com via online or fax. Fee is $31.00 and includes overnight delivery and fee for required use of credit card.

Marriage Certificates

Health and Human Services System, Vital Statistics Section, PO Box 95065, Lincoln, NE 68509-5065 (Courier address: 301 Centennial Mall S, 3rd Floor, Lincoln, NE 68509); 402-471-2871, 402-471-6440, 402-471-8230-Fax; 8AM-5PM.

www.hhs.state.ne.us/ced/nevrinfo.htm

If a certificate is more than 50 years old, a release is not required.

Records are available from 1909 to present. Records are indexed by Soundex code, year and county and are on microfilm from 1956 to present. It takes 30 days before new records are available for inquiry. Records are indexed on microfiche.

Searching: Must have a notarized, signed release from persons of record or immediate family member for investigative purposes. Include the following in your request-names of husband and wife, date of marriage, place or county of marriage, relationship to person of record, reason for information request, wife's maiden name. Also, all requesters must include copy of photo ID.

Access by: mail, phone, fax, in person, online.

Fee & Payment: The fee is $7.00 per record. Fee payee: Vital Records. Prepayment required. Credit cards may only be used for phone expedited service. The file search fee is non-refundable if no records are found. Personal checks accepted. Major credit cards accepted.

Mail search: Turnaround time: 2 to 3 weeks. If this agency receives a search request by overnight mail, they will mail a response within 2 to 3 days. A SASE is requested.

Phone search: See expedited service.

Fax search: The fax number above is for this agency; VitalChek's fax is 402-471-8238.

In person search: Turnaround time is 30 minutes.

Online search: Records may be ordered online from www.vitalchek.com (see expedited services).

Expedited service: Expedited service is available from www.vitalchek.com via online or fax. Fee is $31.00 and includes overnight delivery and fee for required use of credit card. Turnaround time: overnight delivery. Expedited service is available between 9AM and 3PM Central Time.

Divorce Records

Health and Human Services System, Vital Statistics Section, PO Box 95065, Lincoln, NE 68509-5065 (Courier address: 301 Centennial Mall S, 3rd Floor, Lincoln, NE 68509); 402-471-2871, 402-471-6440, 402-471-8230-Fax; 8AM-5PM.

www.hhs.state.ne.us/ced/nevrinfo.htm

If a certificate is more than 50 years, a release is not required.

Records are available from 1909 to present. Records are indexed by Soundex code, year and county and are on microfilm from 1956. It takes 30 days before new records are available for inquiry.

Searching: Must have a signed release from person of record or immediate family member for investigative purposes. Include the following in your request-names of husband and wife, date of divorce, relationship to person of record, reason for information request, county where divorce was granted. Also, all requesters must include copy of photo ID.

Access by: mail, phone, fax, in person, online.

Fee & Payment: Fee is $7.00 per record. Fee payee: Vital Records. Prepayment required. Credit cards may only be used for phone expedited service. The file search fee is non-refundable if no records are found. Personal checks accepted. Major credit cards accepted.

Mail search: Turnaround time: 2 to 3 weeks. If this agency receives a request by overnight mail, they will mail a response within 2-3 days. A SASE is requested.

Phone search: See expedited service.

Fax search: The fax number above is for this agency; VitalChek's fax is 402-471-8238.

In person search: Turnaround time is 20-30 minutes.

Online search: Records may be ordered online from www.vitalchek.com (see expedited services).

Expedited service: Expedited service is available from www.vitalchek.com via online or fax. Fee is $31.00 and includes overnight delivery and fee for required use of credit card. Turnaround time: overnight delivery. Expedited service is available between 9AM and 3PM Central Time.

Workers' Compensation Records

Workers' Compensation Court, PO Box 98908, Lincoln, NE 68509-8908 (Courier address: State Capitol, 13th Floor, Lincoln, NE 68509); 402-471-6468, 800-599-5155 (In-state), 402-471-2700-Fax; 8AM-5PM.

www.wcc.ne.gov

Records are available from 1972 on. It takes 5days before new records are available for inquiry. Records are indexed on microfilm, printout sheets (SS# & name only), computer. Records are normally destroyed after 50 years.

Searching: Must have a release form for medical records. All other records are public record. Include the following in your request-claimant name, Social Security Number, date of birth, date of accident, and docket number if available. A date of injury is required for searches going back more than 10 years.

Access by: mail, fax, in person, online.

Fee & Payment: The agency will charge fees if retrieval and copying fees exceed $20.00 This is at the discretion of the Court, If costs will exceed $50.00 a deposit is required. Fee payee: Workers' Compensation Court. Personal checks accepted. No credit cards accepted.

Mail search: Turnaround time: 4 days.

Fax search: Records may be requested by fax.

In person search: Agency will mail results.

Online search: Access to this Court's orders and decisions is available from the website. Note this is not access to records. Email requests accepted at newcc@wcc.ne.gov.

Driver Records

Department of Motor Vehicles, Driver & Vehicle Records Division, PO Box 94789, Lincoln, NE 68509-4789 (Courier address: 301 Centennial Mall, S, Lincoln, NE 68509); 402-471-3918, 402-471-8694-Fax; 8AM-5PM.

www.dmv.state.ne.us

It is suggested you obtain copies of tickets at the local courts.

Records are available for 5 years for moving violations and suspensions; lifetime for DWIs. Accidents are reported on the record, but fault is not indicated. Surrendered licenses are purged one year after expiration date. It takes 30 days before new records are available for inquiry. Records are normally destroyed after 5 years.

Searching: SSNs will not be released. Only exempt, approved requesters receive the driver's address. The general public cannot get personal data unless notarized authorization from subject and requester presented. The driver's full name and DOB or license number are needed for ordering. Occasional requesters with a permissible use should use the Application for Copy of Driving Record form.

Access by: mail, in person, online.

Fee & Payment: The fee is $3.00 per record. Fee payee: Department of Motor Vehicles. Prepayment required. Personal checks accepted. No credit cards accepted.

Mail search: Turnaround time: 24 hours. A SASE is requested.

In person search: Requesters must produce photo ID, are not charged for a no record found.

Online search: Nebraska outsources all online and tape record requests through Nebrask@ Online at www.nebraska.gov/subscribe.phtml or call 800-747-8177. The system is interactive and open 24 hours a day, 7 days a week. Fee is $3.00 per record. There is an annual fee of $50.00 and a $.12 per minute connect fee or no connect fee if through the Internet.

Vehicle & Vessel Ownership Vehicle Identification,

Department of Motor Vehicles, Driver & Vehicle Records Division, PO Box 94789, Lincoln, NE 68509-4789 (Courier address: 301 Centennial Mall, S, Lincoln, NE 68509); 402-471-8694-Fax; 8AM-5PM.

www.dmv.state.ne.us

Records are available from 1939. Boat ownership information is available from 1997. All motorized boats manufactured after 11/1/72 must be titled. It takes less than 1 day before new records are available for inquiry.

Searching: Only permissible use requesters receive full record data. The general public cannot obtain records, with or without obtain personal data, unless written notarized consent of the subject is provided. Typical items required for search include; full name, VIN or plate number, and year and make.

Access by: mail, in person, online.

Fee & Payment: The fee is $1.00 per record. Lien information appears on the record. Fee payee: Department of Motor Vehicles. Prepayment required. Personal checks accepted. No credit cards accepted.

Mail search: Turnaround time: 7 to 10 days. A SASE is requested.

In person search: Turnaround time is while you wait. "No record founds" are not charged the full amount. Requesters must show photo ID.

Online search: Electronic access is through Nebrask@ Online at www.nebraska.gov/subscribe.phtml. There is a start-up fee addition to the $1.00 per record fee. The system is open 24 hours a day, 7 days a week. Call 800-747-8177 for more information.

Other access: Bulk requesters must be authorized by state officials. Purpose of the request and subsequent usage are reviewed. For more information, call 402-471-3885

Accident Reports

Department of Roads, Accident Records Bureau, Box 94669, Lincoln, NE 68509 (Courier address: 1500 Nebraska Highway 2, Lincoln, NE 68502); 402-479-4645, 402-479-3637-Fax; 7AM-5PM.

www.dor.state.ne.us

Accident reports are required for incidents with property damage in excess of $1,000 or if death or injury.

Records are available from 1978 to 1994 on microfilm; however, fatal accidents are on microfilm since 1956. Records are computerized since 1988. It takes 10 days or more before new records are available for inquiry.

Searching: Individual driver's own reports are not released. Include the following in your request-full name, date of accident, county.

Access by: mail, fax, in person.

Fee & Payment: The fee is $6.00 per record. Fee payee: Accident Records Bureau. Prepayment required. Personal checks accepted. No credit cards accepted.

Mail search: Turnaround time: 1 week to 10 days.

Fax search: Records may be requested by fax.

In person search: Simple requests may be processed immediately.

Other access: Records can be purchased in bulk from the computer database (1988 to present).

Vessel Registration

Records not maintained by a state level agency.

All boats must be registered. Records are found at the county recorder offices. There is no state agency that handles this information.

Voter Registration

Secretary of State, Elections Division-Records, PO Box 94608, Lincoln, NE 68509-4608; 402-471-2555, 402-471-7834-Fax; 8AM-5PM.

www.sos.state.ne.us/elec

Individual look-ups must be done at the county level. It takes 3 days before new records are available for inquiry. Records are indexed on computer.

Searching: The Federal Help America Vote Act of 2002 (HAVA) law requires implementation of a central, computerized, statewide voter registration system by 01/01/2006. The state will comply.

Access by: mail.

Mail search: Turnaround time: 2 to 5 days. You must give SSN and DOB.

Other access: Current law dictates that the database can only be sold for political purposes, and not for commercial purposes. A statewide CD can be purchased for $500.

GED Certificates

NE Dept of Education, Adult Education, PO Box 94987, Lincoln, NE 68509 (Courier address: 301 Centennial Mall S, Lincoln, NE 68509); 402-471-2475, 402-471-8127-Fax; 8AM-5PM.

www.nde.state.ne.us/ADED/home.htm

It takes 1 month before new records are available for inquiry. Records are normally destroyed after records are not destroyed.

Searching: To search, all of the following is required: a signed release, date of birth, all last names used, and SSN. If known, the year and city of test are helpful.

Access by: mail, fax, in person.

Fee & Payment: There is no fee for verification. Copies of transcripts are $2.00. Fee payee: NE Dept of Education. Prepayment required. Money orders are accepted. Personal checks accepted. No credit cards accepted.

Mail search: Turnaround time: 3 to 4 days.

Fax search: Same criteria as mail searching.

In person search: Turnaround time is immediate in most instances.

Hunting and Fishing License Information

Game & Parks Commission, PO Box 30370, Lincoln, NE 68503 (Courier address: 2200 N 33rd St, Lincoln, NE 68503); 402-471-5455, 402-471-6586-Fax; 8AM-5PM.

www.ngpc.state.ne.us

Records are available from 1988 to 2000 on microfiche for Big Game, and 1999 to current year for other hunting and fishing. It takes weeks before new records are available for inquiry. Records are normally destroyed after 5 years (hard copies).

Searching: All information on the face of the license is public information, except for release of SSNs. Include the following in your request-date of birth, name. Date of application helpful.

Access by: mail, phone, in person.

Fee & Payment: There is no search fee.

Mail search: Turnaround time: 1 to 2 days. A SASE is required.

Phone search: Records are available by phone, when personnel available.

In person search: Turnaround immediate, time permitting.

Other access: Database purchase of information is available.

Nebraska State Licensing Agencies

For details about the agency responsible for licensing/certifying/registering an item below or in the Agency Quick Finder section, match an item's number with the number of the agency in the *Licensing Agency Information* section.

Nebraska Licenses Searchable Online

Abstracting Company #4 .... www.abe.state.ne.us/local/company_search.phtml
Abstractor #4 .... www.abe.state.ne.us/local/license_search.phtml
Adult Day Care #30 .... www.hhs.state.ne.us/crl/rosters.htm
Alcohol/Drug Testing #30 .... www.hhs.state.ne.us/lis/lis.asp
Animal Technician #30 .... www.hhs.state.ne.us/lis/lis.asp
Architect #2 .... www.ea.state.ne.us/search/arch.htm
Asbestos Worker/Professional #17 .... www.hhs.state.ne.us/lis/lis.asp
Asbestos-related Occupation #30 .... www.hhs.state.ne.us/lis/lis.asp
Assisted Living Facility #30 .... www.hhs.state.ne.us/crl/rosters.htm
Athletic Trainer #30 .... www.hhs.state.ne.us/lis/lis.asp
Attorney #15 .... www.nebar.com/index.htm
Bank #31 .... www.ndbf.org/searches/fisearch.shtml
Barber School #1 .... www.barbers.state.ne.us/
Check Sales #31 .... www.ndbf.org/searches/fisearch.shtml
Child Care Center / Placing Agency #30 .... www.hhs.state.ne.us/crl/rosters.htm
Chiropractor #30 .... www.hhs.state.ne.us/lis/lis.asp
Collection Agency #26 .... www.sos.state.ne.us/business/collection/col_agn.html
Cosmetologist #30 .... www.hhs.state.ne.us/lis/lis.asp
Cosmetology Salon/School #30 .... www.hhs.state.ne.us/lis/lis.asp
Credit Union #31 .... www.ndbf.org/searches/fisearch.shtml
Debt Management Agency #26 .... www.sos.state.ne.us/business/debt_list.html
Delayed Deposit Service #31 .... www.ndbf.org/searches/fisearch.shtml
Dental Anesthesia Permit #30 .... www.hhs.state.ne.us/lis/lis.asp
Dental Hygienist #30 .... www.hhs.state.ne.us/lis/lis.asp
Dentist #30 .... www.hhs.state.ne.us/lis/lis.asp
Developmentally Disabled Center #30 .... www.hhs.state.ne.us/crl/rosters.htm
Drug Distributor, Wholesale / Facility #30 .... www.hhs.state.ne.us/crl/rosters.htm
Electrologist #30 .... www.hhs.state.ne.us/lis/lis.asp
Electrology Facility #30 .... www.hhs.state.ne.us/lis/lis.asp
Embalmer #30 .... www.hhs.state.ne.us/lis/lis.asp
Emergency Medical Care Facility #30 .... www.hhs.state.ne.us/lis/lis.asp
Engineer #2 .... www.ea.state.ne.us/search/
Environmental Health Specialists #17 .... www.hhs.state.ne.us/lis/lis.asp
Esthetician #30 .... www.hhs.state.ne.us/lis/lis.asp
Esthetician Establishment #30 .... www.hhs.state.ne.us/lis/lis.asp
Fund Transmission #31 .... www.ndbf.org/searches/fisearch.shtml
Funeral Director #30 .... www.hhs.state.ne.us/lis/lis.asp
Funeral Establishment #30 .... www.hhs.state.ne.us/lis/lis.asp
Geologist #7 .... www.geology.state.ne.us/board/roster.pdf
Health Clinic #30 .... www.hhs.state.ne.us/lis/lis.asp
Hearing Aid Dispenser/Fitter #30 .... www.hhs.state.ne.us/lis/lis.asp
Home Health Agency #30 .... www.hhs.state.ne.us/crl/rosters.htm
Hospice #30 .... www.hhs.state.ne.us/crl/rosters.htm
Hospital #30 .... www.nlc.state.ne.us/docs/pilot/pubs/h.html
Insurance Company #14 .... www.nol.org/home/NDOI/company_search/index.html
Inter' Care Facility (mentally retarded) #30 .... www.hhs.state.ne.us/crl/rosters.htm
Investigator, Plainclothes #26 .... www.sos.state.ne.us/business/private_eye/pi_list.html
Investment Advisor/Advisor Rep. #11 .... www.ndbf.org/searches/fisearch.shtml
Labor/Delivery Service/Clinic #30 .... www.hhs.state.ne.us/crl/rosters.htm
Laboratory #30 .... www.hhs.state.ne.us/crl/rosters.htm
Landscape Architect #23 .... www.landarch.state.ne.us/registrants.pdf
Lead Abatement Worker, etc. #17 .... www.hhs.state.ne.us/lis/lis.asp
Liquor Retailers/Whlse/Shippers #19 .... www.lcc.ne.gov/license_search/licsearch.cgi

Lobbyist #8	www.unicam.state.ne.us
Local Anesthesia Certification #30	www.hhs.state.ne.us/lis/lis.asp
Long Term Care Center #30	www.hhs.state.ne.us/crl/rosters.htm
Marriage & Family Therapist #30	www.hhs.state.ne.us/lis/lis.asp
Massage Establishment #30	www.hhs.state.ne.us/lis/lis.asp
Massage Therapy School #30	www.hhs.state.ne.us/lis/lis.asp
Medical Doctor #30	www.hhs.state.ne.us/lis/lis.asp
Mental Health Center #30	www.hhs.state.ne.us/lis/lis.asp
Mentally Retarded Care Service #30	www.hhs.state.ne.us/crl/rosters.htm
Nail Technologist #30	www.hhs.state.ne.us/lis/lis.asp
Notary Public #27	www.sos.state.ne.us
Nurse #30	www.hhs.state.ne.us/lis/lis.asp
Nursing Home #30	www.hhs.state.ne.us/lis/lis.asp
Nursing Home Administrator #30	www.hhs.state.ne.us/lis/lis.asp
Nutrition Therapy, Medical #30	www.hhs.state.ne.us/lis/lis.asp
Occupational Therapist #30	www.hhs.state.ne.us/lis/lis.asp
Optometrist #30	www.hhs.state.ne.us/lis/lis.asp
Osteopathic Physician #30	www.hhs.state.ne.us/lis/lis.asp
Pesticide Applicator/Dealer #18	www.kellysolutions.com/ne/
Pharmacist #30	www.hhs.state.ne.us/lis/lis.asp
Pharmacy #30	www.hhs.state.ne.us/lis/lis.asp
Pharmacy, Mail Order #30	www.hhs.state.ne.us/lis/lis.asp
Physical Therapist #30	www.hhs.state.ne.us/lis/lis.asp
Physician #30	www.hhs.state.ne.us/lis/lis.asp
Physician Assistant #30	www.hhs.state.ne.us/lis/lis.asp
Podiatrist #30	www.hhs.state.ne.us/lis/lis.asp
Polygraph Examiner, Private #26	www.sos.state.ne.us/business/poly_pri.html
Polygraph Examiner, Public #26	www.sos.state.ne.us/business/poly_pub.html
Preschool #30	www.hhs.state.ne.us/crl/rosters.htm
Private Detective #26	www.sos.state.ne.us/business/private_eye/pd_list.html
Private Detective Agency #26	www.sos.state.ne.us/business/private_eye/pd_agenci.html
Psychologist #30	www.hhs.state.ne.us/lis/lis.asp
Public Accountant-CPA #5	www.nbpa.ne.gov/search/index.phtml
Radiographer #30	www.hhs.state.ne.us/lis/lis.asp
Radon Mitigation Specialist/Tech #17	www.hhs.state.ne.us/lis/lis.asp
Real Estate Agent/Sales #25	http://nrec.nol.org/licinfodb/
Real Estate Appraiser #22	www.appraiser.ne.gov/appraiser/listing/
Real Estate Broker #25	http://nrec.nol.org/licinfodb/
Rehabilitation Agency #30	www.hhs.state.ne.us/crl/rosters.htm
Respiratory Care Practitioner #30	www.hhs.state.ne.us/lis/lis.asp
Respite Care Service #30	www.hhs.state.ne.us/crl/rosters.htm
Sales Finance Company #31	www.ndbf.org/searches/fisearch.shtml
Saving & Loan #31	www.ndbf.org/searches/fisearch.shtml
Securities Agent #11	www.ndbf.org/searches/fisearch.shtml
Securities Broker/Dealer #11	www.ndbf.org/searches/fisearch.shtml
Social Worker #30	www.hhs.state.ne.us/lis/lis.asp
Speech-Language Pathol/Audiologist #30	www.hhs.state.ne.us/lis/lis.asp
Substance Abuse Treatment Center #30	www.nlc.state.ne.us/docs/pilot/pubs/h.html
Surveyor, Land #3	www.sso.state.ne.us/bels/
Swimming Pool Operator #30	www.hhs.state.ne.us/lis/lis.asp
Trust Company #31	www.ndbf.org/searches/fisearch.shtml
Veterinarian #30	www.hhs.state.ne.us/lis/lis.asp
Veterinary Technician #30	www.hhs.state.ne.us/lis/lis.asp
Voice Stress Examiner/Analyzer #26	www.sos.state.ne.us/business/voice.html
Water Operator #30	www.hhs.state.ne.us/lis/lis.asp
Water Treatment Plant Operator #17	www.hhs.state.ne.us/lis/lis.asp
Well Driller/Pump Installer #17	www.hhs.state.ne.us/lis/lis.asp
X-ray Unit Portable #30	www.hhs.state.ne.us/lis/lis.asp

Nebraska Licensing Quick Finder

Abstracting Company #4 402-471-2383
Abstractor #4 402-471-2383
Adult Day Care #30 402-471-2115
Aerial Applicator #10 402-471-2371
Air Conditioning/Heating Contr. #12 402-441-7508
Alcohol/Drug Testing #30 402-471-2118
Amusement Ride Inspector #21 402-471-2239
Animal Technician #30 402-471-2118
Architect #2 402-471-2021
Asbestos Worker/Professional #17 402-471-2299
Asbestos-related Occupation #30 402-471-2299
Assisted Living Facility #30 402-471-4970
Athletic Trainer #30 402-471-2299
Attorney #15 .... 800-927-0117, 402-475-7091
Auctioneer #6 402-441-7437
Bank #31 402-471-2171
Barber #1 402-471-2051
Barber School #1 402-471-2051
Boiler&Pressure Vessel Inspector #16 .. 402-471-4721
Boiler Inspection #21 402-471-2230
Boxer #28 402-471-2009
Boxing Promoter #28 402-471-2009
Chauffeur #6 402-441-7437
Check Sales #31 402-471-2171
Child Care Center #30 402-471-2115
Child Caring/Placing Agency #30 402-471-2115
Child Labor #21 402-471-2230
Chiropractor #30 402-471-2299
Collection Agency #26 .... 402-471-8606, 471-2555
Contractor Registration #21 402-595-3095
Contractor, Building #12 402-441-6456
Cosmetologist #30 402-471-2115
Cosmetology Salon/School #30 402-471-2115
Credit Union #31 402-471-2171
Debt Management Agency #26
.... 402-471-8606, 471-2555
Delayed Deposit Service #31 402-471-2171
Dental Anesthesia Permit #30 402-471-2118
Dental Hygienist #30 402-471-2118
Dentist #30 402-471-2118
Developmentally Disabled Center #30 . 402-471-2115
Drug Distributor, Wholesale #30 402-471-2118
Drug Wholesale Facility #30 402-471-2115
Educational Media Specialist/Librarian #13
.... 402-471-0739
Electrician #29 402-471-3550
Electrologist #30 402-471-2115
Electrology Facility #30 402-471-2115
Elevator Inspector/Inspection Manager #21
.... 402-595-2523
Embalmer #30 402-471-2115
Emergency Medical Care Facility #30 .. 402-471-2115
Employment Agency #21 402-595-3095
Engineer #2 402-471-2021
Environmental Health Specialists #17 .. 402-471-2299
Esthetician #30 402-471-2115

Esthetician Establishment #30 402-471-2115
Farm Labor Contractor #21 402-595-3095
Fertilizer Professional/Business #18 402-471-2394
Fire Protection Sprinkler Contr. #12 402-441-6456
Fund Transmission #31 402-471-2171
Funeral Director #30 402-471-2115
Funeral Establishment #30 402-471-2115
Geologist #7 402-471-8383
Health Clinic #30 402-471-2115
Hearing Aid Dispenser/Fitter #30 402-471-2299
Hearing Quality Assurance Screening Test #9
.... 402-471-3593
Home Health Agency #30 402-471-2115
Hospice #30 402-471-2115
Hospital #30 402-471-2115
Insurance Agency/Agent/Broker/Producer #14
.... 402-471-2201
Insurance Company #14 402-471-2201
Insurance Consultant #14 402-471-2201
Insurance Utilizat'n Review Agent #14 .. 402-471-2201
Intermediate Care Facility (Mentally Retarded) #30
.... 402-471-2115
Interpreter for the Hearing Impaired (Nebraska
Registry of Interpreters) #9 402-471-3593
Investigator,plainclothes#26 .402-471-8606, 471-2384
Investment Advisor/Advisor Rep. #11 .. 402-471-3445
Jewelry Dealer, Secondhand #6 402-441-7437
Labor/Delivery Service/Clinic #30 402-471-2115
Laboratory #30 402-471-2115
Landscape Architect #23 402-471-2407
Law Enforcement Officer #20 308-385-6030
Lead Abatement Worker, etc. #17 402-471-2299
Liquor Retail Wholse/ Shippers #19 402-471-2571
Lobbyist #8 402-471-2271
Local Anesthesia Certification #30 402-471-2118
Long Term Care Center #30 402-471-2115
Marriage & Family Therapist #30 402-471-2115
Massage Establishment #30 402-471-2115
Massage Therapy School #30 402-471-2115
Medical Doctor #30 402-471-2118
Mental Health Center #30 402-471-2115
Mentally Retarded Care Service #30 402-471-2115
Nail Technologist #30 402-471-2115
Notary Public #27 402-471-2558
Nurse #30 402-471-2115
Nursing Education Program #30 402-471-2115
Nursing Home #30 402-471-2115
Nursing Home Administrator #30 402-471-2115
Nutrition Therapy, Medical #30 402-471-2115
Occupational Therapist #30 402-471-2299
Optometrist #30 402-471-2118
Osteopathic Physician #30 402-471-2118
Pawnbroker #6 402-441-7437
Pesticide Applicator/Dealer #18 402-471-2394
Pharmacist #30 402-471-2118
Pharmacy #30 402-471-2115

Pharmacy, Mail Order #30 402-471-2115
Physical Therapist #30 402-471-2299
Physician #30 402-471-2118
Physician Assistant #30 402-471-2118
Plant Nursery/Nursery Profession'l #18 402-471-2394
Plumber #12 402-441-6456
Podiatrist #30 402-471-2118
Polygraph Examiner, Private #26 402-471-4070
Polygraph Examiner, Public #26 402-471-4070
Pre-need Seller #14 402-471-2201
Preschool #30 402-471-2115
Private Detective #26 .... 402-471-8606, 471-2384
Private Detective Agency#26 402-471-8606, 471-2384
Psychologist #30 402-471-4905
Public Accountant-CPA #5 402-471-3595
Racing Event/Professional #24 402-471-4155
Radiographer #30 402-471-2118
Radon Mitigation Specialist/Tech. #17 .. 402-471-2299
Real Estate Agent/Sales #25 402-471-2004
Real Estate Appraiser #22 402-471-9015
Real Estate Broker #25 402-471-2004
Rehabilitation Agency #30 402-471-2115
Respiratory Care Practitioner #30 402-471-2299
Respite Care Service #30 402-471-2115
Sales Finance Company #31 402-471-2171
Saving & Loan #31 402-471-2171
School Administrator/Supervisor #13 402-471-0739
School Nurse #13 402-471-0739
Securities Agent #11 402-471-3445
Securities Broker/Dealer #11 402-471-3445
Skin Care Salon #30 402-471-2115
Social Worker #30 402-471-2115
Speech-Language Pathologist/Audiologist #30
.... 402-471-2115
Substance Abuse Treatment Cntr 30 402-471-2115
Surplus Lines Seller #14 402-471-2201
Surveyor, Land #3 402-471-2566
Swimming Pool Operator #30 402-471-2299
Taxi Driver #6 402-441-7437
Teacher #13 402-471-0739
Trust Company #31 402-471-2171
Veterinarian #30 402-471-2118
Veterinary Technician #30 402-471-2115
Voice Stress Examiner/Analyzer #26
.... 402-471-8606, 471-4070
Water Operator #30 402-471-2299
Water Treatment Plant Operator #17 ... 402-471-2299
Well Driller/Pump Installer #17 402-471-2299
Wrestler #28 402-471-2009
Wrestling/Boxing Matches #28 402-471-2009
X-ray Unit Portable #30 402-471-2115

Nebraska Licensing Agency Information

1 Board of Barber Examiners, 301 Centennial Mall S, 6th Fl, Lincoln, NE 68509-4723; 402-471-2051, Fax: 402-471-2052.
www.barbers.state.ne.us

2 Board of Examiners for Engineers & Architects, PO Box 95165, 301 Centennial Mall S 6th Fl, Lincoln, NE 68509-4751; 402-471-2021, Fax: 402-471-0787.
www.ea.state.ne.us
Email: board@nol.org
Search Database at www.ea.state.ne.us

3 Board of Examiners for Land Surveyors, 555 N Cotner Blvd, Lincoln, NE 68505; 402-471-2566, Fax: 402-471-3057.
www.sso.state.ne.us/bels/
Search Database at www.sso.state.ne.us/bels/

4 Abstractors Board of Examiners, PO Box 94944 (1200 N St), Lincoln, NE 68509; 402-471-2383, Fax: 402-471-6575.
www.abe.state.ne.us
Email: mmccull@abe.state.ne.us
Search Database at www.abe.state.ne.us

5 Board of Public Accountancy, PO Box 94725 (140 N 8th St #290), Lincoln, NE 68509-4725; 402-471-3595, Fax: 402-471-4484.
www.nbpa.ne.gov
Email: nbpa01@nol.org
Search Database at
www.nbpa.ne.gov/search/index.phtml

6 Applications & Permits, City Clerk's Office, 555 S 10th St, Lincoln, NE 68508; 402-441-7437, Fax: 402-441-8325.

7 Board of Geologists, PO Box 94844, Lincoln, NE 68509; 402-471-8383, Fax: 402-471-0787.
www.geology.state.ne.us/board/nbg.htm
Email: geology@nol.org
Search Database at
www.geology.state.ne.us/board/roster.pdf

8 Clerk of the Legislature, PO Box 94604, Lincoln, NE 68509-4604; 402-471-2271, Fax: 402-471-2126.
www.unicam.state.ne.us
Email: uio@unicam.state.ne.us
Search Database at www.unicam.state.ne.us

9 Commission for the Deaf & Hard of Hearing, 4600 Valley Rd #420, Lincoln, NE 68510-4844; 402-471-3593, Fax: 402-471-3067.
www.nol.org/home/NCDHH
Email: lstaff@ncdhh.state.ne.us

10 Department of Aeronautics, 3431 Aviation Rd #150 (68524), Lincoln, NE 68501; 402-471-2371, Fax: 402-471-2906.   www.aero.state.ne.us
Email: sonis@mail.state.ne.us

11 Department of Banking & Finance, Bureau of Securities, PO Box 95006 (1200 "N" Street, #311), Lincoln, NE 68509-5006; 402-471-3445.
www.ndbf.org/
Search Database at
www.ndbf.org/searches/fisearch.shtml   Note: The Orders and Actions search page includes state orders and cancelled or denied licenses. The NASD web search site is national.

12 Department of Building & Safety, 555 S 10th St, Lincoln, NE 68508; 402-441-7791, Fax: 402-471-8214.
www.ci.lincoln.ne.us

13 Department of Education, Teacher Accreadiation/Certification Division, 301 Centennial Mall S 6th Fl, Lincoln, NE 68509-4987; 402-471-0739, Fax: 402-471-9735.
www.nde.state.ne.us

14 Department of Insurance, 941 O St #400, Lincoln, NE 68508-3639; 402-471-2201, Fax: 402-471-6559.
www.nol.org/home/NDOI/
Email: consumer_affairs@doi.state.ne.us

15 Nebraska Bar Association, PO Box 81809 (635 S 14th), Lincoln, NE 68501-1809; 800-927-0117, 402-475-7091, Fax: 402-475-7098.
www.nebar.com/index.htm   Note: At website, click on Lawyer Search.

16 Division of Safety & Labor Standards, Boiler Inspectors Section, PO Box 95024, Lincoln, NE 68509; 402-471-4721, Fax: 402-471-5039.
www.dol.state.ne.us/nwd/center.cfm?PRICAT=2& SUBCAT=2C
Email: dburns@dol.state.ne.us

17 Drinking Water & Environmental Sanitation, Credentialing Division, PO Box 95007 (301 Centennial Mall S), Lincoln, NE 68509; 402-471-2299, Fax: 402-471-3577.
www.hhs.state.ne.us
Search Database at www.hhs.state.ne.us/lis/lis.asp
Note: They sell lists, labels and disketts.

18 Department of Agriculture, Bureau of Plant Industry, PO Box 94756 (301 Centennial Mall South), Lincoln, NE 68509; 402-471-2394, Fax: 402-471-6892.
www.kellysolutions.com/ne/
Search Database at
www.agr.state.ne.us/division/bpi/bpi.htm

19 Liquor Control Commission, 301 Centennial Mall S, 5th Fl, Lincoln, NE 68509-5046; 402-471-2571, Fax: 402-471-2814.
www.lcc.ne.gov   Email: nlcc01@nol.org
Search Database at
http://www.lcc.ne.gov/license_search/licsearch.cgi

20 Crime Commission, 3600 N Academy Rd, Grand Island, NE 68801; 308-385-6030, Fax: 308-385-6032.
www.nol.org/home/crimecom
Email: slamken@crimecom.state.ne.us

21 Department of Labor, Office of Safety & Labor Standards, 301 Centennial Mall S, Lower Level, Lincoln, NE 68509-5024; 402-471-2230, Fax: 402-471-5039.
www.dol.state.ne.us
Email: ghirsh@dol.state.ne.us

22 Real Estate Appraiser Board, PO Box 94963, Lincoln, NE 68509-4963; 402-471-9015, Fax: 402-471-9017.
www.appraiser.ne.gov/
Email: mjhass_appraiser.dnr.state.ne.us
Search Database at
www.appraiser.ne.gov/appraiser/listing/

23 Board of Landscape Architects, PO Box 95165, Lincoln, NE 68509-5165; 402-471-2407, Fax: 402-471-0787.
www.landarch.state.ne.us/
Email: landarch@nol.org
Search Database at
www.landarch.state.ne.us/registrants.pdf

24 Racing Commission, 301 Centennial Mall S 6th Fl, Lincoln, NE 68509-5014; 402-471-4155, Fax: 402-471-2339.
www.horseracing.state.ne.us/

25 Real Estate Commission, 1200 N St, Ste 402, Lincoln, NE 68509-4667; 402-471-2004, Fax: 402-471-4492.
www.nrec.state.ne.us
Email: infotech@nrec.state.ne.us
Search Database at http://nrec.nol.org/licinfodb/

26 Secretary of State, Business Services, Licensing Division, PO Box 94608 (State Capitol Rm 2300), Lincoln, NE 68509-4608; 402-471-8606, Fax: 402-471-2530.
www.sos.state.ne.us
Email: sos04@nol.org
Search Database at www.sos.state.ne.us/business/

27 Secretary of State, Notary Division, Rm 1301 State Capitol Bldg, Lincoln, NE 68509-5104; 402-471-2558, Fax: 402-471-4429.
www.sos.state.ne.us/business/notary/
Email: dpester@nol.org

28 Athletic Commission, 301 Centennial Mall S, 1st Fl, Lincoln, NE 68509-4743; 402-471-2009, Fax: 402-471-3396.
www.athcomm.state.ne.us/
Email: contact@athcomm.ne.gov

29 Electrical Division, 800 S 13th St #109, Lincoln, NE 68509; 402-471-3550, Fax: 402-471-4297.
www.electrical.state.ne.us/

30 Health & Human Svcs Regulation & Licensure, Credentialing Division, PO Box 94986, Lincoln, NE 68509-4986; 402-471-2115, Fax: 402-471-3577.
www.hhs.state.ne.us/crl/crlindex.htm
Email: marie.mcclatchey@hhss.state.ne.us
Search Database at www.hhs.state.ne.us/lis/lis.asp
Note: Boarding Homes do not need a license as of 1/1/2001. Domiciliary Facility and Residential Care Facility are now combined into Assisted Living Facility.

31 Department of Banking & Finance, Financial Institutions Divison, PO Box 95006 (1200 "N" Street, #311), Lincoln, NE 68509-5006; 402-471-2171.
www.ndbf.org/
Search Database at
www.ndbf.org/searches/fisearch.shtml

Nebraska Federal Courts

The following list indicates the district and division name for each county in the state.

County/Court Cross Reference

County	Court	County	Court
Adams	Lincoln	Jefferson	Lincoln
Antelope	Lincoln	Johnson	Lincoln
Arthur	North Platte	Kearney	Lincoln
Banner	North Platte	Keith	North Platte
Blaine	North Platte	Keya Paha	North Platte
Boone	Lincoln	Kimball	North Platte
Box Butte	North Platte	Knox	Omaha
Boyd	Lincoln	Lancaster	Lincoln
Brown	North Platte	Lincoln	North Platte
Buffalo	Lincoln	Logan	North Platte
Burt	Omaha	Loup	North Platte
Butler	Lincoln	Madison	Lincoln
Cass	Lincoln (Omaha)	McPherson	North Platte
Cedar	Omaha	Merrick	Lincoln
Chase	North Platte	Morrill	North Platte
Cherry	North Platte	Nance	Lincoln
Cheyenne	North Platte	Nemaha	Lincoln
Clay	Lincoln	Nuckolls	Lincoln
Colfax	Lincoln	Otoe	Lincoln
Cuming	Omaha	Pawnee	Lincoln
Custer	North Platte	Perkins	North Platte
Dakota	Omaha	Phelps	Lincoln
Dawes	North Platte	Pierce	Omaha
Dawson	North Platte	Platte	Lincoln
Deuel	North Platte	Polk	Lincoln
Dixon	Omaha	Red Willow	North Platte
Dodge	Omaha	Richardson	Lincoln
Douglas	Omaha	Rock	North Platte
Dundy	North Platte	Saline	Lincoln
Fillmore	Lincoln	Sarpy	Omaha
Franklin	Lincoln	Saunders	Lincoln
Frontier	North Platte	Scotts. Bluff	North Platte
Furnas	North Platte	Seward	Lincoln
Gage	Lincoln	Sheridan	North Platte
Garden	North Platte	Sherman	Lincoln
Garfield	North Platte	Sioux	North Platte
Gosper	North Platte	Stanton	Omaha (Lincoln)
Grant	North Platte	Thayer	Lincoln
Greeley	Lincoln	Thomas	North Platte
Hall	Lincoln	Thurston	Omaha
Hamilton	Lincoln	Valley	North Platte
Harlan	Lincoln	Washington	Omaha
Hayes	North Platte	Wayne	Omaha
Hitchcock	North Platte	Webster	Lincoln
Holt	Lincoln	Wheeler	Lincoln
Hooker	North Platte	York	Lincoln
Howard	Lincoln		

Standards for Federal Courts: Search fee is $26.00 per item (one party name or case number). Copy fee is $.50 per page. Certification fee is $9.00 per document, double for exemplification, if available. All fees standard unless noted in profile. Mail Search: always enclose a stamped self addressed envelope unless otherwise noted. Most courts accept fax requests or will suggest a copying/search vendor. Before releasing records, all courts require prepayment, unless noted.

Open records are located at the court unless otherwise noted. District courts index by defendant and plaintiff as well as by case number. Bankruptcy courts usually index by debtor and case number. While most courts now have their indexes on computer, many may still maintain index card files as well.

Courts offering internet access via CM-ECF or older RACER, PACER, or Web-PACER systems charge $.08 per page fee unless noted as free. Where PACER is available, the universal sign-up number is 800-676-6856. Find PACER and the US Party/Case Index at http://pacer.psc.uscourts.gov.

US District Court

District of Nebraska

Lincoln Division Court Clerk, PO Box 83468, Lincoln, NE 68501 (courier address: 593 Federal Bldg, 100 Centennial Mall N, Lincoln, NE 68508), 402-437-5225, Fax-402-437-5651. Hours- 8AM-4:45PM. www.ned.uscourts.gov

Counties: Nebraska cases may be filed in any of 3 courts at the attorney's option, except filings in North Platte Division must be during trial session.

Searches & Indexing: Results do not include SSN or DOB. Both computer and card indexes maintained; computer goes back to 1985. New cases in the index 1-2 days after filing date. Records purged yearly.

Fee & Payment: Pay by Visa/MC, money order, cashier's or personal check. Payee: Clerk, US District Court. Prepayment required.

Phone Search: Only docket information available by telephone.

Mail Search: search usually completed- 1-2 days. Include SASE for return.

In Person Search: Fee charged if court performs your search. No self-serve copier available.

E-Services: ECF replaces PACER whose records did go back to late 1990. New records online after 1 day. ECF at https://ecf.ned.uscourts.gov **Opinions Online:** www.nebar.com/resources/opinions/usdist/index.htm.

North Platte Division c/o Lincoln Division, PO Box 83468, Lincoln, NE 68501 (courier address: 593 Federal Bldg, 100 Centennial Mall N, Lincoln, NE 68508), 402-437-5225, Fax-402-437-5651. 8AM-4:45PM. www.ned.uscourts.gov

Counties: Nebraska cases may be filed in any of 3 courts at the attorney's option, except filings in North Platte Division must be during trial session. Some case records may be in the Omaha Division as well as Lincoln Division.

Searches & Indexing: Results do not include SSN or DOB. Computer index back to 2002 is maintained. Records can also be located at Omaha or Lincoln, depending on the judge assigned. New cases in the index 1-2 days after filing date. Records purged yearly. Open records located at Lincoln Division.

Fee & Payment: Pay by Visa/MC, money order, cashier's or personal check. Payee: Clerk, US District Court.

Phone Search: No searching by telephone.

Mail Search: search usually completed- 4 days. Include SASE for return.

In Person Search: permitted. Self-serve copier available - $.50 per page.

E-Services: ECF replaces PACER whose records did go back to late 1990. New records online after 1 day. ECF at https://ecf.ned.uscourts.gov **Opinions Online:** www.nebar.com/resources/opinions/usdist/index.htm.

Omaha Division Court Clerk, 111 S 18th Plaza, Ste 1152, Omaha, NE 68102 (also use mail address for courier delivery), 402-661-7350, Fax-402-661-7387. Hours- 8AM-4:45PM. www.ned.uscourts.gov

Counties: Nebraska cases may be filed in any of 3 courts at the attorney's option, except filings in North Platte Division must be during trial session.

Searches & Indexing: Results do not include SSN or DOB. Both computer and card indexes maintained; computer goes back to 1985. New cases in the index 1-2 days after filing date. Records purged yearly.

Fee & Payment: Pay by money order, cashier's or personal check. Payee: Clerk, US District Court. Prepayment required.

Phone Search: No searching by telephone.

Mail Search: search usually completed- 1-2 days. Include SASE for return.

In Person Search: Fee charged if court performs your search. No self-serve copier available.

E-Services: ECF replaces PACER whose records did go back to late 1990. New records online after 1 day. ECF at https://ecf.ned.uscourts.gov **Opinions Online:** www.nebar.com/resources/opinions/usdist/index.htm.

US Bankruptcy Court

District of Nebraska

Lincoln Division Court Clerk, 460 Federal Bldg, 100 Centennial Mall N, Lincoln, NE 68508 (also use mail address for courier delivery), 402-437-5100, Fax-402-437-5454. Hours- 8AM-4:30PM. www.neb.uscourts.gov

Counties: Adams, Antelope, Boone, Boyd, Buffalo, Butler, Clay, Colfax, Fillmore, Franklin, Gage, Greeley, Hall, Hamilton, Harlan, Holt, Howard, Jefferson, Johnson, Kearney, Lancaster, Madison, Merrick, Nance, Nemaha, Nuckolls, Otoe, Pawnee, Phelps, Platte, Polk, Richardson, Saline, Saunders, Seward, Sherman, Stanton, Thayer, Webster, Wheeler, York. Cases from the North Platte Division assigned here.

Searches & Indexing: All debtor names are indexed for files back to 9/89. Provide full SSN for search; results include only the last 4 digits. Computer index maintained. New cases in the index 1 day after filing date. Records purged every 6 months. District-wide searches available here; this office also maintains records for main bankruptcy office in Omaha.

Fee & Payment: Pay by money order, cashier's or personal check, credit card. No debtor's checks/credit cards accepted. Payee: Clerk, US Bankruptcy Court. Prepayment required.

Phone Search: Only debtor's name, case number, date filed, 341 information, and date discharged and closed is released. Voice Case Information Service available, call VCIS at 800-829-0112 or 402-221-3757.

Mail Search: search usually completed- 1-2 days. SASE not required.

In Person Search: Fee charged if court performs your search. Self-serve copier available for electronic records - $.10 per page.

E-Services: ECF replaces PACER whose records did go back to 9/1989. New records online after 1 day. ECF at https://ecf.neb.uscourts.gov **Opinions Online:** www.neb.uscourts.gov. Click on Case Info, then Nebraska Bankruptcy Opinions.

North Platte Division c/o Lincoln Division, 460 Federal Bldg, 100 Centennial Mall North, Lincoln, NE 68508 (also use mail address for courier delivery), 402-661-7444, Fax-402-661-7492. Hours- 8AM-4:30PM. www.neb.uscourts.gov

Counties: Arthur, Banner, Blaine, Box Butte, Brown, Chase, Cherry, Cheyenne, Custer, Dawes, Dawson, Deuel, Dundy, Frontier, Furnas, Garden, Garfield, Gosper, Grant, Hayes, Hitchcock, Hooker, Keith, Keya Paha, Kimball, Lincoln, Logan, Loup, McPherson, Morrill, Perkins, Red Willow, Rock, Scotts Bluff, Sheridan, Sioux, Thomas, Valley. Cases assigned to Lincoln Division.

Searches & Indexing: Provide full SSN for search; results include only the last 4 digits. New cases in the index 1 day after filing date. Open records located at Lincoln Division.

Fee & Payment: Pay by no business or personal checks accepted. Payee: Clerk, US Bankruptcy Court.

Phone Search: Voice Case Information Service available, call VCIS at 800-829-0112 or 402-221-3757.

Mail Search: search usually completed- same day if possible. SASE not required.

In Person Search: permitted. You may make your own electronic copies - $.10 per page.

E-Services: ECF replaces PACER whose records did go back to 9/1989. New records online after 1 day. ECF at https://ecf.neb.uscourts.gov **Opinions Online:** www.neb.uscourts.gov. Click on Case Info, then Nebraska Bankruptcy Opinions.

Omaha Division Court Clerk, 111 S 18th Plaza, Ste 1125, Omaha, NE 68102 (also use mail address for courier delivery), 402-661-7444, Fax-402-661-7492. Hours- 8AM-4:30PM. www.neb.uscourts.gov

Counties: Burt, Cedar, Cass, Cuming, Dakota, Dixon, Dodge, Douglas, Knox, Pierce, Sarpy, Thurston, Washington, Wayne.

Searches & Indexing: Cases indexed by debtor, creditors, and case number. Provide full SSN for search; results include only the last 4 digits. Computer index maintained. New cases in the index 24 hours after filing date. Records purged every 6 months.

Fee & Payment: Pay by money order, cashier's or personal check. Payee: Clerk, US Bankruptcy Court. Prepayment required.

Phone Search: Only docket information is available by phone. Voice Case Information Service available, call VCIS at 800-829-0112 or 402-221-3757.

Mail Search: search usually completed- 1-2 days. Include SASE for return.

In Person Search: permitted. Make your own electronic copies - $.10 per page.

E-Services: ECF replaces PACER whose records did go back to 9/1989. New records online after 1 day. ECF at https://ecf.neb.uscourts.gov **Opinions Online:** www.neb.uscourts.gov. Click on Case Info, then Nebraska Bankruptcy Opinions.

Nebraska County Courts

Court	Jurisdiction	No. of Courts	How Organized
District Courts*	General	93	12 Districts
County Courts*	Limited	93	11 Districts
Juvenile Courts	Special	3	3 Counties
Workers' Compensation Court	Special	1	

* Profiled in this Sourcebook.

Court	CIVIL								
	Tort	Contract	Real Estate	Min. Claim	Max. Claim	Small Claims	Estate	Eviction	Domestic Relations
District Courts*	X	X	X	$15,000	No Max				X
County Courts*	X	X	X	$0	$15,000	$1800	X	X	X
Juvenile Courts									
Workers' Compensation Court									

Court	CRIMINAL				
	Felony	Misdemeanor	DWI/DUI	Preliminary Hearing	Juvenile
District Courts*	X				
County Courts*		X	X	X	X
Juvenile Courts					X
Workers' Compensation Court					

ADMINISTRATION   Court Administrator, PO Box 98910, Lincoln, NE, 68509-8910; 402-471-3730, Fax: 402-471-2197. http://court.nol.org/AOC

COURT STRUCTURE   The District Court is the court of general jurisdiction. The minimum on civil judgment matters for District Courts is $15,000, however, the State raised the County Court limit on civil matters from $15,000 to $45,000 as of Sept. 1, 2001. As it is less expensive to file civil cases in County Court than in District Court, civil cases in the $15,000 to $45,000 range are more likely to be found in County Court, if after Sept. 1, 2001.

The number of judicial districts went from 21 to the current 12 in July 1992. County Courts have juvenile jurisdiction in all but 3 counties. Douglas, Lancaster, and Sarpy counties have separate Juvenile Courts.

ONLINE ACCESS   An online access subscription service is available for NE District and County courts, except Douglas County District Court. Case details, all party listings, payments and actions taken for criminal, civil, probate, juvenile, and traffic is available. Users must be registered with Nebrask@ Online, there is a start-up fee. The fee is $.60 per record or a flat rate of $300.00 per month. Go to www.nebraska.gov/faqs/justice for more info and how far back records go per county. Supreme Court opinions are available from http://court.nol.org/opinions/.

Currently, Douglas, Lancaster, and Sarpy county courts offer internet access with registration and password required.

ADDITIONAL INFORMATION   Most Nebraska courts require the public to do their own in-person searches and will not respond to written search requests. The State Attorney General has recommended that courts not perform searches because of the time involved and concerns over possible legal liability.

Adams County

County Court PO Box 95, Hastings, NE 68902-0095; phone: 402-461-7143; fax: 402-461-7144; hours 8AM-5PM (CST). *Misdemeanor, Civil Actions Under $45,000, Eviction, Small Claims, Probate.*
Civil Records: Access: In person, online. Visitors must perform in person searches themselves. Court makes copy: $.25 per page; same fee for self serve. Required to search: name, years to search; also helpful: address. Civil cases indexed by defendant. Civil records on index cards and files from 1970s. Online access same as criminal, records date from 10/99 forward, probate from 05/98.
Criminal Records: Access: In person, online. Visitors must perform in person searches themselves. Court makes copy: $.25 per page; same fee for self serve. Required to search: name, years to search; also helpful: DOB, SSN. Criminal records on index cards and files from 1970s. Subscribe to NOL at www.nebraska.gov/service_info.phtml?service_id =147 for court access. $.60 a record fee or $300 per month flat rate. Online criminal and traffic records date from 07/97.
General Information: Public terminal goes back to 1999. No adoption or juvenile records released. Certification fee: $1.00 per page. Payee: Adams County Court. Business checks accepted. Prepayment required.

District Court PO Box 9, Hastings, NE 68902; phone: 402-461-7264; fax: 402-461-7269; hours 8:30AM-5PM (CST). *Felony, Civil Actions Over $15,000.*
http://adamscounty.org/courts/district
Civil Records: Access: In person, online. Visitors must perform in person searches themselves. Court makes copy: $.25 per page. Required to search: name, years to search. Civil cases indexed by defendant, plaintiff; on microfiche from 1800s, 5 yrs on index cards, on docket books from 1800s. Online access same as criminal. Online records date from 07/97.
Criminal Records: Access: In person, online. Visitors must perform in person searches themselves. Court makes copy: $.25 per page. Required to search: name, years to search. Criminal records on microfiche from 1800s, 5 yrs on index cards, on docket books from 1800s. Subscribe to NOL at www.nebraska.gov/service_info.phtml?service_id =147 for court access. $.60 a record fee or $300 per month flat rate. Online records date from 07/97.
General Information: Public terminal has criminal back to - not known and civil back to 7/1997. No juvenile, search warrants or mental health records released. Will not fax documents. Certification fee: $1.00 per page. Prepayment required.

Antelope County

District Court PO Box 45, Neligh, NE 68756; phone: 402-887-4508; fax: 402-887-4870; hours 8:30AM-5PM (CST). *Felony, Civil Actions Over $15,000.*
Civil Records: Access: In person, online. Visitors must perform in person searches themselves. Court makes copy: $.25 per page; same fee for self serve. Required to search: name, years to search. Civil cases indexed by defendant, plaintiff; on index books from 1872, computerized since 1999. Online access same as criminal. Online records date from 03/99.
Criminal Records: Access: In person, online. Visitors must perform in person searches themselves. Court makes copy: $.25 per page; same fee for self serve. Required to search: name, years to search. Criminal records on index books from 1872, computerized since 1999. Subscribe to NOL at www.nebraska.gov/service_info.phtml?service_id =147 for court access. $.60 a record fee or $300 per month flat rate. Online records date from 03/99.

General Information: Public terminal goes back to 1999. No juvenile, sealed, search warrants, or mental health record released. Will fax return specific case file for $1.00 per page. Certification fee: $1.00 per page. Payee: Clerk of District Court. Personal checks accepted. Prepayment required.

Antelope County Court 501 Main, Neligh, NE 68756; phone: 402-887-4650; criminal fax: 402-887-4160; same fax for civil/probate; hours 8:30AM-5PM (CST). *Misdemeanor, Civil Actions Under $45,000, Eviction, Small Claims, Probate.*
Civil Records: Access: In person, online. Visitors must perform in person searches themselves. Court makes copy: $.25 per page; same fee for self serve. Required to search: name, years to search. Civil cases indexed by defendant, plaintiff; on computer from 1994, probate on microfiche from 1800s, civil and small claims indexed from 1983. Online access same as criminal. Online civil and probate records date from 12/99 forward.
Criminal Records: Access: In person, online. Visitors must perform in person searches themselves. Court makes copy: $.25 per page; same fee for self serve. Required to search: name, years to search, DOB, signed release; also helpful: SSN. Criminal index on computer from 1994, indexed from 1800s. Subscribe to NOL at www.nebraska.gov/service_info.phtml?service_id =147 for court access. $.60 a record fee or $300 per month flat rate. Online criminal and traffic records date from 12/99.
General Information: Public use terminal available. No adoption, or sealed records released. Will fax specific case file requests for $1.00 per page. Certification fee: $1.00 plus $.25 per page. Payee: Antelope County Court. Personal checks accepted. Prepayment required.

Arthur County

District & County Court PO Box 126, 205 Fir St, Arthur, NE 69121; phone: 308-764-2203; fax: 308-764-2216; hours 8AM-4PM (MST). *Felony, Misdemeanor, Civil, Eviction, Small Claims, Probate.*
Civil Records: Access: Phone, fax, mail, in person, online. Both court and visitors may perform in person searches themselves. No search fee. Court makes copy: $.20 per page. Required to search: name, years to search. Civil cases indexed by defendant, plaintiff; on index books from 1987, on docket books from 1913. Online access same as criminal. County court online records date from 09/99 forward; District Court records from 06/00. Mail turnaround time 1-2 days.
Criminal Records: Access: Phone, fax, mail, in person, online. Both court and visitors may perform in person searches themselves. No search fee. Court makes copy: $.20 per page. Required to search: name, years to search. Criminal records on index books from 1987, on docket books from 1913. Subscribe to NOL at www.nebraska.gov/service_info.phtml?service_id =147 for court access. $.60 a record fee or $300 per month flat rate. Online criminal and traffic records date from 09/99 forward; District Court records from 06/00. Mail turnaround 1-2 days.
General Information: Public terminal goes back to 1999. No search warrants, juvenile, adoption, mental health, or sealed records released. Will fax documents $1.00 per page. Incoming fax fee $.25. Certification fee: $1.50 first page; $.50 each add'l. Payee: Arthur County Clerk. Personal checks accepted. Prepayment and SASE required.

Banner County

District Court PO Box 67, Harrisburg, NE 69345; phone: 308-436-5265; fax: 308-436-4180; hours 8AM-5PM (MST). *Felony, Civil Actions Over $15,000.*
Civil Records: Access: Fax, mail, in person, online. Both court and visitors may perform in person searches. Search fee: $3.00 per name. Court makes copy: $.50 per page. Required to search: name, years to search; also helpful: address. Civil cases indexed by defendant, plaintiff; on docket books from 1800s. Online access same as criminal, records date from 06/00 forward. Mail turnaround time 5-7 days.
Criminal Records: Access: Fax, mail, in person, online. Both court and visitors may perform in person searches. Search fee: $3.00 per name. Court makes copy: $.50 per page. Required to search: name, years to search, DOB; also helpful: address. Criminal records on docket books from 1800s. Subscribe to NOL at www.nebraska.gov/service_info.phtml?service_id =147 for court access. $.60 a record fee or $300 per month flat rate. Online records date from 06/00 forward. Mail turnaround time 5-7 days.
General Information: Public terminal goes back to 2001. No search warrants, mental health, or sealed records released. Will fax documents $1.00 per page. Certification fee: $1.50 per cert. Payee: Banner County Clerk. Personal checks accepted. Prepayment and SASE required.

Banner County Court PO Box 67, Harrisburg, NE 69345; phone: 308-436-5268; probate phone: 308-436-5268.; fax: 308-436-4180; hours 1-5PM (MST). *Misdemeanor, Civil Actions Under $45,000, Eviction, Small Claims, Probate.*
Civil Records: Access: Mail, in person, online. Both court and visitors may perform in person searches. No search fee. Court makes copy: $.25 per page; same fee for self serve. Required to search: name, years to search. Civil cases indexed by defendant, plaintiff; on register of action cards from 1992, prior on docket books, on computer from 12/2000. Online access same as criminal. Online civil and probate records date from 01/01 forward. Mail turnaround time 4 days from receipt.
Criminal Records: Access: In person, online, mail. Both court and visitors may perform in person searches. No search fee. Court makes copy: $.25 per page; same fee for self serve. Required to search: name, years to search, signed release; also helpful: address, DOB. Criminal records on register of action cards from 1992, prior on docket books, on computer from 6/2000. Subscribe to NOL at www.nebraska.gov/service_info.phtml?service_id =147 for court access. $.60 a record fee or $300 per month flat rate. Online criminal and traffic records date from 04/00 forward. Mail turnaround time 4 days from receipt.
General Information: No public access terminal. No adoption, sealed records released. Certification fee: $1.00. Payee: Banner County Court. Personal checks accepted. Prepayment and SASE required.

Blaine County

District Court Lincoln Ave, Box 136, Brewster, NE 68821; phone: 308-547-2222 x201; fax: 308-547-2228; hours 8AM-4PM (CST). *Felony, Civil Actions Over $15,000.*
www.nol.org/home/DC8/
Civil Records: Access: Fax, mail, in person, online. Search fee: $1.00 per name. Court makes copy: $.25 per page. Required to search: name, years to search. Civil cases indexed by defendant, plaintiff; on index books from late 1800s. Online access same as criminal. Online records date from 06/00 forward. Mail turnaround time 1-2 days.
Criminal Records: Access: Fax, mail, in person, online. Both court and visitors may perform in person searches. Search fee: $1.00 per name. Court makes copy: $.25 per page. Required to search: name, years to search, DOB. Criminal records on index books from late 1800s. Subscribe to NOL at www.nebraska.gov/service_info.phtml?service_id =147 for court access. $.60 a record fee or $300 per month flat rate. Online records date from 06/00 forward. Mail turnaround time 1-2 days.
General Information: Public terminal goes back to 6/2000. No search warrants, mental health, or sealed records released. Will fax documents $1.00 per page. Certification fee: $1.50. Payee: Blaine County Clerk.

Personal checks accepted. Prepayment and SASE required.

Blaine County Court Lincoln Ave, Box 123, Brewster, NE 68821; phone: 308-547-2222 x202; probate phone: x202; criminal fax: 308-547-2228; same fax for civil/probate; hours 8AM-4PM (CST). *Misdemeanor, Civil Actions Under $45,000, Eviction, Small Claims, Probate.*

Civil Records: Access: Phone, fax, mail, in person, online. Only the court performs in person searches; visitors may not. No search fee. Court makes copy: $.25 per page; same fee for self serve. Required to search: name, years to search; also helpful: address. Civil cases indexed by defendant, plaintiff; on index books from 1960. on microfiche prior to 1960. Online access same as criminal. Online civil and probate records date from 01/01 forward. Mail turnaround time 2 days.

Criminal Records: Access: Phone, fax, mail, in person, online. Only the court performs in person searches; visitors may not. No search fee. Court makes copy: $.25 per page; same fee for self serve. Required to search: name, years to search; also helpful: address, DOB, SSN. Criminal records on index books from 1960. on microfiche prior to 1960. Subscribe to NOL at www.nebraska.gov/service_info.phtml?service_id=147 for court access. $.60 a record fee or $300 per month flat rate. Online criminal and traffic records date from 08/00 forward. Mail turnaround time 2 days.

General Information: No public access terminal. No juvenile, adoption, or sealed records released. Will fax documents $1.00 per page. Certification fee: $1.00 per page. Payee: Blaine County Court. Personal checks accepted. Prepayment and SASE required.

Boone County

District Court 222 Fourth St, Albion, NE 68620; phone: 402-395-2057; fax: 402-395-6592; hours 8:30AM-5PM (CST). *Felony, Civil Actions Over $45,000.*

Civil Records: Access: In person, online. Both court and visitors may perform in person searches. Court makes copy: $.25 per page. Required to search: name, years to search. Civil cases indexed by defendant, plaintiff. Civil records in general index and dockets from 1800s, computerized records since 2001. Online access same as criminal. Online records date from 12/99 forward.

Criminal Records: Access: In person, online. Both court and visitors may perform in person searches. Court makes copy: $.25 per page. Required to search: name, years to search; also helpful: DOB. Criminal records in general index and dockets from 1800s, computerized records since 2001. Subscribe at www.nebraska.gov/service_info.phtml?service_id=147 for court access. $.60 a record fee or $300 per month flat rate. Online records date from 12/99 forward.

General Information: Public terminal goes back to 2000. No search warrants, mental health, or sealed records released. Will fax documents $3.00 1st page, $1.00 each add'l. Certification fee: $1.00 per page. Payee: Clerk of District Court. Personal checks accepted. Prepayment required.

Boone County Court 222 S 4th St, Albion, NE 68620; phone: 402-395-6184; fax: 402-395-6592; hours 8AM-5PM (CST). *Misdemeanor, Civil Actions Under $45,000, Eviction, Small Claims, Probate.*

Civil Records: Access: Fax, mail, in person, online. Both court and visitors may perform in person searches. No search fee. Court makes copy: $.25 per page; same fee for self serve. Required to search: name, years to search. Civil cases indexed by defendant, plaintiff; on general index and docket books from late 1800s; computerized back to 2000; probate on microfiche from 1970. Online access same as criminal, records date from 10/00 forward, probate from 01/01. Mail turnaround time 1-2 days. SASE required for large requests.

Criminal Records: Access: Fax, mail, in person, online. Both court and visitors may perform in person searches. No search fee. Court makes copy: $.25 per page; same fee for self serve. Required to search: name, years to search; also helpful: DOB. Criminal records on general index and docket books from late 1800s; computerized back to 2000; probate on microfiche from 1970. Subscribe to NOL at www.nebraska.gov/service_info.phtml?service_id=147 for court access. $.60 a record fee or $300 per month flat rate. Online criminal and traffic records date from 06/00 forward. Mail turnaround time 1-2 days. SASE required for large requests.

General Information: Public terminal goes back to 6/2000. No adoption, or sealed records released. No fee to fax documents. Certification fee: $1.00. Payee: Clerk of County Court. Personal checks accepted. Prepayment and SASE required.

Box Butte County

District Court 515 Box Butte #300, Alliance, NE 69301; phone: 308-762-6293; fax: 308-762-5700; hours 9AM-4PM (MST). *Felony, Civil Actions Over $15,000.*

Civil Records: Access: In person, online. Visitors must perform in person searches themselves. Court makes copy: $.25 per page; same fee for self serve. Required to search: name, years to search. Civil cases indexed by defendant, plaintiff; on general index and docket books from late 1800s. Online access same as criminal. Online records date from 10/97.

Criminal Records: Access: In person, online. Visitors must perform in person searches themselves. Court makes copy: $.25 per page; same fee for self serve. Required to search: name, years to search. Criminal records on general index and docket books from late 1800s. Subscribe to NOL at www.nebraska.gov/service_info.phtml?service_id=147 for court access. $.60 a record fee or $300 per month flat rate. Online records date from 10/97.

General Information: Public terminal goes back to 1890. No mental health, or sealed records released. Will fax specific case file requests for $1.00 per page. Certification fee: $1.00 per page.

Box Butte County Court PO Box 613, Alliance, NE 69301; phone: 308-762-6800; fax: 308-762-2650; hours 8:30AM-5PM (MST). *Misdemeanor, Civil Actions Under $45,000, Eviction, Small Claims, Probate.*

Civil Records: Access: in person, online. Visitors must perform in person searches themselves. Court makes copy: $.25 per page. Required to search: name, years to search. Civil cases indexed by defendant, plaintiff; on microfiche for 10 years, on index cards to docket books from late 1800s; computerized records since 2000. Online access same as criminal. Online records date from 11/00 forward.

Criminal Records: Access: In person, online. Visitors must perform in person searches themselves. Court makes copy: $.25 per page. Required to search: name, years to search, DOB. Criminal records on microfiche for 10 years, on index cards to docket books from late 1800s; computerized records since 2000. Subscribe to NOL at www.nebraska.gov/service_info.phtml?service_id=147 for court access. $.60 a record fee or $300 per month flat rate. Online criminal and traffic records date from 04/00 forward.

General Information: Public terminal goes back to 4/2000. No adoption or sealed records released. Certification fee: $1.00. Payee: Box Butte County Court. Personal checks accepted. Prepayment required.

Boyd County

District Court PO Box 26, Butte, NE 68722; phone: 402-775-2391; fax: 402-775-2146; hours 8:15AM-4PM (CST). *Felony, Civil Actions Over $15,000.*

Civil Records: Access: Mail, fax, in person, online. Both court and visitors may perform in person searches. Search fee: $3.00 per name. Court makes copy: $.25 per page; same fee for self serve. Required to search: name, years to search; also helpful: DOB. Civil cases indexed by defendant, plaintiff; on general index and docket books from late 1800s. Online access same as criminal. Online records date from 07/00. Mail turnaround time 3-4 days.

Criminal Records: Access: Mail, fax, in person, online. Both court and visitors may perform in person searches. Search fee: $3.00 per name. Court makes copy: $.25 per page; same fee for self serve. Required to search: name, years to search, address. Criminal records on general index and docket books from late 1800s. Subscribe to NOL at www.nebraska.gov/service_info.phtml?service_id=147 for court access. $.60 a record fee or $300 per month flat rate. Online records date from 07/00 forward. Mail turnaround time 3-4 days.

General Information: Public terminal goes back to 2000. No search warrants, mental health, or sealed records released. Certification fee: $1.50. Payee: Boyd County Clerk. Personal checks accepted. Prepayment and SASE required.

Boyd County Court PO Box 396, Butte, NE 68722; phone: 402-775-2211; probate phone: 402-775-2211; fax: 402-775-2146; hours 8AM-5PM M,W; Thursday AM (CST). *Misdemeanor, Civil Actions Under $45,000, Eviction, Small Claims, Probate.*

Civil Records: Access: In person, online. Visitors must perform in person searches themselves. Court makes copy: $.25 per page. Required to search: name, years to search; also helpful: address. Civil cases indexed by defendant, plaintiff; on general index and docket books from late 1800s. Online subscription service - see criminal access. Online civil records date from 11/00 forward, probate from 10/00.

Criminal Records: Access: In person, online. Visitors must perform in person searches themselves. Court makes copy: $.25 per page. Required to search: name, years to search; also helpful: address, DOB, SSN. Criminal records on general index and docket books from late 1800s. Subscribe to NOL at www.nebraska.gov/service_info.phtml?service_id=147 for court access. $.60 a record fee or $300 per month flat rate. Online criminal and traffic records date from 08/00.

General Information: No public access terminal. No adoption, juvenile, or sealed records released. Certification fee: $1.00. Payee: Boyd County Court. Personal checks accepted. Prepayment required.

Brown County

District Court 148 W Fourth St, Ainsworth, NE 69210; phone: 402-387-2705; fax: 402-387-0918; hours 8AM-5PM (CST). *Felony, Civil Actions Over $15,000.*

Civil Records: Access: Phone, fax, mail, in person, online. Both court and visitors may perform in person searches. No search fee. Court makes copy: $.10 per page. Required to search: name, years to search; also helpful: address. Civil cases indexed by defendant, plaintiff; on general index and docket books from late 1886s; on computer back to 2000. Online access same as criminal. Online records date from 02/00. Mail turnaround time 3-4 days.

Criminal Records: Access: Fax, mail, in person, online. Both court and visitors may perform in person searches. No search fee. Court makes copy: $.10 per page. Required to search: name, years to search, signed release; also helpful: address, DOB, SSN. Criminal records on general index and docket books from late 1886 on computer back to 2000. Subscribe to NOL at www.nebraska.gov/service_info.phtml?service_id=147 for court access. $.60 a record fee or $300 per month flat rate. Online records date from 02/00. Mail turnaround time 3-4 days.

General Information: Public terminal goes back to 2001. No search warrants, mental health, or sealed records released. Fee to fax documents is $3.00 per page. Certification fee: $2.00 per cert includes copies.

Payee: Clerk of District Court, Brown County. Personal checks accepted. Prepayment and SASE required.

Brown County Court
148 W Fourth St, Ainsworth, NE 69210; phone: 402-387-2864; fax: 402-387-0918; hours 8AM-5PM (CST). *Misdemeanor, Civil Actions Under $45,000, Eviction, Small Claims, Probate.*
Civil Records: Access: In person, online. Both court and visitors may perform in person searches. No search fee. Court makes copy: $.25 per page. Required to search: name, years to search. Civil cases indexed by defendant, plaintiff. Civil records in boxes in office since 1980; on computer since 2001. Online access same as criminal, records date from 04/01 forward, probate from 03/01.
Criminal Records: Access: In person, online. Both court and visitors may perform in person searches. No search fee. Court makes copy: $.25 per page. Required to search: name, years to search, DOB. Criminal records in boxes in office since 1979; on computer since 2000. Subscribe to NOL at www.nebraska.gov/service_info.phtml?service_id=147 for court access. $.60 a record fee or $300 per month flat rate. Online criminal and traffic records date from 08/00.
General Information: Public terminal goes back to 2000. No adoption, juvenile, or sealed records released. Certification fee: $1.00 per page. Payee: Brown County Court. Personal checks accepted. Prepayment required.

Buffalo County

District Court PO Box 520, Kearney, NE 68848; phone: 308-236-1246; fax: 308-233-3693; hours 8AM-5PM (CST). *Felony, Civil Actions Over $15,000.*
Civil Records: Access: In person, online. Both court and visitors may perform in person searches. Court makes copy: $.50 per page; same fee for self serve. Required to search: name, years to search; also helpful: address. Civil cases indexed by defendant, plaintiff; on computer from 1993, on microfiche through 1991, on books from 1800s. Online access same as criminal. Online records date from 05/97.
Criminal Records: Access: In person, online. Visitors must perform in person searches themselves. Court makes copy: $.50 per page; same fee for self serve. Required to search: name, years to search; also helpful: DOB, SSN. Criminal records on computer from 1997; on microfiche 1991-current; on books from 1800s. Subscribe to NOL at www.nebraska.gov/service_info.phtml?service_id=147 for court access. $.60 a record fee or $300 per month flat rate. Online records date from 05/97.
General Information: Public terminal goes back to 1997. No juvenile, mental health, search warrants or sealed records released. Will fax specific case file requests for $3.00 for 1st page, $1.00 each add'l page. Certification fee: $1.00 per doc. Payee: Clerk of District Court. Business checks accepted. Prepayment required.

Buffalo County Court PO Box 520, Kearney, NE 68848; phone: 308-236-1228; criminal phone: 308-236-1231; civil phone: 308-236-3633; probate phone: 308-236-1231; criminal fax: 308-236-1243; same fax for civil/probate; hours 8AM-5PM (CST). *Misdemeanor, Civil Actions Under $45,000, Eviction, Small Claims, Probate.*
Civil Records: Access: In person, online. Visitors must perform in person searches themselves. Court makes copy: $.25 per page. Required to search: name, years to search. Civil cases indexed by defendant, plaintiff; on computer from 4/94, on microfiche, general index, and docket books from late 1800s. Online access same as criminal. Online civil and probate records date from 04/94.
Criminal Records: Access: In person, online. Visitors must perform in person searches themselves. Court makes copy: $.25 per page. Required to search: name, years to search. Criminal

records on computer from 4/94, on microfiche, general index, and docket books from late 1800s. Subscribe to NOL at www.nebraska.gov/service_info.phtml?service_id=147 for court access. $.60 a record fee or $300 per month flat rate. Online criminal and traffic records date from 04/94.
General Information: Public use terminal available. No adoption, or sealed records released. Will not fax documents. Certification fee: $1.00 per seal includes copy fee. Payee: County Court. Personal checks accepted. Prepayment required.

Burt County

District Court 111 N 13th St #11, Tekamah, NE 68061; phone: 402-374-2905; fax: 402-374-2906; hours 8AM-4:30PM (CST). *Felony, Civil Actions Over $15,000.*
Civil Records: Access: Mail, in person, online. Both court and visitors may perform in person searches. No search fee. Court makes copy: $.50 per page. Required to search: name, years to search. Civil cases indexed by defendant, plaintiff; on books from 1800s. Online access same as criminal. Online records date from 03/99. Mail turnaround time 1 day.
Criminal Records: Access: Mail, in person, online. Both court and visitors may perform in person searches. No search fee. Court makes copy: $.50 per page. Required to search: name, years to search; also helpful: DOB, SSN. Criminal records on books from 1800s. Subscribe to NOL at www.nebraska.gov/service_info.phtml?service_id=147 for court access. $.60 a record fee or $300 per month flat rate. Online records date from 03/99. Mail turnaround time 1 day.
General Information: Public terminal goes back to 1999. No mental health records released. Will fax documents to local or toll free line. Certification fee: $2.00 per cert includes copies. Payee: Clerk of District Court. Personal checks accepted. Prepayment and SASE required.

Burt County Court 111 N 13th St, Tekamah, NE 68061; phone: 402-374-2950; fax: 402-374-2951; hours 8AM-4:30PM (CST). *Misdemeanor, Civil Actions Under $45,000, Eviction, Small Claims, Probate.*
Civil Records: Access: In person, online. Visitors must perform in person searches themselves. Court makes copy: $.25 per page. Self serve copy fee: $.25 per page. Required to search: name, years to search, address. Civil cases indexed by defendant, plaintiff; on index cards back to 1867, computerized back to 1998. Online access same as criminal, records date from 03/00 forward, probate from 05/98. Mail turnaround time within 3 days.
Criminal Records: Access: In person, online. Visitors must perform in person searches themselves. Court makes copy: $.25 per page. Self serve copy fee: $.25 per page. Required to search: name, years to search, address, DOB, SSN, signed release. Criminal records on index cards back to 1867, computerized back to 1998. Subscribe to NOL at www.nebraska.gov/service_info.phtml?service_id=147 for court access. $.60 a record fee or $300 per month flat rate. Online criminal and traffic records date from 02/98.
General Information: Public terminal goes back to 1998. No adoption records released. Will not fax documents. Certification fee: $1.00 per page. Payee: County Court. Personal checks accepted. Prepayment required.

Butler County

District Court 451 5th St, David City, NE 68632-1666; phone: 402-367-7460; fax: 402-367-3249; hours 8:30AM-5PM (CST). *Felony, Civil Actions Over $15,000.*
Civil Records: Access: Mail, in person, online. Both court and visitors may perform in person searches. Search fee: $2.00 per name. Court makes copy: $.10 per page. Required to search: name, years to search. Civil cases indexed by defendant, plaintiff; on books.

Online access same as criminal. Online records date from 03/99. Mail turnaround time 1-2 days.
Criminal Records: Access: Mail, in person, online. Both court and visitors may perform in person searches. Search fee: $2.00 per name. Court makes copy: $.10 per page. Required to search: name, years to search; also helpful: DOB, SSN. Criminal records on books. Subscribe to NOL at www.nebraska.gov/service_info.phtml?service_id=147 for court access. $.60 a record fee or $300 per month flat rate. Online records date from 03/99. Mail turnaround time 1-2 days.
General Information: No public access terminal. No juvenile, mental health or protection order records released. No fee to fax documents. Certification fee: $1.50 per document. Payee: District Court. Personal checks accepted. Prepayment and SASE required.

Butler County Court 451 5th St, David City, NE 68632-1666; phone: 402-367-7480; fax: 402-367-3249; hours 8AM-N, 1-5PM (CST). *Misdemeanor, Civil Actions Under $45,000, Eviction, Small Claims, Probate.*
Civil Records: Access: In person, online. Visitors must perform in person searches themselves. Court makes copy: $.25 per page. Required to search: name, years to search. Civil cases indexed by defendant, plaintiff; on computer since 1998, docket books from late 1800s, probate on microfiche. Online access same as criminal, records date from 10/99 forward, probate from 03/98. Note: They can refer requestors to parties who perform searches at the court.
Criminal Records: Access: In person, online. Visitors must perform in person searches themselves. Court makes copy: $.25 per page. Required to search: name, years to search; also helpful: DOB, SSN. Criminal records on computer since 1998, docket books from late 1800s, probate on microfiche. Subscribe to NOL at www.nebraska.gov/service_info.phtml?service_id=147 for court access. $.60 a record fee or $300 per month flat rate. Online criminal and traffic records date from 03/98. Note: They can refer requestors to parties who perform searches at the court.
General Information: Public terminal goes back to 1988. No adoption records released. Some juvenile requires signed release. Certification fee: $1.00. Payee: Butler County Court. Personal checks accepted. Prepayment required.

Cass County

District Court Cass County Courthouse, 346 Main St, Plattsmouth, NE 68048; phone: 402-296-9339; fax: 402-296-9345; hours 8AM-5PM (CST). *Felony, Civil Actions Over $45,000.*
www.cassne.org/distcourt.html
Civil Records: Access: In person, online. Visitors must perform in person searches themselves. Court makes copy: $.25 per page. Required to search: name, years to search. Civil cases indexed by defendant, plaintiff; on index books from 1860s, index on computer since 9/97. Online access same as criminal. Online records date from 08/97.
Criminal Records: Access: In person, online. Visitors must perform in person searches themselves. Court makes copy: $.25 per page. Required to search: name, years to search. Criminal records on index books from 1860s, index on computer since 9/97. Subscribe to NOL at www.nebraska.gov/service_info.phtml?service_id=147 for court access. $.60 a record fee or $300 per month flat rate. Online records date from 08/97.
General Information: Public terminal goes back to 8/1997. Will fax specific case file requests for $1.50 for 1st page; $.50 each add'l. Certification fee: $1.25 per seal. Payee: Clerk of District Court. Prepayment required.

Cass County Court Cass County Courthouse, 346 Main St Rm 301, Plattsmouth, NE 68048; phone: 402-296-9339; probate phone: 402-296-9334; fax: 402-296-5297; hours 8AM-5PM (CST). *Misdemeanor, Civil Actions Under $45,000, Eviction, Small Claims, Probate.*
Civil Records: Access: In person, online. Visitors must perform in person searches themselves. Court makes copy: $.25 per page. Required to search: name, years to search. Civil cases indexed by defendant, plaintiff; on index cards for 5 years then sent to Capital for storage; computerized records since 2000. Online access same as criminal, records date from 01/00 forward, probate from 05/98.
Criminal Records: Access: In person, online. Visitors must perform in person searches themselves. Court makes copy: $.25 per page. Required to search: name, years to search. Criminal records on computer since 1/97. Subscribe to NOL at www.nebraska.gov/service_info.phtml?service_id =147 for court access. $.60 a record fee or $300 per month flat rate. Online criminal and traffic records date from 01/97.
General Information: Public use terminal available. Certification fee: $1.25. Payee: Cass County Court. No personal checks accepted. Prepayment required.

Cedar County

District Court PO Box 796, Hartington, NE 68739-0796; phone: 402-254-6957; fax: 402-254-6954; hours 8AM-5PM (CST). *Felony, Civil Actions Over $45,000.*
Civil Records: Access: In person, online. Visitors must perform in person searches themselves. Court makes copy: $.25 per page. Required to search: name, years to search. Civil cases indexed by defendant, plaintiff. Civil records in books from 1890. Online access same as criminal. Online records date from 11/99.
Criminal Records: Access: In person, online. Visitors must perform in person searches themselves. Court makes copy: $.25 per page. Required to search: name, years to search; also helpful: SSN. Criminal records in books from 1890. Subscribe to NOL at www.nebraska.gov/service_info.phtml?service_id =147 for court access. $.60 a record fee or $300 per month flat rate. Online records date from 11/99.
General Information: Public use terminal available. No mental health records released. Certification fee: $1.00. Payee: District Court. Prepayment required.

Cedar County Court P O Box 695, Hartington, NE 68739; phone: 402-254-7441; fax: 402-254-7447; hours 8AM-5PM (CST). *Misdemeanor, Civil Actions Under $45,000, Eviction, Small Claims, Probate.*
Civil Records: Access: In person, online. Visitors must perform in person searches themselves. Court makes copy: $.25 per page. Required to search: name, years to search. Civil cases indexed by defendant. Civil records on general index, docket books 15 years; some on microfiche to 1983. Online access same as criminal. Online civil and probate records from 11/00 forward.
Criminal Records: Access: In person, online. Visitors must perform in person searches themselves. Court makes copy: $.25 per page. Required to search: name, years to search, offense; also helpful: DOB. Criminal records on general index, docket books since 1983, some on microfiche. Computerized records go back to 2000. Subscribe at www.nebraska.gov/service_info.phtml?service_id =147 for court access. $.60 a record fee or $300 per month flat rate. Online criminal and traffic records date from 06/00.
General Information: Public use terminal available. No juvenile or judge sealed records released. Will fax specific case file requests for $3.00 for 1st page, $1.00 each add'l. Certification fee: $1.00. Payee: Cedar

County Court. Personal checks accepted. Prepayment required.

Chase County

District Court PO Box 1299, Imperial, NE 69033; phone: 308-882-5266; fax: 308-882-5390; hours 8AM-4PM (MST). *Felony, Civil Actions Over $15,000.*
Civil Records: Access: Phone, fax, mail, in person, online. Both court and visitors may perform in person searches. Search fee: $5.00 per name. Court makes copy: $.25 per page; same fee for self serve. Required to search: name, years to search. Civil cases indexed by defendant, plaintiff. Civil records general index, docket books from early 1900s. Online access same as criminal. Online records date from 05/00. Mail turnaround time 5 days.
Criminal Records: Access: Phone, fax, mail, in person, online. Both court and visitors may perform in person searches. Search fee: $5.00 per name. Court makes copy: $.25 per page; same fee for self serve. Required to search: name, years to search; also helpful: DOB, SSN. Criminal records general index, docket books from early 1900s, computerized since 2000. Subscribe to NOL at www.nebraska.gov/service_info.phtml?service_id =147 for court access. $.60 a record fee or $300 per month flat rate. Online records date from 05/00. Mail turnaround time 5 days.
General Information: Public terminal goes back to 2000. Will fax documents $1.00 per page. Certification fee: $1.50. Payee: Chase County Clerk. Personal checks accepted. Prepayment and SASE required.

Chase County Court PO Box 1299, 921 Broadway, Imperial, NE 69033; phone: 308-882-7519; fax: 308-882-7554; hours 8:00AM-4:00PM (MST). *Misdemeanor, Civil Actions Under $45,000, Eviction, Small Claims, Probate.*
Civil Records: Access: In person, online. Both court and visitors may perform in person searches. No search fee. Court makes copy: $.25 per page. Required to search: name, years to search. Civil records on general index, docket books from 1910; prior incomplete. Some probate on microfiche. Online access same as criminal, records date from 11/00 forward, probate from 12/00. Mail turnaround time 1 day.
Criminal Records: Access: In person, online. Both court and visitors may perform in person searches. Court makes copy: $.25 per page. Required to search: name, years to search, DOB. Criminal records on general index, docket books from 1910; prior incomplete. Some probate on microfiche. Subscribe to NOL at www.nebraska.gov/service_info.phtml?service_id =147 for court access. $.60 a record fee or $300 per month flat rate. Online criminal and traffic records date from 09/00.
General Information: Public terminal has criminal back to 9/2000 and civil back to 11/2000. (Terminal located at courthouse.) No adoption, juvenile. Will fax documents to local or toll free line. Certification fee: $1.00 per doc. Payee: Chase County Court. Personal checks accepted. Prepayment required.

Cherry County

District Court 365 N Main St, Valentine, NE 69201; phone: 402-376-1840; fax: 402-376-3830; hours 8:30AM-4:30PM (MST). *Felony, Civil Actions Over $45,000.*
Civil Records: Access: In person, online. Visitors must perform in person searches themselves. Court makes copy: $.25 per page. Required to search: name, years to search; also helpful: address. Civil cases indexed by petitioner, respondent. Civil records on index books from late 1800s. Online access same as criminal. Justice records date from 03/99.
Criminal Records: Access: In person, online. Visitors must perform in person searches themselves. Court makes copy: $.25 per page.

Required to search: name, years to search. Criminal records on index books from late 1800s; computerized records since 1999. Subscribe to NOL at www.nebraska.gov/service_info.phtml?service_id =147 for court access. $.60 a record fee or $300 per month flat rate. Online records date from 03/99.
General Information: Public terminal goes back to 3/1999. No juvenile records. Will not fax documents. Certification fee: $1.00 per page. Payee: Clerk of District Court. Personal checks accepted. Prepayment required.

Cherry County Court 365 N Main St, Valentine, NE 69201; phone: 402-376-2590; fax: 402-376-5942; hours 8AM-5PM (CST). *Misdemeanor, Civil Actions Under $45,000, Eviction, Small Claims, Probate.*
Civil Records: Access: In person, online. Visitors must perform in person searches themselves. Court makes copy: $.25 per page; same fee for self serve. Required to search: name, years to search. Civil cases indexed by defendant. Civil records on docket card file from 1986, general index prior from late 1800s. Online access same as criminal. Online civil and probate records from 11/00 forward.
Criminal Records: Access: In person, online. Visitors must perform in person searches themselves. Court makes copy: $.25 per page; same fee for self serve. Required to search: name, years to search, DOB. Criminal records on docket card file from 1986, general index prior from late 1800s; on computer since 8/2000. Subscribe to NOL at www.nebraska.gov/service_info.phtml?service_id =147 for court access. $.60 a record fee or $300 per month flat rate. Online criminal and traffic records date from 08/20
General Information: Public terminal has criminal back to 8/2000 and civil back to 11/2000. No adoption records released. Juvenile released only to parties involved. Will fax specific case file requests for $3.00 1st page and $1.00 ea add'l. Certification fee: $1.25. Payee: Cherry County Court. Personal checks accepted. Prepayment required.

Cheyenne County

District Court PO Box 217, Sidney, NE 69162; phone: 308-254-2814; fax: 308-254-7832; hours 8AM-N,1-5PM (MST). *Felony, Civil Actions Over $15,000.*
Civil Records: Access: In person, online. Visitors must perform in person searches themselves. Court makes copy: $.50 per page. Required to search: name, years to search. Civil cases indexed by defendant, plaintiff; on general index, docket books going back to late 1800s, on computer since 9/98. Online access same as criminal. Online records date from 08/98.
Criminal Records: Access: In person, online. Visitors must perform in person searches themselves. Court makes copy: $.50 per page. Required to search: name, years to search; also helpful: DOB, SSN. Criminal records on general index, docket books going back to late 1800s, on computer since 9/98. Subscribe to NOL at www.nebraska.gov/service_info.phtml?service_id =147 for court access. $.60 a record fee or $300 per month flat rate. Online records date from 08/98.
General Information: Public terminal goes back to 1997. No mental health or search warrants released. Will fax specific case file requests to local or toll free line. Certification fee: $1.00 per document. Payee: Clerk of District Court. Personal checks not accepted. Prepayment required. Attorneys may be billed.

Cheyenne County Court 1000 10th Ave, Sidney, NE 69162; phone: 308-254-2929; fax: 308-254-2312; hours 8AM-5PM (MST). *Misdemeanor, Civil Actions Under $45,000, Eviction, Small Claims, Probate.*
Civil Records: Access: Fax, mail, in person, online. Both court and visitors may perform in person searches. No search fee. Court makes copy: $.25 per page. Required to search: name, years to search. Civil

cases indexed by defendant, plaintiff; on index books from late 1800s. Online access same as criminal. Online records date from 12/00, including probate. Note: Fax access requires special permission. Mail turnaround time within 1 week.

Criminal Records: Access: Fax, mail, in person, online. Both court and visitors may perform in person searches. No search fee. Court makes copy: $.25 per page. Required to search: name, years to search; also helpful: DOB. Criminal records on index books from late 1800s; computerized records since 2000. Subscribe to NOL at www.nebraska.gov/service_info.phtml?service_id =147 for court access. $.60 a record fee or $300 per month flat rate. Online criminal and traffic records date from 06/00. Mail turnaround time within 1 week.

General Information: Public terminal goes back to 6/2000. No adoption, juvenile, confidential records released. Certification fee: $1.00 per page. Payee: Cheyenne County Court. Personal checks accepted. Prepayment and SASE required.

Clay County

District Court Clerk of The District Court, 111 W Fairfield St, Clay Center, NE 68933; phone: 402-762-3595; fax: 402-762-3604; hours 8:30AM-5PM (CST). *Felony, Civil Actions Over $15,000.*

Civil Records: Access: In person, online. Visitors must perform in person searches themselves. Court makes copy: $.25 per page; same fee for self serve. Required to search: name; also helpful: years to search. Civil cases indexed by defendant, plaintiff; on index books from late 1800s, on microfiche from 1986, computerized since 1998. Online access same as criminal. Online records date from 09/98.

Criminal Records: Access: In person, online. Visitors must perform in person searches themselves. Court makes copy: $.25 per page; same fee for self serve. Required to search: name, DOB; also helpful: years to search, SSN. Criminal records on index books from late 1800s, on microfiche from 1986, computerized since 1998. Subscribe to NOL at www.nebraska.gov/service_info.phtml?service_id =147 for court access. $.60 a record fee or $300 per month flat rate. Online records date from 09/98.

General Information: Public use terminal available. No mental health records released. Will fax documents for $3.00 first page, $1.00 ea add'l. Certification fee: $1.00. Payee: Clerk of District Court. Personal checks accepted.

Clay County Court 111 W Fairfield St, Clay Center, NE 68933; phone: 402-762-3651; fax: 402-762-3250; hours 8:30AM-5PM (CST). *Misdemeanor, Civil Actions Under $45,000, Eviction, Small Claims, Probate, Traffic, Juvenile.*

Civil Records: Access: In person, online. Visitors must perform in person searches themselves. Court makes copy: $.25 per page; same fee for self serve. Required to search: name, years to search. Civil cases indexed by defendant. Civil records in index books from late 1800s, on computer from 4/00. Online access same as criminal. Online records date from 04/00, including probate.

Criminal Records: Access: In person, online. Visitors must perform in person searches themselves. Court makes copy: $.25 per page; same fee for self serve. Required to search: name, years to search; also helpful: DOB, SSN. Criminal records in index books from late 1800s. Subscribe to NOL at www.nebraska.gov/service_info.phtml?service_id =147 for court access. $.60 a record fee or $300 per month flat rate. Online criminal and traffic records date from 04/00.

General Information: Public terminal goes back to 4/2000. No adoption or juvenile records released. Certification fee: $1.00. Payee: Clay County. Personal checks accepted. Prepayment required.

Colfax County

District Court 411 E 11th St, Schuyler, NE 68661; phone: 402-352-8506; fax: 402-352-8550; hours 8:30AM-4:30PM (CST). *Felony, Civil Actions Over $15,000.*
www.colfaxcounty.ne.gov

Civil Records: Access: In person, online. Visitors must perform in person searches themselves. Court makes copy: $.30 per page. Required to search: name, years to search; also helpful: address. Civil cases indexed by defendant, plaintiff; on index books and general index from 1880. Online access same as criminal. Online records date from 04/97. Mail turnaround time 3-4 days.

Criminal Records: Access: In person, online. Visitors must perform in person searches themselves. Court makes copy: $.30 per page. Required to search: name, years to search; also helpful: address, DOB, SSN. Criminal records on index books and general index from 1880. Subscribe to NOL at www.nebraska.gov/service_info.phtml?service_id =147 for court access. $.60 a record fee or $300 per month flat rate. Online records date from 04/97.

General Information: Public terminal goes back to 4/1997. No juvenile or mental health records released. Will fax specific case file requests for $1.00 per page. Certification fee: $1.50. Payee: Clerk of District Court. Business checks accepted; will take local personal check. Prepayment required.

Colfax County Court 411 E 11th St, Box 191, Schuyler, NE 68661; phone: 402-352-8511; fax: 402-352-8535; hours 8AM-4:30PM (CST). *Misdemeanor, Civil Actions Under $45,000, Eviction, Small Claims, Probate.*

Civil Records: Access: In person, online. Visitors must perform in person searches themselves. Court makes copy: $.25 per page. Required to search: name, years to search. Civil cases indexed by defendant, plaintiff; on index books from 1880s; computerized records since 1996. Online access same as criminal, records date from 10/99 forward, probate from 05/98.

Criminal Records: Access: Fax, mail, in person, online. Visitors must perform in person searches themselves. Court makes copy: $.25 per page. Required to search: name, years to search; also helpful: DOB, SSN. Criminal records on index books from 1880s; computerized records since 1996. Subscribe to NOL at www.nebraska.gov/service_info.phtml?service_id =147 for court access. $.60 a record fee or $300 per month flat rate. Online criminal and traffic records date from 10/96.

General Information: Public terminal goes back to 1997. No juvenile records released. Certification fee: $1.00. Payee: Colfax County Court. Personal checks accepted. Prepayment required.

Cuming County

District Court 200 S Lincoln, Rm 200, West Point, NE 68788; phone: 402-372-6004; fax: 402-372-6017; hours 8:30AM-4:30PM (CST). *Felony, Civil Actions Over $15,000.*

Civil Records: Access: Mail, fax, in person, online. Both court and visitors may perform in person searches. Search fee: $10.00 (fax only). Court makes copy: $.25 per page; same fee for self serve. Required to search: name, years to search. Civil cases indexed by defendant, plaintiff. Civil records in books from 1939; on computer back to 2000. Online access same as criminal. Online records date from 11/99.

Criminal Records: Access: Fax, in person, online. Both court and visitors may perform in person searches. Search fee: $10.00 (fax only). Court makes copy: $.25 per page; same fee for self serve. Required to search: name, years to search. Criminal records in books from 1939; on computer back to 2000. Subscribe to NOL at www.nebraska.gov/service_info.phtml?service_id =147 for court access. $.60 a record fee or $300

per month flat rate. Online records date from 11/99.

General Information: Public terminal goes back to 11/1999. No mental health records released. Will fax documents if you provide copy of your check for services. Certification fee: $1.00. No personal checks accepted. Prepayment required.

Cuming County Court 200 S Lincoln, Rm 103, West Point, NE 68788; phone: 402-372-6003; probate phone: 402-372-6003; fax: 402-372-6030; hours 8:30AM-4:30PM (CST). *Misdemeanor, Civil Actions Under $45,000, Eviction, Small Claims, Probate.*

Civil Records: Access: In person, online. Visitors must perform in person searches themselves. Court makes copy: $.25 per page. Required to search: name, years to search. Civil cases indexed by defendant, plaintiff; on index cards, also on computer since 4/2000. Online access same as criminal. Online records date from 04/00, including probate.

Criminal Records: Access: In person, online. Visitors must perform in person searches themselves. Court makes copy: $.25 per page. Required to search: name, years to search; also helpful: DOB, SSN. Criminal records on index cards, also on computer since 4/2000. Subscribe to NOL at www.nebraska.gov/service_info.phtml?service_id =147 for court access. $.60 a record fee or $300 per month flat rate. Online criminal and traffic records date from 03/00.

General Information: Public terminal has criminal back to 1984 and civil back to 1991. (Public terminal located in the District Court office.) No mental health records released. Certification fee: $1.00. Personal checks accepted; ID required. Prepayment required.

Custer County

District Court 431 S 10th Ave, Broken Bow, NE 68822; phone: 308-872-2121; fax: 308-872-5826; hours 9AM-5PM (CST). *Felony, Civil Actions Over $15,000.*

Civil Records: Access: Phone, fax, mail, in person, online. Both court and visitors may perform in person searches. No search fee. Court makes copy: $.25 per page; same fee for self serve. Required to search: name, years to search; also helpful: address. Civil cases indexed by defendant, plaintiff; on index books and docket books from late 1800s; on computer back to 4/1998. Online access same as criminal. Online records date from 03/98. Mail turnaround time 3-4 days.

Criminal Records: Access: Phone, fax, mail, in person, online. Both court and visitors may perform in person searches. No search fee. Court makes copy: $.25 per page; same fee for self serve. Required to search: name, years to search; also helpful: address, DOB, SSN. Criminal records on index books and docket books from late 1800s; on computer back to 4/1998. Subscribe to NOL at www.nebraska.gov/service_info.phtml?service_id =147 for court access. $.60 a record fee or $300 per month flat rate. Online records date from 03/98. Mail turnaround time 3-4 days.

General Information: Public terminal goes back to 4/1998. No search warrants, mental health, or sealed records released. Fee to fax documents is $3.00 per page. Certification fee: $1.25 per page. Payee: Clerk of District Court. Business checks accepted. Prepayment and SASE required.

Custer County Court 431 S 10th Ave, Broken Bow, NE 68822; phone: 308-872-5761; criminal fax: 308-872-6052; same fax for civil/probate; hours 8AM-12 1-5PM (CST). *Misdemeanor, Civil Actions Under $45,000, Eviction, Small Claims, Probate.*

Civil Records: Access: In person, online. Visitors must perform in person searches themselves. Court makes copy: $.25 per page. Required to search: name, years to search. Civil cases indexed by defendant, plaintiff; on computer back to 2000, on index books from 1988, probate from 1986, balance are archived.

Online access same as criminal. Online records date from 1/01, including probate.

Criminal Records: Access: In person, online. Visitors must perform in person searches themselves. Court makes copy: $.25 per page. Required to search: name, years to search. Criminal records on computer back to 2000, index books from 1988, probate from 1986, balance are archived. Subscribe to NOL at www.nebraska.gov/service_info.phtml?service_id =147 for court access. $.60 a record fee or $300 per month flat rate. Online criminal and traffic records date from 7/17/00.

General Information: Public use terminal available. No adoption records released. Certification fee: $1.25. Payee: Custer County Court. Personal checks accepted. Prepayment required.

Dakota County

District Court PO Box 66, Dakota City, NE 68731; phone: 402-987-2115; fax: 402-987-2117; hours 8AM-4:30PM (CST). *Felony, Civil Actions Over $15,000.*

Note: This office will not do name searches.

Civil Records: Access: In person, online. Visitors must perform in person searches themselves. Court makes copy: $.25 per page. Self serve copy fee: $.10 per page. Required to search: name, years to search. Civil cases indexed by defendant, plaintiff; on index books from 1985, prior records archived at NE State Historical Society, Lincoln, NE; computerized records since 1998. Online access same as criminal. Online records date from 03/98.

Criminal Records: Access: Online, in person. Visitors must perform in person searches themselves. Court makes copy: $.25 per page. Self serve copy fee: $.10 per page. Required to search: name, years to search. Criminal records on index books from 1985, prior records archived at NE State Historical Society, Lincoln, NE; computerized records since 1998. Subscribe to NOL at www.nebraska.gov/service_info.phtml?service_id =147 for court access. $.60 a record fee or $300 per month flat rate. Online records date from 03/98.

General Information: Public terminal goes back to 1988. No juvenile or mental health records released. Certification fee: $1.00. Payee: Clerk of District Court. Personal checks accepted. Prepayment and SASE required.

Dakota County Court PO Box 385, 1601 Broadway, Dakota City, NE 68731; phone: 402-987-2145; fax: 402-987-2185; hours 8AM-4:30PM (CST). *Misdemeanor, Civil Actions Under $45,000, Eviction, Small Claims, Probate.*

Civil Records: Access: In person, online, mail, fax. Visitors must perform in person searches themselves. Court makes copy: $.25 per page. Required to search: name, years to search. Civil cases indexed by defendant, plaintiff; on index books from late 1800s. Online access same as criminal, records date from 10/99 forward, probate from 05/98. Mail turnaround time 1 days.

Criminal Records: Access: In person, online, mail, fax. Visitors must perform in person searches themselves. Court makes copy: $.25 per page. Required to search: name, years to search. Criminal records on index books from late 1800s. Subscribe to NOL at www.nebraska.gov/service_info.phtml?service_id =147 for court access. $.60 a record fee or $300 per month flat rate. Online criminal and traffic records date from 10/97. Mail turnaround time 1 days.

General Information: Public terminal goes back to 1998. No adoption or juvenile records released. Certification fee: $1.00. Payee: Dakota County Court. Business checks accepted. Prepayment required.

Dawes County

District Court 451 Main St, Chadron, NE 69337; phone: 308-432-0109; fax: 308-432-0110; hours 8:30AM-4:30PM (MST). *Felony, Civil Actions Over $15,000.*

Civil Records: Access: In person, online. Visitors must perform in person searches themselves. Court makes copy: $.25 per page. Required to search: name, years to search. Civil cases indexed by defendant, plaintiff; on general index, docket books from 1886. Online access same as criminal. Online records date from 08/98.

Criminal Records: Access: Fax, mail, in person, online. Visitors must perform in person searches themselves. Court makes copy: $.25 per page. Required to search: name, years to search. Criminal records on general index, docket books from 1886. Subscribe to NOL at www.nebraska.gov/service_info.phtml?service_id =147 for court access. $.60 a record fee or $300 per month flat rate. Online records date from 08/98.

General Information: Public terminal goes back to 2001. No mental health records released. Certification fee: $1.00. Payee: Clerk of District Court. Personal checks accepted.

Dawes County Court PO Box 806, Chadron, NE 69337; phone: 308-432-0116; fax: 308-432-0118; hours 7:30AM-4:30PM (MST). *Misdemeanor, Civil Actions Under $45,000, Eviction, Small Claims, Probate.*

Civil Records: Access: In person, online. Visitors must perform in person searches themselves. Court makes copy: $.25 per page; same fee for self serve. Required to search: name, years to search. Civil cases indexed by defendant, plaintiff; on case cards, case files kept since 1892; on computer back to 2001. Online access same as criminal. Online civil and probate records from 11/00 forward.

Criminal Records: Access: In person, online. Visitors must perform in person searches themselves. Court makes copy: $.25 per page; same fee for self serve. Required to search: name, years to search, DOB; also helpful: address. Criminal records on case cards, case files kept since 1892; on computer back to 2000. Subscribe to NOL at www.nebraska.gov/service_info.phtml?service_id =147 for court access. $.60 a record fee or $300 per month flat rate. Online criminal and traffic records date from 04/00.

General Information: Public use terminal available. No confidential records released. Certification fee: $1.00. Payee: Dawes County Court. Personal checks accepted. Prepayment required.

Dawson County

District Court PO Box 429, 700 N Washington, Lexington, NE 68850; phone: 308-324-4261; fax: 308-324-3374; hours 8AM-5PM (CST). *Felony, Civil Actions Over $15,000.*

www.dawsoncountyne.net

Civil Records: Access: In person, online. Visitors must perform in person searches themselves. Court makes copy: $.25 per page. Required to search: name, years to search. Civil cases indexed by defendant, plaintiff. Recent civil records on microfiche, some older records on microfilm, index books date to late 1800s. Online access same as criminal. Online records date from 06/97.

Criminal Records: Access: Fax, mail, in person, online. Visitors must perform in person searches themselves. Court makes copy: $.25 per page. Required to search: name, years to search. Recent records on fiche, some older records on microfilm, index books date to late 1800s. Subscribe to NOL at www.nebraska.gov/service_info.phtml?service_id =147 for court access. $.60 a record fee or $300 per month flat rate. Online records date from 06/97.

General Information: Public terminal goes back to 5/1997. No juvenile or mental health records released. Certification fee: $1.00. Payee: Clerk of District Court. Personal checks accepted. Prepayment required.

Dawson County Court 700 N Washington St, Lexington, NE 68850; phone: 308-324-5606; fax: 308-324-9837; hours 8AM-5PM (CST). *Misdemeanor, Civil Actions Under $45,000, Eviction, Small Claims, Probate.*

Note: Court personnel will only search records if specific case # given, turnaround time is 3-5 days.

Civil Records: Access: In person, online. Visitors must perform in person searches themselves. Court makes copy: $.25 per page; same fee for self serve. Required to search: name, years to search; also helpful: address. Civil cases indexed by defendant, plaintiff; on books from late 1800s, docket books 15 years back; on computer since 1998. Online access same as criminal, records date from 10/99 forward, probate from 05/98.

Criminal Records: Access: In person, online. Visitors must perform in person searches themselves. Court makes copy: $.25 per page; same fee for self serve. Required to search: name, years to search, offense, DOB; also helpful: address, SSN. Criminal records on books from late 1800s, docket books 15 years back; on computer since 1998. Subscribe to NOL at www.nebraska.gov/service_info.phtml?service_id =147 for court access. $.60 a record fee or $300 per month flat rate. Online criminal and traffic records date from 05/00.

General Information: Public terminal goes back to late 1997. No adoption or juvenile records released. Will fax specific for $3.00 1st page, $1.00 ea add'l. Certification fee: $1.00. Payee: Dawson County Court. Personal checks or Visa, MC accepted. Prepayment required.

Deuel County

District Court PO Box 327, 718 Third St, Chappell, NE 69129; phone: 308-874-3308/2818; fax: 308-874-3472; hours 8AM-4PM (MST). *Felony, Civil Actions Over $15,000.*

Civil Records: Access: Phone, fax, mail, in person, online. Both court and visitors may perform in person searches. No search fee. Court makes copy: $.50 per page. Required to search: name; also helpful: years to search. Civil cases indexed by defendant, plaintiff; on general index and docket books from late 1800s. Online access same as criminal. Online records date from 05/00. Mail turnaround time 1 week.

Criminal Records: Access: Phone, fax, mail, in person, online. Both court and visitors may perform in person searches. No search fee. Court makes copy: $.50 per page. Self serve copy fee: $.25 per page. Required to search: name; also helpful: years to search, DOB, SSN. Criminal records on general index and docket books from late 1800s. Subscribe to NOL at www.nebraska.gov/service_info.phtml?service_id =147 for court access. $.60 a record fee or $300 per month flat rate. Online records date from 05/00. Mail turnaround time 1 week.

General Information: Public terminal goes back to 2000. No mental health or service discharge records released. No fee to fax documents. Certification fee: $1.50 per page. Payee: Clerk of District Court. Personal checks accepted. Prepayment and SASE required.

Deuel County Court PO Box 514, Chappell, NE 69129; phone: 308-874-2909; fax: 308-874-3472; hours 8AM-4PM (MST). *Misdemeanor, Civil Actions Under $45,000, Eviction, Small Claims, Probate.*

Civil Records: Access: Mail, in person, online. Both court and visitors may perform in person searches. No search fee. Court makes copy: $.25 per page; same fee for self serve. Required to search: name, years to search. Civil cases indexed by defendant, plaintiff; on index cards from 1989, computerized since 2001. Online access same as criminal. Online civil and probate records from 12/00 forward. Mail turnaround time 3 days.

Criminal Records: Access: Mail, in person, online. Both court and visitors may perform in person searches. No search fee. Court makes copy: $.25 per page; same fee for self serve. Required to search: name, years to search, DOB, signed release. Criminal records on index cards from 1989, computerized since 2001. Subscribe to NOL at www.nebraska.gov/service_info.phtml?service_id =147 for court access. $.60 a record fee or $300 per month flat rate. Online criminal and traffic records date from 12/00. Mail turnaround time 3-4 days.

General Information: Public terminal goes back to 12/00. No juvenile records released. Will fax documents. Certification fee: $.25 per page plus $1.00 for seal. Payee: Deuel County Court. No personal checks accepted. Prepayment and SASE required.

Dixon County

District Court PO Box 395, Ponca, NE 68770; phone: 402-755-2881; fax: 402-755-2632; hours 8AM-N, 1-5PM (CST). *Felony, Civil Actions Over $45,000.*

Civil Records: Access: In person, online. Visitors must perform in person searches themselves. Court makes copy: $.25 per page; same fee for self serve. Required to search: name, years to search. Civil cases indexed by defendant, plaintiff; on books from 1876; computerized records go back to 1999. Online access same as criminal. Online records date from 11/99.

Criminal Records: Access: In person, online. Visitors must perform in person searches themselves. Court makes copy: $.25 per page; same fee for self serve. Required to search: name, years to search, DOB. Criminal records on books from 1876; computerized records go back to 1999. Subscribe to NOL at www.nebraska.gov/service_info.phtml?service_id =147 for court access. $.60 a record fee or $300 per month flat rate. Online records date from 11/99.

General Information: Public terminal goes back to 1999. No mental health records released. Will not fax documents. Certification fee: $1.00 per page. Payee: Clerk of District Court. Personal checks accepted. Will bill copy fees.

Dixon County Court PO Box 497, Ponca, NE 68770; phone: 402-755-2355; fax: 402-755-2632; hours 8AM-4:30PM (CST). *Misdemeanor, Civil Actions Under $45,000, Eviction, Small Claims, Probate.*

Civil Records: Access: In person, online. Visitors must perform in person searches themselves. Court makes copy: $.25 per page. Required to search: name, years to search. Civil cases indexed by defendant, plaintiff. Civil records in files, cards from 1987, prior in dockets from 1876, computerized since 2000. Online access same as criminal, records date from 11/01 forward, probate from 01/01.

Criminal Records: Access: In person, online. Visitors must perform in person searches themselves. Court makes copy: $.25 per page. Required to search: name, years to search, DOB. Criminal records in files, cards from 1987, prior in dockets from 1876, computerized since 2000. Subscribe to NOL at www.nebraska.gov/service_info.phtml?service_id =147 for court access. $.60 a record fee or $300 per month flat rate. Online criminal and traffic records date from 07/00.

General Information: Public use terminal available. No adoption or juvenile records released. Certification fee: $1.00. Payee: Dixon County Court. Personal checks accepted. Prepayment required.

Dodge County

District Court PO Box 1237, Fremont, NE 68026; phone: 402-727-2780; fax: 402-727-2773; hours 8:30AM-4:30PM (CST). *Felony, Civil Actions Over $15,000.*

Civil Records: Access: In person, online. Visitors must perform in person searches themselves. Court makes copy: $.25 per page. Required to search: name, years to search. Civil cases indexed by defendant, plaintiff; on general index, docket books from late 1800s; computerized records since 1997. Online access same as criminal. Online records date from 09/97.

Criminal Records: Access: In person, online. Visitors must perform in person searches themselves. Court makes copy: $.25 per page. Required to search: name, years to search. Criminal records on general index, docket books from late 1800s; computerized records since 1997. Subscribe to NOL at www.nebraska.gov/service_info.phtml?service_id =147 for court access. $.60 a record fee or $300 per month flat rate. Online records date from 09/97.

General Information: Public terminal goes back to 7/1997. No mental health records released. Certification fee: $1.50. Payee: District Court. Personal checks accepted. Prepayment required.

Dodge County Court 428 N Broad St, Fremont, NE 68025; phone: 402-727-2755; criminal phone: 402-727-2758; civil phone: 402-727-2756; probate phone: 402-727-2755; criminal fax: 402-727-2762; same fax for civil/probate; hours 8AM-5PM (CST). *Misdemeanor, Civil Actions Under $45,000, Eviction, Small Claims, Probate.*
Note: Probate is separate index at this same address.

Civil Records: Access: In person, online. Visitors must perform in person searches themselves. Court makes copy: $.25 per page; same fee for self serve. Required to search: name, years to search. Civil cases indexed by defendant. Civil records on general index, docket books from early 1900s; on computer back to 1998. Probate on microfilm from early 1900s. Online access same as criminal, records date from 01/00 forward, probate from 05/98.

Criminal Records: Access: In person, online. Visitors must perform in person searches themselves. Court makes copy: $.25 per page; same fee for self serve. Required to search: name, years to search; also helpful: DOB. Criminal records on general index, docket books from early 1900s; on computer back to 1998. Subscribe to NOL at www.nebraska.gov/service_info.phtml?service_id =147 for court access. $.60 a record fee or $300 per month flat rate. Online criminal and traffic records date from 01/20/97.

General Information: Public terminal goes back to 1998. No adoption or juvenile records released. Certification fee: $1.00 per document. Payee: Dodge County Court. Prepayment required.

Douglas County

District Court 1701 Farnam, Hall of Justice, Rm 300, Omaha, NE 68183; phone: 402-444-7018; fax: 402-444-1757; hours 8AM-4:30PM (CST). *Felony, Civil Actions Over $15,000.*
www.co.douglas.ne.us

Civil Records: Access: Mail, in person, online. Both court and visitors may perform in person searches. Search fee: $5.00 per name. Court makes copy: $.50 per page. $1.00 minimum. Add $.50 postage fee. Required to search: name, years to search; also helpful: address. Civil cases indexed by defendant, plaintiff; on computer from 1980, on books back to late 1800s. Access to the Internet system at www.co.douglas.ne.us/cpan/index.htm requires registration and password. Call CPAN at 402-444-7117 for more information. System can be searched by name or case number. Mail turnaround time 1-2 days.

Criminal Records: Access: Mail, in person, online. Visitors must perform in person searches themselves. Search fee: $5.00 per name. Court makes copy: $.50 per page. $1.00 minimum. Add $.50 postage fee. Required to search: name, years to search; also helpful: address, DOB, SSN. Criminal records on computer from 1980, on books back to late 1800s. Access to the Internet system at www.co.douglas.ne.us/cpan/index.htm requires registration and password. Call CPAN at 402-444-7117 for more information. System can be searched by name or case number. Mail turnaround time 1-2 days.

General Information: Public terminal has criminal back to 1981 and civil back to 1974. No juvenile records released. Certification fee: $3.50 for 1-5 pages, $.50 each add'l. Payee: Clerk of District Court. Personal checks accepted. Prepayment and SASE required.

Douglas County Court 1819 Farnam, #F03, Omaha, NE 68183; criminal phone: 402-444-5387; civil phone: 402-444-5424; probate phone: 402-444-7152; criminal fax: 402-444-3608; civil fax: 402-996-8326; probate fax: 402-444-4019; hours 8AM-4:30PM (CST). *Misdemeanor, Civil Actions Under $45,000, Eviction, Small Claims, Probate.*
www.co.douglas.ne.us

Civil Records: Access: Mail, online, in person. Visitors must perform in person searches themselves. Court makes copy: $.25 per page. Self serve copy fee: $.10 per page. Required to search: name, years to search. Civil cases indexed by defendant, plaintiff; on computer from 1987 (small claims), from 1983 (civil). Civil records are purged after about 20 years. Access to the Internet system at www.co.douglas.ne.us/cpan/index.htm requires registration and password. Call CPAN at 402-444-7117 for more information. System can be searched by name or case number. Also, subscribe to NOL at www.nebraska.gov/service_info.phtml?service_id =147 for online court access. $.60 a record fee or $300 per month flat rate, also start-up fee. Note: Online civil records date from 10/18/99 forward, probate from 03/00.

Criminal Records: Access: In person, online. Visitors must perform in person searches themselves. Court makes copy: $.25 per page. Required to search: name, years to search; also helpful: DOB. Criminal records on computer from 1987 (small claims), from 1983 (civil). Civil records are purged after about 20 years. Online access to criminal records is the same as civil. Online criminal and traffic records date from 04/96.

General Information: Public use terminal available. Certification fee: $1.00. Payee: Douglas County Court. Personal checks accepted. Prepayment required.

Dundy County

District Court PO Box 506, 112 Seventh Ave, Benkelman, NE 69021; phone: 308-423-2058; hours 8AM-4PM (MST). *Felony, Civil Actions Over $15,000.*

Civil Records: Access: Phone, mail, in person, online. Both court and visitors may perform in person searches. No search fee. Court makes copy: $1.00 per page. Required to search: name, years to search; also helpful: address. Civil cases indexed by defendant, plaintiff; on index books from late 1800s. Online access same as criminal. Online records date from 8/2000.

Criminal Records: Access: Mail, in person, online. Both court and visitors may perform in person searches. No search fee. Court makes copy: $1.00 per page. Required to search: name, years to search; also helpful: address, DOB, SSN. Criminal records on index books from late 1800s. Subscribe to NOL at www.nebraska.gov/service_info.phtml?service_id =147 for court access. $.60 a record fee or $300 per month flat rate. Online records date from 08/00.

General Information: Public terminal goes back to 8/2000. No juvenile records released. Certification fee: $1.50 plus $.50 each add'l page. Payee: Clerk of District Court. Personal checks accepted. Prepayment required.

Dundy County Court PO Box 378, Benkelman, NE 69021; phone: 308-423-2374; fax: 308-423-2325; hours 8AM-4PM (MST). *Misdemeanor, Civil Actions Under $45,000, Eviction, Small Claims, Probate.*

Civil Records: Access: In person, online. Visitors must perform in person searches themselves. Court makes copy: $.25 per page. Required to search: name, years to search. Civil cases indexed by defendant, plaintiff; on general index, docket books from late 1800s; some probate, civil on microfiche. Online access same as criminal, records date from 11/00 forward, probate from 12/00.

Criminal Records: Access: In person, online. Visitors must perform in person searches themselves. Court makes copy: $.25 per page. Required to search: name, years to search, DOB, signed release; also helpful: address. Criminal records on general index, docket books from late 1800s, computerized since 2001; some probate, civil on microfiche. Subscribe to NOL at www.nebraska.gov/service_info.phtml?service_id=147 for court access. $.60 a record fee or $300 per month flat rate. Online criminal and traffic records date from 08/00.

General Information: Public terminal has criminal back to 2001 and civil back to 2000. No adoption or juvenile records released. Will fax specific case file requests for $3.00 charge for 1st page, $1.00 each add'l page. Certification fee: $1.00 per document. Payee: Dundy County Court. Business checks accepted. Prepayment required.

Fillmore County

District Court PO Box 147, Geneva, NE 68361-0147; phone: 402-759-3811; fax: 402-759-4440; hours 8AM-N, 1-5PM (CST). *Felony, Civil Actions Over $15,000.*
www.fillmorecounty.org

Civil Records: Access: Phone, fax, mail, in person, online. Both court and visitors may perform in person searches. No search fee. Court makes copy: $.35 per page. Required to search: name, years to search. Civil cases indexed by defendant, plaintiff; on index books to late 1800s, last 8 years on computer. Online access same as criminal. Online records date from 06/98. Mail turnaround time 1-5 days.

Criminal Records: Access: Phone, fax, mail, in person, online. Both court and visitors may perform in person searches. No search fee. Court makes copy: $.35 per page. Required to search: name, years to search, DOB. Criminal records on index books to late 1800s, last 8 years on computer. Subscribe to NOL at www.nebraska.gov/service_info.phtml?service_id=147 for court access. $.60 a record fee or $300 per month flat rate. Online records date from 06/98. Mail turnaround time 1-5 days.

General Information: Public terminal goes back to 1998. No juvenile or mental health records released. Will fax documents $2.00 1st page, $1.00 each add'l. Certification fee: $1.00. Payee: Clerk of District Court. Personal checks accepted. Prepayment required. Will bill fax and copy fees, SASE required.

Fillmore County Court PO Box 66, Geneva, NE 68361; phone: 402-759-3514; fax: 402-759-4440; hours 8AM-5PM (CST). *Misdemeanor, Civil Actions Under $51,000, Eviction, Small Claims, Probate.*

Civil Records: Access: Fax, mail, in person, online. Both court and visitors may perform in person searches. No search fee. Court makes copy: $.25 per page. Required to search: name, years to search. Civil cases indexed by defendant, plaintiff; on general index, docket books from late 1800s; probate on microfiche. Online access same as criminal. Online civil and probate records from 02/00 forward. Mail turnaround time 7-8 days.

Criminal Records: Access: Fax, mail, in person, online. Both court and visitors may perform in person searches. No search fee. Court makes copy: $.25 per page. Required to search: name, years to

search. Criminal records on general index, docket books from late 1800s; probate on microfiche. Subscribe to NOL at www.nebraska.gov/service_info.phtml?service_id=147 for court access. $.60 a record fee or $300 per month flat rate. Online criminal and traffic records date from 02/00. Mail turnaround time 7-8 days.

General Information: Public terminal goes back to 2000. No adoption or juvenile records released. Will fax documents $2.00 1st page, $1.00 each add'l. Certification fee: $1.25. Payee: County Court. Personal checks accepted. Prepayment and SASE required.

Franklin County

District Court PO Box 146, 405 15th Ave, Franklin, NE 68939; phone: 308-425-6202; fax: 308-425-6093; hours 8:30AM-4:30PM (CST). *Felony, Civil Actions Over $15,000.*

Civil Records: Access: In person, online. Visitors must perform in person searches themselves. Court makes copy: $1.00 per page. Self serve copy fee: $.25 per page. Required to search: name, years to search. Civil cases indexed by defendant, plaintiff; on index books back to turn of century; on computer back to 2/2000. Online access same as criminal. Online records date from 02/00.

Criminal Records: Access: In person, online. Visitors must perform in person searches themselves. Court makes copy: $1.00 per page. Self serve copy fee: $.25 per page. Required to search: name, years to search. Criminal records on index books back to turn of century; on computer back to 2/2000. Subscribe to NOL at www.nebraska.gov/service_info.phtml?service_id=147 for court access. $.60 a record fee or $300 per month flat rate. Online records date from 02/00.

General Information: Public terminal goes back to 2000. No adoption or juvenile records released. Certification fee: $1.00. Payee: Clerk of District Court or County Clerk. Personal checks accepted. Prepayment required.

Franklin County Court PO Box 174, Franklin, NE 68939; phone: 308-425-6288; fax: 308-425-6289; hours 8:30AM-4:30PM M-F (CST). *Misdemeanor, Civil Actions Under $45,000, Eviction, Small Claims, Probate.*

Note: Court personnel not permitted to do record searches.

Civil Records: Access: In person, online. Visitors must perform in person searches themselves. Court makes copy: $.25 per page. Required to search: name, years to search. Civil cases indexed by defendant, plaintiff; on docket cards since 1988, prior on docket books. Online access same as criminal. Online civil and probate records from 05/00 forward.

Criminal Records: Access: In person, online. Visitors must perform in person searches themselves. Court makes copy: $.25 per page. Required to search: name, years to search. Criminal records on docket cards since 1988, prior on docket books. Subscribe to NOL at www.nebraska.gov/service_info.phtml?service_id=147 for court access. $.60 a record fee or $300 per month flat rate. Online criminal and traffic records date from 05/00.

General Information: Public terminal goes back to 5/2000. No juvenile, adoption records released. Certification fee: $1.25. Payee: Franklin County Court. Personal checks accepted. Prepayment required.

Frontier County

District Court PO Box 40, Stockville, NE 69042; phone: 308-367-8641; hours 9AM-4:30PM (CST). *Felony, Civil Actions Over $15,000.*

Civil Records: Access: Mail, in person, online. Both court and visitors may perform in person searches. No search fee. Court makes copy: $.25 per page. Required to search: name, years to search. Civil cases

indexed by defendant, plaintiff; on general index, docket books from late 1800s; computerized records since 6/00. Online access same as criminal. Online records date from 06/00. Mail turnaround time 5 days.

Criminal Records: Access: Mail, in person, online. Both court and visitors may perform in person searches. No search fee. Court makes copy: $.25 per page. Required to search: name, years to search, DOB, signed release. Criminal records on general index, docket books from late 1800s; computerized records since 6/00. Subscribe to NOL at www.nebraska.gov/service_info.phtml?service_id=147 for court access. $.60 a record fee or $300 per month flat rate. Online records date from 06/00. Mail turnaround time 5 days.

General Information: Public use terminal available. Will fax documents for $3.00 per page. Certification fee: $1.00 per page. Payee: Clerk of District Court. Only cashiers checks and money orders accepted. Prepayment and SASE required.

Frontier County Court PO Box 38, Stockville, NE 69042; phone: 308-367-8629; fax: 308-367-8730; hours 9AM-4:30PM (CST). *Misdemeanor, Civil Actions Under $45,000, Eviction, Small Claims, Probate.*

Civil Records: Access: Fax, mail, in person, online. Both court and visitors may perform in person searches. No search fee. Court makes copy: $.25 per page; same fee for self serve. Required to search: name, years to search. Civil cases indexed by plaintiff. Civil records on general index, docket books from late 1800s; on computer back to 10/2000. Online access same as criminal. Online civil and probate records from 09/00 forward. Mail turnaround time 5 days.

Criminal Records: Access: Fax, mail, in person, online. Both court and visitors may perform in person searches. No search fee. Court makes copy: $.25 per page; same fee for self serve. Required to search: name, years to search, DOB; also helpful-signed release. Criminal records on general index, docket books from late 1800s; on computer back to 10/2000. Subscribe to NOL at www.nebraska.gov/service_info.phtml?service_id=147 for court access. $.60 a record fee or $300 per month flat rate. Online criminal and traffic records date from 09/00. Mail turnaround time 5 days.

General Information: Public use terminal available. No adoption or juvenile records released. Fee to fax documents is $3.00 per page. Certification fee: $1.00 per copy. Payee: County Court. Only cashiers checks and money orders accepted. Prepayment and SASE required.

Furnas County

District Court PO Box 413, Beaver City, NE 68926; phone: 308-268-4015; fax: 308-268-4025; hours 10AM-N, 1-3PM (CST). *Felony, Civil Actions Over $15,000.*

Civil Records: Access: Mail, in person, online. Both court and visitors may perform in person searches. No search fee. Court makes copy: $.25 per page; same fee for self serve. Required to search: name, years to search. Civil cases indexed by defendant, plaintiff. Civil records in general index books and files from late 1800s. Online access same as criminal. Online records date from 04/00. Mail turnaround time 3-4 days.

Criminal Records: Access: Mail, in person, online. Both court and visitors may perform in person searches. No search fee. Court makes copy: $.25 per page; same fee for self serve. Required to search: name, years to search. Criminal records in general index books and files from late 1800s. Subscribe to NOL at www.nebraska.gov/service_info.phtml?service_id=147 for court access. $.60 a record fee or $300 per month flat rate. Online records date from 04/00. Mail turnaround time 3-4 days.

General Information: Public terminal goes back to 2000. No mental health records released. Will fax documents. Certification fee: $1.00. Payee: Clerk of

District Court. Personal checks accepted. Prepayment and SASE required.

Furnas County Court PO Box 373, 912 R St, Beaver City, NE 68926; phone: 308-268-4025; hours 8AM-4PM (CST). *Misdemeanor, Civil Actions Under $45,000, Eviction, Small Claims, Probate.*

Civil Records: Access: In person, online. Visitors must perform in person searches themselves. Court makes copy: $.25 per page; same fee for self serve. Required to search: name, years to search. Civil cases indexed by defendant, plaintiff; on card system from 1984, docket books back to late 1800s. Online access same as criminal. Online civil and probate records from 01/01 forward.

Criminal Records: Access: In person, online. Visitors must perform in person searches themselves. Court makes copy: $.25 per page; same fee for self serve. Required to search: name, years to search; also helpful: DOB. Criminal records on card system from 1984, docket books back to late 1800s. Subscribe to NOL at www.nebraska.gov/service_info.phtml?service_id =147 for court access. $.60 a record fee or $300 per month flat rate. Online criminal and traffic records date from 09/00.

General Information: Public terminal goes back to 9/2000. No adoption, juvenile or sealed records released. Certification fee: $1.00 per page. Payee: County Court. Personal checks accepted. Prepayment required.

Gage County

District Court 612 Grant St, #11, Beatrice, NE 68310-2946; phone: 402-223-1332; fax: 402-223-1313; hours 8AM-5PM (CST). *Felony, Civil Actions Over $45,000.*

Civil Records: Access: Mail, fax, in person, online. Both court and visitors may perform in person searches. No search fee. Court makes copy: $.25 per page. Required to search: name, years to search. Civil cases indexed by defendant, plaintiff; on index books from late 1800s; on computer back to 1997. Online access same as criminal. Online records date from 11/96. Mail turnaround time up to 7-10 days.

Criminal Records: Access: Mail, fax, in person, online. Both court and visitors may perform in person searches. No search fee. Court makes copy: $.25 per page. Required to search: name, years to search, DOB. Criminal records on index books from late 1800s; on computer back to 1997. Subscribe to NOL at www.nebraska.gov/service_info.phtml?service_id =147 for court access. $.60 a record fee or $300 per month flat rate. Online records date from 11/96. Mail turnaround time up to 7-10 days.

General Information: Public terminal goes back to 1997. No juvenile or mental health records released. Will fax documents to local or toll free line. Certification fee: $1.00 per cert. Payee: Clerk of District Court. Personal checks accepted. Prepayment and SASE required.

Gage County Court 612 Grant St, #17, Beatrice, NE 68310-2946; criminal phone: 402-223-1325; civil phone: 402-223-1328; probate phone: 402-223-1327; hours 8AM-5PM (CST). *Misdemeanor, Civil Actions Under $45,000, Eviction, Small Claims, Probate.*

Civil Records: Access: In person, online. Visitors must perform in person searches themselves. Court makes copy: $.25 per page. Required to search: name, years to search. Civil cases indexed by defendant, plaintiff. Civil records go back to 1987; on computer back to 1999. Probate records from 1860, probate on microfiche. Online access same as criminal, records date from 11/16/98 forward, probate from 05/98. Note: Court personnel will not perform name searches.

Criminal Records: Access: Mail, in person, online. Visitors must perform in person searches themselves. No search fee. Court makes copy: $.25 per page. Required to search: name, years to search, DOB. Civil records go back to 1976; on computer

back to 1996. Subscribe to NOL at www.nebraska.gov/service_info.phtml?service_id =147 for court access. $.60 a record fee or $300 per month flat rate. Online criminal and traffic records date from 09/09/96. Note: Court personnel will not perform name searches. Mail turnaround time 1-3 weeks.

General Information: Public terminal goes back to 9/1996. No adoption or juvenile records released. Certification fee: $1.00. Payee: Gage County Court. Personal checks accepted. Prepayment and SASE required.

Garden County

District Court PO Box 486, Oshkosh, NE 69154; phone: 308-772-3924; fax: 308-772-0124; hours 8AM-4PM (MST). *Felony, Civil Actions Over $15,000.*

Civil Records: Access: Fax, mail, in person, online. Both court and visitors may perform in person searches. No search fee. Court makes copy: $.50 per page. Self serve copy fee: $.25 per page. Required to search: name, years to search. Civil cases indexed by defendant, plaintiff. Civil records in files, docket books back to 1910; on computer back to 1998. Online access same as criminal. Online records date from 08/98. Mail turnaround time same day.

Criminal Records: Access: Fax, mail, in person, online. Both court and visitors may perform in person searches. No search fee. Court makes copy: $.50 per page. Self serve copy fee: $.25 per page. Required to search: name, years to search. Criminal records in files, docket books back to 1910; on computer back to 1998. Subscribe to NOL at www.nebraska.gov/service_info.phtml?service_id =147 for court access. $.60 a record fee or $300 per month flat rate. Online records date from 08/98. Mail turnaround time same day.

General Information: Public terminal goes back to 1998. No confidential records released. Will fax documents $2.00 1st page, $1.00 each add'l. Certification fee: $5.00. Payee: Clerk of District Court. Personal checks accepted. Prepayment and SASE required.

Garden County Court PO Box 465, Oshkosh, NE 69154; phone: 308-772-3696; fax: 308-772-0124; hours 8AM-4PM (MST). *Misdemeanor, Civil Actions Under $45,000, Eviction, Small Claims, Probate.*

Civil Records: Access: In person, online. Visitors must perform in person searches themselves. Required to search: name, years to search. Civil cases indexed by defendant, plaintiff; on general index, docket books from 1993, computerized since 1998. Online access same as criminal. Online civil and probate records from 01/01 forward. Note: Phone access limited to short searches.

Criminal Records: Access: In person, online. Visitors must perform in person searches themselves. Required to search: name, years to search. Criminal records on general index, docket books from 1992, computerized since 1998. Subscribe to NOL at www.nebraska.gov/service_info.phtml?service_id =147 for court access. $.60 a record fee or $300 per month flat rate. Online criminal and traffic records date from 06/00.

General Information: No public access terminal. No adoption or juvenile records released. Certification fee: $1.00. Payee: Garden County Court. Personal checks accepted. Prepayment required.

Garfield County

District Court PO Box 218, Burwell, NE 68823; phone: 308-346-4161; hours 9AM-5PM (CST). *Felony, Civil Actions Over $15,000.*

Civil Records: Access: Mail, in person, online. Only the court performs in person searches; visitors may not. Search fee: $5.00. Court makes copy: $.25 per page; same fee for self serve. Required to search: name, years to search; also helpful: address. Civil cases indexed by defendant; on index books

from 1885. Online access same as criminal. Online records date from 07/00. Mail turnaround time 3-4 days.

Criminal Records: Access: Mail, in person, online. Only the court performs in person searches; visitors may not. Search fee: $5.00 per name. Court makes copy: $.25 per page; same fee for self serve. Required to search: name, years to search; also helpful: address, DOB, SSN. Criminal records on index books from 1885. Subscribe to NOL at www.nebraska.gov/service_info.phtml?service_id =147 for court access. $.60 a record fee or $300 per month flat rate. Online records date from 07/00. Mail turnaround time 3-4 days.

General Information: No public access terminal. Will fax documents for $5.00 per page. Certification fee: $1.50. Payee: Clerk of District Court. Personal checks accepted. Prepayment and SASE required.

Garfield County Court PO Box 431, Burwell, NE 68823; phone: 308-346-4123; fax: 308-346-5064; hours 9AM-4PM (CST). *Misdemeanor, Civil Actions Under $45,000, Eviction, Small Claims, Probate.*

Civil Records: Access: Mail, in person, online. Both court and visitors may perform in person searches. No search fee. Court makes copy: $.25 per page. Required to search: name, years to search. Civil cases indexed by defendant. Civil records on index books, from 1885 (probate), 25 years for civil; on computer back to 2000. Online access same as criminal. Online civil and probate records from 10/00 forward. Mail turnaround time within 5 days.

Criminal Records: Access: Mail, in person, online. Both court and visitors may perform in person searches. No search fee. Court makes copy: $.25 per page. Required to search: name, years to search. Criminal record keeping back for 25 years; on computer back to 2000. Subscribe to NOL at www.nebraska.gov/service_info.phtml?service_id =147 for court access. $.60 a record fee or $300 per month flat rate. Online criminal and traffic records date from 07/00. Mail turnaround time within 5 days.

General Information: Public terminal goes back to 2000. No juvenile records released. Will fax documents $3.00 1st page, $1.00 each add'l. Certification fee: $1.00. Payee: County Court. Personal checks accepted. Prepayment and SASE required.

Gosper County

District Court PO Box 136, Elwood, NE 68937; phone: 308-785-2611; fax: 308-785-2300; hours 8:30AM-4:30PM (CST). *Felony, Civil Actions Over $15,000.*

www.co.gosper.ne.us/court.html

Civil Records: Access: In person, online. Visitors must perform in person searches themselves. Court makes copy: $.25 per page. Required to search: name, years to search. Civil cases indexed by defendant, plaintiff. Civil records in general index books since late 1800s. Online access same as criminal. Online records date from 07/00.

Criminal Records: Access: Fax, mail, in person, online. Visitors must perform in person searches themselves. No search fee. Court makes copy: $.25 per page. Required to search: name, years to search; also helpful: DOB. Criminal records in general index books since late 1800s. Subscribe to NOL at www.nebraska.gov/service_info.phtml?service_id =147 for court access. $.60 a record fee or $300 per month flat rate. Online records date from 07/00.

General Information: Public terminal goes back to 2000. No juvenile records or search warrants released. Certification fee: $1.00 per page. Payee: Clerk of District Court. Personal checks accepted. Prepayment required.

Gosper County Court PO Box 55, 507 Smith St, Elwood, NE 68937; phone: 308-785-2531; fax: 308-785-2300; hours 8:30AM-4:30PM (CST). *Misdemeanor, Civil Actions Under $45,000, Eviction, Small Claims, Probate.*

Note: Always call before faxing.

Civil Records: Access: In person, online. Visitors must perform in person searches themselves. Court makes copy: $.25 per page; same fee for self serve. Required to search: name, years to search. Civil cases indexed by defendant, plaintiff; on index cards, docket books kept for 10 years (civil), to late 1800s (probate). Online access same as criminal. Online civil and probate records from 11/00 forward. Note: Mail access limited to short searches.

Criminal Records: Access: In person, online. Visitors must perform in person searches themselves. Court makes copy: $.25 per page; same fee for self serve. Required to search: name, years to search, DOB. Criminal record keeping back for 15 years, 3 years are computerized. Subscribe to NOL at www.nebraska.gov/service_info.phtml?service_id =147 for court access. $.60 a record fee or $300 per month flat rate. Online criminal and traffic records date from 02/00.

General Information: Public terminal goes back to 2000. No adoption or juvenile records released. Certification fee: $1.00. Payee: Gosper County Court. Personal checks accepted. Out of state checks not accepted. Prepayment required.

Grant County

District Court PO Box 139, Hyannis, NE 69350; phone: 308-458-2488; fax: 308-458-2780; hours 8AM-4PM (MST). *Felony, Civil Actions Over $15,000.*

Civil Records: Access: Fax, mail, in person, online. Both court and visitors may perform in person searches. No search fee. Court makes copy: $.20 per page; same fee for self serve. Required to search: name, years to search. Civil cases indexed by defendant, plaintiff; on index books from 1888. Online access same as criminal. Online records date from 06/00. Mail turnaround time 3-4 days.

Criminal Records: Access: Fax, mail, in person, online. Both court and visitors may perform in person searches. No search fee. Court makes copy: $.20 per page; same fee for self serve. Required to search: name, years to search. Criminal records on index books from 1888. Subscribe to NOL at www.nebraska.gov/service_info.phtml?service_id =147 for court access. $.60 a record fee or $300 per month flat rate. Online records date from 06/00. Mail turnaround time 3-4 days.

General Information: No public access terminal. No mental health records released. Will fax documents $.20 per page. Certification fee: $1.50 includes copy fee. Payee: Grant County Clerk. Personal checks accepted. Prepayment and SASE required.

Grant County Court PO Box 97, Hyannis, NE 69350; phone: 308-458-2433; criminal phone: 308-327-5656; civil phone: 308-327-2692; fax: 308-327-5623; hours 11AM-4PM only on 2nd Tues of month (MST). *Misdemeanor, Civil Actions Under $45,000, Eviction, Small Claims, Probate.*

Note: This court will not do record searches by name, etc. but will send and certify copies of specific records.

Civil Records: Access: in person, online. Visitors must perform in person searches themselves. Court makes copy: $.20 per page; same fee for self serve. Required to search: name, years to search; also helpful: address. Civil cases indexed by defendant, plaintiff. Civil records in files, docket books from 1888, computerized since 7/00. Online access same as criminal, records date from 11/00 forward, probate from 01/01. Note: Limited phone searching for specific records.

Criminal Records: Access: In person, online. Visitors must perform in person searches

themselves. Court makes copy: $.20 per page; same fee for self serve. Required to search: name, years to search, DOB; also helpful: address, SSN. Criminal records in files, docket books from 1888, computerized since 7/00. Subscribe to NOL at www.nebraska.gov/service_info.phtml?service_id =147 for court access. $.60 a record fee or $300 per month flat rate. Online criminal and traffic records date from 07/00. Note: Limited phone searching for specific records.

General Information: No public access terminal. No adoption records released. Certification fee: $1.00. Payee: Grant County Court. Personal checks accepted. Prepayment required.

Greeley County

District Court PO Box 287, 101 S Kildare, Greeley, NE 68842; phone: 308-428-3625; fax: 308-428-3022; hours 8AM-N; 1PM-4PM (CST). *Felony, Civil Actions Over $15,000.*

Civil Records: Access: Mail, in person, online. Visitors must perform in person searches themselves. No search fee. Court makes copy: $.25 per page; same fee for self serve. Required to search: name, years to search, address. Civil cases indexed by defendant, plaintiff; on general index books from late 1800s. Online access same as criminal. Online records date from 07/00. Mail turnaround time 1 day.

Criminal Records: Access: Fax, mail, in person, online. Visitors must perform in person searches themselves. No search fee. Court makes copy: $.25 per page; same fee for self serve. Required to search: name, years to search, DOB, signed release. Criminal records on general index books from late 1800s. Subscribe to NOL at www.nebraska.gov/service_info.phtml?service_id =147 for court access. $.60 a record fee or $300 per month flat rate. Online records date from 07/00, Mail turnaround time 1 day.

General Information: Public terminal goes back to 7/2000. No mental health records released. Will fax documents. Certification fee: $1.50 plus $.25 per page. Payee: Clerk of District Court. Only cashiers checks and money orders accepted. Prepayment and SASE required.

Greeley County Court PO Box 302, Greeley, NE 68842; phone: 308-428-2705; criminal phone: 308-428-3995; civil phone: 308-428-3995; probate phone: 308-428-3995; criminal fax: 308-428-6500; same fax for civil/probate; hours 8AM-5PM (CST). *Misdemeanor, Civil Actions Under $45,000, Eviction, Small Claims, Probate.*

Civil Records: Access: In person, online. Visitors must perform in person searches themselves. Court makes copy: $.25 per page. Required to search: name, years to search. Civil cases indexed by defendant, plaintiff; on index cards, kept from late 1800s, computerized since 5/00. Online access same as criminal. Online civil and probate records from 05/00 forward.

Criminal Records: Access: In person, online. Visitors must perform in person searches themselves. Court makes copy: $.25 per page. Required to search: name, years to search. Criminal records on index cards, kept from late 1800s, computerized since 5/00. Subscribe to NOL at www.nebraska.gov/service_info.phtml?service_id =147 for court access. $.60 a record fee or $300 per month flat rate. Online criminal and traffic records date from 05/00.

General Information: Public terminal goes back to 5/2000. No adoption records released. Will fax specific case file requests; fee varies by job. Certification fee: $1.00 per page. Payee: County Court. Only cashiers checks and money orders accepted. Prepayment required.

Hall County

District Court 111 W First St, Box 1926, Grand Island, NE 68802; phone: 308-385-5144; fax: 308-385-5110; hours 8AM-5PM (CST). *Felony, Civil Actions Over $15,000.*

Civil Records: Access: Fax, mail, in person, online. Visitors must perform in person searches themselves. Court makes copy: $.25 per page. Required to search: name, years to search. Civil cases indexed by defendant, plaintiff. Many records on computer since 1985, some on microfilm, original index books back to late 1800s. Online access same as criminal. Online records date from 10/97. Note: Court performs searches for government/law enforcement only. Mail turnaround time 3-4 days.

Criminal Records: Access: Fax, mail, in person, online. Visitors must perform in person searches themselves. Court makes copy: $.25 per page. Required to search: name, years to search. Many records on computer since 1985, some on microfilm, original index books back to late 1800s. Subscribe to NOL at www.nebraska.gov/service_info.phtml?service_id =147 for court access. $.60 a record fee or $300 per month flat rate. Online records date from 10/97. Mail turnaround time 3-4 days.

General Information: Public terminal goes back to 1989. No mental health records released. Fee to fax documents is $3.00 1st page, $1.00 each add'l. Certification fee: $1.00 per cert. Payee: Clerk of District Court. Personal checks accepted. Prepayment and SASE required.

Hall County Court 111 W 1st #1, Grand Island, NE 68801; phone: 308-385-5135; fax: 308-385-5138; hours 8AM-5PM (CST). *Misdemeanor, Civil Actions Under $45,000, Eviction, Small Claims, Probate.*

Civil Records: Access: In person, online. Visitors must perform in person searches themselves. Court makes copy: $.25 per page. Required to search: name, years to search. Civil cases indexed by defendant. Civil records on index books, on computer after 1/24/00. Online access same as criminal, records date from 01/00 forward, probate from 08/98.

Criminal Records: Access: Fax, mail, in person, online. Visitors must perform in person searches themselves. No search fee. Court makes copy: $.25 per page. Required to search: name, years to search, DOB. Criminal records on index books; on computer after 5/19/97. Subscribe to NOL at www.nebraska.gov/service_info.phtml?service_id =147 for court access. $.60 a record fee or $300 per month flat rate. Online criminal and traffic records date from 05/97.

General Information: Public terminal has criminal back to 5/1997 and civil back to 1/2000. No confidential records released. Certification fee: $1.00. Payee: County Court. Personal checks accepted. Prepayment required.

Hamilton County

District Court PO Box 201, Aurora, NE 68818-0201; phone: 402-694-3533; fax: 402-694-2250; hours 8AM-5PM (CST). *Felony, Civil Actions Over $15,000.*

Civil Records: Access: In person, online. Visitors must perform in person searches themselves. Court makes copy: $.25 per page; same fee for self serve. Required to search: name, years to search. Civil cases indexed by defendant, plaintiff; on index books and files from late 1800s. Online access same as criminal. Online records date from 03/98.

Criminal Records: Access: In person, online. Visitors must perform in person searches themselves. Court makes copy: $.25 per page; same fee for self serve. Required to search: name, years to search. Criminal records on index books and files from late 1800s. Subscribe to NOL at www.nebraska.gov/service_info.phtml?service_id =147 for court access. $.60 a record fee or $300 per month flat rate. Online records date from 03/98.

General Information: Public use terminal available. No mental health board hearing records released. Certification fee: $1.00. Payee: Clerk of District Court. Personal checks accepted. Prepayment required.

Hamilton County Court PO Box 323, 1111 13th St, Aurora, NE 68818; phone: 402-694-6188; fax: 402-694-2250; hours 8AM-5PM (CST). *Misdemeanor, Civil Actions Under $45,000, Eviction, Small Claims, Probate.*
Note: Will not do name searches, but will provide specific documents.
Civil Records: Access: In person, online. Visitors must perform in person searches themselves. Court makes copy: $.25 per page. Required to search: name, years to search. Civil cases indexed by defendant, plaintiff. Civil records computerized since 1998, older on docket cards, probate on microfiche from late 1800s. Online access same as criminal, records date from 10/99 forward, probate from 05/98.
Criminal Records: Access: Fax, mail, in person, online. Visitors must perform in person searches themselves. No search fee. Court makes copy: $.25 per page. Required to search: name, years to search. Computerized since 1997. Subscribe to NOL at www.nebraska.gov/service_info.phtml?service_id =147 for court access. $.60 a record fee or $300 per month flat rate. Online criminal and traffic records date from 07/97.
General Information: Public terminal goes back to 4/1998. No adoption records released. Certification fee: $1.00 per page. Payee: Hamilton County Court. Personal checks accepted. Prepayment required.

Harlan County

District Court PO Box 698, Alma, NE 68920; phone: 308-928-2173; fax: 308-928-2079; hours 8:30AM-4:30PM (CST). *Felony, Civil Actions Over $15,000.*
Civil Records: Access: Phone, mail, in person, online. Both court and visitors may perform in person searches. Search fee: $5.00 per name. Court makes copy: $.25 per page; same fee for self serve. Required to search: name, years to search. Civil cases indexed by defendant, plaintiff; on books and in files from late 1800s, on computer back to 3/2000. Online access same as criminal. Online records date from 04/00. Mail turnaround time 1 day.
Criminal Records: Access: Phone, mail, in person, online. Both court and visitors may perform in person searches. Search fee: $5.00 per name. Court makes copy: $.25 per page; same fee for self serve. Required to search: name, years to search. Criminal records on books and in files from late 1800s; on computer back to 3/2000. Subscribe to NOL at www.nebraska.gov/service_info.phtml?service_id =147 for court access. $.60 a record fee or $300 per month flat rate. Online records date from 04/00. Mail turnaround time 1 day.
General Information: Public terminal goes back to 3/2000. No juvenile records released. Certification fee: $1.00. Payee: Clerk of District Court. Personal checks accepted. Prepayment required.

Harlan County Court PO Box 379, Alma, NE 68920; phone: 308-928-2179; fax: 308-928-2170; hours 8:30AM-4:30PM (CST). *Misdemeanor, Civil Actions Under $51,000, Eviction, Small Claims, Probate.*
Civil Records: Access: In person, online. Visitors must perform in person searches themselves. Court makes copy: $.25 per page; same fee for self serve. Required to search: name, years to search; also helpful: address. Civil cases indexed by defendant. Civil records on index cards from 1900; computerized since 2000. Online access same as criminal. Online civil and probate records from 11/00 forward.
Criminal Records: Access: In person, online. Visitors must perform in person searches themselves. Court makes copy: $.25 per page; same fee for self serve. Required to search: name, years to search; also helpful: address, DOB. Criminal records on index cards from 1900, computerized since 2000.

Subscribe to NOL at www.nebraska.gov/service_info.phtml?service_id =147 for court access. $.60 a record fee or $300 per month flat rate. Online criminal and traffic records date from 03/00.
General Information: Public terminal goes back to 2000. (The data is on CD-ROM and available for legal research only.) No adoption records released. Limited access to juvenile records. Certification fee: $1.00. Payee: Harlan County Court. Business checks accepted. Prepayment required. Payment is required at time of search.

Hayes County

District Court PO Box 370, Hayes Center, NE 69032; phone: 308-286-3413; fax: 308-286-3208; hours 8AM-4PM (CST). *Felony, Civil Actions Over $15,000.*
Civil Records: Access: Fax, mail, in person, online. Both court and visitors may perform in person searches. No search fee. Court makes copy: $.25 per page; same fee for self serve. Required to search: name; also helpful: years to search, address. Civil cases indexed by defendant, plaintiff; on index books back to late 1800s. Online access same as criminal. Online records date from 06/00. Mail turnaround time 2 days.
Criminal Records: Access: Fax, mail, in person, online. Both court and visitors may perform in person searches. No search fee. Court makes copy: $.25 per page; same fee for self serve. Required to search: name; also helpful: years to search, address, DOB, SSN. Criminal records on index books back to late 1800s. Subscribe to NOL at www.nebraska.gov/service_info.phtml?service_id =147 for court access. $.60 a record fee or $300 per month flat rate. Online records date from 06/00. Mail turnaround time 2 days.
General Information: Public use terminal available. No sealed records released. Will fax documents to local or toll free line. Certification fee: $4.00. Payee: Clerk of District Court. Personal checks accepted. Prepayment and SASE required.

Hayes County Court PO Box 370, Hayes Center, NE 69032; phone: 308-286-3315; fax: 308-286-3208; hours 9AM-N, 1-4PM Tuesday (Clerk's hours) (CST). *Misdemeanor, Civil Actions Under $45,000, Eviction, Small Claims, Probate.*
Civil Records: Access: Phone, mail, in person, online. Both court and visitors may perform in person searches. No search fee. Court makes copy: $.25 per page; same fee for self serve. Required to search: name, years to search. Civil cases indexed by defendant, plaintiff; on general index books and files back to late 1800s; on computer back to mid-2000. Online access same as criminal, records date from 11/00 forward, probate from 12/00. Mail turnaround time 1 week.
Criminal Records: Access: Phone, mail, in person, online. Both court and visitors may perform in person searches. No search fee. Court makes copy: $.25 per page; same fee for self serve. Required to search: name, years to search, DOB. Criminal records on general index books and files back to late 1800s; on computer back to mid-2000. Subscribe to NOL at www.nebraska.gov/service_info.phtml?service_id =147 for court access. $.60 a record fee or $300 per month flat rate. Online criminal and traffic records date from 08/00. Mail turnaround time 1 week.
General Information: No public access terminal. No juvenile or adoption records released. Certification fee: $1.00. Payee: County Court. Personal checks accepted. Prepayment and SASE required.

Hitchcock County

District Court PO Box 248, 229 E "D" St, Trenton, NE 69044; phone: 308-334-5646; fax: 308-334-5398; hours 8:30AM-4PM (CST). *Felony, Civil Actions Over $15,000.*
www.co.hitchcock.ne.us/court.html

Civil Records: Access: Phone, fax, mail, in person, online. Both court and visitors may perform in person searches. No search fee. Court makes copy: $.50 per page. Required to search: name, years to search. Civil cases indexed by defendant, plaintiff; on books from late 1800s; on computer back to 1999. Online access same as criminal. Online records date from 06/00. Mail turnaround time 2 days.
Criminal Records: Access: Phone, fax, mail, in person, online. Both court and visitors may perform in person searches. No search fee. Court makes copy: $.50 per page. Required to search: name, years to search. Criminal records on books from late 1800s; on computer back to 1999. Subscribe to NOL at www.nebraska.gov/service_info.phtml?service_id =147 for court access. $.60 a record fee or $300 per month flat rate. Online records date from 06/00. Mail turnaround time 2 days.
General Information: Public terminal goes back to 2000. No sealed records released. Will fax documents $3.00 1st page, $1.50 each add'l. Certification fee: $1.00 per cert. Payee: Clerk of District Court. Personal checks accepted. Prepayment and SASE required.

Hitchcock County Court PO Box 248, Trenton, NE 69044; phone: 308-334-5383; hours 8:30AM-4PM (CST). *Misdemeanor, Civil Actions Under $45,000, Eviction, Small Claims, Probate.*
Note: Probate is a separate index at this same address.
Civil Records: Access: Phone, mail, in person, online. Both court and visitors may perform in person searches. No search fee. Court makes copy: $.25 per page; same fee for self serve. Required to search: name, years to search. Civil cases indexed by defendant, plaintiff; on docket books, cards go back to 1960s; on computer back to 2000. Probate records go back to late 1800s. Online access same as criminal. Online civil and probate records from 01/01 forward. Mail turnaround time 2 weeks, limited phone searching- same day.
Criminal Records: Access: Phone, mail, in person, online. Both court and visitors may perform in person searches. No search fee. Court makes copy: $.25 per page; same fee for self serve. Required to search: name, years to search, DOB. Criminal records go back to 1978 approx. on docket books, cards; on computer back to 2000. Subscribe to NOL at www.nebraska.gov/service_info.phtml?service_id =147 for court access. $.60 a record fee or $300 per month flat rate. Online criminal and traffic records date from 09/00. Mail turnaround time 2 weeks, limited phone searching same day
General Information: Public terminal goes back to 2000. (Terminal is across the hall.) No adoption or juvenile records released. Will not fax documents. Certification fee: $1.00. Payee: County Court. Personal checks accepted. Prepayment and SASE required.

Holt County

District Court PO Box 755, 204 N 4th St, O'Neill, NE 68763; phone: 402-336-2840; fax: 402-336-3601; hours 8AM-4:30PM (CST). *Felony, Civil Actions Over $15,000.*
Civil Records: Access: Phone, fax, mail, in person, online. Both court and visitors may perform in person searches. No search fee. Court makes copy: $.20 per page; same fee for self serve. Required to search: name, years to search; also helpful: address. Civil cases indexed by defendant, plaintiff; on docket books and general index books since late 1800, search last 15 years only. Online access same as criminal. Online records date from 6/98. Mail turnaround time 1 week or less.
Criminal Records: Access: Phone, fax, mail, in person, online. Both court and visitors may perform in person searches. No search fee. Court makes copy: $.20 per page; same fee for self serve. Required to search: name, years to search, DOB. Criminal records on docket books and general index books archived since late 1800s, search last 15 years only. Subscribe to NOL at www.nebraska.gov/service_info.phtml?service_id

=147 for court access. $.60 a record fee or $300 per month flat rate. Online records date from 6/98. Mail turnaround time 1 week or less.

General Information: Public terminal has criminal back to 1997 and civil back to 1980s. No juvenile or mental health records released. Will fax documents $3.00 1st page, $1.00 each add'l. Certification fee: $1.00 per page. Payee: Clerk of District Court. Personal checks accepted. Prepayment and SASE required.

Holt County Court 204 N 4th St, O'Neill, NE 68763; phone: 402-336-1662; criminal fax: 402-336-1663; same fax for civil/probate; hours 8AM-4:30PM (CST). *Misdemeanor, Civil Actions Under $45,000, Eviction, Small Claims, Probate.*

Civil Records: Access: In person, online. Visitors must perform in person searches themselves. Court makes copy: $.25 per page. Required to search: name, years to search. Civil cases indexed by defendant. Civil records go back to 1980; on computer back to 2000; probate kept longer. Online access same as criminal, records date from 10/00 forward, probate from 11/00.

Criminal Records: Access: In person, online. Visitors must perform in person searches themselves. Court makes copy: $.25 per page. Required to search: name, years to search, DOB. Criminal records go back to 1920, on computer back to 2000. Subscribe to NOL at www.nebraska.gov/service_info.phtml?service_id =147 for court access. $.60 a record fee or $300 per month flat rate. Online criminal and traffic records date from 07/00.

General Information: Public terminal goes back to 7/2000. No adoption records released. Will not fax documents. Certification fee: $1.00 per page. Payee: Holt County Court. Personal checks accepted. Prepayment required.

Hooker County

District Court PO Box 184, Mullen, NE 69152; phone: 308-546-2244; fax: 308-546-2490; hours 8:30AM-N, 1-4:30PM (MST). *Felony, Civil Actions Over $15,000.*

Civil Records: Access: In person, online. Visitors must perform in person searches themselves. Court makes copy: $1.00 per page. Self serve copy fee: $.25 per page. Required to search: name, years to search. Civil cases indexed by defendant, plaintiff; on index books since late 1800s. Online access same as criminal. Online records date from 06/00.

Criminal Records: Access: In person, online. Visitors must perform in person searches themselves. Court makes copy: $1.00 per page. Self serve copy fee: $.25 per page. Required to search: name, years to search. Criminal records on index books since late 1800s. Subscribe to NOL at www.nebraska.gov/service_info.phtml?service_id =147 for court access. $.60 a record fee or $300 per month flat rate. Online records date from 06/00.

General Information: Public terminal goes back to 6/2000. No mental health records released. Certification fee: $1.50 per cert. Payee: Clerk of District Court. Personal checks accepted. Prepayment required.

Hooker County Court PO Box 184, 305 NW 1st St, Mullen, NE 69152; phone: 308-546-2249; fax: 308-546-2490; hours 8:30AM-4:30PM (MST). *Misdemeanor, Civil Actions Under $45,000, Eviction, Small Claims, Probate.*

Note: Fax number is for sheriff's office.

Civil Records: Access: Fax, mail, in person, online. Only the court performs in person searches; visitors may not. No search fee. Court makes copy: $.25 per page. Required to search: name, years to search. Civil cases indexed by defendant, plaintiff; on index cards and books from late 1800s. Online access same as criminal, records date from 11/99 forward, probate from 08/98. Mail turnaround time 3-4 days.

Criminal Records: Access: Fax, mail, in person, online. Both court and visitors may perform in person searches. No search fee. Court makes copy: $.25 per page. Required to search: name, years to search; also helpful: DOB, SSN. Criminal records on index cards and books from late 1800s, computerized 1998. Subscribe to NOL at www.nebraska.gov/service_info.phtml?service_id =147 for court access. $.60 a record fee or $300 per month flat rate. Online criminal and traffic records date from 08/98. Mail turnaround time 3-4 days.

General Information: No public access terminal. No adoption or juvenile records released. No fee to fax back documents. Certification fee: $1.00 per cert. Payee: County Court. Business checks accepted. Prepayment and SASE required.

Howard County

District Court PO Box 25, 612 Indian St, St Paul, NE 68873; phone: 308-754-4343; fax: 308-754-4125; hours 8AM-5PM (CST). *Felony, Civil Actions Over $15,000.*

Civil Records: Access: In person, online. Both court and visitors may perform in person searches. Court makes copy: $.25 per page. Required to search: name, years to search. Civil cases indexed by defendant, plaintiff; on microfiche from 1986, books prior. Online access same as criminal. Online records date from 06/98.

Criminal Records: Access: Fax, mail, in person, online. Both court and visitors may perform in person searches. No search fee. Court makes copy: $.25 per page. Required to search: name, years to search, DOB. Criminal records on microfiche from 1986, books prior; on computer back to 9/1998. Subscribe to NOL at www.nebraska.gov/service_info.phtml?service_id =147 for court access. $.60 a record fee or $300 per month flat rate. Online records date from 06/98.

General Information: Public terminal has criminal back to 9/1998 and civil back to 2002. No pending case records released. Certification fee: $5.00 per cert. Payee: Clerk of District Court. Personal checks accepted. Prepayment required.

Howard County Court 612 Indian St #6, St Paul, NE 68873; phone: 308-754-4192; fax: 308-754-4727; hours 8AM-N; 1PM-4PM (CST). *Misdemeanor, Civil Actions Under $45,000, Eviction, Small Claims, Probate.*

Civil Records: Access: In person, online. Visitors must perform in person searches themselves. Court makes copy: $.25 per page. Required to search: name, years to search. Civil cases indexed by defendant. Civil records on docket cards since 1982; computerized records since 2000. Online access same as criminal, records date from 05/01 forward, probate from 08/00.

Criminal Records: Access: In person, online. Visitors must perform in person searches themselves. Court makes copy: $.25 per page. Required to search: name, years to search; also helpful: DOB. Criminal records on docket cards since 1982; computerized records since 2000. Subscribe to NOL at www.nebraska.gov/service_info.phtml?service_id =147 for court access. $.60 a record fee or $300 per month flat rate. Online criminal and traffic records date from 08/00.

General Information: Public terminal goes back to 2000. Certification fee: $1.00 per page. Payee: Howard County Court. Business checks accepted. Prepayment required.

Jefferson County

District Court Jefferson County Courthouse, 411 Fourth St, Fairbury, NE 68352; phone: 402-729-2019; fax: 402-729-6596; hours 9AM-5PM (CST). *Felony, Civil Actions Over $15,000.*

Civil Records: Access: Fax, mail, in person, online. Both court and visitors may perform in person

searches. No search fee. Court makes copy: $.25 per page. Required to search: name, years to search. Civil cases indexed by defendant, plaintiff; on index books from 1870s; on computer back to 1996. Online access same as criminal. Online records date from 11/96. Mail turnaround time 1-3 days.

Criminal Records: Access: In person, online. Visitors must perform in person searches themselves. Court makes copy: $.25 per page. Required to search: name, years to search, DOB. Criminal records on index books from 1870s; on computer back to 1996. Subscribe to NOL at www.nebraska.gov/service_info.phtml?service_id =147 for court access. $.60 a record fee or $300 per month flat rate. Online records date from 11/96. Mail turnaround time 1-2 days.

General Information: Public terminal goes back to 1996. No mental health records released. Fee to fax documents is $2.00 per page. Certification fee: $1.00. Payee: Clerk of District Court. Personal checks accepted. Prepayment and SASE required.

Jefferson County Court 411 Fourth St, Fairbury, NE 68352; phone: 402-729-2312; hours 8AM-N, 1-5PM (CST). *Misdemeanor, Civil Actions Under $45,000, Eviction, Small Claims, Probate.*

Note: This court will not longer perform name searches for the public.

Civil Records: Access: In person, online. Visitors must perform in person searches themselves. Court makes copy: $.25 per page. Required to search: name, years to search. Civil cases indexed by defendant, plaintiff; on cards from 1988, prior on docket books; computerized records from 10/1999. Online access same as criminal, records date from 10/99 forward, probate from 05/98.

Criminal Records: Access: In person, online. Visitors must perform in person searches themselves. Court makes copy: $.25 per page. Required to search: name, years to search, DOB, signed release. Criminal records on cards from 1988, prior on docket books; computerized records from 9/1996. Subscribe to NOL at www.nebraska.gov/service_info.phtml?service_id =147 for court access. $.60 a record fee or $300 per month flat rate. Online criminal and traffic records date from 09/96.

General Information: Public terminal has criminal back to 1996 and civil back to 1999. No adoption or sealed records released. Certification fee: $1.00. Payee: County Court. Personal checks accepted. Prepayment required.

Johnson County

District Court PO Box 416, Tecumseh, NE 68450; phone: 402-335-6301; fax: 402-335-6311; hours 8AM-N, 1-4:30PM (CST). *Felony, Civil Actions Over $15,000.*

Civil Records: Access: Mail, in person, online. Both court and visitors may perform in person searches. No search fee. Court makes copy: $.50 per page; same fee for self serve. Required to search: name, years to search. Civil cases indexed by defendant, plaintiff; on index and docket books from late 1800s, microfiche back 7 years. Online access same as criminal. Online civil and probate records from 04/01 forward.

Criminal Records: Access: In person, online. Both court and visitors may perform in person searches. No search fee. Court makes copy: $.50 per page; same fee for self serve. Required to search: name, years to search. Criminal records on index and docket books from late 1800s, microfiche back 7 years. Subscribe to NOL at www.nebraska.gov/service_info.phtml?service_id =147 for court access. $.60 a record fee or $300 per month flat rate. Online records date from 04/00. Mail turnaround time 3 days.

General Information: Public terminal goes back to 1998. No juvenile records released. Fee to fax documents is $2.00 per document. Certification fee: $1.50. Payee: Clerk of District Court. Personal checks accepted. Prepayment required.

Johnson County Court PO Box 285, Tecumseh, NE 68450; phone: 402-335-6313; fax: 402-335-6314; hours 8AM-4:30PM (CST). *Misdemeanor, Civil Actions Under $45,000, Eviction, Small Claims, Probate.*
Note: The court is in the process of computerizing their records.
Civil Records: Access: Mail, in person, online. Both court and visitors may perform in person searches. No search fee. Court makes copy: $.25 per page. Required to search: name, years to search; also helpful: address. Civil cases indexed by defendant, plaintiff; on index cards back 15 years, microfiche back to late 1800s for probate. Online access same as criminal. Online records date from 02/98.
Criminal Records: Access: Mail, in person, online. Both court and visitors may perform in person searches. No search fee. Court makes copy: $.25 per page. Required to search: name, years to search, DOB, signed release; also helpful: address, SSN. Criminal records on index cards back 15 years. Subscribe to NOL at www.nebraska.gov/service_info.phtml?service_id =147 for court access. $.60 a record fee or $300 per month flat rate. Online criminal and traffic records date from 02/98.
General Information: Public terminal goes back to 4/2000. No adoption or juvenile records released. Will not fax documents. Certification fee: $1.00 per page. Payee: County Court. Personal checks accepted. Prepayment required.

Kearney County

District Court PO Box 208, Minden, NE 68959; phone: 308-832-1742; fax: 308-832-0636; hours 8:30AM-5PM (CST). *Felony, Civil Actions Over $15,000.*
Civil Records: Access: In person, online. Visitors must perform in person searches themselves. Court makes copy: $.25 per page. Required to search: name, years to search. Civil cases indexed by defendant, plaintiff. All records on microfilm since 1800s; on computer back to 9/1998. Online access same as criminal. Online records date from 08/98. Note: Mail access to attorneys only.
Criminal Records: Access: In person, online. Visitors must perform in person searches themselves. Court makes copy: $.25 per page. Required to search: name, years to search. Criminal records on microfilm since 1800s; on computer back to 9/1998. Subscribe to NOL at www.nebraska.gov/service_info.phtml?service_id =147 for court access. $.60 a record fee or $300 per month flat rate. Online records date from 08/98.
General Information: Public terminal has only civil records back to 9/1998. No mental health records released. Certification fee: $1.50. Payee: Clerk of District Court. Personal checks accepted. Prepayment required.

Kearney County Court PO Box 377, Minden, NE 68959; phone: 308-832-2719; fax: 308-832-0636; hours 8AM-5PM (CST). *Misdemeanor, Civil Actions Under $45,000, Eviction, Small Claims, Probate.*
Civil Records: Access: In person, online. Visitors must perform in person searches themselves. Court makes copy: $.25 per page. Required to search: name, years to search. Civil cases indexed by defendant. Civil records computerized since 10/99, rest on index cards, some probate on microfiche. Online access same as criminal, records date from 10/99 forward, probate from 05/98.
Criminal Records: Access: In person, online, mail. Visitors must perform in person searches themselves. Court makes copy: $.25 per page. Required to search: name, years to search. Criminal records computerized since 3/97, indexes available since 1988. Subscribe to NOL at www.nebraska.gov/service_info.phtml?service_id =147 for court access. $.60 a record fee or $300 per month flat rate. Online criminal and traffic

records date from 03/97. Mail turnaround time 1 week.
General Information: Public use terminal available. Certification fee: $1.00. Payee: Kearney County Court. Personal checks accepted. Prepayment required. SASE requested.

Keith County

District Court PO Box 686, Ogallala, NE 69153; phone: 308-284-3849; fax: 308-284-3978; hours 8AM-4PM (MST). *Felony, Civil Actions Over $15,000.*
Civil Records: Access: Fax, mail, in person, online. Both court and visitors may perform in person searches. No search fee. Court makes copy: $.25 per page; same fee for self serve. Required to search: name, years to search, DOB. Civil cases indexed by defendant, plaintiff; on index books from late 1800s; on computer back to 1975. Online access same as criminal. Online records date from 06/97. Mail turnaround time 2-3 days.
Criminal Records: Access: Fax, mail, in person, online. Both court and visitors may perform in person searches. No search fee. Court makes copy: $.25 per page; same fee for self serve. Required to search: name, years to search, DOB. Criminal records on index books from late 1800s; on computer back to 1975. Subscribe to NOL at www.nebraska.gov/service_info.phtml?service_id =147 for court access. $.60 a record fee or $300 per month flat rate. Online records date from 06/97. Mail turnaround time 2-3 days.
General Information: Public terminal goes back to 1975. No juvenile or mental health records released. No fee to fax documents. Fee is charged if long distance. Certification fee: $1.00 per cert. Payee: Clerk of District Court. Personal checks accepted. Prepayment required.

Keith County Court PO Box 358, Ogallala, NE 69153; phone: 308-284-3693; fax: 308-284-6825; hours 8AM-5PM (MST). *Misdemeanor, Civil Actions Under $45,000, Eviction, Small Claims, Probate.*
Civil Records: Access: In person, online. Visitors must perform in person searches themselves. Court makes copy: $.25 per page. Required to search: name, years to search. Civil cases indexed by defendant, plaintiff; on index cards, files; computerized records since 1997. Online access same as criminal, records date from 10/99 forward, probate from 05/98.
Criminal Records: Access: In person, online. Visitors must perform in person searches themselves. Court makes copy: $.25 per page. Required to search: name, years to search. Criminal records on index cards, files; computerized records since 1997. Subscribe to NOL at www.nebraska.gov/service_info.phtml?service_id =147 for court access. $.60 a record fee or $300 per month flat rate. Online criminal and traffic records date from 06/97.
General Information: Public use terminal available. No adoption records released. Certification fee: $1.25. Payee: County Court. Local checks only. Prepayment required.

Keya Paha County

District Court PO Box 349, Springview, NE 68778; phone: 402-497-3791; fax: 402-497-3799; hours 8AM-5PM (CST). *Felony, Civil Actions Over $15,000.*
www.co.keya-paha.ne.us
Civil Records: Access: Fax, mail, in person, online. Both court and visitors may perform in person searches. No search fee. Court makes copy: $.25 per page. Legal size copy fee $.30 per page; same fee for self serve. Required to search: name, years to search. Civil cases indexed by defendant, plaintiff; on microfiche 7-9 years, on docket books since late 1800s. Online access same as criminal. Online records date from 07/00. Mail turnaround time 3-4 days.

Criminal Records: Access: Fax, mail, in person, online. Both court and visitors may perform in person searches. No search fee. Court makes copy: $.25 per page. Legal size copy $.30 per page; same fee for self serve. Required to search: name, years to search. Computerized back to 2000, criminal records on microfiche 7-9 years, on docket books since late 1800s. Subscribe to NOL at www.nebraska.gov/service_info.phtml?service_id =147 for court access. $.60 a record fee or $300 per month flat rate. Online records date from 0700. Mail turnaround time 3-4 days.
General Information: Public terminal goes back to 1999. No confidential records released. Will fax documents for $2.00 1st page, $1.00 each add'l. Certification fee: $4.00 per document includes copies. Payee: Clerk of District Court. Personal checks accepted. Prepayment and SASE required.

Keya Paha County Court PO Box 275, Courthouse Ln, Springview, NE 68778; phone: 402-497-3021; probate phone: 402-684-3601; hours varies; 8AM-4PM Mondays (CST). *Misdemeanor, Civil Actions Under $45,000, Eviction, Small Claims, Probate.*
Civil Records: Access: In person, online. Visitors must perform in person searches themselves. Court makes copy: $.25 per page. Required to search: name, years to search; also helpful: address. Civil cases indexed by defendant, plaintiff. Civil records in index books and files, many records on microfiche, back to late 1800s. Online access same as criminal. Online civil and probate records from 01/01 forward.
Criminal Records: Access: In person, online. Visitors must perform in person searches themselves. Court makes copy: $.25 per page. Required to search: name, years to search; also helpful: address, DOB, SSN. Criminal records in index books and files, many records on microfiche, back to late 1800s. Subscribe to NOL at www.nebraska.gov/service_info.phtml?service_id =147 for court access. $.60 a record fee or $300 per month flat rate. Online criminal and traffic records date from 08/00.
General Information: Public terminal goes back to 2000. No juvenile records released. Certification fee: $1.00 per page. Payee: County Clerk. Personal checks accepted; no credit cards. Prepayment required.

Kimball County

District Court 114 E 3rd St, Kimball, NE 69145; phone: 308-235-3591; fax: 308-235-3654; hours 8AM-5PM M-Th, 8AM-4PM F (MST). *Felony, Civil Actions Over $15,000.*
Civil Records: Access: Fax, mail, in person, online. Visitors must perform in person searches themselves. Court makes copy: $.50 per page. Required to search: name, years to search. Civil cases indexed by defendant, plaintiff; on microfiche from 1960 forward, prior in books from early 1900s, computerized since 11/97. Online access same as criminal. Online records date from 10/97.
Criminal Records: Access: Fax, mail, in person, online. Visitors must perform in person searches themselves. Court makes copy: $.50 per page. Required to search: name, years to search; also helpful: DOB. Criminal records on microfiche from 1960 forward, prior in books from early 1900s, computerized since 11/97. Subscribe to NOL at www.nebraska.gov/service_info.phtml?service_id =147 for court access. $.60 a record fee or $300 per month flat rate. Online records date from 10/97.
General Information: Public terminal goes back to 1997. No mental health records released. Certification fee: $1.50. Payee: Clerk of District Court. Personal checks accepted. Prepayment required.

Kimball County Court 114 E 3rd St, Kimball, NE 69145; phone: 308-235-2831; hours 8AM-5PM (MST). *Misdemeanor, Civil Actions Under $45,000, Small Claims, Probate.*
Civil Records: Access: In person, online. Visitors must perform in person searches themselves. Court

makes copy: $.25 per page. Required to search: name, years to search. Civil cases indexed by defendant, plaintiff; on index cards and original files, also state computer. Online access same as criminal. Online civil and probate records from 11/00 forward.

Criminal Records: Access: In person, online. Visitors must perform in person searches themselves. Court makes copy: $.25 per page. Required to search: name, years to search. Criminal records on index cards and original files. Subscribe at www.nebraska.gov/service_info.phtml?service_id =147 for court access. $.60 a record fee or $300 per month flat rate. Online criminal and traffic records date from 04/00.

General Information: Public terminal goes back to 2000. Certification fee: $1.25. Payee: County Court. Only cashiers checks and money orders accepted. Prepayment required.

Knox County

District Court PO Box 126, Center, NE 68724; phone: 402-288-5606; fax: 402-288-5609; hours 8:30AM-4:30PM (CST). *Felony, Civil Actions Over $45,000.*

Civil Records: Access: Fax, mail, person, online. Visitors must perform in person searches themselves. Court makes copy: $.25 per page. Required to search: name, years to search. Civil cases indexed by defendant, plaintiff; on index books from 1874; on computer back to 9/98. Online access same as criminal. Online records date from 09/98.

Criminal Records: Access: Fax, mail, in person, online. Visitors must perform in person searches themselves. Court makes copy: $.25 per page. Required to search: name, years to search; also helpful: DOB. Criminal records on index books from 1874; on computer back to 9/1998. Subscribe to NOL at www.nebraska.gov/service_info.phtml?service_id =147 for court access. $.60 a record fee or $300 per month flat rate. Online records date from 09/98.

General Information: Public terminal goes back to 9/1998. No mental health records released. Certification fee: $1.00. Payee: Clerk of District Court. Personal checks accepted. Prepayment required.

Knox County Court PO Box 125, Center, NE 68724; phone: 402-288-5607; fax: 402-288-5609; hours 8:30AM-4:30PM (CST). *Misdemeanor, Civil Actions Under $45,000, Eviction, Small Claims, Probate.*

Civil Records: Access: In person, online. Visitors must perform in person searches themselves. Court makes copy: $.25 per page; same fee for self serve. Required to search: name, years to search. Civil cases indexed by defendant, plaintiff; on index cards and general docket books from late 1800s; on computer from 8/2000. Online access same as criminal, records date from 11/00 forward, probate from 09/00.

Criminal Records: Access: In person, online. Visitors must perform in person searches themselves. Court makes copy: $.25 per page; same fee for self serve. Required to search: name, years to search; also helpful: DOB. Criminal records on index cards and general docket books from late 1800s; on computer from 8/2000. Subscribe to NOL at www.nebraska.gov/service_info.phtml?service_id =147 for court access. $.60 a record fee or $300 per month flat rate. Online criminal and traffic records date from 08/00.

General Information: Public terminal goes back to 8/2000. No adoption records released. Certification fee: $1.00. Payee: County Court. Personal checks accepted. Prepayment required.

Lancaster County

District Court 575 S Tenth St, Lincoln, NE 68508-2810; phone: 402-441-7328; fax: 402-441-6190; hours 8AM-4:30PM (CST). *Felony, Civil Actions Over $15,000.*

www.ci.lincoln.ne.us/cnty/discrt/index.htm
Civil Records: Access: Mail, in person, online. Visitors must perform in person searches themselves. No search fee. Court makes copy: $.50 per page. Required to search: name, years to search. Civil cases indexed by defendant, plaintiff; on computer from 1984, microfiche from 1900s, docket books from 1800s. Online access same as criminal. Online records date from 06/99. Mail turnaround time 5 days.

Criminal Records: Access: Mail, in person, online. Visitors must perform in person searches themselves. No search fee. Court makes copy: $.50 per page. Required to search: name, years to search, DOB. Criminal records on computer from 1984, microfiche from 1900s, docket books from 1800s. Subscribe to NOL at www.nebraska.gov/service_info.phtml?service_id =147 for court access. $.60 a record fee or $300 per month flat rate. Online records date from 06/99. Mail turnaround time 5 days.

General Information: Public terminal goes back to 1980. No juvenile, mental health or grand jury records released. Will fax documents. Certification fee: $1.00 per cert. Payee: Clerk of District Court. Personal checks accepted. Prepayment required. SASE requested.

Lancaster County Court 575 S 10th, Lincoln, NE 68508; phone: 402-441-7291; hours 8AM-4:30PM (CST). *Misdemeanor, Civil Actions Under $45,000, Eviction, Small Claims, Probate.*

Civil Records: Access: Mail, in person, online. Visitors must perform in person searches themselves. Court makes copy: $.25 per page. Required to search: name, years to search. Civil cases indexed by defendant, plaintiff; on index books back to 1968, computerized since 11/98. Access to the Internet system requires registration and password. Call John at 402-471-3049 for more information. System can be searched by name or case number. A subscription service is at www.nebraska.gov/service_info.phtml?service_id =147. Fee is $.60 a record or $300 per month flat rate, also there is a start-up fee. Note: Online civil records date from 11/16/98 forward, probate from 05/98.

Criminal Records: Access: Mail, in person, online. Visitors must perform in person searches themselves. No search fee. Court makes copy: $.25 per page. Required to search: name, years to search; also helpful: DOB. Criminal records on computer since 2/95; prior records are available if the case number is known. Online access to criminal records is the same as civil. Online criminal and traffic records date from 2/28/95.

General Information: Public terminal goes back to 1995. No adoption records released. Certification fee: $1.00 per cert. Payee: County Court. Personal checks accepted. Visa, MC accepted with $3.00 service charge. Prepayment required.

Lincoln County

District Court PO Box 1616, 301 N Jeffers 3rd Fl, North Platte, NE 69103-1616; phone: 308-534-4350 X301 & X303; hours 8AM-5PM (CST). *Felony, Civil Actions Over $15,000.*

Civil Records: Access: In person, online. Visitors must perform in person searches themselves. Court makes copy: $.25 per page. Required to search: name, years to search. Civil cases indexed by defendant, plaintiff; on computer back to 5/1997; books from 1866. Online access same as criminal. Online records date from 04/97.

Criminal Records: Access: In person, online. Visitors must perform in person searches themselves. Court makes copy: $.25 per page. Required to search: name, years to search. Criminal records on computer back to 5/1997; books from 1866. Subscribe to NOL at www.nebraska.gov/service_info.phtml?service_id =147 for court access. $.60 a record fee or $300 per month flat rate. Online records date from 04/97.

General Information: Public use terminal available. No sealed, court ordered or mental health records released. Certification fee: $1.00. Payee: Clerk of District Court. Personal checks accepted. Prepayment required.

Lincoln County Court PO Box 519, North Platte, NE 69101; phone: 308-534-4350; probate phone: ext 186; fax: 308-534-3525; hours 8AM-5PM (CST). *Misdemeanor, Civil Actions Under $45,000, Eviction, Small Claims, Probate.*

Civil Records: Access: In person, online. Visitors must perform in person searches themselves. Court makes copy: $.25 per page, no fee if record printed from public access terminal. Required to search: name, years to search. Civil cases indexed by defendant, plaintiff. Civil records kept on index books back 20-25 years. Online access same as criminal, records date from 10/99 forward, probate from 05/98.

Criminal Records: Access: In person, online. Visitors must perform in person searches themselves. Court makes copy: $.25 per page, no fee if record printed from public access terminal. Required to search: name, years to search, DOB. Criminal records on computer since 4/97; prior on books back 20 years. Subscribe to NOL at www.nebraska.gov/service_info.phtml?service_id =147 for court access. $.60 a record fee or $300 per month flat rate. Online criminal and traffic records date from 04/97. Note: No fee if record printed from public access terminal.

General Information: Public terminal goes back to 1997. No adoption records released. Certification fee: $1.00. Payee: County Court. Personal checks accepted. Visa, MC, Discover accepted with $3.00 service charge. Prepayment required.

Logan County

District Court PO Box 8, Stapleton, NE 69163; phone: 308-636-2311; fax: 308-636-2333; hours 8:30AM-N; 1PM-4:30PM M-Th; 8:30AM-N; 1PM-4PM F (CST). *Felony, Civil Actions Over $15,000.*

Civil Records: Access: Fax, mail, in person, online. Both court and visitors may perform in person searches. No search fee. Court makes copy: $.25 per page. Required to search: name, years to search. Civil cases indexed by defendant, plaintiff; on docket books; computerized records since 2000. Online access same as criminal. Online records date from 04/97. Mail turnaround time same day.

Criminal Records: Access: Fax, mail, in person, online. Both court and visitors may perform in person searches. No search fee. Court makes copy: $.25 per page. Required to search: name, years to search. Criminal records on docket books; computerized records since 2000. Subscribe to NOL at www.nebraska.gov/service_info.phtml?service_id =147 for court access. $.60 a record fee or $300 per month flat rate. Online records date from 04/97. Mail turnaround time same day.

General Information: Public terminal goes back to 1997. Certification fee: $1.00 per cert plus $.50 per page includes copy. Payee: Clerk of the District Court. Personal checks accepted. Prepayment required. SASE helpful.

Logan County Court PO Box 8, Stapleton, NE 69163; phone: 308-636-2677; hours 8AM-N, 1-4PM Wed (CST). *Misdemeanor, Civil Actions Under $45,000, Eviction, Small Claims, Probate.*

Civil Records: Access: Fax, mail, in person, online. Both court and visitors may perform in person searches. No search fee. Court makes copy: $.25 per page. Required to search: name, years to search; also helpful: address. Civil cases indexed by defendant, plaintiff; on docket books since 1837. Online access same as criminal, records date from 01/00 forward, probate from 09/98. Mail turnaround time 3-4 days.

Criminal Records: Access: Fax, mail, in person, online. Both court and visitors may perform in person searches. No search fee. Court makes copy:

$.25 per page. Required to search: name, years to search, signed release; also helpful: DOB. Criminal records on docket books since 1837. Subscribe to NOL at www.nebraska.gov/service_info.phtml?service_id=147 for court access. $.60 a record fee or $300 per month flat rate. Online criminal and traffic records date from 09/98. Mail turnaround time 3-4 days.

General Information: No public access terminal. Adoption and juvenile records are not released. Fee to fax documents is $3.00 1st page, $1.00 each add'l. Certification fee: $1.00. Payee: County Court. Personal checks accepted. Prepayment and SASE required.

Loup County

District Court PO Box 146, Taylor, NE 68879; phone: 308-942-6035; fax: 308-942-3103; hours 8:30AM-4:30PM M-Th, 8:30AM-N F (CST). *Felony, Civil Actions Over $15,000.*

Civil Records: Access: In person, online. Visitors must perform in person searches themselves. Court makes copy: $.25 per page; same fee for self serve. Required to search: name, years to search. Civil cases indexed by defendant, plaintiff. Civil records in index books from late 1800s. Online access same as criminal. Online records date from 06/00.

Criminal Records: Access: In person, online. Visitors must perform in person searches themselves. Court makes copy: $.25 per page; same fee for self serve. Required to search: name, years to search; also helpful: address, DOB, SSN. Criminal records in index books from late 1800s. Subscribe to NOL at www.nebraska.gov/service_info.phtml?service_id=147 for court access. $.60 a record fee or $300 per month flat rate. Online records date from 06/00.

General Information: Public terminal goes back to 2000. No juvenile or adoption records released. Certification fee: $1.00. Payee: Clerk of District Court. Personal checks accepted. Prepayment required.

Loup County Court PO Box 146, Taylor, NE 68879; phone: 308-942-6035; fax: 308-942-3103; hours 8:30AM-4:30PM M-Th, 8:30AM-N F (CST). *Misdemeanor, Civil Actions Under $45,000, Eviction, Small Claims, Probate.*

Civil Records: Access: In person, online. Visitors must perform in person searches themselves. Court makes copy: $.25 per page; same fee for self serve. Required to search: name, years to search. Civil cases indexed by defendant, plaintiff; on index books since late 1800s. Some records have been filmed and forwarded to state archives. Online access same as criminal, records date from 10/00 forward, probate from 11/00.

Criminal Records: Access: In person, online. Visitors must perform in person searches themselves. Court makes copy: $.25 per page; same fee for self serve. Required to search: name, years to search. Criminal records on index books since late 1800s. Some records have been filmed and forwarded to state archives. Subscribe to NOL at www.nebraska.gov/service_info.phtml?service_id=147 for court access. $.60 a record fee or $300 per month flat rate. Online criminal and traffic records date from 08/00.

General Information: Public use terminal available. Certification fee: $1.00. Payee: County Court. Personal checks accepted. Prepayment required.

Madison County

District Court PO Box 249, Madison, NE 68748; phone: 402-454-3311 X140; fax: 402-454-6528; hours 8AM-5PM (CST). *Felony, Civil Actions Over $45,000.*

Civil Records: Access: In person, online. Visitors must perform in person searches themselves. Court makes copy: $.25 per page. Required to search: name, years to search. Civil cases indexed by defendant,

plaintiff; on microfiche from late 1970s, prior on docket books from 1800s; computerized records go back to 1837. Online access same as criminal. Online records date from 09/97.

Criminal Records: Access: In person, online. Visitors must perform in person searches themselves. Court makes copy: $.25 per page. Required to search: name, years to search. Criminal records on microfiche from late 1970s, prior on docket books from 1800s; computerized records go back to 1987. Subscribe to NOL at www.nebraska.gov/service_info.phtml?service_id=147 for court access. $.60 a record fee or $300 per month flat rate. Online records date from 09/97.

General Information: Public terminal goes back to 9/1997. No mental health records released. Will fax specific case file requests for $1.00 per page if prepaid. Certification fee: $1.50. Payee: Clerk of District Court. Personal checks accepted. Prepayment required.

Madison County Court PO Box 230, Madison, NE 68748; phone: 402-454-3311; criminal phone: x181; civil phone: x142; probate phone: x165; criminal fax: 402-454-3438; same fax for civil/probate; hours 8:30AM-5PM (CST). *Misdemeanor, Civil Actions Under $45,000, Eviction, Small Claims, Probate.*

Civil Records: Access: Mail, in person, online. Visitors must perform in person searches themselves. No search fee. Court makes copy: $.25 per page; same fee for self serve. Required to search: name, years to search. Civil cases indexed by defendant, plaintiff; on computer since 1986, prior on docket book, cards. Online access same as criminal, records date from 01/99 forward, probate from 05/98. Mail turnaround time 5 days.

Criminal Records: Access: Mail, in person, online. Visitors must perform in person searches themselves. No search fee. Court makes copy: $.25 per page; same fee for self serve. Required to search: name, years to search, DOB. Criminal records on computer from 1986. Subscribe to NOL at www.nebraska.gov/service_info.phtml?service_id=147 for court access. $.60 a record fee or $300 per month flat rate. Online criminal and traffic records date from 10/96. Mail turnaround time 5 days.

General Information: No public access terminal. No adoption records released. Will fax documents to local or toll free line. Certification fee: $1.00 per certification. Payee: Madison County Court. Personal checks accepted. Prepayment required.

McPherson County

District Court PO Box 122, Tryon, NE 69167; phone: 308-587-2363; fax: 308-587-2363; hours 8:30AM-N, 1-4:30PM (CST). *Felony, Civil Actions Over $15,000.*

Note: Call before faxing.

Civil Records: Access: Fax, mail, in person, online. Both court and visitors may perform in person searches. No search fee. Court makes copy: $.50 per page; same fee for self serve. Required to search: name, years to search; also helpful: address. Civil cases indexed by defendant, plaintiff; on index books since late 1800s. Online access same as criminal. Online records date from 06/00. Mail turnaround time 3-4 days.

Criminal Records: Access: Fax, mail, in person, online. Both court and visitors may perform in person searches. No search fee. Court makes copy: $.50 per page; same fee for self serve. Required to search: name, years to search; also helpful: address, DOB, SSN. Criminal records on index books since late 1800s. Subscribe to NOL at www.nebraska.gov/service_info.phtml?service_id=147 for court access. $.60 a record fee or $300 per month flat rate. Online records date from 06/00. Mail turnaround time 3-4 days.

General Information: No public access terminal. No adoption records released. Will fax documents

$2.00 1st page, $1.00 each add'l. Certification fee: $1.50 per page. Payee: Clerk of District Court. Business checks accepted. Prepayment and SASE required.

McPherson County Court PO Box 122, Tryon, NE 69167; phone: 308-587-2363; fax: 308-587-2363; hours 8:30AM-N, 1-4:30PM Tu; 8:30AM-N, Th (CST). *Misdemeanor, Civil Actions Under $45,000, Eviction, Small Claims, Probate.*

Note: Call before faxing.

Civil Records: Access: Fax, mail, in person, online. Both court and visitors may perform in person searches. No search fee. Court makes copy: $.25 per page. Required to search: name, years to search; also helpful: address. Civil cases indexed by defendant, plaintiff. Civil records computerized since 6/99, rest on index cards, are not computerized. Online access same as criminal, records date from 01/009 forward, probate from 08/98. Mail turnaround time 3-4 days.

Criminal Records: Access: Fax, mail, in person, online. Both court and visitors may perform in person searches. No search fee. Court makes copy: $.25 per page. Required to search: name, years to search, signed release; also helpful: address, DOB. Criminal records computerized since 8/98. Subscribe to NOL at www.nebraska.gov/service_info.phtml?service_id=147 for court access. $.60 a record fee or $300 per month flat rate. Online criminal and traffic records date from 08/98. Mail turnaround time 3-4 days.

General Information: No public access terminal. Adoption and juvenile records are not released. Fee to fax documents is $3.00 1st page, $1.00 each add'l. Certification fee: $1.00. Payee: County Court. Personal checks accepted. Prepayment and SASE required.

Merrick County

District Court PO Box 27, Central City, NE 68826; phone: 308-946-2461; fax: 308-946-3692; hours 8AM-5PM (CST). *Felony, Civil Actions Over $15,000.*

Civil Records: Access: In person, online. Visitors must perform in person searches themselves. Court makes copy: $.25 per page; same fee for self serve. Required to search: name, years to search. Civil cases indexed by defendant, plaintiff; on index books from 1860; on computer back to 1994. Online access same as criminal. Online records date from 07/94.

Criminal Records: Access: In person, online. Visitors must perform in person searches themselves. Court makes copy: $.25 per page; same fee for self serve. Required to search: name, years to search, signed release. Criminal records on index books from 1860; on computer back to 1994. Subscribe to NOL at www.nebraska.gov/service_info.phtml?service_id=147 for court access. $.60 a record fee or $300 per month flat rate. Online records date from 07/94.

General Information: Public terminal goes back to 7/1994. No probation or mental health records released. Will fax specific case file requests. Certification fee: $1.00. Payee: Clerk of District Court. Personal checks accepted. Prepayment required.

Merrick County Court County Courthouse, PO Box 27, Central City, NE 68826; phone: 308-946-2812; hours 8AM-5PM (CST). *Misdemeanor, Civil Actions Under $45,000, Eviction, Small Claims, Probate.*

Civil Records: Access: In person, online. Visitors must perform in person searches themselves. Court makes copy: $.25 per page. Required to search: name, years to search. Civil cases indexed by defendant, plaintiff; on index books from 1860; on computer back to 1994. Online access same as criminal. Online civil and probate records from 03/94 forward.

Criminal Records: Access: In person, online. Visitors must perform in person searches themselves. Court makes copy: $.25 per page. Required to search: name, years to search, DOB. Criminal records on index books from 1860; on computer back to 1994. Subscribe to NOL at www.nebraska.gov/service_info.phtml?service_id =147 for court access. $.60 a record fee or $300 per month flat rate. Online criminal and traffic records date from 03/94.

General Information: Public terminal goes back to 1/1994. No financial affidavits or sealed records released. Certification fee: $1.00. Payee: County Court. Personal checks accepted. Prepayment required.

Morrill County

District Court PO Box 824, Bridgeport, NE 69336; phone: 308-262-1261; fax: 308-262-1799; hours 8AM-N, 1-4:30PM (MST). *Felony, Civil Actions Over $15,000.*

Civil Records: Access: In person, online. Visitors must perform in person searches themselves. Court makes copy: $.25 per page. Required to search: name, years to search. Civil cases indexed by defendant, plaintiff. Computerized records back to 11/97; civil records on microfilm, books dating back to early 1900. Online access same as criminal. Online records date from 10/97.

Criminal Records: Access: In person, online. Visitors must perform in person searches themselves. Court makes copy: $.25 per page. Required to search: name, years to search. Criminal records on microfilm, books dating back to early 1900. Subscribe to NOL at www.nebraska.gov/service_info.phtml?service_id =147 for court access. $.60 a record fee or $300 per month flat rate. Online records date from 10/97.

General Information: Public terminal goes back to 1997. No mental health records released. Certification fee: $1.00. Payee: Clerk of District Court. Prepayment required.

Morrill County Court PO Box 418, Bridgeport, NE 69336; phone: 308-262-0812; hours 8AM-4:30PM (MST). *Misdemeanor, Civil Actions Under $45,000, Eviction, Small Claims, Probate.*

Civil Records: Access: In person, online. Visitors must perform in person searches themselves. No copy fee. Required to search: name, years to search. Civil cases indexed by defendant, plaintiff; on index books to 1908; probate on microfiche. Online access same as criminal. Online civil and probate records from 01/01 forward.

Criminal Records: Access: In person, online. Visitors must perform in person searches themselves. No copy fee. Required to search: name, years to search. Criminal records on index books to 1908; probate on microfiche. Subscribe to NOL at www.nebraska.gov/service_info.phtml?service_id =147 for court access. $.60 a record fee or $300 per month flat rate. Online criminal and traffic records date from 04/00.

General Information: Public use terminal available. No adoption records released. Certification fee: $1.00. Payee: County Court. Personal checks accepted. Prepayment required.

Nance County

District Court PO Box 338, Fullerton, NE 68638; phone: 308-536-2365; fax: 308-536-2742; hours 8AM-5PM (CST). *Felony, Civil Actions Over $15,000.*

Civil Records: Access: Phone, fax, mail, in person, online. Both court and visitors may perform in person searches. No search fee. Court makes copy: $.25 per page. Required to search: name, years to search; also helpful: address. Civil cases indexed by defendant, plaintiff; on index books from late 1800s. Online access same as criminal. Online records date from 12/99.

Criminal Records: Access: In person, online. Both court and visitors may perform in person searches. No search fee. Court makes copy: $.25 per page. Required to search: name, years to search; also helpful: address, DOB, SSN. Criminal records on index books from late 1800s. Subscribe to NOL at www.nebraska.gov/service_info.phtml?service_id =147 for court access. $.60 a record fee or $300 per month flat rate. Online records date from 12/99. Mail turnaround time 4-5 days.

General Information: Public terminal goes back to 1999. (Public terminal in County Court Office-County will perform searches.) No mental health records released. Will fax documents $1.00 per page plus copy fees. Certification fee: $1.00. Payee: Clerk of District Court. Personal checks accepted. Prepayment and SASE required.

Nance County Court PO Box 837, Fullerton, NE 68638; phone: 308-536-2675; fax: 308-536-2742; hours 8AM-5PM (CST). *Misdemeanor, Civil Actions Under $45,000, Eviction, Small Claims, Probate.*

Civil Records: Access: Fax, mail, in person, online. Both court and visitors may perform in person searches. No search fee. Court makes copy: $.25 per page. Required to search: name, years to search; also helpful: address. Civil cases indexed by defendant, plaintiff; on index cards since late 1800s, computerized since 1/01, probate on microfilm. Online access same as criminal. Online civil and probate records from 08/00 forward. Mail turnaround time 4-5 days.

Criminal Records: Access: Fax, mail, in person, online. Both court and visitors may perform in person searches. No search fee. Court makes copy: $.25 per page. Required to search: name, years to search; also helpful: address, DOB. Criminal records available since 1985, computerized since 2002, probate on microfilm. Subscribe to NOL at www.nebraska.gov/service_info.phtml?service_id =147 for court access. $.60 a record fee or $300 per month flat rate. Online criminal and traffic records date from 08/00. Mail turnaround time 4-5 days.

General Information: Public terminal goes back to 2001. No juvenile, psychological reports or adoption records released. Certification fee: $1.00 per cert. Payee: County Court. Personal checks accepted. Prepayment and SASE required.

Nemaha County

District Court 1824 N St, Auburn, NE 68305; phone: 402-274-3616; fax: 402-274-5583; hours 8AM-5PM (CST). *Felony, Civil Actions Over $15,000.*

Civil Records: Access: In person, mail, online. Both court and visitors may perform in person searches. No search fee. Court makes copy: $.25 per page. Required to search: name, years to search; also helpful: address. Civil cases indexed by defendant, plaintiff; on general index and docket books since the late 1800s; computerized records go back to 1998. Online access same as criminal. Online records date from 6/98. Note: Court will search on a time available basis Mail turnaround time 1 to 3 days.

Criminal Records: Access: In person, mail, online. Both court and visitors may perform in person searches. No search fee. Court makes copy: $.25 per page. Required to search: name, years to search; also helpful: address, DOB, SSN. Criminal records on general index and docket books since1950; computerized records go back to 1998. Subscribe to NOL at www.nebraska.gov/service_info.phtml?service_id =147 for court access. $.60 a record fee or $300 per month flat rate. Online records date from 6/98. Note: Court will only criminal search time permitting. Mail turnaround time 1 to 3 days.

General Information: Public terminal goes back to 6/1998. No mental, juvenile records released. Will fax documents to local or toll free line. Certification fee: $1.00. Payee: Clerk of District Court. Personal checks accepted. Prepayment required.

Nemaha County Court 1824 N St, Auburn, NE 68305; phone: 402-274-3008; criminal fax: 402-274-4605; same fax for civil/probate; hours 8AM-N, 1-5PM (CST). *Misdemeanor, Civil Actions Under $45,000, Eviction, Small Claims, Probate.*

Note: This court also handles adoption, juvenile, and preliminary felony hearings.

Civil Records: Access: In person, online. Visitors must perform in person searches themselves. Court makes copy: $.25 per page. Required to search: name, years to search. Civil cases indexed by defendant, plaintiff; on index books since late 1800s, computerized records go back to 4/2000. Online access same as criminal. Online civil and probate records from 04/00 forward.

Criminal Records: Access: In person, online. Visitors must perform in person searches themselves. Court makes copy: $.25 per page. Required to search: name, years to search; also helpful: DOB, SSN. Criminal records on index books since late 1800s, computerized records go back to 4/2000. Subscribe to NOL at www.nebraska.gov/service_info.phtml?service_id =147 for court access. $.60 a record fee or $300 per month flat rate. Online criminal and traffic records date from 04/00.

General Information: No public access terminal. No adoption records released. Will not fax documents. Certification fee: $1.00 per page. Payee: Clerk of County Court. Personal checks accepted. Prepayment required.

Nuckolls County

District Court PO Box 362, 150 S Main, Nelson, NE 68961; phone: 402-225-4341; fax: 402-225-2373; hours 8:30AM-4:30PM (CST). *Felony, Civil Actions Over $15,000.*

Note: Court's search services not available to employers using employment agencies.

Civil Records: Access: In person, online. Visitors must perform in person searches themselves. Court makes copy: $.25 per page; same fee for self serve. Required to search: name, years to search. Civil cases indexed by defendant, plaintiff; on index books since late 1800s, computerized since 2000. Online access same as criminal. Online records date from 03/00.

Criminal Records: Access: In person, online. Visitors must perform in person searches themselves. Court makes copy: $.25 per page; same fee for self serve. Required to search: name, years to search. Criminal records on index books since late 1800s, computerized since 2000. Subscribe to NOL at www.nebraska.gov/service_info.phtml?service_id =147 for court access. $.60 a record fee or $300 per month flat rate. Online records date from 03/00.

General Information: Public terminal goes back to 2000. Certification fee: $1.00 per cert. Payee: Clerk of District Court. Personal checks accepted. Prepayment required.

Nuckolls County Court PO Box 372, 105 S Main, Nelson, NE 68961; phone: 402-225-2371; fax: 402-225-2373; hours 8AM-4:30PM (CST). *Misdemeanor, Civil Actions Under $45,000, Eviction, Small Claims, Probate.*

Note: Mail access limited to short searches.

Civil Records: Access: In person, online. Visitors must perform in person searches themselves. Court makes copy: $.25 per page; same fee for self serve. Required to search: name, years to search. Civil cases indexed by defendant, plaintiff; on index cards, probate on microfilm. Online access same as criminal, records date from 12/00 forward, probate from 01/01.

Criminal Records: Access: In person, online. Visitors must perform in person searches themselves. Court makes copy: $.25 per page; same fee for self serve. Required to search: name, years to search. Criminal records on index cards, probate on microfilm. Subscribe to NOL at www.nebraska.gov/service_info.phtml?service_id

=147 for court access. $.60 a record fee or $300 per month flat rate. Online criminal and traffic records date from 08/00.

General Information: Public terminal goes back to 2000. No adoption or juvenile records released. Certification fee: $1.00 per cert. Payee: County Court. Personal checks accepted. Prepayment required.

Otoe County

District Court 1021 Central Ave, Rm 209, PO Box 726, Nebraska City, NE 68410; phone: 402-873-9550; fax: 402-873-9583; hours 8AM-5PM Courthouse doors close at 4:30PM (CST). *Felony, Dissolutions, Civil Actions Over $45,000.*

Civil Records: Access: In person, online. Visitors must perform in person searches themselves. Court makes copy: $.50 per page; same fee for self serve. Required to search: name, years to search, address. Civil cases indexed by defendant, plaintiff; on index books from late 1800s, computerized from 8/97. Online access same as criminal. Online records date from 08/97.

Criminal Records: Access: In person, online. Visitors must perform in person searches themselves. Court makes copy: $.50 per page; same fee for self serve. Required to search: name, years to search. Criminal records on index books from late 1800s, computerized from 8/97. Subscribe to NOL at www.nebraska.gov/service_info.phtml?service_id =147 for court access. $.60 a record fee or $300 per month flat rate. Online records date from 08/97.

General Information: Public terminal goes back to 8/1997. Will not fax documents. Certification fee: $1.00. Payee: Clerk of District Court. Personal checks accepted. Prepayment required.

Otoe County Court 1021 Central Ave, Rm 109, PO Box 487, Nebraska City, NE 68410-0487; phone: 402-873-9575; fax: 402-873-9030; hours 8AM-5PM (CST). *Misdemeanor, Civil Actions Under $45,000, Eviction, Small Claims, Probate.*

Civil Records: Access: Phone, fax, mail, in person, online. Only the court performs in person searches; visitors may not. No search fee. Court makes copy: $.25 per page. Required to search: name, years to search. Civil cases indexed by defendant, plaintiff. Civil records go back to 1974; computerized records go to 1999. Online access same as criminal, records date from 10/99 forward, probate from 05/98. Mail turnaround time 2-3 days.

Criminal Records: Access: Fax, mail, in person, online. Both court and visitors may perform in person searches. No search fee. Court makes copy: $.25 per page. Required to search: name, offense; also helpful: years to search, address, DOB. Criminal records go back to 1981; computerized since 1997. Subscribe to NOL at www.nebraska.gov/service_info.phtml?service_id =147 for court access. $.60 a record fee or $300 per month flat rate. Online criminal and traffic records date from 02/97. Mail turnaround time 2-3 days.

General Information: Public terminal has only criminal records. (Public access is at the District Court terminal.) No adoption records released without court order; juvenile records only released with signed release statement. Will fax documents $1.00 per page. Certification fee: $1.00. Payee: County Court. Personal checks accepted. Prepayment and SASE required.

Pawnee County

District Court PO Box 431, Pawnee City, NE 68420; phone: 402-852-2963; criminal phone: 402-852-2969; hours 8AM-4PM (CST). *Felony, Civil Actions Over $15,000.*

Civil Records: Access: Phone, mail, in person, online. Both court and visitors may perform in person searches. Search fee: $3.00 per name. Court makes copy: $.50 per page. Required to search: name, years to search. Civil cases indexed by defendant,

plaintiff; on index books since late 1800s. Online access same as criminal. Online records date from 03/98. Mail turnaround time 2 weeks, limited phone searches immediate.

Criminal Records: Access: Phone, mail, in person, online. Both court and visitors may perform in person searches. Search fee: $3.00 per name. Court makes copy: $.50 per page. Required to search: name, years to search. Criminal records on index books since late 1800s. Subscribe to NOL at www.nebraska.gov/service_info.phtml?service_id =147 for court access. $.60 a record fee or $300 per month flat rate. Online records date from 03/98. Mail turnaround time 2 weeks, limited phone searches immediate.

General Information: Public use terminal available. No mental health records released. Certification fee: $1.00. Payee: Clerk of District Court. Personal checks accepted. Prepayment and SASE required.

Pawnee County Court PO Box 471, Pawnee City, NE 68420; phone: 402-852-2388; fax: 402-852-2388; hours 8AM-Noon; M-Th (CST). *Misdemeanor, Civil Actions Under $45,000, Eviction, Small Claims, Probate.*

Note: Probate requests are accepted by mail.

Civil Records: Access: In person, online. Visitors must perform in person searches themselves. Court makes copy: $.25 per page; same fee for self serve. Required to search: name, years to search; also helpful: address. Civil cases indexed by defendant, plaintiff. Civil records indexed on computer since late 1980s and books back to late 1800s. Online access same as criminal. Online civil and probate records from 06/00 forward.

Criminal Records: Access: In person, online. Visitors must perform in person searches themselves. Court makes copy: $.25 per page; same fee for self serve. Required to search: name, years to search, DOB; also helpful: SSN. Criminal records indexed on computer since late 1980s and books back to late 1800s. Subscribe to NOL at www.nebraska.gov/service_info.phtml?service_id =147 for court access. $.60 a record fee or $300 per month flat rate. Online criminal and traffic records date from 06/00.

General Information: Public terminal goes back to 7/2000. No adoption records released. Certification fee: $1.00. Payee: Pawnee County Court. Personal checks accepted. Prepayment required.

Perkins County

District Court PO Box 156, 200 Lincoln, Grant, NE 69140; phone: 308-352-4643; fax: 308-352-2455; hours 8AM-4PM (MST). *Felony, Civil Actions Over $15,000.*

Civil Records: Access: Fax, mail, in person, online. Both court and visitors may perform in person searches. Search fee: Prepay Fax fee $3.00. Court makes copy: $.50 per page; same fee for self serve. Required to search: name, years to search. Civil cases indexed by defendant, plaintiff; on index books since late 1800s. Online access same as criminal. Online records date from 06/00. Mail turnaround time 2-4 days

Criminal Records: Access: Fax, mail, in person, online. Both court and visitors may perform in person searches. Search fee: Prepay Fax fee $3.00. Court makes copy: $.50 per page; same fee for self serve. Required to search: name, years to search. Criminal records on index books since late 1800s. Subscribe to NOL at www.nebraska.gov/service_info.phtml?service_id =147 for court access. $.60 a record fee or $300 per month flat rate. Online records date from 06/00. Mail turnaround time 2-4 days

General Information: Public terminal goes back to 2000. All records public. Will fax documents for $3.00 prepaid. Certification fee: $1.75 per cert. Payee: Clerk of District Court. Personal checks accepted. Prepayment and SASE required.

Perkins County Court PO Box 222, Grant, NE 69140; phone: 308-352-4415; fax: 308-352-4700; probate fax: same; hours 8AM-4PM (MST). *Misdemeanor, Civil Actions Under $45,000, Eviction, Small Claims, Probate.*

Civil Records: Access: In person, online. Visitors must perform in person searches themselves. Court makes copy: $.25 per page. Required to search: name, years to search. Civil cases indexed by defendant, plaintiff; on index cards from 1987, prior on books; probate on microfilm & hard copy. Online access same as criminal. Online civil and probate records from 11/00 forward. Mail turnaround time 3-4 days.

Criminal Records: Access: In person, online. Visitors must perform in person searches themselves. Court makes copy: $.25 per page. Required to search: name, years to search; also helpful: DOB. Criminal records on index cards from 1987, prior on books; probate on microfilm & hard copy. Subscribe to NOL at www.nebraska.gov/service_info.phtml?service_id =147 for court access. $.60 a record fee or $300 per month flat rate. Online criminal and traffic records date from 06/00.

General Information: Public terminal goes back to 6/2000. No sealed records released. Certification fee: $1.00. Payee: Perkins County Court. Personal checks accepted. Prepayment required.

Phelps County

District Court PO Box 462, Holdrege, NE 68949; phone: 308-995-2281; fax: 308-995-2282; hours 9AM-5PM (CST). *Felony, Civil Actions Over $45,000.*

Civil Records: Access: In person, online. Visitors must perform in person searches themselves. Court makes copy: $.25 per page. Required to search: name, years to search. Civil cases indexed by defendant, plaintiff; on computer from 3/1998, on books back to 1885. Online access same as criminal. Online records date from 03/98.

Criminal Records: Access: In person, online. Visitors must perform in person searches themselves. Court makes copy: $.25 per page. Required to search: name, years to search; also helpful: DOB. Criminal records on computer from 3/1998, on books prior to 1885. Subscribe to NOL at www.nebraska.gov/service_info.phtml?service_id =147 for court access. $.60 a record fee or $300 per month flat rate. Online records date from 03/98.

General Information: Public use terminal available. No mental health, sealed records released. Will fax specific case files to local or toll-free number. Certification fee: $1.00. Payee: Clerk of District Court. Personal checks accepted. Prepayment required.

Phelps County Court PO Box 255, 715 Fifth Ave, Holdrege, NE 68949; phone: 308-995-6561; fax: 308-995-6562; hours 8AM-12;00-1-5PM (CST). *Misdemeanor, Civil Actions Under $45,000, Eviction, Small Claims, Probate.*

Civil Records: Access: In person, online. Visitors must perform in person searches themselves. Court makes copy: $.25 per page. Required to search: name, years to search. Civil cases indexed by defendant, plaintiff. Civil records computerized since 1999, on index cards going back to late 1970s; probate on microfiche to late 1800s. Online access same as criminal, records date from 10/99 forward, probate from 06/98.

Criminal Records: Access: In person, online. Visitors must perform in person searches themselves. Court makes copy: $.25 per page. Required to search: name, years to search, DOB, signed release. Criminal records computerized since 1998, in files to 1987. Subscribe to NOL at www.nebraska.gov/service_info.phtml?service_id =147 for court access. $.60 a record fee or $300 per month flat rate. Online criminal and traffic records date from 06/98.

General Information: Public terminal goes back to 3/1998. No adoption records released. Certification fee: $1.00 per cert. Payee: County Court. Personal checks accepted. Prepayment required.

Pierce County

District Court 111 W Court St, Rm 12, Pierce, NE 68767; phone: 402-329-4335; fax: 402-329-6412; hours 8:30 AM-4:30PM (CST). *Felony, Civil Actions Over $15,000.*

Civil Records: Access: In person, online. Visitors must perform in person searches themselves. Court makes copy: $.25 per page. Required to search: name, years to search. Civil cases indexed by defendant, plaintiff; on index books from 1870s; on computer back to 3/1999. Online access same as criminal. Online records date from 03/99.

Criminal Records: Access: In person, online. Visitors must perform in person searches themselves. Court makes copy: $.25 per page. Required to search: name, years to search; also helpful: address, DOB, SSN. Criminal records on index books from 1870s; on computer back to 3/1999. Subscribe to NOL at www.nebraska.gov/service_info.phtml?service_id =147 for court access. $.60 a record fee or $300 per month flat rate. Online records date from 03/99.

General Information: Public terminal goes back to 3/1999. No mental health records released. Will fax specific case file requests for $3.00 per page. Certification fee: $1.00. Payee: Clerk of District Court. Personal checks accepted. Prepayment required.

Pierce County Court 111 W Court St, Rm 11, Pierce, NE 68767; phone: 402-329-6245; fax: 402-329-6412; hours 8:30AM-4:30PM (CST). *Misdemeanor, Civil Actions Under $45,000, Eviction, Small Claims, Probate.*

Civil Records: Access: In person, online. Visitors must perform in person searches themselves. Court makes copy: $.25 per page; same fee for self serve. Required to search: name, years to search. Civil cases indexed by defendant, plaintiff; on index books back about 15 years, computerized since 5/2000. Online access same as criminal. Online civil and probate records from 05/00 forward.

Criminal Records: Access: In person, online. Visitors must perform in person searches themselves. Court makes copy: $.25 per page; same fee for self serve. Required to search: name, years to search. Criminal records on index books back about 15 years, computerized since 5/00. Subscribe to NOL at www.nebraska.gov/service_info.phtml?service_id =147 for court access. $.60 a record fee or $300 per month flat rate. Online criminal and traffic records date from 05/00.

General Information: Public terminal goes back to 5/2000. No adoption records released. Certification fee: $1.00. Payee: County Court. Personal checks accepted. Prepayment required.

Platte County

District Court PO Box 1188, Columbus, NE 68602-1188; phone: 402-563-4906; fax: 402-562-6718; hours 8:30AM-5PM (CST). *Felony, Civil Actions Over $15,000.*

Civil Records: Access: In person, online. Visitors must perform in person searches themselves. Court makes copy: $.25 per page. Required to search: name, years to search. Civil cases indexed by defendant, plaintiff. Civil records go back to 1800, civil records filed as hard copies; also on computer after 8/1/97. Online access same as criminal. Online records date from 09/97.

Criminal Records: Access: In person, online. Visitors must perform in person searches themselves. Search fee: Same. Court makes copy: $.25 per page. Required to search: name, years to search, DOB. Criminal records go back to 1880's, criminal records filed as hard copies; also on

computer after 8/1/97. Subscribe to NOL at www.nebraska.gov/service_info.phtml?service_id =147 for court access. $.60 a record fee or $300 per month flat rate. Online records date from 09/97.

General Information: Public terminal goes back to 1997. No juvenile or sealed records released. Will not fax documents. Certification fee: $1.00 per certification. Payee: District Court. Only cashiers checks and money orders accepted. Prepayment required.

Platte County Court PO Box 538, Columbus, NE 68602-0538; phone: 402-563-4905; criminal fax: 402-562-8158; same fax for civil/probate; hours 8AM-5PM (CST). *Misdemeanor, Civil Actions Under $45,000, Eviction, Small Claims, Probate.*

Civil Records: Access: In person, online. Visitors must perform in person searches themselves. Court makes copy: $.25 per page. Required to search: name, years to search. Civil cases indexed by defendant, plaintiff; on index books from 1980; on computer back to 1996. Online access same as criminal, records date from 10/99 forward, probate from 05/98.

Criminal Records: Access: In person, online. Visitors must perform in person searches themselves. Court makes copy: $.25 per page. Required to search: name, years to search, DOB. Criminal records on index books from 1980; on computer back to 1996. Subscribe to NOL at www.nebraska.gov/service_info.phtml?service_id =147 for court access. $.60 a record fee or $300 per month flat rate. Online criminal and traffic records date from 10/96.

General Information: Public terminal has criminal back to 10/1996 and civil back to 10/1999. No adoption records released. Will not fax documents. Certification fee: $1.00 for seal. Payee: Platte County Court. Personal checks accepted. Prepayment required.

Polk County

District Court PO Box 447, Osceola, NE 68651; phone: 402-747-3487; fax: 402-747-8299; hours 8AM-N,1-5PM (CST). *Felony, Civil Actions Over $15,000.*

Civil Records: Access: In person, online. Visitors must perform in person searches themselves. Court makes copy: $.25 per page. Required to search: name, years to search. Civil cases indexed by defendant, plaintiff; on index books from 1871. Online access same as criminal. Online records date from 04/98.

Criminal Records: Access: In person, online. Visitors must perform in person searches themselves. Court makes copy: $.25 per page. Required to search: name, years to search, DOB, signed release. Criminal records on index books from 1871. Subscribe to NOL at www.nebraska.gov/service_info.phtml?service_id =147 for court access. $.60 a record fee or $300 per month flat rate. Online records date from 04/98.

General Information: Public terminal has criminal back to 4/1998 and civil back to 4/9/1998. Certification fee: $1.00. Payee: Clerk of District Court. Personal checks accepted. Prepayment required.

Polk County Court PO Box 506, Osceola, NE 68651; phone: 402-747-5371; criminal fax: 402-747-2656; same fax for civil/probate; hours 8AM-5PM (CST). *Misdemeanor, Civil Actions Under $45,000, Eviction, Small Claims, Probate.*

Note: Probate is a separate index at this same address.

Civil Records: Access: In person, online. Visitors must perform in person searches themselves. Court makes copy: $.25 per page; same fee for self serve. Required to search: name, years to search. Civil cases indexed by defendant, plaintiff; on index cards back to late 1970s; probate records back to late 1800s. Online access same as criminal. Online civil and probate records from 01/01 forward.

Criminal Records: Access: In person, online. Visitors must perform in person searches themselves. Court makes copy: $.25 per page; same fee for self serve. Required to search: name, years to search, DOB. Criminal records on index cards to late 1970s; on computer to 8/2000. Subscribe to NOL at www.nebraska.gov/service_info.phtml?service_id =147 for court access. $.60 a record fee or $300 per month flat rate. Online criminal and traffic records date from 08/00.

General Information: Public terminal goes back to 2000. No adoption, juvenile records released. Will fax specific case file requests. Certification fee: $1.00 per seal. Payee: County Court. Personal checks accepted. Prepayment required.

Red Willow County

District Court PO Box 847, 520 Norris Ave, McCook, NE 69001; phone: 308-345-4583; fax: 308-345-7907; hours 8AM-4PM (CST). *Felony, Civil Actions Over $15,000.*

Civil Records: Access: Mail, in person, online. Both court and visitors may perform in person searches. No search fee. Court makes copy: $.50 per page. Required to search: name, years to search. Civil cases indexed by defendant, plaintiff; on index books since 1871, on microfiche since mid 1980s, computerized since 1998. Online access same as criminal. Online records date from 06/98. Mail turnaround time 2-4 days.

Criminal Records: Access: Mail, in person, online. Both court and visitors may perform in person searches. No search fee. Court makes copy: $.50 per page. Required to search: name, years to search. Criminal records on index books since 1871, on microfiche since mid 1980s, computerized since 1998. Subscribe to NOL at www.nebraska.gov/service_info.phtml?service_id =147 for court access. $.60 a record fee or $300 per month flat rate. Online records date from 06/98. Mail turnaround time 2-4 days.

General Information: Public terminal goes back to 1998. Will fax documents $3.00 1st page, $1.00 each add'l. Certification fee: $1.00. Payee: Clerk of District Court. Personal checks accepted. Prepayment and SASE required.

Red Willow County Court PO Box 199, 502 Norris Ave, McCook, NE 69001; phone: 308-345-1904; fax: 308-345-1904; hours 8AM-4PM (CST). *Misdemeanor, Civil Actions Under $45,000, Eviction, Small Claims, Probate.*

Civil Records: Access: Mail, fax, in person, online. Both court and visitors may perform in person searches. No search fee. Court makes copy: $.50 per page. Required to search: name, years to search. Civil cases indexed by defendant, plaintiff; on case files and docket cards since 1984, probate on microfilm since 1977; on computer back to 1998. Online access same as criminal, records date from 01/00 forward, probate from 08/98. Mail turnaround time 2 days.

Criminal Records: Access: Mail, fax, in person, online. Both court and visitors may perform in person searches. No search fee. Court makes copy: $.50 per page. Required to search: name, years to search, DOB. Criminal records on books since 1984; on computer back to 1998. Subscribe to NOL at www.nebraska.gov/service_info.phtml?service_id =147 for court access. $.60 a record fee or $300 per month flat rate. Online criminal and traffic records date from 06/98. Mail turnaround time 2 days.

General Information: Public terminal goes back to 1998. No adoption, juvenile, convictions set aside on misdemeanor offense, sealed records released. Certification fee: $1.00 per cert. Payee: County Court. Personal checks accepted. Prepayment and SASE required.

Richardson County

District Court 1700 Stone St, Falls City, NE 68355; phone: 402-245-2023; fax: 402-245-3725; hours 8:30AM-5PM (CST). *Felony, Civil Actions Over $15,000.*
Civil Records: Access: In person, online. Visitors must perform in person searches themselves. Court makes copy: $.25 per page. Required to search: name, years to search. Civil cases indexed by defendant, plaintiff; on microfiche and at state archives to 1930; on computer back to 1998. Online access same as criminal. Online records date from 02/98.
Criminal Records: Access: In person, online. Visitors must perform in person searches themselves. Court makes copy: $.25 per page. Required to search: name, years to search, DOB, signed release. Criminal records on microfiche and at state archives to 1930; on computer back to 1998. Subscribe to NOL at www.nebraska.gov/service_info.phtml?service_id =147 for court access. $.60 a record fee or $300 per month flat rate. Online records date from 02/98.
General Information: Public use terminal available. No sealed records released. Certification fee: $1.00. Payee: Clerk of District Court. Personal checks accepted. Prepayment required.

Richardson County Court 1700 Stone St Rm 205, Falls City, NE 68355; phone: 402-245-2812; fax: 402-245-3352; hours 8AM-5PM (CST). *Misdemeanor, Civil Actions Under $45,000, Eviction, Small Claims, Probate.*
Civil Records: Access: In person, online. Visitors must perform in person searches themselves. Court makes copy: $.25 per page. Required to search: name, years to search. Civil cases indexed by defendant, plaintiff; on index cards back to 1970s. Online access same as criminal. Online civil and probate records from 11/00 forward.
Criminal Records: Access: In person, online. Visitors must perform in person searches themselves. Court makes copy: $.25 per page. Required to search: name, years to search; also helpful: DOB. Criminal records on index cards back to 1970s. Subscribe to NOL at www.nebraska.gov/service_info.phtml?service_id =147 for court access. $.60 a record fee or $300 per month flat rate. Online criminal and traffic records date from 06/00.
General Information: Public terminal goes back to 2000. No adoption records released. Certification fee: $1.00 per cert. Payee: County Court. Only cashiers checks and money orders accepted. Prepayment required.

Rock County

District Court PO Box 367, 400 State St, Bassett, NE 68714; phone: 402-684-3933; fax: 402-684-2741; hours 9AM-5PM (CST). *Felony, Civil Actions Over $15,000.*
Civil Records: Access: Fax, mail, in person, online. Both court and visitors may perform in person searches. No search fee. Court makes copy: $.25 per page. Required to search: name, years to search. Civil cases indexed by defendant, plaintiff; on index books since 1800s. Online access same as criminal. Online records date from 08/00. Mail turnaround time 1-2 days.
Criminal Records: Access: Fax, mail, in person, online. Both court and visitors may perform in person searches. No search fee. Court makes copy: $.25 per page. Required to search: name, years to search, DOB. Criminal records on index books since 1800s. Subscribe to NOL at www.nebraska.gov/service_info.phtml?service_id =147 for court access. $.60 a record fee or $300 per month flat rate. Online records date from 08/00. Mail turnaround time 1-2 days.
General Information: Public terminal goes back to 2000. No juvenile or sealed records released. Will fax documents for $2.00 1st page and $1.00 each add'l. Certification fee: $1.50 per cert. Payee: Clerk of

District Court. Personal checks accepted. Prepayment and SASE required.

Rock County Court PO Box 249, 400 State St, Bassett, NE 68714; phone: 402-684-3601; fax: 402-684-2741; hours 8AM-5PM (CST). *Misdemeanor, Civil Actions Under $45,000, Eviction, Small Claims, Probate.*
Civil Records: Access: Fax, mail, in person, online. Visitors must perform in person searches themselves. Court makes copy: $.25 per page. Required to search: name, years to search. Civil cases indexed by defendant, plaintiff; on index books from 1800s, index cards from 1985; on computer back to 8/2000. Online access same as criminal. Online civil and probate records from 10/00 forward.
Criminal Records: Access: Fax, mail, in person, online. Visitors must perform in person searches themselves. Court makes copy: $.25 per page. Required to search: name, years to search, DOB. Criminal records on index books from 1800s, index cards from 1985; on computer back to 8/2000. Subscribe to NOL at www.nebraska.gov/service_info.phtml?service_id =147 for court access. $.60 a record fee or $300 per month flat rate. Online criminal and traffic records date from 08/00.
General Information: Public terminal goes back to 2000. Certification fee: $1.50 per cert. Payee: County Court. Personal checks accepted. Prepayment required.

Saline County

District Court Clerk of District Court, PO Box 865, Wilber, NE 68465; phone: 402-821-2823; fax: 402-821-2132; hours 8AM-N, 1-5PM (CST). *Felony, Civil Actions Over $15,000.*
Civil Records: Access: Mail, in person, online. Visitors must perform in person searches themselves. Court makes copy: $.25 per page. Required to search: name, years to search. Civil cases indexed by defendant, plaintiff. Civil records being entered on computer beginning 8/94, index in dockets books from 1800s. Online access same as criminal. Online records date from 07/94.
Criminal Records: Access: Mail, in person, online. Visitors must perform in person searches themselves. Court makes copy: $.25 per page. Required to search: name, years to search; also helpful: DOB. Criminal records being entered on computer beginning 8/94, index in dockets books from 1800s. Subscribe to NOL at www.nebraska.gov/service_info.phtml?service_id =147 for court access. $.60 a record fee or $300 per month flat rate. Online records date from 07/94.
General Information: Public use terminal available. No sealed or mental health records released. Will fax specific for $1.00 1st page $.25 ea add'l, but not name-search documents. Certification fee: $1.00. Payee: Clerk of District Court. Personal checks accepted. Prepayment required.

Saline County Court PO Box 865, 215 S First St, Wilber, NE 68465; phone: 402-821-2131; fax: 402-821-2132; hours 8AM-N; 1PM-5PM (CST). *Misdemeanor, Civil Actions Under $45,000, Eviction, Small Claims, Probate.*
Civil Records: Access: Fax, mail, in person, online. Both court and visitors may perform in person searches. Search fee: $3.00. Court makes copy: $.25 per page. Required to search: name, years to search. Civil cases indexed by defendant, plaintiff; on index books from 1860s; computerized records since 1994. Online access same as criminal. Online civil and probate records from 06/94 forward. Mail turnaround time 2-3 days.
Criminal Records: Access: Fax, mail, in person, online. Both court and visitors may perform in person searches. Search fee: $3.00. Court makes copy: $.25 per page. Required to search: name, years to search. Criminal records on index books from 1860s; computerized since 1994. Subscribe at www.nebraska.gov/service_info.phtml?service_id

=147 for court access. $.60 a record fee or $300 per month flat rate. Online criminal and traffic records date from 07/94. Mail turnaround time 2-3 days.
General Information: Public terminal goes back to 1994. (Available in District Court.) No juvenile or sealed records released. No fee to fax documents. Certification fee: $1.00 per cert. Payee: County Court. Personal checks accepted. Prepayment and SASE required.

Sarpy County

District Court 1210 Golden Gate Dr, #3141, Papillion, NE 68046; phone: 402-593-2267; fax: 402-593-4403; hours 8AM-4:45PM (CST). *Felony, Civil Actions Over $50,000.*
Civil Records: Access: Phone, mail, in person, online. Both court and visitors may perform in person searches. No search fee. Court makes copy: $.75 for 1st page, $.25 each add'l. Required to search: name, years to search. Civil cases indexed by defendant, plaintiff; on computer from 1979 forward, on books prior. Online access same as criminal. Online records date from 12/98. Mail turnaround time 1-2 days.
Criminal Records: Access: Phone, mail, in person, online. Both court and visitors may perform in person searches. No search fee. Court makes copy: $.75 for first page, $.25 each add'l. Required to search: name, years to search. Criminal records on computer from 1979 forward, on books prior. Subscribe to NOL at www.nebraska.gov/service_info.phtml?service_id =147 for court access. $.60 a record fee or $300 per month flat rate. Online records date from 12/98. Note: For phone requests, will only verify from computer index. Mail turnaround time 1-2 days.
General Information: Public terminal goes back to 1979. No mental health or search warrant records released. Certification fee: $1.00. Payee: Clerk of District Court. Only cashiers checks and money orders accepted. Prepayment and SASE required.

Sarpy County Court 1210 Golden Gate Dr, #3142, Papillion, NE 68046; phone: 402-593-5775; fax: 402-593-2193; hours 8AM-4:45PM (CST). *Misdemeanor, Civil Actions Under $50,000, Eviction, Small Claims, Probate.*
www.sarpy.com
Civil Records: Access: Fax, mail, in person, online. Visitors must perform in person searches themselves. Court makes copy: $.25 per page. Required to search: name, years to search. Civil cases indexed by defendant, plaintiff; on computer since 8/97; prior records on docket books and cards from 1800s. Access to internet system requires registration and password. Call John at 402-471-3049 for more information. System can be searched by name or case number. Also, you may subscribe to NOL at www.nebraska.gov/service_info.phtml?service_id =147 for online court access. $.60 a record fee or $300 per month flat rate, also start-up fee. Note: Online civil records date from 10/00 forward, probate from 04/99.
Criminal Records: Access: Fax, mail, in person, online. Visitors must perform in person searches themselves. Court makes copy: $.25 per page. Required to search: name, years to search, DOB. Criminal records on computer since 8/97; prior records on docket books and cards from 1800s. Online access to criminal records is the same as civil. Online criminal and traffic records date from 08/97.
General Information: Public terminal goes back to 1997. No adoption records released. Certification fee: $1.00 per cert. Payee: County Court. Personal checks accepted. Prepayment required.

Saunders County

District Court County Courthouse, 433 N Chestnut, Wahoo, NE 68066; phone: 402-443-8113; fax: 402-443-8170; hours 8AM-5PM (CST). *Felony, Civil Actions Over $15,000.*

Civil Records: Access: In person, online. Visitors must perform in person searches themselves. Court makes copy: $.25 per page. Required to search: name, years to search. Civil cases indexed by defendant, plaintiff; on index books to late 1800s; on computer back to 1998. Online access same as criminal. Online records date from 06/98.

Criminal Records: Access: In person, online. Visitors must perform in person searches themselves. Court makes copy: $.25 per page. Required to search: name, years to search; also helpful: DOB, SSN. Criminal records on index books to late 1800s; on computer back to 1998. Subscribe to NOL at www.nebraska.gov/service_info.phtml?service_id =147 for court access. $.60 a record fee or $300 per month flat rate. Online records date from 06/98.

General Information: Public use terminal available. No mental health records released. Certification fee: $1.00 per copy fee. Payee: Clerk of District Court. Personal checks accepted. Prepayment required.

Saunders County Court 433 N Chestnut, Wahoo, NE 68066; phone: 402-443-8119; fax: 402-443-8121; hours 8AM-5PM (CST). *Misdemeanor, Civil Actions Under $45,000, Eviction, Small Claims, Probate.*

Civil Records: Access: In person, online. Visitors must perform in person searches themselves. Court makes copy: $.25 per page; same fee for self serve. Required to search: name, years to search. Civil cases indexed by defendant, plaintiff; on index books. Online access same as criminal. Online civil and probate records from 11/00 forward.

Criminal Records: Access: In person, online. Visitors must perform in person searches themselves. Court makes copy: $.25 per page; same fee for self serve. Required to search: name, years to search. Criminal records on index books. Subscribe to NOL at www.nebraska.gov/service_info.phtml?service_id =147 for court access. $.60 a record fee or $300 per month flat rate. Online criminal and traffic records from 06/26/00.

General Information: Public terminal has criminal back to 2000 and civil back to 2001. No adoption or sealed records released. Certification fee: $1.00. Payee: County Court. Personal checks accepted. Prepayment required.

Scotts Bluff County

District Court 1725 10th St, PO Box 47, Gering, NE 69341-0047; phone: 308-436-6641; fax: 308-436-6759; hours 8AM-4:30PM (MST). *Felony, Civil Actions Over $15,000.*

Civil Records: Access: In person, online. Visitors must perform in person searches themselves. Court makes copy: $.25 per page. Required to search: name, years to search. Civil cases indexed by defendant, plaintiff; on index books to 1800s; on computer back to 1997. Online access same as criminal.

Criminal Records: Access: In person, online. Visitors must perform in person searches themselves. Court makes copy: $.25 per page. Criminal records on index books to 1800s; on computer back to 1997. Subscribe to NOL at www.nebraska.gov/service_info.phtml?service_id =147 for court access. $.60 a record fee or $300 per month flat rate.

General Information: Public terminal goes back to 1997. No juvenile or mental health records released. Will fax specific case file requests for $3.50 plus copy cost. Certification fee: $1.00 per page. Payee: Clerk of District Court. Business checks accepted. Prepayment required.

Scotts Bluff County Court 1725 10th St, Gering, NE 69341; phone: 308-436-6648; fax: 308-436-6782; hours 8AM-5PM (MST). *Misdemeanor, Civil Actions Under $45,000, Eviction, Small Claims, Probate.*

Civil Records: Access: In person, online. Visitors must perform in person searches themselves. Court makes copy: $.25 per page. Required to search: name, years to search. Civil cases indexed by defendant, plaintiff. Civil records computerized since 2000. Online access same as criminal. Online civil and probate records from 03/01 forward.

Criminal Records: Access: In person, online. Visitors must perform in person searches themselves. Court makes copy: $.25 per page. Required to search: name, years to search, DOB. Criminal records computerized since 2000. Subscribe to NOL at www.nebraska.gov/service_info.phtml?service_id =147 for court access. $.60 a record fee or $300 per month flat rate. Online criminal and traffic records date from 05/00.

General Information: Public terminal goes back to 5/2000. No adoption records released. Certification fee: $1.00 per cert. Payee: County Court. Personal checks accepted. Prepayment required.

Seward County

District Court PO Box 36, Seward, NE 68434; phone: 402-643-4895; fax: 402-643-2950; hours 8AM-5PM (CST). *Felony, Civil Actions Over $15,000.*

Civil Records: Access: In person, online. Visitors must perform in person searches themselves. Court makes copy: $.30 per page. Required to search: name, years to search. Civil cases indexed by defendant, plaintiff; on index books since late 1800s; computerized since 6/98. Online access same as criminal. Online records date from 06/98.

Criminal Records: Access: In person, online. Visitors must perform in person searches themselves. Court makes copy: $.30 per page. Required to search: name, years to search. Criminal records on index books since late 1800s; computerized since 6/98. Subscribe to NOL at www.nebraska.gov/service_info.phtml?service_id =147 for court access. $.60 a record fee or $300 per month flat rate. Online records date from 06/98.

General Information: Public use terminal available. Will fax specific case file requests for $3.00 first page and $1.00 each add'l. Certification fee: $1.00. Personal checks not accepted. Prepayment required.

Seward County Court PO Box 37, 529 Seward St, Seward, NE 68434; phone: 402-643-3341; fax: 402-643-2950; hours 8AM-5PM (CST). *Misdemeanor, Civil Actions Under $45,000, Eviction, Small Claims, Probate.*

Civil Records: Access: Fax, mail, in person, online. Both court and visitors may perform in person searches. No search fee. Court makes copy: $.25 per page. Required to search: name, years to search. Civil cases indexed by defendant, plaintiff; on index books, cards back to 1975, computerized back to 1997. Online access same as criminal, records date from 10/99 forward, probate from 05/98.

Criminal Records: Access: Fax, mail, in person, online. Both court and visitors may perform in person searches. No search fee. Court makes copy: $.25 per page. Required to search: name, years to search. Criminal records on index books, cards back to 1950. Subscribe to NOL at www.nebraska.gov/service_info.phtml?service_id =147 for court access. $.60 a record fee or $300 per month flat rate. Online criminal and traffic records date from 03/97.

General Information: Public terminal goes back to 1997. No adoption, juvenile or sealed records released. Certification fee: $1.00 per cert. Payee: County Court. Personal checks accepted. Prepayment required.

Sheridan County

District Court PO Box 581, Rushville, NE 69360; phone: 308-327-5654; fax: 308-327-5618; hours 8:30AM-4:30PM (MST). *Felony, Civil Actions Over $10,000.*

Civil Records: Access: Mail, fax, in person, online. Both court and visitors may perform in person searches. Search fee: $5.00 per name. Court makes copy: $.10 per page; same fee for self serve. Required to search: name, years to search. Civil cases indexed by defendant, plaintiff; on index and docket books since 1800s, computerized since 1998. Online access same as criminal. Online records date from 08/98. Mail turnaround time 1-2 days.

Criminal Records: Access: Mail, fax, in person, online. Both court and visitors may perform in person searches. Search fee: $5.00 per name. Court makes copy: $.10 per page; same fee for self serve. Required to search: name, years to search, signed release; also helpful: DOB. Criminal records on index and docket books since 1800s, computerized since 1998. Subscribe to NOL at www.nebraska.gov/service_info.phtml?service_id =147 for court access. $.60 a record fee or $300 per month flat rate. Online records date from 08/98. Mail turnaround time 1-2 days.

General Information: Public terminal goes back to 8/1998. No mental health, grand jury records released. Will fax documents to local and toll free lines. Certification fee: $1.00 per case. Payee: Clerk of District Court. Personal checks accepted. SASE required.

Sheridan County Court PO Box 430, Rushville, NE 69360; phone: 308-327-5656; fax: 308-327-5623; hours 8AM-4:30PM (MST). *Misdemeanor, Civil Actions Under $45,000, Eviction, Small Claims, Probate.*

Civil Records: Access: In person, online. Visitors must perform in person searches themselves. No copy fee. Required to search: name, years to search. Civil cases indexed by defendant, plaintiff; on index books, on microfiche from 1920 forward; on computer back to 6/2000. Online access same as criminal. Online civil and probate records from 11/00 forward.

Criminal Records: Access: Fax, mail, in person, online. Visitors must perform in person searches themselves. No search fee. No copy fee. Required to search: name, years to search. Criminal records on index books, on microfiche from 1920 forward; on computer back to 6/2000. Subscribe to NOL at www.nebraska.gov/service_info.phtml?service_id =147 for court access. $.60 a record fee or $300 per month flat rate. Online criminal and traffic records date from 06/00. Mail turnaround time 1-2 days.

General Information: Public terminal has criminal back to 6/12/00 and civil back to 1/2001. No adoption or confidential records released. No fee to fax documents. Faxing available to 800 numbers only. Certification fee: $1.00. Payee: Sheridan County Court. Personal checks accepted. Prepayment and SASE required.

Sherman County

District Court 630 O St, PO Box 456, Loup City, NE 68853; phone: 308-745-1513 x103; fax: 308-745-0297; hours 8:30AM-4:30PM (CST). *Felony, Civil Actions Over $15,000.*

Civil Records: Access: Mail, in person, online. Visitors must perform in person searches themselves. No search fee. Court makes copy: $.50 per page. Self serve copy fee: $.25 per page. Required to search: name, years to search. Civil cases indexed by defendant, plaintiff; on index and docket books since late 1800s; on computer back to 4/2000. Online access same as criminal. Online records date from 04/00. Mail turnaround time 1-2 days.

Criminal Records: Access: Mail, in person, online. Visitors must perform in person searches themselves. No search fee. Court makes copy: $.50 per page. Self serve copy fee: $.25 per page. Required to search: name, years to search. Criminal records on index and docket books since late 1800s; on computer back to 4/2000. Subscribe to NOL at www.nebraska.gov/service_info.phtml?service_id =147 for court access. $.60 a record fee or $300 per month flat rate. Online records date from 04/00. Mail turnaround time 1-2 days.

General Information: Public terminal goes back to 4/17/2000. No mental health records released. Will not fax documents. Certification fee: $1.50. Payee: Clerk of District Court. Personal checks accepted. Prepayment and SASE required.

Sherman County Court 630 O St, PO Box 55, Loup City, NE 68853; phone: 308-745-1513 x102; fax: 308-745-1510; hours 8:30AM-4:30PM (CST). *Misdemeanor, Civil Actions Under $45,000, Eviction, Small Claims, Probate.*

Civil Records: Access: Fax, mail, in person, online. Visitors must perform in person searches themselves. No search fee. Court makes copy: $.50 per page. Self serve copy fee: $.25 per page. Required to search: name, years to search. Civil cases indexed by defendant only. Civil records on index books from late 1800s; on computer back to 5/2000 in DC office. Newer names indexed by defendant only. Online access same as criminal. Online civil and probate records from 05/00 forward. Mail turnaround time 1-2 weeks.

Criminal Records: Access: Fax, mail, in person, online. Visitors must perform in person searches themselves. No search fee. Court makes copy: $.50 per page. Self serve copy fee: $.25 per page. Required to search: name, years to search, DOB. Criminal records on index books from late 1800s; on computer back to 5/2000. Newer names indexed by defendant only. Subscribe to NOL at www.nebraska.gov/service_info.phtml?service_id =147 for court access. $.60 a record fee or $300 per month flat rate. Online criminal and traffic records date from 05/00. Mail turnaround time 1-2 weeks.

General Information: Public terminal goes back to 4/2000. (Terminal located in District Court Office.) No adoption records released. Fee to fax documents is $3.00 1st page; $1.00 each add'l. Certification fee: $1.50 per cert. Payee: Sherman County Court. Business checks accepted. Prepayment and SASE required.

Sioux County

District Court PO Box 158, 325 Main St, Harrison, NE 69346; phone: 308-668-2443; fax: 308-668-2443; hours 8AM-4:30PM (MST). *Felony, Civil Actions Over $15,000.*

Civil Records: Access: Fax, mail, in person, online. Both court and visitors may perform in person searches. No search fee. Court makes copy: $.25 per page; same fee for self serve. Required to search: name, years to search. Civil cases indexed by defendant, plaintiff. Civil records in index and docket books since 1800s; computerized records since 1992. Online access same as criminal. Online records date from 06/00. Mail turnaround time 3-4 days.

Criminal Records: Access: Fax, mail, in person, online. Both court and visitors may perform in person searches. No search fee. Court makes copy: $.25 per page; same fee for self serve. Required to search: name, years to search; also helpful: DOB, SSN. Criminal records in index and docket books since 1800s; computerized records since 1992. Subscribe to NOL at www.nebraska.gov/service_info.phtml?service_id =147 for court access. $.60 a record fee or $300 per month flat rate. Online records date from 06/00. Mail turnaround time 3-4 days.

General Information: Public terminal goes back to 1992. No adoption or sealed records released. Will fax documents for $1.00 per page. Certification fee: $6.00 per page. Payee: Clerk of District Court. Personal checks accepted. Prepayment and SASE required.

Sioux County Court PO Box 158, 325 Main St, Harrison, NE 69346; phone: 308-668-2443; fax: 308-668-2443; hours 8AM-4:30 (MST). *Misdemeanor, Civil Actions Under $45,000, Eviction, Small Claims, Probate.*

Civil Records: Access: Fax, mail, in person, online. Both court and visitors may perform in person searches. No search fee. Court makes copy: $.25 per page; same fee for self serve. Required to search: name, years to search. Civil cases indexed by defendant, plaintiff; on index books from late 1800s. Online access same as criminal. Online civil and probate records from 01/01 forward. Note: This court prefers to take phone requests. Very few civil cases handled each year. Mail turnaround time 3-4 days.

Criminal Records: Access: Fax, mail, in person, online. Both court and visitors may perform in person searches. No search fee. Court makes copy: $.25 per page; same fee for self serve. Required to search: name, years to search. Criminal records on index books from late 1800s. Subscribe to NOL at www.nebraska.gov/service_info.phtml?service_id =147 for court access. $.60 a record fee or $300 per month flat rate. Online criminal and traffic records date from 08/00. Mail turnaround time 3-4 days.

General Information: . iblic terminal goes back to 1992. No sealed, expunged, or adoption records released. Will fax documents for $1.00 per page. Certification fee: $6.00 per page. Payee: County Court. Personal checks accepted. Prepayment and SASE required.

Stanton County

District Court PO Box 347, Stanton, NE 68779; phone: 402-439-2222; fax: 402-439-2200; hours 8:30AM-4:30PM (CST). *Felony, Civil Actions Over $15,000.*

Civil Records: Access: Fax, mail, in person, online. Both court and visitors may perform in person searches. No search fee. Court makes copy: $.50 per page; same fee for self serve. Required to search: name, years to search. Civil cases indexed by defendant, plaintiff; on books from 1867, on computer from 12/1999. Online access same as criminal. Online records date from 12/99. Mail turnaround time 1-2 days, limited phone seraching is immediate.

Criminal Records: Access: Fax, mail, in person, online. Both court and visitors may perform in person searches. No search fee. Court makes copy: $.50 per page; same fee for self serve. Required to search: name, years to search; also helpful: address, DOB, SSN. Criminal records on books from 1867, on computer from 12/1999. Subscribe to NOL at www.nebraska.gov/service_info.phtml?service_id =147 for court access. $.60 a record fee or $300 per month flat rate. Online records date from 12/99. Mail turnaround time 1-2 days, limited phone searching is immediate.

General Information: Public terminal goes back to 12/1999. No juvenile records released. Will fax documents $2.50 1st page, $1.00 each add'l. Certification fee: $1.50 per page. Payee: Clerk of District Court. Personal checks accepted. Prepayment and SASE required.

Stanton County Court 804 Ivy St, PO Box 536, Stanton, NE 68779; phone: 402-439-2221; probate phone: 402-439-2221; fax: 402-439-2229; hours 8:30AM-4:30PM (CST). *Misdemeanor, Civil Actions Under $45,000, Eviction, Small Claims, Probate.*

Civil Records: Access: In person, online. Visitors must perform in person searches themselves. Court makes copy: $.25 per page. Required to search: name, years to search. Civil cases indexed by defendant, plaintiff; on docket cards and books back to 1950s; criminal records go back to 1999, probate on microfilm. Online access same as criminal. Online civil and probate records from 10/00 forward.

Criminal Records: Access: In person, online. Visitors must perform in person searches

themselves. Court makes copy: $.25 per page. Required to search: name, years to search, DOB. Criminal records on docket cards and books back to 1900s; criminal records computerized back to 1999, probate on microfilm. Subscribe to NOL at www.nebraska.gov/service_info.phtml?service_id =147 for court access. $.60 a record fee or $300 per month flat rate. Online criminal and traffic records date from 06/00.

General Information: Public terminal goes back to 7/2000. No adoption records released. Certification fee: $1.00. Payee: Stanton County. Personal checks accepted. Prepayment required.

Thayer County

District Court PO Box 297, Hebron, NE 68370; phone: 402-768-6116; fax: 402-768-6128; hours 8AM-N, 1:00PM-4:30PM (CST). *Felony, Civil Actions Over $15,000.*

Civil Records: Access: In person, online. Visitors must perform in person searches themselves. Court makes copy: $.25 per page. Required to search: name, years to search. Civil cases indexed by defendant, plaintiff; on books from 1900s; computerized records go back 3/2000. Online access same as criminal. Online records date from 03/00.

Criminal Records: Access: Fax, mail, in person, online. Visitors must perform in person searches themselves. No search fee. Court makes copy: $.25 per page. Required to search: name, years to search. Criminal records on books from 1900; computerized records go back 3/2000. Subscribe to NOL at www.nebraska.gov/service_info.phtml?service_id =147 for court access. $.60 a record fee or $300 per month flat rate. Online records date from 03/00. Mail turnaround time 5 days.

General Information: Public terminal goes back to 3/2000. No mental health or sealed records released. Will not fax documents. Certification fee: $1.00. Payee: Thayer County Treasurer. Personal checks accepted. SASE required.

Thayer County Court PO Box 94, Hebron, NE 68370; phone: 402-768-6325; fax: 402-768-7232; hours 8AM-4:30PM (CST). *Misdemeanor, Civil Actions Under $51,000, Eviction, Small Claims, Probate.*

Civil Records: Access: Mail, in person, online. Both court and visitors may perform in person searches. No search fee. Court makes copy: $.25 per page. Required to search: name, years to search, address. Civil cases indexed by defendant, plaintiff; on docket cards from 1871; probate on microfiche. Online access same as criminal. Online civil and probate records from 02/00 forward. Mail turnaround time within 2 weeks.

Criminal Records: Access: Mail, in person, online. Both court and visitors may perform in person searches. No search fee. Court makes copy: $.25 per page. Required to search: name, years to search, DOB. Criminal records on docket cards from 1871; probate on microfiche. Subscribe to NOL at www.nebraska.gov/service_info.phtml?service_id =147 for court access. $.60 a record fee or $300 per month flat rate. Online criminal and traffic records date from 02/00. Mail turnaround time within 2 weeks.

General Information: Public terminal goes back to 2000. No adoption or juvenile records released. Will not fax documents. Certification fee: $1.00. Payee: County Court. Prepayment and SASE required.

Thomas County

District Court PO Box 226, 503 Main St, Thedford, NE 69166; phone: 308-645-2261; fax: 308-645-2623; hours 8AM-N, 1-4PM (CST). *Felony, Civil Actions Over $15,000.*

Civil Records: Access: Fax, mail, in person, online. Both court and visitors may perform in person searches. Search fee: $3.00 per name. Court makes copy: $.25 per page; same fee for self serve. Required to search: name, years to search. Civil cases indexed by defendant, plaintiff. Civil records indexed in books and in case files since 1800s; on computer back to 6/2000. Online access same as criminal. Online records date from 06/00. Mail turnaround time 2 days.

Criminal Records: Access: Fax, mail, in person, online. Both court and visitors may perform in person searches. Search fee: $3.00 per name. Court makes copy: $.25 per page; same fee for self serve. Required to search: name, years to search, DOB; also helpful- SSN, signed release. Criminal records indexed in books and in case files since 1800s; on computer back to 6/2000. Subscribe to NOL at www.nebraska.gov/service_info.phtml?service_id =147 for court access. $.60 a record fee or $300 per month flat rate. Online records date from 06/00. Mail turnaround time 2 days.

General Information: Public terminal goes back to 6/2000. No sealed or juvenile records released. Fee to fax documents is $1.00 per document and $.25 per page. Certification fee: $4.00 per cert. Payee: Clerk of District Court. Personal checks accepted. Prepayment and SASE required.

Thomas County Court PO Box 233, 503 Main St, Thedford, NE 69166; phone: 308-645-2266; fax: 308-645-2623; hours 8AM-N, 1-4PM (CST). *Misdemeanor, Civil Actions Under $45,000, Eviction, Small Claims, Probate.*

Civil Records: Access: Phone, fax, mail, in person, online. Both court and visitors may perform in person searches. No search fee. Court makes copy: $.25 per page; same fee for self serve. Required to search: name, years to search. Civil cases indexed by defendant, plaintiff; on index cards and books from late 1800s. Online access same as criminal, records date from 10/99 forward, probate from 07/98. Mail turnaround time 2 days.

Criminal Records: Access: Fax, mail, in person, online. Both court and visitors may perform in person searches. No search fee. Court makes copy: $.25 per page; same fee for self serve. Required to search: name, years to search, DOB, signed release. Criminal records on index cards and books from late 1800s. Subscribe to NOL at www.nebraska.gov/service_info.phtml?service_id =147 for court access. $.60 a record fee or $300 per month flat rate. Online criminal and traffic records date from 07/98. Mail turnaround time 2 days.

General Information: Public terminal goes back to 6/2000. No adoption or juvenile records released. Certification fee: $1.00 per cert. Payee: County Court. Personal checks accepted. Prepayment and SASE required.

Thurston County

District Court PO Box 216, Pender, NE 68047; phone: 402-385-3318; fax: 402-385-2762; hours 8:30AM-5PM (CST). *Felony, Civil Actions Over $15,000.*

Civil Records: Access: In person, online. Visitors must perform in person searches themselves. Court makes copy: $.25 per page; same fee for self serve. Required to search: name, years to search. Civil cases indexed by defendant, plaintiff; on index books from late 1800s; on computer back to 1998. Online access same as criminal. Online records date from 03/98.

Criminal Records: Access: In person, online. Visitors must perform in person searches themselves. Court makes copy: $.25 per page; same fee for self serve. Required to search: name, years to search. Criminal records on index books from late 1800s; on computer back to 1998. Subscribe to NOL at www.nebraska.gov/service_info.phtml?service_id =147 for court access. $.60 a record fee or $300 per month flat rate. Online records date from 03/98.

General Information: Public terminal goes back to 1998. No mental health records released. Will not fax documents. Certification fee: $1.00 per certification. Payee: Clerk of District Court. No personal checks accepted. Prepayment required.

Thurston County Court County Courthouse, PO Box 129, Pender, NE 68047; phone: 402-385-3136; criminal fax: 402-385-3143; same fax for civil/probate; hours 8:30AM-N,1-5PM (CST). *Misdemeanor, Civil Actions Under $45,000, Eviction, Small Claims, Probate.*

Civil Records: Access: In person, online. Visitors must perform in person searches themselves. Court makes copy: $.25 per page. Self serve copy fee: $.10 per page. Required to search: name, years to search. Civil cases indexed by defendant, plaintiff; on books; probate on microfiche since 1800s; on computer back to 1/2000. Online access same as criminal. Online civil and probate records from 01/00 forward.

Criminal Records: Access: In person, online. Visitors must perform in person searches themselves. Court makes copy: $.25 per page. Self serve copy fee: $.10 per page. Required to search: name, years to search. Criminal records on books per state requirement; on computer back to 1/2000. Subscribe to NOL at www.nebraska.gov/service_info.phtml?service_id =147 for court access. $.60 a record fee or $300 per month flat rate. Online criminal and traffic records date from 01/00.

General Information: Public terminal goes back to 1/2000. No adoption or juvenile records released. Will not fax documents. Certification fee: $1.00 per seal. Payee: County Court. Personal checks accepted. Out of state personal checks not accepted. Prepayment required.

Valley County

District Court 125 S 15th St, Ord, NE 68862; phone: 308-728-3700; fax: 308-728-7725; hours 8AM-5PM (CST). *Felony, Civil Actions Over $15,000.*

Civil Records: Access: Phone, fax, mail, in person, online. Both court and visitors may perform in person searches. No search fee. Court makes copy: $.10 per page. $.15 per page for legal size; same fee for self serve. Required to search: name, years to search. Civil cases indexed by defendant, plaintiff. Civil records in general index books since late 1800s. Online access same as criminal. Online records date from 03/00. Mail turnaround time 3-5 days.

Criminal Records: Access: Fax, mail, in person, online. Both court and visitors may perform in person searches. No search fee. Court makes copy: $.10 per page. $.15 per page for legal size copy; same fee for self serve. Required to search: name, years to search; also helpful: DOB, SSN. Criminal records in general index books since late 1800s; on computer back to 3/2000. Subscribe to NOL at www.nebraska.gov/service_info.phtml?service_id =147 for court access. $.60 a record fee or $300 per month flat rate. Online records date from 03/00. Note: All requests must be in writing. Mail turnaround time 3-5 days.

General Information: Public terminal goes back to 3/2000. Will fax to a toll-free number. Certification fee: $1.00 per page. Payee: Valley County Clerk. Personal checks accepted. Prepayment and SASE required.

Valley County Court 125 S 15th St, Ord, NE 68862; phone: 308-728-3831; fax: 308-728-7725; hours 8AM-5PM (CST). *Misdemeanor, Civil Actions Under $45,000, Eviction, Small Claims, Probate.*

Civil Records: Access: Phone, fax, mail, in person, online. Both court and visitors may perform in person searches. No search fee. Court makes copy: $.25 per page; same fee for self serve. Required to search: name, years to search. Civil cases indexed by defendant, plaintiff; on books and in files since 1890s; probate on microfiche. Online access same as criminal. Online civil and probate records from 05/00 forward. Mail turnaround time 1 week.

Criminal Records: Access: Phone, fax, mail, in person, online. Both court and visitors may perform in person searches. No search fee. Court makes copy: $.25 per page; same fee for self serve. Required to search: name, years to search. Criminal records on books and in files since 1890s; probate on microfiche

Subscribe to NOL at www.nebraska.gov/service_info.phtml?service_id =147 for court access. $.60 a record fee or $300 per month flat rate. Online criminal and traffic records date from 05/00. Mail turnaround time 1 week.

General Information: Public terminal goes back to 5 years. No adoption records released. Will fax documents $3.00 1st page, $1.00 each add'l. Certification fee: $1.25. Payee: Valley County Court. Personal checks accepted. Prepayment and SASE required.

Washington County

District Court PO Box 431, Blair, NE 68008; phone: 402-426-6899; fax: 402-426-6898; hours 8AM-N; 1PM-4:30PM (CST). *Felony, Civil Actions Over $15,000.*

Civil Records: Access: In person, online. Visitors must perform in person searches themselves. Court makes copy: $.25 per page. Required to search: name, years to search. Civil cases indexed by defendant, plaintiff; on index books and in files since 1930s; computerized records since 1997, prior sent to capitol. Online access same as criminal. Online records date from 06/97.

Criminal Records: Access: In person, online. Visitors must perform in person searches themselves. Court makes copy: $.25 per page. Required to search: name, years to search, DOB. Criminal records on index books and in files since 1930s; computerized records since 1997, prior sent to capitol. Subscribe to NOL at www.nebraska.gov/service_info.phtml?service_id =147 for court access. $.60 a record fee or $300 per month flat rate. Online records date from 06/97.

General Information: Public terminal goes back to 7/1997. No juvenile, mental health records released. Certification fee: $1.00. Payee: Clerk of District Court. Personal checks accepted. Prepayment required.

Washington County Court 1555 Colfax St, Blair, NE 68008; phone: 402-426-6833; criminal fax: 402-426-6840; same fax for civil/probate; hours 8AM-4:30PM (CST). *Misdemeanor, Civil Actions Under $45,000, Eviction, Small Claims, Probate.*

Note: Probate records are on a separate index at this address.

Civil Records: Access: In person, online. Visitors must perform in person searches themselves. Court makes copy: $.25 per page; same fee for self serve. Required to search: name, years to search. Civil cases indexed by defendant, plaintiff; on index books, cards; probate on microfilm since 1867; on computer back to 1997. Online access same as criminal, records date from 12/99 forward, probate from 5/98.

Criminal Records: Access: In person, online. Visitors must perform in person searches themselves. Court makes copy: $.25 per page; same fee for self serve. Required to search: name, years to search, DOB, SSN. Criminal records on index books, cards; probate on microfilm since 1867; on computer back to 1997. Subscribe to NOL at www.nebraska.gov/service_info.phtml?service_id =147 for court access. $.60 a record fee or $300 per month flat rate. Online criminal and traffic records date from 2/97.

General Information: Public terminal has criminal back to 2/1997 and civil back to 12/1999. No adoption records released. Will not fax documents. Certification fee: $1.00 per certification. Payee: Washington County Court. Personal checks not accepted. Prepayment required.

Wayne County

District Court 510 Pearl St, Wayne, NE 68787; phone: 402-375-2260; fax: 402-375-0103; hours 8:30AM-5PM (CST). *Felony, Civil Actions Over $15,000.*

http://county.waynene.org/court_system/

Civil Records: Access: In person, online. Visitors must perform in person searches themselves. Court makes copy: $.25 per page. $1.00 minimum; same fee for self serve. Required to search: name, years to search. Civil cases indexed by defendant, plaintiff; on index books from late 1800s, computerized since 3/99. Online access same as criminal. Online records date from 03/99.

Criminal Records: Access: In person, online. Visitors must perform in person searches themselves. Court makes copy: $.25 per page. $1.00 minimum; same fee for self serve. Required to search: name, years to search. Criminal records on index books from late 1800s, computerized since 3/99. Subscribe to NOL at www.nebraska.gov/service_info.phtml?service_id=147 for court access. $.60 a record fee or $300 per month flat rate. Online records date from 03/99.

General Information: Public terminal goes back to 3/1999. No mental health records released. Certification fee: $1.00. Payee: Clerk of District Court. Only cashiers checks and money orders accepted. Prepayment required.

Wayne County Court 510 Pearl St, Wayne, NE 68787; phone: 402-375-1622; hours 8AM-5PM (CST). *Misdemeanor, Civil Actions Under $45,000, Eviction, Small Claims, Probate.*

Civil Records: Access: In person, online. Visitors must perform in person searches themselves. Court makes copy: $.25 per page. Required to search: name, years to search. Civil cases indexed by defendant, plaintiff; on index books, cards from late 1800s. Online same as criminal. Online civil and probate records from 2/2000 forward.

Criminal Records: Access: In person, online. Visitors must perform in person searches themselves. Court makes copy: $.25 per page. Required to search: name, years to search. Criminal records on index books, cards from late 1800s. Subscribe to NOL at www.nebraska.gov/service_info.phtml?service_id=147 for court access. $.60 a record fee or $300 per month flat rate. Online criminal and traffic records date from 2/2000.

General Information: Public use terminal available. No adoption records released. Certification fee: $1.00. Payee: County Court. Personal checks accepted. Prepayment required.

Webster County

District Court 621 N Cedar, Red Cloud, NE 68970; phone: 402-746-2716; fax: 402-746-2710; hours 8:30AM-4:30PM (CST). *Felony, Civil Actions Over $15,000.*

Civil Records: Access: Fax, mail, in person, online. Visitors must perform in person searches themselves. Court makes copy: $1.00 per page. Required to search: name, years to search. Civil cases indexed by defendant, plaintiff. Civil records indexed on microfiche; in files back to 1800s. Online access same as criminal. Online records date from 10/00.

Criminal Records: Access: Fax, mail, in person, online. Visitors must perform in person searches themselves. No search fee. Court makes copy: $1.00 per page. Required to search: name, years to search; also helpful: address, DOB, SSN. Criminal records indexed on microfiche; in files back to 1800s. Subscribe to NOL at www.nebraska.gov/service_info.phtml?service_id=147 for court access. $.60 a record fee or $300 per month flat rate. Online records date from 10/00.

General Information: Public terminal goes back to 10/2000. No mental health records released.

Certification fee: $1.50 per cert. Payee: Clerk of District Court. Personal checks accepted. Prepayment required.

Webster County Court 621 N Cedar, Red Cloud, NE 68970; phone: 402-746-2777; fax: 402-746-2771; probate fax: same; hours 8:30AM-4:30PM (CST). *Misdemeanor, Civil Actions Under $45,000, Eviction, Small Claims, Probate.*

Civil Records: Access: In person, online. Visitors must perform in person searches themselves. Court makes copy: $.25 per page; same fee for self serve. Required to search: name, years to search; also helpful: address. Civil cases indexed by defendant. Civil records on index cards and books; probate on microfiche since late 1930, indexed on computer since 7/00. Online access same as criminal, records date from 01/00 forward, probate from 02/00.

Criminal Records: Access: In person, online. Visitors must perform in person searches themselves. Court makes copy: $.25 per page; same fee for self serve. Required to search: name, years to search, DOB. Criminal records on index cards and books; probate on microfiche since late 1930, indexed on computer since 7/00. Subscribe to NOL at www.nebraska.gov/service_info.phtml?service_id=147 for court access. $.60 a record fee or $300 per month flat rate. Online criminal and traffic records date from 07/00.

General Information: Public use terminal available. No adoption or juvenile records released. Will fax specific case file requests for $3.00 for 1st page; $1.00 each add'l page. Certification fee: $1.00. Payee: County Court. Business checks accepted. Prepayment required.

Wheeler County

District Court PO Box 127, Bartlett, NE 68622; phone: 308-654-3235; fax: 308-654-3470; hours 9AM-N, 1-5PM (CST). *Felony, Civil Actions Over $15,000.*

Civil Records: Access: In person, online. Visitors must perform in person searches themselves. Court makes copy: $.15 per page. Required to search: name, years to search. Civil cases indexed by defendant, plaintiff; on index books from late 1800s. Online access same as criminal. Note: Mail access limited to short searches.

Criminal Records: Access: In person, online. Visitors must perform in person searches themselves. Search fee: $3.00. Court makes copy: $.15 per page. Required to search: name, years to search. Criminal records on index books from late 1800s. Subscribe to NOL at www.nebraska.gov/service_info.phtml?service_id=147 for court access. $.60 a record fee or $300 per month flat rate. Online records date from 07/00.

General Information: Public use terminal available. No juvenile or adoption records released. Will fax specific case file requests for $3.00 per document. Certification fee: $7.00. Payee: Clerk of District Court. Personal checks accepted. Prepayment required.

Wheeler County Court PO Box 127, Bartlett, NE 68622; phone: 308-654-3376; fax: 308-654-3470; hours 10AM-3PM Th, 1st & 2nd Mon (CST). *Misdemeanor, Civil Actions Under $45,000, Eviction, Small Claims, Probate.*

Civil Records: Access: Mail, in person, online. Only the court performs in person searches; visitors may not. Court makes copy: $.25 per page; same fee for self serve. Required to search: name, years to search. Civil cases indexed by defendant, plaintiff; on index books from late 1800s. Online access same as criminal, records date from 1/2001 forward,

probate from 1/02. Mail turnaround time 1-2 weeks.

Criminal Records: Access: Mail, in person, online. Visitors must perform in person searches themselves. Court makes copy: $.25 per page; same fee for self serve. Required to search: name, years to search. Criminal records on index books from late 1800s. Subscribe to NOL at www.nebraska.gov/service_info.phtml?service_id=147 for court access. $.60 a record fee or $300 per month flat rate. Online criminal and traffic records date from 7/2000. Mail turnaround time 1-2 weeks.

General Information: Public terminal goes back to 2000. No adoption records released. Will fax documents $3.00 1st page; $1.00 each add'l. Certification fee: $1.00. Payee: County Court. Personal checks accepted. Prepayment and SASE required.

York County

District Court 510 Lincoln Ave, York, NE 68467; phone: 402-362-4038; fax: 402-362-2577; hours 8:30AM-5PM (CST). *Felony, Civil Actions Over $15,000.*

Note: The SSN does not show up in the computer index, but will show in the case files.

Civil Records: Access: In person, online. Visitors must perform in person searches themselves. Court makes copy: $.25 per page; same fee for self serve. Required to search: name, years to search. Civil cases indexed by defendant, plaintiff; on index books and in files from 1875, computerized go back to 1998. Online access same as criminal. Online records date from 06/98.

Criminal Records: Access: In person, online. Visitors must perform in person searches themselves. Court makes copy: $.25 per page; same fee for self serve. Required to search: name, years to search. Criminal records on index books and in files from 1875, computerized records go back to 1998. Subscribe to NOL at www.nebraska.gov/service_info.phtml?service_id=147 for court access. $.60 a record fee or $300 per month flat rate. Online records date from 06/98.

General Information: Public terminal goes back to 1998. Certification fee: $1.00. Payee: Clerk of District Court. Personal checks accepted. Prepayment required.

York County Court 510 Lincoln Ave, York, NE 68467; phone: 402-362-4925; fax: 402-362-2577; hours 8AM-5PM (CST). *Misdemeanor, Civil Actions Under $45,000, Eviction, Small Claims, Probate.*

Civil Records: Access: In person, online. Visitors must perform in person searches themselves. Court makes copy: $.25 per page. Required to search: name, years to search. Civil cases indexed by defendant, plaintiff; on docket cards, files from 1875. Online access same as criminal, records date from 10/99 forward, probate from 05/98.

Criminal Records: Access: In person, online. Visitors must perform in person searches themselves. Court makes copy: $.25 per page. Required to search: name, years to search. Criminal records on docket cards, files from 1875. Subscribe at www.nebraska.gov/service_info.phtml?service_id=147 for court access. $.60 a record fee or $300 per month flat rate. Online criminal and traffic records date from 03/97.

General Information: Public terminal has only criminal records back to 3/1997. No adoption or sealed records released. Certification fee: $1.00. Payee: York County Court. Prepayment required.

Nebraska Recording Offices

ORGANIZATION: 93 counties, 109 recording offices. The recording officers are County Clerk (UCC and some state tax liens) and Register of Deeds (real estate and most tax liens). Most counties have a combined Clerk/Register office, which are designated "County Clerk" in this section. Sixteen counties have separate offices for County Clerk and for Register of Deeds - Adams, Cass, Dakota, Dawson, Dodge, Douglas, Gage, Hall, Lancaster, Lincoln, Madison, Otoe, Platte, Sarpy, Saunders, and Scotts Bluff. In combined offices, the Register of Deeds is frequently a different person from the County Clerk. 74 counties are in the Central Time Zone (CST) and 19 are in the Mountain Time Zone (MST).

REAL ESTATE RECORDS: Some Nebraska counties will perform real estate searches, including owner of record from the legal description of the property. Address search requests and make checks payable to the Register of Deeds, not the County Clerk. Fees vary.

UCC RECORDS: Financing statements are filed at the state level, and real estate related collateral are filed with the County Clerk. Previously, financing statements could be filed at any county. All non-real estate UCC filings are entered into a statewide database that is accessible from any county office. All but a few counties will perform UCC searches. Use search request form UCC-11. The UCC statute allows for telephone searching. Search fees are usually $4.50 per debtor name. Copy fees vary.

TAX LIEN RECORDS: All federal and some state tax liens are filed with the County Register of Deeds. Some state tax liens on personal property are filed with the County Clerk. Most counties will perform tax lien searches, some as part of a UCC search, and others for a separate fee, usually $4.50 per name in each index. Copy fees vary.

OTHER LIENS: Mechanics, artisans, judgment, motor vehicle, agricultural.

ONLINE ACCESS: Nebrask@online offers online access to Secretary of State's UCC database; registration and a usage fee is required. For information, visit http://www.nebraska.gov/business/egov.phtml. The state treasurer's unclaimed proeprty database is searchable free at www.treasurer.state.ne.us/ie/uphome.asp

---

Adams County Clerk

Register of Deeds, PO Box 2067, Hastings, NE 68902. 402-461-7148; hours: 9AM-5PM. www.adamscounty.org
Record index not computerized. Only the public may search. See Register of Deeds for real estate records. Copy fee $.50 per page. Cert fee- $1.50 per cert plus copy fee. Payee- Adams County Clerk. **Other phones:** Treasurer- 402-461-7120; Appraiser/Auditor- 402-461-7116; Elections- 402-461-7107. **Property tax/Assessor-** 402-461-7116.

Adams County Register of Deeds

Register of Deeds, PO Box 203, Hastings, NE 68902. 402-461-7148; fax-402-461-7154; hours: 9AM-5PM. www.adamscounty.org
All records in one index. Records indexed on a public use terminal back to 1991. Office will perform a UCC search and fed/state tax lien search, but public must search other records themselves. Search fee $1.00 per name per search. Copy fee $1.00 per page for fax, $.50 per page for mail or in-person. Cert fee- $1.50 per page includes copy fee. Payee- Adams County Register of Deeds. **Online access to Property, Treasurer records:** Access real estate or personal property data free at www.nebraskataxesonline.us/taxcollpage1.aspx?county=Adams. **Other phones:** Treasurer- 402-461-7120; Appraiser/Auditor- 402-461-7116; Elections- 402-461-7165; Vital Records- 402-471-2871. **Property tax/Assessor-** 500 W 4th St, Hastings, NE 68902; 402-461-7116.

Antelope County

County Clerk, PO Box 26, Neligh, NE 68756-0026. 402-887-4410; fax-402-887-4719; hours: 8:30AM-5PM.
Records not filed here since 2001. Records indexed on a public use terminal back to 1996. Office will perform a UCC search but public must search other records themselves. General index search fee $3.50 each. Copy fee $.50 per page. $1.00 to fax back. Cert fee- $5.00 per doc plus copy fee. Payee- Antelope County Clerk. **Other phones:** Treasurer- 402-887-4247. **Property tax/Assessor-** 402-887-4515.

Arthur County

County Clerk, Box 126, Arthur, NE 69121-0126. 308-764-2203; fax-308-764-2216; hours: 8AM-N, 1-4PM.
Office personnel or visitors may perform searches. Search fee $5.00 per name. Will not search real estate records. Copy fee $.20 per page. Cert fee- $5.00 per cert. Payee- Arthur County Clerk. **Property tax/Assessor-** 308-764-2203.

Banner County

County Clerk, PO Box 67, Harrisburg, NE 69345-0067. 308-436-5265; fax-308-436-4180; hours: 8AM-N, 1-5PM.
Office personnel or visitors may perform searches. Search fee $3.00 per name. Will not search real estate records. Copy fee $1.00 per page. Payee- Banner County Clerk. **Other phones:** Treasurer- 308-436-5260. **Property tax/Assessor-** 308-436-5265.

Blaine County

County Clerk, PO Box 136, Brewster, NE 68821. 308-547-2222, R/E recording phone-308-547-2222 ext 201, UCC recording phone-308-547-2222; fax-308-547-2228; hours: 8AM-4PM.
All records in one index. Record index not computerized. Only the public may search. General index search fee $1.00 per page. Copy fee $1.00 per page. Cert fee- $1.50 per page plus copy fee. Payee- Blaine County Clerk. **Other phones:** Treasurer- 308-547-2223 ext 202; Elections- 308-547-2222. **Property tax/Assessor-** same address as above. 308-541-2222 ext 201.

Boone County

County Clerk, 222 S. 4th St, Albion, NE 68620-1247. 402-395-2055, UCC recording phone-402-471-4080; fax-402-395-2055; hours: 8:30AM-5PM. www.co.boone.ne.us
Separate indices to search include deed, mortgage, misc, liens, roads. Only the public may search. Copy fee $.25 per page; $.50 if mailed. Cert fee- $1.50 per page plus copy fee. Payee- Boone County Clerk. **Other phones:** Treasurer- 402-395-2513; Elections- 402-395-2055; Vital Records- 402-471-2871/3121. **Property tax/Assessor-** same address as above. 402-395-2045.

Box Butte County

County Clerk, Box 678, Alliance, NE 69301-0678. 308-762-6565, UCC recording phone-402-471-4080 (Sec of State); fax-308-762-2867; hours: 8:30AM-4:30PM. www.co.box-butte.ne.us/
The recording officers are County Clerk (state tax liens) Register of Deeds (real estate and most tax liens). Separate indices to search include deeds, mortgages, miscellaneous, mech liens, incorporations. Record index not computerized. Office will perform a UCC search but public must search other records themselves. UCC search per debtor name- $4.50. Copy fee $.50 per page. Cert fee- $1.00 per page plus copy fee. Payee- Box Butte County Clerk. **Online access to Property, Treasurer records:** Access real estate or personal property data free at www.nebraskataxesonline.us/taxcollpage1.aspx?county=BoxB. **Other phones:** Treasurer- 308-762-6975; Elections- 308-762-6565; Vital Records- 402-471-2871. **Property tax/Assessor-** 308-762-6101.

Boyd County

County Clerk, PO Box 26, Butte, NE 68722. 402-775-2391; fax-402-775-2146; hours: 8:15AM-4PM.
Index: Deeds, Mortgages, Miscellaneous. Record index not computerized. Only the public may search. Copy fee $.25 per copy. Cert fee- $5.00 per page. Payee- County Clerk. **Other phones:** Treasurer- 402-775-2581; Elections- 402-775-2391; Vital Records- 402-775-2391. **Property tax/Assessor-** PO Box 2, Butte, NE 68722; 402-775-2311.

Brown County

County Clerk, 148 W. 4th St.; Courthouse, Ainsworth, NE 69210. 402-387-2705; fax-402-387-0918; hours: 8AM-5PM.
All records in one index. Record index not computerized. Only the public may search. Copy fee $.50, if real estate $.10 per page. Cert fee-$2.00 per page. Payee- Brown County Clerk. **Other phones:** Treasurer- 402-387-2650; Elections-402-387-2705; Secretary of State (UCC)- 402-471-2554. **Property tax/Assessor-** 402-387-1621.

Buffalo County

Register of Deeds, PO Box 1270, Kearney, NE 68848-1270. 308-236-1239, UCC recording phone-402-471-2558; fax-308-236-1291; hours: 8AM-5PM.
Only the public may search. Copy fee $.50 per page. Cert fee- $1.50. Payee- Buffalo County Register of Deeds. **Other phones:** Treasurer- 308-236-1250; Elections- 308-236-1233; Vital Records-402-471-2871. **Property tax/Assessor-** 308-236-1205.

Burt County

County Clerk, PO Box 87, Tekamah, NE 68061. 402-374-2955; fax-402-374-2956; hours: 8AM-4:30PM.
Office personnel or visitors may perform searches. Search fee $4.50 per name. Will not search real estate records. Copy fee $.50 per page. Cert fee- $3.50 per page. Payee- Burt County Clerk. **Other phones:** Treasurer- 402-374-2911; Elections- 402-374-2955. **Property tax/Assessor-** 402-374-2926.

Butler County

Deputy Clerk, PO Box 289, David City, NE 68632-0289. 402-367-7430, R/E recording phone-402-367-7431, UCC recording phone-402-471-4080; fax-402-367-3329; hours: 8:30AM-5PM.
www.co.butler.ne.us/clerk.html
All records in one index. Record index not computerized. Only the public may search. Copy fee $1.00 per filing. **Online access to Assessor Property Search records:** For the Butler County Assessor property search go to http://butler.gisworkshop.com. **Other phones:** Treasurer- 402-367-7450; Elections- 402-367-7430; Vital Records- 402-471-2871. **Property tax/Assessor-** 402-367-7420.

Cass County Clerk

County Clerk, 346 Main St.; Courthouse, Rm 202, Plattsmouth, NE 68048-1964. 402-296-9300; fax-402-296-9332; hours: 8AM-5PM.
Only the public may search. Copy fee $1.00 per page. R/E record copy- $1.50 per page. Cert fee-$5.00 per cert plus copy fee. Payee- Cass County Clerk. **Property tax/Assessor-** 402-296-9310.

Cass County Register of Deeds

Register of Deeds, 346 Main St.; County Courthouse, Plattsmouth, NE 68048-1964. 402-296-9330; fax-402-296-9331; hours: 8AM-5PM. www.cassne.org
They will look at their records when asked if request is not too involved or they have the time. All records in one index. Only the public may search. Copy fee $.50 per page. Cert fee- $1.50 per page plus copy fee. Payee- Register of Deeds. **Other phones:** Treasurer- 402-296-9320; Appraiser/Auditor- 402-296-9310; Elections- 402-296-9306. **Property tax/Assessor-** 402-296-9310.

Cedar County

County Clerk, PO Box 47, Hartington, NE 68739. 402-254-7411, UCC recording phone-402-471-2554; fax-402-254-7410; hours: 8AM-5PM.
www.co.cedar.ne.us
All records in one index. Office will perform a UCC search but public must search other records themselves. Search fee $4.50. Copy fee $.50 per page. Cert fee- $1.50 per doc, plus copy fee. Payee- County Clerk. **Other phones:** Treasurer- 402-254-7421; Elections- 402-254-7411; Vital Records-

402-254-7411. **Property tax/Assessor-** PO Box 668, Hartington, NE 68739; 402-254-7431.

Chase County

County Clerk, Box 1299, Imperial, NE 69033-1299. 308-882-7500; fax-308-882-7552; hours: 8AM-4PM.
www.co.chase.ne.us
Separate indices to search include deeds, mortgages, miscellaneous, oil & gas, articles of inc, federal & state tax liens. Record index not computerized. Office personnel or visitors may perform searches. Search fee $4.50 per name. Copy fee $.25 per page. Cert fee- $1.50 per cert page plus copy fee. Payee- Chase County. **Online access to Property, Treasurer records:** Access real estate or personal property data free at www.nebraskataxesonline.us/taxcollpage1.aspx?county=Chase. **Other phones:** Treasurer- 308-882-7510; Elections- 308-882-7500. **Property tax/Assessor-** 308-882-7506.

Cherry County

County Clerk, Box 120, Valentine, NE 69201-0120. 402-376-2771; fax-402-376-3095; hours: 8:30AM-N, 1-4:30PM.
Separate indices to search include Deeds, mtgs, misc. Record index not computerized. Only the public may search. Copy fee $.25 per page. **Other phones:** Treasurer- 402-376-1580; Elections- 402-376-2771; Vital Records- 402-471-2871. **Property tax/Assessor-** 402-376-1630.

Cheyenne County

County Clerk, PO Box 217, Sidney, NE 69162-0217. 308-254-2141; fax-308-254-4293; hours: 8AM-5PM.
www.co.cheyenne.ne.us
Office will perform a UCC search but public must search other records themselves. UCC search per debtor name- $3.50. Copy fee $1.00 per page mailed; $2.00 per page faxed, prepaid. Cert fee-$1.50 per page. Payee- Cheyenne County Clerk. **Other phones:** Treasurer- 308-254-2733. **Property tax/Assessor-** 308-254-2633.

Clay County

County Clerk, 111 W. Fairfield St, Clay Center, NE 68933-1499. 402-762-3463; fax-402-762-3506; hours: 8:30AM-5PM M-F.
Record index not computerized. Only the public may search. Copy fee $1.00 per page. Cert fee-$1.50 per doc plus copy fee. Payee- County Clerk. **Other phones:** Treasurer- 402-762-3505; Elections-402-762-3463. **Property tax/Assessor-** 402-762-3792.

Colfax County

County Clerk, 411 E. 11th St, Schuyler, NE 68661. 402-352-8504; fax-402-352-8515; hours: 8:30AM-4:30PM. www.colfaxcounty.ne.gov/clerk.html
Separate indices to search include Deeds, Mortgages, Miscellaneous. Only the public may search. Copy fee $.50 per page. R/E or tax lien copy- $.25 per page in office; $1.00 per page by mail. Cert fee- $1.50 per page plus copy fee. Payee- Colfax County Clerk. **Other phones:** Treasurer- 402-352-8519; Appraiser/Auditor- 402-352-8500; Elections- 402-352-8504; Vital Records- 402-471-2871. **Property tax/Assessor-** 411 E 11th St, Schuyler, NE 68661; 402-352-8500.

Cuming County

County Clerk, Box 290, West Point, NE 68788. 402-372-6002; fax-402-372-6013; www.co.cuming.ne.us
Separate indices to search include deeds, mortgages, miscellaneous, wills, mechanics liens, corporations. Office will perform a UCC search but public must search other records themselves. UCC search per debtor name- $4.50. Copy fee $.25 per page. Cert fee- $5.00 per document plus copy fee. **Online to Property, Treasurer records:** Access real estate or personal property data free at www.nebraskataxesonline.us/taxcollpage1.aspx?county=Cuming. **Other phones:** Treasurer- 402-372-

6011; Elections- 402-372-6002. **Property tax/Assessor-** 402-372-6000.

Custer County

County Clerk, 431 S. 10th, Broken Bow, NE 68822. 308-872-5701; hours: 9AM-5PM.
Office personnel or visitors may perform searches. Search fee $3.00 per name. UCC search per debtor name- $3.50. Copy fee $.25 per page. Cert fee-$1.00 per page. Payee- Custer County Clerk. **Other phones:** Treasurer- 308-872-2921. **Property tax/Assessor-** 308-872-2981.

Dakota County

County Register of Deeds, PO Box 511, Dakota City, NE 68731. 402-987-2166, UCC recording phone-402-987-2126; hours: 8AM-4:30PM.
Only the public may search. Copy fee $1.00 per page. Tax lien copy- $.25 per page. Cert fee- $2.50 per cert plus copy fee. Payee- Dakota County Register of Deeds. **Other phones:** Treasurer- 402-987-2131; Elections- 402-987-2126; Vital Records-402-471-2871. **Property tax/Assessor-** 402-987-0264.

Dawes County

County Clerk, 451 Main St; Courthouse, Chadron, NE 69337-2698. 308-432-0100; fax-308-432-5179; hours: 8:30AM-4:30PM.
Separate indices to search include each range has its own index, town has its own index. Record index not computerized. Only the public may search. Separate federal/state combined tax lien search- $3.00 per debtor. Copy fee $1.00 per page. R/E record copy- $.50 per page. Cert fee- $.50 & $1.50 cert fee plus copy fee. Payee- Dawes County Clerk. **Online access to Property, Treasurer records:** Access real estate or personal property data free at www.nebraskataxesonline.us/taxcollpage1.aspx?county=Dawes. **Other phones:** Treasurer- 308-432-0105; Elections- 308-432-0100; Vital Records- 308-432-0100. **Property tax/Assessor-** same address as above. 308-432-0103.

Dawson County Clerk

County Clerk, PO Box 370, Lexington, NE 68850-0370. 308-324-2127, R/E recording phone-308-324-4271; fax-308-324-6106;
Record index not computerized. Office will perform a UCC search but public must search other records themselves. Search fee $4.50. See Register of Deeds for real estate records. Copy fee $.50 per page. Cert fee- $5.00 per form. Payee- Dawson County Clerk. **Other phones:** Treasurer- 308-324-3241; Appraiser/Auditor- 308-324-3471; Elections- 308-324-6106; Vital Records- 308-324-2127. **Property tax/Assessor-** 308-324-3471.

Dawson County Register of Deeds

County Register of Deeds, 700 N. Washington; County Courthouse, Lexington, NE 68850. 308-324-4271; hours: 8AM-N, 1-5PM.
All records in one index. Only the public may search. Copy fee $1.00 per page. Cert fee- $1.50 per page plus copy fee. Payee- Dawson County Register of Deeds. **Other phones:** Treasurer- 308-324-3241. **Property tax/Assessor-** Ruth Meyer-Register of Deeds 308-324-3471.

Deuel County

County Clerk, PO Box 327, Chappell, NE 69129. 308-874-3308; fax-308-874-3472; hours: 8AM-4PM.
Office personnel or visitors may perform searches. Search fee $4.50 per name. Will not search real estate records. Copy fee $.50 per page. Cert fee- $2.00 per cert. Payee- Deuel County Clerk. **Other phones:** Treasurer- 308-874-3307. **Property tax/Assessor-** 308-874-2608.

Dixon County

County Clerk, Box 546, Ponca, NE 68770-0546. 402-755-2208; fax-402-755-4276; hours: 8AM-4:30PM.

Separate indices to search. Will not search real estate records. Will search UCC records, but not tax liens. UCC search per debtor name- $.50 per page. Cert fee- $1.50 per cert, plus copy fee. **Payee**- Dixon County Clerk. **Other phones:** Treasurer- 402-755-2701; Vital Records- 402-471-2871. **Property tax/Assessor**- PO Box 369, Ponca, NE 68770; 402-755-2608.

Dodge County Clerk

County Clerk, 435 North Park; Courthouse - Rm 102, Fremont, NE 68025-4967. 402-727-2767, R/E recording phone-402-727-2735, UCC recording phone-402-471-4080; fax-402-727-2764; hours: 8:30AM-4:30PM.
No searching at this office. See Register of Deeds for real estate records. Copy fee $1.00 per page. Cert fee- $10.00 per page plus copy fee. **Other phones:** Treasurer- 402-727-2750; Appraiser/Auditor- 402-727-3911; Elections- 402-727-2767; Vital Records- 402-471-2871; UCC Searches-County Level- 402-727-2767. **Property tax/Assessor**- 435 North Park, 2nd Fl, Fremont, NE 68025; 402-727-3911.

Dodge County Register of Deeds

County Register of Deeds, 435 North Park, Rm 201, Fremont, NE 68025. 402-727-2735; fax-402-727-2734; hours: 8:30AM-4:30PM. www.registerofdeeds.com
Separate indices to search include alpha grantor/grantee and by legal description. Only the public may search. Office will only lookup specific files. Copy fee $1.00 per page. Cert fee- $1.50 per cert plus copy fee. **Payee**- Dodge County Register of Deeds. **Online access to Real Estate records:** Access to Register of Deeds mortgages database is at the website. Registration is required. The site is under development. **Other phones:** Treasurer- 402-727-2750. **Property tax/Assessor**- 402-727-3911.

Douglas County Clerk

County Clerk, 1819 Farnam St.; Rm H09, Omaha, NE 68183-0008. 402-444-7159; fax-402-444-6456; http://co.douglas.ne.us/explorer.shtml
Office will perform a UCC search but public must search other records themselves. See Register of Deeds for real estate records. UCC search per debtor name- $4.50. **Other phones:** Treasurer- 402-444-7103; Elections- 402-444-8683. **Property tax/Assessor**- 402-444-7060.

Douglas County Register of Deeds

Register of Deeds, 1819 Farnam; Rm H09, Omaha, NE 68183. 402-444-7194; fax-402-444-6693; hours: 8AM-4:30PM. www.co.douglas.ne.us
Only the public may search. Copy fee $.75 per page. Cert fee- $1.50 per page. **Payee**- Register of Deeds. **Online access to Property, Assessor, Marriage records:** Assessor to the county assessor property valuation lookup is free at www.dcassessor.org/valuation.html. Search the clerk/comptroller marriage database free at www.co.douglas.ne.us/dept/Clerk/marriagelicense.htm. **Other phones:** Treasurer- 402-444-7272; Elections- 402-444-7200. **Property tax/Assessor**- 402-444-7060.

Dundy County

County Clerk, PO Box 506, Benkelman, NE 69021-0506. 308-423-2058, R/E recording phone-402-471-4429 Fax# 402-471-4429; hours: 8AM-4PM.
Separate indices to search include deeds, mortgages, misc. Will not search real estate records. Will not search UCC records. Copy fee $1.00 per page. Cert fee- $1.50 per cert plus copy fee. **Payee**- Dundy County Clerk. **Other phones:** Treasurer- 308-423-2346; Vital Records- 402-471-2871. **Property tax/Assessor**- 308-423-2821.

Fillmore County

Register of Deeds, PO Box 307, Geneva, NE 68361-0307. 402-759-4931; fax-402-759-4307; 8AM-5PM. www.fillmorecounty.org/government/gov1.html
The recording officers are County Clerk (Federal and state tax liens) and Register of Deeds (real estate and most tax liens). All records in one index. Office will perform a UCC search but public must search other records themselves. Search fee $4.50. Copy fee $1.00 per page. Cert fee- $1.50 per page. **Payee**- Fillmore County Clerk. **Other phones:** Treasurer- 402-759-3812; Elections- 402-759-4931. **Property tax/Assessor**- 402-759-3613.

Franklin County

County Clerk, PO Box 146, Franklin, NE 68939. 308-425-6202; fax-308-425-6093; hours: 8:30AM-4:30PM.
Only the public may search. Copy fee $1.00 per page. Cert fee- $1.50 per page (Real Estate Records). **Payee**- Franklin County Clerk. **Other phones:** Treasurer- 308-425-6265; Elections- 308-425-6202. **Property tax/Assessor**- 308-425-6229.

Frontier County

County Clerk, PO Box 40, Stockville, NE 69042-0040. 308-367-8641; fax-308-367-8730; hours: 8:30AM-N, 1-5PM. www.co.frontier.ne.us
All records in one index. Records index not computerized. Office personnel or visitors may perform searches. Real estate owner, mortgage, and property transfer searches available. Will search UCC records, tax liens not included in UCC search. UCC search per debtor name- $4.50. Separate federal/state combined tax lien search- $3.00 per debtor. Copy fee $1.00 per page. Cert fee-included in copy fee. **Payee**- Frontier County Register of Deeds. **Other phones:** Treasurer- 308-367-8631; Appraiser/Auditor- 308-367-8637; Elections- 308-367-8641. **Property tax/Assessor**- PO Box 9, Stockville, NE 69042; 308-367-8637.

Furnas County

County Clerk, PO Box 387, Beaver City, NE 68926. 308-268-4145; fax-308-268-3205; hours: 8AM-4PM.
All records in one index. Record index not computerized. Only the public may search. Copy fee $.25 per page. Cert fee- $1.50 per cert plus copy fee. **Payee**- Furnas County Clerk. **Other phones:** Treasurer- 308-268-2195. **Property tax/Assessor**- PO Box 368, Beaver City, NE 68926; 308-268-3145.

Gage County Clerk

County Clerk, PO Box 429, Beatrice, NE 68310-0429. 402-223-1300, R/E recording phone-402-223-1361; fax-402-223-1371; hours: 8AM-5PM. www.co.gage.ne.us/clerk.html
Only the public may search on computer. See Register of Deeds for real estate records. Will search UCC records. UCC search per debtor name- $4.50. **Online access to Property, Assessor records:** Access to property information via the county CIS service is free at http://gage.gisworkshop.com. **Other phones:** Treasurer- 402-223-1315; Appraiser/Auditor- 402-223-1308; Elections- 402-223-1300; Vital Records- 402-223-1300. **Property tax/Assessor**- 612 Grant St, Beatrice, NE 68310; 402-223-1308.

Gage County Register of Deeds

County Register of Deeds, PO Box 337, Beatrice, NE 68310. 402-223-1361; hours: 8AM-4:30PM.
All records in one index. Records indexed on a public use terminal back to 1997. Office will perform a UCC search but public must search other records themselves. UCC search per debtor name- $4.50. Copy fee $.50 per page plus $1.00 for postage & handling when mailed. Cert fee- $1.50 per page plus copy fee. **Payee**- Gage County Register of Deeds. **Online access to Property, Treasurer records:** Access real estate or personal property data free at

www.nebraskataxesonline.us/taxcollpage1.aspx?county=Gage. **Other phones:** Treasurer- 402-223-1315. **Property tax/Assessor**- 402-223-1308.

Garden County

County Clerk, PO Box 486, Oshkosh, NE 69154. 308-772-3924; fax-308-772-0124; hours: 8AM-4PM.
Separate indices to search include deeds, mortgages, misc, or legal descriptions. Record index not computerized. Office will perform a UCC search but public must search other records themselves. UCC search per debtor name- $4.50. Copy fee $.50 per page. Cert fee- $1.50 per page includes copy fee. **Payee**- County Clerk. **Other phones:** Treasurer- 308-772-3622; Elections- 308-772-3924; Vital Records- 402-471-2871. **Property tax/Assessor**- 308-772-4464.

Garfield County

County Clerk, Box 218, Burwell, NE 68823. 308-346-4161; hours: 9AM-N, 1-5PM.
Office will perform a UCC search but public must search other records themselves. Search fee $4.50 per name. Copy fee $1.00 per page. Tax lien copy- $.25. Cert fee- $1.50 per cert. **Payee**- Garfield County Clerk. **Other phones:** Treasurer- 308-346-4125. **Property tax/Assessor**- 308-346-4045.

Gosper County

County Clerk, PO Box 136, Elwood, NE 68937-0136. 308-785-2611; fax-308-785-2300; hours: 8:30AM-4:30PM. www.co.gosper.ne.us
Separate indices to search include deeds, mortgages & miscellaneous. Will not search real estate records. Will search UCC records; search includes tax liens if requested. UCC search per debtor name- $4.50. Tax lien search fee- $.50 per page. Separate state tax lien search- $.50 per page. Separate federal/state combined tax lien search- $3.00 per debtor. Copy fee $.25 per 8 1/2 x 11 page, $.50 per 8 1/2 x 15 page. Cert fee- $10.00 per doc plus copy fee. **Payee**- Gosper County Clerk. **Other phones:** Treasurer- 308-785-2450; Appraiser/Auditor- 308-785-2250; Elections- 308-785-2611; Vital Records- 308-785-2611. **Property tax/Assessor**- 308-785-2250.

Grant County

County Clerk, PO Box 139, Hyannis, NE 69350-0139. 308-458-2488; fax-308-458-2780; hours: 8AM-4PM.
All records in one index. Office personnel or visitors may perform searches. Tax lien search fee- $1.00 per debtor. Federal/state combined tax lien search- $1.50 per debtor. Copy fee $.50 per page. Cert fee- $1.50 per instrument. **Payee**- Grant County Clerk. **Other phones:** Treasurer- 308-458-2422; Appraiser/Auditor- 308-762-2474; Elections- 308-458-2488; Marriages- 308-458-2488. **Property tax/Assessor**- PO Box 139, Hyannis, NE 69350-0139; 308-458-2488.

Greeley County

County Clerk, PO Box 287, Greeley, NE 68842. 308-428-3625; fax-308-428-3022;
Office will perform a UCC search but public must search other records themselves. UCC search per debtor name- $4.50. **Online access to Property, Treasurer records:** Access real estate or personal property data free at www.nebraskataxesonline.us/taxcollpage1.aspx?county=Greeley. **Other phones:** Treasurer- 308-428-3535. **Property tax/Assessor**- 308-428-5310.

Hall County Clerk

County Clerk, 121 S. Pine, Grand Island, NE 68801. 308-385-5080, R/E recording phone-308-385-5040, UCC recording phone-Sec of State; fax-308-385-5084; hours: 8:30AM-5PM. www.hcgi.org
All records in one index. Record index not computerized. Office will perform a UCC search but public must search other records themselves. Search fee $4.50. Copy fee $3.50 per name. Cert fee- $1.50 per page plus copy fee. **Other phones:**

Treasurer- 308-385-5025; Appraiser/Auditor- 308-385-5050; Elections- 308-385-5085; Vital Records- 402-471-2871. **Property tax/Assessor**- same address as above. 308-385-5050.

Hall County Register of Deeds

County Register of Deeds, PO Box 1692, Grand Island, NE 68802-1692. 308-385-5040; fax-308-385-5107; hours: 8:30AM-5PM. www.hcgi.org
All records in one index. Records indexed on a public use terminal back to 1989. Only the public may search. Copy fee $1.00 per page. Cert fee-$1.50 per page plus copy fee. Payee- Hall County Register of Deeds. **Online access to Real Estate, Grantor/Grantee, Deed, Lien, Judgment records:** Access to the county Register of Deeds Document Search is free at http://mapsifter.ci.grand-island.ne.us/mapsifter/advancedlookupform.asp. **Other phones:** Treasurer- 308-385-5025. **Property tax/Assessor**- 308-385-5050.

Hamilton County

County Clerk, Register of Deeds, 1111 13th St, #1; Courthouse, Aurora, NE 68818-2017. 402-694-3443, UCC recording phone-402-471-2554; fax-402-694-2396; hours: 8AM-5PM. www.co.hamilton.ne.us
Separate indices to search include federal and state tax liens. Records indexed on computer back to July, 2004. Office will perform a UCC search but public must search other records themselves. UCC search per debtor name- $4.50. Copy fee $.25 per page. Cert fee- $1.50 plus $1.50 per page includes copy fee. Payee- Hamilton Co. Clerk. **Other phones:** Treasurer- 402-694-2291; Elections- 402-694-3443; Vital Records- 402-471-2871. **Property tax/Assessor**- 402-694-2757.

Harlan County

County Clerk, PO Box 698, Alma, NE 68920-0698. 308-928-2173; fax-308-928-2079; hours: 8:30AM-4:30PM.
Separate indices to search include numerical index (legal description), general index (name). Record index not computerized. Only the public may search. Copy fee $.50, if real estate $.25 per page. Cert fee- $1.00 1st pg; $.25 each add'l page plus copy fee. Payee- Harlan County Clerk. **Other phones:** Treasurer- 308-928-2171. **Property tax/Assessor**- PO Box 379, Alma, NE 68920; 308-928-2177.

Hayes County

County Clerk, PO Box 370, Hayes Center, NE 69032-0370. 308-286-3413; fax-308-286-3208; hours: 8AM-4PM.
Separate indices to search include real estate, mortgage, liens, deeds, misc. Record index not computerized. Office personnel or visitors may perform searches. Search fee $4.50 per name. Copy fee $1.00 per page. Cert fee- $4.00 per cert includes copy fee. Payee- Hayes County Clerk. **Other phones:** Treasurer- 308-286-3214. **Property tax/Assessor**- same address as above. 308-286-3399.

Hitchcock County

County Clerk, PO Box 248, Trenton, NE 69044. 308-334-5646; fax-308-334-5398; hours: 8:30AM-4PM. www.co.hitchcock.ne.us
Separate indices to search include Deeds, mtg, misc. Records indexed on computer. Office will perform a UCC search but public must search other records themselves. Search fee $4.50. Copy fee $.50 per page. Cert fee- $1.50 per page. Payee-Hitchcock County Clerk. **Other phones:** Treasurer-308-334-5544; Appraiser/Auditor- 308-334-5219; Elections- 308-334-5646; Vital Records- 308-334-5646- Marriage Only. **Property tax/Assessor**- PO Box 446, Trenton, NE 69044; 308-334-5219.

Holt County

County Clerk, PO Box 329, O'Neill, NE 68763-0329. 402-336-2250; fax-402-336-1762; hours: 8-4:30PM.

Separate indices to search include section-township-range and cities and villages. Only the public may search. Copy fee $.25 per page. Cert fee- $1.50 per doc plus copy fee. Payee- Register of Deeds. **Other phones:** Treasurer- 402-336-1291. **Property tax/Assessor**- 402-336-1624.

Hooker County

County Clerk, PO Box 184, Mullen, NE 69152. 308-546-2244; fax-308-546-2490; hours: 8:30AM-N, 1-4:30PM.
Separate indices to search include misc, deed, mtg. Record index not computerized. Only the public may search. Copy fee $1.00 per page. Cert fee-$10.00 per page plus copy fee. Payee- Hooker County Clerk. **Other phones:** Treasurer- 308-546-2245; Elections- 308-546-2244. **Property tax/Assessor**- same address as above. 308-546-2244.

Howard County

County Clerk, PO Box 25, St. Paul, NE 68873. 308-754-4343; fax-308-754-4125; hours: 8AM-5PM.
All records in one index. Record index not computerized. Only the public may search. Copy fee $.25 per page. Cert fee- $5.00 per cert includes copy fee. Payee- Howard County Clerk. **Other phones:** Treasurer- 308-754-4852; Elections- 308-754-4343. **Property tax/Assessor**- 308-754-4261.

Jefferson County

County Clerk, 411 4th St; Courthouse, Fairbury, NE 68352-1619. 402-729-5201, UCC recording phone-402-471-2554; fax-402-729-2016; hours: 9AM-N, 1-5PM. www.co.jefferson.ne.us/clerk.html
The recording officers are County Clerk (some state tax liens) and Register of Deeds (real estate and most tax liens). Separate indices to search include deeds, mortgage, misc, also numerical by description. Office will do name lookups, but cannot guarantee searches. R/E record copy- $.50 per page. Cert fee- $1.50 per page plus copy fee. Payee- County Register of Deeds. **Other phones:** Treasurer- 402-729-2411; Elections- 402-729-2323; Vital Records-402-471-2872. **Property tax/Assessor**- same address as above. 402-729-3103.

Johnson County

County Clerk, PO Box 416, Tecumseh, NE 68450. 402-335-6300; fax-402-335-6311; hours: 8AM-12:30PM, 1-4:30PM.
All records in one index. Only the public may search. Copy fee $1.00 per page. Cert fee- $1.50 per page includes copy fee. Payee- Johnson County Clerk. **Other phones:** Treasurer- 402-335-6310; Elections- 402-335-6300. **Property tax/Assessor**- PO Box 356, Tecumseh, NE 68450; 402-335-6303.

Kearney County

County Clerk, PO Box 339, Minden, NE 68959-0339. 308-832-2723; fax-308-832-2729; hours: 8:30AM-5PM.
All records in one index. Record index not computerized. Only the public may search. Copy fee $.50 per page. Cert fee- $3.00 per cert plus copy fee. Payee- Kearney County Clerk. **Other phones:** Treasurer- 308-832-2730. **Property tax/Assessor**- same address as above. 308-832-2625.

Keith County

County Clerk, PO Box 149, Ogallala, NE 69153. 308-284-4726; fax-308-284-6277;
Only the public may search. Office will do a federal tax lien search-no charge. Separate state tax lien-no charge. Tax lien copy- $.50 per page. Cert fee- $1.50 per page. Payee- Keith County Clerk. **Online access to Property, Treasurer records:** Access real estate or personal property data free at www.nebraskataxesonline.us/taxcollpage1.aspx?c

ounty=Keith. **Other phones:** Treasurer- 308-284-3231. **Property tax/Assessor**- 308-284-8040.

Keya Paha County

County Clerk, PO Box 349, Springview, NE 68778. 402-497-3791; fax-402-497-3799; hours: 8AM-N,1-5PM. www.co.keya-paha.ne.us/
Separate indices to search include deeds, mortgages, miscellaneous, District Court index. Office personnel or visitors may perform searches. Search fee $4.00 per name. Copy fee $4.00. R/E or tax lien copy- $.25 per page. Cert fee- $4.00 per cert plus copy fee. Payee- Keya Paha County Clerk. **Other phones:** Treasurer- 402-497-3891; Elections- 402-497-3791. **Property tax/Assessor**-same address as above. 402-497-3791.

Kimball County

County Clerk, 114 E. Third St, Kimball, NE 69145-1296. 308-235-2241; fax-308-235-3654; hours: 8AM-5PM M-Th, 8AM-4PM F. www.co.kimball.ne.us
Separate indices to search include numerical and alphabetical. Record index not computerized. Office will perform a UCC search but public must search other records themselves. Search fee $4.50. Copy fee $1.00 per page. Cert fee- $1.50 per page plus copy fee. Payee- Kimball County Clerk. **Other phones:** Treasurer- 308-235-2242; Elections-308-235-2241; Vital Records- 402-471-2871. **Property tax/Assessor**- same address as above. 308-235-2362.

Knox County Clerk

County Clerk, PO Box 166, Center, NE 68724-0166. 402-288-5604, R/E recording phone-402-288-5613, UCC recording phone-402-288-5604; fax-402-288-5605; hours: 8:30AM-4:30PM. www.co.knox.ne.us
All records in one index. Will not search real estate records. Will search UCC records, but not tax liens. UCC search per debtor name- $4.50. Copy fee $1.00 per page. Cert fee- $.50 per page plus copy fee. Payee- Knox County Register of Deeds. **Other phones:** Treasurer- 402-288-5615; Appraiser/Auditor-402-288-5601; Elections- 402-288-5604. **Property tax/Assessor**- PO Box 87, Center, NE 68724-0087; 402-288-5601.

Lancaster County Clerk

County Clerk, 555 S. 10th St; County-City Bldg, Lincoln, NE 68508-2867. 402-441-7482, R/E recording phone-402-441-7577; fax-402-441-8728; hours: 7:30AM-4:30PM. http://interlink.ci.lincoln.ne.us
Office will perform a UCC search but public must search other records themselves. See Register of Deeds for real estate records. Cert fee- $1.50 per cert plus copy fee. Payee- Lancaster County Clerk. **Online access to Assessor, Recording, Grantor/Grantee, Deed, Judgment, Treasurer, Marriage, Accident, records:** Records on the county Assessor Property Information are free at www.dcassessor.org/valuation.html. Also, search the register of deeds Grantor/Grantee index for free at www.ci.lincoln.ne.us/cnty/deeds/deeds.htm. Search City of Lincoln accident reports at www.ci.lincoln.ne.us/city/police/stats/acc.htm. Also, search treasurer' property info at www.ci.lincoln.ne.us/cnty/treas/property.htm. Search marriages at www.ci.lincoln.ne.us/cnty/clerk/marrsrch.htm. **Other phones:** Treasurer- 402-441-7425; Appraiser/Auditor- 402-441-7463; Elections- 402-441-7311; Vital Records- 402-471-2872. **Property tax/Assessor**- 402-441-7463.

Lancaster County Register of Deeds

Register of Deeds, 555 S. 10th St, Lincoln, NE 68508. 402-441-7577; fax-402-441-7012; hours: 7:30AM-4:30PM. www.mynevadacounty.com/recorder
All records in one index. Records indexed on a public use terminal back to 1867. Only the public may search. Cert fee- $1.50 per page. **Other phones:** Treasurer- 402-441-7425; Vital Records- 402-

441-2871. **Property tax/Assessor**- same address as above. 402-441-7643.

Lincoln County Clerk

County Clerk, 301 N. Jeffers, Rm 101, North Platte, NE 69101. 308-534-4350; fax-308-535-3522; hours: 9AM-5PM. www.co.lincoln.ne.us

Separate indices to search include marriages, corps, misc, election, by department. Office personnel or visitors may perform searches. See Register of Deeds for real estate records. Will search UCC records. UCC search includes state tax liens. UCC search per debtor name- $4.50 (access via state computer). Separate federal/state combined tax lien search- $3.50 per debtor (access via state computer). Copy fee $.50 per page. Cert fee- $5.00 per page plus copy fee. Payee- Lincoln County Clerk. **Other phones:** Treasurer- 308-534-4350; Elections- 308-534-4350. **Property tax/Assessor**- 301 N. Jeffers, Rm 110A, North Platte, NE 69101; 308-534-4350.

Lincoln County Register of Deeds

County Clerk, 301 N. Jeffers, Rm 103, North Platte, NE 69101-3931. 308-534-4350, R/E recording phone-308-534-4350 X 192; fax-308-534-5287; hours: 9AM-5PM.

Separate indices to search include Grantor/Grantee, Deeds, Mtgs, Misc, numerical index. Records indexed on a public use terminal back to 2000. Only the public may search. Copy fee $.50 per page. Cert fee- $1.50 per page. Payee-Lincoln County Register of Deeds. **Online access to Property, Treasurer records:** Access real estate or personal property data free at www.nebraskataxesonline.us/taxcollpage1.aspx?county=Lincoln. **Other phones:** Treasurer- 308-534-4350. **Property tax/Assessor**- 308-534-4350.

Logan County

County Clerk, PO Box 8, Stapleton, NE 69163. 308-636-2311; hours: 8:30AM-4:30PM M,T,W,Th; 8:30AM-4PM F.

Office personnel or visitors may perform searches. Search fee $4.50 per name. Will not search real estate records. Copy fee $1.00 per page. Cert fee- $1.50 per cert plus copy fee. Payee- Logan County Clerk. **Other phones:** Treasurer- 308-636-2441. **Property tax/Assessor**- 308-636-2311.

Loup County

County Clerk, PO Box 187, Taylor, NE 68879-0187. 308-942-3135; fax-308-942-6015; hours: 8:30AM-N, 1-5PM M,T,W,Th; 8:30AM-N F.

Office personnel or visitors may perform searches. Search fee $3.00 per name. Will not search real estate records. UCC search per debtor name- $4.50. Copy fee $.50 per page. Cert fee- $1.00 per page. Payee-Loup County Clerk. **Other phones:** Treasurer- 308-942-3115. **Property tax/Assessor**- 308-942-3135.

Madison County Clerk

County Clerk, PO Box 290, Madison, NE 68748-0290. 402-454-3311 x137, R/E recording phone-402-454-3311 x124, UCC recording phone-402-454-3311 x136; fax-402-454-6682; hours: 8:30AM-5PM. http://co.madison.ne.us/clerk.htm

All records in one index. Records indexed on computer. See Register of Deeds for real estate records. Will search UCC records via the SOS office. UCC search per debtor name- $4.50. Copy fee $.25 per page. **Other phones:** Treasurer- 402-454-3311 x133; Appraiser/Auditor- 402-454-3311; Elections- 402-454-3311 x136; Vital Records- 402-471-2871. **Property tax/Assessor**- PO Box 250, Madison, NE 68748-0250; 402-454-3311 x178.

Madison County Register of Deeds

County Register of Deeds, PO Box 229, Madison, NE 68748. 402-454-3311, R/E recording phone-402-454-3311 x124; fax-402-454-6682; hours: 8:30AM-5PM.

Records indexed on computer back to April 1, 2004. Office will perform a UCC search but public must search other records themselves. UCC search per debtor name- $4.50. Copy fee $1.00 per page. R/E record copy- $.50 per page. Cert fee- $1.50 per page includes copy fee. Payee- Madison County Register of Deeds. **Other phones:** Treasurer-402-454-3311 x133; Elections- 402-454-3311 x136; Vital Records- 402-471-2871. **Property tax/Assessor**-402-454-3311 x178.

McPherson County

County Clerk, PO Box 122, Tryon, NE 69167-0122. 308-587-2363, R/E recording phone-308-587-2242; fax-308-587-2363; hours: 8:30AM-4:30PM.

Separate indices to search include mortgages, deeds or misc. Office will perform a UCC search but public must search other records themselves. UCC search per debtor name- $4.50. Copy fee $.50 per page. Cert fee- $1.50 per page plus copy fee. Payee- McPherson County Clerk. **Other phones:** Treasurer- 308-587-2442. **Property tax/Assessor**- same address as above. 308-587-2363.

Merrick County

County Clerk, PO Box 27, Central City, NE 68826. 308-946-2881, UCC recording phone-The Secretary of State; fax-308-946-2332; hours: 8AM-5PM.

Separate indices to search include deeds, mortgages, miscellaneous, liens (x3), associations. Record index not computerized. Office will perform a pre-1999 UCC search but public must search other records themselves. UCC search per debtor name- $4.50 per page (includes copy fee). Separate federal/state combined tax lien search- $3.00 per debtor. Copy fee $1.00 per page. Cert fee- $5.00 per cert includes copy fee. Payee-Merrick County Clerk. **Other phones:** Treasurer- 308-946-2171; Appraiser/Auditor- Do not have on staff; call Assessor's Office; Elections- 308-946-2881; Vital Records- 402-471-2871. **Property tax/Assessor**-same address as above. 308-946-2443.

Morrill County

County Clerk, PO Box 610, Bridgeport, NE 69336. 308-262-0860; fax-308-262-1469; hours: 8AM-4:30PM.

Only the public may search. Copy fee $.50 per page. Cert fee- $1.50per page. Payee- Morrill County Clerk. **Other phones:** Treasurer- 308-262-1177; Elections- 308-262-0860. **Property tax/Assessor**- 308-262-1534.

Nance County

County Clerk, PO Box 338, Fullerton, NE 68638. 308-536-2331; fax-308-536-2742;

Office personnel or visitors may perform searches. Search fee $5.00 per name. Will not search real estate records. Copy fee $1.00 per page. Cert fee- $1.50 per page. Payee- County Clerk. **Other phones:** Treasurer- 308-536-2165; Elections- 308-536-2331. **Property tax/Assessor**- 308-536-2653.

Nemaha County

County Clerk, 1824 N St; Courthouse, Auburn, NE 68305-2399. 402-274-4213; fax-402-274-4389; hours: 8AM-5PM.

Separate indices to search. Records indexed on computer. Office will perform a UCC or tax lien search but public must search other records themselves. UCC search per debtor name- $4.50. Tax lien search fee- $3.50 per debtor. Copy fee $.25 per page. UCC copy $1.00 per page. Cert fee- $1.50 per cert plus copy fee. Payee- Nemaha County Clerk. **Other phones:** Treasurer- 402-274-3319. **Property tax/Assessor**- 402-274-3820.

Nuckolls County

County Clerk, PO Box 366, Nelson, NE 68961-0366. 402-225-4361; fax-402-225-4301; hours: 8:30AM-4:30PM. www.nuckollscounty.ne.gov

Separate indices to search include deed, mortgage, miscellaneous, liens, veteran records. Office personnel or visitors may perform searches. Will search real estate records as time allows. UCC search per debtor name- $4.50 per written request. Copy fee $1.00 per page. R/E record copy- $.25 per page. If mailed $.50 for 1st page & $.25 each add'l page. Tax lien copy- $.25 to $1.00 per size. Cert fee- $1.50 per page plus copy fee. Payee- Nuckolls County Clerk. **Other phones:** Treasurer- 402-225-4351; Elections- 402-225-4361; Vital Records- 402-225-4361. **Property tax/Assessor**- PO Box 371, Nelson, NE 68961-0371; 402-225-2401.

Otoe County Clerk

Register of Deeds, 1021 Central Ave, Rm 203, Nebraska City, NE 68410-0249. 402-873-9530, UCC recording phone-402-873-9505; fax-402-873-9507; hours: 8AM-4:30PM. www.co.otoe.ne.us/deeds.html

Records indexed on computer. See Register of Deeds for real estate records. Will not search UCC records or tax liens. Copy fee $.50 per page. Cert fee- $1.50 per page. Payee- Register of Deeds. **Other phones:** Treasurer- 402-873-9510; Appraiser/Auditor- 402-873-9522; Elections- 402-873-9505; Vital Records- 402-471-2872. **Property tax/Assessor**- 402-873-9520.

Otoe County Register of Deeds

County Register of Deeds, 1021 Central Ave.; Rm 203, Nebraska City, NE 68410. 402-873-9530; fax-402-873-9507; hours: 8AM-4:30PM.

Separate indices to search include records prior to 5/2002 in index books, deed books, and mortgage books. Records indexed on a public use terminal back to 5/2002. Only the public may search. Copy fee $.50 per page. Cert fee- $1.50 per page plus copy fee. Payee- Otoe County Register of Deeds. **Other phones:** Treasurer- 402-873-9510. **Property tax/Assessor**- 402-873-9520.

Pawnee County

County Clerk, PO Box 431, Pawnee City, NE 68420. 402-852-2962; fax-402-852-2963; hours: 8AM-4PM.

Separate indices to search include Alphabetical and Numerical. Only the public may search. Copy fee $1.00 per page. Cert fee- $5.00 per cert plus copy fee. Payee- Pawnee County Clerk. **Other phones:** Treasurer- 402-852-2380. **Property tax/Assessor**- 402-852-2292.

Perkins County

County Clerk, PO Box 156, Grant, NE 69140-0156. 308-352-4643; fax-308-352-2455; hours: 8AM-4PM.

All records in one index. Record index not computerized. Only the public may search. Office will search if you provide case number. Copy fee $.50 per page. Cert fee- $1.75 per cert plus copy fee. Payee- Perkins County Clerk. **Other phones:** Treasurer- 308-352-4542; Elections- 308-352-4643. **Property tax/Assessor**- 308-352-4938.

Phelps County

County Clerk, PO Box 404, Holdrege, NE 68949-0404. 308-995-4469; fax-308-995-4368; hours: 9AM-5PM. www.phelpsgov.org

Separate indices to search include Deeds, Mortgages, Real Estate by legal description. Records indexed on a public use terminal back to 3/7/2005. Office prefers the visitors do their own searches. Will search real estate records only from legal description. Will search UCC records, but not tax liens. UCC search per debtor name- $4.50. Copy fee $.50 per page. Cert fee- $1.50 per page includes copy fee. Payee- Phelps County Clerk. **Online access to Property, Treasurer records:** Access real estate or personal property data free at www.nebraskataxesonline.us/taxcollpage1.aspx?county=Phelps. **Other phones:** Treasurer- 308-995-6115; Elections- 308-995-4469. **Property tax/Assessor**- 715 Fifth Ave, Holdrege, NE 68949; 308-995-4061.

Pierce County

County Clerk, 111 W. Court; Courthouse - Rm 1, Pierce, NE 68767-1224. 402-329-4225; fax-402-329-6439; 8:30AM-4:30PM. www.co.pierce.ne.us
Office personnel or visitors may perform searches. Search fee $5.00 per name. Will not search real estate records. Copy fee $1.00 per page. Cert fee- $1.50 per cert plus copy fee. Payee- Pierce County Clerk. **Other phones:** Treasurer- 402-329-6335; Elections- 402-329-4225. **Property tax/Assessor-** 402-329-4215.

Platte County Clerk

County Clerk, 2610 14th St, Columbus, NE 68601. 402-563-4904; R/E recording phone-402-563-4911, UCC recording phone-402-563-4904; fax-402-564-4164; hours: 8AM-5PM. www.plattecounty.net
Records indexed on a public use terminal back to 1988. See Register of Deeds for real estate records. Will not search UCC records or tax liens. Copy fee $.50 per page. Cert fee- $4.50 per doc plus copy fee. **Online access to Property, Assessor, Warrant records:** Access to county property tax data free at www.nebraskataxesonline.us/. Access to the sheriff warrant list is free at www.megavision.net/pcsher/Warrant%20List.htm. **Other phones:** Treasurer- 402-563-4913; Elections- 402-563-4908. **Property tax/Assessor-** 402-563-4902.

Platte County Register of Deeds

County Register of Deeds, 2610 14th St, Columbus, NE 68601. 402-563-4911; hours: 8AM-5PM.
Separate indices to search include deeds, mtgs, UCCs, state/federal liens. Records indexed on computer back to 2/2005. Only the public may search. Copy fee $1.00 per page. Cert fee- $1.50 per page. Payee- Platte County Register of Deeds. **Online access to Property, Treasurer records:** Access real estate or personal property data free at www.nebraskataxesonline.us/taxcollpage1.aspx?county=Platte. **Other phones:** Treasurer- 402-563-4913. **Property tax/Assessor-** 402-563-4902.

Polk County

County Clerk, PO Box 276, Osceola, NE 68651-0276. 402-747-5431; fax-402-747-2656; hours: 8AM-5PM.
Separate indices to search include numerical (legal description) and general (alphabetical). Record index not computerized. Only the public may search. Separate federal/state combined tax lien search- $3.00 per debtor. Copy fee $.50 per page. Cert fee- $1.50 per page. Payee- Polk County Clerk. **Other phones:** Treasurer- 402-747-5441; Elections- 402-747-5431; Vital Records- 402-471-2871. **Property tax/Assessor-** PO Box 375, Osceola, NE 68651; 402-747-4491.

Red Willow County

County Clerk, 502 Norris Ave, McCook, NE 69001. 308-345-1552, UCC recording phone-(State Office 402-471-4080); fax-308-345-4460; hours: 8AM-4PM. www.co.red-willow.ne.us/clerk.html
Separate indices to search include legal description and grantor/grantee. Office will perform a UCC search but public must search other records themselves. General search fee $1.50 per debtor. UCC search per debtor name- $4.50. Copy fee $1.00 per page. Cert fee- $1.50 per page includes copy fee. Payee- Red Willow County Clerk. **Other phones:** Treasurer- 308-345-6515; Appraiser/Auditor- 785-475-2072; Elections- 308-345-1552; Vital Records- State Office 402-471-2306). **Property tax/Assessor-** same address as above. 308-345-4388.

Richardson County

County Clerk, 1700 Stone St.; Courthouse, Falls City, NE 68355. 402-245-2911; fax-402-245-2946; hours: 8:30-5PM. www.co.richardson.ne.us/clerk.html
No tax liens filed here. Record index not computerized. Office will perform a UCC and Tax lien search but public must search other records themselves. Search fee $4.50. Copy fee $.50 per page. Cert fee- $5.00 per page plus copy fee. Payee- Richardson County Clerk. **Other phones:** Treasurer- 402-245-3511; Elections- 402-245-2911; Vital Records- 402-245-2535. **Property tax/Assessor-** 402-245-4012.

Rock County

County Clerk, PO Box 367, Bassett, NE 68714. 402-684-3933; fax-402-684-2741; hours: 9AM-N, 1-5PM.
Separate indices to search include deeds, mortgages, miscellaneous. Record index not computerized. Office personnel or visitors may perform searches. General search fee- charge by page found. UCC search per debtor name- $4.50. Federal/state combined tax lien search- $3.00 per debtor. Copy fee $1.00 per page. Cert fee- $4.50 per cert includes copy fee. Payee- Rock County Clerk. **Other phones:** Treasurer- 402-684-3515. **Property tax/Assessor-** PO Box 446, Bassett, NE 68714; 402-684-3831.

Saline County

Real Estate-County Clerk, PO Box 865, Wilber, NE 68465. 402-821-2374, UCC recording phone-402-471-4080 (filed at State level); fax-402-821-3381; hours: 8AM-5PM. www.nol.org/saline
Office will perform a UCC search but public must search other records themselves. UCC search per debtor name- $4.50. Copy fee $1.00 per page. Cert fee- $2.00 per cert. Payee- Saline County Clerk. **Other phones:** Treasurer- 402-821-2375; Elections- 402-821-2374; Vital Records- 402-471-2872 (State Bureau of Vital Statistics). **Property tax/Assessor-** 402-821-2588.

Sarpy County Clerk

County Clerk, 1210 Golden Gate Dr; #1118, Papillion, NE 68046-2895. 402-593-2114; fax-402-593-4360; hours: 8AM-4:45PM M,T,Th,F; 8AM-6PM W. www.sarpy.com
Only the public may search. **Online access to Real Estate records:** Records on the county Property Lookup database are free at www.sarpy.com/assessor/property-search.htm. **Property tax/Assessor-** 402-593-2121.

Sarpy County Register of Deeds

Register of Deeds, 1210 Golden Gate Drive #1118, Papillion, NE 68046. 402-593-2107; fax-402-593-4360; hours: 8AM-5PM. www.sarpy.com
Office personnel or visitors may perform searches. Search fee $4.50 per name. Will not search real estate records. Copy fee $1.00 per page. Tax lien copy- $.50 per page. Cert fee- $1.50 per cert. Payee- Sarpy County Clerk. **Other phones:** Treasurer- 402-436-6621. **Property tax/Assessor-** 402-593-2121.

Saunders County Clerk

County Clerk, PO Box 61, Wahoo, NE 68066-0187. 402-443-8101; fax-402-443-5010; hours: 8AM-5PM.
Office personnel or visitors may perform searches. Search fee $4.50 per name. See Register of Deeds for real estate records. Copy fee $1.00 per page. Cert fee- $5.00 per cert. Payee- Saunders County Clerk. **Property tax/Assessor-** 402-443-5700.

Saunders County Register of Deeds

Register of Deeds, PO Box 184, Wahoo, NE 68066. 402-443-8111; fax-402-443-5010; hours: 8AM-5PM.
All records in one index. Record index not computerized. Only the public may search. Copy fee $1.00 per page. Cert fee- $1.50 per page includes copy fee. Payee- Register of Deeds. **Other phones:** Treasurer- 402-443-8129; Appraiser/Auditor- 402-443-5702; Elections- 402-443-8100. **Property tax/Assessor-** 402-443-5700.

Scotts Bluff County Clerk

Register of Deeds, 1825 10th St; Admin. Office Bldg, Gering, NE 69341. 308-436-6601; fax-308-436-3178; hours: 8AM-4:30PM. www.scottsbluffcounty.org/deedsonline
Records indexed on a public use terminal. Only the public may search. Copy fee $.50 per page. Cert fee- $5.00 per doc plus copy fee. Payee- Scotts Bluff County Clerk. **Property tax/Assessor-** 308-436-6627.

Scotts Bluff County Register of Deeds

County Register of Deeds, 1825 10th St; Admin. Office Bldg, Gering, NE 69341. 308-436-6607; fax-308-436-6609; 8AM-4:30PM. www.scottsbluffcounty.org
Only the public may search. Copy fee $1.00 per page. R/E or tax lien copy- $.50 per page. Cert fee- $1.50 per page. Payee- Scotts Bluff County Register of Deeds. **Online access to Property, Treasurer records:** Access real estate or personal property data free at www.nebraskataxesonline.us/taxcollpage1.aspx?county=Scotts. **Other phones:** Treasurer- 308-436-6621. **Property tax/Assessor-** 308-436-6627.

Seward County

County Clerk, PO Box 190, Seward, NE 68434-0190. 402-643-2883; fax-402-643-9243; hours: 8AM-5PM. http://connectseward.org/cs/
All records in one index. Record index not computerized. Only the public may search. Copy fee $.50 per page. Cert fee- $.50 per page plus copy fee. Payee- Seward County Clerk. **Other phones:** Treasurer- 402-643-4574; Elections- 402-643-2883; Land or Marriage records- 402-643-2883. **Property tax/Assessor-** same address as above. 402-643-3311.

Sheridan County

County Clerk, PO Box 39, Rushville, NE 69360. 308-327-5650; fax-308-327-5624; hours: 8:30AM-4:30PM.
Separate indices to search include general index (alpha) and numeric by legal description. Will not search real estate records. Will search UCC records; search includes tax liens if requested. UCC search per debtor name- $4.50. Separate federal/state combined tax lien search- $3.00 per debtor. Copy fee $1.00 per page. Cert fee- $1.50 per cert plus copy fee. Payee- Sheridan County Clerk. **Other phones:** Treasurer- 308-327-5651. **Property tax/Assessor-** 308-327-5652.

Sherman County

County Clerk, PO Box 456, Loup City, NE 68853-0456. 308-745-1513 x100; fax-308-745-0297; hours: 8:30AM-4:30PM.
Separate indices to search include mortgages, deeds, miscellaneous. Record index not computerized. Only the public may search. UCC search per debtor name-. Copy fee $.50 per page. **Other phones:** Treasurer- 308-745-1513 x101; Elections- 308-745-1513 x100. **Property tax/Assessor-** same address as above. 308-745-0113.

Sioux County

County Clerk, PO Box 158, Harrison, NE 69346. 308-668-2443; fax-308-668-2443; hours: 8AM-4:30PM.
Record index not computerized. Only the public may search. Copy fee $.25 per page. Cert fee- $1.00 per page. Payee- Sioux County Clerk. **Other phones:** Treasurer- 308-668-2422. **Property tax/Assessor-** 308-668-2443.

Stanton County

Register of Deeds, PO Box 347, Stanton, NE 68779-0347. 402-439-2222; fax-402-439-2200; hours: 8:30AM-4:30PM. www.co.stanton.ne.us
All records in one index. Only the public may search. Copy fee $.50 per page. Cert fee- $1.50 per instrument. Payee- County Clerk. **Online access to**

Property, Treasurer records: Access real estate or personal property data free at www.nebraskataxesonline.us/taxcollpage1.aspx?county=Stanton. **Other phones:** Treasurer- 402-439-2223; Elections- 402-439-2222. **Property tax/Assessor-** 402-439-2210.

Thayer County

County Clerk, PO Box 208, Hebron, NE 68370. 402-768-6126; fax-402-768-2129; hours: 8AM-4:30PM.
All records in one index. Records indexed on computer back to 5/2001. Office personnel or visitors may perform searches. Will not search UCCs. Federal/state combined tax lien search- $4.00 per debtor. Copy fee $.25 per page. UCC copy $1.00 per page. Cert fee- $5.00 per cert plus copy fee. Payee- Thayer County Clerk. **Other phones:** Treasurer- 402-768-6227; Appraiser/Auditor- 402-768-6417; Elections- 402-768-6126. **Property tax/Assessor-** PO Box 27, Hebron, NE 68370; 402-768-6417.

Thomas County

County Clerk, PO Box 226, Thedford, NE 69166-0226. 308-645-2261; fax-308-645-2623; hours: 8AM-N, 1-4PM M-Th; 8AM-N, 1-3PM F.
Separate indices to search include Deeds, Mtgs and misc. Record index not computerized. Office will perform a UCC and Tax lien search but public must search other records themselves. Search fee $4.50. Copy fee $1.00 per page. R/E or tax lien copy- $.25 per copy. Cert fee- $5.00 per page plus copy fee. Payee- Thomas County Clerk. **Other phones:** Treasurer- 308-645-2262. **Property tax/Assessor-** 308-645-2261.

Thurston County

County Clerk, PO Box G, Pender, NE 68047. 402-385-2343; fax-402-385-3544; hours: 8:30AM-5PM.
All records in one index. By legal description. Only the public may search. Copy fee $.50 per page. Cert fee- $5.00 per page includes copy fee. Payee- County Clerk. **Other phones:** Treasurer- 402-385-3058; Elections- 402-385-2343. **Property tax/Assessor-** 402-385-2251.

Valley County

County Clerk, 125 S. 15th St, Ord, NE 68862-1499. 308-728-3700; hours: 8AM-5PM.
Separate indices to search include alpha and numerical. Record index not computerized. Only the public may search, as a general rule. General index search fee $5.00 per hour. UCC or tax lien search per debtor name- $4.50. Separate federal/state combined tax lien search- $4.50 per debtor. If you want the image-$.45 per page. Copy fee $1.00 per page; self serve- $.15 per page legal size; $.10 per page letter. Cert fee- $1.50 per cert plus copy fee. Payee- Valley County Clerk. **Other phones:** Treasurer- 308-728-5606. **Property tax/Assessor-** same address as above. 308-728-5081.

Washington County

County Clerk, PO Box 466, Blair, NE 68008. 402-426-6822; fax-402-426-6825; hours: 8AM-4:30PM.
Separate indices to search include numerical indexes by legal description. Only the public may search. Copy fee $.50 per page. Cert fee- $1.50 per page. Payee- Washington County Clerk. **Other phones:** Treasurer- 402-426-6888. **Property tax/Assessor-** 1555 Washington St, Blair, NE 68608; 402-426-6800.

Wayne County

County Clerk, PO Box 248, Wayne, NE 68787-0248. 402-375-2288; fax-402-375-4137; hours: 8:30AM-5PM. http://county.waynene.org
All records in one index. Office personnel or visitors may perform searches. Office does lookup as time permits. UCC search per debtor name- $4.50. Copy fee $1.00 per page. Cert fee- $1.50 per page plus copy fee. Payee- Wayne County Clerk. **Online access to Sheriff Sale, Warrant List records:** Search the sheriff's sales list and warrant list for free at http://county.waynene.org/County_Offices/Sheriff/ **Other phones:** Treasurer- 402-375-3885; Elections- 402-375-2288. **Property tax/Assessor-** 402-375-1979.

Webster County

County Clerk, PO Box 250; County Clerk Office, Red Cloud, NE 68970. 402-746-2716; fax-402-746-2710; hours: 8:30AM-4:30PM.
Index: Computer, Mtg, Deed, and Misc index. Records indexed on a public use terminal back to 11/2004. Only the public may search. Copy fee $1.00 per page. Cert fee- $1.50 per page plus copy fee. Payee- Webster County Clerk. **Other phones:** Treasurer- 402-746-2877; Elections- 402-746-2716; Vital Records- 402-471-2871. **Property tax/Assessor-** 402-746-2717.

Wheeler County

County Clerk, PO Box 127, Bartlett, NE 68622. 308-654-3235; fax-308-654-3470; hours: 9AM-noon, 1-5PM.
Office will perform a UCC search but public must search other records themselves. UCC search per debtor name- $4.50. Copy fee $.50 per page. Cert fee- $7.00 per doc plus copy fee. Payee- Wheeler County Clerk. **Other phones:** Treasurer- 308-654-3236. **Property tax/Assessor-** 308-654-3235.

York County

County Clerk, 510 Lincoln Ave.; Courthouse, York, NE 68467. 402-362-7759; fax-402-362-2651;
Only the public may search, but clerk will inform if UCC exists. Copy fee $1.00 per page. Cert fee- $1.50 per page. **Other phones:** Treasurer- 402-362-4949. **Property tax/Assessor-** 402-362-4926.

Nebraska County Locator

You will usually be able to find the city name in the City/County Cross Reference below. In that case, it is a simple matter to determine the county from the cross reference. However, only the official US Postal Service city names are included in this index. There are an additional 40,000 place names that people use in their addresses. Therefore, we have also included a ZIP/City Cross Reference immediately following the City/County Cross Reference.

If you know the ZIP Code but the city name does not appear in the City/County Cross Reference index, look up the ZIP Code in the ZIP/City Cross Reference, find the city name, then look up the city name in the City/County Cross Reference. For example, you want to know the county for an address of Menands, NY 12204. There is no "Menands" in the City/County Cross Reference. The ZIP/City Cross Reference shows that ZIP Codes 12201-12288 are for the city of Albany. Looking back in the City/County Cross Reference, Albany is in Albany County.

Nebraska City/County Cross Reference

ABIE Butler
ADAMS (68301) Gage(71), Lancaster(22), Otoe(5)
AINSWORTH Brown
ALBION Boone
ALDA Hall
ALEXANDRIA (68303) Thayer(97), Jefferson(2)
ALLEN Dixon
ALLIANCE (69301) Box Butte(97), Sioux(1)
ALMA Harlan
ALVO Cass
AMELIA Holt
AMES Dodge
AMHERST Buffalo
ANGORA Morrill
ANSELMO (68813) Custer(83), Blaine(10), Loup(6)
ANSLEY Custer
ARAPAHOE (68922) Furnas(80), Gosper(19)
ARCADIA (68815) Valley(63), Custer(18), Sherman(17)
ARCHER Merrick
ARLINGTON Washington
ARNOLD (69120) Custer(73), Lincoln(16), Logan(9)
ARTHUR Arthur
ASHBY (69333) Grant(89), Garden(10)
ASHLAND (68003) Saunders(74), Cass(24)
ASHTON (68817) Sherman(91), Howard(8)
ATKINSON Holt
ATLANTA Phelps
AUBURN Nemaha
AURORA (68818) Hamilton(98), Clay(1)
AVOCA (68307) Cass(85), Otoe(15)
AXTELL (68924) Kearney(94), Phelps(5)
AYR Adams
BANCROFT (68004) Cuming(98), Burt(1)
BARNESTON Gage
BARTLETT Wheeler
BARTLEY Red Willow
BASSETT (68714) Rock(71), Holt(25), Brown(1)
BATTLE CREEK Madison
BAYARD (69334) Morrill(63), Scotts Bluff(34), Banner(2)
BEATRICE Gage
BEAVER CITY Furnas
BEAVER CROSSING (68313) Seward(98), York(1)
BEE (68314) Seward(88), Butler(11)
BEEMER Cuming
BELDEN Cedar
BELGRADE (68623) Nance(90), Boone(9)
BELLEVUE (68147) Sarpy(97), Douglas(2)
BELLEVUE Sarpy
BELLWOOD Butler
BELVIDERE Thayer
BENEDICT (68316) York(91), Polk(8)
BENKELMAN Dundy
BENNET (68317) Lancaster(95), Otoe(4)
BENNINGTON (68007) Douglas(92), Washington(7)

BERTRAND (68927) Phelps(78), Gosper(21)
BERWYN Custer
BIG SPRINGS (69122) Deuel(85), Keith(6), Perkins(4), Garden(2)
BINGHAM (69335) Garden(73), Sheridan(26)
BLADEN (68928) Webster(79), Adams(20)
BLAIR Washington
BLOOMFIELD Knox
BLOOMINGTON Franklin
BLUE HILL (68930) Webster(80), Adams(19)
BLUE SPRINGS Gage
BOELUS Howard
BOYS TOWN Douglas
BRADSHAW (68319) York(95), Hamilton(4)
BRADY Lincoln
BRAINARD (68626) Butler(98), Saunders(1)
BREWSTER Blaine
BRIDGEPORT (69336) Morrill(97), Banner(2)
BRISTOW Boyd
BROADWATER Morrill
BROCK Nemaha
BROKEN BOW Custer
BROWNVILLE Nemaha
BRULE (69127) Keith(97), Perkins(2)
BRUNING (68322) Thayer(71), Fillmore(28)
BRUNO (68014) Butler(74), Saunders(25)
BRUNSWICK Antelope
BURCHARD (68323) Pawnee(98), Gage(1)
BURR (68324) Otoe(98), Johnson(1)
BURWELL (68823) Garfield(66), Loup(17), Valley(10), Rock(3)
BUSHNELL Kimball
BUTTE Boyd
BYRON Thayer
CAIRO (68824) Hall(96), Howard(3)
CALLAWAY Custer
CAMBRIDGE (69022) Furnas(73), Frontier(13), Red Willow(10), Gosper(2)
CAMPBELL (68932) Franklin(56), Adams(18), Kearney(15), Webster(9)
CARLETON Thayer
CARROLL Wayne
CEDAR BLUFFS Saunders
CEDAR CREEK Cass
CEDAR RAPIDS (68627) Boone(95), Nance(4)
CENTER Knox
CENTRAL CITY Merrick
CERESCO (68017) Saunders(53), Lancaster(46)
CHADRON Dawes
CHAMBERS (68725) Holt(96), Wheeler(2), Garfield(1)
CHAMPION Chase
CHAPMAN Merrick
CHAPPELL (69129) Deuel(87), Garden(12)
CHESTER Thayer
CLARKS (68628) Merrick(78), Polk(12), Hamilton(9)

CLARKSON (68629) Colfax(73), Stanton(26)
CLATONIA Gage
CLAY CENTER Clay
CLEARWATER (68726) Antelope(94), Holt(5)
CODY Cherry
COLERIDGE Cedar
COLON Saunders
COLUMBUS (68601) Platte(94), Polk(2), Butler(1), Colfax(1)
COLUMBUS Platte
COMSTOCK (68828) Custer(68), Valley(31)
CONCORD Dixon
COOK (68329) Otoe(51), Johnson(47), Nemaha(1)
CORDOVA Seward
CORNLEA Platte
CORTLAND Gage
COTESFIELD (68829) Howard(89), Greeley(10)
COZAD Dawson
CRAB ORCHARD (68332) Johnson(92), Gage(7)
CRAIG (68019) Burt(95), Washington(3), Dodge(1)
CRAWFORD Dawes
CREIGHTON (68729) Knox(89), Antelope(9)
CRESTON (68631) Platte(90), Stanton(10)
CRETE (68333) Saline(90), Lancaster(9)
CROFTON (68730) Knox(76), Cedar(23)
CROOKSTON Cherry
CULBERTSON (69024) Hitchcock(82), Hayes(11), Red Willow(6)
CURTIS (69025) Frontier(83), Lincoln(14), Hitchcock(1)
DAKOTA CITY Dakota
DALTON Cheyenne
DANBURY Red Willow
DANNEBROG (68831) Howard(98), Hall(1)
DAVENPORT (68335) Thayer(68), Nuckolls(24), Fillmore(6)
DAVEY Lancaster
DAVID CITY Butler
DAWSON Richardson
DAYKIN (68338) Jefferson(96), Saline(3)
DE WITT (68341) Saline(58), Gage(41)
DECATUR (68020) Burt(92), Thurston(7)
DENTON (68339) Lancaster(59), Seward(39), Saline(1)
DESHLER Thayer
DEWEESE (68934) Clay(72), Nuckolls(27)
DICKENS Lincoln
DILLER (68342) Jefferson(77), Gage(22)
DIX (69133) Kimball(98), Cheyenne(1)
DIXON (68732) Dixon(98), Cedar(1)
DODGE (68633) Dodge(66), Cuming(20), Colfax(12)
DONIPHAN (68832) Hall(66), Hamilton(33)
DORCHESTER (68343) Saline(78), Seward(21)
DOUGLAS Otoe

DU BOIS (68345) Pawnee(75), Richardson(24)
DUNBAR Otoe
DUNCAN Platte
DUNNING (68833) Blaine(79), Logan(13), Custer(6)
DWIGHT Butler
EAGLE (68347) Cass(71), Otoe(27)
EDDYVILLE (68834) Dawson(83), Custer(16)
EDGAR (68935) Clay(82), Nuckolls(17)
EDISON (68936) Furnas(74), Gosper(14), Greeley(11)
ELBA (68835) Howard(96), Greeley(3)
ELGIN (68636) Antelope(97), Wheeler(1), Boone(1)
ELK CREEK (68348) Johnson(71), Nemaha(19), Pawnee(8)
ELKHORN Douglas
ELLSWORTH (69340) Sheridan(91), Garden(8)
ELM CREEK (68836) Buffalo(79), Phelps(14), Dawson(6)
ELMWOOD Cass
ELSIE (69134) Perkins(92), Chase(6)
ELSMERE (69135) Cherry(52), Brown(47)
ELWOOD (68937) Gosper(83), Dawson(16)
ELYRIA Valley
EMERSON (68733) Dakota(44), Dixon(34), Thurston(20)
EMMET Holt
ENDERS (69027) Chase(96), Dundy(3)
ENDICOTT Jefferson
ERICSON (68637) Wheeler(78), Garfield(22)
EUSTIS (69028) Frontier(63), Dawson(27), Gosper(8)
EWING (68735) Holt(75), Antelope(15), Wheeler(9)
EXETER (68351) Fillmore(81), York(18)
FAIRBURY Jefferson
FAIRFIELD Clay
FAIRMONT (68354) Fillmore(91), York(8)
FALLS CITY Richardson
FARNAM (69029) Dawson(82), Lincoln(17)
FARWELL Howard
FILLEY (68357) Gage(98), Johnson(1)
FIRTH (68358) Lancaster(68), Gage(31)
FORDYCE Cedar
FORT CALHOUN Washington
FOSTER Pierce
FREMONT (68025) Dodge(95), Saunders(4)
FREMONT Dodge
FRIEND (68359) Saline(95), Seward(4)
FULLERTON (68638) Nance(97), Merrick(1)
FUNK Phelps
GARLAND Seward
GENEVA Fillmore
GENOA (68640) Nance(63), Platte(33), Merrick(3)
GERING Scotts Bluff
GIBBON (68840) Buffalo(94), Kearney(5)

GILEAD Thayer
GILTNER Hamilton
GLENVIL (68941) Clay(55), Adams(44)
GOEHNER Seward
GORDON (69343) Sheridan(93), Cherry(6)
GOTHENBURG (69138) Dawson(93), Lincoln(4), Custer(2)
GRAFTON (68365) Fillmore(95), York(4)
GRAND ISLAND (68801) Hall(97), Merrick(2)
GRAND ISLAND Hall
GRANT Perkins
GREELEY Greeley
GREENWOOD (68366) Cass(94), Lancaster(3), Saunders(1)
GRESHAM (68367) York(45), Polk(32), Seward(20), Butler(2)
GRETNA (68028) Sarpy(98), Douglas(1)
GUIDE ROCK (68942) Webster(80), Nuckolls(19)
GURLEY Cheyenne
HADAR Pierce
HAIGLER (69030) Dundy(92), Chase(7)
HALLAM (68368) Lancaster(93), Gage(6)
HALSEY Thomas
HAMLET Hayes
HAMPTON (68843) Hamilton(97), York(2)
HARDY (68943) Nuckolls(99), Thayer(1)
HARRISBURG Banner
HARRISON Sioux
HARTINGTON Cedar
HARVARD (68944) Hamilton(53), Clay(46)
HASTINGS Adams
HAY SPRINGS (69347) Sheridan(65), Dawes(34)
HAYES CENTER Hayes
HAZARD Sherman
HEARTWELL Kearney
HEBRON Thayer
HEMINGFORD (69348) Box Butte(67), Dawes(32)
HENDERSON (68371) York(73), Hamilton(26)
HENDLEY Furnas
HENRY (69349) Scotts Bluff(84), Sioux(15)
HERMAN (68029) Washington(90), Burt(9)
HERSHEY Lincoln
HICKMAN Lancaster
HILDRETH (68947) Franklin(78), Kearney(21)
HOLBROOK (68948) Furnas(71), Gosper(24), Frontier(3)
HOLDREGE (68949) Phelps(98), Harlan(1)
HOLMESVILLE Gage
HOLSTEIN Adams
HOMER Dakota
HOOPER (68031) Dodge(91), Washington(6), Cuming(1)
HORDVILLE Hamilton
HOSKINS (68740) Wayne(89), Stanton(10)
HOWELLS (68641) Colfax(47), Cuming(32), Stanton(20)
HUBBARD Dakota
HUBBELL Thayer
HUMBOLDT (68376) Richardson(86), Nemaha(11), Pawnee(1)
HUMPHREY (68642) Platte(89), Madison(10)
HUNTLEY Harlan
HYANNIS Grant
IMPERIAL (69033) Chase(97), Perkins(2)
INAVALE Webster
INDIANOLA (69034) Red Willow(93), Frontier(6)
INLAND Clay
INMAN Holt
ITHACA Saunders
JACKSON Dakota
JANSEN Jefferson
JOHNSON (68378) Nemaha(92), Johnson(4), Otoe(3)

JOHNSTOWN (69214) Brown(98), Cherry(1)
JULIAN Nemaha
JUNIATA Adams
KEARNEY Buffalo
KENESAW (68956) Adams(80), Buffalo(11), Hall(7)
KENNARD Washington
KEYSTONE (69144) Keith(97), Arthur(2)
KILGORE Cherry
KIMBALL (69145) Kimball(96), Banner(3)
LAKESIDE Sheridan
LAMAR Chase
LAUREL (68745) Cedar(95), Wayne(2), Dixon(1)
LAVISTA (68128) Sarpy(98), Douglas(1)
LAWRENCE (68957) Nuckolls(57), Webster(33), Adams(7), Clay(2)
LEBANON Red Willow
LEIGH (68643) Colfax(47), Platte(35), Stanton(16)
LEMOYNE (69146) Keith(95), Arthur(4)
LESHARA Saunders
LEWELLEN (69147) Keith(61), Garden(37)
LEWISTON Pawnee
LEXINGTON Dawson
LIBERTY (68381) Gage(88), Pawnee(11)
LINCOLN Lancaster
LINDSAY (68644) Platte(83), Madison(16)
LINWOOD (68036) Butler(80), Saunders(19)
LISCO (69148) Garden(85), Morrill(14)
LITCHFIELD (68852) Sherman(90), Custer(9)
LODGEPOLE (69149) Cheyenne(82), Garden(14), Deuel(2)
LONG PINE Brown
LOOMIS Phelps
LORTON Otoe
LOUISVILLE Cass
LOUP CITY Sherman
LYMAN Scotts Bluff
LYNCH (68746) Boyd(84), Holt(15)
LYONS (68038) Burt(93), Cuming(6)
MACY Thurston
MADISON (68748) Madison(93), Stanton(6)
MADRID Perkins
MAGNET Cedar
MALCOLM Lancaster
MALMO Saunders
MANLEY Cass
MARQUETTE Hamilton
MARSLAND Dawes
MARTELL Lancaster
MASKELL Dixon
MASON CITY Custer
MAX Dundy
MAXWELL Lincoln
MAYWOOD (69038) Frontier(85), Lincoln(14)
MC COOK (69001) Red Willow(97), Frontier(1)
MC COOL JUNCTION (68401) York(98), Fillmore(1)
MCGREW Scotts Bluff
MCLEAN Pierce
MEAD Saunders
MEADOW GROVE (68752) Madison(92), Pierce(7)
MELBETA Scotts Bluff
MEMPHIS Saunders
MERNA Custer
MERRIMAN Cherry
MILFORD Seward
MILLER (68858) Buffalo(97), Custer(2)
MILLIGAN Fillmore
MILLS Keya Paha
MINATARE Scotts Bluff
MINDEN Kearney
MITCHELL (69357) Scotts Bluff(95), Sioux(4)

MONROE Platte
MOOREFIELD (69039) Frontier(63), Lincoln(36)
MORRILL (69358) Scotts Bluff(80), Sioux(19)
MORSE BLUFF Saunders
MULLEN Hooker
MURDOCK Cass
MURRAY Cass
NAPER Boyd
NAPONEE (68960) Franklin(78), Harlan(21)
NEBRASKA CITY Otoe
NEHAWKA (68413) Cass(97), Otoe(2)
NELIGH Antelope
NELSON Nuckolls
NEMAHA Nemaha
NENZEL Cherry
NEWCASTLE (68757) Dixon(88), Cedar(11)
NEWMAN GROVE (68758) Madison(64), Platte(21), Boone(13)
NEWPORT (68759) Rock(68), Keya Paha(31)
NICKERSON (68044) Washington(57), Dodge(42)
NIOBRARA Knox
NORFOLK (68701) Madison(95), Stanton(4)
NORFOLK Madison
NORMAN Kearney
NORTH BEND Dodge
NORTH LOUP (68859) Valley(94), Greeley(3), Sherman(1)
NORTH PLATTE Lincoln
OAK (68964) Nuckolls(94), Thayer(5)
OAKDALE Antelope
OAKLAND (68045) Burt(94), Cuming(4)
OBERT Cedar
OCONTO (68860) Custer(94), Dawson(5)
OCTAVIA Butler
ODELL Gage
ODESSA Buffalo
OFFUTT A F B Sarpy
OGALLALA (69153) Keith(97), Perkins(2)
OHIOWA (68416) Fillmore(94), Thayer(5)
OMAHA (68152) Douglas(84), Washington(15)
OMAHA (68157) Sarpy(97), Douglas(2)
OMAHA Douglas
OMAHA Sarpy
ONEILL Holt
ONG (68452) Clay(76), Fillmore(24)
ORCHARD (68764) Antelope(65), Knox(27), Holt(7)
ORD Valley
ORLEANS Harlan
OSCEOLA Polk
OSHKOSH Garden
OSMOND Pierce
OTOE Otoe
OVERTON (68863) Dawson(89), Phelps(10)
OXFORD (68967) Furnas(62), Harlan(37)
PAGE Holt
PALISADE (69040) Hayes(63), Hitchcock(36)
PALMER (68864) Merrick(77), Nance(21)
PALMYRA (68418) Otoe(96), Cass(3)
PANAMA Lancaster
PAPILLION Sarpy
PARKS Dundy
PAWNEE CITY Pawnee
PAXTON (69155) Keith(96), Perkins(2)
PENDER (68047) Thurston(72), Cuming(18), Wayne(9)
PERU (68421) Nemaha(92), Otoe(7)
PETERSBURG (68652) Boone(69), Antelope(30)
PHILLIPS (68865) Hamilton(98), Hall(1)
PICKRELL Gage
PIERCE Pierce

PILGER (68768) Stanton(91), Cuming(4), Wayne(3)
PLAINVIEW (68769) Pierce(79), Antelope(19), Knox(1)
PLATTE CENTER Platte
PLATTSMOUTH Cass
PLEASANT DALE (68423) Seward(82), Lancaster(17)
PLEASANTON (68866) Buffalo(98), Custer(1)
PLYMOUTH (68424) Jefferson(98), Gage(1)
POLK (68654) Polk(66), York(20), Hamilton(12)
PONCA (68770) Dixon(55), Dakota(44)
POTTER (69156) Cheyenne(82), Banner(12), Kimball(4)
PRAGUE Saunders
PRIMROSE (68655) Boone(96), Greeley(3)
PROSSER Adams
PURDUM (69157) Blaine(47), Cherry(34), Thomas(13), Brown(4)
RAGAN Harlan
RANDOLPH (68771) Cedar(57), Pierce(25), Wayne(16)
RAVENNA (68869) Buffalo(94), Sherman(5)
RAYMOND (68428) Lancaster(97), Seward(2)
RED CLOUD Webster
REPUBLICAN CITY Harlan
REYNOLDS Thayer
RICHFIELD Sarpy
RISING CITY Butler
RIVERDALE Buffalo
RIVERTON Franklin
ROCA Lancaster
ROCKVILLE Sherman
ROGERS Colfax
ROSALIE (68055) Thurston(74), Cuming(25)
ROSE (68772) Rock(90), Loup(9)
ROSELAND Adams
ROYAL (68773) Antelope(97), Brown(2)
RULO Richardson
RUSHVILLE Sheridan
RUSKIN (68974) Nuckolls(90), Thayer(9)
SAINT EDWARD (68660) Boone(72), Platte(23), Nance(3)
SAINT HELENA Cedar
SAINT LIBORY (68872) Howard(82), Merrick(17)
SAINT MARY Johnson
SAINT PAUL Howard
SALEM Richardson
SARGENT (68874) Custer(95), Loup(2), Hall(1)
SARONVILLE (68975) Fillmore(55), Clay(44)
SCHUYLER Colfax
SCOTIA (68875) Greeley(95), Howard(4)
SCOTTSBLUFF Scotts Bluff
SCRIBNER Dodge
SENECA (69161) Thomas(63), Cherry(36)
SEWARD Seward
SHELBY (68662) Polk(96), Butler(3)
SHELTON (68876) Buffalo(86), Hall(13)
SHICKLEY (68436) Fillmore(98), Clay(1)
SHUBERT (68437) Richardson(80), Nemaha(19)
SIDNEY Cheyenne
SILVER CREEK (68663) Merrick(41), Polk(39), Nance(17), Platte(1)
SMITHFIELD Gosper
SNYDER Dodge
SOUTH BEND Cass
SOUTH SIOUX CITY Dakota
SPALDING (68665) Greeley(78), Wheeler(21)
SPARKS Cherry
SPENCER (68777) Boyd(86), Holt(13)
SPRAGUE Lancaster

SPRINGFIELD Sarpy
SPRINGVIEW Keya Paha
ST COLUMBANS Sarpy
ST MARY Johnson
STAMFORD (68977) Harlan(68), Furnas(31)
STANTON Stanton
STAPLEHURST Seward
STAPLETON (69163) Logan(72), Lincoln(27)
STEELE CITY Jefferson
STEINAUER (68441) Pawnee(98), Johnson(1)
STELLA (68442) Richardson(83), Nemaha(16)
STERLING (68443) Johnson(92), Otoe(7)
STOCKVILLE Frontier
STRANG Fillmore
STRATTON (69043) Hitchcock(96), Dundy(3)
STROMSBURG (68666) Polk(98), York(1)
STUART Holt
SUMNER (68878) Dawson(94), Custer(5)
SUPERIOR Nuckolls
SURPRISE Butler
SUTHERLAND (69165) Lincoln(84), McPherson(7), Keith(4), Arthur(3)
SUTTON (68979) Clay(87), Fillmore(7), Hamilton(3)

SWANTON Saline
SYRACUSE Otoe
TABLE ROCK (68447) Pawnee(93), Nemaha(4), Johnson(2)
TALMAGE (68448) Otoe(82), Nemaha(10), Johnson(6)
TAYLOR Loup
TECUMSEH Johnson
TEKAMAH Burt
THEDFORD Thomas
THURSTON Thurston
TILDEN (68781) Madison(66), Antelope(26), Pierce(3), Boone(2)
TOBIAS (68453) Saline(88), Jefferson(7), Thayer(3), Fillmore(1)
TRENTON Hitchcock
TRUMBULL (68980) Clay(53), Adams(28), Hamilton(13), Hall(4)
TRYON McPherson
UEHLING Dodge
ULYSSES (68669) Butler(85), Seward(14)
UNADILLA (68454) Otoe(98), Cass(1)
UNION (68455) Cass(98), Otoe(1)
UPLAND (68981) Franklin(85), Kearney(14)
UTICA Seward
VALENTINE (69201) Cherry(98), Merrick(1)
VALLEY (68064) Douglas(93), Saunders(5), Dodge(1)

VALPARAISO (68065) Saunders(53), Lancaster(39), Seward(4), Butler(2)
VENANGO (69168) Perkins(75), Chase(25)
VERDIGRE Knox
VERDON Richardson
VIRGINIA (68458) Gage(89), Pawnee(6), Johnson(3)
WACO (68460) York(98), Seward(1)
WAHOO Saunders
WAKEFIELD (68784) Dixon(60), Wayne(38)
WALLACE (69169) Lincoln(73), Perkins(21), Hayes(4)
WALTHILL Thurston
WALTON (68461) Lancaster(97), Cass(1)
WATERBURY (68785) Dixon(77), Dakota(22)
WATERLOO (68069) Douglas(96), Sarpy(3)
WAUNETA (69045) Chase(47), Dundy(25), Hayes(24), Hitchcock(2)
WAUSA (68786) Knox(92), Cedar(4), Pierce(2)
WAVERLY (68462) Lancaster(98), Cass(1)
WAYNE (68787) Wayne(98), Dixon(1)
WEEPING WATER Cass
WEISSERT Custer
WELLFLEET Lincoln
WEST POINT Cuming

WESTERN (68464) Saline(95), Jefferson(4)
WESTERVILLE Custer
WESTON Saunders
WHITECLAY Sheridan
WHITMAN Grant
WHITNEY Dawes
WILBER (68465) Saline(93), Gage(4), Lancaster(1)
WILCOX (68982) Harlan(31), Kearney(31), Franklin(22), Phelps(14)
WILLOW ISLAND Dawson
WILSONVILLE (69046) Furnas(93), Red Willow(6)
WINNEBAGO Thurston
WINNETOON Knox
WINSIDE Wayne
WINSLOW Dodge
WISNER (68791) Cuming(94), Wayne(4)
WOLBACH (68882) Greeley(50), Howard(39), Nance(8), Boone(2)
WOOD LAKE Cherry
WOOD RIVER Hall
WYMORE Gage
WYNOT (68792) Cedar(97), Dixon(2)
YUTAN Saunders

Nebraska ZIP/City Cross Reference

ZIP	City
68001-68001	ABIE
68002-68002	ARLINGTON
68003-68003	ASHLAND
68004-68004	BANCROFT
68005-68005	BELLEVUE
68007-68007	BENNINGTON
68008-68009	BLAIR
68010-68010	BOYS TOWN
68014-68014	BRUNO
68015-68015	CEDAR BLUFFS
68016-68016	CEDAR CREEK
68017-68017	CERESCO
68018-68018	COLON
68019-68019	CRAIG
68020-68020	DECATUR
68022-68022	ELKHORN
68023-68023	FORT CALHOUN
68025-68026	FREMONT
68028-68028	GRETNA
68029-68029	HERMAN
68030-68030	HOMER
68031-68031	HOOPER
68033-68033	ITHACA
68034-68034	KENNARD
68035-68035	LESHARA
68036-68036	LINWOOD
68037-68037	LOUISVILLE
68038-68038	LYONS
68039-68039	MACY
68040-68040	MALMO
68041-68041	MEAD
68042-68042	MEMPHIS
68044-68044	NICKERSON
68045-68045	OAKLAND
68046-68046	PAPILLION
68047-68047	PENDER
68048-68048	PLATTSMOUTH
68050-68050	PRAGUE
68054-68054	RICHFIELD
68055-68055	ROSALIE
68056-68056	ST COLUMBANS
68057-68057	SCRIBNER
68058-68058	SOUTH BEND
68059-68059	SPRINGFIELD
68061-68061	TEKAMAH
68062-68062	THURSTON
68063-68063	UEHLING
68064-68064	VALLEY
68065-68065	VALPARAISO
68066-68066	WAHOO
68067-68067	WALTHILL
68068-68068	WASHINGTON
68069-68069	WATERLOO
68070-68070	WESTON
68071-68071	WINNEBAGO
68072-68072	WINSLOW
68073-68073	YUTAN
68100-68112	OMAHA
68113-68113	OFFUTT A F B
68114-68122	OMAHA
68123-68123	BELLEVUE
68124-68127	OMAHA
68128-68128	LAVISTA
68130-68132	OMAHA
68133-68133	PAPILLION
68134-68145	OMAHA
68147-68147	BELLEVUE
68152-68198	OMAHA
68301-68301	ADAMS
68303-68303	ALEXANDRIA
68304-68304	ALVO
68305-68305	AUBURN
68307-68307	AVOCA
68309-68309	BARNESTON
68310-68310	BEATRICE
68313-68313	BEAVER CROSSING
68314-68314	BEE
68315-68315	BELVIDERE
68316-68316	BENEDICT
68317-68317	BENNET
68318-68318	BLUE SPRINGS
68319-68319	BRADSHAW
68320-68320	BROCK
68321-68321	BROWNVILLE
68322-68322	BRUNING
68323-68323	BURCHARD
68324-68324	BURR
68325-68325	BYRON
68326-68326	CARLETON
68327-68327	CHESTER
68328-68328	CLATONIA
68329-68329	COOK
68330-68330	CORDOVA
68331-68331	CORTLAND
68332-68332	CRAB ORCHARD
68333-68333	CRETE
68335-68335	DAVENPORT
68336-68336	DAVEY
68337-68337	DAWSON
68338-68338	DAYKIN
68339-68339	DENTON
68340-68340	DESHLER
68341-68341	DE WITT
68342-68342	DILLER
68343-68343	DORCHESTER
68344-68344	DOUGLAS
68345-68345	DU BOIS
68346-68346	DUNBAR
68347-68347	EAGLE
68348-68348	ELK CREEK
68349-68349	ELMWOOD
68350-68350	ENDICOTT
68351-68351	EXETER
68352-68352	FAIRBURY
68354-68354	FAIRMONT
68355-68355	FALLS CITY
68357-68357	FILLEY
68358-68358	FIRTH
68359-68359	FRIEND
68360-68360	GARLAND
68361-68361	GENEVA
68362-68362	GILEAD
68364-68364	GOEHNER
68365-68365	GRAFTON
68366-68366	GREENWOOD
68367-68367	GRESHAM
68368-68368	HALLAM
68370-68370	HEBRON
68371-68371	HENDERSON
68372-68372	HICKMAN
68374-68374	HOLMESVILLE
68375-68375	HUBBELL
68376-68376	HUMBOLDT
68377-68377	JANSEN
68378-68378	JOHNSON
68379-68379	JULIAN
68380-68380	LEWISTON
68381-68381	LIBERTY
68382-68382	LORTON
68401-68401	MC COOL JUNCTION
68402-68402	MALCOLM
68403-68403	MANLEY
68404-68404	MARTELL
68405-68405	MILFORD
68406-68406	MILLIGAN
68407-68407	MURDOCK
68409-68409	MURRAY
68410-68410	NEBRASKA CITY
68413-68413	NEHAWKA
68414-68414	NEMAHA
68415-68415	ODELL
68416-68416	OHIOWA
68417-68417	OTOE
68418-68418	PALMYRA
68419-68419	PANAMA
68420-68420	PAWNEE CITY
68421-68421	PERU
68422-68422	PICKRELL
68423-68423	PLEASANT DALE
68424-68424	PLYMOUTH
68428-68428	RAYMOND
68429-68429	REYNOLDS
68430-68430	ROCA
68431-68431	RULO
68432-68432	SAINT MARY
68432-68432	ST MARY
68433-68433	SALEM
68434-68434	SEWARD
68436-68436	SHICKLEY
68437-68437	SHUBERT
68438-68438	SPRAGUE
68439-68439	STAPLEHURST
68440-68440	STEELE CITY
68441-68441	STEINAUER
68442-68442	STELLA
68443-68443	STERLING
68444-68444	STRANG
68445-68445	SWANTON
68446-68446	SYRACUSE
68447-68447	TABLE ROCK
68448-68448	TALMAGE
68450-68450	TECUMSEH
68452-68452	ONG
68453-68453	TOBIAS
68454-68454	UNADILLA
68455-68455	UNION
68456-68456	UTICA
68457-68457	VERDON
68458-68458	VIRGINIA
68460-68460	WACO
68461-68461	WALTON
68462-68462	WAVERLY
68463-68463	WEEPING WATER
68464-68464	WESTERN
68465-68465	WILBER
68466-68466	WYMORE
68467-68467	YORK
68500-68588	LINCOLN
68601-68602	COLUMBUS
68620-68620	ALBION
68621-68621	AMES
68622-68622	BARTLETT
68623-68623	BELGRADE
68624-68624	BELLWOOD
68625-68625	BOONE
68626-68626	BRAINARD
68627-68627	CEDAR RAPIDS
68628-68628	CLARKS
68629-68629	CLARKSON
68630-68630	CORNLEA
68631-68631	CRESTON
68632-68632	DAVID CITY

68633-68633 DODGE	68770-68770 PONCA	68901-68902 HASTINGS	69120-69120 ARNOLD
68634-68634 DUNCAN	68771-68771 RANDOLPH	68920-68920 ALMA	69121-69121 ARTHUR
68635-68635 DWIGHT	68772-68772 ROSE	68922-68922 ARAPAHOE	69122-69122 BIG SPRINGS
68636-68636 ELGIN	68773-68773 ROYAL	68923-68923 ATLANTA	69123-69123 BRADY
68637-68637 ERICSON	68774-68774 SAINT HELENA	68924-68924 AXTELL	69125-69125 BROADWATER
68638-68638 FULLERTON	68776-68776 SOUTH SIOUX CITY	68925-68925 AYR	69127-69127 BRULE
68640-68640 GENOA	68777-68777 SPENCER	68926-68926 BEAVER CITY	69128-69128 BUSHNELL
68641-68641 HOWELLS	68778-68778 SPRINGVIEW	68927-68927 BERTRAND	69129-69129 CHAPPELL
68642-68642 HUMPHREY	68779-68779 STANTON	68928-68928 BLADEN	69130-69130 COZAD
68643-68643 LEIGH	68780-68780 STUART	68929-68929 BLOOMINGTON	69131-69131 DALTON
68644-68644 LINDSAY	68781-68781 TILDEN	68930-68930 BLUE HILL	69132-69132 DICKENS
68647-68647 MONROE	68783-68783 VERDIGRE	68932-68932 CAMPBELL	69133-69133 DIX
68648-68648 MORSE BLUFF	68784-68784 WAKEFIELD	68933-68933 CLAY CENTER	69134-69134 ELSIE
68649-68649 NORTH BEND	68785-68785 WATERBURY	68934-68934 DEWEESE	69135-69135 ELSMERE
68650-68650 OCTAVIA	68786-68786 WAUSA	68935-68935 EDGAR	69138-69138 GOTHENBURG
68651-68651 OSCEOLA	68787-68787 WAYNE	68936-68936 EDISON	69140-69140 GRANT
68652-68652 PETERSBURG	68788-68788 WEST POINT	68937-68937 ELWOOD	69141-69141 GURLEY
68653-68653 PLATTE CENTER	68789-68789 WINNETOON	68938-68938 FAIRFIELD	69142-69142 HALSEY
68654-68654 POLK	68790-68790 WINSIDE	68939-68939 FRANKLIN	69143-69143 HERSHEY
68655-68655 PRIMROSE	68791-68791 WISNER	68940-68940 FUNK	69144-69144 KEYSTONE
68658-68658 RISING CITY	68792-68792 WYNOT	68941-68941 GLENVIL	69145-69145 KIMBALL
68659-68659 ROGERS	68801-68803 GRAND ISLAND	68942-68942 GUIDE ROCK	69146-69146 LEMOYNE
68660-68660 SAINT EDWARD	68810-68810 ALDA	68943-68943 HARDY	69147-69147 LEWELLEN
68661-68661 SCHUYLER	68812-68812 AMHERST	68944-68944 HARVARD	69148-69148 LISCO
68662-68662 SHELBY	68813-68813 ANSELMO	68945-68945 HEARTWELL	69149-69149 LODGEPOLE
68663-68663 SILVER CREEK	68814-68814 ANSLEY	68946-68946 HENDLEY	69150-69150 MADRID
68664-68664 SNYDER	68815-68815 ARCADIA	68947-68947 HILDRETH	69151-69151 MAXWELL
68665-68665 SPALDING	68816-68816 ARCHER	68948-68948 HOLBROOK	69152-69152 MULLEN
68666-68666 STROMSBURG	68817-68817 ASHTON	68949-68949 HOLDREGE	69153-69153 OGALLALA
68667-68667 SURPRISE	68818-68818 AURORA	68950-68950 HOLSTEIN	69154-69154 OSHKOSH
68669-68669 ULYSSES	68819-68819 BERWYN	68951-68951 HUNTLEY	69155-69155 PAXTON
68701-68702 NORFOLK	68820-68820 BOELUS	68952-68952 INAVALE	69156-69156 POTTER
68710-68710 ALLEN	68821-68821 BREWSTER	68954-68954 INLAND	69157-69157 PURDUM
68711-68711 AMELIA	68822-68822 BROKEN BOW	68955-68955 JUNIATA	69160-69160 SIDNEY
68713-68713 ATKINSON	68823-68823 BURWELL	68956-68956 KENESAW	69161-69161 SENECA
68714-68714 BASSETT	68824-68824 CAIRO	68957-68957 LAWRENCE	69162-69162 SIDNEY
68715-68715 BATTLE CREEK	68825-68825 CALLAWAY	68958-68958 LOOMIS	69163-69163 STAPLETON
68716-68716 BEEMER	68826-68826 CENTRAL CITY	68959-68959 MINDEN	69165-69165 SUTHERLAND
68717-68717 BELDEN	68827-68827 CHAPMAN	68960-68960 NAPONEE	69166-69166 THEDFORD
68718-68718 BLOOMFIELD	68828-68828 COMSTOCK	68961-68961 NELSON	69167-69167 TRYON
68719-68719 BRISTOW	68829-68829 COTESFIELD	68963-68963 NORMAN	69168-69168 VENANGO
68720-68720 BRUNSWICK	68831-68831 DANNEBROG	68964-68964 OAK	69169-69169 WALLACE
68722-68722 BUTTE	68832-68832 DONIPHAN	68966-68966 ORLEANS	69170-69170 WELLFLEET
68723-68723 CARROLL	68833-68833 DUNNING	68967-68967 OXFORD	69171-69171 WILLOW ISLAND
68724-68724 CENTER	68834-68834 EDDYVILLE	68969-68969 RAGAN	69190-69190 OSHKOSH
68725-68725 CHAMBERS	68835-68835 ELBA	68970-68970 RED CLOUD	69201-69201 VALENTINE
68726-68726 CLEARWATER	68836-68836 ELM CREEK	68971-68971 REPUBLICAN CITY	69210-69210 AINSWORTH
68727-68727 COLERIDGE	68837-68837 ELYRIA	68972-68972 RIVERTON	69211-69211 CODY
68728-68728 CONCORD	68838-68838 FARWELL	68973-68973 ROSELAND	69212-69212 CROOKSTON
68729-68729 CREIGHTON	68840-68840 GIBBON	68974-68974 RUSKIN	69214-69214 JOHNSTOWN
68730-68730 CROFTON	68841-68841 GILTNER	68975-68975 SARONVILLE	69216-69216 KILGORE
68731-68731 DAKOTA CITY	68842-68842 GREELEY	68976-68976 SMITHFIELD	69217-69217 LONG PINE
68732-68732 DIXON	68843-68843 HAMPTON	68977-68977 STAMFORD	69218-69218 MERRIMAN
68733-68733 EMERSON	68844-68844 HAZARD	68978-68978 SUPERIOR	69219-69219 NENZEL
68734-68734 EMMET	68845-68845 KEARNEY	68979-68979 SUTTON	69220-69220 SPARKS
68735-68735 EWING	68846-68846 HORDVILLE	68980-68980 TRUMBULL	69221-69221 WOOD LAKE
68736-68736 FORDYCE	68847-68849 KEARNEY	68981-68981 UPLAND	69301-69301 ALLIANCE
68737-68737 FOSTER	68850-68850 LEXINGTON	68982-68982 WILCOX	69331-69331 ANGORA
68738-68738 HADAR	68852-68852 LITCHFIELD	69001-69001 MC COOK	69333-69333 ASHBY
68739-68739 HARTINGTON	68853-68853 LOUP CITY	69020-69020 BARTLEY	69334-69334 BAYARD
68740-68740 HOSKINS	68854-68854 MARQUETTE	69021-69021 BENKELMAN	69335-69335 BINGHAM
68741-68741 HUBBARD	68855-68855 MASON CITY	69022-69022 CAMBRIDGE	69336-69336 BRIDGEPORT
68742-68742 INMAN	68856-68856 MERNA	69023-69023 CHAMPION	69337-69337 CHADRON
68743-68743 JACKSON	68858-68858 MILLER	69024-69024 CULBERTSON	69339-69339 CRAWFORD
68745-68745 LAUREL	68859-68859 NORTH LOUP	69025-69025 CURTIS	69340-69340 ELLSWORTH
68746-68746 LYNCH	68860-68860 OCONTO	69026-69026 DANBURY	69341-69341 GERING
68747-68747 MCLEAN	68861-68861 ODESSA	69027-69027 ENDERS	69343-69343 GORDON
68748-68748 MADISON	68862-68862 ORD	69028-69028 EUSTIS	69345-69345 HARRISBURG
68749-68749 MAGNET	68863-68863 OVERTON	69029-69029 FARNAM	69346-69346 HARRISON
68751-68751 MASKELL	68864-68864 PALMER	69030-69030 HAIGLER	69347-69347 HAY SPRINGS
68752-68752 MEADOW GROVE	68865-68865 PHILLIPS	69031-69031 HAMLET	69348-69348 HEMINGFORD
68753-68753 MILLS	68866-68866 PLEASANTON	69032-69032 HAYES CENTER	69349-69349 HENRY
68755-68755 NAPER	68868-68868 PROSSER	69033-69033 IMPERIAL	69350-69350 HYANNIS
68756-68756 NELIGH	68869-68869 RAVENNA	69034-69034 INDIANOLA	69351-69351 LAKESIDE
68757-68757 NEWCASTLE	68870-68870 RIVERDALE	69035-69035 LAMAR	69352-69352 LYMAN
68758-68758 NEWMAN GROVE	68871-68871 ROCKVILLE	69036-69036 LEBANON	69353-69353 MCGREW
68759-68759 NEWPORT	68872-68872 SAINT LIBORY	69037-69037 MAX	69354-69354 MARSLAND
68760-68760 NIOBRARA	68873-68873 SAINT PAUL	69038-69038 MAYWOOD	69355-69355 MELBETA
68761-68761 OAKDALE	68874-68874 SARGENT	69039-69039 MOOREFIELD	69356-69356 MINATARE
68762-68762 OBERT	68875-68875 SCOTIA	69040-69040 PALISADE	69357-69357 MITCHELL
68763-68763 ONEILL	68876-68876 SHELTON	69041-69041 PARKS	69358-69358 MORRILL
68764-68764 ORCHARD	68878-68878 SUMNER	69042-69042 STOCKVILLE	69360-69360 RUSHVILLE
68765-68765 OSMOND	68879-68879 TAYLOR	69043-69043 STRATTON	69361-69363 SCOTTSBLUFF
68766-68766 PAGE	68880-68880 WEISSERT	69044-69044 TRENTON	69365-69365 WHITECLAY
68767-68767 PIERCE	68881-68881 WESTERVILLE	69045-69045 WAUNETA	69366-69366 WHITMAN
68768-68768 PILGER	68882-68882 WOLBACH	69046-69046 WILSONVILLE	69367-69367 WHITNEY
68769-68769 PLAINVIEW	68883-68883 WOOD RIVER	69101-69103 NORTH PLATTE	

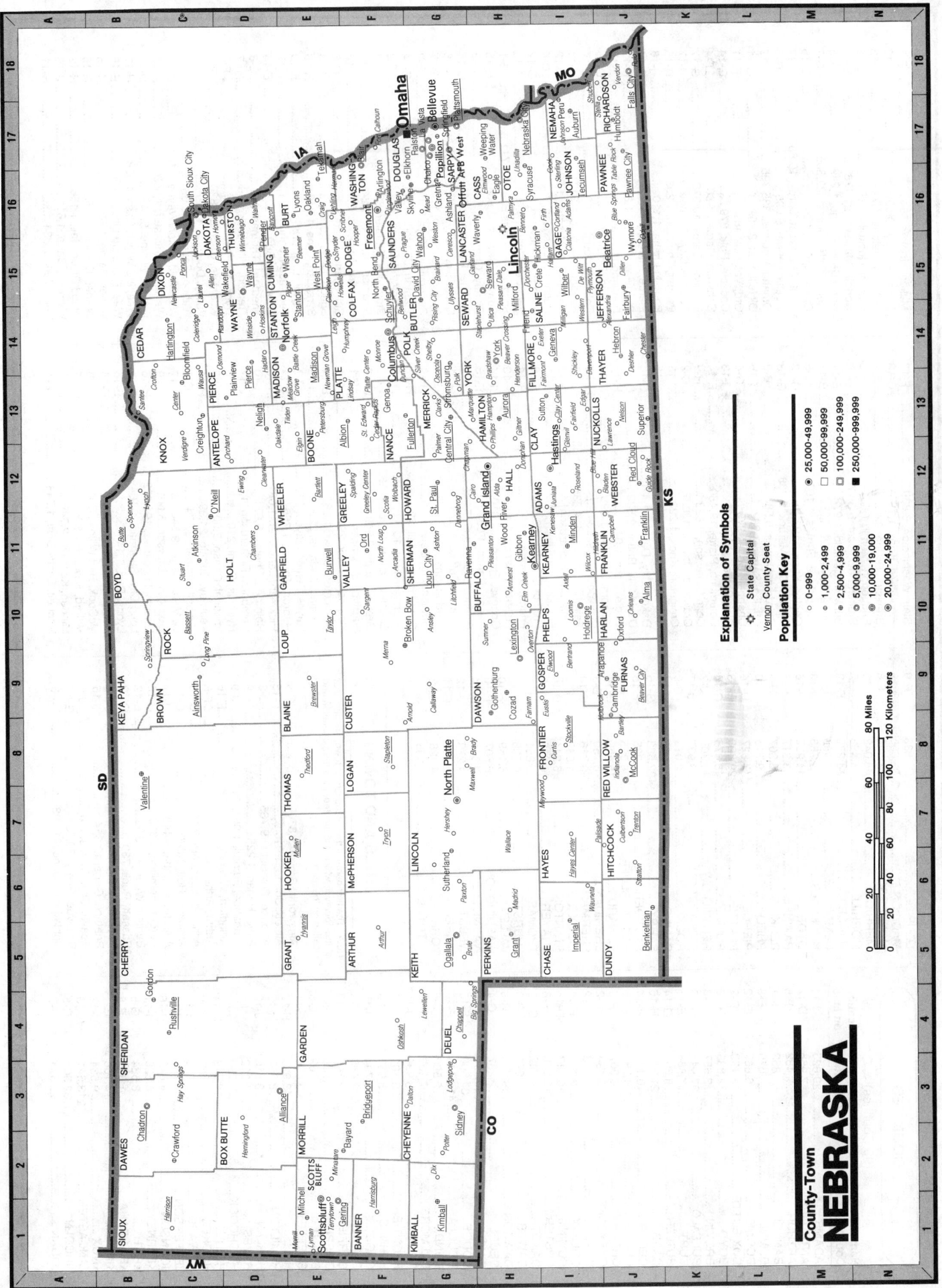

County-Town
NEBRASKA

Explanation of Symbols

⬦ State Capital
⬥ County Seat
<u>Vernon</u> County Seat

Population Key

- ○ 0-999
- ○ 1,000-2,499
- ○ 2,500-4,999
- ◎ 5,000-9,999
- ◉ 10,000-19,000
- ◉ 20,000-24,999
- ◉ 25,000-49,999
- ☐ 50,000-99,999
- ☐ 100,000-249,999
- ■ 250,000-999,999

80 Miles
120 Kilometers

COUNTIES

(93 Counties)

Name of County	Population	Location on Map
ADAMS	29,625	I-11
ANTELOPE	7,965	D-12
ARTHUR	462	F-5
BANNER	852	F-1
BLAINE	675	E-8
BOONE	6,667	E-12
BOX BUTTE	13,130	D-2
BOYD	2,835	B-10
BROWN	3,657	C-8
BUFFALO	37,447	H-10
BURT	7,868	E-16
BUTLER	8,601	G-14
CASS	21,318	H-16
CEDAR	10,131	B-14
CHASE	4,381	I-5
CHERRY	6,307	B-5
CHEYENNE	9,494	F-2
CLAY	7,123	I-12
COLFAX	9,139	F-14
CUMING	10,117	F-15
CUSTER	12,270	F-8
DAKOTA	16,742	C-15
DAWES	9,021	B-3
DAWSON	19,940	H-8
DEUEL	2,237	G-4
DIXON	6,143	C-15
DODGE	34,500	F-15
DOUGLAS	416,444	G-16
DUNDY	2,582	J-5
FILLMORE	7,103	H-13
FRANKLIN	3,938	J-11
FRONTIER	3,101	I-8
FURNAS	5,553	J-9
GAGE	22,794	I-15
GARDEN	2,460	E-3
GARFIELD	2,141	E-10
GOSPER	1,928	I-9
GRANT	769	E-5
GREELEY	3,006	E-11
HALL	48,925	H-12
HAMILTON	8,862	H-13
HARLAN	3,810	J-10
HAYES	1,222	I-6
HITCHCOCK	3,750	J-6
HOLT	12,599	D-11
HOOKER	793	E-6
HOWARD	6,055	G-11
JEFFERSON	8,759	J-14
JOHNSON	4,673	I-16
KEARNEY	6,629	I-11
KEITH	8,584	G-5
KEYA PAHA	1,029	B-8
KIMBALL	4,108	G-1
KNOX	9,534	C-12
LANCASTER	213,641	G-15
LINCOLN	32,508	G-6
LOGAN	878	F-7
LOUP	683	E-9
MADISON	32,655	D-13
MCPHERSON	546	F-6
MERRICK	8,042	G-13
MORRILL	5,423	E-2
NANCE	4,275	F-12
NEMAHA	7,980	I-17
NUCKOLLS	5,786	J-12
OTOE	14,252	H-16
PAWNEE	3,317	J-16
PERKINS	3,367	H-5
PHELPS	9,715	I-10
PIERCE	7,827	D-14
PLATTE	29,820	E-13
POLK	5,675	G-14
RED WILLOW	11,705	J-7
RICHARDSON	9,937	J-17
ROCK	2,019	C-9
SALINE	12,715	I-14
SARPY	102,583	G-16
SAUNDERS	18,285	F-15
SCOTTS BLUFF	36,025	E-1
SEWARD	15,450	G-14
SHERIDAN	6,750	B-3
SHERMAN	3,718	G-10
SIOUX	1,549	B-1
STANTON	6,244	D-14
THAYER	6,635	J-13
THOMAS	851	E-7
THURSTON	6,936	D-15
VALLEY	5,169	F-10
WASHINGTON	16,607	F-16
WAYNE	9,364	D-14
WEBSTER	4,279	J-12
WHEELER	948	E-11
YORK	14,428	G-13
TOTAL	**1,578,385**	

CITIES AND TOWNS

Note: The first name is that of the city or town, second, that of the county in which it is located, then the population and location on the map.

City/Town, County, Population	Map
Ainsworth, Brown, 1,870	C-9
Albion, Boone, 1,916	F-13
Alliance, Box Butte, 9,765	D-3
Alma, Harlan, 1,226	J-10
Arapahoe, Furnas, 1,001	J-9
Arlington, Washington, 1,178	F-16
Arthur, Arthur, 128	F-5
Ashland, Saunders, 2,136	G-16
Atkinson, Holt, 1,380	C-11
Aurora, Hamilton, 3,443	H-13
Auburn, Nemaha, 3,810	I-17
Bartlett, Wheeler, 131	E-12
Bassett, Rock, 739	C-10
Bayard, Morrill, 1,196	E-2
Beatrice, Gage, 12,354	I-15
Beaver City, Furnas, 707	J-9
Bellevue, Sarpy, 30,982	G-17
Benkelman, Dundy, 1,193	J-6
Blair, Washington, 6,860	F-17
Bloomfield, Knox, 1,181	C-13
Brewster, Blaine, 22	E-9
Bridgeport, Morrill, 1,581	F-3
Broken Bow, Custer, 3,778	F-10
Burwell, Garfield, 1,278	E-11
Butte, Boyd, 452	B-11
Cambridge, Furnas, 1,107	J-8
Center, Knox, 112	C-13
Central City, Merrick, 2,868	G-13
Chadron, Dawes, 5,588	B-3
Chalco, Sarpy, 7,337	G-16
Chappell, Deuel, 979	G-4
Clay Center, Clay, 825	I-13
Columbus, Platte, 19,480	F-14
Cozad, Dawson, 3,823	H-9
Crawford, Dawes, 1,115	C-2
Creighton, Knox, 1,223	C-13
Crete, Saline, 4,841	I-15
Dakota City, Dakota, 1,470	C-16
David City, Butler, 2,522	G-15
Eagle, Cass, 1,047	H-16
Elkhorn, Douglas, 1,398	G-16
Elmwood, Cass, 584	I-9
Fairbury, Jefferson, 4,335	J-15
Falls City, Richardson, 4,769	J-18
Franklin, Franklin, 1,112	J-11
Fremont, Dodge, 23,680	F-16
Friend, Saline, 1,111	H-14
Fullerton, Nance, 1,452	F-13
Geneva, Fillmore, 2,310	I-14
Genoa, Nance, 1,082	F-13
Gering, Scotts Bluff, 7,946	E-1
Gibbon, Buffalo, 1,525	H-11
Gordon, Sheridan, 1,803	B-4
Gothenburg, Dawson, 3,232	H-9
Grand Island, Hall, 39,386	H-12
Grant, Perkins, 1,239	H-5
Greeley Center, Greeley, 562	F-12
Gretna, Sarpy, 2,249	G-17
Harrisburg, Banner	F-1
Harrison, Sioux, 291	C-1
Hartington, Cedar, 1,583	B-14
Hastings, Adams, 22,837	I-12
Hayes Center, Hayes, 259	I-7
Hebron, Thayer, 1,765	J-14
Hickman, Lancaster, 1,081	I-15
Holdrege, Phelps, 5,671	I-10
Humboldt, Richardson, 1,003	J-17
Hyannis, Grant, 210	E-5
Imperial, Chase, 2,007	I-5
Kearney, Buffalo, 24,396	H-11
Kimball, Kimball, 2,574	G-1
La Vista, Sarpy, 9,840	G-17
Lexington, Dawson, 6,601	H-9
Lincoln, Lancaster, 191,972	G-17
Loup City, Sherman, 1,104	G-11
Lyons, Burt, 1,144	E-16
Madison, Madison, 2,135	E-14
McCook, Red Willow, 8,112	J-8
Milford, Seward, 1,886	H-15
Minden, Kearney, 2,749	I-11
Mitchell, Scotts Bluff, 1,743	E-1
Mullen, Hooker, 554	E-7
Nebraska City, Otoe, 6,547	H-17
Neligh, Antelope, 1,742	D-13
Nelson, Nuckolls, 627	J-13
Norfolk, Madison, 21,476	E-14
North Bend, Dodge, 1,249	F-15
North Platte, Lincoln, 22,605	G-7
Oakland, Burt, 1,279	E-16
Offutt AFB West, Sarpy, 10,883	G-17
Ogallala, Keith, 5,095	G-5
Omaha, Douglas, 335,795	G-17
O'Neill, Holt, 3,852	C-11
Ord, Valley, 2,481	F-11
Osceola, Polk, 879	G-14
Oshkosh, Garden, 986	F-4
Papillion, Sarpy, 10,372	G-17
Pawnee City, Pawnee, 1,008	J-17
Pender, Thurston, 1,208	D-15
Peru, Nemaha, 1,110	I-18
Pierce, Pierce, 1,615	D-14
Plainview, Pierce, 1,333	D-13
Plattsmouth, Cass, 6,412	G-17
Ponca, Dixon, 877	C-15
Ralston, Douglas, 6,236	G-17
Ravenna, Buffalo, 1,317	H-11
Red Cloud, Webster, 1,204	J-12
Rushville, Sheridan, 1,127	C-4
Saint Paul, Howard, 2,009	G-12
Schuyler, Colfax, 4,052	F-15
Scottsbluff, Scotts Bluff, 13,711	E-1
Seward, Seward, 5,634	H-15
Sidney, Cheyenne, 5,959	G-3
Skyline, Douglas, 2,563	G-16
South Sioux City, Dakota, 9,677	C-16
Springfield, Sarpy, 1,426	G-17
Springview, Keya Paha, 304	B-9
Stanton, Stanton, 1,549	E-14
Stapleton, Logan, 299	F-8
Stockville, Frontier, 32	I-8
Stromsburg, Polk, 1,241	G-14
Superior, Nuckolls, 2,397	J-13
Sutherland, Lincoln, 1,032	G-6
Sutton, Clay, 1,353	I-13
Syracuse, Otoe, 1,646	H-16
Taylor, Loup, 186	E-10
Tecumseh, Johnson, 1,702	I-17
Tekamah, Burt, 1,852	E-16
Thedford, Thomas, 243	E-8
Trenton, Hitchcock, 656	J-7
Tryon, McPherson	F-7
Valentine, Cherry, 2,826	B-8
Valley, Douglas, 1,775	G-16
Wahoo, Saunders, 3,681	G-16
Wakefield, Dixon/Wayne, 1,082	D-15
Waverly, Lancaster, 1,869	G-15
Wayne, Wayne, 5,142	D-15
Weeping Water, Cass, 1,008	H-17
West Point, Cuming, 3,250	E-15
Wilber, Saline, 1,527	I-15
Wisner, Cuming, 1,253	E-15
Wood River, Hall, 1,156	H-12
Wymore, Gage, 1,611	J-16
York, York, 7,884	H-11

Explanation of symbols: ● – Census Designated Place (CDP)

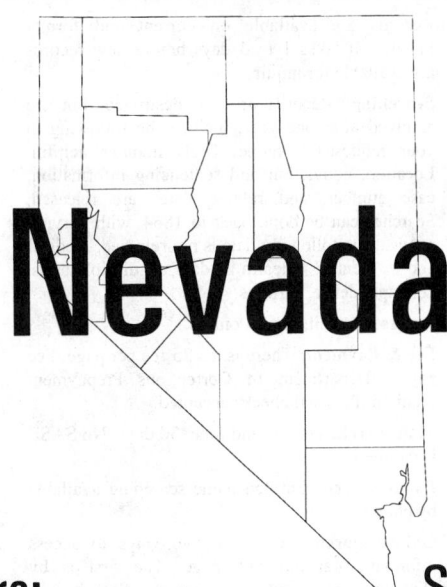

Nevada

General Help Numbers:

Governor's Office
Capitol Building
Carson City, NV 89701
http://gov.state.nv.us

775-684-5670
Fax 775-684-5683
8AM-5PM

Attorney General's Office
100 N Carson St
Carson City, NV 89701
http://ag.state.nv.us

775-684-1100
Fax 775-684-1108
8AM-5PM

Legislative Records
Nevada Legislature
401 S Carson St
Carson City, NV 89701-4747
www.leg.state.nv.us

775-684-6827 (Bill Status)
775-684-6800
Fax 775-684-6663
8AM-5PM

State Archives
100 N Stewart St
Carson City, NV 89701-4285
http://dmla.clan.lib.nv.us/docs/nsla

775-684-3360
Fax 775-684-3330
8AM-5PM M-F

State Specifics:

Capital:	Carson City
	Carson City County
Time Zone:	PST
Number of Counties:	17
Number of Filing Locations:	17
Population:	2,334,771
Web Site:	http://www.nv.gov

State Agencies

Criminal Records

DPS, Record & ID Services, 808 W Nye Lane, Carson City, NV 89703; 775-687-1600, 775-687-1843-Fax; 8AM-5PM.

www.nvrepository.state.nv.us

Records are available if you provide fingerprints and consent of subject. Otherwise, this agency suggests a court record search instead.

Records are available from 1987 and are on computer. Records are maintained indefinitely, unless purged due to court order. It takes 6 hours before new records are available for inquiry. Records are indexed on computer. 56% of all arrests in database have final dispositions recorded, approximately 30% for those arrests within last 5 years.

Searching: This repository maintains all "fingerprintable charges," meaning, essentially, all felony records and DUI and domestic violence. Misdemeanor records are not maintained. 100% of arrest records are fingerprint supported. Include the following in your request-set of fingerprints, signed release, full name. DOB, SSN, sex and race are helpful. The following data is not released: sealed records or juvenile records. Records without dispositions are not released, unless an approved waiver is submitted.

Access by: mail, in person.

Fee & Payment: The fingerprint search fee is $21.00 per individual. If the search requires an FBI fingerprint check (for record checks on occupations concerning children or the elderly, per state statute), the fee is $45.00. Fee payee: Nevada Department of Public Safety Prepayment required. Cash, money order or cashier's check required. No credit cards or personal checks accepted.

Mail search: Turnaround time: 15 working days. No SASE is required.

In person search: Records are still returned by mail.

Statewide Court Records

Supreme Court of Nevada, Administrative Office of the Courts, 201 S Carson St, #250, Carson City, NV 89701-4702; 775-684-1700, 775-684-1723-Fax; 8AM-5PM.

www.nvsupremecourt.us/aoc/aoc.html

Except for certain online research capabilities, all court record access must be done at the local level.

Access by: online.

Online search: The Supreme Court website gives access to opinions and decisions. Some Nevada Courts have internal online computer systems, but only Clark and Washoe Counties offer online access available to the public. A statewide court automation system is being implemented. Clark County justice and municipal courts calendars at http://sandgate.co.clark.nv.us/JusticeCourt/jcCalendarSearch.html.

Sexual Offender Registry

Records and Identification Bureau, Sex Offender Registry, 808 W Nye Lane, Carson City, NV 89703; 775-687-1600 x253, 775-687-1844-Fax; 8AM-5PM.

www.nvsexoffenders.gov

In 1997, the Community Notification of Sex Offenders law was passed (NRS Chapter 179D). There are over 8,700 offenders registered in the state.

Records are available from 1997 forward on computer.

Searching: Based upon NRS 179B.250, the Repository is permitted to share only ZIP Code information. Specific home address information on any convicted sex offender is strictly prohibited. There are less restrictions when requesting data at the local level. Include the following in your request-name, DOB, DL or SSN.

Access by: mail, phone, fax, in person, online.

Fee & Payment: There is no fee. Fee payee: Nevada Highway Patrol. Prepayment required. Money order or cashier's check required. No credit cards or personal checks accepted.

Mail search: Turnaround time: 1 day. No SASE is required.

Phone search: Requests can be made by telephone.

Fax search: Searching by fax permitted.

In person search: Records are still returned by mail.

Online search: Information on the website will include the name, aliases, photograph (where available), conviction information and ZIP Code based on the latest registered address. The website does not contain information on all convicted sex offenders. Information is only provided for sex offenders with a risk assessment score of a TIER Level 3 and certain information regarding a TIER Level 2. Search by name, ZIP Code, or even license plate number.

Incarceration Records

Nevada Department of Corrections, Attn: Records, PO Box 7011, Carson City, NV 89702 (Courier address: 5500 Snyder Ave, Bldg 89, Carson City, NV 89701); 775-887-3285, 775-687-6715-Fax; 8AM-5PM.

www.doc.nv.gov/ncis

Records are available on current and former inmates. It takes 1 to 3 days before new records are available for inquiry.

Searching: Records are not destroyed, but are archived after one year. Include the following in your request-full name; DOC number helpful. Location, conviction and sentencing information, case number, and release dates are released. Searches can be done back to 1864, with varying results. The following data is not released: medical and mental health data, disciplinaries, correspondence, chronos.

Access by: mail, phone, online.

Fee & Payment: There is a $.25 fee per page. Fee payee: Department of Corrections Prepayment required. Personal checks accepted.

Mail search: Turnaround time: 30 days. No SASE is required.

Phone search: Limited name searching available by phone.

Online search: There are two ways to access information at the web page. The first is by clicking on Online Inmate Search or www.doc.nv.gov/ncis/search.php. This will allow you to look up information about a particular individual. If you prefer, you may click on Download Information to obtain text files of all the information available via the Inmate Search. This system contains information about current inmates and those discharged in the past 18 months.

Corporation, Limited Partnerships, Limited Liability Company,

Secretary of State, Records, 202 N Carson City, Carson City, NV 89701-4707; 775-684-5708 (Expedite), 800-486-2880 (Customer Srv), 775-684-5645-Fax; 8AM-5PM.

www.sos.state.nv.us

Records are available since inception of laws. Old, inactive records are purged from computer and archived. New records are available for inquiry immediately. Records are indexed on microfiche, inhouse computer.

Searching: Search requests must be on letterhead or use this agency's form. Form numbers are viewable on the web. To get forms, use their Document-on-Demand System 800-583-9486. Include the following in your request-full name of business, corporation file number. In addition to the articles of incorporation, corporation records include the following information: Annual Lists of Officers & Directors, Prior (merged) names, Inactive and Reserved names, and Resident Agent names.

Access by: mail, phone, fax, in person, online.

Fee & Payment: The search fee is $50.00. The certification fee is $30.00. Copy fees are $2.00 per page. Fee payee: Secretary of State. Prepayment required. Personal checks accepted. Major credit cards accepted.

Mail search: Turnaround time: 1 to 2 weeks. No SASE is required.

Phone search: Staff will give status for corporations and partnerships, corporate officer names, and trademark information.

Fax search: One may request copies by fax, this is considered expedited service, see below.

In person search: Information requests are available.

Online search: Online access is offered on the Internet site for no charge. You can search by corporate name, resident agent, corporate officers, or by file number.

Expedited service: Expedited service is available for mail, fax, phone and in person searches. The expedite search fee is $25.00 There is an additional $75.00 fee for overnight service of copies if 1 to 10 pages, and $125.00 if over 10 pages.

Assumed Name Fictitious Name

Records not maintained by a state level agency.

Records are at the county level.

Trademarks/Servicemarks

Secretary of State, Corporate Expedite Office, 555 E. Washington Ave, #4000, Las Vegas, NV 89101; 702-486-2880, 702-486-2888-Fax; 8AM-5PM.

http://secretaryofstate.biz/comm_rec/trademk/index.htm

Trademark files are kept here and copies of document must be requested from this office. The SOS office in Carson City can look records on computer, but cannot make copies of actual documents in files.

Records are available since inception.

Searching: The same search requirements apply here as in Carson City.

Access by: mail, phone, in person.

Fee & Payment: The search fee is $50.00. Copies are $2.00 per page and $30.00 for certification. Fee payee: NV Secretary of State. Prepayment required. Personal checks accepted. No credit cards accepted.

Mail search: Turnaround time: 1 to 2 weeks.

Phone search: Limited information is offered over the phone.

In person search: Turnaround immediate, time permitting.

Uniform Commercial Code, Federal and State Tax Liens

UCC Division, Secretary of State, 200 N Carson St, Carson City, NV 89701-4069; 775-684-5708, 775-684-5630-Fax; 8AM-5PM.

www.sos.state.nv.us

Federal tax lien search must be requested separately and only contain data on businesses. Tax liens on individuals are filed at the county level. There is no state income tax, thus no recorded state tax liens.

Records are available from 1967 on both computer and microfilm. It takes 1-2 days before new records are available for inquiry. Records are normally destroyed after 6 years.

Searching: Use search request form UCC-11. Include the following in your request-debtor name.

Access by: mail, fax, in person, online.

Fee & Payment: The fee for written request to search a debtor name is $40.00, via the Internet is $20.00. Copies cost $2.00 per page. Fee payee: Secretary of State. Prepayment required. Personal checks accepted. Credit cards accepted: MasterCard, Visa.

Mail search: Turnaround time: 1 to 3 days.

Fax search: See expedited service.

In person search: You may request information in person.

Online search: Searching is available from the web, fee is $20.00, an order form may be downloaded. A commercial system is also available. The PC dial-up system fee is based on hourly rate - $6.50 peak time, $4.50 non-peak time. Includes unlimited access. There is a $50.00 minimum deposit. The system is up from 7 AM to 5 PM.

Expedited service: Expedited service is available for mail and fax request searches. Searches will not be returned by fax. Turnaround time: 2 to 24 hours. Add $75.00 for 1 to 10 copies, $125.00 if 11 or more copies.

Sales Tax Registrations

State does not impose sales tax.

Birth Certificates

Nevada Department of Health, Office of Vital Statistics, 505 E King St, Rm 102, Carson City, NV 89701-4749; 775-684-4242, 775-684-4280 (Message Phone), 877-456-5410 (Orders), 775-684-4156-Fax; 8AM-4PM.

http://health2k.state.nv.us

Records are available from 1911 to present. It takes 30 days of filing before new records are available for inquiry. Records are indexed on microfiche, index cards, inhouse computer, hard copy.

Searching: Birth and death records are considered confidential and not open to the general public. Include the following in your request-full name, names of parents, mother's maiden name, date of birth, place of birth, relationship to person of record, reason for information request. Parents' names are a must to get record.

Access by: mail, phone, fax, in person, online.

Fee & Payment: For a certified copy the fee is $13.00. The fee for a verification only or for a no record found the fee is $8.00. If you wish to purchase using a credit card, there is an additional $5.50 fee. Fee payee: Office of Vital Statistics. Prepayment required. Personal checks accepted. Major credit cards accepted.

Mail search: Turnaround time: 2 to 3 days. No SASE is required.

Phone search: See expedited service.

Fax search: See expedited service.

In person search: Turnaround time 20 minutes.

Online search: Expedited service is available from state designated vendor at www.vitalchek.com.

Expedited service: Expedited service is available for online, phone and fax requests. Add $10.95 for 5 to 7 day service, or $28.45 for 2-5 day service. A credit card is required.

Death Records

Nevada Department of Health, Office of Vital Statistics, 505 E King St, Rm 102, Carson City, NV 89701-4749; 775-684-4242, 775-684-4280 (Message Phone), 877-456-5410 (Orders), 775-684-4156-Fax; 8AM-4PM.

http://health2k.state.nv.us

Records are available from 1911 on. It takes 30 days of filing before new records are available for inquiry. Records are indexed on microfiche, index cards, inhouse computer, hard copy.

Searching: Records are considered confidential, need to state relationship. However, a verification printout with name, date, and location is available to the public. Include the following in your request-full name, date of death, place of death, relationship to person of record, reason for information request.

Access by: mail, phone, fax, in person, online.

Fee & Payment: A certified copy is $10.00. The fee for a verification only or if no record found is $8.00. Fee payee: Office of Vital Statistics. Prepayment required. Personal checks accepted. Major credit cards accepted.

Mail search: Turnaround time: 5 to 10 working days. No SASE is required.

Phone search: See expedited service.

Fax search: See expedited service.

In person search: Turnaround time is 20 minutes.

Online search: Expedited service is available from state designated vendor at www.vitalchek.com.

Expedited service: Expedited service is available for online, phone and fax requests. Add $10.95 for 5 to 7 day service, or $28.45 for 2-5 day service. A credit card is required.

Marriage Certificates, Divorce Records

Access to Records is Restricted.

Nevada Department of Health, Office of Vital Statistics, 505 E King St, Rm 102, Carson City, NV 89701-4749; 775-684-4481.

http://health2k.state.nv.us

Marriage and Divorce records are found at county recorder office of issue and not here. However, this agency has a list of each county agency at http://health2k.state.nv.us/forms/formtypes/statein dex.pdf.

Workers' Compensation Records

Employers Insurance Co of NV, Workers Compensation Insurance, 2550 Paseo Verde Parkway, Henderson, NV 89074-7117; 888-682-6671, 702-671-7175-Fax; 8AM-5PM.

www.eicn.com

Effective 1/1/00, Nevada privatized the business of workers' compensation insurance. The state agency formally named State Industrial Insurance System became a private company. This company holds the records from the state agency.

Records are available from 1940's on. It takes 1 week before new records are available for inquiry. Records are indexed on microfilm, inhouse computer, file folders.

Searching: Must have a signed release from claimant and you must specify what you want from the file. Employers, after a hire, may check records. Older records are kept on microfilm, the records on the in-house computer are for general information only. Include the following in your request-claimant name, Social Security Number. Claim number, date of accident are helpful if known. This office is the phone service center. There are also hard copy records at the Reno office. 9790 Gateway Dr #100, Reno NV 89521. Their fax # is 775-886-1797.

Access by: mail, fax, in person.

Fee & Payment: The fee for a record search is $5.00. Fee is $.50 per page, unless only several copies are required. Fee payee: Employers Insurance Co of NV. Personal checks accepted. No credit cards accepted.

Mail search: Turnaround time: 30 days. A SASE is requested.

Fax search: Fax requests are accepted.

In person search: By going in person, you will only reduce the mail time.

Driver Records

Department of Motor Vehicles, Records Section, 555 Wright Way, Carson City, NV 89711-0250; 775-684-4590, 877-368-7828 (In-state), 775-684-4899-Fax; 8AM-5PM.

www.dmvstat.com

Copies of citations may be obtained at the same address. There is no fee when requesting your own citation, otherwise the fee is $8.00.

Records are available for 3 yrs. Non-moving violations not listed on the driving record for non-CDL drivers. Nevada complies with the Driver's Privacy Protection Act, so personal data is available only to specific users. Records are computer indexed since 1980.

Searching: Authorized users may establish an account by completing the appropriate application. Call 775-684-4590 to request an application. Casual requesters without written consent of subject receive records without personal information. The driver's license number, or name and DOB are needed for a request. The SSN is helpful for searching, but is only released to government agencies. Accidents do not appear on the record.

Access by: mail, phone, fax, online.

Fee & Payment: The fee is $7.00 per record. Fee payee: Nevada Department of Motor Vehicles. Prepayment required. Personal checks accepted. No credit cards accepted.

Mail search: Turnaround time: 10 days. Your request must be on department approved forms. No SASE is required.

Phone search: Phone-in requesters must be pre-approved, are assigned a 5-digit account number and can request up to 5 records at one time over the phone. Call 775-684-4590 for information.

Fax search: Pre-approved accounts may fax requests.

Online search: The state has an FTP type online system available for high volume users. All files received by 5:30 PM are processed and returned at 6:30 PM. Fee is $7.00 per record. Call 775-684-4702 for details.

Vehicle Ownership
Vehicle Identification

Department of Motor Vehicles, Motor Vehicle Record Section, 555 Wright Way, Carson City, NV 89711-0250; 775-684-4590, 775-684-4740-Fax; 8AM-5PM.

www.dmvnv.com

Records are available for the present on computer and on microfilm back to 1980.

Searching: SSNs, withdrawal action, accidents, and information connected to a license plate are not released to the general public. Nevada complies with DPPA and restricts access of records with personal information to permissible users. Requesters must show a legal right to the information or provide written consent or records are released with no personal data.

Access by: mail, phone.

Fee & Payment: The cost is $5.00 per record for current vehicle title or registration information. A vehicle history is $7.00, a title verification letter is also $7.00. Certification is an additional $4.00. Photo copies are $3.00 each. Fee payee: Nevada Department of Motor Vehicles. Prepayment required. Personal checks accepted. No credit cards accepted.

Mail search: Turnaround time: 10 days. Be sure to give as much specific information as possible. Your request must be on department-approved forms. No SASE is required.

Phone search: Phone-in requesters must be pre-approved, are assigned a five-digit account number and can request up to five records at one time over the phone. Call 775-684-4590 for more information. There in-state toll free line is 800-992-7945.

Other access: Database is available for sale to permissible users under DPPA at costs varying from $500 to $2,500.

Accident Reports

Department of Public Safety, Nevada Highway Patrol, 555 Wright Way, Carson City, NV 89711; 775-684-4488, 775-684-4879-Fax; 8AM-5PM.

http://nhp.nv.gov/index.htm

Records are available only for those records at least three years old. It takes 7-10 working days before new records are available for inquiry. Records are indexed on inhouse computer. Records are normally destroyed after 6 years.

Searching: Requests must be in writing. Include the following in your request-full name, date of accident, location of accident, report number. For accidents 3 years old or less, the reports will be found at a regional office (Las Vegas 702-486-4100; Reno 775-688-2500; or Elko 775-753-1111) associated with where the accidents occurred. Same fees apply.

Access by: mail, fax, in person.

Fee & Payment: The fee is $3.50 per report, and report(s) will not be mailed until payment has been received. Fee payee: Nevada Highway Patrol. Prepayment required. Personal checks accepted. No credit cards accepted.

Mail search: Turnaround time: 1 week. Note the turnaround time for the Las Vegas office is often 4 to 6 weeks. A SASE is requested.

Fax search: Fax searching available, but only if pre-paid.

In person search: Turnaround time is immediate if the record is on file.

Vessel Ownership
Vessel Registration

Department of Wildlife Headquarters, Boat Registration, 1100 Valley Rd, Reno, NV 89512-2815; 775-688-1983, 775-688-1509-Fax; 8AM-5PM M-F.

www.ndow.org

Records are available from 1972 to the present and are indexed on computer. All boats must be registered. It takes less than 1 day before new records are available for inquiry.

Searching: To search, one of the following is required: hull ID #, boat #, or name, plus name and address of requester. The following data is not released: Social Security Numbers, phone numbers, email addresses.

Access by: mail, in person.

Fee & Payment: The fee is $5.00 per boat, which includes 1 computer print-out. Photocopies cost $.50 per page. Fee payee: NDOW. Prepayment required. Cash is accepted from in person searchers only. Out-of-state personal checks not accepted. No credit cards accepted.

Mail search: Turnaround time: 4 days. No SASE is required.

In person search: Turnaround time can be immediate if search is not lengthy.

Other access: Information is available on disk, magnetic tape, labels, and printed lists. Fees depend on media type, can be $750 or more.

Voter Registration

Access to Records is Restricted.

Secretary of State, Elections Division, 101 N Carson Street #3, Carson City, NV 89701; 775-684-5705, 775-684-5718-Fax; 8AM-5PM.

http://sos.state.nv.us/nvelection

Presently, records are open to the public at the county level. All data is released except for SSNs. The Federal Help America Vote Act of 2002 (HAVA) law requires implementation of a central, computerized, statewide voter registration system by 01/01/2006. At that time, this office will sell voter registration lists.

GED Certificates

Department of Education, State GED Administrator, 700 E 5th Street, Carson City, NV 89701; 775-687-9104, 775-687-9114-Fax; 8AM-5PM.

www.literacynet.org/nvadulted

These records are not public records and require consent of the examinee.

Records are available from 1948 to present, for GED. This agency holds many limited GED records on individuals tested in the military, federal prison, etc. It takes 2 to 4 weeks before new records are available for inquiry.

Searching: Only "passing scores" were kept from 1948 through 2001. Include the following in your request-name used when tested, location of test, signed release, date of birth, SSN, information about and signature of requester.

Access by: mail, fax, in person.

Fee & Payment: There is no fee.

Mail search: Turnaround time: 7 to 10 days.

Fax search: Same criteria as mail searching.

In person search: Turnaround immediate, if request not lengthy. The agency suggests to first make an appointment.

Hunting and Fishing License Information

Department of Wildlife, Licensing Office, 4600 Kietzke LN, D135, Reno, NV 89502; 775-688-1507, 775-688-1509-Fax; 8AM-5PM.

www.ndow.org

Records are available from 1976 to present on microfiche. It takes 3-6 months before new records are available for inquiry. Records are normally destroyed after 50 years.

Searching: Include the following in your request-full name, date of birth, Social Security Number. The following data is not released: Social Security Numbers or telephone numbers.

Access by: mail.

Fee & Payment: The fee is $5.00 per name per year searched. Fee payee: NDOW Prepayment required with guaranteed funds. No credit cards or personal checks accepted.

Mail search: Turnaround time: 1 to 3 working days. It will help to use their record request form, which you can request by phone. No SASE is required.

Other access: The Department offers mailing lists, labels, magnetic tapes of hunting and fishing license holders for fees ranging from $350 to $1830.

Nevada State Licensing Agencies

For details about the agency responsible for licensing/certifying/registering an item below or in the Agency Quick Finder section, match an item's number with the number of the agency in the *Licensing Agency Information* section.

Nevada Licenses Searchable Online

Ambulatory Surgery Ctr. (Pharm.) #16	https://nvbop.glsuite.us/renewal/glsweb/homeframe.aspx
Architect #2	http://nsbaidrd.state.nv.us/directory.htm
Athletic Promoter, Prof./Amateur) #35	www.boxing.nv.gov/teledir.htm
Attorney #44	www.nvbar.org/find_a_lawyer.asp
Bank #29	http://fid.state.nv.us/banks.htm
Boxing Gym #35	www.boxing.nv.gov/gyms.htm
Boxing Organization #35	www.boxing.nv.gov/teledir.htm
Building Mover #46	http://nscb.sierracat.com/
Carpentry Contractor #46	http://nscb.sierracat.com/
Check Casher #29	http://fid.state.nv.us/check-cashing.htm
Chiropractor #3	http://chirobd.nv.gov/
Collection Agency #29	http://fid.state.nv.us/collection%20agency.htm
Collection Manager #29	http://fid.state.nv.us/Qry_CollectionAgencyManager.asp
Contractor, General #46	http://nscb.sierracat.com/
Court Reporter, Certified #23	http://crptr.state.nv.us/contact.htm
Credit Union #29	http://fid.state.nv.us/credit%20union.htm
Debt Adjuster #29	http://fid.state.nv.us/debt-adjuster.htm
Deferred Deposit Company #29	http://fid.state.nv.us/check-cashing.htm
Dentist / Dental Hygienist #4	www.nvdentalboard.org/database/search.html
Doctor #11	http://medboard.nv.gov/default.asp
Doctor, Disciplinary Action #11	http://medboard.nv.gov/Disciplinary%20Actions/disciplinary_list.htm
Drug Wholesaler/Dist./Mfg. #16	https://nvbop.glsuite.us/renewal/glsweb/homeframe.aspx
Electrical Contractor #46	http://nscb.sierracat.com/
Elevator/Conveyor #46	http://nscb.sierracat.com/
Engineer #19	http://boe.state.nv.us/ROST_HOME.HTM
Engineering, General #46	http://nscb.sierracat.com/
Euthanasia Technician (Animal) #16	https://nvbop.glsuite.us/renewal/glsweb/homeframe.aspx
Fencing #46	http://nscb.sierracat.com/
Financial Development Company #29	http://fid.state.nv.us/development%20co.htm
Fire Protection Contractor #46	http://nscb.sierracat.com/
Fishing Guide #26	www.ndow.org/about/contacts/
Floor/Tile/Carpet Layer #46	http://nscb.sierracat.com/
Fur Dealer #26	www.ndow.org/about/contacts/
Gas Fitter #46	http://nscb.sierracat.com/
GCB Most-Wanted & Banned List #36	http://gaming.state.nv.us/wanted_main.htm
Glazier Contractor #46	http://nscb.sierracat.com/
Heating & Air Conditioning Mechanic #46	http://nscb.sierracat.com/
Hospital Pharmacy, Institutional #16	https://nvbop.glsuite.us/renewal/glsweb/homeframe.aspx
Installment Loan Company #29	http://fid.state.nv.us/installment%20loan.htm
Insulation Installer Contr. #46	http://nscb.sierracat.com/
Insurance Agent #24	www.doi.state.nv.us/PL-ContactUs.htm
Interior Designer #2	http://nsbaidrd.state.nv.us/directory.htm
Landscape Contractor #46	http://nscb.sierracat.com/
Lobbyist #27	www.leg.state.nv.us/lobbyistdb/index.cfm
Marriage & Family Therapist #32	http://marriage.state.nv.us/
Mason #46	http://nscb.sierracat.com/
Medical Device, Equipment or Gas #16	https://nvbop.glsuite.us/renewal/glsweb/homeframe.aspx
Medical Doctor #11	http://medboard.nv.gov/default.asp
Money Transmitter Agent #29	http://fid.state.nv.us/Qry_MTALicensee.asp
Money Transmitter Company #29	http://fid.state.nv.us/money%20transmitter.htm
Narcotic Treatment Center #16	https://nvbop.glsuite.us/renewal/glsweb/homeframe.aspx
Nurse Anesthetist #13	www.nursingboard.state.nv.us/Verification/formLicense.html
Nurse Assistant #13	www.nursingboard.state.nv.us/Verification/formLicense.html
Nurse, Adv'd Practitioner (Pharm) #16	https://nvbop.glsuite.us/renewal/glsweb/homeframe.aspx
Nurse, Adverse Action Report #13	www.nursingboard.state.nv.us/dactions/
Nurse, RN/LPN/Advanced Practice #13	www.nursingboard.state.nv.us/Verification/formLicense.html
Optometrist #50	http://optometry.nv.gov/roster/licenseeinfo.pdf
Osteopathic Physician #15	https://nvboo.glsuite.us/renewal/glsweb/homeframe.aspx
Painter #46	http://nscb.sierracat.com/

Painter/Paper Hanger #46 .... http://nscb.sierracat.com/
Pharmacist/Pharmaceutical Tech #16 .... https://nvbop.glsuite.us/renewal/glsweb/homeframe.aspx
Pharmacy / Pharmacy Practitioner #16 .... https://nvbop.glsuite.us/renewal/glsweb/homeframe.aspx
Physician Assistant #11 .... http://medboard.nv.gov/default.asp
Physician Assistant (Pharm) #16 .... https://nvbop.glsuite.us/renewal/glsweb/homeframe.aspx
Plaster/Lather #46 .... http://nscb.sierracat.com/
Plasterer/Drywall Installer #46 .... http://nscb.sierracat.com/
Playground Builder #46 .... http://nscb.sierracat.com/
Plumber #46 .... http://nscb.sierracat.com/
Podiatrist #18 .... http://podiatry.state.nv.us/
Prison Pharmacy (correctional) #16 .... https://nvbop.glsuite.us/renewal/glsweb/homeframe.aspx
Pump Installer #46 .... http://nscb.sierracat.com/
Refractory/Firebrick Contr. #46 .... http://nscb.sierracat.com/
Residential Designer #2 .... http://nsbaidrd.state.nv.us/directory.htm
Respiratory Care Practitioner #11 .... http://medboard.nv.gov/default.asp
Roofer #46 .... http://nscb.sierracat.com/
Savings & Loan #29 .... http://fid.state.nv.us/savings%20and%20loan.htm
Scientific Collector #26 .... www.ndow.org/about/contacts/
Sewerage Contractor #46 .... http://nscb.sierracat.com/
Sheet Metal Fabricator #46 .... http://nscb.sierracat.com/
Siding Installer #46 .... http://nscb.sierracat.com/
Sign Erector #46 .... http://nscb.sierracat.com/
Solar Contractor #46 .... http://nscb.sierracat.com/
Steel Contractor #46 .... http://nscb.sierracat.com/
Surveyor, Land #19 .... http://boe.state.nv.us/ROST_HOME.HTM
Tank Installer, Pressure/Storage #46 .... http://nscb.sierracat.com/
Thrift Company #29 .... http://fid.state.nv.us/thrift%20company.htm
Trust Company #29 .... http://fid.state.nv.us/trust%20company.htm
Water Well Driller #30 .... http://water.nv.gov/IS/Drillers/wd_queries.htm
Well Driller #46 .... http://nscb.sierracat.com/
Well Driller/Monitor #30 .... http://water.nv.gov/IS/Drillers/wd_queries.htm
Wrecker/Demolisher #46 .... http://nscb.sierracat.com/

Nevada Licensing Quick Finder

Acupuncturist #14 702-837-8921
Adult Day Care #22 775-687-4475
Adult Group Care #22 775-687-4475
Aesthetician #38 702-486-6542
Alcohol & Drug Abuse Center #22 775-687-4475
Alcohol & Drug Abuse Counselor #22.. 775-687-4475
Ambulance Attendant / Permit #22........ 775-687-4475
Ambulatory Surgery Ctr. (Pharm) #16.. 775-850-1440
Animal Technician #21 775-688-1788
Announcer, Athletic Event (Ring) #35 .. 702-486-2575
Appraiser (MVD) #24 702-486-4009
Architect #2 702-486-7300
Athletic Promoter, Prof./Amateur) #35 .. 702-486-2575
Attorney #44 702-382-2200
Audiologist #31 775-857-3500
Auditor #1 775-786-0231
Bank #29 775-684-1830
Barber #45 702-456-4769
Blood Gas Technician/Tech. #22 775-687-4475
Boxer #35 702-486-2575
Boxing Gym #35 702-486-2575
Boxing Organization #35 702-486-2575
Building Mover #46 702-486-1100
Bus Driver #25 775-684-4590
Carpentry Contractor #46 702-486-1100
Casino General Manager #36 775-684-7770
Cemetery #7 702-290-5366
Check Casher #29 775-684-1830
Chiropractor #3 775-688-1921
Claims Adjuster #24 702-486-4009
Clinical Laboratory Technologist #22 .. 775-687-4475
Coach Dealer, Commercial #34 702-486-4590
Collection Agency #29......................... 775-684-1830
Collection Manager #29........................ 775-684-1830
Concrete Contractor #46 702-486-1100
Contractor, General #46 702-486-1100
Cosmetologist #38 702-486-6542
Court Reporter, Certified #23 702-384-1663

Credit Union #29 775-684-1830
Crematorium #7 702-290-5366
Debt Adjuster #29 775-684-1830
Deferred Deposit Company #29........... 775-684-1830
Dentist / Dental Hygienist #4 702-486-7044
Director (Medical Laboratory) #22........ 775-687-4475
Doctor #11 775-688-2559
Doctor, Disciplinary Action #11 775-688-2559
Drug Wholesaler/Dist./Mfg. #16 775-850-1440
Electrical Contractor #46 702-486-1100
Electrologist #38 702-486-6542
Elevator/Conveyor #46 702-486-1100
Embalmer #7 702-290-5366
Emergency Care Center, Independent #22
                              775-687-4475
Emergency Medical Technician #22 775-687-4475
Engineer #19 775-688-1231
Engineering, General #46 702-486-1100
Environmental Health Specialist #42 ... 775-328-2422
ESRD #22 775-687-4475
Euthanasia Technician #21 775-688-1788
Euthanasia Technician (Animal) #16 ... 775-850-1440
Exempt Laboratory #22 775-687-4475
Fencing #46 702-486-1100
Financial Advisor (Investment Advisor) #40
                              702-486-2440
Financial Development Company #29 .. 775-684-1830
Fire Protection Contractor #46 702-486-1100
First Responder EMT #22 775-687-4475
Fishing Guide #26 775-688-1512
Floor/Tile/Carpet Layer #46.................. 702-486-1100
Funeral Director #7 702-290-5366
Fur Dealer #26 775-688-1512
Gaming #36 775-684-7770
Gaming Device Mfg./Dist. #36 775-684-7770
Gaming License Company #36 775-684-7770
Gas Fitter #46 702-486-1100
GCB Most-Wanted & Banned List #36.. 775-684-7770

Glazier Contractor #46 702-486-1100
Groundskeeper/Gardener #28 ..... 775-688-1182x243
Guard Dog Handler #39 775-687-3223
Hair Stylist (Designer) #38 702-486-6542
Health Clinic, Rural #22 775-687-4475
Hearing Aid Specialist #8 702-571-9000
Heating & Air Conditioning Mechanic #46
                              702-486-1100
Histologic Technician #22 775-687-4475
Histotechnologist #22 775-687-4475
Home Health Agency #22 775-687-4475
Homeopathic Physician/Assistant #9.. 702-451-3332
Homeopathic Practitioner,Advanc'd #9 702-451-3332
Hospice #22 775-687-4475
Hospital #22 775-687-4475
Hospital Pharmacy, Institutional #16.... 775-850-1440
IC Emergency Center #22.................... 775-687-4475
Installment Loan Company #29 775-684-1830
Insulation Installer Contr. #46 702-486-1100
Insurance Agent #24 702-486-4009
Interior Designer #2 702-486-7300
Intermediate Care Facility for Mentally Retarded #22
                              775-687-4475
Intermedical Care Facility #22 775-687-4475
Investment Advisor #40....................... 702-486-2440
Kickboxer #35................................... 702-486-2575
Lab Assist./Blood Gas Assist #22 775-687-4475
Laboratory Certification #22 775-687-4475
Laboratory Office Assistant #22 775-687-4475
Laboratory, Medical #22...................... 775-687-4475
Landscape Architect #10..................... 775-530-4602
Landscape Contractor #46................... 702-486-1100
Lobbyist #27 775-684-6800
LPG Gas Distributor/Technician #33 ... 775-687-4890
Manicurist #38 702-486-6542
Marriage & Family Therapist #32......... 702-486-7388
Mason #46.. 702-486-1100
Medical Device, Equipment or Gas #16 775-850-1440

Medical Doctor #11	775-688-2559
Medical Technician #22	775-687-4475
Mixed Martial Arts #35	702-486-2575
Mobile Home Dealer/Limited Dealer#34	702-486-4590
Mobile Home Installer/Mfg. #34	702-486-4590
Mobile Home Salesman #34	702-486-4590
Mobile Home Serviceman/Limited Serviceman #34	702-486-4590
Mobile/Manufactured Home Rebuilder #34	702-486-4590
Mobile/Manufactured Home RME #34	702-486-4590
Money Transmitter Agent #29	775-684-1830
Money Transmitter Company #29	775-684-1830
Narcotic Treatment Center #16	775-850-1440
Notary Public #41	775-684-5749
Nurse Anesthetist #13	888-590-NSBN
Nurse Assistant #13	888-590-NSBN
Nurse, Advanced Practitioner (Pharm) #16	775-850-1440
Nurse, Adverse Action Report #13	800-746-3980
Nurse,RN/LPN/Advanced Practice#13	888-590-NSBN
Nursing Care (Skilled) Facility #22	775-687-4475
Nursing Facility #22	775-687-4475
Nursing Home Administrator #49	702-486-5445
Nursing Pool Operator #22	775-687-4475
Occupational Therapist/Assistant #12	775-857-1700
Optician #5	775-853-1421
Optician Apprentice #5	775-853-1421
Optometrist #50	775-883-8367
Osteopathic Physician #15	702-732-2147
Osteopathic Physician Assistant #15	702-732-2147
Painter #46	702-486-1100
Painter/Paper Hanger #46	702-486-1100
Pathologist Assistant #22	775-687-4475
Patrol Company/Man, Private #39	775-687-3223
Pest Control Applicator/Company #28	775-688-1182x252
Pesticide, Restricted Use #28	775-688-1182x251
Pharmacist/Pharmaceutical Tech. #16	775-850-1440
Pharmacy #16	775-850-1440
Pharmacy Practitioner #16	775-850-1440
Physical Therapist #17	702-876-5535
Physical Therapist Assistant #17	702-876-5535
Physician Assistant #11	775-688-2559
Physician Assistant (Pharm) #16	775-850-1440
Plaster/Lather #46	702-486-1100
Plasterer/Drywall Installer #46	702-486-1100
Playground Builder #46	702-486-1100
Plumber #46	702-486-1100
Podiatrist #18	775-789-2605
Polygraph Examiner #39	775-687-3223
Prison (correctional - Pharm) #16	775-850-1440
Private Investigator #39	775-687-3223
Process Server #39	775-687-3223
Psychologist #20	775-688-1268
Public Accountant-CPA #1	775-786-0231
Pump Installer #46	702-486-1100
Racing #37	775-684-7900
Real Estate Agent/Sales #43	702-486-4033
Real Estate Broker #43	702-486-4033
Referee/Judge/Timekeeper #35	702-486-2575
Refractory/Firebrick Contr. #46	702-486-1100
Rehabilitation Service #22	775-687-4475
Repossessor #39	775-687-3223
Residential Designer #2	702-486-7300
Respiratory Care Practitioner #11	775-688-2559
Roofer #46	702-486-1100
Sanitarian, Public #42	775-328-2418
Savings & Loan #29	775-684-1830
School Administrator #47	702-486-6458
School Counselor #47	702-486-6458
School Librarian #47	702-486-6458
School Program Administrator #47	702-486-6458
Scientific Collector #26	775-688-1512
Securities Broker/Dealer/Branch #40	702-486-2440
Securities Registration #40	702-486-2440
Securities Sales Representative #40	702-486-2440
Sewerage Contractor #46	702-486-1100
Sheet Metal Fabricator #46	702-486-1100
Siding Installer #46	702-486-1100
Sign Erector #46	702-486-1100
Slot Route Operator #36	775-684-7770
Social Worker #6	702-688-2555
Solar Contractor #46	702-486-1100
Speech Pathologist/Audiologist #31	775-857-3500
Steel Contractor #46	702-486-1100
Supervisory Medical Tech.General #22	775-687-4475
Surgical Center, Ambulatory #22	775-687-4475
Surveyor, Land #19	775-688-1231
Tank Installer, Pressure/Storage #46	702-486-1100
Taxi Cab Company (Clark County) #48	702-486-6532
Taxi Driver #48	702-486-6532
Teacher #47	702-486-6458
Thrift Company #29	775-684-1830
Trust Company #29	775-684-1830
Veterinarian #21	775-688-1788
Veterinary Facility #21	775-688-1788
Water Well Driller #30	775-687-3861
Well Driller #46	702-486-1100
Well Driller/Monitor #30	775-687-3861
Wrecker/Demolisher #46	702-486-1100
Wrestler #35	702-486-2575

Nevada Licensing Agency Information

1 Board of Accountancy, 1325 Airmotive Way #220, Reno, NV 89502-3240; 775-786-0231, Fax: 775-786-0234. www.nvaccountancy.com/ Email: cpa@nvaccountancy.com

2 Interior & Residential Design, Board of Interior & Residential Design, 2080 E Flamingo Rd, #225, Las Vegas, NV 89119; 702-486-7300, Fax: 702-486-7304. http://nsbaidrd.state.nv.us/ Email: nsbaidrd@govmail.state.nv.us Search Database at http://nsbaidrd.state.nv.us/directory.htm Note: Phone 702-486-7300 for information about disciplinary actions.

3 Board of Chiropractic Examiners, 4600 Kietzke Ln, M, #245, Reno, NV 89502; 775-688-1921, Fax: 775-688-1920. http://chirobd.nv.gov Email: chirobd@chirobd.nv.gov Search Database at http://chirobd.nv.gov/ Note: Data is presented in a PDF format; click on "Licensed Chiropractic Physicians".

4 Board of Dental Examiners, 6010 S Rainbow Blvd # A-1, Las Vegas, NV 89118; 800-337-3926 or 702-486-7044, Fax: 702-486-7046. www.nvdentalboard.org Email: nsbde@nsbdc.nv.gov Search Database at http://www.nvdentalboard.org/database/search.html

5 Board of Dispensing Opticians, PO Box 19625, Reno, NV 89511-0868; 775-853-1421, Fax: 775-853-1408. http://nvbdo.state.nv.us/ Email: nvbdo@govmail.state.nv.us Note: Complete list is available by mail from the board for a minimal fee.

6 Board of Examiners for Social Workers, 4600 Kietzke Ln, Bldg C, Rm 121, Reno, NV 89502; 775-688-2555, Fax: 775-688-2557.

7 Board of Funeral Directors & Embalmers, 4894 Lone Mt Rd PMB186, Las Vegas, NV 89130; 702-290-5366, Fax: 702-648-5858. http://funeral.state.nv.us

8 Board of Hearing Aid Specialists, PO Box 195, Carson City, NV 89702; 702-571-9000, Fax: 775-267-9374. www.state.nv.us/boards/hearing/

9 Board of Homeopathic Medical Examiners, 3663 Pecos McLeod Int., Las Vegas, NV 89121; 702-451-3332, Fax: 702-451-3332. www.nvbhme.com/contact.html Email: homboard@nevadaclinic.com

10 Board of Landscape Architecture, P. O. Box 17039, Reno, NV 89511; 775-530-4602. http://nsbla.state.nv.us Email: LandscapeBoard@nsbla.nv.gov <LandscapeBoard@nsbla.nv.gov> Search Database at http://nsbla.state.nv.us/Licensed.htm Complete list is available for $5.00 from the Board.

11 Board of Medical Examiners, 1105 Terminal Way, #301, Reno, NV 89510; 775-688-2559, Fax: 775-688-2321. http://medboard.nv.gov Email: nsbme@medboard.nv.gov Search Database at http://medboard.nv.gov/default.asp

12 Board of Occupational Therapy, PO Box 70220, Reno, NV 89570-0220; 775-857-1700, Fax: 775-857-2121. www.nvot.org Email: occtherapy@gbis.com

13 Nevada State Board of Nursing, 2500 W. Sahara Ave #207, Las Vegas, NV 89102-4392; 888-590-6726, 702-486-5800, Consumer hotline-800-746-3980, Lisensure info-888-590-NSBN., Fax: 702-486-5803. www.nursingboard.state.nv.us Email: lasvegas@nsbn.state.nv.us Search Database at www.nursingboard.state.nv.us/Verification/formLicense.html Disciplinary actions and investigations are handled by the Reno office, 5011 Meadowood Mall Way #201, 89502, 800-746-3980.

14 Board of Oriental Medicine, 9775 S Maryland Pkwy, Ste F-280, Reno, NV 89509; 702-837-8921, Fax: 702-914-8921. www.oriental_medicine.state.nv.us Email: sbpark@uissbpark@uisreno.com

15 Board of Osteopathic Medicine, 2860 E Flamingo, #G, Las Vegas, NV 89121; 702-732-2147, Fax: 702-732-2079. www.osteo.state.nv.us Email: osteo@govmail.state.nv.us Search Database at https://nvboo.glsuite.us/renewal/glsweb/homeframe.aspx

16 Board of Pharmacy, 555 Double Eagle Ct #1100, Reno, NV 89511-8991; 775-850-1440, 800-364-2081, Fax: 775-850-1444. https://nvbop.glsuite.us/renewal/glsweb/homeframe.aspx Search Database at https://nvbop.glsuite.us/rene wal/glsweb/homeframe.aspx

17 Physical Therapy Examiners Board, 810 S. Durango Dr #109, Las Vegas, NV 89145; 702-876-5535, Fax: 702-876-2097. http://ptboard.nv.gov Email: atresca@govmail.state.nv.us

18 Board of Podiatry, PO Box 12215, Reno, NV 89510-2215; 775-789-2605.
http://podiatry.state.nv.us/
Email: nvpodiatry@bop.nv.gov
Search Database at http://podiatry.state.nv.us/

19 Board of Professional Engineers & Land Surveyors, 1755 E Plumb Ln, #135, Reno, NV 89502; 775-688-1231, Fax: 775-688-2991.
http://boe.state.nv.us/   Email: jrobins@natinfo.net
Search Database at
http://boe.state.nv.us/ROST_HOME.HTM

20 Board of Psychological Examiners, PO Box 2286 (275 Hill St, #246), Reno, NV 89505-2286; 775-688-1268, Fax: 775-688-1272.
http://psyexam.state.nv.us/
Email: nbop@govmail.state.nv.us

21 Board of Veterinary Medical Examiners, 4600 Kietzke Lane, Bldg O, #265, Reno, NV 89502; 775-688-1788, Fax: 775-688-1808.
Email: vetbbdinfo@govmail.state.nv.us

22 Bureau of Licensure & Certification, Medical Laboratory Services, 1550 College Parkway #158, Carson City, NV 89710; 775-687-4475, Fax: 775-687-6588.   http://health2k.state.nv.us/

23 Certified Court Reporters Board, 3355 Spring Mountain Rd #2, Las Vegas, NV 89102-8631; 702-384-1663, Fax: 702-876-9249.
http://crptr.state.nv.us/index.htm
Email: ccrbnv@juno.com

24 Department of Business & Industry, Insurance Division, 2501 E Sahara Ave, #302, Las Vegas, NV 89104; 702-486-4009, Fax: 702-486-4007.
www.doi.state.nv.us

25 Department of Motor Vehicles & Public Safety, Records Section, 555 Wright Way, Carson City, NV 89711-0250; 775-684-4590, Fax: 775-684-4740.   http://nevadadmv.state.nv.us
Email: jfogliani@dmv.state.nv.us

26 Department of Wildlife, Licensed Wildlife Services, 1100 Valley Rd, Reno, NV 89520; 775-688-1500, Fax: 775-688-1551.
www.ndow.org
Email: tatkinson@ndow.org

27 Director of Legislative Counsel Bureau, 401 S Carson, Carson City, NV 89701-4747; 775-684-6800, Fax: 775-684-6600.
www.leg.state.nv.us/lcb/admin/lobbyist.htm
Email: wiese@icb.state.nv.us
Search Database at
www.leg.state.nv.us/lobbyistdb/index.cfm

28 Department of Agriculture, Pest Control Licensing Division, 350 Capitol Hill, Reno, NV 89502-2923; 775-688-1180, Fax: 775-688-1178.
http://agri.state.nv.us

29 Department of Business & Industry, Divison of Financial Institutions, 406 E 2nd St #3, Carson City, NV 89701;

775-684-1830-Reno; 702-486-4120-Las Vegas, Fax: 775-684-1845-Reno; 702-486-4563-Las Vegas.   http://fid.state.nv.us
Search Database at http://fid.state.nv.us/   Note: Las Vegas office is located at 2501 E. Sahara Ave #300, 89104; phone 702-486-4120.

30 Division of Water Resources, Well Drillers' Advisory Board, 123 W Nye Ln, Capitol Complex Rm 246, Carson City, NV 89706-0818; 775-687-3861, Fax: 775-687-1393.
http://ndwr.state.nv.us
Search Database at
http://water.nv.gov/IS/Drillers/wd_queries.htm

31 Board of Examiners for Audiology & Speech Pathology, PO Box 70550, Reno, NV 89570; 775-857-3500, Fax: 775-857-2121.
http://speech_pathology.state.nv.us

32 Board of Examiners of Marriage & Family Therapists, PO Box 72758, Las Vegas, NV 89170; 702-486-7388, Fax: 702-486-7258.
http://marriage.state.nv.us/

33 Liquefied Petroleum Gas Regulation Board, PO Box 338 (106 E Adams, Rm 216), Carson City, NV 89702; 775-687-4890, Fax: 775-687-3956.
http://lpg.nv.gov   Note: You may email verification requests to lpgasbd@lpg.nv.gov.

34 Attn: Gisele Jordan, Licensing Officer, Manufactured Housing Division, 2501 E Sahara Ave, #205, Las Vegas, NV 89104; 702-486-4590, Fax: 702-486-4309.
www.mhd.state.nv.us
Email: mhlicens@mnd.state.nv.us

35 Athletic Commission, 555 E Washington St #3200, Las Vegas, NV 89101; 702-486-2575, Fax: 702-486-2577.
www.boxing.nv.gov
Email: boxing@boxing.nv.gov

36 Tax & License Division, Gaming Control Board, 1919 E College Pky (PO Box 8003, 89702-8003), Carson City, NV 89706; 775-684-7770.
http://gaming.nv.gov

37 Gaming Control Board, Enforcement Division, 1919 E College Pky, Carson City, NV 89706; 775-684-7900, Fax: 775-687-5362.
http://gaming.state.nv.us

38 Board of Cosmetology, 1785 E Sahara Ave, #255, Las Vegas, NV 89104; 702-486-6542, Fax: 702-369-8064.
www.state.nv.us/cosmetology/
Email: nvcosmbd@govmail.state.nv.us

39 Office of the Attorney General, Private Investigators Licensing Board, 3476 Executive Pointe Way #14, Carson City, NV 89706; 775-687-3223, Fax: 775-687-3226.
http://ag.state.nv.us/faqs/workingaspi.htm
Email: pilbinfo@ag.state.nv.us   Note: Lists only those who want to be listed.

40 Office of the Secretary of State, Securities Division, 555 E Washington Av #5200, Las Vegas, NV 89101; 702-486-2440, Fax: 702-486-2452.
www.sos.state.nv.us/securities

41 Office of the Secretary of State, Notary Division, 101 N Carson St, Carson City, NV 89710-4786; 775-684-5708, Fax: 775-684-5725.
http://sos.state.nv.us/notary/
Email: nvnotary@govmail.state.nv.us

42 Environmental Health Services, Washoe County District Health Department, PO Box 1130 (1001 E 9th St), Reno, NV 89520; 775-328-2434, Fax: 775-328-6176.
www.co.washoe.nv.us/health/ehs/

43 Department of Business & Industry, Real Estate Division, 2501 E Sahara Ave, Las Vegas, NV 89158; 702-486-4033, Fax: 702-486-4275.
www.red.state.nv.us
Email: realest@govmail.state.nv.us

44 State Bar of Nevada, 600 E Charleston Blvd, Las Vegas, NV 89104; 702-382-2200, Fax: 702-385-2878.
www.nvbar.org
Email: pamik@nvbar.org
Search Database at
www.nvbar.org/find_a_lawyer.asp

45 Barbers' Health & Sanitation Board, 4710 E Flamingo Rd, Las Vegas, NV 89121; 702-456-4769 LV (775-688-1988 Reno), Fax: 702-456-1948.
http://barber.state.nv.us

46 Contractors' Board, 9670 Gateway Dr #100, Reno, NV 89521; 775-688-1141-Reno, Fax: 775-688-1271-Reno.
http://nscb.state.nv.us
Email: cntractr@govmail.state.nv.us
Search Database at http://nscb.sierracat.com/
Note: The phone number for the Henderson office is 702-486-1100; fax is 702-486-1190; address is 2310 Corporate Circle #200.

47 Department of Education, Teacher Licensure, 1820 E Sahara, #205, Las Vegas, NV 89104; 702-486-6458, Fax: 702-486-6450.
www.doe.nv.gov
Email: license@nsn.k12.nv.us

48 Taxicab Authority, 1785 E Sahara Ave #200, Las Vegas, NV 89104; 702-486-6532, Fax: 702-486-7350.
http://taxi.state.nv.us
Email: ymoore@taxi.state.nv.us

49 Board of Examiners for Long Term Care Administrators, 3157 N Rainbow Blvd, #313, Las Vegas, NV 89108; 702-486-5445.
http://beltca.nevada.gov/

50 Board of Optometry, PO Box 1824, Carson City, NV 89702; 775-883-8367, Fax 775-883-1938.   http://optometry.nv.gov

Nevada Federal Courts

The following list indicates the district and division name for each county in the state. If the bankruptcy court location is different from the district court, then the location of the bankruptcy court appears in parentheses.

Nevada County/Court Cross Reference

Carson City	Reno	Lincoln	Las Vegas
Churchill	Reno	Lyon	Reno
Clark	Las Vegas	Mineral	Reno
Douglas	Reno	Nye	Las Vegas
Elko	Reno	Pershing	Reno
Esmeralda	Las Vegas	Storey	Reno
Eureka	Reno	Washoe	Reno
Humboldt	Reno	White Pine	Reno
Lander	Reno		

US District Court

Las Vegas Division Court Clerk, Rm 4425, 300 Las Vegas Blvd S, Las Vegas, NV 89101 (also use mail address for courier delivery), 702-464-5400. Hours- 9AM-4PM. www.nvd.uscourts.gov

Counties: Clark, Esmeralda, Lincoln, Nye.

Searches & Indexing: Results do not include SSN or DOB. Computer index maintained back to 1999. New cases in the index same day of filing.

Fee & Payment: Pay by money order, cashier's or personal check. Payee: Clerk, US District Court. Prepayment required.

Phone Search: Only docket information available by phone.

Mail Search: search usually completed- 1-2 days. SASE not required.

In Person Search: Fee charged if court performs your search. No self-serve copier available.

E-Services: PACER online at https://pacer.psc.uscourts.gov/cgi-bin/login/login.pl?court_id=nvdc. Document images available. Currently in the process of implementing CM/ECF.

Reno Division Court Clerk, Rm 301, 400 S Virginia St, Reno, NV 89501 (also use mail address for courier delivery), 775-686-5800, records rm- 775-686-5909, crim dockets- 775-686-5844, civil dockets- 775-686-5845, Fax-702-686-5851. Hours- 9AM-4PM. www.nvd.uscourts.gov

Counties: Carson City, Churchill, Douglas, Elko, Eureka, Humboldt, Lander, Lyon, Mineral, Pershing, Storey, Washoe, White Pine.

Searches & Indexing: Results do not include SSN or DOB. Computer and microfiche indexes maintained. New cases in the index 1-2 days after filing date.

Fee & Payment: Pay by money order, cashier's or personal check. Payee: Clerk, US District Court. Prepayment required.

Phone Search: Only docket information available by phone.

Mail Search: search usually completed- within 1 week. SASE not required.

In Person Search: Fee charged if court performs your search. No self-serve copier available.

E-Services: PACER online at https://pacer.psc.uscourts.gov/cgi-bin/login/login.pl?court_id=nvdc. Document images available. Currently in the process of implementing CM/ECF.

US Bankruptcy Court

Las Vegas Division Court Clerk, 8th Fl, Suite 8112, Lloyd D George Federal Bldg, 300 Las Vegas Blvd South, Las Vegas, NV 89101 (courier address: Clerk's Office, 1st Fl, Lloyd D George Federal Bldg, 300 Las Vegas Blvd South, Las Vegas, NV 89101), 702-388-6257; ECF signup phone-702-388-6931. Hours- 9AM-4PM. www.nvb.uscourts.gov

Counties: Clark, Esmeralda, Lincoln, Nye.

Searches & Indexing: Results include last 4 SSN digits. Both computer and card indexes maintained. New cases in the index 24 hours after filing date. Records purged every 16 months.

Fee & Payment: Pay by money order, cashier's or personal check. No debtor's checks accepted. Payee: Clerk, US Bankruptcy Court.

Phone Search: Voice Case Information Service available, call 800-314-3436 or 702-388-6708.

Mail Search: search usually completed- 1 day. Include SASE for return.

In Person Search: Fee charged if court performs your search. Self-serve copier - $.25 per page.

E-Services: ECF replaces PACER whose records did go back to 9/1993. New records online after 1 day. ECF at https://ecf.nvb.uscourts.gov. Selected documents free at www.nvb.uscourts.gov/docs. **Other Online Access:** Searching records online using RACER has been phased out; ECF account is now required.

Reno Division Court Clerk, Rm 1109, 300 Booth St, Reno, NV 89509 (also use mail address for courier delivery), 775-784-5559. Hours- 9AM-4PM. www.nvb.uscourts.gov

Counties: Carson City, Churchill, Douglas, Elko, Eureka, Humboldt, Lander, Lyon, Mineral, Pershing, Storey, Washoe, White Pine.

Searches & Indexing: Results do not include SSN or DOB. Computer index maintained. New cases in the index 24 hours after filing date. Records purged every 16 months.

Fee & Payment: Pay by money order, cashier's or personal check. No debtor's checks accepted. Payee: Clerk, US Bankruptcy Court.

Phone Search: Voice Case Information Service available, call 800-314-3436 or 702-388-6708.

Mail Search: search usually completed- 3 days. Include SASE for return.

In Person Search: Fee charged if court performs your search. A copy service is available. No self-serve copier available.

E-Services: ECF replaces PACER whose records did go back to 9/1993. New records online after 1 day. ECF at https://ecf.nvb.uscourts.gov. Selected documents free at www.nvb.uscourts.gov/docs. **Other Online Access:** Searching records online using RACER has been phased out; ECF account is now required.

Standards for Federal Courts: Search fee is $26.00 per item (one party name or case number). Copy fee is $.50 per page. Certification fee is $9.00 per document, double for exemplification, if available. All fees standard unless noted in profile. Mail Search: always enclose a stamped self addressed envelope unless otherwise noted. Most courts accept fax requests or will suggest a copying/search vendor. Before releasing records, all courts require prepayment, unless noted.

Open records are located at the court unless otherwise noted. District courts index by defendant and plaintiff as well as by case number. Bankruptcy courts usually index by debtor and case number. While most courts now have their indexes on computer, many may still maintain index card files as well.

Courts offering internet access via CM-ECF or older RACER, PACER, or Web-PACER systems charge $.08 per page fee unless noted as free. Where PACER is available, the universal sign-up number is 800-676-6856. Find PACER and the US Party/Case Index at http://pacer.psc.uscourts.gov.

Nevada County Courts

Court	Jurisdiction	No. of Courts	How Organized
District Courts*	General	17	9 Districts
Justice Courts*	Limited	41	Townships
Municipal Courts	Municipal	17	19 Incorporated Cities/Towns

* Profiled in this Sourcebook.

Court	CIVIL								
	Tort	Contract	Real Estate	Min. Claim	Max. Claim	Small Claims	Estate	Eviction	Domestic Relations
District Courts*	X	X	X	10,000	No Max		X		X
Justice Courts*	X	X	X	$0	$10,000	$3500		X	
Municipal Courts	X	X	X	$0	$3500	$3500			

Court	CRIMINAL				
	Felony	Misdemeanor	DWI/DUI	Preliminary Hearing	Juvenile
District Courts*	X	X	X		X
Justice Courts*		X	X	X	
Municipal Courts					

ADMINISTRATION   Supreme Court of Nevada, Administrative Office of the Courts, Capitol Complex, 201 S Carson Street #250, Carson City, Nevada, 89701; 775-684-1700, Fax: 775-684-1723. www.nvsupremecourt.us/aoc/aoc.html

COURT STRUCTURE   There are 17 District Courts are the courts of general jurisdiction and are within 9 judicial districts. Their minimum civil limit raised from $7,500 to $10,000 on Jan 1, 2005. The Justice Courts are named for the township of jurisdiction. Note that, due to their small populations, some townships no longer have Justice Courts. The Justice Courts handle misdemeanor crime and traffic matters, small claims disputes, evictions, and other civil matters less than $10,000. The justices of the peace also preside over felony and gross misdemeanor arraignments and conduct preliminary hearings to determine if sufficient evidence exists to hold criminals for trial at District Court.

Probate is handled by the District Courts.

ONLINE ACCESS   Some Nevada Courts have internal online computer systems, but only Clark and Washoe counties offer online access to the public. A statewide court automation system is being implemented. The Supreme Court web site gives access to opinions.

Many Clark County justice and municipal courts offer current court calendars at http://sandgate.co.clark.nv.us/JusticeCourt/jcCalendarSearch.html.

ADDITIONAL INFORMATION   Many Nevada Justice Courts are small and have very few records. Their hours of operation vary widely and contact is difficult. It is recommended that requesters call ahead for information prior to submitting a written request or attempting an in-person retrieval.

Carson City County

1st Judicial District Court 885 E Musser St, #3031, Carson City, NV 89701-4775; phone: 775-887-2082; fax: 775-887-2177; hours 9AM-5PM (PST). *Felony, Gross Misdemeanor, Civil Actions Over $10,000, Probate.*
Note: The Justice Courts retain records for minor misdemeanors.
Civil Records: Access: Mail, in person. Only the court performs in person searches; visitors may not. Search fee: $1.00 per name per year. Court makes copy: $1.00 per page. Required to search: name, years to search. Civil cases indexed by defendant, plaintiff. Civil records on computer from

1987, on microfiche and archives from 1861. Mail turnaround time 2-3 days.
Criminal Records: Access: Mail, in person. Only the court performs in person searches; visitors may not. Search fee: $1.00 per name per year. Court makes copy: $1.00 per page. Required to search: name, years to search. Criminal records on computer from 1987, on microfiche and archives from 1861. Mail turnaround time 2-3 days.
General Information: No public access terminal. No sealed or juvenile records released. Will fax documents to local or toll free line. Certification fee: $5.00. Payee: Carson City. Personal check accepted with check guarantee card only. Prepayment and SASE required.

Justice & Municipal Court 885 E Musser St, #2007, Carson City, NV 89701-4775; phone: 775-887-2121; fax: 775-887-2297; hours 8:30AM-5PM (PST). *Misdemeanor, Civil Actions Under $10,000, Eviction, Small Claims.*
Civil Records: Access: Mail, in person. Only the court performs in person searches; visitors may not. Search fee: $1.00 per name per year. Court makes copy: $.30 per page. Required to search: name, years to search. Criminal records on computer alpha index from 1991. Mail turnaround time 1 week.
Criminal Records: Access: Mail, in person. Only the court performs in person searches; visitors may not. Search fee: $1.00 per name per year. Court makes copy: $.30 per page. Required to search: name,

years to search. Criminal records on computer alpha index from 1991. Mail turnaround time 1 week.

General Information: No public access terminal. No sealed, sexual victims, juvenile records released. Will fax documents to local or toll free line. Certification fee: $3.00 per page. Payee: Carson City. Personal checks accepted. Prepayment and SASE required.

Churchill County

3rd Judicial District Court 73 N Maine St, #B, Fallon, NV 89406; phone: 775-423-6080; criminal fax: 775-423-8578; same fax for civil/probate; hours 8AM-N, 1-5PM (PST). *Felony, Gross Misdemeanor, Civil Actions Over $10,000, Probate.*

www.churchillcounty.org/dcourt/

Civil Records: Access: Fax, mail, in person. Only the court performs in person searches; visitors may not. Search fee: $1.00 per name per year. Court makes copy: $1.00 per page. Required to search: name, years to search. Civil cases indexed by defendant, plaintiff. Civil records on computer from 1990, prior on books, microfiche. Mail turnaround time 1-2 days.

Criminal Records: Access: Fax, mail, in person. Only the court performs in person searches; visitors may not. Search fee: $1.00 per name per year. Court makes copy: $1.00 per page. Required to search: name, years to search, DOB; also helpful: SSN. Criminal records on computer from 1990, prior on books, microfiche to 1910. Mail turnaround time 1-2 days.

General Information: No public access terminal. No juvenile, adoption or sealed records released. No fee to fax documents. local or toll free numbers only. Certification fee: $5.00 per document. Payee: Office of Court Clerk. Personal checks accepted. Prepayment and SASE required.

New River Justice Court 71 N Maine St, Fallon, NV 89406; phone: 775-423-2845; fax: 775-423-0472; hours 8AM-5PM (PST). *Misdemeanor, Civil Actions Under $10,000, Eviction, Small Claims.*

www.churchillcounty.org/jcourt/

Note: Fax search requests must be prepaid; use credit card.

Civil Records: Access: Mail, fax, in person. Both court and visitors may perform in person searches. Search fee: $1.00 per name per year. Court makes copy: $.30 per page. Required to search: name, years to search. Civil cases indexed by defendant, plaintiff. Civil records on computer from 1987, prior on microfiche back to 1980. Mail turnaround time 1 day.

Criminal Records: Access: Mail, fax, in person. Both court and visitors may perform in person searches. Search fee: $1.00 per name per year. Court makes copy: $.30 per page. Required to search: name, years to search, DOB. Criminal records on computer from 1987, prior on microfiche back to 1980. Mail turnaround time 1 day.

General Information: No public access terminal. No sealed records released. Will fax search documents to toll-free line. Certification fee: $3.00. Payee: Justice Court. Personal checks or Visa, MC accepted. Prepayment required.

Clark County

8th Judicial District Court PO Box 551601, 200 S 3rd, Las Vegas, NV 89155; phone: 702-455-3156; fax: 702-455-4929; hours 8AM-5PM (PST). *Felony, Gross Misdemeanor, Civil Actions Over $10,000, Probate.*

www.co.clark.nv.us/district_court/courthome.htm

Civil Records: Access: Mail, in person, online. Both court and visitors may perform in person searches. Search fee: $1.00 per name per year, plus copy fees. Fee is per case type. Court makes copy: $1.00 per page; same fee for self serve. Required to search: name, years to search. Civil cases indexed by defendant, plaintiff. Civil records on computer back to

11/90, prior records on microfilm to 1909. Records from the court are free online at http://courtgate.coca.co.clark.nv.us:8490. Search by case number or party name. Probate also available. Note: Clerks will do 1 or 2 names, but if a list is presented, expect to wait 24-48 hours for results. The index does not have personal identifiers, so files must be pulled when doing name searches to insure correct subject. Mail turnaround time 10 working days.

Criminal Records: Access: Mail, in person, online. Both court and visitors may perform in person searches. Search fee: $1.00 per name per year plus copy fees. Fee is per case price. Court makes copy: $1.00 per page; same fee for self serve. Required to search: name, years to search. Criminal records on computer back to 11/90, prior on microfilm to 1909. Online access to criminal records is the same as civil. Clerks will do 1 or 2 names, but if a list is presented, expect to wait 24-48 hours for results. Note: The index does not have personal identifiers, so files must be pulled when doing name searches to insure correct subject. Mail turnaround time 10 working days.

General Information: Public terminal has criminal back to 1/1991 and civil back to 1/1990. No sealed records released. Certification fee: $3.00 per cert. Payee: County Clerk's Office. Personal checks accepted. Prepayment and SASE required.

Boulder Township Justice Court 505 Ave G, Boulder City, NV 89005; phone: 702-455-8000; fax: 702-455-8003; hours 7:30AM-4;30PM M-Th (PST). *Misdemeanor, Civil Actions Under $10,000, Eviction, Small Claims.*

Civil Records: Access: Fax, mail, in person. Both court and visitors may perform in person searches. Search fee: $1.00 per name per year. Court makes copy: $1.00 per page. Required to search: name, years to search; also helpful: address. Civil cases indexed by defendant. Civil records on microfiche varies depending on subject. Current court calendars are at http://sandgate.co.clark.nv.us/JusticeCourt/jcCalendarSearch.html. Mail turnaround time 1 week.

Criminal Records: Access: Fax, mail, in person. Only the court performs in person searches; visitors may not. Search fee: $1.00 per name per year. Court makes copy: $1.00 per page. Required to search: name, years to search, DOB, date of offense; also helpful: SSN. Criminal records on microfiche varies depending on subject. Current court calendars are at http://sandgate.co.clark.nv.us/JusticeCourt/jcCalendarSearch.html. Mail turnaround time 1 week.

General Information: No public access terminal. No financial records released. Certification fee: $3.00. Payee: Justice Court. Personal checks accepted. Prepayment and SASE required.

Bunkerville Justice Court 190 W Virgin St, Bunkerville, NV 89007; phone: 702-346-5711; fax: 702-346-7212; hours 7AM-4;30PM M-Th (PST). *Misdemeanor, Civil Actions Under $10,000, Eviction, Small Claims.*

Civil Records: Access: Mail, in person. Only the court performs in person searches; visitors may not. Search fee: $1.00 per name per year. Court makes copy: $.30 per page. Required to search: name, years to search. Civil cases indexed by case number. Civil records (citations) on computer from 1991, on docket books. Current court calendars are at http://sandgate.co.clark.nv.us/JusticeCourt/jcCalendarSearch.html. Mail turnaround time 2 weeks.

Criminal Records: Access: Mail, in person. Only the court performs in person searches; visitors may not. Search fee: $1.00 per name per year. Court makes copy: $.30 per page. Required to search: name, years to search, DOB; also helpful: SSN. Criminal records (citations) on computer from 1991, on docket books. Current court calendars are at http://sandgate.co.clark.nv.us/JusticeCourt/jcCalendarSearch.html. Mail turnaround time 2 weeks.

General Information: No public access terminal. No sealed or confidential records released. Will fax

documents. Certification fee: $3.00 per cert. Payee: Bunkerville Justice Court. Only cashiers checks and money orders accepted. Prepayment and SASE required.

Goodsprings Township Jean Justice Court PO Box 19155, 1 Main St, Jean, NV 89019; phone: 702-874-1405; fax: 702-874-1612; hours 7AM-4PM M-Th (PST). *Misdemeanor, Civil Actions Under $10,000, Eviction, Small Claims.*

Civil Records: Access: Phone, fax, mail, in person. Only the court performs in person searches; visitors may not. Search fee: $1.00 per name per year. Court makes copy: $.25 per page. Required to search: name, years to search. Civil cases indexed by defendant, plaintiff. Civil records on computer for 6 months, file reports from 1990. Current court calendars are at http://sandgate.co.clark.nv.us/JusticeCourt/jcCalendarSearch.html. Mail turnaround time within 2 weeks.

Criminal Records: Access: Phone, fax, mail, in person. Only the court performs in person searches; visitors may not. Search fee: $1.00 per name per year. Court makes copy: $.25 per page. Required to search: name, years to search, DOB; also helpful: SSN. Criminal records on computer for 6 months, file reports from 1990. Current court calendars are at http://sandgate.co.clark.nv.us/JusticeCourt/jcCalendarSearch.html. Mail turnaround time within 2 weeks.

General Information: No public access terminal. No sealed records released. Certification fee: $2.00 per doc. Payee: Jean Justice Court. Business checks accepted. Prepayment and SASE required.

Henderson Township Justice 243 Water St, Henderson, NV 89015; criminal phone: 702-455-7929; civil phone: 702-455-7978; fax: 702-455-7977; hours 7AM-5:30PM M-Th (PST). *Misdemeanor, Civil Actions Under $10,000, Eviction, Small Claims.*

www.co.clark.nv.us/justicecourt_hd/general_information.htm

Note: Traffic can be reached at 702-455-7980.

Civil Records: Access: Mail, in person. Only the court performs in person searches; visitors may not. Search fee: $1.00 per name per year. Court makes copy: $.30 per page. Required to search: name, years to search, DOB, SSN. Civil cases indexed by defendant. Civil records on index cards and docket books. Evictions kept for 2-6 years; civil and small claims for 6 years. Current court calendars are at http://sandgate.co.clark.nv.us/JusticeCourt/jcCalendarSearch.html. Mail turnaround time 2 weeks.

Criminal Records: Access: Mail, in person. Only the court performs in person searches; visitors may not. Search fee: $1.00 per name per year. Court makes copy: $.30 per page. Required to search: name, years to search, DOB; also helpful: SSN. Criminal records on index cards and docket books. Current court calendars are at http://sandgate.co.clark.nv.us/JusticeCourt/jcCalendarSearch.html. Mail turnaround time 2 weeks.

General Information: No public access terminal. Will not fax documents. Certification fee: $3.00. Payee: Henderson Justice Court. Personal checks accepted. Prepayment and SASE required.

Las Vegas Township Justice PO Box 552511, 200 S 3rd, 2nd Fl, Las Vegas, NV 89155-2511; phone: 702-455-4435; fax: 702-455-4529; hours 8AM-5PM (PST). *Misdemeanor, Civil Actions Under $10,000, Eviction, Small Claims.*

www.co.clark.nv.us/justicecourt_lv/welcome.htm

Civil Records: Access: Phone, fax, mail, in person. Both court and visitors may perform in person searches. Search fee: $1.00 per name per year. Court makes copy: $.30 per page. Required to search: name, years to search. Civil cases indexed by defendant, plaintiff. Civil records go back 8 years. Current court calendars are at http://sandgate.co.clark.nv.us/JusticeCourt/jcCalendarSearch.html. Mail turnaround time 3 weeks.

Criminal Records: Access: Phone, fax, mail, in person. Only the court performs in person searches; visitors may not. Search fee: $1.00 per name per year. Court makes copy: $.30 per page. Required to search: name, years to search, DOB; also helpful: SSN. Criminal records go back 10 years. Current court calendars are at http://sandgate.co.clark.nv.us/JusticeCourt/jcCalendarSearch.html. Mail turnaround time 3 weeks.

General Information: No public access terminal. No sealed, confidential or judge's notes records released. Will fax documents to local or toll free line. Certification fee: $2.00 per doc. Payee: Justice Court, Las Vegas Township. Personal checks accepted. Prepayment and SASE required.

Laughlin Township Justice Court 101
Civic Way, #2, Laughlin, NV 89029; phone: 702-298-4622; fax: 702-298-7508; hours 8AM-4:30PM (T-Fri) (PST). *Misdemeanor, Civil Actions Under $10,000, Eviction, Small Claims.*

Civil Records: Access: Fax, mail, in person. Search fee: $1.00 per name per year. Court makes copy: $.30 per page. Required to search: name, years to search. Civil cases indexed by defendant, plaintiff. Civil records on docket book by name and case number. Current court calendars are at http://sandgate.co.clark.nv.us/JusticeCourt/jcCalendarSearch.html. Mail turnaround time 2 weeks.

Criminal Records: Access: Fax, mail, in person. Only the court performs in person searches; visitors may not. Search fee: $1.00 per name per year. Court makes copy: $.30 per page. Required to search: name, years to search, DOB. Criminal records on computer from 1990, prior in files and must be cross referenced. Current court calendars are at http://sandgate.co.clark.nv.us/JusticeCourt/jcCalendarSearch.html. Mail turnaround time 2 weeks.

General Information: No public access terminal. No sealed records released. Will fax documents to local or toll free line. Certification fee: $2.00 per cert. Payee: Laughlin Justice Court. Personal checks accepted. Prepayment and SASE required.

Mesquite Township Justice Court 500
Hillside Dr, Mesquite, NV 89027-3116; phone: 702-346-5298; fax: 702-346-7319; hours 7AM-5PM M-Th (PST). *Felony, Misdemeanor, Civil Actions Under $10,000, Eviction, Small Claims.*

Civil Records: Access: Fax, mail, in person. Only the court performs in person searches; visitors may not. Search fee: $1.00 per name per year. Court makes copy: $1.00 per page. Required to search: name, years to search. Civil cases indexed by defendant. Criminal records go back to 1989; on computer back to 1996. Current court calendars are at http://sandgate.co.clark.nv.us/JusticeCourt/jcCalendarSearch.html. Mail turnaround time approx. 1-2 weeks.

Criminal Records: Access: Phone, fax, mail, in person. Only the court performs in person searches; visitors may not. Search fee: $1.00 per name per year. Court makes copy: $1.00 per page. Required to search: name, years to search, DOB; also helpful: SSN. Criminal records go back to 1989; on computer back to 1996. Current court calendars are at http://sandgate.co.clark.nv.us/JusticeCourt/jcCalendarSearch.html. Mail turnaround time approx. 1-2 weeks.

General Information: No public access terminal. No sealed records released. Will fax documents for $1.00 per page. Certification fee: $3.00. Payee: Mesquite Justice Court. Only cashiers checks and money orders accepted. Prepayment and SASE required.

Moapa Township Justice Court PO Box
280, 1340 E ComCtr Hwy 168, Moapa, NV 89025; phone: 702-864-2333; fax: 702-864-2585; hours 8AM-5PM M-Th (PST). *Misdemeanor, Civil Actions Under $10,000, Eviction, Small Claims.*
www.co.clark.nv.us

Civil Records: Access: Fax, mail, in person. Only the court performs in person searches; visitors may

not. Search fee: $1.00 per name per year. Court makes copy: $.30 per page. Required to search: name, years to search. Civil cases indexed by defendant, plaintiff. Civil records on computer from 10/90, prior records on index cards and docket books. Archives flooded in 1980s. Current court calendars are at http://sandgate.co.clark.nv.us/JusticeCourt/jcCalendarSearch.html. Mail turnaround time 1-5 days.

Criminal Records: Access: Fax, mail, in person. Only the court performs in person searches; visitors may not. Search fee: $1.00 per name per year. Court makes copy: $.30 per page. Required to search: name, years to search; also helpful: DOB, SSN. Criminal records on computer from 10/90, prior records on index cards and docket books. Archives flooded in 1980s. Current court calendars are at http://sandgate.co.clark.nv.us/JusticeCourt/jcCalendarSearch.html. Mail turnaround time 1-5 days.

General Information: No public access terminal. No sealed records released. No fee to fax documents. Certification fee: $3.00 per cert. Payee: Moapa Township Justice Court. Personal checks accepted. Prepayment and SASE required.

Moapa Valley Township Justice Court
320 N Moapa Valley Blvd, PO Box 337, Overton, NV 89040; phone: 702-397-2840; fax: 702-397-2842; hours 6:30AM-4:30PM M-Th (PST). *Misdemeanor, Civil Actions Under $10,000, Eviction, Small Claims.*

Civil Records: Access: Mail, in person. Only the court performs in person searches; visitors may not. Search fee: $1.00 per name per year. Court makes copy: $.30 per page. Required to search: name, years to search. Civil cases indexed by defendant, plaintiff. Civil records on computer from 1991, prior on docket books. Current court calendars are at http://sandgate.co.clark.nv.us/JusticeCourt/jcCalendarSearch.html. Mail turnaround time approx. 1-2 weeks.

Criminal Records: Access: Mail, in person. Only the court performs in person searches; visitors may not. Search fee: $1.00 per name per year. Court makes copy: $.30 per page. Required to search: name, years to search, DOB; also helpful: SSN. Criminal records on computer from 1991, prior on docket books. Current court calendars are at http://sandgate.co.clark.nv.us/JusticeCourt/jcCalendarSearch.html. Mail turnaround time approx. 1-2 weeks.

General Information: No public access terminal. No sealed records released. Will fax documents for $1.00 per page. Certification fee: $3.00. Payee: Moapa Valley Justice Court. Personal checks accepted. Prepayment and SASE required.

North Las Vegas Township Justice 2428
N Martin L King Blvd, N Las Vegas, NV 89032-3700; phone: 702-455-7802; civil phone: 702-455-7801; fax: 702-455-7831; hours 7:15AM-5:45PM (PST). *Misdemeanor, Civil Actions Under $10,000, Eviction, Small Claims.*

Note: Judge must approve all search requests.

Civil Records: Access: Phone, in person. Visitors must perform in person searches themselves. Search fee: $1.00 per name per year. Court makes copy: $.30 per page. Required to search: name, years to search. Civil cases indexed by defendant, plaintiff. Civil records on docket books, microfilm. Current court calendars are at http://sandgate.co.clark.nv.us/JusticeCourt/jcCalendarSearch.html.

Criminal Records: Access: Phone, mail, in person. Only the court performs in person searches; visitors may not. Search fee: $1.00 per name per year. Court makes copy: $.30 per page. Required to search: name, years to search, DOB, SSN. Criminal records on docket books, microfilm. Current court calendars are at http://sandgate.co.clark.nv.us/JusticeCourt/jcCalendarSearch.html. Mail turnaround time 1-10 days.

General Information: No public access terminal. Certification fee: $3.00 per document. Payee: North

Las Vegas Justice Court. Personal check accepted with bankcard. Prepayment and SASE required.

Searchlight Township Justice PO Box 815,
Searchlight, NV 89046; phone: 702-297-1252; fax: 702-297-1022; hours 7AM-5:30PM M-Th (PST). *Misdemeanor, Civil Actions Under $10,000, Eviction, Small Claims.*

Civil Records: Access: Fax, mail, in person. Only the court performs in person searches; visitors may not. Search fee: $1.00 per name per year. Court makes copy: $1.00 per page. Required to search: name, years to search. Civil cases indexed by defendant, plaintiff. Civil records on computer from 1988, prior to 1988 filed by case number. Current court calendars are at http://sandgate.co.clark.nv.us/JusticeCourt/jcCalendarSearch.html. Mail turnaround time 1-2 weeks.

Criminal Records: Access: Fax, mail, in person. Only the court performs in person searches; visitors may not. Search fee: $1.00 per name per year. Court makes copy: $1.00 per page. Required to search: name, years to search, DOB; also helpful: SSN. Criminal records on computer from 1988, prior to 1988 filed by case number. Current court calendars are at http://sandgate.co.clark.nv.us/JusticeCourt/jcCalendarSearch.html. Mail turnaround time 1-2 weeks.

General Information: No public access terminal. No sealed records released. Certification fee: $2.00 per cert. Payee: Searchlight Justice Court. Personal checks accepted. Prepayment and SASE required.

Douglas County

9th Judicial District Court PO Box 218,
Minden, NV 89423; phone: 775-782-9820; criminal fax: 775-782-9954; same fax for civil/probate; hours 8AM-5PM (PST). *Felony, Gross Misdemeanors, Civil Actions Over $10,000, Probate.*

http://cltr.co.douglas.nv.us/CourtClerk/courtideas/courtclerkhome.htm

Note: Misdemeanors are handled by the East Fork Justice Court and Tahoe Township Justice Court.

Civil Records: Access: Mail, in person. Only the court performs in person searches; visitors may not. Search fee: $1.00 per name per year. Court makes copy: $1.00 per page. Required to search: name, years to search. Civil cases indexed by defendant, plaintiff. Civil records on index cards from 1962, docket books prior to 1962, archived from mid-1850s. On computer back to 1996. Mail turnaround time 2 days.

Criminal Records: Access: Mail, in person. Only the court performs in person searches; visitors may not. Search fee: $1.00 per name per year. Court makes copy: $1.00 per page. Required to search: name, years to search, DOB. Criminal records on index cards from 1962, docket books prior to 1962, archived from mid-1850s. On computer back to 1996. Mail turnaround time 2 days.

General Information: No public access terminal. No sealed records released. Will not fax documents after all payments received. Certification fee: $3.00 per document. Payee: Douglas County Court Clerk. Business checks accepted. Prepayment and SASE required.

East Fork Justice Court PO Box 218,
Minden, NV 89423; phone: 775-782-9955; fax: 775-782-9947; hours 8AM-5PM (PST). *Misdemeanor, Civil Actions Under $10,000, Eviction, Small Claims.*

Civil Records: Access: Mail, in person. Only the court performs in person searches; visitors may not. Search fee: $1.00 per name per year. Court makes copy: $.30 per page. Required to search: name, years to search, DOB or SSN. Civil cases indexed by defendant, plaintiff. Computerized records from 1996. Mail turnaround time 2-4 days.

Criminal Records: Access: Mail, in person. Only the court performs in person searches; visitors may not. Search fee: $1.00 per name per year. Court makes copy: $.30 per page. Required to search: name,

years to search, DOB or SSN. Computerized records from 1996. Mail turnaround time 2-4 days.
General Information: No public access terminal. No sealed records released. Will fax if pre-paid. Certification fee: $3.00. Payee: East Fork Justice Court. Only local personal or business checks accepted. Prepayment and SASE required.

Tahoe Justice Court PO Box 7169, Stateline, NV 89449; phone: 775-586-7200; fax: 775-586-7203; hours 9AM-5PM (PST). *Misdemeanor, Civil Actions Under $10,000, Eviction, Small Claims.*
Civil Records: Access: Phone, mail, in person. Only the court performs in person searches; visitors may not. Search fee: $1.00 per name per year. Court makes copy: $.30 per page. Required to search: name or case number, years to search. Civil cases indexed by defendant, plaintiff. Civil records on index cards from 1985-1995; 1995-present on computer. Prior to 1985 some records in docket books, some on microfilm. Mail turnaround time 2 weeks or less.
Criminal Records: Access: Phone, mail, in person. Only the court performs in person searches; visitors may not. Search fee: $1.00 per name per year. Court makes copy: $.30 per page. Required to search: name or case number, years to search, DOB. Criminal records on docket cards 1985-1995; 1995 to present on computer. Pre-1985 records on books and microfilm. Mail turnaround time 2 weeks.
General Information: No public access terminal. No sealed records released. Certification fee: $3.00 per page. Payee: Tahoe Justice Court. Visa, MC accepted. Prepayment and SASE required.

Elko County

4th Judicial District Court 571 Idaho St, 3rd Fl, Elko, NV 89801; phone: 775-753-4600; criminal fax: 775-753-4610; same fax for civil/probate; hours 9AM-5PM (PST). *Felony, Gross Misdemeanor, Civil Actions Over $10,000, Probate.*
Civil Records: Access: Phone, mail, in person, email. Both court and visitors may perform in person searches. Search fee: $1.00 per name per year. Fee is for years prior to 10/01/91. Court makes copy: $1.00 per page. Self serve copy fee: $.50 per page. Required to search: name, years to search. Civil cases indexed by defendant, plaintiff. Civil records on computer back to 1970; prior on microfilm. Mail turnaround time 1 day.
Criminal Records: Access: Phone, mail, in person. Both court and visitors may perform in person searches. Search fee: $1.00 per name per year. Fee is for years prior to 1980. Court makes copy: $1.00 per page. Self serve copy fee: $.50 per page. Required to search: name, years to search. Criminal records on computer back to 1970; prior primarily on microfilm (including probate). Mail turnaround time 1 day.
General Information: Public terminal goes back to 1970s. No sealed records released. Fee to fax documents is $1.00 per page. Certification fee: $3.00 for cert plus copy fee if court prepares copies; $5.00 cert if you prepare copies. Payee: Elko County Clerk. Personal checks or Visa/MC accepted. Prepayment and SASE required.

Carlin Justice Court PO Box 789, Carlin, NV 89822; phone: 775-754-6321; fax: 775-754-6893; hours 8AM-5PM (PST). *Misdemeanor, Civil Actions Under $10,000, Eviction, Small Claims.*
Civil Records: Access: Mail, in person. Both court and visitors may perform in person searches. Search fee: $1.00 per name per year. Court makes copy: $.30 per page; same fee for self serve. Required to search: name, years to search. Civil cases indexed by defendant, plaintiff. Civil records on computer starting in 1994, prior are in books. Mail turnaround time 1 week.
Criminal Records: Access: Mail, in person. Only the court performs in person searches; visitors may not. Search fee: $1.00 per name per year. Court makes copy: $.30 per page; same fee for self serve. Required to search: name, years to search, DOB, SSN. Criminal records on computer starting in 1994, prior are in books. Mail turnaround time 1 week.

General Information: No public access terminal. Will fax documents if toll free number. Certification fee: $3.00 per document. Payee: Carlin Court. Personal checks accepted. Prepayment and SASE required.

Eastline Justice Court PO Box 2300, West Wendover, NV 89883; phone: 775-664-2305; fax: 775-664-2979; hours 9AM-5PM (PST). *Misdemeanor, Civil Actions Under $10,000, Eviction, Small Claims.*
Civil Records: Access: Mail, in person. Only the court performs in person searches; visitors may not. Search fee: $7.00 per name per year. Court makes copy: $.30 per page. Required to search: name, years to search. Civil cases indexed by defendant. Civil records on computer from 1992, prior on index, docket book. Mail turnaround time 1 week.
Criminal Records: Access: Mail, in person. Only the court performs in person searches; visitors may not. Search fee: $1.00 per name per year. Court makes copy: $.30 per page. Required to search: name, years to search; also helpful: DOB. Criminal records on computer from 1992, prior on index, docket book. Mail turnaround time 1 week.
General Information: No public access terminal. No open case records released. Certification fee: $3.00. Payee: Eastline Justice Court. Only cashiers checks and money orders accepted. Prepayment and SASE required.

Elko Justice Court PO Box 176, Elko, NV 89803; phone: 775-738-8403; fax: 775-738-8416; hours 9AM-N, 1-5PM (PST). *Misdemeanor, Civil Actions Under $10,000, Eviction, Small Claims.*
Civil Records: Access: Fax, mail, in person. Both court and visitors may perform in person searches. Search fee: $1.00 per name per year. Fee is per court. Court makes copy: $.30 per page. Required to search: name, years to search. Civil cases indexed by defendant, plaintiff. Civil records on computer after 1994, on docket books after 1980s, prior in county archives. Mail turnaround time 7-10 days.
Criminal Records: Access: Mail, in person. Both court and visitors may perform in person searches. Search fee: $1.00 per name per year. Fee is per court. Court makes copy: $.30 per page. Required to search: name, years to search; DOB or SSN also required. Criminal records on computer after 1994, on docket books after 1980s, prior in county archives. Mail turnaround time 7-10 days.
General Information: No public access terminal. No confidential evaluations or sealed records released. Certification fee: $3.00. Payee: Elko Justice Court. Personal checks accepted. Prepayment and SASE required.

Jackpot Justice Court PO Box 229, Jackpot, NV 89825; phone: 775-755-2456; fax: 775-755-2455; hours 9AM-N, 1-5PM (PST). *Misdemeanor, Civil Actions Under $10,000, Eviction, Small Claims.*
Civil Records: Access: Mail, in person. Only the court performs in person searches; visitors may not. Search fee: $7.00 per name per year. Court makes copy: $.25 per page. Required to search: name, years to search. Civil cases indexed by defendant. Civil records on docket books per year since 1988; on computer back to 1995. Mail turnaround time 1 week.
Criminal Records: Access: Fax, mail, in person. Only the court performs in person searches; visitors may not. Search fee: $7.00 per name per year. Court makes copy: $.25 per page. Required to search: name, years to search, DOB. Criminal records on docket books per year since 1988; on computer back to 1995. Mail turnaround time 1 week.
General Information: No public access terminal. No fee to fax documents. Certification fee: $3.00. Payee: Jackpot Justice Court. Business checks accepted. Prepayment and SASE required.

Wells Justice Municipal Court PO Box 297, Wells, NV 89835; phone: 775-752-3726; fax: 775-752-3363; hours 9AM-N,1-5PM (PST). *Misdemeanor, Civil Actions Under $10,000, Eviction, Small Claims.*
Civil Records: Access: Mail, in person. Only the court performs in person searches; visitors may not. Search fee: $1.00 per name per year. Court makes copy: $.30 per page. Required to search: name, years to search. Civil cases indexed by defendant, plaintiff. Civil records on computer from 1989, prior on docket books. In person access may require fee for clerical assistance. Mail turnaround time 2 weeks.
Criminal Records: Access: Mail, in person. Only the court performs in person searches; visitors may not. Search fee: $1.00 per name per year. Court makes copy: $.30 per page. Required to search: name, years to search; also DOB or SSN. Criminal records on computer from 1989, prior on docket books. Same as civil. Mail turnaround time 2 weeks.
General Information: No public access terminal. No pending, confidential records released. Certification fee: $3.00. Payee: Wells Justice Court. Personal checks accepted. Prepayment and SASE required.

Jarbidge Justice Court, NV.
Note: This is an "unincorporated ghost town." No criminal or civil cases in more than 20 years. Mostly marriages, fish and game violations. Only 40 year round residents. All records at the Elko Justice Court.

Mountain City Justice Court, NV.
Note: Closed. Records held in Elko Justice Court, 775-738-8403.

Esmeralda County

5th Judicial District Court PO Box 547, Goldfield, NV 89013; phone: 775-485-6309; fax: 775-485-6376; hours 8AM-5PM; Closed 12-1PM (PST). *Felony, Gross Misdemeanor, Civil Actions Over $10,000, Probate.*
Civil Records: Access: Fax, mail, in person. Both court and visitors may perform in person searches. Search fee: $1.00 per name per year. Court makes copy: $1.00 per page. Required to search: name, years to search. Civil cases indexed by defendant, plaintiff. Civil records on docket books from 1800s. Mail turnaround time 2 weeks.
Criminal Records: Access: Fax, mail, in person. Both court and visitors may perform in person searches. Search fee: $1.00. Court makes copy: $1.00 per page. Required to search: name, years to search. Criminal records on docket books from 1800s. Mail turnaround time 2 weeks.
General Information: No public access terminal. No juvenile or pre-sentence records released. Fee to fax documents is $1.00 per page. Certification fee: $3.00. Payee: Esmeralda County Clerk. Personal checks or Visa, MC accepted. Prepayment and SASE required.

Esmeralda Justice Court PO Box 370, Goldfield, NV 89013; phone: 775-485-6359; fax: 775-485-3462; hours 8AM-5PM (PST). *Misdemeanor, Civil Actions Under $10,000, Eviction, Small Claims.*
Civil Records: Access: Phone, fax, mail, in person. Only the court performs in person searches; visitors may not. Search fee: $1.00 per name per year. Court makes copy: $.30 per page. Required to search: name, years to search. Civil cases indexed by plaintiff. Civil records on docket books since 1987. Mail turnaround time 1 day.
Criminal Records: Access: Phone, fax, mail, in person. Only the court performs in person searches; visitors may not. Search fee: $1.00 per name per year. Court makes copy: $.30 per page. Required to search: name, years to search. Criminal records on docket books since 1987. Mail turnaround time 1 day.
General Information: No public access terminal. No sealed records released. Will fax documents $1.00

per page. Certification fee: $3.00. Payee: Justice Court. Only cashiers checks and money orders accepted. Prepayment and SASE required.

Eureka County

7th Judicial District Court PO Box 677, Eureka, NV 89316; phone: 775-237-5262; fax: 775-237-6015; hours 8AM-N, 1-5PM (PST). *Felony, Gross Misdemeanor, Civil Actions Over $10,000, Probate.*
Civil Records: Access: Phone, fax, mail, in person. Both court and visitors may perform in person searches. Search fee: $1.00 per name per year. Court makes copy: $1.00 per page. Required to search: name, years to search. Civil cases indexed by defendant, plaintiff. Civil records archived from 1873. Public can search docket books. Mail turnaround time 1 day.
Criminal Records: Access: Phone, fax, mail, in person. Both court and visitors may perform in person searches. Search fee: $1.00 per name per year. Court makes copy: $1.00 per page. Required to search: name, years to search. Criminal records archived from 1873. Public can search docket books. Mail turnaround time 1 day.
General Information: No public access terminal. No juvenile, sealed records released. Will fax to toll-free number. Certification fee: $5.00 per document. Payee: Eureka County Clerk. Personal checks accepted. Prepayment and SASE required.

Beowawe Justice Court PO Box 211338, Crescent Valley, NV 89821; phone: 775-468-0244; fax: 775-468-0323; hours 8AM-N, 1-5PM (PST). *Misdemeanor, Civil Actions Under $10,000, Eviction, Small Claims.*
Civil Records: Access: Mail, in person. Only the court performs in person searches; visitors may not. Search fee: $1.00 per name per year. Court makes copy: $.30 per page. Required to search: name, years to search. Civil cases indexed by plaintiff. Civil records go back to 2/1994; computerized records go back to 1997. Mail turnaround time 5 days.
Criminal Records: Access: Mail, in person. Only the court performs in person searches; visitors may not. Search fee: $1.00 per name per year. Court makes copy: $.30 per page. Required to search: name, years to search. Criminal records go back to 11/1993; computerized records go back to 1997. Mail turnaround time 5 days.
General Information: No public access terminal. Certification fee: $3.00. Payee: Beowawe Justice Court. Only cashiers checks and money orders accepted. Prepayment and SASE required.

Eureka Justice Court PO Box 496, Eureka, NV 89316; phone: 775-237-5540; fax: 775-237-6016; hours 8AM-N,1-5PM (PST). *Misdemeanor, Civil Actions Under $10,000, Eviction, Small Claims.*
Civil Records: Access: Phone, mail, in person. Only the court performs in person searches; visitors may not. No search fee. Court makes copy: $.50 per page. Required to search: name, years to search. Civil cases indexed by defendant, plaintiff. Civil records on computer since 1995; on docket books, archived from 1940. Mail turnaround time 2 days.
Criminal Records: Access: Phone, mail, in person. Only the court performs in person searches; visitors may not. No search fee. Court makes copy: $.50 per page. Required to search: name, years to search. Criminal records on computer since 1995; on docket books, archived from 1940. Mail turnaround time 2 days.
General Information: No public access terminal. Certification fee: $3.00. Payee: Eureka Justice Court. Only cashiers checks and money orders accepted. Prepayment and SASE required.

Humboldt County

6th Judicial District Court 50 W 5th St, Winnemucca, NV 89445; phone: 775-623-6343; fax: 775-623-6309; hours 8AM-5PM (PST). *Felony, Gross Misdemeanor, Civil Actions Over $10,000, Probate.*
Civil Records: Access: Phone, fax, mail, in person. Both court and visitors may perform in person searches. Search fee: $1.00 per name per year. Court makes copy: $1.00 per page. Required to search: name, years to search. Civil cases indexed by defendant, plaintiff. Civil records on computer from 1984, on microfiche from 1900. Mail turnaround time 1 day.
Criminal Records: Access: Phone, fax, mail, in person. Both court and visitors may perform in person searches. Search fee: $1.00 per name per year. Court makes copy: $1.00 per page. Required to search: name, years to search. Criminal records on computer from 1984, on microfiche from 1900. Mail turnaround time 1 day, immediate if on computer and requested by phone.
General Information: No public access terminal. No adoption, sealed records released. Certification fee: $3.00 per cert. Payee: Humboldt County Clerk. Personal checks accepted. Prepayment and SASE required.

Union Justice Court PO Box 1218, Winnemucca, NV 89446; phone: 775-623-6377; fax: 775-623-6439; hours 8AM-5PM (PST). *Misdemeanor, Civil Actions Under $10,000, Eviction, Small Claims.*
www.hcnv.us/justice/justice_home.htm
Civil Records: Access: Fax, mail, in person. Only the court performs in person searches; visitors may not. Search fee: $1.00 per name per year; minimum of $7.00. Court makes copy: $.30 per page. Required to search: name, years to search; also helpful: address. Civil cases indexed by defendant, plaintiff. Civil records on computer from 1988, prior on docket books. Mail turnaround time 1-2 days.
Criminal Records: Access: Fax, mail, in person. Only the court performs in person searches; visitors may not. Search fee: $1.00 per name per year; minimum of $7.00. Court makes copy: $.30 per page. Required to search: name, years to search, DOB; also helpful: address, SSN. Criminal records on computer from 1988. Mail turnaround time 1-2 days.
General Information: No public access terminal. No fee to fax documents. Certification fee: $3.00 per cert. Payee: Justice Court. Personal checks accepted. Prepayment and SASE required.

McDermitt Justice Court, NV. *Misdemeanor, Civil Actions Under $10,000, Eviction, Small Claims.*
Note: Closed case records are at the Union Justice Court.

Paradise Valley Justice Court, NV. *Misdemeanor, Civil Actions Under $10,000, Eviction, Small Claims.*
www.humboldt-county-nv.net/justice/
Note: Closed case records are at the Union Justice Court.

Lander County

6th Judicial District Court 315 S Humboldt, Battle Mountain, NV 89820; phone: 775-635-5738; criminal fax: 775-635-5761; same fax for civil/probate; hours 8AM-5PM (PST). *Felony, Gross Misdemeanor, Civil Actions Over $10,000, Probate.*
Civil Records: Access: Phone, fax, mail, in person. Only the court performs in person searches; visitors may not. No search fee. Court makes copy: $1.00 per page. Required to search: name, years to search. Civil cases indexed by defendant, plaintiff. Civil records on computer from 1990, on index from 1986-1990, on microfiche until 1985, prior records on docket books. Mail turnaround time 7 days.

Criminal Records: Access: Phone, fax, mail, in person. Only the court performs in person searches; visitors may not. No search fee. Court makes copy: $1.00 per page. Required to search: name, years to search. Criminal records on computer from 1990, on index from 1986-1990, on microfiche until 1985, prior records on docket books. Mail turnaround time 7 days.
General Information: No public access terminal. No juvenile, sealed records released. Fee to fax documents is $1.00 per page. Certification fee: $5.00 per document. Payee: Lander County Clerk. Personal checks accepted. Prepayment and SASE required.

Argenta Justice Court 315 S Humboldt, Battle Mountain, NV 89820; phone: 775-635-5151; fax: 775-635-0604; hours 7:30AM-6PM (PST). *Misdemeanor, Civil Actions Under $10,000, Eviction, Small Claims.*
Civil Records: Access: Phone, mail, in person. Only the court performs in person searches; visitors may not. Search fee: $1.00 per name per year. Court makes copy: $.50 per page. Required to search: name, years to search. Civil cases indexed by defendant, plaintiff. Civil records on computer from 1988, prior on docket books. Mail turnaround time 1 day.
Criminal Records: Access: Phone, mail, in person. Only the court performs in person searches; visitors may not. Search fee: $1.00 per name per year. Court makes copy: $.50 per page. Required to search: name, years to search; also helpful: DOB, SSN. Criminal records on computer from 1988, prior on docket books. Mail turnaround time 1 day.
General Information: No public access terminal. No unserved search warrant records released. Fee to fax documents is $1.00 per page. Certification fee: $1.00 per page. Payee: Argenta Justice Court. Only cashiers checks and money orders accepted. Prepayment and SASE required.

Austin Justice Court PO Box 100, Austin, NV 89310; phone: 775-964-2380; fax: 775-964-2327; hours 8AM-4PM M, 8AM-N T-Th (PST). *Misdemeanor, Civil Actions Under $10,000, Eviction, Small Claims.*
Note: No fees for requests from government agencies.
Civil Records: Access: Phone, mail, fax, in person. Only the court performs in person searches; visitors may not. No search fee. Court makes copy: $.25 per page; same fee for self serve. Required to search: name, years to search. Civil cases indexed by plaintiff and defendant. Civil records on docket books, computerized since 1982. Mail turnaround time 1 week.
Criminal Records: Access: Phone, mail, fax, in person. Only the court performs in person searches; visitors may not. No search fee. Court makes copy: $.25 per page; same fee for self serve. Required to search: name, years to search. Criminal records on computer from 1988, easily available since 1976. Mail turnaround time 1 week.
General Information: No public access terminal. Will fax documents to local or toll free line. No certification fee . Payee: Austin Justice Court. SASE required.

Lincoln County

7th Judicial District Court PO Box 90, Pioche, NV 89043; phone: 775-962-5390; fax: 775-962-5180; hours 9AM-5PM (PST). *Felony, Gross Misdemeanor, Civil Actions Over $10,000, Probate.*
Civil Records: Access: Mail, in person. Both court and visitors may perform in person searches. Search fee: $1.00 per name per year. Court makes copy: $1.00 per page. Required to search: name, years to search. Civil cases indexed by defendant, plaintiff. Civil records on docket books from 1876. Records are computerized since 2001. Mail turnaround time 1-2 days.
Criminal Records: Access: Mail, in person. Both court and visitors may perform in person searches. Search fee: $1.00 per name per year. Court makes copy: $1.00 per page. Required to search: name, years to search. Criminal records on docket books from

1876. Records are computerized since 2001. Mail turnaround time 1-2 days.

General Information: No public access terminal. No juvenile, sealed records released. Fee to fax documents is $1.00 per page. Certification fee: $5.00. Payee: Lincoln County Clerk. Personal checks accepted. Prepayment and SASE required.

Meadow Valley Justice Court
PO Box 36, Pioche, NV 89043; phone: 775-962-5140; fax: 775-962-5559; hours 9AM-5PM (PST). *Misdemeanor, Civil Actions Under $10,000, Eviction, Small Claims.*

Civil Records: Access: Phone, fax, mail, in person. Only the court performs in person searches; visitors may not. No search fee. Court makes copy: none; same fee for self serve. Required to search: name, years to search. Civil cases indexed by defendant, plaintiff. Civil records archived from 1982 on docket books; on computer back to 2000. Mail turnaround time 1-5 days.

Criminal Records: Access: Phone, fax, mail, in person. Only the court performs in person searches; visitors may not. No search fee. Court makes copy: none; same fee for self serve. Required to search: name, years to search. Criminal records are all originals; they go back to 1982; on computer back to 2000. Mail turnaround time 1-5 days.

General Information: No public access terminal. Juvenile records are not released. Will fax documents $3.00 1st page, $1.00 each add'l. No certification fee . Prepayment and SASE required.

Pahranagat Valley Justice Court
PO Box 449, Alamo, NV 89001; phone: 775-725-3357; fax: 775-725-3566; hours 9AM-5PM (PST). *Misdemeanor, Civil Actions Under $10,000, Eviction, Small Claims.*

Civil Records: Access: Fax, mail, in person. Only the court performs in person searches; visitors may not. Search fee: $1.00 per name per year. Court makes copy: $.30 per page. Required to search: name, years to search. Civil cases indexed by defendant. Civil records on docket books to 1980; on computer back to 1997. Mail turnaround time 1-3 days.

Criminal Records: Access: Fax, mail, in person. Only the court performs in person searches; visitors may not. Search fee: $1.00 per name per year. Court makes copy: $.30 per page. Required to search: name, years to search, DOB; also helpful: SSN, signed release. Criminal records on docket books to 1980; on computer back to 1997. Mail turnaround time 1-3 days.

General Information: No public access terminal. No personal notes released. No fee to fax documents. Certification fee: $3.00 per page. Payee: Pahranagat Valley Justice Court. Personal checks accepted. Prepayment and SASE required.

Lyon County

3rd Judicial District Court
27 S Main St, Yerington, NV 89447; phone: 775-463-6503; criminal fax: 775-463-6575; same fax for civil/probate; hours 8AM-5PM (PST). *Felony, Gross Misdemeanor, Civil Actions Over $10,000, Probate.*

Civil Records: Access: Phone, mail, in person. Only the court performs in person searches; visitors may not. Search fee: $1.00 per name per year. Court makes copy: $.25 per page. Required to search: name, years to search. Civil cases indexed by defendant, plaintiff. Civil records on computer back to 1989. Mail turnaround time 1 week for mail requests, immediate for phone requests if on computer.

Criminal Records: Access: Phone, mail, in person. Only the court performs in person searches; visitors may not. Search fee: $1.00 per name per year. Court makes copy: $.25 per page. Required to search: name, years to search. Criminal records on computer back to 1985. Mail turnaround time 1 week for mail requests, immediate for phone requests if on computer.

General Information: No public access terminal. No adoption, juvenile or sealed records released. Will fax documents for $3.00 per page. Certification fee:

$3.00 per document. Payee: Lyon County Clerk. Personal checks accepted. Prepayment and SASE required.

Dayton Township Justice Court
235 Main St, Dayton, NV 89403; phone: 775-246-6233; fax: 775-246-6203; hours 8AM-5PM (PST). *Misdemeanor, Civil Actions Under $10,000, Eviction, Small Claims.*

Civil Records: Access: Phone, fax, mail, in person. Only the court performs in person searches; visitors may not. Search fee: $1.00 per name per year. Court makes copy: $.30 per page. Required to search: name, years to search. Civil cases indexed by defendant, plaintiff. Civil records on computer from 1991, prior on docket books by year. Mail turnaround time within 1 week.

Criminal Records: Access: Phone, fax, mail, in person. Only the court performs in person searches; visitors may not. Search fee: $1.00 per name per year. Court makes copy: $.30 per page. Required to search: name, years to search. Criminal records on computer from 1991, prior on docket books by year. Mail turnaround time within 1 week.

General Information: No public access terminal. No sealed records released. Certification fee: $3.00 per certification. Payee: Dayton Township Justice Court. Personal checks accepted. Prepayment and SASE required.

Fernley Justice Court
565 E Main St, Fernley, NV 89408; phone: 775-575-3355; fax: 775-575-3359; hours 8AM-5PM (PST). *Misdemeanor, Civil Actions Under $10,000, Eviction, Small Claims.*

Civil Records: Access: Phone, mail, in person. Only the court performs in person searches; visitors may not. Search fee: $1.00 per name per year. Court makes copy: $.30 per page. Required to search: name, years to search. Civil cases indexed by defendant, plaintiff. Civil records on computer from 1992, prior on docket books. Mail turnaround time 1 week.

Criminal Records: Access: Phone, mail, in person. Only the court performs in person searches; visitors may not. Search fee: $1.00 per name per year. Court makes copy: $.30 per page. Required to search: name, years to search; also helpful: SSN. Criminal records on computer from 1992, prior on docket books. Mail turnaround time 1 week.

General Information: No public access terminal. No police reports or sealed records released. Certification fee: $2.00 per cert. Payee: Fernley Justice Court. Personal checks accepted. Out of state checks not accepted. Prepayment and SASE required.

Mason Valley Justice Court
30 Nevin Way, Yerington, NV 89447; phone: 775-463-6639; fax: 775-463-6638; hours 8AM-5PM (PST). *Misdemeanor, Civil Actions Under $10,000, Eviction, Small Claims.*

Civil Records: Access: Phone, mail, in person. Only the court performs in person searches; visitors may not. Search fee: $1.00 per name per year. Court makes copy: $.25 per page. Required to search: name, years to search. Civil cases indexed by defendant, plaintiff. Civil records on computer from 1992, archives from 1900s. Mail turnaround time 3 days, immediate for phone requests.

Criminal Records: Access: Phone, mail, in person. Only the court performs in person searches; visitors may not. Search fee: $1.00 per name per year. Court makes copy: $.25 per page. Required to search: name, years to search; also helpful: DOB, SSN. Criminal records on computer from 1992, archives from 1900s. Note: Phone requests are limited to 3 names only. Mail turnaround time 3 days, immediate for phone requests.

General Information: No public access terminal. No police, sheriff reports released. Certification fee: $3.00. Payee: Mason Valley Justice Court. Personal checks not accepted. Prepayment and SASE required.

Smith Valley Justice Court
PO Box 141, Smith, NV 89430; phone: 775-465-2313; fax: 775-465-2153; hours 8AM-N Tues & Fri or by appointment (PST). *Misdemeanor, Civil Actions Under $10,000, Eviction, Small Claims.*

Civil Records: Access: Phone, fax, mail, in person. Only the court performs in person searches; visitors may not. No search fee. Court makes copy: $.25 per page. Required to search: name, years to search; also helpful: address. Civil cases indexed by defendant, plaintiff. Criminal records on computer from 1994. Overall records go back to 1992. Mail turnaround time 1-2 weeks.

Criminal Records: Access: Phone, mail, in person. Only the court performs in person searches; visitors may not. No search fee. Court makes copy: $.25 per page. Required to search: name, years to search; also helpful: address, DOB, SSN. Criminal records on computer from 1994. Overall records go back to 1992. Mail turnaround time 1-2 weeks.

General Information: No public access terminal. Will fax documents for $3.00 per page. Certification fee: $5.00. Payee: Smith Valley Justice Court. Personal checks accepted. Prepayment and SASE required.

Mineral County

5th Judicial District Court
PO Box 1450, Hawthorne, NV 89415; phone: 775-945-2446; criminal fax: 775-945-0706; same fax for civil/probate; hours 8AM-5PM (PST). *Felony, Gross Misdemeanor, Civil Actions Over $10,000, Probate.*

Civil Records: Access: Phone, fax, mail, in person. Both court and visitors may perform in person searches. Search fee: $1.00 per name per year. Court makes copy: $1.00 per page; same fee for self serve. Required to search: name, years to search. Civil cases indexed by defendant, plaintiff. Civil records go back to 1911; computerized records since 1993. Mail turnaround time 1 day.

Criminal Records: Access: Phone, fax, mail, in person. Both court and visitors may perform in person searches. Search fee: $1.00 per name per year. Court makes copy: $1.00 per page; same fee for self serve. Required to search: name, years to search. Criminal records go back to 1911; computerized records since 1993. Mail turnaround time 1 day.

General Information: No public access terminal. No juvenile records released. Will fax documents $1.50 per page. Certification fee: $3.00 per certification. Payee: Mineral County Clerk. Personal checks accepted. Prepayment and SASE required.

Hawthorne Justice Court
PO Box 1660, Hawthorne, NV 89415; phone: 775-945-3859; fax: 775-945-0700; hours 8AM-5PM (PST). *Misdemeanor, Civil Actions Under $10,000, Eviction, Small Claims.*

Note: This court holds records from Schurz Justice Court.

Civil Records: Access: Phone, mail, in person. Both court and visitors may perform in person searches. No search fee. Court makes copy: $.25 per page. Legal size- $1.00 per page. Required to search: name, years to search. Civil cases indexed by defendant. Civil records on computer from 1994, prior on docket books. Mail turnaround time 1-5 days.

Criminal Records: Access: Phone, mail, in person, fax. Both court and visitors may perform in person searches. No search fee. Court makes copy: $.25 per page. Legal size- $1.00 per page. Required to search: name, years to search. Criminal records on computer from 1992. Mail turnaround time 1-5 days.

General Information: No public access terminal. No pending case or sealed records released. No certification fee . Payee: Hawthorne Justice Court. Personal checks accepted. Prepayment and SASE required.

Mina Justice Court, NV.
Note: Court has been closed. All records at the Hawthorne Justice Court.

Schurz Justice Court c/o Hawthorne Justice Ct, PO Box 1660, Hawthorne, NV 89415.
Note: Schurz court closed 1/1/2001; records now housed at Hawthorne Justice Court (see above.)

Nye County

5th Judicial District Court PO Box 1031, Tonopah, NV 89049; phone: 775-482-8131; probate phone: 775-482-8127; fax: 775-482-8133; probate fax: 775-482-8133; hours 8AM-5PM (PST). *Felony, Gross Misdemeanor, Civil Actions Over $10,000, Probate.*
Civil Records: Access: Phone, fax, mail, in person. Only the court performs in person searches; visitors may not. Search fee: $1.00 per name. Court makes copy: $1.00 per page; same fee for self serve. Required to search: name, years to search. Civil records on computer from 1991, on docket books from 1800s, many are microfilmed. Mail turnaround time 1 day.
Criminal Records: Access: Phone, fax, mail, in person. Only the court performs in person searches; visitors may not. Search fee: $1.00 per name. Court makes copy: $1.00 per page; same fee for self serve. Required to search: name, years to search. Criminal records on computer from 1991, on docket books from 1800s, many are microfilmed. Mail turnaround time 1 day.
General Information: No public access terminal. No adoptions or juvenile records released. Will fax documents $2.00 1st page, $1.00 each add'l. Certification fee: $3.00. Payee: Nye County Clerk. Business checks or in state personal checks accepted. Prepayment required. Payment required if more than $15.00. SASE required.

Beatty Justice Court PO Box 805, Beatty, NV 89003; phone: 775-553-2951; fax: 775-553-2136; hours 8AM-5PM (PST). *Misdemeanor, Civil Actions Up to $10.000, Eviction, Small Claims.*
Civil Records: Access: Phone, mail, in person. Only the court performs in person searches; visitors may not. Search fee: $1.00 per name per year. Computer printouts on all civil actions (no way to segregate small claims or evictions) is $0.016 per page. Court makes copy: $.30 per page; same fee for self serve. Required to search: name, years to search. Civil cases indexed by defendant, plaintiff. Civil records on computer from 1989, archived from 1950s, some on docket books. Mail turnaround time 1 week for mail requests, same day for phone requests when possible.
Criminal Records: Access: Phone, mail, in person. Only the court performs in person searches; visitors may not. Search fee: $1.00 per name per year. Court makes copy: $.30 per page; same fee for self serve. Required to search: name, years to search, DOB. Criminal records on computer from 1989. Mail turnaround time 1 week for mail requests, same day for phone requests when possible.
General Information: No public access terminal. No sealed, confidential records released. Will fax documents if all fees paid; fax copies are $0.019 per page (no charge to fax original). If project involves more than 15 minutes time, add'l fees may apply. Certification fee: $3.00 per document. Payee: Beatty Justice Court. Personal checks accepted. Prepayment and SASE required.

Tonopah Justice Court PO Box 1151, Tonopah, NV 89049; phone: 775-482-8155; fax: 775-482-7349; hours 8AM-N, 1-5PM (PST). *Misdemeanor, Civil Actions Under $10,000, Eviction, Small Claims.*
Civil Records: Access: Phone, mail, in person. Only the court performs in person searches; visitors may not. Search fee: $1.00 per name per year. Court makes copy: $.30 per page. Required to search: name, years to search. Civil cases indexed by plaintiff. Civil records on computer from 1992, on archives from 1950s, some on docket books. Mail turnaround time 1-2 weeks.
Criminal Records: Access: Phone, mail, in person. Only the court performs in person searches;

visitors may not. Search fee: $1.00 per name per year. Court makes copy: $.30 per page. Required to search: name, years to search, offense, date of offense; also helpful: DOB, SSN. Criminal records on computer from 1992, on docket books from 1943. Mail turnaround time 1-2 weeks.
General Information: No public access terminal. Will fax documents to local or toll free line. Certification fee: $3.00 per cert. Payee: Tonopah Justice Court. Business checks accepted. Prepayment and SASE required.

Gabbs Justice Court, NV.
Note: This court is closed; any records are now at Tonopah 775-482-8155.

Pershing County

6th Judicial District Court PO Box 820, Lovelock, NV 89419; phone: 775-273-2410; fax: 775-273-2434; hours 9AM-5PM (PST). *Felony, Civil Actions Over $10,000, Probate.*
Note: Misdemeanors are handled by the Lake Township Justice Court.
Civil Records: Access: Phone, fax (3 names or less), mail, in person. Only the court performs in person searches; visitors may not. Search fee: $1.00 per year per name. Court makes copy: $1.00 per page; same fee for self serve. Required to search: name, years to search. Civil cases indexed by defendant, plaintiff. Civil records on computer from 1992, microfilmed from 1919-1938, books from 1919. Court will do up to 3 or more searches by phone Mail turnaround time 1-3 days.
Criminal Records: Access: Phone, fax (3 names or less), mail, in person. Only the court performs in person searches; visitors may not. Search fee: $1.00 per year per name. Court makes copy: $1.00 per page; same fee for self serve. Required to search: name, years to search. Criminal records on computer from 1992, microfilmed from 1919-1938, books from 1919. Court will do up to 3 or more searches by phone. Mail turnaround time 1-3 days.
General Information: No public access terminal. No adoption, juvenile or sealed records released. No fee to fax documents. Certification fee: $3.00. Payee: Pershing County Clerk. Personal checks accepted. Prepayment and SASE required.

Lake Township Justice Court PO Box 8, Lovelock, NV 89419; phone: 775-273-2753; fax: 775-273-0416; hours 8AM-5PM (PST). *Misdemeanor, Civil Actions Under $10,000, Eviction, Small Claims.*
Civil Records: Access: Phone, mail, in person. Visitors must perform in person searches themselves. Search fee: $1.00 per name per year. Court makes copy: $.30 per page. Required to search: name, years to search; also helpful: address. Civil cases indexed by defendant, plaintiff. Civil records on computer from 1988, on docket books prior. Mail turnaround time 2 days.
Criminal Records: Access: Phone, mail, in person. Visitors must perform in person searches themselves. Search fee: $1.00 per name per year. Court makes copy: $.30 per page. Required to search: name, years to search; also helpful: DOB. Criminal records on computer from 1988, on docket books prior. Mail turnaround time 2 days, 30 minutes for phone requests for records prior to 1988.
General Information: Public terminal goes back to 1988. No sealed, driver's history or highway patrol records released. Certification fee: $3.00. Payee: Lake Township Justice Court. Personal checks accepted; ID required. Prepayment and SASE required.

Storey County

1st Judicial District Court PO Drawer D, Virginia City, NV 89440; phone: 775-847-0969; fax: 775-847-0921; hours 9AM-5PM (PST). *Felony, Gross Misdemeanor, Civil Actions Over $10,000, Probate.*
Civil Records: Access: Phone, mail, fax, in person. Both court and visitors may perform in person searches. Search fee: $1.00 per name per year. Court

makes copy: $1.00 per page; same fee for self serve. Required to search: name, years to search. Civil cases indexed by defendant, plaintiff. Civil records on computer since 1992; prior years on books. Search by phone only if paid in advance. Mail turnaround time 1 week; 5 minutes for phone requests when possible.
Criminal Records: Access: Phone, mail, fax, in person. Both court and visitors may perform in person searches. Search fee: $1.00 per name per year. Court makes copy: $1.00 per page; same fee for self serve. Required to search: name, years to search, signed release; also helpful: DOB, SSN. Criminal records on computer since 1992; prior years on books. Search by phone only if pre-paid. Mail turnaround time 1 week; 5 minutes for phone requests when possible.
General Information: No public access terminal. No juvenile or sealed records released. Will fax documents to local or toll free line. Certification fee: $6.00 per document. Payee: Storey County Clerk. Personal checks accepted. Prepayment and SASE required.

Virginia Township Justice Court PO Box 674, Virginia City, NV 89440; phone: 775-847-0962; fax: 775-847-0915; hours 9AM-5PM (PST). *Misdemeanor, Civil Actions Under $10,000, Eviction, Small Claims.*
Civil Records: Access: Phone, mail, in person. Only the court performs in person searches; visitors may not. Search fee: $1.00 per name per year. Court makes copy: $.25 per page. Required to search: name, years to search. Civil cases indexed by defendant, plaintiff. Civil records retained for 7 years, some on docket books. Mail turnaround time 1 week.
Criminal Records: Access: Phone, mail, in person. Both court and visitors may perform in person searches. Search fee: $1.00 per name per year. Court makes copy: $.25 per page. Required to search: name, years to search, DOB; also helpful: SSN. Criminal records on computer since 1988. Mail turnaround time 1 week.
General Information: No public access terminal. Will fax documents to local or toll free line. Certification fee: $3.00. Payee: Justice Court. Personal checks accepted. Prepayment and SASE required.

Washoe County

2nd Judicial District Court PO Box 30083, Reno, NV 89501; phone: 775-328-3110; hours 8AM-5PM (PST). *Felony, Gross Misdemeanor, Civil Actions Over $10,000, Probate.*
www.washoecourts.com
Civil Records: Access: Phone, online, mail, in person. Both court and visitors may perform in person searches. Search fee: $1.00 per name per year. Court makes copy: $1.00 per page. Required to search: name, years to search. Civil cases indexed by defendant, plaintiff. Civil records on computer back to 1984, microfiche from 1983, archives from 1920. CourtConnect online access is at the website. Case data in CourtConnect only limited to cases filed after 1/2000. Calendars also free at website. Note: Phone access limited to computer records. Mail turnaround time 2-4 weeks.
Criminal Records: Access: Phone, online, mail, in person. Both court and visitors may perform in person searches. Search fee: $1.00 per name per year. Court makes copy: $1.00 per page. Required to search: name, years to search. Criminal records on computer back to 1984, microfiche from 1983, archives from 1920. CourtConnect online access is at the website. Case data in CourtConnect only limited to cases filed after 1/2000. Calendars also free at website. Note: Phone access limited to computer records. Mail turnaround time 2-4 weeks.
General Information: Public terminal goes back to 2000. No sealed or juvenile records released. Certification fee: $2.00 per page. Payee: Washoe County District Court, or WCDC. Business checks accepted. Prepayment and SASE required.

Incline Village Justice Court 865 Tahoe Blvd, #301, Incline Village, NV 89451; phone: 775-832-4100; fax: 775-832-4162; hours 9AM-5PM (PST). *Misdemeanor, Civil Actions Under $10,000, Eviction, Small Claims.*
http://207.228.25.168/ijc
Civil Records: Access: Mail, in person. Both court and visitors may perform in person searches. Search fee: $1.00 per name per year. Court makes copy: $.30 per page. Required to search: name, years to search. Civil cases indexed by defendant, plaintiff. Civil records on dockets to 1980's. Mail turnaround time 1-3 days.
Criminal Records: Access: Mail, in person. Both court and visitors may perform in person searches. Search fee: $1.00 per name per year. Court makes copy: $.30 per page. Required to search: name, years to search; also helpful: DOB, SSN. Full dockets of criminal records searchable for 6-7 years, docket sheets available from 1980 to present. Mail turnaround time 1-3 days.
General Information: Public use terminal available. Will fax documents if prepayment received. Certification fee: $3.00. Payee: Justice Court. Personal checks accepted; check guarantee card required. Prepayment required.

Reno Justice Court PO Box 30083, Reno, NV 89520; phone: 775-325-6501; criminal phone: 775-325-6500; criminal fax: 775-325-6510; civil fax: 775-325-6715; hours 8AM-5PM (PST). *Misdemeanor, Civil Actions Under $10,000, Eviction, Small Claims.*
Note: Also hold records for Verdi Justice Court.
Civil Records: Access: Mail, in person. Both court and visitors may perform in person searches. Search fee: $1.00 per name per year. If search requires offsite to storage, additional fees apply. Court makes copy: $.30 per page. Required to search: name, years to search. Civil cases indexed by defendant. Civil records archived from 1982, on docket book; computerized records since 1980. For mail access call first. Court will send form to be filled out & returned with payment. Mail turnaround time 2-5 days.
Criminal Records: Access: Mail, in person. Only the court performs in person searches; visitors may not. Search fee: $1.00 per name per year. Court makes copy: $.30 per page. Required to search: name, years to search; also helpful: DOB, SSN, aliases. Criminal records archived from 1982, on docket books; computerized records since 1980. Same as civil. Mail turnaround time 2-5 days.
General Information: No public access terminal. No sealed records released. Certification fee: $3.00 per page. Payee: Reno Justice Court. Only cashiers checks and money orders accepted. Prepayment and SASE required.

Sparks Justice Court 630 Greenbrae Dr, Sparks, NV 89431; phone: 775-352-3003; fax: 775-352-3004; hours 8AM-5PM (PST). *Misdemeanor, Civil Actions Under $10,000, Eviction, Small Claims.*
http://207.228.25.168/sjc/

Civil Records: Access: Phone, mail, in person. Both court and visitors may perform in person searches. Search fee: $1.00 per name per year. Court makes copy: $.30 per page. Required to search: name, years to search. Civil cases indexed by defendant, plaintiff. Civil records on computer 1990 to present, prior in books and on cards. Case number required to search pre-1990 records. Mail turnaround time 1-3 days.
Criminal Records: Access: Phone, mail, in person. Both court and visitors may perform in person searches. Search fee: $1.00 per name per year. Court makes copy: $.30 per page. Required to search: name, years to search; also helpful: DOB, SSN. Full dockets of criminal records on computer last 6 years, 1990-1996 partially on computer, prior in books and on cards. Case number required to search pre-1990 records. Traffic record search fees are same. Mail turnaround time 1-3 days.
General Information: Public terminal has criminal back to 1993 and civil back to 1990. Will fax documents if prepayment received. Certification fee: $3.00. Payee: Justice Court. Personal checks accepted; check guarantee card required. Prepayment required.

Verdi Justice Court PO Box 30083, Reno, NV 89520; phone: 775-325-6501; criminal phone: 775-325-6500; civil phone: 775-325-6501; hours 8AM-5PM (PST). *Misdemeanor, Civil Actions Under $10,000, Eviction, Small Claims.*
Note: This Verdi court was closed 5/31/2005; all cases and records now at Reno Justice Court, phone and address given here.
Civil Records: Access: Mail, in person. Both court and visitors may perform in person searches. No search fee. No copy fee. Required to search: name, years to search. Civil cases indexed by defendant, plaintiff. Civil records held for at least 20 years. Mail turnaround time 1-3 days.
Criminal Records: Access: Mail, in person. Both court and visitors may perform in person searches. No search fee. No copy fee. Required to search: name, years to search; also helpful: DOB, SSN. Full dockets of criminal records held 20 years. Mail turnaround time 1-3 days.
General Information: No public access terminal. Certification fee: $3.00 per page. Payee: Justice Court. Only cashiers checks and money orders accepted. SASE required.

Wadsworth Justice Court PO Box 68, Wadsworth, NV 89442; phone: 775-575-4585; fax: 775-575-0253; hours 8AM-5PM T,W,Th only (PST). *Misdemeanor, Civil Actions Under $10,000, Eviction, Small Claims.*
Civil Records: Access: Mail, in person. Both court and visitors may perform in person searches. Search fee: $1.00 per name. Court makes copy: $.30 per page. Required to search: name, years to search. Civil cases indexed by defendant, plaintiff. Civil records go back to 1998. Mail turnaround time 1-3 days.
Criminal Records: Access: Mail, in person. Both court and visitors may perform in person searches. Search fee: $1.00 per name. Court makes copy: $.30 per page. Required to search: name, years to search;

also helpful: DOB, SSN. Criminal records go back to 1998. Mail turnaround time 1-3 days.
General Information: No public access terminal. Will fax documents if prepayment received. Certification fee: $3.00 per page. Payee: Justice Court. Personal checks accepted; check guarantee card required. Prepayment required.

White Pine County

Ely Justice Court 801 Clark St, #6, Ely, NV 89301; phone: 775-289-2678; fax: 775-289-3392; hours 9AM-5PM (PST). *Misdemeanor, Civil Actions Under $10,000, Eviction, Small Claims.*
Civil Records: Access: Phone, fax, mail, in person. Only the court performs in person searches; visitors may not. Search fee: $1.00 per name per year. Court makes copy: $.30 per page. Required to search: name, case number, years to search. Civil cases indexed by defendant, plaintiff. Civil records on computer from 1988, archived from 1899. Mail turnaround time 1-5 days.
Criminal Records: Access: Phone, fax, mail, in person. Only the court performs in person searches; visitors may not. Search fee: $1.00 per name per year. Court makes copy: $.30 per page. Required to search: name, case number, years to search; also helpful: DOB, SSN. Criminal records on computer from 1988, archived from 1899. Mail turnaround time 1-5 days.
General Information: No public access terminal. No sealed records released. Will fax documents to toll-free number only. Certification fee: $3.00. Payee: Ely Justice Court. Only cashiers checks and money orders accepted. Prepayment and SASE required.

Lund Justice Court PO Box 87, Lund, NV 89317; phone: 775-238-5400; fax: 775-238-5400; hours 10AM-2:30PM M,W,F (PST). *Misdemeanor, Civil Actions Under $10,000, Eviction, Small Claims.*
Civil Records: Access: Mail, in person. Only the court performs in person searches; visitors may not. Search fee: $1.00 per name per year. Court makes copy: $1.00 per page. Required to search: name, years to search. Civil records only kept in files, archives from 1899. Mail turnaround time 1 day.
Criminal Records: Access: Mail, in person. Only the court performs in person searches; visitors may not. Search fee: $1.00 per name per year. Court makes copy: $1.00 per page. Required to search: name, years to search, DOB; also helpful: SSN. Criminal records only kept in files, archives from 1899. Mail turnaround time 1 day.
General Information: No public access terminal. Will not fax documents. Certification fee: $2.00. Payee: Lund Justice Court. Personal checks accepted. Prepayment and SASE required.

Baker Justice Court PO Box 2, Baker, NV 89311; phone: 775-234-7100. *Misdemeanor, Civil Actions Under $10,000, Eviction, Small Claims.*
Note: This court holds very little records and is rarely open.

Nevada Recording Offices

ORGANIZATION: 16 counties and one independent city, 17 recording offices. The recording officer is County Recorder. Carson City has a separate filing office. The entire state is in the Pacific Time Zone (PST).

REAL ESTATE RECORDS: Most counties will not provide real estate searches. Copies cost $1.00 per page and certification fees are usually $4.00 per document.

UCC RECORDS: Financing statements are filed at the state level, except for real estate related collateral, which are filed with the County Recorder. However, prior to 07/2001, consumer goods and farm collateral were also filed at the County Recorder and these older records can be searched there. Most recording offices will perform UCC searches. Search fees are $15.00 per debtor name using the approved UCC-3 request form and $20.00 using a non-standard form. Copies cost $1.00 per page.

TAX LIEN RECORDS: Federal tax liens on personal property of businesses are filed with the Secretary of State. Federal tax liens on personal property of individuals are filed with the County Recorder. Although not called state tax liens, employment withholding judgments have the same effect and are filed with the County Recorder. Most counties will provide tax lien searches for a fee of $15.00 per name - $20.00 if the standard UCC request form is not used.

OTHER LIENS: Mechanics

ONLINE ACCESS: A number of counties have searchable databases online. A private company, GoverNet, offers online access to Assessor, Treasurer, Recorder and other county databases. Registration is required, sliding monthly and per-hit fees apply. Counties online are Churchill, Clark, Elko, Esmeralda, Eureka, Humboldt, Lander, Lyon, Mineral, Nye, Pershing, Storey, Washoe, and White Pine. System includes access to Secretary of State's Corporation, Partnership, UCC, Fictitious Name, and Federal Tax Lien records. For more information, visit www.governet.net/SurfNV/ or call 208-522-1225.

Carson City

City Recorder, 885 E. Musser St, #1028, Carson City, NV 89701-4775. 775-887-2260, UCC recording phone-775-887-2260 city level or 775-687-4280 St level; fax-775-887-2146; hours: 8AM-5PM. www.carson-city.nv.us/clerk
All records in one index. Records indexed on a public use terminal back to 1985. Office will perform a UCC search but public must search other records themselves. Search fee $40.00. Copy fee $2.00, if tax lien or real estate $1.00 per page. Cert fee- $4.00 per seal. Payee- Carson City Recorder. **Online access to Assessor, Recorder, Treasurer, Real Estate, Marriage, Vital Statistic records:** Access is on goverNet (www.governet.net/surfnv) 208-522-1225; requires registration and fees; see beginning of this section. Also, you may search the city clerk-recorder documents for free at http://207.228.41.46/jwalk/docindex.html. Marriage records are free at http://207.228.41.46/jwalk/marriage.html. **Other phones:** Treasurer- 775-887-2092; Elections- 775-887-2087; Vital Records- 775-684-4242. **Property tax/Assessor-** 201 N Carson St, #6, Carson City, NV 89701; 775-887-2130.

Churchill County

County Recorder, 155 N. Taylor, #131, Fallon, NV 89406-2748. 775-423-6001; fax-775-423-8933; hours: 8AM-5PM. www.churchillcounty.org/recorder/
All records in one index. Office will perform a UCC or tax lien search but public must search other records themselves. UCC search per debtor name- $40.00. Copy fee $1.00 per page; UCC copy $2.00 per page. Cert fee- $4.00 per cert plus copy fee. Payee- Churchill County Recorder. **Online access to Assessor, Property, Recording, Grantor/Grantee, Deed, Judgment, UCC, Lien records:** Access recorder records at www.churchillcounty.org/recorder/. Also, access

assessor property records free at www.churchillcounty.org/assessor/ Go to www.vitalchek.com for vital records. **Other phones:** Treasurer- 775-423-6028; Appraiser/Auditor- 775-423-6584; Elections- 775-423-6028; Vital Records- 775-684-4280 (Birth/Death). **Property tax/Assessor-** 155 N Taylor St. #200, Fallon, NV 89406; 775-423-6584, assessor fax- 775-423-2429.

Clark County (Las Vegas)

County Recorder, PO Box 551510, Las Vegas, NV 89155-1510. 702-455-4336, R/E recording phone-702-455-6566; fax-702-455-5644; www.co.clark.nv.us/recorder/recindex.htm
Only the public may search. Copy fee $1.00 per page. Cert fee- $4.00 per cert plus copy fee. **Online access to Real Estate, Lien, Deed, UCC, Vital Statistic, Marriage, Property Assessor, Fictitious Name, Business License, Inmate, Voter Registration records:** Property records, assessor maps, manufactured housing and road documents on the county Assessor database are free at www.co.clark.nv.us/assessor/Disclaim.htm. Search inmates at www.vinelink.com/index.asp. Marriages: www.co.clark.nv.us/recorder/mar_srch.htm. Property owners on GIS at http://gisgate.co.clark.nv.us. Business licenses: http://sandgate.co.clark.nv.us/businessLicense/businessSearch/blindex.asp. Voters at www.co.clark.nv.us/election/Lookup.asp. Recorder's real estate, UCC and vital recs are at www.co.clark.nv.us/recorder/recindex.htm. UCCs go back to 1986; liens to '84. Search county fictitious names at http://sandgate.co.clark.nv.us:8498/clarkcounty/clerk/clerkSearch.html. **Other phones:** Treasurer- 702-455-4323. **Property tax/Assessor-** 702-455-3891.

Douglas County

County Recorder, PO Box 218, Minden, NV 89423. 775-782-9025; fax-775-783-6413; hours: 9AM-5PM. http://recorder.co.douglas.nv.us
All records in one index. Records indexed on a public use terminal back to 1/1/1983. Office will perform a UCC search but public must search other records themselves. Search fee $20.00 UCC only. Copy fee $1.00 per page. Cert fee- $4.00 per doc, plus copy fee. Payee- Douglas County Recorder. **Online access to Assessor, Real Estate, Property Tax, Recorder, Deed records:** Property records on the Assessor's database are free at www.co.douglas.nv.us/databases/assessors. Also, the clerk/treasurer property tax database is free at www.co.douglas.nv.us/databases/treasurers/. Also, search the recorder's document files for free at www.co.douglas.nv.us/databases/recorders/ Records go back to 1/1/1983. **Other phones:** Treasurer- 775-782-9017; Vital Records- 775-782-9028. **Property tax/Assessor-** 775-782-9830.

Elko County

County Recorder, 571 Idaho St.; Rm 103, Elko, NV 89801-3770. 775-738-6526; fax-775-738-3299; hours: 9AM-5PM.
Index: Marriage records in a separate index. Office will perform a UCC search but public must search other records themselves. UCC search per debtor name- $40.00. Separate federal tax lien search- $20.00 per debtor. Copy fee $1.00 per page. Cert fee- $4.00 per doc plus copy fee. **Online access to Assessor, Treasurer, Recording, Marriage, Personal Property, Property Tax records:** Access to the recorder database including marriages is free at www.elkocountynv.net/recorder.html. Recording records go back to 1984. Access to the assessors database including personal property is free at www.elkocountynv.net/assessor.html. Also, access no longer via the GoverNet system. **Other phones:**

Treasurer- 775-738-5694; Appraiser/Auditor- 775-738-5217; Elections- 775-753-4600; Vital Records- 775-684-4242; Marriages- 775-738-6526. **Property tax/Assessor**- same address as above. 775-738-5217, assessor fax- 775-778-6795.

Esmeralda County

County Recorder, PO Box 458, Goldfield, NV 89013. 775-485-6337; fax-775-485-3524; hours: 8AM-5PM. Office personnel or visitors may perform searches. Search fee $15.00 per name. UCC, search per debtor name- $40.00. Copy fee $2.00 per page. Cert fee- $4.00 per seal. Payee- Esmeralda County Recorder. **Online access to Assessor, Treasurer, Recording, State UCC records:** Access is on goverNet (www.governet.net/surfnv) 208-522-1225; requires registration and fees; see beginning of this section. **Other phones:** Treasurer- 775-485-6367; Appraiser/Auditor- 775-485-6380; Elections- 775-485-6367. **Property tax/Assessor**- 775-485-6380.

Eureka County

County Recorder, PO Box 556, Eureka, NV 89316. 775-237-5263; fax-775-237-5614; hours: 8AM-N, 1-5PM. www.co.eureka.nv.us
All records in one index. Will not search real estate records. Will search UCC records, but not tax liens. UCC search per debtor name- $40.00. Copy fee $1.00 per page. Cert fee- $4.00 per doc plus copy fee. Payee- Eureka County Recorder. **Online access to Assessor, Treasurer, Recorder, Deed, Lien, Judgment, Vital Statistic records:** Assess to the recorders index is free at http://207.212.113.130/docindex.html. Search the treasurer's secured property tax roll at http://207.212.113.130/taxcoll.html. Search the assessor property data at http://207.212.113.130/assessor.html. Also, access is on goverNet (www.governet.net/surfnv) 208-522-1225; requires registration and fees; see beginning of this section. May not be updated regularly. **Other phones:** Treasurer- 775-237-5262; Appraiser/Auditor- 775-237-5270; Elections- 775-237-5262. **Property tax/Assessor**- 775-237-5270.

Humboldt County

County Recorder, 25 W. 4th St, Winnemucca, NV 89445. 775-623-6414, UCC recording phone-775-623-6412; fax-775-623-6337; hours: 8AM-5PM. www.hcnv.us
Separate indices to search include various books-1860's to 1983; Computer-grantor/grantee, 1983 to present Official Records; deeds, deeds of trust, contracts of sales, miscellaneous, probate, et al. Records indexed on a public use terminal back to 1983. Office will perform a UCC search but public must search other records themselves. UCC search per debtor name- $40.00. Copy fee $1.00 per page. Cert fee- $4.00 per cert plus copy fee. Payee- Humboldt County Recorder. **Online access to Inmate records:** The Sheriff's inmate list is free at www.hcsonv.com. **Other phones:** Treasurer- 775-623-6444; Appraiser/Auditor- 775-623-6310; Elections- 775-623-6343; Vital Records- 775-623-6412; 775-623-6414. **Property tax/Assessor**- 50 W 5th St, Winnemucca, NV 89445; 775-623-6310.

Lander County

County Recorder, 315 S. Humboldt, Battle Mountain, NV 89820. 775-635-5173; fax-775-635-8272; hours: 8AM-5PM.
Office will perform a UCC and Tax lien search but public must search other records themselves. Search fee $40.00. Copy fee $1.00 per page. Cert fee- $4.00 per cert plus copy fee. Payee- Lander County Recorder. **Online access to Assessor, Recorder records:** Access is on goverNet

(www.governet.net/surfnv) 208-522-1225; requires registration and fees; see beginning of this section. **Other phones:** Treasurer- 775-635-5127. **Property tax/Assessor**- 775-635-2610.

Lincoln County

County Recorder, PO Box 218, Pioche, NV 89043. 775-962-5495; fax-775-962-5180;
Office personnel or visitors may perform searches. Search fee $20.00 per name. Will not search real estate records. UCC search per debtor name- $40.00. Copy fee $1.00 per page. Cert fee- $4.00 per doc plus copy fee. Payee- Lincon County Recorder. **Other phones:** Treasurer- 775-962-5805. **Property tax/Assessor**- 775-962-5890.

Lyon County

County Recorder, 27 S Main St, Yerington, NV 89447-0927. 775-463-6581; fax-775-463-6585; hours: 8AM-5PM. www.lyon-county.org/recorder/
Will not search real estate records. UCC search per debtor name- $40.00. Federal/state combined tax lien search- $20.00 per debtor. Copy fee $1.00 per page. UCC copy $2.00 per page. Cert fee- $4.00 per page plus copy fees. Payee- Lyon County Recorder. **Online access to Assessor, Recorder, Treasurer, Real Estate, UCC records:** Access recorder records free at www.lyon-county.org/recorder/; records go back to 11/15/1999. Also, access is on goverNet (www.governet.net/surfnv) 208-522-1225; requires registration and fees; see beginning of this section. **Other phones:** Treasurer- 775-463-6502; Appraiser/Auditor- 775-463-6524; Elections- 775-463-6502; Vital Records- 775-463-6581. **Property tax/Assessor**- 775-463-6524.

Mineral County

County Recorder, PO Box 1447, Hawthorne, NV 89415-1447. 775-945-3676; fax-775-945-1749; hours: 8AM-5PM.
Index: Books, computer. Records indexed on a public use terminal back to 1985. Only the public may search. Copy fee $1.00 per page. Cert fee- $4.00 per page plus copy fee. Payee- Mineral County Recorder. **Online access to Assessor, Treasurer, Recording records:** Access is on goverNet (www.governet.net/surfnv) 208-522-1225; requires registration and fees; see beginning of this section. **Other phones:** Treasurer- 775-945-2446. **Property tax/Assessor**- 775-945-3684.

Nye County

County Recorder, PO Box 1111, Tonopah, NV 89049-1111. 775-482-8116; fax-775-482-8111; hours: 8AM-Noon, 1PM-5PM.
Records indexed on a public use terminal. Only the public may search. Copy fee $1.00 per page. Cert fee- $4.00 per cert plus copy fee. Payee- Nye County Recorder. **Online access to Assessor, Treasurer, Recording, Deed records:** Access is on goverNet (www.governet.net/surfnv), phone 208-522-1225; requires registration and fees; see beginning of this section. Also, search for property assessor data for free at www.nyecounty.net/assess/ver2/. **Other phones:** Treasurer- 775-482-8194. **Property tax/Assessor**- 775-482-8174.

Pershing County

County Recorder, PO Box 736, Lovelock, NV 89419-0736. 775-273-2408; fax-775-273-1039; 8AM-5PM.
All records in one index. Records indexed on a public use terminal back to 1986. Office will perform a UCC or tax lien search but public must search other records themselves. UCC search per debtor name- $40.00. Copy fee $1.00 per page. Cert fee- $4.00 per cert plus copy fee. Payee-

Pershing County Recorder. **Online access to Assessor, Treasurer, Recording, Real Estate, Deed, Lien, UCC, Building Permit, Occ. License records:** Access is on goverNet at www.governet.net/surfnv - 208-522-1225; requires registration and fees; see beginning of this section. **Other phones:** Treasurer- 775-273-2208; Appraiser/Auditor- 775-273-2369; Elections- 775-273-2208; Vital Records- 775-273-2408 (marriage only). **Property tax/Assessor**- PO Box 89, Lovelock, NV 89419; 775-273-2369.

Storey County

County Recorder, PO Box 493, Virginia City, NV 89440. 775-847-0967; fax-775-847-1009; hours: 9AM-5PM.
All records in one index. Will not search real estate records. Will search UCC records, but not tax liens. UCC search per debtor name- $20.00. Copy fee $1.00 per page. Cert fee- $4.00 per cert, does not include copy fees. Payee- Storey County Recorder. **Online access to Assessor, Treasurer, Recording records:** Access is on goverNet (www.governet.net/surfnv) 208-522-1225; requires registration and fees; see beginning of this section. This office warns that the database is information only, is not up-to-date nor is audited. **Other phones:** Treasurer- 775-847-0969; Elections- 775-847-0969; Vital Records- 775-847-0969. **Property tax/Assessor**- PO Box 494, Virginia City, NV 89440; 775-847-0961.

Washoe County

County Recorder, PO Box 11130, Reno, NV 89520-0027. 775-328-3661, R/E recording phone-775-328-2230; fax-775-325-8010; hours: 8AM-5PM. www.co.washoe.nv.us/recorder
Office will perform a tax lien search but public must search other records themselves. Search fee $20.00 per debtor. Copy fee $2.00, if tax lien or real estate $1.00 per page. Cert fee- $4.00 per cert plus copy fee. Payee- Washoe County Recorder. **Online access to Assessor, Treasurer, Recording, Grantor/Grantee, Real Estate, Voter Registration, Property Sales, Property Tax, Aircraft, Business Personal Property, Mobile/Manufactured Home records:** Access is on goverNet (www.governet.net/surfnv) 208-522-1225; requires registration & fees, copies made for free; see beginning of this section. Search aircraft, business property, mobile home data free at http://207.228.25.168/assessor/onlinedata.htm Also, access grantor/grantee index free at http://207.228.25.173/icris/splash.jsp; there is a $1.00 per page fee for documents. Free registration required. Download property sales 2003-2005 data free at http://207.228.25.168/assessor/SalesRpt.htm. Search voter registration roll at www.co.washoe.nv.us/voters/regsearch.php~color=grey&text_version=. Property tax at http://207.228.25.168/assessor/cama/index.php; no name searching. **Other phones:** Treasurer- 775-328-2510. **Property tax/Assessor**- 775-328-2277.

White Pine County

County Recorder, 801 Clark St, #1, Ely, NV 89301. 775-289-4567; fax-775-289-9686; hours: 9AM-5PM.
Office will perform a UCC search but public must search other records themselves. UCC search per debtor name- $40.00. Copy fee $2.00 per page. R/E or tax lien copy- $1.00 per page. Cert fee- $4.00 per cert. Payee- White Pine County Recorder. **Online access to Assessor, Recorder records:** Access is on goverNet (www.governet.net/surfnv) 208-522-1225; requires registration and fees; see beginning of this section. **Other phones:** Treasurer- 775-289-4783. **Property tax/Assessor**- 775-289-3016.

Nevada County Locator

You will usually be able to find the city name in the City/County Cross Reference below. In that case, it is a simple matter to determine the county from the cross reference. However, only the official US Postal Service city names are included in this index. There are an additional 40,000 place names that people use in their addresses. Therefore, we have also included a ZIP/City Cross Reference immediately following the City/County Cross Reference.

If you know the ZIP Code but the city name does not appear in the City/County Cross Reference index, look up the ZIP Code in the ZIP/City Cross Reference, find the city name, then look up the city name in the City/County Cross Reference. For example, you want to know the county for an address of Menands, NY 12204. There is no "Menands" in the City/County Cross Reference. The ZIP/City Cross Reference shows that ZIP Codes 12201-12288 are for the city of Albany. Looking back in the City/County Cross Reference, Albany is in Albany County.

Nevada City/County Cross Reference

ALAMO Lincoln
AMARGOSA VALLEY Nye
AUSTIN Lander
BAKER White Pine
BATTLE MOUNTAIN Lander
BEATTY Nye
BLUE DIAMOND Clark
BOULDER CITY Clark
BUNKERVILLE Clark
CAL NEV ARI Clark
CALIENTE Lincoln
CARLIN Elko
CARSON CITY (89706) Carson City(87), Lyon(12)
CARSON CITY Carson City
CARSON CITY Douglas
CRESCENT VALLEY Eureka
CRYSTAL BAY Washoe
DAYTON (89403) Lyon(93), Storey(6)
DEETH Elko
DENIO Humboldt
DUCKWATER White Pine
DYER Esmeralda
EAST ELY White Pine
ELKO Elko
ELY White Pine
EMPIRE Washoe

EUREKA Eureka
FALLON Churchill
FERNLEY (89408) Lyon(97), Churchill(2)
GABBS Nye
GARDNERVILLE Douglas
GENOA Douglas
GERLACH Washoe
GLENBROOK Douglas
GOLCONDA Humboldt
GOLDFIELD Esmeralda
HALLECK Elko
HAWTHORNE Mineral
HENDERSON Clark
HIKO Lincoln
IMLAY Pershing
INCLINE VILLAGE Washoe
INDIAN SPRINGS Clark
JACKPOT Elko
JARBIDGE Elko
JEAN Clark
LAMOILLE Elko
LAS VEGAS Clark
LAUGHLIN Clark
LOGANDALE Clark
LOVELOCK Pershing
LUND White Pine
LUNING Mineral

MANHATTAN Nye
MC DERMITT Humboldt
MC GILL White Pine
MERCURY Nye
MESQUITE Clark
MINA Mineral
MINDEN Douglas
MOAPA Clark
MONTELLO Elko
MOUNTAIN CITY Elko
NELLIS AFB Clark
NIXON Washoe
NORTH LAS VEGAS Clark
OROVADA Humboldt
OVERTON Clark
OWYHEE Elko
PAHRUMP Nye
PANACA Lincoln
PARADISE VALLEY Humboldt
PIOCHE Lincoln
RENO (89521) Washoe(84), Storey(15)
RENO Washoe
ROUND MOUNTAIN Nye
RUBY VALLEY Elko
RUTH White Pine
SCHURZ Mineral
SEARCHLIGHT Clark

SILVER CITY Lyon
SILVER SPRINGS Lyon
SILVERPEAK Esmeralda
SMITH Lyon
SPARKS (89434) Washoe(94), Storey(5)
SPARKS Washoe
SPRING CREEK Elko
STATELINE Douglas
SUN VALLEY Washoe
THE LAKES Clark
TONOPAH Nye
TUSCARORA Elko
VALMY Humboldt
VERDI Washoe
VIRGINIA CITY Storey
WADSWORTH Washoe
WASHOE VALLEY Washoe
WELLINGTON (89444) Lyon(52), Douglas(47)
WELLS Elko
WEST WENDOVER Elko
WINNEMUCCA (89445) Humboldt(91), Pershing(8)
WINNEMUCCA Humboldt
YERINGTON Lyon
ZEPHYR COVE Douglas

Nevada ZIP/City Cross Reference

88901-88901	THE LAKES
88902-88904	LAS VEGAS
88905-88905	THE LAKES
89001-89001	ALAMO
89003-89003	BEATTY
89004-89004	BLUE DIAMOND
89005-89006	BOULDER CITY
89007-89007	BUNKERVILLE
89008-89008	CALIENTE
89009-89009	HENDERSON
89010-89010	DYER
89011-89012	HENDERSON
89013-89013	GOLDFIELD
89014-89016	HENDERSON
89017-89017	HIKO
89018-89018	INDIAN SPRINGS
89019-89019	JEAN
89020-89020	AMARGOSA VALLEY
89021-89021	LOGANDALE
89022-89022	MANHATTAN
89023-89023	MERCURY
89024-89024	MESQUITE
89025-89025	MOAPA
89026-89026	JEAN
89027-89027	MESQUITE
89028-89029	LAUGHLIN
89030-89036	NORTH LAS VEGAS
89039-89039	CAL NEV ARI
89040-89040	OVERTON
89041-89041	PAHRUMP

89042-89042	PANACA
89043-89043	PIOCHE
89044-89044	HENDERSON
89045-89045	ROUND MOUNTAIN
89046-89046	SEARCHLIGHT
89047-89047	SILVERPEAK
89048-89048	PAHRUMP
89049-89049	TONOPAH
89052-89053	HENDERSON
89060-89061	PAHRUMP
89070-89070	INDIAN SPRINGS
89074-89077	HENDERSON
89081-89087	NORTH LAS VEGAS
89101-89162	LAS VEGAS
89163-89163	THE LAKES
89164-89185	LAS VEGAS
89191-89191	NELLIS AFB
89193-89199	LAS VEGAS
89301-89301	ELY
89310-89310	AUSTIN
89311-89311	BAKER
89314-89314	DUCKWATER
89315-89315	EAST ELY
89315-89315	ELY
89316-89316	EUREKA
89317-89317	LUND
89318-89318	MC GILL
89319-89319	RUTH
89402-89402	CRYSTAL BAY
89403-89403	DAYTON

89404-89404	DENIO
89405-89405	EMPIRE
89406-89407	FALLON
89408-89408	FERNLEY
89409-89409	GABBS
89410-89410	GARDNERVILLE
89411-89411	GENOA
89412-89412	GERLACH
89413-89413	GLENBROOK
89414-89414	GOLCONDA
89415-89415	HAWTHORNE
89418-89418	IMLAY
89419-89419	LOVELOCK
89420-89420	LUNING
89421-89421	MC DERMITT
89422-89422	MINA
89423-89423	MINDEN
89424-89424	NIXON
89425-89425	OROVADA
89426-89426	PARADISE VALLEY
89427-89427	SCHURZ
89428-89428	SILVER CITY
89429-89429	SILVER SPRINGS
89430-89430	SMITH
89431-89432	SPARKS
89433-89433	SUN VALLEY
89434-89436	SPARKS
89438-89438	VALMY
89439-89439	VERDI
89440-89440	VIRGINIA CITY

89442-89442	WADSWORTH
89444-89444	WELLINGTON
89445-89446	WINNEMUCCA
89447-89447	YERINGTON
89448-89448	ZEPHYR COVE
89449-89449	STATELINE
89450-89452	INCLINE VILLAGE
89460-89460	GARDNERVILLE
89496-89496	FALLON
89500-89599	RENO
89701-89703	CARSON CITY
89704-89704	WASHOE VALLEY
89705-89721	CARSON CITY
89801-89803	ELKO
89815-89815	SPRING CREEK
89820-89820	BATTLE MOUNTAIN
89821-89821	CRESCENT VALLEY
89822-89822	CARLIN
89823-89823	DEETH
89824-89824	HALLECK
89825-89825	JACKPOT
89826-89826	JARBIDGE
89828-89828	LAMOILLE
89830-89830	MONTELLO
89831-89831	MOUNTAIN CITY
89832-89832	OWYHEE
89833-89833	RUBY VALLEY
89834-89834	TUSCARORA
89835-89835	WELLS
89883-89883	WEST WENDOVER

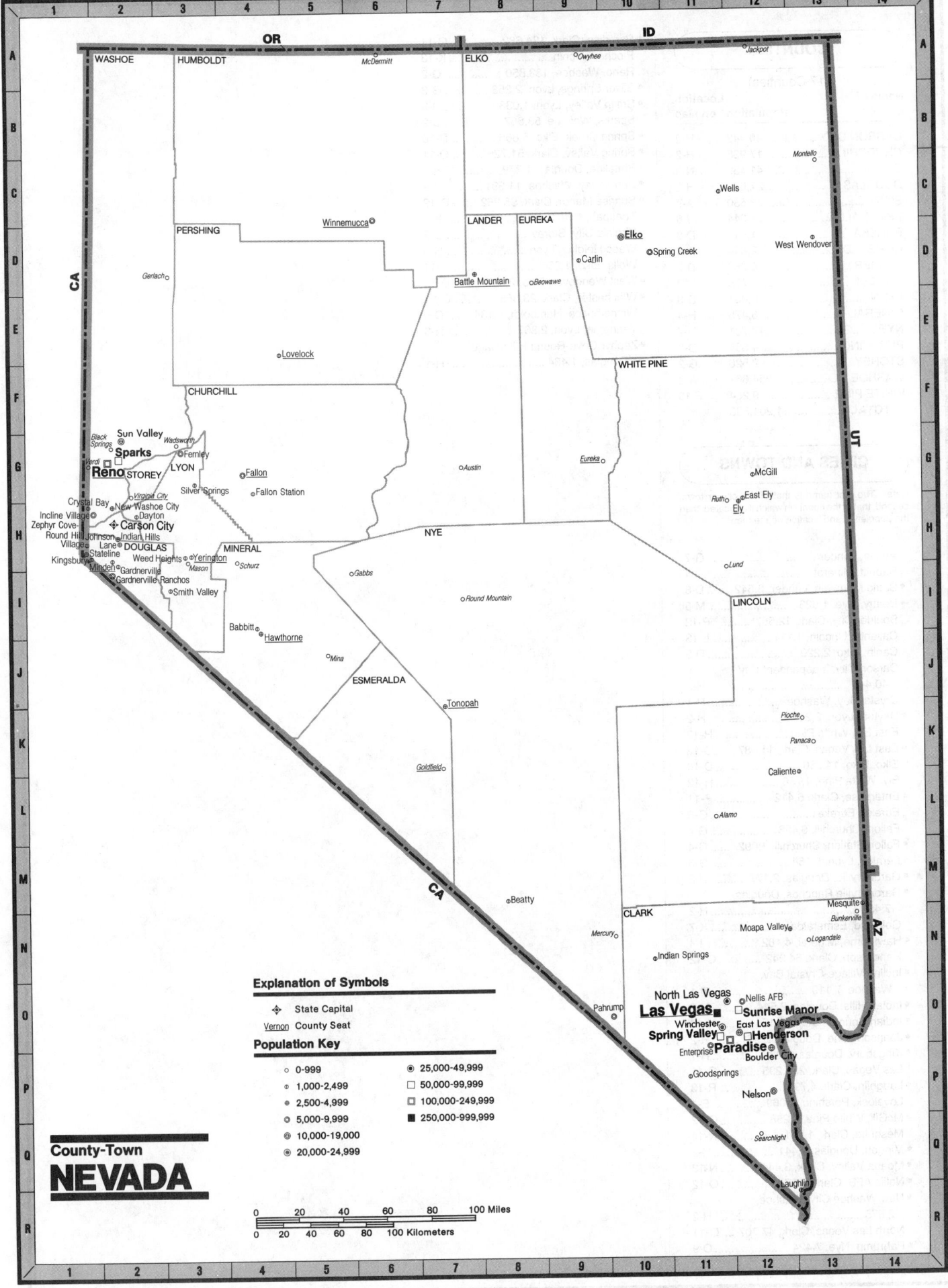

Explanation of Symbols

◈ State Capital
Vernon County Seat

Population Key

○	0-999	⊛	25,000-49,999
⊙	1,000-2,499	☐	50,000-99,999
⊕	2,500-4,999	▢	100,000-249,999
◎	5,000-9,999	■	250,000-999,999
⊛	10,000-19,000		
⊛	20,000-24,999		

County-Town

NEVADA

0 20 40 60 80 100 Miles

0 20 40 60 80 100 Kilometers

Explanation of symbols: • – Census Designated Place (CDP)

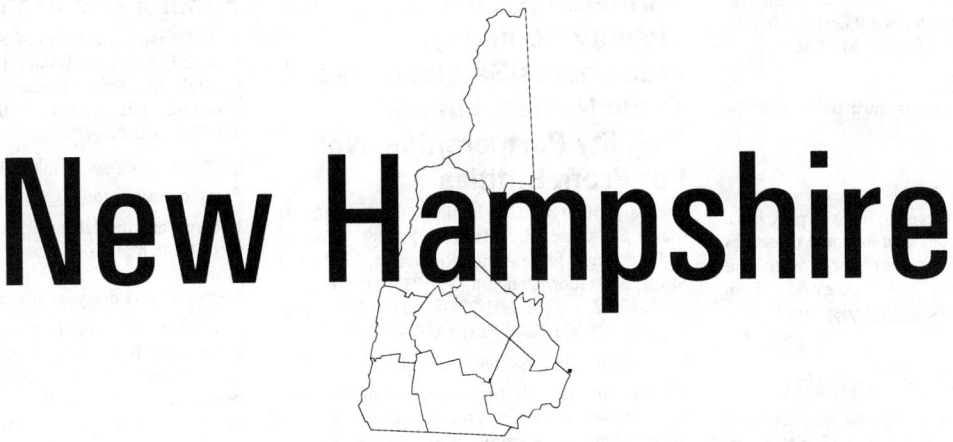

New Hampshire

General Help Numbers:

Governor's Office
State House
25 Capitol St.
Concord, NH 03301-4990
www.state.nh.us/governor/index.html

603-271-2121
Fax 603-271-7680
8AM-5PM

Attorney General's Office
33 Capitol St
Concord, NH 03301-6397
http://doj.nh.gov

603-271-3658
Fax 603-271-2110
8AM-5PM

Legislative Records
New Hampshire State Library
20 Part St
Concord, NH 03301
http://gencourt.state.nh.us/ie

603-271-2239
Fax 603-271-2205
8AM-4:30PM

State Archives
Division of Records Management & Archives
71 S Fruit St
Concord, NH 03301
http://www.sos.nh.gov/archives/

603-271-2236
Fax 603-271-2272
8AM-4:30PM

State Specifics:

Capital:	Concord
	Merrimack County
Time Zone:	EST
Number of Counties:	10
Population:	1,299,500
Web Site:	www.state.nh.us

State Agencies

Criminal Records

State Police Headquarters, Criminal Records, James H. Hayes Bldg,, 33 Hazen Dr, Concord, NH 03305; 603-271-2538, 603-271-2339-Fax; 8:15AM-4:15PM.

www.state.nh.us/safety/nhsp/cr.html

Records are available from circa 1900. It takes 1 day before new records are available for inquiry. 80% of all arrests in database have final dispositions recorded, 90% for those arrests within last 5 years.

Searching: Requester must have "authorization in writing, duly signed and notarized, explicitly allowing the requester to receive such information." Also specify exactly what information is needed. Statutorily-required fingerprint searches include FBI check. Include the following in your request-notarized release, full name, date of birth, any aliases, sex, race. Fingerprint searches are required for certain occupations (i.e. teachers) per state statute. 75% of the records are fingerprint supported. Records without convictions are not released.

Access by: mail, in person.

Fee & Payment: The search fee is $15.00 per name. When required, FBI fingerprint searches are an additional $24.00 Fee payee: NH State Police. Prepayment required. Personal checks accepted. No credit cards accepted.

Mail search: Turnaround time: 1 week. A self addressed envelope is requested.

In person search: In person requests are processed immediately.

Statewide Court Records

Administrative Office of Courts, 2 Noble Dr, Supreme Ct Bldg, Concord, NH 03301-6160; 603-271-2521, 603-271-3977-Fax; 8AM-5PM.

www.courts.state.nh.us

All trial court record access must be done at the local level.

Access by: online.

Online search: While there is no statewide access available for trial court records, the web page has a lot of useful information. Opinions and directives from the Supreme Court, Superior Courts, and District Courts can be accessed from www.courts.state.nh.us/supreme/index.htm

Sexual Offender Registry

State Police Headquarters, Special Investigations Unit-SOR, James H. Hayes Bldg, 33 Hazen Dr, Concord, NH 03305; 603-271-2538, 603-271-6479-Fax; 8:15AM-4:15PM.

www.egov.nh.gov/nsor

A list of all entries in the database can be accessed through local sheriffs' offices.

It takes 1 day before new records are available for inquiry.

Searching: The agency prefers requesters go to the local police departments if the requester does not have Internet access.

Access by: mail, online.

Fee & Payment: There is no search fee.

Mail search: Limited information is available.

Online search: For web access, click on the Offenders Against Children link. This list only contains certain information about registered offenders who have committed certain criminal offenses against children. The list also contains outstanding arrest warrants for any sexual offender or offender against children who did not register.

Incarceration Records

New Hampshire Department of Corrections, Offender Records Office, PO Box 14, Concord, NH 03302; 603-271-1825, 603-271-1867-Fax; 8AM-4PM.

www.nh.gov/nhdoc

Records are available on current and former inmates. It takes up to 3 days before new records are available for inquiry. Records are normally destroyed after 12 years.

Searching: Include the following in your request-full name, DOB helpful. Computerized records go back to 1995. Record requests may also be emailed.

Access by: mail, phone, fax, in person.

Fee & Payment: There is no search fee unless extensive searching or lists are requested.

Mail search: Turnaround time: 1-2 weeks.

Phone search: Call the number above for a phone name search.

Fax search: Requests may be faxed.

In person search: Searchers must present ID and release info.

Corporation, Limited Partnership, Limited Liability Company, Trademarks/Servicemarks, Trade Names, Limited Liability Partnerships, Not For Profit Entities

Secretary of State, Corporation Division, 107 N Main St, Concord, NH 03301-4989 (Courier address: State House Annex Room 341, 25 Capitol Street, 3rd Floor, Concord, NH 03301); 603-271-3246, 603-271-3244, 603-271-8200 (Order Annual Report), 603-271-3247-Fax; 8AM-4:30PM.

www.sos.nh.gov/corporate

Records are available from inception of the laws. Older records and inactive records are stored at the State Archives. Records also include foreign partnerships, investment trusts and cooperatives. New records are available for inquiry immediately. Records are indexed on inhouse computer.

Searching: Include the following in your request-full name of business, specific records needed. In addition to the articles of incorporation, corporation records include the following information: Annual Reports, Officers, Directors, Prior (merged) names, Inactive and Reserved names.

Access by: mail, phone, fax, in person, online.

Fee & Payment: There is no charge for 20 pages or less. If more than 20 pages, the charge is $.50 per page for every page. Certification is $5.00 plus $1.00 per page. Note that they do not print computer screens, but take copies straight from files. Fee payee: Secretary of State. They will invoice for copy fees, but you must pay in advance for certificates of good standing. Fax accounts may be billed monthly. Personal checks accepted. No credit cards accepted.

Mail search: Turnaround time: 1 to 2 days. A SASE is requested.

Phone search: No fee for telephone request. An information line, 603-271-3246, is open from 9AM-3:30PM. You can obtain name, address, incorporation date, and registered agent, check name availability, and request document copies.

Fax search: Fax requests are considered expedited service. Requests received by 2PM will be completed same business day. Fax requests may be invoiced.

In person search: You may request information in person, the agency does the copying.

Online search: A free business name lookup is available at the website. The agency is converting to a new system that will allow purchase of copies and certificates online.

Other access: Corporation, LLC, or trade name monthly Excel files are $50.00 each or $500.00 for a 1 year subscription. A list of all non-profits on file is available for $250.00.

Expedited service: You may fax requests for same day service (if received by 2 PM) for information on company status, details, annual reports (current and past 2 years only), and name availability. You may request 2 names or items per fax. Add $25.00 per document.

Uniform Commercial Code, Federal and State Tax Liens

UCC Division, Secretary of State, 107 N Main St, Concord, NH 03301-4989 (Courier address: 25 Capitol St, State House Annex, 3rd Floor, Concord, NH 03301); 603-271-3276, 9AM-3:30PM (searches).

www.sos.nh.gov/ucc//index.htm

Email questions to UCC@sos.state.nh.us.

Records are available for active filings only. It takes three months or less before new records are available for inquiry. Records are normally destroyed after one year after termination.

Searching: Use search request form UCC-11. In general, tax liens on businesses are filed here and on individuals at the town/county level. It is suggested to search both places. Include the following in your request-debtor name.

Access by: mail, in person, online.

Fee & Payment: Fees is $25.00 per name, copies $1.00 per page. Fee payee: Secretary of State. Prepayment required. Search requests and filings must be prepaid, they will invoice for copies. Personal checks accepted. No credit cards accepted, except if online.

Mail search: Turnaround time: 2 weeks. A SASE is requested.

In person search: See expedited service.

Online search: A commercial site for records is at https://www.sos.nh.gov/uccegov/. Accounts may be established using either automated clearing house (ACH) debit account or credit card. The fee is $27.00 per debtor name, or for $5,000.00 subscription fee unlimited online searches for available for one full year. Users can apply for an ACH (Automated Clearing House) account to be used as a payment option for filings or search.

Expedited service: For in person requests. 24 hour service is $35.00.

Sales Tax Registrations

State does not impose sales tax.

Birth Certificates

Office of Community and Public Health, Bureau of Vital Records, 29 Hazen Dr, Concord, NH 03301-6527; 603-271-4650, 603-271-4654 (Recording), 800-852-3345 x4651 (In-state), 603-223-6614-Fax; 8:30AM-4PM.

www.sos.nh.gov/vitalrecords/index.html

For genealogical purposes, birth records prior less than 100 years old may be released without restriction.

Records are available from 1640 to present. Records are on computer since 1990, indexed since 1948. Records are indexed on microfiche, index cards, computer.

Searching: Must have a signed release from person of record or immediate family member or show proof of "tangible interest." Order forms are available at the website. Include the following in your request-full name, names of parents, mother's maiden name, date of birth, place of birth, relationship to person of record, reason for information request.

Access by: mail, phone, fax, in person, online.

Fee & Payment: The search fee is $12.00 per record and $8.00 for each additional copy of the same record. Fee payee: Treasurer of State of New Hampshire. Prepayment required. Credit cards accepted for expedited service only. Personal checks accepted. Major credit cards accepted.

Mail search: Turnaround time: 4 weeks. A SASE is requested.

Phone search: Must use credit card for additional $6.00 fee.

Fax search: See expedited service.

In person search: Turnaround time while you wait.

Online search: Records may be ordered online from www.vitalchek.com (see expedited services).

Expedited service: Expedited service is available for fax, phone and online orders. Turnaround time: 3 to 4 days. Add $14.50 per package for overnight delivery and $6.00 of use of credit card is required.

Death Records

Office of Community and Public Health, Bureau of Vital Records, 29 Hazen Dr, Concord, NH 03301-6527; 603-271-4650, 603-271-4654 (Recording), 800-852-3345 x4651 (In-state), 603-223-6614-Fax; 8:30AM-4PM.

www.sos.nh.gov/vitalrecords/index.html

For genealogical purposes, death records prior to 1948 may be released without restriction.

Records are available from 1640 to present. Records are computerized since 1990, indexed on computer since 1948. Records are indexed on microfiche, index cards, computer.

Searching: Must have a signed release from immediate family member. Include the following in your request-full name, date of death, place of death, parents' names, relationship to person of record, reason for information request. The following data is not released: cause of death.

Access by: mail, phone, in person, online.

Fee & Payment: The search fee is $12.00 per record, additional copies are $8.00 each. Fee payee: Treasurer of State of New Hampshire. Prepayment required. Credit cards accepted for expedited service only. Personal checks accepted. Major credit cards accepted.

Mail search: Turnaround time: up to 4 weeks. A SASE is requested.

Phone search: Must use a credit card for an additional $6.00 fee.

In person search: Turnaround time while you wait.

Online search: Records may be ordered online from www.vitalchek.com (see expedited services).

Expedited service: Expedited service is available for fax, phone and online orders. Turnaround time: 3 to 4 days. Add $14.50 per package for overnight delivery and $6.00 of use of credit card is required.

Marriage Certificates

Office of Community and Public Health, Bureau of Vital Records & Health Statistics, 29 Hazen Dr, Concord, NH 03301-6527; 603-271-4650, 603-271-4654 (Recording), 800-852-3345 x4651 (In-state), 603-223-6614-Fax; 8:30AM-4PM.

www.sos.nh.gov/vitalrecords/index.html

For genealogical purposes, marriage records prior to 1948 may be released without restriction.

Records are available from 1640 to present. Records are computerized from 1990, indexed on computer since 1948. Records are indexed on microfiche, index cards.

Searching: Must have a signed release from persons of record or immediate family member. Include the following in your request-names of husband and wife, date of marriage, place or county of marriage, relationship to person of record, reason for information request, wife's maiden name.

Access by: mail, phone, in person, online.

Fee & Payment: The search fee is $12.00 per record, each additional copy is $8.00. Fee payee: Treasurer of State of New Hampshire. Prepayment required. Credit cards accepted for expedited service only. Personal checks accepted. Major credit cards accepted.

Mail search: Turnaround time: up to 4 weeks. A SASE is requested. **Phone search:** Must use a credit card for an additional $6.00 fee. **In person search:** Turnaround time while you wait.

Online search: Records may be ordered online from www.vitalchek.com (see expedited services).

Expedited service: Expedited service is available for fax, phone and online orders. Turnaround time: 3 to 5 days. Add $14.50 per package for overnight delivery and $6.00 of use of credit card is required.

Divorce Records

Office of Community and Public Health, Bureau of Vital Records, 29 Hazen Dr, Concord, NH 03301-6527; 603-271-4650, 603-271-4654 (Recording), 800-852-3345 x4651 (In-state), 603-271-3447-Fax; 8:30AM-4PM.

www.sos.nh.gov/vitalrecords/index.html

For genealogical purposes, divorce records prior to 1948 may be released without restriction.

Records are available from 1640 to present. Records are computerized since 1990, indexed on computer since 1948. Records are indexed on microfiche, index cards.

Searching: Must have a signed release from person of record or immediate family member. Include the following in your request-names of husband and wife, date of divorce, year divorce case began, city or town, case number (if known), relationship to person of record, reason for information request.

Access by: mail, phone, fax, in person, online.

Fee & Payment: The search fee is $12.00 per record, additional copies are $8.00 each. Fee payee: Treasurer of State of New Hampshire. Prepayment required. Credit cards accepted for expedited service only. Personal checks accepted. Major credit cards accepted.

Mail search: Turnaround time: up to 4 weeks. A SASE is requested.

Phone search: Must use a credit card for an additional $6.00 fee.

Fax search: No searching by fax.

In person search: Turnaround time while you wait.

Online search: Records may be ordered online from www.vitalchek.com (see expedited services).

Expedited service: Expedited service is available for fax, phone and online orders. Turnaround time: 3 to 5 days. Add $14.50 per package for overnight delivery and $6.00 of use of credit card is required.

Workers' Compensation Records

Labor Department, Workers Compensation Division, 95 Pleasant St, Concord, NH 03301; 603-271-3174, 603-271-6149-Fax; 8AM-4:30PM.

Records are available from 1996 to present. Records prior to 1996 are kept at the State Archives. However, one must go through this office for records. It takes 1-2 weeks before new records are available for inquiry. Records are indexed on microfilm. Records are normally destroyed after 10 years.

Searching: Must have an authorized release from claimant. Include the following in your request-claimant name, Social Security Number, date of accident, place of employment at time of accident.

Access by: mail, fax.

Fee & Payment: There is no search fee, copy fee is $.35 per page. Fee payee: State of NH Prepayment required. Personal checks accepted. No credit cards accepted.

Mail search: Turnaround time: 2 to 3 weeks. A SASE is requested.

Fax search: Same as mail request.

Driver Records

Department of Motor Vehicles, Driving Records, 23 Hazen Dr, Concord, NH 03305; 603-271-2322, 8:15AM-4:15PM.

www.nh.gov/safety/dmv

New Hampshire recommends going to the local courts for copies of tickets or to state Financial Responsibility agency.

Records are available for 5 years for moving violations and 10 for DWIs. Surrendered license information remains on the system at least 5 years after the expiration date. The driver's address is on manually processed records, but not on electronic records. It takes 2 to 3 weeks normally before new records are available for inquiry.

Searching: Use of DSMV Form 505 is recommended. Frequent requesters should establish an account with the state. Include the following in your request-full name, date of birth. Casual (non-permissible use) requesters are required to submit the subject's notarized signature on the Form 505. The license number is not required for a search, but is suggested.

Access by: mail, in person, online.

Fee & Payment: Records are $8.00. If you wish the record certified the fee is $10.00. Fee payee: Department of Safety. Prepayment required. Personal checks accepted. No credit cards accepted.

Mail search: Turnaround time: 5 days. Mail-in requests must include requester's name and address. A SASE is requested.

In person search: Five requests can be processed while you wait.

Online search: Online access is offered for approved commercial accounts. The system is open 22 hours a day. Searches are by license number or by name and DOB. Fee is $8.00 per record. For more information, call the Director's Office.

Other access: Overnight magnetic tape access is available for higher volume users. Minimum order is 50 requests.

Vehicle Ownership
Vehicle Identification

Department of Safety, Bureau of Titles, 23 Hazen Dr, Concord, NH 03305; 603-271-3111 (Bureau of Title), 603-271-2251 (Registration), 603-271-0369-Fax; 8:15AM-4:15PM.

http://nh.gov/safety/dmv/registration/index.html

Requests for registration information should be directed to the Registration Unit, not to the Titles Unit.

Records are available 11 years to present. It takes 2 weeks before new records are available for inquiry. Records are normally destroyed after microfilming.

Searching: The agency will only release to requesters authorized by statute or to casual requesters with a signed release from subject. Include the following in your request-Form DSMV 505. Form requires notarized signature of the requester.

Access by: mail, in person.

Fee & Payment: The fee is $20.00 for a title and lien history and $5.00 for a registration listing and $10.00 if certified. Fee payee: Department of Safety. Prepayment required. Personal checks and major credit cards accepted.

Mail search: Turnaround time: 4 to 5 days.

In person search: Turnaround time while you wait, depending on workload of personnel. Note there are two different counter locations; one for Titles and one for Registration.

Other access: Bulk information is available to approved venders per DPPA. Call 603-271-2314 for information.

Vessel Registration

Department of Safety, Bureau of Registration, Boat Desk, 23 Hazen Dr, Concord, NH 03305; 603-271-2251, 603-271-3242 (Liens), 603-271-1061-Fax; 8:15AM-4:15PM.

Records are available for current and expired registration records. All motorized boats and all sailboats over 12 ft must be registered. Boats are not titled and liens on boats are found at the Secretary of State - 603-271-3242.

Searching: Records are restricted to those authorized by statute. Authorization is stricter than the DPPA requirements. Include the following in your request-owner's name, plate number or VIN is required to search.

Access by: mail, in person.

Fee & Payment: The fee is $5.00 for current year only; add $5.00 for certification. Fee payee: State of New Hampshire. Prepayment required. Personal checks accepted. Visa. MC, AmEx accepted.

Mail search: Turnaround time: timely manner.

In person search: Turnaround time is immediate.

Accident Reports

Department of Safety, Crash Section, 23 Hazen Dr, Concord, NH 03305; 603-271-2128, 8:15AM-4:15PM.

Records are available for 5 years. Records are indexed on computer. It takes 3 to 4 weeks before new records are available for inquiry. Records are normally destroyed after 10 years.

Searching: Access is not open to the public due to Privacy Act, Chapter 295:260:14. This law requires a notarized DSMV 505 Form to be filled out by the subject involved or by an insurance representative licensed to write auto policies in this state. Include the following in your request-full name, date of birth, date of accident, location of accident. It is suggested to include both operators' names in the request.

Access by: mail, in person.

Fee & Payment: The fee is $1.00 per page. With a $5.00 minimum. There is no charge for a "no record found." Requesters are notified of the fee for reports after the report has become available. Fee payee: Department of Safety. Prepayment required. Personal checks and credit cards accepted.

Mail search: Turnaround time: 3 to 4 weeks. A SASE is requested. **In person search:** Over the counter requests are available.

Voter Registration
Access to Records is Restricted.

Secretary of State, Election Division, 107 N. Main Street, Concord, NH 03301; 603-271-3242, 603-271-6316-Fax; 8AM-4:30PM.

www.sos.nh.gov/elections.htm

All records are kept by Town Clerks, records are open. However, the Federal Help America Vote Act of 2002 (HAVA) law requires implementation of a central, computerized, statewide voter registration system by 01/01/2006. The state will comply.

GED Certificates

Adult Education - Dept of Education, GED Testing, 21 S Fruit Street #20, Concord, NH 03301; 603-271-6699, 603-271-3454-Fax; 8AM-4:30PM.

www.ed.state.nh.us/GEDhome.htm

It takes one month before new records are available for inquiry. Records are indexed on microfiche.

Searching: Include the following in your request-Social Security Number, date of birth, year of issue, name at the time, and a signed release. The date is needed since records are filed by year. The signed release is needed for either a verification or transcript.

Access by: mail, fax.

Fee & Payment: The fee is $5.00 for a transcript, there is no fee for a verification. Fee payee: State of New Hampshire. Prepayment required. No credit cards accepted.

Mail search: Turnaround time: 2 days. No SASE is required.

Fax search: You may request verifications by fax.

Hunting and Fishing License Information

Fish & Game Department, Licensing Department, Eleven Hazen Dr, Concord, NH 03301; 603-271-3421, 603-271-5829-Fax; 8AM-4:30PM.

www.wildlife.state.nh.us

Records are available for 3 years back to present. Records are indexed on computer. It takes 2 to 4 months before new records are available for inquiry. Records are indexed on inhouse computer. Records are normally destroyed after 3 years.

Searching: Requests must be in writing using their form. Include the following in your request-full name, date of birth. The following data is not released: financial information.

Access by: mail, fax, in person.

Fee & Payment: There may be a charge of $.10 per page. Fee payee: NH Fish & Game. Prepayment required. Personal checks, Visa, M/C accepted.

Mail search: Turnaround time: 3-5 days. Request must be in writing with payment in advance. A SASE is required.

Fax search: Search requests accepted by fax.

In person search: Written request is require with payment in advance.

Other access: Mailing labels are available at a cost of $25.00 plus $.10 per label.

New Hampshire State Licensing Agencies

For details about the agency responsible for licensing/certifying/registering an item below or in the Agency Quick Finder section, match an item's number with the number of the agency in the *Licensing Agency Information* section.

Licenses Searchable Online

Architect #34	www.state.nh.us/jtboard/arlist.htm
Bank #1	http://webster.state.nh.us/banking/banking.html
Credit Union #1	http://webster.state.nh.us/banking/banking.html
Drug Wholesaler/Manufacturer #27	www.state.nh.us/pharmacy/NH%20Wholesaler%20List.html
Engineer #34	http://nh.neinetwork.com/cgi-bin/professional/nhprof/search.pl
Forester #34	www.state.nh.us/jtboard/forlist.htm
Geologist #34	http://nh.neinetwork.com/cgi-bin/professional/nhprof/search.pl
Liquor Keg Shipper, Direct #35	www.nh.gov/liquor/direct_shippers.shtml
Liquor Product #35	www.nh.gov/liquor/pllicen.shtml
Liquor Stores #35	www.state.nh.us/liquor/stores.shtml
Lobbyist #42	www.sos.nh.gov/lobbyist%20information.htm
Marital Mediator #36	www.nh.gov/marital/mediators.htm
Midwife #24	www.cfmidwifery.org/states/states.asp?ST=38
Nurse, LPN/Practical/Advanced #18	www.nhlicenses.nh.gov/WebLookUp/
Nursing Assistant #18	www.nhlicenses.nh.gov/WebLookUp/
Optometrist #23	www.arbo.org/index.php?action=findanoptometrist
Pharmacist #27	www.state.nh.us/pharmacy/NH%20Pharmacist%20List.html
Pharmacy #27	www.state.nh.us/pharmacy/NH%20Pharmacy%20List.html
Pharmacy Technician #27	www.state.nh.us/pharmacy/NH%20Tech%20List.html
Pharmacy, Mail Order #27	www.state.nh.us/pharmacy/NH%20Mail-Order%20List.html
Physician #19	www.state.nh.us/medicine
Physician Assistant #19	www.state.nh.us/medicine
Public Health Clinic #27	www.state.nh.us/pharmacy/NH%20Clinic%20List.html
Real Estate Agent/Sales/Broker #32	www.nhlicenses.nh.gov/WebLookUp/
Real Estate Appraiser #31	www.asc.gov
Real Estate Firm #32	www.nhlicenses.nh.gov/WebLookUp/
Scientist, Natural #34	http://nh.neinetwork.com/cgi-bin/professional/nhprof/search.pl
Scientist, Wetlands #34	http://nh.neinetwork.com/cgi-bin/professional/nhprof/search.pl
Surveyor, Land #34	www.state.nh.us/jtboard/lsis.htm

New Hampshire Licensing Quick Finder

Accessibility Lift Mechanic #28	603-271-2585
Acupuncturist #10	603-335-1425
Alcohol/Drug Counselor #41	603-271-6100
Ambulance Attendant #22	603-271-7048
Ambulance Service #22	603-271-7048
Architect #34	603-271-2219
Asbestos Abatement Worker #46	603-271-4609
Athletic Trainer #45	603-271-8389
Attorney #43	603-271-2646
Auctioneer #3	603-271-3242
Audiologist #47	603-433-7512
Bail Bondsman #11	603-271-1463
Bail Recovery Agent #11	603-271-1463
Bank #1	603-271-3561
Bank Holding Company #1	603-271-3561
Bank, Cooperative #1	603-271-3561
Barber #4	603-271-3608
Betting Location #48	603-271-2158
Bingo/Lottery Operation #44	603-271-3391
Boiler Inspector #28	603-271-2585
Boxing/Wrestling Contestant #30	603-271-2341
Boxing/Wrestling Manager/Promoter #30	603-271-2341
Boxing/Wrestling Referee/Second/Timekeeper #30	603-271-2341
Canadian Broker/Dealer #11	603-271-1463
Cash Dispensing Machine, Non-bank #1	603-271-3561
Child Care Facility #21	603-271-4624
Child Placing Agency #10	800-852-3345
Chiropractor #14	603-271-4560
Concealed Weapons License, Non-Resident #39	603-271-3575
Corrections Officer #20	603-271-2133
Cosmetologist #4	603-271-3608
Court Reporter #37	603-271-2030
Credit Union #1	603-271-3561
Debt Adjuster #1	603-271-3561
Dental Hygienist #15	603-271-4561
Dentist #15	603-271-4561
Dog Trainer #48	603-271-2158
Drug Wholesaler/Manufacturer #27	603-271-2350
Electrician, Master/Journeyman/Apprentice #29	603-271-3748
Electrologist #12	603-271-4814
Elevator Inspector/ Mechanic #28	603-271-2585
Embalmer #17	603-271-4648
Energy Facility Construction #8	603-271-3503
Energy Facility Site #8	603-271-3503
Engineer #34	603-271-2219
Esthetician #4	603-271-3608
Explosive Storage License #39	603-271-3575
Explosives Competency License #39	603-271-3575
Fire Inspector #38	603-271-2661
Firefighter #38	603-271-2661
Fireworks Competency License #39	603-271-3575
Forester #34	603-271-2219
Foster Family Home #10	800-852-3345
Funeral Director #17	603-271-4648
Geologist #34	603-271-2219
Hearing Aid Dispenser/Fitter #25	603-433-7512
High/Medium Voltage Electrician/Trainee #29	603-271-3748
Horse Trainer #48	603-271-2158
Insurance Adjuster #33	603-271-2261
Insurance Advisor/Consultant #33	603-271-2261

Insurance Agent/Broker #33 603-271-2261
Insurance Company #33 603-271-2261
Investment Advisor #11 603-271-1463
Jockey #48 603-271-2158
Leadworker #46 603-271-4609
Liquor License #35 603-271-3523
Loan Company, Small #1 603-271-3561
Loan Production Office #1 603-271-3561
Lobbyist #42 603-271-3242
Manicurist #4 603-271-3608
Marital Mediator #36 603-271-6593
Marriage & Family Therapist #26 603-271-6762
Mental Health Counselor, Clinical #26 . 603-271-6762
Mortgage (1st) Banker, Non-Depository #1
.... 603-271-3561
Mortgage (1st) Broker #1 603-271-3561
Mortgage (2nd) Home Loan Lender #1 . 603-271-3561
Mortgage Servicer #1 603-271-3561
Motor Vehicle Retail Seller #1 603-271-3561
Motor Vehicle Sales Finance Company #1
.... 603-271-3561
Naturopath #10 603-271-4814
Notary Public #42 603-271-3242
Nurse, LPN/Practical/Advanced #18 ... 603-271-6599
Nursing Assistant #18 603-271-6599
Nursing Home Administrator #16 603-271-6936

Occupational Therapist #45 603-271-8389
Occupational Therapy Assistant #45 ... 603-271-8389
Ophthalmic Dispenser #10 603-271-5127
Optometrist #23 603-271-6936
Pastoral Psychotherapist #26............. 603-271-6762
Pesticide Dealer/Seller #6 603-271-3550
Pesticide Disposal/Labeling #6 603-271-3550
Pesticide User #6 603-271-3550
Pharmacist / Pharmacy #27 603-271-2350
Pharmacy Technician #27 603-271-2350
Physical Therapist #45 603-271-8389
Physical Therapist Assistant #45 603-271-8389
Physician #19 603-271-6936
Physician Assistant #19 603-271-6936
Plumber #9 603-271-3267
Podiatrist #19................................. 603-271-6936
Police Officer/Detective #20 603-271-2133
Private Detective #39 603-271-3575
Psychologist #26 603-271-6762
Public Accountant-CPA #2 603-271-3286
Public Health Clinic #27 603-271-2350
Pump Installer #40........................... 603-271-3503
Racing Owner #48............................ 603-271-2158
Racing Professional #48 603-271-2158
Real Estate Agent/Sales/Broker #32 ... 603-271-6658
Real Estate Appraiser #31 603-271-6186

Real Estate Firm #32 603-271-2702
Residential Care Facility, Children #21 . 603-271-4624
Respiratory Care Practitioner #45........ 603-271-8389
Savings Bank #1 603-271-3561
School Administrator #7 603-271-3871
Scientist, Natural #34 603-271-2219
Scientist, Wetlands #34 603-271-2219
Securities Broker/Dealer/Agent #11..... 603-271-1463
Securities Salesperson #11 603-271-1463
Security Guard #39 603-271-3575
Shorthand Reporter #37..................... 603-271-2030
Social Worker #25............................ 603-433-7512
Social Worker, Clinical #26 603-271-6762
Speech-Language Pathologist #45...... 603-273-8389
Surveyor, Land #34 603-271-2219
Tattoo Establishment/Practitioner #13 .. 603-271-4592
Teacher #7 603-271-3871
Tobacco Law Enforcement #35 603-271-8531
Trust Company #1............................ 603-271-3561
Vendor, Itinerant #30........................ 603- 271-2341
Veterinary Medicine #5 603-271-3706
Vocational Rehabilitation Provider #28 . 603-271-3328
Waste Water Treatment Plant Operator #40
.... 603-271-3503
Water Distribution System Operat'r #40 603-271-3503
Water Well Contractor #40.................. 603-271-3503

New Hampshire Licensing Agency Information

1 Banking Department, 64B Old Suncook Road, Concord, NH 03301; 603-271-3561, Fax: 603-271-1090.
http://webster.state.nh.us/banking/

2 Department of State, Board of Accountancy, 78 Regional Dr Bldg #2
Building Two, Concord, NH 03301; 603-271-3286, Fax: 603-271-8702.
www.state.nh.us/accountancy/index.html
Email: lcollier@boa.state.nh.us

3 Secretary of State, Board of Auctioneers, 107 N Main St., State House Rm 204, Concord, NH 03301; 603-271-3242, Fax: 603-271-6316.
www.nhes.state.nh.us/elmi/licertoccs/auctionr.htm

4 Board of Barbering, Cosmetology & Esthetics, 2 Industrial Park Dr, Concord, NH 03301; 603-271-3608, Fax: 603-271-8889.
http://webster.state.nh.us/cosmet/

5 Board of Veterinary Medicine, PO Box 2042 (25 Capitol St), Concord, NH 03302-2042; 603-271-3706, Fax: 604-271-1109.
www.nh.gov/veterinary
Email: pduncklee@agr.state.nh.us Note: Lists of currently licensed veterinarians are available for $4.00 on diskette or by email. Lists on paper are $.25 per page plus postage.

6 Department of Agriculture, 25 Capitol St 2nd Fl, Concord, NH 03301-2042; 603-271-3551, Fax: 603-271-1109.
http://agriculture.nh.gov/constants/contact.htm

7 Department of Education, Division of Educational Improvement, 101 Pleasant St, State Office Park S, Concord, NH 03301-3860; 603-271-3494, Fax: 603-271-1953.
www.ed.state.nh.us
Email: kcafiero@ed.state.nh.us

8 Department of Environmental Services, Energy Services Division, 6 Hazen Dr. POB 95, Concord, NH 03301; 603-271-3503, Fax: 603-271-8013.
www.des.state.nh.us

9 Plumbing Licensing Board, 21 S Friut St, # 24, Concord, NH 03301-2452; 603-271-3267, Fax: 603-271-6656.
http://webster.state.nh.us/plumbing/
Email: info@plumbing.state.nh

10 Department of Health & Human Svcs, Licensing & Regulative Services, 129 Pleasant, Concord, NH 03301; 800-852-3345, Fax: 603-271-4729.
www.dhhs.state.nh.us/DHHS/Programs+Services/default.htmf
Email: lmeffert@dhhs.state.nh.us

11 Department of State, Bureau of Securities Regulation, State House Rm 204, Concord, NH 03301; 603-271-1463, Fax: 603-271-7933.
www.sos.nh.gov/securities

12 Department of Health & Human Svcs, Advisory Board of Electrologists, 129 Pleasant, Concord, NH 03301; 603-271-4814, Fax: 603-271-5590.
www.dhhs.state.nh.us/DHHS/LRS/CONTACT+INFO/default.htm

13 Department of Health & Human Svcs, Advisory Board of Massage Practitioners, 129 Pleasant, Concord, NH 03301; 603-271-4592, Fax: 603-271-4968.
www.dhhs.state.nh.us/DHHS/LRS/CONTACT+INFO/default.htm

14 Department of Health & Human Svcs, Board of Chiropractic Examiners, 6 Hazen Dr, Concord, NH 03301-6527; 603-271-4560, Fax: 603-271-5199.

15 Department of Health & Human Svcs, Board of Dental Examiners, 2 Industrial Park Dr, Concord, NH 03301-8520; 603-271-4561, Fax: 603-271-6702.
http://webster.state.nh.us/dental/
Email: pthomson@nhsa.state.nh.us

16 Board of Examiners of Nursing Home Administrators, 2 Industrial Park Dr #8, Concord, NH 03301; 603-271-4728, Fax: 603-271-6702.

17 Department of Health & Human Svcs, Board of Funeral Directors & Embalmers, 6 Hazen Dr, Concord, NH 03301-6507; 603-271-4648, Fax: 603-271-3447.
http://webster.state.nh.us/funeral/
Email: funeralbd@dhhs.state.nh.us

18 Department of Health & Human Svcs, Board of Nursing, PO Box 3898, 78 Regional Dr, Bldg B, Concord, NH 03302-3898; 603-271-2323, Fax: 603-271-6605.
www.state.nh.us/nursing/
Email: sgoodness@nursing.state.nh.us
Search Database at
www.nhlicenses.nh.gov/WebLookUp/ Note: They will sell/provide lists. Contact Kathy Crumb at 603-271-2323.

19 NH Board of Medicine, Board of Podiatry, 2 Industrial Park Dr #8, Concord, NH 03301; 603-271-1203, Fax: 603-271-6702.
www.state.nh.us/podiatry/index.html

20 Police Standards & Training Council, 17 Institution Dr, Concord, NH 03301-7413; 603-271-2133.
www.pstc.nh.gov/mission.htm

21 Department of Health & Human Svcs, Bureau of Child Care Licensing, 129 Pleasant St, Brown Bldg, Concord, NH 03301-3857; 603-271-4624, Fax: 603-271-4782.
www.dhhs.state.nh.us/DHHS/BCCL/default.htm
Note: For a $50.00 fee you can receive our area list on disk.

22 Department of Safety, Division of Emergency Medical Services, 10 Hazen Dr, Concord, NH 03305-0003; 603-271-4568, Fax: 603-271-4567.
http://webster.state.nh.us/safety/ems/
Email: tfortier@nhems.mv.com

23 Board of Registration in Optometry, 2 Industrial Park Dr. # 8, Concord, NH 03301; 603-271-2428, Fax: 603-271-6702.
http://webster.state.nh.us/optometry/
Search Database at
www.arbo.org/index.php?action=findanoptometrist

24 Department of Health & Human Svcs, New Hampshire Midwifery Council, 585 Hopkinton Road, Hopkinton, NH 03229; 603-224-0049.
www.cfmidwifery.org/states/states.asp?ST=38

25 New Hampshire Board of Hearing Care Providers, 8 Fillmore Rd., Portsmouth, NH 03801; 603-433-7512.

26 Board of Mental Health Practices, 49 Donovan St, Concord, NH 03301; 603-271-6762, Fax: 603-271-3950.
www.nh.gov/mhpb/
Note: Will do phone verifications.

27 State of New Hampshire, Board of Pharmacy, 57 Regional Dr, Concord, NH 03301-8518; 603-271-2350, Fax: 603-271-2856.
www.state.nh.us/pharmacy
Email: nhpharmacy@nhsa.state.nh.us
Search Database at
www.state.nh.us/pharmacy/database2.html

28 Department of Labor, 95 Pleasant St, State Office Park S, Concord, NH 03301-3836; 603-271-3176, Fax: 603-271-2668.
www.state.nh.us/dol/index.htm

29 Electricians' Licensing Board, 2 Industrial Park Dr (PO Box 646, 03302-0646), Concord, NH 03302-0646; 603-271-3748, Fax: 603-271-2257.
http://webster.state.nh.us/electrician/
Email: inspectors@elecboard.state.nh.us

30 Department of State, Boxing & Wrestling Commission, 234 Webster Street, Manchester, NH 03109; 603- 271-2341, Fax: 603-271-6784.
www.nh.gov/boxing/index.htm

31 Real Estate Appraiser Board, 25 Capitol St, Rm 426, Concord, NH 03301-6312; 603-271-6186, Fax: 603-271-6513.
http://nh.gov/nhreab/
Email: maureen.tully@nhreab.stste.nh.us
Search Database at www.asc.gov Note: Complete lists - $50.00. Individual towns - free, call 603-371-6186.

32 Department of State, Real Estate Commission, 25 Capitol St Rm 434, Concord, NH 03301; 603-271-2701, Fax: 603-271-1039.
www.nh.gov/nhrec
Email: nhrec@nhrec.state.nh.us
Search Database at
www.nhlicenses.nh.gov/WebLookUp/ Note: Lists of salespersons, brokers,and or firms can be purchased by contacting the commission at 603-271-2701.

33 Insurance Department, Division of Licensing, 56 Old Suncook Rd, Concord, NH 03301-7131; 603-271-2261, Fax: 603-271-1406.
http://webster.state.nh.us/insurance/
Email: Requests@ins.state.nh.us

34 Joint Board of Licensure & Certification, 57 Regional Dr, Concord, NH 03301; 603-271-2219, Fax: 603-271-6990.
www.state.nh.us/jtboard/home.htm
Email: llavertu@nhsa.state.nh.us
Search Database at http://nh.neinetwork.com/cgi-bin/professional/nhprof/search.pl Note: All the professions under this Joint Board can be searched at http://nh.neinetwork.com/cgi-bin/professional/nhprof/search.pl.

35 Licensing & Enforcement, Liquor Commission, 10 Commercial St, Concord, NH 03301; 603-271-3523, Fax: 603-271-3758.
http://www.nh.gov/liquor/

36 c/o Judicial Council, Marital Mediator Certification Board, 25 Capitol St Rm 424, Concord, NH 03301; 603-271-6593, Fax: 603-271-1112.
www.nh.gov/marital/index.htm
Search Database at
www.nh.gov/marital/mediators.htm

37 Superior Court Center, 17 Chenell Dr #1, Concord, NH 03301; 603-271-2030, Fax: 603-271-2080.

38 Department of Safety, Division of Fire Standards & Training, 33 Hazen Dr, Concord, NH 03305-0001; 603-271-2661, Fax: 603-271-1091.
www.state.nh.us/safety/fst/index.html
Email: fireacademy@safety.state.nh.us

39 State Police, Permits and License Unit, 10 Hazen Dr, Concord, NH 03305; 603-271-3575.
www.state.nh.us/safety/nhsp/

40 Department of Environmental Services, Water Division, 6 Hazen Dr PO Box 95, Concord, NH 03302-0095; 603-271-3503, Fax: 603-271-2867.
www.des.state.nh.us
Email: pip@des.state.nh.us

41 Bureau of Substance Abuse Services, 105 Pleasant St, Concord, NH 03301; 603-271-6100, Fax: 603-271-6116.

42 Office of Secretary of State, 107 N Main St, State House Rm 204, Concord, NH 03301-4989; 603-271-3242, Fax: 603-271-6316.
http://webster.state.nh.us/sos

43 Supreme Court, Attn: Attorney Registration, 1 Noble Dr, Concord, NH 03301; 603-271-2646, Fax: 603-271-6630.
www.courts.state.nh.us

44 New Hampshire Lottery, Bingo/Lucky 7 Division, Sweepstakes Commission, 14 Integra Dr, Concord, NH 03301-1208; 603-271-3391, Fax: 603-271-1160.
www.state.nh.us/lottery/nhlotto.htm

45 Department of Health & Human Svcs, Office of Allied Health Professions, 2 Industrial Park Dr, Concord, NH 03301-8520; 603-271-8389, Fax: 603-271-6702.
www.dhhs.state.nh.us

46 Department of Health & Human Svcs, Bureau of Health Risk Assessment, 6 Hazen Dr, Concord, NH 03301-6527; 603-271-4609, Fax: 603-271-2667.

47 Board of Hearing Care Providers, Division of Public Health Services, 8 Fillmore Road, Portsmouth, NH 03801; 603-433-7512.

48 Pari-Mutuel Commission, 78 Regional Dr, Bldg 2, Concord, NH 03301; 603-271-2158, Fax: 603-271-3381.
www.nh.gov/parimutuel/

New Hampshire Federal Courts

The following list indicates the district and division name for each county in the state. If the bankruptcy court location is different from the district court, then the location of the bankruptcy court appears in parentheses.

New Hampshire County/Court Cross Reference

Belknap..Concord (Manchester)

Carroll..Concord (Manchester)

Cheshire...Concord (Manchester)

Coos...Concord (Manchester)

Grafton...Concord (Manchester)

Hillsborough.....................................Concord (Manchester)

Merrimack..Concord (Manchester)

Rockingham......................................Concord (Manchester)

Strafford...Concord (Manchester)

Sullivan..Concord (Manchester)

US District Court

Concord Division Court Clerk, Warren B Rudman Courthouse, 55 Pleasant St, #110, Concord, NH 03301 (also use mail address for courier delivery), 603-225-1423. Hours- 8:30AM-4:30PM. www.nhd.uscourts.gov

Counties: Belknap, Carroll, Cheshire, Coos, Grafton, Hillsborough, Merrimack, Rockingham, Strafford, Sullivan.

Searches & Indexing: Results do not include SSN or DOB. Computer index maintained. New cases in the index 24 hours after filing date. Records purged every 2 years.

Fee & Payment: Pay by money order, cashier check, business check. No personal checks. Payee: Clerk, US District Court. Prepayment required.

Phone Search: Only docket information is available by phone.

Mail Search: search usually completed- within 7 days. SASE not required.

In Person Search: Fee charged if court performs your search. Self-serve copier available - $.10 per page.

E-Services: ECF replaces PACER whose records did go back to 1980. New records online after 1 day. ECF at https://ecf.nhd.uscourts.gov **Opinions Online:** www.nhd.uscourts.gov/oo/oo_index.asp.

US Bankruptcy Court

Manchester Division Court Clerk, 1000 Elm St #1001, Manchester, NH 03101 (also use mail address for courier delivery), 603-222-2600, records rm- 603-666-7626, Fax-603-222-2697. Hours- 8:30AM-4:30PM. www.nhb.uscourts.gov

Counties: Belknap, Carroll, Cheshire, Coos, Grafton, Hillsborough, Merrimack, Rockingham, Strafford, Sullivan.

Searches & Indexing: Results include last 4 SSN digits. Both computer and card indexes maintained. New cases in the index 24 hours after filing date. Records purged every 6 months.

Fee & Payment: Pay by Visa/MC, money order, cashier's or personal check. No debtor's checks accepted. Payee: Clerk, US Bankruptcy Court. Prepayment required. Will fax back docket listings up to 5 pages.

Phone Search: Only case number, name, trustee, debtor's attorney and deadlines is released. Voice Case Information Service available, call VCIS at 800-851-8954 or 603-666-7424.

Mail Search: search usually completed- 2 weeks. SASE not required.

In Person Search: Fee charged if court performs your search. Self-serve copier - $.25 per page.

E-Services: ECF replaces PACER whose records did go back to 1989. ECF at https://ecf.nhb.uscourts.gov **Opinions Online:** www.nhb.uscourts.gov/Court_Opinions/court_opinions.html.

Standards for Federal Courts: Search fee is $26.00 per item (one party name or case number). Copy fee is $.50 per page. Certification fee is $9.00 per document, double for exemplification, if available. All fees standard unless noted in profile. Mail Search: always enclose a stamped self addressed envelope unless otherwise noted. Most courts accept fax requests or will suggest a copying/search vendor. Before releasing records, all courts require prepayment, unless noted.

Open records are located at the court unless otherwise noted. District courts index by defendant and plaintiff as well as by case number. Bankruptcy courts usually index by debtor and case number. While most courts now have their indexes on computer, many may still maintain index card files as well.

Courts offering internet access via CM-ECF or older RACER, PACER, or Web-PACER systems charge $.08 per page fee unless noted as free. Where PACER is available, the universal sign-up number is 800-676-6856. Find PACER and the US Party/Case Index at http://pacer.psc.uscourts.gov.

New Hampshire County Courts

Court	Jurisdiction	No. of Courts	How Organized
Superior Courts*	General	11	10 Counties
District Courts*	Limited	37	40 Districts
Probate Courts*	Probate	10	10 Counties
Family Court	Special	8	

* Profiled in this Sourcebook.

						CIVIL			
Court	Tort	Contract	Real Estate	Min. Claim	Max. Claim	Small Claims	Estate	Eviction	Domestic Relations
Circuit Courts*	X	X	X	$1500	No Max				X
District Courts*	X	X	X	$0	$25,000	$5000		X	X
Probate Courts*							X		X
Family Courts									X

			CRIMINAL		
Court	Felony	Misdemeanor	DWI/DUI	Preliminary Hearing	Juvenile
Circuit Courts*	X				
District Courts*		X	X	X	X
Probate Courts*					
Family Courts					X

ADMINISTRATION   Administrative Office of the Courts, Supreme Court Bldg, 2 Noble Dr, Concord, NH, 03301; 603-271-2521, Fax: 603-271-3977. www.courts.state.nh.us/

COURT STRUCTURE   The Superior Court is the court of General Jurisdiction. Felony cases include Class A misdemeanors.

The District Court upper civil limit was increased to $25,000 from $10,000 on 1/1/93. Filing a civil case in the monetary "overlap" area between the Superior Court minimum and the District Court maximum is at the discretion of the filer.

The municipal courts have been closed as the judges retire. The caseload and records are absorbed by the nearest District Court.

ONLINE ACCESS   While there is no statewide access available for trial court records, the web page has a lot of useful information, including opinions and directives form the Supreme Court, Superior Courts, and District Courts. Click on Search..

ADDITIONAL INFORMATION   Fees for searching, copies, and certification are set by the New Hampshire Supreme Court. The fee structure is as follows: Computer search - $10.00 for up to 10 names in one request; $25.00 for 10 or more names in one request; $25.00 per hour for search time beyond one hour. Most courts follow this fee schedule.

Belknap County

Superior Court 64 Court St, Laconia, NH 03246; phone: 603-524-3570; hours 8AM-4:30PM (EST). *Felony, Civil Actions Over $1,500.*
Civil Records: Access: Phone, mail, in person. Only the court performs in person searches; visitors may not. Search fee: $10 up to 10 names, then $25 if 10 or more. Court makes copy: $.50 per page. Required to search: name, years to search. Civil cases indexed by defendant, plaintiff. Civil records on computer from 1/80, index cards from 1900, docket books from 1840. Mail turnaround time 1 week.
Criminal Records: Access: Phone, mail, in person. Only the court performs in person searches; visitors may not. Search fee: $10 up to 10 names,

then $25.00 if 10 or more. Court makes copy: $.50 per page. Required to search: name, years to search; also helpful: DOB, SSN. Criminal records on computer from 1/80, index cards from 1900, docket books from 1840. Mail turnaround time 1 week.
General Information: No adoptions, sealed, juvenile, mental health, expunged, or dismissed records released. Certification fee: $5.00 per doc. Payee: Belknap County Superior Court. Business checks accepted. Prepayment required.

Laconia District Court 26 Academy St, PO Box 1010, Laconia, NH 03247; phone: 603-524-4128; hours 8AM-4PM (EST). *Misdemeanor, Civil Actions Under $25,000, Eviction, Small Claims.*
Note: Includes City of Laconia and the towns of

Meredith, New Hampton, Gilford, Belmont, Alton, Gilmanton, Center Harbor, and Barnstead.
Civil Records: Access: Mail, in person. Only the court performs in person searches; visitors may not. Search fee: $10 for up to 10 names; if pre-5/1992- $25.00. Court makes copy: $.50 per page. Required to search: name, years to search. Civil cases indexed by defendant, plaintiff. Civil records on computer from 5/92, index cards from 7/64. Mail turnaround time 2 weeks.
Criminal Records: Access: Mail, in person. Only the court performs in person searches; visitors may not. Search fee: $10 for up to 10 names; if pre-5/1992- $25.00. Court makes copy: $.50 per page. Required to search: name, years to search, DOB.

Criminal records on computer from 1992, index cards from 7/64. Mail turnaround time 2 weeks.

General Information: No public access terminal. No sealed, juvenile, mental health, expunged or dismissed records released. Will not fax documents. Certification fee: $5.00 per doc. Payee: Laconia District Court. Personal checks accepted. Prepayment and SASE required.

Probate Court 64 Court St, PO Box 1343, Laconia, NH 03247-1343; phone: 603-524-0903; hours 8AM-4PM (EST). *Probate.*

Carroll County

Superior Court 96 Water Village Rd - Box 3, Ossipee, NH 03864-7267; phone: 603-539-2201; hours 8:30AM-4PM (EST). *Felony, Civil Actions Over $1,500.*

Civil Records: Access: Mail, in person. Only the court performs in person searches; visitors may not. Search fee: $10 for up to 10 names; over 10 names- $25.00. Court makes copy: $.50 per page. Required to search: name, years to search. Civil cases indexed by defendant, plaintiff. Civil records on index cards from 1960, index books from 1840. Mail turnaround time same day.

Criminal Records: Access: Mail, in person. Only the court performs in person searches; visitors may not. Search fee: $10 for up to 10 names; over 10 names- $25.00. Court makes copy: $.50 per page. Required to search: name, years to search; also helpful: DOB, SSN. Criminal records on index cards from 1960, index books from 1840. Mail turnaround time same day.

General Information: No public access terminal. No adoptions, sealed, juvenile, mental health, expunged or dismissed records released. Certification fee: $5.00 per doc. Payee: Carroll County Superior Ct. Personal checks accepted. Prepayment and SASE required.

Northern Carroll County District Court PO Box 940, Conway, NH 03818; phone: 603-356-7710; hours 8AM-4PM (EST). *Misdemeanor, Civil Actions Under $25,000, Eviction, Small Claims.*

Note: Includes Towns of Conway, Bartlett, Jackson, Eaton, Chatham, Hart's Location, Albany, Madison and the unincorporated places of Hale's Location, Cutt's Grant, Hadley's Purchase, and portions of Livermore and Waterville.

Civil Records: Access: Mail, in person. Both court and visitors may perform in person searches. Search fee: $10.00 up to 10 names; if pre-10/1992-$25.00. Court makes copy: $.50 per page. Required to search: name, years to search. Civil cases indexed by defendant, plaintiff. Civil records on computer from 1993, on index cards from 1980, on index books from 1954. Mail turnaround time 1 week.

Criminal Records: Access: Mail, in person. Only the court performs in person searches; visitors may not. Search fee: $10.00 up to 10 names. Court makes copy: $.50 per page. Required to search: name, years to search; also helpful: DOB, SSN. Criminal records on computer from 1993, on index cards from 1980, on index books from 1954. Mail turnaround time 1 week.

General Information: No public access terminal. No adoptions, sealed, juvenile, mental health, expunged or dismissed records released. Certification fee: $5.00 per page. Payee: District Court for Northern Carroll County. Personal checks accepted. Prepayment and SASE required.

Southern Carroll County District Court 96 Water Village Rd #2, Ossipee, NH 03864; phone: 603-539-4561; criminal phone: 603-539-4561; civil phone: 603-539-5993; hours 8AM-4PM (EST). *Misdemeanor, Civil Actions Under $25,000, Eviction, Small Claims.*

Note: The former Wolfeboro District Court has been combined with this court. Includes Towns of Ossipee, Tamworth, Freedom, Effingham, Wakefield, Wolfeboro, Brookfield, Tuftonboro, Moultonborough, and Sandwich.

Civil Records: Access: Mail, in person. Only the court performs in person searches; visitors may not. Search fee: $10.00 up to 10 names. Court makes copy: $.50 per page; same fee for self serve. Required to search: name, years to search. Civil cases indexed by defendant, plaintiff. Civil records on computer from 1992, on index cards from 1989. Mail turnaround time 2-3 days.

Criminal Records: Access: Mail, in person. Only the court performs in person searches; visitors may not. Search fee: $10.00 up to 10 names. Court makes copy: $.50 per page; same fee for self serve. Required to search: name, years to search; also helpful: DOB, SSN. Criminal records on computer from 1992, on index cards from 1989. Mail turnaround time 2-3 days.

General Information: No public access terminal. No sealed, juvenile, mental health, expunged or dismissed records released. Certification fee: $5.00. Payee: South Carroll County District Court. Only cashiers checks and money orders accepted. Prepayment and SASE required.

Probate Court 96 Water Village Rd, Box 1, Ossipee, NH 03864; phone: 603-539-4123; fax: 603-539-4761; hours 8:AM-4:00PM (EST). *Probate.*

Cheshire County

Superior Court 12 Court St, Keene, NH 03431; phone: 603-352-6902; hours 8AM-4PM (EST). *Felony, Civil Actions Over $1,500, Family law.*

Note: Probate is a separate office at this same address.

Civil Records: Access: Mail, in person. Only the court performs in person searches; visitors may not. No search fee. Court makes copy: $.50 per page. Self serve copy fee: $.15 per page. Required to search: name, years to search. Civil cases indexed by defendant, plaintiff. Civil records on computer from 1992, on index cards from 1920; records prior to 1918 difficult to access; organized 1769. Mail turnaround time 48 hours.

Criminal Records: Access: Mail, in person. Only the court performs in person searches; visitors may not. Search fee: $10.00 for less than 10 names searched or $25.00 an hour. Court makes copy: $.50 per page. Self serve copy fee: $.15 per page. Required to search: name, years to search, DOB. Criminal records on computer from 1992, criminal records go back to 1900. Mail turnaround time 48 hours.

General Information: No public access terminal. No adoptions, sealed, juvenile, mental health, expunged or dismissed records released. Certification fee: $5.00 per doc. Payee: Clerk of Superior Court. Personal checks accepted. Prepayment and SASE required.

Jaffrey-Peterborough District Court 84 Peterborough St, PO Box 39, Jaffrey, NH 03452-0039; phone: 603-532-8698; hours 8AM-4PM (EST). *Misdemeanor, Civil Actions Under $25,000, Eviction, Small Claims.*

Note: Includes towns of Peterborough, Hancock, Greenville, Greenfield, New Ipswich, Temple, Sharon, Jaffrey, Dublin, Fitzwilliam, and Rindge.

Civil Records: Access: Mail, in person. Only the court performs in person searches; visitors may not. Search fee: $10 for up to 10 names; if pre-1993-$25.00. Court makes copy: $.50 per page. Required to search: name, years to search. Civil cases indexed by defendant, plaintiff. Civil records on computer back to 1993, on index cards from 1980, index books in back room. Mail turnaround time 3-4 weeks.

Criminal Records: Access: Mail, in person. Only the court performs in person searches; visitors may not. Search fee: $10 for up to 10 names; if pre-1993-$25.00. Court makes copy: $.50 per page. Required to search: name, years to search, DOB; also helpful: SSN. Criminal records on computer back to 4/1993, on index cards from 1980, index books stored. Mail turnaround time 3-4 weeks.

General Information: No public access terminal. No sealed, juvenile, mental health records released. Certification fee: $5.00 per cert. Payee: Jaffrey-Peterborough District Court. Personal checks accepted. Prepayment and SASE required.

Keene District Court PO Box 364, Keene, NH 03431; phone: 603-352-2559; hours 8AM-4PM (EST). *Misdemeanor, Civil Actions Under $25,000, Eviction, Small Claims.*

Note: Includes city of Keene and the towns of Stoddard, Westmoreland, Surry, Gilsum, Sullivan, Nelson, Roxbury, Marlow, Swanzey, Marlborough, Winchester, Richmond, Hinsdale, Harrisville, Walpole, Alstead, Troy, and Chesterfield.

Civil Records: Access: Mail, in person. Only the court performs in person searches; visitors may not. Search fee: $10.00 up to 10 names; if pre-1992-$25.00. Court makes copy: $.50 per page. No fee if document is certified. Required to search: name, years to search. Civil cases indexed by defendant, plaintiff. Civil records on computer from 7/92, on index cards from 1980, docket books from 1968 to 1979. Mail turnaround time 5-10 days.

Criminal Records: Access: Mail, in person. Only the court performs in person searches; visitors may not. Search fee: $10.00 up to 10 names; if pre-1992-$25.00. Court makes copy: $.50 per page. No copy fee if document is certified. Required to search: name, DOB, years to search; also helpful: SSN. Criminal records on computer from 7/92, on index cards from 1980, docket books from 1968 to 1979. Mail turnaround time 5-10 days.

General Information: No public access terminal. No sealed, juvenile, mental health or expunged records released. Will not fax documents. Certification fee: $5.00 per doc includes copies. Payee: Keene District Court. Personal checks accepted. Prepayment and SASE required.

Probate Court 12 Court St, Keene, NH 03431; phone: 603-357-7786; hours 8AM-4:00PM (EST). *Probate.*

Coos County

Superior Court 55 School St #301, Lancaster, NH 03584; phone: 603-788-4900; hours 8AM-4PM (EST). *Felony, Civil Actions Over $1,500.*

Civil Records: Access: Mail, in person. Only the court performs in person searches; visitors may not. No search fee. Court makes copy: $.50 per page. Self serve copy fee: $.25 per page. Required to search: name, years to search. Civil cases indexed by defendant, plaintiff. Civil records on computer from 1960; index books from 1887; courthouse burned in 1887, prior records lost (organized 1803). Mail turnaround time 2-3 days.

Criminal Records: Access: Mail, in person. Only the court performs in person searches; visitors may not. No search fee. Court makes copy: $.50 per page. Self serve copy fee: $.25 per page. Required to search: name, years to search, DOB. Criminal records on computer from 1960; index books from 1887. Mail turnaround time 2-3 days.

General Information: No public access terminal. No adoptions, sealed, juvenile, mental health, expunged or dismissed records released. Will not fax documents. Certification fee: $5.00 per cert. Payee: Coos Superior Court. Personal checks accepted. Prepayment and SASE required.

Berlin District Court 220 Main St, Berlin, NH 03570; phone: 603-752-3160; hours 8AM-4PM (EST). *Misdemeanor, Civil Actions Under $25,000, Eviction, Small Claims.*

Note: Includes towns of Berlin, Dummer, and Milan and the unincorporated places of Cambridge and Success.

Civil Records: Access: Mail, in person. Only the court performs in person searches; visitors may not. Search fee: $10.00 up to 10 names; if pre-1993-$25.00. Court makes copy: $.50 per page. Required to search: name, years to search. Civil cases indexed by defendant, plaintiff. Computerized records from 1993, civil records on index cards from 1980, index books from 1970, prior to 1970 archived in basement. Mail turnaround time 1-2 weeks.

Criminal Records: Access: Mail, in person. Only the court performs in person searches; visitors may not. Search fee: $10.00 up to 10 names; if pre-1993- $25.00. Court makes copy: $.50 per page. Required to search: name, years to search, DOB, SSN. Criminal records computerized since 1993, on index cards from 1980, index books from 1970, prior to 1970 archived in basement. Mail turnaround time 1-2 weeks.

General Information: No public access terminal. No sealed, juvenile, mental health, expunged or dismissed records released. Certification fee: $5.00 per cert. Payee: Berlin District Court. Personal checks accepted. Credit cards accepted. Prepayment and SASE required.

Colebrook District Court PO Box 5, 17 Bridge St, Colebrook, NH 03576; phone: 603-237-4229; hours 8AM-N,1-4PM (EST). *Misdemeanor, Civil Actions Under $25,000, Eviction, Small Claims.*

Note: Includes towns of Colebrook, Pittsburg, Clarksville, Wentworth's Location, Errol, Millsfield, Columbia, Stewartstown, Stratford, and unincorp. Dix's Grant,Atkinson & Gilmanton Academy Grant, Second College, Grant, Dixville, Erving's Location, and Odell.

Civil Records: Access: Mail, in person. Only the court performs in person searches; visitors may not. Search fee: $10.00 up to 10 names; if pre-1993- $25.00. Court makes copy: $1.00 per page. Required to search: name, years to search. Civil cases indexed by defendant, plaintiff. Civil records on index cards from 1979, index books from 1964. Mail turnaround time same day.

Criminal Records: Access: Mail, in person. Only the court performs in person searches; visitors may not. Search fee: $10.00 up to 10 names; if pre-1993- $25.00. Court makes copy: $1.00 per page. Required to search: name, years to search, DOB. Criminal records on index cards from 1979, index books from 1964. Mail turnaround time same day.

General Information: No public access terminal. No sealed, juvenile, mental health or expunged records released. Will not fax documents. Certification fee: $5.00 per page. Payee: Colebrook District Court. Personal checks accepted. Prepayment and SASE required.

Gorham District Court PO Box 176, Gorham, NH 03581; phone: 603-466-2454; hours 8AM-4PM (EST). *Misdemeanor, Civil Actions Under $25,000, Eviction, Small Claims.*

Note: Includes towns of Gorham, Shelburne, and Randolph and the unincorporated places of Bean's Purchase, Martin's Location, Green's Grant, Pinkham's Grant, Sargent's Purchase, Thompson & Meserve's Purchase and Low & Burbank's Grant.

Civil Records: Access: Mail, in person. Only the court performs in person searches; visitors may not. Search fee: $25.00 per hour. Electronic searches are $10 for less than 10 names, $25 for 10-25 names. Court makes copy: $.50 per page. Required to search: name, years to search. Civil cases indexed by defendant, plaintiff. Civil records on computer from 1993, on index cards from 1980, index books from 1964. Mail turnaround time 3-4 days.

Criminal Records: Access: Mail, in person. Only the court performs in person searches; visitors may not. Search fee: Same fees as civil. Court makes copy: $.50 per page. Required to search: name, years to search, DOB. Criminal records on computer from 1993, on index cards from 1980. Mail turnaround time 3-4 days.

General Information: No public access terminal. No adoptions, sealed, juvenile, mental health, expunged or dismissed records released. Certification fee: $10.00. Payee: Gorham District Court. Personal checks accepted. Prepayment and SASE required.

Lancaster District Court 55 School St, #201, Lancaster, NH 03584; phone: 603-788-4485; fax: 603-788-2005; hours 8:30AM-4PM (EST). *Misdemeanor, Civil Actions Under $25,000, Eviction, Small Claims.*

Note: Includes Lancaster, Whitefield, Northumberland, Stark, Jefferson, Carroll, Kilkenny, Bean's Grant, Chandler's Purchase and Crawford's Purchase.

Civil Records: Access: Mail, in person. Only the court performs in person searches; visitors may not. Search fee: $10.00 up to 7 names; over 7- $25.00. Electronic search is $10.00. Court makes copy: $.50 per page. Required to search: name, years to search; also helpful: DOB, address. Civil cases indexed by defendant, plaintiff. Civil records on index cards from 1981, index books for public review only, computerized since 1993. Mail turnaround time 1 week.

Criminal Records: Access: Mail, in person. Only the court performs in person searches; visitors may not. Search fee: $10.00 up to 7 names; over 7- $25.00. Electronic search is $10.00. Court makes copy: $.50 per page. Required to search: name, years to search, DOB; also helpful: address. Criminal records on index cards from 1980, index books for public review only, computerized since 1993. Mail turnaround time 1 week.

General Information: No public access terminal. No adoptions, sealed, juvenile, mental health, expunged or dismissed records released. Certification fee: $5.00 per page. Payee: Lancaster District Court. Personal checks accepted. Prepayment and SASE required.

Probate Court 55 School St #104, Lancaster, NH 03584; phone: 603-788-2001; hours 8AM-4PM (EST). *Probate.*

Grafton County

Superior Court 3785 Dartmouth College Hwy, North Haverhill, NH 03774; phone: 603-787-6961; hours 8AM-4:30PM (EST). *Felony, Civil Actions Over $1,500.*

Civil Records: Access: Mail, in person. Only the court performs in person searches; visitors may not. Search fee: $10.00 per request of 10 or less names; $25.00 if over 10 names or if searched manually. Court makes copy: $.50 per page. Required to search: name, years to search. Civil cases indexed by defendant, plaintiff. Civil records on computer back to 1995; on index cards from 1900, index books from 1950. Mail turnaround time 10 days.

Criminal Records: Access: Mail, in person. Only the court performs in person searches; visitors may not. Search fee: $10.00 per request of 10 or less names; $25.00 if over 10 names or if searched manually. Court makes copy: $.50 per page. Required to search: name, years to search; also helpful: DOB, SSN. Criminal records on computer back to 1995; on index cards from 1900. Mail turnaround time 10 days.

General Information: No public access terminal. No sealed records released. Certification fee: $5.00 per cert. Payee: Grafton County Superior Court. Personal checks accepted. Prepayment and SASE required.

Haverhill District Court Grafton County Courthouse, 3785 Dartmouth College Highway - Box 10, North Haverhill, NH 03774; phone: 603-787-6626; hours 8:00AM-4:30PM (EST). *Misdemeanor, Civil Actions Under $25,000, Eviction, Small Claims.*

Note: Includes towns of Haverhill, Bath, Landaff, Benton, Piermont, and Warren.

Civil Records: Access: Mail, in person. Only the court performs in person searches; visitors may not. Search fee: Electronic records search fee- $10.00 per name; 10 or more names- $25.00 each search. Manual search fee is $25.00 per hour. The fee may change to $25.00 per name shortly. Court makes copy: $.50 per page. Required to search: name, years to search. Civil cases indexed by defendant, plaintiff.

Civil records on computer from 1993, on index cards from 1980, index books from 1950s. Mail turnaround time 1-2 days.

Criminal Records: Access: Mail, in person. Only the court performs in person searches; visitors may not. Search fee: Same fees as civil. Court makes copy: $.50 per page. Required to search: name, years to search, DOB. Criminal records on computer from 1993, on index cards from 1980, index books from 1950s. Mail turnaround time 1-2 days.

General Information: No public access terminal. No adoptions, sealed, juvenile, mental health, expunged or dismissed records released. Will fax documents if toll-free number provided. Certification fee: $5.00 per cert includes copy fee. Payee: Haverhill District Court. Personal checks accepted. Prepayment and SASE required.

Lebanon District Court 38 Centerra Parkway, Lebanon, NH 03766; phone: 603-643-3555; hours 8AM-4PM (EST). *Misdemeanor, Civil Actions Under $25,000, Eviction, Small Claims.*

Note: Includes towns of Lebanon, Enfield, Canaan, Grafton, Orange, Hanover, Orford, and Lyme.

Civil Records: Access: Mail, in person. Only the court performs in person searches; visitors may not. Search fee: $10 for up to 10 names; if pre-1993- $25.00. Court makes copy: $.50 per page. Required to search: name, years to search. Civil cases indexed by defendant, plaintiff. Civil records on computer from 1993, on index cards from 1986, index books from 1960s. Mail turnaround time 5 business days.

Criminal Records: Access: Mail, in person. Only the court performs in person searches; visitors may not. Search fee: $10 for up to 10 names; if pre-1993- $25.00. Court makes copy: $.50 per page. Required to search: name, years to search, DOB. Criminal records on computer from 1993, on index cards from 1986, index books from 1960s. Mail turnaround time 5 business days.

General Information: No public access terminal. No sealed, juvenile, mental health or expunged records released. Certification fee: $5.00 per cert. Payee: Lebanon District Court. Personal checks accepted. Prepayment and SASE required.

Littleton District Court 134 Main St, Littleton, NH 03561; phone: 603-444-7750; hours 8AM-4PM (EST). *Misdemeanor, Civil Actions Under $25,000, Eviction, Small Claims.*

Note: Includes towns of Littleton, Monroe, Lyman, Lisbon, Franconia, Bethlehem, Sugar Hill, and Easton.

Civil Records: Access: Mail, in person. Only the court performs in person searches; visitors may not. Search fee: $10.00 up to 10 names; if pre-1993- $25.00. Court makes copy: $.50 per page. Required to search: name, years to search. Civil cases indexed by defendant, plaintiff. Civil records on computer from 1993, index cards from 1985, index books from 1950. Mail turnaround time 3 weeks.

Criminal Records: Access: Mail, in person. Only the court performs in person searches; visitors may not. Search fee: $10.00 up to 10 names; if pre-1993- $25.00. Court makes copy: $.50 per page. Required to search: name, years to search; also helpful: DOB, SSN. Criminal records on computer from 1993, index cards from 1985, index books from 1950. Mail turnaround time 3 weeks.

General Information: No public access terminal. No adoptions, sealed, juvenile, mental health, domestic violence, expunged or dismissed records released. Certification fee: $5.00 per cert. Payee: Littleton District Court. Personal checks accepted. Prepayment and SASE required.

Plymouth District Court 26 Green St, Plymouth, NH 03264; phone: 603-536-3326; hours 8AM-4PM (EST). *Misdemeanor, Civil Actions Under $25,000, Eviction, Small Claims.*

Note: Includes towns of Plymouth, Bristol, Dorchester, Groton, Wentworth, Rumney, Ellsworth, Thornton, Campton, Ashland, Hebron, Holderness, Bridgewater, Alexandria, Lincoln, Woodstock, and portions of Livermore and Waterville.

Civil Records: Access: Mail, in person. Only the court performs in person searches; visitors may not. Search fee: $10.00 up to 10 names back to 1991; complete search back to 1981- $25.00. Court makes copy: $.50 per page. Required to search: name, years to search. Civil cases indexed by defendant, plaintiff. Civil records on computer from 1991, index cards from 1981. Request for an appointment must be made two weeks prior to in person searching. Mail turnaround time one week.

Criminal Records: Access: Mail, in person. Only the court performs in person searches; visitors may not. Search fee: $10.00 up to 10 names back to 1991; complete search back to 1981- $25.00. Court makes copy: $.50 per page. Required to search: name, years to search; also helpful: DOB, SSN. Criminal records on computer from 1991, index cards from 1981. Request for an appointment must be made two weeks prior to in person searching. Mail turnaround time 1 week.

General Information: No sealed, mental health, expunged or dismissed records released. Certification fee: $5.00 per cert. Payee: Plymouth District Court. Personal checks accepted. Prepayment and SASE required.

Probate Court 3785 Dartmouth College Hwy, Box 3, North Haverhill, NH 03774-4936; phone: 603-787-6931; hours 8AM-4PM (EST). *Probate.* www.courts.state.nh.us

Hillsborough County

Superior Court - North District 300 Chestnut St Rm 127, Manchester, NH 03101; phone: 603-669-7410; hours 8:30AM-4PM (EST). *Felony, Civil Actions Over $1,500.*

Civil Records: Access: Mail, in person. Only the court performs in person searches; visitors may not. Search fee: $25.00 per hour. Electronic searches are $10 for less than 10 names, $25 for 10-25 names, then the hourly kicks in. Court makes copy: $.50 per page. Required to search: name, years to search. Civil cases indexed by defendant, plaintiff. Civil records on computer from 5/85, index cards from 1980s, index books from 1900s; organized 1769. Mail turnaround time 3 days.

Criminal Records: Access: Mail, in person. Only the court performs in person searches; visitors may not. Search fee: $25.00 per hour. Electronic searches are $10 for less than 10 names, $25 for 10-25 names, then the hourly kicks in. Court makes copy: $.50 per page. Required to search: name, years to search, DOB. Criminal records on computer from 5/85, index cards from 1980s, index books from 1900s; organized 1769. Mail turnaround time 3 days.

General Information: No public access terminal. No sealed, juvenile, mental health records released. Certification fee: $5.00 per cert. Payee: Hillsborough Superior Court-Northern District. Personal checks accepted. Prepayment and SASE required.

Superior Court - Southern District 30 Spring St, Nashua, NH 03061; phone: 603-883-6461; hours 8AM-4PM (EST). *Felony, Civil Actions Over $1,500.*

Civil Records: Access: Mail, in person. Only the court performs in person searches; visitors may not. Search fee: $10.00 per name. Court makes copy: $.50 per page. Self serve copy fee: $.05 per page. Required to search: name, years to search. Civil cases indexed by defendant, plaintiff. Civil records on computer back to 3/92; overall records go back to 1992. Mail turnaround time 2-3 days.

Criminal Records: Access: Mail, in person. Only the court performs in person searches; visitors may not. Search fee: $10.00 per name. Court makes copy: $.50 per page. Self serve copy fee: $.05 per page. Required to search: name, years to search; also helpful: DOB. Criminal records on computer back to 3/92; overall records go back to 1992. Mail turnaround time 2-3 days.

General Information: No public access terminal. No sealed, juvenile or annulled records released. Will not fax documents. Certification fee: $5.00 per doc.

Payee: Superior Court. Personal checks accepted. Prepayment required.

Goffstown District Court PO Box 129, Goffstown, NH 03045; phone: 603-497-2597; hours 8AM-4PM (EST). *Misdemeanor, Civil Actions Under $25,000, Eviction, Small Claims.*

Note: Includes towns of Goffstown, Weare, New Boston, and Francestown.

Civil Records: Access: Mail, in person. Only the court performs in person searches; visitors may not. Search fee: $10.00 up to 10 names; if over 10 names- $25.00. Court makes copy: $.50 per page. Required to search: name, years to search. Civil cases indexed by defendant, plaintiff. Civil records on computer from 3/92, kept in files prior. Mail turnaround time 2 weeks.

Criminal Records: Access: Mail, in person. Only the court performs in person searches; visitors may not. Search fee: $10.00 up to 10 names; if over 10 names- $25.00. Court makes copy: $.50 per page. Required to search: name, years to search, DOB; also helpful: SSN. Criminal records on computer from 3/92, kept in files prior. Mail turnaround time 2 weeks.

General Information: No public access terminal. No sealed, juvenile, mental health, expunged or dismissed records released. Certification fee: $5.00 per cert. Payee: Goffstown District Court. Personal checks accepted. Prepayment required. SASE helpful.

Hillsborough District Court PO Box 763, Hillsborough, NH 03244; phone: 603-464-5811; hours 8AM-4PM (EST). *Misdemeanor, Civil Actions Under $25,000, Eviction, Small Claims.*

Note: Includes towns of Hillsborough, Deering, Windsor, Antrim, and Bennington.

Civil Records: Access: Mail, in person. Both court and visitors may perform in person searches. Search fee: $10.00 up to 10 names; if pre-1992- $25.00. Court makes copy: $.50 per page. Required to search: name, years to search. Civil cases indexed by defendant, plaintiff. Civil records on computer from 1992, on index cards from 1980, index books from 1960. Appointment required for in person searching. Mail turnaround time 1 week.

Criminal Records: Access: Mail, in person. Both court and visitors may perform in person searches. Search fee: $10.00 up to 10 names; if pre-1992- $25.00. Court makes copy: $.50 per page. Required to search: name, years to search, DOB; also helpful: SSN. Criminal records on computer from 1992, on index cards from 1980, index books from 1960. Mail turnaround time 1 week.

General Information: Public terminal has only civil records back to 1992. No adoptions, sealed, juvenile, mental health, expunged or dismissed records released. Certification fee: $5.00 per cert. Payee: Hillsborough District Court. Personal checks accepted. Prepayment and SASE required.

Manchester District Court PO Box 456, Manchester, NH 03105; phone: 603-624-6510; hours 8AM-4PM (EST). *Misdemeanor, Civil Actions Under $25,000, Eviction, Small Claims.*

Note: Includes city of Manchester.

Civil Records: Access: Mail. Only the court performs in person searches; visitors may not. Search fee: $10.00 up to 10 names; if pre-1992- $25.00. Court makes copy: $.50 per page. Required to search: name, years to search, DOB; also helpful: address. Civil cases indexed by defendant, plaintiff. Civil records on computer from 6/92, on index cards from 1960. All requests must be in writing. Mail turnaround time 2 weeks.

Criminal Records: Access: Mail. Only the court performs in person searches; visitors may not. Search fee: $10.00 up to 10 names; if pre-1992- $25.00. Court makes copy: $.50 per page. Required to search: name, years to search, DOB; also helpful: address. Criminal records on computer from 6/92, on index cards from 1960. All requests must be in writing. Mail turnaround time 2 weeks.

General Information: No public access terminal. No adoptions, sealed, juvenile, mental health,

expunged or dismissed records released. Certification fee: $5.00 per cert. Payee: Manchester District Court. Personal checks accepted. Prepayment and SASE required.

Merrimack District Court PO Box 324, Merrimack, NH 03054-0324; phone: 603-424-9916; hours 8AM-4PM (EST). *Misdemeanor, Civil Actions Under $25,000, Eviction, Small Claims.*

Note: Includes towns of Merrimack, Litchfield, and Bedford.

Civil Records: Access: Mail, in person. Only the court performs in person searches; visitors may not. Search fee: $25 per hour for manual searches; electronic- $10 for up to first 9 names or $25 for first 25 names, then hour rate. Court makes copy: $.50 per page. Required to search: name, years to search. Civil cases indexed by defendant, plaintiff. Civil records on computer from 7/92, on index cards from 1972, index books in archives at Concord. All requests must be in writing. Mail turnaround time 1-2 days.

Criminal Records: Access: Mail, in person. Both court and visitors may perform in person searches. Search fee: Same fees as civil. Court makes copy: $.50 per page. Required to search: name, years to search; also helpful: DOB. Criminal records on computer from 7/92, on index cards from 1972, index books in archives at Concord. All requests must be in writing. Mail turnaround time 1-2 days.

General Information: No public access terminal. No adoptions, sealed, juvenile, mental health, expunged or dismissed records released. Certification fee: $5.00 per doc. Payee: Merrimack District Court. Personal checks accepted. Prepayment and SASE required.

Milford District Court PO Box 943, 180 Elm St, Milford, NH 03055-0943; phone: 603-673-2900; fax: 603-672-5231; hours 8AM-4PM (EST). *Misdemeanor, Civil Actions Under $25,000, Eviction, Small Claims.*

Note: Includes towns of Milford, Brookline, Amherst, Mason, Wilton, Lyndeborough, and Mont Vernon.

Civil Records: Access: Mail, in person. Only the court performs in person searches; visitors may not. Search fee: $10 up to 10 names; if pre-8/1992- $25.00. Court makes copy: $.50 per page. Required to search: name, years to search. Civil cases indexed by defendant, plaintiff. Civil records on computer from 8/92, on index cards from 1950s, prior records may or may not be at old courthouse. Mail turnaround time 7 days.

Criminal Records: Access: Mail, in person. Only the court performs in person searches; visitors may not. Search fee: $10 up to 10 names; if pre-8/1992- $25.00. Court makes copy: $.50 per page. Required to search: name, years to search; also helpful: DOB, SSN. Criminal records on computer from 8/92, on index cards from 1950s, prior records may or may not be at old courthouse. Mail turnaround time 14 days.

General Information: No public access terminal. No adoptions, sealed, juvenile, mental health, expunged or dismissed records released. Certification fee: $5.00 per cert. Payee: Milford District Court. Personal checks accepted. Prepayment and SASE required.

Nashua District Court PO Box 310, Nashua, NH 03061-0310; phone: 603-880-3333; hours 8AM-4PM (EST). *Misdemeanor, Civil Actions Under $25,000, Eviction, Small Claims.*

Note: Includes city of Nashua and the towns of Hudson and Hollis.

Civil Records: Access: Mail, in person. Only the court performs in person searches; visitors may not. Search fee: $10 up to 10 names; if pre-8/1992- $25.00. Court makes copy: $.50 per page. Required to search: name, years to search. Civil cases indexed by defendant, plaintiff. Civil records on computer from 1993, index cards from 1982. All requests must be in writing. Mail turnaround time 5 days.

Criminal Records: Access: Mail, in person. Only the court performs in person searches; visitors may not. Search fee: $10 up to 10 names; if pre-8/1992- $25.00. Court makes copy: $.50 per page. Required to search: name, years to search; also helpful: DOB, SSN. Criminal records on computer from 8/1992, index cards from 1982. All requests must be in writing. Mail turnaround time 5 days.

General Information: No public access terminal. No adoptions, sealed, juvenile, mental health, expunged records released. Certification fee: $5.00 per cert. Payee: Nashua District Court. Personal checks accepted. Prepayment and SASE required.

Probate Court PO Box 387, 30 Spring St, Nashua, NH 03061-0387; phone: 603-882-1231; fax: 603-882-1620; hours 8AM-4PM (EST). *Probate.*

Merrimack County

Superior Court PO Box 2880, Concord, NH 03302-2880; phone: 603-225-5501; hours 8AM-4PM (EST). *Felony, Civil Actions Over $1,500.*

Civil Records: Access: Mail, in person. Only the court performs in person searches; visitors may not. Search fee: $10.00 up to 10 names; if pre-1984- $25.00. Court makes copy: $.50 per page. Required to search: name, years to search. Civil cases indexed by defendant, plaintiff. Civil records on computer from 1983, index cards from 1950, index books from 1800's; organized 1823. Mail turnaround time 2-3 weeks.

Criminal Records: Access: Phone, mail, in person. Only the court performs in person searches; visitors may not. Search fee: $10.00 up to 10 names; if pre-1984- $25.00. Court makes copy: $.50 per page. Required to search: name, years to search, DOB; also helpful: SSN. Criminal records on computer since 1984. Mail turnaround time 2-3 weeks.

General Information: No public access terminal. No adoptions, sealed, juvenile, mental health, expunged or dismissed records released. Certification fee: $5.00 per cert. Payee: Merrimack Superior Court. Personal checks accepted. Prepayment and SASE required.

Concord District Court 32 Clinton St, PO Box 3420, Concord, NH 03302-3420; phone: 603-271-6400; hours 8AM-4PM (EST). *Misdemeanor, Civil Actions Under $25,000, Eviction, Small Claims.*

Note: The former Pittsfield District Court has been combined with this court. Includes city of Concord, and the towns of Loudon, Canterbury, Dunbarton, Bow, Hopkinton, Pittsfield, Chichester, and Epsom.

Civil Records: Access: Mail, in person. Only the court performs in person searches; visitors may not. Search fee: $10.00 up to 10 names; if pre-1989- $25.00. Court makes copy: $.50 per page. Required to search: name, years to search. Civil cases indexed by defendant, plaintiff. Civil records on computer from 1989, index cards from 1978, docket books from 1800. Mail turnaround time 10 days.

Criminal Records: Access: Mail, in person. Only the court performs in person searches; visitors may not. Search fee: $10.00 up to 10 names; if pre-1989- $25.00. Court makes copy: $.50 per page. Required to search: name, years to search, DOB. Criminal records on computer from 1989, index cards from 1978, docket books from 1800. Mail turnaround time 10 days.

General Information: No public access terminal. No sealed, juvenile, mental health, expunged or dismissed records released. Certification fee: $5.00 per cert. Payee: Concord District Court. Personal checks accepted. Prepayment and SASE required.

Franklin District Court 7 Hancock Terrace, Franklin, NH 03235; phone: 603-934-3290; hours 8AM-4PM (EST). *Misdemeanor, Civil Actions Under $25,000, Eviction, Small Claims.*

Note: Includes city of Franklin and the towns of Northfield, Danbury, Andover, Boscawen, Salisbury, Hill, Webster, Sanbornton, and Tilton.

Civil Records: Access: Mail, in person. Only the court performs in person searches; visitors may not. Search fee: $10.00 up to 10 names. Court makes copy: $.50 per page. Required to search: name, years to search. Civil cases indexed by plaintiff. Civil records on computer from 1/91, index cards from 1/80, index books from 1960s. Mail turnaround time 2-3 days.

Criminal Records: Access: Mail, in person. Only the court performs in person searches; visitors may not. Search fee: $10.00 up to 10 names. Court makes copy: $.50 per page. Required to search: name, years to search; also helpful: DOB, SSN. Criminal records on computer from 1/91, index cards from 1/80, index books from 1960s. Mail turnaround time 2-3 days.

General Information: No public access terminal. No adoptions, sealed, juvenile, mental health, expunged or dismissed records released. Certification fee: $5.00 per doc. Payee: Franklin District Court. Personal checks accepted. Prepayment and SASE required.

Henniker District Court 2 Depot St, Henniker, NH 03242; phone: 603-428-3214; hours 8AM-4PM (EST). *Misdemeanor, Civil Actions Under $25,000, Eviction, Small Claims.*

Note: Includes towns of Henniker, Warner, and Bradford.

Civil Records: Access: Mail, in person. Only the court performs in person searches; visitors may not. Search fee: $10.00 up to 10 names; if over 10 names- $25.00. Court makes copy: $.50 per page. Required to search: name, years to search. Civil cases indexed by defendant, plaintiff. Civil records on index cards from 1988, index books from 1960s; on computer back to 1989. Mail turnaround time can take as long as 6 weeks.

Criminal Records: Access: Mail, in person. Only the court performs in person searches; visitors may not. Search fee: $10.00 up to 10 names; if over 10 names- $25.00. Court makes copy: $.50 per page. Required to search: name, years to search, DOB; also helpful: SSN. Criminal records on index cards from 1988, index books from 1960s; on computer back to 1989. Mail turnaround time can take as long as 6 weeks.

General Information: No public access terminal. No adoptions, sealed, juvenile, mental health, expunged or dismissed records released. Certification fee: $5.00 per cert. Payee: Henniker District Court. Personal checks accepted. Prepayment and SASE required.

Hooksett District Court 101 Merrimack, Hooksett, NH 03106; phone: 603-485-9901; hours 8AM-4PM (EST). *Misdemeanor, Civil Actions Under $25,000, Eviction, Small Claims.*

Note: Includes towns of Allenstown, Pembroke, and Hooksett.

Civil Records: Access: Mail, in person. Only the court performs in person searches; visitors may not. Search fee: Electronic $10.00 per name if less than 10 names; if over 10 names- $25.00 each. Manual research is $25.00 per hour. Court makes copy: $.50 per page. Required to search: name, years to search. Civil cases indexed by defendant, plaintiff. Civil records on computer from 1993, on index cards from 1980, index books from 1975. All requests must be in writing. Mail turnaround time 1-2 months.

Criminal Records: Access: Mail, in person. Only the court performs in person searches; visitors may not. Search fee: Same fees as civil. Court makes copy: $.50 per page. Required to search: name, years to search; also helpful: DOB, SSN. Criminal records on computer from 1993, on index cards from 1980, index books from 1975. Mail turnaround time 1-2 months.

General Information: No public access terminal. No sealed, juvenile, mental health, expunged or dismissed records released. Certification fee: $5.00 per page. Cert fee includes copies. Payee: Hooksett District Court. Personal checks accepted. Prepayment and SASE required.

New London District Court PO Box 1966, New London, NH 03257; phone: 603-526-6519; hours 8:30AM-4PM (EST). *Misdemeanor, Civil Actions Under $25,000, Eviction, Small Claims.*

Note: Includes towns of New London, Wilmot, Newbury, and Sutton.

Civil Records: Access: Mail, in person. Only the court performs in person searches; visitors may not. Search fee: $10.00 up to 10 names; if pre-1993- $25.00. Court makes copy: $.50 per page. Required to search: name, years to search. Civil records indexed by defendant, plaintiff. Civil records on computer from 1993, on index cards from 1980, index books from 1970. An appointment is necessary before performing an in person search. Mail turnaround time 1-2 days.

Criminal Records: Access: Mail, in person. Both court and visitors may perform in person searches. Search fee: $10.00 up to 10 names; if pre-1993- $25.00. Court makes copy: $.50 per page. Required to search: name, years to search; also helpful: DOB, SSN. Criminal records on computer from 1993, on index cards from 1980, index books from 1970. An appointment is necessary before performing an in person search. Mail turnaround time 1-2 days.

General Information: No public access terminal. No adoptions, sealed, juvenile, mental health, expunged or dismissed records released. Certification fee: $1.00 per page. Payee: New London District Court. Personal checks accepted. Prepayment and SASE required.

Probate Court 163 N Main St, Concord, NH 03301; phone: 603-224-9589; fax: 603-225-0179; hours 8AM-4:30PM July-Aug: 8AM-4PM (EST). *Probate.*

Rockingham County

Superior Court PO Box 1258, Kingston, NH 03848-1258; phone: 603-642-5256; hours 8AM-4PM (EST). *Felony, Civil Actions Over $1,500.*

Civil Records: Access: Mail, in person. Only the court performs in person searches; visitors may not. Search fee: $10.00 up to 10 names; over 10 names- $25.00. $25.00 per hour for manual searches. Court makes copy: $.50 per page. Self serve copy fee: $.25 per page. Required to search: name, years to search. Civil cases indexed by defendant, plaintiff. Civil records on computer from 1988, index cards from 1920, organized 1769.

Criminal Records: Access: Mail, in person. Only the court performs in person searches; visitors may not. Search fee: $10.00 up to 10 names; over 10 names- $25.00. $25.00 per hour for manual searches. Court makes copy: $.50 per page. Self serve copy fee: $.25 per page. Required to search: name, years to search; also helpful: DOB. Criminal records on computer from 1988, index cards from 1920, organized 1769.

General Information: No public access terminal. No sealed, juvenile, mental health, expunged, annulled records released. Certification fee: $5.00 per cert. Payee: Clerk Superior Court. Personal checks accepted. Prepayment required.

Auburn District Court 5 Priscilla Lane, Auburn, NH 03032; criminal phone: 603-624-2084; civil phone: 603-624-2265; hours 8AM-4PM (EST). *Misdemeanor, Civil Actions Under $25,000, Eviction, Small Claims.*

Note: Includes towns of Auburn, Candia, Deerfield, Northwood, Nottingham, and Raymond.

Civil Records: Access: Mail, in person. Only the court performs in person searches; visitors may not. Search fee: $10.00 up to 10 names; if pre-1993- $25.00. Court makes copy: $.50 per page. Required to search: name, years to search; also helpful: address. Civil cases indexed by defendant, plaintiff. Civil records on computer from 5/92, index cards from 1980, index books from 1968. Mail turnaround time 10 days.

Criminal Records: Access: Mail, in person. Only the court performs in person searches; visitors may not. Search fee: $10.00 up to 10 names; if pre-1993- $25.00. Court makes copy: $.50 per page. Required to search: name, years to search, DOB, signed release. Criminal records on computer from 5/92, index cards from 1980, index books from 1968. Mail turnaround time 10 days.

General Information: No public access terminal. No adoptions, sealed, juvenile, mental health, expunged or dismissed records released. Certification fee: $5.00 per cert. Payee: Auburn District Court. Personal checks accepted. Prepayment and SASE required.

Derry District Court 10 Manning St, Derry, NH 03038; phone: 603-434-4676; hours 8AM-4PM (EST). *Misdemeanor, Civil Actions Under $25,000, Eviction, Small Claims.*

Note: Includes towns of Derry, Londonderry, Chester, and Sandown.

Civil Records: Access: Phone, mail, in person. Only the court performs in person searches; visitors may not. Search fee: $10.00 up to 10 names; if pre-1992-$25.00. Court makes copy: $.50 per page. Required to search: name, years to search. Civil cases indexed by defendant, plaintiff. Civil records on computer from 10/92, on index cards prior. Mail turnaround time 1 week.

Criminal Records: Access: Phone, mail, in person. Only the court performs in person searches; visitors may not. Search fee: $10.00 up to 10 names; if pre-1992- $25.00. Court makes copy: $.50 per page. Required to search: name, years to search; also helpful: DOB, SSN. Criminal records on computer from 10/92, on index cards prior. Mail turnaround time 1 week.

General Information: No public access terminal. No adoptions, sealed, juvenile, mental health, expunged, dismissed or annulment records released. Certification fee: $5.00 per cert. Payee: Derry District Court. Personal checks accepted. Prepayment and SASE required.

Exeter District Court PO Box 1149, Kingston, NH 03848; phone: 603-642-9145; hours 8AM-4PM (EST). *Misdemeanor, Civil Actions Under $25,000, Eviction, Small Claims.*

Note: Relocated to Kingston from Exeter in 2004. Jurisdiction includes towns of Exeter, Newmarket, Stratham, Newfields, Fremont, East Kingston, Kensington, Epping, and Brentwood.

Civil Records: Access: Mail, in person. Only the court performs in person searches; visitors may not. Search fee: $10.00 up to 10 names. Court makes copy: $.50 per page. Required to search: name, years to search; also helpful: address. Civil cases indexed by defendant, plaintiff. Civil records on computer back to 1991. Mail turnaround time 3 days.

Criminal Records: Access: Mail, in person. Both court and visitors may perform in person searches. Search fee: $10.00 up to 10 names. Court makes copy: $.50 per page. Required to search: name, years to search, DOB. Criminal records on computer back to 1991. Mail turnaround time 3 days.

General Information: No public access terminal. No adoptions, sealed, juvenile, mental health, expunged or dismissed records released. Will fax documents to local or toll-free number, must be prepaid. Certification fee: $5.00 per cert. Payee: Exeter District Court. Personal checks accepted. Prepayment and SASE required.

Hampton District Court PO Box 10, Hampton, NH 03843-0010; phone: 603-926-8117; hours 8AM-4PM (EST). *Misdemeanor, Civil Actions Under $25,000, Eviction, Small Claims.*

Note: Includes towns of Hampton, Hampton Falls, North Hampton, South Hampton, and Seabrook.

Civil Records: Access: Mail, in person. Only the court performs in person searches; visitors may not. Search fee: $10.00 up to 10 names; if pre-1991-$25.00. Court makes copy: $.10 per page. Required to search: name, years to search. Civil cases indexed by defendant. Civil records on computer from 4/91, index cards from 1979, index books from 1900s. Mail turnaround time 1 week.

Criminal Records: Access: Mail, in person. Only the court performs in person searches; visitors may not. Search fee: $10.00 up to 10 names; if pre-1991-$25.00. Court makes copy: $.10 per page. Required to search: name, years to search; also helpful: DOB, SSN. Criminal records on computer from 4/91, index

cards from 1979, index books from 1900s. Mail turnaround time 1 week.

General Information: No public access terminal. No adoptions, sealed, juvenile, mental health, expunged or dismissed records released. Certification fee: $5.00 per cert. Payee: Hampton District Court. Personal checks accepted. Prepayment and SASE required.

Plaistow District Court PO Box 129, 14 Elm St, Plaistow, NH 03865; phone: 603-382-4651; fax: 603-382-4952; hours 8AM-4PM (EST). *Misdemeanor, Civil Actions Under $25,000, Eviction, Small Claims.*

Note: Includes towns of Plaistow, Hampstead, Kingston, Newton, Atkinson, and Danville.

Civil Records: Access: Mail, in person. Only the court performs in person searches; visitors may not. Search fee: $10.00 1-9 names; $25.00 for over 9 names. $25.00 per hour manual search fee. Court makes copy: $.50 per page. Required to search: name, years to search. Civil cases indexed by defendant, plaintiff. Civil records on computer from 7/91, index cards from 1980, index books from 1960s. Mail turnaround time 2-3 days.

Criminal Records: Access: Mail, in person. Only the court performs in person searches; visitors may not. Search fee: Same fees as civil. Court makes copy: $.50 per page. Required to search: name, years to search, DOB. Criminal records on computer from 7/91, index cards from 1980, index books from 1960s. Mail turnaround time 2-3 days.

General Information: No public access terminal. No adoptions, sealed, juvenile, mental health, expunged or dismissed records released. Certification fee: $5.00 per cert. Payee: Plaistow District Court. Personal checks accepted. Prepayment and SASE required.

Portsmouth District Court 111 Parrott Ave, Portsmouth, NH 03801; phone: 603-431-2192; hours 8AM-4PM (EST). *Misdemeanor, Civil Actions Under $25,000, Eviction, Small Claims.*

Note: Includes city of Portsmouth and the towns of Newington, Greenland, Rye, and New Castle.

Civil Records: Access: Mail, in person. Only the court performs in person searches; visitors may not. Search fee: $10.00 up to 10 names; if pre-1992-$25.00. Court makes copy: $.50 per page. Required to search: name, years to search. Civil cases indexed by defendant, plaintiff. Civil records on computer from 4/92, docket cards from 1980, index books from 1960s. Mail turnaround time 2-3 days.

Criminal Records: Access: Mail, in person. Only the court performs in person searches; visitors may not. Search fee: $10.00 up to 10 names; if pre-1992-$25.00. Court makes copy: $.50 per page. Required to search: name, years to search; also helpful: DOB, SSN. Criminal records on computer from 4/92, docket cards from 1980, index books from 1960s. Mail turnaround time 2-3 days.

General Information: No public access terminal. No adoptions, sealed, juvenile, mental health, expunged or dismissed records released. Certification fee: $1.00 per page included in search fee plus $.30 per page after first. Payee: Portsmouth District Court. Personal checks accepted. Prepayment and SASE required.

Salem District Court 35 Geremonty Dr, Salem, NH 03079; phone: 603-893-4483; hours 8AM-4PM (EST). *Misdemeanor, Civil Actions Under $25,000, Eviction, Small Claims.*

Note: Includes towns of Salem, Windham, and Pelham.

Civil Records: Access: Mail, in person. Search fee: $10.00 up to 10 names; if pre-1993- $25.00. Court makes copy: $.50 per page. Required to search: name, years to search. Civil cases indexed by defendant, plaintiff. Civil records on computer from 4/92, docket cards from 1980, docket books from 1950. An appointment is necessary before performing an in person search. Mail turnaround time 2-3 weeks.

Criminal Records: Access: Mail, in person. Only the court performs in person searches; visitors may

not. Search fee: $10.00 up to 10 names; if pre-1993-$25.00. Court makes copy: $.50 per page. Required to search: name, years to search, DOB. Criminal records on computer from 4/92, docket cards from 1980, docket books from 1950. Mail turnaround time 2-3 weeks.

General Information: No public access terminal. No adoptions, sealed, juvenile, mental health, expunged or dismissed records released. Certification fee: $5.00 per cert. Payee: Salem District Court. Personal checks accepted. Prepayment and SASE required.

Probate Court PO Box 789, #10 Rt 125, Kingston, NH 03848; phone: 603-642-7117; hours 8AM-4PM (EST). *Probate.*

Strafford County

Superior Court PO Box 799, Dover, NH 03821-0799; criminal phone: 603-742-3065 x305; civil phone: 603-742-3065 x 350; probate phone: 603-742-2550; hours 8:30AM-4PM (EST). *Felony, Civil Actions Over $1,500.*

Civil Records: Access: Mail, in person. Only the court performs in person searches; visitors may not. Search fee: $10.00 for under 10 names; $25.00 over 10 names. Court makes copy: $.50 per page. Self serve copy fee: $.25 per page. Required to search: name, years to search. Civil cases indexed by defendant, plaintiff. Civil records on computer from 3/89, index cards from 1970, index books from 1900s, organized 1769. Mail turnaround time 1 week.

Criminal Records: Access: Mail, in person. Only the court performs in person searches; visitors may not. Search fee: $10.00 for under 10 names; $25.00 over 10 names. Court makes copy: $.50 per page. Self serve copy fee: $.25 per page. Required to search: name, years to search; also helpful: DOB, SSN. Criminal records on computer from 3/89, index cards from 1970, index books from 1900s, organized 1769. Mail turnaround time 1 week.

General Information: No public access terminal. No sealed, juvenile, mental health, expunged or dismissed records released. Certification fee: $5.00 per cert. Cert fee includes copies. Payee: Strafford Superior Court. Personal checks accepted. Prepayment and SASE required.

Dover District Court 25 St Thomas St, Dover, NH 03820; phone: 603-742-7202; fax: 603-742-5956; hours 8AM-4PM (EST). *Misdemeanor, Civil Actions Under $20,000, Eviction, Small Claims.*

Note: Note: Includes City of Dover, Somersworth, and Rollinsford.

Civil Records: Access: Mail, in person. Only the court performs in person searches; visitors may not. Search fee: $10.00 up to 10 names. Court makes copy: $.50 per page. Required to search: name, years to search. Civil cases indexed by defendant, plaintiff. Civil records on computer from 1993, on index cards from 1980, index books from 1970. Mail turnaround time 1-2 days.

Criminal Records: Access: Mail, in person. Only the court performs in person searches; visitors may not. Search fee: $10.00 up to 10 names. Court makes copy: $.50 per page. Required to search: name, years to search, DOB. Criminal records on computer from 1993, on index cards from 1980, index books from 1970. Mail turnaround time 1-2 days.

General Information: No public access terminal. No adoptions, sealed, juvenile, mental health, expunged or dismissed records released. May fax documents. Certification fee: $5.00 per doc. Payee: Dover District Court. Personal checks accepted. Prepayment and SASE required.

Durham District Court 1 Main St, Durham, NH 03824; phone: 603-868-2323; fax: 603-868-2024; hours 8:30AM-4PM (EST). *Misdemeanor, Civil Actions Under $25,000, Eviction, Small Claims.*

Note: Includes towns of Durham, Lee, and Madbury.

Civil Records: Access: Mail, in person. Only the court performs in person searches; visitors may not. Search fee: $10.00 up to 10 names; if pre-1990-

$25.00. Court makes copy: $.50 per page. Required to search: name, years to search. Civil cases indexed by defendant, plaintiff. Civil records on computer back to 1990; index cards from 1980, index books from 1945. Mail turnaround time 4 days.

Criminal Records: Access: Mail, in person. Only the court performs in person searches; visitors may not. Search fee: $10.00 up to 10 names; if pre-1990- $25.00. Court makes copy: $.50 per page. Required to search: name, years to search, DOB; also helpful: SSN. Criminal records on computer back to 1990; index cards from 1980, index books from 1948. Mail turnaround time 4 days.

General Information: No public access terminal. No adoptions, sealed, juvenile, mental health, expunged or dismissed records released. Certification fee: $5.00 per cert. Payee: Durham District Court. Personal checks accepted. Prepayment and SASE required.

Rochester District Court 76 N Main St, Rochester, NH 03867; phone: 603-332-3516; hours 8AM-4PM (EST). *Misdemeanor, Civil Actions Under $25,000, Eviction, Small Claims.*
Note: Includes city of Rochester and the towns of Barrington, Milton, New Durham, Farmington, Strafford, and Middleton.

Civil Records: Access: Mail, in person. Only the court performs in person searches; visitors may not. Search fee: $10.00 up to 10 names; if pre-1990- $25.00. Court makes copy: $.50 per page. Required to search: name, years to search; also helpful DOB. Civil cases indexed by defendant, plaintiff. Civil records on computer from 1989, index cards from 7/80, index books from 1960s. Requests must be in writing. Mail turnaround time 1 week.

Criminal Records: Access: Mail, in person. Only the court performs in person searches; visitors may not. Search fee: $10.00 up to 10 names; if pre-1990- $25.00. Court makes copy: $.50 per page. Required to search: name, years to search; also helpful: DOB. Criminal records on computer from 1989, index cards from 7/80, index books from 1960s. Requests must be in writing. Mail turnaround time 1 week.

General Information: No public access terminal. No sealed, juvenile, mental health, expunged records released. Certification fee: $5.00 per page. Payee: Rochester District Court. Personal checks accepted. Prepayment and SASE required.

Somersworth District Court, NH.
Misdemeanor, Civil Actions Under $25,000, Eviction, Small Claims.
Note: This court combined with the Dover District Court on 11/1/02.

Probate Court PO Box 799, 259 County Farm Rd, Dover, NH 03821-0799; phone: 603-742-2550; hours 8AM-4:30PM (EST). *Probate.*
www.state.nh.us/courts/probate.htm

Sullivan County

Superior Court 22 Main St, Newport, NH 03773; phone: 603-863-3450; hours 8AM-4:00PM (EST). *Felony, Civil Actions Over $1,500.*

Civil Records: Access: Mail, in person. Only the court performs in person searches; visitors may not. Search fee: $25.00 per hour pro-rated manual search; $10.00 for computer search for up to 10 names; $25.00 if over 10 names. Court makes copy: $.50 per page. Self serve copy fee: $.25 per page. Required to search: name, years to search. Civil cases indexed by defendant, plaintiff. Civil records on computer from 1992, on index cards from 1980s, index books from 1800s. Mail turnaround time 1 week.

Criminal Records: Access: Mail, in person. Only the court performs in person searches; visitors may not. Search fee: $25.00 per hour pro-rated manual search; $10.00 for computer search for up to 10 names; $25.00 if over 10 names. Court makes copy: $.50 per page. Self serve copy fee: $.25 per page. Required to search: name, years to search, DOB. Criminal records on computer from 1992, on index cards from 1980s, index books from 1800s. Mail turnaround time 1 week.

General Information: No public access terminal. No adoptions, sealed, juvenile, mental health, expunged or dismissed records released. Will not fax documents. Certification fee: $5.00 for attestation; copies included. Payee: Sullivan County Superior Court. Personal checks accepted. Prepayment and SASE required.

Claremont District Court PO Box 313, Claremont, NH 03743; phone: 603-542-6064; hours 8AM-4PM (EST). *Misdemeanor, Civil Actions Under $25,000, Eviction, Small Claims.*
Note: Includes city of Claremont and the towns of Cornish, Unity, Charlestown, Acworth, Langdon, and Plainfield.

Civil Records: Access: Phone, mail, in person. Only the court performs in person searches; visitors may not. Search fee: $10.00 up to 10 names; if pre-1992- $25.00. Court makes copy: $.50 per page. Required to search: name, years to search, DOB. Civil cases indexed by defendant, plaintiff. Civil records on computer from 10/92, on index cards from 1980, index books from 1960. Mail turnaround time 1 week.

Criminal Records: Access: Phone, mail, in person. Only the court performs in person searches; visitors may not. Search fee: $10.00 up to 10 names; if pre-1992- $25.00. Court makes copy: $.50 per page. Required to search: name, years to search, DOB. Criminal records on computer from 10/92, on index cards from 1980, index books from 1960. Mail turnaround time 1 week.

General Information: No public access terminal. No adoptions, sealed, juvenile, mental health, expunged or dismissed records released. Certification fee: $5.00 per cert. Payee: Claremont District Court. Personal checks accepted. Prepayment and SASE required.

Newport District Court 55 Main St, Newport, NH 03773; phone: 603-863-1832; hours 8AM-4PM (EST). *Misdemeanor, Civil Actions Under $25,000, Eviction, Small Claims.*
Note: Includes towns of Newport, Grantham, Croydon, Springfield, Sunapee, Goshen, Lempster, and Washington.

Civil Records: Access: Mail, in person. Only the court performs in person searches; visitors may not. Search fee: $10.00 up to 10 names; if pre-1993- $25.00. Court makes copy: $.50 per page. Required to search: name, years to search. Civil cases indexed by defendant, plaintiff. Civil records on computer from 1993, on index cards from 1980, index books from 1960s. All requests must be in writing. Mail turnaround time 2-3 days.

Criminal Records: Access: Mail, in person. Only the court performs in person searches; visitors may not. Search fee: $10.00 up to 10 names; if pre-1993- $25.00. Court makes copy: $.50 per page. Required to search: name, years to search, DOB. Criminal records on computer from 1993, on index cards from 1980, index books from 1960s. All requests must be in writing. Mail turnaround time 2-3 days.

General Information: No public access terminal. No adoptions, sealed, juvenile, mental health, expunged or dismissed records released. Certification fee: $1.00 per cert. Payee: Newport District Court. Personal checks accepted. Prepayment and SASE required.

Probate Court PO Box 417, 14 Main St, Newport, NH 03773; phone: 603-863-3150; hours 8AM-4PM (EST). *Probate.*

New Hampshire Recording Offices

ORGANIZATION: 238 cities/towns and 10 counties, 10 recording offices and 242 UCC filing offices. The recording officers are Town/City Clerk (UCC) and Register of Deeds (real estate only). Each town/city profile indicates the county in which the town/city is located. Be careful to distinguish the following names that are identical for both a town/city and a county - Grafton, Hillsborough, Merrimack, Strafford, and Sullivan. Many towns are so small that their mailing addresses are within another town. The following unincorporated towns do not have a Town Clerk, so all liens are located at the corresponding county: Cambridge (Coos), Dicksville (Coos), Green's Grant (Coos), Hale's Location (Carroll), Millsfield (Coos), and Wentworth's Location (Coos). The entire state is in the Eastern Time Zone (EST).

REAL ESTATE RECORDS: Real estate transactions are recorded at the county level, and property taxes are handled at the town/city level. Local town real estate ownership and assessment records are usually located at the Selectman's Office. Each town/city profile indicates the county in which the town/city is located. Most counties will not perform real estate searches. Copy fees vary. Certification fees generally are $2.00 per document.

UCC RECORDS: This was a dual filing state until Revised Article 9. Previously, financing statements were filed at the state level and with the Town/City Clerk, except for consumer goods and farm related collateral, which were filed only with the Town/City Clerk, and real estate related collateral, which was and still is filed with the county Register of Deeds. Most recording offices will perform UCC searches. Use search request form UCC-11. Search fees are usually $5.00 per debtor name using the standard UCC-11 request form and $7.00 using a non-standard form. Copy fees are usually $.75 per page.

TAX LIEN RECORDS: Federal and state tax liens on personal property of businesses are filed with the Secretary of State. Other federal and state tax liens on personal property are filed with the Town/City Clerk. Federal and state tax liens on real property are filed with the county Register of Deeds. There is wide variation in indexing and searching practices among the recording offices. Where a search fee of $7.00 is indicated, it refers to a non-standard request form such as a letter.

OTHER LIENS: Condominium, town tax, mechanics, welfare.

ONLINE ACCESS: The New Hampshire Counties Registry of Deeds website allows free searching of real estate related records for Belknap, Cheshire, Coos, Hillsborough, Rockingham, Strafford and Sullivan counties at www.nhdeeds.com. Also, a private vendor has placed on the Internet the assessor records from a number of towns. Visit http://www.visionappraisal.com/databases/nh/index.htm

Acworth Town

Town Clerk, PO Box 37, Town Clerk, Acworth, NH 03601. 603-835-6879; fax-603-835-7901; hours: 6:30-8PM M-W; 9-11AM Sat.
Record index not computerized. Search fee $10.00 per name. Copy fee $1.00 per page. Cert fee- $10.00. Payee- Town of Acworth. **Other phones:** Treasurer- 603-835-6879. **Property tax/Assessor-** 603-835-6879.

Albany Town

Town Clerk, 19728 NH Route 16, Conway, NH 03818. 603-447-2877; fax-603-447-2877; hours: 8AM-N, M; 4PM-7PM W; 9AM-N Sat.
All records in one index. Record index not computerized. Only the public may search. Real estate records located at Carroll County. Copy fee $1.00 per page. Cert fee- none. Payee- Albany Town Clerk. **Property tax/Assessor-** 603-586-4402.

Alexandria Town

Town Clerk, 45 A Washburn Rd, Alexandria, NH 03222. 603-744-3288, R/E recording phone-603-787-6921; fax-603-744-8577; hours: 8AM-5:30PM M T F, Noon-7PM Th, Closed Wed.
Office personnel or visitors may perform searches. Search fee $10.00 per name. Real estate records located at Grafton County. Copy fee $1.00 per page. Payee- Town of Alexandria. **Other phones:** Treasurer- 603-744-3220; Appraiser/Auditor- 603-744-3220; Elections- 603-744-3288; Vital Records- 602-744-3288. **Property tax/Assessor-** 603-744-3220.

Allenstown Town

Town Clerk, 16 School St, Allenstown, NH 03275. 603-485-4276; fax-603-485-8669; hours: M 8:30-1 & 3-7; T/W 8:30-1 & 3-5; Th 8:30-3; No F. www.allenstown.org
All records in one index. Record index not computerized. Office will perform a UCC search but public must search other records themselves. Search fee $10.00. Real estate records located at Merrimack County. Copy fee $1.00 per page. **Other phones:** Treasurer- 603-485-4276; Elections- 603-485-4276; Vital Records- 603-485-4276. **Property tax/Assessor-** 603-485-4276.

Alstead Town

Town Clerk, Box 65, Alstead, NH 03602. 603-835-2242; fax-603-835-2986; 8AM-4PM,Closed F.
All records in one index. Record index not computerized. Only the office personnel may search. Real estate records located at Cheshire County. Will search UCC records prior to 7/2001. Will not search tax liens. UCC search per debtor name- $10.00. Copy fee $1.00 per page. Cert fee- $3.00 plus copy fee. Payee- Alstead Town Clerk.

Alton Town

Town Clerk, Box 637, Alton, NH 03809. 603-875-2101, R/E recording phone-603-875-5095, UCC recording phone-603-875-2101; fax-603-875-3894; hours: 8:30AM-4:30PM. www.alton.nh.gov
No real estate recordings here. Deeds and tax liens from the county are online at www.nhdeeds.com. All records in one index. Record index not computerized. Agency or visitors may perform searches. Search fee $10.00 per search. Real estate records located at Belknap County. Copy fee $1.00 per page. Tax lien copy- $.25 per page. **Other phones:** Treasurer- 603-875-2161; Appraiser/Auditor- 603-875-0205; Elections- 603-875-2101; Vital Records- 603-875-2101; Tax Collector- 603-875-2171. **Property tax/Assessor-** 603-875-0205.

Amherst Town

Town Clerk, PO Box 960, Amherst, NH 03031. 603-673-6041; fax-603-673-6794; hours: 9AM-3PM M-F; 5:30-8PM Mon.
Record index not computerized. Only the office personnel may search. Search fee $10.00. Real estate records located at Hillsborough County. Copy fee $1.00 per page. Payee- Town of Amherst. **Online access to Assessor records:** Records on the town assessor database are free at http://data.visionappraisal.com/AmherstNH/. Registration is required to view full data. **Other phones:** Treasurer- 603-673-6041. **Property tax/Assessor-** 603-673-6041.

Andover Town

Town Clerk, PO Box 61, Andover, NH 03216. 603-735-5332; fax-603-735-6975; hours: 10AM-1PM T Th, 6:30PM-8:30PM W, 9AM-N Sat.
Office personnel or visitors may perform searches. Search fee $10.00 per name. Real estate records located at Merrimack County. Will search UCC records. Copy fee $1.00 per page. Tax lien copy- $.25 per page. **Other phones:** Treasurer- 603-735-5516; Appraiser/Auditor- 603-735-5332; Vital Records- 603-735-5332. **Property tax/Assessor-** 603-735-5332.

Antrim Town

Town Clerk, PO Box 517, Antrim, NH 03440. 603-588-6785; fax-603-588-2969; hours: 8AM-4PM M-Th. www.antrimnh.org
All records in one index. Record index not computerized. Only the office personnel may

search. Search fee $15.00. Real estate records located at Hillsborough County. Will search UCC records prior to 7/2001 and current liens only. Copy fee $1.00 per page. Cert fee- None. Payee- Antrim Town Clerk.

Ashland Town

Town Clerk, PO Box 517, Ashland, NH 03217. 603-968-4432; fax-603-968-3776; hours: 8AM-4PM.
All records in one index. Record index not computerized. Only the public may search. Real estate records located at Grafton County. Copy fee $1.00 per page.

Atkinson Town

Town Clerk, 21 Academy Ave; Town Hall, Atkinson, NH 03811-2204. 603-362-4920, R/E recording phone-603-642-5526, UCC recording phone-603-271-3242; fax-603-362-5305; hours: 8:30AM-6:30PM M; 8:30AM-4PM T-F. www.town-atkinsonnh.com
Office will perform a UCC search but public must search other records themselves. Real estate records located at Rockingham County. UCC search per debtor name- $15.00. Copy fee $1.00 per page. Payee- Town of Atkinson. **Online access to Property, Real Estate Transfer records:** Access the town property values for free at www.town-atkinsonnh.com/values.htm. Also, search the last three months of real estate transfers and four months of building permits via the main website. **Property tax/Assessor-** 603-362-5266.

Auburn Town

Town Clerk, PO Box 309, Auburn, NH 03032-0309. 603-483-2281; fax-603-483-0518; hours: 8AM-2PM, M,W,TH; 8AM-12PM, F; 6PM-8PM, M Evening.
All records in one index. Record index not computerized. Office will perform a UCC search but public must search other records themselves. Search fee $10.00. Real estate records located at Rockingham County. Copy fee $1.00 per page. **Other phones:** Elections- 603-483-2281; Vital Records- 603-483-2281. **Property tax/Assessor-** same address as above. 603-483-5052.

Barnstead Town

Town Clerk, PO Box 11, Center Barnstead, NH 03225. 603-269-4631;   fax-603-269-4072; www.barnstead.org
Only the office personnel may search. Real estate records located at Belknap County. UCC search per debtor name- $15.00. Copy fee $1.00 per page. **Other phones:** Treasurer- 603-269-4071; Elections- 603-269-4631; Vital Records- 603-269-4631. **Property tax/Assessor-** 603-269-4071.

Barrington Town

Town Clerk, 41 Province Lane, Barrington, NH 03825. 603-664-5476;   fax-603-664-5179;   hours: 8AM-4:15PM M T TH; 4-6PM W; 8AM-Noom F.
All records in one index. Record index not computerized. Only the office personnel may search. Real estate records located at Strafford County. Will search UCC records prior to 7/2001 and current tax liens. UCC search per debtor name- $10.00. Separate federal & state combined tax lien search- $10.00 per debtor. Copy fee $1.00 per page. **Online access to Property, Deed, Grantor/Grantee records:** Records are free on the Stafford county-wide system at www.nhdeeds.com/stfd/web/agree3.htm. Use the subscription service for full data. **Other phones:** Elections- 603-664-5476; Vital Records- 603-664-5476; Tax Collector- 603-664-2230. **Property tax/Assessor-** 603-664-9007.

Bartlett Town

Town Clerk, RFD 1 Box 50, Intervale, NH 03845. 603-356-2300, R/E recording phone-603-356-2950, UCC recording phone-603-356-2300; fax-603-356-2300; hours: 8AM-4PM M-W & F; 8-11AM Sat.
Only the public may search. Copy fee $1.00 per page. Cert fee- None. Payee- Town of Bartlett. **Other phones:** Treasurer- 603-356-2950; Elections-

603-356-2300; Vital Records- 603-356-2300. **Property tax/Assessor-** 603-356-2950.

Bath Town

Town Clerk, PO Box 165, Bath, NH 03740. 603-747-2454; fax-603-747-0497; hours: 8AM-12, 1PM-4PM M,W,Th; 8AM-12, 5:30-8:30PM T.
Record index not computerized. Office will perform a UCC search but public must search other records themselves. Real estate records located at Grafton County. Copy fee $1.00 per page. Payee- Town of Bath. **Other phones:** Treasurer- 603-747-2454; Elections- 603-747-2454; Vital Records- 603-747-2454.

Bedford Town

Town Clerk, 24 N. Amherst Rd, Bedford, NH 03110. 603-472-3550;   fax-603-472-4573;   8AM-4:30PM; (7AM-4:30PM on Tu). www.ci.bedford.nh.us
All records in one index. Records indexed. Office personnel or visitors may perform searches. Real estate records located at Hillsborough County. Will search UCC records prior to 7/2001 and current liens only. UCC search per debtor name- $10.00. Copy fee $1.00 per page. **Online access to Assessor records:** Access assessor data at http://data.visionappraisal.com/BedfordNH/. Free registration for full data. **Other phones:** Elections- 603-472-3550; Vital Records- 603-472-3550. **Property tax/Assessor-** 24 N Amherst Rd, Bedford,NH 03110; 603-472-8104.

Belknap County

Register of Deeds, PO Box 1343, Laconia, NH 03247-1343. 603-527-5420; fax-603-527-5429; hours: 8AM-4PM.
All records in one index. Only the public may search. Copy fee $1.00 per page. Cert fee- $2.00 per doc + $1.00 per page for copy. **Online access to Real Estate, Deed, Mortgage, Lien records:** Access to county register of deeds data is free at www.nhdeeds.com/belk/web/agree5.htm. Online records go back to 1765. To establish an account for copies of documents on line go to www.nhdeeds.com/belk/web/start.htm for account form. **Property tax/Assessor-** Beacon St E, Laconia, NH 03246; not known.

Belmont Town

Town Clerk, PO Box 310, Belmont, NH 03220. 603-267-8302; fax-603-267-8305; hours: 7:30AM-4PM.
All records in one index. Record index not computerized. Office personnel or visitors may perform searches. Search fee $15.00. Real estate records located at Belknap County. Copy fee $1.00 per page. **Online access to Assessor, Property records:** Access to property assessor data is at http://data.visionappraisal.com/BelmontNH/. Does not require a username & password. Simply click on link. **Other phones:** Treasurer- 603-267-8300; Appraiser/Auditor- 603-267-8300; Elections- 603-267-8302; Vital Records- 603-267-8302. **Property tax/Assessor-** 603-267-8300.

Bennington Town

Town Clerk, 7 School St, #101, Bennington, NH 03442. 603-588-2189; fax-603-588-8005; hours: 9AM-N M & Sat; 8:30AM-12:30PM Tu; 4:30-8:30PM Th. http://townofbennington.com/
Agency or visitors may perform searches. Search fee $7.00 per name. Real estate records located at Hillsborough County. UCC search per debtor name- $10.00. Copy fee $1.00 per page. **Property tax/Assessor-** 603-588-2189.

Benton Town

Town Clerk, 110 Flanders Rd, Benton, NH 03785-6402. 603-787-6541, R/E recording phone-603-787-6053, UCC recording phone-603-787-6541; fax-603-787-6646; hours: 6:30-8:30PM Monday night.
Record index not computerized. Office personnel or visitors may perform searches. Search fee $10.00 per name. Real estate records located at

Grafton County. Copy fee $1.00 per page. **Other phones:** Treasurer- 603-787-6004; Appraiser/Auditor- 603-787-6053; Elections- 603-787-2129; Vital Records- 603-787-6541. **Property tax/Assessor-** 603-787-6053.

Berlin City

City Clerk, 168 Main St; City Hall, Berlin, NH 03570. 603-752-2340; fax-603-752-1654; hours: 8:30-N, 1-4:30PM.
All records in one index. Office personnel or visitors may perform searches. Real estate records located at Coos County. UCC search per debtor name- $10.00. Separate federal tax lien search- $7.00 per debtor. Copy fee $1.00 per page. Cert fee- $12.00 per cert plus copy fee. Payee- City of Berlin. **Other phones:** Treasurer- 603-752-1610. **Property tax/Assessor-** same address as above. 603-752-5245.

Bethlehem Town

Town Clerk, PO Box 189, Bethlehem, NH 03574. 603-869-2293, R/E recording phone-603-869-3133, UCC recording phone-603-869-2293; fax-603-869-2280; hours: 4:30-7PM M,W; 9AM-1PM T,Th.
Record index not computerized. Office personnel or visitors may perform searches. Search fee $5.00 per name. Real estate records located at Grafton County. Copy fee $1.00 per page. Payee- Town of Bethlehem. **Other phones:** Treasurer- 603-869-3351; Appraiser/Auditor- 603-869-3351; Elections- 603-869-2293; Vital Records- 603-869-2293. **Property tax/Assessor-** 603-869-3351.

Boscawen Town

Town Clerk, 116 N. Main St, Boscawen, NH 03303. 603-753-9188; fax-603-753-9183; hours: M, Th 8-11AM; 12-4:30; T & W 8-11AM; 12-6:30PM.
All records in one index. Record index not computerized. Only the public may search. Real estate records located at Merrimack County. Copy fee $1.00 per page. **Other phones:** Treasurer- 603-796-2343. **Property tax/Assessor-** 603-753-9188.

Bow Town

Town Clerk, 10 Grandview Rd, Bow, NH 03304-3410. 603-225-2683; fax-603-225-5428; hours: 7:30AM-4:10PM.
Only the public may search. Copy fee $1.00 per page. Payee- Town of Bow. **Online access to Property Assessor records:** Records on the town assessor database are free at http://data.visionappraisal.com/BowNH/. Registration is required to view full data. **Property tax/Assessor-** 603-228-1187x15.

Bradford Town

Town Clerk/Tax Collector, PO Box 607, Bradford, NH 03221-0607. 603-938-2288; fax-603-938-2094; hours: Noon-7PM Mon.; 7AM-5PM Tues; 8AM-5PM Fri.
All records in one index. Record index not computerized. Office will perform a UCC and Tax lien search but public must search other records themselves. Search fee $10.00. Real estate records located at Merrimack County. Copy fee $1.00 per page. Cert fee- $5.00 per page. Payee- Town of Bradford. **Property tax/Assessor-** PO Box 436, Bradford, NH 03221; 603-938-5900.

Brentwood Town

Town Clerk, 1 Dalton Rd, Brentwood, NH 03833. 603-642-6400 x14; fax-603-642-6310; hours: 9AM-4:30PM M-F; 7-9PM T; 9AM-N Sat Sept-May. http://brentwood.town-center.org/static/Gov1.htm
Search fee $10.00 per doc. Copy fee $1.00 per page. Payee- Town of Brentwood. **Other phones:** Treasurer- 603-642-6400 x19; Elections- 603-642-6400 x14; Vital Records- 603-642-6400 x14. **Property tax/Assessor-** 603-642-6400 x10.

Bridgewater Town

Town Clerk, PO Box 419, Plymouth, NH 03264. 603-968-7911; fax-603-968-3506; hours: 6PM-8:30PM T- W; 8:30-10AM 3rd Sat.
Office personnel or visitors may perform searches. Search fee $15.00 per name. Real estate records located at Grafton County. UCC search per debtor name- $10.00. Copy fee $1.00 per page. Cert fee-$15.00 per page. Payee- Town of Bridgewater.

Bristol Town

Town Clerk, 230 Lake St, #A, Bristol, NH 03222-1120. 603-744-8478; fax-603-744-2521; hours: 8:30AM-4PM.
Office will perform a UCC search but public must search other records themselves. Real estate records located at Grafton County. UCC search per debtor name- $10.00. Copy fee $4.00 per page. **Other phones:** Appraiser/Auditor- 603-744-3354; Elections-603-744-8478; Vital Records- 603-744-8478. **Property tax/Assessor-** 603-744-3354.

Brookfield Town

Town Clerk, PO Box 756, Sanbornville, NH 03872. 603-522-3231; fax-603-522-6245; hours: 1-8PM Mon; 8:30AM-1PM Tues.
Separate indices to search include alpha and numerical. Record index not computerized. Search fee $10.00 per name. Real estate records located at Carroll County. UCC search includes tax liens if requested. State tax lien search- $7.00 per debtor. Copy fee $1.00 per page. Cert fee- $10.00.00 per doc plus copy fee. Payee- Town of Brookfield. **Other phones:** Treasurer- 603-522-6756; Appraiser/Auditor- 603-522-0031; Elections- 603-522-3688. **Property tax/Assessor-** same address as above. 603-522-0031.

Brookline Town

Town Clerk, PO Box 336, Brookline, NH 03033. 603-673-8855 x218; fax-603-673-8136; hours: 8AM-2PM M-F, 6PM-9PM W, 9AM-N Last SAT of month. www.brookline.nh.us
Separate indices to search include UCC's. Real estate records located at Hillsborough County. Will search UCC records prior to 7/2001 and current liens only. UCC search per debtor name- $10.00. Copy fee $1.00 per page. Payee- Town of Brookline. **Other phones:** Elections- 603-673-8855 X218; Vital Records- 603-673-8855 X218. **Property tax/Assessor-** PO Box 360, Brookline, NH 03033; 603-673-8855 X216.

Campton Town

Town Clerk, 1307 NH Rte 175, Campton, NH 03223. 603-726-3223; fax-603-726-9817; hours: 9AM-3:30PM.
Record index not computerized. Only the public may search. Real estate records located at Grafton County. Copy fee $1.00 per page. **Other phones:** Appraiser/Auditor- 603-726-3223 x101; Elections- 603-726-3223 X102 or 103. **Property tax/Assessor-** 603-726-3223 x101.

Canaan Town

Town Clerk, PO Box 38, Canaan, NH 03741-0038. 603-523-7106; fax-603-523-4526; hours: 9AM-12 1PM-4PM M,W,F; 9AM-12 T TH.
All records in one index. Records not computerized. Office personnel or visitors may perform searches. Real estate records located at Grafton County. Will search UCC records prior to 7/2001 only. Will not search tax liens. UCC search per debtor name- $10.00. Copy fee $1.00 per page. **Other phones:** Appraiser/Auditor- 603-523-4501; Vital Records- 603-523-7106. **Property tax/Assessor-** 1169 US Rte 4, Canaan, NH 03741; not known.

Candia Town

Town Clerk, 74 High St, Candia, NH 03034-2713. 603-483-5573, R/E recording phone-603-483-8101, UCC recording phone-603-483-5573; fax-603-483-0252; hours: 8:30-11 M, 5PM-8PM T TH, 9AM-1PM W F. www.townofcandianh.org
Index: Vital records on a separate microfilm index. Record index not computerized. Search fee $10.00 per name. Copy fee $1.00 per page. Cert fee-$5.00 plus copy fee. Payee- Pay fees to Town of Canada. **Online access to Assessor records:** Access assessor data at http://data.visionappraisal.com/CandiaNH/. Free registration for full data. **Other phones:** Treasurer-603-483-5140; Appraiser/Auditor- 603-483-8101; Elections- 603-483-5573; Vital Records- 603-483-5573. **Property tax/Assessor-** 74 High St, Candia, NH 03034; 603-483-8101.

Canterbury Town

Town Clerk, PO Box 500, Canterbury, NH 03224. 603-783-9955; fax-603-783-0501; hours: 10AM-2PM M; 11AM-6PM T; 5-8:30PM Th.
Office personnel or visitors may perform searches. Search fee $7.00 per name. Real estate records located at Merrimack County. UCC search per debtor name- $10.00. Copy fee $1.00 per page. Payee- Town of Canterbury.

Carroll County

Register of Deeds, PO Box 163, Ossipee, NH 03864-0163. 603-539-4872; fax-603-539-5239; hours: 9AM-5PM.
All records in one index. Records indexed on a public use terminal back to 1962. Only the public may search. Copy fee $1.00 per page. Cert fee-$1.00 per doc plus copy fee. Payee- Carroll County Register of Deeds.

Carroll Town

Town Clerk, PO Box 88, Twin Mountain, NH 03595-0088. 603-846-5494; fax-603-846-5713; hours: 9AM-N M; 9AM-3PM T,W,Th.
Office will perform a UCC search but public must search other records themselves. Real estate records located at Carroll County. UCC search per debtor name- $10.00. Copy fee $1.00 per page. **Other phones:** Treasurer- 603-846-5754. **Property tax/Assessor-** 603-846-5754.

Center Harbor Town

Town Clerk, PO Box 140, Center Harbor, NH 03226. 603-253-4561; fax-603-253-8420; hours: 9AM-3PM.
All records in one index. Record index not computerized. Office will perform a UCC and Tax lien search but public must search other records themselves. Search fee $10.00. Real estate records located at Belknap County. Copy fee $2.00 per page. Cert fee- $10.00 per page plus copy fee. **Property tax/Assessor-** same address as above. not known.

Charlestown Town

Town Clerk, PO Box 834, Charlestown, NH 03603. 603-826-5821; fax-603-826-5181; hours: 8AM-1PM, 1:30-6PM M; 8AM-1PM, 1:30-4PM T-F.
Search fee $10.00. Real estate records located at Sullivan County. Will search UCC records prior to 7/2001; search includes tax liens if requested. Copy fee $1.00 per page. Payee- Town of Charlestown. **Other phones:** Treasurer- 603-826-4400; Appraiser/Auditor- 603-826-4400; Elections- 603-826-5821; Vital Records- 603-826-5821. **Property tax/Assessor-** PO Box 385, Charlestown, NH 03603; 603-826-4400.

Chatham Town

Town Clerk, 1681 Main Rd, Chatham, NH 03813. 603-694-2043; fax-603-694-2043; hours: 5-7PM T.
Record index not computerized. Office personnel or visitors may perform searches. Search fee $10.00 per name. Real estate records located at Carroll County. Copy fee $1.00 per page. Payee- Town of Chatham. **Other phones:** Treasurer- 603-694-2321; Elections- 603-694-2043; Vital Records- 603-694-2043.

Cheshire County

Register of Deeds, PO Box 584, Keene, NH 03431. 603-352-0403; fax-603-352-7678; hours: 8:30AM-4:30PM.
Separate indices to search include grantor/grantee. Records indexed on a public use terminal back to 1975. Only the public may search. Copy fee $1.00 per page. Cert fee- $2.00 per doc plus copy fee. Payee- Registry of deeds. **Online access to Real Estate, Deed, Mortgage, Lien records:** Access to county register of deeds data is free at www.nhdeeds.com/chsr/web/agree2.htm. Online records go back to 1980. **Other phones:** Treasurer-603-357-0793.

Chester Town

Town Clerk, PO Box 275, Chester, NH 03036. 603-887-3636; fax-603-887-4334; hours: 8AM-12:30PM M,T,Th,F; 8AM-4PM W.
Office personnel or visitors may perform searches. Search fee $5.00 per name. Real estate records located at Rockingham County. Copy fee $.50 per page. Payee- Town of Chester. **Other phones:** Elections- 603-887-4344. **Property tax/Assessor-** 603-887-4045.

Chesterfield Town

Town Clerk, PO Box 64, Chesterfield, NH 03443-0064. 603-363-8071, R/E recording phone-603-363-4624, UCC recording phone-603-363-8071; fax-603-363-8047; hours: 9AM-5:30PM M,W; 5-8PM Th. www.nhchesterfield.com
Office personnel or visitors may perform searches. Search fee $10.00 per name. Real estate records located at Cheshire County. Copy fee $1.00 per page. Cert fee- $4.00 per doc plus copy fee. Payee- Town of Chesterfield. **Other phones:** 603-363-4624; Appraiser/Auditor- 603-363-4624; Elections- 603-363-8071; Vital Records- 603-363-8071. **Property tax/Assessor-** 603-363-4624.

Chichester Town

Town Clerk, 54 Main St, Chichester, NH 03258. 603-798-5808, R/E recording phone-603-798-5350; fax-603-798-3170; hours: 8:30AM-4PM M; 8:30AM-2PM Tu-Th; also 4-7PM Tu.
Office will perform a UCC search but public must search other records themselves. UCC search per debtor name- $10.00. Copy fee $1.00 per page. **Other phones:** Appraiser/Auditor- 603-798-5350; Elections- 603-798-5808; Vital Records- 603-798-5808. **Property tax/Assessor-** 603-798-5350.

Claremont City

City Clerk, 58 Opera House Sq; City Hall, Finance Office, Claremont, NH 03743. 603-542-7003; fax-603-542-7014; hours: 9AM-12:30PM, 1:30-5PM. www.claremontnh.com
All records in one index. Office will perform a UCC search but public must search other records themselves. Real estate records located at Sullivan County. Copy fee $1.00 per page. **Other phones:** Treasurer- 603-542-7000; Elections- 603-542-7003; Vital Records- 603-542-7003. **Property tax/Assessor-** same address as above. 603-542-7004.

Clarksville Town

Town Clerk, 408 NH Route 145, Clarksville, NH 03592. 603-246-7751; fax-603-246-3480; hours: 1-6:30PM M; 9AM-4PM T, Th; 12:30-6:30PM W; 9AM-N F.
The County Register of Deeds records real estate transactions, and the City Clerk records UCC filings. All records in one index. Office personnel or visitors may perform searches. Search fee $10.00 per debtor. Real estate records located at Coos County. Copy fee $1.00 per page. Payee- Town of Clarksville. **Other phones:** Treasurer- 603-246-9648; Appraiser/Auditor- 800-417-2297; Elections- 603-246-7751; Vital Records- 603-246-7751. **Property tax/Assessor-** same address as above. 800-417-2297.

Colebrook Town

Town Clerk, 10 Bridge St, Colebrook, NH 03576. 603-237-5200, R/E recording phone-603-237-4070, UCC recording phone-603-237-5200; fax-603-237-5069; hours: 9AM-5PM M; 9AM-3:30 T-Th; 1-3PM W; 9AM-3:30PM F. www.colebrook-nh.com
UCC search per debtor name- $10.00. Copy fee $1.00 per page. **Other phones:** Treasurer- 603-237-4142; Appraiser/Auditor- 603-237-4142; Elections- 603-237-5200; Vital Records- 603-237-5200. **Property tax/Assessor**- same address as above. 603-237-4070.

Columbia Town

Town Clerk, PO Box 157, Colebrook, NH 03576. 603-237-5255; fax-603-237-8270; hours: 10AM-5PM, M,W; 8AM-3PM, T, F.
Office personnel or visitors may perform searches. Search fee $10.00 per name. Real estate records located at Coos County. Copy fee $1.00 per page.

Concord City

City Clerk, 41 Green St; Rm 2, Concord, NH 03301-4255. 603-225-8500, R/E recording phone-603-228-0101, UCC recording phone-603-271-3242; fax-603-225-8592; hours: 8AM-4:30PM. www.onconcord.com
Office personnel or visitors may perform searches. Search fee $10.00 per name. Real estate records located at Merrimack County. Copy fee $1.00 per page. Cert fee- $5.00 per doc plus copy fee. **Online access to Property Assessor records:** Records on the city assessor database are free at http://data.visionappraisal.com/ConcordNH/. Registration is required to view full data. **Other phones:** Treasurer- 603-225-8540; Appraiser/Auditor- 603-225-8550; Elections- 603-225-8550; Vital Records- 603-225-8550 (Concord); State Vital Records- 603-271-4650. **Property tax/Assessor-** 603-225-8550.

Conway Town

Town Clerk, 1634 E. Main St, Center Conway, NH 03813. 603-447-3822; fax-603-447-1348; hours: 9AM-5PM. http://conwaynh.org
Record index not computerized. Office will perform a UCC and Tax lien search but public must search other records themselves. Search fee $10.00. Real estate records located at Carroll County. Copy fee $1.00 per page. Cert fee- No cert fee. **Other phones:** Treasurer- 603-447-6153; Elections- 603-447-3822; Vital Records- 603-447-3822. **Property tax/Assessor-** same address as above. 603-447-3811.

Coos County

Register of Deeds, 55 School St, #103; Coos County Courthouse, Lancaster, NH 03584. 603-788-2392; fax-603-788-4291; hours: 8AM-4PM.
The County Register of Deeds records real estate and Real Estate/UCC transactions, and the Town/City Clerk records UCC filings. Only the public may search. Copy fee $1.00 per page. R/E record type- $2.00 per page. Cert fee- $1.00 per doc plus copy fee. Payee- County Registry of Deeds. **Online access to Real Estate, Deed, Mortgage, Lien records:** Access to county register of deeds data is free at www.nhdeeds.com/coos/web/start.htm. A subscription is required to print images.

Cornish Town

Town Clerk, PO Box 183, Cornish Flat, NH 03746. 603-675-5207; fax-603-675-5605; hours: 9AM-N M-Th-F; 4PM-7PM M-TH.
Office personnel or visitors may perform searches. General search fee $10.00 per name. Real estate records located at Sullivan County. Tax lien search fee- $20.00 per debtor. Copy fee $1.00 per page.

Croydon Town

Town Clerk, 879 NH Rte 10, Newport, NH 03773. 603-863-7830; fax-603-863-2601; hours: 9AM-1PM M-Th; 6PM-8PM W & Th.
Office will perform a UCC search but public must search other records themselves. Real estate records located at Sullivan County. UCC search per debtor name- $10.00. Copy fee $1.00 per page. Payee-Town of Croydon. **Property tax/Assessor-** 603-863-7830.

Dalton Town

Town Clerk, 741 Dalton Rd, Dalton, NH 03598. 603-837-2096; fax-603-837-9642; hours: 11AM-5:45PM M; 7AM-5PM T,W,Th.
All records in one index. Record index not computerized. Only the office personnel may search. Search fee $10.00. Real estate records located at Coos County. Copy fee $1.00 per page. **Other phones:** Treasurer- 603-837-9802.

Danbury Town

Town Clerk, 23 High St, Danbury, NH 03230. 603-768-5448; fax-603-768-3313; hours: 8AM-4PM M&W; 1-7PM T.
Office will perform a UCC search but public must search other records themselves. Real estate records located at Merrimack County. Copy fee $1.00 per page. Payee- Town of Danbury. **Other phones:** Vital Records- 603-768-5448. **Property tax/Assessor-** same address as above. 603-768-3313.

Danville Town

Town Clerk, PO Box 11, Danville, NH 03819. 603-382-8253; fax-603-382-3363; hours: 8:30AM-1PM M; 3:30-8PM T&Th; 8:30AM-2:30PM W. www.townofdanville.org
All records in one index. Office personnel or visitors may perform searches. Real estate records located at Rockingham County. UCC search per debtor name- $10.00. Separate state tax lien search- $1.00 per property. Copy fee $1.00 per page. **Property tax/Assessor-** same address as above. 603-382-8253 x4.

Deerfield Town

Town Clerk, PO Box 159, Deerfield, NH 03037. 603-463-8811; fax-603-463-2820; hours: 8AM-2:30PM T-F; 8AM-7PM M.
Office will perform a UCC search but public must search other records themselves. Real estate records located at Rockingham County. UCC search per debtor name- $10.00. Copy fee $1.00 per page. **Other phones:** Treasurer- 603-463-8811; Appraiser/Auditor- 603-463-8811; Elections- 603-463-8811; Vital Records- 603-463-8811. **Property tax/Assessor-** 603-463-8811.

Deering Town

Town Clerk, 762 Deering Ctr Rd, Deering, NH 03244. 603-464-3224; fax-603-464-3804; hours: 8;30AM-2;45PM M,T, W, 3PM-6;45PM Th. www.deering.nh.us
All records in one index. Record index not computerized. Only the office personnel may search. Search fee $10.00. Real estate records located at Hillsborough County. Copy fee $1.00 per page. Cert fee- $12.00 per page plus copy fee. Payee- Derring Town Clerk/Tax Collector. **Property tax/Assessor-** same address as above. not known.

Derry Town

Town Clerk, 14 Manning St, Derry, NH 03038. 603-432-6105, R/E recording phone-603-432-6106, UCC recording phone-603-432-6105; fax-603-432-6131; hours: 7AM-4PM M-F; 7AM-7PM W. www.derry.nh.us
All records in one index. Record index not computerized. Office personnel or visitors may perform searches. Real estate records located at Rockingham County. Will search UCC records prior to 7/2001 and current liens only. UCC search per debtor name- $10.00. Separate federal tax lien search-$7.00 per debtor. Separate state tax lien search- $10.00 per debtor. Federal/state combined tax lien search- $10.00 per tax. Copy fee $1.00 per page. **Online access to Assessor, Property records:** Access Derry assessed values database free at http://derry.univers-clt.com. **Other phones:** Treasurer- 603-432-6100; Appraiser/Auditor- 603-432-6104; Elections- 603-432-6105; Vital Records- 603-432-6106. **Property tax/Assessor-** 603-432-6104.

Dorchester Town

Town Clerk, 368 N Dorchester Rd, Dorecester, NH 03266. 603-786-9076; fax-603-786-9431; hours: 9-11AM M; 3-6PM W; 9-11AM last Sat.
Record index not computerized. Only the office personnel may search. Search fee $7.00 per name. Real estate records located at Grafton County. Will search UCC records prior to 7/2001 and current tax liens. UCC search per debtor name- $10.00. Copy fee $1.00 per page. Tax lien copy- $.50 per page. Payee- Town of Dorchester. **Other phones:** Treasurer- 603-786-9076; Elections- 603-786-9076; Vital Records- 603-786-9076. **Property tax/Assessor-** 804 River Rd, Dorchester, NH 03266; 603-523-7658.

Dover City

City Clerk, 288 Central Ave; City Hall, Dover, NH 03820. 603-743-6021; fax-603-516-6666; hours: 8AM-4PM. www.ci.dover.nh.us
All records in one index. Records indexed on computer. Only the office personnel may search. Search fee $10.00. Real estate records located at Strafford County. Copy fee $1.00 per page. **Online access to Property, Deed, Grantor/Grantee records:** Records are free on the Stafford county-wide system at www.nhdeeds.com/stfd/web/agree3.htm. Use the subscription service for full data. **Other phones:** Treasurer- 603-743-6030; Elections- 603-743-6021; Vital Records- 603-743-6021. **Property tax/Assessor-** 603-743-6014.

Dublin Town

Town Clerk, Box 62, Dublin, NH 03444. 603-563-8859; fax-603-563-9221; hours: 8:30AM-4PM M-Th.
Record index not computerized. Office personnel or visitors may perform searches. Search fee $5.00 per name. Real estate records located at Cheshire County. Copy fee $1.00 per page. Tax lien copy-$.25 per page. **Other phones:** Treasurer- 603-563-8544; Appraiser/Auditor- 603-563-8544; Elections- 603-563-8859; Vital Records- 603-563-8859. **Property tax/Assessor-** 603-563-8544.

Dummer Town

Town Clerk, 1420 East Side River Rd, Dummer, NH 03588. 603-449-3408; fax-603-449-3349; hours: by appointment.
Office will perform a UCC search but public must search other records themselves. Real estate records located at Coos County. UCC search per debtor name- $10.00. Copy fee $1.00 per page. Payee-Town of Dummer. **Other phones:** Treasurer- 603-449-3417; Elections- 603-449-3442; Vital Records- 603-449-3408.

Dunbarton Town

Town Clerk, 1011 School St, Dunbarton, NH 03045. 603-774-3547; fax-603-774-5541; hours: 8:30AM-4PM.
Office personnel or visitors may perform searches. Search fee $10.00 per name. Real estate records located at Merrimack County. Copy fee $1.00 per page. **Online access to Assessor records:** Search town assessor database at http://data.visionappraisal.com/DunbartonNH/. Does not require a username & password. Simply click on link. **Property tax/Assessor-** 603-774-3547.

Durham Town

Town Clerk/Tax Collector, 15 Newmarket Rd; Town Hall, Durham, NH 03824-2898. 603-868-5577; fax-603-868-8033; hours: 8AM-5PM. www.ci.durham.nh.us/departments/town_clerk/clerk.html
All records in one index. Record index not computerized. Office will perform a UCC and Tax lien search but public must search other records themselves. Search fee $10.00. Real estate records located at Strafford County. Copy fee $1.00 per page. Tax lien copy- $.75 per copy. **Online access to Property, Deed, Grantor/Grantee, Assessor records:** Records are free on the Stafford county-wide system at www.nhdeeds.com/stfd/web/agree3.htm. Use the subscription service for full data. Also, Assessor data is free at http://data.visionappraisal.com/DurhamNH/. **Other phones:** Treasurer- 603-868-8043; Vital Records- 603-868-5577. **Property tax/Assessor-** same address as above. 603-868-8065.

East Kingston Town

Town Clerk, PO Box 249, East Kingston, NH 03827-0249. 603-642-8794; fax-603-642-8794; hours: 6-8PM Mon&Th; 8AM-2PM T,Th,F; closed Wed. www.eastkingston.org
Real estate records located at Rockingham County. Will search UCC records prior to 7/2001 and current tax liens. UCC search per debtor name- $10.00. Copy fee $1.00 per page. **Other phones:** Treasurer- 603-642-8406; Appraiser/Auditor- 603-642-8406; Elections- 603-642-8794; Vital Records- 603-642-8794. **Property tax/Assessor-** 603-642-8406.

Easton Town

Town Clerk, 1060 Easton Valley Rd, Easton, NH 03580. 603-823-8017; fax-603-823-7780; hours: 9AM-Noon M; 3PM-6PM Th.
Office personnel or visitors may perform searches. Search fee $20.00 per hour. Real estate records located at Grafton County. Copy fee $1.00 per page. Cert fee- $20.00 per page. Payee- Town of Easton.

Eaton Town

Town Clerk, Box 118, Eaton Center, NH 03832. 603-447-2840; fax-603-447-2560; hours: 9AM-11AM M; 7-9PM Tue or by appointment.
All records in one index. Office personnel or visitors may perform searches. Search fee $10.00 per name. Real estate records located at Carroll County. Will search UCC records prior to 7/2001 and current liens only. Copy fee $1.00 per page. Tax lien copy- $3.00 per page. **Property tax/Assessor-** 603-447-2840.

Effingham Town

Town Clerk, PO Box 117, Effingham, NH 03882. 603-539-7551; fax-603-539-7637; hours: 8AM-N, 3PM-7PM T; 8AM-5PM TH; 8AM-N Sat.
Office personnel or visitors may perform searches. Search fee $10.00 per name. Copy fee $.75; tax lien $1.00 per page. Cert fee- $10.00 per cert plus copy fee. Payee- Town of Effingham. **Other phones:** Treasurer- 603-539-7770; Appraiser/Auditor- 603-539-7770; Elections- 603-539-7551; Vital Records- 603-539-7551. **Property tax/Assessor-** 603-539-7770.

Ellsworth Town

Town Clerk, 12 Ellsworth Pond Rd; c/o Donna O'Brien, Plymouth, NH 03223. 603-726-3551; fax-603-726-8994; hours: by appointment only.
Irregular office hours; call and leave message to request appointment. Town Clerk works out of her house. No real estate recordings on record here. Office will perform a UCC search but public must search other records themselves. Real estate records located at Grafton County. UCC search per debtor name- $10.00. Copy fee $1.00 per page. Payee- Town of Ellsworth. **Other phones:** Treasurer- 603-726-8668.

Enfield Town

Town Clerk, PO Box 373, Enfield, NH 03748-0373. 603-632-5001; fax-603-632-5182; hours: 8:30AM-3:30PM M-W & F; 9:30AM-4:30PM T. www.enfield.nh.us
All records in one index. Record index not computerized. Only the office personnel may search. Search fee $15.00 per name. Real estate records located at Grafton County. Copy fee $1.00 per page. Payee- Town of Enfield. **Other phones:** Elections- 603-632-5001; Vital Records- 603-632-5001. **Property tax/Assessor-** same address as above. 603-632-5026.

Epping Town

Town Clerk, 157 Main St, Epping, NH 03042. 603-679-8288; fax-603-679-3002; hours: Noon-8PM M; 9AM-6PM W; 9AM-3PM F.
All records in one index. Only the office personnel may search. Real estate records located at Rockingham County. Will search UCC records prior to 7/2001 only. Will not search tax liens. UCC search per debtor name- $10.00. Copy fee $1.00 per page. Cert fee- $3.00 per page plus copy fee. Payee- Town of Epping. **Other phones:** Appraiser/Auditor- 603-679-5441; Elections- 603-679-8288; Vital Records- 603-679-8288. **Property tax/Assessor-** 157 Main St, Epping, NH 03042; 603-679-5441.

Epsom Town

Town Clerk, PO Box 10, Epsom, NH 03234. 603-736-4825; fax-603-736-8539; hours: 8-1PM;4:30-6:30PM, M;10-3PM T; 8-3PM TH;8-3PM F.
All records in one index. Record index not computerized. Office will perform a UCC search but public must search other records themselves. Search fee $10.00. Real estate records located at Merrimack County. Copy fee $1.00 per page. Tax lien copy- $.50 per page. **Other phones:** Appraiser/Auditor- 603-736-9002. **Property tax/Assessor-** same address as above.

Errol Town

Town Clerk, PO Box 100, Errol, NH 03579. 603-482-3351; fax-603-482-3804; hours: 9AM-11AM M; 5PM-7:30PM, T; 8:30AM-11AM, TH.
All records in one index. Record index not computerized. Office will perform a UCC and Tax lien search but public must search other records themselves. Search fee $5.00. Real estate records located at Coos County. Copy fee $.75; tax lien $1.00 per page. **Other phones:** Treasurer- 603-482-3351; Appraiser/Auditor- 603-482-3351; Elections- 603-482-3351; Vital Records- 603-482-3351. **Property tax/Assessor-** 603-482-3351.

Exeter Town

Town Clerk, 10 Front St, Exeter, NH 03833-2792. 603-778-0591; fax-603-772-4709; hours: 8:30AM-3:30PM. www.exeternh.org/tnclk/index.html
Record index not computerized. Only the office personnel may search. Real estate records located at Rockingham County. Will search UCC records prior to 7/2001 and current liens only. UCC search per debtor name- $10.00. Separate federal tax lien search- $10.00 per search. Copy fee $1.00 per page. Cert fee- $3.00 per page plus copy fee. Payee- Exeter Town Clerk. **Other phones:** Vital Records- 603-778-0591. **Property tax/Assessor-** same address as above. 603-778-0591.

Farmington Town

Town Clerk, 356 Main St; Town Hall, Farmington, NH 03835. 603-755-3657; fax-603-755-9128; hours: 8:30AM-5PM M-W, 8:30AM-7PM Th, 8:30AM-12:30 PM F.
All records in one index. Real estate records located at Strafford County. Will search UCC records prior to 7/2001 and current tax liens. UCC search per debtor name- $10.00. Tax lien search fee- $7.00 per debtor. Separate federal tax lien search- $7.00 per debtor. Copy fee $1.00 per page. Tax lien copy-

$.25 per page. **Online access to Property, Deed, Grantor/Grantee records:** Records are free on the Stafford county-wide system at www.nhdeeds.com/stfd/web/agree3.htm. Use the subscription service for full data. **Other phones:** Treasurer- 603-755-2731; Elections- 603-755-3657; Vital Records- 603-755-3657. **Property tax/Assessor-** 603-755-2774.

Fitzwilliam Town

Town Clerk, PO Box 504, Fitzwilliam, NH 03447-0504. 603-585-7791; fax-603-585-7744; hours: 8:30AM-12:30PM M,W; 1-5PM Thurs; Wed Eve-6-9PM. www.fitzwilliam-nh.gov
Record index not computerized. Only the office personnel may search. Search fee $10.00 per name. Real estate records located at Cheshire County. Copy fee $1.00 per page. **Other phones:** Vital Records- 603-585-7791. **Property tax/Assessor-** PO Box 725, Fitzwilliam, NH 03447-0725; 603-585-7723.

Francestown Town

Town Clerk, PO Box 67, Francestown, NH 03043-0067. 603-547-6251; fax-603-547-2622; hours: 8AM-N, M-Th; 6-8PM M.
Record index not computerized. Office personnel or visitors may perform searches. Search fee $10.00 per name. Real estate records located at Hillsborough County. Copy fee $1.00 per page.

Franconia Town

Town Clerk, PO Box 900, Franconia, NH 03580. 603-823-5237; fax-603-823-5581; hours: 8AM-2PM Tues.; 1-7PM Th.
Office personnel or visitors may perform searches. Search fee $7.00 per name. Real estate records located at Grafton County. UCC search per debtor name- $10.00. Copy fee $1.00 per page. Payee- Town of Franconia.

Franklin City

City Clerk, 316 Central St, Franklin, NH 03235. 603-934-3109; fax-603-934-7413; hours: 8AM-5PM.
All records in one index. Record index not computerized. Only the office personnel may search. Search fee $15.00 per name. Real estate records located at Merrimack County. Copy fee $1.00 per page. Payee- City of Franklin. **Other phones:** Treasurer- 603-934-3900; Appraiser/Auditor- 603-934-5549; Elections- 603-934-3109; Vital Records- 603-934-3109. **Property tax/Assessor-** 603-934-5449.

Freedom Town

Town Clerk, PO Box 457, Freedom, NH 03836. 603-539-8269, R/E recording phone-603-539-4872, UCC recording phone-603-539-6323; fax-603-539-8270; hours: 6:30-8PM Mon & Wed; 9AM-N Sat.
Office will perform a UCC search but public must search other records themselves. Real estate records located at Carroll County. UCC search per debtor name- $15.00. Copy fee $1.00 per page. **Other phones:** Treasurer- 603-539-6323. **Property tax/Assessor-** PO Box 277, Freedom, NH 03836; 603-539-6323.

Fremont Town

Town Clerk, PO Box 120, Fremont, NH 03044. 603-895-8693, R/E recording phone-603-895-2226, UCC recording phone-603-895-8693; fax-603-895-3149; hours: 9AM-N 1-4PM Tu-W; 1-7PM Th; 9AM-N Fri. http://fremont.nh.gov
Records are not computerized. Only the office personnel may search. Real estate records located at Rockingham County. Will search UCC records prior to 7/2001 and current liens only. Tax liens not included in UCC search. UCC search per debtor name- $10.00. Separate federal & state combined tax lien search- $10.00 per search. Copy fee $1.00 per page. **Online to Assessor records:** Search town assessor database at http://data.visionappraisal.com/FremontNH/. Does not require a username & password. Simply click on link. **Other phones:** Treasurer- 603-895-2226;

Appraiser/Auditor- 603-895-2226; Elections- 603-895-8693; Vital Records- 603-895-8693. **Property tax/Assessor-** PO Box 120, 295 Main St, Fremont, NH 03044; 603-895-2226.

Gilford Town

Town Clerk, 47 Cherry Valley Rd; Town Hall, Gilford, NH 03246. 603-527-4713; fax-603-527-4719; hours: 8AM-5PM M-F, 5PM-7PM Th Evenings. www.gilfordnh.org
All records in one index. Office personnel or visitors may perform searches. Search fee $10.00 per name. Real estate records located at Belknap County. UCC search request using non-standard form (per name)- $12.00. Copy fee $1.00 per page. Cert fee- $3.00 per cert includes copy fee. Payee- Town of Gilford. **Other phones:** Elections- 603-527-4713; Vital Records- 603-527-4713; Tax Collector- 603-527-4713. **Property tax/Assessor-** 603-527-4704.

Gilmanton Town

Town Clerk/Tax Collector, PO Box 550, Gilmanton, NH 03237-0550. 603-267-6726; fax-603-267-6701; hours: 9AM-N, 7-8:30PM M; 9AM-4PM W F; 9AM-N Th.
Record index not computerized. Only the office personnel may search. General index search fee $25.00 per hour, $5.00 per name. Tax liens not included in UCC search. UCC search per debtor name- $15.00. Copy fee $1.00 per page. Tax lien copy- $.25 per copy.

Gilsum Town

Town Clerk, PO Box 36, Gilsum, NH 03448. 603-357-0320; fax-603-352-0845; hours: 6PM-8PM Tu; 8AM-N Sat.
No real estate recordings; see tax collector. Office personnel or visitors may perform searches. Search fee $15.00 per name. Real estate records located at Cheshire County. Copy fee $5.00 per page. Cert fee- $5.00 per page plus copy fee. **Property tax/Assessor-** 603-357-0320.

Goffstown Town

Town Clerk, 16 Main St, Goffstown, NH 03045. 603-497-3613; R/E recording phone-603-497-3611, UCC recording phone-603-497-3613; fax-603-497-8993; hours: 8:30AM-4:30PM M,T,F; 8:30AM-N W; 8:30AM-6PM Th. www.ci.goffstown.nh.us
Record index not computerized. Office personnel or visitors may perform searches. Search fee $15.00 per name. Real estate records located at Hillsborough County. Copy fee $1.00 per page. **Other phones:** Treasurer- 603-497-3615; Elections- 603-497-3613; Vital Records- 603-497-3613. **Property tax/Assessor-** 603-497-3611.

Gorham Town

Town Clerk, 20 Park St, Gorham, NH 03581-1694. 603-466-2744; fax-603-466-3100; hours: 8:30AM-N, 1-5PM M,W,F; 8:30AM-1PM, 2-5PM T,Th.
All records in one index. Record index not computerized. Office personnel or visitors may perform searches. Search fee $10.00. Real estate records located at Coos County. Copy fee $1.00 per page. **Other phones:** Treasurer- 603-466-3100; Appraiser/Auditor- 603-466-3322; Elections- 603-466-2744; Vital Records- 603-466-2744. **Property tax/Assessor-** same address as above. 603-466-3322.

Goshen Town

Town Clerk, PO Box 58, Goshen, NH 03752. 603-863-5655; fax-603-863-6139; hours: 8:30AM-N, 1-5PM M,W,F.
Office personnel or visitors may perform searches. Search fee $10.00 per name. Real estate records located at Sullivan County. Copy fee $1.00 per page. Payee- Town of Goshen. **Property tax/Assessor-** 603-863-5080.

Grafton County

Registry of Deeds, 3855 Dartmouth College Hwy, Box 4, North Haverhill, NH 03774-9700. 603-787-6921; fax-603-787-2363; hours: 7:30AM-4:30PM.
All records in one index. Records indexed on a public use terminal back to 1965. Only the public may search. Copy fee $1.00 per page. Cert fee- $2.00 per page plus copy fee. Payee- Grafton County Registry of Deeds. **Online access to Real Estate, Lien records:** Access to the County dial-up service requires a $100 set up fee and $40 per month access fee. Two years of data are kept on system; prior years on CD. Lending agency information available. A fax-back service is in-state only. For further information, call 603-787-6921. **Other phones:** Treasurer- 603-787-6941; Elections- 603-787-6941.

Grafton Town

Town Clerk, PO Box 297, Grafton, NH 03240. 603-523-7270, R/E recording phone-603-523-7700, UCC recording phone-603-523-7270; fax-603-523-4397; hours: 6-8PM M; 9AM-N Wed; 4-7PM F.
All records in one index. Record index not computerized. Office personnel or visitors may perform searches. Search fee $15.00 per name. Real estate records located at Grafton County. Copy fee $1.00 per page. Cert fee- $12.00 for 1st copy; $8 2nd, plus copy fee. Payee- Town of Grafton. **Other phones:** Treasurer- 603-523-7700; Appraiser/Auditor- 603-523-7700; Elections- 603-523-7270; Vital Records- 603-523-7270.

Grantham Town

Town Clerk, PO Box 135, Grantham, NH 03753-0135. 603-863-5608; fax-603-863-4499; hours: 7:30AM-4:30PM M-Th; 7-9PM Tu-W. http://granthamnh.net/
Office personnel or visitors may perform searches. Search fee $10.00 per name. Real estate records located at Sullivan County. Copy fee $1.00 per page. Payee- Town of Grantham. **Other phones:** Treasurer- 603-863-6021; Appraiser/Auditor- 603-863-6021; Elections- 603-863-5608; Vital Records- 603-863-5608. **Property tax/Assessor-** 603-863-6021.

Greenfield Town

Town Clerk, PO Box 256, Greenfield, NH 03047. 603-547-2782; fax-603-547-3004; hours: 6AM-7:30PM M-Th; 2nd & 4th Sat. 9AM-N. http://greenfieldnh.org
Record index not computerized. Office personnel or visitors may perform searches. Search fee $10.00 per name. Real estate records located at Hillsborough County. Copy fee $1.00 per page.

Greenland Town

Town Clerk, PO Box 100, Greenland, NH 03840-0100. 603-431-7111; fax-603-430-3761; hours: 12:00-8PM M; 9AM-4:30PM T-F. www.greenland-nh.com/?dept=clerk
Real estate records located at Rockingham County. Will search UCC records prior to 7/2001 and current liens only. UCC search per debtor name- $10.00. Separate federal tax lien search- $15.00 per debtor. Copy fee $1.00 per page. Cert fee- $1.00. Payee- Greenland Town Clerk. **Online access to Property Assessor records:** Access is via a private company at http://data.visionappraisal.com/GreenlandNH/. Free registration is required to view full data. **Other phones:** Treasurer- 603-431-7111; Appraiser/Auditor- 603-431-7111; Elections- 603-431-7111; Vital Records- 603-431-7111. **Property tax/Assessor-** 603-431-7111.

Greenville Town

Town Clerk, PO Box 354, Greenville, NH 03048-0354. 603-878-4155; fax-603-878-4951; hours: 10AM-N, 1-4PM T,TH; 10AM-N,1-3PM Wed.
Office personnel or visitors may perform searches. Search fee $10.00 per name. Real estate records located at Hillsborough County. Copy fee $1.00 per page. **Property tax/Assessor-** 603-878-2084.

Groton Town

Town Clerk, 63-1 N. Groton Rd, Groton, NH 03241. 603-744-8849; hours: 10AM-6PM M,F;11AM-4PM,W; 10AM-2PM 1st & last Sat.
Record index not computerized. Office will perform a UCC and Tax lien search but public must search other records themselves. Search fee $10.00. Real estate records located at Grafton County. Copy fee $1.00 per page. Payee- Town of Groton.

Hampstead Town

Town Clerk, PO Box 298, Hampstead, NH 03841. 603-329-4100; fax-603-329-7174; hours: 8AM-7PM, M; 8AM-4PM, T,W,TH; 8AM-12PM, F.
Office personnel or visitors may perform searches. Search fee $10.00 per name. Real estate records located at Rockingham County. Copy fee $1.00 per page.

Hampton Falls Town

Town Clerk, 1 Drinkwater Rd; Town Hall, Hampton Falls, NH 03844. 603-926-4618, R/E recording phone-603-929-0828, UCC recording phone-603-926-4618; fax-603-926-1848; hours: 9AM-N, 1-4PM M,T,Th. www.hamptonfalls.org
All records in one index. Search fee $10.00 per name. Real estate records located at Rockingham County. Copy fee $1.00 per page. **Other phones:** Treasurer- 603-929-3613; Elections- 603-926-4618; Vital Records- 603-926-4618; Town Hall- 603-926-7101. **Property tax/Assessor-** 603-929-0828.

Hampton Town

Town Clerk, 100 Winnacunnet Rd, Hampton, NH 03842. 603-926-0406; fax-603-929-5917; hours: 9AM-4PM. www.town.hampton.nh.us
All records in one index. Record index not computerized. Only the office personnel may search. Search fee $10.00 per name. Real estate records located at Rockingham County. Copy fee $1.00 per page. Cert fee- $4.00 per doc plus copy fee. Payee- Town Clerk. **Other phones:** Elections- 603-926-0406; Vital Records- 603-926-0406. **Property tax/Assessor-** 603-929-5923.

Hancock Town

Town Clerk, PO Box 6, Hancock, NH 03449. 603-525-4441; fax-603-525-4427; hours: 9AM-4PM.
All records in one index. Office will perform a UCC search but public must search other records themselves. UCC search per debtor name- $15.00. Copy fee $1.00 per page. **Other phones:** Treasurer- 603-525-4441. **Property tax/Assessor-** same address as above. 603-525-4441.

Hanover Town

Town Clerk, PO Box 483, Hanover, NH 03755-0483. 603-643-0701; fax-603-643-1720; hours: 8:30AM-4:30PM.
Office personnel or visitors may perform searches. Search fee $10.00 per name. Real estate records located at Grafton County. Copy fee $1.00 per page. Cert fee- None. **Other phones:** Treasurer- 603-643-4123. **Property tax/Assessor-** 603-643-0703.

Harrisville Town

Town Clerk, PO Box 284, Harrisville, NH 03450. 603-827-5546; fax-603-827-2917; hours: 2-7PM, T; 4-6:30PM, W; 9-11:30AM Th.
Separate indices to search include paper records. Record index not computerized. Only the office personnel may search. Search fee $10.00 per name. Real estate records located at Cheshire County. Copy fee $2.00 per page. Cert fee- $2.00 per record plus copy fee. Payee- Town Clerk-Harrisville. **Other phones:** Treasurer- 603-827-3431; Elections- 603-827-5546; Vital Records- 603-827-5546.

Hart's Location Town

Town Clerk, 5 Forest Rd, Hart's Location, NH 03812. 603-374-2436; hours: by Appointment.

All records in one index. Office personnel or visitors may perform searches. Search fee $10.00 per name. Real estate records located at Carroll County. Will search UCC records prior to 7/2001 and current tax liens. Copy fee $1.00 per page. Tax lien copy- $15.00 per lien. Payee- Town Clerk of Hart's Location. **Other phones:** Treasurer- 603-383-3605. **Property tax/Assessor-** Northtown Associates, LLC, 1794 Presidential Hwy, Jefferson, NH 03583 603-586-7153.

Haverhill Town

Town Clerk, 2975 Dartmouth College Hwy, N. Haverhill, NH 03774. 603-787-6200, R/E recording phone-603-787-6444, UCC recording phone-603-717-6200; fax-603-787-2226; hours: 9AM-4:30PM.
All records in one index. Record index not computerized. Only the office personnel may search. Search fee $10.00 per name. Real estate records located at Grafton County. Tax lien search-$7.00 per debtor. Copy fee $1.00 per page. Payee- Town of Haverhill. **Other phones:** Treasurer- 603-747-2735; Elections- 603-787-6200; Vital Records-603-787-6200. **Property tax/Assessor-** same address as above. 603-787-6444.

Hebron Town

Town Clerk, PO Box 55, East Hebron, NH 03241. 603-744-7999; fax-603-744-7999; hours: 3-8PM Tu; 9:30-11:30AM Sat. www.hebronnh.org
Real estate records located at Grafton County. Will not search UCC records or tax liens. Copy fee $1.00 per page. Tax lien copy- $.50 per page. Payee- Town of Hebron.

Henniker Town

Town Clerk, 2 Depot Hill Rd, Henniker, NH 03242. 603-428-3240; fax-603-428-4366; hours: 8AM-5:30PM, M; 8AM-N, T; 8AM-4:30PM, W, F.
Real estate records located at Merrimack County. Will search UCC records prior to 7/2001 and current liens only. Tax liens not included in UCC search. UCC search per debtor name- $10.00. Separate federal tax lien search- 10.00. Copy fee $1.00 per page. Cert fee- $12.00. Payee- Henniker Town Clerk. **Other phones:** Elections- 603-428-3240; Vital Records- 603-428-3240. **Property tax/Assessor-** 603-428-3221.

Hill Town

Town Clerk, PO Box 251, Hill, NH 03243. 603-934-3951; fax-603-934-3951; hours: 6-9PM Tues; 9AM-1PM W; 9AM-5PM Th-F.
Separate indices to search. Only the office personnel may search. Real estate records located at Merrimack County. Will search UCC records prior to 7/2001 and current liens only. UCC search per debtor name- $10.00. Copy fee $1.00 per page. Cert fee-$4.00 per doc plus copy fee. Payee- Town of Hill. **Other phones:** Treasurer- 603-934-1094; Elections-603-934-3951; Vital Records- 603-934-3951. **Property tax/Assessor-** 603-934-1094.

Hillsborough County

Registrar of Deeds, PO Box 370, Nashua, NH 03061-0370. 603-882-6933, R/E recording phone-603-882-6933 x115; fax-603-594-4137; hours: 8AM-3:45PM.
All records in one index. Records indexed on a public use terminal back to 1966. Only the public may search. Copy fee $1.00 per page. Cert fee-$2.00 per doc plus copy fee. Payee- Hillsborough County Treasurer. **Online access to Real Estate, Deed, Mortgage, Lien, Grantor/Grantee records:** Access to county register of deeds data is free at www.nhdeeds.com/hils/web/argthc.htm. Online records go back to 1966.

Hillsborough Town

Town Clerk, PO Box 1699, Hillsborough, NH 03244. 603-464-5571; fax-603-464-4270; hours: 9AM-5PM.
Office will perform a UCC search but public must search other records themselves. Real estate records located at Hillsborough County. UCC search per

debtor name- $10.00. Copy fee $5.00 per page. Cert fee- $15.00 per cert. Payee- Hillsborough Town Clerk. **Property tax/Assessor-** 603-464-3877.

Hinsdale Town

Town Clerk, PO Box 31, Hinsdale, NH 03451. 603-336-5719; fax-603-366-5711; hours: 11-4 M-W, 1:30-6:30 1st 2nd TH, other TH 11-4.
All records in one index. Record index not computerized. Office will perform a UCC search but public must search other records themselves. Search fee $10.00. Real estate records located at Cheshire County. Copy fee $1.00 per page. Cert fee-$1.00 per page plus copy fee. Payee- Town of Hinsdale.

Holderness Town

Town Clerk, PO Box 203, Holderness, NH 03245. 603-968-7536; fax-603-968-9954; hours: 8:30AM-4:30PM. www.holderness-nh.gov/
Separate indices to search. Record index not computerized. Office will perform a UCC search but public must search other records themselves. Real estate records located at Grafton County. UCC search per debtor name- $10.00. Copy fee $1.00 per page. R/E record copy- $.50 per page. Tax lien copy- $.25 per page. **Other phones:** Treasurer- 603-968-3537; Elections- 603-968-7536; Vital Records-603-968-7536. **Property tax/Assessor-** same address as above. 603-968-3537.

Hollis Town

Town Clerk, 7 Monument Sq, Hollis, NH 03049-6568. 603-465-2064, R/E recording phone-603-465-7987, UCC recording phone-603-465-2064; fax-603-465-2964; hours: M-W-F 8AM-1PM; Mon Eve. 7-9PM; 1st Sat. 8-11AM. www.hollis.nh.us
Only the office personnel may search. Search fee $10.00 per name. Real estate records located at Hillsborough County. Copy fee $1.00 per page. Cert fee- $10.00 per doc plus copy fee. Payee- Town of Hollis. **Online access to Assessor records:** Access assessor data at http://data.visionappraisal.com/HollisNH/. Does not require a username & password. Simply click on link. **Other phones:** Treasurer- 603-465-6936; Appraiser/Auditor- 603-465-9860; Elections- 603-465-2064; Vital Records- 603-465-2064. **Property tax/Assessor-** 7 Monument Sq, Hollis, NH 03049-6568; 603-465-9860.

Hooksett Town

Town Clerk, 16 N. Main St, Hooksett, NH 03106. 603-485-9534; fax-603-485-4423; hours: 8AM-4:30PM; 8AM-6:30PM W. www.hooksett.org
Office personnel or visitors may perform searches. Search fee $15.00 per name. Real estate records located at Merrimack County. Copy fee $1.00 per page. **Property tax/Assessor-** 603-268-0003.

Hopkinton Town

Town Clerk, PO Box 446, Contoocook, NH 03229-0446. 603-746-3180; fax-603-746-4011; hours: 8AM-4:30PM. www.hopkintonnh.us
Office will perform a UCC search but public must search other records themselves. Real estate records located at Merrimack County. UCC search per debtor name- $10.00. Copy fee $1.00 per page. **Other phones:** Treasurer- 603-746-3180; **Property tax/Assessor-** 603-746-3170.

Hudson Town

Town Clerk, 12 School St, Hudson, NH 03051-4294. 603-886-6003; hours: 8:30AM-4:30PM.
All records in one index. Record index not computerized. Only the office personnel may search. Real estate records located at Hillsborough County. Copy fee $1.00 per page. Payee- Town of Hudson. **Online access to Assessor, Property records:** Access property data free at http://hudsonnh.patriotproperties.com. **Other phones:** Treasurer- 603-886-6000; Vital Records- 603-886-

6003. **Property tax/Assessor-** same address as above. 603-886-6009.

Jackson Town

Town Clerk, PO Box 336, Jackson, NH 03846-0336. 603-383-6248; fax-603-383-6248; hours: 8:30AM-12:30PM T,W,F.
Record index not computerized. Only the office personnel may search. Real estate records located at Carroll County. Will search UCC records prior to 7/2001. Will not search tax liens. UCC search per debtor name- $15.00. Copy fee $5.75 per page. Cert fee- $6.25 per cert includes copy fee. Payee-Jackson Town Clerk. **Property tax/Assessor-** PO Box 268, 54 Main St, Jackson, NH 03846; 603-383-4223.

Jaffrey Town

Town Clerk, 10 Goodnow St, Jaffrey, NH 03452. 603-532-7861; fax-603-532-7862;
Record index not computerized. Office personnel or visitors may perform searches. Search fee $10.00 per name. Real estate records located at Cheshire County. Copy fee $1.00 per page. **Online access to Assessor records:** Search town assessor database at http://data.visionappraisal.com/JaffreyNH/. Does not require a username & password. Simply click on link. **Other phones:** Treasurer- 603-532-7445. **Property tax/Assessor-** 603-532-7445.

Jefferson Town

Town Clerk, 84 Stag Hollow Rd, Jefferson, NH 03583. 603-586-4553; fax-603-586-4553;
Record index not computerized. Office personnel or visitors may perform searches. Search fee $10.00 per name. Real estate records located at Coos County. Copy fee $1.00 per page. **Other phones:** Treasurer- 603-586-4400; Appraiser/Auditor- 603-586-4553; Elections- 603-586-4553; Vital Records- 603-586-4553. **Property tax/Assessor-** 603-586-4553.

Keene City

City Clerk, 3 Washington St, Keene, NH 03431. 603-352-0133, R/E recording phone-603-352-0403, UCC recording phone-603-352-0133; fax-603-357-9884; hours: 8AM-5PM. www.ci.keene.nh.us
Separate indices to search include UCC, federal & state liens, contracts, deeds, leases, easements. Records indexed on computer. Only the office personnel may search. Search fee $10.00 per name. Real estate records located at Cheshire County. Federal tax lien search- $7.00 per debtor. Copy fee $1.00 per page. **Other phones:** Treasurer- 603-357-9801; Appraiser/Auditor- 603-352-2125; Elections-603-352-0133; Vital Records- 603-352-0133. **Property tax/Assessor-** same address as above. 603-352-2125.

Kensington Town

Town Clerk, 95 Amesbury Rd, Rte 150; Town Hall, Kensington, NH 03833. 603-772-5423; fax-603-772-6841; hours: 8:30AM-N M,Tu,Th; 6-8PM Tu-Wed. http://town.kensington.nh.us
Office will perform a UCC or tax lien search but public must search other records themselves. UCC search per debtor name- $10.00. Tax lien search fee- $5.00 per debtor. Copy fee $1.00 per page. **Other phones:** Treasurer- 603-772-5423; Elections-603-772-5423; Vital Records- 603-772-5423. **Property tax/Assessor-** 603-436-5916.

Kingston Town

Town Clerk, PO Box 657, Kingston, NH 03848-0657. 603-642-3112; fax-603-642-3204; hours: 8:30AM-noon, 1-4PM M-F; 7-9PM M, T.
Office will perform a UCC search but public must search other records themselves. Real estate records located at Rockingham County. UCC search per debtor name-$15.00 per search. Copy fee $1.00 per page. **Property tax/Assessor-** 603-642-3342.

Laconia City

City Clerk, PO Box 489, Laconia, NH 03247. 603-527-1265, R/E recording phone-603-527-5420, UCC recording phone-603-527-1265; fax-603-524-1766; hours: 8:30AM-4:30PM.
Office personnel or visitors may perform searches. Search fee $10.00 per name. Real estate records located at Belknap County. Copy fee $1.00 per page. **Online access to Property Assessor records:** Records on the town assessor database are online at http://data.visionappraisal.com/LaconiaNH. Free registration is required for full access. **Other phones:** Treasurer- 603-524-3877; Elections- 603-527-1265; Vital Records- 603-527-1265; Tax Office- 603-527-1269. **Property tax/Assessor-** 603-527-1268.

Lancaster Town

Town Clerk, 25 Main St, Lancaster, NH 03584. 603-788-2306, R/E recording phone-603-788-2392, UCC recording phone-603-788-2306; fax-603-788-2114; hours: 8:30AM-5PM M-TH; 8:30AM-4:30PM F. www.lancasternh.org
Separate indices to search include UCC's and tax liens. Office personnel or visitors may perform searches. Search fee $10.00 per name. Real estate records located at Coos County. Copy fee $1.00 per page. **Other phones:** Treasurer- 603-788-3391; Appraiser/Auditor- 603-788-3391; Elections- 603-788-2306; Vital Records- 603-788-2306. **Property tax/Assessor-** 603-788-3391.

Landaff Town

Town Clerk, PO Box 125, Landaff, NH 03585. 603-838-6220; fax-603-838-6220; hours: 9AM-11AM & 5PM-7PM T.
All records in one index. Record index not computerized. Only the office personnel may search. Search fee $10.00 UCC and tax lien. Real estate records located at Grafton County. Copy fee $1.00 per page. Payee- Town of Landaff. **Other phones:** Treasurer- 603-838-6116; Elections- 603-838-6220; Vital Records- 603-838-6220. **Property tax/Assessor-** 136 Woodfield Dr, Farmington, Me 04938; 207-778-3881.

Langdon Town

Town Clerk, 5 Walker Hill Rd; Langdon Town Hall, Langdon, NH 03602. 603-835-2389; fax-603-835-2389; hours: 10AM-N, 3-6PM T.
Office personnel or visitors may perform searches. Search fee $10.00 per name. Real estate records located at Sullivan County. Copy fee $1.00 per page. Payee- Town of Langdon.

Lebanon City

City Clerk, 51 N. Park St, Lebanon, NH 03766. 603-448-3054; fax-603-448-4891; hours: 8AM-5PM. www.lebcity.com
All records in one index. Record index not computerized. Office will perform a UCC search but public must search other records themselves. Search fee $10.00. Real estate records located at Grafton County. Copy fee $1.00 per page. **Online access to Property Assessor records:** Records from the city assessor database are free at http://data.visionappraisal.com/LEBANONNH/. Free registration is required to view full data. **Other phones:** Elections- 603-448-3054; Vital Records- 603-448-3054. **Property tax/Assessor-** same address as above. 603-448-1499.

Lee Town

Town Clerk, 7 Mast Rd; Town Hall, Lee, NH 03824. 603-659-2964; fax-603-659-7202; hours: 8AM-4PM M, W, F.
All records in one index. Office personnel or visitors may perform searches. Search fee $10.00 per name. Real estate records located at Strafford County. Copy fee $1.00 per page. Cert fee- $1.00. Payee- Lee Town Clerk. **Online access to Property, Deed, Grantor/Grantee records:** Records are free on the Stafford county-wide system at www.nhdeeds.com/stfd/web/agree3.htm. Use the subscription service for full data. **Other phones:** Treasurer- 603-659-5414; Appraiser/Auditor- 603-659-5414; Elections- 603-659-2964; Vital Records- 603-659-2964. **Property tax/Assessor-** 603-659-5414.

Lempster Town

Town Clerk, PO Box 33, East Lempster, NH 03605-0033. 603-863-3213; fax-603-863-8105; hours: 5-8PM Tu,Th; 9AM-N Sat.
All records in one index. Record index not computerized. Real estate records located at Sullivan County. Will search UCC records prior to 7/2001 and current liens only. UCC search per debtor name- $10.00. Copy fee $1.00 per page. **Other phones:** Treasurer- 603-863-3213.

Lincoln Town

Town Clerk, PO Box 39, Lincoln, NH 03251. 603-745-8971; fax-603-745-6743; hours: 8AM-4PM.
Record index not computerized. Office personnel or visitors may perform searches. Search fee $10.00 per name. Real estate records located at Grafton County. Copy fee $1.00 per page. Cert fee- None. Payee- Town of Lincoln. **Other phones:** Treasurer- 603-745-8971. **Property tax/Assessor-** 603-745-2757.

Lisbon Town

Town Clerk, 46 School St, Lisbon, NH 03585. 603-838-2862; fax-603-838-6790; hours: 9AM-N,1-4:30PM.
All records in one index. Record index not computerized. Only the office personnel may search. Search fee $10.00 per name. Real estate records located at Grafton County. Copy fee $1.00 per page. Cert fee- $10.00. Payee- Lisbon Town Clerk. **Other phones:** Vital Records- 603-838-2862. **Property tax/Assessor-** 603-838-6377.

Litchfield Town

Town Clerk, 2 Liberty Way, #3, Litchfield, NH 03052. 603-424-4045, R/E recording phone-603-882-6933, UCC recording phone-603-424-4045; fax-603-424-8154; hours: 10AM-6PM, M; 8AM-3PM, T; 8AM-3PM, W TH F.
All records in one index. Office personnel or visitors may perform searches. Search fee $10.00 per debtor. Real estate records located at Hillsborough County. Will search UCC records prior to 7/2001 only. Copy fee $1.00 per page. Payee- Town of Litchfield. **Other phones:** Vital Records- 603-424-4045. **Property tax/Assessor-** 603-424-4046.

Littleton Town

Town Clerk, 125 Main St; 2nd Fl, Littleton, NH 03561. 603-444-3995 x20, R/E recording phone-603-444-3996x16, UCC recording phone-603-444-3995 x20; fax-603-444-0735; hours: 8:30AM-12:30PM, 1-4PM, M,T, Th, 8-5PM,W, 7AM-N, F. www.townoflittleton.org
Record index not computerized. Office will perform a UCC and Tax lien search but public must search other records themselves. Search fee $10.00. Real estate records located at Grafton County. Copy fee $1.00 per page. Cert fee- $1.00 per page plus copy fee. Payee- Grafton Town Clerk. **Online access to Assessor records:** Search town assessor database at http://data.visionappraisal.com/LittletonNH/. Does not require a username & password. Simply click on link. **Other phones:** Treasurer- 603-444-3995 x11; Elections- 603-444-3995 x20; Vital Records- 603-444-3995 x20. **Property tax/Assessor-** same address as above. 603-444-3995 x16.

Londonderry Town

Town Clerk, 268B Mammoth Rd, Londonderry, NH 03053. 603-432-1100 x195, R/E recording phone-603-432-1100 x135, UCC recording phone-603-432-1100 x195; fax-603-421-9617; hours: 8:30AM-5PM. www.londonderrynh.org
All records in one index. Record index not computerized. Office will perform a UCC search but public must search other records themselves. Search fee $10.00 per name. Copy fee $1.00 per page. Cert fee- none. **Online access to Assessor, Property records:** Access property data free at http://londonderrynh.patriotproperties.com/default.asp.
Other phones: Treasurer- 603-432-1126; Appraiser/Auditor- 603-432-1100 x109; Elections- 603-432-1100 x114; Vital Records- 603-432-1100 x195. **Property tax/Assessor-** same address as above. 603-432-1100 x135.

Loudon Town

Town Clerk, PO Box 7837, Loudon, NH 03301. 603-798-4542, R/E recording phone-603-798-4541, UCC recording phone-603-798-4542; fax-603-798-3539; hours: 8AM-2PM Mon; 3-9PM Tues; 9AM-4PM Wed.
Real estate records located at Merrimack County. Will search UCC records prior to 7/2001 and current liens only. UCC search per debtor name- $10.00. Copy fee $1.00 per page. **Other phones:** Treasurer- 603-798-4541; Elections- 603-798-4542; Vital Records- 603-798-4542. **Property tax/Assessor-** 603-798-4541.

Lyman Town

Town Clerk, 65 Parker Hill Rd, Lyman, NH 03585. 603-838-6113; fax-603-838-6818; hours: 8-11:30AM Mon; 1-4PM Tues; 9AM-N W&Th; call ahead.
All records in one index. Record index not computerized. Only the office personnel may search. Search fee $10.00 per name. Real estate records located at Grafton County. Will search UCC records pre-2000 and tax liens. Copy fee $1.00 per page. **Other phones:** Treasurer- 603-838-6689. **Property tax/Assessor-** 603-838-5900.

Lyme Town

Town Clerk, PO Box 342, Lyme, NH 03768. 603-795-2535, R/E recording phone-603-795-4639 (Selectmen's office); fax-603-795-4637; hours: 9AM-Noon M,T,F,. www.lymenh.gov
Separate indices to search. Office personnel or visitors may perform searches. Search fee $10.00 per name. Real estate records located at Grafton County. Copy fee $1.00 per page. Payee- Town CLerk-Lyme. **Other phones:** Treasurer- 603-795-4639 (Selectmen's office); Elections- 603-795-2535; Vital Records- 603-795-2535. **Property tax/Assessor-** PO Box 126, Lyme, NH 03768; 603-795-4639 (Selectmen's office).

Lyndeborough Town

Town Clerk, PO Box 164, Lyndeborough, NH 03082. 603-654-9653; fax-603-654-5777; hours: 8AM-1PM, 2-7PM M; 8AM-1PM, 2-3PM W.
Record index not computerized. Office personnel or visitors may perform searches. Search fee $10.00 per name. Real estate records located at Hillsborough County. Copy fee $1.00 per page. Tax lien copy- $.50 per page. Payee- Town of Lyndeborough. **Property tax/Assessor-** 603-654-5955.

Madbury Town

Town Clerk, 13 Town Hall Rd, Madbury, NH 03823. 603-742-5131; fax-603-742-2505; hours: 8AM-1PM M W TH.
All records in one index. Only the office personnel may search. Search fee $10.00 per name. Real estate records located at Strafford County. Copy fee $1.00 per page. **Online access to Property, Deed, Grantor/Grantee records:** Records are free on the Stafford county-wide system at www.nhdeeds.com/stfd/web/agree3.htm. Use the subscription service for full data. **Property tax/Assessor-** same address as above. 603-742-5131.

Madison Town

Town Clerk, PO Box 248, Madison, NH 03849. 603-367-9931, R/E recording phone-603-539-4872, UCC recording phone-603-367-9931; fax-603-367-4547; hours: 8AM-4PM M,T,W,F.
All records in one index. Only the office personnel may search. Real estate records located at Carroll County. Copy fee $1.00 per page. **Other phones:** Treasurer- 603-367-4332; Appraiser/Auditor- 603-367-4332; Elections- 603-367-9931; Vital Records- 603-367-9931. **Property tax/Assessor-** same address as above. 603-367-4332.

Manchester City

City Clerk, One City Hall Plaza, Manchester, NH 03101. 603-624-6455, R/E recording phone-603-624-6520, UCC recording phone-603-624-6455; fax-603-624-6481; hours: 8AM-5PM. www.manchesternh.gov
Separate indices to search include assessor's valuation, agendas & minutes, city charter, ordinances, building code, fire safety standards, housing code, zoning ordinance. Office personnel or visitors may perform searches. Search fee $10.00 per debtor. Copy fee $1.00 per page. Payee- City of Manchester. **Other phones:** Treasurer- 603-624-6460; Elections- 603-624-6455; Vital Records- 603-624-6455. **Property tax/Assessor-** same address as above. 603-624-6520.

Marlborough Town

Town Clerk, PO Box 487, Marlborough, NH 03455-0487. 603-876-4529, R/E recording phone-603-876-3751, UCC recording phone-603-876-4529; fax-603-876-4703; hours: 9AM-4:30PM M,T,TH; 9AM-Noon W; 9AM-2PM Fri. www.marlboroughnh.org
Office personnel or visitors may perform searches. Search fee $10.00 per name. Real estate records located at Cheshire County. Copy fee $1.00 per page. **Other phones:** Treasurer- 603-876-3842; Appraiser/Auditor- 603-876-3751; Elections- 603-876-4529; Vital Records- 603-876-4703. **Property tax/Assessor-** 603-876-3751.

Marlow Town

Tax Collector, PO Box 184, Marlow, NH 03456. 603-446-2245; fax-603-446-3806; hours: Tues evening 5-7PM.
Office personnel or visitors may perform searches. Search fee $10.00 per name. Real estate records located at Cheshire County. Copy fee $1.00 per page. **Other phones:** Treasurer- 603-446-2245; Elections-603-446-2245; Vital Records- 603-446-2245.

Mason Town

Town Clerk, 16 Darling Hill Rd, Mason, NH 03048-4717. 603-878-2070; fax-603-878-4892; hours: 1-4PM T; 9AM-N, 7-9PM TH.
Record index not computerized. Office will perform a UCC search but public must search other records themselves. Real estate records located at Hillsborough County. UCC search per debtor name- $10.00. Copy fee $1.00 per page. **Other phones:** Treasurer- 603-878-2070; Appraiser/Auditor- 603-878-2070; Elections- 603-878-3801; Vital Records- 603-878-2070. **Property tax/Assessor-** 603-878-2070.

Meredith Town

Town Clerk, 41 Main St, Meredith, NH 03253-9704. 603-279-4538; fax-603-279-1042; hours: 8AM-5PM. http://meredithnh.org/
All records in one index. Records indexed. Office personnel or visitors may perform searches. Search fee $10.00. Real estate records located at Belknap County. Copy fee $1.00 per page. Cert fee- $5.00 per doc, plus copy fee. Payee- Town of Meredith.

Merrimack County

Register of Deeds, PO Box 248, Concord, NH 03302-0248. 603-228-0101; fax-603-226-0868; hours: 8AM-

4:30PM.
www.merrimackcounty.nh.us.landata.com
All records in one index. Only the public may search. Copy fee $1.00 per page. Cert fee- $2.00 per doc plus copy fee. Payee- Register of Deeds. **Online access to Real Estate, Grantor/Grantee, Deed, Real Estate records:** Access records on the county Registry of Deeds database for free index, images require subscription at www.merrimackcounty.nh.us.landata.com. Indexes are 1920-present, document images, 1945-present. **Other phones:** Treasurer- 603-228-0331; Vital Records- 603-271-4650 (State).

Merrimack Town

Town Clerk, PO Box 27, Merrimack, NH 03054. 603-424-3651; fax-603-424-0461; hours: 8:30AM-4:30PM. www.ci.merrimack.nh.us
All records in one index. Real estate records located at Hillsborough County. Will search UCC records prior to 7/2001; search includes tax liens if requested. UCC search per debtor name- $10.00. Tax lien search fee- $10.00 per debtor. Separate federal tax lien search- $2.00 per debtor. Separate state tax lien search- $2.00 per debtor. Copy fee $1.00 per page. Payee- Town of Merrimack. **Other phones:** Treasurer- 603-424-3531. **Property tax/Assessor-** 603-424-5136.

Middleton Town

Town Clerk, 182 Kings Highway; Middleton Town Offices, Middleton, NH 03887. 603-473-2134; fax-603-473-2577;
Real estate records located at Strafford County. Will search UCC records prior to 7/2001 and current liens only. UCC search per debtor name- $10.00. Tax lien search fee-$15.00 per debtor. Copy fee $1.00 per page. **Online access to Property, Deed, Grantor/Grantee records:** Records are free on the Stafford county-wide system at www.nhdeeds.com/stfd/web/agree.htm. Use the subscription service for full data. **Other phones:** Treasurer- 603-473-2134; Elections- 603-473-2134; Vital Records- 603-473-2134. **Property tax/Assessor-** 603-473-2261.

Milan Town

Town Clerk, PO Box 158, Milan, NH 03588. 603-449-3461; fax-603-449-2624; hours: 9AM-N, 1-5PM T-Th; Mon.9AM-N;1-4PM, eve 6-8PM.
Record index not computerized. Office personnel or visitors may perform searches. Search fee $10.00 per name. Real estate records located at Coos County. Copy fee $1.00 per page.

Milford Town

Town Clerk, 1 Union Sq, Milford, NH 03055. 603-673-3514, 673-3403, R/E recording phone-603-673-3403, UCC recording phone-603-673-3514; fax-603-673-2273; hours: 8AM-3PM. www.milford.nh.gov
Record index not computerized. Only the office personnel may search. Search fee $10.00 per name. Real estate records located at Hillsborough County. Copy fee $1.00 per page. **Other phones:** Treasurer- 603-672-1061; Elections- 603-673-3514; Vital Records- 603-673-3514. **Property tax/Assessor-** 603-672-0525.

Milton Town

Town Clerk, PO Box 180, Milton, NH 03851-0180. 603-652-9414; fax-603-652-4120; hours: 8AM-12:30PM 1:30PM-4:30PM MTF; 8AM-Noon 2PM-7PM Th. www.miltonnh-us.com
All records in one index. Record index not computerized. Only the office personnel may search. General index search fee $10.00 per name. Real estate records located at Strafford County. Federal/state combined tax lien search- $5.00 per debtor + $1.00 per page. Copy fee $1.00 per page. **Online access to Property, Deed, Grantor/Grantee records:** Records are free on the Stafford county-wide system at www.nhdeeds.com/stfd/web/agree3.htm. Use the subscription service for full data. **Other phones:**

Treasurer- 603-652-4501; Elections- 603-652-9414; Vital Records- 603-652-9414. **Property tax/Assessor-** 603-652-4501.

Monroe Town

Treasurer, PO Box 63, Monroe, NH 03771-0063. 603-638-2644; fax-603-638-2021;
Office personnel or visitors may perform searches. Search fee $10.00 per name. Real estate records located at Grafton County. Copy fee $1.00 per page. **Other phones:** Treasurer- 603-638-2644; Appraiser/Auditor- 603-638-2644; Vital Records- 603-638-2644. **Property tax/Assessor-** 603-638-2644.

Mont Vernon Town

Town Clerk, PO Box 417, Mont Vernon, NH 03057. 603-673-9126; fax-603-672-9021; hours: 5-8PM M & W; 9AM-N T & Th. http://town.mont-vernon.nh.us
Office personnel or visitors may perform searches. Real estate records located at Hillsborough County. Will search UCC records prior to 7/2001 only. Will only search Federal tax liens. UCC search per debtor name- $10.00. Copy fee $1.00 per page. **Other phones:** Treasurer- 603-673-6080; Appraiser/Auditor- 603-673-6080; Elections- 603-673-1776; Vital Records- 603-673-9126; Tax Collector- 603-673-6083; Town Hall Fax -603-673-5995. **Property tax/Assessor-** PO Box 444, Mont Vernon, NH 03057; 603-673-6083.

Moultonborough Town

Town Clerk, PO Box 15, Moultonborough, NH 03254. 603-476-2347; fax-603-476-5835; hours: 9AM-N 1-4PM M W F; 9AM-1PM T.
Separate indices to search. Record index not computerized. Only the office personnel may search. Search fee $10.00-$15.00 per name. Copy fee $1.00 per page. **Online access to Assessor records:** Search town assessor database at http://data.visionappraisal.com/MoultonboroughNH/. Free registration for full data. **Other phones:** Treasurer- 603-476-2347; Appraiser/Auditor- 603-476-2347; Elections- 603-476-2347; Vital Records- 603-476-2347. **Property tax/Assessor-** PO Box 139, Moultonborough, NH 03254; 603-476-2347.

Nashua City

City Clerk, 229 Main St, Nashua, NH 03061-2019. 603-589-3010; fax-603-589-3029; hours: 8AM-5PM.
Office personnel or visitors may perform searches. Search fee $10.00 per name. Real estate records located at Hillsborough County. Copy fee $1.00 per page. Payee- Nashua City Clerk. **Online access to Property Assessor records:** Search the City Assessor database for free at www.ci.nashua.nh.us/defaulto.asp?url=/welcome.asp. **Property tax/Assessor-** 603-594-3040.

Nelson Town

Town Clerk, 7 Nelson Common Rd, Nelson, NH 03457. 603-847-9043, R/E recording phone-603-847-0047, UCC recording phone-603-847-9043; fax-603-847-9043; hours: 9AM-N Tu.; 5-8PM W; 9AM-1PM Th.
Record index not computerized. Office will perform a UCC search but public must search other records themselves. Search fee $10.00. Real estate records located at Cheshire County. Copy fee $1.00 per page. **Other phones:** Treasurer- 603-847-0047; Appraiser/Auditor- 603-847-0047; Elections- 603-847-9043; Vital Records- 603-847-9043. **Property tax/Assessor-** same address as above. 603-847-0047.

New Boston Town

Town Clerk, PO Box 250, New Boston, NH 03070-0250. 603-487-5504 x106; fax-603-487-2975; hours: 9AM-4PM M,W,F; 4PM-8PM TH. http://www2.new-boston.nh.us/Pages/NewBostonNH_Clerk/index
All records in one index. Record index not computerized. Office personnel or visitors may

perform searches. Real estate records located at Hillsborough County. Will search UCC records prior to 7/2001 only. Will not search tax liens. UCC search per debtor name- $10.00. Copy fee $1.00 per page. Payee- Town of New Boston. **Other phones:** Treasurer- 603-487-5504 x104; Appraiser/Auditor- 603-487-5504 x101/102; Elections- 603-487-5504 x106; Vital Records- 603-487-5504 x106. **Property tax/Assessor-** 603-487-5504 x 101/102.

New Castle Town

Town Clerk, PO Box 367, New Castle, NH 03854-0367. 603-431-6710; fax-603-433-6198; hours: 9AM-1PM M W; 12PM-5PM Th.
All records in one index. Records indexed on computer back to 1995. Only the office personnel may search. Search fee $10.00. Real estate records located at Rockingham County. Copy fee $1.00 per page. Tax lien copy- $.25 per page. Cert fee- $12.00 per page plus copy fee. Payee- Town of New Castle. **Other phones:** Treasurer- 603-431-6710; Appraiser/Auditor- 603-431-6710; Elections- 603-431-6710; Vital Records- 603-431-6710. **Property tax/Assessor-** P O Box 981, New Castle, NH 03854; 603-431-6710.

New Durham Town

Town Clerk, PO Box 207, New Durham, NH 03855. 603-859-2091; fax-603-859-6644; hours: 9AM-4PM, M-F.
Separate indices to search include name, last year received. Office personnel or visitors may perform searches. Real estate records located at Strafford County. Will search UCC records prior to 7/2001 and current tax liens. UCC search per debtor name- $10.00. Separate federal tax lien search- $10.00 per debtor. Separate state tax lien search- $10.00 per debtor. Copy fee $1.00 per page. Tax lien copy- $.25 per page. Cert fee- $4.00 per page plus copy fee. Payee- Town of New Durham. **Online access to Property, Deed, Grantor/Grantee records:** Records are free on the Stafford county-wide system at www.nhdeeds.com/stfd/web/agree3.htm. Use the subscription service for full data. Assessor data is at http://data.visionappraisal.com/NewDurhamNH/. Does not require a username & password. Simply click on link. **Property tax/Assessor-** 603-859-2091.

New Hampton Town

Town Clerk/Tax Collector, PO Box 538, New Hampton, NH 03256. 603-744-8454; fax-603-744-5106; hours: 7:30AM-11:45PM/1:15PM-4:15 PM M T W F;1-7:30PM Th. www.new-hampton.nh.us
Record index not computerized. Real estate records located at Belknap County. Will search UCC records prior to 7/2001. Will not search tax liens. UCC search per debtor name- $10.00. Copy fee $1.00 per page. **Other phones:** Elections- 603-744-8454; Vital Records- 603-744-8454.

New Ipswich Town

Town Clerk, 661 Turnpike Rd, New Ipswich, NH 03071. 603-878-3567; fax-603-878-3855; hours: 9AM-4PM M,W,Th; 1-7PM Tues.
Record index not computerized. Office will perform a UCC search but public must search other records themselves. Real estate records located at Hillsborough County. UCC search per debtor name- $10.00. Copy fee $1.00 per page. Cert fee- $10.00 per cert plus copy fee. Payee- Town of New Ipswich. **Other phones:** Treasurer- 603-878-2772; Appraiser/Auditor- 603-878-2772; Elections- 603-878-3567; Vital Records- 603-878-3567; Tax Colletor- 603-878-5068. **Property tax/Assessor-** same address as above. 603-878-2772.

New London Town

Town Clerk, PO Box 314, New London, NH 03257-0314. 603-526-4046; fax-603-526-9494; hours: 8:30AM-4PM.
Only the public may search. Copy fee $1.00 per page. **Online access to Property Appraiser records:** Search the town assessor database at http://data.visionappraisal.com/NEWLONDONNH/.
Other phones: Treasurer- 603-526-4821; Elections- 603-526-4046; Vital Records- 603-526-4046. **Property tax/Assessor-** 603-526-4821.

Newbury Town

Town Clerk, PO Box 253, Newbury, NH 03255. 603-763-5326; fax-603-763-5298; hours: 6PM-9PM M; 8:30AM-3:30PM T-F.
Record index not computerized. Office will perform a UCC search but public must search other records themselves. Real estate records located at Merrimack County. UCC search per debtor name- $10.00. Copy fee $1.00 per page. Payee- Town of Newbury. **Online access to Assessor, Property records:** Access to property assessor data is at http://data.visionappraisal.com/NorthHamptonNH/. Free registration required. **Other phones:** Treasurer- 603-763-4940. **Property tax/Assessor-** 603-763-4940.

Newfields Town

Town Clerk, PO Box 300, Newfields, NH 03856-0300. 603-772-5070; fax-603-772-9004; hours: 8:30AM-2:30PM.
All records in one index. Office personnel or visitors may perform searches. Search fee $10.00 per name. Real estate records located at Rockingham County. Copy fee $1.00 per page. **Other phones:** Treasurer- 603-772-7199; Elections- 603-772-5070; Vital Records- 603-772-5070. **Property tax/Assessor-** 603-772-7047.

Newington Town

Town Clerk, 205 Nimble Hill Rd; Town Offices, Newington, NH 03801. 603-436-7640; fax-603-436-7188; hours: 10AM-3PM T,W,Th. www.newington.nh.us
Office personnel or visitors may perform searches. Real estate records located at Rockingham County. Will search UCC records prior to 7/2001 and current liens only. UCC search per debtor name- $10.00. Copy fee $1.00 per page. **Property tax/Assessor-** 603-436-7640.

Newmarket Town

Town Clerk, 186 Main St; Town Hall, Newmarket, NH 03857. 603-659-3073; fax-603-659-3441; hours: 8AM-4:30PM, till 6PM 1st & last Thursdays. www.visionappraisal.com
Office personnel or visitors may perform searches. Search fee $10.00 per name. Real estate records located at Rockingham County. Copy fee $1.00 per page. **Online access to Assessor, Property records:** Access is via a private company at http://data.visionappraisal.com/NewMarketNH/. Apply for a free registered user ID (more data) or search anonymously (less data, no name searching). **Other phones:** Elections- 603-659-3073; Vital Records- 603-659-3073. **Property tax/Assessor-** 603-659-3073.

Newport Town

Town Clerk, 15 Sunapee St, Newport, NH 03773. 603-863-2224; R/E recording phone-603-863-6407, UCC recording phone-603-863-2224; fax-603-863-8008; hours: 8AM-4:30PM.
Office will perform a UCC search but public must search other records themselves. Real estate records located at Sullivan County. UCC search per debtor name- $10.00. Copy fee $1.00 per page. **Other phones:** Treasurer- 603-863-3000; Appraiser/Auditor- 603-863-6407; Elections- 603-863-2224; Vital Records- 603-863-2224. **Property tax/Assessor-** 603-863-6407.

Newton Town

Tax Collector, Box 375, Newton, NH 03858-0375. 603-382-4096; fax-603-382-2596; hours: 8AM-4PM M-W.
All records in one index. Office personnel or visitors may perform searches. Real estate records located at Rockingham County. Will search UCC records prior to 7/2001 and current liens only. Tax liens not included in UCC search. UCC search per debtor name- $15.00. Tax lien search fee- $20.00 per parcel. Separate federal tax lien search- $15.00 per debtor. Separate state tax lien search- $15.00. Federal/state combined tax lien search- $35.00 per parcel. Copy fee $1.00 per page. Cert fee- $2.00 per parcel includes copy fee. Payee- Town of Newton. **Other phones:** Treasurer- 603-382-4405; Appraiser/Auditor- 603-382-4405; Elections- 603-382-4096; Vital Records- 603-382-4096. **Property tax/Assessor-** Town Hall Rd, Newton, NH 03858; 603-382-4405.

North Hampton Town

Town Clerk, PO Box 141, North Hampton, NH 03862-0141. 603-964-6029, R/E recording phone-603-964-8087, UCC recording phone-603-964-6029; fax-603-964-2906; hours: 8:30AM-2PM. www.northhampton-nh.gov
Separate indices to search. Real estate records located at Rockingham County. Will not search UCC records or tax liens. Copy fee $1.00 per page. **Online access to Assessor, Property records:** Access to property assessor data is at http://data.visionappraisal.com/NorthHamptonNH/. Does not require a username & password. Simply click on link. **Other phones:** Treasurer- 603-964-8087; Appraiser/Auditor- 603-964-8087; Elections- 603-964-6029; Vital Records- 603-964-6029. **Property tax/Assessor-** 603-964-8087.

Northfield Town

Town Clerk, 21 Summer St, Northfield, NH 03276. 603-286-4482; fax-603-286-3328; hours: 8:30AM-5PM, Closed Tues.
Only the public may search. Real estate records located at Merrimack County. Copy fee $1.00 per page. Payee- Northfield Town Clerk. **Other phones:** Elections- 603-286-4482; Vital Records- 603-286-4482. **Property tax/Assessor-** 603-286-7039.

Northumberland Town

Town Clerk, 3 State St, Groveton, NH 03582. 603-636-1451; fax-603-636-6098; hours: 8:30AM-4PM.
All records in one index. General index search fee $12.00. UCC search per debtor name- $10.00. Copy fee $1.00 per page. Tax lien copy- $.35 per page. **Other phones:** Appraiser/Auditor- 603-636-1450; Elections- 603-636-1450; Vital Records- 603-636-1450. **Property tax/Assessor-** 603-636-1450.

Northwood Town

Town Clerk, 818 First NH Turnpike, Northwood, NH 03261-0314. 603-942-5586 X201; fax-603-942-9107; hours: 8AM-10AM 11AM-7PM M; 9AM-2PM T F; 9AM-4:30PM TH. www.town.northwood.nh.us
All records in one index. Record index not computerized. Office personnel or visitors may perform searches. General index search fee $10.00 per search. Copy fee $1.00 per page. Cert fee- $12.00 1st copy plus, 1 copy included in copy fee. Payee- Town of Northwood. **Other phones:** Treasurer- 603-942-5586 x211; Appraiser/Auditor- 603-942-5586 x207; Elections- 603-942-5586 x201; Vital Records- 603-942-5586 x201. **Property tax/Assessor-** same address as above. 603-942-5586 x207.

Nottingham Town

Town Clerk, PO Box 114, Nottingham, NH 03290. 603-679-9598, R/E recording phone-603-679-1630, UCC recording phone-603-679-9598; fax-603-679-9598; hours: 4-8PM M,W; 1-5PM T; 9AM-1PM Th,Sat.
Office personnel or visitors may perform searches. Search fee $10.00 per name. Real estate records located at Rockingham County. Copy fee $1.00 per page. Payee- Nottingham Town Clerk. **Other phones:** Elections- 603-679-9598; Vital Records- 603-679-9598; Tax Collector- 603-679-1630. **Property tax/Assessor-** 603-679-5022.

Orford Town

Town Clerk, 59 Archertown Rd.; Clerk's Office, Orford, NH 03777. 603-353-4404; fax-603-353-4889; hours: 2-7PM T; 6-8PM W; 8-11AM Th.
All records in one index. Real estate records located at Grafton County. Will not search UCC records, but will search tax liens. Separate federal tax lien search-$7.00 per debtor. Separate state tax lien search-$7.00 per debtor. Copy fee $1.00 per page. Payee-Town of Orford. **Other phones:** Treasurer- 603-353-4889; Appraiser/Auditor- 603-353-4889; Elections- 603-353-4404; Vital Records- 603-353-4404. **Property tax/Assessor-** PO Box F, Orford, NH 03777; 603-353-4889.

Ossipee Town

Town Clerk, PO Box 67, Center Ossipee, NH 03814. 603-539-2008, R/E recording phone-603-539-4872, UCC recording phone-603-539-2008; fax-603-539-4183; hours: 8:30AM-4:30PM.
Record index not computerized. Office will perform a UCC search but public must search other records themselves. Search fee $15.00. Real estate records located at Carroll County. Copy fee $1.00 per page. Cert fee- $4.00 per page plus copy fee. **Other phones:** Treasurer- 603-539-4181; Elections- 603-539-2008; Vital Records- 603-539-2008. **Property tax/Assessor-** same address as above. 603-539-4181.

Pelham Town

Town Clerk, 6 Village Green, Pelham, NH 03076. 603-635-2040; fax-603-508-3096; hours: 8AM-4PM M,W,Th,F; 8AM-7PM Tu.
Only the office personnel may search. Search fee $10.00 per name. Real estate records located at Hillsborough County Copy fee $1.00 per page. **Online access to Assessor records:** Search town assessor database at http://data.visionappraisal.com/PelhamNH/. Free registration for full data. **Other phones:** Treasurer-603-635-8233; Appraiser/Auditor- 603-635-3317; Elections- 603-635-2040; Vital Records- 603-635-2040. **Property tax/Assessor-** same address as above. 603-635-3317.

Pembroke Town

Town Clerk, 311 Pembroke St, Pembroke, NH 03275. 603-485-4747; fax-603-485-3967; hours: 8-4PM, Th 5PM-8PM.
Record index not computerized. Office personnel or visitors may perform searches. Search fee $10.00 per name. Real estate records located at Merrimack County. Copy fee $1.00 per page. Payee-Pembroke Town Clerk. **Online access to Assessor records:** Access assessor data at http://data.visionappraisal.com/PembrokeNH/. **Property tax/Assessor-** 603-485-4747.

Peterborough Town

Tax Collector, 1 Grove St, Peterborough, NH 03458. 603-924-8010, R/E recording phone-603-924-8000 x103, UCC recording phone-603-924-8000 x105; fax-603-924-8001; hours: 8AM-4:30 M-F; 5-7PM Th. www.townofpeterborough.com
Countywide records can be searched at www.nhdeeds.com. Only the public may search. Copy fee $1.00 per page. **Other phones:** Treasurer-603-924-8000 x103; Elections- 603-924-8000 x105; Vital Records- 603-924-8000 x105. **Property tax/Assessor-** 603-924-8000 x101.

Piermont Town

Town Clerk, PO Box 27, Piermont, NH 03779. 603-272-4840; fax-603-272-4947; hours: 1-7PM Tu,W.
All records in one index. Office personnel will search UCC records or visitors perform searches for other records. Real estate records located at Grafton County. Will search UCC records prior to 7/2001. Will not search tax liens. UCC search per debtor name- $10.00. Copy fee $1.00 per page. Cert fee- $5.00 per name includes copy fee. Payee-

Town Clerk. **Property tax/Assessor-** PO Box 27, Piermont, NH 03779; not known.

Pittsburg Town

Town Clerk, 1526 Main St, Pittsburg, NH 03592. 603-538-6699, R/E recording phone-603-538-6697, UCC recording phone-603-538-6699; fax-603-538-6697; hours: N-6PM,T,8AM-2PM, W, N-4PM. Th.
All records in one index. Record index not computerized. Only the office personnel may search. Search fee $10.00. Real estate records located at Coos County. Copy fee $1.00 per page. Cert fee- $10.00 per doc plus copy fee. Payee- Town of Pittsburg. **Other phones:** Treasurer- 603-538-6697; Elections- 603-538-6699; Vital Records- 603-538-6674; Tax Collector- 603-538-6694. **Property tax/Assessor-** same address as above. 603-538-6697.

Pittsfield Town

Town Clerk, Box 98, Pittsfield, NH 03263-0098. 603-435-6773; fax-603-435-7922; hours: 8AM-6PM M; 8AM-2:30PM T; 8AM-1PM W TH; 2PM-5PM F. www.pittsfield-nh.com
Separate indices to search include UCC, federal tax liens, state tax liens. Only the office personnel may search. Search fee $10.00 per name. Real estate records located at Merrimack County. General copy fee $1.00 per page. Tax lien copy- $.75 per page. Cert fee- $12.00 per cert plus copy fee. **Other phones:** Treasurer- 603-435-6773 or 6774; Appraiser/Auditor- 603-435-6773 or 6774; Elections-603-435-6773 or 6774; Vital Records- 603-435-6773 or 6774. **Property tax/Assessor-** same address as above. 603-435-6773 or 6774.

Plainfield Town

Town Clerk, Box 380 Town Clerk's Office, Meriden, NH 03770. 603-469-3201; fax-603-469-3642; hours: 8AM-4PM M-Th, closed F. www.plainfieldnh.org
Record index not computerized. Office personnel or visitors may perform searches. Search fee $10.00. Real estate records located at Sullivan County. Copy fee $1.00 per filing. Cert fee- $12.00 per page plus copy fee. Payee- Town of Plainfield. **Other phones:** Elections- 603-469-3201; Vital Records- 603-469-3201. **Property tax/Assessor-** same address as above. 603-469-3201.

Plaistow Town

Town Clerk, 145 Main St; Town Hall, #2, Plaistow, NH 03865. 603-382-8129; fax-603-382-7183; hours: 8:30AM-7PM   M,   8:30AM-4:30PM   T-F. www.plaistow.com
All records in one index. Search fee $10.00. Real estate records located at Rockingham County. Copy fee $1.00 per page. **Other phones:** Treasurer- 603-382-8469; Vital Records- 603-382-8129 x16. **Property tax/Assessor-** 603-382-8469.

Plymouth Town

Town Clerk, 6 PO Sq; Town Hall, Plymouth, NH 03264. 603-536-1732; fax-603-536-0036; hours: 8:30AM-4PM.
Office personnel or visitors may perform searches. Search fee $10.00 per name. Real estate records located at Grafton County. Copy fee $.50 per page. Cert fee- None. Payee- Plymouth Town Clerk. **Property tax/Assessor-** 603-536-1731.

Portsmouth City

City Clerk, 1 Junkins Ave, Portsmouth, NH 03801. 603-431-7207, R/E recording phone-603-431-2000, UCC recording phone-603-610-7207; fax-603-427-1526; hours: 8:30AM-5PM. www.cityofportsmouth.com/cityclerk/index.htm
Separate indices to search. Tax lien records only indexed on computer. Office personnel or visitors may perform searches. Search fee $10.00 per name. Real estate records located at Rockingham County. Copy fee $1.00 per page. Cert fee- $5.00 per seal plus $.50 per page copy fee. **Online access to Property Assessor records:** Records on the

Portsmouth Assessed Property Values database are free at www.portsmouthnh.com/realestate/index.cfm. **Other phones:** Treasurer- 603-610-7223; Appraiser/Auditor-603-610-7227; Elections- 603-610-7207; Vital Records- 603-610-7245; Tax Collector- 603-610-7244. **Property tax/Assessor-** same address as above. 603-610-7212.

Randolph Town

Town Hall, 130 Durand Rd, Randolph, NH 03593. 603-466-5771; fax-603-466-9856; hours: 9-11AM M; 7-9PM W.
Records indexed is not computerized. Real estate records located at Coos County. Will search UCC records prior to 7/2001 only. Will not search tax liens. UCC search per debtor name- $5.00. Copy fee $.75 per page. Cert fee- $4.00 per page plus copy fee. Payee- Town of Randolph-Town Clerk. **Other phones:** Treasurer- 603-466-5771; Elections- 603-466-5771; Vital Records- 603-466-5771. **Property tax/Assessor-** same address as above. not known.

Raymond Town

Town Clerk, Epping St; Town Office Bldg, Raymond, NH 03077. 603-895-4735 X110, R/E recording phone-603-895-4735; fax-603-895-0903; hours: 8AM-7PM M; 8AM-4:30PM T-F.
All records in one index. Only the office personnel may search. Real estate records located at Rockingham County. Will search UCC records prior to 7/2001 and current liens only. UCC search per debtor name- $10.00. Separate federal tax lien search- $5.00 per search. Federal/state combined tax lien search-$5.00 per search. Copy fee $1.00 per page. **Online access to Property Assessor records:** Search the town assessor database at http://data.visionappraisal.com/RaymondNH. Free registration is required to view full data. **Other phones:** Treasurer- 603-895-4735; Elections- 603-895-4735; Vital Records- 603-895-4735. **Property tax/Assessor-** 603-895-4735.

Richmond Town

Town Clerk, 105 Old Homestead Hwy, Richmond, NH 03470. 603-239-6202; fax-603-239-6202; hours: 9AM-N, 1-4PM, 6-8PM M; 9AM-N T,Th; 9AM-N, 1-4 W.
Office will perform a UCC search but public must search other records themselves. UCC search per debtor name- $10.00. Copy fee $1.00 per page. Payee- Town of Richmond. **Other phones:** Elections- 603-239-6202; Vital Records- 603-239-6202. **Property tax/Assessor-** 603-239-4232.

Rindge Town

Town Clerk, PO Box 11, Rindge, NH 03461. 603-899-5181 x107, R/E recording phone-603-899-5181 x108, UCC recording phone-603-899-5181 x107; fax-603-899-2101; hours: 9AM-1PM M-Th; 6-8PM Th Eve; 9AM-1PM F. www.town.rindge.nh.us
See Town Tax Collector for property tax liens. All records in one index. Record index not computerized. Only the office personnel may search. Search fee $10.00 per name. Copy fee $1.00 per page. Cert fee- $10.00 per cert includes copy fee. Payee- Town of Rindge. **Online access to Assessor records:** Search town assessor database at http://data.visionappraisal.com/RindgeNH/. Does not require a username & password. Simply click on link. **Other phones:** Treasurer- 603-899-5181 x103; Elections- 603-899-5539; Vital Records- 603-899-5181 x107. **Property tax/Assessor-** PO Box 163, Rindge, NH 03461; 603-899-5181 x102.

Rochester City

City Clerk, 31 Wakefield St; City Hall, Rochester, NH 03867-1917. 603-332-2130; fax-603-335-7565; hours: 8AM-5PM. www.rochesternh.net
Separate indices to search include UCCs and state/federal tax liens. Records no computerized. Office personnel or visitors may perform searches. Search fee $10.00 per name. Real estate records located at Strafford County. UCC record search

includes tax liens. Copy fee $1.00 per page. Cert fee- $4.00 per cert includes copy fee. Payee- City of Rochester. **Online access to Property, Deed, Grantor/Grantee, Assessor records:** Records are free on the Stafford county-wide system at www.nhdeeds.com/stfd/web/agree3.htm. Use the subscription service for full data. Also, access property data free at http://rochesternh.patriotproperties.com/default.asp. **Other phones:** Treasurer- 603-335-7502; Appraiser/Auditor- 603-332-5109; Elections- 603-332-2130; Vital Records- 603-332-2130. **Property tax/Assessor-** 19 Wakefield St, Rochester, NH 03867; 603-332-5109.

Rockingham County

Register of Deeds, PO Box 896, Kingston, NH 03848. 603-642-5526; fax-603-642-8548; hours: 8AM-4PM. For Assessor data, you must contact the Tax Assessor for each town within the county. Only the public may search. Copy fee $1.00 per page. Cert fee- $1.00 per page, plus $1.00 to certify. Payee- Rockingham County Recorder of Deeds. **Online access to Real Estate, Most Wanted, Inmate records:** Access to the register of deeds database is free at www.nhdeeds.com/rock/web/start.htm. Index goes back to 1980. Also, search inmate info on private company website at www.vinelink.com/index.jsp.

Rollinsford Town

Town Clerk, PO Box 309, Rollinsford, NH 03869. 603-742-2510; fax-603-740-0254; hours: 9AM-1PM M,T,W,F; 3-7PM Th. All records in one index. Office personnel or visitors may perform searches. Real estate records located at Strafford County. Will search UCC records prior to 7/2001 and current liens only. Tax liens not included in UCC search. UCC search per debtor name- $10.00. Separate federal tax lien search- $10.00 per debtor. Copy fee $1.00 per page. **Online access to Property, Deed, Grantor/Grantee records:** Records are free on the Stafford county-wide system at www.nhdeeds.com/stfd/web/agree3.htm. Use the subscription service for full data.

Roxbury Town

Town Clerk, 404 Branch Rd, Roxbury, NH 03431. 603-352-4903; hours: 7PM-8PM M. All records in one index. Record index not computerized. Only the office personnel may search. Search fee $10.00 per name. Real estate records located at Cheshire County. Copy fee $1.00 per page. Payee- Town of Roxbury.

Rumney Town

Town Clerk, PO Box 275, Rumney, NH 03266. 603-786-2237; fax-603-786-2237; hours: 4PM-8PM, M; 9AM-2PM, T, W, TH, F. All records in one index. Search fee $5.00 per name. Real estate records located at Grafton County. Copy fee $.75; tax lien $.50 per page. Cert fee- $12.00 per name includes copies. Payee- Town of Rumney. **Other phones:** Treasurer- 603-786-9511; Appraiser/Auditor- 603-786-9511; Elections- 603-786-2237; Vital Records- 603-786-2237. **Property tax/Assessor-** PO Box 220, 79 Depot St, Rumney, NH 03266; 603-786-9511.

Rye Town

Town Clerk, 10 Central Rd, Rye, NH 03870. 603-964-8562; fax-603-964-4132; hours: 8AM-4:30PM. Real estate records located at Rockingham County. Will search UCC records prior to 7/2001 and current liens only. UCC search per debtor name- $10.00. Copy fee $1.00 per page. **Online access to Property Assessor records:** Access is via a private company at http://data.visionappraisal.com/RyeNH. Free registration is required to view full data. **Other phones:** Elections- 603-964-8562; Vital Records- 603-964-8562. **Property tax/Assessor-** 10 Central Rd, Rye, NH 03870; 603-964-5523.

Salem Town

Town Clerk, 33 Geremonty Drive; Municipal Bldg, Salem, NH 03079-3390. 603-890-2110; fax-603-898-1223; hours: 8:30AM-5PM. www.ci.salem.nh.us All records in one index. Record index not computerized. Office personnel or visitors may perform searches. Search fee $10.00. Real estate records located at Rockingham County. Copy fee $2.00 per page. Cert fee- $4.00 per cert plus copy fee. Payee- Town of Salem. **Online access to Property Assessor records:** Records from the town database are free at http://data.visionappraisal.com/SalemNH/. Free registration for full data. **Other phones:** Treasurer- 603-890-2045; Elections- 603-890-2116; Vital Records- 603-890-2116. **Property tax/Assessor-** same address as above. 603-890-2018.

Salisbury Town

Town Clerk, Box 180, Salisbury, NH 03268-0180. 603-648-2473; fax-603-648-6658; hours: 8:30AM-N, 4:30-8:30PM T; 1PM-4PM W. No computerized index. Only the public may search. Real estate records located at Merrimack County. Copy fee $1.00 per page. Cert fee- $1.00 per page plus copy fee. Payee- Town Clerk. **Other phones:** Treasurer- 603-648-2473; Appraiser/Auditor- 603-648-2473; Elections- 603-648-2473; Vital Records- 603-648-2473. **Property tax/Assessor-** 603-648-2473.

Sanbornton Town

Town Clerk, PO Box 124, Sanbornton, NH 03269. 603-286-4034; fax-603-286-9544; hours: 8AM-7:30 M; 8AM-4PM T TH; 8AM-Noon W; 8AM-4PM F. Office personnel or visitors may perform searches. Search fee $10.00 per name. Real estate records located at Belknap County. Copy fee $1.00 per page. **Online access to Assessor, Property records:** Access to assessor property data is at http://data.visionappraisal.com/SanborntonNH/. Free registration for full data. **Property tax/Assessor-** 603-286-8303.

Sandown Town

Town Clerk, 320 Main St; Town Hall, PO Box 583, Sandown, NH 03873-2627. 603-887-4870, R/E recording phone-603-887-3646, UCC recording phone-603-887-4870; fax-603-887-5163; hours: M 8-12PM/2-8PM; T-Th 8-12PM/12:30-3PM; F 8-12PM. www.sandown.us Office personnel or visitors may perform searches. Search fee $15.00 per name. Real estate records located at Rockingham County. Will search UCC records prior to 7/2001 and current liens only. UCC search per debtor name- $10.00. Copy fee $1.00 per page. Cert fee- None. **Other phones:** Treasurer- 603-887-3646; Elections- 603-887-4870; Vital Records- 603-887-4870. **Property tax/Assessor-** 603-887-3646.

Sandwich Town

Town Clerk, PO Box 194, Center Sandwich, NH 03227. 603-284-7113; fax-603-284-6819; hours: Mon. evenings 7-9PM. All records in one index. Record index not computerized. Only the office personnel may search. Search fee $10.00. Real estate records located at Carroll County. General copy fee $1.00 per page. Tax lien copy- $2.00 per page. **Property tax/Assessor-** same address as above. 603-284-7701.

Seabrook Town

Town Clerk, PO Box 476, Seabrook, NH 03874. 603-474-3152, R/E recording phone-603-474-9881, UCC recording phone-603-474-3152; fax-603-474-8007; hours: 9AM-4PM. Property records are online at the county website. All records in one index. Office will perform a UCC search, records prior to 7/2001, but public must search other records themselves. Search fee $15.00

per name. Real estate records located at Rockingham County. Federal/state combined tax lien search- $10.00 per debtor. Copy fee $1.00 per page. Cert fee- $1.00 per page plus copy fee. Payee- Town of Seabrook. **Other phones:** Treasurer- 603-474-8027; Appraiser/Auditor- 603-474-2966; Elections- 603-474-3152; Vital Records- 603-474-3152. **Property tax/Assessor-** same address as above. 603-474-2966.

Sharon Town

Town Clerk, 432 Route 123, Sharon, NH 03458. 603-924-9250; fax-603-924-9250; hours: 6-8PM T. Record index not computerized. Office will perform a UCC search but public must search other records themselves. Real estate records located at Hillsborough County. UCC search per debtor name- $10.00. Copy fee $1.00 per page. Payee- Town of Sharon. **Property tax/Assessor-** 603-924-9250.

Shelburne Town

Town Clerk, 881 N. Rd; Philbrook Farm Inn, Shelburne, NH 03581. 603-466-3831; hours: by appointment. Office will perform a UCC search but public must search other records themselves. Real estate records located at Coos County. UCC search per debtor name- $10.00. Copy fee $1.00 per page. Payee- Town of Shelburne. **Online access to Maps, records:** Access town district maps for free go to www.shelburnenh.com/TR04/TOC.html. **Property tax/Assessor-** 603-466-3926.

Somersworth City

City Clerk, 1 Government Way, Somersworth, NH 03878-9574. 603-692-4262; fax-603-692-9574; hours: 9AM-5PM M,W,F; 8AM-5PM T,Th. All records in one index. Search fee $10.00 per name. Copy fee $1.00 per page. **Online access to Property, Deed, Grantor/Grantee records:** Records are free on the Stafford county-wide system at www.nhdeeds.com/stfd/web/agree3.htm. Use the subscription service for full data. **Other phones:** Vital Records- 603-692-9511. **Property tax/Assessor-** same address as above. 603-692-9520/9518.

South Hampton Town

Town Clerk, 3 Hilldale Ave, South Hampton, NH 03827. 603-394-7696; fax-603-394-7696; hours: 7-8:30PM M,T; 12:30-2PM W; 9:30-11:30AM F. Office will perform a UCC search but public must search other records themselves. Real estate records located at Rockingham County. UCC search per debtor name- $10.00. Copy fee $1.00 per page. Tax lien copy- $.50 per page. Payee- Town of South Hampton.

Springfield Town

Town Clerk, PO Box 22, Springfield, NH 03284. 603-763-4805; fax-603-763-3336; hours: 9AM-N 1-4PM M-W; till 8PM Th; closed Fri. All records in one index. Record index not computerized. Only the office personnel may search. Real estate records located at Sullivan County. UCC search per debtor name- $10.00. Separate federal tax lien search- $10.00 per debtor. Copy fee $1.00 per page. Cert fee- $10.00 per doc plus copy fee. Payee- Springfield Town Clerk. **Property tax/Assessor-** 603-763-4805.

Stark Town

Town Clerk, 1189 Stark Hwy, Stark, NH 03582. 603-636-2118; fax-603-636-6199; hours: 10AM-4PM T,Th. Record index not computerized. Real estate records located at Coos County. General copy fee $1.00 per page. Tax lien copy- $.25 per copy. Payee- Town of Stark. **Other phones:** Treasurer- 603-636-2118; Appraiser/Auditor- 603-636-2118; Elections- 603-636-2118; Vital Records- 603-636-2118. **Property tax/Assessor-** same address as above. 603-636-2118.

Stewartstown Town

Town Clerk, PO Box 119, West Stewartstown, NH 03597-0035. 603-246-3329; fax-603-246-3329; hours: 9:30AM-2PM Tu.; 9AM-4PM M,W, F.
All records in one index. Record index not computerized. Office will perform a UCC search but public must search other records themselves. Real estate records located at Coos County. Copy fee $1.00 per page. Cert fee- $12.00 per page plus copy fee. Payee- Town of Stewartstown. **Property tax/Assessor**- 603-246-3329.

Stoddard Town

Town Clerk, 2175 Route 9, Stoddard, NH 03464. 603-446-2203, R/E recording phone-603-446-3487, UCC recording phone-603-446-2203; fax-603-446-2203; hours: 9AM-2PM 4PM-6PM T TH.
Separate indices to search include recordings, vital statistics. Record index not computerized. Only the office personnel may search. Real estate records located at Cheshire County. Will search UCC records prior to 7/2001 only. Will not search tax liens. UCC search per debtor name- $5.00. Copy fee $1.00 per page. Cert fee- $15.00 per filing includes copy fee. Payee- Town of Stoddard. **Other phones:** Treasurer-603-446-3442; Appraiser/Auditor- 603-446-3326; Elections- 603-446-3326; Vital Records- 603-446-2203. **Property tax/Assessor**- 1450 Route 123 North, Stoddard, NH 03464; 603-446-3326.

Strafford County

Register of Deeds, PO Box 799, Dover, NH 03820. 603-742-1741; fax-603-749-5130;
Office personnel or visitors may perform searches. Search fee $10.00 per name. Will not search real estate records. Copy fee $1.00 per page. **Online access to Real Estate, Deed, Mortgage, Lien, Grantor/Grantee records:** Access to county register of deeds data is free at www.nhdeeds.com/stfd/web/agree3.htm. Online records go back to 1970. **Other phones:** Treasurer-603-742-1458. **Property tax/Assessor**- 603-743-6014.

Strafford Town

Town Clerk, PO Box 169, Strafford, NH 03884-0169. 603-664-2192; fax-603-664-7276; hours: 9AM-1PM, 4-7PM Mon; 9AM-2:30 Tu-Wed.; 9AM-N Th.
All records in one index. Office will perform a UCC or Tax lien search but public must search other records themselves. Search fee $10.00 per name. Real estate records located at Strafford County. Copy fee $1.00 per page. **Online access to Property, Deed, Grantor/Grantee records:** Records are free on the Stafford county-wide system at www.nhdeeds.com/stfd/web/agree3.htm. Use the subscription service for full data.

Stratford Town

Town Clerk, PO Box 366, North Stratford, NH 03590. 603-922-5598; fax-603-922-3317; hours: 9AM-N 4PM-7PM, M; 9AM-N, 4PM-7PM, W.
Records indexed on computer. Only the office personnel may search. Search fee $15.00 per name. Copy fee $.50 per page.

Stratham Town

Town Clerk, 10 Bunker Hill Ave, Stratham, NH 03885. 603-772-4741; fax-603-775-0517; hours: 8:30AM-4PM. www.strathamnh.org
Office will perform a UCC search but public must search other records themselves. Real estate records located at Rockingham County. UCC search per debtor name- $10.00. Copy fee $1.00 per page. **Property tax/Assessor**- 603-772-4741.

Sugar Hill Town

Town Clerk, Box 574, Sugar Hill, NH 03585. 603-823-8516; fax-603-823-8446; hours: 4PM-6PM M; 9AM-1PM T TH.
Only the public may search. Real estate records located at Grafton County. Copy fee $1.00 per page.

Sullivan County

Register of Deeds, PO Box 448, Newport, NH 03773. 603-863-2110; fax-603-863-0013; hours: 8AM-4PM.
This office will not research records for any reason. Records go back to 1827. In NH each town has their own Assessors, tax collectors, etc. If you want tax information you must call the town in which the property is located. Separate indices to search include Grantor/Grantee, Plan index. Only the public may search. Copy fee $1.00. per page. Cert fee- $2.00 per doc plus copy fee. Payee- Register of Deeds. **Online access to Real Estate, Grantor/Grantee, Deed records:** Access to the county Register of Deeds database is free at www.nhdeeds.com/slvn/web/agree7.htm.

Sullivan Town

Town Clerk, 522 South Rd, Sullivan, NH 03445. 603-352-1495, R/E recording phone-603-352-0403; hours: 8AM-9AM.
Office will perform a UCC search but public must search other records themselves. Real estate records located at Cheshire County. Copy fee $1.00 per page. Payee- Lois Woodbury, Town Clerk. **Other phones:** Treasurer- 603-847-2340. **Property tax/Assessor**- PO Box 110, Sullivan, NH 03445; 603-847-9720.

Sunapee Town

Town Clerk, PO Box 303, Sunapee, NH 03782-0303. 603-763-2449; fax-603-763-4608; hours: 9AM-5PM M,T,Th,F; 9AM-1PM W.
Office will perform a UCC search but public must search other records themselves. Real estate records located at Sullivan County. UCC search per debtor name- $25.00. Copy fee $1.00 per page. Payee- Town of Sunapee. **Online access to Assessor records:** Search town assessor database at http://data.visionappraisal.com/SunapeeNH/. Free registration for full data. **Other phones:** Vital Records-603-763-2212. **Property Assessor**- 603-763-2212.

Surry Town

Tax Collector, 1 Village Rd, Surry, NH 03431. 603-352-3075; fax-603-357-4890; Record index not computerized. Only the office personnel may search. Search fee $10.00. Real estate records located at Cheshire County. Copy fee $1.00 per page.

Sutton Town

Town Clerk, PO Box 487, North Sutton, NH 03260-0487. 603-927-4575; fax-603-927-4631; hours: N-6PM M; 8AM-12:30PM T; 8AM-4PM W-Th; 9AM-N last S. www.sutton-nh.gov
All records in one index. Record index not computerized. Only the office personnel may search. Real estate records located at Merrimack County. Copy fee $1.00 per page. Cert fee- $1.00 per page plus copy fee. **Property tax/Assessor**- 603-927-4416.

Swanzey Town

Town Clerk, PO Box 10009, Swanzey, NH 03446. 603-352-7411; fax-603-352-6250; hours: 9AM-5PM.
All records in one index. Record index not computerized. Only the office personnel may search. Search fee $10.00. Real estate records located at Cheshire County. Copy fee $1.00 per page. **Online access to Assessor records:** Access assessor data at http://data.visionappraisal.com/SwanzeyNH/. Free registration for full data. **Assessor**- 603-352-7411.

Tamworth Town

Town Clerk, PO Box 279, Tamworth, NH 03886. 603-323-7971; fax-603-323-2347; hours: 8AM-N, 1-4:30PM T-F.
Office personnel or visitors may perform searches. Search fee $15.00 per name. Real estate records located at Carroll County. Copy fee $1.00 per page. Payee- Town of Tamworth. **Property tax/Assessor**- PO Box 359, Tamworth, NH 03886; 603-323-7525.

Temple Town

Town Clerk, Box 69, Temple, NH 03084. 603-878-3873; fax-603-878-5067; 9AM-2PM- T,W,Th.
Record index not computerized. Only the public may search. Real estate records located at Hillsborough County. Copy fee $1.00 per page. **Other phones:** Treasurer- 603-878-3873; Elections-603-878-3873; Vital Records- 603-878-3873. **Property tax/Assessor**- PO Box 981, Epsom, NH 03234 603-878-2536.

Thornton Town

Town Clerk, 16 Merrill Access Rd, Thornton, NH 03223. 603-726-4232; fax-603-726-2078;
Only the public may search. Copy fee $1.00 per page. **Other phones:** Treasurer- 603-764-9450. **Property tax/Assessor**- 603-726-3223.

Tilton Town

Town Clerk, 257 Main St, Tilton, NH 03276-1207. 603-286-4425; fax-603-286-3519; hours: 8:30AM-4:15PM. www.tiltonnh.org
Record index not computerized. Real estate records located at Belknap County. UCC search per debtor name- $10.00. Copy fee $1.00 per page. **Other phones:** Treasurer- 603-286-4521; Appraiser/Auditor-603-286-4521; Elections- 603-286-4425; Vital Records- 603-286-4425; Land Use- 603-286-7817. **Property tax/Assessor**- 603-286-4521.

Troy Town

Town Clerk, PO Box 249, Troy, NH 03465-0249. 603-242-3845; fax-603-242-3430; hours: 9AM-4:30PM M-W; 1-7PM Th; 9AM-1:30PM Fri. www.town.troy.nh.us
Only the public may search. Real estate records located at Cheshire County. Copy fee $1.00 per page. Payee- Town of Troy. **Other phones:** Vital Records-603-242-3845. **Property tax/Assessor**- PO Box 249, Troy, NH 03465-0249; 603-242-7722.

Tuftonboro Town

Town Clerk, PO Box 98, Center Tuftonboro, NH 03816. 603-569-4539; fax-603-569-4328; hours: 9AM-4PM,M,T,W,F; 9AM-N Th. www.tuftonboro.org
Record index not computerized. Real estate records located at Carroll County. Will search UCC records prior to 7/2001 and current liens only. UCC search per debtor name- $10.00. Separate federal tax lien search-no charge. Copy fee $1.00 per page. Cert fee- $5.00. Payee- Tuftonboro Town Clerk. **Property tax/Assessor**- same address as above. 603-569-4539.

Unity Town

Town Clerk, 13 Center Rd, Unity, NH 03603. 603-542-9665; fax-603-542-9736; hours: M & T 9AM-5PM; Wed 9AM-6PM; Th 8AM-N.
Office personnel or visitors may perform searches. Search fee $10.00 per name. Real estate records located at Sullivan County. Copy fee $1.00 per page. Cert fee- $15.00 per page. **Other phones:** Treasurer-603-542-9665; Elections- 603-542-9665; Vital Records- 603-542-9665. **Property tax/Assessor**- 603-542-9665.

Wakefield Town

Town Clerk, 2 High St, Sanbornville, NH 03872. 603-522-6205 x306, R/E recording phone-603-539-4872; fax-603-522-6794; hours: 8:30-4-T TH F,8:30-12-W,8:30-1:30-SAT. www.wakefieldnh.com
No real estate recordings or UCC recordings. Search fee $10.00 per debtor. Real estate records located at Carroll County. Will search UCC records prior to 7/2001 and current tax liens. Copy fee $1.00 per page. **Other phones:** Treasurer- 603-522-6205; Appraiser/Auditor- 603-522-6205 x300; Elections- 603-522-6205 x306; Vital Records- 603-522-6205 x306. **Property tax/Assessor**- 2 High St, Sanbornville, NH 03072; 603-522-6205 x300.

Walpole Town

Town Clerk, PO Box 756, Walpole, NH 03608. 603-756-3514; fax-603-756-4153; hours: 7AM-4PM T,W,F; 6-7PM W.

Drewsville and North Walpole are in the Town of Walpole. Office will perform a UCC search but public must search other records themselves. Real estate records located at Cheshire County. UCC search per debtor name- $15.00 as time permits. Copy fee $.75 per page. Cert fee- $5.00 per cert plus copy fee. Payee- Town of Walpole. **Property tax/Assessor**- 603-756-3672.

Warner

Town Clerk, PO Box 265, Warner, NH 03278-0265. 603-456-3362, R/E recording phone-603-228-0101, UCC recording phone-603-456-3362; fax-603-456-3576; hours: 8AM-3PM M-TH; 5-7PM T; Closed F. www.warner.nh.us/departments.htm

Office personnel or visitors may perform searches. Search fee $10.00 per name. Real estate records located at Merrimack County. UCC search per debtor name- $15.00. UCC search request using non-standard form (per name)- $20.00. Copy fee $1.00 per page. **Other phones**: Treasurer- 603-456-2298; Appraiser/Auditor- 603-456-2298; Elections- 603-456-3362; Vital Records- 603-456-3362. **Property tax/Assessor**- 603-456-2298.

Warren Town

Town Clerk, PO Box 66, Warren, NH 03279. 603-764-9463, R/E recording phone-603-764-5780; fax-603-764-9315; hours: 4PM-8PM M; 6PM-8PM W.

All records in one index. Record index not computerized. Office will perform a UCC and Tax lien search but public must search other records themselves. Search fee $15.00. Real estate records located at Grafton County. Copy fee $1.00 per page. **Other phones**: Treasurer- 603-764-5780; Appraiser/Auditor- 603-764-5780; Elections- 603-764-5780; Vital Records- 603-764-5780; Tax Collector-603-764-5780. **Property tax/Assessor**- 603-764-5780.

Washington Town

Town Clerk, PO Box 109, Washington, NH 03280-0109. 603-495-3667; fax-603-495-3299; hours: 9AM-3PM F. www.washingtonnh.org

All records in one index. Records indexed. Only the public may search. Search fee $12.00. Real estate records located at Sullivan County. Copy fee $1.00 per page. **Other phones**: Treasurer- 603-495-3667. **Property tax/Assessor**- 7 Halfmoon Pond Rd, Washington, NH 03280; 603-495-3074.

Waterville Valley Town

Town Clerk, Box 500, Waterville Valley, NH 03215. 603-236-4730; fax-603-236-2056; hours: 8AM-4PM.

Separate indices to search include manual search only for town records. Office will perform a UCC search but public must search other records themselves. Search fee $10.00 per name. Real estate records located at Grafton County. Copy fee $1.00 per page. Cert fee- $15.00 per debtor. Payee-Town of Waterville Valley. **Other phones**: Treasurer- 603-236-4730; Appraiser/Auditor- 603-236-4730; Elections- 603-236-4730; Vital Records- 603-236-4730. **Property tax/Assessor**- same address as above. 603-236-4730.

Weare Town

Town Clerk, PO Box 190, Weare, NH 03281-0190. 603-529-7575; fax-603-529-7571; hours: 8AM-4PM M, T, Th, F; 8AM-7PM W. www.town.weare.nh.us

All records in one index. Record index not computerized. Only the office personnel may search. Search fee $15.00 per name. Real estate records located at Hillsborough County. Copy fee $1.00 per page. **Other phones**: Elections- 603-529-7575; Vital Records- 603-529-7575. **Property tax/Assessor**- same address as above. 603-629-1515.

Webster Town

Town Clerk, 945 Battle St, Rte 127, Webster, NH 03303. 603-648-2538, R/E recording phone-603-648-2272, UCC recording phone-603-648-2538; fax-603-648-6055; hours: 9AM-N, 1-4PM M, W; 7-9PM Mon.

All records in one index. Record index not computerized. Only the office personnel may search. Search fee $10.00 per name. Real estate records located at Merrimack County. General copy fee $1.00 per page. Tax lien copy- $5.00 per copy. Cert fee- $10.00 per copy. Payee- Town Clerk of Webster. **Property tax/Assessor**- same address as above. 603-648-2272.

Wentworth Town

Town Clerk, PO Box 2, Wentworth, NH 03282. 603-764-5244; fax-603-764-9362; hours: 12-7PM Tu; 8:30AM-3PM W,Th.

Office personnel or visitors may perform searches. Search fee $10.00 per name. Real estate records located at Grafton County. Copy fee $1.00 per page.

Westmoreland Town

Town Clerk, PO Box 111, Westmoreland, NH 03467. 603-399-7211; fax-603-399-7211; hours: 7-8:30PM M,W; 7:30-2PM M; 7:30-aaAM W.

Index: Records are in 2 indices. Record index not computerized. Office will perform a UCC search but public must search other records themselves. Search fee $10.00 per name. Copy fee $1.00 per page. Payee- Town of Westmoreland. **Other phones**: Treasurer- 603-399-4471; Elections- 603-399-7211; Vital Records- 603-399-7211. **Property tax/Assessor**- PO Box 55, Westmoreland, NH 03467; 603-399-4471.

Whitefield Town

Town Clerk, 7 Jefferson Rd, Whitefield, NH 03598. 603-837-9871; fax-603-837-3148;

Office personnel or visitors may perform searches. Search fee $10.00 per name. Real estate records located at Grafton County. Copy fee $1.00 per page. **Other phones**: Treasurer- 603-837-2551. **Property tax/Assessor**- 603-837-2551.

Wilmot Town

Town Clerk, PO Box 94, Wilmot, NH 03287. 603-526-9639; fax-603-526-2523; hours: 8:30AM-1:30PM T,Th; 4-7PM W, 8AM-N 1st & last Sat.

Office will perform a UCC search but public must search other records themselves. Real estate records located at Merrimack County. UCC search per debtor name- $15.00. Copy fee $.25 per page. Cert fee-None. Payee- Wilmot Town Clerk. **Property tax/Assessor**- 603-526-4802.

Wilton Town

Town Clerk, PO Box 83, Wilton, NH 03086. 603-654-9451; fax-603-654-6663; hours: 9AM-4PM,M,T,F; 9-7PM Th; closed Wed. www.ci.wilton.nh.us

Office personnel or visitors may perform searches. Search fee $7.00 per name. Real estate records located at Hillsborough County. UCC search per debtor name- $10.00. Copy fee $1.00 per page. Cert fee- None. Payee- Town of Wilton. **Property tax/Assessor**- 603-654-9451.

Winchester Town

Town Clerk, 1 Richmond Rd, Winchester, NH 03470. 603-239-6233; fax-603-239-4146; hours: 8AM-5PM. Only the public may search. Real estate records located at Cheshire County Clerk will only give book and page number over the phone. Will not search tax liens. Copy fee $1.00 per page. Cert fee- $2.00 per doc plus copy fee. Payee- Town of Winchester. **Property tax/Assessor**- 603-239-4951.

Windham Town

Town Clerk, PO Box 120, Windham, NH 03087. 603-434-5075, R/E recording phone-603-432-7731, UCC recording phone-603-434-5075; fax-603-425-6582; hours: 8AM-7PM M, 8AM-4PM T W Th F. www.windhamnewhampshire.com

All records in one index. Records index not computerized. Search fee $10.00 per name. Real estate records located at Rockingham County. Copy fee $1.00 per page. Cert fee- $1.00 per page. Payee- Windham Town Clerk. **Other phones**: Treasurer- 603-432-7732; Appraiser/Auditor- 603-434-7530; Elections- 603-434-5075; Vital Records- 603-434-5057. **Property tax/Assessor**- 603-434-7530.

Windsor Town

Town Clerk, 14 White Pond Rd, Windsor, NH 03244. 603-478-3292; fax-603-478-3213; hours: 7PM-9PM W.

Only the public may search. Copy fee $1.00 per page. Payee- Town of Windsor.

Wolfeboro Town

Town Clerk, Box 1207, Wolfeboro, NH 03894. 603-569-5328; fax-603-569-8167; 8AM-1PM, 2-4PM.

Only the public may search. Copy fee $1.00 per page. Payee- Wolfeboro Town Clerk. **Online access to Assessor, Property records**: Access to assessor property data is at http://data.visionappraisal.com/wolfeboroNH/. Free registration for full data. **Other phones**: Appraiser/Auditor- 603-569-8152; Elections- 603-569-5328; Vital Records- 603-569-5328. **Property tax/Assessor**- 603-569-8152.

Woodstock Town

Tax Collector, PO Box 146, North Woodstock, NH 03262. 603-745-9233; fax-603-745-2393; hours: 8:30AM-12:30PM T-Th.

All records in one index. Records indexed on computer. Only the public may search. Real estate records located at Grafton County. Copy fee $1.00 per page. **Other phones**: Treasurer- 603-745-8752; Elections- 603-745-8752; Vital Records- 603-745-8752. **Property tax/Assessor**- 603-745-8752.

New Hampshire County Locator

You will usually be able to find the city name in the City/County Cross Reference below. In that case, it is a simple matter to determine the county from the cross reference. However, only the official US Postal Service city names are included in this index. There are an additional 40,000 place names that people use in their addresses. Therefore, we have also included a ZIP/City Cross Reference immediately following the City/County Cross Reference.

If you know the ZIP Code but the city name does not appear in the City/County Cross Reference index, look up the ZIP Code in the ZIP/City Cross Reference, find the city name, then look up the city name in the City/County Cross Reference.

New Hampshire City/County Cross Reference

ACWORTH Sullivan
ALSTEAD Cheshire
ALTON Belknap
ALTON BAY Belknap
AMHERST Hillsborough
ANDOVER Merrimack
ANTRIM Hillsborough
ASHLAND Grafton
ASHUELOT Cheshire
ATKINSON Rockingham
AUBURN Rockingham
BARNSTEAD (03218) Belknap(97), Strafford(2)
BARRINGTON Strafford
BARTLETT Carroll
BATH Grafton
BEDFORD Hillsborough
BELMONT (03220) Belknap(98), Merrimack(1)
BENNINGTON Hillsborough
BERLIN Coos
BETHLEHEM (03574) Grafton(98), Coos(1)
BOW Merrimack
BRADFORD Merrimack
BRETTON WOODS Coos
BRISTOL Grafton
BROOKLINE Hillsborough
CAMPTON Grafton
CANAAN Grafton
CANDIA Rockingham
CANTERBURY Merrimack
CENTER BARNSTEAD (03225) Belknap(97), Strafford(2)
CENTER CONWAY Carroll
CENTER HARBOR (03226) Belknap(76), Carroll(22)
CENTER OSSIPEE Carroll
CENTER SANDWICH Carroll
CENTER STRAFFORD Strafford
CENTER TUFTONBORO Carroll
CHARLESTOWN Sullivan
CHESTER Rockingham
CHESTERFIELD Cheshire
CHICHESTER Merrimack
CHOCORUA Carroll
CLAREMONT Sullivan
COLEBROOK Coos
CONCORD Merrimack
CONTOOCOOK Merrimack
CONWAY Carroll
CORNISH Sullivan
CORNISH FLAT Sullivan
DANBURY Merrimack
DANVILLE Rockingham
DEERFIELD Rockingham
DERRY Rockingham
DOVER Strafford
DREWSVILLE Cheshire
DUBLIN Cheshire
DUNBARTON Merrimack
DURHAM Strafford
EAST ANDOVER Merrimack
EAST CANDIA Rockingham
EAST DERRY Rockingham
EAST HAMPSTEAD Rockingham
EAST HEBRON Grafton
EAST KINGSTON Rockingham

EAST WAKEFIELD Carroll
EATON CENTER Carroll
ELKINS Merrimack
ENFIELD (03748) Grafton(95), Sullivan(4)
ENFIELD CENTER Grafton
EPPING Rockingham
EPSOM Merrimack
ERROL Coos
ETNA Grafton
EXETER Rockingham
FARMINGTON Strafford
FITZWILLIAM Cheshire
FRANCESTOWN Hillsborough
FRANCONIA Grafton
FRANKLIN Merrimack
FREEDOM Carroll
FREMONT Rockingham
GEORGES MILLS Sullivan
GILFORD Belknap
GILMANTON Belknap
GILMANTON IRON WORKS Belknap
GILSUM Cheshire
GLEN Carroll
GLENCLIFF Grafton
GOFFSTOWN Hillsborough
GORHAM Coos
GOSHEN Sullivan
GRAFTON Grafton
GRANTHAM Sullivan
GREENFIELD Hillsborough
GREENLAND Rockingham
GREENVILLE Hillsborough
GROVETON Coos
GUILD Sullivan
HAMPSTEAD Rockingham
HAMPTON Rockingham
HAMPTON FALLS Rockingham
HANCOCK Hillsborough
HANOVER Grafton
HARRISVILLE Cheshire
HAVERHILL Grafton
HEBRON Grafton
HENNIKER Merrimack
HILL Merrimack
HILLSBORO (03244) Hillsborough(98), Sullivan(1)
HINSDALE Cheshire
HOLDERNESS Grafton
HOLLIS Hillsborough
HOOKSETT Merrimack
HUDSON Hillsborough
INTERVALE Carroll
JACKSON Carroll
JAFFREY Cheshire
JEFFERSON Coos
KEARSARGE Carroll
KEENE Cheshire
KINGSTON Rockingham
LACONIA Belknap
LANCASTER Coos
LEBANON Grafton
LEMPSTER Sullivan
LINCOLN Grafton
LISBON Grafton
LITCHFIELD Hillsborough
LITTLETON Grafton
LOCHMERE Belknap

LONDONDERRY Rockingham
LOUDON Merrimack
LYME Grafton
LYME CENTER Grafton
LYNDEBOROUGH Hillsborough
MADBURY Strafford
MADISON Carroll
MANCHESTER Hillsborough
MARLBOROUGH Cheshire
MARLOW Cheshire
MEADOWS Coos
MELVIN VILLAGE Carroll
MEREDITH Belknap
MERIDEN Sullivan
MERRIMACK Hillsborough
MILAN Coos
MILFORD Hillsborough
MILTON Strafford
MILTON MILLS Strafford
MIRROR LAKE Carroll
MONROE Grafton
MONT VERNON Hillsborough
MOULTONBOROUGH Carroll
MOUNT SUNAPEE Merrimack
MOUNT WASHINGTON Coos
MUNSONVILLE Cheshire
NASHUA Hillsborough
NEW BOSTON Hillsborough
NEW CASTLE Rockingham
NEW DURHAM Strafford
NEW HAMPTON Belknap
NEW IPSWICH Hillsborough
NEW LONDON (03257) Merrimack(98), Sullivan(1)
NEWBURY Merrimack
NEWFIELDS Rockingham
NEWMARKET Rockingham
NEWPORT Sullivan
NEWTON Rockingham
NEWTON JUNCTION Rockingham
NORTH CONWAY Carroll
NORTH HAMPTON Rockingham
NORTH HAVERHILL Grafton
NORTH SALEM Rockingham
NORTH SANDWICH Carroll
NORTH STRATFORD Coos
NORTH SUTTON Merrimack
NORTH WALPOLE Cheshire
NORTH WOODSTOCK Grafton
NORTHWOOD Rockingham
NOTTINGHAM Rockingham
ORFORD Grafton
OSSIPEE Carroll
PELHAM Hillsborough
PETERBOROUGH (03458) Hillsborough(96), Cheshire(3)
PETERBOROUGH Hillsborough
PIERMONT Grafton
PIKE Grafton
PITTSBURG Coos
PITTSFIELD Merrimack
PLAINFIELD Sullivan
PLAISTOW Rockingham
PLYMOUTH Grafton
PORTSMOUTH Rockingham
RANDOLPH Coos
RAYMOND Rockingham

RINDGE Cheshire
ROCHESTER Strafford
ROLLINSFORD Strafford
RUMNEY Grafton
RYE Rockingham
RYE BEACH Rockingham
SALEM Rockingham
SALISBURY Merrimack
SANBORNTON Belknap
SANBORNVILLE Carroll
SANDOWN Rockingham
SEABROOK Rockingham
SILVER LAKE Carroll
SOMERSWORTH Strafford
SOUTH ACWORTH Sullivan
SOUTH EFFINGHAM Carroll
SOUTH NEWBURY Merrimack
SOUTH SUTTON Merrimack
SOUTH TAMWORTH Carroll
SPOFFORD Cheshire
SPRINGFIELD Sullivan
STINSON LAKE Grafton
STODDARD Cheshire
STRAFFORD Strafford
STRATHAM Rockingham
SUGAR HILL Grafton
SULLIVAN Cheshire
SUNAPEE Sullivan
SUNCOOK Merrimack
SWANZEY Cheshire
TAMWORTH Carroll
TEMPLE Hillsborough
TILTON (03276) Belknap(55), Merrimack(44)
TILTON Belknap
TROY Cheshire
TWIN MOUNTAIN Coos
UNION (03887) Strafford(70), Carroll(29)
WALPOLE Cheshire
WARNER Merrimack
WARREN Grafton
WASHINGTON Sullivan
WATERVILLE VALLEY Grafton
WEARE Hillsborough
WENTWORTH Grafton
WEST CHESTERFIELD Cheshire
WEST LEBANON Grafton
WEST NOTTINGHAM Rockingham
WEST OSSIPEE Carroll
WEST PETERBOROUGH Hillsborough
WEST STEWARTSTOWN Coos
WEST SWANZEY Cheshire
WESTMORELAND Cheshire
WHITEFIELD Coos
WILMOT Merrimack
WILTON Hillsborough
WINCHESTER Cheshire
WINDHAM Rockingham
WINNISQUAM Belknap
WOLFEBORO Carroll
WOLFEBORO FALLS Carroll
WONALANCET Carroll
WOODSTOCK Grafton
WOODSVILLE Grafton

New Hampshire ZIP/City Cross Reference

00210-00215	PORTSMOUTH
03031-03031	AMHERST
03032-03032	AUBURN
03033-03033	BROOKLINE
03034-03034	CANDIA
03036-03036	CHESTER
03037-03037	DEERFIELD
03038-03038	DERRY
03040-03040	EAST CANDIA
03041-03041	EAST DERRY
03042-03042	EPPING
03043-03043	FRANCESTOWN
03044-03044	FREMONT
03045-03045	GOFFSTOWN
03046-03046	DUNBARTON
03047-03047	GREENFIELD
03048-03048	GREENVILLE
03049-03049	HOLLIS
03051-03051	HUDSON
03052-03052	LITCHFIELD
03053-03053	LONDONDERRY
03054-03054	MERRIMACK
03055-03055	MILFORD
03057-03057	MONT VERNON
03060-03064	NASHUA
03070-03070	NEW BOSTON
03071-03071	NEW IPSWICH
03073-03073	NORTH SALEM
03076-03076	PELHAM
03077-03077	RAYMOND
03079-03079	SALEM
03082-03082	LYNDEBOROUGH
03084-03084	TEMPLE
03086-03086	WILTON
03087-03087	WINDHAM
03100-03105	MANCHESTER
03106-03106	HOOKSETT
03107-03109	MANCHESTER
03110-03110	BEDFORD
03111-03111	MANCHESTER
03215-03215	WATERVILLE VALLEY
03216-03216	ANDOVER
03217-03217	ASHLAND
03218-03218	BARNSTEAD
03220-03220	BELMONT
03221-03221	BRADFORD
03222-03222	BRISTOL
03223-03223	CAMPTON
03224-03224	CANTERBURY
03225-03225	CENTER BARNSTEAD
03226-03226	CENTER HARBOR
03227-03227	CENTER SANDWICH
03229-03229	CONTOOCOOK
03230-03230	DANBURY
03231-03231	EAST ANDOVER
03232-03232	EAST HEBRON
03233-03233	ELKINS
03234-03234	EPSOM
03235-03235	FRANKLIN
03237-03237	GILMANTON
03238-03238	GLENCLIFF
03240-03240	GRAFTON
03241-03241	HEBRON
03242-03242	HENNIKER
03243-03243	HILL
03244-03244	HILLSBORO
03245-03245	HOLDERNESS
03246-03247	LACONIA
03249-03249	GILFORD
03251-03251	LINCOLN
03252-03252	LOCHMERE
03253-03253	MEREDITH
03254-03254	MOULTONBOROUGH
03255-03255	NEWBURY
03256-03256	NEW HAMPTON
03257-03257	NEW LONDON
03258-03258	CHICHESTER
03259-03259	NORTH SANDWICH

03260-03260	NORTH SUTTON
03261-03261	NORTHWOOD
03262-03262	NORTH WOODSTOCK
03263-03263	PITTSFIELD
03264-03264	PLYMOUTH
03265-03265	ANDOVER
03266-03266	RUMNEY
03268-03268	SALISBURY
03269-03269	SANBORNTON
03272-03272	SOUTH NEWBURY
03273-03273	SOUTH SUTTON
03274-03274	STINSON LAKE
03275-03275	SUNCOOK
03276-03276	TILTON
03278-03278	WARNER
03279-03279	WARREN
03280-03280	WASHINGTON
03281-03281	WEARE
03282-03282	WENTWORTH
03284-03284	SPRINGFIELD
03285-03285	CAMPTON
03287-03287	WILMOT
03289-03289	WINNISQUAM
03290-03290	NOTTINGHAM
03291-03291	WEST NOTTINGHAM
03293-03293	WOODSTOCK
03298-03299	TILTON
03300-03303	CONCORD
03304-03304	BOW
03305-03306	CONCORD
03307-03307	LOUDON
03431-03435	KEENE
03440-03440	ANTRIM
03441-03441	ASHUELOT
03442-03442	BENNINGTON
03443-03443	CHESTERFIELD
03444-03444	DUBLIN
03445-03445	SULLIVAN
03446-03446	SWANZEY
03447-03447	FITZWILLIAM
03448-03448	GILSUM
03449-03449	HANCOCK
03450-03450	HARRISVILLE
03451-03451	HINSDALE
03452-03452	JAFFREY
03455-03455	MARLBOROUGH
03456-03456	MARLOW
03457-03457	MUNSONVILLE
03458-03460	PETERBOROUGH
03461-03461	RINDGE
03462-03462	SPOFFORD
03464-03464	STODDARD
03465-03465	TROY
03466-03466	WEST CHESTERFIELD
03467-03467	WESTMORELAND
03468-03468	WEST PETERBOROUGH
03469-03469	WEST SWANZEY
03470-03470	WINCHESTER
03561-03561	LITTLETON
03570-03570	BERLIN
03574-03574	BETHLEHEM
03575-03575	BRETTON WOODS
03576-03576	COLEBROOK
03579-03579	ERROL
03580-03580	FRANCONIA
03581-03581	GORHAM
03582-03582	GROVETON
03583-03583	JEFFERSON
03584-03584	LANCASTER
03585-03585	LISBON
03586-03586	SUGAR HILL
03587-03587	MEADOWS
03588-03588	MILAN
03589-03589	MOUNT WASHINGTON
03590-03590	NORTH STRATFORD
03592-03592	PITTSBURG
03593-03593	RANDOLPH
03595-03595	TWIN MOUNTAIN

03597-03597	WEST STEWARTSTOWN
03598-03598	WHITEFIELD
03601-03601	ACWORTH
03602-03602	ALSTEAD
03603-03603	CHARLESTOWN
03604-03604	DREWSVILLE
03605-03606	LEMPSTER
03607-03607	SOUTH ACWORTH
03608-03608	WALPOLE
03609-03609	NORTH WALPOLE
03740-03740	BATH
03741-03741	CANAAN
03743-03743	CLAREMONT
03745-03745	CORNISH
03746-03746	CORNISH FLAT
03748-03748	ENFIELD
03749-03749	ENFIELD CENTER
03750-03750	ETNA
03751-03751	GEORGES MILLS
03752-03752	GOSHEN
03753-03753	GRANTHAM
03754-03754	GUILD
03755-03755	HANOVER
03756-03756	LEBANON
03765-03765	HAVERHILL
03766-03766	LEBANON
03768-03768	LYME
03769-03769	LYME CENTER
03770-03770	MERIDEN
03771-03771	MONROE
03772-03772	MOUNT SUNAPEE
03773-03773	NEWPORT
03774-03774	NORTH HAVERHILL
03777-03777	ORFORD
03779-03779	PIERMONT
03780-03780	PIKE
03781-03781	PLAINFIELD
03782-03782	SUNAPEE
03784-03784	WEST LEBANON
03785-03785	WOODSVILLE
03801-03804	PORTSMOUTH
03805-03805	ROLLINSFORD
03809-03809	ALTON
03810-03810	ALTON BAY
03811-03811	ATKINSON
03812-03812	BARTLETT
03813-03813	CENTER CONWAY
03814-03814	CENTER OSSIPEE
03815-03815	CENTER STRAFFORD
03816-03816	CENTER TUFTONBORO
03817-03817	CHOCORUA
03818-03818	CONWAY
03819-03819	DANVILLE
03820-03822	DOVER
03823-03823	MADBURY
03824-03824	DURHAM
03825-03825	BARRINGTON
03826-03826	EAST HAMPSTEAD
03827-03827	EAST KINGSTON
03830-03830	EAST WAKEFIELD
03832-03832	EATON CENTER
03833-03833	EXETER
03835-03835	FARMINGTON
03836-03836	FREEDOM
03837-03837	GILMANTON IRON WORKS
03838-03838	GLEN
03839-03839	ROCHESTER
03840-03840	GREENLAND
03841-03841	HAMPSTEAD
03842-03843	HAMPTON
03844-03844	HAMPTON FALLS
03845-03845	INTERVALE
03846-03846	JACKSON
03847-03847	KEARSARGE
03848-03848	KINGSTON
03849-03849	MADISON
03850-03850	MELVIN VILLAGE
03851-03851	MILTON

03852-03852	MILTON MILLS
03853-03853	MIRROR LAKE
03854-03854	NEW CASTLE
03855-03855	NEW DURHAM
03856-03856	NEWFIELDS
03857-03857	NEWMARKET
03858-03858	NEWTON
03859-03859	NEWTON JUNCTION
03860-03860	NORTH CONWAY
03862-03862	NORTH HAMPTON
03864-03864	OSSIPEE
03865-03865	PLAISTOW
03866-03868	ROCHESTER
03869-03869	ROLLINSFORD
03870-03870	RYE
03871-03871	RYE BEACH
03872-03872	SANBORNVILLE
03873-03873	SANDOWN
03874-03874	SEABROOK
03875-03875	SILVER LAKE
03878-03878	SOMERSWORTH
03882-03882	SOUTH EFFINGHAM
03883-03883	SOUTH TAMWORTH
03884-03884	STRAFFORD
03885-03885	STRATHAM
03886-03886	TAMWORTH
03887-03887	UNION
03890-03890	WEST OSSIPEE
03894-03894	WOLFEBORO
03896-03896	WOLFEBORO FALLS
03897-03897	WONALANCET

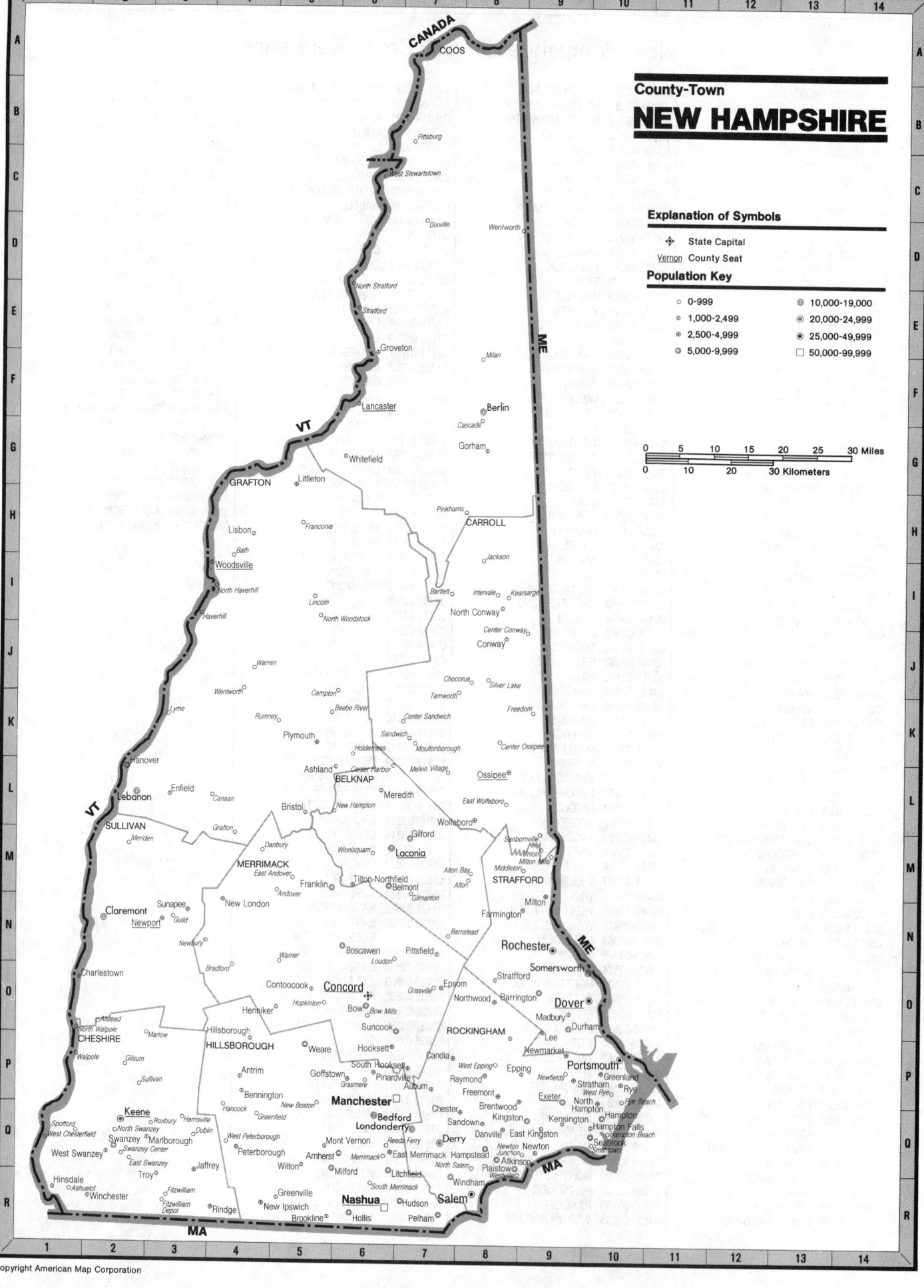

County-Town
NEW HAMPSHIRE

Explanation of Symbols

State Capital
Vernon County Seat

Population Key

○ 0-999
◉ 1,000-2,499
◉ 2,500-4,999
◉ 5,000-9,999

◉ 10,000-19,000
◉ 20,000-24,999
◉ 25,000-49,999
□ 50,000-99,999

Explanation of symbols: ● – Census Designated Place (CDP)   ▲ italics – Townships (shown on the map)   italics – Townships (not shown on the map)

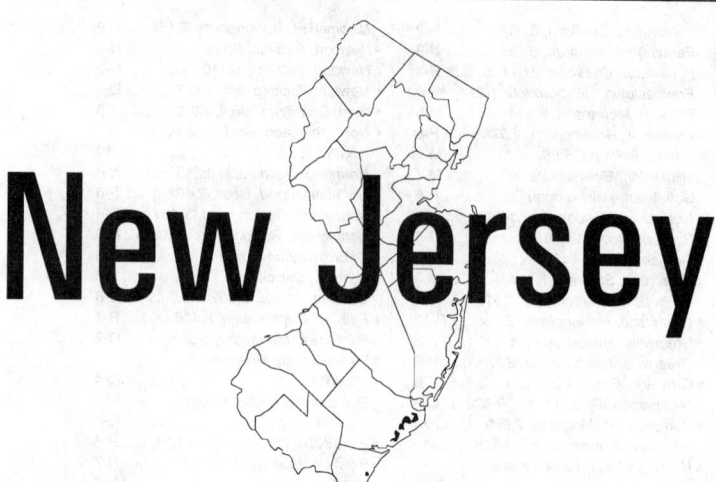

New Jersey

General Help Numbers:

Governor's Office
PO Box 001, 125 W State St
Trenton, NJ 08625-0001
www.state.nj.us/governor

609-292-6000
Fax 609-292-3454
8:30AM-4:30PM

Attorney General's Office
Law & Public Safety Department
PO Box 080, 25 Market St
Trenton, NJ 08625-0080
www.state.nj.us/lps

609-292-8740
Fax 609-292-3508
8:30AM-5PM

Legislative Records
State House Annex, Room B01
PO Box 068
Trenton, NJ 08625-0068
www.njleg.state.nj.us

609-292-4840
Fax 609-777-2440
8:30AM-5PM

State Archives
PO Box 307, 225 W. State Street, L2
Trenton, NJ 08625-0307
www.state.nj.us/state/darm/index.html

609-292-6260
Fax 609-396-2454

8:30AM-4:30PM TU-F

State Specifics:

Capital:	Trenton
	Mercer County
Time Zone:	EST
Number of Counties:	21
Population:	8,698,879
Web Site:	www.state.nj.us

State Agencies

Criminal Records

Division of State Police, Records and Identification Section, PO Box 7068, West Trenton, NJ 08628-0068; 609-882-2000 x2991, 609-530-5780-Fax; 9AM-5PM. www.njsp.org

Records are available from 1921 forward. It takes 1 to 5 days before new records are available for inquiry. Records are indexed on inhouse computer. Records are normally destroyed after verification that subject is no longer alive. 85% of all arrests in database have final dispositions recorded, 95% for those arrests within last 5 years.

Searching: Criminal records are not open to the public but can be obtained by employers, private investigators, screening firms, attorney firms, and the subject. Include the following in your request-date of birth, Social Security Number. A set of fingerprints is optional. The name must match exactly. All requesters, except attorney firms, must submit Form 212 B which must be signed by the subject. Attorney firms require a subpoena. 100% of the records are fingerprint supported. The following data is not released: Juvenile records are restricted. Dismissals, acquittals, not-guilty verdicts are also excluded to the general public. All records are released, including those without dispositions.

Access by: mail, in person.

Fee & Payment: The fee is $18.00 for a name check and $30.00 for a full check with fingerprints. Will not do FBI fingerprint checks. Fee payee: Division of State Police-SBI. Prepayment required. No personal checks or credit cards accepted.

Mail search: Turnaround time: 5 to 10 days.

In person search: Walk-in requests are treated as mail requests. Results are mailed.

Other access: The agency makes available for sale the entire database of public access criminal records. Call 609-292-4681 for details.

Statewide Court Records

Administrative Office of Courts, RJH Justice Complex, 7th Fl, PO Box 037, Trenton, NJ 08625; 609-984-0275, 609-984-6968-Fax; 8:30AM-4:30PM.

www.judiciary.state.nj.us/admin.htm

Supreme and Appellate opinions and current calendars are available at the website. The state has several automated case tracking systems, including case histories. However, this is not accessible directly by the public.

Access by: online.

Online search: Online access to all civil records is available through the ACMS, AMIS, and FACTS systems. The fee is $1.00 per minute of use. For more information, contact the Superior Court Clerk's Office, Electronic Access Program. Write to 25 Market St, CN971, Trenton NJ 08625, or fax 609-292-6564, or call 609-292-4987. Ask for the Inquiry System Guidebook containing hardware and software requirements and an enrollment form. A Superior Court Civil Motion Calendar at www.judiciary.state.nj.us/acms/MOTN/CV0390W0E.ASP or http://lawlibrary.rutgers.edu/search.shtml.

Sexual Offender Registry

Division of State Police, Sexual Offender Registry, PO Box 7068, West Trenton, NJ 08628-0068; 609-882-2000 x2886, 609-538-0544-Fax; 9AM-5PM.

www.njsp.org

Local law enforcement will assist with localized searches. The agency will only provide access to records online.

It takes 1 to 5 days before new records are available for inquiry. Records are indexed on inhouse computer.

Searching: Include the following in your request-name, date of birth.

Access by: online only.

Online search: Data can be searched online at the website. Click on NJ Sex Offender Registry. Search can be done by name, by county or by physical characteristics.

Incarceration Records

New Jersey Department of Corrections, Central Reception & Assignment Facility, PO Box 7450, Trenton, NJ 08628; 609-777-5753, 609-984-2695, 609-777-8369-Fax; 8AM-5PM.

www.state.nj.us/corrections/index.html

Records are available on current and former inmates. It takes 1 day before new records are available for inquiry. Records are normally destroyed after 10 years after release.

Searching: Location, DOC number, physical identifiers, conviction information, and release dates are released. Include the following in your request-full name, DOB and SSN helpful.

Access by: mail, phone, fax, online.

Fee & Payment: Some fees may be involved, depending on extent of research involved. This is decided on a case-by-case basis.

Mail search: Turnaround time: 5 working days.

Phone search: Limited telephone verification.

Fax search: Fax requests can be used in place of phone requests if you have four or more names to search.

Online search: Extensive search capabilities are offered from the website; click on "Offender Search". Offenders on Work Release, Furlough, or in a Halfway House are not necessarily reflected as such in their profile.

Corporation, Limited Liability Company, Fictitious Name, Limited Partnerships

Division of Revenue, Records Unit, PO 450, Trenton, NJ 08646 (Courier address: 225 W State St, 3rd Fl, Trenton, NJ 08608); 609-292-9292, 609-984-6855-Fax; 8:30AM-4:30PM.

www.state.nj.us/treasury/revenue/certcomm.htm

Records are available from inception of laws. New records are available for inquiry immediately. Records are indexed on inhouse computer.

Searching: Include the following in your request-full name of business. In addition to the articles of incorporation, corporation records include the following information: Annual Reports, Amendments, Alternative names, Officers, Directors, Prior (merged) names, and Inactive names. Tradenames are filed at the county level.

Access by: mail, phone, fax, in person, online.

Fee & Payment: A status report is $5.00. Copies are $1.00 per page (except LLC, then $10.00 first and $2.00 each additional). There is a $25.00 ($15.00 if non-profit) fee to certify a document. A Good Standing is $25.00. Fee payee: Treasurer, State of NJ. Prepayment required. Ongoing requesters may set up a pre-paid account. Call 609-633-8255 for more information. Personal checks and major credit cards accepted.

Mail search: Turnaround time: 2 to 3 weeks.

Phone search: See expedited service.

Fax search: See considered expedited service.

In person search: You can look at 3 records per day for no fee. Copies can be provided. The turnaround time is over 1 week.

Online search: Business entities may be searched at https://accessnet.state.nj.us/home.asp. Records are available from the New Jersey Business Gateway Service (NJBGS) website at www.state.nj.us/njbgs. There is no fee to browse the site to locate a name; however fees are involved for copies or status reports. There is also a business list search function at www.state.nj.us/treasury/revenue/searchfile.htm.

Expedited service: Expedited service is available for phone, fax, and in person searches. Turnaround time: 8.5 business hours. Add $15.00 per transaction for corporations, non-profits and LPs and $25.00 per filing for LLCs and LLP. Records may be picked up the next day.

Trademarks/Servicemarks

Department of Treasury, Trademark Division, PO Box 453, Trenton, NJ 08625-0453 (Courier address: 225 W State St, 3rd Floor, Trenton, NJ 08608); 609-292-9292, 609-984-6681-Fax; 8:30AM-5PM.

www.state.nj.us/treasury/revenue

Records are available from the inception of the Division. It takes less than 1 day before new records are available for inquiry. Records are indexed on computer.

Searching: Include the following in your request-trademark/servicemark name, name of owner, date of application. Information returned includes name and address of owner and date of filing.

Access by: mail, in person, online.

Fee & Payment: Search fee is $25.00 for up to 3 names (for name availability). Copies are $1.00 per page. A status is $5.00 per name searched. Fee payee: NJ State Treasurer. Prepayment required. Personal checks and MC, Visa, Discover accepted.

Mail search: Turnaround time: 1 week. A self addressed stamped envelope is appreciated.

In person search: You can take the request in person, but they return the records by mail unless expedited service is requested.

Online search: Search the trade names list free at www.state.nj.us/treasury/revenue/checkbusiness.htm for name availability.

Expedited service: Add $15.00 per document. Turnaround time: next day service.

Uniform Commercial Code

UCC Section, Certification and Status Unit, PO 303, Trenton, NJ 08625 (Courier address: 225 West State St, Trenton, NJ 08618); 609-292-9292, 8AM-5PM.

www.state.nj.us/njbgs

It takes 2 weeks before new records are available for inquiry. Records are indexed on inhouse computer.

Searching: Use search request form UCC-11. Federal tax liens are filed at the county level. State tax liens follow two rules: certificates of debt are filed in Superior Court at Trenton; a warrant of execution is filed at the county level. Include the following in your request-debtor name, address.

Access by: mail, fax, in person, online.

Fee & Payment: The fee is $25.00 for a search certificate per debtor name, $5.00 for non-certified computer printout of any document, copies are $1.00 per page. Fee payee: Treasurer, State of NJ. Prepayment required. Regular requesters can set up a pre-paid account. Personal checks accepted. Credit cards accepted: MasterCard, Visa.

Mail search: Turnaround time: 2 weeks. A SASE is requested.

Fax search: You can order using a credit card; however, results will be mailed or available for pickup by a Courier address.

In person search: Information is mailed, unless you pay the $15.00 expedite fee for quicker service, or pickup later by Courier address.

Online search: Search the UCC index at https://www.state.nj.us/treasury/revenue/dcr/filing/ucc_lead.htm. For a business entity search, go to https://accessnet.state.nj.us/home.asp. Also shows UCC debtor, or other business name without accruing a service charge with the Division of Revenue. However, if you wish to receive status reports or other information services, you will need to pay the applicable statutory fee.

Expedited service: Expedited services is available, when requested, by mail, fax or in person. Turnaround time: 8 1/2 hours. The fee is an additional $15.00 per transaction.

Federal and State Tax Liens

Records not maintained by a state level agency.

Federal tax liens are filed with the county clerk or register of deeds. All state "docket judgment" liens are filed at the Superior Court in Trenton. "Certificates of Debt" are filed at the respective county superior court.

Sales Tax Registrations

Access to Records is Restricted.

Department of Revenue, Sales Tax Licensing, PO Box 252, Trenton, NJ 08646-0252; 609-292-1730, 609-292-4291-Fax; 8:30AM-4:30PM.

www.state.nj.us/treasury/taxation

Sales tax information is considered confidential. Order forms and information about publications are available on this agency's website.

Birth Certificates

Department of Health, Bureau of Vital Statistics, PO Box 370, Trenton, NJ 08625-0370 (Courier address: S Warren St, Room 504, Health & Agriculture Building, Trenton, NJ 08625); 609-292-4087, 877-622-7549 (Credit Card Requests), 609-392-4292-Fax; 8:30AM-4PM.

www.state.nj.us/health/vital/vital.htm

Records are available from 1878 to present. It takes 30 days before new records are available for inquiry. Records are indexed on microfiche.

Searching: The general public is denied access to records unless birth occurred over 80 years ago. You must include the county in your request if it is regarding events before 1903. Include the following in your request-full name, names of parents, mother's maiden name, date of birth, place of birth. Also, requester must submit photo ID and proof of relationship to subject.

Access by: mail, phone, fax, in person, online.

Fee & Payment: The fee is $4.00 per record. Add $2.00 per copy for additional copies. Add $1.00 per year for each additional year searched. The fee for using a credit card is $10.95. Fee payee: New Jersey Department of Health & Senior Services. Prepayment required. Personal checks accepted. Major credit cards accepted.

Mail search: Turnaround time: 6 to 8 weeks.

Phone search: Must use a credit card.

Fax search: Same criteria as phone searching.

In person search: Turnaround time 2 hours.

Online search: Online ordering is available via www.vitalchek.com, a state approved vendor.

Expedited service: Expedited service is available for fax searches. Turnaround time: 2 to 3 days. Add fee of overnight carrier and credit card fee.

Death Records

Department of Health, Bureau of Vital Statistics, PO Box 370, Trenton, NJ 08625-0370 (Courier address: S Warren St, Room 504, Health & Agriculture Building, Trenton, NJ 08625); 609-292-4087, 877-622-7549 (Credit Card Requests), 609-392-4292-Fax; 8:30AM-4PM.

www.state.nj.us/health/vital/vital.htm

Records are available from 1878 to present. It takes 30 days before new records are available for inquiry. Records are indexed on microfiche.

Searching: Cause of death, unless immediate family, is not released. Immediate family and those with a legal interest may obtain a record, unless death occurred over 40 years ago (then considered a genealogical search). Include the following in your request-full name, date of death, place of death, parents names. Submit photo ID and proof of relationship to deceased.

Access by: mail, phone, fax, in person, online.

Fee & Payment: The fee is $4.00 per record. Add $2.00 per copy for additional copies. Add $1.00 per year for each additional year searched. Add $10.95 if credit card is used. Fee payee: NJ Department of Health and Senior Services. Prepayment required. Personal checks accepted. Major credit cards accepted.

Mail search: Turnaround time: 6 to 8 months.

Phone search: Must use a credit card, open 24 hours.

Fax search: Same criteria as phone, turnaround time is 5-12 days.

In person search: Turnaround time 2 hours or less.

Online search: Records can be ordered online from www.vitalcheck.com, a state approved vendor partner.

Expedited service: Expedited service is available for mail, phone and fax searches. Turnaround time: 2 to 3 days. Add carrier fee plus the $10.95 credit card fee.

Marriage Certificates

Department of Health, Bureau of Vital Statistics, PO Box 370, Trenton, NJ 08625-0370 (Courier address: S Warren St, Room 504, Health & Agriculture Building, Trenton, NJ 08625); 609-292-4087, 877-622-7549 (Credit Card Requests), 609-392-4292-Fax; 8:30AM-4PM.

www.state.nj.us/health/vital/vital.htm

Records are available from 1878 to present. It takes 30 days before new records are available for inquiry. Records are indexed on microfiche.

Searching: The general public is denied access to the records unless marriage occurred over 50 years ago. You must include the county in your request if it is regarding events before 1903. Include the following in your request-names of husband and wife, date of marriage, place or county of marriage. Also submit photo ID and proof of relationship to the subject.

Access by: mail, phone, fax, in person, online.

Fee & Payment: The fee is $4.00 per record. Add $2.00 per copy for additional copies. Add $1.00 per year for each additional year searched. The fee to use a credit card is $10.95. Fee payee: New Jersey Department of Health. Prepayment required. Personal checks accepted. Major credit cards accepted.

Mail search: Turnaround time: 6 to 8 weeks.

Phone search: Must use a credit card. Open 24 hours.

Fax search: Same criteria as phone searches.

In person search: Turnaround time 2 hours.

Online search: Records can be ordered online from www.vitalcheck.com, a state approved vendor partner.

Expedited service: Expedited service is available for phone and fax searches. Turnaround time: 2 to 3 days. Add $14.75 carrier fees for overnight shipping and the $10.95 credit card fee. Federal Express 5-7 day service available.

Divorce Records

Clerk of Superior Court, Records Center, PO Box 967, Trenton, NJ 08625-0967 (Courier address: Corner of Jerser & Tremont Streets, Building #2, Trenton, NJ 08625); 609-777-0092, 609-777-0094-Fax; 8:30AM-4PM.

www.judiciary.state.nj.us

Records are available until 9/89. Records after 1989 must be obtained from the Family Division Court in county of occurrence.

Searching: Also provide married name, unless maiden name was used during the marriage. Information on cases that are impounded is not released. Include the following in your request-names of husband and wife, date of divorce, year divorce case began, docket number (if known). No copies are made and no records are retrieved after 3:30PM. The following data is not released: adoption, impound cases.

Access by: mail, fax, in person, online.

Fee & Payment: There is no search fee, but there is a $10.00 certification fee. Fee payee: Clerk of Superior Court. Prepayment required. If you are not sure how many pages the results or your request will be, you may send a blank check with "Not to exceed $25.00" written in the memo. Personal checks accepted. No credit cards accepted.

Mail search: Turnaround time: 2 to 3 weeks. Mail is the preferred request method. A SASE is requested.

Fax search: Requesters must be pre-approved to fax, and only written information is faxed back. Attorneys with charge accounts with the Superior Court can receive copies, without the seal of the court, via fax.

In person search: Turnaround time: while you wait. The Clerk's Office recommends that you not come to the office in person except for emergency requests.

Online search: Records can be ordered online from www.vitalcheck.com, a state approved vendor partner.

Workers' Compensation Records

Labor Department, Division of Workers Compensation, PO Box 381, Trenton, NJ 08625-0381 (Courier address: Labor Building, 6th Floor, John Fitch Plaza, Trenton, NJ 08625); 609-292-6026, 609-292-2515 (General Hotline), 609-984-2515-Fax; 8:30AM-4:30PM.

www.nj.gov/labor/wc/wcindex.html

Records are available for 30 years, then are purged. New records are available for inquiry immediately. Records are indexed on inhouse computer.

Searching: First report of injury-accident is not available to the public. All other records are subject to NJSA 34:15-128 which prohibits the copying of records to all persons not a party to a current related case. Use WC-147 if you want copies of a case. Include the following in your request-claimant name, Social Security Number, date of accident. Use the agency's record request form found at www.nj.gov/labor/wc/forms/wc-147(r7-04).pdf.

Access by: mail, in person, online.

Fee & Payment: There is no search fee. The certified copy fee is $.75 each for first 10 pages; $.50 each for next 10; and $.25 per page over 20. A processing fee of $15.0 is billed, plus any postage costs. Fee payee: Division of Workers' Compensation. Copies can be billed Personal checks accepted. No credit cards accepted.

Mail search: Turnaround time: 1 to 3 weeks. If request is just to know if the person has a claim, the turnaround time is same day. A SASE is requested. Otherwise postage is added to copy fees.

In person search: Turnaround time is same day.

Online search: COURTS on-line is a secure Internet website that provides authorized subscribers access to the Division's database. Possible subscribers include: Insurance Carrier/Law Firms; Court Reporting Firms; and WC Forensic Experts (Physicians).

Driver Records

Motor Vehicle Commission, Driver History Abstract Unit, PO Box 142, Trenton, NJ 08666; 609-984-7771, 609-292-6500 (Forms request), 609-292-7500 (Suspensions), 8AM-4:30PM.

www.state.nj.us/mvc

Copies of tickets are not kept on file and must be obtained from the municipal courts.

Records are available for 5 yrs for the public (complete history for attorneys). Non-moving violations are not reported on the record. Accidents in excess of $500 are reported, but fault is not shown. Driver's address is provided on the record. It takes 3 days to 2 weeks normally before new records are available for inquiry.

Searching: Access of driving records is strict, release to casual requesters is prohibited unless Form DO-21A contains notarized authority from subject. Permissible use requesters should use Form ISM-21. Include the following in your request-full name, DOB and DL. Sex, and eye color are also helpful for manual requests. The driver's license number should be submitted with all requests. The full name, DOB, The following data is not released: Social Security Numbers or medical records.

Access by: mail, in person, online.

Fee & Payment: The current fee is $10.00 for certified mail-in or walk-in requests, and $8.00 for other media including magnetic tape, control cards (100 minimum purchase), and online access. Fee payee: Motor Vehicle Services. Prepayment required. Personal checks accepted. No credit cards accepted.

Mail search: Turnaround time: 2 weeks. A SASE is requested.

In person search: Driving records can obtained at any one of the four Regional Service Centers - Deptford, Wayne, Eatontown, and Trenton.

Online search: Fee is $10.00 per record. Access is limited to insurance, bus and trucking companies, parking authorities, and approved vendors. For more information, call 609-292-4572. NJ drivers may order their own record online at www.state.nj.us/mvc/d_driver_history.html. A user ID number must be obtained first.

Vehicle & Vessel Ownership, Vehicle Identification, Vessel Registration

Motor Vehicle Commission, Certified Information Unit, PO Box 146, Trenton, NJ 08666; 609-292-6500, 888-486-3339 (In-state), 8:30AM-4:30PM.

www.state.nj.us/mvc/cit_title/v_title.html

Ownership and lien records must be ordered from Motor Vehicle Commission, Special Titles, PO Box 017 (Zip is 08666-0017). Lien searches are on current record or particular requests, also can be purchased at $5.00 for each lien history search.

Records are available for 3 years (registration) and 8 years (title). All boats over 12 feet must be titled and registered. Also, this agency maintains records on mobile homes. It takes 3 to 4 months before new records are available for inquiry. Records are normally destroyed after 3 years after expiration.

Searching: SSNs and medical information are not currently released and more restrictions are forthcoming. Casual requesters cannot obtain records. A special request form is required for most searches as follows: ISM/DO-22A for title search, /ISMDO-22 for lien search, and DO-11A for vehicle registration application search.

Access by: mail, in person, online.

Fee & Payment: The fee is $8.00 per record non-certified and $10.00 certified and take 6-8 weeks to process. A lien history search is $5.00 for each lien. A complete title history costs $10.50 and can take as long as 12 weeks to obtain. Fee payee: Motor Vehicle Commission Prepayment required. Personal checks and money orders accepted. No credit cards accepted.

Mail search: Turnaround time: 6 to 8 weeks. Requests must be submitted on Forms mentioned above. **In person search:** Record requests are accepted, but only for title histories and lien searches.

Online search: Limited online access is available for insurance companies, bus and trucking companies, highway/parking authorities, and approved vendors for these businesses. Fees are $4.00 per request for registration record and $8.00 for ownership history. Call 609-292-4572 for more information.

Other access: There is no program for massive/customized bulk look-ups. Each request is looked at on an individual basis. Records are not sold for commercial or political reasons.

Accident Reports

New Jersey State Police, CJRB - Traffic, PO Box 7068, West Trenton, NJ 08628-0068; 609-882-2000 x2234, 8AM-5PM.   www.njsp.org

This profile is only for accidents investigated by the State Police. If investigated by local police, copies must be obtained either from the local PD unit or from the MVC Abstract Unit at PO Box 142, Trenton, NJ 08666. Fee is $10.00 from the MVC.

Records are available for 6 years. Records are computer indexed by driver name and case number. It takes 3 to 4 weeks before new records are available for inquiry. **Searching:** Only the basics of fatal accident reports are available until the full report has been released from the County Prosecutor. While the report is pending, no statements, evidence or photographs can be released without the written consent of the

prosecutor. Include the following in your request-location of accident, date of accident, driver's full name.

Access by: mail, online.

Fee & Payment: Fees: $10.00 for first 3 pages and $2.00 for each additional page with a maximum fee of $16.00. Fee payee: New Jersey State Police Department. Prepayment required. Personal checks or money orders accepted. No credit cards accepted.

Mail search: Turnaround time: 6 to 8 weeks. A SASE is requested.

Online search: No online access to accidents reports is available, however, you may access the Insurance Company Name Codes free online at www.state.nj.us/mvc/cit_insurance/v_insurance_c odes.html. By reading the code on the accident report, you can then use this website to determine the insurance company involved.

Voter Registration
Access to Records is Restricted.

Dept of Law and Public Safety, Division of Elections, PO Box 304, Trenton, NJ 08625 (Courier address: 44 South Clinton Avenue, 7th Floor,); 609-292-3760, 609-777-1280-Fax; 8:30AM-5PM.

www.njelections.org

Until January 2006, records can only be accessed at the county level. While these county agencies may permit individual look-ups, records in mass may only be purchased for political purposes. After 01/06, this agency will have completed a centralized statewide database and will offer bulk access for political purposes.

GED Certificates

GED Testing Program, Dept. of Education - Bureau Adult Ed. & Literacy, PO Box 500, Trenton, NJ 08625-0500; 609-777-0577, 609-777-1050 (Forms), 609-984-0573-Fax; 9AM-4PM.

www.state.nj.us/njded/students/ged

It takes 2 to 4 weeks before new records are available for inquiry.

Searching: GED Information Request Form is required, obtained by calling 609-777-1050 or at www.state.nj.us/njded/students/ged/inforeq.pdf. Include the following in your request-a signed release, date/year of test, SSN, and city of test.

Access by: mail.

Fee & Payment: The fee is $5.00 for a verification or a copy of the transcript. Fee payee: Commissioner of Education. Prepayment required. Money orders and business checks are accepted. No credit cards or personal checks accepted.

Mail search: Turnaround time: up to 4 weeks.

Hunting and Fishing License Information
Records not maintained by a state level agency.

They do not have a central database. You must contact the vendor where the license was purchased. Plans are underway to implement a computerized database by the end of 2006.

New Jersey State Licensing Agencies

For details about the agency responsible for licensing/certifying/registering an item below or in the Agency Quick Finder section, match an item's number with the number of the agency in the *Licensing Agency Information* section.

New Jersey Licenses Searchable Online

Acupuncturist #1	www.state.nj.us/cgi-bin/consumeraffairs/search/searchentry.pl?searchprofession=3251
Alcohol/Drug Counselor #13	www.state.nj.us/cgi-bin/consumeraffairs/search/searchentry.pl?searchprofession=3703
Appraiser, General/Residential #23	www.state.nj.us/cgi-bin/consumeraffairs/search/searchentry.pl?searchprofession=4202
Architect #6	www.state.nj.us/cgi-bin/consumeraffairs/search/searchentry.pl
Athletic Trainer #4	www.state.nj.us/cgi-bin/consumeraffairs/search/searchentry.pl
Audiologist #7	www.state.nj.us/cgi-bin/consumeraffairs/search/search.pl
Barber #9	www.state.nj.us/cgi-bin/consumeraffairs/search/searchentry.pl
Barber Shop #9	www.state.nj.us/cgi-bin/consumeraffairs/search/searchentry.pl
Beautician #9	www.state.nj.us/cgi-bin/consumeraffairs/search/searchentry.pl
Candidate report #43	www.elec.state.nj.us/publicinformation.htm
Cemetery #46	www.state.nj.us/cgi-bin/consumeraffairs/search/searchentry.pl?searchprofession=4701
Cemetery Salesperson #46	www.state.nj.us/cgi-bin/consumeraffairs/search/searchentry.pl?searchprofession=4701
Certificate of Authorization #6	www.state.nj.us/cgi-bin/consumeraffairs/search/searchentry.pl
Charities #3	www.state.nj.us/lps/ca/charfrm.htm
Chiropractor #8	www.state.nj.us/cgi-bin/consumeraffairs/search/searchentry.pl
Contributor, Political #43	www.elec.state.nj.us/publicinformation.htm
Cosmetologist/Hairstylist #9	www.state.nj.us/cgi-bin/consumeraffairs/search/searchentry.pl
Cosmetology/Manicurist Shop #9	www.state.nj.us/cgi-bin/consumeraffairs/search/searchentry.pl
Counselor, Professional #13	www.state.nj.us/cgi-bin/consumeraffairs/search/searchentry.pl
Court Reporter #24	www.state.nj.us/cgi-bin/consumeraffairs/search/searchentry.pl?searchprofession=3000
CPA/Public Accountant #5	www.state.nj.us/cgi-bin/consumeraffairs/search/searchentry.pl?searchprofession=2000
Dental Assistant, Ltd/Registered #10	www.state.nj.us/cgi-bin/consumeraffairs/search/searchentry.pl
Dental Hygienist #10	www.state.nj.us/cgi-bin/consumeraffairs/search/searchentry.pl
Dentist #10	www.state.nj.us/cgi-bin/consumeraffairs/search/searchentry.pl
Electrical Contractor #11	www.state.nj.us/cgi-bin/consumeraffairs/search/searchentry.pl?searchprofession=3400
Embalmer #15	www.state.nj.us/cgi-bin/consumeraffairs/search/searchentry.pl?searchprofession=2
Engineer #20	www.njconsumeraffairs.com/nonmedical/pels.htm
Funeral Home #15	www.state.nj.us/cgi-bin/consumeraffairs/search/searchentry.pl
Funeral Practitioner #15	www.state.nj.us/cgi-bin/consumeraffairs/search/searchentry.pl?searchprofession=2
Hearing Aid Dispenser/Fitter #44	www.state.nj.us/cgi-bin/consumeraffairs/search/searchentry.pl?searchprofession=2253
Home Health Aide #16	www.state.nj.us/cgi-bin/consumeraffairs/search/searchentry.pl
Home Inspection #20	www.njconsumeraffairs.com/nonmedical/pels.htm
Insurance Agent #41	www.nj.gov/dobi/licenseesearch/insurancelicensee.htm
Insurance Public Adjuster #41	www.nj.gov/dobi/licenseesearch/insurancelicensee.htm
Lab Director, Bio-Analytical #14	www.state.nj.us/cgi-bin/consumeraffairs/search/searchentry.pl?searchprofession=2505
Landscape Architect #6	www.state.nj.us/cgi-bin/consumeraffairs/search/searchentry.pl
Lobbyist #43	www.elec.state.nj.us/PublicInformation/GAA_Annual.htm
Manicurist/Manicurist Shop #9	www.state.nj.us/cgi-bin/consumeraffairs/search/searchentry.pl
Marriage & Family Counselor #13	www.state.nj.us/cgi-bin/consumeraffairs/search/searchentry.pl?searchprofession=3703
Marriage Counselor #13	www.state.nj.us/cgi-bin/consumeraffairs/search/searchentry.pl?searchprofession=3703
Midwife #14	www.state.nj.us/cgi-bin/consumeraffairs/search/searchentry.pl?searchprofession=2510
Mortician #15	www.state.nj.us/cgi-bin/consumeraffairs/search/searchentry.pl?searchprofession=2
Nurse, Advance Practice #16	www.state.nj.us/cgi-bin/consumeraffairs/search/searchentry.pl
Nurse-LPN/RN #16	www.state.nj.us/cgi-bin/consumeraffairs/search/searchentry.pl
Occupational Therapist #57	www.state.nj.us/cgi-bin/consumeraffairs/search/searchentry.pl?searchprofession=4601
Occupational Therapy Asst. #57	www.state.nj.us/cgi-bin/consumeraffairs/search/searchentry.pl
Opthalmic Dispenser #51	www.state.nj.us/cgi-bin/consumeraffairs/search/searchentry.pl
Optician/Opthalmic Technician #51	www.state.nj.us/cgi-bin/consumeraffairs/search/searchentry.pl?searchprofession=3102
Optometrist #17	www.state.nj.us/cgi-bin/consumeraffairs/search/searchentry.pl?searchprofession=2701
Orthotist/Prosthetist #52	www.state.nj.us/lps/ca/medical/orthotic.htm
Pharmacist #18	www.state.nj.us/cgi-bin/consumeraffairs/search/searchentry.pl?searchprofession=2801
Physical Therapist/Assistant #19	www.state.nj.us/cgi-bin/consumeraffairs/search/searchentry.pl?searchprofession=4001
Physician #14	www.state.nj.us/cgi-bin/consumeraffairs/search/searchentry.pl?searchprofession=2501
Physician Assistant #14	www.state.nj.us/cgi-bin/consumeraffairs/search/searchentry.pl

Planner, Professional #21 .... www.state.nj.us/cgi-bin/consumeraffairs/search/searchentry.pl?searchprofession=3300
Plumber/Master Plumber #12 .... www.state.nj.us/cgi-bin/consumeraffairs/search/searchentry.pl?searchprofession=3601
Podiatrist #14 .... www.state.nj.us/cgi-bin/consumeraffairs/search/searchentry.pl?searchprofession=2507
Psychologist #22 .... www.state.nj.us/cgi-bin/consumeraffairs/search/searchentry.pl?searchprofession=3
Real Estate Agent/Broker #48 .... www.state.nj.us/dobi/licenseesearch/realestatelicensee.htm
Real Estate Agent/Sales #48 .... www.state.nj.us/dobi/licenseesearch/realestatelicensee.htm
Real Estate Appraiser/Apprentice #23 .... www.state.nj.us/cgi-bin/consumeraffairs/search/searchentry.pl?searchprofession=4202
Real Estate School/ Instructor #48 .... www.state.nj.us/dobi/recskool.htm
Respiratory Therapist #54 .... www.state.nj.us/cgi-bin/consumeraffairs/search/searchentry.pl?searchprofession=4301
Shorthand Reporter #24 .... www.state.nj.us/cgi-bin/consumeraffairs/search/searchentry.pl?searchprofession=3000
Skin Care Specialist/Shop #9 .... www.state.nj.us/cgi-bin/consumeraffairs/search/searchentry.pl
Social Worker #25 .... www.state.nj.us/cgi-bin/consumeraffairs/search/searchentry.pl?searchprofession=4401
Speech-Language Pathologist #7 .... www.state.nj.us/cgi-bin/consumeraffairs/search/search.pl
Surveyor, Land #20 .... www.njconsumeraffairs.com/nonmedical/pels.htm
Tree Expert #55 .... www.state.nj.us/dep/parksandforests/forest/community/cte.html
Veterinarian #26 .... www.state.nj.us/cgi-bin/consumeraffairs/search/searchentry.pl?searchprofession=2901
Viatical Settlement Broker #41 .... www.nj.gov/dobi/licenseesearch/insurancelicensee.htm

New Jersey Licensing Quick Finder

Accountant, Municipal #5 973-504-6380
Acupuncturist #1 609-826-7100
Alcohol/Drug Counselor #13 973-504-6582
Amusement Ride Inspector #45 609-984-7834
Animal Control Officer #59 609-588-3121
Appraiser, General/Residential #23 973-504-6480
Architect #6 973-504-6385
Asbestos Employee/Employer #33 609-633-3760
Asbestos Permit #33 609-633-3760
Athletic Booking Agency #40 973-504-6370
Athletic Trainer #4 609-292-4843
Attorney #49 609-292-8079
Audiologist #7 973-504-6390
Automobile Dealer #42 609-292-4517
Barber #9 973-504-6400
Barber Shop #9 973-504-6400
Beautician #9 973-504-6400
Boiler Operator #34 609-984-3001
Boiler Pressure Vessel & Refrigeration Inspector #45
.... 609-984-7834
Boxer #53 609-292-0317
Boxing Manager #28 609-292-0317
Building Inspector #45 609-984-7834
Candidate report #43 609-292-8700
Career Counselor #40 973-504-6370
Casino #28 609-441-3555
Casino Employee #28 609-441-3015
Cemetery #46 973-504-6553
Cemetery Salesperson #46 973-504-6553
Certificate of Authorization #6 973-504-6385
Charities #3 973-504-6215
Check Casher/Seller #38 609-292-5340
Chiropractor #8 973-504-6395
Club/Cabaret #37 609-984-3231
Collection Agency Bond #36 609-292-9292
Computer Job-Matching Service #40 ... 973-504-6370
Construction Code Official #45 609-984-7834
Contributor, Political #43 609-292-8700
Cosmetologist/Hairstylist #9 973-504-6400
Cosmetology/Manicurist Shop #9 973-504-6400
Counselor, Professional #13 973-504-6582
Court Reporter #24 973-504-6490
CPA/Public Accountant #5 973-504-6380
CPE Sponsor #5 973-504-6380
Crane Operator #34 609-292-5626
Dental Assistant, Ltd/Registered #10 ... 973-504-6405
Dental Hygienist #10 973-504-6405

Dentist #10 973-504-6405
Educational Media Specialist/Librarian #29
.... 609-292-0739
Electrical Contractor #11 973-504-6410
Electrical Inspector #45 609-984-7834
Elevator Inspector #45 609-984-7834
Embalmer #15 609-292-4843
Emergency Medical Svc Provider #32 . 609-633-7777
Emergency Medical Technician #32 609-633-7777
Employment Agency #40 973-504-6370
Engineer #20 973-504-6460
Fire Protection Inspector #45 609-984-7834
Firefighter #58 609-633-6117
Firm #5 973-504-6380
Funeral Home #15 973-504-6425
Funeral Practitioner #15 973-504-6425
Health Care Service Agency #40 973-504-6370
Health Spa #40 973-504-6370
Hearing Aid Dispenser/Fitter #44 973-504-6331
Home Health Aide #16 973-504-6504
Home Inspection #20 973-504-6460
Home Repair Contractor/Seller #39 609-292-3420
Hotel/Motel #37 609-984-3231
Housing Code Official #45 609-984-7834
Inplant Inspector #45 609-984-7834
Inspector of Hotels & Multiple Dwellings Inspector #45
.... 609-984-7834
Insurance Agent #41 609-292-4337
Insurance Public Adjuster #41 609-292-4337
Investment Advisor/Representative #27 973-504-3600
Job Listing Service #40 973-504-6370
Lab Director, Bio-Analytical #14 609-292-4843
Landscape Architect #6 973-504-6385
Lender, Consumer #39 609-292-5340
Librarian #29 609-292-2070
Liquor Control #37 609-984-3231
Liquor Distribution, Plenary Retail/Limited Retail #37
.... 609-984-3231
Liquor Rectifier/Blender #37 609-984-3231
Liquor Retail, Plenary/Seasonal #37 ... 609-984-3231
Liquor Sales,Retail/Limited/Plenary #37 609-984-3231
Liquor Transit, Plenary Retail #37 609-984-3231
Liquor Wholesale, Limited/Plenary #37 609-984-3231
Lobbyist #43 609-292-8700
Manicurist/Manicurist Shop #9 973-504-6400
Marriage & Family Counselor #13 973-504-6582
Marriage Counselor #13 973-504-6582

Mechanical Inspector 1 & 2 Family #45 609-984-7834
Midwife #14 609-292-4843
Modeling & Talent Agency #40 973-504-6370
Mortgage (2nd) Lender #39 609-292-5340
Mortician #15 973-504-6425
Mover/Warehouseman #2 973-504-6512
Notary Public #36 609-292-9292
Nurse, Advance Practice #16 973-504-6504
Nurse-LPN #16 973-504-6504
Nurse-RN #16 973-504-6504
Nursing Home Administrator #50 609-633-9706
Nursing Registry Svc #40 973-504-6370
Occupational Therapist #57 973-504-6570
Occupational Therapy Asst. #57 973-504-6570
Opthalmic Dispenser #51 973-504-6435
Optician/Opthalmic Technician #51 973-504-6435
Optometrist #17 973-504-6440
Orthodontic Assistant, Ltd/ Registered #10
.... 973-504-6405
Orthopedist #14 609-292-4843
Orthotist/Prosthetist #52 973-504-6445
Paramedic #32 609-633-7777
Pesticide Applicator/Operator #31 609-530-4070
Pesticide Dealer #31 609-530-4070
Pharmacist #18 973-504-6450
Pharmacy #18 973-504-6450
Physical Therapist/Assistant #19 973-504-6455
Physician #14 609-292-4843
Physician Assistant #14 609-292-4843
Planner, Professional #21 973-504-6465
Plumber/Master Plumber #12 973-504-6420
Plumbing Inspector #45 609-984-7834
Podiatrist #14 609-292-4843
Private Detective #56 .... 609-882-2000 X2680
Psychologist #22 973-504-6470
Pump Installer #30 609-984-6831
Race Horse #47 609-292-0613
Race Horse Owner/Trainer #47 609-292-0613
Real Estate Agent/Broker #48 609-292-8280
Real Estate Agent/Sales #48 609-292-8280
Real Estate Appraiser/Apprentice #23 . 973-504-6480
Real Estate School/ Instructor #48 609-292-8280
Refrigeration Technician #34 609-984-3001
Respiratory Therapist #54 973-504-6485
Resume Service #40 973-504-6370
School Accountant #5 973-504-6380
School Counselor #29 609-292-0739

School Principal/Admin./Super. #29 609-292-0739	Stable Mate #47 609-292-0613	Veterinarian #26 973-504-6500
School, Accredited #29 609-292-0739	Student Personnel Svc Director #29 609-292-0739	Viatical Settlement Broker #41 609-292-4337
Securities Agent #27 973-504-3600	Surveyor, Land #20 973-504-6460	Waste Water System Operator #30 609-984-6831
Securities Broker/Dealer #27 973-504-3600	Teacher #29 609-292-0739	Weighmaster #35 732-815-4840
Securities Issuer #27 973-504-3600	Temporary Help Agency #40 973-504-6370	Weights & Measures Mechanic #35 .. 732-815-4840
Shorthand Reporter #24 973-504-6490	Theater #37 609-984-3231	Well Driller #30 609-984-6831
Skin Care Specialist/Shop #9 973-504-6400	Ticket Reseller #40 973-504-6370	Wine Wholesaler/Winery #37 609-984-3231
Social Worker #25 973-504-6495	Trademark #36 609-292-9292	
Speech-Language Pathologist #7 973-504-6390	Tree Expert #55 609-292-2532	

New Jersey Licensing Agency Information

1 Board of Medical Examiners, Acupuncture Examining Board, PO Box 183, Trenton, NJ 08625-0183; 609-826-7100.
www.nj.gov/lps/ca/medical/acupuncture.htm
Search Database at
www.state.nj.us/lps/ca/bme/acupdir.htm

2 Division of Consumer Affairs, Regulated Business Section, 124 Halsey St, Newark, NJ 07101; 973-504-6442, Fax: 973-648-2807.
www.state.nj.us/lps/ca
Email: askconsumeraffairs@smtp.lps.state.nj.us

3 Charities Registration Section, Division of Consumer Affairs, PO Box 45021 (124 Halsey St), Newark, NJ 07101; 973-504-6215, Fax: 973-273-8035.
www.state.nj.us/lps/ca
Search Database at
www.state.nj.us/lps/ca/charfrm.htm

4 Board of Medical Examiners, Athletic Training Advisory Commission, 140 E Front St, 2nd Fl, Trenton, NJ 08625-0183; 609-292-4843, Fax: 609-826-7117.
www.state.nj.us/lps/ca/medical.htm

5 Board of Accountancy, PO Box 45000, Newark, NJ 07101; 973-504-6380, Fax: 973-648-2855.
www.state.nj.us/lps/ca/nonmed.htm#acc1
Search Database at
www.state.nj.us/lps/ca/accountancy/accdir.htm

6 Board of Architects, Division of Consumer Affairs, PO Box 45001, Newark, NJ 07101; 973-504-6385, Fax: 973-504-6458.
www.state.nj.us/lps/ca/nonmedical/architects.htm
Search Database at www.state.nj.us/cgi-bin/consumeraffairs/search/searchentry.pl

7 Board of Audiology & Speech Language Pathology, Division of Consumer Affairs, P.O. Pox 45002, 124 Halsey St, Newark, NJ 07101; 973-504-6390, Fax: 973-648-3355.
www.state.nj.us/lps/ca/medical.htm
Search Database at www.state.nj.us/cgi-bin/consumeraffairs/search/search.pl

8 Board of Chiropractic Examiners, Division of Consumer Affairs, PO Box 45004, Newark, NJ 07101; 973-504-6395, Fax: 973-648-3538.
www.state.nj.us/lps/ca/medical.htm
Email: lpygidr@oaq.lps.state.nj.us
Search Database at www.state.nj.us/cgi-bin/consumeraffairs/search/search.pl

9 Board of Cosmetology & Hairstyling, PO Box 45003, Newark, NJ 07101; 973-504-6400, Fax: 973-648-3536.
www.state.nj.us/lps/ca/nonmedical/coshair.htm
Search Database at
www.state.nj.us/lps/ca/director.htm

10 Board of Dentistry, PO Box 45005, 124 Halsey St, Newark, NJ 07101; 973-504-6405, Fax: 973-273-8075.
www.state.nj.us/lps/ca/medical.htm#den3
Search Database at
www.state.nj.us/lps/ca/medical.htm#den3 Note: There is an automated license verification line (need license number) 973-273-8090 with fax back capability for written verifications.

11 Board of Examiners of Electrical Contractors, Division of Consumer Affairs, 124 Halsey St (07102), Newark, NJ 07101; 973-504-6410, Fax: 973-648-3355.
www.state.nj.us/lps/ca/nonmedical/electrical.htm
Email: AskConsumerAffairs@oag.lps.state.nj.us
Search Database at
www.state.nj.us/lps/ca/electric/elecdir.htm

12 Board of Examiners of Master Plumbers, PO Box 45008 (124 Halsey St, 07102), Newark, NJ 07101; 973-504-6420.
www.state.nj.us/lps/ca/home.htm
Search Database at
www.state.nj.us/lps/ca/plumber/plumdir.htm

13 Board of Marriage & Family Therapy Examiners, 124 Halsey St, 6th Fl, Newark, NJ 07101; 973-504-6582.
www.state.nj.us/lps/ca/boards.htm
Search Database at
www.state.nj.us/lps/ca/marriage/pcdir.htm

14 Board of Medical Examiners, PO Box 183, Trenton, NJ 08625-0183; 609-292-4843, Fax: 609-984-3950.
www.state.nj./lps/ca/medical.htm
Search Database at
www.state.nj.us/lps/ca/director.htm

15 Board of Mortuary Science, Division of Consumer Affairs, 124 Halsey St, Newark, NJ 07102; 973-504-6425, Fax: 973-648-2855.
www.state.nj.us/lps/ca/nonmedical/mortuary.htm
Email: lpywidr@oaq.lps.state.nj.us
Search Database at
www.state.nj.us/lps/ca/mort/mortdir.htm

16 Board of Nursing, 124 Halsey St (07102), Newark, NJ 07101; 973-504-6430, Fax: 973-648-3481.
www.state.nj.us/lps/ca/medical/nursing.htm
Email: AskConsumerAffairs@oaq.state.nj.us
Search Database at
www.state.nj.us/lps/ca/medical.htm#nur6

17 Board of Optometrists, Division of Consumer Affairs, 124 Halsey St (07102), Newark, NJ 07101; 973-504-6440, Fax: 973-648-3536.
www.state.nj.us/lps/ca/optometry/optdir.htm
Search Database at
www.state.nj.us/lps/ca/optometry/optdir.htm

18 Board of Pharmacy, PO Box 45013 (124 Halsey St, 07102), Newark, NJ 07101; 973-504-6450, Fax: 973-648-3355.
www.state.nj.us/lps/ca/medical.htm#pharm11
Search Database at
www.state.nj.us/lps/ca/pharm/pharmdir.htm

19 Board of Physical Therapists, 124 Halsey St, Newark, NJ 07101; 973-504-6455, Fax: 973-648-3536.
www.nj.gov/lps/ca/medical/pt.htm
Search Database at
www.state.nj.us/lps/ca/pt/ptdir.htm

20 Board of Professional Engineers & Land Surveyors, 124 Halsey St, 3rd Fl, Newark, NJ 07102; 973-504-6460, Fax: 973-273-8020.
www.njconsumeraffairs.com/nonmedical/pels.htm
Search Database at
www.njconsumeraffairs.com/nonmedical/pels.htm

21 Board of Professional Planners, PO Box 45016 (124 Halsey St, 07102), Newark, NJ 07101; 973-504-6465, Fax: 973-648-3536.
www.state.nj.us/lps/ca/plan/planner.htm
Search Database at
www.state.nj.us/lps/ca/plan/plandir.htm

22 Board of Psychological Examiners, Division of Consumer Affairs, 124 Halsey St, Newark, NJ 07102; 973-504-6470.
www.state.nj.us/lps/ca/medical/psycho.htm
Search Database at
www.state.nj.us/lps/ca/psy/psydir.htm

23 Board of Real Estate Appraisers, Division of Consumer Affairs, PO Box 45032 (124 Halsey St, 07102), Newark, NJ 07101; 973-504-6480, Fax: 973-648-3536. www.state.nj.us/lps/ca
Search Database at
www.state.nj.us/lps/ca/real/realdir.htm

24 Board of Shorthand Reporting, Po Box 45019, Newark, NJ 07101; 973-504-6490.
www.state.nj.us/lps/ca/nonmedical/shorthand.htm
Search Database at
www.state.nj.us/lps/ca/short/shortdir.htm

25 Board of Social Work Examiners, PO Box 45033, Newark, NJ 07101; 973-504-6495, Fax: 973-273-8067.
www.state.nj.us/lps/ca/medical.htm#sw15
Search Database at www.state.nj.us/lps/ca/soc ial/socdir.htm Note: License verification telephone number is 973-273-8090.

26 Board of Veterinary Medical Examiners, PO Box 45033, Newark, NJ 07101; 973-504-6500, Fax: 973-648-3355.
www.state.nj.us/lps/ca/medical/veterinary.htm
Email: ROMANOD@smtd.lps.state.nj.us
Search Database at
www.state.nj.us/lps/ca/vetmed/vetdir.htm

27 Bureau of Securities, PO Box 47029, 153 Halsey St 6th Fl, Newark, NJ 07101; 973-504-3600, Fax: 973-504-3601.
www.state.nj.us/lps/ca/bos.htm

28 Casino Control Commission, Tennessee Ave & Boardwalk, Arcade Bldg, Atlantic City, NJ 08401; 609-441-3000, Fax: 609-441-3752.
www.state.nj.us/casinos

29 Department of Education, Licensing and Credentials, PO Box 500, 100 Riverview Plaza, Trenton, NJ 08625-0500; 609-292-2045, Fax: 609-292-3768.

30 Department of Environmental Protection, Bureau of Water Allocations, PO Box 402 (401 E State St, CN-402), Trenton, NJ 08625; 609-984-6831, Fax: 609-633-1231.
www.state.nj.us/dep/watersupply/well.htm

31 Department of Environmental Protection, Pesticide Control Program, PO Box 411, Trenton, NJ 08625-0411; 609-530-4070, Fax: 609-984-6555.
www.state.nj.us/dep/enforcement/pcp
Email: askDEP@dep.state.nj.us

32 Office of Emergency Medical Svcs, Department of Health, 50 E State St 6th Fl (PO Box 360), Trenton, NJ 08625; 609-633-7777, Fax: 609-633-7954.
www.state.nj.us/health/ems/index.html
Email: ems@doh.state.ny.us   Note: Only disciplinary actions, fines, and enforcement actions are online.

33 Asbestos Control and Licensing, Department of Workforce Dev.; Occupational Safety & Health, PO Box 949 (1 John Fitch Plaza, 3rd Fl), Trenton, NJ 08625-0949; 609-633-3760, Fax: 609-633-0664.

34 Bureau of Boiler & Pressure Vessel Compliance, Department of Community Affairs, PO Box 814 (101 South Broad St), Trenton, NJ 08625-0814; 609-984-3001, Fax: 609-984-1577.

35 Department of Law & Public Safety, Office of Weights & Measures, P.O. Box 490, Avanel, NJ 07001; 732-815-4840, Fax: 732-382-5298.
www.state.nj.us/lps/ca/owm.htm

36 Department of Treasury, Division of Revenue, Notary Section, PO Box 452, West Trenton, NJ 08625; 609-292-9292, Fax: 609-984-6681.
www.state.nj.us/treasury/revenue/dcr/programs/notary.html

37 Division of Alcoholic Beverage Control, 140 E Front St, CN087, Trenton, NJ 08625-0087; 609-984-3230, Fax: 609-633-6078.
www.state.nj.us/lps/abc/licensing.html

38 Division of Banking, Consumer Credit Bureau, 20 W State St CN-040, Trenton, NJ 08625; 609-292-5340, Fax: 609-292-5461.
www.state.nj.us/dobi/bankmnu.shtml

39 Division of Banking, Office of Consumer Finance, 20 W State St CN-040, Trenton, NJ 08625; 609-292-7659, Fax: 609-292-5461.
www.state.nj.us/dobi/index.shtml
Email: lhughes@cobi.state.nj.us

40 Regulated Business Section, Division of Consumer Affairs, PO Box 45028 (124 Halsey St), Newark, NJ 07101; 973-504-6370, Fax: 973-648-2807.
www.njconsumeraffairs.gov/ocp.htm#regulated

41 Division of Insurance, License Processing, PO Box 327 (20 W. State St), Trenton, NJ 08625-0327; 609-292-4337, Fax: 609-984-0092.
www.njdobi.org/insmnu.shtml
Email: inslic@dobi.state.nj.us
Search Database at
www.nj.gov/dobi/licenseesearch/insurancelicensee.htm

42 Division of Motor Vehicles, Dealer Licensing Section, 225 E State St, Trenton, NJ 08666; 609-292-4517, Fax: 609-292-5153.
www.state.nj.us/mvc/bc_licensing/bc_motor_vehicle_dealership_license.html

43 Election Law Enforcement Commission, PO Box 185, CN-185 (28 W State St), Trenton, NJ 08625-0185; 609-292-8700, Fax: 609-292-9854.
www.elec.state.nj.us/

44 Hearing Aid Dispensers Examining Committee, PO Box 45038, Newark, NJ 07101; 973-504-6331, Fax: 973-648-3355.
www.state.nj.us/lps/ca/medical.htm
Search Database at
www.state.nj.us/lps/ca/hear/heardir.htm

45 Department of Community Affairs, Bureau of Code Services, Attn: Licensing Unit, PO Box 816, Trenton, NJ 08625-0816; 609-984-7834, Fax: 609-984-7952.
www.state.nj.us/dca/codes/
Email: codeslicensing@dca.state.nj.us

46 Cemetery Board, PO Box 45036, Newark, NJ 07101; 973-504-6553, Fax: 973-648-3536.
www.state.nj.us/lps/ca/nonmed.htm
Search Database at
www.state.nj.us/lps/ca/director.htm

47 Racing Commission, POB 088 (140 Front St), Trenton, NJ 08625-0080; 609-292-0613, Fax: 609-599-1785.

48 Department of Banking & Insurance, Real Estate Commission, 240 W State St, (PO Box 328), Trenton, NJ 08625-0328; 609-292-8280, Fax: 609-292-0944.
www.state.nj.us/dobi/remnu.htm
Email: realestate@dobi.state.nj.us
Search Database at
www.state.nj.us/dobi/licenseesearch/realestatelicensee.htm

49 Supreme Court, New Jersey Lawyers Fund, PO Box 961, Trenton, NJ 08625; 609-292-8079, Fax: 609-394-3637.
www.judiciary.state.nj.us/cpf/index.htm

50 Nursing Home Administrators Licensing Board, PO Box 367, Trenton, NJ 08625-0367; 609-633-9706, Fax: 609-633-9087.
www.state.nj.us/health/

51 Ophthalmic Dispensers & Ophthalmic Technicians Board, Division of Consumer Affairs, 124 Halsey St, Newark, NJ 07102; 973-504-6435.
www.state.nj.us/lps/ca/medical/ophthalmic.htm
Search Database at
www.state.nj.us/lps/ca/director.htm

52 Orthotics & Prosthetics Board of Examiners, Division of Consumer Affairs, PO Box 45034 (124 Halsey St., Newark, NJ 07112; 973-504-6445, Fax: 973-648-3536.
www.state.nj.us/lps/ca
Search Database at
www.state.nj.us/lps/ca/medical/orthotic.htm

53 Athletic Control Board, 140 E Front St, CN-180, Trenton, NJ 08625-0180; 609-292-0317, Fax: 609-292-3756.

54 Board of Respiratory Care, 122 Halsey St,, Newark, NJ 07101; 973-504-6485, Fax: 973-648-3355.
www.state.nj.us/lps/ca/home.htm
Search Database at
www.state.nj.us/lps/ca/respcare/respdir.htm

55 Forestry Service, 501 E State St CN-404, Trenton, NJ 08625-0404; 609-292-2532, Fax: 609-984-0378.
www.state.nj.us/dep/forestry/community/home.htm
Search Database at
www.state.nj.us/dep/parksandforests/forest/community/cte.html

56 State Police Department, Private Detective Division, River Rd, Trenton, NJ 08628; 609-882-2000 x2680, Fax: 609-637-9583.
www.njsp.org/about/srb.html

57 Occupational Therapy Advisory Council, Division of Consumer Affairs, PO Box 45027 (124 Halsey St), Newark, NJ 07101; 973-504-6570.
www.state.nj.us/lps/ca/home.htm
Email: lpyqidr@oag.lps.state.nj.us
Search Database at
www.state.nj.us/lps/ca/director.htm

58 Department of Community Affairs, Division of Fire Safety, PO Box 809, Trenton, NJ 08625-0809; 609-633-6117, Fax: 609-633-6744.
www.state.nj.us/dca/dfs/

59 Department of Health & Senior Svcs, Infectious & Zoonotic Program, PO Box 369, Trenton, NJ 08625-0369; 609-588-3121, Fax: 609-588-3894.
www.state.nj.us

New Jersey Federal Courts

The following list indicates the district and division name for each county in the state. If the bankruptcy court location is different from the district court, then the location of the bankruptcy court appears in parentheses. For bankruptcies, parts of Burlington County are under the jurisdition of Trenton, other parts Camden.

County/Court Cross Reference

Atlantic	Camden
Bergen	Newark
Burlington	Camden (Camden/Trenton)
Camden	Camden
Cape May	Camden
Cumberland	Camden
Essex	Newark
Gloucester	Camden
Hudson	Newark
Hunterdon	Trenton
Mercer	Trenton
Middlesex	Newark (Trenton/Camden)
Monmouth	Newark (Trenton)
Morris	Newark
Ocean	Trenton
Passaic	Newark
Salem	Camden
Somerset	Trenton
Sussex	Newark
Union	Newark
Warren	Trenton

Standards for Federal Courts: Search fee is $26.00 per item (one party name or case number). Copy fee is $.50 per page. Certification fee is $9.00 per document, double for exemplification, if available. All fees standard unless noted in profile. Mail Search: always enclose a stamped self addressed envelope unless otherwise noted. Most courts accept fax requests or will suggest a copying/search vendor. Before releasing records, all courts require prepayment, unless noted.

Open records are located at the court unless otherwise noted. District courts index by defendant and plaintiff as well as by case number. Bankruptcy courts usually index by debtor and case number. While most courts now have their indexes on computer, many may still maintain index card files as well.

Courts offering internet access via CM-ECF or older RACER, PACER, or Web-PACER systems charge $.08 per page fee unless noted as free. Where PACER is available, the universal sign-up number is 800-676-6856. Find PACER and the US Party/Case Index at http://pacer.psc.uscourts.gov.

US District Court

Camden Division Clerk of Court, PO Box 2797, Camden, NJ 08101 (courier address: Rm 1050, 4th & Cooper Sts, Camden, NJ 08101), 856-757-5021, Fax-856-757-5370. Hours- 9AM-4PM. www.njd.uscourts.gov

Counties: Atlantic, Burlington, Camden, Cape May, Cumberland, Gloucester, Salem.

Searches & Indexing: Computer, microfiche and card indexes maintained. New cases in the index 1-2 days after filing date. Records purged never. District-wide searches available here.

Fee & Payment: Pay by Visa/MC, money order, cashier's or personal check. Payee: Clerk, US District Court. Prepayment required.

Phone Search: Only docket information is available by phone.

Mail Search: search usually completed- 3-4 working days. Include SASE for return.

In Person Search: Fee charged if court performs your search. Searchers can print dockets from the computer. No self-serve copier available.

E-Services: PACER online at http://pacer.njd.uscourts.gov. PACER records go back to 5/1991. New records online after 1 day. ECF at https://ecf.njd.uscourts.gov **Opinions Online:** http://lawlibrary.rutgers.edu/fed/search.html.

Newark Division Court Clerk, ML King, Jr Federal Bldg & US Courthouse, 50 Walnut St, Rm 4015, Newark, NJ 07101 (also use mail address for courier delivery), 973-645-3730, records rm- 973-645-4565. 9AM-4PM. www.njd.uscourts.gov

Counties: Bergen, Essex, Hudson, Middlesex, Morris, Passaic, Sussex, Union. Monmouth County cases here from late 1997-200?; Pre-1997 closed cases remain in Trenton.

Searches & Indexing: Both computer and card indexes maintained. New cases in the index 1-3 days after filing date. Records purged never.

Fee & Payment: Pay by money order, cashier check, business check. No personal checks. Payee: Clerk, US District Court. Prepayment required.

Phone Search: Only docket information available by telephone.

Mail Search: search usually completed- 1 week. Include SASE for return.

In Person Search: Fee charged if court performs your search. No self-serve copier available - $9.00 per page.

E-Services: PACER online at http://pacer.njd.uscourts.gov. PACER records go back to 5/1991. New records online after 1 day. ECF at https://ecf.njd.uscourts.gov **Opinions Online:** http://lawlibrary.rutgers.edu/fed/search.html.

Trenton Division Court Clerk, Clerk, US District Court, 402 E State St, Rm 2020, Trenton, NJ 08608 (also use mail address for courier delivery), 609-989-2065. Hours- 9AM-4PM. www.njd.uscourts.gov

Counties: Hunterdon, Mercer, Monmouth, Ocean, Somerset, Warren. 1997-200? Monmouth County may be found at Newark Division. Pre-1997 closed Monmouth cases remain in Trenton.

Searches & Indexing: Results do not include SSN or DOB. Computer and microfiche indexes maintained; computer back to 1990. New cases in the index several days after filing date. Records purged never. District-wide searches available back to 1920 from Trenton; closed files for Newark division here up to 1997.

Fee & Payment: Pay by Visa/MC, money order, cashier's or personal check. Payee: Clerk, US District Court. Prepayment required.

Phone Search: Only docket information available by phone.

Mail Search: search usually completed- 2 days. SASE not required.

In Person Search: Fee charged if court performs your search. No self-serve copier available.

E-Services: PACER online at http://pacer.njd.uscourts.gov. PACER records go back to 5/1991. New records online after 1 day. ECF at https://ecf.njd.uscourts.gov **Opinions Online:** http://lawlibrary.rutgers.edu/fed/search.html.

US Bankruptcy Court

Camden Division Court Clerk, PO Box 2067, Camden, NJ 08101 (courier address: 401 Market St, 2nd Fl, Camden, NJ 08101), 856-757-5485, Fax-856-757-5425. Hours- 8:30AM-4PM. www.njb.uscourts.gov

Counties: Atlantic, Burlington (partial), Camden, Cape May, Cumberland, Gloucester, Salem. See Trenton Division for remainder of Burlington County

Searches & Indexing: Results include last 4 SSN digits. Computer index maintained. New cases in the index immediately after filing date. Records purged every 6 months.

Fee & Payment: Pay by money order, cashier check, business check. No personal checks. Payee: Clerk, US Bankruptcy Court. Prepayment required.

Phone Search: Only docket information available by phone. Voice Case Information Service available, call VCIS at 877-239-2547 or 973-645-6044.

Mail Search: search usually completed- 2-5 days. Include SASE for return.

In Person Search: Fee charged if court performs your search. No self-serve copier available.

E-Services: ECF replace PACER. Document images available. PACER records go back to 1991. ECF at https://ecf.njb.uscourts.gov **Opinions Online:** www.njb.uscourts.gov/chambers2/index.shtml. Opinions lists are not complete. **Other Online Access:** Calendars free at www.njb.uscourts.gov/hearingdate/index.pl.

Newark Division Court Clerk, PO Box 1352, Newark, NJ 07101-1352 (courier address: ML King Jr Federal Bldg, 50 Walnut St, 3rd Fl, Newark, NJ 07102), 973-645-4764. Hours- 8:30AM-4PM. www.njb.uscourts.gov

Counties: Bergen, Essex, Hudson, Morris, Passaic, Sussex, Union.

Searches & Indexing: Results include last 4 SSN digits. Computer index maintained. New cases in the index immediately after filing date. Records purged every 6 months.

Fee & Payment: Pay by money order, cashier check, business check. No personal checks. Payee: Clerk, US Bankruptcy Court. Prepayment required.

Phone Search: Voice Case Information Service available, call VCIS at 877-239-2547 or 973-645-6044.

Mail Search: search usually completed- 2-5 days. Include SASE for return.

In Person Search: Fee charged if court performs your search. No self-serve copier available.

E-Services: ECF replace PACER. Document images available. PACER records go back to 1991. ECF at https://ecf.njb.uscourts.gov

Opinions Online: www.njb.uscourts.gov/chambers2/index.shtml. Opinions lists are not complete. **Other Online Access:** Calendars free at www.njb.uscourts.gov/hearingdate/index.pl.

Trenton Division Clerk of Court, 402 E State St, 1st Fl, Trenton, NJ 08608 (also use mail address for courier delivery), 609-989-2129, Fax-609-989-0580. Hours- 8:30AM-4PM. www.njb.uscourts.gov

Counties: Burlington (partial), Hunterdon, Mercer, Middlesex, Monmouth, Ocean, Somerset, Warren. See Camden Division for remainder of Burlington County

Searches & Indexing: Results do not include SSN or DOB. Computer index maintained. New cases in the index immediately after filing date. Records purged every 6 months.

Fee & Payment: Pay by money order, cashier check, business check. No personal checks. Payee: Clerk, US Bankruptcy Court. Prepayment required.

Phone Search: Voice Case Information Service available, call 877-239-2547 or 973-645-6044.

Mail Search: search usually completed- 1-2 days. Include SASE for return.

In Person Search: Fee charged if court performs your search. No self-serve copier available.

E-Services: ECF replace PACER. Document images available. PACER records go back to 1991. ECF at https://ecf.njb.uscourts.gov **Opinions Online:** www.njb.uscourts.gov/chambers2/index.shtml. Opinions lists are not complete. **Other Online Access:** Calendars free at www.njb.uscourts.gov/hearingdate/index.pl.

New Jersey County Courts

Court	Jurisdiction	No. of Courts	How Organized
Superior Courts*	General	21	21 Counties/15 Vicinages
Special Civil Part*	Limited	21	21 Counties
Municipal Courts	Municipal	535	
Tax Court	Special	1	

* Profiled in this Sourcebook.

Court	CIVIL								
	Tort	Contract	Real Estate	Min. Claim	Max. Claim	Small Claims	Estate	Eviction	Domestic Relations
Superior Courts*	X	X	X	$15,000	No Max		X		X
Special Civil Part*	X	X	X	$3000	$10,000	$3000		X	
Municipal Courts									
Tax Court									

Court	CRIMINAL				
	Felony	Misdemeanor	DWI/DUI	Preliminary Hearing	Juvenile
Superior Courts*	X				X
Special Civil Part*					
Municipal Courts		X	X		
Tax Court					

ADMINISTRATION Administrative Office of the Courts, RJH Justice Complex, Courts Bldg 7th Fl, PO Box 037, Trenton, NJ, 08625; 609-984-0275, Fax: 609-984-6968. www.judiciary.state.nj.us

COURT STRUCTURE Each Superior Court has 2 divisions; one for the Civil Division and another for the Criminal Division. Search requests should be addressed separately to each division.

The Civil cases in which the amounts in controversy exceeds $15,000 are heard in the Civil Division of Superior Court. Cases in which the amounts in controversy are between $3,000 and $15,000 are heard in the Special Civil Part of the Civil Division. Those in which the amounts in controversy are less than $3,000 also are heard in the Special Civil Part and are known as small claims cases. Probate is handled by Surrogates.

ONLINE ACCESS The Judiciary's civil motion calendar is searchable at http://www.judiciary.state.nj.us/calendars.htm. The database includes all Superior Court Motion Calendars for the Civil Division (Law-Civil Part, Special CivilPart and Chancery-General Equity), and proceeding information for a six-week period (2 weeks prior to the current date and 4 weeks following the current date). Another useful site giving decisions is maintained by the Rutgers law School, go to http://lawlibrary.rutgers.edu/search.shtml.

Also, the state has three computerized case management systems - ACMS, AMIS, and FACTS - which are not open to the general public:

- ACMS (Automated Case Management System) contains data on all active civil cases statewide from the Law Division-Civil Part, Chancery Division-Equity Part, the Special Civil Part statewide, and the Appellate Division.
- AMIS (Archival Management Information System) contains closed civil case information. Records go back to the late 1980s.
- FACTS (Family Automated Case Tracking System) contains information on dissolutions from all counties.

The fee is $1.00 per minute of use, and a $500 collateral account is required. For info or a guidebook containing requirements and an enrollment form, write to: Superior Court Clerk's Office, Electronic Access Program, 25 Market St, CN971, Trenton NJ 08625, FAX 609-292-6564, or call 609-292-4987.

ADDITIONAL INFORMATION

Starting in 2004, Superior Courts have the option of directing civil case inquiries to the main NJ Superior Court, PO Box 971, Trenton, NJ 08625, Attn: Judgment Unit; telephone 609-292-4804. The Judgment Unit will not accept fax requests, but will do a phone search; there is also a public access terminal for case lookups at their office at the Justice Complex, 25 Market St, Trenton.

Criminal searches may be done in person at the court on their public access terminal, but the Superior court now directs non-in person searches to the New Jersey State Police Records and ID Section at 609-882-2000, x2991 or x2918, which are fingerprint-based searches. For information on purchase of the statewide public access criminal records databases, call 609-292-4681.

Note that Cape May County offices are located in City of Cape May Court House, and not in City of Cape May.

Atlantic County

Superior Court - Criminal Division
Criminal Courthouse, 4997 Unami Blvd, Mays Landing, NJ 08330; phone: 609-625-7000; criminal phone: 609-909-8140; fax: 609-645-5875; hours 8:30AM-4:30PM (EST). *Felony.*
www.judiciary.state.nj.us/atlantic/index.htm
Criminal Records: Access: In person only. Visitors must perform in person searches themselves. Court makes copy: $.75 per page. Required to search: name, years to search, DOB; SSN helpful. Criminal records on computer from 1985, prior on docket books and index cards back to 1940.
General Information: Public terminal has only criminal records back to 1985. No sealed, expunged, judges notes, PSI's, or mental illness records released. Certification fee: $5.00. Payee: Treasurer-State of New Jersey. No personal checks accepted. Prepayment required.

Superior Court - Civil Division 1201 Bacharach Blvd, Atlantic City, NJ 08401; phone: 609-625-7000 x3370; fax: 609-645-5875; hours 8:30AM-4:30PM (EST). *Civil Actions Over $15,000, Probate.*
www.judiciary.state.nj.us/atlantic/index.htm
Note: Records location is
Civil Records: Access: Mail, in person, online. No search fee. Court makes copy: $.75 per page 1st 1-10 pages; $.50 per page 11-20 pages; $.25 per page 20 plus pages. Required to search: name, years to search. Civil cases indexed by defendant, plaintiff; on computer from 9/84, on dockets from 1960, prior to 1960 archived. Prior to 1960 records are for public review only (in large books, difficult to find records). Participates in the court records statewide Electronic Access Program; for signup, information and booklet call 609-292-4987. Mail turnaround time 1 day.
General Information: Public terminal has only civil records back to 1985. No sealed, expunged, judges notes, PSI's, or mental illness records released. No certification fee . Payee: Clerk of Special Civil Ct. No personal checks accepted. Prepayment and SASE required.

Superior Court Special Civil Part 1201 Bacharach Blvd, Atlantic City, NJ 08401; phone: 609-345-6700 X3347; fax: 609-343-2326; hours 8:30AM-4:30PM (EST). *Civil Actions Under $15,000, Eviction, Small Claims.*
www.judiciary.state.nj.us/atlantic/index.htm
Civil Records: Access: Mail, online, in person fax. Both court and visitors may perform in person searches. No search fee. Court makes copy: $.75 per page. Required to search: name, years to search. Civil cases indexed by defendant, plaintiff; on computer from 1985 (some from 1987), prior on index books. In order to review index books, call in advance for an appointment. Participates in the court records statewide Electronic Access Program; for signup, information and booklet call 609-292-4987. Mail turnaround time 1 week.
General Information: Public terminal has only civil records back to 1987. No adoption, sealed,

juvenile, expunged, dismissed, or mental health records released. Certification fee: $5.00. Payee: Clerk, Special Civil Part. Personal checks accepted. Prepayment and SASE required.

Bergen County

Superior Court - Criminal Division 10 Main St, Rm 134, Justice Ctr, Hackensack, NJ 07601; phone: 201-527-2445; fax: 201-342-9083; hours 8:30AM-4:30PM (EST). *Felony.*
www.judiciary.state.nj.us/bergen/index.htm
Criminal Records: Access: In person only. Both court and visitors may perform in person searches. No search fee. Court makes copy: $.25. No charge for single copy of criminal record. Required to search: name, years to search. Criminal records on computer from 1973.
General Information: No sealed, expunged, dismissed, judges notes, PSI's, or discovery packets records released. Certification fee: $5.00 per doc. Payee: Bergen County Clerk. Personal checks accepted. Prepayment required.

Superior Court - Civil Division 10 Main St. Rm 119, Justice Ctr, Hackensack, NJ 07601; phone: 201-527-2700 x2; fax: 201-752-4031; hours 8:30AM-4:30PM (EST). *Civil Actions Over $15,000, Probate.*
www.judiciary.state.nj.us/bergen/index.htm
Civil Records: Access: Mail, online, in person. Only the court performs in person searches; visitors may not. Court makes copy: $.50 per page. Required to search: name, years to search. Civil cases indexed by defendant, plaintiff; on computer for 2-5 years, on dockets from 1900s. Participates in the court records statewide Electronic Access Program; for signup, information and booklet call 609-292-4987. Mail turnaround time 1 week.

General Information: No sealed, expunged, dismissed, judges notes, PSI's, or discovery packets records released. Certification fee: $5.00. Payee: Bergen County Clerk. Personal checks accepted. Prepayment and SASE required.

Superior Court Special Civil Part 10 Main St. Rm 430, Justice Ctr, Hackensack, NJ 07601; phone: 201-527-2700 x2; hours 8:30AM-4:30PM (EST). *Civil Actions Under $15,000, Eviction, Small Claims.*
www.judiciary.state.nj.us/bergen/index.htm
Civil Records: Access: Mail, online, in person, phone. Both court and visitors may perform in person searches. Court makes copy: $.75 per page 1st 10 pgs; $.50 each add'l. Required to search: name, years to search. Civil cases indexed by defendant, plaintiff; on computer from 1990, prior on index cards. Participates in the court records statewide Electronic Access Program; for signup, information and booklet call 609-292-4987. Mail turnaround time 2 days to 3 weeks.
General Information: Public terminal has only civil records. (Terminal is located in the law library.) No adoption, sealed, juvenile, expunged, dismissed, or mental illness records released. Will not fax documents. Certification fee: $5.00. Payee: Bergen

County Special Civil Part. Personal checks accepted. Prepayment and SASE required.

Burlington County

Superior Court - Criminal Division 49 Rancocas Rd, Mount Holly, NJ 08060; phone: 609-518-2568; hours 8AM-5PM (EST). *Felony.*
www.judiciary.state.nj.us/burlington/index.htm
Criminal Records: Access: In person only. Visitors must perform in person searches themselves. Court makes copy: $.75 per page for 1st 10 pages; $.50 per page next 10; each add'l $.25. Required to search: name; years to search; also helpful: DOB, SSN. Criminal records on computer from 1986, on docket books from 1954, archived from early 1900s.
General Information: Public terminal has only criminal records. No sealed, expunged, judges notes, PSI's, or discovery packets released. Certification fee: $5.00. Payee: State of New Jersey. Personal checks accepted. Prepayment required.

Superior Court - Civil Division 49 Rancocas Rd, Mount Holly, NJ 08060; phone: 609-518-2815; criminal phone: 609-518-2566; fax: 609-518-2826; hours 8AM-5PM (EST). *Civil Actions Over $15,000, Probate.*
www.judiciary.state.nj.us/burlington/index.htm
Civil Records: Access: Mail, online, in person. Both court and visitors may perform in person searches. No search fee. Court makes copy: $.75 per page for first 10, $.50 per page for next ten, and $.25 per page thereafter. Required to search: name, years to search. Civil cases indexed by defendant, plaintiff. Local judgment records on computer since 1989, all others from 1954 to present. Participates in the court records statewide Electronic Access Program; for signup, information and booklet call 609-292-4987. Mail turnaround time 10 days.

General Information: Public terminal has only civil records back to 1989. No sealed, expunged, judges notes, PSI's, or discovery packets released. Certification fee: $5.00 per doc. Payee: State of New Jersey. Personal checks accepted. Prepayment and SASE required.

Superior Court Special Civil Part 49 Rancocas Rd, Mount Holly, NJ 08060; phone: 609-518-2865; fax: 609-518-2872; hours 8AM-5PM (EST). *Civil Actions Under $15,000, Eviction, Small Claims.*
www.judiciary.state.nj.us/burlington/index.htm
Civil Records: Access: Phone, fax, mail, in person, online. Both court and visitors may perform in person searches. No search fee. Court makes copy: $.75 per page. Fee is for first 10 pages; $.50 per page next 10; each add'l $.25. Required to search: name, years to search. Civil cases indexed by defendant, plaintiff; on computer from 1995, microfilm from 1984, prior on index books by docket number. Participates in the court records statewide Electronic Access Program; for signup, information and booklet call 609-292-4987. Mail turnaround time 1-2 weeks.
General Information: Public terminal has only civil records back to 1995. This court does not handle criminal matters in the Special Civil Part. No

fee to fax documents. Certification fee: $10.00 per doc. Payee: State of New Jersey. Personal checks accepted. Prepayment required.

Camden County

Superior Court - Criminal Division Hall of Justice, 101 S 5th, Camden, NJ 08103; phone: 856-379-2200; criminal phone: x3343; fax: 856-379-2255; hours 8AM-4PM (EST). *Felony.*
www.judiciary.state.nj.us/camden/index.htm
Criminal Records: Access: Mail, fax, in person. Both court and visitors may perform in person searches. No search fee, but a fee is to be implemented soon. No copy fee. Required to search: name, years to search, DOB, SSN. Criminal records on computer from 1986, on docket books from 1970. Mail turnaround time 3 days.
General Information: Public terminal has only criminal records back to 1986. No sealed, expunged, dismissed, judges notes, PSI's or discovery packets records released. No certification fee . Prepayment and SASE required.

Superior Court - Civil Division Hall of Justice, 101 S 5th St, Camden, NJ 08103; phone: 856-379-2200; criminal phone: x3343; fax: 856-379-2255; hours 8:30AM-4:30PM (EST). *Civil Actions Over $15,000, Probate.*
www.judiciary.state.nj.us/camden/index.htm
Civil Records: Access: Mail, online, in person. Both court and visitors may perform in person searches. No search fee. No copy fee. Required to search: name, years to search. Civil cases indexed by defendant, plaintiff; on computer from 1987. Participates in the court records statewide Electronic Access Program; for signup, information or booklet call 609-292-4987. Note: Also, mail or in person judgment searches are directed to Trenton. Mail turnaround time 5 days.
General Information: Public terminal has only civil records back to 1987. No sealed, dismissed, judges notes, or discovery packets records released. Payee: Clerk of Superior Court. Personal checks accepted. Prepayment and SASE required.

Superior Court Special Civil Part Hall of Justice Complex, 101 S. 5th St, Camden, NJ 08103; phone: 856-379-2202; hours 8:30AM-4:30PM (EST). *Civil Actions Under $15,000, Eviction, Small Claims.*
Civil Records: Access: Mail, online, in person. Both court and visitors may perform in person searches. No search fee. Court makes copy: $.75 per page for first ten, $.50 per page for next ten, and $.25 per page thereafter. Required to search: name, years to search. Civil cases indexed by defendant, plaintiff; on computer from 1988. Prior records on docket books. Participates in the court records statewide Electronic Access Program; for signup, information and booklet call 609-292-4987, or contact Admin Office of Court, Hughes Justice Complex, PO Box 981, Trenton, NJ 08625. Note: In person access is limited to one name. Mail turnaround time varies.
General Information: Public terminal has only civil records back to 1988. No adoption, sealed, juvenile, expunged, restricted, or mental health records released. Certification fee: $5.00. Payee: Clerk Special Civil Part. Personal checks accepted. Prepayment required.

Cape May County

Superior Court - Criminal Division 9 N Main St, Superior Court, Cape May Court House, NJ 08210; phone: 609-463-6550; fax: 609-463-6458; hours 8:30AM-4:30PM (EST). *Felony.*
www.judiciary.state.nj.us/atlantic/index.htm
Criminal Records: Access: In person only. Visitors must perform in person searches themselves. Court makes copy: $.75 per page. Required to search: name, years to search, DOB; SSN helpful. Criminal records on computer from 1985; on index books back to 1950.
General Information: Public terminal has only criminal records back to 1985. No sealed,

expunged, dismissed, judges notes, PSI's, or discovery packets records released. Certification fee: $5.00 per doc. Payee: State of New Jersey. Personal checks accepted. Prepayment required.

Superior Court - Civil Division Civil/Equity Division-Law, DN-203, 9 N Main St, Cape May Court House, NJ 08210; phone: 609-463-6506; fax: 609-463-6465; hours 8:30AM-4:30PM (EST). *Civil Actions Over $15,000, Probate.*
www.judiciary.state.nj.us/atlantic/index.htm
Civil Records: Access: Online, in person. Visitors must perform in person searches themselves. Court makes copy: $.75 per pg 1st 10 pgs 11-20, $.50 per pg; over 20 pgs $.25 per pg. Required to search: name, years to search. Civil cases indexed by defendant, plaintiff; on computer from 4/91, on index books and archived from 1900s. Participates in the court records statewide Electronic Access Program; for signup, information and booklet call 609-292-4987. A fee is charged for online access.
General Information: Public terminal has only civil records. No sealed records released. Certification fee: $5.00 per doc. Payee: Clerk of Superior Court. Personal checks accepted. Prepayment required.

Superior Court Special Civil Part DN-203, 9 N. Main St, Cape May Court House, NJ 08210; phone: 609-463-6522; fax: 609-463-6465; hours 8:30AM-4:30PM (EST). *Civil Actions Under $15,000, Eviction, Small Claims.*
www.judiciary.state.nj.us/atlantic/index.htm
Civil Records: Access: Online, in person. Visitors must perform in person searches themselves. Court makes copy: $.75 per page for first ten, $.50 per page for next ten, and $.25 per page thereafter. Required to search: name, years to search; also helpful: address. Civil cases indexed by defendant, plaintiff; on computer from 4/1991, on index from 1973. Participates in the court records statewide Electronic Access Program; for signup, information and booklet 609-292-4987. A fee is charged for remote online access.
General Information: Public terminal has only civil records. No sealed records released. Certification fee: $5.00 if not a party to the action; no cert fee is a party. Payee: Clerk of the Special Civil Part. Personal checks accepted. Prepayment required.

Cumberland County

Superior Court - Criminal Division PO Box 757, Courthouse, Broad/Fayette Strs, Bridgeton, NJ 08302; phone: 856-453-4300; fax: 856-451-7152; hours 8:30AM-4:30PM (EST). *Felony.*
www.judiciary.state.nj.us/gloucester/cum/index.htm
Criminal Records: Access: Mail, in person. Both court and visitors may perform in person searches. Search fee: $4.00 per name. Court makes copy: $.25 per page. Required to search: name, years to search, DOB, SSN, signed release; also helpful: address. Criminal records on computer from 1986, on index from 1900. Mail turnaround time 1 week.
General Information: Public terminal has only criminal records back to 1986. (Terminal in Law Library.) No sealed, expunged, dismissed, judges notes, PSI's, or discovery packets records released. Certification fee: $5.00 per doc. Payee: State of New Jersey, Misc Fund. Personal checks accepted. Prepayment and SASE required.

Superior Court - Civil Division PO Box 757, Bridgeton, NJ 08302; phone: 856-453-4330; criminal phone: 856-453-4300; fax: 856-453-4349; hours 8:30AM-4:30PM (EST). *Civil Actions Over $15,000, Probate.*
www.judiciary.state.nj.us/gloucester/cum/index.htm
Civil Records: Access: Mail, online, in person. Search fee: $4.00 per name. Court makes copy: $.25 per page. Required to search: name, years to search. Civil records on computer from 1986, on index from 1900. Participates in the court records statewide Electronic Access Program; for signup,

information and booklet call 609-292-4987. Mail turnaround time 1 week.
General Information: Public terminal has only civil records back to 1986. No sealed, expunged, dismissed, judges notes, PSI's, or discovery packets records released. Certification fee: $5.00 per doc. Payee: State of New Jersey, Misc Fund. Personal checks accepted. Prepayment and SASE required.

Superior Court Special Civil Part PO Box 10, Bridgeton, NJ 08302; phone: 856-453-4350; fax: 856-453-4349; hours 8:30AM-4:30PM (EST). *Civil Actions Under $15,000, Eviction, Small Claims.*
www.judiciary.state.nj.us/gloucester/cum/index.htm
Civil Records: Access: Phone, mail, online, in person. Only the court performs in person searches; visitors may not. No search fee. Court makes copy: $.75 per page for first ten, $.50 per page for next ten, and $.25 per page thereafter. Required to search: name, years to search. Civil cases indexed by defendant, plaintiff; on computer from 12/89, on docket books from 1949 to 11/89. Participates in the court records statewide Electronic Access Program; for signup, information and booklet call 609-292-4987. Note: Phone access is limited to 1 or 2 searches. Mail turnaround time 1 week.
General Information: No public access terminal. No adoption, sealed, juvenile, expunged, dismissed, or mental illness records released. Certification fee: $5.00. Payee: Clerk, Special Civil Part. Personal checks accepted. Prepayment required. SASE requested.

Essex County

Superior Court - Criminal Division 50 W Market St, Rm 100s, Essex County Court Bldg, Newark, NJ 07102-1681; phone: 973-693-5965, 973-693-5700 (switchboard); hours 8:30AM-4:30PM (EST). *Felony.*
www.judiciary.state.nj.us/essex/index.htm
Criminal Records: Access: Mail, in person. Both court and visitors may perform in person searches. Search fee: $3.00 per name. Court makes copy: $.75 per page. Required to search: name, years to search, DOB, SSN. Criminal records on computer from 1985. Mail turnaround time 1 week.
General Information: Public terminal has only criminal records back to 1985. No sealed, expunged, dismissed, judges notes, PSI's, or discovery packets records released. Will fax documents to local or toll free line. Certification fee: $5.00. Payee: State of New Jersey Judiciary. Only cashiers checks and money orders accepted. Prepayment and SASE required.

Superior Court - Civil Division 465 Dr. Martin Luther King Blvd, Newark, NJ 07102-1681; phone: 973-693-6460; fax: 973-621-1312; hours 8:30AM-4:30PM (EST). *Civil Actions Over $15,000, Probate.*
www.judiciary.state.nj.us/essex/index.htm
Civil Records: Access: Online, in person. Only the court performs in person searches; visitors may not. No search fee. Court makes copy: $.75 per page. Required to search: name, years to search. Civil cases indexed by defendant, plaintiff; on computer from 1984, on index from 1930. Participates in the court records statewide Electronic Access Program; for signup, information and booklet call 609-292-4987. Mail turnaround time 1 week.
General Information: No public access terminal. No sealed, expunged, dismissed, judges notes, PSI's, or discovery packets records released. Will fax documents $3.00 per page. Certification fee: $5.00 per doc. Payee: State of New Jersey Judiciary. Business checks accepted. Prepayment and SASE required.

Superior Court Special Civil Part 465 Martin Luther King Blvd, Newark, NJ 07102; phone: 973-693-6494; 693-6460; fax: 973-621-5914; hours 8:30AM-4:30PM (EST). *Civil Actions Under $15,000, Eviction, Small Claims.*
www.judiciary.state.nj.us/essex/index.htm

Civil Records: Access: Mail, online, in person. Both court and visitors may perform in person searches. No search fee. Court makes copy: $.75 per page. Required to search: name, years to search. Civil cases indexed by defendant, plaintiff; on computer from 1986 and archived back to 1982. Participates in the court records statewide Electronic Access Program; for signup, information and booklet call 609-292-4987. Mail turnaround time 7-10 days.

General Information: No public access terminal. No adoption, sealed, juvenile, expunged, dismissed, or mental illness records released. Fee to fax documents is $.75 per page. No certification fee . Payee: Essex County Special Civil Part. Personal checks accepted. Prepayment and SASE required.

Gloucester County

Superior Court - Criminal Division PO Box 187, 1 N Broad St, Woodbury, NJ 08096; phone: 856-853-3531; hours 8:30AM-4:30 PM (EST). *Felony.*

www.judiciary.state.nj.us/gloucester/glo/index.htm

Criminal Records: Access: Mail, in person. Visitors must perform in person searches themselves. Search fee: $4.00 per name. Court makes copy: $1.00 per page. Required to search: name, years to search, DOB, SSN, signed release. Criminal records on computer from 1982, on index from 1955. Mail turnaround time 1-3 days.

General Information: No public access terminal. No sealed, expunged, dismissed, judges notes, PSI's, or discovery packets records released. Certification fee: $5.00 per doc. Payee: State of New Jersey, Miscellaneous. Personal checks accepted. Prepayment and SASE required.

Superior Court - Civil Division 1 N Broad St, Woodbury, NJ 08096; phone: 856-853-3232; hours 8:30AM-4:30 PM (EST). *Civil Actions Over $15,000, Probate.*

www.judiciary.state.nj.us/gloucester/glo/index.htm

Civil Records: Access: Mail, online, in person. Only the court performs in person searches; visitors may not. Court makes copy: $.75 first 10; $.50 next 10; $.25 each add'l page. Required to search: name, years to search. Civil cases indexed by defendant, plaintiff; on computer from 1988, prior records on county books. Participates in the court records statewide Electronic Access Program; for signup, information and booklet call 609-292-4987. Mail turnaround time ASAP.

General Information: No public access terminal. No sealed, expunged, dismissed, judges notes, PSI's, or discovery packets records released. Certification fee: $1.50. Payee: State of New Jersey. Personal checks accepted. Prepayment and SASE required.

Superior Court Special Civil Part Old Courthouse, 1 N Broad St, Woodbury, NJ 08096; phone: 856-853-3392; fax: 856-853-3416; hours 8:30AM-4:30PM (EST). *Civil Actions Under $15,000, Eviction, Small Claims.*

www.judiciary.state.nj.us/gloucester/glo/index.htm

Civil Records: Access: Mail, online, in person. No search fee. Court makes copy: $.75 per page. Fee is $.50 each after 10 pages. Required to search: name, years to search. Civil cases indexed by defendant, plaintiff; on computer from 8/89, on index books from 1900. Participates in the court records statewide Electronic Access Program; for signup, information and booklet call 609-292-4987.

General Information: No public access terminal. Certification fee: $5.00 per doc. Payee: Clerk, Superior Court of NJ. Personal checks accepted. Prepayment and SASE required.

Hudson County

Superior Court - Criminal Division 595 Newark Ave, Jersey City, NJ 07306; phone: 201-795-6704; fax: 201-217-5210; hours 8:30AM-4:30PM(EST). *Felony.*

www.judiciary.state.nj.us/hudson/index.htm

Criminal Records: Access: Mail, in person. Both court and visitors may perform in person searches.

No search fee. Court makes copy: $.75 per page for 1st 10 pages; $.50 per page next 10; each add'l $.25. Required to search: name, years to search, DOB, SSN. Criminal records on computer from 1985, on index books from 1900. Mail turnaround time 1 week.

General Information: Public terminal has only criminal records back to 1985. No sealed, expunged, dismissed, judges notes, PSI's, or discovery packets records released. Certification fee: $5.00. Uncertified copy of a judgment of conviction-$1.50, Payee: Treasurer, State of New Jersey. Personal checks accepted. Prepayment required.

Superior Court - Civil Division 583 Newark Ave, Jersey City, NJ 07306; phone: 201-217-5162; 201-217-5163 (Records Rm); fax: 201-217-5241; hours 8:30AM-4:30PM (EST). *Civil Actions Over $15,000, Probate.*

www.judiciary.state.nj.us/hudson/index.htm

Civil Records: Access: Mail, in person. Both court and visitors may perform in person searches. No search fee. Court makes copy: $.75 each 1-10 pages; $.50 pages 11-20; $.25 per page over 20. Required to search: name, years to search. Civil cases indexed by defendant, plaintiff; on computer for 18 months after disposition. Mail access is limited to one name. Participates in the court records statewide Electronic Access Program; for signup, information and booklet call 609-292-4987. Mail turnaround time 1 week.

General Information: Public terminal has only civil records. No sealed, expunged, dismissed, judges notes, PSI's, or discovery packets records released. Certification fee: $5.00 per doc. Payee: Clerk of Superior Court. Personal checks accepted. Prepayment required.

Superior Court Special Civil Part 595 Newark Ave, Jersey City, NJ 07306; phone: 201-795-6680; fax: 201-217-5241; hours 8:30AM-4:30PM (EST). *Civil Actions Under $15,000, Eviction, Small Claims.*

www.judiciary.state.nj.us/hudson/index.htm

Civil Records: Access: Online, in person. Visitors must perform in person searches themselves. Court makes copy: $.75 each 1-10 pages, $.50 11-20 pages; $.25 each 20 plus pages. Required to search: name, years to search, address. Civil cases indexed by defendant, plaintiff; on index cards from 1993, prior on docket books. Participates in the court records statewide Electronic Access Program; for signup, information and booklet call 609-292-4987.

General Information: Public terminal has only civil records. No adoptions, sealed, juvenile, expunged, dismissed, or mental illness released. Certification fee: $5.00 per doc. Payee: Clerk, Special Civil Part. Personal checks accepted. Prepayment required.

Hunterdon County

Superior Court - Criminal Division 65 Park Ave, Flemington, NJ 08822; phone: 908-237-5840; fax: 908-237-5841; hours 8:30AM-4:30PM (EST). *Felony.*

www.judiciary.state.nj.us/somerset/index.htm

Criminal Records: Access: Fax, mail, in person. Visitors must perform in person searches themselves. No search fee. Court makes copy: $.75 per page. Required to search: name, years to search, DOB; also helpful: SSN. Criminal records on computer from 1987, prior on index books. Mail turnaround time 1-3 weeks.

General Information: Public terminal has only criminal records back to 1987. No sealed, expunged, dismissed, judges notes, PSI's, or discovery packets records released. Will fax documents, no charge. Certification fee: $5.00 per doc. Payee: State of New Jersey. Personal checks accepted. Prepayment and SASE required.

Superior Court - Civil Division Hunterdon County Justice Ctr, 65 Park Ave, Flemington, NJ 08822; phone: 908-237-5820; probate phone: 908-788-1156; hours 8:30AM-4:30PM (EST). *Civil Actions Over $15,000, Probate.*

www.judiciary.state.nj.us/somerset/index.htm

Note: Probate records are indexed separately and are located on the 2nd Fl Surrogate/Probate office.

Civil Records: Access: Mail, online, in person, phone. Both court and visitors may perform in person searches. No search fee. Court makes copy: $.75 per page 1st 10; $.50 for 2nd 10; $.25 each add'l. Required to search: name, years to search. Civil cases indexed by defendant, plaintiff; on computer since 1990, on index from 1950. Participates in the court records statewide Electronic Access Program; for signup, information and booklet call 609-292-4987. Mail turnaround time 1-2 weeks.

General Information: Public terminal has only civil records back to 1990. No sealed, expunged, dismissed, judges notes, PSI's, or discovery packets records released. Certification fee: $5.00 per doc. Payee: State of New Jersey Judiciary. Personal checks accepted. Prepayment and SASE required.

Superior Court Special Civil Part Hunterdon County Justice Ctr, 65 Park Ave, 2nd Fl, Flemington, NJ 08822; phone: 908-237-5820; fax: 908-237-5821; hours 8:30AM-4:30PM (EST). *Civil Actions Under $15,000, Eviction, Small Claims.*

www.judiciary.state.nj.us/somerset/index.htm

Civil Records: Access: Phone, mail, online, in person. Both court and visitors may perform in person searches. No search fee. Court will do one free search. Court makes copy: $.75 per page for first ten, $.50 per page for next ten, and $.25 per page thereafter. Required to search: name, years to search. Civil cases indexed by defendant, plaintiff; on computer from 1991, on index books from 1900. Participates in the court records statewide Electronic Access Program; for signup, information and booklet call 609-292-4987. Mail turnaround time 1-2 weeks.

General Information: Public terminal has only civil records back to 1991. No protective order files records released. Certification fee: $5.00 per doc. Payee: Superior Court of New Jersey. Personal checks accepted. Prepayment and SASE required.

Mercer County

Superior Court - Criminal Division 209 S. Broad, PO Box 8068, Trenton, NJ 08650-0068; phone: 609-571-4000 x4; hours 8:30AM-4:30PM; Search Hours: 9AM-3:30PM (EST). *Felony.*

www.judiciary.state.nj.us/mercer/index.htm

Criminal Records: Access: In person only. Visitors must perform in person searches themselves. Court makes copy: $.75 per page. $5.00 minimum. Fee less after 10 pages. Required to search: name, years to search, DOB, SSN. Criminal records on computer from 1985, on docket books from 1900s.

General Information: Public terminal has only criminal records back to 1985. No sealed, expunged, judges notes, PSI's, or discovery packets records released. Certification fee: $5.00. Payee: Clerk of Superior Court. Personal checks accepted. Prepayment required.

Superior Court - Civil Division 175 S Broad, PO Box 8068, Trenton, NJ 08650-0068; phone: 609-571-4490; fax: 609-571-4473; hours 8:30AM-4:30PM (EST). *Civil Actions Over $15,000, Probate.*

www.judiciary.state.nj.us/mercer/index.htm

Civil Records: Access: Fax, mail, online, in person. Only the court performs in person searches; visitors may not. No search fee. Court makes copy: $.75 each 1-10 pages; $.50 11-20 pages; $.25 each 20 plus pages. Required to search: name, years to search. Civil cases indexed by defendant, plaintiff; on computer since 1995, archived from 1972, on microfiche from 1965, prior indexed from 1894. Participates in the court records statewide Electronic Access Program; for signup, information and booklet call 609-292-4987. Mail turnaround time up to 2 weeks.

General Information: No public access terminal. No sealed, expunged, dismissed, judges notes, PSI's, or discovery packets records released. Certification fee: $5.00 per doc. Payee: Clerk of Superior Court. Personal checks accepted. Prepayment and SASE required for Civil.

Superior Court Special Civil Part Box 8068, Trenton, NJ 08650; phone: 609-571-4490 x1; fax: 609-571-4489; hours 8:30AM-4:30PM (EST). *Civil Actions Under $15,000, Eviction, Small Claims.*

www.judiciary.state.nj.us/mercer/index.htm

Note: Their record index is located on a public access terminal at the Hughes Justice Center on 25 market St. **Civil Records:** Access: Mail, online, in person. Visitors must perform in person searches themselves. No search fee. Court makes copy: $.75 per page for first ten, $.50 per page for next ten, and $.25 per page thereafter. Required to search: name, years to search. Civil cases indexed by defendant, plaintiff; on computer from 1989, on index from 1984. Participates in the court records statewide Electronic Access Program; for signup, information and booklet call 609-292-4987. Mail turnaround time 1 week.

General Information: Public terminal has only civil records. No adoptions, sealed, juvenile, expunged, dismissed, or mental illness records released. No certification fee . Payee: State of New Jersey. Only cashiers checks and money orders accepted. Prepayment required.

Middlesex County

Superior Court - Criminal Division PO Box 964 (1 JFK Sq), New Brunswick, NJ 08903; phone: 732-981-3128; hours 8:30AM-4:30PM (EST). *Felony.*
www.judiciary.state.nj.us/middlesex/index.htm
Criminal Records: Access: Mail, in person. Both court and visitors may perform in person searches. No search fee. Court makes copy: $.75 per page for 1st 10 pages; $.50 per page next 10; each add'l $.25. Required to search: name and DOB. Criminal records on computer from 1981, prior on index books back to 1956. No name searches. Court will only search if provided with arrest date, summons, complaint or indictment number. Mail turnaround time up to 2 weeks.

General Information: Public terminal has only criminal records. No sealed, expunged, dismissed, judges notes, PSI's, on discovery packets records released. Certification fee: $5.00 per page. Payee: State of New Jersey Judiciary. Cash, personal checks, or money order accepted. Prepayment and SASE required.

Superior Court - Civil Division PO Box 2633, 1 JFK Sq, 2nd Fl Tower, New Brunswick, NJ 08903; phone: 732-981-2464; probate phone: 732-745-3055; hours 8:30AM-4:30PM (EST). *Civil Actions Over $15,000, Probate.*
www.judiciary.state.nj.us/middlesex/index.htm
Civil Records: Access: Mail, online, in person. Both court and visitors may perform in person searches. No search fee. Court makes copy: $.75 first 10, $.50 ea next 10, then $.25 ea. Required to search: name, years to search, if copies needed place request in writing. Civil cases indexed by defendant, plaintiff; on computer from 1992, on docket books from 1940. Participates in the court records statewide Electronic Access Program; for signup, information and booklet call 609-292-4987. Mail turnaround time up to 3 weeks.

General Information: Public terminal has only civil records back to 1992. No sealed, expunged, dismissed, judges notes, PSI's, on discovery packets records released. Certification fee: $5.00. Payee: State of New Jersey, Clerk of Superior Court. Personal checks accepted. Prepayment and SASE required.

Superior Court Special Civil Part PO Box 1146, 1 JKF Sq, 3rd Fl Tower, New Brunswick, NJ 08903; phone: 732-981-2044; fax: 732-981-2078; hours 8:30AM-4:30PM (EST). *Civil Actions Under $15,000, Eviction, Small Claims.*
www.judiciary.state.nj.us/middlesex/index.htm
Civil Records: Access: Mail, online, in person. Both court and visitors may perform in person searches. No search fee. Court makes copy: $.75 per page; 11-20 pages $.50; 20 plus $.25. Required to search: name, years to search. Civil cases indexed by defendant, plaintiff; on computer from 1985, on docket books from 1960. Participates in the court records statewide Electronic Access Program; for signup, information and booklet call 609-292-4987. Mail turnaround time 30 days.

General Information: Public terminal has only civil records back to 1985. No adoption, sealed, juvenile, expunged, dismissed, or mental health records released. Will not fax documents. No certification fee . Payee: Middlesex Special Civil Part. Personal checks accepted. Prepayment required.

Monmouth County

Superior Court - Criminal Division 71 Monument Park, Rm 149, 1st Flr, E Wing, PO Box 1271, Freehold, NJ 07728-1271; phone: 732-677-4300; hours 8:30AM-4:30PM (EST). *Felony.*
www.judiciary.state.nj.us/monmouth/index.htm
Criminal Records: Access: In person only. Visitors must perform in person searches themselves. Court makes copy: $.75 per page for 1st 10 pages; $.50 per page next 10; each add'l $.25. Required to search: name, years to search. Criminal records on computer back to 1990, on index books from 1956.

General Information: Public terminal has only criminal records back to 1986. No sealed or expunged, judges notes, PSI's, or discovery packets records released. Certification fee: $5.00. Cert fee includes copies. Payee: State of New Jersey. Personal checks accepted; ID required. Prepayment required.

Superior Court - Civil Division PO Box 1255, 71 Monument Pk, Freehold, NJ 07728-1255; phone: 732-677-4268; hours 8:30AM-4:30PM (EST). *Civil Actions Over $15,000.*
www.judiciary.state.nj.us/monmouth/index.htm
Civil Records: Access: Mail, online, in person. Visitors must perform in person searches themselves. Court makes copy: $.75. Required to search: name, years to search. Civil cases indexed by defendant, plaintiff; on computer from 1990, on index books from 1956. Participates in the court records statewide Electronic Access Program; for signup, information and booklet call 609-292-4987.
General Information: Public terminal has only civil records. No sealed, expunged, dismissed, judges notes, PSI's, or discovery packets records released. Certification fee: $5.00. Payee: Clerk of Superior Court. Personal checks accepted. Prepayment required.

Superior Court Special Civil Part Courthouse, 71 Monument Pk, PO Box 1270, Freehold, NJ 07728; phone: 732-677-4223; fax: 732-677-4358; hours 8:30AM-4:30PM (EST). *Civil Actions Under $15,000, Eviction, Small Claims.*
www.judiciary.state.nj.us/monmouth/index.htm
Civil Records: Access: Mail, online, in person. Both court and visitors may perform in person searches. No search fee. Court makes copy: $.75 per page. Fee is for first 10 pages; $.50 per page next 10; each add'l $.25. Required to search: name, years to search. Civil cases indexed by defendant, plaintiff; on computer from 1996, on index books from 1985, prior in archives. Participates in the court records statewide Electronic Access Program; for signup, information and booklet call 609-292-4987. Mail turnaround time 1 day to weeks; longer if archived.
General Information: Public terminal has only civil records back to 1985. Certification fee: $5.00 per doc. Payee: Monmouth Special Civil Part.

Personal checks accepted. Prepayment and SASE required.

Morris County

Superior Court - Criminal Division PO Box 910, Washington & Court St, Morristown, NJ 07963-0910; phone: 973-656-4115; criminal phone: 973-656-4169; fax: 973-656-4123; hours 8:30AM-4:30PM (EST). *Felony.*
www.judiciary.state.nj.us/morris/index.htm
Criminal Records: Access: Fax, mail, in person. Both court and visitors may perform in person searches. No search fee. Court makes copy: $.75 per page for 1st 10 pages; $.50 per page next 10; each add'l $.25. Required to search: name, years to search, DOB, SSN, signed release. Criminal records on computer from 1984, on index books from 1966. Mail turnaround time 1 week.
General Information: No public access terminal. No sealed, expunged, dismissed, judges notes, PSI's, or discovery packets records released. Certification fee: $5.00 per doc. Payee: State of New Jersey. Personal checks accepted. Prepayment and SASE required.

Superior Court - Civil Division PO Box 910 (Washington St), Morristown, NJ 07963-0910; phone: 973-656-4115; fax: 973-656-4123; hours 8:30AM-4:30PM (EST). *Civil Actions Over $15,000, Probate.*
www.judiciary.state.nj.us/morris/index.htm
Civil Records: Access: Online, in person. Visitors must perform in person searches themselves. Court makes copy: $.25 per page. Required to search: name, years to search; also helpful: address. Civil cases indexed by defendant, plaintiff; on computer from 1984, on index books from 1966. Participates in the court records statewide Electronic Access Program; for signup, information and booklet call 609-292-4987.

General Information: Public terminal has only civil records back to 1984. No sealed, expunged, dismissed, judges notes, PSI's, or discovery packets records released. Certification fee: $5.00 per doc. Payee: State of New Jersey. Personal checks accepted. Prepayment required.

Superior Court Special Civil Part PO Box 910, Court and Washington Sts, Morristown, NJ 07963-0910; phone: 973-656-4125; fax: 973-656-4123; hours 8:30AM-4:30PM (EST). *Civil Actions Under $15,000, Eviction, Small Claims.*
www.judiciary.state.nj.us/morris/index.htm
Civil Records: Access: Mail, online, in person. Visitors must perform in person searches themselves. Court makes copy: $.75 per page for first 10, $.50 per page for next 10, and $.25 per page thereafter. Self serve copy fee: $.25 per page. Required to search: name, years to search. Civil cases indexed by defendant, plaintiff; on computer from 8/1988, on index books from 1979. Participates in the court records statewide Electronic Access Program; for signup, information and booklet call 609-292-4987. Mail turnaround time 1 week.
General Information: Public terminal has only civil records back to 8/1988. No adoptions, sealed, juvenile, expunged, dismissed, or mental illness records released. Certification fee: $5.00 per doc. Payee: State of New Jersey. Personal checks accepted. Prepayment required.

Ocean County

Superior Court - Criminal Division PO Box 2191, 120 Hooper Ave, Justice Complex, Rm 220, Toms River, NJ 08754-2191; phone: 732-929-2009; fax: 732-506-5067; hours 8:30AM-4:30PM (EST). *Felony.*
www.judiciary.state.nj.us/ocean/index.htm
Criminal Records: Access: Mail, in person, fax. Both court and visitors may perform in person searches. No search fee. Court makes copy: $.75 per page for 1st 10 pages; $.50 per page next 10; each add'l $.25. Required to search: name, years to search;

also helpful: address, DOB, SSN. Criminal records on computer from 1990, on index books from 1920. Mail turnaround time 1 week.

General Information: Public terminal has only criminal records back to 1990. (Terminal allows you to search statewide.) No sealed, expunged, judges notes, PSI's, or discovery packets records released. Will fax reply if no record found documents. Certification fee: $5.00. Payee: NJ State Treasurer. Personal checks accepted. Prepayment required.

Superior Court - Civil Division 118 Washington #121, Toms River, NJ 08754; phone: 732-929-2035; fax: 732-506-5398; hours 8:30AM-4:30PM (EST). *Civil Actions Over $15,000, Probate.*
www.judiciary.state.nj.us/ocean/index.htm

Civil Records: Access: Online, in person. Visitors must perform in person searches themselves. Court makes copy: $.50 per page. Required to search: name, years to search. Civil cases indexed by defendant, plaintiff; on computer from 1989, on index books from 1920. Participates in the court records statewide Electronic Access Program; for signup, information and booklet call 609-292-4987.

General Information: Public terminal has only civil records back to 1989. (Public terminal located at 201 Courthouse Ln.) No certification fee . Payee: Superior Court Clerk. Personal checks accepted. Prepayment required.

Superior Court Special Civil Part 118 Washington St, Toms River, NJ 08754; phone: 732-929-2016; fax: 732-506-5398; hours 8:30AM-4:30PM (EST). *Civil Actions Under $15,000, Eviction, Small Claims.*
www.judiciary.state.nj.us/ocean/index.htm

Civil Records: Access: Online, in person. Both court and visitors may perform in person searches. No search fee. Court makes copy: $.50 per page. Required to search: name, years to search. Civil cases indexed by defendant, plaintiff; on computer from 1985, on index books from 1972, on microfilm prior. Participates in the court records statewide Electronic Access Program; for signup, information and booklet call 609-292-4987. Mail turnaround time 1-2 days.

General Information: Public terminal has only civil records back to 1985. (Terminal located at 201 Courthouse Ln.) No adoptions, sealed, juvenile, expunged, dismissed, or mental illness records released. Certification fee: $5.00 per doc. Payee: Ocean County Special Civil Part. Personal checks accepted. Prepayment required.

Passaic County

Superior Court - Criminal Division 77 Hamilton St. 2nd Fl, Paterson, NJ 07505-2108; phone: 973-247-8403; fax: 973-247-8401; hours 8:30AM-4:30PM (EST). *Felony.*
www.judiciary.state.nj.us/passaic/index.htm

Criminal Records: Access: In person only. Visitors must perform in person searches themselves. No search fee. Court makes copy: $.75 per page for 1st 10 pages; $.50 per page next 10; each add'l $.25. Required to search: name; also helpful: DOB. Criminal records on computer from 1986, on microfiche prior. Note: Court will only retrieve a record if you provide an indictment number, which can be garnered from state police or the public access terminal. Mail turnaround time 3-4 days.

General Information: Public terminal has only criminal records back to 1986. No sealed, expunged, dismissed, judges notes, PSI's, or discovery packets records released. Will fax documents. Certification fee: $5.00 per doc. Payee: Superior Court of New Jersey. Personal checks accepted. Prepayment required.

Superior Court - Civil Division 77 Hamilton St, Ist Fl, Paterson, NJ 07505-2108; phone: 973-247-8000; probate phone: 973-881-4760; hours 8:30AM-4:30PM (EST). *Civil Actions Over $15,000, Probate.*
www.judiciary.state.nj.us/passaic/index.htm

Note: Probate is located on the 2nd Fl with the General Equity Division.

Civil Records: Access: Phone, mail, online, in person. Both court and visitors may perform in person searches. No search fee. Court makes copy: $.25 per page. Required to search: name, years to search. Civil cases indexed by defendant, plaintiff; on computer from 1986, on index books from 1979. Participates in the court records statewide Electronic Access Program; for signup, information and booklet call 609-292-4987. Note: Phone access limited to short searches. Mail turnaround time up to 1 week.

General Information: No public access terminal. No sealed, expunged, dismissed, judges notes, PSI's, or discovery packets records released. Certification fee: $5.00. Payee: State of New Jersey or Clerk of Superior Court. Personal checks accepted. Prepayment required.

Superior Court Special Civil Part 71 Hamilton St, Old Courthouse, 2nd Fl, Paterson, NJ 07505; phone: 973-247-8000; hours 8:30AM-4:30PM (EST). *Civil Actions Under $15,000, Eviction, Small Claims.*
www.judiciary.state.nj.us/passaic/index.htm

Civil Records: Access: Mail, online, in person. Both court and visitors may perform in person searches. No search fee. Court makes copy: $.75 per page. Fee is for first 10 pages; $.50 per page next 10; each add'l $.25. Required to search: name, years to search. Civil cases indexed by defendant, plaintiff; on computer from 1993, on index from 1980, prior archived. Participates in the court records statewide Electronic Access Program; for signup, information and booklet call 609-292-4987. Note: Include your phone number with written requests. It may take up to 2 days for court to retrieve case files. Mail turnaround time 2-3 days.

General Information: Public terminal has only civil records back to 1993. No adoptions, sealed, juvenile, expunged, dismissed, or mental illness records released. Certification fee: $5.00 per doc. Payee: Passaic County Special Civil Part. Personal checks accepted. Prepayment required.

Salem County

Superior Court - Criminal Division PO Box 78, 92 Market St, Salem, NJ 08079-1913; phone: 856-935-7510 x8276; fax: 856-935-8291; hours 8:30AM-4:30PM (EST). *Felony.*
www.judiciary.state.nj.us/gloucester/sal/index.htm

Criminal Records: Access: In person only. Visitors must perform in person searches themselves. Court makes copy: $.25 per page. Required to search: name, years to search, DOB, SSN; indictment number helpful. Criminal records on computer back to 1989; indexed from 1957.

General Information: Public terminal has only criminal records back to 1989. No sealed, expunged, dismissed, judges notes, PSI's, or discovery packets records released. Will not fax documents. Certification fee: $5.00. Payee: State of New Jersey. Personal checks accepted. Prepayment and SASE required.

Superior Court - Civil Division PO Box 29, 92 Market St, Salem, NJ 08079-1913; phone: 856-935-7510 X8214; probate phone: 856-935-7510 X8322; fax: 856-935-6551; hours 8:30AM-4:30PM (EST). *Civil Actions Over $15,000, Probate.*
www.judiciary.state.nj.us/gloucester/sal/index.htm

Note: Probate located at the County Surrogate's office at this 92 Market St address.

Civil Records: Access: In person, online. Both court and visitors may perform in person searches. Court makes copy: $.25 per page. Required to search: name, years to search. Civil cases indexed by defendant, plaintiff; on computer from 1987, indexed from 1953. Participates in the court records statewide Electronic Access Program; for signup, information and booklet call 609-292-4987.

Searches for judgments are directed to the statewide system in Trenton.

General Information: Public terminal has only civil records back to 1987. No sealed, expunged, dismissed, judges notes, PSI's, or discovery packets records released. Certification fee: $5.00 per doc. Payee: Superior Court of NJ. Personal checks accepted. Prepayment required.

Superior Court Special Civil Part PO Box 29 (92 Market St), Salem, NJ 08079; phone: 856-935-7510 x8214; fax: 856-935-6551; hours 8:30AM-4:30PM (EST). *Civil Actions Under $15,000, Eviction, Small Claims.*
www.judiciary.state.nj.us/gloucester/sal/index.htm

Civil Records: Access: Phone, fax, mail, online, in person. Both court and visitors may perform in person searches. No search fee. Court makes copy: $.25 per page. Required to search: name, years to search. Civil cases indexed by defendant, plaintiff; on computer from 1990, on index from 1953. Participates in the court records statewide Electronic Access Program; for signup, information and booklet call 609-292-4987. Mail turnaround time 1-2 days.

General Information: Public terminal has only civil records back to 1990. No adoptions, sealed, juvenile, expunged, dismissed, or mental illness records released. Certification fee: $5.00 per doc. Payee: Special Civil Part. Personal checks accepted. Prepayment required.

Somerset County

Superior Court - Criminal Division PO Box 3000 (20 N Bridge St, 2nd Fl), Somerville, NJ 08876-1262; phone: 908-231-7600; fax: 908-231-5276; hours 8:30AM-4:30PM (EST). *Felony.*
www.judiciary.state.nj.us/somerset/index.htm

Criminal Records: Access: Phone, fax, mail, in person. Both court and visitors may perform in person searches. Search fee: $6.00 per name. Court makes copy: $.75 per page for 1st 10 pages; $.50 per page next 10; each add'l $.25. Required to search: name, years to search, DOB; also helpful: SSN. Criminal records on computer back to 1981, prior on index books. Mail turnaround time 2-3 days.

General Information: Public terminal has only criminal records back to 1981. No sealed, expunged, judges notes, PSI's, or discovery packets records released. Certification fee: $3.00 plus $1.50 per page. Payee: State of New Jersey. Personal checks accepted. Prepayment and SASE required.

Superior Court - Civil Division PO Box 3000, Civil Division, 20 N Bridge St, County Courthouse, Somerville, NJ 08876-1262; phone: 908-231-7054; hours 8:30AM-4:30PM (EST). *Civil Actions, Probate.*
www.judiciary.state.nj.us/somerset/index.htm

Civil Records: Access: Phone, mail, online, in person. Both court and visitors may perform in person searches. No search fee. Court makes copy: $.75 per page. Fee after 1st 10 pages $.50 per pg up to 20 pgs, then $.25 per pg. Required to search: name; also helpful: years to search. Civil cases indexed by defendant, plaintiff; on computer from 1990. Participates in the court records statewide Electronic Access Program; for signup, information and booklet call 609-292-4987. Note: Civil cases are archived 18 months after their last activity. Mail turnaround time 1-2 days.

General Information: Public terminal has only civil records. No sealed, expunged, dismissed, judges notes, PSI's, or discovery packets records released. Certification fee: $5.00 per page. Payee: Superior Court of NJ. Personal checks accepted. Prepayment and SASE required.

Superior Court Special Civil Part PO Box 3000, County Courthouse, Bridge & Main St, Somerville, NJ 08876-1262; phone: 908-231-7014/7015; hours 8:30AM-4:30PM (EST). *Civil Actions Under $15,000, Eviction, Small Claims.*
www.judiciary.state.nj.us/somerset/index.htm

Civil Records: Access: Mail, online, in person. Visitors must perform in person searches themselves. No search fee. Court makes copy: $.75 per page for first ten, $.50 per page for next ten, and $.25 per page thereafter. Required to search: name, years to search. Civil cases indexed by defendant, plaintiff; on computer from 1990, prior on index books. In person access requires an appointment. Participates in the court records statewide Electronic Access Program; for signup, information and booklet call 609-292-4987. Mail turnaround time varies; may be lengthy.

General Information: Public terminal has only civil records. (Terminal at counter provides visitor with book lookup help only.) No adoptions, sealed, juvenile, expunged, dismissed, or mental illness records released. Will not fax documents. No certification fee . Payee: Superior Court of New Jersey. Personal checks accepted. Prepayment and SASE required.

Sussex County

Superior Court - Criminal Division 43-47 High St, Sussex Judicial Ctr, Newton, NJ 07860; phone: 973-579-0696; fax: 973-579-0767; hours 8:30AM-4:30PM (EST). *Felony.*
www.judiciary.state.nj.us/morris/index.htm
Criminal Records: Access: In person only. Visitors must perform in person searches themselves. Court makes copy: $.75 per page for 1st 10 pages; $.50 per page next 10; each add'l $.25. Required to search: name, years to search, DOB, signed release; SSN helpful. Criminal records on computer from 1986, on docket books to 1950s.
General Information: Public terminal has only criminal records. No sealed, expunged, dismissed, judges notes, PSI's, or discovery packets records released. Certification fee: $5.00. Payee: State of New Jersey Judiciary. Only cashiers checks and money orders accepted. Prepayment required.

Superior Court - Civil Division 43-47 High St, Sussex Judicial Ctr, Newton, NJ 07860; phone: 973-579-0914/0915; fax: 973-579-0736; hours 8:30AM-4:30PM (EST). *Civil Actions Over $15,000, Probate.*
www.judiciary.state.nj.us/morris/index.htm
Civil Records: Access: Phone, mail, online, in person. Only the court performs in person searches; visitors may not. No search fee. Court makes copy: $.75 per page for first ten, $.50 per page for next ten, and $.25 per page thereafter. Required to search: name, years to search. Civil cases indexed by defendant, plaintiff; on computer from 1989, on microfiche by plaintiff prior to 1989, closed cases archived yearly and sent to Trenton. Participates in the court records statewide Electronic Access Program; for signup, information and booklet call 609-292-4987. Mail turnaround time up to 1 week.
General Information: No public access terminal. No sealed, expunged, dismissed, judges notes, PSI's, or discovery packets records released. Will not fax documents unless prepaid. Certification fee: $5.00 per doc. Payee: Clerk of Superior Court. Personal checks accepted. Prepayment required.

Superior Court Special Civil Part 43-47 High St, Newton, NJ 07860; phone: 973-579-0918; fax: 973-579-0736; hours 8:30AM-4:30PM (EST). *Civil Actions Under $15,000, Eviction, Small Claims.*
www.judiciary.state.nj.us/morris/index.htm
Civil Records: Access: Phone, fax, mail, online, in person. Both court and visitors may perform in person searches. No search fee. Court makes copy: $.75 per page for first 10; $.50 per page for next 10; each add'l $.25. Required to search: name, years to search. Civil cases indexed by defendant, plaintiff; on computer from mid 1989, on index books from 1940. Participates in the court records statewide Electronic Access Program; for signup,

information and booklet call 609-292-4987. Note: Court will accept name phone and fax search requests for up to 3 names. Mail turnaround time up to 2 weeks.
General Information: No public access terminal. No adoptions, sealed, juvenile, expunged, dismissed, or mental illness records released. Certification fee: $5.00 per doc. Payee: State of New Jersey Judiciary. Personal checks accepted. Prepayment required.

Union County

Superior Court - Criminal Division County Courthouse - Tower Bldg 5th Fl, Elizabeth, NJ 07207; criminal phone: 908-659-3376; civil phone: 908-659-3844; probate phone: 908-527-4280; fax: 908-659-3391; hours 8:30AM-4:30PM (EST). *Felony.*
www.judiciary.state.nj.us/union/index.htm
Criminal Records: Access: In person only. Visitors must perform in person searches themselves. Court makes copy: $.75 per page for 1st 10 pages; $.50 per page next 10; each add'l $.25. Required to search: name, years to search; also helpful: DOB, SSN. Criminal records on computer from 1985, prior on index books from 1960. In person access 9AM-3:30PM. Note: For requests regarding records prior to 1985, contact the NJ State Police for a criminal history sheet, and from the IND/ACC# this court can quickly find the reference in their records.
General Information: Public terminal has only criminal records back to 1985. No sealed, expunged, dismissed, judges notes, PSI's, or discovery packets records released. Will fax documents for you. Certification fee: $5.00 per doc. Payee: State of New Jersey Judiciary. Business checks and money orders accepted. Prepayment required.

Superior Court - Civil Division 2 Broad St, Elizabeth, NJ 07207; phone: 908-659-4176; fax: 908-659-4185; hours 8:30AM-4:30PM (EST). *Civil Actions Over $15,000.*
www.judiciary.state.nj.us/union/index.htm
Civil Records: Access: Phone, mail, online, in person. Visitors must perform in person searches themselves. Court makes copy: $.75 per page for first ten, $.50 per page for next ten, and $.25 per page thereafter. Required to search: name, years to search. Civil cases indexed by defendant, plaintiff; on computer from 1988, prior records archived in Trenton NJ. Participates in the court records statewide Electronic Access Program; for signup, information and booklet call 609-292-4987. Mail turnaround time varies.

General Information: Public terminal has only civil records. No sealed, expunged, dismissed, judges notes, PSI's, or discovery packets records released. Certification fee: $5.00. Payee: Clerk of Superior Court. Personal checks accepted. Prepayment required.

Superior Court Special Civil Part 2 Broad St, Elizabeth, NJ 07207; phone: 908-659-3637/8; fax: 908-659-3663; hours 8:30AM-4:30PM (EST). *Civil Actions Under $15,000, Eviction, Small Claims.*
www.judiciary.state.nj.us/union/index.htm
Civil Records: Access: Phone, mail, online, in person. Both court and visitors may perform in person searches. No search fee. Court makes copy: $.75 per page. Fee is for 1st 10 pages; $.50 per page next 10; each add'l $.25. Required to search: name, years to search. Civil cases indexed by defendant, plaintiff; on computer from 1993, on index books 1965, prior archived. Phone access limited to info after 11/93. Participates in the court records statewide Electronic Access Program; for signup, information and booklet call 609-292-4987. Mail turnaround time varies.
General Information: No public access terminal. No adoptions, sealed, juvenile, expunged, dismissed,

or mental illness records released. No certification fee . Payee: Special Civil Part. Personal checks accepted. Prepayment required.

Warren County

Warren County Superior Court Criminal Case Management Division, PO Box 900, Belvidere, NJ 07823; phone: 908-475-6990; criminal phone: 908-475-6990; civil phone: 908-475-6140; probate phone: 908-475-6223; fax: 908-475-6982; hours 8:30AM-4:30PM (EST). *Felony.*
www.judiciary.state.nj.us/somerset/index.htm
Criminal Records: Access: Phone, mail, fax, in person. Both court and visitors may perform in person searches. Search fee: $6.00 per name. Court makes copy: $.75 each up to 10 pages; $.50 11-20th pages; $.25 each add'l. Required to search: name, years to search, DOB; also helpful: SSN, signed release. Criminal records on computer back 10 years; prior on index cards to 1927. Mail turnaround time 2 days.
General Information: Public terminal has only criminal records back to 1985. No sealed, expunged, dismissed, judges notes, PSI's, or discovery packets records released. Will fax documents to local or toll free line. Certification fee: $5.00. Payee: State of New Jersey Judiciary. Personal checks accepted. Prepayment required.

Superior Court - Civil Division PO Box 900, 314 2nd St, Belvidere, NJ 07823; phone: 908-475-6140; probate phone: 908-475-6223; probate fax: 908-475-6319; hours 8:30AM-4:30PM (EST). *Civil Actions over $15,000, Probate.*
www.judiciary.state.nj.us/somerset/index.htm
Note: Surrogates/Probate court is located at 413 2nd St in the courthouse.
Civil Records: Access: Mail, online, in person. Only the court performs in person searches; visitors may not. No search fee. Court will perform one search no fee. Court makes copy: $.75 per page first 10 pages; $.50 per page next 10; each add'l $.10. Required to search: name, years to search. Civil cases indexed by defendant, plaintiff; on computer from 1990, prior on index books from 1951. Participates in the court records statewide Electronic Access Program; for signup, information and booklet call 609-292-4987. Note: In person access requires an appointment. Mail turnaround time 2 days.
General Information: Public terminal has only civil records back to - closed cases in last 18 months. No sealed, expunged, dismissed, judges notes, PSI's, or discovery packets records released. Certification fee: 1st page free; $5.00 for next 5 pages; add'l pg- $.75. Payee: Superior Court of New Jersey. Personal checks accepted. Prepayment required.

Superior Court Special Civil Part PO Box 900, 413 2nd St, Belvidere, NJ 07823; phone: 908-475-6140; hours 8:30AM-4:30PM (EST). *Civil Actions Under $15,000, Eviction, Small Claims.*
www.judiciary.state.nj.us/somerset/index.htm
Civil Records: Access: Mail, online, in person. Only the court performs in person searches; visitors may not. No search fee. Court will do one search no fee. Court makes copy: $.75 per page for first ten, $.50 per page for next ten, and $.25 per page thereafter. Required to search: name, years to search. Civil cases indexed by defendant, plaintiff; on computer from 10/91, prior on index books from 1951. Participates in the court records statewide Electronic Access Program; for signup, information and booklet call 609-292-4987. Note: In person access requires an appointment. Mail turnaround time 2-3 days.
General Information: No public access terminal. No adoptions, sealed, juvenile, expunged, dismissed, or mental illness records released. No certification fee . Payee: Superior Court of New Jersey. Personal checks accepted. Prepayment and SASE required.

New Jersey Recording Offices

ORGANIZATION: 21 counties, 21 recording offices. The recording officer title varies depending upon the county. It is either Register of Deeds or County Clerk. The Clerk of Circuit Court records the equivalent of some state's tax liens. The entire state is in the Eastern Time Zone (EST).

REAL ESTATE RECORDS: No counties will provide real estate searches. Copy and certification fees vary. Assessment and tax offices are at the municipal level.

UCC RECORDS: Financing statements are filed at the state level, except for real estate related collateral, which are filed with the County Clerk. However, prior to 07/2001, consumer goods and farm collateral were also filed at the County Clerk and these older records can be searched there. About half of the recording offices will perform UCC searches. Use search request form UCC-11. Search fees are usually $25.00 per debtor name and copy fees vary.

TAX LIEN RECORDS: All federal tax liens are filed with the County Clerk/Register of Deeds and are indexed separately from all other liens. State tax liens comprise two categories - certificates of debt are filed with the Clerk of Superior Court (some, called docketed judgments are filed specifically with the Trenton court), and warrants of execution are filed with the County Clerk/Register of Deeds. Few counties will provide tax lien searches. Refer to the County Court section for information about New Jersey Superior Courts.

OTHER LIENS: Judgment, mechanics, bail bond.

ONLINE ACCESS: A statewide database of property tax records can be accessed at http://taxrecords.com. The site is operated by a private company. Also, several county's property assessor and other info is available through a private company; for information, call Infocon at 814-472-6066 or www.ic-access.com.

Atlantic County

County Clerk, 5901 Main St; Courthouse, CN 2005, Mays Landing, NJ 08330-1797. 609-625-4011; fax-609-625-4738; hours: 8:30 AM-6:30 PM M W; 8:30AM-4:30PM T TH F. www.atlanticcountyclerk.org
All records in one index since 2000. Records indexed on a public use terminal back to 1972. Office will perform a UCC search but public must search other records themselves. Search fee $25.00. Copy fee $2.00 per page. Cert fee- $5.00 per cert plus copy fee. Payee- Atlantic County Clerk. **Online access to Property, Assessor, Inmate records:** Access to property data is free at http://tax1.co.monmouth.nj.us/cgi-bin/prc6.cgi. Use username "monm" and password "data" then select county. Also, see online notes in state summary at beginning of section. Also, search inmate info on private company website at www.vinelink.com/index.jsp.

Bergen County

County Clerk, One Bergen County Plaza, Hackensack, NJ 07601. 201-336-7007; hours: 9AM-4PM.
Only the public may search. Copy fee $1.00 per page. Cert fee- $1.00 per page. Payee- Bergen County Clerk. **Online access to Property, Assessor records:** Access to property data is free at http://tax1.co.monmouth.nj.us/cgi-bin/prc6.cgi. Use username "monm" and password "data" then select county. Also, see online notes in state summary at beginning of section. **Other phones:** Treasurer- 201-336-6000. **Property tax/Assessor-** 201-336-6000.

Burlington County

County Clerk, PO Box 6000, Mount Holly, NJ 08060. 609-265-5122; fax-609-265-0696; hours: 8AM-7PM M; 8AM-4PM T-F. www.co.burlington.nj.us/departments/countyclerk/index.htm
Separate indices to search include pre 1965 indexes in book form, UCC's separate index. Records indexed on a public use terminal back to 1965. Only the public may search. Copy fee $2.00 per page. **Online access to Property, Assessor records:** Access to property data is free at http://tax1.co.monmouth.nj.us/cgi-bin/prc6.cgi. Use

username "monm" and password "data" then select county. Also, see online notes in state summary at beginning of section. **Other phones:** Treasurer- 609-265-5018. **Property tax/Assessor-** 609-265-5056.

Camden County

County Clerk, 520 Market St; Courthouse Rm 102, Camden, NJ 08102-1375. 856-225-5300; fax-856-756-2242; hours: 8AM-4PM. www.camdencounty.com
Records indexed on computer back to 1988. Office will perform a UCC search but public must search other records themselves. Computer index available for all real estate transactions after August, 1988 UCC search per debtor name- $25.00 per name. Copy fee $2.00 per page; self serve $.19. Cert fee- $2.00 per cert plus copy fee. Payee- Camden County Clerk. **Online access to Property, Assessor records:** Access to property data is free at http://tax1.co.monmouth.nj.us/cgi-bin/prc6.cgi. Use username "monm" and password "data" then select county. Also, see online notes in state summary at beginning of section. **Property tax/Assessor-** 520 Market St, 3rd Fl, Admin Bldg, Camden, NJ 08102; not known.

Cape May County

County Clerk, PO Box 5000, Cape May Court House, NJ 08210-5000. 609-465-1010; fax-609-465-8625; 8:30AM-4:30PM. www.capemaycountygov.net
All records in one index. Records indexed on computer back to 1996. Only the public may search. Copy fee $2.00 per page. Cert fee- $10.00 per cert plus $1.00 per page. Payee- Cape May County Clerk. **Online access to Real Estate, Recording, Property records:** Property records for Cape May county are free to view online at http://209.204.84.120/ALIS/WW400R.PGM. To print and have full access to documents, registration and login is required. $1.00 per page copy and/or $10.00 certification fees apply to documents. Online documents go back to 1996, images to 2000. For assistance, telephone 609-465-1010. Land Records found at www.capemaycountygov.net. Also, see online notes in state summary at beginning of section. **Other phones:** Treasurer- 609-465-1170; Elections- 609-465-1013; Vital Records- 609-465-1023. **Property tax/Assessor-** same address as above. 609-465-1030.

Cumberland County

County Clerk, PO Box 716, Bridgeton, NJ 08302. 856-453-4864, R/E recording phone-856-453-4860; fax-856-455-1410; hours: 8:30AM-4PM.
All records in one index. Records indexed on a public use terminal back to 1989. Only the public may search. Copy fee $2.00 per page. Cert fee- $10.00 per doc plus $2.00 page fee. Payee- Cumberland County Clerk. **Online access to Property, Assessor records:** Access to property data is free at http://tax1.co.monmouth.nj.us/cgi-bin/prc6.cgi. Use username "monm" and password "data" then select county. Also, see online notes in state summary at beginning of section. **Other phones:** Elections- 856-453-4850. **Property tax/Assessor-** same address as above. 856-451-6699.

Essex County

County Register of Deeds, 465 Martin Luther King Blvd; Hall of Records, Rm 130, Newark, NJ 07102. 973-621-4960, R/E recording phone-973-621-4960 x228, UCC recording phone-973-621-4960 x225; fax-973-621-6114; 9AM-4PM. www.essexregister.com
Separate indices to search include each document type. Only the public may search. Copy fee $.25 per page. Cert fee- $4.00 1st page, $2.00 each add'l page. Payee- Essex County Register. **Online access to Property, Assessor records:** Access to property data is free online at http://tax1.co.monmouth.nj.us/cgi-bin/prc6.cgi. Use username "monm" and password "data" then select county. Also, see online notes in state summary at beginning of section. **Other phones:** Treasurer- 973-621-4997. **Property tax/Assessor-** 50 S Clinton St, East Orange, NJ 07017; 973-395-8525.

Gloucester County

County Clerk, PO Box 129, Woodbury, NJ 08096-0129. 856-853-3230; fax-856-853-3327; hours: 8:30AM-4PM. www.co.gloucester.nj.us
Separate indices to search include mortgage, grantor/grantee. Records indexed on computer, printed indexes separate. Only the public may search. Copy fee $.50 per page. Cert fee- $2.00 per cert plus copy fee. Payee- Gloucester County Clerk. **Online access to Recording, Real Estate,**

Deed, Lien, UCC, Mortgage, Assessor, Property Tax records: Access to property data is free at http://tax1.co.monmouth.nj.us/cgi-bin/prc6.cgi. Use username "monm" and password "data" then select county. Also, see online notes in state summary at beginning of section. Also, land records from the assessor database found free at https://www.landaccess.com/sites/nj/gloucester/. **Other phones:** Treasurer- 856-853-3353; Elections- 856-384-4501; Tax Collector- 856-853-6945. **Property tax/Assessor-** Budd Blvd, Woodbury, NJ 08096; 856-384-6945.

Hudson County

County Clerk, 595 Newark Ave; Rm 105, Jersey City, NJ 07306. 201-795-6571; fax-201-795-5177; hours: 9AM-5PM.
All records in one index. Records indexed on computer back to 1985. Office will perform a UCC search but public must search other records themselves. UCC search per debtor name- $25.00. Copy fee $.25 per page. Cert fee- $10.00 per page $1.50 add'l. Payee- Hudson County Clerk. **Online access to Property, Assessor records:** Access to property data is free at http://tax1.co.monmouth.nj.us/cgi-bin/prc6.cgi. Use username "monm" and password "data" then select county. Also, see online notes in state summary at beginning of section.

Hunterdon County

County Clerk, 71 Main St; Hall of Records, Flemington, NJ 08822. 908-788-1221; fax-908-782-4068; hours: 8:30AM-4PM.
Will not search real estate records. Will search UCC records, but not tax liens. UCC search per debtor name- $25.00. Copy fee $.25 per page. Cert fee- $5.00. Payee- Hunterdon County Clerk. **Online access to Property records:** See online notes in state summary at beginning of section. **Property tax/Assessor-** 908-788-1173.

Mercer County

County Clerk, 209 S. Broad St; Courthouse, Rm 100, Trenton, NJ 08650. 609-989-6466, R/E recording phone-609-989-6487; fax-609-989-1111; hours: 8:30AM-4:30PM. www.mercercounty.org
Separate indices to search. Records indexed on a public use terminal back to August, 24, 1997. Only the public may search. Copy fee $2.00 per page. Cert fee- $10.00 1st page; $1.50 each add'l page plus copy fee. Payee- Mercer County Clerk. **Online access to Property records:** See online notes in state summary at beginning of section. **Other phones:** Treasurer- 609-989-6694; Elections- 609-989-6495; Vital Records- 609-292-4087. **Property tax/Assessor-** 640 S. Broad St, Trenton, NJ 08650; 609-989-6704.

Middlesex County

County Clerk, PO Box 1110, New Brunswick, NJ 08903. 732-745-3204; hours: 8:30AM-4PM. www.co.middlesex.nj.us/countyclerk
Separate indices to search. Only the public may search. Copy fee $2.00 per page. Cert fee- $10.00 per cert includes copy fee. Payee- Middlesex County Clerk. **Online access to Recording, Deed, Lien, Mortgage, Property records:** Access to the county public access system requires registration and password at http://mcrecords.co.middlesex.nj.us/. There is a sign up fee plus $.25 per page, call Bob Receine at 732-745-3769 for more details. Also, search assessor records at http://tax1.co.monmouth.nj.us/cgi-bin/prc6.cgi. Use username "monm" and password "data" then select county. Also, see online notes in state summary at beginning of section. **Other phones:** Treasurer- 732-745-3482. **Property tax/Assessor-** 732-745-3000.

Monmouth County

County Clerk, 33 Mechanic St; Market Yard, Freehold, NJ 07728. 732-431-7324, R/E recording phone-732-431-7321; fax-732-761-9371; hours: 8:30AM-4:30PM. www.visitmonmouth.com
All records in one index. Only the public may search. Copy fee $2.00 per page. Cert fee- $10.00 per cert + $1.50 per page plus copy fee. Payee- Monmouth County Clerk. **Online access to Real Estate, Deed, Mortgage, Grantor/Grantee, Property Tax, Assessor records:** Access to property data is free at http://tax1.co.monmouth.nj.us/cgi-bin/prc6.cgi. Use username "monm" and password "data" then select county. Also, see online notes in state summary at beginning of section. **Other phones:** Treasurer- 732-431-7391; Appraiser/Auditor- 732-431-7404; Elections- 732-431-7780. **Property tax/Assessor-** 1 E Main St, Freehold, NJ 07728; 732-431-7404.

Morris County

County Clerk, PO Box 315, Morristown, NJ 07963-0315. 973-285-6135; fax-973-285-5231; hours: 8AM-4M M-F; 8AM-8PM W. http://clerk.morris.nj.us
Separate indices to search include deeds, mortgage, liens. Records indexed on a public use terminal back to 1968. Only the public may search. Copy fee $.25 per page. Cert fee- $12.00 per doc plus copy fee. Payee- Morris County Clerk. **Online access to Property, Assessor records:** Access to property data is free at http://tax1.co.monmouth.nj.us/cgi-bin/prc6.cgi. Use username "monm" and password "data" then select county. Also, search assessor records at http://tax1.co.monmouth.nj.us/cgi-bin/prc6.cgi. Use username "monm" and password "data" then select county. Also, see online notes in state summary at beginning of section.

Ocean County

County Clerk, PO Box 2191, Toms River, NJ 08754. 732-929-2018; fax-732-349-4336; hours: 8:30AM-4PM. www.oceancountyclerk.com
All records in one index. Records indexed on computer back to 1974. Only the public may search. Copy fee $1.00 per page. Cert fee- $2.00 per doc plus copy fee. Payee- Ocean County Clerk. **Online access to Property Tax, Real Estate, Deed records:** Land records on the County Clerk database are free at www.oceancountyclerk.com/search.htm. Search by parties, document or instrument type, or township. Tax records for Ocean county are also at http://oc.taxrecords.com. Search by name, address or property description. Also, see online notes at beginning of section.

Passaic County

County Clerk Registry Division, 77 Hamilton St; Courthouse, Paterson, NJ 07505. 973-881-4777; hours: 8:30AM-4:30PM; Vault Hours: 7:45AM-5:45PM.
Records indexed on computer from 1989 to present, paper index from 1837-1989. Only the public may search. Copy fee $2.00 per page. Cert fee- $10.00 1st page, $2.00 each add'l page includes copy fee. Payee- Passaic County Clerk. **Property tax/Assessor-** 435 Hamburg Turnpike, Wayne, NJ 07470; 973-720-7399.

Salem County

County Clerk, 92 Market St, Salem, NJ 08079-1911. 856-935-7510 x8218, R/E recording phone-856-935-7510 x8206, UCC recording phone-856-935-7510 x8218; fax-856-935-8882; hours: 8:30AM-4:30PM.
Separate indices to search include books, computer. Records indexed on a public use terminal back to 1990. Only the public may search. Copy fee $2.00 per page; self serve $.25. Cert fee- $5.00 per cert plus copy fee. Payee- Salem County Clerk. **Online access to Property, Assessor records:** Access to property data is free at http://tax1.co.monmouth.nj.us/cgi-bin/prc6.cgi. Use username "monm" and password "data" then select county. Also, see online notes in state summary at beginning of section. **Other phones:** Treasurer- 856-935–9036. **Property tax/Assessor-** 856-935-9231.

Somerset County

County Clerk, PO Box 3000, Somerville, NJ 08876. 908-231-7006; fax-908-253-8853; hours: 8:15AM-4PM. www.co.somerset.nj.us
All records in one index. From 01/01/93 to present computerized, prior in separate indices. Only the public may search. Copy fee $2.00 per page. Cert fee- $2.00 per cert plus copy fee. Payee- Somerset County Clerk. **Online access to Real Estate, Recording, Deed, Property Tax, Assessor records:** Access to the County Clerk's recordings database is free at http://209.92.88.21/. Registration required, or enter as "Guest." Index goes back to 1/93; images back to 6/11/01. Also, access to property data is free at http://tax1.co.monmouth.nj.us/cgi-bin/prc6.cgi. Use username "monm" and password "data" then select county. Also, see online notes in state summary at beginning of section. **Other phones:** Treasurer- 908-231-7000 x7631; Elections- 908-231-7084; Board of Taxation- 908-541-5701. **Property tax/Assessor-** 925 E Main St, Somerville, NJ 08876; not known.

Sussex County

County Clerk, 4 Park Pl; Hall of Records, Newton, NJ 07860-1795. 973-579-0900; fax-973-383-7493; hours: 8:30AM-4:30PM. www.sussexcountyclerk.com
Separate indices to search include liens, deeds, mtgs. Records indexed on a public use terminal back to 1964. Only the public may search. Copy fee $2.00 per page. Cert fee- $5.00 per page plus copy fee. Payee- Sussex County Clerk. **Online access to Property, Assessor, Real Estate, Recording, Deed records:** Access to property data is free at http://tax1.co.monmouth.nj.us/cgi-bin/prc6.cgi. Use username "monm" and password "data" then select county. Also, access recorder records back to 1/1964 at www.landaccess.com/proi/county.jsp?county=njsussex. They may begin charging a $250 sub fee. Also, see online notes in state summary at beginning of section. **Other phones:** Treasurer- 973-579-0330; Elections- 973-579-0950; Administrator- 973-579-0970. **Property tax/Assessor-** 973-579-0970.

Union County

County Clerk, 2 Broad St; Courthouse, Rm 115, Elizabeth, NJ 07207. 908-527-4794, R/E recording phone-908-527-4787, UCC recording phone-908-527-4794; fax-908-558-2589; hours: 8:30AM-4:30PM. http://clerk.ucnj.org
Only the public may search. Copy fee $1.50 per page. Cert fee- $8.00 1st pg; $2.00 each add'l. Payee- Union County Clerk. **Online access to Real Estate, Deed, Property Tax, Assessor records:** Search recorded real estate related documents at http://clerk.ucnj.org/UCPA/DocIndex. Access to property data is free at http://tax1.co.monmouth.nj.us/cgi-bin/prc6.cgi. Use username "monm" and password "data" then select county. **Other phones:** Elections- 908-527-4996.

Warren County

County Clerk, 413 Second St; Courthouse, Belvidere, NJ 07823-1500. 908-475-6211; fax-908-475-6208; hours: 8:30AM-4PM.
Separate indices to search include deeds, mortgages, liens before 7/12/04, since this date all in one. Only the public may search. Copy fee $2.00 per page. Cert fee- $5.00 per doc plus copy fee. Payee- Warren County Clerk. **Other phones:** Treasurer- 908-475-6542; Elections- 908-475-6211. **Property tax/Assessor-** 908-475-6229.

New Jersey County Locator

You will usually be able to find the city name in the City/County Cross Reference below. In that case, it is a simple matter to determine the county from the cross reference. However, only the official US Postal Service city names are included in this index. We have also included a ZIP/City Cross Reference immediately following the City/County Cross Reference.

If you know the ZIP Code but the city name does not appear in the City/County Cross Reference index, look up the ZIP Code in the ZIP/City Cross Reference, find the city name, then look up the city name in the City/County Cross Reference.

New Jersey City/County Cross Reference

ABSECON Atlantic
ADELPHIA Monmouth
ALLAMUCHY Warren
ALLENDALE Bergen
ALLENHURST Monmouth
ALLENTOWN (08501) Monmouth(82), Burlington(10), Mercer(7)
ALLENWOOD Monmouth
ALLOWAY Salem
ALPINE Bergen
ANDOVER Sussex
ANNANDALE Hunterdon
ASBURY (08802) Hunterdon(67), Warren(32)
ASBURY PARK Monmouth
ATCO (08004) Camden(98), Burlington(1)
ATLANTIC CITY Atlantic
ATLANTIC HIGHLANDS Monmouth
AUDUBON Camden
AUGUSTA Sussex
AVALON Cape May
AVENEL Middlesex
AVON BY THE SEA Monmouth
BAPTISTOWN Hunterdon
BARNEGAT Ocean
BARNEGAT LIGHT Ocean
BARRINGTON Camden
BASKING RIDGE (07920) Somerset(98), Morris(1)
BAYONNE Hudson
BAYVILLE Ocean
BEACH HAVEN Ocean
BEACHWOOD Ocean
BEDMINSTER Somerset
BELFORD Monmouth
BELLE MEAD Somerset
BELLEVILLE Essex
BELLMAWR Camden
BELMAR Monmouth
BELVIDERE Warren
BERGENFIELD Bergen
BERKELEY HEIGHTS Union
BERLIN Camden
BERNARDSVILLE Somerset
BEVERLY Burlington
BIRMINGHAM Burlington
BLACKWOOD (08012) Camden(55), Gloucester(44)
BLAIRSTOWN Warren
BLAWENBURG Somerset
BLOOMFIELD Essex
BLOOMINGDALE Passaic
BLOOMSBURY (08804) Hunterdon(70), Warren(29)
BOGOTA Bergen
BOONTON Morris
BORDENTOWN Burlington
BOUND BROOK Somerset
BRADLEY BEACH Monmouth
BRANCHVILLE Sussex
BRICK Ocean
BRIDGEPORT Gloucester
BRIDGETON (08302) Cumberland(93), Salem(6)
BRIDGEWATER Somerset
BRIELLE Monmouth
BRIGANTINE Atlantic
BROADWAY Warren
BROOKSIDE Morris

BROWNS MILLS Burlington
BUDD LAKE Morris
BUENA Atlantic
BURLINGTON Burlington
BUTLER Morris
BUTTZVILLE Warren
CALDWELL Essex
CALIFON (07830) Hunterdon(88), Morris(11)
CAPE MAY Cape May
CAPE MAY COURT HOUSE Cape May
CAPE MAY POINT Cape May
CARLSTADT Bergen
CARTERET Middlesex
CEDAR BROOK Camden
CEDAR GROVE Essex
CEDAR KNOLLS Morris
CEDARVILLE Cumberland
CHANGEWATER Warren
CHATHAM Morris
CHATSWORTH Burlington
CHERRY HILL Camden
CHESTER Morris
CLARK Union
CLARKSBORO Gloucester
CLARKSBURG Monmouth
CLAYTON Gloucester
CLEMENTON Camden
CLIFFSIDE PARK Bergen
CLIFFWOOD Monmouth
CLIFTON Passaic
CLINTON Hunterdon
CLOSTER Bergen
COLLINGSWOOD Camden
COLOGNE Atlantic
COLONIA Middlesex
COLTS NECK Monmouth
COLUMBIA Warren
COLUMBUS Burlington
COOKSTOWN Burlington
CRANBURY (08512) Middlesex(68), Mercer(31)
CRANBURY Middlesex
CRANFORD Union
CREAM RIDGE (08514) Monmouth(70), Ocean(29)
CREAMRIDGE (08514) Monmouth(70), Ocean(29)
CRESSKILL Bergen
CROSSWICKS Burlington
DAYTON Middlesex
DEAL Monmouth
DEEPWATER Salem
DEERFIELD STREET Cumberland
DELAWARE Warren
DELMONT Cumberland
DEMAREST Bergen
DENNISVILLE Cape May
DENVILLE Morris
DIVIDING CREEK Cumberland
DORCHESTER Cumberland
DOROTHY Atlantic
DOVER Morris
DUMONT Bergen
DUNELLEN (08812) Somerset(51), Middlesex(48)
EAST BRUNSWICK Middlesex
EAST HANOVER Morris
EAST ORANGE Essex

EAST RUTHERFORD Bergen
EATONTOWN Monmouth
EDGEWATER Bergen
EDISON Middlesex
EGG HARBOR CITY (08215) Atlantic(94), Burlington(5)
EGG HARBOR TOWNSHIP Atlantic
ELIZABETH Union
ELMER Salem
ELMWOOD PARK Bergen
ELWOOD Atlantic
EMERSON Bergen
ENGLEWOOD Bergen
ENGLEWOOD CLIFFS Bergen
ENGLISHTOWN Monmouth
ESSEX FELLS Essex
ESTELL MANOR Atlantic
EWAN Gloucester
FAIR HAVEN Monmouth
FAIR LAWN Bergen
FAIRFIELD Essex
FAIRTON Cumberland
FAIRVIEW Bergen
FANWOOD Union
FAR HILLS Somerset
FARMINGDALE Monmouth
FLAGTOWN Somerset
FLANDERS Morris
FLEMINGTON Hunterdon
FLORENCE Burlington
FLORHAM PARK Morris
FORDS Middlesex
FORKED RIVER Ocean
FORT LEE Bergen
FORT MONMOUTH Monmouth
FORTESCUE Cumberland
FRANKLIN Sussex
FRANKLIN LAKES Bergen
FRANKLIN PARK Somerset
FRANKLINVILLE Gloucester
FREEHOLD Monmouth
FRENCHTOWN Hunterdon
GARFIELD Bergen
GARWOOD Union
GIBBSBORO Camden
GIBBSTOWN Gloucester
GILLETTE Morris
GLADSTONE Somerset
GLASSBORO Gloucester
GLASSER Sussex
GLEN GARDNER Hunterdon
GLEN RIDGE Essex
GLEN ROCK Bergen
GLENDORA Camden
GLENWOOD Sussex
GLOUCESTER CITY Camden
GOSHEN Cape May
GREAT MEADOWS Warren
GREEN CREEK Cape May
GREEN VILLAGE Morris
GREENDELL Sussex
GREENWICH Cumberland
GRENLOCH Gloucester
HACKENSACK Bergen
HACKETTSTOWN (07840) Warren(82), Morris(17)
HADDON HEIGHTS Camden
HADDONFIELD Camden
HAINESPORT Burlington

HALEDON Passaic
HAMBURG Sussex
HAMMONTON (08037) Atlantic(81), Camden(18)
HAMPTON (08827) Hunterdon(93), Warren(6)
HANCOCKS BRIDGE Salem
HARRINGTON PARK Bergen
HARRISON Hudson
HARRISONVILLE Gloucester
HASBROUCK HEIGHTS Bergen
HASKELL Passaic
HAWORTH Bergen
HAWTHORNE Passaic
HAZLET Monmouth
HEISLERVILLE Cumberland
HELMETTA Middlesex
HEWITT (07421) Passaic(98), Sussex(1)
HIBERNIA Morris
HIGH BRIDGE Hunterdon
HIGHLAND LAKES Sussex
HIGHLAND PARK Middlesex
HIGHLANDS Monmouth
HIGHTSTOWN Mercer
HILLSBOROUGH Somerset
HILLSDALE Bergen
HILLSIDE Union
HO HO KUS Bergen
HOBOKEN Hudson
HOLMDEL Monmouth
HOPATCONG Sussex
HOPE Warren
HOPEWELL (08525) Mercer(92), Hunterdon(6)
HOWELL Monmouth
IMLAYSTOWN Monmouth
IRONIA Morris
IRVINGTON Essex
ISELIN Middlesex
ISLAND HEIGHTS Ocean
JACKSON Ocean
JAMESBURG Middlesex
JERSEY CITY Hudson
JOBSTOWN Burlington
JOHNSONBURG Warren
JULIUSTOWN Burlington
KEANSBURG Monmouth
KEARNY Hudson
KEASBEY Middlesex
KENDALL PARK Middlesex
KENILWORTH Union
KENVIL Morris
KEYPORT (07735) Monmouth(92), Middlesex(7)
KINGSTON Somerset
KIRKWOOD VOORHEES Camden
LAFAYETTE Sussex
LAKE HIAWATHA Morris
LAKE HOPATCONG Morris
LAKEHURST Ocean
LAKEWOOD Ocean
LAMBERTVILLE (08530) Hunterdon(96), Mercer(3)
LANDING Morris
LANDISVILLE Atlantic
LANOKA HARBOR Ocean
LAVALLETTE Ocean
LAWNSIDE Camden
LAYTON Sussex

LEBANON Hunterdon
LEDGEWOOD Morris
LEEDS POINT Atlantic
LEESBURG Cumberland
LEONARDO Monmouth
LEONIA Bergen
LIBERTY CORNER Somerset
LINCOLN PARK Morris
LINCROFT Monmouth
LINDEN Union
LINWOOD Atlantic
LITTLE FALLS Passaic
LITTLE FERRY Bergen
LITTLE SILVER Monmouth
LITTLE YORK Hunterdon
LIVINGSTON Essex
LODI Bergen
LONG BRANCH Monmouth
LONG VALLEY Morris
LONGPORT Atlantic
LUMBERTON Burlington
LYNDHURST Bergen
LYONS Somerset
MADISON Morris
MAGNOLIA Camden
MAHWAH Bergen
MALAGA Gloucester
MANAHAWKIN Ocean
MANASQUAN Monmouth
MANTOLOKING Ocean
MANTUA Gloucester
MANVILLE Somerset
MAPLE SHADE Burlington
MAPLEWOOD Essex
MARGATE CITY Atlantic
MARLBORO Monmouth
MARLTON Burlington
MARMORA Cape May
MARTINSVILLE Somerset
MATAWAN (07747) Monmouth(65),
    Middlesex(34)
MAURICETOWN Cumberland
MAYS LANDING Atlantic
MAYWOOD Bergen
MC AFEE Sussex
MEDFORD Burlington
MENDHAM Morris
MERCHANTVILLE Camden
METUCHEN Middlesex
MICKLETON Gloucester
MIDDLESEX Middlesex
MIDDLETOWN Monmouth
MIDDLEVILLE Sussex
MIDLAND PARK Bergen
MILFORD Hunterdon
MILLBURN Essex
MILLINGTON Morris
MILLTOWN Middlesex
MILLVILLE Cumberland
MILMAY Atlantic
MINE HILL Morris
MINOTOLA Atlantic
MIZPAH Atlantic
MONMOUTH BEACH Monmouth
MONMOUTH JUNCTION Middlesex
MONROE TOWNSHIP Middlesex
MONROEVILLE (08343) Gloucester(58),
    Salem(41)
MONTAGUE Sussex
MONTCLAIR (07043) Essex(96),
    Passaic(3)
MONTCLAIR Essex
MONTVALE Bergen
MONTVILLE Morris
MOONACHIE Bergen
MOORESTOWN Burlington
MORGANVILLE Monmouth
MORRIS PLAINS Morris
MORRISTOWN Morris
MOUNT ARLINGTON Morris
MOUNT EPHRAIM Camden
MOUNT FREEDOM Morris

MOUNT HOLLY Burlington
MOUNT LAUREL Burlington
MOUNT ROYAL Gloucester
MOUNT TABOR Morris
MOUNTAIN LAKES Morris
MOUNTAINSIDE Union
MULLICA HILL Gloucester
MUSICAL HERITAGE Monmouth
NATIONAL PARK Gloucester
NAVESINK Monmouth
NEPTUNE Monmouth
NESHANIC STATION (08853)
    Somerset(86), Hunterdon(13)
NETCONG Morris
NEW BRUNSWICK Middlesex
NEW EGYPT (08533) Ocean(98),
    Burlington(1)
NEW GRETNA Burlington
NEW LISBON Burlington
NEW MILFORD Bergen
NEW PROVIDENCE Union
NEW VERNON Morris
NEWARK Essex
NEWFIELD (08344) Gloucester(65),
    Cumberland(24), Atlantic(6), Salem(3)
NEWFOUNDLAND Passaic
NEWPORT Cumberland
NEWTON Sussex
NEWTONVILLE Atlantic
NORMA Salem
NORMANDY BEACH Ocean
NORTH ARLINGTON Bergen
NORTH BERGEN Hudson
NORTH BRUNSWICK Middlesex
NORTHFIELD Atlantic
NORTHVALE Bergen
NORWOOD Bergen
NUTLEY Essex
OAK RIDGE (07438) Passaic(78),
    Morris(21)
OAKHURST Monmouth
OAKLAND Bergen
OAKLYN Camden
OCEAN CITY Cape May
OCEAN GATE Ocean
OCEAN GROVE Monmouth
OCEAN VIEW Cape May
OCEANPORT Monmouth
OCEANVILLE Atlantic
OGDENSBURG Sussex
OLD BRIDGE Middlesex
OLDWICK Hunterdon
ORADELL Bergen
ORANGE Essex
OSGLI Essex
OXFORD Warren
PALISADES PARK Bergen
PALMYRA Burlington
PARAMUS Bergen
PARK RIDGE Bergen
PARLIN Middlesex
PARSIPPANY Morris
PASSAIC Passaic
PATERSON Passaic
PAULSBORO Gloucester
PEAPACK Somerset
PEDRICKTOWN Salem
PEMBERTON Burlington
PENNINGTON Mercer
PENNS GROVE Salem
PENNSAUKEN Camden
PENNSVILLE Salem
PEQUANNOCK Morris
PERRINEVILLE Monmouth
PERTH AMBOY Middlesex
PHILLIPSBURG Warren
PICATINNY ARSENAL Morris
PINE BEACH Ocean
PINE BROOK Morris
PISCATAWAY Middlesex
PITMAN Gloucester
PITTSTOWN Hunterdon

PLAINFIELD (07063) Union(72),
    Somerset(27)
PLAINFIELD Union
PLAINSBORO Middlesex
PLEASANTVILLE Atlantic
PLUCKEMIN Somerset
POINT PLEASANT BEACH Ocean
POMONA Atlantic
POMPTON LAKES Passaic
POMPTON PLAINS Morris
PORT ELIZABETH Cumberland
PORT MONMOUTH Monmouth
PORT MURRAY Warren
PORT NORRIS Cumberland
PORT READING Middlesex
PORT REPUBLIC Atlantic
POTTERSVILLE Hunterdon
PRINCETON (08540) Mercer(72),
    Middlesex(15), Somerset(12)
PRINCETON JUNCTION Mercer
QUAKERTOWN Hunterdon
QUINTON Salem
RAHWAY Union
RAMSEY Bergen
RANCOCAS Burlington
RANDOLPH Morris
RARITAN Somerset
READINGTON Hunterdon
RED BANK Monmouth
RICHLAND Atlantic
RICHWOOD Gloucester
RIDGEFIELD Bergen
RIDGEFIELD PARK Bergen
RIDGEWOOD Bergen
RINGOES Hunterdon
RINGWOOD Passaic
RIO GRANDE Cape May
RIVER EDGE Bergen
RIVERDALE Morris
RIVERSIDE Burlington
RIVERTON Burlington
ROCHELLE PARK Bergen
ROCKAWAY Morris
ROCKY HILL Somerset
ROEBLING Burlington
ROOSEVELT Monmouth
ROSELAND Essex
ROSELLE Union
ROSELLE PARK Union
ROSEMONT Hunterdon
ROSENHAYN Cumberland
RUMSON Monmouth
RUNNEMEDE Camden
RUTHERFORD Bergen
SADDLE BROOK Bergen
SADDLE RIVER Bergen
SALEM Salem
SAYREVILLE Middlesex
SCHOOLEYS MOUNTAIN Morris
SCOTCH PLAINS Union
SEA GIRT Monmouth
SEA ISLE CITY Cape May
SEASIDE HEIGHTS Ocean
SEASIDE PARK Ocean
SECAUCUS Hudson
SERGEANTSVILLE Hunterdon
SEWAREN Middlesex
SEWELL Gloucester
SHILOH Cumberland
SHORT HILLS Essex
SHREWSBURY Monmouth
SICKLERVILLE (08081) Camden(96),
    Gloucester(3)
SKILLMAN (08558) Somerset(98),
    Mercer(1)
SOMERDALE Camden
SOMERS POINT Atlantic
SOMERSET Somerset
SOMERVILLE (08876) Somerset(98),
    Hunterdon(1)
SOUTH AMBOY Middlesex
SOUTH BOUND BROOK Somerset

SOUTH DENNIS Cape May
SOUTH HACKENSACK Bergen
SOUTH ORANGE Essex
SOUTH PLAINFIELD Middlesex
SOUTH RIVER Middlesex
SOUTH SEAVILLE Cape May
SPARTA Sussex
SPOTSWOOD Middlesex
SPRING LAKE Monmouth
SPRINGFIELD Union
STANHOPE Sussex
STANTON Hunterdon
STEWARTSVILLE Warren
STILLWATER Sussex
STIRLING Morris
STOCKHOLM (07460) Sussex(96),
    Morris(2)
STOCKTON Hunterdon
STONE HARBOR Cape May
STRATFORD Camden
STRATHMERE Cape May
SUCCASUNNA Morris
SUMMIT Union
SUSSEX Sussex
SWARTSWOOD Sussex
SWEDESBORO Gloucester
TEANECK Bergen
TENAFLY Bergen
TENNENT Monmouth
TETERBORO Bergen
THOROFARE Gloucester
THREE BRIDGES Hunterdon
TITUSVILLE Mercer
TOMS RIVER Ocean
TOTOWA Passaic
TOWACO Morris
TOWNSHIP OF WASHINGTON Bergen
TRANQUILITY Sussex
TRENTON (08620) Mercer(85),
    Burlington(14)
TRENTON (08691) Mercer(95),
    Monmouth(4)
TRENTON Burlington
TRENTON Mercer
TUCKAHOE Cape May
TUCKERTON (08087) Ocean(94),
    Burlington(5)
UNION Union
UNION CITY Hudson
VAUXHALL Union
VENTNOR CITY Atlantic
VERNON Sussex
VERONA Essex
VIENNA Warren
VILLAS Cape May
VINCENTOWN Burlington
VINELAND (08360) Cumberland(90),
    Atlantic(5), Gloucester(3)
VINELAND Cumberland
VOORHEES Camden
WALDWICK Bergen
WALLINGTON Bergen
WALLPACK CENTER Sussex
WANAQUE Passaic
WARETOWN Ocean
WARREN Somerset
WASHINGTON Warren
WATCHUNG Somerset
WATERFORD WORKS Camden
WAYNE Passaic
WEEHAWKEN Hudson
WENONAH Gloucester
WEST BERLIN Camden
WEST CREEK Ocean
WEST LONG BRANCH Monmouth
WEST MILFORD Passaic
WEST NEW YORK Hudson
WEST ORANGE Essex
WESTFIELD Union
WESTVILLE Gloucester
WESTWOOD Bergen
WHARTON Morris

WHIPPANY Morris
WHITEHOUSE Hunterdon
WHITEHOUSE STATION Hunterdon
WHITESBORO Cape May
WHITING Ocean
WICKATUNK Monmouth

WILDWOOD Cape May
WILLIAMSTOWN (08094) Gloucester(90),
Atlantic(9)
WILLINGBORO Burlington
WINDSOR Mercer
WINSLOW Camden

WOOD RIDGE Bergen
WOODBINE (08270) Cape May(89),
Atlantic(10)
WOODBRIDGE Middlesex
WOODBURY Gloucester
WOODBURY HEIGHTS Gloucester

WOODCLIFF LAKE Bergen
WOODSTOWN Salem
WRIGHTSTOWN Burlington
WYCKOFF Bergen
ZAREPHATH Somerset

New Jersey ZIP/City Cross Reference

07001-07001 AVENEL	07097-07097 JERSEY CITY	07626-07626 CRESSKILL	07757-07757 OCEANPORT
07002-07002 BAYONNE	07098-07098 AVENEL	07627-07627 DEMAREST	07758-07758 PORT MONMOUTH
07003-07003 BLOOMFIELD	07099-07099 KEARNY	07628-07628 DUMONT	07760-07760 RUMSON
07004-07004 FAIRFIELD	07100-07108 NEWARK	07630-07630 EMERSON	07762-07762 SPRING LAKE
07005-07005 BOONTON	07109-07109 BELLEVILLE	07631-07631 ENGLEWOOD	07763-07763 TENNENT
07006-07007 CALDWELL	07110-07110 NUTLEY	07632-07632 ENGLEWOOD CLIFFS	07764-07764 WEST LONG BRANCH
07008-07008 CARTERET	07111-07111 IRVINGTON	07640-07640 HARRINGTON PARK	07765-07765 WICKATUNK
07009-07009 CEDAR GROVE	07112-07187 NEWARK	07641-07641 HAWORTH	07777-07777 HOLMDEL
07010-07010 CLIFFSIDE PARK	07187-07187 OSGLI	07642-07642 HILLSDALE	07799-07799 EATONTOWN
07011-07015 CLIFTON	07188-07199 NEWARK	07643-07643 LITTLE FERRY	07801-07802 DOVER
07016-07016 CRANFORD	07200-07202 ELIZABETH	07644-07644 LODI	07803-07803 MINE HILL
07017-07019 EAST ORANGE	07203-07203 ROSELLE	07645-07645 MONTVALE	07806-07806 PICATINNY ARSENAL
07020-07020 EDGEWATER	07204-07204 ROSELLE PARK	07646-07646 NEW MILFORD	07820-07820 ALLAMUCHY
07021-07021 ESSEX FELLS	07205-07205 HILLSIDE	07647-07647 NORTHVALE	07821-07821 ANDOVER
07022-07022 FAIRVIEW	07206-07216 ELIZABETH	07648-07648 NORWOOD	07822-07822 AUGUSTA
07023-07023 FANWOOD	07300-07399 JERSEY CITY	07649-07649 ORADELL	07823-07823 BELVIDERE
07024-07024 FORT LEE	07401-07401 ALLENDALE	07650-07650 PALISADES PARK	07825-07825 BLAIRSTOWN
07026-07026 GARFIELD	07403-07403 BLOOMINGDALE	07652-07653 PARAMUS	07826-07826 BRANCHVILLE
07027-07027 GARWOOD	07405-07405 BUTLER	07656-07656 PARK RIDGE	07827-07827 MONTAGUE
07028-07028 GLEN RIDGE	07407-07407 ELMWOOD PARK	07657-07657 RIDGEFIELD	07828-07828 BUDD LAKE
07029-07029 HARRISON	07410-07410 FAIR LAWN	07660-07660 RIDGEFIELD PARK	07829-07829 BUTTZVILLE
07030-07030 HOBOKEN	07416-07416 FRANKLIN	07661-07661 RIVER EDGE	07830-07830 CALIFON
07031-07031 NORTH ARLINGTON	07417-07417 FRANKLIN LAKES	07662-07662 ROCHELLE PARK	07831-07831 CHANGEWATER
07032-07032 KEARNY	07418-07418 GLENWOOD	07663-07663 SADDLE BROOK	07832-07832 COLUMBIA
07033-07033 KENILWORTH	07419-07419 HAMBURG	07666-07666 TEANECK	07833-07833 DELAWARE
07034-07034 LAKE HIAWATHA	07420-07420 HASKELL	07670-07670 TENAFLY	07834-07834 DENVILLE
07035-07035 LINCOLN PARK	07421-07421 HEWITT	07675-07675 WESTWOOD	07836-07836 FLANDERS
07036-07036 LINDEN	07422-07422 HIGHLAND LAKES	07676-07676 TOWNSHIP OF	07837-07837 GLASSER
07039-07039 LIVINGSTON	07423-07423 HO HO KUS	WASHINGTON	07838-07838 GREAT MEADOWS
07040-07040 MAPLEWOOD	07424-07424 LITTLE FALLS	07677-07677 WOODCLIFF LAKE	07839-07839 GREENDELL
07041-07041 MILLBURN	07428-07428 MC AFEE	07688-07688 TEANECK	07840-07840 HACKETTSTOWN
07042-07043 MONTCLAIR	07430-07430 MAHWAH	07699-07699 TETERBORO	07842-07842 HIBERNIA
07044-07044 VERONA	07432-07432 MIDLAND PARK	07701-07701 RED BANK	07843-07843 HOPATCONG
07045-07045 MONTVILLE	07435-07435 NEWFOUNDLAND	07702-07702 SHREWSBURY	07844-07844 HOPE
07046-07046 MOUNTAIN LAKES	07436-07436 OAKLAND	07703-07703 FORT MONMOUTH	07845-07845 IRONIA
07047-07047 NORTH BERGEN	07438-07438 OAK RIDGE	07704-07704 FAIR HAVEN	07846-07846 JOHNSONBURG
07050-07051 ORANGE	07439-07439 OGDENSBURG	07709-07709 ALLENHURST	07847-07847 KENVIL
07052-07052 WEST ORANGE	07440-07440 PEQUANNOCK	07710-07710 ADELPHIA	07848-07848 LAFAYETTE
07054-07054 PARSIPPANY	07442-07442 POMPTON LAKES	07711-07711 ALLENHURST	07849-07849 LAKE HOPATCONG
07055-07055 PASSAIC	07444-07444 POMPTON PLAINS	07712-07712 ASBURY PARK	07850-07850 LANDING
07057-07057 WALLINGTON	07446-07446 RAMSEY	07713-07713 MUSICAL HERITAGE	07851-07851 LAYTON
07058-07058 PINE BROOK	07450-07451 RIDGEWOOD	07715-07715 BELMAR	07852-07852 LEDGEWOOD
07059-07059 WARREN	07452-07452 GLEN ROCK	07716-07716 ATLANTIC HIGHLANDS	07853-07853 LONG VALLEY
07060-07063 PLAINFIELD	07456-07456 RINGWOOD	07717-07717 AVON BY THE SEA	07855-07855 MIDDLEVILLE
07064-07064 PORT READING	07457-07457 RIVERDALE	07718-07718 BELFORD	07856-07856 MOUNT ARLINGTON
07065-07065 RAHWAY	07458-07458 SADDLE RIVER	07719-07719 BELMAR	07857-07857 NETCONG
07066-07066 CLARK	07460-07460 STOCKHOLM	07720-07720 BRADLEY BEACH	07860-07860 NEWTON
07067-07067 COLONIA	07461-07461 SUSSEX	07721-07721 CLIFFWOOD	07863-07863 OXFORD
07068-07068 ROSELAND	07462-07462 VERNON	07722-07722 COLTS NECK	07865-07865 PORT MURRAY
07069-07069 WATCHUNG	07463-07463 WALDWICK	07723-07723 DEAL	07866-07866 ROCKAWAY
07070-07070 RUTHERFORD	07465-07465 WANAQUE	07724-07724 EATONTOWN	07869-07869 RANDOLPH
07071-07071 LYNDHURST	07470-07477 WAYNE	07726-07726 ENGLISHTOWN	07870-07870 SCHOOLEYS MOUNTAIN
07072-07072 CARLSTADT	07480-07480 WEST MILFORD	07727-07727 FARMINGDALE	07871-07871 SPARTA
07073-07073 EAST RUTHERFORD	07481-07481 WYCKOFF	07728-07728 FREEHOLD	07874-07874 STANHOPE
07074-07074 MOONACHIE	07495-07498 MAHWAH	07730-07730 HAZLET	07875-07875 STILLWATER
07075-07075 WOOD RIDGE	07501-07505 PATERSON	07731-07731 HOWELL	07876-07876 SUCCASUNNA
07076-07076 SCOTCH PLAINS	07506-07507 HAWTHORNE	07732-07732 HIGHLANDS	07877-07877 SWARTSWOOD
07077-07077 SEWAREN	07508-07508 HALEDON	07733-07733 HOLMDEL	07878-07878 MOUNT TABOR
07078-07078 SHORT HILLS	07509-07510 PATERSON	07734-07734 KEANSBURG	07879-07879 TRANQUILITY
07079-07079 SOUTH ORANGE	07511-07512 TOTOWA	07735-07735 KEYPORT	07880-07880 VIENNA
07080-07080 SOUTH PLAINFIELD	07513-07533 PATERSON	07737-07737 LEONARDO	07881-07881 WALLPACK CENTER
07081-07081 SPRINGFIELD	07538-07538 HALEDON	07738-07738 LINCROFT	07882-07882 WASHINGTON
07082-07082 TOWACO	07543-07544 PATERSON	07739-07739 LITTLE SILVER	07885-07885 WHARTON
07083-07083 UNION	07601-07602 HACKENSACK	07740-07740 LONG BRANCH	07890-07890 BRANCHVILLE
07086-07086 WEEHAWKEN	07603-07603 BOGOTA	07746-07746 MARLBORO	07901-07902 SUMMIT
07087-07087 UNION CITY	07604-07604 HASBROUCK HEIGHTS	07747-07747 MATAWAN	07920-07920 BASKING RIDGE
07088-07088 VAUXHALL	07605-07605 LEONIA	07748-07748 MIDDLETOWN	07921-07921 BEDMINSTER
07090-07091 WESTFIELD	07606-07606 SOUTH HACKENSACK	07750-07750 MONMOUTH BEACH	07922-07922 BERKELEY HEIGHTS
07092-07092 MOUNTAINSIDE	07607-07607 MAYWOOD	07751-07751 MORGANVILLE	07924-07924 BERNARDSVILLE
07093-07093 WEST NEW YORK	07608-07608 TETERBORO	07752-07752 NAVESINK	07926-07926 BROOKSIDE
07094-07094 SECAUCUS	07620-07620 ALPINE	07753-07754 NEPTUNE	07927-07927 CEDAR KNOLLS
07095-07095 WOODBRIDGE	07621-07621 BERGENFIELD	07755-07755 OAKHURST	07928-07928 CHATHAM
07096-07096 SECAUCUS	07624-07624 CLOSTER	07756-07756 OCEAN GROVE	07930-07930 CHESTER

07931-07931	FAR HILLS
07932-07932	FLORHAM PARK
07933-07933	GILLETTE
07934-07934	GLADSTONE
07935-07935	GREEN VILLAGE
07936-07936	EAST HANOVER
07938-07938	LIBERTY CORNER
07939-07939	LYONS
07940-07940	MADISON
07945-07945	MENDHAM
07946-07946	MILLINGTON
07950-07950	MORRIS PLAINS
07960-07963	MORRISTOWN
07970-07970	MOUNT FREEDOM
07974-07974	NEW PROVIDENCE
07976-07976	NEW VERNON
07977-07977	PEAPACK
07978-07978	PLUCKEMIN
07979-07979	POTTERSVILLE
07980-07980	STIRLING
07981-07999	WHIPPANY
08001-08001	ALLOWAY
08002-08003	CHERRY HILL
08004-08004	ATCO
08005-08005	BARNEGAT
08006-08006	BARNEGAT LIGHT
08007-08007	BARRINGTON
08008-08008	BEACH HAVEN
08009-08009	BERLIN
08010-08010	BEVERLY
08011-08011	BIRMINGHAM
08012-08012	BLACKWOOD
08014-08014	BRIDGEPORT
08015-08015	BROWNS MILLS
08016-08016	BURLINGTON
08018-08018	CEDAR BROOK
08019-08019	CHATSWORTH
08020-08020	CLARKSBORO
08021-08021	CLEMENTON
08022-08022	COLUMBUS
08023-08023	DEEPWATER
08025-08025	EWAN
08026-08026	GIBBSBORO
08027-08027	GIBBSTOWN
08028-08028	GLASSBORO
08029-08029	GLENDORA
08030-08030	GLOUCESTER CITY
08031-08031	BELLMAWR
08032-08032	GRENLOCH
08033-08033	HADDONFIELD
08034-08034	CHERRY HILL
08035-08035	HADDON HEIGHTS
08036-08036	HAINESPORT
08037-08037	HAMMONTON
08038-08038	HANCOCKS BRIDGE
08039-08039	HARRISONVILLE
08040-08040	KIRKWOOD VOORHEES
08041-08041	JOBSTOWN
08042-08042	JULIUSTOWN
08043-08043	VOORHEES
08045-08045	LAWNSIDE
08046-08046	WILLINGBORO
08048-08048	LUMBERTON
08049-08049	MAGNOLIA
08050-08050	MANAHAWKIN
08051-08051	MANTUA
08052-08052	MAPLE SHADE
08053-08053	MARLTON
08054-08054	MOUNT LAUREL
08055-08055	MEDFORD
08056-08056	MICKLETON
08057-08057	MOORESTOWN
08059-08059	MOUNT EPHRAIM
08060-08060	MOUNT HOLLY
08061-08061	MOUNT ROYAL
08062-08062	MULLICA HILL
08063-08063	NATIONAL PARK
08064-08064	NEW LISBON
08065-08065	PALMYRA
08066-08066	PAULSBORO
08067-08067	PEDRICKTOWN
08068-08068	PEMBERTON
08069-08069	PENNS GROVE
08070-08070	PENNSVILLE
08071-08071	PITMAN
08072-08072	QUINTON
08073-08073	RANCOCAS
08074-08074	RICHWOOD
08075-08075	RIVERSIDE
08076-08077	RIVERTON
08078-08078	RUNNEMEDE
08079-08079	SALEM
08080-08080	SEWELL
08081-08081	SICKLERVILLE
08083-08083	SOMERDALE
08084-08084	STRATFORD
08085-08085	SWEDESBORO
08086-08086	THOROFARE
08087-08087	TUCKERTON
08088-08088	VINCENTOWN
08089-08089	WATERFORD WORKS
08090-08090	WENONAH
08091-08091	WEST BERLIN
08092-08092	WEST CREEK
08093-08093	WESTVILLE
08094-08094	WILLIAMSTOWN
08095-08095	WINSLOW
08096-08096	WOODBURY
08097-08097	WOODBURY HEIGHTS
08098-08098	WOODSTOWN
08099-08099	BELLMAWR
08100-08105	CAMDEN
08106-08106	AUDUBON
08107-08107	OAKLYN
08108-08108	COLLINGSWOOD
08109-08109	MERCHANTVILLE
08110-08110	PENNSAUKEN
08201-08201	ABSECON
08202-08202	AVALON
08203-08203	BRIGANTINE
08204-08204	CAPE MAY
08205-08205	ABSECON
08210-08210	CAPE MAY COURT HOUSE
08212-08212	CAPE MAY POINT
08213-08213	COLOGNE
08214-08214	DENNISVILLE
08215-08215	EGG HARBOR CITY
08217-08217	ELWOOD
08218-08218	GOSHEN
08219-08219	GREEN CREEK
08220-08220	LEEDS POINT
08221-08222	LINWOOD
08223-08223	MARMORA
08224-08224	NEW GRETNA
08225-08225	NORTHFIELD
08226-08226	OCEAN CITY
08227-08227	LINWOOD
08230-08230	OCEAN VIEW
08231-08231	OCEANVILLE
08232-08233	PLEASANTVILLE
08234-08234	EGG HARBOR TOWNSHIP
08240-08240	POMONA
08241-08241	PORT REPUBLIC
08242-08242	RIO GRANDE
08243-08243	SEA ISLE CITY
08244-08244	SOMERS POINT
08245-08245	SOUTH DENNIS
08246-08246	SOUTH SEAVILLE
08247-08247	STONE HARBOR
08248-08248	STRATHMERE
08250-08250	TUCKAHOE
08251-08251	VILLAS
08252-08252	WHITESBORO
08260-08260	WILDWOOD
08270-08270	WOODBINE
08302-08302	BRIDGETON
08310-08310	BUENA
08311-08311	CEDARVILLE
08312-08312	CLAYTON
08313-08313	DEERFIELD STREET
08314-08314	DELMONT
08315-08315	DIVIDING CREEK
08316-08316	DORCHESTER
08317-08317	DOROTHY
08318-08318	ELMER
08319-08319	ESTELL MANOR
08320-08320	FAIRTON
08321-08321	FORTESCUE
08322-08322	FRANKLINVILLE
08323-08323	GREENWICH
08324-08324	HEISLERVILLE
08326-08326	LANDISVILLE
08327-08327	LEESBURG
08328-08328	MALAGA
08329-08329	MAURICETOWN
08330-08330	MAYS LANDING
08332-08332	MILLVILLE
08340-08340	MILMAY
08341-08341	MINOTOLA
08342-08342	MIZPAH
08343-08343	MONROEVILLE
08344-08344	NEWFIELD
08345-08345	NEWPORT
08346-08346	NEWTONVILLE
08347-08347	NORMA
08348-08348	PORT ELIZABETH
08349-08349	PORT NORRIS
08350-08350	RICHLAND
08352-08352	ROSENHAYN
08353-08353	SHILOH
08358-08358	CHERRY HILL
08360-08362	VINELAND
08370-08370	RIVERSIDE
08400-08401	ATLANTIC CITY
08402-08402	MARGATE CITY
08403-08403	LONGPORT
08404-08405	ATLANTIC CITY
08406-08406	VENTNOR CITY
08411-08411	ATLANTIC CITY
08501-08501	ALLENTOWN
08502-08502	BELLE MEAD
08504-08504	BLAWENBURG
08505-08505	BORDENTOWN
08510-08510	CLARKSBURG
08511-08511	COOKSTOWN
08512-08512	CRANBURY
08514-08514	CREAMRIDGE
08514-08514	CREAM RIDGE
08515-08515	CROSSWICKS
08518-08518	FLORENCE
08520-08520	HIGHTSTOWN
08525-08525	HOPEWELL
08526-08526	IMLAYSTOWN
08527-08527	JACKSON
08528-08528	KINGSTON
08530-08530	LAMBERTVILLE
08533-08533	NEW EGYPT
08534-08534	PENNINGTON
08535-08535	PERRINEVILLE
08536-08536	PLAINSBORO
08540-08544	PRINCETON
08550-08550	PRINCETON JUNCTION
08551-08551	RINGOES
08553-08553	ROCKY HILL
08554-08554	ROEBLING
08555-08555	ROOSEVELT
08556-08556	ROSEMONT
08557-08557	SERGEANTSVILLE
08558-08558	SKILLMAN
08559-08559	STOCKTON
08560-08560	TITUSVILLE
08561-08561	WINDSOR
08562-08562	WRIGHTSTOWN
08570-08570	CRANBURY
08600-08695	TRENTON
08701-08701	LAKEWOOD
08720-08720	ALLENWOOD
08721-08721	BAYVILLE
08722-08722	BEACHWOOD
08723-08724	BRICK
08730-08730	BRIELLE
08731-08731	FORKED RIVER
08732-08732	ISLAND HEIGHTS
08733-08733	LAKEHURST
08734-08734	LANOKA HARBOR
08735-08735	LAVALLETTE
08736-08736	MANASQUAN
08738-08738	MANTOLOKING
08739-08739	NORMANDY BEACH
08740-08740	OCEAN GATE
08741-08741	PINE BEACH
08742-08742	POINT PLEASANT BEACH
08750-08750	SEA GIRT
08751-08751	SEASIDE HEIGHTS
08752-08752	SEASIDE PARK
08753-08757	TOMS RIVER
08758-08758	WARETOWN
08759-08759	WHITING
08801-08801	ANNANDALE
08802-08802	ASBURY
08803-08803	BAPTISTOWN
08804-08804	BLOOMSBURY
08805-08805	BOUND BROOK
08807-08807	BRIDGEWATER
08808-08808	BROADWAY
08809-08809	CLINTON
08810-08810	DAYTON
08812-08812	DUNELLEN
08816-08816	EAST BRUNSWICK
08817-08820	EDISON
08821-08821	FLAGTOWN
08822-08822	FLEMINGTON
08823-08823	FRANKLIN PARK
08824-08824	KENDALL PARK
08825-08825	FRENCHTOWN
08826-08826	GLEN GARDNER
08827-08827	HAMPTON
08828-08828	HELMETTA
08829-08829	HIGH BRIDGE
08830-08830	ISELIN
08831-08831	JAMESBURG
08831-08831	MONROE TOWNSHIP
08832-08832	KEASBEY
08833-08833	LEBANON
08834-08834	LITTLE YORK
08835-08835	MANVILLE
08836-08836	MARTINSVILLE
08837-08837	EDISON
08840-08840	METUCHEN
08844-08844	HILLSBOROUGH
08846-08846	MIDDLESEX
08848-08848	MILFORD
08850-08850	MILLTOWN
08852-08852	MONMOUTH JUNCTION
08853-08853	NESHANIC STATION
08854-08855	PISCATAWAY
08857-08857	OLD BRIDGE
08858-08858	OLDWICK
08859-08859	PARLIN
08861-08862	PERTH AMBOY
08863-08863	FORDS
08865-08865	PHILLIPSBURG
08867-08867	PITTSTOWN
08868-08868	QUAKERTOWN
08869-08869	RARITAN
08870-08870	READINGTON
08871-08872	SAYREVILLE
08873-08875	SOMERSET
08876-08876	SOMERVILLE
08877-08877	SOUTH RIVER
08878-08879	SOUTH AMBOY
08880-08880	SOUTH BOUND BROOK
08882-08882	SOUTH RIVER
08884-08884	SPOTSWOOD
08885-08885	STANTON
08886-08886	STEWARTSVILLE
08887-08887	THREE BRIDGES
08888-08888	WHITEHOUSE
08889-08889	WHITEHOUSE STATION
08890-08890	ZAREPHATH
08896-08896	RARITAN
08899-08899	EDISON
08901-08901	NEW BRUNSWICK
08902-08902	NORTH BRUNSWICK
08903-08903	NEW BRUNSWICK
08904-08904	HIGHLAND PARK
08905-08989	NEW BRUNSWICK

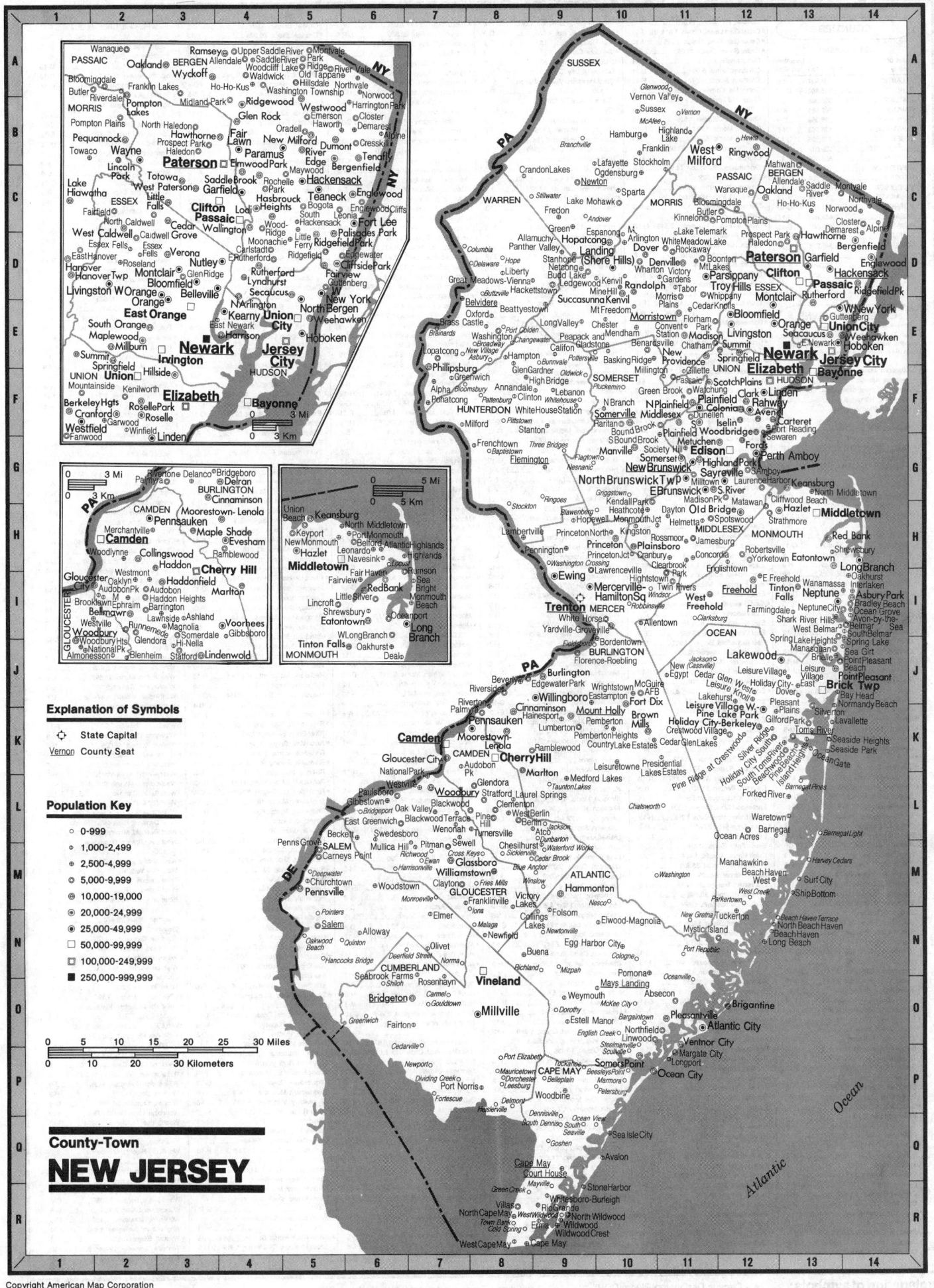

County-Town
NEW JERSEY

COUNTIES

(21 Counties)

Name of County	Population	Location on Map
ATLANTIC	224,327	M-9
BERGEN	825,380	C-12
BURLINGTON	395,066	J-9
CAMDEN	502,824	K-7
CAPE MAY	95,089	P-9
CUMBERLAND	138,053	N-6
ESSEX	778,206	D-12
GLOUCESTER	230,082	M-7
HUDSON	553,099	F-13
HUNTERDON	107,776	F-7
MERCER	325,824	H-9
MIDDLESEX	671,780	H-11
MONMOUTH	553,124	H-12
MORRIS	421,353	C-10
OCEAN	433,203	I-11
PASSAIC	453,060	B-11
SALEM	65,294	M-5
SOMERSET	240,279	F-10
SUSSEX	130,943	A-9
UNION	493,819	F-12
WARREN	91,607	C-8
TOTAL	7,730,188	

CITIES AND TOWNS

Note: The first name is that of the city or town, second, that of the county in which it is located, then the population and location on the map.

Aberdeen, Monmouth, 17,038 ..... G-12
Absecon, Atlantic, 7,298 ..... O-11
Alexandria, Hunterdon, 3,594 ..... F-8
Allamuchy, Warren, 3,484 ..... D-9
• Allamuchy-Panther Valley, Warren, 2,764 ..... D-9
Allendale, Bergen, 5,900 ..... C-13
Allentown, Monmouth, 1,828 ..... I-10
• Alloway, Salem, 1,371 ..... N-6
Alloway, Salem, 2,795 ..... N-6
Almonesson, Gloucester J-2
Alpha, Warren, 2,530 ..... F-7
Alpine, Bergen, 1,716 ..... C-14
Andover, Sussex, 5,438 ..... C-9
• Annandale, Hunterdon, 1,074 ..... F-9
Asbury Park, Monmouth, 16,799 ..... I-14
Ashland, Camden I-3
Atco, Camden L-9
Atlantic City, Atlantic, 37,986 ..... O-11
Atlantic Highlands, Monmouth, 4,629 ..... H-6
Audubon, Camden, 9,205 ..... I-2
Audubon Park, Camden, 1,150 ..... K-7
Avalon, Cape May, 1,809 ..... Q-10
• Avenel, Middlesex, 15,504 ..... F-12
Avon-by-the-Sea, Monmouth, 2,165 ..... I-14
Barnegat, Ocean, 12,235 ..... L-12
• Barnegat, Ocean, 1,160 ..... L-12
Barrington, Camden, 6,774 ..... I-2
Basking Ridge, Somerset E-10
Bass River, Burlington, 1,580 ..... M-11
Bay Head, Ocean, 1,226 ..... J-13
Bayonne, Hudson, 61,444 ..... F-13
Beach Haven, Ocean, 1,475 ..... N-12
• Beach Haven West, Ocean, 4,237 ..... M-12
Beachwood, Ocean, 9,324 ..... K-13
• Beattyestown, Warren, 3,966 ..... E-9
• Beckett, Gloucester, 3,815 ..... M-6
Bedminster, Somerset, 7,086 ..... F-10
Belford, Monmouth H-6
• *Belleville, Essex, 34,213* D-3
Bellmawr, Camden, 12,603 ..... I-2
Belmar, Monmouth, 5,877 ..... I-14
▲ *Belvidere, Warren, 2,669* E-7
Bergenfield, Bergen, 24,458 ..... D-14
Berkeley, Ocean, 37,319 ..... K-13
• *Berkeley Heights, Union, 11,980* F-1
Berlin, Camden, 5,466 ..... L-8
Berlin, Camden, 5,672 ..... L-8
Bernards, Somerset, 17,199 ..... F-10
Bernardsville, Somerset, 6,597 ..... E-10
Bethlehem, Hunterdon, 3,104 ..... F-8
Beverly, Burlington, 2,973 ..... J-8
• Blackwood, Camden, 5,120 ..... L-8
Blackwood Terrace, Gloucester L-7
Blairstown, Warren, 5,331 ..... C-8
Blenheim, Camden J-2
• *Bloomfield, Essex, 45,061* E-12
Bloomingdale, Passaic, 7,530 ..... C-12
Bogota, Bergen, 7,824 ..... C-5
Boonton, Morris, 3,566 ..... D-11
Boonton, Morris, 8,343 ..... D-11
Bordentown, Burlington, 4,341 ..... J-10
Bordentown, Burlington, 7,683 ..... J-10
Bound Brook, Somerset, 9,487 ..... F-11
Bradley Beach, Monmouth, 4,475 ..... I-14
Branchburg, Somerset, 10,888 ..... F-10
• Brass Castle, Warren, 1,419 ..... E-8
• *Brick, Ocean, 66,473* J-13
Bridgeboro, Burlington G-3
Bridgeton, Cumberland, 18,942 ..... O-7
Bridgewater, Somerset, 32,509 ..... F-10
Brielle, Monmouth, 4,406 ..... J-13
Brigantine, Atlantic, 11,354 ..... O-12
Brooklawn, Camden, 1,805 ..... I-2
• Brown Mills, Burlington, 11,429 ..... K-10
• Budd Lake, Morris, 7,272 ..... D-10
Buena, Atlantic, 4,441 ..... N-8
Buena Vista, Atlantic, 7,655 ..... N-9
Burlington, Burlington, 9,835 ..... J-9
▲ *Burlington, Burlington, 12,454* J-9
Butler, Morris, 7,392 ..... C-12
Byram, Sussex, 8,048 ..... D-9
• *Caldwell, Essex, 7,549* D-2
Califon, Hunterdon, 1,073 ..... E-9
Camden, Camden, 87,492 ..... K-7
Cape May, Cape May, 4,668 ..... R-8
• Cape May Court House, Cape May, 4,426 ..... Q-9
Carlstadt, Bergen, 5,510 ..... D-4
• Carneys Point, Salem, 7,686 ..... M-5
Carneys Point, Salem, 8,443 ..... M-5
Carteret, Middlesex, 19,025 ..... F-12
• Cedar Glen Lakes, Ocean, 1,611 ..... J-11
• Cedar Glen West, Ocean, 1,396 ..... J-12
• *Cedar Grove, Essex, 12,053* C-3
Cedar Knolls, Morris E-11
Chatham, Morris, 8,007 ..... E-11
Chatham, Morris, 9,361 ..... E-11
• Cherry Hill, Camden, 69,319 ..... K-8
• *Cherry Hill Township, Camden, 69,348* K-8
Chesilhurst, Camden, 1,526 ..... M-9
Chester, Morris, 1,214 ..... E-10
Chester, Morris, 5,958 ..... E-10
Chesterfield, Burlington, 5,152 ..... J-10
Churchtown, Salem M-5
• *Cinnaminson, Burlington, 14,583* K-8
• *Clark, Union, 14,629* F-12
Clayton, Gloucester, 6,155 ..... M-7
• Clearbrook Park, Middlesex, 2,853 ..... H-11
Clementon, Camden, 5,601 ..... L-8
Cliffside Park, Bergen, 20,393 ..... D-5
• Cliffwood Beach, Monmouth, 3,543 ..... G-12
Clifton, Passaic, 71,742 ..... D-13
Clinton, Hunterdon, 2,054 ..... F-8
Clinton, Hunterdon, 10,816 ..... E-9
Closter, Bergen, 8,094 ..... C-14
• Collings Lakes, Atlantic, 2,046 ..... N-9
Collingswood, Camden, 15,289 ..... H-2
• Colonia, Middlesex, 18,238 ..... F-12
Colts Neck, Monmouth, 8,559 ..... I-13
Commercial, Cumberland, 5,026 ..... P-8
• Concordia, Middlesex, 2,683 ..... H-11
Convent Station, Morris E-11
• Country Lake Estates, Burlington, 4,492 ..... K-10
▲ *Cranbury, Middlesex, 2,500* H-11
• Crandon Lakes, Sussex, 1,177 ..... C-8
• Cranford, Union, 22,624 ..... F-2
Cranford, Union, 22,633 ..... F-2
Cresskill, Bergen, 7,558 ..... B-6
• Crestwood Village, Ocean, 8,030 ..... J-11
• Dayton, Middlesex, 4,321 ..... H-11
Deal, Monmouth, 1,179 ..... J-6
Deerfield, Cumberland, 2,933 ..... O-7
• *Delanco, Burlington, 3,316* G-3
Delaware, Hunterdon, 4,512 ..... G-8
▲ *Delran, Burlington, 13,178* G-4
Demarest, Bergen, 4,800 ..... D-14
Dennis, Cape May, 5,574 ..... P-9
▲ *Denville, Morris, 13,812* D-11
Deptford, Gloucester, 24,137 ..... L-7
Dover, Morris, 15,115 ..... D-10
Dover, Ocean, 76,371 ..... K-12
Downe, Cumberland, 1,702 ..... P-7
Dumont, Bergen, 17,187 ..... B-5
Dunellen, Middlesex, 6,528 ..... F-11
Eagleswood, Ocean, 1,476 ..... M-12
East Amwell, Hunterdon, 4,332 ..... G-9
• *East Brunswick, Middlesex, 43,548* G-11
• East Freehold, Monmouth, 3,842 ..... I-12
▲ *East Greenwich, Gloucester, 5,258* L-7
• *East Hanover, Morris, 9,926* D-1
East Newark, Hudson, 2,157 ..... E-13
East Orange, Essex, 73,552 ..... E-3
East Rutherford, Bergen, 7,902 ..... D-4
East Windsor, Mercer, 22,353 ..... I-11
▲ *Eastampton, Burlington, 4,962* K-9
Eatontown, Monmouth, 13,800 ..... H-13
Edgewater, Bergen, 5,001 ..... D-5
• *Edgewater Park, Burlington, 8,388* J-8
• *Edison, Middlesex, 88,680* G-12
Egg Harbor, Atlantic, 24,544 ..... O-10
Egg Harbor City, Atlantic, 4,583 ..... N-10
Elizabeth, Union, 110,002 ..... F-12
Elk, Gloucester, 3,806 ..... M-7
Elmer, Salem, 1,571 ..... N-7
Elmwood Park, Bergen, 17,623 ..... C-4
Elsinboro, Salem, 1,170 ..... N-5
• Elwood-Magnolia, Atlantic, 1,487 ..... N-10
Emerson, Bergen, 6,930 ..... B-5
Englewood, Bergen, 24,850 ..... D-14
Englewood Cliffs, Bergen, 5,634 ..... C-6
Englishtown, Monmouth, 1,268 ..... H-12
• Erma, Cape May, 2,045 ..... R-9
Espanong, Morris D-10
▲ *Essex Fells, Essex, 2,139* D-2
Estell Manor, Atlantic, 1,404 ..... O-9
Evesham, Burlington, 35,309 ..... L-9
• *Ewing, Mercer, 34,185* I-9
Fair Haven, Monmouth, 5,270 ..... I-6
Fair Lawn, Bergen, 30,548 ..... B-4
Fairfield, Cumberland, 5,699 ..... O-6
• *Fairfield, Essex, 7,615* C-2
• Fairton, Cumberland, 1,359 ..... O-7
Fairview, Bergen, 10,733 ..... D-5
• Fairview, Monmouth, 3,853 ..... I-6
Fanwood, Union, 7,115 ..... G-1
Farmingdale, Monmouth, 1,462 ..... I-13
Flemington, Hunterdon, 4,047 ..... G-9
Florence, Burlington, 10,266 ..... J-9
• Florence-Roebling, Burlington, 8,564 ..... J-9
Florham Park, Morris, 8,521 ..... E-11
Folsom, Atlantic, 2,181 ..... N-9
• Fords, Middlesex, 14,392 ..... G-12
• Forked River, Ocean, 4,243 ..... L-13
• Fort Dix, Burlington, 10,205 ..... J-10
Fort Lee, Bergen, 31,997 ..... C-6
Frankford, Sussex, 5,114 ..... B-10
Franklin, Gloucester, 14,482 ..... N-8
Franklin, Hunterdon, 2,851 ..... F-8
Franklin, Somerset, 42,780 ..... G-10
Franklin, Sussex, 4,977 ..... B-10
Franklin, Warren, 2,404 ..... E-7
Franklin Lakes, Bergen, 9,873 ..... A-3
Franklinville, Gloucester M-7
Fredon, Sussex, 2,763 ..... C-9
Freehold, Monmouth, 10,742 ..... I-12
Freehold, Monmouth, 24,710 ..... I-12
Frelinghuysen, Warren, 1,779 ..... D-9
Frenchtown, Hunterdon, 1,528 ..... G-8
Galloway, Atlantic, 23,330 ..... N-11
Garfield, Bergen, 26,727 ..... D-13
Garwood, Union, 4,227 ..... F-2
Gibbsboro, Camden, 2,383 ..... I-4
• Gibbstown, Gloucester, 3,902 ..... L-6
• Gilford Park, Ocean, 8,668 ..... K-13
Gillette, Morris F-11
Glassboro, Gloucester, 15,614 ..... M-7
Glen Gardner, Hunterdon, 1,665 ..... E-8
• *Glen Ridge, Essex, 7,076* D-3
Glen Rock, Bergen, 10,883 ..... B-4
• Glendora, Camden, 5,201 ..... L-8
Gloucester, Camden, 53,797 ..... L-8
Gloucester City, Camden, 12,649 ..... K-7
• Great Meadows-Vienna, Warren, 1,108 ..... D-8
Green, Sussex, 2,709 ..... C-9
Green Brook, Somerset, 4,460 ..... F-11
Greenwich, Gloucester, 5,102 ..... L-6
▲ *Greenwich, Warren, 1,899* F-7
Guttenberg, Hudson, 8,268 ..... E-13
Hackensack, Bergen, 37,049 ..... C-5
Hackettstown, Warren, 8,120 ..... D-9
▲ *Haddon, Camden, 14,837* I-2
Haddon Heights, Camden, 7,860 ..... I-2
Haddonfield, Camden, 11,628 ..... I-3
▲ *Hainesport, Burlington, 3,249* K-9
Haledon, Passaic, 6,951 ..... B-3
Hamburg, Sussex, 2,566 ..... B-10
Hamilton, Atlantic, 16,012 ..... N-9
Hamilton, Mercer, 86,553 ..... I-9
Hammonton, Atlantic, 12,208 ..... M-9
Hampton, Hunterdon, 1,515 ..... E-8
Hampton, Sussex, 4,438 ..... C-9
• *Hanover, Morris, 11,538* D-1
Harding, Morris, 3,640 ..... E-11
Hardwick, Warren, 1,235 ..... C-8
Hardyston, Sussex, 5,275 ..... B-10
Harmony, Warren, 2,653 ..... E-7
Harrington Park, Bergen, 4,623 ..... B-6
Harrison, Gloucester, 4,715 ..... M-7
Harrison, Hudson, 13,425 ..... E-4
Hasbrouck Heights, Bergen, 11,488 ..... C-5
Haworth, Bergen, 3,384 ..... B-5
Hawthorne, Passaic, 17,084 ..... D-13
Hazlet, Monmouth, 21,976 ..... H-13
• Heathcote, Middlesex, 3,112 ..... H-10
Helmetta, Middlesex, 1,211 ..... H-11
High Bridge, Hunterdon, 3,886 ..... F-8
• Highland Lake, Sussex, 4,550 ..... B-11
Highland Park, Middlesex, 13,279 ..... G-11
Highlands, Monmouth, 4,849 ..... H-6
Hightstown, Mercer, 5,126 ..... I-11
Hillsborough, Somerset, 28,808 ..... G-10
Hillsdale, Bergen, 9,750 ..... A-5
• *Hillside, Union, 21,044* F-3
Hi-Nella, Camden, 1,045 ..... J-3
Ho-Ho-Kus, Bergen, 3,935 ..... C-13
Hoboken, Hudson, 33,397 ..... E-13
• Holiday City-Berkeley, Ocean, 14,293 ..... K-12
• Holiday City-Dover, Ocean, 2,391 ..... J-13
• Holiday City South, Ocean, 5,452 ..... K-12
Holland, Hunterdon, 4,892 ..... F-7
Holmdel, Monmouth, 11,532 ..... H-13
Hopatcong, Sussex, 15,586 ..... D-10
Hope, Warren, 1,719 ..... D-8
Hopewell, Cumberland, 4,215 ..... O-7
Hopewell, Mercer, 1,968 ..... H-9
Hopewell, Mercer, 11,590 ..... H-9
Howell, Monmouth, 38,987 ..... I-13
Independence, Warren, 3,940 ..... E-8
• Irvington, Essex, 59,774 ..... E-3
Irvington, Essex, 61,018 ..... E-3
• Iselin, Middlesex, 16,141 ..... F-12
Island Heights, Ocean, 1,470 ..... K-13
Jackson, Ocean, 33,233 ..... J-11
Jamesburg, Middlesex, 5,294 ..... H-11
Jefferson, Morris, 17,825 ..... C-10
Jersey City, Hudson, 228,537 ..... E-13
Keansburg, Monmouth, 11,069 ..... G-13
Kearny, Hudson, 34,874 ..... E-4
• Kendall Park, Middlesex, 7,127 ..... G-10
Kenilworth, Union, 7,574 ..... F-2
Kenvil, Morris D-10
Keyport, Monmouth, 7,586 ..... H-5
• Kingston, Middlesex, 1,047 ..... H-10
Kingwood, Hunterdon, 3,325 ..... G-8
Kinnelon, Morris, 8,470 ..... C-11
Knowlton, Warren, 2,543 ..... D-8
Lacey, Ocean, 22,141 ..... L-12
Lafayette, Sussex, 1,902 ..... C-10
Lake Hiawatha, Morris C-1
• Lake Mohawk, Sussex, 8,930 ..... C-10
• Lake Telemark, Morris, 1,121 ..... D-11
Lakehurst, Ocean, 3,078 ..... J-12
• Lakewood, Ocean, 26,095 ..... J-13
Lakewood, Ocean, 45,048 ..... J-13
Lambertville, Hunterdon, 3,927 ..... H-8
Landing (Shore Hills), Morris D-10
Laurel Springs, Camden, 2,341 ..... L-8
• Laurence Harbor, Middlesex, 6,361 ..... G-12
Lavallette, Ocean, 2,299 ..... K-13
Lawnside, Camden, 2,841 ..... I-3
Lawrence, Cumberland, 2,433 ..... O-7
Lawrence, Mercer, 25,787 ..... H-9
• Lawrenceville, Mercer, 6,446 ..... H-9
Lebanon, Hunterdon, 1,036 ..... F-9
Lebanon, Hunterdon, 5,679 ..... E-8
Ledgewood, Morris D-10
• Leisure Knoll, Ocean, 2,707 ..... J-12
• Leisure Village, Ocean, 4,295 ..... J-13
• Leisure Village East, Ocean, 1,989 ..... J-13
• Leisure Village West-Pine Lake Park, Ocean, 10,139 ..... K-12
• Leisuretowne, Burlington, 2,552 ..... K-9
• Leonardo, Monmouth, 3,788 ..... H-6
Leonia, Bergen, 8,365 ..... C-5
▲ *Liberty, Warren, 2,493* D-8
Lincoln Park, Morris, 10,978 ..... B-2
• Lincroft, Monmouth, 6,193 ..... I-5
Linden, Union, 36,701 ..... F-12
Lindenwold, Camden, 18,734 ..... J-3
Linwood, Atlantic, 6,866 ..... O-10
Little Egg Harbor, Ocean, 13,333 ..... M-12
• *Little Falls, Passaic, 11,294* C-3
• Little Ferry, Bergen, 9,989 ..... D-5
Little Silver, Monmouth, 5,721 ..... I-6
• *Livingston, Essex, 26,609* E-12
Lodi, Bergen, 22,355 ..... C-4
Logan, Gloucester, 5,147 ..... L-6
Long Beach, Ocean, 3,407 ..... N-12
Long Branch, Monmouth, 28,658 ..... H-14
▲ *Long Hill, Morris, 7,826* F-11
• Long Valley, Morris, 1,744 ..... E-9
Longport, Atlantic, 1,224 ..... P-11
▲ *Lopatcong, Warren, 5,052* F-7
Lower, Cape May, 20,820 ..... R-9
Lower Alloways Creek, Salem, 1,858 ..... N-5
▲ *Lumberton, Burlington, 6,705* K-9
• *Lyndhurst, Bergen, 18,262* D-4
Madison, Morris, 15,850 ..... E-11
• Madison Park, Middlesex, 7,490 ..... G-12
Magnolia, Camden, 4,861 ..... I-3
Mahwah, Bergen C-13
Mahwah, Bergen, 17,905 ..... C-13
• Manahawkin, Ocean, 1,594 ..... M-12
Manalapan, Monmouth, 26,716 ..... I-12
Manasquan, Monmouth, 5,369 ..... J-13
Manchester, Ocean, 35,976 ..... K-11
Mannington, Salem, 1,693 ..... M-6
Mansfield, Burlington, 3,874 ..... J-10
Mansfield, Warren, 7,154 ..... E-8
Mantua, Gloucester, 10,074 ..... M-7
Manville, Somerset, 10,567 ..... G-10
• *Maple Shade, Burlington, 19,211* H-3
Maplewood, Essex, 21,652 ..... E-2
• Maplewood, Essex, 21,756 ..... E-2
Margate City, Atlantic, 8,431 ..... P-11
Marlboro, Monmouth, 27,974 ..... H-12
• Marlton, Burlington, 10,228 ..... I-4
Matawan, Monmouth, 9,270 ..... H-12
Maurice River, Cumberland, 6,648 ..... O-8
• Mays Landing, Atlantic, 2,090 ..... O-10
Maywood, Bergen, 9,473 ..... C-5
• McGuire AFB, Burlington, 7,580 ..... J-10
Medford, Burlington, 20,526 ..... L-9
Medford Lakes, Burlington, 4,462 ..... L-9
Mendham, Morris, 4,537 ..... E-10
Mendham, Morris, 4,890 ..... E-10
• Mercerville-Hamilton Square, Mercer, 26,873 ..... I-9
Merchantville, Camden, 4,095 ..... H-2
Metuchen, Middlesex, 12,804 ..... G-12
Middle, Cape May, 14,771 ..... Q-9
Middlesex, Middlesex, 13,055 ..... F-11
Middletown, Monmouth, 68,183 ..... H-13
Midland Park, Bergen, 7,047 ..... B-4
Milford, Hunterdon, 1,273 ..... F-7
• *Millburn, Essex, 18,630* E-2
Millington, Morris F-11
Millstone, Monmouth, 5,069 ..... I-11
Milltown, Middlesex, 6,968 ..... G-11
Millville, Cumberland, 25,992 ..... O-8
▲ *Mine Hill, Morris, 3,333* D-10
Monmouth Beach, Monmouth, 3,303 ..... I-7
• Monmouth Junction, Middlesex, 1,570 ..... H-10
Monroe, Gloucester, 26,703 ..... M-8
Monroe, Middlesex, 22,255 ..... H-11
Montague, Sussex, 2,832 ..... A-9
• *Montclair, Essex, 37,729* E-12
Montgomery, Somerset, 9,612 ..... G-10
Montvale, Bergen, 6,946 ..... C-14
Montville, Morris, 15,600 ..... D-12
Moonachie, Bergen, 2,817 ..... D-5
Moorestown, Burlington, 16,116 ..... K-8
• Moorestown-Lenola, Burlington, 13,242 ..... K-8
Morris, Morris, 19,952 ..... E-11
Morris Plains, Morris, 5,219 ..... E-11
▲ *Morristown, Morris, 16,189* E-11
Mount Arlington, Morris, 3,630 ..... D-10
Mount Ephraim, Camden, 4,517 ..... I-2
Mount Freedom, Morris E-10
• *Mount Holly, Burlington, 10,639* K-9
Mount Laurel, Burlington, 30,270 ..... K-8
Mount Olive, Morris, 21,282 ..... D-9
Mountain Lakes, Morris, 3,847 ..... D-11
Mountainside, Union, 6,657 ..... F-1
Mullica, Atlantic, 5,896 ..... M-10
• Mullica Hill, Gloucester, 1,117 ..... M-7
• Mystic Island, Ocean, 7,400 ..... N-12
National Park, Gloucester, 3,413 ..... L-7
Navesink, Monmouth H-6
Neptune, Monmouth, 28,148 ..... I-13
Neptune City, Monmouth, 4,997 ..... I-14
Netcong, Morris, 3,311 ..... D-9
New Brunswick, Middlesex, 41,711 ..... G-11
• New Egypt, Ocean, 2,327 ..... J-11
New Hanover, Burlington, 9,546 ..... J-10
New Milford, Bergen, 15,990 ..... B-5
New Monmouth, Monmouth H-5
New Providence, Union, 11,439 ..... E-11
Newark, Essex, 275,221 ..... E-13
Newfield, Gloucester, 1,592 ..... N-8
Newton, Sussex, 7,521 ..... C-9
Normandy Beach, Ocean J-13
North Arlington, Bergen, 13,790 ..... D-4
• North Beach Haven, Ocean, 2,413 ..... N-12
• *North Bergen, Hudson, 48,414* D-5
North Branch, Somerset F-10
• *North Brunswick, Middlesex, 31,287* G-11
• *North Caldwell, Essex, 6,706* C-2
• North Cape May, Cape May, 3,574 ..... R-8
North Haledon, Passaic, 7,987 ..... B-3
North Hanover, Burlington, 9,994 ..... J-10
• North Middletown, Monmouth, 3,160 ..... G-13
North Plainfield, Somerset, 18,820 ..... F-11
North Wildwood, Cape May, 5,017 ..... R-9
Northfield, Atlantic, 7,305 ..... O-11
Northvale, Bergen, 4,563 ..... C-14
Norwood, Bergen, 4,858 ..... C-14
• *Nutley, Essex, 27,099* D-4
• Oak Valley, Gloucester, 4,055 ..... L-7
• Oakhurst, Monmouth, 4,130 ..... J-6
Oakland, Bergen, 11,997 ..... C-12
Oaklyn, Camden, 4,430 ..... I-2
Ocean, Monmouth, 25,058 ..... I-13
Ocean, Ocean, 5,416 ..... L-12
• Ocean Acres, Ocean, 5,587 ..... L-12
Ocean City, Cape May, 15,512 ..... P-10
Ocean Gate, Ocean, 2,078 ..... K-13
• Ocean Grove, Monmouth, 4,818 ..... I-14
Oceanport, Monmouth, 6,146 ..... I-6
Ogdensburg, Sussex, 2,722 ..... C-10
• Old Bridge, Middlesex, 22,151 ..... H-12
Old Bridge, Middlesex, 56,475 ..... H-12
Old Tappan, Bergen, 4,254 ..... A-5
Oldmans, Salem, 1,683 ..... L-5
• Olivet, Salem, 1,315 ..... N-7
Oradell, Bergen, 8,024 ..... B-5
• *Orange, Essex, 29,925* E-12
• Oxford, Warren, 1,767 ..... E-8
Oxford, Warren, 1,790 ..... E-8
Palisades Park, Bergen, 14,536 ..... D-5
Palmyra, Burlington, 7,056 ..... K-8
Paramus, Bergen, 25,067 ..... B-4
Park Ridge, Bergen, 8,102 ..... A-5
• *Parsippany-Troy Hills Township, Morris, 48,478* D-11
Passaic, Passaic, 58,041 ..... D-13
Paterson, Passaic, 140,891 ..... D-13
Paulsboro, Gloucester, 6,577 ..... L-6
Peapack and Gladstone, Somerset, 2,111 ..... E-10
Pemberton, Burlington, 1,367 ..... K-10
Pemberton, Burlington, 31,342 ..... K-10
• Pemberton Heights, Burlington, 2,941 ..... K-10
Pennington, Mercer, 2,537 ..... H-9
Penns Grove, Salem, 5,228 ..... M-5
• Pennsauken, Camden, 34,733 ..... K-8
Pennsauken, Camden, 34,738 ..... K-8
• Pennsville, Salem, 12,218 ..... M-5
Pennsville, Salem, 13,794 ..... M-5
• *Pequannock Township, Morris, 12,844* D-2
Perth Amboy, Middlesex, 41,967 ..... G-12
Phillipsburg, Warren, 15,757 ..... E-7
Pilesgrove, Salem, 3,250 ..... M-6
Pine Beach, Ocean, 1,954 ..... K-13
Pine Hill, Camden, 9,854 ..... L-8
• Pine Ridge at Crestwood, Ocean, 2,372 ..... K-12
Piscataway, Middlesex, 47,089 ..... F-11
Pitman, Gloucester, 9,365 ..... M-7
Pittsgrove, Salem, 8,121 ..... N-7
Plainfield, Union, 46,567 ..... F-11
▲ *Plainsboro, Middlesex, 14,213* H-10
• Pleasant Plains, Ocean, 2,577 ..... K-12
Pleasantville, Atlantic, 16,027 ..... O-11
Plumsted, Ocean, 6,005 ..... J-11
▲ *Pohatcong, Warren, 3,591* F-7
Point Pleasant, Ocean, 18,177 ..... J-13
Point Pleasant Beach, Ocean, 5,112 ..... J-13
• Pomona, Atlantic, 2,624 ..... N-10
Pompton Lakes, Passaic, 10,539 ..... A-2
Pompton Plains, Morris B-2
• Port Monmouth, Monmouth, 3,558 ..... H-6
• Port Norris, Cumberland, 1,701 ..... P-8
• Port Reading, Middlesex, 3,977 ..... F-12
• Presidential Lakes Estates, Burlington, 2,450 ..... K-11
Princeton, Mercer, 12,016 ..... H-10
Princeton, Mercer, 13,198 ..... H-10
• Princeton Junction, Mercer, 2,362 ..... H-10
• Princeton North, Mercer, 4,386 ..... H-10
Prospect Park, Passaic, 5,053 ..... D-13
Quinton, Salem, 2,511 ..... N-6
Rahway, Union, 25,325 ..... F-12
• Ramblewood, Burlington, 6,181 ..... K-9
Ramsey, Bergen, 13,228 ..... A-4
Randolph, Morris, 19,974 ..... E-10
Raritan, Hunterdon, 15,616 ..... G-9
Raritan, Somerset, 5,798 ..... F-10
Readington, Hunterdon, 13,400 ..... F-9
Red Bank, Monmouth, 10,636 ..... H-13
Ridgefield, Bergen, 9,996 ..... D-5
Ridgefield Park, Bergen, 12,454 ..... D-14
Ridgewood, Bergen, 24,152 ..... B-4
Ringwood, Passaic, 12,623 ..... B-12
• Rio Grande, Cape May, 2,505 ..... R-9
River Edge, Bergen, 10,603 ..... B-5
• *River Vale, Bergen, 9,410* A-5
Riverdale, Morris, 2,370 ..... A-2
• *Riverside, Burlington, 7,974* J-8
Riverton, Burlington, 2,775 ..... K-8
• Robertsville, Monmouth, 9,841 ..... H-12
• *Rochelle Park, Bergen, 5,587* C-4
Rockaway, Morris, 19,572 ..... D-11
Rockaway, Morris, 6,243 ..... D-11
Roseland, Essex, 4,847 ..... D-2
Roselle, Union, 20,314 ..... F-2
Roselle Park, Union, 12,805 ..... F-2
• Rosenhayn, Cumberland, 1,053 ..... N-7
• Rossmoor, Middlesex, 3,231 ..... H-11
Roxbury, Morris, 20,429 ..... D-10
Rumson, Monmouth, 6,701 ..... I-6
Runnemede, Camden, 9,042 ..... I-2
Rutherford, Bergen, 17,790 ..... E-13
• *Saddle Brook, Bergen, 13,296* C-4
Saddle River, Bergen, 2,950 ..... A-4
Salem, Salem, 6,883 ..... N-5
Sandyston, Sussex, 1,732 ..... A-9
Sayreville, Middlesex, 34,986 ..... G-12
• *Scotch Plains, Union, 21,160* F-11
Sea Bright, Monmouth, 1,693 ..... I-7
Sea Girt, Monmouth, 2,099 ..... J-14
Sea Isle City, Cape May, 2,692 ..... Q-10
• Seabrook Farms, Cumberland, 1,457 ..... N-7
Seaside Heights, Ocean, 2,366 ..... K-13
Seaside Park, Ocean, 1,871 ..... K-13
Secaucus, Hudson, 14,061 ..... D-5
• Sewaren, Middlesex, 2,569 ..... F-12
Sewell, Gloucester L-7
Shamong, Burlington, 5,765 ..... L-9
• Shark River Hills, Monmouth, 4,228 ..... I-13
Ship Bottom, Ocean, 1,352 ..... M-13
Shrewsbury, Monmouth, 1,098 ..... I-6
Shrewsbury, Monmouth, 3,096 ..... I-6
• Silver Ridge, Ocean, 1,138 ..... K-12
• Silverton, Ocean, 9,175 ..... J-13
• Society Hill, Middlesex, 3,577 ..... G-11
Somerdale, Camden, 5,440 ..... J-3
Somers Point, Atlantic, 11,216 ..... P-10
• Somerset, Somerset, 22,070 ..... G-11
Somerville, Somerset, 11,632 ..... F-10
South Amboy, Middlesex, 7,863 ..... G-12
South Belmar, Monmouth, 1,482 ..... I-14
South Bound Brook, Somerset, 4,185 ..... G-11
South Brunswick, Middlesex, 25,792 ..... H-11
▲ *South Hackensack, Bergen, 2,106* C-5
South Harrison, Gloucester, 1,919 ..... M-6
• *South Orange, Essex, 16,390* E-2
South Plainfield, Middlesex, 20,489 ..... F-11
South River, Middlesex, 13,692 ..... G-11
South Toms River, Ocean, 3,869 ..... K-13
Southampton, Burlington, 10,202 ..... K-10
Sparta, Sussex C-10
Sparta, Sussex, 15,157 ..... C-10
Spotswood, Middlesex, 7,983 ..... H-11
Spring Lake, Monmouth, 3,499 ..... I-14
Spring Lake Heights, Monmouth, 5,341 ..... I-13
Springfield, Burlington, 3,028 ..... J-10
• *Springfield, Union, 13,420* E-12
Stafford, Ocean, 13,325 ..... M-12
Stanhope, Sussex, 3,393 ..... D-9
Stanton, Hunterdon F-9
Stillwater, Sussex, 4,253 ..... C-9
Stockholm, Sussex C-11
Stone Harbor, Cape May, 1,025 ..... R-9
Stow Creek, Cumberland, 1,437 ..... N-6
Stratford, Camden, 7,614 ..... L-8
• Strathmore, Monmouth, 7,060 ..... H-12
• Succasunna-Kenvil, Morris, 11,781 ..... D-10
Summit, Union, 19,757 ..... E-12
Surf City, Ocean, 1,375 ..... M-13
Sussex, Sussex, 2,201 ..... R-10
Swedesboro, Gloucester, 2,024 ..... L-6
Tabernacle, Burlington, 7,360 ..... L-10
Tabor (Mount Tabor), Morris D-11
• *Teaneck, Bergen, 37,825* C-5
Tenafly, Bergen, 13,326 ..... B-6
Tewksbury, Hunterdon, 4,803 ..... E-9
Tinton Falls, Monmouth, 12,361 ..... I-13
• Toms River, Ocean, 7,524 ..... K-13
Totowa, Passaic, 10,177 ..... C-3
Towaco, Morris B-1
Trenton, Mercer, 88,675 ..... I-9
Tuckerton, Ocean, 3,048 ..... N-12
• Turnersville, Gloucester, 3,843 ..... L-8
• Twin Rivers, Mercer, 7,715 ..... I-11
Union, Hunterdon, 5,078 ..... F-8
• *Union, Union, 50,024* F-2
Union Beach, Monmouth, 6,156 ..... H-5
Union City, Hudson, 58,012 ..... E-5
Upper, Cape May, 10,681 ..... P-10
Upper Deerfield, Cumberland, 6,927 ..... N-7
Upper Freehold, Monmouth, 3,277 ..... I-11
Upper Pittsgrove, Salem, 3,140 ..... M-7
Upper Saddle River, Bergen, 7,198 ..... A-4
Ventnor City, Atlantic, 11,005 ..... O-11
Vernon, Sussex, 21,211 ..... B-11
• Vernon Valley, Sussex, 1,696 ..... B-11
• *Verona, Essex, 13,597* D-3
Victory Gardens, Morris, 1,314 ..... D-11
• Victory Lakes, Gloucester, 2,160 ..... N-8
• Villas, Cape May, 8,136 ..... R-8
Vineland, Cumberland, 54,780 ..... N-8
▲ *Voorhees, Camden, 24,559* I-3
Waldwick, Bergen, 9,757 ..... A-4
Wall, Monmouth, 20,244 ..... I-13
Wallington, Bergen, 10,828 ..... C-4
• Wanamassa, Monmouth, 4,530 ..... I-14
Wanaque, Passaic, 9,711 ..... C-12
Wantage, Sussex, 9,487 ..... A-10
• Waretown, Ocean, 1,283 ..... L-13
Warren, Somerset, 10,830 ..... F-11
Washington, Gloucester, 41,960 ..... L-7
Washington, Mercer, 5,815 ..... I-10
Washington, Morris, 15,592 ..... E-9
Washington, Warren, 5,367 ..... E-8
Washington, Warren, 6,474 ..... E-8
• *Washington Township, Bergen, 9,245* A-4
Watchung, Somerset, 5,110 ..... F-11
Waterford, Camden, 10,940 ..... M-9
• *Wayne, Passaic, 47,025* B-2
• *Weehawken, Hudson, 12,385* E-14
Wenonah, Gloucester, 2,331 ..... L-7
West Amwell, Hunterdon, 2,251 ..... H-8
West Belmar, Monmouth, 2,498 ..... I-13
West Berlin, Camden L-8
• *West Caldwell, Essex, 10,422* D-2
West Cape May, Cape May, 1,026 ..... R-8
West Deptford, Gloucester, 19,380 ..... L-7
• West Freehold, Monmouth, 11,166 ..... I-11
West Long Branch, Monmouth, 7,690 ..... I-6
• *West Milford, Passaic, 25,430* B-12
West New York, Hudson, 38,125 ..... E-13
• *West Orange, Essex, 39,103* D-3
West Paterson, Passaic, 10,982 ..... C-3
West Windsor, Mercer, 16,021 ..... I-10
Westampton, Burlington, 6,004 ..... J-9
Westfield, Union, 28,870 ..... F-1
Westmont, Camden I-2
Westville, Gloucester, 4,573 ..... L-7
Westwood, Bergen, 10,446 ..... B-5
▲ *Weymouth, Atlantic, 1,957* O-9
Wharton, Morris, 5,405 ..... D-10
Whippany, Morris D-11
White, Warren, 3,603 ..... E-7
• White Horse, Mercer, 9,397 ..... I-10
• White House Station, Hunterdon, 1,287 ..... F-9
• White Meadow Lake, Morris, 8,002 ..... D-11
• Whitesboro-Burleigh, Cape May, 2,080 ..... R-9
Wildwood, Cape May, 4,484 ..... R-9
Wildwood Crest, Cape May, 3,631 ..... R-9
• Williamstown, Gloucester, 10,891 ..... M-8
• *Willingboro, Burlington, 36,291* J-9
▲ *Winfield, Union, 1,576* F-2
Winslow, Camden, 30,087 ..... M-9
Woodbine, Cape May, 2,678 ..... P-9
• Woodbridge, Middlesex, 17,434 ..... F-12
Woodbridge, Middlesex, 93,086 ..... F-12
Woodbury, Gloucester, 10,904 ..... L-7
Woodbury Heights, Gloucester, 3,392 ..... J-1
Woodcliff Lake, Bergen, 5,303 ..... A-5
Woodland, Burlington, 2,063 ..... L-11
Woodlynne, Camden, 2,547 ..... H-2
Wood-Ridge, Bergen, 7,506 ..... C-4
Woodstown, Salem, 3,154 ..... M-6
Woolwich, Gloucester, 1,459 ..... M-6
Wrightstown, Burlington, 3,843 ..... J-10
• *Wyckoff, Bergen, 15,372* A-3
• Yardville-Groveville, Mercer, 9,248 ..... I-10
• Yorketown, Monmouth, 6,313 ..... M-12

Explanation of symbols:

● – Census Designated Place (CDP)
▲ *italics* – Townships (shown on the map)
● *italics* – Township shown which is also a CDP
italics – Townships (not shown on the map)

New Mexico

General Help Numbers:

Governor's Office
State Capitol, Room 400   505-476-2200
Santa Fe, NM 87503   Fax 505-676-2226
www.governor.state.nm.us   8AM-5PM

Attorney General's Office
PO Drawer 1508   505-827-6000
Santa Fe, NM 87504-1508   Fax 505-827-5826
www.ago.state.nm.us   8AM-5PM

Legislative Records
Legislative Council Service
State Capitol Bldg, Room 411   505-986-4600
Santa Fe, NM 87501   Fax 505-986-4610
http://legis.state.nm.us   8AM-5PM

State Archives
1205 Camino Carlos Rey   505-476-7902
Santa Fe, NM 87505   Fax 505-476-79017909
www.nmcpr.state.nm.us/   8AM-5PM

State Specifics:

Capital:	Santa Fe
	Santa Fe County
Time Zone:	MST
Number of Counties:	33
Population:	1,903,289
Web Site:	www.state.nm.us

State Agencies

Criminal Records

Department of Public Safety, Criminal Records Bureau, PO Box 1628, Santa Fe, NM 87504-1628 (Courier address: 4491 Cerrillos Rd, Santa Fe, NM 87504); 505-827-9181, 505-827-3388-Fax; 8AM-5PM.

www.dps.nm.org

Records are available from 1935 on. It takes 2 to 4 weeks before new records are available for inquiry. Records are indexed on inhouse computer (93%); historical paper records are added to computer once requested. Records are normally destroyed after 99 years. 33% of all arrests in database have final dispositions recorded, 35% for those arrests within last 5 years.

Searching: Fingerprint search requests are not available except for checks for children or elderly-related occupations mandated by state statute, and an FBI search can be done for those groups. The state's records are 100% fingerprint-supported. Include the following in your request-date of birth, Social Security Number, full name, signed release. The signed release from person of record authorizing the State of New Mexico to release records to specific requester must be notarized. A copy of the request form is found at www.dps.nm.org/faq/auth_release_info.pdf. All records are released, including those without dispositions.

Access by: mail, in person, online.

Fee & Payment: The fee is $7.00 per individual. Fee payee: Department of Public Safety. Prepayment required. Must use cashiers check or money order. No credit cards accepted.

Mail search: Turnaround time: 1 to 2 weeks. Turnaround time is for "no record found." If records exist, turnaround time may be 3 to 4 weeks. A SASE is requested.

In person search: If records are found, they may be available in 5 to 7 working days.

Online search: Online access is available from www.osogrande.com/online-services.html, a state-supported agency. The fee is $10.00. You must set up an account to receive a password. When a record is found, a signed release from the subject must then be presented (faxed) to DPS in order to receive the detail page. For more information visit the website mentioned or call 505-345-6555.

Statewide Court Records

Administrative Office of the Courts, 237 Don Gaspar, Rm 25, Santa Fe, NM 87501; 505-827-4800, 505-827-4824-Fax; 8AM-5PM.

www.nmcourts.com

Records are available since 1997, in general. It takes 48 hours before new records are available for inquiry.

Access by: online.

Online search: The www.nmcourts.com website offers free access to District and Magistrate Court case information, except Bernalillo Metro which has its own system. In general, records are available from June 1997 forward. Search by name or case #. The search is inclusive of all participating counties. The website also offers a DWI Offender History tool for researching an individual's DWI history. Search by name or SSN. Supreme Court opinions may be researched at www.supremecourt.nm.org/.

Sexual Offender Registry

Department of Public Safety, Records Bureau, PO Box 1628, Santa Fe, NM 87504-1628 (Courier address: 4491 Cerrillos Rd, Santa Fe, NM 87504); 505-827-9297, 505-827-9193, 505-827-3399-Fax; 8AM-5PM.

www.nmsexoffender.dps.state.nm.us

Records are available from 07/95. It takes 2 to 4 weeks before new records are available for inquiry. Records are normally destroyed after individual moves out of state.

Searching: The work address belonging to a sex offender is released if he/she will come into direct contact with children. The following data is not released: SSN

Access by: mail, phone, online.

Fee & Payment: There is no fee.

Mail search: Turnaround time: 1 to 2 weeks. A SASE is requested.

Phone search: Name searching available by phone.

Online search: The website offers a variety of search methods including by name, county, city, and ZIP Code. The site also offers a complete state list, also an absconder list.

Incarceration Records

New Mexico Corrections Department, Central Records Unit, PO Box 27116, Santa Fe, NM 87502; 505-827-8674, 505-827-8801-Fax; 8AM-5PM.

http://corrections.state.nm.us

Records are available on current and former inmates. It takes 1-3 days before new records are available for inquiry. Records are normally destroyed after 50 years.

Searching: Include the following in your request-name; DOB and SSN are helpful. Location, conviction and sentencing information, behavior, release dates are provided.

Access by: mail, phone, online.

Fee & Payment: Fee is $.50 per copy. Fee payee: NM Department of Corrections Prepayment required. Personal checks accepted, credit cards are not.

Mail search: Turnaround time: 7 to 10 days.

Phone search: Limited name searching available.

Online search: To search at the website, you must first click on Offender Information, then on Offender Search.

Corporation, Limited Liability Company Records

New Mexico Public Regulation Commission, Corporations Bureau, PO Box 1269, Santa Fe, NM 87504-1269 (Courier address: 1120 Paseo de Peralta, Pera Bldg 4th Fl, Rm 413, Santa Fe, NM 87501); 505-827-4502 (Main Number), 800-947-4722 (In-state Only), 505-827-4510 (Good Standing), 505-827-4513 (Copy Request), 505-827-4387-Fax; 8AM-12:00: 1PM-5PM.

www.nmprc.state.nm.us/corporations/corpshome.htm

For Charter Requirement Information call 505-827-4511.

Records are available for all entities. It takes 1-2 days before new records are available for inquiry. Records are indexed on microfilm. Records are normally destroyed after 5 years.

Searching: Include the following in your request-full name of business. In addition to the articles of incorporation, corporation records include the following information: Annual Reports, Officers, Directors, Prior (merged) names, Inactive, Registered and Reserved names. The following data is not released: financial information.

Access by: mail, phone, fax, in person, online.

Fee & Payment: There is no charge for a computer printout. Copies are $1.00 per page with minimum fee of $10.00 for for-profit companies or domestic LLCs and $5.00 for non-profit companies. Certification fee is $25.00, except for non-profits which is $10.00. Fee payee: Public Regulation Commission. Payment is due in 10 days. Personal checks accepted. No credit cards accepted.

Mail search: Turnaround time: 2 days. A SASE is requested.

Phone search: Limited information is given over the phone.

Fax search: Information can be requested by fax, but is returned by mail in 4 to 10 days.

In person search: Call is to schedule viewing time for microfilm.

Online search: There is no charge to view at www.nmprc.state.nm.us/corporations/corpsinquiry.htm. Records can be searched by company name or by director name.

Other access: This agency makes the database available on electronic format using a 3480 tape cartridge. Fee is $3,600, monthly updates available for $600.

Trademarks/Servicemarks, Trade Names

Secretary of State, Trademarks Division, 325 Don Gaspar, #301, Santa Fe, NM 87503; 505-827-3609, 505-827-3611-Fax; 8AM-5PM.

www.sos.state.nm.us/trade.htm

Effective July 1, 1997, New Mexico no longer registers trade names. However, the agency will do searches for records on file.

Records are available from 1980 to present. It takes 1 to 2 days before new records are available for inquiry. Records are indexed on inhouse computer.

Searching: Include the following in your request-trademark/servicemark name. Include your full name, address and telephone number.

Access by: mail, phone, fax, in person.

Fee & Payment: There is no search fee, copies are $.25 a page. Fee payee: Secretary of State. Personal checks accepted. Credit cards not accepted

Mail search: Turnaround time: 2 to 3 days. No SASE is required. No fee for mail request.

Phone search: They will do a computer search and will give you the information over the phone for no fee.

Fax search: There is no fee. Turnaround time: 24 hours.

In person search: No fee for request. Turnaround time is usually immediate.

Uniform Commercial Code

UCC Division, Secretary of State, 325 Don GasparSt #301, Santa Fe, NM 87503; 505-827-3615, 505-827-3611-Fax; 8AM-5PM.

www.sos.state.nm.us/ucc/ucchome.htm

This agency will not conduct in-person searches. You must come in yourself, hire a local search company, request via email (from the web) or conduct your search at the agency website.

Records are available from 1965, but most available records are from 1998 forward. It takes 24 hours before new records are available for inquiry. Records are normally destroyed after six years.

Searching: Please note that all tax liens are filed at the county level. The system does not give information on collateral.

Access by: mail, in person, online.

Fee & Payment: Copies are $1.00 per page, plus $3.00 if certification requested. Fee payee: Secretary of State. Prepayment required. Personal checks accepted. No credit cards accepted.

Mail search: Turnaround time: 3 days. No name requests by mail, you must give specific document number.

In person search: You may use their in-house computer. For appointment only call 505-827-3614. You may view documents for free.

Online search: The website permits searching and provides a form to use to order copies of filings. You can also request records via email.

Other access: Microfilm and images (from 7/99) on disk may be purchased.

Federal and State Tax Liens

Records not maintained by a state level agency.

Records are filed with the Clerk at the county level.

Sales Tax Registrations

Taxation & Revenue Department, Tax Administrative Services Division, PO Box 5374, Santa Fe, NM 87504 (Courier address: Montoya Bldg, 1200 St Francis Drive, Santa Fe, NM 87501); 505-827-0700, 505-827-0614-Fax; 8AM-5PM.

www.state.nm.us/tax

New Mexico does not have a sales tax. It has a gross receipts tax instead.

Records are available from 1996. It takes one week before new records are available for inquiry. Records are normally destroyed after 7 years.

Searching: This agency will only confirm that a business is registered and active. They will provide no other information. Include the following in your request-company name or ID#. The business name is required, the permit number and federal ID are optional.

Access by: mail, in person.

Fee & Payment: There is no search fee, copies are $.05 per page Prepayment is not required. Personal checks accepted. No credit cards accepted.

Mail search: Turnaround time: 6 to 12 weeks. A SASE is requested.

In person search: Simple requests processed immediately.

Expedited service: No expedited service available.

Birth Certificates

Department of Health, Bureau of Vital Records, PO Box 26110, Santa Fe, NM 87502 (Courier address: 1105 South St Francis Dr, Santa Fe, NM 87502); 505-827-0121, 505-827-2338 (Information), 877-284-0963 (Order), 505-984-1048-Fax; 8AM-5:00PM (Counter Service: 8:30AM-4PM).

www.health.state.nm.us

All requesters must sign and date the request. It is a felony to obtain a record fraudulently.

Records are available from 1920 on. New records are available for inquiry immediately. Records are indexed on microfiche, inhouse computer.

Searching: Records available only to immediate family members or those demonstrating legal tangible interest in the desired record. Sealed records (e.g. adoptions and paternity) are unavailable. Include the following in your request-full name, names of parents, mother's maiden name, date of birth, place of birth, relationship to person of record, reason for information request. Signature of requester and physical & mailing addresses are required.

Access by: mail, phone, fax, in person, online.

Fee & Payment: The search fee is $10.00 per record. There is an additional $15.00 fee if you order by phone or by fax for use of a credit card. Fee payee: NM Vital Records. Prepayment required. Personal checks accepted. Major Credit cards accepted only by VitalChek.

Mail search: Turnaround time: 3 weeks. No SASE is required.

Phone search: From VitalChek, see expedited services.

Fax search: From VitalChek, see expedited services. Fax is 877-284-1066

In person search: Turnaround time is usually less than 1/2 hour. Also, counter Service for requesting birth certificates through the Albuquerque Stanford Public Health Office is available Monday through Friday from 9:00 a.m. until 4:00 p.m. The Albuquerque Office is housed at the Stanford Public Health Office at 1111 Stanford NE. The telephone number is 505-841-4185.

Online search: Records can be ordered at www.vitalchek.com, a state designated vendor.

Expedited service: Expedited service is available for online, phone and fax requests. Turnaround time: 24 hours. Add $30.75 for use of credit card fee and delivery service.

Death Records

Department of Health, Bureau of Vital Records, PO Box 26110, Santa Fe, NM 87502 (Courier address: 1105 South St Francis Dr, Santa Fe, NM 87502); 505-827-0121, 505827-2338 (Information), 877-284-0963 (Order), 505-984-1048-Fax; 8AM-5PM (Counter Service: 8:30AM-4PM).

www.health.state.nm.us

Records are available from 1920 to present. New records are available for inquiry immediately. Records are indexed on microfiche, inhouse computer.

Searching: Only immediate family member or a person with tangible interest can receive record. Include the following in your request-full name, date of death, place of death, Social Security Number, relationship to person of record, reason for information request. Age at death and name of mortuary must also be included for search.

Access by: mail, phone, fax, in person, online.

Fee & Payment: The fee is $5.00 per record. An additional fee may be charged if required information is not submitted. Use of credit card is an additional $15.00. Fee payee: NM Vital Records. Prepayment required. Personal checks accepted. Major Credit cards accepted only by VitalChek.

Mail search: Turnaround time: 3 to 4 weeks. No SASE is required.

Phone search: From VitalChek, see expedited services.

Fax search: From VitalChek, see expedited services. Fax is 877-284-1066

In person search: Turnaround time is usually 1 hour or less. The Albuquerque Office is housed at the Stanford Public Health Office at 1111 Stanford NE. The telephone number is (505) 841-4185.

Online search: A free lookup is available at www.rootsweb.com/~usgenweb/nm/nmdi.htm. Records date from 1899 to 1940. Expedited records can be ordered at www.vitalchek.com, a state designated vendor.

Expedited service: Expedited service is available for online, phone and fax requests. Turnaround time: 24 hours. Add $30.75 for use of credit card fee and delivery service.

Marriage Certificates, Divorce Records

Records not maintained by a state level agency.

Marriage and Divorce records are found at county of issue.

Workers' Compensation Records

Access to Records is Restricted.

Workers Compensation Administration, PO Box 27198, Albuquerque, NM 87125-7198 (Courier address: 2410 Centre Ave, SE, Albuquerque, NM 87106); 505-841-6000, 800-255-7965 (In-State Toll Free), 505-841-6060-Fax; 8AM-5PM.

www.state.nm.us/wca

The subject must write the agency, provide proof of ID with a driver's license, and request the record, and pay a copy fee of $.25 per page. Most records are confidential but access is permitted for all parties to a case and other cases involving the same worker. Only upon filing of rejection of a recommended resolution shall records be open to the public.

Driver Records

Motor Vehicle Division, Driver Services Bureau, PO Box 1028, Santa Fe, NM 87504-1028 (Courier address: Joseph M. Montoya Bldg, 1100 S St. Francis Dr, 2nd Floor, Santa Fe, NM 87504); 505-827-2241, 888-683-4636 (Toll Free-Automated), 505-827-4636 (Local-Automated), 505-827-2792-Fax; 8AM-5PM.

www.state.nm.us/tax/mvd

Copies of tickets may be obtained from the same address. There is no fee.

Records are available for 3 years for moving violations; 25 years DWIs. Accidents are not reported on the record and neither are violations less than 10 mph over the limit in 55 or 65 zones. The driver's address is included on the record. It takes 30 to 40 days before new records are available for inquiry.

Searching: The law lists 9 permissible user groups and permits release of records with written consent. Purchasers may not use the information for direct mail solicitation or resell the reports after usage. The full name, DOB and either the license number or SSN is required when ordering. Casual requesters must have signed, notarized consent from subject. The following data is not released: Social Security Numbers, addresses or date of birth.

Access by: mail, phone, in person, online.

Fee & Payment: There is no fee for mail or walk-in requests, as long as requester qualifies. Fee payee: Motor Vehicle Division. Prepayment required. Personal checks accepted. No credit cards accepted.

Mail search: Turnaround time: 5 to 7 days. No fee for manual search. A SASE is requested.

Phone search: Use the toll-free line listed above.

In person search: No fee for manual search. Up to 10 requests can be processed while you wait, the rest must be in writing and left overnight.

Online search: Records are available, for authorized users, from the state's designated vendors - Oso Grande (505-343-7639) www.osogrande.com and Samba (888-94-samba) www.samba.biz. In general, subscription fees are $2.99 per record for interactive, $2.50 per record for batch, plus network or access fees. The systems are open 24 hours a day, batch requesters must wait 24 hours.

Vehicle Ownership
Vehicle Identification,
Vessel Ownership
Vessel Registration

Motor Vehicle Division, Vehicle Services Bureau, PO Box 1028, Santa Fe, NM 87504-1028 (Courier address: Joseph M. Montoya Bldg, 1100 S St. Francis Dr, 2nd Floor, Santa Fe, NM 87504); 505-827-4636, 888-683-4636, 505-827-0395-Fax; 8AM-5PM.

www.state.nm.us/tax/mvd

Records are available for a minimum of 3 years on boats and 6 years on vehicles. All motorized boats, sailboats, and jet skis must be both titled and registered if over 10 ft, and only registered if 10 ft or less. It takes 30 days before new records are available for inquiry.

Searching: Authorized requesters are restricted to 9 user groups and must sign a contract that states purpose of request and subsequent use. Requesters may not use ownership and vehicle information to create a resalable database. Liens on vehicles show the title records. Liens on vessels are filed at the Sec. of State's office. The following data is not released: addresses, Social Security Numbers or date of birth.

Access by: mail, in person, online.

Fee & Payment: There are no fees for mail or in person requests. A vehicle history search (microfilm) goes back 6 years. Fee payee: Department of Motor Vehicles. Prepayment required. Personal checks accepted. No credit cards accepted.

Mail search: Turnaround time: 3 to 4 weeks. A SASE is requested.

In person search: Up to ten requests will be processed while you wait.

Online search: Records are available, for authorized users, from the state's designated vendor - Oso Grande (505-343-7639). Go to www.osogrande.com. In general, fees are $2.50 per records. Authorization must come from the state agency.

Other access: Bulk requests for vehicle or ownership information must be approved by the Director's office. Once a sale is made, further resale is prohibited.

Accident Reports

Department of Public Safety, Attn: Records, PO Box 1628, Santa Fe, NM 87504-1628 (Courier address: New Mexico State Police Complex, 4491 Cerrillos Rd, Santa Fe, NM 87504); 505-827-9181, 505-827-9189-Fax; 8AM-5PM.

www.dps.nm.org

Records are available up to 20 years to present in-house (on computer) and up to 25 years for fatalities. It takes up to 15 days before new records are available for inquiry.

Searching: Arrest information is not released. Include the following in your request-full name, date of accident, county, location of accident.

Access by: mail, phone, in person, online.

Fee & Payment: The fee is $1.00 per page plus $.25 each individual page. There is no fee for a no record found. There is no fee charged for persons directly involved in the accident. Fee payee: Department of Public Safety. Prepayment required. Personal checks accepted.

Mail search: Turnaround time: 2 weeks. A SASE is requested.

Phone search: No fee for telephone request.

In person search: Turnaround time is immediate if incident one year or less old.

Online search: Reports are available at https://www.nmaccidentreports.com/index.jsp. The officer's diagram and narrative is included. There is a $1.00 fee. Credit cards are accepted.

Voter Registration

Access to Records is Restricted.

Secretary of State, Bureau of Elections, 325 Don Gaspar, #300, Santa Fe, NM 87503; 505-827-3621, 800-477-3632, 505-827-8403-Fax; 8AM-5PM.

www.sos.state.nm.us/ELECTNET.HTM

This agency maintains a statewide database and complies with HAVA. The agency does sell statewide lists but only for restricted (political) purposes and not for commercial purposes. Individual look-ups must be done at the county clerk level.

GED Certificates

Department of Education, GED Testing Program, 300 Don Gaspar, Rm 122, Santa Fe, NM 87501-2786; 505-827-6702, 505-827-6616-Fax; 8AM-5PM.

www.sde.state.nm.us/div/ais/assess/ged

Request forms may be downloaded from the website. Unless ordered by the subject, transcripts are mailed directly to institutions or employers only.

Records are available from 1942 to present It takes 45 days before new records are available for inquiry.

Searching: Include the following in your request-name, DOB, SSN, and signed release (for either a verification or signed release).

Access by: mail, fax, in person.

Fee & Payment: There are no fees.

Mail search: Turnaround time: 2 weeks. No SASE is required.

Fax search: Same criteria as mail searching.

In person search: Simple requests may be processed while you wait.

Hunting and Fishing License Information

NM Dept of Game & Fish, PO Box 25112, Santa Fe, NM 87504 (Courier address: #1 Wildlife Way, Santa Fe, NM 87507); 505-476-8000, 800-862-9310, 505-476-8124-Fax; 8AM-12PM; 1PM-5PM.

www.wildlife.state.nm.us

Records are available for last season only. Records are indexed on hard copy.

Searching: Include the following in your request-name.

Access by: mail, in person.

Fee & Payment: Fee is $60 per hour plus $.25 per copy. Fee payee: NM Dept of Fish & Game.

Mail search: Turnaround time: 1 to 2 weeks. Records are available by mail.

In person search: You may do the search yourself for no fee.

New Mexico State Licensing Agencies

For details about the agency responsible for licensing/certifying/registering an item below or in the Agency Quick Finder section, match an item's number with the number of the agency in the *Licensing Agency Information* section.

Licenses Searchable Online

Acupuncturist #26	www.rld.state.nm.us/b&c/Acupuncture/Licensee%20Search/licensee_search.asp
Alcohol Server #14	www.rld.state.nm.us/AGD/Licensee%20Search/licensee_search_servers.asp
Announcer, Athletic Event (Ring) #39	www.rld.state.nm.us/b&c/Athletic%20Comm/Licensee%20Search/licensee_search.asp
Architect #17	www.nmbea.org/People/Aroster.htm
Art Therapist #15	www.rld.state.nm.us/b&c/counseling/Licensee%20Search/licensee_search.asp
Athletic Promoter/Matchmaker #39	www.rld.state.nm.us/b&c/Athletic%20Comm/Licensee%20Search/licensee_search.asp
Athletic Trainer #1	www.rld.state.nm.us/b&c/Athletic%20Trainers/Licensee%20Search/licensee_search.asp
Attorney #20	www.nmbar.org/template.cfm?section=attorney_firm_finder
Audiologist #11	www.rld.state.nm.us/b&c/speech/Licensee%20Search/licensee_search.asp
Bank #48	www.rld.state.nm.us/fid/Licensee%20Search/licensee_search_index.htm
Barber / Barber Shop/School #2	www.rld.state.nm.us/b&c/Barber%20&%20Cosmo/Licensee%20Search/licensee_search.asp
Boiler Operator Journeyman #33	www.contractorsnm.com:8080/search/
Booking Agent #39	www.rld.state.nm.us/b&c/Athletic%20Comm/Licensee%20Search/licensee_search.asp
Boxer/Boxer Mgr./Boxing Judge/Timekeeper #39	www.rld.state.nm.us/b&c/Athletic%20Comm/Licensee%20Search/licensee_search.asp
Cemetery, Endowed/Perpetual Care #48	www.rld.state.nm.us/fid/Licensee%20Search/licensee_search_index.htm
Chiropractor #3	www.rld.state.nm.us/b&c/Chiropractic/Licensee%20Search/licensee_search.asp
Clinical Nurse Specialist #19	www.state.nm.us/nursing/lookup.html
Collection Agency/Manager #48	www.rld.state.nm.us/fid/Licensee%20Search/licensee_search_index.htm
Consumer Credit Grantor/Loaner #48	www.rld.state.nm.us/fid/Licensee%20Search/licensee_search_index.htm
Contractor #13	www.contractorsnm.com:8080/search/
Cosmetologist / Cosmo Shop/School #2	www.rld.state.nm.us/b&c/Barber%20&%20Cosmo/Licensee%20Search/licensee_search.asp
Counseling/Therapy Practice #15	www.rld.state.nm.us/b&c/counseling/Licensee%20Search/licensee_search.asp
Credit Union #48	www.rld.state.nm.us/fid/Licensee%20Search/licensee_search_index.htm
Crematory #12	www.rld.state.nm.us/b&c/thanato/Licensee%20Search/licensee_search_index.asp
Dentist/ Dental Assistant #4	www.rld.state.nm.us/b&c/dental/
Dental Hygienist #4	www.rld.state.nm.us/b&c/dental/
Dietitian/Nutritionist #8	www.rld.state.nm.us
Direct Disposer (Funerary) #12	www.rld.state.nm.us/b&c/thanato/Licensee%20Search/licensee_search_index.asp
Electrologist #2	www.rld.state.nm.us/b&c/Barber%20&%20Cosmo/Licensee%20Search/licensee_search.asp
Electrophysician #2	www.rld.state.nm.us/b&c/Barber%20&%20Cosmo/Licensee%20Search/licensee_search.asp
Engineer #44	www.state.nm.us/java-bin/peps/PEPSBoard/PEPSBoard.jsp
Escrow Company #48	www.rld.state.nm.us/fid/Licensee%20Search/licensee_search_index.htm
Esthetician #2	www.rld.state.nm.us/b&c/Barber%20&%20Cosmo/Licensee%20Search/licensee_search.asp
FSI (Funerary) #12	www.rld.state.nm.us/b&c/thanato/Licensee%20Search/licensee_search_index.asp
Funeral Director/Practitioner/Home #12	www.rld.state.nm.us/b&c/thanato/Licensee%20Search/licensee_search_index.asp
Funeral Service Intern #12	www.rld.state.nm.us/b&c/thanato/Licensee%20Search/licensee_search_index.asp
Hearing Aid Specialist #11	www.rld.state.nm.us/b&c/speech/Licensee%20Search/licensee_search.asp
Hemodialysis Technician #19	www.state.nm.us/nursing/lookup.html
Insurance Agent #23	www.nmprc.state.nm.us/insurance/agents/agentshome.htm
Interior Designer #25	www.rld.state.nm.us/b&c/Interior/Licensee%20Search/licensee_search.asp
Journeyman Contractor #13	www.contractorsnm.com:8080/search/
Landscape Architect #18	www.rld.state.nm.us/b&c/landscape/Licensee%20Search/licensee_search.asp
Loan Company, Small #48	www.rld.state.nm.us/fid/Licensee%20Search/licensee_search_index.htm
Lobbying Organization #32	http://web.state.nm.us/LOBBY/ORG.htm
Lobbyist #32	http://web.state.nm.us/LOBBY/LOB.htm
LPG Gas License #13	www.contractorsnm.com:8080/search/
Manicurist #2	www.rld.state.nm.us/b&c/Barber%20&%20Cosmo/Licensee%20Search/licensee_search.asp
Marriage & Family Therapist #15	www.rld.state.nm.us/b&c/counseling/Licensee%20Search/licensee_search.asp
Martial Arts Contest #39	www.rld.state.nm.us/b&c/Athletic%20Comm/Licensee%20Search/licensee_search.asp
Massage Instr./Practitioner/School #5	www.rld.state.nm.us/b&c/massage/Licensee%20Search/licensee_search.asp
Massage Therapist #5	www.rld.state.nm.us/b&c/massage/Licensee%20Search/licensee_search.asp
Medical Doctor #36	www.docboard.org/nm/
Medication Aide #19	www.state.nm.us/nursing/lookup.html
Mental Health Counselor #15	www.rld.state.nm.us/b&c/counseling/Licensee%20Search/licensee_search.asp
Money Order Agent/Exempt Agent #48	www.rld.state.nm.us/fid/Licensee%20Search/licensee_search_index.htm
Mortgage Co./Loan Broker/Branch #48	www.rld.state.nm.us/fid/Licensee%20Search/licensee_search_index.htm
Motor Vehicle Sales Financer #48	www.rld.state.nm.us/fid/Licensee%20Search/licensee_search_index.htm

Nurse Anesthetist #19	www.state.nm.us/nursing/lookup.html
Nurse Practitioner #19	www.state.nm.us/nursing/lookup.html
Nurse-LPN / RN #19	www.state.nm.us/nursing/lookup.html
Nursing Home Administrator #6	www.rld.state.nm.us/b&c/nhab/Licensee%20Search/licensee_search.asp
Occupational Therapist/Assistant #27	www.rld.state.nm.us/b&c/otb/Licensee%20Search/licensee_search.asp
Optometrist #40	www.rld.state.nm.us/b&c/optometry/Licensee%20Search/licensee_search.asp
Oriental Medicine Doctor #26	www.rld.state.nm.us/b&c/Acupuncture/Licensee%20Search/licensee_search.asp
Osteopathic Physician #7	www.rld.state.nm.us/b&c/osteo/Licensee%20Search/licensee_search.asp
Pharmacist #41	http://ec4.state.nm.us/pharmacy/
Physical Therapist/Assistant #28	www.rld.state.nm.us/b&c/ptb/Licensee%20Search/licensee_search.asp
Physician Assistant #36	www.docboard.org/nm/
Podiatrist #42	www.rld.state.nm.us/b&c/Podiatry/Licensee%20Search/licensee_search.asp
Psychologist #37	www.rld.state.nm.us/b&c/psychology/Licensee%20Search/licensee_search.asp
Psychologist Associate #37	www.rld.state.nm.us/b&c/psychology/Licensee%20Search/licensee_search.asp
Public Accountant-CPA #35	www.rld.state.nm.us/b&c/accountancy/Licensee%20Search/licensee_search.asp
Real Estate Agent/Salesperson #46	http://rld.state.nm.us/b&c/recom/Licensee%20Search/licensee_search.asp
Real Estate Appraiser #49	www.rld.state.nm.us/b&c/reappraisers/Licensee%20Search/licensee_search.asp
Real Estate Broker #46	http://rld.state.nm.us/b&c/recom/Licensee%20Search/licensee_search.asp
Referee #39	www.rld.state.nm.us/b&c/Athletic%20Comm/Licensee%20Search/licensee_search.asp
Respiratory Care Therapist #29	www.rld.state.nm.us/b&c/rcb/Licensee%20Search/licensee_search.asp
Savings & Loan #48	www.rld.state.nm.us/fid/Licensee%20Search/licensee_search_index.htm
School Administrator #24	www.ped.state.nm.us/
School Counselor #24	www.ped.state.nm.us/
Social Worker (LBSW, LI, LM) #10	www.rld.state.nm.us/b&c/socialwk/index.htm
Social Worker, Provisional #10	www.rld.state.nm.us/b&c/socialwk/index.htm
Speech-Language Pathologist #11	www.rld.state.nm.us/b&c/speech/Licensee%20Search/licensee_search.asp
Substance Abuse Counselor/Intern #15	www.rld.state.nm.us/b&c/counseling/Licensee%20Search/licensee_search.asp
Surveyor, Land #44	www.state.nm.us/java-bin/peps/PEPSBoard/PEPSBoard.jsp
Teacher #24	www.ped.state.nm.us/
Trust Company #48	www.rld.state.nm.us/fid/Licensee%20Search/licensee_search_index.htm
Veterinarian/Veterinary Technician #30	newmexicoveterinaryboard.us/
Veterinary Facility #30	newmexicoveterinaryboard.us/
Wrestler #39	www.rld.state.nm.us/b&c/Athletic%20Comm/Licensee%20Search/licensee_search.asp

New Mexico Licensing Quick Finder

Acupuncturist #26	505-476-4630	
Alcohol Server #14	505-476-4875	
Animal Pregnancy Diagnosis #30	505-841-9112	
Announcer, Athletic Event (Ring) #39	505-222-9860	
Architect #17	505-827-6375	
Art Therapist #15	505-476-4610	
Artificial Inseminator #30	505-841-9112	
Athletic Promoter/Matchmaker #39	505-222-9860	
Athletic Trainer #1	505-476-7098	
Attorney #20	505-271-9706	
Audiologist #11	505-476-4640	
Bank #48	505-476-4885	
Barber #2	505-476-4690	
Barber Shop/School #2	505-476-4690	
Bingo/Raffles, Non-profit #14	505-476-4875	
Boiler Operator Journeyman #33	505-452-8311	
Booking Agent #39	505-222-9860	
Boxer #39	505-222-9860	
Boxer Manager #39	505-222-9860	
Boxing Judge/Timekeeper #39	505-222-9860	
Cemetery,Endowed/Perpetuall care#48	505-476-4885	
Chiropractor #3	505-476-7120	
Clinical Nurse Specialist #19	505-841-8340	
Collection Agency/Manager #48	505-476-4885	
Consumer Credit Grantor/Loan Company #48	505-476-4885	
Contractor #13	505-467-4700	
Cosmetologist #2	505-476-4690	
Cosmetology Shop/School #2	505-476-4690	
Counseling/Therapy Practice #15	505-476-4610	
Credit Union #48	505-476-4885	
Crematory #12	505-476-4870	
Dentist / Dental Assistant #4	505-476-4680	
Dental Hygienist #4	505-476-4680	
Dietitian/Nutritionist #8	505-476-7053	
Direct Disposer (Funerary) #12	505-476-4870	
Dispensing Physician #41	505-222-9830	
Electrologist #2	505-827-7550	
Electrophysician #2	505-476-4690	
Emergency Medical Technician #22	505-476-7701	
Engineer #44	505-827-7561	
Escrow Company #48	505-476-4885	
Esthetician #2	505-476-4690	
Fireworks Distributor Class C or B #31	505-827-3761	
Fireworks Manufacturer 1.4G #31	505-827-3761	
Fireworks Vendor (Retail, Wholse) #31	505-827-3761	
FSI (Funerary) #12	505-476-4870	
Funeral Director/Practitioner #12	505-476-4870	
Funeral Home #12	505-476-4870	
Funeral Service Intern #12	505-476-4870	
Gambling, Non-Profit #14	505-476-4875	
Hearing Aid Specialist #11	505-476-4640	
Hemodialysis Technician #19	505-841-8340	
Insurance Agent #23	505-827-4637	
Interior Designer #25	505-476-4865	
Investment Advisor/Representative #32	505-476-4580	
Journeyman Contractor #13	505-467-4700	
Landscape Architect #18	505-476-4600	
Liquor Distributor #14	505-476-4875	
Loan Company, Small #48	505-476-4885	
Lobbying Organization #32	505-476-4580	
Lobbyist #32	505-476-4580	
LPG Gas License #13	505-467-4700	
Manicurist #2	505-476-4690	
Manufactured Housing Dealer/Broker #47	505-476-4770	
Manufactured Housing Installer/Repairman #47	505-476-4770	
Manufactured Housing Manuf. #47	505-476-4770	
Manufactur'd Housing Salesperson#47	505-476-4770	
Marriage & Family Therapist #15	505-476-4610	
Martial Arts Contest #39	505-222-9860	
Massage Instr./Practitioner/School #5	505-476-4870	
Massage Therapist #5	505-476-4870	
Medical Doctor #36	505-827-6784	
Medical Researcher #41	505-222-9830	
Medical Wholesale Company #41	505-222-9830	
Medication Aide #19	505-841-8340	
Mental Health Counselor #15	505-476-4610	
Midwife #34	505-476-8908	
Midwife (CNM) #34	505-476-8908	
Money Order Agent/Company/Exempt Agent #48	505-476-4885	
Mortgage Company/Loan Broker/Branch #48	505-476-4885	
Motor Vehicle Sales Finance Company #48	505-476-4885	
Notary Public #43	505-827-3605	
Nuclear Medicine Technologist #38	505-476-3264	
Nurse Anesthetist #19	505-841-8340	
Nurse Practitioner #19	505-841-8340	
Nurse-LPN #19	505-841-8340	
Nurse-RN #19	505-841-8340	

Nursing Home Administrator #6 505-476-4660
Occupational Therapist/Assistant #27 ..505-476-4596
Optometrist #40 505-476-4660
Oriental Medicine Doctor #26 505-476-4630
Osteopathic Physician #7 505-476-4695
Osteopathic Physician Assistant #7 505-476-4695
Patrol Operator, Private #9 505-476-4650
Pest Management Consultant #21 505-646-2133
Pesticide Applicator/Operator #21........505-646-2133
Pesticide Dealer #21 505-646-2133
Pharmacist #41 505-222-9830
Pharmacy, Non-Residential #41...........505-222-9830
Physical Therapist/Assistant #28 505-476-4596
Physician Assistant #36......................505-827-6784
Podiatrist #42 505-476-4695
Polygraph Examiner #9 505-476-4650

Private Investigator #9.......................505-476-4650
Psychologist #37 505-476-4607
Psychologist Associate #37................505-476-4607
Public Accountant-CPA #35 505-841-9108
Racing #45 505-841-6400
Radiation Therapy Technologist #38 ...505-476-3264
Radiologic Technologist #38 505-476-3264
Real Estate Agent/Salesperson #46 ...505-476-4512
Real Estate Appraiser #49 505-476-4611
Real Estate Broker #46 505-476-4512
Referee #39 505-222-9860
Respiratory Care Therapist #29 505-476-7121
Savings & Loan #48 505-476-4885
School Administrator #24 505-827-6587
School Counselor #24 505-827-6587
Securities Broker/Dealer #32 505-476-4580

Securities Division Agent #32 505-476-4580
Securities Sales Representative #32 ...505-476-4580
Security Guard #9 505-476-4650
Shorthand Reporter #16......................505-821-1440
Social Worker (LBSW, LI, LM) #10 505-476-4890
Social Worker, Provisional #10 505-476-4890
Speech-Language Pathologist #11......505-476-4640
Substance Abuse Couns./Intern #15 ...505-476-4610
Surveyor, Land #44 505-827-7561
Teacher #24 505-827-6587
Trust Company #48............................505-476-4885
Veterinarian/Veterinary Technician #30505-841-9112
Veterinary Facility #30.......................505-841-9112
Waste Water System Operator #38 505-476-3264
Wrestler #39 505-222-9860

New Mexico Licensing Agency Information

1 Regulation & Licensing Dept., Athletic Trainers Board, POB 2055 (2055 S Pacheco St #300), Santa Fe, NM 87505; 505-476-7098, Fax: 505-476-7094. www.rld.state.nm.us/b&c/Athletic%20Trainers/index.htm　Email: AthleticTrainerBoard@state.nm.us Search Database at www.rld.state.nm.us/b&c/Athletic%20Trainers/Licensee%20Search/licensee_search.asp

2 Regulation & Licensing Dept., Board of Barbers & Cosmetologists, 2550 Cerrillos Rd, Santa Fe, NM 87505-3206; 505-476-4690, Fax: 505-476-4645. www.rld.state.nm.us/b&c/Barber%20&%20Cosmo/index.htm　Search Database at www.rld.state.nm.us/b&c/Barber%20&%20Cosmo/Licensee%20Search/licensee_search.asp

3 Regulation & Licensing Dept., Board of Chiropractic Examiners, 2550 Cerrillos Rd 2nd Fl, Santa Fe, NM 87504; 505-476-4695, Fax: 505-476-4545. www.rld.state.nm.us/b&c/Chiropractic/index.htm Email: ChiroBoard@state.nm.us　Search Database at www.rld.state.nm.us/b&c/Chiropractic/Licensee%20Search/licensee_search.asp　Note: The lists provided online do not include sanctions.

4 Regulation & Licensing Dept., Board of Dental Health Care, PO Box 25101, Santa Fe, NM 87504-5101; 505-476-4680, Fax: 505-476-7095. www.rld.state.nm.us/b&c/dental/index.htm Email: Cynthia.Salazar@state.nm.us Search Database at www.rld.state.nm.us/b&c/dental/

5 Regulation & Licensing Dept., Massage Therapy Board, 2550 Cerrillos Road, Santa Fe, NM 87505; 505-476-4870, Fax: 505-476-7095. www.rld.state.nm.us/b&c/massage/index.htm Email: MassageBoard@state.nm.us　Search data at www.rld.state.nm.us/b&c/massage/Licnesee%20Search/licensee_search.asp

6 Regulation & Licensing Dept., Nursing Home Administrators Board, 2550 Cerrillos Rd, Santa Fe, NM 87505-3260; 505-476-4660. www.rld.state.nm.us/b&c/nhab/index.htm Email: NursingHomeAdminBd@state.nm.us Search Database at www.rld.state.nm.us/b&c/nhab/Licensee%20Search/licensee_search.asp

7 Regulation & Licensing Dept., Board of Osteopathic Medical Examiners, 2550 Cerrillos Rd, Santa Fe, NM 87505-3260; 505-476-4695, Fax: 505-476-4665. www.rld.state.nm.us/b&c/osteo/index.htm Email: OsteoBoard@state.nm.us Search Database at www.rld.state.nm.us/b&c/osteo/Licensee%20Search/licensee_search.asp

8 Regulation & Licensing Dept., Nutrition & Dietetics Practice Board, 2550 Cerrillos Rd, Santa Fe, NM 87505-3206; 505-476-7053, Fax: 505-476-7094.　www.rld.state.nm.us Email: NutritionDieteticsBd@state.nm.us

9 Regulation & Licensing Dept., Private Investigators & Polygraph Board, 2550 Cerrillos Rd, Santa Fe, NM 87505-3260; 505-476-4650, Fax: 505-476-4645. www.rld.state.nm.us/b&c/pipolygraph/index.htm Email: PIPolygraphBd@state.nm.us

10 Regulation & Licensing Dept., Social Work Examiners Board, 2550 Cerrillos Rd, Santa Fe, NM 87505-3206; 505-476-4890, Fax: 505-476-4620. www.rld.state.nm.us/b&c/socialwk/index.htm Email: SocialWorkBoard@state.nm.us Search Database at www.rld.state.nm.us/b&c/socialwk/index.htm Note: Verification $5.00 for first 5 names; $1.00 each addl. name. Lists, lables,or disc available.

11 Regulation & Licensing Dept., Speech, Language, Audiology, & Hearing Aid Board, 2550 Cerrillos Rd, Santa Fe, NM 87505-3260; 505-476-4640, Fax: 505-476-4620. www.rld.state.nm.us/b&c/speech/index.htm Email: Speech/Hearing@state.nm.us Search Database at www.rld.state.nm.us/b&c/speech/Licensee%20Search/licensee_search.asp

12 Regulation & Licensing Dept., Thanatopractice Board, 2550 Cerrillos Rd, Santa Fe, NM 87505-3260; 505-476-4870, Fax: 505-476-4665. www.rld.state.nm.us/b&c/thanato/ Email: FuneralBoard@state.nm.us　Search Database at www.rld.state.nm.us/b&c/thanato/Licensee%20Search/licensee_search_index.asp

13 Regulation & Licensing Dept., Construction Industries Division, 2550 Cerrillos Rd, Sante Fe, NM 87505-3260; 505-467-4700, Fax: 505-765-5670. http://rld.state.nm.us/cid　Email: rldcide@state.nm.us Search Database at www.contractorsnm.com:8080/search/

14 Regulation & Licensing Dept., Alcohol & Gaming Division, 2550 Cerrillos Rd, Santa Fe, NM 87505-3260; 505-476-4875, Fax: 505-476-4595. www.rld.state.nm.us/agd/index.htm Email: agd@state.nm.us

15 Regulation & Licensing Dept., Counseling & Therapy Practice Board, 2550 Cerrillos Rd, Sante Fe, NM 87505-3260; 505-476-4610, Fax: 505-476-4633. www.rld.state.nm.us/b&c/counseling/index.htm Email: CounselingBoard@state.nm.us Search Database at www.rld.state.nm.us/b&c/counseling/Licensee%20Search/licensee_search.asp

16 Board Governing Recording of Judicial Proceedings, PO Box 92648, Albuquerque, NM 87199-2648; 505-821-1440, Fax: 505-821-2940.

17 Board of Examiners for Architects, PO Box 509, Santa Fe, NM 87504; 505-827-6375, Fax: 505-827-6373.　www.nmbea.org Search Database at www.nmbea.org/People/Aroster.htm

18 Board of Landscape Architects, 2550 Cerrillos Rd, Santa Fe, NM 87505-3260; 505-476-4600, Fax: 505-476-7087. www.rld.state.nm.us/b&c/landscape/index.htm Email: LandscapeArchitects@state.nm.us Search Database at www.rld.state.nm.us/b&c/landscape/Licensee%20Search/licensee_search.asp

19 Board of Nursing, 6301 Indian School NE #710, Albuquerque, NM 87110; 505-841-8340, Fax: 505-841-8347. www.state.nm.us/nursing Email: boardifnursing@state.nm.us Search Database at www.state.nm.us/nursing/lookup.html

20 Board of Bar Examiners, 9420 Indian School NE, Albuquerque, NM 87112; 505-271-9706, Fax: 505-271-9768. www.nmexam.org　Email: info@nmexam.org Search Database at www.nmbar.org/template.cfm?section=attorney_firm_finder

21 Department of Agriculture, Pesticide Management Bureau, MSC 3AQ, PO Box 30005 MSC 3AQ, Las Cruces, NM 88003-8005; 505-646-2133, Fax: 505-646-5977. http://nmdaweb.nmsu.edu/DIVISIONS/AES/pest.html　Email: webmastr@nmsu.edu

22 Department of Health, Injury Prevention & EMS Bureau, 2500 Cerrillos Rd, Santa Fe, NM 87505; 505-476-7701, Fax: 505-476-7810.

23 Department of Insurance, Insurance Licensing Division, PO Box 1269, Santa Fe, NM 87504; 505-827-4637, Fax: 505-827-4551. www.nmprc.state.nm.us/insurance/agents/agentshome.htm

24 Education Department, Professional Licensure, 300 Don Gaspar, Education Bldg, Santa Fe, NM 87501-2786; 505-827-6587, Fax: 505-827-6696. www.sde.state.nm.us

25 Regulation & Licensing Dept., Board of Interior Design, 2550 Cerrillos Rd, Santa Fe, NM 87505-3260; 505-476-4865, Fax: 505-827-7087. www.rld.state.nm.us/b&c/Interior/index.htm Email: InteriorDesignBd@state.nm.us Search Database at www.rld.state.nm.us/b&c/Interior/Licensee%20Search/licensee_search.asp

26 Regulation & Licensing Dept., Acupuncture & Oriental Medicine Board, 2550 Cerrillos Rd, Santa Fe, NM 87505-3260; 505-476-4630, Fax: 505-476-4545. www.rld.state.nm.us/b&c/acupuncture/index.htm Email: AcuOrMedBoard@state.nm.us Search Database at www.rld.state.nm.us/b&c/Acupuncture/Licensee%20Search/licensee_search.asp

27 Regulation & Licensing Dept., Occupational Therapy Board, 2550 Cerrillos Rd, Santa Fe, NM 87505-3206; 505-476-4596, Fax: 505-476-4655. www.rld.state.nm.us/b&c/otb/index.htm Email: OccupationalTherapy@state.nm.us Search Database at www.rld.state.nm.us/b&c/otb/Licensee%20Search/licensee_search.asp

28 Regulation & Licensing Dept., Physical Therapy Board, P.O. Box 25101, Santa Fe, NM 87504-5101; 505-476-4596, Fax: 505-476-4655. www.rld.state.nm.us/b&c/ptb/index.htm Email: PhysicalThearpy@state.nm.us Search Database at www.rld.state.nm.us/b&c/ptb/Licensee%20Search/licensee_search.asp

29 Regulation & Licensing Dept., Repiratory Care Advisory Board, 2550 Cerrillos Rd, Santa Fe, NM 87505; 505-476-4660, Fax: 505-476-7095. www.rld.state.nm.us/b&c/rcb/index.htm Email: respiratorycarebd@state.mt.us Search Database at www.rld.state.nm.us/b&c/rcb/Licensee%20Search/licensee_search.asp

30 Board of Veterinary Medicine, 7301 Jefferson St. NE Ste C, Albuquerque, NM 87109-4363; 505-841-9112, Fax: 505-841-9127. www.newmexicoveterinaryboard.us/ Search Database at www.newmexicoveterinaryboard.us/ To search, click on "license verification" at the website.

31 State Fire Marshal, Public Regulation Commission, 142 West Palace Ave, P.O. Box 1269, Santa Fe, NM 87504; 505-827-3761, Fax: 505-827-3778.

32 Securities Division, Regulation and Licensing Dept., 2550 Cerrillos Rd, Santa Fe, NM 87505-3260; 505-476-4580, Fax: 505-984-0617. www.rld.state.nm.us/Securities/index.htm Email: rldsd@state.nm.us

33 Boiler Operator Journeyman Licensing Board, c/o Contractor Licensing Services, 3211 Coors Blvd SW #A3, Albuquerque, NM 87121; 505-452-8311, Fax: 505-452-8310. www.contractorsnm.com Search Database at www.contractorsnm.com:8080/search/

34 Maternal Health Program, Public Health, PO Box 26110, Santa Fe, NM 87502; 505-476-8908, Fax: 505-476-8909. Email: rimav@doh.state.nm.us Search Database at www.health.state.nm.us/midwife-roster.html

35 Regulation & Licensing Dept., Accountancy Board, 5200 Oakland NE, Suite D, Albuquerque, NM 87113; 505-841-9108, Fax: 505-841-9101. www.rld.state.nm.us/b&c/accountancy/ Email: publicaccountancyboard@state.nm.us Search data at www.rld.state.nm.us/b&c/accountancy/Licensee%20Search/licensee_search.asp

36 Board of Medical Examiners, 2055 S. Pacheco St., Building 400, Santa Fe, NM 87505; 505-476-7220, Fax: 505-476-7237. www.state.nm.us/nmbme/ Search Database at www.docboard.org/nm/

37 Regulation & Licensing Dept., Board of Psychologist Examiners, 2550 Cerrillos Rd, Santa Fe, NM 87505; 505-476-4607, Fax: 505-827-7017. www.rld.state.nm.us/b&c/psychology/index.htm Email: psychologistexaminers@state.nm.us Search Database at www.rld.state.nm.us/b&c/psychology/Licensee%20Search/licensee_search.asp

38 Environment Department, Radiation Protection Program, 1190 Saint Francis Dr, Santa Fe, NM 87502; 505-476-3264, Fax: 505-476-3015. www.nmenv.state.nm.us Email: stephen_sanchez@nmenv.state.nm.us

39 Regulation & Licensing Dept., Athletic Commission, 2550 Cerrillos Rd, Santa Fe, NM 87505-3260; 505-222-9860, Fax: 505-827-7095. www.rld.state.nm.us/b&c/Athletic%20Comm/ Email: henrietta.leos@state.nm.us Search Database at www.rld.state.nm.us/b&c/Athletic%20Comm/Licensee%20Search/licensee_search.asp

40 Regulation & Licensing Dept., Board of Examiners in Optometry, 2550 Cerrillos Road, Santa Fe, NM 87505-3260; 505-476-4660, Fax: 505-476-4620. www.rld.state.nm.us/b&c/optometry/index.htm Email: optometrybd@state.nm.us Search Database at www.rld.state.nm.us/b&c/optometry/Licensee%20Search/licensee_search.asp

41 Regulation & Licensing Dept., Pharmacy Board, 5200 Oakland NE Suite A, Albuquerque, NM 87113; 505-222-9830, Fax: 505-222-9845. www.state.nm.us/pharmacy Email: NMBOP@nm-us.campuscwix.net Search Database at http://ec4.state.nm.us/pharmacy/

42 Regulation & Licensing Dept., Podiatry Board, 2550 Cerrillos Rd, Santa Fe, NM 87505-3260; 505-476-4695, Fax: 505-476-4545. www.rld.state.nm.us/b&c/Podiatry/index.htm Email: PodiatryBoard@state.nm.us Search Database at www.rld.state.nm.us/b&c/Podiatry/Licensee%20Search/licensee_search.asp

43 Secretary of State, Notary Public Section, State Capitol North Ste300, Santa Fe, NM 87503; 505-827-3600, Fax: 505-827-3634. www.sos.state.nm.us Email: nm.notary@state.nm.us

44 Professional Engineers & Surveyors Board, 4001 Office Court Dr, # 902-904, Santa Fe, NM 87507-4962; 505-827-7561, Fax: 505-827-7566. www.state.nm.us/pepsboard Search Database at www.state.nm.us/java-bin/peps/PEPSBoard/PEPSBoard.jsp

45 Racing Commission, 300 San Mateo Blvd NE, #110, Albuquerque, NM 87108; 505-841-6400, Fax: 505-841-6413. http://nmrc.state.nm.us/ Email: nmrc@state.nm.us

46 Regulation & Licensing Dept., Real Estate Commission, 2550 Cerrillos Road, Santa Fe, NM 87504; 505- 476-4512 800-801-7505, Fax: 505-476-4511. www.state.nm.us/nmrec Email: nmrec@state.nm.us Search Database at http://rld.state.nm.us/b&c/recom/Licensee%20Search/licensee_search.asp

47 Regulation & Licensing Dept., Manufactured Housing Division, 2550 Cerrillos Rd, Santa Fe, NM 87505-3260; 505-476-4770, Fax: 505-827-7074. www.rld.state.nm.us/mhd/index.htm Email: MHD@state.nm.us

48 Regulation & Licensing Dept., Financial Institutions Division, 2550 Cerrillos Rd 3rd Floor, Santa Fe, NM 87505-3260; 505-476-4885, Fax: 505-476-4670. www.rld.state.nm.us/fid/index.htm Email: rldfid@state.nm.us Search Database at www.rld.state.nm.us/fid/Licensee%20Search/licensee_search_index.htm

49 Regulation & Licensing Dept., Real Estate Appraisers Board, 2550 Cerrillos Rd, Santa Fe, NM 87505-3260; 505-476-4611, Fax: 505-476-4645. www.rld.state.nm.us/b&c/reappraisers/index.htm Email: RobertaPerea@state.nm.us Search Database at www.rld.state.nm.us/b&c/reappraisers/Licensee%20Search/licensee_search.asp

New Mexico Federal Courts

The following list indicates the district and division name for each county in the state.

New Mexico County/Court Cross Reference

County	Division	County	Division
Bernalillo	Albuquerque	McKinley	Albuquerque
Catron	Albuquerque	Mora	Albuquerque
Chaves	Albuquerque	Otero	Albuquerque
Cibola	Albuquerque	Quay	Albuquerque
Colfax	Albuquerque	Rio Arriba	Albuquerque
Curry	Albuquerque	Roosevelt	Albuquerque
De Baca	Albuquerque	San Juan	Albuquerque
Dona Ana	Albuquerque	San Miguel	Albuquerque
Eddy	Albuquerque	Sandoval	Albuquerque
Grant	Albuquerque	Santa Fe	Albuquerque
Guadalupe	Albuquerque	Sierra	Albuquerque
Harding	Albuquerque	Socorro	Albuquerque
Hidalgo	Albuquerque	Taos	Albuquerque
Lea	Albuquerque	Torrance	Albuquerque
Lincoln	Albuquerque	Union	Albuquerque
Los Alamos	Albuquerque	Valencia	Albuquerque
Luna	Albuquerque		

US District Court

Albuquerque Division Court Clerk, 333 Lomas Blvd NW #270, Albuquerque, NM 87102-2274 (also use mail address for courier delivery), 505-348-2000, records rm- 505-348-2020, Fax- 505-348-2028. Hours- 8:30AM-N, 1-4:30PM. www.nmcourt.fed.us/dcdocs

Counties: All counties in New Mexico. Cases may be assigned to any of 3 divisions - Santa Fe (505-988-6481), Las Cruces (505-528-1400), and Roswell (505-625-2388). Santa Fe and Las Cruces have searchable records; Roswell does not.

Searches & Indexing: Inquirer's phone number and years to search required. Search records 1990 to present by plaintiff name. Search prior records by defendant or case number. Results do not include SSN or DOB. Computer index maintained back to 1992. New cases in the index 2 days after filing date. Records purged every 6 months.

Fee & Payment: Pay by money order, cashier's or personal check. Payee: Clerk, US District Court. Prepayment required.

Phone Search: Only docket information available by phone.

Mail Search: search usually completed- 24 hours. SASE not required.

In Person Search: Fee charged if court performs your search. Copying available from copy service. No self-serve copier available.

E-Services: Register for free online searching. This court utilizes ACE (Advanced Court Engineering), not the US Courts standard CM/ECF system. Submit a written request for an ACE user name and password in order to freely access court records, docket reports, court opinions. See www.nmcourt.fed.us/web/DCDOCS/files/accountr equest.html. Court does not participate in the U.S. party case index. No PACER access to this court. ECF at www.nmcourt.fed.us/dcdocs - click on Electronic Filing.

US Bankruptcy Court

Albuquerque Division Court Clerk, PO Box 546, Albuquerque, NM 87103-0546 (courier address: 3rd Fl, Rm 316, 421 Gold Ave SW, Albuquerque, NM 87102), 505-348-2500, Fax- 505-348-2473. Hours- 8:30AM-4:30PM. www.nmcourt.fed.us/bkdocs

Counties: All counties in New Mexico. Judges do travel to Las Cruces and Roswell, however, bankruptcy records are not searchable at those courthouses.

Searches & Indexing: Results include last 4 SSN digits. Both computer and card indexes maintained; on computer back to 5/26/1987. New cases in the index 24 hours after filing date.

Fee & Payment: Pay by Visa/MC, money order, cashier's or personal check. No debtor's checks accepted. Payee: Clerk, US Bankruptcy Court. Prepayment required.

Phone Search: Index, docket and claim information is released via phone. Voice Case Information Service available, call VCIS at 888-435-7822 or 505-348-2444.

Mail Search: search usually completed- 8 business days. Fee is charged only when a case file search is required. Include SASE for return.

In Person Search: Fee charged if court performs your search. There is a contract copy service, fax service and other related services located here. Copy service available by FAX; all 505-842-9836. No self-serve copier available.

E-Services: PACER online at http://pacer.nmb.uscourts.gov. PACER records go back to 7/1991. New records online after 1 day. Currently in the process of implementing CM/ECF. **Other Online Access:** Submit a written request for an ACE (Advanced Court Engineering) user name and password in order to freely access court records, docket, and court opinions. See www.nmcourt.fed.us/web/BCDOCS/bcindex.html.

Standards for Federal Courts: Search fee is $26.00 per item (one party name or case number). Copy fee is $.50 per page. Certification fee is $9.00 per document, double for exemplification, if available. All fees standard unless noted in profile. Mail Search: always enclose a stamped self addressed envelope unless otherwise noted. Most courts accept fax requests or will suggest a copying/search vendor. Before releasing records, all courts require prepayment, unless noted.

Open records are located at the court unless otherwise noted. District courts index by defendant and plaintiff as well as by case number. Bankruptcy courts usually index by debtor and case number. While most courts now have their indexes on computer, many may still maintain index card files as well.

Courts offering internet access via CM-ECF or older RACER, PACER, or Web-PACER systems charge $.08 per page fee unless noted as free. Where PACER is available, the universal sign-up number is 800-676-6856. Find PACER and the US Party/Case Index at http://pacer.psc.uscourts.gov.

New Mexico County Courts

Court	Jurisdiction	No. of Courts	How Organized
District Courts*	General	30	13 Districts
Magistrate Courts*	Limited	54	32 Magistrate Districts
Metropolitan Court of Bernalillo County*	Municipal	1	
Municipal Courts	Municipal	81	
Probate Courts	Probate	30	33 Counties

* Profiled in this Sourcebook.

Court	CIVIL								
	Tort	Contract	Real Estate	Min. Claim	Max. Claim	Small Claims	Estate	Eviction	Domestic Relations
District Courts*	X	X	X	$0	No Max	$10000	X		X
Magistrate Courts*	X	X	X	$0	$10000	$10000		X	
Metropolitan Court of Bernalillo County*	X	X	X	$0	$10000	$10000			
Municipal Courts									
Probate Courts*							X		

Court	CRIMINAL				
	Felony	Misdemeanor	DWI/DUI	Preliminary Hearing	Juvenile
District Courts*	X				X
Magistrate Courts*		X	X	X	
Metropolitan Court of Bernalillo County*		X	X	X	
Municipal Courts		Petty	X		
Probate Courts*					

ADMINISTRATION Administrative Office of the Courts, 237 Don Gaspar, Rm 25, Santa Fe, NM, 87501; 505-827-4800, Fax: 505-827-4824. www.nmcourts.com/aoc.htm

COURT STRUCTURE The 30 District Courts in 13 districts are the courts of general jurisdiction. The Magistrate Courts handle civil cases up to $10,000, and are refered to as Small Claims. Also, the Bernalillo Metropolitan Court has jurisdiction in cases up to $10,000. Municipal Courts handle petty misdemeanors, DWI/DUI, traffic violations and other municipal ordinance violations.

ONLINE ACCESS The www.nmcourts.com web site offers free access to District and Magistrate Court case information, except Bernalillo Metro (see below). In general, records are available from June 1997 forward. The web site also offers a DWI Offender History tool for researching an individual's DWI history. Search by name or SSN. Supreme Court opinions may be researched at http://www.supremecourt.nm.org/.

A commercial online service is available for the Metropolitan Court of Bernalillo County. There is a $35.00 set up fee, a connect time fee based on usage. The system is available 24 hours a day. Call 505-345-6555 for more information.

ADDITIONAL INFORMATION There are some "shared" courts in New Mexico, with one county handling cases arising in another. Records are held at the location(s) indicated in the text.

PROBATE COURTS County Clerks handle "informal" (uncontested) probate cases, and the District Courts handle "formal" (contested) probate cases.

Bernalillo County

2nd Judicial District Court PO Box 488, Albuquerque, NM 87103; phone: 505-841-7425 (Administration); criminal phone: 505-841-7542; civil phone: 505-841-7451; criminal fax: 505-841-7463; civil fax: 505-841-7446; hours 8AM-5PM (MST). *Felony, Civil.*
www.seconddistrictcourt.com
Civil Records: Access: Mail, online, in person. Both court and visitors may perform in person searches. Search fee: $1.50 per name. Court makes copy: $.35 per page. Required to search: name, years to search. Civil cases indexed by defendant, plaintiff; on computer from 1984, prior on docket books/microfiche. Online access is free at www.nmcourts.com. Most data goes back to 6/1997. Mail turnaround time up to 10 days.
Criminal Records: Access: Mail, online, in person. Both court and visitors may perform in person searches. Search fee: $1.50 per name. Court makes copy: $.35 per page. Required to search: name, years to search; also helpful: DOB, SSN. Criminal records on computer from 1979, prior on docket books/microfiche. Online access to criminal records is free at www.nmcourts.com. Most data goes back to 6/1997. Mail turnaround time up to 10 days.
General Information: Public use terminal available. No sequestered or juvenile records released. Certification fee: $1.50. Payee: Clerk of the Court. Only cashiers checks and money orders accepted. Prepayment and SASE required.

Metropolitan Court 401 Lomas NW, Albuquerque, NM 87102; phone: 505-841-8151/841-8160; fax: 505-222-4800; hours 8AM-5PM (MST). *Misdemeanor, Civil Actions Under $10,000, Eviction, Small Claims.*
www.metrocourt.state.nm.us
Note: Records phone is 505-841-8240.
Civil Records: Access: Phone, fax, mail, online, in person. Both court and visitors may perform in person searches. No search fee. Court makes copy: $.50 per page. Computer printouts are $1.00 per page. Required to search: name, years to search. Civil cases indexed by defendant, plaintiff; on computer from 1987. Max. 5 years back except uncollected judgments which stay open 14 years from date of judgment. Access Metropolitan court civil records online at www.osogrande.com. There is set up fee plus a per minute charge based on usage. For information or to obtain an account call 505-345-6555. Also, search Metro Court civil case records free at www.metrocourt.state.nm.us. Mail turnaround time 3-5 days.
Criminal Records: Access: Phone, fax, mail, online, in person. Both court and visitors may perform in person searches. No search fee. Court makes copy: $.50 per page. Computer printout $1.00 per page. Required to search: name, SSN; also helpful: DOB. Criminal records on computer from 1983. Search Metro Court criminal case records free at www.metrocourt.state.nm.us/docket_help.htm. Mail turnaround time 3-5 days.
General Information: Public terminal goes back to 1987. No pre-sentence reports, psychological evaluations, confidential records released. Certification fee: $1.50. Payee: Metro Court. Personal checks or Visa, MC accepted. Prepayment and SASE required.

County Clerk #1 Civic Plaza NW, 6th Fl, Albuquerque, NM 87102; phone: 505-768-4247; fax: 505-768-5180; hours 8AM-4:30PM (MST). *Probate.*
www.bernco.gov/live/departments.asp?dept=2317

Catron County

7th Judicial District Court PO Drawer 1129, Socorro, NM 87801; phone: 505-835-0050 x10; fax: 505-838-5217; hours 8AM-4PM (MST). *Felony, Civil.*
Note: This court is also responsible for Socorro County.

Civil Records: Access: Phone, fax, mail, online, in person. Both court and visitors may perform in person searches. No search fee. Court makes copy: $.35 per page. Required to search: name, years to search. Civil cases indexed by defendant, plaintiff; on microfiche and hard copies from 1925; on computer back to 1997. Access to court records from 1997 forward is free at www.nmcourts.com. Mail turnaround time 1 day.
Criminal Records: Access: Phone, fax, mail, online, in person. Both court and visitors may perform in person searches. No search fee. Court makes copy: $.35 per page. Required to search: name, years to search, DOB; also helpful-SSN, signed release. Criminal records on microfiche and hard copies from 1925; on computer back to 1997. Online access to criminal records is free at www.nmcourts.com. Mail turnaround time 1 day.
General Information: Public use terminal available. No sequestered records released. Will fax documents to local or toll free line. Certification fee: $2.50 per cert. Payee: District Court Clerk. Business checks accepted. Prepayment and SASE required.

Quemado Magistrate Court PO Box 283, Quemado, NM 87829; phone: 505-773-4604; fax: 505-773-4688; hours 8AM-5PM (MST). *Misdemeanor, Civil Actions Under $10,000, Eviction, Small Claims.*
Civil Records: Access: Mail, fax, in person, online. Only the court performs in person searches. No search fee. Court makes copy: $.10 per page. Required to search: name, years to search; also helpful-DOB, SSN, address. Records computerized since 1997. Access to court records from 1997 forward is free at www.nmcourts.com. Mail turnaround time 1-2 weeks.
Criminal Records: Access: Mail, fax, in person, online. Only the court performs in person searches. No search fee. Court makes copy: $.10 per page. Required to search: name, years to search, DOB; also helpful: SSN. Records computerized since 1997. Online access to criminal records is free at www.nmcourts.com. Mail turnaround time 1-2 weeks.
General Information: No public access terminal. Fee to fax documents is $1.00 per page. Certification fee: $.50 per page includes copy fee. Payee: Magistrate Court. Prepayment required.

Reserve Magistrate Court PO Box 447, Reserve, NM 87830; phone: 505-533-6474; fax: 505-533-6623; hours 8AM-5PM (MST). *Misdemeanor, Civil Actions Under $10,000, Eviction, Small Claims.*
Civil Records: Access: Mail, fax, in person, online. Both court and visitors may perform in person searches. No search fee. Court makes copy: $.50 each; same fee for self serve. Required to search: name, years to search, address, other names used. Records computerized since 1996. Access to court records from 1997 forward is free at www.nmcourts.com. Mail turnaround 1 week.
Criminal Records: Access: Mail, fax, in person, online. Both court and visitors may perform in person searches. No search fee. Court makes copy: $.50 each; same fee for self serve. Required to search: name, years to search; also helpful: DOB, SSN. Records computerized since 1996. Online access to criminal records is free at www.nmcourts.com. Mail turnaround time 1 week.
General Information: Public terminal goes back to 1996. Will fax for $.50 per page. Certification fee: $1.00 per page includes copy fee. Payee: Magistrate Court. Prepayment required.

County Clerk PO Box 197, Reserve, NM 87830; phone: 505-533-6400; hours 8AM-4;30PM (MST). *Probate.*
Note: Local Probate Judge-505-533-6247, PO Box 663, Reserve NM, 87830 by appointment.

Chaves County

5th Judicial District Court Box 1776, Roswell, NM 88202; phone: 505-622-2212; criminal phone: x16, x17; civil phone: x18; fax: 505-624-9510; hours 8AM-N,1-5PM (MST). *Felony, Civil.*
www.fifthdistrictcourt.com
Civil Records: Access: Online, in person. Visitors must perform in person searches themselves. Court makes copy: $.35 per page; same fee for self serve. Required to search: name, years to search. Civil cases indexed by defendant, plaintiff; on computer from 1996, on microfiche and archived from 1891. Access to court records from 1997 forward is free at www.nmcourts.com.
Criminal Records: Access: Online, in person. Visitors must perform in person searches themselves. Court makes copy: $.35 per page; same fee for self serve. Required to search: name, years to search, DOB, aliases. Criminal records on computer from 1996, on microfiche and archived from 1891. Online access to criminal records is free at www.nmcourts.com.
General Information: Public terminal goes back to 1996. No sequestered records released. Will fax documents, sometimes. Certification fee: $1.50 per document. Payee: District Court Clerk. Only cashiers checks and money orders accepted. Prepayment required.

Magistrate Court 200 E 4th St, Roswell, NM 88201; phone: 505-624-6088; fax: 505-624-6092; hours 8AM-4PM M, T, Th, F; 9AM-4PM W (MST). *Misdemeanor, Civil Actions Under $10,000, Eviction, Small Claims.*
www.nmcourts.com
Civil Records: Access: Online, in person. Both court and visitors may perform in person searches. Court makes copy: $.50 per page. Access to court records from 1997 forward is free at www.nmcourts.com.
Criminal Records: Access: Online, in person. Both court and visitors may perform in person searches. Court makes copy: $.50 per page. Required to search: name, years to search, DOB; also helpful: SSN. Online access to criminal records is free at www.nmcourts.com.
General Information: Public terminal goes back to 1997. Prepayment required.

County Clerk Box 580, #1 St Mary's Pl #110, Roswell, NM 88202; phone: 505-624-6614; fax: 505-624-6523; hours 7AM-5PM (MST). *Probate.*

Cibola County

13th Judicial District Court Box 758, Grants, NM 87020; phone: 505-287-8831; criminal fax: 505-285-5755; same fax for civil/probate; hours 8AM-5PM (MST). *Felony, Civil, Probate.*
Civil Records: Access: Fax, mail, online, in person. Both court and visitors may perform in person searches. Search fee: $5.00 per name. Court makes copy: $.35 per page; same fee for self serve. Required to search: name, years to search. Civil cases indexed by defendant, plaintiff; on microfiche from 1981; prior to 1981 belong to Valencia County. Access to court records from 1997 forward is free at www.nmcourts.com. Mail turnaround 2-3 days.
Criminal Records: Access: Fax, mail, online, in person. Search fee: $5.00 per name. Court makes copy: $.35 per page; same fee for self serve. Required to search: name, years to search. Criminal records on microfiche from 1981. Online access to criminal records is free at www.nmcourts.com. Mail turnaround time 2-3 days.
General Information: No public access terminal. No sequestered records released. Will fax documents; unless a toll-free number provided, fee is $2.50 in-state; $5.00 out-of-state. Certification fee: $1.50 per page. Payee: District Court Clerk. Only cashier checks or money orders accepted. Prepayment required.

Magistrate Court 515 W High, Grants, NM 87020; phone: 505-285-4605; fax: 505-285-6485; hours 8AM-4PM (MST). *Misdemeanor, Civil Actions Under $10,000, Eviction, Small Claims.*
Civil Records: Access: Fax, mail, in person, online. Both court and visitors may perform in person searches. Court makes copy: $.50. Access to court records from 1997 forward free at www.nmcourts.com. Mail turnaround 1-2 weeks.
Criminal Records: Access: Fax, mail, in person, online. Only the court performs in person searches. No search fee. Court makes copy: $.50. Required to search: name, years to search. Online access to criminal records is free at www.nmcourts.com. Mail turnaround 2 weeks.
General Information: SASE required.

County Clerk PO Box 190, 515 W. High St, Grants, NM 87020; phone: 505-285-2552; fax: 505-285-2539; hours 8AM-5PM (MST). *Probate.*

Colfax County

8th Judicial District Court Box 160, Raton, NM 87740; phone: 505-445-5585; fax: 505-445-2626; hours 8AM-4PM (MST). *Felony, Civil.*
Civil Records: Access: Phone, mail, online, in person. Both court and visitors may perform in person searches. No search fee. Court makes copy: $.35 per page; same fee for self serve. Required to search: name, years to search. Civil cases indexed by defendant, plaintiff. Civil records archived from 1912. Access to court records from 1997 forward is free at www.nmcourts.com. Pleadings are unavailable. Mail turnaround time 1 week.
Criminal Records: Access: Phone, mail, online, in person. Both court and visitors may perform in person searches. No search fee. Court makes copy: $.35 per page; same fee for self serve. Required to search: name, years to search; also helpful: DOB, SSN. Criminal records archived from 1912; computerized records go back to 1996/97. Online access to criminal records is free at www.nmcourts.com. Pleadings are unavailable. Mail turnaround time 1 week.
General Information: Public terminal goes back to 1997. No adoption, mental, guardianship, children's cases records released. Fee to fax documents is $2.00 per page. Certification fee: $1.50. Payee: District Court. Business checks accepted. Prepayment and SASE required.

Cimarron Magistrate Court PO Drawer 367, Highway 21, Cimarron, NM 87714; phone: 505-376-2634; fax: 505-376-9108; hours 8:30AM-3PM alternating Weds only (MST). *Misdemeanor, Civil Actions Under $10,000, Eviction, Small Claims.*
Note: On days when this court is not in session, you may call the Springer Magistrate Court at 505-483-2417.
Civil Records: Access: In person, mail, online. Visitors must perform in person searches themselves. No search fee. No copy fee. Required to search: Name, years to search; also helpful: DOB. Records searchable from 3/97 on computer. Access to court records from 1997 forward is free at www.nmcourts.com. Mail turnaround 10 days.
Criminal Records: Access: In person, mail, online. Visitors must perform in person searches themselves. No search fee. No copy fee. Required to search: name, years to search; also helpful: DOB. Records searchable from 3/97 on computer, except DUI. Online access to criminal records is free at www.nmcourts.com. Mail turnaround 10 days.
General Information: No public access terminal. No certification fee .

Raton Magistrate Court PO Box 68, Raton, NM 87740; phone: 505-445-2220; fax: 505-445-8966; hours 8AM-N, 1-4PM (MST). *Misdemeanor, Civil Actions Under $10,000, Eviction, Small Claims.*
Civil Records: Access: Phone, mail, fax, in person, online. Only the court performs in person searches. No search fee. Court makes copy: $.50. Required to search: name, years to search; also helpful: DOB,

SSN. Records held for 14 years. Access to court records from 1997 forward is free at www.nmcourts.com. Mail turnaround time within 1 week.
Criminal Records: Access: Phone, mail, fax, in person, online. Only the court performs in person searches. No search fee. Court makes copy: $.50. Required to search: name, years to search; also helpful: DOB, SSN. Online access to criminal records is free at www.nmcourts.com. Mail turnaround time within 1 week.
General Information: No public access terminal. Prepayment required.

Springer Magistrate Court 300 Colbert Ave. PO Box 760, Springer, NM 87747; phone: 505-483-2417; fax: 505-483-0127; hours 8AM-4PM (MST). *Misdemeanor, Civil Actions Under $10,000, Eviction, Small Claims.*
Civil Records: Access: Online, in person. Both court and visitors may perform in person searches. No search fee. No copy fee. Required to search: name, years to search; also helpful: DOB. On computer back to 3/1997. Access to court records from 1997 forward is free at www.nmcourts.com.
Criminal Records: Access: Online, in person. Both court and visitors may perform in person searches. No copy fee. Required to search: name, years to search; also helpful: DOB, SSN. On computer back to 3/1997, DUI kept longer. Online access to criminal records is free at www.nmcourts.com.
General Information: No public access terminal. Certification fee: No charge.

County Clerk PO Box 159, 230 N 3rd St, Raton, NM 87740; phone: 505-445-5551; fax: 505-445-4031; hours 8AM-5PM (MST). *Probate.*

Curry County

9th Judicial District Court Curry County Courthouse, 700 N Main, #11, Clovis, NM 88101; phone: 505-762-9148; fax: 505-763-5160; hours 8AM-4PM (MST). *Felony, Civil.*
www.nmcourts9thjdc.com
Civil Records: Access: Online, in person. Visitors must perform in person searches themselves. Court makes copy: $.35 per page. Required to search: name, years to search, address. Civil cases indexed by defendant, plaintiff; on computer from 1997, on microfiche and archived from 1910. Access to court records from 1997 forward is free at www.nmcourts.com.
Criminal Records: Access: Online, in person. Visitors must perform in person searches themselves. Court makes copy: $.35 per page. Required to search: name, years to search; also helpful: SSN. Criminal records on computer from 1997, on microfiche and archived from 1910. Online access to criminal records is free at www.nmcourts.com.
General Information: Public terminal goes back to 1997. No adoptions, insanity, sequestered, neglect or abuse released. Certification fee: $1.50. Payee: 9th Judicial District Court. Only cashiers checks and money orders accepted. Prepayment required.

Magistrate Court 221 Pile, Clovis, NM 88101; phone: 505-762-3766; fax: 505-769-1437; hours 8AM-4PM (MST). *Misdemeanor, Civil Actions Under $10,000, Eviction, Small Claims.*
Civil Records: Access: Phone, mail, online, in person. Only the court performs in person searches. Court makes copy: $.50 per page. Access to court records from 1997 forward is free at www.nmcourts.com. Mail turnaround time 1 week.
Criminal Records: Access: Phone, mail, fax, online, in person. Only the court performs in person searches. No search fee. Court makes copy: $.50 per page. Required to search: name, years to search; also helpful: DOB, SSN. Online access to criminal records is free at www.nmcourts.com. Mail turnaround time 1 week.

General Information: No public access terminal. Certification fee: $.50 per page. Only cashiers checks and money orders accepted. Prepayment required.

De Baca County

10th Judicial District Court Box 910, Ft. Sumner, NM 88119; phone: 505-355-2896; fax: 505-355-2899; hours 8AM-4:30PM (MST). *Felony, Civil.*
Civil Records: Access: Phone, mail, online, in person. Only the court performs in person searches. No search fee. Court makes copy: $.35 per page; same fee for self serve. Required to search: name, years to search. Civil cases indexed by defendant, plaintiff; on index cards and docket books archived from 1917; on computer since 1997. Access to court records from 1997 forward is free at www.nmcourts.com. Mail turnaround time 2 days.
Criminal Records: Access: Phone, mail, online, in person. Only the court performs in person searches. No search fee. Court makes copy: $.35 per page; same fee for self serve. Required to search: name, years to search. Criminal records on index cards and docket books archived from 1917; on computer since 1997. Online access to criminal records is free at www.nmcourts.com. Mail turnaround time 2 days.
General Information: No public access terminal. No mental, adoptions, or juvenile released. Fee to fax documents is $1.00 per page. Certification fee: $1.50 per cert. Payee: District Court. Only cashiers checks and money orders accepted. Prepayment and SASE required.

Magistrate Court Box 24, Ft Sumner, NM 88119; phone: 505-355-7371; fax: 505-355-7149; hours 8AM-5PM (MST). *Misdemeanor, Civil Actions Under $10,000, Eviction, Small Claims.*
Civil Records: Access: In person, mail, online. Both court and visitors may perform in person searches. No search fee. Court makes copy: $.50 per page. Required to search: name, COB; SSN is helpful. Online records go back to 1997. Access to court records from 1997 forward is free at www.nmcourts.com. Mail turnaround 1 week.
Criminal Records: Access: In person, mail, online. Both court and visitors may perform in person searches. No search fee. Court makes copy: $1.00 per page. Required to search: name, years to search, DOB, SSN. Online records go back to 1997. Online access to criminal records is free at www.nmcourts.com. Mail turnaround time 1 week.
General Information: Public terminal goes back to 1997. Will fax documents. Prepayment required.

County Clerk 514 Ave C, PO Box 347, Ft. Sumner, NM 88119; phone: 505-355-2601; fax: 505-355-2441; hours 8AM-N, 1-4:30PM (MST). *Probate.*

Dona Ana County

3rd Judicial District Court 201 W Picacho, #A, Las Cruces, NM 88005; phone: 505-523-8200; fax: 505-523-8290; hours 8AM-N, 1-5PM (MST). *Felony, Civil.*
www.thirddistrictcourt.com/
Note: They also handle Domestic cases.
Civil Records: Access: Mail, online, in person. Both court and visitors may perform in person searches. Search fee: $1.50 per name. Court makes copy: $.35 per page; same fee for self serve. Required to search: name, years to search. Civil cases indexed by defendant, plaintiff; on computer from 1986 (clerk's index 1986 to 9/96), on microfiche and archived from 1912. Access to court records from 1997 forward is free at www.nmcourts.com. Mail turnaround time 2-3 days.
Criminal Records: Access: Mail, online, in person. Both court and visitors may perform in person searches. Search fee: $1.50 per name. Court makes copy: $.35 per page; same fee for self serve. Required to search: name, years to search; also helpful: DOB, SSN. Criminal records on computer from 1986 (clerk's index 1977 to 9/96), on microfiche and archived from 1912. Online access to criminal

records is free at www.nmcourts.com. Mail turnaround time 2-3 days.

General Information: Public terminal goes back to 9/1996. No adoption, mental health, or juvenile released. Certification fee: $1.50. Payee: 3rd Judicial District. Only cashiers checks and money orders accepted. Prepayment and SASE required.

Anthony Magistrate Court PO Box 1259, Anthony, NM 88021; phone: 505-233-3147; fax: 505-822-0113; hours 8AM-N, 1-5PM (MST). *Misdemeanor, Civil Actions Under $10,000, Eviction, Small Claims.*

Civil Records: Access: Online, mail, in person. Only the court performs in person searches. No search fee. Access to court records from 1997 forward is free at www.nmcourts.com.

Criminal Records: Access: Online, mail, in person. Only the court performs in person searches. No search fee. Required to search: name, years to search, DOB, SSN. Online access to criminal records is free at www.nmcourts.com.

General Information: No certification fee .

Hatch Magistrate Court PO Box 896, Hatch, NM 87937; phone: 505-267-5202; fax: 505-267-5088; hours 8:30AM-4PM Monday (MST). *Misdemeanor, Civil Actions Under $10,000, Eviction, Small Claims.*

Note: Note that this court is only open on Mondays.

Civil Records: Access: Mail, in person, online. Only the court performs in person searches. No search fee. Court makes copy: $.50 per page. Access to court records from 1997 forward is free at www.nmcourts.com. Mail turnaround time 1 week.

Criminal Records: Access: Mail, in person, online. Only the court performs in person searches. No search fee. Court makes copy: $.50 per page. Required to search: name, years to search, DOB, SSN. Online access to criminal records is free at www.nmcourts.com. Mail turnaround time 1 week.

General Information: No public access terminal. No certification fee . Payee: Magistrate Court. Only cashiers checks and money orders accepted. SASE required.

Las Cruces Magistrate Court 151 N Church, Las Cruces, NM 88001; phone: 505-524-2814; civil phone: 505-647-3816; fax: 505-525-2951; hours 8AM-4PM (MST). *Misdemeanor, Civil Actions Under $10,000, Eviction, Small Claims.*

Civil Records: Access: Fax, mail, in person, online. Both court and visitors may perform in person searches. No search fee. Court makes copy: $.50, if done by court $1.00. Self serve copy fee: $.50 per page. Access to court records from 1997 forward is free at www.nmcourts.com. Mail turnaround time same day.

Criminal Records: Access: Fax, mail, in person, online. Both court and visitors may perform in person searches. No search fee. Court makes copy: $1.00 per page. Self serve copy fee: $.50 per page. Required to search: name, years to search; also helpful: DOB, SSN. Online access to criminal records is free at www.nmcourts.com. Mail turnaround time same day.

General Information: Public use terminal available. No certification fee . Payee: Magistrate Court.

County Clerk c/o Third Judicial District, 201 W Picacho #A, Los Cruces, NM 88005; phone: 505-523-8200; fax: 505-523-8290; hours 8AM-N, 1-5PM (MST). *Probate.*

Eddy County

5th Judicial District Court 102 N Canal St #240, Carlsbad, NM 88220; phone: 505-885-4740; criminal phone: x20; civil phone: x23; fax: 505-887-7095; hours 8AM-N, 1-5PM (MST). *Felony, Civil.* www.fifthdistrictcourt.com

Civil Records: Access: In person, online. Visitors must perform in person searches themselves. Court makes copy: $.35 per page. Required to search: name, years to search. Civil cases indexed by defendant.

Civil records on computer from 1986, microfiche from 1891. Access to court records from 1997 forward is free at www.nmcourts.com/disclaim.html, or via the court website above.

Criminal Records: Access: In person, online. Visitors must perform in person searches themselves. No search fee. Court makes copy: $.35 per page. Required to search: name, years to search, SSN or DOB. Criminal records on computer from 1986, microfiche from 1900s. Online access to criminal records is free at www.nmcourts.com.

General Information: Public terminal goes back to 1997. No adoption, SS case w/children, or guardianship released. Will fax specific case file requests if urgent for $1.00 per page. Certification fee: $1.50 per pleading. Payee: District Court Clerk. Only cashiers checks, money orders and law firm checks only. Prepayment required.

Artesia Magistrate Court 109 N 15th St, Artesia, NM 88210; phone: 505-746-2481; fax: 505-746-6763; hours 8AM-4PM (MST). *Misdemeanor, Civil Actions Under $10,000, Eviction, Small Claims.*

Note: This court also handles preliminary felonies, traffic, and DUI cases.

Civil Records: Access: Phone, mail, online. Only the court performs in person searches. No search fee. Court makes copy: $.50. Records available from 1992, computerized since 1996. Access to court records from 1997 forward is free at www.nmcourts.com. Mail turnaround time 1-2 days.

Criminal Records: Access: Phone, mail, online. Only the court performs in person searches. No search fee. Court makes copy: $.50. Required to search: name, years to search; also helpful: DOB, SSN. Records computerized since 1996. Online access to criminal records is free at www.nmcourts.com. Mail turnaround time 1-2 days.

General Information: No public access terminal. Certification fee: $.50 per page. Prepayment required.

Carlsbad Magistrate Court 1949 S Canal St, Carlsbad, NM 88220; phone: 505-885-3218; fax: 505-887-3460; hours 8AM-4PM (MST). *Misdemeanor, Civil Actions Under $10,000, Eviction, Small Claims.*

Civil Records: Access: Phone, mail, fax, in person, online. Only the court performs in person searches. No search fee. Court makes copy: $.50 per page. Required to search: name, DOB, SSN, address, other names used. Records held 14 years, computerized since 1996. Access to court records from 1997 forward is free at www.nmcourts.com. Mail turnaround time 1-4 days.

Criminal Records: Access: Online, mail, in person. Visitors must perform in person searches themselves. No search fee. Court makes copy: $.50 per page. Required to search: name, years to search, DOB, SSN, other names used. Records held 3 years, computerized since 1996. Online access to criminal records is free at www.nmcourts.com. Mail turnaround time 1-5 days.

General Information: No public access terminal. Certification fee: $.50 per page.

County Clerk Eddy County Probate Judge, 101 W. Green #312, Carlsbad, NM 88220; phone: 505-885-3383; fax: 505-234-1793; hours 8AM-5PM (MST). *Probate.*

Grant County

6th Judicial District Court Box 2339, Silver City, NM 88062; phone: 505-538-3250; fax: 505-388-5439; hours 8AM-4PM M-F (MST). *Felony, Civil.*

Civil Records: Access: Fax, mail, online, in person. Both court and visitors may perform in person searches. No search fee. Court makes copy: $.35 per page. Required to search: name, years to search. Civil cases indexed by defendant, plaintiff; on microfiche from 1912-1987, on books from 1987; on computer

back to 1996. Access to court records from 1997 forward is free at www.nmcourts.com. Mail turnaround time 1-3 days.

Criminal Records: Access: Fax, mail, online, in person. Both court and visitors may perform in person searches. No search fee. Court makes copy: $.35 per page. Required to search: name, years to search. Criminal records on microfiche from 1912-1987, on books from 1987; on computer back to 1996. Online access to criminal records is free at www.nmcourts.com. Mail turnaround time 1-3 days.

General Information: Public use terminal available. No adoptions, guardianship or abuse records released. Fee to fax documents is $2.50 per page. Certification fee: $1.50. Payee: District Court Clerk. Only cashiers checks and money orders accepted. Prepayment and SASE required.

Bayard Magistrate Court PO Box 125, Bayard, NM 88023; phone: 505-537-3042; fax: 505-537-7365; hours 8AM-5PM (MST). *Misdemeanor, Civil Actions Under $10,000, Eviction, Small Claims.*

Civil Records: Access: Mail, fax, in person, online. Only the court performs in person searches. Court makes copy: $1.00. Civil records go back to 1992. Access to court records from 1997 forward is free at www.nmcourts.com. Mail turnaround time 10 days.

Criminal Records: Access: Mail, fax, in person, online. Only the court performs in person searches. No search fee. Court makes copy: $1.00. Required to search: name, years to search. Criminal records go back to 1999. Online access to criminal records is free at www.nmcourts.com. Mail turnaround time 10 days.

General Information: No public access terminal. Certification fee: $1.00. Prepayment required.

Silver City Magistrate Court 1620 E Pine St, Silver City, NM 88061; phone: 505-538-3811; fax: 505-538-8079; hours 8AM-5PM (MST). *Misdemeanor, Civil Actions Under $10,000, Eviction, Small Claims.*

Civil Records: Access: Mail, fax, in person, online. Only the court performs in person searches. Court makes copy: $.50 per page. Required to search: years to search, DOB, SSN. Records computerized since 1995. Access to court records from 1997 forward is free at www.nmcourts.com. Mail turnaround time 2 days.

Criminal Records: Access: Mail, fax, in person, online. Only the court performs in person searches. No search fee. Court makes copy: $.50 per page. Required to search: name, years to search, DOB; also helpful: SSN. Records held here from 1988, computerized since 6/16/95. Online access to criminal records is free at www.nmcourts.com. Mail turnaround time 2 days.

General Information: No public access terminal. Will fax for $1.00 per page. Payee: Magistrate Court. Prepayment required.

County Clerk P O Box 898, 1400 Hwy 180 E, Silver City, NM 88062; phone: 505-574-0042; fax: 505-574-0076; hours 8AM-5PM (MST). *Probate.*

Note: Access to court records from 1997 forward are free online at www.nmcourts.com/disclaim.html.

Guadalupe County

4th Judicial District Court 420 Parker Ave #5, Guadalupe County Courthouse, Santa Rosa, NM 88435; phone: 505-472-3888; fax: 505-472-4451; hours 8AM-N; 1PM-5PM (MST). *Felony, Civil.*

Civil Records: Access: Online, in person. Visitors must perform in person searches themselves. Court makes copy: $.35 per page; same fee for self serve. Required to search: name, years to search. Civil cases indexed by defendant, plaintiff; on docket books from 1912. Access to court records from 1997 forward is free at www.nmcourts.com.

Criminal Records: Access: Online, in person. Visitors must perform in person searches themselves. Court makes copy: $.35 per page; same

fee for self serve. Required to search: name, years to search, DOB; also helpful: SSN. Criminal records on docket books from 1912. Online access to criminal records is free at www.nmcourts.com.
General Information: Public terminal goes back to 1997. No adoption, insanity, juvenile, guardianship records released. Certification fee: $1.50. Payee: District Court Clerk Office. Only cashiers checks and money orders accepted. Prepayment required.

Santa Rosa Magistrate Court 603 Parker Ave, Santa Rosa, NM 88435; phone: 505-472-3237; fax: 505-472-3592; hours 8AM-4PM (MST). *Misdemeanor, Civil Actions Under $10,000, Eviction, Small Claims.*
Civil Records: Access: Online, mail, in person. Only the court performs in person searches. Court makes copy: $.50 per page. Access to court records from 1997 forward is free at www.nmcourts.com. Mail turnaround time 7 days.
Criminal Records: Access: Online, mail, in person. Only the court performs in person searches. No search fee. Court makes copy: $.50 per page. Required to search: name, years to search, DOB, offense, date of offense; also helpful: SSN. Online access to criminal records is free at www.nmcourts.com. Mail turnaround time 7 days.
General Information: No public access terminal. No certification fee . Prepayment and SASE required.

Vaughn Magistrate Court c/o Santa Rosa Justice Court, 603 Parker Av, Santa Rosa, NM 88435; phone: 505-584-2345; fax: 505-472-3592; hours 8AM-4PM (MST). *Misdemeanor, Civil Actions Under $10,000, Eviction, Small Claims.*
Note: The Vaughn court is only open the 2nd Wednesday of the month. It is located at 8th & Calle De Carill, Vaughn, NM 88353. Most records are at Santa Rosa (phone # given here).
Civil Records: Access: Mail, in person, online. Both court and visitors may perform in person searches. No search fee. Court makes copy: $.50 per page. Access to court records from 1997 forward is free at www.nmcourts.com. Mail turnaround time 7 days.
Criminal Records: Access: Mail, in person, online. Visitors must perform in person searches themselves. No search fee. Court makes copy: $.50 per page. Required to search: name, years to search. Online access to criminal records is free at www.nmcourts.com. Mail turnaround time 7 days.
General Information: No public access terminal. No certification fee . Prepayment and SASE required.

County Clerk 420 Parker Ave, #1,Courthouse, Santa Rosa, NM 88435; phone: 505-472-3791; fax: 505-472-4791; hours 8AM-N, 1-5PM (MST). *Probate.*

Harding County

10th Judicial District Court Box 1002, Mosquero, NM 87733; phone: 505-673-2252; fax: 505-673-0333; hours 9AM-3PM M-W,F (MST). *Felony, Civil.*
Civil Records: Access: Phone, fax, mail, online, in person. Only the court performs in person searches. No search fee. Court makes copy: $.35 per page; same fee for self serve. Required to search: name; also helpful: years to search. Civil cases indexed by defendant, plaintiff; on books from 1927. Computerized records go back to 1997. Access to court records from 1997 forward is free at www.nmcourts.com. Mail turnaround 1 week.
Criminal Records: Access: Phone, fax, mail, online, in person. Only the court performs in person searches. No search fee. Court makes copy: $.35 per page; same fee for self serve. Required to search: name, DOB, SSN; also helpful: years to search. Criminal records on books from 1927. Computerized records go back to 1997. Online access to criminal records is free at www.nmcourts.com. Mail turnaround time 1 week.
General Information: No public access terminal. No adoption records released. Will fax documents for $1.00 per page. Certification fee: $1.50. Payee:

District Court Clerk. Business checks accepted from attorneys only. No personal checks. Prepayment and SASE required.

Magistrate Court Box 9, Roy, NM 87743; phone: 505-485-2549; fax: 505-485-2407; hours 8AM-4PM (MST). *Misdemeanor, Civil Actions Under $10,000, Eviction, Small Claims.*
Civil Records: Access: Mail, phone, in person, online. Both court and visitors may perform in person searches. Court makes copy: $.50 per page. Required to search: name, DOB, years to search, other names used; also helpful-SSN, address. Records computerized since 1996. Access to court records from 1997 forward is free at www.nmcourts.com. Mail turnaround time 2 days.
Criminal Records: Access: Mail, phone, in person, online. Both court and visitors may perform in person searches. No search fee. Court makes copy: $.50 per page. Required to search: name, years to search, DOB; also helpful: address, SSN. Records computerized since 1996. Online access to criminal records is free at www.nmcourts.com. Mail turnaround time 2 days.
General Information: Public terminal goes back to 1997. Will fax documents. Payee: Magistrate Court. Prepayment required.

County Clerk County Clerk, Box 1002, 35 Pine St, Mosquero, NM 87733; phone: 505-673-2301; fax: 505-673-2922; hours 8AM-4PM (MST). *Probate.*

Hidalgo County

6th Judicial District Court PO Box 608, Lordsburg, NM 88045; phone: 505-542-3411; fax: 505-542-3481; hours 8AM-N, 1-5PM (MST). *Felony, Civil.*
Civil Records: Access: Phone, fax, mail, online, in person. Only the court performs in person searches. No search fee. Court makes copy: $.35 per page. Required to search: name, years to search. Civil cases indexed by defendant, plaintiff; on microfiche and archived from 1920. Access to court records from 1997 forward is free at www.nmcourts.com. Mail turnaround 3-5 days.
Criminal Records: Access: Phone, fax, mail, online, in person. Only the court performs in person searches. No search fee. Court makes copy: $.35 per page. Required to search: name, years to search; also helpful: alias. Criminal records on microfiche and archived from 1920. Online access to criminal records is free at www.nmcourts.com. Mail turnaround time 3-5 days.
General Information: No public access terminal. No juvenile or adoption records released. Fee to fax documents is $5.00 per document; will only fax documents to toll-free numbers. Certification fee: $1.50. Payee: District Court Clerk. Business checks accepted. No personal checks accepted. Prepayment and SASE required.

Magistrate Court 420 Wabash Ave, Lordsburg, NM 88045; phone: 505-542-3582; criminal phone: 505-542-3596; hours 8AM-5PM (MST). *Misdemeanor, Civil Actions Under $10,000, Eviction, Small Claims.*
www.nmcourts.com
Civil Records: Access: Online, mail, in person. Only the court performs in person searches. No search fee. Court makes copy: $.50. Access to court records from 1997 forward is free at www.nmcourts.com. Mail turnaround 1 week.
Criminal Records: Access: Mail, in person, fax, online. Only the court performs in person searches. No search fee. Court makes copy: $.50. Required to search: name, years to search; also helpful: DOB, SSN. Online access to criminal records is free at www.nmcourts.com. Mail turnaround time 1 week.
General Information: No public access terminal. Fee to fax document is $1.00 per page. No certification fee . Payee: Magistrate Court. Only cashiers checks and money orders accepted. Prepayment and SASE required.

County Clerk 300 S Shakespeare, Lordsburg, NM 88045; phone: 505-542-9213; fax: 505-542-3193; hours 8AM-5PM (MST). *Probate.*

Lea County

5th Judicial District Court 100 N. Main, #6-C, Lovington, NM 88260; phone: 505-396-8571; fax: 505-396-2428; hours 8AM-5PM (MST). *Felony, Civil.*
www.fifthdistrictcourt.com
Civil Records: Access: Online, in person. Both court and visitors may perform in person searches. No search fee. Court makes copy: $.35 per page; same fee for self serve. Required to search: name, years to search. Civil cases indexed by defendant, plaintiff; on computer from 1990, on microfiche from 1912. Access to court records from 1997 forward is free at www.nmcourts.com. Mail turnaround time 1-3 days.
Criminal Records: Access: Online, in person. Both court and visitors may perform in person searches. No search fee. Court makes copy: $.35 per page; same fee for self serve. Required to search: name, years to search. Criminal records on computer from 1997, on microfiche from 1912. Online access to criminal records is free at www.nmcourts.com.
General Information: Public terminal goes back to 1990. No adoptions, mental, abuse records released. Certification fee: $1.50 per cert. Payee: District Court Clerk. Only cashiers checks and money orders accepted. Prepayment required.

Eunice Magistrate Court PO Box 240, Eunice, NM 88231; phone: 505-394-3368; fax: 505-394-3335; hours 8AM-4PM M,W,F (MST). *Misdemeanor, Civil Actions Under $10,000, Eviction, Small Claims.*
Civil Records: Access: Online, mail, in person. Only the court performs in person searches. No search fee. Court makes copy: $1.00. Access to court records from 1997 forward is free at www.nmcourts.com. Mail turnaround time 3 days.
Criminal Records: Access: Online, mail, in person. Only the court performs in person searches. No search fee. Court makes copy: $1.00. Required to search: name, years to search, DOB; also helpful: SSN. Online access to criminal records is free at www.nmcourts.com. Mail turnaround time 3 days.
General Information: No public access terminal. Certification fee: $.50 per page. Payee: Magistrate Court. Business checks accepted. SASE required.

Hobbs Magistrate Court 2110 N Alto Dr, Hobbs, NM 88240-3455; phone: 505-397-3621; fax: 505-393-9121; hours 8AM-4PM (MST). *Misdemeanor, Civil Actions Under $10,000, Eviction, Small Claims.*
www.nmcourts.com
Civil Records: Access: Online, mail, in person. Only the court performs in person searches. Court makes copy: none; same fee for self serve. Required to search: name, years to search, signed release, address, other names used; DOB, SSN helpful. Civil records held 14 years, computerized since early 2002. Access to court records from 1997 forward is free at www.nmcourts.com. Mail turnaround time 7 days for mail; 3 days for fax.
Criminal Records: Access: Online, mail, in person. Only the court performs in person searches. No search fee. Court makes copy: $.50 per page; same fee for self serve. Required to search: name, years to search, DOB; SSN and signed release helpful. Criminal records held 1 year after disposition; computerized since early 2002. Online access to criminal records is free at www.nmcourts.com. Mail turnaround 3-5 days.
General Information: No public access terminal. Will fax documents to local or toll free line. No certification fee Certification included in copy fee. Prepayment required.

Jal Magistrate Court PO Box 507, Jal, NM 88252; phone: 505-395-2740; fax: 505-395-2595; hours 8-4pm T,Th (MST). *Misdemeanor, Civil Actions Under $10,000, Eviction, Small Claims.*
Note: All record requests must be in writing.
Civil Records: Access: Mail, in person, online. Only the court performs in person searches. No search fee. Court makes copy: $.50. Access to court records from 1997 forward is free at www.nmcourts.com. Mail turnaround time 3 days.
Criminal Records: Access: Mail, in person, online. Only the court performs in person searches. No search fee. Court makes copy: $.50. Required to search: name, years to search, DOB; also helpful: SSN. Online access to criminal records is free at www.nmcourts.com. Mail turnaround time 3 days.
General Information: No public access terminal. Will fax documents for $1.00 per page. Certification fee: $.50 per page. SASE required.

Lovington Magistrate Court 100 W Central, #D, Lovington, NM 88260; phone: 505-396-6677; fax: 505-396-6163; hours 8AM-4PM (MST). *Misdemeanor, Civil Actions Under $10,000, Eviction, Small Claims.*
www.nmcourts.com
Civil Records: Access: Phone, fax, mail, in person, online. Both court and visitors may perform in person searches. No search fee. Court makes copy: $.50. Required to search: name, years to search. Access to court records from 1997 forward is free at www.nmcourts.com. Mail turnaround 3 days.
Criminal Records: Access: Phone, fax, mail, in person, online. Both court and visitors may perform in person searches. No search fee. Court makes copy: $.50. Required to search: name, years to search, DOB. Online access to criminal records is free at www.nmcourts.com. Mail turnaround time 3 days.
General Information: Public use terminal available. Will fax documents per arrangement. Certification fee: $.50 per page. Payee: Magistrate Court. Business checks accepted. Prepayment and SASE required.

Tatum Magistrate Court PO Box 918, Tatum, NM 88267; phone: 505-398-5300; fax: 505-398-5310; hours 8AM-4PM (MST). *Misdemeanor, Civil Actions Under $10,000, Eviction, Small Claims.*
Civil Records: Access: Phone, mail, fax, in person, online. Both court and visitors may perform in person searches. No search fee. Court makes copy: $.50 per page. Required to search: name, signed release, address, other names used. Civil records indexed by case number. Access to court records from 1997 forward is free at www.nmcourts.com. Mail turnaround time 5 days.
Criminal Records: Access: Phone, mail, fax, in person, online. Both court and visitors may perform in person searches. No search fee. Court makes copy: $.50 per page. Required to search: name, years to search, DOB, SSN, signed release; also helpful: address. Criminal records go back to 1996. All DWI case are on file forever. Online access to criminal records is free at www.nmcourts.com. Note: Phone access only on cases with final disposition. Mail turnaround time 5 days.
General Information: No public access terminal. Certification fee: $2.00 per document. Payee: Magistrate Court. Prepayment and SASE required.

County Clerk Box 1507, 100 N Main St, Lovington, NM 88260; phone: 505-396-8668; fax: 505-396-3293; hours 8AM-5PM (MST). *Probate.*
www.leacounty-nm.net

Lincoln County

12th Judicial District Court Box 725, Carrizozo, NM 88301; phone: 505-648-2432; fax: 505-648-2581; hours 8AM-5PM (MST). *Felony, Civil.*
www.12thdistrict.net
Civil Records: Access: Online, mail, in person. Both court and visitors may perform in person searches. No search fee. Court makes copy: $.35 per page. Required to search: name, years to search. Civil cases indexed by defendant, plaintiff; on computer from

1991, docket books from 1960, microfiche to 1960. Access to court records from 1997 forward is free at www.nmcourts.com.
Criminal Records: Access: Online, in person. Both court and visitors may perform in person searches. Court makes copy: $.35 per page. Required to search: name, years to search. Criminal records on computer from 1991, docket books from 1960, microfiche to 1960. Online access to criminal records is free at www.nmcourts.com.
General Information: No juvenile, adoption, or mental records released. Will fax documents to toll free number. Certification fee: $1.50 per stamp. Payee: District Court Clerk. Business checks accepted. Prepayment required.

Carrizozo Magistrate Court 310 11th St, Carrizozo, NM 88301; phone: 505-648-2380; civil phone: 505-378-7022; fax: 505-648-2695; hours 8AM-Noon; 1-4PM (MST). *Misdemeanor, Civil Actions Under $10,000, Eviction, Small Claims.*
Civil Records: Access: Mail, in person, online. Both court and visitors may perform in person searches. No search fee. Court makes copy: $.50 per page. Access to court records from 1997 forward is free at www.nmcourts.com. Mail turnaround time 3 days.
Criminal Records: Access: Fax, in person, mail, online. Visitors must perform in person searches themselves. Search fee: $7.00 per name, if more than 1 name. Court makes copy: $.50 per page. Required to search: name, years to search; also helpful: DOB, SSN. Online access to criminal records for past 10 years is free at www.nmcourts.com. Mail turnaround time 3 days.
General Information: No public access terminal. No certification fee . Payee: Magistrate Court. SASE required.

Ruidoso Magistrate Court 301 W Highway 70 #2, Ruidoso, NM 88345; phone: 505-378-7022; fax: 505-378-8508; hours 8AM-4PM (MST). *Misdemeanor, Civil Actions Under $10,000, Eviction, Small Claims.*
Civil Records: Access: Online, mail, in person. Both court and visitors may perform in person searches. No search fee. Court makes copy: $.50 per page. Access to court records from 1997 forward is free at www.nmcourts.com. Mail turnaround time 3 days.
Criminal Records: Access: Online, mail, in person. Visitors must perform in person searches themselves. Court makes copy: $.50 per page. Required to search: name, years to search; also helpful: DOB, SSN. Online access to criminal records is free at www.nmcourts.com. Mail turnaround time 3 days.
General Information: No certification fee . Payee: Magistrate Court.

County Clerk PO Box 338, Carrizozo, NM 88301; phone: 505-648-2394; fax: 505-648-2576; hours 8AM-5PM (MST). *Probate.*
Note: This court will do searches.

Los Alamos County

1st Judicial District Court c/o Santa Fe 1st District Court, PO Box 2268, Santa Fe, NM 87504.
http://firstdistrictcourt.com
Note: All civil and criminal cases handled by Santa Fe District Court.

Magistrate Court 1319 Trinity Dr, Los Alamos, NM 87544; phone: 505-662-2727; criminal fax: 505-661-6258; same fax for civil/probate; hours 8AM-4PM (MST). *Misdemeanor, Civil Actions Under $10,000, Eviction, Small Claims.*
Civil Records: Access: Online, in person. Only the court performs in person searches. No search fee. Court makes copy: $.50 per page. Required to search: name, years to search, address, other names used, signed release. 1997 records forward are on database. Access to court records from 1997 forward is free at www.nmcourts.com.

Criminal Records: Access: Online, in person. Only the court performs in person searches. Court makes copy: $.50 per page. Required to search: name, years to search, address, DOB, signed release; also helpful: SSN. Normally destroyed after 1 years from closure; except DWIs. Online access to criminal records is free at www.nmcourts.com.
General Information: No public access terminal. Will fax documents for $1.00 per page.

County Clerk-Probate PO Box 30, 2300 Trinity Dr, Rm 100, Los Alamos, NM 87544; phone: 505-662-8010; fax: 505-662-8008; hours 8AM-5PM (MST). *Probate.*

Luna County

6th Judicial District Court Luna County Courthouse, Rm 40, Deming, NM 88030; phone: 505-546-9611; fax: 505-546-0971; hours 8AM-4PM (MST). *Felony, Civil.*
www.nmcourts.com
Civil Records: Access: Mail, online, in person. Both court and visitors may perform in person searches. Court makes copy: $.35 per page; same fee for self serve. Required to search: name, years to search. Civil cases indexed by defendant, plaintiff; on microfiche from 1911; on computer back to 1997. Access to court records from 1997 forward is free at www.nmcourts.com. Mail turnaround time 5 days.
Criminal Records: Access: Mail, online, in person. Both court and visitors may perform in person searches. Court makes copy: $.35 per page; same fee for self serve. Required to search: name, years to search. Criminal records on microfiche from 1911; on computer back to 1997. Online access to criminal records is free at www.nmcourts.com. Mail turnaround time 5 days.
General Information: Public terminal goes back to 1987. No adoptions, mental, sequestered or juvenile records released. Will fax documents for $.35 per page. Certification fee: $1.50 per document. Payee: District Court Clerk. Only cashiers checks and money orders accepted. Prepayment and SASE required.

Magistrate Court 912 S Silver St, Deming, NM 88030; phone: 505-546-9321; fax: 505-546-4896; hours 8AM-N, 1-5PM (MST). *Misdemeanor, Civil Actions Under $10,000, Eviction, Small Claims.*
www.nmcourts.com
Civil Records: Access: Mail, in person, online. Only the court performs in person searches. No search fee. Court makes copy: $.50 per page includes certification. Access to court records from 1997 forward is free at www.nmcourts.com. Mail turnaround time 2-3 days.
Criminal Records: Access: Mail, in person, online. Only the court performs in person searches. No search fee. Court makes copy: $.50 per page includes certification. Required to search: name, years to search. Online access to criminal records is free at www.nmcourts.com. Mail turnaround time 2-3 days.
General Information: No public access terminal. Will fax documents for $1.00 per page. No certification fee . Payee: Luna Magistrate Court. Prepayment and SASE required.

County Clerk PO Box 1838, 110 N Gold, Deming, NM 88031; phone: 505-546-0491; fax: 505-544-4187; hours 8AM-5PM (MST). *Probate.*
Note: There can be some probate cases (those in dispute) at the District Court level.

McKinley County

11th Judicial District Court 201 W. Hill, Rm 4, Gallup, NM 87301; phone: 505-863-6816; fax: 505-722-3401; hours 8AM-N, 1-5PM (MST). *Felony, Civil.*
Civil Records: Access: Phone, mail, online, in person. Both court and visitors may perform in person searches. No search fee. Court makes copy: $.35 per page; same fee for self serve. Required to search: name, years to search. Civil cases indexed by defendant, plaintiff; on computer from 1989, on

microfiche from 1923. Access to court records from 1997 forward is free at www.nmcourts.com. One name only by phone. Mail turnaround 3-5 days.

Criminal Records: Access: Phone, mail, online, in person. Both court and visitors may perform in person searches. No search fee. Court makes copy: $.35 per page; same fee for self serve. Required to search: name, years to search, DOB; also helpful: SSN. Criminal records on computer from 1989, on microfiche from 1923. Online access to criminal records is free at www.nmcourts.com. Note: Will search one name only by phone. Mail turnaround time 3-5 days.

General Information: Public terminal goes back to 1988. No adoption or juvenile records released. Fee to fax documents is $5.00 per call. Certification fee: $1.50. Payee: McKinley County District Court. No personal checks accepted. Prepayment and SASE required.

Magistrate Court 285 Boardman Dr, Gallup, NM 87301; phone: 505-722-6636; fax: 505-863-3510; hours 8AM-4PM (MST). *Misdemeanor, Civil Actions Under $10,000, Eviction, Small Claims.*
Note: Felony preliminary hearings held here.
Civil Records: Access: Online, in person. Only the court performs in person searches. Court makes copy: $.50 per page. Access to court records from 1997 forward is free at www.nmcourts.com.
Criminal Records: Access: Online, in person. Only the court performs in person searches. Court makes copy: $.50 per page. Required to search: name, years to search, DOB; also helpful: SSN. Online access to criminal records is free at www.nmcourts.com.
General Information: No public access terminal. No certification fee . Prepayment required.

Thoreau Magistrate Court PO Box 37, Thoreau, NM 87323; phone: 505-862-7871; hours 8:30AM-4PM Once a month on a Friday (MST). *Misdemeanor, Civil Actions Under $10,000, Eviction, Small Claims.*
Note: Note this court is open once a month on a Friday. Call the clerk anytime at 505-772-6636 x1008; ask for Deloria.
Civil Records: Access: Mail, in person, online. Only the court performs in person searches. Access to records from 1997 forward free at www.nmcourts.com. Mail turnaround 1-2 weeks.
Criminal Records: Access: Mail, in person, online. Only the court performs in person searches. No search fee. Required to search: name, years to search, DOB; also helpful: SSN. Online access to criminal records is free at www.nmcourts.com. Mail turnaround 1-2 weeks.
General Information: No public access terminal. Prepayment required.

County Clerk PO Box 1268, Gallup, NM 87305; phone: 505-863-6866; fax: 505-863-1419; hours 8AM-5PM (MST). *Probate.*

Mora County

4th Judicial District Court PO Box 1540, Las Vegas, NM 87701; phone: 505-425-7281; criminal phone: x25; civil phone: x25; fax: 505-454-8611; hours 8AM-N, 1-4PM (MST). *Felony, Civil.*
Note: Mora District Court records maintained in Las Vegas.
Civil Records: Access: Online, in person. Only the court performs in person searches. No search fee. Court makes copy: $.35 per page; same fee for self serve. Required to search: name, years to search. Civil cases indexed by defendant, plaintiff; on microfiche from 1912, archived before 1912. Access to court records from 1997 to present free at www.nmcourts.com.
Criminal Records: Access: Online, in person, fax. Both court and visitors may perform in person searches. No search fee. Court makes copy: $.35 per page; same fee for self serve. Required to search: name, years to search, DOB or SSN. Criminal records on microfiche from 1912, archived before 1912. Online access to criminal records 1997 to present free at www.nmcourts.com.

General Information: No public access terminal. No adoptions, insanity, guardianship, abuse, neglect or juvenile records released. Will fax documents for $1.00 per page to local or toll-free number, $2.00 per page long distance. Certification fee: $1.50 per seal. Payee: 4th Judicial District Court. Only cashiers checks and money orders accepted. Prepayment required.

Magistrate Court PO Box 131, Mora, NM 87732; phone: 505-387-2937 x3; hours 8AM-4PM (MST). *Misdemeanor, Civil Actions Under $10,000, Eviction, Small Claims.*
Civil Records: Access: Online, in person. Both court and visitors may perform in person searches. No search fee. Court makes copy: $.50 per page. Access to court records from 1997 forward is free at www.nmcourts.com.
Criminal Records: Access: Online, in person. Both court and visitors may perform in person searches. Court makes copy: $.50 per page. Required to search: name, years to search. Online access to criminal records is free at www.nmcourts.com.
General Information: No public access terminal. No certification fee . Payee: Magistrate Court. Only cashiers checks and money orders accepted. Prepayment required.

Probate Court PO Box 580, Mora, NM 87732; phone: 505-387-5014; hours 8AM-5PM Mon (MST). *Probate.*

Otero County

12th Judicial District Court 1000 New York Ave, Rm 209, Alamogordo, NM 88310-6940; phone: 505-437-7310; fax: 505-434-8886; hours 8AM-5PM (MST). *Felony, Civil.*
www.12thdistrict.net
Civil Records: Access: Online, mail, in person. Visitors must perform in person searches themselves. Court makes copy: $.35 per page; same fee for self serve. Required to search: name, years to search. Civil cases indexed by defendant, plaintiff; on computer from 1991, on microfiche from 1926. Access to court records from 1997 forward is free at www.nmcourts.com. Also, current court dockets are at the court website. Note: Phone & mail access limited to 5 names each.
Criminal Records: Access: Online, mail, in person. Visitors must perform in person searches themselves. Court makes copy: $.35 per page; same fee for self serve. Required to search: name, years to search. Criminal records on computer from 1991, on microfiche from 1926. Online access to criminal records is free at www.nmcourts.com. Note: Phone & mail access limited to 5 names each. Only court performs searches prior to March 1986.
General Information: Public use terminal available. No sealed, adoption records released. Certification fee: $1.50. Payee: District Court. Only cashiers checks, cash and money orders accepted. Prepayment required.

Magistrate Court 263 Robert H Bradley Dr, Alamogordo, NM 88310-8288; phone: 505-437-9000 x256; fax: 505-439-1365; hours 8AM-4PM (MST). *Misdemeanor, Civil Actions Under $10,000, Eviction, Small Claims.*
Civil Records: Access: Online, mail, in person. Only the court performs in person searches. No search fee. Court makes copy: $.50 per page. Records placed in storage after one year. Access to court records from 1997 forward is free at www.nmcourts.com. Mail turnaround 1-2 weeks.
Criminal Records: Access: Online, mail, in person. Only the court performs in person searches. No search fee. Court makes copy: $.50 per page. Required to search: name, years to search, DOB; also helpful: SSN. Records placed in storage after one year. Online access to criminal records is free at www.nmcourts.com. Mail turnaround time 1-2 weeks.
General Information: No public access terminal. Will fax documents for $1.00 per page. Certification

fee: $1.00 per page. Payee: Magistrate Court. Prepayment and SASE required.

County Clerk 1000 New York Ave, Rm 108, Alamogordo, NM 88310-6932; phone: 505-437-4942; fax: 505-443-2922; hours 7:30AM-6PM (MST). *Probate.*

Quay County

10th Judicial District Court Box 1067, Tucumcari, NM 88401; phone: 505-461-2764; fax: 505-461-4498; hours 8AM-5PM (MST). *Felony, Civil.*
Civil Records: Access: Phone, fax, mail, online, in person. Both court and visitors may perform in person searches. No search fee. Court makes copy: $.35 per page; same fee for self serve. Required to search: name, years to search. Civil cases indexed by defendant, plaintiff; on hard copy file from 1995 to present, microfiche 1912 to 1994, archived from 1911, on computer back to 1997. Access to court records from 1997 forward is free at www.nmcourts.com. Mail turnaround time same day.
Criminal Records: Access: Phone, fax, mail, online, in person. Both court and visitors may perform in person searches. No search fee. Court makes copy: $.35 per page; same fee for self serve. Required to search: name; also helpful: years to search, DOB, SSN. Criminal records on hard copy file from 1995 to present, microfiche 1912 to 1994, archived from 1911, on computer back to 1997. Online access to criminal records is free at www.nmcourts.com. Mail turnaround time same day.
General Information: Public terminal goes back to 1912. No adoptions, juvenile, insanity records released. Will fax documents $2.00 1st page, $1.00 each add'l. Certification fee: $1.50. Payee: District Court Clerk. Only cashiers checks and money orders accepted. Prepayment and SASE required.

Tucumcari Magistrate Court PO Box 1301, Tucumcari, NM 88401; phone: 505-461-1700; fax: 505-461-4522; hours 8AM-4PM; 9AM-5PM Tues (MST). *Misdemeanor, Civil Actions Under $10,000, Eviction, Small Claims.*
Note: San Jon Magistrate Court (closed) records are found here.
Civil Records: Access: Online, in person. Only the court performs in person searches. Court makes copy: $.50 per page. Access to court records from 1997 forward is free at www.nmcourts.com.
Criminal Records: Access: Online, in person. Only the court performs in person searches. Court makes copy: $.50 per page. Required to search: name, years to search, DOB, SSN. Online access to criminal records is free at www.nmcourts.com.
General Information: No public access terminal.

County Clerk 300 S 3rd St, PO Box 1225, Tucumcari, NM 88401; phone: 505-461-0510; fax: 505-461-0513; hours 8AM-N, 1-5PM (MST). *Probate.*

Rio Arriba County

1st Judicial District Court c/o Santa Fe 1st District Court, PO Box 2268, Santa Fe, NM 87504; phone: 505-476-0189; fax: 505-827-5055; hours 8AM-4PM (MST). *Felony, Misdemeanor, Probate.*
http://firstdistrictcourt.com
Note: Most all major civil and criminal cases are handled by Santa Fe District Court.

Rio Arriba Magistrate Court - Division 1 PO Box 538, 1332 Hwy 17, Chama, NM 87520; phone: 505-756-2278; fax: 505-756-2477; hours 8AM-N, 1-5PM (MST). *Misdemeanor, Civil Actions Under $10,000, Eviction, Small Claims.*
Civil Records: Access: Mail, fax, in person, online. Both court and visitors may perform in person searches. No search fee. Court makes copy: $.50 per page. Required to search: name, years to search. On computer back to 1997. Access to court records from 1997 forward is free at www.nmcourts.com. Mail turnaround time 1 week.

Criminal Records: Access: Mail, fax, in person, online. Only the court performs in person searches. No search fee. Court makes copy: $.50 per page. Required to search: name, years to search. On computer back to 1997. Online access to criminal records is free at www.nmcourts.com. Mail turnaround time 1 week.

General Information: No public access terminal. No certification fee .

Rio Arriba Magistrate Court - Division 2
410 Paseo de Onate, Espanola, NM 87532; phone: 505-753-2532; fax: 505-753-4802; hours 8AM-4PM (MST). *Misdemeanor, Civil Actions Under $10,000, Eviction, Small Claims.*

Civil Records: Access: Mail, in person, online. Only the court performs in person searches. Court makes copy: $.50 per page; same fee for self serve. Access to court records from 1997 forward is free at www.nmcourts.com. Mail turnaround time 3 days.

Criminal Records: Access: Mail, in person, online. Only the court performs in person searches. No search fee. Court makes copy: $.50 per page. Required to search: name, years to search. Online access to criminal records is free at www.nmcourts.com. Mail turnaround within 1 week.

General Information: No public access terminal.

County Clerk PO Box 158, 7 Main St, Tierra Amarilla, NM 87575; phone: 505-588-7724; fax: 505-588-7418; hours 8AM-5PM (MST). *Probate.*
Note: Access to court records are free online at www.nmcourts.com/disclaim.html.

Roosevelt County

9th Judicial District Court
109 W 1st St, #207, Portales, NM 88130; phone: 505-356-4463; fax: 505-359-2140; hours 8AM-4PM (MST). *Felony, Civil.*
www.nmcourts9thjdc.com

Civil Records: Access: Online, in person. Visitors must perform in person searches themselves. Court makes copy: $.35 per page; same fee for self serve. Required to search: name, years to search. Civil cases indexed by defendant, plaintiff; on microfiche from 1912, archived before 1912. Access to court records from 1997 forward is free at www.nmcourts.com.

Criminal Records: Access: Online, in person. Visitors must perform in person searches themselves. Court makes copy: $.35 per page; same fee for self serve. Required to search: name, years to search. Criminal records on microfiche from 1912, archived before 1912. Online access to criminal records is free at www.nmcourts.com.

General Information: No public access terminal. No adoption, guardianship, insanity records released. Certification fee: $1.50. Payee: 9th Judicial District Court. Only cashiers checks and money orders accepted. Prepayment required.

Magistrate Court
42427 US Hwy 70, Portales, NM 88130; phone: 505-356-8569; fax: 505-359-6883; hours 8AM-4PM (MST). *Misdemeanor, Civil Actions Under $10,000, Eviction, Small Claims, Felonies.*
www.nmcourts.com

Civil Records: Access: Phone, mail, fax, in person, online. Only the court performs in person searches. Court makes copy: $.50 per page; same fee for self serve. Records computerized since 1995. Access to court records from 1997 forward is free at www.nmcourts.com. Mail turnaround time 5 days.

Criminal Records: Access: Phone, mail, fax, in person, online. Only the court performs in person searches. No search fee. Court makes copy: $.50 per page; same fee for self serve. Required to search: name, DOB; also helpful: SSN. Records computerized since 1995. Online access to criminal records is free at www.nmcourts.com. Mail turnaround time 5 days.

General Information: No public access terminal. Will fax documents $1.00 per page. Certification fee: $1.00. Prepayment required.

County Clerk Roosevelt County Courthouse, 109 W 1st, Portales, NM 88130; phone: 505-356-8562; fax: 505-356-3560; hours 8AM-5PM (MST). *Probate.*

San Juan County

11th Judicial District Court
103 S Oliver, Aztec, NM 87410; phone: 505-334-6151; fax: 505-334-1940; hours 8AM-N, 1-5PM (MST). *Felony, Civil.*

Civil Records: Access: Online, in person. Visitors must perform in person searches themselves. Court makes copy: $.35 per page; same fee for self serve. Required to search: name, years to search; also helpful: address. Civil cases indexed by defendant, plaintiff; on computer from 1986, on microfiche from 1925; cardfile from 1912. Access to court records from 1997 forward is free at www.nmcourts.com.

Criminal Records: Access: Online, in person, mail, fax. Both court and visitors may perform in person searches. Court makes copy: $.35 per page; same fee for self serve. Required to search: name, years to search, DOB; also helpful: address, SSN. Criminal records on computer from 1986, on microfiche from 1925; cardfile from 1912. Online access to criminal records is free at www.nmcourts.com. Court will not perform search before 1986. Mail turnaround time 3 days.

General Information: Public use terminal available. No adoptions, insanity, sealed, expunged records released. Will fax documents for $.35 per page. Certification fee: $1.50 per page. Payee: Eleventh District Court. No personal or out-of-state checks accepted. Prepayment and SASE required.

Aztec Magistrate Court
200 Gossett, Aztec, NM 87410; phone: 505-334-9479; fax: 505-334-2178; hours 8AM-4PM (MST). *Misdemeanor, Civil Actions Under $10,000, Eviction, Small Claims.*

Civil Records: Access: Online, in person. Both court and visitors may perform in person searches. Court makes copy: $.50 per page. Access to court records from 1997 forward is free at www.nmcourts.com.

Criminal Records: Access: Online, in person. Both court and visitors may perform in person searches. Court makes copy: $.50 per page. Required to search: name, years to search; also helpful: DOB, SSN. Online access to criminal records is free at www.nmcourts.com.

General Information: Public use terminal available. No certification fee .

Farmington Magistrate Court
950 W Apache St, Farmington, NM 87401; phone: 505-326-4338; criminal phone: x103; civil phone: x109; fax: 505-325-2618; hours 8AM-4PM (MST). *Misdemeanor, Civil Actions Under $10,000, Eviction, Small Claims.*
www.nmcourts.com

Civil Records: Access: Online, in person. Both court and visitors may perform in person searches. No search fee. Court makes copy: $.50 per page; $1.00 per page if computer generated; same fee for self serve. Required to search: name, DOB, SSN; also helpful-years to search, other names used, address. Civil records go back 12 years for open cases. Closed case records go back to 6-30-03. Access to court records from 1997 forward is free at www.nmcourts.com. Mail turnaround up to 4 days.

Criminal Records: Access: Online, in person. Both court and visitors may perform in person searches. Court makes copy: $.50 per page; same fee for self serve. Required to search: name, years to search, DOB; also helpful: SSN. Criminal records go back to 6-30-03; DWI's 1986. Online access to criminal records is free at www.nmcourts.com.

General Information: No public access terminal. Will fax documents for $1.00 per page. No certification fee . Prepayment required.

County Clerk PO Box 550, 100 S Oliver,#200, Aztec, NM 87410; phone: 505-334-9471; fax: 505-334-3635; hours 7AM-5:30PM (MST). *Probate.*

San Miguel County

4th Judicial District Court
PO Box 1540, Las Vegas, NM 87701; phone: 505-425-7281; fax: 505-454-8611; hours 8AM-N, 1-5PM (MST). *Felony, Civil, Probate.*
Note: Also handles cases for Mora County.

Civil Records: Access: Phone, mail, online, in person, fax. Only the court performs in person searches. No search fee, but SASE or postage must be supplied for mail back documents. Court makes copy: $.35 per page. Required to search: name, years to search. Civil cases indexed by defendant, plaintiff; on microfiche from 1939, prior archived. All requests must be in writing. Access to court records from 1997 forward is free at www.nmcourts.com.

Criminal Records: Access: Online, in person. Only the court performs in person searches. Court makes copy: $.35 per page. Required to search: name, years to search. Criminal records on microfiche from 1930, prior archived, computerized 1997 to present. Online access to criminal records is free at www.nmcourts.com.

General Information: No adoptions, insanity, juvenile records released. Will fax for $1.00 if local, $2.00 if long distance. Certification fee: $1.50 per document. Payee: 4th Judicial District Court Clerk. Only cashiers checks and money orders accepted, unless a law firm. Prepayment and SASE required.

Magistrate Court
1927 7th St, Las Vegas, NM 87701-4957; phone: 505-425-5204; fax: 505-425-0422; hours 8AM-4PM (MST). *Misdemeanor, Civil Actions Under $10,000, Eviction, Small Claims.*

Civil Records: Access: Fax, online, in person. Only the court performs in person searches. No search fee. Court makes copy: $.50 per page. Required to search: name, years to search. Access to court records from 1997 forward is free at www.nmcourts.com.

Criminal Records: Access: Fax, online, in person. Only the court performs in person searches. No search fee. Court makes copy: $.50 per page. Required to search: name, years to search, DOB; also helpful: address, SSN. Online access to criminal records is free at www.nmcourts.com.

General Information: No certification fee .

County Clerk San Miguel County Clerk, 500 W National Ave, #113, Las Vegas, NM 87701; phone: 505-425-9331; fax: 505-454-1799; hours 8AM-N, 1-5PM, M-Th, 8AM-4PM, Fri (MST). *Probate.*

Sandoval County

13th Judicial District Court
100 Avenida De Justicia, Bernalillo, NM 87004; phone: 505-867-2376; fax: 505-867-5161; hours 8AM-N, 1-5PM (MST). *Felony, Civil.*

Civil Records: Access: Fax, mail, online, in person. Both court and visitors may perform in person searches. Search fee: $5.00 search fee. Court makes copy: $.35 per page. Microfilm copies $.50 per page (1991 and prior). Required to search: name, years to search. Civil cases indexed by defendant, plaintiff. Civil records indexed on computer back to 11/96; prior on microfiche. Access to court records from 1997 forward is free at www.nmcourts.com. Mail turnaround time 2-3 days.

Criminal Records: Access: Fax, mail, online, in person. Both court and visitors may perform in person searches. Search fee: $5.00 per name. Court makes copy: $.35 per page. Microfilm copies $.50 per page 1991 and prior. Required to search: name, years to search. Criminal records on computer back to 11/96. Online access to criminal records is free at www.nmcourts.com. Mail turnaround 2-3 days.

General Information: No public access terminal. No adoption, neglect and abuse records released. Fee to fax documents is $2.50 per page. Out of state $5.00 per page. Certification fee: $1.50 per page. Payee: 13th Judicial District Court. Business checks accepted, no personal checks. Prepayment required.

Bernalillo Magistrate Court PO Box 818, Bernalillo, NM 87004; phone: 505-867-5202 x2-6; fax: 505-867-0970; hours 8AM-4PM (MST). *Misdemeanor, Civil Actions Under $10,000, Eviction, Small Claims.*

Civil Records: Access: Mail, fax, in person, online. Both court and visitors may perform in person searches. No search fee. Court makes copy: $.50 per page. Civil records go back to 12/1996; prior destroyed. Access to court records from 1997 forward is free at www.nmcourts.com. Mail turnaround time 1-2 weeks.

Criminal Records: Access: Online, mail, in person. Visitors must perform in person searches themselves. No search fee. Court makes copy: $.50 per page. Required to search: name, years to search. Criminal records go back to 12/1996; prior destroyed. Online access to criminal records is free at www.nmcourts.com. Mail turnaround 1-2 weeks.

General Information: Public use terminal available. Certification fee: $.50 per page. Payee: Magistrate Court.

Cuba Magistrate Court PO Box 1497, Cuba, NM 87013; phone: 505-289-3519; fax: 505-289-3013; hours 8AM-4PM (MST). *Misdemeanor, Civil Actions Under $10,000, Eviction, Small Claims.*

Civil Records: Access: Online, in person. Visitors must perform in person searches themselves. Access to court records from 1997 forward is free at www.nmcourts.com.

Criminal Records: Access: Online, in person. Visitors must perform in person searches themselves. Required to search: name, years to search. Online access to criminal records is free at www.nmcourts.com.

General Information: Public terminal has criminal back to 3 years and civil back to 14 years.

Probate Court PO Box 40, 711 Camino del Pueblo, Bernalillo, NM 87004; phone: 505-867-7647; civil phone: 505-867-7645; fax: 505-867-9365; hours 8AM-5PM (MST). *Probate.*

Santa Fe County

First Judicial District Court Box 2268, Santa Fe, NM 87504; phone: 505-476-0189; fax: 505-827-5055; hours 8AM-4PM (MST). *Felony, Civil.* http://firstdistrictcourt.com

Note: Because this court also handles the counties of Los Alamos and Rio Arriba, you must indicate which county you are searching.

Civil Records: Access: Phone, mail, online, in person. Both court and visitors may perform in person searches. No search fee. Court makes copy: $.35 per page; same fee for self serve. Required to search: name, years to search. Civil cases indexed by defendant, plaintiff; on computer from 1984, older records on docket books. Request must be in writing. Access to index of court records from 1997 forward is free at www.nmcourts.com. Mail turnaround time 2 days.

Criminal Records: Access: Phone, mail, online, in person. Both court and visitors may perform in person searches. No search fee. Court makes copy: $.35 per page; same fee for self serve. Required to search: name, years to search; also helpful: DOB, SSN. Criminal records on computer from 1984, older records on docket books. Online access to index of criminal records is free at www.nmcourts.com. Mail turnaround time 2 days.

General Information: Public use terminal available. No adoption, juvenile, mental or abuse records released. Certification fee: $1.50 per seal. Payee: First Judicial District Court. Business checks accepted if law firm. Prepayment and SASE required.

Pojoaque Magistrate Court, NM; phone: 505-498-9914; hours 8AM-N,1-5PM (MST). *Misdemeanor, Civil Actions Under $10,000, Eviction, Small Claims.*

Note: The Court In Pojoaque is often closed; the clerk can be contacted at the Santa Fe Magistrate Court, 505-476-0189 (address above).

Santa Fe Magistrate Court 2056 Galisteo St, Santa Fe, NM 87505; phone: 505-984-9914; fax: 505-986-5866; hours 8AM-4PM (MST). *Misdemeanor, Civil Actions Under $10,000, Eviction, Small Claims.*

Note: Also, the clerk for the Pojoaque Magistrate Court may be contacted here.

Civil Records: Access: Fax, mail, in person, online. Both court and visitors may perform in person searches. No search fee. Court makes copy: $.50 per page. Required to search: Name, years to search. Civil records on computer back to 1997. Access to court records from 1997 forward is free at www.nmcourts.com. Mail turnaround 1 week.

Criminal Records: Access: Fax, mail, in person, online. Both court and visitors may perform in person searches. No search fee. Court makes copy: $.50 per page. Required to search: name, years to search, DOB; also helpful: SSN. Criminal records on computer back to 1997. Online access to criminal records is free at www.nmcourts.com. Mail turnaround time 1 week.

General Information: No public access terminal. No certification fee .

County Clerk Box 276, Santa Fe, NM 87504-0276; phone: 505-986-6279; fax: 505-986-6362; hours 8AM-5PM (MST). *Probate.*

Sierra County

7th Judicial District Court PO Box 3009, Truth or Consequences, NM 87901; phone: 505-894-7167; fax: 505-894-7168; hours 8AM-4PM (MST). *Felony, Civil.*

Civil Records: Access: Fax, mail, online, in person. Both court and visitors may perform in person searches. No search fee. Court makes copy: $.35 per page. Required to search: name, years to search, address. Civil cases indexed by defendant, plaintiff; on microfiche from 1920, archived before 1920. Access to court records from 1997 forward is free at www.nmcourts.com. Mail turnaround time 2 days.

Criminal Records: Access: Fax, mail, online, in person. Both court and visitors may perform in person searches. No search fee. Court makes copy: $.35 per page. Required to search: name, years to search, address, SSN. Criminal records on microfiche from 1920, archived before 1920. Online access to criminal records is free at www.nmcourts.com. Mail turnaround time 2 days.

General Information: Public use terminal available. No adoptions, insanity, juvenile, guardianship records released. Certification fee: $1.50. Payee: Sierra County District Court. Only cashiers checks and money orders accepted. Prepayment and SASE required.

Magistrate Court 155 W Barton, Truth or Consequences, NM 87901; phone: 505-894-3051; fax: 505-894-0476; hours 8AM-4PM (MST). *Misdemeanor, Civil Actions Under $10,000, Eviction, Small Claims.*

Civil Records: Access: Online, in person. Both court and visitors may perform in person searches. Court makes copy: $.50 per page. Access to court records from 1997 forward is free at www.nmcourts.com.

Criminal Records: Access: Online, in person. Both court and visitors may perform in person searches. Court makes copy: $.50 per page. Required to search: name, years to search. Online access to criminal records is free at www.nmcourts.com.

General Information: No public access terminal. No certification fee .

County Clerk 100 N Date St, Probate Records, Truth or Consequences, NM 87901; phone: 505-894-2840; fax: 505-894-2516; hours 8AM-5PM (MST). *Probate.*

Socorro County

7th Judicial District Court District Court, PO Drawer 1129, Socorro, NM 87801; phone: 505-835-0050 x10; fax: 505-838-5217; hours 8AM-4PM

(MST). *Felony, Civil Actions Over $7,500, Probate.* Note: Although case hearings and trials are held here, all civil and criminal case files are housed at the Catron County District Court at the address above. The physical address for this court is 200 Church St, Socorro.

Magistrate Court 102 Winkler St, Socorro, NM 87801; phone: 505-835-2500; fax: 505-838-0428; hours 8AM-4PM (MST). *Misdemeanor, Civil Actions Under $10,000, Eviction, Small Claims.*

Civil Records: Access: Mail, in person, online. Only the court performs in person searches. No search fee. Court makes copy: $.50 per page. Required to search: name, years to search, address, other names used. Civil records on computer back to 1997; judgments back 14 years or until satisfied. Access to court records from 1997 forward is free at www.nmcourts.com. Mail turnaround 1-5 days.

Criminal Records: Access: Mail, in person, online. Only the court performs in person searches. No search fee. Court makes copy: $.50 per page. Required to search: name, years to search, other names used; also helpful-DOB, SSN. Criminal records on computer back to 1997; files destroyed 2 years after closure. Online access to criminal records is free at www.nmcourts.com. Mail turnaround 1-5 days.

General Information: No public access terminal. Will fax documents to gov't agencies only. Certification fee: $1.00. Payee: Magistrate Court. SASE required.

County Clerk 200 Church St, PO Box I, Socorro, NM 87801; phone: 505-835-0423; fax: 505-835-1043; hours 8AM-5PM (MST). *Probate.*

Taos County

8th Judicial District Court 105 Albright St, #H, Taos, NM 87571; phone: 505-758-3173 x1; fax: 505-751-1281; hours 8AM-4PM (MST). *Felony, Civil.*

Civil Records: Access: In person, online. Visitors must perform in person searches themselves. Court makes copy: $.35 per page. Required to search: name, years to search. Civil cases indexed by defendant, plaintiff; on computer since 1993, books since 1912, microfiche from 1912-1980. Access to court records from 1993 forward is free at www.nmcourts.com.

Criminal Records: Access: In person, online. Visitors must perform in person searches themselves. Court makes copy: $.35 per page. Required to search: name, years to search, DOB; also helpful: signed release, SSN. Criminal records on computer since 1993, books since 1912, microfiche from 1912-1950. Online access to criminal records is free at www.nmcourts.com.

General Information: No public access terminal. No adoption, juvenile, abuse or sequestered case records released. Certification fee: $1.50 per cert. Payee: District Court. Only cashiers checks and money orders accepted. Prepayment required.

Questa Magistrate Court PO Box 586, State Rd 522 and Hwy 230, Questa, NM 87556; phone: 505-586-0761; fax: 505-586-0428; hours 8AM-5PM Tu/Th; Wed 8AM-4PM; closed Fri (MST). *Misdemeanor, Civil Actions Under $10,000, Eviction, Small Claims.* www.nmcourts.com

Civil Records: Access: Mail, in person, online. Both court and visitors may perform in person searches. No search fee. Court makes copy: $.50 per page. Required to search: name, signed release, address. Civil records go back to 1984. Access to court records from 1997 forward is free at www.nmcourts.com. Mail turnaround time 14 days.

Criminal Records: Access: Online, mail, in person. Both court and visitors may perform in person searches. No search fee. Court makes copy: $.50 per page. Required to search: name, years to search; also helpful: DOB, SSN. Criminal records go back to 1998. Online access to criminal records is free at www.nmcourts.com. Mail turnaround time 14 days.

General Information: Public terminal has criminal back to 1999 and civil back to 1984. Fee to fax documents is $1.00 per page. Certification fee: $3.00 per copy. Payee: Taos Circuit Court. Prepayment required.

Taos Magistrate Court 920 Salazar Rd, #B, Taos, NM 87571; phone: 505-758-4030; fax: 505-751-0983; hours 8AM-4PM (MST). *Misdemeanor, Civil Actions Under $10,000, Eviction, Small Claims.*

Civil Records: Access: Online, in person. Both court and visitors may perform in person searches. Court makes copy: $.50 per page. Civil records go back to 1997. Access to court records from 1997 forward is free at www.nmcourts.com.

Criminal Records: Access: Online, in person. Both court and visitors may perform in person searches. Court makes copy: $.50 per page. Required to search: name, years to search, DOB; also helpful: SSN. Criminal records go back to 1997. Online access to criminal records is free at www.nmcourts.com.

General Information: No public access terminal. Certification fee: $.50 per page. Prepayment required.

County Clerk 105 Albright, #D, Taos, NM 87551; phone: 505-758-8266; hours 8AM-N; 1-5PM (MST). *Probate.*

Torrance County

7th Judicial District Court County Courthouse, PO Box 78, Estancia, NM 87016; phone: 505-384-2974; fax: 505-384-2229; hours 8AM-4PM (MST). *Felony, Civil.*
www.nmcourts.com

Civil Records: Access: Mail, online, in person. Both court and visitors may perform in person searches. No search fee. Court makes copy: $.35 per page. Required to search: name, years to search. Civil cases indexed by defendant, plaintiff; on hard copy until filmed, microfiche from 1912; on computer back to 1997. Access to court records from 1997 forward is free at www.nmcourts.com. Mail turnaround time one week.

Criminal Records: Access: Mail, online, in person. Both court and visitors may perform in person searches. No search fee. Court makes copy: $.35 per page. Required to search: name, years to search; also helpful: SSN, DOB. Criminal records on hard copy until filmed, microfiche from 1912; on computer back to 1997. Online access to criminal records is free at www.nmcourts.com. Mail turnaround time 1 week.

General Information: Public terminal goes back to 1997. No juvenile, neglect, adoption, mental health records released. Will fax documents to local or toll free line. Certification fee: $1.50 per cert. Payee: Seventh Judicial District Court. Only cashiers checks and money orders accepted. Prepayment and SASE required.

Estancia Magistrate Court Neil Mertz Judicial Complex, PO Box 274, Estancia, NM 87016; phone: 505-384-2926; fax: 505-384-3157; hours 8AM-4PM (MST). *Misdemeanor, Civil Actions Under $10,000, Eviction, Small Claims.*
Note: All record requests must be in writing.
Civil Records: Access: Mail, fax, in person, online. Both court and visitors may perform in person searches. Court makes copy: $.50 per page. Closed case files maintained 1 year then archived, record index on computer since 1997. Access to court records from 1997 forward is free at www.nmcourts.com. Mail turnaround 3-5 days.
Criminal Records: Access: Mail, fax, in person, online. Both court and visitors may perform in person searches. No search fee. Court makes copy: $.50 per page. Required to search: name, years to search; also helpful: DOB, SSN. Closed case files maintained 1 years then destroyed 1 year from date of closure, record index on computer since 1997. Online access to criminal records is free at

www.nmcourts.com. Mail turnaround time up to 3 days.

General Information: Public terminal goes back to 1997. Will fax documents for $1.00 per page. Certification fee: $.50. Payee: Magistrate court. Prepayment required.

Moriarty Magistrate Court PO Box 2027, Moriarty, NM 87035; phone: 505-832-4476; fax: 505-832-1563; hours 8AM-4PM (MST). *Misdemeanor, Civil Actions Under $10,000, Eviction, Small Claims.*

Civil Records: Access: Mail, fax, mail, in person, online. Both court and visitors may perform in person searches. No search fee. Court makes copy: $.50 per page. Closed case files maintained 1 year, record index on computer since 1997. Access to court records from 1997 forward is free at www.nmcourts.com. Mail turnaround time up to 3 days.

Criminal Records: Access: Online, mail, in person. Both court and visitors may perform in person searches. No search fee. Court makes copy: $.50 per page. Required to search: name, years to search; also helpful: DOB, SSN. Closed case files maintained 1 year, record index on computer since 1997. Online access to criminal records is free at www.nmcourts.com. Mail turnaround time 3 days.

General Information: Public terminal goes back to 2/1997. Prepayment required.

County Clerk PO Box 767, 205 9th St and Allen, Estancia, NM 87016; phone: 505-246-4735; fax: 505-384-4080; hours 8AM-5PM (MST). *Probate.*

Union County

8th Judicial District Court Box 310, Clayton, NM 88415; phone: 505-374-9577; fax: 505-374-2089; hours 8AM-N, 1-5PM (MST). *Felony, Civil.*
Civil Records: Access: Mail, online, in person. Both court and visitors may perform in person searches. No search fee. Court makes copy: $.35 per page; same fee for self serve. Required to search: name, years to search. Civil cases indexed by defendant, plaintiff; on cards from 1981. Computerized records go to 1997. Access to court records from 1997 forward is free at www.nmcourts.com. Mail turnaround time 1-2 days.

Criminal Records: Access: Mail, online, in person. Both court and visitors may perform in person searches. No search fee. Court makes copy: $.35 per page; same fee for self serve. Required to search: name, years to search. Criminal records on docket sheets from 1981. Computerized records go to 1997. Online access to criminal records is free at www.nmcourts.com. Mail turnaround time 1-2 days.

General Information: Public terminal goes back to 1997. No adoption, juvenile records released. Will fax documents for $.35 per page. Certification fee: $1.50 per cert. Payee: Clerk of District Court. Only cashiers checks and money orders accepted. Prepayment and SASE required.

Magistrate Court 836 Main St, Clayton, NM 88415; phone: 505-374-9472; fax: 505-374-9368; hours 8AM-N, 12:30-4:30PM (MST). *Misdemeanor, Civil Actions Under $10,000, Eviction, Small Claims.*
www.nmcourts.com/
Note: The court also handles preliminary felony hearings and felony probable cause.
Civil Records: Access: Online, mail, in person. Both court and visitors may perform in person searches. Court makes copy: $.50 per page. Records available since 6/31/87, computerized since 3/13/97. Access to court records from 1997 forward is free at www.nmcourts.com. Mail turnaround time 2 days.
Criminal Records: Access: Online, mail, in person. Both court and visitors may perform in person searches. No search fee. Court makes copy: $.50 per page. Required to search: name, years to search; also helpful: address, DOB, SSN. Records computerized

since 3/13/97. Online access to criminal records is free at www.nmcourts.com. Mail turnaround time 2 days.

General Information: No public access terminal. Prepayment required.

County Clerk PO Box 430, 100 Court St, Clayton, NM 88415; phone: 505-374-9491; fax: 505-374-9591; hours 9AM-5PM (MST). *Probate.*

Valencia County

13th Judicial District Court Box 1089, Los Lunas, NM 87031; phone: 505-865-4291; fax: 505-865-8801; hours 8AM-5PM (MST). *Felony, Civil.*
Civil Records: Access: Fax, mail, online, in person. Both court and visitors may perform in person searches. Search fee: $5.00 for up to 2 names, $10.00 for 3-10 names. Court makes copy: $.35 per page. Required to search: name, years to search. Civil cases indexed by defendant, plaintiff; on microfiche from 1915. Access to court records from 1997 forward is free at www.nmcourts.com. Mail turnaround time 2 days.

Criminal Records: Access: Mail, online, in person. Both court and visitors may perform in person searches. Search fee: $5.00 fee for 2 names, $10.00 for 3-10 names. Court makes copy: $.35 per page. Required to search: name, years to search. Criminal records on microfiche from 1915. Online access to criminal records is free at www.nmcourts.com. Mail turnaround time 2 days.

General Information: Public terminal goes back to 1997. No adoptions or juvenile records released. Will fax documents for $2.50 in-state; $5.00 out-of-state. Certification fee: $1.50 per cert. Payee: 13th Judicial District Court. Only cashiers checks and money orders accepted. SASE required.

Belen Magistrate Court 901 W Castillo, Belen, NM 87002; phone: 505-864-7509; fax: 505-864-9532; hours 8AM-4PM (MST). *Misdemeanor, Civil Actions Under $10,000, Eviction, Small Claims.*

Civil Records: Access: Online, mail, in person. Only the court performs in person searches. Court makes copy: $.50 per page. Access to court records from 1997 forward is free at www.nmcourts.com. Mail turnaround time 1 day.

Criminal Records: Access: Online, mail, in person. Only the court performs in person searches. No search fee. Court makes copy: $.50 per page. Required to search: name, years to search, DOB, date of offense; also helpful: address, SSN. Online access to criminal records is free at www.nmcourts.com. Mail turnaround time 1 day.

Los Lunas Magistrate Court 1206 Main St, Los Lunas, NM 87031; phone: 505-865-4637; fax: 505-865-0639; hours 8AM-4PM (MST). *Misdemeanor, Civil Actions Under $10,000, Eviction, Small Claims.*

Civil Records: Access: Online, mail, in person. Only the court performs in person searches. No search fee. Court makes copy: $.50 per page. Access to court records from 1997 forward is free at www.nmcourts.com. Mail turnaround time 3-5 days.

Criminal Records: Access: Online, mail, in person. Only the court performs in person searches. No search fee. Court makes copy: $.50 per page. Required to search: name, years to search, DOB; also helpful: SSN. Online access to criminal records is free at www.nmcourts.com. Mail turnaround time 3-5 days.

General Information: No public access terminal. Certification fee: $1.00 per copy. Prepayment required.

County Clerk PO Box 969, 444 Luna Ave, Los Lunas, NM 87031; phone: 505-866-2073; fax: 505-866-2023; hours 8AM-4:30PM (MST). *Probate.*
www.co.valencia.nm.us/Clerk.htm

New Mexico Recording Offices

ORGANIZATION: 33 counties, 33 recording offices. The recording officer is County Clerk. Most counties maintain a grantor/grantee index and a miscellaneous index. The entire state is in the Mountain Time Zone (MST).

REAL ESTATE RECORDS: Most counties will not perform real estate searches. Copy and certification fees vary.

UCC RECORDS: Financing statements are filed at the state level, except for real estate related collateral, which are filed with the County Clerk. However, prior to 07/2001, consumer goods and farm collateral were also filed at the County Clerk and these older records can be searched there. Only a few recording offices will perform UCC searches. Use search request form UCC-11. Search and copy fees vary widely.

TAX LIEN RECORDS: All federal and state tax liens are filed with the County Clerk. Most counties will not provide tax lien searches.

OTHER LIENS: Judgment, mechanics, lis pendens, contractors, hospital.

ONLINE ACCESS: Several counties offer online access, but there is no statewide system.

Bernalillo County

County Clerk, PO Box 542, Albuquerque, NM 87103-0542. 505-768-4090, R/E recording phone-505-768-4268; fax-505-768-4190; hours: 8AM-5PM. www.bernco.gov/live/depts_and_offices.asp
Records indexed on a public use terminal back to 1982. Only the public may search. Copy fee $1.00 per page. R/E record copy- $.50 per page. Cert fee- $.50 per doc plus copy fee. Payee- Bernalillo County. **Online access to Real Estate, Property Assessor records:** Search assessor records at www.bernco.gov/property/default.asp?qpaction=search _form&type=situs. Also, the recorders data and Grantor/Grantee index is at http://cyclops.bernco.gov/splash.jsp. Free registration and password required. For more information call 505-768-4090. **Other phones:** Treasurer- 505-768-4031. **Property tax/Assessor-** 505-222-3700.

Catron County

County Clerk, PO Box 197, Reserve, NM 87830-0197. 505-533-6400; fax-505-533-6400; hours: 8AM-4:30PM. www.mylocalgov.com/catroncountynm
May provide unofficial searches as a courtesy, and if mail and copy fees prepaid. All records in one index. Only the public may search. Will not do official UCC records searches but may honor unofficial mail requests. Copy fee $1.00 per page if mailed. Cert fee- $1.00 per doc plus copy fee. Payee- Catron County Clerk. **Other phones:** Treasurer- 505-533-6384; Elections- 505-533-6400. **Property tax/Assessor-** PO Box 416, Reserve, NM 87830; 505-533-6577.

Chaves County

County Clerk, PO Box 580, Roswell, NM 88202-0580. 505-624-6614; fax-505-624-6523; hours: 7AM-5PM. Separate indices to search include Computer and old records in Books. Records indexed on a public use terminal back to 1983. Only the public may search. General copy fee $1.00 per page. R/E or tax lien copy- $.25 per page. Cert fee- $1.00 per cert plus copy fee. Payee- Chaves County Clerk. **Other phones:** Treasurer- 505-624-6618; Appraiser/Auditor- 505-624-6603; Elections- 505-624-6614; Vital Records- 505-827-0121. **Property tax/Assessor-** 505-624-6603.

Cibola County

County Clerk, PO Box 190, Grants, NM 87020. 505-287-2539, R/E recording phone-505-285-2539; fax-505-285-2562; hours: 8AM-5PM.
All records in one index. Records indexed on computer. Only the public may search. Copy fee $1.00 per page. Cert fee- $2.00 per doc plus copy fee. Payee- Cibola County Clerk. **Other phones:** Treasurer- 505-285-2520; Elections- 505-285-2540. **Property tax/Assessor-** 505-285-2527.

Colfax County

County Clerk, PO Box 159, Raton, NM 87740-0159. 505-445-5551; fax-505-445-4031; hours: 8AM-5PM. All records in one index. Records indexed on a public use terminal. Only the public may search. Copy fee $1.00 per sheet. R/E record copy- $.35 per page. Tax lien copy- $.25 per page. Cert fee- $1.00 per doc plus copy fee. Payee- Colfax County Clerk. **Other phones:** Treasurer- 505-445-3171; Elections- 505-445-5551; Vital Records- 505-445-5551. **Property tax/Assessor-** PO Box 427, Raton, NM 87740; 505-445-2341.

Curry County

County Clerk, PO Box 1168, Clovis, NM 88102-1168. 505-763-5591; fax-505-763-4232; hours: 8AM-5PM. All records in one index. Records indexed on a public use terminal back to /1986. Only the public may search. Copy fee $1.00 per page. R/E or tax lien copy- $.25 per page. Cert fee- $1.00 per doc + $.25 per page plus copy fee. Payee- Curry County Clerk. **Other phones:** Treasurer- 505-763-3931; Appraiser/Auditor- 505-763-6581; Elections- 505-763-5591; Vital Records- 505-827-0121. **Property tax/Assessor-** 700 N Main St, #6, Clovis, NM 88101 505-763-5731.

De Baca County

County Clerk, PO Box 347, Fort Sumner, NM 88119. 505-355-2601; fax-505-355-2441; hours: 8AM-N, 1-4:30PM.
All records in one index. Record index not computerized. Only the public may search. Copy fee $.30 per page. Cert fee- $1.50 per doc plus copy fee. Payee- De Baca County Clerk. **Other phones:** Treasurer- 505-355-7395; Appraiser/Auditor- 505-355-7448; Elections- 505-355-2601. **Property tax/Assessor-** 505-355-7448.

Dona Ana County

County Clerk, 251 W. Amador, Rm 103, Las Cruces, NM 88005-2893. 505-647-7421, R/E recording phone-505-647-7420; fax-505-647-7464; hours: 8AM-5PM. www.co.dona-ana.nm.us
All records in one index. Records indexed on a public use terminal back to 1979. Only the public may search. Copy fee $1.00 per page. R/E or tax lien copy- $.25 per page. Cert fee- $1.50 per doc plus copy fee. Payee- Dona Ana County Clerk. **Online access to Assessor, Real Estate, Deed, Personal Property records:** Access the deeds database free at www.co.dona-ana.nm.us/search/deeds/. Also, access the Real Property database free at www.co.dona-ana.nm.us/search/realprop/. **Other phones:** Treasurer- 505-647-7433; Appraiser/Auditor- 505-647-7400; Elections- 505-647-7466; Vital Records- 505-827-0121. **Property tax/Assessor-** 505-647-7400.

Eddy County

County Clerk, 101 W. Greene St, Rm 312, Carlsbad, NM 88220. 505-885-3383; fax-505-234-1793; hours: 8AM-5PM.
Only the public may search. Copy fee $.50 per page. Cert fee- $1.00 per doc, plus copy fee. **Other phones:** Treasurer- 505-885-3913; Appraiser/Auditor- 505-885-3813; Elections- 505-885-3383; Vital Records- 505-827-0121. **Property tax/Assessor-** 505-885-3813.

Grant County

County Clerk, PO Box 898, Silver City, NM 88062. 505-574-0042; fax-505-574-0076; hours: 8AM-5PM. All records in one index. Records indexed on a public use terminal back to 1978. Only the public may search. Copy fee $.25. Cert fee- $1.00 per page plus copy fee. Payee- Grant County Clerk. **Other phones:** Treasurer- 505-574-0055; Appraiser/Auditor- 505-574-0030; Elections- 505-574-0042; Vital Records- 505-574-0042. **Property tax/Assessor-** 1400 Hwy 180 E, Silver City, NM 88062; 505-574-0030.

Guadalupe County

County Clerk, 420 Parker Ave, #1; Courthouse, Santa Rosa, NM 88435. 505-472-3791; fax-505-472-4791; hours: 8AM-N, 1-5PM.
Separate indices to search include deeds, miscellaneous, mortgages, judgments, marriage licenses. Records indexed on a public use terminal back to 1993; earlier years being added. Only the public may search. Copy fee $1.00 per page if mailed back; $.50 in person. Cert fee- $3.00 per doc plus copy fee. Payee- Guadalupe Co.Clerk. **Other phones:** Treasurer- 505-472-3133; Appraiser/Auditor- 505-472-3738; Elections- 505-472-3741; Vital Records- 505-472-3211. **Property tax/Assessor-** 505-472-3738.

Harding County

County Clerk, PO Box 1002, Mosquero, NM 87733-1002. 505-673-2301; fax-505-673-2922; hours: 8AM-4PM. www.hardingcounty.org
NM Vital Statistics, 1105 St Francis Dr PO Box 26110, Santa Fe, NM 87502. Separate indices to search include mortgage, oil & gas, quit claim deeds, plats, patents, warranty deed all in real estate and miscellaneous. Records indexed on computer from 1989. Only the public may search. General copy fee $.50 per page. Record copys-$.25 if from book; $.50 if from microfiche or color copy. Cert fee- $1.00 per doc plus $.50 per page plus copy fee. Payee- Harding County Clerk. **Other phones:** Treasurer- 505-673-2928; Appraiser/Auditor- 505-673-2926; Elections- 505-673-2301; Vital Records- 505-827-0121 (Info-505-827-2338). **Property tax/Assessor-** 505-673-2926.

Hidalgo County

County Clerk, 300 Shakespeare St, Lordsburg, NM 88045. 505-542-9213; fax-505-542-3193; hours: 8AM-5PM.
Record index not computerized. Only the public may search. Copy fee $.25 per page. Cert fee- $1.25 per cert in person; $1.50 per page if mailed. Payee- Hidalgo County Clerk. **Other phones:** Treasurer- 505-542-9313. **Property tax/Assessor-** same address as above. 505-542-3433.

Lea County

County Clerk, PO Box 1507, Lovington, NM 88260. 505-396-8614, R/E recording phone-505-396-8531; fax-505-396-3293; hours: 8AM-5PM. www.leacounty.net/Clerk.htm
Records indexed on a public use terminal back to 1982. Only the public may search. Copy fee none 1st 5 pages, $.50 per page each add'l. **Other phones:** Elections- 505-396-8531. **Property tax/Assessor-** 505-396-8527.

Lincoln County

County Clerk, PO Box 338, Carrizozo, NM 88301. 505-648-2394; fax-505-648-2576; hours: 8AM-5PM.
All records in one index. Office personnel (will look-up by name only) or visitors may perform searches. Will search for brief real estate records. Will search UCC records and tax liens. Copy fee $.25 per page. Cert fee- $1.50 plus copy fee. Payee- Lincoln County Clerk. **Online access to Assessor, Property records:** Access to the assessor property records is free at www.lincolncountynm.net/ACCESS[1].htm. Registration, software, username and password is required. Follow prompts at website. **Other phones:** Treasurer- 505-648-2397; Appraiser/Auditor- 505-648-2306; Elections- 505-648-2331; Vital Records- 505-648-2394; Manager- 505-648-2385. **Property tax/Assessor-** 505-648-2306.

Los Alamos County

County Clerk, PO Box 30, Los Alamos, NM 87544. 505-662-8010; fax-505-662-8008; hours: 7:30AM-5PM.
Separate indices to search. Only the public may search. Copy fee $2.00, if tax lien or real estate $1.00 per page. Cert fee- $1.00 per cert plus copy fee. Payee- Los Alamos County Clerk. **Other phones:** Treasurer- 505-662-8070; Elections- 505-662-8011; Vital Records- 505-827-2338. **Property tax/Assessor-** 505-662-8030.

Luna County

County Clerk, PO Box 1838, Deming, NM 88031-1838. 505-546-0491; fax-505-546-4708; hours: 8AM-5PM.
All records in one index. Records indexed on a public use terminal back to 1977. Only the public may search. Copy fee $.50 per page. Cert fee- $1.00 per doc, plus copy fee. Payee- Luna County Clerk. **Other phones:** Treasurer- 505-546-0401; Elections- 505-546-0491; Vital Records- 505-827-0121 (Santa Fe, NM). **Property tax/Assessor-** 505-546-0404.

McKinley County

County Clerk, PO Box 1268, Gallup, NM 87301. 505-863-6866; fax-505-863-1419; hours: 8AM-5PM.
Separate indices to search include Grantor/Grantee, books, Microfiche. Records indexed on a public use terminal back to 8/1/1989. Only the public may search. General copy fee $1.00 per page. R/E record copy- $.35 per page. Tax lien copy- $.50 per page. Cert fee- $2.00 per cert plus copy fee. Payee- McKinley County Clerk. **Other phones:** Treasurer- 505-722-4459; Appraiser/Auditor- 505-863-3032; Elections- 505-722-4469; Vital Records- 505-821-0121. **Property tax/Assessor-** same address as above. 505-863-3032.

Mora County

County Clerk, PO Box 360, Mora, NM 87732-0360. 505-387-2448; fax-505-387-9023; hours: 8AM-N, 1-5PM.
Separate indices to search include grantor/grantee. Records indexed on computer from 1/2000 to 5/2003. Office personnel or visitors may perform searches. General index search fee $10.00 per name per 10 years. Copy fee $1.00 per page. Cert fee- $3.00 per document plus copy fee. **Other phones:** Treasurer- 505-387-2756; Appraiser/Auditor- 505-387-5289; Elections- 505-387-2448. **Property tax/Assessor-** 505-387-5289.

Otero County

County Clerk, 1000 New York Ave; Rm 108, Alamogordo, NM 88310-6932. 505-437-4942; fax-505-443-2922; 7:30AM-6PM. www.co.otero.nm.us
All records in one index. Records indexed on computer back to 1985. Only the public may search. Copy fee $.25 per page. Cert fee- $1.00 per page plus copy fee. Payee- Otero County Clerk. **Other phones:** Treasurer- 505-437-2030; Elections-505-437-4942; Vital Records- 505-437-0121. **Property tax/Assessor-** 505-437-5310.

Quay County

County Clerk, PO Box 1225, Tucumcari, NM 88401-1225. 505-461-0510; fax-505-461-0513; hours: 8AM-5PM.
All records in one index. Records indexed on a public use terminal back to 1980. Office will perform a UCC search but public must search other records themselves. Search fee $5.00. Copy fee $.50 per page. Cert fee- $1.50 per page. Payee- Quay County Clerk. **Other phones:** Treasurer- 505-461-0470; Appraiser/Auditor- 505-461-1760; Elections- 505-461-0510; Vital Records- 505-827-2338. **Property tax/Assessor-** PO Box 1227, Tucumcari, NM 88401; 505-461-1760.

Rio Arriba County

County Clerk, PO Box 158, Tierra Amarilla, NM 87575. 505-753-1780; fax-505-588-7418; hours: 8AM-5PM.
Records indexed on a public use terminal back to 1997 (computer located in Assessor's office next door). Only the public may search. Copy fee $1.00 per page. Cert fee- $.50 per cert plus copy fee. Payee- Rio Arriba County Clerk. **Other phones:** Treasurer- 505-588-7727. **Property tax/Assessor-** 505-588-7726.

Roosevelt County

County Clerk, 101 W. First; Rm 106, Portales, NM 88130. 505-356-8562; fax-505-356-3560; hours: 8AM-5PM. www.rooseveltcounty.com
Separate indices to search include real property, mortgage deeds, oil & gas, mineral deed, warranty deeds, miscellaneous records, plats, surveys, marriage license. Records indexed on computer back to 1986. Only the public may search. Copy fee $1.00 per page. R/E or tax lien copy- $.50 per page. Cert fee- $1.00 per page plus copy fee. Payee- Roosevelt County Clerk. **Other phones:** Treasurer- 505-356-4081. **Property tax/Assessor-** 505-356-6971.

San Juan County

County Clerk, PO Box 550, Aztec, NM 87410. 505-334-9471; fax-505-334-3635; hours: 7AM-5:30PM. www.sjcounty.net/Dpt/Clerk/_Default.asp
All records in one index. Only the public may search. Copy fee $1.00 per page. Real estate record or tax lien copy- $.50 per page. Cert fee- $1.00 per cert plus copy fee. Payee- County Clerks Office. **Online access to Real Estate, Assessor records:** Access to county real estate tax data is free at www.sjcounty.net/SJCTaxes/. **Other phones:** Treasurer- 505-334-9421; Appraiser/Auditor- 505-334-6157; Elections- 505-334-9471. **Property**

tax/Assessor- 100 S. Oliver Dr. #400, Aztec, NM 87410; 505-334-6157.

San Miguel County

County Clerk, Courthouse, Las Vegas, NM 87701. 505-425-9331; fax-505-454-1799; hours: 8AM-5PM.
Only the public may search. Copy fee $.50 per copy. Cert fee- $2.00 per copy. Payee- San Miguel County. **Other phones:** Treasurer- 505-425-9376; Elections- 505-425-9331; Vital Records- 505-425-9368. **Property tax/Assessor-** 505-454-4980.

Sandoval County

County Clerk, PO Box 40, Bernalillo, NM 87004. 505-867-7572; fax-505-771-8610; hours: 8AM-5PM.
Records indexed on a public use terminal back to 1985. Only the public may search. General index search fee $5.00 per 5 years search. Copy fee $.25; R/E or tax lien $1.00 per page. Cert fee- $.75 per doc plus copy fee. **Other phones:** Treasurer- 505-867-7581; Appraiser/Auditor- 505-867-7503; Elections- 505-867-7577; Vital Records- 505-841-4185. **Property tax/Assessor-** 505-867-7562.

Santa Fe County

County Clerk, PO Box 1985, Santa Fe, NM 87504-1985. 505-986-6280; fax-505-995-2767; hours: 8AM-5PM. www.co.santa-fe.nm.us
All records in one index. Records indexed on a public use terminal back to 1991. Office personnel or visitors may perform searches. Office will do phone search form 1991-present. No search fee if found on computer. Copy fee $.50 per page; $.75 if from microfilm. R/E or tax lien copy- $.75 per copy, microfilm xerox-$.50. Cert fee- $1.50 per doc plus $.50 per page, plus copy fee. Payee-Santa Fe County Clerk. **Online access to Assessor, Property, Real Estate, Grantor/Grantee records:** Access to county property data at http://216.161.39.9/wick/Query1CompactHTMLInput.html requires Location ID or Tax Account ID that is found on a county tax bill. Also, access to recorder's grantor/grantee index available by subscription, username and password required; call Mary Quintana at 505-986-6375 or 6329. **Other phones:** Treasurer- 505-986-6245; Appraiser/Auditor- 505-986-6300; Elections- 505-986-6287; Vital Records- 505-827-0121. **Property tax/Assessor-** PO Box 126, 102 Grant Ave, Santa Fe, NM 87504; 505-986-6308.

Sierra County

County Clerk, 100 Date St, Truth or Consequences, NM 87901. 505-894-2840; fax-505-894-2516; hours: 8AM-5PM.
If asked, this agency will look in computer to see what is there for you, but they are not bonded to do searches. All records in one index. Records indexed on a public use terminal back to the mid 1980's. Office personnel or visitors may perform searches. Will not search UCC records. Copy fee $.50 per copy. Cert fee- $1.00 per cert plus copy fee. Payee-Sierra County Clerk. **Other phones:** Treasurer- 505-894-3524; Elections- 505-894-2840; Vital Records- 505-827-2338. **Property tax/Assessor-** same address as above. 505-894-2589.

Socorro County

County Clerk, PO Box I, Socorro, NM 87801. 505-835-3263, R/E recording phone-505-835-0423; fax-505-835-1043; hours: 8AM-5PM.
All records in one index. Records indexed on a public use terminal back to 1989. Only the public may search. Copy fee $.25 per page. Cert fee-$2.00 per page plus copy fee. Payee- Socorro County. **Other phones:** Treasurer- 505-835-1701; Appraiser/Auditor- 505-835-0714; Elections- 505-835-0423; Vital Records- 505-835-0423. **Property tax/Assessor-** 505-835-0714.

Taos County

County Clerk, 105 Albright St, #D, Taos, NM 87571. 505-737-6380; fax-505-737-6390; hours: 8AM-5PM. All records in one index. Records indexed on a public use terminal back to 1980. Only the public may search. Copy fee $.25 per page. Cert fee- $1.50 per cert plus copy fee. Payee- Taos County Clerk. **Other phones:** Treasurer- 505-737-6360; Appraiser/Auditor- 505-737-6360; Elections- 505-737-6400; Tax Collector- 505-7376340. **Property tax/Assessor-** 505-751-8651.

Torrance County

County Clerk, PO Box 48, Estancia, NM 87016. 505-246-4735; fax-505-384-4080; hours: 8AM-5PM. All records in one index. Records indexed on a public use terminal back to 1985. Only the public may search. Copy fee $1.00 per page. Cert fee- $1.00 per doc plus copy fee. Payee- Torrance County Clerk. **Other phones:** Treasurer- 505-246-4787. **Property tax/Assessor-** 505-246-4727.

Union County

County Clerk, PO Box 430, Clayton, NM 88415. 505-374-9491; fax-505-374-9591; hours: 9AM-5PM. All records in one index. Will not search real estate records. Will not search UCC records or tax liens. Copy fee $.50 per page. Cert fee- $1.00 per page. **Other phones:** Treasurer- 505-374-2331; Appraiser/Auditor- 505-374-9441; Elections- 505-374-9491. **Property tax/Assessor-** same address as above. 505-374-9441.

Valencia County

County Clerk, PO Box 969, Los Lunas, NM 87031. 505-866-2073; fax-505-866-2023; hours: 8AM-4:30PM.
www.co.valencia.nm.us/CntyAgencies.htm
All records in one index. Records indexed on computer back to 1989, prior in indexes by date and letter. Only the public may search. General copy fee $1.00 if mail request; $.50 if in person. R/E or tax lien copy- $2.50 per copy. Cert fee- $2.50 plus copy fee. Payee- County Clerk. **Other phones:** Treasurer- 505-866-2090; Elections- 505-866-2080; Vital Records- 505-841-4100. **Property tax/Assessor-** PO Box 909, Los Lunas, NM 87031; 505-866-2065.

New Mexico County Locator

You will usually be able to find the city name in the City/County Cross Reference below. In that case, it is a simple matter to determine the county from the cross reference. However, only the official US Postal Service city names are included in this index. There are an additional 40,000 place names that people use in their addresses. Therefore, we have also included a ZIP/City Cross Reference immediately following the City/County Cross Reference.

If you know the ZIP Code but the city name does not appear in the City/County Cross Reference index, look up the ZIP Code in the ZIP/City Cross Reference, find the city name, then look up the city name in the City/County Cross Reference. For example, you want to know the county for an address of Menands, NY 12204. There is no "Menands" in the City/County Cross Reference. The ZIP/City Cross Reference shows that ZIP Codes 12201-12288 are for the city of Albany. Looking back in the City/County Cross Reference, Albany is in Albany County.

New Mexico City/County Cross Reference

ABIQUIU Rio Arriba
ALAMOGORDO Otero
ALBUQUERQUE Bernalillo
ALBUQUERQUE Sierra
ALCALDE Rio Arriba
ALGODONES Sandoval
ALTO Lincoln
AMALIA Taos
AMISTAD Union
ANGEL FIRE Colfax
ANIMAS Hidalgo
ANTHONY (88021) Dona Ana(98), Otero(1)
ANTON CHICO Guadalupe
ARAGON Catron
ARENAS VALLEY Grant
ARREY Sierra
ARROYO HONDO Taos
ARROYO SECO Taos
ARTESIA Eddy
AZTEC San Juan
BARD Quay
BAYARD Grant
BELEN Valencia
BELL RANCH San Miguel
BELLVIEW Curry
BENT Otero
BERINO Dona Ana
BERNALILLO Sandoval
BINGHAM Socorro
BLANCO San Juan
BLOOMFIELD San Juan
BLUEWATER Cibola
BOSQUE (87006) Socorro(83), Valencia(16)
BOSQUE FARMS Valencia
BRIMHALL McKinley
BROADVIEW (88112) Quay(60), Curry(39)
BUCKHORN Grant
BUENA VISTA Mora
BUEYEROS Harding
CABALLO Sierra
CANJILON Rio Arriba
CANNON AFB Curry
CANONES Rio Arriba
CAPITAN Lincoln
CAPROCK Lea
CAPULIN Union
CARLSBAD Eddy
CARRIZOZO (88301) Lincoln(80), Torrance(20)
CARSON Taos
CASA BLANCA Cibola
CAUSEY Roosevelt
CEBOLLA Rio Arriba
CEDAR CREST Bernalillo
CEDARVALE Torrance
CERRILLOS Santa Fe
CERRO Taos
CHACON Mora
CHAMA Rio Arriba
CHAMBERINO Dona Ana
CHAMISAL Taos

CHAPARRAL (88081) Dona Ana(74), Otero(25)
CHIMAYO Rio Arriba
CHURCH ROCK McKinley
CIMARRON Colfax
CLAUNCH Socorro
CLAYTON Union
CLEVELAND Mora
CLIFF Grant
CLINES CORNERS Torrance
CLOUDCROFT Otero
CLOVIS Curry
COCHITI LAKE Sandoval
COCHITI PUEBLO Sandoval
COLUMBUS Luna
CONCHAS DAM San Miguel
CONTINENTAL DIVIDE McKinley
CORDOVA Rio Arriba
CORONA Lincoln
CORRALES (87048) Sandoval(85), Bernalillo(14)
COSTILLA Taos
COUNSELOR Sandoval
COYOTE Rio Arriba
CROSSROADS Lea
CROWNPOINT McKinley
CUBA Sandoval
CUBERO Cibola
CUCHILLO Sierra
CUERVO Guadalupe
DATIL Catron
DEMING Luna
DERRY Sierra
DES MOINES Union
DEXTER Chaves
DIXON Rio Arriba
DONA ANA Dona Ana
DORA Roosevelt
DULCE Rio Arriba
DURAN Torrance
EAGLE NEST Colfax
EDGEWOOD (87015) Santa Fe(69), Torrance(17), Bernalillo(12)
EL PRADO Taos
EL RITO Rio Arriba
ELEPHANT BUTTE Sierra
ELIDA (88116) Roosevelt(94), Chaves(5)
EMBUDO Rio Arriba
ENCINO (88321) Torrance(70), Guadalupe(29)
ESPANOLA Rio Arriba
ESTANCIA Torrance
EUNICE Lea
FAIRACRES Dona Ana
FARMINGTON San Juan
FAYWOOD Grant
FENCE LAKE Cibola
FLORA VISTA San Juan
FLOYD (88118) Roosevelt(94), Curry(5)
FLYING H Chaves
FOLSOM Union
FORT BAYARD Grant
FORT STANTON Lincoln

FORT SUMNER De Baca
FORT WINGATE McKinley
FRUITLAND San Juan
GALLINA Rio Arriba
GALLUP McKinley
GALLUP San Juan
GAMERCO McKinley
GARFIELD Dona Ana
GARITA San Miguel
GILA Grant
GLADSTONE Union
GLENCOE Lincoln
GLENRIO Quay
GLENWOOD Catron
GLORIETA Santa Fe
GONZALES RANCH San Miguel
GRADY (88120) Quay(57), Curry(42)
GRANTS Cibola
GRENVILLE Union
GUADALUPITA Mora
HACHITA Grant
HAGERMAN Chaves
HANOVER Grant
HATCH Dona Ana
HERNANDEZ Rio Arriba
HIGH ROLLS MOUNTAIN PARK Otero
HILLSBORO Sierra
HOBBS Lea
HOLLOMAN AIR FORCE BASE Otero
HOLMAN Mora
HONDO Lincoln
HOPE (88250) Chaves(62), Eddy(37)
HOUSE Quay
HURLEY Grant
ILFELD San Miguel
ISLETA Bernalillo
JAL Lea
JAMESTOWN McKinley
JARALES Valencia
JEMEZ PUEBLO Sandoval
JEMEZ SPRINGS Sandoval
KENNA Roosevelt
KIRTLAND San Juan
KIRTLAND AFB Bernalillo
LA JARA Sandoval
LA JOYA Socorro
LA LOMA Guadalupe
LA LUZ Otero
LA MADERA Rio Arriba
LA MESA Dona Ana
LA PLATA San Juan
LAGUNA Cibola
LAKE ARTHUR (88253) Chaves(96), Eddy(3)
LAKEWOOD Eddy
LAMY Santa Fe
LAS CRUCES Dona Ana
LAS TABLAS Rio Arriba
LAS VEGAS San Miguel
LEDOUX Mora
LEMITAR Socorro
LINDRITH Rio Arriba
LINGO Roosevelt

LLANO Taos
LOCO HILLS Eddy
LOGAN Quay
LORDSBURG Hidalgo
LOS ALAMOS Los Alamos
LOS LUNAS Valencia
LOS OJOS Rio Arriba
LOVING Eddy
LOVINGTON Lea
LUMBERTON Rio Arriba
LUNA Catron
MAGDALENA Socorro
MALAGA Eddy
MALJAMAR Lea
MAXWELL Colfax
MAYHILL (88339) Otero(77), Chaves(22)
MC ALISTER Quay
MC DONALD Lea
MC INTOSH Torrance
MEDANALES Rio Arriba
MELROSE (88124) Curry(83), Quay(11), Roosevelt(5)
MENTMORE McKinley
MESCALERO Otero
MESILLA Dona Ana
MESILLA PARK Dona Ana
MESQUITE Dona Ana
MEXICAN SPRINGS McKinley
MIAMI Colfax
MILAN Cibola
MILLS Harding
MILNESAND Roosevelt
MIMBRES Grant
MONTEZUMA San Miguel
MONTICELLO Sierra
MONUMENT Lea
MORA Mora
MORIARTY Torrance
MOSQUERO Harding
MOUNT DORA Union
MOUNTAINAIR Torrance
MULE CREEK Grant
NAGEEZI San Juan
NARA VISA Quay
NAVAJO (87328) McKinley(87), San Juan(12)
NAVAJO DAM San Juan
NEW LAGUNA Cibola
NEWCOMB San Juan
NEWKIRK Guadalupe
NOGAL Lincoln
OCATE Mora
OIL CENTER Lea
OJO CALIENTE Taos
OJO FELIZ Mora
OJO SARCO Rio Arriba
ORGAN Dona Ana
OROGRANDE Otero
PAGUATE Cibola
PECOS San Miguel
PENA BLANCA Sandoval
PENASCO Taos
PEP Roosevelt

PERALTA Valencia
PETACA Rio Arriba
PICACHO Lincoln
PIE TOWN Catron
PINEHILL Cibola
PINON (88344) Chaves(84), Otero(15)
PINOS ALTOS Grant
PLACITAS Sandoval
PLAYAS Hidalgo
POLVADERA Socorro
PONDEROSA Sandoval
PORTALES Roosevelt
PREWITT (87045) McKinley(78), Cibola(22)
PUEBLO OF ACOMA Valencia
QUAY Quay
QUEMADO Catron
QUESTA Taos
RADIUM SPRINGS Dona Ana
RAINSVILLE Mora
RAMAH (87321) Cibola(57), McKinley(42)
RANCHOS DE TAOS Taos
RATON Colfax
RED RIVER Taos
REDROCK Grant
REGINA Sandoval
REHOBOTH McKinley
RESERVE Catron
RIBERA San Miguel
RINCON Dona Ana
RIO RANCHO Sandoval
ROCIADA (87742) Mora(68), San Miguel(31)
RODARTE Taos

RODEO Hidalgo
ROGERS Roosevelt
ROSWELL Chaves
ROWE San Miguel
ROY Harding
RUIDOSO Lincoln
RUIDOSO DOWNS Lincoln
RUTHERON Rio Arriba
SACRAMENTO Otero
SAINT VRAIN Curry
SALEM Dona Ana
SAN ACACIA Socorro
SAN ANTONIO Socorro
SAN CRISTOBAL Taos
SAN FIDEL Cibola
SAN JON Quay
SAN JOSE San Miguel
SAN JUAN PUEBLO Rio Arriba
SAN MATEO Cibola
SAN MIGUEL Dona Ana
SAN PATRICIO Lincoln
SAN RAFAEL Cibola
SAN YSIDRO Sandoval
SANDIA PARK (87047) Bernalillo(70), Sandoval(18), Santa Fe(11)
SANOSTEE San Juan
SANTA CLARA Grant
SANTA CRUZ Santa Fe
SANTA FE Santa Fe
SANTA ROSA Guadalupe
SANTA TERESA Dona Ana
SANTO DOMINGO PUEBLO Sandoval
SAPELLO San Miguel
SEBOYETA Cibola

SEDAN Union
SENA San Miguel
SENECA Union
SERAFINA San Miguel
SHEEP SPRINGS San Juan
SHIPROCK San Juan
SILVER CITY Grant
SMITH LAKE McKinley
SOCORRO Socorro
SOLANO Harding
SPRINGER Colfax
STANLEY Santa Fe
STEAD Union
SUNLAND PARK Dona Ana
SUNSPOT Otero
TAIBAN (88134) De Baca(72), Roosevelt(20), Quay(8)
TAJIQUE Torrance
TAOS Taos
TAOS SKI VALLEY Taos
TATUM Lea
TERERRO San Miguel
TESUQUE Santa Fe
TEXICO Curry
THOREAU McKinley
TIERRA AMARILLA Rio Arriba
TIJERAS Bernalillo
TIMBERON Otero
TINNIE Lincoln
TOHATCHI McKinley
TOME Valencia
TORREON Torrance
TRAMPAS Taos
TREMENTINA San Miguel

TRES PIEDRAS Taos
TRUCHAS Rio Arriba
TRUTH OR CONSEQUENCES Sierra
TUCUMCARI Quay
TULAROSA Otero
TYRONE Grant
UTE PARK Colfax
VADITO Taos
VADO Dona Ana
VALDEZ Taos
VALLECITOS Rio Arriba
VALMORA Mora
VANADIUM Grant
VANDERWAGEN McKinley
VAUGHN Guadalupe
VEGUITA Socorro
VELARDE Rio Arriba
VILLANUEVA San Miguel
WAGON MOUND Mora
WATERFLOW San Juan
WATROUS Mora
WEED Otero
WHITE SANDS MISSILE RANGE Dona Ana
WHITES CITY Eddy
WILLARD Torrance
WILLIAMSBURG Sierra
WINSTON Sierra
YATAHEY McKinley
YESO De Baca
YOUNGSVILLE Rio Arriba
ZUNI McKinley

New Mexico ZIP/City Cross Reference

87001-87001	ALGODONES
87002-87002	BELEN
87004-87004	BERNALILLO
87005-87005	BLUEWATER
87006-87006	BOSQUE
87007-87007	CASA BLANCA
87008-87008	CEDAR CREST
87009-87009	CEDARVALE
87010-87010	CERRILLOS
87011-87011	CLAUNCH
87012-87012	COYOTE
87013-87013	CUBA
87014-87014	CUBERO
87015-87015	EDGEWOOD
87016-87016	ESTANCIA
87017-87017	GALLINA
87018-87018	COUNSELOR
87020-87020	GRANTS
87021-87021	MILAN
87022-87022	ISLETA
87023-87023	JARALES
87024-87024	JEMEZ PUEBLO
87025-87025	JEMEZ SPRINGS
87026-87026	LAGUNA
87027-87027	LA JARA
87028-87028	LA JOYA
87029-87029	LINDRITH
87031-87031	LOS LUNAS
87032-87032	MC INTOSH
87034-87034	PUEBLO OF ACOMA
87035-87035	MORIARTY
87036-87036	MOUNTAINAIR
87037-87037	NAGEEZI
87038-87038	NEW LAGUNA
87040-87040	PAGUATE
87041-87041	PENA BLANCA
87042-87042	PERALTA
87043-87043	PLACITAS
87044-87044	PONDEROSA
87045-87045	PREWITT
87046-87046	REGINA
87047-87047	SANDIA PARK
87048-87048	CORRALES
87049-87049	SAN FIDEL
87050-87050	SAN MATEO
87051-87051	SAN RAFAEL
87052-87052	SANTO DOMINGO PUEBLO
87053-87053	SAN YSIDRO
87055-87055	SEBOYETA
87056-87056	STANLEY
87057-87057	TAJIQUE
87059-87059	TIJERAS
87060-87060	TOME
87061-87061	TORREON
87062-87062	VEGUITA
87063-87063	WILLARD
87064-87064	YOUNGSVILLE
87068-87068	BOSQUE FARMS
87070-87070	CLINES CORNERS
87072-87072	COCHITI PUEBLO
87083-87083	COCHITI LAKE
87100-87116	ALBUQUERQUE
87117-87117	KIRTLAND AFB
87118-87123	ALBUQUERQUE
87124-87124	RIO RANCHO
87125-87140	ALBUQUERQUE
87144-87144	RIO RANCHO
87151-87158	ALBUQUERQUE
87174-87174	RIO RANCHO
87176-87201	ALBUQUERQUE
87300-87305	GALLUP
87310-87310	BRIMHALL
87311-87311	CHURCH ROCK
87312-87312	CONTINENTAL DIVIDE
87313-87313	CROWNPOINT
87315-87315	FENCE LAKE
87316-87316	FORT WINGATE
87317-87317	GAMERCO
87319-87319	MENTMORE
87320-87320	MEXICAN SPRINGS
87321-87321	RAMAH
87322-87322	REHOBOTH
87323-87323	THOREAU
87324-87324	GALLUP
87325-87325	TOHATCHI
87326-87326	VANDERWAGEN
87327-87327	ZUNI
87328-87328	NAVAJO
87347-87347	JAMESTOWN
87357-87357	PINEHILL
87364-87364	SHEEP SPRINGS
87365-87365	SMITH LAKE
87375-87375	YATAHEY
87401-87402	FARMINGTON
87410-87410	AZTEC
87412-87412	BLANCO
87413-87413	BLOOMFIELD
87415-87415	FLORA VISTA
87416-87416	FRUITLAND
87417-87417	KIRTLAND
87418-87418	LA PLATA
87419-87419	NAVAJO DAM
87420-87420	SHIPROCK
87421-87421	WATERFLOW
87455-87455	NEWCOMB
87461-87461	SANOSTEE
87499-87499	FARMINGTON
87500-87509	SANTA FE
87510-87510	ABIQUIU
87511-87511	ALCALDE
87512-87512	AMALIA
87513-87513	ARROYO HONDO
87514-87514	ARROYO SECO
87515-87515	CANJILON
87516-87516	CANONES
87517-87517	CARSON
87518-87518	CEBOLLA
87519-87519	CERRO
87520-87520	CHAMA
87521-87521	CHAMISAL
87522-87522	CHIMAYO
87523-87523	CORDOVA
87524-87524	COSTILLA
87525-87525	TAOS SKI VALLEY
87527-87527	DIXON
87528-87528	DULCE
87529-87529	EL PRADO
87530-87530	EL RITO
87531-87531	EMBUDO
87532-87533	ESPANOLA
87535-87535	GLORIETA
87536-87536	GONZALES RANCH
87537-87537	HERNANDEZ
87538-87538	ILFELD
87539-87539	LA MADERA
87540-87540	LAMY
87541-87541	LAS TABLAS
87543-87543	LLANO
87544-87545	LOS ALAMOS
87547-87547	LUMBERTON
87548-87548	MEDANALES
87549-87549	OJO CALIENTE
87550-87550	OJO SARCO
87551-87551	LOS OJOS
87552-87552	PECOS
87553-87553	PENASCO
87554-87554	PETACA
87556-87556	QUESTA
87557-87557	RANCHOS DE TAOS
87558-87558	RED RIVER
87560-87560	RIBERA
87561-87561	RODARTE
87562-87562	ROWE
87563-87563	RUTHERON
87564-87564	SAN CRISTOBAL
87565-87565	SAN JOSE
87566-87566	SAN JUAN PUEBLO
87567-87567	SANTA CRUZ
87568-87568	SENA
87569-87569	SERAFINA
87571-87571	TAOS
87573-87573	TERERRO
87574-87574	TESUQUE
87575-87575	TIERRA AMARILLA
87576-87576	TRAMPAS
87577-87577	TRES PIEDRAS
87578-87578	TRUCHAS
87579-87579	VADITO
87580-87580	VALDEZ
87581-87581	VALLECITOS
87582-87582	VELARDE
87583-87583	VILLANUEVA

87592-87594 SANTA FE
87701-87701 LAS VEGAS
87710-87710 ANGEL FIRE
87711-87711 ANTON CHICO
87712-87712 BUENA VISTA
87713-87713 CHACON
87714-87714 CIMARRON
87715-87715 CLEVELAND
87718-87718 EAGLE NEST
87722-87722 GUADALUPITA
87723-87723 HOLMAN
87724-87724 LA LOMA
87725-87725 LEDOUX
87728-87728 MAXWELL
87729-87729 MIAMI
87730-87730 MILLS
87731-87731 MONTEZUMA
87732-87732 MORA
87733-87733 MOSQUERO
87734-87734 OCATE
87735-87735 OJO FELIZ
87736-87736 RAINSVILLE
87740-87740 RATON
87742-87742 ROCIADA
87743-87743 ROY
87745-87745 SAPELLO
87746-87746 SOLANO
87747-87747 SPRINGER
87749-87749 UTE PARK
87750-87750 VALMORA
87752-87752 WAGON MOUND
87753-87753 WATROUS
87801-87801 SOCORRO
87815-87815 BINGHAM
87820-87820 ARAGON
87821-87821 DATIL
87823-87823 LEMITAR
87824-87824 LUNA
87825-87825 MAGDALENA
87827-87827 PIE TOWN
87828-87828 POLVADERA
87829-87829 QUEMADO
87830-87830 RESERVE
87831-87831 SAN ACACIA
87832-87832 SAN ANTONIO
87901-87901 TRUTH OR CONSEQUENCES
87910-87910 ALBUQUERQUE
87930-87930 ARREY
87931-87931 CABALLO
87932-87932 CUCHILLO
87933-87933 DERRY
87935-87935 ELEPHANT BUTTE
87936-87936 GARFIELD

87937-87937 HATCH
87939-87939 MONTICELLO
87940-87940 RINCON
87941-87941 SALEM
87942-87942 WILLIAMSBURG
87943-87943 WINSTON
88000-88001 LAS CRUCES
88002-88002 WHITE SANDS MISSILE RANGE
88003-88007 LAS CRUCES
88008-88008 SANTA TERESA
88009-88009 PLAYAS
88011-88012 LAS CRUCES
88020-88020 ANIMAS
88021-88021 ANTHONY
88022-88022 ARENAS VALLEY
88023-88023 BAYARD
88024-88024 BERINO
88025-88025 BUCKHORN
88026-88026 SANTA CLARA
88027-88027 CHAMBERINO
88028-88028 CLIFF
88029-88029 COLUMBUS
88030-88031 DEMING
88032-88032 DONA ANA
88033-88033 FAIRACRES
88034-88034 FAYWOOD
88036-88036 FORT BAYARD
88038-88038 GILA
88039-88039 GLENWOOD
88040-88040 HACHITA
88041-88041 HANOVER
88042-88042 HILLSBORO
88043-88043 HURLEY
88044-88044 LA MESA
88045-88045 LORDSBURG
88046-88046 MESILLA
88047-88047 MESILLA PARK
88048-88048 MESQUITE
88049-88049 MIMBRES
88051-88051 MULE CREEK
88052-88052 ORGAN
88053-88053 PINOS ALTOS
88054-88054 RADIUM SPRINGS
88055-88055 REDROCK
88056-88056 RODEO
88058-88058 SAN MIGUEL
88061-88062 SILVER CITY
88063-88063 SUNLAND PARK
88065-88065 TYRONE
88072-88072 VADO
88073-88073 VANADIUM
88081-88081 CHAPARRAL
88101-88102 CLOVIS

88103-88103 CANNON AFB
88111-88111 BELLVIEW
88112-88112 BROADVIEW
88113-88113 CAUSEY
88114-88114 CROSSROADS
88115-88115 DORA
88116-88116 ELIDA
88118-88118 FLOYD
88119-88119 FORT SUMNER
88120-88120 GRADY
88121-88121 HOUSE
88122-88122 KENNA
88123-88123 LINGO
88124-88124 MELROSE
88125-88125 MILNESAND
88126-88126 PEP
88130-88130 PORTALES
88132-88132 ROGERS
88133-88133 SAINT VRAIN
88134-88134 TAIBAN
88135-88135 TEXICO
88136-88136 YESO
88201-88203 ROSWELL
88210-88211 ARTESIA
88213-88213 CAPROCK
88220-88221 CARLSBAD
88230-88230 DEXTER
88231-88231 EUNICE
88232-88232 HAGERMAN
88240-88244 HOBBS
88250-88250 HOPE
88252-88252 JAL
88253-88253 LAKE ARTHUR
88254-88254 LAKEWOOD
88255-88255 LOCO HILLS
88256-88256 LOVING
88260-88260 LOVINGTON
88262-88262 MC DONALD
88263-88263 MALAGA
88264-88264 MALJAMAR
88265-88265 MONUMENT
88266-88266 OIL CENTER
88267-88267 TATUM
88268-88268 WHITES CITY
88301-88301 CARRIZOZO
88310-88311 ALAMOGORDO
88312-88312 ALTO
88314-88314 BENT
88316-88316 CAPITAN
88317-88317 CLOUDCROFT
88318-88318 CORONA
88319-88319 DURAN
88321-88321 ENCINO
88322-88322 FLYING H

88323-88323 FORT STANTON
88324-88324 GLENCOE
88325-88325 HIGH ROLLS MOUNTAIN PARK
88330-88330 HOLLOMAN AIR FORCE BASE
88336-88336 HONDO
88337-88337 LA LUZ
88338-88338 LINCOLN
88339-88339 MAYHILL
88340-88340 MESCALERO
88341-88341 NOGAL
88342-88342 OROGRANDE
88343-88343 PICACHO
88344-88344 PINON
88345-88345 RUIDOSO
88346-88346 RUIDOSO DOWNS
88347-88347 SACRAMENTO
88348-88348 SAN PATRICIO
88349-88349 SUNSPOT
88350-88350 TIMBERON
88351-88351 TINNIE
88352-88352 TULAROSA
88353-88353 VAUGHN
88354-88354 WEED
88355-88355 RUIDOSO
88401-88401 TUCUMCARI
88410-88410 AMISTAD
88411-88411 BARD
88412-88412 BUEYEROS
88414-88414 CAPULIN
88415-88415 CLAYTON
88416-88416 CONCHAS DAM
88417-88417 CUERVO
88418-88418 DES MOINES
88419-88419 FOLSOM
88421-88421 GARITA
88422-88422 GLADSTONE
88423-88423 GLENRIO
88424-88424 GRENVILLE
88426-88426 LOGAN
88427-88427 MC ALISTER
88429-88429 MOUNT DORA
88430-88430 NARA VISA
88431-88431 NEWKIRK
88432-88432 SANTA ROSA
88433-88433 QUAY
88434-88434 SAN JON
88435-88435 SANTA ROSA
88436-88436 SEDAN
88437-88437 SENECA
88438-88438 STEAD
88439-88439 TREMENTINA
88441-88441 BELL RANCH

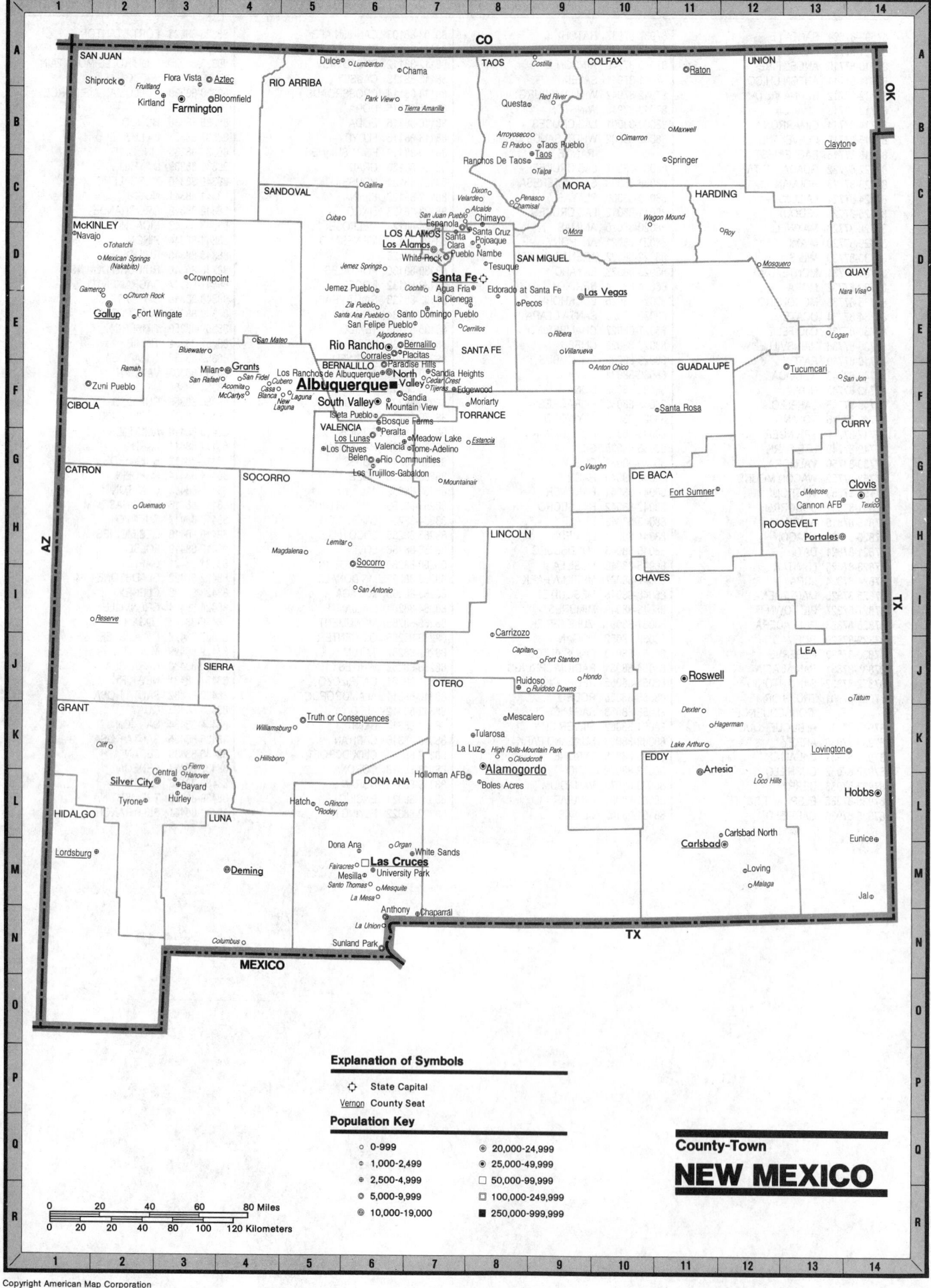

NEW MEXICO

County-Town

Explanation of Symbols

◇ State Capital

Vernon County Seat

Population Key

○ 0-999	◉ 20,000-24,999
◉ 1,000-2,499	◉ 25,000-49,999
◉ 2,500-4,999	☐ 50,000-99,999
◎ 5,000-9,999	☐ 100,000-249,999
◉ 10,000-19,000	■ 250,000-999,999

0   20   40   60   80 Miles

0   20   20   40   80   100   120 Kilometers

Explanation of symbols: ● – Census Designated Place (CDP)

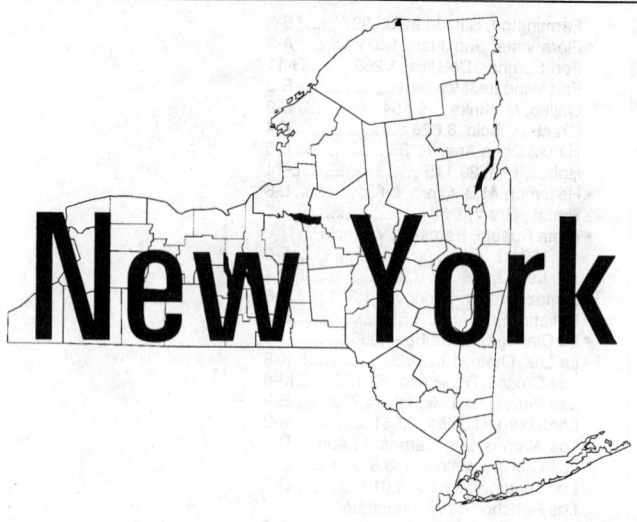

General Help Numbers:

Governor's Office
Executive Chamber, State Capitol   518-474-8390
Albany, NY 12224   Fax 518-474-1513
www.state.ny.us/governor

Attorney General's Office
State Capitol   518-474-7330
Albany, NY 12224-0341   Fax 518-473-9909
www.oag.state.ny.us   9AM-5:30PM

Legislative Records
State Capitol   518-455-2312
State Street Rm 317   Fax 518-426-6841
Albany, NY 12247   9AM-5PM
www.senate.state.ny.us

State Archives
Empire State Plaza   518-474-8955
Cultural Education Center, 11D40   Fax 518-473-9985
Albany, NY 12230   9AM-5PM
http://www.nysarchives.org/gindex.shtml

State Specifics:

Capital: Albany
Albany County

Time Zone: EST

Number of Counties: 62

Population: 19,227,088

Web Site: www.state.ny.us

State Agencies

Criminal Records

Access to Records is Restricted.

Division of Criminal Justice Services, 4 Tower Place, Albany, NY 12203; 518-457-6043, 518-457-6550-Fax; 8AM-5PM.

www.criminaljustice.state.ny.us

Records are only released pursuant to court order, subpoena, to entities authorized by statute, or to person of record. 99% of records are fingerprint supported. The public must search at the county court level. One may obtain their own personal criminal history record review by requesting a Record Review Packet from DCJS, and following

the directions for the completion and submission of a fingerprint card to DCJS along with a fee of $50.00.

Statewide Court Records

NY State Office of Court Administration, New York City Office, 25 Beaver St, New York, NY 10004; 212-428-2100, 212-428-2990, 212-428-2190-Fax; 9AM-5PM.

www.courts.state.ny.us

The details below primarily refer to criminal court cases. The OCA mandates that all criminal record requests made to county Supreme Court Clerks

and City Courts be forwarded to this office for processing.

It takes 24 hours in NYC and 7 days rest of state before new records are available for inquiry.

Searching: Most counties provide felony case information back to 1981. Notable exceptions are New York (1987), Richmond (1987), and Kings (1987). NYS town and village court criminal disposition data contains approx. 20% of cases since 2003. Include the following in your request-name, DOB, and SASE. Conviction and "pending" records are reported. The following data is not released: misdemeanor records prior to 2003.

Access by: mail, in person, online.

Fee & Payment: The fee for a statewide search is $52.00. Fee payee: NYS Office of Court Administration Prepayment or pre-approved account required. Personal checks accepted. Credit cards are not accepted.

Mail search: Turnaround time: 2 days or more. The search is a statewide search.

In person search: Records may be requested at this office and picked up the next day.

Online search: The OCA offers online or email access to approved requesters for criminal records. Call the OCA for details on how to set up an account. The fee is $52.00 per record. Civil Supreme Court case information for open cases is available for all 62 New York counties through https://iapps.courts.state.ny.us/caseTrac/jsp/ecourt. htm. Go to www.nycourts.gov/ctapps for appellate case summaries. Also, state Civil Court Commercial Division decisions are searchable at http://decisions.courts.state.ny.us/nyscomdiv/searc h/comdivintro.htm.

Expedited service: Current criminal docket info for 13 counties is available also.

Sexual Offender Registry

Division of Criminal Justice Srvs, Sexual Offender Registry, 4 Tower Place, Rm 604, Albany, NY 12203; 518-457-6326 x1, 800-262-3257 x2 (Verification), 518-485-5805-Fax; 8AM-5PM.

www.criminaljustice.state.ny.us/nsor/index.htm

Please note that a federal court injunction currently prohibits the release of information on this web site concerning sex offenders who committed their crime prior to January 21, 1996 and were assigned a risk level prior to January 1, 2000.

Records are available back to 01/22/96. It takes 1 day before new records are available for inquiry.

Searching: Local law enforcement is required to maintain the database for the public to view upon request. Include the following in your request- name, and one of following if by mail, fax or phone: SSN, DOB, DL# or exact address. Email questions to infodcjs@dcjs.state.ny.us.

Access by: mail, phone, fax, online.

Fee & Payment: There is no fee to use the 800 telephone.

Mail search: Turnaround time: 1 week.

Phone search: Search requests can be done over the phone. Lengthy lists must be mailed.

Fax search: Will respond to a toll free or local fax line.

Online search: The sex offender registry Level 3 can be searched at the website. Requesters are required to register. Please note that a federal court injunction currently prohibits the release of information on this web site concerning sex offenders who committed their crime prior to January 21, 1996 and were assigned a risk level prior to January 1, 2000.

Incarceration Records

New York Department of Correctional Services, Building 2 - Central Files, 1220 Washington Ave, Albany, NY 12226-2050; 518-457-5000, 518-457-8126 (Contact phone), 518-457-4966-Fax; hours-8AM-4PM.

www.docs.state.ny.us

Written requests should be directed to FOIA Unit.

Records are available on current and former inmates. It takes 1 to 20 days before new records are available for inquiry.

Searching: Include the following in your request- full name; the DOB, SSN, and DIN (inmate number) are helpful. Location, DIN number, conviction and sentencing information, and release dates are provided.

Access by: mail, phone, fax, online.

Fee & Payment: There is no search fee. Copy fee is $.25 per page

Mail search: Turnaround time: 7 to 10 days. A SASE is requested.

Phone search: Limited name searching by phone is available from the agency. For information on the location of a NYS prison inmate, call 518-457-5000 during normal business hours.

Fax search: Requests accepted via fax

Online search: Computerized inmate information is available from the Inmate Lookup at http://nysdocslookup.docs.state.ny.us/kinqw00 or follow "inmate lookup" link at main site. Records go back to early 1970s. To acquire inmate DIN number, you may call 518-457-5000. The site is open, in general, from Mon. thru Sat. 2:00 a.m.-11:00 p.m. & Sun. 4:00 a.m. thru 11:00 p.m.

Corporation, Limited Partnership, Limited Liability Company, Limited Liability Partnerships

Division of Corporations, Department of State, 41 State St, Albany, NY 12231; 518-473-2492 (General Information), 900-835-2677 (Corporate Searches), 518-474-1418-Fax; 8AM-4:30PM.

www.dos.state.ny.us

Information available includes date of incorporation, subsequent filings, status, principle business location, registered agent, service of process address, number and type of stock shares entitled to issue, and biennial statements w/addresses.

Records are available from inception. Information on active entities is automated. Records on entities inactive prior to 1978 are not automated and require additional research. New records are available for inquiry immediately.

Searching: All data is considered public information. Include the following in your request- full name of business.

Access by: mail, phone, fax, in person, online.

Fee & Payment: There is no fee for basic information up to 5 names. Over 5 names, the fee is $5.00 per name. For documents, the certification fee is $10.00, $25.00 if SOS seal is required. The fee is $5.00 for every name availability checked. Fee payee: New York Department of State. Payments must be by check, money order, credit card or drawdown account. If amount is over $500, funds must be certified. VISA/MasterCard accepted.

Mail search: Turnaround time: 1 week. A SASE is requested.

Phone search: Call 1-900-TEL-CORP. You may search up to 5 names per call for a flat rate charge of $4.00 per call.

Fax search: Fax requests accepted.

In person search: The general public may obtain copies of documents and certificates under seal while they wait ONLY if expedited fees are paid.

Online search: A commercial account can be set up for direct access. Fee is $.75 per transaction through a drawdown account. There is an extensive amount of information available including historical information. Also, the Division's corporate and business entity database may be accessed via the Internet without charge at http://appsext5.dos.state.ny.us/corp_public/CORP SEARCH.ENTITY_SEARCH_ENTRY. The web has not-for-profit corporations, limited partnerships, limited liability companies and limited liability partnerships as well.

Other access: You may submit an email search request at corporations@dos.state.ny.us.

Expedited service: Expedited service is available for in person, mail and fax for searching and filing. Fees are $150 for 2-hour service; $75 for same day service and $25 for 24-hour service.

Trademarks/Servicemarks

Department of State, Miscellaneous Records Unit, 41 State St, Albany, NY 12231; 518-474-4770, 518-473-0730-Fax; 8AM-4:30PM.

http://dos.state.ny.us

Records are available for past 10 years. It takes 1 to 2 weeks before new records are available for inquiry. Records are normally destroyed after one year when expired.

Searching: Searches are only done on registered marks, not on pending marks. You need to provide written description of design or features of the mark.

Access by: mail, phone, fax, in person.

Fee & Payment: The first two requests by mail, fax, or phone are free. Additional requests cost $5.00 per search. Fee payee: New York Department of State. Prepayment required. Payments of more than $500.00 must be certified check or money order; personal checks accepted for amounts less than $500.00 Personal checks accepted. No credit cards accepted.

Mail search: Turnaround time: 2 to 3 days. A SASE is requested.

Phone search: Limited verification information is available.

Fax search: Turnaround time is 2-3 days. There is a $.50 fee per page to return results by fax.

In person search: No fee for request. You can request 1 search in person.

Other access: New marks can be photocopied and sent out on a regular monthly basis. Fees are determined by numbers of marks.

Uniform Commercial Code, Federal and State Tax Liens

Department of State, UCC Unit - Records, 41 State Street, Albany, NY 12231-0001; 518-474-4763, 518-474-5418, 518-474-4478-Fax; 8AM-4:30PM.

www.dos.state.ny.us/corp/uccfaq.html

Records are available from 1964. Records are computerized from 1/96. Records are indexed on computer, microfilm.

Searching: Use search request form UCC-11. Federal tax liens on businesses will be included. Lists of state tax liens (warrants) are available, but must be searched separately on premises. Federal tax liens on individuals are filed at the county level. Include the following in your request-debtor name. It is suggested for written requests that the form be 5" x 8" or use the UCC-11.

Access by: mail, in person, online.

Fee & Payment: UCC search is $25.00 per debtor name, one name per UCC-11 form. Individual debtor names should list addresses. The copy fee is $5.00 per file number, add $5.00 to certify. You can search state tax liens, in person, at no charge. Fee payee: Department of State. Prepayment required. All checks over $500.00 must be certified. The department will certify search listings for an additional $25.00. Credit cards (VISA & MC) are accepted.

Mail search: Turnaround time: 2 days. No SASE is required.

In person search: You may request information in person.

Online search: Free access is available at http://appsext4.dos.state.ny.us/pls/ucc_public/web_search.main_frame. Seach financing statements and federal tax lien notices by by debtor name, or secured party name, or by filing number and date. Document images can be provided. Revised Article 9 of the Uniform Commercial Code can be accessed through the New York State Senate's Website at www.senate.state.ny.us.

Other access: This agency offers its database for sale on microfilm.

Sales Tax Registrations

Sales Tax Registration Bureau, WA Harriman Campus, Building 8, Rm 957, Albany, NY 12227; 800-972-1233, 518-435-2974-Fax; 7AM-5PM.

www.nystax.gov

Records are available for current records only. Records are computerized since 1970. It takes 20 days before new records are available for inquiry.

Searching: This agency will confirm that a business is registered and release the legal name. Include the following in your request-business name. They will also search by tax permit number or federal tax number.

Access by: mail, phone, fax, in person.

Mail search: Turnaround time: 2 to 3 weeks. A SASE is requested. No fee for mail request.

Phone search: No fee for telephone request.

Fax search: Fax searching available.

In person search: No fee for request.

Birth Certificates

Vital Records Section, Certification Unit, 800 N Pearl St, Albany, NY 12204-1842; 518-474-3038, 518-474-3077, 877-854-4481 (Searching), 877-854-4607-Fax; 8:30AM-4:30PM.

www.health.state.ny.us/nysdoh/consumer/vr.htm

For records from New York City information, see that profile. Records may be ordered online from a vendor website www.vitalchek.com.

Records are available from 1881 on. New records are available for inquiry immediately. Records are indexed on microfiche, inhouse computer.

Searching: May only obtain your own or a dependent child's records, without notarized release. They will not return records to a PO Box or an "in care of." Include the following in your

request-full name, names of parents, mother's maiden name, date of birth, place of birth, relationship to person of record, reason for information request. Requester must show or include valid identification or 2 items showing proof of address (utility or telephone bill, etc.)

Access by: mail, phone, fax, in person.

Fee & Payment: The fee is $30.00 for searching and additional $15.00 if priority handling requested. Add $11.95 if credit card used (phone and Internet searching only). Fee payee: New York State Department of Health. Prepayment required. Personal checks accepted. Major credit cards accepted.

Mail search: Turnaround time: 1 month. Turnaround time will be 2 weeks if you send your request by Express Mail, or if you pay an additional $15.00 for priority handling. A SASE is requested.

Phone search: See expedited service.

Fax search: See expedited service.

In person search: Results are still returned by mail.

Expedited service: Expedited service is available for phone and fax searches. Add $15.00 for priority handling and $11.95 for use of credit card.

Death Records

Vital Records Section, Certification Unit, 800 N Pearl St, Albany, NY 12204-1842 (Courier address: PO Box 2602, Albany, NY 12220-2602); 518-474-3038, 518-474-3077, 518-474-9168-Fax; 8:30AM-4:30PM.

www.health.state.ny.us/nysdoh/consumer/vr.htm

For New York City, see the separate entry. Records may be ordered online from website via Vitalchek.

Records are available from 1880 on. New records are available for inquiry immediately. Records are indexed on microfiche, inhouse computer.

Searching: You must show cause why record is needed on letterhead, if not member of the immediate family. Include the following in your request-full name, date of death, place of death, relationship to person of record, reason for information request, and telephone number. Requester must show or include valid identification.

Access by: mail, phone, fax, in person, online.

Fee & Payment: The fee is $30.00 for searching and additional $15.00 if priority handling requested. Add $11.95 if credit card used (phone and Internet searching only). Fee payee: New York State Department of Health. Prepayment required. Personal checks accepted. Major credit cards accepted.

Mail search: Turnaround time: 1 month. Turnaround time will be 2 weeks if you send your request by Express Mail, or if you pay an additional $15.00 for priority handling. A SASE is requested.

Phone search: See expedited service.

Fax search: Same criteria as phone searches, use 518-432-6286.

In person search: Turnaround time shortened by mail time only.

Online search: Online ordering is available via an approved third party vendor, go to www.vitalcheck.com.

Expedited service: Expedited service is available for mail, phone and fax searches. Turnaround time: 7 to 10 days. Add priority and credit card fees.

Marriage Certificates

Vital Records Section, Certification Unit, 800 N Pearl St, Albany, NY 12204-1842 (Courier address: PO Box 2602, Albany, NY 12220-2602); 518-474-3038, 518-474-3077, 8:30AM-4:30PM.

www.health.state.ny.us/nysdoh/consumer/vr.htm

For New York City information, see the separate entry. Records may be ordered online from website via Vitalchek.

Records are available from 1881 on. New records are available for inquiry immediately. Records are indexed on microfiche, inhouse computer.

Searching: Must have a notarized release from persons of record or immediate family member for investigative purposes. Include the following in your request-names of husband and wife, date of marriage, place or county of marriage, relationship to person of record, reason for information request, wife's maiden name. Requester must show or include valid identification.

Access by: mail, phone, fax, in person, online.

Fee & Payment: The fee is $30.00 for searching and additional $15.00 if priority handling requested. Add $11.95 if credit card used (phone and Internet searching only). Fee payee: New York State Department of Health. Prepayment required. Personal checks accepted. Major credit cards accepted.

Mail search: Turnaround time: 1 month. Turnaround time will be 2 weeks if you send your request by Express Mail, or if you pay an additional $15.00 for priority handling. A SASE is requested.

Phone search: See expedited service.

Fax search: Same criteria as general searches, use 518-432-6286. Turnaround time is 1 week.

In person search: Turnaround time shortened by mail time only.

Online search: Online ordering is available via an approved third party vendor, go to www.vitalcheck.com.

Expedited service: Expedited service is available for mail, phone and fax searches. Turnaround time: 7 to 10 days. Add priority and credit card fees.

Divorce Records

Vital Records Section, Certification Unit, 800 N Pearl St, Albany, NY 12204-1842 (Courier address: PO Box 2602, Albany, NY 12220-2602); 518-474-3038, 518-474-3077, 8:30AM-4:30PM.

www.health.state.ny.us/nysdoh/consumer/vr.htm

To obtain a copy of a divorce decree prior to 1963,, visit the county court where the document was filed.

Records are available from 1963 on. New records are available for inquiry immediately. Records are indexed on microfiche, inhouse computer.

Searching: If you are not a party to the divorce you must have a court order to obtain records or show legal cause. Include the following in your request-names of husband and wife, date of divorce, place of divorce, relationship to person of record, reason for information request, and your telephone number.

Access by: mail, phone, fax, in person, online.

Fee & Payment: The fee is $30.00 for searching and additional $15.00 if priority handling requested. Add $11.95 if credit card used (phone and Internet searching only). Fee payee: New York State Department of Health. Prepayment required. Personal checks accepted. Major credit cards accepted.

Mail search: Turnaround time: 1 month. Turnaround time will be 2 weeks if you send your request by Express Mail, or if you pay an additional $15.00 for priority handling. A SASE is requested.

Phone search: See expedited service.

Fax search: Same criteria as phone searches, use 518-432-6286.

In person search: Turnaround time shortened by mail time only.

Online search: Online ordering is available via an approved third party vendor, go to www.vitalcheck.com.

Expedited service: Expedited service is available for mail, phone and fax searches. Turnaround time: 7 to 10 days. Add priority and credit card fees.

Birth Certificate, Death Records-New York City

Department of Health, Bureau of Vital Records, 125 Worth St, Box 4, Rm 133, New York, NY 10013; 212-788-4520, 212-442-1999, 212-962-6105-Fax; 9AM-4PM.

www.nyc.gov/html/doh

Records may be ordered online from an approved vendor at www.vitalcheck.com. The fax number if calling outside NYC is 800-908-9146.

Records are available from 1910 to present for birth and from 1949 forward for death. For prior records, call Municipal Archives at 212-788-8580. It takes 2 months before new records are available for inquiry. Records are indexed on microfiche, inhouse computer.

Searching: Must have a notarized signed release from immediate family member. Include a copy of your photo ID. Include the following in your request-full name, date of birth, date of death, place of birth, place of death, reason for information request, name of the hospital. Parents' names are also required, mother's maiden name for birth.

Access by: mail, phone, fax, in person, online.

Fee & Payment: The fee is $15.00 per record plus $5.50 if using a credit card. Only those parties appearing on the birth record may order via a credit card. All other parties must order by mail or in-person and show cause or reason for the request. Fee payee: Department of Health. Prepayment required. Personal checks accepted. Major credit cards accepted.

Mail search: Allow 3-4 weeks for a birth record and 8-10 weeks for a death record. A SASE is requested.

Phone search: Online ordering is thru a message system. Use of a credit card is required. The automated voice ordering system, is available 24 hours a day, seven days a week.

Fax search: Same criteria as phone searching.

In person search: Turnaround time is usually while you wait.

Online search: Records may be requested via www.vitalchek.com. Use of credit card is required.

Expedited service: Expedited service is available for phone, fax searches. Turnaround time: 1 to 2 days. Add $12.50 for overnight delivery service.

Marriage Certificates-New York City

Office of the City Clerk, Municipal Building, 1 Centre St, Rm 252 South, New York, NY 10007; 212-669-8090, 9AM-4:30PM (till 1PM on F).

http://nycmarriagebureau.com

Marriage records before 1930 are available for $15.00 plus $2.00 for each borough searched. After 1930, one must visit the City Clerk's Office in borough where marriage was performed.

Records are available from 1930 to present. In person requests from 1996 to present. Prior records must be obtained from the Manhattan Office.

Searching: Current records (50 years or less) are not public information and are only available to the parties involved or their authorization or to legal representatives for litigation purposes. Otherwise, records are open. Include the following in your request-names and DOBs of parties, date of marriage, relationship of requester to involved parties, government issued photo ID of requester.

Access by: mail, in person.

Fee & Payment: There is a $15.00 search fee for the first year searched, then $2.00 add'l for each add'l year searched. Certification is another $10.00. Fee payee: City Clerk of New York Prepayment required. No personal checks accepted, except attorneys.

Mail search: Turnaround time: 6-8 weeks. Requesters must use the agency form. Call to have a copy mailed or download from the web.

In person search: Simple requests may be processed while you wait.

Workers' Compensation Records

NY Workers' Compensation Board, Office of General Counsel, 20 Park Street # 401, Albany, NY 12207; 518-474-6670, 9AM-5PM.

www.wcb.state.ny.us

The Board maintains eleven district offices located in Albany, Binghamton, Brooklyn, Buffalo, Hauppague, Hempstead, Manhattan, Peekskill, Queens, Rochester and Syracuse.

Records are available for up to 18 years after the case is closed. Older records are destroyed. New records are available for inquiry immediately. Records are indexed on inhouse computer. Records are normally destroyed after a limited time.

Searching: Must have a original signed Form OC-110-V (available from web site) or notarized release from claimant naming requesting party. It is a misdemeanor to request records for employment purposes. Include the following in your request-claimant name, Social Security Number, claim number, date of accident. File copies of records are not released for employment purposes, even with a signed release.

Access by: mail, in person, online.

Fee & Payment: Copies are $.25 each. Fee payee: Workers' Compensation Board. Prepayment required. Personal checks accepted. No credit cards accepted.

Mail search: Turnaround time: varies. No SASE is required. Include proper authorization and identification.

In person search: Visitors may make in person requests with proper authorization and identification. Turnaround time varies.

Online search: Proof of coverage is available at www.wcb.state.ny.us/design/framework/ebiz.htm.

Driver Records

Department of Motor Vehicles, MV-15 Processing, 6 Empire State Plaza, Room 430, Albany, NY 12228; 518-473-5595, 800-225-5368 (In-state), 8AM-5PM.

www.nydmv.state.ny.us

Records are available for 3 years in addition to the current year for moving violations, 10 years for DWIs, and indefinitely for open (4 years for closed) suspensions. Most non-moving violations are not shown on record. It takes a few days after conviction before new records are available for inquiry. Records are normally destroyed after 5 years from expiration.

Searching: New York restricts the release of personal information on driving records to casual requesters. However, they will provide a "masked" abstract that contains no personal information. This record is only available from the DMV Albany Central Office. Include the following in your request-DL# or ID#, name, and DOB. Use Form MV-15, if consent of driver is given use Form MV-15GC. The forms can be downloaded from the web.

Access by: mail, phone, in person, online.

Fee & Payment: The fee is $6.00 per record, $5.00 if electronic. The Form MV-15 lists all fees. Fee payee: Department of Motor Vehicles. Prepayment required. Escrow accounts can be set up for high volume users. Personal checks accepted. No credit cards accepted.

Mail search: Turnaround time: 4 to 6 weeks. Form MV-15 is required when ordering. A SASE is requested.

Phone search: Drivers wishing to obtain their own record or account holders may call. The DL# or name, DOB and sex are required when ordered. Payment by a credit card is required and an additional $5.00 is charged.

In person search: Records can be ordered from most any county-operated motor vehicle office and at the state offices in Albany. A photo ID of the requester and use of Form MV-15C is required.

Online search: NY has implemented a "Dial-In Inquiry" system which enables customers to obtain data within 24 hours a day. The DL# or name, DOB and sex are required to retrieve. The systems works off of a pre-paid bank. The fee is $5.00 per record. For more information, visit www.nysdmv.com/dialin.htm. Note: You can use your Dial-in Search Account to request DMV records by mail.

Other access: This agency offers a program to employers whereby This agency will notify the employers when an event is posted to an employee's record. To find out about the "LENS" program, visit www.nysdmv.com/lens.htm.

Vehicle Ownership
Vehicle Identification
Vessel Ownership
Vessel Registration

Department of Motor Vehicles, MV-15 processing, 6 Empire State Plaza, Room 430, Albany, NY 12228; 518-474-0710, 518-474-8510, 8AM-5PM.

www.nydmv.state.ny.us

Records are available for a minimum of 4 years on computer. All motorized vessels must be registered. Titles on boats are issued for model year 1987 and newer, if boat is at least 14 ft long. New records are available for inquiry immediately.

Searching: Generally, vehicle and ownership information is available. However, accessed is restricted in adherence to the Drivers' Privacy Protection Act and casual requesters cannot obtain records without consent. Use of Form MV-15 required. To obtain consent, use MV-15GC, The forms are downloadable from the website.

Access by: mail, in person, online.

Fee & Payment: Mail requests are $6.00 per record, online inquiries are $5.00 per record. A complete price list is on Form MV-15. Fee payee: Commissioner of Motor Vehicles. Prepayment required. For information regarding deposit accounts, call 518-474-4293. Personal checks accepted. No credit cards accepted.

Mail search: Turnaround time: 2 to 4 weeks. Include copy of requester's ID. Mail to MV-15 Form Processing for fastest turnaround time. A SASE is requested.

In person search: Documents may be requested at the counter, but cannot be picked up (or mailed) until the next day.

Online search: New York offers plate, VIN and ownership data through the same network discussed in the Driving Records Section. The system is interactive and open 24 hours a day. The fee is $5.00 per record. All accounts must be approved, requesters must follow DPPS guidelines. Call 518-474-4293 or visit www.nysdmv.com/dialin.htm for more information.

Accident Reports

DMV Certified Document Center, Accident Report Section, PO Box 2086, Albany, NY 12228-2086; 518-474-0710, 8AM-4:30PM.

www.nysdmv.com/dmvfaqs.htm#accident

The DMV has copies of accident reports, but requester may also call or visit the local police agency or precinct where the accident occurred, or the State Police troop headquarters where the accident was reported

Records are available for 4 years to present. It takes 180 days after date of accident before new records are available for inquiry. Records are indexed on inhouse computer. Records are normally destroyed after 4 years.

Searching: Records are open to the public, but request must be in writing. Use of Form MV-198C is suggested, downloadable from web. Release of records is restricted based on the Drivers' Privacy Protection Act. Include the following in your request-date of accident, location of accident, full name. Provide driver's address, if known.

Access by: mail, phone, fax.

Fee & Payment: The fees are $6.00 per search and $15.00 per accident report. Express mail is given priority. Fee payee: Commissioner of Motor Vehicle. Prepayment required. Personal checks accepted. No credit cards accepted.

Mail search: Turnaround time: 2 to 3 weeks. No SASE is required.

Phone search: There is an additional $5.00 fee if processed by phone.

Fax search: Fax requests accepted from ongoing accounts.

Voter Registration
Access to Records is Restricted.

State Board of Elections, 40 Steuben Street,, Albany, NY 12207-2108; 518-474-6220, 518-486-4068-Fax; 9AM-5PM.

www.elections.state.ny.us

Records may only be viewed or purchased at the county level. Purchases are restricted for political purposes only. The Federal Help America Vote Act of 2002 (HAVA) law requires implementation of a central, computerized, statewide voter registration system by 01/01/2006. At that time, this office will sell voter registration lists.

GED Certificates

NY State Education Dept, GED Testing, PO Box 7348, Albany, NY 12224-0348; 518-474-5906, 518-474-3041-Fax; 8AM-4:30PM.

www.emsc.nysed.gov/ged

The web page at www.emsc.nysed.gov/ged/otherserv.shtml gives detailed instruction and forms needed to obtain test results.

Records are available from 1985 to present. It takes 4 to 6 weeks, if paper before new records are available for inquiry.

Searching: Include the following in your request-full name when tested, data and location of test, SSN, DOB, signature of the testee.

Access by: mail, phone, in person.

Fee & Payment: There is no fee for verification. Copies of transcripts are $4.00 each. Copies of diplomas are $10.00 each. Fee payee: NY State Education Dept. Prepayment required. Money orders are accepted. Personal checks not accepted. No credit cards accepted.

Mail search: Turnaround time: 3 to 4 weeks. No SASE is required. Use "Attachment G" found on the web page.

Phone search: Phone verification service is provided if the transcript ID number or SSN is provided.

In person search: The hours of operation are Monday through Friday, 1:00 pm through 3:00 pm. The window is located in the New York State Education Building Annex, 89 Washington Avenue in Albany, at the Hawk Street entrance.

Expedited service: Will expedite if you provide a prepaid express envelope.

Hunting and Fishing License Information

DEC - Fish & Wildlife Division, Records Access Officer, 625 Broadway, Albany, NY 12233-1016; 518-402-8845, 518-402-2209-Fax; 8:30AM-4:45PM.

www.dec.state.ny.us/website/dfwmr

Access by: mail, fax, in person.

Fee & Payment: There is no search fee, copies are $.25 per page. Fee payee: DEC Prepayment required.

Mail search: Turnaround time: 1-2 days.

Fax search: Requests accepted by fax.

In person search: Turnaround while you wait.

New York State Licensing Agencies

For details about the agency responsible for licensing/certifying/registering an item below or in the Agency Quick Finder section, match an item's number with the number of the agency in the *Licensing Agency Information* section.

New York Licenses Searchable Online

Accountant, CPA/Public #19 .... www.op.nysed.gov/opsearches.htm#nme
Acupuncturist/Acupuncturist Assist. #19 .... www.op.nysed.gov/opsearches.htm#nme
Addiction Treatment Center #31 .... www.oasas.state.ny.us/atc/atc.htm
Adult Care Med. Facility #38 .... www.health.state.ny.us/nysdoh/acf/map.htm
Adult Care Suspended List #38 .... www.health.state.ny.us/nysdoh/acf/memorandum.htm
Alarm Installer #10 .... http://appsext5.dos.state.ny.us/lcns_public/lcns_query.lic_name_search_frm
Alcohol Abuse Provider #31 .... http://aps.oasas.state.ny.us/providers/
Alcohol Beverage Bond Company #46 .... http://abc.state.ny.us/JSP/content/bonds.jsp
Alcohol Distiller/Whlser/Mfg #46 .... http://abc.state.ny.us/JSP/query/PublicQueryInstructPage.jsp
Alcohol Service Establishment #46 .... http://abc.state.ny.us/JSP/query/PublicQueryInstructPage.jsp
Apartment Information Vendor #10 .... http://appsext5.dos.state.ny.us/lcns_public/lcns_query.lic_name_search_frm
Apartment Manager/Vendor/Agent #10 .... http://appsext5.dos.state.ny.us/lcns_public/lcns_query.lic_name_search_frm
Apartment Sharing Manager #10 .... http://appsext5.dos.state.ny.us/lcns_public/lcns_query.lic_name_search_frm
Appearance Enhancement Business #10 .... http://appsext5.dos.state.ny.us/lcns_public/lcns_query.lic_name_search_frm
Appearance Enhancer #10 .... http://appsext5.dos.state.ny.us/lcns_public/lcns_query.lic_name_search_frm
Architect #19 .... www.op.nysed.gov/opsearches.htm#nme
Armored Car/Car Carrier #10 .... http://appsext5.dos.state.ny.us/lcns_public/lcns_query.lic_name_search_frm
Athlete Agent #10 .... http://appsext5.dos.state.ny.us/lcns_public/lcns_query.lic_name_search_frm
Athletic Trainer #19 .... www.op.nysed.gov/opsearches.htm#nme
Attorney #18 .... www.nycourts.gov/attorneys/registration/index.shtml
Audiologist #19 .... www.op.nysed.gov/opsearches.htm#nme
Backflow Prevention Device Tester #13 .... www.health.state.ny.us
Bail Enforcement Agent #10 .... http://appsext5.dos.state.ny.us/lcns_public/lcns_query.lic_name_search_frm
Bank Branches, Foreign #23 .... www.banking.state.ny.us/sifbranc.htm
Bank Representative Office, Foreign #23 .... www.banking.state.ny.us/silicrepo.htm
Bank, Domestic / Foreign #23 .... www.banking.state.ny.us/sifagen.htm
Banker, Private #23 .... www.banking.state.ny.us/siprivat.htm
Banking Regulatory Action #23 .... www.banking.state.ny.us/ra.htm
Barber Apprentice #10 .... http://appsext5.dos.state.ny.us/lcns_public/lcns_query.lic_name_search_frm
Barber/Barber Shop #10 .... http://appsext5.dos.state.ny.us/lcns_public/lcns_query.lic_name_search_frm
Bottled Water Facility #13 .... www.health.state.ny.us
Budget Planner #23 .... www.banking.state.ny.us/sibudget.htm
Bulk Water Facility #13 .... www.health.state.ny.us
Check Casher #23 .... www.banking.state.ny.us/sicheckc.htm
Chiropractor #19 .... www.op.nysed.gov/opsearches.htm#nme
Cigarette/Tobacco Whlse/Retailer #52 .... http://www7.nystax.gov/CGTX/cgtxHome
Cigarette/Tobacco Tax Agent #52 .... http://www7.nystax.gov/CGTX/cgtxHome
Cosmetologist #10 .... http://appsext5.dos.state.ny.us/lcns_public/lcns_query.lic_name_search_frm
Court Reporter #19 .... www.op.nysed.gov/opsearches.htm#nme
Credit Union #23 .... www.banking.state.ny.us/sicredit.htm
Day Care, Farm Worker (ABCD) #29 .... www.agmkt.state.ny.us/programs/childdev.html
DEC Permit Application #11 .... www.dec.state.ny.us/apps/envapps/index.cfm?view=wizard
Dental Hygienist #19 .... www.op.nysed.gov/opsearches.htm#nme
Dentist/Dental Assistant #19 .... www.op.nysed.gov/opsearches.htm#nme
Dietitian #19 .... www.op.nysed.gov/opsearches.htm#nme
Dispatch Facility (Alarm/Secur'y/Fire) #10 .... http://appsext5.dos.state.ny.us/lcns_public/lcns_query.lic_name_search_frm
Dog License #27 .... www.agmkt.state.ny.us/AI/dog_pwd.htm
Domestic Out of State Bank Ofc. #23 .... www.banking.state.ny.us/sioosrep.htm
Engineer #19 .... www.op.nysed.gov/opsearches.htm#nme
Environmental Permit #11 .... www.dec.state.ny.us/apps/envapps/index.cfm?view=wizard
Esthetics Specialist #10 .... http://appsext5.dos.state.ny.us/lcns_public/lcns_query.lic_name_search_frm
Farm Products Dealer #26 .... www.agmkt.state.ny.us/AP/LicFarmProdDealersList.asp
Foreign Banking Agency #23 .... www.banking.state.ny.us/sifagen.htm
Greenhouse #26 .... www.agmkt.state.ny.us/nurseryDealers.html
Guard Dog Agency #10 .... http://appsext5.dos.state.ny.us/lcns_public/lcns_query.lic_name_search_frm
Guard/Patrol Agency #10 .... http://appsext5.dos.state.ny.us/lcns_public/lcns_query.lic_name_search_frm

Hair Styling, Natural #10	http://appsext5.dos.state.ny.us/lcns_public/lcns_query.lic_name_search_frm
Hearing Aid Dealer #10	http://appsext5.dos.state.ny.us/lcns_public/lcns_query.lic_name_search_frm
HMO (Insurance) #12	www.ins.state.ny.us/tocol4.htm
Holding Company #23	www.banking.state.ny.us/siholdmu.htm
Insurance Company #12	www.ins.state.ny.us/tocol4.htm
Interior Designer #19	www.op.nysed.gov/opsearches.htm#nme
Investment Company Article XII #23	www.banking.state.ny.us/siinvest.htm
Landscape Architect #19	www.op.nysed.gov/opsearches.htm#nme
Lender, Licensed #23	www.banking.state.ny.us/silicend.htm
Lobbyist #16	www.nylobby.state.ny.us/lobby_data.html
Lottery Claim Center #47	www.nylottery.org/ny/nyStore/cgi-bin/ProdSubEV_Cat_333605_NavRoot_306.htm#lcc
Massage Therapist #19	www.op.nysed.gov/opsearches.htm#nme
Medical Doctor #19	www.op.nysed.gov/opsearches.htm#nme
Medical Examiner, Independent #57	www.wcb.state.ny.us/content/main/hcpp/wc09000ime.htm
Med. Facility, Worker's Comp App'vd #57	www.wcb.state.ny.us/content/main/hcpp/wc09000.htm
Mentally Retarded Facility/Service #49	www.omr.state.ny.us/ws/servlets/WsAdminServlet
Midwife #19	www.op.nysed.gov/opsearches.htm#nme
Minority/Woman-owned Business #35	http://205.232.252.35/
Money Transmitter #23	www.banking.state.ny.us/simoneyt.htm
Mortgage Banker #23	www.banking.state.ny.us/simbanke.htm
Mortgage Broker #23	www.banking.state.ny.us/simbroke.htm
Nail Technologist #10	http://appsext5.dos.state.ny.us/lcns_public/lcns_query.lic_name_search_frm
Notary Public #10	http://appsext5.dos.state.ny.us/lcns_public/lcns_query.lic_name_search_frm
Nurse #19	www.op.nysed.gov/opsearches.htm#nme
Nurse-LPN, RPN #19	www.op.nysed.gov/opsearches.htm#nme
Nursery, Plant #26	www.agmkt.state.ny.us/nurseryDealers.html
Nutritionist #19	www.op.nysed.gov/opsearches.htm#nme
Occupational Therapist/Assistant #19	www.op.nysed.gov/opsearches.htm#nme
Off-Track Betting #15	http://licensing.racing.state.ny.us/license.cfm
Ophthalmic Dispenser #19	www.op.nysed.gov/opsearches.htm#nme
Optometrist #19	www.op.nysed.gov/opsearches.htm#nme
Pesticide Business #2	www.dec.state.ny.us/website/dshm/pesticid/appman.htm#top
Pesticide Distributor #2	www.dec.state.ny.us/website/dshm/pesticid/appman.htm#top
Pesticide/Commercial Applicator #2	www.dec.state.ny.us/website/dshm/pesticid/appman.htm#top
Pharmacist #19	www.op.nysed.gov/opsearches.htm#nme
Physical Therapist/Assistant #19	www.op.nysed.gov/opsearches.htm#nme
Physician #19	www.op.nysed.gov/opsearches.htm#nme
Physician Assistant #19	www.op.nysed.gov/opsearches.htm#nme
Physicians Specialist Assistant #19	www.op.nysed.gov/opsearches.htm#nme
Plant Dealer #26	www.agmkt.state.ny.us/nurseryDealers.html
Podiatrist #19	www.op.nysed.gov/opsearches.htm#nme
Premium Finance Company #23	www.banking.state.ny.us/sipremfi.htm
Private Investigator #10	http://appsext5.dos.state.ny.us/lcns_public/lcns_query.lic_name_search_frm
Psychiatrist #19	www.nyspsych.org
Psychologist #19	www.op.nysed.gov/opsearches.htm#nme
Public Accountant-CPA #19	www.op.nysed.gov/opsearches.htm#nme
Racing Occupation #15	http://licensing.racing.state.ny.us/license.cfm
Radiologic Technology School #14	www.health.state.ny.us/nysdoh/radtech/schlist2.htm
Radon Testing Lab #14	www.wadsworth.org/labcert/elap/radon.html
Real Estate Agent/Broker/Office #10	http://appsext5.dos.state.ny.us/lcns_public/lcns_query.lic_name_search_frm
Real Estate Appraiser #10	http://appsext5.dos.state.ny.us/lcns_public/lcns_query.lic_name_search_frm
Respiratory Therapist/Therapy Tech. #19	www.op.nysed.gov/opsearches.htm#nme
Safe Deposit Company #23	www.banking.state.ny.us/sisafede.htm
Sales Finance Company #23	www.banking.state.ny.us/sisalesf.htm
Savings & Loan #23	www.banking.state.ny.us/sisavloa.htm
Savings Bank #23	www.banking.state.ny.us/sisaving.htm
School, Non-Degree/Proprietary #34	www.highered.nysed.gov/bpss/directory_main_page.htm
Security & Fire Alarm Installer #10	http://appsext5.dos.state.ny.us/lcns_public/lcns_query.lic_name_search_frm
Security Guard #10	http://appsext5.dos.state.ny.us/lcns_public/lcns_query.lic_name_search_frm
Social Worker #19	www.op.nysed.gov/opsearches.htm#nme
Speech Pathologist/Audiologist #19	www.op.nysed.gov/opsearches.htm#nme
State Telecommunication Contrac'r #37	www.ogs.state.ny.us/purchase/telecomContracts.asp
Substance Abuse Provider #31	http://aps.oasas.state.ny.us/providers/
Summer Camp for Mental Retarded #49	www.omr.state.ny.us/hp_camp_directory.jsp
Surveyor, Land #19	www.op.nysed.gov/opsearches.htm#nme

Teacher #17 .... www.highered.nysed.gov/tcert/respublic/ocvs.htm
Telemarketer Business #10 .... http://appsext5.dos.state.ny.us/lcns_public/lcns_query.lic_name_search_frm
Trust Company #23 .... www.banking.state.ny.us/sibank.htm
Uniform Procedures Act Permit #11 .... www.dec.state.ny.us/apps/envapps/index.cfm?view=wizard
Upholster & Bedding Industry #10 .... http://appsext5.dos.state.ny.us/lcns_public/lcns_query.lic_name_search_frm
Veterinarian/Veterinary Technician #19 ...... www.op.nysed.gov/opsearches.htm#nme
Water Supply Permit #11 .... www.dec.state.ny.us/apps/envapps/index.cfm?view=wizard
Water Treatment Plant Operator #13 .... www.health.state.ny.us
Waxing Establishment/Oper/Tech #10 .... http://appsext5.dos.state.ny.us/lcns_public/lcns_query.lic_name_search_frm
Weights/Measures Local Office #28 .... www.agmkt.state.ny.us/WM/wmdirlst.html
Woman-owned Business #35 .... http://205.232.252.35/
Workers Comp 3rd Party Admin. #57 .... www.wcb.state.ny.us/content/main/SiLr/sec50_3bd.pdf
Workers Comp Claim Representitive #57 ...... www.wcb.state.ny.us/content/main/SiLr/sec24a.pdf
Workers Comp PPO Applicant #57 .... www.wcb.state.ny.us/content/main/ppopage/ppotrak1.pdf

New York Licensing Quick Finder

Accident/health Insurer #12 518-474-6623
Accountant, CPA/Public #19 518-474-3817
Acupuncturist/Acupuncturist Assistant #19
.... 518-474-3817
Addiction Counselor#31 800-482-9564,518-485-2057
Addiction Treatment Center #31 518-457-4384
Adoption Agency #24 800-345-5437
Adult Care Med. Facility #38 518-408-1219
Adult Care Suspended List #38 518-408-1219
Adult Family Home #24 518-474-7112
Aircraft Take-off from Thruway Permit #55
.... 518-436-3079
Alarm Installer #10 518-474-4429
Alcohol Abuse Provider #31 518-457-4384
Alcohol Beverage Bond Company #46 . 212-961-8385
Alcohol Distiller/Whlser/Mfg #46 212-961-8385
Alcohol Service Establishment #46 212-961-8385
Alcohol Service Permit #46 212-961-8385
Alcohol/Substance Abuse Counselor #31
.... 800-482-9564, 518-485-2057
Alcoholic Beverage Distributor #52 800-225-5829
Alternative Fueling Site #37 518-862-1090
Ambulance Service #7 518-402-0996
Ambulatory Service, Mentally Retarded #49
.... 518-473-9689
Amusement Device #9 518-457-2735
Animal Disposal Plant #27 518-457-5459
Animal Transport Service #27 518-457-5459
Animals, Lab Permit #41 518-485-5378
Apartment Information Vendor #10 518-474-4429
Apartment Manager/Vendor/Agent #10. 518-474-4429
Apartment Sharing Manager #10 518-474-4429
Apiary #26 518-457-2087
Apparel Mfg Industry Certificate #9 518-457-1942
Appearance Enhancement Buss.#10.... 518-474-4429
Appearance Enhancement Prof. #10 518-474-4429
Aquaculture-related Permit #11 631-444-0483
Architect #19 518-474-3817
Armored Car/Car Carrier #10 518-474-4429
Asbestos Handler #9 518-457-2735
Asbestos Safety Trainer #39 518-402-7940
Athlete Agent #10 518-474-4429
Athletic Trainer #19 518-474-3817
ATM Machine #23.....877-BANK-NYS, 212-709-1511
Attorney #18 212-428-2800
Audiologist #19 518-474-3817
Backflow Prevention Device Tester #13 518-402-7712
Bail Bond Agent #12 518-474-6630
Bail Enforcement Agent #10 518-474-4429
Bank Branches, Foreign #23
.... 877-BANK-NYS, 212-709-1559
Bank Representative Office, Foreign #23
.... 877-BANK-NYS, 212-709-1559
Bank, Domestic #23 .877-BANK-NYS, 212-709-1503
Bank, Foreign #23 .. 877-BANK-NYS, 212-709-1559
Banker, Private #23 .. 877-BANK-NYS, 212-709-1503

Banking Regulatory Action #23 .... 877-BANK-NYS
Barber Apprentice #10 518-474-4429
Barber/Barber Shop #10 518-474-4429
Bathing Beach #40 518-402-7600
Bedding Manufacturing #10 518-474-4429
Beer/Malt Beverage Distributor #52 800-225-5829
Blaster #9 518-457-2735
Blood Alcohol Analyzer #41 518-474-0005
Blood Bank #41 518-485-5378
Boat Launch Sites #50 518-474-0445
Boating Permit (State Park) #50 518-474-0445
Boiler Inspector #8 518-457-2722
Bottled Water Facility #13 518-402-7712
Boxer #21 212-417-5700
Boxing/Wrestling-related Prof. #21 212-417-5700
Breath Analysis Operator #41 518-474-2821
Brewer #46 212-961-8385
Budget Planner #23 .. 877-BANK-NYS, 212-709-5498
Building Permit #10 518-474-4429
Bulk Water Facility #13 518-402-7712
Business School Agent/Teacher #34 .. 518-474-3969
Canal Recreational Vessel Permit #32 . 518-436-2894
Care Facility (Family Board-sponsored) #25
.... 518-473-4630
Casino Employee #15 .... 518-453-8460 X2
Charitable Annuity #12 212-480-4778
Charitable Gaming #15 .... 518-453-8460 X2
Charity, Registered #44 212-416-8430
Check Casher #23 .... 877-BANK-NYS, 212-709-5494
Chemical Dependence Operation #31 .. 518-457-4384
Children's Overnight Camp #40 518-402-7600
Chiropractor #19 518-474-3817
Cigarette/Tobacco Whlse/Retailer #52 800-225-5829
Cigarette/Tobacco Tax Agent #52 800-225-5829
Clinical Lab Director/Assistant #41 518-485-5378
Clinical Lab/Blood Bank #41 518-485-5378
Coastal/Marine-related Permit #11 631-444-0470
Coin Processor #10 518-474-4429
Commercial Vessel (Canal) #32 518-471-5010
Commodity Investment Advisor #1 212-416-8222
Community Residence, Mental Health #48
.... 518-474-5570
Condominium #45 212-416-8122
Construction Permit #36 518-474-1314
Construction Plans Purchased #36 518-474-1314
Controlled Substance Dispenser #42... 518-402-0707
Controlled Substance Lab/Importer #42 518-402-0707
Controlled Substance Mfg/Dist/Exporter #42
.... 518-402-0707
Controlled Substance Researcher #42 . 518-402-0707
Cooperative Insurance Co., Advance/Premium #12
.... 212-480-5565
Cooperative, Housing #45 212-416-8122
Cosmetologist #10 518-474-4429
Court Reporter #19 518-474-3817
Crane Operator #9 518-457-2735

Credit Union #23 ...... 877-BANK-NYS, 212-709-1511
Cytotechnologist #41 518-485-5378
Day Care Center #24 518-474-7112
Day Care, Farm Worker (ABCD) #29 .. 518-457-7076
Day Service Program #24 518-474-7112
DEC Permit Application #11 518-402-8985
Dental Hygienist #19 518-474-3817
Dentist/Dental Assistant #19 518-474-3817
Diagnostic/Treatment Center/Clinic #22 518-402-0911
Dietitian #19 518-474-3817
Dispatch Facility (Alarm/Security/Fire) #10
.... 518-474-4429
Dog License #27 519-457-2728
Dog/Cat Breeder #27 518-457-2728
Domestic Out of State Bank Rep. Ofc. #23
.... 877-BANK-NYS
Domestic Violence Facility #24 518-474-7112
Drugs/Pharm. Devices, Mfg/Whsle/Dist. #19
.... 518-474-3817
Electrician, Master #10 518-474-4429
Emergency Medical Technician #7 518-402-0996
Employment Agency/Manager #9 212-352-6079
Engineer #19 518-474-3817
Engineering Corporation #19 518-474-3817
English as a Second Language School #34
.... 518-474-3969
Environmental Permit #11 518-402-8985
Esthetics Specialist #10 518-474-4429
Euthanize Dogs/Cats #42 518-402-0707
Excavate/Remove/Dispose of Material #37
.... 518-474-2195
Excess Line Broker #12 518-474-6630
Explosive Registration/Handling #9 518-457-2735
Explosives Transportation (Thruway) #55
.... 518-436-3079
Falconer #11 518-402-8843
Family Program, Interim #24 518-474-7112
Family/Group Day Care #24 518-474-7112
Farm Labor Camp/Commissary/Store#9 518-457-4321
Farm Products Dealer #26 518-457-1954
Farmworker Specialty Certification #29 518-457-7076
Feed Facility #29 519-457-5457
Fertilizer Distributor #26 518-457-2087
Firearms Manufacturer #51 518-457-2627
First Responder #7 518-402-0996
Fish Processor #29 518-457-5459
Fishing Guide #3 518-402-8838
Food Inspector #29 518-457-5459
Food Processor #29 518-457-7139
Food Salvager #29 518-457-1215
Food Service Establishment #40 518-402-7630
Food Store, Retail #29 518-457-1215
Foreign Banking Agency #23
.... 877-BANK-NYS, 212-709-1559
Foster Care #24 518-474-7112
Franchise Sales #1 212-416-8222

Franchise, Approved #1 212-416-8222
Fraternal Benefit Society #12 212-480-5027
Fund Raider, Professional #44 518-486-9797
Fund Raising Counsel #44 518-473-2374
Funeral Home/Director #6 518-402-0785
Game Bird Breeder #11 518-402-8985
Games of Chance Registration #10 518-474-4429
Greenhouse #26 518-457-2087
Guard Dog Agency #10 518-474-4429
Guard/Patrol Agency #10 518-474-4429
Guide, Camping/Fishing/Hiking/Hunting #3 518-402-8838
Guide. Rock/Ice Climbing #3 518-402-8838
Hair Styling, Natural #10 518-474-4429
Hauling Permit, Specialty (thruway) #55 518-436-2793
Health Care Plan, Prepaid #43 518-473-4842
Health Club #10 518-474-4429
Hearing Aid Dealer #10 518-474-4429
Heating Oil Seller #53 800-225-5829
Highway Use Tax Registration #53 800-748-3676
Hiking Guide #3 518-402-8838
HMO (Insurance) #12 518-474-6630
HMO (Medical Operation) #43 518-473-4842
Holding Company #23 877-BANK-NYS, 212-709-1503
Home Care Service #38 518-408-1219
Home Health Agency #38 518-408-1219
Home Health Aide Training #38 518-408-1219
Homeworker Industrial Distributor #9 212-352-6032
Hospice #38 518-408-1219
Hospital #38 518-408-1219
Hotel/Motel Name Certificate #10 518-474-4429
Hunting Guide #3 518-402-8838
Insurance Adjuster #12 518-474-6630
Insurance Agent/Consultant/Broker 12 518-474-6630
Insurance Appraiser #12 518-474-6630
Insurance Company #12 518-474-6630
Insurance Cont. Educ. Provider #12 518-474-6630
Interior Designer #19 518-474-3817
Investment Advisor #1 212-416-8222
Investment Company Article XII #23 .... 877-BANK-NYS, 212-709-1503
Juvenile Detention Facility #25 518-473-4630
Kosher Food #30 718-722-2852
Landscape Architect #19 518-474-3817
Laser Operator, Mobile #9 518-457-2735
Lender, Licens'd #23 . 877-BANK-NYS, 212-709-5496
Loan Broker #33 518-270-2200
Lobbyist #16 518-474-7126
Lottery Agent/Ticket Seller #47 518-388-3300
Lottery Claim Center #47 518-388-3300
LPG-related #53 800-225-5829
Mass Gathering #40 518-402-7600
Massage Therapist #19 518-474-3817
Medicaid Managed Care Service #43 518-473-4842
Medical Certificate of Authorization #57 518-474-2036
Medical Delivery System, Integrat'd #43 518-473-4842
Medical Disciplinary Action #22 800-663-6114
Medical Doctor #19 518-474-3817
Medical Examiner, Independent #57 .... 518) 402-6190
Medical Facility, Worker's Comp App'vd #57 518-474-2036
Medical Personnel Profile #22 888-338-6999
Mental Health Facility #48 518-474-5570
Mentally Retarded Health Facility/Service #49 518-473-9689
Midwife #19 518-474-3817
Migrant Farmworker Housing Facility #40 518-402-7600
Milk-related Dealer/Service #27 518-457-5731
Mining/Exploration, State-owned Land #37 518-473-1288
Minority/Woman-owned Business #35 . 518-292-5250
Mobile Home Park #40 518-402-7600
Money Transmit'r #23 . 877-BANK-NYS, 212-709-5494
Mortgage Banker #23 877-BANK-NYS, 212-709-5574
Mortgage Broker #23 . 877-BANK-NYS, 212-709-5574
Mortgage Guaranty InsuranceAgent #12 518-474-6630

Mover #56 518-457-6236
Municipal Health Benefit Plan #12 212-480-5245
Nail Technologist #10 518-474-4429
Notary Public #10 518-474-4429
Nurse - LPN / RPN #19 518-474-3817
Nursery, Plant #26 518-457-2087
Nurses' Aide #5 518-474-3817
Nursing Home #38 518-408-1219
Nursing Home Administrator #5 518-474-3817
Nutritionist #19 518-474-3817
Occupational Therapist/Assistant #19 .. 518-474-3817
Off-Track Betting #15 .... 518-453-8460 X2
Ophthalmic Dispenser #19 518-474-3817
Optometrist #19 518-474-3817
Paramedic #7 518-402-0996
Passenger Motor Carrier #56 518-457-6503
Patient Service Center #41 518-485-5378
Pesticide Business #2 518-402-8748
Pesticide Distributor #2 518-402-8748
Pesticide/Commercial Applicator #2 518-402-8748
Pet Cemetery/Crematory #10 518-474-4429
Pet Dealer #27 518-457-7749
Pet Food Producer #29 519-457-5457
Petroleum/Fuel Product Dealer/Handler #53 800-225-5829
Pharmacist / Pharmacy #19 518-474-3817
Physical Therapist/Assistant #19 518-474-3817
Physician #19 518-474-3817
Physician Assistant #19 518-474-3817
Physicians Specialist Assistant #19 518-474-3817
Phytosanitarian #26 518-457-2087
Pistol Permit #51 518-457-2627
Plant Dealer #26 518-457-2087
Podiatrist #19 518-474-3817
Premium Finance Company #23 .... 877-BANK-NYS, 212-709-5498
Private Investigator #10 518-474-4429
Private School, Mentally Retarded #49 . 518-473-9689
Promoter, Entertainment #54 800-225-5829
Psychiatrist /Psychologist #19 518-474-3817
Public Accountant-CPA #19 518-474-3817
Public Vessel (State Waters) #50 518-474-0445
Racetrack #15 .... 518-453-8460 X2
Racing Occupation #15 .... 518-453-8460 X2
Radiation Device, General-use #9 518-457-1202
Radiation Materials Permit #14 518-402-7550
Radiation Safety Officer #14 518-402-7580
Radiation Therapy Technologist #14 518-402-7580
Radiologic Technologist #14 518-402-7580
Radiologic Technology School #14 518-402-7580
Radon Testing Lab #14 518-402-7580
Rafting Guide, Whitewater #3 518-402-8838
Railroad/Steamboat Policeman #10 518-457-1932
Real Estate Agent/Broker/Office #10 518-474-4429
Real Estate Appraiser #10 518-474-4429
Real Estate Investment Trust #45 212-416-8122
Real Estate Offering, Registered #45 .. 212-416-8122
Real Estate Syndication #45 212-416-8122
Recreational Vehicle #50 518-474-0445
Regatta/Marina #50 518-474-0445
Reinsurance Intermediary #12 518-474-6630
Re-insurer #12 518-474-6623
Renderer #29 518-457-1215
Rental Agency, Limited #12 518-474-6630
Residential Facility #24 518-474-7112
Respiratory Therapist/Therapy Technician #19 518-474-3817
Restaurant Brewer #46 212-961-8385
Rock and Ice Climbing Guide #3 518-402-8838
Safe Deposit Company #23 .... 877-BANK-NYS, 212-709-1503
Sales Finance Company #23 .... 877-BANK-NYS, 212-709-5496
Sales Tax Permit #54 800-225-5829
Savings & Loan #23 .. 877-BANK-NYS, 212-709-1511
Savings Bank #23 ..... 877-BANK-NYS, 212-709-1511
School Administrator/Supervisor #17 518-474-3901

School Counselor #17 518-474-3901
School Media Specialist #17 518-474-3901
School, Non-Degree Granting/Proprietary #34 518-474-3969
School, Private #34 518-474-3969
School, Private, Dir./Teacher #34 518-474-3969
Scientific Collection #11 631-444-0483
Securities Broker/Dealer/Seller#1 212-416-8222
Security & Fire Alarm Installer #10 518-474-4429
Security Guard #10 518-474-4429
Self-Insured Carrier Rep. #57 518-402-6190
Shellfish-related Permit #11 631-444-0483
Short Hand Reporter #19 518-474-3817
Show, Permit to Operate #54 800-225-5829
Ski Tow #9 518-457-2131
Slaughterhouse #27 518-457-5459
Snowmobile Event #50 518-474-0445
Snowmobile Instructor #50 518-474-0445
Social Worker #19 518-474-3817
Solicitor (Fund Raising) #44 518-486-9797
Special Event, Serving Alcohol #46 212-961-8385
Specialty Food Producer #29 519-457-1215
Speech Pathologist/Audiologist #19 518-474-3817
Sporting License #11 518-402-8843
Sportsman License, Lifetime #11 518-402-8843
State Bid Result #36 518-474-1314
State Telecommunication Contr. #37 518-473-2658
Stevedore #20 212-742-9280
Stock Life Insurer #12 212-480-5038
Substance Abuse Provider #31 518-457-4384
Summer Camp / Mental Retarded #49 . 518-473-9689
Summer Day Camp #40 518-402-7600
Surveyor, Land #19 518-474-3817
Swimming Pool, Public/Group #40 518-402-7600
Takeover Statement, Registration #1 .. 212-416-8222
Tandem Trailer Permit (Thruway) #55 .. 518-436-3150
Teacher #17 518-474-3901
Teacher, Proprietary School #34 518-474-3969
Telemarketer Business #10 518-474-4429
Terminal Operator #53 800-225-5829
Theatrical Syndication #1 212-416-8222
Ticket Distributor #1 212-416-8222
Tour Vessel #32 518-471-5010
Trading Stamp Registration #10 518-474-4429
Tramway #9 518-457-2131
Trapper #11 518-402-8843
Traveling Summer Day Camp #40 518-402-7600
Treatment Center/Clinic #22 518-402-0911
Trust Company #23 .. 877-BANK-NYS, 212-709-1503
Underwater Land Lease #37 518-474-2195
Uniform Procedures Act Permit #11 518-402-8985
Upholster & Bedding Industry #10 518-474-4429
Utilization Mgmt. Registration#43 518-473-4842
Vessel Operator, Recreational/Touring #50 518-474-0445
Veterinarian/Veterinary Technician #19 518-474-3817
Viatical Settlement Broker #12 518-474-6630
Warehouse, Food #29 518-457-1215
Warehouse, Refrigerated #29 518-457-1215
Waste Water Treatment Plant Oper. #4518-402-8177
Water Supply Permit #11 518-402-8985
Water Treatment Plant Operator #13 518-402-7712
Waxing Establishment/Oper/Tech #10 518-474-4429
Weighmaster #28 518-457-3146
Weights/Measures Local Office #28 518-457-3146
Wildlife Collector #11 518-402-8985
Wildlife Rehabilitator #11 518-402-8985
Window Cleaning Equipment #9 518-457-1536
Woman-owned Business #35 518-292-5250
Workers Comp 3rd Party Admin. #57 .... 518 402-6190
Workers Comp Claim Rep. #57 .... 518 402-6190
Workers Comp PPO Applicant #57 518-402-6190
Workers' Comp Preferred Provider #43518-473-4842
Workplace Safety/Loss Prevention Consultant #9 518-457-2735
Wrestler #21 212-417-5700
Youth Shelter, Runaway/Homeless #24518-474-7112

New York Licensing Agency Information

1 Department of Law, Bureau of Investor Protection & Securities, 120 Broadway, 23rd Floor, New York, NY 10271; 212-416-8222, Fax: 212-416-8816. www.oag.state.ny.us

2 Department of Environmental Conservation, Bureau of Pesticide Management, 625 Broadway, Albany, NY 12233-7254; 518-402-8748, Fax: 518-402-9024. www.dec.state.ny.us Search Database at www.dec.state.ny.us/website/dshm/pesticid/appma n.htm#top   Note: Permits are issued from various regional offices.

3 Department of Environmental Conservation, Division of Forest Protection & Fire Mgmt., 625 Broadway, 8th Fl, Albany, NY 12233-2560; 518-402-8838, Fax: 518-485-8458. www.dec.state.ny.us/website/protection/rangers/fr guid6.html Email: dpaeweb@gw.dec.state.ny.us

4 Department of Environmental Conservation, Division of Water, Bureau of Watershed Compliance, 625 Broadway, Albany, NY 12233-3506; 518-402-8155, Fax: 518-402-8177. www.dec.state.ny.us Email: Webmaster@gw.dec.state.ny.us

5 Board of Examiners of Nursing Home Administrators, Bureau of Professional Credentialling, 161 Delaware Av, Delmar, NY 10254; 518-478-1060.

6 Department of Health, Bureau of Funeral Directing, 433 River St #303, Troy, NY 12180-2299; 518-402-0785, Fax: 518-402-0784.

7 Department of Health, Emergency Medical Services, 433 River St, #303, Troy, NY 12180; 518-402-0996, Fax: 518-402-0985. www.health.state.ny.us/nysdoh/ems/main.htm

8 Department of Labor, Boiler Safety Bureau, Bldg 12, Rm 165, Albany, NY 12240-0102; 518-457-2722, Fax: 518-485-9077.

9 Department of Labor, License & Certificate Unit, State Office Bldg Campus 12 Rm 166, Albany, NY 12240; 518-457-2735, Fax: 518-457-8452. www.labor.state.ny.us/

10 Department of State, Division of Licensing Services, 84 Holland Ave, Albany, NY 12208-3490; 518-474-4429, Fax: 518-473-6648. www.dos.state.ny.us/lcns/licensing.html Email: info@dos.state.ny.us Search Database at http://appsext5.dos.state.ny.us/l cns_public/lcns_query.lic_name_search_frm

11 Department of Environmental Conservation, Offices of Fish, Wildlife and Marine Resources, 625 Broadway, Albany, NY 12233-4750; 518-402-8985, Fax: 518-402-9027. www.dec.state.ny.us/website/dfwmr/index.html Email: fwinfo@gw.dec.state.ny.us <fwinfo@gw.dec.state.ny.us>

12 Insurance Department, Licensing Bureau Agency, One Commerce Plaza, Albany, NY 12257; 518-474-6630. www.ins.state.ny.us Email: licensing@ins.state.ny.us

13 Department of Health, Bureau of Water Supply Protection, 547 River Street, Flanigan Square, Rm 400, Troy, NY 12180; 518-402-7712, 800-458-1158 xt27650., Fax: 518-402-7599. www.health.state.ny.us/nysdoh/water/operate/oper ate.htm

14 Department of Health, Bureau of Environmental Radiation Protection, 547 River St, Flanigan Sq, Room 530, Troy, NY 12180-2216; 518-402-7580, Fax: 518-402-7575. www.health.state.ny.us/nysdoh/radtech/radtech.ht m   Email: berp@health.state.ny.us Search Database at www.health.state.ny.us/nys doh/radtech/radtech.htm

15 Racing & Wagering Board, 1 Watervliet Av Extension #2, Albany, NY 12206; 518-453-8460 x2, Fax: 518-453-8492. www.racing.state.ny.us Search Database at http://licensing.racing.state.ny.us/license.cfm

16 Temporary Commission on Lobbying, Agency Bldg #2, 17th Fl, Albany, NY 12223-1254; 518-474-7126, Fax: 518-473-6492. www.nylobby.state.ny.us Email: lobcom@emi.com Search Database at www.nylobby.state.ny.us/lobby_data.html

17 State Education Department, Office of Teaching, 5N Education Bldg, Albany, NY 12234; 518-474-3901, Fax: 518-473-0271. www.highered.nysed.gov/tcert/ Search Database at www.highered.nysed.gov/tcert/respublic/ocvs.htm

18 Unified Court System, Attorney Registration Unit, PO Box 2806, Church Street Station, New York, NY 10008; 212-428-2800, Fax: 212-428-2804. www.nycourts.gov   Email: attyreg@courts.state.ny.us Search Database at www.nycourts.gov/attorney s/registration/index.shtml

19 Education Department, Office of the Professions, 89 Washington Ave, State Education Bldg, 2nd Fl, Albany, NY 12234; 518-474-3817, attendant available 9-11:45AM and 12:45-4:30PM ESTTDD 518-473-1426. www.op.nysed.gov   Email: op4info@mail.nysed.gov Search Database at www.op.nysed.gov/opsearches.htm#nme

20 Division of Licenings & EIC, Waterfront Commission of New York Harbor, 39 Broadway, 4th Fl, New York, NY 10006; 212-742-9280, Fax: 212-905-9249. www.wcnynj.org

21 State Athletic Commission, Department of State, 123 Williams St, 20th Fl, New York, NY 10038; 212-417-5700, Fax: 212-417-4987. www.dos.state.ny.us/athletic/ Email: athletic@dos.state.ny.us

22 Department of Health, Office of Professional Medical Conduct, 433 River St. #303, Troy, NY 12180; 800-663-6114, 518-402-0836. www.health.state.ny.us/nysdoh/opmc/main.htm Email: opmc@health.state.ny.us Search Database at http://w3.health.state.ny.us/opmc/factions.nsf

23 State Banking Department, Licensed Financial Services Division, One State St, 3rd Fl, New York, NY 10004-1417; 877-BANK-NYS, Fax: 212-709-3582.   www.banking.state.ny.us Search at www.banking.state.ny.us/supinst.htm

24 Office of Children and Family Services, Legal Division, 52 Washington St, Rensselaer, NY 12144; 518-474-7112.   www.ocfs.state.ny.us

25 Office of Children and Family Services, Detention/Voluntary Agency Services Unit, 52 Washington St, Rensselaer, NY 12144; 518-473-4630. www.ocfs.state.ny.us

26 Department of Agriculture and Markets, Division of Plant Industry, 10B Airline Dr, Albany, NY 12235; 1-800-554-4501. www.agmkt.state.ny.us/   Note: User name and password required for dog license search.

27 Department of Agriculture and Markets, Division of Animal Industry, 10 B Airline Dr., Albany, NY 12235; 518-457-3502, Fax: 518-485-5816. www.agmkt.state.ny.us/AI/AIHome.html

28 Department of Agriculture and Markets, Division of Weights and Measures, 10B Airline Dr, Albany, NY 12235-0001; 518-457-3146. www.agmkt.state.ny.us/WM/WMHome.html Email: agmweigh@agmkt.state.ny.us

29 Department of Agriculture and Markets, Division of Food Safety and Inspection, 1 Winners Circle, Albany, NY 12235; 518-457-1215, Fax: 518-457-8892. www.agmkt.state.ny.us/FS/FSHome.html

30 Department of Agriculture and Markets, Division of Kosher Law Enforcement, 55 Hanson Pl, Brooklyn, NY 11217; 718-722-2852. www.agmkt.state.ny.us/KO/KOHome.html

31 Office of Alcoholism and Substance Abuse Services, Bureau of Professional Development, 1450 Western Ave, Albany, NY 12203-3526; 518-473-3460. www.oasas.state.ny.us/www/home.cfm Email: Certification@oasas.state.ny.us

32 State Canal Corporation, Interchange 23, Rte 9W, Albany, NY 12201; 518-436-2700. www.canals.state.ny.us/

33 Office of the State Comptroller, Office of Unclaimed Funds, 110 State St, 8th Fl, Albany, NY 12236; 518-270-2200. www.osc.state.ny.us

34 State Education Department, Bureau of Proprietary School Supervision, Education Building Annex, Rm 974, Albany, NY 12234; 518-474-3969. www.highered.nysed.gov/bpss/ Email: bpss@mail.nysed.gov

35 Empire State Development, Division of Minority and Women's Business Development, 30 S Pearl St, Albany, NY 12245; 518-292-5250. www.nylovesbiz.com/Small_and_Growing_Busin esses/mwbe.asp Search Database at http://205.232.252.35/   Note: A second office is at 633 3rd Av, NY, NY 10017, phone 212-803-2414.

36 State Office of General Services, Design and Construction, Corning Tower, Albany, NY 12242; 518-474-1314.
Email: design.construction @ogs.state.ny.us

37 State Office of General Services, Real Estate Development, 26th Fl Tower Bldg, Empire State Plaza, Albany, NY 12242; 518-474-2195.
www.ogs.state.ny.us/default.asp
Email: real.property @ogs.state.ny.us

38 Department of Health, Office of Health Systems Management, 161 Delaware Ave, Delmar, NY 12054; 518-408-1219.
Email: acfinfo@health.state.ny.us

39 State Department of Health, Bureau of Environmental Health, 547 River St, Rm 230, Flanagan Sq, Troy, NY 12180; 518-402-7940, Fax: 518-402-7949.

40 State Department of Health, Bureau of Community Environmental Health and Food Protection, 547 River St. Flanagan Sq, Rm 515, Troy, NY 12180; 518-402-7600.
www.health.state.ny.us/nysdoh/environ/phone.htm

41 State Department of Health, Wadsworth Center, Empire State Plaza, Concourse Level, Rm. E324, Albany, NY 12201-0509; 518-474-0005.
www.health.state.ny.us

42 Department of Health, Bureau of Narcotic Enforcement, 433 River St, Troy, NY 12180; 518-402-0707, Fax: 518-402-0709.
www.health.state.ny.us

43 State Department of Health, Bureau of Managed Care Certification & Surveillance, Corning Tower Bldg, Empire State Plaza, Rm 1911, Albany, NY 12237-0062; 518-473-4842.
www.health.state.ny.us/nysdoh/mancare/mcmain.htm

44 Office of the Attorney General, Charities Bureau, 120 Broadway, 3rd Fl, New York, NY 10271; 212-416-8430.
www.oag.state.ny.us/charities/charities.html
Email: Charities.Bureau@oag.state.ny.us Note: There is a second office at the State Capitol in Albany, in telephone area code 518.

45 Office of the Attorney General, Bureau of Real Estate Finance, 120 Broadway, New York, NY 10271; 212-416-8122, Fax: 212-416-8179.
www.oag.state.ny.us/realestate/realestate.html

46 State Liquor Authority, Divison of Alcoholic Beverage Control, 317 Lenox Ave, New York, NY 10027; 212-961-8385, Fax: 212-961-8283.
www.abc.state.ny.us
Search Database at
http://abc.state.ny.us/JSP/query/PublicQueryInstructPage.jsp Note: The Agency maintains three zone offices located in New York City, Albany (518-474-3114) and Buffalo (716-847-3035) and one satellite office in Syracuse (315-428-4198). Public Affairs office is 212-961-8300.

47 New York Lottery, 1 Broadway Center, Schenectady, NY 12301-7500; 518-388-3300, Fax: 518-388-3403.
www.nylottery.org/index.php

48 State Office of Mental Health, Bureau of Inspection and Certification, 44 Holland Ave, Albany, NY 12229; 518-474-5570, Fax: 518-486-5587.

49 Office of Mental Retardation and Developmental Disabilities, Developmental Disabilities Service Office, 44 Holland Ave, Albany, NY 12229; 518-473-9689, Fax: 518-474-1335.
www.omr.state.ny.us Note: There is also a New York City Office at 75 Morton St, 212-229-3231.

50 State Parks, Recreation and Historic Preservation, Bureau of Marine and Recreational Vehicles, Agency Building 1, 11th Fl, Empire State Plaza, Albany, NY 12238; 518-474-0445, Fax: 518-486-7378.
Snowmobiles must be registered with state DMV.

51 State Police, BCI Section; Firearms Section, 1220 Washington Ave, Bldg 22, Albany, NY 12226; 518) 457-2627.
www.troopers.state.ny.us
Email: PIOOFFIC@troopers.state.ny.us

52 Department of Taxation and Finance, Registration and Bonding Tax Unit, Building 8, Rm 855, State Campus, Albany, NY 12227; 800-225-5829, Fax: 518-457-9807.
www.tax.state.ny.us/sbc/

53 Department of Taxation & Finance, Registration & Data Services Bureau, Commodities Tax Unit, Building 8, Rm 400, State Campus, Albany, NY 12227; 800-225-5829.
www.tax.state.ny.us

54 Department of Taxation & Finance, Sales Tax Registration Unit, Building 8, Rm 431, State Campus, Albany, NY ; 800-225-5829.
www.tax.state.ny.us

55 State Thruway Authority, Department Traffic Management, 200 Southern Blvd, Albany, NY 12201-0189; 518-436-3079.
www.thruway.state.ny.us/commercial/index.html

56 State Department of Transportation, Passenger and Freight Safety Division, 50 Wolf Rd. Pod 53, Albany, NY 12232; 518-457-1016.
www.dot.state.ny.us

57 State Workers' Compensation Board, Health Provider Administration, 100 Broadway-Menands, Albany, NY 12241; 866-750-5157, Fax: 518-473-9166.
www.wcb.state.ny.us www.wcb.state.ny.us

New York Federal Courts

The following list indicates the district and division name for each county in the state. If the bankruptcy court location is different from the district court, then the location of the bankruptcy court appears in parentheses.

New York County/Court Cross Reference

County	District	Division
Albany	Northern	Albany
Allegany	Western	Buffalo
Bronx	Southern	New York City
Broome	Northern	Binghamton (Utica)
Cattaraugus	Western	Buffalo
Cayuga	Northern	Syracuse (Utica)
Chautauqua	Western	Buffalo
Chemung	Western	Rochester
Chenango	Northern	Binghamton (Utica)
Clinton	Northern	Albany-varies
Columbia	Northern (Southern)	Albany (Poughkeepsie)
Cortland	Northern	Syracuse (Utica)
Delaware	Northern	Binghamton (Utica)
Dutchess	Southern	White Plains (Poughkeepsie)
Erie	Western	Buffalo
Essex	Northern	Albany -varies
Franklin	Northern	Albany-varies (Albany)
Fulton	Northern	Utica (Albany)
Genesee	Western	Buffalo
Greene	Northern (Southern)	Albany (Poughkeepsie)
Hamilton	Northern	Utica
Herkimer	Northern	Utica
Jefferson	Northern	Albany-varies (Albany)
Kings	Eastern	Brooklyn
Lewis	Northern	Albany-varies (Utica)
Livingston	Western	Rochester
Madison	Northern	Syracuse (Utica)
Monroe	Western	Rochester
Montgomery	Northern	Utica (Albany)
Nassau	Eastern	Brooklyn (Westbury)
New York	Southern	New York City
Niagara	Western	Buffalo
Oneida	Northern	Utica
Onondaga	Northern	Syracuse (Utica)
Ontario	Western	Rochester
Orange	Southern	White Plains (Poughkeepsie)
Orleans	Western	Buffalo
Oswego	Northern	Syracuse (Utica)
Otsego	Northern	Binghamton (Utica)
Putnam	Southern	White Plains (Poughkeepsie)
Queens	Eastern	Brooklyn
Rensselaer	Northern	Albany
Richmond	Eastern	Brooklyn
Rockland	Southern	White Plains
Saratoga	Northern	Albany
Schenectady	Northern	Albany
Schoharie	Northern	Albany
Schuyler	Western	Rochester
Seneca	Western	Rochester
St. Lawrence	Northern	Albany-varies (Albany)
Steuben	Western	Rochester
Suffolk	Eastern	Central Islip
Sullivan	Southern	White Plains (Poughkeepsie)
Tioga	Northern	Binghamton (Utica)
Tompkins	Northern	Syracuse (Utica)
Ulster	Northern (Southern)	Albany (Poughkeepsie)
Warren	Northern	Albany
Washington	Northern	Albany
Wayne	Western	Rochester
Westchester	Southern	White Plains
Wyoming	Western	Buffalo
Yates	Western	Rochester

Standards for Federal Courts: Search fee is $26.00 per item (one party name or case number). Copy fee is $.50 per page. Certification fee is $9.00 per document, double for exemplification, if available. All fees standard unless noted in profile. Mail Search: always enclose a stamped self addressed envelope unless otherwise noted. Most courts accept fax requests or will suggest a copying/search vendor. Before releasing records, all courts require prepayment, unless noted.

Open records are located at the court unless otherwise noted. District courts index by defendant and plaintiff as well as by case number. Bankruptcy courts usually index by debtor and case number. While most courts now have their indexes on computer, many may still maintain index card files as well.

Courts offering internet access via CM-ECF or older RACER, PACER, or Web-PACER systems charge $.08 per page fee unless noted as free. Where PACER is available, the universal sign-up number is 800-676-6856. Find PACER and the US Party/Case Index at http://pacer.psc.uscourts.gov.

US District Court

Eastern District of New York

Brooklyn Division Clerk of Court, 225 Cadman Plaza E, Rm 130, Brooklyn Courthouse, Brooklyn, NY 11201 (also use mail address for courier delivery), 718-260-2600, records rm- 718-260-2285, crim dockets- 718-260-2610, civil dockets- 718-260-2610. Hours- 8:30AM-5PM. www.nyed.uscourts.gov

Counties: Kings, Queens, Richmond. Cases from Nassau and Suffolk may also be filed here (but paper records and cases are heard in Central Islip Div.), but all records are available electronically through PACER from this Brooklyn Division.

Searches & Indexing: Results do not include SSN or DOB. Computer index maintained back to 1982. New cases in the index 2 days after filing date. Records purged never. Case records for Suffolk and Nassau counties are not physically located here - see Central Islip Division.

Fee & Payment: Pay by Visa/MC, money order, cashier's or personal check. Payee: Clerk, US District Court. Prepayment required.

Phone Search: No searching by telephone.

Mail Search: search usually completed- 1-2 days. SASE not required.

In Person Search: Fee charged if court performs your search. Self-serve copier - $.25 per page.

E-Services: ECF replaces PACER. This system includes electronic records from Suffolk and Nassau Counties, Long Island. PACER records go back to 1/1990. New records online after 1 day. ECF at https://ecf.nyed.uscourts.gov. Decisions of Interest and Cases of Interest at www.nyed.uscourts.gov. **Other Online Access:** Access to court calendars at www.nyed.uscourts.gov/cgi-bin/caldir.pl.

Central Islip Division Court Clerk, 100 Federal Plaza, Central Islip, NY 17722-4438 (also use mail address for courier delivery), 631-712-6000, records rm- 631-712-6032. Hours- 8:30AM-5PM. www.nyed.uscourts.gov

Counties: Nassau, Suffolk. Cases from these counties may be filed in Brooklyn Division, but heard in Central Islip. Central Islip cases can be found on Brooklyn's PACER system.

Searches & Indexing: Results do not include SSN or DOB. Computer and card indexes maintained; computer index back to 1980, 1990. New cases in the index 2 days after filing date. Records purged never.

Fee & Payment: Pay by Visa/MC, money order, cashier's or personal check. Payee: Clerk, US District Court. Prepayment required.

Phone Search: Some limited docket information is available by phone.

Mail Search: search usually completed- 1-2 days. Include SASE for return.

In Person Search: Fee charged if court performs your search. Self-serve copier - $.25 per page.

E-Services: ECF replaces PACER whose records did go back to 1/1990. New records online after 1 day. ECF at https://ecf.nyed.uscourts.gov. Decisions of Interest and Cases of Interest at www.nyed.uscourts.gov. **Other Online Access:** Access to court calendars at www.nyed.uscourts.gov/cgi-bin/caldir.pl.

US Bankruptcy Court

Eastern District of New York

Brooklyn Division Court Clerk, 271 Cadman Plaza East, Brooklyn, NY 11201 (also use mail address for courier delivery), 718-330-2188. Hours- 9AM-4:30PM. www.nyeb.uscourts.gov

Counties: Kings, Queens, Richmond. Kings and Queens County Chapter 11 cases may also be assigned to Westbury. Other Queens County cases may be assigned to Westbury Division. Nassau County Chapter 11 cases may be assigned here. This office relocating to 271 Cadman Plaza East on Sept. 23, 2005.

Searches & Indexing: Results do not include SSN or DOB. Computer index maintained; older cases indexed on microfiche. New cases in the index 1 day after filing date. Records purged yearly.

Fee & Payment: Pay by money order, cashier check, business check. No personal checks. Payee: Clerk, US Bankruptcy Court. Prepayment required.

Phone Search: Only docket information is available by phone. Voice Case Information Service available, call VCIS at 800-252-2537 or 718-852-5726.

Mail Search: search usually completed- 1-2 weeks. SASE not required.

In Person Search: Fee charged if court performs your search. Self-serve copier - $.10 per page.

E-Services: ECF replaces PACER whose records did go back to 1991. New records online after 1 day. ECF at https://ecf.nyeb.uscourts.gov **Opinions Online:** www.nyeb.uscourts.gov/jud_o pinions/search.php. Opinions date back to 4/2004. **Other Online Access:** Access calendars free at www.nyeb.uscourts.gov/calendars.htm.

Central Islip Division Court Clerk, Long Island Federal Courthouse, 290 Federal Plaza, 2nd Fl, Central Islip, NY 11722 (also use mail address for courier delivery), 631-712-6200. Hours- 9AM-4:30PM. www.nyeb.uscourts.gov

Counties: Suffolk, Nassau.

Searches & Indexing: Results include last 4 SSN digits. Computer index maintained. New cases in the index 1-2 days after filing date. Records purged yearly.

Fee & Payment: Pay by money order, cashier's or personal check. No debtor's checks accepted. Payee: Clerk, US Bankruptcy Court. Prepayment required. Enclose a FedEx package for expedited service.

Phone Search: Basic docket data only available by phone. Voice Case Information Service available, call VCIS at 800-252-2537 or 718-852-5726.

Mail Search: search usually completed- 1 week. SASE not required.

In Person Search: Fee charged if court performs your search. Self-serve copier available - $.10 per page.

E-Services: ECF replaces PACER whose records did go back to 1991. New records online after 1 day. ECF at https://ecf.nyeb.uscourts.gov **Opinions Online:** www.nyeb.uscourts.gov/jud_o pinions/search.php. Opinions date back to 4/2004. **Other Online Access:** Access calendars free at www.nyeb.uscourts.gov/calendars.htm.

US District Court

Northern District of New York

Albany Division Court Clerk, 445 Broadway, Rm 509, James T Foley Courthouse, Albany, NY 12207-2924 (also use mail address for courier delivery), 518-257-1800. Hours- 9AM-4PM. www.nynd.uscourts.gov

Counties: Albany, Clinton, Columbia, Essex, Greene, Rensselaer, Saratoga, Schenectady, Schoharie, Ulster, Warren, Washington. This court provides the judges (and physical case records) for Plattsburgh Division - Clinton, Essex, Franklin counties - although cases are often assigned to Syracuse, Utica or Binghamton Divisions on occasion.

Searches & Indexing: Case indexes on computer terminal in any Northern District Division. Results include last 4 SSN digits, also birth year. Both computer and card indexes maintained. New cases in the index 1 day after filing date.

Fee & Payment: Pay by money order, cashier's or personal check. Payee: Clerk, US District Court. Prepayment required.

Phone Search: No searching by telephone.

Mail Search: search usually completed- 1-2 days. SASE not required.

In Person Search: Fee charged if court performs your search. No self-serve copier available.

E-Services: ECF replaces PACER whose records did go back to 6/1991. New records online after 1 day. ECF at https://ecf.nynd.uscourts.gov **Opinions Online:** www.nysd.uscourts.gov/co urtweb/PubMain.htm. Selected Rulings only.

Binghamton Division Court Clerk, 15 Henry St, Binghamton, NY 13902 (also use mail address for courier delivery), 607-773-2893, civil dockets- 607-773-2638. Hours- 9AM-4PM. www.nynd.uscourts.gov

Counties: Broome, Chenango, Delaware, Jefferson, Lewis, Otsego, St. Lawrence, Tioga. This court provides the judges (and physical case records) for the Watertown Division - Jefferson, Lewis and St Lawrence counties - although cases are often assigned to Syracuse, Utica or especially Albany Divisions.

Searches & Indexing: Case indexes on computer terminal in any Northern District Division. Results include last 4 SSN digits, also birth year. Computer index maintained. New cases in the index 1 day after filing date. Open records may be located at this court.

Fee & Payment: Pay by Visa/MC, money order, cashier's or personal check. Payee: Clerk, US District Court. Prepayment required.

Phone Search: Only docket information is available by phone.

Mail Search: search usually completed- 1-2 days. Include SASE for return.

In Person Search: Fee charged if court performs your search. No self-serve copier available.

E-Services: ECF replaces PACER whose records did go back to 6/1991. New records online after 1 day. ECF at https://ecf.nynd.uscourts.gov **Opinions Online:** www.nysd.uscourts.gov/co urtweb/PubMain.htm. Selected Rulings only.

Syracuse Division Court Clerk, PO Box 7367, Syracuse, NY 13261-7367 (courier address: 100 S Clinton St, Syracuse, NY 13261), 315-234-8500, records rm- 315-234-8544, Fax-315-234-8501. Hours- 9AM-4PM. www.nynd.uscourts.gov

Counties: Cayuga, Cortland, Madison, Onondaga, Oswego, Tompkins. May also have some cases from Watertown Division - Jefferson, Lewis, or St Lawrence counties - and rarely from Clinton, Essex, Franklin counties.

Searches & Indexing: Case indexes on computer terminal in any Northern District Division. Results do not include SSN or DOB. Computer index maintained; criminal goes back to 1994, civil to 1991. New cases in the index 1 day after filing date.

Fee & Payment: Pay by Visa/MC (in person only), money order, cashier's or personal check. Payee: Clerk, US District Court. Prepayment required.

Phone Search: Only docket information is available by phone.

Mail Search: search usually completed- 1-2 days. Include SASE for return.

In Person Search: Fee charged if court performs your search. No self-serve copier available.

E-Services: ECF replaces PACER whose records did go back to 6/1991. New records online immediately. ECF at https://ecf.nynd.uscourts.gov **Opinions Online:** www.nysd.uscourts.gov/courtweb/PubMain.htm. Selected rulings only.

Utica Division Court Clerk, Alexander Pirnie Bldg, 10 Broad St, Utica, NY 13501 (also use mail address for courier delivery), 315-793-8151, records rm- x8. Hours- 9AM-4PM. www.nynd.uscourts.gov

Counties: Fulton, Hamilton, Herkimer, Montgomery, Oneida. May also have some cases from Watertown Division - Jefferson, Lewis, or St Lawrence counties - and rarely from Clinton, Essex, Franklin counties.

Searches & Indexing: Case indexes on computer terminal in any Northern District Division (As of 1995, Albany, Binghamton and Syracuse no longer send their physical records to Utica). Results do not include SSN or DOB. Computer and card indexes available; computer back to 1996. New cases in the index 1 day after filing date. Records purged every 6 months. Closed case records from the other 3 Northern district courts are assembled here before going to New York Records Center.

Fee & Payment: Pay by Visa/MC, money order, cashier's, business or personal check. Payee: Clerk, US District Court. Prepayment required.

Phone Search: Only computerized Information back to 1991 is available by phone.

Mail Search: search usually completed- 1 week. SASE not required.

In Person Search: Fee charged if court performs your search. No self-serve copier available.

E-Services: ECF replaces PACER whose records did go back to 6/1991. New records online after 1 day. ECF at https://ecf.nynd.uscourts.gov **Opinions   Online:** www.nysd.uscourts.gov/courtweb/PubMain.htm. Selected rulings only.

US Bankruptcy Court

Northern District of New York

Albany Division Court Clerk Office, 445 Broadway #330, James T Foley Courthouse, Albany, NY 12207 (also use mail address for courier delivery), 518-257-1661, records rm- 518-257-1650.   Hours-   9AM-4PM. www.nynb.uscourts.gov

Counties: Albany, Clinton, Essex, Franklin, Fulton, Jefferson, Montgomery, Rensselaer, Saratoga, Schenectady, Schoharie, St. Lawrence, Warren, Washington.

Searches & Indexing: Both computer and card indexes maintained. New cases in the index 48 hours after filing date.

Fee & Payment: Pay by Visa/MC (in person only), no business or personal checks accepted. Payee: Clerk, US Bankruptcy Court. Prepayment required.

Phone Search: Only docket information is available by phone. Voice Case Information Service available, call VCIS at 800-206-1952.

Mail Search: search usually completed- 1-2 days. If case number is not known, the turnaround time may be as long as 5 days. Include SASE for return.

In Person Search: Fee charged if court performs your search. No self-serve copier available.

E-Services: ECF replaces PACER whose records did go back to 1992. New records online after 1 day. ECF at https://ecf.nynb.uscourts.gov **Opinions Online:** www.nynb.uscourts.gov/decisions.htm. **Other Online Access:** Access weekly calendars free at www.nynb.uscourts.gov/usbc/calendar/calendar.html.

Utica Division Court Clerk, Rm 230, 10 Broad St, Utica, NY 13502 (also use mail address for courier delivery), 315-793-8101, Fax-315-793-8128. Hours- 9AM-4PM. www.nynb.uscourts.gov

Counties: Broome, Cayuga, Chenango, Cortland, Delaware, Hamilton, Herkimer, Lewis, Madison, Oneida, Onondaga, Otsego, Oswego, Tioga, Tompkins.

Searches & Indexing: As of 1/1995, Jefferson and St. Lawrence Counties moved to Albany Division from Utica, while Broome, Chenango, Delaware, Otsego, Tioga and Tompkins Counties moved to Utica Division from Albany. Results include SSN. Both computer and card indexes maintained. New cases in the index 24 hours after filing date.

Fee & Payment: Pay by Visa/MC (in person only), money order, cashier's or personal check. No debtor's checks accepted. Payee: Clerk, US Bankruptcy Court.

Phone Search: Only docket information is available by phone. Voice Case Information Service available, call VCIS at 800-206-1952.

Mail Search: search usually completed- 5 days. SASE not required.

In Person Search: Fee charged if court performs your search. No self-serve copier available.

E-Services: ECF replaces PACER whose records did go back to 1992. New records online after 1 day. ECF at https://ecf.nynb.uscourts.gov **Opinions Online:** www.nynb.uscourts.gov/decisions.htm. **Other Online Access:** Access weekly calendars free at www.nynb.uscourts.gov/usbc/calendar/calendar.html.

US District Court

Southern District of New York

New York City Division Court Clerk, 500 Pearl St, New York, NY 10007 (also use mail address for courier delivery), 212-805-0136, records rm- Open recs: 212-805-0710; Closed recs: 212-805-0715. Hours- 8:30AM-5PM. www.nysd.uscourts.gov

Counties: Bronx, New York. A 2nd courthouse at 40 Centre St is an Appellate Division with some District Cases heard there; search both at Pearl St location. Some cases from the counties in the White Plains Division are also assigned to this New York Division.

Searches & Indexing: Results do not include SSN or DOB. Computer index maintained. New cases in the index 2 days after filing date. Records purged every 6 months.

Fee & Payment: Pay by no business or personal checks accepted. Payee: Clerk of Court, S.D.N.Y. Prepayment required.

Phone Search: Only docket information is available by phone.

Mail Search: search usually completed- 1-2 weeks. Include SASE for return.

In Person Search: Fee charged if court performs your search. Self-serve copier available - $.25 per page.

E-Services: ECF replaces PACER whose records did go back to early 1990. New records online after 1 day. ECF at https://ecf.nysd.uscourts.gov **Opinions Online:** www.nysd.uscourts.gov/courtweb. Search selected rulings online using CourtWeb. Adobe Acrobat Reader required to download and view rulings.

White Plains Division Court Clerk, 300 Quarropas St, US Courthouse, White Plains, NY 10601 (also use mail address for courier delivery), 914-390-4100.   Hours-   8:30AM-5PM. www.nysd.uscourts.gov

Counties: Dutchess, Orange, Putnam, Rockland, Sullivan, Westchester. Some cases may be assigned to New York Division.

Searches & Indexing: Results do not include SSN or DOB. Computer index maintained back to 1999. Indexes automated since 1983. New cases in the index 2 days after filing date. Records purged every 6 months.

Fee & Payment: Pay by Visa/MC, no business or personal checks accepted. Attorney checks accepted. Payee: Clerk of Court, S.D.N.Y. Prepayment required.

Phone Search: No searching by telephone.

Mail Search: search usually completed- 1-2 days. Include SASE for return.

In Person Search: Fee charged if court performs your search. Self-serve copier available - $.15 per page.

E-Services: ECF replaces PACER whose records did go back to early 1990. New records online after 1 day. ECF at https://ecf.nysd.uscourts.gov **Opinions Online:** www.nysd.uscourts.gov/courtweb. Search selected rulings online using CourtWeb. Adobe Acrobat Reader required to download and view rulings.

US Bankruptcy Court

Southern District of New York

New York Division Court Clerk, Rm 534, 1 Bowling Green, New York, NY 10004-1408 (also use mail address for courier delivery), 212-668-2870. Hours- 9AM-4PM. www.nysb.uscourts.gov

Counties: Bronx, New York.

Searches & Indexing: Results include last 4 SSN digits. Both computer and card indexes maintained. New cases in the index 1-3 days after filing date. Records purged every 6 months.

Fee & Payment: Pay by money order, cashier check, business check. No personal checks. Payee: Clerk, Bankruptcy Court. Prepayment required.

Phone Search: This court only reveals whether a case is pending via phone. Voice Case Information Service available, call VCIS at 212-668-2772.

Mail Search: search usually completed- 2-3 days. SASE not required.

In Person Search: permitted. Self-serve copier available - $.25 per page.

E-Services: ECF replaces PACER whose records did go back to 6/1991. New records online after 1 day. ECF at http://ecf.nysb.uscourts.gov **Other Online Access:** Judges Bernstein, Gerber, Gonzales calendars at http://216.220.101.146/calendar/. All other judge calendars on ECF system.

Poughkeepsie Division Court Clerk, 176 Church St, Poughkeepsie, NY 12601 (also use mail address for courier delivery), 845-452-4200, Fax-845-452-8375. Hours- 8:30AM-5PM. www.nysb.uscourts.gov

Counties: Columbia, Dutchess, Greene, Orange, Putnam, Sullivan, Ulster.

Searches & Indexing: Results include last 4 SSN digits. Both computer and card indexes maintained. New cases in the index immediately after filing date. Records purged every 6 months.

Fee & Payment: Pay by money order, cashier check, business check. No personal checks. Payee: Clerk, Bankruptcy Court. Prepayment required.

Phone Search: This court only reveals whether a case is pending via phone. Voice Case Information Service available, call VCIS at 212-668-2772.

Mail Search: search usually completed- 3 days. SASE not required.

In Person Search: Fee charged if court performs your search. Self-serve copier - $.15 per page.

E-Services: ECF replaces PACER whose records did go back to 6/1991. New records online after 1 day. ECF at http://ecf.nysb.uscourts.gov **Other Online Access:** Judges Bernstein, Gerber, Gonzales calendars at http://216.220.101.146/calendar/. All other judge calendars on ECF system.

White Plains Division Court Clerk, 300 Quarropas St, White Plains, NY 10601 (also use mail address for courier delivery), 914-390-4060. Hours- 8:30AM-5PM. www.nysb.uscourts.gov

Counties: Rockland, Westchester.

Searches & Indexing: Results include last 4 SSN digits. Computer, microfiche and card indexes maintained. New cases in the index immediately after filing date. Records purged every 6 months. District-wide searches available for cases back to 1991.

Fee & Payment: Pay by Visa/MC (in person only), money order, business check. No personal or debtor's checks accepted. Payee: Clerk, US Bankruptcy Court. Prepayment required.

Phone Search: This court only reveals whether a case is pending via phone. Voice Case Information Service available, call VCIS at 212-668-2772.

Mail Search: search usually completed- 1-2 days. Include SASE for return. **In Person Search:** Fee charged if court performs your search. Self-serve copier - $.15 per page.

E-Services: ECF replaces PACER whose records did go back to 6/1991. New records online after 1 day. ECF at http://ecf.nysb.uscourts.gov **Other Online Access:** Judges Bernstein, Gerber, Gonzales calendars at http://216.220.101.146/calendar/. All other judge calendars on ECF system.

US District Court

Western District of New York

Buffalo Division Court Clerk, Rm 304, 68 Court St, Buffalo, NY 14202 (use mail address for courier delivery), 716-551-4211, Fax-716-551-4850. 9AM-5PM. www.nywd.uscourts.gov

Counties: Allegany, Cattaraugus, Chautauqua, Erie, Genesee, Niagara, Orleans, Wyoming. Prior to 1982, this division included what is now the Rochester Division.

Searches & Indexing: Results do not include SSN or DOB. Computer index maintained; criminal back to 1990. New cases in the index 2 days after filing date. Records purged never.

Fee & Payment: Pay by money order, cashier's or personal check. Payee: Clerk, US District Court. Prepayment required. **Phone Search:** No searching by telephone. **Mail Search:** search usually completed- 1-2 days. SASE not required.

In Person Search: Fee charged if court performs your search. No self-serve copier available.

E-Services: ECF replaces PACER whose records did go back to 1992. New records online after 1 day. ECF at https://ecf.nywd.uscourts.gov **Opinions Online:** www.nywd.uscourts.gov/decision/decision.php.

Rochester Division Court Clerk, Rm 2120, 100 State St, Rochester, NY 14614 (also use mail address for courier delivery), 585-613-4000, Fax-585-613-4035. Hours- 9AM-5PM. www.nywd.uscourts.gov **Counties:** Chemung, Livingston, Monroe, Ontario, Schuyler, Seneca, Steuben, Wayne, Yates.

Searches & Indexing: Division established in 1981. Results do not include SSN or DOB. Computer index maintained back to 1995. New cases in the index 1 day after filing date. Records purged never. Cases closed back to 1996 also held here. Earlier case records and indexes held in Buffalo Division, Erie County.

Fee & Payment: Pay by money order, cashier's or personal check. Payee: Clerk, US District Court. Prepayment required. Will fax documents; call for instructions. **Phone Search:** Simple docket information available by phone.

Mail Search: search usually completed- 1-2 days. Mail searches including years prior to 1982 will be forwarded to Buffalo Division. SASE not required.

In Person Search: Fee charged if court performs your search. No self-serve copier available.

E-Services: ECF replaces PACER whose records did go back to 1992. New records online after 1 day. ECF at https://ecf.nywd.uscourts.gov **Opinions Online:** www.nywd.uscourts.gov/decision/decision.php.

US Bankruptcy Court

Western District of New York

Buffalo Division Court Clerk, Olympic Towers, 300 Pearl St #250, Buffalo, NY 14202-2501 (also use mail address for courier delivery), 716-551-4130. Hours- 8AM-4:30PM. www.nywb.uscourts.gov

Counties: Allegany, Cattaraugus, Chautauqua, Erie, Genesee, Niagara, Orleans, Wyoming.

Searches & Indexing: Results include last 4 SSN digits. Both computer and card indexes maintained. New cases in the index 24 hours after filing date. Records purged never.

Fee & Payment: Pay by money order, cashier check, business check. No personal checks. Payee: Clerk, US Bankruptcy Court. Prepayment required.

Phone Search: Only docket information is available by phone. Voice Case Information Service available, call VCIS at 800-776-9578 or 716-551-5311. **Mail Search:** search usually completed- 2-3 days. Include SASE for return. **In Person Search:** Fee charged if court performs your search. No self-serve copier available.

E-Services: ECF replaces PACER whose records did go back to 8/1987. New records online after 1 day. ECF at https://ecf.nywb.uscourts.gov **Opinions Online:** www.nywb.uscourts.gov/decisions/. **Other Online Access:** Calendars free at www.nywb.uscourts.gov/calendars.php.

Rochester Division Court Clerk, Rm 1220, 100 State St, Rochester, NY 14614 (also use mail address for courier delivery), 585-613-4200. Hours- 8AM-5PM. www.nywb.uscourts.gov

Counties: Chemung, Livingston, Monroe, Ontario, Schuyler, Seneca, Steuben, Wayne, Yates.

Searches & Indexing: Results include last 4 SSN digits. Computer and microfiche indexes maintained. New cases in the index 24 hours after filing date. Records purged never. District-wide searches available back to 9/1987.

Fee & Payment: Pay by money order, cashier check, business check. No personal checks. Payee: Clerk, Bankruptcy Court. Prepayment required.

Phone Search: Only docket information is available by phone. Voice Case Information Service available, call VCIS at 800-776-9578 or 716-551-5311.

Mail Search: search usually completed- 1-2 days. Include SASE for return.

In Person Search: Fee charged if court performs your search. No self-serve copier available.

E-Services: ECF replaces PACER whose records did go back to 8/1987. New records online after 1 day. ECF at https://ecf.nywb.uscourts.gov **Opinions Online:** www.nywb.uscourts.gov/decisions/. **Other Online Access:** Calendars free at www.nywb.uscourts.gov/calendars.php

New York County Courts

Court	Jurisdiction	No. of Courts	How Organized
Supreme Courts*	General	11	12 Districts
County Courts*	General	2	57 Counties
Combined Courts*	General	57	
City Courts*	Limited	61	61 Cities (outside of NYC)
District Courts*	Limited	10	Nassau, Suffolk Counties
Civil /Criminal Courts of the City of New York*	Municipal	6	Boroughs
Town and Village Justice Courts	Municipal	2173	
Surrogates' Courts*	Probate	62	62 Counties and Boroughs
Court of Claims	Limited	1	
Family Courts	Special	62	62 Counties and Boroughs

* Profiled in this Sourcebook.

Court	CIVIL								
	Tort	Contract	Real Estate	Min. Claim	Max. Claim	Small Claims	Estate	Eviction	Domestic Relations
Supreme Courts*	X	X	X	$25,000	No Max				X
County Courts*	X	X	X	$0	$25,000				
City Courts*	X	X	X	$0	$15,000	$3000		X	
District Courts*	X	X	X	$0	$15,000	$3000		X	
Civil /Criminal Courts of the City of New York*	X	X	X	$0	$25,000	$3000		X	
Town and Village Justice Courts	X	X	X	$0	$3000	$3000			
Surrogates' Courts*							X		X
Court of Claims	X	X	X	$0	No Max				
Family Courts									X

Court	CRIMINAL				
	Felony	Misdemeanor	DWI/DUI	Preliminary Hearing	Juvenile
Supreme Courts*	X				
County Courts*				X	
City Courts*	X	X	X	X	
District Courts*		X	X	X	
Civil /Criminal Courts of the City of New York*		X	X	X	
Town and Village Justice Courts		X	X	X	
Surrogates' Courts*					
Court of Claims					
Family Courts					X

ADMINISTRATION   Office of Court Administration, 25 Beaver St, New York, NY 10004, 212-428-2700. www.courts.state.ny.us

COURT STRUCTURE   "Supreme and County Courts" are the highest trial courts in the state, equivalent to Circuit or District Courts in other states. New York's Supreme and County Courts may be administered together or separately; when separate, there is a clerk for each. Supreme and/or County Courts are not appeals courts. Supreme Courts handle civil cases (usually civil cases over $25,000 but there are many exceptions). County Courts handle felony cases, and in many counties, these County Courts also handle misdemeanors.

City Courts handle misdemeanors and lower-value civil cases, small claims, and eviction cases. Not all counties have City Courts, thus cases there fall to the Supreme and County Courts respectively, or, in a many counties, to the small Town and Village Courts, which can number in the dozens within a county.

The staff at NY Superior, County, and City Courts are NY state employees. However, in some counties (usually smaller NY counties), the clerk for Supreme and County Courts may also be the "County Clerk" - these duo-role clerks are employed partly by the county, and partly by the state, which creates a question of whose "directives" and rules do they follow in regard to court record search procedures. More below.

Records for Supreme and County Courts are maintained by the County Clerks, who are county employees. There are exceptions. In New York City - with its five boroughs - the courts records are administered directly by the state OCA (Office of Court Administration). Also, there are a small number of upstate counties where the Supreme Court OR County Court records are maintained by their court clerk (state employee), and only an index list of cases and defendants is provided to the County Clerk (county employee).

You will find separate entries for "County Clerks" for most NY counties in this edition. While the County Clerks are not courts, they do hold court records and the methods for searching at the County Clerk office are far different from searching at the Courts themselves. In counties where the County Clerk and the Chief Court Clerk are one in the same, you will find only the standard Supreme & County Court listing. In other counties - where the Supreme and County Courts direct all searches to the County Clerk - you will find the information for searching at the County Clerk office.

In some NY counties, the address for the County Clerk is the same as for the Supreme and County Courts. Exceptions are noted in the court profiles, and a separate profile is provided that lists the County Clerk and the "County" rules for a "countywide record search." Note also that, due to limitations in the receiving of records from the Chief Court Clerks, the County Clerk may only be able to do a civil record search, or, rarely, only a criminal record search. Each county is going to be different.

City Courts - While all City Courts are administered by state employees, there are a few City Courts that will do a city-only record check despite the edict to state employees that they must direct record searches to the OCA for the statewide record check. Records from City Courts do not go to the County Clerk. Records from City Courts go directly to the OCA.

In at least 20 New York Counties, misdemeanor records are only available at city, town, or village courts. This is also true of small claims and eviction records. Town and Village Courts are be listed at the end of each county section.

Now you have an overview of the confusing array of NY courts. You may have concluded that record searching would be a daunting task if you did not have the individual court profiles, updated progressively, provided here to aid you. You may also conclude that an accurate search for misdemeanor records is nearly impossible as there are over 1200 Town and Village Courts in NY which may or may not be accurately reporting their case records.

**COURT RECORD
SEARCHES
FROM THE OCA**

OCA will perform an electronic search for criminal history information from a database of criminal case records from all boroughs and all counties including Supreme Courts, County Courts, and City Courts. At press time, it is not clear that all City Courts submit all misdemeanors to this database. The search fee, payable by check, is $52.00 per name. The search is available by mail or in-person (6 to 24-hour turnaround time), or high volume requesters may order online with email return (same day if ordered by 2:30 pm). The Criminal History Record Search Unit can be reached at 212-428-2943 or www.nycourts.gov/apps/chrs.

Direct mail and in person requests to: Office of Court Administration (OCA), Criminal History Search, 25 Beaver St, 8th Floor, New York, NY 10004.

Please note that nearly all the City Courts no longer do criminal record searchs and send misdemeanor record requesters to the OCA for the $52.00 statewide record search.

We have indicated the counties where the County Clerks (and a limited number of Supreme and County Court Clerks) continue to provide countywide criminal record searches. We have also indicated when the County Clerk or Chief Clerk instructs criminal record searches to contact OCA. This information is subject to change, and does.

We urge those entities that use criminal records to utilize the services of professional researchers found in the *National Directory of Local Court and County Record Retrievers*.

ONLINE ACCESS

In addition to the $52.00 statewide mail or in-person record search that has been explained above, the OCA offers online access to "approved requesters" for criminal records. Requesters receive information back via email. Call the OCA for details on how to set up an account. The fee is the same $52.00 per record.

Civil Supreme Court case information is available for all 62 New York counties through the court system's website - `http://e.courts.state.ny.us`. Select decisions from New York Supreme Criminal Court and other criminal courts are also available. There is no charge for this information.

Also at `http://e.courts.state.ny.us`, you may search for future court dates for defendants in these 21 criminal courts: Bronx Criminal Court, Bronx Supreme Court, Dutchess County Court, Buffalo City Court, Erie County Court, Kings Criminal Court, Kings Supreme Court, Nassau County Court, Nassau District Court, New York Criminal Court, New York Supreme Court, Orange County Court, Putnam County, Queens Criminal Court, Queens Supreme Court, Richmond Criminal Court, Richmond Supreme Court, Rockland County Court, Suffolk County Court, Suffolk District Court, Westchester County Court.

**ADDITIONAL
INFORMATION**

In all but a few NY counties, the Supreme and County Court records are maintained in some format in the County Clerk's office, which (with the exception of New York City and its boroughs) may index civil cases by defendant, whereas the courts themselves maintain only a plaintiff index. And, while most criminal courts in the state are indexed by defendant and plaintiff, many New York City courts are indexed by plaintiff only.

Almost all County Courts (felony records) will provide a Certificate of Disposition. This Certificate is a certified document from the court that indicates the disposition of a case. The fee for a Certificate of Disposition is either $5.00 or $6.00, depending upon the county. To obtain a Certificate of Disposition, you must prepay, you must include the name and an exact as possible date (either the disposition date or the arrest date - this requirement varies from county to county), or provide the case number. Some counties also ask for a signed release (this and other details will be noted in the individual court profiles.)

Certification fees can vary depending on how the clerk office interprets the rules. Fortunately, most court clerk offices will simply apply a flat $5.00 per document certification fee, however, at some offices, if a document is more than 4 pages, then an add'l $1.25 per page is added for certification. If the certified document is to be mailed, the certification fee may be $6.00, the additional $1.00 of the certification fee going for no purpose if you have provided a SASE, and hopefully they will charge you only the $5.00 cert fee if you have provided that SASE.

Probate is handled by Surrogate Courts. Surrogate Courts may also hear Domestic Relations cases in some counties.

📖 📖 📖 📖 📖 📖 📖

Albany County

County Clerk Courthouse, Rm 128, 16 Eagle St, Albany, NY 12207; phone: 518-487-5118; fax: 518-487-5099; hours 9AM-5PM (4:30 cut-off time) (EST). *Felony, Civil.*

www.albanycounty.com/clerk

Note: Countywide search requests made to the County Clerk are processed in the manner described below.

Civil Records: Access: Mail, in person. Both court and visitors may perform in person searches. Search fee: $5.00 per name. Fee is for each two years requested. Court makes copy: $.65 per page; minimum $1.30. Required to search: name, years to search. Civil cases indexed by defendant, plaintiff; on computer from 1981, prior in books. Mail turnaround time 1-3 days.

Criminal Records: Access: Mail, in person, online. Both court and visitors may perform in person searches. Search fee: $5.00 per name. Fee is per two years requested. Court makes copy: $.65 per page; minimum $1.30. Required to search: name, years to search, DOB. Criminal records on computer from 1981, prior in books. Search requests must be in writing. Access to current cases is at http://iapps.courts.state.ny.us/webcrim_attorney/Login. Mail turnaround time 1-3 days.

General Information: Public terminal goes back to 1980. No sealed, expunged, adoption, sex offense, juvenile, mental health or divorce records released. Will not fax documents. Certification fee: $5.00. Payee: County Clerk. Personal checks accepted. Prepayment required. SASE appreciated.

Supreme & County Court Courthouse, Rm 102, 16 Eagle St, Albany, NY 12207; phone: 518-487-5010; fax: 518-487-5020; hours 9AM-5PM (EST). *Felony, Civil.*

Note: Court-clerks direct record search requests to the OCA for a $52.00 statewide record check. For county only search requests, see the County Clerk in separate listing. Also, online access to current cases is available at http://e.courts.state.ny.us/.

Albany City Court - Civil Part City Hall, Rm 209, Albany, NY 12207; phone: 518-434-5115; fax: 518-434-5034; hours 8:30AM-5PM (EST). *Civil Actions Under $15,000, Eviction, Small Claims.*

Civil Records: Access: Mail, in person. Only the court performs in person searches; visitors may not. No search fee. Court makes copy: $1.30 for first page, $.65 each add'l. Required to search: name, years to search. Civil cases indexed by plaintiff. Civil records on computer from 1993, records go back 25 years. Mail turnaround time varies.

General Information: No public access terminal. No code enforcement records released. Will fax documents. Certification fee: $6.00 per document. Payee: Albany City Court. Business checks accepted. Prepayment and SASE required.

Albany City Court - Misdemeanors 1 Morton Ave, Albany, NY 12202; phone: 518-462-6714; fax: 518-447-8778; hours 8:30AM-4:30PM (EST). *Misdemeanor.*

Criminal Records: Access: Mail, in person. Only the court performs in person searches; visitors may not. Search fee: $5.00 per name per certificate of disposition. Court makes copy: court claims that they do not make copies, call AOC. Required to search: name, years to search, DOB. Criminal records on computer since mid-'93, on index cards prior. Searching will depend on which clerk you talk to. Some may forward you to OCA in NYC, while others may search for free or $5.00 per name. Mail turnaround time 1-5 days.

General Information: No public access terminal. No sealed, expunged, adoption, sex offense, juvenile, or mental health records released without a signed release. Certification fee: $5.00 per doc. Payee: Albany City Court Criminal Part. Business checks accepted. Prepayment and SASE required.

Cohoes City Court PO Box 678, 97 Mohawk St, Cohoes, NY 12047-0678; phone: 518-233-2133; fax: 518-233-8202; hours 8AM-4PM (EST). *Misdemeanor, Civil Actions Under $15,000, Eviction, Small Claims.*

Civil Records: Access: In person only. Only the court performs in person searches; visitors may not. No search fee. Court makes copy: $.25 per page. Required to search: name, years to search. Civil cases indexed by defendant, plaintiff; on computer from 1/95, prior in books, on cards. Note: This court recommends searching for judgments through the County Clerk's office.

Criminal Records: Access: None. Court makes copy: $.25 per page. Will not permit access to records. All name searches forwarded to OCA for $52.00 statewide search unless specific docket number given.

General Information: No public access terminal. No sealed or expunged records released. Certification fee: $5.00. Payee: City Court. Only cashiers checks and money orders accepted. Prepayment required.

Watervliet City Court 2 15th St, Watervliet, NY 12189; phone: 518-270-3803; fax: 518-270-3812; hours 8AM-3PM (EST). *Misdemeanor, Civil Actions Under $15,000, Eviction, Small Claims.*

Civil Records: Access: Phone, fax, mail, in person. Only the court performs in person searches; visitors may not. Search fee: $5.00 per name per 2 year period. Court makes copy: $.65 per page. Required to search: name, years to search. Civil cases indexed by plaintiff. Civil records on computer from 1991, prior on index cards back to 1975. Mail turnaround time 1-2 weeks.

Criminal Records: Access: Mail, in person. Only the court performs in person searches; visitors may not. Court makes copy: $.65 per page. Required to search: name, years to search, DOB. Criminal records on computer from 1991, prior on index cards back to 1975. All name searches forwarded to OCA for $52.00 statewide search, unless specific docket number given to this court. Mail turnaround time 1-2 weeks.

General Information: No public access terminal. Fee to fax documents is $5.00 per document. Certification fee: $6.00 per document. Payee: City Court. Business checks accepted. Prepayment and SASE required.

Surrogate's Court 16 Eagle St, #125, Courthouse, Albany, NY 12207; phone: 518-487-5393; fax: 518-487-5087; hours 9AM-5PM (EST). *Probate.*

Note: Search fee is $30.00 for up to 25 year search; $90 if over.

Albany Town/Village Courts - *misdemeanor or civil records:* Altamont Village- 518-861-8554; Berne Town- 518-872-1448; Bethlehem Town- 518-439-9717; Coeymans Town- 518-756-8480; Colonie Town- 518-783-2714; Green Island Town- 518-273-0661; Guilderland Town- 518-356-1980; Knox Town- 518-872-2551; Menands Village- 518-434-3992; New Scotland Town- 518-475-0493; Ravena Village- 518-756-2313; Rensselaerville Town- 518-239-4225; Voorheesville Village- 518-765-5524; Westerlo Town- 518-797-3239.

Allegany County

County Clerk 7 Court St, Belmont, NY 14813; phone: 585-268-9270; fax: 585-268-9659; hours 9AM-N, 1-5PM; Summer- 8:30AM-N, 12:30-4PM (EST). *Civil.*

Note: Felony records in Allegany County are managed by the County-Court Clerk (not the County Clerk) who directs search requests to OCA for $52.00 statewide search.

Civil Records: Access: In person, online. Visitors must perform in person searches themselves. Court makes copy: $.65 per page; $1.30 minimum. Required to search: name, years to search. Civil cases indexed by defendant. Civil records on computer back to 1992; prior on docket books. Access to current/pending Supreme Court civil cases is at http://e.courts.state.ny.us/. Mail turnaround time 7-10 days.

General Information: Public terminal has only civil records back to 1992. No sealed records released. No fee to fax documents. Will fax to toll free numbers only. Certification fee: $5.00 per doc. Over 5 pgs, add $1.25 each add'l page. Payee: County Clerk. Personal checks accepted. Prepayment required.

Supreme & County Court 7 Court St, Belmont, NY 14813; phone: 585-268-5813; fax: 585-268-7090; hours 9AM-5PM; 8:30AM-4PM Summer hours (EST). *Felony, Civil.*

Note: Direct civil record requests to County Clerk, see separate listing. The County-Court directs criminal search requests to the OCA for a $52.00 statewide record check. Access to current/pending civil cases is available at http://e.courts.state.ny.us/.

Surrogate's Court Courthouse, 7 Court St, Belmont, NY 14813; phone: 585-268-5815; fax: 585-268-7090; hours 9AM-5PM Sept-May; 8:30AM-4PM June-Aug (EST). *Probate.*

Allegany Town/Village Courts - *misdemeanor or civil records:* Alfred Town- 607-587-8524; Alfred Village- 607-587-9142; Allen Town; Alma Town- 585-593-4021; Almond Town- 607-276-6665; Amity Town- 585-268-5305; Andover Town- 607-478-8446; Andover Village- 607-478-8446; Angelica Town- 585-466-7928; Angelica Village- 585-466-7928; Belfast Town- 585-365-2623; Belmont Village; Birdsall Town; Bolivar Town- 585-928-1860; Bolivar Village- 585-928-2234; Burns Town- 607-545-6509; Caneadea Town- 585-365-8240; Centerville Town- 585-567-8424; Clarksville Town- 585-968-2031; Cuba Town- 585-968-1690; Friendship Town- 585-973-7566; Genesee Town- 585-928-2178; Granger Town; Grove Town- 607-545-8664; Hume Town- 585-567-2666; Independence Town- 607-356-3608; New Hudson Town- 585-968-2179; Rushford Town- 585-437-2206; Scio Town- 585-593-5777; Ward Town- 585-593-7300; Wellsville Town- 585-593-1750; Wellsville Village- 585-593-5609; West Almond Town- 607-276-2629; Willing Town; Wirt Town- 585-928-2130.

Bronx Borough

Supreme Court - Civil Division 851 Grand Concourse, Mezzanine, Rm 118, Bronx, NY 10451; phone: 718-590-3648 Clerk; fax: 718-590-8122; hours 9AM-5PM (EST). *Civil Actions Over $25,000.*

www.courts.state.ny.us/courts/12jd/

Civil Records: Access: In person, online. Both court and visitors may perform in person searches. Court makes copy: $.25 per page. Self serve copy fee: $.15 per page. Required to search: name, years to search. Civil cases indexed by defendant, plaintiff; on computer since 2001; prior records on archives. Archives are offsite. Access to current/pending civil cases and some closed cases is at http://e.courts.state.ny.us/. Mail turnaround time 7-10 days.

General Information: Public terminal has only civil records back to 1996. No marriage or divorce records released. Certification fee: $8.00 per document. Payee: Bronx County Clerk. Only cashiers checks and money orders accepted. Prepayment and SASE required.

Supreme Court - Criminal Division 851 Grand Concourse, Rm 123, Bronx, NY 10451; phone: 718-590-3803; criminal phone: 718-590-2854; fax: 718-590-3708; hours 9AM-5PM (EST). *Felony.*

www.courts.state.ny.us/courts/12jd/

Criminal Records: Access: In person only. Both court and visitors may perform in person searches. Court makes copy: $.75 per page. Self serve copy fee: $.15 per page. Required to search: name, years to search, DOB. Criminal records on computer back to 1977, prior on microfiche. Search online for future court appearances at http://iapps.courts.s

tate.ny.us/webcrim_attorney/Login Note: Unless a specific docket number given here, criminal record name search requests are directed to OCA for $52.00 statewide search. Mail turnaround time 4-6 weeks.

General Information: Public terminal has only criminal records back to 1995. No sealed, expunged, juvenile or sex offense records released. Will not fax documents. Certification fee: $10.00 per doc (may be $6.00). Payee: Bronx County Clerk. Only cashiers checks and money orders accepted. Prepayment and SASE required.

Civil Court of the City of New York - Bronx Branch
851 Grand Concourse, Window 6, Basement, Bronx, NY 10451; phone: 718-590-3601, 718-590-3597 records room; hours 9AM-5PM (EST). *Civil Actions Under $25,000, Eviction, Small Claims.*

www.courts.state.ny.us/courts/12jd/

Note: Evictions phone- 718-463-3000. Small claims- 718-590-2693.

Civil Records: Access: Phone, in person. Visitors must perform in person searches themselves. No search fee. Self serve copy fee: $.25 per page. Required to search: name, years to search. Civil cases indexed by defendant, plaintiff. Small claims in docket books. Civil records in books, file cards back to the 1970's; computerized records since 1998. Records archived after five years, requiring 4-8 weeks (four to eight weeks) to requisition. To view files, call ahead so that clerk can schedule a time and have files available. Please use their request form.
General Information: Public terminal has only civil records back to 1998. Certification fee: $6.00 per doc. Payee: Clerk of the Court. Only money orders and cash accepted. Prepayment required.

Supreme Court - Criminal Div. - Misdemeanors
Central Clerk's Office, 215 E 161st St, Bronx, NY 10451; phone: 718-590-2853; hours 9AM-1PM, 2-5PM (EST). *Misdemeanor.*

www.courts.state.ny.us/courts/12jd/criminal.shtml

Criminal Records: Access: In person, online. Only the court performs in person searches; visitors may not. No search fee. Required to search: name, years to search, DOB. Some criminal records on computer back to 1976, prior on microfiche. Search online for future court appearances at http://iapps.courts.state.ny.us/webcrim_attorney/Login Access records on the statewide CHRS system; fee is $52.00 per statewide search per name; call 212-428-2943 for info and sign-up or visit www.courts.state.ny.us/apps/chrs/. Note: Unless a specific docket number given, all criminal record name search requests are directed to the OCA for statewide record search, $52.00 search fee.
General Information: No public access terminal. No sealed, expunged, juvenile or sex offense records released. Certification fee: $10.00 per doc. Payee: Bronx Supreme Court. Only cashiers checks and money orders accepted. Prepayment and SASE required.

Surrogate's Court
851 Grand Concourse, #321, Bronx, NY 10451; phone: 718-590-4515; fax: 718-537-5158; hours 9AM-5PM (EST). *Probate.*

Broome County

County Clerk
PO Box 2062, Broome County Clerk, County Office Bldg, Binghamton, NY 13902; phone: 607-778-2255; fax: 607-778-2243; hours 8AM-5PM; 7:30AM-4PM June-August (EST). *Felony, Civil.*

www.gobcclerk.com

Countywide search requests made to the County Clerk are processed in the manner described below.

Civil Records: Access: Fax, mail, in person, online. Both court and visitors may perform in person searches. Search fee: $5.00 per name. Fee is per 2 years searched, 10 years maximum. Court makes copy: $.65 per page. $1.30 minimum. Required to

search: name, years to search. Civil cases indexed by defendant, plaintiff; on computer from 1987, prior in books. Access to current/pending civil cases and some closed cases is at http://e.courts.state.ny.us/. Access to civil (judgment) records are available; for registration information on the county clerk online system, call Danielle at 607-778-2377. Also, search court and judgment indexes free at www.gobcclerk.com/cgi/Official_Search_Types.html/input; records go back to 1987. Mail turnaround time 5 days.

Criminal Records: Access: Fax, mail, in person, online. Both court and visitors may perform in person searches. Search fee: $5.00 per name. Fee is per 2 years searched, 10 year maximum. Court makes copy: $.65 per page, $1.30 minimum. Required to search: name, years to search, DOB. Criminal records on computer from 1987, prior in books. Online access to criminal records may be available; for online date and registration information on the county clerk online system, call Danielle at 607-778-2377. Also, search index for criminal actions include in civil actions 1987 to present free at www.gobcclerk.com/cgi/Official_Search_Types.html/input. Mail turnaround time 3-5 days.
General Information: Public terminal goes back to 1986. No sealed or youthful offender records released. Will fax documents for $1.00 per page. Certification fee: $5.20 per 8-page document includes copy fee. Payee: Broome County Clerk. No personal checks over $1000.00. Prepayment and SASE required.

Supreme & County Court
PO Box 1766, 92 Court St, County Courthouse, Binghamton, NY 13902; phone: 607-778-2448; fax: 607-778-6426; hours 8AM-5PM; 8AM-4PM June-August (EST). *Felony, Civil.*

Note: The Supreme Court directs criminal record search requests to the OCA for processing. Countywide search requests can be made to the County Clerk, see separate listing.

Binghamton City Court
Governmental Plaza, Binghamton, NY 13901; phone: 607-772-7006; fax: 607-772-7041; hours 9AM-5PM (EST). *Misdemeanor, Civil Actions Under $15,000, Eviction, Small Claims.*

Civil Records: Access: Phone, mail, in person. Both court and visitors may perform in person searches. No search fee. Court makes copy: $.65 per page; $1.30 minimum. Required to search: name, years to search. Civil cases indexed by defendant. Civil records on computer from 1990, prior in books, index cards. In person searching only for 04/21/99 forward. Mail turnaround time 1-2 weeks.
Criminal Records: Access: Mail, in person. Only the court performs in person searches; visitors may not. Court makes copy: $.65 per page; $1.30 minimum. Required to search: notarized signature of requester (mail searches only), name, years to search, DOB. Criminal records on computer from 1990. Note: Unless a specific docket number given, all criminal record name search requests are directed to the OCA for statewide record search, $52.00 search fee. Mail turnaround time 1-2 weeks.
General Information: Public terminal has only civil records back to 1996. No sealed records released. Will not fax documents. Certification fee: $5.00 per certificate. Payee: Binghamton City Court. Only cashiers checks and money orders accepted. Prepayment and SASE required.

Surrogate's Court
PO Box 1766, 92 Court St, Binghamton, NY 13902; phone: 607-778-2111; fax: 607-778-2308; hours 9AM-5PM; 8AM-4PM July-Sept (EST). *Probate.*

Note: $25 record search fee.

Broome Town/Village Courts - *misdemeanor or civil records:* Barker Town- 607-648-6961; Binghamton Town- 607-772-0357; Chenango Town- 607-722-4191; Colesville Town- 607-693-1172; Conklin Town- 607-775-5244; Deposit Village- 607-467-4240; Dickinson Town- 607-723-9403; Endicott Village- 607-757-2483; Fenton Town- 607-648-4801;

Johnson City Village- 607-798-0002; Kirkwood Town- 607-775-2653; Lisle Town- 607-849-4685; Maine Town- 607-862-3427; Nanticoke Town- 607-692-4041; Sanford Town- 607-467-2516; Triangle Town- 607-692-7013; Union Town- 607-786-2965; Vestal Town- 607-748-1514; Windsor Town- 607-655-1973.

Cattaraugus County

County Clerk
303 Court St, Little Valley, NY 14755; phone: 716-938-9111 x2297; probate phone: x2327; fax: 716-938-6004; hours 9AM-5PM (EST). *Felony, Civil.*
Note: Countywide search requests made to the County Clerk are processed in the manner described below.

Civil Records: Access: Mail, in person, online. Both court and visitors may perform in person searches. Search fee: $5.00 per name. Fee is per 2 years searched. Court makes copy: $1.00 per page. Required to search: name, years to search. Civil cases indexed by defendant, plaintiff; on computer from 1989, prior in books, index cards from 1900. Access to current/pending Supreme Court civil cases is at http://e.courts.state.ny.us/. Mail turnaround time 2-3 days.

Criminal Records: Access: Mail, in person. Both court and visitors may perform in person searches. Search fee: $5.00 per name. Fee is per 2 years searched. Court makes copy: $1.00 per page. Required to search: name, years to search, DOB. Criminal records on computer from 1989, prior in books, index cards from 1900. Mail turnaround time 2-3 days.
General Information: Public terminal has only civil records back to 1990, judgments to 1987. No sealed or youthful offender records released. Will fax documents to local or toll free line for $3.00 add'l per page. Certification fee: $5.00. Payee: County Clerk. Business checks accepted. Prepayment required.

Supreme & County Court
303 Court St, Little Valley, NY 14755; phone: 716-938-9111 x2378; fax: 716-938-6413; hours 9AM-5PM (EST). *Felony, Civil.*

Note: Court-clerks direct search requests to the OCA for a $52.00 statewide record check. For a countywide search, see the County Clerk in separate listing. Access to current/pending Supreme Court civil cases is available at http://e.courts.state.ny.us/.

Olean City Court
PO Box 631, 101 E State St, Olean, NY 14760; phone: 716-376-5620; fax: 716-376-5623; hours 8:30AM-4:30PM (EST). *Misdemeanor, Civil Actions Under $15,000, Eviction, Small Claims.*

Civil Records: Access: Mail, in person. Only the court performs in person searches; visitors may not. Search fee: $5.00 per name. Court makes copy: $1.00 per page. Required to search: name, years to search, signed release; also helpful-case number. Civil cases indexed by defendant or docket number. Civil records on docket books. Mail turnaround time 1 week.

Criminal Records: Access: None. Search fee: A Certificate of Disposition is $6.00. Court makes copy: $1.00 per page. Criminal records on computer from 1990, prior in books. Note: Unless a specific docket number given, all criminal record name search requests are directed to the OCA for statewide record search, $52.00 search fee. Mail turnaround time 4-5 days.
General Information: No public access terminal. No sealed or youthful offender records released. Will fax documents to local or toll free line, if pre-paid. Certification fee: $6.00. Payee: Olean City Court. Business checks accepted if in-state. Prepayment and SASE required.

Salamanca City Court
Municipal Center, 225 Wildwood Ave, Salamanca, NY 14779; phone: 716-945-4153; fax: 716-945-2362; hours 8AM-4PM (EST). *Misdemeanor, Civil Actions Under $15,000, Eviction, Small Claims.*

Civil Records: Access: Mail, in person. Only the court performs in person searches; visitors may not. No search fee. Court makes copy: $.50 per page; same fee for self serve. Required to search: name, years to search. Civil cases indexed by defendant. Civil records on dockets from 1930s; on computer back to 1995. Mail turnaround time 1-2 weeks.

Criminal Records: Access: Mail, in person. Only the court performs in person searches; visitors may not. Search fee: A Certificate of Disposition is $6.00; release required. Court makes copy: $.50 per page; same fee for self serve. Required to search: name, years to search, DOB, case number. Criminal records on dockets from 1930s; on computer back to 1995. Unless a specific docket number given, all criminal record name search requests are directed to the OCA for a $52.00 statewide record search. Mail turnaround time 1-2 weeks.

General Information: No public access terminal. No sealed records released. Will fax documents. Certification fee: $6.00 per doc. Payee: Salamanca City Court. No personal checks accepted. Prepayment and SASE required.

Surrogate's Court 303 Court St, Little Valley, NY 14755; phone: 716-938-9111ext 2327; fax: 716-938-6983; hours 9AM-5PM (EST). *Probate.*
Note: Public can search, but if court has to search there is a fee.

Cattaraugus Town/Village Courts - *misdemeanor or civil records:* Allegany Town- 716-373-3670; Allegany Village- 716-373-1460; Ashford Town; Carrollton Town- 716-925-7772; Coldspring Town- 716-354-5752; Conewango Town- 716-358-9321, 716-358-9152; Dayton Town- 716-532-3758; East Otto Town; Ellicottville Town- 716-699-2240; Ellicottville Village- 716-699-2900; Farmersville Town- 716-676-3030; Franklinville Town- 716-676-3077; Freedom Town- 716-492-0961; Great Valley Town- 716-945-4200; Hinsdale Town- 716-557-2478; Humphrey Town- 716-945-1010; Ischua Town- 716-557-2236; Leon Town- 716-296-8132; Little Valley Town- 716-938-6882; Lyndon Town- 716-676-9928; Machias Town- 716-353-8207; Mansfield Town; Napoli Town- 716-938-9492; New Albion Town- 716-257-5387; Olean Town- 716-373-0582; Otto Town- 716-257-9623; Perrysburg Town- 716-532-4090; Persia Town- 716-532-4042; Portville Town- 716-933-6658; Portville Village- 716-933-6288; Randolph Town- 716-358-4515; Red House Town; Salamanca Town; South Dayton Village- 716-988-3833; South Valley Town- 716-354-5854; Yorkshire Town- 716-492-1640.

Cayuga County

County Clerk 160 Genesee St, Attn: County Clerk, Auburn, NY 13021; phone: 315-253-1271; fax: 315-253-1653; hours 9AM-5PM Sept-June; 8AM-4PM July-Aug (EST). *Felony, Misdemeanor, Civil.*
Note: If you have a specific case number, you can search countywide at the County Clerk office. This County Clerk will not do a felony record name search.

Civil Records: Access: Mail, in person, online. Both court and visitors may perform in person searches. Search fee: $5.00 per name per 5 years searched. Court makes copy: $.65 per page; $1.30 minimum. Required to search: name, years to search. Civil cases indexed by defendant, plaintiff; on computer from 1986, prior in books. Access to current/pending Supreme Court civil cases is at http://e.courts.state.ny.us/.

Criminal Records: Access: In person only. Visitors must perform in person searches themselves. Court makes copy: $.65 per page; $1.30 minimum. Required to search: name, years to search, DOB. Criminal records names are computerized since 1980s. Unless a specific case file number is given, access to records, including name searching, must be done at the OCA in New York City. The fees are $52.00 for a statewide search. In person search is on computer only.

General Information: Public terminal has criminal back to 1980s and civil back to 1987. No sealed records released. Will not fax back documents. Certification fee: $5.00 per doc. Payee: County Clerk. Personal checks accepted. Prepayment and SASE required.

Supreme & County Court 154 Genesee St, Auburn, NY 13021-3424; phone: 315-255-4320; fax: 315-255-4322; hours 9AM-5PM Sept-June; 8AM-4PM July-Aug (EST). *Felony, Misdemeanor, Civil.*
Note: The County Clerk provides county only record searches, see separate entry. Also, access to current/pending Supreme Court civil cases is available at http://e.courts.state.ny.us/.

Auburn City Court 157 Genesee St, Auburn, NY 13021-3434; phone: 315-253-1570; fax: 315-253-1085; hours 8AM-4PM (EST). *Misdemeanor, Civil Actions Under $15,000, Eviction, Small Claims.*

Civil Records: Access: In person only. Only the court performs in person searches; visitors may not. No search fee. Court makes copy: $.65 per page; $1.30 minimum. Required to search: name, years to search. Civil cases indexed by defendant. Civil records on computer from 1986.

Criminal Records: Access: None. Search fee: A Certificate of Disposition is $5.00. Court makes copy: $.65 per page; $1.30 minimum. The court refuses to permit access to records unless specific case file given. Searchers must use the OCA $52.00 statewide search.

General Information: No public access terminal. No sealed, expunged, adoption, sex offense, juvenile or mental health records released. Certification fee: $6.00 per doc. Payee: City Court Clerk. No personal checks. Prepayment required.

Surrogate's Court Courthouse, 152 Genesee St, Auburn, NY 13021-3471; phone: 315-255-4316; fax: 315-255-4322; hours 8:30AM-4:30PM; Summer hours 8AM-4:00PM (EST). *Probate.*

Cayuga Town/Village Courts - *misdemeanor or civil records:* Aurelius Town- 315-255-0065; Brutus Town- 315-834-6618; Cato Town- 315-626-6904; Cato Village- 315-626-2397; Conquest Town; Fleming Town- 315-252-8988; Genoa Town- 315-364-6722; Ira Town- 315-626-3500; Ledyard Town- 315-364-5708; Locke Town; Mentz Town- 315-776-8692; Meridian Village- 315-626-6904; Montezuma Town- 315-776-9163; Moravia Town- 315-497-0968; Moravia Village- 315-497-0968; Niles Town- 315-497-0066; Owasco Town- 315-255-0446; Port Byron Village- 315-776-9692; Scipio Town- 315-364-5325; Semperonius Town- 315-496-2376; Sennett Town- 315-253-7748; Springport Town- 315-889-5020; Sterling Town- 315-865-5508; Summerhill Town- 315-497-3496; Throop Town- 315-252-7373; Venice Town- 315-364-6875; Victory Town- 315-626-6817; Weedsport Village- 315-834-8634.

Chautauqua County

County Clerk Courthouse, PO Box 170, Mayville, NY 14757; phone: 716-753-4331; probate phone: 716-753-4339; fax: 716-753-4293; hours 9AM-5PM/Summer 8:30AM-4:30PM (EST). *Felony, Civil.*

www.co.chautauqua.ny.us/clerk/clerkframe.htm
Note: Non in-person felony record requests are managed by the Supreme Court clerk who directs searches to OCA for $52.00 statewide search.

Civil Records: Access: In person, online. Visitors must perform in person searches themselves. Court makes copy: $4.00 per doc; add $1.00 per page after first 4. Required to search: name, years to search. Access to current/pending Supreme Court civil cases is at http://e.courts.state.ny.us/.

Criminal Records: Access: In person only. Visitors must perform in person searches themselves. Court makes copy: $4.00 per doc; add $1.00 per page after first 4. Required to search: name, years to search, DOB. Criminal records on court's computer system

from 8/1987. A Certificate of Conviction can be ordered for $5.00. Note: Court will not search felony records.

General Information: Public terminal goes back to 8/1997. No sealed records released. Will not fax documents. Certification fee: Same as copy fee. Payee: County Clerk. Prepayment required.

Supreme & County Court - Criminal Courthouse, PO Box 292, Mayville, NY 14757; phone: 716-753-4266; fax: 716-753-4993; hours 9AM-5PM/Summer 8:30AM-4:30PM (EST). *Felony.*
Note: Misdemeanor records are maintained by city, town and village courts. The County-court directs search requests to the OCA for a $52.00 statewide record check.

Supreme & County Court - Civil PO Box 170, 1 N Erie St, Mayville, NY 14757; phone: 716-753-4331; civil phone: 716-753-4976; fax: 716-753-4293; hours 9AM-5PM; Summer 8:30AM-4:30PM (EST). *Civil.*

www.co.chautauqua.ny.us/clerk/clerkframe.htm
Note: Supreme Court Clerk phone is 716-753-4266 but they do not have the records.

Civil Records: Access: In person, online. Visitors must perform in person searches themselves. No search fee. Court makes copy: $4.00. Add $1.00 per page after first 4. Required to search: name, years to search. Civil cases indexed by plaintiff. Civil records in docket books or cards; on computer back to 8/1/1997. Access to current/pending Supreme Court civil cases is at http://e.courts.state.ny.us/. Mail turnaround time 1-2 days.

General Information: Public terminal has only civil records back to 8/1997. (Terminal located in the county clerk office.) No sealed records released. Will not fax documents. Certification fee: Cert fee included in copy fee. Payee: Chautauqua County Clerk. Personal checks accepted. Prepayment required.

Dunkirk City Court City Hall, 342 Central Ave, Dunkirk, NY 14048; phone: 716-366-2055; fax: 716-366-3622; hours 9AM-5PM (EST). *Misdemeanor, Civil Actions Under $15,000, Eviction, Small Claims.*

Civil Records: Access: Mail, in person. Only the court performs in person searches; visitors may not. No search fee. Court makes copy: $.65 per page; $1.30 minimum. Required to search: name, years to search. Civil cases indexed by defendant. Civil records on computer back to 1990, prior in books. Make appointment to search.

Criminal Records: Access: None. Search fee: A Certificate of Disposition is $6.00. Court makes copy: $.65 per page; $1.30 minimum. Required to search: name, DOB, arrest date (for Cert of Disposition). The court refuses to permit access to records unless specific case file given. It is suggested to send requests to OCA for $52.00 statewide search. Also, record checks from local Police Dept.- 716-366-2266. Mail turnaround time 1 week.

General Information: No public access terminal. No sealed, expunged, adoption, sex offense, juvenile or mental health records released. Certification fee: $6.00 per doc. Payee: Dunkirk City Court. Only cashiers checks and money orders accepted. Prepayment and SASE required.

Jamestown City Court City Hall, Jamestown, NY 14701; phone: 716-483-7561/7562; fax: 716-483-7519; hours 8:30AM-5PM (EST). *Misdemeanor, Civil Actions Under $15,000, Eviction, Small Claims.*

Civil Records: Access: Fax, mail, in person. Both court and visitors may perform in person searches. Search fee: $5.00 per name per 2 years searched. Court makes copy: $.65 per page. Required to search: name, years to search. Civil cases indexed by defendant. Civil records on computer back to 1989, prior in books.

Criminal Records: Access: None. Only the court performs in person searches; visitors may not. Court makes copy: $.65 per page. Required to search:

Name, DOB. Criminal records on computer back to 1989, prior in books to 1965. The court refuses to permit access to records unless specific case file given. It is suggested to send requests to OCA for $52.00 statewide search. Mail turnaround time 1 week.

General Information: No public access terminal. No sealed records released. Will fax documents to local or toll free line. Certification fee: $6.00 per document. Payee: City Court. Business checks accepted. Prepayment and SASE required.

Surrogate's Court PO Box C, 3 N Erie St, Gerace Office Bldg, Mayville, NY 14757; phone: 716-753-4339; fax: 716-753-4600; hours 9AM-5PM SUMMER-8;30-4;30,JULY-SEPT3 (EST). *Probate.*

Chautauqua Town/Village Courts - *misdemeanor or civil records:* Arkwright Town-716-679-4445; Brocton Village- 716-792-4189; Busti Town- 716-763-4695; Carroll Town- 716-569-5365; Charlotte Town- 716-962-2004; Chautauqua Town- 716-753-5245; Cherry Creek Town- 716-296-5721; Clymer Town- 716-355-6331; Dunkirk Town-716-366-3945; Ellery Town- 716-386-2521; Ellicott Town- 716-665-5319; Ellington Town- 716-287-2026; Fredonia Village- 716-679-2312; French Creek Town- 716-355-8801; Gerry Town- 716-985-5323; Hanover Town- 716-934-4770; Harmony Town- 716-488-1178; Kiantone Town- 716-488-0383; Mina Town- 716-769-7555; North Harmony Town- 716-789-3445; Poland Town- 716-267-3809; Pomfret Town- 716-672-6867; Portland Town- 716-792-4111; Ripley Town- 716-736-7575; Sheridan Town- 716-672-2600; Sherman Town- 716-761-6770; Silver Creek Village- 716-934-3558; Stockton Town; Villenova Town- 716-988-3678; Westfield Town- 716-326-6255; Westfield Village- 716-326-6135.

Chemung County

Supreme & County Court - Criminal PO Box 588, Hazlett Bldg, 6th Fl, Elmira, NY 14902-0588; phone: 607-737-2084; probate phone: 607-737-2873; hours 9AM-5PM (EST). *Felony.*

Note: See County Clerk for Supreme court civil case records.

Criminal Records: Access: Mail, in person. Only the court performs in person searches; visitors may not. Search fee: $5.00 for every 2 years searched or $20.00 for a seven year search. Searches with both maiden and married names are considered two searches. Court makes copy: $.65 per page; same fee for self serve. Required to search: name, years to search, DOB, SSN. Criminal records in docket books back to 1979. Mail turnaround time 4-6 weeks.

General Information: No public access terminal. No sealed, divorce or adoption records released. Will fax documents to local or toll free line. Certification fee: $5.00. Payee: County Clerk. Personal checks accepted. Prepayment and SASE required.

County Clerk PO Box 588, 210 Lake St, Elmira, NY 14902; phone: 607-737-2920; fax: 607-737-2897; hours 8:30AM-4:30PM (EST). *Civil.*

www.chemungcounty.com

Note: Search requests made to the County Clerk are processed in the manner described below.

Civil Records: Access: Mail, fax, in person, online. Both court and visitors may perform in person searches. Search fee: $5.00 per name. Fee is per 2 years searched. Court makes copy: $.65 per page. $1.30 minimum. Self serve copy fee: $.65 per page. Required to search: name, years to search. Civil cases indexed by defendant, plaintiff; on computer from 1994, prior in books to 1800s. Access to current/pending Supreme Court civil cases is at http://e.courts.state.ny.us/. Mail turnaround time 1-2 days.

General Information: No public access terminal. No sealed, divorce or adoption records released. Will fax documents for $1.00 per page. Certification fee: $5.00 up to 4 pages, $1.25 each add'l page, includes

copies. Payee: County Clerk. Personal checks accepted. Prepayment and SASE required.

Elmira City Court 317 E Church St, Elmira, NY 14901; phone: 607-737-5681; fax: 607-737-5820; hours 8AM-4PM (EST). *Misdemeanor, Civil Actions Under $15,000, Eviction, Small Claims.*

Civil Records: Access: In person only. Visitors must perform in person searches themselves. Court makes copy: $.65 per page; $1.30 minimum. Required to search: name, years to search. Civil cases indexed by defendant. Civil records on computer back to 1997; prior records on index cards.

Criminal Records: Access: None. Search fee: A Certificate of Disposition is $5.00. Court makes copy: $.65 per page; $1.30 minimum. Required to search: name, years to search, date of arrest (for Cert of Disposition). Criminal records on computer back to 1987; prior on books. Court does not permit access to records unless specific case file given. Send requests to OCA for $52.00 statewide search.

General Information: Public terminal has only civil records back to 1997. No sealed records released. Will fax documents to local or toll free line. Certification fee: $5.00 per doc. Payee: Elmira City Court. Personal checks accepted. Prepayment required.

Surrogate's Court PO Box 588, 224 Lake St, Elmira, NY 14902; phone: 607-737-2946/2819; fax: 607-737-2874; hours 9AM-5PM; July-Sept 3-8:30AM-4:30PM (EST). *Probate.*

Chemung Town/Village Courts - *misdemeanor or civil records:* Ashland Town- 607-398-7119; Baldwin Town- 607-398-7208; Big Flats Town- 607-562-8443 x233; Catlin Town- 607-739-5598; Chemung Town- 607-529-3322; Elmira Heights Village- 607-737-6750; Elmira Town- 607-734-5971; Erin Town- 607-739-3313; Horseheads Town- 607-739-2113; Horseheads Village- 607-739-0158; Millport Village- 631-286-0327x22; Southport Town- 607-734-4446; Van Etten Town- 607-589-4929; Veteran Town- 607-739-3337; Wellsburg Village- 315-846-5222.

Chenango County

County Clerk County Office Bldg, 1st Fl, 5 Court St, Norwich, NY 13815-1676; phone: 607-337-1450; hours 8:30AM-5PM (EST). *Felony, Civil.*

Note: Countywide search requests made to the County Clerk are processed in the manner described below.

Civil Records: Access: Mail, in person, online. Both court and visitors may perform in person searches. Search fee: $5.00 per name. Fee is per 2 years searched. Court makes copy: $.65 per page. $1.30 minimum. Required to search: name, years to search. Civil cases indexed by defendant, plaintiff; on computer from 1994, prior in books since 1880. Access to current/pending Supreme Court civil cases is at http://e.courts.state.ny.us/. Mail turnaround time 1 week.

Criminal Records: Access: Mail, in person. Both court and visitors may perform in person searches. Search fee: $5.00 per name. Fee is per 2 years searched. Court makes copy: $.65 per page, $1.30 minimum. Required to search: name, years to search, DOB. Criminal records in docket books. Mail turnaround time 1 week.

General Information: Public terminal has criminal back to 2004 and civil back to 1994. No sealed, expunged, adoption, sex offense, juvenile or mental health records released. Certification fee: $1.25 per page, $5.00 minimum. Payee: County Clerk. Personal checks accepted. Prepayment and SASE required.

Supreme & County Court County Office Bldg, 5 Court St, Norwich, NY 13815-1676; phone: 607-337-1457; hours 8:30AM-5PM (EST). *Felony, Civil.*

Note: Direct all search requests to the County Clerk office, see separate listing. Online access to current/pending Supreme Court civil cases is available at http://e.courts.state.ny.us/.

Norwich City Court 1 Court Plaza, Norwich, NY 13815; phone: 607-334-1224; fax: 607-334-8494; 8:30AM-4:30PM (EST). *Misdemeanor, Civil Actions Under $15,000, Eviction, Small Claims.*

Civil Records: Access: Fax, mail, in person. Only the court performs in person searches; visitors may not. No search fee. Court makes copy: $.65 per page; minimum $1.30. Required to search: name, years to search. Civil cases indexed by defendant. Civil records on computer from 1990, prior in books. Mail turnaround time 5-7 days.

Criminal Records: Access: In person only. Only the court performs in person searches; visitors may not. Search fee: Clerk here will provide $5.00 Certificate of Disposition only. Court makes copy: $.65 per page; minimum $1.30. Court directs criminal record searchers to OCA for $52.00 statewide search. Mail turnaround time 5-7 days.

General Information: No public access terminal. No sealed, expunged, adoption, sex offense, juvenile or mental health records released. Will fax documents to local or toll free line. Certification fee: $5.00 per doc. Payee: Norwich City Court. Business checks accepted. Prepayment and SASE required.

Surrogate's Court County Office Bldg, 5 Court St, Norwich, NY 13815; phone: 607-337-1822/1827; fax: 607-337-1834; hours 8:30AM-4:30PM (EST). *Probate.*

Chenango Town/Village Courts - *misdemeanor or civil records:* Afton Town; Bainbridge Town & Village- 607-967-7465; Columbus Town; Coventry Town - 607-656-8602; Earlville Village- 315-691-6020; German Town; Greene Town- 607-656-4333; Greene Village- 607-656-4544; Guilford Town- 607-895-6818; Lincklaen Town- 315-852-6128; New Berlin Town- 607-847-8962; New Berlin Village-607-847-6249; North Norwich Town- 607-334-5994; Norwich Town- 607-337-2301; Otselic Town- 315-653-7201; Oxford Town & Village- 607-843-9772; Oxford Village- 607-843-9772; Pharsalia Town- 607-647-5203; Pitcher Town- 607-863-4929; Plymouth Town; Preston Town- 607-334-9334; Sherburne Town & Village- 607-674-4827; Smithville Town-607-656-7969; Smyrna Town- no phone.

Clinton County

County Clerk County Government Ctr, 137 Margaret St, 1st Fl, Plattsburgh, NY 12901; phone: 518-565-4701; fax: 518-565-4718; hours 8AM-5PM (EST). *Civil.* Note: This County Clerk does not have a separate index of felony records; see the Supreme and County Court.

Civil Records: Access: In person, online. Visitors must perform in person searches themselves. Court makes copy: $.65 per page. Required to search: name, years to search. Civil cases indexed by defendant and plaintiff. Civil records in docket books up to 2003; on computer from 2003 to present. Online access to current/pending civil cases is free at http://e.courts.state.ny.us/descCaseSearch.html.

General Information: No public access terminal. No sealed or sex case records released. Will fax specific case file requests to local or toll free line. Certification fee: $1.25 per page, minimum $5.00. Payee: County Clerk. Personal checks accepted. Prepayment required.

Supreme & County Court County Government Ctr, 137 Margaret St, #311, Plattsburgh, NY 12901; phone: 518-565-4715; fax: 518-565-4708; hours 9AM-N, 1-5PM (EST). *Felony, Civil.*

Note: The County Court directs criminal search requests to the OCA for a $52.00 statewide record check. Civil records are with the County Clerk, see separate listing. Online access to current/pending civil cases is available at http://e.courts.state.ny.us.

Plattsburg City Court 24 US Oval, Plattsburgh, NY 12903; phone: 518-563-7870; fax: 518-563-3124; hours 8AM-4PM (EST). *Misdemeanor, Civil Actions Under $15,000, Eviction, Small Claims.*

Civil Records: Access: Mail, in person. Only the court performs in person searches; visitors may not. Search fee: $16.00 for computerized search. Court makes copy: $.65 per page. Required to search: name, years to search. Civil cases indexed by defendant. Civil records on computer back to 1986, prior in books.

Criminal Records: Access: None. Court makes copy: $.65 per page. Records available here since 1986. The court will not support name searches unless specific case file given. Searchers must use the statewide search. Mail turnaround same day.

General Information: No public access terminal. No sealed records released. Certification fee: $5.00 per certificate. Payee: City Court. Only cashiers checks and money orders accepted. Prepayment and SASE required.

Surrogate's Court 137 Margaret St, #315, Plattsburgh, NY 12901-2933; phone: 518-565-4630; fax: 518-565-4769; hours 8AM-5PM (EST). *Probate.*

Clinton Town/Village Courts - *misdemeanor or civil records:* Altona Town- 518-236-7035; Au Sable Town- 518-834-6095; Beekmantown Town- 518-563-9930; Black Brook Town- 518-647-5412; Champlain Town- 518-298-2043; Champlain Village- 518-298-4088; Chazy Town- 518-846-8600; Clinton Town- 518-497-6042; Dannemora Town- 518-492-9751; Dannemora Village- 518-492-7000; Ellenburg Town- 518-594-7177; Keeseville Village- 518-834-9590; Mooers Town- 518-236-7927; Peru Town- 518-643-2745; Plattsburgh Town- 518-562-6870; Rouses Point Village- 518-297-6648 x334; Saranac Town- 518-293-6666; Schuyler Falls Town- 518-563-1129.

Columbia County

County Clerk 560 Warren St, Hudson, NY 12534; phone: 518-828-3339; fax: 518-828-5299; hours 9AM-5PM (EST). *Felony, Civil.*

Note: Countywide search requests made to the County Clerk are processed in the manner described below.

Civil Records: Access: Mail, in person, online. Both court and visitors may perform in person searches. Search fee: $5.00 per name. Fee is per 2 years searched. Court makes copy: $.65 per page. Self serve copy fee: $.25 per page. Required to search: name, years to search. Civil cases indexed by defendant. Civil records on computer from 1993, prior on cards to 1985. Access to current/pending Supreme Court civil cases is at http://e.courts.state.ny.us/. Supreme and County courts are actually located at 401 Union in Hudson, but records for both courts are located at the County Clerk's Office as listed above. Mail turnaround time 1 week.

Criminal Records: Access: Mail, in person. Both court and visitors may perform in person searches. Search fee: $5.00 per name. Fee is for 10 years searched. Court makes copy: $.65 per page. Self serve copy fee: $.25 per page. Required to search: name, years to search. Criminal records on computer from 1993, prior on cards to 1985. Supreme and County courts are actually located at 401 Union in Hudson, but records for both courts are located at the County Clerk's Office as listed above. Mail turnaround time 3 weeks.

General Information: Public use terminal available. No sealed records released. Certification fee: $4.00. Payee: County Clerk. Personal checks accepted. Prepayment and SASE required.

Supreme & County Court 401 Union St, Hudson, NY 12534; phone: 518-828-7858; hours 9AM-5PM (EST). *Felony, Civil.*

Note: Direct countywide search requests to the County Clerk, see separate listing. Also, access to current/pending Supreme Court civil cases is available at http://e.courts.state.ny.us/.

Hudson City Court 427 Warren St, Hudson, NY 12534; phone: 518-828-3100; fax: 518-828-3628; hours 8AM-3:45PM (EST). *Misdemeanor, Civil Actions Under $15,000, Eviction, Small Claims.*
www.nycourts.gov/courts/3jd/

Civil Records: Access: Fax, mail, in person. Only the court performs in person searches; visitors may not. Search fee: $16.00 per name. Court makes copy: $.65 per page. Required to search: name, years to search; also helpful: address. Civil cases indexed by defendant, plaintiff; on computer from 1991, prior in books.

Criminal Records: Access: None. Court makes copy: $.65 per page. Required to search: name, years to search, DOB. Criminal records on computer from 1991, prior in books. Note: This court directs criminal records search requests to the OCA for a $52.00 statewide record check. Mail turnaround time 1 week.

General Information: No public access terminal. No sealed, expunged, adoption, sex offense, juvenile or mental health records released. Will fax documents to local or toll free line. Certification fee: $5.00. Payee: Hudson City Court. Business checks accepted. Prepayment and SASE required.

Surrogate's Court Courthouse, 401 Union St, Hudson, NY 12534; phone: 518-828-0414; fax: 518-828-1603; hours 9AM-5PM (EST). *Probate.*

Columbia Town/Village Courts - *misdemeanor or civil records:* Ancram Town- 518-329-6512; Austerlitz Town- 518-392-3260; Canaan Town- 518-781-3144; Chatham Town- 518-392-5440; Chatham Village- 518-392-9476; Claverack Town- 518-672-4468; Clermont Town- 518-537-6868 x503/x505; Copake Town- 518-329-4042; Gallatin Town- 518-398-7690; Germantown Town- 518-537-6687; Ghent Town- 518-392-4644; Greenport Town- 518-828-4656; Hillsdale Town- 518-325-5073; Kinderhook Town- 518-784-2506; Kinderhook Village- 518-784-2233; Livingston Town- 518-851-7210; New Lebanon Town- 518-794-9456; Philmont Village- 518-672-4886; Stockport Town- 518-828-9389; Stuyvesant Town; Taghkanic Town- 518-329-3030; Valatie Village- 518-758-9838.

Cortland County

County Clerk 46 Greenbush St, #101, Cortland, NY 13045; phone: 607-753-5021; hours 8:30PM-4:30PM (EST). *Felony, Civil.*

Note: Countywide search requests made to the County Clerk are processed in the manner described below.

Civil Records: Access: Mail, in person, online. Both court and visitors may perform in person searches. Search fee: $5.00 per name per 2 year search. Court makes copy: $.65 per page, minimum $1.30. Required to search: name, years to search. Civil cases indexed by defendant, plaintiff; on computer from 5/94, prior in books. Access to current/pending Supreme Court civil cases and some closed cases is at http://e.courts.state.ny.us/. Also, online access at https://cclerk.cortland-co.org/index.asp gives judgments and other county clerk records. Login using "public" as user name and password. A subscription service is also available Mail turnaround time 2 days.

Criminal Records: Access: Mail, in person. Only the court performs in person searches; visitors may not. Search fee: $5.00 per name per 2 years. Court makes copy: $.65 per page, minimum $1.30. Required to search: name, years to search, DOB. Criminal records in books. Mail turnaround time 2 days.

General Information: No public access terminal. No sealed or youthful offender records released. Will not fax documents. Certification fee: $1.25 per page, $5.00 minimum. Payee: County Clerk. Personal checks accepted. Prepayment and SASE required.

Supreme & County Court 46 Greenbush St, #301, Cortland, NY 13045; phone: 607-753-5013, 753-5500; fax: 607-753-5378; hours 9AM-5PM (in July/Aug 8:30AM-4:30PM) (EST). *Felony, Civil.*

www.cortland-co.org/cc/index.htm

Note: Direct record search requests to the County Clerk, see separate listing. Also, access to current/pending Supreme Court civil cases and some closed cases is at http://e.courts.state.ny.us/.

Cortland City Court 25 Court St, Cortland, NY 13045; phone: 607-753-1811; fax: 607-753-9932; hours 8:30AM-4:30PM (EST). *Misdemeanor, Civil Actions Under $15,000, Eviction, Small Claims.*

Civil Records: Access: Mail, in person. Only the court performs in person searches; visitors may not. Search fee: $5.00 per name per 2 years. Court makes copy: $.65 per page; $1.30 minimum. Required to search: name, years to search. Civil cases indexed by defendant. Civil records on computer from 1991, prior in books. Mail turnaround time 10 days.

Criminal Records: Access: Mail, in person. Only the court performs in person searches; visitors may not. Search fee: For violations only- $5.00 per name per 2 years. Certificate of Disposition- $5.00. Court makes copy: $.65 per page; $1.30 minimum. Required to search: name, years to search, DOB. Criminal records on computer from 1991, prior in books. The court does not permit access to "fingerprintable records" unless specific case file given. You must send requests to OCA for $52.00 statewide search. Mail turnaround time 10 days.

General Information: No public access terminal. No sealed records released. Will fax documents to local or toll free line. Certification fee: $6.00 per doc; may be $5.00 if in person. Payee: Cortland City Court. Only cashiers checks and money orders accepted. Prepayment and SASE required.

Surrogate's Court 46 Greenbush St, #301, Cortland, NY 13045; phone: 607-753-5355; fax: 607-756-3409; hours 9AM-5PM; 8:30-4:30 July-Sept 3 (EST). *Probate.*
www.courts.state.ny.us/6jd/

Cortland Town/Village Courts - *misdemeanor or civil records:* Cincinnatus Town- 607-863-4220; Cortlandville Town- 607-756-2352; Cuyler Town; Freetown Town- 607-849-3306; Harford Town- 518-632-9151; Homer Town- 607-749-2326; Homer Village- 607-749-2326; Lapeer Town- 607-849-3808; Marathon Town; Preble Town- 607-749-2377; Scott Town- 607-749-2902; Solon Town; Taylor Town- 607-863-3556; Truxton Town- 607-842-6291; Virgil Town- 607-835-6587; Willet Town- 607-863-3261.

Delaware County

County Clerk 3 Court St, Delhi, NY 13753; phone: 607-746-2123; fax: 607-746-6924; hours 8:30AM-5PM (EST). *Felony, Civil.*

Note: Countywide search requests made to the County Clerk are processed in the manner described below.

Civil Records: Access: Mail, in person, online. Both court and visitors may perform in person searches. Search fee: $10.00 per name. Court makes copy: $1.00 per page. Required to search: name, years to search. Civil cases indexed by defendant. Civil records in books. Access to current/pending Supreme Court civil cases and some closed cases is at http://e.courts.state.ny.us/. Mail turnaround time 2 days.

Criminal Records: Access: Mail, in person. Both court and visitors may perform in person searches. Search fee: $10.00 per name. Court makes copy: $1.00 per page. Required to search: name, years to search, DOB. Criminal records in books. Misdemeanor records are maintained by city, town and village courts. Mail turnaround time 2 days.

General Information: No public access terminal. No sealed records released. Certification fee: $4.00 for up to 4 pages, then $1.00 per page. Payee: County Clerk. Personal checks accepted. Prepayment and SASE required.

Supreme & County Court 3 Court St, Delhi, NY 13753; phone: 607-746-2131; fax: 607-746-3253; hours 9AM-5PM (EST). *Felony, Civil.*

Note: Direct record search requests to the County Clerk, see separate listing. Access to current/pending Supreme Court civil cases and some closed cases is available at http://e.courts.state.ny.us/.

Surrogate's Court 3 Court St, Delhi, NY 13753; phone: 607-746-2126; fax: 607-746-2288; hours 9AM-5PM (EST). *Probate.*

Delaware Town/Village Courts - *misdemeanor or civil records:* Andes Town- 845-676-3550; Bovina Town; Colchester Town; Davenport Town; Delhi Town- 607-746-7278; Deposit Town- 607-467-3233; Franklin Town- 607-829-3440; Hamden Town- 607-746-6660; Hancock Town- 607-637-3651; Hancock Village- 607-637-5789; Harpersfield Town- 607-652-5060; Kortright Town- 607-538-9319; Masonville Town; Meredith Town- 607-746-2431; Middletown Town- 845-586-2575; Roxbury Town- 607-588-7507; Sidney Town- 607-561-2309; Sidney Village- 607-561-2309; Stamford Town- 607-538-1825; Stamford Village- 607-652-6671; Tompkins Town- 607-865-4949; Walton Town- 607-865-5182; Walton Village- 607-865-6150.

Dutchess County

County Clerk 22 Market St, Poughkeepsie, NY 12601-3203; phone: 845-486-2139 (records); 486-2120 (main); hours 9AM-5PM (EST). *Felony, Civil.*

www.dutchessny.gov/dcclerk.htm

Note: Countywide search requests made to the County Clerk are processed in the manner described below.

Civil Records: Access: Mail, in person, online. Visitors must perform in person searches themselves. Search fee: $5.00 per name. Court makes copy: $.65 per page; $1.30 minimum. Self serve copy fee: $.25 per page. Required to search: name, years to search. Civil cases indexed by defendant, plaintiff. Civil records in books back to 1847; on computer back to 1986. Access to current/pending Supreme Court civil cases is at http://e.courts.state.ny.us/.

Criminal Records: Access: Mail, in person. Both court and visitors may perform in person searches. Search fee: $5.00 per name per 2 years. Court makes copy: $.65 per page; $1.30 minimum. Self serve copy fee: $.25 per page. Required to search: name, years to search, aliases. Criminal records go back to 1847; on computer back to 1987. Note: They will only create a certificate if their staff performs the search. Mail turnaround time 2 weeks.

General Information: Public use terminal available. No sealed or youthful offender records released. Will not fax documents. Certification fee: $5.00 per doc for 4 pages ($6.00 if mailed); add $1.25 each add'l page. Payee: Dutchess County Clerk. Personal checks accepted. Prepayment and SASE required.

Supreme & County Court 10 Market St, Poughkeepsie, NY 12601-3203; phone: 845-486-2260; hours 9AM-5PM (EST). *Felony, Civil.*

Note: For countywide record search, see the County Clerk, otherwise this court recommends the $52.00 statewide search via the OCA. Also, access to current/pending civil cases is available at http://e.courts.state.ny.us/. Pending criminal cases also available.

Beacon City Court One Municipal Plaza, #2, Beacon, NY 12508; phone: 845-838-5030; fax: 845-838-5041; hours 8AM-4PM (EST). *Misdemeanor, Civil Actions Under $15,000, Eviction, Small Claims.*

Civil Records: Access: Mail, in person. Both court and visitors may perform in person searches. No search fee. An electronic search is $16.00. Court makes copy: $.65 per page; $1.30 minimum. Required to search: name, DOB, years to search; also helpful- address. Civil cases indexed by defendant, plaintiff; on computer from 1996, prior in books and cards.

Criminal Records: Access: None. No criminal searching at this court. Search fee: A Certificate of Disposition is $5.00, signed release required. Court makes copy: $.65 per page; $1.30 minimum. The court refuses to permit access to records unless specific case file given. Searchers must use the $52.00 statewide OCA search.

General Information: Public terminal goes back to 1996. No sealed or youthful offender records released. Certification fee: $5.00 for criminal; $6.00 if civil. Payee: City Court of Beacon. Only cashiers checks and money orders accepted. Prepayment required.

Poughkeepsie City Court Civic Center Plaza, PO Box 300, Poughkeepsie, NY 12602; phone: 845-451-4091; fax: 845-485-6795; hours 8AM-4PM (EST). *Misdemeanor, Civil Actions Under $15,000, Eviction, Small Claims.*

Civil Records: Access: Mail, in person. Both court and visitors may perform in person searches. Search fee: $5.00 per name per 2 years searched. $5.00 for certificate of disposition. Court makes copy: $.65 per page. Required to search: name, years to search. Civil cases indexed by defendant. Civil records on computer from 1993.

Criminal Records: Access: In person only. Court makes copy: $.65 per page. Criminal records on computer from 1990. Direct criminal records search requests to OCA for $52.00 statewide search. Must go through state in order to get a certified disposition. Mail turnaround time 1 week.

General Information: No public access terminal. No sealed, expunged, adoption, sex offense, juvenile or mental health records released. Certification fee: $5.00. Payee: Poughkeepsie City Court. Only cashiers checks and money orders accepted. Prepayment and SASE required.

Surrogate's Court 10 Market St, Poughkeepsie, NY 12601; phone: 845-486-2235; fax: 845-486-2234; hours 9AM-5PM (EST). *Probate.*

Dutchess Town/Village Courts - *misdemeanor or civil records:* Amenia Town- 845-373-7017; Beekman Town- 845-724-5581; Clinton Town- 845-266-5988; Dover Town- 845-832-3461; East Fishkill Town- 845-226-4229; Fishkill Town- 845-831-7860; Fishkill Village; Hyde Park Town- 845-229-2606/229-5210; La Grange Town- 845-452-1837; Milan Town- 845-758-6960; Millbrook Village- 845-677-8277; Millerton Village- 518-789-3080; North East Town- 518-789-3080; Pawling Town- 845-855-3516; Pawling Village- 845-855-5602; Pine Plains Town- 518-398-7194; Pleasant Valley Town- 845-635-2856; Poughkeepsie Town- 845-485-3690/3696; Red Hook Town- 845-758-4611/758-4609; Red Hook Village- 845-758-4113; Rhinebeck Town- 845-876-3858; Rhinebeck Village- 845-876-4119; Stanford Town- 845-868-2269/2258; Tivoli Village- 845-757-3219; Union Vale Town- 845-724-3288/724-5600; Wappinger Town- 845-297-6070; Wappingers Falls Village- 845-297-6777; Washington Town- 845-677-6366.

Erie County

County Clerk 25 Delaware Ave, 1st Fl, Buffalo, NY 14202; phone: 716-858-8865; criminal phone: 716-858-7877; fax: 716-858-6550; hours 9AM-5PM; usually closed 1 hour for lunch but time varies (EST). *Felony, Civil.*

www.erie.gov/depts/government/clerk/civil_criminal.phtml

Note: Countywide search requests made to the County Clerk are processed in the manner described below. Office now located near the 94 Franklin St entrance in old section of courthouse.

Civil Records: Access: Mail, in person, online. Both court and visitors may perform in person searches. Search fee: $5.00 per name per 2 years. Court makes copy: $1.00 per page. Required to search: name, years to search. Civil cases indexed by defendant. Civil records on computer from 1994, prior in books back to 1900's. Online access to the county clerk's database of civil matters is free at http://ecclerk.erie.gov. Records go back to 2/1994. Also, access to current/pending Supreme Court civil cases is at http://e.courts.state.ny.us/.

Criminal Records: Access: In person only. No search fee. Court makes copy: $1.00 per page. Required to search: name, years to search, DOB. Criminal records in books back to 1900's. No

misdemeanors located here. Mail requests are directed to the OCA for $52.00 statewide record search. Mail turnaround time 3-4 days.

General Information: Public terminal has only civil records back to 1994. No sealed records released. Will not fax documents. Certification fee: $5.00 per doc. Payee: County Clerk. Personal checks accepted. Prepayment and SASE required.

Supreme & County Court 25 Delaware Ave, Ground Fl, Buffalo, NY 14202; phone: 716-845-9301; fax: 716-851-3293; hours 9AM-5PM (EST). *Felony, Civil.*

www.erie.gov

Note: Court directs felony search requests to the OCA for a $52.00 statewide record check. See also County Clerk for access. Access to current/pending Supreme Court civil cases available at http://e.courts.state.ny.us/, also search pending criminal appearances.

Buffalo City Court 50 Delaware Ave, Buffalo, NY 14202; phone: 716-845-2689; criminal phone: 716-845-2661; civil phone: 716-845-2662; criminal fax: 716-847-8257; civil fax: 716-856-4670; hours 9AM-5PM (EST). *Misdemeanor, Civil Actions Under $15,000, Eviction, Small Claims.*

Civil Records: Access: In person only. Both court and visitors may perform in person searches. Court makes copy: $.65 per page; $1.30 minimum. Required to search: name, years to search. Civil cases indexed by defendant, plaintiff. Criminal records on computer back to 1983, prior in books back to 1974.

Criminal Records: Access: In person only. Only the court performs in person searches; visitors may not. However, clerk will do Certificate of Disposition for $5.00 per name. Court makes copy: $.65 per page; $1.30 minimum. Required to search: name, DOB, date of offense. Criminal records on computer back to 1983, prior in books back to 1974. Search online for future court appearances at http://iapps.courts.state.ny.us/webcrim_attorney/Login Note: No general searches are performed; criminal requests directed to OCA in NYC for $52.00 statewide search.

General Information: No public access terminal. No sealed or youthful offender records released. Certification fee: $6.00 per cert. Payee: City Court. Business checks accepted.

Lackawanna City Court 714 Ridge Rd, Rm 225, Lackawanna, NY 14218; phone: 716-827-6486; criminal phone: 716-827-6487; civil phone: 716-827-6661; fax: 716-825-1874; hours 8:30AM-4:30PM (EST). *Misdemeanor, Civil Actions Under $15,000, Eviction, Small Claims.*

Civil Records: Access: Mail, in person. Only the court performs in person searches; visitors may not. Search fee: $16.00 per name. Court makes copy: $1.00 per page. Required to search: name; also helpful: years to search. Civil cases indexed by defendant. Civil records on computer from 1994, prior on docket books. Mail access available to government agencies only.

Criminal Records: Access: None. Court makes copy: $1.00 per page. Criminal records on computer from 1994, prior on docket books. The court refuses to permit access to court records unless specific case file given. It is suggested to send requests to OCA for $52.00 statewide search. Mail turnaround time 2-3 days.

General Information: No public access terminal. No sealed or youthful offender records released. Will not fax documents. Certification fee: $6.00 per document. Payee: City Court. Only cashiers checks and money orders accepted. Prepayment and SASE required.

Tonawanda City Court 200 Niagara St, Tonawanda, NY 14150; phone: 716-693-3484; fax: 716-693-1612; hours 9AM-4PM (EST). *Misdemeanor, Civil Actions Under $15,000, Eviction, Small Claims, Criminal.*

Civil Records: Access: Mail, in person. Only the court performs in person searches; visitors may not. No search fee. Court makes copy: $.65 per page, minimum $1.30. Required to search: name, years to search. Civil cases indexed by defendant, plaintiff; on computer since 1997, prior on index cards, in books. Mail turnaround time 3-5 days.

Criminal Records: Access: Mail, in person. Only the court performs in person searches; visitors may not. Search fee: $5.00 per name. A Certificate of Disposition is $5.00. Court makes copy: $.65 per page, minimum $1.30. Required to search: name, years to search (case number, arrest date if Cert of Disposition). Criminal records on computer since 1986, prior on index cards, in books. As a rule, the court will not permit access to its records unless specific case file given. It is suggested to send requests to OCA for $52.00 statewide search. However, court will search older records for the fee listed below. Mail turnaround time 3-5 days.
General Information: No public access terminal. No sealed records released. Certification fee: $5.00. Payee: City Court of Tonawanda. Business checks accepted. Prepayment required.

Surrogate's Court 92 Franklin St, Buffalo, NY 14202; phone: 716-854-2560; hours 9AM-5PM (EST). *Probate.*

Dutchess Town/Village Courts - *misdemeanor or civil records:* Amenia Town- 845-373-7017; Beekman Town- 845-724-5581; Clinton Town- 845-266-5988; Dover Town- 845-832-3461; East Fishkill Town- 845-226-4229; Fishkill Town- 845-831-7860; Fishkill Village; Hyde Park Town- 845-229-2606/229-5210; La Grange Town- 845-452-1837; Milan Town- 845-758-6960; Millbrook Village- 845-677-8277; Millerton Village- 518-789-3080; North East Town- 518-789-3080; Pawling Town- 845-855-3516; Pawling Village- 845-855-5602; Pine Plains Town- 518-398-7194; Pleasant Valley Town- 845-635-2856; Poughkeepsie Town- 845-485-3690/3696; Red Hook Town- 845-758-4611/758-4609; Red Hook Village- 845-758-4113; Rhinebeck Town- 845-876-3858; Rhinebeck Village- 845-876-4119; Stanford Town- 845-868-2269/2258; Tivoli Village- 845-757-3219; Union Vale Town- 845-724-3288/724-5600; Wappinger Town- 845-297-6070; Wappingers Falls Village- 845-297-6777; Washington Town- 845-677-6366.

Essex County

County Clerk PO Box 247, 7559 Court St, Essex County Government Ctr, Elizabethtown, NY 12932; criminal phone: 518-873-3370; civil phone: 518-873-3600, 518-873-3601; criminal fax: 518-873-3376; civil fax: 518-873-3548; hours 8AM-5PM (EST). *Civil, Felony.*

Note: County Clerk will not do felony record searches for County-Court felony records; clerk will only do civil. You may search felony books in person.

Civil Records: Access: Mail, in person, online. Both court and visitors may perform in person searches. No search fee. Court makes copy: $.65 per page; $1.30 minimum. Self serve copy fee: $.65 per page. Required to search: name, years to search. Civil cases indexed by defendant, plaintiff; on computer from 11/93, prior in books. Access to current/pending Supreme Court civil cases is at http://e.courts.state.ny.us/.
Criminal Records: Access: In person only. Visitors must perform in person searches themselves. Court makes copy: $.65 per page; $1.30 minimum. Self serve copy fee: $.65 per page. Required to search: name, years to search, DOB. Criminal records on computer from 1950s, prior in books; you may search the books.
General Information: Public terminal has only civil records back to 1993. No sealed or youthful offender records released. Will not fax documents. Certification fee: $1.00 per page; minimum $5.00. Payee: Essex County Clerk. Personal checks accepted. Prepayment and SASE required.

Supreme & County Court PO Box 217, 7559 Court St, Essex County Government Ctr, Elizabethtown, NY 12932; criminal phone: 518-873-3370; civil phone: 518-873-3600; fax: 518-873-3376; hours 8AM-5PM (EST). *Felony, Civil.*

Note: County-court directs criminal searches to the OCA for $52.00 statewide record check. Countywide record checks can be made at County Clerk, see separate listing. Access to current/pending Supreme Court civil cases available at http://e.courts.state.ny.us/.

Surrogate's Court 7559 Court St, PO Box 505, Elizabethtown, NY 12932; phone: 518-873-3384; fax: 518-873-3731; hours 9AM-5PM (EST). *Probate.*

Essex Town/Village Courts - *misdemeanor or civil records:* Chesterfield Town- 518-834-9211; Crown Point Town- 518-597-4144; Elizabethtown Town- 518-873-2047; Essex Town- 518-963-8016; Jay Town- 518 647 2204; Keene Town- 518-576-4444; Lake Placid Village- 518-523-2004; 2141; Lewis Town- 518-873-3204; Minerva Town- 518-251-2869; Moriah Town- 518-546-9955; Newcomb Town- 518-582-2010; North Elba Town- 518-523-9516; North Hudson Town- 518-532-0587; Schroon Town- 518-532-0569; St Armand Town- 518-891-3189; Ticonderoga Town- 518-585-7141; Westport Town- 518-962-4882; Willsboro Town- 518-963-8933; Wilmington Town- 518-946-2105.

Franklin County

County Clerk 355 W Main St, Attn: County Clerk, Malone, NY 12953-1817; phone: 518-481-1681; hours 9AM-5PM; 8AM-4PM Summer hours (EST). *Felony, Civil.*

Note: Felony records are managed by the Supreme Court clerk who directs search requests to OCA for a $52.00 statewide search. However, felony record index is accessible in person here (at Courty Clerk Office) on the public access terminal.

Civil Records: Access: Mail, in person, online. Visitors must perform in person searches themselves. Search fee: $5.00 per name per 2 years. Court makes copy: $.65 per page; same fee for self serve. Required to search: name, years to search. Civil cases indexed by defendant. Civil index of dockets on computer from 1996, prior in file folders in Clerk's office. Access to current/pending Supreme Court civil cases is at http://e.courts.state.ny.us/.
Criminal Records: Access: In person only. Visitors must perform in person searches themselves. Court makes copy: $.65 per page; same fee for self serve. Required to search: name, years to search, DOB. Criminal records on computer from 1962.
General Information: Public terminal goes back to 1966. (There are separate terminals for criminal records and civil records.) No sealed or youthful offender records released. Certification fee: $1.00 per page, 5 page minimum. Payee: County Clerk. Personal checks accepted. Prepayment and SASE required.

Supreme & County Court 355 W Main St, Court Clerk, Malone, NY 12953-1817; phone: 518-481-1748; criminal phone: 518-481-1749; civil phone: 518-481-1681; fax: 518-483-9143; hours 9AM-5PM; 8AM-4PM Summer hours (EST). *Felony, Civil.*

Note: Supreme court directs criminal search requests to the OCA for a $52.00 statewide record check. Search civil records at County Clerk, see separate listing.

Criminal Records: Access: Mail, in person. Visitors must perform in person searches themselves. No search fee. Court makes copy: $.65 per page. Required to search: name, years to search, DOB. Criminal records on computer from 1962. Note: Unless you search here in person, all criminal record name search requests are directed to the OCA for statewide record search, $52.00 search fee. Mail turnaround time 1 week.

General Information: Public terminal has only criminal records back to 1962. No sealed or youthful offender records released. Will fax specific case file requests for $2.60 per page. Certification fee: $1.00 per page, 5 page minimum. Payee: County Clerk. Personal checks accepted. Prepayment and SASE required.

Surrogate's Court 355 W Main St, #3223, Malone, NY 12953-1817; phone: 518-481-1736 & 1737; fax: 518-483-7583; hours 8AM-5PM Summer; 8:00-4PM June-Aug (EST). *Probate.*

Franklin Town/Village Courts - *misdemeanor or civil records:* Altamont Town- 518-359-9278; Bangor Town- 518-481-6570; Bellmont Town- 518-425-3349; Bombay Town- 518-358-9939; Brandon Town- 518-327-3202; Brighton Town- 518-327-3202; Burke Town- 518-483-5497; Chateaugay Town- 518-497-6931; Constable Town- 518-481-6113; Dickinson Town- 518-856-0201; Duane Town- 518-483-0386; Fort Covington Town- 518-358-2796; Franklin Town- 518-891-2189; Harrietstown Town- 518-891-4500; Malone Town- 518-481-6634; Malone Village- 518-483-5210; Moira Town- 518-529-2080; Santa Clara Town- 518-891-1919; Saranac Lake Village- 518-891-4423; Tupper Lake Village- 518-359-9161; Waverly Town- 518-856-9249; Westville Town- 518-358-2499, 518-358-3432.

Fulton County

Supreme & County Court 223 W Main St, County Bldg, Johnstown, NY 12095; phone: 518-736-5539 (court) 518-736-5555 (county clerk); civil phone: 518-736-5555; fax: 518-762-5078; hours 9AM-5PM (EST). *Felony, Civil.*

www.courts.state.ny.us
Note: Hamilton County Supreme Court cases are heard here. Supreme court clerk directs criminal search requests to the OCA for a $52.00 statewide record check, however the County Clerk office (same location) may permit in person criminal record search requests.

Civil Records: Access: Phone, mail, fax, in person, online. Both court and visitors may perform in person searches. Search fee: $16.00 per name. Court makes copy: $1.00 per page. Self serve copy fee: $.50 per page. Required to search: name, years to search. Civil cases indexed by defendant, plaintiff. Civil records computerized since 1994. Access to current/pending Supreme Court civil cases is at http://e.courts.state.ny.us/. Mail turnaround time same day.
Criminal Records: Access: In person only. Only the court performs in person searches; visitors may not. Search fee: $5.00 if search done in archives. Court makes copy: $1.00 per page. Self serve copy fee: $.50 per page. Required to search: name, years to search, DOB. Criminal records in file folders since 1915, computerized since 1977. Mail turnaround time 1 week.
General Information: No public access terminal. No sealed, expunged, adoption, sex offense, juvenile or mental health records released. Will fax documents after payment received. Certification fee: $4.00 per page. Payee: County Clerk. Business checks accepted. Prepayment and SASE required.

Gloversville City Court 3 Frontage Rd, City Hall, Gloversville, NY 12078; phone: 518-773-4527; fax: 518-773-4599; hours 8AM-4PM; window closes at 3:30 (EST). *Misdemeanor, Civil Actions Under $15,000, Eviction, Small Claims.*

Civil Records: Access: Mail, in person. Only the court performs in person searches; visitors may not. No search fee. Court makes copy: $.65 per page; $1.30 minimum. Required to search: name, years to search. Civil cases indexed by plaintiff. Civil records in books; on computer since. Mail turnaround time less than 1 week.
Criminal Records: Access: None. However, a Certificate of Disposition is $5.00. Court makes copy: $.65 per page; $1.30 minimum. Required to search:

name, years to search, charge, date of arrest or sentence. The court refuses to permit access to records unless specific case file given. Searchers must use the OCA $52.00 statewide search. Mail turnaround time 2 weeks.

General Information: No public access terminal. No sealed, youthful offender records released. Certification fee: $5.00 per doc criminal; $6.00 if civil,. Payee: Gloversville City Court. Only cashiers checks and money orders accepted. Prepayment and SASE required.

Johnstown City Court 33-41 E Main St, Johnstown, NY 12095; phone: 518-762-0007; fax: 518-762-2720; hours 8AM-4PM (EST). *Misdemeanor, Civil Actions Under $15,000, Eviction, Small Claims.*

Civil Records: Access: Mail, in person. Only the court performs in person searches; visitors may not. Search fee: $16.00 per name. Court makes copy: $.65 per page, $1.30 minimum. Required to search: name, years to search. Civil cases indexed by plaintiff. Civil records in file folders, computerized since 1995.

Criminal Records: Access: None. Only the court performs in person searches; visitors may not. Court makes copy: $.65 per page, $1.30 minimum. Required to search: name, years to search, DOB. Criminal records on computer from 1990. The court does not permit access to court records unless specific case file given. Requesters are directed to OCA for $52.00 statewide search. Mail turnaround time 1 month.

General Information: No public access terminal. No sealed or youthful offender records released. Will not fax documents. Certification fee: $5.00 per document includes copy fee. Payee: City Court. Only cashiers checks and money orders accepted. Prepayment and SASE required.

Surrogate's Court 223 W Main St, Johnstown, NY 12095; phone: 518-736-5685; fax: 518-762-6372; hours 9AM-5PM (8AM-4PM July-August) (EST). *Probate.*

Fulton Town/Village Courts - *misdemeanor or civil records:* Bleeker Town- 518-725-0859; Broadalbin Town- 518-883-5131; Broadalbin Village- 518-883-3353; Ephratah Town- 518-568-7560; Johnstown Town- 518-762-6904; Mayfield Town- 518-661-5225; Oppenheim Town- 518-568-2662; Perth Town- 518-843-6977; Stratford Town- 315-429-8341.

Genesee County

County Clerk PO Box 379, Attn: County Clerk, 15 Main St, County Clerk, Batavia, NY 14021-0379; phone: 585-344-2550; criminal phone: x2243; civil phone: x2242; fax: 585-344-8521; hours 8:30AM-5PM (EST). *Felony, Civil.*

Note: Countywide felony search requests made to the County Clerk are processed in the manner described below.

Civil Records: Access: Mail, in person, online. Both court and visitors may perform in person searches. Search fee: $10.00 per name per 5 year period. Court makes copy: $1.30 for first page, $.65 each add'l. Required to search: name, years to search; also helpful: address. Civil cases indexed by defendant, plaintiff; indexed by defendant only prior to 1995. Civil records in books from 1802; on computer back to 1995. Access to current/pending Supreme Court civil cases is at http://e.courts.state.ny.us/. Mail turnaround time same or next day.

Criminal Records: Access: Fax, mail, in person. Both court and visitors may perform in person searches. Search fee: $10.00 per name per 5 year period, $15.00 for 6-10 years, $20.00 for 11-20 years. Court makes copy: $1.30 for first page, $.65 each add'l. Required to search: name, years to search, DOB; also helpful: SSN. Criminal records in books from 1802; on computer back to 1995. Note: With fax requests, include a photocopy of your fee payment check and they will entertain your search

request and speed up the process. Mail turnaround time 1-3 days.

General Information: Public terminal goes back to 1/1995. No sealed, expunged, adoption, sex offense, juvenile or mental health records released. Fee to fax documents is $5.00 per document; no charge if to a toll free number. Certification fee: $4.00 plus $.50 per page in excess of 8 pages. Payee: County Clerk. Personal checks accepted. Prepayment and SASE required.

Supreme & County Court PO Box 379, Attn: County-Court Clerk, 15 Main St, County-Court Clerk, Batavia, NY 14021-0379; phone: 585-344-2550 x2239; civil phone: x2243 for records info; hours 8:30AM-5PM (EST). *Felony, Civil.*

Note: The County Court directs criminal search requests to the OCA for a $52.00 statewide record check. See also County Clerk, see separate listing. Access to current/pending Supreme Court civil cases is available at http://e.courts.state.ny.us/.

Batavia City Court Genesee County Courts Facility, 1 W Main St, Batavia, NY 14020; phone: 585-344-2550 x2416, 2417, 2418; fax: 585-344-8556; hours 9AM-5PM (EST). *Misdemeanor, Civil Actions Under $15,000, Eviction, Small Claims.*

Civil Records: Access: Fax, mail, in person. Both court and visitors may perform in person searches. Search fee: $6.00 per name. Court makes copy: $.50 per page. Required to search: name, years to search. Civil cases indexed by plaintiff. Civil records on computer from 1990, in books from 1957. Mail turnaround time 1-3 days.

Criminal Records: Access: Mail, in person. Only the court performs in person searches; visitors may not. Search fee: A Certificate of Disposition is available for $6.00. Court makes copy: $.50 per page. Required to search: name, years to search, DOB. Criminal records on computer from 1993, in books from 1947. Note: All criminal record name search requests are directed to the OCA for statewide record search, $52.00 search fee. Mail turnaround time 1-3 days.

General Information: No public access terminal. No sealed, expunged, sex offense or mental health records released. Will fax documents to local or toll free line only. Certification fee: $6.00 per seal. Payee: City Court. Only cashiers checks and money orders accepted. Prepayment and SASE required.

Surrogate's Court 1 W Main St, Batavia, NY 14020; phone: 585-344-2550 x2237; fax: 585-344-8517; hours 9AM-5PM; June-Sept 3-8:30AM-4:30PM (EST). *Probate.*

Note: $30.00 search fee.

Genesee Town/Village Courts - *misdemeanor or civil records:* Alabama Town; Alexander Town- 585-591-0908; Batavia Town- 585-343-1729; Bergen Town- 585-494-1121; Bethany Town- 585-343-3325; Byron Town- 585-548-7123; Corfu Village- 585-599-3327; Darien Town- 585-547-2274 x21; Elba Town- 585-757-9200; Leroy Town & Village- 585-768-6910; Oakfield Town- 585-948-5835 x3; Pavilion Town- 585-584-3850; Pembroke Town- 585-599-4817; Stafford Town- 585-344-4020.

Greene County

Supreme & County Court County Clerk, Courthouse, 411 Main St, Catskill, NY 12414; phone: 518-719-3255, (county clerk) 518-943-2230 (court clerk); fax: 518-719-3284; hours 9AM-5PM; 8:30AM-4:30PM June-Aug hours (EST). *Felony, Civil.*

Note: Search requests are processed by the County Clerk office in the manner described below. Courts are located at 320 Main St. Fax to the court clerk office is 518-943-2146.

Civil Records: Access: In person, online. Both court and visitors may perform in person searches. No search fee. Court makes copy: $1.00 per page. Required to search: name, years to search. Civil cases indexed by defendant, plaintiff. Civil records in file folder, computerized since 6/13/97. Access to

current/pending Supreme Court civil cases is at http://e.courts.state.ny.us/.

Criminal Records: Access: In person. Only the court performs in person searches; visitors may not. Search fee: $17.50 per name for 7-20 years. May also do search for $5.00 per name for 2 years. Court makes copy: $1.00 per page. Required to search: name, years to search, DOB. Criminal records on index cards.

General Information: Public terminal has only civil records back to 1999 for index. No sealed or youthful offender records released. Will not fax back documents. Certification fee: $5.00 per doc. Payee: County Clerk. Personal checks accepted. Prepayment required.

Surrogate's Court Courthouse, 320 Main St, Catskill, NY 12414; phone: 518-943-2484; fax: 518-943-1864; hours 9AM-5PM (EST). *Probate.*

Greene Town/Village Courts - *misdemeanor or civil records:* Ashland Town- 518-734-3636; Athens Town- 518-945-3360; Athens Village- 518-945-3002; Cairo Town- 518-622-3388; Catskill Town- 518-943-2142; Catskill Village- 518-943-9544; Coxsackie Town- 518-731-6934; Coxsackie Village- 518-731-2225; Durham Town- 518-239-8260; Greenville Town- 518-966-4873; Halcott Town- 845-254-6441; Hunter Town- 518-589-6150; Hunter Village- 518-263-4288; Jewett Town- 518-263-4626; Lexington Town- 518-989-6303; New Baltimore Town- 518-756-2079; Prattsville Town- 518-299-3125; Windham Town- 518-734-3431.

Hamilton County

County Clerk & County Court Hamilton County Clerk, PO Box 204, Rte 8, Lake Pleasant, NY 12108; phone: 518-548-7111; hours 8:30AM-4:30PM (EST). *Felony, Civil.*

Note: Countywide record search requests are processed in the manner described below. Civil cases are heard in Fulton County (518-736-5539, Patricia, for info). Once closed, civil case records are returned to Hamilton County clerk.

Civil Records: Access: Mail, phone, in person, online. Both court and visitors may perform in person searches. No search fee. Court makes copy: $.65 per page. $1.30 minimum. Required to search: name, years to search. Civil cases indexed by defendant. Civil records in books, records go back to 1850's. Access to current/pending Supreme Court civil cases is at http://e.courts.state.ny.us/. Mail turnaround time 2-3 days.

Criminal Records: Access: Mail, in person. Only the court performs in person searches; visitors may not. Search fee: $5.00 per name. Fee is per two years searched. Court makes copy: $.65 per page, $1.30 minimum. Required to search: name, years to search, DOB. Criminal records go back to 1878; no computerized records. Note: Record search request must be in writing. Mail turnaround time 2-3 days.

General Information: No public access terminal. No sealed or youthful offender records released. Fee to fax documents is $1.00 per document. Certification fee: $1.25 per page; $5.00 minimum. Payee: Hamilton County Clerk. Personal checks accepted. Prepayment required.

Supreme Court Hamilton County Clerk, PO Box 204, Rte 8, Lake Pleasant, NY 12108; phone: 518-548-7111 (Hamilton county clerk) 518-736-5539 (Fulton court clerk); hours 8:30AM-4:30PM (EST). *Civil.*

Note: Supreme court (civil cases) in Hamilton County are heard in Fulton County. Civil records eventually returned to Hamilton County Clerk once the case is completed in Fulton. Original filings made in Hamilton, but subsequent filings usually made at Fulton.

Civil Records: Access: Mail, fax, phone, in person, online. Both court and visitors may perform in person searches. No search fee. Court makes copy: $.65 per page. $1.30 minimum. Required to search: name, years to search. Civil cases indexed by defendant. Civil records in books, records go back to 1850's. Access to current/pending Supreme Court civil cases is at http://e.courts.state.ny.us/. Mail turnaround time 2-3 days.

General Information: Public terminal has only civil records. (Hamilton County civil cases heard in Fulton County may be available on Fulton County civil records computer system. No public terminal in Hamilton County.) No sealed or youthful offender records released. Fee to fax documents is $1.00 per document. Certification fee: $1.00 per page; $5.00 minimum. Payee: Hamilton County Clerk. Personal checks accepted. Prepayment required.

Surrogate's Court PO Box 780, 79 White Birch Lane, Indian Lake, NY 12842; phone: 518-648-5411; fax: 518-648-6286; hours 8:30AM-4:30PM (EST). *Probate.*

Note: Court is located in Hamilton County Ofc. Bldg.

Hamilton Town/Village Courts - *misdemeanor or civil records:* Arietta Town- 518-548-6203; Benson Town; Caroga Town- 518-835-4211; Hope Town- 518-924-4302; Indian Lake Town- 518-648-6226; Inlet Town- 315-357-6121; Lake Pleasant Town- 518-548-3625; Long Lake Town- 518-624-3761; Morehouse Town; Wells Town- 518-924-9285/924-7407.

Herkimer County

County Clerk 109 Mary St, Herkimer County Office Bldg, Herkimer, NY 13350-1993; phone: 315-867-1133; fax: 315-867-1349; hours 9AM-5PM Sept-May; 8:30AM-4PM June-Aug (EST). *Felony, Civil.*

Note: Countywide search requests made to the County Clerk are processed in the manner described below.

Civil Records: Access: Mail, in person, online. Both court and visitors may perform in person searches. Search fee: $5.00 per name per 2 year period. Court makes copy: $.65 per page, $1.30 minimum. Required to search: name, years to search. Civil cases indexed by defendant, plaintiff; on index books since 1800s. Access to current/pending Supreme Court civil cases is at http://e.courts.state.ny.us/. Mail turnaround time varies/asap.

Criminal Records: Access: mail, in person. Both court and visitors may perform in person searches. Search fee: $5.00 per name per 2 year period. Court makes copy: $.65 per page, $1.30 minimum. Required to search: name, years to search, DOB. Criminal records on index books since 1800s. Mail turnaround time varies/ASAP.

General Information: Public terminal has criminal back to 1800s. and civil back to mid-1990s. No sealed, expunged, adoption, sex offense, juvenile or mental health records released. Will fax back documents, fax fee is same amount as copy fee total. Certification fee: 1-4 pages is $5.00; $1.25 each add'l page. Payee: County Clerk. Personal checks accepted. Prepayment and SASE required.

Supreme & County Court 301 N Washington St, Herkimer, NY 13350-1993; criminal phone: 315-867-1282; civil phone: 315-867-1209; fax: 315-866-1802; hours 9AM-5PM; 8:30AM-4PM Summer hours (EST). *Felony, Civil.*

Note: The County Court clerk directs felony requests to the OCA for a $52.00 statewide record check. See also separate listing for County Clerk. Access to current/pending Supreme Court civil cases is available at http://e.courts.state.ny.us/.

Little Falls City Court 659 E Main St, Little Falls, NY 13365; phone: 315-823-1690; fax: 315-823-1623; hours 8:30AM-4:30PM (EST). *Misdemeanor, Civil Actions Under $15,000, Eviction, Small Claims.*

Civil Records: Access: Mail, fax, in person. Only the court performs in person searches; visitors may not. Search fee: $5.00 per name. Court makes copy: $.65 per page; minimum $1.30. Required to search: name, years to search. Civil cases indexed by defendant. Civil records go back to 1973; on computer back to 4/02. Mail turnaround time 1 week.

Criminal Records: Access: Mail, in person. Only the court performs in person searches; visitors may not. Search fee: $5.00 per name. Court makes copy: $.65 per page; minimum $1.30. Required to search: name, years to search, DOB, signed release. Criminal records go back to 1948; on computer back to 4/02. Mail turnaround time 1 week.

General Information: No public access terminal. No sealed, expunged, adoption, sex offense, juvenile or mental health records released. Will fax documents to local or toll free line. Certification fee: $5.00 per document. Payee: City Court. Only cashiers checks and money orders accepted. Prepayment and SASE required.

Surrogate's Court 301 N Washington St, #5550, Herkimer, NY 13350; phone: 315-867-1170; fax: 315-866-1722; hours 9AM-5PM Sept-May; 8:00AM-4PM June-Aug (EST). *Probate.*

Herkimer Town/Village Courts - *misdemeanor or civil records:* Cold Brook Village- 315-826-3432; Columbia Town- 315-866-1309; Danube Town- 315-823-4210; Fairfield Town- 315-823-2747; Frankfort Town- 315-895-7267; Frankfort Village- 315-894-8513; German Flatts Town- 315-866-3571; Herkimer Town- 315-866-1280; Herkimer Village- 315-866-0604; Ilion Village- 315-894-4175; Litchfield Town; Little Falls Town- 315-823-1202; Manheim Town- 315-429-9631; Middleville Village- 315-823-2747; Newport Town; Newport Village- 315-845-8938; Norway Town- 315-845-8272; Ohio Town- 315-826-3466; Poland Town- 315-826-3432; Russia Town- 315-826-3432; Salisbury Town- 315-429-8581; Schuyler Town- 315-733-1093; Stark Town- 315-858-2091; Warren Town; Webb Town- 315-369-3321; Winfield Town- 315-822-4555.

Jefferson County

Supreme & County Court Jefferson County Clerk's Office-Court Records, 175 Arsenal St, County Bldg, Watertown, NY 13601-3783; phone: 315-785-3200 County Clerk; probate phone: 315-785-3019; fax: 315-785-5145; hours 9AM-5PM; 8:30AM-4PM July-Aug Summer hours (EST). *Felony, Civil.*

www.co.jefferson.ny.us/Jefflive.nsf/cclerk

Note: Countywide record search requests are processed in the manner described below by the County Clerk.

Civil Records: Access: In person, online. Visitors must perform in person searches themselves. Court makes copy: $.65 per page; $1.30 minimum; same fee for self serve. Required to search: name, years to search. Civil cases indexed by defendant, plaintiff; on computer back to 1/1992; prior in books from 1805 by first defendant name only. Access to current/pending Supreme Court civil cases is at http://e.courts.state.ny.us/. Note: Civil phone for the Supreme Court clerk 315-785-7912.

Criminal Records: Access: Mail, in person. Both court and visitors may perform in person searches. Search fee: $5.00 per name. Fee is per 2 years searched. Court makes copy: $.65 per page; $1.30 minimum; same fee for self serve. Required to search: name, years to search; also helpful: DOB, signed release. Criminal records on computer back to 1/1992; prior in books from 1805 by first defendant name only. Note: Phone for the county court clerk is 315-785-3044. Mail turnaround time 1 week.

General Information: Public terminal goes back to 1992. No sealed, expunged, adoption, sex offense, juvenile or mental health records released. Will fax specific case file requests. Certification fee: $.65 per page, $5.20 minimum. With copies: $1.25 per page, $5.00 minimum. Payee: County Clerk of Jefferson County. Personal checks accepted. Prepayment and SASE required.

Watertown City Court 245 Washington St, Municipal Bldg, Watertown, NY 13601; phone: 315-785-7785; fax: 315-785-7818; hours 8:30AM4:30PM (EST). *Misdemeanor, Civil Actions Under $15,000, Eviction, Small Claims.*

Civil Records: Access: Mail, in person. Only the court performs in person searches; visitors may not. Search fee: $6.00 per name. Fee is per name & docket. Court makes copy: $.65 per page. Required to search: name, years to search. Civil cases indexed by defendant. Civil records in docket books. Mail turnaround time 1 day.

Criminal Records: Access: None. Court makes copy: $.65 per page. Criminal records in docket books. The court refuses to permit access to court records unless specific case file given. It is mandatory to send requests to OCA for $52.00 statewide search. Mail turnaround time same day.

General Information: No public access terminal. No sealed records released. Will fax documents to local or toll free line. Certification fee: $6.00. Payee: City Court. Only cashiers checks and money orders accepted. Prepayment and SASE required.

Surrogate's Court County Court Complex, 163 Arsenal St, 3rd Fl, Watertown, NY 13601-2562; phone: 315-785-3019; fax: 315-785-5194; hours 8:20AM-4:30PM Sept-May; 8:30AM-4PM June-Aug (EST). *Probate.*

Jefferson Town/Village Courts - *misdemeanor or civil records:* Adams Town- 315-583-5085; Adams Village- 315-232-2124; Alexandria Bay Village- 315-482-4786; Alexandria Town- 315-482-9637; Antwerp Town- 315-659-8989; Brownville Town- 315-639-6266; Brownville Village- 315-639-6266; Cape Vincent Town- 315-654-3883; Carthage Village- 315-493-2890; Champion Town- 315-493-2687; Clayton Town and Village- 315-686-2427; Ellisburg Town- 315-846-9216; Glen Park Village- 315-639-6266; Henderson Town- 315-938-5614; Hounsfield Town- 315-646-2030; LeRay Town- 315-629-0228; Lorraine Town- 315-232-2548; Lyme Town- 315-893-7544; Orleans Town- 315-658-2272; Pamelia Town- 315-785-9794; Philadelphia Town- 315-642-3421; Philadelphia Village- 315-642-3452; Rodman Town- 315-232-4029; Rutland Town- 315-788-1265; Sackets Harbor Village- 315-646-3548; Theresa Town- 315-628-5046; Theresa Village- 315-628-5424; Watertown Town; West Carthage Village- 315-493-6345; Wilna Town- 315-493-2771; Worth Town- no phone.

Kings Borough

Supreme Court - Civil Division 360 Adams St, #189, Brooklyn, NY 11201; phone: 718-643-5894; fax: 718-643-8187; hours 9AM-3PM for records (EST). *Civil Actions Over $25,000.*

www.courts.state.ny.us/courts/2jd/kings.shtml#sup

Note: In person - see Window #9.

Civil Records: Access: Mail, in person, online. Visitors must perform in person searches themselves. Search fee: $10.00 per name per 2 years. Court makes copy: $.65 per page; $1.30 minimum. Required to search: name, years to search; also requested by clerk- index number. Civil cases indexed by defendant. Civil records on computer back to 1993; in books, on microfiche back to 1900's. Access to current/pending Supreme Court civil cases is at http://e.courts.state.ny.us/. Note: Picture ID required for in person searchers for matrimonial cases.

General Information: Public terminal has only civil records back to 1993. No sealed, expunged, adoption, sex offense, juvenile or mental health records released. Certification fee: $8.00 per doc. $25.00 for exemplification. Payee: County Clerk. Only cashiers checks and money orders accepted. Prepayment and SASE required.

Supreme Court - Criminal 120 Schermerhorn St, Brooklyn, NY 11210; phone: 718-643-4044; hours 9:30AM-1, 2-4:30PM (EST). *Felony, Misdemeanor.*

www.courts.state.ny.us/courts/2jd/kings.shtml#sup

Note: This court does not perform criminal searches; In person searches can be performed at OCA, 25 Beaver St, NYC, 212-428-2810. Also, search online for future court appearances at http://e.courts.state.ny.us.

Civil Court of the City of New York - Kings Branch

141 Livingston St, Brooklyn, NY 11201; phone: 718-643-5069/643-8133 Clerk; hours 9AM-5PM (EST). *Civil Actions Under $25,000, Eviction, Small Claims.*

www.courts.state.ny.us/courts/2jd/kings.shtml#sup

Civil Records: Access: In person only. Visitors must perform in person searches themselves. Self serve copy fee: $.15 per page. Required to search: name, years to search. Civil cases indexed by plaintiff. Civil records on computer from 1987 for small claims, 1990 for tenant/landlord, and from 1/1998 for civil.
General Information: Public terminal has only civil records back to 1998. (Terminal has Landlord/tenant, civil, and small claims since 1998.) All records public. Certification fee: $6.00 per doc. Payee: NYC Civil Court. Only cashiers checks and money orders accepted. Prepayment required.

Surrogate's Court

2 Johnson St, Brooklyn, NY 11201; phone: 718-643-5262; fax: 718-643-6237; hours 9AM-5PM (EST). *Probate.*

Lewis County

Supreme & County Court

Courthouse, County Clerk, PO Box 232, Lowville, NY 13367; phone: 315-376-5333 (County); 315-376-5380 (Supreme); fax: 315-376-3768; hours 8:30AM-4:30PM (EST). *Felony, Civil.*

Note: Countywide search requests are processed in the manner described below.

Civil Records: Access: Mail, in person, online. Both court and visitors may perform in person searches. Search fee: $10.00 per name. Court makes copy: $.65 per page; same fee for self serve. Required to search: name, years to search. Civil cases indexed by defendant only. Civil records on index cards from 1935. Access to current/pending Supreme Court civil cases is at http://e.courts.state.ny.us/. Mail turnaround time 2 days.
Criminal Records: Access: Mail, in person. Both court and visitors may perform in person searches. Search fee: $10.00 per name. Court makes copy: $.65 per page; same fee for self serve. Required to search: name, years to search. Criminal records on index cards from 1935. Mail turnaround time 2 days.
General Information: Public terminal goes back to 2002. No sealed, youthful offender or sex abuse case records released. Will fax documents for $1.00 per page. Certification fee: $5.00 per document. Payee: County Clerk. Personal checks accepted. Prepayment and SASE required.

Surrogate's Court

Courthouse, 7660 State St, Lowville, NY 13367; phone: 315-376-5344; fax: 315-376-4145; hours 8:30AM-4:30PM; Jun-July-Aug 8;30-4PM (EST). *Probate.*

Note: Search Fee is $25 for under 25 years to $70 for over 70 years.

Lewis Town/Village Courts - *misdemeanor or civil records:* Croghan Town- 315-346-1272; Denmark Town; Diana Town- 315-543-2628; Greig Town; Harrisburg Town- 315-688-4193; Lewis Town; Leyden Town- 315-348-6215; Lowville Town- 315-376-8070; Lowville Village- 315-376-2834; Lyonsdale Town; Martinsburg Town- 315-376-2458; New Bremen Town- 315-376-3752; Osceola Town- 315-245-1610; Pinckney Town; Port Leyden Village- 315-348-6215; Turin Town- 315-348-6313; Watson Town- 315-376-3866; West Turin Town- 315-397-2231.

Livingston County

County Clerk

6 Court St, Rm 201, Geneseo, NY 14454; phone: 585-243-7010; fax: 585-243-7928; hours 8:30AM-4:30PM Oct-May; 8AM-4PM June-Sept (EST). *Felony, Civil.*

Note: Countywide search requests made to the County Court Clerk are processed in the manner described below.

Civil Records: Access: Phone, mail, fax, in person, online. Both court and visitors may perform in person searches. Search fee: $2.50 per name per year if a written request. Court makes copy: $.65 per page. Required to search: name, years to search. Civil cases indexed by defendant only. Civil records on computer since 1996. Plaintiff index available only on computer searches. Access to current/pending Supreme Court civil cases is at http://e.courts.state.ny.us/. Mail turnaround time same day.
Criminal Records: Access: Phone, mail, fax, in person. Both court and visitors may perform in person searches. Search fee: $2.50 per name per year if a written request. Phone requests: will search computer records back to 1996 only for no fee, but only a few requests. Court makes copy: $.65 per page. Required to search: name, years to search. Criminal records on computer since 1996. Misdemeanor records are maintained by city, town and village courts. Note: Fax requests accepted with payment. Mail turnaround time same day.
General Information: Public use terminal available. No sealed or youthful offender records released. Will not fax documents unless prepaid or to a toll-free number. Certification fee: $5.00 up to 4 pages, $1.25 each add'l page. Payee: County Clerk. Personal checks and money orders accepted. Prepayment and SASE required.

Supreme & County Court

2 Court St, Geneseo, NY 14454; phone: 585-243-7060; fax: 585-243-7067; 9AM-5PM (EST). *Felony, Civil.*

Note: County-Court directs felony search requests to the OCA for a $52.00 statewide search fee. See also County Clerk in separate listing. Access to current/pending Supreme Court civil cases is available at http://e.courts.state.ny.us/.

Surrogate's Court

2 Court St, Geneseo, NY 14454; phone: 585-243-7095; fax: 585-243-7583; hours 9AM-5PM (EST). *Probate.*

Note: Search records over 25 years old is $70.00 search fee; if under 25 years old then $25.00 fee.

Livingston Town/Village Courts - *misdemeanor or civil records:* Avon Town- 585-226-2130; Avon Village- 585-226-3660; Caledonia Village- 585-538-9810; Conesus Town- 585-346-3130; Dansville Village- 585-335-2460; Geneseo Town & Village- 585-243-4530; Groveland Town- 585-243-3782; Leicester Town- 585-382-9419; Lima Town- 585-582-1011; Livonia Town- 585-346-3710; Mount Morris Town- 585-658-2333; Mount Morris Village- 585-658-3249; North Dansville Village- 585-335-2460; Nunda Village- 585-468-5558; Ossian Town- 585-335-8040; Portage Town; Sparta Town; Springwater Town- 585-669-2635; West Sparta Town- 585-335-2907; York Town- 585-243-0666.

Madison County

County Clerk

County Office Bldg, PO Box 668, Wampsville, NY 13163; phone: 315-366-2261; probate phone: 315-366-2392; fax: 315-366-2615; hours 9AM-5PM (EST). *Felony, Civil.*

Note: Countywide search requests made to the County Clerk are processed in the manner described below.

Civil Records: Access: Mail, in person, online. Both court and visitors may perform in person searches. Search fee: $5.00 per name. Fee is per 5 years searched. Court makes copy: $1.00 per page. Required to search: name, years to search. Civil cases indexed by defendant. Judgment records on computer from 1992, prior in books. Access to current/pending Supreme Court civil cases and

some closed cases is at http://e.courts.state.ny.us/. Mail turnaround time 1 day.
Criminal Records: Access: Mail, in person. Only the court performs in person searches; visitors may not. Search fee: $5.00 per name per 5 years. Court makes copy: $1.00 per page. Required to search: name, years to search, DOB. Criminal records on computer to 1989, previous years in books. Mail turnaround time 2 days.
General Information: Public terminal has only civil records back to 1977. No sealed, expunged, adoption, sex offense, juvenile or mental health records released. Certification fee: Minimum $5.00; $1.00 per page if over 4 pages. Payee: County Clerk. Personal checks accepted. Prepayment and SASE required.

Supreme & County Court

PO Box 545, Wampsville, NY 13163; phone: 315-366-2267; fax: 315-366-2267; 9AM-5PM (EST). *Felony, Civil.*

www.nycourts.gov/6jd/CountyMaps/madison

Note: Direct countywide search requests to County Clerk, see separate listing. Access to current/pending Supreme Court civil cases and some closed cases is available at http://e.courts.state.ny.us/. Misdemeanor records maintained by city, town, village courts.

Oneida City Court

109 N Main St, Oneida, NY 13421; phone: 315-363-1310; fax: 315-363-3230; hours 8:30AM-4:30PM (EST). *Misdemeanor, Civil Actions Under $15,000, Eviction, Small Claims.*

Civil Records: Access: Mail, in person. Only the court performs in person searches; visitors may not. Search fee: $5.00 per name per 2 years searched. Court makes copy: $.65 per page. Required to search: name, years to search. Civil cases indexed by plaintiff. Civil records on computer from 1990, prior in books back to 1950s. Mail turnaround time 1-2 days.
Criminal Records: Access: Mail, in person. Search fee: $52.00 statewide search fee. Court makes copy: $.65 per page. Criminal records on computer back to 1989; prior in books back to 1950s. All criminal record search requests made to the Court Clerk are forwarded to the OCA for processing (see Introduction). Mail turnaround time 1-2 days.
General Information: No public access terminal. No sealed, expunged, sex offense, mental health or youthful offender records released. Will fax documents to local or toll free line. Certification fee: $6.00 per document. Payee: City Court. Personal checks accepted. Prepayment and SASE required.

Surrogate's Court

PO Box 607, 138 N Court St, Wampsville, NY 13163; phone: 315-366-2392; fax: 315-366-2539; hours 9AM-5PM (EST). *Probate.*

Madison Town/Village Courts - *misdemeanor or civil records:* Brookfield Town- 315-899-5856; Canastota Village- 315-697-9410; Cazenovia Town- 315-655-5631; Cazenovia Village- 315-655-4011; Chittenango Village- 315-687-3937; De Ruyter Town- 315-852-9650; Eaton Town- 315-684-9111; Fenner Town- 315-655-2705; Georgetown Town- 315-837-4795; Hamilton Town- 315-824-3508; Hamilton Village- 315-824-3508; Lebanon Town- 315-837-4835; Lenox Town- 315-697-9410; Lincoln Town- 315-697-7018; Madison Town- 315-893-7544; Morrisville Village- 315-684-3154; Nelson Town- 315-655-8582; Smithfield Town; Stockbridge Town- 315-495-6660; Sullivan Town- 315-687-3347; Wampsville Village- 315-363-5810.

Monroe County

County Clerk

County Office Bldg, County Clerk Office, 39 W Main St #101, Rochester, NY 14614; phone: 585-428-5151; fax: 585-428-4698; hours 9AM-5PM (EST). *Felony, Civil.*

www.clerk.co.monroe.ny.us

Note: Countywide search requests made to the County Clerk are processed in the manner described below.

Civil Records: Access: Fax, mail, online, in person. Both court and visitors may perform in person searches. Search fee: $5.00 per name per 2 years.

Court makes copy: $.65 per page. $1.30 minimum. Required to search: name, years to search. Civil cases indexed by defendant. Civil records on computer since 6/93, prior in books. Online access to felony, civil, and divorce records free online at www.clerk.co.monroe.ny.us. Records go back to 6/1993, and earlier film images are being added. Call 585-428-5151 for username, password, or more information. Note: Also, access to current Supreme court cases and some closed cases is at http://e.courts.state.ny.us/. Mail turnaround time 2 weeks.

Criminal Records: Access: Fax, mail, online, in person. Both court and visitors may perform in person searches. Search fee: $5.00 per name; fee is per 2 years searched. A $5.00 blanket index search is also available. Court makes copy: $.65 per page, $1.30 minimum. Required to search: name, years to search, DOB. Criminal records on computer since 6/93, prior in books. Online access to criminal records is the same as civil. Mail turnaround time 2 weeks.

General Information: Public terminal goes back to 1993. No sealed, divorce records, confidential files released. Certification fee: $5.00 up to 4 pages, $1.25 each add'l page; includes copy fee. Payee: County Clerk. Personal checks accepted. Prepayment and SASE required.

Supreme & County Court 545 Hall of Justice, 99 Exchange Blvd, Rochester, NY 14614; phone: 585-428-5001; 9AM-5PM (EST). *Felony, Civil.*

www.clerk.co.monroe.ny.us

Note: Direct countywide search requests to the County Clerk, see separate listing. Online access to courts records free online at www.clerk.co.monroe.ny.us. Current Supreme court cases and some closed cases is available at http://e.courts.state.ny.us/.

Rochester City Court - Civil 99 Exchange Blvd, Hall of Justice, Rm 6, Rochester, NY 14614; phone: 585-428-2444; fax: 585-428-2588; hours 9AM-5PM (EST). *Civil Actions Under $15,000, Eviction, Small Claims.*

www.courts.state.ny.us/courts/7jd/rochester/index.shtml

Civil Records: Access: In person. Both court and visitors may perform in person searches. No search fee. Court makes copy: $.65 per page; $1.30 minimum. Required to search: name, years to search. Civil cases indexed by defendant, plaintiff; on computer from 1983, prior in books from 1973.

General Information: Public terminal has only civil records back to 1983. No sealed, expunged, probation reports, adoption, sex offense, juvenile or mental health records released. Will not fax documents. Certification fee: $6.00 per document. Only cashiers checks and money orders accepted. Prepayment required.

Rochester City Court - Criminal 150 S Plymouth, Rm 123, Public Safety Bldg, Rochester, NY 14614; phone: 585-428-2447; fax: 585-428-2732; hours 8:30AM-5PM (EST). *Misdemeanor.*

Criminal Records: Access: In person. Search fee: Certificate of disposition is $5.00. Court makes copy: $1.00 per page; none for Certificate of Disposition. Required to search: Name, years to search, date (for Certificate of Disposition). Criminal records on computer since 1986, prior on books from 1973. The court directs name searches to the OCA for $52.00 statewide search, unless specific docket number given. Note: In person searches limited to pending and current cases on the public access terminal. Mail turnaround time 1 week.

General Information: Public terminal has only criminal records. No sealed, expunged, probation reports, adoption, sex offense, juvenile or mental health records released. No certification fee . Payee: City Court. Only cashiers checks and money orders accepted. Prepayment required.

Surrogate's Court Hall of Justice, Rm 541, 99 Exchange Blvd, Rochester, NY 14614; phone: 585-428-5200; fax: 585-428-2650; hours 9AM-5PM (EST). *Probate.*

Note: Includes estates, adoptions, guardianships.

Monroe Town/Village Courts - *misdemeanor or civil records:* Brighton Town- 585-473-8849; Chili Town- 585-889-1999; Clarkson Town- 585-637-1134; East Rochester Town- 585-385-2576; Fairport Village- 585-223-0316; Gates Town- 585-247-6106; Greece Town- 585-227-3155; Hamlin Town- 585-964-8641; Henrietta Town- 585-359-2640; Honeoye Falls Village- 585-624-1711; Irondequoit Town- 585-336-6040; Mendon Town- 585-624-6064; Ogden Town; Parma Town- 585-392-9470; Penfield Town- 585-377-8623; Perinton Town- 585-223-0770; Pittsford Town- 585-248-6238; Riga Town- 585-293-3884; Rush Town- 585-533-1312; Sweden Town; Webster Town- 585-872-7020/7022; Wheatland Town- 585-889-3074 x4.

Montgomery County

County Clerk PO Box 1500, 64 E Broadway, County Office Bldg, Fonda, NY 12068; phone: 518-853-8113; hours 9AM-5PM; 8:30AM-4PM Summer hrs (EST). *Felony, Misdemeanor, Civil.*

Note: Countywide search requests made to the County Clerk are processed in the manner described below.

Civil Records: Access: Mail, in person, online. Both court and visitors may perform in person searches. Search fee: $5.00 per name per 2 years. Court makes copy: $1.00 per page. Required to search: name, years to search, address. Civil cases indexed by defendant, plaintiff. Civil records in books and on index cards back to 1965; on computer back to 1992. Access to current/pending Supreme Court civil cases is at http://e.courts.state.ny.us/.

Criminal Records: Access: In person only. Visitors must perform in person searches themselves. Court makes copy: $1.00 per page. Required to search: name, years to search, DOB. Criminal records on computer back to 1992; file index back to 1965. Clerk directs criminal searches to OCA for $52.00 statewide search.

General Information: Public terminal has only civil records back to 1992. No sealed or youthful offender records released. Certification fee: $4.00 per doc. Payee: County Clerk. Personal checks accepted. Prepayment and SASE required.

Supreme & County Court PO Box 1500, 53 Broadway - County Courthouse, Fonda, NY 12068; civil phone: 518-853-4516; fax: 518-853-3596; hours 9AM-5PM (EST). *Felony, Misdemeanor, Civil.*

Note: See County Clerk for civil search. See state OCA for $52.00 felony search. Court keeps its own Misdemeanor cases only; also search city, town, village courts. Access to current/pending Supreme Ct. civil cases is available at http://e.courts.state.ny.us/.

Amsterdam City Court Public Safety Bldg, Rm 208, One Guy Park Ave Ext, Amsterdam, NY 12010; phone: 518-842-9510; fax: 518-843-8474; hours 8AM-4PM (EST). *Misdemeanor, Civil Actions Under $15,000, Eviction, Small Claims.*

Civil Records: Access: Mail, in person. Only the court performs in person searches; visitors may not. Search fee: $16.00 per name. Court makes copy: $.65 per page. Required to search: name, years to search. Civil cases indexed by defendant. Civil records on computer since 1995, prior on index cards. Mail turnaround time 1 week.

Criminal Records: Access: Mail, in person. Only the court performs in person searches; visitors may not. Search fee: A Certificate of Disposition from this court is $6.00. Court makes copy: $.65 per page. Required to search: name, DOB, years to search. Criminal records on computer from 11/93, prior on index cards. Note: All criminal record name search requests are directed to the OCA for statewide record search, $52.00 search fee. This court does

not have access to county records. Mail turnaround time 1 week.

General Information: No public access terminal. No sealed, expunged, adoption, sex offense, juvenile or mental health records released. Will fax documents to local or toll free line. Certification fee: $10.00 per document. Payee: City Court. Only cashiers checks and money orders accepted. Prepayment and SASE required.

Surrogate's Court 58 Broadway, PO Box 1500, Fonda, NY 12068; phone: 518-853-8108; fax: 518-853-8230; hours 9AM-5PM (EST). *Probate.*

Montgomery Town/Village Courts - *misdemeanor or civil records:* Amsterdam Town- 518-842-7411; Canajoharie Town- 518-673-3013; Canajoharie Village- 518-673-5116; Charleston Town- 518-922-7661; Florida Town- 518-843-6468; Fultonville Village- 518-853-3166; Glen Town- 518-853-4825; Minden Town- 518-568-2728 or 518-993-5180; Mohawk Town- 518-853-3031; Palatine Town- 518-673-1003; Root Town- 518-673-3549; St Johnsville Justice Court- 518-568-2662; St Johnsville Village- 518-568-5298.

Nassau County

County Clerk 240 Old Country Rd, Mineola, NY 11501; phone: 516-571-2272; hours 9AM-5PM (EST). *Felony, Civil Actions Over $15,000.*

www.co.nassau.ny.us/clerk/

Note: Holds records for Supreme Court and County Court. As a rule, this office directs felony record search requests to the OCA for the $52.00 statewide search, however, the records department can perform in person felony searches as described below.

Civil Records: Access: Mail, in person, online. Both court and visitors may perform in person searches. Search fee: $25.00 for judgment search. Court makes copy: $.65 per page; $1.30 minimum. Self serve copy fee: $.25 per page. Required to search: name, years to search. Civil cases indexed by defendant, plaintiff; on computer from 1992, prior in books. Search supreme court decisions for free at www.co.nassau.ny.us/clerk/search.html. Note: Answers to record search questions-Bob Grabel at County Clerk's office- 516-571-1448. Mail turnaround time 1-2 weeks.

Criminal Records: Access: In person only. Court makes copy: $.65 per page; $1.30 minimum. Self serve copy fee: $.25 per page. Required to search: name, DOB. Note: The county clerk has felony case "minutes" from the County Court, but "minutes" data is only accessible by attorney's with a written letter of request. For full records, contact the County Court.

General Information: Public terminal has only civil records back to 1992. No sealed, expunged, adoption, sex offense, juvenile or mental health records released. Certification fee: $5.00 per doc includes 4 copy pgs; $1.25 each add'l page. Includes copy fee. Payee: Nassau County Clerk's Office. Personal checks accepted. Prepayment and SASE required.

Supreme Court Supreme Court Bldg, 100 Supreme Court Dr, Mineola, NY 11501; civil phone: 516-571-2906; hours 9AM-5PM (EST). *Civil Actions Over $15,000.*

www.co.nassau.ny.us/clerk/

Note: All physical records are maintained at the County Clerk's Office (see entry for County Clerk) 240 Old Country Rd, Mineola, 516-571-2272.

County Court 262 Old Country Rd, Mineola, NY 11501; phone: 516-571-2802; fax: 516-571-2160; hours 9AM-5PM (EST). *Felony.*

www.co.nassau.ny.us/clerk/

Criminal Records: Access: In person only. Only the court performs in person searches; visitors may not. Search fee: $16.00 plus $2.00 here per year 1982 and prior only. Otherwise use the $52.00 statewide search if done by OCA. Court makes copy: $.65 per page, $1.30 minimum. Required to search: name, years to search, DOB. Criminal records on computer from 1982, prior in archives or on microfilm. Search online for future court appearances at http://iapps.courts.state.ny.us/webcrim_attorney/Login The County Court clerk directs felony search requests to the OCA for a statewide record search. However, the court will search pre-1982 records, which are on books only. Note: Also, for "minutes," you may contact records section of the County Clerk office at 240 Old Country Rd, Mineola, NY, 11501, 516-571-2272. Minutes records are restricted to attorneys only. Mail turnaround time up to 3 weeks for pre-1982 records only.

General Information: No public access terminal. No sealed, expunged, sex offense, juvenile, or mental health records released. Certification fee: $5.20. Payee: Clerk of Court. Only cashiers checks and money orders accepted. Prepayment required.

District Court - 1st & 2nd Districts
99 Main St, Hempstead, NY 11550; phone: 516-572-2355; civil phone: 516-572-2266; hours 9AM-5PM (EST). *Misdemeanor, Civil Actions Under $15,000, Eviction, Small Claims.*

Note: Small Claims phone- 516-572-2261. All records for 2nd District are separate prior to 1980. 1st District handles Misdemeanor case records.

Civil Records: Access: In person only. Only the court performs in person searches; visitors may not. Search fee: Fee varies, but no guarantee when search will get done. Court makes copy: $.65 per page; $1.30 minimum. Required to search: name, years to search. Civil cases indexed by defendant, plaintiff; on computer back to 1980, prior in books back to 1960.

Criminal Records: Access: None. However, clerk will perform Certificate of Disposition search for $5.00 per name. Court makes copy: $.65 per page; $1.30 minimum. Criminal records on computer back to 1980, prior in books back to 1960. The court refuses to permit access to court records unless specific case file given. It is suggested to send requests to OCA for $52.00 statewide search. Search online for future court appearances at http://e.courts.state.ny.us.

General Information: Public terminal has only criminal records back to - new in 2005. No sealed records released. Certification fee: $5.00. Payee: Clerk of Court. Only cashiers checks and money orders accepted. Prepayment required.

District Court - 3rd District
435 Middle Neck Rd, Great Neck, NY 11023; phone: 516-571-8400/8401; fax: 516-571-8403; hours 9AM-4:30PM (EST). *Misdemeanor, Civil Actions Under $15,000, Eviction, Small Claims.*

Note: Court has records only for its district. Records include Town of North Hempstead ordinance violations.

Civil Records: Access: In person only. Only the court performs in person searches; visitors may not. Court makes copy: $.65 per page, $1.30 minimum. Required to search: name, years to search. Civil cases indexed by defendant, plaintiff; on computer from 1989, prior in books.

Criminal Records: Access: None. Only the court performs in person searches; visitors may not. However, clerk will perform a Certificate of Disposition search for $6.00 per name. Court makes copy: $.65 per page, $1.30 minimum. Required to search: name, years to search, DOB. Criminal records on computer from 1989, prior in books. Misdemeanor records are ordinance violations-only minor misdemeanors found here. For a full criminal search, the court suggest the OCA for $52.00 statewide search.

General Information: No public access terminal. No sealed, expunged, sex offense, juvenile or mental health records released. Certification fee: $6.00 per doc. Payee: Clerk of Court. Only cashiers checks and money orders accepted. Prepayment required.

District Court - 4th District
99 Main St, Hempstead, NY 11550; phone: 516-572-2355; hours 9AM-4;30PM (EST). *Civil Actions Under $15,000, Eviction, Small Claims.*

Note: Court closed until further notice. Records at District Court 1st & 2nd District in Hempstead, 516-572-2355.

Glen Cove City Court
13 Glen St, Glen Cove, NY 11542; phone: 516-676-0109; fax: 516-676-1570; hours 9AM-5PM (EST). *Misdemeanor, Civil Actions Under $15,000, Eviction, Small Claims.*

Civil Records: Access: Mail, fax, in person. Only the court performs in person searches; visitors may not. Search fee: $16.00 per name. Court makes copy: $.65 per page; minimum $1.30. Required to search: name, years to search. Civil records go back to 1970; on computer back to 1996.

Criminal Records: Access: None. Court makes copy: $.65 per page; minimum $1.30. Criminal records go back to 1966; on computer back to 1996. The court refuses to permit access to court records unless specific case file given. It is suggested to send requests to OCA for $52.00 statewide search.

General Information: No public access terminal. No sealed, expunged, adoption, sex offense, juvenile or mental health records released. Certification fee: $5.00. Payee: Glen Cove City Court. Only cashiers checks and money orders accepted. Prepayment and SASE required.

Long Beach City Court
1 W Chester St, Long Beach, NY 11561; phone: 516-431-1000; fax: 516-889-3511; hours 9AM-5PM (EST). *Misdemeanor, Civil Actions Under $15,000, Eviction, Small Claims, Traffic.*

Civil Records: Access: Mail, in person. Only the court performs in person searches; visitors may not. Search fee: $16.00 if case number not known; Best to get Certificate of Disposition for $5.00, then get case numbers. Court makes copy: $.65 per copy, $1.30 minimum. Required to search: name, years to search.

Criminal Records: Access: None. Search fee: $5.00 for Certificate of Disposition. Court makes copy: $.65 per page, $1.30 minimum. Criminal records on computer from 1997. The court will not permit access to court records unless specific case file given. First, get Cert. of Disposition. It is suggested to send requests to OCA for $52.00 statewide search. Mail turnaround time 2 days.

General Information: No public access terminal. No sealed, expunged, adoption, sex offense, juvenile or mental health records released. Certification fee: $6.00 per doc. Payee: City Court of Long Beach. Only cashiers checks and money orders accepted. Prepayment required.

Surrogate's Court
262 Old Country Rd, Mineola, NY 11501; phone: 516-571-2082; fax: 516-571-3864; hours 9AM-4;45PM (EST). *Probate.*

Nassau Town/Village Courts - *misdemeanor or civil records:* Atlantic Beach Village- 516-371-4552; Brookville Village- 516-922-8191; Cove Neck Village- 516-624-7715x1; East Rockaway Village; East Williston Village- 516-922-9154; Farmingdale Village- 516-293-2292; Garden City Village- 516-742-9886; Hempstead Village- 516-489-3400; Kings Point Village- 516-482-7872; Lake Success Village- 516-482-7430; Lattingtown Village- 516-681-9271; Lawrence Village- 516-239-9166; Malverne Village- 516-599-1200; Manorhaven Village- 516- 883-7000; Munsey Park Village- 516-365-7790; Oyster Bay Cove Village- 516-681-9271; Plandome Heights Village- 516-627-1748; Plandome Manor Village- 516-627-3701; Plandome Village- 516-627-1748; Rockville Centre Village- 516-678-9233; Stewart Manor Village- 516-354-1800; Upper Brookville Village- 516-676-5619; Valley Stream Village- 516-825-4200; Westbury Village- 516-334-1700.

New York Borough

Supreme Court - Civil Division
County Clerk, 60 Centre St, Rm 103, New York City, NY 10007; phone: 646-386-5955; civil phone: 646-386-5942 records; hours 9AM-3PM (EST). *Civil Actions.*

www.nycourts.gov/supctmanh/

Note: Record search requests are managed by the County Clerk office; information here is for that County Clerk office.

Civil Records: Access: In person, online. Both court and visitors may perform in person searches. Court makes copy: $.25 per page. Required to search: name, years to search. Civil cases indexed by defendant, plaintiff; on computer from 1993, prior in books; records go back to 1971. Access to current/pending Supreme Court civil cases is at http://e.courts.state.ny.us/. Search decisions at http://portal.courts.state.ny.us/pls/portal30/CMS_DEV.DECISIONS_NDAWCASE.show_parms.

General Information: Public terminal has only civil records back to 1993. (Terminal located in Rm 103B.) Certification fee: $8.00 per doc. Payee: County Clerk. Only cashiers checks. Attorney checks, and money orders accepted; no credit cards. Prepayment required.

Supreme Court - Criminal Division
100 Centre St, Rm 1000, New York, NY 10013; phone: 646-386-4000; criminal phone: 646-386-3860 correspondence sec.; fax: 212-374-3177; hours 9AM-5PM (EST). *Felony, Misdemeanor.*

Note: The Court will only process mail or in person requests for specific documents or papers related to felony cases.

Criminal Records: Access: Mail, in person. Visitors must perform in person searches themselves. No search fee if in person. A Certificate of Disposition is $10.00. Court makes copy: not known. Self serve copy fee: $.15 per page. Required to search: name, years to search, DOB (case number or other date identifier is required for a Certificate of Disposition). Criminal records on computer from 1977, prior records archived. Search online for future court appearances at http://http://iapps.courts.state.ny.us/webcrim_attorney/Login.state.ny.us. Note: Written requests for name searches must be directed to OCA for $52.00 statewide record search. Will accept requests for specific documents via fax or via email at asknyscr@courts.state.ny.us. Mail turnaround time- 1 day.

General Information: No public access terminal. No sealed, expunged, adoption, sex offense, juvenile or mental health records released. Certification fee: $8.00 per document. Payee: Office of Court Administration. No personal checks or credit cards accepted. Prepayment required.

Civil Court of the City of New York
111 Centre St, New York, NY 10013; phone: 646-386-5600; fax: 212-374-5709; hours 9AM-5PM (EST). *Civil Actions Under $25,000, Eviction, Small Claims.*

Civil Records: Access: Mail, in person, phone. Visitors must perform in person searches themselves. No copy fee. Required to search: name, years to search; also helpful: address. Civil cases indexed by plaintiff; computerized records since 1994. Landlord/Tenant records on computer from 1984, civil from 1994, prior in books. Records are archived after 3 years; search by defendant available only from 6/94 on. Mail turnaround time varies.

General Information: Public terminal has only civil records back to 1994. no sealed records released. Certification fee: $6.00 per doc. Payee: Clerk of Civil Court. Only cashiers checks and money orders accepted. Attorney's and certified checks accepted. Prepayment and SASE required.

Surrogate's Court
31 Chambers St, New York City, NY 10007; phone: 212-374-8233, 374-8232; hours 9AM-5PM (EST). *Probate.*

www.courts.state.ny.us/courts/nyc/surrogates/index.shtml

Niagara County

County Clerk 175 Hawley St, Lockport, NY 14094; phone: 716-439-7030; criminal phone: 716-439-7030; civil phone: 716-439-7029; probate phone: 716-439-7135; fax: 716-439-7066; hours 9AM-5PM; 8:30AM-4:30PM Summer Hours (EST). *Felony, Civil Actions Over $25,000.*

Note: County Clerk maintains records for the Supreme Court (civil) and the County Court (felony).

Civil Records: Access: Mail, fax, in person, online. Both court and visitors may perform in person searches. Search fee: $5.00 per name per 2 years. Court makes copy: $1.00 per page. Required to search: name, years to search. Civil cases indexed by defendant. Civil records in index books back to 1950, computerized since 1997. Access to current/pending Supreme Court civil cases is at http://e.courts.state.ny.us/. Note: Will accept fax requests if payment arrangement is made in advance. Mail turnaround time 3-5 days.

Criminal Records: Access: Mail, fax, in person. Both court and visitors may perform in person searches. Search fee: $5.00 per name per 2 years. Court makes copy: $1.00 per page. Required to search: name, years to search, DOB. Criminal records on computer since 1/97; prior records in books. Note: Will accept fax requests if payment arrangement is made in advance. Mail turnaround time 3-5 days.

General Information: Public terminal goes back to 1997. No sealed or youthful offender records released. Will fax documents for add'l $3.00 per name. Certification fee: $5.00 minimum; up to 5 pages. Payee: County Clerk. Personal checks and money orders accepted. Prepayment required.

Supreme Court 775 3rd St, Niagara Falls, NY 14302; phone: 716-278-1800; fax: 716-278-1809; hours 9AM-5PM (EST). *Civil Actions Over $25,000.*

Note: All records are maintained at County Clerk office, 175 Hawley St, Lockport, NY 14094, 716-439-7030. Also, access to current/pending Supreme Court civil cases is available at http://e.courts.state.ny.us/.

County Court Courthouse, 175 Hawley St, Lockport, NY 14094; phone: 716-439-7022; fax: 716-439-7066; hours 9AM-5PM (EST). *Felony, Civil Actions Under $25,000.*

Note: All records are maintained at County Clerk office, 175 Hawley St, Lockport, NY 14094, 716-439-7030.

Lockport City Court One Locks Plaza, Municipal Bldg, Lockport, NY 14094; criminal phone: 716-439-6671; civil phone: 716-439-6660; fax: 716-439-6684; hours 8AM-4:30PM (EST). *Misdemeanor, Civil Actions Under $15,000, Eviction, Small Claims.*

Civil Records: Access: Phone, fax, mail, in person. Both court and visitors may perform in person searches. Search fee: $16.00 per name. Court makes copy: $1.00 per page. Required to search: name, years to search. Civil cases indexed by defendant. Civil records on computer from 1988, prior in books from 1900s.

Criminal Records: Access: None. Court makes copy: $1.00 per page. Criminal records in books from 1977 forward; computerized since 1988. The court refuses to permit access to criminal records unless specific case file given. It is suggested to send requests to OCA for $52.00 statewide search. Mail turnaround time 1 week.

General Information: No public access terminal. No sealed, expunged, adoption, sex offense, juvenile or mental health records released. Will fax documents to local or toll free line. Certification fee: $5.00. Payee: City Court of Lockport. Only cashiers checks and money orders accepted. Prepayment and SASE required.

Niagara Falls City Court 520 Hyde Park Blvd, Public Safety Bldg, Niagara Falls, NY 14301; phone: 716-278-9800; criminal phone: 716-278-9800; civil phone: 716-278-9860; fax: 716-278-9809; hours 8:30AM-4:30PM (EST). *Misdemeanor, Civil Actions Under $15,000, Eviction, Small Claims.*

Civil Records: Access: Mail, in person. Both court and visitors may perform in person searches. Search fee: $5.00 per name for 2 years; computer search is $16.00. Court makes copy: $1.00 per page. Required to search: name, years to search. Civil cases indexed by defendant. Civil records on microfilm from 1985, in books since 1970. Mail turnaround time 7-10 working days.

Criminal Records: Access: Mail, in person. Only the court performs in person searches; visitors may not. Search fee: A certificate of Disposition is $5.00. Court makes copy: $1.00 per page. Criminal records in books from 1970. Note: The court refuses to permit access to criminal court records unless specific case file given. All criminal record name search requests are directed to the OCA for statewide record search, $52.00 search fee. Mail turnaround time 7-10 working days.

General Information: No public access terminal. No sealed, expunged, adoption, sex offense, juvenile or mental health records released. Payee: City Court of Niagara Falls. No checks accepted. Prepayment and SASE required.

North Tonawanda City Court 216 Payne Ave, City Hall, North Tonawanda, NY 14120; phone: 716-693-1010; fax: 716-743-1754; hours 8AM-5PM (EST). *Misdemeanor, Civil Actions Under $15,000, Eviction, Small Claims.*

Civil Records: Access: Mail, in person. Only the court performs in person searches; visitors may not. Search fee: $5.00 for transcript. Court makes copy: $1.00 per page. Required to search: name, years to search. Civil cases indexed by defendant. Civil records on computer from 1993, prior in books. Mail turnaround time 2-5 days.

Criminal Records: Access: Mail, in person. Only the court performs in person searches; visitors may not. Search fee: $5.00 per name. Court makes copy: $1.00 per page. Required to search: Name, exact date of arrest, DOB. Criminal records on computer from 1986, prior in books. This court will do a criminal search but they warn that the date of arrest must be included. The court suggests to send requests to OCA for $52.00 statewide search. Mail turnaround time 2-5 days.

General Information: No public access terminal. No sealed, expunged, adoption, sex offense, juvenile or mental health records released. Will fax documents for $5.00 fee. Certification fee: $5.00 per document. Payee: City Court. Only cashiers checks and money orders accepted. Prepayment required. SASE requested.

Surrogate's Court Niagara's County Courthouse, 175 Hawley St, Lockport, NY 14094; phone: 716-439-7130/7131; fax: 716-439-7319; hours 9AM-5PM, Reg Hrs, 8:30AM-4;30 June 27-Sept 5, (EST). *Probate.*

Niagara Town/Village Courts - *misdemeanor or civil records:* Barker Village- 716-795-9193; Cambria Town- 716-433-7664; Hartland Town- 716-735-7239; Lewiston Town- 716-754-8213; Lockport Town- 716-439-9528; Newfane Town- 716-778-9292; Niagara Town- 716-215-1480; Pendleton Town- 716-625-8833; Porter Town- 716-745-7036 x6; Royalton Town- 716-772-2588; Somerset Town- 716-795-9193; Wheatfield Town- 716-694-6793; Wilson Town- 716-751-0549; Wilson Village- 716-751-0549.

Oneida County

County Clerk 800 Park Ave, Utica, NY 13501; criminal phone: 315-798-5797; civil phone: 315-798-5776; fax: 315-798-6440; hours 8:30AM-5PM, 8:30AM-4:30PM Summer hours (EST). *Felony, Civil.*

Note: Countywide search requests made to the County Clerk are processed in the manner described below.

Civil Records: Access: Mail, fax, in person, online. Both court and visitors may perform in person searches. Search fee: $5.00 per name. Fee is for 2 year search. Court makes copy: $.65 per page, $5.00 minimum. Self serve copy fee: $.65 per page, $5.20 minimum. Required to search: name, years to search. Civil cases indexed by defendant, plaintiff; on computer from 1992, prior in books by plaintiff only. Access to current/pending Supreme Court civil cases is at http://e.courts.state.ny.us/. Mail turnaround time 1 week.

Criminal Records: Access: Mail, fax, in person. Both court and visitors may perform in person searches. Search fee: $5.00 per name. Fee is for 2 years searched. Court makes copy: $.65 per page, $5.00 minimum. Self serve copy fee: $.65 per page, $5.20 minimum. Required to search: name, years to search, DOB, signed release. Criminal records on computer from 1992, prior in books by defendant only. Mail turnaround time 1 week.

General Information: Public terminal has criminal back to 1992 and civil back to 1974. No sealed, expunged, adoption, sex offense, juvenile or mental health records released. Will fax documents for $1.00 per page. Certification fee: $5.00 includes copy fee. Payee: County Clerk. Personal checks accepted. Prepayment and SASE required.

Supreme & County Court 200 Elizabeth St, Utica, NY 13501; phone: 315-798-5889; hours 9AM-5PM; 8:30AM-4PM Summer hours (EST). *Felony, Civil.*

Note: Direct record search requests to the County Clerk, see separate listing. Also, access to current/pending Supreme Court civil cases is available at http://e.courts.state.ny.us/.

Rome City Court 100 W Court St, Rome, NY 13440; phone: 315-337-6440; fax: 315-338-0343; hours 8:30AM-4:30PM; 8:30AM-4PM Summer Hours (EST). *Misdemeanor, Civil Actions Under $15,000, Eviction, Small Claims.*

Civil Records: Access: In person only. Only the court performs in person searches; visitors may not. Search fee: $5.00 per name per 2 years. Court makes copy: $.65 per page, $1.30 minimum. Required to search: name, years to search. Civil cases indexed by defendant, plaintiff. Civil records in books and some on computer.

Criminal Records: Access: In person. Only the court performs in person searches; visitors may not. Search fee: A Certificate of Disposition is $6.00. Court makes copy: $.65 per page, $1.30 minimum. Required to search: name, years to search, (case number, arrest date for Cert. of Disposition). As a rule, this court does not permit access to court records unless specific case file given. It is suggested to send requests to OCA for $52.00 statewide search. However, aware that the state system does not include certain "violation" records, this court does allow an in person hand search.

General Information: No public access terminal. No sealed or youthful offender records released. Will fax documents to local or toll free line. Certification fee: $5.00 per doc. Payee: Rome City Court. Only cashiers checks and money orders accepted. Prepayment required.

Sherrill City Court 373 Sherrill Rd, Sherrill, NY 13461; phone: 315-363-0996; fax: 315-363-1176; hours 8AM-4PM (EST). *Misdemeanor, Civil Actions Under $15,000, Eviction, Small Claims.*

Civil Records: Access: Mail, in person. Only the court performs in person searches; visitors may not. Search fee: $5.00 per name per 2 year period. Court makes copy: $.65 per page. Required to search: name, years to search. Civil cases indexed by defendant only. Civil records in books since 1988, rest archived. Mail turnaround time 1-2 days.

Criminal Records: Access: Mail, in person. Only the court performs in person searches; visitors may not. Search fee: $5.00 per name per 2 year period. Also, a Certificate of Disposition is $6.00. Court makes copy: $.65 per page. Required to search: name, DOB, years to search. Criminal records in books since 1800s. Though the court will do a name search of their records, they suggest to send requests to OCA for $52.00 statewide search. Mail turnaround time 1-2 days.

General Information: No public access terminal. No sealed, expunged, adoption, sex offense, juvenile or mental health records released. Will not fax documents. Certification fee: $6.00 per document. Payee: Sherrill City Court. Personal checks accepted. Prepayment required. SASE requested.

Utica City Court 411 Oriskany St W, Utica, NY 13502; criminal phone: 315-724-8227; civil phone: 315-724-8157; criminal fax: 315-724-0762; civil fax: 315-792-8038; hours 8:30AM-4:30PM (EST). *Misdemeanor, Civil Actions Under $15,000, Eviction, Small Claims.*

Civil Records: Access: In person only. Both court and visitors may perform in person searches. No search fee. Court makes copy: $.65 per page. $1.30 minimum. Required to search: name, years to search, address. Civil cases indexed by defendant. Civil records in books from 1900s, computerized records back to 1980's.

Criminal Records: Both court and visitors may perform in person searches. Court makes copy: $.65 per page. $1.30 minimum. Required to search: name, years to search, address. Criminal records in books from 1900s, computerized records back to 1980's. The court refuses to permit access to court records unless specific case file given. It is suggested to send requests to OCA for $52.00 statewide search.

General Information: No public access terminal. No sealed, expunged, adoption, sex offense, juvenile or mental health records released. Certification fee: $5.00 per cert. Payee: City Court of Utica. Only cashiers checks and money orders accepted. Prepayment required.

Surrogate's Court Oneida County Office Bldg 8th Fl, 800 Park Ave, Utica, NY 13501; phone: 315-797-9230; fax: 315-797-9237; hours 8:30AM-4:30PM Sept-May; 8:30AM-4PM June-Aug (EST). *Probate.*

Oneida Town/Village Courts - *misdemeanor or civil records:* Annsville Town- 315-336-1295; Augusta Town- 315-821-6314; Ava Town- 315-942-5669; Boonville Town- 315-943-2071; Boonville Village- 315-943-2070; Bridgewater Town- 315-822-5909; Camden Town- 315-245-0817; Deerfield Town- 315-724-0413; Florence Town; Floyd Town- 315-865-4256; Forestport Town- 315-392-2801; Kirkland Town- 315-853-4538; Lee Town- 315-336-1585; Marcy Town; Marshall Town- 315-841-8525; New Hartford Town- 315-732-5924; New Hartford Village- 315-732-5924; New York Mills Village- 315-736-7811; Oriskany Village- 315-736-6349; Paris Town- 315-839-6208; Remsen Town- 315-831-5332; Sangerfield Town- 315-841-4108; Steuben Town; Sylvan Beach Village- 315-762-4246; Trenton Town- 315-896-4510; Vernon Town & Village- 315-829-4481; Verona Town- 315-363-4394; Vienna Town- 315-245-2191; Waterville Village- 315-841-8007; Western Town- 315-827-4928; Westmoreland Town- 315-853-4333; Whitesboro Village- 315-736-4353; Whitestown Town- 315-736-1251.

Onondaga County

County Clerk 401 Montgomery St, Rm 200, Syracuse, NY 13202; phone: 315-435-2229; criminal phone: 315-435-2236; civil phone: 315-435-2234; fax: 315-435-3455; hours 8AM-5PM (EST). *Felony, Civil.*
Note: Countywide search requests made to the County Clerk are processed in the manner described below. All requests must be in writing.

Civil Records: Access: Mail, in person, online. Both court and visitors may perform in person searches. Search fee: $2.50 per name per year. Court makes copy: $.65 per page. $1.30 minimum. Required to search: name, years to search. Civil cases indexed by defendant, plaintiff; on computer from 1989, prior in books but can only search by plaintiff name. Access to current/pending Supreme Court civil cases is at http://e.courts.state.ny.us/. Mail time 2-3 days.

Criminal Records: Access: Mail, in person. Both court and visitors may perform in person searches. Search fee: $2.50 per name per year. Court makes copy: $.65 per page, $1.30 minimum. Required to search: name, years to search; also helpful: DOB. Criminal records computerized from 1990, prior in books. Mail turnaround time 2-3 days.

General Information: Public terminal has criminal back to 1990 and civil back to 1989. No sealed, divorce, judgment or sexual abuse records released. Will not fax documents. Certification fee: $5.00 minimum; $1.25 per page over 4. Payee: County Clerk. Personal checks accepted; $60.00 limit. Prepayment and SASE required.

Supreme Court 401 Montgomery St, 3rd Fl, Syracuse, NY 13202; phone: 315-671-1030; fax: 315-671-1176; hours 8:30AM-4PM (EST). *Civil.*

Note: Search requests to Supreme Court forwarded to the OCA for processing. Countywide only searches can be performed at the County Clerk, see separate listing. Access to current/pending Supreme Court civil cases is available at http://e.courts.state.ny.us/.

County Court 505 S State St, Syracuse, NY 13202; phone: 315-671-1020; fax: 315-671-1191; hours 8:30AM-4PM (EST). *Felony.*

Note: Search requests made to County-Court are forwarded to the OCA for processing of $52.00 statewide record search. Countywide only searches can be performed at the County Clerk office, see separate listing.

Syracuse City Court 505 S State St, Rm 130, Syracuse, NY 13202-2104; phone: 315-671-2773; criminal phone: 315-671-2760; civil phone: 315-671-2782; criminal fax: 315-671-2744; civil fax: 315-671-2741; hours 8:30AM-4:30PM (EST). *Misdemeanor, Civil Actions Under $15,000, Eviction, Small Claims.*
www.nycourts.gov/courts/5jd/onondaga/syracuse
Note: Small claims phone is 315-671-2784; fax is 315-671-2741.

Civil Records: Access: Phone, fax, mail, in person. Only the court performs in person searches; visitors may not. Search fee: $16.00 per name. Court makes copy: $.65 per page. $1.30 minimum. Required to search: name, years to search; also helpful: address. Civil cases indexed by defendant, plaintiff or index number. Civil records on computer from 1993, from 1980-2000 on fiche or microfilm. Mail turnaround time 1-2 weeks.

Criminal Records: Access: Phone, fax, mail, in person. Only the court performs in person searches; visitors may not. Court makes copy: $.65 per page. $1.30 minimum. Required to search: name, years to search, DOB; also helpful: offense. Criminal records from 1960 to present are on either computer, dockets or manual books. If the case file is in electronic format, the court will direct searchers to the OCA statewide record search. Otherwise, search fee is $5.00 for each 2 years searched. Mail turnaround time 1-2 weeks.

General Information: No public access terminal. No sealed, expunged, adoption, sex offense, juvenile or mental health records released. Certification fee: $6.00 Civil cert fee; criminal records searched manually are certified as part of search fee. Payee: Syracuse City Court. Only cashiers checks, money orders and attorney checks accepted. Prepayment and SASE required.

Surrogate's Court Onondaga Courthouse, Rm 209, 401 Montgomery St, Syracuse, NY 13202; phone: 315-671-2100; fax: 315-671-1162; hours 8:30AM-4:30PM (EST). *Probate.*
http://surrogate5th.courts.state.ny.us/public/
Search Surrogate Court records online at the website.

Onondaga Town/Village Courts - *misdemeanor or civil records:* Baldwinsville Village- 315-635-6355; Camillus Town- 315-487-7066; Cicero Town- 315-699-8478; Clay Town- 315-652-3800; De Witt Town- 315-446-9180; East Syracuse Village- 315-437-3541; Elbridge Town- 315-689-7380; Fabius Town; Fayetteville Village- 315-637-8070; Geddes Town- 315-468-3613; Jordan Village- 315-689-3483; La Fayette Town- 315-677-9350; Liverpool Village- 315-457-5379 x3; Lysander Town- 315-638-1308; Manlius Town- 315-637-3251; Manlius Village- 315-682-7245; Marcellus Town- 315-673-3269 x3; Minoa Village- 315-656-2203; North Syracuse Justice Court- 315-458-4695; Onondaga Town- 315-469-1674; Otisco Town- 315-696-6771; Pompey Town- 315-682-9877; Salina Town- 315-457 4252; Skaneateles Town- 315-685-5880; Solvay Village- 315-952-1374; Spafford Town- 315-673-0710; Tully Town- 315-696-5884; Van Buren Town- 315-635-3523.

Ontario County

County Clerk 20 Ontario St, Municipal Bldg, Canandaigua, NY 14424; criminal phone: 585-393-2953; civil phone: 585-396-4205; fax: 585-393-2951; hours 8:30AM-5PM (EST). *Felony, Civil.*
Note: Felony search requests made to the County Court Clerk are processed in the manner described below.

Civil Records: Access: Fax, mail, in person, online. Both court and visitors may perform in person searches. No search fee. Court makes copy: $.65 per page, minimum $1.30; same fee for self serve. Required to search: name, years to search. Civil cases indexed by defendant, plaintiff; on computer from 1992, records go back to 1887. Access to current/pending Supreme Court civil cases is at http://e.courts.state.ny.us/. Online decisions go back to 2001; search by firm or attorney name. Mail turnaround time 1 week.

Criminal Records: Access: Fax, mail, in person. Both court and visitors may perform in person searches. Search fee: $5.00 per name. Court makes copy: $.65 per page, minimum $1.30; same fee for self serve. Required to search: name, years to search; also helpful-DOB. Criminal records on computer from 1990, records go back to 1919. Mail turnaround time 1 week.

General Information: Public terminal has criminal back to 1990 and civil back to 1992. No sealed, youthful offender, sex abuse, sex crime, divorce or sealed records released. Will fax civil search documents for fee of $1.50 1st page; $1.00 per add'l page. There is no fax fee to fax criminal search documents. Certification fee: $5.20 minimum if you prepare ($.65 each copy); $5.00 minimum if they prepare ($1.25 each copy). Payee: County Clerk. Personal checks accepted. Prepayment and SASE required.

Supreme & County Court 27 N Main St, Rm 130, Canandaigua, NY 14424-1447; phone: 585-396-4239; criminal phone: 585-396-4025; fax: 585-396-4576; hours 9AM-5PM (EST). *Felony, Civil.*
http://www.nycourts.gov/courts/7jd

Note: Direct search requests to the County Clerk, see separate listing. Also, access to current/pending Supreme Court civil cases is available at http://e.courts.state.ny.us/.

Canandaigua City Court 2 N Main St, City Hall, Canandaigua, NY 14424-1448; phone: 585-396-5011; fax: 585-396-5012; hours 8AM-4PM (EST). *Misdemeanor, Civil Actions Under $15,000, Eviction, Small Claims.*
www.courts.state.ny.us

Civil Records: Access: Mail, in person. Only the court performs in person searches; visitors may not. Search fee: $5.00 per two years searched. Court makes copy: $.65 per page; minimum $1.30. Required to search: name, years to search. Civil cases indexed by defendant, plaintiff; on computer from 1986, prior in books from 1960. Books are not kept on-site.

Criminal Records: Access: None. Court makes copy: $.65 per page; minimum $1.30. Criminal records on computer from 1986, prior in books from 1960. Books not kept on-site. The court refuses to permit access to court records unless specific case file given. It is suggested to send requests to OCA for $52.00 statewide search. Mail turnaround time 1 week.

General Information: No public access terminal. No sealed, expunged, adoption, sex offense, juvenile or mental health records released. Certification fee: $5.00 per document includes copy fee. Payee: Canandaigua City Court. Only cashiers checks and money orders accepted. Prepayment and SASE required.

Geneva City Court 255 Exchange St, Public Safety Bldg, Geneva, NY 14456; phone: 315-789-6560; fax: 315-781-2802; hours 8AM-4PM (EST). *Misdemeanor, Civil Actions Under $15,000, Eviction, Small Claims.*
Civil Records: Access: Mail, in person. Only the court performs in person searches; visitors may not. Search fee: $16.00 per name. Court makes copy: $1.00 per page. Required to search: name, years to search. Civil cases indexed by plaintiff. Civil records on computer from 1992, prior in books. Mail turnaround time 1 week.
Criminal Records: Access: None. Court makes copy: $1.00 per page. Criminal records on computer from 1992, prior in books. The court refuses to permit access to court records unless specific case file given. It is suggested to send requests to OCA for $52.00 statewide search.
General Information: No public access terminal. No youthful offender records released. Will fax documents to local or toll free line. Certification fee: $5.00 per doc. Payee: City Court. Only cashiers checks and money orders accepted. Prepayment and SASE required.

Surrogate's Court 27 N Main St, Canandaigua, NY 14424-1447; phone: 585-396-4055; fax: 585-396-4576; hours 9AM-5PM (EST). *Probate.*

Ontario Town/Village Courts - *misdemeanor or civil records:* Bristol Town- 585-229-4523; Canadice Town- 585-367-3590; Canandaigua Town- 585-394-9040; Clifton Springs Village- 315-462-3048; East Bloomfield Town- 585-657-7248; Farmington Town- 315-986-3113 or 8195; Geneva Town- 315-789-1100; Gorham Town- 585-526-6298; Hopewell Town- 585-394-1963 x6; Manchester Town- 585-289-3010 x103 & x111; Naples Town- 585-374-2111; Phelps Town- 315-548-2090; Richmond Town; Seneca Town- 585-526-4780; South Bristol Town- 585-374-6355; Victor Town- 585-924-5775; West Bloomfield Town Court.

Orange County

County Clerk 255 Main St, Goshen, NY 10924; phone: 845-291-3080; fax: 845-291-2691; hours 9AM-5PM (EST). *Felony, Civil.*
Note: Search requests made to the County Clerk are processed in the manner described below.
Civil Records: Access: Fax, mail, in person. Both court and visitors may perform in person searches. Search fee: $2.50 per name; $5.00 per 2 years. Court makes copy: $.65 per page. Self serve copy fee: $.25 per page. Required to search: name, years to search. Civil cases indexed by defendant, plaintiff; on computer from 1993; prior indexed only by plaintiff. Mail turnaround time 2 weeks.
Criminal Records: Access: Fax, mail, in person. Both court and visitors may perform in person searches. Search fee: $2.50 per name per year. Court makes copy: $.65 per page. Self serve copy fee: $.25

per page. Required to search: name, years to search, DOB. Criminal records on computer since 1993; prior on index Rolodex cards. Mail turnaround time 2 weeks.
General Information: Public terminal goes back to 8/1993. No sealed records released. Will not fax documents. Certification fee: $5.00 plus $1.25 per page after first 4. Payee: County Clerk. Business checks accepted. Prepayment and SASE required.

Supreme & County Court 255 Main St, Goshen, NY 10924; criminal phone: 845-291-3100; civil phone: 845-291-3111; hours 9AM-5PM (EST). *Felony, Civil.*
Note: Direct search requests to County Clerk; see separate listing. The County-Court (criminal court) is at 285 Main St, but records at County Clerk office. Search future criminal court appearances and civil cases online at http://e.courts.state.ny.us.

Middletown City Court 2 James St, Middletown, NY 10940; phone: 845-346-4050; fax: 845-343-5737; hours 8:30AM-4PM (EST). *Misdemeanor, Civil Actions Under $15,000, Eviction, Small Claims.*
Civil Records: Access: Mail, in person. Both court and visitors may perform in person searches. No search fee; prior to 1994 is $5.00 per name per 2 year search. Court makes copy: $.65 per page. $1.30 minimum. Required to search: name, years to search. Civil cases indexed by defendant, plaintiff; on computer from 1994, prior on cards. Mail turnaround time 1 week.
Criminal Records: Access: None. Court makes copy: $.65 per page, $1.30 minimum. Criminal records on computer from 1986, prior on cards. The court refuses to permit access to court records unless specific case file given. It is suggested to send requests to OCA for $52.00 statewide search. Mail turnaround time 2-3 weeks.
General Information: No public access terminal. No sealed or youthful offender records released. Certification fee: $5.00 per doc. Payee: City Court of Middletown. Only cashiers checks and money orders accepted. Prepayment and SASE required.

Newburgh City Court 57 Broadway, Newburgh, NY 12550; phone: 845-565-3208; criminal phone: 845-565-3208; civil phone: 845-565-3074; hours 8AM-4PM (EST). *Misdemeanor, Civil Actions Up to $15,000, Eviction, Small Claims.*
Civil Records: Access: Mail, in person. Only the court performs in person searches; visitors may not. Search fee: $6.00 per name per 2 years. Court makes copy: $.65 per page. Required to search: name, years to search; also helpful- case caption. Civil cases indexed by defendant. Civil records on computer from 1997, prior in docket books or on index cards.
Criminal Records: Access: None. Court makes copy: $.65 per page. Criminal records on computer from 1986. The court refuses to permit access to court records unless specific case file given. It is suggested to send requests to OCA for $52.00 statewide search.
General Information: No public access terminal. No sealed, youthful offender or sex abuse victim records released. Will fax documents to local or toll free line. Certification fee: $6.00 per doc includes copy fee. Payee: Newburgh City Court. Only cashiers checks and money orders accepted. Prepayment and SASE required.

Port Jervis City Court 14-18 Hammond St, Port Jervis, NY 12771-2495; phone: 845-858-4034; fax: 845-858-9883; hours 9AM-5PM (EST). *Misdemeanor, Civil Actions Under $15,000, Eviction, Small Claims.*
Civil Records: Access: Mail, in person. Both court and visitors may perform in person searches. No search fee. Court makes copy: $.65 per page, $1.30 minimum. Required to search: name, years to search. Civil cases indexed by defendant. Civil records on dockets from 1978, computerized since 1996. Mail turnaround time 3 weeks.

Criminal Records: Access: Mail, in person. Search fee: $5.00 per name per 2 years for "violations" only, no misdemeanors. Court makes copy: $.65 per page, $1.30 minimum. Required to search: Name, years to search. Criminal records on dockets from 1978, computerized since 1996. The court refuses to permit access to misdemeanor records unless specific case file given. It is suggested to send requests to OCA for $52.00 statewide search. Mail turnaround time 3 weeks.
General Information: No public access terminal. No sealed, expunged, adoption, sex offense, juvenile or mental health records released. Will not fax documents. Certification fee: $6.00. Payee: City Court of Port Jervis. Only cashiers checks and money orders accepted. Prepayment and SASE required.

Surrogate's Court 30 Park Pl, Surrogate's Courthouse, Goshen, NY 10924; phone: 845-291-2193; fax: 845-291-2196; hours 9AM-5PM; Vault closes at 4PM (EST). *Probate.*

Orange Town/Village Courts - *misdemeanor or civil records:* Blooming Grove Town- 845-496-7631; Chester Town- 845-469-9541; Chester Village- 845-469-8584; Cornwall Town- 845-534-8717; Crawford Town- 845-744-2435; Deerpark Town- 845-856-2928; Florida Village- 845-651-4940; Goshen Town- 845-294-6477; Goshen Village- 845-294-5826; Greenville Town- 845-856-0564; Greenwood Lake Village- 845-477-9218; Hamptonburgh Town- 845-427-5432; Harriman Village- 845-782-6853; Highlands Town- 845-446-8666; Maybrook Village- 845-427-2224; Minisink Town- 845-726-3700; Monroe Town- 845-783-9733; Montgomery Town- 845-457-2620; Montgomery Village- 845-457-9037; Mount Hope Town- 845-386-5303; New Windsor Town- 845-563-4682; Newburgh Town- 845-564-0960; Otisville Village- 845-386-1004; Tuxedo Park Village- 845-928-2311; Tuxedo Town- 845-351-5655; Walden Village- 845-778-1632; Wallkill Town- 845-692-7822; Warwick Town- 845-986-1128; Warwick Village- 845-986-7044; Washingtonville Village- 845-496-9797; Wawayanda Town- 845-355-5706; Woodbury Court- 845-928-2311.

Orleans County

County Clerk Courthouse, Attn: County Clerk, 3 S Main, Albion, NY 14411-9998; phone: 585-589-5334; fax: 585-589-0181; hours 9AM-5PM; July/Aug is 8:30AM-4PM) (EST). *Civil.*
Note: For felony records see the County-Court clerk at the Supreme and County Court in separate listing.

Civil Records: Access: Mail, in person, online. Both court and visitors may perform in person searches. Search fee: $5.00 per name. Fee is for 2 year search. Court makes copy: $1.00 per page; same fee for self serve. Required to search: name, years to search. Civil cases indexed by defendant. Civil records in books to 1940s; on computer back to 1998. Access to current/pending Supreme Court civil cases is at http://e.courts.state.ny.us. Mail turnaround 1 week.
Criminal Records: Access: Mail, in person. Search fee: $52.00 OCA statewide search. Court makes copy: $1.00 per page; same fee for self serve. Required to search: name, years to search, DOB. Criminal records in books to 1940s; on computer back to 1993. Note: The clerk will only pull specific case files. All criminal record name search requests are directed to the OCA for statewide record search, $52.00 search fee. Mail turnaround time 1 week.
General Information: No public access terminal. No sealed or divorce records released. Will fax documents. Certification fee: $4.00 plus $1.00 per page after first 4. Payee: County Clerk. Personal checks accepted. Prepayment and SASE required.

Supreme & County Court Courthouse, 3 S Main, Albion, NY 14411-9998; phone: 585-589-4457; fax: 585-589-0632; hours 9AM-5PM (EST). *Felony, Civil.*
Note: The court directs felony search requests to the OCA for a $52.00 statewide record search. Access civil records through the County Clerk, see separate

entry. Access to current/pending Supreme Court civil cases is available at http://e.courts.state.ny.us/.

Surrogate's Court 3 S Main St, Albion, NY 14411; phone: 585-589-4457; fax: 585-589-0632; hours 9AM-5PM (EST). *Probate.*

Orleans Town/Village Courts - *misdemeanor or civil records:* Albion Town- 585-589-7048 x18; Albion Village- 585-589-2335; Barre Town- 585-589-5100; Carlton Town- 585-682-4517; Clarendon Justice Court- 585-638-6371 x5; Gaines Town- 585-589-4592; Kendall Town- 716-659-2341; Medina Village- 585-798-4875; Murray Town- 585-638-7048; Ridgeway Town- 585-798-3282; Shelby Town- 585-798-3120; Yates Town- 585-765-9603.

Oswego County

County Clerk 46 E Bridge St, Oswego, NY 13126; phone: 315-349-8616; fax: 315-349-8692; hours 9AM-5PM (EST). *Felony, Civil.*
Note: Countywide search requests made to the County Court Clerk are processed in the manner described below.

Civil Records: Access: In person, online. Visitors must perform in person searches themselves. Court makes copy: $.65 per page, $1.30 minimum. Required to search: name, years to search. Civil cases indexed by defendant and plaintiff. Civil records on computer from 1/90, prior in books from 1896. Access to current/pending Supreme Court civil cases is at http://e.courts.state.ny.us/.
Criminal Records: Access: Mail, in person. Only the court performs in person searches; visitors may not. Search fee: $5.00 per name for every 2 years searched. Court makes copy: $.65 per page, $1.30 minimum. Required to search: name, years to search, DOB, signed release. Criminal records on computer from 1973; prior in docket books from 1939. Mail turnaround time 2-3 days.
General Information: Public terminal has only civil records back to 1990. No sealed, youthful offender or divorce records released. Will not fax documents. Certification fee: $5.00 minimum, includes 4 pages copies; $1.25 per page after 4. Payee: County Clerk. Personal checks accepted up to $200.00. Prepayment and SASE required.

Supreme & County Court 46 E Bridge St, Oswego, NY 13126; phone: 315-349-3280; hours 9AM-4PM (EST). *Felony, Civil.*
Note: Direct search requests to the County Clerk, see separate listing. Also, access to current/pending Supreme Court civil cases is available at http://e.courts.state.ny.us/.

Fulton City Court 141 S 1st St, Fulton, NY 13069; phone: 315-593-8400; hours 8:30AM-4:30PM; Summer 8:30AM-4PM (EST). *Misdemeanor, Civil Actions Under $15,000, Eviction, Small Claims.*
Civil Records: Access: Mail, in person. Only the court performs in person searches; visitors may not. No search fee. Court makes copy: $.65 per page; $1.30 minimum. Required to search: name, years to search. Civil cases indexed by defendant. Civil records on dockets from 1991; computerized records since 1998. Mail turnaround time 2 weeks or less.
Criminal Records: Access: None. Criminal records go back to 1918, computerized records since 1997, criminal records on dockets from 1987. The court refuses to permit access to court records unless specific case file given. It is suggested to send requests to OCA for $52.00 statewide search.
General Information: No public access terminal. No sealed, expunged, adoption, sex offense, juvenile or mental health records released. Will fax documents to a local or toll free line. Certification fee: $6.00 per doc. Payee: Fulton City Court. Only cashiers checks and money orders accepted. Prepayment required.

Oswego City Court Conway Municipal Bldg, 20 W Oneida St, Oswego, NY 13126; phone: 315-343-0415; fax: 315-343-0531; hours 8:30AM-5PM (EST). *Misdemeanor, Civil Actions Under $15,000, Eviction, Small Claims.*
Civil Records: Access: Mail, in person. Only the court performs in person searches; visitors may not. No search fee. Court makes copy: $.65 per page. Required to search: name, years to search. Civil cases indexed by defendant. Civil records on computer from 1987, prior in books.
Criminal Records: Access: None. Court makes copy: $.65 per page. Criminal records on computer from 1987, prior in books. The court refuses to permit access to court records unless specific case file given. It is suggested to send requests to OCA for $52.00 statewide search. Mail turnaround time 3-4 days.
General Information: No sealed or youthful offender records released. Certification fee: $6.00 plus $.65 per page after first. Payee: Oswego City Court. Only cashiers checks and money orders accepted. Prepayment and SASE required.

Surrogate's Court Courthouse, 25 E Oneida St, Oswego, NY 13126; phone: 315-349-3295; fax: 315-349-8514; hours 9AM-4:30PM Sept-May; 8:30AM-4 PM June-Aug (EST). *Probate.*

Oswego Town/Village Courts - *misdemeanor or civil records:* Albion Town- 315-298-6325; Amboy Town- 315-964-1165; Boylston Town; Constantia Town- 315-623-7713; Granby Town- 315-598-2958; Hannibal Town- 315-564-6037; Hastings Town- 315-676-4317; Mexico Town- 315-963-3785; Minetto Town- 315-343-2393; New Haven Town- 315-963-8886; Orwell Town- 315-298-3236; Oswego Town- 315-343-7249; Palermo Town- 315-593-2333; Parish Town- 315-625-4592; Pulaski Village- 315-298-7431; Redfield Town- 315-599-7125, 599-8825; Richland Town- 315-298-5174; Sandy Creek Town- 315-387-5456; Schroeppel Town- 315-695-6177; Scriba Town- 315-343-3250; Volney Town- 315-598-7082; West Monroe Town- 315-676-3522; Williamstown Town- 315-964-2279.

Otsego County

County Clerk 197 Main St, Public Office Bldg, Cooperstown, NY 13326; phone: 607-547-4276; hours 9AM-5PM; 8AM-5PM Summer hours (EST). *Felony, Civil.*
Note: Countywide search requests made to the county clerk are processed in the manner described below.
Civil Records: Access: Mail, in person, online. Both court and visitors may perform in person searches. Search fee: $5.00 per name. Court makes copy: $1.00 per page. Required to search: name, years to search. Civil cases indexed by defendant. Civil records on computer back to 1997; prior in books. Access to current/pending Supreme Court civil cases is at http://e.courts.state.ny.us/. Mail turnaround time 1-2 days.
Criminal Records: Access: Mail, in person. Both court and visitors may perform in person searches. Search fee: $5.00 per name. Court makes copy: $1.00 per page. Required to search: name, years to search, address, DOB. Criminal records on computer back to 1997; prior in books. Note: Misdemeanor records are maintained by city, town and village courts. In person criminal record searches should be performed over at the Supreme and County Court office at the courthouse. Mail turnaround time 1-2 days.
General Information: Public terminal has only civil records. No sealed, expunged, adoption, sex offense, juvenile or mental health records released. Will fax documents on criminal cases. Certification fee: $4.00. Payee: County Clerk. Business checks accepted. Prepayment and SASE required.

Supreme & County Court 193 Main St, Courthouse, Cooperstown, NY 13326; phone: 607-547-4364; probate phone: 607-547-4213; fax: 607-547-7567; hours 9AM-5PM; 8AM-4PM Summer hours (EST). *Felony, Civil.*
www.nycourts.gov/6jd/CountyMaps/default.html
Note: In person criminal index searches can be made at this address. Direct all other types of search requests to the County Clerk office, see separate listing. Access to current/pending Supreme Court civil cases is available at http://e.courts.state.ny.us/.

Oneonta City Court 81 Main St, Oneonta, NY 13820; phone: 607-432-4480; fax: 607-432-2328; hours 8AM-4PM (EST). *Misdemeanor, Civil Actions Under $15,000, Eviction, Small Claims.*
Civil Records: Access: Mail, in person. Only the court performs in person searches; visitors may not. Search fee: $5.00 per name per 2 years. Court makes copy: $.65 per page. $1.30 minimum. Required to search: name, years to search. Civil cases indexed by defendant. Civil records on computer from 1987, prior in books. Mail turnaround time 2 days.
Criminal Records: Access: None. Only the court performs in person searches; visitors may not. Search fee: A Certificate of Disposition is available for $5.00. Court makes copy: $.65 per page, $1.30 minimum. Required to search: Name, case number, signed release. A release form is available from the clerk. Most records go back 6 years; DWAI 10 years. The court does not permit access to county records unless a specific case file number given. To name search, requesters must use the OCA statewide search. Note: Only the court performs Certificate of Disposition searches only. Mail turnaround time 1 day.
General Information: No public access terminal. No sealed or youthful offender records released. Certification fee: $5.00 per page. Payee: Oneonta City Court. Prefers certified funds only. Prepayment and SASE required.

Surrogate's Court Surrogate's Office, 197 Main St, Cooperstown, NY 13326; phone: 607-547-4338; fax: 607-547-7566; hours 9AM-N, 1-5PM, Reg Hrs, 8AM-4PM July -Aug (EST). *Probate.*

Otsego Town/Village Courts - *misdemeanor or civil records:* Burlington Town; Butternuts Town- 607-783-2758; Cherry Valley Town- 607-264-8324; Cherry Valley Village- 607-264-3791; Cooperstown Village- 607-547-9597; Decatur Town- 607-397-7365; Edmeston Town- 607-965-9823; Exeter Town- 315-858-3905; Hartwick Town- 607-293-8133; Laurens Town Court & Village- 607-433-1053; Maryland Town- 607-638-9495; Middlefield Town- 607-547-2126; Milford Town- 607-286-7773; Morris Town Court & Village- 607-263-2224; New Lisbon Town- 607-965-8627; Oneonta Town- 607-432-0124; Otego Town- 607-988-2698; Otsego Town- 607-547-5689; Pittsfield Town- 607-847-6524; Plainfield Town; Richfield Springs Village- 315-858-2048; Richfield Town- 315-858-2830; Roseboom Town- 607-264-3293; Springfield Town- 315-858-1508; Unadilla Town- 607-369-7458; Westford Town- 607-397-9210; Worcester Town- 607-397-8476.

Putnam County

County Clerk 40 Gleneida Ave, County Clerk Office, Carmel, NY 10512; phone: 845-225-3641 X306; fax: 845-228-0231; hours 9AM-5PM; 8AM-4PM Summer hours (EST). *Felony, Civil.*
Note: Coauntywide search requests made to the County Court Clerk are processed in the manner described below.
Civil Records: Access: Mail, in person, online. Both court and visitors may perform in person searches. Search fee: $5.00 per name. Fee is per 2 years searched. Court makes copy: $1.00 per page. Self serve copy fee: $.25 per page. Required to search: name, years to search. Civil cases indexed by defendant, plaintiff; on computer from 4/93, prior in books. Access to current/pending Supreme Court

civil cases is at http://e.courts.state.ny.us/. Mail turnaround time 2 days.

Criminal Records: Access: Mail, in person. Both court and visitors may perform in person searches. Search fee: $5.00 per name per certificate of disposition. Court makes copy: $1.00 per page. Self serve copy fee: $.25 per page. Required to search: name, years to search, DOB. Criminal records computerized since 1983. Mail turnaround time 2 days.

General Information: Public terminal goes back to 1983. No sealed or youthful offender records released. Certification fee: $4.00. Payee: County Clerk. Personal checks accepted. Prepayment and SASE required.

Supreme & County Court 40 Gleneida Ave, Supreme and County Court, Carmel, NY 10512; phone: 845-225-3641 X336; hours 9AM-5PM (EST). *Felony, Civil.*

Note: For a county only record search, see the county clerk, see separate listing. Search online for future court appearances and for current/pending Supreme Court civil cases at http://e.courts.state.ny.us.

Surrogate's Court Historic Courthouse, 44 Gleneida Ave, Carmel, NY 10512; phone: 845-225-3641 X295; fax: 845-228-5761; hours 9AM-5PM (EST). *Probate.*

Otsego Town/Village Courts - *misdemeanor or civil records:* Burlington Town; Butternuts Town- 607-783-2758; Cherry Valley Town- 607-264-8324; Cherry Valley Village- 607-264-3791; Cooperstown Village- 607-547-9597; Decatur Town- 607-397-7365; Edmeston Town- 607-965-9823; Exeter Town- 315-858-3905; Hartwick Town- 607-293-8133; Laurens Town Court & Village- 607-433-1053; Maryland Town- 607-638-9495; Middlefield Town- 607-547-2126; Milford Town- 607-286-7773; Morris Town Court & Village- 607-263-2224; New Lisbon Town- 607-965-8627; Oneonta Town- 607-432-0124; Otego Town- 607-988-2698; Otsego Town- 607-547-5689; Pittsfield Town- 607-847-6524; Plainfield Town; Richfield Springs Village- 315-858-2048; Richfield Town- 315-858-2830; Roseboom Town- 607-264-3293; Springfield Town- 315-858-1508; Unadilla Town- 607-369-7458; Westford Town- 607-397-9210; Worcester Town- 607-397-8476.

Queens Borough

Supreme Court - Civil Division 88-11 Sutphin Blvd, #106, Jamaica, NY 11435; phone: 718-298-1000, 718-298-0615 Records Rm; fax: 718-520-2204 Admin; hours 9AM-5PM, no cashier transactions after 4:45PM (EST). *Civil Actions Over $25,000.*

www.courts.state.ny.us/courts/11jd/index.shtml

Civil Records: Access: Mail, in person, online. Both court and visitors may perform in person searches. Search fee: $10.00 per name. Fee is for first two years; add $5.00 per add'l 2 years. Court makes copy: $4.00 per document. Required to search: name, years to search, address. Civil cases indexed by plaintiff. Civil records on computer from 1992, prior in books back through 1980s. Access to current/pending Supreme Court civil cases is at http://e.courts.state.ny.us/. Mail turnaround 1 week.

General Information: Public terminal has only civil records back to 1992. No marriage or incompetence records released. Identification required to review confidential matrimonial case records. Certification fee: $8.00 per doc. Payee: County Clerk. Only cashiers checks and money orders accepted. Prepayment and SASE required.

Supreme Court - Criminal Division 125-01 Queens Blvd, Kew Gardens, NY 11415; phone: 718-520-3542; hours 9:30AM-4:30PM (EST). *Felony, Misdemeanor.*

www.courts.state.ny.us/11jd/queens/

Criminal Records: Access: None. Court makes copy: $.15 per page. Search online for future court appearances at http://iapps.courts.state.ny.us/webcrim_attorney/Login All criminal record search requests made to the Supreme Court Clerk are forwarded to the OCA for processing - see NY Court Section Introduction.

General Information: Public terminal has only criminal records. Certification fee: $8.00 for 1st page, $1.00 each add'l. Payee: County Clerk. Personal checks accepted. Prepayment and SASE required.

Supreme Court - Long Is. City 25-10 Court Sq, Long Island City, NY 11101; phone: 718-520-3934; fax: 718-520-2539; hours 9AM-5PM (EST). *Civil Actions over $25,000.*

Note: Trials only here; Criminal records available at Kew Gardens Criminal Court only; Court recommends the OCA $52.00 statewide criminal search. Civil cases available only at Jamaica Civil Court only.

Civil Court of the City of New York - Queens Branch 89-17 Sutphin Blvd, Jamaica, NY 11435; phone: 718-262-7100; civil phone: 212-791-6000; hours 9AM-5PM (EST). *Civil Actions Under $25,000, Eviction, Small Claims.*

Note: Housing court information telephone number is 212-791-6070.

Civil Records: Access: In person only. Visitors must perform in person searches themselves. Court makes copy: $.25 per page. Required to search: name, years to search. Civil cases indexed by plaintiff. Civil records on computer from 1997, prior in books.

General Information: Public terminal has only civil records. (Housing and civil.) No sealed, youthful offender or sex victim records released. Certification fee: $6.00. Payee: Clelrk of Civil Court. Only cashiers checks and money orders accepted. Prepayment and SASE required.

Surrogate's Court 88-11 Sutphin Blvd, Jamaica, NY 11435; phone: 718-298-0500; hours 9AM-1PM, 2-5PM (EST). *Probate.*

Rensselaer County

County Clerk 105 3rd St, Troy, NY 12180; phone: 518-270-4080; fax: 518-271-7998; hours 8:30AM-5PM (EST). *Felony, Civil.*

www.rensco.com

Note: Countywide record search requests made to the county clerk are processed in the manner described below.

Civil Records: Access: Mail, in person, online. Visitors must perform in person searches themselves. Search fee: $10.00 per name. Court makes copy: $1.00 per page. Self serve copy fee: $.25 per page. Required to search: name, years to search. Civil cases indexed by plaintiff pre-1996; by defendant & plaintiff after 1996. Civil records on computer back to 1997; prior in books to 1930s. Access to current/pending Supreme Court civil cases is at http://e.courts.state.ny.us/. Mail turnaround time 1 week.

Criminal Records: Access: Mail, in person. Only the court performs in person searches; visitors may not. Search fee: $5.00 per name per 2 years. Court makes copy: $1.00 per page. Required to search: name, years to search; also helpful- DOB. Criminal records on computer back to 1986; prior in books to 1976. Mail turnaround time 1 week.

General Information: Public terminal has only civil records back to 1997. No sealed, open/pending cases, youthful offender records released. Will not fax documents. Certification fee: $4.00 per cert includes 8 copy pages. Payee: County Clerk. Personal checks accepted. Prepayment and SASE required.

Supreme & County Court 80 2nd St, Troy, NY 12180; phone: 518-270-3711; hours 8:30AM-5PM (EST). *Felony, Civil.*

Note: Direct all search requests to the County Clerk office, see separate listing.

Rensselaer City Court City Hall, Rensselaer, NY 12144; phone: 518-462-6751; fax: 518-462-3307; hours 8AM-3:30PM (EST). *Misdemeanor, Civil Actions Under $15,000, Eviction, Small Claims, Traffic.*

Civil Records: Access: Mail, in person. Only the court performs in person searches; visitors may not. Court makes copy: $.50 per page. Required to search: name, years to search. Civil cases indexed by defendant. Civil records in books back 15 years; on computer back 5 years. Note: All record name search requests are directed to the OCA for statewide record search, $52.00 search fee. Mail turnaround time 72 hours.

Criminal Records: Access: Mail, in person. Only the court performs in person searches; visitors may not. Search fee: $6.00 for a Certificate of Disposition only. Court makes copy: $.50 per page. Required to search: name, years to search, DOB, signed release. Criminal records in books go back 15 years; on computer back 9 years. Note: Court will only confirm convictions with Certificate of Disposition. All criminal record name search requests are directed to the OCA for statewide record search, $52.00 search fee. Mail turnaround time 72 hours.

General Information: No public access terminal. No sealed, expunged, adoption, sex offense, juvenile or mental health records released. Will not fax documents. Certification fee: $6.00. Payee: Rensselaer City Court. Only cashiers checks and money orders accepted. Prepayment required.

Troy City Court 51 State St, 2nd Fl, Troy, NY 12180; phone: 518-271-1602; fax: 518-274-2816; hours 9AM-3:30PM (EST). *Misdemeanor.*

Criminal Records: Access: In person only. Only the court performs in person searches; visitors may not. Search fee: $5.00 per name for certificate of disposition. Court makes copy: copies not made in court office. Required to search: name, years to search, DOB, aliases, offense. Criminal records on computer from 1989, prior in books. Note: Court will only confirm convictions. Name search requests are directed to the state OCA for a $52.00 statewide record check.

General Information: No public access terminal. No sealed records released. Certification fee: $5.00 per doc. Payee: City Court. Personal checks accepted. Prepayment required.

Surrogate's Court County Courthouse, 80 2nd St, Troy, NY 12180; phone: 518-270-3724; fax: 518-272-5452; hours 9AM-5PM (EST). *Probate.*

Rensselaer Town/Village Courts - *misdemeanor or civil records:* Berlin Town- 518-658-2020; Brunswick Town- 518-279-3461; Castleton-on-Hudson Village- 518-732-2211; East Greenbush Town- 518-477-5412; Grafton Town- 518-279-3565; Hoosick Falls Village- 518-686-4399; Hoosick Town- 518-686-3335; Nassau Town- 518-766-2813; Nassau Village- 518-766-3044; North Greenbush Town- 518-283-2789 x28 or x29; Petersburgh Town- 518-658-3777; Pittstown Town- 518-753-4076, 753-4222 x 30; Poestenkill Town- 518-283-5100; Sand Lake Town- 518-674-3033; Schaghticoke Town- 518-753-6915; Schodack Town- 518-477-9390; Stephentown Town- 518-733-5636.

Richmond County

Supreme Court - Civil Division 130 Stuyvesant Pl, c/o Richmond County Clerk, Staten Island, NY 10301; phone: 718-390-5389 Court Desk; civil phone: 718-390-5352; hours 9AM-5PM (EST). *Civil Actions Over $25,000.*

Civil Records: Access: In person, online. Visitors must perform in person searches themselves. Self serve copy fee: $.25 per page. Required to search: name, years to search. Civil cases indexed by plaintiff. Civil records on computer back to 1993. Access to current/pending Supreme Court civil cases is at http://e.courts.state.ny.us/.

General Information: Public terminal has only civil records back to 1993. No matrimonial records released. Will not fax documents. Certification fee: $8.00. Payee: Richmond County Clerk. Only attorney's checks and money orders accepted. Prepayment required.

Supreme Court - Criminal Division 18 Richmond Terrace, Rm 110, Staten Island, NY 10301; phone: 718-390-5352 option2, 718-390-5280; hours 9AM-5PM (EST). *Felony, Misdemeanor.*

Criminal Records: Access: Mail, in person. Visitors must perform in person searches themselves. Search fee: $5.00 Certificate of Disposition. Court makes copy: $.50 per page. Required to search: name, years to search, DOB. A notarized signed release is required for access to sealed records. Criminal records on computer back to 1975, prior archived back to 1960. Access is for Certificate of Disposition only; this office does not allow in person or mail access to case files without a specific case number. All criminal record name search requests directed to the OCA for statewide record search, $52.00 search fee. Search online for future court appearances at http://e.courts.state.ny.us. Mail turnaround time 1-2 days.

General Information: No public access terminal. No sealed or youthful offender records released unless to subject. Will not fax documents. Certification fee: $10.00 per doc. Payee: County Clerk, Richmond County. Only cashiers checks and money orders accepted. Prepayment and SASE required.

Civil Court of the City of New York - Richmond Branch 927 Castleton Ave, Staten Island, NY 10310; phone: 718-390-5417/5419; fax: 718-390-8108; hours 9AM-5PM (EST). *Civil Actions Under $25,000, Eviction, Small Claims.*

Civil Records: Access: In person only. Visitors must perform in person searches themselves. Self serve copy fee: $.15 per page. Required to search: name. Civil cases indexed by plaintiff. Civil records on computer since 1999; prior on books.

General Information: Public terminal has only civil records back to 1999. No sealed records released. Certification fee: $6.00 per doc includes copies. Payee: Clerk Civil Court. Only cashiers checks and money orders accepted. Prepayment and SASE required.

Surrogate's Court 18 Richmond Terrace, Rm 201, Staten Island, NY 10301; phone: 718-390-5400; fax: 718-390-8741; hours 9AM-5PM (EST). *Probate.*

Rockland County

County Clerk 1 S. Main #100, New City, NY 10956; phone: 845-638-5070; criminal phone: x3; civil phone: x4; fax: 845-638-5647; hours 7AM-6:30PM M-Th, 7AM-5:30PM Fri (EST). *Felony, Civil.*

www.rocklandcountyclerk.com

Note: Countywide search requests made to the county clerk are processed here. Misdemeanor records maintained by city, town, village courts, but this clerk may have a misdemeanor record if your provide an index number.

Civil Records: Access: Mail, online, in person. Both court and visitors may perform in person searches. Search fee: $5.00 per each 2 years. Court makes copy: $1.00 per page. Self serve copy fee: $.25 per page. Required to search: name, years to search. Civil indexed by defendant, plaintiff. Civil records on computer from 1982. Online access to county clerk index is free at www.rocklandcountyclerk.com/court_records.html . Online includes civil judgments, real estate records, tax warrants. Free registration required. Call 845-638-5221 for info. Also, access to current Supreme court cases is at http://e.courts.state.ny.us. Mail turnaround time 10 days.

Criminal Records: Access: Mail, online, in person. Both court and visitors may perform in person

searches. Search fee: $5.00 each 2 years. Court makes copy: $1.00 per page. Self serve copy fee: $.25 per page. Required to search: name, years to search. Criminal records on computer from 1982. Online access to county clerk index is free at www.rocklandcountyclerk.com/court_records.html . Index includes criminal records back to 1982. Free registration required. Also, access to current Supreme court cases is at http://e.courts.state.ny.us. Mail turnaround time 10 days.

General Information: Public terminal goes back to 1982. No detention records release. Will not fax documents. Certification fee: $1.25 per page; $5.00 minimum. Payee: County Clerk. Personal checks accepted. Prepayment and SASE required.

Supreme & County Court 1 S Main St, #200, New City, NY 10956; criminal phone: 845-638-5363; civil phone: 845-638-5393; hours 9AM-5PM (EST). *Felony, Civil.*

Note: Direct all search requests to the County Clerk office, see separate listing. Online access to current/pending Supreme Court civil cases is available at http://e.courts.state.ny.us/. See also county clerk for online access. County-Court is located in #400.

Surrogate's Court 1 S Main St, #270, New City, NY 10956; phone: 845-638-5330; fax: 845-638-5632; hours 9AM-5PM (EST). *Probate.*

Rockland Town/Village Courts - *misdemeanor or civil records:* Chestnut Ridge Village- 845-425-3108; Clarkstown Town- 845-639-5960; Grand View-on-Hudson Village- 845-358-4148; Haverstraw Town- 845-947-0020; Haverstraw Village- 845-947-4063; Hillburn Village- 845-357-2036; New Hempstead Village- 845-354-8101; New Square Village- 845-354-1313; Nyack Village- 845-358-4464; Orangetown Town- 845-359-5100; Piermont Village- 845-359-0345; Ramapo Town- 845-357-5100; Sloatsburg Village- 845-753-2727; South Nyack Village- 845-358-5078; Spring Valley Village- 845-573-5820; Stony Point Town- 845-786-2506; Suffern Village- 845-357-6424; Upper Nyack Village- 845-358-0202; Wesley Hills Village- 845-354-0404; West Haverstraw Village- 845-947-1013.

Saratoga County

County Clerk 40 McMaster St, Ballston Spa, NY 12020; phone: 518-885-2213 X4410; fax: 518-884-4726; hours 8AM-5PM (EST). *Civil.*

Note: This County Clerk does not have a separate index of felony records; see the Supreme and County Court.

Civil Records: Access: Mail, in person, online. Both court and visitors may perform in person searches. Search fee: $5.00 per name per 2 years. Court makes copy: $1.25 per page. Self serve copy fee: $.50 per page. Required to search: name, years to search; also helpful: address. Civil cases indexed by defendant, plaintiff; on computer from 3/88, prior in books. Access to current/pending Supreme Court civil cases is at http://e.courts.state.ny.us/. Mail turnaround time 3-4 days.

General Information: Public terminal has only civil records back to 1987. No youthful offender or divorce records released. Will not fax documents. Certification fee: $5.00 per cert includes 4 copy pages. Payee: County Clerk. Personal checks accepted. Prepayment and SASE required.

Supreme & County Court 30 McMaster St, Ballston Spa, NY 12020; phone: 518-885-2224; hours 9AM-5PM (EST). *Felony, Civil.*

Note: Misdemeanor records are maintained by city, town and village courts.

Civil Records: Access: In person, online. Both court and visitors may perform in person searches. See the separate County Clerk entry for Supreme court civil case records. Access to current/pending Supreme Court civil cases is available at http://e.courts.state.ny.us/.

Criminal Records: Access: Mail, in person. Both court and visitors may perform in person searches. Search fee: $5.00 per name per 2 years. Court makes copy: $1.25 per page. Self serve copy fee: $.50 per page. Required to search: name, years to search, DOB; also helpful: address. Criminal records not computerized here, on books only. The County-Court directs criminal search requests to the OCA for a $52.00 statewide record check, however, you may search in person at the County-Court clerk office, as described below. However, the court will provide a Certificate of Disposition for $5.00, which is prepared by the County Clerk office.

General Information: Public terminal has only civil records. (Civil records terminal is in County Clerk office.) No youthful offender or divorce records released. Certification fee: $5.00 for 1st 4 pages, $1.25 each add'l. Payee: County Court Clerk. Personal checks accepted. Prepayment required.

Mechanicville City Court 36 N Main St, Mechanicville, NY 12118; phone: 518-664-9876; fax: 518-664-8606; hours 8AM-4PM (EST). *Misdemeanor, Civil Actions Under $15,000, Eviction, Small Claims.*

Civil Records: Access: Mail, in person. Both court and visitors may perform in person searches. No search fee. Court makes copy: $.65 per page; $1.30 minimum. Required to search: name, years to search. Civil cases indexed by defendant. Civil records on computer since 1/94; records go back to 1900.

Criminal Records: Access: None. Only the court performs in person searches; visitors may not. No search fee. Court makes copy: $.65 per page; $1.30 minimum. Criminal records on computer from 9/93; records go back to 1900. The court refuses to permit access to court records unless specific case file given. Court directs searchers to OCA for $52.00 statewide search. Mail turnaround time 1 day.

General Information: No public access terminal. No sealed, expunged, adoption, sex offense, juvenile or mental health records released. Will fax documents to local or toll free line. Certification fee: $5.00 per document. Payee: City Court. Personal checks accepted. Prepayment and SASE required.

Saratoga Springs City Court City Hall, 474 Broadway, Saratoga Springs, NY 12866; phone: 518-581-1797; fax: 518-584-3097; hours 8AM-4PM (EST). *Misdemeanor, Civil Actions Under $15,000, Eviction, Small Claims.*

Civil Records: Access: Mail, in person. Only the court performs in person searches; visitors may not. Search fee: $5.00 per name per 2 years or $16.00 computer search back to 10/94. Court makes copy: $1.30 1st page; $.65 each add'l. Required to search: name, years to search. Civil cases indexed by defendant. Civil records on computer back to 10/94; prior records on index cards.

Criminal Records: Access: None. Court makes copy: $1.30 1st page; $.65 each add'l. Criminal records on computer back to 8/93. The court refuses to permit access to its records. The court directs requests to OCA for the $52.00 statewide search.

General Information: No public access terminal. Sealed files not released. Will not fax documents. Certification fee: $5.00. Payee: City Court. Only cashiers checks and money orders accepted. Prepayment and SASE required.

Surrogate's Court 30 McMaster St, Bldg 3, Ballston Spa, NY 12020; phone: 518-884-4722; fax: 518-884-4774; hours 9AM-5PM (EST). *Probate.*

Saratoga Town/Village Courts - *misdemeanor or civil records:* Ballston Spa Village- 518-885-8559; Ballston Town- 518-885-8559; Charlton Town- 518-384-0152 x201; Clifton Park Town- 518-371-6668; Corinth Town- 518-654-6991; Day Town- 518-696-3789; Edinburg Town; Galway Town- 518-882-6070; Galway Village- 518-882-6070; Greenfield Town- 518-893-7432 x310; Hadley Town- 518-696-4379 x33; Halfmoon Town- 518-371-7410; Malta Town- 518-899-6121; Milton Town- 518-885-9267; Moreau Town- 518-793-3188; Northumberland

Town- 518-745-0178; Providence Town; Saratoga Town- 518-695-6887; Stillwater Town- 518-664-6946; Stillwater Village- 518-664-5392; Waterford Town- 518-237-6788; Wilton Town- 518-587-1980.

Schenectady County

County Clerk 620 State St, Attn: County Clerk, Schenectady, NY 12305; phone: 518-388-4222; fax: 518-388-4224; hours 9AM-4PM (EST). *Civil.*
Note: For felony records see the County-Court clerk at the Supreme and County Court in separate listing.

Civil Records: Access: Mail, in person, online. Both court and visitors may perform in person searches. Search fee: $5.00 per name. Fee is per 2 years searched. Court makes copy: $1.00 per page off of computer. Self serve copy fee: $.25 per page. Required to search: name, years to search. Civil cases indexed by plaintiff. Civil records on computer from 1989, prior on index cards. In person access is only here at the County Clerk, not the Supreme Court Clerk. Access to current/pending Supreme Court civil cases is at http://e.courts.state.ny.us/. Mail turnaround time 4 days. Will expedite requests if requested.
General Information: Public terminal has only civil records back to 1988. No sealed, youthful offenders, infant compromise or divorce records released. Will fax documents if all fees are paid, or to a toll-free number. Certification fee: $4.00 includes copy fee. Payee: County Clerk. Personal checks accepted. Prepayment and SASE required.

Supreme & County Court 612 State St, Schenectady, NY 12305; phone: 518-388-4322; fax: 518-388-4520; hours 9AM-5PM; 8:30-4:30 PM Summer hours (EST). *Felony, Civil.*
Note: Direct civil record requests to County Clerk, see separate listing. Access to current/pending civil cases is available at http://e.courts.state.ny.us/.
Civil Records: Access: In person only. Both court and visitors may perform in person searches. Search fee: $5.00 per name per 2 years searched, if searched at County Clerk office. Court makes copy: $1.00 per page if on computer. Self serve copy fee: $.25 per page. Required to search: name, years to search. Civil cases indexed by plaintiff. Civil records on computer from 1989, prior on index cards.
Criminal Records: Access: Mail, in person. Both court and visitors may perform in person searches. Search fee: $5.00 per name per 2 years searched. Court makes copy: $.50 per page. Required to search: name, years to search, DOB. Criminal records on computer from 1989, prior in index books. The County-Court Clerk gives itself the option of referring criminal record search requests to the OCA for processing for $52.00 fee, or doing the search themselves. Court will also do a Certificate of Disposition for $5.00 each. Mail turnaround time 4 days.
General Information: No public access terminal. No sealed, youthful offenders, infant compromise or divorce records released. Notarized, signed release required to access sealed records. Certification fee: $5.00 per doc. Payee: County Clerk. Personal checks accepted. Prepayment and SASE required.

Schenectady City Court - Civil Jay St, City Hall, #215, Schenectady, NY 12305; phone: 518-382-5077; fax: 518-382-5080; hours 8AM-4PM (EST). *Civil Actions Under $15,000, Eviction, Small Claims.*
Civil Records: Access: Mail, in person. Only the court performs in person searches; visitors may not. Search fee: $16.00 per name. Court makes copy: $.50 per page. Required to search: name, years to search. Civil cases indexed by defendant. Civil records on computer from 1998, prior in books. Mail turnaround time 2 weeks.
General Information: No public access terminal. No sealed or youthful offender records released. Certification fee: $6.00. Payee: City Court. Only cashiers checks and money orders accepted. Prepayment and SASE required.

Schenectady City Court - Criminal 531 Liberty St, Schenectady, NY 12305; phone: 518-382-5239; fax: 518-382-5241; hours 8AM-4PM (EST). *Misdemeanor.*
Criminal Records: Access: None. Search fee: A certificate of Disposition is $6.00. Court makes copy: $.50 per page. Required to search: Name, DOB, case number. Criminal records on computer from 1981, prior in books. The court directs name searches to the OCA for $52.00 statewide search, unless specific docket number given.
General Information: No public access terminal. No sealed or youthful offender records released. Certification fee: $6.00. Payee: City Court. Only cashiers checks and money orders accepted. Prepayment required.

Surrogate's Court 612 State St, Judicial Bldg, Schenectady, NY 12305; phone: 518-425-8455; fax: 518-377-6378; hours 9AM-5PM (EST). *Probate.*
Note: New phone number late 2005 or early 2006 is 518-425-8455.

Schenectady Town/Village Courts - *misdemeanor or civil records:* Duanesburg Town- 518-895-8922; Glenville Town; Niskayuna Town- 518-386-4560; Princetown Town- 518-357-4047; Rotterdam Town- 518-355-7911; Scotia Village- 518-374-2099.

Schoharie County

Supreme & County Court PO Box 549, 284 Main St, Attn: County Clerk, Schoharie, NY 12157; phone: 518-295-8316 (County Clerk); 518-295-8342 (Supreme); fax: 518-295-8338; hours 8:30AM-5PM (EST). *Felony, Civil, Misdemeanor, Eviction, Small Claims.*
Note: Direct search requests to the County Clerk who processes requests in the manner described below.
Civil Records: Access: Fax, mail, in person, online. Both court and visitors may perform in person searches. Search fee: $5.00 per name. Court makes copy: $.50 per page; same fee for self serve. Required to search: name, years to search. Civil cases indexed by defendant, plaintiff; on computer from 1994, prior in books. Access to current/pending Supreme Court civil cases is at http://e.courts.state.ny.us/. Mail turnaround time 24-48 hours.
Criminal Records: Access: Fax, mail, in person. Both court and visitors may perform in person searches. Search fee: $5.00 per name. Court makes copy: $.50 per page; same fee for self serve. Required to search: name, years to search, DOB or SSN. Criminal records in books back to 1930; on computer back to 2000. Mail turnaround time 24-48 hours.
General Information: Public terminal has criminal back to 2000 and civil back to 1994. No sealed criminal or divorce records released. Fee to fax documents is $1.00 per page unless provided toll-free number. Certification fee: $4.00. Payee: County Clerk. Personal checks accepted. Prepayment and SASE required.

Surrogate's Court Courthouse, 290 Main St, PO Box 669, Schoharie, NY 12157; phone: 518-295-8387; fax: 518-295-8451; hours 9AM-5PM (EST). *Probate.*

Schoharie Town/Village Courts - *misdemeanor or civil records:* Blenheim Town- 518-827-6115; Broome Town- 518-827-5074; Carlisle Town- 518-234-3486; Cobleskill Town & Village- 518-234-7886; Conesville Town- 607-588-7211; Esperance Town- 518-875-6109; Esperance Village- 518-875-6109; Fulton Town- 518-827-6695; Gilboa Town- 607-588-7526; Jefferson Town- 607-652-2109; Middleburgh Town- 518-827-7433; Middleburgh Village- 518-827-5143; Richmondville Town- 518-294-8851; Schoharie Town & Village- 518-295-7879; Seward Town; Sharon Town- 518-284-3419; Summit Town- 518-287-1194; Wright Town- 518-872-9726.

Schuyler County

County Clerk Courthouse, 105 9th St, Unit 8, Watkins Glen, NY 14891; phone: 607-535-8133; hours 9AM-5PM (EST). *Felony, Civil.*
Note: Countywide search requests made to the county clerk are processed in the manner described below.

Civil Records: Access: Phone, mail, in person, online. Both court and visitors may perform in person searches. Search fee: $5.00 per name; a single name search is performed for free via telephone. Court makes copy: $.65 per page. Required to search: name, years to search. Civil cases indexed by defendant. Civil records are indexed in books; on computer back to 1987. Access to current/pending Supreme Court civil cases and some closed cases is at http://e.courts.state.ny.us/. Mail turnaround time 2-3 days.
Criminal Records: Access: Phone, mail, in person. Only the court performs in person searches; visitors may not. Search fee: $5.00 per name; a single name search is performed for free via telephone. Court makes copy: $.65 per page. Required to search: name, years to search, DOB. Criminal records are indexed in books; on computer back to 1987. Misdemeanors go back to 1971. Mail turnaround time 2-3 days.
General Information: No public access terminal. No sealed or youthful offender records released. No fax at this office. Certification fee: $5.00. This includes copy fee for first 4 pages, thereafter it is $1.00 per page, copies included. Payee: County Clerk. Personal checks accepted. Prepayment and SASE required.

Supreme & County Court Courthouse, 105 9th St, #38, Watkins Glen, NY 14891; criminal phone: 607-535-7015; civil phone: 607-535-7760; fax: 607-535-4918; hours 9AM-5PM (EST). *Felony, Civil.*
Note: Court-clerks direct record search requests to the OCA for a $52.00 statewide record check. For county only search requests (including free), see the County Clerk in separate listing. Online access to current cases is at http://e.courts.state.ny.us/.

Surrogate's Court County Courthouse, 105 9th St, Watkins Glen, NY 14891; phone: 607-535-7144; fax: 607-535-4918; hours 9AM-5PM (EST). *Probate.*

Schuyler Town/Village Courts - *misdemeanor or civil records:* Catharine Town- 607-594-2273; Cayuta Town- 607-594-2507; Dix Town- 607-535-5103; Hector Town- 607-546-5286; Montour Falls Village- 607-535-7362; Montour Town- 607-535-2467; Odessa Village- 607-594-2273; Orange Town- 607-962-7558; Reading Town; Tyrone Town; Watkins Glen Village- 607-535-9717.

Seneca County

County Clerk 1 DiPronio Dr, County Office Bldg, Attn: Seneca County Clerk, Waterloo, NY 13165-1396; phone: 315-539-1771; fax: 315-539-3789; hours 8:30AM-5PM (EST). *Felony, Civil.*
Note: Countywide search requests made to the county clerk are processed in the manner described below.

Civil Records: Access: Mail, in person, online. Both court and visitors may perform in person searches. Search fee: $10.00 per name. Court makes copy: $.65 per page. Self serve copy fee: $.40 per page. Required to search: name, years to search. Civil cases indexed by defendant. Civil records on computer since 3/1997; prior records in books. Access to current/pending Supreme court civil cases and some closed cases is at http://e.courts.state.ny.us. Mail turnaround time 1 week.
Criminal Records: Access: Mail, in person. Both court and visitors may perform in person searches. Search fee: $10.00 per name. Court makes copy: $.65 per page. Self serve copy fee: $.40 per page. Required to search: name, years to search, signed release. Criminal records on computer since 3/1997; prior records in books. Mail turnaround time 1 week.

General Information: Public use terminal available. No divorce records released. Will fax documents to local or toll free line. Certification fee: $5.00. Payee: Seneca County Clerk. Personal checks accepted. Prepayment and SASE required.

Supreme & County Court 48 W Williams St, Courthouse, Waterloo, NY 13165; phone: 315-539-7021; fax: 315-539-7929; hours 9AM-5PM (EST). *Felony, Civil.*

Note: Direct all search requests to the County Clerk office, see separate listing. Online access to current/pending Supreme Court civil cases is available at http://e.courts.state.ny.us/.

Surrogate's Court 48 W Williams St, Waterloo, NY 13165; phone: 315-539-7531; fax: 315-539-3267; hours 9AM-5PM (EST). *Probate.*

Seneca Town/Village Courts - *misdemeanor or civil records:* Covert Town- 607-387-3790; Fayette Town- 315-585-6282; Junius Town- 315-539-4667; Lodi Town- 607-582-7730; Ovid Town- 607-869-9845; Romulus Town- 607-869-9650; Seneca Falls Town- 315-568-9234; Tyre Town- 315-568-1221; Varick Town- 315-585-6018; Waterloo Town- 315-539-3213; Waterloo Village- 315-539-2512.

St. Lawrence County

Supreme & County Court 48 Court St, Canton, NY 13617-1169; phone: 315-379-2237 (county clerk); 315-379-2219 (Court Clerk); probate: 315-379-2217; fax: 315-379-2302; hours 8:30AM-4:30PM (Thurs til 7PM) (EST). *Felony, Civil.*

Note: Direct all search requests to the County Clerk office; information given here is for that County Clerk office.

Civil Records: Access: Fax, mail, in person, online. Both court and visitors may perform in person searches. Search fee: $5.00 per name. Court makes copy: $.65 per page. Required to search: name, years to search. Civil cases indexed by defendant, plaintiff. Civil records go back to 1986; on computer since 1990, prior in books. Access to current/pending Supreme Court civil cases is at http://e.courts.state.ny.us/. Mail turnaround time 2-3 days.
Criminal Records: Access: Fax, mail, in person. Both court and visitors may perform in person searches. Search fee: $5.00 per name. Court makes copy: $.65 per page; same fee for self serve. Required to search: name, years to search, DOB. Criminal records on computer since 1985, prior in books. Misdemeanor records are maintained by city, town and village courts. Mail turnaround time 2-3 days.
General Information: Public terminal has criminal back to 1985 and civil back to 1986. No sealed or divorce records released. Will fax documents $4.00 per document; no fee to toll-free numbers. Certification fee: $5.00. Payee: County Clerk. Personal checks accepted. Prepayment and SASE required.

Ogdensburg City Court 330 Ford St, Ogdensburg, NY 13669; phone: 315-393-3941; fax: 315-393-6839; hours 8AM-4PM (EST). *Misdemeanor, Civil Actions Under $15,000, Eviction, Small Claims.*
Civil Records: Access: Mail, in person. Only the court performs in person searches; visitors may not. No search fee. Court makes copy: $.50 per page. Required to search: name, years to search. Civil cases indexed by defendant. Civil records on computer since 1995; prior records in books. Mail turnaround time 1 week.
Criminal Records: Access: None. Search fee: A Certificate of Disposition is $6.00. Court makes copy: $.50 per page. Computerized records go back to 1992; archives back to 19th Century. The court does not permit access to county records unless a specific case file number given. Requesters must use the $52.00 OCA statewide search. Mail turnaround time 1 week.

General Information: No public access terminal. No youthful offender records released. Certification fee: $5.00. Payee: City Court. Business checks accepted. Prepayment and SASE required.

Surrogate's Court 48 Court St, Surrogate Bldg, Canton, NY 13617; phone: 315-379-2217/9427; fax: 315-379-2372; hours 9AM-5PM Sept-June; 8AM-4PM July-Aug (EST). *Probate.*

St Lawrence Town/Village Courts - *misdemeanor or civil records:* Brasher Town- 315-389-4223 x5; Canton Town- 315-379-9844; Canton Village- 315-379-9844; Clare Town- 315-386-3084; Clifton Town- 315-848-5522; Colton Town- 315-262-2380; De Peyster Town- 315-344-7259; DeKalb Town- 315-347-2119; Depeyster Town- 315-344-7259; Edwards Town- 315-562-8113; Fine Town- 315-848-3413; Fowler Town- 315-287-0045; Gouverneur Town- 315-287-4623; Gouverneur Village- 315-287-0850; Hammond Town- 315-324-5321; Hopkinton Town- 315-328-4187; Lawrence Town- 315-389-4487; Lisbon Town- 315-393-0489; Louisville Town- 315-764-1424; Macomb Town- 315-578-2212; Madrid Town- 315-322-5760; Massena Town & Village- 315-769-5431; Morristown Town- 315-375-4148; Norfolk Town- 315-384-4721; Oswegatchie Town- 315-344-2400; Parishville Town- 315-268-1722; Piercefield Town- 518-359-7544; Pierrepont Town- 315-379-0415; Pitcairn Town- 315-543-2111; Potsdam Town- 315-265-4318; Potsdam Village- 315-265-5890; Rossie Town- 315-324-5166; Russell Town- 315-347-4824; Stockholm Justice Court- 315-389-5171; Waddington Town- 315-388-5629.

Steuben County

Supreme & County Court 3 E Pulteney Sq - County Clerk, Bath, NY 14810; phone: 607-776-9631 x3203; fax: 607-664-2158; hours 8:30AM-5PM (EST). *Felony, Civil.*
Note: Direct all search requests to the County Clerk office; information given here is for that County Clerk office.

Civil Records: Access: Fax, mail, in person, online. Both court and visitors may perform in person searches. Search fee: $10.00 per name. Court makes copy: $.65 per page, minimum $1.30; same fee for self serve. Required to search: name, years to search. Civil cases indexed by defendant. Civil records on computer from 1960, in book from 1931, prior archived. Access to current/pending Supreme Court civil cases is at http://e.courts.state.ny.us/. Mail turnaround time 1 day.
Criminal Records: Access: Fax, mail, in person. Both court and visitors may perform in person searches. Search fee: $10.00 per name. Court makes copy: $.65 per page, minimum $1.30; same fee for self serve. Required to search: name, years to search, DOB, SSN. Criminal records on computer from 1984, in book from 1931, prior archived. Mail turnaround time 1 day.
General Information: Public terminal has only civil records back to 1960. No sealed, expunged, adoption, sex offense, juvenile or mental health records released. Will fax documents for $3.00 per doc plus $1.00 per page. Certification fee: $5.00. Payee: County Clerk. Personal checks accepted. Prepayment and SASE required.

Corning City Court 12 Civic Center Plaza, Corning, NY 14830-2884; phone: 607-936-4111; fax: 607-936-0519; hours 8AM-4PM (EST). *Misdemeanor, Civil Actions Under $15,000, Eviction, Small Claims.*
Civil Records: Access: Mail, in person. Only the court performs in person searches; visitors may not. Search fee: Fees subject to change; call for details. Court makes copy: $.65 per page; $1.30 minimum. Required to search: name, years to search. Civil cases indexed by defendant. Civil records on computer from 1986, prior in books. Note: Request must be in writing.

Criminal Records: Access: none. Court makes copy: $.65 per page; $1.30 minimum. Criminal records on computer from 1986, prior in books. The court refuses to permit access to court records unless specific case file given. Requesters are directed to OCA for $52.00 statewide search.
General Information: No public access terminal. No sealed or youthful offender records released. Will fax documents to local or toll free line. Certification fee: $5.00. Payee: Corning City Court. Prepayment and SASE required.

Hornell City Court PO Box 627 (82 Main St), Hornell, NY 14843-0627; phone: 607-324-7531; fax: 607-324-6325; hours 8AM-4PM (EST). *Misdemeanor, Civil Actions Under $15,000, Eviction, Small Claims.*

www.nycourts.gov/courts/7jd/hornell/index.shtml
Civil Records: Access: Fax, mail, in person. Only the court performs in person searches; visitors may not. No search fee. Court makes copy: $.65 per page. Required to search: name, years to search, DOB. Civil cases indexed by defendant, plaintiff; on computer from 1985, prior in books, folders and index cards go back 25 years.
Criminal Records: Access: None. Court makes copy: $.65 per page, minimum $1.30, maximum $30.00. Criminal records on computer from 1985, records go back 25 years. The court will not permit access to court records. The court directs requesters to OCA for $52.00 statewide search.
General Information: No public access terminal. No sealed or sexual offense records released. Will fax documents to a local or toll free line. Certification fee: $6.00. Payee: Hornell City Court. Only cashiers checks and money orders accepted. Prepayment required.

Surrogate's Court 3 E Pulteney Sq, Bath, NY 14810-1598; phone: 607-776-7126; fax: 607-776-4987; hours 9AM-5PM (EST). *Probate.*

Steuben Town/Village Courts - *misdemeanor or civil records:* Addison Town- 607-359-3615; Avoca Town Court Court- 607-566-2093; Bath Town & Village- 607-776-3192; Bradford Town- 607-583-4270; Cameron Town; Campbell Town- 607-527-8244; Canisteo Town; Caton Town- 607-524-6772; Cohocton Town; Corning Town- 607-936-9062; Dansville Town- 607-295-9917; Erwin Justice Court- 607-936-3122; Fremont Town- 607-324-0798; Greenwood Town- 607-225-4654 x3; Hammondsport Village- 607-569-2709; Hartsville Town- 607-698-2305; Hornby Town- 607-962-0683; Hornellsville Town- 607-295-7768; Howard Town- 607-566-2554; Jasper Town- 607-792-3338; Lindley Town- 607-523-8816; Prattsburgh Town- 607-522-3761; Pulteney Town; Rathbone Town; Savona Village; Thurston Town; Troupsburg Town- 607-525-6403; Tuscarora Town- 607-359-2360; Urbana Town- 607-569-3738; Wayland Town & Village- 585-728-3504; Wayne Town- 607-292-3450; West Union Town; Wheeler Town- 607-776-7208; Woodhull Town- 607-458-5178.

Suffolk County

Supreme & County Court - Main 310 Centre Dr, Attn: Court Actions, Riverhead, NY 11901; phone: 631-852-3793, 631-852-1462 county; criminal phone: 631-852-2016; civil phone: 631-852-3793; fax: 631-852-2004; hours 9AM-5PM (EST). *Felony, Civil.*

www.courts.state.ny.us/courts/10jd/suffolk/supreme.shtml

Civil Records: Access: Mail, in person, online. Both court and visitors may perform in person searches. Search fee: $5.00 per name. Fee is per 2 years searched. Court makes copy: $1.25 per page. Self serve copy fee: $.25 per page. Required to search: name, years to search. Civil cases indexed by defendant, plaintiff; on computer back to 4/84; prior in books. Access to civil actions is free at www.co.suffolk.ny.us/clerk/clerkapp/index.htm
Access to current/pending Supreme court civil

cases and some closed cases is at http://e.courts.state.ny.us/. Mail turnaround time 7-10 days.

Criminal Records: Access: Mail, in person. Both court and visitors may perform in person searches. Search fee: $52.00 statewide record search through OCA for 1985 to present; $5.00 per name per 2 years searched if prior to 1985. Court makes copy: $1.25 per page. Self serve copy fee: $.25 per page. Required to search: name, years to search, DOB. Criminal records on computer back to 1984. Note: Court usually restricts searcher's number of records pulled to 10 per day. Mail turnaround time 7-10 days.

General Information: Public terminal has criminal back to 1984 and civil back to 1985. No sealed or divorce records released. Certification fee: $5.00 per cert. Payee: County Clerk. Personal checks accepted. Prepayment and SASE required.

Supreme & County Court - Central Islip
400 Carleton Ave, Central Islip, NY 11722; phone: 631-853-5423; hours 9AM-5PM (EST). *Felony, Civil.*

www.courts.state.ny.us/courts/10jd/suffolk/index.shtml
Note: Records are at the Supreme Court in Riverhead only.

1st District Court - Criminal
400 Carleton Ave, Central Islip, NY 11722; phone: 631-853-5356/4562; hours 8:30AM-4:30PM (EST). *Misdemeanor.*

http://courts.state.ny.us/courts/10jd/suffolk/dist/

Criminal Records: Access: In person only. Only the court performs in person searches; visitors may not. Court makes copy: $.65 per page. Required to search: Name, DOB. Criminal records go back to 1961; on computer back to 3/2000. Court will pull record if docket number and proper identifiers are provided. Online access to active criminal court dates only listed by defendant or docket are free at http://e.courts.state.ny.us/crims; login as guest. Since court does not permit access to court records unless specific case file is given, name search requesters are directed to send requests to OCA for $52.00 statewide search. Note: Also, a Suffolk County only search is through the local Police Dept- 631-852-6015.

General Information: No public access terminal. No sealed or youthful offender records released. Certification fee: $6.00 per doc. Payee: District Court Clerk. Personal checks accepted with proper ID. Prepayment required.

2nd District Court
375 Commack Rd, Deer Park, NY 11702; phone: 631-854-1950; hours 9AM-1PM, 2-5PM (EST). *Minor Misdemeanors, Civil Actions Under $15,000, Eviction, Small Claims.*

http://courts.state.ny.us/courts/10jd/suffolk/
Note: Very low misdemeanor cases are heard here. Also handles Babylon Town ordinance cases. Use your paid receipt for a civil search from any Suffolk District Court to search at any other Suffolk District courts for free.

Civil Records: Access: Mail, in person. Only the court performs in person searches; visitors may not. Search fee: $16.00 per name. Court makes copy: $.65 per page. Required to search: name, years to search. Civil cases indexed by plaintiff. Civil records on computer from 1989, prior in books, on cards. Mail turnaround time 2 weeks.

Criminal Records: Access: In person. Only the court performs in person searches; visitors may not. Search fee: $6.00 for Certificate of Disposition only. Court makes copy: $.65 per page. Required to search: name, years to search. Criminal records on computer from 1989, prior in books, on cards. Online access to criminal court dates only listed by defendant are free at http://e.courts.state.ny.us/crims. Court performs $6.00 Certificate of Disposition only, but does not recommend it due to their very limited number of case files. Note: Court does not permit access to

court records unless specific case file given. Requesters are to direct name search requests to OCA for $52.00 statewide search. Mail turnaround time 1 week.

General Information: No public access terminal. No sealed or youthful offender records released. Certification fee: $6.00 per doc. Payee: Clerk of Court. Only cashiers checks and money orders accepted. Prepayment and SASE required.

3rd District Court
1850 New York Ave, Huntington Station, NY 11746; phone: 631-854-4545; fax: 631-854-4549; hours 9AM-1PM, 2-4:30PM (EST). *Misdemeanor, Civil Actions Under $15,000, Eviction, Small Claims.*

http://courts.state.ny.us/courts/10jd/suffolk/
Note: Use your paid receipt for a civil search from any Suffolk District Court to search at any other Suffolk District courts for free.

Civil Records: Access: Mail, in person. Only the court performs in person searches; visitors may not. Search fee: $16.00 per name. Court makes copy: $.65 per page. Required to search: name, years to search. Civil cases indexed by defendant. Civil records on computer from 1988, prior in books, on microfilm. Note: This court suggests a wider civil record search be performed at the County Clerk office. This court's civil records are indexed by key letters "HU"

Criminal Records: Access: In person only. Only the court performs in person searches; visitors may not. Search fee: $6.00 for Certificate of Disposition only. Court makes copy: $.65 per page. Required to search: name, years to search, DOB, SSN, signed release. Criminal records on computer from 1988, prior in books, on microfilm. Only minor misdemeanor records located here. Direct search requests to OCA for the $52.00 statewide record search for 1985 to present. For older records, you may search here in person; fees dependent on scope of search.

General Information: No public access terminal. No sealed records released. Certification fee: $6.00 per doc. Payee: Clerk of the Court. Business and personal checks accepted. Prepayment required.

4th District Court
North County Complex Bldg C158, Hauppauge, NY 11787; criminal phone: 631-853-5357; civil phone: 631-853-5400; fax: 631-853-5951; hours 9AM-5PM (EST). *Misdemeanor, Civil Actions Under $15,000, Eviction, Small Claims.*

http://courts.state.ny.us/courts/10jd/suffolk/
Note: Use your paid receipt for a civil search from any Suffolk District Court to search at any other Suffolk District courts for free.

Civil Records: Access: Mail, in person. Only the court performs in person searches; visitors may not. Search fee: $16.00 per name. Court makes copy: $.65 per page. Required to search: name, years to search. Civil cases indexed by defendant, plaintiff; on computer from 1987, prior in books.

Criminal Records: Access: None. Only the court performs in person searches; visitors may not. Court makes copy: $.65 per page. Required to search: name, years to search, DOB. Criminal records on computer from 1987, prior in books. Online access to criminal court dates only listed by defendant are free at http://e.courts.state.ny.us/crims. Note: All name searches forwarded to OCA for $52.00 statewide search unless specific docket number given. Mail turnaround time 1-2 weeks.

General Information: No public access terminal. No sealed records released. Will not fax documents. Certification fee: $6.00. Payee: Clerk of Court. Personal checks accepted. Prepayment and SASE required.

6th District Court
150 W Main St, Patchogue, NY 11772; phone: 631-854-1440; fax: 631-854-1444; hours 9AM-1PM, 2-4:30PM (EST). *Misdemeanor, Civil Actions Under $15,000, Eviction, Small Claims.*

http://courts.state.ny.us/courts/10jd/suffolk/

Note: Use your paid receipt for a civil search from any Suffolk District Court to search at any other Suffolk District courts for free. Misdemeanor records here cover only Brookhaven Town Ordinance violations.

Civil Records: Access: Mail, in person. Both court and visitors may perform in person searches. Search fee: $16.00 per name. Court makes copy: $.65 per page. Required to search: name, years to search. Civil records on computer from 1989, prior on microfilm.

Criminal Records: Access: Mail, in person. Both court and visitors may perform in person searches. Search fee: $6.00 for Certificate of Disposition only. Court makes copy: $.65 per page. Criminal records on computer from 1992, prior on microfilm. Online access to criminal court dates only listed by defendant are free at http://e.courts.state.ny.us/crims. All name searches forwarded to OCA for $52.00 statewide search unless specific docket number given. Mail turnaround time 3 days.

General Information: Public use terminal available. (Currently adding terminals.) No sealed or youthful offender records released. Will fax back documents no fee. Certification fee: $6.00 per doc includes copies. Payee: Clerk of Court. Personal checks accepted, no credit cards. Prepayment and SASE required.

Suffolk District Courts 1 & 5 - Civil
3105-1 Veterans Memorial Hwy, Ronkonkoma, NY 11779-7614; phone: 631-854-9676 (1st); 631-854-9673 (5th); fax: 631-854-9681; hours 9AM-1PM, 2-5PM (EST). *Civil Actions Under $15,000, Eviction, Small Claims.*

http://courts.state.ny.us/courts/10jd/suffolk/
Note: Use your paid receipt for a civil search from any Suffolk District Court to search at any other Suffolk District courts for free.

Civil Records: Access: Mail, in person. Only the court performs in person searches; visitors may not. Search fee: $16.00 per name. Court makes copy: $1.30 for one page, $.65 each for 2 or more pages. Required to search: name, years to search. Civil cases indexed by defendant. Civil records on computer back to 1989, prior in books back to 1969. Mail turnaround time 2 weeks.

General Information: Public terminal has only civil records back to 1989. No sealed or youthful offender records released. Will fax documents for no fee. Certification fee: $6.00 per page includes copy fee. Payee: Clerk of the Court. Cash, checks and money orders accepted. Prepayment and SASE required.

Surrogate's Court
320 Centre Dr, Riverhead, NY 11901; phone: 631-852-1745; fax: 631-852-1414; hours 9AM-4:30PM (EST). *Probate.*

Suffolk Town/Village Courts - *misdemeanor or civil records:* Asharoken Village- 631-261-8677; Belle Terre Village; East Hampton Town- 631-324-4134; Greenport Village- 631-477-0248; Head of the Harbor Village- 631-584-5550; Islandia Village- 631-348-0470; Lake Grove Justice Court- 631-585-2008; Lloyd Harbor Village; Nissequogue Village- 631-862-8576; Ocean Beach Village- 631-583-0104; Old Field Village- 631-941-9416; Patchogue Village- 631-475-2753; Poquott Village- 631-331-0402; Port Jefferson Village- 631-802-2120; Quogue Village Justice Court- 631-653-9400; Riverhead Justice Court- 631-727-3200; Shelter Island Town- 631-749-8989; Shoreham Village- 631-821-0680; Southampton Town Court- 631-283-6017; Southampton Village- 631-204-2140; Southold Town- 631-765-1852; West Hampton Dunes Village- 631-288-6571; Westhampton Beach Village- 631-288-1654.

Sullivan County

County Clerk 100 North St, Sullivan Gov't Ctr, Monticello, NY 12701; phone: 845-794-3000 x3012; hours 9AM-5PM (EST). *Felony, Civil.*
Note: Countywide search requests made to the county clerk are processed in the manner described below.

Civil Records: Access: Mail, in person, online. Both court and visitors may perform in person searches. Search fee: $5.00 per name. Court makes copy: $1.00 per page; $.50 if off computer. Self serve copy fee: $.25 per page. Required to search: name, years to search. Civil cases indexed by plaintiff. Civil records on computer from 1990, prior in books from 1800s. Access to current/pending Supreme Court civil cases is at http://e.courts.state.ny.us/. Note: This office searches off the computer only. Mail turnaround time 1-2 weeks.
Criminal Records: Access: In person only. Only the court performs in person searches; visitors may not. No search fee. A Certificate of Disposition is $6.00. Court makes copy: $1.00 per page; $.50 if off computer. Self serve copy fee: $.25 per page. Required to search: name, years to search, DOB. Criminal records go back to 1967; on computer back to 4/1990. For mail requests, the County-Court directs criminal search requests to the OCA for a $52.00 statewide record check. Note: For in person requests, first name search the County Clerk index for case numbers. To retrieve case records, take case numbers to the Supreme & County Court (see separate listing) County-Court clerk who will pull case records for you.
General Information: Public terminal has only civil records back to 1990. No sealed, expunged, adoption, sex offense, juvenile or mental health records released. Certification fee: $5.20 if certification of prepared copy. Payee: County Clerk for civil; to Court Clerk for criminal. Personal checks accepted. Prepayment required.

Supreme & County Court County Courthouse, 414 Broadway, Monticello, NY 12701; phone: 845-794-4066; probate phone: 845-794-3000 x3450; hours 9AM-5PM (EST). *Felony, Civil, Misdemeanor.*
Note: Civil records and criminal record index are maintained at County Clerk's office, see separate listing. However, actual felony records are located here at County-Court Clerk office.
Civil Records: Access: Mail, in person, online. Both court and visitors may perform in person searches. Search fee: $16.00 per case. Court makes copy: $.65 per page, maximum of $40.00 per file. Required to search: name, years to search. Civil cases indexed by plaintiff. Civil records on computer from 1990, prior in books from 1800s. Access to current/pending Supreme Court civil cases is at http://e.courts.state.ny.us/. Note: Perform civil searches at the Court Clerk office.
Criminal Records: Access: In person only. Visitors must perform in person searches themselves. Court makes copy: $.65 per page, maximum of $40.00 per file. Required to search: name, years to search, DOB. Criminal records go back to 1967; on computer back to 4/1990. For mail requests, the County-Court directs criminal search requests to the OCA for a $52.00 statewide record check. For in person searches, first find the case index number by performing a search at the County Clerk office (see separate entry), then ask the County-Court clerk office (address above) for the case file.
General Information: Public terminal goes back to 4/1990. No sealed, expunged, adoption, sex offense, juvenile or mental health records released. Certification fee: $5.20 per 8 pages. Payee: County Clerk for civil; to Court Clerk for criminal. Personal checks accepted. Prepayment required.

Surrogate's Court County Government Ctr, 100 North St, Monticello, NY 12701; phone: 845-794-3000 X3450/3451; fax: 845-794-0310; hours 9AM-5PM may be closed for lunch 12;00-1PM (EST). *Probate.*

Sullivan Town/Village Courts - *misdemeanor or civil records:* Bethel Town- 845-583-7420; Bloomingburg Justice Court- 845-733-1400; Callicoon Town- 845-482-5390 x301; Cochecton Town; Delaware Justice Court- 845-887-5849; Fallsburg Town- 845-434-4574; Forestburgh Town- 845-794-0611 x 20; Fremont Town- 845-687-4883; Highland Town- 845-557-8132; Liberty Justice Court- 845-292-0290; Liberty Town- 845-292-6980; Lumberland Town- 845-858-8548; Mamakating Town; Monticello Village- 845-794-1222; Neversink Town- 845-985-7685 x311; Rockland Town- 607-498-4320; Thompson Town- 845-794-7130; Tusten Town- 845-252-3310 x13.

Tioga County

Court Clerk PO Box 307, 16 Court St, Owego, NY 13827; phone: 607-687-8660; fax: 607-687-8686; hours 9AM-5PM (EST). *Civil, Felony.*
Note: Countywide civil record search requests made to the county clerk are processed in the manner described below. County clerk has only a paper index list of felony proceedings. Felony records are managed by the County-Court Clerk, see separate listing.

Civil Records: Access: In person, online. Visitors must perform in person searches themselves. Court makes copy: $.50 per page. Self serve copy fee: $.25 per page. Required to search: name, years to search. Civil cases indexed by defendant. Civil records in books. Visitor can search in County Clerk's Office. Access to current/pending Supreme Court civil cases is at http://e.courts.state.ny.us/. Mail turnaround time varies.
General Information: Public terminal has only civil records back to 9/2003. No sealed, expunged, adoption, sex offense, juvenile or mental health records released. Will not fax documents. Certification fee: $5.00 per doc includes copy fee. Payee: County Clerk. Personal checks accepted. Prepayment and SASE required.

Supreme & County Court PO Box 307, 16 Court St, Owego, NY 13827; phone: 607-687-0544; fax: 607-687-3240; hours 8:30AM-4:30PM (EST). *Felony.*
Note: For civil records, see County Clerk. Also, access to current/pending Supreme Court civil cases is available at http://e.courts.state.ny.us/.
Criminal Records: Access: In person only. Both court and visitors may perform in person searches. No search fee if in person search. Court makes copy: $.50 per page. Required to search: name, years to search, DOB. Criminal records in books since 1970s; earlier records stored off-site. Note: Felony records are managed by the County-Court Clerk who directs search requests to OCA for $52.00 statewide search. You may also search County-court clerk felony files in person; details below.
General Information: No public access terminal. No sealed, expunged, sex offense, or juvenile records released. Certification fee: $5.00. Payee: County Clerk. Personal checks accepted. Prepayment required.

Surrogate's Court PO Box 10, 20 Court St, Owego, NY 13827; phone: 607-687-1303; fax: 607-687-3240; hours 9AM-5PM (EST). *Probate.*
Note: Court is located in the County Court Annex Bldg.

Tioga Town/Village Courts - *misdemeanor or civil records:* Barton Town- 607-565-8609; Berkshire Town; Candor Town & Village- 607-659-3175; Newark Valley Town- 607-642-8746; Nichols Town- 607-642-5278; Owego Town- 607-687-2822; Owego Village- 607-687-2236; Richford Town; Spencer Town; Spencer Village- 607-589-4310; Tioga Town- 607-687-9577; Waverly Village- 607-565-4771.

Tompkins County

Supreme & County Court Tomkins County Clerk, 320 N Tioga St, Ithaca, NY 14850; phone: 607-274-5431 (County Clerk); 607-272-0466 (Count Clerks); criminal phone: 607-274-5453; civil phone: 607-274-5453; fax: 607-274-5445; hours 9AM-5PM (Court Clerks have Summer hours-8:30AM-4:30PM) (EST). *Felony, Civil.*
Note: Direct all search requests to the County Clerk office; information given here is for that County Clerk office.
Civil Records: Access: Fax, mail, in person, online. Both court and visitors may perform in person searches. Search fee: $5.00 per name if court does search. Fee is per 2 years searched. Court makes copy: $.65 per page, $1.30 minimum; same fee for self serve. Required to search: name, years to search. Civil cases indexed by defendant, plaintiff. Civil records in books. Access to current/pending Supreme Court civil cases is at http://e.courts.state.ny.us/. Note: Before faxing, you must first be approved with a credit account. Mail turnaround time 1-2 days.
Criminal Records: Access: Fax, mail, in person. Only the court performs in person searches; visitors may not. Search fee: $5.00 per name if court does search. Fee is per 2 years searched. Court makes copy: $.65 per page, $1.30 minimum; same fee for self serve. Required to search: name, years to search, signed release; also helpful: DOB, SSN. Felony records in books. Note: Before faxing, you must first be approved with a credit account. Mail turnaround time 1-2 days.
General Information: Public terminal has only civil records back to 7/7/1999. No sealed, expunged, adoption, sex offense, juvenile or mental health records released. Will fax documents to local or toll free line. Certification fee: $5.00 per document. Payee: County Clerk. Personal checks accepted. Prepayment and SASE required.

Ithaca City Court 118 E Clinton St, Ithaca, NY 14850; phone: 607-273-2263; fax: 607-277-3702; hours 8AM-4PM (EST). *Misdemeanor, Civil Actions Under $15,000, Eviction, Small Claims.*
www.nycourts.gov/ithaca/city
Civil Records: Access: Fax, mail, in person. Only the court performs in person searches; visitors may not. Search fee: $16.00 per name. For records prior to 1996, fee is $5.00 per each 2 year period searched. Court makes copy: $1.30 for 1st page; $.65 per add'l page. Required to search: name, years to search. Civil cases indexed by defendant. Civil records on computer since 1996; prior records in books.
Criminal Records: Access: None. Court makes copy: $1.30 for 1st page; $.65 per add'l page. Criminal records on computer from 1990, prior in books. The court refuses to permit access to court records unless specific case file given. State policy requires requests be send to OCA for $52.00 statewide search.
General Information: No public access terminal. No sealed, youthful offender records released. Will fax documents to local or toll free line. Certification fee: $5.00. Payee: City Court. Only cashiers checks and money orders accepted. Prepayment and SASE required.

Surrogate's Court P O Box 70, 320 N Tioga St, Ithaca, NY 14851; phone: 607-277-0622; fax: 607-256-2572; hours 9AM-5PM, Reg Hrs, Summer 8;30AM-4;30PM July 5-Sept 5 (EST). *Probate.*

Tompkins Town/Village Courts - *misdemeanor or civil records:* Caroline Town- 607-539-7796; Cayuga Heights Village- 607-257-3944; Danby Town- 607-277-4788; Dryden Town- 607-844-8621; Enfield Town- 607-272-6490; Freeville Village- 607-844-8470; Groton Town- 607-898-5273; Ithaca Town- 607-273-1721; Lansing Town- 607-533-4776; Newfield Town- 607-564-9571; Ulysses Town- 607-387-5411.

Ulster County

County Clerk PO Box 1800, 244 Fair St, Kingston, NY 12401; phone: 845-340-3288 (Clerk); 845-340-3000 (Switchboard); fax: 845-340-3299; hours 9AM-4:45PM (EST). *Felony, Civil.*

www.co.ulster.ny.us

Note: Countywide search requests made to the County Clerk are processed in the manner described below.

Civil Records: Access: Phone, mail, in person. Both court and visitors may perform in person searches. Search fee: $5.00 per name per 2 years searched; county clerk may perform 1 search from 1987 forward for free over phone. Court makes copy: $1.25 per page, minimum $5.00. Self serve copy fee: $.65 per page, 2 page minimum. Required to search: name, years to search. Civil cases indexed by defendant, plaintiff; on computer from 1987, in books from 1920s, prior archived. Access to current Supreme court cases is at https://iapps.courts.state.ny.us/caseTrac/jsp/ecourt.htm Mail turnaround time 5 days.

Criminal Records: Access: Phone, mail, in person. Both court and visitors may perform in person searches. Search fee: $5.00 per name. Fee is per 2 years searched. Court makes copy: $1.25 per page, minimum $5.00. Self serve copy fee: $.65 per page, 2 page minimum. Required to search: name, years to search. Criminal records on computer from 1987, in books from 1920s, prior archived. Mail turnaround time 5 days.

General Information: Public terminal goes back to 1987. No sealed, expunged, adoption, sex offense, juvenile or mental health records released. Certification fee: $5.00. Payee: Ulster County Clerk. Personal checks accepted. Prepayment required.

Supreme & County Court 285 Wall St, Kingston, NY 12401; phone: 845-340-3377; hours 9AM-5PM (EST). *Felony, Civil.*

Note: The Court Clerk directs record search requests to the County Clerk, see separate listing. Online access to current Supreme court cases are available at http://e.courts.state.ny.us/.

Kingston City Court One Garraghan Dr, Kingston, NY 12401; phone: 845-338-2974; hours 8:30AM-4PM (EST). *Misdemeanor, Civil Actions Under $15,000, Eviction, Small Claims.*

Civil Records: Access: Mail, in person. Only the court performs in person searches; visitors may not. Search fee: $5.00 per name per 2 years. If pre-1995, fee is $16.00. Court makes copy: $1.00 per page. Required to search: name, years to search. Civil cases indexed by plaintiff. Civil records on computer from 1995. Overall records go back to 1983. Request must be in writing. Mail turnaround time 2 weeks.

Criminal Records: Access: Mail. Only the court performs in person searches; visitors may not. Court makes copy: $1.00 per page. Required to search: Name, years to search, DOB. Criminal records on computer from 1995. Overall records go back to 1983. The court does not permit access to court records unless specific case file given. Requesters are directed to send requests to OCA for $52.00 statewide search. Mail turnaround time 2 weeks.

General Information: No public access terminal. No sealed or youthful offender records released. Will not fax documents. Certification fee: $5.00. Payee: City Court. No personal checks accepted. Prepayment and SASE required.

Surrogate's Court PO Box 1800, 240 Fair St, Kingston, NY 12402; phone: 845-340-3348; fax: 845-340-3352; hours 9AM-5PM (EST). *Probate.*

Ulster Town/Village Courts - *misdemeanor or civil records:* Crawford Town; Denning Town- 845-985-2411; Ellenville Village- 845-647-7080; Esopus Town- 845-331-5776; Gardiner Town- 845-255-9675x0017; Hardenburgh Town- 845-586-3135; Hurley Town- 845-331-9229; Kingston Town- 845-336-8853; Lloyd Town- 845-691-7544; Marbletown Town- 845-687-4328; Marlborough Town- 845-795-5100; New Paltz Town- 845-255-0100; Olive Town- 845-657-2320; Plattekill Town- 845-883-5805; Rochester Town- 845-626-2522; Rosendale Town- 845-658-3696; Saugerties Town- 845-246-9989, 246-2800; Saugerties Village- 845-246-3958, 246-2321; Shandaken Town- 845-688-5005; Shawangunk Town- 845-895-2611; Ulster Town- 845-382-1737; Wawarsing Town- 845-647-6560; Woodstock Town- 845-679-6345.

Warren County

County Clerk 1340 State Route 9, Attn: County Clerk, Lake George, NY 12845; phone: 518-761-6426; fax: 518-761-6551; hours 9AM-5PM (EST). *Civil, Felony.*

Note: Countywide civil record search requests made to the county clerk are processed in the manner described below.

Civil Records: Access: Mail, in person, online. Both court and visitors may perform in person searches. Search fee: $5.00 per name for each 2 years. Court makes copy: $.65 per page. Required to search: name, years to search. Civil cases indexed by plaintiff. Civil records index on computer from 1917 to present. Access to current/pending Supreme Court civil cases is at http://e.courts.state.ny.us.

Criminal Records: Access: In person only. Both court and visitors may perform in person searches. No search fee. Court makes copy: $.65 per page. Required to search: name, years to search, DOB. Criminal records not on computer, on index from 1929. The Court clerk office will not do Certificate of Conviction reports. They may direct you to the sheriff's office for record searches, but first call sheriff's office at 518-743-2500. Note: First, name search the County Clerk index of dispositions for case numbers. To retrieve case records, take case numbers to the Supreme & County Court (see separate listing) County-Court clerk who will pull cases records for you. Mail turnaround time 2-5 days.

General Information: Public terminal has only civil records back to 1900s. No adoption, juvenile or mental health records released. Certification fee: $5.00 for 1st four pages, $1.25 each add'l page. Payee: Warren County Clerk. Personal checks accepted. Prepayment and SASE required.

Supreme & County Court 1340 State Rte 9, Lake George, NY 12845; phone: 518-761-6430/6431; hours 9AM-4:30 (EST). *Felony.*

Note: Direct civil searches to County Clerk only, see separate entry. Also, a criminal record disposition index is maintained at County Clerk's office. However, actual felony records are located here at Supreme & County Court County-Court Clerk office.

Criminal Records: Access: Mail, in person. Both court and visitors may perform in person searches. No search fee. Court makes copy: $.50 per page. Required to search: name, years to search, DOB, SSN, signed release. Criminal records on computer from 1986, prior on index from 1929. For mail requests, the County-Court directs criminal search requests to the OCA for a $52.00 statewide record check. Note: For in person requests, first name search the County Clerk index for case numbers. To retrieve case records, take case numbers to the Supreme & County Court (see separate listing) County-Court clerk who will pull cases records for you. Mail turnaround time same day.

General Information: Public terminal has only criminal records back to 1987. (Terminal located in county clerk office.) No adoption, juvenile or mental health records released. Certification fee: $5.00 for 1st 4 pages, $1.25 each add'l. Payee: Warren County Clerk. Personal checks accepted. Prepayment and SASE required.

Glens Falls City Court 42 Ridge St, Glens Falls, NY 12801; phone: 518-798-4714; fax: 518-798-0137; hours 8:30AM-4:30PM (EST). *Misdemeanor, Civil Actions Under $15,000, Eviction, Small Claims.*

Civil Records: Access: None. Only the court performs in person searches; visitors may not. Court makes copy: $.65 per page; $1.30 minimum. Required to search: name, years to search. Civil cases indexed by defendant, plaintiff. Civil records go back to 1975; on computer from 1987, prior on microfilm. This court will only provide record is a case number is provided. Because judgment releases are not always filed with this court, the court will not name search. This court will refer you to the County Clerk for civil searches. Mail turnaround time 24 hours.

Criminal Records: Access: None. Court makes copy: $.65 per page; $1.30 minimum. Criminal records go back to the late 1960's; on computer from 1990, prior on microfilm. The court does not permit access to court records unless specific case file given. Requesters are directed to OCA for $52.00 statewide search.

General Information: No public access terminal. No sealed records released. Will fax documents to local or toll free line. Certification fee: $6.00 per document. Payee: City Court. Only cashiers checks and money orders accepted. Prepayment required.

Surrogate's Court 1340 State Rte 9, County Municipal Ctr, Lake George, NY 12845; phone: 518-761-6514/6515/6512; fax: 518-761-6511; hours 9AM-5PM (EST). *Probate.*

Note: When faxing, it may be necessary to fax to extension 6511.

Warren Town/Village Courts - *misdemeanor or civil records:* Bolton Town- 518-644-2202; Chester Justice Ciurt- 518-494-3133; Hague Town- 518-543-6161; Horicon Town- 518-494-7958; Johnsburg Town- 518-251-3011; Lake George Town- 518-668-5420; Lake Luzerne Town- 518-696-4294; Queensbury Town- 518-745-5571; Stony Creek Town- 518-696-3575; Thurman Town- 518-623-9660; Warrensburg Town- 518-623-9776.

Washington County

County Clerk 383 Broadway, Bldg A, Fort Edward, NY 12828; phone: 518-746-2170; fax: 518-746-2166; hours 8:30AM-4:30PM (EST). *Civil.*

Note: For felony records see the County-Court clerk at the Supreme and County Court in separate listing.

Civil Records: Access: Mail, in person, online. Visitors must perform in person searches themselves. No search fee. Generally, court will answer mailed civil records requests but you must at least provide year to search. Court makes copy: $1.00 per page. Self serve copy fee: $.50 per page. Required to search: name, years to search. Civil cases indexed by defendant. Civil records on books from 1800s. Access to current/pending Supreme Court civil cases and some closed cases are at http://e.courts.state.ny.us/. Mail turnaround time 1-2 days.

General Information: Public terminal has only civil records. No sealed or youthful offender records released. Will not fax documents. Certification fee: $5.00 per doc. Payee: County Clerk. Business checks accepted. Prepayment and SASE required.

Supreme & County Court 383 Broadway, Fort Edward, NY 12828; criminal phone: 518-746-2521; civil phone: 518-746-2520; fax: 518-746-5219; hours 8:30AM-4:30PM (EST). *Felony, Civil.*

Civil Records: Access: In person, online. Direct civil record search requests to the County Clerk, see separate listing. Access to current/pending Supreme Court civil cases and some closed cases is at http://e.courts.state.ny.us/.

Criminal Records: Access: In person only. Visitors must perform in person searches themselves. No search fee if you search; $5.00 for Certificate of Disposition. Court makes copy: $1.00 per page. Required to search: name, years to search. Criminal records on books from 1800s, on computer back to late 1989. Note: All criminal record name search requests are directed to the OCA for the $52.00 statewide record search.

General Information: Public terminal has only criminal records back to late 1989. No sealed or youthful offender records released. Certification fee: none at this court office. Payee: County Clerk. Business checks accepted at county clerk office. Prepayment required.

Surrogate's Court 383 Broadway, Fort Edward, NY 12828; phone: 518-746-2546; fax: 518-746-2547; hours 8:30AM-4:30PM (EST). *Probate.*

Washington Town/Village Courts – *misdemeanor or civil records:* Argyle Town- 518-638-8681; Cambridge Town- 518-677-2444; Cambridge Village- 518-677-2414; Dresden Town- 518-499-2040; Easton Town- 518-692-0027; Ft Ann Town- 518-639-8929; Ft Edward Town & Village- 518-747-2252; Granville Town- 518-642-9243; Granville Village- 518-642-9386; Greenwich Town & Village- 518-692-7611; Hampton Town- 518-282-9830; Hartford Town- 518-632-5255; Hebron Town- 518-854-9300; Hudson Falls Village- 518-747-3292; Jackson Town- 518-677-8896; Kingsbury Town- 518-747-2188; Putnam Town- 518-547-8317; Salem Town & Village- 518-854-9215; White Creek Town- 518-677-8545; Whitehall Town- 518-499-0772; Whitehall Village- 518-499-0772.

Wayne County

Supreme & County Court 9 Pearl St, PO Box 608, Lyons, NY 14489-0608; phone: 315-946-7470; probate phone: 315-946-5430; fax: 315-946-5978; 9AM-5PM *Felony, Civil, Eviction, Small Claims.*
Note: Direct all search requests to the County Clerk office; information given here is for that County Clerk office.
Civil Records: Access: Phone, fax, mail, in person, email, online. Both court and visitors may perform in person searches. Search fee: $5.00 per name per every 2 years. Court makes copy: $.65 per page; $1.30 minimum. Self serve copy fee: $.25 per page. Required to search: name, years to search. Civil cases indexed by defendant, plaintiff; on computer back to 1985, prior in books. Access to current/pending Supreme Court civil cases is at http://e.courts.state.ny.us/. Mail turnaround time 5-7 days.
Criminal Records: Access: Fax, mail, in person. Both court and visitors may perform in person searches. Search fee: $5.00 per name uncertified back to 1979. $5.00 per name for every 2 years certified search. Court makes copy: $.65 per page; $1.30 minimum. Self serve copy fee: $.25 per page. Required to search: name, years to search, DOB; also helpful: gender. Criminal records on computer back to 1979. Mail turnaround time 5-7 days.
General Information: Public terminal has criminal back to 1979 and civil back to 1985. No matrimonial records released. Fees to fax documents: long distance within Wayne County $2.00 1st page, $1.00 each add'l page; long distance outside Wayne County $3.00 1st page, $1.00 each add'l page; no fax charge for 800 number. Certification fee: $5.00 up to 4 pages, $1.25 each add'l page includes copy fee. Payee: County Clerk. Personal checks accepted. Prepayment required. SASE requested.

Surrogate's Court 54 Broad St, #106, Hall of Justice, Lyons, NY 14489; phone: 315-946-5430; fax: 315-946-5433; hours 9AM-5PM *Probate.*

Wayne Town/Village Courts - *misdemeanor or civil records:* Arcadia Town- 315-331-8020; Butler Town- 315-594-2719; Galen Town- 315-923-9375; Huron Town- 315-594-6511; Lyons Town- 315-946-4076; Lyons Village- 315-946-4565; Macedon Town- 315-986-5932; Macedon Village- 315-986-1597; Marion Town- 315-926-4461; Newark Village- 315-331-5139; Ontario Justice Court- 315-524-6511 x7; Palmyra Town- 315-597-5431; Rose Town- 315-587-4418; Savannah Town- 315-365-2811; Sodus Point Village- 315-483-9660; Sodus Town- 315-483-6807; Walworth Town; Williamson Town- 315-589-8250; Wolcott Town- 315-594-8257; Wolcott Village- 315-594-6437.

Westchester County

County Clerk 110 Dr Martin L King Blvd, Rm 330, White Plains, NY 10601; phone: 914-995-3070; fax: 914-995-3172; hours 8AM-5:30PM (EST). *Felony, Civil.*
www.westchesterclerk.com
Note: Countywide search requests made to the County Clerk are processed in the manner described below.
Civil Records: Access: Mail, in person, online. Both court and visitors may perform in person searches. Search fee: $5.00 per name per 2 years. Court makes copy: $.65 per page. Self serve copy fee: $.65 per page. Required to search: name, years to search. Civil cases indexed by defendant, plaintiff; on computer from 1986, prior in books from 1847. Access to current/pending Supreme court civil cases and some closed cases is at https://iapps.courts.state.ny.us/caseTrac/jsp/ecourt.htm Also, access judgments on the county clerk database search site at http://ccpv.westchesterclerk.com. Search is free, but registration and fees for images. Mail turnaround time 1 week.
Criminal Records: Access: Mail, in person, online. Both court and visitors may perform in person searches. Search fee: $5.00 per name per 2 years. Court makes copy: $.65 per page. Self serve copy fee: $.65 per page. Required to search: name, years to search. Criminal records on computer from 1986, prior in books from 1847. Access criminal records on the county clerk database search site at http://ccpv.westchesterclerk.com. Search if free, but registration and fees for images. Mail turnaround time 1 week.
General Information: Public terminal goes back to 1986. No sealed, expunged, adoption, sex offense, juvenile or mental health records released. Will not fax documents. Certification fee: $5.00 per doc. Payee: County Clerk. Personal checks accepted. Prepayment and SASE required.

Supreme & County Court 111 Dr Martin L King Blvd, Rm 803, White Plains, NY 10601; criminal phone: 914-824-5400; civil phone: 914-9824-5300; hours 9AM-5PM (EST). *Felony, Civil.*
www.westchesterclerk.com and www.courts.state.ny.us/courts/9jd/Westchester/supremecounty.shtml
Note: Direct search requests to the County Clerk, see separate listing, otherwise requests are directed to the OCA for the $52.00 statewide record search.

Mt Vernon City Court Ronald Blackwood Bldg, 2 Roosevelt Square, 2nd Fl, Mt Vernon, NY 10550-2019; phone: 914-665-2400; criminal phone: 914-665-2409; fax: 914-699-1230; hours 8:30AM-5PM (payments to 4PM only) (EST). *Misdemeanor, Civil Actions Under $15,000, Eviction, Small Claims.*
Note: Small claims: 665-2404; Landlord/Tenant: 665-2402; Traffic: 665-2405.
Civil Records: Access: Mail, in person. Only the court performs in person searches; visitors may not. No search fee. Court makes copy: $1.30 1st page, $.65 each add'l page. Required to search: name, years to search; also helpful: address. Civil cases indexed by defendant, plaintiff; on computer since 1986, prior in books. Mail turnaround time 1 week.
Criminal Records: Access: In person only. Only the court performs in person searches; visitors may not. Court makes copy: $1.30 1st page, $.65 each add'l. Criminal records on computer since 1986, prior in books. Mail turnaround time minimum 2 weeks.
General Information: No public access terminal. No sealed records released. Will not fax documents. Certification fee: $6.00. Payee: City Court. Only cashiers checks and money orders accepted. Prepayment and SASE required.

New Rochelle City Court 475 North Ave, New Rochelle, NY 10801; criminal phone: 914-654-2311; civil phone: 914-654-2299; fax: 914-654-0344; hours 9AM-5PM (EST). *Misdemeanor, Civil Actions Under $15,000, Small Claims.*
www.courts.state.ny.us/courts/9jd/Westchester/NewRochelle.shtml
Civil Records: Access: Mail, in person. Only the court performs in person searches; visitors may not. Search fee: $16.00 per name. Court makes copy: $1.00 per page. Required to search: name, years to search. Civil records go back 20 years.
Criminal Records: Access: None. Court makes copy: $1.00 per page. The court does not permit access to court records unless specific case file given. Requesters are directed to OCA for $52.00 statewide search.
General Information: No public access terminal. No sealed records released. Certification fee: $6.00 per document. Payee: City Court of New Rochelle. Prepayment required.

Peekskill City Court 2 Nelson Ave, Peekskill, NY 10566; phone: 914-737-3405; fax: na/; hours 9AM-5PM (EST). *Misdemeanor, Civil Actions Under $15,000, Eviction, Small Claims.*
Civil Records: Access: Mail, in person. Only the court performs in person searches; visitors may not. No search fee. Court makes copy: $1.30 for 1st page; $.65 per add'l page. Required to search: name, years to search. Civil cases indexed by plaintiff. Civil records on computer back to 1994, prior in books. Note: Request must be in writing.
Criminal Records: Court makes copy: $1.30 for 1st page; $.65 per add'l page. Required to search: name, years to search, DOB. Criminal records on computer back to 1990, prior on cards. The court does not permit access to court records unless specific case file given. Requesters are directed to OCA for $52.00 statewide search. Mail turnaround time 0-5 days.
General Information: No public access terminal. No sealed records released. Will not fax documents. Certification fee: $6.00 per doc. Payee: Peekskill City Court. Only cash, cashiers checks or money orders accepted. Prepayment and SASE required.

Rye City Court 21 McCullough Pl, Rye, NY 10580; phone: 914-967-1599; fax: 914-967-3308; hours 8:30AM-4:30PM (EST). *Misdemeanor, Civil Actions Under $15,000, Eviction, Small Claims.*
Civil Records: Access: Fax, mail, in person. Only the court performs in person searches; visitors may not. No search fee. Court makes copy: $.50 per page. Required to search: name, years to search. Civil cases indexed by plaintiff. Civil records on computer from 1994, prior on index cards. Mail turnaround 1 month.
Criminal Records: Access: In person only. Only the court performs in person searches; visitors may not. Court makes copy: $.50 per page. Required to search: DOB, years to search. Criminal records on computer from 1986. The court will perform limited name searches. It is suggested to send requests to OCA for $52.00 statewide search. Mail turnaround time 1 month.
General Information: No public access terminal. No sealed records released. Certification fee: $5.00 per cert. Payee: City Court. Only cashiers checks and money orders accepted. Prepayment and SASE required.

White Plains City Court 77 S Lexington Ave, White Plains, NY 10601; phone: 914-824-5675; fax: 914-422-6058; hours 8:30AM-4:30PM (EST). *Misdemeanor, Civil Actions Under $15,000, Eviction, Small Claims.*
Civil Records: Access: Mail, fax, in person. Only the court performs in person searches; visitors may not. Search fee: $16.00 per name. Court makes copy: $1.00 for 1st page; $.50 each add'l. Required to search: name, years to search. Civil cases indexed by defendant. Civil records on docket cards and computer. Mail turnaround time 1-2 days.

Criminal Records: Access: In person only. Court makes copy: $1.00 for 1st page; $.50 each add'l. Criminal records on computer from 1988, prior on cards. The court does not permit access to court records unless specific case file given. Requesters are directed to OCA for $52.00 statewide search.
General Information: No public access terminal. No sealed, youthful offender or sex case records released. Will fax documents no fee, if prepaid. Certification fee: $6.00 per doc. Payee: City Court. Only cashiers checks and money orders accepted. Prepayment and SASE required.

Yonkers City Court 100 S Broadway, Yonkers, NY 10701; criminal phone: 914-377-6352; civil phone: 914-377-6376; fax: 914-377-6966; hours 9AM-3:30PM (EST). *Misdemeanor, Civil Actions Under $15,000, Eviction, Small Claims.*
Civil Records: Access: Mail, in person. Only the court performs in person searches; visitors may not. Search fee: $16.00 per name. No copy fee. Required to search: name, years to search. Civil cases indexed by plaintiff. Civil records on computer since 1/95. Mail turnaround time 2-3 weeks.
Criminal Records: Access: Mail, in person. Search fee: $16.00, if specific case # given. No copy fee. Criminal records on computer since 1993. The court does not permit access to court records unless specific case file given. Requesters are directed to the OCA for $52.00 statewide search. Mail turnaround time 2-3 weeks.
General Information: No public access terminal. No sealed records released. Certification fee: $5.00 per document. Payee: City Court. Only cashiers checks and money orders accepted. Prepayment required.

Surrogate's Court 140 Grand St, 8th Fl, White Plains, NY 10601; phone: 914-824-5656; fax: 914-995-3728; hours 9AM-4PM (EST). *Probate.*

Westchester Town/Village Courts - *misdemeanor or civil records:* Ardsley Village- 914-693-1703; Bedford Town- 914-666-6965; Briarcliff Manor Village- 914-944-2788; Bronxville Village- 914-337-2454; Buchanan Village- 914-737-1033; Cortlandt Town- 914-734-1090; Croton-on-Hudson Village- 914-271-6266; Dobbs Ferry Village- 914-693-6161; Eastchester Town- 914-771-3354; Elmsford Village- 914-592-8949; Greenburgh Town- 914-682-5365; Harrison Town- 914-835-2000 x3; Hastings-on-Hudson Village- 914-478-3403; Irvington Village- 914-591-7095; Larchmont Village- 914-834-1826; Lewisboro Justice Court- 914-763-5417; Mamaroneck Town- 914-381-7875; Mamaroneck Village- 914-777-7710; Mount Kisco Town- 914-241-7033; Mount Pleasant Town- 914-742-2354; New Castle Justice Court- 914-238-4726; North Castle Justice Court- 914-273-8627; North Salem Town- 914-669-9691; North Tarrytown Village- 914-631-2783; Ossining Town- 914-762-8562; Ossining Village- 914-941-3067; Pelham Town- 914-738-7030; Pleasantville Village- 914-769-2027; Port Chester Justice Court- 914-939-8220; Pound Ridge Justice Court- 914-764-5511; Rye Town- 914-939-3305; Scarsdale Village- 914-722-1120/1123; Somers Town- 914-277-8225; Tarrytown Village- 914-631-5215; Tuckahoe Village- 914-961-4787; Yorktown Town- 914-962-6216.

Wyoming County

Supreme & County Court 143 N Main St, #104, Warsaw, NY 14569; phone: 585-786-8810 county clerk, 585-786-2253 (court clerks); fax: 585-786-3703; hours 9AM-5PM (EST). *Felony, Civil.*
Note: Direct all search requests to the County Clerk office; information given here is for that County Clerk office. Supreme and County Court office is at 147 Main St.
Civil Records: Access: Phone, fax, mail, in person, online. Both court and visitors may perform in person searches. Search fee: $5.00 per name. Court makes copy: $1.00 per page. Self serve copy fee: $.50 per page. Required to search: name, years to search. Civil cases indexed by defendant. Civil records on computer back to 2/14/2001; prior on books. Access to current/pending Supreme court civil cases and some closed cases are at http://e.courts.state.ny.us/. Mail turnaround time 2-3 days.
Criminal Records: Access: Phone, fax, mail, in person. Only the court performs in person searches; visitors may not. Search fee: $10.00 for 1-5 years searched per name; 6-10 years is $15.00; 11-20 years is $20.00. Court makes copy: $.50 per page. Required to search: name, years to search, DOB. Criminal records in books. Note: Address requests to County Clerk. Mail turnaround time 2-3 days.
General Information: Public terminal has only civil records back to 2001. No sealed, divorce or sexual abuse records released. Fee to fax documents is $1.00 per page. Certification fee: $5.00. Payee: County Clerk. Personal checks accepted. Prepayment and SASE required.

Surrogate's Court 147 N Main St, Warsaw, NY 14569; phone: 585-786-3148; hours 9AM-5PM (EST). *Probate.*

Wyoming Town/Village Courts - *misdemeanor or civil records:* Arcade Justice Court- 585-492-4479; Arcade Town- 585-492-4479; Attica Town; Attica Village- 585-591-2957; Bennington Town- 716-652-5585; Castile Town- 585-493-5875; Covington Town- 585-584-3565; Eagle Town- 585-322-7667; Gainesville Town; Genesee Falls Town; Java Town- 585-457-3233; Middlebury Town- 585-495-6300; Orangeville Town- 585-786-2883; Perry Town & Village- 585-237-2149; Pike Town- 585-493-5140; Sheldon Town- 585-535-7644; Silver Springs Village- 585-493-3395; Warsaw Town & Village- 585-786-3361; Wethersfield Town- 585-457-3384.

Yates County

County Clerk 417 Liberty St, #1107, Penn Yan, NY 14527; phone: 315-536-5120; fax: 315-536-5545; hours 9AM-5PM; (8:30AM-4:30PM in July & Aug) (EST). *Felony, Civil.*
Note: Countywide search requests made to the County Clerk are processed in the manner described here, also see Supreme & County Court.

Civil Records: Access: In person, online. Both court and visitors may perform in person searches. Court makes copy: $.65 per page, $1.30 minimum. Required to search: name, years to search. Civil cases indexed by defendant, plaintiff. Civil record indices on computer back to 1/88, prior in books. Access to current/pending Supreme Court civil cases is at http://e.courts.state.ny.us/.
Criminal Records: Access: Mail, fax, in person. Both court and visitors may perform in person searches. Search fee: $10.00 per name. Court makes copy: $.65 per page, $1.30 minimum. Required to search: name, years to search. Criminal records on book index; not computerized. Mail turnaround time 2-3 days.
General Information: Public terminal has only civil records. No divorce records outside parties involved, sealed records released. Will fax specific case file requests for $2.00 a page to non-toll-free number. Certification fee: $1.25 per page, $5.00 minimum. Payee: Yates County Clerk. Personal checks accepted. Prepayment and SASE required.

Supreme & County Court 415 Liberty St, Penn Yan, NY 14527; phone: 315-536-5126/5129; hours 9AM-5PM; 8:30AM-4:30PM Summer Hours (EST). *Felony, Civil.*
Note: Direct civil search requests to the County Clerk office or http://e.courts.state.ny.us. This court directs felony searches to OCA for a $52.00 statewide search, however, a countywide search can be made at the County Clerk office, see separate listing.

Surrogate's Court 415 Liberty St, Penn Yan, NY 14527; phone: 315-536-5130; fax: 315-536-5190; hours 9AM-5PM (EST). *Probate.*

Yates Town/Village Courts - *misdemeanor or civil records:* Barrington Town- 607-243-8959; Benton Town- 315-536-2320; Dundee Village- 607-243-5551; Italy Town- 585-374-6194; Jerusalem Town- 315-595-6102; Middlesex Town- 585-554-3607; Milo Town- 585-531-8816; Penn Yan Village- 315-536-7243; Potter Town- 585-554-6758; Starkey Town; Torrey Town Court.

New York Recording Offices

ORGANIZATION: 62 counties, 62 recording offices. Recording officers are County Clerk (New York City Register in the counties of Bronx, Kings, New York, and Queens). Entire state is in the Eastern Time Zone (EST).

REAL ESTATE RECORDS: Some counties will perform real estate searches. Certified copy fees are usually $1.00 per page with a $4.00 minimum. Tax records are located at the Treasurer's Office.

UCC RECORDS: This was a dual filing state. Financing statements were filed both at the state level and with the County Clerk, except for consumer goods, cooperatives (as in cooperative apartments), farm related and real estate related collateral, which were filed only with the County Clerk. Effective 07/2001, only real estate related collateral is filed at the county, but searches may still be done on all the records prior to 07/2001. All counties will perform UCC searches. Use search request form UCC-11. Search fees are $25.00 per debtor name. Copies usually cost $5.00 per document.

TAX LIEN RECORDS: Federal tax liens on personal property of businesses are filed with the Secretary of State. Other federal tax liens are filed with the County Clerk. State tax liens are filed with the County Clerk, with a master list - called state tax warrants - available at the Secretary of State's office. Federal tax liens are usually indexed with UCC Records. State tax liens are usually indexed with other miscellaneous liens and judgments. Some counties include federal tax liens as part of a UCC search, and others will search tax liens for a separate fee, or not search at all. Search fees and copy fees vary.

OTHER LIENS: Judgment, mechanics, welfare, hospital, matrimonial, wage assignment, lis pendens.

ONLINE ACCESS: A handful of counties and towns offering free Internet access to assessor records, and the number is growing. The NYC Register now offers free access to borough real estate records.

Albany County

County Clerk, 32 N Russell Rd, Albany, NY 12206. 518-487-5120; fax-518-487-5099; hours: 9AM-4:45PM. www.albanycounty.com/clerk
General index search fee $5.00 per name per 2 years. UCC search per debtor name- $25.00. Separate federal tax lien search- $25.00 per debtor. Separate state tax lien search- $5.00 per debtor per 2 years. Copy fee $.65 per page; $1.30 minimum. Cert fee- $5.00 per doc plus copy fee. Payee-Albany County Clerk. **Online to Real Estate, Deed, Mortgage, Recording, Assessor, Property Tax, Naturalization records:** Deeds and mortgages free at https://access.albanycounty.com/clerk/deedsandmortgages/. A private company offers property assessment data online at www.uspdr.com/consumer/ownersearch.asp. Also, search county naturalization records free at www.albanycounty.com/departments/achor/. **Other phones:** Treasurer- 518-447-7070; Elections- 518-487-5060; Vital Records- 518-434-5045. **Property tax/Assessor-** 518-487-5350.

Allegany County

County Clerk, 7 Court St; Courthouse, Belmont, NY 14813-0087. 585-268-9270; fax-585-268-9659; hours: 9AM-5PM (June-August 8:30AM-4PM). www.alleganyco.com
Records indexed on a public use terminal back to 1992. Only the public may search. Copy fee $5.00 per document. Cert fee- $5.00 per doc plus copy fee. Payee- Allegany County Clerk. **Other phones:** Treasurer- 585-268-9282; Elections- 585-268-9294; Vital Records- each town/village have their own vital records. **Property tax/Assessor-** 585-268-9381.

Bronx County

City Register, 1932 Arthur Ave, Bronx, NY 10457. 718-579-6827; hours: 9AM-4PM.
Office will perform a UCC search but public must search other records themselves. UCC search per debtor name- $25.00. Copy fee $5.00 per document. Cert fee- $5.00 per doc plus copy fee. Payee- NYC Dept. of Finance. **Online access to Real Estate, Lien, Deed, Judgment, UCC, Deed, Mortgage, Tax Assessor, Property records:** Recording data from the City Register are free at http://a836-acris.nyc.gov/scripts/docsearch.dll/index. Also, for deeper financial data back 10 years, subscribe to the NYC Dept of Finance dial-up system; fee-$250 monthly and $5.00 per item. For info/signup, call

Richard Reskin 718-935-6523. Also, property assessment rolls from NYC's Dept. of Finance are free at http://nyc.gov/html/dof/html/home/home.shtml. No name searching. Also, they offer daily downloads for borough-wide transactions of UCCs, Fed Liens, deeds, real estate. Also, a private company offers property assessment data online at www.uspdr.com/consumer/ownersearch.asp. **Property tax/Assessor-** 718-579-6879.

Broome County

County Clerk, PO Box 2062, Binghamton, NY 13902-2062. 607-778-2451, R/E recording phone-607-778-2255; fax-607-778-2243; hours: 8AM-5PM (Memorial Day to Labor Day-7:30AM-4PM). www.gobroomecounty.com/clerk/index.php
Separate indices to search include searches by name not particular documents. Records indexed on a public use terminal. Office will perform a UCC search but public must search other records themselves. Search fee $5.00 per 2 years. UCC search per debtor name- $25.00. Copy fee $5.00 per UCC document. R/E or tax lien copy- $.65 per page. Cert fee- $5.20 per doc includes first 8 pages, add'l pages $.65 per page each. Payee-Broome County Clerk. **Online access to Property, Deed, Mortgage, Recording, Real Estate, Lien, Judgment, Court Index records:** A private company offers property assessment data online at www.uspdr.com/consumer/ownersearch.asp. Also, search the clerk's indexes free at www.gobcclerk.com/cgi/Official_Search_Types.html/input. Online misc, liens records go back to 1989, deeds & mortgages go back to 1963 and court records (civil and criminal) from 1985 to present. **Other phones:** Treasurer- 607-778-2161; Elections- 607-778-2172; Secretary- 607-778-2377. **Property tax/Assessor-** 607-778-2169.

Cattaraugus County

County Clerk, 303 Court St, Little Valley, NY 14755. 716-938-9111; fax-716-938-6009; hours: 9AM-5PM. www.cattco.org
Index: Deeds, Mtgs, Civil Actions, Judgmts lis Pend, Misc Records, Consolidated Liens, Fed. Tax Liens. Records indexed on computer. Office personnel or visitors may perform searches. Search fee $5.00 per 2 years. Will not search real estate records. UCC and tax lien copy fee $5.00, real estate $1.00 per document. Cert fee- $5.00 per doc plus copy fee. Payee- County Clerk. **Online access**

to Real Estate, Tax Assessor, Most Wanted, Warrant, Land records: Records on the City of Olean assessor database are free at www.cityofolean.com/Assessor/main.htm. Also, you may search for property info on the interactive map at www.cattco.org/real_property/parcel_news.asp. Also, a private company offers property assessment data online at www.uspdr.com/consumer/ownersearch.asp. **Other phones:** Treasurer- 716-938-9111. **Property tax/Assessor-** 716-938-9111.

Cayuga County

County Clerk, 160 Genesee St, Auburn, NY 13021. 315-253-1271; fax-315-253-1653; www.co.cayuga.ny.us/clerk
Office personnel or visitors may perform searches. Search fee $5.00 per name. Will not search real estate records. Copy fee $1.00 per page. R/E record copy-$.65 per page, $1.30 minimum. Cert fee- $5.00 per doc plus copy fee. Payee- Cayuga County Clerk. **Online to Property, Assessor, Real Estate, Deed, Lien records:** Search real estate, deeds and liens at www.landaccess.com/proi/county.jsp?county=nycayuga. Subscription fee is $440 per year or $40 per month, plus $5.00 per image, credit cards accepted. Index goes back to 1972; images back to 1993. **Other phones:** Treasurer- 315-253-1211; Elections- 315-253-1285; Vital Records- 315-255-4100. **Property tax/Assessor-** 315-253-1270.

Chautauqua County

County Clerk, PO Box 170, Mayville, NY 14757-0170. 716-753-4331; fax-716-753-4293; hours: 8:30AM-4:30PM. www.co.chautauqua.ny.us
Office will perform a UCC search but public must search other records themselves. UCC search per debtor name- $25.00. Copy fee $5.00 per document. Cert fee- $5.00 per doc plus copy fee. Payee- Chautauqua County Clerk. **Property tax/Assessor-** 716-661-7223.

Chemung County

County Clerk, PO Box 588, Elmira, NY 14902-0588. 607-737-2920; fax-607-737-2897; 8:30Am-4:30PM. www.chemungcounty.com/bin/site/templates/splash.asp
All records in one index. Records indexed on computer back to 1992. Office personnel or visitors may perform searches. Search fee $5.00 per 2 years. UCC and tax lien copy fee $5.00, real estate $.65 per document. Cert fee- $5.00 per doc plus copy fee. Minimum charge $5.00 over 5

pages, $1.25 per page. Payee- Chemung County Clerk. **Other phones:** Treasurer- 607-737-2927; Elections- 607-737-5475; Vital Records- 607-737-2018. **Property tax/Assessor-** 607-737-2988.

Chenango County

County Clerk, 5 Court St, Norwich, NY 13815. 607-337-1452, R/E recording phone-607-337-1450 (County Clerks Office); fax-607-337-1455; hours: 8:30AM-5PM. www.co.chenango.ny.us
No phone searches accepted. Will search real estate records. Will search UCC records, search includes federal tax liens if requested. UCC search per debtor name- $25.00. Tax lien search fee- $25.00 per debtor. Copy fee $5.00 per document. R/E or tax lien copy- $.65 per page, $1.30 minimum. Cert fee- $5.00 per doc plus copy fee. Payee- Chenango County Clerk. **Online access to Property records:** A private company offers property assessment data online at www.uspdr.com/consumer/ownersearch.asp. **Other phones:** Treasurer- 607-337-1414. **Property tax/Assessor-** 607-337-1490.

Clinton County

County Clerk, 137 Margaret St #101; Government Ctr, Plattsburgh, NY 12901-2974. 518-565-4700, UCC 518-565-4846; fax-518-565-4718; 8AM-5PM. www.co.clinton.ny.us/Departments/CC/CCHome.htm
Separate indices to search include deeds, mortgages, satisfaction of mortgage, assignment of mortgage. Records indexed on a public use terminal. Office will perform a UCC search but public must search other records themselves. UCC search per debtor name- $25.00. Copy fee $5.00 per document. R/E record copy- $.65 per page, $1.30 minimum. Tax lien copy- $1.00 per page. Cert fee- $1.25 per page includes copy fee, $5.00 minimum. Payee- Clinton County Clerk. **Other phones:** Treasurer- 518-565-4730; Elections- 518-565-4740; Vital Records- 518-565-7702. **Property tax/Assessor-** 137 Margaret St, Real Property Office, Plattsburgh, NY 12901; 518-565-4760.

Columbia County

County Clerk, 560 Warren St, Hudson, NY 12534. 518-828-3339; fax-518-828-5299; hours: 9AM-5PM.
Office will perform a UCC search but public must search other records themselves. UCC search per debtor name- $25.00. Copy fee $5.00 per document. R/E or tax lien copy- $.25 per page. Cert fee- $4.00 per doc plus copy fee. Payee- Columbia County Clerk. **Online access to Property records:. Other phones:** Treasurer- 518-828-0513; Elections- 518-828-3115. **Property tax/Assessor-** 518-828-7334.

Cortland County

County Clerk, 46 Greenbush St #101, Cortland, NY 13045-3702. 607-753-5021; fax-607-758-5500; hours: 9AM-5PM. http://www2.cortland-co.org
All records in one index. Records indexed on a public use terminal back to 1986. Office personnel or visitors may perform searches. General index search fee $28.00 plus $3.00 per page; $.50 extra for references on prior instruments. Copy fee $.65 per page. Tax lien copy- $10.00 per document. Cert fee- $5.00 per doc plus copy fee. **Online access to Property, Deed, Mortgage, Civil, Judgment, UCC, Lien, Fictitious Business Name records:** Online access at https://cclerk.cortland-co.org/index.asp gives judgments and other county clerk records. Login using "public" as user name and password. A subscription service is also available Also, a private company offers property assessment data online at www.uspdr.com/consumer/ownersearch.asp. **Other phones:** Treasurer- 607-753-5070; Elections- 607-753-5032; Vital Records- 607-756-6521. **Property tax/Assessor-** 607-753-5040 (Real Property).

Delaware County

County Clerk, PO Box 426, Delhi, NY 13753. 607-746-2123; fax-607-746-6924; hours: 8:30AM-5PM.

Office will perform a UCC search but public must search other records themselves. Search fee $25.00. Copy fee $5.00 per document. R/E or tax lien copy- $.50 per page. Cert fee- $5.00 per doc plus copy fee. Payee- Delaware County Clerk. **Online access to Property records:** A private company offers property assessment data online at www.uspdr.com/consumer/ownersearch.asp. **Other phones:** Treasurer- 607-746-2121; Elections- 607-746-2315. **Property tax/Assessor-** 607-746-3747.

Dutchess County

County Clerk, 22 Market St, Poughkeepsie, NY 12601. 845-486-2120, UCC recording phone-845-486-2125; fax-845-486-2138; hours: 9AM-4:45PM. www.dutchessny.gov
Office will perform a UCC search but public must search other records themselves. UCC search per debtor name- $2.00 per name per year. Copy fee $5.00 per document. Cert fee- $5.00 per doc plus copy fee. Payee- Dutchess County Clerk. **Other phones:** Treasurer- 845-431-2025; Elections- 845-486-2480. **Property tax/Assessor-** 845-431-2140.

Erie County

County Clerk, 25 Delaware Ave; County Hall, Buffalo, NY 14202. 716-858-6724, UCC recording phone-716-858-6425; fax-716-858-6550; http://ecclerk.erie.gov
For information about searches, call 716-858-8785. Office personnel or visitors may perform searches. General index search fee $5.00 per 2 years. UCC search per debtor name- $25.00. Copy fee $5.00 per document. R/E or tax lien copy- $1 per page. Cert fee- $4.00 per doc plus copy fee. Payee- Erie County Clerk. **Online access to Recording, Deed, Mortgage, Judgment, Property records:** Access to the county clerk's database index and images is at http://ecclerk.erie.gov/CGI-BIN/DB2WWW/RECORDS.mbr/RECORDS. A private company offers property assessments at www.uspdr.com/consumer/ownersearch.asp. Also, find property data on the mapping site at www.co.chautauqua.ny.us. **Other phones:** Treasurer- 716-858-3236. **Property/Assessor-** 716-858-8322.

Essex County

County Clerk, PO Box 247, Elizabethtown, NY 12932. 518-873-3601; fax-518-873-3548; hours: 8AM-5PM. www.co.essex.ny.us
Each town has its own assessor. Separate indices to search include deeds, mortgages, APA's, assets & sats. All are researchable. Will not search real estate records. Will search UCC records; search includes tax liens if requested. UCC search per debtor name- $40.00. General copy fee $5.00 per document or name. R/E record copy- $1.25 per page after 4 if certified. Cert fee- $1.25 per page if over 4 pages, flat fee of $5.00 if under 4 pages plus copy fee. Payee- Essex County Clerk. **Online access to Property records:** A private company offers property assessment data online at www.uspdr.com/consumer/ownersearch.asp. **Other phones:** Treasurer- 518-873-3310; Elections- 518-873-3474. **Property tax/Assessor-** 518-873-3390.

Franklin County

County Clerk, PO Box 70, Malone, NY 12953. 518-481-1681; fax-518-483-9143; hours: 8AM-PM June-Aug; 9AM-5PM Sept-May.
All records in one index from 4/1/2000 to present. Records indexed on a public use terminal back to 1959 for deeds. Office will perform a UCC search including federal tax liens but public must search other records themselves. UCC search per debtor name- $25.00. Copy fee $5.00 per document. Cert fee- $5.00 per doc plus copy fee. Payee- Franklin County Clerk. **Other phones:** Treasurer- 518-481-1516; Elections- 518-481-1662; Vital Records- 518-481-1671. **Property tax/Assessor-** 355 W Main St, Malone, NY 12953; 518-481-1502.

Fulton County

County Clerk, PO Box 485, Johnstown, NY 12095. 518-736-5555; fax-518-762-3839; hours: 9AM-5PM. Office personnel or visitors may perform searches. Search fee $5.00 per name. Will not search real estate records. UCC search per debtor name- $25.00. Copy fee $5.00 per document. Cert fee- $5.00 per doc plus copy fee. **Online to Auditor, Real Estate, Deed, UCC records:** Search auditor information at http://66.194.132.76/, recorder documents at www.landaccess.com/sites/oh/disclaimer.php?county=ohfulton. **Other phones:** Treasurer- 518-736-5580; Elections- 518-736-5526; Vital Records- 518-736-5555. **Property tax/Assessor-** 518-736-5510.

Genesee County

County Clerk, PO Box 379, Batavia, NY 14021-0379. 585-344-2550 x2443, R/E recording phone-585-344-2550 x2242, UCC recording phone-585-344-2550 x2243; fax-585-344-8551; hours: 8:30AM-5PM. www.co.genesee.ny.us
Records indexed on a public use terminal back to 1984 (deeds/mortgages). Search fee $10.00 for 5 years per name; 11-20 years- $20.00. Will not search real estate records. UCC search includes federal tax liens and is $25.00 per name. Separate judgment search/tax lien search-$5.00 per debtor per 5 years. Copy fee $.65 per page, $1.30 minimum. Cert fee- $5.00 per doc plus copy fee. Payee- Genesee County Clerk. **Online access to Property records:** A private company offers property assessment data online at www.uspdr.com/consumer/ownersearch.asp. **Other phones:** Treasurer- 585-344-2550 x2210; Elections- 585-344-2550 x2206. **Property tax/Assessor-** 15 Main St, Batavia, NY 14020; 585-344-2550 x2219.

Greene County

County Clerk, PO Box 446, Catskill, NY 12414. 518-719-3255; fax-518-719-3284; hours: 9AM-5PM (June-Aug. 8:30AM-4:30PM).
www.greenegovernment.com/department/clerk/index.htm
Separate indices to search include land, judgments, lis pendens, civil action, UCC, Fed liens. Records indexed on a public use terminal back to 1992. Office will perform a UCC search but public must search other records themselves. UCC search per debtor name- $25.00. Copy fee $1.00 per page or $5.00 per document. Cert fee- $5.00 per doc plus copy fee. Payee- Greene County Clerk. **Online access to Property records:. Other phones:** Treasurer- 518-719-3530; Elections- 518-719-3550. **Property tax/Assessor-** 411 Main St, 4th Fl, Catskill, NY 12414; 518-719-3525.

Hamilton County

County Clerk, PO Box 204, Lake Pleasant, NY 12108. 518-548-7111; fax-518-548-9740; 8:30AM-4:30PM. Separate indices to search include deeds, mortgages, miscellaneous records, court orders, lis pendens, APA permits & judgments. Office will perform a UCC search but public must search other records themselves. Will search UCC records only if search form presented and proper fee paid. UCC search per debtor name- $25.00. Copy fee $5.00. Copy fee $.65 per page, minimum $1.30 per document. Cert fee- $1.00 per page, minimum $5.00 plus copy fee. Payee- Hamilton County Clerk. **Online access to Property records:** A private company offers property assessment data online at www.uspdr.com/consumer/ownersearch.asp. **Other phones:** Treasurer- 518-548-7911. **Property tax/Assessor-** PO Box 168, Lake Pleasant, NY 12108; 518-548-5531.

Herkimer County

County Clerk, 109 Mary St, #1111, Herkimer, NY 13350. 315-867-1137; fax-315-867-1349; hours: 9AM-5PM; Summer- 8:30AM-4PM.
Index: Pre-1991 records indexed by doc type; 1991 forward in global and real estate indices. Office will perform a UCC or tax lien search but public must search other records themselves.

Search fee $25.00 per debtor name. Tax lien fee is for 2 years searched. Copy fee $5.00 per document. Cert fee- $10.00 per doc plus copy fee. Payee- Herkimer County Clerk. **Online access to Property records:** A private company offers property assessment data online at www.uspdr.com/consumer/ownersearch.asp. **Other phones:** Treasurer- 315-867-1153; Elections- 315-867-1102.

Jefferson County

County Clerk, 175 Arsenal St, Watertown, NY 13601-2555. 315-785-3081; fax-315-785-5145; hours: 9AM-5PM; 8:30AM-4PM July & August.
All land records indexed from 10/2002. Search fee $5.00 per 2 years per name. Will search limited real estate records. UCC search per debtor name- $25.00. UCC and tax lien copy fee $5.00, real estate $1.00 per page. Cert fee- $4.00 per doc plus copy fee. Payee- Jefferson County Clerk. **Online access to Property records:** A private company offers property assessment data online at www.uspdr.com/consumer/ownersearch.asp. Also property assessment data offered online at www.co.jefferson.ny.us. **Other phones:** Treasurer- 315-785-3055; Elections- 315-785-5119. **Property tax/Assessor-** 175 Arsenal St, Watertown, NY 13601; 315-785-3074.

Kings County

County Clerk, 210 Joralemon St; Municipal Bldg, 1st Fl, Rm 2, Brooklyn, NY 11201. 718-802-3589; fax-718-802-3745; hours: 9AM-4PM.
Office personnel or visitors may perform searches. Search fee $25.00 per name. Will not search real estate records. Copy fee $5.00 per document. Cert fee- $5.00 per doc plus copy fee. Payee- NYC Dept. of Finance. **Online access to Real Estate, Lien, Deed, Judgment, UCC, Deed, Mortgage, Tax Assessor, Property records:** Recording data from the City Register free at http://a836-acris.nyc.gov/scripts/docsearch.dll/index. Also, for deeper financial data back 10 years, subscribe to the NYC Dept of Finance dial-up system; fee-$250 monthly and $5.00 per item. For info/signup, call Richard Reskin 718-935-6523. Also, property assessment rolls from NYC's Dept. of Finance are free at http://nyc.gov/html/dof/html/home/home.shtml. No name searching. Also, a private company offers property assessment data online at www.uspdr.com/consumer/ownersearch.asp. **Other phones:** Treasurer- 718-669-2746. **Property tax/Assessor-** 718-802-3560.

Lewis County

County Clerk, PO Box 232, Lowville, NY 13367-0232. 315-376-5333; fax-315-376-3768; hours: 8:30AM-4:30PM. http://lewiscountyny.org
All records in one index. Records indexed on computer back to 1980. Office personnel or visitors may perform searches. Search fee $10.00 unless otherwise indicated. Will not search real estate records. Will search UCC records. UCC search includes federal tax liens. UCC search per debtor name- $25.00. UCC and tax lien copy fee $5.00, real estate $.65 per document. Cert fee- $5.00 per doc includes copies. Payee- Lewis County Clerk. **Online access to Property, Assessor records:** A private company offers property assessment data online at www.uspdr.com/consumer/ownersearch.asp. **Other phones:** Treasurer- 315-376-5326; Elections- 315-376-5329. **Property tax/Assessor-** 315-376-5356.

Livingston County

County Clerk, 6 Court St, Rm 201; Government Ctr, Geneseo, NY 14454-1043. 585-243-7010; fax-585-243-7928; hours: 8:30AM-4:30PM Oct 1-May 30; 8AM-4PM June 1-Sept 30.
Office will perform a UCC search but public must search other records themselves. UCC search per debtor name- $25.00. Copy fee $5.00 per document. Cert fee- $5.00 per doc plus copy fee. Payee- Livingston County Clerk. **Other phones:**

Treasurer- 585-243-7050. **Property tax/Assessor-** 585-243-7192.

Madison County

County Clerk, PO Box 668, Wampsville, NY 13163. 315-366-2261, UCC recording phone-315-366-2262; fax-315-366-2615; hours: 9AM-4:45PM.
All records in one index. Records indexed on computer back to 1966. Office personnel or visitors may perform searches. General index search fee $5.00 per name per 5 years. Copy fee $5.00 per document. Cert fee- $5.00 per doc includes copy fee unless over 5 pages. **Online access to Property records:** A private company offers property assessment data online at www.uspdr.com/consumer/ownersearch.asp. **Other phones:** Treasurer- 315-366-2371; Elections- 315-366-2231. **Property tax/Assessor-** County Office Bldg, Wampsville, NY 13163; 315-366-2346.

Monroe County

County Clerk, 39 W. Main St, Rochester, NY 14614. 585-428-5151; fax-585-428-5447; hours: 9AM-5PM. www.monroecounty.gov/org34.asp
Records indexed on a public use terminal back to 1982. Office personnel or visitors may perform searches. Search fee $5.00 for two years. Copy fee $.65 per page. Cert fee- $5.00 per doc plus copy fee. **Online access to Land, Judgment, UCC, Lien, Court, Property records:** Access the county clerk database online at www.clerk.co.monroe.ny.us. Includes mortgages, deeds, court records; free registration. Land records back to 1984. Liens, judgments, UCCS back to 5/1989. Court records - civil, felony, divorce - go back to June, 1993. Earlier microfilm images are being added as time permits. Also, a private company offers property assessment data online at www.uspdr.com/consumer/ownersearch.asp. **Other phones:** Treasurer- 585-428-5290; Elections- 585-428-4550; Vital Records- 585-274-6141. **Property tax/Assessor-** 585-428-5290.

Montgomery County

County Clerk, PO Box 1500, Fonda, NY 12068-1500. 518-853-8111; hours: 8:30AM-4PM.
Records indexed on a public use terminal. Office personnel or visitors may perform searches. General index search fee $5.00 per 2 years. Will search real estate records if in writing. UCC search per debtor name- $40.00. Separate federal/state combined tax lien search- $25.00 per 2 years. Copy fee $1.00 per page. Cert fee- $5.00 per doc plus copy fee. Payee- Montgomery County Clerk. **Online access to Property records:** A private company offers property assessment data online at www.uspdr.com/consumer/ownersearch.asp. **Other phones:** Treasurer- 518-853-8175; Elections- 518-853-8181.

Nassau County

County Clerk, 240 Old Country Rd, Mineola, NY 11501. 516-571-2272; fax-516-742-4099; hours: 9AM-4:45PM.
www.co.nassau.ny.us/clerk/index.html
Office personnel or visitors may perform searches. Search fee $25.00 per name. Copy fee $5.00 per document. Cert fee- $10.00 per doc plus copy fee. Payee- Nassau County Clerk. **Online access to Real Estate, Assessor, Recording, Property records:** Access to the county assessor tax data for free at www.mynassauproperty.com. No name searching. Also, access to recorder images is through a private company at www.courthousedirect.com/pac-info/. Fee for data. **Other phones:** Treasurer- 516-571-5021. **Property tax/Assessor-** 516-571-2490.

New York County

City Register, 66 John St; Rm 202, New York, NY 10007. 212-361-7550; hours: 8:30④PM.
Only the public may search. Copy fee $5.00 per document. Cert fee- $5.00 per doc plus copy fee. Payee- NYC Dept of Finance. **Online access to Real**

Estate, Lien, Judgment, UCC, Deed, Mortgage, Tax Assessor records: Recording data from the City Register is free at http://a836-acris.nyc.gov/scripts/docsearch.dll/index. Also, for deeper financial data back 10 years, subscribe to the NYC Dept of Finance dial-up system; fee-$250 monthly and $5.00 per item. For info/signup, call Rich Reskin 718-935-6523. Aassessment roll searches at http://nycserv.nyc.gov/nycproperty/nynav/jsp/selectbbl.jsp; no name searching. Also, search assessments free at www.uspdr.com/consumer/ownersearch.asp. **Other phones:** Treasurer- 212-669-3913. **Property tax/Assessor-** 212-669-2387.

Niagara County

County Clerk, PO Box 461, Lockport, NY 14095. 716-439-7022, R/E recording phone-716-439-7031, UCC recording phone-716-439-7307; fax-716-439-7066; hours: 9AM-5PM (Summer 8:30AM-4:30PM).
Records indexed on a public use terminal back to 1980's. Office personnel or visitors may perform searches. Search fee $5.00 per name per 2 year search. UCC search per debtor name- $25.00. UCC search request if there is real estate as collateral $40.00. Copy fee $5.00 per document. R/E or tax lien copy- $1.00 per page. Cert fee- $5.00 per doc includes copy fee (if document is 5 pages or less). Payee- Niagara County Clerk. **Online access to Real Estate, Recording, Deed, Mortgage, Lien, Judgment records:** A private company offers access to recorder documents at http://www2.landaccess.com/niagara_ny. Username and password required; register online. **Other phones:** Treasurer- 716-439-7007; Elections- 716-438-4040; Vital Records- 716-439-6676. **Property tax/Assessor-** 59 Park Ave, Lockport, NY 14094; 716-439-7077.

Oneida County

County Clerk, 800 Park Ave, Utica, NY 13501. 315-798-5792; fax-315-798-6440; hours: 8:30AM-5PM. www.oneidacounty.org/index1.htm
All records in one index. Records indexed on office computer back to 1974. Real estate record owner and mortgage searches available. Will search UCC records, search includes federal tax liens if requested. UCC search per debtor name- $25.00. Separate federal and or state tax lien search-$25.00 per debtor. Copy fee $.65 per page; $1.30 minimum. Cert fee- $5.00 per doc plus copy fee. Payee- Oneida County Clerk. **Online access to Property records:** A private company offers property assessment data online at www.uspdr.com/consumer/ownersearch.asp. **Other phones:** Treasurer- 315-798-5750; Elections- 315-798-5763; Vital Records- 315-798-5833. **Property tax/Assessor-** 315-798-5750.

Onondaga County

County Clerk, 401 Montgomery St, Rm 200, Syracuse, NY 13202. 315-435-2226 or 2241, R/E recording phone-315-435-8250, UCC recording phone-315-435-8200; fax-315-435-3455; hours: 8AM-5PM. www.ongov.net
Office personnel or visitors may perform searches. Search fee $25.00 per name. Copy fee $5.00 per document. Cert fee- $5.00 per doc plus copy fee. **Online access to Assessor, Property, GIS-mapping, Inmate records:** Access county property data free at http://ocfintax.ongov.net/imate/search.aspx; to access City of Syracuse property data free, go to http://ocfintax.ongov.net/imateSyr/search.aspx. Also search for property dta free on the GIS-mapping page at www.maphost.com/syracuse%2Donondaga/main.asp. Click on "Query" and then "Find Tax Parcels." Also, access sheriff's county inmate list at http://w3cor.ongov.net:26001/inmate_lookup. **Property tax/Assessor-** 315-448-8280 (City Syr), 315-435-2426 (outside city).

Ontario County

County Clerk, 20 Ontario St.; Ontario County Muni. Bldg, Canandaigua, NY 14424. 585-396-4200; fax-

585-393-2951; hours: 8:30AM-5PM. www.co.ontario.ny.us
All records in one index. Records indexed on a public use terminal back to 1973. Office will perform a UCC search but public must search other records themselves. UCC search per debtor name- $25.00. UCC and tax lien copy fee $5.00, real estate $.65 per page. Cert fee- $5.00 per doc up to 4 pages, $1.25 each add'l page includes copy fee. Payee- Ontario County Clerk. **Online access to Property records:** A private company offers property assessment data online at www.uspdr.com/consumer/ownersearch.asp. **Other phones:** Treasurer- 585-396-4432; Elections- 585-396-4005.

Orange County

County Clerk, 255 Main St, Goshen, NY 10924. 845-291-2690, R/E recording 845-291-3062; fax-845-291-2691; hours: 9AM-5PM. www.co.orange.ny.us
Office personnel or visitors may perform searches. General search fee $2.50 per name. UCC search per debtor name- $25.00. Copy fee $5.00 per document. R/E record copy- $1.00 per page 1st 4 pages, $.50 each add'l page. Cert fee- $5.00 per doc plus copy fee. Payee- Orange County Clerk. **Other phones:** Treasurer- 845-291-2485; Elections- 845-291-2444. **PropertyAssessor-** 845-291-2480.

Orleans County

County Clerk, 3 S. Main St; Courthouse Sq, Albion, NY 14411-1498. 585-589-5334; fax-585-589-0181; hours: 8:30AM-4PM July-Aug; 9AM-5PM Sept-June. www.orleansny.com
Index: Pre-3/98 records in books. Records indexed on a public use terminal back to 3/98. Will lookup one or two real estate records only. UCC search per debtor name- $7.00. Copy fee $1.00 per page. Cert fee- $4.00 per doc includes 4 copy pages. **Online access to Property, Assessor records:** A private company offers property assessment data online at www.uspdr.com/consumer/ownersearch.asp. **Other phones:** Treasurer- 585-589-5353; Elections- 585-589-7004; **Property tax/Assessor-** 585-589-5400, assessor fax- 585-589-5505.

Oswego County

County Clerk, 46 E. Bridge St, Oswego, NY 13126. 315-349-8385; fax-315-343-8383; hours: 9AM-5PM. Office personnel or visitors may perform searches. Search fee $25.00 per name. Copy fee $5.00 per document. Cert fee- $5.00 per doc plus copy fee. Payee- Oswego County Clerk. **Other phones:** Treasurer- 315-349-8393. **Property tax/Assessor-** 315-349-8315.

Otsego County

County Clerk, PO Box 710, Cooperstown, NY 13326-0710. 607-547-4278, R/E recording phone-607-547-4277, UCC recording phone-607-547-4278; fax-607-547-7544; hours: 9AM-5PM Sept-June; 9AM-4PM July-Aug.
Records indexed on a public use terminal back to 1997. Office will perform a UCC and Tax lien search but public must search other records themselves. Search fee $25.00. Copy fee $5.00 per document. R/E record copy- $1.00 per page. Cert fee- $5.00 per doc plus copy fee. Payee- County Clerk. **Online access to Property records:** A private company offers property assessment data online at www.uspdr.com/consumer/ownersearch.asp. **Other phones:** Treasurer- 607-547-4235; Appraiser/Auditor-each town has own; Elections- 607-547-4247. **Property tax/Assessor-** 607-547-4222.

Putnam County

County Clerk, 40 Gleneida Ave, Carmel, NY 10512. 845-225-3641, R/E recording phone-845-225-3641 x304, x305, UCC recording phone-845-225-3641 x300; fax-845-228-0231; hours: 9AM-5PM (Summer 8AM-4PM).
Office personnel or visitors may perform searches. Search fee $5.00 per 2 years. UCC search per debtor name- $25.00. Copy fee $5.00 per document. R/E or tax lien copy- $1.00. Cert fee- $5.00 per doc plus copy fee. Payee- Putnam County Clerk. **Online access to Real Estate, UCC, Lien, Property records:** recorder records are accessible through a private online service at www.landaccess.com; Registration is required. **Other phones:** Treasurer- 845-225-3641 x321; Elections-845-278-6970. **Property tax/Assessor-** 845-225-3641 x310.

Queens County

City Register, 144-06 94th Ave, Jamaica, NY 11435. 718-298-7000; hours: 9AM-4PM.
Office will perform a UCC search but public must search other records themselves. UCC search per debtor name- $25.00. Copy fee $5.00 per document. Cert fee- $5.00 per doc plus copy fee. Payee- New York City Department of Finance. **Online access to Real Estate, Lien, Deed, Judgment, UCC, Deed, Mortgage, Tax Assessor records:** Recording data from the City Register are free at http://a836-acris.nyc.gov/scripts/docsearch.dll/index. Also, for deeper financial data back 10 years, subscribe to the NYC Dept of Finance dial-up system; fee-$250 monthly and $5.00 per item. For info/signup, call Richard Reskin 718-935-6523. Also, property assessment rolls from NYC's Dept. of Finance are free at http://nyc.gov/html/dof/html/home/home.shtml. No name searching. **Property tax/Assessor-** 718-658-4626.

Rensselaer County

County Clerk, Courthouse; Congress & 2nd St, Troy, NY 12180. 518-270-4080; fax-518-271-7998; hours: 8:30AM-5PM.
Office will perform a UCC search but public must search other records themselves. Will search deeds and mortgages with name and year. UCC search per debtor name- $25.00. Copy fee $5.00 per document. R/E record copy- $1.00 per page. Cert fee- $5.00 per doc plus copy fee. Payee- Rensselaer County Clerk. **Online access to Property, Assessor, Deed, Lien, Real Estate records:** Search real estate deeds and liens at www.nylandrecords.com. Registration is now required. Commercial users can subscribe for $25.00 per month and $.25 per search; Personal users can purchase documents for $5.00 each, no monthly fee. **Other phones:** Treasurer- 518-270-2751. **Property tax/Assessor-** 518-270-2751.

Richmond County

County Clerk, 130 Stuyvesant Pl, Staten Island, NY 10301. 718-390-5386, R/E recording phone-718-390-5387, UCC recording phone-718-390-5386; hours: 9AM-5PM.
Office will perform a UCC search but public must search other records themselves. UCC search per debtor name- $25.00. Copy fee $5.00 per document. Cert fee- $5.00 per doc plus copy fee. Payee- Richmond County Clerk. **Online access to Real Estate, Lien, Deed, Judgment, UCC, Deed, Mortgage, Tax Assessor records:** Recording data from the City Register are free at http://a836-acris.nyc.gov/scripts/docsearch.dll/index. Also, for deeper financial data back 10 years, subscribe to the NYC Dept of Finance dial-up system; fee-$250 monthly and $5.00 per item. For info/signup, call Richard Reskin 718-935-6523. Property assessment rolls from NYC's Dept. of Finance are free at http://nycserv.nyc.gov/nycproperty/nynav/jsp/selectbbl.jsp. No name searching. **Property tax/Assessor-** 718-815-8511.

Rockland County

County Clerk, 1 S. Main St #100, New City, NY 10956. 845-638-5070, R/E recording phone-845-638-5069, UCC recording phone-845-708-7180; fax-845-638-5647; hours: 7AM-6:30PM M-Th; 7AM-5:30PM F. www.rocklandcountyclerk.com
All records in one index. Records indexed on a public use terminal back to 1932. Office personnel or visitors may perform searches. Search fee $5.00 for every 2 years. Copy fee $5.00 per document. R/E record copy- $1.00 per page. Cert fee- $5.00 per doc includes 1 free copy. Payee- Rockland County Clerk. **Online access to Real Estate, Lien, Deed, Court, Recording records:** Access is the county clerk's records index is free at www.rocklandcountyclerk.com/court_records.html. Includes criminal records back to 1982, civil judgments, real estate records, tax warrants. View images back to 6/96, and more are being added. Call Paul Pipearto at 845-638-5221 for more information. Also, search for parcel info on the GIS site at http://idsigis.com/rockland/start.asp?tfw=400. Click on Start Search and "Search by Owner." Also, a private company offers property assessment data online at www.uspdr.com/consumer/ownersearch.asp. **Other phones:** Elections- 845-638-5712. **Property tax/Assessor-** 845-638-5131.

Saratoga County

County Clerk, 40 McMaster St, Ballston Spa, NY 12020. 518-885-2213 ext 4411; fax-518-884-4726; hours: Search hours: 8AM-5PM; Recording hours: 8-?.
Records indexed on a public use terminal back to 1987. Office will perform a UCC search but public must search other records themselves. Search fee $5.00 per 2 years. UCC and tax lien copy fee $5.00, real estate $1.25 per page. Cert fee- $5.00 includes 4 pages. Payee- Saratoga County Clerk. **Online access to Property records:** A private company offers property assessment data online at www.uspdr.com/consumer/ownersearch.asp. **Other phones:** Treasurer- 518-885-4724. **Property tax/Assessor-** 518-885-5381 x455.

Schenectady County

County Clerk, 620 State St, Schenectady, NY 12305-2114. 518-388-4220; fax-518-388-4224; hours: 9AM-5PM.
Office personnel or visitors may perform searches. General search fee $5.00 per 2 years. UCC search per debtor name- $25.00 + $5.00 per document. Copy fee $1.00 per page. Cert fee- $5.00 per doc plus copy fee. **Other phones:** Treasurer- 518-388-4262. **Property tax/Assessor-** 518-388-4247.

Schoharie County

County Clerk, PO Box 549, Schoharie, NY 12157. 518-295-8316; fax-518-295-8338; hours: 8:30AM-5PM. www.schohariecounty-ny.gov/CountyWebSite/CountyClerk/CountyClerkHome.jsp
Index: Indices prior to 1/1/1994 are in books. Records indexed on a public use terminal back to 1989. Office personnel or visitors may perform searches. General index search fee $5.00 per name. Will search UCC records. UCC search per debtor name- $25.00. Separate federal tax lien search-$7.00 per 2 years. Copy fee $.50 per page except maps. Cert fee- $4.00 per doc plus copy fee. **Online access to Property records:** A private company offers property assessment data online at www.uspdr.com/consumer/ownersearch.asp. **Other phones:** Treasurer- 518-295-8386; Elections- 518-295-8326. **Property tax/Assessor-** PO Box 308, Schoharie, NY 12157; 518-295-7141.

Schuyler County

County Clerk, 105 Ninth St Unit 8; County Office Bldg, Watkins Glen, NY 14891. 607-535-8133; hours: 9AM-5PM.
Will not search real estate records. Will search UCC records, but not tax liens. UCC search per debtor name- $25.00. Copy fee $5.00 per document. R/E or tax lien copy- $.65 per page. Cert fee- $5.00 per doc plus copy fee. Payee- Schuyler County Clerk. **Online access to Property records:** A private company offers property assessment data online at www.uspdr.com/consumer/ownersearch.asp. **Other phones:** Treasurer- 607-535-8181. **Property tax/Assessor-** 607-535-8118.

Seneca County

County Clerk, 1 DiPronio Drive, Waterloo, NY 13165. 315-539-1771, R/E recording phone-315-539-1770, UCC recording-315-539-1772; fax-315-539-3789; hours: 8:45AM-4:45PM. www.co.seneca.ny.us
All records in one index. Records indexed on a public use terminal back to 1967. Office will perform a UCC and tax lien search but public must search other records themselves. UCC search including tax liens per debtor name- $25.00. Copy fee $5.00 per document. Cert fee- $5.00 per doc includes copy fee. Payee- Seneca County Clerk. **Online access to Property records:** A private company offers property assessment data online at www.uspdr.com/consumer/ownersearch.asp. **Other phones:** Treasurer- 315-539-1738; Appraiser/Auditor- 315-539-1718; Elections- 315-539-1762. **Property tax/Assessor-** 315-539-1720.

St. Lawrence County

County Clerk, 48 Court St, Canton, NY 13617-1198. 315-379-2237; fax-315-379-2302; hours: 8:30AM-4:30PM. www.co.st-lawrence.ny.us/CoTOC2.htm
Office will perform a UCC search but public must search other records themselves. UCC search per debtor name- $25.00. Copy fee $5.00 per document. R/E or tax lien copy- $.65 per page. Cert fee- $5.00 per doc plus copy fee. Payee- St. Lawrence County Clerk. **Other phones:** Treasurer- 315-379-2234; Appraiser/Auditor- 315-379-2272; Elections- 315-379-2202. **Property tax/Assessor-** 315-379-2272.

Steuben County

County Clerk, 3 E. Pulteney Sq; County Office Bldg, Bath, NY 14810. 607-776-9631 x3210, R/E recording phone-607-776-9631 x3203; fax-607-776-7158; hours: 8:30AM-4PM. www.steubencony.org
Office personnel or visitors may perform searches. Search fee $20.00 per name. Copy fee $5.00 per document. R/E or tax lien copy- $.65 per page. Cert fee- $5.00 per doc plus copy fee. Payee- Steuben County Clerk. **Online access to Property records:** Search Real Property Assessment Roll free online at www.erwinny.org/ertxsrch.htm. **Other phones:** Treasurer- 607-776-9631 x2488. **Property tax/Assessor-** 607-324-3074.

Suffolk County

Clerk's Office, 310 Center Drive, Riverhead, NY 11901-3392. 631-852-2048 or 2099, R/E recording phone-631-852-2043, UCC recording phone-631-852-2038; fax-631-852-2004; hours: 8AM-5PM.
Office will perform a UCC search but public must search other records themselves. UCC search per debtor name- $25.00. Copy fee $5.00 per document. Cert fee- $10.00 per doc plus copy fee. Payee- Suffolk County Clerk. **Other phones:** Treasurer- 631-852-1500. **Property tax/Assessor-** 631-852-1551.

Sullivan County

County Clerk, PO Box 5012, Monticello, NY 12701. 845-794-3000 x3152; hours: 9AM-5PM.
Index: Computer system A.C.S. Records indexed on a public use terminal back to 1990. Office will perform a UCC search but public must search other records themselves. Search fee $5.00. UCC search $25.00. Will not search real estate records. Tax liens not included in UCC search. Copy fee $1.00 per document. Cert fee- $5.20 per doc plus copy fee. Payee- Sullivan County Clerk. **Online access to Property records:** A private company offers property assessment data online at www.uspdr.com/consumer/ownersearch.asp. **Other phones:** Treasurer- 845-794-3000. **Property tax/Assessor-** 845-794-3000 x5014.

Tioga County

County Clerk, PO Box 307, Owego, NY 13827. 607-687-8660; fax-607-687-8686; hours: 9AM-5PM.
Office will perform a UCC search but public must search other records themselves. UCC search per debtor name- $25.00 per name. General copy fee $5.00 per document. Tax lien copy- $.50 per page; by mail- $5.00 per document. Cert fee- $5.00 per doc plus copy fee. Payee- Tioga County Clerk. **Other phones:** Treasurer- 607-687-8670; Elections- 607-687-8261; Real Property Tax- 607-687-8661.

Tompkins County

County Clerk, 320 N. Tioga St; Main Courthouse, Ithaca, NY 14850-4284. 607-274-5431; fax-607-274-5445; hours: 8:30AM-5PM. www.tompkins-co.org
All records in one index. Records indexed on a public use terminal back to 1968. Office personnel or visitors may perform searches. Will search UCC records. UCC search includes federal tax liens. UCC search per debtor name- $25.00. Separate federal tax lien search- $4.50 per debtor. Separate state tax lien search- $5.00 per debtor. Copy fee $5.00 per document. R/E record copy- $.50 per page, $1.00 minimum. Cert fee- $5.00 per doc plus copy fee. Payee- Tompkins County Clerk. **Online access to Real Estate, Assessor records:** Access to property records on the ImageMate system at www.tompkins-co.org/assessment/online.html has two levels: basic free and a registration/password fee-based full system. There is no name searching on the free version. The fee service is $20 monthly or $200 per year. For info or registration for the latter, email assessment@tompkins-co.org. Property assessment data online at www.uspdr.com/consumer/ownersearch.asp. **Other phones:** Treasurer- 607-274-5545; Elections- 607-274-5522; Vital Records- 607-274-642. **Property tax/Assessor-** 128 E Buffalo St, Ithaca, Ny 14850; 607-274-5517.

Ulster County

County Clerk, PO Box 1800, Kingston, NY 12402-0800. 845-340-3288; fax-845-340-3299; hours: 9AM-4:45PM. www.co.ulster.ny.us
All records in one index. Records indexed on a public use terminal back to 1984. Office personnel or visitors may perform searches. General index search fee $5.00 per 2 years. Real estate owner, mortgage, and property transfer searches available. Will search UCC records, tax liens not included in UCC search. UCC search per debtor name- $25.00. UCC and tax lien copy fee $5.00, real estate $.65 per document. Cert fee- $5.00 per doc plus copy fee. Payee- Ulster County Clerk. **Online access to Real Estate, Lien, Property Tax, Voter Registration, Court records:** Two sources exist. Access to county online records requires a $33.33 (under 25 transactions) or $44.55 monthly fee; 12 month agreement required. Land Records date back to 7/1987. Includes county court records back to 1984. Lending agency information is available. For info, contact Valerie Harris at 845-334-5367. Also, a private company offers property assessment data at www.uspdr.com/consumer/ownersearch.asp. **Other phones:** Treasurer- 845-340-3431; Elections- 845-340-5470. **Property tax/Assessor-** 845-340-3490.

Warren County

County Clerk, 1340 State Route 9; Municipal Ctr, Lake George, NY 12845. 518-761-6426; fax-518-761-6551; hours: 9AM-5PM.
Office personnel or visitors may perform searches. Search fee $5.00 per name. Will not search real estate records. UCC search per debtor name- $25.00. General copy fee $5.00 per document. Tax lien copy- $1.25 per document. Cert fee- $5.00 per doc plus copy fee. Payee- Warren County Clerk. **Online access to Property records:.** **Property tax/Assessor-** 518-761-6465.

Washington County

County Clerk, 383 Broadway, Bldg A, Fort Edward, NY 12828. 518-746-2170, UCC recording 518-746-2176; fax-518-746-2177; hours: 8:30AM-4:30PM.
All records in one index. Records indexed on a public use terminal back to 3/1/2004. Office will perform a UCC search but public must search other records themselves. UCC search per debtor name- $25.00. Copy fee $5.00 per document. Cert fee- $5.00 per 10 pages. Payee- Washington County Clerk. **Other phones:** Treasurer- 518-746-2220; Elections- 518-746-2180. **Property tax/Assessor-** 518-746-2130 (Real Property Tax).

Wayne County

County Clerk, PO Box 608, Lyons, NY 14489-0608. 315-946-7470; fax-315-946-5978; hours: 9AM-5PM. www.co.wayne.ny.us
Office personnel or visitors may perform searches. Search fee $25.00 per name. General copy fee $5.00 per document. Tax lien copy- $5.00 per dot for Fed, $.65 per page State. Cert fee- $5.00 per doc plus copy fee. Payee- Wayne County Clerk. **Other phones:** Treasurer- 315-946-7443; Elections- 315-946-7400. **Property tax/Assessor-** 315-946-5916.

Westchester County

County Clerk, 110 Dr. Martin Luther King Jr. Blvd, White Plains, NY 10601. 914-995-3098; fax-914-995-3172; hours: 8AM-4:30PM.
Office personnel or visitors may perform searches. Search fee $25.00 per name. Will not search real estate records. Copy fee $5.00 per document. Cert fee- $10.00 per doc plus copy fee. Payee- Westchester County Clerk. **Online access to Property, Recordings, Deed, Land, Fictitious Names, Judgment, Lien, UCC records:** Access to the clerk's land record database is free at http://ccpv.westchesterclerk.com/StartMain.asp. There is also an advanced search that features images; registration is required. **Property tax/Assessor-** 914-422-1223.

Wyoming County

County Clerk, 143 N Main St, #104, Warsaw, NY 14569. 585-786-8810; fax-585-786-3703; hours: 9AM-5PM. www.wyomingco.net
All records in one index. Records indexed on a public use terminal. Office will perform a UCC search but public must search other records themselves. Search fee $25.00. Copy fee $5.00 per document. R/E or tax lien copy- $.50 per document. Cert fee- $5.00 per doc. Payee- Wyoming County Clerk. **Online access to Real Estate, Recording, Property, Registered Sex Offenders records:** recorder records are accessible through a private online service at www.landaccess.com; fees and registration are required. Also, a private company offers property assessment data online at www.uspdr.com/consumer/ownersearch.asp. Also, Registered Sex Offenders list is accessible at www.geocities.com/wyomingso1/. **Other phones:** Treasurer- 585-786-8812; Elections- 585-786-8931. **Property tax/Assessor-** 585-786-8828.

Yates County

County Clerk, 417 Liberty St #1107, Penn Yan, NY 14527. 315-536-5120; fax-315-536-5545; hours: 9AM-5PM Sept-June; 8:30AM-4:30PM July-August. www.yatescounty.org
Separate indices to search include land records (deed, mortgage, etc maintained in one index on computer); books separate index, miscellaneous, real estate transfer records all in separate indexes. Office will perform a UCC search but public must search other records themselves. UCC search per debtor name- $25.00. Copy fee $5.00 per document. R/E record copy- $.65 per page, minimum $1.30. Federal Tax lien copy- $5.00 per page. Cert fee- $1.25 per page. Payee- Yates County Clerk. **Online access to Property records:** A private company offers property assessment data online at www.uspdr.com/consumer/ownersearch.asp. **Other phones:** Treasurer- 315-536-5192; Elections- 315-536-5135. **Property tax/Assessor-** 417 Liberty St, #1093, Penn Yan, NY 14527; 315-536-5165.

New York County Locator

You will usually be able to find the city name in the City/County Cross Reference below. In that case, it is a simple matter to determine the county from the cross reference. However, only the official US Postal Service city names are included in this index. There are an additional 40,000 place names that people use in their addresses. Therefore, we have also included a ZIP/City Cross Reference immediately following the City/County Cross Reference.

If you know the ZIP Code but the city name does not appear in the City/County Cross Reference index, look up the ZIP Code in the ZIP/City Cross Reference, find the city name, then look up the city name in the City/County Cross Reference. For example, you want to know the county for an address of Menands, NY 12204. There is no "Menands" in the City/County Cross Reference. The ZIP/City Cross Reference shows that ZIP Codes 12201-12288 are for the city of Albany. Looking back in the City/County Cross Reference, Albany is in Albany County.

New York City/County Cross Reference

ACCORD Ulster
ACRA Greene
ADAMS Jefferson
ADAMS BASIN Monroe
ADAMS CENTER Jefferson
ADDISON Steuben
ADIRONDACK Warren
AFTON (13730) Chenango(93), Broome(6)
AKRON (14001) Erie(92), Niagara(3), Genesee(3)
ALABAMA Genesee
ALBANY Albany
ALBERTSON Nassau
ALBION Orleans
ALCOVE Albany
ALDEN (14004) Erie(92), Wyoming(5), Genesee(2)
ALDER CREEK Oneida
ALEXANDER Genesee
ALEXANDRIA BAY Jefferson
ALFRED Allegany
ALFRED STATION (14803) Allegany(89), Steuben(10)
ALLEGANY Cattaraugus
ALLENTOWN Allegany
ALMA Allegany
ALMOND Allegany
ALPINE Schuyler
ALPLAUS Schenectady
ALTAMONT Albany
ALTMAR Oswego
ALTON Wayne
ALTONA Clinton
AMAGANSETT Suffolk
AMAWALK Westchester
AMENIA Dutchess
AMITYVILLE Suffolk
AMSTERDAM (12010) Montgomery(95), Schenectady(3), Fulton(1)
ANCRAM Columbia
ANCRAMDALE Columbia
ANDES Delaware
ANDOVER (14806) Allegany(83), Steuben(16)
ANGELICA Allegany
ANGOLA Erie
ANNANDALE ON HUDSON Dutchess
ANTWERP Jefferson
APALACHIN Tioga
APPLETON Niagara
APULIA STATION Onondaga
AQUEBOGUE Suffolk
ARCADE (14009) Wyoming(91), Cattaraugus(8)
ARDEN Orange
ARDSLEY Westchester
ARDSLEY ON HUDSON Westchester
ARGYLE Washington
ARKPORT (14807) Steuben(79), Allegany(20)
ARKVILLE (12406) Delaware(93), Ulster(6)
ARMONK Westchester
ASHLAND Greene
ASHVILLE Chautauqua

ATHENS Greene
ATHOL Warren
ATHOL SPRINGS Erie
ATLANTA Steuben
ATLANTIC BEACH Nassau
ATTICA (14011) Wyoming(91), Genesee(8)
AU SABLE FORKS (12912) Clinton(98), Essex(1)
AUBURN Cayuga
AURIESVILLE Montgomery
AURORA Cayuga
AUSTERLITZ Columbia
AVA Oneida
AVERILL PARK Rensselaer
AVOCA Steuben
AVON Livingston
BABYLON Suffolk
BAINBRIDGE (13733) Chenango(98), Delaware(1)
BAKERS MILLS Warren
BALDWIN Nassau
BALDWIN PLACE (10505) Westchester(83), Putnam(16)
BALDWINSVILLE Onondaga
BALLSTON LAKE Saratoga
BALLSTON SPA Saratoga
BALMAT St. Lawrence
BANGALL Dutchess
BANGOR Franklin
BARKER (14012) Niagara(95), Orleans(4)
BARNEVELD Oneida
BARRYTOWN Dutchess
BARRYVILLE Sullivan
BARTON Tioga
BASOM (14013) Genesee(98), Erie(1)
BATAVIA Genesee
BATH Steuben
BAY SHORE Suffolk
BAYPORT Suffolk
BAYSIDE Queens
BAYVILLE Nassau
BEACON Dutchess
BEAR MOUNTAIN Rockland
BEARSVILLE Ulster
BEAVER DAMS (14812) Schuyler(46), Chemung(30), Steuben(22)
BEAVER FALLS Lewis
BEDFORD Westchester
BEDFORD HILLS Westchester
BELFAST Allegany
BELLEVILLE Jefferson
BELLMORE Nassau
BELLONA Yates
BELLPORT Suffolk
BELLVALE Orange
BELMONT Allegany
BEMUS POINT Chautauqua
BERGEN (14416) Genesee(89), Monroe(9)
BERKSHIRE (13736) Tioga(94), Broome(4)
BERLIN Rensselaer
BERNE Albany
BERNHARDS BAY Oswego
BETHEL Sullivan
BETHPAGE Nassau

BIBLE SCHOOL PARK Broome
BIG FLATS (14814) Chemung(85), Steuben(14)
BIG INDIAN Ulster
BILLINGS Dutchess
BINGHAMTON Broome
BLACK CREEK Allegany
BLACK RIVER Jefferson
BLAUVELT Rockland
BLISS (14024) Wyoming(92), Allegany(7)
BLODGETT MILLS Cortland
BLOOMFIELD Ontario
BLOOMING GROVE Orange
BLOOMINGBURG (12721) Sullivan(93), Orange(6)
BLOOMINGDALE Essex
BLOOMINGTON Ulster
BLOOMVILLE Delaware
BLOSSVALE Oneida
BLUE MOUNTAIN LAKE Hamilton
BLUE POINT Suffolk
BOHEMIA Suffolk
BOICEVILLE Ulster
BOLIVAR Allegany
BOLTON LANDING Warren
BOMBAY Franklin
BOONVILLE Oneida
BOSTON Erie
BOUCKVILLE Madison
BOUQUET Essex
BOVINA CENTER Delaware
BOWMANSVILLE Erie
BRADFORD (14815) Schuyler(65), Steuben(34)
BRAINARD Rensselaer
BRAINARDSVILLE Franklin
BRANCHPORT (14418) Yates(90), Steuben(9)
BRANT Erie
BRANT LAKE Warren
BRANTINGHAM Lewis
BRASHER FALLS St. Lawrence
BREESPORT Chemung
BRENTWOOD Suffolk
BREWERTON Onondaga
BREWSTER Putnam
BRIARCLIFF MANOR Westchester
BRIDGEHAMPTON Suffolk
BRIDGEPORT (13030) Madison(56), Onondaga(43)
BRIDGEWATER Oneida
BRIER HILL St. Lawrence
BRIGHTWATERS Suffolk
BROADALBIN (12025) Fulton(84), Saratoga(15)
BROCKPORT Monroe
BROCTON Chautauqua
BRONX Bronx
BRONX New York
BRONXVILLE Westchester
BROOKFIELD Madison
BROOKHAVEN Suffolk
BROOKLYN Kings

BROOKTONDALE (14817) Tompkins(94), Tioga(5)
BROOKVIEW Rensselaer
BROWNVILLE Jefferson
BRUSHTON Franklin
BUCHANAN Westchester
BUFFALO Erie
BULLVILLE Orange
BURDETT Schuyler
BURKE Franklin
BURLINGHAM Sullivan
BURLINGTON FLATS Otsego
BURNT HILLS (12027) Saratoga(83), Schenectady(16)
BURT Niagara
BUSKIRK Rensselaer
BYRON (14422) Genesee(97), Orleans(2)
CADYVILLE Clinton
CAIRO Greene
CALCIUM Jefferson
CALEDONIA (14423) Livingston(98), Monroe(1)
CALLICOON Sullivan
CALLICOON CENTER Sullivan
CALVERTON Suffolk
CAMBRIA HEIGHTS Queens
CAMDEN Oneida
CAMERON Steuben
CAMERON MILLS Steuben
CAMILLUS Onondaga
CAMPBELL Steuben
CAMPBELL HALL Orange
CANAAN Columbia
CANAJOHARIE Montgomery
CANANDAIGUA Ontario
CANASERAGA (14822) Allegany(88), Livingston(11)
CANASTOTA Madison
CANDOR Tioga
CANEADEA Allegany
CANISTEO Steuben
CANTON St. Lawrence
CAPE VINCENT Jefferson
CARLE PLACE Nassau
CARLISLE Schoharie
CARMEL Putnam
CAROGA LAKE Fulton
CARTHAGE (13619) Lewis(97), St. Lawrence(2)
CASSADAGA Chautauqua
CASSVILLE Oneida
CASTILE Wyoming
CASTLE CREEK Broome
CASTLE POINT Dutchess
CASTLETON ON HUDSON Rensselaer
CASTORLAND Lewis
CATO (13033) Cayuga(96), Onondaga(2)
CATSKILL Greene
CATTARAUGUS Cattaraugus
CAYUGA Cayuga
CAYUTA (14824) Schuyler(72), Chemung(27)
CAZENOVIA (13035) Madison(96), Onondaga(3)

CEDARHURST Nassau
CELORON Chautauqua
CEMENTON Greene
CENTER MORICHES Suffolk
CENTEREACH Suffolk
CENTERPORT Suffolk
CENTERVILLE Allegany
CENTRAL BRIDGE Schoharie
CENTRAL ISLIP Suffolk
CENTRAL SQUARE Oswego
CENTRAL VALLEY Orange
CERES Allegany
CHADWICKS Oneida
CHAFFEE (14030) Erie(76), Cattaraugus(17), Wyoming(6)
CHAMPLAIN Clinton
CHAPPAQUA Westchester
CHARLOTTEVILLE Schoharie
CHASE MILLS St. Lawrence
CHATEAUGAY Franklin
CHATHAM Columbia
CHAUMONT Jefferson
CHAZY Clinton
CHELSEA Dutchess
CHEMUNG Chemung
CHENANGO BRIDGE Broome
CHENANGO FORKS Broome
CHERRY CREEK Chautauqua
CHERRY PLAIN Rensselaer
CHERRY VALLEY Otsego
CHESTER Orange
CHESTERTOWN Warren
CHICHESTER Ulster
CHILDWOLD St. Lawrence
CHIPPEWA BAY St. Lawrence
CHITTENANGO (13037) Madison(98), Onondaga(1)
CHURCHVILLE Monroe
CHURUBUSCO Clinton
CICERO Onondaga
CINCINNATUS Cortland
CIRCLEVILLE Orange
CLARENCE Erie
CLARENCE CENTER (14032) Erie(98), Niagara(1)
CLARENDON Orleans
CLARK MILLS Oneida
CLARKSON Monroe
CLARKSVILLE Albany
CLARYVILLE (12725) Sullivan(57), Ulster(42)
CLAVERACK Columbia
CLAY Onondaga
CLAYTON Jefferson
CLAYVILLE (13322) Herkimer(91), Oneida(8)
CLEMONS Washington
CLEVELAND (13042) Oswego(53), Oneida(46)
CLEVERDALE Warren
CLIFTON PARK Saratoga
CLIFTON SPRINGS Ontario
CLIMAX Greene
CLINTON Oneida
CLINTON CORNERS Dutchess
CLINTONDALE Ulster
CLOCKVILLE Madison
CLYDE (14433) Wayne(94), Seneca(5)
CLYMER Chautauqua
COBLESKILL Schoharie
COCHECTON Sullivan
COCHECTON CENTER Sullivan
COEYMANS Albany
COEYMANS HOLLOW (12046) Albany(90), Greene(9)
COHOCTON Steuben
COHOES Albany
COLD BROOK (13324) Herkimer(98), Hamilton(1)
COLD SPRING Putnam
COLD SPRING HARBOR Suffolk
COLDEN Erie

COLLIERSVILLE Otsego
COLLINS Erie
COLLINS CENTER Erie
COLTON St. Lawrence
COLUMBIAVILLE Columbia
COMMACK Suffolk
COMSTOCK Washington
CONESUS Livingston
CONEWANGO VALLEY (14726) Cattaraugus(90), Chautauqua(10)
CONGERS Rockland
CONKLIN Broome
CONNELLY Ulster
CONSTABLE Franklin
CONSTABLEVILLE Lewis
CONSTANTIA Oswego
COOPERS PLAINS Steuben
COOPERSTOWN Otsego
COPAKE Columbia
COPAKE FALLS Columbia
COPENHAGEN Lewis
COPIAGUE Suffolk
CORAM Suffolk
CORBETTSVILLE Broome
CORFU (14036) Genesee(97), Erie(2)
CORINTH Saratoga
CORNING (14830) Steuben(98), Chemung(1)
CORNING Steuben
CORNWALL Orange
CORNWALL ON HUDSON Orange
CORNWALLVILLE Greene
CORTLAND (13045) Cortland(91), Cayuga(6), Tompkins(1)
CORTLANDT MANOR Westchester
COSSAYUNA Washington
COTTEKILL Ulster
COWLESVILLE (14037) Wyoming(75), Erie(24)
COXSACKIE Greene
CRAGSMOOR Ulster
CRANBERRY LAKE St. Lawrence
CRARYVILLE Columbia
CRITTENDEN Erie
CROGHAN Lewis
CROMPOND Westchester
CROPSEYVILLE Rensselaer
CROSS RIVER Westchester
CROTON FALLS Westchester
CROTON ON HUDSON Westchester
CROWN POINT Essex
CUBA (14727) Allegany(79), Cattaraugus(20)
CUDDEBACKVILLE (12729) Orange(88), Sullivan(11)
CUTCHOGUE Suffolk
CUYLER (13050) Cortland(95), Onondaga(4)
DALE Wyoming
DALTON (14836) Livingston(57), Allegany(42)
DANNEMORA Clinton
DANSVILLE (14437) Livingston(90), Steuben(8)
DARIEN CENTER (14040) Genesee(87), Wyoming(12)
DAVENPORT (13750) Delaware(98), Otsego(1)
DAVENPORT CENTER Delaware
DAYTON Cattaraugus
DE KALB JUNCTION St. Lawrence
DE LANCEY Delaware
DE PEYSTER St. Lawrence
DE RUYTER (13052) Madison(52), Chenango(27), Cortland(18), Onondaga(1)
DEANSBORO Oneida
DEER PARK Suffolk
DEER RIVER Lewis
DEFERIET Jefferson
DELANSON (12053) Schenectady(86), Albany(13)

DELEVAN Cattaraugus
DELMAR Albany
DELPHI FALLS Onondaga
DENMARK Lewis
DENVER Delaware
DEPAUVILLE Jefferson
DEPEW Erie
DEPOSIT (13754) Broome(70), Delaware(29)
DERBY Erie
DEWITTVILLE Chautauqua
DEXTER Jefferson
DIAMOND POINT Warren
DICKINSON CENTER Franklin
DOBBS FERRY Westchester
DOLGEVILLE (13329) Herkimer(95), Fulton(4)
DORMANSVILLE Albany
DOVER PLAINS Dutchess
DOWNSVILLE Delaware
DRESDEN Yates
DRYDEN (13053) Tompkins(83), Cortland(16)
DUANESBURG Schenectady
DUNDEE (14837) Yates(74), Schuyler(20), Steuben(4)
DUNKIRK Chautauqua
DURHAM Greene
DURHAMVILLE Oneida
EAGLE BAY Herkimer
EAGLE BRIDGE Rensselaer
EAGLE HARBOR Orleans
EARLTON Greene
EARLVILLE (13332) Chenango(97), Madison(2)
EAST AMHERST Erie
EAST AURORA Erie
EAST BERNE Albany
EAST BETHANY (14054) Genesee(91), Wyoming(8)
EAST BLOOMFIELD Ontario
EAST BRANCH Delaware
EAST CHATHAM Columbia
EAST CONCORD Erie
EAST DURHAM Greene
EAST FREETOWN Cortland
EAST GREENBUSH Rensselaer
EAST GREENWICH Washington
EAST HAMPTON Suffolk
EAST HOMER Cortland
EAST ISLIP Suffolk
EAST JEWETT Greene
EAST MARION Suffolk
EAST MEADOW Nassau
EAST MEREDITH Delaware
EAST MORICHES Suffolk
EAST NASSAU (12062) Columbia(98), Rensselaer(1)
EAST NORTHPORT Suffolk
EAST NORWICH Nassau
EAST OTTO Cattaraugus
EAST PALMYRA Wayne
EAST PEMBROKE Genesee
EAST PHARSALIA Chenango
EAST QUOGUE Suffolk
EAST RANDOLPH Cattaraugus
EAST ROCHESTER Monroe
EAST ROCKAWAY Nassau
EAST SCHODACK Rensselaer
EAST SETAUKET Suffolk
EAST SPRINGFIELD Otsego
EAST SYRACUSE Onondaga
EAST WILLIAMSON Wayne
EAST WORCESTER Otsego
EASTCHESTER Westchester
EASTPORT Suffolk
EATON Madison
EDEN Erie
EDMESTON Otsego
EDWARDS St. Lawrence
ELBA (14058) Genesee(95), Orleans(4)
ELBRIDGE Onondaga

ELDRED Sullivan
ELIZABETHTOWN Essex
ELIZAVILLE Columbia
ELKA PARK Greene
ELLENBURG Clinton
ELLENBURG CENTER Clinton
ELLENBURG DEPOT Clinton
ELLENVILLE Ulster
ELLICOTTVILLE Cattaraugus
ELLINGTON Chautauqua
ELLISBURG Jefferson
ELMA Erie
ELMHURST Queens
ELMIRA Chemung
ELMONT Nassau
ELMSFORD Westchester
ENDICOTT (13760) Broome(90), Tioga(9)
ENDICOTT Broome
ENDWELL Broome
ERIEVILLE Madison
ERIN Chemung
ESOPUS Ulster
ESPERANCE Montgomery
ETNA Tompkins
EVANS MILLS Jefferson
FABIUS Onondaga
FAIR HAVEN (13064) Oswego(94), Onondaga(5)
FAIRFIELD Herkimer
FAIRPORT Monroe
FALCONER Chautauqua
FALLSBURG Sullivan
FANCHER Orleans
FAR ROCKAWAY Queens
FARMERSVILLE STATION (14060) Allegany(53), Cattaraugus(46)
FARMINGDALE (11735) Nassau(71), Suffolk(28)
FARMINGDALE Nassau
FARMINGTON Ontario
FARMINGVILLE Suffolk
FARNHAM Erie
FAYETTE Seneca
FAYETTEVILLE Onondaga
FELTS MILLS Jefferson
FERNDALE Sullivan
FEURA BUSH Albany
FILLMORE Allegany
FINDLEY LAKE Chautauqua
FINE St. Lawrence
FISHERS Ontario
FISHERS ISLAND Suffolk
FISHERS LANDING Jefferson
FISHKILL Dutchess
FISHS EDDY Delaware
FLEISCHMANNS (12430) Greene(59), Delaware(40)
FLORAL PARK (11001) Nassau(90), Queens(9)
FLORAL PARK Nassau
FLORAL PARK Queens
FLORIDA Orange
FLUSHING Queens
FLY CREEK Otsego
FONDA (12068) Montgomery(98), Fulton(1)
FORESTBURGH Sullivan
FORESTPORT Oneida
FORESTVILLE Chautauqua
FORT ANN Washington
FORT COVINGTON Franklin
FORT DRUM Jefferson
FORT EDWARD (12828) Washington(53), Saratoga(46)
FORT HUNTER Montgomery
FORT JACKSON St. Lawrence
FORT JOHNSON Montgomery
FORT MONTGOMERY Orange
FORT PLAIN (13339) Montgomery(73), Herkimer(15), Fulton(11)
FRANKFORT Herkimer
FRANKLIN Delaware
FRANKLIN SPRINGS Oneida

FRANKLIN SQUARE Nassau
FRANKLINVILLE (14737) Cattaraugus(98), Allegany(1)
FREDONIA Chautauqua
FREEDOM (14065) Cattaraugus(54), Allegany(45)
FREEHOLD Greene
FREEPORT Nassau
FREEVILLE Tompkins
FREMONT CENTER Sullivan
FREWSBURG (14738) Chautauqua(88), Cattaraugus(11)
FRIENDSHIP Allegany
FULTON Oswego
FULTONHAM Schoharie
FULTONVILLE Montgomery
GABRIELS Franklin
GAINESVILLE Wyoming
GALLUPVILLE Schoharie
GALWAY Saratoga
GANSEVOORT Saratoga
GARDEN CITY Nassau
GARDINER Ulster
GARNERVILLE Rockland
GARRATTSVILLE Otsego
GARRISON Putnam
GASPORT Niagara
GENESEO Livingston
GENEVA (14456) Ontario(92), Seneca(6)
GENOA Cayuga
GEORGETOWN (13072) Madison(96), Chenango(3)
GEORGETOWN Chenango
GERMANTOWN Columbia
GERRY Chautauqua
GETZVILLE Erie
GHENT Columbia
GILBERTSVILLE Otsego
GILBOA Schoharie
GLASCO Ulster
GLEN AUBREY Broome
GLEN COVE Nassau
GLEN HEAD Nassau
GLEN OAKS Queens
GLEN SPEY Sullivan
GLEN WILD Sullivan
GLENFIELD Lewis
GLENFORD Ulster
GLENHAM Dutchess
GLENMONT Albany
GLENS FALLS Warren
GLENWOOD Erie
GLENWOOD LANDING Nassau
GLOVERSVILLE Fulton
GODEFFROY Orange
GOLDENS BRIDGE Westchester
GORHAM Ontario
GOSHEN Orange
GOUVERNEUR St. Lawrence
GOWANDA (14070) Cattaraugus(57), Erie(42)
GRAFTON Rensselaer
GRAHAMSVILLE (12740) Sullivan(86), Ulster(13)
GRAND GORGE (12434) Delaware(92), Schoharie(7)
GRAND ISLAND Erie
GRANITE SPRINGS Westchester
GRANVILLE Washington
GREAT BEND Jefferson
GREAT NECK Nassau
GREAT RIVER Suffolk
GREAT VALLEY Cattaraugus
GREENE (13778) Chenango(66), Broome(33)
GREENFIELD CENTER Saratoga
GREENFIELD PARK Ulster
GREENHURST Chautauqua
GREENLAWN Suffolk
GREENPORT Suffolk
GREENVALE Nassau
GREENVILLE Greene

GREENWICH Washington
GREENWOOD Steuben
GREENWOOD LAKE Orange
GREIG Lewis
GROTON (13073) Tompkins(98), Cayuga(1)
GROVELAND Livingston
GUILDERLAND Albany
GUILDERLAND CENTER Albany
GUILFORD Chenango
HADLEY Saratoga
HAGAMAN Montgomery
HAGUE Warren
HAILESBORO St. Lawrence
HAINES FALLS Greene
HALCOTTSVILLE Delaware
HALL Ontario
HAMBURG Erie
HAMDEN Delaware
HAMILTON Madison
HAMLIN (14464) Monroe(97), Orleans(2)
HAMMOND St. Lawrence
HAMMONDSPORT (14840) Steuben(97), Schuyler(2)
HAMPTON Washington
HAMPTON BAYS Suffolk
HANCOCK Delaware
HANKINS Sullivan
HANNACROIX Greene
HANNAWA FALLS St. Lawrence
HANNIBAL Oswego
HARFORD Cortland
HARPERSFIELD Delaware
HARPURSVILLE Broome
HARRIMAN Orange
HARRIS Sullivan
HARRISON Westchester
HARRISVILLE (13648) St. Lawrence(84), Lewis(15)
HARTFORD Washington
HARTSDALE Westchester
HARTWICK Otsego
HARTWICK SEMINARY Otsego
HASTINGS Oswego
HASTINGS ON HUDSON Westchester
HAUPPAUGE Suffolk
HAVERSTRAW Rockland
HAWTHORNE Westchester
HECTOR Schuyler
HELENA St. Lawrence
HELMUTH Erie
HEMLOCK (14466) Ontario(58), Livingston(41)
HEMPSTEAD Nassau
HENDERSON Jefferson
HENDERSON HARBOR Jefferson
HENRIETTA Monroe
HENSONVILLE Greene
HERKIMER Herkimer
HERMON St. Lawrence
HEUVELTON St. Lawrence
HEWLETT Nassau
HICKSVILLE Nassau
HIGH FALLS Ulster
HIGHLAND Ulster
HIGHLAND FALLS Orange
HIGHLAND LAKE Sullivan
HIGHLAND MILLS Orange
HIGHMOUNT Ulster
HILLBURN Rockland
HILLSDALE Columbia
HILTON Monroe
HIMROD Yates
HINCKLEY Oneida
HINSDALE Cattaraugus
HOBART Delaware
HOFFMEISTER Hamilton
HOGANSBURG Franklin
HOLBROOK Suffolk
HOLLAND Erie
HOLLAND PATENT Oneida
HOLLEY (14470) Orleans(97), Monroe(2)

HOLLOWVILLE Columbia
HOLMES (12531) Dutchess(82), Putnam(17)
HOLTSVILLE Suffolk
HOMER (13077) Cortland(92), Onondaga(4), Cayuga(2)
HONEOYE Ontario
HONEOYE FALLS (14472) Monroe(90), Livingston(6), Ontario(2)
HOOSICK Rensselaer
HOOSICK FALLS Rensselaer
HOPEWELL JUNCTION (12533) Dutchess(98), Putnam(1)
HOPKINTON St. Lawrence
HORNELL Steuben
HORSEHEADS Chemung
HORTONVILLE Sullivan
HOUGHTON Allegany
HOWELLS Orange
HOWES CAVE Schoharie
HUBBARDSVILLE Madison
HUDSON Columbia
HUDSON FALLS Washington
HUGHSONVILLE Dutchess
HUGUENOT Orange
HULETTS LANDING Washington
HUME Allegany
HUNT (14846) Livingston(75), Allegany(24)
HUNTER Greene
HUNTINGTON Suffolk
HUNTINGTON STATION Suffolk
HURLEY Ulster
HURLEYVILLE Sullivan
HYDE PARK Dutchess
ILION Herkimer
INDIAN LAKE Hamilton
INDUSTRY Monroe
INLET Hamilton
INTERLAKEN Seneca
INWOOD Nassau
INWOOD Queens
IONIA (14475) Ontario(93), Monroe(6)
IRVING (14081) Chautauqua(50), Erie(47), Cattaraugus(2)
IRVINGTON Westchester
ISLAND PARK Nassau
ISLANDIA Suffolk
ISLIP Suffolk
ISLIP TERRACE Suffolk
ITHACA Tompkins
JACKSONVILLE Tompkins
JAMAICA Queens
JAMESPORT Suffolk
JAMESTOWN Chautauqua
JAMESVILLE Onondaga
JASPER Steuben
JAVA CENTER Wyoming
JAVA VILLAGE Wyoming
JAY Essex
JEFFERSON (12093) Schoharie(73), Delaware(26)
JEFFERSON VALLEY Westchester
JEFFERSONVILLE Sullivan
JERICHO Nassau
JEWETT Greene
JOHNSBURG Warren
JOHNSON Orange
JOHNSON CITY Broome
JOHNSONVILLE Rensselaer
JOHNSTOWN Fulton
JORDAN (13080) Onondaga(87), Cayuga(12)
JORDANVILLE Herkimer
KANONA Steuben
KATONAH Westchester
KATTSKILL BAY Warren
KAUNEONGA LAKE Sullivan
KEENE Essex
KEENE VALLEY Essex
KEESEVILLE (12944) Clinton(92), Essex(7)
KEESEVILLE Clinton

KENDALL (14476) Orleans(95), Monroe(4)
KENNEDY (14747) Chautauqua(90), Cattaraugus(9)
KENOZA LAKE Sullivan
KENT Orleans
KERHONKSON Ulster
KEUKA PARK Yates
KIAMESHA LAKE Sullivan
KILL BUCK Cattaraugus
KILLAWOG Broome
KINDERHOOK Columbia
KING FERRY Cayuga
KINGS PARK Suffolk
KINGSTON Ulster
KIRKVILLE (13082) Madison(57), Onondaga(42)
KIRKWOOD Broome
KNAPP CREEK Cattaraugus
KNOWLESVILLE Orleans
KNOX Albany
KNOXBORO Oneida
LA FARGEVILLE Jefferson
LA FAYETTE Onondaga
LACONA Oswego
LAGRANGEVILLE Dutchess
LAKE CLEAR Franklin
LAKE GEORGE Warren
LAKE GROVE Suffolk
LAKE HILL Ulster
LAKE HUNTINGTON Sullivan
LAKE KATRINE Ulster
LAKE LUZERNE Warren
LAKE PEEKSKILL Putnam
LAKE PLACID Essex
LAKE PLEASANT Hamilton
LAKE VIEW Erie
LAKEMONT Yates
LAKEVILLE Livingston
LAKEWOOD Chautauqua
LANCASTER Erie
LANESVILLE Greene
LANSING (14882) Tompkins(98), Cayuga(1)
LARCHMONT Westchester
LATHAM Albany
LAUREL Suffolk
LAURENS Otsego
LAWRENCE Nassau
LAWRENCEVILLE St. Lawrence
LAWTONS Erie
LAWYERSVILLE Schoharie
LE ROY (14482) Genesee(95), Livingston(3)
LEBANON Madison
LEBANON SPRINGS Columbia
LEE CENTER Oneida
LEEDS Greene
LEICESTER (14481) Livingston(98), Wyoming(1)
LEON Cattaraugus
LEONARDSVILLE Madison
LEVITTOWN Nassau
LEW BEACH (12753) Ulster(58), Sullivan(38), Delaware(4)
LEWIS Essex
LEWISTON Niagara
LEXINGTON Greene
LIBERTY Sullivan
LILY DALE Chautauqua
LIMA (14485) Livingston(93), Ontario(6)
LIMERICK Jefferson
LIMESTONE Cattaraugus
LINCOLNDALE Westchester
LINDENHURST Suffolk
LINDLEY Steuben
LINWOOD Genesee
LISBON St. Lawrence
LISLE Broome
LITTLE FALLS Herkimer
LITTLE GENESEE Allegany
LITTLE VALLEY Cattaraugus
LITTLE YORK Cortland

LIVERPOOL Onondaga
LIVINGSTON Columbia
LIVINGSTON MANOR (12758)
   Sullivan(91), Ulster(7)
LIVONIA (14487) Livingston(93), Ontario(6)
LIVONIA CENTER Livingston
LOCH SHELDRAKE Sullivan
LOCKE (13092) Tompkins(97), Cayuga(2)
LOCKPORT Niagara
LOCKWOOD (14859) Tioga(59),
   Chemung(40)
LOCUST VALLEY Nassau
LODI Seneca
LONG BEACH Nassau
LONG EDDY (12760) Delaware(67),
   Sullivan(32)
LONG ISLAND CITY Queens
LONG LAKE Hamilton
LORRAINE Jefferson
LOWMAN Chemung
LOWVILLE (13367) Lewis(94), Herkimer(5)
LYCOMING Oswego
LYNBROOK Nassau
LYNDONVILLE (14098) Orleans(98),
   Niagara(1)
LYON MOUNTAIN Clinton
LYONS (14489) Wayne(95), Ontario(2),
   Seneca(2)
LYONS FALLS Lewis
LYSANDER Onondaga
MACEDON (14502) Wayne(97), Monroe(2)
MACHIAS Cattaraugus
MADISON (13402) Madison(98), Oneida(1)
MADRID St. Lawrence
MAHOPAC (10541) Putnam(93),
   Westchester(6)
MAHOPAC FALLS Putnam
MAINE Broome
MALDEN BRIDGE Columbia
MALDEN ON HUDSON Ulster
MALLORY Oswego
MALONE Franklin
MALVERNE Nassau
MAMARONECK Westchester
MANCHESTER Ontario
MANHASSET Nassau
MANLIUS (13104) Onondaga(98),
   Madison(1)
MANNSVILLE Jefferson
MANORVILLE Suffolk
MAPLE SPRINGS Chautauqua
MAPLE VIEW Oswego
MAPLECREST Greene
MARATHON (13803) Cortland(94),
   Broome(5)
MARCELLUS Onondaga
MARCY Oneida
MARGARETVILLE (12455) Delaware(96),
   Ulster(3)
MARIETTA Onondaga
MARILLA Erie
MARION Wayne
MARLBORO (12542) Ulster(93), Orange(6)
MARTINSBURG Lewis
MARTVILLE (13111) Cayuga(87),
   Oswego(12)
MARYKNOLL Westchester
MARYLAND Otsego
MASONVILLE Delaware
MASSAPEQUA Nassau
MASSAPEQUA PARK Nassau
MASSENA St. Lawrence
MASTIC Suffolk
MASTIC BEACH Suffolk
MATTITUCK Suffolk
MATTYDALE Onondaga
MAYBROOK (12543) Orange(98),
   Dutchess(1)
MAYFIELD Fulton
MAYVILLE Chautauqua
MC CONNELLSVILLE Oneida
MC DONOUGH Chenango

MC GRAW Cortland
MC LEAN Tompkins
MECHANICVILLE (12118) Saratoga(98),
   Rensselaer(1)
MECKLENBURG Schuyler
MEDFORD Suffolk
MEDINA Orleans
MEDUSA Albany
MELLENVILLE Columbia
MELROSE Rensselaer
MELVILLE Suffolk
MEMPHIS Onondaga
MENDON Monroe
MERIDALE Delaware
MERIDIAN Cayuga
MERRICK Nassau
MEXICO Oswego
MID HUDSON Orange
MID ISLAND Suffolk
MIDDLE FALLS Washington
MIDDLE GRANVILLE Washington
MIDDLE GROVE Saratoga
MIDDLE ISLAND Suffolk
MIDDLE VILLAGE Queens
MIDDLEBURGH (12122) Albany(57),
   Schoharie(42)
MIDDLEPORT (14105) Niagara(94),
   Orleans(3), Genesee(1)
MIDDLESEX Yates
MIDDLETOWN (10940) Orange(98),
   Sullivan(1)
MIDDLETOWN Orange
MIDDLEVILLE Herkimer
MILFORD Otsego
MILL NECK Nassau
MILLBROOK Dutchess
MILLER PLACE Suffolk
MILLERTON (12546) Dutchess(96),
   Columbia(3)
MILLPORT (14864) Chemung(85),
   Schuyler(14)
MILLWOOD Westchester
MILTON Ulster
MINEOLA Nassau
MINERVA Essex
MINETTO Oswego
MINEVILLE Essex
MINOA Onondaga
MODEL CITY Niagara
MODENA Ulster
MOHAWK Herkimer
MOHEGAN LAKE Westchester
MOIRA Franklin
MONGAUP VALLEY Sullivan
MONROE Orange
MONSEY Rockland
MONTAUK Suffolk
MONTEZUMA Cayuga
MONTGOMERY Orange
MONTICELLO Sullivan
MONTOUR FALLS Schuyler
MONTROSE Westchester
MOOERS Clinton
MOOERS FORKS Clinton
MORAVIA Cayuga
MORIAH Essex
MORIAH CENTER Essex
MORICHES Suffolk
MORRIS Otsego
MORRISONVILLE Clinton
MORRISTOWN St. Lawrence
MORRISVILLE Madison
MORTON Orleans
MOTTVILLE Onondaga
MOUNT KISCO Westchester
MOUNT MARION Ulster
MOUNT MORRIS Livingston
MOUNT SINAI Suffolk
MOUNT TREMPER Ulster
MOUNT UPTON (13809) Chenango(66),
   Otsego(33)
MOUNT VERNON Westchester

MOUNT VISION Otsego
MOUNTAIN DALE Sullivan
MOUNTAINVILLE Orange
MUMFORD Monroe
MUNNSVILLE (13409) Madison(92),
   Oneida(7)
NANUET Rockland
NAPANOCH Ulster
NAPLES (14512) Ontario(75), Yates(19),
   Steuben(3)
NARROWSBURG Sullivan
NASSAU Rensselaer
NATURAL BRIDGE (13665) Jefferson(96),
   Lewis(3)
NEDROW Onondaga
NELLISTON Montgomery
NESCONSET Suffolk
NEVERSINK Sullivan
NEW BALTIMORE Greene
NEW BERLIN Chenango
NEW CITY Rockland
NEW HAMPTON Orange
NEW HARTFORD Oneida
NEW HAVEN Oswego
NEW HYDE PARK (11040) Nassau(96),
   Queens(3)
NEW HYDE PARK Nassau
NEW KINGSTON Delaware
NEW LEBANON Columbia
NEW LISBON Otsego
NEW MILFORD Orange
NEW PALTZ Ulster
NEW ROCHELLE Westchester
NEW RUSSIA Essex
NEW SUFFOLK Suffolk
NEW WINDSOR Orange
NEW WOODSTOCK (13122)
   Onondaga(65), Madison(34)
NEW YORK New York
NEW YORK MILLS Oneida
NEWARK (14513) Wayne(98), Ontario(1)
NEWARK VALLEY (13811) Tioga(93),
   Broome(6)
NEWBURGH Orange
NEWCOMB Essex
NEWFANE Niagara
NEWFIELD Tompkins
NEWPORT Herkimer
NEWTON FALLS St. Lawrence
NEWTONVILLE Albany
NIAGARA FALLS Niagara
NIAGARA UNIVERSITY Niagara
NICHOLS Tioga
NICHOLVILLE St. Lawrence
NINEVEH Broome
NIOBE Chautauqua
NIVERVILLE Columbia
NORFOLK St. Lawrence
NORTH BABYLON Suffolk
NORTH BANGOR Franklin
NORTH BAY Oneida
NORTH BLENHEIM Schoharie
NORTH BOSTON Erie
NORTH BRANCH Sullivan
NORTH BROOKFIELD Madison
NORTH CHATHAM Columbia
NORTH CHILI Monroe
NORTH CLYMER Chautauqua
NORTH COHOCTON Steuben
NORTH COLLINS Erie
NORTH CREEK Warren
NORTH EVANS Erie
NORTH GRANVILLE Washington
NORTH GREECE Monroe
NORTH HOOSICK Rensselaer
NORTH HUDSON Essex
NORTH JAVA Wyoming
NORTH LAWRENCE St. Lawrence
NORTH NORWICH Chenango
NORTH PITCHER Chenango
NORTH RIVER Warren
NORTH ROSE Wayne

NORTH SALEM Westchester
NORTH TONAWANDA Niagara
NORTHPORT Suffolk
NORTHVILLE Fulton
NORTON HILL Greene
NORWICH Chenango
NORWOOD St. Lawrence
NUNDA Livingston
NYACK Rockland
OAK HILL Greene
OAKDALE Suffolk
OAKFIELD Genesee
OAKS CORNERS Ontario
OBERNBURG Sullivan
OCEAN BEACH Suffolk
OCEANSIDE Nassau
ODESSA Schuyler
OGDENSBURG St. Lawrence
OLCOTT Niagara
OLD BETHPAGE Nassau
OLD CHATHAM Columbia
OLD FORGE Herkimer
OLD WESTBURY Nassau
OLEAN Cattaraugus
OLIVEBRIDGE Ulster
OLIVEREA Ulster
OLMSTEDVILLE Essex
ONCHIOTA Franklin
ONEIDA (13421) Madison(84), Oneida(15)
ONEONTA Otsego
ONTARIO (14519) Wayne(96), Monroe(3)
ONTARIO CENTER Wayne
ORAN Onondaga
ORANGEBURG Rockland
ORCHARD PARK Erie
ORIENT Suffolk
ORISKANY Oneida
ORISKANY FALLS (13425) Oneida(97),
   Madison(2)
ORWELL Oswego
OSSINING Westchester
OSWEGATCHIE St. Lawrence
OSWEGO Oswego
OTEGO (13825) Otsego(93), Delaware(6)
OTISVILLE (10963) Orange(97),
   Sullivan(2)
OTTO Cattaraugus
OUAQUAGA Broome
OVID Seneca
OWASCO Cayuga
OWEGO Tioga
OWLS HEAD Franklin
OXBOW Jefferson
OXFORD Chenango
OYSTER BAY Nassau
PAINTED POST (14870) Steuben(97),
   Schuyler(2)
PALATINE BRIDGE Montgomery
PALENVILLE Greene
PALISADES Rockland
PALMYRA (14522) Wayne(89), Ontario(10)
PANAMA Chautauqua
PARADOX Essex
PARIS Oneida
PARISH Oswego
PARISHVILLE St. Lawrence
PARKSVILLE Sullivan
PATCHOGUE Suffolk
PATTERSON Putnam
PATTERSONVILLE Schenectady
PAUL SMITHS Franklin
PAVILION (14525) Genesee(61),
   Wyoming(33), Livingston(5)
PAWLING Dutchess
PEARL RIVER Rockland
PECONIC Suffolk
PEEKSKILL Westchester
PELHAM Westchester
PENFIELD Monroe
PENN YAN Yates
PENNELLVILLE Oswego
PERKINSVILLE Steuben

PERRY Wyoming
PERRYSBURG Cattaraugus
PERRYVILLE Madison
PERU Clinton
PETERBORO Madison
PETERSBURG Rensselaer
PHELPS (14532) Ontario(94), Seneca(5)
PHILADELPHIA Jefferson
PHILLIPSPORT Sullivan
PHILMONT Columbia
PHOENICIA Ulster
PHOENIX (13135) Oswego(87),
    Onondaga(12)
PIERCEFIELD St. Lawrence
PIERMONT Rockland
PIERREPONT MANOR Jefferson
PIFFARD Livingston
PIKE Wyoming
PINE BUSH (12566) Ulster(58),
    Orange(37), Sullivan(3)
PINE CITY (14871) Chemung(83),
    Steuben(16)
PINE HILL Ulster
PINE ISLAND Orange
PINE PLAINS (12567) Dutchess(92),
    Columbia(7)
PINE VALLEY Chemung
PISECO Hamilton
PITCHER (13136) Chenango(96),
    Cortland(3)
PITTSFORD Monroe
PLAINVIEW Nassau
PLAINVILLE Onondaga
PLATTEKILL Ulster
PLATTSBURGH Clinton
PLEASANT VALLEY Dutchess
PLEASANTVILLE Westchester
PLESSIS Jefferson
PLYMOUTH Chenango
POESTENKILL Rensselaer
POINT LOOKOUT Nassau
POLAND (13431) Oneida(90), Herkimer(9)
POMONA Rockland
POMPEY Onondaga
POND EDDY Sullivan
POOLVILLE Madison
POPLAR RIDGE Cayuga
PORT BYRON Cayuga
PORT CHESTER Westchester
PORT CRANE Broome
PORT EWEN Ulster
PORT GIBSON Ontario
PORT HENRY Essex
PORT JEFFERSON Suffolk
PORT JEFFERSON STATION Suffolk
PORT JERVIS Orange
PORT KENT Essex
PORT LEYDEN Lewis
PORT WASHINGTON Nassau
PORTAGEVILLE (14536) Wyoming(74),
    Allegany(25)
PORTER CORNERS Saratoga
PORTLAND Chautauqua
PORTLANDVILLE Otsego
PORTVILLE (14770) Cattaraugus(75),
    Allegany(24)
POTSDAM St. Lawrence
POTTERSVILLE Warren
POUGHKEEPSIE Dutchess
POUGHQUAG Dutchess
POUND RIDGE Westchester
PRATTS HOLLOW Madison
PRATTSBURGH (14873) Steuben(98),
    Yates(1)
PRATTSVILLE (12468) Greene(95),
    Delaware(4)
PREBLE (13141) Cortland(63),
    Onondaga(36)
PRESTON HOLLOW (12469) Greene(95),
    Albany(4)
PROSPECT Oneida
PULASKI Oswego

PULTENEY Steuben
PULTNEYVILLE Wayne
PURCHASE Westchester
PURDYS Westchester
PURLING Greene
PUTNAM STATION Washington
PUTNAM VALLEY Putnam
PYRITES St. Lawrence
QUAKER STREET Schenectady
QUEENS VILLAGE Queens
QUEENSBURY Warren
QUOGUE Suffolk
RAINBOW LAKE Franklin
RANDOLPH Cattaraugus
RANSOMVILLE Niagara
RAQUETTE LAKE Hamilton
RAVENA Albany
RAY BROOK Essex
RAYMONDVILLE St. Lawrence
READING CENTER Schuyler
RED CREEK (13143) Wayne(98),
    Cayuga(1)
RED HOOK Dutchess
REDFIELD Oswego
REDFORD Clinton
REDWOOD Jefferson
REMSEN Oneida
REMSENBURG Suffolk
RENSSELAER Rensselaer
RENSSELAER FALLS St. Lawrence
RENSSELAERVILLE Albany
RETSOF Livingston
REXFORD (12148) Saratoga(96),
    Schenectady(3)
REXVILLE (14877) Steuben(98),
    Allegany(1)
RHINEBECK Dutchess
RHINECLIFF Dutchess
RICHBURG Allegany
RICHFIELD SPRINGS Otsego
RICHFORD (13835) Tioga(57),
    Broome(29), Cortland(12)
RICHLAND Oswego
RICHMOND HILL Queens
RICHMONDVILLE (12149) Schoharie(97),
    Otsego(2)
RICHVILLE St. Lawrence
RIDGE Suffolk
RIFTON Ulster
RIPARIUS Warren
RIPLEY Chautauqua
RIVERHEAD Suffolk
ROCHESTER Monroe
ROCK CITY FALLS Saratoga
ROCK HILL Sullivan
ROCK STREAM (14878) Schuyler(71),
    Yates(28)
ROCK TAVERN Orange
ROCKAWAY PARK Queens
ROCKLAND M P C Rockland
ROCKVILLE CENTRE Nassau
ROCKY POINT Suffolk
RODMAN Jefferson
RODMAN Lewis
ROME Oneida
ROMULUS Seneca
RONKONKOMA Suffolk
ROOSEVELT Nassau
ROOSEVELTOWN St. Lawrence
ROSCOE (12776) Sullivan(74),
    Delaware(25)
ROSE Wayne
ROSEBOOM Otsego
ROSENDALE Ulster
ROSLYN Nassau
ROSLYN HEIGHTS Nassau
ROSSBURG Allegany
ROTTERDAM JUNCTION Schenectady
ROUND LAKE Saratoga
ROUND TOP Greene
ROUSES POINT Clinton
ROXBURY Delaware

RUBY Ulster
RUSH Monroe
RUSHFORD Allegany
RUSHVILLE (14544) Yates(54),
    Ontario(45)
RUSSELL St. Lawrence
RYE Westchester
SABAEL Hamilton
SACKETS HARBOR Jefferson
SAG HARBOR Suffolk
SAGAPONACK Suffolk
SAINT BONAVENTURE Cattaraugus
SAINT JAMES Suffolk
SAINT JOHNSVILLE (13452)
    Montgomery(59), Fulton(40)
SAINT REGIS FALLS Franklin
SALAMANCA Cattaraugus
SALISBURY CENTER Herkimer
SALISBURY MILLS Orange
SALT POINT Dutchess
SANBORN Niagara
SAND LAKE Rensselaer
SANDUSKY Cattaraugus
SANDY CREEK Oswego
SANGERFIELD Oneida
SARANAC Clinton
SARANAC LAKE (12983) Franklin(82),
    Essex(17)
SARANAC LAKE Franklin
SARATOGA SPRINGS Saratoga
SARDINIA Erie
SAUGERTIES Ulster
SAUQUOIT (13456) Oneida(93),
    Herkimer(6)
SAVANNAH Wayne
SAVONA Steuben
SAYVILLE Suffolk
SCARSDALE Westchester
SCHAGHTICOKE Rensselaer
SCHENECTADY (12309) Schenectady(92),
    Albany(6)
SCHENECTADY Schenectady
SCHENEVUS Otsego
SCHODACK LANDING (12156)
    Rensselaer(91), Columbia(8)
SCHOHARIE Schoharie
SCHROON LAKE Essex
SCHUYLER FALLS Clinton
SCHUYLER LAKE Otsego
SCHUYLERVILLE Saratoga
SCIO Allegany
SCIPIO CENTER Cayuga
SCOTTSBURG Livingston
SCOTTSVILLE Monroe
SEA CLIFF Nassau
SEAFORD Nassau
SELDEN Suffolk
SELKIRK Albany
SENECA CASTLE Ontario
SENECA FALLS Seneca
SENNETT Cayuga
SEVERANCE Essex
SHANDAKEN (12480) Ulster(71),
    Greene(28)
SHARON SPRINGS (13459)
    Schoharie(94), Montgomery(5)
SHEDS Madison
SHELTER ISLAND Suffolk
SHELTER ISLAND HEIGHTS Suffolk
SHENOROCK Westchester
SHERBURNE (13460) Chenango(98),
    Madison(1)
SHERIDAN Chautauqua
SHERMAN Chautauqua
SHERRILL Oneida
SHINHOPPLE Delaware
SHIRLEY Suffolk
SHOKAN Ulster
SHOREHAM Suffolk
SHORTSVILLE Ontario
SHRUB OAK Westchester
SHUSHAN Washington

SIDNEY (13838) Delaware(94), Otsego(5)
SIDNEY CENTER Delaware
SILVER BAY Warren
SILVER CREEK Chautauqua
SILVER LAKE Wyoming
SILVER SPRINGS Wyoming
SINCLAIRVILLE Chautauqua
SKANEATELES (13152) Onondaga(92),
    Cayuga(7)
SKANEATELES FALLS Onondaga
SLATE HILL Orange
SLATERVILLE SPRINGS Tompkins
SLINGERLANDS Albany
SLOANSVILLE Schoharie
SLOATSBURG Rockland
SMALLWOOD Sullivan
SMITHBORO Tioga
SMITHS LANDING Greene
SMITHTOWN Suffolk
SMITHVILLE FLATS (13841) Cortland(80),
    Chenango(14), Broome(4)
SMYRNA Chenango
SODUS Wayne
SODUS CENTER Wayne
SODUS POINT Wayne
SOLSVILLE Madison
SOMERS Westchester
SONYEA Livingston
SOUND BEACH Suffolk
SOUTH BETHLEHEM Albany
SOUTH BUTLER Wayne
SOUTH BYRON Genesee
SOUTH CAIRO Greene
SOUTH COLTON St. Lawrence
SOUTH DAYTON (14138)
    Cattaraugus(65), Chautauqua(34)
SOUTH EDMESTON Otsego
SOUTH FALLSBURG Sullivan
SOUTH GLENS FALLS Saratoga
SOUTH JAMESPORT Suffolk
SOUTH KORTRIGHT Delaware
SOUTH LIMA Livingston
SOUTH NEW BERLIN Chenango
SOUTH OTSELIC Chenango
SOUTH PLYMOUTH Chenango
SOUTH RUTLAND Jefferson
SOUTH SALEM Westchester
SOUTH SCHODACK Rensselaer
SOUTH WALES Erie
SOUTH WESTERLO Albany
SOUTHAMPTON Suffolk
SOUTHFIELDS Orange
SOUTHOLD Suffolk
SPARKILL Rockland
SPARROW BUSH (12780) Orange(82),
    Sullivan(17)
SPECULATOR Hamilton
SPENCER (14883) Tioga(79),
    Tompkins(20)
SPENCERPORT Monroe
SPENCERTOWN Columbia
SPEONK Suffolk
SPRAKERS Montgomery
SPRING BROOK Erie
SPRING GLEN Ulster
SPRING VALLEY Rockland
SPRINGFIELD CENTER Otsego
SPRINGVILLE (14141) Erie(94),
    Cattaraugus(5)
SPRINGWATER (14560) Ontario(51),
    Livingston(49)
STAATSBURG Dutchess
STAFFORD Genesee
STAMFORD (12167) Delaware(76),
    Schoharie(23)
STANFORDVILLE Dutchess
STANLEY (14561) Ontario(94), Yates(5)
STAR LAKE St. Lawrence
STATEN ISLAND Richmond
STEAMBURG Cattaraugus
STELLA NIAGARA Niagara
STEPHENTOWN Rensselaer

STERLING Cayuga
STERLING FOREST Orange
STILLWATER Saratoga
STITTVILLE Oneida
STOCKTON Chautauqua
STONE RIDGE Ulster
STONY BROOK Suffolk
STONY CREEK Warren
STONY POINT Rockland
STORMVILLE Dutchess
STOTTVILLE Columbia
STOW Chautauqua
STRATFORD (13470) Fulton(77), Herkimer(22)
STRYKERSVILLE (14145) Wyoming(92), Erie(7)
STUYVESANT Columbia
STUYVESANT FALLS Columbia
SUFFERN Rockland
SUGAR LOAF Orange
SUGARBUSH Franklin
SUMMIT Schoharie
SUMMITVILLE Sullivan
SUNDOWN Ulster
SURPRISE Greene
SWAIN Allegany
SWAN LAKE Sullivan
SYLVAN BEACH Oneida
SYOSSET Nassau
SYRACUSE Onondaga
TABERG Oneida
TALLMAN Rockland
TANNERSVILLE Greene
TAPPAN Rockland
TARRYTOWN Westchester
THENDARA Herkimer
THERESA Jefferson
THIELLS Rockland
THOMPSON RIDGE Orange
THOMPSONVILLE Sullivan
THORNWOOD Westchester
THOUSAND ISLAND PARK Jefferson
THREE MILE BAY Jefferson
TICONDEROGA Essex
TILLSON Ulster
TIOGA CENTER Tioga
TIVOLI (12583) Dutchess(62), Columbia(37)
TOMKINS COVE Rockland
TONAWANDA Erie
TREADWELL Delaware
TRIBES HILL Montgomery
TROUPSBURG Steuben
TROUT CREEK Delaware
TROY Albany
TROY Rensselaer
TRUMANSBURG (14886) Tompkins(61), Schuyler(26), Seneca(12)
TRUXTON (13158) Cortland(97), Madison(2)
TUCKAHOE Westchester
TULLY (13159) Onondaga(82), Cortland(17)
TUNNEL Broome

TUPPER LAKE (12986) Franklin(94), St. Lawrence(5)
TURIN Lewis
TUXEDO PARK Orange
TYRONE Schuyler
ULSTER PARK Ulster
UNADILLA Otsego
UNION HILL Wayne
UNION SPRINGS Cayuga
UNIONDALE Nassau
UNIONVILLE Orange
UPPER JAY Essex
UPTON Suffolk
UTICA (13501) Oneida(97), Herkimer(2)
UTICA Oneida
VAILS GATE Orange
VALATIE Columbia
VALHALLA Westchester
VALLEY COTTAGE Rockland
VALLEY FALLS Rensselaer
VALLEY STREAM Nassau
VALOIS (14888) Schuyler(82), Seneca(17)
VAN BUREN POINT Chautauqua
VAN ETTEN (14889) Chemung(87), Schuyler(6), Tioga(5)
VAN HORNESVILLE (13475) Herkimer(82), Otsego(17)
VARYSBURG Wyoming
VERBANK Dutchess
VERMONTVILLE Franklin
VERNON Oneida
VERNON CENTER Oneida
VERONA Oneida
VERONA BEACH Oneida
VERPLANCK Westchester
VERSAILLES Cattaraugus
VESTAL Broome
VICTOR (14564) Ontario(97), Monroe(2)
VICTORY MILLS Saratoga
VOORHEESVILLE Albany
WACCABUC Westchester
WADDINGTON St. Lawrence
WADHAMS Essex
WADING RIVER Suffolk
WAINSCOTT Suffolk
WALDEN Orange
WALES CENTER Erie
WALKER VALLEY Ulster
WALLKILL (12589) Ulster(78), Orange(21)
WALTON Delaware
WALWORTH Wayne
WAMPSVILLE Madison
WANAKENA St. Lawrence
WANTAGH Nassau
WAPPINGERS FALLS Dutchess
WARNERS Onondaga
WARNERVILLE Schoharie
WARRENSBURG Warren
WARSAW Wyoming
WARWICK Orange
WASHINGTON MILLS Oneida
WASHINGTONVILLE Orange
WASSAIC Dutchess
WATER MILL Suffolk

WATERFORD Saratoga
WATERLOO Seneca
WATERPORT Orleans
WATERTOWN Jefferson
WATERVILLE (13480) Oneida(95), Madison(4)
WATERVLIET Albany
WATKINS GLEN Schuyler
WAVERLY (14892) Tioga(91), Chemung(8)
WAWARSING Ulster
WAYLAND (14572) Steuben(79), Livingston(20)
WAYNE Schuyler
WEBSTER Monroe
WEBSTER CROSSING Livingston
WEEDSPORT (13166) Cayuga(97), Onondaga(2)
WELLESLEY ISLAND Jefferson
WELLS Hamilton
WELLS BRIDGE Otsego
WELLSBURG Chemung
WELLSVILLE Allegany
WEST BABYLON Suffolk
WEST BLOOMFIELD Ontario
WEST BURLINGTON Otsego
WEST CAMP Ulster
WEST CHAZY Clinton
WEST CLARKSVILLE Allegany
WEST COPAKE Columbia
WEST COXSACKIE Greene
WEST DANBY Tompkins
WEST DAVENPORT Delaware
WEST EATON Madison
WEST EDMESTON (13485) Madison(74), Otsego(24)
WEST EXETER Otsego
WEST FALLS Erie
WEST FULTON Schoharie
WEST HARRISON Westchester
WEST HAVERSTRAW Rockland
WEST HEMPSTEAD Nassau
WEST HENRIETTA Monroe
WEST HURLEY Ulster
WEST ISLIP Suffolk
WEST KILL Greene
WEST LEBANON Columbia
WEST LEYDEN (13489) Lewis(98), Oneida(1)
WEST MONROE Oswego
WEST NYACK Rockland
WEST ONEONTA Otsego
WEST PARK Ulster
WEST POINT Orange
WEST SAND LAKE Rensselaer
WEST SAYVILLE Suffolk
WEST SHOKAN Ulster
WEST STOCKHOLM St. Lawrence
WEST VALLEY Cattaraugus
WEST WINFIELD (13491) Herkimer(90), Otsego(6), Oneida(2)
WESTBROOKVILLE Sullivan
WESTBURY Nassau
WESTDALE (13483) Oneida(97), Oswego(2)

WESTERLO Albany
WESTERN Oneida
WESTERNVILLE Oneida
WESTFIELD Chautauqua
WESTFORD Otsego
WESTHAMPTON Suffolk
WESTHAMPTON BEACH Suffolk
WESTMORELAND Oneida
WESTONS MILLS Cattaraugus
WESTPORT Essex
WESTTOWN Orange
WEVERTOWN Warren
WHALLONSBURG Essex
WHIPPLEVILLE Franklin
WHITE LAKE Sullivan
WHITE PLAINS Westchester
WHITE SULPHUR SPRINGS Sullivan
WHITEHALL Washington
WHITESBORO Oneida
WHITESVILLE (14897) Allegany(93), Steuben(6)
WHITNEY POINT Broome
WILLARD Seneca
WILLET (13863) Cortland(98), Broome(1)
WILLIAMSON Wayne
WILLIAMSTOWN Oswego
WILLISTON PARK Nassau
WILLOW Ulster
WILLSBORO Essex
WILLSEYVILLE (13864) Tioga(67), Tompkins(32)
WILMINGTON (12997) Saratoga(84), Essex(15)
WILSON Niagara
WINDHAM Greene
WINDSOR Broome
WINGDALE Dutchess
WINTHROP St. Lawrence
WITHERBEE Essex
WOLCOTT Wayne
WOODBOURNE (12788) Sullivan(97), Ulster(2)
WOODBURY Nassau
WOODGATE Oneida
WOODHULL Steuben
WOODMERE Nassau
WOODRIDGE Sullivan
WOODSTOCK Ulster
WOODVILLE Jefferson
WORCESTER Otsego
WURTSBORO Sullivan
WYANDANCH Suffolk
WYNANTSKILL Rensselaer
WYOMING (14591) Wyoming(87), Genesee(12)
YAPHANK Suffolk
YONKERS Westchester
YORK Livingston
YORKSHIRE Cattaraugus
YORKTOWN HEIGHTS Westchester
YORKVILLE Oneida
YOUNGSTOWN Niagara
YOUNGSVILLE Sullivan
YULAN Sullivan

New York ZIP/City Cross Reference

00401-00401	PLEASANTVILLE	
00501-00544	HOLTSVILLE	
06390-06390	FISHERS ISLAND	
09002-09894	APO or FPO	
10000-10292	NEW YORK	
10300-10314	STATEN ISLAND	
10400-10499	BRONX	
10501-10501	AMAWALK	
10502-10502	ARDSLEY	
10503-10503	ARDSLEY ON HUDSON	
10504-10504	ARMONK	
10505-10505	BALDWIN PLACE	
10506-10506	BEDFORD	
10507-10507	BEDFORD HILLS	
10509-10509	BREWSTER	
10510-10510	BRIARCLIFF MANOR	
10511-10511	BUCHANAN	
10512-10512	CARMEL	
10514-10514	CHAPPAQUA	
10516-10516	COLD SPRING	
10517-10517	CROMPOND	
10518-10518	CROSS RIVER	
10519-10519	CROTON FALLS	
10520-10521	CROTON ON HUDSON	
10522-10522	DOBBS FERRY	
10523-10523	ELMSFORD	
10524-10524	GARRISON	
10526-10526	GOLDENS BRIDGE	
10527-10527	GRANITE SPRINGS	
10528-10528	HARRISON	
10530-10530	HARTSDALE	
10532-10532	HAWTHORNE	
10533-10533	IRVINGTON	
10535-10535	JEFFERSON VALLEY	
10536-10536	KATONAH	
10537-10537	LAKE PEEKSKILL	
10538-10538	LARCHMONT	
10540-10540	LINCOLNDALE	
10541-10541	MAHOPAC	
10542-10542	MAHOPAC FALLS	
10543-10543	MAMARONECK	
10545-10545	MARYKNOLL	
10546-10546	MILLWOOD	
10547-10547	MOHEGAN LAKE	
10548-10548	MONTROSE	
10549-10549	MOUNT KISCO	
10550-10559	MOUNT VERNON	
10560-10560	NORTH SALEM	
10562-10562	OSSINING	
10566-10566	PEEKSKILL	
10567-10567	CORTLANDT MANOR	
10570-10572	PLEASANTVILLE	
10573-10573	PORT CHESTER	
10576-10576	POUND RIDGE	
10577-10577	PURCHASE	
10578-10578	PURDYS	

Zip Range	Place
10579-10579	PUTNAM VALLEY
10580-10581	RYE
10583-10583	SCARSDALE
10587-10587	SHENOROCK
10588-10588	SHRUB OAK
10589-10589	SOMERS
10590-10590	SOUTH SALEM
10591-10592	TARRYTOWN
10594-10594	THORNWOOD
10595-10595	VALHALLA
10596-10596	VERPLANCK
10597-10597	WACCABUC
10598-10598	YORKTOWN HEIGHTS
10600-10603	WHITE PLAINS
10604-10604	WEST HARRISON
10605-10650	WHITE PLAINS
10700-10705	YONKERS
10706-10706	HASTINGS ON HUDSON
10707-10707	TUCKAHOE
10708-10708	BRONXVILLE
10709-10709	EASTCHESTER
10710-10710	YONKERS
10800-10802	NEW ROCHELLE
10803-10803	PELHAM
10804-10805	NEW ROCHELLE
10901-10901	SUFFERN
10910-10910	ARDEN
10911-10911	BEAR MOUNTAIN
10912-10912	BELLVALE
10913-10913	BLAUVELT
10914-10914	BLOOMING GROVE
10915-10915	BULLVILLE
10916-10916	CAMPBELL HALL
10917-10917	CENTRAL VALLEY
10918-10918	CHESTER
10919-10919	CIRCLEVILLE
10920-10920	CONGERS
10921-10921	FLORIDA
10922-10922	FORT MONTGOMERY
10923-10923	GARNERVILLE
10924-10924	GOSHEN
10925-10925	GREENWOOD LAKE
10926-10926	HARRIMAN
10927-10927	HAVERSTRAW
10928-10928	HIGHLAND FALLS
10930-10930	HIGHLAND MILLS
10931-10931	HILLBURN
10932-10932	HOWELLS
10933-10933	JOHNSON
10940-10943	MIDDLETOWN
10949-10950	MONROE
10951-10951	ROCKLAND M P C
10952-10952	MONSEY
10953-10953	MOUNTAINVILLE
10954-10954	NANUET
10956-10956	NEW CITY
10958-10958	NEW HAMPTON
10959-10959	NEW MILFORD
10960-10960	NYACK
10962-10962	ORANGEBURG
10963-10963	OTISVILLE
10964-10964	PALISADES
10965-10965	PEARL RIVER
10968-10968	PIERMONT
10969-10969	PINE ISLAND
10970-10970	POMONA
10973-10973	SLATE HILL
10974-10974	SLOATSBURG
10975-10975	SOUTHFIELDS
10976-10976	SPARKILL
10977-10977	SPRING VALLEY
10979-10979	STERLING FOREST
10980-10980	STONY POINT
10981-10981	SUGAR LOAF
10982-10982	TALLMAN
10983-10983	TAPPAN
10984-10984	THIELLS
10985-10985	THOMPSON RIDGE
10986-10986	TOMKINS COVE
10987-10987	TUXEDO PARK
10988-10988	UNIONVILLE
10989-10989	VALLEY COTTAGE
10990-10990	WARWICK
10992-10992	WASHINGTONVILLE
10993-10993	WEST HAVERSTRAW
10994-10995	WEST NYACK
10996-10997	WEST POINT
10998-10998	WESTTOWN
11001-11002	FLORAL PARK
11003-11003	ELMONT
11004-11004	GLEN OAKS
11005-11005	FLORAL PARK
11010-11010	FRANKLIN SQUARE
11020-11027	GREAT NECK
11030-11030	MANHASSET
11040-11044	NEW HYDE PARK
11050-11055	PORT WASHINGTON
11096-11096	INWOOD
11099-11099	NEW HYDE PARK
11100-11120	LONG ISLAND CITY
11200-11256	BROOKLYN
11300-11359	FLUSHING
11359-11359	BAYSIDE
11360-11379	FLUSHING
11379-11379	MIDDLE VILLAGE
11380-11380	FLUSHING
11380-11380	ELMHURST
11381-11390	FLUSHING
11400-11411	JAMAICA
11411-11411	CAMBRIA HEIGHTS
11412-11418	JAMAICA
11418-11418	RICHMOND HILL
11419-11427	JAMAICA
11427-11427	QUEENS VILLAGE
11428-11428	JAMAICA
11428-11428	QUEENS VILLAGE
11429-11499	JAMAICA
11501-11501	MINEOLA
11507-11507	ALBERTSON
11509-11509	ATLANTIC BEACH
11510-11510	BALDWIN
11514-11514	CARLE PLACE
11516-11516	CEDARHURST
11518-11518	EAST ROCKAWAY
11520-11520	FREEPORT
11530-11536	GARDEN CITY
11542-11542	GLEN COVE
11545-11545	GLEN HEAD
11547-11547	GLENWOOD LANDING
11548-11548	GREENVALE
11549-11551	HEMPSTEAD
11552-11552	WEST HEMPSTEAD
11553-11553	UNIONDALE
11554-11554	EAST MEADOW
11555-11556	UNIONDALE
11557-11557	HEWLETT
11558-11558	ISLAND PARK
11559-11559	LAWRENCE
11560-11560	LOCUST VALLEY
11561-11561	LONG BEACH
11563-11564	LYNBROOK
11565-11565	MALVERNE
11566-11566	MERRICK
11568-11568	OLD WESTBURY
11569-11569	POINT LOOKOUT
11570-11571	ROCKVILLE CENTRE
11572-11572	OCEANSIDE
11575-11575	ROOSEVELT
11576-11576	ROSLYN
11577-11577	ROSLYN HEIGHTS
11579-11579	SEA CLIFF
11580-11583	VALLEY STREAM
11588-11588	UNIONDALE
11590-11590	WESTBURY
11592-11592	ROCKVILLE CENTRE
11593-11595	WESTBURY
11596-11596	WILLISTON PARK
11597-11597	WESTBURY
11598-11598	WOODMERE
11599-11599	GARDEN CITY
11600-11694	FAR ROCKAWAY
11694-11694	ROCKAWAY PARK
11695-11695	FAR ROCKAWAY
11696-11696	INWOOD
11697-11697	FAR ROCKAWAY
11701-11701	AMITYVILLE
11702-11702	BABYLON
11703-11703	NORTH BABYLON
11704-11704	WEST BABYLON
11705-11705	BAYPORT
11706-11706	BAY SHORE
11707-11707	WEST BABYLON
11708-11708	AMITYVILLE
11709-11709	BAYVILLE
11710-11710	BELLMORE
11713-11713	BELLPORT
11714-11714	BETHPAGE
11715-11715	BLUE POINT
11716-11716	BOHEMIA
11717-11717	BRENTWOOD
11718-11718	BRIGHTWATERS
11719-11719	BROOKHAVEN
11720-11720	CENTEREACH
11721-11721	CENTERPORT
11722-11722	CENTRAL ISLIP
11724-11724	COLD SPRING HARBOR
11725-11725	COMMACK
11726-11726	COPIAGUE
11727-11727	CORAM
11729-11729	DEER PARK
11730-11730	EAST ISLIP
11731-11731	EAST NORTHPORT
11732-11732	EAST NORWICH
11733-11733	EAST SETAUKET
11735-11737	FARMINGDALE
11738-11738	FARMINGVILLE
11739-11739	GREAT RIVER
11740-11740	GREENLAWN
11741-11741	HOLBROOK
11742-11742	HOLTSVILLE
11743-11743	HUNTINGTON
11745-11745	SMITHTOWN
11746-11746	HUNTINGTON STATION
11747-11747	MELVILLE
11749-11749	FARMINGVILLE
11749-11749	ISLANDIA
11750-11750	HUNTINGTON STATION
11751-11751	ISLIP
11752-11752	ISLIP TERRACE
11753-11753	JERICHO
11754-11754	KINGS PARK
11755-11755	LAKE GROVE
11756-11756	LEVITTOWN
11757-11757	LINDENHURST
11758-11758	MASSAPEQUA
11760-11760	HAUPPAUGE
11760-11760	ISLANDIA
11762-11762	MASSAPEQUA PARK
11763-11763	MEDFORD
11764-11764	MILLER PLACE
11765-11765	MILL NECK
11766-11766	MOUNT SINAI
11767-11767	NESCONSET
11768-11768	NORTHPORT
11769-11769	OAKDALE
11770-11770	OCEAN BEACH
11771-11771	OYSTER BAY
11772-11772	PATCHOGUE
11773-11773	SYOSSET
11774-11774	FARMINGDALE
11775-11775	MELVILLE
11776-11776	PORT JEFFERSON STATION
11777-11777	PORT JEFFERSON
11778-11778	ROCKY POINT
11779-11779	RONKONKOMA
11780-11780	SAINT JAMES
11782-11782	SAYVILLE
11783-11783	SEAFORD
11784-11784	SELDEN
11786-11786	SHOREHAM
11787-11787	SMITHTOWN
11788-11788	HAUPPAUGE
11789-11789	SOUND BEACH
11790-11790	STONY BROOK
11791-11791	SYOSSET
11792-11792	WADING RIVER
11793-11793	WANTAGH
11794-11794	STONY BROOK
11795-11795	WEST ISLIP
11796-11796	WEST SAYVILLE
11797-11797	WOODBURY
11798-11798	WYANDANCH
11801-11802	HICKSVILLE
11803-11803	PLAINVIEW
11804-11804	OLD BETHPAGE
11805-11805	MID ISLAND
11815-11819	HICKSVILLE
11853-11853	JERICHO
11854-11855	HICKSVILLE
11901-11901	RIVERHEAD
11930-11930	AMAGANSETT
11931-11931	AQUEBOGUE
11932-11932	BRIDGEHAMPTON
11933-11933	CALVERTON
11934-11934	CENTER MORICHES
11935-11935	CUTCHOGUE
11937-11937	EAST HAMPTON
11939-11939	EAST MARION
11940-11940	EAST MORICHES
11941-11941	EASTPORT
11942-11942	EAST QUOGUE
11944-11944	GREENPORT
11946-11946	HAMPTON BAYS
11947-11947	JAMESPORT
11948-11948	LAUREL
11949-11949	MANORVILLE
11950-11950	MASTIC
11951-11951	MASTIC BEACH
11952-11952	MATTITUCK
11953-11953	MIDDLE ISLAND
11954-11954	MONTAUK
11955-11955	MORICHES
11956-11956	NEW SUFFOLK
11957-11957	ORIENT
11958-11958	PECONIC
11959-11959	QUOGUE
11960-11960	REMSENBURG
11961-11961	RIDGE
11962-11962	SAGAPONACK
11963-11963	SAG HARBOR
11964-11964	SHELTER ISLAND
11965-11965	SHELTER ISLAND HEIGHTS
11967-11967	SHIRLEY
11968-11969	SOUTHAMPTON
11970-11970	SOUTH JAMESPORT
11971-11971	SOUTHOLD
11972-11972	SPEONK
11973-11973	UPTON
11975-11975	WAINSCOTT
11976-11976	WATER MILL
11977-11977	WESTHAMPTON
11978-11978	WESTHAMPTON BEACH
11980-11980	YAPHANK
12007-12007	ALCOVE
12008-12008	ALPLAUS
12009-12009	ALTAMONT
12010-12010	AMSTERDAM
12015-12015	ATHENS
12016-12016	AURIESVILLE
12017-12017	AUSTERLITZ
12018-12018	AVERILL PARK
12019-12019	BALLSTON LAKE
12020-12020	BALLSTON SPA
12022-12022	BERLIN
12023-12023	BERNE
12024-12024	BRAINARD
12025-12025	BROADALBIN
12026-12026	BROOKVIEW
12027-12027	BURNT HILLS
12028-12028	BUSKIRK
12029-12029	CANAAN
12031-12031	CARLISLE
12032-12032	CAROGA LAKE
12033-12033	CASTLETON ON HUDSON
12035-12035	CENTRAL BRIDGE
12036-12036	CHARLOTTEVILLE
12037-12037	CHATHAM

12040-12040 CHERRY PLAIN	12150-12150 ROTTERDAM JUNCTION	12448-12448 LAKE HILL	12545-12545 MILLBROOK
12041-12041 CLARKSVILLE	12151-12151 ROUND LAKE	12449-12449 LAKE KATRINE	12546-12546 MILLERTON
12042-12042 CLIMAX	12153-12153 SAND LAKE	12450-12450 LANESVILLE	12547-12547 MILTON
12043-12043 COBLESKILL	12154-12154 SCHAGHTICOKE	12451-12451 LEEDS	12548-12548 MODENA
12045-12045 COEYMANS	12155-12155 SCHENEVUS	12452-12452 LEXINGTON	12549-12549 MONTGOMERY
12046-12046 COEYMANS HOLLOW	12156-12156 SCHODACK LANDING	12453-12453 MALDEN ON HUDSON	12550-12552 NEWBURGH
12047-12047 COHOES	12157-12157 SCHOHARIE	12454-12454 MAPLECREST	12553-12553 NEW WINDSOR
12050-12050 COLUMBIAVILLE	12158-12158 SELKIRK	12455-12455 MARGARETVILLE	12555-12555 MID HUDSON
12051-12051 COXSACKIE	12159-12159 SLINGERLANDS	12456-12456 MOUNT MARION	12561-12561 NEW PALTZ
12052-12052 CROPSEYVILLE	12160-12160 SLOANSVILLE	12457-12457 MOUNT TREMPER	12563-12563 PATTERSON
12053-12053 DELANSON	12161-12161 SOUTH BETHLEHEM	12458-12458 NAPANOCH	12564-12564 PAWLING
12054-12054 DELMAR	12162-12162 SOUTH SCHODACK	12459-12459 NEW KINGSTON	12565-12565 PHILMONT
12055-12055 DORMANSVILLE	12163-12163 SOUTH WESTERLO	12460-12460 OAK HILL	12566-12566 PINE BUSH
12056-12056 DUANESBURG	12164-12164 SPECULATOR	12461-12461 OLIVEBRIDGE	12567-12567 PINE PLAINS
12057-12057 EAGLE BRIDGE	12165-12165 SPENCERTOWN	12462-12462 OLIVEREA	12568-12568 PLATTEKILL
12058-12058 EARLTON	12166-12166 SPRAKERS	12463-12463 PALENVILLE	12569-12569 PLEASANT VALLEY
12059-12059 EAST BERNE	12167-12167 STAMFORD	12464-12464 PHOENICIA	12570-12570 POUGHQUAG
12060-12060 EAST CHATHAM	12168-12169 STEPHENTOWN	12465-12465 PINE HILL	12571-12571 RED HOOK
12061-12061 EAST GREENBUSH	12170-12170 STILLWATER	12466-12466 PORT EWEN	12572-12572 RHINEBECK
12062-12062 EAST NASSAU	12172-12172 STOTTVILLE	12468-12468 PRATTSVILLE	12574-12574 RHINECLIFF
12063-12063 EAST SCHODACK	12173-12173 STUYVESANT	12469-12469 PRESTON HOLLOW	12575-12575 ROCK TAVERN
12064-12064 EAST WORCESTER	12174-12174 STUYVESANT FALLS	12470-12470 PURLING	12577-12577 SALISBURY MILLS
12065-12065 CLIFTON PARK	12175-12175 SUMMIT	12471-12471 RIFTON	12578-12578 SALT POINT
12066-12066 ESPERANCE	12176-12176 SURPRISE	12472-12472 ROSENDALE	12580-12580 STAATSBURG
12067-12067 FEURA BUSH	12177-12177 TRIBES HILL	12473-12473 ROUND TOP	12581-12581 STANFORDVILLE
12068-12068 FONDA	12179-12183 TROY	12474-12474 ROXBURY	12582-12582 STORMVILLE
12069-12069 FORT HUNTER	12184-12184 VALATIE	12475-12475 RUBY	12583-12583 TIVOLI
12070-12070 FORT JOHNSON	12185-12185 VALLEY FALLS	12477-12477 SAUGERTIES	12584-12584 VAILS GATE
12071-12071 FULTONHAM	12186-12186 VOORHEESVILLE	12480-12480 SHANDAKEN	12585-12585 VERBANK
12072-12072 FULTONVILLE	12187-12187 WARNERVILLE	12481-12481 SHOKAN	12586-12586 WALDEN
12073-12073 GALLUPVILLE	12188-12188 WATERFORD	12482-12482 SOUTH CAIRO	12588-12588 WALKER VALLEY
12074-12074 GALWAY	12189-12189 WATERVLIET	12483-12483 SPRING GLEN	12589-12589 WALLKILL
12075-12075 GHENT	12190-12190 WELLS	12484-12484 STONE RIDGE	12590-12590 WAPPINGERS FALLS
12076-12076 GILBOA	12192-12192 WEST COXSACKIE	12485-12485 TANNERSVILLE	12592-12592 WASSAIC
12077-12077 GLENMONT	12193-12193 WESTERLO	12486-12486 TILLSON	12593-12593 WEST COPAKE
12078-12078 GLOVERSVILLE	12194-12194 WEST FULTON	12487-12487 ULSTER PARK	12594-12594 WINGDALE
12082-12082 GRAFTON	12195-12195 WEST LEBANON	12489-12489 WAWARSING	12600-12604 POUGHKEEPSIE
12083-12083 GREENVILLE	12196-12196 WEST SAND LAKE	12490-12490 WEST CAMP	12701-12701 MONTICELLO
12084-12084 GUILDERLAND	12197-12197 WORCESTER	12491-12491 WEST HURLEY	12719-12719 BARRYVILLE
12085-12085 GUILDERLAND CENTER	12198-12198 WYNANTSKILL	12492-12492 WEST KILL	12720-12720 BETHEL
12086-12086 HAGAMAN	12200-12288 ALBANY	12493-12493 WEST PARK	12721-12721 BLOOMINGBURG
12087-12087 HANNACROIX	12300-12345 SCHENECTADY	12494-12494 WEST SHOKAN	12722-12722 BURLINGHAM
12089-12089 HOOSICK	12401-12402 KINGSTON	12495-12495 WILLOW	12723-12723 CALLICOON
12090-12090 HOOSICK FALLS	12404-12404 ACCORD	12496-12496 WINDHAM	12724-12724 CALLICOON CENTER
12092-12092 HOWES CAVE	12405-12405 ACRA	12498-12498 WOODSTOCK	12725-12725 CLARYVILLE
12093-12093 JEFFERSON	12406-12406 ARKVILLE	12501-12501 AMENIA	12726-12726 COCHECTON
12094-12094 JOHNSONVILLE	12407-12407 ASHLAND	12502-12502 ANCRAM	12727-12727 COCHECTON CENTER
12095-12095 JOHNSTOWN	12409-12409 BEARSVILLE	12503-12503 ANCRAMDALE	12729-12729 CUDDEBACKVILLE
12106-12106 KINDERHOOK	12410-12410 BIG INDIAN	12504-12504 ANNANDALE ON HUDSON	12732-12732 ELDRED
12107-12107 KNOX	12411-12411 BLOOMINGTON	12506-12506 BANGALL	12733-12733 FALLSBURG
12108-12108 LAKE PLEASANT	12412-12412 BOICEVILLE	12507-12507 BARRYTOWN	12734-12734 FERNDALE
12110-12111 LATHAM	12413-12413 CAIRO	12508-12508 BEACON	12736-12736 FREMONT CENTER
12113-12113 LAWYERSVILLE	12414-12414 CATSKILL	12510-12510 BILLINGS	12737-12737 GLEN SPEY
12114-12114 LEBANON SPRINGS	12415-12415 CEMENTON	12511-12511 CASTLE POINT	12738-12738 GLEN WILD
12115-12115 MALDEN BRIDGE	12415-12415 SMITHS LANDING	12512-12512 CHELSEA	12739-12739 GODEFFROY
12116-12116 MARYLAND	12416-12416 CHICHESTER	12513-12513 CLAVERACK	12740-12740 GRAHAMSVILLE
12117-12117 MAYFIELD	12417-12417 CONNELLY	12514-12514 CLINTON CORNERS	12741-12741 HANKINS
12118-12118 MECHANICVILLE	12418-12418 CORNWALLVILLE	12515-12515 CLINTONDALE	12742-12742 HARRIS
12120-12120 MEDUSA	12419-12419 COTTEKILL	12516-12516 COPAKE	12743-12743 HIGHLAND LAKE
12121-12121 MELROSE	12420-12420 CRAGSMOOR	12517-12517 COPAKE FALLS	12745-12745 HORTONVILLE
12122-12122 MIDDLEBURGH	12421-12421 DENVER	12518-12518 CORNWALL	12746-12746 HUGUENOT
12123-12123 NASSAU	12422-12422 DURHAM	12520-12520 CORNWALL ON HUDSON	12747-12747 HURLEYVILLE
12124-12124 NEW BALTIMORE	12423-12423 EAST DURHAM	12521-12521 CRARYVILLE	12748-12748 JEFFERSONVILLE
12125-12125 NEW LEBANON	12424-12424 EAST JEWETT	12522-12522 DOVER PLAINS	12749-12749 KAUNEONGA LAKE
12128-12128 NEWTONVILLE	12427-12427 ELKA PARK	12523-12523 ELIZAVILLE	12750-12750 KENOZA LAKE
12130-12130 NIVERVILLE	12428-12428 ELLENVILLE	12524-12524 FISHKILL	12751-12751 KIAMESHA LAKE
12131-12131 NORTH BLENHEIM	12429-12429 ESOPUS	12525-12525 GARDINER	12752-12752 LAKE HUNTINGTON
12132-12132 NORTH CHATHAM	12430-12430 FLEISCHMANNS	12526-12526 GERMANTOWN	12753-12753 LEW BEACH
12133-12133 NORTH HOOSICK	12431-12431 FREEHOLD	12527-12527 GLENHAM	12754-12754 LIBERTY
12134-12134 NORTHVILLE	12432-12432 GLASCO	12528-12528 HIGHLAND	12758-12758 LIVINGSTON MANOR
12135-12135 NORTON HILL	12433-12433 GLENFORD	12529-12529 HILLSDALE	12759-12759 LOCH SHELDRAKE
12136-12136 OLD CHATHAM	12434-12434 GRAND GORGE	12530-12530 HOLLOWVILLE	12760-12760 LONG EDDY
12137-12137 PATTERSONVILLE	12435-12435 GREENFIELD PARK	12531-12531 HOLMES	12762-12762 MONGAUP VALLEY
12138-12138 PETERSBURG	12436-12436 HAINES FALLS	12533-12533 HOPEWELL JUNCTION	12763-12763 MOUNTAIN DALE
12139-12139 PISECO	12438-12438 HALCOTTSVILLE	12534-12534 HUDSON	12764-12764 NARROWSBURG
12140-12140 POESTENKILL	12439-12439 HENSONVILLE	12537-12537 HUGHSONVILLE	12765-12765 NEVERSINK
12141-12141 QUAKER STREET	12440-12440 HIGH FALLS	12538-12538 HYDE PARK	12766-12766 NORTH BRANCH
12143-12143 RAVENA	12441-12441 HIGHMOUNT	12540-12540 LAGRANGEVILLE	12767-12767 OBERNBURG
12144-12144 RENSSELAER	12442-12442 HUNTER	12541-12541 LIVINGSTON	12768-12768 PARKSVILLE
12147-12147 RENSSELAERVILLE	12443-12443 HURLEY	12542-12542 MARLBORO	12769-12769 PHILLIPSPORT
12148-12148 REXFORD	12444-12444 JEWETT	12543-12543 MAYBROOK	12770-12770 POND EDDY
12149-12149 RICHMONDVILLE	12446-12446 KERHONKSON	12544-12544 MELLENVILLE	12771-12771 PORT JERVIS

12775-12775 ROCK HILL	12884-12884 VICTORY MILLS	12994-12994 WHALLONSBURG	13125-13125 ORAN
12776-12776 ROSCOE	12885-12885 WARRENSBURG	12995-12995 WHIPPLEVILLE	13126-13126 OSWEGO
12777-12777 FORESTBURGH	12886-12886 WEVERTOWN	12996-12996 WILLSBORO	13129-13129 GEORGETOWN
12778-12778 SMALLWOOD	12887-12887 WHITEHALL	12997-12997 WILMINGTON	13130-13130 OWASCO
12779-12779 SOUTH FALLSBURG	12901-12903 PLATTSBURGH	12998-12998 WITHERBEE	13131-13131 PARISH
12780-12780 SPARROW BUSH	12910-12910 ALTONA	13020-13020 APULIA STATION	13132-13132 PENNELLVILLE
12781-12781 SUMMITVILLE	12911-12911 KEESEVILLE	13021-13024 AUBURN	13133-13133 PERRYVILLE
12782-12782 SUNDOWN	12912-12912 AU SABLE FORKS	13026-13026 AURORA	13134-13134 PETERBORO
12783-12783 SWAN LAKE	12913-12913 BLOOMINGDALE	13027-13027 BALDWINSVILLE	13135-13135 PHOENIX
12784-12784 THOMPSONVILLE	12914-12914 BOMBAY	13028-13028 BERNHARDS BAY	13136-13136 PITCHER
12785-12785 WESTBROOKVILLE	12915-12915 BRAINARDSVILLE	13029-13029 BREWERTON	13137-13137 PLAINVILLE
12786-12786 WHITE LAKE	12916-12916 BRUSHTON	13030-13030 BRIDGEPORT	13138-13138 POMPEY
12787-12787 WHITE SULPHUR SPRINGS	12917-12917 BURKE	13031-13031 CAMILLUS	13139-13139 POPLAR RIDGE
12788-12788 WOODBOURNE	12918-12918 CADYVILLE	13032-13032 CANASTOTA	13140-13140 PORT BYRON
12789-12789 WOODRIDGE	12919-12919 CHAMPLAIN	13033-13033 CATO	13141-13141 PREBLE
12790-12790 WURTSBORO	12920-12920 CHATEAUGAY	13034-13034 CAYUGA	13142-13142 PULASKI
12791-12791 YOUNGSVILLE	12921-12921 CHAZY	13035-13035 CAZENOVIA	13143-13143 RED CREEK
12792-12792 YULAN	12922-12922 CHILDWOLD	13036-13036 CENTRAL SQUARE	13144-13144 RICHLAND
12801-12801 GLENS FALLS	12923-12923 CHURUBUSCO	13037-13037 CHITTENANGO	13145-13145 SANDY CREEK
12803-12803 SOUTH GLENS FALLS	12924-12924 KEESEVILLE	13039-13039 CICERO	13146-13146 SAVANNAH
12804-12804 QUEENSBURY	12926-12926 CONSTABLE	13040-13040 CINCINNATUS	13147-13147 SCIPIO CENTER
12808-12808 ADIRONDACK	12927-12927 CRANBERRY LAKE	13041-13041 CLAY	13148-13148 SENECA FALLS
12809-12809 ARGYLE	12928-12928 CROWN POINT	13042-13042 CLEVELAND	13150-13150 SENNETT
12810-12810 ATHOL	12929-12929 DANNEMORA	13043-13043 CLOCKVILLE	13151-13151 SHEDS
12811-12811 BAKERS MILLS	12930-12930 DICKINSON CENTER	13044-13044 CONSTANTIA	13152-13152 SKANEATELES
12812-12812 BLUE MOUNTAIN LAKE	12932-12932 ELIZABETHTOWN	13045-13045 CORTLAND	13153-13153 SKANEATELES FALLS
12814-12814 BOLTON LANDING	12933-12933 ELLENBURG	13050-13050 CUYLER	13154-13154 SOUTH BUTLER
12815-12815 BRANT LAKE	12934-12934 ELLENBURG CENTER	13051-13051 DELPHI FALLS	13155-13155 SOUTH OTSELIC
12816-12816 CAMBRIDGE	12935-12935 ELLENBURG DEPOT	13052-13052 DE RUYTER	13156-13156 STERLING
12817-12817 CHESTERTOWN	12936-12936 ESSEX	13053-13053 DRYDEN	13157-13157 SYLVAN BEACH
12819-12819 CLEMONS	12937-12937 FORT COVINGTON	13054-13054 DURHAMVILLE	13158-13158 TRUXTON
12820-12820 CLEVERDALE	12938-12938 FORT JACKSON	13055-13055 EAST FREETOWN	13159-13159 TULLY
12821-12821 COMSTOCK	12938-12938 NORTH LAWRENCE	13056-13056 EAST HOMER	13160-13160 UNION SPRINGS
12822-12822 CORINTH	12939-12939 GABRIELS	13057-13057 EAST SYRACUSE	13162-13162 VERONA BEACH
12823-12823 COSSAYUNA	12940-12940 HOPKINTON	13060-13060 ELBRIDGE	13163-13163 WAMPSVILLE
12824-12824 DIAMOND POINT	12941-12941 JAY	13061-13061 ERIEVILLE	13164-13164 WARNERS
12826-12826 EAST GREENWICH	12942-12942 KEENE	13062-13062 ETNA	13165-13165 WATERLOO
12827-12827 FORT ANN	12943-12943 KEENE VALLEY	13063-13063 FABIUS	13166-13166 WEEDSPORT
12828-12828 FORT EDWARD	12944-12944 KEESEVILLE	13064-13064 FAIR HAVEN	13167-13167 WEST MONROE
12831-12831 GANSEVOORT	12945-12945 LAKE CLEAR	13065-13065 FAYETTE	13200-13210 SYRACUSE
12832-12832 GRANVILLE	12946-12946 LAKE PLACID	13066-13066 FAYETTEVILLE	13211-13211 MATTYDALE
12833-12833 GREENFIELD CENTER	12949-12949 LAWRENCEVILLE	13068-13068 FREEVILLE	13212-13290 SYRACUSE
12834-12834 GREENWICH	12950-12950 LEWIS	13069-13069 FULTON	13301-13301 ALDER CREEK
12835-12835 HADLEY	12952-12952 LYON MOUNTAIN	13071-13071 GENOA	13302-13302 ALTMAR
12836-12836 HAGUE	12953-12953 MALONE	13072-13072 GEORGETOWN	13303-13303 AVA
12837-12837 HAMPTON	12955-12955 LYON MOUNTAIN	13073-13073 GROTON	13304-13304 BARNEVELD
12838-12838 HARTFORD	12956-12956 MINEVILLE	13074-13074 HANNIBAL	13305-13305 BEAVER FALLS
12839-12839 HUDSON FALLS	12957-12957 MOIRA	13076-13076 HASTINGS	13308-13308 BLOSSVALE
12841-12841 HULETTS LANDING	12958-12958 MOOERS	13077-13077 HOMER	13309-13309 BOONVILLE
12842-12842 INDIAN LAKE	12959-12959 MOOERS FORKS	13078-13078 JAMESVILLE	13310-13310 BOUCKVILLE
12843-12843 JOHNSBURG	12960-12960 MORIAH	13080-13080 JORDAN	13312-13312 BRANTINGHAM
12844-12844 KATTSKILL BAY	12961-12961 MORIAH CENTER	13081-13081 KING FERRY	13313-13313 BRIDGEWATER
12845-12845 LAKE GEORGE	12962-12962 MORRISONVILLE	13082-13082 KIRKVILLE	13314-13314 BROOKFIELD
12846-12846 LAKE LUZERNE	12964-12964 NEW RUSSIA	13083-13083 LACONA	13315-13315 BURLINGTON FLATS
12847-12847 LONG LAKE	12965-12965 NICHOLVILLE	13084-13084 LA FAYETTE	13316-13316 CAMDEN
12848-12848 MIDDLE FALLS	12966-12966 NORTH BANGOR	13085-13085 LEBANON	13317-13317 CANAJOHARIE
12849-12849 MIDDLE GRANVILLE	12967-12967 NORTH LAWRENCE	13087-13087 LITTLE YORK	13318-13318 CASSVILLE
12850-12850 MIDDLE GROVE	12968-12968 ONCHIOTA	13088-13090 LIVERPOOL	13319-13319 CHADWICKS
12851-12851 MINERVA	12968-12968 SUGARBUSH	13092-13092 LOCKE	13320-13320 CHERRY VALLEY
12852-12852 NEWCOMB	12968-12968 ONCHIOTA	13093-13093 LYCOMING	13321-13321 CLARK MILLS
12853-12853 NORTH CREEK	12969-12969 OWLS HEAD	13094-13094 LYSANDER	13322-13322 CLAYVILLE
12854-12854 NORTH GRANVILLE	12970-12970 PAUL SMITHS	13101-13101 MC GRAW	13323-13323 CLINTON
12855-12855 NORTH HUDSON	12972-12972 PERU	13102-13102 MC LEAN	13324-13324 COLD BROOK
12856-12856 NORTH RIVER	12973-12973 PIERCEFIELD	13103-13103 MALLORY	13325-13325 CONSTABLEVILLE
12857-12857 OLMSTEDVILLE	12974-12974 PORT HENRY	13104-13104 MANLIUS	13326-13326 COOPERSTOWN
12858-12858 PARADOX	12975-12975 PORT KENT	13107-13107 MAPLE VIEW	13327-13327 CROGHAN
12859-12859 PORTER CORNERS	12976-12976 RAINBOW LAKE	13108-13108 MARCELLUS	13328-13328 DEANSBORO
12860-12860 POTTERSVILLE	12977-12977 RAY BROOK	13110-13110 MARIETTA	13329-13329 DOLGEVILLE
12861-12861 PUTNAM STATION	12978-12978 REDFORD	13111-13111 MARTVILLE	13331-13331 EAGLE BAY
12862-12862 RIPARIUS	12979-12979 ROUSES POINT	13112-13112 MEMPHIS	13332-13332 EARLVILLE
12863-12863 ROCK CITY FALLS	12980-12980 SAINT REGIS FALLS	13113-13113 MERIDIAN	13333-13333 EAST SPRINGFIELD
12864-12864 SABAEL	12981-12981 SARANAC	13114-13114 MEXICO	13334-13334 EATON
12865-12865 SALEM	12982-12982 SARANAC LAKE	13115-13115 MINETTO	13335-13335 EDMESTON
12866-12866 SARATOGA SPRINGS	12985-12985 SCHUYLER FALLS	13116-13116 MINOA	13336-13336 FAIRFIELD
12870-12870 SCHROON LAKE	12986-12986 TUPPER LAKE	13117-13117 MONTEZUMA	13337-13337 FLY CREEK
12871-12871 SCHUYLERVILLE	12987-12987 UPPER JAY	13118-13118 MORAVIA	13338-13338 FORESTPORT
12872-12872 SEVERANCE	12989-12989 VERMONTVILLE	13119-13119 MOTTVILLE	13339-13339 FORT PLAIN
12873-12873 SHUSHAN	12990-12990 WADHAMS	13120-13120 NEDROW	13340-13340 FRANKFORT
12874-12874 SILVER BAY	12991-12991 BANGOR	13121-13121 NEW HAVEN	13341-13341 FRANKLIN SPRINGS
12878-12878 STONY CREEK	12992-12992 WEST CHAZY	13122-13122 NEW WOODSTOCK	13342-13342 GARRATTSVILLE
12879-12879 NEWCOMB	12993-12993 WESTPORT	13123-13123 NORTH BAY	13343-13343 GLENFIELD
12883-12883 TICONDEROGA	12994-12994 BOUQUET	13124-13124 NORTH PITCHER	13345-13345 GREIG

13346-13346 HAMILTON	13490-13490 WESTMORELAND	13681-13681 RICHVILLE	13832-13832 PLYMOUTH
13348-13348 HARTWICK	13491-13491 WEST WINFIELD	13682-13682 RODMAN	13833-13833 PORT CRANE
13349-13349 HARTWICK SEMINARY	13492-13492 WHITESBORO	13683-13683 ROOSEVELTOWN	13834-13834 PORTLANDVILLE
13350-13350 HERKIMER	13493-13493 WILLIAMSTOWN	13684-13684 RUSSELL	13835-13835 RICHFORD
13352-13352 HINCKLEY	13494-13494 WOODGATE	13685-13685 SACKETS HARBOR	13837-13837 SHINHOPPLE
13353-13353 HOFFMEISTER	13495-13495 YORKVILLE	13687-13687 SOUTH COLTON	13838-13838 SIDNEY
13354-13354 HOLLAND PATENT	13500-13599 UTICA	13688-13688 SOUTH RUTLAND	13839-13839 SIDNEY CENTER
13355-13355 HUBBARDSVILLE	13601-13601 WATERTOWN	13690-13690 STAR LAKE	13840-13840 SMITHBORO
13357-13357 ILION	13602-13602 FORT DRUM	13691-13691 THERESA	13841-13841 SMITHVILLE FLATS
13360-13360 INLET	13603-13603 WATERTOWN	13692-13692 THOUSAND ISLAND PARK	13842-13842 SOUTH KORTRIGHT
13361-13361 JORDANVILLE	13605-13605 ADAMS	13693-13693 THREE MILE BAY	13843-13843 SOUTH NEW BERLIN
13362-13362 KNOXBORO	13606-13606 ADAMS CENTER	13694-13694 WADDINGTON	13844-13844 SOUTH PLYMOUTH
13363-13363 LEE CENTER	13607-13607 ALEXANDRIA BAY	13695-13695 WANAKENA	13845-13845 TIOGA CENTER
13364-13364 LEONARDSVILLE	13608-13608 ANTWERP	13696-13696 WEST STOCKHOLM	13846-13846 TREADWELL
13365-13365 LITTLE FALLS	13609-13609 BALMAT	13697-13697 WINTHROP	13847-13847 TROUT CREEK
13367-13367 LOWVILLE	13610-13610 RODMAN	13698-13698 WOODVILLE	13848-13848 TUNNEL
13368-13368 LYONS FALLS	13611-13611 BELLEVILLE	13699-13699 POTSDAM	13849-13849 UNADILLA
13401-13401 MC CONNELLSVILLE	13612-13612 BLACK RIVER	13730-13730 AFTON	13850-13851 VESTAL
13402-13402 MADISON	13613-13613 BRASHER FALLS	13731-13731 ANDES	13856-13856 WALTON
13403-13403 MARCY	13614-13614 BRIER HILL	13732-13732 APALACHIN	13859-13859 WELLS BRIDGE
13404-13404 MARTINSBURG	13615-13615 BROWNVILLE	13733-13733 BAINBRIDGE	13860-13860 WEST DAVENPORT
13406-13406 MIDDLEVILLE	13616-13616 CALCIUM	13734-13734 BARTON	13861-13861 WEST ONEONTA
13407-13407 MOHAWK	13617-13617 CANTON	13736-13736 BERKSHIRE	13862-13862 WHITNEY POINT
13408-13408 MORRISVILLE	13618-13618 CAPE VINCENT	13737-13737 BIBLE SCHOOL PARK	13863-13863 WILLET
13409-13409 MUNNSVILLE	13619-13619 CARTHAGE	13738-13738 BLODGETT MILLS	13864-13864 WILLSEYVILLE
13410-13410 NELLISTON	13620-13620 CASTORLAND	13739-13739 BLOOMVILLE	13865-13865 WINDSOR
13411-13411 NEW BERLIN	13621-13621 CHASE MILLS	13740-13740 BOVINA CENTER	13900-13905 BINGHAMTON
13413-13413 NEW HARTFORD	13622-13622 CHAUMONT	13743-13743 CANDOR	14001-14001 AKRON
13415-13415 NEW LISBON	13623-13623 CHIPPEWA BAY	13744-13744 CASTLE CREEK	14003-14003 ALABAMA
13416-13416 NEWPORT	13624-13624 CLAYTON	13745-13745 CHENANGO BRIDGE	14004-14004 ALDEN
13417-13417 NEW YORK MILLS	13625-13625 COLTON	13746-13746 CHENANGO FORKS	14005-14005 ALEXANDER
13418-13418 NORTH BROOKFIELD	13626-13626 COPENHAGEN	13747-13747 COLLIERSVILLE	14006-14006 ANGOLA
13419-13419 WESTERN	13627-13627 DEER RIVER	13748-13748 CONKLIN	14008-14008 APPLETON
13420-13420 OLD FORGE	13628-13628 DEFERIET	13749-13749 CORBETTSVILLE	14009-14009 ARCADE
13421-13421 ONEIDA	13630-13630 DE KALB JUNCTION	13750-13750 DAVENPORT	14010-14010 ATHOL SPRINGS
13424-13424 ORISKANY	13631-13631 DENMARK	13751-13751 DAVENPORT CENTER	14011-14011 ATTICA
13425-13425 ORISKANY FALLS	13632-13632 DEPAUVILLE	13752-13752 DE LANCEY	14012-14012 BARKER
13426-13426 ORWELL	13633-13633 DE PEYSTER	13753-13753 DELHI	14013-14013 BASOM
13428-13428 PALATINE BRIDGE	13634-13634 DEXTER	13754-13754 DEPOSIT	14020-14021 BATAVIA
13429-13429 PARIS	13635-13635 EDWARDS	13755-13755 DOWNSVILLE	14024-14024 BLISS
13431-13431 POLAND	13636-13636 ELLISBURG	13756-13756 EAST BRANCH	14025-14025 BOSTON
13432-13432 POOLVILLE	13637-13637 EVANS MILLS	13757-13757 EAST MEREDITH	14026-14026 BOWMANSVILLE
13433-13433 PORT LEYDEN	13638-13638 FELTS MILLS	13758-13758 EAST PHARSALIA	14027-14027 BRANT
13434-13434 PRATTS HOLLOW	13639-13639 FINE	13760-13761 ENDICOTT	14028-14028 BURT
13435-13435 PROSPECT	13640-13640 WELLESLEY ISLAND	13762-13762 ENDWELL	14029-14029 CENTERVILLE
13436-13436 RAQUETTE LAKE	13641-13641 FISHERS LANDING	13763-13763 ENDICOTT	14030-14030 CHAFFEE
13437-13437 REDFIELD	13642-13642 GOUVERNEUR	13774-13774 FISHS EDDY	14031-14031 CLARENCE
13438-13438 REMSEN	13643-13643 GREAT BEND	13775-13775 FRANKLIN	14032-14032 CLARENCE CENTER
13439-13439 RICHFIELD SPRINGS	13645-13645 HAILESBORO	13776-13776 GILBERTSVILLE	14033-14033 COLDEN
13440-13449 ROME	13646-13646 HAMMOND	13777-13777 GLEN AUBREY	14034-14034 COLLINS
13450-13450 ROSEBOOM	13647-13647 HANNAWA FALLS	13778-13778 GREENE	14035-14035 COLLINS CENTER
13452-13452 SAINT JOHNSVILLE	13648-13648 HARRISVILLE	13780-13780 GUILFORD	14036-14036 CORFU
13454-13454 SALISBURY CENTER	13649-13649 HELENA	13782-13782 HAMDEN	14037-14037 COWLESVILLE
13455-13455 SANGERFIELD	13650-13650 HENDERSON	13783-13783 HANCOCK	14038-14038 CRITTENDEN
13456-13456 SAUQUOIT	13651-13651 HENDERSON HARBOR	13784-13784 HARFORD	14039-14039 DALE
13457-13457 SCHUYLER LAKE	13652-13652 HERMON	13786-13786 HARPERSFIELD	14040-14040 DARIEN CENTER
13459-13459 SHARON SPRINGS	13654-13654 HEUVELTON	13787-13787 HARPURSVILLE	14041-14041 DAYTON
13460-13460 SHERBURNE	13655-13655 HOGANSBURG	13788-13788 HOBART	14042-14042 DELEVAN
13461-13461 SHERRILL	13656-13656 LA FARGEVILLE	13790-13790 JOHNSON CITY	14043-14043 DEPEW
13464-13464 SMYRNA	13657-13657 LIMERICK	13794-13794 KILLAWOG	14047-14047 DERBY
13465-13465 SOLSVILLE	13658-13658 LISBON	13795-13795 KIRKWOOD	14048-14048 DUNKIRK
13466-13466 SOUTH EDMESTON	13659-13659 LORRAINE	13796-13796 LAURENS	14051-14051 EAST AMHERST
13468-13468 SPRINGFIELD CENTER	13660-13660 MADRID	13797-13797 LISLE	14052-14052 EAST AURORA
13469-13469 STITTVILLE	13661-13661 MANNSVILLE	13801-13801 MC DONOUGH	14054-14054 EAST BETHANY
13470-13470 STRATFORD	13662-13662 MASSENA	13802-13802 MAINE	14055-14055 EAST CONCORD
13471-13471 TABERG	13664-13664 MORRISTOWN	13803-13803 MARATHON	14056-14056 EAST PEMBROKE
13472-13472 THENDARA	13665-13665 NATURAL BRIDGE	13804-13804 MASONVILLE	14057-14057 EDEN
13473-13473 TURIN	13666-13666 NEWTON FALLS	13806-13806 MERIDALE	14058-14058 ELBA
13475-13475 VAN HORNESVILLE	13667-13667 NORFOLK	13807-13807 MILFORD	14059-14059 ELMA
13476-13476 VERNON	13668-13668 NORWOOD	13808-13808 MORRIS	14060-14060 FARMERSVILLE STATION
13477-13477 VERNON CENTER	13669-13669 OGDENSBURG	13809-13809 MOUNT UPTON	14061-14061 FARNHAM
13478-13478 VERONA	13670-13670 OSWEGATCHIE	13810-13810 MOUNT VISION	14062-14062 FORESTVILLE
13479-13479 WASHINGTON MILLS	13671-13671 OXBOW	13811-13811 NEWARK VALLEY	14063-14063 FREDONIA
13480-13480 WATERVILLE	13672-13672 PARISHVILLE	13812-13812 NICHOLS	14065-14065 FREEDOM
13482-13482 WEST BURLINGTON	13673-13673 PHILADELPHIA	13813-13813 NINEVEH	14066-14066 GAINESVILLE
13483-13483 WESTDALE	13674-13674 PIERREPONT MANOR	13814-13814 NORTH NORWICH	14067-14067 GASPORT
13484-13484 WEST EATON	13675-13675 PLESSIS	13815-13815 NORWICH	14068-14068 GETZVILLE
13485-13485 WEST EDMESTON	13676-13676 POTSDAM	13820-13820 ONEONTA	14069-14069 GLENWOOD
13486-13486 WESTERNVILLE	13677-13677 PYRITES	13825-13825 OTEGO	14070-14070 GOWANDA
13487-13487 WEST EXETER	13678-13678 RAYMONDVILLE	13826-13826 OUAQUAGA	14072-14072 GRAND ISLAND
13488-13488 WESTFORD	13679-13679 REDWOOD	13827-13827 OWEGO	14075-14075 HAMBURG
13489-13489 WEST LEYDEN	13680-13680 RENSSELAER FALLS	13830-13830 OXFORD	14079-14079 HELMUTH

14080-14080 HOLLAND	14101-14101 MACHIAS	14113-14113 NORTH JAVA	14134-14134 SARDINIA
14081-14081 IRVING	14102-14102 MARILLA	14120-14120 NORTH TONAWANDA	14135-14135 SHERIDAN
14082-14082 JAVA CENTER	14103-14103 MEDINA	14125-14125 OAKFIELD	14136-14136 SILVER CREEK
14083-14083 JAVA VILLAGE	14105-14105 MIDDLEPORT	14126-14126 OLCOTT	14138-14138 SOUTH DAYTON
14085-14085 LAKE VIEW	14107-14107 MODEL CITY	14127-14127 ORCHARD PARK	14139-14139 SOUTH WALES
14086-14086 LANCASTER	14108-14108 NEWFANE	14129-14129 PERRYSBURG	14140-14140 SPRING BROOK
14091-14091 LAWTONS	14109-14109 NIAGARA UNIVERSITY	14130-14130 PIKE	14141-14141 SPRINGVILLE
14092-14092 LEWISTON	14110-14110 NORTH BOSTON	14131-14131 RANSOMVILLE	14143-14143 STAFFORD
14094-14095 LOCKPORT	14111-14111 NORTH COLLINS	14132-14132 SANBORN	14144-14144 STELLA NIAGARA
14098-14098 LYNDONVILLE	14112-14112 NORTH EVANS	14133-14133 SANDUSKY	14145-14145 STRYKERSVILLE
14150-14151 TONAWANDA	14507-14507 MIDDLESEX	14716-14716 BROCTON	14813-14813 BELMONT
14166-14166 VAN BUREN POINT	14508-14508 MORTON	14717-14717 CANEADEA	14814-14814 BIG FLATS
14167-14167 VARYSBURG	14510-14510 MOUNT MORRIS	14718-14718 CASSADAGA	14815-14815 BRADFORD
14168-14168 VERSAILLES	14511-14511 MUMFORD	14719-14719 CATTARAUGUS	14816-14816 BREESPORT
14169-14169 WALES CENTER	14512-14512 NAPLES	14720-14720 CELORON	14817-14817 BROOKTONDALE
14170-14170 WEST FALLS	14513-14513 NEWARK	14721-14721 CERES	14818-14818 BURDETT
14171-14171 WEST VALLEY	14514-14514 NORTH CHILI	14722-14722 CHAUTAUQUA	14819-14819 CAMERON
14172-14172 WILSON	14515-14515 NORTH GREECE	14723-14723 CHERRY CREEK	14820-14820 CAMERON MILLS
14173-14173 YORKSHIRE	14516-14516 NORTH ROSE	14724-14724 CLYMER	14821-14821 CAMPBELL
14174-14174 YOUNGSTOWN	14517-14517 NUNDA	14726-14726 CONEWANGO VALLEY	14822-14822 CANASERAGA
14200-14280 BUFFALO	14518-14518 OAKS CORNERS	14727-14727 CUBA	14823-14823 CANISTEO
14300-14305 NIAGARA FALLS	14519-14519 ONTARIO	14728-14728 DEWITTVILLE	14824-14824 CAYUTA
14410-14410 ADAMS BASIN	14520-14520 ONTARIO CENTER	14729-14729 EAST OTTO	14825-14825 CHEMUNG
14411-14411 ALBION	14521-14521 OVID	14730-14730 EAST RANDOLPH	14826-14826 COHOCTON
14413-14413 ALTON	14522-14522 PALMYRA	14731-14731 ELLICOTTVILLE	14827-14827 COOPERS PLAINS
14414-14414 AVON	14525-14525 PAVILION	14732-14732 ELLINGTON	14830-14831 CORNING
14415-14415 BELLONA	14526-14526 PENFIELD	14733-14733 FALCONER	14836-14836 DALTON
14416-14416 BERGEN	14527-14527 PENN YAN	14735-14735 FILLMORE	14837-14837 DUNDEE
14418-14418 BRANCHPORT	14529-14529 PERKINSVILLE	14736-14736 FINDLEY LAKE	14838-14838 ERIN
14420-14420 BROCKPORT	14530-14530 PERRY	14737-14737 FRANKLINVILLE	14839-14839 GREENWOOD
14422-14422 BYRON	14532-14532 PHELPS	14738-14738 FREWSBURG	14840-14840 HAMMONDSPORT
14423-14423 CALEDONIA	14533-14533 PIFFARD	14739-14739 FRIENDSHIP	14841-14841 HECTOR
14424-14424 CANANDAIGUA	14534-14534 PITTSFORD	14740-14740 GERRY	14842-14842 HIMROD
14425-14425 FARMINGTON	14536-14536 PORTAGEVILLE	14741-14741 GREAT VALLEY	14843-14843 HORNELL
14427-14427 CASTILE	14537-14537 PORT GIBSON	14742-14742 GREENHURST	14844-14845 HORSEHEADS
14428-14428 CHURCHVILLE	14538-14538 PULTNEYVILLE	14743-14743 HINSDALE	14846-14846 HUNT
14429-14429 CLARENDON	14539-14539 RETSOF	14744-14744 HOUGHTON	14847-14847 INTERLAKEN
14430-14430 CLARKSON	14541-14541 ROMULUS	14745-14745 HUME	14850-14853 ITHACA
14432-14432 CLIFTON SPRINGS	14542-14542 ROSE	14747-14747 KENNEDY	14854-14854 JACKSONVILLE
14433-14433 CLYDE	14543-14543 RUSH	14748-14748 KILL BUCK	14855-14855 JASPER
14435-14435 CONESUS	14544-14544 RUSHVILLE	14749-14749 KNAPP CREEK	14856-14856 KANONA
14437-14437 DANSVILLE	14545-14545 SCOTTSBURG	14750-14750 LAKEWOOD	14857-14857 LAKEMONT
14441-14441 DRESDEN	14546-14546 SCOTTSVILLE	14751-14751 LEON	14858-14858 LINDLEY
14442-14442 EAGLE HARBOR	14547-14547 SENECA CASTLE	14752-14752 LILY DALE	14859-14859 LOCKWOOD
14443-14443 EAST BLOOMFIELD	14548-14548 SHORTSVILLE	14753-14753 LIMESTONE	14860-14860 LODI
14444-14444 EAST PALMYRA	14549-14549 SILVER LAKE	14754-14754 LITTLE GENESEE	14861-14861 LOWMAN
14445-14445 EAST ROCHESTER	14550-14550 SILVER SPRINGS	14755-14755 LITTLE VALLEY	14863-14863 MECKLENBURG
14449-14449 EAST WILLIAMSON	14551-14551 SODUS	14756-14756 MAPLE SPRINGS	14864-14864 MILLPORT
14450-14450 FAIRPORT	14554-14554 SODUS CENTER	14757-14757 MAYVILLE	14865-14865 MONTOUR FALLS
14452-14452 FANCHER	14555-14555 SODUS POINT	14758-14758 NIOBE	14867-14867 NEWFIELD
14453-14453 FISHERS	14556-14556 SONYEA	14759-14759 NORTH CLYMER	14868-14868 NORTH COHOCTON
14454-14454 GENESEO	14557-14557 SOUTH BYRON	14760-14760 OLEAN	14869-14869 ODESSA
14456-14456 GENEVA	14558-14558 SOUTH LIMA	14766-14766 OTTO	14870-14870 PAINTED POST
14461-14461 GORHAM	14559-14559 SPENCERPORT	14767-14767 PANAMA	14871-14871 PINE CITY
14462-14462 GROVELAND	14560-14560 SPRINGWATER	14769-14769 PORTLAND	14872-14872 PINE VALLEY
14463-14463 HALL	14561-14561 STANLEY	14770-14770 PORTVILLE	14873-14873 PRATTSBURGH
14464-14464 HAMLIN	14563-14563 UNION HILL	14772-14772 RANDOLPH	14874-14874 PULTENEY
14466-14466 HEMLOCK	14564-14564 VICTOR	14774-14774 RICHBURG	14876-14876 READING CENTER
14467-14467 HENRIETTA	14568-14568 WALWORTH	14775-14775 RIPLEY	14877-14877 REXVILLE
14468-14468 HILTON	14569-14569 WARSAW	14776-14776 ROSSBURG	14878-14878 ROCK STREAM
14469-14469 BLOOMFIELD	14571-14571 WATERPORT	14777-14777 RUSHFORD	14879-14879 SAVONA
14470-14470 HOLLEY	14572-14572 WAYLAND	14778-14778 SAINT BONAVENTURE	14880-14880 SCIO
14471-14471 HONEOYE	14580-14580 WEBSTER	14779-14779 SALAMANCA	14881-14881 SLATERVILLE SPRINGS
14472-14472 HONEOYE FALLS	14584-14584 WEBSTER CROSSING	14781-14781 SHERMAN	14882-14882 LANSING
14474-14474 INDUSTRY	14585-14585 WEST BLOOMFIELD	14782-14782 SINCLAIRVILLE	14883-14883 SPENCER
14475-14475 IONIA	14586-14586 WEST HENRIETTA	14783-14783 STEAMBURG	14884-14884 SWAIN
14476-14476 KENDALL	14588-14588 WILLARD	14784-14784 STOCKTON	14885-14885 TROUPSBURG
14477-14477 KENT	14589-14589 WILLIAMSON	14785-14785 STOW	14886-14886 TRUMANSBURG
14478-14478 KEUKA PARK	14590-14590 WOLCOTT	14786-14786 WEST CLARKSVILLE	14887-14887 TYRONE
14479-14479 KNOWLESVILLE	14591-14591 WYOMING	14787-14787 WESTFIELD	14888-14888 VALOIS
14480-14480 LAKEVILLE	14592-14592 YORK	14788-14788 WESTONS MILLS	14889-14889 VAN ETTEN
14481-14481 LEICESTER	14600-14694 ROCHESTER	14801-14801 ADDISON	14891-14891 WATKINS GLEN
14482-14482 LE ROY	14701-14704 JAMESTOWN	14802-14802 ALFRED	14892-14892 WAVERLY
14485-14485 LIMA	14706-14706 ALLEGANY	14803-14803 ALFRED STATION	14893-14893 WAYNE
14486-14486 LINWOOD	14707-14707 ALLENTOWN	14804-14804 ALMOND	14894-14894 WELLSBURG
14487-14487 LIVONIA	14708-14708 ALMA	14805-14805 ALPINE	14895-14895 WELLSVILLE
14488-14488 LIVONIA CENTER	14709-14709 ANGELICA	14806-14806 ANDOVER	14896-14896 WEST DANBY
14489-14489 LYONS	14710-14710 ASHVILLE	14807-14807 ARKPORT	14897-14897 WHITESVILLE
14502-14502 MACEDON	14711-14711 BELFAST	14808-14808 ATLANTA	14898-14898 WOODHULL
14504-14504 MANCHESTER	14712-14712 BEMUS POINT	14809-14809 AVOCA	14900-14975 ELMIRA
14505-14505 MARION	14714-14714 BLACK CREEK	14810-14810 BATH	
14506-14506 MENDON	14715-14715 BOLIVAR	14812-14812 BEAVER DAMS	

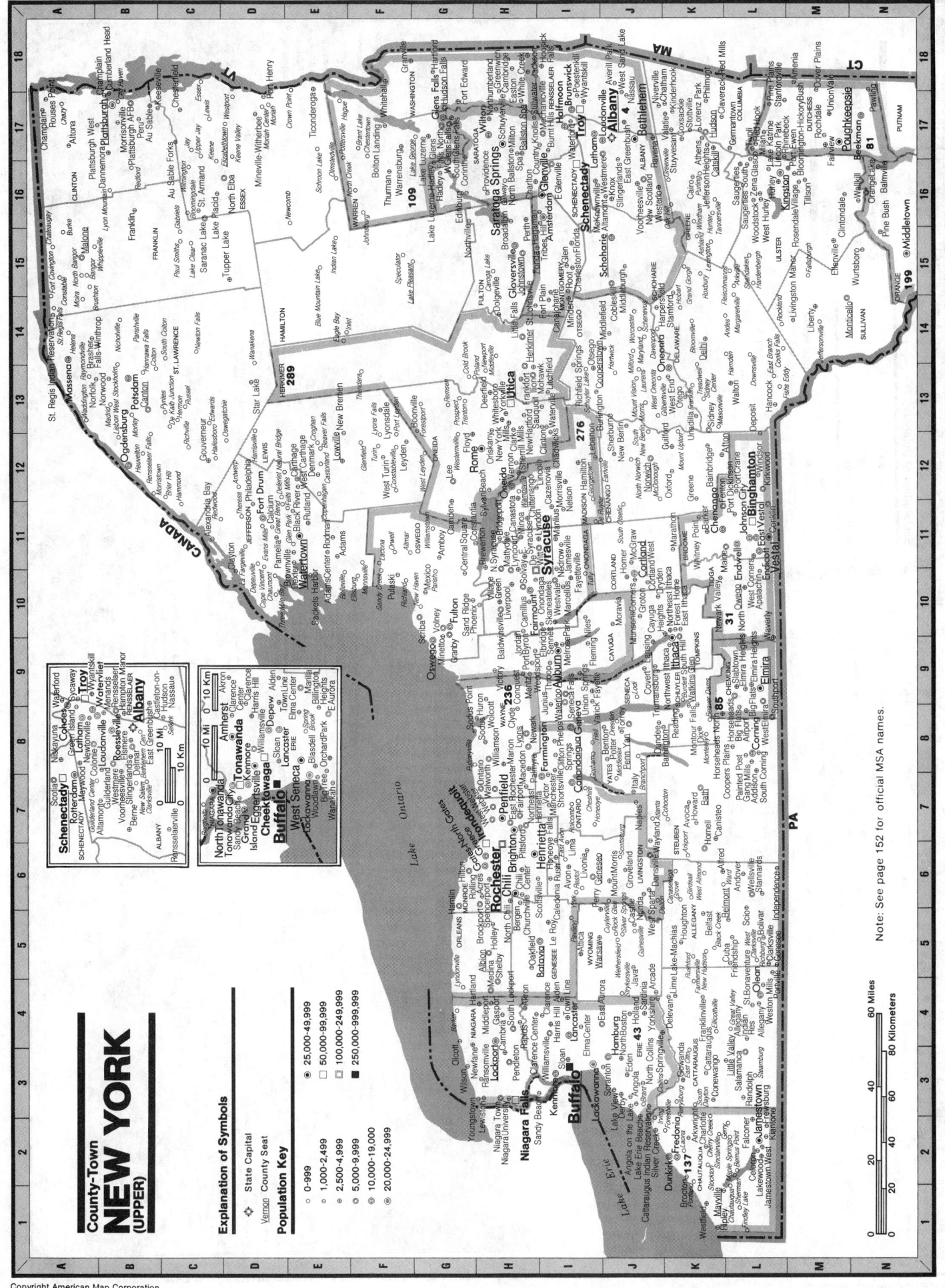

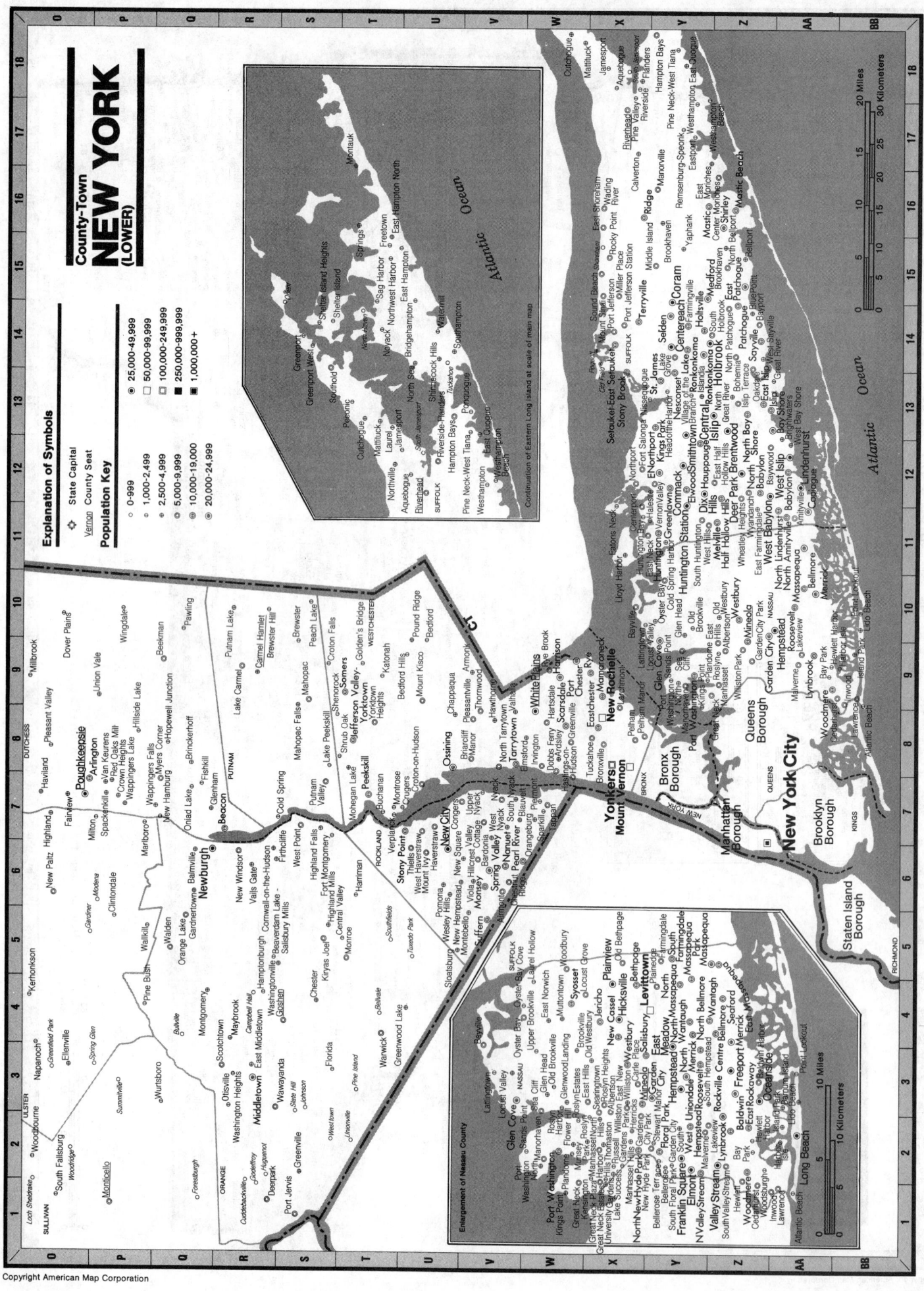

Explanation of symbols:

● – Census Designated Place (CDP)

▲ *italics* – Township (shown on the map)

● *italics* – Township shown which is also a CDP

italics – Township (not shown on the map)

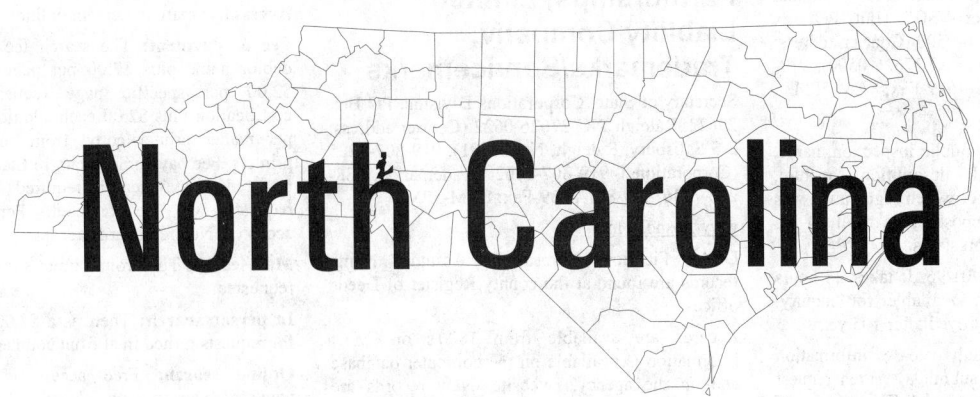

General Help Numbers:

Governor's Office

20301 Mail Service Center
Raleigh, NC 27699-0301
www.governor.state.nc.us

919-733-4240
Fax 919-715-3175
8AM-6PM

Attorney General's Office

Justice Department
9001 Mail Service Center
Raleigh, NC 27699-9001
www.jus.state.nc.us

919-716-6400
Fax 919-716-6750
8AM-5PM

Legislative Records

North Carolina General Assembly
16 W. Jones Street, Rm 2226
Raleigh, NC 27603
www.ncleg.net

919-733-7779
919-733-7778
8:30AM-5:30PM

State Archives

Archives & History Division
109 E Jones St
Raleigh, NC 27601-2807
www.ah.dcr.state.nc.us

919-807-7280
Fax 919-733-8807
8AM-5:30PM TU-F, 9-5 SA

State Specifics:

Capital:	Raleigh
	Wake County
Time Zone:	EST
Number of Counties:	100
Population:	8,541,221
Web Site:	www.ncgov.com

State Agencies

Criminal Records

Access to Records is Restricted.

State Bureau of Investigation, C.I.I.S., PO Box 29500, Raleigh, NC 27626 (Courier address: 3320 Garner Rd, Raleigh, NC 27626-0500); 919-662-4500, 919-662-4380-Fax; 8AM-5PM.

http://sbi.jus.state.nc.us

This agency and the Administrative Office of the Courts (AOC) have implemented a computer-to-computer interface, which provides all users with the capability to access statewide Clerk of Court criminal records. Record access is limited to criminal justice and other government agencies authorized by law. Employers are denied access unless subject is in a business designated to receive records (i.e. health or child care). Contact agency for proper paperwork.

Statewide Court Records

Administrative Office of Courts, PO Box 2448, Raleigh, NC 27602-2448 (Courier address: 227 Fayatteville St Mall, Raleigh, NC 27601); 919-733-7107, 919-715-5779-Fax; 8AM-5PM.

www.nccourts.org/Courts

All trial court research for record copies must be done at the local level.

Access by: online.

Online search: The state AOC has public access on its Virtual Private Network for approved requesters. Charges are based on screens viewed, rather than a specific fee per name. As we go to press, there is a question if the DOB will be taken off this system. A lessor valued product known as the Criminal Extract is available, but does not have the depth and quality of data as the network described above. Call 919-716-5088 for details on the programs. For current calendars, go to http://www1.aoc.state.nc.us/www/. Also, appellate and supreme court opinions are available at www.aoc.state.nc.us/www/public/html/opinions.htm.

Sexual Offender Registry

State Bureau of Investigation, Criminal Information & Ident Sect - SOR Unit, PO Box 29500, Raleigh, NC 27626-0500 (Courier address: 3320 Garner Rd, Raleigh, NC 27626-0500); 919-662-4500 x6257, 919-662-4619-Fax; 8AM-5PM.

http://sbi.jus.state.nc.us

Records are available for public inspection; name, sex, address, physical description, picture, conviction date, offense for which registration was required, the sentence imposed as a result of the conviction, and registration status.

Records are available 01/01/96. It takes 24 hours before new records are available for inquiry. Records are normally destroyed after 105 years.

Searching: This office only releases information online. They suggest to submit a written request for the information to the sheriff. The identity of the victim cannot be released. A sheriff may charge a reasonable fee The following data is not released: victim information.

Access by: mail, in person, online.

Mail search: Turnaround time: 24 hours. SASE is required. Records are available by mail.

In person search: Records may be viewed in person at this office or at local law enforcement offices. There is a public access terminal.

Online search: Search Level 3 records at the website. Search by name or geographic region.

Other access: Agency can provide data on CD-ROM.

Incarceration Records

North Carolina Department of Corrections, Combined Records, 2020 Yonkers Road, 4226 MSC, Raleigh, NC 27699-4226; 919-716-3200, 919-716-3986-Fax; 8AM-4:30PM.

www.doc.state.nc.us

Records are available on current and former inmates. It takes up to 10 days before new records are available for inquiry. Records are normally destroyed after 10 years (paper copies).

Searching: Computer records go back to 1973. Include the following in your request-full name. the DOB, SSN and DOC number are helpful. Location, physical identifiers, conviction and sentencing information, and release dates are provided.

Access by: mail, phone, fax, in person, online.

Fee & Payment: The fee for copies is $1.00 for first page and $.25 each add'l. Fee payee: NC Dept of Corrections Personal checks are accepted.

Mail search: Turnaround time: 1 to 2 days.

Phone search: Name searching available by phone.

Fax search: Search requests accepted by fax.

In person search: Walk-in requesters are serviced.

Online search: The web access allows searching by name or ID number for public information on inmates, probationers, or parolees since 1973. Also, a private company offers free web access to inmates at www.vinelink.com/index.jsp including state, DOC, and county jail systems.

Corporation, Limited Partnerships, Limited Liability Company, Trademarks/Servicemarks

Secretary of State, Corporations Division, PO Box 29622, Raleigh, NC 27626-0622 (Courier address: 2 S Salisbury, Raleigh, NC 27601); 919-807-2225 (Corporations), 919-807-2162 (Trademarks), 888-246-7636, 919-807-2039-Fax; 8AM-5PM.

www.sosnc.com

DBAs, Fictitious Names and Assumed Name records are found at the county Register of Deeds offices.

Records are available from 1800's on. Most information is available on the computer database and on the agency's website. New records are available for inquiry immediately. Records are normally destroyed after records are not destroyed.

Searching: Information is open to the public. Will only expedite the filing of documents, not for searches. Include the following in your request-full name of business. Information contained in filings includes officers' names and addresses; registered agent; principal office; date of incorporation; and nature of the business.

Access by: mail, phone, fax, in person, online.

Fee & Payment: There is no search fee. Copies are $1.00 per page. Document certification is $15.00. Electronic certification is $10.00. Fee payee: Secretary of State. Prepayment required. Personal checks accepted. Credit cards accepted.

Mail search: Turnaround time: 2-3 days. Expect 6-10 day turnaround time for corporation documents, 2-3 day turnaround time for trademark documents. SASE helpful.

Phone search: Copies may be ordered over the telephone.

Fax search: They will invoice.

In person search: Turnaround time is immediate. There is a public access terminal to view records.

Online search: The website offers a free search of status, corporate documents, and search by registered agent. The trademark database is not available online.

Other access: This agency makes database information available for purchase via an FTP site. Contact Bonnie Elek at 919-807-2196 for details.

Uniform Commercial Code, Federal Tax Liens

UCC Division, Secretary of State, PO Box 29626, Raleigh, NC 27626-0626 (Courier address: 2 South Salisbury St, Raleigh, NC 27602); 919-807-2111, 919-807-2119, 919-807-2120-Fax; 8AM-5PM.

www.secretary.state.nc.us/UCC

Email questions to uccmail@sosnc.com.

Records are available from 1967. Records are computerized since 1985. It takes 72 hours before new records are available for inquiry. Records are normally destroyed after six years from lapse date.

Searching: Use search request form UCC-11. The search includes federal tax liens on businesses since 1985 if you request (add $5.00). You may search federal tax liens separately. Federal tax liens on individuals and all state tax liens are filed at Superior Courts. Include the following in your

request-debtor name. Name will be searched as submitted; name variation printouts will be given.

Access by: mail, in person, online.

Fee & Payment: The search fee is $38.00 per debtor name plus $2.00 per page for copies or $2.00 per specific page request. $6.25 for certification plus $2.00 each additional page. $.50 per reader printer copy, from customer reader printers. Fee payee: Secretary of State. Prepayment required. Prepayment is required. Underpayment requests will be rejected. Personal checks accepted. No credit cards accepted.

Mail search: Turnaround time: 3 days. A SASE is requested.

In person search: There is a $2.00 fee per page for requests turned in at front counter.

Online search: Free access is available at www.secretary.state.nc.us/ucc/. Click on "UCC research" or "Tax Liens." Search by ID number or debtor name. Also, you may search tax liens at www.secretary.state.nc.us/taxliens.

Other access: The UCC or tax lien database can be purchased on either a weekly or monthly basis via an FTP site. For more information, call 919-807-2196.

State Tax Liens

Records not maintained by a state level agency.

Tax lien data is found at the county level.

Sales Tax Registrations

Revenue Department, Sales & Use Tax Division, PO Box 25000, Raleigh, NC 27640 (Courier address: 501 N Wilmington Street, Raleigh, NC 27604); 877-252-3052, 919-733-5750-Fax; 8AM-5PM.

www.dor.state.nc.us

Searching: Include the following in your request-name or account # or federal ID.

Access by: mail, online.

Mail search: Records are available by mail.

Online search: Delinquent debtors are shown at www.dor.state.nc.us/collect/delinquent.html.

Birth Certificates

Center for Health Statistics, Vital Records Branch, 1903 Mail Service Center, Raleigh, NC 27699-1903 (Courier address: 225 N McDowell St, Raleigh, NC 27603); 919-733-3526, 800-669-8310 (Credit Card Orders), 919-829-1359-Fax; 8AM-4PM.

http://vitalrecords.dhhs.state.nc.us

Anyone can order an non-certified copy of a record. Only family members can order a certified copy. The fee is the same.

Records are available from 1913 to present. Prior to 1913, the state did not keep records of births. Recent records must be obtained at the county level. It takes 180 days after birth before new records are available for inquiry. Records are indexed on microfiche, inhouse computer.

Searching: Investigative searches are permitted, but only non-certified copies are provided. Otherwise, requester must state relationship to subject and why record is needed. Include the following in your request-full name, names of parents, mother's maiden name, date of birth, place of birth. The following data is not released: adoption records or medical records.

Access by: mail, phone, fax, in person, online.

Fee & Payment: Search fee is $10.00 per 5 years searched. Add $9.95 for using a credit card. Add $5.00 per copy for additional copies. Add $15.00 for in person requests. Fee payee: North Carolina Vital Records. Prepayment required. Credit cards accepted for expedited service only. Personal checks accepted. Credit cards accepted only by VitalChek.

Mail search: Turnaround time: 2 weeks.

Phone search: See expedited service.

Fax search: See expedited service.

In person search: Walk-in services in the lobby is only for simple certificate requests. All other services (such as amending a certificate) will be conducted by appointment only. The walk-in service entails an additional $15.00 fee.

Online search: See expedited service.

Expedited service: Expedited service is available using a credit card via a state-designated vendor - www.vitalchek. Total fee is $55.45 and includes use of credit card and express delivery.

Death Records

Dept of Environment, Health & Natural Resources, Vital Records Section, 1903 Mail Service Center, Raleigh, NC 27699-1903 (Courier address: 225 N McDowell St, Raleigh, NC 27603); 919-733-3526, 800-669-8310 (Credit card orders), 919-829-1359-Fax; 8AM-4PM.

http://vitalrecords.dhhs.state.nc.us

Non-certified records may be obtained by the public; certified copies can only be purchased by family members. The fee is the same for either record.

Records are available from 1930 to present. Recent records must be obtained at the county level. It takes 180 days after death before new records are available for inquiry. Records are indexed on microfiche, inhouse computer.

Searching: Investigative searches are permitted, but only non-certified copies are provided. Include the following in your request-full name, date of death, place of death. SSN is helpful.

Access by: mail, phone, fax, in person, online.

Fee & Payment: The search fee is $15.00 for each 5 years searched. Add $9.95 for using a credit card. Add $5.00 per copy for additional copies. Add $15.00 for in person requests. Fee payee: North Carolina Vital Records. Prepayment required. Credit cards accepted for phone service only. Personal checks accepted. Credit cards accepted only by VitalChek.

Mail search: Turnaround time: 2 weeks.

Phone search: See expedited service.

Fax search: See expedited service.

In person search: Walk-in services in the lobby is only for simple certificate requests. All other services (such as amending a certificate) will be conducted by appointment only. The walk-in service entails an additional $15.00 fee.

Online search: See expedited service.

Expedited service: Expedited service is available using a credit card via a state-designated vendor - www.vitalchek. Total fee is $55.45 and includes use of credit card and express delivery.

Marriage Certificates

Dept of Environment, Health & Natural Resources, Vital Records Section, 1903 Mail Service Center, Raleigh, NC 27699-1903 (Courier address: 225 N McDowell St, Raleigh, NC 27603); 919-733-3526, 800-669-8310 (Credit card orders), 919-829-1359-Fax; 8AM-4PM.

http://vitalrecords.dhhs.state.nc.us

Non-certified copies may be purchased by the public. Certified copies can be obtained by family members. The fee is the same for either report.

Records are available from 1962 to present. Recent records must be obtained at the county level. It takes 8 months before new records are available for inquiry. Records are indexed on microfiche, inhouse computer.

Searching: Investigative searches are permitted, but only non-certified copies are provided. Include the following in your request-names of husband and wife, date of marriage, place or county of marriage.

Access by: mail, phone, fax, in person, online.

Fee & Payment: The search fee is $15.00 for each 5 years searched. Add $9.95 for using a credit card (expedited service only). Add $5.00 per copy for additional copies. Add $15.00 for in person requests. Fee payee: North Carolina Vital Records. Prepayment required. Personal checks accepted. Credit cards accepted only by VitalChek.

Mail search: Turnaround time: 2 weeks.

Phone search: See expedited service.

Fax search: See expedited service.

In person search: Walk-in services in the lobby is only for simple certificate requests. All other services (such as amending a certificate) will be conducted by appointment only. The walk-in service entails an additional $15.00 fee.

Online search: See expedited service.

Expedited service: Expedited service is available using a credit card via a state-designated vendor - www.vitalchek. Total fee is $55.45 and includes use of credit card and express delivery.

Divorce Records

Dept of Environment, Health & Natural Resources, Vital Records Section, 1903 Mail Service Center, Raleigh, NC 27699-1903 (Courier address: 225 N McDowell St, Raleigh, NC 27603); 919-733-3526, 800-669-8310 (Credit card orders), 919-829-1359-Fax; 8AM-4PM.

http://vitalrecords.dhhs.state.nc.us

Non-certified copies are available to the public, certified copies to family members. The fee is the same for either report.

Records are available from 1958 to present. Recent records must be obtained at the county level. It takes up to 1 year before new records are available for inquiry. Records are indexed on microfiche, inhouse computer.

Searching: Investigative searches are permitted, but only non-certified copies are provided. Include the following in your request-names of husband and wife, date of divorce, place of divorce, case number (if known).

Access by: mail, phone, fax, in person, online.

Fee & Payment: The search fee is $15.00 for each 5 years searched. Add $9.95 for using a credit card (expedited only) . Add $5.00 per copy for additional copies. Add $15.00 for in person

requests. Fee payee: North Carolina Vital Records. Prepayment required. Personal checks accepted. Credit cards accepted only by VitalChek.

Mail search: Turnaround time: 2 weeks.

Phone search: See expedited service.

Fax search: See expedited service.

In person search: Walk-in services in the lobby is only for simple certificate requests. All other services (such as amending a certificate) will be conducted by appointment only. The walk-in service entails an additional $15.00 fee.

Online search: See expedited service.

Expedited service: Expedited service is available using a credit card via a state-designated vendor - www.vitalchek. Total fee is $55.45 and includes use of credit card and express delivery.

Workers' Compensation Records

NC Industrial Commission, Worker's Comp Records, 4340 Mail Service Center, Raleigh, NC 27699-4340; 919-807-2500, 800-688-8349 (Claims Questions), 919-715-0282-Fax; 8AM-5PM.

www.comp.state.nc.us

One may search the Workers' Compensation Name Search System at the web to find the addresses of employers, insurance companies, third party administrators, and the parties responsible for workers' compensation coverage at the time of an accident.

Records are available from 1980. From 1997 back records are purged and stored in warehouse. It takes 24 hours before new records are available for inquiry.

Searching: Searches require a signed release or statement of purpose of request on letterhead. Only parties to claim will be allowed access. Per federal law, records may not be used for pre-employment screening.

Access by: mail, in person, online.

Fee & Payment: There is no search fee. There is no copy fee unless the file is over 20 pages, then the fee is $1.00 per page (over 20). Fee payee: NC Industrial Commission. Personal checks accepted. No credit cards accepted.

Mail search: Turnaround time: 2 to 3 days.

In person search: Generally turnaround time is immediate, unless the case is closed and records must be researched.

Online search: Extensive information about employers and insurerss may be searched online at www.comp.state.nc.us/iwcnss/. This site also gives access to court decisions involving worker's comp.

Driver Records

Division of Motor Vehicles, Driver License Records, 3113 MSC, Raleigh, NC 27699; 919-715-7000, 8AM-5PM.

www.ncdot.org/dmv/driver_services

Records available include a limited three year (insurance purposes) and a seven year (employment purposes) record.

Records are available for 5 yrs or more for moving violations, 10 yrs or more for DWIs and suspensions. Surrendered license records are kept for 1 yr after the expiration date. This state utilizes two point systems-one for the DMV, one for insurance purposes. It takes minutes before new records are available for inquiry. Records are normally destroyed after 10 years, if not renewed.

Searching: Form DL-DPPA-1 is required. Casual requesters cannot obtain records without consent. Include the following in your request-driver's license number, full name, SSN, date of birth. Search modes will look at the driver's license number first, then SSN, the name and DOB as a secondary search. The following data is not released: medical information.

Access by: mail, in person, online.

Fee & Payment: The current fee is $5.00 per record. Certified records are an additional $2.00. Fee payee: NC Division of Motor Vehicles. Prepayment required. Personal checks accepted. No credit cards accepted.

Mail search: Turnaround time: 10business days.

In person search: Up to 2 requests will be processed across the counter; the rest are available the next day.

Online search: To qualify for online availability, a client must be an insurance agent or insurance company support organization. The mode is interactive and is open from 7 AM to 10 PM. The DL# and name are needed when ordering. Records are $5.00 each. A minimum $500 security deposit is required. Call 919-861-3062 for details.

Other access: Magnetic tape for high volume batch users is available. Requests must be pre-paid.

Vehicle Ownership Vehicle Identification

Division of Motor Vehicles, Registration/Correspondence Unit, 1100 New Bern Ave, Rm 100, Raleigh, NC 27697-0001; 919-715-7000, 8AM-5PM.

www.dmv.dot.state.nc.us

Records are available from their first records for title records (on microfilm). Computer records are purged periodically according to plate activity. Records are maintained for mobile homes and boat trailers, also.

Searching: The agency is in compliance with DPPA. Casual requesters receive records without personal information. Include the following in your request-vehicle description, name, and signed release of subject on Form MVR-605A if not an ongoing requester.

Access by: mail, in person.

Fee & Payment: The fee is $1.00 per record (includes lien data) or $5.00 for a certified record. Fee payee: Department of Motor Vehicles. Prepayment required. Personal checks accepted. No credit cards accepted.

Mail search: Turnaround time: 3 days. The use of Form MVR-605A is helpful. The request requires the requester's signature. A SASE is requested.

In person search: Turnaround time is while you wait if you have the correct authorization.

Other access: North Carolina offers a bulk retrieval of ownership and registration information on magnetic tape. A written request specifying the purpose and details of the request is required. Request must comply with DPPA. For more information, call 919-861-3062

Accident Reports

Division of Motor Vehicles, Traffic Records Section, 3105 Mail Service Center, Raleigh, NC 27699-3105; 919-861-3098, 919-733-9605-Fax; 8AM-5PM.

www.ncdot.org/dmv/other_services/recordsstatistics/copyCrashReport.html

Records are available from 1986 to present on computer, from 1995 to present on microfiche. Hard copies are available from 1995. It takes 24 hours or less before new records are available for inquiry.

Searching: Records are not released on minor drivers. Using Form TR-67A, the requester should submit at least one of the names of the owner or driver, the county of occurrence, date of occurrence, and the exception under which he/she qualifies to receive personal information in accordance with DPPA.

Access by: mail, in person.

Fee & Payment: The fee is $4.00 for a certified copy or no cost for a non-certified copy. Fee payee: Division of Motor Vehicles. Prepayment required. Personal checks accepted. No credit cards accepted.

Mail search: Turnaround time: 5 days.

In person search: Turnaround time is immediate .

Other access: Bulk file purchase is available.

Vessel Ownership Vessel Registration

North Carolina Wildlife Resources Commission, Transaction Management, 1709 Mail Service Center, Raleigh, NC 27699-1709 (Courier address: 322 Chapanoke Road, Raleigh, NC 27603); 800-628-3773, 919-662-4379-Fax; 8AM-5PM.

http://216.27.49.98

Records are available from 1970 and are computerized. This is an optional title state. Lien information will show if the vessel is titled. All motorized boats, including jet skis, and sailboats over 14 ft must be registered. New records are available for inquiry immediately.

Searching: Include the following in your request-Name, signed release. Submit the name or registration number or hull number.

Access by: mail, fax.

Fee & Payment: There is no search fee.

Mail search: Turnaround time: 1 to 2 weeks.

Fax search: Turnaround time is several days.

Other access: The agency sells a CD-ROM disk with registration information for $20.00 per disk.

Voter Registration

State Board of Elections, PO Box 27255, Raleigh, NC 27611-7255; 919-733-7173, 919-715-0135-Fax; 8AM-5PM.

www.sboe.state.nc.us

There is a statewide online system for record access. Records are open to the public, subject to certain legal limitations.

Searching: Include the following in your request-sufficient data to define the records needed.

Access by: mail, phone, fax, in person, online.

Fee & Payment: The only fees are for either specialized reports or for actual costs to reproduces the records in the desired format.

Mail search: Turnaround time is variable, depending on workload.

Phone search: Records are available by phone.

Fax search: Records are available by fax.

In person search: Simple requests may be processed while you wait.

Online search: Online access to voter registration records is available free at www.app.sboe.state.nc.us/votersearch/seimsvot.htm. A DOB is needed.

Other access: Most records are sold in CD format or sent via email. The maximum fee is $25.00. Request forms are available at the webpage. This is the most prompt access to records, other than in person.

GED Certificates

Department of Community Colleges, GED Office, 5016 Mail Service Center, Raleigh, NC 27699-5016; 919-807-7137, 919-807-7172-Fax; 8AM-5PM.

www.ncccs.cc.nc.us

Records are available from the 1940s, from 09/77 on microfilm. It takes less than 1 day before new records are available for inquiry.

Searching: There are no fees for verification or copies of transcripts. A request form is found at www.ncccs.cc.nc.us/Basic_Skills/requestFormForGedOrGedScores.htm, Include the following in your request-signed release, Social Security Number, date of birth, signature of the subject. The year and place of the test is helpful.

Access by: mail, fax, in person.

Mail search: Turnaround time: 1 week.

Fax search: Request form may be faxed. Indicate if you merely need a "yes/no" answer.

In person search: No fee for request.

Hunting and Fishing License Information

Wildlife Resource Commission, Archdale Bldg, 512 N Salisbury Street, Raleigh, NC 27604-0118; 919-662-4370, 919-661-4878-Fax; 8AM-5PM.

http://216.27.49.98

Records are available for the past three years. It takes 1 day before new records are available for inquiry.

Searching: Requests must be in writing.

Access by: mail, fax.

Fee & Payment: The fee is $20.00 per list. Fee payee: NC Wildlife Resources Commission

Mail search: Turnaround time: 3 days or less. You may call them after mailing your request.

Fax search: You may have to call back for results, once you have faxed the request.

Other access: CD lists are available for hunting/fishing license holders, either all counties or selected counties. The fee is $20.00. This agency also has vessel owners data.

North Carolina State Licensing Agencies

For details about the agency responsible for licensing/certifying/registering an item below or in the Agency Quick Finder section, match an item's number with the number of the agency in the *Licensing Agency Information* section.

North Carolina Licenses Searchable Online

Acupuncturist #40	http://ncaaom.org/directory.php
Amusement Device #24	www.nclabor.com/elevator/elevator.htm
Architect #3	www.member-base.com/ncbarch/public/lic/searchdb.asp
Architectural Firm #3	www.member-base.com/ncbarch/public/firms/searchdb.asp
Athletic Trainer #38	www.ncbate.org/trainers.html
Attorney #45	www.ncbar.com/home/member_directory.asp
Auction Company #2	www.ncalb.org/scripts/members.asp
Auctioneer Disciplinary Action #2	www.ncalb.org/scripts/disciplinaryaction.asp
Auctioneer/Auctioneer Apprentice #2	www.ncalb.org/scripts/members.asp
Bank #17	https://www.nccob.org/Online/brts/BanksAndTrusts.aspx
Boiler/Pressure Vessel Inspector #24	www.nclabor.com/boiler/boiler.htm
Building Inspector #23	www.ncdoi.com/OSFM/Documents/Engineering/InspectionDirectories/InspectorsByJurisdiction.pdf
Charitable/Sponsor Organization #52	www.secretary.state.nc.us/csl/Search.aspx
Check Casher #17	https://www.nccob.org/Online/CCS/CompanyListing.aspx
Clinical Social Worker #15	www.ncswboard.org/search.asp
Consumer Financer #17	https://www.nccob.org/online/CFS/CFSCompanyListing.aspx
Contractor, General #32	www.nclbgc.org/lic_fr.html
Cosmetology Disciplinary Action #55	www.cosmetology.state.nc.us/newsletter/Disciplinary.pdf
Counselor, Professional #13	www.ncblpc.org/search.php
Crematory #7	www.ncbfs.org/dir_crematoriesdb.htm
Dental Hygienist #42	www.ncdentalboard.org/ncdbe_search.asp
Dentist #42	www.ncdentalboard.org/ncdbe_search.asp
Electrical Contractor/Inspector #6	www.ncbeec.org/LicSearch.asp
Elevator Inspector #24	www.nclabor.com/elevator/elevator.htm
Embalmer #7	www.ncbfs.org/dir_licenseedb.htm
Engineer #48	www.member-base.com/ncbels-vs/public/searchdb.asp
Engineering/Surveying Firm #48	www.member-base.com/ncbels-vs/public/searchdb.asp
Fire Marshall #23	www.ncdoi.com/OSFM/Documents/FireRescueCommission/NCCFMAList.pdf
Fire Sprinkler Contractor #31	www.nclicensing.org/OnlineReg.htm
Fire Sprinkler Inspection Contr./Tech #31	www.nclicensing.org/OnlineReg.htm
Forester #54	http://members.aol.com/ncbrf/roster_index.htm
Fund Raiser Consultant/Solicitor #52	www.secretary.state.nc.us/csl/Search.aspx
Funeral Chapel #7	www.ncbfs.org/dir_chapeldb.htm
Funeral Director/Service #7	www.ncbfs.org/dir_licenseedb.htm
Funeral Home #7	www.ncbfs.org/dir_funeralhomedb.htm
Funeral Trainee #7	www.ncbfs.org/dir_traineesdb.htm
Funeral Transport/Removal Svc #7	www.ncbfs.org/Transport%20and%20Removal%20Services.doc
Geologist #46	www.ncblg.org/licensees.html
Hearing Aid Dispenser/Fitter #43	www.nchalb.org/cgi-bin/sho_memb.pl
Heating Contractor #31	www.nclicensing.org/OnlineReg.htm
HMO #23	http://infoportal.ncdoi.net/cmp_lookup.jsp
Insurance Company #23	http://infoportal.ncdoi.net/cmp_lookup.jsp
Insurer, Life/Health #23	http://infoportal.ncdoi.net/filelookup.jsp?divtype=3
Insurer, Property/Casualty #23	http://infoportal.ncdoi.net/filelookup.jsp?divtype=2
Investment Representative/Advisor #26	www.sosnc.com/
Landscape Architect #46	www.ncbola.org/rosternew.html
Loan Officer #17	https://www.nccob.com/online/LicenseSearch.aspx
Lobbyist #51	www.secretary.state.nc.us/Lobbyists/LSearch.aspx
Manuf'd Housing Retailer/Mfg/Contr. #23	www.ncdoi.com/OSFM/Home/Marshal.asp?PARAMSection=sidManufacturedBuilding&PARAMCategory=cidMBManufacturedHousing&PARAMSubCategory=scidHousingDirectory
Medical Doctor/Physician #47	www.ncmedboard.org/Clients/NCBOM/Public/NCBOMLicenseeSearch.aspx
Money Transmitter #17	https://www.nccob.org/Online/MTS/MTSCompanyListing.aspx
Mortgage Lender/Broker #17	https://www.nccob.com/online/licensesearch.aspx
Nurse Practitioner #47	www.ncmedboard.org/Clients/NCBOM/Public/NCBOMLicenseeSearch.aspx

Nurse-LPN #8	https://www.ncbon.com/Lic-verif.asp
Nursing Home Administrator #5	www.ncbenha.org/searchdb.asp
Occ. Therapist/Therapist Assistant #9	www.ncbot.org/fpdb/otimport.html
Optometrist #18	www.ncoptometry.org/verify/index.asp
Osteopathic Physician #47	www.ncmedboard.org/Clients/NCBOM/Public/NCBOMLicenseeSearch.aspx
Pesticide Applicator #16	www.ncagr.com/aspzine/Fooddrug/data/advsearch.asp
Pesticide Dealer/Consultant #16	www.ncagr.com/aspzine/Fooddrug/data/advsearch.asp
Pharmacist #11	www.ncbop.org/namesAA.asp
Pharmacy Technician #11	www.ncbop.org/Names01.asp
Pharmacy/Physician Pharmacy #11	www.ncbop.org/pharmacyAA.asp
Physical Therapist #49	www.ncptboard.org/search.asp
Physical Therapist Assistant #49	www.ncptboard.org/search.asp
Physician Assistant #47	www.ncmedboard.org/Clients/NCBOM/Public/NCBOMLicenseeSearch.aspx
Plumber #31	www.nclicensing.org/OnlineReg.htm
Podiatrist #12	www.ncbpe.org/search.php
Psychological Associate #36	www.ncpsychologyboard.org/search.htm
Psychologist #36	www.ncpsychologyboard.org/search.htm
Public Accountant-CPA #37	www.cpaboard.state.nc.us
RAL #17	https://www.nccob.org/online/RALS/RALSCompanyListing.aspx
Real Estate Agent/Broker/Dealer #39	www.memberbase.com/ncrec-new/licdb/indv/searchdb.asp
Real Estate Firm #39	www.memberbase.com/ncrec-new/licdb/firms/searchdb.asp
Sanitarian #14	www.rsboard.com/rsweb/directory/directory.htm
Securities Agent/Broker #26	www.sosnc.com/
Social Worker #15	www.ncswboard.org/search.asp
Social Worker Manager #15	www.ncswboard.org/search.asp
Soil Scientist #22	www.ncblss.org/director.html
Speech Pathologist/Audiologist #30	www.ncboeslpa.org
Surveyor, Land #48	www.member-base.com/ncbels-vs/public/searchdb.asp
Trust Company #17	https://www.nccob.org/Online/brts/BanksAndTrusts.aspx

North Carolina Licensing Quick Finder

Acupuncturist #40	919-773-0530
Alarm Installer #1	919-875-3611
Alarm System Business #1	919-875-3611
Alcoholic Beverage Control #20	919-779-0700
Ambulance Attendant #21	919-855-3750
Amusement Device #24	919-733-7166
Anesthetist Nurse #8	919-782-3211x252
Architect #3	919-733-9544
Architectural Firm #3	919-733-9544
Armed Security Guard #53	919-875-3611
Armored Car #53	919-875-3611
Athletic Agent #51	919-807-2156
Athletic Trainer #38	919-821-4980
Attorney #45	919-828-4886
Auction Company #2	919-567-2844
Auctioneer Disciplinary Action #2	919-567-2844
Auctioneer/Auctioneer Apprentice #2	919-567-2844
Bail Bond Runner #23	919-733-7487
Bank #27	919-508-5973
Bank #17	919-733-3016
Barber Inspector/Instructor #4	919-715-1159
Barber/Barber Apprentice #4	919-715-1159
Beauty Shop/Salon #55	919-733-4117
Boiler/Pressure Vessel Inspector #24	919-733-7166
Bondsman, Professional/Surety #23	919-733-7487
Building Inspector #23	919-661-5880
Cemetery #19	919-981-2536
Cemetery Salesperson #19	919-981-2536
Charitable/Sponsor Organization #52	919-807-2214
Check Casher #17	919-733-3016
Chiropractor #41	704-793-1342
Clinical Nurse Specialist #8	919-782-3211x252
Clinical Social Worker #15	336-625-1679
Consumer Financer #17	919-733-3016
Contractor, General #32	919-571-4183

Cosmetologist Instructor/Apprentice/Practitioner #55	919-733-4117
Cosmetology Disciplinary Action #55	919-733-4117
Counselor, Professional #13	919-661-0820
Counter Intelligence Service #53	919-875-3611
Courier Service #53	919-875-3611
Crematory #7	919-733-9380
Dental Hygienist #42	919-678-8223
Dentist #42	919-678-8223
DME (Rx Device) #11	919-942-4454
EDM #21	919-855-3750
Electrical Contractor/Inspector #6	919-733-9042
Elevator Inspector #24	919-733-7166
Embalmer #7	919-733-9380
Emergency Medical Service #21	919-855-3750
Emergency Medical Technician #21	919-855-3750
Engineer #48	919-791-2000
Engineering/Surveying Firm #48	919-791-2000
Esthetician Instructor/Apprentice/Practitioner #55	919-733-4117
Family Therapist #33	919-772-6600
Fire Marshall #23	919-661-5880
Fire Sprinkler Contractor #31	919-875-3612
Fire Sprinkler Inspection Contr. #31	919-875-3612
Fire Sprinkler Inspection Technic'n #31	919-875-3612
Fire Sprinkler Maintenance Technician #31	919-875-3612
Fire/Rescue Instructor #23	919-661-5880
Firearms Trainer #53	919-875-3611
Forester #54	919-847-5441
Fund Raiser Consultant/Solicitor #52	919-807-2214
Funeral Chapel #7	919-733-9380
Funeral Director/Service #7	919-733-9380
Funeral Home #7	919-733-9380
Funeral Pre-Need Seller #7	919-733-9380
Funeral Trainee #7	919-733-9380

Funeral Transport/Removal Svc #7	919-733-9380
Fur Dealer #25	919-661-4872
Game Bird Propagator #25	919-661-4872
Geologist #46	919-850-9669
Guard Dog Service #53	919-875-3611
Hearing Aid Dispenser/Fitter #43	252-752-6382
Heating Contractor #31	919-875-3612
HMO #23	919-733-7487
Home Inspector #23	919-661-5880
Hospital #21	919-855-3750
Hunting Preserve Operator #25	919-661-4872
Insurance Agent #23	919-981-5244 option 1
Insurance Company #23	919-981-5244 option 1
Insurer, Life/Health #23	919-733-7487
Insurer, Property/Casualty #23	919-733-7487
Investment Representative/Advisor #26	919-733-3924
Jailer #56	919-716-6460
Landscape Architect #46	919-850-9088
Librarian, Public #28	919-733-2570
Loan Officer #17	919-733-3016
Lobbyist #51	919-807-2156
Manicurist Instructor/Apprentice/Practitioner #55	919-733-4117
Manufactured Housing Retailer/Mfg/Contr. #23	919-733-7487
Marriage & Family Therapist #33	919-772-6600
Medical Doctor/Physician #47	919-326-1100
Medical Program Director #21	919-855-3750
Medical Responder #21	919-855-3750
Midwife Nurse #8	919-782-3211x244
Money Transmitter #17	919-733-3016
Mortgage Lender/Broker #17	919-733-3016
Notary Public #44	919-733-3406
Nurse Practitioner #8	919-782-3211x244
Nurse Practitioner #47	919-326-1100
Nurse-LPN #8	919-782-3211

Nursing Home #21	919-855-3750	
Nursing Home Administrator #5	919-571-4164	
Occupational Therapist/Therapist Assistant #9	919-832-1380	
Optician #10	919-733-9321	
Optometrist #18	910-285-3160	
Osteopathic Physician #47	919-326-1100	
Paramedic #21	919-855-3750	
Pesticide Applicator #16	919-733-3556	
Pesticide Dealer/Consultant #16	919-733-3556	
Pharmacist #11	919-942-4454	
Pharmacy/Physician Pharmacy #11	919-942-4454	
Physical Therapist #49	919-490-6393	
Physical Therapist Assistant #49	919-490-6393	

Physician Assistant #47	919-326-1100
Plumber #31	919-875-3612
Podiatrist #12	919-861-5583
Polygraph Examiner #53	919-875-3611
Private Investigator #53	919-875-3611
Psychological Associate #36	828-262-2258
Psychologist #36	828-262-2258
Public Accountant-CPA #37	919-733-4222
RAL #17	919-733-3016
Real Estate Agent/Broker/Dealer #39	919-875-3700 x772
Real Estate Firm #39	919-875-3700 x772
Sanitarian #14	910-608-0196
Securities Agent/Broker #26	919-733-3924

Security Guard & Patrol #53	919-875-3611
Shorthand Reporter #29	919-733-2927
Social Worker #15	336-625-1679
Social Worker Manager #15	336-625-1679
Soil Scientist #22	919-851-8963
Solid Waste Facility Operator #34	919-733-0379
Speech Pathologist/Audiologist #30	336-272-1828
Surveyor, Land #48	919-791-2000
Taxidermist #25	919-661-4872
Unarmed Security Guard #53	919-875-3611
Veterinarian #50	919-854-5601
Veterinary Technician #50	919-854-5601
Waste Water Treatment Plant Oper. #34	919-733-0379
Wildlife Collector #25	919-661-4872

North Carolina Licensing Agency Information

1 Alarm Systems Licensing Board, 1631 Midtown Pl #104, Raleigh, NC 27609; 919-875-3611, Fax: 919-875-3609.
Email: PPSASL@ncdoj.com

2 Auctioneer Licensing Board, 602 Stellata Drive, Fuquay-Varina, NC 27526; 919-567-2844, Fax: 919-567-2865.
www.ncalb.org   Email: info@ncalb.org
Search Database at
www.ncalb.org/scripts/members.asp

3 Board of Architecture, 127 Hargett St #304, Raleigh, NC 27601; 919-733-9544, Fax: 919-733-1272.   www.ncbarch.org
Email: ncba@earthlink.net
Search Database at www.ncbarch.org/dbase.asp
Note: Mailing lists are also available, see "Directory" section at main website.

4 Board of Barber Examiners, 2321 Crabtree Blvd #110, Raleigh, NC 27604-2260; 919-715-1159, Fax: 919-715-4669.

5 Board of Examiners for Nursing Home Administrators, 3733 National Drive #228, Raleigh, NC 27612; 919-571-4164, Fax: 919-571-4166.   www.ncbenha.org
Search Database at
www.ncbenha.org/searchdb.asp

6 Public Board of Examiners of Electrical Contractors, PO Box 18727 (1299 Front St.), Raleigh, NC 27619; 919-733-9042, Fax: 919-733-6105.
www.ncbeec.org
Email: info@ncbeec.org
Search Database at
www.ncbeec.org/LicSearch.asp

7 Board of Funeral Service, 1033 Wade Avenue #108, Raleigh, NC 27605-1158; 919-733-9380, Fax: 919-733-8271.
http://ncbfs.org/
Email: wpharris@ncbfs.org
Search Database at www.ncbfs.org/directory.htm

8 Board of Nursing, PO Box 2129 (3724 National Dr.), Raleigh, NC 27602; 919-782-3211, Fax: 919-781-9461.   www.ncbon.com
Search Database at https://www.ncbon.com/Lic-verif.asp

9 Board of Occupational Therapy, PO Box 2280, Raleigh, NC 27602; 919-832-1380, Fax: 919-833-1059.
www.ncbot.org
Email: administrator@ncbot.org
Search Database at
www.ncbot.org/fpdb/otimport.html

10 Board of Opticians, PO Box 25336, Raleigh, NC 27611-5336; 919-733-9321, Fax: 919-733-0040.

11 Board of Pharmacy, PO Box 4560, Chapel Hill, NC 27515-4560; 919-942-4454, Fax: 919-967-5757.
http://www.ncbop.org/default1.asp
Email: csmith@ncboq.org

12 Board of Podiatry Examiners, 1500 Sunday Dr #102, Raleigh, NC 27607-5151; 919-861-5583, Fax: 919-787-4916.
www.ncbpe.org
Email: info@ncbpe.org
Search Database at www.ncbpe.org/search.php

13 Board of Licensed Professional Counselors, PO Box 1369, Garner, NC 27529; 919-661-0820, Fax: 919-779-5642.
www.ncblpc.org
Search Database at www.ncblpc.org/search.php
There is a $4.00 per name fee for verification request. Verifications are not given via phone.

14 Board of Sanitarian Examiners, 7171 Brown Summit Rd, Browns Summit, NC 27214; 910-608-0196, Fax: 910-608-0448.
www.rsboard.com
Email: rsboardcb@earthlink.net
Search Database at
www.rsboard.com/rsweb/directory/directory.htm

15 NC Social Work Certification & Licensure Board, PO Box 1043, Asheboro, NC 27204; 336-625-1679, Fax: 336-625-4246.
www.ncswboard.org   Email: swboard@asheboro.com
Search Database at
www.ncswboard.org/search.asp

16 Department of Agriculture, Pesticide Section, 1090 Mail Service Ctr. (2109 Blue Ridge Rd), Raleigh, NC 27699-1090; 919-733-3556, Fax: 919-733-9796.
www.ncagr.com/pesticide Search data at www.ncagr.com/aspzine/Fooddrug/data/advsearch.asp

17 Department of Commerce, Commission of Banks, 4309 Mail Service Center (316 W. Edenton St), Raleigh, NC 27699; 919-733-3016, Fax: 919-733-6918.   www.nccob.org/
Search Database at www.nccob.org/

18 Board of Examiners in Optometry, 109 N. Graham Street, Wallace, NC 28466; 910-285-3160, Fax: 910-285-4546.
www.ncoptometry.org
Email: info@ncoptometry.org
Search Database at
www.ncoptometry.org/verify/index.asp

19 Department of Commerce, Cemetery Commission, 1001 Navaho Dr St101, Raleigh, NC 27609; 919-981-2536, Fax: 919-981-2538.

20 Alcoholic Beverage Control Commission, 4307 Mail Service Center, Raleigh, NC 27699-4307; 919-779-0700, Fax: 919-662-3583.
www.ncabc.com

21 Department of Health & Human Services, Division of Family Services, 2701 Mail Service Center (701 Barbour Drive), Raleigh, NC 27699-2701; 919-855-3750, Fax: 919-733-2757.
www.dhhs.state.nc.us/
Email: ed.browning@ncmail.net

22 Board For Licensing of Soil Scientists, 659 Cary Towne Blvd, PMB 281, , Cary, NC 27511; 919-851-8963.
www.ncblss.org
Email: ncblss@earthlink.net
Search Database at www.ncblss.org

23 Department of Insurance, 430 N. Salisbury Street, Raleigh, NC 27603; 919-733-7487,.
www.ncdoi.com   Note: There is a telephone Automated Verification Service available at 919-981-5244.

24 Department of Labor, 1101 Mail Service Center, Raleigh, NC 27601-1092; 919-733-7166.
www.dol.state.nc.us

25 Department of Natural Resources & Environment, Wildlife Resources Commission, 512 N Salisbury St, Raleigh, NC 27604-1188; 919-661-4872, Fax: 919-773-2955.
www.ncwildlife.org/fs_index_01_license.htm

26 Department of State, NC Secretary of State, P O Box 29622, Raleigh, NC 27626; 919-733-3924, Fax: 919-821-0818.
www.sosnc.com/
Email: secdiv@sosnc.com
Search Database at www.sosnc.com/

27 Department of State Treasurer, Investment & Banking Division, 3250 N Salisbury St, Raleigh, NC 27603; 919-508-5176, Fax: 919-508-5167.
www.treasurer.state.nc.us

28 Division of State Library, Department of Cultural Resources, 109 E Jones St, Raleigh, NC 27601-2807; 919-733-2570, Fax: 919-733-8714.
http://statelibrary.dcr.state.nc.us

29 Examiners for Court Reporting Standards & Testing, PO Box 2448 (2 E Morgan St), Raleigh, NC 27602; 919-733-7107, Fax: 919-715-5779.

30 Examiners for Speech Pathologists & Audiologists, PO Box 16885, Greensboro, NC 27416-0885; 336-272-1828, Fax: 336-272-4353. www.ncboeslpa.org
Email: ncboe@bellsouth.net
Search Database at www.ncboeslpa.org

31 Board of Examiners of Plumbing, Heating & Fire Sprinkler Contractors, 1109 Dresser Court, Raleigh, NC 27609; 919-875-3612, Fax: 919-875-3616.
www.nclicensing.org   Email: info@nclicensing.org
Search Database at www.nclicensing.org/OnlineReg.htm

32 Licensing Board for General Contractors, PO Box 17187 (3739 National Dr #225), Raleigh, NC 27619; 919-571-4183, Fax: 919-571-4703. www.nclbgc.net
Search Database at www.nclbgc.org/lic_fr.html

33 Marital & Family Therapy Certification Board, 1001 S. Marshall St, #5, Winston-Salem, NC 27101; 919-772-6600, Fax: 919-772-6007. www.nclmft.org
Email: mftlb@nc.rr.com

34 Water Treatment Facility Operators, Certification Board, 1635 Mail Service Center, Raleigh, NC 27699-1635; 919-733-0379, Fax: 919-715-2726.

35 Board of Electrolysis Examiners, POBox 34, 2 Centerview Dr., Greensboro, NC 27407; 336-856-1010.

36 Psychology Board, 895 State Farm Road #101, Boone, NC 28607; 828-262-2258, Fax: 828-265-8611.   www.ncpsychologyboard.org
Email: ncpsybd@charter.net
Search Database at www.ncpsychologyboard.org/search.htm

37 Board of CPA Examiners, PO Box 12827 (1101 Oberlin Rd, #104), Raleigh, NC 27605-2827; 919-733-4222, Fax: 919-733-4209. www.cpaboard.state.nc.us
Search Database at www.cpaboard.state.nc.us

38 Board of Athletic Trainer Examiners, PO Box 10769, Raleigh, NC 27605; 919-821-4980, Fax: 919-833-5743.   www.ncbate.org
Search Database at www.ncbate.org/trainers.html

39 Real Estate Commission, P.O. Box 17100 (1313 Navaho Dr), Raleigh, NC 27619-7100; 919-875-3700.
www.ncrec.state.nc.us
Email: records@ncrec.state.nc.us
Search Database at www.ncrec.state.nc.us/licensees/licensees.asp
Note: Online database contains only active licensees.

40 Acupuncture Licensing Board, PO Box 10686, Raleigh, NC 27605; 919-773-0530, Fax: 919-833-5743.   http://ncaaom.org
Search Database at http://ncaaom.org/directory.php

41 Board of Chiropractic Examiners, 174 Church St N, Concord, NC 28025; 704-793-1342.
http://ncchiroboard.com/
Email: ncchirobrd@juno.com

42 Board of Dental Examiners, 15100 Weston Parkway, Suite 101, Cary, NC 27513; 919-678-8223, Fax: 919-678-8472.
www.ncdentalboard.org
Email: info@ncdentalboard.org
Search Database at www.ncdentalboard.org/ncdbe_search.asp

43 Board of Hearing Aid Dealers & Fitters, 2462 Stantonsburg Rd #214, Greenville, NC 27834; 252-752-6382, Fax: 252-752-6305.
www.nchalb.org
Email: info@nchalb.org
Search Database at www.nchalb.org/cgi-bin/sho_memb.pl

44 Secretary of State, Notary Public Section, PO Box 29622, Raleigh, NC 27626-0622; 919-807-2131.
www.sosnc.com
Email: noarty@sosnc.com

45 North Carolina State Bar, Board of Law Examiners, PO Box 25908 (208 Fayetteville St Mall), Raleigh, NC 27611; 919-828-4620, Fax: 919-821-9168.   www.ncbar.com/index.asp
Email: ncbar@bellsouth.net
Search Database at www.ncbar.com/home/member_directory.asp

46 Landscape Architecture & Geologists Board, PO Box 41225 (3733 Benson Dr), Raleigh, NC 27629; 919-850-9669, Fax: 919-872-1598.
www.ncbola.org
Email: ncbla@bellsouth.net
Search Database at www.ncbola.org/rosternew.html

47 Board of Medical Examiners, PO Box 20007 (1201 Front St, 27609), Raleigh, NC 27619; 919-326-1100, Fax: 919-326-1131.
www.ncmedboard.org
Email: info@ncmedboard.org
Search Database at www.ncmedboard.org/find.htm

48 Board of Examiners for Prof Engineers & Land Surveyors, 4601 Six Forks Rd, # 310, Raleigh, NC 27609; 919-791-2000, Fax: 919-791-2012.
www.ncbels.org
Email: lbpeace@ncbels.org
Search Database at www.member-base.com/ncbels-vs/public/searchdb.asp

49 Examining Board of Physical Therapy, 18 W Colony Pl #140, Durham, NC 27705; 919-490-6393, Fax: 919-490-5106.
www.ncptboard.org
Email: NCPTBoard@mindspring.com
Search Database at www.ncptboard.org/search.asp
Note: Licensure lists for PT & PTA may be obtained for $60.00 each (disk or labels).

50 Veterinary Medical Board, PO Box 37549, Raleigh, NC 27627-7549; 919-854-5601, Fax: 919-854-5606.
www.ncvmb.org

51 Secretary of State, Lobbyist Registration, 2 N Salisbury St (PO Box 29622), Raleigh, NC 27626-0622; 919-807-2156, Fax: 919-807-2160.
www.secstate.state.nc.us/
Email: mkelly@mail.secstate.state.nc.us
Search Database at www.secretary.state.nc.us/Lobbyists/LSearch.aspx

52 Secretary of State, Charitable Solicitation Licensing Section, PO Box 29622, Raleigh, NC 27626-0525; 919-807-2214, Fax: 919-807-2220.
www.sosnc.com/
Email: csl@sosnc.com
Search Database at www.secretary.state.nc.us/csl/Search.aspx

53 Private Protective Svcs Board, 1631 Midtown Pl #104, Raleigh, NC 27609; 919-875-3611, Fax: 919-875-3609.
www.ncdoj.com/law_enforcement/cle_pps_licensing.jsp
Email: PPSASL@ncdoj.com

54 Board of Registration of Forresters, PO Box 27393, Raleigh, NC 27611; 919-847-5441, Fax: 919-847-5441.
http://members.aol.com/ncbrf/index.htm
Email: ncbrf@aol.com
Search Database at http://members.aol.com/ncbrf/roster_index.htm

55 Board of Cosmetic Arts Examiners, 1201 Front St., #110, Raleigh, NC 27609; 919-733-4117, Fax: 919-733-4127.
www.cosmetology.state.nc.us

56 Department of Justice, Attorney General's Office, Sheriff's Standard Division, PO Drawer 629, Raleigh, NC 27602; 919-716-6460, Fax: 919-716-6753.

North Carolina Federal Courts

The following list indicates the district and division name for each county in the state. If the bankruptcy court location is different from the district court, then the location of the bankruptcy court appears in parentheses.

County/Court Cross Reference

County	District	Division
Alamance	Middle	Greensboro
Alexander	Western	Statesville (Charlotte)
Alleghany	Western	Statesville (Charlotte)
Anson	Western	Charlotte
Ashe	Western	Statesville (Charlotte)
Avery	Western	Asheville (Charlotte)
Beaufort	Eastern	Greenville-Eastern (Wilson)
Bertie	Eastern	Elizabeth City (Wilson)
Bladen	Eastern	Wilmington (Wilson)
Brunswick	Eastern	Wilmington (Wilson)
Buncombe	Western	Asheville (Charlotte)
Burke	Western	Asheville (Charlotte)
Cabarrus	Middle	Greensboro (Winston-Salem)
Caldwell	Western	Statesville (Charlotte)
Camden	Eastern	Elizabeth City (Wilson)
Carteret	Eastern	Greenville-Eastern (Wilson)
Caswell	Middle	Greensboro
Catawba	Western	Statesville (Charlotte)
Chatham	Middle	Greensboro
Cherokee	Western	Bryson City (Charlotte)
Chowan	Eastern	Elizabeth City (Wilson)
Clay	Western	Bryson City (Charlotte)
Cleveland	Western	Asheville (Charlotte)
Columbus	Eastern	Wilmington (Wilson)
Craven	Eastern	Greenville-Eastern (Wilson)
Cumberland	Eastern	Greenville-Eastern (Wilson)
Currituck	Eastern	Elizabeth City (Wilson)
Dare	Eastern	Elizabeth City (Wilson)
Davidson	Middle	Greensboro (Winston-Salem)
Davie	Middle	Greensboro (Winston-Salem)
Duplin	Eastern	Wilmington (Wilson)
Durham	Middle	Greensboro
Edgecombe	Eastern	Raleigh (Wilson)
Forsyth	Middle	Greensboro (Winston-Salem)
Franklin	Eastern	Raleigh
Gaston	Western	Charlotte
Gates	Eastern	Elizabeth City (Wilson)
Graham	Western	Bryson City (Charlotte)
Granville	Eastern	Raleigh
Greene	Eastern	Greenville-Eastern (Wilson)
Guilford	Middle	Greensboro
Halifax	Eastern	Greenville-Eastern (Wilson)
Harnett	Eastern	Raleigh
Haywood	Western	Asheville (Charlotte)
Henderson	Western	Asheville (Charlotte)
Hertford	Eastern	Elizabeth City (Wilson)
Hoke	Middle	Greensboro
Hyde	Eastern	Greenville-Eastern (Wilson)
Iredell	Western	Statesville (Charlotte)
Jackson	Western	Bryson City (Charlotte)
Johnston	Eastern	Raleigh
Jones	Eastern	Greenville-Eastern (Wilson)
Lee	Middle	Greensboro
Lenoir	Eastern	Greenville-Eastern (Wilson)
Lincoln	Western	Statesville (Charlotte)
Macon	Western	Bryson City (Charlotte)
Madison	Western	Asheville (Charlotte)
Martin	Eastern	Greenville-Eastern (Wilson)
McDowell	Western	Asheville (Charlotte)
Mecklenburg	Western	Charlotte
Mitchell	Western	Asheville (Charlotte)
Montgomery	Middle	Greensboro
Moore	Middle	Greensboro
Nash	Eastern	Raleigh (Wilson)
New Hanover	Eastern	Wilmington (Wilson)
Northampton	Eastern	Elizabeth City (Wilson)
Onslow	Eastern	Wilmington (Wilson)
Orange	Middle	Greensboro
Pamlico	Eastern	Greenville-Eastern (Wilson)
Pasquotank	Eastern	Elizabeth City (Wilson)
Pender	Eastern	Wilmington (Wilson)
Perquimans	Eastern	Elizabeth City (Wilson)
Person	Middle	Greensboro
Pitt	Eastern	Greenville-Eastern (Wilson)
Polk	Western	Asheville (Charlotte)
Randolph	Middle	Greensboro
Richmond	Middle	Greensboro
Robeson	Eastern	Wilmington (Wilson)
Rockingham	Middle	Greensboro
Rowan	Middle	Greensboro (Winston-Salem)
Rutherford	Western	Asheville (Charlotte)
Sampson	Eastern	Wilmington (Wilson)
Scotland	Middle	Greensboro
Stanly	Middle	Greensboro (Winston-Salem)
Stokes	Middle	Greensboro (Winston-Salem)
Surry	Middle	Greensboro (Winston-Salem)
Swain	Western	Bryson City (Charlotte)
Transylvania	Western	Asheville (Charlotte)
Tyrrell	Eastern	Elizabeth City (Wilson)
Union	Western	Charlotte
Vance	Eastern	Raleigh
Wake	Eastern	Raleigh
Warren	Eastern	Raleigh
Washington	Eastern	Elizabeth City (Wilson)
Watauga	Western	Statesville (Charlotte)
Wayne	Eastern	Raleigh (Wilson)
Wilkes	Western	Statesville (Charlotte)
Wilson	Eastern	Raleigh (Wilson)
Yadkin	Middle	Greensboro (Winston-Salem)
Yancey	Western	Asheville (Charlotte)

Standards for Federal Courts: See New York or North Dakota Federal Courts section for information on Federal Courts standards and fees.

US District Court

Eastern District of North Carolina

Eastern Division Court Clerk, Rm 209, 201 S Evans St, Greenville, NC 27858-1137 (also use mail address for courier delivery), 252-830-6009, crim dockets- 252-856-4370, Fax-252-830-2793. Hours- 8:30AM-4:30PM. www.nced.uscourts.gov

Counties: Beaufort, Carteret, Craven, Edgecombe, Greene, Halifax, Hyde, Jones, Lenoir, Martin, Pamlico, Pitt.

Searches & Indexing: Results do not include SSN or DOB. Computer index maintained back to 9/1998. New cases in the index same day if possible after filing. Records purged as deemed necessary. Civil records retained 2 years. All criminal records after 1979 forwarded to Raleigh.

Fee & Payment: Pay by money order, cashier check, business check. In state personal checks also accepted. Payee: Clerk, US District Court. Prepayment required.**Phone Search:** Limited docket information available by phone. **Mail Search:** search usually completed- 1 week. Include SASE for return. **In Person Search:** Fee charged if court performs your search. Self-serve copier - $.50 per page.

E-Services: RACER system is administered by PACER, see www.nced.uscourts.gov/Racer.htm for record access. PACER toll-free: 800-995-0313. PACER local phone: 919-856-4768. PACER records go back to 1989. New records online after 3 days. In process of implementing CM/ECF.

Northern Division c/o Raleigh Division, PO Box 25670, Raleigh, NC 27611 (courier address: Rm 574, 310 New Bern Ave, Raleigh, NC 27601), 919-645-1700. Hours- 8:30AM-4:30PM. www.nced.uscourts.gov

Counties: Bertie, Camden, Chowan, Currituck, Dare, Gates, Hertford, Northampton, Pasquotank, Perquimans, Tyrrell, Washington.

Searches & Indexing: Cases indexed by name and case number. Results include last 4 SSN digits, also birth year. Records purged as deemed necessary. Open records located at Raleigh Div.

Fee & Payment: Pay by money order, cashier's or personal check. **Phone Search:** No searching by telephone. **Mail Search:** search usually completed- 2 days. SASE not required. **In Person Search:** No self-serve copier available.

E-Services: RACER system is administered by PACER, see www.nced.uscourts.gov/Racer.htm for record access. PACER toll-free: 800-995-0313. PACER local phone: 919-856-4768. PACER records go back to 1989. New records online after 3 days. In process of implementing CM/ECF.

Southern Division Court Clerk, 2 Princess St, Rm 239, Alton Lennon Federal Bldg, Wilmington, NC 28401 (also use mail address for courier delivery), 910-815-4663, Fax-910-815-4518. 8:30AM-4:30PM. www.nced.uscourts.gov

Bladen, Brunswick, Columbus, Duplin, New Hanover, Onslow, Pender, Robeson, Sampson.

Searches & Indexing: Results do not include SSN or DOB. Both computer and card indexes

maintained; computer back to 1993. New cases in the index 1 day after filing date. Closed civil records retained for 2 years.

Fee & Payment: Pay by money order, cashier's or personal check. Payee: Clerk, US District Court. Prepayment required. **Phone Search:** Phone searches are available for information from 1992 to the present. **Mail Search:** search usually completed- 10 days. SASE not required. **In Person Search:** Fee charged if court performs your search. Self-serve copier - $.50 per page.

E-Services: RACER system is administered by PACER, see www.nced.uscourts.gov/Racer.htm for record access. PACER toll-free: 800-995-0313. PACER local phone: 919-856-4768. PACER records go back to 1989. New records online after 3 days. In process of implementing CM/ECF.

Western Division Clerk's Office, PO Box 25670, Raleigh, NC 27611 (courier address: Rm 574, 310 New Bern Ave, Raleigh, NC 27601), 919-645-1700, Fax-919-645-1750. Hours- 8:30AM-4:30PM. www.nced.uscourts.gov

Counties: Cumberland, Franklin, Granville, Harnett, Johnston, Nash, Vance, Wake, Warren, Wayne, Wilson.

Searches & Indexing: Records from Fayetteville, which handled Cumberland and Harnett counties, are maintained here. Results include last 4 SSN digits, also birth year. Both computer and card indexes maintained. New cases in the index 1 day after filing date. Records purged as deemed necessary. District-wide searches available here back to 1979 for criminal records.

Fee & Payment: Pay by money order, cashier check, business check. In state personal checks also accepted. Payee: Clerk, US District Court. Prepayment required. **Phone Search:** Only docket information is available by phone. **Mail Search:** search usually completed- 2 days. SASE not required. **In Person Search:** Fee charged if court performs your search. No self-serve copier.

E-Services: RACER system is administered by PACER, see www.nced.uscourts.gov/Racer.htm for record access. PACER toll-free: 800-995-0313. PACER local phone: 919-856-4768. PACER records go back to 1989. New records online after 3 days. In process of implementing CM/ECF.

US Bankruptcy Court

Eastern District of North Carolina

Raleigh Division Court Clerk, PO Box 1441, Raleigh, NC 27602 (courier address: Rm 209, Century Station Bldg, 300 Fayetteville St Mall, Raleigh, NC 27601), 919-856-4752. Hours- 8:30AM-4:30PM. www.nceb.uscourts.gov

Counties: Franklin, Granville, Harnett, Johnston, Vance, Wake, Warren.

Searches & Indexing: Results include last 4 SSN digits. Computer index maintained. New cases in the index immediately after filing date.

Fee & Payment: Pay by Visa/MC (from companies only), money order, cashier check, business check. No personal checks. Payee: Clerk, US Bankruptcy Court. Prepayment required.

Phone Search: Voice Case Information Service available, call 888-847-9138 or 919-856-4618. **Mail Search:** search usually completed- 2-3 days. Include SASE for return. **In Person Search:** Fee charged if court performs your search. Self-serve copier available - $.25 per page.

E-Services: ECF replaces PACER. ECF at https://ecf.nceb.uscourts.gov. For info on their electronic noticing and filing system using court watch.com- www.nceb.uscourts.gov/efiling.htm. **Opinions Online:** http://207.41.17.205. Selected significant decisions back to 2000. **Other Online Access:** Old free RACER system no longer available. Search calendars free at www.nceb.uscourts.gov/calendars.php.

Wilson Division Court Clerk, PO Drawer 2807, Wilson, NC 27894-2807 (courier address: The Thomas Milton Moore Bldg, 1760-A Parkwood Blvd, Wilson, NC), 252-237-0248. 8:30AM-4:30PM. www.nceb.uscourts.gov

Counties: Beaufort, Bertie, Bladen, Brunswick, Camden, Carteret, Chowan, Columbus, Craven, Cumberland, Currituck, Dare, Duplin, Edgecombe, Gates, Greene, Halifax, Hertford, Hyde, Jones, Lenoir, Martin, Nash, New Hanover, Northampton, Onslow, Pamlico, Pasquotank, Pender, Perquimans, Pitt, Robeson, Sampson, Tyrrell, Washington, Wayne, Wilson.

Searches & Indexing: Results include last 4 SSN digits. Computer index maintained. New cases in the index 1 day after filing date.

Fee & Payment: Pay by Visa/MC, money order, cashier check, business check. No personal checks. Payee: Clerk, US Bankruptcy Court. Prepayment required. **Phone Search:** Only major dates such as 341 date, discharge date and entry date is released. Voice Case Information Service available, call 888-513-9765 or 252-234-7655. **Mail Search:** search usually completed- 2-3 days. Include SASE for return. **In Person Search:** Fee charged if court performs search. Self-serve copier - $.25 per page.

E-Services: ECF replaces PACER. ECF at https://ecf.nceb.uscourts.gov. For info on their electronic noticing and filing system using court watch.com, www.nceb.uscourts.gov/efiling.htm **Opinions Online:** http://207.41.17.205. Selected significant decisions back to 2000. **Other Online Access:** Search calendars free at www.nceb.uscourts.gov/calendars.php.

US District Court

Middle District of North Carolina

Greensboro Division Clerk's Office, PO Box 2708, Greensboro, NC 27402 (courier address: Rm 401, 324 W Market St, Greensboro, NC 27401), 336-332-6000, records rm- 336-332-6030, crim dockets- 336-332-6020. Hours- 8AM-5PM. www.ncmd.uscourts.gov **Counties:** Alamance, Cabarrus, Caswell, Chatham, Davidson, Davie, Durham, Forsyth, Guilford, Hoke, Lee, Montgomery, Moore, Orange, Person, Randolph, Richmond, Rockingham, Rowan, Scotland, Stanly, Stokes, Surry, Yadkin. All other district divisions abolished as of 7/1997.

Searches & Indexing: Results do not include SSN or DOB. Both computer and card indexes maintained; computer goes back to 1990. New cases in the index 1 day after filing date. Records purged never.

Fee & Payment: Pay by Visa/MC, money order, cashier check, business check. In state personal checks also accepted. Payee: Clerk, US District Court. Prepayment required. **Phone Search:** Only docket info is available by case number via phone. **Mail Search:** search usually completed- 7 days. SASE not required. **In Person:** Fee charged if court performs search. No self-serve copier.

E-Services: ECF replaces PACER. Document images available. PACER records go back to 9/1991. New records online after 1 day. ECF at https://ecf.ncmd.uscourts.gov **Opinions Online:** www.ncmd.uscourts.gov. **Other Online Access:** Access calendars at www.ncmd.uscourts.gov.

US Bankruptcy Court

Middle District of North Carolina

Greensboro Division Court Clerk, PO Box 26100, Greensboro, NC 27420-6100 (courier address: 101 S Edgeworth St, Greensboro, NC 27401), 336-333-5647. www.ncmb.uscourts.gov

Counties: Includes Durham Division records. Alamance, Caswell, Chatham, Durham, Guilford, Hoke, Lee, Montgomery, Moore, Orange, Person, Randolph, Richmond, Rockingham, Scotland.

Searches & Indexing: Results include last 4 SSN digits. Computer index maintained. New cases in the index 1-2 days after filing date.

Fee & Payment: Pay by money order, cashier's or personal check. No debtor's checks accepted. Payee: Clerk, US Bankruptcy Court. Prepayment required. **Phone Search:** Only basic docket information is available via phone. Voice Case Information Service available, call VCIS at 888-319-0455 or 336-333-5532. **Mail Search:** search usually completed- 1-2 days. Include SASE for return. **In Person Search:** Fee charged if court performs your search. No self-serve copier.

E-Services: ECF replaces PACER whose records did go back to 1992. New records online after 1 day. ECF at https://ecf.ncmb.uscourts.gov. ECF images go back to 1999. **Opinions Online:** http://www1.ncmb.uscourts.gov/opinions/search/Main.cfm. **Other Online Access:** Current calendars free at http://www1.ncmb.uscourts.gov/calendar/pdf_cal.cfm.

Winston-Salem Division Court Clerk, 226 S Liberty St, Winston-Salem, NC 27101 (also use mail address for courier delivery), 336-631-5340, Hours- 8AM-5PM. www.ncmb.uscourts.gov

Counties: Cabarrus, Davidson, Davie, Forsyth, Rowan, Stanly, Stokes, Surry, Yadkin.

Searches & Indexing: Results include last 4 SSN digits. Both computer and card indexes maintained. New cases in the index 2 days after filing date. Records purged every 2 years.

Fee & Payment: Pay by money order, cashier's or personal check. No debtor's checks accepted. Payee: Clerk, US Bankruptcy Court. Prepayment required. **Phone Search:** Basic docket data only is available by phone. Voice Case Information Service available, call 888-319-0455 or 336-333-5532. **Mail Search:** search usually completed- 1-2 days. Include SASE for return. **In Person Search:** Fee charged if court performs your search. No self-serve copier available.

E-Services: ECF replaces PACER. Document images back to 1999 available. PACER records go back to 1992. New records online after 1 day. ECF at https://ecf.ncmb.uscourts.gov. ECF images go back to 1999. **Opinions Online:** http://www1.ncmb.uscourts.gov/opinions/search/Main.cfm. **Other Online Access:** Current calendars free at http://www1.ncmb.uscourts.gov/calendar/pdf_cal.cfm.

US District Court

Western District of North Carolina

Asheville Division Clerk of the Court, Rm 309, US Courthouse Bldg, 100 Otis St, Asheville, NC 28801-2611 (use mail address for courier delivery), 828-771-7200, Fax-828-271-4343. Hours- 8:30AM-12:30PM, 1:30-4PM. www.ncwd.uscourts.gov

Counties: Avery, Buncombe, Burke, Cleveland, Haywood, Henderson, Madison, McDowell, Mitchell, Polk, Rutherford, Transylvania, Yancey. This Division now houses records from Shelby Division, which is closed. Asheville Division also holds records for Bryson City Div.

Searches & Indexing: Office also handles records for Bryson City and Shelby Divisions. Results do not include SSN or DOB. Both computer and card indexes maintained. Not all records are entered into the in house automated system. New cases in the index 1 day after filing date.

Fee & Payment: Pay by money order, cashier's or personal check. Payee: Clerk, US District Court. Prepayment required. **Phone Search:** Only docket information is available by phone. **Mail Search:** search completed- 7 days. Include SASE for return. **In Person Search:** Fee if court performs your search. Self-serve copier - $.50 per page.

E-Services: WebPACER replaced by CM-ECF system. PACER records go back to 1991. New records online immediately. ECF at https://ecf.ncwd.uscourts.gov **Other Online Access:** Calendars free at https://ecf.ncwd.uscourts.gov/cgi-bin/NCWD_GetPublicCal.pl.

Bryson City Division c/o Asheville Division, Clerk of the Court, Rm 309, US Courthouse, 100 Otis St, Asheville, NC 28801-2611 (also use mail address for courier delivery), 828-771-7200. www.ncwd.uscourts.gov **Counties:** Cherokee, Clay, Graham, Jackson, Macon, Swain.

Searches & Indexing: Cases indexed by and case number. Results do not include SSN or DOB. Open records located at Asheville Division.

Fee & Payment: Pay by no business or personal checks accepted. **Phone Search:** No searching by telephone. **Mail Search:** Include SASE for return. **In Person Search:** No self-serve copier.

E-Services: WebPACER replaced by CM-ECF system. PACER records go back to 1991. New records online immediately. ECF at https://ecf.ncwd.uscourts.gov **Other Online Access:** Calendars free at https://ecf.ncwd.uscourts.gov/cgi-bin/NCWD_GetPublicCal.pl.

Charlotte Division Clerk of Court, Rm 210, 401 W Trade St, Charlotte, NC 28202 (also use mail address for courier delivery), 704-350-7400. Hours- 8:30AM-4PM. www.ncwd.uscourts.gov

Counties: Anson, Gaston, Mecklenburg, Union.

Searches & Indexing: Results do not include SSN or DOB. Computer index maintained. New cases in the index 1-2 days after filing date. District-wide searches available here back to 1950.

Fee & Payment: Pay by money order, cashier's or personal check. Payee: Clerk, US District Court. Prepayment required. **Phone Search:** Only docket information is available by phone. **Mail Search:** search usually completed- 7-10 days. SASE not required. **In Person Search:** Fee charged if court performs your search. No self-serve copier.

E-Services: WebPACER replaced by CM-ECF system. New records online immediately. ECF at https://ecf.ncwd.uscourts.gov **Other Online Access:** Calendars free at https://ecf.ncwd.uscourts.gov/cgi-bin/NCWD_GetPublicCal.pl.

Statesville Division Court Clerk, 200 W Broad St #100, Statesville, NC 28677 (also use mail address for courier delivery), 704-883-1000, Fax-704-873-0903. Hours- 8:30AM-12:30PM, 1:30-4:30PM. www.ncwd.uscourts.gov

Counties: Alexander, Alleghany, Ashe, Caldwell, Catawba, Iredell, Lincoln, Watauga, Wilkes.

Searches & Indexing: Results do not include SSN or DOB. Both computer and card indexes maintained; computer index back to 1993. New cases in the index 2 days after filing date. Records purged when space runs out.

Fee & Payment: Pay by money order, cashier's or personal check. No credit cards. Payee: Clerk, US District Court. Prepayment required. **Phone Search:** Only docket information is available by phone. **Mail Search:** search usually completed- 2 days. SASE not required. **In Person Search:** Fee charged if court performs your search. Self-serve copier - - current fee is not known - per page.

E-Services: WebPACER replaced by CM-ECF system. PACER records go back to 1991. New records online immediately. ECF at https://ecf.ncwd.uscourts.gov **Other Online Access:** Calendars free at https://ecf.ncwd.uscourts.gov/cgi-bin/NCWD_GetPublicCal.pl.

US Bankruptcy Court

Western District of North Carolina

Charlotte Division Court Clerk, PO Box 34189, Charlotte, NC 28234-4189 (courier address: 401 W Trade St, Charlotte, NC 28202), 704-350-7500. Hours- 8:30AM-4:30PM. www.ncwb.uscourts.gov

Counties: Alexander, Alleghany, Anson, Ashe, Avery, Buncombe, Burke, Caldwell, Catawba, Cherokee, Clay, Cleveland, Gaston, Graham, Haywood, Henderson, Iredell, Jackson, Lincoln, Macon, Madison, McDowell, Mecklenburg, Mitchell, Polk, Rutherford, Swain, Transylvania, Union, Watauga, Wilkes, Yancey. There are five offices within this division; records for all may be searched here or at Asheville: 100 Otis St #112, Asheville, NC 28801, 828-771-7300.

Searches & Indexing: Results include last 4 SSN digits. Computer index maintained. New cases in the index 1-2 days after filing date. Records purged every 2 years.

Fee & Payment: Pay by money order, cashier check, business check. No personal or debtor's checks accepted. Payee: Clerk, US Bankruptcy Court. Prepayment required. **Phone Search:** Only docket information available by telephone. Voice Case Information Service available, call 800-884-9868 or 704-350-7505. **Mail Search:** search usually completed- 7-10 days. Include SASE for return. **In Person Search:** Fee charged if court performs your search. No self-serve copier.

E-Services: ECF replaces PACER whose records did go back to 1992. New records online after 1 day. ECF at https://ecf.ncwb.uscourts.gov **Opinions Online:** www.ncwb.uscourts.gov/opinions/opinions.html. Select New Cases or Miscellaneous Cases. **Other Online Access:** Calendars are free at www.ncwb.uscourts.gov

North Carolina County Courts

Court	Jurisdiction	No. of Courts	How Organized
Superior Courts*	General	0	46 Districts
District Courts*	Limited	0	39 Districts
Combined Courts*		100	

* Profiled in this Sourcebook.

Court	CIVIL								
	Tort	Contract	Real Estate	Min. Claim	Max. Claim	Small Claims	Estate	Eviction	Domestic Relations
Superior Courts*	X	X	X	$10,000	No Max		X		
District Courts*	X	X	X	$0	$10,000	4100		X	X

Court	CRIMINAL				
	Felony	Misdemeanor	DWI/DUI	Preliminary Hearing	Juvenile
Superior Courts*	X				
District Courts*		X	X	X	X

ADMINISTRATION   Administrative Office of the Courts, Justice Bldg, PO Box 2448, Raleigh, NC, 27602; 919-733-7107, Fax: 919-715-5779. www.nccourts.org

COURT STRUCTURE   The Superior Court is the court of general jurisdiction, the District Court is limited. The counties combine the courts, thus searching is done through one court, not two, within the county. Small claims court is part of the District Court Division. It handles civil cases where a plaintiff requests assignment to a magistrate and the amount in controversy is $4,000 or less. The principal relief sought in small claims court is money, the recovery of specific personal property, or summary ejectment (eviction).

ONLINE ACCESS   The state AOC has public access on its Virtual Private Network for approved requesters. Charges are based on screens viewed rather than a specific fee per name. There is a question if the DOB will be taken off this system. A lessor valued product known as the Criminal Extract is available, but does not have the depth and quality of data as the network described above. Call 919-716-5088 for details on the programs. For current civil and criminal calendars, go to http://www1.aoc.state.nc.us/www/. Appellate and supreme court opinions at www.aoc.state.nc.us/www/public/html/opinions.htm.

ADDITIONAL INFORMATION   Many courts recommend that civil searches be done in person or by a retriever and that only criminal searches be requested in writing (for a $10.00 search fee, which is certified in most jurisdictions). Many courts have archived their records prior to 1968 in the Raleigh State Archives, 919-807-7280. A list of companies offering North Carolina criminal records online can be accessed at www.nccourts.org/Citizens/GoToCourt/ Default.asp?topic=1

PROBATE COURTS   Probate is handled by County Clerks.

Alamance County

Superior-District Court - Criminal 212 W Elm St, #105, Graham, NC 27253; phone: 336-438-1001; hours 8AM-5PM (EST). *Felony, Misdemeanor.*
www.aoc.state.nc.us/www/public/courts/alamance.html
Note: Search civil and criminal court calendars at www1.aoc.state.nc.us/www/calendars.html.
Criminal Records: Access: Mail, in person. Both court and visitors may perform in person searches. Search fee: $10.00 per name. Court makes copy: $2.00 for 1st page, $.25 each add'l. Required to search: name, years to search, DOB; also helpful: address, SSN. Records on computer since 1985, on index cards back to 1975. Mail turnaround time 1 week.
General Information: Public terminal has only criminal records back to 3/1985. No sealed case records released. Certification fee: None; $3.00 if you perform search in person. Payee: Clerk of Superior

Court. Only cashiers checks and money orders accepted. Prepayment required.
Superior-District Court - Civil 1 Court Square, Graham, NC 27253; phone: 336-438-1013; probate phone: 336-438-1008; fax: 336-570-6988; hours 8AM-5PM (EST). *Civil, Eviction, Small Claims, Probate.*
Note: Search civil and criminal court calendars at www1.aoc.state.nc.us/www/calendars.html.
Civil Records: Access: In person only. Visitors must perform in person searches themselves. Court makes copy: $2.00 for first page, $.25 each add'l. Required to search: name, years to search. Civil cases indexed by defendant, plaintiff. Civil records computerized since 1988, prior indexed on books.
General Information: Public terminal has only civil records. No adoptions, sealed cases, juvenile, or mental records released. Certification fee: None; $3.00 if you perform search in person. Prepayment required.

Alexander County

Superior-District Court PO Box 100, Taylorsville, NC 28681; phone: 828-632-2215; fax: 828-632-3550; hours 8AM-5PM (EST) *Felony, Misdemeanor, Civil, Eviction, Small Claims, Probate.*
www.aoc.state.nc.us/www/public/courts/alexander.htm
Note: Search civil and criminal court calendars at www1.aoc.state.nc.us/www/calendars.html.
Civil Records: Access: Mail, in person. Both court and visitors may perform in person searches. Search fee: $5.00 per name. Court makes copy: $.25 per page; same fee for self serve. Required to search: name, years to search, address. Civil cases indexed by defendant, plaintiff, on computer since 10/1989, prior on books to 1865. Mail turnaround time 1-3 days.
Criminal Records: Access: Mail, in person. Both court and visitors may perform in person searches. Search fee: $10.00 per name. Court makes copy: $.25 per page; same fee for self serve. Required to search:

name, years to search, address, DOB, SSN. Records on computer since 10/1989, prior on books to 1865. Mail turnaround time 1-3 days.

General Information: Public terminal goes back to 1989. No adoptions, sealed cases, juvenile, sex offenders, mental, expunged records released. Certification fee: None; $3.00 if you perform search in person. Payee: Clerk of Superior Court. Business checks accepted. Prepayment and SASE required.

Alleghany County

Superior-District Court PO Box 61, Sparta, NC 28675; phone: 336-372-8949; fax: 336-372-4899; hours 8AM-5PM *Felony, Misdemeanor, Civil, Eviction, Small Claims, Probate.*

www.aoc.state.nc.us/www/public/courts/alleghany.html

Note: Search civil and criminal court calendars at www1.aoc.state.nc.us/www/calendars.html

Civil Records: Access: In person only. Visitors must perform in person searches themselves. Court makes copy: $2.00 for first page, $.25 each add'l. Required to search: name, years to search; also helpful: address. Civil cases indexed by defendant, plaintiff, on computer from 11/1988, index books prior.

Criminal Records: Access: Fax, mail, in person. Both court and visitors may perform in person searches. Search fee: $10.00 per name. Court makes copy: $2.00 for first page, $.25 each add'l. Required to search: name, years to search, DOB; also helpful: address, SSN. Records on computer from 11/ 1988, index books prior. Mail turnaround time 2 days.

General Information: Public terminal goes back to 1988. No adoptions, sealed cases, juvenile, mental or expunged records released. Certification fee: None; $3.00 if you perform search in person. Payee: Clerk of Superior Court. Business checks accepted. Prepayment and SASE required.

Anson County

Superior-District Court PO Box 1064 (114 N Greene St), Wadesboro, NC 28170; phone: 704-694-2314; fax: 704-695-1161; hours 8AM-5PM (EST). *Felony, Misdemeanor, Civil, Eviction, Small Claims, Probate.*

www.aoc.state.nc.us/www/public/courts/anson.htm

Note: Search civil and criminal court calendars at www1.aoc.state.nc.us/www/calendars.html.

Civil Records: Access: Mail, in person. Visitors must perform in person searches themselves. Search fee: $10.00 per name. Court makes copy: $2.00 for first page, $.25 each add'l. Required to search: name, years to search. Civil cases indexed by defendant, plaintiff, on computer since 11/1989, in books prior. Mail turnaround time 2-5 days.

Criminal Records: Access: Mail, in person. Only the court performs in person searches. Search fee: $10.00 per name. Court makes copy: $2.00 for first page, $.25 each add'l. Required to search: name, years to search, DOB; also helpful: SSN. Records on computer since 10/89, on microfilm 1982-89, in books prior. Mail turnaround time 2-5 days.

General Information: Public terminal has only civil records. (Estates/Special Proceedings only.) No adoptions, sealed cases, juvenile, mental, or expunged records released. Certification fee: None; $3.00 if you perform search in person. Payee: Clerk of Superior Court. Business checks accepted. Prepayment and SASE required.

Ashe County

Superior-District Court 150 Government Circle #3100, Jefferson, NC 28640-9378; phone: 336-246-5641; fax: 336-246-4276; hours 8AM-5PM (EST). *Felony, Misdemeanor, Civil, Eviction, Small Claims, Probate.*

www.aoc.state.nc.us/www/public/courts/ashe.html

Note: Search civil and criminal court calendars at www1.aoc.state.nc.us/www/calendars.html.

Civil Records: Access: Mail, in person. Both court and visitors may perform in person searches. Search fee: $5.00 per name. Court makes copy: $2.00

for first page, $.25 each add'l; same fee for self serve. Required to search: name, years to search. Civil cases indexed by defendant, plaintiff, on computer from 12/89, on index books back to 1900s. Mail turnaround time 1-3 days.

Criminal Records: Access: Mail, in person. Both court and visitors may perform in person searches. Search fee: $10.00 per name. Court makes copy: $2.00 for first page, $.25 each add'l; same fee for self serve. Required to search: name, years to search. Records on computer from 12/89, on index books back to 1900s. Note: Court will search records after 1988; visitors or researchers must search themselves for records prior to 1988. Mail turnaround time 1-3 days.

General Information: Public terminal has criminal back to 1988 and civil back to 1989. No adoptions, sealed cases, juvenile, sex offenders, mental or expunged records released. Certification fee: None; $3.00 if you perform search in person. Payee: Clerk of Superior Court. Only cashiers checks and money orders accepted. Prepayment required.

Avery County

Superior-District Court PO Box 115, Newland, NC 28657; phone: 828-733-2900; fax: 828-733-8410; hours 8AM-4:30PM (EST). *Felony, Misdemeanor, Civil, Eviction, Small Claims, Probate.*

www.aoc.state.nc.us/www/public/courts/avery.htm

Note: Search civil and criminal court calendars at www1.aoc.state.nc.us/www/calendars.html.

Civil Records: Access: In person only. Visitors must perform in person searches themselves. Court makes copy: $2.00 first page, $.25 ea add'l; same fee for self serve. Required to search: name, years to search; also helpful: address. Civil cases indexed by defendant, plaintiff, on computer since 1988, on index books to 1968.

Criminal Records: Access: Mail, in person. Both court and visitors may perform in person searches. Search fee: $10.00 per name. Court makes copy: $2.00 first page, $.25 ea add'l. Required to search: name, years to search; also helpful: address. Records on computer from 11/88; on cards and books back to 1968. Mail turnaround time 2-3 days.

General Information: Public terminal has criminal back to 11/1988 and civil back to 10/88. No adoptions, sealed cases, juvenile, sex offenders, mental or expunged records released. Certification fee: None; $3.00 if you perform search in person. Payee: Clerk of Superior Court. Only cashiers checks and money orders accepted. Prepayment required. Will bill copy fees.

Beaufort County

Superior-District Court PO Box 1403, Washington, NC 27889; phone: 252-946-5184; civil phone: 252-974-7817; fax: 252-946-6448; hours 8:30AM-5:30PM (EST). *Felony, Misdemeanor, Civil, Eviction, Small Claims, Probate.*

www.aoc.state.nc.us/www/public/courts/beaufort.html

Note: Search civil and criminal court calendars at www1.aoc.state.nc.us/www/calendars.html.

Civil Records: Access: In person only. Visitors must perform in person searches themselves. Court makes copy: $2.00 for 1st page, $.25 each add'l. Required to search: name, years to search, address. Civil cases indexed by defendant, plaintiff, on computer since 6/87, docket books to 1800s.

Criminal Records: Access: Mail, in person. Both court and visitors may perform in person searches. Search fee: $10.00 per name. Court makes copy: $2.00 for first page, $.25 each add'l. Required to search: name, years to search, address, DOB, SSN. Records on computer since 6/87, docket books to 1800s. Mail turnaround time 5 days.

General Information: Public terminal has only criminal records back to 1987. No adoptions, sealed cases, juvenile, sex offenders, mental or expunged records released. Certification fee: None; $3.00 if you perform search in person. Payee: Clerk of Superior

Court. Business checks accepted, personal checks are not. Prepayment required.

Bertie County

Superior-District Court PO Box 370, Windsor, NC 27983; phone: 252-794-3039; fax: 252-794-2482; hours 8AM-5PM (EST). *Felony, Misdemeanor, Civil, Eviction, Small Claims, Probate.*

www.aoc.state.nc.us/www/public/courts/bertie.html

Note: Search civil and criminal court calendars at www1.aoc.state.nc.us/www/calendars.html.

Civil Records: Access: In person only. Both court and visitors may perform in person searches. No search fee. Court makes copy: $2.00 for 1st pg of each document, $.25 each add'l. Required to search: name, years to search. Civil cases indexed by defendant, plaintiff, on computer from 11/96, prior on books to 1968. Note: Court will do a civil search if it is conjunction with a criminal search.

Criminal Records: Access: Mail, in person. Both court and visitors may perform in person searches. Search fee: $10.00 per name. Court makes copy: $2.00 for 1st page, $.25 each add'l. Required to search: name, years to search, DOB; also helpful: address, SSN. Records on computer from 3/89, prior on books to 1968. Mail turnaround time 1-2 days.

General Information: Public terminal has criminal back to 3/1989 and civil back to 6/1989. No adoptions, sealed cases, juvenile, mental, expunged records released. Fee to fax documents is $1.00 1st page; $.25 each add'l. No certification fee Court will not certify any in person searches. Payee: Clerk of Superior Court. Only cashiers checks and money orders accepted. Prepayment required. SASE requested.

Bladen County

Superior-District Court PO Box 2619, Elizabethtown, NC 28337; criminal phone: 910-862-2818; civil phone: 910-862-2143; probate phone: 910-862-4911; fax: 910-862-6131; hours 8:30AM-5PM (EST). *Felony, Misdemeanor, Civil, Eviction, Small Claims, Probate.*

www.aoc.state.nc.us/www/public/courts/bladen.html

Note: Search civil and criminal court calendars at www1.aoc.state.nc.us/www/calendars.html.

Civil Records: Access: In person only. Visitors must perform in person searches themselves. Court makes copy: $2.00 for first page, $.25 each add'l. Required to search: name, years to search. Civil cases indexed by defendant, plaintiff, on computer since 1989, prior on judgment books back to 1896 (fire).

Criminal Records: Access: Mail, in person. Both court and visitors may perform in person searches. Search fee: $10.00 per name. Court makes copy: $2.00 for first page, $.25 each add'l. Required to search: name, years to search, DOB. Records on computer from 5/89, on books to 1968. Mail turnaround time 5 days.

General Information: Public use terminal available. No adoptions, sealed cases, juvenile, sex offenders, mental or expunged records released. Certification fee: None; $3.00 if you perform search in person. Payee: Clerk of Superior Court. Only cashiers checks and money orders accepted. Prepayment required.

Brunswick County

Superior-District Court 310 Goverment Ctr Dr, Unit 1, Attn: Clerk, Bolivia, NC 28422; criminal phone: 910-253-8512; civil phone: 910-253-8502; probate phone: 910-253-8505; fax: 910-253-7652; 8:30AM-5:00PM (EST). *Felony, Misdemeanor, Civil, Eviction, Small Claims, Probate.*

www.aoc.state.nc.us/www/public/courts/brunswick.html

Note: Search civil and criminal court calendars at www1.aoc.state.nc.us/www/calendars.html.

Civil Records: Access: In person only. Visitors must perform in person searches themselves. Court makes copy: $2.00 for first page, $.25 each add'l. Required to search: name, years to search. Civil cases indexed by defendant, plaintiff, on computer since 1989, prior on books to 1968.

Criminal Records: Access: Mail, in person. Both court and visitors may perform in person searches. Search fee: $10.00 per name. Court makes copy: $2.00 for first page, $.25 each add'l. Required to search: name, years to search. Records on computer since 1989, prior on books to 1968. Mail turnaround time 1-2 days.

General Information: Public terminal goes back to 1989. No adoptions, sealed cases, juvenile, mental or expunged records. Certification fee: $5.00 per doc. Payee: Clerk of Court. Business checks accepted. Prepayment required.

Buncombe County

Superior-District Court 60 Court Plaza, Asheville, NC 28801; phone: 828-232-2605; criminal phone: 828-232-2677; civil phone: 828-232-2636; probate phone: 828-232-2694; criminal fax: 828-232-2646; civil fax: 828-251-6257; hours 8:30AM-5PM (EST). *Felony, Misdemeanor, Civil, Eviction, Small Claims, Probate.*
www.nccourts.org/County/Buncombe/Default.asp
Note: Search civil and criminal court calendars at www1.aoc.state.nc.us/www/calendars.html.
Civil Records: Access: Mail, fax, in person. Both court and visitors may perform in person searches. Search fee: $10.00 per name. Court makes copy: $2.00 for first page, $.25 each add'l. Required to search: name, years to search. Civil cases indexed by defendant, plaintiff, on computer since 1/88; on books or dockets to 1915; judgment books in archives. Mail turnaround time 1 week.
Criminal Records: Access: Mail, fax, in person. Both court and visitors may perform in person searches. Search fee: $10.00 per name. Court makes copy: $2.00 for first page, $.25 each add'l. Required to search: name, years to search, DOB. Records on computer since 11/82; on books or dockets to 12/70. Mail turnaround time 1 week.
General Information: Public terminal has criminal back to 12/82 and civil back to 1988. No adoptions, sealed cases, juvenile, sex offenders, mental or expunged records required. Fee to fax documents is $1.00 1st page; $.25 each add'l. Certification fee: $3.00 per page. Payee: Clerk of Court. Only cashiers checks and money orders accepted. Prepayment and SASE required.

Burke County

Superior-District Court PO Box 796, Morganton, NC 28680; phone: 828-432-2800; civil phone: 828-432-2805; fax: 828-438-5460; hours 8AM-5PM (EST). *Felony, Misdemeanor, Civil, Eviction, Small Claims, Probate.*
www.aoc.state.nc.us/www/public/courts/burke.html
Note: Search civil and criminal court calendars at www1.aoc.state.nc.us/www/calendars.html.
Civil Records: Access: Mail, in person. Visitors must perform in person searches themselves. Search fee: $10.00 per name. Court makes copy: $1.25 for 1st page, $.25 each add'l. Required to search: name, years to search; also helpful: address. Civil cases indexed by defendant, plaintiff, on computer since 10/1988, on index books to 1890s.
Criminal Records: Access: Mail, in person. Both court and visitors may perform in person searches. Search fee: $10.00 per name. Court makes copy: $1.25 for 1st page, $.25 each add'l. Required to search: name, years to search, DOB; also helpful: address, SSN. Records on computer since 6/1986, on cards or books back to 1900s. Mail turnaround time 1-2 days.
General Information: Public terminal has criminal back to 6/1986 and civil back to 10/1988. No adoptions, sealed cases, juvenile, sex offenders, mental or expunged records released. Fee to fax documents is $3.00 per document. Certification fee: $5.00 per doc. Payee: Clerk of Court. Business checks accepted. Prepayment and SASE required.

Cabarrus County

Superior-District Court PO Box 70, 77 Union St, Concord, NC 28026-0070; phone: 704-786-4137 (Estates & Special Proceed); criminal phone: 704-786-4138 (Superior); 786-4211 (Dist.); civil phone: 704-786-4201; hours 8:30AM-5PM (EST). *Felony, Misdemeanor, Civil, Eviction, Small Claims, Probate.*
www.aoc.state.nc.us/www/public/courts/cabarrus.htm
Note: Search civil and criminal court calendars at www1.aoc.state.nc.us/www/calendars.html.
Civil Records: Access: In person only. Visitors must perform in person searches themselves. Court makes copy: $2.00 for first page, $.25 each add'l. Required to search: name, years to search; also helpful: address. Civil cases indexed by defendant, plaintiff. Civil records go back to 1900s; on computer since 2/13/89.
Criminal Records: Access: Mail, in person. Both court and visitors may perform in person searches. Search fee: $10.00 per name. Court makes copy: $2.00 for first page, $.25 each add'l. Required to search: name, DOB; also helpful: address, SSN, maiden name. Criminal records go back to 12/70; on computer back to 1/85. Mail turnaround time 2-3 days.
General Information: Public terminal has criminal back to 1985 and civil back to 1989. No adoptions, sealed cases, juvenile, sex offenders, mental or expunged records released. Certification fee: None; $3.00 if you perform search in person. Payee: Clerk of Superior Court. Only cashiers checks and money orders accepted. Prepayment required.

Caldwell County

Superior-District Court PO Box 1376, Lenoir, NC 28645; phone: 828-757-1373; fax: 828-757-1479; hours 8AM-5PM (EST). *Felony, Misdemeanor, Civil, Eviction, Small Claims, Probate.*
www.aoc.state.nc.us/www/public/courts/caldwell.html
Note: Search civil and criminal court calendars at www1.aoc.state.nc.us/www/calendars.html.
Civil Records: Access: In person only. Visitors must perform in person searches themselves. Court makes copy: $2.00 for first page, $.25 each add'l; same fee for self serve. Required to search: name, years to search. Civil cases indexed by defendant, plaintiff, on computer since 11/1988, prior on books to 1849.
Criminal Records: Access: Mail, in person. Both court and visitors may perform in person searches. Search fee: $10.00 per name. Court makes copy: $2.00 for first page, $.25 each add'l. Required to search: name. Records on computer from 8/86, prior in books to 1966. Mail turnaround time 1-2 days.
General Information: Public terminal has criminal back to 8/1986 and civil back to 11/88. No adoptions, sealed cases, juvenile, sex offenders, mental or expunged records released. Fee to fax documents is $2.00 1st page; $.25 each add'l. Certification fee: None; $3.00 if you perform search in person. Payee: Clerk of Superior Court. Only cashiers checks and money orders accepted. Prepayment required.

Camden County

Superior-District Court PO Box 219, 117 N Hwy 343, Camden, NC 27921; phone: 252-331-4871; criminal 252-331-4871 x270 (Superior), x269 (District); civil 252-331-4871 x272 (District & Superior); probate: 252-331-4871 x273; fax: 252-331-4827; hours 8AM-5PM (EST). *Felony, Misdemeanor, Civil, Eviction, Small Claims, Probate.*
www.aoc.state.nc.us/www/public/courts/camden.html
Note: Small Claims ext 268. Search court calendars at www1.aoc.state.nc.us/www/calendars.html.
Civil Records: Access: In person only. Visitors must perform in person searches themselves. Court makes copy: $2.00 for first page, $.25 each add'l; same fee for self serve. Required to search: name,

years to search. Civil cases indexed by defendant, plaintiff, on computer since 11/27/1989, prior on index books to 1966.
Criminal Records: Access: Mail, fax, in person. Both court and visitors may perform in person searches. Search fee: $10.00 per name. Court makes copy: $2.00 for first page, $.25 each add'l; same fee for self serve. Required to search: name, years to search, DOB. Records on computer since 11/27/1989, prior on index books to 1966. Note: Fax search requests must be prepaid. Mail turnaround time 1-2 days.
General Information: Public terminal has criminal back to 1990 and civil back to 1989. No adoptions, sealed cases, juvenile, sex offenders, mental or expunged records released. Will fax documents for no fee. Certification fee: None; $3.00 if you perform search in person. Payee: Clerk of Superior Court. Business checks accepted. Prepayment required.

Carteret County

Superior-District Court - Carteret County Courthouse Square, Beaufort, NC 28516; phone: 252-728-8500; fax: 252-728-6502; hours 8AM-5PM (EST). *Felony, Misdemeanor, Civil, Eviction, Small Claims, Probate.*
www.aoc.state.nc.us/www/public/courts/carteret.html
Note: Search civil and criminal court calendars at www1.aoc.state.nc.us/www/calendars.html.
Civil Records: Access: In person only. Visitors must perform in person searches themselves. Court makes copy: $2.00 for first page, $.25 each add'l. Required to search: name, years to search. Civil cases indexed by defendant, plaintiff, on computer back to 1988, prior on books to 1800s.
Criminal Records: Access: Mail, fax, in person. Both court and visitors may perform in person searches. Search fee: $10.00 per name. Court makes copy: $2.00 for first page, $.25 each add'l. Required to search: name, years to search; also helpful: address, DOB, SSN. Records on computer back to 1/87, prior on cards and books to 1800s. Mail turnaround time 1-2 days.
General Information: Public terminal has criminal back to 1987 and civil back to 1988. No adoptions, sealed cases, juvenile, sex offenders, mental or expunged records released. Certification fee: None; $3.00 if you perform search in person. Payee: Clerk of Superior Court. Business checks accepted. Prepayment required.

Caswell County

Superior-District Court PO Drawer 790, Yanceyville, NC 27379; phone: 336-694-4171; fax: 336-694-7338; hours 8:30AM-5PM (EST). *Felony, Misdemeanor, Civil, Eviction, Small Claims, Probate.*
www.aoc.state.nc.us/www/public/courts/caswell.html
Note: Search civil and criminal court calendars at www1.aoc.state.nc.us/www/calendars.html.
Civil Records: Access: In person only. Visitors must perform in person searches themselves. Court makes copy: $2.00 for first page, $.25 each add'l; same fee for self serve. Required to search: name, years to search. Civil cases indexed by defendant, plaintiff, on computer from 3/89 to present, on index books back to 1970, prior records in civil summons book.
Criminal Records: Access: Mail, in person. Both court and visitors may perform in person searches. Search fee: $10.00 per name. Court makes copy: $2.00 for first page, $.25 each add'l; same fee for self serve. Required to search: name, years to search, DOB; also helpful: address. Records on computer since 5/88, prior on books and cards. Mail turnaround time 1-2 days.
General Information: Public terminal has criminal back to 5/18/1988 and civil back to 3/1989. No adoptions, sealed cases, juvenile, mental or expunged records released. Certification fee: None; $3.00 if you perform search in person. Payee: Clerk of Superior Court. Business checks accepted. Prepayment and SASE required.

Catawba County

Superior-District Court PO Box 790, Newton, NC 28658; phone: 828-466-6100; criminal phone: 828-466-6106; civil phone: 828-466-6104; probate phone: 828-466-6103; fax: 828-465-8975; hours 8AM-5PM (EST). *Felony, Misdemeanor, Civil, Eviction, Small Claims, Probate.*
www.co.catawba.nc.us/state/clerk/clerklst.asp
Note: Search civil and criminal court calendars at www1.aoc.state.nc.us/www/calendars.html.
Civil Records: Access: In person only. Visitors must perform in person searches themselves. Court makes copy: $2.00 for first page, $.25 each add'l. Required to search: name, years to search. Civil cases indexed by defendant, plaintiff, on computer since 3/1988, prior on books.
Criminal Records: Access: Mail, in person. Both court and visitors may perform in person searches. Search fee: $10.00 per name. Court makes copy: $2.00 for first page, $.25 each add'l. Required to search: name, years to search, DOB. Records on computer since 4/85, on books to 1966, archived prior. Mail turnaround time 5 days.
General Information: Public terminal has criminal back to 4/1985 and civil back to 1988. No adoptions, sealed cases, juvenile, sex offenders, mental or expunged records released. Certification fee: $3.00 includes copies, but if over $3.00 worth of copies, add on add'l copy fee. Payee: Clerk of Court. Only cashiers checks and money orders accepted. Prepayment and SASE required.

Chatham County

Superior-District Court PO Box 369, 12 East St, Pittsboro, NC 27312; phone: 919-542-3240; fax: 919-542-1402; hours 8AM-5PM (EST). *Felony, Misdemeanor, Civil, Eviction, Small Claims, Probate.*
www.nccourts.org/County/Chatham/Default.asp
Note: Search civil and criminal court calendars at www1.aoc.state.nc.us/www/calendars.html.
Civil Records: Access: In person only. Both court and visitors may perform in person searches. No search fee. Court makes copy: $2.00 for 1st page, $.25 each add'l. Required to search: name, years to search. Civil cases indexed by defendant, plaintiff, on computer since 4/1989, prior on books, archived 1968 back in Raleigh. Search civil court calendars at www1.aoc.state.nc.us/www/calendars/Civil.html.
Criminal Records: Access: Mail, in person. Both court and visitors may perform in person searches. Search fee: $10.00 per name. Court makes copy: $2.00 for 1st page, $.25 each add'l. Required to search: name, years to search; also helpful: address, DOB, SSN. Records on computer since 7/1987, prior on books or cards to 1968. Search criminal court calendars at www1.aoc.state.nc.us/www/calendars/Criminal.html. Mail turnaround time 1 day.
General Information: Public terminal has criminal back to 7/1987 and civil back to 4/1989. No adoptions, sealed cases, juvenile, sex offenders, mental or expunged records released. Certification fee: None; $3.00 if you perform search in person. Will not certify civil. Payee: Clerk of Superior Court. No personal checks accepted. Prepayment required.

Cherokee County

Superior-District Court 75 Peachtree St, Rm 201, Murphy, NC 28906; phone: 828-837-2522; fax: 828-837-8178; hours 8AM-5PM (EST). *Felony, Misdemeanor, Civil, Eviction, Small Claims, Probate.*
www.aoc.state.nc.us/www/public/courts/cherokee.html
Note: Search civil and criminal court calendars at www1.aoc.state.nc.us/www/calendars.html.
Civil Records: Access: Phone, fax, mail, in person. Both court and visitors may perform in person searches. No search fee. Court makes copy: $2.00 for first page, $.25 each add'l. Required to search: name, years to search, address. Civil cases indexed by

defendant, plaintiff, on computer since 5/89, on index books to 1867. Mail turnaround time 1-2 days.
Criminal Records: Access: Mail, in person. Only the court performs in person searches. Search fee: $10.00 per name. Court makes copy: $2.00 for first page, $.25 each add'l. Required to search: name, years to search, DOB. Records on computer since 5/89, index cards to 1985, index books to 1966. Note: There is no public access terminal for searching criminal records. Mail turnaround time 1-2 days.
General Information: Public terminal has only civil records. No adoptions, sealed cases, juvenile or mental records released. Fee to fax documents is $2.00 1st page, $.25 each add'l. Will fax to toll-free number for no charge. Certification fee: None; $3.00 if you perform search in person. Payee: Clerk of Superior Court. No personal checks accepted. Prepayment and SASE required.

Chowan County

Superior-District Court Clerk of Superior Ct; N.C. Courier Box 106319, PO Box 588, Edenton, NC 27932; phone: 252-482-2323; criminal fax: 252-482-2190; same fax for civil/probate; hours 9AM-5PM (EST). *Felony, Misdemeanor, Civil, Eviction, Small Claims, Probate.*
www.nccourts.org/County/Chowan/Default.asp
Note: Search civil and criminal court calendars at www1.aoc.state.nc.us/www/calendars.html.
Civil Records: Access: In person only. Visitors must perform in person searches themselves. Court makes copy: $2.00 for first page, $.25 each add'l. Required to search: name, years to search; also helpful: address. Civil cases indexed by defendant, plaintiff, on computer since 1990, prior on books to 1800s.
Criminal Records: Access: Mail, in person. Both court and visitors may perform in person searches. Search fee: $10.00 per name. Court makes copy: $2.00 for first page, $.25 each add'l. Required to search: name, years to search, DOB; also helpful: address, SSN. Records on computer from 1/90, prior as civil. Mail turnaround time 3-5 days.
General Information: Public terminal goes back to 1990. No adoptions, sealed cases, juvenile, sex offenders, mental or expunged records released. Will not fax documents. Certification fee: None; $3.00 if you perform search in person. Payee: Clerk of Superior Court. Only cashiers checks and money orders accepted. Prepayment and SASE required.

Clay County

Superior-District Court PO Box 506, 25 Herbert St, Hayesville, NC 28904; phone: 828-389-8334; fax: 828-389-3329; hours 8AM-5PM (EST). *Felony, Misdemeanor, Civil, Eviction, Small Claims, Probate.*
www.aoc.state.nc.us/www/public/courts/clay.html
Note: Search civil and criminal court calendars at www1.aoc.state.nc.us/www/calendars.html.
Civil Records: Access: In person only. Visitors must perform in person searches themselves. Court makes copy: $2.00 for 1st page, $.25 each add'l. Required to search: name, years to search; also helpful: address. Civil cases indexed by defendant, plaintiff, on computer since 1989, on books since 1888.
Criminal Records: Access: Fax, mail, in person. Only the court performs in person searches. Search fee: $10.00 per name. Court makes copy: $2.00 for 1st page, $.25 each add'l. Required to search: name, years to search, DOB; also helpful: address, SSN. Records on computer back to 1989, on books since 1888. Mail turnaround time 1-2 days.
General Information: Public terminal has only civil records back to 1989. No adoptions, sealed cases, juvenile, sex offenders, mental or expunged records released. Fee to fax documents is $.25 per page. Certification fee: None; $3.00 if you perform search in person. Payee: Clerk of Court. Business checks accepted. Prepayment and SASE required.

Cleveland County

Superior-District Court 100 Justice Pl, Shelby, NC 28150; phone: 704-484-4862; hours 8AM-5PM (EST). *Felony, Misdemeanor, Civil, Eviction, Small Claims, Probate.*
Note: Search civil and criminal court calendars at www1.aoc.state.nc.us/www/calendars.html.
Civil Records: Access: In person only. Visitors must perform in person searches themselves. Court makes copy: $2.00 for 1st page, $.25 each add'l; same fee for self serve. Required to search: name, years to search. Civil cases indexed by defendant, plaintiff, on computer since 1988, books to 1968, archived prior.
Criminal Records: Access: Mail, in person. Both court and visitors may perform in person searches. Search fee: $10.00 per name. Court makes copy: $2.00 for 1st page, $.25 each add'l; same fee for self serve. Required to search: name, years to search, DOB; also helpful: address, SSN. Records on computer since 6/86, on books to 1972, archived prior. Mail turnaround time 1-2 days.
General Information: Public terminal has criminal back to 6/1988 and civil back to 1988. No adoptions, sealed cases, juvenile, sex offenders, mental or expunged records released. Will not fax back documents. Certification fee: None; $3.00 if you perform search in person. Payee: Clerk of Superior Court. No out-of-state checks accepted. Prepayment required. SASE requested.

Columbus County

Superior-District Court PO Box 1587, Whiteville, NC 28472; criminal phone: 910-641-3020; civil phone: 910-641-3000; probate phone: 910-641-3010; fax: 910-641-3027; hours 8AM-5PM (EST). *Felony, Misdemeanor, Civil, Eviction, Small Claims, Probate.*
www.aoc.state.nc.us/www/public/courts/columbus.html
Note: Search civil and criminal court calendars at www1.aoc.state.nc.us/www/calendars.html.
Civil Records: Access: Mail, fax, in person. Visitors must perform in person searches themselves. Court makes copy: $2.00 1st page, $.25 each add'l; same fee for self serve. Required to search: name, years to search; also helpful: address. Civil cases indexed by defendant, plaintiff, on computer from 1989, prior on books to 1968. Mail turnaround time 2-5 days.
Criminal Records: Access: Mail, fax, in person. Both court and visitors may perform in person searches. Search fee: $10.00 per name. Court makes copy: $2.00 1st page, $.25 each add'l; same fee for self serve. Required to search: name, years to search, DOB; also helpful: address, SSN. Records on computer from 1987, prior on books or cards to 1968. Mail turnaround time 2-5 days.
General Information: Public terminal has criminal back to 6/1987 and civil back to 5/1989. No adoptions, sealed, juvenile, sex offender, mental, expunged or dismissed. Will not fax documents. Certification fee: None; $3.00 if you perform search in person. Payee: Clerk of Superior Court. Only cashiers checks and money orders accepted. Prepayment and SASE required.

Craven County

Superior-District Court PO Box 1187, New Bern, NC 28563; phone: 252-514-4774; criminal phone: 352-514-4777; civil phone: 252-514-4860; fax: 252-514-4891; hours 8AM-5PM (EST). *Felony, Misdemeanor, Civil, Eviction, Small Claims, Probate.*
www.aoc.state.nc.us/www/public/courts/craven.htm
Note: Search civil and criminal court calendars at www1.aoc.state.nc.us/www/calendars.html.
Civil Records: Access: Mail, in person. Both court and visitors may perform in person searches. Search fee: $7.50 per name. Court makes copy: $2.00 for first page, $.25 each add'l. Required to search: name, years to search; also helpful: address. Civil cases indexed by defendant, plaintiff, on computer

from 10/88, prior to 1968 are archived. Mail turnaround time 1-2 days.

Criminal Records: Access: Mail, in person. Both court and visitors may perform in person searches. Search fee: $10.00 per name. Court makes copy: $2.00 for first page, $.25 each add'l. Required to search: name, years to search, DOB; also helpful: address, SSN. Records on computer since 1/87, prior on books and cards to 1968. Mail turnaround time 1-2 days.

General Information: Public use terminal available. No adoptions, sealed cases, juvenile, sex offenders, mental, expunged, or dismissed. Certification fee: None; $3.00 if you perform search in person. Payee: Clerk of Superior Court. Only cashiers checks and money orders accepted. Prepayment and SASE required.

Cumberland County

Superior-District Court PO Box 363, Fayetteville, NC 28302; phone: 910-678-2902; criminal phone: 910-678-2906; civil phone: 910-678-2909; probate phone: 910-678-2904; hours 8AM-5PM (EST). *Felony, Misdemeanor, Civil, Eviction, Small Claims, Probate.*

www.aoc.state.nc.us/district12/

Note: Search civil and criminal court calendars at www1.aoc.state.nc.us/www/calendars.html.

Civil Records: Access: Mail, in person, online. Both court and visitors may perform in person searches. Search fee: $10.50 per name. Court makes copy: $2.00 1st page, $.50 ea add'l. Required to search: name, years to search; also helpful: address. Civil cases indexed by defendant, plaintiff, on computer since 1988, books back to 1956. Search civil court calendars at www1.aoc.state.nc.us/www/calendars.html. Mail turnaround time 5-10 days.

Criminal Records: Access: Mail, in person, online. Both court and visitors may perform in person searches. Search fee: $10.00 per name. Court makes copy: $2.00 1st page, $.50 ea add'l. Required to search: name, years to search; also helpful: address, DOB, SSN. Records on computer since 5/82, books and cards to 1920s. Search criminal court calendars at www1.aoc.state.nc.us/www/calendars.html. Mail turnaround time 2 weeks.

General Information: Public terminal has criminal back to 1982 and civil back to 7/88. No adoptions, sealed cases, juvenile, sex offenders, mental or expunged records released. Certification fee: $3.00. Cert fee includes copies. Payee: Clerk of Superior Court. Business checks accepted. Prepayment required.

Currituck County

Superior-District Court PO Box 175, Currituck, NC 27929; phone: 252-232-2010; fax: 252-232-3722; hours 8AM-5PM (EST). *Felony, Misdemeanor, Civil, Eviction, Small Claims, Probate.*

www.aoc.state.nc.us/www/public/courts/currituck.html

Note: Search civil and criminal court calendars at www1.aoc.state.nc.us/www/calendars.html.

Civil Records: Access: In person only. Both court and visitors may perform in person searches. Court makes copy: $2.00 for first page, $.25 each add'l. Required to search: name, years to search. Civil cases indexed by defendant, plaintiff, on computer back to 11/27/89, books to 1968, prior archived.

Criminal Records: Access: Mail, in person. Both court and visitors may perform in person searches. Search fee: $10.00 per name. Court makes copy: $2.00 for first page, $.25 each add'l. Required to search: name, years to search, DOB; also helpful-SSN, signed release. Records on computer back to 11/27/89, books to 1968, prior archived. Mail search requests must be on letterhead and include signed release.

General Information: Public terminal goes back to 1990. No adoptions, sealed cases, juvenile, sex offenders, mental or expunged records released.

Certification fee: None; $2.00 if you perform search in person. Payee: Clerk of Superior Court. Only cashiers checks and money orders accepted. Prepayment required.

Dare County

Superior-District Court PO Box 1849, Manteo, NC 27954; phone: 252-475-9100; fax: 252-473-1620; hours 8:30AM-5PM (EST). *Felony, Misdemeanor, Civil, Eviction, Small Claims, Probate.*

www.aoc.state.nc.us/www/public/courts/dare.htm

Note: Search civil and criminal court calendars at www1.aoc.state.nc.us/www/calendars.html.

Civil Records: Access: Phone, mail, in person. Both court and visitors may perform in person searches. Search fee: $10.00 per name. Court makes copy: $2.00 for first page, $.25 each add'l; same fee for self serve. Required to search: name, years to search; also helpful: address. Civil cases indexed by defendant, plaintiff, on computer since 1985, on books to 1966. Mail turnaround time 2 days.

Criminal Records: Access: Mail, in person. Both court and visitors may perform in person searches. Search fee: $10.00 per name. Court makes copy: $2.00 for first page, $.25 each add'l; same fee for self serve. Required to search: name, years to search, DOB. Records on computer since 1987, on books and cards to 1966. Mail turnaround time 2 days.

General Information: Public terminal has criminal back to 1989 and civil back to 1987. No adoptions, sealed cases, juvenile, sex offenders, mental or expunged records released. Fee to fax documents is $.25 per page. Certification fee: None; $3.00 if you perform search in person. Payee: Superior District Court. Business checks accepted. No personal checks accepted. Prepayment required.

Davidson County

Superior-District Court PO Box 1064, 110 W Center St, Lexington, NC 27293-1064; phone: 336-249-0351; fax: 336-249-6951; hours 8AM-5PM (EST). *Felony, Misdemeanor, Civil, Eviction, Small Claims, Probate.*

www.aoc.state.nc.us/www/public/courts/davidson.html

Note: Search civil and criminal court calendars at www1.aoc.state.nc.us/www/calendars.html.

Civil Records: Access: In person only. Visitors must perform in person searches themselves. Court makes copy: $2.00 for first page, $.25 each add'l. Self serve copy fee: no charge for computer printouts. Required to search: name, years to search; also helpful: address. Civil cases indexed by defendant, plaintiff, on computer since 5/16/1988, prior on books.

Criminal Records: Access: Fax, mail, in person. Both court and visitors may perform in person searches. Search fee: $10.00 per name. Court makes copy: $2.00 for first page, $.25 each add'l. Self serve copy fee: no charge for computer printouts. Required to search: name, years to search; also helpful: address, DOB, SSN. Records on computer since 10/1985, on books and cards to 1952. Mail turnaround time 2-3 days.

General Information: Public terminal goes back to 1985. No adoptions, sealed cases, juvenile, sex offenders, mental or expunged records released. Certification fee: None; $3.00 if you perform search in person. Payee: Clerk of Superior Court. Business checks accepted. No credit cards accepted. Prepayment required. SASE requested.

Davie County

Superior-District Court 140 S Main St, Mocksville, NC 27028; criminal phone: 336-751-3508; civil phone: 336-751-3507; probate phone: 336-751-3508; fax: 336-751-4720; hours 8:30AM-5PM (EST). *Felony, Misdemeanor, Civil, Eviction, Small Claims, Probate.*

www.aoc.state.nc.us/www/public/courts/davie.html

Note: Search civil and criminal court calendars at www1.aoc.state.nc.us/www/calendars.html.

Civil Records: Access: Mail, in person. Both court and visitors may perform in person searches. Search fee: $10.00 per name. Court makes copy: $2.00 for first page, $.25 each add'l; same fee for self serve. Required to search: name, years to search. Civil cases indexed by defendant, plaintiff, on computer back to 10/89; on books to 1970. Mail turnaround time 5 days.

Criminal Records: Access: Mail, in person. Both court and visitors may perform in person searches. Search fee: $10.00 per name. Court makes copy: $2.00 for first page, $.25 each add'l; same fee for self serve. Required to search: name, years to search, DOB, signed release. Records on computer back to 10/89; on books to 1970. Mail turnaround time 5 days.

General Information: Public terminal goes back to 11/89. No adoptions, sealed cases, juvenile, sex offenders, mental or expunged records released. Certification fee: None; $3.00 if you perform search in person. Payee: Clerk of Superior Court. Personal checks accepted. Prepayment and SASE required.

Duplin County

Superior-District Court PO Box 189, 112 Duplin St, Kenansville, NC 28349; criminal phone: 910-296-2306; civil phone: 910-296-1686; fax: 910-296-2310; hours 8AM-5PM (EST). *Felony, Misdemeanor, Civil, Eviction, Small Claims, Probate.*

www.aoc.state.nc.us/www/public/courts/duplin.htm

Note: Search civil and criminal court calendars at www1.aoc.state.nc.us/www/calendars.html.

Civil Records: Access: Phone, fax, mail, in person. Both court and visitors may perform in person searches. Search fee: $5.00 per name. Phone search is free index check. Court makes copy: $2.00 for 1st page, $.25 each add'l. Required to search: name, years to search. Civil cases indexed by defendant, plaintiff, on computer since 1989, prior on books to early 1900s. Mail turnaround time 1-2 days.

Criminal Records: Access: Mail, in person. Both court and visitors may perform in person searches. Search fee: $10.00 per name. Court makes copy: $2.00 for 1st page, $.25 each add'l. Required to search: name, years to search, DOB. Records on computer since 5/1988, on cards and books to 1927. Mail turnaround time 1-2 days.

General Information: Public terminal has criminal back to 5/1988 and civil back to 1989. No adoptions, sealed cases, juvenile, sex offenders, mental or expunged records released. Will fax documents to local or toll free line. Certification fee: None; $3.00 if you perform search in person. Payee: Clerk of Superior Court. No personal checks or credit cards accepted. Prepayment and SASE required.

Durham County

Superior-District Court 201 E Main St, Durham, NC 27702; criminal phone: 919-564-7270; civil phone: 919-564-7050; hours 8:30AM-5PM (EST). *Felony, Misdemeanor, Civil, Eviction, Small Claims, Probate.*

www.nccourts.org/County/Durham/Default.asp

Note: Search civil and criminal court calendars at www1.aoc.state.nc.us/www/calendars.html.

Civil Records: Access: In person only. Visitors must perform in person searches themselves. Court makes copy: $2.00 for first page, $.25 each add'l. Required to search: name, years to search; also helpful: address. Civil cases indexed by defendant, plaintiff, on computer since 1/88, on books to late 1800s.

Criminal Records: Access: Mail, in person. Both court and visitors may perform in person searches. Search fee: $10.00 per name. Court makes copy: $2.00 for first page, $.25 each add'l. Required to search: name, years to search, DOB; also helpful: address. Criminal records on microfiche since 1982, prior on books to 1979. Mail turnaround time 3-4 days.

General Information: Public use terminal available. No adoptions, sealed cases, juvenile, sex offenders, mental or expunged records released. Will not fax documents. Certification fee: None; $3.00 if you perform search in person. Payee: Clerk of Superior Court. Only cashiers checks and money orders accepted. Prepayment and SASE required.

Edgecombe County

Superior-District Court PO Drawer 9, 301 St Andrews St, Tarboro, NC 27886; criminal phone: 252-823-2056; civil phone: 252-823-6161; fax: 252-823-1278; hours 8AM-5PM (EST). *Felony, Misdemeanor, Civil, Eviction, Small Claims, Probate.*

www.aoc.state.nc.us/www/public/courts/edgecombe.htm

Note: Search civil and criminal court calendars at www1.aoc.state.nc.us/www/calendars.html.

Civil Records: Access: In person only. Visitors must perform in person searches themselves. Court makes copy: $2.00 for first page, $.25 each add'l. Required to search: name, years to search, address. Civil cases indexed by defendant, plaintiff, on computer since 1988.

Criminal Records: Access: Mail, in person. Both court and visitors may perform in person searches. Search fee: $10.00 per name. Court makes copy: $2.00 for first page, $.25 each add'l. Required to search: name, years to search, DOB; also helpful: former names. Records on computer since 4/87, on books and cards to 1900s. Mail turnaround 1-2 days.

General Information: Public terminal has criminal back to 1987 and civil back to 1988. No adoptions, sealed cases, juvenile, sex offenders, mental or expunged records required. Certification fee: None; $3.00 if you perform search in person. Payee: Clerk of Superior Court. Only certified check or money order accepted. Prepayment required.

Forsyth County

Superior-District Court PO Box 20099, Winston Salem, NC 27120-0099; phone: 336-761-2250; criminal phone: 336-761-2366; civil phone: 336-761-2280; probate phone: 336-761-2471; criminal fax: 336-761-2018; same fax for civil/probate; hours 8AM-5PM (EST). *Felony, Misdemeanor, Civil, Eviction, Small Claims, Probate.*

www.aoc.state.nc.us/www/public/courts/forsyth.html

Note: Search civil and criminal court calendars at www1.aoc.state.nc.us/www/calendars.html.

Civil Records: Access: Mail, in person. Both court and visitors may perform in person searches. Search fee: $5.00 per name. Court makes copy: $2.00 for 1st page, $.25 each add'l. Required to search: name, years to search. Civil cases indexed by defendant, plaintiff, on computer since 4/1988, prior on books to 1968, on microfiche prior. Mail turnaround time 1-2 days.

Criminal Records: Access: Mail, in person. Both court and visitors may perform in person searches. Search fee: $10.00 per name found ($5.00 if not found). Court makes copy: $2.00 for 1st page, $.25 each add'l. Required to search: name, years to search, DOB. Records on computer since 10/1983, prior on books to 1968, on microfiche prior. Mail turnaround time 1-2 days.

General Information: Public terminal has criminal back to 10/1983 and civil back to 4/1988. No adoptions, sealed cases, juvenile, sex offenders, mental or expunged records released. Will not fax documents. Certification fee: None; $3.00 if you perform search in person. Payee: Clerk of Superior Court. Business checks accepted. Prepayment and SASE required.

Franklin County

Superior-District Court 102 S Main St, Louisburg, NC 27549; phone: 919-496-5104; fax: 919-496-0407; hours 8:30AM-5PM (EST). *Felony, Misdemeanor, Civil, Eviction, Small Claims, Probate.*

www.nccourts.org/County/Franklin/Default.asp

Note: Search civil and criminal court calendars at www1.aoc.state.nc.us/www/calendars.html.

Civil Records: Access: Mail, in person. Visitors must perform in person searches themselves. Court makes copy: $2.00 for first page, $.25 each add'l. Self serve copy fee: $.25 per page. Required to search: name, years to search; also helpful: address. Civil cases indexed by defendant, plaintiff, on computer since 6/1989, prior on books. Mail turnaround time 1-2 days.

Criminal Records: Access: Mail, in person. Both court and visitors may perform in person searches. Search fee: $10.00 per name. Court makes copy: $2.00 for first page, $.25 each add'l. Self serve copy fee: $.25 per page. Required to search: name, years to search, DOB; also helpful: address. Records on computer since 1980, on index books back to 1968. Mail turnaround time 1-2 days.

General Information: Public terminal goes back to 1980. No adoptions, sealed cases, juvenile, mental or expunged records released. Certification fee: None; $3.00 if you perform search in person. Payee: Clerk of Superior Court. Personal checks accepted. Prepayment required. SASE requested.

Gaston County

Superior-District Court Gaston County Court House, 325 N Marietta St. #1004, Gastonia, NC 28052-2331; phone: 704-852-3100; fax: 704-852-3267; hours 8:30AM-5PM (EST). *Felony, Misdemeanor, Civil, Eviction, Small Claims, Probate.*

www.nccourts.org/County/Gaston/Default.asp

Note: Search civil and criminal court calendars at www1.aoc.state.nc.us/www/calendars.html.

Civil Records: Access: In person only. Visitors must perform in person searches themselves. Court makes copy: $2.00 first page; $.25 addl page. Required to search: name, years to search; also helpful: address. Civil cases indexed by defendant, plaintiff, on computer since 1988, prior on books to 1891.

Criminal Records: Access: Mail, in person. Both court and visitors may perform in person searches. Search fee: $10.00 per name. Court makes copy: $2.00 first page; $.25 each add'l. Required to search: name, address, DOB; also helpful: years to search, SSN. Criminal records on criminal terminal from 1/83, on books and microfilm to 1973. Mail turnaround time 1-2 days.

General Information: Public use terminal available. No adoptions, sealed cases, juvenile, mental or expunged records released. Certification fee: None; $3.00 if you perform search in person. Payee: Clerk of Superior Court. No out of state checks accepted. Prepayment required.

Gates County

Superior-District Court PO Box 31, Gatesville, NC 27938; phone: 252-357-1365; fax: 252-357-1047; hours 8AM-5PM (EST). *Felony, Misdemeanor, Civil, Eviction, Small Claims, Probate.*

www.aoc.state.nc.us/www/public/courts/gates.html

Note: Search civil and criminal court calendars at www1.aoc.state.nc.us/www/calendars.html.

Civil Records: Access: In person only. Visitors must perform in person searches themselves. Court makes copy: $2.00 for first page, $.25 each add'l. Required to search: name, years to search; also helpful: address. Civil cases indexed by defendant, plaintiff, on computer since 1990, prior on books to 1966.

Criminal Records: Access: Mail, in person. Only the court performs in person searches. Search fee: $10.00 per name. Court makes copy: $2.00 for 1st page, $.25 each add'l. Required to search: name, years to search, DOB; also helpful: address, SSN. Records on computer since 1990, prior on books to 1966. Mail turnaround time 1-2 days.

General Information: Public terminal has only civil records. No adoptions, sealed cases, juvenile,

sex offenders, mental or expunged records released. Certification fee: None; $3.00 if you perform search in person. Payee: Clerk of Superior Court. Business checks accepted. Prepayment required.

Graham County

Superior-District Court PO Box 1179, Robbinsville, NC 28771; phone: 828-479-7986; criminal phone: X7975; civil phone: X7974; fax: 828-479-6417; hours 8AM-5PM (EST). *Felony, Misdemeanor, Civil, Eviction, Small Claims, Probate.*

www.aoc.state.nc.us/www/public/courts/graham.html

Note: Search civil and criminal court calendars at www1.aoc.state.nc.us/www/calendars.html.

Civil Records: Access: In person only. Visitors must perform in person searches themselves. Court makes copy: $1.50 for first page, $.25 each add'l. Required to search: name, years to search. Civil cases indexed by defendant, plaintiff, on computer since 1989, on books since 1920s.

Criminal Records: Access: Mail, in person. Both court and visitors may perform in person searches. Search fee: $10.00 per name. Court makes copy: $1.50 for first page, $.25 each add'l. Required to search: name, years to search; also helpful: address, DOB, SSN. Records on computer since 1984, on books to 1920s. Mail turnaround time 3-5 days.

General Information: Public terminal has criminal back to 1984 and civil back to 1989. No adoptions, sealed cases, juvenile, sex offenders, mental or expunged records released. Certification fee: None; $3.00 if you perform search in person. Payee: Clerk of Superior Court. Only cashiers checks and money orders accepted. Prepayment and SASE required.

Granville County

Superior-District Court Courthouse, 101 Main St, Oxford, NC 27565; phone: 919-693-2649; fax: 919-693-8944. *Felony, Misdemeanor, Civil, Eviction, Small Claims, Probate.*

www.nccourts.org/County/Granville/Default.asp

Note: Search civil and criminal court calendars at www1.aoc.state.nc.us/www/calendars.html.

Civil Records: Access: In person only. Court makes copy: $2.00 for 1st page, $.25 each add'l. Required to search: name, years to search; also helpful: address. Civil cases indexed by defendant, plaintiff, on computer since 6/12/1989, on books to 1968, prior files destroyed. Mail turnaround time 1 day.

Criminal Records: Access: Mail, in person. Both court and visitors may perform in person searches. Search fee: $10.00 per name. Court makes copy: $2.00 for 1st page, $.25 each add'l. Required to search: name, years to search, DOB; also helpful: address. Records on computer since 3/1988, prior on books on cards to 1968. Mail turnaround time 1 day.

General Information: Public terminal has criminal back to 3/1988 and civil back to 6/1989. No adoptions, sealed cases, juvenile, mental or expunged records released. Will not fax documents. Certification fee: None; $3.00 if you perform search in person. Payee: Clerk of Superior Court. No personal checks or credit cards accepted. Prepayment required. SASE helpful.

Greene County

Superior-District Court PO Box 675, Snow Hill, NC 28580; phone: 252-747-3505; criminal fax: 252-742-2700; same fax for civil/probate; hours 8AM-5PM (EST). *Felony, Misdemeanor, Civil, Eviction, Small Claims, Probate.*

www.nccourts.org/County/Greene/Default.asp

Note: Search civil and criminal court calendars at www1.aoc.state.nc.us/www/calendars.html.

Civil Records: Access: In person only. Visitors must perform in person searches themselves. Court makes copy: $2.00 for first page, $.25 each add'l; same fee for self serve. Required to search: name, years to search; also helpful: address. Civil cases indexed by defendant, plaintiff, on computer since 10/1989, prior on books to 1865.

Criminal Records: Access: Mail, in person. Both court and visitors may perform in person searches. Search fee: $10.00 per name. Court makes copy: $2.00 for first page, $.25 each add'l; same fee for self serve. Required to search: name, years to search; also helpful: address, DOB, SSN. Records on computer since 10/1989, prior on books to 1865. Mail turnaround time 1-2 days.

General Information: Public terminal has criminal back to 1989 and civil back to 1986. No adoptions, sealed cases, juvenile, sex offenders, mental or expunged records released. Will fax documents if you pay copy fee. Certification fee: None; $3.00 if you perform search in person. Payee: Clerk of Superior Court. Business checks accepted. Prepayment required.

Guilford County

Superior-District Court PO Box 3008, 201 S Eugene St, Greensboro, NC 27402; criminal phone: 336-574-4307; civil phone: 336-574-4305; hours 8AM-5PM (EST). *Felony, Misdemeanor, Civil, Eviction, Small Claims, Probate.*

www.aoc.state.nc.us/www/public/courts/guilford.html
Note: Search civil and criminal court calendars at www1.aoc.state.nc.us/www/calendars.html.
Civil Records: Access: In person only. Visitors must perform in person searches themselves. Court makes copy: $2.00 for 1st pg, $.25 each add'l. Required to search: name, years to search; also helpful: address. Civil cases indexed by defendant, plaintiff, on computer since 9/88, on books to late 1800s.
Criminal Records: Access: Mail, in person. Both court and visitors may perform in person searches. Search fee: $10.00 per name. Court makes copy: $2.00 for 1st page, $.25 each add'l. Required to search: name, years to search, DOB; also helpful: address, full name. Records on computer since 5/83, on cards and books to late 1800s. Mail turnaround time 1 week.

General Information: Public terminal has criminal back to 5/1983 and civil back to 9/1988. No adoptions, sealed cases, juvenile, sex offenders, mental or expunged records released. Certification fee: None; $3.00 if you perform search in person. Payee: Clerk of Superior Court. Only cashiers checks and money orders accepted. Prepayment and SASE required.

Halifax County

Superior-District Court PO Box 66, Halifax, NC 27839; phone: 252-583-5061; fax: 252-583-1005; hours 8:30AM-5PM (EST). *Felony, Misdemeanor, Civil, Eviction, Small Claims, Probate.*

www.aoc.state.nc.us/data/HALIFAX/index.html
Note: Search civil and criminal court calendars at www1.aoc.state.nc.us/www/calendars.html.
Civil Records: Access: In person only. Visitors must perform in person searches themselves. Court makes copy: $2.00 for first page, $.25 each add'l. Required to search: name, years to search; also helpful: address. Civil cases indexed by defendant, plaintiff, on computer since 1988, on books to 1968, prior archived.
Criminal Records: Access: Mail, in person. Both court and visitors may perform in person searches. Search fee: $10.00 per name. Court makes copy: $2.00 for first page, $.25 each add'l. Required to search: name, years to search; also helpful: address, DOB, SSN. Records on computer since 1988, on books to 1968, prior archived. Mail turnaround time 1-2 days.

General Information: Public terminal goes back to 1988. No adoptions, sealed cases, juvenile, sex offenders, mental or expunged records released. Certification fee: None; $3.00 if you perform search in person. Payee: Clerk of Superior Court. Business checks accepted. Prepayment required.

Harnett County

Superior-District Court 301 W Cornelius Blvd, Lillington, NC 27546; phone: 910-814-4600; criminal phone: 910-814-4601; civil phone: 910-814-4602; probate phone: 910-814-4603; fax: 910-893-3683; hours 8:30AM-5PM (EST). *Felony, Misdemeanor, Civil, Eviction, Small Claims, Probate.*

www.aoc.state.nc.us/www/public/courts/harnett.html
Note: Search civil and criminal court calendars at www1.aoc.state.nc.us/www/calendars.html.
Civil Records: Access: In person only. Visitors must perform in person searches themselves. Court makes copy: $2.00 for first page, $.25 each add'l. Required to search: name, years to search; also helpful: address. Civil cases indexed by defendant, plaintiff, on computer since 4/17/1989, prior on books from 1938.
Criminal Records: Access: Mail, in person. Both court and visitors may perform in person searches. Search fee: $10.00 per name. Court makes copy: $2.00 for first page, $.25 each add'l. Required to search: name, years to search; also helpful: address, DOB, SSN. Records on computer since 5/87, on books from 1968. Mail turnaround time 1 week-10 days.

General Information: Public terminal has criminal back to 5/1987 and civil back to 4/1989. No adoptions, sealed cases, juvenile, mental or expunged records released. Will fax documents for $2.00 1st page and $.25 each addl page. Certification fee: None; $3.00 if you perform search in person. Payee: Clerk of Superior Court. Only cashiers checks and money orders accepted. Prepayment and SASE required.

Haywood County

Superior-District Court 285 N. Main, #1500, Waynesville, NC 28786; phone: 828-454-6501; criminal phone: 828-454-6341; fax: 828-456-4937; hours 8AM-5PM (EST). *Felony, Misdemeanor, Civil, Eviction, Small Claims, Probate.*

www.aoc.state.nc.us/www/public/courts/haywood.html
Note: Search civil and criminal court calendars at www1.aoc.state.nc.us/www/calendars.html.
Civil Records: Access: Mail, in person. Both court and visitors may perform in person searches. Search fee: $10.00. Court makes copy: $2.00 for first page, $.25 each add'l. Required to search: name, years to search; also helpful: address. Civil cases indexed by defendant, plaintiff, on computer since 10/13/1988, prior on books to 1955. Mail turnaround time 1-2 days.
Criminal Records: Access: Mail, in person. Both court and visitors may perform in person searches. Search fee: $10.00 per name. Court makes copy: $2.00 for first page, $.25 each add'l. Required to search: name, years to search, DOB; also helpful: address, SSN. Records on computer from 5/87, on books or cards from 1800s. Mail turnaround time 1-2 days.

General Information: Public terminal has criminal back to 10/1981 and civil back to 10/88. No adoptions, sealed cases, juvenile, sex offenders, mental or expunged records released. Certification fee: None; $3.00 if you perform search in person. Payee: Clerk of Superior Court. Only cashiers checks and money orders accepted. Prepayment and SASE required.

Henderson County

Superior-District Court PO Box 965, Hendersonville, NC 28793; criminal phone: 828-697-4859; civil phone: 828-697-4851; probate phone: 828-697-4868; hours 8:30AM-5PM (EST). *Felony, Misdemeanor, Civil, Eviction, Small Claims, Probate.*

www.aoc.state.nc.us/www/public/courts/henderson.html
Note: Search civil and criminal court calendars at www1.aoc.state.nc.us/www/calendars.html.

Civil Records: Access: Mail, in person. Both court and visitors may perform in person searches. Court makes copy: $2.00 per 1st page. Required to search: name, years to search; also helpful: address. Civil cases indexed by defendant, plaintiff, on computer back to 1988, prior on books to 1968. Mail turnaround time 1 week.
Criminal Records: Access: Mail, in person. Both court and visitors may perform in person searches. Search fee: $10.00 per name. Court makes copy: $2.00 1st page; $.25 each add'l. Required to search: name, years to search, DOB; also helpful: address, SSN. Records on computer back to 9/89, prior on books to 1968. Mail turnaround time 1 week.

General Information: Public terminal has criminal back to 9/86 and civil back to 10/88. No adoptions, sealed cases, juvenile, sex offenders, mental or expunged records released. Certification fee: None; $3.00 if you perform search in person. Payee: Clerk of Superior Court. Personal checks accepted. Prepayment and SASE required.

Hertford County

Superior-District Court PO Box 86, Winton, NC 27986; phone: 252-358-7845; fax: 252-358-0793; hours 8AM-5PM (EST). *Felony, Misdemeanor, Civil, Eviction, Small Claims, Probate.*

www.aoc.state.nc.us/www/public/courts/hertford.html
Note: Search civil and criminal court calendars at www1.aoc.state.nc.us/www/calendars.html.
Civil Records: Access: In person only. Visitors must perform in person searches themselves. Court makes copy: $2.00 for first page, $.25 each add'l. Required to search: name, years to search; also helpful: address. Civil cases indexed by defendant, plaintiff, on computer back to 4/1989, prior on index cards and judgment books to 1968.
Criminal Records: Access: Mail, in person. Both court and visitors may perform in person searches. Search fee: $10.00 per name. Court makes copy: $2.00 for first page, $.25 each add'l. Required to search: name, years to search, DOB; also helpful: address, SSN. Records on computer back to 4/1989, prior on index cards or judgment books to 1968. Mail turnaround time 1-2 days.

General Information: Public terminal goes back to 1989. No adoptions, sealed cases, juvenile, sex offenders, mental or expunged records released. Certification fee: None; $3.00 if you perform search in person. Payee: Clerk of Superior Court. Only cashiers checks and money orders accepted. Prepayment required. SASE helpful.

Hoke County

Superior-District Court PO Drawer 1569, Raeford, NC 28376; phone: 910-875-3728; fax: 910-904-1708; hours 8:30AM-5PM (EST). *Felony, Misdemeanor, Civil, Eviction, Small Claims, Probate.*

www.aoc.state.nc.us/www/public/courts/hoke.html
Note: Search civil and criminal court calendars at www1.aoc.state.nc.us/www/calendars.html.
Civil Records: Access: In person only. Visitors must perform in person searches themselves. Court makes copy: $2.00 for first page, $.25 each add'l. Required to search: name, years to search; also helpful: address. Civil cases indexed by defendant, plaintiff, on computer since 10/89, on books to 1967.
Criminal Records: Access: Mail, in person. Both court and visitors may perform in person searches. Search fee: $10.00 per name. Court makes copy: $2.00 for first page, $.25 each add'l. Required to search: name, years to search, DOB; also helpful: address, SSN. Records on computer since 10/89, on books to 1967. Mail turnaround time 1-2 days.

General Information: Public use terminal available. No adoptions, sealed cases, juvenile, mental or expunged records released. Will not fax documents. Certification fee: None; $3.00 if you perform search in person. Payee: Clerk of Superior Court. Business checks accepted. Prepayment and SASE required.

Hyde County

Superior-District Court PO Box 337, Swanquarter, NC 27885; phone: 252-926-4101; fax: 252-926-1002; hours 8:00AM-5:00PM (EST). *Felony, Misdemeanor, Civil, Eviction, Small Claims, Probate.*
www.aoc.state.nc.us/www/public/courts/hyde.html
Note: Search civil and criminal court calendars at www1.aoc.state.nc.us/www/calendars.html.
Civil Records: Access: Mail, in person. Both court and visitors may perform in person searches. Search fee: $5.00 per name. Court makes copy: $2.00 for 1st page, $.25 each add'l; same fee for self serve. Required to search: name, years to search. Civil cases indexed by defendant, plaintiff, on computer since 7/89, on books to 1968; estate and special proceedings back to 1996. Mail turnaround time 2 days.
Criminal Records: Access: Mail, in person. Both court and visitors may perform in person searches. Search fee: $10.00 per name. Court makes copy: $2.00 for 1st page, $.25 each add'l; same fee for self serve. Required to search: name, years to search, DOB; also helpful- signed release. Records on computer since 7/89, on books to 1968. Mail turnaround time 2 days
General Information: Public terminal has criminal back to 1989 and civil back to 1996. No adoptions, sealed cases, juvenile, sex offenders, mental, involuntary commitments, or expunged records released. Will fax documents if copy fee is paid. Certification fee: None; $3.00 if you perform search in person. Payee: Clerk of Superior Court. Only cashiers checks and money orders accepted. Prepayment and SASE required.

Iredell County

Superior-District Court PO Box 186, Statesville, NC 28687; criminal phone: 704-878-4204; civil phone: 704-878-4306; probate phone: 704-878-4311; fax: 704-878-3261; hours 8:30AM-5PM (EST). *Felony, Misdemeanor, Civil, Eviction, Small Claims, Probate.*
www.aoc.state.nc.us/www/public/courts/iredell.htm
Note: Search civil and criminal court calendars at www1.aoc.state.nc.us/www/calendars.html.
Civil Records: Access: Mail, in person. Both court and visitors may perform in person searches. Search fee: $10.00 per name. Court makes copy: $2.00 for first page, $.25 each add'l. Required to search: name, years to search. Civil cases indexed by defendant, plaintiff, on computer since 1985, in books since, 1786, on microfiche since 1939. Mail turnaround time 2 days.
Criminal Records: Access: Mail, in person. Both court and visitors may perform in person searches. Search fee: $10.00 per name. Court makes copy: $2.00 for first page, $.25 each add'l. Required to search: name, years to search, DOB. Records on computer since 1985, prior on books and cards to 1970. Mail turnaround time 2 days.
General Information: Public terminal goes back to 1985. No adoptions, sealed cases, juvenile, sex offenders, mental or expunged records released. Will fax documents to local or toll free line, will not fax certified . Certification fee: None; $3.00 if you perform search in person. Payee: Clerk of Superior Court. Only cashiers checks and money orders accepted. Prepayment and SASE required.

Jackson County

Superior-District Court 401 Grindstaff Cove Rd, Sylva, NC 28779; phone: 828-586-7512; criminal fax: 828-586-9009; same fax for civil/probate; hours 8:30AM-5PM (EST). *Felony, Misdemeanor, Civil, Eviction, Small Claims, Probate.*
www.aoc.state.nc.us/www/public/courts/jackson.html
Note: Search civil and criminal court calendars at www1.aoc.state.nc.us/www/calendars.html.
Civil Records: Access: In person only. Visitors must perform in person searches themselves. Court makes copy: $2.00 for first page, $.25 each add'l;

same fee for self serve. Required to search: name, years to search; also helpful: address. Civil cases indexed by defendant, plaintiff, on computer since 5/29/1989, prior on books from 1966.
Criminal Records: Access: Mail, in person. Both court and visitors may perform in person searches. Search fee: $10.00 per name. Court makes copy: $2.00 for first page, $.25 each add'l; same fee for self serve. Required to search: name, years to search, DOB; also helpful: address, SSN. Records on computer since 5/29/1989, prior on books from 1966. Mail turnaround time 1-2 days.
General Information: Public terminal goes back to 5/1989. No adoptions, sealed cases, juvenile, mental or expunged records released. Will not fax documents. Certification fee: $10.00 per document includes copies. Payee: Clerk of Superior Court. Only cashiers checks and money orders accepted. Prepayment and SASE required.

Johnston County

Superior-District Court PO Box 297, Smithfield, NC 27577; phone: 919-934-3192; criminal fax: 919-934-5857; same fax for civil/probate; hours 8AM-5PM (EST). *Felony, Misdemeanor, Civil, Eviction, Small Claims, Probate.*
www.nccourts.org/County/Johnston/Default.asp
Note: Search civil and criminal court calendars at www1.aoc.state.nc.us/www/calendars.html. Probate is in a separate index at this courthouse.
Civil Records: Access: In person only. Visitors must perform in person searches themselves. Court makes copy: $2.00 for 1st page, $.25 each add'l. Required to search: name, years to search; also helpful: address. Civil cases indexed by defendant, plaintiff, on computer since 1989, prior on books to 1930s.
Criminal Records: Access: Mail, in person. Both court and visitors may perform in person searches. Search fee: $10.00 per name. Court makes copy: $2.00 for 1st page, $.25 each add'l. Required to search: name, DOB; also helpful: years to search, address, SSN. Records on computer from 5/86, prior on books and cards to 1968. Mail turnaround time 1-2 days.
General Information: Public use terminal available. No adoptions, sealed cases, juvenile, sex offenders, mental or expunged records released. Will fax documents. Certification fee: $3.00 per document unless copy fee exceeds $3.00, then no cert fee. Payee: Clerk of Superior Court. Business checks accepted. Prepayment required. SASE requested.

Jones County

Superior-District Court PO Box 280, Trenton, NC 28585; phone: 252-448-7351; fax: 252-448-1607; hours 8AM-5PM (EST). *Felony, Misdemeanor, Civil, Eviction, Small Claims, Probate.*
www.nccourts.org/County/Jones/Default.asp
Note: Search civil and criminal court calendars at www1.aoc.state.nc.us/www/calendars.html.
Civil Records: Access: In person only. Visitors must perform in person searches themselves. Court makes copy: $2.00 for first page, $.25 each add'l. Required to search: name, years to search. Civil cases indexed by defendant, plaintiff, on computer since 1989, prior on microfilm. Mail turnaround time 5 days.
Criminal Records: Access: Mail, in person. Both court and visitors may perform in person searches. Search fee: $10.00 per name. Court makes copy: $2.00 for first page, $.25 each add'l. Required to search: name, years to search, DOB. Records on computer since 1989, prior on microfilm. Mail turnaround time 5 days.
General Information: Public use terminal available. No adoptions, sealed cases, juvenile, sex offenders, mental or expunged records released. Will not fax documents. Certification fee: None; $3.00 if you perform search in person. Payee: Clerk of Court. Only

cashiers checks and money orders accepted. Prepayment and SASE required.

Lee County

Superior-District Court PO Box 4209, 1400 S Horner Blvd, Sanford, NC 27331; phone: 919-708-4400; criminal phone: 919-708-4407; civil phone: 919-708-4402; probate phone: 919-708-4417; fax: 919-775-3483; hours 8AM-5PM (EST). *Felony, Misdemeanor, Civil, Eviction, Small Claims, Probate.*
www.nccourts.org/County/Lee/Default.asp
Note: Search civil and criminal court calendars at www1.aoc.state.nc.us/www/calendars.html.
Civil Records: Access: In person only. Visitors must perform in person searches themselves. Court makes copy: $2.00 for 1st page, $.25 each add'l. Required to search: name, years to search. Civil cases indexed by defendant, plaintiff, on computer since 1989, prior on books to 1967, index to 1907.
Criminal Records: Access: Mail, in person. Both court and visitors may perform in person searches. Search fee: $10.00 per name. Court makes copy: $2.00 for 1st page, $.25 each add'l. Required to search: name, years to search, DOB. Records on computer since 6/87, prior on books to 12/68, index to criminal actions books from 8/84 to 6/87. Mail turnaround time 1-3 days.
General Information: Public terminal has criminal back to 6/1987 and civil back to 1989. No adoptions, sealed cases, juvenile, sex offenders, mental or expunged records released. Certification fee: $3.00 per doc. Payee: Clerk of Superior Court. Only cashiers checks and money orders accepted. Prepayment required.

Lenoir County

Superior-District Court PO Box 68, Kinston, NC 28502-0068; phone: 252-527-6231; fax: 252-527-9154; hours 8AM-5PM (EST). *Felony, Misdemeanor, Civil, Eviction, Small Claims, Probate.*
www.nccourts.org/County/Lenoir/Default.asp
Note: Search civil and criminal court calendars at www1.aoc.state.nc.us/www/calendars.html.
Civil Records: Access: In person only. Both court and visitors may perform in person searches. Court makes copy: $2.00 for first page, $.25 each add'l; same fee for self serve. Required to search: name, years to search; also helpful: address. Civil cases indexed by defendant, plaintiff, on computer since 10/24/1988, prior on books to 1900s, prior destroyed due to fire.
Criminal Records: Access: Mail, in person. Only the court performs in person searches. Search fee: $10.00 per name. Court makes copy: $2.00 for first page, $.25 each add'l; same fee for self serve. Required to search: name, years to search, DOB; also helpful: address. Records on computer since 8/86, prior records on books and cards to 1925. Mail turnaround time 1-2 days.
General Information: Public terminal has only civil records back to 1988. No adoptions, sealed cases, juvenile, sex offenders, mental or expunged records released. Will fax documents to local or toll free line. Certification fee: None; $3.00 if you perform search in person. Payee: Clerk of Superior Court. Only cashiers checks and money orders accepted. Prepayment and SASE required.

Lincoln County

Superior-District Court PO Box 8, Lincolnton, NC 28093; criminal phone: 704-736-8561; civil phone: 704-736-8563; probate phone: 704-736-8565; fax: 704-736-8718; hours 8:30AM-5PM (EST). *Felony, Misdemeanor, Civil, Eviction, Small Claims, Probate.*
www.nccourts.org/County/Lincoln/Default.asp
Note: Search civil and criminal court calendars at www1.aoc.state.nc.us/www/calendars.html.
Civil Records: Access: In person only. Visitors must perform in person searches themselves. Court

makes copy: $2.00 for first page, $.25 each add'l. Required to search: name, years to search. Civil cases indexed by defendant, plaintiff, on computer since 11-1-87, in books since mid-1800s, on microfiche from 1-1-68 to present.

Criminal Records: Access: Mail, in person. Both court and visitors may perform in person searches. Search fee: $10.00 per name. Court makes copy: $2.00 for first page, $.25 each add'l. Required to search: name, years to search, DOB. Records on computer since 1987, prior on books and cards to 1968. Mail turnaround time 2 days to 1 week.

General Information: Public use terminal available. No adoptions, sealed cases, juvenile, sex offenders, mental or expunged records released. Certification fee: None; $3.00 if you perform search in person. Payee: Clerk of Court. Business checks accepted. No personal checks accepted. Prepayment and SASE required.

Macon County

Superior-District Court PO Box 288, 5 W Main St, Franklin, NC 28744; phone: 828-349-2000; fax: 828-369-2515; hours 8:30AM-5PM (EST). *Felony, Misdemeanor, Civil, Eviction, Small Claims, Probate.*

www.nccourts.org/County/Macon/Default.asp
Note: Search civil and criminal court calendars at www1.aoc.state.nc.us/www/calendars.html.
Civil Records: Access: In person only. Visitors must perform in person searches themselves. Court makes copy: $.25 per page; same fee for self serve. Required to search: name, years to search; also helpful: address. Civil cases indexed by defendant, plaintiff, on computer since 5/1989, prior on books to 1968.
Criminal Records: Access: Mail, in person. Only the court performs in person searches. Search fee: $10.00 per name. Court makes copy: $.25 per page; same fee for self serve. Required to search: name, DOB; also helpful: years to search, address. Records on computer since 5/1989, prior on books to 1968. Mail turnaround time 1-2 days.
General Information: Public terminal goes back to 5/1989. No adoptions, sealed cases, juvenile, sex offenders, mental or expunged records released. Certification fee: None; $3.00 if you perform search in person. Payee: Clerk of Superior Court. No personal checks accepted. Prepayment required.

Madison County

Superior-District Court PO Box 217, Marshall, NC 28753; phone: 828-649-2531; fax: 828-649-2829; hours 8AM-5PM (EST). *Felony, Misdemeanor, Civil, Eviction, Small Claims, Probate.*

www.aoc.state.nc.us/www/public/courts/madison.htm
Note: Search civil and criminal court calendars at www1.aoc.state.nc.us/www/calendars.html.
Civil Records: Access: In person only. Visitors must perform in person searches themselves. Court makes copy: $2.00 for first page, $.25 each add'l. Required to search: name, years to search; also helpful: address. Civil cases indexed by defendant, plaintiff, on computer back to 10/88, prior on books to 1968.
Criminal Records: Access: Mail, in person. Visitors must perform in person searches themselves. Search fee: $10.00 per name. Court makes copy: $2.00 for first page, $.25 each add'l. Required to search: name, DOB; also helpful: years to search. Records on computer since 10/88, prior on books to 1968. Mail turnaround time 1-2 days.
General Information: Public terminal goes back to 10/1988. No adoptions, sealed cases, juvenile, sex offenders, mental, expunged, or dismissed records released. Certification fee: None; $3.00 if you perform search in person. Payee: Clerk of Superior Court. Only cashiers checks and money orders accepted. Prepayment required.

Martin County

Superior-District Court PO Box 807, Williamston, NC 27892; phone: 252-792-2515; fax: 252-792-6668; hours 8AM-5PM (EST). *Felony, Misdemeanor, Civil, Eviction, Small Claims, Probate.*

www.aoc.state.nc.us/www/public/courts/martin.html
Note: Search civil and criminal court calendars at www1.aoc.state.nc.us/www/calendars.html.
Civil Records: Access: Mail, in person. Both court and visitors may perform in person searches. Search fee: $10.00 per name. Court makes copy: $2.00 for first page, $.25 each add'l. Required to search: name, years to search, address. Civil cases indexed by defendant, plaintiff. Civil records go back to 1800s, civil records on computer since 1989, in books since 1968. Mail turnaround time 1 week.
Criminal Records: Access: Mail, in person. Both court and visitors may perform in person searches. Search fee: $10.00 per name. Court makes copy: $2.00 for first page, $.25 each add'l. Required to search: name, years to search, address, DOB; also helpful: SSN. Criminal records go back to 1800s Records on computer since 1996 in books since 1968. Mail turnaround time 1 week.
General Information: Public use terminal available. No adoptions, sealed cases, juvenile, mental or expunged records released. Certification fee: None; $3.00 if you perform search in person. Payee: Clerk of Court. Only cashiers checks and money orders accepted. Prepayment and SASE required.

McDowell County

Superior-District Court 21 S Main St, Marion, NC 28752; phone: 828-652-7717 x201; criminal phone: 828-652-7717 x228; civil phone: 828-652-7717 x208; fax: 828-659-2641; hours 8:30AM-5PM (EST). *Felony, Misdemeanor, Civil, Eviction, Small Claims, Probate.*

www.aoc.state.nc.us/www/public/courts/mcdowell.html
Note: Search civil and criminal court calendars at www1.aoc.state.nc.us/www/calendars.html.
Civil Records: Access: Mail, in person. Both court and visitors may perform in person searches. No search fee. Court makes copy: $1.50 for first page, $.25 each add'l. Required to search: name, years to search; also helpful: address. Civil cases indexed by defendant, plaintiff, on computer since 11/88, prior on books to 1930. Mail turnaround time 1-2 days.
Criminal Records: Access: Mail, in person. Both court and visitors may perform in person searches. Search fee: $10.00 per name. Court makes copy: $1.50 for first page, $.25 each add'l. Required to search: name, DOB; also helpful: years to search, address, SSN. Records on computer since 10/1987, prior on books to 1968. Mail turnaround time 1-2 days.
General Information: Public use terminal available. No adoptions, sealed cases, juvenile, sex offenders, mental or expunged records released. Certification fee: None; $3.00 if you perform search in person. Payee: Clerk of Superior Court. Business checks accepted. Prepayment and SASE required.

Mecklenburg County

Superior-District Court 800 E 4th St, PO Box 37971, Charlotte, NC 28237; criminal phone: 704-347-7809; civil phone: 704-347-7814; hours 8AM-5PM (EST). *Felony, Misdemeanor, Civil, Eviction, Small Claims, Probate.*

www.nccourts.org/County/Mecklenburg/Default.asp
Note: Search civil and criminal court calendars at www1.aoc.state.nc.us/www/calendars.html.
Civil Records: Access: In person only. Visitors must perform in person searches themselves. Court makes copy: $1.50 for first page, $.25 each add'l. Required to search: name. Civil cases indexed by defendant, plaintiff, on computer since 4/1988, prior on books to 1940s.
Criminal Records: Access: Mail, in person. Both court and visitors may perform in person searches.

Search fee: $10.00 per name. Court makes copy: $1.50 for first page, $.25 each add'l. Required to search: name, years to search, address, DOB; also helpful. Records on computer from 1/83, prior on cards and books to 1930s. Mail turnaround time 1-2 days.
General Information: Public use terminal available. No adoptions, sealed cases, juvenile, sex offenders, mental or expunged records released. Certification fee: None; $3.00 if you perform search in person. Payee: Clerk of Superior Court. Only cashiers checks and money orders accepted. Prepayment required. SASE requested.

Mitchell County

Superior-District Court PO Box 402, 328 Longview Dr, Bakersville, NC 28705; phone: 828-688-2161; fax: 828-688-2168; hours 8:30AM-5PM (EST). *Felony, Misdemeanor, Civil, Eviction, Small Claims, Probate.*

www.clerkofcourt.org
Note: Search civil and criminal court calendars at www1.aoc.state.nc.us/www/calendars.html.
Civil Records: Access: In person only. Both court and visitors may perform in person searches. Court makes copy: $2.00 for first page, $.25 each add'l. Required to search: name, years to search; also helpful: address. Civil cases indexed by defendant, plaintiff, on computer since 1988, prior on books since 1968. Mail turnaround time 1-2 days.
Criminal Records: Access: Mail, in person. Both court and visitors may perform in person searches. Search fee: $10.00 per name. Court makes copy: $2.00 for first page, $.25 each add'l. Required to search: name, years to search, DOB, SSN; also helpful: address. Records on computer since 1988, prior on books since 1968. Mail turnaround time 1-2 days.
General Information: Public terminal goes back to 1988. No adoptions, sealed cases, juvenile, sex offenders, mental or expunged records released. Certification fee: None; $3.00 if you perform search in person. Payee: Superior-District Court. Business checks accepted. Prepayment and SASE required.

Montgomery County

Superior-District Court PO Box 527, Troy, NC 27371; phone: 910-576-4211; hours 8:30AM-5PM (EST). *Felony, Misdemeanor, Civil, Eviction, Small Claims, Probate.*

www.nccourts.org/County/Montgomery/Default.asp
Note: Search civil and criminal court calendars at www1.aoc.state.nc.us/www/calendars.html. Address mail to Clerk of Superior Court.
Civil Records: Access: In person only. Visitors must perform in person searches themselves. Court makes copy: $2.00 for 1st pg, $.25 per page thereafter. Self serve copy fee: $.25 per page. Required to search: name, years to search. Civil cases indexed by defendant, plaintiff, on computer since 4/1989, on books to 170, archived in Raleigh to 1843, prior records destroyed in fire.
Criminal Records: Access: Phone, fax, mail, in person. Both court and visitors may perform in person searches. Search fee: $10.00 per name. Court makes copy: $2.00 for 1st page, $.25 each add'l; same fee for self serve. Required to search: name, years to search, address, DOB, signed release. Records on computer since 4/1989, on books to 170, archived in Raleigh to 1843, prior records destroyed in fire. Mail turnaround time 1-2 days.
General Information: Public terminal has only criminal records back to 1988. No adoptions, sealed cases, juvenile, sex offenders, mental or expunged records released. Certification fee: None; $3.00 if you perform search in person. Payee: Clerk of Superior Court. Only cashiers checks and money orders accepted. Prepayment required.

Moore County

Superior-District Court PO Box 936, Carthage, NC 28327; phone: 910-947-2396; fax: 910-947-1444; hours 8AM-5PM (EST). *Felony, Misdemeanor, Civil, Eviction, Small Claims, Probate.*
www.nccourts.org/County/Moore/Default.asp
Note: Search civil and criminal court calendars at www1.aoc.state.nc.us/www/calendars.html.
Civil Records: Access: Mail, in person. Both court and visitors may perform in person searches. No search fee. Court makes copy: $2.00 for first page, $.25 each add'l. Civil cases indexed by defendant, plaintiff, on computer since 3/1989, prior on books, older records in basement. Mail turnaround time 2-4 days.
Criminal Records: Access: Mail, in person. Both court and visitors may perform in person searches. Search fee: $10.00 per name. Court makes copy: $2.00 for first page, $.25 each add'l. Required to search: name, years to search, DOB, signed release; also helpful: address, SSN. Records on computer since 3/1989, prior on books to 1968, older records in basement. Mail turnaround time 2-4 days.
General Information: Public terminal has criminal back to 1989 and civil back to 1987. No adoptions, sealed cases, juvenile, mental or expunged records released. Certification fee: None; $3.00 if you perform search in person. Payee: Clerk of Superior Court. Only cashiers checks and money orders accepted. Prepayment required.

Nash County

Superior-District Court PO Box 759, 234 W Washignton St, Nashville, NC 27856; phone: 252-459-4081; criminal phone: 252-459-4085; fax: 252-459-6050; hours 8AM-5PM (EST). *Felony, Misdemeanor, Civil, Eviction, Small Claims, Probate.*
www.aoc.state.nc.us/www/public/courts/nash.html
Note: Search civil and criminal court calendars at www1.aoc.state.nc.us/www/calendars.html.
Civil Records: Access: In person only. Both court and visitors may perform in person searches. Court makes copy: $2.00 for 1st page, $.25 each add'l. Required to search: name, years to search; also helpful: address. Civil cases indexed by defendant, plaintiff, on computer since 6/1988, prior in books. Mail turnaround time 1 week.
Criminal Records: Access: Mail, in person. Both court and visitors may perform in person searches. Search fee: $10.00 per name. Court makes copy: $2.00 for 1st page, $.25 each add'l. Required to search: name, years to search, DOB; also helpful: address. Records on computer since 5/1980, prior on books and cards dating back to late 1800s. Mail turnaround time 1 week.
General Information: Public terminal has criminal back to 1980 and civil back to 6/1988. No adoptions, sealed cases, juvenile, mental or expunged records released. Certification fee: None; $3.00 if you perform search in person. Payee: Clerk of Superior Court. Only cashiers checks and money orders accepted. Prepayment and SASE required.

New Hanover County

Superior-District Court PO Box 2023, Wilmington, NC 28402; phone: 910-341-1111; criminal phone: 910-341-1301; probate phone: 910-341-1304; fax: 910-251-2676; hours 8AM-5PM (EST). *Felony, Misdemeanor, Civil, Eviction, Small Claims, Probate.*
www.nccourts.org/County/NewHanover/Default.asp
Note: Search civil and criminal court calendars at http://www1.aoc.state.nc.us/www/calendars.html.
Civil Records: Access: In person only. Visitors must perform in person searches themselves. Court makes copy: $2.00 for first page, $.25 each add'l. Required to search: name, years to search; also helpful: address. Civil cases indexed by defendant, plaintiff, on computer since 1988, on books to late 1800s.

Criminal Records: Access: Mail, in person. Both court and visitors may perform in person searches. Search fee: $10.00 per name. Court makes copy: $2.00 for first page, $.25 each add'l. Required to search: name, years to search, DOB; also helpful: address, SSN. Records on computer since 11/83, prior on books and files to late 1800s. Mail turnaround time 1-2 days.
General Information: Public use terminal available. No adoptions, sealed cases, juvenile, sex offenders, mental or expunged records released. Certification fee: None; $3.00 if you perform search in person. Payee: Clerk of Superior Court. Only cashiers checks and money orders accepted. Prepayment and SASE required.

Northampton County

Superior-District Court PO Box 217, Jackson, NC 27845; phone: 252-534-1631; fax: 252-534-1308; hours 8:30AM-5PM (EST). *Felony, Misdemeanor, Civil, Eviction, Small Claims, Probate.*
www.aoc.state.nc.us/www/public/courts/northampton.html
Note: Search civil and criminal court calendars at www1.aoc.state.nc.us/www/calendars.html.
Civil Records: Access: Mail, in person. Both court and visitors may perform in person searches. No search fee. Court makes copy: $2.00 for first page, $.25 each add'l. Required to search: name, years to search; also helpful: address. Civil cases indexed by defendant, plaintiff, on computer back to 1993, prior on books to 1968. Mail turnaround time 3-10 days
Criminal Records: Access: Mail, in person. Search fee: $10.00 per name. Court makes copy: $2.00 for first page, $.25 each add'l. Required to search: name, years to search, DOB; also helpful: address, SSN. Records on computer back to 1989, prior on books to 1968. Mail turnaround time 3-10 days
General Information: Public terminal goes back to 1989. No adoptions, sealed cases, juvenile, sex offenders, mental or expunged records released. Certification fee: None; $3.00 if you perform search in person. Payee: Clerk of Superior Court. Business checks accepted. Prepayment required.

Onslow County

Superior-District Court 625 Court St, Jacksonville, NC 28540; phone: 910-455-4458; hours 8AM-5PM (EST). *Felony, Misdemeanor, Civil, Eviction, Small Claims, Probate.*
www.aoc.state.nc.us/www/public/courts/onslow.htm
Note: Search civil and criminal court calendars at www1.aoc.state.nc.us/www/calendars.html.
Civil Records: Access: In person only. Visitors must perform in person searches themselves. Court makes copy: $2.0 for 1st page, $.25 each add'l; same fee for self serve. Required to search: name, years to search; also helpful: address. Civil cases indexed by defendant, plaintiff, on computer since 1988, prior on books to 1920s.
Criminal Records: Access: Mail, in person. Both court and visitors may perform in person searches. Search fee: $10.00 per name. Court makes copy: $2.00 for 1st page, $.25 each add'l; same fee for self serve. Required to search: name, years to search, DOB; also helpful: address, SSN. Records on computer since 2/83, prior on books to 1920s. Mail turnaround time 1-2 days.
General Information: Public use terminal available. No adoptions, sealed cases, juvenile, sex offenders, mental or expunged records released. Certification fee: None; $3.00 if you perform search in person. Payee: Clerk of Superior Court. Business checks accepted. Prepayment required.

Orange County

Superior-District Court 106 E Margaret Lane, Hillsborough, NC 27278; criminal phone: 919-245-2200; civil phone: 919-245-2210; probate phone: 919-245-2214; fax: 919-644-3043; hours 8AM-5PM (EST). *Felony, Misdemeanor, Civil, Eviction, Small Claims, Probate.*

www.nccourts.org
Note: Search civil and criminal court calendars at www1.aoc.state.nc.us/www/calendars.html.
Civil Records: Access: In person only. Both court and visitors may perform in person searches. Court makes copy: $1.50 for first page, $.25 each add'l. Required to search: name, years to search; also helpful: address. Civil cases indexed by defendant, plaintiff, on computer since 5/1989, prior on books to early 1800s.
Criminal Records: Access: Mail, in person. Both court and visitors may perform in person searches. Search fee: $10.00 per name. Court makes copy: $1.50 for first page, $.25 each add'l. Required to search: name, years to search, DOB; also helpful: address, SSN, race, sex. computer records go to 3/87. Mail turnaround time 1-3 days.
General Information: Public terminal has criminal back to 1987 and civil back to 1989. No adoptions, sealed cases, juvenile, sex offenders, mental or expunged records released. Certification fee: None; $3.00 if you perform search in person. Payee: Clerk of Superior Court. Only cashiers checks and money orders accepted. Prepayment and SASE required.

Pamlico County

Superior-District Court PO Box 38, Bayboro, NC 28515; criminal phone: 252-745-6001; civil phone: 252-745-6000; probate phone: 252-745-6003; criminal fax: 252-745-6018; same fax for civil/probate; hours 8AM-5PM (EST). *Felony, Misdemeanor, Civil, Eviction, Small Claims, Probate.*
www.aoc.state.nc.us/www/public/courts/pamlico.html
Note: Search civil and criminal court calendars at www1.aoc.state.nc.us/www/calendars.html.
Civil Records: Access: Mail, in person. Both court and visitors may perform in person searches. Court makes copy: $2.00 for 1st page, $.25 each add'l. Required to search: name, years to search, address. Civil cases indexed by defendant, plaintiff., records go back to 1988; Records on computer since 9/89, prior on books to 1968. Mail turnaround 1-2 days.
Criminal Records: Access: Mail, in person. Both court and visitors may perform in person searches. Search fee: $10.00 per name. Court makes copy: $2.00 for 1st page, $.25 each add'l. Required to search: name, years to search, DOB. Records on computer since 9/84, prior on books to 1968. Mail turnaround time 1-2 days.
General Information: Public use terminal available. No adoptions, sealed cases, juvenile, sex offenders, mental or expunged records released. Will fax documents to local or toll free line. Certification fee: None; $3.00 if you perform search in person. Payee: Clerk of Court. Only cashiers checks and money orders accepted. Prepayment and SASE required.

Pasquotank County

Superior-District Court PO Box 449, Elizabeth City, NC 27907-0449; phone: 252-331-4751; fax: 252-331-4826; hours 8AM-5PM (EST). *Felony, Misdemeanor, Civil, Eviction, Small Claims, Probate.*
www.nccourts.org/
Note: Search civil and criminal court calendars at www1.aoc.state.nc.us/www/calendars.html.
Civil Records: Access: In person only. Visitors must perform in person searches themselves. Court makes copy: $2.00 for first page, $.25 each add'l; same fee for self serve. Required to search: name, years to search; also helpful: address. Civil cases indexed by defendant, plaintiff, on computer since 3/6/1989, books prior to 1800s (some in Raleigh).
Criminal Records: Access: Mail, in person. Both court and visitors may perform in person searches. Search fee: $10.00 per name. Court makes copy: $2.00 for first page, $.25 each add'l; same fee for self serve. Required to search: name, years to search, DOB; also helpful: address, SSN, race, sex. Records on computer since 4/88, prior on books and microfiche. Mail turnaround time 2 days.

General Information: Public terminal has criminal back to 1989 and civil back to 1993. No adoptions, sealed cases, juvenile, sex offenders, mental or expunged records released. Certification fee: None; $3.00 if you perform search in person. Payee: Clerk of Superior Court. Business checks accepted. Prepayment required.

Pender County

Superior-District Court PO Box 310, Burgaw, NC 28425; phone: 910-259-1229; fax: 910-259-1292; hours 8:30AM-5PM (EST). *Felony, Misdemeanor, Civil, Eviction, Small Claims, Probate.*
www.nccourts.org/County/Pender/Default.asp
Note: Search civil and criminal court calendars at www1.aoc.state.nc.us/www/calendars.html.
Civil Records: Access: In person only. Visitors must perform in person searches themselves. Court makes copy: $2.00 for first page, $.25 each add'l; same fee for self serve. Required to search: name, years to search; also helpful: address. Civil cases indexed by defendant, plaintiff, on computer since 9/89, prior in books from 1875.
Criminal Records: Access: Fax, mail, in person. Both court and visitors may perform in person searches. Search fee: $10.00 per name. Court makes copy: $2.00 for first page, $.25 each add'l; same fee for self serve. Required to search: name, years to search, DOB; also helpful: address, SSN. Records on computer since 9/89, prior in books from 1968. Mail turnaround time 1 week.
General Information: Public terminal has criminal back to 7/89 and civil back to 1989. No adoptions, sealed cases, juvenile, sex offenders, mental or expunged records released. Will fax documents $2.00 1st page, $.25 each add'l. Certification fee: None; $3.00 if you perform search in person. Payee: Clerk of Superior Court. Business checks accepted. Prepayment required.

Perquimans County

Superior-District Court PO Box 33, 128 N Church St, Hertford, NC 27944; phone: 252-426-1505; fax: 252-426-1901; hours 8AM-5PM (EST). *Felony, Misdemeanor, Civil, Eviction, Small Claims, Probate.*
www.nccourts.org/County/Perquimans/Default.asp
Note: Search civil and criminal court calendars at www1.aoc.state.nc.us/www/calendars.html.
Civil Records: Access: In person only. Visitors must perform in person searches themselves. Court makes copy: $2.00 for 1st page, $.25 each add'l. Required to search: name, years to search. Civil cases indexed by defendant, plaintiff, on computer since 1989, prior in books to 1966, rest archived and must be searched in person only.
Criminal Records: Access: Mail, in person. Both court and visitors may perform in person searches. Search fee: $10.00 per name. Court makes copy: $2.00 for 1st page, $.25 each add'l. Required to search: name, years to search, DOB. Records on computer since 1989, prior in books to 12/1966, rest archived and must be searched in person only. Mail turnaround time 1-2 days.
General Information: Public terminal goes back to 10/23/89. No adoptions, sealed cases, juvenile, sex offenders, mental or expunged records released. Certification fee: None; $3.00 if you perform search in person. Payee: Clerk of Superior Court. Only cashiers checks and money orders accepted. Prepayment required.

Person County

Superior-District Court 105 S Main St, Roxboro, NC 27573; criminal phone: 336-597-0556; civil phone: 336-597-0554; fax: 336-597-0568; hours 8:30AM-5PM (EST). *Felony, Misdemeanor, Civil, Eviction, Small Claims, Probate.*
www.aoc.state.nc.us/www/public/courts/person.html
Note: Search civil and criminal court calendars at www1.aoc.state.nc.us/www/calendars.html.

Civil Records: Access: In person only. Both court and visitors may perform in person searches. Court makes copy: $2.00 for 1st page, $.25 each add'l. Required to search: name, years to search. Civil cases indexed by defendant, plaintiff, on microfiche since 4/89, prior in index books to 1968.
Criminal Records: Access: Mail, in person. Both court and visitors may perform in person searches. Search fee: $10.00 per name. Court makes copy: $1.50 for first page, $.25 each add'l. Required to search: name, years to search, DOB. Records on computer since 3/88, index cards and books prior to 1968. Mail turnaround time 1-2 days.
General Information: Public terminal has criminal back to 3/1988 and civil back to 4/1989. No adoptions, sealed cases, juvenile, sex offenders, mental or expunged records released. Certification fee: None; $3.00 if you perform search in person. Payee: Clerk of Superior Court. Business checks accepted. Prepayment and SASE required.

Pitt County

Superior - District Court PO Box 6067, 100 W Third St, Greenville, NC 27835; phone: 252-695-7100; criminal phone: 252-695-7117; civil phone: 252-695-7150; fax: 252-695-7376; hours 8AM-5PM (EST). *Felony, Misdemeanor, Civil, Eviction, Small Claims, Probate.*
www.aoc.state.nc.us/www/public/courts/pitt.htm
Note: Search civil and criminal court calendars at www1.aoc.state.nc.us/www/calendars.html.
Civil Records: Access: In person only. Visitors must perform in person searches themselves. Court makes copy: $2.00 for 1st page, $.25 each add'l. Required to search: name, years to search; also helpful: address. Civil cases indexed by defendant, plaintiff, on computer back to 1988, on books to 1968.
Criminal Records: Access: Mail, in person. Both court and visitors may perform in person searches. Search fee: $10.00 per name. Court makes copy: $2.00 for 1st page, $.25 each add'l. Required to search: name, years to search, DOB; also helpful: address, SSN. Records on computer back to 2/85, on books and cards to early 1900s. Mail turnaround time 1-2 days.
General Information: Public terminal has criminal back to 2/1985 and civil back to 1988. No adoptions, sealed cases, juvenile, sex offenders, mental or expunged records released. Certification fee: None; $3.00 if you perform search in person. Payee: Clerk of Court. Cashiers check or money order only. Prepayment required.

Polk County

Superior-District Court PO Box 38, Columbus, NC 28722; phone: 828-894-8231; fax: 828-894-5752; hours 8AM-5PM (EST). *Felony, Misdemeanor, Civil, Eviction, Small Claims, Probate.*
www.aoc.state.nc.us/www/public/courts/polk.html
Note: Search civil and criminal court calendars at www1.aoc.state.nc.us/www/calendars.html.
Civil Records: Access: Mail, in person. Both court and visitors may perform in person searches. Search fee: $5.00 per name. Court makes copy: $2.00 for 1st page, $.25 each add'l; same fee for self serve. Required to search: name, years to search. Civil cases indexed by defendant, plaintiff, on computer since 5/89, prior on books to 1968. Mail turnaround time 1-2 days.
Criminal Records: Access: Mail, in person. Both court and visitors may perform in person searches. Search fee: $10.00 per name. Court makes copy: $2.00 for 1st page, $.25 each add'l. Required to search: name, years to search, DOB. Records on computer since 5/89, prior on books to 1968. Mail turnaround time 1-2 days.
General Information: Public use terminal available. No adoptions, sealed cases, juvenile, sex offenders, mental, expunged or dismissed records released. Certification fee: None; $3.00 if you perform search in person. Payee: Clerk of Superior Court. Business checks accepted. Prepayment and SASE required.

Randolph County

Superior-District Court 176 E Salisbury St #201, Asheboro, NC 27203; phone: 336-328-3000; criminal phone: 336-328-3005; civil phone: 336-328-3004; fax: 336-328-3131; hours 8AM-5PM (EST). *Felony, Misdemeanor, Civil, Eviction, Small Claims, Probate.*
www.nccourts.org/County/Randolph/Default.asp
Note: Search civil and criminal court calendars at www1.aoc.state.nc.us/www/calendars.html.
Civil Records: Access: In person only. Visitors must perform in person searches themselves. Court makes copy: $2.00 for first page, $.25 each add'l. Required to search: name, years to search. Civil cases indexed by defendant, plaintiff, on computer since 2/89, prior on books to 1800s.
Criminal Records: Access: Mail, in person. Only the court performs in person searches. Search fee: $10.00 per name. Court makes copy: $2.00 for first page, $.25 each add'l. Required to search: name, years to search, address, DOB. Records on computer since 6/85, prior on books and cards from 1970 to 1981. Microfilm from 1981 to 6/85. Mail turnaround time 1-2 days.
General Information: No public access terminal. No adoptions, sealed cases, juvenile, sex offenders, mental or expunged records released. Will not fax documents. Certification fee: None; $3.00 if you perform search in person. Payee: Clerk of Superior Court. Only cashiers checks and money orders accepted. Prepayment and SASE required.

Richmond County

Superior-District Court 114 E Franklin St #103, Rockingham, NC 28379; criminal phone: 910-997-9101; civil phone: 910-997-9102; fax: 910-997-9126; hours 8AM-5PM (EST). *Felony, Misdemeanor, Civil, Eviction, Small Claims, Probate.*
www.aoc.state.nc.us/www/public/courts/richmond.htm
Note: Search civil and criminal court calendars at www1.aoc.state.nc.us/www/calendars.html.
Civil Records: Access: In person only. Visitors must perform in person searches themselves. Court makes copy: $2.00 for first page, $.25 each add'l; same fee for self serve. Required to search: name, years to search; also helpful- address. Civil cases indexed by defendant, plaintiff, on computer since 4/89, prior on books since 1968.
Criminal Records: Access: Mail, in person. Both court and visitors may perform in person searches. Search fee: $10.00 per name. Court makes copy: $2.00 for first page, $.25 each add'l; same fee for self serve. Required to search: name, years to search, DOB; also helpful: address, SSN. Records on computer since 1977, cards to 1977, books to 1940, prior archived. Mail turnaround time 1-2 days.
General Information: Public use terminal available. No adoptions, sealed cases, juvenile, sex offenders, mental or expunged records released. Certification fee: None; $3.00 if you perform search in person. Payee: Clerk of Superior Court. Business checks accepted. Prepayment and SASE required.

Robeson County

Superior-District Court PO Box 1084, Lumberton, NC 28359; phone: 910-737-5035; criminal phone: 910-671-3395; civil phone: 910-671-3372; fax: 910-618-5598; hours 8:15AM-5:15PM (EST). *Felony, Misdemeanor, Civil, Eviction, Small Claims, Probate.*
www.aoc.state.nc.us/www/public/courts/robeson.html
Note: Search civil and criminal court calendars at www1.aoc.state.nc.us/www/calendars.html.
Civil Records: Access: In person only. Visitors must perform in person searches themselves. Court makes copy: $2.00 for first page, $.25 each add'l. Required to search: name, years to search; also helpful: address. Civil cases indexed by defendant, plaintiff, on computer since 1988, prior on books since 1966.

Criminal Records: Access: Mail, in person. Both court and visitors may perform in person searches. Search fee: $10.00 per name. Court makes copy: $2.00 for first page, $.25 each add'l. Required to search: name, years to search; also helpful: address, DOB. Records on computer since 1983, index books prior. Mail turnaround time 1-2 days.

General Information: Public terminal has criminal back to 1983 and civil back to 1988. No sealed cases, juvenile, sex offenders, mental or expunged records released. Will not fax documents. Certification fee: $3.00 if you perform search; Exemplification is $10.00. Payee: Clerk of Superior Court. Business checks accepted. Prepayment and SASE required.

Rockingham County

Superior-District Court PO Box 127, Wentworth, NC 27375; phone: 336-342-8700; criminal phone: 336-342-8706; civil phone: 336-342-8722; probate phone: 336-342-8703; fax: 336-616-1991; hours 8AM-5PM (EST). *Felony, Misdemeanor, Civil, Eviction, Small Claims, Probate.*

www.aoc.state.nc.us/www/public/courts/rockingham.html

Note: Search civil and criminal court calendars at www1.aoc.state.nc.us/www/calendars.html.

Civil Records: Access: In person only. Both court and visitors may perform in person searches. Court makes copy: $2.00 for first page, $.25 each add'l; same fee for self serve. Required to search: name, years to search. Civil cases indexed by defendant, plaintiff, on computer since 2/89, prior on books.

Criminal Records: Access: Mail, in person. Both court and visitors may perform in person searches. Search fee: $10.00 per name. Court makes copy: $2.00 for first page, $.25 each add'l; same fee for self serve. Required to search: name, years to search, DOB. Records on computer since 5/85, prior on cards and books. Mail turnaround time 1-2 days.

General Information: Public terminal has criminal back to 1985 and civil back to 1989. No adoptions, sealed cases, juvenile, sex offenders, mental or expunged records released. Certification fee: None; $3.00 if you perform search in person. Cert fee includes copies. Payee: Clerk of Superior Court. Only cashiers checks and money orders accepted. Prepayment required.

Rowan County

Superior-District Court PO Box 4599, 210 N Main St, Salisbury, NC 28145; phone: 704-639-7505; civil phone: x130; probate phone: 704-639-7680; hours 8AM-5PM (EST). *Felony, Misdemeanor, Civil, Eviction, Small Claims, Probate.*

www.aoc.state.nc.us/www/public/courts/rowan.html

Note: Search civil and criminal court calendars at http://www1.aoc.state.nc.us/www/calendars.html.

Civil Records: Access: In person only. Both court and visitors may perform in person searches. Court makes copy: $2.00 for 1st page, $.25 each add'l. Required to search: name, years to search; also helpful: address. Civil cases indexed by defendant, plaintiff, on computer since 1989, prior on books to 1800s.

Criminal Records: Access: Mail, in person. Both court and visitors may perform in person searches. Search fee: $10.00 per name. Court makes copy: $2.00 for 1st page, $.25 each add'l. Required to search: name, DOB; also helpful: years to search, address, SSN. Records on computer from 5/85, prior on books and cards to 1970. Mail turnaround time 1-3 days.

General Information: Public terminal has criminal back to 1985 and civil back to 1989. No adoptions, sealed cases, juvenile, sex offenders, mental or expunged records released. Certification fee: None; $3.00 per page if you perform search in person. Payee: Clerk of Superior Court. Business checks accepted. Prepayment required.

Rutherford County

Superior-District Court PO Box 630, 229 N Main St, Rutherfordton, NC 28139; phone: 828-286-3243; criminal phone: 828-286-3243; civil phone: 828-286-9136; fax: 828-286-4322; hours 8:30AM-5PM (EST). *Felony, Misdemeanor, Civil, Eviction, Small Claims, Probate.*

www.aoc.state.nc.us/www/public/courts/rutherford.htm

Note: Search civil and criminal court calendars at www1.aoc.state.nc.us/www/calendars.html.

Civil Records: Access: In person only. Visitors must perform in person searches themselves. Court makes copy: $2.00 for 1st page, $.25 each add'l. Required to search: name, years to search; also helpful: address. Civil cases indexed by defendant, plaintiff, on computer 10/1988, prior on books, some records to 1700s.

Criminal Records: Access: Mail, in person. Both court and visitors may perform in person searches. Search fee: $10.00 per name. Court makes copy: $2.00 for 1st page, $.25 each add'l. Required to search: name, years to search, DOB; also helpful: address, SSN. Records on computer since 6/87, prior on microfiche and books dating to 1800s. Mail turnaround time 1-2 days.

General Information: Public terminal has criminal back to 6/1987 and civil back to 10/1988. No adoptions, sealed cases, juvenile, sex offenders, mental or expunged records released. Certification fee: None; $3.00 if you perform search in person. Payee: Clerk of Superior Court. No business checks accepted. Prepayment and SASE required.

Sampson County

Superior-District Court Courthouse, Clinton, NC 28328; phone: 910-592-5191; fax: 910-592-5502; hours 8AM-5PM (EST). *Felony, Misdemeanor, Civil, Eviction, Small Claims, Probate.*

www.sampsoncountyclerkofcourt.org

Note: Search civil and criminal court calendars at www1.aoc.state.nc.us/www/calendars.html.

Civil Records: Access: In person only. Visitors must perform in person searches themselves. Court makes copy: $2.00 for first page, $.25 each add'l. Required to search: name, years to search; also helpful: address. Civil cases indexed by defendant, plaintiff, on computer since 1989, prior on books.

Criminal Records: Access: Phone, mail, in person. Both court and visitors may perform in person searches. Search fee: $10.00 per name. Court makes copy: $2.00 for first page, $.25 each add'l. Required to search: name, years to search, DOB; also helpful: address, SSN. Records on computer since 7/87, prior on books. Mail turnaround time 1-2 days.

General Information: Public use terminal available. No adoptions, sealed cases, juvenile, sex offenders, mental or expunged records released. Will fax documents. Certification fee: None; $3.00 if you perform search in person. Payee: Clerk of Superior Court. No personal checks accepted. Prepayment required. SASE requested.

Scotland County

Superior-District Court PO Box 769, Laurinburg, NC 28353; phone: 910-277-3240; criminal phone: 910-277-3250; civil phone: 910-277-3265; probate phone: 910-277-3260; criminal fax: 910-277-3261; same fax for civil/probate; hours 8:30AM-5PM (EST). *Felony, Misdemeanor, Civil, Eviction, Small Claims, Probate.*

www.aoc.state.nc.us/www/public/courts/scotland.html

Note: Small claims phone is 910-277-3244. Search civil and criminal court calendars at www1.aoc.state.nc.us/www/calendars.html.

Civil Records: Access: Mail, in person. Both court and visitors may perform in person searches. Search fee: $5.00 per name. Court makes copy: $2.00 for 1st page, $.25 each add'l. Required to search: name, years to search. Civil cases indexed by defendant, plaintiff, on computer since 1988, in books since 1966, on microfiche since 1984. Search civil

and criminal court calendars at www1.aoc.state.nc.us/www/calendars.html. Mail turnaround time 1-2 days.

Criminal Records: Access: Mail, in person. Both court and visitors may perform in person searches. Search fee: $10.00 per name. Court makes copy: $2.00 for 1st page, $.25 each add'l. Required to search: name, years to search, DOB; SSN helpful. Records on computer since 1988, in books 1966-1988, on microfiche 1984-1988. Search civil and criminal court calendars at www1.aoc.state.nc.us/www/calendars.html. Mail turnaround time 1-2 days.

General Information: Public terminal has criminal back to 1988 and civil back to 1989. No adoptions, sealed cases, juvenile, sex offenders, mental or expunged records released. Will not fax documents. Certification fee: None; $3.00 if you perform search in person. Payee: Clerk of Court. Only cashiers checks and money orders accepted. Prepayment and SASE required.

Stanly County

Superior-District Court PO Box 668, 201 S 2nd St, Albemarle, NC 28002-0668; phone: 704-982-2161; criminal phone: x176; fax: 704-982-8107; hours 8:30AM-5PM (EST). *Felony, Misdemeanor, Civil, Eviction, Small Claims, Probate.*

www.aoc.state.nc.us/www/public/courts/stanly.htm

Note: Search civil and criminal court calendars at www1.aoc.state.nc.us/www/calendars.html.

Civil Records: Access: In person only. Visitors must perform in person searches themselves. Court makes copy: $2.00 for 1st page, $.25 each add'l. Required to search: name, years to search; also helpful: address. Civil cases indexed by defendant, plaintiff, on computer since 1989, books to 1968.

Criminal Records: Access: Mail, in person. Both court and visitors may perform in person searches. Search fee: $10.00 per name. Court makes copy: $2.00 for 1st page, $.25 each add'l. Required to search: name, years to search, DOB. Records on computer since 1989, books to 1968. Mail turnaround time 1-2 days.

General Information: Public terminal goes back to 1989. No adoptions, sealed cases, juvenile, sex offenders, mental or expunged records released. Certification fee: None; $3.00 if you perform search in person. Payee: Clerk of Superior Court. Only cashiers checks and money orders accepted. Prepayment and SASE required.

Stokes County

Superior-District Court PO Box 250, 1012 Main St, Danbury, NC 27016; phone: 336-593-9173; fax: 336-593-5459; hours 8AM-5PM (EST). *Felony, Misdemeanor, Civil, Eviction, Small Claims, Probate.*

www.aoc.state.nc.us/www/public/courts/stokes.html

Note: Search civil and criminal court calendars at www1.aoc.state.nc.us/www/calendars.html.

Civil Records: Access: In person only. Visitors must perform in person searches themselves. Court makes copy: $2.00 for 1st page, $.25 each add'l. Required to search: name, years to search; also helpful: address. Civil cases indexed by defendant, plaintiff, on computer since 9/1988, prior on books to early 1900s.

Criminal Records: Access: Mail, in person. Both court and visitors may perform in person searches. Search fee: $10.00 per name. Court makes copy: $2.00 for 1st page, $.25 each add'l. Required to search: name, years to search; also helpful: address, DOB. Records on computer since 9/1988, prior on books to early 1900s. Mail turnaround time 1 week.

General Information: Public terminal goes back to 9/1988. No adoptions, sealed cases, juvenile, sex offenders, mental or expunged records released. Certification fee: None; $3.00 if you perform search in person. Payee: Clerk of Superior Court. Only cashiers checks and money orders accepted. Prepayment and SASE required.

Surry County

Superior-District Court PO Box 345, Dobson, NC 27017; phone: 336-386-3700; hours 8AM-5PM (EST). *Felony, Misdemeanor, Civil, Eviction, Small Claims, Probate.*

www.aoc.state.nc.us/www/public/courts/surry.html

Note: Search civil and criminal court calendars at www1.aoc.state.nc.us/www/calendars.html.

Civil Records: Access: In person, mail. Visitors must perform in person searches themselves. Court makes copy: $1.50 for first page, $.25 each add'l. Required to search: name, years to search, DOB; also helpful: address. Civil cases indexed by defendant, plaintiff, on computer since 10/88, on books to 1970, must know township for earlier records. Mail turnaround time 1-2 days.

Criminal Records: Access: Mail, in person. Both court and visitors may perform in person searches. Search fee: $10.00 per name. Court makes copy: $1.50 for first page, $.25 each add'l. Required to search: name, years to search, DOB. Records on computer since 10/88, on books to 1970, must know township for earlier records. Mail turnaround 1-2 days.

General Information: Public terminal goes back to 1987. No adoptions, sealed cases, juvenile, sex offenders, mental or expunged records released. Certification fee: None; $3.00 if you perform search in person. Payee: Clerk of Superior Court. Business checks accepted. No personal checks or credit cards. Prepayment and SASE required.

Swain County

Superior-District Court Clerk of Superior Court, PO Box 1397, Bryson City, NC 28713; phone: 828-488-2288; fax: 828-488-9360; hours 8:30AM-5PM (EST). *Felony, Misdemeanor, Civil, Eviction, Small Claims, Probate.*

www.aoc.state.nc.us/www/public/courts/swain.html

Note: Search civil and criminal court calendars at www1.aoc.state.nc.us/www/calendars.html.

Civil Records: Access: In person only. Both court and visitors may perform in person searches. Court makes copy: $2.00 first page, $.25 ea add'l. Self serve copy fee: $.25 per page. Required to search: name, years to search. Civil cases indexed by defendant, plaintiff, on computer since 5/1989, prior on books to 1920.

Criminal Records: Access: In person only. Both court and visitors may perform in person searches. Search fee: Court may charge a search fee. Court makes copy: $2.00 first page, $.25 ea add'l. Self serve copy fee: $.25 per page. Required to search: name, years to search, DOB; also helpful-SSN, signed release. Records on computer back to 1989, prior on books to 1969.

General Information: Public terminal has criminal back to 8/1984 and civil back to 5/8/89. No adoptions, sealed cases, juvenile, mental or expunged records released. Will fax specific case file for $10.00 per page. Fee must be paid in advance. Certification fee: $1.00 for first page, $.25 each add'l. Payee: Clerk of Superior Court. Only cashiers checks and money orders accepted. Prepayment required.

Transylvania County

Superior-District Court 12 E Main St, Brevard, NC 28712; phone: 828-884-3120; fax: 828-883-2161; hours 8AM-5PM (EST). *Felony, Misdemeanor, Civil, Eviction, Small Claims, Probate.*

www.aoc.state.nc.us/www/public/courts/transylvania.html

Note: Search civil and criminal court calendars at www1.aoc.state.nc.us/www/calendars.html.

Civil Records: Access: In person only. Visitors must perform in person searches themselves. Court makes copy: $2.00 for 1st page, $.25 each add'l. Required to search: name, years to search; also helpful: address. Civil cases indexed by defendant, plaintiff, on computer from 11/99, on books from 1968.

Criminal Records: Access: Mail, in person. Visitors must perform in person searches themselves. Search fee: $10.00 per name. Fee is for certified record check. Court makes copy: $2.00 for 1st page, $.25 each add'l. Required to search: name, years to search, DOB; also helpful: address, SSN. Records on computer from 6/89, on books 1968-1989. Mail turnaround time 1-3 days.

General Information: Public terminal has criminal back to 6/1989 and civil back to 11/1989. No adoptions, sealed cases, juvenile, mental or expunged records released. Certification fee: None; $3.00 if you perform search in person. Payee: Clerk of Superior Court. Personal checks accepted. Prepayment and SASE required.

Tyrrell County

Superior-District Court PO Box 406, Columbia, NC 27925; phone: 252-796-6281; fax: 252-796-0008; hours 8:30AM-5PM (EST). *Felony, Misdemeanor, Civil, Eviction, Small Claims, Probate.*

www.aoc.state.nc.us/www/public/courts/tyrrell.html

Note: Search civil and criminal court calendars at www1.aoc.state.nc.us/www/calendars.html.

Civil Records: Access: In person only. Visitors must perform in person searches themselves. Court makes copy: $2.00 for 1st page, $.25 each add'l. Required to search: name, years to search; also helpful: address. Civil cases indexed by defendant, plaintiff, on computer since 10/89, prior on microfilm to 1968.

Criminal Records: Access: Mail, in person. Both court and visitors may perform in person searches. Search fee: $10.00 per name. Court makes copy: $2.00 for 1st page, $.25 each add'l. Required to search: name, years to search, DOB; also helpful: address, SSN. Records on computer since 10/89, prior on books to 1968. Mail turnaround time 1-2 days.

General Information: Public terminal has criminal back to 1990 and civil back to 1996. No adoptions, sealed cases, juvenile, sex offenders, mental records expunged. Certification fee: None; $3.00 if you perform search in person. Payee: Clerk of Superior Court. Business checks accepted. No personal checks or credit cards. Prepayment required.

Union County

Superior-District Court PO Box 5038, Monroe, NC 28111; phone: 704-296-4600; hours 8AM-5PM (EST). *Felony, Misdemeanor, Civil, Eviction, Small Claims, Probate.*

www.aoc.state.nc.us/www/public/courts/union.htm

Note: Search civil and criminal court calendars at www1.aoc.state.nc.us/www/calendars.html.

Civil Records: Access: In person only. Visitors must perform in person searches themselves. Court makes copy: $2.00 for 1st page, $.25 each add'l. Required to search: name, years to search; also helpful: address. Civil cases indexed by defendant, plaintiff, on computer since 1987, prior on books to 1968.

Criminal Records: Access: Mail, in person. Both court and visitors may perform in person searches. Search fee: $10.00 per name. Court makes copy: $2.00 for 1st page, $.25 each add'l. Required to search: name, years to search; also helpful: address, DOB, SSN. Criminal record on computer since 1987, prior on books to 1968. Mail turnaround time 1-2 weeks.

General Information: Public terminal goes back to 1987. No adoptions, sealed cases, juvenile, sex offenders, mental or expunged records released. Certification fee: None; $3.00 if you perform search in person. Payee: Clerk of Superior Court. Will accept local business checks. Prepayment required.

Vance County

Superior-District Court 156 Church St. #101, Henderson, NC 27536; phone: 252-738-9000; hours 8AM-5PM (EST). *Felony, Misdemeanor, Civil, Eviction, Small Claims, Probate.*

www.nccourts.org/County/Vance/Default.asp

Note: Search civil and criminal court calendars at www1.aoc.state.nc.us/www/calendars.html.

Civil Records: Access: In person only. Visitors must perform in person searches themselves. Court makes copy: $2.00 for 1st page, $.25 each add'l. Required to search: name, years to search; also helpful: address. Civil cases indexed by defendant, plaintiff, on computer since 1989, prior on books to 1881.

Criminal Records: Access: Mail, in person. Both court and visitors may perform in person searches. Search fee: $10.00 per name. Court makes copy: $2.00 for 1st page, $.25 each add'l. Required to search: name, years to search, address, DOB; also helpful: SSN. Records on computer to 12/80, prior on books and cards to 1881. Mail turnaround time 1-2 days.

General Information: Public terminal goes back to 1979. No adoptions, sealed cases, juvenile, sex offenders, mental or expunged records released. Certification fee: None; $3.00 if you perform search in person. Payee: Clerk of Superior Court. Business checks accepted. Prepayment required.

Wake County

Superior-District Court PO Box 351, Raleigh, NC 27602; phone: 919-755-4105; criminal phone: 919-755-4112; civil phone: 919-755-4108; probate phone: 919-755-4116; criminal fax: 919-835-3039; civil fax: 919-755-4124; hours 8:30AM-5:00PM (EST). *Felony, Misdemeanor, Civil, Eviction, Small Claims, Probate.*

http://web.co.wake.nc.us/courts

Note: Search civil and criminal court calendars at www1.aoc.state.nc.us/www/calendars.html.

Civil Records: Access: In person only. Visitors must perform in person searches themselves. Court makes copy: $2.00 for first page, $.25 each add'l. Required to search: name, years to search. Civil cases indexed by defendant, plaintiff, on computer since 1988, prior on books to 1920s.

Criminal Records: Access: Mail, in person. Both court and visitors may perform in person searches. Search fee: $10.00 per name. Court makes copy: $2.00 for first page, $.25 each add'l. Required to search: name, years to search. Records on computer from 5/82, prior on books and cards from 1968. Mail turnaround time 3 days.

General Information: Public use terminal available. Juvenile, judicial waivers, involuntary commitments are confidential. No sealed cases, juvenile, mental or expunged records released. Certification fee: None; $3.00 if you perform search in person. Payee: Clerk of Superior Court. Business checks accepted with prior registration. No personal checks accepted. Prepayment required.

Warren County

Superior-District Court PO Box 709, Warrenton, NC 27589; phone: 252-257-3261; criminal fax: 252-257-5529; same fax for civil/probate; hours 8:30AM-5PM (EST). *Felony, Misdemeanor, Civil, Eviction, Small Claims, Probate.*

www.aoc.state.nc.us/www/public/courts/warren.htm

Note: Search civil and criminal court calendars at www1.aoc.state.nc.us/www/calendars.html.

Civil Records: Access: In person only. Visitors must perform in person searches themselves. Court makes copy: $2.00 for first page, $.25 each add'l; same fee for self serve. Required to search: name, years to search. Civil cases indexed by defendant, plaintiff, on computer since 1989, prior on books to 1968.

Criminal Records: Access: Mail, in person. Both court and visitors may perform in person searches.

Search fee: $10.00 per name. Court makes copy: $2.00 for first page, $.25 each add'l; same fee for self serve. Required to search: name, years to search, DOB. Records on computer from 5/81, prior on books to 1968. Mail turnaround time 1-2 days.

General Information: Public terminal has criminal back to 1981 and civil back to 1989. No adoptions, sealed cases, juvenile, sex offenders, mental or expunged records released. Will fax documents for $2.00 per page fax fee. Certification fee: None; $3.00 if you perform search in person. Payee: Clerk of Superior Court. Business checks accepted. Prepayment required.

Washington County

Superior-District Court PO Box 901, Plymouth, NC 27962; phone: 252-793-3013; fax: 252-793-1081; hours 8AM-5PM (EST). *Felony, Misdemeanor, Civil, Eviction, Small Claims, Probate.*
www.aoc.state.nc.us/www/public/courts/washington.html
Note: Search civil and criminal court calendars at www1.aoc.state.nc.us/www/calendars.html.
Civil Records: Access: In person only. Visitors must perform in person searches themselves. Court makes copy: $2.00 for first page, $.25 each add'l; same fee for self serve. Required to search: name, years to search. Civil cases indexed by defendant, plaintiff, on computer back to 12/89, prior on books.
Criminal Records: Access: Mail, in person. Both court and visitors may perform in person searches. Search fee: $10.00 per name. Court makes copy: $2.00 for first page, $.25 each add'l; same fee for self serve. Required to search: name, years to search; also helpful: address, DOB, SSN. Records on computer back to 12/89, prior on books. Mail turnaround time 2-3 days.
General Information: Public terminal goes back to 12/89. No adoptions, sealed, juvenile, mental health, expunged records released. Certification fee: None; $3.00 if you perform search in person. Payee: Clerk of Court. Business checks accepted. Prepayment and SASE required.

Watauga County

Superior-District Court Courthouse #13, 842 W King St, Boone, NC 28607-3525; phone: 828-265-5364; criminal phone: 828-265-5430; civil phone: 828-265-5432; probate phone: 828-265-5443; fax: 828-262-5753; hours 8AM-5PM (EST). *Felony, Misdemeanor, Civil, Eviction, Small Claims, Probate.*
www.aoc.state.nc.us/www/public/courts/watauga.htm
Note: Search civil and criminal court calendars at www1.aoc.state.nc.us/www/calendars.html.
Civil Records: Access: In person only. Visitors must perform in person searches themselves. Court makes copy: $2.00 for first page, $.25 each add'l; same fee for self serve. Required to search: name, years to search. Civil cases indexed by defendant, plaintiff, on computer since 12/5/88, on books to 1872, prior destroyed by fire.
Criminal Records: Access: Mail, in person. Both court and visitors may perform in person searches. Search fee: $10.00 per name. Court makes copy: $2.00 for first page, $.25 each add'l; same fee for self serve. Required to search: name, years to search, DOB, SSN. Records on computer from 11/88, prior on cards and books to 1968. Mail turnaround time 1-2 days.
General Information: Public terminal goes back to 1988. No adoptions, sealed, juvenile, sex offenders, mental, expunged or dismissed records released. Certification fee: None; $3.00 if you perform search in person. Payee: Clerk of Court. Only cashiers checks and money orders accepted. Prepayment required. SASE requested.

Wayne County

Superior-District Court 224 E Walnut St, Rm 230, Goldsboro, NC 27530; phone: 919-731-7910; criminal phone: 919-731-7910; civil phone: 919-731-7919; probate phone: 919-731-7921; fax: 919-731-2037; hours 8AM-5PM (EST). *Felony, Misdemeanor, Civil, Eviction, Small Claims, Probate.*
www.nccourts.org/County/Wayne/Default.asp
Note: Search civil and criminal court calendars at www1.aoc.state.nc.us/www/calendars.html.
Civil Records: Access: In person only. Both court and visitors may perform in person searches. Court makes copy: $2.00 for first page, $.25 each add'l; same fee for self serve. Required to search: name, years to search; also helpful: address. Civil cases indexed by defendant, plaintiff, on computer since 7-18-88, on books since 1968, open to public prior.
Note: The court will not do a search unless book and page number or a year of judgment given.
Criminal Records: Access: Mail, in person. Both court and visitors may perform in person searches. Search fee: $10.00 per name. Court makes copy: $2.00 for first page, $.25 each add'l; same fee for self serve. Required to search: name, years to search, DOB; also helpful: address, SSN, aliases. Records on computer since 7-18-88, on books since 1985, open to public prior. Mail turnaround time 1-2 days.
General Information: Public terminal goes back to 1985. No adoptions, sealed, juvenile, sex offenders, mental, expunged or dismissed. Certification fee: None; $3.00 if you perform search in person. Payee: Clerk of Superior Court. Business checks accepted. Prepayment required. SASE requested.

Wilkes County

Superior-District Court 500 Courthouse Drive, #1115, Wilkesboro, NC 28697; criminal phone: 336-667-5266; civil phone: 336-667-1201; hours 8AM-5PM (EST). *Felony, Misdemeanor, Civil, Eviction, Small Claims, Probate.*
www.nccourts.org/County/Wilkes/
Note: Search civil and criminal court calendars at www1.aoc.state.nc.us/www/calendars.html.
Civil Records: Access: In person only. Visitors must perform in person searches themselves. Court makes copy: $2.00 for 1st page, $.25 each add'l. Required to search: name, years to search. Civil cases indexed by defendant, plaintiff, on computer since 12/88, prior on books to early 1900s.
Criminal Records: Access: Mail, in person. Both court and visitors may perform in person searches. Search fee: $10.00 per name. Court makes copy: $2.00 for 1st page, $.25 each add'l. Required to search: name, years to search, DOB; also helpful: address. Records on computer since 12/88, prior on books to early 1900s. Mail turnaround time 1-2 days.
General Information: No adoptions, sealed cases, juvenile, sex offenders, mental or expunged records released. Certification fee: None; $3.00 if you perform search in person. Payee: Clerk of Superior Court. Only cashiers checks and money orders accepted. Prepayment required. SASE requested.

Wilson County

Superior-District Court PO Box 1608, Wilson, NC 27894; phone: 252-291-7500; civil phone: 252-291-7502; probate phone: 252-291-7502; criminal fax: 252-291-8049; civil fax: 252-291-8635; hours 9AM-5PM (EST). *Felony, Misdemeanor, Civil, Eviction, Small Claims, Probate.*
www.aoc.state.nc.us/www/public/courts/wilson.html
Note: Search civil and criminal court calendars at www1.aoc.state.nc.us/www/calendars.html.
Civil Records: Access: In person only. Visitors must perform in person searches themselves. Court makes copy: $2.00 for first page, $.25 each add'l. Required to search: name, years to search; also helpful: address. Civil cases indexed by defendant,

plaintiff, on computer since 8/88, prior on books to 1968, public viewing from 1915 to 1968.
Criminal Records: Access: Mail, fax, in person. Both court and visitors may perform in person searches. Search fee: $10.00 per name. Court makes copy: $2.00 for first page, $.25 each add'l. Required to search: name, years to search, DOB; also helpful: address, SSN. Records on computer since 5/86, Index cards to 9/76, books to 1918. Mail turnaround time 2-4 days.
General Information: Public terminal has criminal back to 5/1986 and civil back to 10/89. No adoptions, sealed cases, juvenile, sex offenders, mental, or expunged records released. Will not fax documents. Certification fee: None; $3.00 if you perform search in person. Payee: Clerk of Court. Only cashiers checks and money orders accepted. Prepayment required. SASE requested.

Yadkin County

Superior-District Court PO Box 95, Yadkinville, NC 27055; phone: 336-679-8838; fax: 336-679-4378; hours 8AM-5PM (EST). *Felony, Misdemeanor, Civil, Eviction, Small Claims, Probate.*
www.aoc.state.nc.us/www/public/courts/yadkin.htm
Note: Search civil and criminal court calendars at www1.aoc.state.nc.us/www/calendars.html.
Civil Records: Access: In person only. Visitors must perform in person searches themselves. Court makes copy: $2.00 for first page, $.25 each add'l. Required to search: name, years to search; also helpful: address. Civil cases indexed by defendant, plaintiff, on computer since 8/89, prior on books to 1970.
Criminal Records: Access: Mail, in person. Both court and visitors may perform in person searches. Search fee: $10.00 per name. Court makes copy: $2.00 for first page, $.25 each add'l. Required to search: name, years to search, DOB; also helpful: address. Records on computer since 8/89, prior on books to 1970. Mail turnaround time 1-2 days.
General Information: Public use terminal available. No adoptions, sealed cases, juvenile, sex offenders, mental or expunged records released. Certification fee: None; $3.00 if you perform search in person. Payee: Clerk of Superior Court. Business checks accepted. Prepayment and SASE required.

Yancey County

Superior-District Court 110 Town Square, Burnsville, NC 28714; phone: 828-682-2122; fax: 828-682-6296; hours 8:30AM-5PM (EST). *Felony, Misdemeanor, Civil, Eviction, Small Claims, Probate.*
www.aoc.state.nc.us/www/public/courts/yancey.htm
Note: Search civil and criminal court calendars at www1.aoc.state.nc.us/www/calendars.html.
Civil Records: Access: In person only. Visitors must perform in person searches themselves. Court makes copy: $2.00 for 1st page, $.25 each add'l. Required to search: name, years to search; also helpful: address. Civil cases indexed by defendant, plaintiff, on computer since 1988, prior on books.
Criminal Records: Access: Mail, in person. Only the court performs in person searches. Search fee: $10.00 per name. Court makes copy: $2.00 for 1st page, $.25 each add'l. Required to search: name, years to search, DOB; also helpful: address, SSN. Records on computer since 1988, prior on books. Mail turnaround time depends on ease of access, can take up to 2 weeks.
General Information: Public terminal has only civil records back to 1988. No adoptions, sealed cases, juvenile, sex offenders, mental, expunged or dismissed records released. Certification fee: None; $3.00 if you perform search in person. Payee: Clerk of Superior Court. Business checks accepted. No personal checks or credit cards. Prepayment required.

North Carolina Recording Offices

ORGANIZATION: 100 counties, 100 recording offices. The recording officers are Register of Deeds and Clerk of Superior Court (tax liens). The entire state is in the Eastern Time Zone (EST).

REAL ESTATE RECORDS: Counties will not perform real estate searches. Copy fees are usually $1.00 per page. Certification usually costs $5.00 for the first page and $2.00 for each additional page of a document.

UCC RECORDS: This was a dual filing state. Financing statements are were both at the state level and with the Register of Deeds, except for consumer goods, farm related and real estate related collateral. As of 7/1/2001, only real estate related collateral is filed at the county level. All counties will perform UCC searches on the records recorded prior to 7/1/2001. Use search request form UCC-11. Search fees were raised in 2001 to $30.00 per debtor name. Copies usually cost $1.00 per page.

TAX LIEN RECORDS: Federal tax liens on personal property of businesses are filed with the Secretary of State. Other federal and all state tax liens are filed with the county Clerk of Superior Court, not with the Register of Deeds. (Oddly, even tax liens on real property are also filed with the Clerk of Superior Court, not with the Register of Deeds.)

OTHER LIENS: Judgment, mechanics (all at Clerk of Superior Court).

ONLINE ACCESS: A growing number of counties offer free access to assessor and real estate records via the web.

Alamance County

Register of Deeds, PO Box 837, Graham, NC 27253. 336-570-6565; hours: 8AM-5PM. www.alamance-nc.com
No tax liens filed here. Office will perform a UCC search for records prior to 7/2001, but public must search other records themselves. Search fee $30.00 per debtor name. Copy fee $1.00 per page. Cert fee- $5.00 per cert plus copy fee. Payee- Alamance County Register of Deeds. **Other phones:** Treasurer- 336-570-1318. **Property tax/Assessor-** 124 W Elm St, Graham, NC 27253; 336-228-1318.

Alexander County

Register of Deeds, 75 First St SW; #1, Taylorsville, NC 28681-2504. 828-632-3152, R/E recording phone-704-632-3152; fax-828-632-1119; hours: 8AM-5PM.
No tax liens filed here. Office will perform a UCC search but public must search other records themselves. Copy fee $1.00 per page. Cert fee- $5.00 1st pg, $1.00 each add'l. Payee- Alexander County Register of Deeds.

Alleghany County

Register of Deeds, PO Box 186, Sparta, NC 28675. 336-372-4342; fax-336-372-2061; hours: 8AM-5PM. www.alleghanycounty-nc.gov
No tax liens filed here. All records in one index. Records indexed on a public use terminal back to 1989. Office will perform a UCC search but public must search other records themselves. Search fee $30.00. Copy fee $1.00 per page. R/E record copy- $.25 per copy. Cert fee- $3.00 1st pg, $2.00 each add'l. Payee- Alleghany County Register of Deeds. **Online access to Real Estate, Grantor/Grantee, Property, GIS records:** Access to the Register of Deeds database is free at www.allcorod.com. Click on "View & Search records online." Records go back to 1/1/1993. Also, search for property information on a GIS mapping site at http://arcims.webgis.net/nc/Alleghany/default.asp. To name search click on Quick Search. **Other phones:** Treasurer- 336-372-4179; Appraiser/Auditor- 336-372-8291; Elections- 336-372-4557; Vital Records- 336-372-4342. **Property tax/Assessor-** PO Box 1027, Sparta, NC 28675; 336-372-8291.

Anson County

Register of Deeds, PO Box 352, Wadesboro, NC 28170-0352. 704-694-3212, UCC recording phone-704-694-7594; fax-704-694-6135; hours: 8:30AM-5PM. www.co.anson.nc.us/services.php
No tax liens filed here. All records in one index index if recorded after 8/1/1989; prior records are in a deed index or deed of trust index. Records

indexed on a public use terminal back to 8/1/1989. Office will perform a UCC search but public must search other records themselves. UCC search per debtor name- $30.00. Copy fee $1.00 per page. R/E record copy- $.25 per page. Cert fee- $5.00 1st page, $2.00 each add'l page, plus copy fee. Payee- Anson County Register of Deeds. **Online access to Assessor, Real Estate, 911 Address Converter, Tax Collection records:** Records on the county Online Tax Inquiry System are free at www.co.anson.nc.us/pubcgi/taxinq. A tax collections search at www.co.anson.nc.us/pubcgi/colinq/. Also, there is an 911 address converter at www.co.anson.nc.us/pubcgi/911addresslookup/. **Other phones:** Treasurer- 704-694-6219; Appraiser/Auditor- 704-694-3072; Elections- 704-694-7593; Vital Records- 704-694-7593. **Property tax/Assessor-** Assessor, Courthouse Basement, Wadesboro, NC 28170; 704-694-2918.

Ashe County

Register of Deeds, 150 Government Circle, #2300, Jefferson, NC 28640. 336-219-2540; fax-336-219-2596; hours: 8AM-4:30PM. www.ashencrod.org
No tax liens filed here. All records in one index. Records indexed on a public use terminal back to 1995. Office will perform a UCC search but public must search other records themselves. UCC search per debtor name- $30.00. Copy fee $1.00 per page for maps. R/E record copy- $.25 per page. Cert fee- $5.00 1st page, $2.00 each add'l plus copy fee. Payee- Ashe County Register of Deeds. **Online access to Assessor, Real Estate, Grantor/Grantee, Property records:** Access to the register of deeds real estate data is free at www.ashencrod.org/Opening.asp. Full index goes back to 1/1995; images to 8/1940. Also, access to records on the county Tax Parcel Information System is free at http://arcims2.webgis.net/ashe/default.asp. Click on the "Search" button. **Other phones:** Treasurer- 336-219-2560; Appraiser/Auditor- 336-219-2554; Elections- 336-219-2570; Vital Records- 336-219-2540. **Property tax/Assessor-** 336-219-2554.

Avery County

Register of Deeds, PO Box 87, Newland, NC 28657. 828-733-8260; fax-828-733-8261; hours: 8AM-4:30PM. www.averyrod.com
No tax liens filed here. Records indexed on a public use terminal back to 1995. Office will perform a UCC search but public must search other records themselves. Search fee $38.00. Copy fee $1.00 per page. R/E record copy- $.25 per page. Cert fee- $5.00 per cert plus $2.00 each add'l. Payee- Avery County Register of Deeds. **Online access to Recording, Grantor/Grantee, Property records:**

Search the recorders database free at www.averyrod.com/view/disclaimer.html. Also, search for property info on the GIS site for free at http://arcims2.webgis.net/avery/default.asp. To name search click on Quick Search. **Other phones:** Treasurer- 828-732-8200. **Property tax/Assessor-** 828-733-8216.

Beaufort County

Register of Deeds, PO Box 514, Washington, NC 27889. 252-946-2323; hours: 8:30AM-5PM.
No tax liens filed here. Records indexed on a public use terminal back to 1995. Office will perform a UCC search for records from 2000-7/2001, but public must search other records themselves. UCC search per debtor name- $30.00. Copy fee $1.00 per page. R/E record copy- $.25 per page. Cert fee- $5.00 1st page; $2.00 each add'l page plus copy fee. Payee- Beaufort County Register of Deeds. **Other phones:** Vital Records- 252-946-2323.

Bertie County

Register of Deeds, PO Box 340, Windsor, NC 27983. 252-794-5309; fax-252-794-5374; 8:30AM-5PM.
No tax liens filed here. Separate indices to search. Records indexed on a public use terminal back to 1983. Office will perform a UCC search but public must search other records themselves. UCC search per debtor name- $30.00. Copy fee $1.00 per copy. Cert fee- $5.00 1st page, $2.00 each add'l page. Payee- Register of Deeds. **Other phones:** Elections- 252-794-5306; Vital Records- 252-794-5309. **Property tax/Assessor-** 252-794-5310.

Bladen County

Register of Deeds, PO Box 247, Elizabethtown, NC 28337. 910-862-6710; fax-910-862-6714; hours: 8:30AM-5PM. www.bladeninfo.org
No tax liens filed here. All records in one index. Records indexed on a public use terminal from 1988-2005. Office will perform a UCC search but public must search other records themselves. UCC search per debtor name- $30.00. Copy fee $.25 per page. Cert fee- $5.00 1st page; $2.00 each add'l page includes copy fee. Payee- Register of Deeds. **Online access to Real Estate, Grantor/Grantee, Deed records:** Access unofficial register of deeds site at www.withersravenel.com/deeds/; search comprehensive index or direct images. **Other phones:** Elections- 910-862-6951; Vital Records- 910-862-6710. **Property tax/Assessor-** 910-862-6748.

Brunswick County

Register of Deeds, PO Box 87, Bolivia, NC 28422-0087. 877-625-9310, 910-253-2690, R/E recording phone-910-253-4371; fax-910-253-2703; hours: 8:30AM-4:45PM. http://rod.brunsco.net No tax liens filed here. Office will perform a UCC search but public must search other records themselves. UCC search per debtor name- $30.00. Copy fee $.25 per page. Mail request must include copy fee plus SASE. **Online access to Recording, Deed records:** Access to the recorder database is free at http://rod.brunsco.net. Free registration, logon and password are required. Records are updated on the 10th, 20th, and 30th of the month. Also, search the tax administration data for free at www.brunsconctax.org/. **Other phones:** Treasurer- 910-253-4331. **Property tax/Assessor-** 910-253-4351.

Buncombe County

Register of Deeds, 60 Court Plaza, Rm 110, Asheville, NC 28801-3563. 828-250-4300, R/E recording phone-828-250-4305, UCC recording phone-828-250-4302; fax-828-255-5829; hours: 8:30AM-5PM. www.buncombecounty.org No tax liens filed here. Office will perform a UCC search but public must search other records themselves. UCC search per debtor name- $38.00. Copy fee $2.00 per page. Cert fee- $6.25 per cert. **Online access to Assessor, Property Tax, Real Estate, Recording, Marriage, Death, Corporation, Fictitious Name, Deed, UCC records:** Access to county Register of Deeds records is free at http://registerofdeeds.buncombecounty.org/resolution/login.asp. Free registration is required; includes marriages, deaths, fictitious names, deeds. Also, county assessor tax records are free at www.buncombetax.org/lookup/default.html Also, Secretary of State UCC site is www.secretary.state.nc.us/ucc/. **Other phones:** Appraiser/Auditor- 828-250-4900; Elections- 828-250-4200; Vital Records- 828-250-4301. **Property tax/Assessor-** 828-250-4940.

Burke County

Register of Deeds, PO Box 936, Morganton, NC 28680. 828-438-5450, UCC recording phone-828-438-5456; fax-828-438-5463; hours: 8AM-5PM. www.co.burke.nc.us No tax liens filed here. Index: In books. Records indexed on a public use terminal back to 1988. Office will perform a UCC search but public must search other records themselves. Search fee $38.00. Copy fee $.15 per page. Cert fee- $5.00 per page plus $2.00 each add'l copy. Payee- Burke County Register of Deeds. **Online access to Property, Assessor records:** Access to the property information is free on the GIS mapping site at http://arcims.webgis.net/nc/Burke/default.asp. To name search click on Quick Search. **Other phones:** Treasurer- 828-438-5446; Appraiser/Auditor- 828-438-5403; Elections- 828-433-1703; Vital Records- 828-438-5453; Liens/Judgments- 828-432-2804. **Property tax/Assessor-** 828-438-5444.

Cabarrus County

Register of Deeds, PO Box 707, Concord, NC 28026. 704-920-2112; fax-704-920-2898; hours: 8AM-5PM. www.cabarruscounty.us No tax liens filed here. All records in one index. Records indexed on a public use terminal back to 1983. Office will perform a UCC search but public must search other records themselves. UCC search per debtor name- $30.00. Copy fee $.25 per page. Cert fee- $5.00 1st page, $2.00 each add'l page, including copies. **Online access to Assessor, Real Estate, Recorder, Deed, Lien, Grantor/Grantee, UCC, Tax Roll, Deliq Tax list records:** Access to the recorder records is free at www.cabarrusncrod.org by two methods: full system or image-only system. You can name search the former; book & page number required for the latter. Land records go back to 1983; images to 2001. Also, search the tax assessor database for free online at http://166.82.128.222/ParcelInfo.html. Also, search the tax bill scroll for free at http://co.cabarrus.nc.us/TaxScroll/index.html. Also, search delinquent tax list free at

www.cabarruscounty.us/Pages/Tax/DelinquenttaxListing.pdf. **Property tax/Assessor-** 704-920-2166.

Caldwell County

Register of Deeds, 905 West Ave N.W.; County Office Bldg, Lenoir, NC 28645. 828-757-1399, R/E recording phone-828-757-1311; fax-828-757-1294; hours: 8AM-5PM. www.co.caldwell.nc.us No tax liens filed here. Records indexed on a public use terminal back to 1971. Only the public may search. Copy fee $1.00 per page. Cert fee- $5.00 1st page, $2.00 each add'l page includes copy fee. Payee- Register of Deeds. **Online access to Property, Assessor, Real Estate, Birth, Death, Marriage, Notary, Business Name records:** Records on the county GIS map server site are free at http://maps.co.caldwell.nc.us. Click on "Start Spatial-data Explorer" then find query field at bottom of next page. Also, access to register of deeds recording data is for free at http://rod.co.caldwell.nc.us/resolution/. Choose advanced or simple search; online registration is required. **Other phones:** Vital Records- 828-757-1310.

Camden County

Register of Deeds, PO Box 190, Camden, NC 27921. 252-338-1919; fax-225-338-1758; hours: 8AM-5PM. No tax liens filed here. Records indexed on a public use terminal back to 1998. Only the public may search. Copy fee $1.00 per page. Cert fee- $5.00 per cert. Payee- Camden County Register of Deeds. **Property tax/Assessor-** 252-338-0066.

Carteret County

Register of Deeds, Courthouse Sq, Beaufort, NC 28516-1898. 252-728-8474; fax-252-728-7693; hours: 8AM-5PM. www.co.carteret.nc.us No tax liens filed here. Office will perform a UCC search but public must search other records themselves. UCC search per debtor name- $38.00. Copy fee $1.00 per page. Cert fee- $5.00 add'l $2.00 per page. Payee- Carteret County Register of Deeds. **Other phones:** Vital Records- 252-728-8474.

Caswell County

Register of Deeds, PO Box 98, Yanceyville, NC 27379. 336-694-4197; fax-336-694-1405; hours: 8AM-5PM. www.caswellrod.org All records in one index. Records indexed on computer back to 10/2000. Office will perform a UCC search but public must search other records themselves. Search fee $38.00. Copy fee $1.00 per page. R/E record copy- $.50 per page. Cert fee- $5.00 1st pg, $2.00 each add'l plus copy fee. Payee- Caswell County Register of Deeds. **Online access to Property, Map, Grantor/Grantee records:** Access property data free at http://arcims.webgis.net/nc/caswell/. Also, to search for grantor/grantee (online documents) for free go to www.caswellrod.com/index.html. **Property tax/Assessor-** 336-694-4194.

Catawba County

Register of Deeds, PO Box 65, Newton, NC 28658-0065. 828-465-1573; fax-828-465-1573; hours: 8AM-5PM. www.catawbacountync.gov No tax liens filed here. All records in one index. Office will perform a UCC search but public must search other records themselves. Copy fee $.50 per page; self serve $.25. Cert fee- $5.00 1st page, $2.00 each add'l page. Payee- Catawba County Register of Deeds. **Online access to Assessor, Property, Grantor/Grantee, Real Estate, Deed records:** Records on the Catawba County Geographic Information System database are free at www.gis.catawba.nc.us/. Click on "Online Mapping" then choose "Real Estate" then search using query fields. Also, access register of deeds information free at http://204.211.226.33/rod/index.html. **Other phones:** Elections- 828-464-2424. **Property tax/Assessor-** 828-465-8421.

Chatham County

Register of Deeds, PO Box 756, Pittsboro, NC 27312. 919-542-8235; hours: 8AM-4:30PM. www.chathamncrod.org No tax liens filed here. Separate indices to search include grantor/grantee, index books. Records indexed on a public use terminal back to 1987. Office will perform a UCC search but public must search other records themselves. UCC search per debtor name- $30.00. Copy fee $1.00 per page. R/E record copy- $.25 per page. Cert fee- $5.00 1st pg, $2.00 each add'l includes copy fee. Payee- Chatham County Register of Deeds. **Other phones:** Treasurer- 919-542-8210; Appraiser/Auditor- 919-542-8287; Elections- 919-542-8206; Vital Records- 919-542-8235; County Manager- 919-542-8200. **Property tax/Assessor-** 919-542-8250.

Cherokee County

Register of Deeds, 53 Peachtree St, Murphy, NC 28906. 828-837-2613; fax-828-837-8414; www.cherokeecounty-nc.org No tax liens filed here. Office will perform a UCC search but public must search other records themselves. UCC search per debtor name- $30.00. Copy fee $.25 per page. Cert fee- $5.00 per doc plus copy fee. **Other phones:** Elections- 828-837-6670. **Property tax/Assessor-** 828-837-6626.

Chowan County

Register of Deeds, PO Box 487, Edenton, NC 27932-0487. 252-482-2619; hours: 8AM-5PM. No tax liens filed here. All records in one index. Office will perform a UCC search but public must search other records themselves. UCC search per debtor name- $38.00. Copy fee $.25 per page; $.50 if mailed; $2.00 each if UCC page. R/E record copy- $.50 per page. Cert fee- $5.00 1st pg, $2.00 each add'l. Payee- Chowan County Register of Deeds. **Property tax/Assessor-** PO Box 1030, Edenton, NC 27932; 252-482-8486.

Clay County

Register of Deeds, PO Box 118, Hayesville, NC 28904. 828-389-0087; fax-828-389-9749; hours: 8AM-5PM. No tax liens filed here. All records in one index. Records indexed on a public use terminal back to 1995. Office will perform a UCC search but public must search other records themselves. UCC search per debtor name- $38.00. Copy fee $1.00 per page. R/E record copy- $.25 per page. Cert fee- $5.00 1st pg, $2.00 each add'l includes copy fee. Payee- Clay County Register of Deeds. **Online access to Land, Property, Assessor, Recorder, Deed records:** Access to property and deeds indexes and images is via a private company at www.titlesearcher.com. Fee/registration required. **Property tax/Assessor-** 828-389-1266.

Cleveland County

Register of Deeds, PO Box 1210, Shelby, NC 28151-1210. 704-484-4834; fax-704-484-4909; hours: 8AM-5PM. www.clevelandcounty.com No tax liens filed here. All records in one index. Office will perform a UCC search but public must search other records themselves. Search fee $30.00. Copy fee $1.00 per page. Cert fee- $5.00 per page, $2.00 each add'l. Payee- Cleveland County Register of Deeds. **Online access to Real Estate, Assessor, Real Estate, Grantor/Grantee records:** Access to property data free at http://arcims2.webgis.net/nc/Cleveland/default.asp. Also, access to grantor/grantee index is free at http://cleveland.parker-lowe.net/view/softlic.html. **Other phones:** Treasurer- 704-484-4807; Vital Records- 704-484-4834. **Property tax/Assessor-** same address as above. 704-484-4847.

Columbus County

Register of Deeds, PO Box 1086, Whiteville, NC 28472-1086. 910-640-6625; fax-910-640-2547; hours: 8:30AM-5PM.

No tax liens filed here. Only the public may search. Copy fee $1.00 per page. Cert fee- $5.00. Payee- Columbus County Register of Deeds. **Online access to Recording, Deed, Lien, Real Estate, Assumed Name, Corporation, UCC records:** Access to the Recorder's database is free at http://216.64.106.43/. User-ID is "public" and you should be able to logon for free. **Property tax/Assessor**- 910-640-6635.

Craven County

Register of Deeds, 226 Pollock St, New Bern, NC 28560. 252-636-6617; fax-252-636-1937; hours: 8AM-5PM. www.co.craven.nc.us
No tax liens filed here. All records in one index. Records indexed on a public use terminal back to 1995. Office will perform a UCC search but public must search other records themselves. Search fee $38.00. Copy fee $1.00 per page. R/E record copy- $.25 per page. Cert fee- $5.00 per doc plus copy fee. Payee- Register of Deeds. **Online access to Real Estate, Recording, Deed, Tax Assessor, Boat, Mobile Home, Foreclosure, GIS records:** Access to the county Public Inquiry System is free at www.co.craven.nc.us/depts/reg/regwwwdisclaimer.htm . Also, access to assessor and property data is free at http://gismaps2.cravencounty.com/maps/map.asp.
Other phones: Treasurer- 252-636-6603; Appraiser/Auditor- 252-636-6640; Elections- 252-636-6610; Vital Records- 252-636-6617. **Property tax/Assessor**- same address as above. 252-636-6605.

Cumberland County

Register of Deeds, PO 2039, Fayetteville, NC 28302-2039. 910-678-7775, R/E recording phone-910-678-7783, UCC recording phone-910-678-7718; fax-910-323-1456; hours: 8AM-5PM. www.ccrod.org
No tax liens filed here. Records indexed on computer back to 1978. Office will perform a UCC search but public must search other records themselves. UCC search per debtor name- $30.00. Copy fee $1.00 per page. Cert fee- $5.00 1st pg, $2.00 each add'l, includes copy fee. Payee- Cumberland County Register of Deeds. **Online access to Land, Deed, Recording, UCC, Property Tax, Assessor, GIS records:** Search two systems free at www.ccrodinternet.org. The land records index and images go back to 1978; images go back to 1/21/1972; UCCs are from 1995 to 6/29/2001. Also, the county tax assessor real estate search is free at http://mainfr.co.cumberland.nc.us/oasearch.htm. Also, search property data free on the GIS mapping site at http://152.31.99.8/. Click on Search on the Parcel Viewer. **Other phones:** Appraiser/Auditor- 910-678-7507; Elections- 910-678-7733; Vital Records- 910-678-7767. **Property tax/Assessor**- 117 Dick St, Rm 530, Fayetteville, NC 28302; 910-678-7507, assessor fax-910-678-7582.

Currituck County

Register of Deeds, PO Box 71, Currituck, NC 27929. 252-232-3297; fax-252-232-3906; hours: 8AM-5PM. www.visitcurrituck.com
No tax liens filed here. Records indexed on computer back to 8/1977. Office will perform a UCC search but public must search other records themselves. UCC search per debtor name- $30.00. Copy fee $1.00 per page. R/E record copy- $.25 per page. $1.00 per page to mail. Cert fee- $5.00 per cert, $2.00 per page. Payee- Currituck County Register of Deeds. **Property tax/Assessor**- 252-232-3005.

Dare County

Register of Deeds, PO Box 70, Manteo, NC 27954. 252-473-3438, R/E recording phone-252-475-5970; hours: 8:30AM-5PM. www.co.dare.nc.us
No tax liens filed here. All records in one index. Will not search real estate records. Will search UCC records prior to 7/2001 and current fixture (land) files. UCC search per debtor name- $38.00. Copy fee $1.00 per page. R/E record copy- $.25 per page. Cert fee-$5.00 per cert plus copy fee. Payee- Dare County Register of Deeds. **Online access to Assessor, Real**

Estate, Marriage, UCC records: Assessor records are at www.co.dare.nc.us/public/TaxInquiry.htm. Other records are free at www.co.dare.nc.us/public/index.htm. Real estate from 1976 forward, UCC from 1989 forward, and marriage from 1990 forward. Additionally, tax files can be downloaded from this site.
Other phones: Treasurer- 252-475-5930; Appraiser/Auditor- 252-475-5940; Elections- 252-475-5630; Vital Records- 252-475-5970. **Property tax/Assessor**- PO Box 1000, Manteo, NC 27954; 252-475-5952.

Davidson County

Register of Deeds, PO Box 464, Lexington, NC 27293-0464. 336-242-2150; fax-336-238-2318; hours: 8AM-5PM. www.co.davidson.nc.us
No tax liens filed here. All records in one index. Records indexed on a public use terminal back to 1990. Only the public may search. Copy fee $1.00 per page. R/E record copy- $1.00 1st page, $.25 each add'l page. Cert fee- $5.00 per doc includes copy fee. Payee- Register of deeds. **Online access to Property, Assessor, Real Estate records:** Records on the county Tax Dept database are free at www.co.davidson.nc.us/Tax/1252.asp. Also, search for property info on the GIS mapping site for free at http://arcims2.webgis.net/davidson/default.asp. To name search click on Quick Search. **Other phones:** Vital Records- 336-242-2150.

Davie County

Register of Deeds, 123 S. Main St, Mocksville, NC 27028. 336-634-2513; hours: 8:30AM-5PM. www.co.davie.nc.us
No tax liens filed here. Office will perform a UCC search but public must search other records themselves. UCC search per debtor name- $30.00. Copy fee $.25 per page. Cert fee- $5.00 1st pg, $2.00 each add'l. Payee- Davie County Register of Deeds. **Online access to Real Estate, GIS-mapping records:** Access to county property data on the GIS-mapping site is free at www.roktech.net/DavieNC/. Click on "Start Spatial Data Explorer" then search at bottom of page. **Property tax/Assessor**- 336-634-3416.

Duplin County

Register of Deeds, PO Box 970, Kenansville, NC 28349. 910-296-2108; fax-910-296-2344; hours: 8AM-5PM. http://rod.duplincounty.org
No tax liens filed here. All records in one index. Records indexed on a public use terminal back to 1982. Office will perform a UCC search but public must search other records themselves. Search fee $30.00. Copy fee $1.00 by mail, $.25 per page in person. Cert fee- $5.00 1st page; $2.00 each add'l page. Payee- Register of Deeds. **Online access to Real Property, Deed, Mortgage, Marriage, Death, Notary, Military Discharge records:** Access to the Register's multiple databases is free at http://rod.duplincounty.org. **Other phones:** Treasurer-910-296-2104; Appraiser/Auditor- 910-296-2110; Elections- 910-296-2170; Vital Records- 910-296-2108. **Property tax/Assessor**- 910-296-2110.

Durham County

Register of Deeds, PO Box 1107, Durham, NC 27702. 919-560-0480; fax-919-560-0497; hours: 8:30AM-5PM. www.co.durham.nc.us
No tax liens filed here. Records indexed on a public use terminal. Office will perform a UCC search but public must search other records themselves. UCC search per debtor name- $30.00. Copy fee $1.00 per page; from computer $.10. Cert fee-$5.00 1st page, $2.00 per add'l page. Payee- Register of Deeds. **Online access to Real Estate, Deed, Judgment, Recording, Voter Registration, Feeod/Lodging, GIS, Inmate records:** Access to the Register of Deeds database is free at http://207.4.222.118 or http://rodweb.co.durham.nc.us/. Access to the tax assessor data is free at www.co.durham.nc.us/departments/txad/TaxDB/. Search property records from the GIS mapping site free

at http://gisweb2.ci.durham.nc.us/sdx/. After the disclaimer, click on "Spatial Data Explorer" to search. Also, search voter registration free at www.co.durham.nc.us/departments/elec/votersearch/VoterRecSearch.cfm. Find all searchable record types at www.co.durham.nc.us/common/PublRecordsdB.cfm.
Other phones: Vital Records- 919-560-7670 (births/deaths); Vital Records (Marriages)- 919-560-0480. **Property tax/Assessor**- 200 E Main St, Durham, NC 27702; 919-560-0300.

Edgecombe County

Register of Deeds, PO Box 386, Tarboro, NC 27886. 252-641-7924; fax-252-641-1771; hours: 7:30AM-5:30PM M-TH; 7:30AM-5PM F.
No tax liens filed here. All records in one index. Office will perform a UCC search but public must search other records themselves. UCC search per debtor name- $38.00 1-2 pcs, 3-10 $45.00, $2.00 ea addl pg. Copy fee $.10 per sheet, $.25 per page. R/E record copy- $1.00 2st page; $.10 each add'l page if SASE provided. Cert fee- $5.00 1st page; $2.00 each add'l page includes copy fee. Payee- Register of Deeds. **Other phones:** Treasurer- 252-641-7834; Appraiser/Auditor- 252-641-7858; Elections- 252-641-7854; Vital Records- 252-641-7924. **Property tax/Assessor**- 201 St. Andrew St, Tarboro, NC 27886; 252-641-7855.

Forsyth County

Register of Deeds, PO Box 20639, Winston-Salem, NC 27120-0639. 336-703-2700; fax-336-727-2341; hours: 8AM-5PM. www.forsyth.cc
No tax liens filed here. All records in one index. Records indexed on a public use terminal back to 1965. Office will perform a UCC search but public must search other records themselves. UCC search per debtor name- $30.00. Copy fee $1.00 per page. Cert fee- No fee for certification plus copy fee. Payee- Forsyth County Register of Deeds. **Online access to Real Estate, Recording, Property, Deed, Lien, Lien List, Voter Registration records:** Access to the county Geo-Data Explorer database is free online at www.co.forsyth.nc.us/Tax/geodata.aspx. Click on "Launch Geo-Data Explorer." Address and Parcel ID searching only. Includes Board of Adjustment and building permit records. Also, Register of Deed records are on CD-ROM. Also, search tax liens by name lists free at www.forsyth.cc/Tax/advertisement.aspx. Search voter registration records free at www.co.forsyth.nc.us/elections/voterLookup.aspx. Also, access to property and deeds indexes and images is via a private company at www.titlesearcher.com or support@TitleSearcher.com. Fee/registration required; monthly and per day access available. **Other phones:** Treasurer- 336-727-2655; Vital Records- 336-703-2700. **Property tax/Assessor**- 336-703-2300.

Franklin County

Register of Deeds, PO Box 545, Louisburg, NC 27549-0545. 919-496-3500; fax-919-496-1457; hours: 8AM-5PM. www.co.franklin.nc.us
No tax liens filed here. All records in one index. Records indexed on a public use terminal back to January 1, 1979. Office will perform a UCC search but public must search other records themselves. UCC search per debtor name- $30.00. Copy fee $1.00 per page. R/E record copy- $.25 per page. Cert fee- $2.00 per notary plus copy fee. **Online access to Real Property records:** Access to the county spatial data explorer database is free at www.co.franklin.nc.us/docs/frame_tax.htm. Search the gis map or click on "text search" for name searching. **Other phones:** Elections- 919-496-3710. **Property tax/Assessor**- 919-496-1497.

Gaston County

Register of Deeds, PO Box 1578, Gastonia, NC 28053. 704-862-7681, R/E recording phone-704-866-3181, UCC recording phone-704-862-7583; fax-704-862-7519; hours: 8:30AM-5PM. www.co.gaston.nc.us
No tax liens filed here. Separate indices to search include Corporations, Ordinances, and Vital

Records. Records indexed on a public use terminal back to 1960 real estate. Only the public may search. Copy fee $1.00 per page. Cert fee- $5.00 for 1st pg, $2.00 each add'l pg. Payee- Gaston County Register of Deeds. **Other phones:** Treasurer- 704-866-3034; Appraiser/Auditor- 704-810-5809; Elections- 704-864-5858; Vital Records- 704-862-7687; Deed Room- 704-862-7683. **Property tax/Assessor-** same address. 704-810-5838.

Gates County

Register of Deeds, PO Box 471, Gatesville, NC 27938-0471. 252-357-0850; fax-252-357-0850; hours: 9AM-5PM.
No tax liens filed here. Office will perform a UCC search but public must search other records themselves. UCC search per debtor name- $30.00. **Other phones:** Treasurer- 252-357-1240; Appraiser/Auditor- 252-357-1360; Elections- 252-357-1780; Vital Records- 252-357-0850. **Property tax/Assessor-** 252-357-1360.

Graham County

Register of Deeds, PO Box 406, Robbinsville, NC 28771-0406. 828-479-7971; fax-828-479-7971; hours: 8;30AM-5PM.
All records in one index. Only the public may search. Copy fee $1.00 per page. Cert fee- $5.00 per page plus $2.00 each add'l. **Other phones:** Treasurer- 828-479-7962; Appraiser/Auditor- 828-479-7963; Elections- 828-479-7969; Vital Records- 828-479-7971. **Property tax/Assessor-** 828-479-7965.

Granville County

Register of Deeds, PO Box 427, Oxford, NC 27565. 919-693-6314; hours: 8:30AM-5PM.
No tax liens filed here. All records in one index. Records indexed on a public use terminal back to 1975. Office will perform a UCC search for records prior to 7/2001, but public must search other records themselves. UCC search per debtor name- $30.00. Copy fee $1.00 per page. R/E record copy- $1.00 1st page, $.25 each add'l page. Cert fee- $5.00 1st page, $2.00 each add'l page. Payee- Register of Deeds. **Other phones:** Treasurer- 919-603-1301 (Finance); Elections- 919-693-2515; Vital Records- 919-693-6314. **Property tax/Assessor-** 919-693-4181.

Greene County

Register of Deeds, PO Box 86, Snow Hill, NC 28580. 252-747-3620, R/E recording phone-919-747-3620; hours: 8AM-5PM.
No tax liens filed here. All records in one index. Record index not computerized. Only the public may search. Copy fee $1.00 per page. Cert fee- $5.00 1st pg, $2.00 each add'l. Payee- Greene County Register of Deeds.

Guilford County

Register of Deeds, PO Box 1467, High Point, NC 27261-1467. 336-845-7931, R/E recording phone-336-845-6935; hours: 8AM-5PM. www.guilforddeeds.com
No tax liens filed here. All records in one index. Records indexed on a public use terminal back to 1982. Office will perform a UCC search but public must search other records themselves. UCC search per debtor name- $30.00. Copy fee $1.00 per page. Cert fee- $5.00 1st page, $2.00 each add'l plus copy fee. Payee- Guilford County Register of Deeds. **Online access to Recorder, Assessor, Property, UCC, Vital Statistic records:** Access to the county e-gov databases is free at www.co.guilford.nc.us/egov/index.html. Also, you may search Birth, Death, Marriage, and military records directly at www.co.guilford.nc.us/novation/rodvrpub.html. Search page found at www.co.guilford.nc.us/government/deeds/. **Other phones:** Appraiser/Auditor- 336-845-3330; Elections- 336-845-3836; Vital Records- 336-845-7931. **Property tax/Assessor-** same address. 336-845-7911.

Halifax County

Register of Deeds, PO Box 67, Halifax, NC 27839-0067. 252-583-2101; fax-252-583-1273; hours: 8:30AM-5PM. www.halifaxnc.com/halinav.html
No tax liens filed here. All records in one index. Records indexed on a public use terminal back to 1976. Office will perform a UCC search but public must search other records themselves. UCC search per debtor name- $38.00. Copy fee $.25 per page. Cert fee- $5.00 1st page, $2.00 each add'l page plus copy fee. Payee- Register of Deeds. **Other phones:** Treasurer- 252-583-3771; Appraiser/Auditor- 252-583-2121; Elections- 252-583-4391; Vital Records- 252-583-2101. **Property tax/Assessor-** same address as above. 252-583-2121.

Harnett County

Register of Deeds, 305 W Cornelius Harnett Blvd #200, Lillington, NC 27546. 910-893-7540; fax-910-814-3841; hours: 8AM-5PM. http://rod.harnett.org
No tax liens filed here. All records in one index. Records indexed on a public use terminal back to 1986. Office will perform a UCC search but public must search other records themselves. Search fee $30.00. Copy fee $1.00 per page. R/E record copy-$.10 per page. Cert fee- $5.00 1st pg, $2.00 each add'l. Payee- Harnett County Register of Deeds. **Online access to Real Estate, Grantor/Grantee, Vital Statistic, Military Discharge, UCC records:** County real estate and property tax information is free online at http://rod.harnett.org. Search Births, Deaths, Marriages, military discharges, UCCs and official public records. **Other phones:** Treasurer- 910-893-7557; Elections- 910-893-7553; Vital Records- 910-893-7542. **Property tax/Assessor-** same address as above. 910-893-7520.

Haywood County

Register of Deeds, 215 N Main St; Courthouse, Waynesville, NC 28786. 828-452-6635; fax-828-452-6762; hours: 8AM-5PM. www.haywoodnc.net
No tax liens filed here. All records in one index. Office will perform a UCC search but public must search other records themselves. Search fee $30.00. Copy fee $1.00 per page. Cert fee- None per page plus copy fee. Payee- Haywood County Register of Deeds. **Online access to Real Estate, Deed, Property, GIS-mapping records:** Records on the Register of Deeds database are free at http://rodweb.gov.co.haywood.nc.us. Real estate records go back to 1986. Also, search for property data on the GIS-mapping site for free at www.undersys.com/cweb/haywood.html. **Property tax/Assessor-** same address as above. 828-452-6641.

Henderson County

Register of Deeds, 200 N. Grove St, #129, Hendersonville, NC 28792. 828-697-4901; hours: 9AM-5PM.
No tax liens filed here. All records in one index. Records indexed on a public use terminal back to 1979. Only the public may search. Copy fee $.25 per page. Cert fee- $5.00 1st pg, $2.00 add'l. Payee- Henderson County Register of Deeds. **Online access to Real Estate, GIS-mapping records:** Search property records at the GIS site free at www.hendersoncountync.org/gis/. **Other phones:** Vital Records- 828-697-4901. **Property tax/Assessor-** 828-697-4870.

Hertford County

Register of Deeds, PO Box 36, Winton, NC 27986. 252-358-7850; fax-252-358-7914; hours: 8:30AM-5PM. www.co.hertford.nc.us/
No tax liens filed here. Office will perform a UCC search but public must search other records themselves. UCC search per debtor name- $30.00. **Other phones:** Treasurer- 252-358-7815; Elections- 252-358-7812; Vital Records- 252-358-7850. **Property tax/Assessor-** 252-358-7810.

Hoke County

Register of Deeds, 113 Campus Ave, Raeford, NC 28376. 910-875-2035, UCC recording phone-910-875-0235; fax-910-875-9554; hours: 8AM-5PM. www.hokencrod.org
No tax liens filed here. All records in one index. Records indexed on computer back to late 1992. Office will perform a UCC search but public must search other records themselves. UCC search per debtor name- $30.00. Copy fee $1.00 per page. Cert fee- $5.00 includes copy fee. Payee- Hoke County Register of Deeds. **Online access to Real estate, Recorder, Deed, Lien records:** Access recorder data for free at www.hokencrod.org/Opening.asp. Land records index goes back to 7/1992; images back to 12/1994. **Other phones:** Appraiser/Auditor- 910-875-8751; Elections- 910-875-8751; Vital Records- 910-875-2035. **Property tax/Assessor-** 227 N Main St, Raeford, NC 28376; 910-875-8751.

Hyde County

Register of Deeds, PO Box 294, Swan Quarter, NC 27885. 252-926-4181, R/E recording phone-252-926-3011; fax-252-926-3710; www.hyderod.com
No tax liens filed here. Office will perform a UCC search but public must search other records themselves. UCC search per debtor name- $30.00. Payee- Hyde County Register of Deeds. **Online access to Real Property, Grantor/Grantee records:** Access to the Register of Deeds real property records is free at www.hyderod.com/view/disclaimer.html. **Other phones:** Treasurer- 252-926-4101. **Property tax/Assessor-** 252-926-5151.

Iredell County

Register of Deeds, PO Box 904, Statesville, NC 28687. 704-872-7468; fax-704-878-3055; hours: 8AM-5PM. www.co.iredell.nc.us
No tax liens filed here. Office will perform a UCC search but public must search other records themselves. UCC search per debtor name- $30.00. Copy fee $1.00 per page. Cert fee- $5.00 1st page, $2.00 each add'l page. Payee- Iredell County Register of Deeds. **Online access to Real Estate, Recorder, Vital Statistic, Property Appraisal, Pre-2001 UCC, Permit records:** Access recorder records at www.co.iredell.nc.us/resolution/. Registration required. Also, search property appraisal cards free at www.co.iredell.nc.us/apprcard/. Access county permits and inspection history records free at www.mspection.com/counties/iredell/search.asp. Also, search property data free on the GI-mapping site at www.co.iredell.nc.us/Gismaps.asp. Once on the map page, click on the binoculars to text search. **Property tax/Assessor-** 704-872-3021.

Jackson County

Register of Deeds, 401 Grindstaff Cove Rd. #103, Sylva, NC 28779. 828-586-7530; fax-828-586-6879; hours: 8AM-5PM. www.jacksonnc.org
No tax liens filed here. Separate indices to search. Records indexed on a public use terminal back to 1991. Only the public may search. Copy fee $1.00 per page if mailed; self serve- $.30 per page. R/E record copy- $3.00 per document; $.30 self serve. Cert fee- $5.00 1st page; $2.00 each add'l page. Payee- Register of Deeds. **Other phones:** Treasurer- 828-586-7501; Appraiser/Auditor- 828-586-7542; Vital Records- 828-568-7530. **Property tax/Assessor-** 828-586-4055.

Johnston County

Register of Deeds, PO Box 118, Smithfield, NC 27577. 919-989-5160; fax-919-989-5728; hours: 8AM-5PM. www.johnstonnc.com
No tax liens filed here. Records indexed on a public use terminal back to 1940. Only the public may search. Copy fee $.10 per page. Cert fee- $5.00 1st pg, $2.00 each add'l. Payee- Johnston County Register of Deeds. **Online access to Real Estate, UCC, Deed records:** Access to Register's indexes is free at http://johnstonnc.com/deedsearch. Land records

go back to 1972; UCCs back to 7/1997. **Other phones:** Elections- 919-989-5095; Vital Records- 919-989-5161; Deed Vault- 919-989-5165.

Jones County

Register of Deeds, PO Box 189, Trenton, NC 28585-0189. 252-448-2551; fax-252-448-1357; hours: 8AM-5PM. www.jonesrod.com

No tax liens filed here. All records in one index. Only the public may search, except UCC. Will search UCC records prior to 7/2001 and current fixture (land) files. UCC search per debtor name- $30.00. Copy fee $1.00 per page. R/E record copy- $.25 per page. Cert fee- $5.00 1st pg, $2.00 each add'l, includes copy fee. Payee- Jones County Register of Deeds. **Online access to Real Estate, Deed, GIS, Map records:** Access recorded documents and maps free at www.jonesrod.com/maps.html. **Other phones:** Vital Records- 252-448-2551. **Property tax/Assessor-** 252-448-2546.

Lee County

Register of Deeds, PO Box 2040, Sanford, NC 27331-2040. 919-718-4585, UCC recording phone-919-718-4588; fax-919-718-4586; hours: 8AM-5PM. www.leencrod.org/Opening.asp

No tax liens filed here. All records in one index. Records indexed on computer. Only the public may search. Copy fee $1.00 per page. R/E record copy- $.25 per copy. Cert fee- $5.00 for 1st pg, $2.00 each add'l pg. Payee- Register of Deeds. **Online access to Real Estate, Grantor/Grantee, Deed, Lien records:** Access to the Register of Deeds index and images are free at www.leencrod.org/welcome.asp. Land record index goes back to 1985; images to 1971. Plat images go back to 1975. **Other phones:** Appraiser/Auditor- 919-718-4661; Elections- 919-776-0515; Vital Records- 919-718-4585. **Property tax/Assessor-** 919-718-4600.

Lenoir County

Register of Deeds, PO Box 3289, Kinston, NC 28502. 252-559-6420; fax-252-523-6139; hours: 8:30AM-5PM.

No tax liens filed here. Office will perform a UCC search but public must search other records themselves. UCC search per debtor name- $30.00. Copy fee $1.00 per page. **Other phones:** Treasurer- 252-527-7174; Vital Records- 252-559-6420. **Property tax/Assessor-** 252-527-7174.

Lincoln County

Register of Deeds, PO Box 218, Lincolnton, NC 28093-0218. 704-736-8530, R/E recording phone-704-736-8535, UCC recording phone-704-736-8533; fax-704-732-9049; hours: 8AM-5PM. www.co.lincoln.nc.us

No tax liens filed here. Office will perform a UCC search but public must search other records themselves. UCC search per debtor name- $30.00. Copy fee $1.00 per page. Cert fee- $5.00 per doc plus $2.00 per page. Payee- Register of Deeds. **Online access to Real Estate, Deed, Lien, Mapping, UCC, Property Tax records:** Tax and property information is free at www.lincolncounty.org/County/faq.htm. Enable browser for Java. Grantor/Grantee indices go back to 1993. Images go back to Book 186. Search either of the 2 databases. Also, access to the county GIS Land System is free at www.co.lincoln.nc.us/County/gisd.htm. At the website, under Data Tools, click on Search. **Other phones:** Elections- 704-736-8480; Vital Records- 704-736-8530. **Property tax/Assessor-** 704-736-8540.

Macon County

Register of Deeds, 5 W. Main St, Franklin, NC 28734. 828-349-2095, R/E recording phone-828-524-6421; fax-828-349-6382;

No tax liens filed here. Office will perform a UCC search but public must search other records themselves. UCC search per debtor name- $30.00. **Online access to Property, Deed Image records:**

Access to county property data is free at http://63.167.19.252/dbp/deed.asp. **Other phones:** Elections- 828- 349-2034. **Property tax/Assessor-** 828-524-6421.

Madison County

Register of Deeds, PO Box 66, Marshall, NC 28753. 828-649-3131; hours: 8:30AM-5PM. www.madisonrod.com

No tax liens filed here. Records indexed on a public use terminal back to 1995. Office will perform a UCC search but public must search other records themselves. Search fee $30.00. General copy fee $3.00 1st page, $1.00 each add'l. R/E record copy- $.25 per page. Cert fee- $5.00 1st pg, $2.00 each add'l. Payee- Madison County Register of Deeds. **Online access to Real Estate, Recorder, Grantor/Grantee records:** Access real property records free at www.madisonrod.com/view/disclaimer.html, . **Other phones:** Treasurer- 828-649-2521; Appraiser/Auditor- 828-649-3014; Elections- 828-649-3731; Vital Records- 828-649-3131. **Property tax/Assessor-** 828-649-3014.

Martin County

Register of Deeds, PO Box 348, Williamston, NC 27892. 252-792-1683; fax-252-792-1684; hours: 8AM-5PM.

No tax liens filed here. All records in one index. Office will perform a UCC search (only if a UCC-11 is filed), but public must search other records themselves. UCC search per debtor name- $38.00. Copy fee $.25 per sheet. Cert fee- $5.00 1st page, $2.00 each add'l page plus copy fee. Payee- Martin County Register of Deeds. **Other phones:** Elections- 252-792-5845; Vital Records- 252-792-1683; Collector- 252-792-2167; Finance -252-792-3345. **Property tax/Assessor-** 305 E. Main St, Williamston, NC 27892; 252-792-1031.

McDowell County

Register of Deeds, 21 S. Main St; Courthouse, Marion, NC 28752-3992. 828-652-4727; fax-828-652-1537; hours: 8:30AM-5PM.

No tax liens filed here. Separate indices to search include plats & highway right of ways. Office will perform a UCC search but public must search other records themselves. UCC search per debtor name- $30.00. Copy fee $.35 per page, $1.00 if mailed. Cert fee- $14.00 add'l $3.00 plus copy fee. Payee- McDowell County Register of Deeds. **Online access to Land, Deed records:** Access to property and deeds indexes and images is via a private company at www.titlesearcher.com. Fee/registration required; see state introduction. Images go back to 1/1971. **Other phones:** Treasurer- 828-652-7121; Elections- 828-652-7121; Vital Records- 828-652-4727. **Property tax/Assessor-** 10 E Court St, Marion, NC 28752; 828-652-7121.

Mecklenburg County

Register of Deeds, 720 E. 4th St, #103, Charlotte, NC 28202. 704-336-2443; fax-704-336-7699; hours: 8:30AM-4:30PM. http://meckrod.hartic.com

Office will perform a UCC search but public must search other records themselves. UCC search per debtor name- $30.00. Copy fee $1.00 per page. Cert fee- $4.00 1st pg, $2.00 each add'l. Payee- Mecklenburg County Register of Deeds. **Online access to Assessor, Real Estate, Grantor/Grantee, Judgment, Lien, Vital Statistic, Personal Property, Accident Report records:** Access to birth, death, marriage, recordings, judgments, liens, and grantor/grantee indices are free at http://meckrod.hartic.com/default.asp. There is also a real estate lookup at http://meckcama.co.mecklenburg.nc.us/relookup/. Also, online access to the assessors records for real estate, personal property, and tax bills are free at http://mcmf.co.mecklenburg.nc.us:3007/cics/txar/txar00 i/. Search warrants at http://mcmf.co.mecklenburg.nc.us:3007/cjcr01w/cjjl/we

bnull Sheriff's inmate lookup is at www.charmeck.org/Departments/MCSO/Divisions/In mate+Information/InmateLookup.htm. Accident reports are at http://accident.ci.charlotte.nc.us/index.htm.

Mitchell County

Register of Deeds, 26 Crimson Laurel Cir. #4, Bakersville, NC 28705-9510. 828-688-2139, R/E recording phone-828-688-2139 x318; fax-828-688-3666; hours: 8AM-5PM. www.mitchellrod.com/

No tax liens filed here. All records in one index. Will not search real estate records. Will search UCC records prior to 7/2001 and current fixture (land) files. UCC search per debtor name- $30.00. Copy fee $1.00 per page. Cert fee- $5.00 for 1st page, $2 each add'l (includes copy fee). Payee- Mitchell County Register of Deeds. **Online access to Granter/Grantee Index records:** Search records at www.mitchellrod.com/view/disclaimer.html. **Other phones:** Treasurer- 828-688-2139 x325; Appraiser/Auditor- 828-688-2139 x315; Elections- 828-688-3101; Vital Records- 828-688-2139 x318. **Property tax/Assessor-** 828-688-2139 x315.

Montgomery County

Register of Deeds, PO Box 695, Troy, NC 27371-0695. 910-576-4271; fax-910-576-2209; hours: 8AM-5PM. www.montgomeryrod.com

No tax liens filed here. Office will perform a UCC search but public must search other records themselves. Search fee $38.00. Copy fee $1.00 per page. R/E record copy- $.25 per page. Cert fee- $5.00 1st pg, $3.00 each add'l. Payee- Montgomery County Register of Deeds. **Other phones:** Treasurer- 910-572-4221; Appraiser/Auditor- 910-576-4311; Elections- 910-572-2024; Vital Records- 910-576-4271. **Property tax/Assessor-** PO Box 614, Troy, NC 27371; 910-576-4311.

Moore County

Register of Deeds, PO Box 1210, Carthage, NC 28327. 910-947-6370, R/E recording phone-910-947-6372; fax-910-947-6396; hours: 8AM-5PM. http://rod.moorecountync.gov

No tax liens filed here. All records in one index. Records indexed on a public use terminal back to 7/1/88. Office will perform a UCC search but public must search other records themselves. UCC search per debtor name- $30.00. Copy fee $1.00 per copy. Cert fee- $5.00 1st page, $2.00 each add'l page plus copy fee. **Online access to Real Estate, Lien, Grantor/Grantee, Vital Statistic (no images), Property Tax, Land Record, Restaurant Grade records:** Access to the public record databases at www.co.moore.nc.us/main/page.asp?rec=/pages/proper tyinfo/propertyinfo.asp. Also, access Register of Deeds grantor/grantee index free at http://rod.moorecountync.gov. **Other phones:** Treasurer- 910-947-6310; Appraiser/Auditor- 910-947-6412; Elections- 910-947-3868; Vital Records- 910-947-6370.

Nash County

Register of Deeds, PO Box 974, Nashville, NC 27856. 252-459-9836, UCC recording phone-252-459-9825; fax-252-459-9889; hours: 8AM-4:30PM. www.deeds.co.nash.nc.us

No tax liens filed here. Office will perform a UCC search but public must search other records themselves. UCC search per debtor name- $38.00. Copy fee $1.00 per page. Cert fee- $5.00 1st page, $2.00 each add'l page. **Online access to Real Estate, Real Property, Fixture Filings records:** No fee required but must have your own user ID and password for this site. www.deeds.co.nash.nc.us/resolution . **Other phones:** Vital Records- 252-459-9839. **Property tax/Assessor-** 252-459- 9824.

New Hanover County

Register of Deeds, 216 N. 2nd St, Wilmington, NC 28401. 910-798-4530; fax-910-798-4586; hours: 8AM-5PM. www.nhcgov.com

Until further notice, real estate records are located at 216 N 2nd St. Records indexed on a public use terminal back to 1969. Only the public may search. Copy fee $1.00 per page. Cert fee- $5.00 1st page; $2.00 each add'l page. **Online access to Real Estate, Assessor, Grantor/Grantee, Lien, UCC, Judgment, Marriage, Military Discharge records:** Access to the Register of Deeds database is free at http://srvrodweb.nhcgov.com. Also, online access to the real estate tax database is free at www.nhcgov.com/Oasinq/Oasinput.jsp. Also, you may search for property information on the GIS-mappings site at www.nhcgov.com/GIS/GISservices.asp. **Other phones:** Elections- 910-798-4060; Vital Records- 910-798-4547.

Northampton County

Register of Deeds, PO Box 128, Jackson, NC 27845. 252-534-2511; fax-252-534-1580; hours: 8AM-5PM. No tax liens filed here. Office will perform a UCC search but public must search other records themselves. UCC search per debtor name- $30.00. Copy fee $1.00 per page. R/E record copy- $.25 per page. Cert fee- $5.00 1st pg, $2.00 each add'l. Payee- Northampton County Register of Deeds. **Property tax/Assessor**- 252-534-2511.

Onslow County

Register of Deeds, 109 Old Bridge St, Jacksonville, NC 28540. 910-347-3451; fax-910-347-3340; hours: 8AM-5PM.
http://co.onslow.nc.us/register_of_deeds
No tax liens filed here. Office will perform a old UCC search but public must search other records themselves. UCC search per debtor name- $30.00. Copy fee $1.00 per page. Cert fee- $5.00 1st page, $2 each add'l page. Payee- County Register of Deeds. **Online access to Real Estate, GIS, Assessor records:** Access is to property information is free at www.roktech.net/onslow/. Enter the site and name search using the advanced search in the Parcel Query box. **Property tax/Assessor**- 39 Tallman St, Tax Admin/Collector, Jacksonville, NC 28540; 910-989-2200, assessor fax- 910-455-4579.

Orange County

Register of Deeds, PO Box 8181, Hillsborough, NC 27278-8181. 919-732-8181, R/E recording phone-919-245-2675; fax-919-644-3018; hours: 8AM-5PM. www.co.orange.nc.us/deeds/
No tax liens filed here. Separate indices to search include vital and non-vitals. Records indexed on a public use terminal back to 1932 for non-vitals. Office will perform a UCC search but public must search other records themselves. UCC search per debtor name- $38.00 3 pgs, $45.00 3-10 pgs, $2.00 each add'l pg. Copy fee $1.00 per page. Cert fee- $5.00 1st 5 pages, $.50 each add'l page. **Online access to Property records:** Access to property records on the GIS mapping site is free at http://gis.co.orange.nc.us/gisdisclaimer.htm . **Other phones:** Elections- 919-245-2350. **Property tax/Assessor**- same address. 919-245-2101.

Pamlico County

Register of Deeds, PO Box 433, Bayboro, NC 28515. 252-745-4421; fax-252-745-7020; hours: 8AM-5PM. www.pamlicorod.com
No tax liens filed here. Separate indices to search. Records indexed on a public use terminal back to 6/1/1988. Office will perform a UCC search but public must search other records themselves. UCC search per debtor name- $30.00. Copy fee $1.00 per page. R/E record copy- $.25 per page. Cert fee- $5.00 1st pg, $2.00 each add'l plus copy fee. Payee- Pamlico County Register of Deeds. **Property tax/Assessor**- 252-745-4125 x33.

Pasquotank County

Register of Deeds, PO Box 154, Elizabeth City, NC 27907-0154. 252-335-4367; fax-252-335-5106; hours: 8AM-5PM.

www.co.pasquotank.nc.us/departments/rod/default .htm
No tax liens filed here. Office will perform a UCC search but public must search other records themselves. UCC search per debtor name- $30.00. **Online access to Property, Assessor, Recording, Deed, Grantor/Grantee records:** Access recorder data free at http://pasquotankrod.com/view/disclaimer.html. Also, access to the county tax parcel database is free at http://207.4.214.118/departments/gis/taxsearch.php . **Other phones:** Treasurer- 252-335-4580; Elections- 252-335-1739; Vital Records- 252-335-4367. **Property tax/Assessor**- 252-338-5169.

Pender County

Register of Deeds, PO Box 43, Burgaw, NC 28425. 910-259-1225; fax-910-259-1299; hours: 8AM-4;30PM. www.pender-county.com/Departments/rod/
No tax liens filed here. All records in one index. Records indexed on a public use terminal back to 1/1/1990. Only the public may search. Copy fee $1.00 per page. Cert fee- $5.00 1st page, $2.00 add'l. Payee- Pender County Register of Deeds. **Online access to Property, Assessor, Real Estate, Grantor/Grantee, Deed records:** Access recorder data free with registration at http://pender-county.com/~testsite/. This is a test site; web address may change. Also, access to property data on the Oasis-Webview system is $49.00 per quarter at www.undersys.com/penderord.html. **Other phones:** Elections- 910-259-1225; Vital Records- 910-259-1458. **Property tax/Assessor**- 910-259-1222.

Perquimans County

Register of Deeds, PO Box 74, Hertford, NC 27944. 252-426-5660; fax-252-426-7443; hours: 8AM-5PM. No tax liens filed here. Office will perform a UCC search but public must search other records themselves. UCC search per debtor name- $30.00. Copy fee $1.00 per page. Cert fee- $3.00 1st pg, $1.00 each add'l. Payee- Perquimans County Register of Deeds. **Property tax/Assessor**- 252-426-5564.

Person County

Register of Deeds, Courthouse Sq, Roxboro, NC 27573. 336-597-1733; hours: 8:30AM-5PM. www.personrod.com/
No tax liens filed here. All records in one index. Only the public may search except UCC. Will search UCC records prior to 7/2001. UCC search per debtor name- $30.00. Copy fee $1.00 per page. Cert fee- $5.00 for 1st page; $2.00 each add'l, includes copy fees. Payee- Person County Register of Deeds. **Online access to Real Estate, Recording, Grantor/Grantee records:** Access to county real estate records is free at www.personrod.com/view/disclaimer.html. Index goes back to 1/1/1995. **Other phones:** Elections- 336-597-1727; Vital Records- 336-597-1733; Deed Vault- 336-597-1729. **Property tax/Assessor**- Courthouse Sq, Rm 102, Roxboro, NC 27573; 336-597-1712.

Pitt County

Register of Deeds, PO Box 35, Greenville, NC 27835-0035. 252-902-1650, R/E recording phone-252-830-4138; hours: 8AM-5PM. www.co.pitt.nc.us/depts/
No tax liens filed here. Office will perform a UCC search but public must search other records themselves. UCC search per debtor name- $30.00. Copy fee $1.00 per page. Cert fee- $5.00 1st pg, $2.00 each add'l. Payee- Pitt County Register of Deeds. **Property tax/Assessor**- 252-830-4138.

Polk County

Register of Deeds, PO Box 308, Columbus, NC 28722. 828-894-8450; fax-828-894-5781; hours: 8:30-5PM. www.polkrod.com
No tax liens filed here. Records indexed on a public use terminal back to 1994. Only the public may search. Copy fee $.25 per page. Cert fee- $5.00 per

page plus copy fee. Payee- Polk County Register of Deeds. **Other phones:** Treasurer- 828-894-8500. **Property tax/Assessor**- 828-894-8500.

Randolph County

Register of Deeds, PO Box 4458, Asheboro, NC 27204. 336-318-6960; hours: 8AM-5PM. www.co.randolph.nc.us
No tax liens filed here. All records in one index. Records indexed. Office will perform a UCC search but public must search other records themselves. Will not search real estate records. UCC search per debtor name- $30.00. Copy fee $1.00 per page. R/E record copy- $.50 per page. Cert fee- $5.00 1st page, $2.00 each add'l page. Payee- Randolph County Register of Deeds. **Online access to Real Property records:** Access to the county GIS database is free at www.co.randolph.nc.us/gis.htm. In the "Search functions" on the map page, click on "parcel owner." Real Estate records access at www.randrod.com. **Other phones:** Vital Records- 336-318-6960. **Property tax/Assessor**- 725 McDowell Rd, Asheboro, NC 27204; not known.

Richmond County

Register of Deeds, 114 E Franklin St,; #101, Rockingham, NC 28379-3601. 910-997-8250; fax-910-997-8499; hours: 8AM-5PM.
No tax liens filed here. All records in one index, except Military Discharges. Records indexed on a public use terminal back to 1995. Office will perform a UCC search but public must search other records themselves. Search fee $30.00. Copy fee $1.00 per page. Cert fee- $5.00 1st page; $2.00 each add'l page. Payee- Register of Deeds. **Online access to Property records:** Access to County property records is via a subscription service; registration and fees are required. For information, call 334-344-3333. **Other phones:** Elections- 910-997-8254; Vital Records- 910 997-8251. **Property tax/Assessor**- P O Box 1644, Rockingham, NC 28379; 910-997-8274.

Robeson County

Register of Deeds, 500 N. Elm St; Courthouse, Rm 102, Lumberton, NC 28358. 910-671-3046, R/E recording phone-910-671-3043, UCC recording phone-910-671-3046; fax-910-671-3041; hours: 8:15AM-5:15PM. http://rod.co.robeson.nc.us
No tax liens filed here. Index: UCCs in Real Estate Fixture Filings only after 7/1/2001; prior UCCs in separate file. Records indexed on a public use terminal. Office will perform a search of UCC records prior to 7/2001 and current fixture (land) files, but public must search other records themselves. UCC search per debtor name- $38.00 per request. Price vary by the amount of requests. Copy fee $1.00 per page. **Online access to Real Estate, Recorder, Deed, Grantor/Grantee, Land, Property, Assessor records:** Access to recorder data is free at http://rod.co.robeson.nc.us/search.php. Also, Assessor is planning to have property records available through a GIS-mapping site; check at www.co.robeson.nc.us/departments/tax/index.htm. Also, access to property and deeds indexes and images is via a private company at www.titlesearcher.com. Fee/registration required. **Other phones:** Elections- 910-671-3080; Vital Records- 910-671-4045; Deed Vault- 910-671-3049. **Property tax/Assessor**- 500 N. Elm St #101, Lumberton, NC 28358; 910-671-3060.

Rockingham County

Register of Deeds, PO Box 56, Wentworth, NC 27375-0056. 336-342-8820; fax-336-342-6209; hours: 8AM-5PM. www.rockinghamcorod.org
No tax liens filed here. Office will perform a UCC search but public must search other records themselves. UCC search per debtor name- $30.00. Copy fee $1.00 per page. R/E record copy- $.25 per sheet. Cert fee- $5.00 1st pg, $2.00 each add'l. Payee- Rockingham County Register of Deeds. **Online access to Land, Grantor/Grantee, Judgment,**

Tax Sale, Property, GIS records: Access to Register of Deeds database is free at www.rockinghamcorod.org. Land indexes 1996 to present; and record images 1984 to present; plats 1907 to present. Also, online access to real estate (1996 forward) and tax appraiser data is free at www.co.rockingham.nc.us/taxinfo2.html. Also, search property data free at the GIS site at http://arcims.webgis.net/nc/rockingham/default.asp. To name search, click on Quick Search. Also, online access to the tax sales property is at www.co.rockingham.nc.us/forecl.htm. **Other phones:** Treasurer- 336-342-8120; Appraiser/Auditor- 336-342-8280; Elections- 336-342-8107; Vital Records- 336-342-8820. **Property tax/Assessor-** 336-342-8280.

Rowan County

Register of Deeds, PO Box 2568, Salisbury, NC 28145. 704-638-3102; hours: 8AM-5PM. www.co.rowan.nc.us/rod
No tax liens filed here. All records in one index. Records indexed on a public use terminal back to 1975. Only the public may search. Copy fee $1.00 per page. R/E record copy- $.50 per page. Cert fee- $5.00 1st pg, $2.00 each add'l. Payee- Rowan County Register of Deeds. **Online access to Real Estate, Recording, Property records:** Access to the Register of Dees land records database is free at http://rod.co.rowan.nc.us. Records go back to 1975; financing statements back to 1993; images back to 2000 (eventually to 1990). Also, access to the county GIS mapping site is free at http://arcims2.webgis.net/nc/Rowan/default.asp. To name search click on Quick Search. **Other phones:** Treasurer- 704-633-3871; Elections- 704-633-6231. **Property tax/Assessor-** 704-633-4601.

Rutherford County

Register of Deeds, PO Box 551, Rutherfordton, NC 28139. 828-287-6155; fax-828-287-1229; hours: 8:30AM-5PM.
No tax liens filed here. All records in one index. Records indexed on a public use terminal back to 1974. Only the public may search. Copy fee $1.00 per page. Cert fee- $5.00 per cert plus copy fee. Payee- Rutherford County Register of Deeds. **Online access to Property, Tax Map records:** Access property data free at http://arcims.webgis.net/nc/rutherford/. **Property tax/Assessor-** 828-287-6215.

Sampson County

Register of Deeds, Main St.; Courthouse, Rm 107, Clinton, NC 28329. 910-592-8026; fax-910-592-1803; hours: 8AM-5PM. www.sampsonrod.org
No tax liens filed here. All records in one index. Records indexed on a public use terminal back to 1988. Office will perform a UCC search but public must search other records themselves. UCC search per debtor name- $38.00. Copy fee $1.00 per page. R/E record copy- $.50 per page. Cert fee- $5.00 1st page; $2.00 each add'l page plus copy fee. Payee- Sampson County Register of Deeds. **Online access to Real Estate, Recorder, Deed, Grantor/Grantee records:** Access to county Register of Deeds land data is free at www.sampsonrod.org. Index goes back to 1988. **Other phones:** Vital Records- 910-592-8026.

Scotland County

Register of Deeds, PO Box 769, Laurinburg, NC 28353. 910-277-2575, UCC recording phone-910 277-2575; fax-910-277-3185; hours: 8AM-5PM.
No tax liens filed here. Office will perform a UCC search but public must search other records themselves. UCC search per debtor name- $30.00. Copy fee $1.00 per copy. R/E record copy- $.25 per page. Cert fee- $5.00 1st page; $2.00 each add'l page. Payee- Scotland County Register of Deeds. **Other phones:** Treasurer- 910-277-2410; Appraiser/Auditor- 910-277-2566; Elections- 910-277-2595; Vital Records- 910-277-2575. **Property tax/Assessor-** 910-277-3270.

Stanly County

Register of Deeds, PO Box 97, Albemarle, NC 28002-0097. 704-986-3640; hours: 8:30AM-5PM. www.co.stanly.nc.us
No tax liens filed here. Only the public may search, except UCC. Will not search real estate records. Will search UCC records prior to 7/2001. UCC search per debtor name- $38.00. Copy fee $1.00 per page. Cert fee- $5.00 1st pg, $2.00 each add'l. Payee- Stanly County Register of Deeds. **Online access to Real Estate, Grantor/Grantee, Deed records:** Access the Register of Deeds index at http://66.101.143.145/login.asp?password=stqn342&accountid=stanlyhome. **Other phones:** Treasurer- 704-986-3618; Appraiser/Auditor- 704-986-3629; Elections- 704-986-3647; Vital Records- 704-986-3640. **Property tax/Assessor-** 704-586-3626.

Stokes County

Register of Deeds, PO Box 67, Danbury, NC 27016. 336-593-2811; fax-336-593-9360; hours: 8:30AM-5PM. www.stokescorod.org
No tax liens filed here. All records in one index. Records indexed on a public use terminal back to1993. Office will perform a UCC search but public must search other records themselves. Will search UCC records prior to 7/2001 and current fixture (land) files only. UCC search per debtor name- $38.00. Copy fee $1.00 per page. R/E record copy- $.50 per page by mail, $.25 in person. Cert fee- $5.00 1st page; $2.00 each add'l page. Payee- Register of Deeds. **Online access to Grantor/Grantee, Deed, UCC, Property records:** Access to the Register of Deeds Remote Access site is free at www.stokescorod.org/welcome.asp. Land records go back to 1993, images to mid-1970; UCCs back to 1994. Also, access to property info on the GIS mapping site is free at http://arcims2.webgis.net/stokes/default.asp. To name search click on Quick Search. **Other phones:** Appraiser/Auditor- 336-593-2811; Elections- 336-593-2811; Vital Records- 336-593-2811. **Property tax/Assessor-** 336-593-2811.

Surry County

Register of Deeds, PO Box 303, Dobson, NC 27017-0303. 336-401-8150, R/E recording phone-336-386-9201; fax-336-401-8151; hours: 8:15AM-5PM. www.co.surry.nc.us
No tax liens filed here. Separate indices to search include real estate, vitals. Only the public may search. Copy fee $1.00 per page. **Online access to Property, Tax Map records:** Access property data free at http://arcims.webgis.net/nc/surry/default.asp. Click on Quicksearch. Tax maps also located at this site. **Other phones:** Treasurer- 336-386-9230; Elections- 336-401-8225. **Property tax/Assessor-** 336-401-8100.

Swain County

Register of Deeds, PO Box 1183, Bryson City, NC 28713. 828-488-9273 x207, R/E recording phone-828-488-9273 x205; fax-828-488-6947; hours: 8:30AM-5PM. www.swaincounty.org/page5.html
Office will perform a UCC search but public must search other records themselves. UCC search per debtor name- $30.00. Copy fee $1.00 per page. **Other phones:** Elections- 828-488-6177; Vital Records- 828-488-9273 x205. **Property tax/Assessor-** 828-488-9273 x223.

Transylvania County

Register of Deeds, 12 E Main St; Courthouse, Brevard, NC 28712. 828-884-3162; hours: 8:30AM-5PM. www.landofsky.org
No tax liens filed here. All records in one index. Office personnel or visitors may perform searches. No search fee unless extensive research needed. Will search UCC records prior to July 1, 2001. UCC search per debtor name- $30.00. Copy fee $.25 per page. Cert fee- $5.00 1st page, $2.00 each add'l. Vital records are $10.00 ea. Payee- Transylvania County Register of Deeds. **Online access to Real**

Estate, Deed records: Access real estate records at www.titlesearcher.com. Images are viewable back to 12/30/2003, indices back to 1/3/1973. **Other phones:** Treasurer- 828-884-3104; Appraiser/Auditor- 828-884-3200; Elections- 828-884-3114; Vital Records- 828-884-3162. **Property tax/Assessor-** 828-884-3200.

Tyrrell County

Register of Deeds, PO Box 449, Columbia, NC 27925. 252-796-2901; fax-252-796-0148; hours: 9AM-5PM. www.tyrrellrod.com
No tax liens filed here. Records indexed on a public use terminal back to 1997. Only the public may search. Copy fee $1.00 per page. R/E record copy- $.25 per page. Cert fee- $5.00 for 1st pg, $2.00 each add'l pg. Payee- Register of Deeds. **Online access to Real Estate, Grantor/Grantee, Deed records:** Access to Register of Deeds real estate records is free at www.tyrrellrod.com/view/disclaimer.html. Records go back to 1997; images are from Book 137 forward. **Other phones:** Elections- 252-796-0775. **Property tax/Assessor-** 252-796-1371.

Union County

Register of Deeds, PO Box 248, Monroe, NC 28111-0248. 704-283-3727, UCC recording phone-704-283-3610; hours: 8AM-5PM. www.unionconcord.org
No tax liens filed here. Separate indices to search include deeds and mortgages before 1990. Records indexed on a public use terminal back to 6/15/1993. Office will perform a UCC search but public must search other records themselves. Will not search real estate records. UCC search per debtor name- $30.00. Copy fee $1.00 per page. Cert fee- $5.00 1st pg, $2.00 each add'l plus copy fee. Payee- Union County Register of Deeds. **Other phones:** Vital Records- 704-283-3610; Land Records- 704-283-3728.

Vance County

Register of Deeds, 122 Young St; Courthouse, #F, Henderson, NC 27536. 252-738-2110; hours: 8:30AM-5PM.
No tax liens filed here. All records in one index. Record index not computerized. Office will perform a UCC search but public must search other records themselves. UCC search per debtor name- $30.00. Copy fee $.25 per page. Cert fee- $5.00 per cert for 1st page, $2.00 each add'l page plus copy fee. Payee- Vance County Register of Deeds.

Wake County

Register of Deeds, PO Box 1897, Raleigh, NC 27602. 919-856-5460, UCC recording phone-919-856-5464; fax-919-856-5467; hours: 8:30AM-5:15PM. http://web.co.wake.nc.us/rdeeds/
No tax liens filed here. All records in one index. Records indexed on computer. Office will perform a UCC search but public must search other records themselves. Search fee $30.00. Copy fee $1.00 per page. Cert fee- $5.00 1st page, $2.00 each add'l page. Payee- Wake County Register of Deeds. **Online access to Real Estate, Assessor, Deed, Judgment, Lien, Voter Registration records:** Records from the County Department of Revenue are downloadable by township for free at http://web.co.wake.nc.us/revenue/wcmap.html. Also, a free real estate property search is at http://aws1.co.wake.nc.us/realestate/search.asp. Also, online access to the Register of Deeds database is free at http://rodweb01.co.wake.nc.us/books/genext/genextsearch.asp. Records go back to 10/1953. Registered voters can be found at http://msweb03.co.wake.nc.us/bordelec/Waves/WavesOptions.asp. Also, access to Town of Cary property info is free http://arcims2.webgis.net/nc/cary/default.asp. **Other phones:** Treasurer- 919-856-6600; Vital Records- 919-733-3526. **Property tax/Assessor-** 919-856-6600.

Warren County

Register of Deeds, PO Box 506, Warrenton, NC 27589. 252-257-3265; fax-252-257-7011; 8:30AM-5PM. No tax liens filed here. Only the public may search. Copy fee $.25 per page. Cert fee- $5.00. Payee- Warren County Register of Deeds. **Other phones:** Treasurer- 252-257-3337; 2nd Fax- 252-257-7011. **Property tax/Assessor-** 252-257-4158.

Washington County

Register of Deeds, PO Box 1007, Plymouth, NC 27962. 252-793-2325; fax-252-793-6982; hours: 8:30AM-5PM. www.washingtoncountygov.com No tax liens filed here. Only the public may search. Copy fee $1.00 per page. R/E record copy- $.25 per page. Cert fee- $5.00 1st pg, $2.00 each add'l. Payee- Washington County Register of Deeds. **Property tax/Assessor-** same address as above. 252-793-1176.

Watauga County

Register of Deeds, 842 W. King St, #9, Boone, NC 28607-3585. 828-265-8052, UCC recording phone-828-265-8056; fax-828-265-7632; hours: 8AM-5PM. www.wataugacounty.org/deeds/index.html No tax liens filed here. Only the public may search. Copy fee $.50 per page. Cert fee- $5.00 per page plus copy fee,1st copy, add'l $2.00. **Online access to Grantor/Grantee, Deed, UCC, Assessor, Property records:** Access to register of deeds database is free at www.wataugacounty.org/deeds/disclaimer.shtml. Also, online access to county tax search data is free at www.wataugacounty.org/tax/search_tax.shtml. Also, search Town of Blowing Rock property info at http://arcims2.webgis.net/blowingrock/default.asp. To name search click on Quick Search. **Other phones:** Appraiser/Auditor- 828-265-8141; Elections- 828-265-8061; Vital Records- 828-265-8052. **Property tax/Assessor-** 828-265-8036.

Wayne County

Register of Deeds, 224-226 E Walnut St, Goldsboro, NC 27530. 919-731-1449; fax-919-731-1441; hours: 8AM-5PM. www.waynegov.com

No tax liens filed here. Separate indices to search include real estate, CRP, vitals, financing statements, military discharge. Office personnel or visitors may perform searches. Search fee- none. Will not do title work. Copy fee $1.25 per page. Cert fee- $5.00 per cert plus copy fee. Payee- Wayne County Register of Deeds. **Online access to Real Estate, Deed, Grantor/Grantee, Property Tax, Assessor records:** Access to the registers CRP, financing statement, and real estate (to 1969) databases are free at http://152.34.232.92/resolution/ or via www.waynegov.com/departments/rod/disclaimer.asp. Real Estate may only include 1969-1994; others are current. Also, access property records free at www.waynegov.com/departments/tax/taxinquiry/. Only available 8AM-5PM. **Property tax/Assessor-** PO Box 1495, Goldsboro, NC 27533; 919-731-1461.

Wilkes County

Register of Deeds, 500 Courthouse Dr, #1000, Wilkesboro, NC 28697. 336-651-7351; hours: 8:30AM-5PM. No tax liens filed here. All records in one index. Office will perform a UCC search for records prior to 7/2001, but public must search other records themselves. UCC search per debtor name- $30.00. Copy fee $1.00 per page. R/E record copy- $1.00 per page if mailed; $.25 per page otherwise. Cert fee- $5.00 1st pg, $2.00 each add'l plus copy fee. Payee- Wilkes County Register of Deeds. **Online access to Property, GIS-mapping records:** Access to property data is free on the GIS-mapping site at www.undersys.com/wilkesweb/wilkes.html. **Other phones:** Vital Records- 336-651-7351.

Wilson County

Register of Deeds, PO Box 1728, Wilson, NC 27893. 252-399-2935; fax-252-399-2942; hours: 8AM-5PM. www.wilson-co.com/rod.html No tax liens filed here. All records in one index. Records indexed on a public use terminal back to 1974. Office will perform a UCC search but public must search other records themselves. Search fee $30.00. Copy fee $1.00 per page. $.25 each reader printer copy from customer. R/E record copy- $.50

per copy. **Online access to Assessor, Real Estate, Voter Registration, Property, Deed records:** Records on the county Geo-link property tax database are free at www.wilson-co.com/intro.html. Records on the county registered voter database are at www.wilson-co.com/wcbe_search.cfm. Also, search the Register of Deeds search site at www.wilson-co.com/wcjav_begin.html. If using property search function, username or password required; deeds section does not. Search voter registration records at www.wilson-co.com/wcbe_search.cfm. **Other phones:** Treasurer- 252-399-2902; Elections- 252-399-2836; Vital Records- 252-399-2935. **Property tax/Assessor-** 252-399-2901.

Yadkin County

Register of Deeds, PO Box 211, Yadkinville, NC 27055. 336-679-4225; fax-336-679-3239; hours: 8AM-5PM. www.yadkincounty.gov/RegDeed.htm No tax liens filed here. All records in one index. Records indexed on a public use terminal back to 1993. Office will perform a UCC search but public must search other records themselves. UCC search per debtor name- $38.00. Copy fee $1.00 per page. R/E record copy- $.25 per page. Cert fee- $10.00 per cert plus copy fee. Payee- Yadkin County Register of Deeds. **Other phones:** Treasurer- 336-679-4223; Appraiser/Auditor- 336-679-2308; Elections- 336-679-4227; Vital Records- 336-679-4225. **Property tax/Assessor-** 336-679-4221.

Yancey County

Register of Deeds, Courthouse, Rm #4; 110 Town Sq, Burnsville, NC 28714. 828-682-2174, R/E recording phone-704-682-2174; fax-828-682-4520; hours: 8:30AM-5PM. No tax liens filed here. All records in one index. Records indexed on a public use terminal back to 1995. Only the public may search. Copy fee $1.00 per page to copy and mail. Copy fee onsite is $.25 per page. Cert fee- $5.00 1st pg, $2.00 each add'l page, includes copy fee. Payee- Yancey County Register of Deeds.

North Carolina County Locator

You will usually be able to find the city name in the City/County Cross Reference below. In that case, it is a simple matter to determine the county from the cross reference. However, only the official US Postal Service city names are included in this index. There are an additional 40,000 place names that people use in their addresses. Therefore, we have also included a ZIP/City Cross Reference immediately following the City/County Cross Reference.

If you know the ZIP Code but the city name does not appear in the City/County Cross Reference index, look up the ZIP Code in the ZIP/City Cross Reference, find the city name, then look up the city name in the City/County Cross Reference. For example, you want to know the county for an address of Menands, NY 12204. There is no "Menands" in the City/County Cross Reference. The ZIP/City Cross Reference shows that ZIP Codes 12201-12288 are for the city of Albany. Looking back in the City/County Cross Reference, Albany is in Albany County.

North Carolina City/County Cross Reference

ABERDEEN (28315) Moore(76), Hoke(23)
ADVANCE Davie
AHOSKIE Hertford
ALAMANCE Alamance
ALBEMARLE Stanly
ALBERTSON Duplin
ALEXANDER Buncombe
ALEXIS Gaston
ALLIANCE Pamlico
ALMOND Swain
ALTAMAHAW Alamance
ANDREWS Cherokee
ANGIER (27501) Harnett(73), Johnston(25), Wake(1)
ANSONVILLE Anson
APEX (27523) Wake(66), Chatham(33)
APEX Wake
AQUONE Macon
ARAPAHOE Pamlico
ARARAT Surry
ARDEN (28704) Buncombe(91), Henderson(8)
ASH Brunswick
ASHEBORO Randolph
ASHEVILLE Buncombe
ATKINSON Pender
ATLANTIC Carteret
ATLANTIC BEACH Carteret
AULANDER (27805) Bertie(68), Hertford(31)
AURORA Beaufort
AUTRYVILLE (28318) Sampson(87), Cumberland(12)
AVON Dare
AYDEN (28513) Pitt(94), Greene(5)
AYDLETT Currituck
BADIN Stanly
BAHAMA Durham
BAILEY (27807) Nash(64), Wilson(35)
BAKERSVILLE Mitchell
BALSAM Jackson
BALSAM GROVE Transylvania
BANNER ELK (28604) Watauga(61), Avery(38)
BARBER Rowan
BARCO Currituck
BARIUM SPRINGS Iredell
BARNARDSVILLE Buncombe
BARNESVILLE Robeson
BAT CAVE Henderson
BATH Beaufort
BATTLEBORO (27809) Nash(53), Edgecombe(46)
BAYBORO Pamlico
BEAR CREEK Chatham
BEAUFORT Carteret
BELEWS CREEK Forsyth
BELHAVEN Beaufort
BELLARTHUR Pitt
BELMONT Gaston
BELVIDERE (27919) Perquimans(89), Chowan(6), Gates(3)

BENNETT (27208) Chatham(95), Moore(2), Randolph(1)
BENSON (27504) Johnston(97), Harnett(2)
BESSEMER CITY Gaston
BETHANIA Forsyth
BETHEL (27812) Pitt(95), Edgecombe(4)
BEULAVILLE (28518) Duplin(90), Onslow(9)
BISCOE (27209) Montgomery(81), Moore(18)
BLACK CREEK Wilson
BLACK MOUNTAIN Buncombe
BLADENBORO (28320) Bladen(91), Columbus(8)
BLANCH Caswell
BLOUNTS CREEK Beaufort
BLOWING ROCK Watauga
BOILING SPRINGS Cleveland
BOLIVIA Brunswick
BOLTON (28423) Columbus(95), Bladen(4)
BONLEE Chatham
BOOMER Wilkes
BOONE Watauga
BOONVILLE Yadkin
BOSTIC Rutherford
BRASSTOWN (28902) Clay(94), Cherokee(5)
BREVARD Transylvania
BRIDGETON Craven
BROADWAY (27505) Harnett(80), Lee(19)
BROWNS SUMMIT Guilford
BRUNSWICK Columbus
BRYSON CITY Swain
BUIES CREEK Harnett
BULLOCK (27507) Granville(93), Vance(6)
BUNN Franklin
BUNNLEVEL Harnett
BURGAW Pender
BURLINGTON (27217) Alamance(92), Caswell(7)
BURLINGTON Alamance
BURNSVILLE Yancey
BUTNER Granville
BUTTERS Bladen
BUXTON Dare
BYNUM Chatham
CALABASH Brunswick
CALYPSO Duplin
CAMDEN Camden
CAMERON (28326) Harnett(45), Moore(34), Lee(20)
CAMP LEJEUNE Onslow
CANDLER Buncombe
CANDOR Montgomery
CANTON Haywood
CAROLEEN Rutherford
CAROLINA BEACH New Hanover
CARRBORO Orange
CARTHAGE Moore
CARY (27519) Wake(97), Durham(1)
CARY Wake
CASAR (28020) Cleveland(85), Rutherford(14)

CASHIERS Jackson
CASTALIA (27816) Nash(76), Franklin(23)
CASTLE HAYNE New Hanover
CATAWBA Catawba
CEDAR FALLS Randolph
CEDAR GROVE Orange
CEDAR ISLAND Carteret
CEDAR MOUNTAIN Transylvania
CERRO GORDO Columbus
CHADBOURN Columbus
CHAPEL HILL (27517) Chatham(40), Orange(39), Durham(20)
CHAPEL HILL (27516) Orange(87), Chatham(12)
CHAPEL HILL Orange
CHARLOTTE (28215) Mecklenburg(94), Cabarrus(5)
CHARLOTTE Mecklenburg
CHEROKEE Swain
CHERRY POINT Craven
CHERRYVILLE (28021) Gaston(85), Lincoln(11), Cleveland(3)
CHIMNEY ROCK Rutherford
CHINA GROVE Rowan
CHINQUAPIN (28521) Duplin(95), Onslow(4)
CHOCOWINITY Beaufort
CLAREMONT Catawba
CLARENDON Columbus
CLARKTON (28433) Bladen(67), Columbus(32)
CLAYTON Johnston
CLEMMONS (27012) Forsyth(75), Davidson(24)
CLEVELAND (27013) Rowan(90), Iredell(9)
CLIFFSIDE Rutherford
CLIMAX (27233) Randolph(66), Guilford(33)
CLINTON Sampson
CLYDE Haywood
COATS Harnett
COFIELD Hertford
COINJOCK Currituck
COLERAIN Bertie
COLFAX Guilford
COLLETTSVILLE (28611) Caldwell(94), Avery(6)
COLUMBIA Tyrrell
COLUMBUS Polk
COMFORT Jones
COMO Hertford
CONCORD Cabarrus
CONETOE Edgecombe
CONNELLYS SPRINGS (28612) Burke(98), Catawba(1)
CONOVER Catawba
CONWAY Northampton
COOLEEMEE Davie
CORAPEAKE Gates
CORDOVA Richmond
CORNELIUS Mecklenburg
COROLLA Currituck
COUNCIL Bladen

COVE CITY Craven
CRAMERTON Gaston
CRANBERRY Avery
CREEDMOOR (27522) Granville(89), Wake(10)
CRESTON Ashe
CRESWELL (27928) Washington(96), Tyrrell(3)
CROSSNORE Avery
CROUSE (28033) Lincoln(90), Gaston(9)
CRUMPLER Ashe
CULBERSON Cherokee
CULLOWHEE Jackson
CUMBERLAND Cumberland
CUMNOCK Lee
CURRIE Pender
CURRITUCK Currituck
DALLAS Gaston
DANA Henderson
DANBURY Stokes
DAVIDSON (28036) Mecklenburg(73), Cabarrus(25), Iredell(1)
DAVIDSON Mecklenburg
DAVIS Carteret
DEEP GAP Watauga
DEEP RUN (28525) Lenoir(89), Duplin(10)
DELCO Columbus
DENTON (27239) Davidson(77), Randolph(22)
DENVER (28037) Lincoln(83), Catawba(16)
DILLSBORO Jackson
DOBSON Surry
DOVER (28526) Craven(83), Jones(13), Lenoir(2)
DREXEL Burke
DUBLIN Bladen
DUDLEY Wayne
DUNN (28334) Harnett(63), Sampson(28), Johnston(6), Cumberland(1)
DUNN Harnett
DURANTS NECK Perquimans
DURHAM (27707) Durham(98), Orange(1)
DURHAM (27713) Durham(98), Chatham(1)
DURHAM Durham
EAGLE ROCK (27523) Wake(66), Chatham(33)
EAGLE SPRINGS Moore
EARL Cleveland
EAST BEND Yadkin
EAST FLAT ROCK Henderson
EAST SPENCER Rowan
EDEN Rockingham
EDENTON Chowan
EDNEYVILLE Henderson
EDWARD Beaufort
EFLAND Orange
ELIZABETH CITY Pasquotank
ELIZABETHTOWN Bladen
ELK PARK Avery
ELKIN (28621) Surry(64), Wilkes(35)
ELLENBORO Rutherford
ELLERBE Richmond

ELM CITY (27822) Wilson(89), Nash(6),
   Edgecombe(3)
ELON COLLEGE (27244) Alamance(95),
   Guilford(4)
EMERALD ISLE Carteret
ENFIELD Halifax
ENGELHARD Hyde
ENKA Buncombe
ENNICE Alleghany
ERNUL Craven
ERWIN Harnett
ETHER Montgomery
ETOWAH Henderson
EURE Gates
EVERETTS Martin
EVERGREEN Columbus
FAIR BLUFF Columbus
FAIRFIELD (27826) Hyde(87), Tyrrell(12)
FAIRMONT Robeson
FAIRVIEW Buncombe
FAISON (28341) Sampson(77), Duplin(22)
FAITH Rowan
FALCON Cumberland
FALKLAND Pitt
FALLSTON Cleveland
FARMVILLE Pitt
FAYETTEVILLE (28304) Cumberland(98),
   Hoke(1)
FAYETTEVILLE (28312) Cumberland(91),
   Bladen(8)
FAYETTEVILLE Cumberland
FERGUSON Wilkes
FLAT ROCK Henderson
FLEETWOOD Ashe
FLETCHER (28732) Henderson(76),
   Buncombe(22)
FONTANA DAM Graham
FOREST CITY Rutherford
FORT BRAGG Cumberland
FOUNTAIN (27829) Wilson(72), Pitt(22),
   Edgecombe(5)
FOUR OAKS (27524) Johnston(97),
   Wayne(2)
FRANKLIN Macon
FRANKLINTON (27525) Franklin(74),
   Granville(25)
FRANKLINVILLE Randolph
FREMONT (27830) Wayne(95), Wilson(4)
FRISCO Dare
FUQUAY VARINA (27526) Wake(71),
   Harnett(28)
GARLAND (28441) Sampson(59),
   Bladen(39)
GARNER (27529) Wake(77), Johnston(22)
GARYSBURG Northampton
GASTON Northampton
GASTONIA Gaston
GATES Gates
GATESVILLE Gates
GERMANTON (27019) Stokes(74),
   Forsyth(25)
GERTON Henderson
GIBSON Scotland
GIBSONVILLE (27249) Guilford(63),
   Alamance(28), Caswell(5),
   Rockingham(2)
GLADE VALLEY Alleghany
GLEN ALPINE Burke
GLENDALE SPRINGS Ashe
GLENDON Moore
GLENVILLE Jackson
GLENWOOD McDowell
GLOUCESTER Carteret
GODWIN (28344) Sampson(80),
   Cumberland(19)
GOLD HILL (28071) Rowan(49),
   Cabarrus(29), Stanly(21)
GOLDSBORO Wayne
GOLDSTON Chatham
GRAHAM Alamance
GRANDY Currituck
GRANITE FALLS Caldwell

GRANITE QUARRY Rowan
GRANTSBORO Pamlico
GRASSY CREEK (28631) Ashe(98),
   Alleghany(1)
GRAYSON Ashe
GREEN MOUNTAIN Yancey
GREENMOUNTAIN Yancey
GREENSBORO Guilford
GREENVILLE Pitt
GRIFTON (28530) Pitt(46), Lenoir(26),
   Craven(23), Greene(3)
GRIMESLAND (27837) Pitt(94), Beaufort(5)
GROVER Cleveland
GULF Chatham
GUMBERRY Northampton
HALIFAX Halifax
HALLSBORO Columbus
HAMILTON Martin
HAMLET (28345) Richmond(98),
   Scotland(1)
HAMPSTEAD Pender
HAMPTONVILLE (27020) Yadkin(76),
   Wilkes(17), Iredell(6)
HARBINGER Currituck
HARKERS ISLAND Carteret
HARMONY (28634) Iredell(93), Davie(6)
HARRELLS (28444) Bladen(53),
   Sampson(44), Duplin(1)
HARRELLSVILLE Hertford
HARRIS Rutherford
HARRISBURG Cabarrus
HASSELL Martin
HATTERAS Dare
HAVELOCK Craven
HAW RIVER Alamance
HAYESVILLE Clay
HAYS Wilkes
HAZELWOOD Haywood
HENDERSON (27537) Vance(94),
   Franklin(3), Warren(1)
HENDERSON Vance
HENDERSONVILLE Henderson
HENRICO (27842) Northampton(97),
   Warren(2)
HENRIETTA Rutherford
HERTFORD Perquimans
HICKORY (28601) Catawba(96),
   Caldwell(2)
HICKORY (28602) Catawba(95), Burke(4)
HICKORY Catawba
HIDDENITE (28636) Alexander(96),
   Iredell(3)
HIGH POINT (27265) Guilford(76),
   Davidson(22), Forsyth(1)
HIGH POINT (27263) Randolph(59),
   Guilford(40)
HIGH POINT Guilford
HIGH SHOALS Gaston
HIGHFALLS Moore
HIGHLANDS Macon
HILDEBRAN (28637) Burke(98),
   Catawba(1)
HILLSBOROUGH (27278) Orange(96),
   Durham(3)
HOBBSVILLE (27946) Gates(97),
   Chowan(1)
HOBGOOD (27843) Halifax(90),
   Edgecombe(8)
HOBUCKEN Pamlico
HOFFMAN (28347) Richmond(92),
   Moore(7)
HOLLISTER Halifax
HOLLY RIDGE (28445) Onslow(57),
   Pender(42)
HOLLY SPRINGS (27540) Wake(89),
   Harnett(10)
HOOKERTON (28538) Greene(79),
   Lenoir(20)
HOPE MILLS Cumberland
HORSE SHOE Henderson
HOT SPRINGS Madison
HUBERT Onslow

HUDSON Caldwell
HUNTERSVILLE Mecklenburg
HURDLE MILLS (27541) Person(50),
   Orange(49)
HUSK Ashe
ICARD Burke
INDIAN TRAIL Union
INGOLD Sampson
IRON STATION (28080) Lincoln(98),
   Gaston(1)
IVANHOE (28447) Sampson(35),
   Pender(32), Bladen(31)
JACKSON Northampton
JACKSON SPRINGS (27281) Moore(58),
   Montgomery(35), Richmond(6)
JACKSONVILLE Onslow
JAMESTOWN Guilford
JAMESVILLE Martin
JARVISBURG Currituck
JEFFERSON (28640) Ashe(97), Wilkes(2)
JONAS RIDGE Burke
JONESVILLE (28642) Yadkin(93),
   Wilkes(6)
JULIAN (27283) Guilford(85), Randolph(14)
KANNAPOLIS (28083) Cabarrus(73),
   Rowan(26)
KANNAPOLIS Cabarrus
KELFORD Bertie
KELLY Bladen
KENANSVILLE Duplin
KENLY (27542) Wilson(50), Johnston(44),
   Wayne(5)
KERNERSVILLE (27284) Forsyth(93),
   Guilford(4), Davidson(2)
KERNERSVILLE Forsyth
KILL DEVIL HILLS Dare
KING (27021) Stokes(97), Forsyth(2)
KINGS MOUNTAIN Cleveland
KINSTON (28501) Lenoir(97), Jones(2)
KINSTON Lenoir
KIPLING Harnett
KITTRELL (27544) Vance(89),
   Granville(10)
KITTY HAWK Dare
KNIGHTDALE Wake
KNOTTS ISLAND Currituck
KURE BEACH New Hanover
LA GRANGE (28551) Lenoir(66),
   Wayne(26), Greene(6)
LAKE JUNALUSKA Haywood
LAKE LURE Rutherford
LAKE TOXAWAY Transylvania
LAKE WACCAMAW Columbus
LAKEVIEW Moore
LANDIS Rowan
LANSING Ashe
LASKER Northampton
LATTIMORE Cleveland
LAUREL HILL Scotland
LAUREL SPRINGS (28644) Alleghany(58),
   Ashe(38), Wilkes(2)
LAURINBURG Scotland
LAWNDALE (28090) Cleveland(90),
   Lincoln(9)
LAWSONVILLE Stokes
LEASBURG Caswell
LEICESTER Buncombe
LELAND Brunswick
LEMON SPRINGS Lee
LENOIR (28645) Caldwell(98), Wilkes(1)
LENOIR Caldwell
LEWISTON WOODVILLE Bertie
LEWISVILLE Forsyth
LEXINGTON Davidson
LIBERTY (27298) Randolph(59),
   Alamance(30), Guilford(8), Chatham(1)
LILESVILLE Anson
LILLINGTON Harnett
LINCOLNTON (28092) Lincoln(94),
   Gaston(4), Catawba(1)
LINCOLNTON Lincoln

LINDEN (28356) Cumberland(68),
   Harnett(31)
LINVILLE Avery
LINVILLE FALLS Burke
LINWOOD Davidson
LITTLE SWITZERLAND McDowell
LITTLETON (27850) Halifax(83),
   Warren(16)
LOCUST Stanly
LONGISLAND Catawba
LONGWOOD Brunswick
LOUISBURG Franklin
LOWELL Gaston
LOWGAP Surry
LOWLAND Pamlico
LUCAMA Wilson
LUMBER BRIDGE (28357) Robeson(54),
   Hoke(45)
LUMBERTON Robeson
LYNN Polk
MACCLESFIELD (27852) Wilson(81),
   Edgecombe(18)
MACON Warren
MADISON (27025) Rockingham(73),
   Stokes(26)
MAGGIE VALLEY Haywood
MAGNOLIA (28453) Duplin(73),
   Sampson(26)
MAIDEN Catawba
MAMERS Harnett
MANNS HARBOR Dare
MANSON (27553) Vance(65), Warren(34)
MANTEO Dare
MAPLE Currituck
MAPLE HILL (28454) Pender(77),
   Onslow(22)
MARBLE Cherokee
MARGARETTSVILLE Northampton
MARIETTA Robeson
MARION McDowell
MARS HILL (28754) Madison(88),
   Yancey(11)
MARSHALL Madison
MARSHALLBERG Carteret
MARSHVILLE (28103) Union(98), Anson(1)
MARSTON (28363) Scotland(57),
   Richmond(42)
MATTHEWS (28105) Mecklenburg(97),
   Union(2)
MATTHEWS (28104) Union(93),
   Mecklenburg(6)
MATTHEWS Mecklenburg
MAURY Greene
MAXTON (28364) Robeson(73),
   Scotland(26)
MAYODAN Rockingham
MAYSVILLE (28555) Onslow(75),
   Jones(24)
MC ADENVILLE Gaston
MC FARLAN Anson
MC GRADY Wilkes
MC LEANSVILLE Guilford
MCCAIN Hoke
MCCUTCHEON FIELD Onslow
MEBANE (27302) Alamance(60),
   Orange(26), Caswell(13)
MERRITT Pamlico
MERRY HILL Bertie
MICAVILLE Yancey
MICRO Johnston
MIDDLEBURG Vance
MIDDLESEX (27557) Johnston(51),
   Nash(46), Wilson(1)
MIDLAND (28107) Cabarrus(88),
   Mecklenburg(6), Stanly(3), Union(1)
MIDWAY PARK Onslow
MILL SPRING (28756) Polk(97),
   Rutherford(2)
MILLERS CREEK Wilkes
MILTON (27305) Caswell(98), Person(1)
MILWAUKEE Northampton
MINERAL SPRINGS Union

MINNEAPOLIS Avery
MISENHEIMER Stanly
MOCKSVILLE Davie
MONCURE Chatham
MONROE Union
MONTEZUMA Avery
MONTREAT Buncombe
MOORESBORO (28114) Rutherford(54),
   Cleveland(45)
MOORESVILLE (28115) Iredell(86),
   Rowan(13)
MOORESVILLE Iredell
MORAVIAN FALLS Wilkes
MOREHEAD CITY Carteret
MORGANTON Burke
MORRISVILLE (27560) Wake(94),
   Durham(5)
MORVEN Anson
MOUNT AIRY (27030) Surry(97), Stokes(2)
MOUNT GILEAD (27306) Richmond(59),
   Montgomery(40)
MOUNT HOLLY Gaston
MOUNT MOURNE Iredell
MOUNT OLIVE (28365) Wayne(65),
   Duplin(30), Sampson(4)
MOUNT PLEASANT Cabarrus
MOUNT ULLA (28125) Rowan(94),
   Iredell(5)
MOUNTAIN HOME Henderson
MOYOCK Currituck
MURFREESBORO (27855) Hertford(96),
   Northampton(3)
MURPHY Cherokee
NAGS HEAD Dare
NAKINA Columbus
NAPLES Henderson
NASHVILLE Nash
NEBO (28761) McDowell(83), Burke(16)
NEW BERN (28560) Craven(89),
   Pamlico(10)
NEW BERN (28562) Craven(96), Jones(3)
NEW BERN Craven
NEW HILL (27562) Wake(55),
   Chatham(43)
NEW LONDON (28127) Stanly(60),
   Montgomery(33), Davidson(5)
NEWELL Mecklenburg
NEWLAND (28657) Avery(88), Burke(11)
NEWPORT Carteret
NEWTON Catawba
NEWTON GROVE (28366) Sampson(81),
   Johnston(18)
NORLINA Warren
NORMAN Richmond
NORTH WILKESBORO Wilkes
NORTHSIDE Granville
NORWOOD Stanly
OAK CITY Martin
OAK ISLAND Brunswick
OAK RIDGE Guilford
OAKBORO Stanly
OCEAN ISLE BEACH Brunswick
OCRACOKE Hyde
OLD FORT McDowell
OLIN Iredell
OLIVIA Harnett
ORIENTAL Pamlico
ORRUM Robeson
OTTO Macon
OXFORD (27565) Granville(92), Vance(6),
   Person(1)
PALMYRA Halifax
PANTEGO Beaufort
PARKTON (28371) Robeson(83),
   Cumberland(16)
PARMELE Martin
PATTERSON Caldwell
PAW CREEK Mecklenburg
PEACHLAND (28133) Anson(90), Union(9)
PELHAM (27311) Caswell(93),
   Rockingham(6)
PEMBROKE Robeson

PENDLETON Northampton
PENLAND Mitchell
PENROSE (28766) Transylvania(78),
   Henderson(21)
PFAFFTOWN Forsyth
PIKEVILLE (27863) Wayne(70),
   Greene(29)
PILOT MOUNTAIN (27041) Surry(67),
   Stokes(32)
PINE HALL Stokes
PINE LEVEL Johnston
PINEBLUFF Moore
PINEHURST Moore
PINEOLA Avery
PINETOPS Edgecombe
PINETOWN Beaufort
PINEVILLE Mecklenburg
PINEY CREEK Alleghany
PINK HILL (28572) Duplin(55), Lenoir(36),
   Jones(7)
PINNACLE Stokes
PISGAH FOREST Transylvania
PITTSBORO Chatham
PLEASANT GARDEN (27313) Guilford(59),
   Randolph(40)
PLEASANT HILL Northampton
PLUMTREE Avery
PLYMOUTH Washington
POINT HARBOR Currituck
POLKTON Anson
POLKVILLE Cleveland
POLLOCKSVILLE (28573) Jones(98),
   Craven(1)
POPE A F B Cumberland
POPLAR BRANCH Currituck
POTECASI Northampton
POWELLS POINT Currituck
POWELLSVILLE Bertie
PRINCETON (27569) Johnston(88),
   Wayne(11)
PROCTORVILLE Robeson
PROSPECT HILL Caswell
PROVIDENCE Caswell
PURLEAR Wilkes
RAEFORD Hoke
RALEIGH (27603) Wake(98), Johnston(1)
RALEIGH (27613) Wake(97), Durham(2)
RALEIGH Wake
RAMSEUR Randolph
RANDLEMAN (27317) Randolph(98),
   Guilford(1)
RED OAK Nash
RED SPRINGS (28377) Robeson(62),
   Hoke(37)
REIDSVILLE (27320) Rockingham(90),
   Caswell(9)
REIDSVILLE Rockingham
REX Robeson
RHODHISS Caldwell
RICH SQUARE Northampton
RICHFIELD (28137) Rowan(50), Stanly(49)
RICHLANDS (28574) Onslow(94),
   Duplin(3), Jones(2)
RIDGECREST Buncombe
RIDGEWAY Warren
RIEGELWOOD (28456) Columbus(51),
   Bladen(42), Brunswick(6)
ROANOKE RAPIDS Halifax
ROARING GAP Alleghany
ROARING RIVER Wilkes
ROBBINS Moore
ROBBINSVILLE Graham
ROBERSONVILLE (27871) Pitt(83),
   Martin(16)
ROCKINGHAM Richmond
ROCKWELL (28138) Rowan(81),
   Cabarrus(18)
ROCKY MOUNT (27803) Nash(89),
   Wilson(10)
ROCKY MOUNT Edgecombe
ROCKY MOUNT Nash
ROCKY POINT Pender

RODANTHE Dare
RODUCO Gates
ROLESVILLE Wake
RONDA Wilkes
ROPER Washington
ROSE HILL (28458) Duplin(69),
   Sampson(30)
ROSEBORO (28382) Sampson(80),
   Cumberland(19)
ROSMAN Transylvania
ROUGEMONT (27572) Orange(40),
   Person(31), Durham(23), Granville(4)
ROWLAND Robeson
ROXBORO Person
ROXOBEL Bertie
RUFFIN (27326) Rockingham(60),
   Caswell(40)
RURAL HALL (27045) Forsyth(94),
   Stokes(5)
RURAL HALL Forsyth
RUTHERFORD COLLEGE Burke
RUTHERFORDTON Rutherford
SAINT PAULS (28384) Robeson(87),
   Bladen(11)
SALEMBURG Sampson
SALISBURY Rowan
SALTER PATH Carteret
SALUDA (28773) Polk(84), Henderson(15)
SALVO Dare
SANDY RIDGE Stokes
SANFORD (27330) Lee(91), Chatham(6)
SANFORD (27332) Lee(58), Harnett(41)
SANFORD Lee
SAPPHIRE (28774) Jackson(72),
   Transylvania(27)
SARATOGA Wilson
SAXAPAHAW Alamance
SCALY MOUNTAIN Macon
SCOTLAND NECK Halifax
SCOTTS Iredell
SCOTTVILLE Ashe
SCRANTON Hyde
SEABOARD (27876) Northampton(88),
   Pitt(11)
SEAGROVE (27341) Randolph(69),
   Moore(20), Montgomery(10)
SEALEVEL Carteret
SEDALIA Guilford
SELMA Johnston
SEMORA (27343) Person(67), Caswell(32)
SEVEN SPRINGS (28578) Wayne(69),
   Lenoir(17), Duplin(13)
SEVERN Northampton
SHALLOTTE Brunswick
SHANNON (28386) Robeson(61),
   Hoke(38)
SHARPSBURG Nash
SHAWBORO (27973) Camden(72),
   Currituck(27)
SHELBY Cleveland
SHERRILLS FORD (28673) Catawba(97),
   Lincoln(2)
SHILOH Camden
SILER CITY (27344) Chatham(98),
   Randolph(1)
SILOAM Surry
SIMPSON Pitt
SIMS (27880) Wilson(92), Nash(7)
SKYLAND Buncombe
SMITHFIELD Johnston
SMYRNA Carteret
SNEADS FERRY Onslow
SNOW CAMP (27349) Alamance(78),
   Chatham(21)
SNOW HILL Greene
SOPHIA Randolph
SOUTH BRUNSWICK Brunswick
SOUTH MILLS Camden
SOUTHERN PINES Moore
SOUTHMONT Davidson
SOUTHPORT Brunswick
SPARTA Alleghany

SPEED Edgecombe
SPENCER Rowan
SPINDALE Rutherford
SPRING HOPE Nash
SPRING LAKE (28390) Harnett(53),
   Cumberland(46)
SPRUCE PINE Mitchell
STACY Carteret
STALEY (27355) Randolph(71),
   Chatham(28)
STANFIELD Stanly
STANLEY (28164) Gaston(78), Lincoln(21)
STANTONSBURG (27883) Wilson(70),
   Wayne(18), Greene(11)
STAR (27356) Montgomery(85), Moore(14)
STATE ROAD (28676) Wilkes(95), Surry(4)
STATESVILLE Iredell
STEDMAN Cumberland
STELLA (28582) Onslow(63), Carteret(36)
STEM Granville
STOKES Pitt
STOKESDALE (27357) Rockingham(67),
   Guilford(32)
STONEVILLE Rockingham
STONEWALL Pamlico
STONY POINT Alexander
STOVALL Granville
STUMPY POINT Dare
SUGAR GROVE Watauga
SUMMERFIELD (27358) Guilford(67),
   Rockingham(32)
SUNBURY Gates
SUNSET BEACH Brunswick
SUPPLY Brunswick
SWANNANOA Buncombe
SWANQUARTER Hyde
SWANSBORO (28584) Carteret(60),
   Onslow(39)
SWEPSONVILLE Alamance
SYLVA Jackson
TABOR CITY Columbus
TAPOCO Graham
TAR HEEL Bladen
TARAWA TERRACE Onslow
TARBORO Edgecombe
TAYLORSVILLE Alexander
TEACHEY Duplin
TERRELL Catawba
THOMASVILLE (27360) Davidson(94),
   Randolph(5)
THOMASVILLE Davidson
THURMOND Wilkes
TILLERY Halifax
TIMBERLAKE (27583) Person(98),
   Orange(1)
TOAST Surry
TOBACCOVILLE (27050) Forsyth(85),
   Stokes(14)
TODD (28684) Ashe(53), Watauga(46)
TOPTON (28781) Macon(51),
   Cherokee(48)
TOWNSVILLE Vance
TRAPHILL Wilkes
TRENTON Jones
TRINITY Randolph
TRIPLETT Watauga
TROUTMAN Iredell
TROY (27371) Montgomery(86),
   Randolph(13)
TRYON Polk
TUCKASEGEE Jackson
TURKEY Sampson
TURNERSBURG Iredell
TUXEDO Henderson
TYNER Chowan
UNION GROVE Iredell
UNION MILLS Rutherford
VALDESE Burke
VALE (28168) Lincoln(55), Catawba(43)
VALLE CRUCIS Watauga
VANCEBORO (28586) Craven(87), Pitt(6),
   Beaufort(5)

VANDEMERE Pamlico
VASS Moore
VAUGHAN Warren
VILAS Watauga
WACO Cleveland
WADE Cumberland
WADESBORO Anson
WAGRAM Scotland
WAKE FOREST (27587) Wake(94),
   Granville(3), Franklin(2)
WAKE FOREST Wake
WAKULLA Robeson
WALKERTOWN Forsyth
WALLACE (28466) Duplin(78), Pender(20),
   Sampson(1)
WALLBURG Davidson
WALNUT COVE (27052) Stokes(89),
   Forsyth(10)
WALSTONBURG (27888) Wilson(51),
   Greene(45), Pitt(2)
WANCHESE Dare
WARNE Clay
WARRENSVILLE Ashe

WARRENTON (27589) Warren(97),
   Franklin(2)
WARSAW Duplin
WASHINGTON (27889) Beaufort(97),
   Pitt(2)
WATHA Pender
WAVES Dare
WAXHAW Union
WAYNESVILLE Haywood
WEAVERVILLE (28787) Buncombe(95),
   Madison(4)
WEBSTER Jackson
WELCOME Davidson
WELDON Halifax
WENDELL (27591) Wake(77),
   Johnston(22)
WENTWORTH Rockingham
WEST END Moore
WEST JEFFERSON Ashe
WESTFIELD Surry
WHITAKERS (27891) Nash(90),
   Edgecombe(8), Halifax(1)
WHITE OAK Bladen

WHITE PLAINS Surry
WHITEHEAD Alleghany
WHITEVILLE Columbus
WHITSETT Guilford
WHITTIER Jackson
WILBAR Wilkes
WILKESBORO Wilkes
WILLARD (28478) Pender(96),
   Sampson(3)
WILLIAMSTON Martin
WILLISTON Carteret
WILLOW SPRING (27592) Wake(52),
   Johnston(43), Harnett(3)
WILMINGTON (28411) New Hanover(88),
   Pender(11)
WILMINGTON Brunswick
WILMINGTON New Hanover
WILSON (27896) Wilson(84), Nash(15)
WILSON Wilson
WILSONS MILLS Johnston
WINDSOR Bertie
WINFALL Perquimans
WINGATE Union

WINNABOW Brunswick
WINSTON SALEM (27127) Forsyth(89),
   Davidson(10)
WINSTON SALEM Forsyth
WINSTON-SALEM Forsyth
WINTERVILLE Pitt
WINTON Hertford
WISE Warren
WOODLAND (27897) Northampton(92),
   Hertford(7)
WOODLEAF Rowan
WRIGHTSVILLE BEACH New Hanover
YADKINVILLE Yadkin
YANCEYVILLE Caswell
YOUNGSVILLE (27596) Franklin(87),
   Wake(8), Granville(3)
ZEBULON (27597) Wake(76), Franklin(14),
   Johnston(4), Nash(4)
ZIONVILLE (28698) Watauga(98), Ashe(1)
ZIRCONIA Henderson

North Carolina ZIP/City Cross Reference

27006-27006	ADVANCE
27007-27007	ARARAT
27008-27008	BARBER
27009-27009	BELEWS CREEK
27010-27010	BETHANIA
27011-27011	BOONVILLE
27012-27012	CLEMMONS
27013-27013	CLEVELAND
27014-27014	COOLEEMEE
27016-27016	DANBURY
27017-27017	DOBSON
27018-27018	EAST BEND
27019-27019	GERMANTON
27020-27020	HAMPTONVILLE
27021-27021	KING
27022-27022	LAWSONVILLE
27023-27023	LEWISVILLE
27024-27024	LOWGAP
27025-27025	MADISON
27027-27027	MAYODAN
27028-27028	MOCKSVILLE
27030-27030	MOUNT AIRY
27031-27031	WHITE PLAINS
27040-27040	PFAFFTOWN
27041-27041	PILOT MOUNTAIN
27042-27042	PINE HALL
27043-27043	PINNACLE
27045-27045	RURAL HALL
27046-27046	SANDY RIDGE
27047-27047	SILOAM
27048-27048	STONEVILLE
27049-27049	TOAST
27050-27050	TOBACCOVILLE
27051-27051	WALKERTOWN
27052-27052	WALNUT COVE
27053-27053	WESTFIELD
27054-27054	WOODLEAF
27055-27055	YADKINVILLE
27094-27099	RURAL HALL
27100-27100	WINSTON-SALEM
27100-27100	WINSTON SALEM
27100-27100	WINSTON-SALEM
27101-27199	WINSTON SALEM
27201-27201	ALAMANCE
27202-27202	ALTAMAHAW
27203-27205	ASHEBORO
27207-27207	BEAR CREEK
27208-27208	BENNETT
27209-27209	BISCOE
27212-27212	BLANCH
27213-27213	BONLEE
27214-27214	BROWNS SUMMIT
27215-27220	BURLINGTON
27228-27228	BYNUM
27229-27229	CANDOR
27230-27230	CEDAR FALLS
27231-27231	CEDAR GROVE
27233-27233	CLIMAX
27235-27235	COLFAX
27237-27237	CUMNOCK
27239-27239	DENTON
27242-27242	EAGLE SPRINGS
27243-27243	EFLAND
27244-27244	ELON COLLEGE
27247-27247	ETHER
27248-27248	FRANKLINVILLE
27249-27249	GIBSONVILLE
27251-27251	GLENDON
27252-27252	GOLDSTON
27253-27253	GRAHAM
27256-27256	GULF
27258-27258	HAW RIVER
27259-27259	HIGHFALLS
27260-27265	HIGH POINT
27278-27278	HILLSBOROUGH
27281-27281	JACKSON SPRINGS
27282-27282	JAMESTOWN
27283-27283	JULIAN
27284-27285	KERNERSVILLE
27288-27289	EDEN
27291-27291	LEASBURG
27292-27295	LEXINGTON
27298-27298	LIBERTY
27299-27299	LINWOOD
27301-27301	MC LEANSVILLE
27302-27302	MEBANE
27305-27305	MILTON
27306-27306	MOUNT GILEAD
27310-27310	OAK RIDGE
27311-27311	PELHAM
27312-27312	PITTSBORO
27313-27313	PLEASANT GARDEN
27314-27314	PROSPECT HILL
27315-27315	PROVIDENCE
27316-27316	RAMSEUR
27317-27317	RANDLEMAN
27320-27323	REIDSVILLE
27325-27325	ROBBINS
27326-27326	RUFFIN
27330-27332	SANFORD
27340-27340	SAXAPAHAW
27341-27341	SEAGROVE
27342-27342	SEDALIA
27343-27343	SEMORA
27344-27344	SILER CITY
27349-27349	SNOW CAMP
27350-27350	SOPHIA
27351-27351	SOUTHMONT
27355-27355	STALEY
27356-27356	STAR
27357-27357	STOKESDALE
27358-27358	SUMMERFIELD
27359-27359	SWEPSONVILLE
27360-27361	THOMASVILLE
27370-27370	TRINITY
27371-27371	TROY
27373-27373	WALLBURG
27374-27374	WELCOME
27375-27375	WENTWORTH
27376-27376	WEST END
27377-27377	WHITSETT
27379-27379	YANCEYVILLE
27395-27499	GREENSBORO
27501-27501	ANGIER
27502-27502	APEX
27503-27503	BAHAMA
27504-27504	BENSON
27505-27505	BROADWAY
27506-27506	BUIES CREEK
27507-27507	BULLOCK
27508-27508	BUNN
27509-27509	BUTNER
27510-27510	CARRBORO
27511-27513	CARY
27514-27517	CHAPEL HILL
27518-27519	CARY
27520-27520	CLAYTON
27521-27521	COATS
27522-27522	CREEDMOOR
27523-27523	EAGLE ROCK
27523-27523	APEX
27524-27524	FOUR OAKS
27525-27525	FRANKLINTON
27526-27526	FUQUAY VARINA
27527-27528	CLAYTON
27529-27529	GARNER
27530-27534	GOLDSBORO
27536-27537	HENDERSON
27539-27539	APEX
27540-27540	HOLLY SPRINGS
27541-27541	HURDLE MILLS
27542-27542	KENLY
27543-27543	KIPLING
27544-27544	KITTRELL
27545-27545	KNIGHTDALE
27546-27546	LILLINGTON
27549-27549	LOUISBURG
27551-27551	MACON
27552-27552	MAMERS
27553-27553	MANSON
27555-27555	MICRO
27556-27556	MIDDLEBURG
27557-27557	MIDDLESEX
27559-27559	MONCURE
27560-27560	MORRISVILLE
27562-27562	NEW HILL
27563-27563	NORLINA
27564-27564	NORTHSIDE
27565-27565	OXFORD
27568-27568	PINE LEVEL
27569-27569	PRINCETON
27570-27570	RIDGEWAY
27571-27571	ROLESVILLE
27572-27572	ROUGEMONT
27573-27574	ROXBORO
27576-27576	SELMA
27577-27577	SMITHFIELD
27581-27581	STEM
27582-27582	STOVALL
27583-27583	TIMBERLAKE
27584-27584	TOWNSVILLE
27586-27586	VAUGHAN
27587-27588	WAKE FOREST
27589-27589	WARRENTON
27591-27591	WENDELL
27592-27592	WILLOW SPRING
27593-27593	WILSONS MILLS
27594-27594	WISE
27596-27596	YOUNGSVILLE
27597-27597	ZEBULON
27599-27599	CHAPEL HILL
27600-27699	RALEIGH
27700-27722	DURHAM
27801-27804	ROCKY MOUNT
27805-27805	AULANDER
27806-27806	AURORA
27807-27807	BAILEY
27808-27808	BATH
27809-27809	BATTLEBORO
27810-27810	BELHAVEN
27811-27811	BELLARTHUR
27812-27812	BETHEL
27813-27813	BLACK CREEK
27814-27814	BLOUNTS CREEK
27816-27816	CASTALIA
27817-27817	CHOCOWINITY
27818-27818	COMO
27819-27819	CONETOE
27820-27820	CONWAY
27821-27821	EDWARD
27822-27822	ELM CITY
27823-27823	ENFIELD
27824-27824	ENGELHARD
27825-27825	EVERETTS
27826-27826	FAIRFIELD
27827-27827	FALKLAND

27828-27828 FARMVILLE	27935-27935 EURE	28088-28088 LANDIS	28351-28351 LAUREL HILL
27829-27829 FOUNTAIN	27936-27936 FRISCO	28089-28089 LATTIMORE	28352-28353 LAURINBURG
27830-27830 FREMONT	27937-27937 GATES	28090-28090 LAWNDALE	28355-28355 LEMON SPRINGS
27831-27831 GARYSBURG	27938-27938 GATESVILLE	28091-28091 LILESVILLE	28356-28356 LINDEN
27832-27832 GASTON	27939-27939 GRANDY	28092-28093 LINCOLNTON	28357-28357 LUMBER BRIDGE
27833-27836 GREENVILLE	27941-27941 HARBINGER	28097-28097 LOCUST	28358-28360 LUMBERTON
27837-27837 GRIMESLAND	27942-27942 HARRELLSVILLE	28098-28098 LOWELL	28361-28361 MCCAIN
27838-27838 GUMBERRY	27943-27943 HATTERAS	28101-28101 MC ADENVILLE	28362-28362 MARIETTA
27839-27839 HALIFAX	27944-27944 HERTFORD	28102-28102 MC FARLAN	28363-28363 MARSTON
27840-27840 HAMILTON	27946-27946 HOBBSVILLE	28103-28103 MARSHVILLE	28364-28364 MAXTON
27841-27841 HASSELL	27947-27947 JARVISBURG	28104-28106 MATTHEWS	28365-28365 MOUNT OLIVE
27842-27842 HENRICO	27948-27948 KILL DEVIL HILLS	28107-28107 MIDLAND	28366-28366 NEWTON GROVE
27843-27843 HOBGOOD	27949-27949 KITTY HAWK	28108-28108 MINERAL SPRINGS	28367-28367 NORMAN
27844-27844 HOLLISTER	27950-27950 KNOTTS ISLAND	28109-28109 MISENHEIMER	28368-28368 OLIVIA
27845-27845 JACKSON	27953-27953 MANNS HARBOR	28110-28112 MONROE	28369-28369 ORRUM
27846-27846 JAMESVILLE	27954-27954 MANTEO	28114-28114 MOORESBORO	28370-28370 PINEHURST
27847-27847 KELFORD	27956-27956 MAPLE	28115-28117 MOORESVILLE	28371-28371 PARKTON
27848-27848 LASKER	27957-27957 MERRY HILL	28119-28119 MORVEN	28372-28372 PEMBROKE
27849-27849 LEWISTON WOODVILLE	27958-27958 MOYOCK	28120-28120 MOUNT HOLLY	28373-28373 PINEBLUFF
27850-27850 LITTLETON	27959-27959 NAGS HEAD	28123-28123 MOUNT MOURNE	28374-28374 PINEHURST
27851-27851 LUCAMA	27960-27960 OCRACOKE	28124-28124 MOUNT PLEASANT	28375-28375 PROCTORVILLE
27852-27852 MACCLESFIELD	27962-27962 PLYMOUTH	28125-28125 MOUNT ULLA	28376-28376 RAEFORD
27853-27853 MARGARETTSVILLE	27964-27964 POINT HARBOR	28126-28126 NEWELL	28377-28377 RED SPRINGS
27854-27854 MILWAUKEE	27965-27965 POPLAR BRANCH	28127-28127 NEW LONDON	28378-28378 REX
27855-27855 MURFREESBORO	27966-27966 POWELLS POINT	28128-28128 NORWOOD	28379-28380 ROCKINGHAM
27856-27856 NASHVILLE	27967-27967 POWELLSVILLE	28129-28129 OAKBORO	28382-28382 ROSEBORO
27857-27857 OAK CITY	27968-27968 RODANTHE	28130-28130 PAW CREEK	28383-28383 ROWLAND
27858-27858 GREENVILLE	27969-27969 RODUCO	28133-28133 PEACHLAND	28384-28384 SAINT PAULS
27859-27859 PALMYRA	27970-27970 ROPER	28134-28134 PINEVILLE	28385-28385 SALEMBURG
27860-27860 PANTEGO	27972-27972 SALVO	28135-28135 POLKTON	28386-28386 SHANNON
27861-27861 PARMELE	27973-27973 SHAWBORO	28136-28136 POLKVILLE	28387-28388 SOUTHERN PINES
27862-27862 PENDLETON	27974-27974 SHILOH	28137-28137 RICHFIELD	28390-28390 SPRING LAKE
27863-27863 PIKEVILLE	27976-27976 SOUTH MILLS	28138-28138 ROCKWELL	28391-28391 STEDMAN
27864-27864 PINETOPS	27978-27978 STUMPY POINT	28139-28139 RUTHERFORDTON	28392-28392 TAR HEEL
27865-27865 PINETOWN	27979-27979 SUNBURY	28144-28147 SALISBURY	28393-28393 TURKEY
27866-27866 PLEASANT HILL	27980-27980 TYNER	28150-28152 SHELBY	28394-28394 VASS
27867-27867 POTECASI	27981-27981 WANCHESE	28159-28159 SPENCER	28395-28395 WADE
27868-27868 RED OAK	27982-27982 WAVES	28160-28160 SPINDALE	28396-28396 WAGRAM
27869-27869 RICH SQUARE	27983-27983 WINDSOR	28163-28163 STANFIELD	28397-28397 WAKULLA
27870-27870 ROANOKE RAPIDS	27985-27985 WINFALL	28164-28164 STANLEY	28398-28398 WARSAW
27871-27871 ROBERSONVILLE	27986-27986 WINTON	28166-28166 TROUTMAN	28399-28399 WHITE OAK
27872-27872 ROXOBEL	28001-28002 ALBEMARLE	28167-28167 UNION MILLS	28401-28412 WILMINGTON
27873-27873 SARATOGA	28006-28006 ALEXIS	28168-28168 VALE	28420-28420 ASH
27874-27874 SCOTLAND NECK	28007-28007 ANSONVILLE	28169-28169 WACO	28421-28421 ATKINSON
27875-27875 SCRANTON	28009-28009 BADIN	28170-28170 WADESBORO	28422-28422 BOLIVIA
27876-27876 SEABOARD	28010-28010 BARIUM SPRINGS	28173-28173 WAXHAW	28423-28423 BOLTON
27877-27877 SEVERN	28012-28012 BELMONT	28174-28174 WINGATE	28424-28424 BRUNSWICK
27878-27878 SHARPSBURG	28016-28016 BESSEMER CITY	28200-28299 CHARLOTTE	28425-28425 BURGAW
27879-27879 SIMPSON	28017-28017 BOILING SPRINGS	28301-28306 FAYETTEVILLE	28428-28428 CAROLINA BEACH
27880-27880 SIMS	28018-28018 BOSTIC	28307-28307 FORT BRAGG	28429-28429 CASTLE HAYNE
27881-27881 SPEED	28019-28019 CAROLEEN	28308-28308 POPE A F B	28430-28430 CERRO GORDO
27882-27882 SPRING HOPE	28020-28020 CASAR	28309-28309 FAYETTEVILLE	28431-28431 CHADBOURN
27883-27883 STANTONSBURG	28021-28021 CHERRYVILLE	28310-28310 FORT BRAGG	28432-28432 CLARENDON
27884-27884 STOKES	28023-28023 CHINA GROVE	28311-28314 FAYETTEVILLE	28433-28433 CLARKTON
27885-27885 SWANQUARTER	28024-28024 CLIFFSIDE	28315-28315 ABERDEEN	28434-28434 COUNCIL
27886-27886 TARBORO	28025-28027 CONCORD	28318-28318 AUTRYVILLE	28435-28435 CURRIE
27887-27887 TILLERY	28031-28031 CORNELIUS	28319-28319 BARNESVILLE	28436-28436 DELCO
27888-27888 WALSTONBURG	28032-28032 CRAMERTON	28320-28320 BLADENBORO	28438-28438 EVERGREEN
27889-27889 WASHINGTON	28033-28033 CROUSE	28323-28323 BUNNLEVEL	28439-28439 FAIR BLUFF
27890-27890 WELDON	28034-28034 DALLAS	28324-28324 BUTTERS	28441-28441 GARLAND
27891-27891 WHITAKERS	28035-28036 DAVIDSON	28325-28325 CALYPSO	28442-28442 HALLSBORO
27892-27892 WILLIAMSTON	28037-28037 DENVER	28326-28326 CAMERON	28443-28443 HAMPSTEAD
27893-27896 WILSON	28038-28038 EARL	28327-28327 CARTHAGE	28444-28444 HARRELLS
27897-27897 WOODLAND	28039-28039 EAST SPENCER	28328-28329 CLINTON	28445-28445 HOLLY RIDGE
27906-27909 ELIZABETH CITY	28040-28040 ELLENBORO	28330-28330 CORDOVA	28446-28446 INGOLD
27910-27910 AHOSKIE	28041-28041 FAITH	28331-28331 CUMBERLAND	28447-28447 IVANHOE
27915-27915 AVON	28042-28042 FALLSTON	28332-28332 DUBLIN	28448-28448 KELLY
27916-27916 AYDLETT	28043-28043 FOREST CITY	28333-28333 DUDLEY	28449-28449 KURE BEACH
27917-27917 BARCO	28051-28056 GASTONIA	28334-28335 DUNN	28450-28450 LAKE WACCAMAW
27919-27919 BELVIDERE	28070-28070 HUNTERSVILLE	28337-28337 ELIZABETHTOWN	28451-28451 LELAND
27920-27920 BUXTON	28071-28071 GOLD HILL	28338-28338 ELLERBE	28452-28452 LONGWOOD
27921-27921 CAMDEN	28072-28072 GRANITE QUARRY	28339-28339 ERWIN	28453-28453 MAGNOLIA
27922-27922 COFIELD	28073-28073 GROVER	28340-28340 FAIRMONT	28454-28454 MAPLE HILL
27923-27923 COINJOCK	28074-28074 HARRIS	28341-28341 FAISON	28455-28455 NAKINA
27924-27924 COLERAIN	28075-28075 HARRISBURG	28342-28342 FALCON	28456-28456 RIEGELWOOD
27925-27925 COLUMBIA	28076-28076 HENRIETTA	28343-28343 GIBSON	28457-28457 ROCKY POINT
27926-27926 CORAPEAKE	28077-28077 HIGH SHOALS	28344-28344 GODWIN	28458-28458 ROSE HILL
27927-27927 COROLLA	28078-28078 HUNTERSVILLE	28345-28345 HAMLET	28459-28459 SHALLOTTE
27928-27928 CRESWELL	28079-28079 INDIAN TRAIL	28347-28347 HOFFMAN	28460-28460 SNEADS FERRY
27929-27929 CURRITUCK	28080-28080 IRON STATION	28348-28348 HOPE MILLS	28461-28461 SOUTHPORT
27930-27930 DURANTS NECK	28081-28083 KANNAPOLIS	28349-28349 KENANSVILLE	28462-28462 SUPPLY
27932-27932 EDENTON	28086-28086 KINGS MOUNTAIN	28350-28350 LAKEVIEW	28463-28463 TABOR CITY

ZIP Range	Location	ZIP Range	Location	ZIP Range	Location	ZIP Range	Location
28464-28464	TEACHEY	28582-28582	STELLA	28662-28662	PINEOLA	28730-28730	FAIRVIEW
28465-28465	OAK ISLAND	28583-28583	STONEWALL	28663-28663	PINEY CREEK	28731-28731	FLAT ROCK
28466-28466	WALLACE	28584-28584	SWANSBORO	28664-28664	PLUMTREE	28732-28732	FLETCHER
28467-28467	CALABASH	28585-28585	TRENTON	28665-28665	PURLEAR	28733-28733	FONTANA DAM
28468-28468	SUNSET BEACH	28586-28586	VANCEBORO	28666-28666	ICARD	28734-28734	FRANKLIN
28469-28469	OCEAN ISLE BEACH	28587-28587	VANDEMERE	28667-28667	RHODHISS	28735-28735	GERTON
28470-28470	SOUTH BRUNSWICK	28589-28589	WILLISTON	28668-28668	ROARING GAP	28736-28736	GLENVILLE
28471-28471	WATHA	28590-28590	WINTERVILLE	28669-28669	ROARING RIVER	28737-28737	GLENWOOD
28472-28472	WHITEVILLE	28594-28594	EMERALD ISLE	28670-28670	RONDA	28738-28738	HAZELWOOD
28478-28478	WILLARD	28601-28603	HICKORY	28671-28671	RUTHERFORD COLLEGE	28739-28739	HENDERSONVILLE
28479-28479	WINNABOW	28604-28604	BANNER ELK	28672-28672	SCOTTVILLE	28740-28740	GREENMOUNTAIN
28480-28480	WRIGHTSVILLE BEACH	28605-28605	BLOWING ROCK	28673-28673	SHERRILLS FORD	28740-28740	GREEN MOUNTAIN
28501-28504	KINSTON	28606-28606	BOOMER	28674-28674	NORTH WILKESBORO	28741-28741	HIGHLANDS
28508-28508	ALBERTSON	28607-28607	BOONE	28675-28675	SPARTA	28742-28742	HORSE SHOE
28509-28509	ALLIANCE	28609-28609	CATAWBA	28676-28676	STATE ROAD	28743-28743	HOT SPRINGS
28510-28510	ARAPAHOE	28610-28610	CLAREMONT	28677-28677	STATESVILLE	28744-28744	FRANKLIN
28511-28511	ATLANTIC	28611-28611	COLLETTSVILLE	28678-28678	STONY POINT	28745-28745	LAKE JUNALUSKA
28512-28512	ATLANTIC BEACH	28612-28612	CONNELLYS SPRINGS	28679-28679	SUGAR GROVE	28746-28746	LAKE LURE
28513-28513	AYDEN	28613-28613	CONOVER	28680-28680	MORGANTON	28747-28747	LAKE TOXAWAY
28515-28515	BAYBORO	28614-28614	CRANBERRY	28681-28681	TAYLORSVILLE	28748-28748	LEICESTER
28516-28516	BEAUFORT	28615-28615	CRESTON	28682-28682	TERRELL	28749-28749	LITTLE SWITZERLAND
28518-28518	BEULAVILLE	28616-28616	CROSSNORE	28683-28683	THURMOND	28750-28750	LYNN
28519-28519	BRIDGETON	28617-28617	CRUMPLER	28684-28684	TODD	28751-28751	MAGGIE VALLEY
28520-28520	CEDAR ISLAND	28618-28618	DEEP GAP	28685-28685	TRAPHILL	28752-28752	MARION
28521-28521	CHINQUAPIN	28619-28619	DREXEL	28686-28686	TRIPLETT	28753-28753	MARSHALL
28522-28522	COMFORT	28621-28621	ELKIN	28687-28687	STATESVILLE	28754-28754	MARS HILL
28523-28523	COVE CITY	28622-28622	ELK PARK	28688-28688	TURNERSBURG	28755-28755	MICAVILLE
28524-28524	DAVIS	28623-28623	ENNICE	28689-28689	UNION GROVE	28756-28756	MILL SPRING
28525-28525	DEEP RUN	28624-28624	FERGUSON	28690-28690	VALDESE	28757-28757	MONTREAT
28526-28526	DOVER	28625-28625	STATESVILLE	28691-28691	VALLE CRUCIS	28758-28758	MOUNTAIN HOME
28527-28527	ERNUL	28626-28626	FLEETWOOD	28692-28692	VILAS	28760-28760	NAPLES
28528-28528	GLOUCESTER	28627-28627	GLADE VALLEY	28693-28693	WARRENSVILLE	28761-28761	NEBO
28529-28529	GRANTSBORO	28628-28628	GLEN ALPINE	28694-28694	WEST JEFFERSON	28762-28762	OLD FORT
28530-28530	GRIFTON	28629-28629	GLENDALE SPRINGS	28695-28695	WHITEHEAD	28763-28763	OTTO
28531-28531	HARKERS ISLAND	28630-28630	GRANITE FALLS	28696-28696	WILBAR	28765-28765	PENLAND
28532-28532	HAVELOCK	28631-28631	GRASSY CREEK	28697-28697	WILKESBORO	28766-28766	PENROSE
28533-28533	CHERRY POINT	28632-28632	GRAYSON	28698-28698	ZIONVILLE	28768-28768	PISGAH FOREST
28537-28537	HOBUCKEN	28633-28633	LENOIR	28699-28699	SCOTTS	28770-28770	RIDGECREST
28538-28538	HOOKERTON	28634-28634	HARMONY	28701-28701	ALEXANDER	28771-28771	ROBBINSVILLE
28539-28539	HUBERT	28635-28635	HAYS	28702-28702	ALMOND	28772-28772	ROSMAN
28540-28541	JACKSONVILLE	28636-28636	HIDDENITE	28703-28703	AQUONE	28773-28773	SALUDA
28542-28542	CAMP LEJEUNE	28637-28637	HILDEBRAN	28704-28704	ARDEN	28774-28774	SAPPHIRE
28543-28543	TARAWA TERRACE	28638-28638	HUDSON	28705-28705	BAKERSVILLE	28775-28775	SCALY MOUNTAIN
28544-28544	MIDWAY PARK	28639-28639	HUSK	28707-28707	BALSAM	28776-28776	SKYLAND
28545-28545	MCCUTCHEON FIELD	28640-28640	JEFFERSON	28708-28708	BALSAM GROVE	28777-28777	SPRUCE PINE
28546-28546	JACKSONVILLE	28641-28641	JONAS RIDGE	28709-28709	BARNARDSVILLE	28778-28778	SWANNANOA
28547-28547	CAMP LEJEUNE	28642-28642	JONESVILLE	28710-28710	BAT CAVE	28779-28779	SYLVA
28551-28551	LA GRANGE	28643-28643	LANSING	28711-28711	BLACK MOUNTAIN	28780-28780	TAPOCO
28552-28552	LOWLAND	28644-28644	LAUREL SPRINGS	28712-28712	BREVARD	28781-28781	TOPTON
28553-28553	MARSHALLBERG	28645-28645	LENOIR	28713-28713	BRYSON CITY	28782-28782	TRYON
28554-28554	MAURY	28646-28646	LINVILLE	28714-28714	BURNSVILLE	28783-28783	TUCKASEGEE
28555-28555	MAYSVILLE	28647-28647	LINVILLE FALLS	28715-28715	CANDLER	28784-28784	TUXEDO
28556-28556	MERRITT	28648-28648	LONGISLAND	28716-28716	CANTON	28785-28786	WAYNESVILLE
28557-28557	MOREHEAD CITY	28649-28649	MC GRADY	28717-28717	CASHIERS	28787-28787	WEAVERVILLE
28560-28564	NEW BERN	28650-28650	MAIDEN	28718-28718	CEDAR MOUNTAIN	28788-28788	WEBSTER
28570-28570	NEWPORT	28651-28651	MILLERS CREEK	28719-28719	CHEROKEE	28789-28789	WHITTIER
28571-28571	ORIENTAL	28652-28652	MINNEAPOLIS	28720-28720	CHIMNEY ROCK	28790-28790	ZIRCONIA
28572-28572	PINK HILL	28653-28653	MONTEZUMA	28721-28721	CLYDE	28791-28793	HENDERSONVILLE
28573-28573	POLLOCKSVILLE	28654-28654	MORAVIAN FALLS	28722-28722	COLUMBUS	28800-28816	ASHEVILLE
28574-28574	RICHLANDS	28655-28655	MORGANTON	28723-28723	CULLOWHEE	28901-28901	ANDREWS
28575-28575	SALTER PATH	28656-28656	NORTH WILKESBORO	28724-28724	DANA	28902-28902	BRASSTOWN
28577-28577	SEALEVEL	28657-28657	NEWLAND	28725-28725	DILLSBORO	28903-28903	CULBERSON
28578-28578	SEVEN SPRINGS	28658-28658	NEWTON	28726-28726	EAST FLAT ROCK	28904-28904	HAYESVILLE
28579-28579	SMYRNA	28659-28659	NORTH WILKESBORO	28727-28727	EDNEYVILLE	28905-28905	MARBLE
28580-28580	SNOW HILL	28660-28660	OLIN	28728-28728	ENKA	28906-28906	MURPHY
28581-28581	STACY	28661-28661	PATTERSON	28729-28729	ETOWAH	28909-28909	WARNE

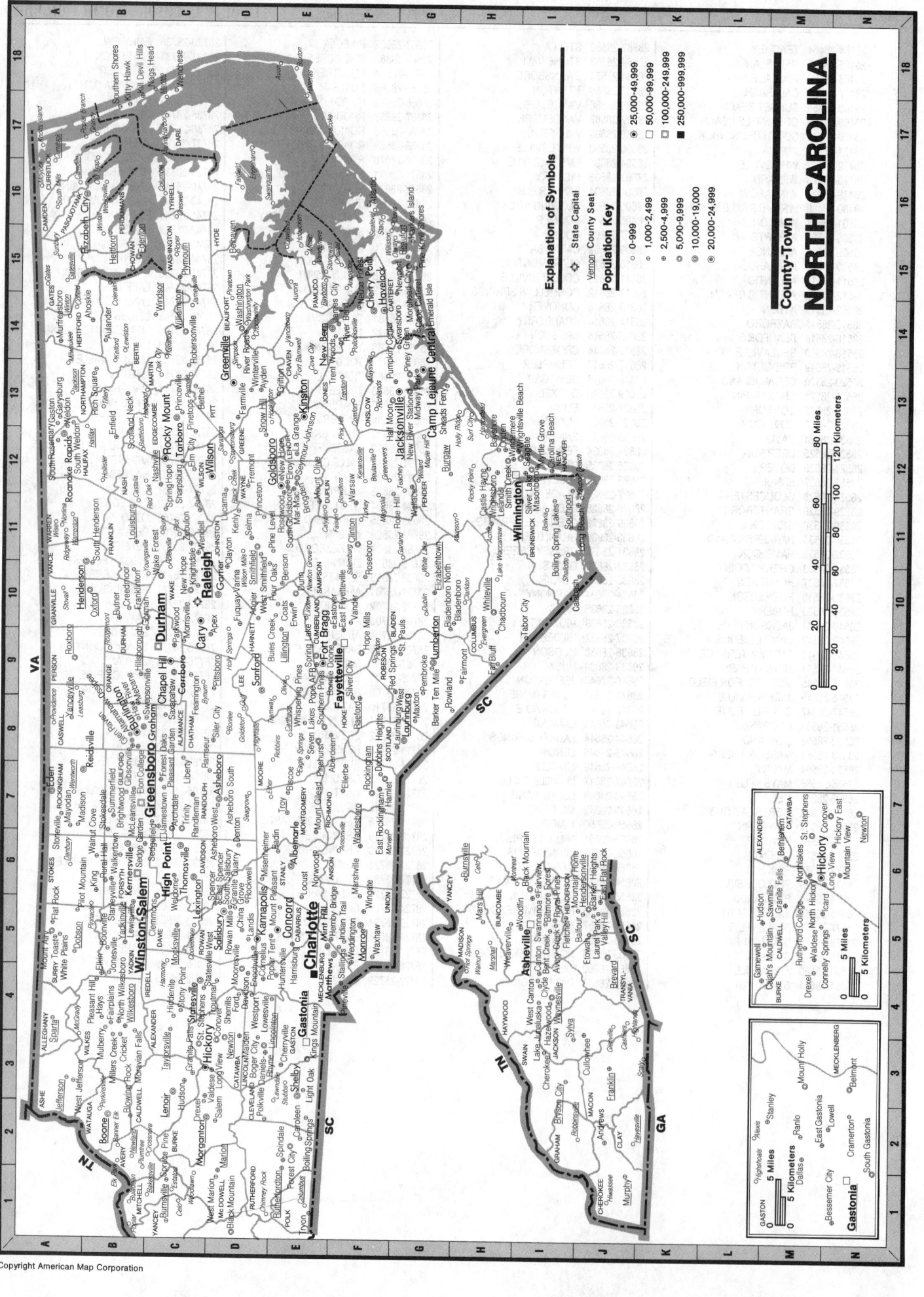

NORTH CAROLINA
County-Town

Explanation of Symbols

✤ State Capital
Vernon ⊙ County Seat

Population Key

⊙ 0-999
○ 1,000-2,499
⊕ 2,500-4,999
⊙ 5,000-9,999
⊛ 10,000-19,000
⊛ 20,000-24,999

⊛ 25,000-49,999
□ 50,000-99,999
▣ 100,000-249,999
■ 250,000-999,999

COUNTIES

(100 Counties)

Name of County	Population	Location on Map
ALAMANCE	108,213	C-8
ALEXANDER	27,544	C-3
ALLEGHANY	9,590	A-3
ANSON	23,474	F-6
ASHE	22,209	A-2
AVERY	14,867	B-2
BEAUFORT	42,283	D-14
BERTIE	20,388	B-13
BLADEN	28,663	F-9
BRUNSWICK	50,985	I-11
BUNCOMBE	174,821	H-5
BURKE	75,744	C-2
CABARRUS	98,935	E-5
CALDWELL	70,709	B-2
CAMDEN	5,904	A-15
CARTERET	52,556	F-14
CASWELL	20,693	A-8
CATAWBA	118,412	D-3
CHATHAM	38,759	C-8
CHEROKEE	20,170	J-1
CHOWAN	13,506	B-15
CLAY	7,155	J-2
CLEVELAND	84,714	D-2
COLUMBUS	49,587	H-9
CRAVEN	81,613	E-13
CUMBERLAND	274,566	E-9
CURRITUCK	13,736	A-16
DARE	22,746	C-17
DAVIDSON	126,677	C-6
DAVIE	27,859	C-5
DUPLIN	39,995	E-11
DURHAM	181,835	B-9
EDGECOMBE	56,558	C-12
FORSYTH	265,878	B-6
FRANKLIN	36,414	B-11
GASTON	175,093	E-3
GATES	9,305	A-14
GRAHAM	7,196	I-2
GRANVILLE	38,345	A-10
GREENE	15,384	D-12
GUILFORD	347,420	B-7
HALIFAX	55,516	A-12
HARNETT	67,822	D-9
HAYWOOD	46,942	H-4
HENDERSON	69,285	I-5
HERTFORD	22,523	A-14
HOKE	22,856	F-8
HYDE	5,411	D-15
IREDELL	92,931	C-4
JACKSON	26,846	I-3
JOHNSTON	81,306	D-11
JONES	9,414	E-13
LEE	41,374	D-9
LENOIR	57,274	E-12
LINCOLN	50,319	D-3
MACON	23,499	J-2
MADISON	16,953	H-5
MARTIN	25,078	C-13
MCDOWELL	35,681	D-1
MECKLENBURG	511,433	E-4
MITCHELL	14,433	B-1
MONTGOMERY	23,346	E-7
MOORE	59,013	D-7
NASH	76,677	B-12
NEW HANOVER	120,284	I-12
NORTHAMPTON	20,798	A-13
ONSLOW	149,838	F-13
ORANGE	93,851	B-9
PAMLICO	11,372	E-14
PASQUOTANK	31,298	A-15
PENDER	28,855	G-11
PERQUIMANS	10,447	B-15
PERSON	30,180	A-9
PITT	107,924	D-13
POLK	14,416	E-1
RANDOLPH	106,546	C-7
RICHMOND	44,518	E-7
ROBESON	105,179	F-9
ROCKINGHAM	86,064	A-7
ROWAN	110,605	C-5
RUTHERFORD	56,918	D-1
SAMPSON	47,297	E-10
SCOTLAND	33,754	F-8
STANLY	51,765	E-6
STOKES	37,223	A-6
SURRY	61,704	A-4
SWAIN	11,268	I-3
TRANSYLVANIA	25,520	J-4
TYRRELL	3,856	C-16
UNION	84,211	F-5
VANCE	38,892	A-10
WAKE	423,380	C-10
WARREN	17,265	A-11
WASHINGTON	13,997	C-15
WATAUGA	36,952	B-2
WAYNE	104,666	D-12
WILKES	59,393	B-3
WILSON	66,061	C-12
YADKIN	30,488	B-4
YANCEY	15,419	C-1
TOTAL	6,628,637	

CITIES AND TOWNS

Note: The first name is that of the city or town, second, that of the county in which it is located, then the population and location on the map.

Aberdeen, Moore, 2,700 ... E-8
Ahoskie, Hertford, 4,391 ... B-14
Albemarle, Stanly, 14,939 ... E-6
• Altamahaw-Ossipee, Alamance, 1,076 ... B-8
Andrews, Cherokee, 2,551 ... J-2
Angier, Harnett, 2,235 ... D-10
Apex, Wake, 4,968 ... D-9
Archdale, Guilford/Randolph, 6,913 ... C-7
Asheboro, Randolph, 16,362 ... D-7
Asheville, Buncombe, 61,607 ... I-5
Atlantic Beach, Carteret, 1,938 ... F-15
Aulander, Bertie, 1,209 ... B-14
• Avery Creek, Buncombe, 1,144 ... J-5
Ayden, Pitt, 4,740 ... D-13
• Badin, Stanly, 1,481 ... E-6
Bakersville, Mitchell, 332 ... C-1
• Balfour, Henderson, 1,118 ... J-5
• Barker Heights, Henderson, 1,137 ... J-5
• Barker Ten Mile, Robeson, 1,087 ... G-9
Bayboro, Pamlico, 733 ... E-15
• Bayshore, New Hanover, 1,661 ... H-12
Beaufort, Carteret, 3,808 ... G-15
Belhaven, Beaufort, 2,269 ... D-15
Belmont, Gaston, 8,434 ... N-3
Benson, Johnston, 2,810 ... E-10
• Bent Creek, Buncombe, 1,487 ... I-5
Bessemer City, Gaston, 4,698 ... N-1
Bethel, Pitt, 1,842 ... C-13
• Bethlehem, Alexander, 3,186 ... M-6
Biltmore Forest, Buncombe, 1,327 ... I-5
Biscoe, Montgomery, 1,484 ... E-7
Black Mountain, Buncombe, 5,418 ... I-6
Bladenboro, Bladen, 1,821 ... G-10
Bladenboro North, Bladen ... G-10
Blowing Rock, Caldwell/Watauga, 1,257 ... B-2
• Boger City, Lincoln, 1,373 ... D-3
Boiling Spring Lakes, Brunswick, 1,650 ... I-12
Boiling Springs, Cleveland, 2,445 ... E-2
• Bonnie Doone, Cumberland, 3,893 ... F-9
Boone, Watauga, 12,915 ... B-2
Boonville, Yadkin, 1,009 ... B-5
Brevard, Transylvania, 5,388 ... J-5
Brightwood, Guilford ... B-7
• Brogden, Wayne, 3,246 ... E-12
Bryson City, Swain, 1,145 ... I-3
• Buies Creek, Harnett, 2,085 ... E-10
Burgaw, Pender, 1,807 ... G-12
Burlington, Alamance, 39,498 ... B-8
Burnsville, Yancey, 1,482 ... C-1
• Butner, Granville, 4,679 ... B-10
Cajah's Mountain, Caldwell, 2,429 ... M-5
Calabash, Brunswick, 1,210 ... I-11
Camden, Camden ... A-16
• Camp Lejeune Central, Onslow, 36,716 ... G-13
Canton, Haywood, 3,790 ... I-4
Cape Carteret, Carteret, 1,008 ... G-14
Caroleen, Rutherford ... E-2
Carolina Beach, New Hanover, 3,630 ... I-12
Carrboro, Orange, 11,553 ... C-9
Carthage, Moore, 976 ... E-8
Cary, Wake, 43,858 ... C-10
• Castle Hayne, New Hanover, 1,182 ... H-12
Chadbourn, Columbus, 2,005 ... H-9
Chapel Hill, Durham/Orange, 38,719 ... C-9
Charlotte, Mecklenburg, 395,934 ... E-4
Cherokee, Swain ... I-3
Cherry Point, Craven ... F-14
Cherryville, Gaston, 4,756 ... E-3
China Grove, Rowan, 2,732 ... D-5
Clayton, Johnston, 4,756 ... D-10
Clemmons, Forsyth, 6,020 ... C-6
Clinton, Sampson, 8,204 ... F-11
Clyde, Haywood, 1,041 ... I-4
Coats, Harnett, 1,493 ... E-10
Columbia, Tyrrell, 836 ... C-16
Columbus, Polk, 812 ... E-1
Concord, Cabarrus, 27,347 ... E-5
Connelly Springs, Burke, 1,349 ... N-5
Conover, Catawba, 5,465 ... D-3
Cornelius, Mecklenburg, 2,581 ... D-4
Cramerton, Gaston, 2,371 ... N-2
Creedmoor, Granville, 1,504 ... B-10
• Cricket, Wilkes, 2,015 ... B-3
• Cullowhee, Jackson, 4,029 ... J-4
Currituck, Currituck ... A-16
Dallas, Gaston, 3,012 ... M-2
Danbury, Stokes, 119 ... A-6
Daniels-Rhyne, Lincoln ... D-3
Davidson, Iredell/Mecklenburg, 4,046 ... D-4
Denton, Davidson, 1,292 ... D-6
Dobbins Heights, Richmond, 1,144 ... F-7
Dobson, Surry, 1,195 ... A-5
Drexel, Burke, 1,746 ... C-2
Dunn, Harnett, 8,336 ... E-10
Durham, Durham/Orange, 136,611 ... C-9
East Fayetteville, Cumberland ... F-10
• East Flat Rock, Henderson, 3,218 ... J-5
East Gastonia, Gaston ... N-2
• East Rockingham, Richmond, 4,158 ... F-7
East Spencer, Rowan, 2,055 ... D-5
• Eastover, Cumberland, 1,243 ... F-10
Eden, Rockingham, 15,238 ... A-7
Edenton, Chowan, 5,268 ... B-15
Elizabeth City, Camden/Pasquotank, 14,292 ... A-16
Elizabethtown, Bladen, 3,704 ... G-10
Elkin, Surry/Wilkes, 3,790 ... B-4
Ellerbe, Richmond, 1,132 ... F-7
Elm City, Wilson, 1,624 ... C-12
Elon College, Alamance, 4,394 ... B-8
• Elroy, Wayne, 4,028 ... E-12
Emerald Isle, Carteret, 2,434 ... G-14
Enfield, Halifax, 3,082 ... B-12
• Enochville, Rowan, 2,901 ... D-5
Erwin, Harnett, 4,061 ... E-10
• Etowah, Henderson, 1,997 ... J-5
Fair Bluff, Columbus, 1,068 ... H-9
Fairmont, Robeson, 2,489 ... H-9
• Fairplains, Wilkes, 2,339 ... B-4
• Fairview, Buncombe, 1,830 ... I-6
Farmville, Pitt, 4,392 ... D-13
Fayetteville, Cumberland, 75,695 ... F-9
• Fearrington, Chatham, 1,101 ... C-8
• Flat Rock, Surry, 1,812 ... A-5
Fletcher, Henderson, 2,787 ... I-5
Forest City, Rutherford, 7,475 ... E-2
• Forest Oaks, Guilford, 3,054 ... C-7
• Fort Bragg, Cumberland, 34,744 ... E-9
Four Oaks, Johnston, 1,308 ... D-10
Franklin, Macon, 2,873 ... J-3
Franklinton, Franklin, 1,615 ... B-10
Fremont, Wayne, 1,710 ... D-12
Fuquay-Varina, Wake, 4,562 ... D-10
Gamewell, Caldwell, 3,357 ... M-5
Garner, Wake, 14,967 ... D-10
Garysburg, Northampton, 1,057 ... A-13
Gaston, Northampton, 1,003 ... A-13
Gastonia, Gaston, 54,732 ... E-3
Gatesville, Gates, 308 ... A-15
Gibsonville, Alamance/Guilford, 3,441 ... B-8
• Glen Raven, Alamance, 2,616 ... B-8
Goldsboro, Wayne, 40,709 ... E-12
• Gorman, Durham, 1,090 ... C-10
Graham, Alamance, 10,426 ... B-8
Granite Falls, Caldwell, 3,253 ... C-3
Granite Quarry, Rowan, 1,646 ... D-5
Greensboro, Guilford, 183,521 ... B-7
Greenville, Pitt, 44,972 ... D-13
Grifton, Lenoir/Pitt, 2,393 ... E-13
• Half Moon, Onslow, 6,306 ... F-13
Halifax, Halifax, 327 ... B-12
Hamlet, Richmond, 6,196 ... F-7
• Harkers Island, Carteret, 1,759 ... G-15
Harrisburg, Cabarrus, 1,625 ... E-5
Havelock, Craven, 20,268 ... F-14
Haw River, Alamance, 1,855 ... B-8
Hayesville, Clay, 279 ... J-2
• Hays, Wilkes, 1,522 ... B-4
Hazelwood, Haywood, 1,678 ... I-4
• Hemby Bridge, Union, 2,876 ... E-5
Henderson, Vance, 15,655 ... A-10
Hendersonville, Henderson, 7,284 ... J-5
Hertford, Perquimans, 2,105 ... B-15
Hickory, Burke/Catawba, 28,301 ... C-3
Hickory East, Catawba ... N-6
Hiddenite, Alexander ... C-4
High Point, Davidson/Forsyth/Guilford/ Randolph, 69,496 ... C-6
Hillsborough, Orange, 4,263 ... B-9
Hope Mills, Cumberland, 8,184 ... F-9
Hudson, Caldwell, 2,819 ... C-3
Huntersville, Mecklenburg, 3,014 ... E-4
• Icard, Burke, 2,553 ... N-5
Indian Trail, Union, 1,942 ... F-5
Jackson, Northampton, 592 ... A-13
Jacksonville, Onslow, 30,013 ... G-13
• James City, Craven, 4,279 ... F-14
Jamestown, Guilford, 2,600 ... C-7
Jefferson, Ashe, 1,300 ... A-3
Jonesville, Yadkin, 1,549 ... B-4
Kannapolis, Cabarrus/Rowan, 29,696 ... D-5
Kenansville, Duplin, 856 ... F-12
Kenly, Johnston/Wilson, 1,549 ... D-11
Kernersville, Forsyth/Guilford, 10,836 ... B-6
Kill Devil Hills, Dare, 4,238 ... B-17
King, Forsyth/Stokes, 4,059 ... B-6
Kings Mountain, Cleveland/Gaston, 8,763 ... E-3
Kinston, Lenoir, 25,295 ... E-13
Kitty Hawk, Dare, 1,937 ... B-17
Knightdale, Wake, 1,884 ... C-10
La Grange, Lenoir, 2,805 ... E-12
• Lake Junaluska, Haywood, 2,482 ... I-4
Landis, Rowan, 2,333 ... D-5
Landis Northeast, Rowan ... D-5
Laurel Park, Henderson, 1,322 ... J-5
Laurinburg, Scotland, 11,643 ... G-8
Laurinburg West, Scotland ... G-8
Leland, Brunswick, 1,801 ... H-12
Lenoir, Caldwell, 14,192 ... C-3
• Lewisville, Forsyth, 3,206 ... B-5
Lexington, Davidson, 16,581 ... C-6
Liberty, Randolph, 2,047 ... C-8
• Light Oak, Cleveland, 1,339 ... E-3
Lillington, Harnett, 2,048 ... E-9
Lincolnton, Lincoln, 6,847 ... D-3
Locust, Stanly, 1,940 ... E-6
Long Beach, Brunswick, 3,816 ... I-11
Long View, Burke/Catawba, 3,229 ... D-3
Louisburg, Franklin, 3,037 ... B-11
Lowell, Gaston, 2,704 ... N-2
• Lowesville, Lincoln, 1,092 ... D-4
Lumberton, Robeson, 18,601 ... G-9
Madison, Rockingham, 2,371 ... A-7
Maiden, Catawba/Lincoln, 2,574 ... D-3
Manteo, Dare, 991 ... C-17
• Mar-Mac, Wayne, 3,282 ... E-12
Marion, McDowell, 4,765 ... D-1
Mars Hill, Madison, 1,611 ... H-5
Marshall, Madison, 809 ... H-5
Marshville, Union, 2,020 ... F-5
• Masonboro, New Hanover, 7,010 ... I-12
Matthews, Mecklenburg, 13,651 ... E-5
Maxton, Robeson/Scotland, 2,373 ... G-8
Mayodan, Rockingham, 2,471 ... A-7
• McLeansville, Guilford, 1,154 ... B-7
Mebane, Alamance/Orange, 4,754 ... B-8
Midway Park, Onslow ... G-13
• Millers Creek, Wilkes, 1,787 ... B-3
Mint Hill, Mecklenburg, 11,567 ... E-5
Misenheimer, Stanly ... D-6
Mocksville, Davie, 3,399 ... C-5
Monroe, Union, 16,127 ... F-5
Mooresville, Iredell, 9,317 ... D-4
• Moravian Falls, Wilkes, 1,736 ... B-3
Morehead City, Carteret, 6,046 ... G-15
Morganton, Burke, 15,085 ... C-2
Morrisville, Durham/Wake, 1,022 ... C-9
Mount Airy, Surry, 7,156 ... A-5
Mount Gilead, Montgomery, 1,336 ... E-7
Mount Holly, Gaston, 7,710 ... M-3
Mount Olive, Duplin/Wayne, 4,582 ... E-11
Mount Pleasant, Cabarrus, 1,027 ... E-5
• Mountain Home, Henderson, 1,898 ... J-5
• Mountain View, Catawba, 3,697 ... N-6
• Mulberry, Wilkes, 2,339 ... B-4
Murfreesboro, Hertford, 2,580 ... A-14
Murphy, Cherokee, 1,575 ... J-1
• Myrtle Grove, New Hanover, 4,275 ... I-12
Nags Head, Dare, 1,838 ... C-18
Nashville, Nash, 3,617 ... C-12
• Neuse Forest, Craven, 1,110 ... F-14
New Bern, Craven, 17,363 ... E-14
• New Hope, Wake, 5,694 ... C-10
• New Hope, Wayne, 4,491 ... E-12
• New River Station, Onslow, 9,732 ... G-13
Newland, Avery, 645 ... B-2
Newport, Carteret, 2,516 ... F-15
Newton, Catawba, 9,304 ... D-3
• North Hickory, Catawba, 4,299 ... M-6
North Wilkesboro, Wilkes, 3,384 ... B-4
• Northlakes, Caldwell, 1,219 ... M-6
Norwood, Stanly, 1,617 ... E-6
• Ogden, New Hanover, 3,228 ... H-12
Oxford, Granville, 7,913 ... B-10
• Parkwood, Durham, 4,123 ... C-9
Pembroke, Robeson, 2,241 ... G-9
Pilot Mountain, Surry, 1,181 ... A-5
Pine Knoll Shores, Carteret, 1,360 ... G-15
Pine Level, Johnston, 1,217 ... E-11
Pinehurst, Moore, 5,103 ... E-8
Pinetops, Edgecombe, 1,514 ... C-12
Pineville, Mecklenburg, 2,970 ... F-4
• Piney Green, Onslow, 8,999 ... G-13
Pittsboro, Chatham, 1,436 ... D-9
• Pleasant Garden, Guilford, 2,228 ... C-7
• Pleasant Hill, Wilkes, 1,114 ... B-4
Plymouth, Washington, 4,328 ... C-15
Polkville, Cleveland, 1,514 ... D-2
• Pope AFB, Cumberland, 2,857 ... E-9
• Poplar Tent, Cabarrus, 3,872 ... E-5
Princeton, Johnston, 1,181 ... D-11
Princeville, Edgecombe, 1,652 ... C-13
• Pumpkin Center, Onslow, 2,857 ... G-13
Raeford, Hoke, 3,469 ... F-8
Raleigh, Wake, 207,951 ... C-10
Ramseur, Randolph, 1,186 ... D-7
Randleman, Randolph, 2,612 ... C-7
Ranlo, Gaston, 1,650 ... M-2
Red Springs, Robeson, 3,799 ... G-9
Reidsville, Rockingham, 12,183 ... A-7
Rich Square, Northampton, 1,058 ... B-13
River Bend, Craven, 2,408 ... F-14
• River Road, Beaufort, 3,892 ... D-15
Roanoke Rapids, Halifax, 15,722 ... A-12
Robbinsville, Graham, 709 ... J-2
Robersonville, Martin, 1,940 ... C-13
Rockingham, Richmond, 9,399 ... F-7
Rockwell, Rowan, 1,598 ... D-5
Rocky Mount, Edgecombe/Nash, 48,997 ... C-12
Rose Hill, Duplin, 1,287 ... F-12
Roseboro, Sampson, 1,441 ... F-10
Rowan Mill, Rowan ... D-5
Rowland, Robeson, 1,139 ... G-8
Roxboro, Person, 7,332 ... A-9
• Royal Pines, Buncombe, 4,418 ... I-5
Rural Hall, Forsyth, 1,652 ... B-6
Rutherford College, Burke, 1,126 ... M-5
Rutherfordton, Rutherford, 3,617 ... E-1
Saint Pauls, Robeson, 1,992 ... G-9
• Saint Stephens, Catawba, 8,734 ... M-7
• Salem, Burke, 2,271 ... D-2
Salisbury, Rowan, 23,087 ... D-5
Sanford, Lee, 14,475 ... D-9
Sawmills, Caldwell, 4,088 ... M-5
• Saxapahaw, Alamance, 1,178 ... C-8
Scotland Neck, Halifax, 2,575 ... B-13
• Seagate, New Hanover, 5,444 ... H-12
• Sedge Garden, Forsyth, 2,784 ... B-6
Sedgefield, Guilford ... C-7
Selma, Johnston, 4,600 ... D-11
• Seven Lakes, Moore, 2,049 ... E-7
Seymour-Johnson, Wayne ... E-12
Sharpsburg, Edgecombe/Nash/Wilson, 1,536 ... C-12
Shelby, Cleveland, 14,669 ... E-3
• Sherrills Ford, Catawba, 3,185 ... D-4
Siler City, Chatham, 4,808 ... D-8
• Silver City, Hoke, 1,343 ... F-8
• Silver Lake, New Hanover, 4,071 ... I-12
• Smith Creek, New Hanover, 7,461 ... H-12
Smithfield, Johnston, 7,540 ... D-11
• Sneads Ferry, Onslow, 2,031 ... G-13
Snow Hill, Greene, 1,378 ... D-12
• South Gastonia, Gaston, 5,487 ... N-2
South Goldsboro, Wayne ... E-12
• South Henderson, Vance, 1,374 ... B-10
• South Rosemary, Halifax, 1,955 ... A-12
South Salisbury, Rowan ... D-5
• South Weldon, Halifax, 1,640 ... A-13
Southern Pines, Moore, 9,129 ... E-8
Southern Shores, Dare, 1,447 ... B-17
Southport, Brunswick, 2,369 ... I-12
Sparta, Alleghany, 1,957 ... A-4
Spencer, Rowan, 3,219 ... D-5
Spindale, Rutherford, 4,040 ... E-2
Spring Hope, Nash, 1,221 ... C-11
Spring Lake, Cumberland, 7,524 ... E-9
Spruce Pine, Mitchell, 2,010 ... C-1
Stallings, Union, 2,132 ... F-5
Stanley, Gaston, 2,823 ... M-2
• Stanleyville, Forsyth, 4,779 ... B-6
Statesville, Iredell, 17,567 ... C-4
Stokesdale, Guilford, 2,134 ... B-7
Stoneville, Rockingham, 1,109 ... A-7
• Stony Point, Alexander/Iredell, 1,286 ... C-4
• Summerfield, Guilford, 2,051 ... B-7
• Swannanoa, Buncombe, 3,538 ... I-5
Swanquarter, Hyde ... D-16
Swansboro, Onslow, 1,165 ... G-14
• Swepsonville, Alamance, 1,195 ... B-8
Sylva, Jackson, 1,809 ... I-3
Tabor City, Columbus, 2,330 ... I-9
Tarboro, Edgecombe, 11,037 ... C-13
Taylorsville, Alexander, 1,566 ... C-4
Thomasville, Davidson, 15,915 ... C-6
• Toast, Surry, 2,125 ... A-5
Trent Woods, Craven, 2,366 ... F-14
Trenton, Jones, 248 ... F-13
• Trinity, Randolph, 5,469 ... C-7
Troutman, Iredell, 1,493 ... D-4
Troy, Montgomery, 3,404 ... E-7
Tryon, Polk, 1,680 ... E-1
Valdese, Burke, 3,914 ... C-3
• Valley Hill, Henderson, 1,802 ... J-5
• Vander, Cumberland, 1,179 ... F-10
Wadesboro, Anson, 3,645 ... F-6
Wake Forest, Wake, 5,769 ... C-10
Walkertown, Forsyth, 1,200 ... B-6
Wallace, Duplin/Pender, 2,939 ... G-12
Walnut Cove, Stokes, 1,088 ... B-6
• Wanchese, Dare, 1,380 ... C-18
Warrenton, Warren, 949 ... A-11
Warsaw, Duplin, 2,859 ... F-11
Washington, Beaufort, 9,075 ... D-14
Waxhaw, Union, 1,294 ... F-5
Waynesville, Haywood, 6,758 ... I-4
Weaverville, Buncombe, 2,107 ... H-5
Weddington, Mecklenburg/Union, 3,803 ... F-5
• Welcome, Davidson, 3,377 ... C-6
Weldon, Halifax, 1,392 ... A-13
Wendell, Wake, 2,822 ... C-11
Wentworth, Rockingham ... A-7
• West Canton, Haywood, 1,119 ... I-4
West Jefferson, Ashe, 1,002 ... A-3
• West Marion, McDowell, 1,291 ... D-1
• West Smithfield, Johnston, 2,411 ... E-11
• Westport, Lincoln, 1,280 ... D-4
Whispering Pines, Moore, 1,243 ... E-8
• White Plains, Surry, 1,027 ... A-5
Whiteville, Columbus, 5,078 ... H-10
Wilkesboro, Wilkes, 2,573 ... B-4
Williamston, Martin, 5,503 ... C-14
Wilmington, New Hanover, 55,530 ... H-12
Wilson, Wilson, 36,930 ... D-12
• Windemere, New Hanover, 4,604 ... H-12
Windsor, Bertie, 2,056 ... C-14
Wingate, Union, 2,821 ... F-5
Winston-Salem, Forsyth, 143,485 ... B-6
Winterville, Pitt, 2,816 ... D-13
Winton, Hertford, 796 ... A-14
Woodfin, Buncombe, 2,736 ... I-5
• Wrightsboro, New Hanover, 4,752 ... H-12
Wrightsville Beach, New Hanover, 2,937 ... H-12
Yadkinville, Yadkin, 2,525 ... B-5
Yanceyville, Caswell, 1,973 ... A-8
Zebulon, Wake, 3,173 ... C-11

Explanation of symbols: • – Census Designated Place (CDP)

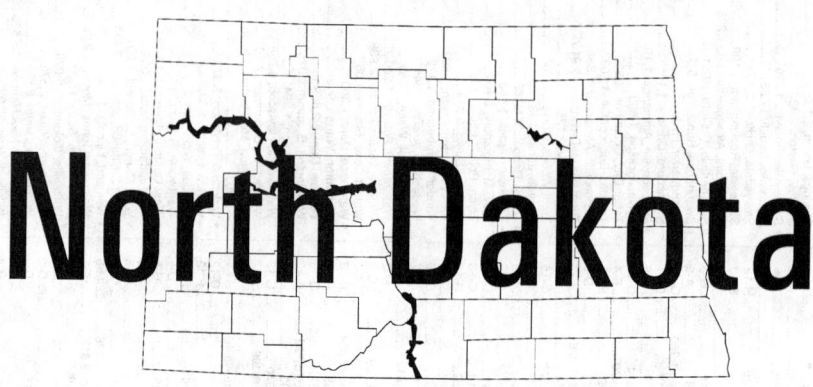

General Help Numbers:

Governor's Office
State Capitol Dept.101   701-328-2200
600 E Boulevard Ave, 1st Floor   Fax 701-328-2205
Bismarck, ND 58505-0001   8AM-5PM
www.governor.state.nd.us

Attorney General's Office
State Capitol - Dept 125   701-328-2210
600 E Boulevard Ave   Fax 701-328-2226
Bismarck, ND 58505-0040   8AM-5PM
www.ag.state.nd.us

Legislative Records
North Dakota Legislative Council   701-328-2916
600 E Blvd Ave   Fax 701-328-3615
Bismarck, ND 58505   8AM-5PM
www.state.nd.us/lr

State Archives
State Archives &   701-328-2666
Historical Research Library   Fax 701-328-3710
N Dakota Heritage Center, 612 E Blvd Ave   8AM-5PM
Bismarck, ND 58505-0830
www.state.nd.us/hist/sal.htm

State Specifics:

Capital: Bismark
Burleigh County

Time Zone: CST

Number of Counties: 53

Population: 634,366

Web Site: http://discovernd.com

State Agencies

Criminal Records

Bureau of Criminal Investigation, Criminal Records Section, PO Box 1054, Bismarck, ND 58502-1054 (Courier address: 4205 N State St, Bismarck, ND 58501); 701-328-5500, 701-328-5510-Fax; 8AM-5PM.

www.ag.state.nd.us

Records are available from 1930 to present. It takes 6 to 10 days before new records are available for inquiry. Records are indexed on computer if DOB is 1940 to present; prior in paper files.

Records are normally destroyed after (records maintained indefinitely). 86% of all arrests in database have final dispositions recorded, 78% for those arrests within last 5 years.

Searching: Subject will be notified of the request. Include the following in your request-signed release from subject, name, DOB, current address, Social Security Number. Fingerprint searches are not available to public. 100% of the records are fingerprint-supported. The following data is not released: cases dismissed or scaled After three years, only records with convictions are released.

Charges that are dismissed or sealed are not released.

Access by: mail, in person.

Fee & Payment: The search fee is $15.00 per name. Fee payee: ND Attorney General. Prepayment required. Personal checks accepted. No credit cards accepted.

Mail search: Turnaround time: 3 to 5 days. No SASE is required.

In person search: Turnaround time while you wait.

Statewide Court Records

Court Administrator, North Dakota Supreme Court, 600 E Blvd Ave, Dept 180, Bismarck, ND 58505-0530; 701-328-4216, 701-328-2092-Fax; 8AM-5PM.

www.ndcourts.com

There is no statewide service for trial courts. Except for certain online research capabilities, all court record access must be done at the local level.

Access by: online.

Online search: You may search ND Supreme Court dockets and opinions at the website. Search by docket number, party name, or anything else that may appear in the text. Records are from 1982 forward. You may subscribe to receive e-mail notification when new Opinions are posted to the North Dakota Supreme Court website, and to be informed when Supreme Court Notices (of proposed or new rules, and the like) are posted.

Sexual Offender Registry

Bureau of Criminal Investigation, SOR Unit, PO Box 1054, Bismarck, ND 58502-1054 (Courier address: 4205 N State St, Bismarck, ND 58501); 701-328-5500, 701-328-5510-Fax; 8AM-5PM.

www.ndsexoffender.com

Records are available from 1991. It takes 6 to 10 days before new records are available for inquiry.

Searching: Offender information may be requested by city, county, or the entire state.

Access by: mail, phone, fax, in person, online.

Fee & Payment: There is no fee.

Mail search: Turnaround time: 1 to 2 days. No SASE is required.

Phone search: Limited name searching available. Call for lists.

Fax search: Fax requests accepted.

In person search: Turnaround time while you wait.

Online search: Access is available from the website. The online listings include offenders who are identified as lifetime registrants as defined by law, or have been designated as high-risk offenders by the Attorney General's Risk Level Committee.

Incarceration Records

Department of Corrections and Rehabilitation, Records Clerk, PO Box 5521, Bismarck, ND 58506 (Courier address: 3100 E Railroad Ave, Bismarck, ND 58506); 701-328-6122, 701-328-6640-Fax; 8AM-5PM.

www.state.nd.us/docr

Employees of the Prisons Division may not disclose inmate information except as granted in North Dakota Century Code 12-47-36.

Records are available on current and former inmates. It takes about 3 days before new records are available for inquiry. Records are normally destroyed after 7 years after discharge.

Searching: Include the following in your request-first and last name. DOB is helpful. Location, conviction and sentencing information, and release dates are provided.

Access by: mail, phone, fax.

Fee & Payment: There is no fee.

Mail search: Turnaround time: 5 to 7 days. Requests in writing must be specific about information requested.

Phone search: Searching available by telephone.

Fax search: May request via the fax.

Corporation, Limited Liability Company, Limited Partnership, Limited Liability Partnership, Trademarks/Servicemarks, Fictitious Name, Assumed Name

Secretary of State, Business Information/ Registration, 600 E Boulevard Ave, Dept 108, Bismarck, ND 58505-0500; 701-328-4284, 800-352-0867, 701-328-2992-Fax; 8AM-5PM.

www.nd.gov/sos/businessserv

Records are available from 1890's on. Records are computerized since 1989. Records inactive prior to 1989 are maintained by state archives, and may take as long as two weeks to search. New records are available for inquiry immediately. Records are indexed on index cards, inhouse computer.

Searching: Include the following in your request-full name of business. In addition to the articles of incorporation, corporation records include the following information: Annual Reports, Officers, Directors, DBAs, Prior (merged) names, Inactive names, and Reserved names. The following data is not released: financial information.

Access by: mail, phone, fax, in person, online.

Fee & Payment: There is a search fee of $5.00 if a written confirmation is required or if data must be retrieved from the archives. Copies cost $1.00 for each 4 pages or fraction thereof. Certification is an additional $15.00. Fee payee: Secretary of State. Prepayment required. Personal checks and MasterCard, Visa, Discover accepted.

Mail search: Turnaround time: 3 to 5 days. No SASE is required.

Phone search: There is no fee for verbal confirmation on an active record, otherwise there is a $5.00 fee.

Fax search: Same fees as phone searching. Turnaround time is 1-3 days if written confirmation required. Add $1.00 per page for fax results.

In person search: No fee on active records, $5.00 fee on inactive records or if in archives. Turnaround time is usually while you wait.

Online search: The Secretary of State's registered business database may be viewed at the Internet for no charge. Documents are not available online. Records include corporations, limited liability companies, limited partnerships, limited liability partnerships, limited liability limited partnerships, partnership fictitious names, trade names, trademarks, and real estate investment trusts. The database includes all active records and records inactivated within past twelve months. Access by the first few words of a business name, a significant word in a business name, or by the record ID number assigned. If questions, email sosbir@state.nd.us.

Other access: This agency provides a database purchase program. Cost is $35.00 per database and processing fees vary for type of media.

Uniform Commercial Code, Federal and State Tax Liens

UCC Division, Secretary of State, 600 E Boulevard Ave Dept 108, Bismarck, ND 58505-0500; 701-328-3662, 701-328-4214-Fax; 8AM-5PM.

www.nd.gov/sos/businessserv/centralindex/index.html

The state has a Central Indexing System which allows UCC and tax lien searches at this office or at any of the county Register of Deeds (53).

Records are available from 1966. Records are computerized on index statewide since 1992. It takes less than 1 day before new records are available for inquiry. Records are indexed on inhouse computer. Records are normally destroyed after 1 year after expiration date.

Searching: Use search request form UCC-11. Include the following in your request-debtor name.

Access by: mail, phone, fax, in person, online.

Fee & Payment: The search fee is $7.00 for the first 5 entries and $2.00 for each additional 5 entries or fraction thereof. A copy request with certificate is $7.00 for first 3 copies and $2.00 for each additional. All tax liens will show on the record request. Fee payee: Secretary of State. Will invoice, if requested. Monthly billing is offered to ongoing requesters. Personal checks and MasterCard, Visa, Discover accepted.

Mail search: Turnaround time: 1 day. A SASE is requested.

Phone search: General information is available without charge.

Fax search: There is an additional fee of $3.00 (maximum 20 pages) to return by fax. Please allow 20 minutes to 1 hour.

In person search: You may request information in person.

Online search: There is a limited free public search and a commercial system for professionals. Sign-up for access to the Central Indexing System includes an annual subscription $150 fee and a one-time $50.00 registration fee. The UCC-11 fee (normally $7.00) applies, but documents will not be certified. Searches include UCC-11 information listing and farm product searches.

Other access: The agency offers bulk access on IBM cartridge or paper copy. Call for details.

Sales Tax Registrations

Office of State Tax Commissioner, Sales & Special Taxes Division, State Capitol, 600 E Boulevard Ave, Bismarck, ND 58505-0599; 701-328-3470, 701-328-0336-Fax; 8AM-5PM.

www.state.nd.us/taxdpt

Records are available from 1999 to present, including inactive records. It takes hours before new records are available for inquiry. Records are indexed on computer. Records are normally destroyed after 6 years.

Searching: This agency will only confirm if a business is registered and active. They will provide no other information as it is confidential. Include the following in your request-business name. They will also search by tax permit number or owner name.

Access by: mail, phone, fax, online.

Mail search: Turnaround time: 7 to 10 days. A SASE is requested. No fee for mail request.

Phone search: No fee for telephone request.

Fax search: There is no fee.

Online search: A permit number may be verified online at website. System indicates valid permit registered to company name.

Birth Certificates

ND Department of Health, Vital Records, State Capitol, 600 E Blvd, Dept 301, Bismarck, ND 58505-0200; 701-328-2360, 701-328-1850-Fax; 7:30AM-5PM.

www.vitalnd.com

Records are available from 1870 on. New records are available for inquiry immediately. Records are indexed on inhouse computer.

Searching: Must have a signed release from person of record if it is an out-of-wedlock birth. If under 18, parent or legal guardian signature needed. Include the following in your request-full name, names of parents, mother's maiden name, date of birth, place of birth, relationship to person of record, reason for information request.

Access by: mail, fax, in person, online.

Fee & Payment: The fee is $7.00 per name. Add $4.00 per name for second copies. Fee payee: North Dakota Department of Health. Prepayment required. Personal checks and MasterCard, Visa, Discover accepted.

Mail search: Turnaround time: 3 to 5 days. No SASE is required.

Fax search: Use of credit card required. Turnaround time is same day if received by 10AM and request is marked for FedEx or UPS.

In person search: Turnaround time is less than 15 minutes.

Online search: Records may be ordered online from the Internet site or from vitalchek.com. Records are not returned online.

Expedited service: Expedited service is available for fax or online searches. Turnaround time: overnight delivery. Expedited service options are available using a credit card and an additional $13.00 fee for shipping.

Death Records

ND Department of Health, Vital Records, State Capitol, 600 E Blvd, Dept 301, Bismarck, ND 58505-0200; 701-328-2360, 701-328-1850-Fax; 7:30AM-5PM.

www.vitalnd.com

Records are available from 1881 on. Early records are few. New records are available for inquiry immediately. Records are indexed on inhouse computer.

Searching: Cause of death not shown on copy of Death Certificate if not a family member. Include the following in your request-full name, date of death, place of death, relationship to person of record, reason for information request.

Access by: mail, fax, in person, online.

Fee & Payment: The fee is $5.00 per name. Add $2.00 per name for second copies. Fee payee: North Dakota Department of Health. Prepayment required. Personal checks and MasterCard, Visa, Discover accepted.

Mail search: Turnaround time: 3 to 5 days. A SASE is requested.

Fax search: This is considered expedited service. Turnaround time is same day if received by 10AM noon and request is marked for FedEx or UPS.

In person search: Turnaround time is 10 to 15 minutes.

Online search: Records may be ordered online from the Internet site.

Expedited service: Expedited service is available for fax searches. Turnaround time: overnight delivery. Expedited service options are available using a credit card and an additional $13.00 fee for shipping.

Marriage Certificates

ND Department of Health, Vital Records, State Capitol, 600 E Blvd, Dept 301, Bismarck, ND 58505-0200; 701-328-2360, 701-328-1850-Fax; 7:30AM-5PM.

www.vitalnd.com

Records are available from July 1, 1925 to present. New records are available for inquiry immediately. Records are indexed on inhouse computer.

Searching: Include the following in your request-names of husband and wife, date of marriage, place or county of marriage, relationship to person of record, reason for information request, wife's maiden name.

Access by: mail, fax, in person, online.

Fee & Payment: The fee is $5.00 per name. Add $2.00 per name for second copies. Fee payee: North Dakota Department of Health. Prepayment required. Personal checks accepted. Major credit cards accepted.

Mail search: Turnaround time: 3 to 5 days. No SASE is required.

Fax search: Turnaround time is same day if received by 10 AM and request is being returned by FedEx or UPS.

In person search: Turnaround time is 10 to 15 minutes.

Online search: Records may be ordered online from the Internet site.

Expedited service: Expedited service is available for fax or online searches. Turnaround time: overnight delivery. Expedited service options are available using a credit card and an additional $13.00 fee for shipping.

Divorce Records

Access to Records is Restricted.

ND Department of Health, Vital Records, State Capitol, 600 E Blvd, Dept 301, Bismarck, ND 58505-0200; 701-328-2360, 701-328-1850-Fax; 7:30AM-5PM. www.vitalnd.com

Copies of divorce records can only be obtained from the county recorder in the county in which the divorce or annulment was decreed. This office will assist in determining what county to contact. Their index contains records from July 1, 1949 to present. Call or e-mail to vitalrec@state.nd.us.

Workers' Compensation Records

Workforce Safety & Insurance, Workers' Compensation Records, PO Box 5585, Bismarck ND 58506-5585 (Courier address: 1600 East Century Avenue, Suite 1, Bismarck, ND 58503-

0644); 701-328-3800, 800-777-5033, 701-328-3750-Fax; 7:30AM-5PM.

www.workforcesafety.com

Records are available from 1919 but more reliable information is from 1975 on. It takes 24 hours before new records are available for inquiry. Records are indexed on inhouse computer.

Searching: Must have a signed release from person of record stating exactly what information is requested. Include the following in your request-claimant name, Social Security Number, date of birth. Also, a signed release by the subject is required, unless the requester is involved within the case.

Access by: mail.

Fee & Payment: Copies are $.35 per page. There is no search fee, unless file needs to be retrieved from off-site, then $5.00 is charged. Fee payee: Workforce Safety & Enforcement Prepayment required. Personal checks accepted.

Mail search: Turnaround time: 5 days. A SASE is requested.

Driver Records

Department of Transportation, Driver License & Traffic Safety Division, 608 E Boulevard Ave, Bismarck, ND 58505-0700; 701-328-2603, 701-328-2435-Fax; 8AM-5PM.

www.state.nd.us/dot

Copies of tickets must be obtained from the local courts.

Records are available for 3 yrs for moving violations, DWI and suspensions. Records available to the public show neither violations less than 2 points nor accidents. The record will not show driver's address to casual requesters without consent. It takes 1 day before new records are available for inquiry. Records are normally destroyed after three years.

Searching: The Division sends an additional copy of the abstract to the driver whose record was requested, accompanied by a statement identifying the requester. Include the following in your request-license number, name, and DOB are required when ordering, but "two out of three" may produce a "hit.". Written requests must also include reason for request.

Access by: mail, in person, online.

Fee & Payment: The fee is $3.00 per record. Fee payee: Driver License & Traffic Safety. Prepayment required. Personal checks and MasterCard, Visa, Discover accepted.

Mail search: Turnaround time: 3 days. A SASE is requested.

In person search: Up to eight requests will be processed while you wait.

Online search: The web offers record ordering at https://secure.apps.state.nd.us/dot/dlts/dlos/welcome.htm. Fee is $3.00 per record, record is returned by mail. If you are not ordering your own record, you must qualify per DPPA. Ongoing, approved commercial accounts may request records with personal information via a commercial system. There is a minimum of 100 requests per month. For more information, call 701-328-4790.

Other access: Magnetic tape ordering is available for high volume users.

Vehicle Ownership
Vehicle Identification

Department of Transportation, Records Section/Motor Vehicle Div., 608 E Boulevard Ave, Bismarck, ND 58505-0780; 701-328-2725, 701-328-1487-Fax; 8AM-4:50PM.

www.state.nd.us/dot

Records on mobile homes are also maintained by this agency.

Records are available from 1911 for license plate numbers. It takes 10 to 14 days before new records are available for inquiry. Records are normally destroyed after they are imaged.

Searching: Records are available with the prior authorization. Personal information is not released to casual requesters without consent. A written request or use of Form SFN-51269A is required and found at the web page. Requester must initial one of 12 categories. The following data is not released: Social Security Numbers or medical records.

Access by: mail, fax, in person.

Fee & Payment: The fee is $3.00 per vehicle (includes lien data). There is a fee for a no record found. Fee payee: Motor Vehicle Division. Prepayment required. Personal checks accepted. Credit cards accepted: MasterCard, Visa.

Mail search: Turnaround time: same day. A SASE is helpful.

Fax search: fax requesting is available for pre-approved commercial accounts.

In person search: The state may limit the number of requests processed immediately, if busy.

Other access: North Dakota offers bulk or batch retrieval of VIN or ownership information of vehicles. The requester must explain purpose and intent; however, there are no restrictions placed upon requests of a legal nature. Customized or special runs are available.

Accident Reports

Driver License & Traffic Safety Division, Traffic Records Section, 608 E Boulevard Ave, Bismarck, ND 58505-0780; 701-328-4352, 701-328-2601, 701-328-2435-Fax; 8AM-5PM.

www.state.nd.us/dot

Records are available from 1998. Records are computer indexed since 1998. It takes 1-2 months before new records are available for inquiry. Records are normally destroyed after 5 years.

Searching: The front page which includes drivers, witnesses, and insurance information, can be ordered by anyone with a written request. The investigating officer's report is also only to parties involved or their legal representative or insurer. Include the following in your request-date of accident, location of accident, full name of at least one driver, reason for information request.

Access by: mail, in person.

Fee & Payment: Fee is $2.00 for front page record (drivers, witnesses, etc.). Add $5.00 to receive the investigating officer's report. Fee

payee: Driver License & Traffic Safety Division. Prepayment required. Personal checks accepted. Credit cards accepted: MasterCard, Visa.

Mail search: Turnaround time: 5 days. A SASE is requested.

In person search: Turnaround time while you wait.

Vessel Ownership
Vessel Registration

North Dakota Game & Fish Department, Boat Registrations, 100 N Bismarck Expressway, Bismarck, ND 58501; 701-328-6335, 701-328-6374-Fax; 8AM-5PM.

www.state.nd.us/gnf

Liens are filed at same locations as UCCs. Owners of any watercraft propelled by motors must register their vessels with the Game and Fish Department. No titles are issued by this agency.

Records are available from 1975 to present. Records are computer indexed for the last five years. It takes 2 weeks. before new records are available for inquiry. Records are normally destroyed after 10 years.

Searching: Include the following in your request-one of the following is required: hull ID #, registration #, decal #, or name. The agency does NOT follow DPPA. All records are open to the public.

Access by: mail, phone, fax, in person, online.

Fee & Payment: There is no fee for 1-2 names.

Mail search: Turnaround time: 1 day. No SASE is required.

Phone search: Records are available by phone.

Fax search: Results can be faxed, mailed, or phone.

In person search: Turnaround time is usually immediate.

Online search: There is a free public inquiry system at https://secure.apps.state.nd.us/gnf/inquiry/pubsysinq-boat.htm (or access it via the agency web page). One can also search lottery hunting permit applications and hunter safety listings.

Other access: A printed list is available of all registered vessels.

Voter Registration
Access to Records is Restricted.

Secretary of State, Elections Division, 600 E Boulevard Ave Dept 108, Bismarck ND 58505-0500; 701-328-4146, 701-328-2992-Fax; 8AM-5PM.

www.nd.gov/sos/electvote

Currently, records are maintained at the county level by the County Auditors in poll books. Records are open to the public. Although, the Federal Help America Vote Act of 2002 (HAVA) law requires implementation of a central, computerized, statewide voter registration system

by 01/01/2006, this state agency will not comply, the agency is exempt.

GED Certificates

Department of Public Instruction, GED Testing - CKEN-11, 600 E Blvd Ave, Bismarck, ND 58505-0440; 701-328-2393, 701-328-4770-Fax; 8AM-4:30PM.

www.dpi.state.nd.us/adulted/index.shtm

Searching: A verification will only verify that a test was taken, but not if the subject passed the test. Include the following in your request-name, signed release, Social Security Number, date of birth.

Access by: mail, fax, in person, online.

Fee & Payment: There is no fee for a verification (yes or no) and a $2.00 fee for a copy of a transcript. Fee payee: Dept of Public Instruction. Prepayment required. Money orders and business checks accepted. No credit cards accepted.

Mail search: Turnaround time: 1 week. No SASE is required.

Fax search: Used only for verification of a "yes or no" request.

In person search: Picture ID required.

Online search: One may request records via email at JMarcell@state.nd.us. There is no fee, unless a transcript is ordered.

Hunting and Fishing License Information

ND Game & Fish Department, 100 N Bismarck Expressway, Bismarck, ND 58501-5095; 701-328-6300, 701-328-6335 (Licensing), 701-328-6352-Fax; 8AM-5PM.

www.state.nd.us/gnf

Records are available from 1992 on computer. Big Game Lottery Permits are only available for the current season. Records are indexed on inhouse computer.

Searching: Include the following in your request-full name, date of birth, Social Security Number. This agency also registers boats.

Access by: mail, fax, in person, online.

Fee & Payment: There is no search fee.

Mail search: Turnaround time: 1 to 3 days. A SASE is requested.

Fax search: Same criteria as mail searches.

In person search: You can go in and access their records. They also make the boat registrations available.

Online search: From the web site, one can search to see if a person has been chosen (lottery) for a specific hunt or passed hunter safety. Go to Public Inquiry System.

Other access: They sell mailing lists. Call Paul Schadewald at 701-328-6328 for more information.

North Dakota State Licensing Agencies

For details about the agency responsible for licensing/certifying/registering an item below or in the Agency Quick Finder section, match an item's number with the number of the agency in the *Licensing Agency Information* section.

North Dakota Licenses Searchable Online

Alcoholic Beverage Control #3	www.ag.state.nd.us/Licensing/Beverage/Beverage.htm
Amusement Device, Coin-Operated #3	www.ag.state.nd.us/Licensing/Amusement/Amusement.htm
Asbestos-related Occupation #27	www.health.state.nd.us/AQ/IAQ/ASB/cntr.pdf
Attorney #41	www.court.state.nd.us/court/lawyers/index/frameset.htm
Bank, Commercial #20	www.state.nd.us/dfi/regulate/reg/regulated.asp
Charitable Solicitation #39	www.state.nd.us/sec/charitableorg/search.htm
Collection Agency #20	www.state.nd.us/dfi/regulate/reg/regulated.asp
Consumer Finance Company #20	www.state.nd.us/dfi/regulate/reg/regulated.asp
Contractor #27	www.health.state.nd.us/AQ/IAQ/ASB/cntr.pdf
Contractor/General Contractor #39	www.state.nd.us/sec/licensing/search.html
Credit Union #20	www.state.nd.us/dfi/regulate/reg/regulated.asp
Debt Collector #20	www.state.nd.us/dfi/regulate/reg/regulated.asp
Deferred Presentment Provider #20	www.state.nd.us/dfi/regulate/reg/regulated.asp
Drug Mfg./Wholesaler #14	www.nodakpharmacy.com
Engineer #36	www.ndpelsboard.org
Fireworks, Wholesale #3	www.ag.state.nd.us/Licensing/Fireworks/Fireworks.htm
Gaming #3	www.ag.state.nd.us/Gaming/listorg.PDF
Gaming Distributor #3	www.ag.state.nd.us/Gaming/distlist.PDF
Gaming Manufacturer #3	www.ag.state.nd.us/Gaming/manlst.PDF
Grain Buyer #34	www.psc.state.nd.us/jurisdiction/grain-entities.html
Grain Warehouse/Elevator #34	www.psc.state.nd.us/jurisdiction/grain-entities.html
Investment Advisor #40	www.ndsecurities.com
Land Surveyor #36	www.ndpelsboard.org
Livestock Agent #19	www.agdepartment.com/Programs/Livestock/Agents.html
Livestock Auction Market #19	www.agdepartment.com/Programs/Livestock/markets.html
Livestock Dealer #19	www.agdepartment.com/Programs/Livestock/Dealers.html
Lobbyist #39	www.state.nd.us/sec/lobbylegislate/lobbying/reg-mnu.html
Medical Doctor #47	www.ndbomex.com/SearchPage.asp
Money Broker Firm #20	www.state.nd.us/dfi/regulate/reg/regulated.asp
Nurse Assistant #31	www.ndbon.org
Nurse-Advanced Practice #31	www.ndbon.org
Nurse-LPN / RN #31	www.ndbon.org
Optometrist #49	www.ndsbopt.org/directory.asp
Osteopathic Physician #47	www.ndbomex.com/SearchPage.asp
Pharmacist / Pharmacy #14	www.nodakpharmacy.com
Pharmacy Technician/Intern #14	www.nodakpharmacy.com
Physician Assistant #47	www.ndbomex.com/SearchPage.asp
Polygraph Examiner #3	www.ag.state.nd.us/Licensing/Polygraph/Polygraph.htm
Private Investigation Agency #33	www.state.nd.us/pisb/holders.html
Private Investigator #33	www.state.nd.us/pisb/holders.html
Public Accountant-CPA #42	www.state.nd.us/ndsba/database/sbasearch.asp
Public Accounting Firm #42	www.state.nd.us/ndsba/database/sbasearch.asp
Racing #3	www.ndracingcommission.com/Forms.htm
Sale of Check #20	www.state.nd.us/dfi/regulate/reg/regulated.asp
Securities Agent/Dealer #40	www.ndsecurities.com
Security Provider/Company #33	www.state.nd.us/pisb/holders.html
Social Worker #18	http://secure.ebigpicture.com/ndbswe/live/public.asp
Soil Classifier #17	www.soilsci.ndsu.nodak.edu/soilclassifiers/pscand.htm
Speech-Language Patholog't/Audi't #12	http://governor.state.nd.us/boards/bcpublicsearch.asp?searchtype=member
Tobacco, Retail/Wholesale #3	www.ag.state.nd.us/Licensing/Tobacco/Tobacco.htm
Transient Merchant #3	www.ag.state.nd.us/Licensing/Transient/TransientMerchant.htm
Trust Company #20	www.state.nd.us/dfi/regulate/reg/regulated.asp
Water Well Driller/Well Pump & Pitless Unit #50	www.health.state.nd.us/wq/gw/wells.htm
Well Contractor, Monitoring #50	www.health.state.nd.us/wq/gw/wells.htm

North Dakota Licensing Quick Finder

Abstractor/Abstractor Company #1 701-947-2446
Adoption Service #22 701-328-4805
Aerial Applicator #30 701-328-9650
Aircraft Dealer #30 701-328-9650
Aircraft Registration #30 701-328-9650
Alcoholic Beverage Control #3 701-328-2329
Amusement Device, Coin-Operated #3 701-328-2329
Architect #43 701-223-3184
Asbestos-related Occupation #27 701-328-5188
Athletic Trainer #5.......................... 701-857-3486
Attorney #41 701-328-4201
Auction Clerk #34 701-328-2400
Auctioneer #34 701-328-2400
Bank, Commercial #20 701-328-9933
Barber #6 701-223-5186
Barber Shop #6.............................. 701-223-5186
Boxer/Boxing Professional #38 701-328-3665
Broker, Corporate #28 .... 701-328-3548 x2
Charitable Solicitation #39.............. 701-328-3665
Chiropractor #7 701-352-1690
Coal Mine, Surface #34 701-328-2400
Collection Agency #20 701-328-9933
Consumer Finance Company #20........ 701-328-9933
Contractor #27 701-328-5188
Contractor/General Contractor #39 701-328-3665
Cosmetologist/Cosmetologist Instructor #8
.... 701-224-9800
Counselor, Addiction #4 701-255-1439
Counselor, Professional #9 701-667-5969
Credit Union #20............................ 701-328-9933
Crematorium #44............................ 701-873-7700
Day Care Service #22 701-328-4809
Debt Collector #20.......................... 701-328-9933
Deferred Presentment Provider #20..... 701-328-9933
Dental Assistant #10........................ 701-258-8600
Dental Hygienist #10 701-258-8600
Dentist #10.................................... 701-258-8600
Dietitian/Nutritionist #11.................. 701-746-9171
Drug Mfg./Wholesaler #14.............. 701-328-9535
Electrician #25................................ 701-328-9522
Electrician Apprentice #25................ 701-328-9522
Embalmer #44................................ 701-873-7700
Employment Agency (Permanent Placing) #23
.... 701-328-2660
Engineer #36 701-258-0786

Esthetician #8................................ 701-224-9800
Fireworks, Wholesale #3.................. 701-328-2329
Fishing Guide #26 701-328-6300
Foster Care Program #22................ 701-328-3587
Fund Raiser, Professional #39............ 701-328-3665
Funeral Director #44........................ 701-873-7700
Funeral Home #44 701-873-7700
Gaming #3 701-328-2329
Gaming Distributor #3 701-328-2329
Gaming Manufacturer #3.................. 701-328-2329
Grain Buyer #34 701-328-2400
Grain Warehouse/Elevator #34.......... 701-328-2400
Hearing Aid Dealer/Fitter #45............ 701-237-9977
Hunting Guide #26.......................... 701-328-6300
Hunting/Fishing Guide Combo #26 701-328-6300
Insurance Agency/Agent #28 ...... 701-328-3548 x2
Insurance Broker #28.............. 701-328-3548 x2
Investment Advisor #40.................... 701-328-4698
Kickboxer #38................................ 701-328-3665
Laboratory Clinician #52.................. 701-530-0199
Land Surveyor #36 701-258-0786
Livestock Agent #19........................ 701-328-4761
Livestock Auction Market #19............ 701-328-4761
Livestock Dealer #19........................ 701-328-4761
Lobbyist #39 701-328-3665
Manicurist #8 701-224-9800
Massage Therapist #46.................... 701-872-4895
Medical Doctor #47........................ 701-328-6500
Money Broker Firm #20.................... 701-328-9933
Mortician #44 701-873-7700
Notary Public #39 701-328-2901
Nurse Assistant #31 701-328-9780
Nurse-Advanced Practice #31 701-328-9777
Nurse-LPN/RN #31.......................... 701-328-9777
Nursing Home Administrator #13........ 701-222-4867
Nutritionist #11.............................. 701-746-9171
Occupational Therapist #48.............. 701-250-0847
Occupational Therapy Assistant #48 .. 701-250-0847
Oil & Gas Broker #40 701-328-2910
Oil & Gas Wellhead Welder #40........ 701-328-2910
Optometrist #49.............................. 701-225-9333
Osteopathic Physician #47................ 701-328-6500
Pharmacist / Pharmacy #14.............. 701-328-9535
Pharmacy Technician/Intern #14 701-328-9535
Physical Therapist/Assistant #51 701-352-0125

Physician Assistant #47 701-328-6500
Plumber Journeyman/Apprentice/Master #32
.... 701-328-9977
Podiatrist #15 701-234-8770
Polygraph Examiner #3.................... 701-328-2329
Private Investigation Agency #33........ 701-222-3063
Private Investigator #33 701-222-3063
Psychologist #16............................ 701-250-8691
Public Accountant-CPA #42.............. 800-532-5904
Public Accounting Firm #42 800-532-5904
Racing #3 701-328-4633
Real Estate Agent/Broker #35 701-328-9749
Respiratory Care Practitioner #37...... 701-222-1564
Sale of Check #20 701-328-9933
School Counselor/Designate #24 701-328-2260
School Media Specialist #24.............. 701-328-2260
School Principal/Assistant #24............ 701-328-2260
School Superintendent/Assistant #24 .. 701-328-2260
Securities Agent/Dealer #40 701-328-4698
Security Employee #33 701-222-2063
Security Provider/Company #33 701-222-3063
Sewer & Water Contractor/Installer #32701-328-9977
Social Worker #18.......................... 701-222-0255
Soil Classifier #17............................ 701-530-2020
Speech-Language Pathologist/Audiologist #12
.... 701-777-4421
Taxidermist #26.............................. 701-328-6300
Teacher #24 701-328-2260
Telecommunications Company #34..... 701-328-2400
Telecommunications Personnel #34.... 701-328-2400
Tobacco, Retail/Wholesale #3 701-328-2329
Transient Merchant #3 701-328-2329
Trust Company #20.......................... 701-328-9933
Veterinarian #29 701-328-9540
Veterinary Technician #29 701-328-9540
Waste Water System Operator #21 701-328-5211
Water Conditioning Contractor/Installer #32
.... 701-328-9977
Water Distribution System Operatr #21 701-328-5211
Water Well Driller #50...................... 701-328-2754
Water Well Pump & Pitless Unit #50.... 701-328-2754
Weather Modifier #2........................ 701-328-2788
Weighing Device Company #34.......... 701-328-2400
Weighing Device Tester #34.............. 701-328-2400
Well Contractor, Monitoring #50 701-328-2754

North Dakota Licensing Agency Information

1 Abstractors Board of Examiners, PO Box 551, New Rockford, ND 58356; 701-947-2446, Fax: 701-947-2443. http://governor.state.nd.us/boards/boards-query.asp?Board_ID=1

2 Atmospheric Resource Board, Water Commission, 900 E Boulevard Ave, Bismarck, ND 58505; 701-328-4940, Fax: 701-328-4749. www.swc.state.nd.us/index.html

3 Attorney General's Office, Licensing Division, 600 E Boulevard Ave, Dept 125, Bismarck, ND 58505-0040; 701-328-4848, Fax: 701-328-3535. www.ag.state.nd.us

4 Board of Addiction Counseling Examiners, PO Box 975, Bismarck, ND 58502-0975; 701-255-1439, Fax: 701-224-9824. www.ndbace.org Email: ndbace@aptnd.com The Board can sell lists for $20.00. Can be sent by email, labels or a list.

5 Board of Athletic Trainers, 413 22nd Street, PO Box 5020, Valley City, ND 58702; 701-857-3486. http://governor.state.nd.us/boards/boards-query.asp?Board_ID=12

6 Board of Barber Examiners, 1210 West Coulee Road, Bismarck, ND 58501; 701-223-5186.

7 c/o Jerry Blanchard, Board of Chiropractic Examiners, PO Box 185, Grafton, ND 58237; 701-352-1690, Fax: 701-352-2258.

8 Board of Cosmetology, PO Box 2177 (1102 S Washington #200), Bismarck, ND 58502; 701-224-9800, Fax: 701-222-8756. Email: cosmo@gcentral.com

9 Board of Counselor Examiners, 2112 10th Av SE, Mandan, ND 58554-5066; 701-667-5969. www.sendit.nodak.edu/ndbce/ Email: ndbce@btigate.com

10 Board of Dental Examiners, PO Box 7246, Bismarck, ND 58507-7246; 701-258-8600, Fax: 701-224-9824. www.nddentalboard.org Email: ndsbde@aptnd.com Note: Lists available on disk, labels, email, or printed.

11 Board of Dietetic Practice, PO Box 6142, Grand Forks, ND 58206-6142; 701-777-2539, Fax: 701-777-3268. http://governor.state.nd.us/boards/boards-query.asp?Board_ID=33

12 Board of Examiners in Audiology/Speech Pathology, 720 4th St N, Fargo, ND 58122; 701-777-4421, Fax: 701-777-4365. http://governor.state.nd.us/boards/boards-query.asp?Board_ID=14

13 Board of Examiners in Nursing Home Adminstrators, 1900 N 11th St, Bismarck, ND 58501-1914; 701-222-4867, Fax: 701-223-0977. www.ndboenha.org Email: bev@ndltca.org

14 Board of Pharmacy, PO Box 1354, Bismarck, ND 58502-1354; 701-328-9535, Fax: 701-258-9312. www.nodakpharmacy.com Email: ndboph@btinet.net

15 Dr. Mathews, Board of Podiatric Medicine, 2400 32nd Ave S, Fargo, ND 58103; 701-234-8770.

16 Board of Psychologist Examiners, PO Box 7458, Bismarck, ND 58507-7458; 701-250-8691, Fax: 701-250-8611. www.governor.state.nd.us/boards/boards-query.asp?Board_ID=88

17 Board of Registry for Professional Soil Classifier, 202 E Divide Ave, Bismarck, ND 58501; 701-530-2020.
www.governor.state.nd.us/boards/
Email: mike.ulmer@nd.udsa.gov

18 Board of Social Worker Examiners, PO Box 914, Bismarck, ND 58502-0914; 701-222-0255, Fax: 701-224-9824.
www.ndbswe.com
Email: ndbswe@aptnd.com Note: Also sell lists for $100.00 by email, disk list or labels - for continuing ed or research purposes only.

19 Department of Agriculture, Livestock & Pesticide Programs, 600 E Boulevard Ave,Dept 602, Bismarck, ND 58505-0020; 701-328-2231, Fax: 701-328-4567. www.agdepartment.com
Email: wcarlson@state.nd.us Search Database at www.agdepartment.com/Programs/Livestock/Livestock.html

20 Department of Financial Institutions, 2000 Schafer St. #G, Bismarck, ND 58501-1204; 701-328-9933, Fax: 701-328-9955.
www.discovernd.com/dfi
Email: dfi@state.nd.us Search Database at www.state.nd.us/dfi/regulate/reg/regulated.asp

21 Department of Health, Municipal Facilities, 1200 Missouri Av, Bismarck, ND 58506-5520; 701-328-5211, Fax: 701-328-5200.
www.health.state.nd.us/MF/

22 Department of Human Services, Children & Family Services, 600 E Boulevard Ave, Bismarck, ND 58505-0250; 701-328-2310, Fax: 701-328-2359. www.state.nd.us/humanservices

23 Department of Labor, 600 E Blvd Ave, Dept 406, Bismarck, ND 58505-0340; 701-328-2660, Fax: 701-328-2031.
www.state.nd.us/labor/services/ea-licensing/
Email: labor@state.nd.us

24 Department of Public Instruction, 600 E Boulevard Ave, 1st Fl-Judicial Wing, Bismarck, ND 58505-0440; 701-328-2260, Fax: 701-328-2461. www.dpi.state.nd.us

25 Electrical Board, PO Box 857 (721 Memorial Highway), Bismarck, ND 58502; 701-328-9522, Fax: 701-328-9524.
www.state.nd.us/electric
Email: electric@state.nd.us

26 Game & Fish Department, 100 N Bismarck Exprwy, Bismarck, ND 58501-5095; 701-328-6300, Fax: 701-328-6352.
www.state.nd.us/gnf/ Email: ndgf@state.nd.us

27 Department of Health, Asbestos Control Program, PO Box 5520 (1200 Missouri Ave), Bismarck, ND 58506-5520; 701-328-5188, Fax: 701-328-5200.
www.health.state.nd.us/AQ/IAQ/ASB/
Email: kwangler@state.nd.us

28 Insurance Department, Producer/Agent Information, 600 E Boulevard Ave, Capitol Bldg, 1st Fl, Bismarck, ND 58505-0320; 701-328-2440, Fax: 701-328-4880.
www.state.nd.us/ndins Email: insuranc@state.nd.us

29 Board of Veterinarian Examiners, PO Box 5001, Bismarck, ND 58502-5001; 701-328-9540, Fax: 701-224-0435.
Email: ndbvme@state.nd.us

30 Aeronautics Commission, PO Box 5020, Bismarck, ND 58502-5020; 701-328-9650, Fax: 701-328-9656.
www.state.nd.us/ndaero/
Email: ndaero@state.nd.us

31 Board of Nursing, 919 S 7th St #504, Bismarck, ND 58504-5881; 701-328-9777, Fax: 701-328-9785. www.ndbon.org

32 State Board of Plumbing, 204 W Thayer Av, Bismarck, ND 58501; 701-328-9977, Fax: 701-328-9979.
http://governor.state.nd.us/boards/boards-query.asp?Board_ID=83
Email: ndplumb@state.nd.us

33 Private Investigation & Security Board, Private Investigators Licensing, 513 E Bismarck Expy, #5, Bismarck, ND 58504-6577; 701-222-3063, Fax: 701-222-3063. www.state.nd.us/pisb
Email: ndpisb@midco.net Search Database at www.state.nd.us/pisb/holders.html

34 Public Service Commission, 600 E Boulevard Ave, Dept 408, Bismarck, ND 58505-0480; 701-328-2400, Fax: 701-328-2410.
www.psc.state.nd.us Email: skr@psc.state.nd.us
Search Database at
www.psc.state.nd.us/jurisdiction/grain-entities.html Note: Lists are provided online.

35 Real Estate Commission, PO Box 727, Bismarck, ND 58502-0727; 701-328-9749, Fax: 701-328-9750.
Email: pjergenson@state.nd.us

36 Registration for Prof. Engineers & Land Surveyors, PO Box 1357, Bismarck, ND 58502-1357; 701-258-0786, Fax: 701-258-7471.
www.ndpelsboard.org
Email: brdofreg@bt.igate.net

37 Respiratory Care Examining Board, PO Box 2223, Bismarck, ND 58502; 701-222-1564, Fax: 701-255-9149.
www.governor.state.nd.us/boards/boards-query.asp?Board_ID=96
Email: ndsbrc@btigate.com

38 Secretary of State, Athletic Commissioner, Licensing Division, 600 East Blvd Ave, Dept 108, Bismarck, ND 58505-0040; 701-328-2900, Fax: 701-328-1690.
www.nd.gov/sos/ Email: sosadlic@state.nd.us

39 Secretary of State, Licensing Division, 600 East Blvd Ave, Dept 108, Bismarck, ND 58505-0500; 701-328-3665, Fax: 701-328-1690.
www.state.nd.us/sec/
Email: sosadlic@state.nd.us

40 Securities Department, 600 E Blvd Ave, Dept 414, State Capitol, 5th Fl, Bismarck, ND 58505-0510; 701-328-2910, Fax: 701-328-2946.
www.ndsecurities.com
Email: ndsecurities@state.nd.us
Search Database at http://pdpi.nasdr.com/PDPI/

41 State Board of Law Examiners, 600 E Boulevard Ave, Dept. 180, Bismarck, ND 58505-0530; 701-328-4201, Fax: 701-328-4480.
www.ndcourts.com/lawyers/
Search Database at
www.court.state.nd.us/court/lawyers/index/framest.htm

42 Board of Accountancy, 2701 S Columbia Rd, Grand Forks, ND 58201-6029; 800-532-5904, Fax: 701-775-7430. www.state.nd.us/ndsba
Email: ndsba@state.nd.us
Search Database at
www.state.nd.us/ndsba/database/sbasearch.asp

43 Board of Architects, PO Box 7370, Bismarck, ND 58507-7370; 701-223-3184, Fax: 701-223-8154. www.governor.state.nd.us/

44 Board of Funeral Service, PO Box 633, Devil's Lake, ND 58301; 701-662-2511, Fax: 701-662-2501. Email: sfh@westriv.com

45 Board of Hearing Instrument Specialists, 825 25th St SW, Fargo, ND 58103; 701-237-9977.
http://governor.state.nd.us/boards/boards-query.asp?Board_ID=47

46 Board of Massage, PO Box 218, Beach, ND 58621; 701-872-4895, Fax: 701-872-4895.
www.ndboardofmassage.com
Email: k_wojahn@yahoo.com

47 Board of Medical Examiners, 418 E. Broadway #12, Bismarck, ND 58501; 701-328-6500, Fax: 701-328-6505. www.ndbomex.com
Email: medbd@tic.bisman.com
Search Database at
www.ndbomex.com/SearchPage.asp Note: Order form needed. For bulk users, a $15.00 setup fee plus $.05 per name billed after order is filled.

48 Board of Occupational Therapy Practice, PO Box 4005, Bismarck, ND 58502-4005; 701-250-0847, Fax: 701-224-9824.
www.ndotboard.com/
Email: ndotboard@aptnd.com

49 Board of Optometry, 341 1st St E, Dickinson, ND 58601; 701-483-9141, Fax: 701-483-9501.
www.ndsbopt.org
Email: ndsbopt@dickinson.ctctel.com
Search Database at www.ndsbopt.org/directory.asp

50 Board of Water Well Contractors, 900 E Boulevard Ave, Bismarck, ND 58505; 701-328-2754, Fax: 701-328-3696.
http://governor.state.nd.us/boards/boards-query.asp?Board_ID=111

51 Examining Committee of Physical Therapists, PO Box 69, Grafton, ND 58237; 701-352-0125, Fax: 701-352-3093. Email: ndsecpt@qft.midco.net

52 Board of Clinical Laboratory Practice, PO Box 4103, Bismarck, ND 58502-4103; 701-530-0199, Fax: 701-224-9824. www.ndclinlab.com/
Email: ndbclp@aptnd.com

North Dakota Federal Courts

The following list indicates the district and division name for each county in the state. If the bankruptcy court location is different from the district court, then the location of the bankruptcy court appears in parentheses.

North Dakota County/Court Cross Reference

County	Court	County	Court
Adams	Bismarck-Southwestern (Fargo)	McLean	Bismarck-Southwestern (Fargo)
Barnes	Fargo-Southeastern (Fargo)	Mercer	Bismarck-Southwestern (Fargo)
Benson	Grand Forks-Northeastern (Fargo)	Morton	Bismarck-Southwestern (Fargo)
Billings	Bismarck-Southwestern (Fargo)	Mountrail	Minot-Northwestern (Fargo)
Bottineau	Minot-Northwestern (Fargo)	Nelson	Grand Forks-Northeastern (Fargo)
Bowman	Bismarck-Southwestern (Fargo)	Oliver	Bismarck-Southwestern (Fargo)
Burke	Minot-Northwestern (Fargo)	Pembina	Grand Forks-Northeastern (Fargo)
Burleigh	Bismarck-Southwestern (Fargo)	Pierce	Minot-Northwestern (Fargo)
Cass	Fargo-Southeastern (Fargo)	Ramsey	Grand Forks-Northeastern (Fargo)
Cavalier	Grand Forks-Northeastern (Fargo)	Ransom	Fargo-Southeastern (Fargo)
Dickey	Fargo-Southeastern (Fargo)	Renville	Minot-Northwestern (Fargo)
Divide	Minot-Northwestern (Fargo)	Richland	Fargo-Southeastern (Fargo)
Dunn	Bismarck-Southwestern (Fargo)	Rolette	Minot-Northwestern (Fargo)
Eddy	Fargo-Southeastern (Fargo)	Sargent	Fargo-Southeastern (Fargo)
Emmons	Bismarck-Southwestern (Fargo)	Sheridan	Minot-Northwestern (Fargo)
Foster	Fargo-Southeastern (Fargo)	Sioux	Bismarck-Southwestern (Fargo)
Golden Valley	Bismarck-Southwestern (Fargo)	Slope	Bismarck-Southwestern (Fargo)
Grand Forks	Grand Forks-Northeastern (Fargo)	Stark	Bismarck-Southwestern (Fargo)
Grant	Bismarck-Southwestern (Fargo)	Steele	Fargo-Southeastern (Fargo)
Griggs	Fargo-Southeastern (Fargo)	Stutsman	Fargo-Southeastern (Fargo)
Hettinger	Bismarck-Southwestern (Fargo)	Towner	Grand Forks-Northeastern (Fargo)
Kidder	Bismarck-Southwestern (Fargo)	Traill	Grand Forks-Northeastern (Fargo)
La Moure	Fargo-Southeastern (Fargo)	Walsh	Grand Forks-Northeastern (Fargo)
Logan	Bismarck-Southwestern (Fargo)	Ward	Minot-Northwestern (Fargo)
McHenry	Minot-Northwestern (Fargo)	Wells	Minot-Northwestern (Fargo)
McIntosh	Bismarck-Southwestern (Fargo)	Williams	Minot-Northwestern (Fargo)
McKenzie	Minot-Northwestern (Fargo)		

Standards for Federal Courts: Search fee is $26.00 per item (one party name or case number). Copy fee is $.50 per page. Certification fee is $9.00 per document, double for exemplification, if available. All fees standard unless noted in profile. Mail Search: always enclose a stamped self addressed envelope unless otherwise noted. Most courts accept fax requests or will suggest a copying/search vendor. Before releasing records, all courts require prepayment, unless noted.

Open records are located at the court unless otherwise noted. District courts index by defendant and plaintiff as well as by case number. Bankruptcy courts usually index by debtor and case number. While most courts now have their indexes on computer, many may still maintain index card files as well.

Courts offering internet access via CM-ECF or older RACER, PACER, or Web-PACER systems charge $.08 per page fee unless noted as free. Where PACER is available, the universal sign-up number is 800-676-6856. Find PACER and the US Party/Case Index at http://pacer.psc.uscourts.gov.

US District Court

Bismarck - Southwestern Division
Court Clerk, PO Box 1193, Bismarck, ND 58502 (courier address: 220 E Rosser Ave, Rm 476, Bismarck, ND 58501), 701-530-2300, Fax-701-530-2312. www.ndd.uscourts.gov

Counties: Adams, Billings, Bowman, Burleigh, Dunn, Emmons, Golden Valley, Grant, Hettinger, Kidder, Logan, McIntosh, McLean, Mercer, Morton, Oliver, Sioux, Slope, Stark.

Searches & Indexing: Results do not include SSN or DOB. Computer index maintained. Records on computer and also stored as hard copies. New cases in the index 24 hours after filing date. Records purged never.

Fee & Payment: Pay by money order, cashier check, in-state business or personal check. Payee: Clerk, US District Court. Court will bill for copies. Will fax documents $1.50 per page.

Phone Search: Only docket information is available by phone.

Mail Search: search usually completed- 1 week. SASE not required.

In Person Search: Fee charged if court performs your search. No self-serve copier available.

E-Services: PACER online at http://pacer.ndd.uscourts.gov. PACER records go back to 10/1990. New records online after 1 day. Currently in the process of implementing CM/ECF. **Opinions Online:** www.ndd.uscourts.gov/DNDOpinions/JudgesOpinions.htm. **Other Online Access:** Calendars free at www.ndd.uscourts.gov/CAL/CourtCal.htm.

Fargo - Southeastern Division
Court Clerk, PO Box 870, Fargo, ND 58107 (courier address: 655 1st Ave N, Fargo, ND 58102), 701-297-7000, Fax-701-297-7005. Hours- 8AM-12, 1-5PM. www.ndd.uscourts.gov

Counties: Barnes, Cass, Dickey, Eddy, Foster, Griggs, La Moure, Ransom, Richland, Sargent, Steele, Stutsman. Rolette County cases prior to 1995 may be located here.

Searches & Indexing: Results do not include SSN or DOB. Both computer and card indexes maintained; computer index back to 1992. Civil cases prior to 10/90 on index cards. All criminal records on cards. Current records on computer; also stored as hard copies. New cases in the index 1 day after filing date. Records purged never.

Fee & Payment: Pay by money order, cashier check, in-state business or personal check. Payee: Clerk, US District Court. Prepayment required. Will fax documents $.50 per page, prepaid.

Phone Search: Only docket information is available by phone.

Mail Search: search usually completed- 1 week. SASE not required.

In Person Search: Fee charged if court performs your search. No self-serve copier available.

E-Services: PACER online at http://pacer.ndd.uscourts.gov. PACER records go back to 10/1990. New records online after 1 day. Currently in the process of implementing CM/ECF. **Opinions Online:** www.ndd.uscourts.gov/DNDOpinions/JudgesOpinions.htm. **Other Online Access:** Calendars free at www.ndd.uscourts.gov/CAL/CourtCal.htm.

Grand Forks - Northeastern Division
c/o Fargo-Southeastern Division, 102 N 4th St, Grand Forks, ND 58201 (courier address: 655 1st Ave N, Fargo, ND 58102), 701-297-7000. www.ndd.uscourts.gov

Counties: Benson, Cavalier, Grand Forks, Nelson, Pembina, Ramsey, Towner, Traill, Walsh. Grand Forks office now unstaffed.

Searches & Indexing: Cases indexed by and case number. Results do not include SSN or DOB. Records purged never. Open records located at Fargo-SE Division.

Fee & Payment: Pay by no business or personal checks accepted.

Phone Search: No searching by telephone.

In Person Search permitted. No self-serve copier.

E-Services: PACER online at http://pacer.ndd.uscourts.gov. PACER records go back to 10/1990. New records online after 1 day. Currently in the process of implementing CM/ECF. **Opinions Online:** www.ndd.uscourts.gov/DNDOpinions/JudgesOpinions.htm. **Other Online Access:** Calendars free at www.ndd.uscourts.gov/CAL/CourtCal.htm.

Minot - Northwestern Division
c/o Bismarck Division, PO Box 1193, Bismarck, ND 58502 (courier address: 100 1st St SW, Minot, ND 58701), 701-839-6251, records rm- 701-530-2300, Fax-701-530-2312. Hours- 8:30AM-4:30PM. www.ndd.uscourts.gov

Counties: Bottineau, Burke, Divide, McHenry, McKenzie, Mountrail, Pierce, Renville, Rolette, Sheridan, Ward, Wells, Williams. Case records from Rolette County prior to 1995 may be located in Fargo-Southeastern Division.

Searches & Indexing: Cases indexed by and case number. Results do not include SSN or DOB. Records purged never. Open records located at Bismarck Division.

Fee & Payment: Pay by money order, cashier's, business or personal check. Payee: District Court.

Phone Search: No searching by telephone.

Mail Search: SASE not required.

In Person Search permitted. No self-serve copier.

E-Services: PACER online at http://pacer.ndd.uscourts.gov. PACER records go back to 10/1990. New records online after 1 day. Currently in the process of implementing CM/ECF. **Opinions Online:** www.ndd.uscourts.gov/DNDOpinions/JudgesOpinions.htm. **Other Online Access:** Calendars free at www.ndd.uscourts.gov/CAL/CourtCal.htm.

US Bankruptcy Court

Fargo Division
Court Clerk, 655 1st Ave N, #210, Fargo, ND 58102-4932 (also use mail address for courier delivery), 701-297-7100, Fax-701-297-7105. Hours- 8AM-4:30PM. www.ndb.uscourts.gov

Counties: All counties in North Dakota.

Searches & Indexing: Results include last 4 SSN digits. Computer index maintained. New cases in the index 1 day after filing date.

Fee & Payment: Pay by money order, cashier check, business check. No personal checks. Payee: Clerk, US Bankruptcy Court. Prepayment required. Fax available in emergencies for $.50 per page sending or receiving.

Phone Search: Only docket information available by telephone. Voice Case Information Service available, call VCIS at 701-297-7166.

Mail Search: search usually completed- 1 day. SASE not required.

In Person Search: Fee charged if court performs your search. No self-serve copier available.

E-Services: PACER online at http://pacer.ndd.uscourts.gov. PACER records go back to 1991. New records online after 1 day. ECF at https://ecf.ndb.uscourts.gov **Other Online Access:** RACER is no longer available, replaced by newer PACER system.

North Dakota County Courts

Court	Jurisdiction	No. of Courts	How Organized
District Courts*	General	53	7 Judicial Districts
Municipal Courts	Municipal	76	76 Cities

* Profiled in this Sourcebook.

Court	CIVIL								
	Tort	Contract	Real Estate	Min. Claim	Max. Claim	Small Claims	Estate	Eviction	Domestic Relations
District Courts*	X	X	X	$0	No Max	$5000	X	X	X
Municipal Courts									

Court	CRIMINAL				
	Felony	Misdemeanor	DWI/DUI	Preliminary Hearing	Juvenile
District Courts*	X	X	X	X	X
Municipal Courts			X		

ADMINISTRATION   State Court Administrator, North Dakota Judiciary, 600 E Blvd, 1st Floor Judicial Wing, Dept. 180, Bismarck, ND, 58505-0530; 701-328-4216, Fax: 701-328-2092. www.ndcourts.com or www.court.state.nd.us

COURT STRUCTURE   In 1995, the County Courts merged with the District Courts statewide. County court records are maintained by the 53 District Court Clerks in the seven judicial districts. We recommend stating "include all County Court cases" in search requests. There are 76 Municipal Courts that handle traffic cases.

ONLINE ACCESS   A statewide computer system for internal purposes is in operation in most counties. You may now search North Dakota Supreme Court dockets and opinions at www.ndcourts.com. Search by docket number, party name, or anything else that may appear in the text. Records are from 1982 forward. Email notification of new opinions is also available.

ADDITIONAL INFORMATION   In the summer of 1997, the standard search fee in District Courts increased to $10.00 per name, and the certification fee increased to $10.00 per document. The standard copy fee is $.50 per page, but many courts charge only $.25.

Adams County

Southwest Judicial District Court 602 Adams Ave, PO Box 469, Hettinger, ND 58639; phone: 701-567-2460; criminal fax: 701-567-2910; same fax for civil/probate; hours 8:30AM-5PM (MST). *Felony, Misdemeanor, Civil, Eviction, Small Claims, Probate.*

Note: Search requests must be in writing.

Civil Records: Access: Fax, mail, in person. Both court and visitors may perform in person searches. Search fee: $10.00 per name. Court makes copy: $.25 per page. Required to search: name, years to search; also helpful: address. Civil cases indexed by defendant, plaintiff; on index cards from 1990, on docket books in vault from 1900s. Mail turnaround time 1-2 days.

Criminal Records: Access: Fax, mail, in person. Both court and visitors may perform in person searches. Search fee: $10.00 per name. Court makes copy: $.25 per page. Required to search: name, years to search, DOB; also helpful: address. Criminal records on index cards from 1990, on docket books in vault from 1900s. Mail turnaround time 1-2 days.

General Information: No public access terminal. No adoptions, sealed, juvenile, mental health, expunged, DV or dismissed records released. Fee to fax documents is $3.00 1st 2 pages, $.50 each add'l. Certification fee: $10.00 per document. Payee: Clerk of District Court. Personal checks accepted. Prepayment and SASE required.

Barnes County

Southeast Judicial District Court PO Box 774, Valley City, ND 58072; phone: 701-845-8512; fax: 701-845-1341; hours 8AM-5PM (CST). *Felony, Misdemeanor, Civil, Eviction, Small Claims, Probate.*

Civil Records: Access: Fax, mail, in person. Both court and visitors may perform in person searches. Search fee: $10.00 per name. Court makes copy: $.25 per page; same fee for self serve. Required to search: name, years to search; also helpful: address. Civil cases indexed by defendant, plaintiff; on index books from early 1900s; on computer back to 1996. Mail turnaround time 1-2 days.

Criminal Records: Access: Fax, mail, in person. Both court and visitors may perform in person searches. Search fee: $10.00 per name. Court makes copy: $.25 per page; same fee for self serve. Required to search: name, years to search; also helpful: address, DOB, SSN. Criminal records maintained here for 10 years, archived on index books from early 1900s; on computer back to 1996. Mail turnaround time 1-2 days.

General Information: Public terminal goes back to 1996. No adoptions, paternity, sealed, juvenile, mental health, expunged or dismissed records released. Will fax documents $10.00 per doc. Certification fee: $10.00. $5.00 for second copy. Payee: Clerk of District Court. Personal checks accepted. Prepayment and SASE required.

Benson County

Northeast Judicial District Court PO Box 213, Minnewaukan, ND 58351; phone: 701-473-5345; fax: 701-473-5571; hours 8:30AM-4:30PM (CST). *Felony, Misdemeanor, Civil, Eviction, Small Claims, Probate.*

Civil Records: Access: Fax, mail, in person. Only the court performs in person searches; visitors may not. Search fee: $10.00 per name. Court makes copy: $.25 per page. Required to search: name, years to search; also helpful: address. Civil cases indexed by defendant, plaintiff; on docket books and index books from early 1900s, on index cards from 6/10/91. Mail turnaround time 5 days.

Criminal Records: Access: Fax, mail, in person. Only the court performs in person searches; visitors may not. Search fee: $10.00 per name. Court makes copy: $.25 per page. Required to search: name, years to search, DOB, signed release; also helpful: address. Criminal records on docket books and index books from early 1900s, on index cards from 6/10/91. Signed release required for juvenile cases. Mail turnaround time 5 days.

General Information: No public access terminal. No adoptions, sealed, juvenile, mental health, expunged or dismissed records released. Will fax documents for $1.00 per page. Certification fee: $10.00 per doc includes copy fee. Payee: Benson County Court. Personal checks accepted. Prepayment and SASE required.

Billings County

Southwest Judicial District Court PO Box 138, Medora, ND 58645; phone: 701-623-4492; fax: 701-623-4896; hours 9AM-N, 1-5PM (MST). *Felony, Misdemeanor, Civil, Eviction, Small Claims, Probate.*

Civil Records: Access: Fax, mail, in person. Both court and visitors may perform in person searches. Search fee: $10.00 per name. Court makes copy: $1.00 per page. Self serve copy fee: $.25 per page. Required to search: name, years to search; also helpful: address. Civil cases indexed by defendant, plaintiff; on index books from 1800s. Mail turnaround time 1 day.

Criminal Records: Access: Fax, mail, in person. Both court and visitors may perform in person searches. Search fee: $10.00 per name. Court makes copy: $1.00 per page. Self serve copy fee: $.25 per page. Required to search: name, years to search; also helpful: address, DOB, SSN. Criminal records in books. Mail turnaround time 1 day.

General Information: No public access terminal. No adoptions, sealed, juvenile, mental health, expunged or dismissed records released. Will fax documents for $2.00 1st 4 pages, $.50 each add'l. Certification fee: $10.00 plus $5.00 each add'l page. Payee: Clerk of District Court. No out-of-state checks accepted unless pre-approved. Prepayment and SASE required.

Bottineau County

Northeast Judicial District Court 314 W 5th St, Bottineau, ND 58318; phone: 701-228-3618; fax: 701-228-2336; hours 8:30AM-5PM (CST). *Felony, Misdemeanor, Civil, Eviction, Small Claims, Probate.*

Civil Records: Access: Fax, mail, in person. Only the court performs in person searches; visitors may not. Search fee: $10.00 per name. Court makes copy: $.25 per page. Required to search: name, years to search; also helpful: address. Civil cases indexed by defendant, plaintiff; on index cards from 1987, on docket books from 1972. Mail turnaround time 1 day.

Criminal Records: Access: Fax, mail, in person. Only the court performs in person searches; visitors may not. Search fee: $10.00 per name. Court makes copy: $.25 per page. Required to search: name, years to search; also helpful: address, DOB, SSN. Criminal records on docket books from 1885. Mail turnaround time 1 day.

General Information: No adoptions, paternity, sealed, juvenile, mental health, expunged or dismissed records released. Will fax documents $4.00 for 1st page, $2.00 each add'l. Certification fee: $10.00 per doc. Payee: Clerk of the Court. Personal checks accepted. Prepayment and SASE required.

Bowman County

Southwest Judicial District Court PO Box 379, Bowman, ND 58623; phone: 701-523-3450; criminal fax: 701-523-5443; same fax for civil/probate; hours 8:00AM-N, 1-4:30PM (MST). *Felony, Misdemeanor, Civil, Eviction, Small Claims, Probate.*

Civil Records: Access: Mail, in person, phone, fax. Both court and visitors may perform in person searches. Search fee: $10.00 per name. Court makes copy: $.50 per page. Required to search: name, years to search; also helpful: address. Civil cases indexed by defendant, plaintiff; on dockets from 1907; computerized records back to 1995. Mail turnaround time 1-2 days.

Criminal Records: Access: Mail, in person. Both court and visitors may perform in person searches. Search fee: $10.00 per name. Court makes copy: $.50 per page. Required to search: name, years to search, DOB; also helpful: address. Criminal records on microfiche from 1978, on dockets from 1907; computerized records back to 1995. Mail turnaround time 1-2 days.

General Information: No public access terminal. No adoptions, sealed, juvenile, mental health, expunged or dismissed records released. Will fax documents to local or toll free line. Certification fee: $10.00 per document; add'l document copies $5.00 each. Payee: Clerk of Court. Personal checks accepted. Prepayment and SASE required.

Burke County

Northwest Judicial District Court PO Box 219, Bowbells, ND 58721; phone: 701-377-2718; fax: 701-377-2020; hours 8:30AM-N, 1-5 PM (CST). *Felony, Misdemeanor, Civil, Eviction, Small Claims, Probate.*

Civil Records: Access: Fax, mail, in person. Both court and visitors may perform in person searches. Search fee: $10.00 if a written reply is required. Court makes copy: $.50 per page. Required to search: name, years to search; also helpful: address. Civil cases indexed by defendant, plaintiff. Civil records for county civil, probate, and district from 1910, county criminal and small claims from 1980. Mail turnaround time 1-3 days.

Criminal Records: Access: Fax, mail, in person. Both court and visitors may perform in person searches. Search fee: $10.00 if a written reply is required. Court makes copy: $.50 per page. Required to search: name, years to search; also helpful: address, DOB, SSN. Criminal records for county civil, probate, and district from 1910, county criminal and small claims from 1980. Mail turnaround time 1-3 days.

General Information: No public access terminal. No adoptions, sealed, juvenile, mental health, expunged or dismissed records released. Fee to fax documents is $2.00 per page. Certification fee: $10.00 per doc includes copies. Payee: Clerk of Court. Personal checks accepted. Prepayment required.

Burleigh County

South Central Judicial District Court PO Box 1055, Bismarck, ND 58502; phone: 701-222-6690; civil phone: 701-222-6690; probate phone: 701-222-6690; fax: 701-221-6756; probate fax: 701-221-3756; hours 8AM-5PM (CST). *Felony, Misdemeanor, Civil, Eviction, Small Claims, Probate.*

Civil Records: Access: Mail, in person. Both court and visitors may perform in person searches. Search fee: $10.00 per name. Court makes copy: $.10 per page; $1.00 minimum. Required to search: name; also helpful: years to search. Civil cases indexed by defendant, plaintiff; on computer back to 1/91; in books from 1800s. Mail turnaround time 2 days.

Criminal Records: Access: Mail, in person. Both court and visitors may perform in person searches. Search fee: $10.00 per name. Court makes copy: $.10 per page; $1.00 minimum. Required to search: name; also helpful: years to search, address, DOB, SSN. Criminal records on computer back to 1/91; in books from early 1900s. Mail turnaround time 1-2 days.

General Information: No adoptions, sealed, juvenile, mental health, expunged or dismissed records released. Will fax documents to local or toll free line. Certification fee: $10.00 plus $5.00 each add'l Cert copy. Payee: Clerk of Court. Personal checks accepted. Prepayment and SASE required.

Cass County

East Central Judicial District Court PO Box 2806, Fargo, ND 58108; criminal phone: 701-241-5660; civil phone: 701-241-5645; probate phone: 701-241-5655; fax: 701-241-5636; hours 8AM-5PM (CST). *Felony, Misdemeanor, Civil, Eviction, Small Claims, Probate.*

Civil Records: Access: Mail, fax, in person, online. Both court and visitors may perform in person searches. Search fee: $10.00 per name. Court makes copy: $.10 per page. $1.00 minimum. Required to search: name, years to search; also helpful: address. Civil cases indexed by defendant, plaintiff; on computer from 1988, on index books from late 1800s. Probate is online at www.lib.ndsu.nodak.edu/ndirs/databases/probate.php. There is no fee. Mail turnaround time 3-5 days.

Criminal Records: Access: Mail, fax, in person. Both court and visitors may perform in person searches. Search fee: $10.00 per name. Court makes copy: $.10 per page. $1.00 minimum. Required to search: name, years to search; also helpful: address, DOB, SSN. Criminal records on computer from 1988, on index cards from 1980. Mail turnaround time 3-5 days.

General Information: Public terminal goes back to 1988. No adoptions, sealed, juvenile, mental health, expunged or dismissed records released. Certification fee: $10.00 per doc includes copy fee. Payee: Clerk of District Court. Personal checks accepted. Prepayment and SASE required.

Cavalier County

Northeast Judicial District Court 901 Third St, Langdon, ND 58249; phone: 701-256-2124; fax: 701-256-3468; hours 8:30AM-4:30PM (CST). *Felony, Misdemeanor, Civil, Eviction, Small Claims, Probate.*

Civil Records: Access: Fax, mail, in person. Only the court performs in person searches; visitors may not. Search fee: $10.00 per name. Court makes copy: $.25 per page. Required to search: name, years to search; also helpful: address. Civil cases indexed by defendant, plaintiff. Civil records going on computer, prior stored. Mail turnaround time 1 week.

Criminal Records: Access: Fax, mail, in person. Only the court performs in person searches; visitors may not. Search fee: $10.00 per name. Court makes copy: $.25 per page. Required to search: name, years to search; also helpful: address, DOB, SSN. Criminal records for District Court on index books from 1937, for County Court on index books from 1983, prior stored. Mail turnaround time 1 week.

General Information: No public access terminal. No adoptions, sealed, juvenile, mental health, expunged or dismissed records released. No fee to fax documents. Certification fee: $10.00. Payee: Clerk of Court. Personal checks accepted. Prepayment and SASE required.

Dickey County

Southeast Judicial District Court Clerk of Court, PO Box 336, Ellendale, ND 58436; phone: 701-349-3249 X4; criminal fax: 701-349-3560; same fax for civil/probate; hours 9AM-N, 1-5PM (CST). *Felony, Misdemeanor, Civil, Eviction, Small Claims, Probate.*

Civil Records: Access: Mail, in person. Only the court performs in person searches; visitors may not. Search fee: $10.00 per name. Court makes copy: $.25 per page. Required to search: name, years to search; also helpful: address. Civil cases indexed by defendant, plaintiff; on index books to 1983; 1997-present. Probate from 1800s. Old district court records have no index and are very hard to search. Mail turnaround time 1-2 days.

Criminal Records: Access: Mail, in person. Only the court performs in person searches; visitors may not. Search fee: $10.00 per name. Court makes copy: $.25 per page. Required to search: name, years to search, DOB; also helpful: address, SSN. Criminal records on index books to 1983, 1997- present. Old district court records have no index and are very hard to search. Mail turnaround time 1-2 days.

General Information: No public access terminal. No adoptions, sealed, juvenile, mental health, expunged or dismissed records released. Will fax documents to local or toll free line. Certification fee: $10.00 per document. Payee: Clerk of Court. Personal checks accepted. Prepayment required.

Divide County

Northwest Judicial District Court PO Box 68, Crosby, ND 58730; phone: 701-965-6831; fax: 701-965-6943; hours 8:30AM-N, 1-5PM (CST). *Felony, Misdemeanor, Civil, Eviction, Small Claims, Probate.*

Civil Records: Access: Fax, mail, in person. Only the court performs in person searches; visitors may not. Search fee: $10.00 per name. Court makes copy: $.25 per page. $1.00 minimum. Required to search: name, years to search; also helpful: address. Civil cases indexed by defendant, plaintiff; on index books from 1910. Visitor can check for judgments. Records for eviction, small claims and probate are an additional $10.00 if full certification needed. Mail turnaround time 1-2 days.

Criminal Records: Access: Fax, mail, in person. Only the court performs in person searches; visitors may not. Search fee: $10.00 per name. Court makes copy: $.25 per page. $1.00 minimum. Required to search: name, years to search; also helpful: address, DOB, SSN. Criminal records on index books from 1910. Mail turnaround time 1-2 days.

General Information: No public access terminal. No adoptions, sealed, juvenile, mental health, expunged or dismissed records released. Will fax documents $3.00 1st page, $1.00 each add'l. Also a charge of $1.00 per incoming fax page. Certification fee: $10.00 per doc. Payee: Clerk of District Court. Personal checks accepted. Prepayment and SASE required.

Dunn County

District Court PO Box 136, Manning, ND 58642-0136; phone: 701-573-4447; criminal fax: 701-573-4444; same fax for civil/probate; hours 8AM-N,12:30-4:30PM (MST). *Felony, Misdemeanor, Civil, Small Claims, Probate.*

Civil Records: Access: Fax, mail, in person. Both court and visitors may perform in person searches. Search fee: $10.00 per name. Court makes copy: $2.00 plus $.50 each page for mailed copies. Self serve copy fee: $.25 per page. Required to search: name, years to search; also helpful: address. Civil cases indexed by defendant, plaintiff; on plaintiff/defendant index cards from 1988, on docket books from 1900s, on computer since 1/97. Fax requests must fax copy of the check to be mailed. Mail turnaround time 2 days.

Criminal Records: Access: Fax, mail, in person. Both court and visitors may perform in person searches. Search fee: $10.00 per name. Court makes copy: $2.00 plus $.50 each page mailed copies. Self serve copy fee: $.25 per page. Required to search: name, years to search, DOB; also helpful: address, SSN. Criminal records on plaintiff/defendant index cards from 1988, on docket books from 1900s, on computer since 1/97. Fax requesters must fax copy of the check, which can be mailed. Mail turnaround time 2 days.

General Information: Public terminal goes back to 1/1997. Adoptions, paternity, juvenile, mental health, deferred impositions, and termination of parental rights are restricted access files. Will fax documents $2.00 plus $1.00 per page. Certification fee: $10.00 per document includes copy fee. Payee: Dunn County Clerk of Court. In state personal checks accepted. Prepayment required.

Eddy County

Southeast Judicial District Court 524 Central Ave, New Rockford, ND 58356; phone: 701-947-2813 x2013; fax: 701-947-2067; hours 8AM-4PM (CST). *Felony, Misdemeanor, Civil, Eviction, Small Claims, Probate.*

Civil Records: Access: Fax, mail, in person. Only the court performs in person searches; visitors may not. Search fee: $10.00 per name. Court makes copy: $1.00 per document. Required to search: name, years to search; also helpful: address. Civil cases indexed by defendant, plaintiff; on index cards from 4/92, on index books from early 1900s. All requests must be in writing. Mail turnaround time 1-2 days.

Criminal Records: Access: Fax, mail, in person. Only the court performs in person searches; visitors may not. Search fee: $10.00 per name. Court makes copy: $1.00 per document. Required to search: name, years to search; also helpful: address, DOB, SSN. Criminal records on index cards from 4/92, on index books from early 1900s. All requests must be in writing. Mail turnaround time 1-2 days.

General Information: No public access terminal. No adoptions, sealed, juvenile, mental health, expunged or dismissed records released. Fee to fax documents is $4.00 1st 3 pages, $1.00 each add'l page. Certification fee: $10.00. Payee: Eddy County District Court. Personal checks accepted. Prepayment and SASE required.

Emmons County

South Central Judicial District Court PO Box 905, Linton, ND 58552; phone: 701-254-4812; criminal fax: 701-254-4012; same fax for civil/probate; hours 8:30AM-N, 1-5PM (CST). *Felony, Misdemeanor, Civil, Eviction, Small Claims, Probate.*

Civil Records: Access: Fax, mail, in person. Only the court performs in person searches; visitors may not. Search fee: $10.00 per name. Court makes copy: $.20 per page. Required to search: name, years to search; also helpful: address. Civil cases indexed by defendant, plaintiff; on index cards from 1988, on index books from 1914, on computer back to 1995. Mail turnaround time 1-2 days.

Criminal Records: Access: Fax, mail, in person. Only the court performs in person searches; visitors may not. Search fee: $10.00 per name. Court makes copy: $.20 per page. Required to search: name, years to search, DOB; also helpful: address, SSN. Criminal records on index books back to 1983; on computer back to 1995. Mail turnaround time 1-2 days.

General Information: No public access terminal. No adoptions, sealed, juvenile, mental health, expunged or dismissed records released. Fee to fax documents is $3.00 1st page, $1.00 each add'l. Certification fee: $10.00 per document. Payee: Clerk of Courts. Personal checks accepted. Prepayment and SASE required.

Foster County

Southeast Judicial District Court PO Box 257, Carrington, ND 58421; phone: 701-652-1001; fax: 701-652-2173; hours 8:30AM-4:30PM (CST). *Felony, Misdemeanor, Civil, Eviction, Small Claims, Probate.*

Civil Records: Access: Mail, in person. Both court and visitors may perform in person searches. Search fee: $10.00 per name if court performs search. Court makes copy: $1.00 per page; same fee for self serve. Required to search: name, years to search; also helpful: address. Civil cases indexed by defendant, plaintiff; on index books from early 1900s. Mail turnaround time 1-2 days.

Criminal Records: Access: Mail, in person. Both court and visitors may perform in person searches. Search fee: $10.00 per name if court performs search. Court makes copy: $1.00 per page; same fee for self serve. Required to search: name, years to search, DOB; also helpful: address. Criminal records

available for past 10 years. Mail turnaround time 1-2 days.

General Information: No public access terminal. No adoptions, sealed, juvenile, mental health, expunged or dismissed records released. Will fax documents $3.00 per doc. Certification fee: $10.00. Payee: Clerk of Courts. Personal checks accepted. Prepayment and SASE required.

Golden Valley County

Southwest Judicial District Court PO Box 9, Beach, ND 58621-0009; phone: 701-872-3713; fax: 701-872-4383; hours 8AM-N, 1-4PM (MST). *Felony, Misdemeanor, Civil, Eviction, Small Claims, Probate.*

Civil Records: Access: Fax, mail, in person. Only the court performs in person searches; visitors may not. Search fee: $10.00 per name. Court makes copy: $.50 per page. Required to search: name, years to search; also helpful: address. Civil cases indexed by defendant, plaintiff; on index cards from 1987, on index books from 1913 to 1960. From 1960 to 1987, records are hard to find; there is no indexing and files are filed by number. Fax request must include copy of check. Mail turnaround time 3-4 days.

Criminal Records: Access: Fax, mail, in person. Only the court performs in person searches; visitors may not. Search fee: $10.00 per name. Court makes copy: $.50 per page. Required to search: name, years to search, DOB; also helpful: address, SSN. Criminal records on index cards from 1987, on index books from 1913 to 1960. From 1960 to 1987, records are hard to find; there is no indexing and files are filed by number. Fax request must include copy of check. Statewide records on computer since 04/04/03. Mail turnaround time 3-4 days.

General Information: No public access terminal. No adoptions, sealed, juvenile, mental health, expunged or dismissed records released. Will fax documents $1.00 per page. Certification fee: $10.00. Payee: Clerk of Court. Personal checks accepted. Prepayment and SASE required.

Grand Forks County

Northeast Central Judicial District Court PO Box 5939, Grand Forks, ND 58206-5939; phone: x; criminal phone: 701-787-2700; civil phone: 701-787-2715; probate phone: 701-787-2715; criminal fax: 701-787-2701; civil fax: 701-787-2716; probate fax: 701-787-2716; hours 8AM-5PM (CST). *Felony, Misdemeanor, Civil, Eviction, Small Claims, Probate.*

Civil Records: Access: Mail, in person. Both court and visitors may perform in person searches. Search fee: $10.00 per name. Court makes copy: $.10 per page; $1.00 minimum. Required to search: name, years to search; also helpful: address. Civil cases indexed by defendant, plaintiff; on computer from 10/91, on index books from early 1900s. Mail turnaround time 1-2 days.

Criminal Records: Access: Mail, in person. Both court and visitors may perform in person searches. Search fee: $10.00 per name. Court makes copy: $.10 per page; $1.00 minimum. Required to search: name, years to search, DOB, signed release; also helpful: address, SSN. Criminal records on computer from 10/91, on index books from early 1900s. Mail turnaround time 1-2 days.

General Information: Public use terminal available. No adoptions, sealed, juvenile, mental health, expunged or dismissed records released. Will fax documents for no charge. Certification fee: $10.00. Payee: Clerk of District Court. Personal checks accepted. Prepayment and SASE required.

Grant County

South Central Judicial District Court PO Box 258, Carson, ND 58529; phone: 701-622-3615; fax: 701-622-3717; hours 8AM-N, 12:30-4PM (MST). *Felony, Misdemeanor, Civil, Eviction, Small Claims, Probate.*

Civil Records: Access: Fax, mail, in person. Both court and visitors may perform in person searches. Search fee: $10.00 per name. Court makes copy: $.25 per page. Required to search: name, years to search; also helpful: address. Civil cases indexed by defendant, plaintiff; on index cards from 1990, on docket books in vault from 1900s. Mail turnaround time 1 day.

Criminal Records: Access: Fax, mail, in person. Both court and visitors may perform in person searches. Search fee: $10.00 per name. Court makes copy: $.25 per page. Required to search: name, years to search; also helpful: address, DOB, SSN. Criminal records on index cards from 1990, on docket books in vault from 1900s. Mail turnaround time 1 day.

General Information: No public access terminal. No adoptions, sealed, juvenile, mental health, expunged or dismissed records released. Will fax documents $3.00 per doc. Certification fee: $10.00 per doc includes copy fee. Payee: Clerk of Grant County Court. Personal checks accepted. Prepayment required.

Griggs County

Southeast Judicial District Court PO Box 326, Cooperstown, ND 58425; phone: 701-797-2772; fax: 701-797-3587; hours 8AM-N, 1-4:30PM (CST). *Felony, Misdemeanor, Civil, Eviction, Small Claims, Probate.*

Civil Records: Access: Fax, mail, in person. Both court and visitors may perform in person searches. Search fee: $10.00 per name. Court makes copy: $.25 per page. Required to search: name, years to search; also helpful: address. Civil cases indexed by defendant, plaintiff. Civil records in docket books from 1890 to 2001 and UCIS 2001 to present. Phone access discouraged. Mail turnaround time 1-2 days.

Criminal Records: Access: Fax, mail, in person. Both court and visitors may perform in person searches. Search fee: $10.00 per name. Court makes copy: $.25 per page. Required to search: name, years to search; also helpful: address, DOB, SSN. Criminal records on docket books from 1890 to 2001 and UCIS 2001 to present. Phone access discouraged. Mail turnaround time 1-2 days.

General Information: No public access terminal. No adoptions, sealed, juvenile, mental health, expunged or dismissed records released. Will fax documents $1.00 per page. Incoming fax- $1.00 per page; free for state attorneys. Certification fee: $10.00. Payee: Clerk of Courts. Personal checks accepted. Prepayment and SASE required.

Hettinger County

Southwest Judicial District Court PO Box 668, Mott, ND 58646; phone: 701-824-2645; fax: 701-824-2717; hours 8AM-N, 1-4:30PM (MST). *Felony, Misdemeanor, Civil, Eviction, Small Claims, Probate.*

Civil Records: Access: Fax, mail, in person. Both court and visitors may perform in person searches. Search fee: $10.00 per name. Court makes copy: $.25 per page. Required to search: name, years to search; also helpful: address. Civil cases indexed by defendant, plaintiff; on index cards from 1987, on index books from 1908. Mail turnaround time 1 day.

Criminal Records: Access: Fax, mail, in person. Both court and visitors may perform in person searches. Search fee: $10.00 per name. Court makes copy: $.25 per page. Required to search: name, years to search, DOB; also helpful: address. Criminal records on index cards from 1987, on index books from 1908. Mail turnaround time 1 day.

General Information: No public access terminal. No adoptions, sealed, juvenile, mental health, expunged or dismissed records released. Will fax documents $3.00 per doc. Fee is for up to 20 pages. Certification fee: $10.00 per doc includes copies. Payee: Hettinger Court Clerk. Personal checks accepted. Prepayment and SASE required.

Kidder County

District Court PO Box 66, Steele, ND 58482; phone: 701-475-2632; fax: 701-475-2202; hours 9AM-5PM (CST). *Felony, Misdemeanor, Civil, Eviction, Small Claims, Probate.*

Civil Records: Access: Fax, mail, in person. Both court and visitors may perform in person searches. Search fee: $10.00 per name. Court makes copy: $1.00 per document. Required to search: name, years to search; also helpful: address. Civil cases indexed by defendant, plaintiff; on index book from 1800s, on computer since 1990. Mail turnaround time 1-2 days.

Criminal Records: Access: Mail, in person. Both court and visitors may perform in person searches. Search fee: $10.00 per name. Court makes copy: $1.00 per document. Required to search: name, years to search, DOB; also helpful: address. Records on index book from 1900s, on computer since 1990. Mail turnaround time 1-2 days.

General Information: Public terminal goes back to 1990. No adoptions, sealed, juvenile, mental health, expunged or dismissed records released. Will fax documents for $3.00 plus the copy fee. Certification fee: $10.00. Payee: Clerk of Court. Personal checks accepted. Prepayment and SASE required.

La Moure County

Southeast Judicial District Court PO Box 128, LaMoure, ND 58458; phone: 701-883-5193; criminal fax: 701-883-4240; same fax for civil/probate; hours 8:30AM-N, 1-4:30PM (CST). *Felony, Misdemeanor, Civil, Eviction, Small Claims, Probate.*

Civil Records: Access: Fax, mail, in person. Both court and visitors may perform in person searches. Search fee: $10.00 per name. Court makes copy: $.25 for first page, $.10 each add'l. Required to search: name, years to search; also helpful: address. Civil cases indexed by defendant, plaintiff; on docket books from 1800s; on computer back to 2002. Mail turnaround time usually same day.

Criminal Records: Access: Fax, mail, in person. Both court and visitors may perform in person searches. Search fee: $10.00 per name. Court makes copy: $.25 for first page, $.10 each add'l. Required to search: name, years to search; also helpful: address, DOB. Felony records go back to 1987; misdemeanors back 15 years. Mail turnaround time 1 day.

General Information: No public access terminal. No adoptions, sealed, juvenile, mental health, expunged or dismissed records released. Will not fax documents without pre-payment or copy of payment check. Certification fee: $10.00. Payee: Clerk of Court. Personal checks accepted. Prepayment and SASE required.

Logan County

South Central Judicial District Court PO Box 6, Napoleon, ND 58561; phone: 701-754-2751; criminal fax: 701-754-2270; same fax for civil/probate; hours 8:30AM-4:30PM (CST). *Felony, Misdemeanor, Civil, Eviction, Small Claims, Probate.*

Civil Records: Access: Fax, mail, in person. Both court and visitors may perform in person searches. Search fee: $10.00 per name. Court makes copy: $10.00 per document. Required to search: name, years to search; also helpful: address, signed release. Civil cases indexed by defendant, plaintiff; on index books from 1884. Mail turnaround time 1-2 days.

Criminal Records: Access: Fax, mail, in person. Only the court performs in person searches; visitors may not. Search fee: $10.00 per name. Court makes copy: $10.00 per document. Required to search: name, years to search, DOB; also helpful: address, signed release. Criminal records on index books from 1890. Mail turnaround time 1-2 days.

General Information: No public access terminal. No adoptions, sealed, juvenile, mental health, expunged or dismissed records released. Fee to fax documents is $3.00 1st page, $1.00 each add'l.

Certification fee: $10.00 per document. Payee: Clerk of Court. Business checks accepted. Prepayment and SASE required.

McHenry County

Northeast Judicial District Court PO Box 117, Towner, ND 58788; phone: 701-537-5729; criminal fax: 701-537-5969; same fax for civil/probate; hours 8AM-4:30PM (CST). *Felony, Misdemeanor, Civil, Eviction, Small Claims, Probate.*

Note: Probate in a separate index at this same address.

Civil Records: Access: Fax, mail, in person. Both court and visitors may perform in person searches. Search fee: $10.00 per name. Court makes copy: $.25 per page. Required to search: name, years to search; also helpful: address. Civil cases indexed by defendant, plaintiff; on index cards from 1991, on index books from 1905. Mail turnaround time 1-2 days.

Criminal Records: Access: Fax, mail, in person. Both court and visitors may perform in person searches. Search fee: $10.00 per name. Court makes copy: $.25 per page. Required to search: name, years to search; also helpful: address, DOB, SSN. Criminal records on index cards from 1991, on index books from 1905. Mail turnaround time 1-2 days.

General Information: No public access terminal. No adoptions, sealed, juvenile, mental health, expunged or dismissed records released. Will fax documents $1.00 1st page, $.25 each add'l. Certification fee: $10.00 includes copies. Payee: Clerk of Courts. Personal checks accepted. Prepayment and SASE required.

McIntosh County

South Central Judicial District Court PO Box 179, Ashley, ND 58413; phone: 701-288-3450; fax: 701-288-3671; hours 8AM-4:30PM (CST). *Felony, Misdemeanor, Civil, Eviction, Small Claims, Probate.*

Civil Records: Access: Phone, fax, mail, in person. Visitors must perform in person searches themselves. Search fee: $10.00 per name. Court makes copy: $.25 per page; same fee for self serve. Required to search: name, years to search; also helpful: address. Civil cases indexed by defendant, plaintiff; on index cards from 1987, on index books from 1930s. Mail turnaround time 1-2 days.

Criminal Records: Access: Fax, mail, in person. Both court and visitors may perform in person searches. Search fee: $10.00 per name. Court makes copy: $.25 per page; same fee for self serve. Required to search: name, years to search, DOB; also helpful: address. Criminal records on index cards from 1987, on index books from 1930s. Mail turnaround time 1-2 days.

General Information: Public terminal goes back to 1995. No adoptions, sealed, juvenile, mental health, expunged or dismissed records released. Will fax documents to local or toll free line. Certification fee: $10.00 per doc. Payee: Clerk of Court. Only cashiers checks and money orders accepted. Prepayment required.

McKenzie County

Northwest Judicial District Court PO Box 524, Watford City, ND 58854; phone: 701-444-3452; fax: 701-444-3916; hours 8:30AM-N, 1-5PM (CST). *Felony, Misdemeanor, Civil, Eviction, Small Claims, Probate.*

Civil Records: Access: Mail, in person. Both court and visitors may perform in person searches. Search fee: $10.00 per name. Court makes copy: $.25 per page. Required to search: name, years to search; also helpful: address, SSN. Civil cases indexed by defendant, plaintiff; on computer back to 1/96. Mail turnaround time 1-2 days.

Criminal Records: Access: Mail, in person. Only the court performs in person searches; visitors may not. Search fee: $10.00 per name. Court makes copy: $.25 per page. Required to search: name, years to search, DOB, SSN. Criminal records on computer back to 12/87; on books back to 1908. Mail turnaround time 1-2 days.

General Information: No public access terminal. No adoptions, juvenile, mental health, expunged or dismissed records released. Fee to fax documents is $2.00 per page. Certification fee: $10.00 per document. Payee: Clerk of Court, McKenzie County. Personal checks accepted. Prepayment and SASE required.

McLean County

South Central Judicial District Court PO Box 1108, Washburn, ND 58577; phone: 701-462-8541; criminal fax: 701-462-8212; same fax for civil/probate; hours 8AM-N, 12:30-4:30PM (CST). *Felony, Misdemeanor, Civil, Eviction, Small Claims, Probate.*

Civil Records: Access: Mail, in person. Both court and visitors may perform in person searches. Search fee: $10.00 per name. Court makes copy: $.10 per page, $1.00 minimum. Self serve copy fee: $.10 per page. Required to search: name, years to search; also helpful: address. Civil cases indexed by defendant, plaintiff; on index books from early 1900s; on computer back to 1996. Mail turnaround time 1-2 days.

Criminal Records: Access: Mail, in person. Both court and visitors may perform in person searches. Search fee: $10.00 per name. Court makes copy: $.10 per page, $1.00 minimum. Self serve copy fee: $.10 per page. Required to search: name, years to search, DOB; also helpful: address, SSN. Criminal records on index cards from 1983, on index books from early 1900s; on computer back to 1996. Mail turnaround time 1-2 days.

General Information: Public terminal goes back to 1996. No adoptions, sealed, juvenile, mental health, expunged or deferred imposition dismissed records released. Will fax documents to toll free line. Certification fee: $10.00 per document. Payee: Clerk of Courts. Personal checks accepted. Prepayment and SASE required.

Mercer County

District Court PO Box 39, Stanton, ND 58571; phone: 701-745-3262; fax: 701-745-3710; hours 8AM-4PM (MST). *Felony, Misdemeanor, Civil, Eviction, Small Claims, Probate.*

Civil Records: Access: Fax, mail, in person. Both court and visitors may perform in person searches. Search fee: $10.00 per name. Court makes copy: $.25 per page; same fee for self serve. Required to search: name, years to search; also helpful: address. Civil cases indexed by defendant, plaintiff; on index cards from 1979, on index books from 1889, computerized since 1990. Mail turnaround time 1-2 days.

Criminal Records: Access: Fax, mail, in person. Both court and visitors may perform in person searches. Search fee: $10.00 per name. Court makes copy: $.25 per page; same fee for self serve. Required to search: name, years to search, signed release; also helpful: address, DOB, SSN. Criminal records on index cards from 1979, on index books from 1889, computerized since 1990. Mail turnaround time 1-2 days.

General Information: Public terminal goes back to 1992. No adoptions, sealed, juvenile, mental health, expunged or dismissed records released. Will fax documents $5.00 per doc. Certification fee: $10.00. Payee: Mercer County Clerk of Court. Personal checks accepted. Prepayment and SASE required.

Morton County

South Central Judicial District Court 210 2nd Ave NW, Mandan, ND 58554; phone: 701-667-3358; criminal phone: 701-667-3355; fax: 701-667-3474; hours 8AM-5PM (MST). *Felony, Misdemeanor, Civil, Eviction, Small Claims, Probate.*

Civil Records: Access: Mail, in person. Both court and visitors may perform in person searches.

Search fee: $10.00 per name. Fee is for written search request. Court makes copy: $.35 per page. Self serve copy fee: $.25 per page. Required to search: name, years to search; also helpful: address. Civil cases indexed by defendant, plaintiff; on computer from 1990; on index books from 1985. Mail turnaround time 1-2 days.

Criminal Records: Access: Mail, in person. Both court and visitors may perform in person searches. Search fee: $10.00 per name. Fee is for written search request. Court makes copy: $.35 per page. Self serve copy fee: $.25 per page. Required to search: name, years to search, DOB; also helpful: address. Criminal records on computer from 1990, on index books from 1985. Mail turnaround time 1-2 days.

General Information: Public terminal goes back to 1990. No adoptions, sealed, juvenile, mental health, expunged or dismissed records released. Will fax case files to local or toll free number. Certification fee: $10.00. Cert fee includes copies. Payee: Clerk of District Court. Personal checks accepted. Prepayment and SASE required.

Mountrail County

Northwest County District Court PO Box 69, Stanley, ND 58784; phone: 701-628-2915; criminal fax: 701-628-2276; same fax for civil/probate; hours 8:30AM-4:30PM (CST). *Felony, Misdemeanor, Civil, Eviction, Small Claims, Probate.*

Note: Probate is a separate index at this same address.

Civil Records: Access: Mail, in person, fax, phone. Both court and visitors may perform in person searches. Search fee: $10.00 per name. Fee is for written search. Court makes copy: $.30 per page. Required to search: name, years to search; also helpful: address. Civil cases indexed by defendant, plaintiff; on index books from 1909; on computer back to 1998. Mail turnaround time 1-2 days.

Criminal Records: Access: Mail, in person. Both court and visitors may perform in person searches. Search fee: $10.00 per name. Fee is for written search. Court makes copy: $.30 per page. Required to search: name, years to search, DOB. Criminal records on index books from 1909; on computer back to 1998. Mail turnaround time 1-2 days.

General Information: Public terminal goes back to 1998. No adoptions, sealed, juvenile, mental health, expunged or dismissed records released. No fee to fax documents. Certification fee: $10.00 per document includes copy fee. Payee: Clerk of District Court. Personal checks accepted. Prepayment required.

Nelson County

Northeast Central Judicial District Court Nelson County Recorder-Clerk of Court, 210 B Ave W, #203, Lakota, ND 58344-7410; phone: 701-247-2462; criminal fax: 701-247-2412; same fax for civil/probate; hours 8:30AM-N; 1PM-4:30PM (CST). *Felony, Misdemeanor, Civil, Eviction, Small Claims, Probate.*

Civil Records: Access: Fax, mail, in person, email. Both court and visitors may perform in person searches. Search fee: $10.00 per name. Court makes copy: $1.00 per 4-page document; $.25 each add'l page. Required to search: name, years to search; also helpful: address. Civil cases indexed by defendant, plaintiff; on index books from 1883. Will accept email record requests at rstevens@pioneer.state.nd.us. Mail turnaround time 1-2 days.

Criminal Records: Access: Fax, mail, in person, email. Both court and visitors may perform in person searches. Search fee: $10.00 per name. Court makes copy: $1.00 per 4-page document; $.25 each add'l page. Required to search: name, years to search, DOB; also helpful: address, SSN. Criminal records on index books from 1883. Will accept email record requests at rstevens@pioneer.state.nd.us. Mail turnaround time 1-2 days.

General Information: Public terminal has criminal back to 2002 and civil back to 10 years for judgments, 20 if renewed. No adoptions, sealed,

juvenile, mental health, expunged or dismissed records released. Will fax documents $3.00 per doc. Certification fee: $10.00 includes copies. Payee: Clerk of Courts. Personal checks accepted. Prepayment and SASE required.

Oliver County

South Central Judicial District Court Box 125, Center, ND 58530; phone: 701-794-8777; fax: 701-794-3476; hours 8AM-4PM (CST). *Felony, Misdemeanor, Civil, Eviction, Small Claims, Probate.*

Civil Records: Access: Fax, mail, in person. Both court and visitors may perform in person searches. Search fee: $10.00 per name. Court makes copy: $.25 per page. Required to search: name, years to search; also helpful: address. Civil cases indexed by defendant. Civil records on docket books from 1920s. Mail turnaround time 1-2 days.

Criminal Records: Access: Fax, mail, in person. Both court and visitors may perform in person searches. Search fee: $10.00 per name. Court makes copy: $.25 per page. Required to search: name, years to search, DOB; also helpful: address. Criminal records on docket books from 1920s. Mail turnaround time 1-2 days.

General Information: Public terminal goes back to 1995. No adoptions, sealed, juvenile, mental health, expunged or dismissed records released. Will fax documents $1.00 1st page, $.50 each add'l. Certification fee: $10.00 per doc includes copies. Payee: Clerk of Court. Personal checks accepted. Prepayment and SASE required.

Pembina County

Pembina County District Court 301 Dakota St West #6, Cavalier, ND 58220-4100; phone: 701-265-4373; criminal fax: 701-265-4876; same fax for civil/probate; hours 8:30AM-5PM (CST). *Felony, Misdemeanor, Civil, Eviction, Small Claims, Probate.*

Civil Records: Access: Fax, mail, in person. Both court and visitors may perform in person searches. Search fee: $10.00 per name. Court makes copy: $.25 per page. Required to search: name, years to search; also helpful: address, DOB, SSN. Civil cases indexed by defendant, plaintiff; on index books from 1880s; computerized records go back to 1992. Mail turnaround time 1-2 days.

Criminal Records: Access: Fax, mail, in person. Both court and visitors may perform in person searches. Search fee: $10.00 per name. Court makes copy: $.25 per page. Required to search: name, years to search, DOB; also helpful: address, SSN. Felony records kept for 21 years, misdemeanor for 15 years; computerized records go back to 1997. Mail turnaround time 1-2 days.

General Information: Public terminal has criminal back to 1997 and civil back to 1995. No adoptions, sealed, juvenile, mental health, expunged or dismissed records released. Will fax documents to local or toll free line. Certification fee: $10.00 per document includes copy fee. Payee: Pembina County Clerk of Court. Personal checks accepted. Prepayment required. SASE requested.

Pierce County

Northeast Judicial District Court PO Box 258, 240 SE 2nd St, Rugby, ND 58368; phone: 701-776-6161; criminal fax: 701-776-5707; same fax for civil/probate; hours 9AM-5PM (CST). *Felony, Misdemeanor, Civil, Eviction, Small Claims, Probate.*

Civil Records: Access: Fax, mail, in person. Both court and visitors may perform in person searches. Search fee: $10.00 per name. Court makes copy: $.25 per page. Required to search: name, years to search. Civil cases indexed by defendant, plaintiff; on computer from 1996, on index books and docket books from early 1900s. Mail turnaround time 1-2 days.

Criminal Records: Access: Fax, mail, in person. Both court and visitors may perform in person searches. Search fee: $10.00 per name. Court makes copy: $.25 per page. Required to search: name, years to search, DOB; also helpful: SSN. Criminal records on computer from 1996, on index books and docket books from early 1900s. Mail turnaround time 1-2 days.

General Information: Public terminal has criminal back to 1996 and civil back to 1996. (Civil records include only judgments.) No adoptions, sealed, juvenile, mental health, expunged or dismissed records released. Will not fax documents. Certification fee: $10.00 per document; $5.00 for an add'l copy. Payee: Clerk of Courts. Personal checks accepted. Prepayment required. SASE helpful.

Ramsey County

District Court 524 4th Ave #4, Devils Lake, ND 58301; phone: 701-662-1309; fax: 701-662-1303; hours 8AM-N; 1:00PM-5:00PM (CST). *Felony, Misdemeanor, Civil, Eviction, Small Claims, Probate.*

Civil Records: Access: Mail, in person. Both court and visitors may perform in person searches. Search fee: $10.00 per name. Court makes copy: $.10 per page. Required to search: name; also helpful: years to search. Civil cases indexed by defendant, plaintiff; on index cards from 1985, on index books from early 1900s. Mail turnaround time 1-2 days.

Criminal Records: Access: Mail, in person. Both court and visitors may perform in person searches. Search fee: $10.00 per name. Court makes copy: $.10 per page. Required to search: name; also helpful: years to search, address, DOB, SSN. Criminal records on index cards from 1985, on index books from early 1900s. Mail turnaround time 1-2 days.

General Information: Public terminal goes back to 1997. No adoptions, sealed, juvenile, mental health, expunged or dismissed records released. No fee to fax documents. Fax only available to businesses. Certification fee: $10.00 per doc includes copies. Payee: Clerk of Courts. Personal checks accepted. Prepayment and SASE required.

Ransom County

Southeast Judicial District Court PO Box 626, Lisbon, ND 58054; phone: 701-683-5823 X120; criminal phone: 701-683-5823 x142; fax: 701-683-5826; hours 8:30AM-5PM (CST). *Felony, Misdemeanor, Civil, Eviction, Small Claims, Probate.*

Civil Records: Access: Fax, mail, in person. Both court and visitors may perform in person searches. Search fee: $10.00 per name. Court makes copy: $.20 per page. Required to search: name, years to search; also helpful: address. Civil cases indexed by defendant, plaintiff. Civil records computerized from 2000. Mail turnaround time 3-4 days.

Criminal Records: Access: Fax, mail, in person. Both court and visitors may perform in person searches. Search fee: $10.00 per name. Court makes copy: $.20 per page. Required to search: name, years to search, DOB; also helpful: address. Criminal records computerized from 2000. Mail turnaround time 3-4 days.

General Information: No public access terminal. No adoptions, sealed, juvenile, mental health, expunged or dismissed records released. No fee to fax documents. Certification fee: $10.00. Payee: Clerk of Court. Personal checks accepted. Prepayment and SASE required.

Renville County

Northeast Judicial District Court PO Box 68, Mohall, ND 58761; phone: 701-756-6398; fax: 701-756-6398; hours 9AM-4:30PM (CST). *Felony, Misdemeanor, Civil, Eviction, Small Claims, Probate.*

Civil Records: Access: Fax, mail, in person. Both court and visitors may perform in person searches. Search fee: $10.00 per name. Court makes copy: $.25

per page. Required to search: name, years to search; also helpful: address. Civil cases indexed by defendant, plaintiff; on index books from 1910. Mail turnaround time 1-2 days.

Criminal Records: Access: Fax, mail, in person. Both court and visitors may perform in person searches. Search fee: $10.00 per name. Court makes copy: $.25 per page. Required to search: name, years to search, DOB; also helpful: address. Criminal records on computer from 1/88, on index books from 1910 but not reliable before 1940. Mail turnaround time 1-2 days.

General Information: No public access terminal. No adoptions, sealed, juvenile, mental health, expunged or dismissed records released. Will fax documents $3.00 1st page, $1.00 each add'l. Certification fee: $10.00 per doc. Payee: Clerk of Courts. Personal checks accepted. Prepayment and SASE required.

Richland County

Southeast Judicial District Court 418 2nd Ave North, Wahpeton, ND 58074; phone: 701-671-1524; fax: 701-671-1512; hours 8AM-5PM (CST). *Felony, Misdemeanor, Civil, Eviction, Small Claims, Probate.*

Civil Records: Access: Mail, fax, in person. Both court and visitors may perform in person searches. Search fee: $10.00 per name. Court makes copy: $.10 per page; $1.00 minimum. Required to search: name, years to search; also helpful: address. Plaintiff and defendant names required to search. Civil records on index cards and computer. Plaintiff and defendant names required to search. Mail turnaround time 1-2 days.

Criminal Records: Access: Mail, fax, in person. Both court and visitors may perform in person searches. Search fee: $10.00 per name. Court makes copy: $.10 per page; $1.00 minimum. Required to search: name, years to search, DOB, SSN; also helpful: address. Criminal records on docket books and computer. Mail turnaround time 1-2 days.

General Information: Public terminal goes back to 1998. No adoptions, sealed, juvenile, mental health, expunged or dismissed records released. Will fax documents to toll-free number, otherwise fee is $.25 per page, $1.00 minimum. Certification fee: $10.00. Payee: Clerk of District Court. Personal checks accepted. Prepayment and SASE required.

Rolette County

Northeast Judicial District Court PO Box 460, Rolla, ND 58367; phone: 701-477-3816; fax: 701-477-8594; hours 8:30AM-4:30PM (CST). *Felony, Misdemeanor, Civil, Eviction, Small Claims, Probate.*

Civil Records: Access: Fax, mail, in person. Both court and visitors may perform in person searches. Search fee: $10.00 per name. Court makes copy: $.50 per page. Self serve copy fee: $.50 per page. Required to search: name, years to search; also helpful: address. Civil cases indexed by defendant, plaintiff, stored since 1889; computerized since 2000. Mail turnaround time 1-2 days.

Criminal Records: Access: Fax, mail, in person. Both court and visitors may perform in person searches. Search fee: $10.00 per name. Court makes copy: $.50 per page. Self serve copy fee: $.50 per page. Required to search: name, years to search; also helpful: address, DOB, SSN. Criminal records on dockets from 1970, computerized since 2000. Prior to 1970, records hard to find and not very accurate. Mail turnaround time 1-2 days.

General Information: No public access terminal. No adoptions, sealed, juvenile, mental health, expunged or dismissed records released. Will fax documents $5.00 per doc. Certification fee: $10.00. Payee: Clerk of Court. Business checks accepted. Prepayment and SASE required.

Sargent County

Southeast Judicial District Court PO Box 176 (355 Main St), Forman, ND 58032; phone: 701-724-6241 X115; fax: 701-724-6244; hours 9AM-N, 12:30-4:30PM (CST). *Felony, Misdemeanor, Civil, Eviction, Small Claims, Probate.*

Civil Records: Access: Fax, mail, in person. Both court and visitors may perform in person searches. Search fee: $10.00 per name. Court makes copy: $.10 per page; same fee for self serve. Required to search: name, years to search; also helpful: address. Civil cases indexed by defendant. Civil records on books from early 1800s. Mail turnaround time 1-2 days.

Criminal Records: Access: Fax, mail, in person. Both court and visitors may perform in person searches. Search fee: $10.00 per name. Court makes copy: $.10 per page; same fee for self serve. Required to search: name, years to search; also helpful-DOB. Criminal records on books from early 1800s. Mail turnaround time 1-2 days.

General Information: No public access terminal. No adoptions, sealed, juvenile, mental health, expunged or dismissed records released. Will fax documents $3.00 1st page, $1.00 each add'l. Certification fee: $10.00. Payee: Clerk of Court. Personal checks accepted. Prepayment required.

Sheridan County

South Central Judicial District Court PO Box 409, McClusky, ND 58463; phone: 701-363-2207; fax: 701-363-2953; hours 9AM-N, 1-5PM (CST). *Felony, Misdemeanor, Civil, Eviction, Small Claims, Probate.*

Civil Records: Access: Mail, in person. Both court and visitors may perform in person searches. Search fee: $10.00 per name. Court makes copy: $.25 per page; same fee for self serve. Required to search: name, years to search; also helpful: address. Civil cases indexed by defendant, plaintiff; on index books from 1909. Mail turnaround time 1-2 days.

Criminal Records: Access: Mail, in person. Both court and visitors may perform in person searches. Search fee: $10.00 per name. Court makes copy: $.25 per page; same fee for self serve. Required to search: name, years to search, signed release; also helpful: address, DOB, SSN. Criminal records on index books from 1909. Mail turnaround time 1-2 days.

General Information: Public terminal goes back to 1909. No adoptions, sealed, juvenile, mental health, expunged or dismissed records released. Certification fee: $10.00. Payee: Clerk of District Court. Business checks accepted. Prepayment required.

Sioux County

South Central Judicial District Court Box L, Fort Yates, ND 58538; phone: 701-854-3853; fax: 701-854-3854; hours 9AM-4:30PM (CST). *Felony, Misdemeanor, Civil, Eviction, Small Claims, Probate.*

Civil Records: Access: Mail, in person. Both court and visitors may perform in person searches. Search fee: $10.00 per name per year. Court makes copy: $.50 per page. Required to search: name, years to search; also helpful: address. Civil cases indexed by defendant, plaintiff; on index books from 1914. Mail turnaround time 1-2 days.

Criminal Records: Access: Mail, in person. Both court and visitors may perform in person searches. Search fee: $10.00 per name per year. Court makes copy: $.50 per page. Required to search: name, years to search; also helpful: address, DOB, SSN. Criminal records on index books from 1914. Mail turnaround time 1-2 days.

General Information: No public access terminal. No adoptions, sealed, juvenile, mental health, expunged or dismissed records released. Fee to fax documents is $3.00 per document. Certification fee: $10.00 per doc includes copies. Payee: Clerk of Court. Personal checks accepted. Prepayment and SASE required.

Slope County

Southwest Judicial District Court PO Box JJ, Amidon, ND 58620; phone: 701-879-6275; fax: 701-879-6278; hours 8:00AM-N; 1:00PM-5:00PM (MST). *Felony, Misdemeanor, Civil, Eviction, Small Claims, Probate.*

Civil Records: Access: Fax, mail, in person. Both court and visitors may perform in person searches. Search fee: $10.00 per name. Court makes copy: $.50 per page. Self serve copy fee: $.25 per page. Required to search: name, years to search; also helpful: address. Civil cases indexed by defendant, plaintiff; on index cards from 1989. Mail turnaround time 1-2 days.

Criminal Records: Access: Fax, mail, in person. Both court and visitors may perform in person searches. Search fee: $10.00 per name. Court makes copy: $.50 per page. Self serve copy fee: $.25 per page. Required to search: name, years to search, DOB; also helpful: address. Criminal records on index books from 1915. Mail turnaround time 1-2 days.

General Information: No public access terminal. No adoptions, sealed, juvenile, mental health, expunged or dismissed records released. Will fax documents $3.00 per doc. Certification fee: $10.00. Payee: Clerk of Court. Personal checks accepted. Prepayment and SASE required.

Stark County

District Court 51 Third St #106, Dickinson, ND 58602; phone: 701-227-3184; criminal: 701-227-3180; civil: 701-227-3182; fax: 701-227-3181; fax: 701-227-3185; hours 8AM-5PM (MST). *Felony, Misdemeanor, Civil, Eviction, Small Claims, Probate.*

Civil Records: Access: Mail, in person. Both court and visitors may perform in person searches. Search fee: $10.00 per name. Court makes copy: $.10 per page; $1.00 minimum. Self serve copy fee: $.10 per page. Required to search: name, years to search. Civil cases indexed by defendant, plaintiff; on computer since 1/92, index cards since 1800s. Mail turnaround time 1-2 days.

Criminal Records: Access: Mail, in person. Both court and visitors may perform in person searches. Search fee: $10.00 per name. Court makes copy: $.10 per page; $1.00 minimum. Self serve copy fee: $.10 per page. Required to search: name, years to search, DOB; also helpful: SSN. Criminal records on computer since 1/92, index cards since 1800s. Mail turnaround time 1-2 days.

General Information: Public terminal goes back to 1992. No adoptions, sealed, juvenile, mental health, expunged or dismissed records. Will fax documents for $.25 per page, $1.00 minimum. Certification fee: $10.00. Payee: Clerk of Court. Personal checks accepted. Prepayment and SASE required.

Steele County

East Central Judicial District Court PO Box 296, Finley, ND 58230; phone: 701-524-2152; fax: 701-524-1325; hours 8AM-N; 1-4:30PM (CST). *Felony, Misdemeanor, Civil, Eviction, Small Claims, Probate.*

Civil Records: Access: Mail, in person. Only the court performs in person searches; visitors may not. Search fee: $10.00 per name. Court makes copy: $1.00 per page. Required to search: name, years to search; also helpful: address. Civil cases indexed by defendant, plaintiff; on docket books from approx 1894. Mail turnaround time 1-2 days.

Criminal Records: Access: Mail, in person. Only the court performs in person searches; visitors may not. Search fee: $10.00 per name. Court makes copy: $1.00 per page. Required to search: name, years to search, DOB, signed release; also helpful: address. Criminal records on docket books from approx 1894. Mail turnaround time 1-2 days.

General Information: No public access terminal. No adoptions, sealed, juvenile, mental health, expunged or dismissed records released. Certification fee: $10.00. Payee: Clerk of Court. Business checks accepted. Prepayment and SASE required.

Stutsman County

Southeast Judicial District Court 511 2nd Ave SE, Jamestown, ND 58401; phone: 701-252-9042; probate phone: 701-251-6331; fax: 701-251-1006; hours 8AM-5PM (CST). *Felony, Misdemeanor, Civil, Eviction, Small Claims, Probate.*

Civil Records: Access: Mail, fax, in person. Only the court performs in person searches; visitors may not. Search fee: $10.00 per name. Court makes copy: $.20 per page, minimum charge is $1.00. Required to search: name, years to search; also helpful: address. Civil records on computer back to 1/87, on index books from 1800s. Mail turnaround time 1-2 days.

Criminal Records: Access: Mail, fax, in person. Only the court performs in person searches; visitors may not. Search fee: $10.00 per name. Court makes copy: $.20 per page, minimum charge is $1.00. Required to search: name, years to search, DOB; also helpful: address. Criminal records on computer back to 1/96, on index books from 1800s. Mail turnaround time 1-2 days.

General Information: No public access terminal. No adoptions, sealed, juvenile, mental health, expunged or dismissed records released. Will fax documents to local or toll free line. Certification fee: $10.00. Payee: Clerk of Court. Personal checks accepted. Prepayment and SASE required.

Towner County

Northeast Judicial District Court Box 517, Cando, ND 58324; phone: 701-968-4340 x3; fax: 701-968-4344; hours 8:30AM-N; 1:00PM-5:00PM (CST). *Felony, Misdemeanor, Civil, Eviction, Small Claims, Probate.*

Civil Records: Access: Fax, mail, in person. Only the court performs in person searches; visitors may not. Search fee: $10.00 per name. Court makes copy: $1.00 per page. Required to search: name, years to search; also helpful: address. Civil cases indexed by defendant, plaintiff; on index books from 1800s, computerized since 1998. Mail turnaround time 1-2 days.

Criminal Records: Access: Fax, mail, in person. Only the court performs in person searches; visitors may not. Search fee: $10.00 per name. Court makes copy: $1.00 per page. Required to search: name, years to search; also helpful: address, DOB, SSN. Records computerized since 1998. Mail turnaround time 1-2 days.

General Information: No adoptions, sealed, juvenile, mental health, expunged or dismissed records released. Will fax documents $3.00 per doc. Certification fee: $10.00. Payee: Clerk of District Court. Personal checks accepted. Prepayment and SASE required.

Traill County

East Central Judicial District Court PO Box 805, Hillsboro, ND 58045; phone: 701-636-4454; fax: 701-636-5124; hours 8AM-4:30PM (CST). *Felony, Misdemeanor, Civil, Eviction, Small Claims, Probate.*

Civil Records: Access: Phone, fax, mail, in person. Only the court performs in person searches; visitors may not. Search fee: $10.00 per name. Court makes copy: $.25 per page. Required to search: name, years to search; also helpful: address. Civil cases indexed by defendant, plaintiff; on index books from 1800s. Mail turnaround time 1-2 days.

Criminal Records: Access: Phone, fax, mail, in person. Only the court performs in person searches; visitors may not. Search fee: $10.00 per name. Court makes copy: $.25 per page. Required to search: name, years to search; also helpful: address, DOB, SSN. Criminal records on index books from 1800s. Mail turnaround time 1-2 days.

General Information: No public access terminal. No adoptions, sealed, juvenile, mental health, expunged or dismissed records released. Will fax documents $1.00 per page. Certification fee: $10.00 per doc includes copies. Payee: Clerk of Court.

Personal checks accepted. Prepayment and SASE required.

Walsh County

Northeast Judicial District Court Clerk of District Court, 600 Cooper Ave, Grafton, ND 58237; phone: 701-352-0350; fax: 701-352-4466; hours 8:30AM-5PM (CST). *Felony, Misdemeanor, Civil, Eviction, Small Claims, Probate.*

Civil Records: Access: Mail, in person. Both court and visitors may perform in person searches. Search fee: $10.00 per name. Court makes copy: $.10 per page; $1.00 minimum. Required to search: name, years to search; also helpful: address. Civil cases indexed by defendant, plaintiff; on index books from early 1900s; on computer from 11/97. Mail turnaround time 2-3 days.

Criminal Records: Access: Mail, in person. Both court and visitors may perform in person searches. Search fee: $10.00 per name. Court makes copy: $.10 per page; $1.00 minimum. Required to search: name, years to search, DOB; also helpful: address, SSN. Criminal records on index books from early 1900s; on computer from 11/97. Mail turnaround time 2-3 days.

General Information: Public terminal goes back to 11/97. No adoptions, sealed, juvenile, mental health, expunged or dismissed records released. Fee to fax documents is $5.00 per document. Certification fee: $10.00, then $5.00 each add'l copy. Payee: Clerk of Court. Personal checks accepted. Prepayment and SASE required.

Ward County

Northwest Judicial District Court PO Box 5005, Minot, ND 58702-5005; criminal phone: 701-857-6610; civil phone: 701-857-6600; probate phone: 701-857-6620; fax: 701-857-6623; hours 8AM-4:30PM (CST). *Felony, Misdemeanor, Civil, Eviction, Small Claims, Probate.*

Civil Records: Access: Mail, in person. Both court and visitors may perform in person searches. Search fee: $10.00 per name. Court makes copy: $.10 per page, minimum $1.00. Self serve copy fee: $.10 per page. Required to search: name, years to search; also helpful: address. Civil cases indexed by defendant, plaintiff; on index cards from 1990, on index books from 1800s; computerized records go back to 1994. Mail turnaround time 5 days.

Criminal Records: Access: Mail, in person. Both court and visitors may perform in person searches. Search fee: $10.00 per name. Court makes copy: $.10 per page; minimum $1.00. Self serve copy fee: $.10 per page. Required to search: name, years to search; also helpful: address, DOB, SSN. Criminal records on index cards from 1990, on index books from 1800s; computerized records go back to 1994. Mail turnaround time 5 days.

General Information: Public terminal goes back to 1994. No adoptions, sealed, juvenile, mental health, expunged or dismissed records released. Certification fee: $10.00. Payee: Clerk of District Court. Business checks accepted. Prepayment and SASE required.

Wells County

Southeast Judicial District Court PO Box 155, Fessenden, ND 58438; phone: 701-547-3122; criminal fax: 701-547-3840; same fax for civil/probate; hours 8AM-4:30PM (CST). *Felony, Misdemeanor, Civil, Eviction, Small Claims, Probate.*

Civil Records: Access: Mail, in person. Only the court performs in person searches; visitors may not. Search fee: $10.00 per name. Court makes copy: $1.00 per document. Required to search: name, years to search; also helpful: address. Civil cases indexed by defendant, plaintiff; on index books. Mail turnaround time same day.

Criminal Records: Access: Mail, in person. Only the court performs in person searches; visitors may not. Search fee: $10.00 per name. Court makes copy: $1.00 per document. Required to search: name, years to search; also helpful: address, DOB, SSN. Criminal records on index books from 1980. Mail turnaround time 1-2 days.

General Information: No public access terminal. No adoptions, sealed, juvenile, mental health, expunged or dismissed records released. Will fax documents to local or toll free line. Certification fee: $10.00 per doc includes copies. Payee: District Court. Personal checks accepted. Prepayment and SASE required.

Williams County

Northwest Judicial District Court PO Box 2047, Williston, ND 58802; phone: 701-774-4374; criminal phone: 701-774-4377; fax: 701-774-4379; hours 8AM-5PM (CST). *Felony, Misdemeanor, Civil, Eviction, Small Claims, Probate.*

Civil Records: Access: Mail, in person. Both court and visitors may perform in person searches. Search fee: $10.00 per name. Court makes copy: $.10 per page, $1 minimum; same fee for self serve. Required to search: name, years to search; also helpful: address. Civil cases indexed by defendant, plaintiff. Civil records computerized since 1/98, on index cards from 1/92, on index books from 1899. Mail turnaround time 1-2 days.

Criminal Records: Access: Mail, in person. Both court and visitors may perform in person searches. Search fee: $10.00 per name. Court makes copy: $.10 per page; $1 minimum; same fee for self serve. Required to search: name, years to search; also helpful: address, DOB, SSN. Criminal records computerized since 1/98, on index cards from 1/92, on index books from 1899. Mail turnaround time 1-2 days.

General Information: Public terminal goes back to 1998. No adoptions, sealed, juvenile, mental health, expunged or dismissed records released. Will fax documents. Certification fee: $10.00. Payee: Clerk of Court. Personal checks accepted. Prepayment and SASE required.

North Dakota Recording Offices

ORGANIZATION:	53 counties, 53 recording offices. The recording officer is the Register of Deeds. The entire state is in the Central Time Zone (CST).
REAL ESTATE RECORDS:	Some counties will perform real estate searches by name or by legal description. Copy fees are usually $1.00 per page. Certified copies usually cost $5.00 for the first page and $2.00 for each additional page. Copies may be faxed.
UCC RECORDS:	Since 07/1/2001, all financing statements must be filed at the state level, except for real estate related collateral, which are filed only with the Register of Deeds. Previously, the state was a dual filing state and reocrd could be filed at either place. The good news is that all counties access a statewide computer database of filings and will perform UCC searches. Use search request form UCC-11. Various search options are available, including by federal tax identification number or Social Security number The search with copies costs $7.00 per debtor name, including three pages of copies and $1.00 per additional page. Copies may be faxed for an additional fee of $3.00.
TAX LIEN RECORDS:	Federal tax liens on personal property of businesses are filed with the Secretary of State. Other federal and all state tax liens are filed with the county Register of Deeds. All counties will perform tax lien searches. Some counties automatically include business federal tax liens as part of a UCC search because they appear on the statewide database. (Be careful - federal tax liens on individuals may only be in the county lien books, not on the statewide system.) Separate searches are usually available at $5.00-7.00 per name. Copy fees vary. Copies may be faxed.
OTHER LIENS:	Mechanics, judgment, hospital, repair, egg cutter.
ONLINE ACCESS:	The North Dakota Recorders Information Network (NDRIN) is a electronic central repository representing a number of ND counties - 32 currently with more being added - participating and offering Internet access to to records, indices and images. There is a $100 set-up fee and $50 monthly with $1.00 charge per image printed. Register or request information via the website at www.ndrin.com

Adams County

County Recorder, PO Box 469, Hettinger, ND 58639-0469. 701-567-2460; fax-701-567-2910; hours: 8:30AM-N, 1-5PM.
Office personnel or visitors may perform searches. Search fee $10.00 per name. UCC copy request with certificate per debtor name- $7.00. Copy fee $1.00 per document. Cert fee- $5.00 1st page; $2.00 each add'l. Payee- Adams County Recorder. **Other phones:** Treasurer- 701-567-2537; Elections- 701-567-4363. **Property tax/Assessor-** 701-567-2900.

Barnes County

Register of Deeds, 230 4th St NW, #201, Valley City, ND 58072. 701-845-8506, UCC recording phone-701-845-8507; fax-701-845-8538; hours: 8AM-5PM.
Participates in the ND Recorders Information Network, www.ndrin.com. Office personnel or visitors may perform searches. Search fee $7.00+ per name. Will not search real estate records. Copy fee $1.00 per page. Cert fee- $5.00 per page, $2.00 each add'l. Payee- Barnes County Recorders. **Online access to Real Estate records:** Subscription access the recorder's land records via NDRIN's central repository at www.ndrin.com. See section introduction. **Other phones:** Treasurer- 701-845-8505; Elections- 701-845-8500; Vital Records- 701-845-8512. **Property tax/Assessor-** 701-845-8515.

Benson County

County Recorder, PO Box 193, Minnewaukan, ND 58351. 701-473-5345, R/E recording phone-701-473-5332; fax-701-473-5571;
Office personnel or visitors may perform searches. General index search fee $7.00. Copy fee $2.00 per copy. **Online access to Real Estate records:** Subscription access the recorder's land records via NDRIN's central repository at www.ndrin.com. See section introduction. **Other phones:** Treasurer- 701-473-5458; Elections- 701-473-5340; Vital Records-

701-473-5345. **Property tax/Assessor-** 701-473-5524.

Billings County

County Recorder, PO Box 138, Medora, ND 58645-0138. 701-623-4491; fax-701-623-4896; hours: 8AM-N; 1PM-5PM.
All records in one index. Search fee $7.00 per name. Will not search real estate records. Copy fee $1.00 per page; $.25 self serve. Cert fee- $5.00 for 1st pg,$1.00 each add'l pg. Payee- Billings County. **Online access to Real Estate records:** Subscription access the recorder's land records via NDRIN's central repository at www.ndrin.com. See section introduction. **Other phones:** Treasurer- 701-623-4484; Elections- 701-623-4377. **Property tax/Assessor-** 701-623-4810.

Bottineau County

County Recorder, 314 W. 5th St, Bottineau, ND 58318-1265. 701-228-2786; fax-701-228-3658; hours: 8:30AM-5PM.
All records in one index. Records indexed on a public use terminal back to 7/1997. Office will perform a tax lien search but public must search other records themselves. Search fee $7.00 per debtor. Copy fee $1.00 per page. Cert fee- $7.00 1st pg; $1.00 each add'l page. **Other phones:** Treasurer- 701-228-2035; Elections- 701-228-2225.

Bowman County

County Recorder, PO Box 379, Bowman, ND 58623. 701-523-3450; fax-701-523-5443; hours: 8AM-4:30PM.
Records indexed on a public use terminal back to 10/7/2004. Office personnel or visitors may perform searches. Search fee $7.00 1st hour, $25.00 after 1 hour. Copy fee $1.00 per record. Cert fee- $5.00 1st page; $2.00 each add'l page. Payee- County Recorder. **Other phones:** Treasurer- 701-523-3665; Appraiser/Auditor- 701-523-3129; Elections- 701-523-3130; Vital Records- 701-328-

2360; Auditor- 701-523-3130. **Property tax/Assessor-** PO Box 453, Bowman, ND 58623; 701-523-3129.

Burke County

County Recorder, PO Box 219, Bowbells, ND 58721-0219. 701-377-2818; fax-701-377-2020; hours: 8:30AM-5PM.
Office personnel or visitors may perform searches. Search fee $7.00 per name. Copy fee $1.00 per page. R/E record copy- $.50 per page. Cert fee- $5.00 for 1st page; $2.00 each add'l. Payee- County Recorder. **Other phones:** Treasurer- 701-377-2917; Appraiser/Auditor- 701-377-2661; Elections- 701-377-2861; Vital Records- 701-377-2718. **Property tax/Assessor-** 701-377-2661.

Burleigh County

County Recorder, PO Box 5518, Bismarck, ND 58506-5518. 701-222-6749; fax-701-222-6717; hours: 8AM-5PM. www.ndrin.com
All records in one index. Records indexed on computer back to 10/7/96/. Office will perform a UCC search but public must search other records themselves. Search fee $7.00 per name minimum. Copy fee $1.00 per page. **Online access to Real Estate, Treasurer/Auditor, Property records:** Subscription access the recorder's land records via NDRIN's central repository at www.ndrin.com. See section introduction. Also, access to treasurer and auditor property data is free at https://burleigh.nd.ezgov.com/ezproperty/review_search.jsp. No name searching. **Other phones:** Treasurer- 701-222-6696; Appraiser/Auditor- 701-222-6691; Elections- 701-222-6718; Vital Records- 701-328-2360. **Property tax/Assessor-** same address as above. 701-222-6691.

Cass County

Register of Deeds, PO Box 2806, Fargo, ND 58108-2806. 701-241-5622, R/E recording phone-701-241-5620; fax-701-241-5621; hours: 8AM-5PM.
Records indexed on computer back to 1992. Office personnel or visitors may perform searches. Search

fee $7.00 per name. Copy fee $1.00 per page. Tax lien copy- $2.00. Cert fee- $5.00 per cert. Payee- Cass County Register of Deeds. **Online access to Real Estate records:** Subscription access the recorder's land records via NDRIN's central repository at www.ndrin.com. See section introduction. **Other phones:** Treasurer- 701-241-5611; Elections- 701-241-5601. **Property tax/Assessor-** 701-241-5611.

Cavalier County

County Recorder, 901 3rd St #13, Langdon, ND 58249. 701-256-2136; fax-701-256-2566; hours: 8:30AM-4:30PM.
Participates in the ND Recorders Information Network, www.ndrin.com. All records in one index. Office personnel or visitors may perform searches. Will not search real estate records. Will search UCC records. UCC copy request with certificate per debtor name- $7.00. Copy fee $1.00 per UCC. **Online access to Real Estate records:** Subscription access the recorder's land records via NDRIN's central repository at www.ndrin.com. See section introduction. **Other phones:** Treasurer- 701-256-2549; Elections- 701-256-2229; Vital Records- 701-256-2124. **Property tax/Assessor-** 901 3rd St, Langdon, ND 58249; 701-256-2229.

Dickey County

Register of Deeds, PO Box 148, Ellendale, ND 58436. 701-349-3249; fax-701-349-4639; hours: 8AM-4:30PM.
Office personnel or visitors may perform searches. Search fee $7.00 per name. Copy fee $1.00 per page. Tax lien copy- $3.00. Cert fee- $5.00 per cert. Payee- Dickey County. **Other phones:** Elections- 701-349-3249. **Property tax/Assessor-** 701-349-3218.

Divide County

Register of Deeds, PO Box 68, Crosby, ND 58730. 701-965-6661; fax-701-965-6943; hours: 8:30AM-N, 1-5PM.
Office personnel or visitors may perform searches. Search fee $7.00 per name. Will not search real estate records. Copy fee $2.00 per page. Cert fee- $5.00 per cert. Payee- Webster County Recorder. **Other phones:** Treasurer- 701-965-6312; Elections- 701-965-6351. **Property tax/Assessor-** 701-965-6351.

Dunn County

Register of Deeds, PO Box 106, Manning, ND 58642-0106. 701-573-4443; fax-701-573-4444; hours: 8AM-N, 12:30-4:30PM. www.ndrin.com
All records in one index. Records indexed on a public use terminal back to 1908. Only the public may search. Copy fee $1.00 per copy. Cert fee- $10.00 per cert plus copy fee. Payee- Dunn County Recorder. **Online access to Real Estate records:** Subscription access the recorder's land records via NDRIN's central repository at www.ndrin.com. See section introduction. **Other phones:** Treasurer- 701-573-4446; Elections- 701-573-4448 (Auditor); Vital Records- 701-328-2360. **Property tax/Assessor-** 701-573-4445.

Eddy County

Register of Deeds, 524 Central Ave, New Rockford, ND 58356-1698. 701-947-2813; fax-701-947-2067; hours: 8AM-N; 12:30-4:00PM.
Office personnel or visitors may perform searches. Search fee $10.00 per name. Will not search real estate records. Copy fee $.25 per page. Cert fee- $10.00 per cert. Payee- Eddy County. **Other phones:** Treasurer- 701-947-5315; Elections- 701-947-2434. **Property tax/Assessor-** 701-947-5220.

Emmons County

County Recorder, PO Box 905, Linton, ND 58552. 701-254-4812; fax-701-254-4012; hours: 8:30AM-N, 1PM-5PM.
Index: Two separate indices to search. Record index not computerized. Office personnel (minimal) or visitors may perform searches. Will

not search real estate records. Will search UCC records. UCC copy request with certificate per debtor name- $7.00. Copy fee $1.00 per page. Cert fee- $10.00 per cert plus copy fee. Payee- Emmons County Recorder. **Other phones:** Treasurer- 701-254-4802; Elections- 701-254-4807. **Property tax/Assessor-** 701-254-4417.

Foster County

Recorder, PO Box 76, Carrington, ND 58421. 701-652-2491; fax-701-652-2173; hours: 8:30AM-4:30PM.
Office personnel or visitors may perform searches. Search fee- varies. R/E record copy- $1.00 per document. Cert fee- $5.00 for 1st page/$2.00 per add'l pages. Payee- Foster County Recorder. **Online access to Real Estate records:** Subscription access the recorder's land records via NDRIN's central repository at www.ndrin.com. See section introduction. **Other phones:** Treasurer- 701-652-2322; Elections- 701-652-2441. **Property tax/Assessor-** 701-652-2441.

Golden Valley County

County Recorder, PO Box 130, Beach, ND 58621-0130. 701-872-3713; fax-701-872-4383; hours: 8AM-N, 1PM-4PM.
Separate indices to search include grantor/grantee, deeds, misc, mortgagor/mortgatee, corner monument records. Records indexed on a public use terminal. Office will perform a UCC search, (if "all" is checked on request form, than tax liens will be searched), but public must search other records themselves. UCC copy request with certificate per debtor name- $7.00. Copy fee $1.00 per page. Cert fee- $5.00 1st page, $2.00 each add'l page. Payee- County Recorder. **Online access to Real Estate records:** Subscription access the recorder's land records via NDRIN's central repository at www.ndrin.com. See section introduction. **Other phones:** Treasurer- 701-872-4411; Elections- 701-872-4331; Vital Records- 701-328-2360; Auditor- 701-872-4331. **Property tax/Assessor-** PO Box 67, Beach, ND 58621; 701-872-4673.

Grand Forks County

Register of Deeds, PO Box 5066, Grand Forks, ND 58206. 701-780-8259, R/E recording phone-701-780-8200; fax-701-780-8212; hours: 8AM-5PM. www.co.grand-forks.nd.us/homepage.htm
Office will perform a UCC search but public must search other records themselves. UCC copy request with certificate per debtor name- $7.00. **Online access to Real Estate, Recording, Deed, Death, Judgment, Lien records:** Access to county property information is free at www.co.grand-forks.nd.us/search.htm. Also, access to the recorder's database is free at www.co.grand-forks.nd.us/recorders%20search.htm. **Other phones:** Treasurer- 701-780-8295; Elections- 701-780-8200. **Property tax/Assessor-** 701-780-8261.

Grant County

Register of Deeds, PO Box 258, Carson, ND 58529. 701-622-3544; fax-701-622-3717; hours: 8AM-4PM.
Office personnel or visitors may perform searches. Search fee $7.00 per name. Will not search real estate records. Copy fee $1.00 per page. Cert fee- $10.00 per cert. Payee- Grant County Register of Deeds. **Other phones:** Treasurer- 701-622-3422; Elections- 701-622-3275. **Property tax/Assessor-** 701-622-3275.

Griggs County

Register of Deeds, PO Box 237, Cooperstown, ND 58425. 701-797-2771; fax-701-797-3587; hours: 8AM-N, 1-4:30PM.
Participates in the ND Recorders Information Network, www.ndrin.com. Office personnel or visitors may perform searches. Search fee $11.00 per name. Will not search real estate records. Copy fee $1.00 per page. Cert fee- $5.00 per cert. Payee- Griggs County Register of Deeds. **Online access to Real Estate records:** Subscription access the recorder's

land records via NDRIN's central repository at www.ndrin.com. See section introduction. **Other phones:** Treasurer- 701-797-2411; Elections- 701-797-3117. **Property tax/Assessor-** 701-797-3211.

Hettinger County

County Recorder, PO Box 668, Mott, ND 58646. 701-824-2545/2645, R/E recording phone-701-824-2545; fax-701-824-2717;
Office personnel or visitors may perform searches. Search fee $7.00 per name. Will not search real estate records. Copy fee - varies. R/E record copy- $1.00 per copy. Cert fee- $7.00 1st pg; $2.00 each add'l page. **Other phones:** Treasurer- 701-824-2655; Appraiser/Auditor- 701-824-2515; Elections- 701-824-2515; Vital Records- 701-824-2545. **Property tax/Assessor-** 701-824-2515.

Kidder County

County Recorder, PO Box 66, Steele, ND 58482. 701-475-2632; fax-701-475-2202; hours: 9AM-12PM; 1-5PM.
All records in one index. Records indexed on computer back to 1992-93. Office will perform a UCC search but public must search other records themselves. UCC copy request with certificate per debtor name- $7.00. Copy fee $1.00 per page. Cert fee- $5.00 1st page; $2.00 each add'l page plus copy fee. Payee- County Recorder. **Online access to Real Estate records:** Subscription access the recorder's land records via NDRIN's central repository at www.ndrin.com. See section introduction. **Other phones:** Treasurer- 701-475-2632; Elections- 701-475-2632. **Property tax/Assessor-** 701-475-2632.

La Moure County

County Recorder, PO Box 128, La Moure, ND 58458-0128. 701-883-5301 x6; fax-701-883-4220; hours: 8:30AM-N, 1-4:30PM. http://lamoco.drtel.net/countyrecorder.html
All records in one index. Office personnel or visitors may perform searches. General index search fee $28.00 per hour, after 1st hour free. UCC copy request with certificate per debtor name- $7.00 per 5 entities. Separate federal tax lien search- $7.00 per debtor per 5 entries. Separate state tax lien search- $7.00 per debtor. Federal/state combined tax lien search- $7.00 per debtor. Copy fee $1.00 per document up to 10 pages, $.10 per page after. Cert fee- $10.00 1st page, $3.00 each add'l page includes copy fee. Payee- County Recorder. **Other phones:** Treasurer- 701-883-5101; Elections- 701-883-5301. **Property tax/Assessor-** 701-883-5301.

Logan County

County Recorder, PO Box 6, Napoleon, ND 58561-0006. 701-754-2751; fax-701-754-2270; hours: 8:30AM-N, 1-4:30PM.
Record index not computerized. Office will perform a UCC search but public must search other records themselves. Search fee $7.00 per name. Copy fee $1.00 per page after 1st 3 pages free. Cert fee- $7.00 1st 3 pgs, $2.00 each add'l. Payee- Logan County Recorder. **Other phones:** Treasurer- 701-754-2286; Elections- 701-754-2425. **Property tax/Assessor-** 301 Broadway, Napoleon, ND 58561; 701-754-2239.

McHenry County

County Recorder, PO Box 149, Towner, ND 58788. 701-537-5634; fax-701-537-5969; hours: 8AM-N, 1-4:30PM.
Office personnel or visitors may perform searches. Search fee $7.00 per debtor for 1st 3 pages; $2.00 each add'l page. R/E record copy- $1.00 per copy. **Online access to Real Estate records:** Subscription access the recorder's land records via NDRIN's central repository at www.ndrin.com. See section introduction. **Other phones:** Treasurer- 701-537-5731; Elections- 701-537-5724; Vital Records- 701-537-5729. **Property tax/Assessor-** 701-537-5359.

McIntosh County

County Recorder, PO Box 179, Ashley, ND 58413. 701-288-3589/3450, R/E recording phone-701-288-3589; fax-701-288-3671; hours: 8AM-4:30PM.
All records in one index. Search fee $7.00. Copy fee $1.00 per page. Cert fee- $5.00 plus $2.00 each add'l page. Payee- County Recorder. **Online access to Real Estate records:** Subscription access the recorder's land records via NDRIN's central repository at www.ndrin.com. See section introduction. **Other phones:** Treasurer- 701-288-3342; Elections- 701-288-3347. **Property tax/Assessor-** 701-288-3347.

McKenzie County

County Recorder, PO Box 523, Watford City, ND 58854. 701-444-3453; fax-701-844-3902; hours: 8:30AM-5PM. www.4eyes.net/county.htm
All records in one index. Records indexed on a public use terminal back to 2000. Office will perform a UCC and Tax lien search but public must search other records themselves. Search fee $7.00. Copy fee $1.00 per page. Cert fee- $5.00 1st page plus $2.00 each add'l page. Payee- County Recorder. **Online access to Real Estate records:** Access the recorder's land records 5/1998 to present by subscription via NDRIN's central repository at www.ndrin.com. See section introduction. **Other phones:** Treasurer- 701-444-3457; Appraiser/Auditor-701-444-6852; Elections- 701-444-3616; Vital Records- 701-444-3452. **Property tax/Assessor-** 701-444-6852.

McLean County

County Recorder, PO Box 1108, Washburn, ND 58577-1108. 701-462-8541 x226/5, R/E recording phone-701-462-8541 X226, x225, UCC recording phone-701-462-8541; fax-701-462-3633; hours: 8AM-N,   12:30-4:30PM. www.visitmcleancounty.com
All records in one index. Will search records depending on nature of request; prefers visitors do their own searches. Will search UCC records including tax liens. UCC copy request with certificate per debtor name- $7.00 (includes 1st 3 pages; Add' pages are $2.00 each. Copy fee $1.00 per page. R/E record copy- $.50 per page. Cert fee- $5.00 per page plus $2.00 each add'l document page. Payee- McLean County Recorder. **Online access to Real Estate records:** Subscription access the recorder's land records is via NDRIN's central repository at www.ndrin.com. See section introduction. **Other phones:** Treasurer- 701-462-8541 x223; Elections- 701-462-8541 x216; Vital Records- 701-462-8541 x228. **Property tax/Assessor-** 701-462-8541 x220.

Mercer County

County Recorder, PO Box 39, Stanton, ND 58571. 701-745-3272; fax-701-745-3364; hours: 8AM-4PM.
Office personnel or visitors may perform searches. Search fee $7.00 per name. Will not search real estate records. **Other phones:** Treasurer- 701-745-3323; Elections- 701-745-3292. **Property tax/Assessor-** 701-745-3294.

Morton County

Register of Deeds, 210 2nd Ave, Mandan, ND 58554. 701-667-3305; fax-701-667-3453; hours: 8AM-5PM.
Participates in the ND Recorders Information Network, www.ndrin.com. Office personnel or visitors may perform searches. Search fee $7.00 per name. Will not search real estate records. General copy fee $2.00 per page. Tax lien copy- $1.00. Cert fee- $5.00 per cert. Payee- Morton County Register of Deeds. **Online access to Real Estate records:** Subscription access the recorder's land records via www.ndrin.com. See section introduction. **Other phones:** Treasurer- 701-667-3310; Elections-701-667-3300; Auditor- 701-667-3300. **Property tax/Assessor-** 701-667-3300.

Mountrail County

Register of Deeds, PO Box 69, Stanley, ND 58784. 701-628-2945; fax-701-628-2276;
Separate indices to search. Record index not computerized. Office will perform a UCC search but public must search other records themselves. UCC copy request with certificate per debtor name- $7.00. Copy fee $1.00 1st page; $.50 each add'l. Cert fee- $5.00 1st page plus $2.00 each add'l page, plus copy fee. **Other phones:** Treasurer-701-628-2935; Elections- 701-628-2145. **Property tax/Assessor-** 701-826-2425.

Nelson County

County Recorder, 210 B Ave. West, #203, Lakota, ND 58344. 701-247-2433; fax-701-247-2412; hours: 8AM-N, 1PM-4:30PM.
Participates in the ND Recorders Information Network, www.ndrin.com. Separate indices to search include deed/misc, mortgage. Office will perform a UCC search but public must search other records themselves. UCC or tax lien copy request (per debtor name)- $7.00. Copy fee $1.00 per page. Cert fee- UCC $7.00 per 5 entries, includes copy fee. Payee- Nelson County Recorder. **Online access to Real Estate records:** Subscription access the recorder's land records via NDRIN's central repository at www.ndrin.com. See section introduction. **Other phones:** Treasurer- 701-247-2453; Elections- 701-247-2463; Vital Records- 701-247-2462. **Property tax/Assessor-** 210 B Ave West, #303, Lakota, ND 58344; 701-247-2840.

Oliver County

Register of Deeds, PO Box 125, Center, ND 58530-0125. 701-794-8777; fax-701-794-3476; hours: 8AM-N, 1-4PM.
Office personnel or visitors may perform searches. Search fee $7.00 per name. Will search real estate records. Will not search tax liens. Copy fee $1.00 per page. R/E record copy- $.25 per page. Cert fee- $5.00 per cert. Payee- County Recorder. **Other phones:** Treasurer- 701-794-8737; Elections- 701-794-8721. **Property tax/Assessor-** 701-794-8721.

Pembina County

Clerk/Recorder, 301 Dakota St W. #10, Cavalier, ND 58220. 701-265-4373; fax-701-265-4876; hours: 8AM-5PM. www.pembinacountynd.gov
Office personnel or visitors may perform searches. Search fee $7.00 per name. Will not search real estate records. Copy fee $1.00 per page. Cert fee- $5.00 1st page, $2.00 each add'l page. Payee- Pembina County. **Online access to Real Estate records:** Subscription access the recorder's land records via NDRIN's central repository at www.ndrin.com. See section introduction. **Other phones:** Treasurer- 701-265-4465; Elections- 701-265-4231. **Property tax/Assessor-** 701-265-4697.

Pierce County

Register of Deeds, 240 S.E. 2nd St, Rugby, ND 58368. 701-776-5206; fax-701-776-5707; hours: 9AM-5PM.
Office personnel or visitors may perform searches. Search fee $7.00 per name. Will not search real estate records. UCC copy request with certificate per debtor name- $15.00. Copy fee $1.00 per page. Cert fee- $7.00 per cert. Payee- Pierce County Register of Deeds. **Online access to Real Estate records:** Subscription access the recorder's land records via NDRIN's central repository at www.ndrin.com. See section introduction. **Other phones:** Treasurer- 701-776-6841; Elections- 701-776-5225. **Property tax/Assessor-** 701-776-5225.

Ramsey County

Register of Deeds, 524 4th Ave #30, Devils Lake, ND 58301. 701-662-7018; fax-701-662-7093; hours: 8AM-5PM. www.co.ramsey.nd.us
Office personnel or visitors may perform searches. Search fee $7.00 per name. Will not search real estate records. Copy fee $1.00 per page. R/E record copy-$2.00 per document. Cert fee- $7.00 per page. Payee- Ramsey County Recorder. **Online access to Real Estate records:** Subscription access the recorder's land records via NDRIN's central repository at www.ndrin.com. See section introduction. **Other phones:** Treasurer- 701-662-7021; Elections- 701-662-7007; Vital Records- 701-662-7018. **Property tax/Assessor-** 701-662-7012.

Ransom County

County Recorder, PO Box 666, Lisbon, ND 58054-0666. 701-683-5823x115, R/E recording phone-701-683-5823 x115; fax-701-683-5827; 8:30AM-5PM.
Participates in the ND Recorders Information Network, www.ndrin.com. All records in one index. Records indexed on a public use terminal. Office will perform a UCC search but public must search other records themselves. Search fee $7.00. Copy fee $1.00 per filing. Cert fee- $5.00 1st page, #2.00 each add'l. Payee- Ransom County Recorder. **Online access to Real Estate records:** Subscription access the recorder's land records via NDRIN's central repository at www.ndrin.com. See section introduction. **Other phones:** Treasurer- 701-683-5823 x118; Elections- 701-683-5823 x113; Vital Records- 701-683-5823 x 120. **Property tax/Assessor-** PO Box 830, Lisbon, ND 58054; 701-683-5823 x111.

Renville County

Register of Deeds, PO Box 68, Mohall, ND 58761-0068. 701-756-6398; fax-701-756-7158; hours: 9AM-4:30PM. www.renvillecounty.org
Will not search real estate records. Will search UCC records. UCC search includes federal tax liens. UCC copy request with certificate per debtor name-$7.00. Separate state tax lien search- $5.00 per debtor. Copy fee $1.00 per page after 1st 3 pages free. Cert fee- $7.00 1st pg, $3.00 each add'l. Payee- Renville County Register of Deeds. **Other phones:** Treasurer- 701-756-6304; Appraiser/Auditor-701-756-6304; Elections- 701-756-6301; Vital Records- 701-756-6398. **Property tax/Assessor-** 701-756-6304.

Richland County

County Recorder, 418 2nd Ave North; Courthouse, Wahpeton, ND 58075-4400. 701-642-7800; fax-701-642-7820; hours: 8AM-5PM.
All records in one index. Records indexed on a public use terminal back to 12/1993. Office personnel or visitors may perform searches. Will search real estate records. Will search UCC records and tax liens. UCC copy request with certificate per debtor name- $7.00 for 1st 5 entries. Copy fee $1.00 per page. Cert fee- $7.00 1st page; $2.00 each add'l page. Payee- County Recorder. **Online access to Real Estate records:** Subscription access the recorder's land records via NDRIN's central repository at www.ndrin.com. See section introduction. **Other phones:** Treasurer- 701-642-7705; Elections- 701-642-7700; Vital Records- 701-642-7800. **Assessor-** same address as above. 701-642-7805.

Rolette County

Recorder, PO Box 276, Rolla, ND 58367. 701-477-3166; fax-701-477-5770; hours: 8:30AM-4:30PM.
Office personnel or visitors may perform searches. Search fee $7.00 per name. Copy fee $1.00 per page. Cert fee- $7.00 per 1st page; $2.00 each add'l page includes copy fee. Payee- Recorder. **Online access to Real Estate records:** Subscription access the recorder's land records via NDRIN's central repository at www.ndrin.com. See section introduction. **Other phones:** Treasurer- 701-477-3207; Elections-701-477-5665; Vital Records- 701-477-3166. **Property tax/Assessor-** 701-477-5665.

Sargent County

Register of Deeds, PO Box 176, Forman, ND 58032-0176. 701-724-6241, R/E recording phone-701-724-6241 x117; fax-701-724-6244;
Office personnel or visitors may perform searches. Search fee $7.00 per name. Will not search real estate

records. Copy fee $1.00 per copy. Cert fee- $5.00 per doc plus copy fee. Payee- County Recorder. **Online access to Real Estate records:** Subscription access the recorder's land records via NDRIN's central repository at www.ndrin.com. See section introduction. **Other phones:** Treasurer- 701-724-6241 x13,14; Elections- 701-724-6241. **Property tax/Assessor-** 701-724-6241 x15.

Sheridan County

Register of Deeds, PO Box 668, McClusky, ND 58463-0668. 701-363-2207; fax-701-363-2953; hours: 9AM-N, 1-5PM.
Office personnel or visitors may perform searches. Search fee $7.00 per name. Copy fee $1.00 per page. Cert fee- $5.00 1st page, $2.00 each add'l page. Payee- Sheridan County Recorder. **Other phones:** Treasurer- 701-363-2206; Elections- 701-363-2205; Vital Records- 603-895-2207. **Property tax/Assessor-** 701-363-2201.

Sioux County

Sioux County Recorder, PO Box L, Fort Yates, ND 58538. 701-854-3853; fax-701-854-3854; hours: 8AM-4:30PM.
All records in one index. Record index not computerized. Office personnel or visitors may perform searches. Search fee $7.50. Will not search real estate records. Copy fee $2.00 per page. Cert fee- $5.00. Payee- Sioux County Recorder. **Other phones:** Treasurer- 701-854-3853; Elections- 701-854-3481; Vital Records- 701-854-3853. **Property tax/Assessor-** 701-854-3481.

Slope County

County Recorder, PO Box JJ, Amidon, ND 58620-0445. 701-879-6275; fax-701-879-6278;
Office will perform a UCC search but public must search other records themselves. UCC copy request with certificate per debtor name- $7.00. R/E or tax lien copy- $.50 per page. Cert fee- $10.00 per name. Payee- County Recorder. **Online access to Real Estate records:** Subscription access the recorder's land records via NDRIN's central repository at www.ndrin.com. See section introduction. **Other phones:** Treasurer- 701-879-6272; Elections- 701-879-6276. **Property tax/Assessor-** 701-879-6370.

Stark County

County Recorder, 51 3rd St E, Dickinson, ND 58601. 701-456-7645; fax-701-456-7628; hours: 8AM-5PM.
Office personnel or visitors may perform searches. Search fee $7.00 per name. Will not search real estate records. Copy fee $1.00 per page. Payee- Stark County Recorder. **Online access to Real Estate records:** Subscription access the recorder's land records via NDRIN's central repository at www.ndrin.com. See section introduction. **Other phones:** Elections- 701-456-7630; Vital Records- 701-456-7645. **Property tax/Assessor-** 701-456-7671.

Steele County

Recorder of Deeds, PO Box 296, Finley, ND 58230. 701-524-2152, R/E recording phone-701-524-2790; fax-701-524-1325; hours: 8AM-N, 1-4:30PM.
All records in one index. Record index not computerized. Only the office personnel may

search. Search fee $7.00 minimum. Copy fee $1.00 per page. Cert fee- $10.00 1st page, $3.00 add'l. Payee- Steele County Recorder of Deeds. **Online access to Real Estate records:** Subscription access the recorder's land records via NDRIN's central repository at www.ndrin.com. See section introduction. **Other phones:** Treasurer- 701-524-2890; Elections- 701-524-2110. **Property tax/Assessor-** 701-524-2110.

Stutsman County

County Recorder, 511 2nd Ave S.E.; Courthouse, Jamestown, ND 58401. 701-252-9034; fax-701-251-1603; hours: 8AM-5PM.
Participates in the ND Recorders Information Network, www.ndrin.com. Separate indices to search include all documents with legal descriptions are indexed in their tract index books. Miscellaneous docs indexed in book "V", etc if they don't have a legal description on them. Records indexed on a public use terminal back to 11/1/1996 (for information only). Office will perform a UCC search but public must search other records themselves. UCC copy request with certificate per debtor name- $7.00. Copy fee $1.00 per 4 pages plus $3.00 fax. Cert fee- $7.00 per cert plus $2.00 per page after 1st. Payee- Stutsam County Recorder. **Online access to Real Estate records:** Subscription access the recorder's land records via NDRIN's central repository at www.ndrin.com. See section introduction. **Other phones:** Treasurer- 701-252-9036; Elections- 701-252-9035; Vital Records- 701-252-9034. **Property tax/Assessor-** same address as above. 701-252-9032.

Towner County

Recorder, PO Box 517, Cando, ND 58324. 701-968-4340 x5; fax-701-968-4344; hours: 8:30AM-5PM.
Office personnel or visitors may perform searches. Search fee $7.00 per name. Will not search real estate records. Copy fee $1.00 per page. Cert fee- $7.00 per doc; $1.00 each add'l page. **Other phones:** Treasurer- 701-968-4347; Elections- 701-968-4340. **Property tax/Assessor-** 701-968-4352.

Traill County

County Recorder, PO Box 399, Hillsboro, ND 58045. 701-636-4457, R/E recording phone-701-436-4457; fax-701-636-4457; hours: 8AM-N, 12:30-4:30PM.
Office personnel or visitors may perform searches. Search fee $7.00 per name. **Other phones:** Treasurer- 701-436-4459; Elections- 701-436-4458; Vital Records- 701-436-4454. **Property tax/Assessor-** 701-436-5950.

Walsh County

County Recorder, 600 Cooper Ave; Courthouse, Grafton, ND 58237. 701-352-2380; fax-701-352-3340; hours: 8AM-N, 12:30-4:30PM.
Separate indices to search include deed, mortgage indexes where the legal descriptions eradicate the property locations. Records indexed on computer back to 1997. Office will perform a UCC search and tax lien search, but public must search other records themselves. Search fee $7.00 for 1st 5, $2.00 each add'l. Copy fee $1.00 per page. Cert fee- $5.00 1st page, $2.00 each add'l plus copy

fee. Payee- Walsh County Recorder. **Online access to Real Estate records:** Subscription access the recorder's land records via NDRIN's central repository at www.ndrin.com. See section introduction. **Other phones:** Treasurer- 701-352-2541; Elections- 701-352-2851; Vital Records- 701-352-2380. **Assessor-** same address as above. 701-352-1077.

Ward County

County Recorder, PO Box 5005, Minot, ND 58705-5005. 701-857-6410, R/E recording phone-701-857-6420; fax-701-857-6414; hours: 8AM-4:30PM.
Office personnel or visitors may perform searches. Search fee $7.00 per name. Will not search real estate records. Copy fee $1.00 per page. Cert fee- $7.00 per cert. Payee- Ward County Register of Deeds. **Online access to Real Estate, Property Tax records:** Subscription access the recorder's land records via NDRIN's central repository at www.ndrin.com. See section introduction. Also, access to property tax data is free at www.co.ward.nd.us/ext/PropertyTax.htm. **Other phones:** Elections- 701-857-6420. **Property tax/Assessor-** 701-857-6430.

Wells County

County Recorder, PO Box 125, Fessenden, ND 58438-0125. 701-547-3141; fax-701-547-3719; 8AM-N, 12:30-4PM. http://mylocalgov.com/wellscountynd
Office personnel or visitors may perform searches. Search fee $7.00 for first 5 entries; $2.00 each add'l entry. Copy fee $1.00 per page. Cert fee- $7.00 for 1st page; $2.00 each add'l. Payee- Well County Recorder. **Online access to Real Estate records:** Subscription access the recorder's land records via NDRIN's central repository at www.ndrin.com. See section introduction. **Other phones:** Treasurer- 701-547-3161; Elections- 701-547-3521; Vital Records- 701-547-3122; State Vital Records- 701-328-2360. **Property tax/Assessor-** 701-547-3220.

Williams County

Recorder, PO Box 2047, Williston, ND 58802-2047. 701-577-4540; fax-701-577-4535; hours: 8AM-5PM. www.williamsnd.com
Participates in the ND Recorders Information Network, www.ndrin.com. Only the public may search. Copy fee $1.00 per page. R/E record copy- $.50 per page. Cert fee- $5.00 1st page; $2.00 each add'l page. Payee- Williams County Recorder. **Online access to Property Tax, Treasurer, Real Estate records:** Access to the county property tax data is free at www.williamsnd.com/taxes/search/default.asp. Also, subscription access the recorder's land records via NDRIN's central repository at www.ndrin.com. See section introduction. **Other phones:** Treasurer- 701-577-4530; Elections- 701-577-4500; Vital Records- 701-577-4580. **Property tax/Assessor-** 701-577-4555.

North Dakota County Locator

You will usually be able to find the city name in the City/County Cross Reference below. In that case, it is a simple matter to determine the county from the cross reference. However, only the official US Postal Service city names are included in this index. There are an additional 40,000 place names that people use in their addresses. Therefore, we have also included a ZIP/City Cross Reference immediately following the City/County Cross Reference. If you know the ZIP Code but the city name does not appear in the City/County Cross Reference index, look up the ZIP Code in the ZIP/City Cross Reference, find the city name, then look up the city name in the City/County Cross Reference.

North Dakota City/County Cross Reference

ABERCROMBIE Richland
ABSARAKA Cass
ADAMS Walsh
AGATE Rolette
ALAMO (58830) Williams(60), Divide(39)
ALEXANDER McKenzie
ALFRED La Moure
ALICE Cass
ALMONT (58520) Morton(73), Grant(26)
ALSEN Cavalier
AMBROSE Divide
AMENIA Cass
AMIDON (58620) Slope(97), Billings(2)
ANAMOOSE (58710) McHenry(61), Sheridan(22), Pierce(16)
ANETA (58212) Nelson(63), Griggs(25), Grand Forks(9), Steele(1)
ANTLER Bottineau
ARDOCH Walsh
ARENA (58412) Burleigh(98), Kidder(1)
ARGUSVILLE Cass
ARNEGARD McKenzie
ARTHUR Cass
ARVILLA Grand Forks
ASHLEY (58413) McIntosh(93), Dickey(6)
AYR Cass
BALDWIN Burleigh
BALFOUR McHenry
BALTA Pierce
BANTRY McHenry
BARNEY Richland
BARTON Pierce
BATHGATE Pembina
BEACH (58621) Golden Valley(96), McKenzie(2)
BELCOURT Rolette
BELFIELD (58622) Stark(72), Billings(27)
BENEDICT (58716) McLean(81), Ward(18)
BERLIN (58415) La Moure(98), Dickey(1)
BERTHOLD (58718) Ward(73), Mountrail(23), Renville(2)
BEULAH (58523) Mercer(94), Oliver(5)
BINFORD (58416) Griggs(97), Nelson(2)
BISBEE (58317) Towner(95), Rolette(3)
BISMARCK Burleigh
BLAISDELL Mountrail
BLANCHARD Traill
BOTTINEAU Bottineau
BOWBELLS (58721) Burke(96), Ward(3)
BOWBELLS Burke
BOWDON (58418) Wells(92), Kidder(7)
BOWMAN (58623) Bowman(91), Slope(8)
BRADDOCK (58524) Emmons(67), Kidder(21), Burleigh(10)
BREMEN Wells
BRINSMADE Benson
BROCKET (58321) Ramsey(50), Nelson(27), Walsh(21)
BUCHANAN Stutsman
BUFFALO Cass
BURLINGTON Ward
BUTTE (58723) Sheridan(44), McLean(44), McHenry(11)
BUXTON Traill
CALEDONIA Traill
CALVIN (58323) Cavalier(71), Towner(28)
CANDO Towner
CANNON BALL Sioux
CARPIO (58725) Renville(53), Ward(46)

CARRINGTON (58421) Foster(95), Stutsman(2), Wells(1)
CARSON Grant
CARTWRIGHT McKenzie
CASSELTON Cass
CATHAY Wells
CAVALIER Pembina
CAYUGA Sargent
CENTER Oliver
CHAFFEE Cass
CHASELEY (58423) Wells(84), Kidder(15)
CHRISTINE (58015) Richland(97), Cass(2)
CHURCHS FERRY (58325) Ramsey(61), Benson(38)
CLEVELAND Stutsman
CLIFFORD (58016) Traill(66), Steele(33)
COGSWELL Sargent
COLEHARBOR McLean
COLFAX Richland
COLUMBUS Burke
COOPERSTOWN Griggs
COURTENAY (58426) Stutsman(98), Foster(1)
CRARY Ramsey
CROSBY Divide
CRYSTAL Pembina
CRYSTAL SPRINGS Kidder
CUMMINGS Traill
DAHLEN (58224) Nelson(95), Walsh(4)
DAVENPORT Cass
DAWSON Kidder
DAZEY (58429) Barnes(97), Griggs(2)
DEERING (58731) McHenry(95), Ward(4)
DENHOFF Sheridan
DES LACS Ward
DEVILS LAKE Ramsey
DICKEY La Moure
DICKINSON (58601) Stark(96), Dunn(3)
DICKINSON Stark
DODGE (58625) Dunn(70), Mercer(29)
DONNYBROOK (58734) Ward(42), Mountrail(38), Renville(19)
DOUGLAS (58735) Ward(58), McLean(41)
DOYON Ramsey
DRAKE (58736) McHenry(88), Sheridan(11)
DRAYTON (58225) Pembina(87), Walsh(12)
DRISCOLL (58532) Burleigh(75), Kidder(24)
DUNN CENTER Dunn
DUNSEITH (58329) Rolette(83), Bottineau(16)
ECKELSON Barnes
EDGELEY (58433) La Moure(89), Dickey(10)
EDINBURG (58227) Walsh(62), Pembina(32), Cavalier(5)
EDMORE (58330) Ramsey(93), Walsh(4), Cavalier(2)
EGELAND Towner
ELGIN Grant
ELLENDALE Dickey
EMERADO Grand Forks
ENDERLIN (58027) Ransom(74), Cass(19), Barnes(5)
EPPING Williams
ERIE Cass
ESMOND (58332) Benson(87), Pierce(12)

FAIRDALE (58229) Walsh(75), Cavalier(20), Ramsey(3)
FAIRFIELD Billings
FAIRMOUNT Richland
FARGO Cass
FESSENDEN Wells
FINGAL (58031) Barnes(60), Cass(39)
FINLEY Steele
FLASHER (58535) Morton(78), Grant(21)
FLAXTON Burke
FORBES Dickey
FORDVILLE (58231) Walsh(73), Grand Forks(26)
FOREST RIVER (58233) Walsh(90), Grand Forks(9)
FORMAN Sargent
FORT RANSOM (58033) Ransom(98), La Moure(1)
FORT RICE Morton
FORT TOTTEN Benson
FORT YATES Sioux
FORTUNA Divide
FOXHOLM Ward
FREDONIA (58440) Logan(70), McIntosh(29)
FULLERTON Dickey
GACKLE (58442) Logan(85), Stutsman(14)
GALESBURG (58035) Traill(60), Cass(25), Steele(14)
GARDENA Bottineau
GARDNER Cass
GARRISON McLean
GILBY Grand Forks
GLADSTONE (58630) Stark(75), Dunn(24)
GLASSTON Pembina
GLEN ULLIN (58631) Morton(80), Grant(11), Mercer(7), Oliver(1)
GLENBURN (58740) Renville(70), Ward(25), Bottineau(1), McHenry(1)
GLENFIELD (58443) Foster(98), Griggs(1)
GOLDEN VALLEY Mercer
GOLVA Golden Valley
GOODRICH (58444) Sheridan(94), Burleigh(5)
GRACE CITY (58445) Foster(87), Eddy(12)
GRAFTON Walsh
GRAND FORKS Grand Forks
GRAND FORKS AFB Grand Forks
GRANDIN (58038) Cass(75), Traill(25)
GRANVILLE McHenry
GRASSY BUTTE (58634) McKenzie(92), Billings(7)
GREAT BEND Richland
GRENORA (58845) Williams(57), Divide(42)
GUELPH Dickey
GWINNER Sargent
HAGUE Emmons
HALLIDAY (58636) Dunn(97), Mercer(2)
HAMBERG Wells
HAMILTON Pembina
HAMPDEN (58338) Ramsey(54), Cavalier(45)
HANKINSON Richland
HANNAFORD (58448) Griggs(98), Barnes(1)
HANNAH Cavalier
HANSBORO Towner
HARVEY (58341) Wells(88), Pierce(9), Benson(1)

HARWOOD Cass
HATTON (58240) Traill(73), Steele(16), Grand Forks(10)
HAVANA Sargent
HAZELTON Emmons
HAZEN (58545) Mercer(94), Oliver(5)
HEATON (58450) Wells(86), Kidder(13)
HEBRON (58638) Morton(77), Mercer(9), Stark(8), Dunn(3)
HEIMDAL Wells
HENSEL Pembina
HENSLER Oliver
HETTINGER Adams
HILLSBORO Traill
HOOPLE (58243) Walsh(88), Pembina(12)
HOPE (58046) Steele(73), Barnes(23), Cass(3)
HORACE Cass
HUNTER (58048) Cass(95), Traill(4)
HURDSFIELD (58451) Wells(97), Sheridan(2)
INKSTER (58244) Grand Forks(96), Walsh(3)
JAMESTOWN Stutsman
JESSIE Griggs
JOLIETTE Pembina
JUD (58454) La Moure(80), Stutsman(19)
KARLSRUHE McHenry
KATHRYN (58049) Barnes(77), Ransom(16), La Moure(5)
KEENE McKenzie
KENMARE (58746) Ward(76), Renville(12), Burke(10)
KENSAL (58455) Stutsman(81), Foster(18)
KIEF (58747) Sheridan(70), McHenry(29)
KILLDEER (58640) Dunn(97), McKenzie(1)
KINDRED (58051) Cass(79), Richland(20)
KINTYRE (58549) Emmons(58), Logan(37), Kidder(3)
KNOX Benson
KRAMER (58748) Bottineau(96), McHenry(3)
KULM (58456) La Moure(77), Dickey(16), McIntosh(6)
LAKOTA (58344) Nelson(96), Ramsey(3)
LAMOURE (58458) La Moure(98), Dickey(1)
LANGDON Cavalier
LANKIN Walsh
LANSFORD (58750) Bottineau(64), Renville(35)
LARIMORE Grand Forks
LAWTON (58345) Ramsey(61), Walsh(38)
LEEDS (58346) Benson(92), Towner(7)
LEFOR Stark
LEHR (58460) McIntosh(55), Logan(44)
LEITH Grant
LEONARD (58052) Cass(80), Richland(15), Ransom(3)
LIDGERWOOD (58053) Richland(84), Sargent(15)
LIGNITE Burke
LINTON Emmons
LISBON Ransom
LITCHVILLE (58461) Barnes(74), La Moure(25)
LUVERNE (58056) Barnes(56), Steele(30), Griggs(12)
MADDOCK (58348) Benson(92), Wells(7)
MAIDA Cavalier

MAKOTI (58756) Ward(78), Mountrail(15), McLean(5)
MANDAN Morton
MANDAREE (58757) McKenzie(52), Dunn(47)
MANFRED Wells
MANNING (58642) Dunn(93), Billings(6)
MANTADOR Richland
MANVEL Grand Forks
MAPLETON Cass
MARION (58466) La Moure(77), Barnes(20), Stutsman(1)
MARMARTH (58643) Bowman(67), Slope(32)
MARSHALL Dunn
MARTIN (58758) Sheridan(66), Pierce(17), Wells(15)
MAX (58759) Ward(56), McLean(43)
MAXBASS Bottineau
MAYVILLE Traill
MCCANNA Grand Forks
MCCLUSKY Sheridan
MCGREGOR (58755) Williams(65), Divide(26), Burke(8)
MCHENRY (58464) Foster(52), Eddy(40), Griggs(7)
MCKENZIE Burleigh
MCLEOD (58057) Richland(72), Ransom(28)
MCVILLE Nelson
MEDINA (58467) Stutsman(94), Kidder(5)
MEDORA (58645) Billings(93), Golden Valley(6)
MEKINOCK Grand Forks
MENOKEN Burleigh
MERCER (58559) McLean(88), Sheridan(11)
MERRICOURT Dickey
MICHIGAN Nelson
MILNOR (58060) Sargent(80), Ransom(18)
MILTON (58260) Cavalier(93), Walsh(6)
MINNEWAUKAN (58351) Benson(95), Ramsey(4)
MINOT Ward
MINOT AFB Ward
MINTO (58261) Walsh(87), Grand Forks(12)
MOFFIT (58560) Burleigh(82), Emmons(17)
MOHALL (58761) Renville(72), Bottineau(27)
MONANGO Dickey
MONTPELIER (58472) Stutsman(69), La Moure(30)
MOORETON Richland
MOTT (58646) Hettinger(97), Adams(2)
MOUNTAIN (58262) Pembina(95), Cavalier(4)

MUNICH (58352) Cavalier(93), Towner(6)
MYLO Rolette
NAPOLEON Logan
NECHE Pembina
NEKOMA Cavalier
NEW ENGLAND (58647) Hettinger(66), Slope(26), Stark(7)
NEW LEIPZIG (58562) Grant(88), Hettinger(7), Adams(3)
NEW ROCKFORD (58356) Eddy(94), Wells(3), Foster(1)
NEW SALEM (58563) Morton(81), Oliver(17)
NEW TOWN (58763) Mountrail(77), McKenzie(22)
NEWBURG (58762) Bottineau(85), McHenry(14)
NIAGARA (58266) Grand Forks(82), Nelson(17)
NOME (58062) Barnes(80), Ransom(19)
NOONAN Divide
NORTHWOOD (58267) Grand Forks(98), Steele(1)
NORWICH (58768) McHenry(54), Ward(45)
OAKES (58474) Dickey(96), Sargent(3)
OBERON Benson
ORISKA Barnes
ORRIN Pierce
OSNABROCK Cavalier
OVERLY Bottineau
PAGE (58064) Cass(89), Barnes(8), Steele(1)
PALERMO Mountrail
PARK RIVER Walsh
PARSHALL (58770) Mountrail(82), McLean(17)
PEKIN Nelson
PEMBINA Pembina
PENN Ramsey
PERTH (58363) Towner(85), Rolette(14)
PETERSBURG Nelson
PETTIBONE (58475) Kidder(94), Stutsman(5)
PILLSBURY Barnes
PINGREE Stutsman
PISEK Walsh
PLAZA (58771) Mountrail(78), Ward(18), McLean(2)
PORTAL Burke
PORTLAND (58274) Traill(85), Steele(14)
POWERS LAKE (58773) Burke(73), Mountrail(26)
RALEIGH Grant
RAY Williams
REEDER (58649) Adams(85), Hettinger(7), Bowman(6)
REGAN Burleigh
REGENT (58650) Hettinger(94), Adams(5)

REYNOLDS (58275) Grand Forks(57), Traill(42)
RHAME (58651) Bowman(69), Slope(30)
RICHARDTON (58652) Stark(89), Dunn(10)
RIVERDALE McLean
ROBINSON Kidder
ROCKLAKE Towner
ROGERS Barnes
ROLETTE (58366) Rolette(97), Pierce(2)
ROLLA (58367) Rolette(91), Towner(8)
ROSEGLEN McLean
ROSS Mountrail
RUGBY (58368) Pierce(95), McHenry(2), Benson(2)
RUSO (58778) McLean(95), McHenry(4)
RUTLAND Sargent
RYDER (58779) McLean(54), Ward(45)
SAINT ANTHONY Morton
SAINT JOHN Rolette
SAINT MICHAEL Benson
SAINT THOMAS Pembina
SANBORN Barnes
SARLES (58372) Towner(51), Cavalier(48)
SAWYER Ward
SCRANTON (58653) Bowman(90), Slope(9)
SELFRIDGE Sioux
SELZ Pierce
SENTINEL BUTTE Golden Valley
SHARON Steele
SHELDON (58068) Ransom(98), Cass(1)
SHERWOOD (58782) Renville(95), Bottineau(4)
SHEYENNE (58374) Eddy(59), Benson(31), Wells(8)
SHIELDS Grant
SOLEN (58570) Morton(58), Sioux(41)
SOURIS Bottineau
SOUTH HEART Stark
SPIRITWOOD (58481) Stutsman(51), Barnes(48)
STANLEY (58784) Mountrail(95), Burke(4)
STANTON (58571) Mercer(76), Oliver(23)
STARKWEATHER (58377) Ramsey(81), Towner(11), Cavalier(7)
STEELE Kidder
STERLING Burleigh
STIRUM (58069) Sargent(95), Ransom(4)
STRASBURG Emmons
STREETER (58483) Stutsman(66), Logan(21), Kidder(12)
SURREY Ward
SUTTON (58484) Griggs(81), Foster(18)
SYKESTON (58486) Wells(92), Stutsman(7)
TAPPEN Kidder
TAYLOR (58656) Stark(83), Dunn(16)

THOMPSON Grand Forks
TIOGA (58852) Williams(91), Mountrail(8)
TOKIO Benson
TOLLEY (58787) Renville(96), Ward(3)
TOLNA (58380) Nelson(47), Eddy(43), Benson(8)
TOWER CITY (58071) Cass(80), Barnes(19)
TOWNER (58788) McHenry(95), Pierce(4)
TRENTON Williams
TROTTERS Golden Valley
TURTLE LAKE McLean
TUTTLE Kidder
UNDERWOOD McLean
UNION Cavalier
UPHAM (58789) McHenry(90), Bottineau(9)
VALLEY CITY Barnes
VELVA (58790) McHenry(92), Ward(7)
VENTURIA McIntosh
VERONA (58490) La Moure(86), Ransom(13)
VOLTAIRE McHenry
WAHPETON Richland
WALCOTT Richland
WALES Cavalier
WALHALLA (58282) Pembina(86), Cavalier(13)
WARWICK (58381) Benson(53), Eddy(46)
WASHBURN McLean
WATFORD CITY McKenzie
WEBSTER Ramsey
WEST FARGO Cass
WESTHOPE Bottineau
WHEATLAND Cass
WHITE EARTH (58794) Mountrail(98), Williams(1)
WILDROSE (58795) Divide(52), Williams(47)
WILLISTON Williams
WILLOW CITY (58384) Bottineau(65), Pierce(17), McHenry(11), Rolette(5)
WILTON (58579) McLean(51), Burleigh(48)
WIMBLEDON (58492) Barnes(78), Stutsman(12), Griggs(8)
WING Burleigh
WISHEK (58495) McIntosh(84), Logan(15)
WOLFORD (58385) Pierce(91), Rolette(8)
WOODWORTH Stutsman
WYNDMERE Richland
YORK (58386) Benson(74), Pierce(25)
YPSILANTI (58497) Stutsman(93), Barnes(6)
ZAHL (58856) Williams(65), Divide(34)
ZAP Mercer
ZEELAND McIntosh

North Dakota ZIP/City Cross Reference

58001-58001 ABERCROMBIE	58031-58031 FINGAL	58057-58057 MCLEOD	58204-58205 GRAND FORKS AFB
58002-58002 ABSARAKA	58032-58032 FORMAN	58058-58058 MANTADOR	58206-58208 GRAND FORKS
58003-58003 ALICE	58033-58033 FORT RANSOM	58059-58059 MAPLETON	58210-58210 ADAMS
58004-58004 AMENIA	58035-58035 GALESBURG	58060-58060 MILNOR	58212-58212 ANETA
58005-58005 ARGUSVILLE	58036-58036 GARDNER	58061-58061 MOORETON	58213-58213 ARDOCH
58006-58006 ARTHUR	58038-58038 GRANDIN	58062-58062 NOME	58214-58214 ARVILLA
58007-58007 AYR	58039-58039 GREAT BEND	58063-58063 ORISKA	58216-58216 BATHGATE
58008-58008 BARNEY	58040-58040 GWINNER	58064-58064 PAGE	58218-58218 BUXTON
58009-58009 BLANCHARD	58041-58041 HANKINSON	58065-58065 PILLSBURY	58219-58219 CALEDONIA
58011-58011 BUFFALO	58042-58042 HARWOOD	58067-58067 RUTLAND	58220-58220 CAVALIER
58012-58012 CASSELTON	58043-58043 HAVANA	58068-58068 SHELDON	58222-58222 CRYSTAL
58013-58013 CAYUGA	58045-58045 HILLSBORO	58069-58069 STIRUM	58223-58223 CUMMINGS
58014-58014 CHAFFEE	58046-58046 HOPE	58071-58071 TOWER CITY	58224-58224 DAHLEN
58015-58015 CHRISTINE	58047-58047 HORACE	58072-58072 VALLEY CITY	58225-58225 DRAYTON
58016-58016 CLIFFORD	58048-58048 HUNTER	58074-58076 WAHPETON	58227-58227 EDINBURG
58017-58017 COGSWELL	58049-58049 KATHRYN	58077-58077 WALCOTT	58228-58228 EMERADO
58018-58018 COLFAX	58051-58051 KINDRED	58078-58078 WEST FARGO	58229-58229 FAIRDALE
58021-58021 DAVENPORT	58052-58052 LEONARD	58079-58079 WHEATLAND	58230-58230 FINLEY
58027-58027 ENDERLIN	58053-58053 LIDGERWOOD	58081-58081 WYNDMERE	58231-58231 FORDVILLE
58029-58029 ERIE	58054-58054 LISBON	58102-58126 FARGO	58233-58233 FOREST RIVER
58030-58030 FAIRMOUNT	58056-58056 LUVERNE	58201-58203 GRAND FORKS	58235-58235 GILBY

ZIP Range	City	ZIP Range	City	ZIP Range	City	ZIP Range	City
58236-58236	GLASSTON	58367-58367	ROLLA	58495-58495	WISHEK	58704-58705	MINOT AFB
58237-58237	GRAFTON	58368-58368	RUGBY	58496-58496	WOODWORTH	58707-58707	MINOT
58238-58238	HAMILTON	58369-58369	SAINT JOHN	58497-58497	YPSILANTI	58710-58710	ANAMOOSE
58239-58239	HANNAH	58370-58370	SAINT MICHAEL	58501-58507	BISMARCK	58711-58711	ANTLER
58240-58240	HATTON	58372-58372	SARLES	58520-58520	ALMONT	58712-58712	BALFOUR
58241-58241	HENSEL	58373-58373	SELZ	58521-58521	BALDWIN	58713-58713	BANTRY
58243-58243	HOOPLE	58374-58374	SHEYENNE	58523-58523	BEULAH	58716-58716	BENEDICT
58244-58244	INKSTER	58377-58377	STARKWEATHER	58524-58524	BRADDOCK	58718-58718	BERTHOLD
58246-58246	JOLIETTE	58379-58379	TOKIO	58528-58528	CANNON BALL	58720-58720	BLAISDELL
58249-58249	LANGDON	58380-58380	TOLNA	58529-58529	CARSON	58721-58721	BOWBELLS
58250-58250	LANKIN	58381-58381	WARWICK	58530-58530	CENTER	58722-58722	BURLINGTON
58251-58251	LARIMORE	58382-58382	WEBSTER	58531-58531	COLEHARBOR	58723-58723	BUTTE
58253-58253	MCCANNA	58384-58384	WILLOW CITY	58532-58532	DRISCOLL	58725-58725	CARPIO
58254-58254	MCVILLE	58385-58385	WOLFORD	58533-58533	ELGIN	58727-58727	COLUMBUS
58255-58255	MAIDA	58386-58386	YORK	58535-58535	FLASHER	58728-58728	BOWBELLS
58256-58256	MANVEL	58401-58405	JAMESTOWN	58537-58537	FORT RICE	58730-58730	CROSBY
58257-58257	MAYVILLE	58411-58411	ALFRED	58538-58538	FORT YATES	58731-58731	DEERING
58258-58258	MEKINOCK	58412-58412	ARENA	58540-58540	GARRISON	58733-58733	DES LACS
58259-58259	MICHIGAN	58413-58413	ASHLEY	58541-58541	GOLDEN VALLEY	58734-58734	DONNYBROOK
58260-58260	MILTON	58415-58415	BERLIN	58542-58542	HAGUE	58735-58735	DOUGLAS
58261-58261	MINTO	58416-58416	BINFORD	58544-58544	HAZELTON	58736-58736	DRAKE
58262-58262	MOUNTAIN	58418-58418	BOWDON	58545-58545	HAZEN	58737-58737	FLAXTON
58265-58265	NECHE	58420-58420	BUCHANAN	58547-58547	HENSLER	58738-58738	FOXHOLM
58266-58266	NIAGARA	58421-58421	CARRINGTON	58549-58549	KINTYRE	58739-58739	GARDENA
58267-58267	NORTHWOOD	58422-58422	CATHAY	58551-58551	LEITH	58740-58740	GLENBURN
58269-58269	OSNABROCK	58423-58423	CHASELEY	58552-58552	LINTON	58741-58741	GRANVILLE
58270-58270	PARK RIVER	58424-58424	CLEVELAND	58553-58553	MCKENZIE	58744-58744	KARLSRUHE
58271-58271	PEMBINA	58425-58425	COOPERSTOWN	58554-58554	MANDAN	58746-58746	KENMARE
58272-58272	PETERSBURG	58426-58426	COURTENAY	58558-58558	MENOKEN	58747-58747	KIEF
58273-58273	PISEK	58427-58427	CRYSTAL SPRINGS	58559-58559	MERCER	58748-58748	KRAMER
58274-58274	PORTLAND	58428-58428	DAWSON	58560-58560	MOFFIT	58750-58750	LANSFORD
58275-58275	REYNOLDS	58429-58429	DAZEY	58561-58561	NAPOLEON	58752-58752	LIGNITE
58276-58276	SAINT THOMAS	58430-58430	DENHOFF	58562-58562	NEW LEIPZIG	58755-58755	MCGREGOR
58277-58277	SHARON	58431-58431	DICKEY	58563-58563	NEW SALEM	58756-58756	MAKOTI
58278-58278	THOMPSON	58432-58432	ECKELSON	58564-58564	RALEIGH	58757-58757	MANDAREE
58279-58279	UNION	58433-58433	EDGELEY	58565-58565	RIVERDALE	58758-58758	MARTIN
58281-58281	WALES	58436-58436	ELLENDALE	58566-58566	SAINT ANTHONY	58759-58759	MAX
58282-58282	WALHALLA	58438-58438	FESSENDEN	58568-58568	SELFRIDGE	58760-58760	MAXBASS
58301-58301	DEVILS LAKE	58439-58439	FORBES	58569-58569	SHIELDS	58761-58761	MOHALL
58310-58310	AGATE	58440-58440	FREDONIA	58570-58570	SOLEN	58762-58762	NEWBURG
58311-58311	ALSEN	58441-58441	FULLERTON	58571-58571	STANTON	58763-58763	NEW TOWN
58313-58313	BALTA	58442-58442	GACKLE	58572-58572	STERLING	58765-58765	NOONAN
58315-58315	BARTON	58443-58443	GLENFIELD	58573-58573	STRASBURG	58768-58768	NORWICH
58316-58316	BELCOURT	58444-58444	GOODRICH	58575-58575	TURTLE LAKE	58769-58769	PALERMO
58317-58317	BISBEE	58445-58445	GRACE CITY	58576-58576	UNDERWOOD	58770-58770	PARSHALL
58318-58318	BOTTINEAU	58447-58447	GUELPH	58577-58577	WASHBURN	58771-58771	PLAZA
58319-58319	BREMEN	58448-58448	HANNAFORD	58579-58579	WILTON	58772-58772	PORTAL
58320-58320	BRINSMADE	58450-58450	HEATON	58580-58580	ZAP	58773-58773	POWERS LAKE
58321-58321	BROCKET	58451-58451	HURDSFIELD	58581-58581	ZEELAND	58775-58775	ROSEGLEN
58323-58323	CALVIN	58452-58452	JESSIE	58601-58602	DICKINSON	58776-58776	ROSS
58324-58324	CANDO	58454-58454	JUD	58620-58620	AMIDON	58778-58778	RUSO
58325-58325	CHURCHS FERRY	58455-58455	KENSAL	58621-58621	BEACH	58779-58779	RYDER
58327-58327	CRARY	58456-58456	KULM	58622-58622	BELFIELD	58781-58781	SAWYER
58328-58328	DOYON	58458-58458	LAMOURE	58623-58623	BOWMAN	58782-58782	SHERWOOD
58329-58329	DUNSEITH	58460-58460	LEHR	58625-58625	DODGE	58783-58783	SOURIS
58330-58330	EDMORE	58461-58461	LITCHVILLE	58626-58626	DUNN CENTER	58784-58784	STANLEY
58331-58331	EGELAND	58463-58463	MCCLUSKY	58627-58627	FAIRFIELD	58785-58785	SURREY
58332-58332	ESMOND	58464-58464	MCHENRY	58630-58630	GLADSTONE	58787-58787	TOLLEY
58335-58335	FORT TOTTEN	58465-58465	MANFRED	58631-58631	GLEN ULLIN	58788-58788	TOWNER
58337-58337	HAMBERG	58466-58466	MARION	58632-58632	GOLVA	58789-58789	UPHAM
58338-58338	HAMPDEN	58467-58467	MEDINA	58634-58634	GRASSY BUTTE	58790-58790	VELVA
58339-58339	HANSBORO	58469-58469	MERRICOURT	58636-58636	HALLIDAY	58792-58792	VOLTAIRE
58341-58341	HARVEY	58471-58471	MONANGO	58638-58638	HEBRON	58793-58793	WESTHOPE
58342-58342	HEIMDAL	58472-58472	MONTPELIER	58639-58639	HETTINGER	58794-58794	WHITE EARTH
58343-58343	KNOX	58474-58474	OAKES	58640-58640	KILLDEER	58795-58795	WILDROSE
58344-58344	LAKOTA	58475-58475	PETTIBONE	58641-58641	LEFOR	58801-58802	WILLISTON
58345-58345	LAWTON	58476-58476	PINGREE	58642-58642	MANNING	58830-58830	ALAMO
58346-58346	LEEDS	58477-58477	REGAN	58643-58643	MARMARTH	58831-58831	ALEXANDER
58348-58348	MADDOCK	58478-58478	ROBINSON	58644-58644	MARSHALL	58833-58833	AMBROSE
58351-58351	MINNEWAUKAN	58479-58479	ROGERS	58645-58645	MEDORA	58835-58835	ARNEGARD
58352-58352	MUNICH	58480-58480	SANBORN	58646-58646	MOTT	58838-58838	CARTWRIGHT
58353-58353	MYLO	58481-58481	SPIRITWOOD	58647-58647	NEW ENGLAND	58843-58843	EPPING
58355-58355	NEKOMA	58482-58482	STEELE	58649-58649	REEDER	58844-58844	FORTUNA
58356-58356	NEW ROCKFORD	58483-58483	STREETER	58650-58650	REGENT	58845-58845	GRENORA
58357-58357	OBERON	58484-58484	SUTTON	58651-58651	RHAME	58847-58847	KEENE
58359-58359	ORRIN	58486-58486	SYKESTON	58652-58652	RICHARDTON	58849-58849	RAY
58360-58360	OVERLY	58487-58487	TAPPEN	58653-58653	SCRANTON	58852-58852	TIOGA
58361-58361	PEKIN	58488-58488	TUTTLE	58654-58654	SENTINEL BUTTE	58853-58853	TRENTON
58362-58362	PENN	58489-58489	VENTURIA	58655-58655	SOUTH HEART	58854-58854	WATFORD CITY
58363-58363	PERTH	58490-58490	VERONA	58656-58656	TAYLOR	58856-58856	ZAHL
58365-58365	ROCKLAKE	58492-58492	WIMBLEDON	58657-58657	TROTTERS		
58366-58366	ROLETTE	58494-58494	WING	58701-58703	MINOT		

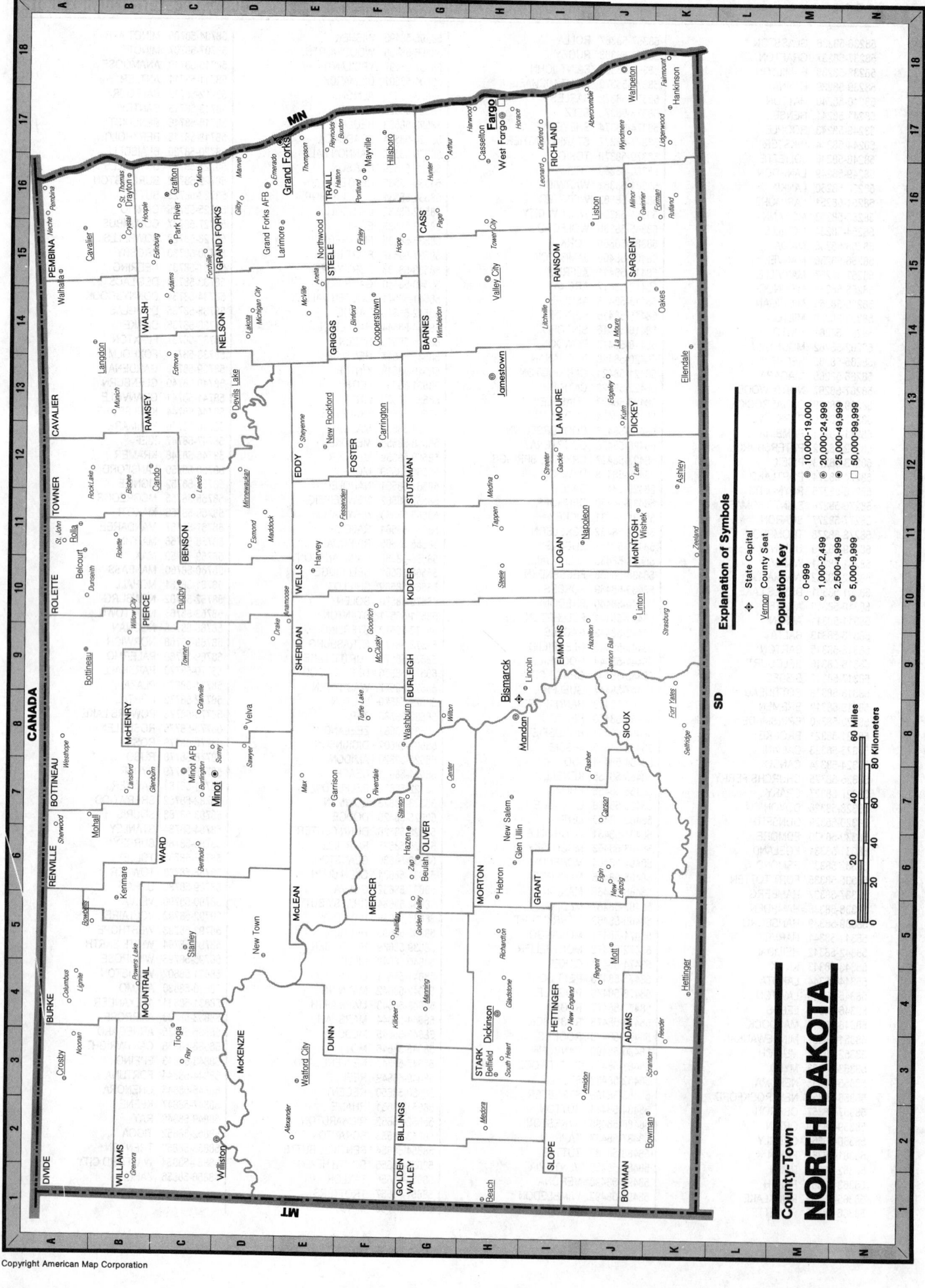

NORTH DAKOTA

County-Town

Explanation of Symbols

✦ State Capital

Vernon County Seat

Population Key

Symbol	Population
○	0-999
⊙	1,000-2,499
⊛	2,500-4,999
⊚	5,000-9,999
⊗	10,000-19,000
⊛	20,000-24,999
⊙	25,000-49,999
□	50,000-99,999

60 Miles
80 Kilometers

CITIES AND TOWNS

Note: The first name is that of the city or town, second, that of the county in which it is located, then the population and location on the map.

Explanation of symbols: ● – Census Designated Place (CDP)

General Help Numbers:

Governor's Office
77 S High St, 30th Floor   614-466-3555
Columbus, OH 43215   Fax 614-466-9354
http://governor.ohio.gov   8AM-5PM

Attorney General's Office
State Office Tower   614-466-4320
30 E Broad St, 17th Floor   Fax 614-644-6135
Columbus, OH 43215-3428   8AM-5PM
www.ag.state.oh.us

Legislative Records
Ohio House of Representatives   614-466-9745
77 S High Street   Fax 614-644-8744
Columbus, OH 43266   8:30AM-5PM
www.legislature.state.oh.us

State Archives
Archives/Library   614-297-2300
1982 Velma Ave   Fax 614-297-2546
Columbus, OH 43211-2497   9AM-5PM TH-SA: 10-5 SU
www.ohiohistory.org/ar_tools.html

State Specifics:

Capital:	Columbus Franklin County
Time Zone:	EST
Number of Counties:	88
Population:	11,459,011
Web Site:	www.ohio.gov

State Agencies

Criminal Records

Ohio Bureau of Investigation, Civilian Background Section, PO Box 365, London, OH 43140 (Courier address: 1560 State Rte 56, London, OH 43140); 740-845-2000 (General Info), 740-845-2375 (Civilian Background Cks), 740-845-2633-Fax; 8AM-4:45PM.

www.webcheck.ag.state.oh.us

The state has an innovative system over the web for electronic transfer of fingerprints. See Online Access below.

Records are available from 1921 on. Records from 1960's on are computerized and the agency is in

the process of computerizing older records. It takes 5 days, 15 with fingerprints before new records are available for inquiry. Records are indexed on inhouse computer. Records are normally destroyed after (records maintained indefinitely). 62% of all arrests in database have final dispositions recorded.

Searching: All record requests must include a fingerprint card: name searches are not performed. Include the following in your request-witnessed signed release from subject, fingerprints, name DOB, SSN. 100% of the records are fingerprint supported. Records without dispositions are not released. Escalating misdemeanors are released.

These is any offense classified as a misdemeanor on the first offense and a felony on subsequent offense.

Access by: mail, online.

Fee & Payment: The search fee is $15.00 per record. Statutorily-required checks may include an FBI fingerprint check for an additional $24.00. Fee payee: Treasurer - State of Ohio. Prepayment required. No credit cards accepted.

Mail search: Turnaround time: 30 days. No SASE is required.

Online search: WebCheck is an Internet-based request program for civilian background checks for school districts, education associations, children's hospitals, and public institutions. Results are NOT returned via the Internet. Turnaround time is 2 days. Agencies can send fingerprint images and other data via the Internet using a single digit fingerprint scanner and a driver's license magnetic strip reader. Within two business days, the school or daycare center will receive their results of their background check requests.

Statewide Court Records

Administrative Director, Supreme Court of Ohio, 65 S Front Street, Columbus, OH 43215-3431; 614-387-9000, 800-826-9010, 614-387-9410 (Case Management), 614-387-9419-Fax; 8AM-5PM.

www.sconet.state.oh.us

This office does not provide access to county court records. Except for certain online research capabilities, all trial court record access must be done at the local level.

Access by: online.

Online search: Appellate and Supreme Court opinions may be researched from the website. Go to www.sconet.state.oh.us/rod/newpdf/.

Sexual Offender Registry

Ohio Bureau of Investigation, Sexual Offender Registry, PO Box 365, London, OH 43140 (Courier address: 1560 State Rte 56 SW, London, OH 43140); 740-845-2221, 740-845-2223, 866-406-4534, 740-845-2633-Fax; 8AM-4:45PM.

www.esorn.ag.state.oh.us/Secured/p1.aspx

O.R.C. 2950.13 requires that the public eSORN database contain information on every person convicted as an adult and registered in the state registry of sex offenders and child-victim offenders.

Searching: The database that contains information regarding all registered sex offenders in the State of Ohio is known as eSORN. The individual county sheriff's representatives are best situated to provide local sex offender and registration information.

Access by: online.

Online search: Search online eSORN at www.esorn.ag.state.oh.us/Secured/p21_2.aspx. Users can search by offender name, zip code, county and / or school district. The site is linked to all 88 of Ohio's sheriff's offices and all 32 Ohio correctional facility records offices

Incarceration Records

Ohio Department of Rehabilitation and Correction, Bureau of Records Management, 1050 Freeway Drive, N., Columbus, OH 43229; 614-752-1076, 614-752-1159 x3 (Inmate Records), 614-752-1086-Fax; 8:30AM-5PM M-F.

www.drc.state.oh.us

Records are available on current and former inmates, except online is current only. It takes 1 to 5 days before new records are available for inquiry. Records are normally destroyed after 10 years.

Searching: Include the following in your request-first and last name or Offender Number. The DOB and SSN are helpful. Location, physical identifiers, conviction and sentencing information, and release dates are provided.

Access by: mail, phone, fax, online.

Mail search: Turnaround time: 1 to 2 weeks. No SASE is required.

Phone search: Record inquiry available by phone. To obtain information on offenders previously under the supervision of the Department, call 614-752-1159 and choose option 3.

Fax search: Fax requests are accepted.

Online search: From the website, in the Select a Destination box, select Offender Search. You can search by name or inmate number. The Offender Search includes all offenders currently incarcerated or under some type of Department supervision (parole, post-release control, or transitional control).

Corporation, Fictitious Name, Limited Partnership, Assumed Name, Trademarks/Servicemarks, Limited Liability Company

Secretary of State, Corporate Records Access, PO Box 130, Columbus, OH 43216 (Courier address: 30 E Broad Street, 16th Fl, Columbus, OH 43215); 877-767-3453, 614-466-3910, 614-466-3899-Fax; 8AM-5PM.

www.sos.state.oh.us/sos/businessservices/corp.aspx

Information regarding officers is available from the Department of Taxation at 614-438-5339, but the requester must obtain the Charter # from this agency.

Records are available from the 1800's. New records are available for inquiry immediately. Records are indexed on microfilm, index cards, inhouse computer.

Searching: This agency also holds records for Real Estate Trusts, Business Trusts, Churches, and Not-for Profits. Include the following in your request-full name of business. Use the request form for certified documents (available from web). In addition to the articles of incorporation, corporation records include the following information: Annual Reports, Prior (merged) names, Inactive and Reserved names.

Access by: mail, phone, fax, in person, online.

Fee & Payment: The certification fee is $5.00, a Good Standing is also $5.00. Copy fees are no charge up to 34 pages, $1.05 for the 35th, and $.03 per copy thereafter. There is no fee for a corporate printout of limited information. Fee payee: Secretary of State. Prepayment required. Personal checks accepted. No credit cards accepted.

Mail search: Turnaround time: 2 days. No SASE is required.

Phone search: They will release limited information over the phone.

Fax search: No fee, turnaround time is 2 days. Do not fax for plain copy requests.

In person search: There is no fee to look at records.

Online search: The agency provides free Internet searching for business and corporation records at www.sos.state.oh.us/sos/businessservices/corp.aspx?Section=104. The site also includes UCC and campaign finance. Images are available, as well as Good Standings.

Other access: This agency makes the database available for purchase, call for details.

Uniform Commercial Code

UCC Records, Secretary of State, PO Box 2795, Columbus, OH 43216 (Courier address: 30 E Broad Street, Columbus, OH 43215); 877-767-3453, 614-466-3910, 614-466-2892-Fax; 8AM-5PM.

www.sos.state.oh.us/sos/ucc/ucc.aspx

Records are available for only current or active filings. Records are indexed on inhouse computer.

Searching: Use search form UCC-11. All tax liens are filed at the county level. Include the following in your request-debtor name. Be sure to include the words "any and all addresses" in your search request.

Access by: mail, phone, fax, in person, online.

Fee & Payment: The search fee is $20.00 per debtor name, copies included. Fee payee: Secretary of State. Prepayment required. Personal checks accepted. No credit cards accepted.

Mail search: Turnaround time: 2 days.

Phone search: Calls are limited to 10 filings, 3 debtor names per call. There is no charge for verbal information.

Fax search: Only available for prepaid accounts.

In person search: Simple requests may be processed while you wait.

Online search: The Internet site offers free online access to records. Search by debtor, secured party, or financing statement number.

Other access: The complete database is available on electronic media with weekly updates. Call for current pricing.

Federal and State Tax Liens

Records not maintained by a state level agency.

Records are not housed by a state agency. You must secure from the local county recorder offices.

Sales Tax Registrations

Access to Records is Restricted.

Taxation Department, Sale & Use Tax Division, 30 E Broad St, 20th Floor, Columbus, OH 43215; 614-466-7351, 888-405-4039, 614-466-4977-Fax; 8AM-5PM M-F.

http://tax.ohio.gov

This agency refuses to release any information about registrants.

Birth Certificates

Ohio Department of Health, Bureau of Vital Statistics, PO Box 15098, Columbus, OH 43215-0098 (Courier address: 246 N High St, 1st Fl, Revenue Room, Columbus, OH 43215); 614-466-2531, 877-828-3101, 877-553-2439-Fax; 7:45AM-4:30PM.

http://www2.odh.ohio.gov/VitStats/vsmain1.htm

Records are available from 1908 to present. Records from 12/20/08 to 12/44 are at the Ohio Historical Society at 614-297-2510. It takes 3 months before new records are available for inquiry.

Searching: Include the following in your request-full name, names of parents including mother's maiden name, date of birth, city and county of birth.

Access by: mail, fax, in person, online.

Fee & Payment: A certified copy of $15.00. If year is not known the search fee is $3.00 for each 10 years searched per name spelling. Fee payee: Treasurer, State of Ohio Prepayment required. Personal checks accepted. Credit cards accepted only by VitalChek.

Mail search: Turnaround time: 4 to 12 weeks. No SASE is required.

Fax search: See expedited service below.

In person search: Turnaround time 7 to 10 days.

Online search: Records can be ordered from a state-designated vendor - www.vitalchek.com. See expedited service below.

Expedited service: For online, fax and phone requests. Turnaround time: 2 to 3 days. This is available from VitalChek.com. There is an additional $9.95 fee to use a credit card, add $14.75 for overnight shipping costs if desired.

Death Records

Ohio Department of Health, Bureau of Vital Statistics, PO Box 15098, Columbus, OH 43215-0098 (Courier address: 246 N High Street, 1st Fl, Revenue Room, Columbus, OH 43215); 614-466-2531, 877-828-3101, 877-553-2439-Fax; 7:45AM-4:30PM.

http://www2.odh.ohio.gov/VitStats/vsmain1.htm

Records are available from 1954 to present. Death records from 1908 to 1953 are found at Ohio Historical Society, 1982 Velma Ave, Columbus, OH 43211. Records prior to 1908 are located at the county level. It takes 3 months before new records are available for inquiry.

Searching: Requests must be in writing. Include the following in your request-full name, date of death, city and county of death.

Access by: mail, fax, in person, online.

Fee & Payment: A certified copy of $15.00. If year is not known the search fee is $3.00 for each 10 years searched per name spelling. Fee payee: Treasurer, State of Ohio. Prepayment required. Personal checks accepted. Credit cards accepted only by VitalChek.

Mail search: Turnaround time: 4 to 12 weeks. No SASE is required.

Fax search: See expedited service.

In person search: Turnaround time is 7 to 10 days.

Online search: The Ohio Historical Society Death Certificate Index Searchable Database at www.ohiohistory.org/dindex/ permits searching by name, county, index. Data is available from 1913 to 1937 only. Records can be ordered from a state-designated vendor - www.vitalchek.com. See expedited service below.

Expedited service: For fax, online and phone requests. Turnaround time: 2 to 3 days. This is available from VitalChek.com. There is an additional $9.95 fee to use a credit card, add $14.75 for overnight shipping costs if desired.

Marriage Certificates, Divorce Records

Access to Records is Restricted.

Ohio Department of Health, Bureau of Vital Statistics, PO Box 15098, Columbus, OH 43215-0098; 614-466-2531.

http://www2.odh.ohio.gov/VitStats/vsmain1.htm

Marriage and Divorce records are found at county of issue. This agency will only do a search of the index from 1953 forward. To request a 10-year search, a $3 fee is assessed for every 10-year period searched.

Workers' Compensation Records

Bureau of Workers Compensation, Customer Contact Center - Records Mgr, 30 W Spring St, 10th, Columbus, OH 43215-2241; 800-644-6292, 614-728-3210 (Records), 614-752-4732-Fax; 7:30AM-5:30PM.

www.ohiobwc.com

Records are available for the past 10 years. Records are indexed on inhouse computer. Records are normally destroyed after 10 years if records are inactive.

Searching: All information is public except injured worker medical report and information pertaining to the employer's financial condition. Include the following in your request-claimant name, Social Security Number or claim number. Claim number is helpful. All requests must be in writing.

Access by: mail, phone, fax, in person, online.

Fee & Payment: There is no search fee, copy fee is $.05 per page. Fee payee: Ohio Bureau of Workers Compensation. Prepayment required. Personal checks accepted. No credit cards accepted.

Mail search: Turnaround time: 1 week. A SASE is requested.

Phone search: They will provide the information immediately unless file is lengthy or excessive.

Fax search: Service is available with a 24 hour turnaround time.

In person search: Call for location of records before going in because there are 22 different office locations.

Online search: Injured workers, injured worker designees, representatives and managed care organizations (MCOs) can view a list of all claims associated with a given SSN, but are limited to viewing only the claims with which they are associated. Employers, their representatives or designees, and managed care organizations can view a list of all claims associated to their BWC policy number. Medical providers can view all claims associated with any given SSN. Access is through the website listed above.

Other access: Bulk data is released to approved accounts; however, the legal department must approve requesters. The agency has general information available on a website.

Driver Records

Department of Public Safety, Bureau of Motor Vehicles, 1970 W Broad St, Columbus, OH 43223-1102; 614-752-7600, 614-752-7987-Fax; 8AM-5:30PM M-T-W; 8AM-4:30PM TH-F.

www.ohiobmv.com

Copies of tickets are available from the Bureau of Motor Vehicles, Transcript Records, PO Box 16520, Columbus 43266-0020. The fee is $1.00 per page.

Records are available for 3 years for moving violations, DWI's and suspensions. Records are purged from public view after 3 years; insurance laws require 36 months of availability. It takes 2 to 5 weeks before new records are available for inquiry.

Searching: Use Request Form BMV1173 (downloaded from Internet). If requester does not have permissible use per DPPA, Form BMV 5008 is also required, which requires notarized consent of subject. Records w/o personal information are not released to the public. Include the following in your request-driver's license number, full name, date of birth, Social Security Number. Driver's address is included as part of the search report for permissible requesters, except for requests received from California. The following data is not released: mental health records, SSNs unless provided by requester (except government agency requesters).

Access by: mail, phone, fax, in person, online.

Fee & Payment: The fee is $2.00 per record. A license status check is available for $2.00. Fee payee: Treasurer, State of Ohio. Prepayment required. Personal checks accepted. No credit cards accepted.

Mail search: Turnaround time: 1 to 3 days. A SASE is requested.

Phone search: Qualified, pre-approved accounts may order by phone. There is a $200.00 deposit.

Fax search: Same criteria as phone searches.

In person search: Up to eight records will be processed by this location while you wait. Record requests are also processed at regional offices.

Online search: The Online Abstract System by FTP is suggested for requesters who order 100 or more motor vehicle reports per day in batch mode. The DL# or SSN and name are needed when ordering. Fee is $2.00 per record. For more information, call Fiscal Srvs at 614-752-2091.

Other access: Overnight CD service is available for larger accounts.

Vehicle Ownership
Vehicle Identification

Bureau of Motor Vehicles, Motor Vehicle Title Records, 1970 W Broad St, Columbus, OH 43223-1102; 614-752-7671, 614-752-8929-Fax; 7:30AM-4:45PM.

www.ohiobmv.com

Records are available for the current year plus six. It takes 1 to 2 days normally before new records are available for inquiry.

Searching: Use Record Request Form 1173 (downloadable from Internet). If requester does not have permissible use per DPPA, Form BMV 5008 is also required, which requires notarized consent of subject. Records w/o personal information are not released to the public. Include the following in your request-name, year, make VIN, license plate number if known. Lien information is not recorded on vehicle registration records in Ohio. The following data is not released: Social Security Numbers, unless included in request.

Access by: mail, phone, fax, in person, online.

Fee & Payment: The fee is $2.00 or each record searched. Fee payee: Treasurer, State of Ohio. Prepayment required. Personal checks accepted. No credit cards accepted.

Mail search: Turnaround time: 1 to 3 days. A SASE is requested.

Phone search: There is a pre-paid Search Account for addresses only. Call Fiscal Section at 614-752-2091 to establish an account.

Fax search: Records are available only for pre-approved accounts with funds on file.

In person search: There may be a limit on the number of requests processed immediately, most are not available until the next day.

Online search: Ohio offers online access through AAMVAnet. All requesters must comply with a contractual agreement prior to release of data, which complies with DPPA regulations. Fee is $2.00 per record. Call 614-752-7671 for more information. The website offers free access to title records for vehicles and watercraft. No personal information is release. Search by title number or ID. Also search at https://www.dps.state.oh.us/atps/. **Other access:** Bulk records are available for purchase, per DPPA guidelines.

Accident Reports

Department of Public Safety, OSHP Central Records, 1st Fl, PO Box 182074, Columbus, OH 43218-2074; 614-466-3536, 614-644-9749-Fax; 8AM-4:45PM.

http://statepatrol.ohio.gov/crash.htm

Records are available for 5 years to present. Crash records are indexed on computer. It takes 7 to 10 days before new records are available for inquiry. Records are normally destroyed after 5 years.

Searching: OSHP will assist to find correct report, but will not accept phone orders. Include the following in your request-full name, date of accident county of occurrence, or crash number if known. Submitting the driver's license number or SSN is very helpful for reports older than 2001. The following data is not released: Social Security Numbers.

Access by: mail, in person, online.

Fee & Payment: The fee is $4.00 per record. There is a charge for a no record found. Fee payee: Ohio State Highway Patrol Prepayment required. Personal checks accepted. No credit cards accepted.

Mail search: Turnaround time: 3-4 weeks.

In person search: Public access terminals are available in the lobby. Turnaround time is immediate if the record is on file. Assistance is available.

Online search: Crash reports purchased online will be sent to your e-mail account the same day. Crash photographs purchased online will be sent in the mail. Online crash reports are available for crashes that occurred on or after August 5, 2001. Crash reports prior to August 5, 2001 are available by mail-in request. Reports must be purchased using a credit card.

Vessel Ownership, Vessel Registration

NRD-Division of Watercraft, Titles and Registration, 2045 Morse Rd, Columbus, OH 43229; 614-265-6480, 877-426-2837 (Titles), 614-784-5987-Fax; 8AM-5PM.

www.dnr.state.oh.us/watercraft

Liens are included on title histories, but you must first request the lien history in writing.

Records are available from 1960 to the present. Records are indexed on computer for the last 3 years. Any boat operated on public waters must be registered. All boats 14 ft or longer or having a 10+ hp motor must be titled.

Searching: To search, one of the following is required: name, hull ID #, registration #, or serial #. The following data is not released: Social Security Numbers.

Access by: mail, phone, fax, in person.

Fee & Payment: There is no search fee for registration records. There is a $2.00 fee for a title search. Fee payee: Division of Watercraft. Prepayment required. Personal checks accepted. No credit cards accepted.

Mail search: Turnaround time: 2 to 4 days. No SASE is required.

Phone search: There is a limit of five names per call for registration information.

Fax search: Same criteria as mail searching.

In person search: Simple requests may be processed while you wait.

Voter Registration

Secretary of State, Elections Division, 180 E Broad St, 15th Fl, Columbus, OH 43215; 614-466-2585, 614-752-4360-Fax; 8AM-5PM.

www.sos.state.oh.us

Records are open. This agency will sell the voter file to individuals and businesses. Single name search requests are better served at the local level.

Records are available for a limited number of years. It takes 1 day before new records are available for inquiry.

Searching: The agency suggests that all individual requests be done at the county Board of Elections.

Access by: mail, in person.

Fee & Payment: There is no fee, unless lists or extensive research is involved. Fee payee: Secretary of State. Prepayment required. No credit cards accepted.

Mail search: Turnaround time: 1 week to 10 days. No SASE is required.

In person search: The state is not prepared to handle look-ups, but will assist as necessary.

Other access: Records may be purchased in a variety of formats. Lists are arranged in alpha order within precinct, unless otherwise indicated. For further information, contact Audrey Hatchett at (614) 466-8895.

GED Certificates

GED Transcript Office, 25 S Front St, 1st Fl, Columbus, OH 43215-4183; 614-466-1577, 614-752-9445-Fax; 8AM-4:30PM.

www.ode.state.oh.us/curriculum-assessment/assessment/ged

Students may review their test scores online.

Records are available from 1984 to present. Prior records are on microfilm. It takes 3 to 4 weeks before new records are available for inquiry.

Searching: A request form for a transcript copy is found at the webpage. Include the following in your request-date of birth, Social Security Number, signed release, approx date of test. DOB, city of test, previous names are helpful.

Access by: mail, fax, in person.

Fee & Payment: There is no fee for a verification, a $5.00 fee is charged for a copy of a transcript. Fee payee: Oh Testing Services Prepayment required. Personal checks not accepted. No credit cards accepted.

Mail search: Turnaround time: 7 to 10 days. No SASE is required.

Fax search: Same criteria as mail searching.

In person search: Simple requests may be processed while you wait.

Hunting and Fishing License Information

Ohio Department of Natural Resources, Division of Wildlife, 2045

Morse Rd, Columbus, OH 43229; 614-265-6300, 8AM-5PM.

www.dnr.state.oh.us/wildlife/default.htm

Records are open to the public.

Records are available since 1999. Many records are not computerized, but the records that are computerized go back to 1999. It takes 2 days before new records are available for inquiry. Records are normally destroyed after 3 years.

Searching: Request must be in writing, suggest placing "Attn: Law Section" on envelope. Include the following in your request-SSN, DOB. The following data is not released: SSN, DOB

Access by: mail.

Fee & Payment: There is no fee for simple requests, but the agency will charge for extensive search requests involving the paper records.

Mail search: Turnaround time: 1 to 3 days.

Other access: Current and previous year of licenses can be purchased for $50 on CD, one for hunting and one for fishing.

Ohio State Licensing Agencies

For details about the agency responsible for licensing/certifying/registering an item below or in the Agency Quick Finder section, match an item's number with the number of the agency in the *Licensing Agency Information* section.

Ohio Licenses Searchable Online

Accounting Firm #1	http://acc.ohio.gov/lookup.html
Acupuncturist #28	https://license.ohio.gov/lookup/default.asp
Anesthesiologist Assistant #28	https://license.ohio.gov/lookup/default.asp
Architect #2	www.arc.ohio.gov//license/query.asp
Athletic Trainer #29	https://license.ohio.gov/lookup/default.asp
Attorney (State) #44	www.sconet.state.oh.us/atty_reg/Public_AttorneyInformation.asp
Audiologist/Audiologist Aide #8	https://license.ohio.gov/lookup/default.asp
Backflow Prevention Assembly Insp. #34	www.com.state.oh.us/dic/plans/scripts/bkfloqy.htm
Backflow Tester #14	www.com.state.oh.us/dic/plans/scripts/bkfloqy.htm
Bank #17	https://www.com.state.oh.us/dfi/fiin_apps/license/default.aspx?vType=MB
Barber School #26	www.state.oh.us/brb/barbsch.htm
Boiler Contractor #38	www.com.state.oh.us/dic/scripts/boilerctrqy.htm
Cemetery #15	https://www.com.state.oh.us/real/scripts/searchcriteria.htm
Check Cashing / Lending Service #17	https://www.com.state.oh.us/dfi/fiin_apps/license/default.aspx?vType=MB
Child Care Type A or B House #19	www.odjfs.state.oh.us/cdc/query.asp
Child Day Care Facility #19	www.odjfs.state.oh.us/cdc/query.asp
Chiropractor #9	http://chirobd.ohio.gov/
Clinical Nurse Specialist #6	www.nursing.ohio.gov/verification.stm
Coil Cleaner (Liquor/Beverage) #27	www.state.oh.us/com/liquor/liquor13.htm
Consumer Finance Company #17	https://www.com.state.oh.us/dfi/fiin_apps/license/default.aspx?vType=MB
Contractor #14	www.com.state.oh.us/dic/scripts/ociebqy.htm
Cosmetic Therapist #28	https://license.ohio.gov/lookup/default.asp
Cosmetologist / Mgr Cosmetologist / Instructor #4	https://license.ohio.gov/lookup/default.asp
Counselor #11	http://cswmft.ohio.gov/query.asp
Day Camp, Children's #19	www.odjfs.state.oh.us/cdc/query.asp
Dental Assistant Radiologist #33	www.dental.ohio.gov/license/query.stm
Dental Hygienist #33	www.dental.ohio.gov/license/query.stm
Dentist #33	www.dental.ohio.gov/license/query.stm
Dialysis Technician #6	www.nursing.ohio.gov/verification.stm
Dietitian #31	www.dietetics.ohio.gov
Drug Wholesaler/Distributor #7	http://pharmacy.ohio.gov/license.htm
Electrical Safety Inspector #3	www.com.state.oh.us/dic/default.htm
Electrician #14	www.com.state.oh.us/dic/scripts/ociebqy.htm
Emergency Medical Technician #22	https://www.dps.state.oh.us/ems/cert.asp
Engineer #23	www.ohiopeps.org/files/license_lookup.html
Engineering/Surveying Company #23	www.ohiopeps.org/files/license_lookup.html
Esthetician/Managing Esthetician #4	https://license.ohio.gov/lookup/default.asp
Fire Protection System Designer #3	www.com.state.oh.us/dic/default.htm
Firefighter/Firefighter Instructor #22	https://www.dps.state.oh.us/ems/cert.asp
Foreign Real Estate Property #15	https://www.com.state.oh.us/real/scripts/searchcriteria.htm
Heating/Refrigeration (HVAC) #14	www.com.state.oh.us/dic/scripts/ociebqy.htm
Horse Racing Facility/Owner #41	http://racing.ohio.gov/license.stm
Hydronic-related Occupation #14	www.com.state.oh.us/dic/scripts/ociebqy.htm
Insurance Agent #20	www.ohioinsurance.gov/ConsumServ/ocs/agentloc.asp
Landscape Architect #2	www.arc.ohio.gov//license/query.asp
Legislative Agent/Agent Employer #30	www.jlec-olig.state.oh.us/agent_search_form.cfm
Liquor Distributor #27	www.state.oh.us/com/liquor/liquor15.htm
Liquor License #27	www.state.oh.us/com/liquor/phone.txt
Liquor License Cancellation #27	www.liquorcontrol.ohio.gov/canceled.txt
Liquor Permit / Liquor Store #27	www.liquorcontrol.ohio.gov/phone.txt
Lobbyist/Lobbyist Employer #30	www.jlec-olig.state.oh.us/agent_search_form.cfm
Manicuring/Esthetician Instructor #4	https://license.ohio.gov/lookup/default.asp
Manicurist/Managing Manicurist #4	https://license.ohio.gov/lookup/default.asp
Marriage and Family Therapist #11	http://cswmft.ohio.gov/query.asp
Massage Therapist #28	https://license.ohio.gov/lookup/default.asp
Mechanotherapist #28	https://license.ohio.gov/lookup/default.asp
Medical Doctor #28	https://license.ohio.gov/lookup/default.asp

Midwife Nurse #6	www.nursing.ohio.gov/verification.stm
Mortgage Broker #17	https://www.com.state.oh.us/dfi/fiin_apps/license/default.aspx?vType=MB
Naprapath #28	https://license.ohio.gov/lookup/default.asp
Nurse Anesthetist #6	www.nursing.ohio.gov/verification.stm
Nurse Practitioner #6	www.nursing.ohio.gov/verification.stm
Nurse-RN/LPN #6	www.nursing.ohio.gov/verification.stm
Occupational Therapist/Assistant #29	https://license.ohio.gov/lookup/default.asp
Ocularist/Ocularist Apprentice #39	https://license.ohio.gov/lookup/default.asp
Optical Dispenser #39	https://license.ohio.gov/lookup/default.asp
Optician/Optician Apprentice #39	https://license.ohio.gov/lookup/default.asp
Optometrist #37	www.optometry.ohio.gov/query.asp
Optometrist, Diagnostic/Therapeutic #37	www.optometry.ohio.gov/query.asp
Osteopathic Physician #28	https://license.ohio.gov/lookup/default.asp
Pawnbroker #17	https://www.com.state.oh.us/dfi/fiin_apps/license/default.aspx?vType=MB
Pesticide Applicator/Operator/Dealer #40	www.ohioagriculture.gov/pubs/divs/plnt/plnt-licensing.stm
Pesticide Private Applicator #40	www.ohioagriculture.gov/pubs/divs/plnt/plnt-licensing.stm
Pharmacist #7	http://pharmacy.ohio.gov/license.htm
Pharmacy/Pharmacy Dispensary #7	http://pharmacy.ohio.gov/license.htm
Physical Therapist/Assistant #29	https://license.ohio.gov/lookup/default.asp
Physician Assistant #28	https://license.ohio.gov/lookup/default.asp
Plumber #14	www.com.state.oh.us/dic/scripts/ociebqy.htm
Plumbing Inspector #3	www.com.state.oh.us/odoc/dic/default.htm
Podiatrist #28	https://license.ohio.gov/lookup/default.asp
Polygraph Examiner #46	http://polygraph.org/states/oape/directory.htm
Precious Metals Dealer #17	https://www.com.state.oh.us/dfi/fiin_apps/license/default.aspx?vType=MB
Premium Finance Company #17	https://www.com.state.oh.us/dfi/fiin_apps/license/default.aspx?vType=MB
Prescriptive Authority #6	www.nursing.ohio.gov/verification.stm
Private Investigator #15	https://www.com.state.oh.us/real/scripts/searchcriteria.htm
Psychologist #36	https://license.ohio.gov/lookup/default.asp?division=83
Public Accountant-CPA #1	http://acc.ohio.gov/lookup.html
Racetrack-related Occupation #41	http://racing.ohio.gov/license.stm
Racing Permit #41	http://racing.ohio.gov/license.stm
Real Estate Agent/Sales/Broker #15	https://www.com.state.oh.us/real/scripts/searchcriteria.htm
Real Estate Appraiser #15	https://www.com.state.oh.us/real/scripts/searchcriteria.htm
Respiratory Therapist/Student #42	https://license.ohio.gov/lookup/default.asp
Savings & Loan Association / Savings Bank #17	https://www.com.state.oh.us/dfi/fiin_apps/license/default.aspx?vType=MB
School Psychologist #36	https://license.ohio.gov/lookup/default.asp?division=83
Securities Filing #16	www.securities.state.oh.us/secu_apps/offering/disclaimer.aspx
Security Guard #15	https://www.com.state.oh.us/real/scripts/searchcriteria.htm
Social Worker #11	http://cswmft.ohio.gov/query.asp
Speech Pathologist/Audiologist #8	https://license.ohio.gov/lookup/default.asp
Storage Tank Corrective Action #34	https://www.com.state.oh.us/sfm/bustr/CorrectiveActions.htm
Surveyor, Land #23	www.ohiopeps.org/files/license_lookup.html
Teacher/Teacher's Aide #43	https://www.ode.state.oh.us/Teaching-Profession/Teacher/Certification_Licensure/certifact.asp
Underground Storage Tank #34	https://www.com.state.oh.us/sfm/bustr/PublicInquiry.htm
Underground Tank Inspector #34	https://www.com.state.oh.us/sfm/bustr/PDFs/Data/WEBInspectorList
Underground Tank Installer #34	https://www.com.state.oh.us/odoc/sfm/bustr/PDFs/Data/WEBInstallerList
Underground Tank Instructor #34	hhttps://www.com.state.oh.us/sfm/bustr/PDFs/TrainerApprovedlist.xls
Veterinarian/Veterinary Tech #45	www.ovmlb.ohio.gov/

Ohio Licensing Quick Finder

Accounting Firm #1 ... 614-466-4135	Bank #17 ... 614-728-8400	Child Care Type A or B House #19 ... 614-466-3822
Acupuncturist #28 ... 614-466-3934	Barber / Barber Instructor #26 ... 614-466-5003	Child Day Care Facility #19 ... 614-466-3822
Adoption Agency #19 ... 614-466-9274	Barber School / Shop #26 ... 614-466-5003	Children's Residential Center #19 ... 614-466-5392
Adult Care Home #18 ... 614-466-7713	Bedding/Furniture Dealer/Dist. #38 ... 614-644-2233	Children's Services Agency #19 ... 614-466-5392
Airline Liquor Permit #27 ... 614-644-2360	Bedding/Furniture Mfg/Renovator #38 .. 614-644-2233	Chiropractor #9 ... 614-644-7032
Anesthesiologist Assistant #28 ... 614-466-3934	Boiler Contractor #38 ... 614) 644-2223	Clinical Nurse Specialist #6 ... 614-466-3947
Architect #2 ... 614-466-2316	Boiler Inspector #34 ... 614-644-2223	Coil Cleaner (Liquor/Beverage) #27 .. 614-644-2360
Athlete Agent #32 ... 216-518-9497	Boiler Operator #34 ... 614-644-2223	Consumer Finance Company #17 ... 614-728-8400
Athletic Trainer #29 ... 614-466-3774	Boxer/Boxing Professional #32 ... 216-518-9497	Contractor #14 ... 614-644-3493
Attorney (Bar Assoc./by type) #13 ... 800-282-6556	Boxing Event #32 ... 216-518-9497	Cosmetic Therapist #28 ... 614-466-3934
Attorney (State) #44 ... 614-466-1553	Building Inspector #3 ... 614-644-2613	Cosmetologist/Mgr'g Cosmetologist #4 614-644-3834
Audiologist/Audiologist Aide #8 ... 614-466-3145	Building Official #3 ... 614-644-2613	Cosmetology Instructor #4 ... 614-644-3834
Backflow Prevention Inspector #34 ... 614-644-2223	Cemetery #15 ... 216-787-3100	Counselor #11 ... 614-466-0912
Backflow Tester #14 ... 614-644-2223	Check Cashing / Lending Service #17 . 614-728-8400	Crematory #5 ... 614-466-4252

Dairy Farm #12	614-466-5550
Day Camp, Childrens #19	614-466-3822
Dental Assistant Radiologist #33	614-466-2580
Dental Hygienist #33	614-466-2580
Dentist #33	614-466-2580
Dialysis Technician #6	614-466-3947
Dietitian #31	614-466-3291
Drug Wholesaler/Distributor #7	614-466-4143
Electrical Safety Inspector #3	614-644-2613
Electrical Safety Trainee #3	614-644-2613
Electrician #14	614-644-3493
Elevator Inspector #38	614-644-3524
Embalmer/Embalming Facility #5	614-466-4252
Emergency Medical Tech. Instr. #22	614-466-9447
Emergency Medical Technician #22	614-466-9447
Engineer #23	614-466-3650
Engineering/Surveying Company #23	614-466-3650
Esthetician/Managing Esthetician #4	614-644-3834
Explosives #34	614-752-7126
Family Foster Home #19	614-466-5392
Fire Alarm & Detection Inspector #34	614-644-7126
Fire Extinguisher Inspector #34	614-644-7126
Fire Extinguisher Equip. Inspector #34	614-644-7126
Fire Protection System Designer #3	614-644-2613
Firefighter/Firefighter Instructor #22	614-466-9447
Fireworks Exhibitor/Assistant #34	614-752-7126
Fishing Guide #21	419-625-8062
Foreign Real Estate Property #15	614-466-4100
Funeral Director/Funeral Home #5	614-466-4252
Group Home Operator #19	614-466-5392
Health Care Facility #18	614-466-7713
Hearing Aid Dealer/Fitter #25	614-466-5215
Heating/Refrigeration (HVAC) #14	614-644-3493
Horse Racing Facility/Owner #41	614-466-2757
Hotel/Motel #34	614-752-7126
Hydronic-related Occupation #14	614-644-3493
Independent Living Arranger #19	614-466-9274
Insurance Agent #20	614-644-2665
Insurance Broker, Non-Resident #20	614-644-2665
Insurance Solicitor #20	614-644-2665
Investment Advisor/Advisor Rep. #16	614-644-3466
Landscape Architect #2	614-466-2316
Legislative Agent/Agent Employer #30	614-728-5100
Liquor Distributor #27	614-644-2360

Liquor License #27	614-644-2360
Liquor License Cancellation #27	614-644-2360
Liquor Permit / Liquor Store #27	614-644-2360
Lobbyist/Lobbyist Employer #30	614-728-5100
Lottery Retailer #35	216-787-3200
Manicuring/Esthetician Instructor #4	614-644-3834
Manicurist/Managing Manicurist #4	614-644-3834
Marriage and Family Therapist #11	614-466-0912
Massage Therapist #28	614-466-3934
Mechanical Inspector #3	614-644-2613
Mechanotherapist #28	614-466-3934
Medical Doctor #28	614-466-3934
Midwife Nurse #6	614-466-3947
Milk Hauler #12	614-466-5550
Milk Processor/Producer/Plant #12	614-466-5550
Milk Tester/Sampler #12	614-466-5550
Mortgage Broker #17	614-728-8400
Naprapath #28	614-466-3934
Notary Public #10	614-644-4559
Nurse Anesthetist #6	614-466-3947
Nurse Practitioner #6	614-466-3947
Nurse-RN/LPN #6	614-466-3947
Nursing Home #18	614-466-7713
Nursing Home Administrator #18	614-466-5114
Occupational Therapist/Assistant #29	614-466-3774
Ocularist/Ocularist Apprentice #39	614-466-9709
Optical Dispenser #39	614-466-9709
Optician/Optician Apprentice #39	614-466-9709
Optometrist #37	614-466-5115
Osteopathic Physician #28	614-466-3934
Pawnbroker #17	614-728-8400
Pesticide Applicator Business #40	614-728-6987
Pesticide-related Occupation #40	614-728-6987
Pharmacist #7	614-466-4143
Pharmacy/Pharmacy Dispensary #7	614-466-4143
Physical Therapist/Assistant #29	614-466-3774
Physician Assistant #28	614-466-3934
Plan Examiner #3	614-644-2613
Plumber #14	614-644-3493
Plumbing Inspector #3	614-644-2613
Podiatrist #28	614-466-3934
Polygraph Examiner #46	614-645-4174
Precious Metals Dealer #17	614-728-8400
Premium Finance Company #17	614-466-2221

Prescriptive Authority #6	614-466-3947
Pressure Piping Inspector #34	614-644-2223
Private Investigator #15	614-466-4130
Psychologist #36	614-466-8808
Public Accountant-CPA #1	614-466-4135
Public Adjuster #20	614-644-2665
Racetrack-related Occupation #41	614-466-2757
Racing Permit #41	614-466-2757
Real Estate Agent/Broker/Sales #15	614-466-4100
Real Estate Appraiser #15	216-787-3100
Residential Care Facility #18	614-466-7713
Residential Parenting Organization #19	614-466-9274
Respiratory Therapist/Student #42	614-752-9218
Savings & Loan Association #17	614-728-8400
Savings Bank #17	614-728-8400
School Counselor #43	614-466-3593
School Principal/Administrator #43	614-466-3593
School Psychologist #36	614-466-8808
School Treasurer/Business Mgr. #43	614-466-3593
Scientific Collection Permit #21	614-265-6320
Securities Filing #16	614-644-3466
Securities Salesperson/Dealer #16	614-644-3466
Security Guard #15	614-466-4130
Social Worker #11	614-466-0912
Solid Waste Facility Operator #24	614-644-2621
Speech Pathologist Aide #8	614-466-3145
Speech Pathologist/Audiologist #8	614-466-3145
Sprinkler Equipment Inspector #34	614-644-7126
Sprinkler Inspector #3	614-644-2613
Sprinkler, Fire Alarm, Hazardous Designer #3	614-644-2613
Steam Engineer #34	614-644-2223
Steam, Stationary #34	614-644-2223
Storage Tank Corrective Action #34	614-752-7921
Surveyor, Land #23	614-466-3650
Teacher/Teacher's Aide #43	614-466-3593
Tough-Person Promoter #32	216-518-9497
Tour Promoter #34	614-644-2223
Travel Agent #34	614-644-2223
Underground Tan-related Occupation #34	614-752-7921
Veterinarian/Veterinary Tech. #45	614-644-5281
Water Supply Equipment Inspct. #34	614-644-2223

Ohio Licensing Agency Information

1 Accountancy Board of Ohio, 77 S High St, 18th Fl, Columbus, OH 43215-6128; 614-466-4135, Fax: 614-466-2628. www.state.oh.us/acc Search Database at http://acc.ohio.gov/lookup.html

2 Architects Board of Ohio, 77 S High St, 16th Fl, Columbus, OH 43266-0303; 614-466-2316, Fax: 614-644-9048. www.arc.ohio.gov/ Email: cmharch@aol.com Search Database at www.arc.ohio.gov//license/query.asp

3 Department of Commerce, Board of Building Standards, 6606 Tussing Rd (PO Box 4009), Reynoldsburg, OH 43068; 614-644-2613, Fax: 614-644-3147. www.com.state.oh.us/dic/dicbbs.htm Email: jwbrant@com.state.oh.us Search Database at www.com.state.oh.us/dic/default.htm

4 Board of Cosmetology, Suite 101 Southland Mall, 3700 South High Street, Columbus, OH 43207-4041; 614-466-3834, Fax: 614-466-6880. http://cos.ohio.gov Email: ohiocosbd@cos.state.oh.us Search Database at https://license.ohio.gov/lookup/default.asp

5 Board of Embalmers & Funeral Directors of Ohio, 77 S High St, 16th Fl, Columbus, OH 43215-6108; 614-466-4252, Fax: 614-728-6825. www.state.oh.us/fun Email: oh.emb.bd@exchange.state.oh.us

6 Board of Nursing, 17 S High St #400, Columbus, OH 43215; 614-466-3947, Fax: 614-466-0388. www.nursing.ohio.gov Search Database at www.nursing.ohio.gov/verification.stm Note: Must search by license number or SSN. Prescriptive authority needs name or COA#.

7 Board of Pharmacy, 77 S High St, 17th Fl, Columbus, OH 43266-0320; 614-466-4143, Fax: 614-752-4836. http://pharmacy.ohio.gov/index.htm Email: agent.licensing@wvinsurance.gov Search Database at http://pharmacy.ohio.gov/license.htm

8 Board of Speech Pathology & Audiology, 77 S High St, 16th Fl, Columbus, OH 43215; 614-466-3145, Fax: 614-995-2286. www.slpaud.ohio.gov/ Email: michael.setty@splaud.state.oh.us Search Database at https://license.ohio.gov/lookup/default.asp

9 Chiropractic Board, 77 S High St, 16th Fl, Columbus, OH 43215-6108; 614-644-7032, Fax: 614-752-2539. www.state.oh.us/chr/ Email: chirobd@mail.peps.state.oh.us Search Database at http://chirobd.ohio.gov/

10 Commission Clerk, PO Box 1658, Columbus, OH 43215; 614-644-4559, Fax: 614-644-8820. www.sos.state.oh.us/sos/info/notaryCommission.aspx

11 Counselor & Social Worker Board, 77 S High St, 16th Fl, Columbus, OH 43266-0340; 614-466-0912, Fax: 614-728-7790. www.state.oh.us/csw Email: csw_hackett@ohio.gov Search Database at http://cswmft.ohio.gov/query.asp

12 Department of Agriculture, 8995 E Main St, Reynoldsburg, OH 43068-3399; 614-466-5550, Fax: 614-728-2652. www.state.oh.us/agr/ Email: agri@odant.agri.state.oh.us

13 State Bar Association, 1700 Lake Shore Dr, Columbus, OH 43204; 800-282-6556, 614-487-2050, Fax: 614-487-1008. www.ohiobar.org Email: osba@ohiobar.org

14 Ohio Department of Commerce, Construction Industry Examination Board, 6606 Tussing Rd, Reynoldsburg, OH 43068-9009; 614-644-3493, Fax: 614-728-1200.
www.com.state.oh.us/dic/default.htm
Search Database at
www.com.state.oh.us/dic/scripts/ociebqy.htm

15 Department of Commerce, Division of Real Estate & Professional Licensing, 77 S High St, 20th Fl, Columbus, OH 43215-6133; 614-466-4190, Fax: 614-644-0584.
www.com.state.oh.us/real
Email: repld@com.state.oh.us   Search data- https://www.com.state.oh.us/real/scripts/searchcriteria.htm

16 Department of Commerce, Division of Securities, 77 S High St, 22nd Fl, Columbus, OH 43215-0548; 614-644-7381, Fax: 614-466-3316.
www.securities.state.oh.us

17 Department of Commerce, Division of Financial Institutions, 77 S High St, 21st Fl, Columbus, OH 43266-0121; 614-728-8400, Fax: 614-466-1631.
www.com.state.oh.us/dfi/default.htm
Email: WebMaster@com.state.oh.us
Search Database at
https://www.com.state.oh.us/dfi/fiin_apps/license/default.aspx?vType=MB

18 Department of Health, Health Care Facility Program, PO Box 118, Columbus, OH 43216-0118; 614-466-5114, Fax: 614-466-0271.
www.ohiobenha.org/

19 Office For Children & Families, Bureau of Family Svcs, 255 E Main, 3rd Fl, Columbus, OH 43215; 614-466-9274, Fax: 614-728-6726.
http://jfs.ohio.gov/ocf/

20 Department of Insurance, 2100 Stella Ct, Columbus, OH 43215-1067; 614-644-2665, Fax: 614-644-3475.
www.ohioinsurance.gov
Search Database at www.ohioinsurance.gov/ConsumServ/ocs/agentloc.asp

21 Department of Natural Resources, 2045 Morse Rd, Bldg G, Columbus, OH 43229; 1-800-945-3543, Fax: 614-262-1143.
www.dnr.state.oh.us/wildlife/default.htm

22 Department of Public Safety, Emergency Medical Services Division, PO Box 182073, Columbus, OH 43218-2073; 614-466-9447, Fax: 614-466-9461.
http://ems.ohio.gov
Email: rnrucker@dps.state.oh.us
Search Database at
https://www.dps.state.oh.us/ems/cert.asp

23 Engineers & Surveyors Board, 77 S High St, 16th Fl, Rm 1698, Columbus, OH 43266-0314; 614-466-3650, Fax: 614-728-3059.
www.ohiopeps.org
Email: board@mail.peps.state.oh.us
Search Database at
www.ohiopeps.org/files/license_lookup.html

24 Hazardous Waste Facility Board, 122 S Front St, Columbus, OH 43215; 614-644-2621, Fax: 614-728-5315.
www.epa.state.oh.us/dsiwm

25 Hearing Aid Dealers & Fitters Board, 246 N High St (PO Box 118), Columbus, OH 43216-0118; 614-466-5215, Fax: 614-466-8692.
Email: hearing@gw.odh.state.oh.us

26 Licensing Boards, Barber Board, 77 S High St, 16th Fl, Columbus, OH 43215; 614-466-5003, Fax: 614-387-1694.   www.state.oh.us/brb

27 Division of Liquor Control, 6606 Tussing Rd, Reynoldsburg, OH 43068-9005; 614-644-2360, Fax: 614-644-2480.
www.state.oh.us/com/liquor/liquororiginal.htm
Email: agencyops@liquor.state.oh.us

28 Medical Board of Ohio, 77 S High St, 17th Fl, Columbus, OH 43266-0315; 614-466-3934, Fax: 614-728-5946.
www.med.ohio.gov
Email: kay.rieve@med.state.oh.us
Search Database at
https://license.ohio.gov/lookup/default.asp

29 OTPTAT - Occupational Therapy - Physical Therapy Board, 77 S High St, 16th Fl, Columbus, OH 43266-0317; 614-466-3774, Fax: 614-995-0816.   http://otptat.ohio.gov/
Search Database at
https://license.ohio.gov/lookup/default.asp

30 Office of Legislative Inspector General, 50 W Broad St, #1308, Columbus, OH 43215-3365; 614-728-5100, Fax: 614-728-5074.
www.jlec-olig.state.oh.us
Email: info@jlec-olig.state.oh.us
Search Database at www.jlec-olig.state.oh.us/agent_search_form.cfm

31 Board of Dietetics, 77 S High St, 18th Fl, Columbus, OH 43266-0337; 614-466-3291, Fax: 614-728-0723.   www.dietetics.ohio.gov
Email: obd_mavko@ohio.gov

32 Boxing Commission, 242 Federal Plaza West, Youngstown, OH 44503; 330-797-2556.
Email: paul.amodio@exchange.state.oh.us

33 Dental Board, 77 S High St, 18th Fl, Columbus, OH 43215-6135; 614-466-2580, Fax: 614-752-8995.
www.state.oh.us/den   Search Database at
www.dental.ohio.gov/license/query.stm

34 Ohio Department of Commerce, Testing and Registration, PO Box 4009 , (6606 Tussing Rd), Reynoldsburg, OH 43068-9009; 614-644-2223, Fax: 614-644-2428.
www.com.state.oh.us/odoc/dic/default.htm
Email: ic@com.state.oh.us
Search Database at
www.com.state.oh.us/dic/default.htm

35 Lottery Commission, 615 W Superior Ave, NW Frank J. Lausche Bldg, Cleveland, OH 44113; 216-787-3200, Fax: 216-787-3718.
www.ohiolottery.com
Email: olcwebmail@olc.state.oh.us

36 State Board of Psychology, 77 S High St, Ste 1830, Columbus, OH 43215-6108; 614-466-8808, Fax: 614-728-7081.   www.state.oh.us/psy
Email: optometry.board@exchange.state.oh.us
Search Database at
www.psychology.ohio.gov/LicenseLookup/query.asp   Note: If "SP" is part of a license number, that indicates a "school psychologist."

37 Board of Optometry, 77 S High St, 16th Fl, Columbus, OH 43215-6108; 614-466-5115, Fax: 614-644-3937.
www.optometry.ohio.gov/
Email: optometry.board@exchange.state.oh.us
Search Database at
www.optometry.ohio.gov/query.asp   Note: Will sell rosters and labels on disk.

38 Ohio Department of Commerce, Industrial Complaince Division; Operations & Maintenance, 6606 Tussing Rd (PO Box 4009), Reynoldsburg, OH 43068-9009;
614-644-3964, Fax: 614-644-8658.
www.com.state.oh.us/odoc/dic/dicbedding.htm

39 Optical Dispensers Board, 77 S High St, 16th Fl, Columbus, OH 43215-6108; 614-466-9709, Fax: 614-995-5392.
www.optical.ohio.gov/
Email: ohioopticalboard@hotmail.com
Search Database at
https://license.ohio.gov/lookup/default.asp

40 Pesticide Regulations, 8995 E Main St, Reynoldsburg, OH 43068-3399; 614-728-6200, Fax: 614-728-4235.   www.ohioagriculture.gov/
Search Database at www.ohioagriculture.gov/pubs/divs/plnt/plnt-licensing.stm

41 Racing Commission, 77 S High St, 18th Fl, Columbus, OH 43215-6108; 614-466-2757, Fax: 614-466-1900.
www.state.oh.us/rac/keypersonnel.stm
Search Database at
http://racing.ohio.gov/license.stm

42 Respiratory Care Board, 77 S High St, 16th Fl, Columbus, OH 43215-6108; 614-752-9218, Fax: 614-728-8691.
http://respiratorycare.ohio.gov/
Email: rcb.logsdon@rcb.state.oh.us
Search Database at
https://license.ohio.gov/lookup/default.asp

43 Department of Education, Office of Certification/Licensure, 25 S Front St, Columbus, OH 43215-4183; 614-466-3593, Fax: 614-466-1999.   https://www.ode.state.oh.us
Search data at https://www.ode.state.oh.us/Teaching-Profession/Teacher/Certification_Licensure/certifact.asp

44 Supreme Court, Attorney Registration Section, 65 S Front St, 5th Fl, Columbus, OH 43215; 614-387-9320, Fax: 614-387-9323.
www.sconet.state.oh.us/Atty_Reg/
Email: attyreg@sconet.state.oh.us
Search Database at www.sconet.state.oh.us/atty_reg/Public_AttorneyInformation.asp

45 Veterinary Medical Board, 77 S High St, 16th Fl, Columbus, OH 43266-0116; 614-644-5281, Fax: 614-644-9038.
www.ovmlb.ohio.gov/
Email: info@ovmlb.state.oh.us
Search Database at www.ovmlb.ohio.gov/   Note: Searching will be available at search site.

46 Association of Polygraph Examiners, c/o Phillip Osborne, Columbus PD, 120 Marconi Blvd. 7th Fl, Columbus, OH 43215; 614-645-4174, Fax: 614-781-0257.
http://polygraph.org/states/oape/index.htm
Email: posborne@insight.rr.com
Search Database at
http://polygraph.org/states/oape/directory.htm

Ohio Federal Courts

The following list indicates the district and division name for each county in the state. If the bankruptcy court location is different from the district court, then the location of the bankruptcy court appears in parentheses.

Ohio County/Court Cross Reference

County	District	Division
Adams	Southern	Cincinnati
Allen	Northern	Toledo
Ashland	Northern	Cleveland (Canton)
Ashtabula	Northern	Cleveland (Youngstown)
Athens	Southern	Columbus
Auglaize	Northern	Toledo
Belmont	Southern	Columbus
Brown	Southern	Cincinnati
Butler	Southern	Cincinnati (Dayton)
Carroll	Northern	Akron (Canton)
Champaign	Southern	Dayton
Clark	Southern	Dayton
Clermont	Southern	Cincinnati
Clinton	Southern	Cincinnati (Dayton)
Columbiana	Northern	Youngstown
Coshocton	Southern	Columbus
Crawford	Northern	Cleveland (Canton)
Cuyahoga	Northern	Cleveland
Darke	Southern	Dayton
Defiance	Northern	Toledo
Delaware	Southern	Columbus
Erie	Northern	Toledo
Fairfield	Southern	Columbus
Fayette	Southern	Columbus
Franklin	Southern	Columbus
Fulton	Northern	Toledo
Gallia	Southern	Columbus
Geauga	Northern	Cleveland
Greene	Southern	Dayton
Guernsey	Southern	Columbus
Hamilton	Southern	Cincinnati
Hancock	Northern	Toledo
Hardin	Northern	Toledo
Harrison	Southern	Columbus
Henry	Northern	Toledo
Highland	Southern	Cincinnati
Hocking	Southern	Columbus
Holmes	Northern	Akron (Canton)
Huron	Northern	Toledo
Jackson	Southern	Columbus
Jefferson	Southern	Columbus
Knox	Southern	Columbus
Lake	Northern	Cleveland
Lawrence	Southern	Cincinnati
Licking	Southern	Columbus
Logan	Southern	Columbus
Lorain	Northern	Cleveland
Lucas	Northern	Toledo
Madison	Southern	Columbus
Mahoning	Northern	Youngstown
Marion	Northern	Toledo
Medina	Northern	Cleveland (Akron)
Meigs	Southern	Columbus
Mercer	Northern	Toledo
Miami	Southern	Dayton
Monroe	Southern	Columbus
Montgomery	Southern	Dayton
Morgan	Southern	Columbus
Morrow	Southern	Columbus
Muskingum	Southern	Columbus
Noble	Southern	Columbus
Ottawa	Northern	Toledo
Paulding	Northern	Toledo
Perry	Southern	Columbus
Pickaway	Southern	Columbus
Pike	Southern	Columbus
Portage	Northern	Akron
Preble	Southern	Dayton
Putnam	Northern	Toledo
Richland	Northern	Cleveland (Canton)
Ross	Southern	Columbus
Sandusky	Northern	Toledo
Scioto	Southern	Cincinnati
Seneca	Northern	Toledo
Shelby	Southern	Dayton
Stark	Northern	Akron (Canton)
Summit	Northern	Akron
Trumbull	Northern	Youngstown
Tuscarawas	Northern	Akron (Canton)
Union	Southern	Columbus
Van Wert	Northern	Toledo
Vinton	Southern	Columbus
Warren	Southern	Cincinnati (Dayton)
Washington	Southern	Columbus
Wayne	Northern	Akron (Canton)
Williams	Northern	Toledo
Wood	Northern	Toledo
Wyandot	Northern	Toledo

Standards for Federal Courts: Search fee is $26.00 per item (one party name or case number). Copy fee is $.50 per page. Certification fee is $9.00 per document, double for exemplification, if available. All fees standard unless noted in profile. Mail Search: always enclose a stamped self addressed envelope unless otherwise noted. Most courts accept fax requests or will suggest a copying/search vendor. Before releasing records, all courts require prepayment, unless noted.

Open records are located at the court unless otherwise noted. District courts index by defendant and plaintiff as well as by case number. Bankruptcy courts usually index by debtor and case number. While most courts now have their indexes on computer, many may still maintain index card files as well.

Courts offering internet access via CM-ECF or older RACER, PACER, or Web-PACER systems charge $.08 per page fee unless noted as free. Where PACER is available, the universal sign-up number is 800-676-6856. Find PACER and the US Party/Case Index at http://pacer.psc.uscourts.gov.

US District Court

Northern District of Ohio

Akron Division Court Clerk, 568 US Courthouse, 2 S Main St, Akron, OH 44308 (also use mail address for courier delivery), 330-375-5705, records rm- 330-375-5407. Hours- 9AM-4PM. www.ohnd.uscourts.gov

Counties: Carroll, Holmes, Portage, Stark, Summit, Tuscarawas, Wayne. Northern District is on a central draw- a case may be assigned here or at Cleveland or Youngstown. Cases filed prior to 1995 for counties in the Youngstown Division may be located here.

Searches & Indexing: Results include last 4 SSN digits only. Computer index maintained. New cases in the index immediately after filing date. Records purged never. Open cases may be located in other district divisions depending on the judge assigned.

Fee & Payment: Pay by money order, cashier's or personal check. Payee: Clerk, US District Court. Prepayment required.

Phone Search: Only docket information is available by phone.

Mail Search: search usually completed- 1-2 days. Include SASE for return.

In Person Search: Fee charged if court performs your search. Self-serve copier available - $.10 per page.

E-Services: ECF replaces PACER. Many cases prior to the indicated dates are also online. PACER records go back to 1/ 1990. ECF at https://ecf.ohnd.uscourts.gov **Other Online Access:** Make copy requests at www.ohnd.uscourts.gov/Clerk_s_Office/Copy_Request/copy_request.html. Read "Notable Cases at www.ohnd.uscourts.gov/Clerk_s_Office/Notable_Cases/index.html.

Cleveland Division Court Clerk, 801 W Superior Ave, Cleveland, OH 44114-1830 (also use mail address for courier delivery), 216-357-7000, records rm- 216-357-7040. Hours- 9AM-4PM. www.ohnd.uscourts.gov

Counties: Ashland, Ashtabula, Crawford, Cuyahoga, Geauga, Lake, Lorain, Medina, Richland. Cases prior to 7/1995 for the counties of Ashland, Crawford, Medina and Richland are located in the Akron Division. Cases filed prior to 1995 from the counties in the Youngstown Division may be located here. Northern District is on a central draw- rarely a case may be located to Youngstown or Akron Divisions.

Searches & Indexing: Results do not include SSN or DOB. Computer index maintained. New cases in the index immediately after filing date. Records purged never. Open cases may be located in other district divisions depending on the judge assigned.

Fee & Payment: Pay by money order, cashier's or personal check. Payee: Clerk, US District Court. Prepayment required.

Phone Search: Only docket information is available by phone.

Mail Search: search usually completed- 1-2 days. SASE not required.

In Person Search: Fee charged if court performs your search.

E-Services: ECF replaces PACER. Many cases prior to the indicated dates are also online. PACER records go back to 1/1990. ECF at https://ecf.ohnd.uscourts.gov **Other Online Access:** Make copy requests at www.ohnd.uscourts.gov/Clerk_s_Office/Copy_Request/copy_request.html. Read "Notable Cases" at www.ohnd.uscourts.gov/Clerk_s_Office/Notable_Cases/index.html.

Toledo Division Court Clerk, 114 US Courthouse, 1716 Spielbusch Ave, Toledo, OH 43624 (also use mail address for courier delivery), 419-259-6412. Hours- 9AM-4PM. www.ohnd.uscourts.gov

Counties: Allen, Auglaize, Defiance, Erie, Fulton, Hancock, Hardin, Henry, Huron, Lucas, Marion, Mercer, Ottawa, Paulding, Putnam, Sandusky, Seneca, Van Wert, Williams, Wood, Wyandot. This is known as the Western Division of the Northern District.

Searches & Indexing: Results do not include SSN or DOB. Computer index maintained back to 1990. New cases in the index 1 day after filing date. Records purged never.

Fee & Payment: Pay by Visa/MC, money order, cashier's or personal check. Payee: Clerk, US District Court. Prepayment required.

Phone Search: Only docket information is available by phone.

Mail Search: search usually completed- 1-2 days. Include SASE for return.

In Person Search: Fee charged if court performs your search. No self-serve copier available.

E-Services: ECF replaces PACER. Many cases prior to the indicated dates are also online. PACER records go back to 1/1990. ECF at https://ecf.ohnd.uscourts.gov **Other Online Access:** Make copy requests at www.ohnd.uscourts.gov/Clerk_s_Office/Copy_Request/copy_request.html. Read "Notable Cases at www.ohnd.uscourts.gov/Clerk_s_Office/Notable_Cases/index.html.

Youngstown Division Court Clerk, 337 Federal Bldg, 125 Market St, Youngstown, OH 44503-1780 (also use mail address for courier delivery), 330-746-1906, Fax-330-746-2027. Hours- 9AM-4PM. www.ohnd.uscourts.gov

Counties: Columbiana, Mahoning, Trumbull. This division was re-activated in the middle of 1995. Older cases will be found in Akron or Cleveland. Northern District is on a central draw- a case may be assigned here or at Cleveland or Akron.

Searches & Indexing: Results do not include SSN or DOB. Computer index maintained back to 1991. New cases in the index immediately after filing date. Records purged never. Open cases may be located in other district divisions depending on the judge assigned.

Fee & Payment: Pay by Visa/MC, money order, cashier's or personal check. Payee: Clerk, US District Court. Prepayment required.

Phone Search: Only docket information is available by phone.

Mail Search: search usually completed- 2-3 days. Include SASE for return.

In Person Search: Fee charged if court performs your search. No self-serve copier available.

E-Services: ECF replaces PACER. Many cases prior to the indicated dates are also online. PACER records go back to 1/1990. ECF at https://ecf.ohnd.uscourts.gov **Other Online Access:** Make copy requests at www.ohnd.uscourts.gov/Clerk_s_Office/Copy_Request/copy_request.html. Read "Notable Cases at www.ohnd.uscourts.gov/Clerk_s_Office/Notable_Cases/index.html.

US Bankruptcy Court

Northern District of Ohio

Akron Division Court Clerk, 455 US Courthouse, 2 S Main, Akron, OH 44308 (also use mail address for courier delivery), 330-375-5840. Hours- 9AM-4PM. www.ohnb.uscourts.gov

Counties: Medina, Portage, Summit.

Searches & Indexing: Results include SSN. Both computer and card indexes maintained. New cases in the index 1-2 days after filing date. Case records closed before 1993 were sent to Chicago Records Center. In Spring 1995, 1994 and after closed cases sent to Dayton.

Fee & Payment: Pay by Visa/MC, money order, cashier's or personal check. Payee: Clerk, US Bankruptcy Court. Prepayment required.

Phone Search: Voice Case Information Service available, call 800-898-6899 or 330-489-4731.

Mail Search: search usually completed- 5 days. Include SASE for return.

In Person Search: Fee charged if court performs your search. Self-serve copier - $.25 per page.

E-Services: ECF replaces PACER whose records did go back to 1/1985. New records online after 1 day. ECF at https://ecf.ohnb.uscourts.gov **Opinions Online:** www.ohnb.uscourts.gov. These judges' postings include calendars and opinions.

Canton Division Court Clerk, Frank T Bow Federal Bldg, 201 Cleveland Ave SW, Canton, OH 44702 (also use mail address for courier delivery), 330-489-4426, Fax-330-489-4434. Hours- 9AM-4PM. www.ohnb.uscourts.gov

Counties: Ashland, Carroll, Crawford, Holmes, Richland, Stark, Tuscarawas, Wayne.

Searches & Indexing: Results include last 4 SSN digits. Computer index back to 1990 maintained. Records indexed on cards 1982-1989; journalized in books 1984-1990. New cases in the index 48 hours after filing date. Prior to 1995, closed cases sent to Chicago Records Center; case records now sent to Dayton Records Center every few years.

Fee & Payment: Pay by Visa/MC, money order, cashier's or personal check. No debtor's checks accepted. Payee: Clerk, US Bankruptcy Court. Prepayment required.

Phone Search: Voice Case Information Service available, call 800-898-6899 or 330-489-4731.

Mail Search: search usually completed- 1-7 days. Include SASE for return.

In Person Search: Fee charged if court performs your search. Self-serve copier available - $.25 per page.

E-Services: ECF replaces PACER whose records did go back to 6/1990. New records online after 1 day. ECF at https://ecf.ohnb.uscourts.gov **Opinions Online:** www.ohnb.uscourts.gov. These judges' postings include calendars and opinions.

Cleveland Division Court Clerk, 201 Superior Ave, E, Cleveland, OH 44114-1233 (also use mail address for courier delivery), 216-615-4300, Fax-216-615-4363. Hours- 9AM-4PM. www.ohnb.uscourts.gov

Counties: Cuyahoga, Geauga, Lake, Lorain.

Searches & Indexing: Results include SSN. Computer, microfiche and card indexes maintained. New cases in the index immediately after filing date. Records purged every few years. Prior to 1995, closed cases sent to Chicago Records Center; case records now sent to Dayton Records Center.

Fee & Payment: Pay by money order, personal check. No debtor's checks accepted. Payee: Clerk, US Bankruptcy Court.

Phone Search: Voice Case Information Service available, call VCIS at 800-898-6899 or 330-489-4731.

Mail Search: search usually completed- 1 week. Include SASE for return.

In Person Search: Fee charged if court performs your search. Outside copy service available. No self-serve copier available.

E-Services: ECF replaces PACER whose records did go back to 1/1985. New records online after 1 day. ECF at https://ecf.ohnb.uscourts.gov **Opinions Online:** www.ohnb.uscourts.gov. These judges' postings include calendars and opinions.

Toledo Division Court Clerk, Rm 411, 1716 Spielbusch Ave, Toledo, OH 43624 (also use mail address for courier delivery), 419-259-6440. Hours- 9AM-4PM. www.ohnb.uscourts.gov

Counties: Allen, Auglaize, Defiance, Erie, Fulton, Hancock, Hardin, Henry, Huron, Lucas, Marion, Mercer, Ottawa, Paulding, Putnam, Sandusky, Seneca, Van Wert, Williams, Wood, Wyandot.

Searches & Indexing: Results do not include SSN or DOB. Computer index maintained. After 2002 all cases on ECF; no paper files. New cases in the index immediately after filing date.

Fee & Payment: Pay by money order, cashier check, business check. No personal checks. Payee: Clerk, Bankruptcy Court. Prepayment required.

Phone Search: Voice Case Information Service available, call VCIS at 800-898-6899 or 330-489-4731.

Mail Search: search usually completed- within 2 days. Include SASE for return.

In Person Search: Fee charged if court performs your search. No self-serve copier available.

E-Services: ECF replaces PACER whose records did go back to 1/1985. New records online after 1 day. ECF at https://ecf.ohnb.uscourts.gov **Opinions Online:** www.ohnb.uscourts.gov. These judges' postings include calendars and opinions.

Youngstown Division Court Clerk, 10 E Commerce St, US Courthouse, Youngstown, OH 44501 (also use mail address for courier delivery), 330-746-7027. Hours- 9AM-4PM. www.ohnb.uscourts.gov

Counties: Ashtabula, Columbiana, Mahoning, Trumbull.

Searches & Indexing: Cases indexed by debtor, creditors, and case number. Results include last 4 SSN digits. A card index is maintained. New cases in the index 24 hours after filing date. Prior to 1995, closed cases sent to Chicago Records Center; case records now sent to Dayton Records Center every few years.

Fee & Payment: Pay by Visa/MC, money order, cashier check, business check. No personal checks. Payee: Clerk, US Bankruptcy Court. Prepayment required.

Phone Search: Voice Case Information Service available, call VCIS at 800-898-6899 or 330-489-4731.

Mail Search: search usually completed- 2 days. SASE not required.

In Person Search: Fee charged if court performs your search. No self-serve copier available.

E-Services: ECF replaces PACER whose records did go back to 1/1985. New records online after 1 day. ECF at https://ecf.ohnb.uscourts.gov **Opinions Online:** www.ohnb.uscourts.gov. These judges' postings include calendars and opinions.

US District Court

Southern District of Ohio

Cincinnati Division Clerk, US District Court, Potter Stewart Courthouse Rm 103, 100 E 5th St, Cincinnati, OH 45202 (also use mail address for courier delivery), 513-564-7500, Fax-513-564-7505. Hours- 8:30AM-5PM. www.ohsd.uscourts.gov

Counties: Adams, Brown, Butler, Clermont, Clinton, Hamilton, Highland, Lawrence, Scioto, Warren

Searches & Indexing: Results do not include SSN or DOB. Computer index maintained back to 1970. New cases in the index immediately after filing date. Records purged never.

Fee & Payment: Pay by Visa/MC, money order, cashier's or personal check, cash. Payee: Clerk, US District Court. Prepayment required. Give FedEx account number for expedited copy delivery.

Phone Search: Only docket information is available by phone.

Mail Search: search usually completed- 3-4 working days. SASE not required.

In Person Search: Fee charged if court performs your search. No self-serve copier available.

E-Services: ECF replaces PACER whose records did go back to 1994. New records online after 1 day. ECF at https://ecf.ohsd.uscourts.gov **Opinions Online:** www.ohsd.uscourts.gov/opinions.htm.

Columbus Division Court Clerk, Office of the Clerk, Rm 260, 85 Marconi Blvd, Columbus, OH 43215 (also use mail address for courier delivery), 614-719-3000, Fax-614-719-3005. Hours- 8AM-5PM. www.ohsd.uscourts.gov

Counties: Athens, Belmont, Coshocton, Delaware, Fairfield, Fayette, Franklin, Gallia, Guernsey, Harrison, Hocking, Jackson, Jefferson, Knox, Licking, Logan, Madison, Meigs, Monroe, Morgan, Morrow, Muskingum, Noble, Perry, Pickaway, Pike, Ross, Union, Vinton, Washington.

Searches & Indexing: Results do not include SSN or DOB. Computer, microfiche and card indexes maintained. Microfiche index goes back to 1982. New cases in the index 1-2 days after filing date. Records purged never. District-wide searches available here.

Fee & Payment: Pay by money order, cashier check, business check. No personal checks. Payee: Clerk, US District Court. Prepayment required.

Phone Search: Only docket information is available by phone.

Mail Search: search usually completed- 1-2 days. Include SASE for return.

In Person Search: Fee charged if court performs your search. No self-serve copier available.

E-Services: ECF replaces PACER whose records did go back to 1994. New records online after 1 day. ECF at https://ecf.ohsd.uscourts.gov **Opinions Online:** www.ohsd.uscourts.gov/opinions.htm.

Dayton Division Court Clerk Office, 200 W 2nd, Federal Bldg, Rm 712, Dayton, OH 45402 (also use mail address for courier delivery), 937-512-1400. 9AM-4PM. www.ohsd.uscourts.gov

Counties: Champaign, Clark, Darke, Greene, Miami, Montgomery, Preble, Shelby.

Searches & Indexing: Results do not include SSN or DOB. Both computer, microfiche and card indexes maintained. Computer has only open and pending cases back to 1/90. Public can use a view box for cases filed present-day. New cases in the index 1 day after filing date. Records purged never.

Fee & Payment: Pay by money order, cashier check, business check. No personal checks. Payee: Clerk, US District Court. Prepayment required. Provide a wide envelope for return of documents.

Phone Search: By phone, court only reveals whether a case has been filed. Court does not respond to phone requests involving copy work.

Mail Search: search usually completed- 1-2 days. Include SASE for return.

In Person Search: Fee charged if court performs your search. No self-serve copier available.

E-Services: ECF replaces PACER whose records did go back to 1994. New records online after 1 day. ECF at https://ecf.ohsd.uscourts.gov **Opinions Online:** www.ohsd.uscourts.gov/opinions.htm.

US Bankruptcy Court

Southern District of Ohio

Cincinnati Division Court Clerk, Atrium Two, Suite 800, 221 E Fourth St, Cincinnati, OH 45202 (also use mail address for courier delivery), 513-684-2572. Hours- 9AM-4PM. www.ohsb.uscourts.gov

Counties: Adams, Brown, Clermont, Hamilton, Highland, Lawrence, Scioto and part of Butler.

Searches & Indexing: Results include last 4 SSN digits. Computer index maintained. New cases in the index 2 days after filing date. Records purged every 6 months. Paper records kept 2 years.

Fee & Payment: Pay by Visa/MC - from law firms only, money order, cashier check, business check. No personal checks or debtor checks accepted. Payee: Clerk, US Bankruptcy Court.

Phone Search: Voice Case Information Service available, call VCIS at 800-726-1004 or 937-225-2544.

Mail Search: search usually completed- 1-2 days. Include SASE for return.

In Person Search: Fee charged if court performs your search. No self-serve copier available.

E-Services: ECF replaces PACER whose records did go back to 1990. New records online after 1 day. ECF at https://ecf.ohsb.uscourts.gov **Opinions Online:** www.ohsb.uscourts.gov/OHSB/OpNet/search.aspx. **Other Online Access:** PDF lists pf judges' current schedules free at www.ohsb.uscourts.gov/OHSB/hsnet/hearingschedulejudges.aspx.

Columbus Division Court Clerk, 170 N High St, Columbus, OH 43215 (also use mail address for courier delivery), 614-469-6638. Hours- 9AM-5PM. www.ohsb.uscourts.gov

Counties: Athens, Belmont, Coshocton, Delaware, Fairfield, Fayette, Franklin, Gallia, Guernsey, Harrison, Hocking, Jackson, Jefferson, Knox, Licking, Logan, Madison, Meigs, Monroe, Morgan, Morrow, Muskingum, Noble, Perry, Pickaway, Pike, Ross, Union, Vinton, Washington.

Searches & Indexing: Cases indexed by and case number. Results include last 4 SSN digits. Computer index maintained. New cases in the index 1 day after filing date. Records purged every 6 months.

Fee & Payment: Pay by money order, cashier check, business check. No personal or debtor's checks accepted. Payee: Clerk, US Bankruptcy Court.

Phone Search: Voice Case Information Service available, call VCIS at 800-726-1006.

Mail Search: search usually completed- 1-2 days. SASE not required.

In Person Search: permitted. Court also offers on-site copy service to provide copies, fee does not exceed $.50 per page. Call West Coast Copy Svc., 614-228-8812. No self-serve copier available.

E-Services: ECF replaces PACER whose records did go back to 1990. New records online after 1 day. ECF at https://ecf.ohsb.uscourts.gov **Opinions Online:** www.ohsb.uscourts.gov/OHSB/OpNet/search.aspx. **Other Online Access:** PDF lists pf judges' current schedules free at www.ohsb.uscourts.gov/OHSB/hsnet/hearingschedulejudges.aspx.

Dayton Division Court Clerk, 120 W 3rd St, Dayton, OH 45402 (also use mail address for courier delivery), 937-225-2516, Fax-937-225-7574. Hours- 9AM-4PM. www.ohsb.uscourts.gov

Counties: Butler, Champaign, Clark, Clinton, Darke, Greene, Miami, Montgomery, Preble, Shelby, Warren; parts of Butler County are handled by Cincinnati Division.

Searches & Indexing: Results include last 4 SSN digits. Computer index maintained. New cases in the index immediately after filing date. Records purged every 6 months.

Fee & Payment: Pay by money order, cashier check, in-state business check. No personal checks. Payee: Clerk, US Bankruptcy Court.

Phone Search: Only docket information is available by phone. Voice Case Information Service available, call VCIS at 800-726-1004 or 937-225-2544.

Mail Search: search usually completed- 1-2 days. Include SASE for return.

In Person Search: Fee charged if court performs your search. No self-serve copier available.

E-Services: ECF replaces PACER whose records did go back to 1990. New records online after 1 day. ECF at https://ecf.ohsb.uscourts.gov **Opinions Online:** www.ohsb.uscourts.gov/OHSB/OpNet/search.aspx. **Other Online Access:** PDF lists pf judges' current schedules free at www.ohsb.uscourts.gov/OHSB/hsnet/hearingschedulejudges.aspx

Ohio County Courts

Court	Jurisdiction	No. of Courts	How Organized
Court of Common Pleas*	General	88	county
County Courts*	Limited	47	
Municipal Courts*	Municipal	118	
Mayors Courts	Municipal	400	
Court of Claims	Special	1	

* Profiled in this Sourcebook.

Court	CIVIL								
	Tort	Contract	Real Estate	Min. Claim	Max. Claim	Small Claims	Estate	Eviction	Domestic Relations
Court of Common Pleas*	X	X	X	$3000/ $10,000	No Max		X		X
County Courts*	X	X	X	$0	$15,000	$3000		X	
Municipal Courts*	X	X	X	$0	$15,000	$3000		X	
Mayors Courts									
Court of Claims					No Max				

Court	CRIMINAL				
	Felony	Misdemeanor	DWI/DUI	Preliminary Hearing	Juvenile
Court of Common Pleas*	X		Juvenile		X
County Courts*		X	X	X	
Municipal Courts*		X	X	X	
Mayors Courts		X	X		
Court of Claims					

ADMINISTRATION Administrative Director, Supreme Court of Ohio, 65 S Front Street, Columbus, OH 43215-3431; 614-387-9000, Fax: 614-387-9419. www.sconet.state.oh.us

COURT STRUCTURE The Court of Common Pleas is the general jurisdiction court and County Courts have limited jurisdiction. Effective July 1, 1997, the dollar limits for civil cases in County and Municipal Courts were raised as follows: County Court - from $3,000 to $15,000; Municipal Court - from $10,000 to $15,000. In addition the small claims limit was raised from $2,000 to $3,000.

Effective in 2001, Ohio Common Pleas Courts may name their own civil action limits, though most of these courts elect not to make changes. In effect, these Common Pleas courts may take any civil cases. However, civil maximum limits for Ohio's County Courts and Municipal Courts remains the same: $15,000.

ONLINE ACCESS There is no statewide computer system, but a number of counties offer online access. Appellate and Supreme Court opinions may be researched from the web site.

PROBATE COURTS Probate courts are separate from the Court of Common Pleas, but Probate Court phone numbers are given with that court in each county.

Adams County

Common Pleas Court 110 W Main, Rm 207, West Union, OH 45693; phone: 937-544-2344; probate phone: 937-544-2921; fax: 937-544-8271; probate fax: 937-544-8911; hours 8:30AM-4PM (EST). *Felony, Civil Actions Over $3,000, Probate.*
Civil Records: Access: In person only. Visitors must perform in person searches themselves. Court makes copy: $.25 per page. Required to search: name, years to search. Civil cases indexed by defendant, plaintiff; on computer from 4/1993, prior in books, archived from 1910.
Criminal Records: Access: Mail, in person. Visitors must perform in person searches themselves. Search fee: $10.00 per name. Court makes copy: $.25 per page. Required to search: name, years to search, signed release; also helpful: DOB, SSN. Criminal records on computer from 4/93, prior in books, archived from 1910.
General Information: Public terminal goes back to 1993. Will fax documents to local or toll free line. Certification fee: $1.00 per page, includes copy. Payee: Clerk of Court. Personal checks accepted. Prepayment required.

County Court 110 W Main, Rm 25, West Union, OH 45693; phone: 937-544-2011; fax: 937-544-8911; hours 8AM-4PM (EST). *Misdemeanor, Civil Actions Under $15,000, Small Claims.*
Civil Records: Access: Mail, in person. Both court and visitors may perform in person searches. Search fee: $10.00 per name. Court makes copy: $.50 per page. Required to search: name, years to search. Civil cases indexed by defendant, plaintiff; on computer from 3/93, index from 1958, prior on dockets and microfilm. Mail turnaround 1-2 days.
Criminal Records: Access: Mail, in person. Both court and visitors may perform in person searches. Search fee: $10.00 per name. Court makes copy: $.50 per page. Required to search: name, years to search; also helpful: SSN. Criminal records on computer from 3/93, index from 1958, prior on dockets and microfilm. Mail turnaround time 1-2 days.
General Information: Public terminal goes back to 1993. Certification fee: $1.00. Payee: Adams County Court. Business checks accepted. Prepayment and SASE required.

Allen County

Common Pleas Court PO Box 1243, 301 N Main, Lima, OH 45802; phone: 419-228-3700; fax: 419-222-8427; hours 8AM-4:30PM (EST). *Felony, Civil Actions Over $15,000, Probate.*
www.co.allen.oh.us
Note: Probate is a separate court at this address.
Civil Records: Access: In person, online. Visitors must perform in person searches themselves. Court makes copy: $1.00 for first page, $.25 each add'l. Required to search: name; also helpful: years to search, address. Civil cases indexed by defendant, plaintiff; on computer back to 1986; in books and archived prior. Online access to civil records is the same as criminal, see below.
Criminal Records: Access: In person, online. Visitors must perform in person searches themselves. Court makes copy: $1.00 for first page, $.25 each add'l. Required to search: name, years to search; also helpful: address, DOB, SSN. Criminal records on computer back to 1986; in books and archived prior. Online access is free at http://65.17.134.12/pa/pa.urd/pamw6500.display. Records go back to 12/1/1988.
General Information: Public use terminal available. No secret indictment records released. Certification fee: $3.00. Payee: Clerk of Court. Personal checks accepted. Prepayment required.

Lima Municipal Court PO Box 1529, 109 N Union St, Lima, OH 45802; phone: 419-221-5275; civil phone: 419-221-5250; criminal fax: 419-998-5526; civil fax: 419-998-5517; hours 8AM-5PM (EST). *Misdemeanor, Civil Actions Under $15,000, Eviction, Small Claims.*
www.limamunicipalcourt.org
Civil Records: Access: Phone, fax, mail, in person, email, online. Both court and visitors may perform in person searches. No search fee. Court makes copy: $.25 per page. Required to search: name, years to search; also helpful: address. Civil cases indexed by defendant, plaintiff; on computer from 4/1990, microfilm from 1975, books and archived prior. Search index information from the website, click on Case Inquiry. Mail turnaround time same day.
Criminal Records: Access: Phone, fax, mail, in person, email, online. Both court and visitors may perform in person searches. No search fee. Court makes copy: $.25 per page. Required to search: name, years to search; also helpful: address, DOB, SSN. Criminal records on computer from 4/90, microfilm from 1975, books and archived prior. Search index information from the website, click on Case Inquiry. Mail turnaround time same day.
General Information: Public terminal goes back to 4/1990. Fee to fax documents is $.25 per page. Certification fee: $2.00. Payee: Clerk of Court. Business checks or Visa, MC accepted. Prepayment and SASE required.

Ashland County

Common Pleas Court 142 W 2nd St, Ashland, OH 44805; phone: 419-282-4242; probate phone: 419-282-4284; fax: 419-282-4240; hours 8AM-4PM (EST). *Felony, Civil Actions Over $10,000, Probate.*
www.ashlandcounty.org/clerkofcourts
Probate court is a separate court at the same address.
Civil Records: Access: In person, online. Visitors must perform in person searches themselves. Court makes copy: $.10 per page. Required to search: name or case number. Civil cases indexed by defendant, plaintiff; on microfilm from 1800s. Access records at www.ashlandcountycpcourt.org. Computerized court records go back to 6/7/1995.
Criminal Records: Access: In person, online. Visitors must perform in person searches themselves. No search fee. Court makes copy: $.10 per page. Required to search: name or case number. Criminal records on microfilm from 1800s. Access records at www.ashlandcountycpcourt.org. Computerized court records go back to 6/7/1995.
General Information: Public terminal goes back to 6/1995. Certification fee: $1.00 per page includes copy fee. Payee: Clerk of Court. Personal checks accepted. Prepayment required.

Ashland Municipal Court 1209 E Main St, Ashland, OH 44805; phone: 419-289-8137x; fax: 419-289-8545; hours 8AM-5PM (EST). *Misdemeanor, Civil Actions Under $15,000, Eviction, Small Claims.*
www.ashland-ohio.com
Civil Records: Access: Phone, mail, fax, in person. Both court and visitors may perform in person searches. No search fee. Court makes copy: $.10 per page. Required to search: name, years to search. Civil cases indexed by defendant, plaintiff; on docket keys from 1952, computerized since 1995. Mail turnaround time 1-3 days.
Criminal Records: Access: Phone, mail, fax, in person. Both court and visitors may perform in person searches. No search fee. Court makes copy: $.10 per page. Required to search: name, years to search, SSN. Criminal records on docket books from 1952, computerized since 1995. Mail turnaround time 1-3 days.
General Information: Public terminal goes back to 10/94. Fee to fax documents is $1.00 per page. Certification fee: $1.00. Payee: Municipal Court. Personal checks accepted. Prepayment and SASE required.

Ashtabula County

Common Pleas Court 25 W Jefferson St, Jefferson, OH 44047; phone: 440-576-3637; probate phone: 440-576-3451; fax: 440-567-2819; hours 8AM-N clerk hours (EST). *Felony, Civil Actions Over $10,000, Probate.* Probate is a separate office at the same location. Probate fax is 440-576-3633.
Civil Records: Access: In person. Visitors must perform in person searches themselves. Court makes copy: $.25 per page. Required to search: name, years to search; also helpful: address. Civil cases indexed by defendant, plaintiff; on computer back to 5/93, in books to the 1800s. Access to records are free at http://courts.co.ashtabula.oh.us/pa.htm.
Criminal Records: Access: In person, online. Visitors must perform in person searches themselves. No search fee. Court makes copy: $.25 per page. Required to search: name, years to search; also helpful: address, DOB, SSN. Criminal records on computer back to 5/93, in books to the 1800s. Access to records are free at http://courts.co.ashtabula.oh.us/pa.htm.
General Information: Public terminal goes back to 5/1993. No expungments released. Will not fax documents. Certification fee: $1.00 per page. Payee: Clerk of Court. Personal checks accepted. Prepayment required.

County Court Eastern Division 25 W Jefferson St, Jefferson, OH 44047; phone: 440-576-3617; fax: 440-576-3441; hours 8AM-4:30PM (EST). *Misdemeanor, Civil Actions Under $15,000, Eviction, Small Claims.*
www.ashtabula.oh.us
Civil Records: Access: Mail, fax, in person, online. Both court and visitors may perform in person searches. No search fee. Court makes copy: $.50 per page. Required to search: name, years to search. Civil cases indexed by defendant, plaintiff; on computer since 1/9/95; in books to 1960s. Access to records are free at http://courts.co.ashtabula.oh.us/pa.htm. Mail turnaround time 1-2 days.
Criminal Records: Access: Mail, fax, in person, online. Both court and visitors may perform in person searches. No search fee. Court makes copy: $.50 per page; same fee for self serve. Required to search: name, years to search, DOB or SSN. Criminal records on computer since 1/9/95; in books to 1960s. Access to records are free at http://courts.co.ashtabula.oh.us/pa.htm. Mail turnaround time 1-2 days.
General Information: Public terminal goes back to 1995. Fee to fax documents is $.50 per page. Certification fee: $1.50. Payee: Eastern County Court. Only cashiers checks and money orders accepted. Prepayment and SASE required.

County Court Western Division 117 W Main St, Geneva, OH 44041; phone: 440-466-1184; fax: 440-466-7171; hours 8AM-4:30PM Mon; 8AM-N T-F (EST). *Misdemeanor, Civil Actions Under $15,000, Small Claims.*
Civil Records: Access: In person, mail, fax, online. Visitors must perform in person searches themselves. No search fee. Court makes copy: $.25 per page. Required to search: name, years to search. Civil cases indexed by defendant, plaintiff; on computer back to 1995; prior records on docket books. Access to records is free at http://courts.co.ashtabula.oh.us/pa.htm. Mail turnaround time 72 hours.
Criminal Records: Access: In person, mail, fax, online. Visitors must perform in person searches themselves. No search fee. Court makes copy: $.25 per page. Required to search: name, years to search, DOB, SSN, signed release. Criminal records on computer back to 1995; prior records on docket books. Access to records is free at http://courts.co.ashtabula.oh.us/pa.htm. Mail turnaround time 72 hours.
General Information: Public terminal has criminal back to 1995 and civil back to 1995. No confidential records released. Will not fax documents. No certification fee . Payee: Western County Court. Only cashiers checks and money orders accepted. Prepayment and SASE required.

Ashtabula Municipal Court 110 W 44th St, Ashtabula, OH 44004; phone: 440-992-7110; fax: 440-998-5786; hours 8AM-4:30PM (EST). *Misdemeanor, Civil Actions Under $15,000, Eviction, Small Claims.*

www.ashtabulamunicipalcourt.com

Note: 440-992-7109 gives a directory.

Civil Records: Access: In person, online. Visitors must perform in person searches themselves. Court makes copy: $1.00 per page. Required to search: name, years to search. Civil cases indexed by defendant, plaintiff; on computer from 1992, books to 1971. Access to court cases free at web.

Criminal Records: Access: In person, online. Visitors must perform in person searches themselves. Court makes copy: $1.00 per page. Required to search: name, years to search, DOB, SSN, signed release. Criminal records on computer from 1992, books to 1971. Online access to court cases, including traffic, free at the webpage.

General Information: Public terminal goes back to 1988. No expunged records released. Will fax specific case files for $1.00 per document. Certification fee: $5.00 includes copy fee. Payee: Municipal Court. Personal checks accepted. Prepayment required.

Athens County

Common Pleas Court PO Box 290, Athens, OH 45701-0290; phone: 740-592-3242; probate phone: 740-592-3251; hours 8AM-4PM (EST). *Felony, Civil Actions Over $10,000, Probate.*

www.athenscountycpcourt.org

Civil Records: Access: In person, online. Visitors must perform in person searches themselves. Court makes copy: $.10 per page. Self serve copy fee: $.10 per page. Required to search: name, years to search; also helpful: address. Civil cases indexed by defendant, plaintiff; on computer back to 1/92; prior in books. Online access to the CP court records are free   at www.athenscountycpcourt.org/genrlmnu.htm.

Criminal Records: Access: In person, online. Visitors must perform in person searches themselves. Court makes copy: $.10 per page. Self serve copy fee: $.10 per page. Required to search: name, years to search; also helpful: address, DOB, SSN. Criminal records on computer back to 1/92; prior in books. Online access to criminal records is the same as civil.

General Information: Public terminal goes back to 1992. Certification fee: $1.00. Payee: Clerk of Court. Business checks accepted. Prepayment required.

Athens Municipal Court City Hall, 8 E Washington St, Athens, OH 45701; phone: 740-592-3328; fax: 740-592-3331; hours 8AM-4PM (EST). *Misdemeanor, Civil Actions Under $15,000, Eviction, Small Claims.*

Civil Records: Access: Mail, in person, online. Visitors must perform in person searches themselves. No search fee. Court makes copy: $.05 per page. Required to search: name, years to search; also helpful: address. Civil cases indexed by defendant, plaintiff; on computer back to 1994, prior in books. Search by name or case number at http://docket.webxsol.com/athens/index.html. Records available from 1992. Mail turnaround time 10 days.

Criminal Records: Access: Mail, in person, online. Visitors must perform in person searches themselves. No search fee. Court makes copy: $.05 per page. Required to search: name, years to search; also helpful: address, DOB, SSN. Criminal records on computer back to 7/1993, prior in books to 1974. Search by name or case number at http://docket.webxsol.com/athens/index.html. Records available from 1992. Mail turnaround time 10 days.

General Information: Public terminal goes back to 1988. No expunged or sealed records released. Certification fee: $1.00 per page. Payee: ACMC.

Personal checks or Visa, MC accepted. Prepayment required.

Auglaize County

Common Pleas Court PO Box 409, Wapakoneta, OH 45895; phone: 419-739-6765; probate phone: 419-739-6778; criminal fax: 419-738-7953; civil fax: 419-738-7953; probate fax: 419-739-7563; hours 8AM-4:30PM (EST). *Felony, Civil Actions Over $10,000, Probate.*

Note: Probate is a separate index at 201 Willippi St #103.

Civil Records: Access: In person only. Visitors must perform in person searches themselves. Court makes copy: $.25 per page. Required to search: name, years to search; also helpful: address. Civil cases indexed by defendant, plaintiff; on dockets from 1850, computerized since 2/00.

Criminal Records: Access: In person only. Visitors must perform in person searches themselves. Court makes copy: $.25 per page. Required to search: name, years to search; also helpful: address, DOB, SSN. Criminal records on dockets from 1850, computerized since 2/00.

General Information: Public terminal goes back to 2/2000. Fee to fax specific case file is $2.00 per page, plus $.25 each copy fee. Certification fee: $1.00 per document. Payee: Clerk of Court. Personal checks accepted. Prepayment required.

Auglaize County Municipal Court PO Box 409, Wapakoneta, OH 45895; criminal: 419-739-6766; civil: 419-739-7953; fax: 419-738-7953; hours 8AM-4:30PM (EST). *Misdemeanor, Civil Actions Under $15,000, Eviction, Small Claims.*

Civil Records: Access: In person only. Visitors must perform in person searches themselves. Court makes copy: $.25 per page. Required to search: name, years to search; also helpful: address. Civil cases indexed by defendant, plaintiff; on computer from 4/1994, docket back to 1976.

Criminal Records: Access: In person only. Visitors must perform in person searches themselves. Court makes copy: $.25 per page. Required to search: name, years to search, signed release; also helpful: address, DOB, SSN. Criminal records on computer from 10/1993, docket back to 1976.

General Information: Public terminal has criminal back to 1993 and civil back to 1994. No records released. Certification fee: $2.00. Payee: Clerk of Court. Personal checks accepted. Prepayment required.

Belmont County

Common Pleas Court Belmont County Clerk of Courts, Main St, Courthouse, St Clairsville, OH 43950; phone: 740-695-2121; civil phone: 740-695-2169; probate phone: 740-695-2121 X202; hours 8:30AM-4:30PM (EST). *Felony, Civil Actions Over $3,000, Probate.*

Civil Records: Access: Mail, in person. Both court and visitors may perform in person searches. Search fee: $3.00 per name. Court makes copy: $1.00 per page. Required to search: name, years to search. Civil cases indexed by defendant, plaintiff. Civil records in books, archived from 1896; computerized from 1995. Mail turnaround time 1 day.

Criminal Records: Access: Mail, in person. Both court and visitors may perform in person searches. Search fee: $3.00 per name. Court makes copy: $1.00 per page. Required to search: name, years to search. Criminal records in books, archived from 1896; computerized from 1995. Mail turnaround time 1 day.

General Information: Public terminal has criminal back to - not known and civil back to 5/1995. No secret criminal records released. Will fax documents to local or toll free line. Certification fee: $5.00. Payee: Clerk of Court. Personal checks accepted. Prepayment and SASE required.

County Court Eastern Division 400 W 26th St, Bellaire, OH 43906; phone: 740-676-4490; fax: 740-671-6100; hours 8AM-4PM (EST). *Misdemeanor, Civil Actions Under $15,000, Small Claims.*

Civil Records: Access: Mail, in person. Both court and visitors may perform in person searches. No search fee. No copy fee. Required to search: name, years to search. Civil cases indexed by defendant, plaintiff; on computer from 9/1994, books to 1950s. Mail access for attorneys only.

Criminal Records: Access: Mail, in person. Both court and visitors may perform in person searches. No search fee. No copy fee. Required to search: name, years to search; also helpful: DOB, SSN. Criminal records on computer from 9/1994, books to 1950s.

General Information: Public terminal goes back to 1994. No sealed or confidential records released. Certification fee: $1.00 per page. Payee: Eastern Division. Only cashiers checks and money orders accepted. Prepayment and SASE required.

County Court Northern Division PO Box 40, Martins Ferry, OH 43935; phone: 740-633-3147; fax: 740-633-6631; hours 8AM-4PM (EST). *Misdemeanor, Civil Actions Under $15,000, Small Claims.*

Civil Records: Access: Mail, fax, in person. Both court and visitors may perform in person searches. No search fee. Court makes copy: none; same fee for self serve. Required to search: name, years to search. Civil cases indexed by defendant, plaintiff; on computer from 6/1994, books to 1950s. Mail turnaround time 5-7 days.

Criminal Records: Access: Mail, fax, in person. Both court and visitors may perform in person searches. No search fee. Court makes copy: none; same fee for self serve. Required to search: name, years to search, DOB; also helpful: SSN, sex, signed release. Criminal records on computer from 6/1994, books to 1950s. Mail turnaround 5-7 days.

General Information: Public terminal goes back to 1999. Will fax documents for no fee. No certification fee .

County Court Western Division 147 W Main St, St Clairsville, OH 43950; phone: 740-695-2875; fax: 740-695-7285; hours 8AM-4PM (EST). *Misdemeanor, Civil Actions Under $15,000, Small Claims.*

Civil Records: Access: Fax, mail, in person. Both court and visitors may perform in person searches. No search fee. No copy fee. Required to search: name, years to search, address. Civil cases indexed by defendant, plaintiff; on computer from 1994, books to 1950s. Mail turnaround time 2 days.

Criminal Records: Access: Fax, mail, in person. Both court and visitors may perform in person searches. No search fee. No copy fee. Required to search: name, years to search, address, DOB, SSN. Criminal records on computer from 1994, books to 1950s. Mail turnaround time 1 week.

General Information: Public terminal goes back to 1994. Pending case information not released. No fee to fax documents. No certification fee . Payee: Western Division Court. Only cashiers checks, money orders accepted. Prepayment and SASE required.

Brown County

Common Pleas Court 101 S Main, Georgetown, OH 45121; phone: 937-378-3100; probate phone: 937-378-6549; fax: 937-378-4212; hours 7:30AM-4:30PM (EST). *Felony, Civil Actions Over $3,000, Probate.*

Civil Records: Access: in person only. Visitors must perform in person searches themselves. Court makes copy: $.10 per page; same fee for self serve. Required to search: name, years to search; also helpful: address. Civil cases indexed by defendant, plaintiff; on computer since 1995, in books to 1860s.

Criminal Records: Access: In person only. Visitors must perform in person searches themselves. Court makes copy: $.10 per page; same fee for self serve. Required to search: name, years to search; also helpful: address, DOB, SSN. Criminal records on computer since 1995, in books to 1860s.

General Information: Public terminal goes back to 1995. No criminal expungement records released. Will not fax specific case file. Certification fee: $1.00 per certification. Payee: Clerk of Court. Personal checks accepted. Prepayment required.

County Municipal Court 770 Mount Orab Pike, Georgetown, OH 45121; phone: 937-378-6358; hours 7:30AM-4:00PM (EST). *Misdemeanor, Civil Actions Under $15,000, Eviction, Small Claims.*

www.browncountycourt.org

Civil Records: Access: Mail, in person, online. Both court and visitors may perform in person searches. No search fee. Court makes copy: $.10 per page. Required to search: name, years to search. Civil cases indexed by defendant, plaintiff. Civil records in books to 1958, computerized since 1995. Access free at www.browncountycourt.org/search.html.

Criminal Records: Access: Mail, in person, online. Both court and visitors may perform in person searches. No search fee. Court makes copy: $.10 per page. Required to search: name, years to search, DOB; also helpful: SSN. Criminal records in books to 1958, computerized since 1995. Access free at www.browncountycourt.org/search.html.

General Information: Public terminal goes back to 1995. Will not fax documents. No certification fee . Payee: Brown County Municipal Court. Only cashiers checks and money orders accepted. Prepayment and SASE required.

Butler County

Common Pleas Court 315 High St, General Division, Government Services Ctr, 3rd Fl, Hamilton, OH 45011; phone: 513-887-3278; probate phone: 513-887-3294; fax: 513-887-3089; hours 8:30AM-4:30PM (EST). *Felony, Civil Actions Over $3,000, Probate.*

www.butlercountyclerk.org

Note: Government Service Center phone number is 513-887-3288.

Civil Records: Access: Online, in person. Visitors must perform in person searches themselves. Court makes copy: $.25 per page. Required to search: name, years to search. Civil cases indexed by defendant, plaintiff; on computer from 1988, records go back to 1987. Access to records free at www.butlercountyclerk.org/pa/pa.urd/pamw6500-display. Search by name, dates, or case number and type. Access to Probate Court records free at http://66.117.197.22/index.cfm?page=courtRecords Search the Estate or Guardianship databases.

Criminal Records: Access: Online, in person. Visitors must perform in person searches themselves. Court makes copy: $.25 per page. Required to search: name, years to search, DOB; also helpful: SSN. Criminal records on computer from 1988, prior in books. Online access to criminal records is the same as civil.

General Information: Public terminal goes back to 4/1988. Certification fee: $2.00. Cert fee includes copy fee, fee is per page. Payee: Butler County Clerk of Court. Personal checks accepted. Prepayment required.

County Court Area #1 118 W High, Oxford, OH 45056; phone: 513-523-4748; fax: 513-523-4737; hours 8AM-5PM (EST). *Misdemeanor, Civil Actions Under $15,000, Small Claims.*

Civil Records: Access: Phone, mail, in person. Both court and visitors may perform in person searches. No search fee. No copy fee. Required to search: name, years to search. Civil cases indexed by defendant, plaintiff; on index back to 1983. Mail turnaround time 3 days.

Criminal Records: Access: Mail, in person, phone. Both court and visitors may perform in person searches. No search fee. No copy fee. Required to search: name, years to search, DOB. Criminal records on index back to 1983. Mail turnaround 1-5 days.

General Information: Public terminal goes back to 1993. No sealed records released. No certification fee . SASE required.

County Court Area #2 Butler County Courthouse, 101 High St, 1st Fl, Hamilton, OH 45011; phone: 513-887-3459; fax: 513-887-3568; hours 8AM-5PM (EST). *Misdemeanor, Civil Actions Under $15,000, Small Claims.*

Note: Probate is a separate index located on Courthouse 2nd Fl.

Civil Records: Access: Phone, in person. Visitors must perform in person searches themselves. No search fee. No copy fee. Required to search: name, years to search. Civil cases indexed by defendant, plaintiff; on computer from 1993, books to 1983.

Criminal Records: Access: Phone, in person, mail. Visitors must perform in person searches themselves. No search fee. No copy fee. Required to search: name, years to search. Criminal records on computer from 1993, books to 1983. Mail turnaround time 2 days.

General Information: Public terminal goes back to 1993. No sealed records released. No certification fee . Only cashiers checks and money orders accepted. Prepayment and SASE required.

County Court Area #3 9577 Beckett Rd #300, West Chester, OH 45069; phone: 513-867-5070; fax: 513-777-0558; hours 8:AM-5PM (EST). *Misdemeanor, Civil Actions Under $15,000, Small Claims.*

Civil Records: Access: Mail, in person. Both court and visitors may perform in person searches. No search fee. Court makes copy: $.10 per page. Required to search: name, years to search. Civil cases indexed by defendant, plaintiff; on computer from 1993, books to 1983. Mail turnaround 2-3 days.

Criminal Records: Access: Mail, in person. Both court and visitors may perform in person searches. No search fee. No copy fee. Required to search: name, years to search. Criminal records on computer from 1993, books to 1983. Mail turnaround 2-3 days.

General Information: Public terminal goes back to 7/1993. Certification fee: $1.00. Payee: Area #3 Court. Personal checks accepted. Prepayment and SASE required.

Hamilton Municipal Court 345 High St, #2, Hamilton, OH 45011; phone: 513-785-7300; fax: 513-785-7315; hours 8AM-5PM (EST). *Misdemeanor, Civil Actions Under $15,000, Small Claims.*

www.hamiltonmunicipalcourt.org

Civil Records: Access: Mail, in person, online. Both court and visitors may perform in person searches. No search fee. Court makes copy: $.05 per page. Required to search: name, years to search. Civil cases indexed by defendant, plaintiff; on computer from 1993, books to 1983. Record access free at www.hamiltonmunicipalcourt.org.

Criminal Records: Access: Mail, in person, online. Both court and visitors may perform in person searches. No search fee. Court makes copy: $.05 per page. Required to search: name, years to search. Criminal records on computer from 1993, books to 1983. Record access free at www.hamiltonmunicipalcourt.org.

General Information: Public terminal goes back to 1992. No sealed records released. Will fax documents to local or toll free line. No certification fee . Prepayment required.

Carroll County

Common Pleas Court PO Box 367, Carrollton, OH 44615; phone: 330-627-4886; probate phone: 330-627-2323; fax: 330-627-6437; hours 8AM-4PM (EST). *Felony, Civil Actions Over $15,000, Probate.*

Note: Probate Court address is 119 Public Sq, Courthouse, Carrollton, OH.

Civil Records: Access: In person only. Visitors must perform in person searches themselves. Court makes copy: $.05 per page. Required to search: name,

years to search. Civil cases indexed by defendant, plaintiff. Civil records in books to 1900s.

Criminal Records: Access: In person only. Visitors must perform in person searches themselves. Court makes copy: $.05 per page. Required to search: name, years to search; also helpful: DOB, SSN. Criminal records in books to 1900s.

General Information: Public terminal goes back to 3/2000. Will fax specific case file for $2.00 for 1st page plus $1.00 each add'l page. Certification fee: $1.00 per document. Payee: Clerk of Court. Personal checks accepted in person with photo ID. Prepayment required.

County Court 119 S Lisbon St, #301, Carrollton, OH 44615; phone: 330-627-5049; fax: 330-627-3662; hours 8AM-4PM (EST). *Misdemeanor, Civil Actions Under $15,000, Small Claims, Evictions.*

Civil Records: Access: In person only. Visitors must perform in person searches themselves. Court makes copy: $.25 per page. Required to search: name, years to search. Civil cases indexed by defendant, plaintiff. Civil records in books from 1958; on computer since 11/95.

Criminal Records: Access: In person only. Visitors must perform in person searches themselves. Court makes copy: $.25 per page. Required to search: name, years to search, DOB. Criminal records in books from 1958; on computer since 11/95.

General Information: Public terminal goes back to 1995. No confidential records released. Certification fee: $2.00. Payee: Carroll County Court. Personal checks accepted. Prepayment required.

Champaign County

Common Pleas Court 200 N Main St, Urbana, OH 43078; phone: 937-484-1000; criminal phone: 937-484-1047; civil phone: 937-484-1047; probate phone: 937-484-1028; hours 8AM-4PM (EST). *Felony, Civil Actions Over $10,000, Probate.*

Civil Records: Access: Phone, mail, in person. Visitors must perform in person searches themselves. No search fee. Court makes copy: $.25 per page. Required to search: name, years to search. Civil cases indexed by defendant, plaintiff; on computer from 6/92, books to late 1800s. Will only do phone or mail searches with a case number. Even in this situation, requesters are limited to 10 files per month if acting as a retriever.

Criminal Records: Access: Phone, mail, in person. Visitors must perform in person searches themselves. No search fee. Court makes copy: $.25 per page. Required to search: name, years to search, DOB, SSN, signed release. Criminal records on computer from 6/92, books to late 1800s. Will only do mail or phone searches with a case number. Even in this situation, requesters are limited to 10 files per month if acting as a retriever.

General Information: Public terminal goes back to 1992. All records are public. Will fax documents for $1.00 per page fee. Certification fee: $1.00 per certification. Payee: Clerk of Court. Personal checks over $10.00 not accepted. Prepayment and SASE required.

Champaign County Municipal Court PO Box 85, Urbana, OH 43078; phone: 937-653-7376; hours 8AM-4PM (EST). *Misdemeanor, Civil Actions Under $15,000, Eviction, Small Claims.*

Civil Records: Access: Mail, in person. Both court and visitors may perform in person searches. No search fee. Court makes copy: $.25 per page. Required to search: name, years to search. Civil cases indexed by defendant, plaintiff; on computer from 6/1993, books to late 1800s. Mail turnaround 2-3 days.

Criminal Records: Access: Mail, in person. Both court and visitors may perform in person searches. No search fee. Court makes copy: $.25 per page. Required to search: name, years to search; also helpful: DOB, SSN. Criminal records on computer from 6/1993, books to late 1800s. Mail turnaround time 2-3 days.

General Information: No public access terminal. No sealed records released. Will not fax documents. Certification fee: $2.50 per page includes copies. Payee: Municipal Court. Only cashiers checks and money orders accepted. Prepayment and SASE required.

Clark County

Common Pleas Court 101 N Limestone St, Springfield, OH 45502; phone: 937-328-2458; 937-328-4648 (Domestic); probate phone: 937-328-2434; fax: 937-328-2436; hours 8AM-4:30PM (EST). *Felony, Civil Actions Over $10,000, Probate.* www.clarkcountyohio.gov/courts/index.htm
Note: Probate Court and records at 50 W Columbia St, 5th Fl.
Civil Records: Access: In person, online. Visitors must perform in person searches themselves. Court makes copy: $.25 per page. Required to search: name, years to search. Civil cases indexed by defendant. Civil records on computer back to 1990, prior in index books. Online access to clerk's records is free at http://12.150.181.49/.
Criminal Records: Access: In person, online. Visitors must perform in person searches themselves. Court makes copy: $.25 per page. Required to search: name, years to search. Criminal records on computer back to 1990, prior in index books. Online access to clerk's records are free at http://12.150.181.49/. The Sheriff's most wanted list is found at www.clarkcountysheriff.com.
General Information: Public terminal goes back to 1990. Will fax specific case file requests for $2.00 fee. Certification fee: $1.00. Payee: Clerk of Court. Business checks accepted. Prepayment required.

Clark County Municipal Court 50 E Columbia St, Springfield, OH 45502; phone: 937-328-3700; criminal phone: 937-328-3726; civil phone: 937-328-3715; hours 8AM-5PM (EST). *Misdemeanor, Civil Actions Under $15,000, Eviction, Small Claims.*
www.clerkofcourts.municipal.co.clark.oh.us
Civil Records: Access: Phone, mail, in person, online. Both court and visitors may perform in person searches. No search fee. Court makes copy: $.50 per page. Self serve copy fee: none. Required to search: name, years to search. Civil cases indexed by defendant, plaintiff; on computer since 5/90; prior records go back to 6/87. Online access to case information is free at www.clerkofcourts.municipal.co.clark.oh.us/web/welcome.nsf/HomePage?OpenForm. Images available back to 1/2003. Name searching on "New Cases;" other types require a case number. Records available since 03/90. Mail turnaround time 2-3 days.
Criminal Records: Access: Mail, in person, online. Both court and visitors may perform in person searches. No search fee. Court makes copy: $.50 per page. Self serve copy fee: none. Required to search: name, years to search; also helpful: DOB, SSN. Criminal records on computer since 3/90; prior records go back to 6/87. Access to criminal records is the same as civil. Mail turnaround time 2-3 days.
General Information: Public terminal goes back to 5/1990. Will fax documents in an emergency only. Certification fee: $2.00 includes copy fee. Payee: Clerk of Court. Personal checks not accepted. Prepayment and SASE required.

Clermont County

Common Pleas Court 270 Main St, Batavia, OH 45103; phone: 513-732-7130; probate phone: 513-732-7243; fax: 513-732-7050; hours 8:30AM-4:30PM (EST). *Felony, Civil Actions Over $10,000, Probate.* Probate court is located at 76 S Riverside Dr, Batavia 45103.
Civil Records: Access: In person, online. Visitors must perform in person searches themselves. Court makes copy: $.10 per page. Required to search: name, years to search; also helpful: address. Civil cases indexed by defendant, plaintiff; on computer from

1987, some on microfiche from 1920s, index books from 1959. Online access to civil records is the same as criminal, see following.
Criminal Records: Access: In person, online. Visitors must perform in person searches themselves. Court makes copy: $.10 per page. Required to search: name, years to search, DOB; also helpful: address, SSN. Criminal records on computer from 1987, some on microfiche from 1920s, index books from 1959. Online access to court records is free at www.clermontclerk.org/Case_Access.htm. Online records go back to 1/1998. Includes later Municipal Court records. Note: Clerk refers criminal record requests to the Sheriff (513-732-7500) who will do searches for $20.00 per name.
General Information: Public terminal goes back to 1987. Certification fee: $1.00 per page. Payee: Clerk of Court. Business checks accepted. Prepayment required.

Clermont County Municipal Court 4430 State Rt 222, Batavia, OH 45103; criminal phone: 513-732-7290; civil phone: 513-732-7292; fax: 513-732-7831; hours 8AM-5PM (EST). *Misdemeanor, Civil Actions Under $15,000, Eviction, Small Claims.*
www.clermontclerk.org
Civil Records: Access: Mail, in person, online. Visitors must perform in person searches themselves. No search fee. Court makes copy: $.25 per page. Required to search: name, years to search. Civil cases indexed by defendant, plaintiff. Computerized records from 5/96, civil records in books and microfiche from 1959, docket books to 1800s. Online access to court records is the same as criminal, see following.
Criminal Records: Access: Mail, in person, online. Visitors must perform in person searches themselves. No search fee. Court makes copy: $.25 per page. Required to search: name, years to search, DOB; also helpful: SSN. Computerized records back to 5/96, criminal records in books and microfiche from 1957, docket books to 1800s. Online access to court records is free at www.clermontclerk.org/Case_Access.htm. Online records go back to 5/1/1996. Includes Common Pleas court records.
General Information: Public use terminal available. Certification fee: $4.00. Payee: Clerk of Court. Only cashiers checks and money orders accepted. Prepayment and SASE required.

Clinton County

Common Pleas Court 46 S South St, Wilmington, OH 45177; phone: 937-382-2316; probate phone: 937-382-2280; fax: 937-383-3455; probate fax: 937-383-1158; hours 7:30AM-4:30PM (EST). *Felony, Civil Actions Over $15,000, Probate.* Note: Probate fax is 937-383-1158; hours are 8AM-4:30PM.
Civil Records: Access: Fax, mail, in person. Both court and visitors may perform in person searches. No search fee. Court makes copy: $.25 per page. Required to search: name, years to search; also helpful: address. Civil cases indexed by defendant, plaintiff; on computer since 1995; prior in books to 1810. Mail turnaround time 1 week.
Criminal Records: Access: Mail, in person. Both court and visitors may perform in person searches. Search fee: $5.00 per name. Court makes copy: $.25 per page. Required to search: name, years to search, DOD, SSN; also helpful: address. Criminal records on computer since 1995; prior in books to 1810. Mail turnaround time 1 week.
General Information: Public terminal goes back to 1995. No confidential records released. Will fax documents for $5.00 per name. Certification fee: $1.00. Payee: Clerk of Court. Personal checks accepted. Prepayment and SASE required.

Clinton County Municipal Court 69 N South St, PO Box 71, Wilmington, OH 45177; phone: 937-382-8985; fax: 937-383-0130; hours 8AM-4PM (EST). *Misdemeanor, Civil Actions Under $15,000, Eviction, Small Claims.*
Civil Records: Access: Fax, mail, in person, online. Both court and visitors may perform in person searches. No search fee. Court makes copy: $.25 per page. Required to search: name, years to search. Civil cases indexed by defendant, plaintiff. Civil records in books from 1960; computerized records go back to 1995. Search court records online at www.clintonmunicourt.org/search.html. Mail turnaround time 1 day.
Criminal Records: Access: Fax, mail, in person, online. Both court and visitors may perform in person searches. No search fee. Court makes copy: $.25 per page. Required to search: name, years to search, DOB; also helpful: SSN. Criminal records in books from 1960; computerized records go back to 1995. Search court records online at www.clintonmunicourt.org/search.html. Mail turnaround time 1 day.
General Information: Public terminal goes back to 1994. Will fax documents to local or toll free line. No certification fee . Payee: Clerk of Court. Only cashiers checks and money orders accepted. Prepayment and SASE required.

Columbiana County

Common Pleas Court 105 S Market St, Lisbon, OH 44432; phone: 330-424-7777; fax: 330-424-3960; hours 8AM-4PM (EST). *Felony, Civil Actions Over $15,000, Probate.*
www.ccclerk.org
Civil Records: Access: In person, online. Visitors must perform in person searches themselves. Court makes copy: $.05 per page; same fee for self serve. Required to search: name, years to search; also helpful: address. Civil cases indexed by defendant, plaintiff; on computer since 1993; prior in books from 1968, archived back to 1800s. Access free to index civil docket records and probate at www.ccclerk.org/case_access.htm.
Criminal Records: Access: In person, online. Visitors must perform in person searches themselves. No search fee. Court makes copy: $.05 per page; same fee for self serve. Required to search: name, years to search, DOB; also helpful: address, SSN. Criminal records on computer since 1993; prior in books from 1968, archived back to 1800s. Free online access to all county court index and docket records is at www.ccclerk.org/case_access.htm.
General Information: Public terminal goes back to 03/93. Certification fee: $1.00 per page. Payee: Clerk of Court. Personal checks accepted. Prepayment required.

Municipal Court Eastern Area 31 N Market St, East Palestine, OH 44413; phone: 330-426-3774; fax: 330-426-6328; hours 8AM-4PM (EST). *Misdemeanor, Civil Actions Under $15,000, Small Claims.*
www.ccclerk.org/the_courts.htm
Civil Records: Access: In person, online. Visitors must perform in person searches themselves. Court makes copy: $.25 per page. Required to search: name, years to search. Civil cases indexed by defendant, plaintiff. Civil records in books from 1950s, archived from 1800s, recent records computerized. Online access free to all county court index and docket records at www.ccclerk.org/the_courts.htm.
Criminal Records: Access: In person, online. Visitors must perform in person searches themselves. No search fee. Court makes copy: $.25 per page. Required to search: name, years to search. Criminal records in books from 1950s, archived from 1800s, recent records computerized. Free online access to all county court index and docket records at www.ccclerk.org/the_courts.htm.
General Information: Public terminal goes back to 1994. Will fax specific case file requests to toll-free line. Certification fee: $1.00 per page. Payee: Clerk of

Court. Only cashiers checks and money orders accepted. Prepayment required.

Municipal Court Northwest Area 130 Penn Ave, Salem, OH 44460; phone: 330-332-0297; fax: 330-332-0904; hours 8AM-4PM (EST). *Misdemeanor, Civil Actions Under $15,000, Small Claims.*

www.ccclerk.org

Civil Records: Access: In person, online. Both court and visitors may perform in person searches. Court makes copy: $.25 per page. Required to search: name, years to search. Civil cases indexed by defendant, plaintiff. Civil records in books from 1950s, archived from 1800s, computerized since 11/94. Online access free to all county court index and docket records at www.ccclerk.org/the_courts.htm.

Criminal Records: Access: Mail, in person, online. Both court and visitors may perform in person searches. No search fee. Court makes copy: $.25 per page. Required to search: name, years to search; also helpful: DOB. Criminal records in books from 1950s, archived from 1800s, computerized back to 11/94. Free online access to all county court index and docket records at www.ccclerk.org/the_courts.htm. Mail turnaround time 2-3 days.

General Information: Public terminal goes back to 11/1994. (Some older cases may be available if any subsequent action has taken place.) Will only fax to government agencies. Certification fee: $1.00 per page includes copy fee. Payee: Northwest Area Court. Only cashiers checks and money orders accepted. Prepayment and SASE required.

Municipal Court Southwest Area 41 N Park Ave, Lisbon, OH 44432; phone: 330-424-5326; fax: 330-424-6658; hours 8AM-4PM (EST). *Misdemeanor, Civil Actions Under $15,000, Small Claims.*

www.ccclerk.org/the_courts.htm

Civil Records: Access: In person, online. Visitors must perform in person searches themselves. Court makes copy: $.50 per page. Self serve copy fee: $.05 per page. Required to search: name, years to search. Civil cases indexed by defendant, plaintiff. Civil records in books from 1950s, archived back to 1800s; on computer back to 1994. Online access free to all county court index and docket records at www.ccclerk.org/the_courts.htm.

Criminal Records: Access: In person, online. Visitors must perform in person searches themselves. No search fee. Court makes copy: $.50 per page. Self serve copy fee: $.05 per page. Required to search: name, years to search; also helpful: DOB, SSN. Criminal records in books from 1950s, archived back to 1800s; on computer back to 1994. Free online access to all county court index and docket records at www.ccclerk.org/the_courts.htm.

General Information: Public terminal goes back to 1994. No expungment records released. Will not fax documents. Certification fee: $1.00 per page. Payee: Southwest Court. Only cashiers checks and money orders accepted. Prepayment required.

East Liverpool Municipal Court 126 W 6th St, East Liverpool, OH 43920; phone: 330-385-5151; fax: 330-385-1566; hours 8AM-4PM (EST). *Misdemeanor, Civil Actions Under $15,000, Eviction, Small Claims.*

www.eastliverpool.com/court.html

Civil Records: Access: Phone, fax, mail, in person, online. Both court and visitors may perform in person searches. No search fee. Court makes copy: $.25 per page. Required to search: name, years to search. Civil cases indexed by defendant, plaintiff. Civil records in books from 1968, archived back to 1800s, computerized since 11/92. Online access free to all county court index and docket records at www.ccclerk.org/the_courts.htm. Mail turnaround time 1-2 days.

Criminal Records: Access: Phone, fax, mail, in person, online. Both court and visitors may perform in person searches. No search fee. Court makes copy: $.25 per page. Required to search: name, years

to search, signed release; also helpful: DOB, SSN. Criminal records in books from 1968, archived back to 1800s, computerized since 11/92. Free access to all county court index at www.ccclerk.org/the_courts.htm. Mail turnaround time 1-2 days.

General Information: Public terminal goes back to 1992. No expungment records released. No fee to fax documents. Certification fee: $3.00 each includes copy fee. Copy fee may also apply if more than 4 pages. Payee: East Liverpool Municipal Court. No business or personal checks accepted. Prepayment and SASE required.

Coshocton County

Common Pleas Court 318 Main St, Coshocton, OH 43812; phone: 740-622-1456; probate phone: 740-622-1837; probate fax: 740-623-6514; hours 8AM-4PM (EST). *Felony, Civil Actions Over $10,000, Probate.*

Note: Probate is a separate index at 426 Main St.

Civil Records: Access: Mail, in person. Both court and visitors may perform in person searches. No search fee. Court makes copy: $.25 per page; same fee for self serve. Required to search: name, years to search. Civil cases indexed by defendant, plaintiff. Civil records in books, microfilm back to 1985, archived back to 1800s; on computer back to 1998. Mail turnaround time 2 days.

Criminal Records: Access: Mail, in person. Both court and visitors may perform in person searches. No search fee. Court makes copy: $.25 per page; same fee for self serve. Required to search: name, years to search, DOB; also helpful: SSN. Criminal records in books, microfilm back to 1985, archived back to 1800s; on computer back to 1998. Mail turnaround time 2 days.

General Information: Public terminal goes back to 1998. No expunged records released. Will not fax documents. Certification fee: $1.00 per page. Payee: Clerk of Court. Personal checks accepted. Prepayment required.

Coshocton Municipal Court 760 Chesnut St, Coshocton, OH 43812; phone: 740-622-2871; fax: 740-623-5928; hours 8AM-4:30PM M-W F; 8AM-N Th (EST). *Misdemeanor, Civil Actions Under $15,000, Eviction, Small Claims.*

www.coshoctonmunicipalcourt.com

Civil Records: Access: Phone, fax, mail, in person, online. Both court and visitors may perform in person searches. No search fee. Court makes copy: $1.00 per page. Required to search: name, years to search. Civil cases indexed by defendant, plaintiff; on computer from 1989, books to 1952. Online access to civil records at website. Search by name, case number, attorney, date. Mail turnaround same day.

Criminal Records: Access: Phone, fax, mail, in person, online. Both court and visitors may perform in person searches. No search fee. Court makes copy: $1.00 per page. Required to search: name, years to search; also helpful: DOB, SSN. Criminal records on computer from 1989, books to 1952. Online access to criminal records is the same as civil. Search by name, attorney, citation or case number. Mail turnaround time same day.

General Information: Public terminal goes back to 1989. No expunged records released. No fee to fax documents. Certification fee: $5.00. Payee: Clerk of Court. Personal checks accepted. Prepayment required. SASE requested.

Crawford County

Common Pleas Court 112 E Mansfield St, #204, Bucyrus, OH 44820; phone: 419-562-2766; probate phone: 419-562-8891; fax: 419-562-8011; probate fax: 419-563-1920; hours 8:30AM-4:30PM (EST). *Felony, Civil Actions Over $3,000, Probate.*

www.crawford-co.org/Clerk/default.html

Note: Probate is a separate index, separate office-Probate Court.

Civil Records: Access: Phone, mail, in person, online. Both court and visitors may perform in

person searches. No search fee. No copy fee. Required to search: name, years to search. Civil cases indexed by defendant, plaintiff; on computer back to 1990, some on microfiche and index books from 1800s. Online access to Common Pleas court records is free at www.crawford-co.org/Clerk/default.html and click on "Internet Inquiry." Mail turnaround time usually same day.

Criminal Records: Access: Mail, in person, online. Both court and visitors may perform in person searches. No search fee. No copy fee. Required to search: name, years to search, DOB, SSN. Criminal records on computer back to 1990, some on microfiche and index books from 1800s. Online access to criminal cases is the same as civil. Mail turnaround time 1-2 days.

General Information: Public terminal goes back to 2/1990. No divorce investigations. Will fax documents for no fee. Certification fee: $1.00 per page includes copy fee. Payee: Clerk of Court. Personal checks accepted. Prepayment and SASE required.

Crawford County Municipal Court PO Box 550, Bucyrus, OH 44820; phone: 419-562-2731; fax: 419-562-7064; hours 8:30AM-4:30PM (EST). *Misdemeanor, Civil Actions Under $15,000, Eviction, Small Claims.*

Civil Records: Access: Phone, fax, mail, in person. Both court and visitors may perform in person searches. No search fee. Court makes copy: $.10 per page. Required to search: name, years to search. Civil cases indexed by defendant, plaintiff. Civil records in books to 1978. Mail turnaround within 1 week.

Criminal Records: Access: Mail, in person. Both court and visitors may perform in person searches. No search fee. Court makes copy: $.10 per page. Required to search: name, years to search, DOB. Criminal records in books to 1978; on computer back to 1996. Mail turnaround time within 1 week.

General Information: Public terminal goes back to 1996. No counseling report records released. Will fax documents to toll free line. Certification fee: $2.00. Crawford county business checks accepted. Prepayment required.

Crawford County Municipal Court Eastern Division 301 Harding Way E, Galion, OH 44833; phone: 419-468-6819; fax: 419-468-6828; hours 8AM-5PM (EST). *Misdemeanor, Civil Actions Under $15,000, Eviction, Small Claims.*

Civil Records: Access: Mail, in person. Both court and visitors may perform in person searches. No search fee. Court makes copy: $.10 per page. Required to search: name, years to search. Civil cases indexed by defendant, plaintiff. Civil records in books to 1800s. Mail turnaround time 2-3 days.

Criminal Records: Access: Mail, in person. Both court and visitors may perform in person searches. No search fee. Court makes copy: $.10 per page. Required to search: name, years to search, DOB, SSN, signed release. Criminal records in books to 1800s. Mail turnaround time 2-3 days.

General Information: Public terminal goes back to 1996. Certification fee: $3.00. Payee: Municipal Court. Only cashiers checks and money orders accepted. Prepayment and SASE required.

Cuyahoga County

Common Pleas Court - General Division 1200 Ontario St, Cleveland, OH 44113; phone: 216-443-8560; criminal phone: 216-443-7985; civil phone: 216-443-7960; probate phone: 216-443-8764; fax: 216-443-5424; hours 8:30AM-4:30PM (EST). *Felony, Civil Actions Over $10,000, Probate.*

www.cuyahoga.oh.us/common/default.htm

Note: Probate is a separate division with separate records and personnel.

Civil Records: Access: Phone, mail, in person, online. Both court and visitors may perform in person searches. Search fee: $5.00 per name. Court makes copy: $.25 per page. Required to search: name, years to search; also helpful: address. Civil cases indexed by defendant, plaintiff; on index and dockets from 1968, archived from 1800s; computerized since 1975. Online access to Common Please civil courts; click on Civil Case Dockets at http://cpdocket.cuyahoga.oh.us/cjisjs/servlet/cjis.urd/run/cmsw101. Access or Probate is at http://probate.cuyahogacounty.us/pa/. Note: Phone requests to 216-443-7966. Address mail requests to Gerald Fuerst, 1st Floor, Index Dept.

Criminal Records: Access: In person, online. Visitors must perform in person searches themselves. Court makes copy: $.25 per page. Required to search: name, years to search; also helpful: address, DOB, SSN. Criminal records on index and dockets from 1968, archived from 1800s; computerized since 1975. Online access to criminal records dockets is free at http://cpdocket.cuyahoga.oh.us/cjisjs/servlet/cjis.urd/run/cmsw101. Note: Criminal Dept on 2nd Floor. Any phone requests must have case number.

General Information: Public terminal goes back to 1970. No expungments or sealed records released. Certification fee: $1.00 per page. Payee: Clerk of Court. Business checks accepted. Prepayment and SASE required.

Cleveland Municipal Court - Civil Division
1200 Ontario St, Cleveland, OH 44113; phone: 216-664-4870; fax: 216-664-4065; hours 8AM-3:50PM (EST). *Civil Actions Under $15,000, Eviction, Small Claims.*

http://clevelandmunicipalcourt.org/home.html
Note: Court plans to have online access to case information.

Civil Records: Access: Fax, mail, in person. Both court and visitors may perform in person searches. Court makes copy: $.25 per page. Required to search: name, years to search; also helpful: address. Civil cases indexed by defendant, plaintiff; on computer from 1988, docket books and index from 1950s, prior archived. Mail turnaround time 2 days.

General Information: Public terminal has civil records back to 1990. Certification fee: $1.00 per page. Payee: Municipal Court. Personal checks accepted. Prepayment and SASE required.

Cleveland Municipal Court - Criminal Division
1200 Ontario St, Cleveland, OH 44113; phone: 216-664-3268; hours 8AM-3:50PM (EST). *Misdemeanor.*

http://clevelandmunicipalcourt.org/home.html
Note: The court plan to have online access to case information in the near future.

Criminal Records: Access: In person. Both court and visitors may perform in person searches. No search fee. Court makes copy: $.25 per page. Required to search: name, years to search, DOB, SSN, signed release. Criminal records on computer since 1988, on books to 1950s, archived prior. Mail turnaround time 3-4 days.

General Information: No public access terminal. No adoption or juvenile records released. Certification fee: $3.00. Payee: Municipal Court. Personal checks accepted. Prepayment and SASE required.

Bedford Municipal Court
165 Center Rd, Bedford, OH 44146; phone: 440-232-3420; fax: 440-232-2510; hours 8:30AM-4:30PM (EST). *Misdemeanor, Civil Actions Under $15,000, Eviction, Small Claims.*

www.bedfordmuni.com
Civil Records: Access: Fax, mail, in person, online. Both court and visitors may perform in person searches. No search fee. Court makes copy: $.05 per page. Required to search: name, years to search. Civil cases indexed by defendant, plaintiff; on computer from 1990 docket books and index from 1970s, prior archived. Access index to court records at the web page. Mail turnaround time 3 days.

Criminal Records: Access: Fax, mail, in person, online. Both court and visitors may perform in person searches. No search fee. Court makes copy: $.05 per page. Required to search: name, years to search. Criminal records on computer from 2000, docket books and index from 1970s, prior archived.

Access index to court records at the web page. Mail turnaround time 3 days.

General Information: Public terminal has criminal back to 2000 and civil back to 1990. No fee to fax documents. Certification fee: $2.00. Payee: Municipal Court. Only cashiers checks and money orders accepted. Prepayment and SASE required.

Berea Municipal Court
11 Berea Commons, Berea, OH 44017; criminal phone: 440-826-5862; civil phone: 440-826-5860; criminal fax: 440-234-2768; civil fax: 440-891-3387; hours 8AM-4:30PM (EST). *Misdemeanor, Civil Actions Under $15,000, Eviction, Small Claims.*

Note: Traffic fax is same number as criminal fax.

Civil Records: Access: Mail, in person, online. Both court and visitors may perform in person searches. No search fee. Court makes copy: $1.00 per page. Required to search: name, years to search. Civil cases indexed by defendant, plaintiff; on computer back to 1991, prior in books and archived. Search docket information at the website. Mail turnaround time 1 week-10 days.

Criminal Records: Access: Mail, in person, online. Both court and visitors may perform in person searches. Search fee: $5.00 per name. Court makes copy: $1.00 per page. Required to search: name, years to search; also helpful: address, DOB, SSN. Criminal records on computer back to 1991, prior in books and archived. Search docket information at the website. Mail turnaround time 1 week-10 days.

General Information: No public access terminal. No probation records released. No fee to fax documents. Certification fee: $5.00 per doc. Payee: Berea Municipal Court. Personal checks or Visa, MC accepted. Prepayment and SASE required.

Cleveland Heights Municipal Court
40 Severance Cir, Cleveland Heights, OH 44118; phone: 216-291-4901; fax: 216-291-2459; hours 8AM-5PM (EST). *Misdemeanor, Civil Actions Under $15,000, Eviction, Small Claims.*

www.clevelandheightscourt.com
Civil Records: Access: Online, in person. Visitors must perform in person searches themselves. Court makes copy: $.10 per page. Required to search: name, years to search; also helpful: address. Civil cases indexed by defendant, plaintiff; on computer from 1990, prior in books to 1980. Civil docket records for Municipal Court are on the website. Search by name or case number.

Criminal Records: Access: Online, in person. Visitors must perform in person searches themselves. Court makes copy: $.10 per page. Required to search: name, years to search; also helpful: address, DOB, SSN. Criminal records on computer from 1990, prior in books to 1980s. Online access to criminal records is the same as civil.

General Information: Public terminal goes back to 1990. No expungments or search warrant records released. Certification fee: $3.00. Payee: Municipal Court. Personal checks or Visa, MC accepted. Visa, MC in person only. Prepayment required.

East Cleveland Municipal Court
14340 Euclid Ave, East Cleveland, OH 44112; phone: 216-681-2021/2022; hours 8:30AM-4:30PM (EST). *Misdemeanor, Civil Actions Under $15,000, Eviction, Small Claims.*

Civil Records: Access: In person only. Visitors must perform in person searches themselves. Court makes copy: $1.00 per page. Required to search: name, years to search. Civil cases indexed by defendant, plaintiff. Civil records go back to 1979; on computer from 1989, docket books and index from 1950s, prior archived.

Criminal Records: Access: Mail, in person. Visitors must perform in person searches themselves. No search fee. Court makes copy: $1.00 per page. Required to search: name, years to search, DOB, SSN, signed release; also helpful: address. Criminal records on computer from 1997, docket books and index from 1950s, prior archived. Address mail requests to Police Record Room. Mail turnaround time 1-2 weeks.

General Information: No public access terminal. Certification fee: $3.00. Payee: Municipal Court. Personal checks not accepted on criminal cases. Prepayment and SASE required.

Euclid Municipal Court
555 E 222 St, Euclid, OH 44123-2099; phone: 216-289-2888; fax: 216-289-8254; hours 8:30AM-4:30PM (EST). *Misdemeanor, Civil Actions Under $15,000, Eviction, Small Claims.*

Civil Records: Access: Mail, in person. Both court and visitors may perform in person searches. Search fee: $5.00 per name. Court makes copy: $.05 per page. Required to search: name, years to search. Civil cases indexed by defendant, plaintiff; on computer from 2004, docket books and index from 1950s, prior archived. Mail turnaround time 1 week.

Criminal Records: Access: Mail, in person. Both court and visitors may perform in person searches. Search fee: $5.00 per name. Court makes copy: $.05 per page. Required to search: name, years to search, DOB; also helpful: address, SSN. Criminal records on computer from 1995, docket books and index from 1950s, prior archived. Mail turnaround time 1 week.

General Information: Public use terminal available. No expunged records released. Certification fee: $5.00 but normally included in search fee. Payee: Municipal Court. Personal checks accepted. Prepayment and SASE required.

Garfield Heights Municipal Court
5555 Turney Rd, Garfield Heights, OH 44125; phone: 216-475-1900; fax: 216-475-3087; hours 8:30AM-4:30PM (EST). *Misdemeanor, Civil Actions Under $15,000, Eviction, Small Claims.*

www.ghmc.org
Civil Records: Access: Phone, mail, in person, online. Both court and visitors may perform in person searches. No search fee. Court makes copy: $.05 per page. Required to search: name, years to search; also helpful: address. Civil cases indexed by defendant, plaintiff; on computer from 11/91, docket books and index from 1996, prior archived. Online access is limited to current dockets; search by name, date or case number at www.ghmc.org/docket.html. Note: Phone access depends on age of case. Mail turnaround 2 weeks.

Criminal Records: Access: Phone, mail, in person, online. Both court and visitors may perform in person searches. No search fee. Court makes copy: $.05 per page. Required to search: name, years to search, DOB; also helpful: address, SSN, signed release. Criminal records on computer from 1996, docket books and index from 1995, prior archived. Online access to criminal records is the same as civil. Mail turnaround time 2 weeks.

General Information: Public terminal goes back to 1999. No expunged records released. Certification fee: $1.00 per page. Cert fee includes copies. Payee: Municipal Court. Personal checks accepted. Prepayment and SASE required.

Lakewood Municipal Court
12650 Detroit Ave, Lakewood, OH 44107; phone: 216-529-6700; fax: 216-529-7687; hours 8AM-5PM (EST). *Misdemeanor, Civil Actions Under $15,000, Eviction, Small Claims.*

www.lakewoodcourtoh.com
Civil Records: Access: Phone, fax, mail, in person, online. Both court and visitors may perform in person searches. No search fee. Court makes copy: $.25 per page. Required to search: name, years to search; also helpful: address. Civil cases indexed by defendant, plaintiff; on computer from 1987, prior in books. Weekly dockets only are at www.lakewoodcourtoh.com/CourtDockets.htm. Mail turnaround time 1 week.

Criminal Records: Access: Fax, mail, in person, online. Both court and visitors may perform in person searches. No search fee. Court makes copy: $.25 per page. Required to search: name, years to search, DOB; also helpful: address, SSN. Criminal records on computer since 1983, prior in books. Weekly dockets only are at

www.lakewoodcourtoh.com/CourtDockets.htm.
Mail turnaround time 1 week.
General Information: No public access terminal. No confidential records released. No fee to fax documents. Local faxing only. Certification fee: $3.00. Payee: Municipal Court. Personal checks accepted. Prepayment and SASE required.

Lyndhurst Municipal Court 5301 Mayfield Rd, Lyndhurst, OH 44124; phone: 440-461-6500; fax: 440-442-1910; hours 8:30AM-5PM M-Th; -4PM F (EST). *Misdemeanor, Civil Actions Under $15,000, Eviction, Small Claims.*
www.lyndhurstmunicipalcourt.org
Civil Records: Access: Mail, in person. Both court and visitors may perform in person searches. No search fee. Court makes copy: $.25 per page. Required to search: name, years to search; also helpful: address. Civil cases indexed by defendant, plaintiff; on computer from 1991, prior in books. Mail turnaround time 1 week.
Criminal Records: Access: Mail, in person. Both court and visitors may perform in person searches. No search fee. Court makes copy: $.25 per page. Required to search: name, years to search, signed release; also helpful: address, DOB, SSN, location. Criminal records on computer from 1991, prior in books. Mail turnaround time 1 week.
General Information: No public access terminal. Will fax documents to local or toll free line. Certification fee: $10.00 per page. Payee: Municipal Court. Personal checks accepted. Prepayment and SASE required.

Parma Municipal Court 5555 Powers Blvd, Parma, OH 44125; phone: 440-887-7400; fax: 440-887-7485; hours 8:30AM-4:30PM (EST). *Misdemeanor, Civil Actions Under $15,000, Eviction, Small Claims.*
Note: The court is making changes to block the SSN from appearing on record requests.
Civil Records: Access: Phone, fax, mail, in person. Both court and visitors may perform in person searches. Search fee: $1.00 for copy. Court makes copy: $.05 per page. Required to search: name, years to search; also helpful: address. Civil cases indexed by defendant, plaintiff; on computer from 1993, prior in books to 1977. Mail turnaround time up to 1 week.
Criminal Records: Access: Phone, fax, mail, in person. Both court and visitors may perform in person searches. Search fee: $1.00 for copy. Court makes copy: $.05 per page. Required to search: name, years to search, DOB; also helpful: address, SSN. Criminal records on computer from 1993, prior in books to 1992. Mail turnaround time up to 1 week.
General Information: Public terminal has only civil records back to 1993. Certification fee: $1.00. Payee: Municipal Court. Personal checks accepted. Prepayment and SASE required.

Rocky River Municipal Court 21012 Hilliard Blvd, Rocky River, OH 44116; phone: 440-333-0066; fax: 440-356-5613; hours 8:30AM-4:30PM (EST). *Misdemeanor, Civil Actions Under $15,000, Eviction, Small Claims.*
www.rrcourt.net
Civil Records: Access: Phone, fax, mail, in person, online. Visitors must perform in person searches themselves. No search fee. Court makes copy: $.10 per page. Required to search: name, years to search. Civil cases indexed by defendant, plaintiff; on computer from 1987, prior in books to 1977. Public access to record index at the web page. Mail turnaround time 2 days.
Criminal Records: Access: Phone, fax, mail, in person, online. Visitors must perform in person searches themselves. No search fee. Court makes copy: $.10 per page. Required to search: name, years to search, DOB. Criminal records on computer back to 1987, prior in books to 1977. Public access to record index is at the web page. Mail turnaround time 2 days.
General Information: Public terminal has criminal back to 1/1988 and civil back to 6/1987. Will fax documents to toll free line. Certification fee: $10.00.

Payee: Municipal Court. Personal checks accepted. Prepayment and SASE required.

Shaker Heights Municipal Court 3355 Lee Rd, Shaker Heights, OH 44120; phone: 216-491-1300; fax: 216-491-1314; hours 8:30AM-4:30PM (EST). *Misdemeanor, Civil Actions Under $15,000, Eviction, Small Claims.*
www.shakerheightscourt.org
Note: Criminal Clerk open until 6:30PM on Mondays.
Civil Records: Access: Mail, fax, in person, onliine. Both court and visitors may perform in person searches. No search fee. Court makes copy: $.05 per page; same fee for self serve. Required to search: name, years to search; also helpful: address. Civil cases indexed by defendant, plaintiff; on computer from 6/86, prior in books for at least 25 years. Search case records and dockets at www.shakerheightscourt.org/home/. Mail turnaround time 2 days.
Criminal Records: Access: Phone, fax, mail, in person, online. Both court and visitors may perform in person searches. No search fee, however complete dockets are $10.00. Court makes copy: $.05 per page; same fee for self serve. Required to search: name, years to search, DOB or SSN. Criminal records on computer from 06/86, prior in books. For records prior to 1986 provide month & year to search. Search case records and dockets at www.shakerheightscourt.org/home/. Note: Phone access limited to gov't agencies. Mail turnaround time 2 days.
General Information: No public access terminal. No medical or LEADS print-out records released. Fee to fax documents is $.50 per page. Certification fee: $5.00 per document. Payee: Shaker Heights Municipal Court. Personal checks accepted. Credit cards accepted: Visa, MC, AmEx. Visa, MC, Amex, accepted in person only. Prepayment and SASE required.

South Euclid Municipal Court 1349 S Green Rd, South Euclid, OH 44121; phone: 216-381-2880; fax: 216-381-1195; hours 8:30AM-5PM (EST). *Misdemeanor, Civil Actions Under $15,000, Eviction, Small Claims.*
Civil Records: Access: Phone, fax, mail, in person. Both court and visitors may perform in person searches. No search fee. Court makes copy: no charge for 1st 10 pages, then $.10 per copy. Required to search: name, years to search; also helpful: address. Civil cases indexed by defendant, plaintiff; on computer back to 10/97; prior in docket books to 1960s. Mail turnaround time up to 1 week.
Criminal Records: Access: Mail, in person. Both court and visitors may perform in person searches. No search fee. Court makes copy: no charge for 1st 10 pages, then $.10 per copy. Required to search: name, years to search, DOB, SSN; also helpful: address. Records on computer back to 10/97; prior in docket books to 1960s. Mail turnaround up to 1 week.
General Information: Public terminal goes back to 10/1997. Will fax documents to local or toll free line. Certification fee: $1.00 per page. Includes copies but if over 10 pages, add $.10 per page. Payee: Clerk of Court, South Euclid Municipal Court. Personal checks accepted. Visa/MC accepted in person only. Prepayment and SASE required.

Darke County

Common Pleas Court Courthouse, Greenville, OH 45331; phone: 937-547-7335; probate phone: 937-547-7345; fax: 937-547-7305; hours 8:30AM-4:30PM (EST). *Felony, Civil Actions Over $15,000, Probate.* Probate is a separate court located at 300 Garst Ave.
Civil Records: Access: Mail, in person. Both court and visitors may perform in person searches. Search fee: $5.00 per name. Court makes copy: $.25 per page; same fee for self serve. Required to search: name, years to search. Civil cases indexed by defendant, plaintiff. Civil records in books to 1832, on microfiche from 1940s, computerized since 1993. Mail turnaround time 1-2 days.

Criminal Records: Access: Mail, in person. Both court and visitors may perform in person searches. Search fee: $5.00 per name. Court makes copy: $.25 per page; same fee for self serve. Required to search: name, years to search. Criminal records in books to 1832, on microfiche from 1940s, computerized since 1987. Mail turnaround time 1-2 days.
General Information: Public terminal has criminal back to 1988 and civil back to 1993. No secret indictment records released. Will fax documents to local or toll free line. Certification fee: $1.00. Payee: Clerk of Court. Business checks accepted. Prepayment and SASE required.

County Municipal Court Courthouse, Greenville, OH 45331-1990; phone: 937-547-7340; fax: 937-547-7378; hours 8:30AM-4:30PM (EST). *Misdemeanor, Civil Actions Under $15,000, Small Claims.*
Civil Records: Access: Mail, in person. Both court and visitors may perform in person searches. Search fee: $5.00 per name. Court makes copy: $.25 per page. Required to search: name, years to search. Civil cases indexed by defendant, plaintiff. Civil records in books since 1959, computerized since 1996. Mail turnaround time 1 week.
Criminal Records: Access: Mail, in person. Both court and visitors may perform in person searches. Search fee: $5.00 per name. Court makes copy: $.25 per page. Required to search: name, years to search, DOB; also helpful: SSN. Criminal records in books since 1959. Mail turnaround time 1 week.
General Information: Public terminal goes back to 1996. No sealed or confidential records released. Will fax documents for a fee. Certification fee: $5.00 includes copy fee. Payee: Clerk of Court, Darke County. Only cashiers checks and money orders accepted. Visa, MC accepted. Prepayment and SASE required.

Defiance County

Common Pleas Court PO Box 716, Defiance, OH 43512; phone: 419-782-1936; probate phone: 419-782-4181; fax: 419-782-2739; hours 8:30AM-4:30PM (EST). *Felony, Civil Actions Over $10,000, Probate.*
Note: Common Pleas Court records managed by Clerk of Courts. Probate is a separate office.
Civil Records: Access: Phone, in person. Visitors must perform in person searches themselves. No search fee. Court makes copy: $.25 per page; same fee for self serve. Required to search: name, years to search; also helpful: address. Civil cases indexed by defendant, plaintiff; on computer since 1995. Most recent records are kept here.
Criminal Records: Access: Phone, in person. Visitors must perform in person searches themselves. No search fee. Court makes copy: $.25 per page; same fee for self serve. Required to search: name, years to search; also helpful: address, DOB, SSN. Criminal records on computer since 1995; prior records on docket books.
General Information: Public terminal goes back to 1995. Will fax documents $3.00 1st page, $1.00 each add'l. Certification fee: $1.00 per pleading or page of a pleading,. Payee: Clerk of Court. Personal checks accepted. Prepayment required.

Defiance Municipal Court 324 Perry St, Defiance, OH 43512; phone: 419-782-5756; criminal phone: 419-782-5756; civil phone: 419-782-4092; fax: 419-782-2018; hours 7AM-5PM (EST). *Misdemeanor, Civil Actions Under $15,000, Eviction, Small Claims.*
Civil Records: Access: Mail, in person. Both court and visitors may perform in person searches. Search fee: $9.00 per name. Fee only for records in storage. Court makes copy: $.50 per page. Required to search: name, years to search; also helpful: DOB, SSN, address. Civil cases indexed by defendant, plaintiff; on computer from 12/89, prior in books to 1958. Search fee if record on computer- $.10 per computer page. Mail turnaround time approx. 5 days.

Criminal Records: Access: Mail, in person. Both court and visitors may perform in person searches. Search fee: $9.00 per name, but only for records from storage. Court makes copy: $.50 per page. Required to search: name, years to search; also helpful: address, DOB, SSN. Criminal records on computer from 10/89, prior in books to 1958. Search fee if record on computer- $.10 per computer page. Mail turnaround time approx. 5 days.

General Information: Public terminal goes back to 2/1989. (Terminal only available M,W,F 1-4:45PM and Tu & Thur 7AM-4:45PM.) No confidential records released. Will fax documents. Certification fee: $1.00 per page. Payee: Municipal Court. Personal checks accepted. Credit cards accepted. Prepayment and SASE required.

Delaware County

Common Pleas Court 91 N Sandusky, Delaware, OH 43015; phone: 740-833-2500; probate phone: 740-833-2680; fax: 740-833-2499; hours 8:30AM-4:30PM (EST). *Felony, Civil Actions Over $15,000, Probate.*

www.delawarecountyclerk.org

Note: Probate Court is separate and located at 88 N Sandusky St; Probate hours are 8:30AM-4:30PM. Fax number for Probate is not available.

Civil Records: Access: Mail, in person, online. Both court and visitors may perform in person searches. No search fee. Court makes copy: $.10 per page; same fee for self serve. Required to search: name, years to search; also helpful: address. Civil cases indexed by defendant, plaintiff; on computer from 1992, prior books go back to 1800s. Access to court records is free at www.delawarecountyclerk.org. Probate court index from 1852 to 1920 is free at www.midohio.net/dchsdcgs/probate.html. Mail turnaround time 1-2 days.

Criminal Records: Access: Mail, in person. Both court and visitors may perform in person searches. No search fee. Court makes copy: $.10 per page; same fee for self serve. Required to search: name, years to search, DOB; also helpful: address, SSN. Criminal records on computer from 1992, prior books go back to 1800s. Access to court records is free at www.delawarecountyclerk.org. Search the sheriff's county database of sex offenders, deadbeat parents, and most wanted list for free at www.delawarecountysheriff.com. Mail turnaround time 1-2 days.

General Information: Public terminal goes back to 1992. No grand jury proceedings or expungment records released. Will not fax documents. Certification fee: $1.00. Payee: Clerk of Court. Personal checks accepted. Prepayment and SASE required.

Delaware Municipal Court 70 N Union St, Delaware, OH 43015; phone: 740-548-6707; criminal phone: 740-368-1555; civil phone: 740-368-1550; fax: 740-368-1583; hours 8AM-4:30PM (EST). *Misdemeanor, Civil Actions Under $15,000, Eviction, Small Claims.*

www.municipalcourt.org

Civil Records: Access: Phone, mail, in person, online. Both court and visitors may perform in person searches. No search fee. Court makes copy: $.05 per page. Required to search: name, years to search. Civil cases indexed by defendant, plaintiff; on computer from 1992, prior in books. Municipal courts records are at www.municipalcourt.org:81/connection/court/. Mail turnaround time 1-2 weeks.

Criminal Records: Access: Phone, mail, in person, online. Both court and visitors may perform in person searches. No search fee. Court makes copy: $.05 per page. Required to search: name, years to search, DOB; also helpful: SSN. Criminal records on computer from 1992, prior in books. Misdemeanor and traffic case records are free at www.municipalcourt.org:81/connection/court/look up.xsp?in=ct. Also, search the court's DUI list at

www.municipalcourt.org/main_dui.asp. Mail turnaround time 1-2 weeks.

General Information: Public use terminal available. No assessment results or probation records released. Will not fax documents. Certification fee: $1.00. Payee: Delaware Municipal Court. Delaware County personal checks accepted. Prepayment and SASE required.

Erie County

Common Pleas Court 323 Columbus Ave, 1st Fl, Sandusky, OH 44870; phone: 419-627-7705; probate phone: 419-627-7759; hours 8AM-4PM M-Th/8AM-5PM F (EST). *Felony, Civil Actions Over $10,000, Probate.*

Civil Records: Access: In person only. Visitors must perform in person searches themselves. Court makes copy: $.25 per page. Required to search: name, years to search. Civil cases indexed by defendant, plaintiff; on books.

Criminal Records: Access: In person only. Visitors must perform in person searches themselves. Court makes copy: $.25 per page. Required to search: name, years to search, DOB, SSN, signed release. Criminal records on books; computerized records since 2001.

General Information: Public terminal goes back to 4/2000. Passports and expungments not released. Certification fee: $1.00 for 1st page, $.25 each add'l. Payee: Clerk of Court. Personal checks accepted. Prepayment required.

Erie County Court 150 W Mason Rd, Milan, OH 44846; phone: 419-499-4689; fax: 419-499-3300; hours 8AM-4PM (EST). *Misdemeanor, Civil Actions Under $15,000, Small Claims.*

Civil Records: Access: Mail, in person. Only the court performs in person searches. No search fee. Court makes copy: $.10 per page; same fee for self serve. Required to search: name, years to search; also helpful: address. Civil cases indexed by defendant, plaintiff; on computer back to 1990, microfiche back to 1982. Mail turnaround time 3-4 days.

Criminal Records: Access: Mail, in person. Only the court performs in person searches. No search fee. Court makes copy: $.10 per page; same fee for self serve. Required to search: name, years to search; also helpful: address, DOB. Criminal records on computer back to 1990, microfiche back to 1982. Mail turnaround time 3-4 days.

General Information: No public access terminal. No sealed records released. No certification fee . Payee: Erie County Court. No checks accepted. Prepayment and SASE required.

Sandusky Municipal Court 222 Meigs St, Sandusky, OH 44870; phone: 419-627-5926; criminal phone: 419-627-5975; civil phone: 419-627-5914; fax: 419-627-5950; hours 7AM-4PM (EST). *Misdemeanor, Civil Actions Under $15,000, Eviction, Small Claims.*

Civil Records: Access: Phone, fax, mail, in person. Both court and visitors may perform in person searches. No search fee. Court makes copy: $.10 per page. Required to search: name, years to search; also helpful: case number. Civil cases indexed by defendant, plaintiff; on computer from 1987, prior in books. Mail turnaround time 3-4 days.

Criminal Records: Access: Phone, fax, mail, in person. Both court and visitors may perform in person searches. No search fee. Court makes copy: $.10 per page. Required to search: name, years to search, DOB; also helpful: SSN, case number. Criminal records on computer from 1987, prior in books. Mail turnaround time 3-4 days.

General Information: Public terminal goes back to 1987. No pending, Juvenile crimes of violence records, or expunged records released. Will fax documents for $0.10 per page. Certification fee: $4.00. Payee: Sandusky Municipal Court. Prepayment required. SASE requested.

Vermilion Municipal Court 687 Decatur St, Vermilion, OH 44089; phone: 440-967-6543; fax: 440-967-1467; hours 8AM-4PM (EST). *Misdemeanor, Civil Actions Under $15,000, Eviction, Small Claims.*

www.vermilionmunicipalcourt.org

Note: This court handles cases from both Erie and Lorain counties.

Civil Records: Access: Fax, mail, in person, online. Both court and visitors may perform in person searches. No search fee. Court makes copy: none, but $1.00 per page fee for a computer printout. Required to search: name, years to search. Civil cases indexed by defendant, plaintiff; on computer from 1992, prior in books. Online access to municipal court records is at the website. Mail turnaround time 1-5 days.

Criminal Records: Access: Fax, mail, in person, online. Both court and visitors may perform in person searches. No search fee. Court makes copy: none, but $1.00 per page fee for a computer printout. Required to search: name, years to search, DOB; also helpful: SSN. Criminal records on computer from 1992, prior in books. Online access to criminal records is the same as civil. Mail turnaround time 1-5 days.

General Information: Public terminal goes back to 1992. Certification fee: $2.00 includes copies. Payee: Vermilion Municipal Court. Only cashiers checks and money orders accepted. Visa, MC accepted. Prepayment and SASE required.

Fairfield County

Common Pleas Court 224 E Main, Clerk's Office, Lancaster, OH 43130-0370; phone: 740-687-7030; probate phone: 740-687-7093; hours 8AM-4PM (EST). *Felony, Civil Actions Over $10,000, Probate.*

www.fairfieldcountyclerk.com

Note: Probate Court is separate from this court but at the same address.

Civil Records: Access: In person, online. Visitors must perform in person searches themselves. Court makes copy: $.05 per page. Required to search: name, years to search; also helpful: address. Civil cases indexed by defendant, plaintiff; on computer from 10/93, in books to 1970, prior archived to 1800s. Online access to County Clerk's court records database is free at www.fairfieldcountyclerk.com/Search/.

Criminal Records: Access: In person, online. Visitors must perform in person searches themselves. Court makes copy: $.05 per page. Required to search: name, years to search; also helpful: address, DOB, SSN. Criminal records on computer from 10/93, in books to 1970, prior archived to 1800s. Online access to County Clerk's court records database is free at www.fairfieldcountyclerk.com/Search/.

General Information: Public terminal goes back to 10/1993. No adoption or juvenile records released. Certification fee: $5.00 per doc. Payee: Clerk of Court. Personal checks accepted. Credit cards accepted: Visa. Credit cards not accepted over the phone. Prepayment required.

Fairfield County Municipal Court PO Box 2390, Lancaster, OH 43130; phone: 740-687-6621; fax: 740-681-5014; hours 8AM-4PM (EST). *Misdemeanor, Civil Actions Under $15,000, Eviction, Small Claims.*

www.fairfieldcountymunicipalcourt.org

Civil Records: Access: Mail, in person, online. Both court and visitors may perform in person searches. No search fee. No copy fee. Required to search: name, years to search. Civil cases indexed by defendant, plaintiff; on computer from 1990, prior in books. Cases may be searched online from the website. Mail turnaround time 2 days.

Criminal Records: Access: Mail, in person, online. Both court and visitors may perform in person searches. No search fee. No copy fee. Required to search: name, years to search. Criminal records on computer from 1989, prior in books. Cases may be searched online from the website. Mail turnaround time 2 days.

General Information: Public terminal goes back to 10/89. Will fax documents to local or toll free line. Certification fee: $1.00. Payee: Fairfiled County Court. Personal checks accepted. Prepayment and SASE required.

Fayette County

Common Pleas Court 110 E Court St, Washington Court House, OH 43160; phone: 740-335-6371; probate phone: 740-335-0640; fax: 740-333-3522; hours 9AM-4PM (EST). *Felony, Civil Actions Over $10,000, Probate.*
Note: Probate is a separate court.
Civil Records: Access: Mail, in person. Visitors must perform in person searches themselves. No search fee. Court makes copy: $.25 per page; same fee for self serve. Required to search: name, years to search. Civil cases indexed by defendant, plaintiff; on computer from 1992, prior in books to 1800s. Mail turnaround time varies.
Criminal Records: Access: Mail, in person. Visitors must perform in person searches themselves. No search fee. Court makes copy: $.25 per page; same fee for self serve. Required to search: name, years to search, DOB, SSN. Criminal records on computer from 1992, prior in books to 1800s. Mail turnaround time varies.
General Information: Public terminal goes back to 1/1992. No records released. Fee to fax documents is $1.00 per page, plus $2.00 for cover page. Certification fee: $1.00 per cert. Payee: Clerk of Court. Personal checks accepted. Prepayment and SASE required.

Municipal Court Washington Courthouse, 119 N Main St, Washington Court House, OH 43160; phone: 740-636-2350; fax: 740-636-2359; hours 8AM-4PM (EST). *Misdemeanor, Civil Actions Under $15,000, Eviction, Small Claims.*
www.wayneohio.org/public_access.html
Civil Records: Access: Mail, in person, online. Both court and visitors may perform in person searches. No search fee. No copy fee. Required to search: name, years to search. Civil cases indexed by defendant, plaintiff; on computer from 1990, prior in books to 1950s. Free search of record index at http://216.29.108.131/search.htm. Mail turnaround time 1 week.
Criminal Records: Access: Mail, in person, online. Both court and visitors may perform in person searches. No search fee. No copy fee. Required to search: name, years to search, DOB; also helpful: SSN. Criminal records on computer from 1990, prior in books to 1950s. Free search of record index at http://216.29.108.131/search.htm. Mail turnaround time 1 week.
General Information: Public terminal goes back to 1990. No records protected by the privacy act released. Will not fax documents. Certification fee: $5.00 per document includes copies. Payee: Clerk of Court. Only cashiers checks and money orders accepted. Prepayment and SASE required.

Franklin County

Common Pleas Court 369 S High St, Columbus, OH 43215-6311; phone: 614-462-3600; criminal phone: 614-462-3650; civil phone: 614-462-3621; probate phone: 614-462-3894; criminal fax: 614-462-5371; civil fax: 614-462-4325; hours 8AM-5PM (EST). *Felony, Civil Actions Over $15,000.*
www.franklincountyclerk.com
Civil Records: Access: Online, in person. Visitors must perform in person searches themselves. Court makes copy: $.10 per page. Self serve copy fee: none. Required to search: name, years to search. Civil cases indexed by defendant, plaintiff. Civil records go back to 1820. Access records via the website. Java-enable web browser required.
Criminal Records: Access: In person only. Both court and visitors may perform in person searches.

No search fee. Court makes copy: $.10 per page. Self serve copy fee: none. Required to search: name, years to search. Criminal records available since 1935.
General Information: Public terminal has criminal back to 1980 and civil back to 1995. No psych, adoption or estate tax records released. Certification fee: $1.00 per page. Payee: Franklin County Clerk of Courts. Only cashiers checks and money orders accepted. Prepayment required.

Franklin County Municipal Court - Civil Division 375 S High St, 3rd Fl, Columbus, OH 43215; phone: 614-645-7220; civil phone: 614-645-8161-file room; fax: 614-645-6919; hours 8AM-5PM (EST). *Civil Actions Under $15,000, Eviction, Small Claims.*
www.fcmcclerk.com
Civil Records: Access: Phone, fax, mail, online, in person. Both court and visitors may perform in person searches. No search fee. Court makes copy: first 25 copies free, then $.05 each. Required to search: name, years to search. Civil cases indexed by defendant, plaintiff; on computer from 1992, prior in books to 1974. Records from the Clerk of Court Courtview database free online at www.fcmcclerk.com/pa/pa.htm. Search by name or case number. Mail turnaround time 2-3 days.
General Information: Public terminal has only civil records back to 1992. No sealed or expunged records released. Will fax documents for free. Certification fee: none. Payee: Franklin County Municipal Court. Personal checks or Visa, MC, Discover accepted. Prepayment and SASE required.

Franklin County Municipal Court - Criminal Division 375 S High St, 2nd Fl, Columbus, OH 43215; phone: 614-645-7657; fax: 614-645-6036; hours Open 24 hours a day (EST). *Misdemeanor.*
www.fcmcclerk.com
Criminal Records: Access: Mail, online, in person. Both court and visitors may perform in person searches. No search fee. Court makes copy: $.25 per page. Required to search: name, years to search; also helpful: DOB, SSN. Criminal records go back to 1987; on computer back to 1992. Criminal and traffic records from the Clerk of Court Courtview database free online at www.fcmcclerk.com/pa/pa.htm. Search by name, SSN, dates, ticket, DL or case numbers. Mail turnaround time 7 days.
General Information: Public terminal has only criminal records back to 1992. No sealed or expunged records released. Certification fee: $1.00 per page. Payee: Franklin County Municipal Court. Personal checks or Visa, MC accepted. Prepayment and SASE required.

Probate Court 373 S High St, 22nd Fl, Columbus, OH 43215-6311; phone: 614-462-3894; fax: 740-462-7422; hours 8AM-4;30PM (EST). *Probate.*
Note: Search online at www.co.franklin.oh.us/probate/ProbateSearch.html.

Fulton County

Common Pleas Court 210 S Fulton, Wauseon, OH 43567; phone: 419-337-9230; probate phone: 419-337-9242; hours 8:30AM-4:30PM (EST). *Felony, Civil Actions Over $3,000, Probate.*
Civil Records: Access: In person only. Visitors must perform in person searches themselves. Court makes copy: $.25 per page first 25 pages, then $.13 next 75 pages, then $.06 thereafter. Required to search: name, years to search. Civil cases indexed by defendant, plaintiff; on computer from 9/88, prior in books to 1968, archived to 1800s.
Criminal Records: Access: In person only. Visitors must perform in person searches themselves. Court makes copy: $.25 per page first 25 pages, then $.13 next 75 pages, then $.06 thereafter. Required to search: name, years to search, DOB; SSN helpful. Criminal records on computer from 9/88, prior in books to 1968, archived to 1800s.

General Information: Public terminal goes back to 9/1988. Certification fee: $1.00 per page. Payee: Mary Gype Clerk of Court. Personal checks accepted. Prepayment required.

County Court Eastern District 204 S Main St, Swanton, OH 43558; phone: 419-826-5636; fax: 419-825-3324; hours 8:30AM-4:30PM (EST). *Misdemeanor, Civil Actions Under $15,000, Small Claims.*
www.fultoncountyoh.com/courts.htm
Civil Records: Access: Mail, fax, in person. Both court and visitors may perform in person searches. No search fee. Court makes copy: none, but must supply own paper for copies. Required to search: name, years to search. Civil cases indexed by defendant, plaintiff; on computer from 1988, prior in books. Mail turnaround time 2 weeks.
Criminal Records: Access: Mail, in person. Only the court performs in person searches. No search fee. Court makes copy: none, but must supply own paper for copies. Required to search: name, years to search, DOB; signed release requested. Criminal records on computer from 1988, prior in books. Mail turnaround time 2 weeks.
General Information: No public access terminal. No pending case records released. Will fax documents for no fee. No certification fee . Only cashiers checks and money orders accepted. SASE required.

County Court Western District 224 S Fulton St, Wauseon, OH 43567; phone: 419-337-9212; criminal fax: 419-337-9286; same fax for civil/probate; hours 8:30AM-4:30PM (EST). *Misdemeanor, Civil Actions Under $15,000, Small Claims.*
Civil Records: Access: Mail, in person. Both court and visitors may perform in person searches. No search fee. Court makes copy: $.10 per page. Required to search: name, years to search. Civil cases indexed by defendant, plaintiff; on computer from 1989, prior in books. In-person searchers should call first; Tuesdays are court day and computers in use. Mail turnaround time 2-3 days.
Criminal Records: Access: Mail, in person. Both court and visitors may perform in person searches. No search fee. Court makes copy: $.10 per page. Required to search: name, years to search, DOB; also helpful: SSN. Criminal records on computer after 1988, indexed by name and DOB. In-person searchers should call first; be aware Tuesdays are busy and hard to get on computer to search. Mail turnaround time 2-3 days.
General Information: Public terminal goes back to 1988. No pending case records released. Will fax documents for no fee. Certification fee: $1.00 includes copies. Payee: County Court Western District. No personal checks. Prepayment and SASE required.

Gallia County

Common Pleas Court - Gallia County Courthouse 18 Locust St, Rm 1290, Gallipolis, OH 45631-1290; phone: 740-446-4612 x223; probate phone: 740-446-4612 x240; fax: 740-441-2094; hours 8AM-4PM (EST). *Felony, Civil Actions Over $10,000, Probate.*
Note: Probate is in room 1293
Civil Records: Access: In person only. Visitors must perform in person searches themselves. Court makes copy: $.25 per page. Required to search: name, years to search. Civil cases indexed by defendant, plaintiff; on computer from 7/91, in books to 1968, archived to 1800s.
Criminal Records: Access: In person only. Visitors must perform in person searches themselves. Court makes copy: $.25 per page. Required to search: name, years to search. Criminal records on computer from 7/91, in books to 1968, archived to 1800s.
General Information: Public terminal goes back to 7/1991. No records released. Will fax copies for $1.00 per page if pre-paid. Certification fee: $1.00. Payee: Clerk of Court. Personal checks accepted. Prepayment required.

Gallipolis Municipal Court 518 2nd Ave, Gallipolis, OH 45631; phone: 740-446-9400; fax: 740-441-2070; hours 7:30AM-5PM (EST). *Misdemeanor, Civil Actions Under $15,000, Eviction, Small Claims.*

Civil Records: Access: Phone, mail, in person. Both court and visitors may perform in person searches. No search fee. Court makes copy: $.10 per page; same fee for self serve. Required to search: name, years to search; also helpful: address. Civil cases indexed by defendant, plaintiff; on computer from 8/93, prior in books. Mail turnaround time 1 week.

Criminal Records: Access: Phone, mail, in person. Both court and visitors may perform in person searches. No search fee. Court makes copy: $.10 per page; same fee for self serve. Required to search: name, years to search; also helpful: address, DOB, SSN. Criminal records on computer from 8/93, prior in books. Mail turnaround time 1 week.

General Information: Public terminal goes back to 1993. No expunged records released. Will not fax documents. Certification fee: $2.00. Payee: Municipal Court. Personal checks accepted. Prepayment and SASE required.

Geauga County

Common Pleas Court Clerk of Court, 100 Short Court, Chardon, OH 44024; phone: 440-285-2222 X2380; probate phone: 440-285-2222 X2000; fax: 440-286-2127; hours 8AM-4:30PM (EST). *Felony, Civil Actions Over $10,000, Probate.*

www.co.geauga.oh.us

Civil Records: Access: In person, online. Visitors must perform in person searches themselves. Court makes copy: $.25 per page. Required to search: name, years to search. Civil cases indexed by defendant, plaintiff; on computer from 1990, in books from 1968, prior archived. Online access is free from the Clerk of Courts at www.co.geauga.oh.us/departments/clerk_of_courts/docket/Courtintro.asp. Online records go back to 1990. Includes domestic cases.

Criminal Records: Access: In person, online. Visitors must perform in person searches themselves. Court makes copy: $.25 per page. Required to search: name, years to search. Criminal records on computer from 1990, in books from 1968, prior archived. Online access is free from the Clerk of Courts at www.co.geauga.oh.us/departments/clerk_of_courts/docket/Courtintro.asp. Online records go back to 1990.

General Information: Public use terminal available. no sealed records released. Will not fax documents. Certification fee: $1.00. Cert fee includes copy fee. Payee: Clerk of Court. Personal checks accepted. Credit cards accepted. Prepayment required.

Chardon Municipal Court 111 Water St, Chardon, OH 44024; phone: 440-286-2670/2684; criminal phone: 440-286-2670; civil phone: 440-286-2684; fax: 440-286-2679; hours 8AM-4:30PM (EST). *Misdemeanor, Civil Actions Under $15,000, Eviction, Small Claims.*

www.co.geauga.oh.us/departments/muni_court.htm

Civil Records: Access: Mail, in person, online. Both court and visitors may perform in person searches. No search fee. Court makes copy: $.25 per page. Required to search: name, years to search; also helpful: address. Civil cases indexed by defendant, plaintiff; on computer from 1990, prior in books. Search court records free at www.auditor.co.geauga.oh.us/pa/. Mail turnaround time 2-4 days.

Criminal Records: Access: Mail, in person, online. Both court and visitors may perform in person searches. No search fee. Court makes copy: $.25 per page. Required to search: name, years to search; also helpful: address, DOB, SSN. Criminal records on computer from 1988, prior in books to 1965. Search court records free at www.auditor.co.geauga.oh.us/pa/. Mail turnaround time 2-4 days.

General Information: Public terminal goes back to 1990. (Available 8AM-4:30PM; 2 hour maximum.) No expunged records released. Will fax documents to local or toll free line. Certification fee: $1.50 per request. Payee: Chardon Municipal Court. Personal checks or Visa, MC accepted. Accepted for criminal only. Prepayment and SASE required.

Greene County

Common Pleas Court PO Box 156, 45 N Detroit St, Xenia, OH 45385; phone: 937-562-5290; probate phone: 937-376-5280; civil/criminal fax: 937-562-5309; probate fax: 937-376-5316; hours 8AM-4:30PM (EST). *Felony, Civil Actions Over $10,000, Probate.*

www.co.greene.oh.us/clerk.htm

Note: Probate is separate court at same physical address; closes at 4PM.

Civil Records: Access: In person, online. Visitors must perform in person searches themselves. Court makes copy: $.25 per page. Required to search: name, years to search. Civil cases indexed by defendant, plaintiff; on computer from 1982, prior in books and on microfiche. Online access to clerk of court records is free at http://198.30.12.230/pa/pa.htm. Search by name or case number.

Criminal Records: Access: In person, online. Visitors must perform in person searches themselves. No search fee. Court makes copy: $.25 per page. Required to search: name, years to search; also helpful: DOB, SSN, case number. Criminal records on computer from 1982, prior in books and on microfiche. Online access to clerk of court records is free at http://198.30.12.230/pa/pa.htm. Search by name or case number.

General Information: Public terminal goes back to 1982. No sealed records released. Will fax specific case file requests for $2.00 per page. Certification fee: $1.00 per page includes copy fee. Payee: Clerk of Court. Personal checks accepted; no credit cards. Prepayment required.

Fairborn Municipal Court 1148 Kauffman Ave, Fairborn, OH 45324; criminal phone: 937-754-3040; civil phone: 937-754-3044; fax: 937-879-4422; hours 7:30AM-4:30PM (EST). *Misdemeanor, Civil Actions Under $20,000, Eviction, Small Claims.*

http://ci.fairborn.oh.us/Court/municipal_court.htm

Civil Records: Access: Mail, in person, online. Both court and visitors may perform in person searches. No search fee. Court makes copy: $.25 per page. Required to search: name, years to search; also helpful: address. Civil cases indexed by defendant, plaintiff; on computer from 1991, records go back to 1976. The web page offers free online access to civil, misdemeanor and traffic records. Mail turnaround time 1 week.

Criminal Records: Access: Mail, in person, online. Both court and visitors may perform in person searches. No search fee. Court makes copy: $.25 per page. Required to search: name, years to search, SSN; also helpful: address, DOB. Criminal records on computer from mid 1991, records go back to 1976. Online access same as civil. Mail turnaround time 1 week.

General Information: Public use terminal available. Will not fax documents. Certification fee: $2.00. Payee: Municipal Court. Personal checks accepted. Prepayment and SASE required.

Xenia Municipal Court 101 N Detroit, Xenia, OH 45385; phone: 937-376-7294; 376-7297 (Civil Clerk); fax: 937-376-7288; hours 8AM-4:30PM (EST). *Misdemeanor, Civil Actions Under $15,000, Eviction, Small Claims.*

http://xmcwa.ci.xenia.oh.us

Civil Records: Access: Mail, in person, online. Both court and visitors may perform in person searches. Search fee: $10.00 per name. Court makes copy: $.10 per page. Required to search: name, years to search; also helpful: address. Civil cases indexed by defendant, plaintiff; on computer from 1994, prior in

books to 1966. Online access to Municipal Court records is free through CourtView at http://xmcwa.ci.xenia.oh.us. Mail turnaround time 2-3 days.

Criminal Records: Access: Mail, in person, online. Both court and visitors may perform in person searches. Search fee: $10.00 per name. Court makes copy: $.10 per page. Required to search: name, years to search; also helpful: address, DOB, SSN. Criminal records on computer from 1994, prior in books to 1966. Access to criminal records is the same as civil. Mail turnaround time 2-3 days.

General Information: Public terminal goes back to 1/1994. No search warrant records released. No fee to fax documents. Certification fee: $2.00 includes copies. Payee: Municipal Court. Business checks or Visa, MC accepted. Visa, MC. Prepayment and SASE required.

Guernsey County

Common Pleas Court 801 E Wheeling Ave D-300, Cambridge, OH 43725; phone: 740-432-9230; probate phone: 740-432-9262; fax: 740-432-7807; hours 8:30AM-4PM (EST). *Felony, Civil Actions Over $10,000, Probate.*

www.guernseycountycpcourt.org

Note: Probate is a separate division with separate records and personnel.

Civil Records: Access: Online, in person. Visitors must perform in person searches themselves. Court makes copy: $.25 per page. Required to search: name, years to search. Civil cases indexed by defendant, plaintiff; on computer from 1990, prior in books, archived to 1800s. Access case index data online at the website.

Criminal Records: Access: Online, in person. Visitors must perform in person searches themselves. Court makes copy: $.25 per page. Required to search: name, years to search, DOB. Criminal records on computer from 1990, prior in books, archived to 1800s. Access case index data online at the website.

General Information: Public use terminal available. No expunged records released. Certification fee: $2.00. Payee: Clerk of Court. Personal checks accepted. Prepayment required.

Cambridge Municipal Court 134 Southgate Pky, Cambridge, OH 43725; phone: 740-439-5585; criminal phone: x226; civil phone: x240; fax: 740-439-5666; hours 8:30AM-4:30PM (EST). *Misdemeanor, Civil Actions Under $15,000, Eviction, Small Claims.*

Civil Records: Access: Mail, in person, fax. Both court and visitors may perform in person searches. No search fee. No copy fee. Required to search: name, years to search; also helpful: address. Civil cases indexed by defendant, plaintiff; on computer from 1988, prior in books. Fax civil court requests to 740-439-9405. Mail turnaround time 3-5 days.

Criminal Records: Access: Mail, in person, fax. Visitors must perform in person searches themselves. No search fee. No copy fee. Required to search: name, years to search, DOB, SSN; also helpful: address. Criminal records on computer from 1988, prior in books. Mail turnaround time 3-5 days.

General Information: Public use terminal available. No confidential records released. Will fax documents to toll-free number only. Certification fee: $2.00. Payee: Cambridge Municipal Court. Personal checks or Visa, MC accepted. Prepayment and SASE required.

Hamilton County

Common Pleas Court 1000 Main St, Rm 315, Cincinnati, OH 45202; criminal phone: 513-946-5677; civil phone: 513-946-5635; probate phone: 513-946-3580; hours 8AM-4PM (EST). *Felony, Civil Actions Over $10,000, Probate.*

www.courtclerk.org

Note: Probate is separate court.

Civil Records: Access: Mail, online, in person. Both court and visitors may perform in person searches. No search fee. Court makes copy: $.10 per page; same fee for self serve. Required to search: name, years to search. Civil cases indexed by defendant, plaintiff. Civil records indexed on computer since 1960s, prior in books and files. Records from the court clerk are free online at the website or www.courtclerk.org/queries.htm. Online civil index goes back to 1991. Also, search probate records free at www.probatect.org/case_search/casesearch.asp. Mail turnaround time 2-3 days.

Criminal Records: Access: Mail, online, in person. Both court and visitors may perform in person searches. No search fee. Court makes copy: $.10 per page; same fee for self serve. Required to search: name, years to search, signed release; also helpful: DOB, SSN. Criminal records indexed on computer since 1960s, prior in books and files. Online access to criminal records is the same as civil. Online criminal index goes back to 1986. Mail turnaround time 2-3 days.

General Information: Public use terminal available. Criminal histories not released. Certification fee: $1.00. Payee: Clerk of Court. Personal checks accepted. Credit cards accepted. Prepayment and SASE required.

Hamilton County Municipal Court - Civil

1000 Main St, Rm 115, Cincinnati, OH 45202; phone: 513-946-5700; criminal phone: 513-946-6029; fax: 513-946-5710; hours 8AM-4PM (EST). *Civil Actions Under $15,000, Eviction, Small Claims.*

www.courtclerk.org

Civil Records: Access: Fax, mail, online, in person. Both court and visitors may perform in person searches. No search fee. Court makes copy: $.25 per page. $5.00 for docket sheet. Required to search: name; also helpful: years to search. Civil cases indexed by defendant, plaintiff; on computer from 1989, prior on microfilm. Records from the court clerk are free online at the website or www.courtclerk.org/queries.htm. Mail turnaround time 5 days.

General Information: Public terminal has only civil records back to 1989. No expungement records released. No fee to fax documents. Certification fee: $5.00. Payee: Clerk of Courts. Personal checks or Visa, MC accepted. Prepayment required.

Hamilton County Municipal Court - Criminal

1000 Sycamore St #111, Cincinnati, OH 45202; phone: 513-946-6029/6040; hours 8AM-4PM (EST). *Misdemeanor.*

www.courtclerk.org

Criminal Records: Access: In person, online. Visitors must perform in person searches themselves. No search fee. Court makes copy: $.10 per page. Required to search: name, years to search, DOB; also helpful: SSN. Criminal records on computer back to 2000, prior on microfiche back to 1973. Records from the court clerk are free online at www.courtclerk.org/queries.htm

General Information: Public terminal has only criminal records back to 1999. No certification fee . Payee: Clerk of Courts. Personal checks accepted. Visa/MC accepted. Prepayment required.

Hancock County

Common Pleas Court 300 S Main St, Findlay, OH 45840; phone: 419-424-7037/7008; probate phone: 419-424-7079; hours 8:30AM-4:30PM (EST). *Felony, Civil Actions Over $10,000, Probate.*

www.co.hancock.oh.us/commonpleas/

Civil Records: Access: Mail, in person, online. Both court and visitors may perform in person searches. Search fee: $10.00 per name. Court makes copy: $.25 per page. Required to search: name, years to search. Civil cases indexed by defendant, plaintiff; on computer from 1985, microfiche from 1974, dockets archived to 1800s. Search records online back to 1985 at web page. Mail turnaround time 1-2 days.

Criminal Records: Access: Mail, in person, online. Both court and visitors may perform in person searches. Search fee: $10.00 per name. Court makes copy: $.25 per page. Required to search: name, years to search. Criminal records on computer from 1985, microfiche from 1974, dockets archived to 1800s. Search records online back to 1985 at web page. Mail turnaround time 1-2 days.

General Information: Public terminal goes back to 1985. No home investigations, medical records released. Certification fee: $1.00 per page. Payee: Clerk of Court. Personal checks accepted. Prepayment and SASE required.

Findlay Municipal Court

PO Box 826, Findlay, OH 45839; criminal phone: 419-424-7141; civil phone: 419-424-7143; fax: 419-424-7803; hours 8AM-5PM; 8AM-7PM Tuesday only (EST). *Misdemeanor, Civil Actions Under $15,000, Eviction, Small Claims.*

www.ci.findlay.oh.us/municourt/

Civil Records: Access: Mail, in person, online. Both court and visitors may perform in person searches. Search fee: $2.00 per name/SSN. Court makes copy: $.25 per page; same fee for self serve. Required to search: name, years to search. Civil cases indexed by defendant, plaintiff; on computer from 1984. Online access from www.ci.findlay.oh.us/municourt/searchcivildocket .asp?pageId=71.

Criminal Records: Access: Mail, in person, online. Both court and visitors may perform in person searches. Search fee: $2.00 per name/SSN. Court makes copy: $.25 per page; same fee for self serve. Required to search: name, years to search, DOB, SSN. Criminal records on computer from 1984. Online access same as civil.

General Information: Public terminal goes back to 1984. Will not fax documents. Certification fee: $1.00. Payee: Findlay Municipal Court. Local (Hancock County) personal checks accepted. Visa, MC accepted. Prepayment and SASE required.

Hardin County

Common Pleas Court Courthouse, #310, Kenton, OH 43326; phone: 419-674-2278; probate phone: 419-674-2230; fax: 419-674-2273; hours 8:30AM-4PM (EST). *Felony, Civil Actions Over $15,000.*

Civil Records: Access: Mail, in person. Both court and visitors may perform in person searches. Search fee: $5.00 per name. Court makes copy: $.25 per page; same fee for self serve. Required to search: full name, years to search, SSN, DOB, reason for request. Civil cases indexed by defendant, plaintiff. Current records on computer as of 1/95. Overall records go back to 1885. Mail turnaround time 2-4 days.

Criminal Records: Access: Mail, fax, in person. Both court and visitors may perform in person searches. Search fee: $5.00 per name. Court makes copy: $.25 per page; same fee for self serve. Required to search: full name, years to search, SSN, DOB, reason for request. Current records on computer as of 1/95. Overall records go back to 1885. Mail turnaround time 2-4 days.

General Information: Public terminal goes back to 10/1994. Will fax documents $2.00 1st page, $1.00 each add'l. Certification fee: $1.00 per page. Payee: Clerk of Court. Business checks accepted. Prepayment and SASE required.

Hardin County Municipal Court

PO Box 250, Kenton, OH 43326; phone: 419-674-4362; fax: 419-674-4096; hours 8:30AM-4PM (EST). *Misdemeanor, Civil Actions Under $15,000, Eviction, Small Claims.*

Civil Records: Access: Mail, in person. Both court and visitors may perform in person searches. Search fee: $5.00. Court makes copy: $.25 per page. Required to search: name, years to search. Civil cases indexed by defendant, plaintiff; on computer since 1989, prior on books. Mail turnaround time 1-2 days.

Criminal Records: Access: Mail, in person, online. Both court and visitors may perform in person searches. Search fee: $5.00 per name. Court makes copy: $.25 per page. Required to search: name, years to search; also helpful: SSN. Criminal records on computer since 1989, prior on books. Mail turnaround time 1-2 days.

General Information: Public terminal goes back to 1989. Will fax documents to local or toll-free number. Certification fee: $2.00 per page includes copies. Payee: Hardin County Municipal Court. Business checks accepted. Prepayment and SASE required.

Harrison County

Common Pleas Court 100 W Market, Cadiz, OH 43907; phone: 740-942-8500; criminal phone: 740-942-8863; probate phone: 740-942-8868; fax: 740-942-3006; probate fax: 740-942-8483; hours 8:30AM-4:30PM (EST). *Felony, Civil Actions Over $15,000, Probate.*

Note: Probate records in separate index at this same address.

Civil Records: Access: Phone, fax, mail, in person. Both court and visitors may perform in person searches. No search fee. Court makes copy: $.25 per page. Required to search: name, years to search; also helpful: address. Civil cases indexed by defendant, plaintiff; on computer since 1994, in books to 1800s.

Criminal Records: Access: In person only. Visitors must perform in person searches themselves. Court makes copy: $.25 per page. Required to search: name, years to search; also helpful: address, DOB, SSN. Criminal records on computer since 1994, in books to 1800s.

General Information: Public terminal goes back to 1994. No secret records released. Will fax documents $.25 per page. Certification fee: $1.00. Payee: Clerk of Court. Personal checks accepted. Prepayment and SASE required.

Harrison County Court

Courthouse, 100 W Market St, Cadiz, OH 43907; phone: 740-942-8865; fax: 740-942-3541; hours 8:00AM-4:30PM (EST). *Misdemeanor, Civil Actions Under $15,000, Small Claims.*

Civil Records: Access: In person only. Visitors must perform in person searches themselves. Court makes copy: $1.00 per page; same fee for self serve. Required to search: name, years to search. Civil cases indexed by defendant, plaintiff. Civil records in books; on computer back to 2/2000 (older records being added).

Criminal Records: Access: In person only. Visitors must perform in person searches themselves. Court makes copy: $1.00 per page; same fee for self serve. Required to search: name, years to search, DOB; SSN helpful. Criminal records in books; on computer back to 2/2000 (older records being added).

General Information: Public terminal goes back to 2/2000. Will fax specific case file. Certification fee: $6.00 per document. Payee: Harrison County Court. Only cashiers checks and money orders accepted. Prepayment required.

Henry County

Common Pleas Court PO Box 70, 660 N Perry St #302, Napoleon, OH 43545; phone: 419-592-5926; criminal phone: 419-592-5886; civil phone: 419-592-5886; probate phone: 419-592-7771; criminal fax: 419-592-5888; civil fax: 419-592-5888; probate fax: 419-592-7000; hours 8:30AM-4:30PM (EST). *Felony, Civil Actions Over $15,000, Probate.*

Note: Probate Court is same address, office #203. Probate copies are $1.00 per page.

Civil Records: Access: Fax, mail, in person. Visitors must perform in person searches themselves. No search fee. Court makes copy: $.25 per page 1st 25 pages; $.12 each up to 75 pages. Required to search: name, years to search. Civil cases indexed by defendant, plaintiff; on computer from 10/94, prior in books. Mail turnaround time 3 days.

Criminal Records: Access: Fax, mail, in person. Visitors must perform in person searches themselves. No search fee. Court makes copy: $.25 per page 1st 25 pages; $.12 each up to 75 pages. Required to search: name, years to search. Criminal records on computer from 10/94, prior in books. Mail turnaround time 3 days.

General Information: Public use terminal available. No adoption or mental records released. Will fax documents $3.00 1st page, $1.00 each add'l. Certification fee: $1.00 per page. Payee: Henry County Clerk of Courts. Personal checks accepted. Prepayment and SASE required.

Napoleon Municipal Court
PO Box 502, Napoleon, OH 43545; phone: 419-592-2851; fax: 419-592-1805; hours 8AM-5PM (EST). *Misdemeanor, Civil Actions Under $15,000, Eviction, Small Claims.*

Civil Records: Access: Phone, fax, mail, in person. Both court and visitors may perform in person searches. No search fee. Court makes copy: $.05 per page. Required to search: name, years to search. Civil cases indexed by defendant, plaintiff; on computer from 1990, prior in books. Mail turnaround time 1-2 days.

Criminal Records: Access: Phone, fax, mail, in person. Both court and visitors may perform in person searches. No search fee. Court makes copy: $.05 per page. Required to search: name, years to search, DOB; also helpful: SSN. Criminal records on computer from 1990, prior in books. Mail turnaround time 1-2 days.

General Information: No public access terminal. No alcohol treatment records released. Will fax documents for no fee. Certification fee: $1.00. Payee: Clerk of Court. Personal checks or Visa, MC accepted. Prepayment and SASE required.

Highland County

Common Pleas Court
PO Box 821, Hillsboro, OH 45133; phone: 937-393-9957; probate phone: 937-393-9981; fax: 937-393-9878; hours 8AM-4:30PM (EST). *Felony, Civil Actions Over $10,000, Probate.*

Note: Probate is a separate court.

Civil Records: Access: Mail, fax, in person. Both court and visitors may perform in person searches. No search fee. Court makes copy: $.10 per page; same fee for self serve. Required to search: name, years to search; also helpful: address. Civil cases indexed by defendant, plaintiff. Civil records in books since 1800s; on computer since 1995. Mail turnaround time usually same day.

Criminal Records: Access: Mail, fax, in person. Both court and visitors may perform in person searches. No search fee. Court makes copy: $.10 per page; same fee for self serve. Required to search: name, years to search, DOB, signed release; also helpful: SSN. Criminal records in books since 1800s; on computer since 1990. Mail turnaround time same day.

General Information: Public terminal has criminal back to 1984 and civil back to 1995. No sealed records released. Will fax documents to local or toll free line. Certification fee: $1.00 per page. Payee: Clerk of Court. Personal checks accepted. SASE required.

Hillsboro County Municipal Court
130 Homestead Ave, Hillsboro, OH 45133; phone: 937-393-3022; fax: 937-393-0517; hours 7AM-3:30PM M,T,Th,F; 7AM-N W (EST). *Misdemeanor, Civil Actions Under $15,000, Eviction, Small Claims.*
www.hillsboroohio.net

Civil Records: Access: Phone, fax, mail, in person, online. Only the court performs in person searches. No search fee. Court makes copy: $.15 per page. Required to search: name, years to search. Civil cases indexed by defendant, plaintiff; on computer from 1991, prior in books. Online access is same as criminal, see below. Mail turnaround time 1-2 days.

Criminal Records: Access: Phone, fax, mail, in person, Online. Only the court performs in person searches. No search fee. Court makes copy: $.15 per page. Required to search: name, years to search, DOB, SSN. Criminal records on computer from 1991, prior in books. Online access is free at http://24.123.13.34/. Mail turnaround time 1-2 days.

General Information: No public access terminal. No expunged records released. No fee to fax documents. Local or toll free calls only. No certification fee . Payee: Hillsboro Municipal Court. Personal checks accepted. Prepayment required.

Hocking County

Common Pleas Court
PO Box 108, Logan, OH 43138; phone: 740-385-2616; probate phone: 740-385-3022; fax: 740-385-1822; hours 8AM-4PM (EST). *Felony, Civil Actions Over $10,000.*

Note: Probate is a separate court at the number given.

Civil Records: Access: Fax, mail, in person. Both court and visitors may perform in person searches. No search fee. Court makes copy: $.10 per page, plus $10.00 if extensive - entire case. Required to search: name, years to search; also helpful: address. Civil cases indexed by defendant, plaintiff; on computer since 1996, in books to late 1800s. Mail turnaround time 1-2 days.

Criminal Records: Access: Fax, mail, in person. Both court and visitors may perform in person searches. No search fee. Court makes copy: $.10 per page, plus $10.00 if extensive - entire case. Required to search: name, years to search; also helpful: address, DOB, SSN. Criminal records date back to 1980 on docket books. Mail turnaround time 1-2 days.

General Information: Public terminal goes back to 1996. No secret records released. Will fax documents $1.00 per page. Certification fee: $1.00 per page. Payee: Clerk of Court. Business checks accepted. Prepayment and SASE required.

Hocking County Municipal Court
PO Box 950, County Courthouse, 1st Fl, Logan, OH 43138-1278; phone: 740-385-2250; fax: 740-385-3826; hours 8:30AM-4PM (EST). *Misdemeanor, Civil Actions Under $15,000, Eviction, Small Claims.*
www.hockingcountymunicipalcourt.com

Civil Records: Access: Mail, in person, fax. Both court and visitors may perform in person searches. No search fee. Court makes copy: $.10 per page. Required to search: name, years to search. Civil cases indexed by defendant, plaintiff; on computer from 1991, prior in books. Mail turnaround time 1-2 days.

Criminal Records: Access: Mail, in person, fax. Both court and visitors may perform in person searches. No search fee. Court makes copy: $.10 per page. Required to search: name, years to search, DOB, SSN (signed release if for a housing check). Criminal records on computer from 1991 prior in books. Mail turnaround time 1-2 days.

General Information: No public access terminal. Certification fee: $1.00 per page. Payee: Hocking County Municipal Court. Personal checks accepted. Prepayment and SASE required.

Holmes County

Common Pleas Court
1 E Jackson St, #306, Millersburg, OH 44654; phone: 330-674-1876; probate phone: 330-674-5881; fax: 330-674-0289; hours 8:30AM-4:30PM (EST). *Felony, Civil Actions Over $10,000, Probate.*

Note: Juvenile and probate court at #201, on second floor.

Civil Records: Access: Fax, mail, in person. Both court and visitors may perform in person searches. Search fee: $5.00 per name. Court makes copy: $.10 per page. Required to search: name, years to search; also helpful: address. Civil cases indexed by defendant, plaintiff; on computer from 6/30/94, prior in books to 1850. Mail turnaround time 1-2 days.

Criminal Records: Access: Fax, mail, in person. Both court and visitors may perform in person

searches. Search fee: $5.00 per name. Court makes copy: $.10 per page. Required to search: name, years to search; also helpful: address, DOB, SSN. Criminal records on computer from 6/30/94, prior in books to 1850. Mail turnaround time 1-2 days.

General Information: Public terminal goes back to 1994. No expunged records released. Fee to fax documents is $1.00 per page. Certification fee: $1.00 per document. Payee: Clerk of Court. Personal checks accepted. Prepayment and SASE required.

County Court
1 E Jackson St, #101, Millersburg, OH 44654; phone: 330-674-4901; fax: 330-674-5514; hours 8:30AM-4:30PM (EST). *Misdemeanor, Civil Actions Under $15,000, Small Claims.*

Civil Records: Access: Phone, fax, mail, in person. Both court and visitors may perform in person searches. Search fee: $1.00 per name. Court makes copy: $.25 1-10 pages; $.10 each add'l. Required to search: name, years to search. Civil cases indexed by defendant, plaintiff. Civil records in books going back to 1813; computerized records since 1994. Phone & fax access limited to 1 name. Mail turnaround time 2-5 days.

Criminal Records: Access: Phone, fax, mail, in person. Both court and visitors may perform in person searches. Search fee: $1.00 per name. Court makes copy: $.25 each 1-10 pages; $.10 each add'l. Required to search: name, years to search. Criminal records in books going back to 1813; computerized records since 1994. Same as civil. Mail turnaround time 2-5 days.

General Information: Public terminal goes back to 1994. No search warrant records released. Certification fee: $1.00 per page. Payee: Holmes County Court. Personal checks accepted. Prepayment and SASE required.

Huron County

Common Pleas Court
Clerk of Courts, 2 E Main St, Norwalk, OH 44857; phone: 419-668-5113; probate phone: 419-668-4383; fax: 419-663-4048; hours 8AM-4:30PM (EST). *Felony, Civil Actions Over $10,000, Probate.*
www.huroncountyclerk.com

Note: Probate is separate court at this same address.

Civil Records: Access: In person, online. Both court and visitors may perform in person searches. Court makes copy: $.10 per page; same fee for self serve. Required to search: name, years to search; also helpful: address. Civil cases indexed by defendant, plaintiff; on computer from 1989, prior in books and on microfiche. Search court dockets and public records free at the website or http://64.186.204.42/search.shtml.

Criminal Records: Access: In person, online. Both court and visitors may perform in person searches. Search fee: $1.00 per name. Court makes copy: $.10 per page; same fee for self serve. Required to search: name, years to search, offense, date of offense; also helpful: address, DOB, SSN. Criminal records on computer since 1989, records from 1985 to present in actual files, 1930 to 1985 on microfiche. Search court dockets and public records free at the website or http://64.186.204.42/search.shtml.

General Information: Public terminal goes back to 1989. No secret records released. Will fax specific case file requests for $2.00 per fax plus $1.00 per page. Certification fee: $1.00. Payee: Clerk of Court. Personal checks accepted. Prepayment required.

Bellevue Municipal Court
3000 Seneca Industrial Pky, Bellevue, OH 44811; phone: 419-483-5880; fax: 419-484-8060; hours 8:30AM-4:30PM (EST). *Misdemeanor, Civil Actions Under $15,000, Eviction, Small Claims.*

Note: Jurisdiction includes City of Bellevue, Towns of Lyme and Strongs Ridge, and York township in Sandusky County.

Civil Records: Access: Phone, mail, in person. Both court and visitors may perform in person searches. No search fee. Court makes copy: no fee if less than 5 copies; add'l copy fee varies. Required to search: name, years to search. Civil cases indexed by defendant, plaintiff; on index from 1988, prior in books. Will only do phone searching if not busy. Mail turnaround time 3-7 days.

Criminal Records: Access: Phone, mail, in person. Both court and visitors may perform in person searches. No search fee. Court makes copy: no fee if less than 5 copies. Required to search: name, years to search, DOB; also helpful: SSN. Criminal records on computer from 8/93. Court searches back 10 years only. Use an abstractor to go back further. Mail turnaround time 3-7 days.

General Information: No public access terminal. Will fax documents to local or toll free line. Certification fee: $1.00. Payee: Bellevue Municipal Court. Only cashiers checks and money orders accepted. Prepayment and SASE required.

Norwalk Municipal Court 45 N Linwood, Norwalk, OH 44857; phone: 419-663-6750; fax: 419-663-6749; hours 8:30AM-4:30PM (EST). *Misdemeanor, Civil Actions Under $15,000, Eviction, Small Claims.*

www.norwalkmunicourt.com

Civil Records: Access: Fax, mail, in person. Both court and visitors may perform in person searches. Search fee: $1.00 per name. Court makes copy: $.05 per page. Required to search: name, years to search; also helpful: address. Civil cases indexed by defendant, plaintiff; on computer from 7/88; prior on docket book to 1976. Mail turnaround time 2-7 days.

Criminal Records: Access: Fax, mail, in person. Both court and visitors may perform in person searches. Search fee: $1.00 per name. Court makes copy: $.05 per page. Required to search: name, years to search, DOB, SSN; also helpful: address. Criminal records on computer from 7/88, prior on docket books to 1976. Mail turnaround time 2-7 days.

General Information: Public terminal goes back to 1988. Fee to fax documents is $1.00 per page. Certification fee: $1.00 per page. Payee: Municipal Court. Personal checks accepted. Prepayment and SASE required.

Jackson County

Common Pleas Court 226 Main St, Jackson, OH 45640; phone: 740-286-2006; probate phone: 740-286-1401; fax: 740-286-4061; hours 8AM-4PM (EST). *Felony, Civil Actions Over $10,000, Probate.*
Civil Records: Access: In person only. Both court and visitors may perform in person searches. No search fee. Court makes copy: $.10 per page. Required to search: name, years to search; also helpful: address. Civil cases indexed by defendant, plaintiff. Civil records go back to 1800s, computerized since 6/20/97. Mail turnaround time varies.

Criminal Records: Access: In person only. Both court and visitors may perform in person searches. Search fee: Searches only performed in emergency situations. Court makes copy: $.10 per page. Required to search: name, years to search; also helpful: address, DOB, SSN. Criminal records go back to 1/83; computerized since 06/20/97.

General Information: Public terminal goes back to 6/1997. No juvenile or search warrant record released. Will fax documents for $3.00 fee. Certification fee: $1.00. Payee: Clerk of Court. Personal checks accepted. Prepayment required.

Jackson County Municipal Court 350 Portsmouth St, #101, Jackson, OH 45640-1764; phone: 740-286-2718; fax: 740-286-0679; hours 8AM-4PM (EST). *Misdemeanor, Civil Actions Under $15,000, Eviction, Small Claims.*
Civil Records: Access: In person only. Visitors must perform in person searches themselves. Court makes copy: $.10 per page. Required to search: name, years to search. Civil cases indexed by defendant, plaintiff. Civil records in books readily available for 8-10 years, prior archived.

Criminal Records: Access: In person only. Visitors must perform in person searches themselves. Court makes copy: $.10 per page. Required to search: name,

years to search, DOB, SSN. Criminal records in books readily available for 8-10 years, prior archived.

General Information: Public terminal goes back to 1997. No victim records released. Will not fax specific case file. No certification fee . Payee: Clerk of Municipal Court. Only cashiers checks and money orders accepted. Prepayment required.

Jefferson County

Common Pleas Court PO Box 1326, 301 Market St, Steubenville, OH 43952; phone: 740-283-8583; probate phone: 740-283-8554; hours 8:30AM-4:30PM (EST). *Felony, Civil Actions Over $500, Probate.*
Note: Probate is at PO Box 649.

Civil Records: Access: Mail, in person. Both court and visitors may perform in person searches. Search fee: $5.00 per name. Court makes copy: $.25 per page. Required to search: name, years to search. Civil cases indexed by defendant, plaintiff; on computer back 10 years or so, prior archived. Computerized domestic records go back to 1972. Mail turnaround time 1-3 days.

Criminal Records: Access: Mail, in person. Both court and visitors may perform in person searches. Search fee: $5.00 per name. Court makes copy: $.25 per page. Required to search: name, years to search, DOB; also helpful-SSN. Criminal records on books for 10 years or so, prior archived. Mail turnaround time 1-2 days.

General Information: Public terminal has criminal back to 1988 and civil back to 1995. No sealed records released. Will not fax documents. Certification fee: $1.00 per page, includes copy fee. Payee: Jefferson County Clerk of Courts. Business checks accepted. Prepayment and SASE required.

County Court #1 1007 Franklin Ave, Toronto, OH 43964; phone: 740-537-2020; fax: 740-537-1866; hours 8AM-4PM (EST). *Misdemeanor, Civil Actions Under $15,000, Small Claims.*
Civil Records: Access: Mail, in person. Both court and visitors may perform in person searches. Search fee: $5.00 per name. No copy fee. Self serve copy fee: $.25 per page. Required to search: name, years to search. Civil cases indexed by defendant, plaintiff. Civil records in books, dating from 1813, computerized records from 6/98. Mail turnaround time 1-2 days.

Criminal Records: Access: Mail, in person. Both court and visitors may perform in person searches. Search fee: $5.00 per name. No copy fee. Self serve copy fee: $.25 per page. Required to search: name, years to search, DOB, also helpful: SSN, sex, signed release. Criminal records in books, dating from 1813, computerized records from 6/98. Mail turnaround time 1-2 days.

General Information: Public terminal goes back to 6/1998. All records are public. Will fax documents to local or toll free line. No certification fee . Payee: Jefferson County Court #1. Only cashiers checks and money orders accepted. SASE required.

County Court #2 PO Box 2207, Wintersville, OH 43953; phone: 740-264-7644; fax: 740-264-3909; hours 8AM-4PM (EST). *Misdemeanor, Civil Actions Under $15,000, Small Claims.*
Civil Records: Access: Mail, in person. Both court and visitors may perform in person searches. Search fee: $5.00 per name. Court makes copy: $.25 per page. Required to search: name, years to search. Civil cases indexed by defendant, plaintiff; on computer back to 1998; in books from 1950s, prior archived. Mail turnaround time 1-2 days.

Criminal Records: Access: Mail, in person. Both court and visitors may perform in person searches. Search fee: $5.00 per name. Court makes copy: $.25 per page. Required to search: name, years to search, DOB or SSN. Criminal records on computer back to 1998; in books from 1950s, prior archived. Mail turnaround time 1-2 days.

General Information: Public terminal goes back to 1998. Will fax documents to local or toll free line. Certification fee: $1.00 per page. Payee: County Court

#2. Only cashiers checks and money orders accepted. Prepayment and SASE required.

County Court #3 PO Box 495, Dillonvale, OH 43917; phone: 740-769-2903; fax: 740-769-7640; hours 8AM-4PM (EST). *Misdemeanor, Civil Actions Under $15,000, Small Claims.*
Civil Records: Access: Mail, fax, in person. Both court and visitors may perform in person searches. Search fee: $5.00. Court makes copy: $1.00 per page. Required to search: name, years to search. Civil cases indexed by defendant, plaintiff; on computer from 1998, prior manual dockets. Mail turnaround time 1-2 days.

Criminal Records: Access: Mail, in person. Both court and visitors may perform in person searches. Search fee: $5.00. Court makes copy: $1.00 per page. Required to search: name, years to search, DOB; also helpful: SSN. Criminal records on computer from 1998, prior manual dockets. Mail turnaround time 1-2 days.

General Information: Public terminal goes back to 1998. Will fax documents for $1.00 per page. Certification fee: $1.00. Payee: County Court #3. Only cashiers checks and money orders accepted. Prepayment and SASE required.

Steubenville Municipal Court 123 S 3rd St, Steubenville, OH 43952; phone: 740-283-6000 x2200; fax: 740-283-6167; hours 8:30AM-4PM (EST). *Misdemeanor, Civil Actions Under $15,000, Eviction, Small Claims.*

www.ci.steubenville.oh.us/courts/

Note: Email questions to municipalcourt@cityofsteubenville.us.

Civil Records: Access: Mail, in person. Both court and visitors may perform in person searches. No search fee. Court makes copy: $1.00 per page. Required to search: name, years to search; also helpful: address. Civil cases indexed by defendant, plaintiff; on computer from 1991, prior in books. Mail turnaround time 10-14 days.

Criminal Records: Access: Mail, in person. Both court and visitors may perform in person searches. No search fee. Court makes copy: $1.00 per page. Required to search: name, years to search; also helpful: address, DOB, SSN. Criminal records on computer from 1991, prior in books. Mail turnaround time 10-14 days.

General Information: No public access terminal. No expunged records released. Will fax documents to local or toll free line. Certification fee: $2.00. Payee: Steubenville Municipal Court. Only cashiers checks and money orders accepted. Prepayment and SASE required.

Knox County

Common Pleas Court Knox County Clerk of Courts, 117 E High St, #201, Mt Vernon, OH 43050; phone: 740-393-6788; probate phone: 740-393-6798; hours 8AM-4PM (EST). *Felony, Civil Actions Over $10,000.*

www.knoxcountyclerk.org

Note: Probate is a separate office located at 111 E High St.

Civil Records: Access: Online, in person. Visitors must perform in person searches themselves. Court makes copy: $.10 per page. Required to search: name, years to search. Civil cases indexed by defendant, plaintiff; on computer since 9/86, on microfilm from 1960, prior archived. Search court index, dockets, calendars free online at www.knoxcountycpcourt.org. Search by name or case number.

Criminal Records: Access: Online, in person. Visitors must perform in person searches themselves. Court makes copy: $.10 per page. Required to search: name, years to search. Criminal records on computer since 9/86, on microfilm from 1960, prior archived. Online access to criminal records is the same as civil.

General Information: Public terminal goes back to 1986. If exact case number given, clerk will return pages by fax for $3.00 1st page and $1.00 each add'l.

Certification fee: $1.00. Payee: Knox County Clerk of Courts. Personal checks accepted.

Mount Vernon Municipal Court 5 N Gay St, Mount Vernon, OH 43050; phone: 740-393-9510; fax: 740-393-5349; hours 8AM-4PM (EST). *Misdemeanor, Civil Actions Under $15,000, Eviction, Small Claims.*

www.mountvernonmunicipalcourt.org

Civil Records: Access: Phone, fax, mail, in person, online. Both court and visitors may perform in person searches. No search fee. No copy fee. Required to search: name, years to search. Civil cases indexed by defendant, plaintiff; on computer back to 6/89, prior in books. Access to the clerk's civil records are free at www.mountvernonmunicipalcourt.org/cmiflash/court/home.html. Mail turnaround time 1 week.

Criminal Records: Access: Phone, fax, mail, in person, online. Both court and visitors may perform in person searches. No search fee. No copy fee. Required to search: name, years to search. Criminal records on computer from 06/89, prior in books. Access to the clerk's criminal and traffic records are free at www.mountvernonmunicipalcourt.org/cmiflash/court/home.html, Mail turnaround time 1 week.

General Information: No public access terminal. Will fax documents. No certification fee . Payee: Mt Vernon Municipal Ct. Personal checks accepted. Credit cards accepted in some cases. SASE required.

Probate Court 111 E High St, Mt Vernon, OH 43050; phone: 740-393-6796; fax: 740-393-6832; hours 8AM-4PM (EST). *Probate.*

Lake County

Common Pleas Court PO Box 490, Painesville, OH 44077; phone: 440-350-2626; probate phone: 440-350-2624; hours 8AM-4:30PM (EST). *Felony, Civil Actions Over $10,000, Probate.*

www.lakecountyohio.org

Civil Records: Access: In person, online. Visitors must perform in person searches themselves. Court makes copy: $.05 per page. Required to search: name, years to search; also helpful: address. Civil cases indexed by defendant, plaintiff; on computer from 1990, microfilm from 1960, prior archived. Online access to court records, dockets, and quick index are free at http://clerk.lakecountyohio.org/clerk/. Includes domestic and appeals cases. Access probate online at http://probate.lakecountyohio.org/probate/.

Criminal Records: Access: In person, online. Visitors must perform in person searches themselves. Court makes copy: $.05 per page. Required to search: name, years to search; also helpful: address, DOB, SSN. Criminal records on computer from 1990, microfilm from 1960, prior archived. Online access to criminal records is the same as civil.

General Information: Public terminal goes back to 1998. No adoption or juvenile records released. Will not fax documents. Certification fee: $1.00. Payee: Clerk of Court. Business checks accepted. Prepayment required.

Mentor Municipal Court 8500 Civic Center Blvd, Mentor, OH 44060-2418; criminal phone: 440-974-5744; civil phone: 440-974-5745; fax: 440-974-5742; hours 8AM-4PM daily except Wed 8AM-6PM (EST). *Misdemeanor, Civil Actions Under $15,000, Eviction, Small Claims.*

Civil Records: Access: In person only. Visitors must perform in person searches themselves. Court makes copy: $1.00 per page. Required to search: name. Civil cases indexed by defendant, plaintiff. Civil records go back to 1972; on computer back to 11/1995.

Criminal Records: Access: In person only. Visitors must perform in person searches themselves. Court makes copy: $1.00 per page. Required to search: name, years to search; also helpful: DOB. Criminal

records go back to 1972; on computer back to 11/1995.

General Information: Public terminal goes back to 1995. Will not fax specific case file. Certification fee: None, just copy fee. Payee: Mentor Municipal Court. Only cashiers checks and money orders accepted. Prepayment required.

Painesville Municipal Court PO Box 601, 7 Richmond St, Painesville, OH 44077; phone: 440-392-5900; fax: 440-352-0028; hours 8AM-4:30PM (EST). *Misdemeanor, Civil Actions Under $15,000, Eviction, Small Claims.*

www.pmcourt.com

Note: Probation fax is 440-639-4932.

Civil Records: Access: Fax, mail, in person, online. Visitors must perform in person searches themselves. No search fee. Court makes copy: $1.00 first page. $.20 each addl. Required to search: name, years to search; also helpful: address. Civil cases indexed by defendant, plaintiff; on computer from 7/90 (all divisions), prior on books or archived. Free online access to records at www.pmcourt.com/search.html. Mail turnaround time 1 week.

Criminal Records: Access: Fax, mail, in person, online. Visitors must perform in person searches themselves. No search fee. Court makes copy: $1.00 first page. $.20 each add'l. Required to search: name, years to search, address; also helpful: DOB, SSN. Criminal records on computer from 7/90 (all divisions), prior on books or archived. Free online access to records at www.pmcourt.com/search.html. Mail turnaround time 1 week.

General Information: Public terminal goes back to 1990. Will fax documents: local $1.00 per page; long distance $3.00 per page. Certification fee: $2.00 plus $1.00 per page after first. Payee: Municipal Court. Personal checks or Visa, MC accepted. Prepayment and SASE required.

Willoughby Municipal Court One Public Square, Willoughby, OH 44094-7888; phone: 440-953-4150; criminal phone: 440-953-4150; civil phone: 440-953-4170; fax: 440-953-4149; hours 7:30AM-4:30 PM (till 7:30 on Mon) (EST). *Misdemeanor, Civil Actions Under $15,000, Eviction, Small Claims.*

www.willoughbycourt.com

Note: This court serves these communities: Eastlake, Kirtland, Kirtland Hills, Lakeland Community College, Lakeline, Timberlake, Waite Hill, Wickliffe, Willoughby, Willoughby Hills, and Willowick.

Civil Records: Access: Mail, in person. Both court and visitors may perform in person searches. No search fee. Court makes copy: $.25 per page. Required to search: name, years to search. Civil cases indexed by defendant. Civil records on docket books since 1960, computerized back to 1986. Mail turnaround time 2-3 days.

Criminal Records: Access: Mail, in person. Both court and visitors may perform in person searches. No search fee. Court makes copy: $.25 per page. Required to search: name; also helpful: DOB, SSN. Criminal records in docket books since 1960, computerized back to 1988. Mail turnaround time 2-3 days.

General Information: Public use terminal available. Certification fee: $1.00 per page. Payee: Willoughby Municipal Court. Personal checks accepted. Prepayment required.

Lawrence County

Common Pleas Court Clerk of the Courts, PO Box 208, Ironton, OH 45638; phone: 740-533-4355/4329; probate phone: 740-533-4343; fax: 740-533-4383; hours 8:30AM-4PM (EST). *Felony, Civil Actions.*

www.lawrencecountyclkofcrt.org

Note: Probate is a separate court at Veterans Square in Ironton.

Civil Records: Access: In person, online. Visitors must perform in person searches themselves. Court makes copy: $.25 per page. Required to search: name, years to search; also helpful: address. Civil cases indexed by defendant, plaintiff; on computer back to 6/88, prior in books going back to 1800s. Online access to civil records is free at the website.

Criminal Records: Access: In person, online. Visitors must perform in person searches themselves. No search fee. Court makes copy: $.25 per page. Required to search: name, years to search; also helpful: address, DOB, SSN. Criminal records on computer back to 1/88, prior in books going back to 1800s. Online access to criminal records is free at www.lawrencecountyclkofcrt.org.

General Information: Public terminal goes back to 1988. Will fax specific case file requests. No certification fee . Payee: Clerk of Court. Personal checks accepted. Prepayment required.

Lawrence County Municipal Court PO Box 126, Chesapeake, OH 45619; phone: 740-867-3128/3127; fax: 740-867-3547; hours 8:30AM-4PM (EST). *Misdemeanor, Civil Actions Under $15,000, Eviction, Small Claims.*

Civil Records: Access: Phone, fax, mail, in person. Both court and visitors may perform in person searches. Search fee: $5.00 per name. Court makes copy: $.25 per page; same fee for self serve. Required to search: name, years to search. Civil cases indexed by defendant, plaintiff; on computer from 1991. Mail turnaround time 7-10 days.

Criminal Records: Access: Phone, fax, mail, in person. Both court and visitors may perform in person searches. Search fee: $5.00 per name. Court makes copy: $.25 per page; same fee for self serve. Required to search: name, years to search, DOB; also helpful: SSN. Criminal records on computer from 1991. Mail turnaround time 7-10 days.

General Information: No public access terminal. All records public. Certification fee: $2.00. Payee: Lawrence County Municipal Court. Personal checks accepted. Prepayment and SASE required.

Ironton Municipal Court PO Box 237, Ironton, OH 45638; phone: 740-532-3062; fax: 740-533-6088; hours 8:30AM-4PM (EST). *Misdemeanor, Civil Actions Under $15,000, Eviction, Small Claims.*

Note: Searches of the index books only allowed Wed and Fri.

Civil Records: Access: Mail, in person. Both court and visitors may perform in person searches. No search fee. No copy fee. Required to search: name, years to search; also helpful: address. Civil cases indexed by defendant, plaintiff; on computer from 7/89, prior in books. Mail turnaround time 1-2 weeks.

Criminal Records: Access: Mail, in person. Both court and visitors may perform in person searches. No search fee. No copy fee. Required to search: name, years to search; also helpful: address, DOB, SSN. Criminal records on computer from 7/89, prior in books. Note: Searches of the index books only allowed Wed and Fri. Mail turnaround time 1-2 weeks.

General Information: Public terminal goes back to 1989. Certification fee: $1.00 per page includes copy fee. Payee: Municipal Court. Prepayment and SASE required.

Licking County

Common Pleas Court PO Box 4370, Newark, OH 43058-4370; phone: 740-349-6171; probate phone: 740-349-6141; fax: 740-349-6945; hours 8AM-4:30PM (EST). *Felony, Civil Actions Over $15,000, Probate.*

www.lcounty.com/clerkofcourts/

Note: Probate court has a separate clerk at the same address.

Civil Records: Access: In person, online. Visitors must perform in person searches themselves. Court makes copy: $.05 per page. Required to search: name, years to search; also helpful: address. Civil cases indexed by defendant, plaintiff; on computer from 1992, prior in books. The county clerk's office offers free Internet access to current records at the website. Click on "Courtview 2000."

Criminal Records: Access: In person, online. Visitors must perform in person searches themselves. No search fee. Court makes copy: $.05 per page. Required to search: name, years to search, DOB; also helpful: address, SSN. Criminal records on computer from 1992, prior in books. The county clerk's office offers free Internet access to current records at the website. Click on "Courtview 2000"

General Information: Public terminal goes back to 2/1992. No sealed records released. Certification fee: $1.00. Payee: Clerk of Court. Business checks accepted. Prepayment required.

Licking County Municipal Court 40 W
Main St, Newark, OH 43055; criminal phone: 740-349-6627; civil phone: 740-349-6631; fax: 740-345-4250; hours 8AM-4:30PM (EST). *Misdemeanor, Civil Actions Under $15,000, Eviction, Small Claims.*

www.ci.newark.oh.us/city/municipalcourt/municourt.asp

Civil Records: Access: Phone, fax, mail, in person, online. Both court and visitors may perform in person searches. No search fee. Court makes copy: $.05 per page; same fee for self serve. Required to search: name, years to search. Civil cases indexed by defendant, plaintiff; on computer from 1990, prior in books. Online access to Municipal Court records is free at http://67.141.197.6/connection/court/. Mail turnaround time 2-3 days.

Criminal Records: Access: Phone, fax, mail, in person, online. Both court and visitors may perform in person searches. No search fee. Court makes copy: $.05 per page; same fee for self serve. Required to search: name, years to search. Criminal records on computer from 1990, prior in books. Online access to criminal records is the same as civil. Mail turnaround time 2-3 days.

General Information: Public terminal goes back to 1990. No sealed records released. Will not fax documents. Certification fee: $2.00 per page. Payee: Licking County Municipal Court. Personal checks accepted. Prepayment and SASE required.

Logan County

Common Pleas Court 101 S Main St, Rm 18,
Bellefontaine, OH 43311-2097; phone: 937-599-7261; criminal phone: 937-599-7256; civil phone: 937-599-7275; probate phone: 937-599-7274; criminal fax: 937-292-4175; civil fax: 937-599-7281; probate fax: 937-599-7297; hours 8:30AM-4:30PM (EST). *Felony, Civil Actions Over $10,000, Probate.*

http://co.logan.oh.us/clerkofcourts/
Note: Probate is separate index and office.
Civil Records: Access: In person only. Visitors must perform in person searches themselves. Court makes copy: $.05 per page after first 25 pages. Required to search: name, years to search; also helpful: address. Civil cases indexed by defendant, plaintiff; on computer from 6/88, prior in books to 1943.

Criminal Records: Access: In person only. Visitors must perform in person searches themselves. Court makes copy: $.05 per page after first 25 pages. Required to search: name, years to search, DOB; also helpful: address, SSN. Criminal records on computer from 6/88, prior in books to 1943.

General Information: Public terminal goes back to 6/1988. All records public. Will fax specific case file for $2.00 for 1st page, $1.00 each add'l page. Certification fee: $1.00 per page includes copy fee. Payee: Clerk of Court. Only cashiers checks and money orders accepted. Prepayment required.

Bellefontaine Municipal Court 226 W
Columbus Ave, Bellefontaine, OH 43311; phone: 937-599-6127; fax: 937-599-2488; hours 8AM-4:30PM (EST). *Misdemeanor, Civil Actions Under $15,000, Eviction, Small Claims.*

Civil Records: Access: In person, fax, mail. Visitors must perform in person searches themselves. Court makes copy: $.05 per page. Required to search: name, years to search. Civil cases indexed by defendant, plaintiff; on computer from 1986, prior in books. Mail turnaround time 1-2 days.

Criminal Records: Access: In person, fax, mail. Visitors must perform in person searches themselves. Court makes copy: $.05 per page. Required to search: name, years to search, DOB, SSN, signed release; also helpful: address. Criminal records on computer from 1986, prior in books. Mail turnaround time 1-2 days.

General Information: Public terminal goes back to 1984. All records are public. Certification fee: $1.00 per cert. Payee: Bellefontaine Municipal Court. Local checks or Visa, MC accepted. Accepted for traffic & criminal only. Prepayment and SASE required.

Lorain County

Common Pleas Court 225 Court St, Elyria,
OH 44035; phone: 440-329-5536; criminal phone: 440-329-5538; civil phone: 440-329-5536; probate phone: 440-329-5175; criminal fax: 440-329-5404; probate fax: 440-328-2157; hours 8AM-4:30PM (EST). *Felony, Civil Actions Over $10,000, Probate.*

www.loraincounty.com/clerk
Note: Probate is a separate index in Rm #611.
Civil Records: Access: Online, in person. Both court and visitors may perform in person searches. No search fee. Court makes copy: $.10 per page. Required to search: name, years to search. Civil cases indexed by defendant, plaintiff; on computer from 1988, prior in books archived to 1800s. Some records on microfiche to 1824. The website offers free access to indices and dockets for civil and domestic relationship cases. Access probate records at www.loraincounty.com/probate/search.shtml. Note: Court will not do index searching, but they will pull specified records.

Criminal Records: Access: Online, in person. Both court and visitors may perform in person searches. Court makes copy: $.10 per page. Required to search: name, years to search. Criminal records on computer from 1988, prior in books archived to 1800s. Some records on microfiche to 1960. Online access to criminal records is the same as civil. Note: Court will not do index searching, but they will pull specified records.

General Information: Public terminal goes back to 1988. No juvenile records released. Certification fee: $1.00. Payee: Clerk of Court. Personal checks accepted. Prepayment required.

Avon Lake Municipal Court 32855 Walker
Rd, Avon Lake, OH 44012; phone: 440-930-4103; fax: 440-930-4128; hours 8:30AM-4:30PM (EST). *Misdemeanor, Civil Actions Under $15,000, Eviction, Small Claims.*

Civil Records: Access: Phone, mail, in person. Both court and visitors may perform in person searches. No search fee. Court makes copy: $.10 per page. Required to search: name, years to search. Civil cases indexed by defendant, plaintiff; on computer from 5/92, records go back to 1976. Mail turnaround time 1-2 days.

Criminal Records: Access: Phone, mail, in person. Both court and visitors may perform in person searches. No search fee. Court makes copy: $.10 per page. Required to search: name, years to search, DOB; also helpful: SSN. Criminal records on computer from 7/92, records go back to 1976. Mail turnaround time 1-2 days.

General Information: Public terminal goes back to 5/92. No non-public records released. Fee to fax documents is $3.00 per document. Certification fee:

$1.00. Payee: Avon Lake Municipal Court. Personal checks accepted. Prepayment and SASE required.

Elyria Municipal Court 328 Broad St, Elyria,
OH 44035; phone: 440-323-5743; criminal phone: 440-323-1328; criminal fax: 440-323-8095; civil fax: 440-323-0785; hours 8AM-4:30PM (EST). *Misdemeanor, Civil Actions Under $15,000, Eviction, Small Claims.*

www.elyriamunicourt.org
Civil Records: Access: Fax, mail, online, in person. Both court and visitors may perform in person searches. No search fee. No copy fee. Required to search: name, years to search; also helpful: address. Civil cases indexed by defendant, plaintiff. Civil records in books to 1956, computer from 1996. Search at the Internet site, also you can request information by email to civil@elyriamunicourt.org. Mail turnaround time 5 days.

Criminal Records: Access: Fax, mail, in person, online. Both court and visitors may perform in person searches. No search fee. No copy fee. Required to search: name, years to search; also helpful: address, DOB, SSN. Criminal records in books to 1956, computer from 1996. Search misdemeanor and traffic records at the website, also send email requests to crtr@elyriamunicourt.org. Mail turnaround time 5 days.

General Information: Public use terminal available. All records are public. Certification fee: $2.00. Personal checks accepted. SASE required.

Lorain Municipal Court 200 W Erie Ave,
Lorain, OH 44052; phone: 440-204-2140; fax: 440-204-2146; hours 8:30AM-4:30PM (EST). *Misdemeanor, Civil Actions Under $15,000, Eviction, Small Claims.*

www.lorainmunicourt.org
Civil Records: Access: Online, in person. Visitors must perform in person searches themselves. Court makes copy: $.25 per page. Required to search: name, years to search; also helpful: address. Civil cases indexed by defendant, plaintiff. Civil records in books. Access municipal court records free at www.lorainmunicourt.org/search.shtml. Search by name, date, case number, driver license number or attorney.

Criminal Records: Access: Online, in person. Visitors must perform in person searches themselves. Court makes copy: $.25 per page. Required to search: name, years to search; also helpful: address, DOB, SSN. Criminal records in books. Online access to criminal records is the same as civil.

General Information: Public terminal goes back to 8/1998. No certification fee . Payee: Municipal Court. Prepayment required.

Oberlin Municipal Court 85 S Main St,
Oberlin, OH 44074; phone: 440-775-1751; fax: 440-775-0619; hours 8AM-4PM (EST). *Misdemeanor, Civil Actions Under $15,000, Eviction, Small Claims.*

www.oberlinmunicipalcourt.org
Civil Records: Access: In person, online. Visitors must perform in person searches themselves. Court makes copy: $.10 per page. Required to search: name, years to search; also helpful: address. Civil cases indexed by defendant, plaintiff; on computer from 1991, prior in books. Access case information free online at http://65.120.95.142/connection/court/index.xsp.

Criminal Records: Access: In person, online. Visitors must perform in person searches themselves. Court makes copy: $.10 per page. Required to search: name, years to search; also helpful: address, DOB, SSN. Criminal records on computer from 1991, prior in books. Access case information free online at http://65.120.95.142/connection/court/index.xsp.

General Information: Public terminal goes back to 1991. Certification fee: none. Payee: Oberlin

Municipal Court. Business checks or Visa, MC accepted. Prepayment required.

Vermilion Municipal Court 687 Decatour St, Vermilion, OH 44089-1152; phone: 440-967-6543; fax: 440-967-1467; hours 8AM-4PM (EST). *Misdemeanor, Civil Actions Under $15,000, Eviction, Small Claims.*

www.vermilionmunicipalcourt.org

Note: This court handles cases from both Erie and Lorain counties.

Civil Records: Access: Fax, mail, in person, online. Both court and visitors may perform in person searches. No search fee. No copy fee. Required to search: name, years to search; also helpful: address. Civil cases indexed by defendant, plaintiff; on computer since late 1991, indexed in books since 1966. Online access to municipal court records is at the website or directly at www.vermilionmunicipalcourt.org/search.html.

Criminal Records: Access: Fax, mail, in person, online. Both court and visitors may perform in person searches. No search fee. No copy fee. Required to search: name, years to search; also helpful: SSN. Criminal records on computer since late 1991, indexed in books since 1966. Online access to criminal records is the same as civil.

General Information: Public terminal goes back to 1991. no addresses, victim info or confidential report records released. No fee to fax documents. Certification fee: $2.00 includes copies. Payee: Municipal Court. Personal checks or Visa, MC accepted. Prepayment required.

Lucas County

Common Pleas Court 700 Adams, Courthouse, Toledo, OH 43624; phone: 419-213-4483, 4484; criminal phone: 419-213-4480; civil phone: 419-213-4493; probate phone: 419-213-4775; criminal fax: 419-213-4487; probate fax: call for number; hours 8AM-4:45PM (EST). *Felony, Civil Actions Over $10,000, Probate.*

www.co.lucas.oh.us/default.asp?RequestedAlias=clerk

Note: Probate records must be searched separately; probate hours are 8:30-4:30.

Civil Records: Access: Fax, mail, in person, online. Both court and visitors may perform in person searches. Search fee: $2.00 per name. Court makes copy: $.05 per page; same fee for self serve. Required to search: name, years to search. Civil cases indexed by defendant, plaintiff. Civil records computer from 1987, records go back to 1948, prior in books and on film. Online access to clerk of courts dockets is free at www.co.lucas.oh.us/Clerk/dockets.asp. Online records go back to 9/1997. Search probate records at www.lucas-co-probate-ct.org/. Mail turnaround time 3 days.

Criminal Records: Access: Fax, mail, in person, online. Both court and visitors may perform in person searches. Search fee: $5.00 per name. Court makes copy: $.05 per page; same fee for self serve. Required to search: name, years to search, DOB, SSN; also helpful: sex, signed release. Criminal records computer from 1987, records go back to 1948, prior in books and on film. Online access to clerk of courts dockets is free at www.co.lucas.oh.us/Clerk/dockets.asp. Online record go back to 9/1997. Search sex offenders at www.lucascountysheriff.org/sheriff/disclaimer.asp. Mail turnaround time 3 days.

General Information: Public use terminal available. No expunged records released. Will fax documents for $3.00 transmittal fee plus copy fees. Certification fee: $1.00. Payee: Clerk of Court. Only cashiers checks and money orders accepted. Prepayment required.

Maumee Municipal Court 400 Conant St, Maumee, OH 43537-3397; criminal phone: 419-897-7136; civil phone: 419-897-7145; fax: 419-897-7129; hours 8AM-4:30PM (EST). *Misdemeanor, Civil Actions Under $15,000, Eviction, Small Claims.*

www.maumee.org/municipal/default.htm

Civil Records: Access: Phone, fax, mail, in person, online. Only the court performs in person searches. No search fee. Court makes copy: none, up to 20 pages; $.05 per page over 20. Required to search: name; also helpful: years to search. Civil cases indexed by defendant, plaintiff. Civil records in docket books since 1964, on computer since 1989. Online access to the interactive web court system database is free at www.maumee.org/municipal/caseinfo.htm. Online includes civil, criminal, traffic. Mail turnaround time 1 week.

Criminal Records: Access: Phone, fax, mail, in person, online. Only the court performs in person searches. No search fee. Court makes copy: none, up to 20 pages; $.05 per page over 20. Required to search: name, years to search, DOB; also helpful: SSN. Criminal records in docket books since 1964, on computer since 1987. Online access to criminal records is the same as civil. Mail turnaround time 1 week.

General Information: No public access terminal. Will fax documents for no fee. Certification fee: $1.00 per page up to 20 pages includes copy fee. Payee: Maumee Municipal Court. Personal checks or Visa, MC accepted. Credit cards not accepted for phone orders. Prepayment required.

Oregon Municipal Court 5330 Seaman Rd, Oregon, OH 43616; criminal phone: 419-698-7173; civil phone: 419-698-7008; fax: 419-698-7013; hours 8:30AM-4:30PM (EST). *Misdemeanor, Civil Actions Under $15,000, Eviction, Small Claims, Traffic.*

www.ci.oregon.oh.us/ctydpt/court/court.htm

Civil Records: Access: Phone, fax, mail, in person, email. Both court and visitors may perform in person searches. No search fee. Court makes copy: $.15 for 1st page, $.10 each add'l. Required to search: name, years to search. Civil cases indexed by defendant, plaintiff; on books since 1960, computerized since 1989. Mail turnaround time 1-2 days.

Criminal Records: Access: Phone, fax, mail, in person. Both court and visitors may perform in person searches. No search fee. Court makes copy: $.15 for first page, $.10 each add'l. Required to search: name, years to search; also helpful: DOB, SSN. Criminal records on books since 1960, computerized since 1989. Mail turnaround time 1-2 days.

General Information: No public access terminal. No fee to fax documents; must be local call. Certification fee: $2.50 for 1st page, $.10 each add'l. Payee: Oregon Municipal Court. Personal checks accepted. Visa, MC cards accepted for criminal records only. For in person searching only. Prepayment and SASE required.

Sylvania Municipal Court 6700 Monroe St, Sylvania, OH 43560-1995; phone: 419-885-8975; criminal phone: 419-885-8975; civil phone: 419-885-8985; fax: 419-885-8987; hours 7:30AM-4PM (EST). *Misdemeanor, Civil Actions Under $15,000, Eviction, Small Claims.*

www.sylvaniacourt.com

Civil Records: Access: Fax, mail, in person, online. Visitors must perform in person searches themselves. No search fee. Court makes copy: $.10 per page. Required to search: name, years to search. Civil cases indexed by defendant, plaintiff; on books since 1964, computerized since 1987. Online access free at http://63.164.246.229/. Mail turnaround time 1 week.

Criminal Records: Access: Fax, mail, in person, online. Visitors must perform in person searches themselves. No search fee. Court makes copy: $.10

per page. Required to search: name, years to search, DOB, SSN. Criminal records on books since 1964, computerized since 1987. Online access free at http://63.164.246.229/ Mail turnaround time 1 week.

General Information: Public use terminal available. Will fax documents to local or toll free line. Certification fee: $2.00 per page. Payee: Clerk of Court. Business checks accepted. Prepayment required.

Toledo Municipal Court 555 N Erie St, Toledo, OH 43624-1391; phone: 419-245-1926 (Small Claims); criminal phone: 419-936-3650; civil phone: 419-245-1927; fax: 419-245-1801; hours 8AM-4:30PM civil; 6AM-6PM M-F, 6-11:30AM Sat crim & traffic (EST). *Misdemeanor, Civil Actions Under $15,000, Eviction, Small Claims.*

www.tmc-clerk.com

Note: A second web site is at www.toledomunicipalcourt.org.

Civil Records: Access: Mail, fax, in person, email. Both court and visitors may perform in person searches. No search fee. Court makes copy: $.20 per page. Self serve copy fee: $.15 per page. Required to search: name, years to search. Civil cases indexed by defendant. Civil records on computer back to 1986, prior in books since 1960s. The daily docket is online at the website. Direct email requests to clerk@tmc-clerk.com. Mail turnaround time 3 to 5 days.

Criminal Records: Access: Mail, fax, in person, email, online. Both court and visitors may perform in person searches. No search fee. Court makes copy: $.20 per page. Self serve copy fee: $.25 per page. Required to search: name, years to search, DOB, SSN; also helpful: address. Criminal records on computer back to 1985, prior in books since 1960s. The daily docket is online at the website. Direct email requests to clerk@tmc-clerk.com. Note: Have either date of birth or SSN to request a search. Mail turnaround time 3 to 5 days.

General Information: Public terminal has criminal back to 1980 and civil back to 1986. (Terminal also has traffic records back to 1978.) No expunged records released. Certification fee: $6.00. Payee: Toledo Municipal Court. Personal checks and credit cards accepted for criminal records only. Prepayment and SASE required.

Madison County

Common Pleas Court PO Box 557, London, OH 43140; phone: 740-852-9776; probate phone: 740-852-0756; fax: 740-845-1778; hours 8AM-4PM (EST). *Felony, Civil Actions Over $10,000, Probate.*

Civil Records: Access: In person, online. Visitors must perform in person searches themselves. Court makes copy: $.25 per page. Required to search: name, years to search. Civil cases indexed by defendant, plaintiff. Civil records in books since 1981. Search probate records (not civil records) at www.madisonprobate.org/Search/.

Criminal Records: Access: In person only. Visitors must perform in person searches themselves. Court makes copy: $.25 per page. Required to search: name, years to search; also helpful: address, DOB, SSN. Criminal records in books since 1981.

General Information: Public terminal goes back to 2/2001. No secret indictment records released. No certification fee . Payee: Clerk of Court. Personal checks accepted. Prepayment required.

Madison County Municipal Court PO Box 646, 1 N Main St, London, OH 43140; phone: 740-852-1669; fax: 740-852-0812; hours 8AM-4PM (EST). *Misdemeanor, Civil Actions Under $15,000, Eviction, Small Claims.*

Civil Records: Access: Phone, fax, mail, in person. Both court and visitors may perform in person searches. No search fee. Court makes copy: $.25 per page. Required to search: name, years to search. Civil cases indexed by defendant, plaintiff; on computer from 1989, prior in books indexed from 1958. Mail turnaround time up to 1 week.

Criminal Records: Access: Phone, fax, mail, in person. Both court and visitors may perform in person searches. No search fee. Court makes copy: $.25 per page. Required to search: name, years to search, DOB; also helpful: SSN. Criminal records on computer from 1989, prior in books indexed from 1958. Mail turnaround time up to 1 week.

General Information: Public terminal goes back to 1985. No probation records released. No fee to fax documents. Certification fee: $1.00 per cert. Payee: Madison County Municipal Court. Only cashiers checks and money orders accepted. Prepayment and SASE required.

Mahoning County

Common Pleas Court 120 Market St, Youngstown, OH 44503; phone: 330-740-2103; probate phone: 330-740-2312; fax: 330-740-2105; hours 8AM-4PM (EST). *Felony, Civil Actions Over $15,000, Probate.*

Civil Records: Access: In person, online. Visitors must perform in person searches themselves. Court makes copy: $.10 per page. Required to search: name, years to search; also helpful: address. Civil cases indexed by defendant, plaintiff; on computer from 1989, prior in books indexed from 1946. For online access, see criminal section.

Criminal Records: Access: Mail, in person, online. Both court and visitors may perform in person searches. No search fee. Court makes copy: $.10 per page. Required to search: name, years to search; also helpful: address, DOB, SSN. Criminal records on computer from 1989, prior in books indexed from 1946. Access integrated justice system cases back to 1989 free at http://courts.mahoningcountyoh.gov/. Attorney searching also available. Mail turnaround time 1 week.

General Information: Public terminal goes back to 1989. No secret indictment records released. Will fax documents $2.00 1st page, $1.00 each add'l. Certification fee: $1.00 per cert. Payee: Clerk of Court. Personal checks accepted. Prepayment and SASE required.

County Court #2 127 Boardman Canfield Rd, Boardman, OH 44512; phone: 330-726-5546; fax: 330-740-2035; hours 8:30AM-4PM (EST). *Misdemeanor, Civil Actions Under $15,000, Small Claims.*

http://courts.mahoningcountyoh.gov

Civil Records: Access: Mail, fax, in person, online. Both court and visitors may perform in person searches. No search fee. Court makes copy: $.10 per page. Required to search: name, years to search. Civil cases indexed by defendant, plaintiff. Civil records in books and dockets from 1960; on computer back to 1995. For online access, see criminal section. Mail turnaround time 5-10 days.

Criminal Records: Access: Mail, fax, in person, online. Both court and visitors may perform in person searches. No search fee. Court makes copy: $.10 per page. Required to search: name, years to search, DOB, SSN, signed release. Criminal records in books and dockets from 1960; on computer back to 1995. Access integrated justice system cases back to 1989 free at http://courts.mahoningcountyoh.gov/. Attorney searching also available. Note: Court will not perform party names searches for in-person requesters. Mail turnaround time 5-10 days.

General Information: Public terminal goes back to 1995. Expunged records are not released. Certification fee: $1.00 per cert. Payee: County Court #2. Personal checks accepted. Prepayment and SASE required.

County Court #3 605 E Ohio Ave, Sebring, OH 44672; phone: 330-938-9873; fax: 330-938-6518; hours 8:30AM-4PM (EST). *Misdemeanor, Civil Actions Under $15,000, Small Claims.*

Civil Records: Access: Mail, in person, online. Both court and visitors may perform in person searches. No search fee. Court makes copy: $.10 per page.

Required to search: name, years to search. Civil cases indexed by defendant, plaintiff. Civil records in books from 1958; on computer back to 8/95. For online access, see criminal section Mail turnaround time 1 week.

Criminal Records: Access: Mail, in person, online. Both court and visitors may perform in person searches. No search fee. Court makes copy: $.10 per page. Required to search: name, years to search, DOB; also helpful: SSN. Criminal records in books from 1989; on computer back to 8/95. Access integrated justice system cases back to 1989 free at http://courts.mahoningcountyoh.gov/. Attorney searching also available. Mail turnaround time 1 week.

General Information: Public use terminal available. No expunged records released. Certification fee: $1.00 per page. Payee: Mahoning County Court #3. Personal checks accepted. Prepayment and SASE required.

County Court #4 6000 Mahoning Ave, Youngstown, OH 44515-2288; phone: 330-740-2001; fax: 330-740-2036; hours 8:30AM-4PM (EST). *Misdemeanor, Civil Actions Under $15,000, Small Claims.*

Civil Records: Access: Fax, mail, in person, online. Both court and visitors may perform in person searches. No search fee. Court makes copy: $.10 per page. Required to search: name, years to search. Civil cases indexed by defendant, plaintiff. Civil records in books from the 1940s, on microfiche recent; computerized records since 1996. For online access, see criminal section. Note: Phone, fax and mail access limited to out of town requests. Mail turnaround time same day.

Criminal Records: Access: Fax, mail, in person, online. Both court and visitors may perform in person searches. No search fee. Court makes copy: $.10 per page. Required to search: name, years to search, DOB, SSN, signed release. Criminal records in books from the 1940s, on microfiche rec; computerized records since 1996. Access integrated justice system cases back to 1989 free at http://courts.mahoningcountyoh.gov/. Attorney searching also available. Mail turnaround time same day.

General Information: Public terminal goes back to 1996. No expunged records released. Will fax documents $2.00 1st page, $.50 each add'l. Certification fee: $1.00 per cert. Payee: County Court #4. Personal checks accepted. Prepayment and SASE required.

County Court #5 72 N Broad St, Canfield, OH 44406; phone: 330-533-3643; fax: 330-740-2034; hours 8:30AM-4PM (EST). *Misdemeanor, Civil Actions Under $15,000, Small Claims.*

Civil Records: Access: In person, online. Visitors must perform in person searches themselves. No search fee. Court makes copy: $.10 per page. Required to search: name, years to search; also helpful: address. Civil cases indexed by defendant, plaintiff; on computer since 1995; overall records go back to 1991. For online access, see criminal section.

Criminal Records: Access: Fax, mail, in person, online. Both court and visitors may perform in person searches. Search fee: $5.00 per name. Fee includes certification. Court makes copy: $.10 per page. Required to search: name, years to search; also helpful: DOB, SSN. Criminal records on computer since 1995; overall records go back to 1991. Access integrated justice system cases back to 1989 free at http://courts.mahoningcountyoh.gov/. Attorney searching also available. Mail turnaround time 1-2 days.

General Information: Public terminal goes back to 1995. No LEADS printout records released. Will fax documents $2.00 1st page, $1.00 each add'l. Certification fee: $1.00 per page. Payee: County Court #5. Only cashiers checks and money orders accepted. Prepayment and SASE required.

Campbell Municipal Court 351 Tenney Ave, Campbell, OH 44405; phone: 330-755-2165; fax: 330-750-3058; hours 8AM-4PM (EST). *Misdemeanor, Civil Actions Under $15,000, Eviction, Small Claims.*

Civil Records: Access: Fax, mail, in person. Only the court performs in person searches. No search fee. Court makes copy: $.50 per page. Required to search: name, years to search. Civil cases indexed by defendant, plaintiff. Civil records in books from 1950s; on computer back to 1999. Mail and fax access limited to short searches. Mail turnaround time depends on workload.

Criminal Records: Access: Fax, mail, in person. Only the court performs in person searches. No search fee. Court makes copy: $.50 per page. Required to search: name, years to search; also helpful: DOB, SSN, signed release. Criminal records in books from 1950s; on computer back to 7/1999. Mail turnaround time depends on workload.

General Information: No public access terminal. No sealed records released. Will fax documents to police agencies only. Certification fee: $20.00 includes copies. Payee: Campbell Municipal Court. Only cashiers checks and money orders accepted. Prepayment and SASE required.

Struthers Municipal Court 6 Elm St, Struthers, OH 44471; phone: 330-755-1800; criminal phone: x114; civil phone: x113; fax: 330-755-2790; hours 8AM-4PM; Public access only on Tuesday and Thursday (EST). *Misdemeanor, Civil Actions Under $15,000, Eviction, Small Claims.*

Civil Records: Access: Mail, in person. Both court and visitors may perform in person searches. No search fee. Court makes copy: $.25 per page; same fee for self serve. Required to search: name, years to search. Civil cases indexed by defendant, plaintiff. Civil records in books since 1965; on computer since 1996. Mail turnaround time 2-3 days.

Criminal Records: Access: Mail, in person. Both court and visitors may perform in person searches. No search fee. Court makes copy: $.25 per page; same fee for self serve. Required to search: name, years to search; also helpful: SSN, DOB, signed release. Criminal records in books since 1965; on computer since 1996. Mail turnaround time 2-3 days.

General Information: Public terminal goes back to 1996. (Terminal up on Tuesdays and Thursdays.) No pending case records released. Will fax documents no fee. Certification fee: $10.00. Payee: Municipal Court. Only cashiers checks and money orders accepted. Prepayment and SASE required.

Youngstown Municipal Court - Civil Records PO Box 6047, Youngstown, OH 44501-6047; phone: 330-742-8863; fax: 330-742-8786; hours 8AM-4PM (EST). *Civil Actions Under $15,000, Eviction, Small Claims.*

Civil Records: Access: Phone, fax, mail, in person, online. Both court and visitors may perform in person searches. No search fee. Court makes copy: $.10 per page. Required to search: name, years to search; also helpful: address. Civil cases indexed by defendant, plaintiff. Civil records in books since 1970; on computer since 1998. Access integrated justice system cases back to 1989 free at http://courts.mahoningcountyoh.gov/. Attorney searching also available. Mail turnaround time 1-2 days.

General Information: Public terminal has only civil records back to 1998. (Records are small claims and traffic.) All records are public. Certification fee: $1.00. Cert fee includes copies. Payee: Municipal Court. Personal checks accepted. Prepayment and SASE required.

Youngstown Municipal Court - Criminal Records 26 S Phelps St, Youngstown, OH 44503; phone: 330-742-8860; fax: 330-742-8786; hours 8AM-4PM (EST). *Misdemeanor.*

Criminal Records: Access: Fax, mail, in person, online. Both court and visitors may perform in person searches. No search fee. Court makes copy: $1.00 per page. Required to search: name, years to search, DOB; also helpful: SSN. Criminal records go back to 1966; kept available since 1994 on docket books, microfiche; also on computer since 1998. Access integrated justice system cases back to 1989 free at http://courts.mahoningcountyoh.gov/. Attorney searching also available. Mail turnaround time 1 day.

General Information: Public terminal has only criminal records back to 1998. No records released. Will fax documents to local or toll free line. Certification fee: $1.00. Payee: Municipal Court. Cashiers checks and money orders accepted. SASE required.

Marion County

Common Pleas Court 100 N Main St, Marion, OH 43301-1823; phone: 740-223-4270; probate phone: 740-232-4260; fax: 740-223-4279; hours 8:30AM-4:30PM (EST). *Felony, Civil Actions Over $10,000.*

Civil Records: Access: Mail, in person. Visitors must perform in person searches themselves. Court makes copy: $.10 per page; same fee for self serve. Required to search: name, years to search. Civil cases indexed by defendant, plaintiff; on computer from 1991, prior in books since 1886. Mail is only used if you have the case number and request a specific document. Mail turnaround time 1-3 days.

Criminal Records: Access: Mail, in person. Visitors must perform in person searches themselves. Court makes copy: $.10 per page; same fee for self serve. Required to search: name, years to search; also helpful: DOB, SSN. Criminal records on computer from 1991, prior in books since 1886. Mail is only used if you have the case number and request a specific document. Mail turnaround time 1-3 days.

General Information: Public terminal goes back to 1991. No sealed, expunged records released. Fee to fax documents is $2.00 per transmission and $1.00 per page. Certification fee: $1.00. Payee: Marion County Clerk of Courts. Personal checks accepted. Prepayment and SASE required.

Marion Municipal Court 233 W Center St, Marion, OH 43302-0326; phone: 740-387-0439; criminal phone: 740-382-4031; civil phone: 740-383-5515; fax: 740-382-5274; hours 8:30AM-4:30PM (EST). *Misdemeanor, Civil Actions Under $15,000, Eviction, Small Claims.*

Civil Records: Access: In person only. Visitors must perform in person searches themselves. Court makes copy: $.25 per page. Required to search: name, years to search. Civil cases indexed by defendant, plaintiff; on computer since 1995.

Criminal Records: Access: Mail, in person. Both court and visitors may perform in person searches. No search fee. Court makes copy: $.25 per page. Required to search: name, years to search; also helpful: DOB, SSN. Criminal records on computer from 1986, prior in books. Mail turnaround time 7 days.

General Information: No public access terminal. Certification fee: $5.00. Payee: Municipal Court. Only cashiers checks and money orders accepted. Prepayment and SASE required.

Medina County

Common Pleas Court 93 Public Square, Medina, OH 44256; phone: 330-725-9720; criminal phone: 330-725-9721; civil phone: 330-725-9722; probate phone: 330-725-9703; fax: 330-764-8454; hours 8AM-4:30PM (EST). *Felony, Civil Actions Over $10,000, Probate.*

www.medinacommonpleas.com

Note: Probate is a separate office at this address.

Civil Records: Access: Mail, in person, online. Both court and visitors may perform in person searches. No search fee. Court makes copy: $.25 per page. Required to search: name, years to search. Civil cases indexed by defendant, plaintiff; on computer from 10/92, in books to early 1960s, prior archived. Online access is the same as criminal, see below. Mail turnaround time 1-2 days.

Criminal Records: Access: Mail, in person, online. Both court and visitors may perform in person searches. No search fee. Court makes copy: $.25 per page. Required to search: name, years to search. Criminal records on computer from 10/92, in books to early 1960s, prior archived. Search court documents, motion dockets, sexual predator judgments and court notices at the web page. Mail turnaround time 1-2 days.

General Information: Public terminal has criminal back to 1991 and civil back to 1992. Will not fax documents. Certification fee: $1.00 per page. Payee: Clerk of Court. Personal checks accepted. Prepayment and SASE required.

Medina Municipal Court 135 N Elmwood, Medina, OH 44256; phone: 330-723-3287; fax: 330-225-1108; hours 8AM-4:30PM (EST). *Misdemeanor, Civil Actions Under $15,000, Eviction, Small Claims.*

www.medinamunicipalcourt.org

Civil Records: Access: Mail, online, in person. Both court and visitors may perform in person searches. Court makes copy: $.25 per page. Required to search: name, years to search. Civil cases indexed by defendant, plaintiff; on computer from 1986, prior in books. There are two systems, one is via the website, and the other is dial-up system. Both contain records from 1986 to present. Access to the dial-up system requires ProComm Plus. There are no fees. Search by name or case number. Note: The computer access number is 330-723-4337. For more information, call Rich Armstrong at 330-723-3287, ext. 230. Mail turnaround 7-14 days.

Criminal Records: Access: Mail, online, in person. Visitors must perform in person searches themselves. No search fee. Court makes copy: $.25 per page. Required to search: name, years to search; also helpful: address, DOB, SSN. Criminal records on computer from 1986, prior in books. Online access to traffic records is the same as civil. Mail turnaround time 7-14 days.

General Information: Public terminal goes back to 1987. No expunged records released. Certification fee: $1.50. Payee: Municipal Court. Personal checks accepted. Visa, MC accepted for criminal and traffic records only. Prepayment and SASE required.

Wadsworth Municipal Court 120 Maple St, Wadsworth, OH 44281-1825; phone: 330-335-1596; fax: 330-335-2723; hours 8AM-4PM (EST). *Misdemeanor, Civil Actions Under $15,000, Eviction, Small Claims.*

www.wadsworthmunicipalcourt.com/main.htm

Note: Covers Villages of Gloria Glens, Lodi, Seville, Westfield Center; Townships of: Guilford, Harrisville, Homer, Sharon, Wadsworth, and Westfield.

Civil Records: Access: Fax, mail, in person. Both court and visitors may perform in person searches. No search fee. Court makes copy: $.05 per page after first 25 pages. Required to search: name, years to search. Civil cases indexed by defendant, plaintiff; on computer from 3/90, prior in books. Mail turnaround time 2-4 days.

Criminal Records: Access: Fax, mail, in person. Both court and visitors may perform in person searches. No search fee. Court makes copy: $.05 per page after first 25 pages. Required to search: name, years to search; also helpful: address, DOB, SSN. Criminal records on computer from 3/90, prior in books. Mail turnaround time up to 1 week.

General Information: Public terminal goes back to 1990. No search warrant records released. No fee to fax documents. Local faxing only. Certification fee: $1.00. Payee: Wadsworth Municipal Court. Personal checks accepted. Prepayment and SASE required.

Meigs County

Common Pleas Court Clerk, PO Box 151, Pomeroy, OH 45769; phone: 740-992-6439; probate phone: 740-992-3096; fax: 740-992-3828; hours 8:30AM-4:30PM (EST). *Felony, Civil Actions Over $3,000, Probate.*

Note: Probate fax is 740-992-6727.

Civil Records: Access: In person only. Visitors must perform in person searches themselves. Court makes copy: $.25 per page. Required to search: name, years to search; also helpful: address. Civil cases indexed by defendant, plaintiff; on computer since 1996, in books to 1800s.

Criminal Records: Access: In person only. Visitors must perform in person searches themselves. Court makes copy: $.25 per page. Required to search: name, years to search, DOB; also helpful: SSN. Criminal records on computer since 1996, in books to 1800s.

General Information: Public terminal goes back to 1996. No secret records released. Will fax specific document to local or toll-free number. Certification fee: $1.00. Payee: Clerk of Court. Personal checks accepted. Prepayment required.

Meigs County Court 2nd St Courthouse, Pomeroy, OH 45769; phone: 740-992-2279; fax: 740-992-4570; hours 8:30AM-4:30PM (EST). *Misdemeanor, Civil Actions Under $15,000, Small Claims.*

Civil Records: Access: In person only. Visitors must perform in person searches themselves. Court makes copy: $.25 per page. Required to search: name, years to search. Civil cases indexed by defendant, plaintiff; on computer from 8/90, prior in docket books. Phone access limited to records from 1990 to present.

Criminal Records: Access: In person only. Visitors must perform in person searches themselves. Court makes copy: $.25 per page. Required to search: name, years to search, DOB, SSN, signed release. Criminal records on computer from 8/90, prior in docket books. Phone access limited to records from 1990 to present.

General Information: No public access terminal. No sealed records released. Will not fax specific case file. Certification fee: $2.00 includes copy fee. Payee: Meigs County Court. Personal checks accepted. Prepayment required.

Mercer County

Common Pleas Court 101 N Main St, Rm 205, PO Box 28, Celina, OH 45822; phone: 419-586-6461; probate phone: 419-586-2418; fax: 419-586-5826; probate fax: 419-586-4506; hours 8:30AM-4PM (EST). *Felony, Civil Actions Over $10,000, Probate.*

Note: Probate records located at 101 N Main ST, Rm 306-307.

Civil Records: Access: In person only. Visitors must perform in person searches themselves. Court makes copy: $.25 per page. Required to search: name, years to search; also helpful: address. Civil cases indexed by defendant, plaintiff; on computer back to 1997, microfiche up to and including 1985, prior in books.

Criminal Records: Access: In person only. Visitors must perform in person searches themselves. Court makes copy: $.25 per page. Required to search: name, years to search; also helpful: address, DOB, SSN. Criminal records on computer back to 1997, microfiche up to and including 1985, prior in books.

General Information: Public terminal goes back to 1997. No juvenile or sealed records released. Will fax specific document for $3.00 for 1st page; $1.00 for each add'l page. Certification fee: $1.00. Payee: Clerk of Court. Personal checks accepted. Prepayment required.

Celina Municipal Court PO Box 362, Celina, OH 45822; phone: 419-586-6491; fax: 419-586-4735; hours 8AM-5PM (EST). *Misdemeanor, Civil Actions Under $15,000, Eviction, Small Claims.*

Civil Records: Access: Fax, mail, in person. Both court and visitors may perform in person searches. No search fee. Court makes copy: $.05 per page. Required to search: name, years to search; also helpful: address. Civil cases indexed by defendant, plaintiff; on computer from 1990, prior in books. Mail turnaround time 2-3 days.

Criminal Records: Access: Fax, mail, in person. Both court and visitors may perform in person searches. No search fee. Court makes copy: $.05 per page. Required to search: name, years to search; also helpful: address, DOB, SSN. Criminal records are on computer since 1989, prior found in books and files. Mail turnaround time 2-3 days.

General Information: Public terminal has criminal back to 1989 and civil back to 1990. No confidential information released. Will fax documents to local or toll free line. Certification fee: $1.00 per page. Payee: Municipal Court. Personal checks accepted. Prepayment and SASE required.

Miami County

Common Pleas Court & Court of Appeals Safety Bldg, 201 W Main St, 3rd Fl, Troy, OH 45373; phone: 937-440-6010; probate phone: 937-440-6050; civil/criminal fax: 937-440-6011; probate fax: 937-440-3529; hours 8AM-4PM (EST). *Felony, Civil Actions Over $10,000, Probate.*

www.onthesquare.com/muni/index.htm

Note: Probate is a separate division on the 2nd Fl.

Civil Records: Access: Fax, mail, in person. Both court and visitors may perform in person searches. Search fee: $5.00 per name. Court makes copy: $.25 per page. Required to search: name, years to search; also helpful: address. Civil cases indexed by defendant, plaintiff. Civil records in books for past 30 years, prior are archived; on computer since 1984. Mail turnaround time 1-2 days.

Criminal Records: Access: Fax, mail, in person. Both court and visitors may perform in person searches. Search fee: $5.00 per name. Court makes copy: $.25 per page. Required to search: name, years to search, DOB, SSN; also helpful: address. Criminal records in books for past 30 years, prior are archived; on computer since 1984. Mail turnaround time 1-2 days.

General Information: Public terminal goes back to 1989. No expunged or sealed records released. Will fax documents $1.00 per doc. Certification fee: $1.00. Payee: Miami County Clerk of Courts. Personal checks accepted. Prepayment required.

Miami County Municipal Court 201 W Main St, Troy, OH 45373; phone: 937-440-3910; criminal phone: 937-440-3910; civil phone: 937-440-3918; fax: 937-440-3911; hours 8AM-4PM (EST). *Misdemeanor, Civil Actions Under $15,000, Eviction, Small Claims.*

www.co.miami.oh.us/muni/index.htm

Note: If the SSN is not provided by the party doing the search, the court personnel will mask the SSN before providing copies.

Civil Records: Access: Mail, in person, online. Both court and visitors may perform in person searches. Search fee: $5.00 per name. Court makes copy: $.25 per page. Self serve copy fee: none. Required to search: name, years to search. Civil cases indexed by defendant, plaintiff. Civil records in books go back 25 years; on computer back to 11/89. Online access to records is free at www.co.miami.oh.us/pa/index.htm. Mail turnaround time 2-3 days.

Criminal Records: Access: Mail, in person, online. Both court and visitors may perform in person searches. Search fee: $5.00 per name. Court makes copy: $.25 per page. Self serve copy fee: none. Required to search: name, years to search, SSN. Criminal records on computer back to 1985, prior in books. Online access to records is free at www.co.miami.oh.us/pa/index.htm. Mail turnaround time 2-3 days.

General Information: Public terminal has criminal back to 1986 and civil back to 11/1989. No search warrant records released. Will fax documents for no fee. Certification fee: $2.00 per page. Payee: Municipal Court. Visa, MC accepted. Prepayment and SASE required.

Monroe County

Common Pleas Court 101 N Main St, Rm 26, Woodsfield, OH 43793; phone: 740-472-0761; probate phone: 740-472-1654; fax: 740-472-2549; hours 8:30AM-4:30PM (EST). *Felony, Civil Actions Over $3,000, Probate.*

Note: Probate is a separate index at a separate office.

Civil Records: Access: In person only. Visitors must perform in person searches themselves. Court makes copy: $.25 per page. Required to search: name, years to search; also helpful: address. Civil cases indexed by defendant, plaintiff. Civil records in books since 1800; computerized records from 11/18/02 to present.

Criminal Records: Access: Mail, fax, in person. Both court and visitors may perform in person searches. Search fee: $2.00 per name. Clerk of Courts will search more than one name but we do charge $2.00 per name!!!. Court makes copy: $.25 per page. Required to search: name, years to search; also helpful: address, DOB, SSN. Criminal records in books since 1800; computerized records from 11/18/02 to present. The court will not do party names searches for in-person requesters. Mail turnaround time 3 days.

General Information: Public terminal goes back to 11/2002. No secret indictment records released. Fee to fax documents is $2.00 per page. Certification fee: $1.00 per page. Payee: Clerk of Court. Personal checks accepted. Prepayment and SASE required.

County Court 101 N Main St, Rm 35, Woodsfield, OH 43793; phone: 740-472-5181; fax: 740-472-2526; hours 9AM-4:30PM (EST). *Misdemeanor, Civil Actions Under $15,000, Small Claims.*

Civil Records: Access: Phone, mail, in person. Both court and visitors may perform in person searches. No search fee. No copy fee. Required to search: name, years to search. Civil cases indexed by defendant, plaintiff. Civil records in books, indexed back to 1950; on computer back to 8/1999. Mail turnaround time 1-2 days.

Criminal Records: Access: Phone, mail, in person. Both court and visitors may perform in person searches. No search fee. No copy fee. Required to search: name, years to search. Criminal records in books, indexed back to 1979; on computer back to 1999. Mail turnaround time 1-2 days.

General Information: Public use terminal available. No certification fee . SASE required.

Montgomery County

Common Pleas Court 41 N Perry St, Dayton, OH 45422; phone: 937-225-4536; criminal phone: 937-225-4536 x4; civil phone: 937-225-4512; probate phone: 937-225-4640; criminal fax:; civil fax: 937-496-7220; hours 8:30AM-4:30PM (EST). *Felony, Civil Actions Over $10,000, Probate.*

www.clerk.co.montgomery.oh.us

Civil Records: Access: Fax, mail, in person, online. Both court and visitors may perform in person searches. Court makes copy: $.10 per page. Required to search: name, years to search; also helpful: address. Civil cases indexed by defendant, plaintiff; on computer from 1970s, prior in books. Online access to the Courts county-wide PRO system is free at www.clerk.co.montgomery.oh.us/legal/records.cfm. Note: Address mail requests to Montgomery County Clerk of Court "Civil Records."

Criminal Records: Access: In person, online. Visitors must perform in person searches themselves. Court makes copy: $.10 per page. Required to search: name, years to search; also helpful: address, DOB, SSN. Criminal records on computer from 1970s, prior in books. Online access to criminal and traffic records is the same as civil.

General Information: Public terminal has criminal back to 1997 and civil back to 1997. No sealed records released. Certification fee: $1.00 per page. Cert fee includes copies. Payee: Clerk of Court. Personal checks accepted. Prepayment required.

County Court - Area 1 195 S Clayton Rd, New Lebanon, OH 45345-9601; phone: 937-687-9099; fax: 937-687-7119; hours 8AM-4PM; (10PM-7PM, M); (9-4PM, F) (EST). *Misdemeanor, Civil Actions Under $15,000, Small Claims.*

www.clerk.co.montgomery.oh.us

Civil Records: Access: Mail, in person, online. Both court and visitors may perform in person searches. No search fee. Court makes copy: $.10 per page. Required to search: name, years to search. Civil cases indexed by defendant, plaintiff; on computer from 2/92, prior in books, Archives 937-225-6366. Search county-wide records online at www.clerk.co.montgomery.oh.us/areacourt/pro/. Mail turnaround time 2-3 days.

Criminal Records: Access: Mail, in person, online. Both court and visitors may perform in person searches. No search fee. Court makes copy: $.10 per page. Required to search: name, years to search; also helpful: SSN. Criminal records on computer from 2/92, prior in books, Archives 937-225-6366. Online access to criminal records is the same as civil. Mail turnaround time 2-3 days.

General Information: No public access terminal. No medical, PSI report or LEADS print-out records released. Certification fee: $1.00. Payee: Montgomery County Court Area One. Only cashiers checks and money orders accepted. Prepayment and SASE required.

County Court - Area 2 6111 Taylorsville Rd, Huber Heights, OH 45424; phone: 937-496-7231; fax: 937-496-7236; hours 8Am-4PM M-W; N-7PM Th; 9AM-4PM F (EST). *Misdemeanor, Civil Actions Under $15,000, Small Claims under $3,000.*

Civil Records: Access: Phone, fax, mail, in person, online, email. Both court and visitors may perform in person searches. No search fee. Court makes copy: $.25 per page. Required to search: name, years to search; also helpful: address. Civil cases indexed by defendant, plaintiff; on computer from 1992, prior in books to 1974. Search county-wide records online at www.clerk.co.montgomery.oh.us/areacourt/pro/. Mail turnaround time 2-7 days.

Criminal Records: Access: Phone, fax, mail, in person, online, email. Both court and visitors may perform in person searches. No search fee. Court makes copy: $.25 per page. Required to search: name, years to search; also helpful: address, DOB, SSN. Criminal records on computer from 1992, prior in books to 1974. Online access to criminal records is the same as civil. Mail turnaround time 2-7 days.

General Information: Public terminal goes back to 1991. No confidential, forensic evaluation or medical records released. No fee to fax documents. Certification fee: $1.00 per cert. Payee: County Court Area Two. Business checks and credit cards accepted. Prepayment and SASE required.

Dayton Municipal Court - Civil Division 301 W 3rd St, PO Box 968, Dayton, OH 45402-0968; phone: 937-333-4471; fax: 937-333-4468; hours 8AM-4:30PM (EST). *Civil Actions Under $15,000, Eviction, Small Claims.*

www.daytonmunicipalcourt.org

Civil Records: Access: Phone, fax, mail, in person, online. Both court and visitors may perform in person searches. No search fee. Court makes copy: $.25 per page. Required to search: name, years to search; also helpful: address. Civil cases indexed by defendant, plaintiff; on computer back to 1998, prior in books to 1977. Online access to municipal court records is free at www.daytonmunicipalcourt.org/scripts/rgw.dll/Docket; includes traffic and criminal. Mail turnaround time 2-3 days.

General Information: Public terminal has only civil records back to 1998. No expunged case records released. No certification fee . Payee: Clerk of Court. Personal checks accepted. Prepayment and SASE required.

Dayton Municipal Court - Criminal Division 301 W 3rd St, Rm 331, Dayton, OH 45402; phone: 937-333-4315; fax: 937-333-4490; hours 8AM-4:30PM (EST). *Misdemeanor.*

www.daytonmunicipalcourt.org

Criminal Records: Access: In person, online. Visitors must perform in person searches themselves. Court makes copy: $.10 per page. Required to search: name, years to search, DOB; also helpful: address, SSN, signed release. Criminal records on computer back to 1992, prior in books. Online access to municipal court records is free at www.daytonmunicipalcourt.org/scripts/rgw.dll/Docket; includes traffic and civil. Note: Phone access is limited.

General Information: Public terminal has only criminal records back to 1992. All records are public. No certification fee . Payee: Dayton Municipal Court. Personal checks or Visa, MC accepted. Prepayment required.

Kettering Municipal Court 3600 Shroyer Rd, Kettering, OH 45429; phone: 937-296-2461; fax: 937-534-7017; hours 8:30AM-4:30PM (EST). *Misdemeanor, Civil Actions Under $15,000, Eviction, Small Claims.*

Civil Records: Access: Phone, mail, fax, in person. Both court and visitors may perform in person searches. No search fee. Court makes copy: $.05 per page. Required to search: name, years to search. Civil cases indexed by defendant, plaintiff; on computer from 1989, prior in books. Mail turnaround time 1-5 days.

Criminal Records: Access: Phone, mail, in person. Both court and visitors may perform in person searches. No search fee. Court makes copy: $.05 per page. Required to search: name, years to search, DOB; also helpful: SSN. Criminal records on computer from 1988. Mail turnaround time 1-5 days.

General Information: No public access terminal. No expungment records released. Will fax documents to local or toll free line. Certification fee: $2.50 per page. Payee: Kettering Municipal Court. Business checks, attorney checks or Visa, MC accepted. SASE required.

Miamisburg Municipal Court 10 N 1st St, Miamisburg, OH 45342; phone: 937-866-2203; criminal fax: 937-866-0135; same fax for civil/probate; hours 8AM-4PM (EST). *Misdemeanor, Civil Actions Under $15,000, Eviction, Small Claims.*

www.miamisburgcourts.com

Civil Records: Access: Mail, in person. Both court and visitors may perform in person searches. No search fee. Court makes copy: $.25 per page. Required to search: name, years to search; also helpful: address. Civil cases indexed by defendant, plaintiff; on computer from 1988, prior in books. Call in advance to schedule in person searching. Mail request requires SASE. Mail turnaround time 1-2 weeks.

Criminal Records: Access: Mail, in person. Only the court performs in person searches. No search fee. Court makes copy: $.25 per page. Required to search: name, years to search; also helpful: address, DOB, SSN. Criminal records on computer from 1988, prior in books. Call in advance to schedule in person searching. Mail request requires SASE. Mail turnaround time 1-2 weeks.

General Information: No public access terminal. No police reports, search warrants with no returns records released. Will fax documents to local or toll free line. No certification fee . Payee: Clerk of Court. Personal checks accepted. Prepayment and SASE required.

Oakwood Municipal Court 30 Park Ave, Dayton, OH 45419; phone: 937-293-3058; fax: 937-297-2939; hours 8:30AM-4PM (EST). *Misdemeanor, Civil Actions Under $15,000, Eviction, Small Claims.*

Civil Records: Access: Mail, in person. Only the court performs in person searches. No search fee.

Court makes copy: $.05 per page. Required to search: name, years to search; also helpful: address. Civil cases indexed by defendant, plaintiff. Civil records in books since 1976. Mail turnaround time 1-2 weeks.

Criminal Records: Access: Mail, in person. Only the court performs in person searches. No search fee. Court makes copy: $.05 per page. Required to search: name, years to search; also helpful: address, DOB, SSN. Criminal records in books since 1976. Address mail search requests to the Police Records Section. Mail turnaround time 1-2 weeks.

General Information: No public access terminal. No sealed, expunged or confidential records released. Will fax documents to local or toll free line. No certification fee . Local checks accepted. SASE required.

Vandalia Municipal Court PO Box 429, 245 James Bohanan Dr, Justice Center, 2nd Fl, Vandalia, OH 45377; phone: 937-898-3996; fax: 937-898-6648; hours 8AM-4PM (EST). *Misdemeanor, Civil Actions Under $15,000, Eviction, Small Claims.*

www.vandaliacourt.com

Civil Records: Access: Phone, fax, mail, in person, online. Both court and visitors may perform in person searches. Search fee: $1.00 per page for complete print out. Court makes copy: $1.00 per page. Required to search: name, years to search. Civil cases indexed by defendant, plaintiff; on computer from 1986, prior in books. Search records, including traffic, at http://64.108.110.4/cmiflash/court/. Mail turnaround time 7 days.

Criminal Records: Access: Fax, mail, in person, online. Both court and visitors may perform in person searches. No search fee. Court makes copy: $1.00 per page. Required to search: name, years to search, DOB, SSN. Criminal records on computer from 1986, prior in books. Search records, including traffic, at http://64.108.110.4/cmiflash/court/. Mail turnaround time 7 days.

General Information: Public use terminal available. No medical, psychological reports or domestic violence report records released. No certification fee . Payee: Clerk of Court. Business checks or credit cards accepted. Prepayment and SASE required.

Dayton Municipal Court - Traffic Division PO Box 10700, 301 W 3rd St, Dayton, OH 45402; phone: 937-333-4313; fax: 937-333-7558; hours 8AM-4:30PM (EST). *Misdemeanor.*

www.daytonmunicipalcourt.org

Note: It is difficult for the court to provide case information prior to 1995. Search dockets free online at www.daytonmunicipalcourt.org/scripts/rgw.dll/Docket.

Morgan County

Common Pleas Court 19 E Main St, McConnelsville, OH 43756; phone: 740-962-4752; probate phone: 740-962-2861; fax: 740-962-4589; hours 8AM-4PM M-Th; 8AM-5PM F (EST). *Felony, Civil Actions Over $3,000, Probate.*

Note: Above number is for Clerk. The Common Pleas Court can be reached at 740-962-3371.

Civil Records: Access: Mail, in person. Visitors must perform in person searches themselves. Search fee: $2.00 per name. No copy fee. Required to search: name, years to search; also helpful: address. Civil cases indexed by defendant, plaintiff. Civil records in books, some back to 1850. Mail turnaround time 1-3 days.

Criminal Records: Access: Mail, in person. Both court and visitors may perform in person searches. Search fee: $2.00 per name. No copy fee. Required to search: name, years to search; also helpful: address, DOB, SSN. Criminal records in books, some back to 1850. Mail turnaround time 1-3 days.

General Information: Public use terminal available. No secret indictment records released. Certification fee: $1.00 per page. Payee: Clerk of Court. Personal checks accepted. Prepayment and SASE required.

Morgan County Court 37 E Main St, McConnelsville, OH 43756; phone: 740-962-4031; fax: 740-962-2895; hours 8AM-4PM (EST). *Misdemeanor, Civil Actions Under $15,000, Small Claims.*

Civil Records: Access: Fax, mail, in person. Both court and visitors may perform in person searches. No search fee. Court makes copy: $.10 per page; same fee for self serve. Required to search: name, years to search. Civil cases indexed by defendant, plaintiff. Civil records in books from 1950, computerized since 12/02. Mail turnaround time 1-2 days.

Criminal Records: Access: Fax, mail, in person. Both court and visitors may perform in person searches. No search fee. Court makes copy: $.10 per page; same fee for self serve. Required to search: name, years to search, DOB; also helpful: SSN. Criminal records in books from 1950, computerized since 12/02. Mail turnaround time 1-2 days.

General Information: Public terminal goes back to 12/02. No fee to fax documents. Certification fee: $1.00. Payee: Morgan County Court. Personal checks accepted. Prepayment and SASE required.

Morrow County

Common Pleas Court 48 E High St, Mount Gilead, OH 43338; phone: 419-947-2085; probate phone: 419-947-5575; fax: 419-947-5421; hours 8AM-4:30PM (EST). *Felony, Civil Actions Over $3,000, Probate.*

Civil Records: Access: Phone, fax, mail, in person. Both court and visitors may perform in person searches. No search fee. Court makes copy: $.25 per page; same fee for self serve. Required to search: name, years to search; also helpful: address. Civil cases indexed by defendant, plaintiff. Civil records in books from 1960, computerized since 1/02. Mail turnaround time 1 day.

Criminal Records: Access: Phone, fax, mail, in person. Both court and visitors may perform in person searches. No search fee. Court makes copy: $.25 per page; same fee for self serve. Required to search: name, years to search; also helpful: address, DOB, SSN. Criminal records in books from 1960, computerized since 1/02. Mail turnaround time 1 day.

General Information: Public terminal goes back to 2001. Certification fee: $1.00. Payee: Clerk of Court. Personal checks accepted. Prepayment and SASE required.

Municiapl Court 48 E High St, Mount Gilead, OH 43338; phone: 419-947-5045; fax: 419-947-9161; hours 7:30AM-5PM (EST). *Misdemeanor, Civil Actions Under $15,000, Small Claims.*

Civil Records: Access: Phone, fax, mail, in person. Both court and visitors may perform in person searches. No search fee. Court makes copy: $1.00 per page. Required to search: name, years to search; also helpful-DOB or SSN. Civil cases indexed by defendant, plaintiff; on computer back to 1997, indexed on books from 1970s, archived from 1800s. Mail turnaround time 1-2 days.

Criminal Records: Access: Phone, fax, mail, in person. Both court and visitors may perform in person searches. No search fee. Court makes copy: $1.00 per page. Required to search: name, years to search, DOB, SSN. Criminal records on computer since 1990, indexed on books from 1970s, archived from 1800s. Mail turnaround time 1-2 days.

General Information: No public access terminal. No confidential records released. Certification fee: $2.00 per cert.

Muskingum County

Common Pleas Court 401 Main St, Zanesville, OH 43701; phone: 740-455-7104; probate phone: 740-455-7113; hours 8:30AM-4:30PM (EST). *Felony, Civil Actions, Probate.*

Note: As of 1/1/2001, there is no dollar limit on civil actions; prior, the civil action minimum was $15,000. This court reports it hopes to be online by beginning of 2006. Probate is separate index at this same address.

Civil Records: Access: Mail, in person. Both court and visitors may perform in person searches. No search fee. Court makes copy: $.25 per page; same fee for self serve. Required to search: name, years to search; also helpful: address. Civil cases indexed by defendant, plaintiff. Civil records in original files back to 1800s. Mail turnaround time 2 weeks.

Criminal Records: Access: Mail, in person. Both court and visitors may perform in person searches. No search fee. Court makes copy: $.25 per page; same fee for self serve. Required to search: name, years to search, DOB; also helpful: address, SSN. Criminal records on docket books to 1960, original files back to 1800s. Mail turnaround time 2 weeks.

General Information: Public terminal goes back to 10/17/1994. No grand jury records released. Will not fax documents. Certification fee: $1.00 per page include copy fee. Payee: Clerk of Court. Personal checks or Visa/MC accepted. Prepayment and SASE required.

County Court 27 N 5th St, Zanesville, OH 43701; phone: 740-455-7138; fax: 740-455-7157; hours 8AM-4PM (EST). *Misdemeanor, Civil Actions Under $15,000, Small Claims.*

www.muskingumcountycourt.org

Civil Records: Access: Fax, mail, in person, online. Both court and visitors may perform in person searches. No search fee. Court makes copy: $.25 per page. Required to search: name, years to search; also helpful: address. Civil cases indexed by defendant, plaintiff. Civil records in books from 1958; on computer back to 1995. Access to county court records is free at www.muskingumcountycourt.org/sear.html. Mail turnaround time up to 1 week.

Criminal Records: Access: Fax, mail, in person, online. Both court and visitors may perform in person searches. No search fee. Court makes copy: $.25 per page. Required to search: name, years to search, DOB; also helpful: address, SSN. Criminal records in books from 1958; on computer back to 1995. Access to county court records is free at www.muskingumcountycourt.org/sear.html. Mail turnaround time up to 1 week.

General Information: Public terminal goes back to 1995. No expunged records released. No fee to fax documents. Fax available in emergency only. Certification fee: $1.00 per page includes copy fee. Payee: Muskingum County Clerk. Personal checks accepted. Prepayment and SASE required.

Zanesville Municipal Court PO Box 566, 332 South St, Zanesville, OH 43702; phone: 740-454-3269; fax: 740-455-0739; hours 9AM-4:30PM; 9AM-N Thur (EST). *Misdemeanor, Civil Actions Under $15,000, Eviction, Small Claims.*

www.coz.org/municipal_court.cfm

Civil Records: Access: Mail, in person, online. Both court and visitors may perform in person searches. No search fee. No copy fee. Required to search: name, years to search; also helpful: address. Civil cases indexed by defendant, plaintiff; on computer since 1987. Online access same as criminal, see below. Mail turnaround time 1 day.

Criminal Records: Access: Mail, in person, fax, online. Both court and visitors may perform in person searches. No search fee. No copy fee. Required to search: name, years to search; also helpful: address, DOB, SSN. Criminal records on computer since 1993. Online access is free at http://216.29.90.62/connection/court/. Also includes traffic and civil. Mail turnaround time 1 day.

General Information: Public terminal has criminal back to 1993 and civil back to 1986. Certification fee: $1.00 per page include copies. Payee: Municipal Court. Personal checks accepted. Prepayment and SASE required.

Noble County

Common Pleas Court 350 Courthouse, Caldwell, OH 43724; phone: 740-732-4408; probate phone: 740-732-5047; fax: 740-732-0100; hours 8AM-4PM M-W; 8AM-Noon Th; 8AM-6PM F (EST). *Felony, Civil Actions Over $3,000.*

Note: Probate is a separate office at 270 Courthouse, in Caldwell.

Civil Records: Access: Phone, fax, mail, in person. Both court and visitors may perform in person searches. No search fee. Court makes copy: $.25 per page; same fee for self serve. Required to search: name, years to search; also helpful: address. Civil cases indexed by defendant, plaintiff. Civil records in books, archived back to mid-1800s. Recent civil records are computerized. Mail turnaround time 1-2 days.

Criminal Records: Access: Phone, fax, mail, in person. Both court and visitors may perform in person searches. No search fee. Court makes copy: $.25 per page; same fee for self serve. Required to search: name, years to search; also helpful: address, DOB, SSN. Criminal records in books, archived back to 1800s. Recent civil records are computerized. Mail turnaround time 1-2 days.

General Information: Public terminal goes back to 7/1997. No sealed records released. No fee to fax documents. Certification fee: $1.00 per page. Payee: Clerk of Court. Personal checks accepted. Will bill all court rule copies. SASE required.

Noble County Court 100 Courthouse, Caldwell, OH 43724; phone: 740-732-5795; fax: 740-732-1435; hours 8:30AM-4PM M-W,F; 8:30-N Th (EST). *Misdemeanor, Civil Actions Under $15,000, Small Claims.*

Civil Records: Access: Phone, fax, mail, in person. Both court and visitors may perform in person searches. No search fee. Court makes copy: $.25 per page; same fee for self serve. Required to search: name, years to search. Civil cases indexed by defendant, plaintiff. Civil records in books since 1960, on computer back to 2002. Mail turnaround time same day.

Criminal Records: Access: Fax, mail, in person. Both court and visitors may perform in person searches. No search fee. Court makes copy: $.25 per page; same fee for self serve. Required to search: name, years to search, DOB; also helpful- SSN, signed release. Criminal records in books since 1960; on computer back to 2002. Mail turnaround time same day.

General Information: Public terminal goes back to 2002. Will fax documents to local or toll free line. Certification fee: $5.00 per document. Payee: County Court. Only cashiers checks and money orders accepted. Prepayment and SASE required.

Ottawa County

Common Pleas Court 315 Madison St, 3rd Fl, Port Clinton, OH 43452; phone: 419-734-6755 (General Division); probate phone: 419-734-6830; hours 8:30AM-4:30PM (EST). *Felony, Civil Actions Over $10,000, Probate.*

www.ottawacocpcourt.com

Note: Probate is a separate court at 315 Madison St, Rm 306.

Civil Records: Access: In person only. Visitors must perform in person searches themselves. Court makes copy: $.15 per page. Required to search: name, years to search; also helpful: address. Civil cases indexed by defendant, plaintiff; on computer from 8/89, prior in books to 1842.

Criminal Records: Access: In person only. Visitors must perform in person searches themselves. Court makes copy: $.15 per page. Required to search: name, years to search; also helpful: address, DOB, SSN. Criminal records on computer from 8/89, prior in books to 1842.

General Information: Public terminal goes back to 8/1989. No sealed records released. Will fax specific case for $3.00. Certification fee: $1.00. Payee: Clerk

of Courts. Personal checks accepted. Prepayment required.

Ottawa County Municipal Court 1860 E Perry St, Port Clinton, OH 43452; phone: 419-734-4143; fax: 419-732-2862; hours 8:30AM-4:30PM (EST). *Misdemeanor, Civil Actions Under $15,000, Eviction, Small Claims.*

www.ottawacountymunicipalcourt.com

Civil Records: Access: In person, online. Visitors must perform in person searches themselves. Court makes copy: $.10 per page. Required to search: name, years to search; also helpful: address. Civil cases indexed by defendant, plaintiff; on computer from 1989, prior in books. Record index is at www.ottawacountymunicipalcourt.com/search.html. Includes small claims.

Criminal Records: Access: In person, online. Visitors must perform in person searches themselves. Court makes copy: $.10 per page. Required to search: name, years to search, DOB; also helpful: address, SSN. Criminal records on computer from 1989, prior in books. Record index is at www.ottawacountymunicipalcourt.com/search.html. Includes traffic.

General Information: Public use terminal available. No sealed records released. Certification fee: $3.00. Payee: Ottawa County Municipal Court. Only cashiers checks and money orders accepted. Prepayment required.

Paulding County

Common Pleas Court 115 N Williams St, Rm 104, Paulding, OH 45879; phone: 419-399-8210; probate phone: 419-339-8256; civil/criminal fax: 419-399-8248; probate fax: 419-399-8261; hours 8AM-4PM (EST). *Felony, Civil Actions Over $3,000, Probate.*

Note: Probate in separate index at this address.

Civil Records: Access: Fax, mail, in person. Visitors must perform in person searches themselves. Search fee: $5.00 per name. Court makes copy: $.25 per page. Required to search: name, years to search. Civil cases indexed by defendant, plaintiff. Civil records in books, archived from 1800s. Mail turnaround time same day.

Criminal Records: Access: Fax, mail, in person. Both court and visitors may perform in person searches. Search fee: $5.00 per name. Court makes copy: $.25 per page. Required to search: name, years to search; also helpful: address, DOB, SSN. Criminal records in books, archived from 1800s. Mail turnaround time same day.

General Information: Public terminal goes back to 12/2/2002. No mental, adoption records released. No fee to fax documents. Certification fee: $1.00. Payee: Clerk of Court. Personal checks accepted. Prepayment and SASE required.

County Court 201 E Carolina St, #2, Paulding, OH 45879; phone: 419-399-2792; fax: 419-399-3421; hours 8AM-4PM (EST). *Misdemeanor, Civil Actions Under $15,000, Small Claims.*

www.pauldingcountycourt.com

Civil Records: Access: Fax, mail, in person. Both court and visitors may perform in person searches. Search fee: $5.00 per name. Court makes copy: $.50 per page. Required to search: name, years to search; also helpful: address. Civil cases indexed by defendant, plaintiff. Civil records in books since 1985; computerized records since 1997. Access to civil records is at www.pauldingcountycourt.com/. Mail turnaround time 2-4 days.

Criminal Records: Access: Fax, mail, in person. Both court and visitors may perform in person searches. Search fee: $5.00 per name. Court makes copy: $.50 per page. Required to search: name, years to search; also helpful: address, DOB, SSN. Criminal records in books since 1985; computerized records since 1997. Access to criminal records is at www.pauldingcountycourt.com/. Mail turnaround time 2-4 days.

General Information: Public use terminal available. No fee to fax documents. Certification fee: $2.00. Payee: County Court. Personal checks not accepted. Prepayment and SASE required.

Perry County

Common Pleas Court PO Box 67, New Lexington, OH 43764; phone: 740-342-1022; probate phone: 740-342-1493; fax: 740-342-5527; hours 8AM-4PM (EST). *Felony, Civil Actions Over $3,000, Probate.*

www.lawrencecountyclkofcrt.org

Civil Records: Access: In person only. Visitors must perform in person searches themselves. Court makes copy: $.05 per page. Required to search: name, years to search; also helpful: address. Civil cases indexed by defendant, plaintiff; on computer since 3/96, in case files prior, indexed from 1940.

Criminal Records: Access: In person only. Visitors must perform in person searches themselves. Court makes copy: $.05 per page. Required to search: name, years to search; also helpful: address, DOB, SSN. Criminal records on computer since 3/96, in case files prior, indexed from 1940.

General Information: Public terminal goes back to 1996. Certification fee: $1.00 per cert. Payee: Clerk of Court. Personal checks accepted. Prepayment required.

Perry County Court PO Box 207, New Lexington, OH 43764-0207; phone: 740-342-3156; fax: 740-342-2188; hours 8:30AM-4:30PM M,W,F (EST). *Misdemeanor, Civil Actions Under $15,000, Small Claims.*

Civil Records: Access: In person only. Visitors must perform in person searches themselves. Court makes copy: $1.00 per page; same fee for self serve. Required to search: name, years to search. Civil cases indexed by defendant, plaintiff. Civil records in books 10 to 12 years, computerized since 4/97.

Criminal Records: Access: In person only. Visitors must perform in person searches themselves. Court makes copy: $1.00 per page; same fee for self serve. Required to search: name, years to search, DOB, SSN, signed release. Criminal records in books 10 to 12 years, computerized since 4/97.

General Information: Public terminal goes back to 1997. All records are public. Certification fee: $1.00. Payee: Perry County Court. Personal checks accepted. Prepayment required.

Pickaway County

Common Pleas Court County Courthouse, 207 Court St, PO Box 270, Circleville, OH 43113; phone: 740-474-5231; probate phone: 740-474-3950; fax: 740-477-3976; hours 8AM-4PM (EST). *Felony, Civil Actions Over $10,000, Probate.*

www.pickawaycountycpcourt.org

Note: Probate is a separate index and separate address.

Civil Records: Access: Mail, in person, online. Both court and visitors may perform in person searches. No search fee. Court makes copy: $.25 per page. Required to search: name, years to search; also helpful: address. Civil cases indexed by defendant. Civil records on computer back to 1988, indexed to 1940s, archived from 1800s. Search docket information at the website. Mail turnaround time 2-3 days.

Criminal Records: Access: Mail, in person, online. Both court and visitors may perform in person searches. No search fee. Court makes copy: $.25 per page. Required to search: name, years to search; also helpful: address, DOB, SSN. Criminal records on computer back to 1988, indexed to 1940s, archived from 1800s. Search docket information at the website. Mail turnaround time 2-3 days.

General Information: Public terminal goes back to 1988. Will not fax documents. Certification fee: $1.00 per page. Payee: Clerk of Court. Prepayment and SASE required.

Circleville Municipal Court PO Box 128, Circleville, OH 43113; phone: 740-474-3171; fax: 740-477-8291; hours 8AM-4PM (EST). *Misdemeanor, Civil Actions Under $15,000, Eviction, Small Claims.*

www.circlevillecourt.com

Civil Records: Access: Phone, fax, mail, in person, online. Both court and visitors may perform in person searches. No search fee. Court makes copy: $.50 per page. Required to search: name, years to search. Civil cases indexed by defendant, plaintiff; on computer from 1989, prior in books. Search online at www.circlevillecourt.com/AccessCourtRecords.asp. Mail turnaround time 1-2 days.

Criminal Records: Access: Phone, fax, mail, in person, online. Both court and visitors may perform in person searches. No search fee. Court makes copy: $.50 per page. Required to search: name, years to search; also helpful: SSN. Criminal records on computer from 1987, prior in books to 1983. Search online at www.circlevillecourt.com/AccessCourtRecords.asp. Mail turnaround time 1-2 days.

General Information: Public use terminal available. No warrant records released. No certification fee . Payee: Circleville Municipal Court. Personal checks or Visa, MC accepted. Prepayment and SASE required.

Pike County

Common Pleas Court 100 E 2nd St, 2nd Fl, Waverly, OH 45690; phone: 740-947-2715; probate phone: 740-947-2560; fax: 740-947-1729; hours 8:30AM-4PM (EST). *Felony, Civil Actions Over $15,000, Probate.*

Note: Probate is a separate court at 230 Waverly Plaza, #600.

Civil Records: Access: Mail, in person. Visitors must perform in person searches themselves. Search fee: $2.00 per name. Court makes copy: $.25 per page. Required to search: name, years to search; also helpful: address. Civil cases indexed by defendant, plaintiff. Civil records in books to 1815; on computer back to 1999.

Criminal Records: Access: Mail, in person. Visitors must perform in person searches themselves. Search fee: $2.00 per name. Court makes copy: $.25 per page. Required to search: name, years to search; also helpful: address, DOB, SSN. Criminal records in books to 1815; on computer back to 1999.

General Information: Public terminal goes back to 11/1999. No grand jury secret indictment records released. Certification fee: $1.00 per cert. Payee: Clerk of Court. Personal checks accepted. Prepayment required.

Pike County Court 230 Waverly Plaza, #900, Waverly, OH 45690; criminal phone: 740-947-4003; fax: 740-747-7644; hours 8:30AM-4PM (EST). *Misdemeanor, Civil Actions Under $15,000, Small Claims.*

Civil Records: Access: Phone, fax, mail, in person. Both court and visitors may perform in person searches. No search fee. No copy fee. Required to search: name, years to search. Civil cases indexed by defendant, plaintiff. Civil records in books indexed to 1958, computerized since 1996. Mail turnaround time 1 week.

Criminal Records: Access: Phone, fax, mail, in person. Both court and visitors may perform in person searches. No search fee. No copy fee. Required to search: name, years to search. Criminal records in books indexed to 1958, computerized since 1996. Mail turnaround time 1 week.

General Information: Public terminal goes back to 12/1996. No sealed or expunged records released. Will fax documents to local or toll free line. No certification fee . Payee: Pike County Court. Personal checks accepted. Prepayment and SASE required.

Portage County

Common Pleas Court PO Box 1035, Ravenna, OH 44266; phone: 330-297-3644; criminal phone: 330-297-3647; civil phone: 330-297-3644; probate phone: 330-297-3874; fax: 330-297-4554; hours 8AM-4PM (EST). *Felony, Civil Actions Over $15,000, Probate.*

Note: Probate Court address is 203 W Main, Ravenna, OH 44266.

Civil Records: Access: In person, online. Visitors must perform in person searches themselves. Court makes copy: $.10 per page; same fee for self serve. Required to search: name, years to search; also helpful: address. Civil cases indexed by defendant, plaintiff; on computer back to 11/1991, prior in books to 1977; Judgments back to 1/1982. For records from 1992 forward, go to http://67.39.103.41/pa/pa.htm.

Criminal Records: Access: In person, online. Visitors must perform in person searches themselves. No search fee. Court makes copy: $.10 per page; same fee for self serve. Required to search: name, years to search; also helpful: address, DOB. Criminal records index on computer back to 1977, cases back to 1/1991; prior in books. For records from 1992 forward, go to http://67.39.103.41/pa/pa.htm. (Direct questions about online access to Pam Christy at 330-297-3646.)

General Information: Public terminal goes back to 11/1991 for cases, to 1977 for index. Will fax specific case file requests for $1.00 per page. Certification fee: $1.00 per page includes copy fee. Payee: Clerk of Court. Personal checks accepted. Prepayment required. Monthly accounts available.

Portage County Municipal Court PO Box 958, Ravenna, OH 44266; criminal phone: 330-297-3639; civil phone: 330-297-3635; criminal fax: 330-297-5867; civil fax: 330-297-3526; hours 8AM-4PM (EST). *Misdemeanor, Civil Actions Under $15,000, Eviction, Small Claims.*

www.co.portage.oh.us

Civil Records: Access: Mail, in person, online. Visitors must perform in person searches themselves. Search fee: $5.00. Court makes copy: $.10 per page. Required to search: name, years to search; also helpful: address. Civil cases indexed by defendant, plaintiff; on computer from 1992. For records from 1992 forward, go to http://67.39.103.41/pa/pa.htm. Mail turnaround time 2 days.

Criminal Records: Access: Mail, in person, online. Visitors must perform in person searches themselves. Search fee: $5.00. Court makes copy: $.10 per page. Required to search: name, years to search; also helpful: address, DOB, SSN. Criminal records on computer from 1992. For records from 1992 forward, go to http://67.39.103.41/pa/pa.htm. (Direct questions about online access to Pam Christy at 330-297-3646.) Mail turnaround time 2 days.

General Information: Public terminal has only civil records back to 1991. No records released. Certification fee: $1.00. Payee: Municipal Court. Personal checks accepted. Prepayment required.

Portage Municipal Court - Kent Branch 214 S Water, Kent, OH 44240; phone: 330-678-9170; criminal phone: 330-678-9100; civil phone: 330-678-9170; fax: 330-677-9944; hours 8AM-4PM (EST). *Misdemeanor, Civil Actions Under $15,000, Eviction, Small Claims.*

www.co.portage.oh.us

Civil Records: Access: In person, online. Court makes copy: $.10 per page; same fee for self serve. Required to search: name, years to search; also helpful: address. Civil cases indexed by defendant, plaintiff; on computer from 1992, prior in books. For records from 1992 forward, go to http://67.39.103.41/pa/pa.htm.

Criminal Records: Access: In person, online. Both court and visitors may perform in person searches. Search fee: $5.00 per name. Court makes copy: $.10

per page; same fee for self serve. Required to search: name, years to search; also helpful: address, DOB, SSN. Criminal records on computer from 1992, prior in books. For records from 1992 forward, go to http://67.39.103.41/pa/pa.htm. (Direct questions about online access to Pam Christy at 330-297-3646.)

General Information: Public terminal goes back to 1992. No expunged records released. Will fax case file for $1.00 per page. Certification fee: $1.00. Payee: Portage County Municipal Court. Personal checks and Visa/MC cards accepted (plus 4% fee). Accepted for criminal only, and only if "in person". Prepayment required.

Preble County

Common Pleas Court 101 E Main, 3rd Fl, Eaton, OH 45320; phone: 937-456-8160; 456-8165 (common pleas); probate phone: 937-456-8138; fax: 937-456-9548; hours 8AM-4:30PM (EST). *Felony, Civil, Probate.*

Note: Probate office is separate from this court.

Civil Records: Access: In person only. Visitors must perform in person searches themselves. Court makes copy: $.50 per page. Required to search: name, years to search; also helpful: address. Civil cases indexed by defendant, plaintiff; on computer from 11/89, prior in books indexed to 1940s.

Criminal Records: Access: Mail, in person. Both court and visitors may perform in person searches. Search fee: $3.00 per name. Court makes copy: $.50 per page. Required to search: name, years to search; also helpful: address, DOB, SSN. Criminal records on computer from 11/89, prior in books indexed to 1940s. Mail turnaround time 1 day.

General Information: Public use terminal available. No secret records released. No certification fee . Payee: Clerk of Court. Personal checks accepted. Prepayment and SASE required.

Eaton Municipal Court PO Box 65 (101 E Main St), Eaton, OH 45320; phone: 937-456-4941/6204; fax: 937-456-4685; hours 8AM-4:30PM (EST). *Misdemeanor, Civil Actions Under $15,000, Eviction, Small Claims.*

www.eatonmunicipalcourt.com

Civil Records: Access: Mail, in person, online. Both court and visitors may perform in person searches. No search fee. Court makes copy: $1.00 per page. Required to search: name, years to search. Civil cases indexed by defendant, plaintiff; on computer from 1989, prior in books indexed to 1959. Search by name or case number at the website. Records back to 1989. Mail turnaround time 1 week.

Criminal Records: Access: Mail, in person, online. Both court and visitors may perform in person searches. No search fee. Court makes copy: $1.00 per page. Required to search: name, years to search; also helpful: SSN. Criminal records on computer from 1989, prior in books indexed to 1959. Search by name or case number at the website. Computerized records begin in 1992 for civil, criminal and traffic cases. Mail turnaround time 1 week.

General Information: Public terminal goes back to 1989. No driving records released. Certification fee: $1.00. Payee: Eaton Municipal Court. Personal checks or Visa, MC accepted. Prepayment and SASE required.

Putnam County

Common Pleas Court 245 E Main, Rm 301, Ottawa, OH 45875; phone: 419-523-3110; probate phone: 419-523-3012; civil/criminal fax: 419-523-5284; probate fax: 419-523-9291; hours 8:30AM-4:30PM (EST). *Felony, Civil Actions Over $10,000, Probate.*

Note: Probate is a separate court at Rm 204.

Civil Records: Access: Fax, mail, in person. Both court and visitors may perform in person searches. Search fee: $10.00 per name. Court makes copy: $.25 per page. Required to search: name, years to search. Civil cases indexed by defendant, plaintiff; on

computer from 1992 indexed on docket books to 1800s. Mail turnaround time 1-4 days.

Criminal Records: Access: Fax, mail, in person. Both court and visitors may perform in person searches. Search fee: $10.00 per name. Court makes copy: $.25 per page. Required to search: name, years to search; also helpful: address, DOB, SSN. Criminal records on computer from 1992 indexed on docket books to 1800s. Mail turnaround time 1-4 days.

General Information: Public terminal goes back to 1992. No sealed records released. Will fax documents for $3.00 per transmission plus $1.00 per page. Certification fee: $1.00 per certification. Payee: Clerk of Court. Putnam County personal checks accepted. Prepayment and SASE required.

Putnam County Court 245 E Main, Rm 303, Ottawa, OH 45875; phone: 419-523-3110; fax: 419-523-5284; hours 8:30AM-4:30PM (EST). *Misdemeanor, Civil Actions Under $10,000, Small Claims.*

Civil Records: Access: Mail, in person, fax. Both court and visitors may perform in person searches. Search fee: $10.00 per name. Court makes copy: $.25 per page. Required to search: name, years to search. Civil cases indexed by defendant, plaintiff. Civil records go back to 1800s; computerized records go back to 1992. Mail turnaround time 48 hours.

Criminal Records: Access: Mail, in person. Both court and visitors may perform in person searches. Search fee: $10.00 per name. Court makes copy: $.25 per page. Required to search: name, years to search. Criminal records go back to 1826; computerized records go back to 1992. Mail turnaround time 48 hours.

General Information: Public terminal goes back to 1992. Will fax documents for $3.00 per fax plus $1.00 per page. Certification fee: $1.00 per page. Payee: Clerk of Court. Only cashiers checks and money orders accepted. Prepayment and SASE required.

Richland County

Common Pleas Court 50 Park Ave E, 2nd Fl, PO Box 127, Mansfield, OH 44901; phone: 419-774-5549; probate phone: 419-755-5583; hours 8AM-4PM (EST). *Felony, Civil Actions Over $10,000, Probate.*

www.richlandcountyoh.us/coc.htm

Note: Court website is www.richlandcountyoh.us/cpc.htm.

Civil Records: Access: Mail, fax, in person, online. Both court and visitors may perform in person searches. No search fee. Court makes copy: $.25 per page. Required to search: name, years to search; also helpful: address. Civil cases indexed by defendant, plaintiff; on computer from 1989, prior in books and on microfiche to 1960. Access to civil records is at www.richlandcountyoh.us/courtv.htm.

Criminal Records: Access: Mail, in person. Both court and visitors may perform in person searches. No search fee. Court makes copy: $.25 per page. Required to search: name, years to search, DOB, SSN, signed release; also helpful: address. Criminal records on computer from 1991, prior in books and on microfiche to 1960. Access to criminal records at www.richlandcountyoh.us/courtv.htm.

General Information: Public use terminal available. No sealed records released. Certification fee: $5.00. Payee: Clerk of Court. Personal checks accepted. Prepayment required.

Mansfield Municipal Court PO Box 1228, Mansfield, OH 44901; phone: 419-755-9617; criminal phone: 419-755-9634; civil phone: 419-755-9637; criminal fax: 419-755-9647; civil fax: 419-755-9641; hours 8AM-4PM (EST). *Misdemeanor, Civil Actions Under $15,000, Eviction, Small Claims.*

Civil Records: Access: Phone, fax, mail, in person, online. Both court and visitors may perform in person searches. No search fee. Court makes copy: $.25 per page. Required to search: name, years to

search; also helpful: address. Civil cases indexed by defendant, plaintiff. Criminal records on computer from 1989. Overall records go back to 1940. Phone & fax access limited to short searches. Online access at www6.mapstrategies.com/mansfield/index.html for records from 1992 forward. Mail turnaround time 2-3 days.

Criminal Records: Access: Phone, fax, mail, in person, online. Both court and visitors may perform in person searches. No search fee. Court makes copy: $.25 per page. Required to search: name, years to search; also helpful: address, DOB, SSN. Criminal records on computer from 1989. Overall records go back to 1940. Online access at www6.mapstrategies.com/mansfield/index.html for records from 1992 forward. Mail turnaround time 2-3 days.

General Information: Public terminal has criminal back to 10/1989 and civil back to 1990. No lead print out records released. No fee to fax documents. Certification fee: $1.00 per page. Payee: Clerk of Court or Mansfield Municipal Court. Personal checks accepted. Prepayment and SASE required.

Ross County

Common Pleas Court County Courthouse, 2 N Paint St, #A, Chillicothe, OH 45601; phone: 740-702-3010; probate phone: 740-774-1179; fax: 740-702-3018; hours 8AM-4PM (EST). *Felony, Civil Actions Over $10,000, Probate.*

www.co.ross.oh.us

Civil Records: Access: In person online. Both court and visitors may perform in person searches. No search fee. Court makes copy: $.05 per page; same fee for self serve. Required to search: name, years to search; also helpful: address. Civil cases indexed by defendant, plaintiff; on computer from 1989, prior in books to 1800s. Search records back to 11/89 at the website.

Criminal Records: Access: In person, online. Both court and visitors may perform in person searches. No search fee. Court makes copy: $.05 per page; same fee for self serve. Required to search: name, years to search; also helpful: address, DOB, SSN. Criminal records on computer from 1989, prior in books to 1800s. Search records back to 11/89 at the website.

General Information: Public terminal goes back to 11/89. No secret indictment records released. Will fax documents to local or toll free line. Certification fee: $1.00. Payee: Clerk of Court. Personal checks accepted. Prepayment required.

Chillicothe Municipal Court 26 S Paint St, Chillicothe, OH 45601; phone: 740-773-3515; fax: 740-774-1101; hours 7:30AM-4:30PM (EST). *Misdemeanor, Civil Actions Under $15,000, Eviction, Small Claims.*

www.chillicothemunicipalcourt.org

Civil Records: Access: Mail, in person, online. Both court and visitors may perform in person searches. No search fee. Court makes copy: $.05 per page. Required to search: name, years to search; also helpful: address. Civil cases indexed by defendant, plaintiff; on computer from 6/93, prior in books. Search docket information from http://216.201.21.130/Search/. Mail turnaround time 10 days.

Criminal Records: Access: Mail, in person, online. Both court and visitors may perform in person searches. No search fee. Court makes copy: $.05 per page. Required to search: name, years to search, DOB, SSN; also helpful: address. Criminal records on computer from 6/93, prior in books. Search docket information from http://216.201.21.130/Search/. Mail turnaround time 10 days.

General Information: Public terminal goes back to 6/93. No confidential records released. Will not fax documents. Certification fee: $1.00 per page includes $.05 copy fee. Payee: Municipal Court. Business checks accepted. Prepayment and SASE required.

Sandusky County

Common Pleas Court 100 N Park Ave, #320, Fremont, OH 43420; phone: 419-334-6161/6163; probate phone: 419-334-6217; civil/criminal fax: 419-334-6164; probate fax: 419-334-6210; hours 8AM-4:30PM (EST). *Felony, Civil Actions Over $3,000, Probate.*

Note: Probate index is a separate office, Suite 224.

Civil Records: Access: In person only. Visitors must perform in person searches themselves. Court makes copy: $.10 per page. Required to search: name, years to search; also helpful: address. Civil cases indexed by defendant, plaintiff; on computer from 1988, prior in books to 1800s.

Criminal Records: Access: In person only. Visitors must perform in person searches themselves. Court makes copy: $.10 per page. Required to search: name, years to search; also helpful: address, DOB, SSN. Criminal records on computer from 1988, prior in books to 1800s.

General Information: Public use terminal available. No search warrant records released. Certification fee: $1.00 per page. Payee: Clerk of Court. Personal checks accepted. Prepayment required.

County Court #1 PO Box 267, 847 E McPherson Hwy, Clyde, OH 43410; phone: 419-547-0915; fax: 419-547-9198; hours 8AM-4:30PM (EST). *Misdemeanor, Civil Actions Under $15,000, Small Claims.*

www.co.sandusky.oh.us

Civil Records: Access: Phone, fax, mail, in person. Both court and visitors may perform in person searches. No search fee. Court makes copy: $.10 per page; same fee for self serve. Required to search: name, years to search; also helpful: address. Civil cases indexed by defendant, plaintiff; on computer from 1998, prior in books for 25 years. Mail turnaround time 2-3 days.

Criminal Records: Access: Phone, fax, mail, in person. Both court and visitors may perform in person searches. No search fee. Court makes copy: $.10 per page; same fee for self serve. Required to search: name, years to search, DOB, SSN; also helpful: address. Criminal records on computer from 1998, prior in books for 25 years. Mail turnaround time 2-3 days.

General Information: No public access terminal. No fee to fax documents to toll-free number. Certification fee: $1.00. Cert fee includes copies. Payee: Sandusky County Court. Personal checks or Visa, MC accepted. Prepayment and SASE required.

County Court #2 215 W Main St, Woodville, OH 43469; phone: 419-849-3961; fax: 419-849-3932; hours 8AM-4:30PM (EST). *Misdemeanor, Civil Actions Under $15,000, Small Claims.*

www.sandusky-county.org

Civil Records: Access: Phone, fax, mail, in person. Both court and visitors may perform in person searches. No search fee. Court makes copy: $.10 per page. Required to search: name, years to search; also helpful: address. Civil cases indexed by defendant, plaintiff. Civil records go back to 1983; on computer back to 1998. Mail turnaround time 10 days; by phone 3 hours.

Criminal Records: Access: Phone, fax, mail, in person. Only the court performs in person searches. No search fee. Court makes copy: $.10 per page. Required to search: name, years to search, DOB, SSN. Criminal records go back to 1995; on computer back to 1998. Mail turnaround time 10 days; by phone 3 hours.

General Information: No public access terminal. No confidential records released. Will fax documents $5.00 per doc. Certification fee: $1.00 per page. Payee: County Court. Personal checks or Visa, MC accepted. Prepayment and SASE required.

Fremont Municipal Court
PO Box 886, Fremont, OH 43420-0071; phone: 419-332-1579; fax: 419-332-1570; hours 8AM-4:30PM (EST). *Misdemeanor, Civil Actions Under $15,000, Eviction, Small Claims.*

Civil Records: Access: Fax, mail, in person. Both court and visitors may perform in person searches. No search fee. Court makes copy: $.10 per page. Required to search: name, years to search. Civil cases indexed by defendant, plaintiff. Civil records in books from 1960, computerized since 1992. Mail turnaround time 2 days.

Criminal Records: Access: Fax, mail, in person. Both court and visitors may perform in person searches. No search fee. Court makes copy: $.10 per page. Required to search: name, years to search; also helpful: DOB, SSN. Criminal records in books from 1960, computerized since 1992. Mail turnaround time 2 days.

General Information: Public terminal goes back to 1992. No fee to fax documents. Local faxing only. Certification fee: $1.00 per page. Cert fee includes copy fee. Payee: Fremont Municipal Court. Only cashiers checks and money orders accepted. Prepayment required.

Scioto County

Common Pleas Court 602 7th St, Rm 205, Portsmouth, OH 45662; phone: 740-355-8226; probate phone: 740-355-8243; fax: 740-354-2057; hours 8AM-4:30PM (EST). *Felony, Civil Actions Over $15,000, Probate.*

www.sciotocountycpcourt.org

Note: Probate is a separate index at the same address in Rm 201.

Civil Records: Access: In person, online. Both court and visitors may perform in person searches. Court makes copy: $1.00 per page. Required to search: name, years to search; also helpful: address. Civil cases indexed by defendant, plaintiff; on computer from 1986, dockets to 1800s. Online access to civil records is free at www.sciotocountycpcourt.org/search.htm. Search by court calendar, quick index, general index or docket sheet.

Criminal Records: Access: In person, online. Both court and visitors may perform in person searches. No search fee. Court makes copy: $1.00 per page. Required to search: name, years to search; also helpful: address, DOB. Criminal records on computer from 1986, dockets to 1800s. Online access to criminal records is the same as civil.

General Information: Public terminal goes back to 1/1986. No sealed or secret records released. Will fax specific case file requests for $1.00 per page. Certification fee: $1.00 per page. Payee: Clerk of Court. Personal checks accepted. Prepayment required.

Portsmouth Municipal Court 728 2nd St, Portsmouth, OH 45662; phone: 740-354-3283; fax: 740-353-6645; hours 8AM-4PM (EST). *Misdemeanor, Civil Actions Under $15,000, Eviction, Small Claims.*

www.portsmouth-municipal-court.com

Civil Records: Access: Fax, mail, in person, online. Both court and visitors may perform in person searches. Search fee: No fee for computer records search 1989 forward. Court makes copy: $.50 per page. Required to search: name, years to search. Civil cases indexed by defendant, plaintiff. Criminal records go back to 1985; on computer back to 1995. Online access is free at www.portsmouth-municipal-court.com/disc.html. Mail turnaround time 2-3 days; older records up to 2 weeks.

Criminal Records: Access: Fax, mail, in person, online. Both court and visitors may perform in person searches. Search fee: $20.00 per name if search includes years prior to 1989. No fee for computer records search 1989 forward. Court makes copy: $.50 per page. Required to search: name, years to search, SSN. Criminal records go back to 1985; on computer back to 1995. Online access to criminal

records is free at www.portsmouth-municipal-court.com/disc.html. Mail turnaround time 2-3 days; older records up to 2 weeks.

General Information: Public terminal goes back to 11/1989. No competency hearing, protection order records released. No fee to fax documents. Certification fee: $1.00 per page. Payee: Portsmouth Municipal Court. Prepayment and SASE required.

Seneca County

Common Pleas Court 117 E Market, Tiffin, OH 44883; phone: 419-447-0671; probate phone: 419-447-3121; fax: 419-443-7919; hours 8:30AM-4:30PM (EST). *Felony, Civil Actions Over $10,000, Probate.*

Note: Probate records with Clerk of Courts, #4101

Civil Records: Access: In person, online. Both court and visitors may perform in person searches. Court makes copy: $.10 per page; same fee for self serve. Required to search: name, years to search; also helpful: address. Civil cases indexed by defendant, plaintiff; on computer from 1/93, prior in books to 1900s, archived to 1800s. Dockets are searchable online at www.senecaco.org/clerk/default.html. Click on Internet Inquiry. Mail turnaround time usually 1 day.

Criminal Records: Access: In person, online. Both court and visitors may perform in person searches. No search fee. Court makes copy: $.10 per page; same fee for self serve. Required to search: name, years to search, SSN, date of offense. Criminal records on computer from 1/93, prior in books to 1900s, archived to 1800s. Dockets are searchable online at www.senecaco.org/clerk/default.html. Click on Internet Inquiry.

General Information: Public terminal goes back to 1/1993. (Terminal located in the Recorder's Office; docket sheets can be printed out for $.10 per page in clerk's office.) No sealed records released. Will fax specific case file requests for $2.00 per transmission. Certification fee: $1.00 per page. Payee: Clerk of Court. Personal checks accepted. Prepayment required.

Fostoria Municipal Court PO Box 985, Fostoria, OH 44830; phone: 419-435-8139; fax: 419-435-1150; hours 8:30AM-5PM; W 8:30AM-N (EST). *Misdemeanor, Civil Actions Under $15,000, Eviction, Small Claims.*

Civil Records: Access: Phone, fax, mail, in person. Both court and visitors may perform in person searches. No search fee. Court makes copy: $.10 per page. Required to search: name, years to search. Civil cases indexed by defendant, plaintiff. Civil records computerized since 1987. Mail turnaround time 1-2 days.

Criminal Records: Access: Phone, fax, mail, in person. Both court and visitors may perform in person searches. No search fee. Court makes copy: $.10 per page. Required to search: name, years to search; also helpful: SSN. Criminal records computerized since 1987. Mail turnaround time 1-2 days.

General Information: Public terminal has criminal back to 1987 and civil back to 1987. No fee if faxed to local or toll free number. Certification fee: $1.00 per page includes copies. Payee: Fostoria Municipal Court. Personal checks accepted. Prepayment required.

Tiffin Municipal Court PO Box 694, Tiffin, OH 44883; phone: 419-448-5412; criminal phone: 419-448-5411; civil phone: 419-448-5418; fax: 419-448-5419; hours 8:30AM-4:30PM (EST). *Misdemeanor, Civil Actions Under $15,000, Eviction, Small Claims.*

Civil Records: Access: Fax, mail, in person. Both court and visitors may perform in person searches. No search fee. Court makes copy: $.05 per page; same fee for self serve. Required to search: name, years to search; also helpful: address. Civil cases indexed by defendant, plaintiff; on computer from 8/90, prior in books. Mail turnaround time 3 days.

Criminal Records: Access: Fax, mail, in person. Both court and visitors may perform in person searches. No search fee. Court makes copy: $.05 per page; same fee for self serve. Required to search: name, years to search, DOB, SSN, signed release; also helpful: address. Criminal records on computer from 8/90, prior in books. Mail turnaround time 3 days.

General Information: Public terminal goes back to 8/90. No expunged records released. Fee to fax documents is $.25 per page. Certification fee: $1.00. Payee: Municipal Court. Personal checks accepted. Prepayment and SASE required.

Shelby County

Common Pleas Court PO Box 809, Sidney, OH 45365; phone: 937-498-7221; fax: 937-498-4840; hours 8AM-4PM (EST). *Felony, Civil Actions Over $10,000, Probate.*

http://co.shelby.oh.us/commonpleas/

Civil Records: Access: Fax, mail, in person. Both court and visitors may perform in person searches. Search fee: $1.00 per name. Court makes copy: $.10 per page. Required to search: name, years to search; also helpful: address. Civil cases indexed by defendant, plaintiff; on computer from 1987, on indexes from 1819. Mail turnaround time 5 days.

Criminal Records: Access: Mail, in person. Visitors must perform in person searches themselves. Search fee: $1.00 per name. Court makes copy: $.10 per page. Required to search: name, years to search DOB, SSN; also helpful: address. Criminal records on computer from 1987, on indexes from 1819. Mail turnaround time 5 days.

General Information: Public terminal goes back to 1987. No grand jury tapes released. Fee to fax documents is $3.00 per page. Certification fee: $4.00. Payee: Shelby County Clerk of Courts. Personal checks accepted. Prepayment and SASE required.

Sidney Municipal Court 201 W Poplar, Sidney, OH 45365; phone: 937-498-0011; fax: 937-498-8179; hours 8AM-4:30PM (EST). *Misdemeanor, Civil Actions Under $15,000, Eviction, Small Claims.*

www.sidneyoh.com

Note: Send mail requests to the address above; phone and in person searches are made at the court at 110 W Court St.

Civil Records: Access: Phone, fax, mail, in person. Both court and visitors may perform in person searches. No search fee. Court makes copy: $.10 per page. Required to search: name, years to search. Civil cases indexed by defendant, plaintiff; on computer from 1988; prior on books to 1958. Mail turnaround time 2 days.

Criminal Records: Access: Phone, fax, mail, in person. Both court and visitors may perform in person searches. No search fee. Court makes copy: $.10 per page. Required to search: name, years to search; also helpful: address, DOB, SSN. Criminal records on computer from 1988; prior on books to 1958. Mail turnaround time 2 days.

General Information: Public terminal goes back to 1993. Confidential and probation records are not released. Will fax documents to toll-free number only, no charge. Certification fee: $1.00 per page. Cert fee includes copies. Payee: Municipal Court. Personal checks accepted. Prepayment and SASE required.

Stark County

Common Pleas Court - Civil Division PO Box 21160, Canton, OH 44701; phone: 330-451-7795; fax: 330-451-7066; hours 8:30AM-4:30PM (EST). *Civil Actions Over $15,000.*

www.starkclerk.org

Civil Records: Access: Phone, fax, mail, in person, online. Both court and visitors may perform in person searches. No search fee. Court makes copy: $.10 per page; same fee for self serve. Required to search: name, years to search. Civil cases indexed by defendant, plaintiff; on computer from 1985, prior in books from 1940s. A access to the county online case docket database is free at www.starkcourt.org/docket/index.html. Search by name or case number. Mail turnaround up to 1 week.

General Information: Public terminal has only civil records back to 1985. No sealed records released. Fee to fax documents is $2.00 for 1st page, $1.00 each add'l. Certification fee: $1.00. Payee: Clerk of Court. Personal checks accepted. Prepayment and SASE required.

Alliance Municipal Court 470 E Market St, Rm 16, Alliance, OH 44601; phone: 330-823-6600; criminal fax: 330-829-2230; civil fax: 330-829-2231; hours 8:30AM-4:30PM (EST). *Misdemeanor, Civil Actions Under $15,000, Eviction, Small Claims.*

www.starkcountycjis.org/alliance/

Note: Jurisdiction includes Alliance, Lexington, Marlboro, Washington, Paris, Uniontown, Minerva, Limaville, and Roberstville.

Civil Records: Access: Fax, mail, in person, online. Both court and visitors may perform in person searches. No search fee. Court makes copy: $.25 per page. Required to search: name. Civil cases indexed by defendant, plaintiff. Civil records go back to 1993. Search the Online Case Docket of the Alliance Court at www.starkcountycjis.org/alliance/docket/search_large_frame.html Mail turnaround time 1 day.

Criminal Records: Access: Fax, mail, in person, online. Both court and visitors may perform in person searches. No search fee. Court makes copy: $.25 per page. Required to search: name, years to search; also helpful: DOB, SSN. computerized since 1991. Search the Online Case Docket of the Massillon Court at www.starkcountycjis.org/alliance/docket/search_large_frame.html, includes traffic and misdemeanor records. Mail turnaround time 1 day.

General Information: Public terminal goes back to 1993. No fee to fax documents. Certification fee: $3.00 per page. Payee: Alliance Municipal Court. Personal checks accepted. Prepayment required.

Common Pleas Court - Criminal Division PO Box 21160, Canton, OH 44701-1160; phone: 330-451-7929; fax: 330-451-7066; hours 8:30AM-4:30PM (EST). *Felony.*

www.starkclerk.org

Criminal Records: Access: Mail, in person, online. Both court and visitors may perform in person searches. No search fee. Court makes copy: $.10 per page. Required to search: name, years to search, DOB, SSN. Criminal records on computer back to 1985, prior in books to 1940s. Online access to the county online case docket database is free at www.starkcourt.org/docket/index.html. Search by name, case number or SSN. Mail turnaround time up to 2 weeks.

General Information: Public terminal goes back to 1985. No secret indictments, expungment records released. Will fax documents. Certification fee: $1.00 include copy fee. Payee: Clerk of Courts. Personal checks accepted. Prepayment and SASE required.

Canton Municipal Court 218 Cleveland Ave SW, PO Box 24218, Canton, OH 44702-4218; phone: 330-489-3203; criminal fax: 330-489-3372; civil fax: 330-489-3075; hours 8AM-4:30PM (EST). *Misdemeanor, Civil Actions Under $15,000, Eviction, Small Claims.*

www.cantoncourt.org

Note: Jurisdiction includes Canton, North Canton, Louisville, Lake, Plain, Nimishillen, Osnaburg, Pike, Sandy, Hartville, East Canton, Myers Lake, East Sparta, Waynesburg, and Magnolia.

Civil Records: Access: Phone, fax, mail, in person, online. Both court and visitors may perform in person searches. No search fee. Court makes copy: $.25 per page; same fee for self serve. Required to search: name, years to search. Civil cases indexed by defendant, plaintiff; on computer from 1991, prior in books to 1928. Search docket information at www.cantoncourt.org/docket.html. Mail turnaround time 1-2 days.

Criminal Records: Access: Phone, fax, mail, in person, online. Both court and visitors may perform in person searches. No search fee. Court makes copy: $.25 per page; same fee for self serve. Required to search: name, years to search; also helpful: DOB, SSN. Criminal records on computer from 1986, books to 1928. Search docket information at www.cantoncourt.org/docket.html. Includes traffic. Mail turnaround time 1-2 days.

General Information: Public use terminal available. No sealed records released. No fee to fax documents. Certification fee: $1.00. Payee: Municipal Court. Personal checks accepted. Prepayment and SASE required.

Massillon Municipal Court PO Box 1040, 2 James Duncan Plaza, Massillon, OH 44646-1040; phone: 330-830-2591; criminal phone: 330-830-1732; civil phone: 330-830-1731; fax: 330-830-3648; hours 8:30AM-4:30PM (EST). *Misdemeanor, Civil Actions Under $15,000, Eviction, Small Claims.*

www.massilloncourt.org

Note: Jurisdiction includes Massillon, Canal Fulton, Bethlehem, Jackson, Lawrence, Perry, Sugarcreek, Tuscarawas, Beach City, Brewster, Hills and Dales, Navarre, and Wilmot.

Civil Records: Access: Fax, mail, in person, online. Both court and visitors may perform in person searches. No search fee. Court makes copy: $.05 per page. Required to search: name. Civil cases indexed by defendant, plaintiff; on docket books from 1986, computerized since 1991. Search the Online Case Docket of the Massillon Court at www.massilloncourt.org. Mail turnaround time 1 week.

Criminal Records: Access: Fax, mail, in person, online. Both court and visitors may perform in person searches. No search fee. Court makes copy: $.05 per page. Required to search: name, years to search; also helpful: DOB, SSN. computerized since 1991. Search the Online Case Docket of the Massillon Court at the website, includes traffic and misdemeanor records. Mail turnaround time 1 week.

General Information: Public use terminal available. No fee to fax documents. Certification fee: $2.00 per page. Payee: Massillon Municipal Court. Personal checks accepted. Prepayment required.

Summit County

Common Pleas Court 209 S High St, Akron, OH 44308; phone: 330-643-2201 (Divorce); criminal phone: 330-643-2282; civil phone: 330-643-2217; probate phone: 330-643-2350; fax: 330-643-7772; hours 9:30AM-4:15PM (EST). *Felony, Civil Actions Over $10,000, Probate.*

www.cpclerk.co.summit.oh.us

Note: For faster service, mail requests to Clerk at 53 University Ave, Akron 44308. Probate is a separate court.

Civil Records: Access: Mail, in person, online. Both court and visitors may perform in person searches. No search fee. Court makes copy: $.05 per page. Required to search: name, years to search. Civil cases indexed by defendant, plaintiff; on computer from 1982, prior in books, some microfiche. Access to county clerk of courts records is free at www.cpclerk.co.summit.oh.us. Click on "Case Search." Access to probate records at http://probatecourt.summitoh.net/CaseAccess.htm. Mail turnaround time 1 week.

Criminal Records: Access: Mail, in person, online. Both court and visitors may perform in person searches. Search fee: $2.00 per name. Court makes copy: $.05 per page. Required to search: name, years to search, DOB; also helpful: SSN. Criminal records on computer from 1982, prior in books, some microfiche. Access to county clerk of courts records is free at www.cpclerk.co.summit.oh.us.

Click on "Case Search." Mail turnaround time 1 week.

General Information: Public terminal goes back to 1982. No secret indictment records released. Certification fee: $1.00 per page. Payee: Clerk of Court. Only cashiers checks and money orders accepted. Prepayment and SASE required.

Akron Municipal Court 217 S High St, Rm 837, Akron, OH 44308; criminal phone: 330-375-2570; civil phone: 330-375-2920; fax: 330-375-2024; hours 8AM-4:30PM (EST). *Misdemeanor, Civil Actions Under $15,000, Eviction, Small Claims.*

http://courts.ci.akron.oh.us

Civil Records: Access: Fax, mail, in person, online. Both court and visitors may perform in person searches. No search fee. Court makes copy: $.25 per page. Required to search: name, years to search. Civil cases indexed by defendant, plaintiff; on computer from 1988, prior in books to 1975. Online access to court records is free at http://courts.ci.akron.oh.us/disclaimer.htm. Mail turnaround time up to 1 week.

Criminal Records: Access: Fax, mail, in person, online. Both court and visitors may perform in person searches. No search fee. Court makes copy: $.25 per page. Required to search: name, years to search, DOB, SSN. Criminal records on computer from 1988, prior in books to 1960. Online access to court records is free at http://courts.ci.akron.oh.us/disclaimer.htm. Mail turnaround time up to 1 week.

General Information: Public terminal goes back to 1988. No sealed records released. Will not fax documents. Certification fee: $1.00 per page. Payee: Municipal Court. Personal checks accepted. Prepayment and SASE required.

Barberton Municipal Court Municipal Bldg, 576 W Park Ave, Barberton, OH 44203-2584; phone: 330-753-2261; fax: 330-848-6779; hours 8AM-4:30PM (civ); Crim/traffic to 8PM (EST). *Misdemeanor, Civil Actions Under $15,000, Eviction, Small Claims.*

www.cityofbarberton.com/clerkofcourts

Civil Records: Access: Phone, fax, mail, in person, online. Both court and visitors may perform in person searches. No search fee. Court makes copy: $.10 per page. Required to search: name, years to search. Civil cases indexed by defendant, plaintiff. Civil records computerized since 1994. Online records for Barberton, Green, Norton, Franklin, Clinton, Copley and Coventry are free at http://24.123.45.19/. Mail turnaround time 1 week.

Criminal Records: Access: Phone, fax, mail, in person, online. Both court and visitors may perform in person searches. No search fee. Court makes copy: $.10 per page. Required to search: name, years to search; also helpful: DOB, SSN. Criminal records computerized since 1994. Online records for Barberton, Green, Norton, Franklin, Clinton, Copley and Coventry are free at http://24.123.45.19/. Mail turnaround time 1 week.

General Information: Public use terminal available. No fee to fax documents. Certification fee: $1.00 per page. Payee: Barberton Municipal Court. Personal checks accepted. Prepayment required.

Cuyahoga Falls Municipal Court 2310 2nd St, Cuyahoga Falls, OH 44221; phone: 330-971-8110; criminal phone: 330-971-8109; civil phone: 330-971-8108; fax: 330-971-8114; hours 8AM-8PM (Criminal), 8AM-4:30PM (Civil) (EST). *Misdemeanor, Civil Actions Under $15,000, Eviction, Small Claims.*

www.cfmunicourt.com

Civil Records: Access: Phone, mail, in person, online. Both court and visitors may perform in person searches. No search fee. Court makes copy: $.05 per page. Required to search: name, years to search. Civil cases indexed by defendant, plaintiff, or case number. Civil records indexed back to 1954.

Court docket information is free at the website. Mail turnaround time 1 week.

Criminal Records: Access: Phone, mail, in person, online. Both court and visitors may perform in person searches. No search fee. Court makes copy: $.05 per page. Required to search: name or case number. Criminal records indexed back to 1954. Court docket information is free at the website. Mail turnaround time 1 week.

General Information: Public terminal goes back to 1992. Will not fax documents. Certification fee: $1.00 per page includes copy. Payee: Cuyahoga Falls Municipal Court. Business checks accepted. Prepayment required.

Trumbull County

Common Pleas Court 161 High St, Warren, OH 44481; phone: 330-675-2557; criminal phone: 330-675-3058; civil phone: 330-675-2557; probate phone: 330-675-2521; fax: 330-675-2563; hours 8:30AM-4:30PM (EST). *Felony, Civil Actions Over $10,000, Probate.*

www.clerk.co.trumbull.oh.us

Civil Records: Access: Phone, mail, in person, online. Both court and visitors may perform in person searches. Search fee: $5.00 per name. Court makes copy: $.10 per page; same fee for self serve. Required to search: name, years to search. Civil cases indexed in books from 1977, archived from 1800s; on computer back to 5/96. Online access to court records is free at www.clerk.co.trumbull.oh.us/search.htm. Records go back to May, 1996. Online access to probate court records is free at www.trumbullprobate.org/paccessfront.htm. Mail turnaround time 1 week.

Criminal Records: Access: Mail, in person, online. Both court and visitors may perform in person searches. Search fee: $5.00 per name. Court makes copy: $.10 per page; same fee for self serve. Required to search: name, years to search, DOB, SSN, signed release. Criminal records indexed in books from 1977, archived from 1800s; on computer back to 5/96. Online access to criminal records is the same as civil. Mail turnaround time 1 week.

General Information: Public terminal goes back to 5/1996. No secret or sealed records released. Will not fax documents. Certification fee: $1.00 per page. Payee: Clerk of Court. Business checks accepted. Prepayment and SASE required.

Trumbull County Court Central 180 N Mecca St, Cortland, OH 44410; phone: 330-637-5023; fax: 330-637-5021; hours 8AM-4PM (EST). *Misdemeanor, Civil Actions Under $15,000, Eviction, Small Claims.*

Civil Records: Access: Phone, fax, mail, in person. Both court and visitors may perform in person searches. No search fee. Court makes copy: $.25 per page; same fee for self serve. Required to search: name, years to search. Records available since 1983. Mail turnaround time 1-2 days

Criminal Records: Access: Phone, fax, mail, in person. Both court and visitors may perform in person searches. No search fee. Court makes copy: $.25 per page; same fee for self serve. Required to search: name, years to search; also helpful: DOB, SSN. Same record keeping as civil. Mail turnaround time 1-2 days

General Information: Public terminal goes back to 1993. No fee to fax documents. Local faxing only. Certification fee: $2.00 per page. Payee: Trumbull County Court Central. Personal checks or Visa, MC accepted. In person only. Prepayment required.

Trumbull County Court East 7130 Brookwood Dr, Brookfield, OH 44403; phone: 330-448-1726; fax: 330-448-6310; hours 8:30AM-4:30PM (EST). *Misdemeanor, Civil Under $15,000, Eviction, Small Claims.*

Civil Records: Access: Phone, fax, mail, in person. Both court and visitors may perform in person searches. No search fee. Court makes copy: $.25 per

page; same fee for self serve. Required to search: name, years to search. Civil records go back to 1994. Mail turnaround time 1-2 days.

Criminal Records: Access: Phone, fax, mail, in person. Both court and visitors may perform in person searches. No search fee. Court makes copy: $.25 per page; same fee for self serve. Required to search: name, years to search; also helpful: DOB, SSN. Criminal Records in docket books since 1990, computerized since 1994. Mail turnaround time 1-2 days.

General Information: No public access terminal. No fee to fax documents. Local faxing only. Certification fee: $1.00 per page, if "non-copies" are used, then $2.00 per page. Payee: Trumbull County Court East. Personal checks or Visa, MC accepted. Prepayment required.

Girard Municipal Court City Hall, 100 N Market St, #A, Girard, OH 44420-2559; criminal phone: 330-545-0069; civil phone: 330-545-3177; fax: 330-545-7045; hours 8AM-4PM (EST). *Misdemeanor, Civil Actions Under $15,000, Eviction, Small Claims.*

Note: Traffic records: 330-545-3049.

Civil Records: Access: Fax, mail, in person. Both court and visitors may perform in person searches. No search fee. Court makes copy: 1st 10 free; $.10 per page each add'l. Required to search: name, years to search. Civil cases indexed by defendant, plaintiff; on books since 1964, computerized since 9/96. Mail turnaround time 1 week.

Criminal Records: Access: Fax, mail, in person. Both court and visitors may perform in person searches. No search fee. Court makes copy: 1st 10 pages free; each add'l page $.10. Required to search: name, years to search; also helpful: DOB, SSN. Criminal records on books since 1964, computerized since 9/96. Mail turnaround time 1 week.

General Information: Public terminal goes back to 9/1996. No fee to fax documents. Certification fee: $10.00 per document includes copy fee. Payee: Girard Municipal Court. Business checks accepted. Prepayment and SASE required.

Newton Falls Municipal Court 19 N Canal St, Newton Falls, OH 44444-1302; phone: 330-872-0302; criminal phone: 330-872-0232; civil phone: 330-872-0232; fax: 330-872-3899; hours 7:30AM-4:00PM (EST). *Misdemeanor, Civil Actions Under $15,000, Eviction, Small Claims.*

www.newtonfallscourt.com

Civil Records: Access: Fax, mail, in person, online. Only the court performs in person searches. No search fee. Court makes copy: $.10 per page. Required to search: name, years to search. Civil cases indexed by defendant, plaintiff. Civil records in books since 1970, computerized since 1992. Search record index free at www.newtonfallscourt.com/Search/. Mail turnaround time varies, but usually 1 week or less.

Criminal Records: Access: Fax, mail, in person, online. Only the court performs in person searches. No search fee. Court makes copy: $.10 per page. Required to search: name, years to search; also helpful: DOB, SSN. Criminal records in books since 1970, computerized since 1992. Search record index free at www.newtonfallscourt.com/Search/. Mail turnaround time varies, but usually 1 week or less.

General Information: No public access terminal. No fee to fax documents. Local faxing only. Certification fee: $1.00 per page. Payee: Newton Falls Municipal Court. Only cashiers checks and money orders accepted. Prepayment required.

Niles Municipal Court 15 E State St, Niles, OH 44446-5051; phone: 330-652-5863; fax: 330-544-9025; hours 8AM-4PM (EST). *Misdemeanor, Civil Actions Under $15,000, Eviction, Small Claims.*

Civil Records: Access: Fax, mail, in person. Both court and visitors may perform in person searches. No search fee. Court makes copy: $.25 per page. Required to search: name, years to search. Civil cases indexed by defendant, plaintiff; on computer since

10/96, in books since 1990, in storage from 1930. Mail turnaround times will vary.

Criminal Records: Access: Fax, mail, in person. Both court and visitors may perform in person searches. No search fee. Court makes copy: $.25 per page. Required to search: name, years to search; also helpful: DOB, SSN. Criminal records on computer since 10/96, in books since 1990, in storage from 1930. Mail turnaround times will vary.

General Information: Public use terminal available. No fee to fax documents. Local faxing only. No certification fee . Payee: Niles Municipal Court. Only cashiers checks and money orders accepted. Prepayment required.

Warren Municipal Court PO Box 1550, 141 South St SE, Warren, OH 44482; phone: 330-841-2525; criminal phone: 330-841-2525 x105-110; civil phone: 330-841-2525 x112-115; fax: 330-841-2760; hours 8AM-4:30PM (EST). *Misdemeanor, Civil Actions Under $15,000, Eviction, Small Claims.*

Civil Records: Access: Fax, mail, in person. Both court and visitors may perform in person searches. No search fee. Court makes copy: $.05 per page. Required to search: name, years to search; also helpful: address. Civil cases indexed by defendant, plaintiff; on computer since 1995; prior in books to 1978. Mail turnaround time 1-5 days.

Criminal Records: Access: Fax, mail, in person. Both court and visitors may perform in person searches. No search fee. Court makes copy: $.05 per page. Required to search: name, years to search; DOB, SSN, signed release; also helpful: address. Criminal records on computer since 1995; prior in books to 1978. Mail turnaround time 1-5 days.

General Information: Public terminal goes back to 1995. (Public cannot print copies from terminal.) No open case records released. No fee to fax documents. Certification fee: $1.00 per document. Payee: Warren Municipal Court. Personal checks or Visa, MC accepted. Prepayment and SASE required.

Tuscarawas County

Common Pleas Court PO Box 628, 125 E High, New Philadelphia, OH 44663; phone: 330-365-3243; probate phone: 330-365-3266; fax: 330-343-4682; hours 8AM-4:30PM (EST). *Felony, Civil Actions Over $15,000, Probate.*

www.co.tuscarawas.oh.us
Note: Probate is a separate court at 101 E High Ave.

Civil Records: Access: In person, online. Visitors must perform in person searches themselves. Court makes copy: $.10 per page. Required to search: name, years to search; also helpful: address. Civil cases indexed by defendant, plaintiff; on computer from 1987, prior in books to 1808, archived prior. Search dockets online at www.co.tuscarawas.oh.us/ClerkofCourts/DocketSearch.htm.

Criminal Records: Access: In person, online. Visitors must perform in person searches themselves. No search fee. Court makes copy: $.10 per page. Required to search: name, years to search; also helpful: address, DOB, SSN. Criminal records go back to 1868, criminal records on computer from 1987, prior in books to 1808, archived prior. Search dockets online at www.co.tuscarawas.oh.us/ClerkofCourts/DocketSearch.htm

General Information: Public terminal goes back to 1986. Will fax specific case file requests for $2.00 transmission fee plus $1.00 per page. Certification fee: $1.00 per page. Payee: Clerk of Court. Personal checks or Visa, MC accepted. Visa, MC. Prepayment required.

County Court 220 E 3rd, Uhrichsville, OH 44683; phone: 740-922-4795; fax: 740-922-7020; hours 8AM-4:30PM (EST). *Misdemeanor, Civil Actions Under $15,000, Small Claims.*
Note: Probation Office phone: 740-922-3653 & 922-4360. Probation Office hours: 8AM-4:30PM.

Civil Records: Access: Fax, mail, in person, fax, online. Both court and visitors may perform in person searches. No search fee. Court makes copy: $.10 per page. Required to search: name, years to

search. Civil cases indexed by defendant, plaintiff. Civil cases go back to 19700's, civil records on computer from 2/94, prior in books. Search dockets only online at www.co.tuscarawas.oh.us/ClerkofCourts/DocketSearch.htm. Mail turnaround time 1-2 days.

Criminal Records: Access: Fax, mail, in person, online. Both court and visitors may perform in person searches. No search fee. Court makes copy: $.10 per page. Required to search: name, years to search, DOB; also helpful: SSN. Criminal records on computer from 2/94, prior in books. Search dockets only online at www.co.tuscarawas.oh.us/ClerkofCourts/DocketSearch.htm Mail turnaround time 1-2 days.

General Information: Public terminal goes back to 1992. No fee to fax documents. Local faxing only. No certification fee . Payee: Tuscarawas County Court. Only Tuscarawas County personal checks accepted. Prepayment and SASE required.

New Philadelphia Municipal Court 166 E High Ave, New Philadelphia, OH 44663; phone: 330-343-6797; criminal phone: 330-343-6797; civil phone: 330-343-6797; fax: 330-364-6885; hours 8AM-4:30PM (EST). *Misdemeanor, Civil Actions Under $15,000, Eviction, Small Claims.*

www.npmunicipalcourt.org/
Note: The New Philadelphia Municipal Court has territorial jurisdiction in the municipal corporations of New Philadelphia and Dover, and the villages of Baltic, Bolivar, Midvale, Mineral City, Roswell, Stonecreek, Strasburg, Sugarcreek, and Zoar.

Civil Records: Access: Mail, in person. Visitors must perform in person searches themselves. Court makes copy: $.05 per page after first 10 free. Required to search: name, years to search. Civil cases indexed by defendant, plaintiff; on computer back to 4/91, prior in books to 1976.

Criminal Records: Access: In person only. Visitors must perform in person searches themselves. Court makes copy: $.05 per page after first 10 free. Required to search: name, years to search, SSN. Records on computer back to 4/91, prior in books to 1976.

General Information: Public terminal goes back to 4/1991. Certification fee: $1.00 per page. Payee: Municipal Court. Personal checks accepted. Credit cards accepted in person: Visa, MC. Prepayment and SASE required.

Union County

Common Pleas Court County Courthouse, Clerk of Courts, 215 W 5th, 2nd Fl, Marysville, OH 43040; phone: 937-645-3006; criminal phone: 937-645-3140; civil phone: 937-645-3145; probate phone: 937-645-3029; fax: 937-645-3162; hours 8:30AM-4PM (EST). *Felony, Civil Actions Over $10,000, Probate.*

www.co.union.oh.us/Clerk_of_Courts/clerk_of_courts.html
Note: Forms are available at the website. Probate is located at the same address, separate office. Probate fax is 937-645-3160.

Civil Records: Access: In person, online. Visitors must perform in person searches themselves. Court makes copy: $.10 per page. Required to search: name, years to search; also helpful: address. Civil cases indexed by defendant, plaintiff; on computer from 1990, records go back to 1850. Online access to the court clerk's public record and index is free at http://www3.co.union.oh.us/clerkofcourts/. Records go back to 1/1990, older records added as accessed. Images go back to 1/2002.

Criminal Records: Access: In person, online. Visitors must perform in person searches themselves. Search fee: $5.00 per name. Court makes copy: $.10 per page. Required to search: name, years to search, DOB, SSN; also helpful: address. Criminal records on computer from 1990, records go back to 1850. Online access to the court clerk's public record and index is free at http://www3.co.union.oh.us/clerkofcourts/.

Records go back to 1/1990, older records added as accessed. Images go back to 1/2002.

General Information: Public terminal goes back to 1990. Will fax specific case file requests for $1.00 per page. Certification fee: $1.00 per page. Payee: Clerk of Court. Only cashiers checks and money orders accepted. Prepayment required.

Marysville Municipal Court City Hall Bldg, 125 E 6th St, Marysville, OH 43040; phone: 937-644-9102; fax: 937-644-1228; hours 8AM-4PM (EST). *Misdemeanor, Civil Actions Under $15,000, Eviction, Small Claims.*

Civil Records: Access: Phone, fax, mail, in person. Both court and visitors may perform in person searches. No search fee. Court makes copy: $.20 per page after first 5 copies. Required to search: name, years to search. Civil cases indexed by defendant, plaintiff; on computer from 1989, prior on microfilm. Mail turnaround time 1-2 days.

Criminal Records: Access: Phone, fax, mail, in person. Both court and visitors may perform in person searches. No search fee. Court makes copy: $.20 per page after first 5 copies. Required to search: name, years to search; also helpful: SSN. Criminal records on computer from 1989, prior on microfilm. Mail turnaround time 1-2 days.

General Information: Public terminal goes back to 1989. No probation records released. No fee to fax documents. No certification fee . SASE required.

Van Wert County

Common Pleas Court 305 Courthouse, 121 E Main St, Van Wert, OH 45891; phone: 419-238-6935; criminal phone: 419-238-1022; civil phone: 419-238-1022; probate phone: 419-238-0027; fax: 419-238-2874; hours 8AM-4PM (EST). *Felony, Civil Actions, Probate.*

www.vwcommonpleas.org
Note: Fax number for Common Pleas Clerk is 419-238-4760. Probate records are at 108 Main St, Van Wert, OH 45891.

Civil Records: Access: In person only. Visitors must perform in person searches themselves. Court makes copy: $.20 per page. Required to search: name, years to search. Civil cases indexed by defendant, plaintiff. Some early records on microfiche, have docket books and files, indexed on computer since 5/98. Court calendars available online.

Criminal Records: Access: In person only. Visitors must perform in person searches themselves. Court makes copy: $.20 per page. Required to search: name, years to search; also helpful: address, DOB, SSN. Some early years on microfiche, have docket books and files, indexed on computer since 5/98. Court calendar available online.

General Information: Public terminal goes back to 5/1998. All records public. Certification fee: $1.00. Payee: Clerk of Court. Personal checks accepted. Prepayment required.

Van Wert Municipal Court 124 S Market, Van Wert, OH 45891; phone: 419-238-5767; hours 8AM-4PM (EST). *Misdemeanor, Civil Actions Under $15,000, Eviction, Small Claims.*

http://vanwert.org/gov/court/index.htm

Civil Records: Access: Mail, in person. Both court and visitors may perform in person searches. No search fee. Court makes copy: $1.00 per page. Required to search: name, years to search. Civil cases indexed by defendant, plaintiff; on computer from 1989. Mail turnaround time 1-2 days.

Criminal Records: Access: Mail, in person. Both court and visitors may perform in person searches. No search fee. Court makes copy: $1.00 per page. Required to search: name, years to search; also helpful: SSN. Criminal records on computer from 1989. Mail turnaround time 1-2 days.

General Information: Public terminal goes back to 1988. Fee to fax documents is $1.00 per page. Certification fee: $1.00. Payee: Municipal Court. Personal checks accepted. Prepayment and SASE required.

Vinton County

Common Pleas Court County Courthouse, 100 E Main St, McArthur, OH 45651; phone: 740-596-3001; probate phone: 740-596-3438; fax: 740-596-9611; hours 8:30AM-4PM M-F (EST). *Felony, Civil Actions Over $3,000, Probate.*

Civil Records: Access: In person only. Both court and visitors may perform in person searches. No search fee. Court makes copy: $.25 per page. Required to search: name, years to search. Civil cases indexed by defendant, plaintiff. Civil records in books since 1850.

Criminal Records: Access: In person only. Both court and visitors may perform in person searches. No search fee. Court makes copy: $.25 per page. Required to search: name, years to search; also helpful: DOB, SSN. Criminal records in books since 1850.

General Information: Public terminal goes back to 1/1998. No sealed records released. Certification fee: $2.00. Payee: Clerk of Court. Personal checks accepted. Prepayment required.

Vinton County Court County Courthouse, McArthur, OH 45651; phone: 740-596-5000; fax: 740-596-9721; hours 8:30AM-4PM (EST). *Misdemeanor, Civil Actions Under $15,000, Small Claims $3,000.*

Civil Records: Access: In person only. Both court and visitors may perform in person searches. No search fee. No copy fee. Required to search: name, years to search. Civil cases indexed by defendant, plaintiff. Civil records in books from 1980s, archived from 1800s.

Criminal Records: Access: In person only. Both court and visitors may perform in person searches. No search fee. No copy fee. Required to search: name, years to search, DOB; SSN helpful. Criminal records in books from 1980s, archived from 1800s.

General Information: No public access terminal. Will not fax specific case file. Certification fee: No fee for certification.

Warren County

Common Pleas Court PO Box 238, Lebanon, OH 45036; phone: 513-695-1120; probate phone: 513-695-1180; civil/criminal fax: 513-695-2965; probate fax: 513-695-2945; hours 8:30AM-4:30PM (EST). *Felony, Civil Actions Over $3,000, Probate.*

www.co.warren.oh.us/clerkofcourt/
Note: Probate located at 570 Justice Dr.

Civil Records: Access: Phone, mail, in person, online. Both court and visitors may perform in person searches. Search fee: $4.00 per name. Court makes copy: $.20 per page. Required to search: name, years to search. Civil cases indexed by defendant, plaintiff; on computer from 1974, archived from 1850. Access to court records is free at www.co.warren.oh.us/clerkofcourt/search/index.htm. Index goes back to 1980. Mail turnaround time 1-4 days.

Criminal Records: Access: Mail, in person, online. Both court and visitors may perform in person searches. Search fee: $4.00 per name. Court makes copy: $.20 per page. Required to search: name, years to search, DOB, signed release; also helpful: SSN. Criminal records on computer from 1974, archived from 1850. Access to court records is free at www.co.warren.oh.us/clerkofcourt/search/index.htm. Index goes back to 1980. Mail turnaround time 1-4 days.

General Information: Public terminal goes back to 1974. Will fax documents for $2.00 per fax plus $1.00 per page. Certification fee: $1.00 per page. Payee: Clerk of Court. Personal checks accepted. Prepayment and SASE required.

County Court 550 Justice Dr, Lebanon, OH 45036; criminal phone: 513-695-1370; civil phone: 513-695-1371; fax: 513-695-2990; hours 8AM-4:30PM (EST). *Misdemeanor, Civil Actions Under $15,000, Small Claims under $3000.*

www.co.warren.oh.us/countycourt

Civil Records: Access: Phone, mail, in person. Both court and visitors may perform in person searches. No search fee. Court makes copy: $.05 per page. Required to search: name, years to search; also helpful: address. Civil cases indexed by defendant, plaintiff; on computer from 1990, prior in books. Note: No in person searches on Tuesdays or Thursdays. Mail turnaround time 1-2 weeks.

Criminal Records: Access: Phone, mail, in person. Both court and visitors may perform in person searches. No search fee. Court makes copy: $.05 per page. Required to search: name, years to search, DOB; also helpful: SSN, address. Criminal records on computer from 1990, prior in books. Note: No in person searches on Tuesdays or Thursdays. Mail turnaround time 1-2 weeks.

General Information: Public use terminal available. Will not fax documents. No certification fee . Warren County checks accepted. Visa/MC accepted. Prepayment and SASE required.

Franklin Municipal Court 1 Benjamin Franklin Way, Franklin, OH 45005; phone: 937-746-2858; fax: 937-743-7751; hours 8:30AM-5PM (EST). *Misdemeanor, Civil Actions Under $15,000, Eviction, Small Claims.*

Civil Records: Access: Phone, mail, in person. Both court and visitors may perform in person searches. No search fee. Court makes copy: $.50 per page. Required to search: name, years to search. Civil cases indexed by defendant, plaintiff; on computer back to 1990. Mail turnaround time 1-2 days.

Criminal Records: Access: Phone, mail, in person. Both court and visitors may perform in person searches. No search fee. Court makes copy: $.50 per page. Required to search: name, years to search, signed release; also helpful: DOB, SSN. Criminal records on computer back to 1990. Mail turnaround time 1-2 days.

General Information: No public access terminal. Will fax documents. Certification fee: $5.00 per document. Payee: Franklin Municipal Court. Personal checks accepted. In person only. Prepayment required.

Lebanon Muncipal Court City Bldg, 50 S Broadway, Lebanon, OH 45036-1777; phone: 513-932-3060; fax: 513-933-7212; hours 8AM-4PM (EST). *Misdemeanor, Civil Actions, Eviction, Small Claims.*

Civil Records: Access: Fax, mail, in person. Both court and visitors may perform in person searches. No search fee. Court makes copy: $.25 per page; first 6 pages free. Required to search: name, years to search. Civil cases indexed by defendant, plaintiff; on books since 1956, computerized since 1990. Mail turnaround time 2 days.

Criminal Records: Access: Fax, mail, in person. Both court and visitors may perform in person searches. No search fee. Court makes copy: $.25 per page; first 6 pages free. Required to search: name, years to search; also helpful: DOB, SSN. Criminal records on books since 1956, computerized since 1990. Mail turnaround time 2 days.

General Information: Public terminal goes back to 1989. No fee to fax documents. Local faxing only. No certification fee.

Mason Municipal Court 5950 S Mason Montgomery Rd, Mason, OH 45040-3712; phone: 513-398-7901; fax: 513-459-8085; hours 7:30AM-4PM (EST). *Misdemeanor, Civil Actions Under $15,000, Eviction, Small Claims.*

www.masonmunicipalcourt.org

Civil Records: Access: Phone, fax, mail, in person, online. Both court and visitors may perform in person searches. No search fee. Self serve copy fee: $.25 per page. Required to search: name, years to search. Civil cases indexed by defendant, plaintiff. Civil records in docket books since 1985, computerized since 1988. Online access to court records is free at http://courtconnect.masonmunicipalcourt.org/connection/court/. Mail turnaround time 1-2 weeks.

Criminal Records: Access: Phone, fax, mail, in person, online. Both court and visitors may perform in person searches. No search fee. Self serve copy fee: $.25 per page. Required to search: name, years to search; also helpful: SSN. Criminal records in docket books since 1985, computerized since 1988. Online access to court records is free at http://courtconnect.masonmunicipalcourt.org/connection/court/. Mail turnaround time 1-2 weeks.

General Information: No public access terminal. No fee to fax documents. Local faxing only. Certification fee: $3.00 per page. Payee: Mason Municipal Court. Only cashiers checks and money orders accepted. Visa, MC accepted. In person criminal searching only. Prepayment required.

Washington County

Common Pleas Court 205 Putnam St, Marietta, OH 45750; phone: 740-373-6623; hours 8AM-4:15PM (EST). *Felony, Civil Actions Over $10,000, Probate.*

www.washingtongov.org
Note: Probate is separate index at this same address.

Civil Records: Access: In person only. Visitors must perform in person searches themselves. Court makes copy: $.10 per page if 10 pages or over. Self serve copy fee: $.10 per page. Required to search: name, years to search. Civil cases indexed by defendant, plaintiff; on computer since 1985, microfilm to 1977, index in books prior to 1795.

Criminal Records: Access: In person only. Visitors must perform in person searches themselves. Court makes copy: $.10 per page if 10 pages or over. Self serve copy fee: $.10 per page. Required to search: name, years to search. Criminal records on computer since 1985, microfilm to 1977, index in books prior to 1795.

General Information: Public terminal goes back to 1985. No sealed, expunged records released. Will not fax specific case file. Certification fee: $1.00 per page, includes copy fee if less than 10 pages. Payee: Clerk of Court. Personal checks and credit cards accepted. Prepayment required.

Marietta Municipal Court PO Box 615, 301 Putnam, Marietta, OH 45750; phone: 740-373-4474; fax: 740-373-2547; hours 8AM-5PM (EST). *Misdemeanor, Civil Actions Under $15,000, Eviction, Small Claims.*

www.mariettacourt.com

Civil Records: Access: Mail, in person, online. Both court and visitors may perform in person searches. No search fee. Court makes copy: $.05 per page. Required to search: name, years to search. Civil cases indexed by defendant, plaintiff; on computer from 11/91, prior in books. Online access to from 1992 of court dockets is free at www.mariettacourt.com. Mail turnaround time 1 week.

Criminal Records: Access: Mail, in person, online. Both court and visitors may perform in person searches. No search fee. Court makes copy: $.05 per page. Required to search: name, years to search. Criminal records on computer from 11/91, prior in books to 1975. Online access to criminal records is the same as civil. Mail turnaround time 1 week.

General Information: Public use terminal available. Certification fee: $1.50. Payee: Municipal Court. Personal checks accepted. Prepayment and SASE required.

Wayne County

Common Pleas Court PO Box 507, Wooster, OH 44691; phone: 330-287-5590; probate phone: 330-287-5575; fax: 330-287-5416; hours 8AM-4:30PM (EST). *Felony, Civil Actions Over $15,000, Probate.*

http://waynecountyclerkofcourts.org
Note: Probate is a separate court at same address.

Civil Records: Access: Mail, in person, online. Visitors must perform in person searches themselves. No search fee. Court makes copy: $.05 per page. Required to search: name, years to search. Civil cases indexed by defendant, plaintiff; on computer since 1995, in books to 1800s. Online access same as criminal, see below. Note: No name searches are performed by mail. Mail turnaround time 1 week.

Criminal Records: Access: Mail, in person, online. Visitors must perform in person searches themselves. No search fee. Court makes copy: $.05 per page. Required to search: name, years to search. Criminal records on computer since 1995, in books to 1800s. Online access free at www.wayneohio.org/public_access.html; probate index included. Your web browser must be Active-X enabled, Mail turnaround time 1 week.

General Information: Public terminal goes back to 1995. No grand jury indictment records released. Will not fax documents. Certification fee: $2.00. Payee: Clerk of Court. Personal checks accepted. Prepayment required.

Wayne County Municipal Court Clerk

215 N Grant St, Wooster, OH 44691-4817; phone: 330-287-5650; fax: 330-263-4043; hours 8AM-4:30PM (EST). *Misdemeanor, Civil Actions Under $15,000, Eviction, Small Claims.*

www.waynecountyclerkofcourts.org

Civil Records: Access: In person, online. Visitors must perform in person searches themselves. Court makes copy: $.05 per page. Required to search: name, years to search. Civil cases indexed by defendant, plaintiff; on computer back to 9/94; in books from 1975. Online access is same as criminal, see below.

Criminal Records: Access: In person, online. Visitors must perform in person searches themselves. No search fee. Court makes copy: $.05 per page. Required to search: name, years to search, offense, date of offense. Criminal records on computer back to 9/94; in books from 1975. Access free at www.wayneohio.org/public_access.html. Your web browser must be Active-X enabled,

General Information: Public terminal goes back to 9/1994. Will fax specific case file requests. Certification fee: $1.00 per page and includes copy fee. Payee: Wayne County Municipal Court. In state personal checks accepted. Prepayment required.

Williams County

Common Pleas Court 1 Courthouse Sq, Clerk of Court of Common Pleas, Bryan, OH 43506; phone: 419-636-1551; probate phone: 419-636-1548; fax: 419-636-7877; hours 8:30AM-4:30PM (EST). *Felony, Civil Actions Over $10,000, Probate.* Note: Probate Court is at the same address.

Civil Records: Access: Phone, fax, mail, in person. Both court and visitors may perform in person searches. No search fee. Court makes copy: $.25 per page; same fee for self serve. Required to search: name, years to search. Civil cases indexed by defendant, plaintiff; on computer from 1988, records go back to 1840. Mail turnaround time 1-2 days.

Criminal Records: Access: Mail, in person. Both court and visitors may perform in person searches. No search fee. Court makes copy: $.25 per page; same fee for self serve. Required to search: name, years to search. Criminal records on computer from 1988, records go back to 1840. Mail turnaround 1-2 days.

General Information: Public terminal goes back to 4/1998. No expunged records released. Will fax documents. Certification fee: $1.00 per page. Payee: Clerk of Court. Personal checks accepted. Prepayment and SASE required.

Bryan Municipal Court PO Box 546, 1399 E High St, Bryan, OH 43506; phone: 419-636-6939; fax: 419-636-3417; hours 8:30AM-4:30PM (EST). *Misdemeanor, Civil Actions Under $15,000, Eviction, Small Claims.*

Civil Records: Access: Fax, mail, in person. Both court and visitors may perform in person searches. No search fee. No copy fee. Required to search: name, years to search. Civil cases indexed by defendant, plaintiff; on computer from 1988, prior in books to 1966, indexed prior. Mail turnaround time 5 days.

Criminal Records: Access: Fax, mail, in person. Both court and visitors may perform in person searches. No search fee. No copy fee. Required to search: name, years to search, DOB; also helpful: SSN. Criminal records on computer from 1988, prior in books to 1966, indexed prior. Mail turnaround time 5 days.

General Information: Public terminal goes back to 1988. Will fax documents $2.00. Certification fee: $2.00 per page. Payee: Municipal Court. Personal checks or Visa, MC accepted. Prepayment and SASE required.

Wood County

Common Pleas Court Courthouse Sq, Bowling Green, OH 43402; phone: 419-354-9280; probate phone: 419-354-9230; fax: 419-354-9241; probate fax: 419-354-9357; hours 8:30AM-4:30PM (EST). *Felony, Civil Actions Over $10,000, Probate.* Note: Probate record searching is separate, with separate fees.

Civil Records: Access: Phone, fax, mail, in person, online. Both court and visitors may perform in person searches. Search fee: $3.00 per name. Court makes copy: $.25 per page first 25 pages, $.10 thereafter. Required to search: name, years to search. Civil cases indexed by defendant, plaintiff; on computer from 7/90, in books and on microfilm from 1800s, docket books, journals and microfilm back to 1800s. Search probate records online at www.probate-court.co.wood.oh.us. Mail turn around time same day.

Criminal Records: Access: Fax, mail, in person. Both court and visitors may perform in person searches. Search fee: $3.00 per name. Court makes copy: $.25 per page first 25 pages, $.10 thereafter. Required to search: name, years to search; also helpful: SSN. Criminal records on computer from 7/90, in books and on microfilm from 1980, docket books, journals and microfilm back to 1800s. Mail turnaround time same day.

General Information: Public use terminal available. No adoption commitment, parental rights, juvenile, mental illness records released. No fee to fax documents. Certification fee: $1.00. Payee: Common Pleas Court. Business checks accepted. Prepayment and SASE required.

Bowling Green Municipal Court PO Box 326, Bowling Green, OH 43402; phone: 419-352-5263; fax: 419-352-9407; hours 8:30AM-4:30PM (EST). *Misdemeanor, Civil Actions Under $15,000, Eviction, Small Claims.*

www.bgcourt.org

Civil Records: Access: Phone, fax, mail, in person, online. Both court and visitors may perform in person searches. No search fee. Court makes copy: $.05 per page. Required to search: name, years to search. Civil cases indexed by defendant, plaintiff; on computer from 1988. Access is free to civil records at http://157.134.164.156/cmiflash/court/ Mail turnaround time 3 days.

Criminal Records: Access: Phone, fax, mail, in person, online. Both court and visitors may perform in person searches. No search fee. Court makes copy: $.05 per page. Required to search: name, years to search, DOB; also helpful: SSN. Criminal records on computer from 1988. Free access to criminal and traffic records from http://157.134.164.156/cmiflash/court/ Mail turnaround time 3 days.

General Information: Public terminal goes back to 1988. No fee to fax documents. Local faxing only. Certification fee: $1.00 per page. Payee: Municipal Court. Personal checks or Visa, MC accepted. SASE required.

Perrysburg Municipal Court 300 Walnut St, Perrysburg, OH 43551; criminal phone: 419-872-7900; civil phone: 419-872-7910; fax: 419-872-7905; hours 8AM-4:30PM M, W-F; 8AM-6:30PM Tu (EST). *Misdemeanor, Civil Actions Under $15,000, Eviction, Small Claims.*

www.perrysburgcourt.com

Civil Records: Access: Phone, fax, mail, online, in person. Both court and visitors may perform in person searches. Search fee: $3.00 per name. Fee is $15.00 to look in closed, stored files. Court makes copy: $.10 per page; same fee for self serve. Required to search: name, years to search; also helpful: address. Civil cases indexed by defendant, plaintiff; on computer from 1989, prior in books to 1982, archived from 1972. Online access to court records is free at www.perrysburgcourt.com/disc.html. Mail turnaround time 2 days.

Criminal Records: Access: Phone, fax, mail, online, in person. Both court and visitors may perform in person searches. Search fee: $3.00 per name. Fee is $15.00 to look in closed, stored files. Court makes copy: $.10 per page; same fee for self serve. Required to search: name, years to search; also helpful: DOB, SSN. Criminal records on computer from 1989, prior in books to 1982, archived from 1972. Online access to court records is free at www.perrysburgcourt.com/disc.html. Mail turnaround time 2 days.

General Information: No public access terminal. No expunged records released. Fee to fax documents is $5.00 per document. Certification fee: $3.00 per cert. Payee: Municipal Court. Personal checks or Visa, MC accepted. Not accepted over the phone. Prepayment and SASE required.

Wyandot County

Common Pleas Court 109 S Sandusky Ave, Rm 31, Upper Sandusky, OH 43351; phone: 419-294-1432; probate phone: 419-294-2302; fax: 419-294-6414; hours 8:30AM-4:30PM (EST). *Felony, Civil Actions Over $10,000, Probate.*

www.co.wyandot.oh.us/clerk/index.html

Civil Records: Access: In person only. Visitors must perform in person searches themselves. Court makes copy: $.25 per page; same fee for self serve. Required to search: name, years to search. Civil cases indexed by defendant, plaintiff; on computer from 1990, prior in books from late 1800s.

Criminal Records: Access: Fax, mail, in person, phone. Both court and visitors may perform in person searches. No search fee. Court makes copy: $.25 per page; same fee for self serve. Required to search: name, years to search; also helpful: SSN. Criminal records on computer from 1990, prior in books from late 1800s. Mail turnaround 1-2 days.

General Information: Public terminal goes back to 1/1990. No fee to fax documents. Certification fee: $1.00 per page. Payee: Clerk of Court. Personal checks accepted. Prepayment and SASE required.

Upper Sandusky Municipal Court 119 N 7th St, Upper Sandusky, OH 43351; phone: 419-294-3354; criminal phone: ask for probation dept; civil phone: ask for civil; fax: 419-209-0474; hours 8AM-4:30PM (EST). *Misdemeanor, Civil Actions Under $15,000, Eviction, Small Claims.*

Civil Records: Access: Mail, in person. Both court and visitors may perform in person searches. Search fee: $10.00 per name found. No copy fee. Self serve copy fee: $.50 per page. Required to search: name, years to search. Civil cases indexed by defendant, plaintiff; on computer from 5/90, prior in books. Mail turnaround time 1-2 days.

Criminal Records: Access: Mail, in person. Both court and visitors may perform in person searches. Search fee: $10.00 per name found. No copy fee. Self serve copy fee: $.50 per page. Required to search: name, years to search; also helpful: SSN. Criminal records on computer from 5/90, prior in books. Mail turnaround time 1-2 days.

General Information: No public access terminal. No sealed records released. Will fax documents for $10.00 per name, includes copies. The $.50 per page self-serve copy fee includes certification. Certification fee: $1.00 per page includes copy fee. Payee: Upper Sandusky. Personal checks or Visa, MC accepted. Not accepted over the phone. Prepayment and SASE required.

Ohio Recording Offices

ORGANIZATION: 88 counties, 88 recording offices. The recording officer is County Recorder and Clerk of Common Pleas Court (state tax liens). The entire state is in the Eastern Time Zone (EST).

REAL ESTATE RECORDS: Counties will not perform real estate searches. Copy fees are usually $2.00 per page. Certification usually costs $1.00 per document. Tax records are located at the Auditor's Office.

UCC RECORDS: This was a dual filing state. Financing statements were filed both at the state level and with the County Recorder, except for consumer goods, farm related and real estate related collateral, which were filed only with the County Recorder. As of 7/1/2001, only real estate related collateral is filed at the county level. All counties will perform UCC searches. Use search request form UCC-11. Search fees are usually $20.00 per debtor name. Copies usually cost $2.00 per page.

TAX LIEN RECORDS: All federal tax liens are filed with the County Recorder. All state tax liens are filed with the Clerk of Common Pleas Court. Refer to County Court section for information about Ohio courts. Federal tax liens are filed in the "Official Records" of each county. Most counties will not perform a federal tax lien search.

OTHER LIENS: Mechanics, workers compensation, judgment.

ONLINE ACCESS: A growing number of Ohio counties offer online access via the Internet to assessor/real estate data.

Adams County

County Recorder, 110 W. Main; Courthouse, West Union, OH 45693. 937-544-2513, R/E recording phone-937-258-3315 or 544-5051, UCC recording phone-937-258-3315; fax-937-544-4616; 8AM-4PM. Office personnel or visitors may perform searches. Search fee $20.00 per name. Will not search real estate records. Copy fee $2.00 per page. Cert fee-$1.00 per cert plus copy fee. Payee- Adams County Recorder. **Online access to Property Tax, Sex Offender records:** Access to the treasurer and auditor property tax data is free at http://adamspropertymax.governmaxa.com/propertymax/rover30.asp. **Other phones:** Treasurer- 937-544-2317; Appraiser/Auditor- 937-544-2364; Elections-937-544-2633; Vital Records- 937-544-5547. **Property tax/Assessor-** 937-544-2364.

Allen County

County Recorder, PO Box 1243, Lima, OH 45802. 419-223-8517; fax-419-222-8427; hours: 8:30AM-4:30PM. www.co.allen.oh.us/rec.php
All records in one index. Records indexed on a public use terminal back to 1989. Only the public may search. Copy fee $2.00 per page. Cert fee-$1.00 per cert plus copy fee. Payee- Allen County Recorder. **Online access to Property, Auditor, Property Sale, Cemetery, War Casualty, Death records:** Access to the auditor property data is free at www.allencountyauditorohio.com/Allen208/LandRover.asp Also, search cemetery, war, and death records free at www.delphos-ohio.com/history/cemeteri.htm. **Other phones:** Treasurer- 419-223-8515.

Ashland County

County Recorder, 142 W. 2nd St.; Courthouse, Ashland, OH 44805-2193. 419-282-4238; fax-419-281-5715; hours: 8AM-4PM. www.ashlandcounty.org/recorder/index.htm
All records in one index. Only the public may search. Copy fee $2.00 per page. Cert fee- $1.00 per cert plus copy fee. Payee- Ashland County Recorder. **Online access to Real Estate, Auditor, Property Sale, Sex Offender records:** Access property records on the Auditor's database free at www.ashlandcoauditor.org. Also, search the county sex offender list for free at www.ashlandcounty.org/sheriff/offenders.cfm. **Other phones:** Treasurer- 419-282-4229; Appraiser/Auditor- 419-282-4330; Elections- 419-282-4224; Vital Records- 419-282-4226. **Property tax/Assessor-** same address as above. 419-282-4330.

Ashtabula County

County Recorder, 25 W. Jefferson St, Jefferson, OH 44047. 440-576-3762; fax-440-576-3231; hours: 8AM-4:30PM. www.co.ashtabula.oh.us
All records in one index. Records indexed on computer back to 1984. Office personnel searches UCC, otherwise visitors perform searches. Can give specific real estate information - filed date, deed volume/page, etc.- over phone. Will search UCC records, but not tax liens. UCC search per debtor name- $20.00. Copy fee $2.00 per page. Cert fee-$1.00 per cert plus copy fee. **Online access to Real Estate, Auditor, Property Sale records:** Property records on the county Auditor's database are free at www.ashtabulacountyauditor.org/ashtabula208/LandRover.asp. **Other phones:** Treasurer- 440-576-3727; Appraiser/Auditor- 440-576-3789; Elections- 440-576-6915; Vital Records- 440-576-3627; Auditor- 440-576-3783. **Property tax/Assessor-** same address as above. 440-576-3789.

Athens County

County Recorder, 15 S Court St, Rm 236, Athens, OH 45701. 740-592-3228; fax-740-592-3229; hours: 8AM-4PM. www.athenscountygovernment.com
Office will perform a UCC search but public must search other records themselves. Search fee $20.00 per name. Copy fee $2.00 per page. Cert fee-$1.00 per cert plus copy fee. **Online access to Property, Deed, UCC, Inmate, Mapping records:** Access to county land and UCC records is free at www.landaccess.com. Records go back to 1/1981. Also, search the GIS mapping site by name at http://132.235.241.200/website/athens_v1/viewer.htm. Also, search the inmate list for free at http://xw.textdata.com:81/cgi/progcgi.exe?program=search. **Other phones:** Treasurer- 740-592-3231; Appraiser/Auditor- 740-592-3223; Elections- 740-592-3201; Vital Records- 740-592-3251; Auditor- 740-592-3223; Microfilm Dept -740-592-3271. **Property tax/Assessor-** 740-592-3223.

Auglaize County

County Recorder, 209 S Blackhoof St; Rm 103, Wapakoneta, OH 45895-1972. 419-739-6735; fax-419-739-6736; hours: 8AM-4:30PM.
Office will perform a UCC search but public must search other records themselves. UCC search per debtor name- $20.00. Copy fee $2.00 per page. Cert fee- $1.00 per cert plus copy fee. **Online access to Property, Assessor, Recorder, Real Estate, Deed, Lien, UCC records:** Access county property data for free at http://auglaizeauditor.ddti.net/. Also, search recorder data free online at www.landaccess.com/sites/oh/auglaize/index.php. **Other phones:** Treasurer- 419-739-6745; Elections-419-739-6720; Auditor- 419-739-6705.

Belmont County

County Recorder, 101 Main St; Courthouse, Rm 105, St. Clairsville, OH 43950. 740-699-2121; fax-740-699-2140 x198; hours: 8:30AM-4:30PM. www.belmontcountyohio.org
All records in one index. Records indexed on a public use terminal back to 1992. Office will perform a UCC search but public must search other records themselves. Search fee $20.00 flat fee. Copy fee $2.00 per page. Cert fee- $1.00 per cert plus copy fee. Payee- Belmont County Recorder. **Online access to Deed, Property records:** Access to recorder deed information is free at www.belmontcountyohio.org/recorder/index.html. Also, search auditor records at www.belmontcountyohio.org/auditor.htm. Also, land records from the assessor database found free at www.landaccess.com/. **Other phones:** Treasurer- 740-695-2120 x211; Auditor- 740-695-2120 x257. **Property tax/Assessor-** 740-699-2130.

Brown County

County Recorder, PO Box 149, Georgetown, OH 45121. 937-378-6478; fax-937-378-2848; 8AM-4PM. Office will perform a UCC search but public must search other records themselves. UCC search per debtor name- $20.00. Copy fee $2.00 per page. Cert fee- $1.00 per cert plus copy fee. Payee- Brown County Recorder. **Online access to Property, Deed, UCC records:** Access to recordings is free at www.landaccess.com/sites/oh/brown/index.php. **Other phones:** Treasurer- 937-378-6705; Appraiser/Auditor- 937-378-6398.

Butler County

County Recorder, 130 High St, Hamilton, OH 45011. 513-887-3192; fax-513-887-3198; hours: 8AM-4:30PM. http://66.117.197.5/recorder/
All records in one index. Records indexed on a public use terminal back to 1987. Only the public may search. Copy fee $2.00 per page. Cert fee-$1.00 per cert. Payee- Butler County Recorder. **Online access to Property, Deed, UCC, Probate, Voter Registration, Tax Sale, Sex Offender records:** County voter records are at www.butlercountyohio.org/elections/search/search.asp. County probate records are at www.butlercountyohio.org/probate/estate.cfm. Search auditor records at http://propertysearch.butlercountyohio.org/butler/. Also, access county land and UCC records free at www.landaccess.com. Records go back

to 1/1987. Also, http://66.117.197.5/recorder/index.c fm?page=regLand_search offers access to recorded documents free; must download software. Also, search county available property at www.butlercounty.biz/Si tes.html. The sheriff's tax sale and sex offender lists are at www.butlersheriff.org. Search vendors at www.butlercountyauditor.org/vl_search.cfm. **Other phones:** Treasurer- 513-887-3181; Appraiser/Auditor- 513-887-3147; Elections- 513-887-3700; Vital Records- 513-863-1770; Auditor- 513-887-3295. **Property tax/Assessor-** same address as above. 513-887-3154.

Carroll County

County Recorder, PO Box 550, Carrollton, OH 44615-0550. 330-627-4545; fax-330-627-4295; hours: 8AM-4PM. www.ohiorecorders.com
Office will perform a UCC search but public must search other records themselves. UCC search per debtor name- $20.00. Copy fee $2.00 per page. Cert fee- $1.00 per doc, plus copy fee. Payee- Carroll County Recorder. **Online access to Auditor, Property records:** Access to the Auditor's property data is free at http://carrollpropertymax.governm axa.com/propertymax/rover30.asp. **Other phones:** Treasurer- 330-627-4221; Appraiser/Auditor- 330-627-2250; Elections- 330-627-2610. **Property tax/Assessor-** 330-327-2250.

Champaign County

County Recorder, 512 S US Hwy 68 #B200, Urbana, OH 43078. 937-484-1630; fax-937-484-1628; hours: 8AM-4PM. www.co.champaign.oh.us/auditor/
Office will perform a UCC search but public must search other records themselves. UCC search per debtor name- $20.00. Copy fee $2.00 per page. Cert fee- $1.00 per cert plus copy fee. **Online access to Real Estate records:** Auditor real estate data is free at http://champaignoh.ddti.net/. **Other phones:** Treasurer- 937-484-1640; Auditor- 937-652-2264.

Clark County

County Recorder, PO Box 1406, Springfield, OH 45501. 937-328-2445; fax-937-328-4620; hours: 8AM-4:30PM. www.co.clark.oh.us/
Only the public may search. Copy fee $2.00 per page. Cert fee- $1.00 per cert plus copy fee. Payee- Clark County Recorder. **Online access to Property, Deed, UCC, Sheriff Real Estate Sale, Tax Sale, Sex Offender records:** Access to county land and UCC records is free at www.landaccess.com. Records go back to 1/1988. Also, the sheriff's real estate sale, tax sale, sex offender and most wanted lists are at www.clarkcountysheriff.com. Also, search cemeteries free at www.geocities.com/Heartland/Garden/34 58/Cemeteries.htm. Search obituaries at http://guardian.ccpl.lib.oh.us/obits/. **Other phones:** Treasurer- 937-328-2432; Auditor- 937-328-2423.

Clermont County

County Recorder, 101 E. Main St, Batavia, OH 45103-2958. 513-732-7236; fax-513-732-7891; hours: 8AM-4:30PM. http://recorder.co.clermont.oh.us/
Office will perform a UCC search but public must search other records themselves. Will not search real estate records. UCC search per debtor name- $20.00. Separate federal tax lien search-will do over phone for free but only a couple names. Copy fee $2.00 per page. Cert fee- $1.00 per doc plus copy fee. Payee- Clermont County Treasurer. **Online access to Property, Deed, UCC, Property Tax, Auditor, Sex Offender, Child Support records:** Records from the auditor's county property database are free at www.clermontauditorrealestate.org. Also, free access to the recorder's property, deed, and UCC records is at www.landaccess.com. Also, search county sex offenders database free at www.clermontsheriff.org/registered_sex_offenders.htm Search child support wants at www.clermontsupportskids.org. **Other phones:** Treasurer- 513-732-7254; Elections- 513-732-7275; Auditor- 513-732-7150; Commissioners -513-732-7300. **Property tax/Assessor-** 513-732-7150.

Clinton County

County Recorder, 46 S. South St; Courthouse, Wilmington, OH 45177. 937-382-2067; fax-937-382-8097; hours: 8AM-4PM.
www.co.clinton.oh.us/default.htm
All records in one index. Records indexed on a public use terminal back to 1981. Office will perform a UCC search but public must search other records themselves. UCC search per debtor name- $20.00. Copy fee $2.00 per page. Cert fee- $1.00 per page plus copy fee. Payee- Clinton County Recorder. **Online access to Auditor, Property records:** Access the Auditor's property database for free at www.co.clinton.oh.us/audi tor/iView/iView.asp. **Other phones:** Treasurer- 937-382-2224; Elections- 937-382-3537; Vital Records- 937-382-3829; Auditor- 937-382-2250.

Columbiana County

County Recorder, 105 S. Market St.; County Courthouse, Rm 104, Lisbon, OH 44432. 330-424-9517 x641; fax-330-424-5067; hours: 8AM-4PM.
All records in one index. Records indexed on a public use terminal back to 1983. Office will perform a UCC search but public must search other records themselves. Search fee $20.00. Copy fee $2.00; customer makes copy $.25 per page. Cert fee- $2.00 per cert plus copy fee. Payee- Columbiana County Recorder. **Online access to Real Estate, Auditor, Forfeited Land Sale records:** Property records on the Auditor's database are free at www.columbianacntyauditor.org/columbv208/LandRo ver.asp. Both the Auditor and Sheriff's sales can be accessed here.

Coshocton County

County Recorder, PO Box 817, Coshocton, OH 43812. 740-622-2817; fax-740-295-7352; hours: 8AM-4PM.
www.co.coshocton.oh.us/
Records indexed on a public use terminal back to 1980. Only the public may search. Copy fee $2.00 per page. Cert fee- $1.00 per cert plus copy fee. Payee- County Recorder. **Online access to Property, Deed, UCC, Auditor, Property Tax, Sex Offender records:** Access to county land and UCC records is free at www.landaccess.com. Records go back to 1/1980. Also, search property tax records for free at www.coshcoauditor.org; click on "Property Search." The sex offender list can be searched at www.coshoctonsheriff.com/sexualpred.cfm. **Other phones:** Treasurer- 740-622-2713; Elections- 740-622-1117; Auditor- 740-622-1243.

Crawford County

County Recorder, 112 E. Mansfield St #206, Bucyrus, OH 44820-0788. 419-562-6961; fax-419-562-6061; hours: 8:30-4:30PM.
All records in one index. Only the public may search. Copy fee $2.00 per page. Cert fee- $1.00 per cert plus copy fee. Payee- Crawford County Recorder. **Online access to Auditor, Real Estate, Dog Tag records:** Access to the auditor database is free at www.crawford-co.org/auditor/default.html. **Other phones:** Treasurer- 419-562-7861; Appraiser/Auditor- 419-562-7941; Elections- 419-562-8721. **Property tax/Assessor-** same address as above. not known.

Cuyahoga County

County Recorder, 1219 Ontario St; Rm 220, Cleveland, OH 44113. 216-443-7316, R/E recording phone-216-443-7300, 216-443-8194, UCC recording phone-216-443-7300; fax-216-443-8193; hours: 8:30AM-4:30PM. http://recorder.cuyahogacounty.us
Office personnel or visitors may perform searches. General index search fee $4.00 per 15 minutes. Will not do federal tax lien search. UCC search per debtor name- $20.00. Copy fee $2.00 per page. Cert fee- $1.00 per cert plus copy fee. Payee- Cuyahoga County Recorder. **Online access to Auditor, Probate, Marriage, Real Estate, Tax Lien, Recording, Cemetery, Most Wanted, Sexual Predator records:** Access the Recorders database free at http://recorder.cuyahogacounty.us. The Recorder's data includes land documents from 1925-2003. Search the auditor property database at http://auditor.cuyahogacounty.us/repi/default.asp. Also, search 22 categories of Probate records including marriages free at http://probate.cuyahogacounty.us/pa/. Obits and death notices are at www.cleveland.co m/obits/archives/. Also, sexual predators, most wanted lists, and foreclosure sales are at www.cuyahogacoun ty.us/sheriff/default.htm. Cemeterys at www.geocit ies.com/micheledanielle/cemetery.html. Vendors at https://auditor.cuyahogacounty.us/genservices/vendorLi st_report.asp. **Other phones:** Appraiser/Auditor- 216-443-7092; Vital Records- 216-664-2317.

Darke County

County Recorder, 504 S Broadway; Courthouse, Greenville, OH 45331. 937-547-7390; hours: 8:30AM-4:30PM. www.co.darke.oh.us/links.htm
Separate indices to search include abstract indexes, soldier discharges. Records indexed on a public use terminal back to 6/96 (scanning 8/1/2000). Office will perform a UCC search but public must search other records themselves. Search fee $20.00 plus $4.00 each name. Copy fee $2.00 per copy. Cert fee- $1.00 per doc, plus copy fee. Payee- Darke County Recorder. **Online access to Real Estate, Property Tax records:** Property and property tax records on the Darke County database are free at http://darkepropertymax.governmax.com/propertymax/ rover30.asp?. **Other phones:** Treasurer- 937-547-7365; Elections- 937-548-1835; Vital Records- 937-547-7361; Auditor- 937-547-7310; Probate Court -937-547-7345.

Defiance County

County Recorder, 221 Clinton St; Courthouse, Defiance, OH 43512. 419-782-4741; fax-419-782-3421; hours: 8:30AM-4:30PM. www.defiance-county.com/recorder.html
Separate indices to search include up until 1997 they had separate indexes, beginning 1997 they have Official Records. Office will perform a UCC search but public must search other records themselves. UCC search per debtor name- $20.00. Copy fee $2.00 per page; self serve $.25. Cert fee- $1.00 per cert plus copy fee. Payee- Defiance County Recorder. **Online access to Auditor, Real Estate records:** Assess to the auditor real estate data is at www.defiance-county.com/realestatesearch.html. Call 800-875-3953 or 419-784-3111 for necessary password. **Other phones:** Treasurer- 419-782-8741; Appraiser/Auditor- 419-784-3111. **Property tax/Assessor-** same address as above. 419-784-3111.

Delaware County

County Recorder, 140 N Sandusky St, Delaware, OH 43015. 740-833-2460; fax-740-833-2459; hours: 8:30AM-4:30PM. www.co.delaware.oh.us
All records in one index. Only the public may search. Copy fee $2.00 per page. Cert fee- $1.00 per cert plus copy fee. Payee- Delaware County Recorder. **Online access to Real Estate, Deed, UCC Auditor, Property Sale, Sheriff Sale, Most Wanted, Sex Offender, DUI records:** Access to the Recorder's data plus UCCs is free at www.landaccess.com. Also, access to auditor's property and sales data is free at www.delawarecountyauditor.org/propertymax/rover30. asp?. Also, Sheriff sales, Most Wanted, Sex Offender information is free at www.delawarecountysheriff.com. Also, search the municipal court DUI list at www.municipalcourt.org/main_dui.asp. Also, search cemeteries at http://delcohist.tripod.com/burials.htm.

Erie County

County Recorder, 247 Columbus Ave.; Erie County Office Bldg, Rm 225, Sandusky, OH 44870-2635. 419-627-7686, R/E recording phone-419-627-7661, UCC recording phone-419-627-7686; fax-419-627-6639; hours: 8AM-4PM. www.erie-county-ohio.net/officials.htm

Separate indices to search include prior to 1990 are indexed in different categories. Records indexed on computer back to 1990. Office will perform a UCC search but public must search other records themselves. UCC search per debtor name- $20.00. Copy fee $2.00 per page; self serve $.10. Cert fee- $1.00 per doc plus copy fee. Payee- Erie County Recorder. **Online access to Auditor, Property, Recording, Deed records:** Access the auditor property database for free at www.erie.iviewtaxmaps.com/iView/iView.asp. Access recorded documents at www.co-erie-oh-us-recorder.com. **Other phones:** Treasurer- 419-627-7201; Appraiser/Auditor- 419-627-7746; Auditor- 419-627-7741.

Fairfield County

County Recorder, PO Box 2420, Lancaster, OH 43130-5420. 740-687-7100; fax-740-687-7104; hours: 8AM-N, 1-4PM. www.co.fairfield.oh.us
Separate indices to search include deed, mortgage, miscellaneous, UCC, release, lease, OR. Records indexed on a public use terminal back to 8/1996. Only the public may search. Copy fee $2.00 per page. Cert fee- $1.00 per cert plus copy fee. Payee- Fairfield County Recorder. **Online access to Property, Deed, UCC, Auditor, Property Sale, Inmate, Sex Offender records:** Access to county land and UCC records is free at www.landaccess.com. Records go back to 8/1996. Also, online access to the Auditor's property and sales database is free at http://realestate.co.fairfield.oh.us/. Also, access to the sheriff's real estate sale list and sex offenders list is free at www.sheriff.fairfield.oh.us/. Search inmates list at http://xw.textdata.com:81/cgi/progcgi.exe?program=search3. **Other phones:** Treasurer- 740-687-7094; Auditor- 740-687-7090.

Fayette County

County Recorder, 133 S Main St; Courthouse Bldg, Washington Court House, OH 43160-1393. 740-335-1770; fax-740-333-3521; hours: 9AM-4PM. www.fayette-co-oh.com
Search fee $20.00 per name. Will not search real estate records. Will search UCC records, but not tax liens. Copy fee $2.00 per page; $.25 self serve. Cert fee- $1.00 per cert plus copy fee. Payee- Recorder. **Online access to Recorder, Deed, Lien, Auditor, Property, Sale, Sex Offender, Sheriff Sale records:** Search the auditor's database for property data at http://fayettepropertymax.governmax.com/propertymax/rover30.asp. Also, access to recorders index database is through a private company for free at www.landaccess.com. Images go back to 5/20/02. Also, search the sheriff's lists for free at www.faycoso.com. **Other phones:** Treasurer- 740-335-4961; Elections- 740-335-1190; Vital Records- 740-335-5910. **Property tax/Assessor-** 740-335-6461.

Franklin County

County Recorder, 373 S. High St; 18th Fl, Columbus, OH 43215-6307. 614-462-3930, 614-462-3378, R/E recording phone-614-462-3930, UCC recording phone-614-462-3937; fax-614-462-4299; hours: 8:AM-5PM. www.co.franklin.oh.us/recorder/
Office will perform a UCC search but public must search other records themselves. UCC search per debtor name- $20.00. Copy fee $2.00 per page. Cert fee- $1.00 per cert plus copy fee. **Online access to Recorder, Property, Auditor, Unclaimed Funds, Marriage, Treasurer Refund, Most Wanted, Sheriff Sale, Sex Offender records:** Access to the recorders data is free at www.co.franklin.oh.us/recorder/documents.html. Free registration required. Search veterans graves at www.co.franklin.oh.us/main/vetsTransPage.htm. Search marriage licenses back to 1995 at www.co.franklin.oh.us/recorder/. Search unclaimed funds at www.franklincountyohio.gov/clerk/UnclaimedFunds.htm. Most wanted, sex offenders, sheriff sales at www.faycoso.com Also, auditor's property data is at http://franklin.governmaxa.com/propertymax/rover30.asp. Other county/municipal databases are

free at www.co.franklin.oh.us. **Other phones:** Auditor-614-462-3894.

Fulton County

County Recorder, 152 S Fulton St #175, Wauseon, OH 43567. 419-337-9232; fax-419-337-9282; hours: 8:30AM-4:30PM. www.fultoncountyoh.com
Records indexed on computer back to 8/1995. Office will perform a UCC search but public must search other records themselves. Search fee $20.00. Copy fee $2.00 per page, self serve $.25 per page. Cert fee- $1.00 per cert plus copy fee. Payee- Fulton County Recorder. **Online access to Property, Deed, Recorder, UCC, Auditor, Real Estate records:** Access to property, deed, and UCC records is to be free online at www.landaccess.com/sites/oh/disclaimer.php?county=ohfulton. Also, search the auditor property data for free at http://fultonpropertymax.governmax.com/propertymax/rover30.asp. **Other phones:** Treasurer- 419-337-9252; Elections- 419-335-6841; Auditor- 419-337-9200.

Gallia County

County Recorder, 18 Locust St; Rm 1265, Gallipolis, OH 45631-1265. 740-446-4612 x248, R/E recording phone-740-446-4612 x246, UCC recording phone-740-446-4612; fax-740-446-4804; hours: 8AM-4PM. www.galliacounty.org/government/government.html
Separate indices to search include deeds, mortgages, liens & miscellaneous, financing statements. Records indexed on computer. Office will perform a UCC search but public must search other records themselves. UCC search per debtor name- $20.00. Copy fee $2.00 per page. Cert fee- $1.00 per cert plus copy fee. Payee- Gallia County Recorder. **Online access to Property, Real Estate, Most Wanted, Sex Offender, Inmate records:** Property records on the county auditor real estate database are free at http://galliaauditor.ddti.net. Click on "attributes" for property information; click on "sales" to search by real estate attributes. Also, search the sheriff's database for inmates, sex offenders, ner'do'wells, etc at www.galliasheriff.org. **Other phones:** Treasurer- 740-446-6004; Auditor- 740-446-4612 x218. **Property tax/Assessor-** 740-446-4612 x218.

Geauga County

County Recorder, 231 Main St, #1C; Courthouse Annex, Chardon, OH 44024-1235. 440-285-2222 x3680; hours: 8AM-4:30PM. www.co.geauga.oh.us
All records in one index. Only the public may search, unless proper UCC form submitted. Will not search real estate records. Will search UCC records. UCC search per debtor name- $20.00. Copy fee $2.00 per page; $.10 self serve. Cert fee- $1.00 per cert plus copy fee. Payee- Geauga County Recorder. **Online access to Delinquent Property Tax, Tax Sale, Auditor, Property, Most Wanted, Sex Offender records:** Search the Auditor's property data at www.co.geauga.oh.us/departments/auditor/ag/. No name searching. Also, search the auditor's records at www.auditor.co.geauga.oh.us/ag/. Also, search the sheriff's tax sale, most wanted and sex offender lists for free at www.sheriff.geauga.oh.us. **Other phones:** Treasurer- 440-285-2222 x3850; Appraiser/Auditor- 440-285-2222 x4490; Elections- 440-285-2222 x4020; Vital Records- 440-285-2222 x6407. **Property tax/Assessor-** 231 Main St #1A, Chardon, OH 44024; 440-285-2222 x3450.

Greene County

County Recorder, PO Box 100, Xenia, OH 45385-0100. 937-376-5270, R/E recording phone-937-562-5270, UCC recording phone-937-562-5275; fax-937-376-5386; hours: 8AM-4:30PM. www.co.greene.oh.us/recorder.htm
Separate indices to search include books. Records indexed on a public use terminal back to 1984. Office will perform a UCC search but public must search other records themselves. Search fee $20.00. Copy fee $2.00 per page, self serve $.50 per page. Cert fee- $1.00 per cert plus copy fee. Payee- Greene County Recorder. **Online access to**

Real Estate, Auditor, Recording, Deed, Mortgage, Grantor/Grantee, Sheriff Sale, Sex Offender records: Access to the recorders data is free at www.co.greene.oh.us/recorder/documentSearch.asp. Also, records on the county Internet Map Server are free at www.co.greene.oh.us/gismapserver.htm. Click on "Click here to enter. Server Site #1". Data includes owner, address, valuation, taxes, sales data, and parcel ID number. Also, search the sheriff's sales and sex offender list at www.co.greene.oh.us/sheriff/. **Other phones:** Treasurer- 937-562-5017; Appraiser/Auditor- 937-562-5278; Elections- 937-562-5261; Vital Records- 937-562-5686; Auditor- 937-562-5065. **Property tax/Assessor-** 15 Greene St, Xenia, OH 45385; 937-562-5017.

Guernsey County

County Recorder, 627 Wheeling Ave #305, Cambridge, OH 43725. 740-432-9275; fax-740-439-6258; hours: 8AM-4PM.
Office will perform a UCC search but public must search other records themselves. UCC search per debtor name- $20.00. Copy fee $2.00 per page. Cert fee- $1.00 per cert plus copy fee. Payee- Guernsey County Recorder. **Online access to Sex Offender records:** Search for sex offenders at www.guernseysheriff.com/sexoffenders.htm. **Other phones:** Treasurer- 740-432-9278; Appraiser/Auditor- 740-432-9243; Elections- 740-432-2680; Vital Records- 740-432-3577. **Property tax/Assessor-** 627 Wheeling Ave, Cambridge, OH 43725; 740-432-9243.

Hamilton County

County Recorder, 138 E Court St; Rm 101-A, Cincinnati, OH 45202. 513-946-4570; fax-513-946-4577; hours: 8AM-4PM. http://recordersoffice.hamilton-co.org
All records in one index. Will not search real estate records. Will search UCC records, UCC search does not include tax liens. UCC search per debtor name- $20.00. Separate federal tax lien search- $.50 per page. This agency will not do a state tax lien search. Copy fee $2.00 per page. Cert fee- $1.00 per page plus copy fee. Payee- Hamilton County Recorder. **Online access to Real Estate, Lien, Recording, Lien, Deed, Mortgage, UCC, Auditor, Sex Offender, Most Wanted, Missing, Sheriff Sale. Marriage records:** Access to recorder records is free at http://recordersoffice.hamilton-co.org. Search the marriage license database at www.probatect.org/case_search/cs-scripts/ml_Input.asp. Also, online access to the auditor's tax records database is free at www.hamiltoncountyauditor.org./realestate/. Also, search probate records back to 1/2000 at www.probatect.org/case_search/cs-scripts/pimain.html. Also, search lists for most wanted, sex offender, deadbeat parents, missing persons, and sheriff's sale on the sheriff's site under "Public Services" at www.hcso.org. **Other phones:** Treasurer- 513-946-4800; Appraiser/Auditor- 513-946-4000.

Hancock County

County Recorder, 300 S. Main St; Courthouse, Findlay, OH 45840. 419-424-7091; fax-419-423-3017; hours: 8:30AM-4:30PM.
http://co.hancock.oh.us/recorder/recorder.htm
Separate indices to search prior to 1986. Only the public may search. Copy fee $2.00 per page; self serve $.15. Cert fee- $1.00 per cert plus copy fee. Payee- Hancock County Recorder. **Online access to Property, Auditor, Sex Offender, Real estate, Recorder, Deed, UCC records:** Search the auditor's property database free at http://hancock.iviewauditor.com. No name searching. Also, access to recorder records is free at www.landaccess.com. Index goes back to 1986; images to 12/19/2000. Also, search the sheriff's sex offender list at www.hancocksheriff.org/info/sexoffenders.htm. **Other phones:** Treasurer- 419-424-7213; Appraiser/Auditor- 419-424-7015; Elections- 419-422-3245; Vital Records- 419-424-7869; Auditor- 419-424-

7083. **Property tax/Assessor-** same address as above. not known.

Hardin County

County Recorder, One Courthouse Sq; #220, Kenton, OH 43326. 419-674-2250; fax-419-675-2802; hours: 8:30AM-4PM; 8:30AM-5PM F. www.co.hardin.oh.us
All records in one index. Office will perform a UCC search but public must search other records themselves. Search fee $20.00. Copy fee $.25 per page; fax back- $2.00 per page. Cert fee- $2.00 per cert plus copy fee. Payee- Hardin County Recorder. **Online access to Auditor, Property, Sex Offender records:** Property records from the county database are at www.co.hardin.oh.us. Click on "Real Estate Internet Inquiry." Also, check a dog tag number for its owner's name here. **Other phones:** Treasurer- 419-674-2246; Auditor- 419-674-2239.

Harrison County

County Recorder, 100 W. Market St; Courthouse, Cadiz, OH 43907. 740-942-8869; fax-740-942-4693; hours: 8:30AM-4:30PM. www.harrisoncountyohio.org/
Separate indices to search include grantor/grantee from 12/31/94, abstracts from 1812-current, computer from 1994-current. Records indexed on a public use terminal back to 1994. Office will perform a UCC search only if in writing, but public must search other records themselves. UCC search per debtor name- $20.00. Copy fee $2.00 per page. Cert fee- $1.00 per cert plus copy fee. Payee- Harrison County Recorder. **Other phones:** Treasurer- 740-942-8864; Elections- 740-942-8866; Vital Records- 740-942-8868; Auditor- 740-942-8861; Engineer -740-942-8867.

Henry County

County Recorder, 660 N. Perry St.; Courthouse, Rm 202, Napoleon, OH 43545-1747. 419-592-1766; fax-419-592-1652; hours: 8:30AM-4:30PM. www.henrycountyohio.com
All records in one index. Records indexed on a public use terminal back to 1990. Office will perform a UCC search but public must search other records themselves. UCC search per debtor name- $20.00. Copy fee $2.00 per page; $.10 per page. Cert fee- $1.00 per cert plus copy fee. Payee- Henry County Recorder. **Online access to Land, Recording, Lien, Deed, Sheriff Sale, Sex Offender records:** Access recorder data free at www.landaccess.com/sites/oh/disclaimer.php?county=ohhenry. Also, search county sex offender and sheriff sales lists for free at www.henrycountysheriff.com. **Other phones:** Treasurer- 419-592-1851; Elections- 419-592-7956; Vital Records- 419-599-5545. **Property tax/Assessor-** 419-492-1956.

Highland County

County Recorder, PO Box 804, Hillsboro, OH 45133. 937-393-9954; fax-937-393-5855; hours: 8:30AM-4PM. www.ohiorecorders.com
Office personnel or visitors may perform searches. General search fee $2.00 per name. Will not search real estate records. UCC search per debtor name- $20.00. Copy fee $2.00 per item/page. Cert fee- $1.00 per cert plus copy fee. Payee- Highland County Recorder. **Online access to Property, Deed, UCC, Auditor, Property Sale, Sex Offender, Sheriff Sale records:** Access to recorders database is free at www.landaccess.com/sites/oh/highland/index.php. Also, search the auditor's data for free at http://highlandpropertymax.governmaxa.com/propertymax/rover30.asp. The sheriff's sex offender and sales lists are free at www.highlandcoso.com/rso.htm. **Other phones:** Treasurer- 937-393-9951; Appraiser/Auditor- 937-393-1915; Elections- 937-393-9961; Vital Records- 937-393-1941. **Property tax/Assessor-** 937-393-1915.

Hocking County

County Recorder, PO Box 949, Logan, OH 43138-0949. 740-385-2031; fax-740-385-0377; hours: 8:30AM - 4PM. www.co.hocking.oh.us/
All records in one index. Office will perform a UCC search but public must search other records themselves. UCC search per debtor name- $20.00. Copy fee $2.00 per page. Cert fee- $1.00 per cert plus copy fee. Payee- Recorder. **Online access to Property, Auditor, Sexual Offender, Inmate records:** Access to the auditor's real estate data (and dog tag ownership) is free at www.realestate.co.hocking.oh.us. Also, search the sheriff list of sexual offenders at www.hockingsheriff.org. Search the county list of inmates at http://xw.textdata.com:81/cgi/progcgi.exe?program=search3. **Other phones:** Treasurer- 740-385-3517; Appraiser/Auditor- 740-385-2127; Elections- 740-380-8683; Vital Records- 740-385-3030; Clerk of Courts- 740-385-2616. **Property tax/Assessor-** 740-385-2127.

Holmes County

County Recorder, PO Box 213, Millersburg, OH 44654. 330-674-5916; fax-330-674-0782; hours: 8AM-4:30PM.
Office will perform a UCC search but public must search other records themselves. UCC search per debtor name- $20.00. Copy fee $2.00 per page. Cert fee- $1.00 per cert plus copy fee. Payee- Holmes County Recorder. **Online access to Property, Auditor, Sale records:** Access to the auditor's property data is free at www.holmescountyauditor.org. **Other phones:** Treasurer- 330-674-1896; Auditor- 330-674-1896.

Huron County

County Recorder, PO Box 354, Norwalk, OH 44857. 419-668-1916; fax-419-663-4052; hours: 8AM-4:30PM. www.huroncountyrecorder.org
All records in one index. Records indexed on a public use terminal back to 1986. Office will perform a UCC search but public must search other records themselves. UCC search per debtor name- $20.00. Copy fee $2.00 per page. Cert fee- $1.00 per cert plus copy fee. **Online access to Property, Auditor, Sale records:** Access to the auditor data is free at www.huroncountyauditor.org. **Other phones:** Treasurer- 419-668-2090; Elections- 419-668-8238; Vital Records- 419-668-1652; Auditor- 419-668-4304. **Property tax/Assessor-** 12 E Main St, Norwalk, OH 44857; 419-668-4304.

Jackson County

County Recorder, 226 E. Main St.; Courthouse, #1, Jackson, OH 45640. 740-286-1919; hours: 8AM-4PM.
Records indexed on computer, fiche and abstract books. Will not search real estate records. Will search UCC records. Will not do federal tax lien search. UCC search per debtor name- $20.00. Copy fee $2.00 per page. Cert fee- $1.00 per cert plus copy fee. Payee- Jackson County Recorder. **Online access to Inmates, Sex Offender records:** Access to the county inmate search is free online at http://xw.textdata.com:81/cgi/progcgi.exe?program=search3. **Other phones:** Treasurer- 740-286-2402; Elections- 740-286-2905; Auditor- 740-286-4231.

Jefferson County

County Recorder, 301 Market St, Steubenville, OH 43952. 740-283-8566; fax-740-283-4007; hours: 8:30AM-4:30PM.
Office will perform a UCC search but public must search other records themselves. UCC search per debtor name- $20.00. Copy fee $2.00 per page. Cert fee- $2.00 per cert plus copy fee. Payee- Jefferson County Recorder. **Online access to Property, Auditor records:** Access to the county auditor property data is free at http://public.jeffersoncountyoh.com/tax/. **Other**

phones: Treasurer- 614-283-8511; Auditor- 614-283-8511. **Property tax/Assessor-** 614-283-8518.

Knox County

County Recorder, 117 E. High St, Mount Vernon, OH 43050. 740-393-6755; hours: 8AM-4PM. www.recorder.co.knox.oh.us
Only the office personnel may search. UCC search per debtor name- $20.00. Copy fee $2.00 per page. Cert fee- $1.00 per cert plus copy fee. Payee- Knox County Recorder. **Online access to Real Estate, Recorder, Deed, Financing Statement, Plat, Map records:** Access records online at www.recorder.co.knox.oh.us/Resolution/default.asp. **Other phones:** Treasurer- 740-393-6735; Appraiser/Auditor- 740-393-6750; Elections- 740-393-6716; Vital Records- 740-393-2200; Records Center 740-393-6781-. **Property tax/Assessor-** 740-397-6291.

Lake County

County Recorder, PO Box 490, Painesville, OH 44077-0490. 440-350-2510, UCC recording phone-440-350-2511; fax-440-350-5940; hours: 8AM-4PM. www.lakecountyrecorder.org/recorders/
All records in one index. Only the public may search. Copy fee $2.00 per page. Cert fee- $1.00 per doc plus copy fee. Payee- Lake County Recorder. **Online access to Recording, Lien, Deed, UCC, Land Bank Sale records:** Access to the Recorder's Document Index database is free at www.lakecountyrecorder.org/recorders/search/index.asp. Records go back to 1986. UCCs are index only. Also, access to the treasurer and auditor's real estate databases is free at www.lake.iviewauditor.com. Also, access Land Bank sales at www.lakecountyohio.org/auditor/index.htm and click on "Land Bank Sales". **Other phones:** Treasurer- 440-350-2517; Elections- 440-350-2700; Vital Records- 440-350-2549; Auditor- 440-350-2528.

Lawrence County

County Recorder, PO Box 77, Ironton, OH 45638. 740-533-4314; fax-740-533-4411; hours: 8AM-4PM. http://64.193.97.62/
Separate indices to search include deeds to 1982, Liens to 1981, mtgs to 1988. Records indexed on computer. Office will perform a UCC search but public must search other records themselves. Search fee $20.00. Copy fee $2.00 per page. Cert fee- $1.00 per cert plus copy fee. **Online access to Auditor, Property, Real Estate, Deed, Lien, Recording records:** Access to the recorders database is free at http://lawcorec-gw.clohwireless.com/idxweb/indexing/idx_name_search.asp?. Deeds go back to 1982; mortgages to 1988; liens back to 1981. Also, the auditor's data is free online at www.lawrencecountyauditor.org. Search county death index by years on a private site at www.lawrencecountyohio.com/deaths/index/. **Other phones:** Treasurer- 740-533-4304; Elections- 740-533-4320; Vital Records- 740-532-2172. **Property tax/Assessor-** same address as above. 740-533-4310.

Licking County

County Recorder, PO Box 520, Newark, OH 43058. 740-349-6060, R/E recording phone-740-670-5301; fax-740-349-1415; hours: 8:30AM-4:30PM. www.lcounty.com/rec/
Office will perform a UCC search but public must search other records themselves. UCC search per debtor name- $20.00. Copy fee $2.00 per page. Cert fee- $2.00 per cert plus copy fee. Payee- Licking County Recorder. **Online access to Real Estate, Tax Lien, Recording, Property Tax, Cemetery, Genealogy, Sex Offender records:** Access to the recorders database is free at www.lcounty.com/recordings/. Records with images go back to 1997. Also, online access to the Assessor's county property database is free at http://www2.lcounty.com/licking208/LandRover.asp?. Search the sheriff's sex offender lists for free at

www.lcounty.com/sheriff/sex_offenders/. Also, search cemetery names free on private company site at www.rootsweb.com/~cemetery/ohio/licking.htm. Search the genealogy site for the county at www.rootsweb.com/~ohlickin/#data. **Other phones:** Treasurer- 740-670-5010; Appraiser/Auditor- 740-670-5040; Elections- 740-670-5080. **Property tax/Assessor-** 740-670-5040.

Logan County

County Recorder, 100 S Madriver; #A, Bellefontaine, OH 43311-2075. 937-599-7201; fax-937-599-7287; hours:8:30AM-4:30PM.

www.co.logan.oh.us/recorder/index.html

All records in one index. Only the public may search, but clerk searches UCC. Tax liens not included in UCC search. UCC search per debtor name- $20.00. Copy fee $2.00 per page. Cert fee-$1.00 per cert plus copy fee. Payee- Logan County Recorder. **Online access to Real Estate, Auditor, Recording, Deed, Lien, Jail Inmate, Sex Offender records:** Records on the County Auditor's database are free at http://www2.co.logan.oh.us/logan208/LandRover.asp. Also, online access to the recorders database is free at http://www3.co.logan.oh.us/recordmax401/record40.asp. Click on "Document Search." Also, search the sheriff's inmate and sex offender lists at www.co.logan.oh.us/sheriff/. **Other phones:** Treasurer-937-599-7223; Elections- 937-599-7255; Auditor- 937-599-7213.

Lorain County

County Recorder, 226 Middle Ave, Elyria, OH 44035. 440-329-5148, UCC recording phone-440-329-514; fax-440-329-5477; hours: 8AM-4:30PM. www.loraincounty.com/recorder

Separate indices to search. Records indexed on a public use terminal back to 1992. Office personnel or visitors may perform searches. Search fee $15.00 per name. Real Estate search fee-$10.00 per name. Copy fee $6.00 per page. Cert fee- $6.00 1st page, $3.00 each add'l page includes copy fee. **Online access to Real Estate, Lien, Auditor, Property Sale, Sheriff Sale, Sex Offender records:** Access to the county assessor database is free at www.loraincounty.com/recorder/register. Free registration is required. Also, access records on the County Auditor's database for a fee at www.loraincountyauditor.org/lorain208/LandRover.asp. Search the sex offender and sheriff sales lists for free at www.loraincountysheriff.com. **Other phones:** Appraiser/Auditor- 440-329-5207. **Property tax/Assessor-** 500 W Temple, Los Angeles, CA 90012; not known.

Lucas County

County Recorder, 1 Government Ctr #700; Jackson St, Toledo, OH 43604. 419-213-4400; fax-419-213-4284; hours: 8AM-5PM. www.co.lucas.oh.us/

All records in one index. Records indexed on a public use terminal back to 1985. Only the public may search, but clerk searches UCC. UCC search per debtor name- $20.00. Copy fee $2.00 per page. Cert fee- $2.00 per cert plus copy fee. Payee-Lucas County Recorder. **Online access to Real Estate, Auditor, Sex Offender records:** Property records on the County Auditor's Real Estate Information System (AREIS) database are free at www.co.lucas.oh.us/Areis/areismain.asp. This replaces the old system. Also, access to recorder real estate records is free with registration at www.co.lucas.oh.us/recordings/logon.asp. Search the sheriff's sex offender list at www.lucascountysheriff.org/sheriff/disclaimer.asp.

Other phones: Treasurer- 419-213-4303; Vital Records- 419-213-4100; Auditor- 419-213-4420.

Madison County

County Recorder, 1 N Main St, Rm 40; Courthouse, London, OH 43140. 740-852-1854; fax-740-845-1776; hours: 8AM-4PM. www.co.madison.oh.us

All records in one index. Records indexed on a public use terminal back to 5/1/1994. Only the public may search. Copy fee $2.00 per page. Cert fee- $1.00 per cert plus copy fee. Payee- Madison County Recorder. **Online access to Real Estate, Auditor, Deed, UCC, Recording, Sex Offender, Sheriff Sale records:** Records on the County Auditor's database are free at www.co.madison.oh.us/auditor/iView/iView.asp. Also, online access to county land and UCC records is free at www.landaccess.com/sites/oh/madison/index.php. Records go back to 5/1994. Also, access to the sheriff's sale and sex offender lists are at www.madisonsheriff.org. **Other phones:** Treasurer-740-852-1936; Auditor- 740-852-9717.

Mahoning County

County Recorder, PO Box 928, Youngstown, OH 44501. 330-740-2345; fax-330-740-2347; www.mahoningcountygov.com/dept_recorder.htm

Separate indexes. Records indexed on a public use terminal back to 1985. Only the public may search. Copy fee $.10 per page. Cert fee- $1.00 per cert plus copy fee. **Online access to Real Estate, Auditor, Property Sale, Deed, UCC, Lien, Judgment, Recording records:** Access to recorder's property, deed, and UCC records is to be free at www.landaccess.com/sites/oh/mahoning/index.php. Records go back to 1985. Also, property tax records on the County Auditor's database are free at www.mahoningcountyauditor.org. **Other phones:** Treasurer- 330-740-2460; Appraiser/Auditor- 330-740-2010; Elections- 330-783-2474; Vital Records- 330-743-3333 x231; Auditor- 330-740-2010. **Property tax/Assessor-** 330-740-2010.

Marion County

County Recorder, 222 W Center St, Marion, OH 43302-3646. 740-223-4100; fax-740-223-4109; hours: 8:30AM-4:30PM. www.co.marion.oh.us

All records in one index. Records indexed on computer from 1983 on; images from July 1995 on; separate records prior to 1983; deed, mortgage, miscellaneous, mechanics lien and military. Only the public may search with beginning help of staff. Will search real estate records. Will search UCC records, but not tax liens. UCC search per debtor name- $20.00. Copy fee $2.00 per page. Copies at cost if customer is able to print copy-$.10 per page. Cert fee- $1.00 per cert plus copy fee. Payee-Marion County Recorder. **Online access to Real Estate, Auditor records:** Access to the county auditor real estate database is free at www.co.marion.oh.us. Click on "Real Estate Inquiry.". **Other phones:** Treasurer- 740-223-4030; Appraiser/Auditor- 740-223-4020; Elections- 740-223-4090; Auditor- 740-223-4020. **Property tax/Assessor-** 740-223-4020.

Medina County

County Recorder, 144 N. Broadway; County Admin. Bldg, Medina, OH 44256-2295. 330-725-9782; hours: 8AM-4:30PM. www.recorder.co.medina.oh.us

All records in one index. Office will perform a UCC search but public must search other records themselves. UCC search per debtor name- $20.00. Copy fee $2.00 per page. Cert fee- $1.00 per cert plus copy fee. Payee- Medina County Recorder. **Online access to Real Estate, Auditor, Property Transfer, Sex Offender, records:** Access to indexes 1983 to present on the recorder database is free at www.recorder.co.medina.oh.us/fcquery.htm. Also, online access to property records on the Medina County Auditor database are free online at www.medinacountyauditor.org/pptylook.htm. Also, search property transfers online at www.medinacountyauditor.org/trbytd2.htm. Also, find a lost dog's owner online at www.medinacountyauditor.org/finddog.htm. The sheriff's sex offender list is via www.medinasheriff.com; the county tax sale list is at www.medinacountyauditor.org/sheriff.htm#delinq. **Property tax/Assessor-** 330-725-9754.

Meigs County

County Recorder, 100 E. Second St; Courthouse, Pomeroy, OH 45769. 740-992-3806; fax-740-992-2867; hours: 8:30AM-4:30PM.

Records indexed on a public use terminal back to 1994. Only the public may search. Copy fee $2.00 per page. Cert fee- $1.00 per cert plus copy fee. Payee- Meigs County Recorder. **Other phones:** Treasurer- 740-992-2004; Appraiser/Auditor- 740-992-2004; Auditor- 740-992-5290.

Mercer County

County Recorder, 101 N. Main St; Courthouse Sq, Rm 203, Celina, OH 45822. 419-586-4232; fax-419-586-3541; hours: 8:30AM-5PM M; 8:30AM-4PM T-F. www.mercercountyohio.org

All records in one index. Only the public may search. Copy fee $2.00 per page. Cert fee- $1.00 per cert plus copy fee. Payee- Mercer County Recorder. **Online access to Real Estate, Auditor, Property Sale records:** Access property records on County Auditor Real Estate database free at www.mercercountyohio.org/auditor/ParcelSearch/. **Other phones:** Treasurer- 419-586-2259; Appraiser/Auditor- 419-586-6402; Elections- 419-586-2215; Auditor- 419-586-2259.

Miami County

County Recorder, PO Box 653, Troy, OH 45373. 937-440-6040, R/E recording phone-937-440-5925, UCC recording phone-937-440-6040; fax-937-440-6041; hours: 7:30AM-4:30PM.

All records in one index. Records indexed on a public use terminal back to 7/1/1997. Office will perform a UCC search but public must search other records themselves. Search fee $20.00. Copy fee $2.00 per page. Cert fee- $1.00 per cert plus copy fee. Payee- Miami County Recorder. **Other phones:** Treasurer- 937-440-6045; Appraiser/Auditor-937-440-5925; Elections- 937-440-3900; Auditor- 937-440-5925. **Property tax/Assessor-** same address as above. 937-440-5925.

Monroe County

County Recorder, PO Box 152, Woodsfield, OH 43793-0152. 740-472-5264; fax-740-472-2523; hours: 8AM-4PM.

Separate indices to search include mortgage, deed, lease indexes. Record index not computerized. Office will perform a UCC search but public must search other records themselves. UCC search per debtor name- $20.00. Copy fee $2.00 per page. Cert fee- $1.00 per cert includes copy fee. Payee-Monroe County Recorder. **Other phones:** Treasurer-740-472-1521; Auditor- 740-472-0873. **Property tax/Assessor-** 740-472-0763.

Montgomery County

County Recorder, PO Box 972, Dayton, OH 45422. 937-225-4275; fax-937-225-5980; hours: 8AM-4:30PM. www.mcrecorder.org

Separate indices to search include document type, address, owners name, legal description. Records indexed on a public use terminal back to 1980. Only the public may search. Copy fee $2.00 per page. Cert fee- $1.00 per cert plus copy fee. **Online access to Property, Real Estate, Lien, Recording, Auditor records:** Access to the recorders data is free at www.mcrecorder.org/search_selection.cfm. Also, search the auditor's property records for free at www.mcauditor.org/realestate/. Also, property tax records on the county treasurer real estate tax information database are free at www.mctreas.org. also, search the sheriff's site for missing persons, property sales, and sex offenders at www.co.montgomery.oh.us/Sheriff/. **Other phones:** Appraiser/Auditor- 937-225-4002.

Morgan County

County Recorder, 155 E Main St, RM 160, McConnelsville, OH 43756. 740-962-4051; fax-740-962-3364; hours: 8AM-4PM.

Separate indices before 1/1994. Records indexed on computer back to 1/1994. Only the public may search. Copy fee $2.00 per page, self serve $.25 per page. Cert fee- $1.00 per cert plus copy fee. Payee- Morgan County Recorder. **Online access to Property, Auditor, Inmate records:** Access to the auditor property data is free at http://morgancountyauditor.org. Use Quick search or Attribute Search. Also, search the county past inmate list online for free at http://xw.textdata.com:81/cgi/progcgi.exe?program=search3. Engineer-www.morgancoengineer.com. **Other phones:** Treasurer- 740-962-3561; Elections- 740-962-3116; Vital Records- 740-962-4572; Auditor- 740-962-4475; Engineer -740-962-3171. **Property tax/Assessor-** 155 E Main St, RM 217, McConnelsville, OH 43756; not known.

Morrow County

County Recorder, 48 E. High St, Mount Gilead, OH 43338. 419-947-3060; fax-419-947-3709; hours: 8AM-4PM.
www.morrowcounty.info/morrowoff.htm
All records in one index. Records indexed on a public use terminal back to 1994. Office will perform a UCC search but public must search other records themselves. Search fee $20.00. Copy fee $2.00 per page. Cert fee- $2.00 per cert plus copy fee. Payee- Morrow County Recorder. **Online access to Real Estate, Appraisal, Property Sale records:** Access to the county auditor database is free at http://auditor.co.morrow.oh.us/iView. Includes property sales data. **Other phones:** Treasurer- 419-947-6070; Appraiser/Auditor- 419-946-4060. **Property tax/Assessor-** same address as above. 419-947-6070.

Muskingum County

County Recorder, PO Box 2333, Zanesville, OH 43702-2333. 740-455-7107; fax-740-455-7943; hours: 8:30AM-4:30PM.
http://recorder.muskingumcounty.org/recorder1024.htm
All records in one index. Records indexed on a public use terminal back to 1976. Office will perform a UCC search but public must search other records themselves. Search fee $20.00. Copy fee $2.00 per page; self serve $.25 per page. Cert fee- $1.00 per cert plus copy fee. Payee- Muskingum County Recorder. **Online access to Real Estate, Assessor, Sheriff Sale, Sex Offender records:** Records on auditor database are free at www.muskingumcountyauditor.org/iView/iView.asp. Also, the sheriff's site provides sale lists and sex offender info at www.ohiomuskingsheriff.org. **Other phones:** Treasurer- 740-455-7118; Appraiser/Auditor- 740-455-7109; Elections- 740-455-7120; Auditor- 740-455-7109. **Property tax/Assessor-** 401 Main St, Zanesville, OH 43702; 740-455-7109.

Noble County

County Recorder, 260 Courthouse, Rm 2E, Caldwell, OH 43724. 740-732-4319; hours: 8AM-4PM M-W; 8-N Th; 8AM-6PM Fri.
Separate indices to search include from 1992 back to 1851; deed, mortgage, lease, federal tax liens, mechanics liens & UCC's. One index from 1992 to present. Records indexed on a public use terminal back to 1992. Office will perform a UCC search (no certification of UCC searches by county recorders, and only with UCC-11 form), but public must search other records themselves. UCC search per debtor name- $20.00. Copy fee $2.00 per page. Payee- Noble County Recorder. **Other phones:** Treasurer- 740-732-2457; Elections- 740-732-2057; Vital Records- 740-732-5047.

Ottawa County

County Recorder, 315 Madison St; Rm 204, Port Clinton, OH 43452. 419-734-6730, R/E recording phone-419-734-6735; fax-419-734-6919; hours: 8:30AM-4:30PM.

Office will perform a UCC search but public must search other records themselves. UCC search per debtor name- $20.00. Copy fee $2.00 per page. Cert fee- $1.00 per cert plus copy fee. Payee-Ottawa County Recorder. **Online access to Property, Auditor, Cemetery, Sex Offender records:** Access to the auditor's property database is free at www.ottawacountyauditor.org. Also, search cemetery registrations for free on private company website at www.rootsweb.com/~cemetery/ohio/ottawa.htm. Search the sheriff's sex offender list for free at www.ottawacountysheriff.org/som.html. **Other phones:** Treasurer- 419-734-6750; Appraiser/Auditor-419-734-6740; Vital Records- 419-734-6800.

Paulding County

County Recorder, 115 N Williams St, Paulding, OH 45879. 419-399-8275; fax-419-399-2862; hours: 8AM-4PM.
Separate indices to search include direct, reverse, geographic. Will not search real estate records. Will search UCC records, but not tax liens. UCC search per debtor name- $20.00. Copy fee $2.00 per page. Cert fee- $1.00 per cert plus copy fee. Payee-County Recorder. **Online access to Real Estate, Recorder, Deed, Lien, UCC records:** Access recorder data free at www.landaccess.com/sites/oh/disclaimer.php?county=ohpaulding. **Other phones:** Treasurer- 419-399-9280; Appraiser/Auditor- 419-399-8205; Elections- 419-399-8230; Vital Records- 419-399-3921. **Property tax/Assessor-** 419-399-8205.

Perry County

County Recorder, PO Box 147, New Lexington, OH 43764. 740-342-2494, R/E recording phone-740-342-2444, UCC recording phone-740-342-2494; fax-740-342-5539; hours: 8:30AM-4:30PM.
All records in one index. Records indexed on a public use terminal back to 1983. Office will perform a UCC search but public must search other records themselves. Search fee $20.00. Copy fee $2.00 per page. Cert fee- $1.00 per cert plus copy fee. Payee- Perry County Recorder. **Online access to Inmate records:** Access to the county inmates search is free online at http://xw.textdata.com:81/cgi/progcgi.exe?program=search3. **Other phones:** Treasurer- 740-342-1235; Auditor- 740-342-2074.

Pickaway County

County Recorder, 207 S. Court St, Circleville, OH 43113. 740-474-5826; fax-740-477-6361; hours: 8AM-4PM.
All records in one index. Records indexed on a public use terminal back to 1990. Office will perform a UCC search but public must search other records themselves. Search fee $20.00 per name. Copy fee $2.00 per page. Cert fee- $1.00 per doc plus copy fee. Payee- Pickaway County Recorder. **Online access to Property, Auditor, Real Estate, Recorder, Deed, UCC records:** Access to the county auditor property data is free at http://pickaway.iviewauditor.com/iView/. Also, search the recorder database free at www.landaccess.com/sites/oh/pickaway/index.php. **Other phones:** Treasurer- 740-474-2370; Elections- 740-474-1100; Auditor- 740-474-4765. **Property tax/Assessor-** same address as above. 740-474-4765.

Pike County

County Recorder, 230 Waverly Plaza #500; Courthouse, Waverly, OH 45690. 740-947-2622; fax-740-947-7997; hours: 8:30AM-4PM.
Records indexed on a public use terminal back to 7/1992. Office personnel or visitors may perform searches. Search fee $20.00. Copy fee $2.00 per copy. Cert fee- $1.00 per cert plus copy fee. Payee- Pike County Recorder. **Online access to Recorder, Deed, Lien, UCC, Real Estate, Auditor, Inmate records:** Access to the recorder's database is free at www.landaccess.com/sites/oh/pike/index.php. Also, access to the county auditor property tax data is

free at http://207.90.76.229/pikeweb/browser/. Also, search the inmate list for free at http://xw.textdata.com:81/cgi/progcgi.exe?program=search3. **Other phones:** Treasurer- 740-947-2713; Auditor- 614-947-2713. **Property tax/Assessor-** 740-947-4125.

Portage County

County Recorder, 449 S. Meridian St, Ravenna, OH 44266. 330-297-3554, R/E recording phone-330-297-3553; fax-330-297-7349; hours: 8AM-4:30PM.
www.co.portage.oh.us
All records in one index. Records indexed form 1984 to current. Will not search real estate records. Will search UCC records, but not tax liens. UCC search per debtor name- $20.00. Copy fee $2.00 per page. Cert fee- $1.00 per cert plus copy fee. Payee- Portage County Recorder. **Online access to Property, Auditor, Property Sale, Sheriff Sale, Sex Offender records:** Access to the auditor's property records is free at http://portagepropertymax.govemmaxa.com/propertymax/rover30.asp. Also, access to the sheriff's property sales and sex offender lists is free at www.co.portage.oh.us. **Other phones:** Treasurer- 330-297-3586; Appraiser/Auditor- 330-297-3569. **Property tax/Assessor-** 449 S. Meridian St, Ravenna, OH 44266; not known.

Preble County

County Recorder, PO Box 371, Eaton, OH 45320-0371. 937-456-8173; fax-none; hours: 8AM-4:30PM.
www.ohiorecorders.com
All records in one index. Records indexed on computer back to 12/1999. Office will perform a UCC search but public must search other records themselves. UCC search per debtor name- $20.00. Copy fee $2.00 per page. Cert fee- $1.00 per cert plus copy fee. Payee- Preble County Recorder. **Online access to Real Estate, Auditor records:** Property records on the County Auditor's database are free at www.preblecountyauditor.org/preble208/LandRover.asp. **Other phones:** Treasurer- 937-456-8141; Elections- 937-456-8117. **Property tax/Assessor-** 101 E Main St, Eaton, OH 45320; 937-456-8148.

Putnam County

County Recorder, 245 E. Main St; Courthouse - #202, Ottawa, OH 45875-1959. 419-523-6490; fax-419-523-4403; hours: 8:30AM-4:30PM.
All records in one index. Will not search real estate records. Will search UCC records, but not tax liens. UCC search per debtor name- $20.00. Copy fee $2.00 per copy. Cert fee- $1.00 per cert plus copy fee. Payee- Putnam County Recorder. **Online access to Property, Auditor, Property Sale records:** Access to the county auditor property data is free at www.putnam.iviewauditor.com/iView.asp. **Other phones:** Appraiser/Auditor- 419-523-6686; Elections- 419-523-3343.

Richland County

County Recorder, 50 Park Ave East, Mansfield, OH 44902. 419-774-5602/5600, R/E recording phone-419-774-5599, UCC recording phone-419-774-5601; fax-419-774-5603; hours: 8AM-4PM.
www.richlandcountyauditor.org
Index: Kept in Books Before 4/4/1989. Records indexed on computer back to 1989. Office will perform a UCC search but public must search other records themselves. Search fee $20.00. Copy fee $2.00 per page. Cert fee- $1.00 per cert plus copy fee. Payee- Richland County Recorder. **Online access to Real Estate, Auditor, Deed, UCC, Property Sale, Sheriff Sale, Sex Offender records:** Property records from the County Auditor database are free at www.richlandcountyauditor.org. Also, online access to county land and UCC records is free at www.landaccess.com. Records go back to 4/1989. Also, search the sheriff sales and sex offender lists for free at www.sheriffrichlandcounty.com. **Other phones:** Treasurer- 419-774-5622; Appraiser/Auditor- 419-774-

5503; Elections- 419-774-5530; Vital Records- 419-774-4500. **Property tax/Assessor-** 419-774-5502.

Ross County

County Recorder, PO Box 6162, Chillicothe, OH 45601. 740-702-3000; fax-740-702-3006; hours: 8:30AM-4:30PM. www.co.ross.oh.us/
Office will perform a UCC search but public must search other records themselves. UCC search per debtor name- $20.00. Copy fee $2.00 per page. Cert fee- $2.00 per cert plus copy fee. Payee- Ross County Recorder. **Online access to Property, Deed, UCC, Auditor, Recorder records:** Access to county land, recording and UCC records is free at www.landaccess.com. Records go back to 1/1974. Also, access to the auditor's property and sales data is free at www.co.ross.oh.us/auditor/iView/iView.asp. **Other phones:** Treasurer- 740-702-3080; Appraiser/Auditor- 740-702-3080. **Property tax/Assessor-** 740-702-3080.

Sandusky County

County Recorder, 100 N. Park Ave.; Courthouse, Fremont, OH 43420-2477. 419-334-6226; hours: 8AM-4:30PM. www.sandusky-county.org/County_Recorder.asp
All records in one index. Records indexed on a public use terminal back to 1996. Office will perform a UCC search but public must search other records themselves. UCC search per debtor name- $20.00. Copy fee $2.00 per page. Cert fee- $1.00 per cert plus $2.00 per page copy. Payee-Sandusky County Recorder. **Online access to Property, Auditor, Treasurer records:** Access to county auditor and treasurer property data is free at http://ohsanduskypropertymax.governmaxa.com/proper tymax/rover30.asp. Click on "Property Search" and choose to search by name. **Other phones:** Treasurer- 419-334-6233; Auditor- 419-334-6123.

Scioto County

County Recorder, 602 7th St, Rm 110; Rm 110, Portsmouth, OH 45662-3950. 740-355-8304; fax-740-353-7358; hours: 8AM-4:30PM. www.sciotocountyohio.com
All records in one index. Records indexed on a public use terminal back to June, 1996. Only the public may search. Copy fee $2.00 per page. Cert fee- $1.00 per cert plus copy fee. Payee- Recorder. **Online access to Property, Auditor records:** Access to the auditor's property data is free at www.sciotocountyauditor.org; click on Proeprty Search. **Other phones:** Treasurer- 740-355-8296; Appraiser/Auditor- 740-355-8264; Elections- 740-355-8217; City Birth or Death- 740-353-5153; County Birth or Death -740-354-3241. **Property tax/Assessor-** 602 7th St Rm 103, Portsmouth, OH 45662; 740-355-8264.

Seneca County

County Recorder, 109 S. Washington St #2104, Tiffin, OH 44883. 419-447-4434; hours: 8:30AM-4:30PM.
All records in one index. Only the public may search, except UCC. UCC search per debtor name- $20.00. Copy fee $2.00 per page. Cert fee- $1.00 per cert plus copy fee. Payee- Seneca County Recorder. **Online access to Property, Most Wanted, Missing Person records:** Access the sheriff's missing person and most wanted lists is free at www.bright.net/~senecaso/. Also, property data may be accessible via www.landaccess.com. **Other phones:** Treasurer- 419-447-1584; Appraiser/Auditor- 419-447-0692; Vital Records- 419-447-3691. **Property tax/Assessor-** 419-447-1584.

Shelby County

County Recorder, 129 E. Court St; Shelby County Annex, Sidney, OH 45365. 937-498-7270; fax-937-498-7272; hours: 8AM-4:30PM. www.co.shelby.oh.us/Recorder.asp
Office will perform a UCC search but public must search other records themselves. UCC search per debtor name- $20.00 to start search. Copy fee

$2.00 per page. Cert fee- $1.00 per doc plus copy fee. Payee- Shelby County Recorder. **Online access to Sheriff's sales and Sex Offender records:** Access to the sheriff's sales and sex offender lists is free at http://shelbycountysheriff.com/index2.htm. **Other phones:** Treasurer- 937-498-7281; Appraiser/Auditor- 937-498-7202; Elections- 937-498-7208 or 7209; Vital Records- 937-498-7249 (Birth & Death Certificates); Probate (Wills)- 937-498-7263; Clerk of Courts-Divorce & judgments -937-498-7221.

Stark County

County Recorder, 110 Central Plaza South; #170, Canton, OH 44702-1409. 330-451-7443, R/E recording phone-330-451-7443 x4464, UCC recording phone-330-451-7443 x7933; fax-330-451-7394; hours: 8:30AM-4:30PM (Recording: 8:30AM-4PM). www.co.stark.oh.us
Office will perform a UCC search but public must search other records themselves. UCC search per debtor name- $20.00. Copy fee $2.00 per page. Cert fee- $1.00 per cert plus copy fee. Payee- Stark County Recorder. **Online access to Real Estate, Deed, Recording, Auditor, Property, Sheriff Sale, Delinquent Taxpayer, Sex Offender, Unclaimed Funds records:** Access to the recorder's database is free at www.recorder.co.stark.oh.us/DTS/. Chose from simple, advanced or instrument search. Also, search the auditor's property data for free at www.auditor.co.stark.oh.us/AUDsearch.asp. Also, a weekly delinquent taxpayers list is at www.starktaxes.com/list.cgi. Access to sheriff sales lists are at www.sheriff.co.stark.oh.us/RealEstate.htm. Sex offenders list at www.sheriff.co.stark.oh.us/OffenderLinks.htm. Louisville City library obituary list may be at www.louisville.lib.oh.us/genealogy/; may be temp. down. **Other phones:** Treasurer- 330-451-7814; Appraiser/Auditor- 330-451-7814.

Summit County

Fiscal Officer, Recording Department, 175 S Main St, Akron, OH 44308-1355. 330-643-2720, UCC recording phone-330-643-8143; hours: 7:30AM-4PM. www.co.summit.oh.us/fiscaloffice
Index: Pre-1988 indices include deed, mortgage, miscellaneous, etc. Records indexed on a public use terminal back to 1988. Office will perform a UCC search but public must search other records themselves. UCC search per debtor name- $20.00. Copy fee $2.00 per page. Cert fee- $1.00 per document plus copy fee. Payee- Summit County Fiscal Officer. **Online access to Real Estate, Auditor, Property Tax, Recording, Deed, Sex Offender, Most Wanted, Sheriff Sale, Dog records:** Tax map information from the county fiscal officer is free at http://scids.summitoh.net/default2.htm; choose Internet map server, then Parcel search. Also property appraisal, images and tax information are at above site. Access to full images requires registration, password. Call Data Ctr Help Desk at 330-643-2013 for info/sign-up. Also search property tax records at http://megatron.summitoh.net/summit/html/webintg.html. Recorder images are at www.summitoh.net/rec/html/rcd5.html. Password required; obtain password from Fiscal Officer. No name searching. Also search sex offenders, most wanted, and sheriff tax sale lists for free at www.co.summit.oh.us/sheriff. **Other phones:** Treasurer- 330-643-2587; Appraiser/Auditor- 330-643-2638; Fiscal Officer- 330-643-2630.

Trumbull County

County Recorder, 160 High St NW, Warren, OH 44481. 330-675-2401, UCC recording phone-330-675-2798; fax-330-675-2404; hours: 8:30AM-4:30PM. www.tcrecorder.co.trumbull.oh.us
All records in one index. Records indexed on a public use terminal back to 1985. Office will perform a UCC search (at low priority), but public must search other records themselves. UCC search per debtor name- $20.00. Copy fee $2.00 per page. Cert fee- $1.00 per seal plus copy fee. Payee-

Trumbull County Recorder. **Online access to Auditor, Property Tax, Recording, Deed, Mortgage, Lien, Unclaimed Funds, Warrant records:** Access to the recorder's database requires free registration at http://tcrecorder.co.trumbull.oh.us/index.cfm. Also, search property data free online at http://208.4.223.96:7036/propertysearch/ureca_asp/index.htm. Also, unclaimed funds list from probate court is at www.trumbullprobate.org/UnclaimedFunds.htm. The Sheriff's warrants list is at www.sheriff.co.trumbull.oh.us/warrants.htm. **Other phones:** Treasurer- 330-675-2736; Appraiser/Auditor- 330-675-2420; Elections- 330-675-4050; Auditor- 330-675-2420.

Tuscarawas County

County Recorder, 125 E. High Ave, New Philadelphia, OH 44663. 330-365-3284; fax-330-365-3281; hours: 8AM-4:30PM. www.co.tuscarawas.oh.us
Office will perform a UCC search but public must search other records themselves. UCC search per debtor name- $20.00. Copy fee $2.00 per page. Cert fee- $1.00 per cert plus copy fee. Payee-Tuscarawas County Recorder. **Online access to Real Estate, Delinquent Tax List records:** County real estate records are free at www.co.tuscarawas.oh.us/tusca208/LandRover.asp. The auditor's delinquent tax list is updated in September. **Other phones:** Treasurer- 330-365-3254; Appraiser/Auditor- 330-365-3220; Auditor- 330-364-8811 x220.

Union County

County Recorder, 233 W. Sixth St, Marysville, OH 43040. 937-645-3032; fax-937-642-3397; hours: 8:30AM-4PM. www.co.union.oh.us/Recorder/recorder.html
All records in one index. Records indexed on a public use terminal back to 1998. Only the public may search. Copy fee $2.00, Self serve $.25 per page. Cert fee- $1.00 per cert plus copy fee. Payee-Union County Recorder. **Online access to Auditor, Property Tax, Real Estate, Recording, Delinquent Taxpayer records:** Access to the Auditors tax assessment/property records database and the appraiser property information database is free at http://www3.co.union.oh.us/PropInfoGuide.htm. Also search for property information via the online GIS map. Search recorded documents at www.co.union.oh.us/Recorder/disclaimer.htm. Search the treasurers' list of delinquent taxpayers at www.co.union.oh.us/Treasurer/List_of_Delinquent_Taxpayers/list_of_delinquent_taxpayers.html. **Other phones:** Treasurer- 937-645-3029; Auditor- 937-645-3003.

Van Wert County

County Recorder, 121 E Main St; Courthouse - Rm 206, Van Wert, OH 45891-1729. 419-238-2558; fax-419-238-5410; hours: 8:30AM-5PM M; 8:30AM-4PM T-F. www.ohiorecorders.com
Separate indices to search include geographic index, plus daily and grantor/grantee index. Only the public may search. Copy fee $2.00 per page includes lookup; $.20 self serve. Cert fee- $2.00 per cert, $1.00 for certified stamp. Payee- Van Wert County Recorder. **Online access to Property, Deed, UCC, Recording, Auditor records:** Access to county land and UCC records is free at www.landaccess.com. Index go back to 1/1994, copies of document back to 10/1997. Also, access to the auditor's property records is free at http://realestate.co.vanwert.oh.us. **Other phones:** Treasurer- 419-238-5177; Appraiser/Auditor- 419-238-0843; Elections- 419-238-4192; Vital Records- 419-238-0808; Auditor- 419-238-0843; Micrographics - 419-238-0466. **Property tax/Assessor-** 121 E Main St, Van Wert, OH 45891; 419-238-0843.

Vinton County

County Recorder, 100 E Main St, McArthur, OH 45651. 740-596-4314; fax-740-596-2265; hours: 8:30AM-4PM.

All records in one index. Will not search real estate records. Will search UCC records, but not tax liens. UCC search per debtor name- $20.00. Copy fee $2.00 per page. Cert fee- $1.00 per page. Payee- Vinton County Recorder. **Online access to Inmate records:** Access to the county past inmate list is free at http://xw.textdata.com:81/cgi/progcgi.exe?program=search3. **Other phones:** Treasurer- 740-596-4571; Appraiser/Auditor- 740-596-4571; Elections- 740-596-4571; Vital Records- 740-596-5480; Auditor- 740-596-4571. **Property tax/Assessor**- 100 E Main St, McArthur, OH 45651; 740-596-4571.

Warren County

County Recorder, 406 Justice Dr, Lebanon, OH 45036. 513-695-1382, UCC recording phone-513-695-2638; fax-513-695-2949; hours: 8AM-4:30PM. www.co.warren.oh.us
All records in one index. Records indexed on a public use terminal back to 1990. Only the public may search. Copy fee $2.00 per page. Cert fee- $3.00 per page (must copy entire doc). Payee- Recorder. **Online access to Property, Auditor, Mapping, Sex Offender records:** Access to the county auditor database is free at www.co.warren.oh.us/auditor/property_search/index.htm. Also, search the sheriff's sex offender list at www.wcsooh.org/sheriff/sex_offenders_disclaimer.htm. Recorders Records access since 1979 found at www.co.warren.oh.us/recorder. **Other phones:** Treasurer- 513-695-1300; Appraiser/Auditor- 513-695-1218; Elections- 513-695-1358; Vital Records- 513-695-1815; Auditor- 513-695-1235. **Property tax/Assessor**- same address as above. 513-695-1235.

Washington County

County Recorder, 205 Putnam St; Courthouse, Marietta, OH 45750. 740-373-6623 x235 or 236, R/E recording phone-740-373-6623 x235; fax-740-373-9643; hours: 8AM-5PM. www.ohiorecorders.com
All records in one index since 1996. Records indexed on a public use terminal back to 12/ 1984. Will not search real estate records. Will search UCC records, but not tax liens. UCC search per debtor name- $20.00. Copy fee $2.00 per page. Cert fee-

$2.00 per page plus copy fee. **Online access to Property, Auditor, Deed, UCC, Recorder, Real Estate records:** Access to the county auditor's property search database is free at www.washingtoncountyauditor.org. Also, access to property, deed, and UCC records is free at www.landaccess.com/sites/oh/washington/index.php. **Other phones:** Treasurer- 740-373-6623 x256; Auditor- 740-373-6623 x263.

Wayne County

County Recorder, 428 W Liberty St, Wooster, OH 44691-5097. 330-287-5460; fax-330-287-5685; hours: 8AM-4:30PM. www.co.wayne.oh.us
Separate indices to search include official records discharges, plats back to 1996. Records indexed on computer back to 1988. Office will perform a UCC search but public must search other records themselves. UCC search per debtor name- $20.00. Copy fee $2.00 per page. $.25 per computer page. Cert fee- $1.00 per cert plus copy fee. Payee- Wayne County Recorder. **Online access to Property, Auditor, Sex Offender, Late Taxpayer records:** Access to the auditor's property data should be free at www.waynecountyauditor.org. The late taxpayer list should soon be appear at the treasurer's website, www.co.wayne.oh.us. Also, search the sheriff's sex offender list for free at www.waynecountysheriff.com/sexoffenders.htm. **Other phones:** Treasurer- 330-287-5450; Elections- 330-287-5480; Auditor- 330-287-5430.

Williams County

County Recorder, 1 Courthouse Sq, Bryan, OH 43506. 419-636-3259; hours: 8:30AM-4:30PM. www.co.williams.oh.us
All records in one index. Records indexed on a public use terminal back to 10/25/1999. Office will perform a UCC search but public must search other records themselves. UCC search per debtor name- $20.00. Copy fee $2.00 per page; self serve $.25. Cert fee- $1.00 per cert plus copy fee. Payee- Williams County Recorder. **Online access to Property, Auditor, Property Sale, Real Estate, Deed, Lien, UCC records:** Access to the auditor's property data is free at www.co.williams.oh.us/realesta

te/LandRover.asp. Also, search recorder records free at www.landaccess.com/sites/oh/williams/index.php. **Other phones:** Auditor- 419-636-5639.

Wood County

County Recorder, 1 Courthouse Sq, Bowling Green, OH 43402-2427. 419-354-9140; hours: 8:30AM-4:30PM. www.co.wood.oh.us/recorder
All records in one index. Records indexed on a public use terminal back to 1985. Only the public may search. Copy fee $2.00 per page. Cert fee- $1.00 per cert plus copy fee. Payee- Wood County Recorder. **Online access to Property, Auditor, Obituary, Treasurer Tax records:** Access to the auditor's property data is free at http://auditor.co.wood.oh.us/. No name searching. Also, search the treasurer's tax data for free at http://woodtaxcollector.governmax.com/collectmax/collect30.asp? Also, search the library's obituaries from 1848 to present for free at http://wcdpl.lib.oh.us/databases/obitsearch.asp. **Other phones:** Treasurer- 419-354-9130; Appraiser/Auditor- 419-354-9150; Elections- 419-354-9120; Vital Records- 419-354-9130. **Property tax/Assessor**- 419-354-9150.

Wyandot County

County Recorder, 109 S. Sandusky Ave.; Courthouse, Upper Sandusky, OH 43351. 419-294-1442; fax-419-294-6405; hours: 8:30AM-4:30PM.
Separate indices to search include "official" since 5.1993; prior in grantor/grantee index. Office will perform a UCC search but public must search other records themselves. UCC search per debtor name- $20.00. Copy fee $2.00 per page. Cert fee- $1.00 per cert plus copy fee. Payee- Wyandot County. **Online access to Property, Auditor records:** Access to the Auditor's real estate database is free at www.co.wyandot.oh.us/auditor/default.html. Click on "Real Estate Internet Inquiry." Also may search dog tags. **Other phones:** Treasurer- 419-294-2131; Elections- 419-294-1226; Vital Records- 419-294-2302. **Property tax/Assessor**- same address as above. 419-294-1531, assessor fax- 419-209-0408.

Ohio County Locator

You will usually be able to find the city name in the City/County Cross Reference below. In that case, it is a simple matter to determine the county from the cross reference. However, only the official US Postal Service city names are included in this index. There are an additional 40,000 place names that people use in their addresses. Therefore, we have also included a ZIP/City Cross Reference immediately following the City/County Cross Reference.

If you know the ZIP Code but the city name does not appear in the City/County Cross Reference index, look up the ZIP Code in the ZIP/City Cross Reference, find the city name, then look up the city name in the City/County Cross Reference. For example, you want to know the county for an address of Menands, NY 12204. There is no "Menands" in the City/County Cross Reference. The ZIP/City Cross Reference shows that ZIP Codes 12201-12288 are for the city of Albany. Looking back in the City/County Cross Reference, Albany is in Albany County.

Ohio City/County Cross Reference

ABERDEEN (45101) Brown(97), Adams(2)
ADA (45810) Hardin(94), Hancock(2), Allen(2)
ADAMSVILLE Muskingum
ADDYSTON Hamilton
ADELPHI Ross
ADENA (43901) Jefferson(77), Harrison(12), Belmont(10)
ADRIAN Seneca
AKRON Summit
ALBANY (45710) Athens(59), Meigs(23), Vinton(16)
ALEXANDRIA Licking
ALGER (45812) Hardin(93), Allen(6)
ALLEDONIA Belmont
ALLIANCE (44601) Stark(90), Mahoning(6), Columbiana(2)
ALPHA Greene
ALVADA (44802) Seneca(61), Hancock(38)
ALVORDTON Williams
AMANDA (43102) Fairfield(90), Hocking(7), Pickaway(1)
AMELIA Clermont
AMESVILLE (45711) Athens(91), Washington(6), Morgan(2)
AMHERST Lorain
AMLIN Franklin
AMSDEN Seneca
AMSTERDAM (43903) Carroll(54), Jefferson(45)
ANDOVER Ashtabula
ANNA Shelby
ANSONIA Darke
ANTWERP (45813) Paulding(98), Defiance(1)
APPLE CREEK Wayne
ARCADIA Hancock
ARCANUM (45304) Darke(98), Preble(1)
ARCHBOLD (43502) Fulton(89), Henry(9)
ARLINGTON Hancock
ASHLAND (44805) Ashland(98), Richland(1)
ASHLEY (43003) Delaware(73), Morrow(26)
ASHTABULA Ashtabula
ASHVILLE Pickaway
ATHENS Athens
ATTICA (44807) Seneca(86), Huron(13)
ATWATER (44201) Portage(96), Stark(3)
AUGUSTA Carroll
AURORA (44202) Portage(89), Summit(8), Geauga(2)
AUSTINBURG Ashtabula
AVA Noble
AVON Lorain
AVON LAKE Lorain
B F GOODRICH CO Summit
BAINBRIDGE (45612) Ross(69), Pike(20), Highland(9)
BAKERSVILLE Coshocton
BALTIC (43804) Holmes(52), Tuscarawas(25), Coshocton(21)
BALTIMORE Fairfield
BANNOCK Belmont
BARBERTON Summit

BARLOW Washington
BARNESVILLE Belmont
BARTLETT Washington
BARTON Belmont
BASCOM Seneca
BATAVIA Clermont
BATH Summit
BAY VILLAGE Cuyahoga
BEACH CITY (44608) Stark(75), Tuscarawas(24)
BEACHWOOD Cuyahoga
BEALLSVILLE (43716) Monroe(73), Belmont(26)
BEAVER (45613) Pike(82), Jackson(17)
BEAVERDAM Allen
BEDFORD Cuyahoga
BELLAIRE Belmont
BELLBROOK Greene
BELLE CENTER (43310) Logan(75), Hardin(24)
BELLE VALLEY Noble
BELLEFONTAINE Logan
BELLEVUE (44811) Huron(41), Sandusky(41), Seneca(11), Erie(6)
BELLVILLE (44813) Richland(85), Knox(7), Morrow(6)
BELMONT Belmont
BELMORE Putnam
BELOIT (44609) Mahoning(60), Columbiana(39)
BELPRE Washington
BENTON RIDGE Hancock
BENTONVILLE Adams
BEREA Cuyahoga
BERGHOLZ (43908) Jefferson(95), Carroll(4)
BERKEY (43504) Lucas(95), Fulton(4)
BERLIN Holmes
BERLIN CENTER Mahoning
BERLIN HEIGHTS Erie
BETHEL (45106) Clermont(86), Brown(13)
BETHESDA Belmont
BETTSVILLE Seneca
BEVERLY (45715) Washington(97), Morgan(2)
BIDWELL Gallia
BIG PRAIRIE (44611) Holmes(94), Wayne(5)
BIRMINGHAM Erie
BLACKLICK Franklin
BLADENSBURG Knox
BLAINE Belmont
BLAKESLEE Williams
BLANCHESTER (45107) Clinton(83), Warren(8), Clermont(4), Brown(3)
BLISSFIELD Coshocton
BLOOMDALE (44817) Wood(91), Hancock(8)
BLOOMINGBURG Fayette
BLOOMINGDALE (43910) Jefferson(96), Harrison(3)
BLOOMVILLE (44818) Seneca(62), Crawford(37)
BLUE CREEK (45616) Adams(82), Scioto(17)

BLUE ROCK (43720) Muskingum(91), Morgan(8)
BLUFFTON (45817) Allen(82), Hancock(15), Putnam(1)
BOLIVAR (44612) Tuscarawas(95), Stark(4)
BOTKINS (45306) Shelby(95), Auglaize(4)
BOURNEVILLE Ross
BOWERSTON (44695) Harrison(56), Carroll(43)
BOWERSVILLE Greene
BOWLING GREEN Wood
BRADFORD (45308) Darke(54), Miami(45)
BRADNER (43406) Wood(92), Sandusky(7)
BRADY LAKE Portage
BRECKSVILLE (44141) Cuyahoga(93), Summit(6)
BREMEN (43107) Fairfield(92), Hocking(5), Perry(2)
BREWSTER Stark
BRICE Franklin
BRIDGEPORT Belmont
BRILLIANT Jefferson
BRINKHAVEN (43006) Coshocton(40), Holmes(40), Knox(19)
BRISTOLVILLE Trumbull
BROADVIEW HEIGHTS Cuyahoga
BROADWAY Union
BROOKFIELD Trumbull
BROOKPARK Cuyahoga
BROOKVILLE Montgomery
BROWNSVILLE Licking
BRUNSWICK Medina
BRYAN (43506) Williams(93), Defiance(6)
BUCHTEL Athens
BUCKEYE LAKE Licking
BUCKLAND Auglaize
BUCYRUS Crawford
BUFFALO Guernsey
BUFORD Highland
BURBANK (44214) Wayne(72), Medina(27)
BURGHILL Trumbull
BURGOON (43407) Sandusky(97), Seneca(2)
BURKETTSVILLE Mercer
BURTON Geauga
BUTLER (44822) Richland(60), Knox(38)
BYESVILLE Guernsey
CABLE Champaign
CADIZ (43907) Harrison(98), Jefferson(1)
CAIRO Allen
CALDWELL (43724) Noble(97), Morgan(1)
CALEDONIA (43314) Marion(87), Morrow(6), Crawford(5)
CAMBRIDGE Guernsey
CAMDEN Preble
CAMERON Monroe
CAMP DENNISON Hamilton
CAMPBELL Mahoning
CANAL FULTON (44614) Stark(97), Summit(1), Wayne(1)
CANAL WINCHESTER (43110) Franklin(73), Fairfield(26)
CANFIELD Mahoning

CANTON (44720) Stark(92), Summit(7)
CANTON (44730) Stark(98), Carroll(1)
CANTON Stark
CARBON HILL Hocking
CARBONDALE Athens
CARDINGTON (43315) Morrow(93), Marion(6)
CAREY (43316) Wyandot(84), Seneca(13), Hancock(1)
CARROLL Fairfield
CASSTOWN (45312) Miami(98), Champaign(1)
CASTALIA (44824) Erie(96), Sandusky(3)
CATAWBA Clark
CECIL (45821) Paulding(89), Defiance(10)
CEDARVILLE (45314) Greene(98), Clark(1)
CELINA Mercer
CENTERBURG (43011) Knox(69), Morrow(11), Delaware(10), Licking(7)
CHAGRIN FALLS (44022) Cuyahoga(77), Geauga(22)
CHAGRIN FALLS Geauga
CHANDLERSVILLE Muskingum
CHARDON (44024) Geauga(97), Lake(2)
CHARM Holmes
CHATFIELD Crawford
CHAUNCEY Athens
CHERRY FORK Adams
CHESAPEAKE Lawrence
CHESHIRE (45620) Gallia(96), Meigs(3)
CHESTER Meigs
CHESTERHILL (43728) Morgan(96), Athens(3)
CHESTERLAND Geauga
CHESTERVILLE Morrow
CHICKASAW Mercer
CHILLICOTHE Ross
CHILO Clermont
CHIPPEWA LAKE Medina
CHRISTIANSBURG Champaign
CINCINNATI (45241) Hamilton(72), Butler(26), Warren(1)
CINCINNATI (45244) Hamilton(57), Clermont(42)
CINCINNATI (45246) Hamilton(92), Butler(7)
CINCINNATI (45249) Hamilton(96), Warren(3)
CINCINNATI (45255) Hamilton(64), Clermont(35)
CINCINNATI Clermont
CINCINNATI Hamilton
CIRCLEVILLE Pickaway
CLARINGTON Monroe
CLARKSBURG (43115) Ross(77), Pickaway(22)
CLARKSVILLE (45113) Clinton(62), Warren(37)
CLAY CENTER Ottawa
CLAYTON Montgomery
CLEVELAND Cuyahoga
CLEVES Hamilton
CLIFTON Greene
CLINTON (44216) Summit(89), Stark(9)

CLOVERDALE (45827) Putnam(84), Paulding(15)
CLYDE (43410) Sandusky(96), Seneca(3)
COAL RUN Washington
COALTON Jackson
COLDWATER Mercer
COLERAIN Belmont
COLLEGE CORNER Butler
COLLINS (44826) Huron(84), Erie(15)
COLLINSVILLE Butler
COLTON Henry
COLUMBIA STATION Lorain
COLUMBIANA (44408) Columbiana(85), Mahoning(14)
COLUMBUS Delaware
COLUMBUS Franklin
COLUMBUS GROVE (45830) Putnam(79), Allen(20)
COMMERCIAL POINT Pickaway
CONESVILLE (43811) Coshocton(98), Muskingum(1)
CONNEAUT Ashtabula
CONOVER (45317) Champaign(47), Miami(40), Shelby(11)
CONTINENTAL (45831) Putnam(96), Defiance(2), Paulding(1)
CONVOY (45832) Van Wert(98), Paulding(1)
COOLVILLE (45723) Athens(87), Meigs(10), Washington(1)
CORNING (43730) Perry(97), Morgan(2)
CORTLAND Trumbull
COSHOCTON Coshocton
COVINGTON Miami
CREOLA (45622) Vinton(97), Hocking(2)
CRESTLINE (44827) Crawford(90), Richland(9)
CRESTON (44217) Wayne(89), Medina(10)
CROOKSVILLE (43731) Perry(85), Morgan(14)
CROTON (43013) Licking(98), Delaware(1)
CROWN CITY (45623) Gallia(83), Lawrence(16)
CUBA Clinton
CUMBERLAND (43732) Guernsey(74), Noble(16), Muskingum(6), Morgan(2)
CURTICE (43412) Lucas(56), Ottawa(43)
CUSTAR (43511) Wood(72), Henry(27)
CUTLER (45724) Washington(98), Athens(1)
CUYAHOGA FALLS Summit
CYGNET Wood
CYNTHIANA Pike
DALTON (44618) Wayne(92), Stark(7)
DAMASCUS Mahoning
DANVILLE Knox
DAYTON (45434) Greene(98), Montgomery(1)
DAYTON (45440) Montgomery(62), Greene(37)
DAYTON (45458) Montgomery(92), Warren(5), Greene(1)
DAYTON (45459) Montgomery(98), Greene(1)
DAYTON Greene
DAYTON Montgomery
DE GRAFF (43318) Logan(79), Champaign(20)
DECATUR Brown
DEERFIELD Portage
DEERSVILLE Harrison
DEFIANCE (43512) Defiance(95), Paulding(3)
DELLROY Carroll
DELPHOS (45833) Allen(56), Van Wert(40), Putnam(3)
DELTA Fulton
DENNISON (44621) Tuscarawas(90), Harrison(8), Carroll(1)
DERBY Pickaway
DERWENT Guernsey

DESHLER (43516) Henry(81), Wood(12), Putnam(4), Hancock(1)
DEXTER CITY Noble
DIAMOND (44412) Portage(80), Mahoning(19)
DILLONVALE (43917) Jefferson(68), Belmont(31)
DOLA Hardin
DONNELSVILLE Clark
DORSET Ashtabula
DOVER Tuscarawas
DOYLESTOWN (44230) Wayne(97), Medina(2)
DRESDEN (43821) Muskingum(86), Coshocton(13)
DUBLIN (43017) Franklin(87), Delaware(11)
DUNBRIDGE Wood
DUNCAN FALLS Muskingum
DUNDEE (44624) Tuscarawas(60), Holmes(27), Wayne(11)
DUNKIRK Hardin
DUPONT Putnam
EAST CLARIDON Geauga
EAST FULTONHAM Muskingum
EAST LIBERTY (43319) Logan(96), Union(3)
EAST LIVERPOOL Columbiana
EAST PALESTINE Columbiana
EAST ROCHESTER (44625) Columbiana(81), Carroll(18)
EAST SPARTA (44626) Stark(94), Tuscarawas(5)
EAST SPRINGFIELD Jefferson
EASTLAKE Lake
EATON Preble
EDGERTON (43517) Williams(78), Defiance(21)
EDISON Morrow
EDON Williams
ELDORADO Preble
ELGIN Van Wert
ELKTON Columbiana
ELLSWORTH Mahoning
ELMORE (43416) Ottawa(93), Sandusky(6)
ELYRIA Lorain
EMPIRE Jefferson
ENGLEWOOD (45322) Montgomery(97), Miami(2)
ENON Clark
ETNA Licking
EUCLID Cuyahoga
EVANSPORT Defiance
FAIRBORN (45324) Greene(96), Clark(3)
FAIRFIELD Butler
FAIRLAWN Summit
FAIRPOINT Belmont
FAIRVIEW Guernsey
FARMDALE Trumbull
FARMER Defiance
FARMERSVILLE (45325) Montgomery(96), Preble(3)
FAYETTE (43521) Fulton(97), Williams(2)
FAYETTEVILLE (45118) Brown(94), Highland(2), Clermont(2)
FEESBURG Brown
FELICITY (45120) Clermont(73), Brown(26)
FINDLAY Hancock
FLAT ROCK Seneca
FLEMING Washington
FLETCHER Miami
FLUSHING (43977) Belmont(80), Harrison(19)
FOREST (45843) Hardin(61), Wyandot(19), Hancock(18)
FORT JENNINGS (45844) Putnam(90), Allen(4), Van Wert(4)
FORT LORAMIE (45845) Shelby(95), Auglaize(3)
FORT RECOVERY (45846) Mercer(84), Darke(15)
FORT SENECA Seneca

FOSTORIA (44830) Seneca(65), Hancock(17), Wood(16)
FOWLER Trumbull
FRANKFORT Ross
FRANKLIN Warren
FRANKLIN FURNACE (45629) Scioto(93), Lawrence(6)
FRAZEYSBURG (43822) Muskingum(61), Licking(19), Coshocton(12), Knox(6)
FREDERICKSBURG (44627) Wayne(68), Holmes(31)
FREDERICKTOWN (43019) Knox(84), Morrow(14)
FREEPORT (43973) Guernsey(52), Harrison(46)
FREMONT Sandusky
FRESNO (43824) Coshocton(91), Tuscarawas(8)
FRIENDSHIP Scioto
FULTON Morrow
FULTONHAM Muskingum
GALENA Delaware
GALION (44833) Crawford(85), Morrow(9), Richland(3), Marion(1)
GALLIPOLIS Gallia
GALLOWAY (43119) Franklin(95), Madison(4)
GAMBIER Knox
GARRETTSVILLE (44231) Portage(88), Geauga(10)
GATES MILLS (44040) Cuyahoga(98), Geauga(1)
GENEVA (44041) Ashtabula(98), Lake(1)
GENOA (43430) Ottawa(94), Wood(3), Sandusky(1)
GEORGETOWN (45121) Brown(98), Clermont(1)
GERMANTOWN (45327) Montgomery(97), Preble(1)
GETTYSBURG Darke
GIBSONBURG (43431) Sandusky(98), Wood(1)
GIRARD Trumbull
GLANDORF Putnam
GLENCOE Belmont
GLENFORD (43739) Perry(64), Licking(35)
GLENMONT (44628) Holmes(61), Knox(38)
GLOUSTER (45732) Athens(92), Perry(5), Hocking(2)
GNADENHUTTEN Tuscarawas
GOMER Allen
GORDON Darke
GOSHEN (45122) Clermont(91), Warren(8)
GRAFTON Lorain
GRAND RAPIDS (43522) Wood(48), Lucas(45), Henry(6)
GRAND RIVER Lake
GRANVILLE Licking
GRATIOT Licking
GRATIS Preble
GRAYSVILLE (45734) Monroe(78), Washington(21)
GRAYTOWN Ottawa
GREEN Summit
GREEN CAMP Marion
GREEN SPRINGS (44836) Seneca(65), Sandusky(34)
GREENFIELD (45123) Highland(55), Ross(25), Fayette(18)
GREENFIELD Highland
GREENFORD Mahoning
GREENTOWN Stark
GREENVILLE Darke
GREENWICH (44837) Huron(75), Richland(12), Ashland(12)
GRELTON Henry
GROVE CITY Franklin
GROVEPORT (43125) Franklin(98), Pickaway(1)
GROVEPORT Franklin

GROVER HILL (45849) Paulding(63), Van Wert(34), Putnam(1)
GUYSVILLE (45735) Athens(94), Meigs(5)
GYPSUM Ottawa
HALLSVILLE Ross
HAMDEN Vinton
HAMERSVILLE (45130) Brown(89), Clermont(10)
HAMILTON Butler
HAMLER Henry
HAMMONDSVILLE (43930) Jefferson(83), Columbiana(16)
HANNIBAL Monroe
HANOVERTON Columbiana
HARBOR VIEW Lucas
HARLEM SPRINGS Carroll
HARPSTER (43323) Wyandot(93), Marion(6)
HARRISBURG Franklin
HARRISON Hamilton
HARRISVILLE Harrison
HARROD (45850) Allen(81), Hardin(12), Auglaize(6)
HARTFORD Trumbull
HARTVILLE (44632) Stark(95), Portage(4)
HARVEYSBURG Warren
HASKINS Wood
HAVERHILL Scioto
HAVILAND Paulding
HAYDENVILLE Hocking
HAYESVILLE Ashland
HEBRON Licking
HELENA Sandusky
HICKSVILLE (43526) Defiance(96), Paulding(3)
HIGGINSPORT Brown
HIGHLAND Highland
HILLIARD Franklin
HILLSBORO (45133) Highland(97), Pike(2)
HINCKLEY Medina
HIRAM (44234) Portage(55), Geauga(44)
HOCKINGPORT Athens
HOLGATE (43527) Henry(89), Defiance(10)
HOLLAND Lucas
HOLLANSBURG Darke
HOLLOWAY Belmont
HOLMESVILLE Holmes
HOMER Licking
HOMERVILLE Medina
HOMEWORTH (44634) Columbiana(80), Stark(19)
HOOVEN Hamilton
HOPEDALE (43976) Harrison(98), Jefferson(1)
HOPEWELL (43746) Muskingum(90), Licking(10)
HOUSTON Shelby
HOWARD Knox
HOYTVILLE Wood
HUBBARD Trumbull
HUDSON (44236) Summit(98), Portage(1)
HUDSON Summit
HUNTSBURG (44046) Geauga(98), Ashtabula(1)
HUNTSVILLE Logan
HURON Erie
IBERIA Morrow
INDEPENDENCE Cuyahoga
IRONDALE (43932) Jefferson(92), Columbiana(7)
IRONTON (45638) Lawrence(94), Scioto(5)
IRWIN (43029) Union(75), Madison(24)
ISLE SAINT GEORGE Ottawa
JACKSON Monroe
JACKSON CENTER (45334) Shelby(88), Auglaize(7), Logan(3)
JACKSONTOWN Licking
JACKSONVILLE Athens
JACOBSBURG Belmont
JAMESTOWN (45335) Greene(95), Clinton(2), Fayette(1)

JASPER Pike
JEFFERSON Ashtabula
JEFFERSONVILLE Fayette
JENERA (45841) Hancock(94), Hardin(5)
JEROMESVILLE (44840) Ashland(98), Wayne(1)
JERRY CITY Wood
JERUSALEM (43747) Monroe(64), Belmont(35)
JEWELL Defiance
JEWETT (43986) Harrison(91), Carroll(8)
JOHNSTOWN (43031) Licking(97), Delaware(2)
JUNCTION CITY Perry
KALIDA Putnam
KANSAS (44841) Seneca(69), Sandusky(30)
KEENE Coshocton
KELLEYS ISLAND Erie
KENSINGTON (44427) Columbiana(57), Carroll(42)
KENT (44240) Portage(98), Summit(1)
KENT Portage
KENTON Hardin
KERR Gallia
KETTLERSVILLE Shelby
KIDRON Wayne
KILBOURNE Delaware
KILLBUCK (44637) Holmes(83), Coshocton(16)
KIMBOLTON (43749) Guernsey(92), Coshocton(4), Tuscarawas(2)
KINGS MILLS Warren
KINGSTON (45644) Ross(64), Pickaway(35)
KINGSVILLE Ashtabula
KINSMAN (44428) Trumbull(96), Ashtabula(3)
KIPLING Guernsey
KIPTON Lorain
KIRBY Wyandot
KIRKERSVILLE Licking
KITTS HILL Lawrence
KUNKLE Williams
LA RUE (43332) Marion(90), Hardin(7), Wyandot(1)
LACARNE Ottawa
LAFAYETTE Allen
LAFFERTY Belmont
LAGRANGE Lorain
LAINGS Monroe
LAKE MILTON (44429) Mahoning(98), Portage(1)
LAKEMORE Summit
LAKESIDE MARBLEHEAD Ottawa
LAKEVIEW (43331) Logan(94), Auglaize(4), Hardin(1)
LAKEVILLE (44638) Holmes(79), Ashland(14), Wayne(7)
LAKEWOOD Cuyahoga
LANCASTER Fairfield
LANGSVILLE Meigs
LANSING Belmont
LATHAM Pike
LATTY Paulding
LAURA (45337) Miami(86), Darke(13)
LAURELVILLE (43135) Hocking(75), Ross(12), Pickaway(11)
LEAVITTSBURG Trumbull
LEBANON Warren
LEES CREEK Clinton
LEESBURG (45135) Highland(77), Fayette(15), Clinton(6)
LEESVILLE Carroll
LEETONIA Columbiana
LEIPSIC (45856) Putnam(97), Henry(2)
LEMOYNE Wood
LEWIS CENTER Delaware
LEWISBURG Preble
LEWISTOWN Logan
LEWISVILLE Monroe

LIBERTY CENTER (43532) Henry(89), Fulton(7), Lucas(3)
LIMA (45806) Allen(94), Auglaize(5)
LIMA Allen
LIMAVILLE Stark
LINDSEY (43442) Sandusky(96), Ottawa(3)
LISBON Columbiana
LITCHFIELD (44253) Medina(82), Lorain(17)
LITHOPOLIS Fairfield
LITTLE HOCKING (45742) Washington(91), Athens(8)
LOCKBOURNE (43137) Franklin(51), Pickaway(48)
LODI Medina
LOGAN (43138) Hocking(98), Perry(1)
LONDON Madison
LONDONDERRY Ross
LONG BOTTOM Meigs
LORAIN Lorain
LORE CITY Guernsey
LOUDONVILLE (44842) Ashland(89), Holmes(9)
LOUISVILLE Stark
LOVELAND (45140) Clermont(40), Hamilton(30), Warren(29)
LOWELL (45744) Morgan(54), Washington(40), Noble(5)
LOWELLVILLE Mahoning
LOWER SALEM (45745) Noble(73), Monroe(14), Washington(12)
LUCAS (44843) Richland(97), Ashland(2)
LUCASVILLE (45648) Scioto(70), Pike(29)
LUCASVILLE Scioto
LUCKEY (43443) Wood(98), Sandusky(1)
LUDLOW FALLS Miami
LYNCHBURG (45142) Highland(90), Clinton(9)
LYNX Adams
LYONS Fulton
MACEDONIA Summit
MACKSBURG (45746) Noble(80), Washington(19)
MADISON Lake
MAGNETIC SPRINGS Union
MAGNOLIA (44643) Stark(42), Tuscarawas(36), Carroll(20)
MAINEVILLE (45039) Warren(98), Hamilton(1)
MALAGA Monroe
MALINTA Henry
MALTA Morgan
MALVERN Carroll
MANCHESTER Adams
MANSFIELD (44904) Richland(89), Morrow(10)
MANSFIELD Richland
MANTUA (44255) Portage(86), Geauga(13)
MAPLE HEIGHTS Cuyahoga
MAPLEWOOD Shelby
MARATHON Clermont
MARENGO (43334) Morrow(94), Delaware(5)
MARIA STEIN (45860) Mercer(98), Darke(1)
MARIETTA Washington
MARK CENTER Defiance
MARSHALLVILLE (44645) Wayne(97), Stark(2)
MARTEL Marion
MARTIN (43445) Ottawa(69), Lucas(30)
MARTINS FERRY Belmont
MARTINSBURG Knox
MARTINSVILLE Clinton
MARYSVILLE Union
MASON Warren
MASSILLON Stark
MASURY Trumbull
MAUMEE Lucas
MAXIMO Stark
MAYNARD Belmont
MC ARTHUR Vinton

MC CLURE (43534) Henry(97), Wood(2)
MC COMB (45858) Hancock(97), Putnam(2)
MC CONNELSVILLE Morgan
MC CUTCHENVILLE (44844) Wyandot(65), Seneca(34)
MC DERMOTT Scioto
MC DONALD (44437) Trumbull(97), Mahoning(2)
MC GUFFEY Hardin
MECHANICSBURG (43044) Champaign(81), Clark(12), Madison(5)
MECHANICSTOWN Carroll
MEDINA Medina
MEDWAY Clark
MELMORE Seneca
MELROSE Paulding
MENDON (45862) Mercer(92), Auglaize(7)
MENTOR Lake
MESOPOTAMIA Trumbull
METAMORA Fulton
MIAMISBURG Montgomery
MIAMITOWN Hamilton
MIAMIVILLE Clermont
MIDDLE BASS Ottawa
MIDDLE POINT Van Wert
MIDDLEBRANCH Stark
MIDDLEBURG Logan
MIDDLEFIELD (44062) Geauga(80), Trumbull(16), Ashtabula(2)
MIDDLEPORT Meigs
MIDDLETOWN Butler
MIDLAND (45148) Clinton(93), Brown(6)
MIDVALE Tuscarawas
MILAN (44846) Erie(92), Huron(7)
MILFORD Clermont
MILFORD CENTER (43045) Union(95), Champaign(4)
MILLBURY (43447) Wood(80), Ottawa(19)
MILLEDGEVILLE Fayette
MILLER CITY Putnam
MILLERSBURG (44654) Holmes(97), Coshocton(2)
MILLERSPORT (43046) Fairfield(91), Licking(8)
MILLFIELD Athens
MILTON CENTER Wood
MINERAL CITY (44656) Tuscarawas(96), Carroll(3)
MINERAL RIDGE (44440) Trumbull(83), Mahoning(16)
MINERVA (44657) Stark(50), Carroll(34), Columbiana(14)
MINFORD Scioto
MINGO Champaign
MINGO JUNCTION Jefferson
MINSTER (45865) Auglaize(78), Shelby(20)
MOGADORE (44260) Portage(70), Summit(24), Stark(5)
MONCLOVA Lucas
MONROE Butler
MONROEVILLE (44847) Huron(70), Erie(29)
MONTEZUMA Mercer
MONTPELIER Williams
MONTVILLE (44064) Geauga(97), Ashtabula(2)
MORRAL (43337) Marion(83), Wyandot(16)
MORRISTOWN Belmont
MORROW Warren
MOSCOW Clermont
MOUNT BLANCHARD (45867) Hancock(94), Wyandot(5)
MOUNT CORY (45868) Hancock(96), Putnam(3)
MOUNT EATON Wayne
MOUNT GILEAD Morrow
MOUNT HOPE Holmes
MOUNT LIBERTY Knox
MOUNT ORAB Brown

MOUNT PERRY (43760) Perry(66), Muskingum(29), Licking(3)
MOUNT PLEASANT Jefferson
MOUNT SAINT JOSEPH Hamilton
MOUNT STERLING (43143) Madison(75), Pickaway(16), Fayette(7)
MOUNT VERNON Knox
MOUNT VICTORY (43340) Hardin(89), Union(10)
MOWRYSTOWN Highland
MOXAHALA Perry
MUNROE FALLS Summit
MURRAY CITY Hocking
NANKIN Ashland
NAPOLEON (43545) Henry(98), Defiance(1)
NASHPORT (43830) Muskingum(88), Licking(11)
NASHVILLE Holmes
NAVARRE (44662) Stark(97), Wayne(2)
NEAPOLIS Lucas
NEFFS Belmont
NEGLEY Columbiana
NELSONVILLE (45764) Athens(88), Hocking(11)
NEVADA (44849) Wyandot(87), Crawford(12)
NEVILLE Clermont
NEW ALBANY Franklin
NEW ATHENS Harrison
NEW BAVARIA (43548) Henry(94), Defiance(2), Putnam(2)
NEW BLOOMINGTON Marion
NEW BREMEN (45869) Auglaize(91), Shelby(4), Mercer(4)
NEW CARLISLE (45344) Clark(82), Miami(14), Montgomery(2)
NEW CONCORD (43762) Muskingum(82), Guernsey(17)
NEW HAMPSHIRE Auglaize
NEW HAVEN Huron
NEW HOLLAND (43145) Pickaway(66), Fayette(33)
NEW KNOXVILLE (45871) Auglaize(77), Shelby(22)
NEW LEBANON Montgomery
NEW LEXINGTON Perry
NEW LONDON (44851) Huron(82), Lorain(12), Ashland(4)
NEW MADISON Darke
NEW MARSHFIELD (45766) Athens(89), Vinton(10)
NEW MATAMORAS (45767) Monroe(66), Washington(33)
NEW MIDDLETOWN Mahoning
NEW PARIS (45347) Preble(93), Darke(6)
NEW PHILADELPHIA Tuscarawas
NEW PLYMOUTH (45654) Vinton(72), Hocking(27)
NEW RICHMOND Clermont
NEW RIEGEL Seneca
NEW RUMLEY Harrison
NEW SPRINGFIELD (44443) Mahoning(95), Columbiana(4)
NEW STRAITSVILLE (43766) Perry(84), Hocking(15)
NEW VIENNA (45159) Clinton(95), Highland(4)
NEW WASHINGTON (44854) Crawford(95), Seneca(4)
NEW WATERFORD Columbiana
NEW WESTON (45348) Darke(98), Mercer(1)
NEWARK Licking
NEWBURY Geauga
NEWCOMERSTOWN (43832) Tuscarawas(84), Coshocton(13), Guernsey(2)
NEWTON FALLS (44444) Trumbull(94), Portage(4), Mahoning(1)
NEWTONSVILLE Clermont
NEY Defiance

NILES Trumbull
NORTH BALTIMORE (45872) Wood(98), Hancock(1)
NORTH BEND Hamilton
NORTH BENTON (44449) Portage(52), Mahoning(47)
NORTH BLOOMFIELD Trumbull
NORTH FAIRFIELD Huron
NORTH GEORGETOWN Columbiana
NORTH HAMPTON Clark
NORTH JACKSON Mahoning
NORTH KINGSVILLE Ashtabula
NORTH LAWRENCE (44666) Stark(80), Wayne(19)
NORTH LEWISBURG (43060) Union(51), Champaign(34), Logan(14)
NORTH LIMA Mahoning
NORTH OLMSTED Cuyahoga
NORTH RIDGEVILLE Lorain
NORTH ROBINSON Crawford
NORTH ROYALTON Cuyahoga
NORTH STAR Darke
NORTHFIELD Summit
NORTHWOOD Wood
NORWALK (44857) Huron(98), Erie(1)
NORWICH Muskingum
NOVA (44859) Ashland(92), Lorain(7)
NOVELTY Geauga
OAK HARBOR (43449) Ottawa(97), Sandusky(2)
OAK HILL (45656) Jackson(87), Gallia(7), Lawrence(4)
OAKWOOD Paulding
OBERLIN Lorain
OCEOLA Crawford
OHIO CITY Van Wert
OKEANA Butler
OKOLONA Henry
OLD FORT Seneca
OLD WASHINGTON Guernsey
OLMSTED FALLS Cuyahoga
ONTARIO Richland
ORANGEVILLE Trumbull
OREGON Lucas
OREGONIA Warren
ORIENT (43146) Pickaway(76), Franklin(21), Madison(1)
ORRVILLE Wayne
ORWELL (44076) Ashtabula(91), Trumbull(8)
OSGOOD Darke
OSTRANDER (43061) Delaware(82), Union(17)
OTTAWA Putnam
OTTOVILLE Putnam
OTWAY (45657) Scioto(80), Adams(17), Pike(2)
OVERPECK Butler
OWENSVILLE Clermont
OXFORD Butler
PAINESVILLE Lake
PALESTINE Darke
PANDORA (45877) Putnam(93), Allen(4), Hancock(1)
PARIS Stark
PARKMAN Geauga
PATASKALA Licking
PATRIOT Gallia
PAULDING Paulding
PAYNE Paulding
PEDRO Lawrence
PEEBLES (45660) Adams(87), Pike(10), Highland(2)
PEMBERTON Shelby
PEMBERVILLE Wood
PENINSULA Summit
PERRY Lake
PERRYSBURG Wood
PERRYSVILLE (44864) Ashland(61), Richland(38)
PETERSBURG (44454) Mahoning(84), Columbiana(15)

PETTISVILLE Fulton
PHILLIPSBURG Montgomery
PHILO Muskingum
PICKERINGTON Fairfield
PIEDMONT (43983) Belmont(57), Guernsey(29), Harrison(14)
PIERPONT Ashtabula
PIKETON Pike
PINEY FORK Jefferson
PIONEER Williams
PIQUA (45356) Miami(96), Shelby(3)
PITSBURG Darke
PLAIN CITY (43064) Madison(52), Union(45), Franklin(1)
PLAINFIELD Coshocton
PLEASANT CITY (43772) Guernsey(58), Noble(41)
PLEASANT HILL Miami
PLEASANT PLAIN (45162) Warren(97), Clermont(2)
PLEASANTVILLE (43148) Fairfield(90), Perry(9)
PLYMOUTH (44865) Richland(49), Huron(45), Crawford(4)
POLK Ashland
POMEROY Meigs
PORT CLINTON Ottawa
PORT JEFFERSON Shelby
PORT WASHINGTON (43837) Tuscarawas(96), Guernsey(3)
PORT WILLIAM Clinton
PORTAGE Wood
PORTLAND Meigs
PORTSMOUTH Scioto
POTSDAM Miami
POWELL (43065) Delaware(85), Franklin(14)
POWHATAN POINT (43942) Belmont(92), Monroe(7)
PROCTORVILLE Lawrence
PROSPECT (43342) Marion(91), Delaware(6), Union(2)
PUT IN BAY Ottawa
QUAKER CITY (43773) Guernsey(54), Noble(39), Belmont(2), Monroe(2)
QUINCY (43343) Logan(89), Champaign(6), Shelby(3)
RACINE Meigs
RADCLIFF Vinton
RADNOR Delaware
RANDOLPH Portage
RARDEN (45671) Scioto(66), Pike(20), Adams(8), Fairfield(4)
RAVENNA Portage
RAWSON Hancock
RAY (45672) Vinton(68), Jackson(26), Ross(4)
RAYLAND (43943) Jefferson(96), Belmont(3)
RAYMOND Union
REEDSVILLE Meigs
REESVILLE Clinton
RENO Washington
REPUBLIC Seneca
REYNOLDSBURG (43068) Franklin(74), Licking(18), Fairfield(7)
REYNOLDSBURG Franklin
RICHFIELD Summit
RICHMOND Jefferson
RICHMOND DALE Ross
RICHWOOD (43344) Union(96), Delaware(2)
RIDGEVILLE CORNERS Henry
RIDGEWAY (43345) Hardin(61), Logan(38)
RIO GRANDE Gallia
RIPLEY Brown
RISINGSUN (43457) Wood(69), Sandusky(26), Seneca(4)
RITTMAN (44270) Wayne(94), Medina(5)
ROBERTSVILLE Stark
ROCK CAMP Lawrence
ROCK CREEK Ashtabula

ROCKBRIDGE Hocking
ROCKFORD (45882) Mercer(94), Van Wert(5)
ROCKY RIDGE Ottawa
ROCKY RIVER Cuyahoga
ROGERS Columbiana
ROME Ashtabula
ROOTSTOWN Portage
ROSEVILLE (43777) Muskingum(55), Perry(44)
ROSEWOOD Champaign
ROSS Butler
ROSSBURG Darke
ROSSFORD Wood
ROUNDHEAD Hardin
RUDOLPH Wood
RUSHSYLVANIA (43347) Logan(89), Hardin(10)
RUSHVILLE (43150) Fairfield(67), Perry(32)
RUSSELLS POINT Logan
RUSSELLVILLE Brown
RUSSIA Shelby
RUTLAND Meigs
SABINA (45169) Clinton(98), Fayette(1)
SAINT CLAIRSVILLE Belmont
SAINT HENRY Mercer
SAINT JOHNS Auglaize
SAINT LOUISVILLE Licking
SAINT MARYS Auglaize
SAINT PARIS Champaign
SALEM (44460) Columbiana(88), Mahoning(11)
SALESVILLE (43778) Guernsey(97), Noble(2)
SALINEVILLE (43945) Columbiana(71), Carroll(19), Jefferson(9)
SANDUSKY Erie
SANDYVILLE Tuscarawas
SARAHSVILLE Noble
SARDINIA Brown
SARDIS Monroe
SAVANNAH Ashland
SCIO (43988) Harrison(71), Carroll(28)
SCIOTO FURNACE Scioto
SCOTT (45886) Van Wert(55), Paulding(45)
SCOTTOWN (45678) Lawrence(80), Gallia(19)
SEAMAN (45679) Adams(92), Highland(7)
SEBRING Mahoning
SEDALIA Madison
SENECAVILLE (43780) Guernsey(69), Noble(30)
SEVEN MILE Butler
SEVILLE Medina
SHADE (45776) Meigs(52), Athens(47)
SHADYSIDE Belmont
SHANDON Butler
SHARON CENTER Medina
SHARPSBURG Athens
SHAUCK Morrow
SHAWNEE Perry
SHEFFIELD LAKE Lorain
SHELBY (44875) Richland(97), Crawford(2)
SHERRODSVILLE (44675) Carroll(70), Tuscarawas(29)
SHERWOOD Defiance
SHILOH (44878) Richland(90), Huron(6), Ashland(3)
SHORT CREEK Harrison
SHREVE (44676) Wayne(82), Holmes(17)
SIDNEY Shelby
SINKING SPRING Highland
SMITHFIELD Jefferson
SMITHVILLE Wayne
SOLON Cuyahoga
SOMERDALE Tuscarawas
SOMERSET Perry
SOMERVILLE Butler

SOUTH BLOOMINGVILLE (43152) Hocking(81), Vinton(18)
SOUTH CHARLESTON (45368) Clark(97), Greene(2)
SOUTH LEBANON Warren
SOUTH POINT Lawrence
SOUTH SALEM Ross
SOUTH SOLON (43153) Madison(76), Fayette(10), Clark(7), Greene(4)
SOUTH VIENNA Clark
SOUTH WEBSTER (45682) Scioto(96), Jackson(2)
SOUTHINGTON (44470) Trumbull(98), Portage(1)
SPARTA Morrow
SPENCER (44275) Medina(93), Lorain(6)
SPENCERVILLE (45887) Allen(75), Auglaize(14), Van Wert(7), Mercer(2)
SPRING HILL NURSERIES Miami
SPRING VALLEY Greene
SPRINGBORO Warren
SPRINGFIELD (45502) Clark(97), Champaign(2)
SPRINGFIELD Clark
STAFFORD Monroe
STERLING Wayne
STEUBENVILLE Jefferson
STEWART Athens
STEWARTSVILLE Belmont
STILLWATER Tuscarawas
STOCKDALE Pike
STOCKPORT (43787) Morgan(92), Washington(7)
STOCKPORT Morgan
STONE CREEK (43840) Coshocton(70), Tuscarawas(29)
STONY RIDGE Wood
STOUT (45684) Scioto(67), Adams(32)
STOUTSVILLE (43154) Fairfield(78), Pickaway(21)
STOW Summit
STRASBURG Tuscarawas
STRATTON Jefferson
STREETSBORO Portage
STRONGSVILLE Cuyahoga
STRUTHERS Mahoning
STRYKER (43557) Williams(81), Henry(12), Fulton(5)
SUGAR GROVE (43155) Fairfield(74), Hocking(25)
SUGARCREEK (44681) Tuscarawas(77), Holmes(22)
SULLIVAN (44880) Ashland(81), Lorain(15), Medina(2)
SULPHUR SPRINGS Crawford
SUMMERFIELD (43788) Noble(76), Monroe(23)
SUMMIT STATION Licking
SUMMITVILLE Columbiana
SUNBURY (43074) Delaware(98), Licking(1)
SWANTON (43558) Fulton(57), Lucas(42)
SYCAMORE (44882) Wyandot(65), Crawford(29), Seneca(5)
SYCAMORE VALLEY Monroe
SYLVANIA Lucas
SYRACUSE Meigs
TALLMADGE (44278) Summit(97), Portage(2)
TARLTON Pickaway
TERRACE PARK Hamilton
THE PLAINS Athens
THOMPSON (44086) Geauga(79), Lake(15), Ashtabula(5)
THORNVILLE (43076) Perry(45), Licking(30), Fairfield(23)
THURMAN (45685) Gallia(72), Jackson(27)
THURSTON Fairfield
TIFFIN Seneca
TILTONSVILLE Jefferson
TIPP CITY (45371) Miami(98), Montgomery(1)

TIPPECANOE (44699) Harrison(72), Tuscarawas(24), Guernsey(2)
TIRO Crawford
TOLEDO (43605) Lucas(97), Wood(2)
TOLEDO Lucas
TOLEDO Wood
TONTOGANY Wood
TORCH Athens
TORONTO Jefferson
TREMONT CITY Clark
TRENTON Butler
TRIMBLE Athens
TRINWAY Muskingum
TROY Miami
TUPPERS PLAINS Meigs
TUSCARAWAS Tuscarawas
TWINSBURG Summit
UHRICHSVILLE (44683) Tuscarawas(91), Harrison(8)
UNION CITY Darke
UNION FURNACE Hocking
UNIONPORT Jefferson
UNIONTOWN (44685) Stark(51), Summit(48)
UNIONVILLE Ashtabula
UNIONVILLE CENTER Union
UNIOPOLIS Auglaize
UPPER SANDUSKY Wyandot
UTICA (43080) Licking(70), Knox(29)
VALLEY CITY (44280) Medina(95), Lorain(4)
VAN BUREN Hancock
VAN WERT Van Wert
VANDALIA Montgomery
VANLUE Hancock
VAUGHNSVILLE Putnam
VENEDOCIA (45894) Van Wert(96), Mercer(2)
VERMILION (44089) Erie(56), Lorain(43)
VERONA Preble
VERSAILLES Darke
VICKERY (43464) Sandusky(76), Erie(23)
VIENNA Trumbull

VINCENT Washington
VINTON Gallia
WADSWORTH Medina
WAKEFIELD Pike
WAKEMAN (44889) Huron(58), Erie(31), Lorain(10)
WALBRIDGE Wood
WALDO (43356) Marion(77), Delaware(14), Morrow(7)
WALHONDING (43843) Coshocton(65), Knox(34)
WALNUT CREEK Holmes
WAPAKONETA (45895) Auglaize(98), Logan(1)
WARNOCK Belmont
WARREN (44481) Trumbull(98), Mahoning(1)
WARREN Trumbull
WARSAW (43844) Coshocton(95), Knox(4)
WASHINGTON COURT HOUSE (43160) Fayette(98), Ross(1)
WASHINGTONVILLE Columbiana
WATERFORD (45786) Washington(93), Morgan(6)
WATERLOO (45688) Lawrence(93), Gallia(6)
WATERTOWN Washington
WATERVILLE Lucas
WAUSEON Fulton
WAVERLY (45690) Pike(92), Ross(7)
WAYLAND Portage
WAYNE Wood
WAYNESBURG (44688) Stark(88), Carroll(11)
WAYNESFIELD (45896) Auglaize(77), Hardin(11), Allen(10)
WAYNESVILLE Warren
WELLINGTON Lorain
WELLSTON Jackson
WELLSVILLE Columbiana
WEST ALEXANDRIA (45381) Preble(93), Montgomery(6)
WEST CHESTER Butler

WEST ELKTON Preble
WEST FARMINGTON (44491) Trumbull(82), Geauga(14), Portage(2)
WEST JEFFERSON Madison
WEST LAFAYETTE Coshocton
WEST LIBERTY (43357) Logan(75), Champaign(24)
WEST MANCHESTER (45382) Preble(77), Darke(22)
WEST MANSFIELD (43358) Logan(57), Union(42)
WEST MILLGROVE Wood
WEST MILTON Miami
WEST POINT Columbiana
WEST PORTSMOUTH Scioto
WEST RUSHVILLE Fairfield
WEST SALEM (44287) Wayne(63), Ashland(29), Medina(6)
WEST UNION Adams
WEST UNITY (43570) Williams(94), Fulton(5)
WESTERVILLE Delaware
WESTERVILLE Franklin
WESTFIELD CENTER Medina
WESTLAKE Cuyahoga
WESTON Wood
WESTVILLE Champaign
WHARTON Wyandot
WHEELERSBURG Scioto
WHIPPLE Washington
WHITE COTTAGE Muskingum
WHITEHOUSE Lucas
WICKLIFFE Lake
WILBERFORCE Greene
WILKESVILLE Vinton
WILLARD Huron
WILLIAMSBURG Clermont
WILLIAMSFIELD Ashtabula
WILLIAMSPORT (43164) Pickaway(95), Ross(4)
WILLIAMSTOWN Hancock
WILLISTON Ottawa
WILLOUGHBY Lake

WILLOW WOOD Lawrence
WILLSHIRE (45898) Van Wert(70), Mercer(29)
WILMINGTON Clinton
WILMOT (44689) Holmes(70), Stark(29)
WINCHESTER (45697) Adams(62), Brown(25), Highland(12)
WINDHAM (44288) Portage(98), Trumbull(1)
WINDSOR (44099) Ashtabula(87), Geauga(12)
WINESBURG Holmes
WINGETT RUN (45789) Washington(96), Monroe(3)
WINONA Columbiana
WINTERSVILLE Jefferson
WOLF RUN Jefferson
WOODSFIELD Monroe
WOODSTOCK (43084) Champaign(91), Union(8)
WOODVILLE (43469) Sandusky(93), Ottawa(5), Wood(1)
WOOSTER Wayne
WREN Van Wert
XENIA Greene
YELLOW SPRINGS (45387) Greene(92), Clark(7)
YORKSHIRE (45388) Darke(95), Mercer(2), Shelby(2)
YORKVILLE (43971) Jefferson(65), Belmont(34)
YOUNGSTOWN (44505) Mahoning(65), Trumbull(34)
YOUNGSTOWN Mahoning
ZALESKI Vinton
ZANESFIELD Logan
ZANESVILLE Muskingum
ZOAR Tuscarawas

Ohio ZIP/City Cross Reference

43001-43001	ALEXANDRIA
43002-43002	AMLIN
43003-43003	ASHLEY
43004-43004	BLACKLICK
43005-43005	BLADENSBURG
43006-43006	BRINKHAVEN
43007-43007	BROADWAY
43008-43008	BUCKEYE LAKE
43009-43009	CABLE
43010-43010	CATAWBA
43011-43011	CENTERBURG
43013-43013	CROTON
43014-43014	DANVILLE
43015-43015	DELAWARE
43016-43017	DUBLIN
43018-43018	ETNA
43019-43019	FREDERICKTOWN
43021-43021	GALENA
43022-43022	GAMBIER
43023-43023	GRANVILLE
43025-43025	HEBRON
43026-43026	HILLIARD
43027-43027	HOMER
43028-43028	HOWARD
43029-43029	IRWIN
43030-43030	JACKSONTOWN
43031-43031	JOHNSTOWN
43032-43032	KILBOURNE
43033-43033	KIRKERSVILLE
43035-43035	LEWIS CENTER
43036-43036	MAGNETIC SPRINGS
43037-43037	MARTINSBURG
43040-43041	MARYSVILLE
43044-43044	MECHANICSBURG
43045-43045	MILFORD CENTER
43046-43046	MILLERSPORT

43047-43047	MINGO
43048-43048	MOUNT LIBERTY
43050-43050	MOUNT VERNON
43054-43054	NEW ALBANY
43055-43058	NEWARK
43060-43060	NORTH LEWISBURG
43061-43061	OSTRANDER
43062-43062	PATASKALA
43064-43064	PLAIN CITY
43065-43065	POWELL
43066-43066	RADNOR
43067-43067	RAYMOND
43068-43069	REYNOLDSBURG
43070-43070	ROSEWOOD
43071-43071	SAINT LOUISVILLE
43072-43072	SAINT PARIS
43073-43073	SUMMIT STATION
43074-43074	SUNBURY
43076-43076	THORNVILLE
43077-43077	UNIONVILLE CENTER
43078-43078	URBANA
43080-43080	UTICA
43081-43082	WESTERVILLE
43083-43083	WESTVILLE
43084-43084	WOODSTOCK
43085-43085	COLUMBUS
43086-43086	WESTERVILLE
43093-43093	NEWARK
43098-43098	HEBRON
43099-43099	BLACKLICK
43101-43101	ADELPHI
43102-43102	AMANDA
43103-43103	ASHVILLE
43105-43105	BALTIMORE
43106-43106	BLOOMINGBURG
43107-43107	BREMEN

43109-43109	BRICE
43110-43110	CANAL WINCHESTER
43111-43111	CARBON HILL
43112-43112	CARROLL
43113-43113	CIRCLEVILLE
43115-43115	CLARKSBURG
43116-43116	COMMERCIAL POINT
43117-43117	DERBY
43119-43119	GALLOWAY
43123-43123	GROVE CITY
43125-43125	GROVEPORT
43126-43126	HARRISBURG
43127-43127	HAYDENVILLE
43128-43128	JEFFERSONVILLE
43130-43132	LANCASTER
43135-43135	LAURELVILLE
43136-43136	LITHOPOLIS
43137-43137	LOCKBOURNE
43138-43138	LOGAN
43140-43140	LONDON
43142-43142	MILLEDGEVILLE
43143-43143	MOUNT STERLING
43144-43144	MURRAY CITY
43145-43145	NEW HOLLAND
43146-43146	ORIENT
43147-43147	PICKERINGTON
43148-43148	PLEASANTVILLE
43149-43149	ROCKBRIDGE
43150-43150	RUSHVILLE
43151-43151	SEDALIA
43152-43152	SOUTH BLOOMINGVILLE
43153-43153	SOUTH SOLON
43154-43154	STOUTSVILLE
43155-43155	SUGAR GROVE
43156-43156	TARLTON
43157-43157	THURSTON

43158-43158	UNION FURNACE
43160-43160	WASHINGTON COURT HOUSE
43162-43162	WEST JEFFERSON
43163-43163	WEST RUSHVILLE
43164-43164	WILLIAMSPORT
43195-43199	GROVEPORT
43200-43299	COLUMBUS
43301-43307	MARION
43310-43310	BELLE CENTER
43311-43311	BELLEFONTAINE
43314-43314	CALEDONIA
43315-43315	CARDINGTON
43316-43316	CAREY
43317-43317	CHESTERVILLE
43318-43318	DE GRAFF
43319-43319	EAST LIBERTY
43320-43320	EDISON
43321-43321	FULTON
43322-43322	GREEN CAMP
43323-43323	HARPSTER
43324-43324	HUNTSVILLE
43325-43325	IBERIA
43326-43326	KENTON
43330-43330	KIRBY
43331-43331	LAKEVIEW
43332-43332	LA RUE
43333-43333	LEWISTOWN
43334-43334	MARENGO
43335-43335	MARTEL
43336-43336	MIDDLEBURG
43337-43337	MORRAL
43338-43338	MOUNT GILEAD
43340-43340	MOUNT VICTORY
43341-43341	NEW BLOOMINGTON
43342-43342	PROSPECT

43343-43343 QUINCY	43532-43532 LIBERTY CENTER	43773-43773 QUAKER CITY	43970-43970 WOLF RUN
43344-43344 RICHWOOD	43533-43533 LYONS	43777-43777 ROSEVILLE	43971-43971 YORKVILLE
43345-43345 RIDGEWAY	43534-43534 MC CLURE	43778-43778 SALESVILLE	43972-43972 BANNOCK
43346-43346 ROUNDHEAD	43535-43535 MALINTA	43779-43779 SARAHSVILLE	43973-43973 FREEPORT
43347-43347 RUSHSYLVANIA	43536-43536 MARK CENTER	43780-43780 SENECAVILLE	43974-43974 HARRISVILLE
43348-43348 RUSSELLS POINT	43537-43537 MAUMEE	43782-43782 SHAWNEE	43976-43976 HOPEDALE
43349-43349 SHAUCK	43540-43540 METAMORA	43783-43783 SOMERSET	43977-43977 FLUSHING
43350-43350 SPARTA	43541-43541 MILTON CENTER	43786-43786 STAFFORD	43981-43981 NEW ATHENS
43351-43351 UPPER SANDUSKY	43542-43542 MONCLOVA	43787-43787 STOCKPORT	43983-43983 PIEDMONT
43356-43356 WALDO	43543-43543 MONTPELIER	43788-43788 SUMMERFIELD	43984-43984 NEW RUMLEY
43357-43357 WEST LIBERTY	43545-43545 NAPOLEON	43789-43789 SYCAMORE VALLEY	43985-43985 HOLLOWAY
43358-43358 WEST MANSFIELD	43547-43547 NEAPOLIS	43791-43791 WHITE COTTAGE	43986-43986 JEWETT
43359-43359 WHARTON	43548-43548 NEW BAVARIA	43793-43793 WOODSFIELD	43988-43988 SCIO
43360-43360 ZANESFIELD	43549-43549 NEY	43802-43802 ADAMSVILLE	43989-43989 SHORT CREEK
43402-43403 BOWLING GREEN	43550-43550 OKOLONA	43803-43803 BAKERSVILLE	44001-44001 AMHERST
43406-43406 BRADNER	43551-43552 PERRYSBURG	43804-43804 BALTIC	44003-44003 ANDOVER
43407-43407 BURGOON	43553-43553 PETTISVILLE	43805-43805 BLISSFIELD	44004-44005 ASHTABULA
43408-43408 CLAY CENTER	43554-43554 PIONEER	43811-43811 CONESVILLE	44010-44010 AUSTINBURG
43410-43410 CLYDE	43555-43555 RIDGEVILLE CORNERS	43812-43812 COSHOCTON	44011-44011 AVON
43412-43412 CURTICE	43556-43556 SHERWOOD	43821-43821 DRESDEN	44012-44012 AVON LAKE
43413-43413 CYGNET	43557-43557 STRYKER	43822-43822 FRAZEYSBURG	44017-44017 BEREA
43414-43414 DUNBRIDGE	43558-43558 SWANTON	43824-43824 FRESNO	44021-44021 BURTON
43416-43416 ELMORE	43560-43560 SYLVANIA	43828-43828 KEENE	44022-44023 CHAGRIN FALLS
43420-43420 FREMONT	43565-43565 TONTOGANY	43830-43830 NASHPORT	44024-44024 CHARDON
43430-43430 GENOA	43566-43566 WATERVILLE	43832-43832 NEWCOMERSTOWN	44026-44026 CHESTERLAND
43431-43431 GIBSONBURG	43567-43567 WAUSEON	43836-43836 PLAINFIELD	44028-44028 COLUMBIA STATION
43432-43432 GRAYTOWN	43569-43569 WESTON	43837-43837 PORT WASHINGTON	44030-44030 CONNEAUT
43433-43433 GYPSUM	43570-43570 WEST UNITY	43840-43840 STONE CREEK	44032-44032 DORSET
43434-43434 HARBOR VIEW	43571-43571 WHITEHOUSE	43842-43842 TRINWAY	44033-44033 EAST CLARIDON
43435-43435 HELENA	43600-43615 TOLEDO	43843-43843 WALHONDING	44035-44036 ELYRIA
43436-43436 ISLE SAINT GEORGE	43616-43616 OREGON	43844-43844 WARSAW	44039-44039 NORTH RIDGEVILLE
43437-43437 JERRY CITY	43617-43617 TOLEDO	43845-43845 WEST LAFAYETTE	44040-44040 GATES MILLS
43438-43438 KELLEYS ISLAND	43618-43618 OREGON	43901-43901 ADENA	44041-44041 GENEVA
43439-43439 LACARNE	43619-43619 NORTHWOOD	43902-43902 ALLEDONIA	44044-44044 GRAFTON
43440-43440 LAKESIDE MARBLEHEAD	43620-43699 TOLEDO	43903-43903 AMSTERDAM	44045-44045 GRAND RIVER
43441-43441 LEMOYNE	43701-43702 ZANESVILLE	43905-43905 BARTON	44046-44046 HUNTSBURG
43442-43442 LINDSEY	43711-43711 AVA	43906-43906 BELLAIRE	44047-44047 JEFFERSON
43443-43443 LUCKEY	43713-43713 BARNESVILLE	43907-43907 CADIZ	44048-44048 KINGSVILLE
43445-43445 MARTIN	43716-43716 BEALLSVILLE	43908-43908 BERGHOLZ	44049-44049 KIPTON
43446-43446 MIDDLE BASS	43717-43717 BELLE VALLEY	43909-43909 BLAINE	44050-44050 LAGRANGE
43447-43447 MILLBURY	43718-43718 BELMONT	43910-43910 BLOOMINGDALE	44052-44053 LORAIN
43449-43449 OAK HARBOR	43719-43719 BETHESDA	43912-43912 BRIDGEPORT	44054-44054 SHEFFIELD LAKE
43450-43450 PEMBERVILLE	43720-43720 BLUE ROCK	43913-43913 BRILLIANT	44055-44055 LORAIN
43451-43451 PORTAGE	43721-43721 BROWNSVILLE	43914-43914 CAMERON	44056-44056 MACEDONIA
43452-43452 PORT CLINTON	43722-43722 BUFFALO	43915-43915 CLARINGTON	44057-44057 MADISON
43456-43456 PUT IN BAY	43723-43723 BYESVILLE	43916-43916 COLERAIN	44060-44061 MENTOR
43457-43457 RISINGSUN	43724-43724 CALDWELL	43917-43917 DILLONVALE	44062-44062 MIDDLEFIELD
43458-43458 ROCKY RIDGE	43725-43725 CAMBRIDGE	43920-43920 EAST LIVERPOOL	44064-44064 MONTVILLE
43460-43460 ROSSFORD	43727-43727 CHANDLERSVILLE	43925-43925 EAST SPRINGFIELD	44065-44065 NEWBURY
43462-43462 RUDOLPH	43728-43728 CHESTERHILL	43926-43926 EMPIRE	44067-44067 NORTHFIELD
43463-43463 STONY RIDGE	43730-43730 CORNING	43927-43927 FAIRPOINT	44068-44068 NORTH KINGSVILLE
43464-43464 VICKERY	43731-43731 CROOKSVILLE	43928-43928 GLENCOE	44070-44070 NORTH OLMSTED
43465-43465 WALBRIDGE	43732-43732 CUMBERLAND	43930-43930 HAMMONDSVILLE	44072-44073 NOVELTY
43466-43466 WAYNE	43733-43733 DERWENT	43931-43931 HANNIBAL	44074-44074 OBERLIN
43467-43467 WEST MILLGROVE	43734-43734 DUNCAN FALLS	43932-43932 IRONDALE	44076-44076 ORWELL
43468-43468 WILLISTON	43735-43735 EAST FULTONHAM	43933-43933 JACOBSBURG	44077-44077 PAINESVILLE
43469-43469 WOODVILLE	43736-43736 FAIRVIEW	43934-43934 LANSING	44080-44080 PARKMAN
43501-43501 ALVORDTON	43738-43738 FULTONHAM	43935-43935 MARTINS FERRY	44081-44081 PERRY
43502-43502 ARCHBOLD	43739-43739 GLENFORD	43937-43937 MAYNARD	44082-44082 PIERPONT
43504-43504 BERKEY	43740-43740 GRATIOT	43938-43938 MINGO JUNCTION	44084-44084 ROCK CREEK
43505-43505 BLAKESLEE	43746-43746 HOPEWELL	43939-43939 MOUNT PLEASANT	44085-44085 ROME
43506-43506 BRYAN	43747-43747 JERUSALEM	43940-43940 NEFFS	44086-44086 THOMPSON
43510-43510 COLTON	43748-43748 JUNCTION CITY	43941-43941 PINEY FORK	44087-44087 TWINSBURG
43511-43511 CUSTAR	43749-43749 KIMBOLTON	43942-43942 POWHATAN POINT	44088-44088 UNIONVILLE
43512-43512 DEFIANCE	43750-43750 KIPLING	43943-43943 RAYLAND	44089-44089 VERMILION
43515-43515 DELTA	43752-43752 LAINGS	43944-43944 RICHMOND	44090-44090 WELLINGTON
43516-43516 DESHLER	43754-43754 LEWISVILLE	43945-43945 SALINEVILLE	44092-44092 WICKLIFFE
43517-43517 EDGERTON	43755-43755 LORE CITY	43946-43946 SARDIS	44093-44093 WILLIAMSFIELD
43518-43518 EDON	43756-43756 MC CONNELSVILLE	43947-43947 SHADYSIDE	44094-44094 WILLOUGHBY
43519-43519 EVANSPORT	43757-43757 MALAGA	43948-43948 SMITHFIELD	44095-44095 EASTLAKE
43520-43520 FARMER	43758-43758 MALTA	43950-43950 SAINT CLAIRSVILLE	44096-44096 WILLOUGHBY
43521-43521 FAYETTE	43759-43759 MORRISTOWN	43951-43951 LAFFERTY	44097-44097 EASTLAKE
43522-43522 GRAND RAPIDS	43760-43760 MOUNT PERRY	43952-43952 STEUBENVILLE	44099-44099 WINDSOR
43523-43523 GRELTON	43761-43761 MOXAHALA	43953-43953 WINTERSVILLE	44100-44106 CLEVELAND
43524-43524 HAMLER	43762-43762 NEW CONCORD	43960-43960 STEWARTSVILLE	44107-44107 LAKEWOOD
43525-43525 HASKINS	43764-43764 NEW LEXINGTON	43961-43961 STRATTON	44108-44115 CLEVELAND
43526-43526 HICKSVILLE	43766-43766 NEW STRAITSVILLE	43962-43962 SUMMITVILLE	44116-44116 ROCKY RIVER
43527-43527 HOLGATE	43767-43767 NORWICH	43963-43963 TILTONSVILLE	44117-44117 EUCLID
43528-43528 HOLLAND	43768-43768 OLD WASHINGTON	43964-43964 TORONTO	44118-44121 CLEVELAND
43529-43529 HOYTVILLE	43770-43770 STOCKPORT	43966-43966 UNIONPORT	44122-44122 BEACHWOOD
43530-43530 JEWELL	43771-43771 PHILO	43967-43967 WARNOCK	44123-44123 EUCLID
43531-43531 KUNKLE	43772-43772 PLEASANT CITY	43968-43968 WELLSVILLE	44124-44130 CLEVELAND

Zip Range	City
44131-44131	INDEPENDENCE
44132-44132	EUCLID
44133-44133	NORTH ROYALTON
44134-44135	CLEVELAND
44136-44136	STRONGSVILLE
44137-44137	MAPLE HEIGHTS
44138-44138	OLMSTED FALLS
44139-44139	SOLON
44140-44140	BAY VILLAGE
44141-44141	BRECKSVILLE
44142-44142	BROOKPARK
44143-44144	CLEVELAND
44145-44145	WESTLAKE
44146-44146	BEDFORD
44147-44147	BROADVIEW HEIGHTS
44149-44149	STRONGSVILLE
44177-44199	CLEVELAND
44201-44201	ATWATER
44202-44202	AURORA
44203-44203	BARBERTON
44210-44210	BATH
44211-44211	BRADY LAKE
44212-44212	BRUNSWICK
44214-44214	BURBANK
44215-44215	CHIPPEWA LAKE
44216-44216	CLINTON
44217-44217	CRESTON
44221-44223	CUYAHOGA FALLS
44224-44224	STOW
44230-44230	DOYLESTOWN
44231-44231	GARRETTSVILLE
44232-44232	GREEN
44233-44233	HINCKLEY
44234-44234	HIRAM
44235-44235	HOMERVILLE
44236-44238	HUDSON
44240-44240	KENT
44241-44241	STREETSBORO
44242-44243	KENT
44250-44250	LAKEMORE
44251-44251	WESTFIELD CENTER
44253-44253	LITCHFIELD
44254-44254	LODI
44255-44255	MANTUA
44256-44259	MEDINA
44260-44260	MOGADORE
44262-44262	MUNROE FALLS
44264-44264	PENINSULA
44265-44265	RANDOLPH
44266-44266	RAVENNA
44270-44270	RITTMAN
44272-44272	ROOTSTOWN
44273-44273	SEVILLE
44274-44274	SHARON CENTER
44275-44275	SPENCER
44276-44276	STERLING
44278-44278	TALLMADGE
44280-44280	VALLEY CITY
44281-44282	WADSWORTH
44285-44285	WAYLAND
44286-44286	RICHFIELD
44287-44287	WEST SALEM
44288-44288	WINDHAM
44300-44317	AKRON
44318-44318	B F GOODRICH CO
44319-44334	AKRON
44334-44334	FAIRLAWN
44372-44399	AKRON
44401-44401	BERLIN CENTER
44402-44402	BRISTOLVILLE
44403-44403	BROOKFIELD
44404-44404	BURGHILL
44405-44405	CAMPBELL
44406-44406	CANFIELD
44408-44408	COLUMBIANA
44410-44410	CORTLAND
44411-44411	DEERFIELD
44412-44412	DIAMOND
44413-44413	EAST PALESTINE
44415-44415	ELKTON
44416-44416	ELLSWORTH
44417-44417	FARMDALE
44418-44418	FOWLER
44420-44420	GIRARD
44422-44422	GREENFORD
44423-44423	HANOVERTON
44424-44424	HARTFORD
44425-44425	HUBBARD
44427-44427	KENSINGTON
44428-44428	KINSMAN
44429-44429	LAKE MILTON
44430-44430	LEAVITTSBURG
44431-44431	LEETONIA
44432-44432	LISBON
44436-44436	LOWELLVILLE
44437-44437	MC DONALD
44438-44438	MASURY
44439-44439	MESOPOTAMIA
44440-44440	MINERAL RIDGE
44441-44441	NEGLEY
44442-44442	NEW MIDDLETOWN
44443-44443	NEW SPRINGFIELD
44444-44444	NEWTON FALLS
44445-44445	NEW WATERFORD
44446-44446	NILES
44449-44449	NORTH BENTON
44450-44450	NORTH BLOOMFIELD
44451-44451	NORTH JACKSON
44452-44452	NORTH LIMA
44453-44453	ORANGEVILLE
44454-44454	PETERSBURG
44455-44455	ROGERS
44460-44460	SALEM
44470-44470	SOUTHINGTON
44471-44471	STRUTHERS
44473-44473	VIENNA
44481-44488	WARREN
44490-44490	WASHINGTONVILLE
44491-44491	WEST FARMINGTON
44492-44492	WEST POINT
44493-44493	WINONA
44500-44599	YOUNGSTOWN
44601-44601	ALLIANCE
44606-44606	APPLE CREEK
44607-44607	AUGUSTA
44608-44608	BEACH CITY
44609-44609	BELOIT
44610-44610	BERLIN
44611-44611	BIG PRAIRIE
44612-44612	BOLIVAR
44613-44613	BREWSTER
44614-44614	CANAL FULTON
44615-44615	CARROLLTON
44617-44617	CHARM
44618-44618	DALTON
44619-44619	DAMASCUS
44620-44620	DELLROY
44621-44621	DENNISON
44622-44622	DOVER
44624-44624	DUNDEE
44625-44625	EAST ROCHESTER
44626-44626	EAST SPARTA
44627-44627	FREDERICKSBURG
44628-44628	GLENMONT
44629-44629	GNADENHUTTEN
44630-44630	GREENTOWN
44631-44631	HARLEM SPRINGS
44632-44632	HARTVILLE
44633-44633	HOLMESVILLE
44634-44634	HOMEWORTH
44636-44636	KIDRON
44637-44637	KILLBUCK
44638-44638	LAKEVILLE
44639-44639	LEESVILLE
44640-44640	LIMAVILLE
44641-44641	LOUISVILLE
44643-44643	MAGNOLIA
44644-44644	MALVERN
44645-44645	MARSHALLVILLE
44646-44648	MASSILLON
44650-44650	MAXIMO
44651-44651	MECHANICSTOWN
44652-44652	MIDDLEBRANCH
44653-44653	MIDVALE
44654-44654	MILLERSBURG
44656-44656	MINERAL CITY
44657-44657	MINERVA
44659-44659	MOUNT EATON
44660-44660	MOUNT HOPE
44661-44661	NASHVILLE
44662-44662	NAVARRE
44663-44663	NEW PHILADELPHIA
44665-44665	NORTH GEORGETOWN
44666-44666	NORTH LAWRENCE
44667-44667	ORRVILLE
44669-44669	PARIS
44670-44670	ROBERTSVILLE
44671-44671	SANDYVILLE
44672-44672	SEBRING
44675-44675	SHERRODSVILLE
44676-44676	SHREVE
44677-44677	SMITHVILLE
44678-44678	SOMERDALE
44679-44679	STILLWATER
44680-44680	STRASBURG
44681-44681	SUGARCREEK
44682-44682	TUSCARAWAS
44683-44683	UHRICHSVILLE
44685-44685	UNIONTOWN
44687-44687	WALNUT CREEK
44688-44688	WAYNESBURG
44689-44689	WILMOT
44690-44690	WINESBURG
44691-44691	WOOSTER
44693-44693	DEERSVILLE
44695-44695	BOWERSTON
44697-44697	ZOAR
44699-44699	TIPPECANOE
44700-44799	CANTON
44801-44801	ADRIAN
44802-44802	ALVADA
44803-44803	AMSDEN
44804-44804	ARCADIA
44805-44805	ASHLAND
44807-44807	ATTICA
44809-44809	BASCOM
44811-44811	BELLEVUE
44813-44813	BELLVILLE
44814-44814	BERLIN HEIGHTS
44815-44815	BETTSVILLE
44816-44816	BIRMINGHAM
44817-44817	BLOOMDALE
44818-44818	BLOOMVILLE
44820-44820	BUCYRUS
44822-44822	BUTLER
44824-44824	CASTALIA
44825-44825	CHATFIELD
44826-44826	COLLINS
44827-44827	CRESTLINE
44828-44828	FLAT ROCK
44829-44829	FORT SENECA
44830-44830	FOSTORIA
44833-44833	GALION
44836-44836	GREEN SPRINGS
44837-44837	GREENWICH
44838-44838	HAYESVILLE
44839-44839	HURON
44840-44840	JEROMESVILLE
44841-44841	KANSAS
44842-44842	LOUDONVILLE
44843-44843	LUCAS
44844-44844	MC CUTCHENVILLE
44845-44845	MELMORE
44846-44846	MILAN
44847-44847	MONROEVILLE
44848-44848	NANKIN
44849-44849	NEVADA
44850-44850	NEW HAVEN
44851-44851	NEW LONDON
44853-44853	NEW RIEGEL
44854-44854	NEW WASHINGTON
44855-44855	NORTH FAIRFIELD
44856-44856	NORTH ROBINSON
44857-44857	NORWALK
44859-44859	NOVA
44860-44860	OCEOLA
44861-44861	OLD FORT
44862-44862	ONTARIO
44864-44864	PERRYSVILLE
44865-44865	PLYMOUTH
44866-44866	POLK
44867-44867	REPUBLIC
44870-44871	SANDUSKY
44874-44874	SAVANNAH
44875-44875	SHELBY
44878-44878	SHILOH
44880-44880	SULLIVAN
44881-44881	SULPHUR SPRINGS
44882-44882	SYCAMORE
44883-44883	TIFFIN
44887-44887	TIRO
44888-44888	WILLARD
44889-44889	WAKEMAN
44890-44890	WILLARD
44900-44999	MANSFIELD
45001-45001	ADDYSTON
45002-45002	CLEVES
45003-45003	COLLEGE CORNER
45004-45004	COLLINSVILLE
45005-45005	FRANKLIN
45011-45013	HAMILTON
45014-45014	FAIRFIELD
45015-45015	HAMILTON
45018-45018	FAIRFIELD
45020-45026	HAMILTON
45030-45030	HARRISON
45032-45032	HARVEYSBURG
45033-45033	HOOVEN
45034-45034	KINGS MILLS
45036-45036	LEBANON
45039-45039	MAINEVILLE
45040-45040	MASON
45041-45041	MIAMITOWN
45042-45044	MIDDLETOWN
45050-45050	MONROE
45051-45051	MOUNT SAINT JOSEPH
45052-45052	NORTH BEND
45053-45053	OKEANA
45054-45054	OREGONIA
45055-45055	OVERPECK
45056-45056	OXFORD
45061-45061	ROSS
45062-45062	SEVEN MILE
45063-45063	SHANDON
45064-45064	SOMERVILLE
45065-45065	SOUTH LEBANON
45066-45066	SPRINGBORO
45067-45067	TRENTON
45068-45068	WAYNESVILLE
45069-45069	WEST CHESTER
45070-45070	WEST ELKTON
45071-45071	WEST CHESTER
45073-45099	MONROE
45101-45101	ABERDEEN
45102-45102	AMELIA
45103-45103	BATAVIA
45105-45105	BENTONVILLE
45106-45106	BETHEL
45107-45107	BLANCHESTER
45110-45110	BUFORD
45111-45111	CAMP DENNISON
45112-45112	CHILO
45113-45113	CLARKSVILLE
45114-45114	CUBA
45115-45115	DECATUR
45118-45118	FAYETTEVILLE
45119-45119	FEESBURG
45120-45120	FELICITY
45121-45121	GEORGETOWN
45122-45122	GOSHEN
45123-45123	GREENFIELD
45130-45130	HAMERSVILLE
45131-45131	HIGGINSPORT
45132-45132	HIGHLAND
45133-45133	HILLSBORO
45135-45135	LEESBURG
45138-45138	LEES CREEK
45140-45140	LOVELAND

ZIP Range	City	ZIP Range	City	ZIP Range	City	ZIP Range	City
45142-45142	LYNCHBURG	45358-45358	PITSBURG	45681-45681	SOUTH SALEM	45820-45820	CAIRO
45144-45144	MANCHESTER	45359-45359	PLEASANT HILL	45682-45682	SOUTH WEBSTER	45821-45821	CECIL
45145-45145	MARATHON	45360-45360	PORT JEFFERSON	45683-45683	STOCKDALE	45822-45822	CELINA
45146-45146	MARTINSVILLE	45361-45361	POTSDAM	45684-45684	STOUT	45826-45826	CHICKASAW
45147-45147	MIAMIVILLE	45362-45362	ROSSBURG	45685-45685	THURMAN	45827-45827	CLOVERDALE
45148-45148	MIDLAND	45363-45363	RUSSIA	45686-45686	VINTON	45828-45828	COLDWATER
45150-45150	MILFORD	45365-45365	SIDNEY	45687-45687	WAKEFIELD	45830-45830	COLUMBUS GROVE
45152-45152	MORROW	45366-45366	SPRING HILL NURSERIES	45688-45688	WATERLOO	45831-45831	CONTINENTAL
45153-45153	MOSCOW	45367-45367	SIDNEY	45690-45690	WAVERLY	45832-45832	CONVOY
45154-45154	MOUNT ORAB	45368-45368	SOUTH CHARLESTON	45692-45692	WELLSTON	45833-45833	DELPHOS
45155-45155	MOWRYSTOWN	45369-45369	SOUTH VIENNA	45693-45693	WEST UNION	45835-45835	DOLA
45156-45156	NEVILLE	45370-45370	SPRING VALLEY	45694-45694	WHEELERSBURG	45836-45836	DUNKIRK
45157-45157	NEW RICHMOND	45371-45371	TIPP CITY	45695-45695	WILKESVILLE	45837-45837	DUPONT
45158-45158	NEWTONSVILLE	45372-45372	TREMONT CITY	45696-45696	WILLOW WOOD	45838-45838	ELGIN
45159-45159	NEW VIENNA	45373-45373	TROY	45697-45697	WINCHESTER	45839-45840	FINDLAY
45160-45160	OWENSVILLE	45377-45377	VANDALIA	45698-45698	ZALESKI	45841-45841	JENERA
45162-45162	PLEASANT PLAIN	45378-45378	VERONA	45699-45699	LUCASVILLE	45843-45843	FOREST
45164-45164	PORT WILLIAM	45380-45380	VERSAILLES	45701-45701	ATHENS	45844-45844	FORT JENNINGS
45165-45165	GREENFIELD	45381-45381	WEST ALEXANDRIA	45710-45710	ALBANY	45845-45845	FORT LORAMIE
45166-45166	REESVILLE	45382-45382	WEST MANCHESTER	45711-45711	AMESVILLE	45846-45846	FORT RECOVERY
45167-45167	RIPLEY	45383-45383	WEST MILTON	45712-45712	BARLOW	45848-45848	GLANDORF
45168-45168	RUSSELLVILLE	45384-45384	WILBERFORCE	45713-45713	BARTLETT	45849-45849	GROVER HILL
45169-45169	SABINA	45385-45385	XENIA	45714-45714	BELPRE	45850-45850	HARROD
45171-45171	SARDINIA	45387-45387	YELLOW SPRINGS	45715-45715	BEVERLY	45851-45851	HAVILAND
45172-45172	SINKING SPRING	45388-45388	YORKSHIRE	45716-45716	BUCHTEL	45853-45853	KALIDA
45174-45174	TERRACE PARK	45389-45389	CHRISTIANSBURG	45717-45717	CARBONDALE	45854-45854	LAFAYETTE
45176-45176	WILLIAMSBURG	45390-45390	UNION CITY	45719-45719	CHAUNCEY	45855-45855	LATTY
45177-45177	WILMINGTON	45401-45490	DAYTON	45720-45720	CHESTER	45856-45856	LEIPSIC
45200-45299	CINCINNATI	45500-45506	SPRINGFIELD	45721-45721	COAL RUN	45858-45858	MC COMB
45301-45301	ALPHA	45601-45601	CHILLICOTHE	45723-45723	COOLVILLE	45859-45859	MC GUFFEY
45302-45302	ANNA	45612-45612	BAINBRIDGE	45724-45724	CUTLER	45860-45860	MARIA STEIN
45303-45303	ANSONIA	45613-45613	BEAVER	45727-45727	DEXTER CITY	45861-45861	MELROSE
45304-45304	ARCANUM	45614-45614	BIDWELL	45729-45729	FLEMING	45862-45862	MENDON
45305-45305	BELLBROOK	45616-45616	BLUE CREEK	45730-45730	JACKSON	45863-45863	MIDDLE POINT
45306-45306	BOTKINS	45617-45617	BOURNEVILLE	45732-45732	GLOUSTER	45864-45864	MILLER CITY
45307-45307	BOWERSVILLE	45618-45618	CHERRY FORK	45734-45734	GRAYSVILLE	45865-45865	MINSTER
45308-45308	BRADFORD	45619-45619	CHESAPEAKE	45735-45735	GUYSVILLE	45866-45866	MONTEZUMA
45309-45309	BROOKVILLE	45620-45620	CHESHIRE	45739-45739	HOCKINGPORT	45867-45867	MOUNT BLANCHARD
45310-45310	BURKETTSVILLE	45621-45621	COALTON	45740-45740	JACKSONVILLE	45868-45868	MOUNT CORY
45311-45311	CAMDEN	45622-45622	CREOLA	45741-45741	LANGSVILLE	45869-45869	NEW BREMEN
45312-45312	CASSTOWN	45623-45623	CROWN CITY	45742-45742	LITTLE HOCKING	45870-45870	NEW HAMPSHIRE
45314-45314	CEDARVILLE	45624-45624	CYNTHIANA	45743-45743	LONG BOTTOM	45871-45871	NEW KNOXVILLE
45315-45315	CLAYTON	45628-45628	FRANKFORT	45744-45744	LOWELL	45872-45872	NORTH BALTIMORE
45316-45316	CLIFTON	45629-45629	FRANKLIN FURNACE	45745-45745	LOWER SALEM	45873-45873	OAKWOOD
45317-45317	CONOVER	45630-45630	FRIENDSHIP	45746-45746	MACKSBURG	45874-45874	OHIO CITY
45318-45318	COVINGTON	45631-45631	GALLIPOLIS	45750-45750	MARIETTA	45875-45875	OTTAWA
45319-45319	DONNELSVILLE	45633-45633	HALLSVILLE	45760-45760	MIDDLEPORT	45876-45876	OTTOVILLE
45320-45320	EATON	45634-45634	HAMDEN	45761-45761	MILLFIELD	45877-45877	PANDORA
45321-45321	ELDORADO	45636-45636	HAVERHILL	45764-45764	NELSONVILLE	45879-45879	PAULDING
45322-45322	ENGLEWOOD	45638-45638	IRONTON	45766-45766	NEW MARSHFIELD	45880-45880	PAYNE
45323-45323	ENON	45640-45640	JACKSON	45767-45767	NEW MATAMORAS	45881-45881	RAWSON
45324-45324	FAIRBORN	45642-45642	JASPER	45768-45768	NEWPORT	45882-45882	ROCKFORD
45325-45325	FARMERSVILLE	45643-45643	KERR	45769-45769	POMEROY	45883-45883	SAINT HENRY
45326-45326	FLETCHER	45644-45644	KINGSTON	45770-45770	PORTLAND	45884-45884	SAINT JOHNS
45327-45327	GERMANTOWN	45645-45645	KITTS HILL	45771-45771	RACINE	45885-45885	SAINT MARYS
45328-45328	GETTYSBURG	45646-45646	LATHAM	45772-45772	REEDSVILLE	45886-45886	SCOTT
45329-45329	GORDON	45647-45647	LONDONDERRY	45773-45773	RENO	45887-45887	SPENCERVILLE
45330-45330	GRATIS	45648-45648	LUCASVILLE	45775-45775	RUTLAND	45888-45888	UNIOPOLIS
45331-45331	GREENVILLE	45650-45650	LYNX	45776-45776	SHADE	45889-45889	VAN BUREN
45332-45332	HOLLANSBURG	45651-45651	MC ARTHUR	45777-45777	SHARPSBURG	45890-45890	VANLUE
45333-45333	HOUSTON	45652-45652	MC DERMOTT	45778-45778	STEWART	45891-45891	VAN WERT
45334-45334	JACKSON CENTER	45653-45653	MINFORD	45779-45779	SYRACUSE	45893-45893	VAUGHNSVILLE
45335-45335	JAMESTOWN	45654-45654	NEW PLYMOUTH	45780-45780	THE PLAINS	45894-45894	VENEDOCIA
45336-45336	KETTLERSVILLE	45656-45656	OAK HILL	45781-45781	TORCH	45895-45895	WAPAKONETA
45337-45337	LAURA	45657-45657	OTWAY	45782-45782	TRIMBLE	45896-45896	WAYNESFIELD
45338-45338	LEWISBURG	45658-45658	PATRIOT	45783-45783	TUPPERS PLAINS	45897-45897	WILLIAMSTOWN
45339-45339	LUDLOW FALLS	45659-45659	PEDRO	45784-45784	VINCENT	45898-45898	WILLSHIRE
45340-45340	MAPLEWOOD	45660-45660	PEEBLES	45786-45786	WATERFORD	45899-45899	WREN
45341-45341	MEDWAY	45661-45661	PIKETON	45787-45787	WATERTOWN	45944-45999	CINCINNATI
45342-45342	MIAMISBURG	45662-45662	PORTSMOUTH	45788-45788	WHIPPLE		
45343-45343	MIAMISBURG	45663-45663	WEST PORTSMOUTH	45789-45789	WINGETT RUN		
45344-45344	NEW CARLISLE	45669-45669	PROCTORVILLE	45801-45807	LIMA		
45345-45345	NEW LEBANON	45670-45670	RADCLIFF	45808-45808	BEAVERDAM		
45346-45346	NEW MADISON	45671-45671	RARDEN	45809-45809	GOMER		
45347-45347	NEW PARIS	45672-45672	RAY	45810-45810	ADA		
45348-45348	NEW WESTON	45673-45673	RICHMOND DALE	45812-45812	ALGER		
45349-45349	NORTH HAMPTON	45674-45674	RIO GRANDE	45813-45813	ANTWERP		
45350-45350	NORTH STAR	45675-45675	ROCK CAMP	45814-45814	ARLINGTON		
45351-45351	OSGOOD	45677-45677	SCIOTO FURNACE	45815-45815	BELMORE		
45352-45352	PALESTINE	45678-45678	SCOTTOWN	45816-45816	BENTON RIDGE		
45353-45353	PEMBERTON	45679-45679	SEAMAN	45817-45817	BLUFFTON		
45354-45354	PHILLIPSBURG	45680-45680	SOUTH POINT	45819-45819	BUCKLAND		
45356-45356	PIQUA						

County-Town
OHIO

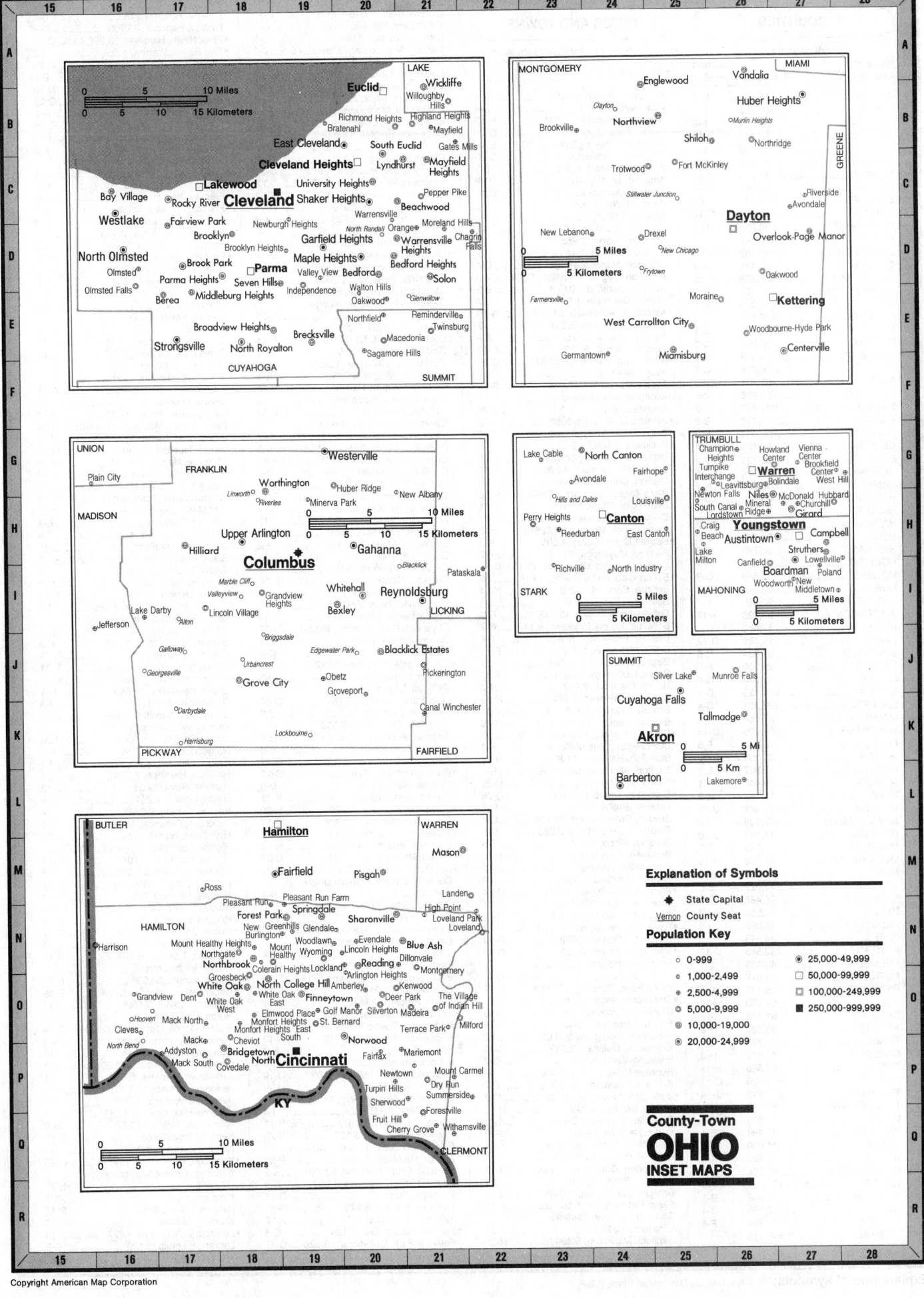

County-Town OHIO INSET MAPS

COUNTIES

(88 Counties)

Name of County	Population	Location on Map
ADAMS	25,371	M-4
ALLEN	109,755	E-3
ASHLAND	47,507	F-9
ASHTABULA	99,821	B-13
ATHENS	59,549	L-9
AUGLAIZE	44,585	F-2
BELMONT	71,074	I-12
BROWN	34,966	M-4
BUTLER	291,479	J-1
CARROLL	26,521	G-12
CHAMPAIGN	36,019	H-3
CLARK	147,548	I-4
CLERMONT	150,187	M-3
CLINTON	35,415	K-4
COLUMBIANA	108,276	E-13
COSHOCTON	35,427	G-9
CRAWFORD	47,870	E-7
CUYAHOGA	1,412,140	B-11
DARKE	53,619	G-1
DEFIANCE	39,350	C-1
DELAWARE	66,929	G-6
ERIE	76,779	C-7
FAIRFIELD	103,461	J-8
FAYETTE	27,466	J-5
FRANKLIN	961,437	I-7
FULTON	38,498	B-2
GALLIA	30,954	N-9
GEAUGA	81,129	C-12
GREENE	136,731	J-4
GUERNSEY	39,024	H-11
HAMILTON	866,228	K-1
HANCOCK	65,536	D-4
HARDIN	31,111	F-4
HARRISON	16,085	G-12
HENRY	29,108	D-3
HIGHLAND	35,728	L-5
HOCKING	25,533	K-7
HOLMES	32,849	G-9
HURON	56,240	D-7
JACKSON	30,230	L-7
JEFFERSON	80,298	F-13
KNOX	47,473	G-9
LAKE	215,499	B-12
LAWRENCE	61,834	N-8
LICKING	128,300	H-7
LOGAN	42,310	G-4
LORAIN	271,126	D-9
LUCAS	462,361	B-4
MADISON	37,068	H-5
MAHONING	264,806	D-13
MARION	64,274	F-5
MEDINA	122,354	D-10
MEIGS	22,987	L-9
MERCER	39,443	F-1
MIAMI	93,182	H-3
MONROE	15,497	J-12
MONTGOMERY	573,809	J-2
MORGAN	14,194	J-10
MORROW	27,749	F-7
MUSKINGUM	82,068	I-10
NOBLE	11,336	J-12
OTTAWA	40,029	B-6
PAULDING	20,488	D-1
PERRY	31,557	J-9
PICKAWAY	48,255	J-6
PIKE	24,249	L-5
PORTAGE	142,585	D-12
PREBLE	40,113	J-1
PUTNAM	33,819	D-2
RICHLAND	126,137	E-8
ROSS	69,330	K-6
SANDUSKY	61,963	C-6
SCIOTO	80,327	M-6
SENECA	59,733	D-7
SHELBY	44,915	H-3
STARK	367,585	F-11
SUMMIT	514,990	C-11
TRUMBULL	227,813	C-14
TUSCARAWAS	84,090	H-11
UNION	31,969	G-5
VAN WERT	30,464	E-1
VINTON	11,098	K-8
WARREN	113,909	K-3
WASHINGTON	62,254	K-10
WAYNE	101,461	F-10
WILLIAMS	36,956	B-1
WOOD	113,269	D-4
WYANDOT	22,254	F-5
TOTAL	10,847,115	

CITIES AND TOWNS

Note: The first name is that of the city or town, second, that of the county in which it is located, then the population and location on the map.

Aberdeen, Brown, 1,329 ... W-4
Ada, Hardin, 5,413 ... E-4
Addyston, Hamilton, 1,198 ... P-17
Akron, Summit, 223,019 ... D-11
Alliance, Mahoning/Stark, 23,376 ... E-12
Amberley, Hamilton, 3,108 ... O-20
Amelia, Clermont, 1,837 ... L-3
Amherst, Lorain, 10,332 ... C-9
Andover, Ashtabula, 1,216 ... B-14
Anna, Shelby, 1,164 ... G-3
Ansonia, Darke, 1,279 ... H-1
Antwerp, Paulding, 1,677 ... D-1
Arcanum, Darke, 1,953 ... I-2
Archbold, Fulton, 3,440 ... B-2
Arlington, Hancock, 1,267 ... E-4
Arlington Heights, Hamilton, 1,084 ... O-20
Ashland, Ashland, 20,079 ... E-9
Ashley, Delaware, 1,059 ... G-7
Ashtabula, Ashtabula, 21,633 ... A-13
Ashville, Pickaway, 2,254 ... J-7
Athens, Athens, 21,265 ... K-9
Aurora, Portage, 9,192 ... C-12
• Austintown, Mahoning, 32,371 ... G-25
Avon, Lorain, 7,337 ... C-9
Avon Lake, Lorain, 15,066 ... B-10
Avondale, Montgomery ... C-27
Avondale, Stark ... G-23
• Bainbridge, Geauga, 3,602 ... C-12
• Ballville, Sandusky, 3,083 ... C-6
Baltimore, Fairfield, 2,971 ... I-8
Barberton, Summit, 27,623 ... L-24
Barnesville, Belmont, 4,326 ... H-12
Batavia, Clermont, 1,700 ... L-3
Bay Village, Cuyahoga, 17,000 ... C-16
Beach City, Stark, 1,051 ... F-11
Beachwood, Cuyahoga, 10,677 ... C-21
Beavercreek, Greene, 33,626 ... J-3
• Beckett Ridge, Butler, 4,505 ... K-2
Bedford, Cuyahoga, 14,822 ... E-20
Bedford Heights, Cuyahoga, 12,131 ... D-20
• Beechwood Trails, Licking, 1,875 ... I-8
Bellaire, Belmont, 6,028 ... H-14
Bellbrook, Greene, 6,511 ... J-3
Bellefontaine, Logan, 12,142 ... G-4
Bellevue, Huron/Sandusky, 8,146 ... C-7
Bellville, Richland, 1,568 ... F-8
Beloit, Mahoning, 1,037 ... E-13
Belpre, Washington, 6,796 ... K-11
Berea, Cuyahoga, 19,051 ... E-17
Bethel, Clermont, 2,407 ... M-3
Bethesda, Belmont, 1,161 ... H-13
Beverly, Washington, 1,444 ... J-11
Bexley, Franklin, 13,088 ... I-19
• Blacklick Estates, Franklin, 10,080 ... J-20
Blanchester, Clinton/Warren, 4,206 ... K-3
Blue Ash, Hamilton, 11,860 ... N-21
Bluffton, Allen/Hancock, 3,367 ... E-4
• Boardman, Mahoning, 38,596 ... H-26
• Bolindale, Trumbull, 2,827 ... G-26
Botkins, Shelby, 1,340 ... G-3
Bowling Green, Wood, 28,176 ... C-4
Bradford, Darke/Miami, 2,005 ... H-2
Bradner, Wood, 1,093 ... C-5
Bratenahl, Cuyahoga, 1,356 ... B-19
Brecksville, Cuyahoga, 11,818 ... E-19
Bremen, Fairfield, 1,386 ... J-8
• Brentwood, Jefferson, 3,568 ... G-14
Brewster, Stark, 2,307 ... F-11
Bridgeport, Belmont, 2,318 ... H-14
• Bridgetown North, Hamilton, 11,748 ... P-17
Brilliant, Jefferson, 1,672 ... G-14
• Brimfield, Portage, 3,223 ... D-12
Broadview Heights, Cuyahoga, 12,219 ... C-11
Brook Park, Cuyahoga, 22,865 ... D-17
• Brookfield Center, Trumbull, 1,396 ... G-27
Brooklyn, Cuyahoga, 11,706 ... D-18
Brooklyn Heights, Cuyahoga, 1,450 ... D-19
Brookville, Montgomery, 4,621 ... I-2
Brunswick, Medina, 28,230 ... D-10
Bryan, Williams, 8,348 ... C-2
Buckeye Lake, Licking, 2,986 ... I-8
Bucyrus, Crawford, 13,496 ... E-7
• Burlington, Lawrence, 3,003 ... O-8
Burton, Geauga, 1,349 ... B-12
Byesville, Guernsey, 2,435 ... I-11
Cadiz, Harrison, 3,439 ... G-13
• Calcutta, Columbiana, 1,212 ... F-14
Caldwell, Noble, 1,786 ... I-11
Cambridge, Guernsey, 11,748 ... H-11
Camden, Preble, 2,210 ... J-1
Campbell, Mahoning, 10,038 ... H-27
Canal Fulton, Stark, 4,157 ... E-11
Canal Winchester, Fairfield/Franklin, 2,617 ... I-21
Canfield, Mahoning, 5,409 ... H-25
Canton, Stark, 84,161 ... E-12
Cardington, Morrow, 1,770 ... G-7
Carey, Wyandot, 3,684 ... E-5
Carlisle, Montgomery/Warren, 4,872 ... J-2
Carrollton, Carroll, 3,042 ... F-13
Cedarville, Greene, 3,210 ... J-4
Celina, Mercer, 9,650 ... F-1
Centerburg, Knox, 1,323 ... G-7
Centerville, Montgomery, 21,082 ... E-27
Chagrin Falls, Cuyahoga, 4,146 ... D-22
• Champion Heights, Trumbull, 4,665 ... C-13
Chardon, Geauga, 4,446 ... B-12
• Cherry Grove, Hamilton, 4,972 ... Q-21
Chesapeake, Lawrence, 1,073 ... O-8
• Chesterland, Geauga, 2,078 ... B-12
Cheviot, Hamilton, 9,616 ... O-18
Chillicothe, Ross, 21,923 ... K-6
Chillicothe West, Ross ... K-6
• Chocktou Lake, Madison, 1,234 ... I-6
• Churchill, Trumbull, 2,691 ... D-14
Cincinnati, Hamilton, 364,040 ... L-2
Circleville, Pickaway, 11,666 ... J-7
Cleveland, Cuyahoga, 505,616 ... C-11
Cleveland Heights, Cuyahoga, 54,052 ... C-20
Cleves, Hamilton, 2,208 ... L-1
Clinton, Summit, 1,175 ... E-11
Clyde, Sandusky, 5,776 ... C-7
Coal Grove, Lawrence, 2,251 ... N-8
Coldwater, Mercer, 4,335 ... G-1
Colerain Heights, Hamilton ... N-18
Columbiana, Columbiana/Mahoning, 4,961 ... E-14
Columbus, Fairfield/Franklin, 632,910 ... H-7
Columbus Grove, Putnam, 2,231 ... E-3
Conneaut, Ashtabula, 13,241 ... A-14
Continental, Putnam, 1,214 ... D-3
Convoy, Van Wert, 1,200 ... E-1
Copley, Summit ... D-11
Cortland, Trumbull, 5,666 ... C-14
Coshocton, Coshocton, 12,193 ... G-10
• Covedale, Hamilton, 6,669 ... L-1
Covington, Miami, 2,603 ... H-2
Craig Beach, Mahoning, 1,402 ... D-13
Crestline, Crawford/Richland, 4,934 ... E-7
Creston, Wayne, 1,848 ... E-10
Cridersville, Auglaize, 1,885 ... F-3
Crooksville, Perry, 2,601 ... I-9
• Crystal Lakes, Clark, 1,613 ... I-3
Cuyahoga Falls, Summit, 48,950 ... J-25
Dalton, Wayne, 1,377 ... E-11
Danville, Knox, 1,001 ... G-9
• Day Heights, Clermont, 2,812 ... L-2
Dayton, Montgomery, 182,044 ... J-3
De Graff, Logan, 1,331 ... G-4
Deer Park, Hamilton, 6,181 ... O-20
Defiance, Defiance, 16,768 ... C-2
Delaware, Delaware, 20,030 ... G-6
Delphos, Allen/Van Wert, 7,093 ... E-2
Delta, Fulton, 2,849 ... B-3
Dennison, Tuscarawas, 3,282 ... G-12
• Dent, Hamilton, 6,416 ... O-17
Deshler, Henry, 1,876 ... D-3
• Devola, Washington, 2,736 ... K-11
• Dillonvale, Hamilton, 4,209 ... N-20
Dover, Tuscarawas, 11,329 ... F-11
Doylestown, Wayne, 2,668 ... E-11
Dresden, Muskingum, 1,581 ... H-10
• Drexel, Montgomery, 5,143 ... D-24
• Dry Run, Hamilton, 5,389 ... P-21
Dublin, Delaware/Franklin/Union, 16,366 ... H-6
Duncan Falls, Muskingum ... I-10
East Canton, Stark, 1,742 ... H-25
East Cleveland, Cuyahoga, 33,096 ... B-20
East Liverpool, Columbiana, 13,654 ... F-14
East Liverpool North, Columbiana ... F-14
East Palestine, Columbiana, 5,168 ... E-14
Eastlake, Lake, 21,161 ... B-11
Eaton, Preble, 7,396 ... J-1
• Eaton Estates, Lorain, 1,586 ... C-10
Edgerton, Williams, 1,896 ... C-1
• Edgewood, Ashtabula, 5,189 ... A-13
Elida, Allen, 1,486 ... E-3
Elmore, Ottawa, 1,334 ... C-6
Elmwood Place, Hamilton, 2,937 ... O-19
Elyria, Lorain, 56,746 ... C-9
Englewood, Montgomery, 11,432 ... B-24
Enon, Clark, 2,605 ... I-4
Euclid, Cuyahoga, 54,875 ... B-11
Evendale, Hamilton, 3,175 ... N-20
Fairborn, Greene, 31,300 ... I-3
Fairfax, Hamilton, 2,029 ... P-20
Fairfield, Butler/Hamilton, 39,729 ... K-2
• Fairfield Beach, Fairfield, 1,084 ... I-8
Fairhope, Stark ... G-25
Fairlawn, Summit, 5,779 ... D-11
Fairport Harbor, Lake, 2,978 ... A-12
• Fairview Lanes, Erie, 1,120 ... C-8
Fairview Park, Cuyahoga, 18,028 ... C-17
Fayette, Fulton, 1,248 ... B-2
Findlay, Hancock, 35,703 ... D-4
• Finneytown, Hamilton, 13,096 ... O-19
• Five Points, Warren, 1,554 ... J-2
Flushing, Belmont, 1,042 ... H-13
Forest, Hardin, 1,594 ... E-5
Forest Park, Hamilton, 18,609 ... N-19
• Forestville, Hamilton, 9,185 ... Q-21
Fort Loramie, Shelby, 1,042 ... G-2
• Fort McKinley, Montgomery, 9,740 ... C-25
Fort Recovery, Mercer, 1,313 ... G-1
Fort Shawnee, Allen, 4,128 ... F-3
Fostoria, Hancock/Seneca/Wood, 14,983 ... D-5
Frankfort, Ross, 1,065 ... K-6
Franklin, Warren, 11,026 ... J-2
• Franklin Furnace, Scioto, 1,212 ... N-7
Frazeysburg, Muskingum, 1,165 ... H-9
Fredericktown, Knox, 2,443 ... G-8
Fremont, Sandusky, 17,648 ... C-6
• Fruit Hill, Hamilton, 4,101 ... Q-20
Gahanna, Franklin, 27,791 ... H-20
Galion, Crawford, 11,859 ... F-7
Gallipolis, Gallia, 4,831 ... M-9
Gambier, Knox, 2,073 ... G-8
Garfield Heights, Cuyahoga, 31,739 ... D-19
Garrettsville, Portage, 2,014 ... C-13
Gates Mills, Cuyahoga, 2,508 ... B-21
Geneva, Ashtabula, 6,597 ... A-13
Geneva-on-the-Lake, Ashtabula, 1,626 ... A-13
Genoa, Ottawa, 2,262 ... B-5
Georgetown, Brown, 3,627 ... M-4
Germantown, Montgomery, 4,916 ... E-24
Gibsonburg, Sandusky, 2,579 ... C-6
Girard, Trumbull, 11,304 ... D-14
Glendale, Hamilton, 2,445 ... N-19
• Glenmoor, Columbiana, 2,307 ... F-14
Glouster, Athens, 2,001 ... J-9
Gnadenhutten, Tuscarawas, 1,226 ... G-12
Golf Manor, Hamilton, 4,154 ... O-20
Goshen, Clermont ... L-3
Grafton, Lorain, 3,344 ... C-9
• Grandview, Hamilton, 1,301 ... O-16
Grandview Heights, Franklin, 7,010 ... I-18
Granville, Licking, 4,353 ... H-8
• Granville South, Licking, 1,124 ... H-8
Green, Summit, 3,553 ... E-11
• Green Meadows, Clark, 2,526 ... I-4
Green Springs, Sandusky/Seneca, 1,446 ... D-6
Greenfield, Highland, 5,172 ... K-5
Greenhills, Hamilton, 4,393 ... N-19
• Greensburg, Summit, 3,306 ... E-11
• Greentown, Stark, 1,856 ... E-11
Greenville, Darke, 12,863 ... H-1
Greenwich, Huron, 1,442 ... D-8
• Groesbeck, Hamilton, 6,684 ... O-18
Grove City, Franklin, 19,661 ... I-6
Groveport, Franklin, 2,948 ... J-20
Hamilton, Butler, 61,368 ... K-2
• Harbor Hills, Licking, 1,372 ... I-8
Harrison, Hamilton, 7,518 ... K-1
Hartville, Stark, 2,031 ... E-12
Heath, Licking, 7,231 ... H-8
Hebron, Licking, 2,076 ... I-8
Hicksville, Defiance, 3,664 ... C-1
High Point, Hamilton ... N-21
Highland Heights, Cuyahoga, 6,249 ... B-21
Hilliard, Franklin, 11,796 ... H-17
Hillsboro, Highland, 6,235 ... L-5
Hiram, Portage, 1,330 ... C-12
Holgate, Henry, 1,290 ... D-3
• Holiday Valley, Clark, 1,243 ... I-2
Holland, Lucas, 1,210 ... B-4
• Howland Center, Trumbull, 6,732 ... C-27
Howland Corners, Trumbull ... C-14
Hubbard, Trumbull, 8,248 ... D-14
Huber Heights, Miami/Montgomery, 38,696 ... B-27
• Huber Ridge, Franklin, 5,255 ... G-19
Hudson, Summit, 5,159 ... D-11
Huron, Erie, 7,030 ... C-8
Independence, Cuyahoga, 6,500 ... D-19
Ironton, Lawrence, 12,751 ... N-8
Jackson, Jackson, 6,144 ... L-8
Jackson Center, Shelby, 1,398 ... G-3
Jamestown, Greene, 1,794 ... J-4
Jefferson, Ashtabula, 3,331 ... A-13
Jefferson, Madison, 4,505 ... I-6
Jeffersonville, Fayette, 1,281 ... J-5
Johnstown, Licking, 3,237 ... H-8
Kent, Portage, 28,835 ... D-12
Kenton, Hardin, 8,356 ... F-5
• Kenwood, Hamilton, 7,469 ... O-20
Kettering, Greene/Montgomery, 60,569 ... E-27
Kingston, Ross, 1,153 ... K-7
Kirtland, Lake, 5,881 ... B-12
Krumroy, Summit ... D-11
• La Croft, Columbiana, 1,427 ... F-14
Lagrange, Lorain, 1,199 ... D-9

Explanation of symbols: • – Census Designated Place (CDP)

Lake Cable, Stark G-23
• Lake Darby, Franklin, 2,798 I-16
Lake Milton, Mahoning D-13
Lakemore, Summit, 2,684 L-26
Lakeview, Logan, 1,056 G-4
Lakewood, Cuyahoga, 59,718 C-11
Lancaster, Fairfield, 34,507 J-8
• Landen, Warren, 9,263 K-2
Leavittsburg, Trumbull C-13
Lebanon, Warren, 10,453 K-3
Leesburg, Highland, 1,063 K-5
Leetonia, Columbiana, 2,070 E-14
Leipsic, Putnam, 2,203 D-3
Lewisburg, Preble, 1,584 I-2
Lexington, Richland, 4,124 F-8
Liberty Center, Henry, 1,084 C-3
Lima, Allen, 45,549 F-3
Lincoln Heights, Hamilton, 4,805 N-20
• Lincoln Village, Franklin, 9,958 I-17
Lisbon, Columbiana, 3,037 E-14
Lockland, Hamilton, 4,357 N-6
Lodi, Medina, 3,042 D-10
Logan, Hocking, 6,725 J-8
• Logan Elm Village, Pickaway, 1,287 J-7
London, Madison, 7,807 I-5
Lorain, Lorain, 71,245 C-9
Lorain South, Lorain C-9
Lordstown, Trumbull, 3,404 D-13
Loudonville, Ashland/Holmes, 2,915 F-9
Louisville, Stark, 8,087 E-12
Loveland, Clermont/Hamilton/Warren, 9,990 N-22
• Loveland Park, Hamilton/Warren, 1,357 N-22
Lowellville, Mahoning, 1,349 H-28
• Lucasville, Scioto, 1,575 M-7
Lynchburg, Highland, 1,212 L-4
Lyndhurst, Cuyahoga, 15,982 C-21
Macedonia, Summit, 7,509 E-20
Mack, Hamilton O-17
• Mack North, Hamilton, 2,816 O-17
• Mack South, Hamilton, 5,767 P-17
Madeira, Hamilton, 9,141 O-20
Madison, Lake, 2,477 A-13
Malvern, Carroll, 1,112 F-12
Manchester, Adams, 2,223 N-5
Manchester, Summit E-11
Mansfield, Richland, 50,627 E-8
Mantua, Portage, 1,178 C-12
Maple Heights, Cuyahoga, 27,089 D-20
• Maple Ridge, Mahoning, 1,018 E-13
Mariemont, Hamilton, 3,118 P-20
Marietta, Washington, 15,026 K-12
Marion, Marion, 34,075 F-6
Marion East, Marion F-6
Martins Ferry, Belmont, 7,990 H-14
Marysville, Union, 9,656 H-5
Mason, Warren, 11,452 K-2
Massillon, Stark, 31,007 E-11
Matamoras, Washington, 1,002 J-13
Maumee, Lucas, 15,561 B-4
Mayfield, Cuyahoga, 3,462 B-21
Mayfield Heights, Cuyahoga, 19,847 C-21
McArthur, Vinton, 1,541 L-8
McComb, Hancock, 1,544 D-4
McConnelsville, Morgan, 1,804 J-10
McDonald, Trumbull, 3,526 D-14
Mechanicsburg, Champaign, 1,803 H-5
Medina, Medina, 19,231 D-10
Mentor, Lake, 47,358 B-12
Mentor-on-the-Lake, Lake, 8,271 B-12
Miamisburg, Montgomery, 17,834 E-25
Middleburg Heights, Cuyahoga, 14,702 E-17
Middlefield, Geauga, 1,898 C-12
Middleport, Meigs, 2,725 L-10
Middletown, Butler/Warren, 46,022 J-2
Milan, Erie/Huron, 1,464 C-8
Milford, Clermont/Hamilton, 5,660 L-3
Millbury, Wood, 1,081 B-5
Millersburg, Holmes, 3,051 F-10
Millersport, Fairfield, 1,010 I-8
• Mineral Ridge, Mahoning/Trumbull, 3,928 D-14
Minerva, Carroll/Columbiana/Stark, 4,318 F-13
Minerva Park, Franklin, 1,463 H-19
Mingo Junction, Jefferson, 4,297 G-14
Minster, Auglaize, 2,650 G-2
Mogadore, Portage/Summit, 4,008 D-12
• Monfort Heights East, Hamilton, 3,661 O-18
• Monfort Heights South, Hamilton, 4,587 O-18
Monroe, Butler/Warren, 4,490 K-2
Monroeville, Huron, 1,381 D-7
Montgomery, Hamilton, 9,753 N-21
Montpelier, Williams, 4,299 B-1
• Montrose-Ghent, Summit, 4,906 D-11
Moraine, Montgomery, 5,989 E-26
Moreland Hills, Cuyahoga, 3,354 D-21
Morrow, Warren, 1,206 K-3
• Mount Carmel, Clermont, 4,462 L-2
Mount Gilead, Morrow, 2,846 I-7
Mount Healthy, Hamilton, 7,580 N-18
• Mount Healthy Heights, Hamilton, 3,863 N-18
Mount Orab, Brown, 1,929 L-4
• Mount Repose, Clermont, 3,093 L-2
Mount Sterling, Madison, 1,647 J-6
Mount Vernon, Knox, 14,550 G-8
• Mulberry, Clermont, 2,856 L-2
Munroe Falls, Summit, 5,359 J-26
Napoleon, Henry, 8,884 C-3
Navarre, Stark, 1,635 F-11
• Neffs, Belmont, 1,213 H-13
Nelsonville, Athens, 4,563 K-9
New Albany, Franklin, 1,621 H-21
New Boston, Scioto, 2,717 M-7
New Bremen, Auglaize, 2,558 G-2
New Burlington, Hamilton N-19
New Carlisle, Clark, 6,049 I-3
New Concord, Muskingum, 2,086 H-11
New Lebanon, Montgomery, 4,323 J-2
New Lexington, Perry, 5,117 J-9
New London, Huron, 2,642 D-8
New Miami, Butler, 2,555 K-2
New Middletown, Mahoning, 1,912 E-14
New Paris, Preble, 1,801 I-1
New Philadelphia, Tuscarawas, 15,698 G-11
New Richmond, Clermont, 2,408 M-2
New Washington, Crawford, 1,057 E-7
New Waterford, Columbiana, 1,278 E-14
Newark, Licking, 44,389 H-8
Newburgh Heights, Cuyahoga, 2,310 D-19
Newcomerstown, Tuscarawas, 4,012 G-11
Newton Falls, Trumbull, 4,866 D-13
Newtown, Hamilton, 1,589 P-21
Niles, Trumbull, 21,128 D-13
North Baltimore, Wood, 3,139 D-4
North Canton, Stark, 14,748 G-23
North College Hill, Hamilton, 11,002 O-18
• North Folk Village, Ross, 1,247 K-7
North Industry, Stark I-24
North Kingsville, Ashtabula, 2,672 A-14
North Lewisburg, Champaign, 1,160 H-5
• North Madison, Lake, 8,699 A-13
North Mount Vernon-Academia, Knox G-8
North Olmsted, Cuyahoga, 34,204 D-16
North Ridgeville, Lorain, 21,564 C-10
North Royalton, Cuyahoga, 23,197 E-18
• North Zanesville, Muskingum, 2,121 I-10
• Northbrook, Hamilton, 11,471 N-18
Northfield, Summit, 3,624 E-20
• Northgate, Hamilton, 7,864 N-18
• Northridge, Clark, 5,939 I-4
• Northridge, Montgomery, 9,448 B-26
• Northview, Montgomery, 10,337 B-25
Northwood, Wood, 5,506 B-5
Norton, Summit/Wayne, 11,477 D-11
Norwalk, Huron, 14,731 D-8
Norwood, Hamilton, 23,674 P-20
Oak Harbor, Ottawa, 2,637 B-6
Oak Hill, Jackson, 1,831 M-8
Oakwood, Cuyahoga, 3,392 E-20
Oakwood, Montgomery, 8,957 D-26
Oberlin, Lorain, 8,191 C-9
Obetz, Franklin, 3,167 J-19
Olmsted, Cuyahoga D-16
Olmsted Falls, Cuyahoga, 6,741 D-16
Ontario, Richland, 4,026 F-8
Orange, Cuyahoga, 2,810 D-21
Oregon, Lucas, 18,334 B-5
Orrville, Wayne, 7,712 E-10
Orwell, Ashtabula, 1,258 B-13
Ottawa, Putnam, 3,999 D-3
Ottawa Hills, Lucas, 4,543 B-5
• Overlook-Page Manor, Montgomery, 13,242 D-27
Owensville, Clermont, 1,019 L-3
Oxford, Butler, 18,937 K-1
Painesville, Lake, 15,699 B-12
Pandora, Putnam, 1,009 E-4
• Park Layne, Clark, 4,795 I-3
Parma, Cuyahoga, 87,876 C-11
Parma Heights, Cuyahoga, 21,448 D-18
Pataskala, Licking, 3,046 H-22
Paulding, Paulding, 2,605 D-2
Payne, Paulding, 1,244 D-1
Peebles, Adams, 1,782 M-5
Pemberville, Wood, 1,279 C-5
Pepper Pike, Cuyahoga, 6,185 C-21
Perry, Lake, 1,012 A-12
• Perry Heights, Stark, 9,055 H-23
Perrysburg, Wood, 12,551 B-5
Pickerington, Fairfield/Franklin, 5,668 I-21
• Pigeon Creek, Summit, 1,008 D-11
Piketon, Pike, 1,717 L-6
Pioneer, Williams, 1,287 B-2
Piqua, Miami, 20,612 H-3
Plain City, Madison/Union, 2,278 H-6
• Pleasant Grove, Muskingum, 2,001 I-10
Pleasant Hill, Miami, 1,066 H-2
• Pleasant Run, Hamilton, 4,964 N-18
• Pleasant Run Farm, Hamilton, 4,545 N-18
Plymouth, Huron/Richland, 1,942 E-8
Poland, Mahoning, 2,992 H-27
Pomeroy, Meigs, 2,259 L-10
Port Clinton, Ottawa, 7,106 B-7
• Portage Lakes, Summit, 13,373 E-11
Portsmouth, Scioto, 22,676 N-7
Powell, Delaware, 2,154 H-6
Powhatan Point, Belmont, 1,807 I-13
Prospect, Marion, 1,148 G-6
Ravenna, Portage, 12,069 D-12
Reading, Hamilton, 12,038 N-20
Reedurban, Stark H-23
Reminderville, Summit, 2,163 E-22
Reno Beach, Lucas B-6
Reynoldsburg, Fairfield/Franklin/Licking, 25,748 I-21
Richfield, Summit, 3,117 D-11
Richmond Heights, Cuyahoga, 9,611 B-20
Richville, Stark E-11
Richwood, Union, 2,186 G-5
Ripley, Brown, 1,816 N-4
Rittman, Medina/Wayne, 6,147 E-10
Riverside, Montgomery, 1,471 C-27
Rockford, Mercer, 1,119 F-1
Rocky River, Cuyahoga, 20,410 C-17
• Rosemount, Scioto, 1,926 M-7
Roseville, Muskingum/Perry, 1,847 I-9
• Ross, Butler, 2,124 K-1
Rossford, Wood, 5,861 B-5
Russells Point, Logan, 1,504 G-4
Sabina, Clinton, 2,662 K-4
Sagamore Hills, Summit E-20
Saint Bernard, Hamilton, 5,344 O-19
Saint Clairsville, Belmont, 5,162 H-13
Saint Henry, Mercer, 1,907 G-1
Saint Marys, Auglaize, 8,441 F-2
Saint Paris, Champaign, 1,842 H-3
Salem, Columbiana, 12,233 E-13
Salineville, Columbiana/Jefferson, 1,474 F-13
Sandusky, Erie, 29,764 C-7
• Sandusky South, Erie, 6,336 C-7
• Sciotodale, Scioto, 1,128 M-7
Seaman, Adams, 1,013 M-5
Sebring, Mahoning, 4,848 E-13
Seven Hills, Cuyahoga, 12,339 D-19
Seville, Medina, 1,810 D-10
Shadyside, Belmont, 3,934 I-14
Shaker Heights, Cuyahoga, 30,831 C-20
Sharon West, Trumbull C-14
Sharonville, Butler/Hamilton, 13,153 N-20
• Shawnee Hills, Greene, 2,199 J-4
Sheffield, Lorain, 1,943 C-9
Sheffield Lake, Lorain, 9,825 B-10
Shelby, Richland, 9,564 E-8
• Sherwood, Hamilton, 3,709 P-20
• Shiloh, Montgomery, 11,607 B-25
Shreve, Wayne, 1,584 F-10
Sidney, Shelby, 18,710 G-3
Silver Lake, Summit, 3,052 J-25
Silverton, Hamilton, 5,859 O-20
Smithville, Wayne, 1,354 E-10
Solon, Cuyahoga, 18,548 D-21
Somerset, Perry, 1,390 I-9
South Amherst, Lorain, 1,765 C-9
• South Canal, Trumbull, 1,319 H-25
South Charleston, Clark, 1,626 I-5
South Euclid, Cuyahoga, 23,866 B-20
South Lebanon, Warren, 2,696 K-3
South Middle, Butler, 3,491 K-1
South Point, Lawrence, 3,823 O-8
South Russell, Geauga, 3,402 C-12
South Zanesville, Muskingum, 1,969 I-10
Spencerville, Allen, 2,288 F-2
Springboro, Montgomery/Warren, 6,590 J-3
Springdale, Hamilton, 10,621 N-19
Springfield, Clark, 70,487 I-4
Steubenville, Jefferson, 22,125 G-14
• Stony Prairie, Sandusky, 1,536 C-6
Stow, Summit, 27,702 D-11
Strasburg, Tuscarawas, 1,995 F-11
Streetsboro, Portage, 9,932 C-12
Strongsville, Cuyahoga, 35,308 C-10
Struthers, Mahoning, 12,284 H-27
Stryker, Williams, 1,468 B-2
Sugarcreek, Tuscarawas, 2,062 F-11
• Summerside, Clermont, 4,573 L-2
• Summit Station, Licking, 1,380 H-7
Sunbury, Delaware, 2,046 H-7
Swanton, Fulton/Lucas, 3,557 B-4
Sylvania, Lucas, 17,301 B-5
Tallmadge, Summit, 14,870 J-26
Terrace Park, Hamilton, 2,133 O-21
• The Plains, Athens, 2,644 K-9
The Village of Indian Hill, Hamilton, 5,383 O-21
Tiffin, Seneca, 18,604 D-6
Tiltonsville, Jefferson, 1,517 H-14
Tipp City, Miami, 6,027 I-3
Toledo, Lucas, 332,943 B-5
Toronto, Jefferson, 6,127 G-14
Trenton, Butler, 6,189 K-2
Trotwood, Montgomery, 8,816 C-24
Troy, Miami, 19,478 H-3
• Turnpike Interchange, Trumbull, 1,188 H-25
• Turpin Hills, Hamilton, 4,927 P-20
Twinsburg, Summit, 9,606 E-21
Uhrichsville, Tuscarawas, 5,604 G-12
Union, Montgomery, 5,501 I-2
Union City, Darke, 1,984 H-1
• Uniontown, Stark, 3,074 E-12
University Heights, Cuyahoga, 14,790 C-20
Upper Arlington, Franklin, 34,128 H-6
Upper Sandusky, Wyandot, 5,906 E-6
Urbana, Champaign, 11,353 H-4
Urichsville, Tuscarawas G-11
Utica, Knox/Licking, 1,997 H-8
Valley View, Cuyahoga, 2,137 D-19
Van Wert, Van Wert, 10,891 E-2
Vandalia, Montgomery, 13,882 A-26
Vermilion, Erie/Lorain, 11,127 C-9
Versailles, Darke, 2,351 H-2
• Vienna Center, Trumbull, 1,067 G-27
Vincent, Lorain C-9
Wadsworth, Medina, 15,718 D-11
Walbridge, Wood, 2,736 B-5
Walton Hills, Cuyahoga, 2,371 E-20
Wapakoneta, Auglaize, 9,214 F-3
Warren, Trumbull, 50,793 C-13
Warrensville, Cuyahoga D-20
Warrensville Heights, Cuyahoga, 15,745 D-21
Washington, Fayette, 12,983 J-5
Waterville, Lucas, 4,517 B-4
Wauseon, Fulton, 6,322 B-3
Waverly City, Pike, 4,477 L-7
Waynesburg, Stark, 1,068 F-12
Waynesville, Warren, 1,949 J-3
Wellington, Lorain, 4,140 D-9
Wellston, Jackson, 6,049 L-8
Wellsville, Columbiana, 4,532 F-13
West Alexandria, Preble, 1,460 J-2
West Carrollton City, Montgomery, 14,403 E-25
• West Hill, Trumbull, 2,954 G-27
West Lafayette, Coshocton, 2,129 G-10
West Liberty, Logan, 1,613 G-4
West Milton, Miami, 4,348 I-2
• West Portsmouth, Scioto, 3,551 M-6
West Salem, Wayne, 1,534 E-9
West Union, Adams, 3,096 M-5
West Unity, Williams, 1,677 B-2
Westerville, Delaware/Franklin, 30,269 G-5
Westlake, Cuyahoga, 27,018 C-16
Weston, Wood, 1,716 C-4
• Wheelersburg, Scioto, 5,113 N-7
• White Oak, Hamilton, 12,430 O-18
• White Oak East, Hamilton, 3,544 O-18
• White Oak West, Hamilton, 2,879 O-18
Whitehall, Franklin, 20,572 I-21
Whitehouse, Lucas, 2,528 B-4
Wickliffe, Lake, 14,558 B-21
• Wilberforce, Greene, 2,639 J-4
Willard, Huron, 6,210 D-7
Williamsburg, Clermont, 2,322 L-3
Willoughby, Lake, 20,510 B-11
Willoughby Hills, Lake, 8,427 B-21
Willowick, Lake, 15,269 B-11
Wilmington, Clinton, 11,199 K-4
Windham, Portage, 2,943 D-13
Wintersville, Jefferson, 4,102 G-14
• Withamsville, Clermont, 2,834 L-2
• Woodbourne-Hyde Park, Montgomery, 7,837 E-26
Woodlawn, Hamilton, 2,674 N-19
Woodsfield, Monroe, 2,832 I-13
Woodville, Sandusky, 1,953 C-5
Woodworth, Mahoning E-14
Wooster, Wayne, 22,191 E-10
Worthington, Franklin, 14,869 G-18
• Wright-Patterson AFB, Greene/Montgomery, 8,579 I-3
Wyoming, Hamilton, 8,128 N-19
Xenia, Greene, 24,664 J-4
Yellow Springs, Greene, 3,973 I-4
Yorkville, Belmont/Jefferson, 1,246 H-14
Youngstown, Mahoning/Trumbull, 95,732 D-14
Zanesville, Muskingum, 26,778 I-10

Explanation of symbols: • – Census Designated Place (CDP)

General Help Numbers:

Governor's Office

State Capitol, Suite 212
Oklahoma City, OK 73105
http://www.governor.state.ok.us

405-521-2342
Fax 405-521-3353
8AM-5PM

Attorney General's Office

2300 N Lincoln, #112
Oklahoma City, OK 73105
www.oag.state.ok.us/
explorer.index.html

405-521-3921
Fax 405-521-6246
8:30AM-5PM

Legislative Records

Oklahoma Legislature, State Capitol,
Bill Status Info-Rm B-30, Copies-Rm 310
Oklahoma City, OK 73105
www.lsb.state.ok.us

405-521-5642
Fax 405-521-5507
8:30AM-4:30PM

State Archives

Archives & Records Mgt Divisions
200 NE 18th
Oklahoma City, OK 73105-3298
www.odl.state.ok.us

405-522-3577
Fax 405-525-7804
8AM-5PM

State Specifics:

Capital:	Oklahoma City Oklahoma County
Time Zone:	CST
Number of Counties:	77
Population:	3,523,553
Web Site:	www.state.ok.us

State Agencies

Criminal Records

OK State Bureau of Investigation, Criminal History Reporting, 6600 N Harvey, Oklahoma City, OK 73116; 405-848-6724, 405-879-2503-Fax; 8:30AM-4:30PM.

www.osbi.state.ok.us

A record request form is available at the website. Questions may be directed to sda@osbi.state.ok.us.

Records are available from 1925 on. Records are maintained indefinitely. It takes 5 to 7 days before new records are available for inquiry. 35% of all arrests in database have final dispositions recorded, 47% for those arrests within last 5 years.

Searching: Include the following in your request-DOB or approximate age. The SSN, sex or race are helpful and provide a better search, but not required. Fingerprints are optional. 100% of the records are fingerprint-supported. The following data is not released: juvenile records. Arrest records without dispositions are released if the party was fingerprinted. Computer searches include arrests without dispositions.

Access by: mail, fax, in person.

Fee & Payment: The fee for a computer name search is $15.00. The fee for the fingerprint search is $19.00. Copies are $.25 per page. Fee payee: O.S.B.I. Prepayment required. Personal checks not accepted. MasterCard, Visa, Discover accepted.

Mail search: Turnaround time: 2 weeks. A SASE is requested.

Fax search: Use of credit card and their "Credit Card Fax Form" is required. Call to have them fax you the form or download from web.

In person search: Name requests take 20 minutes, fingerprint searches take up to ten days to process.

Statewide Court Records

Administrative Office of Courts, 1915 N Stiles, #305, Oklahoma City, OK 73105; 405-521-2450, 405-521-6815-Fax; 8AM-5PM.

www.oscn.net

Access by: online.

Online search: Free Internet access is available for District Courts in 12 populous counties and all Appellate courts at www.oscn.net. Both civil and criminal docket information is available for the counties involved. Also, the Oklahoma District Court Records free website at www.odcr.com offers searching from over 50 District Courts. More counties are being added as they are readied; they hope to eventually feature all OK District Courts. Please note many of the county records in this system do not go back 7 years.

Sexual Offender Registry

Oklahoma Department of Corrections, Sex Offender Registry, 2901 N Classen Blvd, Ste 200, Oklahoma City, OK 73106; 405-962-6104, 8AM-5PM.

www.doc.state.ok.us/DOCS/offender_info.htm

It takes 7 days before new records are available for inquiry.

Access by: mail, online.

Fee & Payment: The copy fee is $.25 per page.

Mail search: Turnaround time: 1-3 days. Names searches and geographic lists are available by mail.

Online search: Searching is available from the website. The Sex Offender Lookup only lists lifetime (habitual and aggravated) sex offenders, all others have not been put on the site yet. There are a number of search options.

Incarceration Records

Oklahoma Department of Corrections, Offender Records, PO Box 11400, Oklahoma City, OK 73136 (Courier address: 3400 Martin Luther King Avenue, Oklahoma City, OK 73136); 405-425-2500, 405-425-2608-Fax; 8AM-4:30PM.

www.doc.state.ok.us

Records are available on current and former inmates. It takes 10 days before new records are available for inquiry.

Searching: Records are maintained indefinitely. Include the following in your request-provide first and last name, but the DOB, SSN and DOC number helpful. You can search online by either the name or DOC number. Location, DOC number, physical identifiers, conviction and sentencing information, and release dates are provided. The following data is not released: SSN, offender home address.

Access by: mail, phone, fax, online.

Mail search: Turnaround time: 5 to 10 working days.

Phone search: Limited phone searching available.

Fax search: May request via the fax.

Online search: At the main website, click on Offender Information. The online system is shut down from 3AM until 3:30 AM.

Corporation, Limited Liability Company, Limited Partnership, Trademark, Limited Liability Partnership Records

Secretary of State, Business Records Department, 2300 N Lincoln Blvd, Rm 101, Oklahoma City, OK 73105-4897; 405-522-4582 (Records), 900-733-2428 (Records), 405-521-3771-Fax; 8AM-5PM.

www.sos.state.ok.us

Officers are available from the Franchise Tax Dept. of the Oklahoma Tax Commission, 405-521-3161.

Records are available from late 1800's on. Older records are kept at the State Archives. Most recent records are maintained on a PC-based system. New records are available for inquiry immediately.

Searching: The search includes correct name, status, date of registration, service agent and address, state of domicile, authorized shares and par value, amendments, name changes, mergers, and trade names. The records do not include owner names and addresses. Include the following in your request-full name of business. Records include: corporations, limited partnerships, limited liability companies, limited liability partnerships, certificate of partnership fictitious name for general partnerships and trade names.

Access by: mail, phone, fax, in person, online.

Fee & Payment: The search fee is $5.00. Copies are provided by the Certification Dept at $1.00 per page. Fee payee: Secretary of State. Prepayment required. Personal checks accepted. Credit cards access for online, fax and phone requests.

Mail search: Turnaround time: 1 to 2 days. A SASE is requested.

Phone search: Dial 1-900-733-2424. The fee is $5.00 per call and you are allowed up to 3 record searches per call. Dial 405-522-4582 for verbal information using a credit card. $5.00 also applies.

Fax search: Turnaround time 1 to 2 days.

In person search: There is no fee to search records on a public access terminal.

Online search: Visit SOONERAccess at https://www.sooneraccess.state.ok.us/ for free searches on business entities, including registered agents and Trademarks. Customers may also order and receive status certificates as well as certified and plain copies.

Uniform Commercial Code

UCC Central Filing Office, Oklahoma County Clerk, 320 R.S. Kerr Ave, County Office Bldg, Rm 105, Oklahoma City, OK 73102; 405-713-1521, 405-713-1810-Fax; 8AM-5PM.

www.oklahomacounty.org/countyclerk

This county agency is the central filing agency for the state.

Records are available for since 2/91 on UCC, 10 years on tax liens on computer. Records are on microfiche from 1977 to present. It takes 2 to 3 days before new records are available for inquiry. Records are normally destroyed after one year from lapse.

Searching: Use search request form UCC-11, the national standard form. Include the following in your request-debtor name.

Access by: mail, in person, online.

Fee & Payment: The search fee is $10.00 per debtor name, the copy fee is $1.00 per page, to certify the document add $1.00 per page. Fee payee: Oklahoma County Clerk. Prepayment required. Personal checks accepted. No credit cards accepted, but may start in late 2004.

Mail search: Turnaround time: 2 days.

In person search: Unless time permits, most record requests must be picked up the next day.

Online search: Records of all UCC financing statements may be viewed free on the Internet at www.oklahomacounty.org/coclerk/default.htm. Neither certified searches nor record requests are accepted at the web. Search by debtor or secured party.

Other access: The entire database is available on microfilm or computer tapes, prices start at $500.

Federal and State Tax Liens

Records not maintained by a state level agency.

All state tax liens and federal tax liens are filed at the local level. Federal tax liens on businesses are filed with the Clerk of Oklahoma County.

Sales Tax Registrations

Taxpayer Assistance, Sales Tax Registration Records, 2501 N Lincoln Blvd, Oklahoma City, OK 73194; 405-521-3160, 405-521-3200, 405-521-3826-Fax; 7:30AM-4:30PM.

www.oktax.state.ok.us/salesuse.html

Records are available for the most recent 10 years on computer, microfilmed back to the 1970's.

Searching: This agency will provide any information found on the face of the permit-business name, address, tax permit number, and SIC code. Payment history is not released. Include the following in your request-permit number or business name. They will also search by owner name, federal tax ID, or by tax permit number.

Access by: mail, phone, in person.

Fee & Payment: No search fees, but there is a copy fee of $.25 per page. Fee payee: Oklahoma Tax Commission. Prepayment required. If the card is used, there is an additional fee equal to 1.35% of the purchase. Personal checks accepted. No credit cards accepted.

Mail search: Turnaround time: within 2 weeks. A SASE is requested.

Phone search: Tax permit numbers can be verified by phone, via an automated system.

In person search: Copies cost $.25 per page.

Other access: Current sales tax permit holders are permitted to purchase the sales tax database on microfiche or on 3.5 inch floppies. The annual subscription is $150.00 and is updated monthly.

Birth Certificates

State Department of Health, Vital Records Service, PO Box 53551, Oklahoma City, OK 73152-3551 (Courier address: 1000 NE 10th St, Oklahoma City, OK 73117); 405-271-4040, 405-271-1646 (Order Line), 405-232-3311-Fax; 8:30AM-4PM.

www.health.state.ok.us/program/vital/brec.html

Records are available from 1908 on. Records are computerized since 1930. New records are available for inquiry immediately. Records are indexed on inhouse computer.

Searching: Must have a signed release from person of record or immediate family member. Include the following in your request-full name, names of parents, mother's maiden name, date of birth, place of birth, reason for information request, and copy of ID of requester. Also, daytime phone number.

Access by: mail, phone, fax, in person.

Fee & Payment: Fee is $10.00, a "Heirloom" record is $35.00. Fee payee: Oklahoma State Health Department. Prepayment required. Personal checks accepted. Credit cards accepted: MasterCard, Visa.

Mail search: Turnaround time: 1 to 2 weeks. A SASE is requested.

Phone search: See expedited service.

Fax search: See expedited service.

In person search: Turnaround time is while you wait.

Expedited service: Expedited service is available for fax and phone searches. Turnaround time: 1-2 days. Add $17.00 for express delivery. Use of credit card required, for an additional $10.95 fee.

Death Records

State Department of Health, Vital Records Service, PO Box 53551, Oklahoma City, OK 73152-3551 (Courier address: 1000 NE 10th St, Oklahoma City, OK 73117); 405-271-4040, 405-271-1646 (Order Line), 405-232-3311-Fax; 8:30AM-4PM.

www.health.state.ok.us/program/vital/brec.html

Records are available from October 1908 on. Records are computerized since 1930. New records are available for inquiry immediately. Records are indexed on microfiche, inhouse computer.

Searching: Records are open to the public. Include the following in your request-full name, date of death, place of death, copy of ID of requester. Also, daytime phone number.

Access by: mail, phone, fax, in person.

Fee & Payment: Fee is $10.00 per record. Fee payee: Oklahoma State Health Department. Prepayment required. Personal checks accepted. No credit cards accepted.

Mail search: Turnaround time: 1 to 2 weeks. A SASE is requested.

Phone search: See expedited service.

Fax search: See expedited service.

In person search: Turnaround time is while you wait.

Expedited service: Expedited service is available for fax and phone searches. Turnaround time: 1-2 days. Add $17.00 for express delivery. Use of credit card required, for an additional $10.95 fee.

Marriage Certificates, Divorce Records

Records not maintained by a state level agency.

Marriage and Divorce records are found at county level. The record should be requested from the county courthouse in the county where the marriage or divorce was filed or granted.

Workers' Compensation Records

Workers Compensation Court, Records, 1915 N Stiles Ave, Oklahoma City, OK 73105-4918; 405-522-8600, 405-522-8640 (Records Dept), 800-269-5353 (Enforcement), 405-552-6471-Fax; 8AM-5PM.

www.owcc.state.ok.us

Records are available since 1989 on computer. Index to case files are on print-outs and cards since the 1930's. It takes one day before new records are available for inquiry. Records are normally destroyed after ten years.

Searching: Claims information is considered public record. Anyone having a correct case number can access and review files. There are 2 searches involved-1st to get case number, then to do search. Any requests must be on their forms. Pending cases are available. Include the following in your request-claimant name, Social Security Number, claim number, date of birth, date of accident. To get the claim number, send a written request (Attn: Prior Claims) on their "Request for Information Form," and they will notify you of the case number. With a case number, you can request copies, but you must use their form.

Access by: mail, in person.

Fee & Payment: Using their "Request for Information Form" (index card), include a $1.00 search fee to get the case number, unless you are statutorily exempt. The copy fee is $1.00 for the first page and $.50 each add'l page if done by staff; $.25 if by searcher. Fee payee: Workers' Compensation Court. Prepayment required. In-state businesses can set up charge accounts for copies only; payment due within 30 days. Personal checks accepted. No credit cards accepted.

Mail search: Turnaround time: 5 days. Frequent requesters should set up an account. If payment not included, party will be billed and funds must be received before documents are mailed. A SASE is requested.

In person search: One may search on the in-house computer in the basement level and also request and review a file ($1.00 per file). Files are pulled for the public from 8:15AM to 4:45PM.

Other access: PDF versions of most forms are available at the website.

Driver Records

MVR Desk, Records Management Division, PO Box 11415, Oklahoma City, OK 73136-0415 (Courier address: 3600 Martin Luther King Blvd, Rm 206, Oklahoma City, OK 73111); 405-425-2262, 8AM-4:45PM.

www.dps.state.ok.us/dls/default.htm

Copies of tickets may be obtained for $.25 per page from the address listed above. Most tickets are two pages. For certification of copies, add $3.00.

Records are available for 3 years for moving violations, DWIs and suspensions. All violations, except speeding less than ten mph over the limit, appear on the driving record. Accidents are reported if there is a conviction of citation. It takes 10 days to 6 months before new records are available for inquiry.

Searching: Information is available for law enforcement purposes. Anyone else requesting an MVR for another person is required to submit a

consent to release records form signed by both parties. Ask for a State of Oklahoma Records Request Form. Include the following in your request-full name and date of birth, or driver's license number. Requesters can also visit "local tag agencies" to obtain record information. The following data is not released: medical records, Social Security Numbers, addresses or personal information (height, weight, sex, eye color, etc.).

Access by: mail, in person, online.

Fee & Payment: The fee is $10.00 per driving record. There is a full fee for a no record found. Online access is slightly higher ($12.50). Fee payee: Department of Public Safety. Prepayment required. Personal checks not accepted. No credit cards accepted.

Mail search: Turnaround time: 1 week to 10 days. This agency offers a monthly billing system for high volume requesters. A SASE is requested.

In person search: Records may be requested at any Oklahoma Tag Agency statewide. Up to ten requests may be processed in one day or less. Many Tag Agency offices across the state will sell records.

Online search: Online access is available for qualified, approved users through www.youroklahoma.com. This is a batch mode process with plans for interactive service in the future. The $12.50 fee includes a $2.50 service fee. For further information, call 800-955-3468.

Vehicle Ownership
Vehicle Identification
Vessel Ownership
Vessel Registration

Oklahoma Tax Commission, Motor Vehicle Division, Attn: Research, 2501 N Lincoln Blvd, Oklahoma City, OK 73194; 405-521-3770, 7:30AM-4:30PM.

www.oktax.state.ok.us/mvhome.html

Records are available for 3 years (registration records); the state keeps title records internally for 20 years. All watercraft must be titled and registered. All motors in excess of 10 HP must be titled. Lien information appears on title records. It takes 2 up to 5 weeks before new records are available for inquiry.

Searching: Records are not released to casual requesters. Approved requesters must use the Vehicle Information Request Form 769 completed front and back. (available at web page) Name searches are not performed. The title number, VIN or current plate number is needed for a search. Actual signature on each form required.

Access by: mail, in person.

Fee & Payment: Current ownership/lienholder data is $1.00. A computer generated title history is $5.00 (models 1992 & newer), a microfilm title history is $7.50, and a certified microfilm title history is $10.00. Fee payee: Oklahoma Tax Commission, MVD. Prepayment required. Personal checks accepted. No credit cards accepted.

Mail search: Turnaround time: 7 to 10 days.

In person search: Turnaround time is while you wait, depending on the workload.

Other access: Oklahoma does not offer bulk delivery of vehicle and ownership information except for purposes such as vehicle recall.

Accident Reports

Department of Public Safety, Records Management Division, PO Box 11415, Oklahoma City, OK 73136 (Courier address: 3600 Martin Luther King Blvd, Room 206, Oklahoma City, OK 73111); 405-425-2192, 405-425-2046-Fax; 8AM-4:45PM.

www.dps.state.ok.us

This agency refers to these reports as Collision Reports. Reports are held 60 days before release to the public.

Records are available for 3 years to present. It takes 10 to 14 days before new records are available for inquiry. Records are indexed on inhouse computer.

Searching: Include the following in your request-date of accident, location of accident, full name, county. Qualified requesters include those uses listed under DPPA and members of the media.

Access by: mail, phone, in person.

Fee & Payment: The fee is $7.00 for an uncertified copy and $10.00 for a certified copy. There is no charge for a no record found. Fee payee: Department of Public Safety. Prepayment required. Personal checks accepted. No credit cards accepted.

Mail search: Turnaround time: 24 hours. A SASE is requested.

Phone search: No fee for telephone request. This agency will reveal whether there is an accident over the phone. No other information will be revealed over the phone.

In person search: Normal turnaround time is while you wait.

Voter Registration

State Election Board, PO Box 53156, Oklahoma City, OK 73152 (Courier address: State Capitol-Rm B6, Oklahoma City, OK 73105); 405-521-2391, 405-521-6457-Fax; 8AM-5PM.

www.elections.state.ok.us

Records are available for 4 years. It takes 7 to 10 days before new records are available for inquiry.

Searching: Records are open to the public and can be accessed at both the state and county levels. Include the following in your request-subject name, address and DOB. The following data is not released: phone numbers.

Access by: mail, phone, fax, in person, online.

Fee & Payment: There is no fee for look-ups. Fee payee: OK State Election Board Certified funds or cashier's checks are preferred for database sales. A 2-week hold is placed on order paid for using personal check. No credit cards accepted.

Mail search: Turnaround time: 2 to 5 days. No SASE is required.

Phone search: Limited information is given, depending on staff availability.

Fax search: Same criteria as mail search.

In person search: Simple requests may be processed while you wait.

Online search: A searchable online database is not available, but requests may be emailed to elections@oklaosf.state.ok.us.

Other access: A statewide database can be purchased on CD for a fee of $150. Large counties are available on CD for $50-75, and smaller counties or precincts or district are available on disk for $10-35.

GED Records

State Dept of Education, Lifelong Learning, 2500 N Lincoln Blvd, Rm 115, Oklahoma City, OK 73105; 405-521-3321, 405-522-5394 (Fax) .

http://sde.state.ok.us

Searching: To search, all of the following is required: name, approximate year of test, date of birth, and SSN.

Access by: mail, phone, fax, in person.

Fee & Payment: There is no fee for a verification. There is a $5.00 fee to obtain a transcript, each additional duplicate is $5.00. Fee payee: State Dept of Education. Prepayment required. Money orders and business checks are accepted. No credit cards accepted.

Mail search: Turnaround time: 1 to 2 days. No SASE is required, but helpful.

Phone search: This is for verification only.

Fax search: The will accept requests for verifications only, not for transcripts.

In person search: Turnaround time is typically 30 minutes for verification.

Hunting and Fishing License Information

Access to Records is Restricted.

Department of Wildlife Conservation, Fish & Game Records, PO Box 53465, Oklahoma City, OK 73152; 405-521-3852, 405-521-6535-Fax; 8AM-4:30PM.

www.wildlifedepartment.com

They have a central database, but do not release information to the public.

Oklahoma State Licensing Agencies

For details about the agency responsible for licensing/certifying/registering an item below or in the Agency Quick Finder section, match an item's number with the number of the agency in the *Licensing Agency Information* section.

Oklahoma Licenses Searchable Online

Accounting Firm #15....................................www.youroklahoma.com/oab/search.php
Alarm Company/Company Employee #37 .www.health.state.ok.us/program/ol/OklahomaLicensedAlarmCompanies.pdf
Architect #23...www.youroklahoma.com/architects/search.php?searchtype=0
Athletic Trainer/Apprentice #8 ....www.okmedicalboard.org/display.php?content=md_search_advanced:md_search_advanced
Attorney #28 ....www.oklahomafindalawyer.com/find
Audiologist #6 ....www.obespa.state.ok.us/License%20Data.htm
Bank #35 ....www.state.ok.us/~osbd/
Consumer Finance Company #20..............www.okdocc.state.ok.us/
Credit Services Organization #20...............www.okdocc.state.ok.us/
Credit Union #35..www.state.ok.us/~osbd/
Dental Laboratory #29 ....www.dentist.state.ok.us/lists/index.htm
Dentist/Dental Assistant/Hygenist #29 ....www.dentist.state.ok.us/lists/index.htm
Dietitian/Provisional Dietitian #8 ....www.okmedicalboard.org/display.php?content=md_search_advanced:md_search_advanced
Electrologist #8 ....www.okmedicalboard.org/display.php?content=md_search_advanced:md_search_advanced
Engineer #13 ....www.pels.state.ok.us/roster/index.html
Funeral Home #5.......................................www.okfuneral.com/funeralhomedirectory/index.htm
Health Spa #20..www.okdocc.state.ok.us/
Home Inspector #37 ....www.health.state.ok.us/program/ol/homeinspectorlist.pdf
Investment Company #34...........................www.securities.state.ok.us/_private/DB_Query/Corp_Fin_Search.htm
Landscape Architect #23...........................www.youroklahoma.com/architects/search.php?searchtype=1
Lobbyist #42 ....www.state.ok.us/~ethics/lobbyist.html
Medical Doctor #8......................................www.okmedicalboard.org/display.php?content=md_search_advanced:md_search_advanced
Midwife, Nurse #30...................................www.youroklahoma.com/nursing/verify/
Money Order Agent #35 ....www.state.ok.us/~osbd/
Mortgage Broker #20.................................www.okdocc.state.ok.us/
Notary Public #26 ....https://www.sooneraccess.state.ok.us/notary/notary_search-menu.asp
Nurse Anesthetist / Clinical Specialist #30 ..www.youroklahoma.com/nursing/verify/
Nurse-RN / LPN / Advanced Pract. #30 .....www.youroklahoma.com/nursing/verify/
Occupational Therapist/Assistant #8 ....www.okmedicalboard.org/display.php?content=md_search_advanced:md_search_advanced
Optometrist #7 ....www.arbo.org/index.php?action=findanoptometrist
Orthotist/Prosthetist #8 ....www.okmedicalboard.org/display.php?content=md_search_advanced:md_search_advanced
Osteopathic Physician #10 ....www.docboard.org/ok/df/oksearch.htm
Pawnbroker #20 ....www.okdocc.state.ok.us/
Payday Lender #20 ....www.okdocc.state.ok.us/
Pedorthist #8 ....www.okmedicalboard.org/display.php?content=md_search_advanced:md_search_advanced
Perfusionist #8..www.okmedicalboard.org/display.php?content=md_search_advanced:md_search_advanced
Pesticide Applicator / Dealers #27..............http://kellysolutions.com/ok/
Pesticide Certification/Registration #27......http://kellysolutions.com/ok/
Pharmacy Intern / Technician #11 ....http://lv.pharmacy.state.ok.us/osbpinquire/
Physical Therapist/Assistant #8..................www.okmedicalboard.org/display.php?content=md_search_advanced:md_search_advanced
Physician Assistant #8...............................www.okmedicalboard.org/display.php?content=md_search_advanced:md_search_advanced
Podiatrist #12..www.okmedicalboard.org/display.php?content=md_search_advanced:md_search_advanced
Precious Metals & Gem Dealer #20 ....www.okdocc.state.ok.us/
Private Investigator Person/Agency #19 ....www.opia.com/find_a_pi/default.asp
Prosthetist #8..www.okmedicalboard.org/display.php?content=md_search_advanced:md_search_advanced
Public Accountant-CPA #15 ....www.youroklahoma.com/oab/search.php
Real Estate Agent/Broker/Sales/Corp #38 ..www.orec.state.ok.us/agents2.html
Real Estate Appraiser #33.........................www.asc.gov/content/category1/appr_by_state.asp
Rent to Own Dealer #20 ....www.okdocc.state.ok.us/
Respiratory Care Practitioner #8 ....www.okmedicalboard.org/display.php?content=md_search_advanced:md_search_advanced
Savings & Loan Association #35 ....www.state.ok.us/~osbd/
Speech Pathologist #6...............................www.obespa.state.ok.us/License%20Data.htm
Surveyor, Land #13 ....www.pels.state.ok.us/roster/index.html
Trust Company #35....................................www.state.ok.us/~osbd/

Oklahoma Licensing Quick Finder

Accounting Firm #15	405-521-2397
Advanced Registered Nurse Practitioner #30	405-962-1800
Alarm Company #37	405-271-5217
Alarm Company Employee #37	405-271-5217
Alcohol & Drug Influence Tester #17	405-425-2460
Animal Technician #18	405-524-9006
Architect #23	405-949-2383
Asbestos Abatement Worker #44	405-528-1500 x326
Athletic Trainer/Apprentice #8	405-848-6841 x113
Attorney #28	405-416-7000
Audiologist #6	405-524-4955
Bail Bondsman #32	405-521-6610
Bank #35	405-521-2783
Barber Instructor #37	405-271-5217
Barber Shop #37	405-271-5217
Barber/Barber Apprentice #37	405-271-5217
Beauty School #4	405-521-2441
Beauty Shop/Salon #4	405-521-2441
Blacksmith #31	405-943-6472
Building Inspector #37	405-271-5217
Burglar Alarm Salesman #37	405-271-5217
Burglar Alarm Service/Installer #37	405-271-5217
Cemetery #35	405-521-2783
Certified Nurse Midwife #30	405-962-1800
Certified Registered Nurse Anesthetist #30	405-962-1800
Children & Youth Agency, Private/Public #21	405-521-3561
Chiropractor #3	405-524-6223
Clinical Nurse Specialist #30	405-962-1800
Consumer Finance Company #20	405-521-3653
Cosmetician/Dry Hair Stylist #4	405-521-2441
Cosmetology Instructor #4	405-521-2441
Cosmetology Student/Apprentice #4	405-521-2441
Counselor LPC/LM&T #43	405-271-6030
Credit Services Organization #20	405-521-3653
Credit Union #35	405-521-2783
Dental Hygienist #29	405-524-9037/ 1-866-534-9037
Dental Lab #29	405-524-9037/ 1-866-534-9037
Dentist/Dental Asst #29	405-524-9037/1-866-534-9037
Dietitian/Provisional Dietitian #8	405-848-6841 x113
Electrical Contractor #37	405-271-5217
Electrical Inspector #37	405-271-5217
Electrician, Journeyman #37	405-271-5217
Electrologist #8	405-848-6841 x113
Embalmer #5	405-522-1790
Emergency Medical Technician #37	405-271-4240
Engineer #13	405-521-2874
Facial Operator School/Instructor #4	405-521-2441
Facial Operator/Esthetician #4	405-521-2441
Feed/Seed #27	405-522-5894
Fertilizer #27	405-522-5985
Firearm Permit for Ret'd Police Officer #19	405-425-2484
Forester #16	405-522-6147
Funeral Director #5	405-522-1790
Funeral Home #5	405-522-1790
Ground Water & Observation Water Well Driller #39	405-530-8800
Groundwater Right Permitting #39	405-530-8800
Hairbraider #4	405-521-2441
Health Spa #20	405-521-3653
Hearing Aid Dealer/Fitter #37	405-271-5217
Home Inspector #37	405-271-5217
Horse Racing #31	405-943-6472
Horse Racing Professional #31	405-943-6472
Insurance Adjuster #32	405-521-2828
Insurance Agent/Representative #32	405-521-2828
Insurance Consultant #32	405-521-2828
Investment Adviser #34	405-280-7700
Investment Adviser Rep #34	405-280-7700
Investment Company #34	405-280-7700
Issuer Agent #34	405-280-7700
Jockey / Jockey Agent #31	405-943-6472
Journeyman #36	405-271-5217
Land Sales Agent #34	405-280-7700
Landscape Architect #23	405-949-2383
Liquor Industry #1	405-521-3484
Lobbyist #42	405-521-3451
LPG-Liquefied Petroleum Dealer/Mfg./Mgr #25	405-521-2458
LPG-Liquefied Petroleum System Installer #25	405-521-2458
Manicurist #4	405-521-2441
Mechanical Contractor #36	405-271-5217
Mechanical Inspector #36	405-271-5217
Medical Doctor #8	405-848-6841 x113
Mining Operation #22	405-521-3859
Money Order Agent #35	405-521-2783
Mortgage Broker #20	405-521-3653
Notary Public #26	405-521-2516
Nurse-RN/LPN #30	405-962-1800
Nursery, Plant #27	405-522-5953
Nursing Home Administrator #2	405-521-0991
Occupational Therapist/Assistant #8	405-848-6841 x113
Optometrist #7	405-733-7836
Orthotist/Prosthetist #8	405-848-6841 x113
Osteopathic Physician #10	405-528-8625
Pawnbroker #20	405-521-3653
Payday Lender #20	405-521-3653
Pedorthist #8	405-848-6841 x113
Perfusionist #8	405-848-6841 x113
Pesticide Applicator #27	405-522-5984
Pesticide Certification/Registration #27	405-522-5950
Pesticide Dealers #27	405-522-5984
Pharmacist / Pharmacy #11	405-521-3815
Pharmacy Intern #11	405-521-3815
Pharmacy Technician #11	405-521-3815
Physical Therapist/Assistant #8	405-848-6841 x113
Physician Assistant #8	405-848-6841 x113
Placement Agency #21	405-521-3561
Plumbing Contractor/Inspector #36	405-271-5217
Podiatrist #12	405-848-6841
Police Officer #19	405-425-2755
Polygraph Examiner/Intern #40	405-425-2772
Polygraph Operator #19	405-425-2778
Precious Metals & Gem Dealer #20	405-521-3653
Private Investigator Individual/Agency #19	405-425-2775
Prosthetist #8	405-848-6841 x113
Psychologist #14	405-524-9094
Public Accountant-CPA #15	405-521-2397
Pump Installer #39	405-530-8800
Real Estate Agent/Broker/Sales #38	405-521-3387
Real Estate Appraiser #33	405-521-6636
Real Estate Corp./Partnership #38	405-521-3387
Rent to Own Dealer #20	405-521-3653
Residential Child Care Facility #21	405-521-3561
Respiratory Care Practitioner #8	405-848-6841 x113
Sanitarian/Environmental Special't #37	405-271-5217
Savings & Loan Association #35	405-521-2783
School Accreditation #41	405-521-3301
School Transportation #41	405-521-3301
Securities Broker-Dealer #34	405-280-7700
Security Guard/Agency #19	405-425-2775
Self Defense Act Instructor #19	405-425-2760
Shorthand Reporter #9	405-521-2450
Social Worker #24	405-946-7230
Speech Pathologist #6	405-524-4955
Surface Water Right Permit #39	405-530-8800
Surveyor, Land #13	405-521-2874
Teacher #41	405-521-3301
Trust Company #35	405-521-2783
Veterinarian #18	405-524-9006
Veterinary Technician #18	405-524-9006
Waste Water Operator #36	405-702-1000
Weights & Measures, Agricultural #27	405-522-5870
Well Driller/Monitor #39	405-530-8800

Oklahoma Licensing Agency Information

1 Alcoholic Beverage Laws Enforcement Commission, 4545 N Lincoln Blvd, #270, Oklahoma City, OK 73105; 405-521-3484, Fax: 405-521-6578. www.able.state.ok.us Email: ablecomm@mhs.oklaosf.state.ok.us

2 Board for Nursing Home Administrators, 3033 N Walnut, #100E, Oklahoma City, OK 73105; 405-521-0991, Fax: 405-528-3483. Email: jclark@oklaosf.state.ok.us

3 Board of Chiropractic Examiners, 201 N.E. 38th Terrace, Suite 3, Oklahoma City, OK 73105; 405-524-6223, Fax: 405-524-9542. www.state.ok.us/~chiro/obce.htm Email: bkelly@chiro.state.ok.us

4 Board of Cosmetology, 2401 NW 23rd St #84, Oklahoma City, OK 73107-2431; 405-521-2441, Fax: 405-521-2440. www.state.ok.us/~cosmo

5 Board of Embalmers & Funeral Directors, 4545 N Lincoln Blvd, #175, Oklahoma City, OK 73105; 405-522-1790, Fax: 405-522-1797.

www.okfuneral.com   Email: info@okfuneral.com

6 Board of Examiners for Speech Pathology/Audiology, P.O. Box 53592 (3700 N Classen Blvd, #248, 73118), Oklahoma City, OK 73152-3592; 405-524-4955, Fax: 405-524-4985. www.obespa.state.ok.us Email: obespa@oklaosf.state.ok.us   Search Database at www.obespa.state.ok.us/License%20Data.htm

7 Board of Examiners in Optometry, 6912 E Reno Ave #302, Midwest City, OK 73110-2162; 405-733-7836, Fax: 405-741-3060. www.state.ok.us/~optometry Email: optboard@oklaosf.state.ok.us Search Database at www.arbo.org/index.php?action=findanoptometrist

8 Board of Medical Licensure & Supervision, 5104 N Francis, #C (POB 18256 OK, OK 73154), Oklahoma City, OK 73118-0256; 405-848-6841 x113, Fax: 405-848-8240. www.okmedicalboard.org/index.php Email: licensing@okmedicalboard.org Search Database at www.okmedicalboard.org/index.php ("Find a Doctor")

9 Board of Official Shorthand Reporters, 1915 N Stiles, Rm 305, Oklahoma City, OK 73105; 405-521-2450, Fax: 405-521-9688. www.oscn.net

10 Board of Osteopathic Examiners, 4848 N Lincoln, #100, Oklahoma City, OK 73105; 405-528-8625, Fax: 405-557-0653. www.docboard.org/ok/ok.htm Search Database at www.docboard.org/ok/df/oksearch.htm

11 Oklahoma Board of Pharmacy, 4545 N Lincoln Blvd #112, Oklahoma City, OK 73105-3488; 405-521-3815, Fax: 405-521-3758.
www.pharmacy.state.ok.us/
Email: pharmacy@oklaosf.state.ok.us

12 Board of Podiatry, 5104 N Francis, #C, Oklahoma City, OK 73154-0256;
405-848-6841, Fax: 405-848-8240.
Email: executive@osbmis.state.ok.us
Search Database at
www.okmedicalboard.org/display.php?content=md_search_advanced:md_search_advanced Note: May purchase information on discs or hardcopy.

13 Board of Professional Engineers & Land Surveyors, 201 NE 27th St, Oklahoma City, OK 73105; 405-521-2874, Fax: 405-523-2135.
www.pels.state.ok.us
Email: okpels@pels.state.ok.us
Search Database at
www.pels.state.ok.us/roster/index.html

14 Board of Psychologists Examiners, 201 NE 38th Terr #3, Oklahoma City, OK 73105; 405.524.9094.
www.youroklahoma.com/agencies/contact.php?page=135

15 Board of Public Accountancy, 4545 N Lincoln Blvd, #165, Oklahoma City, OK 73105; 405-521-2397, Fax: 405-521-3118.
www.youroklahoma.com/oab/
Email: okaccybd@oklaosf.state.ok.us
Search Database at
www.youroklahoma.com/oab/search.php

16 Board of Registration for Foresters, 2800 N Lincoln Blvd, Agriculture Bldg, Oklahoma City, OK 73105-4298; 405-522-6147,
Fax: 405-522-4583.
Email: kurt@oda.state.ok.us Note: Will provide list of registered foresters.

17 Board of Tests for Alcohol & Drug Influence, PO Box 11415, Oklahoma City, OK 73136-0415; 405-425-2460, Fax: 405-425-2490.
www.youroklahoma.com/bot/
Email: msample@dos.state.ok.us

18 Board of Veterinary Medical Examiners, 201 NE 38th Terr. #1, Oklahoma City, OK 73105; 405-524-9006, Fax: 405-524-9012.
www.okvetboard.com
Email: information@okvetboard.com

19 Council on Law Enforcement Education & Training, 3530 N Martin Luther King Ave, Oklahoma City, OK 73136-0476; 405-425-2750, Fax: 405-425-2773.
www.cleet.state.ok.us
Email: nfloyd@cleet.state.ok.us

20 Department of Consumer Credit, 4545 N Lincoln Blvd, #104, Oklahoma City, OK 73105; 405-521-3653, Fax: 405-521-6740.
www.okdocc.state.ok.us/
Email: kbanks@okdocc.state.ok.us
Search Database at www.okdocc.state.ok.us/

21 Department of Human Services, PO Box 25352, Oklahoma City, OK 73125; 405-521-3561, Fax: 405-522-2564.
www.okdhs.org/childcare/

22 Department of Mines, Mining Commission, 4040 N Lincoln, #107, Oklahoma City, OK 73105; 405-521-3859, Fax: 405-427-9646.
www.odl.state.ok.us/sginfo/oksg/ok_mines.htm

23 Board of Governors/Licensed Architects & Landscape Architects, PO Box 53430 (3555 NW 58th St #640), Oklahoma City, OK 73152; 405-949-2383, Fax: 405-949-1690.
www.youroklahoma.com/architects/

24 Licensed Social Workers Registration Board, 5104 North Francis, Suite E, Oklahoma City, OK 73112; 405-946-7230, Fax: 405-942-1070.
www.state.ok.us/~osblsw/
Email: socialwork@oswb.state.ok.us

25 Liquefied Petroleum Gas Board, 2101 N Lincoln Blvd, Jim Thorpe Bldg, Rm B-45, Oklahoma City, OK 73105-4990; 405-521-2458, Fax: 405-521-6037.
Email: lpgasinfo@lpgas.state.ok.us

26 Office of Secretary of State, Notary Public Department, 2300 N. Lincoln Blvd., Suite 101, Oklahoma City, OK 73105; 405-521-2516, Fax: 405-522-3555.
www.sos.state.ok.us
Email: mary.a.watts@oklaosf.state.ok.us
Search Database at
https://www.sooneraccess.state.ok.us/notary/notary_search-menu.asp

27 Department of Agriculture, Food & Forestry, Plant Industry & Comsumer Services Division, 2800 N Lincoln Blvd, Oklahoma City, OK 73105-4298; 405-521-3864, Fax: 405-922-0909.
www.oda.state.ok.us/pics-home.htm

28 Bar Association, Attorney Certification, 1901 Lincoln Blvd, Oklahoma City, OK 73105; 405-416-7000, Fax: 405-524-7001.
www.okbar.org
Email: jennyg@okbar.org
Search Database at
www.oklahomafindalawyer.com/find Note: They sell labels @ $.15 per name.

29 Board of Dentistry, 201 N.E. 38th Terr, #2, Oklahoma City, OK 73105; 405-524-9037, Fax: 405-524-2223.
www.state.ok.us/~dentist/
Email: dentist@oklaosf.state.ok.us
Search Database at
www.dentist.state.ok.us/lists/index.htm

30 Board of Nursing, 2915 N Classen Blvd, #524, Oklahoma City, OK 73106;
405-962-1800, Fax: 405-962-1821.
www.youroklahoma.com/nursing/
Email: oklahoma@ncsbn.org
Search Database at
www.youroklahoma.com/nursing/verify/

31 Horse Racing Commission, 2401 NW 23rd St, #78, Oklahoma City, OK 73107; 405-943-6472, Fax: 405-943-6474.
www.state.ok.us/~ohrc
Email: ohrc@socket.net

32 Insurance Department, PO Box 53408 (2401 N.W. 23 St #28), Oklahoma City, OK 73152-3408; 405-521-2828, Fax: 405-521-6652.
www.oid.state.ok.us Note: Tulsa office is 3105 E. Skelly Dr #305, Tulsa OK 74105, 918/747-7700.

33 Real Estate Appraiser Board, PO Box 53408, Oklahoma City, OK 73152-3408; 405-521-6636, Fax: 405-522-6909.
www.oid.state.ok.us/agentbrokers/index.html
Email: reab@insurance.state.ok.us

34 Securities Commission, Department of Securities, 120 N Robinson, 1st National Center #860, Oklahoma City, OK 73102; 405-280-7700, Fax: 405-280-7742.
www.securities.state.ok.us
Email: jku@securities.state.ok.us

35 Banking Department, 4545 N Lincoln Blvd, #164, Oklahoma City, OK 73105-3427; 405-521-2782, Fax: 405-522-2993.
www.state.ok.us/~osbd
Search Database at www.state.ok.us/~osbd

36 Department of Environmental Quality, 707 N Robinson, Oklahoma City, OK 73102; 405-702-1000, Fax: 405-702-1001.
www.deq.state.ok.us/

37 Department of Health, Occupational Licensing, 1000 NE 10th St, Oklahoma City, OK 73117-1299; 405-271-5600, Fax: 405-271-5254.
www.health.state.ok.us
Email: rockym@health.state.ok.us
Search Database at
www.health.state.ok.us/program/ol/info.html

38 Real Estate Commission, 2401 NW 23rd St #18, Oklahoma City, OK 73107; 405-521-3387, Fax: 405-521-2189.
www.orec.state.ok.us
Email: orec.help@orec.state.ok.us
Search Database at
www.orec.state.ok.us/agents2.html

39 Water Resources Board, 3800 N Classen Blvd, Oklahoma City, OK 73118; 405-530-8800, Fax: 405-530-8900.
www.owrb.state.ok.us

40 Polygraph Examiners Board, PO Box 11476, Oklahoma City, OK 73136-0476; 405-425-2778, Fax: 405-425-7314.

41 Department of Education, 2500 N Lincoln Blvd, Oklahoma City, OK 73105-4599; 405-521-3301, Fax: 405-521-6205.
www.sde.state.ok.us/home/defaultie.html

42 Ethics Commission, Lobbyist Registration, Sec. of State, 2300 N Lincoln Blvd, RM B5, Oklahoma City, OK 73105-4812; 405-521-3451, Fax: 405-521-4905.
www.ethics.state.ok.us/
Search Database at
www.state.ok.us/~ethics/lobbyist.html

43 Department of Health, Professional Counselor Licensing, 1000 NE 10th, Oklahoma City, OK 73117-1299; 405-271-6030, Fax: 405-271-1918.
www.health.state.ok.us

44 Department of Labor, Asbestos Division, 4001 N Lincoln Blvd, Oklahoma City, OK 73105-5212; 405-528-1500, Fax: 405-528-3412.
www.state.ok.us/~okdol/asbestos/asbestos%20FAQ.htm

Oklahoma Federal Courts

The following list indicates the district and division name for each county in the state. If the bankruptcy court location is different from the district court, then the location of the bankruptcy court appears in parentheses.

Oklahoma County/Court Cross Reference

County	District	Court
Adair	Eastern	Muskogee (Okmulgee)
Alfalfa	Western	Oklahoma City
Atoka	Eastern	Muskogee (Okmulgee)
Beaver	Western	Oklahoma City
Beckham	Western	Oklahoma City
Blaine	Western	Muskogee (Okmulgee)
Bryan	Eastern	Muskogee (Okmulgee)
Caddo	Western	Oklahoma City
Canadian	Western	Oklahoma City
Carter	Eastern	Muskogee (Okmulgee)
Cherokee	Eastern	Muskogee (Okmulgee)
Choctaw	Eastern	Muskogee (Okmulgee)
Cimarron	Western	Oklahoma City
Cleveland	Western	Oklahoma City
Coal	Eastern	Muskogee (Okmulgee)
Comanche	Western	Oklahoma City
Cotton	Western	Oklahoma City
Craig	Northern	Tulsa
Creek	Northern	Tulsa
Custer	Western	Oklahoma City
Delaware	Northern	Tulsa
Dewey	Western	Oklahoma City
Ellis	Western	Oklahoma City
Garfield	Western	Oklahoma City
Garvin	Western	Oklahoma City
Grady	Western	Oklahoma City
Grant	Western	Oklahoma City
Greer	Western	Oklahoma City
Harmon	Western	Oklahoma City
Harper	Western	Oklahoma City
Haskell	Eastern	Muskogee (Okmulgee)
Hughes	Eastern	Muskogee (Okmulgee)
Jackson	Western	Oklahoma City
Jefferson	Western	Oklahoma City
Johnston	Eastern	Muskogee (Okmulgee)
Kay	Western	Oklahoma City
Kingfisher	Western	Oklahoma City
Kiowa	Western	Oklahoma City
Latimer	Eastern	Muskogee (Okmulgee)
Le Flore	Eastern	Muskogee (Okmulgee)
Lincoln	Western	Oklahoma City
Logan	Western	Oklahoma City
Love	Eastern	Muskogee (Okmulgee)
Major	Western	Oklahoma City
Marshall	Eastern	Muskogee (Okmulgee)
Mayes	Northern	Tulsa
McClain	Western	Oklahoma City
McCurtain	Eastern	Muskogee (Okmulgee)
McIntosh	Eastern	Muskogee (Okmulgee)
Murray	Eastern	Muskogee (Okmulgee)
Muskogee	Eastern	Muskogee (Okmulgee)
Noble	Western	Oklahoma City
Nowata	Northern	Tulsa
Okfuskee	Eastern	Muskogee (Okmulgee)
Oklahoma	Western	Oklahoma City
Okmulgee	Eastern	Muskogee (Okmulgee)
Osage	Northern	Tulsa
Ottawa	Northern	Tulsa
Pawnee	Northern	Tulsa
Payne	Western	Oklahoma City
Pittsburg	Eastern	Muskogee (Okmulgee)
Pontotoc	Eastern	Muskogee (Okmulgee)
Pottawatomie	Western	Oklahoma City
Pushmataha	Eastern	Muskogee (Okmulgee)
Roger Mills	Western	Oklahoma City
Rogers	Northern	Tulsa
Seminole	Eastern	Muskogee (Okmulgee)
Sequoyah	Eastern	Muskogee (Okmulgee)
Stephens	Western	Oklahoma City
Texas	Western	Oklahoma City
Tillman	Western	Oklahoma City
Tulsa	Northern	Tulsa
Wagoner	Eastern	Muskogee (Okmulgee)
Washington	Northern	Tulsa
Washita	Western	Oklahoma City
Woods	Western	Oklahoma City
Woodward	Western	Oklahoma City

Standards for Federal Courts: Search fee is $26.00 per item (one party name or case number). Copy fee is $.50 per page. Certification fee is $9.00 per document, double for exemplification, if available. All fees standard unless noted in profile. Mail Search: always enclose a stamped self addressed envelope unless otherwise noted. Most courts accept fax requests or will suggest a copying/search vendor. Before releasing records, all courts require prepayment, unless noted.

Open records are located at the court unless otherwise noted. District courts index by defendant and plaintiff as well as by case number. Bankruptcy courts usually index by debtor and case number. While most courts now have their indexes on computer, many may still maintain index card files as well.

Courts offering internet access via CM-ECF or older RACER, PACER, or Web-PACER systems charge $.08 per page fee unless noted as free. Where PACER is available, the universal sign-up number is 800-676-6856. Find PACER and the US Party/Case Index at http://pacer.psc.uscourts.gov.

US District Court

Eastern District of Oklahoma

Muskogee Division Clerk of Court, PO Box 607, Muskogee, OK 74401 (courier address: 101 N 5th, Rm 208, Muskogee, OK 74401), 918-684-7920, Fax-918-684-7902. Hours- 8AM-4:30PM. www.oked.uscourts.gov

Counties: Adair, Atoka, Bryan, Carter, Cherokee, Choctaw, Coal, Haskell, Hughes, Johnston, Latimer, Le Flore, Love, McCurtain, McIntosh, Marshall, Murray, Muskogee, Okfuskee, Okmulgee, Pittsburg, Pontotoc, Pushmataha, Seminole, Sequoyah, Wagoner.

Searches & Indexing: Results do not include SSN or DOB. Both computer and card indexes maintained; criminal index back to 1994, civil to 1992. New cases in the index 1 day after filing date. Records purged never.

Fee & Payment: Pay by money order, cashier check, business check. No personal checks. Payee: Clerk, US District Court. Will bill law firms.

Phone Search: Only docket information is available by phone.

Mail Search: search usually completed- 2-3 weeks. SASE not required.

In Person Search: Fee charged if court performs your search. Self-serve copier - $.50 per page.

E-Services: PACER online at http://pacer.oked.uscourts.gov. PACER toll-free: 866-863-3767. PACER local phone: 918-687-2166. PACER records go back to 1996. New records online after 1 day. ECF at https://ecf.oked.uscourts.gov

US Bankruptcy Court

Eastern District of Oklahoma

Okmulgee Division Court Clerk, PO Box 1347, Okmulgee, OK 74447 (courier address: PO & Federal Bldg, 111 W 4th St, Rm 229, Okmulgee, OK 74447), 918-758-0126, Fax-918-756-9248. Hours- 8:30AM-4:30PM. www.okeb.uscourts.gov

Counties: Adair, Atoka, Bryan, Carter, Cherokee, Choctaw, Coal, Haskell, Hughes, Johnston, Latimer, Le Flore, Love, Marshall, McCurtain, McIntosh, Murray, Muskogee, Okfuskee, Okmulgee, Pittsburg, Pontotoc, Pushmataha, Seminole, Sequoyah, Wagoner.

Searches & Indexing: Results include last 4 SSN digits. Computer index maintained. New cases in the index immediately after filing date. Records purged every 6 months.

Fee & Payment: Pay by money order, cashier's or personal check. No debtor's checks accepted. Payee: Clerk, US Bankruptcy Court. Prepayment required. Will fax back $2.00 per page.

Phone Search: Only docket information available by phone. Voice Case Information Service available, call 877-377-1221 or 918-756-8617.

Mail Search: search usually completed- 1-2 days. Include SASE for return.

In Person Search: Fee charged if court performs your search. No self-serve copier available.

E-Services: ECF replaces PACER whose records did go back to 1986. New records online after 1 day. ECF at https://ecf.okeb.uscourts.gov. Document images available. **Other Online Access:** Calendars available free http://pacer.okeb.uscourts.gov/calendars.html

US District Court

Northern District of Oklahoma

Tulsa Division Court Clerk, 411 US Courthouse, 333 W 4th St, Tulsa, OK 74103 (also use mail address for courier delivery), 918-699-4700, Fax-918-699-4756. Hours- 8:30AM-4:30PM. www.oknd.uscourts.gov

Counties: Craig, Creek, Delaware, Mayes, Nowata, Osage, Ottawa, Pawnee, Rogers, Tulsa, Washington.

Searches & Indexing: Results do not include SSN or DOB. Computer index maintained. New cases in the index immediately after filing date.

Fee & Payment: Pay by Visa/MC (in person only), money order, cashier's or personal check,

cash. Payee: Clerk, US District Court. Prepayment required.

Phone Search: Only docket information is available by phone.

Mail Search: search usually completed- 1-2 days. Include SASE for return.

In Person Search: Fee charged if court performs your search. Self-serve copier - $.10 per page.

E-Services: PACER online at www.oknd.uscourts.gov/perl/bkplog.html. PACER records go back to 1992. New records online after 1 day. ECF at https://ecf.oknd.uscourts.gov. Electronic filings began 2/2005.

US Bankruptcy Court

Northern District of Oklahoma

Tulsa Division Court Clerk, 224 S Boulder Ave #105, Tulsa, OK 74103 (also use mail address for courier delivery), phone- 918-699-4000, Fax-918-699-4045. Hours- 8:30AM-4:30PM. www.oknb.uscourts.gov

Counties: Craig, Creek, Delaware, Mayes, Nowata, Osage, Ottawa, Pawnee, Rogers, Tulsa, Washington.

Searches & Indexing: Results include last 4 SSN digits only. Both computer and card indexes maintained. New cases in the index same day if possible after filing date. Records purged never. District-wide searches available here.

Fee & Payment: Pay by money order, cashier's or personal check. No debtor's checks accepted. Payee: Clerk, US Bankruptcy Court. Prepayment required. Will fax back results for fee.

Phone Search: Limited docket info given by phone, and only if it takes a minimum amount of time. Voice Case Information Service available, call VCIS at 888-501-6977 or 918-699-4001.

Mail Search: search usually completed- 2 days. SASE required.

In Person Search: Fee charged if court performs your search.

E-Services: ECF replaces PACER whose records did go back to 1990. New records online after 1 day. ECF at https://ecf.oknb.uscourts.gov. Document images available 1998-present. **Other Online Access:** WebPACER at www.oknb.uscourts.gov/perl/bkplog.html. Racer system data has a 24-hour lag time; WebPACER does not. Also search judgment book free at www.oknb.uscourts.gov/court_information/judgment/judgments.htm. Search opinions and calendars by judge name free at main website.

US District Court

Western District of Oklahoma

Oklahoma City Division Clerk of Court, Rm 1210, 200 NW 4th St, Oklahoma City, OK 73102 (also use mail address for courier delivery), 405-609-5000, records rm- 405-609-5029, Fax-405-609-5099. Hours- 8:30AM-4:30PM. www.okwd.uscourts.gov

Counties: Alfalfa, Beaver, Beckham, Blaine, Caddo, Canadian, Cimarron, Cleveland,

Comanche, Cotton, Custer, Dewey, Ellis, Garfield, Garvin, Grady, Grant, Greer, Harmon, Jackson, Jefferson, Kay, Kingfisher, Kiowa, Lincoln, Logan, McClain, Major, Noble, Oklahoma, Payne, Pottawatomie, Roger Mills, Stephens, Texas, Tillman, Washita, Woods, Woodward.

Searches & Indexing: Computer and microfiche indexes maintained. New cases in the index immediately after filing date. Records purged never. District-wide searches available here back to 1907.

Fee & Payment: Pay by money order, cashier's or personal check. Payee: Clerk, US District Court.

Phone Search: Information relating to docket entries is given via phone.

Mail Search: search usually completed- 2-3 days. SASE not required.

In Person Search: Fee charged if court performs your search. Self-serve copier - $.10 per page.

E-Services: ECF replaces PACER and RACER. PACER records go back to 1991. ECF at https://ecf.okwd.uscourts.gov

US Bankruptcy Court

Western District of Oklahoma

Oklahoma City Division Court Clerk, 1st Fl, Old Post Office Bldg, 215 Dean A McGee Ave, Oklahoma City, OK 73102 (also use mail address for courier delivery), phone- 405-609-5700, Fax-405-609-5752. Hours- 8:30AM-4:30PM. www.okwb.uscourts.gov

Counties: Alfalfa, Beaver, Beckham, Blaine, Caddo, Canadian, Cimarron, Cleveland, Comanche, Cotton, Custer, Dewey, Ellis, Garfield, Garvin, Grady, Grant, Greer, Harmon, Harper, Jackson, Jefferson, Kay, Kingfisher, Kiowa, Lincoln, Logan, Major, McClain, Noble, Oklahoma, Payne, Pottawatomie, Roger Mills, Stephens, Texas, Tillman, Washita, Woods, Woodward.

Searches & Indexing: Cases also indexed by SSN. Computer index maintained. New cases in the index 24 hours after filing date. Records purged every 6 months.

Fee & Payment: Pay by money order, cashier's or personal check. No debtor's checks accepted. Payee: Clerk, US Bankruptcy Court.

Phone Search: Docket information available by phone. Voice Case Information Service available, call VCIS at 800-872-1348 or 405-231-4768.

Mail Search: search usually completed- same day if possible. Include SASE for return.

In Person Search: Fee charged if court performs your search. No self-serve copier available.

E-Services: No PACER access for this court; free searching available. No PACER access to this court. ECF at https://ecf.okwb.uscourts.gov **Opinions Online:** www.okwb.uscourts.gov:8008/. **Other Online Access:** Internet access to court records is free at www.okcbankr.com; registration and username required. For information, call 405-609-5700 or 405-609-5746. Also, monthly calendars available by judges' names at www.okwb.uscourts.gov/Chambers.htm

Oklahoma County Courts

Court	Jurisdiction	No. of Courts	How Organized
District Courts*	General	82	26 Districts
Municipal Courts of Record	Municipal	2	
Municipal Courts Not of Record	Municipal	340	
Workers' Compensation Court	Special	1	

* Profiled in this Sourcebook.

CIVIL									
Court	Tort	Contract	Real Estate	Min. Claim	Max. Claim	Small Claims	Estate	Eviction	Domestic Relations
District Courts*	X	X	X	$0	No Max	$4500	X	X	X
Municipal Courts of Record									
Municipal Courts Not of Record									
Workers' Compensation Court									

CRIMINAL					
Court	Felony	Misdemeanor	DWI/DUI	Preliminary Hearing	Juvenile
District Courts*	X	X	X	X	X
Municipal Courts of Record			X		
Municipal Courts Not of Record			X		
Workers' Compensation Court					

ADMINISTRATION Administrative Director of Courts, 1915 N Stiles #305, Oklahoma City, OK, 73105; 405-521-2450, Fax: 405-521-6815. www.oscn.net

COURT STRUCTURE There are 82District Courts in 26 judicial districts. Cities with populations in excess of 200,000 (Oklahoma City and Tulsa) have municipal criminal courts of record. Cities with less than 200,000 do not have such courts.

The small claims limit was raised from $3000 to $4500 in 1998.

ONLINE ACCESS Free Internet access is available for District Courts in 12 counties and all Appellate courts at www.oscn.net. Both civil and criminal docket information is available for the counties invoved. Also, search the Oklahoma Supreme Court Network from site.

Case information is available in bulk form for downloading to computer. For information, call the Administrative Director of Courts, 405-521-2450.

Also, the Oklahoma District Court Records free website at www.odcr.com offers searching for over 50 District Courts. More counties are being added as they are readied; they hope to eventually feature all OK District Courts. Please note many of the county records in this system do not go back 7 years.

Adair County

15th Judicial District Court PO Box 426 (220 W Division), Stilwell, OK 74960; phone: 918-696-7633; fax: 918-696-5365; hours 8AM-4:30PM (CST). *Felony, Misdemeanor, Civil, Eviction, Small Claims, Probate.*

Civil Records: Access: Phone, fax, mail, in person. Both court and visitors may perform in person searches. Search fee: $5.00 per name. Fee is for 7 year search. Court makes copy: $1.00 for first page, $.50 each add'l. Required to search: name, years to search. Civil cases indexed by defendant, plaintiff. Civil records archived since 1907. Mail turnaround time 1 day.

Criminal Records: Access: Phone, fax, mail, in person. Both court and visitors may perform in person searches. Search fee: $5.00 per name. Fee is for 7 year search. Court makes copy: $1.00 for first page, $.50 each add'l. Required to search: name, years to search, DOB; also helpful: SSN. Criminal records archived since 1907. Mail turnaround time 1 day.

General Information: No public access terminal. No juvenile, mental health or guardianship records released. Will fax documents to local or toll free line. Certification fee: $.50 per page. Payee: Adair County Court Clerk. Personal checks accepted. Prepayment and SASE required.

Alfalfa County

4th Judicial District Court County Courthouse, 300 S Grand, Cherokee, OK 73728; phone: 580-596-3523; hours 8:30AM-4:30PM (CST). *Felony, Misdemeanor, Civil, Eviction, Small Claims, Probate.*
Civil Records: Access: Mail, in person. Both court and visitors may perform in person searches. Search fee: $5.00 per name. Court makes copy: $1.00 for first page, $.50 each add'l. Required to search: name, years to search. Civil cases indexed by defendant, plaintiff. Civil records archived to 1907; on computer back to 1998. Mail turnaround same day.
Criminal Records: Access: Mail, in person. Both court and visitors may perform in person searches. Search fee: $5.00 per name. Court makes copy: $1.00 for first page, $.50 each add'l. Required to search: name, years to search. Records archived to 1907; on computer back to 1998. Mail turnaround time 1 day.
General Information: Public terminal back to 1998. No confidential or guardianship records released. Fee to fax documents is $4.00 per page; $2.00 each add'l. Certification fee: $.50 per instrument. Payee: Court Clerk. Only cashiers checks and money orders accepted. Prepayment and SASE required.

Atoka County

25th Judicial District Court 200 E Court St, Atoka, OK 74525; phone: 580-889-3565; probate phone: 580-889-3565; hours 8:30AM-4:30PM (CST). *Felony, Misdemeanor, Civil, Eviction, Small Claims, Probate.*
Civil Records: Access: Mail, in person, online. Both court and visitors may perform in person searches. Search fee: $5.00 per name. Court makes copy: $1.00 for first page, $.50 each add'l. Required to search: name, years to search. Civil cases indexed by defendant, plaintiff; on computer back to 1998; prior on books. Free court records from 1/1998 to present online at www.odcr.com; updated monthly. Mail turnaround time 1-2 days.
Criminal Records: Access: Mail, in person, online. Both court and visitors may perform in person searches. Search fee: $5.00 per name. Court makes copy: $1.00 for first page, $.50 each add'l. Required to search: name, years to search, DOB or SSN. Criminal records on books from 1920; on computer back to 1998. Free court records from 1/1998 to present online at www.odcr.com; updated monthly. Mail turnaround time 1-2 days.
General Information: Public terminal goes back to 1998. No adoption, mental health or juvenile records released. Certification fee: $.50 per page. Payee: Court Clerk. Personal checks accepted. Prepayment and SASE required.

Beaver County

1st Judicial District Court PO Box 237 (111 W 2nd), Beaver, OK 73932; phone: 580-625-3191; hours 9AM-5PM (CST). *Felony, Misdemeanor, Civil, Eviction, Small Claims, Probate.*
Civil Records: Access: Phone, mail, in person, online. Both court and visitors may perform in person searches. Search fee: $5.00 per name. Court makes copy: $1.00 for first page, $.50 each add'l. Required to search: name, years to search. Civil cases indexed by defendant, plaintiff; on microfilm and archives from late 1800s, computerized back to 1997. Free court records from 6/1/1997 to present online at www.odcr.com; updated monthly. Mail turnaround time 3 days.
Criminal Records: Access: Mail, in person, online. Both court and visitors may perform in person searches. Search fee: $5.00 per name. Court makes copy: $1.00 for first page, $.50 each add'l. Required to search: name, years to search. Criminal records on microfilm and archives from late 1800s, computerized back to 1997. Free court records from 6/1/1997 to present online at www.odcr.com; updated monthly. Mail turnaround time 1-3 days.

Beckham County

2nd Judicial District Court PO Box 520 (302 E Main St), Sayre, OK 73662; phone: 580-928-3330; fax: 580-928-9278; hours 9AM-5PM (CST). *Felony, Misdemeanor, Civil, Eviction, Small Claims, Probate.*
Civil Records: Access: Fax, mail, in person, online. Both court and visitors may perform in person searches. Search fee: $5.00 per name. Court makes copy: $1.00 for first page, $.50 each add'l; same fee for self serve. Required to search: name, years to search. Civil cases indexed by defendant, plaintiff; on microfiche back to 1907; on computer to 1997. Free record access 01/00 to present at www.odcr.com; updated daily. Mail turnaround time 2 weeks.
Criminal Records: Access: Fax, mail, in person, online. Both court and visitors may perform in person searches. Search fee: $5.00 per name. Court makes copy: $1.00 for first page, $.50 each add'l; same fee for self serve. Required to search: name, years to search. Criminal records on microfiche; on computer back to 1997. Free court records from 1/2000 to present online at www.odcr.com; updated daily. Mail turnaround time 2 weeks.
General Information: Public terminal goes back to 1996. No juvenile, adoption or expunged records released. Fee to fax documents is $1.00 per page. Certification fee: $.50 per page. Payee: Court clerk. Personal checks accepted. Prepayment and SASE required.

Blaine County

4th Judicial District Court 212 N Weigle St, Watonga, OK 73772; phone: 580-623-5970; fax: 580-623-4781; hours 8AM-4PM (CST). *Felony, Misdemeanor, Civil, Eviction, Small Claims, Probate.*
Civil Records: Access: Fax, mail, in person, online. Both court and visitors may perform in person searches. Search fee: $5.00 per name. Court makes copy: $1.00 for first page, $.50 each add'l. Required to search: name, years to search. Civil cases indexed by defendant, plaintiff. Civil records archived from 1900; on computer back to 1998. Free court records from 8/1998 to present online at www.odcr.com; updated daily. Mail turnaround time 7-10 days.
Criminal Records: Access: Fax, mail, in person, online. Both court and visitors may perform in person searches. Search fee: $5.00 per name. Court makes copy: $1.00 for first page, $.50 each add'l. Required to search: name, years to search. Criminal records archived from 1900; on computer back to 1998. Free court records from 8/1998 to present online at www.odcr.com; updated daily. Mail turnaround time 7-10 days.
General Information: Public terminal goes back to 7/1998. No juvenile or expunged records released. Certification fee: $.50 per page. Payee: Court Clerk. Personal checks accepted. Prepayment and SASE required.

Bryan County

19th Judicial District Court Courthouse 3rd Fl, 402 W Evergreen St, Durant, OK 74701; phone: 580-924-1446; hours 8:00AM-12:00PM,1:00PM-5:00PM (CST). *Felony, Misdemeanor, Civil, Eviction, Small Claims, Probate.*
Civil Records: Access: Mail, in person, online. Both court and visitors may perform in person searches. Search fee: $5.00 per name. Court makes copy: $1.00 for first page, $.50 each add'l. Required to search: name, years to search, DOB. Civil cases indexed by defendant, plaintiff. Civil records archived from 1907; on computer back to 1994. Free court records from 7/1/1994 to present online at www.odcr.com; updated daily. Mail turnaround time 2 days.

General Information: Public use terminal available. No adoption, mental health or juvenile records released. Certification fee: $.50 per page. Payee: Court Clerk. Personal checks accepted. Prepayment and SASE required.

Criminal Records: Access: Mail, in person, online. Both court and visitors may perform in person searches. Search fee: $5.00 per name. Court makes copy: $1.00 for first page, $.50 each add'l. Required to search: name, DOB, SSN, signed release. Criminal records archived from 1907; on computer back to 1994. Free court records from 7/1/1994 to present online at www.odcr.com; updated daily. Mail turnaround time 2 days.
General Information: Public terminal goes back to 1994. No juvenile, mental health records released. Certification fee: $.50 per page. Payee: Bryan County Court Clerk. Only cashiers checks, money orders accepted. Prepayment and SASE required.

Caddo County

6th Judicial District Court PO Box 10 (201 W Oklahoma Ave), Anadarko, OK 73005; phone: 405-247-3393; hours 8:30AM-4:30PM (CST). *Felony, Misdemeanor, Civil, Eviction, Small Claims, Probate.*
Civil Records: Access: Mail, in person, online. Both court and visitors may perform in person searches. Search fee: $10.00 per hour. Court makes copy: $1.00 for first page, $.50 each add'l. Required to search: name, years to search. Civil cases indexed by defendant, plaintiff; on computer since 1997; prior on docket books to 1901. Free court records from 1/1997 to present online at www.odcr.com; updated monthly. Mail turnaround time 1 week.
Criminal Records: Access: Mail, in person, online. Both court and visitors may perform in person searches. Search fee: $10.00 per hour. Court makes copy: $1.00 for first page, $.50 each add'l. Required to search: name, years to search. Records on computer since 1997, prior on docket books to 1901. Free court records from 1/1997 to present online at www.odcr.com; updated monthly. Mail turnaround time 1 week.
General Information: Public use terminal available. No adoption, mental health, juvenile, and some guardianship records released. Certification fee: $.50 per page. Payee: Court Clerk. No foreign checks accepted. Prepayment required. SASE helpful.

Canadian County

26th Judicial District Court PO Box 730 (301 N Choctaw St), El Reno, OK 73036; phone: 405-262-1070; hours 8AM-4:30PM (CST). *Felony, Misdemeanor, Civil, Eviction, Small Claims, Probate.* Use ext 167 for civil; 165 for criminal; and 170 for probate.
Civil Records: Access: Mail, online, in person. Both court and visitors may perform in person searches. Search fee: $5.00 per name. Court makes copy: $1.00 for first page, $.50 each add'l. Required to search: name, years to search. Civil cases indexed by defendant, plaintiff; on computer back to 1993, archived from 1907. Access to court dockets free at www.oscn.net/applications/oscn/casesearch.asp. Dockets back to 3/1993. Mail turnaround 2-3 days.
Criminal Records: Access: Mail, online, in person. Both court and visitors may perform in person searches. Search fee: $5.00 per name. Court makes copy: $1.00 for first page, $.50 each add'l. Required to search: name, years to search, DOB or SSN. Criminal records on computer back to 1993, archived from 1907. Online access to criminal dockets is same as civil. Mail turnaround time 2-3 days.
General Information: Public terminal goes back to 1993. No expunged criminal cases, juvenile, adoption records released. Certification fee: $.50 per page. Payee: Court Clerk. Personal checks accepted. Prepayment required.

Carter County

20th Judicial District Court PO Box 37, Court Clerk, First & B Southwest, Court Clerk, Ardmore, OK 73402; phone: 580-223-5253; hours 8AM-N, 1-5PM (CST). *Felony, Misdemeanor, Civil, Eviction, Small Claims, Probate.*
www.brightok.net/cartercounty/CarterCountyCourtClerk.html

Civil Records: Access: Mail, in person. Both court and visitors may perform in person searches. Search fee: $5.00 per name. Court makes copy: $1.00 for first page, $.50 each add'l; same fee for self serve. Required to search: name, years to search. Civil cases indexed by defendant, plaintiff. Civil records archived from 1907; on computer back to 1997. Free court records from 1/1997 to present online at www.odcr.com; updated monthly. Also, only current week dockets are online at clerk's website. Mail turnaround time 2 weeks.

Criminal Records: Access: Mail, in person, online. Both court and visitors may perform in person searches. Search fee: $5.00 per name. Court makes copy: $1.00 for first page, $.50 each add'l; same fee for self serve. Required to search: name, years to search. Criminal records archived from 1907; on computer back to 1997. Free court records from 1/1997 to present online at www.odcr.com; updated monthly. Also, only current week dockets and bench warrants are online at this clerk's website. Mail turnaround time 2 weeks.

General Information: Public terminal goes back to 1997. No juvenile, mental health, or adoption records released. The copy room is filled with Elvis memorabilia. Certification fee: $.50 per page. Payee: Carter County Court Clerk. Personal checks accepted. Prepayment and SASE required.

Cherokee County

15th Judicial District Court 213 W Delaware, Rm 302, Tahlequah, OK 74464; phone: 918-456-0691; fax: 918-458-6587; hours 8AM-4:30PM (CST). *Felony, Misdemeanor, Civil, Eviction, Small Claims, Probate.*

Civil Records: Access: Phone, mail, in person, online. Both court and visitors may perform in person searches. Search fee: $5.00 per name. Court makes copy: $1.00 for first page, $.50 each add'l. Required to search: name, years to search. Civil cases indexed by defendant, plaintiff; on microfiche from 1907 (civil, probate, vital), computerized since 1997. Free court records from 1/1997 to present online at www.odcr.com; updated daily. Mail turnaround time 1-2 days.

Criminal Records: Access: Phone, mail, in person, online. Both court and visitors may perform in person searches. Search fee: $5.00 per name. Court makes copy: $1.00 for first page, $.50 each add'l. Required to search: name, years to search, DOB. Criminal records kept from 1907. Free court records from 1/1997 to present online at www.odcr.com; updated daily. Mail turnaround time 1-2 days.

General Information: Public use terminal available. No juvenile, adoption or mental health released. Certification fee: $.50 per page. Payee: Court Clerk. Personal checks accepted. Prepayment and SASE required.

Choctaw County

17th Judicial District Court 300 E Duke, Hugo, OK 74743; phone: 580-326-7554 & 7555; criminal fax: 580-326-0291; same fax for civil/probate; hours 8AM-4PM (CST). *Felony, Misdemeanor, Civil, Eviction, Small Claims, Probate.*

Civil Records: Access: Phone, fax, mail, in person. Both court and visitors may perform in person searches. Search fee: $10.00 per name. Court makes copy: $1.00 for first page, $.50 each add'l; same fee for self serve. Required to search: name, years to search. Civil cases indexed by defendant, plaintiff. Civil records archived from 1907. Mail turnaround time 1 day.

Criminal Records: Access: Phone, fax, mail, in person. Both court and visitors may perform in person searches. Search fee: $10.00 per name. Court makes copy: $1.00 for first page, $.50 each add'l; same fee for self serve. Required to search: name, years to search, DOB. Criminal records archived from 1907. Mail turnaround time 1 day.

General Information: Public use terminal available. No juvenile, adoption, guardianship, wills or expunged records released. Will fax documents $7.50 fee. Certification fee: $.50 document. Payee: Court Clerk. Personal checks accepted. Prepayment and SASE required.

Cimarron County

1st Judicial District Court PO Box 788, Boise City, OK 73933; phone: 580-544-2221; fax: 580-544-2006; hours 9AM-N,1-5PM (CST). *Felony, Misdemeanor, Civil, Eviction, Small Claims, Probate.*

Civil Records: Access: Phone, mail, in person. Only the court performs in person searches; visitors may not. No search fee. Court makes copy: $1.00 for first page, $.50 each add'l. Required to search: name, years to search. Civil cases indexed by defendant, plaintiff. Civil records archived from 1907; on computer back to 8/2001. Mail turnaround time 1 day.

Criminal Records: Access: Phone, mail, in person. Only the court performs in person searches; visitors may not. No search fee. Court makes copy: $1.00 for first page, $.50 each add'l. Required to search: name, years to search. Criminal records archived from 1907. Mail turnaround time 1 day.

General Information: No public access terminal. No juvenile, adoption or mental health records released. Will fax documents for $1.00 per page. Certification fee: $.50 per page. Payee: Court Clerk. Personal checks accepted. Prepayment required. SASE requested.

Cleveland County

21st Judicial District Court - Civil Branch 200 S Peters, Norman, OK 73069; phone: 405-321-6402; hours 8AM-5PM (CST). *Civil, Eviction, Small Claims, Probate.*

Civil Records: Access: Mail, online, in person. Both court and visitors may perform in person searches. No search fee. Court makes copy: $1.00 for first page, $.50 each add'l. Required to search: name, years to search. Civil cases indexed by defendant, plaintiff; on computer from 1989, on microfiche from 1800s, archived since 1970. Access to court dockets is free at www.oscn.net/applications/oscn/casesearch.asp. Dockets back to 1/1989. Mail turnaround time 8 days.

General Information: Public terminal has only civil records. No expunged, sealed records released. Certification fee: $.50 per page. Payee: Court Clerk. Personal checks accepted. Prepayment and SASE required.

21st Judicial District Court - Criminal 200 S Peters, Norman, OK 73069; phone: 405-321-6402; hours 8AM-5PM (CST). *Felony, Misdemeanor.*

Criminal Records: Access: Mail, online, in person. Both court and visitors may perform in person searches. No search fee. Court makes copy: $1.00 for first page, $.50 each add'l. Required to search: name, years to search. Records computerized from 1989, microfiche from 1800s. Access dockets free at www.oscn.net/applications/oscn/casesearch.asp. Dockets go back to 1/1989. Mail takes 7-10 days.

General Information: Public terminal has only criminal records. No juvenile, adoption, or guardianship records released. Certification fee: $.50 per page. Payee: Cleveland County Court Clerk. Local personal checks accepted. Prepayment required.

Coal County

25th Judicial District Court 4 N Main St, Coalgate, OK 74538; phone: 580-927-2281; hours 8AM-4PM (CST). *Felony, Misdemeanor, Civil, Eviction, Small Claims, Probate.*

Civil Records: Access: Mail, in person. Visitors must perform in person searches themselves. No search fee. Court makes copy: $1.00 for first page, $.50 each add'l. Required to search: name, years to search. Civil cases indexed by defendant, plaintiff. Civil records archived since 1907; computerized back to 1999. Mail turnaround time 2-3 days.

Criminal Records: Access: Mail, in person. Visitors must perform in person searches themselves. No search fee. Court makes copy: $1.00 for first page, $.50 each add'l. Required to search: name, years to search. Criminal records archived since 1907; computerized back to 1999. Mail turnaround time 2-3 days.

General Information: Public use terminal available. No juvenile, adoption, mental health, guardianship, wills or expunged records released. Certification fee: $.50 per page. Certification included in copy fee. Payee: Court Clerk. Only cashiers checks and money orders accepted. Prepayment and SASE required.

Comanche County

5th Judicial District Court 315 SW 5th St, Rm 504, Lawton, OK 73501-4390; criminal phone: 580-355-4017; civil phone: 580-581-4565; hours 8AM-5PM (CST). *Felony, Misdemeanor, Civil, Eviction, Small Claims, Probate.*

Note: Traffic and marriage licenses also handled here. Small claims, licenses, Juvenile phone is 580-250-5093

Civil Records: Access: Phone, mail, online, in person. Only the court performs in person searches; visitors may not. Search fee: $10.00 per name. Court makes copy: $1.00 for 1st page, $.50 each add'l. Required to search: name, years to search. Civil cases indexed by defendant, plaintiff; on computer from 8/88, prior in books to 1901. Online access to court dockets is free at www.oscn.net/applications/oscn/casesearch.asp. Dockets go back to 8/1988. Mail turnaround time 1 day.

Criminal Records: Access: Mail, online, in person. Only the court performs in person searches; visitors may not. Search fee: $10.00 per name. Court makes copy: $1.00 for 1st page, $.50 each add'l. Required to search: name, years to search; also helpful: DOB, SSN. Records computerized from 8/88, prior in books to 1901. Access to court dockets free at www.oscn.net/applications/oscn/casesearch.asp. Dockets go back to 8/1988. Mail turnaround time 1 day.

General Information: No public access terminal. No juvenile, mental health, adoption or some probate records released. Will not fax documents. Certification fee: $.50 per page includes copy fee. Payee: District Court Clerk. Business checks accepted. Prepayment and SASE required.

Cotton County

5th Judicial District Court 301 N Broadway, Walters, OK 73572; phone: 580-875-3029; hours 8AM-4PM (CST). *Felony, Misdemeanor, Civil, Eviction, Small Claims, Probate.*

Civil Records: Access: Mail, in person, online. Both court and visitors may perform in person searches. Search fee: $5.00 per name. Court makes copy: $1.00 for first page, $.50 each add'l. Required to search: name, years to search. Civil cases indexed by defendant, plaintiff. Civil records archived from 1912; computerized back to 1997. Free court records from 1/1997 to present online at www.odcr.com; updated daily. Mail turnaround time 2 days.

Criminal Records: Access: Mail, in person, online. Both court and visitors may perform in person searches. Search fee: $5.00 per name. Court makes copy: $1.00 for first page, $.50 each add'l. Required to search: name, years to search, DOB. Criminal records archived from 1912; computerized back to 1997. Free court records from 1/1997 to present online at www.odcr.com; updated daily. Mail turnaround time 2 days.

General Information: Public terminal goes back to 1997. No adoption, juvenile, and some guardianship records released. Certification fee: $.50 per page. Payee: Court Clerk. Personal checks accepted. Prepayment required.

Craig County

12th Judicial District Court 301 W Canadian, Vinita, OK 74301; phone: 918-256-6451; hours 8:30AM-4:30PM (CST). *Felony, Misdemeanor, Civil, Eviction, Small Claims, Probate.*

Note: SSNs are released to the public on criminal case matters, but not for civil cases.

Civil Records: Access: Mail, in person, online. Both court and visitors may perform in person searches. Search fee: $5.00 per name. Court makes copy: $1.00 for first page, $.50 each add'l; same fee for self serve. Required to search: name, years to search. Civil cases indexed by defendant, plaintiff; on microfilm from 1902; on computer since 4/97. Free court records from 4/1/1997 to present online at www.odcr.com; updated daily. Mail turnaround time 1-3 days.

Criminal Records: Access: Mail, in person, online. Both court and visitors may perform in person searches. Search fee: $5.00 per name. Court makes copy: $1.00 for first page, $.50 each add'l; same fee for self serve. Required to search: name, years to search; also helpful: SSN, DOB, sex. Criminal records on microfilm from 1902; on computer since 4/97. Free court records from 4/1/1997 to present online at www.odcr.com; updated daily. Mail turnaround time 1-3 days.

General Information: Public terminal goes back to 1985. No mental, guardianship, adoption, or juvenile records released. Certification fee: $.50 per page includes copy fee. Payee: Court Clerk. Personal checks accepted. Prepayment and SASE required.

Creek County

24th Judicial District Court - Sapulpa 222 E Dewey Ave, #201, Sapulpa, OK 74066; phone: 918-227-2525; criminal fax: 918-227-5030; same fax for civil/probate; hours 8AM-5PM (CST). *Felony, Misdemeanor, Civil, Eviction, Small Claims, Probate.*

Note: All three courts in this county should be searched, there is not overall countywide database.

Civil Records: Access: In person, online. Visitors must perform in person searches themselves. Court makes copy: $1.00 for first page, $.50 each add'l. Required to search: name, years to search; also helpful: address. Civil cases indexed by defendant, plaintiff. Computerized records back to 1998, civil records on docket books and files back to 1907. Free court records from 3/1998 to present online at www.odcr.com; updated daily.

Criminal Records: Access: In person, online. Visitors must perform in person searches themselves. No search fee. Court makes copy: $1.00 for first page, $.50 each add'l. Required to search: name, years to search; also helpful: address, DOB, SSN. Criminal records on docket books and files. They go back "many years, no exact date known". Free court records from 3/1998 to present online at www.odcr.com; updated daily.

General Information: Public use terminal available. No juvenile, mental health, or adoption records released. Will not fax documents. Certification fee: $.50 per page. Payee: Creek County Court Clerk. Personal checks accepted. Prepayment required.

24th Judicial District Court - Bristow PO Box 1055, Bristow, OK 74010; phone: 918-367-5537; fax: 918-367-5055; hours 8AM-5PM (CST). *Felony, Misdemeanor, Civil, Eviction, Small Claims, Probate.*

Note: All three courts in this county should be searched, there is not overall countywide database.

Civil Records: Access: In person, mail, online. Both court and visitors may perform in person searches. Court makes copy: $1.00 for first page, $.50 each add'l. Required to search: name, years to search; also helpful: address. Civil cases indexed by defendant, plaintiff. Computerized records back to Computerized records back to 1998, civil records on docket books and files back to 1907. Free court records from 10/25/1999 to present online at www.odcr.com; updated daily. Mail turnaround time 1-2 days.

Criminal Records: Access: In person, mail, online. Both court and visitors may perform in person searches. Court makes copy: $1.00 for first page, $.50 each add'l. Required to search: name, years to search; also helpful: address, DOB, SSN. Criminal records on docket books and files. They go back "many years, no

exact date known". Free court records from 10/25/1999 to present online at www.odcr.com; updated daily. Mail turnaround time 1-2 days.

General Information: No public access terminal. No juvenile, mental health, or adoption records released. Certification fee: $.50 per page. Payee: Creek County Court Clerk. Personal checks accepted. Prepayment required.

24th Judicial District Court - Drumright PO Box 1118, Drumright, OK 74030; phone: 918-352-2575; hours 8AM-5PM (CST). *Felony, Misdemeanor, Civil, Eviction, Small Claims, Probate.*

Note: All three courts in this county should be searched, there is not overall countywide database.

Civil Records: Access: In person, mail, online. Visitors must perform in person searches themselves. Court makes copy: $1.00 for first page, $.50 each add'l. Required to search: name, years to search; also helpful: address. Civil cases indexed by defendant, plaintiff; on docket books and files back at least 20 years. Free court records from 11/15/2004 to present online at www.odcr.com; updated daily.

Criminal Records: Access: In person, mail, online. Visitors must perform in person searches themselves. Court makes copy: $1.00 for first page, $.50 each add'l. Required to search: name, years to search; also helpful: address, DOB, SSN. Criminal records on docket books and files. They go back "many years, no exact date known". Free court records from 11/15/2004 to present online at www.odcr.com; updated daily.

General Information: No public access terminal. No juvenile, mental health, or adoption records released. Certification fee: $.50 per page. Payee: Creek County Court Clerk. Personal checks accepted. Prepayment required.

Custer County

2nd Judicial District Court PO Box D, 675 B St, Arapaho, OK 73620; phone: 580-323-3233; criminal fax: 580-331-1121; same fax for civil/probate; hours 8AM-4PM (CST). *Felony, Misdemeanor, Civil, Eviction, Small Claims, Probate.*

Civil Records: Access: In person, online. Visitors must perform in person searches themselves. Court makes copy: $1.00 first page of doc, $.50 each add'l. Required to search: name, years to search; also helpful: address. Civil cases indexed by defendant, plaintiff. Civil records go back to 1900's; records on computer go back to 1/95. Free court records from 8/1/2001 to present online at www.odcr.com; updated daily.

Criminal Records: Access: Mail, in person, online. Both court and visitors may perform in person searches. Search fee: $5.00 per name. Court makes copy: $1.00 first page of doc, $.50 each add'l. Required to search: name, years to search; also helpful: DOB, SSN. Criminal records go back to 1900's; records on computer go back to 1/95. Free court records from 8/1/2001 to present online at www.odcr.com; updated daily. Mail turnaround time 2-3 days.

General Information: Public terminal goes back to 1995. No adoptions, juvenile, or mental records released. Will fax specific case file requests to local or toll free line. Certification fee: $.50 per page. Payee: Court Clerk. Personal checks accepted. Prepayment required. SASE requested.

Delaware County

13th Judicial District Court Box 407 (Whitehead & Krause St), Jay, OK 74346; phone: 918-253-4420; hours 8AM-4:30PM (CST). *Felony, Misdemeanor, Civil, Eviction, Small Claims, Probate.*

Civil Records: Access: Mail, in person, online. Both court and visitors may perform in person searches. Search fee: $5.00 per name. Court makes copy: $1.00 for 1st page, $.50 each add'l. Self serve copy fee: $.10 per page. Required to search: name, years to search.

Civil cases indexed by defendant, plaintiff; on computer since 1996 and on microfilm from 1913. Free court records from 6/1/1991 to present online at www.odcr.com; updated daily. Mail turnaround time 1-2 days.

Criminal Records: Access: Mail, in person, online. Both court and visitors may perform in person searches. Search fee: $5.00 per name. Court makes copy: $1.00 for 1st page, $.50 each add'l. Self serve copy fee: $.10 per page. Required to search: name, years to search; also helpful: DOB, SSN. Criminal records on computer since 1991. Free court records from 6/1/1991 to present online at www.odcr.com; updated daily. Mail turnaround time 1-2 weeks.

General Information: Public terminal has criminal back to 1991 and civil back to 1996. No juvenile, adoption, guardianship or search warrant records released. Will fax documents. Certification fee: $.50 per page. Payee: Delaware County Court Clerk. Business checks accepted. Prepayment required. SASE requested.

Dewey County

4th Judicial District Court Box 278 (Broadway & Ruble), Taloga, OK 73667; phone: 580-328-5521; hours 8AM-4PM (CST). *Felony, Misdemeanor, Civil, Small Claims, Probate.*

Civil Records: Access: Mail, in person. Both court and visitors may perform in person searches. No search fee. Court makes copy: $1.00 for first page, $.50 each add'l. Required to search: name, years to search. Civil cases indexed by defendant, plaintiff. Civil records archived from late 1800s, computerized records go back to 1995. All requests must be in writing. Mail turnaround time usually same day.

Criminal Records: Access: Mail, in person. Both court and visitors may perform in person searches. No search fee. Court makes copy: $1.00 for first page, $.50 each add'l. Required to search: name, years to search; also helpful: SSN. Criminal records archived from late 1800s, computerized records go back to 1995. All requests must be in writing. Mail turnaround time 2 days.

General Information: Public terminal goes back to 1995. No expunged, adoption, mental, guardianship, juvenile records released. Certification fee: $.50 per page. Payee: Dewey County Court Clerk. Personal checks accepted. Prepayment required. SASE requested.

Ellis County

2nd Judicial District Court Box 217, 100 S Washington St, Arnett, OK 73832; phone: 580-885-7255; hours 8:30AM-4:30PM (CST). *Felony, Misdemeanor, Civil, Eviction, Small Claims, Probate.* Probate is a separate index at this address.

Civil Records: Access: Phone, mail, in person, online. Both court and visitors may perform in person searches. No search fee. Court makes copy: $1.00 for first page, $.50 each add'l. Required to search: name, years to search. Civil cases indexed by defendant, plaintiff; on docket books from 1900. Online access to court dockets is free at www.oscn.net/applications/oscn/casesearch.asp. Mail turnaround time 1 day.

Criminal Records: Access: Phone, mail, in person, online. Both court and visitors may perform in person searches. Search fee: $5.00 per name. Court makes copy: $1.00 for first page, $.50 each add'l. Required to search: name, years to search; also helpful: SSN. Criminal records on docket books from 1900. Online access to court dockets is free at www.oscn.net/applications/oscn/casesearch.asp. Mail turnaround time 1 day.

General Information: Public use terminal available. No expunged records released. Will fax documents to local or toll free line. Certification fee: $.50 per page. Payee: Ellis County Court Clerk. Personal checks accepted. Prepayment and SASE required.

Garfield County

4th Judicial District Court 114 W Broadway, Enid, OK 73701-4024; phone: 580-237-0232; hours 8AM-4:30PM (CST). *Felony, Misdemeanor, Civil, Eviction, Small Claims, Probate.*

Civil Records: Access: Mail, online, in person. Both court and visitors may perform in person searches. Search fee: $5.00 per name. Court makes copy: $1.00 for first page, $.50 each add'l. Required to search: name, years to search. Civil cases indexed by defendant, plaintiff; on computer from 3-89, on microfiche from 1893. Online access to court dockets is free at www.oscn.net/applications/oscn/casesearch.asp. Dockets go back to 3/1989

Criminal Records: Access: Mail, online, in person. Both court and visitors may perform in person searches. Search fee: $5.00 per name. Court makes copy: $1.00 for first page, $.50 each add'l. Required to search: name, years to search, SSN. Records computerized from 1989, on microfiche from 1893. Online access to criminal dockets is same as civil.

General Information: Public terminal goes back to 1989. No juvenile, mental health, or adoption records released. Certification fee: $.50 per page. Payee: Court Clerk. Personal checks accepted. Prepayment and SASE required.

Garvin County

21st Judicial District Court PO Box 239, 201 W Grant, Pauls Valley, OK 73075; phone: 405-238-5596; fax: 405-238-1138; hours 8:30AM-4:30PM (CST). *Felony, Misdemeanor, Civil, Eviction, Small Claims, Probate.*

Civil Records: Access: Mail, in person, online. Both court and visitors may perform in person searches. Search fee: $10.00 per name. SASE enclosed. Court makes copy: $1.00 for first page, $.50 each add'l. Required to search: name, years to search. Civil cases indexed by defendant, plaintiff; on computer since 1994, docket books from 1907. Access court records from 6/1/1995 to present free at www.odcr.com; updated daily. Mail turnaround time 1 day.

Criminal Records: Access: Mail, in person, online. Both court and visitors may perform in person searches. Search fee: $10.00 per name. SASE enclosed. Court makes copy: $1.00 for first page, $.50 each add'l. Required to search: name, years to search; also helpful: SSN, DOB. Criminal records on computer since 1994, docket books from 1907. Online access to criminal dockets and records is same as civil. Mail turnaround time 1 day.

General Information: Public use terminal available. No juvenile, adoption or guardianship released. Will fax documents to local or toll free line. Certification fee: $.50 per page. Payee: Garvin County Court Clerk. Only cashiers checks and money orders accepted. Prepayment and SASE required.

Grady County

6th Judicial District Court PO Box 605 (4th & Choctaw Ave), Chickasha, OK 73023; phone: 405-224-7446; hours 8AM-4:30PM (CST). *Felony, Misdemeanor, Civil, Eviction, Small Claims, Probate.*

Civil Records: Access: In person only. Visitors must perform in person searches themselves. Court makes copy: $1.00 for first page, $.50 each add'l. Required to search: name, years to search. Civil cases indexed by defendant, plaintiff; on microfiche from 1982, archived from 1907.

Criminal Records: Access: In person only. Visitors must perform in person searches themselves. Court makes copy: $1.00 for first page, $.50 each add'l. Required to search: name, years to search; also helpful: address, DOB, SSN. Criminal records on microfiche from 1982, archived from 1907.

General Information: Public terminal goes back to 1996. No juvenile, adoption, guardianship or mental health records released. Certification fee: $.50 per page. Payee: Court Clerk. Personal checks accepted. Prepayment required.

Grant County

4th Judicial District Court 112 E Guthrie, Medford, OK 73759; phone: 580-395-2828; hours 8AM-4:30PM (CST). *Felony, Misdemeanor, Civil, Eviction, Small Claims, Probate.*

Civil Records: Access: Mail, in person. Both court and visitors may perform in person searches. Search fee: $5.00 per name. Court makes copy: $1.00 for first page, $.50 each add'l. Required to search: name, years to search. Civil cases indexed by defendant, plaintiff. Civil records archived from 1893, in books since 1898. Mail turnaround time 1-3 days.

Criminal Records: Access: Mail, in person. Both court and visitors may perform in person searches. Search fee: $5.00 per name. Court makes copy: $1.00 for first page, $.50 each add'l. Required to search: name, years to search; also helpful: SSN. Criminal records archived from 1893, in books since 1898. Mail turnaround time 1-3 days.

General Information: Public terminal goes back to 1997. No juvenile, adoption, mental health, some guardianship or wills released. Certification fee: $.50 per page. Payee: Court Clerk. No out of state personal checks accepted. Prepayment required. SASE helpful.

Greer County

3rd Judicial District Court PO Box 216 (Courthouse Sq), Mangum, OK 73554; phone: 580-782-3665; fax: 580-782-4026; hours 9AM-5PM (CST). *Felony, Misdemeanor, Civil, Eviction, Small Claims, Probate.*

Civil Records: Access: Mail, in person. Both court and visitors may perform in person searches. Search fee: $5.00 per name. Court makes copy: $1.00 for first page, $.50 each add'l. Required to search: name, years to search. Civil cases indexed by defendant, plaintiff; on docket books from 1901; on computer back to 1997. Mail turnaround time 1-2 days.

Criminal Records: Access: Mail, in person. Both court and visitors may perform in person searches. Search fee: $5.00 per name. Court makes copy: $1.00 for first page, $.50 each add'l. Required to search: name, years to search, DOB; also helpful: SSN. Criminal records on docket books from 1901; on computer back to 1997. Mail turnaround time 1-2 days.

General Information: Public use terminal available. No juvenile, mental health, adoption or guardianship records released. Fee to fax documents is $1.00 per document. Certification fee: $.50 per page. Payee: Court Clerk. Only cash, cashiers checks or money orders accepted. Prepayment and SASE required.

Harmon County

3rd Judicial District Court 114 W Hollis, Hollis, OK 73550; phone: 580-688-3617; criminal fax: 580-688-2900; same fax for civil/probate; hours 8AM-5PM (CST). *Felony, Misdemeanor, Civil, Eviction, Small Claims, Probate.*

Civil Records: Access: Mail, fax, in person. Both court and visitors may perform in person searches. Search fee: $5.00 per name. Court makes copy: $1.00 for first page, $.50 each add'l. Required to search: name, years to search. Civil cases indexed by defendant, plaintiff; on docket books from 1909; on computer since 1999. Mail turnaround time 1-2 days.

Criminal Records: Access: Mail, fax, in person. Both court and visitors may perform in person searches. Search fee: $5.00 per name. Court makes copy: $1.00 for first page, $.50 each add'l. Required to search: name, years to search; also helpful: DOB, SSN, sex. Criminal records on docket books from 1909; on computer since 1999. Mail turnaround time 1-2 days.

General Information: No public access terminal. No juvenile, adoption, mental health, or guardianship records released. Will fax documents if prepaid or you provide proof of payment, facsimile of check, etc. Certification fee: $.50 per page. Payee: Harmon County Court Clerk. Personal checks accepted. Prepayment required. SASE requested.

Harper County

1st Judicial District Court Box 347 (311 SE 1st St), Buffalo, OK 73834; phone: 580-735-2010; hours 8AM-4PM (CST). *Felony, Misdemeanor, Civil, Eviction, Small Claims, Probate.*

Civil Records: Access: Mail, in person. Both court and visitors may perform in person searches. Search fee: $5.00 per name. Court makes copy: $1.00 for 1st page, $.50 each add'l. Required to search: name, years to search. Civil cases indexed by defendant, plaintiff; on docket books from 1907. Mail turnaround time 3 or 4 days.

Criminal Records: Access: Mail, in person. Both court and visitors may perform in person searches. Search fee: $5.00 per name. Court makes copy: $1.00 for 1st page, $.50 each add'l. Required to search: name, years to search. Criminal records on docket books from 1907. Mail turnaround time 3 or 4 days.

General Information: No public access terminal. No adoption, juvenile, conservatorship, mental health, guardianship, or expunged records released. Will fax documents for no fee. Certification fee: $.50 per page. Payee: Harper County Court Clerk. Personal checks not accepted. Cashier's check or money order. Prepayment required. SASE requested.

Haskell County

16th Judicial District Court 202 E Main, Stigler, OK 74462; phone: 918-967-3323; fax: 918-967-2819; hours 8AM-4:30PM (CST). *Felony, Misdemeanor, Civil, Eviction, Small Claims, Probate.*

Civil Records: Access: Phone, fax, mail, in person, online. Both court and visitors may perform in person searches. Search fee: $5.00. Court makes copy: $1.00 for first page, $.50 each add'l. Required to search: name, years to search. Civil cases indexed by defendant, plaintiff. Civil records archived from 1907, they are in the process of placing files on microfiche starting with 1994; computerized since 1997. Free court records from 11/1/1997 to present online at www.odcr.com; updated daily. Mail turnaround time 1 week.

Criminal Records: Access: Phone, fax, mail, in person, online. Both court and visitors may perform in person searches. Search fee: $5.00. Court makes copy: $1.00 for first page, $.50 each add'l. Required to search: name, years to search; also helpful: SSN. Criminal records archived from 1907, they are in the process of placing files on microfiche starting with 1994; computerized since 1997. Access to the OK Dist. Ct. Records site is free at www.odcr.com. Mail turnaround time 1 week.

General Information: Public terminal goes back to 1997. No juvenile, adoption or mental health records released. Certification fee: $2.00. Payee: Haskell County Court Clerk. Personal checks accepted. SASE required.

Hughes County

22nd Judicial District Court 200 N Broadway, Box 32, Holdenville, OK 74848; phone: 405-379-3384; hours 8AM-4:30PM (CST). *Felony, Misdemeanor, Civil, Eviction, Small Claims, Probate.*

Note: Probate is a separate index at this same address.

Civil Records: Access: Mail, in person, online. Both court and visitors may perform in person searches. Search fee: $5.00 per name. Court makes copy: $1.00 for first page, $.50 each add'l. Required to search: name, years to search. Civil cases indexed by defendant, plaintiff. Civil records archived from 1907, computerized records go back to 1998. Free court records from 12/1998 to present online at www.odcr.com; updated daily. Mail turnaround time 2 days.

Criminal Records: Access: Mail, in person, online. Both court and visitors may perform in person searches. Search fee: $5.00 per name. Court makes copy: $1.00 for first page, $.50 each add'l. Required to search: name, years to search; also helpful: SSN. Criminal records archived from 1907. Free court records from 12/1998 to present online at www.odcr.com; updated daily. Mail turnaround time 2 days.

General Information: Public terminal goes back to 1998. No juvenile or adoption records released. Will not fax documents. Certification fee: $.50 per page. Payee: Hughes County Court Clerk. Personal checks accepted. Prepayment and SASE required.

Jackson County

3rd Judicial District Court PO Box 616, 101 N Main, Rm 303, County Courthouse, Altus, OK 73522; phone: 580-482-0448; hours 8AM-4PM (CST). *Felony, Misdemeanor, Civil, Eviction, Small Claims, Probate.*

Civil Records: Access: Mail, in person. Both court and visitors may perform in person searches. Search fee: $5.00 per name. Court makes copy: $1.00 for first page, $.50 each add'l. Self serve copy fee: $1.00 per page. Required to search: name, years to search. Civil records indexed by defendant, plaintiff. Civil records archived from early 1900; computerized records since 7/97. Mail turnaround time 3-4 days.

Criminal Records: Access: Mail, in person. Both court and visitors may perform in person searches. Search fee: $5.00 per name. Court makes copy: $1.00 for first page, $.50 each add'l. Self serve copy fee: $1.00 per page. Required to search: name, years to search; also helpful: SSN. Criminal records archived from early 1900; computerized records since 7/97. Mail turnaround time 3-4 days.

General Information: Public terminal goes back to 1997. No adoption, juvenile, mental health, or guardianship records released. Certification fee: $.50 per page. Payee: Jackson County Court Clerk. Business checks accepted. Prepayment and SASE required.

Jefferson County

5th Judicial District Court 220 N Main, Rm 302, Waurika, OK 73573; phone: 580-228-2961; fax: 580-228-2185; hours 8AM-4PM (CST). *Felony, Misdemeanor, Civil, Eviction, Small Claims, Probate.*

Civil Records: Access: Mail, in person, online. Both court and visitors may perform in person searches. Search fee: $5.00 per name. Court makes copy: $1.00 for first page, $.50 each add'l. Required to search: name, years to search, DOB or SSN. Civil cases indexed by defendant, plaintiff; on docket books from 1907; on computer since 10/1997. Free court records from 1/1998 to present online at www.odcr.com; updated monthly. Mail turnaround time 1 week.

Criminal Records: Access: Mail, in person, online. Both court and visitors may perform in person searches. Search fee: $5.00 per name. Court makes copy: $1.00 for first page, $.50 each add'l. Required to search: name, years to search, DOB; also helpful: SSN. Criminal records on docket books from 1907; on computer since 10/1997. Free court records from 1/1998 to present online at www.odcr.com; updated monthly. Mail turnaround time 1 week.

General Information: Public terminal goes back to 10/97. No juvenile, adoption or guardianship records released. Certification fee: $.50 per page. Payee: Court Clerk. Personal checks accepted. Prepayment and SASE required.

Johnston County

20th Judicial District Court 403 W Main, #201, Tishomingo, OK 73460; phone: 580-371-3281; hours 8:30AM-4:30PM (CST). *Felony, Misdemeanor, Civil, Eviction, Small Claims, Probate.*

Civil Records: Access: Phone, mail, in person. Both court and visitors may perform in person searches. Search fee: $5.00 per name. Court makes copy: $1.00 for first page, $.50 each add'l. Required to search: name, years to search. Civil cases indexed by defendant, plaintiff; on docket books from 1907; on computer back to 1997. All requests must be in writing. Mail turnaround time 2 days.

Criminal Records: Access: Mail, in person. Both court and visitors may perform in person searches. Search fee: $5.00 per name. Court makes copy: $1.00 for first page, $.50 each add'l. Required to search: name, years to search; also helpful: DOB, SSN. Criminal records on docket books from 1907; on computer back to 1997. All requests must be in writing. Mail turnaround time 2 days.

General Information: Public use terminal available. No juvenile or mental health records released. Certification fee: $.50 per page. Payee: Court. Personal checks accepted. Prepayment and SASE required.

Kay County

8th Judicial District Court Box 428, Newkirk, OK 74647; phone: 580-362-3350; hours 8:00AM-4:30PM (CST). *Felony, Misdemeanor, Civil, Eviction, Small Claims, Probate.*
www.courthouse.kay.ok.us/home.html
Note: This courthouse holds the closed case files for the satellite courts in Ponca City (580-762-2148) and Blackwell (580-363-2080).

Civil Records: Access: Mail, in person, online. Both court and visitors may perform in person searches. Search fee: $5.00 per name. Court makes copy: $1.00 for first page, $.50 each add'l. Required to search: name, years to search. Civil cases indexed by defendant, plaintiff; on microfiche and original records; computerized records since 1995. Free court records from 5/1/1995 to present online at www.odcr.com; updated daily. Blackwell and Ponca City online goes back to 1/1997. Mail turnaround time 1 day.

Criminal Records: Access: Mail, in person, online. Both court and visitors may perform in person searches. Search fee: $5.00 per name. Court makes copy: $1.00 for first page, $.50 each add'l. Required to search: name, years to search; also helpful: DOB, SSN. Criminal records on microfiche and original records; computerized records since 1995. Free court records from 5/1/1995 to present online at www.odcr.com; updated daily. Blackwell and Ponca City online goes back to 1/1997. Mail turnaround time 1 day.

General Information: Public terminal goes back to 1995. No juvenile, adoption, mental health, or sealed records released. Will not fax documents. Certification fee: $.50 per page. Payee: Kay County Court Clerk. Personal checks accepted. Prepayment required.

Kingfisher County

4th Judicial District Court Box 328, 101 S Main St, Kingfisher, OK 73750; phone: 405-375-3813; hours 8:00AM-4:30PM (CST). *Felony, Misdemeanor, Civil, Eviction, Small Claims, Probate.*

Civil Records: Access: Phone, mail, in person, online. Both court and visitors may perform in person searches. Search fee: $5.00. Court makes copy: $1.00 for first page, $.50 each add'l. Required to search: name, years to search. Civil cases indexed by defendant, plaintiff. Civil records archived from 1900, computerized since 1998. Free court records from 10/1/1997 to present online at www.odcr.com; updated daily. Mail turnaround time 1-2 days.

Criminal Records: Access: Mail, in person, online. Both court and visitors may perform in person searches. Search fee: $5.00. Court makes copy: $1.00 for first page, $.50 each add'l. Required to search: name, years to search; also helpful: SSN. Criminal records archived from 1900, computerized since 1998. Free court records from 10/1/1997 to present online at www.odcr.com; updated daily. Mail turnaround time 1-2 days.

General Information: Public terminal goes back to 1998. No juvenile, mental or guardianship records released. Certification fee: $.50 per page. Payee: Court Clerk. Personal checks accepted. Prepayment required.

Kiowa County

3rd Judicial District Court Box 854 (316 S Main St), Hobart, OK 73651; phone: 580-726-5125; probate phone: 580-726-5125; fax: 580-726-2340; hours 9AM-5PM (CST). *Felony, Misdemeanor, Civil, Eviction, Small Claims, Probate.*

Civil Records: Access: Phone, mail, in person. Both court and visitors may perform in person searches. Search fee: $5.00 per name. Court makes copy: $1.00 for first page, $.50 each add'l. Required to search: name, years to search. Civil cases indexed by defendant, plaintiff. Civil records archived from 1900, computerized records from 1996. Mail turnaround time 1-2 days.

Criminal Records: Access: Phone, mail, in person. Both court and visitors may perform in person searches. Search fee: $5.00 per name. Court makes copy: $1.00 for first page, $.50 each add'l. Required to search: name, years to search; also helpful: SSN. Criminal records archived from 1900, computerized records from 1996. Mail turnaround time 1-2 days.

General Information: Public terminal goes back to 1992. No juvenile or adoptions records released. Certification fee: $.50 per page. Payee: Court Clerk. Only cashiers checks and money orders accepted. Prepayment and SASE required.

Latimer County

16th Judicial District Court 109 N Central, Rm 200, Wilburton, OK 74578; phone: 918-465-2011; hours 8AM-4:30PM (CST). *Felony, Misdemeanor, Civil, Eviction, Small Claims, Probate.*

Civil Records: Access: Phone, mail, in person, online. Both court and visitors may perform in person searches. Search fee: $5.00 per name. Court makes copy: $1.00 for first page, $.50 each add'l. Required to search: name, years to search. Civil cases indexed by defendant, plaintiff; in original files from 1907, computerized from 1999. Free court records from 11/1999 to present online at www.odcr.com; updated monthly. Mail turnaround time 2 days.

Criminal Records: Access: Mail, in person, online. Both court and visitors may perform in person searches. Search fee: $5.00 per name. Court makes copy: $1.00 for first page, $.50 each add'l. Required to search: name, years to search; also helpful: DOB, SSN. Criminal records in original files from 1907, computerized from 1999. Free court records from 11/1999 to present online at www.odcr.com; updated monthly. Mail turnaround time 2 days.

General Information: Public terminal goes back to 1999. No guardianship or juvenile records released. Will not fax documents. Certification fee: $.50 per page. Payee: Latimer County Court Clerk. Personal checks accepted. Prepayment required. Will bill search fee to law firms.

Le Flore County

16th Judicial District Court PO Box 688, 100 S Broadway, Poteau, OK 74953; phone: 918-647-3181; hours 8AM-4:30PM (CST). *Felony, Misdemeanor, Civil, Eviction, Small Claims, Probate.*

Civil Records: Access: Mail, in person, online. Both court and visitors may perform in person searches. Search fee: $5.00 per name. Court makes copy: $1.00 for first page, $.50 each add'l. Required to search: name, years to search. Civil cases indexed by defendant, plaintiff; on computer since 7/1997; prior records archived since 1904 in files and books. Free court records from 7/1/1997 to present online at www.odcr.com; updated daily. Mail turnaround time 1 week.

Criminal Records: Access: Mail, in person, online. Both court and visitors may perform in person searches. Search fee: $5.00 per name. Court makes copy: $1.00 for first page, $.50 each add'l. Required to search: name, years to search; also helpful: SSN. Criminal records on computer since 7/1997; prior records archived since 1904 in files and books. Free court records from 7/1/1997 to present online at www.odcr.com; updated daily. Mail turnaround time 1 week.

General Information: Public terminal goes back to 1997. No juvenile, adoptions, mental health or guardian records released. Certification fee: $.50 per page. Payee: Court Clerk. Personal checks accepted. Prepayment and SASE required.

Lincoln County

23rd Judicial District Court PO Box 307 (811 Manvel Ave), Chandler, OK 74834; phone: 405-258-1309; fax: 405-258-3067; hours 8:30AM-4:30PM (CST). *Felony, Misdemeanor, Civil, Eviction, Small Claims, Probate.*
Civil Records: Access: Mail, in person, online. Both court and visitors may perform in person searches. Search fee: $5.00 per name. Court makes copy: $1.00 for first page, $.50 each add'l. Self serve copy fee: $.15 per page. Required to search: name, years to search. Civil cases indexed by defendant, plaintiff. Civil records archived since 1891. Free court records from 7/1/1994 to present online at www.odcr.com; updated daily. Mail turnaround time can take 30 days or more. Record searching is a low priority.
Criminal Records: Access: Mail, in person, online. Both court and visitors may perform in person searches. Search fee: $5.00 per name. Court makes copy: $1.00 for first page, $.50 each add'l. Self serve copy fee: $.15 per page. Required to search: name, years to search, DOB, signed release; also helpful: SSN. Criminal records archived since 1891. Free court records from 7/1/1994 to present online at www.odcr.com; updated daily. Mail turnaround time can take 30 days or more. Record searching is a low priority.
General Information: Public terminal goes back to 7/1994. No juvenile, adoption or guardianship records released. Will not fax documents. No certification fee. Payee: Court Clerk. Personal checks accepted. Prepayment and SASE required.

Logan County

9th Judicial District Court 301 E Harrison, Rm 201, Guthrie, OK 73044; phone: 405-282-0123; hours 8:30AM-4:30PM (CST). *Felony, Misdemeanor, Civil, Eviction, Small Claims, Probate.* Probate is a separate index at this address.
Civil Records: Access: Mail, in person, online. Both court and visitors may perform in person searches. Search fee: $5.00 per name. Court makes copy: $1.00 for first page, $.50 each add'l. Required to search: name, years to search. Civil cases indexed by defendant, plaintiff; on microfiche from 1907. www.oscn.net/applications/oscn/start.asp. There is no fee. Mail turnaround time 7-10 days.
Criminal Records: Access: Mail, in person, online. Both court and visitors may perform in person searches. Search fee: $5.00 per name. Court makes copy: $1.00 for first page, $.50 each add'l. Required to search: name, years to search; also helpful: SSN, DOB. Criminal records on microfiche from 1907. www.oscn.net/applications/oscn/start.asp. There is no fee. Mail turnaround time 7-10 days.
General Information: Public use terminal available. No juvenile, mental health or adoption records released. Will not fax documents. Certification fee: $.50 per page includes copy fee. Payee: Court Clerk. Personal checks accepted. Prepayment required. SASE requested.

Love County

20th Judicial District Court 405 W Main, Marietta, OK 73448; phone: 580-276-2235; hours 8AM-4:30PM (CST). *Felony, Misdemeanor, Civil, Eviction, Small Claims, Probate.*
Civil Records: Access: Mail, in person. Both court and visitors may perform in person searches. Search fee: $5.00 per name. Court makes copy: $1.00 for first page, $.50 each add'l. Required to search: name, years to search. Civil cases indexed by defendant, plaintiff; on docket books from 1907,

computer records back to 1997. Mail turnaround time 1-2 days.
Criminal Records: Access: Mail, in person. Both court and visitors may perform in person searches. Search fee: $5.00 per name. Court makes copy: $1.00 for first page, $.50 each add'l. Required to search: name, years to search; also helpful: DOB, SSN. Records on docket books from 1907, computer records back to 1997. Mail turnaround 1-2 days.
General Information: Public terminal goes back to 4/1997. No juvenile or adoptions records released. Certification fee: $.50 per page. Payee: Court Clerk. Only cashiers checks and money orders accepted. Prepayment and SASE required.

Major County

4th Judicial District Court 500 E Broadway, Fairview, OK 73737; phone: 580-227-4690; fax: 580-227-1275; hours 8:30AM-4:30PM (CST). *Felony, Misdemeanor, Civil, Small Claims, Probate.*
Civil Records: Access: Phone, fax, mail, in person, online. Both court and visitors may perform in person searches. Search fee: $5.00 per name. Fee is per book. Court makes copy: $1.00 for first page, $.50 each add'l. Required to search: name, years to search. Civil cases indexed by defendant, plaintiff; on docket books from 1907, on microfiche from 1970, on computer back to 1997. Free court records from 1/1/1998 to present online at www.odcr.com; updated monthly. Mail turnaround time 3 days.
Criminal Records: Access: Phone, fax, mail, in person, online. Both court and visitors may perform in person searches. Search fee: $5.00 per name. Fee is per book. Court makes copy: $1.00 for first page, $.50 each add'l. Required to search: name, years to search, DOB; also helpful: SSN. Criminal records on docket books from 1907, on microfiche from 1970; on computer back to 1997. Free court records from 1/1/1998 to present online at www.odcr.com; updated monthly. Mail turnaround time 3 days.
General Information: Public terminal goes back to 1997. No juvenile, adoptions or mental records released. Will fax documents to local or toll free line. Certification fee: $.50 per page. Payee: Court Clerk. Personal checks accepted. Prepayment required. Will bill attorneys or firms with previous credit paid. SASE required.

Marshall County

20th Judicial District Court Box 58, Madill, OK 73446; phone: 580-795-3278 X240; hours 8:30AM-5PM (CST). *Felony, Misdemeanor, Civil, Eviction, Small Claims, Probate.*
Civil Records: Access: In person, online Mail, in person. Both court and visitors may perform in person searches. Search fee: $5.00. Court makes copy: $1.00 for first page, $.50 each add'l. Required to search: name, years to search. Civil cases indexed by defendant, plaintiff; on docket books from 1907; computerized since 1997. Free court records from 1/1/1998 to present online at www.odcr.com; updated daily. Mail turnaround time 3 days.
Criminal Records: Access: Mail, in person, online. Both court and visitors may perform in person searches. Search fee: $5.00. Court makes copy: $1.00 for first page, $.50 each add'l. Required to search: name, years to search, DOB, SSN, signed release. Criminal records on docket books from 1907; computerized since 1997. Free court records from 1/1/1998 to present online at www.odcr.com; updated daily. Mail turnaround time 3 days.
General Information: Public use terminal available. No juvenile, adoptions, mental health or guardianship records released. Certification fee: $3.00. Payee: Court Clerk. Personal checks accepted. Prepayment and SASE required.

Mayes County

12th Judicial District Court 1 Court Pl #200, County Court Clerk, Pryor, OK 74361; criminal phone: 918-825-0133; civil phone: 918-825-2185; fax: 918-825-4415; hours 9AM-5PM (CST). *Felony, Misdemeanor, Civil, Eviction, Small Claims, Probate.*
Civil Records: Access: Phone, mail, in person, online. Both court and visitors may perform in person searches. Search fee: $1.00 per name per year. Search fee is payable to employee doing research after hours. Court makes copy: $1.00 for first page, $.50 each add'l. Required to search: name, years to search. Civil cases indexed by defendant, plaintiff. Civil records archived from 1907 on microfilm, computerized since 1998. Free court records from 7/1/1998 to present online at www.odcr.com; updated daily. Mail turnaround time 1 week.
Criminal Records: Access: Phone, mail, in person, online. Both court and visitors may perform in person searches. Search fee: $1.00 per name per year. Search fee is payable to employee doing research after hours. Court makes copy: $1.00 for first page, $.50 each add'l. Required to search: name, years to search; also helpful: DOB, SSN. Criminal records archived from 1907 on microfilm, computerized since 1998. Free court records from 1/1/1998 to present online at www.odcr.com; updated daily. Mail turnaround time 1 week.
General Information: Public terminal goes back to 7/1998. No mental, adoption, most juvenile, and some reports in guardianship records not released. Will not fax documents. Certification fee: $.50 per page. Payee: Clerk of Court. Personal checks accepted. Prepayment and SASE required.

McClain County

21st Judicial District Court 121 N 2nd, Rm 231, Purcell, OK 73080; phone: 405-527-3221; hours 8AM-4:30PM (CST). *Felony, Misdemeanor, Civil, Eviction, Small Claims, Probate.*
Note: Probate is a separate index at this same address.
Civil Records: Access: Mail, in person, online. Both court and visitors may perform in person searches. Search fee: $10.00 per name. Court makes copy: $1.00 for 1st page, $.50 each add'l. Required to search: name, years to search. Civil cases indexed by defendant, plaintiff; on docket books and cards from 1907, computerized since 1/97. Free court records from 1/1997 to present online at www.odcr.com; updated daily. Mail turnaround time 2 days.
Criminal Records: Access: Mail, in person, online. Both court and visitors may perform in person searches. Search fee: $10.00 per name. Court makes copy: $1.00 for 1st page, $.50 each add'l. Required to search: name, years to search; also helpful: DOB, SSN. Criminal records kept in individual docket files. Free court records from 1/1997 to present online at www.odcr.com; updated daily. Mail turnaround time 2 days.
General Information: Public terminal goes back to 1997. No adoptions, mental health or juvenile records released. Will not fax documents. Certification fee: $.50 per document. Payee: Court Clerk. Personal checks accepted. Prepayment and SASE required.

McCurtain County

17th Judicial District Court Box 1378 (108 N Central Ave), Idabel, OK 74745; phone: 580-286-3693; fax: 580-286-7095; hours 8AM-4PM (CST). *Felony, Misdemeanor, Civil, Eviction, Small Claims, Probate.*
Civil Records: Access: Mail, in person, online. Both court and visitors may perform in person searches. Search fee: $5.00 per name. Court makes copy: $2.00 per page. Required to search: name, years to search. Civil cases indexed by defendant, plaintiff; on docket books from 1907; on computer back to 1998. Free court records from 6/1/1998 to present online at www.odcr.com; updated monthly. Mail turnaround time 1 day.

Criminal Records: Access: Mail, in person, online. Both court and visitors may perform in person searches. Search fee: $5.00. Court makes copy: $2.00 per page. Required to search: name, years to search; also helpful: SSN. Criminal records on docket books from 1907; on computer back to 1998. Free court records from 6/1/1998 to present online at www.odcr.com; updated monthly. Mail turnaround time 1 day.

General Information: Public terminal goes back to 1998. No adoptions, guardianship or juvenile records released. Certification fee: $.50 per page. Payee: Court Clerk. Personal checks accepted. Prepayment and SASE required.

McIntosh County

18th Judicial District Court Box 426 (110 N 1st St), Eufaula, OK 74432; phone: 918-689-2282; hours 8AM-4PM (CST). *Felony, Misdemeanor, Civil, Eviction, Small Claims, Probate.*

Civil Records: Access: Mail, in person, online. Both court and visitors may perform in person searches. Search fee: $5.00 per name. Court makes copy: $1.00 for first page, $.50 each add'l. Required to search: name, years to search. Civil cases indexed by defendant, plaintiff; on microfilm since 1907; computerized back to May 1996. Free court records from 5/1/1996 to present online at www.odcr.com; updated monthly. Mail turnaround time 3 days.

Criminal Records: Access: Mail, in person. Both court and visitors may perform in person searches. Search fee: $5.00 per name. Court makes copy: $1.00 for first page, $.50 each add'l. Required to search: name, years to search; also helpful: SSN, DOB. Criminal records on microfilm since 1947; computerized back to May 1996. Online same as civil Mail turnaround time 3 days.

General Information: Public use terminal available. No adoptions, mental health, guardianship or juvenile records released. Will not fax documents. Certification fee: $.50 per page. Payee: Court. No personal checks accepted; use cashier's check or money order. Prepayment and SASE required.

Murray County

20th Judicial District Court Box 578, 10th & Wyandotte St, Sulphur, OK 73086; phone: 580-622-3223; 8AM-4:30PM (CST). *Felony, Misdemeanor, Civil, Eviction, Small Claims, Probate.*

Civil Records: Access: Mail, in person, online. Both court and visitors may perform in person searches. Search fee: $5.00 per name. Court makes copy: $1.00 for first page, $.50 each add'l. Required to search: name, years to search; also helpful: DOB. Civil cases indexed by defendant, plaintiff; on docket books from 1907, from 1973 back records are on microfilm; computerized back to 1997. Free court records from 1/1/1998 to present online at www.odcr.com; updated monthly. Mail turnaround time 2 days, immediate if easily accessible.

Criminal Records: Access: Mail, in person, online. Both court and visitors may perform in person searches. Search fee: $5.00 per name. Court makes copy: $1.00 for first page, $.50 each add'l. Required to search: name, years to search; also helpful: SSN, DOB. Criminal records on docket books from 1907, from 1973 back records are on microfilm; computerized back to 1997. Free court records from 1/1/1998 to present online at www.odcr.com; updated monthly. Mail turnaround time 2 days, immediate if easily accessible.

General Information: Public terminal goes back to 9/1997. No mental health, guardianship, juvenile or adoption records released. Will not fax documents. Certification fee: $5.00. Payee: Murray County Court Clerk. Personal checks accepted. Prepayment and SASE required.

Muskogee County

15th Judicial District Court Box 1350 (200 State St), Muskogee, OK 74402; phone: 918-682-7873; criminal fax: 918-684-1694/1696; same fax for civil/probate; hours 8AM-4:30PM (CST). *Felony, Misdemeanor, Civil, Eviction, Small Claims, Probate.* Probate is separate index at this address.

Civil Records: Access: Mail, in person, online. Both court and visitors may perform in person searches. Search fee: $10.00 per name. Court makes copy: $1.00 for 1st page, $.50 each add'l. Required to search: name, years to search. Civil cases indexed by defendant, plaintiff; on docket books from 1907. Free court records from 1/3/2003 to present online at www.odcr.com; updated daily. Mail turnaround time 2-3 days.

Criminal Records: Access: Mail, in person, online. Both court and visitors may perform in person searches. Search fee: $10.00 per name. Court makes copy: $1.00 for 1st page, $.50 each add'l. Required to search: name, years to search, DOB; also helpful: SSN. Criminal records on docket books from 1907. Free court records from 1/3/2003 to present online at www.odcr.com; updated daily. Mail turnaround time 2-3 days.

General Information: Public terminal goes back to 2003. No adoptions, mental health, guardianship or juvenile records released. Will fax documents. No certification fee. Payee: Court Clerk. Personal checks accepted. Prepayment and SASE required.

Noble County

8th Judicial District Court 300 Courthouse Dr, Box 14, Perry, OK 73077; phone: 580-336-5187; hours 8AM-4:30PM (CST). *Felony, Misdemeanor, Civil, Eviction, Small Claims, Probate.*

Note: Probate is separate index at this same address.

Civil Records: Access: Mail, in person, online. Both court and visitors may perform in person searches. Search fee: $5.00 per name. Court makes copy: $1.00 for first page, $.50 each add'l. Required to search: name, years to search. Civil cases indexed by defendant, plaintiff; on microfiche from 1893; computerized back to 1997. Free court records from 1/1997 to present online at www.odcr.com; updated daily. Mail turnaround time 1 day.

Criminal Records: Access: Mail, in person, online. Both court and visitors may perform in person searches. Search fee: $5.00 per name. Court makes copy: $1.00 for first page, $.50 each add'l. Required to search: name, years to search, DOB; also helpful: address, SSN. Criminal records on microfiche from 1893; computerized back to 1997. Free court records from 1/1997 to present online at www.odcr.com; updated daily. Mail turnaround time 1 day.

General Information: Public terminal goes back to 1997. No adoptions, mental health, guardianship or juvenile records released. Will not fax documents. Certification fee: $.50 per instrument. Payee: Noble County Court Clerk. Personal checks accepted. Prepayment required. SASE appreciated.

Nowata County

11th Judicial District Court 229 N Maple, Nowata, OK 74048; phone: 918-273-0127; hours 8AM-4:30PM (CST). *Felony, Misdemeanor, Civil, Eviction, Small Claims, Probate.*

Civil Records: Access: Mail, in person, online. Both court and visitors may perform in person searches. Search fee: $5.00 per name. Court makes copy: $1.00 for first page, $.50 each add'l. Required to search: name, years to search. Civil cases indexed by defendant, plaintiff; on docket books from 1907; on computer since 1998. Probate is separate index. Free court records from 7/1/1998 to present online at www.odcr.com; updated monthly. Mail turnaround time 1 day.

Criminal Records: Access: Mail, in person, online. Both court and visitors may perform in person searches. Search fee: $5.00 per name. Court makes copy: $1.00 for first page, $.50 each add'l. Required to search: name, years to search; also helpful: SSN. Criminal records on docket books from 1907; on computer since 1998. Free court records from 7/1/1998 to present online at www.odcr.com; updated monthly. Mail turnaround time 1 day.

General Information: Public terminal goes back to 1998. No adoptions, mental health, guardianship or juvenile records released. Will fax documents to local or toll free line. Certification fee: $.50 per page. Payee: Court Clerk. Personal checks accepted. Prepayment required. SASE requested.

Okfuskee County

24th Judicial District Court Box 30 (3rd & Atlanta St), Okemah, OK 74859; phone: 918-623-0525; fax: 918-623-2687; hours 8:30AM-4:30PM (CST). *Felony, Misdemeanor, Civil, Eviction, Small Claims, Probate.*

Civil Records: Access: Mail, in person, online. Both court and visitors may perform in person searches. Search fee: $5.00 per name. Court makes copy: $1.00 for first page, $.50 each add'l. Required to search: name, years to search. Civil cases indexed by defendant, plaintiff; in files and docket books from 1907, computerized since 1996. Free court records from 1/1997 to present online at www.odcr.com; updated monthly. Mail turnaround time 3 days.

Criminal Records: Access: Mail, in person, online. Both court and visitors may perform in person searches. Search fee: $5.00 per name. Court makes copy: $1.00 for first page, $.50 each add'l. Required to search: name, years to search; also helpful: SSN. Criminal records in files and docket books from 1907, computerized since 1996. Free court records from 1/1997 to present online at www.odcr.com; updated monthly. Mail turnaround time 3 days.

General Information: Public use terminal available. No adoptions, mental health, guardianship or juvenile released. Will fax documents to local or toll free line. Certification fee: $.50 per document. Payee: Court Clerk. Personal checks accepted. Prepayment and SASE required.

Oklahoma County

District Court 320 Robert S Kerr St, Rm 409, Oklahoma City, OK 73102; phone: 405-713-1705; criminal phone: 405-713-1713; civil phone: 405-713-1725; probate phone: 405-713-1725; hours 8AM-5PM (CST). *Felony, Misdemeanor, Civil, Eviction, Small Claims, Probate.*

Note: Small claims: 405-713-1738.

Civil Records: Access: Mail, online, in person. Both court and visitors may perform in person searches. Search fee: Lengthy searches are $5.00 per half hour, otherwise no search fee. Court makes copy: $1.00 for 1st page, $.50 each add'l. Required to search: name, years to search. Civil cases indexed by defendant, plaintiff; on microfiche from 1980, prior archived. Online access to court dockets is free at www.oscn.net/applications/oscn/casesearch.asp. Civil dockets go back to 12/1984. Mail turnaround time 5-10 days.

Criminal Records: Access: Mail, online, in person. Both court and visitors may perform in person searches. Search fee: Lengthy searches $5.00 per half hour; commercial purpose searches: $25.00. Court makes copy: $1.00 for 1st page, $.50 each add'l. Required to search: name, years to search, DOB; also helpful: SSN. Criminal records on microfiche from 1980, prior archived. Online access to criminal dockets is same as civil. Criminal dockets go back to 9/1988. The sheriff's current inmates and warrants list is free at www.oklahomacounty.org/cosheriff/. Mail turnaround time 5-10 days.

General Information: Public terminal goes back to 1986. No juvenile, sealed, or expunged records released. Certification fee: $.50 per doc. Payee: District Court Clerk. Personal checks accepted. Prepayment and SASE required.

Okmulgee County

24th Judicial District Court - Henryetta Branch 115 S 4th, Henryetta, OK 74437; phone: 918-652-7142; fax: 918-650-0287; hours 8AM-4:30PM (CST). *Felony, Misdemeanor, Civil, Eviction, Small Claims, Probate.*

Note: You must search both courts in this county, records are not co-mingled.
Civil Records: Access: Limited phone, mail, in person, online. Both court and visitors may perform in person searches. Court makes copy: $1.00 for first page, $.50 each add'l; same fee for self serve. Required to search: name, years to search. Civil cases indexed by defendant, plaintiff; on microfiche from 1970, computerized since 1997. Free court records from 1/1998 to present online at www.odcr.com; updated monthly. Mail turnaround time 1-2 days.
Criminal Records: Access: Mail, in person, online. Both court and visitors may perform in person searches. Search fee: $5.00 per name. Court makes copy: $1.00 for first page, $.50 each add'l; same fee for self serve. Required to search: name, years to search; also helpful: SSN. Criminal records on microfiche from 1970, books to 6-5-79, computerized since 1997. Free court records from 1/1998 to present online at www.odcr.com; updated monthly. Mail turnaround time 1-2 days.
General Information: Public terminal goes back to 1997. No expunged or guardianship records released. Will fax documents for $1.00 1st page; $.50 each page thereafter. Payment in advance. Certification fee: $.50 per page. Payee: Court Clerk. Business checks accepted. Prepayment and SASE required.

24th Judicial District Court - Okmulgee Branch 314 W 7th, Okmulgee, OK 74447; phone: 918-756-3042; fax: 918-758-1237; hours 8AM-4:30PM (CST). *Felony, Misdemeanor, Civil, Eviction, Small Claims, Probate.*
Civil Records: Access: Phone, mail, in person, online. Both court and visitors may perform in person searches. Search fee: $5.00 per name. Court makes copy: $1.00 for first page, $.50 each add'l. Required to search: name, years to search. Civil cases indexed by defendant, plaintiff; on microfiche from 1986, archived from 1907, computerized since 1997. Free court records from 1/1998 to present online at www.odcr.com; updated monthly. Mail turnaround time 1-2 days.
Criminal Records: Access: Phone, mail, in person, online. Both court and visitors may perform in person searches. Search fee: $5.00 per name. Court makes copy: $1.00 for first page, $.50 each add'l. Required to search: name, years to search; also helpful: SSN. Criminal records on microfiche from 1986, archived from 1907, computerized since 1997. Free court records from 1/1998 to present online at www.odcr.com; updated monthly. Mail turnaround time 1-2 days.
General Information: Public terminal goes back to 1997. No juvenile, mental health, adoption or guardianship records released. Certification fee: $.50 per page. Payee: Court Clerk. Business checks accepted. Prepayment required. SASE requested.

Osage County

10th Judicial District Court County Courthouse, 600 Grandview, Pawhuska, OK 74056; phone: 918-287-4104; hours 9AM-5PM (CST). *Felony, Misdemeanor, Civil, Eviction, Small Claims, Probate, Divorce.*
Civil Records: Access: Mail, in person, online. Both court and visitors may perform in person searches. Search fee: $5.00 per name. Court makes copy: $1.00 for first page, $.50 each add'l. Required to search: name, years to search; also helpful: address. Civil cases indexed by defendant, plaintiff. Civil records archived from 1969. Free court records from 1/1996 to present online at www.odcr.com; updated daily. Mail turnaround time 2 days.
Criminal Records: Access: Mail, in person, online. Both court and visitors may perform in person searches. Search fee: $5.00 per name. Court makes copy: $1.00 for first page, $.50 each add'l. Required to search: name, years to search; also helpful: address. Criminal records archived from 1969. Free court records from 1/1996 to present online at www.odcr.com; updated daily. Mail turnaround time 2 days.

General Information: Public use terminal available. No juvenile or adoption records released. Will not fax documents. Certification fee: $.50 per page. Payee: Court Clerk. Only cashiers checks and money orders accepted. Prepayment and SASE required.

Ottawa County

13th Judicial District Court 102 E Central Ave, #300, Miami, OK 74354; phone: 918-542-2801; hours 9:00AM-5:00PM (CST). *Felony, Misdemeanor, Civil, Eviction, Small Claims, Probate.*
Civil Records: Access: Phone, mail, in person, online. Both court and visitors may perform in person searches. Search fee: $5.00 per name. Court makes copy: $1.00 for first page, $.50 each add'l; same fee for self serve. Required to search: name, years to search. Civil cases indexed by defendant, plaintiff; on docket books or cards from 1907, recent records computerized. Free court records from 9/1/1997 to present online at www.odcr.com; updated daily. Mail turnaround time 1-2 days.
Criminal Records: Access: Mail, in person, online. Both court and visitors may perform in person searches. Search fee: $5.00. Court makes copy: $1.00 for first page, $.50 each add'l; same fee for self serve. Required to search: name, years to search; also helpful: SSN. Criminal records on docket books or cards from 1907, recent records computerized. Free court records from 9/1/1997 to present online at www.odcr.com; updated daily. Mail turnaround time 1-2 days.
General Information: Public terminal goes back to 1997. No juvenile, mental health, adoption or guardianship records released. Will not fax documents. Certification fee: $.50 per page includes copy fee. Payee: Clerk of Court. Money orders accepted. Prepayment and SASE required.

Pawnee County

14th Judicial District Court Courthouse, 500 Harrison St, Pawnee, OK 74058; phone: 918-762-2547; 8AM-4:30PM (CST). *Felony, Misdemeanor, Civil, Eviction, Small Claims, Probate.*
Civil Records: Access: Mail, in person, online. Both court and visitors may perform in person searches. Search fee: $5.00. Court makes copy: $1.00 for first page, $.50 each add'l. Required to search: name, years to search. Civil cases indexed by defendant, plaintiff; on docket sheets to 1975, computerized from 1997. Free court records from 1/1997 to present online at www.odcr.com; updated daily. Mail turnaround time 1-3 days.
Criminal Records: Access: Mail, in person, online. Both court and visitors may perform in person searches. Search fee: $5.00. Court makes copy: $1.00 for first page, $.50 each add'l. Required to search: name, years to search; also helpful: SSN. Criminal records on docket sheets to 1975, computerized from 1997. Free court records from 1/1997 to present online at www.odcr.com; updated daily. Mail turnaround time 1-3 days.
General Information: Public terminal goes back to 1997. No sealed records released. Certification fee: $.50 per page. Payee: Court Clerk. Personal checks accepted. Prepayment and SASE required.

Payne County

9th Judicial District Court 606 S Husband, Rm 308, Stillwater, OK 74074; phone: 405-372-4774; 8AM-5PM (CST). *Felony, Misdemeanor, Civil, Eviction, Small Claims, Probate.*
Civil Records: Access: Mail, online, in person. Both court and visitors may perform in person searches. Search fee: $5.00 plus $1.00 per name per year. Court makes copy: $1.00 for first page, $.50 each add'l. Required to search: name, years to search. Cases indexed by defendant, plaintiff; on docket books from late 1800s, from 1994 on computer. Access to dockets free at www.oscn.net/applications/oscn/casesearch.asp. Dockets back to 1/1994. Mail turnaround 2 days.

Criminal Records: Access: Mail, online, in person. Both court and visitors may perform in person searches. Search fee: $5.00 per name per year. Court makes copy: $1.00 for first page, $.50 each add'l. Required to search: name, years to search, DOB, SSN, signed release. Criminal records on docket books from late 1800s, as of 1994 on computer. Online access to criminal dockets is same as civil. Mail turnaround time 2 days.
General Information: Public terminal goes back to 1994. No sealed records, juveniles or adoption records released. Certification fee: $1.50 per page. Payee: Clerk of Court. Personal checks accepted. Prepayment and SASE required.

Pittsburg County

18th Judicial District Court Box 460, 115 E Carl Albert Pky, McAlester, OK 74502; phone: 918-423-4859; hours 8AM-5PM (CST). *Felony, Misdemeanor, Civil, Eviction, Small Claims, Probate.*
Civil Records: Access: Mail, in person, online. Both court and visitors may perform in person searches. Search fee: $5.00 per name. Court makes copy: $1.00 for first page, $.50 each add'l; same fee for self serve. Required to search: name, years to search. Civil cases indexed by defendant, plaintiff; on microfiche since 1907; on computer since 1997. Free court records from 7/1/1997 to present online at www.odcr.com; updated monthly. Mail turnaround time 1-2 days.
Criminal Records: Access: Mail, in person, online. Both court and visitors may perform in person searches. Search fee: $5.00 per name. Court makes copy: $1.00 for first page, $.50 each add'l; same fee for self serve. Required to search: name, years to search, DOB. Criminal records on microfiche since 1907; on computer since 1997. Free court records from 7/1/1997 to present online at www.odcr.com; updated monthly. Mail turnaround time 1-2 days.
General Information: Public terminal goes back to 1997. No juvenile, adoptions, mental health or guardianship records released. Will not fax documents. Certification fee: $.50 per page. Payee: Court Clerk. Prepayment and SASE required.

Pontotoc County

22nd Judicial District Court Box 427 (120 W 13th), Ada, OK 74820; phone: 580-332-5763; hours 8AM-N; 1-5PM (CST). *Felony, Misdemeanor, Civil, Eviction, Small Claims, Probate.*
Civil Records: Access: Mail, in person, online. Both court and visitors may perform in person searches. Search fee: $5.00 per name. Court makes copy: $1.00 for first page, $.50 each add'l. Required to search: name, years to search. Civil cases indexed by defendant, plaintiff; on card index from 1907; on computer back to 1997. Free court records from 1/1997 to present online at www.odcr.com; updated monthly. Mail turnaround time 2 days.
Criminal Records: Access: Mail, in person, monthly. Both court and visitors may perform in person searches. Search fee: $5.00 per name. Court makes copy: $1.00 for first page, $.50 each add'l. Required to search: name, years to search; also helpful: DOB, SSN. Criminal records on card index from 1907; on computer back to 1990. Free court records from 1/1997 to present online at www.odcr.com; updated monthly. Mail turnaround time 2 days.
General Information: Public terminal has criminal back to 1987 and civil back to 1997. No juvenile, adoptions, mental health or guardianship records released. Certification fee: $.50 per page. Payee: Clerk of Court. Personal checks accepted. Must prepay if out of state. Prepayment and SASE required.

Pottawatomie County

23rd Judicial District Court 325 N Broadway, Shawnee, OK 74801; phone: 405-273-3624; fax: 405-878-5525; hours 8:30AM-N, 1-5 PM (CST). *Felony, Misdemeanor, Civil, Eviction, Small Claims, Probate.*

Civil Records: Access: Mail, in person, online. Both court and visitors may perform in person searches. Search fee: $5.00 per name. Court makes copy: $1.00 for first page, $.50 each add'l. Required to search: name, years to search. Civil cases indexed by defendant, plaintiff; on computer from 7/97; prior records on book of names from 1906. Free court records from 7/1/1997 to present online at www.odcr.com; updated daily. Mail turnaround time 2 weeks or less.

Criminal Records: Access: Mail, in person, online. Both court and visitors may perform in person searches. Search fee: $5.00 per name. Court makes copy: $1.00 for first page, $.50 each add'l. Required to search: name, years to search; also helpful: SSN. Records computerized from 7/97; prior records on book of names from 1960. Free court records from 7/1/1997 to present online at www.odcr.com; updated daily. Mail turnaround time 2 weeks or less.

General Information: Public use terminal available. No juvenile, adoptions, mental health or guardianship records released. Certification fee: $.50 per. page. Payee: Court Clerk. Personal checks accepted. Prepayment required. SASE requested.

Pushmataha County

17th Judicial District Court Pushmataha County Courthouse, 302 SW B, Antlers, OK 74523; phone: 580-298-2274; hours 8AM-4:30PM (CST). *Felony, Misdemeanor, Civil, Eviction, Small Claims, Probate.*

Civil Records: Access: Mail, in person, online. Both court and visitors may perform in person searches. Search fee: $5.00 per name. Court makes copy: $1.00 for first page, $.50 each add'l. Required to search: name, years to search. Civil cases indexed by defendant, plaintiff; on docket book from 1907. Online access to court dockets is free at www.oscn.net/applications/oscn/casesearch.asp. Mail turnaround time 1 day.

Criminal Records: Access: Mail, in person, online. Both court and visitors may perform in person searches. Search fee: $5.00 per name. Court makes copy: $1.00 for first page, $.50 each add'l. Required to search: name, years to search; also helpful: SSN. Criminal records on docket book from 1907. Online access to court dockets is free at www.oscn.net/applications/oscn/casesearch.asp. Mail turnaround time 1 day.

General Information: No public access terminal. No juvenile or adoption records released. Certification fee: $.50 per page includes copy fee. Payee: Court Clerk. Personal checks accepted. Prepayment and SASE required.

Roger Mills County

2nd Judicial District Court Box 409 (LL Males Blvd & Broadway), Cheyenne, OK 73628; phone: 580-497-3361; criminal fax: 580-497-2167; same fax for civil/probate; hours 8AM-4:30PM (CST). *Felony, Misdemeanor, Civil, Eviction, Small Claims, Probate.*

Civil Records: Access: Phone, mail, in person, online. Both court and visitors may perform in person searches. No search fee. Court makes copy: $1.00 for first page, $.50 each add'l. Required to search: name, years to search. Civil cases indexed by defendant, plaintiff; on computer since 1992, in books since 1893. Online access to court dockets is free at www.oscn.net/applications/oscn/casesearch.asp. Mail turnaround time 1 day.

Criminal Records: Access: Phone, mail, fax, in person, online. Both court and visitors may perform in person searches. No search fee. Court makes copy: $1.00 for first page, $.50 each add'l. Required to search: name, years to search, DOB; also helpful: SSN. Criminal records on computer since 1992, in books since 1893. Online access is the same as civil. Mail turnaround time 1 day.

General Information: Public terminal has criminal back to - not known and civil back to 5 years. No adoption, juvenile, mental health or guardianship

records released. Will fax documents for $1.00 per page. Certification fee: $.50 per certification. Payee: Court Clerk. Personal checks accepted. Prepayment and SASE required.

Rogers County

12th Judicial District Court Box 839 (219 S Missouri), Claremore, OK 74018; phone: 918-341-5711; hours 8AM-4:30PM (CST). *Felony, Misdemeanor, Civil, Eviction, Small Claims, Probate.*

Civil Records: Access: Phone, mail, online, in person. Both court and visitors may perform in person searches. No search fee, but phone and mail requests require case number. Court makes copy: $1.00 for first page, $.50 each add'l; same fee for self serve. Required to search: name, years to search. Civil cases indexed by defendant, plaintiff; in card index since 1907, some computerized. Online access to court dockets is free at www.oscn.net/applications/oscn/casesearch.asp. Dockets go back to 7/1997. Mail turnaround 1 day.

Criminal Records: Access: Phone, mail, online, in person. Both court and visitors may perform in person searches. No search fee, but phone and mail requests require case number. Court makes copy: $1.00 for first page, $.50 each add'l; same fee for self serve. Required to search: name, years to search, DOB; also helpful: SSN. Criminal records on card index since 1907, some computerized. Online access to criminal dockets is the same as civil. Mail turnaround time 1 day.

General Information: Public terminal goes back to 7/1997. No juvenile or adoption records released. Certification fee: $.50 per page. Payee: Court Clerk. Personal checks accepted. Prepayment and SASE required.

Seminole County

22nd Judicial District Court - Seminole Branch Box 1320 (401 Main St), Seminole, OK 74868; phone: 405-382-3424; fax: 405-382-9440; hours 8AM-N, 1-4PM (CST). *Civil, Small Claims, Probate.*

Note: Criminal records are now maintained at Seminole County Court Clerk, PO Box 130, Wewoka, OK, 405-257-6236.

Civil Records: Access: Phone, fax, mail, in person. Only the court performs in person searches; visitors may not. Search fee: $5.00 per name. Court makes copy: $1.00 for first page, $.50 each add'l. Required to search: name, years to search. Civil cases indexed by defendant, plaintiff; on index cards from 1931, probate from 1969; on computer back to 1996. Mail turnaround time 1 to 2 days.

General Information: No public access terminal. Certification fee: $.50 per page. Payee: Court Clerk. Only cashiers checks and money orders accepted. Prepayment and SASE required.

22nd Judicial District Court - Wewoka Branch Box 130 (120 S Wewoka Ave), Wewoka, OK 74884; phone: 405-257-6236; hours 8AM-4PM (CST). *Felony, Misdemeanor, Civil, Eviction, Small Claims, Probate.*

Note: Probate records in separate books, but on same computer system.

Civil Records: Access: Mail, in person, online. Both court and visitors may perform in person searches. Search fee: $5.00 per name. Court makes copy: $1.00 for first page, $.50 each add'l; same fee for self serve. Required to search: name, years to search. Civil cases indexed by defendant, plaintiff; in dexed on computer since 1995; prior records on books to 1907. Free court records from 1/1995 to present online at www.odcr.com; updated daily. Mail turnaround time 1 day.

Criminal Records: Access: Mail, in person, online. Both court and visitors may perform in person searches. Search fee: $5.00 per name. Court makes copy: $1.00 for first page, $.50 each add'l; same fee for self serve. Required to search: name, years to search; also helpful: SSN. Criminal records indexed

on computer since 1995; prior records on books to 1908. Free court records from 1/1995 to present online at www.odcr.com; updated daily. Mail turnaround time 1 day.

General Information: Public terminal goes back to 1995. (Includes probate.) No juvenile or adoption records released. Will fax documents to toll-free number only. Certification fee: $.50 per page. Payee: Court Clerk. Personal checks accepted. Prepayment and SASE required.

Sequoyah County

15th Judicial District Court 120 E Chickasaw, Sallisaw, OK 74955; phone: 918-775-4411; criminal fax: 918-775-1223; same fax for civil/probate; hours 8AM-4PM (CST). *Felony, Misdemeanor, Civil, Eviction, Small Claims, Probate.*

Note: Probate is a separate office at this same address.

Civil Records: Access: Mail, in person, online. Both court and visitors may perform in person searches. Search fee: $5.00 per name. Court makes copy: $1.00 for first page, $.50 each add'l; same fee for self serve. Required to search: name, years to search. Civil cases indexed by defendant, plaintiff; in files and dockets from 1907; on computer back to 1997. Free court records from 7/1/1997 to present online at www.odcr.com; updated daily. Mail turnaround time 1 week.

Criminal Records: Access: Phone, mail, in person, online. Both court and visitors may perform in person searches. Search fee: $5.00 per name. Court makes copy: $1.00 for first page, $.50 each add'l; same fee for self serve. Required to search: name, years to search; also helpful: SSN. Some criminal records on computer back to 1997, prior in files and dockets. Free court records from 7/1/1997 to present online at www.odcr.com; updated daily. Mail turnaround time 1 week.

General Information: Public terminal goes back to 1997. No juvenile, adoptions, mental health or guardianship records released. Will fax documents to toll-free or local number. No certification fee . Payee: Court Clerk. Personal checks accepted. Prepayment required. Will bill mail requests. SASE required.

Stephens County

5th Judicial District Court 101 S 11th St, Rm 301, Duncan, OK 73533; phone: 580-470-2000; hours 8:30AM-4:30PM (CST). *Felony, Misdemeanor, Civil, Eviction, Small Claims, Probate.*

Civil Records: Access: Mail, in person, online. Both court and visitors may perform in person searches. Search fee: $5.00 per name. Court makes copy: $1.00 for first page, $.50 each add'l. Required to search: name, years to search. Civil cases indexed by defendant, plaintiff; on computer from 10/95; prior records on docket books from 1907. Free court records from 1/1996 to present online at www.odcr.com; updated monthly. Mail turnaround time 1 day.

Criminal Records: Access: Mail, in person, online. Both court and visitors may perform in person searches. Search fee: $5.00 per name. Court makes copy: $1.00 for first page, $.50 each add'l. Required to search: name, years to search; also helpful: address, DOB, SSN. Records computerized from 10/95; prior records on docket books from 1907. Free access to records /1996 to present at www.odcr.com; updated monthly. Mail turnaround time 1 day.

General Information: Public terminal goes back to 1996. No juvenile, adoptions, mental or guardianship records released. Certification fee: $.50 per page. Payee: Stephens County 5th Judicial Court. Personal checks not accepted. Prepayment and SASE required.

Texas County

1st Judicial District Court Box 1081 (319 N Main St), Guymon, OK 73942; phone: 580-338-3003; 9AM-5PM (CST). *Felony, Misdemeanor, Civil, Eviction, Small Claims, Probate.*

Civil Records: Access: Mail, in person, online. Both court and visitors may perform in person searches. Search fee: $5.00 per name. Court makes copy: $.50 per page; same fee for self serve. Required to search: name, years to search. Civil cases indexed by defendant, plaintiff; on microfiche from 1976, archived prior, computerized since 3/95. Free court records from 1/15/1995 to present online at www.odcr.com; updated daily. Mail turnaround time 5 days; 1 day for phone.

Criminal Records: Access: Mail, in person, online. Both court and visitors may perform in person searches. Search fee: $5.00 per name. Court makes copy: $.50 per page; same fee for self serve. Required to search: name, years to search; also helpful: SSN. Criminal records on microfiche from 1976, archived prior, computerized since 3/95. Free court records from 1/15/1995 to present online at www.odcr.com; updated daily. Mail turnaround time 5 days; 1 day for phone.

General Information: Public terminal goes back to 5/1995. No juvenile, adoptions, mental health or guardianship records released. Will fax documents. Certification fee: $.50 per pleading or instrument. Payee: Court Clerk. Personal checks accepted. Prepayment and SASE required.

Tillman County

3rd Judicial District Court Box 116 (Main & Gladstone), Frederick, OK 73542; phone: 580-335-3023; fax: 580-335-5613; hours 8AM-4PM (CST). *Felony, Misdemeanor, Civil, Eviction, Small Claims, Probate.*

Civil Records: Access: Mail, in person. Both court and visitors may perform in person searches. Search fee: $5.00 per name. Court makes copy: $1.00 for first page, $.50 each add'l. Required to search: name, years to search. Civil cases indexed by defendant, plaintiff; on docket books from 1907; on computer back to 1998. Mail turnaround time 1 day.

Criminal Records: Access: Mail, in person. Both court and visitors may perform in person searches. Search fee: $5.00 per name. Court makes copy: $1.00 for first page, $.50 each add'l. Required to search: name, years to search, DOB; also helpful: SSN. Criminal records on docket books from 1907; on computer back to 1998. Mail turnaround time 1 day.

General Information: Public terminal goes back to 1998. No expunged records released. Will fax documents to local or toll-free number. Certification fee: $1.00. Payee: District Court. Business checks accepted. Prepayment required. Will bill law firms. SASE required.

Tulsa County

14th Judicial District Court 500 S Denver Ave, Tulsa, OK 74103-3832; phone: 918-596-5000; criminal phone: 918-596-5471; civil phone: 918-596-5436; probate phone: 918-596-5440; hours 8:30AM-5PM (CST). *Felony, Misdemeanor, Civil, Eviction, Small Claims, Probate.*

Civil Records: Access: Mail, online, in person. Both court and visitors may perform in person searches. Search fee: $5.00 per name. Court makes copy: $1.00 for first page, $.50 each add'l. Required to search: name, years to search. Civil cases indexed by defendant, plaintiff; on computer from 1984, on microfiche from 1907, archived from 1907. Online access to court dockets is free at www.oscn.net/applications/oscn/casesearch.asp. Civil dockets go back to 10/1984. Mail turnaround time 1 week.

Criminal Records: Access: Mail, online, in person. Both court and visitors may perform in person searches. Search fee: $5.00 per name. Court makes copy: $1.00 for first page, $.50 each add'l. Required to search: name, years to search; also helpful: SSN. Records computerized from 1984, on microfiche from 1907, archived from 1907. Online access to criminal dockets is same as civil. Criminal dockets go back to 1/1988. Mail turnaround time 1 week.

General Information: Public terminal goes back to 1984. No juvenile, adoption or guardianship records released. Certification fee: $.50 per page. Payee: Court Clerk. Will accept attorney personal checks. Prepayment and SASE required.

Wagoner County

15th Judicial District Court Box 249 (302 E Cherokee St), Wagoner, OK 74477; phone: 918-485-4508; hours 8:00AM-4:30PM (CST). *Felony, Misdemeanor, Civil, Eviction, Small Claims, Probate.*

Civil Records: Access: Mail, in person, online. Both court and visitors may perform in person searches. Search fee: $5.00 per name. Court makes copy: $1.00 for first page, $.50 each add'l. Required to search: name, years to search. Civil cases indexed by defendant, plaintiff; on docket books from 1980; on computer back to 1997. Free court records from 1/1990 to present online at www.odcr.com; updated daily. Mail turnaround time 1-2 days for civil, longer for criminal.

Criminal Records: Access: Mail, in person, online. Both court and visitors may perform in person searches. Search fee: $5.00 per name if assisted. Court makes copy: $1.00 for first page, $.50 each add'l. Required to search: name, years to search; also helpful: SSN. Criminal records are in files and dockets back to 1907; on computer back to 1997. Free court records from 1/1990 to present online at www.odcr.com; updated daily. Mail turnaround time 1-2 days for civil, longer for criminal.

General Information: Public terminal goes back to 1990. No juvenile, mental health, adoption or guardianship records released. Certification fee: $.50 per page. Payee: Court Clerk. Personal checks accepted. Prepayment and SASE required.

Washington County

11th Judicial District Court 420 S Johnstone, Rm 101, Bartlesville, OK 74003; phone: 918-337-2870; fax: 918-337-2897; hours 8AM-5PM (CST). *Felony, Misdemeanor, Civil, Eviction, Small Claims, Probate.*

Civil Records: Access: Fax, mail, in person, online. Both court and visitors may perform in person searches. Search fee: $5.00 per name. Court makes copy: $1.00 for first page, $.50 each add'l. Required to search: name, years to search. Civil cases indexed by defendant, plaintiff; on docket books from 1907; computerized records since 1995. Free court records from 1/1999 to present online at www.odcr.com; updated daily. Mail turnaround time 2-4 days.

Criminal Records: Access: Fax, mail, in person, online. Both court and visitors may perform in person searches. Search fee: $5.00 per name. Court makes copy: $1.00 for first page, $.50 each add'l. Required to search: name, years to search, signed release; also helpful: DOB, SSN. Criminal records on docket books from 1907; computerized records since 1997. Free court records from 1/1999 to present online at www.odcr.com; updated daily. Mail turnaround time 2-4 days.

General Information: Public use terminal available. No juvenile, mental health, adoption or guardianship records released. Will fax documents to local or toll free line. Certification fee: $.50 per page. Payee: Court Clerk. Personal checks accepted. Prepayment required.

Washita County

2nd Judicial District Court Box 397 (111 E Main St), Cordell, OK 73632; phone: 580-832-3836; fax: 580-832-4123; hours 8AM-4PM (CST). *Felony, Misdemeanor, Civil, Small Claims, Probate.*

Civil Records: Access: Mail, in person, online. Both court and visitors may perform in person searches. Search fee: $5.00 per name. Court makes copy: $1.00 for first page, $.50 each add'l. Required to search: name, years to search. Civil cases indexed by defendant, plaintiff; on computer since 1998; prior records on microfiche from 1980s & on docket books

from 1892. Free court records from 10/1/1997 to present online at www.odcr.com; updated daily. Mail turnaround time same day.

Criminal Records: Access: Mail, in person, online. Both court and visitors may perform in person searches. Search fee: $5.00 per name. Court makes copy: $1.00 for first page, $.50 each add'l. Required to search: name, years to search; also helpful: DOB, SSN, aliases. Criminal records on computer since 1998; prior records on microfiche from 1980s & on docket books from 1892. Free court records from 10/1/1997 to present online at www.odcr.com; updated daily. Mail turnaround time same day.

General Information: Public terminal goes back to 1998. No juvenile, mental health, adoption or guardianship records released. Will fax documents for $1.00 per page. Certification fee: $.50 per page or $5.00 authenticated certificate. Payee: Court Clerk. Personal checks accepted. Prepayment and SASE required.

Woods County

4th Judicial District Court Box 924, 407 Government St, Alva, OK 73717; phone: 580-327-3119; hours 9AM-5PM (CST). *Felony, Misdemeanor, Civil, Eviction, Small Claims, Probate.*

Civil Records: Access: Mail, in person, online. Both court and visitors may perform in person searches. Search fee: $5.00 per name. Court makes copy: $1.00 for first page, $.50 each add'l. Required to search: name, years to search. Civil cases indexed by defendant, plaintiff; on docket books from 1890. Free court records from 7/2002 to present online at www.odcr.com; updated monthly. Mail turnaround time 2 days.

Criminal Records: Access: Mail, in person, online. Both court and visitors may perform in person searches. Search fee: $5.00 per name. Court makes copy: $1.00 for first page, $.50 each add'l. Required to search: name, years to search. Criminal records on computer since 1987, on dockets and cards from 1890s. Free court records from 7/2002 to present online at www.odcr.com; updated monthly. Mail turnaround time 2 days.

General Information: Public terminal goes back to 2002. No juvenile, mental health, adoption or guardianship records released. Will not fax documents. Certification fee: $.50 per page. Payee: Clerk of Court. Personal checks accepted. Prepayment and SASE required.

Woodward County

4th Judicial District Court 1600 Main St, Woodward, OK 73801; phone: 580-256-3413; hours 9AM-5PM (CST). *Felony, Misdemeanor, Civil, Eviction, Small Claims, Probate.*

Civil Records: Access: Mail, in person. Both court and visitors may perform in person searches. Search fee: $5.00 per name. Court makes copy: $1.00 for first page, $.50 each add'l; same fee for self serve. Required to search: name, years to search. Civil cases indexed by defendant, plaintiff; on docket books from 1890, on microfiche from 1989; on computer from 1997. Mail turnaround time 1-2 days unless older cases found.

Criminal Records: Access: Mail, in person. Both court and visitors may perform in person searches. Search fee: $5.00 per name. Court makes copy: $1.00 for first page, $.50 each add'l; same fee for self serve. Required to search: name, years to search; also helpful: DOB, SSN. Criminal records on docket books from 1890, on microfiche from 1989; on computer from 1997. Mail turnaround time 1-2 days unless older cases found.

General Information: Public terminal goes back to 1997. No mental, juvenile, adoption, guardianship records released. Fee to fax documents is 1.00 per document. Certification fee: $.50 per page. $5.00 for whole file. Payee: Court Clerk. Personal checks accepted. Prepayment and SASE required.

Oklahoma Recording Offices

ORGANIZATION: 77 counties, 77 recording offices. The recording officer is County Clerk. The entire state is in the Central Time Zone (CST).

REAL ESTATE RECORDS: Many counties will perform real estate searches by legal description. Copy fees are usually $1.00 per page. Certification usually costs $1.00 per document.

UCC RECORDS: Financing statements are filed centrally with the County Clerk of Oklahoma County. Prior to 7/2001, consumer goods, farm related, and real estate related collateral were dual filed with the local County Clerk as well as the County Clerk of Oklahoma County. Now only real estate related collateral is filed at the local level. All counties will perform UCC searches. Use search request form UCC-4. Search fees vary from usually $5.00 to $10.00 per debtor name for a written request and $3.00 per name by telephone. Copies usually cost $1.00 per page.

TAX LIEN RECORDS: Federal tax liens on personal property of businesses are filed with the County Clerk of Oklahoma County, which is the central filing office for the state. Other federal and all state tax liens are filed with the County Clerk. Usually state and federal tax liens on personal property are filed in separate indexes. Some counties will perform tax lien searches. Search fees vary.

OTHER LIENS: Judgment, mechanics, physicians, hospital.

ONLINE ACCESS: Very little is available online from the counties directly. A private company - OKAssessors.com - provides subscription access to assessor indices and property images from all but 6 Oklahoma counties, see. www.okassessor.com, or call 800-535-6467 or email tracy@okassessor.com for information. Generally, all records are within 90 days of current. Sub packages: $30 per county or 10 counties $150 or $250 for entire state except for Cleveland, Garfield, Osage, Rogers, Texas and Washington counties, which are not yet available.

Adair County

County Clerk, PO Box 169, Stilwell, OK 74960. 918-696-7198; fax-918-696-2603; hours: 8AM-4:30PM.
All records in one index. Records indexed on computer back to 1978, full records back to 1983-4. Office personnel or visitors may perform searches. General index search fee $5.00 per instrument. UCC search includes tax liens. Copy fee $1.00 per page. Cert fee- $2.00 per page plus copy fee. Payee- Adair County Clerk. **Other phones:** Treasurer- 918-696-7551; Elections- 918-696-7221. **Property tax/Assessor-** Adair County Courthouse, Stilwell, OK 74960; 918-696-2012.

Alfalfa County

County Clerk, 300 S. Grand, Cherokee, OK 73728. 580-596-3158; hours: 8:30AM-4:30PM.
May search real estate records depending on situation. Will search UCC records, search includes tax liens. UCC search per debtor name- $10.00. Copy fee $1.00 per page. Cert fee- $1.00 per page plus copy fee. Payee- Alfalfa County Clerk. **Other phones:** Treasurer- 580-596-3148; Elections- 580-596-2718. **Property tax/Assessor-** same address as above. 580-596-2145.

Atoka County

County Clerk, 200 E. Court St, Atoka, OK 74525. 580-889-5157; fax-580-889-5063; hours: 8:30AM-4:30PM.
Separate indices to search include m&m liens, UCC's, federal tax liens, judgments, state tax liens. Record index not computerized. Office personnel or visitors may perform searches. Search fee $10.00 per name. Copy fee $1.00 per page. Cert fee- $1.00 per cert includes copy fee. Payee- Atoka County Clerk. **Other phones:** Treasurer- 580-889-5283; Elections- 580-889-5297. **Property tax/Assessor-** same address as above. 580-889-6036.

Beaver County

County Clerk, PO Box 338, Beaver, OK 73932-0338. 580-625-3141, R/E recording phone-580-625-3418; fax-580-625-3430; hours: 8AM-5PM.
All records in one index. Records indexed on computer back to 1998. Office personnel or visitors may perform searches. No search fee for general index. Copy fee $1.00 per page. Cert fee- $1.00 per page plus copy fee. Payee- Beaver County Clerk. **Other phones:** Treasurer- 580-625-3161; Elections- 580-625-4742. **Property tax/Assessor-** 580-625-3116.

Beckham County

County Clerk, PO Box 428, Sayre, OK 73662-0428. 580-928-3383; fax-580-928-5220; hours: 9AM-5PM.
Index: Numerous indexes to search. Search fee $10.00. Will not search real estate records. Copy fee $1.00 per page. Cert fee- $1.00 per page plus copy fee. Payee- Beckham County Clerk. **Other phones:** Treasurer- 580-928-2589. **Property tax/Assessor-** 580-928-3329.

Blaine County

County Clerk, PO Box 138, Watonga, OK 73772. 580-623-5890; fax-580-623-5009; hours: 8AM-4PM.
Office personnel or visitors may perform searches. Search fee $3.00 per name. Copy fee $1.00 per page. Cert fee- $1.00 per doc plus copy fee. Payee- County Clerk. **Other phones:** Treasurer- 580-623-5007; Elections- 580-623-5518; Vital Records- 405-271-4040. **Property tax/Assessor-** 580-623-5123.

Bryan County

County Clerk, PO Box 1789, Durant, OK 74702. 580-924-2202; fax-580-924-2289; hours: 8AM-5PM.
Index: Indices arranged by legal descriptions. Search fee $5.00 per name. Will search real estate records as time permits. Copy fee $1.00 per copy. Cert fee- $1.00 per impression. Payee- County Clerk. **Online access to Real Estate Recording, Deed records:** Access recording office land data at www.etitlesearch.com; registration required, fee based on usage. **Other phones:** Treasurer- 580-924-0748; Appraiser/Auditor- 580-924-2166; Elections- 580-924-3228. **Property tax/Assessor-** 402 W Evergreen, Durant, OK 74702; 580-924-2166.

Caddo County

County Clerk, PO Box 68, Anadarko, OK 73005. 405-247-6609; fax-405-247-6510; hours: 8:30AM-4:30PM.
Separate indices to search include computer and index. Records indexed on a public use terminal back to 1993. Only the public may search. Copy fee $1.00 per page. Cert fee- $1.00 per doc plus copy fee. Payee- Caddo County Clerk. **Other phones:** Treasurer- 405-247-5151; Elections- 405-247-5001; Vital Records- 405-271-4040; Real Estate- 405-247-6510. **Property tax/Assessor-** 405-247-2477.

Canadian County

County Clerk, PO Box 458, El Reno, OK 73036. 405-262-1070 ext123; fax-405-422-2411; www.canadiancounty.org
Office will perform a UCC search but public must search other records themselves. UCC search per debtor name- $10.00. Copy fee $1.00 per page. Cert fee- $1.00 per doc plus copy fee. Payee- Canadian County Clerk. **Online access to Land, Grantor/Grantee, Deed, Lien, Judgment records:** Access to recorders database is free http://landrecords.canadiancounty.org/coclerk/deeds/default.asp. Records go back to 1/2000. **Other phones:** Treasurer- 405-262-1070 x250. **Property tax/Assessor-** 405-262-1070 x269.

Carter County

County Clerk, PO Box 1236, Ardmore, OK 73402. 580-223-8162; hours: 8AM-5PM. www.brightok.net/chickasaw/ardmore/county/coclerk.html
All records in one index. Only the public may search. Copy fee $1.00 per page. Cert fee- $1.00 per doc plus copy fee. Payee- Carter County Clerk. **Online access to Assessor, Unsolved Case records:** The sheriff's unsolved mysteries page is free at www.brightok.net/cartercounty/UnsolvedMysteries.html. Search the county assessor database for free at www.cartercountyassessor.org/disclaim.htm. **Other phones:** Treasurer- 580-223-9467. **Property tax/Assessor-** 580-223-9594, 800-231-8668 x594 (in county).

Cherokee County

County Clerk, 213 W. Delaware; Rm 200, Tahlequah, OK 74464. 918-456-3171, UCC recording phone-918-458-6512; fax-918-458-6508; hours: 8AM-4:30PM (Recording hours 8AM-4PM).
Separate indices to search include warranty deeds, mortgage & miscellaneous. Records indexed on a public use terminal back to 1998. Office personnel or visitors may perform searches. General index search fee $5.00 per name. Copy fee $1.00 per page. Cert fee- $1.50 per cert plus copy fee. Payee-

Cherokee County Clerk. **Other phones:** Treasurer-918-456-3321; Elections- 918-456-2261. **Property tax/Assessor-** same address as above. 918-456-3201.

Choctaw County

County Clerk, 300 E, Duke; Courthouse, Hugo, OK 74743. 580-326-3778; fax-580-326-6787; hours: 8AM-4PM.

Separate indices to search. Records indexed on computer back to April, 2001. Office personnel or visitors may perform searches. Search fee $5.00 per name. UCC search per debtor name- $10.00. Copy fee $1.00 per page. Cert fee- $1.00 per cert plus copy fee. Payee- County Clerk. **Other phones:** Treasurer- 580-326- 6142; Elections- 580-326-5164; Vital Records- 580-271-4040. **Property tax/Assessor-** same address as above. 580-326-2358.

Cimarron County

County Clerk, PO Box 145, Boise City, OK 73933. 580-544-2251; fax-580-544-2251; hours: 8AM-N, 1-5PM.

All records in one index. Record index not computerized. Office personnel or visitors may perform searches. General index search fee $12.00 per hour. Copy fee $1.00 per page. Cert fee- $1.00 per doc plus copy fee. Payee- Cimarron County Clerk. **Other phones:** Treasurer- 580-544-2261; Elections- 580-544-3377. **Property tax/Assessor-** 580-544-2701.

Cleveland County

County Clerk, 641 E Robinson #300, Norman, OK 73071. 405-366-0240, UCC recording phone-405-366-0234; fax-405-366-0229; hours: 8:15AM-4:45PM. http://search.cogov.net/okclev/

Separate indices to search include real estate, M&M, federal tax, fictitious names, UCC's, military discharges (discharges are NOT available for public access). Office will perform a UCC search but public must search other records themselves. UCC search per debtor name- $10.00. Copy fee $1.00 per page. Cert fee- $1.00 per doc plus copy fee. Payee- County Clerk. **Online access to Recording, Lien, Judgment, UCC, Fictitious Name, Military Discharge records:** Access to the Clerk Index is free at http://search.cogov.net/okclev/default.asp. For access to Tax Liens, Real Estate, UCC, Physician Liens and Mechanic Liens go to clevelandcountyclerk.net. **Other phones:** Treasurer- 405-366-0217; Appraiser/Auditor-405-366-0230; Elections- 405-366-0210; Vital Records- 405-271-4040. **Property tax/Assessor-** 641 E Robinson #100, Norman, OK, 73071; 405-366-0230.

Coal County

County Clerk, 4 N. Main; #1, Coalgate, OK 74538. 580-927-2103; fax-580-927-4003; hours: 8AM-4PM. Office will perform a UCC search but public must search other records themselves. UCC search per debtor name- $10.00. Copy fee $1.00 per page. Cert fee- $1.00 per instrument plus copy fee. Payee- Coal County Clerk. **Other phones:** Treasurer- 580-927-3121; Elections- 580-927-3456; Vital Records- 580-927-2281. **Property tax/Assessor-** 4 N Main #5, Coalgate, OK 74538; 580-927-3123.

Comanche County

County Clerk, 315 SW 5th; Rm 304, Lawton, OK 73501-4347. 580-355-5214; hours: 8:30AM-5PM. Office will perform a UCC search but public must search other records themselves. UCC search per debtor name- $10.00. Copy fee $1.00 per page. Cert fee- $1.00 per doc plus copy fee. Payee- Comanche County Clerk. **Other phones:** Treasurer- 580-355-5763; Elections- 580-353-1880; Vital Records- 405-271-4040. **Property tax/Assessor-** 580-355-1052.

Cotton County

County Clerk, 301 N. Broadway, Walters, OK 73572. 580-875-3026; fax-580-875-3756; hours: 8AM-4PM. Separate indices to search include tract indexes by hand, grantor/grantee indexes on computer. Records indexed on computer back to 1986. Only the public may search. Copy fee $1.00 per page. Cert fee- $1.00 per doc plus copy fee. Payee-Cotton County Clerk. **Other phones:** Treasurer- 580-875-3264; Elections- 580-875-3403; Vital Records-405-271-4040. **Property tax/Assessor-** same address as above. 580-875-3289.

Craig County

County Clerk, PO Box 397, Vinita, OK 74301. 918-256-2507; fax-918-256-3617; hours: 8:30AM-4:30PM.

Separate indices to search include grantor/grantee, land tract. Office personnel or visitors may perform searches. Search fee $10.00 per name. Copy fee $1.00 per page. Cert fee- $2.00 1st page; $1.00 each add'l. **Other phones:** Treasurer- 918-256-2286; Elections- 918-256-7559. **Property tax/Assessor-** 918-256-8766.

Creek County

County Clerk, 317 E. Lee #100, Sapulpa, OK 74066. 918-227-6306, R/E recording phone-918-224-4084, UCC recording phone-918-227-6306; hours: 8AM-5PM.

Record index not computerized. Office will perform a UCC search but public must search other records themselves. UCC search per debtor name- $5.00. Copy fee $1.00 per page. Cert fee- $1.00 per cert plus copy fee. Payee- Creek County Clerk. **Other phones:** Treasurer- 918-227-4501; Mapping- 918-227-6357. **Property tax/Assessor-** same address as above. 918-224-4508.

Custer County

County Clerk, PO Box 300, Arapaho, OK 73620. 580-323-1221; fax-580-323-4421; hours: 8AM-4PM. All records in one index. Record index not computerized. Office personnel or visitors may perform searches. Search fee $3.00 per name. Copy fee $1.00 per page. Cert fee- $1.00 per doc plus copy fee. Payee- County Clerk. **Other phones:** Treasurer- 580-323-2292; Elections- 580-323-2291; Vital Records- 580-323-4040. **Property tax/Assessor-** 580-323-3271.

Delaware County

County Clerk, PO Box 309, Jay, OK 74346. 918-253-4520; fax-918-253-8352; hours: 8AM-4:30PM. www.delawareclerk.org

All records in one index. Records indexed on a public use terminal back to 1987. Search fee $10.00 per name written; $3.00 per name verbal. Will not search real estate records. Copy fee $1.00 per page. Cert fee- $1.00 per cert plus copy fee. Payee-Delaware County Clerk. **Online access to Real Estate, Deed, Recorder records:** Access land records index free at www.okcountyrecords.com or http://okcountyrecords.com/search.php?County=021. Subscription required for images; $10.00 per month. **Other phones:** Treasurer- 918-253-4533; Elections-918-253-8762; Court Clerk- 918-253-4420. **Property tax/Assessor-** 918-328-5561.

Dewey County

County Clerk, PO Box 368, Taloga, OK 73667. 580-328-5361; fax-580-328-5652; hours: 8AM-4PM. Separate indices to search include judgments. Will not search real estate records. Will search UCC records, but not tax liens. UCC search per debtor name- $10.00. Copy fee $1.00 per page. Cert fee- $1.00 per cert plus copy fee. Payee- Dewey County Clerk. **Other phones:** Treasurer- 580-328-5501. **Property tax/Assessor-** PO Box 235, Taloga, OK 73667; 580-328-5561.

Ellis County

, PO Box 197, Arnett, OK 73832. 580-885-7301; fax-580-885-7258; hours: 8:30AM-4:30PM.

All records in one index. Office personnel or visitors may perform searches. Will search real estate records. Copy fee $1.00 per page. Cert fee- $1.00 per page plus copy fee. Payee- Ellis County Clerk. **Other phones:** Treasurer- 580-885-7670; Elections-580-885-7721; Vital Records- 580-885-7301. **Property tax/Assessor-** PO Box 276, Arnett, OK 73832; 580-885-7975.

Garfield County

County Clerk, PO Box 1664, Enid, OK 73702-1664. 580-237-0226; fax-580-249-5951; hours: 8AM-4:30PM.

All records in one index. Only the public may search. Copy fee $1.00 per page. Cert fee- $1.00 per page plus copy fee. Payee- Garfield County Clerk. **Other phones:** Treasurer- 580-237-0246; Appraiser/Auditor- 580-237-0220; Elections- 580-237-6016; Court Clerk- 580-237-0232. **Property tax/Assessor-** 114 W Broadway, Rm 106, Enid, OK 73703; 580-237-0220.

Garvin County

County Clerk, PO Box 926, Pauls Valley, OK 73075. 405-238-2772; fax-405-238-6283; hours: 8:30-4:30PM.

Office will perform a UCC search but public must search other records themselves. UCC search per debtor name- $5.00. Copy fee $1.00 per page. Cert fee- $1.00 per cert. Payee- Garvin County Clerk. **Other phones:** Treasurer- 405-238-7301. **Property tax/Assessor-** 405-238-2409.

Grady County

County Clerk, PO Box 1009, Chickasha, OK 73023. 405-224-7388; fax-405-222-4506; hours: 8AM-4:30PM.

Separate indices to search include 6 rural, 2 town. Records indexed on a public use terminal back to 1989. Office will perform a UCC search but public must search other records themselves. UCC search per debtor name- $5.00. Copy fee $1.00 per page. Cert fee- $1.00 per doc plus copy fee. Payee-County Clerk. **Online access to Assessor, Property records:** Access assessor property data free at www.gradycountyassessor.org/search.stm; for full data, registration and $25.00 monthly fee required. **Other phones:** Treasurer- 405-224-5337; Elections- 405-224-1430; Vital Records- 405-271-4040. **Property tax/Assessor-** 326 Choctaw St, Chickasha, OK 73023; 405-224-4361.

Grant County

County Clerk, 112 E. Guthrie St #102, Medford, OK 73759. 580-395-2274; fax-580-395-2086; hours: 8AM-4:30PM.

Office personnel or visitors may perform searches. Search fee $5.00 per name. Will not search real estate records. Copy fee $1.00 per page. Cert fee- $1.00 per cert plus copy fee. Payee- Grant County Clerk. **Other phones:** Treasurer- 580-395-2284; Elections-580-395-2862. **Property tax/Assessor-** 580-395-2844.

Greer County

County Clerk, PO Box 207, Mangum, OK 73554. 580-782-3664; fax-580-782-3803; hours: 8AM-4PM. Index: Indexes; Mtg, Deeds, Misc, Fed & State Tax liens, Judgments, and M & M Liens. Office will perform a UCC search but public must search other records themselves. General index search fee $5.00. Copy fee $1.00 per page. Cert fee- $1.00 per page plus copy fee. Payee- Greer County Clerk. **Other phones:** Treasurer- 580-782-5515; Appraiser/Auditor- 580-782-2454; Elections- 580-782-2307; Vital Records- 405-271-4040. **Property tax/Assessor-** 106 E Jefferson,Rm14, Mangum, OK 73554; 580-782-2740.

Harmon County

County Clerk, 114 W Hollis; Courthouse, Hollis, OK 73550. 580-688-3658; fax-580-688-9784; hours: 8AM-N, 1-5PM.
All records in one index. Office personnel or visitors may perform searches. Search fee $5.00 per name. Property transfer searches available. Will search UCC records, tax liens not included in UCC search. Copy fee $1.00 per page. Cert fee- $2.00 per doc plus copy fee. Payee- Harmon County Clerk. **Other phones:** Treasurer- 580-882-3566. **Property tax/Assessor-** 114 W Hollis, Hollis, OK 73550; 580-882-2529.

Harper County

County Clerk, PO Box 369, Buffalo, OK 73834. 580-735-2012; fax-580-735-2612; hours: 8AM-4PM.
Separate indices to search. Office personnel or visitors may perform searches. General index search fee $10.00. Will search real estate records. Will search UCC records; search includes tax liens if requested. UCC search per debtor name- $10.00. Copy fee $1.00 per page. Cert fee- $1.00 per page plus copy fee. Payee- Harper County Clerk. **Other phones:** Treasurer- 580-735-2442; Elections- 580-735-2313; Court Clerk- 580-735-0010. **Property tax/Assessor-** 580-735-2343.

Haskell County

County Clerk, 202 E. Main; Courthouse, Stigler, OK 74462. 918-967-2884; fax-918-967-2885; hours: 8AM-4:30PM.
Records indexed on computer back to 1994. Office personnel or visitors may perform searches. Search fee $10.00 written; $3.00 phone. Copy fee $1.00 per page. Cert fee- $1.00 per page plus copy fee. Payee- Haskell County Clerk. **Other phones:** Treasurer- 918-967-2441; Elections- 918-967-8792. **Property tax/Assessor-** same address as above. 918-967-2611.

Hughes County

County Clerk, 200 N. Broadway ST. #5, Holdenville, OK 74848-3400. 405-379-5487; fax-405-379-6890; hours: 8AM-4:30PM.
All records in one index. Only the public may search. Copy fee $1.00 per page. Cert fee- $1.00 per seal. Payee- Hughes County Clerk. **Other phones:** Treasurer- 405-379-5371; Elections- 405-379-2174. **Property tax/Assessor-** same address as above. 405-379-3862.

Jackson County

County Clerk, PO Box 515, Altus, OK 73522. 580-482-4070; fax-none; hours: 8AM-4PM.
Separate indices to search include taxes, deeds, mortgages. Records indexed on computer back to 2004. Office personnel or visitors may perform searches. General index search fee $10.00 per person. Copy fee $1.00 per page. Cert fee- $1.00 per cert plus copy fee. Payee- Jackson County Clerk. **Other phones:** Treasurer- 580-482-4371; Elections- 580-482-2370; Vital Records- 580-482-4070. **Property tax/Assessor-** 101 N Main, Rm 201, Altus, OK 73521; 580-482-0787.

Jefferson County

County Clerk, 220 N. Main; Courthouse - Rm 103, Waurika, OK 73573. 580-228-2029; fax-580-228-3418; hours: 8AM-4PM.
All records in one index. Record index not computerized. Only the office personnel may search. Search fee $5.00. Will not search real estate records. Copy fee $1.00 per page. Cert fee- $1.00 per page plus copy fee. Payee- Jefferson County Clerk. **Other phones:** Treasurer- 580-228-2967; Elections- 580-228-3150. **Property tax/Assessor-** 580-228-2377.

Johnston County

County Clerk, 403 W. Main; Rm 101, Tishomingo, OK 73460. 580-371-3184; fax-580-371-3662; hours: 8:30AM-4:30PM.
Office personnel or visitors may perform searches. Search fee $10.00 unless otherwise indicated. Limited real estate owner, mortgage, and property transfer searches available. Tax lien search fee- $3.00 per debtor for uncertified verbal search. Copy fee $1.00 per page. Cert fee- $1.00 per page plus copy fee. Payee- Johnston County Clerk. **Other phones:** Treasurer- 580-371-3082; Elections- 580-371-3670; Vital Records- 580-271-4040. **Property tax/Assessor-** 403 W. Main #102, Tishomingo, OK 73460; 580-371-3645.

Kay County

County Clerk, PO Box 450, Newkirk, OK 74647-0450. 580-362-2537; fax-580-362-3300; hours: 8AM-4:30PM.
All records in one index. Records indexed on a public use terminal. Office personnel or visitors may perform searches. Search fee $10.00 per name. Copy fee $1.00 per page. Cert fee- $1.00 per page plus copy fee. Payee- Kay County Clerk. **Other phones:** Treasurer- 580-362-2523; Elections- 580-362-2130. **Property tax/Assessor-** 580-362-2566.

Kingfisher County

County Clerk, 101 S. Main, Rm #3, Kingfisher, OK 73750. 405-375-3887; fax-405-375-6033; hours: 8AM-4:30PM.
Office will perform a UCC search but public must search other records themselves. UCC search per debtor name- $10.00. Copy fee $1.00 per page. Cert fee- $1.00 per doc plus copy fee. Payee- Judy Grellner, County Clerk. **Other phones:** Treasurer- 405-375-3827; Appraiser/Auditor- 405-375-3884; Elections- 405-375-3895. **Property tax/Assessor-** 405-375-3884.

Kiowa County

County Clerk, PO Box 73, Hobart, OK 73651-0073. 580-726-5286; fax-580-726-6033; hours: 9AM-5PM.
All records in one index. Records indexed on a public use terminal. Office will perform a UCC search but public must search other records themselves. UCC search per debtor name- $10.00. Copy fee $1.00 per page. Cert fee- $1.00 per doc, plus copy fee. Payee- Kiowa County Clerk. **Other phones:** Treasurer- 580-726-2362; Elections- 580-726-2509. **Property tax/Assessor-** P O Box 853 580-726-2150.

Latimer County

County Clerk, 109 N Central; Rm 103, Wilburton, OK 74578. 918-465-3543; fax-918-465-4001; hours: 8AM-4:30PM.
Office personnel or visitors may perform searches. Search fee $10.00 per name. Copy fee $1.00 per page. Cert fee- $1.00 per cert. Payee- Latimer County Clerk. **Other phones:** Treasurer- 918-465-3450. **Property tax/Assessor-** 918-465-3031.

Le Flore County

County Clerk, PO Box 218, Poteau, OK 74953-0218. 918-647-5738; fax-918-647-8930; hours: 8AM-4:30PM.
Office personnel or visitors may perform searches. Search fee $5.00 per name. Will not search real estate records. Will search UCC records. UCC search per debtor name- $10.00. Copy fee $1.00 per page. Cert fee- None. Payee- Le Flore County Clerk. **Online access to Real Estate, Deed, Recorder records:** Access land records index free at www.okcountyrecords.com or http://okcountyrecords.com/search.php. Subscription required for images; $10.00 per month. **Other phones:** Treasurer- 918-647-3525; Elections- 918-647-3701. **Property tax/Assessor-** 918-647-3652.

Lincoln County

County Clerk, PO Box 126, Chandler, OK 74834-0126. 405-258-1264; fax-405-258-0439; hours: 8:30AM-4:30PM.
Separate indices to search include judgments, trust, tax liens, etc. Office personnel or visitors may perform searches. General index search fee $3.00 per legal. Property transfer searches available. UCC search per debtor name- $10.00 for written request. Will do a verbal search for $3.00. Copy fee $1.00 per page. Cert fee- $1.00 per page plus copy fee. Payee- Lincoln County Clerk. **Online access to Real Estate Recording, Deed records:** Access land records at http://etitlesearch.com. You can do a name search; choose from $25.00 monthly subscription or per click account. **Other phones:** Treasurer- 405-258-1491; Elections- 405-258-1349. **Property tax/Assessor-** same address as above. 405-258-1209.

Logan County

County Clerk, 301 E. Harrison; #102, Guthrie, OK 73044-4999. 405-282-0266; fax-405-282-0267; hours: 8:30AM-4:30PM.
All records in one index. Record index not computerized. Only the public may search. Offers only a very limited search of real estate records. Copy fee $1.00 per page. Cert fee- $1.00 per cert plus copy fee. Payee- Logan County Clerk. **Other phones:** Treasurer- 405-282-3154; Elections- 405-282-1900; Vital Records- 405-271-4040. **Property tax/Assessor-** 405-282-3509.

Love County

County Clerk, 405 W. Main; Rm 203, Marietta, OK 73448. 580-276-3059; hours: 8AM-N, 12:30-4:30PM.
Office personnel or visitors may perform searches. Will not search real estate records. UCC search per debtor name- $10.00. Separate federal/state combined tax lien search- no charge. Copy fee $1.00 per page. Cert fee- $1.00 per cert. Payee- Love County Clerk. **Other phones:** Treasurer- 580-276-2360. **Property tax/Assessor-** 580-276-3059.

Major County

County Clerk, PO Box 379, Fairview, OK 73737-0379. 580-227-4732, R/E recording phone-580-227-3918; fax-580-227-2736; hours: 8:30AM-4:30PM.
All records in one index. Office will perform a UCC search but public must search other records themselves. Search fee $5.00 per name. Copy fee $1.00 per page. Cert fee- $1.00. Payee- Major County Clerk. **Other phones:** Treasurer- 580-227-4782. **Property tax/Assessor-** 500 E Broadway, Fairview, OK 73737; 580-227-4821.

Marshall County

County Clerk, Marshall County Courthouse; Rm 101, Madill, OK 73446. 580-795-3220; fax-580-795-7596; hours: 8:30AM-N, 12:30-5PM.
Real estate record owner searches available; legal description and name required. Will search UCC records; search includes tax liens if requested. UCC search per debtor name- $10.00. Separate federal/state combined tax lien search-no charge. Copy fee $1.00 per page. Cert fee- $1.00 per cert, copies not included. Payee- Marshall County Clerk. **Other phones:** Treasurer- 580-795-2463; Appraiser/Auditor- 580-795-2398; Elections- 580-795-5460. **Property tax/Assessor-** Marshall County Courthouse, Rm 105, Madill, OK 73446; 580-795-2398.

Mayes County

County Clerk, 1 Court Place #120, Pryor, OK 74361. 918-825-2426; fax-918-825-3803; hours: 9AM-5PM.
All records in one index. Office personnel or visitors may perform searches. If office personnel searches they are not guaranteed. Search fee $10.00 per debtor; phone searches-$3.00 per search. Copy fee $1.00 per page. Cert fee- $1.00

per doc, plus copy fee. Payee- Mayes County Clerk. **Other phones:** Treasurer- 918-825-0160; Appraiser/Auditor- 918-825-0625; Elections- 918-825-1826. **Property tax/Assessor-** 1 Court Pl #110, Pryor, OK 74361; 918-825-0625.

McClain County

County Clerk, PO Box 629, Purcell, OK 73080-0629. 405-527-3360; hours: 8AM-4:30PM.
All records in one index. Records indexed on computer with name for anything filed after June, 1994. All indexing is hand done on index books. Office personnel or visitors may perform searches. Search fee $3.00. Real estate owner, mortgage, and property transfer searches available. Will search UCC records and tax liens. Copy fee $1.00 per page. Cert fee- $1.00 per cert plus copy fee. Payee- McClain County Clerk. **Other phones:** Treasurer- 405-527-3261; Elections- 405-527-3121. **Property tax/Assessor-** 405-527-3520.

McCurtain County

County Clerk, PO Box 1078, Idabel, OK 74745. 580-286-2370, R/E recording phone-580-286-2370x100; fax-580-286-7040; hours: 8AM-4PM.
All records in one index. Records indexed on a public use terminal back to 3/15/2001. Office will perform a UCC and Tax Lien search but public must search other records themselves. Search fee $10.00. Copy fee $1.00 per page. Cert fee- $1.00 per cert plus copy fee. Payee- McCurtain County Clerk. **Other phones:** Treasurer- 580-286-5128; Vital Records- 405-271-5600; Voter Registrar- 580-286-7405. **Property tax/Assessor-** same address as above, Idabel, OK 74745; 580-286-5272.

McIntosh County

County Clerk, PO Box 110, Eufaula, OK 74432-0110. 918-689-2741; fax-918-689-3385; hours: 8AM-4PM.
Index: indices are separated by township and range. Record index not computerized. Search fee $10.00. Will not search real estate records. Copy fee $1.00 per page. Cert fee- $1.00 plus copy fee. Payee- McIntosh County County Clerk. **Other phones:** Treasurer- 918-689-2491. **Property tax/Assessor-** 918-689-2611.

Murray County

County Clerk, PO Box 442, Sulphur, OK 73086. 580-622-3920; fax-580-622-6209; hours: 8AM-4:30PM.
All records in one index. Records indexed on a public use terminal back to 1990. Office will perform a UCC search but public must search other records themselves. Search fee $5.00. Copy fee $1.00 per page. Cert fee- $1.00 per cert plus copy fee. Payee- Murray County Clerk. **Other phones:** Treasurer- 580-622-5622; Elections- 580-622-3800. **Property tax/Assessor-** 580-622-3433.

Muskogee County

County Clerk, PO Box 1008, Muskogee, OK 74402. 918-682-7781; hours: 8AM-4:30PM.
Office personnel or visitors may perform searches. Search fee $10.00 per name. Will not search real estate records. Copy fee $1.00 per page. Cert fee- $1.00 per cert plus copy fee. Payee- Muskogee County Clerk. **Other phones:** Treasurer- 918-682-0811. **Property tax/Assessor-** 918-682-8781.

Noble County

County Clerk, 300 Courthouse Dr, Box 11; Courthouse, Rm 201, Perry, OK 73077. 580-336-2141; fax-580-336-2481; hours: 8AM-4:30PM.
Record index not computerized. Office personnel or visitors may perform searches. Search fee $10.00. Copy fee $1.00 per page. Cert fee- $1.00 per page. Payee- Noble County Clerk. **Other phones:** Treasurer- 580-336-2026; Elections- 580-336-3527. **Property tax/Assessor-** 580-336-2185.

Nowata County

County Clerk, 229 N. Maple, Nowata, OK 74048. 918-273-2480; fax-918-273-2481; hours: 8AM-4:30PM.
Index: All records searchable except for DD-214 and personal. Office will perform a UCC search but public must search other records themselves. Search fee $10.00 per name. Copy fee $1.00 per page. Cert fee- $1.00 per instrument plus copy fee. Payee- Nowata County Clerk. **Other phones:** Treasurer- 918-273-3562; Elections- 918-273-0710; Vital Records- 918-273-0127. **Property tax/Assessor-** same address as above. 918-273-0581.

Okfuskee County

County Clerk, PO Box 108, Okemah, OK 74859-0108. 918-623-1724; fax-918-623-0739; hours: 8AM-4PM.
All records in one index. Office personnel or visitors may perform searches. Will search UCC records and tax liens. UCC search per debtor name- $10.00. Copy fee $1.00 per page. Cert fee- $1.00 per seal plus copy fee. Payee- County Clerk. **Other phones:** Treasurer- 918-623-1494; Elections- 918-623-0105; Vital Records- 405-271-4040. **Property tax/Assessor-** PO Box 601, Okemah, OK 74859; 918-623-1535.

Oklahoma County

County Clerk, 320 Robert S. Kerr Ave; UCC Filing Ofc - Rm 107, Oklahoma City, OK 73102. 405-713-1522, R/E recording phone-405-713-1540, UCC recording phone-405-713-1522; fax-405-713-1810; hours: 8AM-5PM. www.oklahomacounty.org
The OK UCC Central Filing Office is operated by the OK County Clerk's Office. All records in one index. Records indexed on a public use terminal back to 1961. Office will perform a UCC search but public must search other records themselves. Search fee $10.00. Copy fee $1.00 per page. Cert fee- 1.00 per page. Payee- Oklahoma County Clerk. **Online access to Real Estate, Assessor, Grantor/Grantee, UCC, Property Tax, Inmate, Sex Offender, Most Wanted records:** Assessor and property information on the county assessor database are free at www.oklahomacounty.org/assessor/disclaim.htm. Real estate, UCC, grantor/grantee records on the county clerk database are free at www.oklahomacounty.org/coclerk. Also, search the treasurer's property info at www.oklahomacounty.org/Treasurer/searches/default2.asp. Also, search the sheriff lists of inmates, wanted, and sex offenders at www.oklahomacounty.org/sheriff/default.htm. **Other phones:** Treasurer- 405-713-1300; Appraiser/Auditor- 405-713-1200; Elections- 405-713-1515. **Property tax/Assessor-** 405-278-3838.

Okmulgee County

County Clerk, PO Box 904, Okmulgee, OK 74447-0904. 918-756-0788; fax-918-758-1261; hours: 8AM-4:30PM.
Separate indices to search include Federal tax lien, M&M liens, liens, judgments. Office personnel or visitors may perform searches, depending on type of record. General index search fee $5.00 per legal. If extensive, an hourly rate will be charged. Will search real estate records. Will search UCC records and tax liens. UCC search per debtor name- $5.00 pr name. Tax lien search fee- $5.00 per debtor. Copy fee $1.00 per page. Cert fee- $1.00 per instrument. **Other phones:** Treasurer- 918-756-3848; Elections- 918-756-2365; Vital Records- 405-271-4040. **Property tax/Assessor-** 314 W 7th, #103, Okmulgee, OK 74447; 918-758-0303.

Osage County

County Clerk, PO Box 87, Pawhuska, OK 74056. 918-287-3136; fax-918-287-4979; hours: 8:30AM-5PM.
Separate indices to search include Tax Liens, Judgments, Mechanics Liens. Will not search real estate records. Will search UCC records, but not tax liens. UCC search per debtor name- $10.00. Copy fee $1.00 per page. Cert fee- $1.00 per cert plus copy fee. Payee- Osage County Clerk. **Other phones:** Treasurer- 918-287-3101; Appraiser/Auditor-918-287-3448; Elections- 918-287-3036. **Property tax/Assessor-** 600 Grandview, Rm 101, Pawhuska, OK 74056; 918-287-3448.

Ottawa County

County Clerk, 102 E. Central; #203, Miami, OK 74354-7043. 918-542-3332; fax-918-542-8260; hours: 9AM-N,1-5PM; Recording until 4PM.
Index: books, organized by legal description. Records indexed on a public use terminal back to 1995. Office will perform a UCC search but public must search other records themselves. Search fee $10.00. Copy fee $1.00 per page. Cert fee- $1.00 per cert plus copy fee. Payee- Ottawa County Clerk. **Other phones:** Treasurer- 918-542-8232; Elections- 918-542-2893; Vital Records- 918-571-2600. **Property tax/Assessor-** same address as above. 918-542-9418.

Pawnee County

County Clerk, 500 Harrison St.; Courthouse, Rm 202, Pawnee, OK 74058. 918-762-2732; fax-918-762-6404; hours: 8AM-4:30PM.
Separate indices by townships. Office will perform a UCC search but public must search other records themselves. UCC search per debtor name- $10.00. Copy fee $1.00 per page. Cert fee- $1.00 per cert plus copy fee. Payee- Pawnee County Clerk. **Other phones:** Treasurer- 918-762-2418; Elections- 918-762-2125. **Property tax/Assessor-** 500 Harrison St. Courthouse Rm 201, Pawnee, OK 74058; 918-762-2402.

Payne County

County Clerk, 315 W 6th Ave #202, Stillwater, OK 74074. 405-747-8310, R/E recording phone-405-747-8345, UCC recording phone-405-747-8310; fax-405-747-8304; hours: 8AM-5PM. www.okcountyrecords.com
Separate indices to search include sec township rng and by additions. Records indexed on a public use terminal back 12 years. Office personnel or visitors may perform searches. Search fee $5.00 per name. Copy fee $1.00 per page. Cert fee- $1.00 per cert plus copy fee. Payee- Payne County Clerk. **Online access to Real Estate, Deed, Recorder records:** Access land records index free at www.okcountyrecords.com or http://okcountyrecords.com/search.php. Subscription required for images; $10.00 per month. **Other phones:** Treasurer- 405-747-9411; Appraiser/Auditor- 405-747-8300; Vital Records- 405-271-4040; 405-747-8344. **Property tax/Assessor-** 315 W 6th Ave, #101, Stillwater, OK 74074; 405-747-8300.

Pittsburg County

County Clerk, PO Box 3304, McAlester, OK 74502. 918-423-6865; fax-918-423-7304; hours: 8AM-5PM.
Separate indices to search. Records indexed on computer. Office personnel or visitors may perform searches. Search fee $5.00 per name. Copy fee $1.00 per page. Cert fee- $1.00 per page. Payee- Pittsburg County Clerk. **Other phones:** Treasurer- 918-423-6895. **Property tax/Assessor-** 918-423-4726.

Pontotoc County

County Clerk, PO Box 1425, Ada, OK 74820. 580-332-1425; fax-580-332-9509; hours: 8AM-5PM. www.pontotoccountyclerk.org/
All records in one index. Records indexed on a public use terminal back to 1992. Office personnel or visitors may perform searches. Search fee $10.00 per name. Will not search real estate records. Copy fee $1.00 per page. Cert fee- $1.00 per cert. **Online access to Recording, Land, UCC, Judgment, Lien, Military records:** Access to the recorders records is free on the website. To search, login as guest and password a21b23. Password is case sensitive. **Other phones:** Treasurer- 580-332-0183; Elections- 580-332-4534; Vital Records- 405-271-5600. **Property tax/Assessor-** 580-332-0317.

Pottawatomie County

County Clerk, PO Box 576, Shawnee, OK 74802. 405-273-8222; fax-405-275-6898; hours: 8:30AM-5PM. All records in one index. Records indexed on a public use terminal back to 1985. Office personnel or visitors may perform searches. Search fee $5.00. Copy fee $1.00 per page. Cert fee- $1.00 per doc plus copy fee. Payee- County Clerk. **Other phones:** Treasurer- 405-273-0213; Elections- 405-273-8367. **Property tax/Assessor-** same address as above. 405-275-4740.

Pushmataha County

County Clerk, 302 SW 'B', Antlers, OK 74523. 580-298-3626; fax-580-298-8452; hours: 8AM-4:30PM. Office will perform a UCC search but public must search other records themselves. UCC search per debtor name- $5.00. Copy fee $1.00 per page. Cert fee- $2.00 per page. Payee- Pushmataha County Clerk. **Other phones:** Treasurer- 580-298-2580; Appraiser/Auditor- 580-298-3504; Elections- 580-298-3292; County Clerk- 580-298-2274. **Property tax/Assessor-** 580-298-3504.

Roger Mills County

County Clerk, PO Box 708, Cheyenne, OK 73628. 580-497-3395, R/E recording phone-580-497-3366 or 3395; fax-580-497-3488; hours: 9AM-4:30PM. Only the public may search. Copy fee $1.00 per page. Cert fee- $1.00. Payee- Roger Mills County Clerk. **Other phones:** Treasurer- 580-497-3349; Elections- 580-497-3330. **Property tax/Assessor-** 580-497-3350.

Rogers County

County Clerk, PO Box 1210, Claremore, OK 74018. 918-341-2518; fax-918-341-4529; hours: 8AM-5PM. www.rogerscounty.org
Separate indices to search include land, liens, judgment, legal description. Search fee $10.00 per name. Will not search real estate records. Copy fee $1.00 per page. Cert fee- $1.00 per cert plus copy fee. Payee- Rogers County Clerk. **Online access to Assessor, Property Tax, Treasurer, Tax Roll, Real Estate Recording records:** Access to the assessor database is free at www.rogerscounty.org/search.html. Also, you may search the treasurers tax roll database free at www.rogerscounty.org/treasurer/search.html. Also, access land records at http://etitlesearch.com; for registration and subscription, call 870-856-3055. **Other phones:** Treasurer- 918-341-3159; Appraiser/Auditor- 918-341-0200; Elections- 918-314-2965; Vital Records- 405-271-4040. **Property tax/Assessor-** 219 S Missouri, Rm 1-108, Claremore, OK 74017; 918-341-3290.

Seminole County

County Clerk, PO Box 1180, Wewoka, OK 74884. 405-257-2501; fax-405-257-6422; hours: 8AM-4PM. Office personnel or visitors may perform searches. Search fee $10.00 per name. Will not search real estate records. Copy fee $1.00 per page. Cert fee- $1.00 per instrument. Payee- Seminole County Clerk. **Other phones:** Treasurer- 405-257-6262. **Property tax/Assessor-** 405-257-3371.

Sequoyah County

County Clerk, 120 E. Chickasaw, Sallisaw, OK 74955. 918-775-4516; fax-918-775-1218; hours: 8-4. All records in one index. Records indexed on a public use terminal back to 1988. Office will perform a UCC search but public must search other records themselves. Tax liens not included in UCC search. UCC search per debtor name- $5.00.

Separate federal tax lien search- $5.00 per debtor. Copy fee $1.00 per page. Cert fee- $1.00 per doc plus copy fee. Payee- Pay fees to Seg. Co Clerk. **Other phones:** Treasurer- 918-775-9321; Elections- 918-775-2614. **Property tax/Assessor-** 117 S Oak, Sallisaw, OK 74955; 918-775-2062.

Stephens County

County Clerk, 101 S. 11th St, Rm 203, Duncan, OK 73533-4758. 580-255-0977; fax-580-255-0991; hours: 8:30AM-4:30PM.
All records in one index. Only the public may search. Copy fee $1.00 per page. Cert fee- $1.00 per page plus copy fee. Payee- Stephens County Clerk. **Online access to Real Estate, Deed, Recorder records:** Access land records index free at www.okcountyrecords.com or http://okcountyrecords.com/search.php. Subscription required for images; $10.00 per month. **Other phones:** Treasurer- 580-255-0728. **Property tax/Assessor-** 580-255-1542.

Texas County

County Clerk, PO Box 197, Guymon, OK 73942-0197. 580-338-3141; fax-580-338-4311; hours: 9AM-5PM. Records indexed on a public use terminal back to 1986. Office will perform a UCC search but public must search other records themselves. UCC search per debtor name- $5.00. Copy fee $1.00 per page. Cert fee- $1.00 per cert plus copy fee. Payee-Texas County Clerk. **Other phones:** Treasurer- 580-338-7050; Elections- 580-338-7644; Vital Records- 405-271-4040. **Property tax/Assessor-** 580-338-3060.

Tillman County

County Clerk, PO Box 992, Frederick, OK 73542. 580-335-3421; fax-580-335-3795; hours: 8AM-4PM. www.oklahomacounty.org/countyclerk
Separate indices to search include deed, mortgage, miscellaneous, platted and unplattted legal descriptions, judgments, state tax lien and federal tax liens. Record index not computerized. Office will perform a UCC search but public must search other records themselves. Search fee $10.00 per name. Copy fee $1.00 per page. Cert fee- $1.00 per cert plus copy fee. Payee- County Clerk. **Other phones:** Treasurer- 580-335-3425; Elections- 580-335-2287; Vital Records- 405-271-4040. **Property tax/Assessor-** 205 N 10th, Frederick, OK 73542; 580-335-3424.

Tulsa County

County Clerk, 500 S. Denver Ave; County Admin. Bldg, Rm 120, Tulsa, OK 74103-3832. 918-596-5801, UCC recording phone-918-596-5864; fax-918-596-5867; hours: 8:30AM-5PM. www.tulsacounty.org
All records in one index. Records indexed on a public use terminal back to 1979. Only the public may search. Copy fee $1.00 per page. Cert fee- $1.00 per doc plus copy fee. Payee- County Clerk. **Online access to Assessor, Treasurer, Recording, Deed, Property, Inmate records:** Access to Tulsa County's Land Records System requires an approved user agreement, username and password http://lrmis.tulsacounty.org/. Monthly access fee is $40.00 and 1st trial month is free. Records go back to 1979. For more information or signup, contact Dorise at 918-596-5206 or LRMISHelp@tulsacounty.org. Also, search inmate info on private company website at www.vinelink.com/index.jsp. **Other phones:** Treasurer- 918-596-5030. **Property tax/Assessor-** 918-596-5828.

Wagoner County

County Clerk, PO Box 156, Wagoner, OK 74477. 918-485-2216; fax-918-485-7709; hours: 8AM-4:30PM. Office will perform a UCC search but public must search other records themselves. UCC search per debtor name- $5.00. Copy fee $1.00 per page. Cert fee- $1.00 per seal. Payee- Wagoner County Clerk. **Other phones:** Treasurer- 918-485-2149; Elections- 918-485-2142. **Property tax/Assessor-** 918-485-2367.

Washington County

County Clerk, 420 S Johnstone, #100, Bartlesville, OK 74003. 918-337-2840, R/E recording phone-918-337-2834; fax-918-337-2894; hours: 8AM-5PM. www.countycourthouse.org
Office personnel or visitors may perform searches. Will not search real estate records. UCC search per debtor name- $5.00. **Online access to Land, Deed, Mortgage, Lien, Sex Offender records:** Access to the recorders database is free at www.countycourthouse.org/countyclerk/disclaimer.htm Also, access to the sex offenders registry is free at www.countycourthouse.org/registry/index.htm. **Other phones:** Treasurer- 918-337-2810; Elections- 918-337-2850. **Property tax/Assessor-** 918-337-2830.

Washita County

County Clerk, PO Box 380, Cordell, OK 73632. 580-832-3548; fax-580-832-3526; hours: 8AM-4PM. Record index not computerized. Office will perform a UCC search but public must search other records themselves. Search fee $5.00. Will not search real estate records. Tax liens included in UCC search. UCC search per debtor name- $10.00. Copy fee $1.00 per page. Cert fee- $1.00 per page plus copy fee. Payee- Washita County Clerk. **Other phones:** Treasurer- 580-832-2667; Elections- 580-832-3658. **Property tax/Assessor-** 580-832-2468.

Woods County

County Clerk, PO Box 386, Alva, OK 73717-0386. 580-327-0998, R/E recording phone-580-327-6229, UCC recording phone-580-327-0998; fax-580-327-6222; hours: 9AM-5PM.
All records in one index. Record index not computerized. Office will perform a UCC and Tax lien search but public must search other records themselves. Search fee $5.00. Copy fee $1.00 per page. Cert fee- $1.00 per instrument. Payee-Woods County Clerk. **Other phones:** Treasurer- 580-327-0308; Elections- 580-327-1452. **Property tax/Assessor-** 580-327-3118.

Woodward County

County Clerk, 1600 Main St, #8, Woodward, OK 73801-3051. 580-254-6800, R/E recording phone-580-256-3625; fax-580-254-6840; hours: 9AM-5PM.
All records in one index. Records indexed on computer back to 11/19/2003. Office personnel or visitors may perform searches. Search fee $5.00 per name. Copy fee $1.00 per page. Cert fee- $1.00 per cert plus copy fee. Payee- Woodward County Clerk. **Other phones:** Treasurer- 580-254-7404. **Property tax/Assessor-** same address as above. 580-254-5061.

Oklahoma County Locator

You will usually be able to find the city name in the City/County Cross Reference below. In that case, it is a simple matter to determine the county from the cross reference. However, only the official US Postal Service city names are included in this index. There are an additional 40,000 place names that people use in their addresses. Therefore, we have also included a ZIP/City Cross Reference immediately following the City/County Cross Reference.

If you know the ZIP Code but the city name does not appear in the City/County Cross Reference index, look up the ZIP Code in the ZIP/City Cross Reference, find the city name, then look up the city name in the City/County Cross Reference. For example, you want to know the county for an address of Menands, NY 12204. There is no "Menands" in the City/County Cross Reference. The ZIP/City Cross Reference shows that ZIP Codes 12201-12288 are for the city of Albany. Looking back in the City/County Cross Reference, Albany is in Albany County.

Oklahoma - City/County Cross Reference

ACHILLE Bryan
ADA Pontotoc
ADAIR (74330) Mayes(97), Craig(2)
ADAMS Texas
ADDINGTON Jefferson
AFTON (74331) Delaware(62), Ottawa(35), Craig(1)
AGRA (74824) Lincoln(88), Payne(11)
ALBANY Bryan
ALBERT Caddo
ALBION Pushmataha
ALDERSON Pittsburg
ALEX (73002) Grady(82), McClain(17)
ALINE (73716) Alfalfa(62), Woods(30), Major(6)
ALLEN (74825) Pontotoc(78), Hughes(21)
ALTUS Jackson
ALTUS AFB Jackson
ALVA Woods
AMBER Grady
AMES (73718) Major(68), Garfield(29), Kingfisher(1)
AMORITA Alfalfa
ANADARKO Caddo
ANTLERS Pushmataha
APACHE (73006) Caddo(52), Comanche(47)
ARAPAHO Custer
ARCADIA (73007) Oklahoma(73), Logan(26)
ARDMORE Carter
ARKOMA Le Flore
ARNETT (73832) Ellis(91), Woodward(8)
ASHER Pottawatomie
ATOKA Atoka
ATWOOD Hughes
AVANT Osage
BACHE Pittsburg
BALKO Beaver
BARNSDALL Osage
BARTLESVILLE (74003) Washington(85), Osage(14)
BARTLESVILLE Washington
BATTIEST McCurtain
BEAVER Beaver
BEGGS Okmulgee
BENNINGTON Bryan
BESSIE Washita
BETHANY Oklahoma
BETHEL McCurtain
BIG CABIN (74332) Craig(87), Mayes(10), Rogers(1)
BILLINGS (74630) Noble(75), Garfield(22), Kay(1)
BINGER Caddo
BISON Garfield
BIXBY Tulsa
BLACKWELL Kay
BLAIR (73526) Jackson(90), Greer(9)
BLANCHARD (73010) McClain(62), Grady(37)
BLANCO Pittsburg
BLOCKER Pittsburg

BLUEJACKET (74333) Ottawa(90), Craig(9)
BOISE CITY Cimarron
BOKCHITO Bryan
BOKOSHE Le Flore
BOLEY Okfuskee
BOSWELL (74727) Choctaw(90), Bryan(9)
BOWLEGS Seminole
BOWRING Osage
BOYNTON (74422) Okmulgee(55), Muskogee(44)
BRADLEY (73011) Grady(98), Garvin(1)
BRAGGS Muskogee
BRAMAN Kay
BRAY Stephens
BRISTOW Creek
BROKEN ARROW Tulsa
BROKEN ARROW Wagoner
BROKEN BOW McCurtain
BROMIDE Johnston
BUFFALO Harper
BUNCH (74931) Cherokee(59), Adair(36), Sequoyah(3)
BURBANK Osage
BURLINGTON Alfalfa
BURNEYVILLE Love
BURNS FLAT Washita
BUTLER Custer
BYARS (74831) McClain(87), Pontotoc(9), Garvin(2)
BYRON Alfalfa
CACHE Comanche
CADDO (74729) Atoka(76), Bryan(23)
CALERA Bryan
CALUMET Canadian
CALVIN Hughes
CAMARGO Dewey
CAMERON Le Flore
CANADIAN Pittsburg
CANEY Atoka
CANTON (73724) Blaine(66), Dewey(33)
CANUTE Washita
CAPRON (73725) Woods(79), Alfalfa(20)
CARDIN Ottawa
CARMEN (73726) Alfalfa(82), Woods(17)
CARNEGIE (73015) Caddo(92), Washita(7)
CARNEY Lincoln
CARRIER Garfield
CARTER Beckham
CARTWRIGHT Bryan
CASHION (73016) Kingfisher(57), Logan(40), Canadian(1)
CASTLE Okfuskee
CATOOSA (74015) Rogers(71), Wagoner(26), Tulsa(1)
CEMENT (73017) Grady(66), Caddo(26), Comanche(6)
CENTRAHOMA Coal
CHANDLER Lincoln
CHATTANOOGA (73528) Comanche(62), Tillman(37)
CHECOTAH McIntosh
CHELSEA (74016) Rogers(93), Mayes(3), Nowata(1), Craig(1)

CHEROKEE Alfalfa
CHESTER (73838) Major(89), Woodward(10)
CHEYENNE Roger Mills
CHICKASHA Grady
CHOCTAW (73020) Oklahoma(97), Cleveland(2)
CHOUTEAU (74337) Mayes(94), Wagoner(5)
CLAREMORE (74019) Rogers(98), Mayes(1)
CLAREMORE Rogers
CLARITA Coal
CLAYTON (74536) Pushmataha(96), Pittsburg(2), Latimer(1)
CLEARVIEW Okfuskee
CLEO SPRINGS (73729) Major(88), Woods(9), Alfalfa(2)
CLEVELAND Pawnee
CLINTON (73601) Custer(97), Washita(2)
COALGATE Coal
COLBERT Bryan
COLCORD Delaware
COLEMAN (73432) Johnston(86), Atoka(13)
COLLINSVILLE (74021) Tulsa(77), Rogers(19), Washington(3)
COLONY (73021) Washita(63), Caddo(36)
COMANCHE Stephens
COMMERCE Ottawa
CONCHO Canadian
CONNERVILLE Johnston
COOKSON Cherokee
COPAN (74022) Washington(96), Osage(3)
CORDELL Washita
CORN Washita
COUNCIL HILL (74428) McIntosh(60), Muskogee(39)
COUNTYLINE Stephens
COVINGTON Garfield
COWETA Wagoner
COYLE (73027) Payne(53), Logan(46)
CRAWFORD Roger Mills
CRESCENT (73028) Logan(93), Kingfisher(6)
CROMWELL Seminole
CROWDER Pittsburg
CUSHING (74023) Payne(96), Lincoln(3)
CUSTER CITY Custer
CYRIL Caddo
DACOMA (73731) Woods(93), Alfalfa(6)
DAISY (74540) Atoka(75), Pushmataha(25)
DAVENPORT Lincoln
DAVIDSON Tillman
DAVIS (73030) Murray(97), Garvin(2)
DEER CREEK Grant
DELAWARE Nowata
DEPEW (74028) Creek(98), Lincoln(1)
DEVOL Cotton
DEWAR Okmulgee
DEWEY Washington
DIBBLE McClain
DILL CITY Washita
DISNEY Mayes

DOUGHERTY Murray
DOUGLAS Garfield
DOVER Kingfisher
DRUMMOND (73735) Garfield(98), Major(1)
DRUMRIGHT (74030) Creek(98), Payne(1)
DUKE (73532) Jackson(94), Greer(4)
DUNCAN Stephens
DURANT Bryan
DURHAM Roger Mills
DUSTIN (74839) Hughes(80), Okfuskee(14), McIntosh(4)
EAGLETOWN McCurtain
EAKLY Caddo
EARLSBORO (74840) Pottawatomie(80), Seminole(19)
EDMOND (73034) Oklahoma(77), Logan(22)
EDMOND Oklahoma
EL RENO Canadian
ELDORADO (73537) Jackson(95), Harmon(4)
ELGIN Comanche
ELK CITY Beckham
ELMER Jackson
ELMORE CITY Garvin
ENID Garfield
ERICK Beckham
EUCHA Delaware
EUFAULA (74432) McIntosh(92), Pittsburg(7)
FAIRFAX Osage
FAIRLAND Ottawa
FAIRMONT Garfield
FAIRVIEW Major
FANSHAWE Le Flore
FARGO (73840) Ellis(66), Woodward(33)
FAXON (73540) Comanche(97), Cotton(2)
FAY (73646) Blaine(44), Dewey(41), Custer(14)
FELT Cimarron
FINLEY Pushmataha
FITTSTOWN Johnston
FITTSTOWN Pontotoc
FITZHUGH Pontotoc
FLETCHER Comanche
FORGAN Beaver
FORT COBB Caddo
FORT GIBSON (74434) Muskogee(97), Wagoner(1)
FORT SILL Comanche
FORT SUPPLY (73841) Woodward(83), Ellis(13), Harper(3)
FORT TOWSON (74735) Choctaw(74), Pushmataha(25)
FOSS (73647) Washita(88), Custer(11)
FOSTER (73434) Stephens(59), Garvin(40)
FOX Carter
FOYIL Rogers
FRANCIS Pontotoc
FREDERICK Tillman
FREEDOM (73842) Woods(66), Woodward(24), Harper(9)
GAGE (73843) Ellis(95), Beaver(4)

GANS Sequoyah
GARBER Garfield
GARVIN McCurtain
GATE (73844) Beaver(51), Harper(48)
GEARY (73040) Blaine(69), Canadian(28), Adair(1)
GENE AUTRY Carter
GERONIMO (73543) Comanche(96), Cotton(3)
GLENCOE (74032) Payne(82), Pawnee(11), Noble(6)
GLENPOOL (74033) Tulsa(93), Creek(6)
GOLDEN McCurtain
GOLTRY (73739) Alfalfa(87), Garfield(12)
GOODWELL Texas
GORE (74435) Sequoyah(88), Muskogee(11)
GOTEBO (73041) Kiowa(79), Washita(20)
GOULD Harmon
GOWEN Latimer
GRACEMONT Caddo
GRAHAM Carter
GRANDFIELD Tillman
GRANITE Greer
GRANT Choctaw
GREENFIELD Blaine
GROVE Delaware
GUTHRIE Logan
GUYMON Texas
HAILEYVILLE Pittsburg
HALLETT Pawnee
HAMMON (73650) Roger Mills(74), Custer(25)
HANNA McIntosh
HARDESTY Texas
HARRAH (73045) Oklahoma(82), Lincoln(12), Pottawatomie(4)
HARTSHORNE (74547) Pittsburg(97), Latimer(2)
HASKELL (74436) Muskogee(59), Okmulgee(30), Wagoner(10)
HASTINGS (73548) Stephens(39), Jefferson(34), Cotton(25)
HAWORTH McCurtain
HAYWOOD Pittsburg
HEADRICK Jackson
HEALDTON Carter
HEAVENER Le Flore
HELENA Alfalfa
HENDRIX Bryan
HENNEPIN (73444) Carter(75), Garvin(12), Murray(12)
HENNESSEY (73742) Kingfisher(96), Garfield(3)
HENRYETTA (74437) Okmulgee(98), McIntosh(1)
HILLSDALE Garfield
HINTON (73047) Caddo(76), Canadian(23)
HITCHCOCK (73744) Blaine(92), Kingfisher(7)
HITCHITA McIntosh
HOBART Kiowa
HODGEN Le Flore
HOLDENVILLE Hughes
HOLLIS Harmon
HOLLISTER Tillman
HOMINY Osage
HONOBIA (74549) Le Flore(94), Pushmataha(5)
HOOKER Texas
HOPETON Woods
HOWE Le Flore
HOYT Haskell
HUGO Choctaw
HULBERT Cherokee
HUNTER (74640) Garfield(93), Grant(6)
HYDRO (73048) Caddo(44), Custer(36), Blaine(18)
IDABEL McCurtain
INDIAHOMA Comanche
INDIANOLA Pittsburg
INOLA (74036) Rogers(96), Mayes(3)

ISABELLA Major
JAY Delaware
JENKS Tulsa
JENNINGS (74038) Pawnee(63), Creek(36)
JET Alfalfa
JONES Oklahoma
KANSAS (74347) Delaware(97), Cherokee(2)
KAW CITY Kay
KELLYVILLE Creek
KEMP Bryan
KEMP CPO Bryan
KENEFIC (74748) Johnston(67), Bryan(18), Atoka(13)
KENTON Cimarron
KEOTA (74941) Haskell(85), Le Flore(14)
KETCHUM Mayes
KEYES Cimarron
KIAMICHI - HONOBIA CPO (74549) Le Flore(94), Pushmataha(5)
KIEFER Creek
KINGFISHER Kingfisher
KINGSTON Marshall
KINTA Haskell
KIOWA (74553) Pittsburg(71), Atoka(28)
KNOWLES Beaver
KONAWA (74849) Seminole(86), Pottawatomie(13)
KREBS Pittsburg
KREMLIN Garfield
LAHOMA (73754) Garfield(90), Major(9)
LAMAR Hughes
LAMONT (74643) Grant(92), Kay(7)
LANE Atoka
LANGLEY Mayes
LANGSTON Logan
LAVERNE (73848) Beaver(50), Harper(47), Ellis(2)
LAWTON Comanche
LEBANON Marshall
LEEDEY (73654) Dewey(62), Roger Mills(28), Custer(9)
LEFLORE Le Flore
LEHIGH (74556) Atoka(60), Coal(40)
LENAPAH Nowata
LEON Love
LEONARD Tulsa
LEQUIRE Haskell
LEXINGTON Cleveland
LINDSAY (73052) Garvin(63), McClain(31), Grady(4)
LOCO Stephens
LOCUST GROVE (74352) Mayes(82), Sequoyah(14), Wagoner(1)
LOGAN Beaver
LONE GROVE Carter
LONE WOLF (73655) Kiowa(97), Greer(2)
LONGDALE (73755) Blaine(62), Major(31), Dewey(6)
LOOKEBA Caddo
LOVELAND Tillman
LOYAL Kingfisher
LUCIEN (73757) Noble(84), Garfield(15)
LUCIEN CPO (73757) Noble(84), Garfield(15)
LUTHER (73054) Oklahoma(77), Lincoln(14), Logan(7)
MACOMB (74852) Pottawatomie(96), Cleveland(3)
MADILL (73446) Marshall(97), Carter(1)
MANCHESTER (73758) Grant(81), Alfalfa(18)
MANGUM (73554) Greer(98), Harmon(1)
MANITOU Tillman
MANNFORD (74044) Creek(69), Pawnee(30)
MANNSVILLE (73447) Johnston(97), Marshall(2)
MARAMEC (74045) Pawnee(98), Payne(1)
MARBLE CITY Sequoyah
MARIETTA Love

MARLAND Noble
MARLOW (73055) Stephens(87), Grady(10), Comanche(2)
MARSHALL (73056) Garfield(65), Logan(29), Kingfisher(4)
MARTHA Jackson
MAUD (74854) Pottawatomie(60), Seminole(39)
MAY (73851) Ellis(51), Harper(48)
MAYFIELD Beckham
MAYSVILLE (73057) Garvin(78), McClain(21)
MAZIE Mayes
MC LOUD (74851) Pottawatomie(74), Cleveland(15), Lincoln(10)
MCALESTER Pittsburg
MCCURTAIN (74944) Haskell(87), Le Flore(12)
MCLOUD (74851) Pottawatomie(74), Cleveland(15), Lincoln(10)
MEAD Bryan
MEDFORD Grant
MEDICINE PARK Comanche
MEEKER (74855) Lincoln(89), Pottawatomie(10)
MEERS Comanche
MENO Major
MERIDIAN Logan
MIAMI Ottawa
MILBURN Johnston
MILFAY Creek
MILL CREEK (74856) Johnston(91), Murray(8)
MILLERTON McCurtain
MINCO (73059) Grady(72), Canadian(14), Caddo(13)
MOFFETT Sequoyah
MONROE Le Flore
MOODYS Cherokee
MOORELAND Woodward
MORRIS Okmulgee
MORRISON Noble
MOUNDS (74047) Okmulgee(51), Creek(28), Tulsa(20)
MOUNTAIN PARK (73559) Kiowa(69), Comanche(30)
MOUNTAIN VIEW Kiowa
MOYERS Pushmataha
MULDROW Sequoyah
MULHALL (73063) Logan(83), Payne(16)
MUSE Le Flore
MUSKOGEE Muskogee
MUSTANG Canadian
MUTUAL Woodward
NARDIN (74646) Kay(89), Grant(10)
NASH (73761) Grant(93), Garfield(6)
NASHOBA Pushmataha
NEWALLA (74857) Cleveland(75), Oklahoma(23), Pottawatomie(1)
NEWCASTLE McClain
NEWKIRK Kay
NICOMA PARK Oklahoma
NINNEKAH Grady
NOBLE Cleveland
NORMAN (73072) Cleveland(95), McClain(4)
NORMAN Cleveland
NORTH MIAMI Ottawa
NOWATA Nowata
OAKHURST Tulsa
OAKS (74359) Delaware(63), Cherokee(36)
OAKWOOD (73658) Dewey(90), Blaine(9)
OCHELATA (74051) Washington(98), Osage(1)
OILTON Creek
OKARCHE (73762) Kingfisher(51), Canadian(48)
OKAY Wagoner
OKEENE (73763) Blaine(89), Major(7), Kingfisher(2)

OKEMAH (74859) Okfuskee(93), Seminole(6)
OKLAHOMA CITY (73128) Oklahoma(87), Canadian(12)
OKLAHOMA CITY (73169) Oklahoma(66), Cleveland(33)
OKLAHOMA CITY (73179) Oklahoma(86), Canadian(13)
OKLAHOMA CITY Cleveland
OKLAHOMA CITY Oklahoma
OKMULGEE Okmulgee
OKTAHA Muskogee
OLUSTEE Jackson
OMEGA (73764) Kingfisher(60), Blaine(39)
OOLOGAH Rogers
ORLANDO (73073) Logan(77), Garfield(19), Noble(2), Payne(1)
OSAGE Osage
OSCAR Jefferson
OVERBROOK (73453) Love(64), Carter(35)
OWASSO (74055) Tulsa(72), Rogers(27)
PADEN Okfuskee
PANAMA Le Flore
PANOLA Latimer
PAOLI (73074) Garvin(86), McClain(13)
PARK HILL Cherokee
PAULS VALLEY Garvin
PAWHUSKA Osage
PAWNEE Pawnee
PEGGS (74452) Cherokee(88), Mayes(11)
PERKINS (74059) Payne(96), Lincoln(3)
PERNELL Garvin
PERRY Noble
PHAROAH Okfuskee
PICHER Ottawa
PICKENS McCurtain
PIEDMONT (73078) Canadian(98), Oklahoma(1)
PITTSBURG Pittsburg
PLATTER Bryan
POCASSET (73079) Grady(91), Caddo(8)
POCOLA Le Flore
PONCA CITY (74604) Kay(70), Osage(29)
PONCA CITY Kay
POND CREEK Grant
PORTER Wagoner
PORUM (74455) Muskogee(80), McIntosh(19)
POTEAU Le Flore
PRAGUE (74864) Lincoln(74), Pottawatomie(25)
PRESTON Okmulgee
PROCTOR Adair
PRUE Osage
PRYOR Mayes
PURCELL McClain
PUTNAM (73659) Dewey(98), Custer(1)
QUAPAW Ottawa
QUINTON (74561) Pittsburg(78), Haskell(21)
RALSTON (74650) Pawnee(65), Osage(34)
RAMONA Washington
RANDLETT Cotton
RATLIFF CITY (73481) Carter(90), Stephens(6), Garvin(2)
RATLIFF CITY Carter
RATTAN Pushmataha
RAVIA Johnston
RED OAK Latimer
RED ROCK (74651) Noble(96), Pawnee(3)
REDBIRD Wagoner
RENTIESVILLE McIntosh
REYDON Roger Mills
RINGLING (73456) Jefferson(65), Carter(25), Love(8)
RINGOLD (74754) McCurtain(67), Pushmataha(30), Choctaw(2)
RINGWOOD Major
RIPLEY Payne
ROCKY (73661) Washita(97), Kiowa(2)

ROFF (74865) Pontotoc(91), Garvin(5), Murray(3)
ROLAND Sequoyah
ROOSEVELT (73564) Kiowa(97), Comanche(2)
ROSE (74364) Delaware(85), Mayes(12), Cherokee(1)
ROSSTON Harper
RUFE McCurtain
RUSH SPRINGS (73082) Grady(96), Comanche(3)
RYAN Jefferson
S COFFEYVILLE (74072) Nowata(97), Craig(2)
SAINT LOUIS Pottawatomie
SALINA (74365) Mayes(81), Delaware(18)
SALLISAW Sequoyah
SAND SPRINGS (74063) Tulsa(74), Osage(20), Creek(5)
SAPULPA (74066) Creek(98), Tulsa(1)
SAPULPA Creek
SASAKWA (74867) Seminole(95), Hughes(4)
SAVANNA Pittsburg
SAWYER Choctaw
SAYRE (73662) Beckham(97), Roger Mills(2)
SCHULTER Okmulgee
SEILING Dewey
SEMINOLE Seminole
SENTINEL Washita
SHADY POINT Le Flore
SHAMROCK Creek
SHARON Woodward
SHATTUCK Ellis
SHAWNEE Pottawatomie
SHIDLER (74652) Osage(96), Kay(3)
SKIATOOK (74070) Osage(60), Tulsa(30), Washington(9)
SLICK Creek
SMITHVILLE (74957) Le Flore(78), McCurtain(21)
SNOW Pushmataha
SNYDER (73566) Kiowa(88), Tillman(11)

SOPER Choctaw
SOUTHARD Blaine
SPARKS Lincoln
SPAVINAW (74366) Mayes(89), Delaware(10)
SPENCER Oklahoma
SPENCERVILLE (74760) Choctaw(65), Pushmataha(34)
SPERRY (74073) Tulsa(65), Osage(34)
SPIRO Le Flore
SPRINGER Carter
STERLING Comanche
STIDHAM McIntosh
STIDHAM COUNTRY CPU McIntosh
STIGLER (74462) Haskell(98), Pittsburg(1)
STILLWATER (74075) Payne(97), Noble(2)
STILLWATER Payne
STILWELL Adair
STONEWALL (74871) Pontotoc(93), Coal(2), Adair(2), Johnston(1)
STRANG Mayes
STRATFORD (74872) Garvin(58), Pontotoc(34), McClain(6)
STRINGTOWN Atoka
STROUD (74079) Lincoln(96), Creek(2)
STUART (74570) Hughes(56), Pittsburg(42), Coal(1)
SULPHUR Murray
SWEETWATER Roger Mills
SWINK Choctaw
TAFT Muskogee
TAHLEQUAH Cherokee
TALALA (74080) Rogers(82), Washington(17)
TALIHINA (74571) Le Flore(60), Latimer(33), Pushmataha(5)
TALOGA Dewey
TATUMS Carter
TECUMSEH Pottawatomie
TEMPLE Cotton
TERLTON (74081) Pawnee(94), Creek(5)
TERRAL Jefferson
TEXHOMA (73949) Cimarron(55), Texas(45)

TEXOLA Beckham
THACKERVILLE Love
THOMAS (73669) Custer(94), Blaine(3), Dewey(2)
TIPTON Tillman
TISHOMINGO Johnston
TONKAWA Kay
TRYON Lincoln
TULLAHASSEE Wagoner
TULSA (74106) Tulsa(94), Osage(5)
TULSA (74108) Tulsa(87), Wagoner(12)
TULSA (74116) Tulsa(62), Rogers(37)
TULSA (74127) Tulsa(60), Osage(39)
TULSA (74132) Tulsa(63), Creek(36)
TULSA Creek
TULSA Tulsa
TUPELO Coal
TURPIN (73950) Beaver(84), Texas(15)
TUSKAHOMA (74574) Pushmataha(51), Latimer(48)
TUSSY Carter
TUTTLE Grady
TWIN OAKS Delaware
TYRONE Texas
UNION CITY Canadian
VALLIANT (74764) McCurtain(90), Choctaw(9)
VELMA Stephens
VERA Washington
VERDEN (73092) Grady(75), Caddo(24)
VERNON McIntosh
VIAN Sequoyah
VICI (73859) Dewey(79), Woodward(17), Ellis(2)
VINITA Craig
VINSON (73571) Harmon(95), Greer(4)
WAGONER Wagoner
WAINWRIGHT Muskogee
WAKITA Grant
WALTERS (73572) Cotton(96), Comanche(3)
WANETTE (74878) Pottawatomie(88), Cleveland(11)
WANN (74083) Nowata(98), Washington(1)

WAPANUCKA (73461) Johnston(92), Atoka(7)
WARDVILLE (74576) Atoka(50), Pittsburg(50)
WARNER Muskogee
WASHINGTON McClain
WASHITA Caddo
WASHITA CPO Caddo
WATONGA Blaine
WATSON McCurtain
WATTS (74964) Adair(84), Delaware(15)
WAUKOMIS Garfield
WAURIKA Jefferson
WAYNE McClain
WAYNOKA (73860) Woods(91), Major(8)
WEATHERFORD (73096) Custer(97), Washita(2)
WEBBERS FALLS Muskogee
WELCH Craig
WELEETKA (74880) Okfuskee(97), Okmulgee(2)
WELLING Cherokee
WELLSTON (74881) Lincoln(90), Logan(9)
WELTY Okfuskee
WESTVILLE Adair
WETUMKA (74883) Hughes(98), Okfuskee(1)
WEWOKA Seminole
WHEATLAND Oklahoma
WHITEFIELD Haskell
WHITESBORO Le Flore
WILBURTON Latimer
WILLOW (73673) Greer(92), Beckham(7)
WILSON (73463) Carter(98), Love(1)
WISTER (74966) Le Flore(96), Latimer(3)
WOODWARD Woodward
WRIGHT CITY McCurtain
WYANDOTTE (74370) Ottawa(91), Delaware(8)
WYNNEWOOD Garvin
WYNONA Osage
YALE Payne
YUKON Canadian

Oklahoma - ZIP/City Cross Reference

73001-73001	ALBERT	73034-73034	EDMOND	73068-73068	NOBLE	73430-73430	BURNEYVILLE
73002-73002	ALEX	73035-73035	ELMORE CITY	73069-73072	NORMAN	73432-73432	COLEMAN
73003-73003	EDMOND	73036-73036	EL RENO	73073-73073	ORLANDO	73433-73433	ELMORE CITY
73004-73004	AMBER	73037-73037	NORMAN	73074-73074	PAOLI	73434-73434	FOSTER
73005-73005	ANADARKO	73038-73038	FORT COBB	73075-73075	PAULS VALLEY	73435-73435	FOX
73006-73006	APACHE	73039-73039	FOSTER	73076-73076	PERNELL	73436-73436	GENE AUTRY
73007-73007	ARCADIA	73040-73040	GEARY	73077-73077	PERRY	73437-73437	GRAHAM
73008-73008	BETHANY	73041-73041	GOTEBO	73078-73078	PIEDMONT	73438-73438	HEALDTON
73009-73009	BINGER	73042-73042	GRACEMONT	73079-73079	POCASSET	73439-73439	KINGSTON
73010-73010	BLANCHARD	73043-73043	GREENFIELD	73080-73080	PURCELL	73440-73440	LEBANON
73011-73011	BRADLEY	73044-73044	GUTHRIE	73081-73081	RATLIFF CITY	73441-73441	LEON
73012-73012	BRAY	73045-73045	HARRAH	73082-73082	RUSH SPRINGS	73442-73442	LOCO
73013-73013	EDMOND	73046-73046	HENNEPIN	73083-73083	EDMOND	73443-73443	LONE GROVE
73014-73014	CALUMET	73047-73047	HINTON	73084-73084	SPENCER	73444-73444	HENNEPIN
73015-73015	CARNEGIE	73048-73048	HYDRO	73085-73085	YUKON	73446-73446	MADILL
73016-73016	CASHION	73049-73049	JONES	73086-73086	SULPHUR	73447-73447	MANNSVILLE
73017-73017	CEMENT	73050-73050	LANGSTON	73087-73087	TATUMS	73448-73448	MARIETTA
73018-73018	CHICKASHA	73051-73051	LEXINGTON	73088-73088	TUSSY	73449-73449	MEAD
73019-73019	NORMAN	73052-73052	LINDSAY	73089-73089	TUTTLE	73450-73450	MILBURN
73020-73020	CHOCTAW	73053-73053	LOOKEBA	73090-73090	UNION CITY	73453-73453	OVERBROOK
73021-73021	COLONY	73054-73054	LUTHER	73091-73091	VELMA	73455-73455	RAVIA
73022-73022	CONCHO	73055-73055	MARLOW	73092-73092	VERDEN	73456-73456	RINGLING
73023-73023	CHICKASHA	73056-73056	MARSHALL	73093-73093	WASHINGTON	73458-73458	SPRINGER
73024-73024	CORN	73057-73057	MAYSVILLE	73094-73094	WASHITA	73459-73459	THACKERVILLE
73025-73025	COUNTYLINE	73058-73058	MERIDIAN	73094-73094	WASHITA CPO	73460-73460	TISHOMINGO
73026-73026	NORMAN	73059-73059	MINCO	73095-73095	WAYNE	73461-73461	WAPANUCKA
73027-73027	COYLE	73061-73061	MORRISON	73096-73096	WEATHERFORD	73463-73463	WILSON
73028-73028	CRESCENT	73062-73062	MOUNTAIN VIEW	73097-73097	WHEATLAND	73476-73476	PERNELL
73029-73029	CYRIL	73063-73063	MULHALL	73098-73098	WYNNEWOOD	73481-73481	RATLIFF CITY
73030-73030	DAVIS	73064-73064	MUSTANG	73099-73099	YUKON	73487-73487	TATUMS
73031-73031	DIBBLE	73065-73065	NEWCASTLE	73100-73199	OKLAHOMA CITY	73488-73488	TUSSY
73032-73032	DOUGHERTY	73066-73066	NICOMA PARK	73401-73403	ARDMORE	73491-73491	VELMA
73033-73033	EAKLY	73067-73067	NINNEKAH	73425-73425	COUNTYLINE	73501-73502	LAWTON

ZIP Range	City	ZIP Range	City	ZIP Range	City	ZIP Range	City
73503-73503	FORT SILL	73669-73669	THOMAS	73945-73945	HOOKER	74344-74345	GROVE
73505-73507	LAWTON	73673-73673	WILLOW	73946-73946	KENTON	74346-74346	JAY
73520-73520	ADDINGTON	73701-73706	ENID	73947-73947	KEYES	74347-74347	KANSAS
73521-73522	ALTUS	73716-73716	ALINE	73949-73949	TEXHOMA	74349-74349	KETCHUM
73523-73523	ALTUS AFB	73717-73717	ALVA	73950-73950	TURPIN	74350-74350	LANGLEY
73526-73526	BLAIR	73718-73718	AMES	73951-73951	TYRONE	74352-74352	LOCUST GROVE
73527-73527	CACHE	73719-73719	AMORITA	74001-74001	AVANT	74353-74353	MAZIE
73528-73528	CHATTANOOGA	73720-73720	BISON	74002-74002	BARNSDALL	74354-74355	MIAMI
73529-73529	COMANCHE	73722-73722	BURLINGTON	74003-74006	BARTLESVILLE	74358-74358	NORTH MIAMI
73530-73530	DAVIDSON	73723-73723	BYRON	74008-74008	BIXBY	74359-74359	OAKS
73531-73531	DEVOL	73724-73724	CANTON	74009-74009	BOWRING	74360-74360	PICHER
73532-73532	DUKE	73725-73725	CAPRON	74010-74010	BRISTOW	74361-74362	PRYOR
73533-73536	DUNCAN	73726-73726	CARMEN	74011-74014	BROKEN ARROW	74363-74363	QUAPAW
73537-73537	ELDORADO	73727-73727	CARRIER	74015-74015	CATOOSA	74364-74364	ROSE
73538-73538	ELGIN	73728-73728	CHEROKEE	74016-74016	CHELSEA	74365-74365	SALINA
73539-73539	ELMER	73729-73729	CLEO SPRINGS	74017-74019	CLAREMORE	74366-74366	SPAVINAW
73540-73540	FAXON	73730-73730	COVINGTON	74020-74020	CLEVELAND	74367-74367	STRANG
73541-73541	FLETCHER	73731-73731	DACOMA	74021-74021	COLLINSVILLE	74368-74368	TWIN OAKS
73542-73542	FREDERICK	73733-73733	DOUGLAS	74022-74022	COPAN	74369-74369	WELCH
73543-73543	GERONIMO	73734-73734	DOVER	74023-74023	CUSHING	74370-74370	WYANDOTTE
73544-73544	GOULD	73735-73735	DRUMMOND	74026-74026	DAVENPORT	74401-74403	MUSKOGEE
73546-73546	GRANDFIELD	73736-73736	FAIRMONT	74027-74027	DELAWARE	74421-74421	BEGGS
73547-73547	GRANITE	73737-73737	FAIRVIEW	74028-74028	DEPEW	74422-74422	BOYNTON
73548-73548	HASTINGS	73738-73738	GARBER	74029-74029	DEWEY	74423-74423	BRAGGS
73549-73549	HEADRICK	73739-73739	GOLTRY	74030-74030	DRUMRIGHT	74425-74425	CANADIAN
73550-73550	HOLLIS	73741-73741	HELENA	74031-74031	FOYIL	74426-74426	CHECOTAH
73551-73551	HOLLISTER	73742-73742	HENNESSEY	74032-74032	GLENCOE	74427-74427	COOKSON
73552-73552	INDIAHOMA	73743-73743	HILLSDALE	74033-74033	GLENPOOL	74428-74428	COUNCIL HILL
73553-73553	LOVELAND	73744-73744	HITCHCOCK	74034-74034	HALLETT	74429-74429	COWETA
73554-73554	MANGUM	73746-73746	HOPETON	74035-74035	HOMINY	74430-74430	CROWDER
73555-73555	MANITOU	73747-73747	ISABELLA	74036-74036	INOLA	74431-74431	DEWAR
73556-73556	MARTHA	73749-73749	JET	74037-74037	JENKS	74432-74432	EUFAULA
73557-73557	MEDICINE PARK	73750-73750	KINGFISHER	74038-74038	JENNINGS	74434-74434	FORT GIBSON
73558-73558	MEERS	73753-73753	KREMLIN	74039-74039	KELLYVILLE	74435-74435	GORE
73559-73559	MOUNTAIN PARK	73754-73754	LAHOMA	74041-74041	KIEFER	74436-74436	HASKELL
73560-73560	OLUSTEE	73755-73755	LONGDALE	74042-74042	LENAPAH	74437-74437	HENRYETTA
73561-73561	OSCAR	73756-73756	LOYAL	74043-74043	LEONARD	74438-74438	HITCHITA
73562-73562	RANDLETT	73757-73757	LUCIEN	74044-74044	MANNFORD	74440-74440	HOYT
73564-73564	ROOSEVELT	73757-73757	LUCIEN CPO	74045-74045	MARAMEC	74441-74441	HULBERT
73565-73565	RYAN	73758-73758	MANCHESTER	74046-74046	MILFAY	74442-74442	INDIANOLA
73566-73566	SNYDER	73759-73759	MEDFORD	74047-74047	MOUNDS	74444-74444	MOODYS
73567-73567	STERLING	73760-73760	MENO	74048-74048	NOWATA	74445-74445	MORRIS
73568-73568	TEMPLE	73761-73761	NASH	74050-74050	OAKHURST	74446-74446	OKAY
73569-73569	TERRAL	73762-73762	OKARCHE	74051-74051	OCHELATA	74447-74447	OKMULGEE
73570-73570	TIPTON	73763-73763	OKEENE	74052-74052	OILTON	74450-74450	OKTAHA
73571-73571	VINSON	73764-73764	OMEGA	74053-74053	OOLOGAH	74451-74451	PARK HILL
73572-73572	WALTERS	73766-73766	POND CREEK	74054-74054	OSAGE	74452-74452	PEGGS
73573-73573	WAURIKA	73768-73768	RINGWOOD	74055-74055	OWASSO	74454-74454	PORTER
73575-73575	DUNCAN	73770-73770	SOUTHARD	74056-74056	PAWHUSKA	74455-74455	PORUM
73601-73601	CLINTON	73771-73771	WAKITA	74058-74058	PAWNEE	74456-74456	PRESTON
73620-73620	ARAPAHO	73772-73772	WATONGA	74059-74059	PERKINS	74457-74457	PROCTOR
73622-73622	BESSIE	73773-73773	WAUKOMIS	74060-74060	PRUE	74458-74458	REDBIRD
73624-73624	BURNS FLAT	73801-73802	WOODWARD	74061-74061	RAMONA	74459-74459	RENTIESVILLE
73625-73625	BUTLER	73832-73832	ARNETT	74062-74062	RIPLEY	74460-74460	SCHULTER
73626-73626	CANUTE	73834-73834	BUFFALO	74063-74063	SAND SPRINGS	74461-74461	STIDHAM
73627-73627	CARTER	73835-73835	CAMARGO	74066-74067	SAPULPA	74461-74461	STIDHAM COUNTRY CPU
73628-73628	CHEYENNE	73838-73838	CHESTER	74068-74068	SHAMROCK	74462-74462	STIGLER
73632-73632	CORDELL	73840-73840	FARGO	74070-74070	SKIATOOK	74463-74463	TAFT
73638-73638	CRAWFORD	73841-73841	FORT SUPPLY	74071-74071	SLICK	74464-74465	TAHLEQUAH
73639-73639	CUSTER CITY	73842-73842	FREEDOM	74072-74072	S COFFEYVILLE	74466-74466	TULLAHASSEE
73641-73641	DILL CITY	73843-73843	GAGE	74073-74073	SPERRY	74467-74467	WAGONER
73642-73642	DURHAM	73844-73844	GATE	74074-74078	STILLWATER	74468-74468	WAINWRIGHT
73644-73644	ELK CITY	73847-73847	KNOWLES	74079-74079	STROUD	74469-74469	WARNER
73645-73645	ERICK	73848-73848	LAVERNE	74080-74080	TALALA	74470-74470	WEBBERS FALLS
73646-73646	FAY	73849-73849	LOGAN	74081-74081	TERLTON	74471-74471	WELLING
73647-73647	FOSS	73851-73851	MAY	74082-74082	VERA	74472-74472	WHITEFIELD
73648-73648	ELK CITY	73852-73852	MOORELAND	74083-74083	WANN	74477-74477	WAGONER
73650-73650	HAMMON	73853-73853	MUTUAL	74084-74084	WYNONA	74501-74502	MCALESTER
73651-73651	HOBART	73855-73855	ROSSTON	74085-74085	YALE	74521-74521	ALBION
73654-73654	LEEDEY	73857-73857	SHARON	74100-74194	TULSA	74522-74522	ALDERSON
73655-73655	LONE WOLF	73858-73858	SHATTUCK	74301-74301	VINITA	74523-74523	ANTLERS
73656-73656	MAYFIELD	73859-73859	VICI	74330-74330	ADAIR	74525-74525	ATOKA
73658-73658	OAKWOOD	73860-73860	WAYNOKA	74331-74331	AFTON	74526-74526	BACHE
73659-73659	PUTNAM	73901-73901	ADAMS	74332-74332	BIG CABIN	74528-74528	BLANCO
73660-73660	REYDON	73931-73931	BALKO	74333-74333	BLUEJACKET	74529-74529	BLOCKER
73661-73661	ROCKY	73932-73932	BEAVER	74335-74335	CARDIN	74530-74530	BROMIDE
73662-73662	SAYRE	73933-73933	BOISE CITY	74337-74337	CHOUTEAU	74531-74531	CALVIN
73663-73663	SEILING	73937-73937	FELT	74338-74338	COLCORD	74533-74533	CANEY
73664-73664	SENTINEL	73938-73938	FORGAN	74339-74339	COMMERCE	74534-74534	CENTRAHOMA
73666-73666	SWEETWATER	73939-73939	GOODWELL	74340-74340	DISNEY	74535-74535	CLARITA
73667-73667	TALOGA	73942-73942	GUYMON	74342-74342	EUCHA	74536-74536	CLAYTON
73668-73668	TEXOLA	73944-73944	HARDESTY	74343-74343	FAIRLAND	74538-74538	COALGATE

74540-74540 DAISY	74543-74543 FINLEY	74546-74546 HAILEYVILLE	74548-74548 HAYWOOD
74542-74542 ATOKA	74545-74545 GOWEN	74547-74547 HARTSHORNE	74549-74549 HONOBIA
74549-74549 KIAMICHI - HONOBIA CPO	74720-74720 ACHILLE	74827-74827 ATWOOD	74877-74877 VERNON
74552-74552 KINTA	74721-74721 ALBANY	74829-74829 BOLEY	74878-74878 WANETTE
74553-74553 KIOWA	74722-74722 BATTIEST	74830-74830 BOWLEGS	74880-74880 WELEETKA
74554-74554 KREBS	74723-74723 BENNINGTON	74831-74831 BYARS	74881-74881 WELLSTON
74555-74555 LANE	74724-74724 BETHEL	74832-74832 CARNEY	74882-74882 WELTY
74556-74556 LEHIGH	74726-74726 BOKCHITO	74833-74833 CASTLE	74883-74883 WETUMKA
74557-74557 MOYERS	74727-74727 BOSWELL	74834-74834 CHANDLER	74884-74884 WEWOKA
74558-74558 NASHOBA	74728-74728 BROKEN BOW	74835-74835 CLEARVIEW	74901-74901 ARKOMA
74559-74559 PANOLA	74729-74729 CADDO	74836-74836 CONNERVILLE	74902-74902 POCOLA
74560-74560 PITTSBURG	74730-74730 CALERA	74837-74837 CROMWELL	74930-74930 BOKOSHE
74561-74561 QUINTON	74731-74731 CARTWRIGHT	74838-74838 SHAWNEE	74931-74931 BUNCH
74562-74562 RATTAN	74733-74733 COLBERT	74839-74839 DUSTIN	74932-74932 CAMERON
74563-74563 RED OAK	74734-74734 EAGLETOWN	74840-74840 EARLSBORO	74935-74935 FANSHAWE
74565-74565 SAVANNA	74735-74735 FORT TOWSON	74842-74842 FITTSTOWN	74936-74936 GANS
74567-74567 SNOW	74736-74736 GARVIN	74843-74843 FITZHUGH	74937-74937 HEAVENER
74569-74569 STRINGTOWN	74737-74737 GOLDEN	74844-74844 FRANCIS	74939-74939 HODGEN
74570-74570 STUART	74738-74738 GRANT	74845-74845 HANNA	74940-74940 HOWE
74571-74571 TALIHINA	74740-74740 HAWORTH	74848-74848 HOLDENVILLE	74941-74941 KEOTA
74572-74572 TUPELO	74741-74741 HENDRIX	74849-74849 KONAWA	74942-74942 LEFLORE
74574-74574 TUSKAHOMA	74743-74743 HUGO	74850-74850 LAMAR	74943-74943 LEQUIRE
74576-74576 WARDVILLE	74745-74745 IDABEL	74851-74851 MC LOUD	74944-74944 MCCURTAIN
74577-74577 WHITESBORO	74747-74747 KEMP	74851-74851 MCLOUD	74945-74945 MARBLE CITY
74578-74578 WILBURTON	74747-74747 KEMP CPO	74852-74852 MACOMB	74946-74946 MOFFETT
74601-74604 PONCA CITY	74748-74748 KENEFIC	74854-74854 MAUD	74947-74947 MONROE
74630-74630 BILLINGS	74750-74750 MILLERTON	74855-74855 MEEKER	74948-74948 MULDROW
74631-74631 BLACKWELL	74752-74752 PICKENS	74856-74856 MILL CREEK	74949-74949 MUSE
74632-74632 BRAMAN	74753-74753 PLATTER	74857-74857 NEWALLA	74951-74951 PANAMA
74633-74633 BURBANK	74754-74754 RINGOLD	74859-74859 OKEMAH	74953-74953 POTEAU
74636-74636 DEER CREEK	74755-74755 RUFE	74860-74860 PADEN	74954-74954 ROLAND
74637-74637 FAIRFAX	74756-74756 SAWYER	74862-74862 PHAROAH	74955-74955 SALLISAW
74640-74640 HUNTER	74759-74759 SOPER	74863-74863 FITTSTOWN	74956-74956 SHADY POINT
74641-74641 KAW CITY	74760-74760 SPENCERVILLE	74864-74864 PRAGUE	74957-74957 SMITHVILLE
74643-74643 LAMONT	74761-74761 SWINK	74865-74865 ROFF	74959-74959 SPIRO
74644-74644 MARLAND	74764-74764 VALLIANT	74866-74866 SAINT LOUIS	74960-74960 STILWELL
74646-74646 NARDIN	74766-74766 WRIGHT CITY	74867-74867 SASAKWA	74962-74962 VIAN
74647-74647 NEWKIRK	74801-74804 SHAWNEE	74868-74868 SEMINOLE	74963-74963 WATSON
74650-74650 RALSTON	74818-74818 SEMINOLE	74869-74869 SPARKS	74964-74964 WATTS
74651-74651 RED ROCK	74820-74821 ADA	74871-74871 STONEWALL	74965-74965 WESTVILLE
74652-74652 SHIDLER	74824-74824 AGRA	74872-74872 STRATFORD	74966-74966 WISTER
74653-74653 TONKAWA	74825-74825 ALLEN	74873-74873 TECUMSEH	
74701-74702 DURANT	74826-74826 ASHER	74875-74875 TRYON	

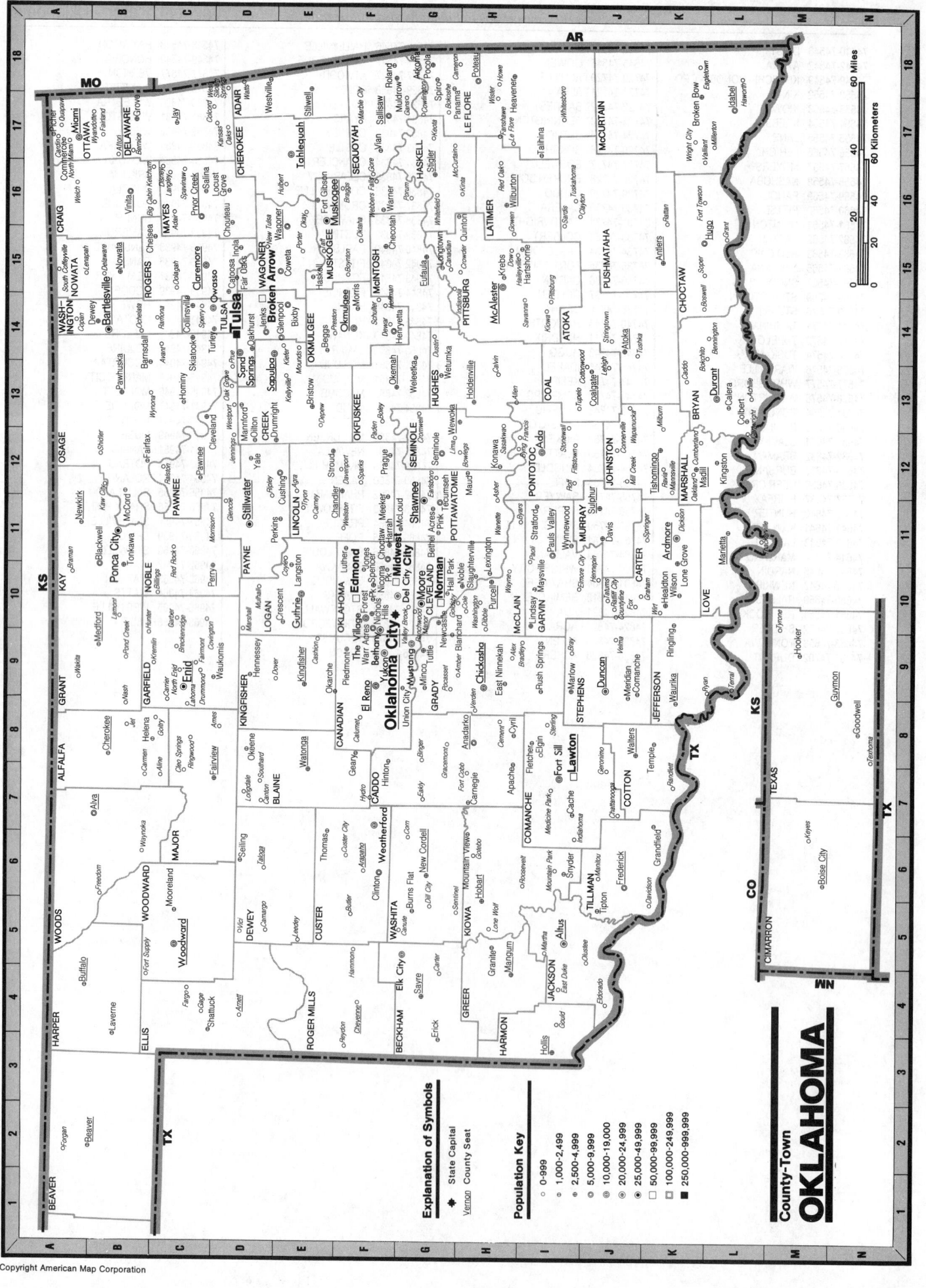

OKLAHOMA

County-Town

Explanation of Symbols

✦ State Capital

<u>Vernon</u> County Seat

Population Key

- ○ 0-999
- ◦ 1,000-2,499
- ◦ 2,500-4,999
- ◉ 5,000-9,999
- ◉ 10,000-19,999
- ◉ 20,000-24,999
- ◉ 25,000-49,999
- □ 50,000-99,999
- ▢ 100,000-249,999
- ■ 250,000-999,999

COUNTIES

(77 Counties)

Name of County	Population	Location on Map
ADAIR	18,421	D-17
ALFALFA	6,416	A-7
ATOKA	12,778	I-14
BEAVER	6,023	A-1
BECKHAM	18,812	G-3
BLAINE	11,470	E-7
BRYAN	32,089	K-13
CADDO	29,550	F-7
CANADIAN	74,409	F-8
CARTER	42,919	J-10
CHEROKEE	34,049	D-16
CHOCTAW	15,302	K-14
CIMARRON	3,301	M-5
CLEVELAND	174,253	G-10
COAL	5,780	I-13
COMANCHE	111,486	I-6
COTTON	6,651	J-7
CRAIG	14,104	A-15
CREEK	60,915	D-12
CUSTER	26,897	E-5
DELAWARE	28,070	B-17
DEWEY	5,551	D-5
ELLIS	4,497	B-3
GARFIELD	56,735	B-8
GARVIN	26,605	I-10
GRADY	41,747	G-8
GRANT	5,689	A-8
GREER	6,559	H-4
HARMON	3,793	H-3
HARPER	4,063	A-3
HASKELL	10,940	G-16
HUGHES	13,023	G-13
JACKSON	28,764	I-4
JEFFERSON	7,010	K-8
JOHNSTON	10,032	J-12
KAY	48,056	A-10
KINGFISHER	13,212	D-8
KIOWA	11,347	H-5
LATIMER	10,333	H-16
LE FLORE	43,270	E-17
LINCOLN	29,216	E-11
LOGAN	29,011	D-10
LOVE	8,157	L-10
MAJOR	8,055	C-6
MARSHALL	10,829	K-12
MAYES	33,366	C-15
McCLAIN	22,795	H-10
McCURTAIN	33,433	J-17
McINTOSH	16,779	F-15
MURRAY	12,042	I-11
MUSKOGEE	68,078	E-16
NOBLE	11,045	B-10
NOWATA	9,992	A-14
OKFUSKEE	11,551	F-12
OKLAHOMA	599,611	F-10
OKMULGEE	36,490	E-14
OSAGE	41,645	A-12
OTTAWA	30,561	A-17
PAWNEE	15,575	C-11
PAYNE	61,507	D-10
PITTSBURG	40,581	H-14
PONTOTOC	34,119	I-12
POTTAWATOMIE	58,760	G-11
PUSHMATAHA	10,997	J-15
ROGER MILLS	4,147	E-3
ROGERS	55,170	B-14
SEMINOLE	25,412	G-12
SEQUOYAH	33,828	F-16
STEPHENS	42,299	I-8
TEXAS	16,419	M-7
TILLMAN	10,384	J-5
TULSA	503,341	D-14
WAGONER	47,883	D-15
WASHINGTON	48,066	A-14
WASHITA	11,441	F-5
WOODS	9,103	A-5
WOODWARD	18,976	B-5
TOTAL	3,145,585	

CITIES AND TOWNS

Note: The first name is that of the city or town, second, that of the county in which it is located, then the population and location on the map.

Ada, Pontotoc, 15,820 I-12
Altus, Jackson, 21,910 I-5
Alva, Woods, 5,495 B-7
Anadarko, Caddo, 6,586 G-8
Antlers, Pushmataha, 2,524 K-15
Apache, Caddo, 1,591 H-8
Arapaho, Custer, 802 F-6
Ardmore, Carter, 23,079 K-11
Arkoma, Le Flore, 2,393 G-18
Arnett, Ellis, 547 D-4
Atoka, Atoka, 3,298 J-14
Barnsdall, Osage, 1,316 B-13
Bartlesville, Osage/Washington, 34,256 B-14
Beaver, Beaver, 1,584 B-2
Beggs, Okmulgee, 1,150 E-14
Bethany, Oklahoma, 20,075 F-9
Bethel Acres, Pottawatomie, 2,505 G-11
Bixby, Tulsa/Wagoner, 9,502 E-14
Blackwell, Kay, 7,538 B-10
Blanchard, Grady/McClain, 1,922 G-9
Boise City, Cimarron, 1,509 M-6
Bristow, Creek, 4,062 E-13
Broken Arrow, Tulsa/Wagoner, 58,043 D-14
Broken Bow, McCurtain, 3,961 K-17
Buffalo, Harper, 1,312 A-4
Burns Flat, Washita, 1,027 G-5
Cache, Comanche, 2,251 I-7
Calera, Bryan, 1,536 L-13
Carnegie, Caddo, 1,593 H-7
Catoosa, Rogers, 2,954 D-15
Chandler, Lincoln, 2,596 F-12
Checotah, McIntosh, 3,290 F-15
Chelsea, Rogers, 1,620 C-15
Cherokee, Alfalfa, 1,787 B-8
Cheyenne, Roger Mills, 948 F-4
Chickasha, Grady, 14,988 H-9
Choctaw, Oklahoma, 8,545 F-11
Chouteau, Mayes, 1,771 D-16
Claremore, Rogers, 13,280 C-15
Cleveland, Pawnee, 3,156 C-13
Clinton, Custer/Washita, 9,298 F-6
Coalgate, Coal, 1,895 J-13
Colbert, Bryan, 1,043 L-13
Collinsville, Rogers/Tulsa, 3,612 C-14
Comanche, Stephens, 1,695 J-9
Commerce, Ottawa, 2,426 A-17
Coweta, Wagoner, 6,159 E-15
Crescent, Logan, 1,236 E-10
Cushing, Payne, 7,218 E-12
Cyril, Caddo, 1,072 H-8
Davis, Garvin/Murray, 2,543 J-11
Del City, Oklahoma, 23,928 G-10
Dewey, Washington, 3,326 B-14
Drumright, Creek/Payne, 2,799 D-12
Duncan, Stephens, 21,732 J-9
Durant, Bryan, 12,823 L-13
East Ninnekah, Grady, 1,016 H-9
Edmond, Oklahoma, 52,315 F-10
El Reno, Canadian, 15,414 F-9
Elk City, Beckham, 10,428 G-5
Enid, Garfield, 45,309 C-9
Erick, Beckham, 1,083 G-3
Eufaula, McIntosh, 2,652 G-15
Fair Oaks, Rogers/Wagoner, 1,133 D-15
Fairfax, Osage, 1,749 B-12
Fairview, Major, 2,936 D-7
Fletcher, Comanche, 1,002 I-8
Forest Park, Oklahoma, 1,249 F-10
Fort Gibson, Muskogee, 3,359 E-16
Fort Sill, Comanche, 12,107 I-7
Frederick, Tillman, 5,221 J-6
Geary, Blaine/Canadian, 1,347 F-8
Glenpool, Tulsa, 6,688 E-14
Goodwell, Texas, 1,065 N-8
Grandfield, Tillman, 1,224 K-7
Granite, Greer, 1,844 H-5
Grove, Delaware, 4,020 B-17
Guthrie, Logan, 10,518 E-10
Guymon, Texas, 7,803 N-8
Hall Park, Cleveland, 1,090 G-10
Harrah, Oklahoma, 4,206 F-11
Hartshorne, Pittsburg, 2,120 I-15
Haskell, Muskogee, 2,143 E-15
Healdton, Carter, 2,872 K-10
Heavener, Le Flore, 2,601 H-18
Helena, Alfalfa, 1,043 B-8
Hennessey, Kingfisher, 1,902 D-9
Henryetta, Okmulgee, 5,872 F-14
Hinton, Caddo, 1,233 F-8
Hobart, Kiowa, 4,305 G-5
Holdenville, Hughes, 4,792 H-13
Hollis, Harmon, 2,584 I-3
Hominy, Osage, 2,342 C-13
Hooker, Texas, 1,551 M-9
Hugo, Choctaw, 5,978 K-15
Idabel, McCurtain, 6,957 L-17
Inola, Rogers, 1,444 D-15
Jay, Delaware, 2,220 C-17
Jenks, Tulsa, 7,493 D-14
Jones, Oklahoma, 2,424 F-10
Kingfisher, Kingfisher, 4,095 E-9
Kingston, Marshall, 1,237 L-12
Konawa, Seminole, 1,508 H-12
Krebs, Pittsburg, 1,955 H-15
Langston, Logan, 1,471 E-10
Laverne, Harper, 1,269 B-3
Lawton, Comanche, 80,561 J-7
Lexington, Cleveland, 1,776 H-10
Lindsay, Garvin, 2,947 I-10
Locust Grove, Mayes, 1,326 D-16
Lone Grove, Carter, 4,114 K-11
Longtown, Pittsburg, 1,641 G-15
Luther, Oklahoma, 1,560 F-11
Madill, Marshall, 3,069 K-12
Mangum, Greer, 3,344 H-4
Mannford, Creek/Pawnee/Tulsa, 1,826 D-13
Marietta, Love, 2,306 L-11
Marlow, Stephens, 4,416 I-9
Maud, Pottawatomie/Seminole, 1,204 H-12
Maysville, Garvin, 1,203 I-10
McAlester, Pittsburg, 16,370 H-15
● McCord, Osage, 2,170 B-12
McLoud, Pottawatomie, 2,493 G-11
Medford, Grant, 1,172 B-9
Meeker, Lincoln, 1,003 F-11
Meridian, Stephens, 1,471 J-9
Miami, Ottawa, 13,142 A-17
Midwest City, Oklahoma, 52,267 F-10
Minco, Grady, 1,411 G-9
Moore, Cleveland, 40,318 G-10
Mooreland, Woodward, 1,157 C-5
Morris, Okmulgee, 1,216 F-14
Mountain View, Kiowa, 1,086 H-6
Muldrow, Sequoyah, 2,889 F-18
Muskogee, Muskogee, 37,708 E-15
Mustang, Canadian, 10,434 G-9
New Cordell, Washita, 2,903 G-6
Newcastle, McClain, 4,214 G-10
Newkirk, Kay, 2,168 A-11
Nichols Hills, Oklahoma, 4,020 F-10
Nicoma Park, Oklahoma, 2,353 F-10
Noble, Cleveland, 4,710 H-10
Norman, Cleveland, 80,071 G-10
Nowata, Nowata, 3,896 B-15
● Oakhurst, Creek/Tulsa, 3,030 D-14
Oilton, Creek, 1,060 D-12
Okarche, Canadian/Kingfisher, 1,160 E-9
Okeene, Blaine, 1,343 D-8
Okemah, Okfuskee, 3,085 F-13
Oklahoma City, Canadian/Cleveland/ McClain/Oklahoma/Pottawatomie, 444,719 F-10
Okmulgee, Okmulgee, 13,441 F-14
Owasso, Rogers/Tulsa, 11,151 C-14
Panama, Le Flore, 1,528 G-18
Pauls Valley, Garvin, 6,150 I-11
Pawhuska, Osage, 3,825 B-13
Pawnee, Pawnee, 2,197 C-12
Perkins, Payne, 1,925 E-11
Perry, Noble, 4,978 D-10
Picher, Ottawa, 1,714 A-17
Piedmont, Canadian/Kingfisher, 2,522 F-9
Pink, Pottawatomie, 1,020 G-11
Pocola, Le Flore, 3,664 G-18
Ponca City, Kay/Osage, 26,359 B-11
Poteau, Le Flore, 7,210 H-18
Prague, Lincoln, 2,308 F-12
Pryor Creek, Mayes, 8,327 C-16
Purcell, Cleveland/McClain, 4,784 H-10
Quinton, Pittsburg, 1,133 G-16
Ringling, Jefferson, 1,250 K-10
Roland, Sequoyah, 2,481 F-18
Rush Springs, Grady, 1,229 I-9
Salina, Mayes, 1,153 C-16
Sallisaw, Sequoyah, 7,122 F-17
Sand Springs, Osage/Tulsa, 15,346 D-14
Sapulpa, Creek, 18,074 D-13
Sayre, Beckham, 2,881 G-4
Seiling, Dewey, 1,031 D-6
Seminole, Seminole, 7,071 G-12
Shattuck, Ellis, 1,454 C-4
Shawnee, Pottawatomie, 26,017 G-11
Skiatook, Osage/Tulsa, 4,910 C-14
Slaughterville, Cleveland, 1,843 H-10
Snyder, Kiowa, 1,619 I-6
Spencer, Oklahoma, 3,972 F-10
Spiro, Le Flore, 2,146 G-18
Stigler, Haskell, 2,574 G-16
Stillwater, Payne, 36,676 D-11
Stilwell, Adair, 2,663 E-18
Stratford, Garvin, 1,404 I-11
Stroud, Creek/Lincoln, 2,666 E-12
Sulphur, Murray, 4,824 J-11
Tahlequah, Cherokee, 10,398 E-17
Talihina, Le Flore, 1,297 I-17
Taloga, Dewey, 415 D-6
Tecumseh, Pottawatomie, 5,750 G-11
Temple, Cotton, 1,223 K-8
The Village, Oklahoma, 10,353 F-10
Thomas, Custer, 1,246 E-7
Tipton, Tillman, 1,043 J-5
Tishomingo, Johnston, 3,116 K-12
Tonkawa, Kay, 3,127 B-10
Tulsa, Osage/Rogers/Tulsa, 367,302 D-14
● Turley, Tulsa, 2,930 G-9
Tuttle, Grady, 2,807 G-9
Union City, Canadian, 1,000 G-9
Vian, Sequoyah, 1,414 F-17
Vinita, Craig, 5,804 B-16
Wagoner, Wagoner, 6,894 E-15
Walters, Cotton, 2,519 J-8
Warner, Muskogee, 1,479 F-16
Warr Acres, Oklahoma, 9,288 F-10
Watonga, Blaine, 3,408 E-7
Waukomis, Garfield, 1,322 C-8
Waurika, Jefferson, 2,088 K-8
Weatherford, Custer, 10,124 F-7
Weleetka, Okfuskee, 1,112 G-14
Westville, Adair, 1,374 D-18
Wetumka, Hughes, 1,427 G-13
Wewoka, Seminole, 4,050 H-13
Wilburton, Latimer, 3,092 H-16
Wilson, Carter, 1,639 K-10
Woodward, Woodward, 12,340 C-5
Wynnewood, Garvin, 2,451 I-11
Yale, Payne, 1,392 D-12
Yukon, Canadian, 20,935 F-9

Explanation of symbols: ● – Census Designated Place (CDP)

General Help Numbers:

Governor's Office

State Capitol Bldg.   503-373-1027
900 Court St NE   Fax 503-373-6827
Salem, OR 97301-4047   8AM-5PM
www.governor.state.or.us

Attorney General's Office

Department of Justice   503-378-4400
1162 Court St NE   Fax 503-378-4017
Salem, OR 97310   8AM-5PM
www.doj.state.or.us

Legislative Records

Oregon Legislative Assembly, Legislative Publications,
900 Court St, #49   503-986-1180
Salem, OR 97310   Fax 503-373-1527
www.leg.state.or.us   8AM-5PM

State Archives

Archives Division   503-373-0701
800 Summer St NE   Fax 503-373-0953
Salem, OR 97301   8AM-4:45PM
http://arcweb.sos.state.or.us

State Specifics:

Capital:	Salem Marion County
Time Zone:	PST
Number of Counties:	36
Population:	3,594,586
Web Site:	www.oregon.gov

State Agencies

Criminal Records

Oregon State Police, Unit 11, Identification Services Section, PO Box 4395, Portland, OR 97208-4395 (Courier address: 3772 Portland Rd NE, Bldg C, Salem, OR 97303); 503-378-3070, 503-378-2121-Fax; 8AM-5PM M-F.

http://egov.oregon.gov/OSP/ID

Records are available from 1941 on and are computerized. It takes up to 8 days before new records are available for inquiry. Records are indexed on inhouse computer. 100% of arrest records are fingerprint supported. Records are normally destroyed after (records maintained indefinitely). Approximately 50% of all arrests in database have final dispositions recorded.

Searching: Three types of searches exist: open records search, own record search, and statutorily-required search. The latter can include an FBI fingerprint check for an additional $24.00 fee. Include the following in your request-name, date of birth, last known address. Submitting the SSN is helpful, but not required. Fingerprints are required only when subject submits the request. If record exists, person of record will be notified of the request and the record will not be released for 14 additional days. Open record information includes all records with convictions and also all arrests within the past year without disposition. Statutorily-required record searches and own record searches include all records.

Access by: mail, fax, online.

Fee & Payment: Open record search fee is $10.00 per individual name. If someone is submitting a search on oneself, the fee is $33.00 and fingerprints are required. Statutorily-required searches are $28.00 plus FBI fingerprint fee, if required. $5.00 fee to notarize. Fee payee: Oregon State Police. Prepayment required. Personal checks accepted. No credit cards accepted.

Mail search: Turnaround time: 5 days if clean. Records with hits can take up to 3 weeks to return.

Fax search: Requesters must be pre-approved, however records are not returned by fax.

Online search: A web based site is available for requesting and receiving criminal records. Website is ONLY for high-volume requesters who must be pre-approved. Results are posted as "No Record" or "In Process" ("In Process" means a record will be mailed in 14 days). Use the "open records" link to get into the proper site. Fee is $10.00 per record. Call 503-373-1808 x230 to receive the application, or visit the website.

Statewide Court Records

Court Administrator, Supreme Court Bldg, 1163 State St, Salem, OR 97301-2563; 503-986-5500, 503-986-5503-Fax; 8AM-5PM.

www.ojd.state.or.us/osca The Appellate Courts office is located at 1163 State St.

Access by: online.

Online search: Appellate opinions are found at www.publications.ojd.state.or.us/. Online computer access is available through the Oregon Judicial Information Network (OJIN) which includes almost all cases filed in the Oregon state courts. There is a one-time setup fee of $295.00 plus usage fees of $10-13.00 per hour. The database contains criminal, civil, small claims, probate, and some but not all juvenile records. However, it does not contain any records from municipal nor county courts. For further information visit www.ojd.state.or.us/ojin, or call 800-858-9658 or 503-986-5588.

Other access: Purchase of bulk record is also available, call for details.

Sexual Offender Registry

Oregon State Police, SOR Unit, 255 Capitol St NE, 4th Fl, Salem, OR 97310; 503-378-3720, 503-363-5475-Fax; 8AM-5PM. www.osp.state.or.us

It takes up to 8 days before new records are available for inquiry. Records are normally destroyed after 1 year after death of the offender.

Searching: Include the following in your request-name and DOB.

Access by: mail, phone, fax.

Fee & Payment: There is no fee.

Mail search: Turnaround time: up to 3 weeks. **Phone search:** You can request a list or do a name check by phone. **Fax search:** Requests accepted via fax.

Incarceration Records

Oregon Department of Corrections, Offender Information & Sentence Computation, PO Box 5670, Wilsonville, OR 97070-5670 (Courier address: 24499 SW Grahams Ferry Rd, Bldg Z, Wilsonville, OR 97070); 503-570-6900, 503-570-6902-Fax; 8AM-4PM. www.doc.state.or.us

Records are available on current and former inmates. It takes up to 4 days before new records are available for inquiry. Records are normally destroyed after being microfilmed after final discharge.

Searching: Include the following in your request-full name; DOB and SID# helpful. Location, SID number, physical identifiers, conviction and sentencing information, release dates provided.

Access by: mail, phone, fax, online.

Fee & Payment: Fees are charged for copies as follows: $.50 for paper, $1.25 from microfilm.

Mail search: Turnaround time: 2 to 4 weeks.

Phone search: Name searching permitted by phone. **Fax search:** Same criteria as mail.

Online search: No online offender searching is available from this agency; there is a "Corrections Most Wanted" list in the pull down menu box. A private company offers free web access at www.vinelink.com/index.jsp; includes state, DOC, and most county jails. Also, use imate.info@doc.state.or.us to request by email.

Other access: Bulk sale of information is available. Contact ISSD.

Corporation, Limited Partnership, Trademarks/Servicemarks, Fictitious Name, Assumed Name, Limited Liability Company Records

Corporation Division, Public Service Building, 255 Capital St NE, #151, Salem, OR 97310-1327; 503-986-2317, 503-378-4381-Fax; 8AM-5PM.

www.filinginoregon.com

Records are available on the computer screen for 20 years after inactive. Assumed names are only available for 5 years after inactive. The records prior to 20 years ago are stored in the State Archives back to the 1800's for corporations only. New records are available for inquiry immediately. Records are indexed on microfilm, inhouse computer.

Searching: All information is public record. Include the following in your request-full name of business. In addition to the articles of incorporation, corporation records include the following information: last annual report, Prior (merged) names, Articles of Amendment.

Access by: mail, phone, fax, in person, online.

Fee & Payment: There is no search fee. Copies cost $5.00 per business name or $15.00 if certified, otherwise there is a $1.00 fee per business name for a computer printout. A Good Standing certificate is $10.00. Fee payee: Corporation Division. Prepayment required. Personal checks accepted. Credit cards accepted: MasterCard, Visa.

Mail search: Turnaround time: 7 to 10 days. A SASE is requested.

Phone search: There is a limit of 3 searches per phone call. **Fax search:** Requesters must use a credit card, turnaround time is 5 days or less. **In person search:** Turnaround time while you wait.

Online search: There is free access at the website for business registry information. Search by name or business registry number. Displays active and inactive records.

Other access: A subscription service for new business lists on email, diskettes and CDs of the database are available for $15.00 per month or $180.00 for an annual subscription. Call 503-986-2343 for more information.

Uniform Commercial Code, Federal and State Tax Liens

UCC Division, Attn: Records, 255 Capitol St NE, Suite 151, Salem, OR 97310-1327; 503-986-2200 x6, 503-373-1166-Fax; 8AM-5PM.

www.filinginoregon.com/ucc/index.htm

State tax liens on personal property are filed here; state tax liens on real property are filed at the county level.

Records are available on microfiche to 1963. It takes 2 to 4 days before new records are available for inquiry.

Searching: Use search request form UCC-11. The search includes tax liens filed here. Include the following in your request-debtor name.

Access by: mail, fax, in person, online.

Fee & Payment: The search fee is $10.00 per name, with copies is $15.00 per name. A document number request is $5.00. A state seal certificate is $15.00. CD service is $20.00 per CD. Special research projects are $20.00 per hour. Fee payee: Secretary of State. Prepayment required. Personal checks accepted. Credit cards accepted: MasterCard, Visa.

Mail search: Turnaround time: 1 to 4 days. **Fax search:** A credit card is required. Results are mailed. **In person search:** Searches done while you wait. **Online search:** UCC index information and filings can be obtained for free from the website. You can search by debtor name or by lien number. You can also download forms from here.

Other access: Monthly UCC information is released via e-mail, FTP or CD. Prices start at $15.00 per month or $150.00 annually for new filings, or $200 per month for all active filings. For more info, call Program Services at 503-986-2212.

Sales Tax Registrations

State does not impose sales tax.

Birth Certificates

Department of Human Services, Vital Records, PO Box 14050, Portland, OR 97293-0050 (Courier address: 800 NE Oregon St, #205, Portland, OR 97232); 503-731-4108, 503-731-4095 (Recorded Message), 503-234-8417-Fax; 8AM-4:30PM.

http://oregon.gov/DHS/ph/chs/order/index.shtml

Records are available for 07/1903 to present. There are some delayed filed, unindexed records with DOBs from 1885 to 1904. Birth indexes prior to 1903 years available at the State Archives. It takes 2 to 4 weeks before new records are available for inquiry.

Searching: Investigative searches must have a signed, notarized release from person of record or immediate family member, unless record over 100 years old. Records only available to legal guardians & legal representatives with proof of such Include the following in your request-full name, names of parents, mother's full maiden name, date of birth, place of birth, relationship to person of record. Must request "long form" if time of birth, hospital or physician's names is needed. The following data is not released: original birth record prior to adoption, except to adoptee over age of 21.

Access by: mail, phone, fax, in person, online.

Fee & Payment: The search fee is $20.00. Add $15.00 for each additional copy. Fee payee: DHS Vital Records Prepayment required. Personal checks accepted. Major credit cards accepted.

Mail search: Turnaround time: 2 to 3 weeks. Express mail requests are handled immediately. No SASE is required.

Phone search: See expedited service. **Fax search:** See expedited service. **In person search:** Turnaround time is under 20 minutes.

Online search: Order records online at www.vitalchek.com, a state designated vendor.

Expedited service: Fax and phone orders are billed to credit cards and processed the same day. There is an additional $12.50 service fee. Turnaround time: same or next day. Add fee for delivery service.

Death Records

Department of Human Services, Vital Records, PO Box 14050, Portland, OR 97293-0050 (Courier address: 800 NE Oregon St, #205, Portland, OR 97232); 503-731-4108, 503-731-4095 (Recorded Message), 503-234-8417-Fax; 8AM-4:30PM.

http://oregon.gov/DHS/ph/chs/order/index.shtml

Records are available for 07/1903 years to present. It takes 2 to 4 weeks before new records are available for inquiry.

Searching: Investigative searches must have a signed, notarized release from immediate family member or legal representative or person with a personalor property right. After 50 years, a record becomes public record and there are no restrictions. Include the following in your request- full name, date of death, place of death, relationship to person of record, reason for information request. The name of the spouse is helpful. The date of birth is helpful for common names.

Access by: mail, phone, fax, in person, online.

Fee & Payment: The search fee is $20.00 and additional copies are $15.00 each. Fee payee: DHS Vital Records. Prepayment required. Personal checks accepted. Major credit cards accepted.

Mail search: Turnaround time: 2 to 3 weeks. Express mail requests are processed immediately. No SASE is required.

Phone search: See expedited service.

Fax search: See expedited service.

In person search: Turnaround time is within 20 minutes.

Online search: Search records from 1903-1930 at www.heritagetrailpress.com/Death_Index/. You may order directly on Vital Chek's web page at www.VitalChek.com.

Other access: Indexes are available at many state libraries.

Expedited service: Phone and fax orders require use of a credit card and an additional $12.50 service fee. Turnaround time is generally in 24 hours. Turnaround time: same or next day. Carrier chosen to return documents determines fees.

Marriage Certificates

Department of Human Services, Vital Records, PO Box 14050, Portland, OR 97293-0050 (Courier address: 800 NE Oregon St, #205, Portland, OR 97232); 503-731-4108, 503-731-4095 (Recorded Message), 503-234-8417-Fax; 8AM-4:30PM.

http://oregon.gov/DHS/ph/chs/order/index.shtml

Records are available from 1910 to present. Early records are in an abbreviated form called "Return of Marriage." Records from 1906 to 1910 are in State Archives. It takes 4 to 8 weeks before new records are available for inquiry.

Searching: Records less than 50 years old are only available to family members, legal representatives or those with a personal or property right. Include the following in your request-names of husband and wife, date of marriage, place or county of marriage, and reason for request. Include daytime phone number and as many identifiers as possible.

Access by: mail, phone, fax, in person, online.

Fee & Payment: The search fee is $20.00, additional copies $15.00 per record. Fee payee: DHS Vital Records Prepayment required. Personal checks accepted. Major credit cards accepted.

Mail search: Turnaround time: 2 to 3 weeks. If request is expressed, it will be answered ASAP. No SASE is required.

Phone search: See expedited service.

Fax search: See expedited service.

In person search: Turnaround time is usually within 20 minutes.

Online search: Order online via www.vitalchek.com, a state approved vendor.

Other access: Many state libraries offer record indexes.

Expedited service: There is an additional $12.50 quick service search fee per telephone or fax order. Use of a credit card is required. Turnaround time: same or next day. Additional fees will be added, depending on carrier. For mail requests, enclose a prepaid, self-addressed envelope for overnight carrier.

Divorce Records

Department of Human Services, Vital Records, PO Box 14050, Portland, OR 97293-0050 (Courier address: 800 NE Oregon St, #205, Portland, OR 97232); 503-731-4108, 502-731-4095 (Recorded Message), 503-234-8417-Fax; 8AM-4:30PM.

http://oregon.gov/DHS/ph/chs/order/index.shtml

Records are available from 1925 to present. It takes 4 to 8 weeks before new records are available for inquiry.

Searching: Records less than 50 years old are only available to family members, legal representatives or those with a personal or property right. Include the following in your request-date of divorce. Also include names of husband and wife, and reason for request.

Access by: mail, phone, fax, in person, online.

Fee & Payment: The search fee is $20.00, additional copies are $15.00 each. Fee payee: DHS Vital Records. Prepayment required. For a mail request, enclose a prepaid, self-addressed envelope for overnight carrier. Personal checks accepted. Major credit cards accepted.

Mail search: Turnaround time: 2 to 3 weeks. Send request by overnight delivery and it will be processed ASAP. No SASE is required.

Phone search: See expedited service. **Fax search:** See expedited services. **In person search:** Turnaround time is usually within 20 minutes.

Online search: Order records online at www.vitalchek.com, a state designated vendor.

Other access: Indexes are available in many Oregon libraries.

Expedited service: There is an additional $12.50 service fee for ordering by fax, phone or online and you must use a credit card. Turnaround time: same or next day.

Workers' Compensation Records

Department of Consumer & Business Srvs, Workers Compensation Division, PO Box 14480, Salem, OR 97309-0405 (Courier address: 350 Winter Street NE Rm 27, Salem, OR 97301-3879); 503-947-7818, 503-947-7993 (TTY), 503-945-7630-Fax; 8AM-5PM M-F.

www.oregonwcd.org

Records are available from 1996 to present. It takes 4 days or less before new records are available for inquiry. Records are indexed on inhouse computer.

Searching: Per ORS 192.502(18), claims records are exempt from public disclosure. Access to records is at the discretion of the Director. In general, those with a legitimate business purpose are granted access. Include the following in your request-claimant name, Social Security Number, claim number, name and address of requester. A signed release by subject is honored. The website features rules, bulletins, forms, and publications.

Access by: mail, fax, in person, online.

Fee & Payment: The Department has the authority to charge for staff time and resources for any record request. Records releases only after disclosure requirements are met. Fee payee: DCBS. Prepayment required. Personal checks accepted. No credit cards accepted.

Mail search: Turnaround time: 14 days. No SASE is required. **Fax search:** Fax requests are accepted if disclosure requirements are met. Completed report may be mailed back. **In person search:** Completed report may need to be mailed back. Turnaround time: 1 to 14 days.

Online search: A search of employers that have coverage, and employers that have coverage ending soon is found at www.oregonwcd.org/compliance/ecu/empcoverage.html.

Other access: State is allowed to deliver data in other forms to parties that qualify under ORS 192.502(19).

Expedited service: Will expedite if requester agrees to payment.

Driver Records

Driver and Motor Vehicle Services, Record Services, 1905 Lana Ave, NE, Salem, OR 97314; 503-945-5000, 503-945-5425-Fax; 8AM-5PM.

www.oregondmv.com

Oregon differentiates between "employment" and "non-employment" records. Ongoing requesters with a permissible use and qualify to receive personal information per state law may establish a Record Inquiry Account.

Records are available for 3 years for accidents, 5 years for minor convictions; 10 years for DUIs and major convictions; and 3 or 5 years after reinstatement for suspensions. If CMV related, 55 years. It takes 2-3 weeks normally before new records are available for inquiry.

Searching: Permissible use requesters may open a Record Inquiry Account and are then approved to access via one of the automated systems. Casual requesters who do not present written consent may receive a "sanitized record." Include the following in your request-full name, date of birth, driver's license number. A driver's license report is available which lists the driver's name, address, date of birth, license number, issue and expiration dates, original business date, restrictions, status, and, if applicable, the ID card expiration date. The following data is not released: medical information, SSNs, photos.

Access by: mail, phone, fax.

Fee & Payment: Fee for a 3 year non-employment driving record is $1.50; $2.00 for a 3 year employment driving record; $3.00 for a "court print" record; $1.50 per record for a driver license information report. There is a charge of $1.50 for no record found. Fee payee: DMV Services. Prepayment required, unless account holder. Personal checks accepted; no credit cards.

Mail search: Turnaround time: 1 day from receipt. A record request form and record fee list is available online. No SASE is required.

Phone search: Oregon offers "IVR" (DMV's Interactive Voice Response System) to approved accounts. IRV reads information from computer files in a human sounding voice. A variety of records are available on IVR 24 hours a day. Call 503-945-7950 for more information.

Fax search: Records are available by fax, but only for approved account holders.

Other access: The agency offers an automated "flag program" that informs customers of activity on a name list. Call the Automated Reporting Service at 503-945-5428/5427.

Vehicle Ownership, Vehicle Identification

Driver and Motor Vehicle Services, Record Services Unit, 1905 Lana Ave, NE, Salem, OR 97314; 503-945-5000, 503-945-5425-Fax; 8AM-5PM. www.oregondmv.com

Ongoing requesters with a permissible use and qualify for personal information per state law may establish a Record Inquiry Account.

Records are available from 1963 to present. Vehicle title and registration records are archived on microfilm and microfiche. It takes 2-3 weeks from issue before new records are available for inquiry.

Searching: Title and registration ownership records are open to the public, for a fee. By law, only certain entities may receive records with personal info. Casual requesters cannot obtain records with personal information without written consent of subject. Include the following in your request-name and DOB, or VIN or plate. The following data is not released: medical information, SSNs.

Access by: mail, phone, fax.

Fee & Payment: Vehicle record prints are $4.00, information given orally is $2.50 (to account holders). A complete vehicle title history is $22.50. An insurance information search is $10.00. Generally, $2.50 is charged if no record is found. Fee payee: Driver & Motor Services (DMV). Prepayment required unless account holder. Personal checks accepted; no credit cards.

Mail search: Turnaround time: 1 day. A SASE is helpful. **Phone search:** The automated system called "IVR" is open 24 hours a day. An account is necessary. Call 503-945-7950 for more information. **Fax search:** No searching by fax.

Other access: Bulk lists available on cartridge to qualified accounts. Call 503-945-7590 for more information.

Accident Reports

Driver & Motor Vehicle Services Division, Accident Reports & Information, 1905 Lana Ave, NE, Salem, OR 97314; 503-945-5098, 503-945-5267-Fax; 8AM-5PM. www.oregondmv.com

Police reports filed with the DMV are available. Copies of individual's reports are not, but information is provided in letter form to those involved or representing someone involved.

Records are available for 5 years to present. It takes 2-4 weeks before new records are available for inquiry.

Searching: Qualified requesters include legal representatives, involved insurance companies and those involved with property damage or injury. Include the following in your request-full name, date of accident, location of accident. The police report is provided without personal information unless the requester qualifies for personal information under OR law.

Access by: mail, phone, fax, in person.

Fee & Payment: The fee is $8.50 for a police accident report. There is $8.50 charge for a "no record found." The letter described above is no charge to qualified requesters; certification is $13.00 however. Information letters (from personal reports) are $12.50 each. Fee payee: DMV Services. Prepayment required. Personal checks accepted. No credit cards accepted.

Mail search: Turnaround time: 3 to 5 days. No SASE is required.

Phone search: This is only available for pre-approved accounts.

Fax search: This is only available for account holders. Same fees and turnaround time (3-5 days).

In person search: Turnaround time will vary, record may not be available same day.

Other access: Bulk release of police accident reports is available for sale to qualified requesters. Records are unsorted and include all counties.

Vessel Ownership Vessel Registration

Oregon State Marine Board, Records, PO Box 14145, Salem, OR 97309 (Courier address: 435 Commercial St NE, #400, Salem, OR 97301); 503-378-8587, 503-378-4597-Fax; 8AM-5PM M-F.

www.boatoregon.com

Lien information is shown on the title records.

Records are available from 1997 to present for titles. Records are indexed on computer for the last 3 years. Records are on microfiche from the 1978 to the present. Titles and registrations are issued on all motorized boats and on sailboats 12 ft and over. It takes two days before new records are available for inquiry.

Searching: Extremely large pleasure boats which move along the OR-WA-CA border for 60 days or more are sometimes documented with the US Coast Guard. Call 800-799-8362 for more information. To search, one of the following is required: name, Oregon #, or hull ID #. Requests can be made via e-mail, from the website,

Access by: mail, phone, fax, in person.

Fee & Payment: There is no fee for one search. Fees for lists are dependent on the time involved. Fee payee: State Marine Board. Prepayment required. Personal checks accepted. No credit cards accepted.

Mail search: Turnaround time: 7 to 10 days. No SASE is required. **Phone search:** Limited registration information is released over the phone. **Fax search:** Records are available by fax. **In person search:** If the search is lengthy, the results will be returned by mail.

Other access: An opt out provision is in effect if mailing lists are requested. Records are available on CD. Fee is $165, no credit cards accepted. For more information, call 503-378-8587, ext 232.

Voter Registration

Access to Records is Restricted.

Secretary of State, Elections Division, 141 State Capitol, Salem, OR 97310; 503-986-1518, 503-373-7414-Fax; 8AM-5PM.
www.sos.state.or.us/elections/elechp.htm

Records are maintained at the county level and cannot be purchased for commercial reasons. The state plans on having a statewide voter registration database in place in 2006.

GED Certificates

Dept of Community Colleges/ Workforce Development, Oregon GED Program, 255 Capitol St NE, Salem, OR 97310; 503-378-8648 x369, 503-378-8434-Fax; 8AM-5PM M-F.

www.odccwd.state.or.us

A request form is available at the webpage. Use their search button and type in GED, or email to request a form.

Searching: To verify, the following is a required: name at time of test, date/year of test, DOB, and SSN. If a copy of a transcript is requested, include the above plus a signed release and fee.

Access by: mail, phone, in person, online.

Fee & Payment: There is no fee for verification. Copies of transcripts are $5.00 each. Fee payee: Oregon GED Program Prepayment required. Money orders are accepted. Personal checks accepted. No credit cards accepted.

Mail search: Turnaround time: 7 to 10 days. No SASE is required. **Phone search:** Will verify over phone for employers, schools and agencies. **In person search:** Turnaround time is typically 5 minutes.

Online search: For records from 2002 forward, online access is available with the access code provided by the testing center.

Hunting and Fishing License Information

Fish & Wildlife Department, Licensing Division, 3406 Cherry Ave NE, Salem, OR 97303; 503-947-6100, 503-947-6117-Fax; 8AM-5PM.

www.dfw.state.or.us

Records are available from 1996 on computer. It takes 24 hours before new records are available for inquiry. Records normally destroyed after 6 years.

Searching: Include the following in your request-full name, DOB. Fishing licenses and hunting licenses are in the same building in different divisions. The following data is not released: phone numbers or Social Security Numbers.

Access by: mail, fax, in person.

Fee & Payment: The fee for a search is $10.00 for a certified record. If extensive research involved, $28.00 per hour charged, billed in 15 minute increments. Copy fee is $.25 per page first 10, then $.50 per page. Fee payee: O.D.F.W. Prepayment required. Personal checks and MasterCard, Visa, Discover accepted.

Mail search: Turnaround time: 1 to 3 days. No SASE is required. **Fax search:** Same fees and turnaround time as mail requests. Fax fee is $.30 per page if returned. **In person search:** Records are usually returned by mail.

Other access: This agency will release bulk data on list or CD for a fee. Call 503-947-6265..

Oregon State Licensing Agencies

For details about the agency responsible for licensing/certifying/registering an item below or in the Agency Quick Finder section, match an item's number with the number of the agency in the *Licensing Agency Information* section.

Oregon Licenses Searchable Online

Acupuncturist #29	http://egov.oregon.gov/BME/liccred.shtml
Airport/Aircraft Landing Area #3	www.aviation.state.or.us/Aviation/municipal_airports.shtml
Animal Feed (Livestock) #22	http://oregon.gov/ODA/oda_licenses.shtml
Animal Food Processor #22	http://oregon.gov/ODA/oda_licenses.shtml
Architect #6	http://new.orbae.com/index.php?option=com_obae
Architectural Firm #6	http://new.orbae.com/index.php?option=com_obae
Athletic Trainer #49	https://elite.hlo.state.or.us/elitepublic/LPRBrowser.aspx
Attorney #43	www.osbcle.org/members/start.asp
Audiologist #33	www.bspa.state.or.us/directory/ALPHA.htm
Auditor, Municipal #5	http://boahost.com/egovlicsearch.lasso
Bakery #23	http://oregon.gov/ODA/oda_licenses.shtml
Body Piercer #7	http://159.121.106.128/
Boiler Welder #19	www.oregonbcd.org/licensesearch.html
Boilermaker #19	www.oregonbcd.org/licensesearch.html
Brand (Livestock) #22	http://oregon.gov/ODA/oda_licenses.shtml
Brand Inspector #22	http://oregon.gov/ODA/oda_licenses.shtml
Building Official #19	www.oregonbcd.org/licensesearch.html
Building Service Mechanic #19	www.oregonbcd.org/licensesearch.html
Chiropractor/Chiropractic Assistant #8	http://obce.alcsoftware.com/liclookup.php
Christmas Tree Grower #25	http://oregon.gov/ODA/oda_licenses.shtml
Construction Contractor/Subcontr. #21	www.ccb.state.or.us/New_Web/new_search_bak.htm
Cosmetologist #7	http://159.121.106.128/
Counselor, Professional #28	www.oblpct.state.or.us/OBLPCT/type.shtml
Dairy Establishment #23	http://oregon.gov/ODA/oda_licenses.shtml
Dental Hygienist #51	http://egov.oregon.gov/Dentistry/licensee_lookup.shtml
Dentist #51	http://egov.oregon.gov/Dentistry/licensee_lookup.shtml
Denture Technologist #49	https://elite.hlo.state.or.us/elitepublic/LPRBrowser.aspx
Denturist #9	https://elite.hlo.state.or.us/elitepublic/LPRBrowser.aspx
Diagnostic Radiologic Technologist #39	www.obrt.state.or.us
Diagnostic/Therapeutic Technologist #39	www.obrt.state.or.us
Dietitian #11	http://bld.oregonlookups.com/
Dog Racing Occupation #42	http://licenseinfo.oregon.gov/
Egg Handler/Breaker #23	http://oregon.gov/ODA/oda_licenses.shtml
Electrical Installation #19	www.oregonbcd.org/licensesearch.html
Electrician #19	www.oregonbcd.org/licensesearch.html
Electrician, Maintenance #19	www.oregonbcd.org/licensesearch.html
Elevator Journeyman, Limited #19	www.oregonbcd.org/licensesearch.html
Energy Technician, Ltd./Restricted #19	www.oregonbcd.org/licensesearch.html
Engineer #10	www.osbeels.org
Facial Technician/Technologist #7	http://159.121.106.128/
Fertilizer/Mineral/Lime Registrant #24	http://oregon.gov/ODA/oda_licenses.shtml
Florist #25	http://oregon.gov/ODA/oda_licenses.shtml
Food Establishment, Retail #23	http://oregon.gov/ODA/oda_licenses.shtml
Food Exporter/Processing Facility #23	http://oregon.gov/ODA/oda_licenses.shtml
Food Producer/Distributor #23	http://oregon.gov/ODA/oda_licenses.shtml
Food Storage Facility #23	http://oregon.gov/ODA/oda_licenses.shtml
Frozen Desert-related Industry #23	http://oregon.gov/ODA/oda_licenses.shtml
Geologist #12	www.open.org/~osbge/registrants.htm
Geologist, Engineering #12	www.open.org/~osbge/registrants.htm
Greenhouse Grower, Herbaceous #25	http://oregon.gov/ODA/oda_licenses.shtml
Hair Stylist #7	http://159.121.106.128/
Heliport #3	www.aviation.state.or.us/Aviation/municipal_airports.shtml
Horse Racing Occupation #42	http://licenseinfo.oregon.gov/
Inspector, Building Code #19	www.oregonbcd.org/licensesearch.html

Inspector, Structural/Mechanical #19	www.oregonbcd.org/licensesearch.html
Insurance Agent / Adjuster / Consultant #27	http://www4.cbs.state.or.us/ex/ins/inslic/agent/
Insurance Agency #27	www.cbs.state.or.us/external/imd/database/inslic/agency_main.htm
Insurance Company #27	www.cbs.state.or.us/external/imd/database/inslic/comp_main.htm
Landscape Business #21	https://orlsc.glsuite.us/renewal/glsweb/homeframe.aspx
Landscaper #25	http://oregon.gov/ODA/oda_licenses.shtml
Livestock-Related Business #22	http://oregon.gov/ODA/oda_licenses.shtml
Manicurist/Nail Technician #7	https://elite.hlo.state.or.us/elitepublic/LPRBrowser.aspx
Manufact'd Housing Construction #19	www.oregonbcd.org/licensesearch.html
Marriage & Family Therapist #28	www.oblpct.state.or.us/OBLPCT/type.shtml
Massage Therapist #38	www.oregonmassage.org/liclookup.php
Measuring Devices #20	http://oda.state.or.us/dbs/search.lasso#msd
Medical Doctor/Surgeon #29	http://egov.oregon.gov/BME/liccred.shtml
Midwife #49	https://elite.hlo.state.or.us/elitepublic/LPRBrowser.aspx
Milk Hauler/Milk Stabilizat'n/Handler #23	http://oregon.gov/ODA/oda_licenses.shtml
Motor Fuel Quality #20	http://oda.state.or.us/dbs/search.lasso#msd
Naturopathic Physician #34	www.obne.state.or.us/OBNE/FindADoctor.shtml
Non-Alcoholic Beverage Plant #23	http://oregon.gov/ODA/oda_licenses.shtml
Nurse #13	http://mscfprod1.iservices.state.or.us/nursinglu/LicenseLookup.cfm
Nurse-LPN #13	http://mscfprod1.iservices.state.or.us/nursinglu/LicenseLookup.cfm
Nursery Dealer #25	http://oregon.gov/ODA/oda_licenses.shtml
Nursery Stock/Native Plants Collec'r #25	http://oregon.gov/ODA/oda_licenses.shtml
Nursing Assistant #13	http://mscfprod1.iservices.state.or.us/nursinglu/LicenseLookup.cfm
Nursing Home Administrator #35	www.nhabd.state.or.us/directory/index.htm
Occupational Therapist #36	http://159.121.112.98/directory/ALPHAOT.htm
Occupational Therapy Assistant #36	http://159.121.112.98/directory/ALPHAAOT.htm
Oil Module #19	www.oregonbcd.org/licensesearch.html
Optometrist #14	www.oregonobo.org/doctorinfo.htm
Oral Pathology Endorsement #9	https://elite.hlo.state.or.us/elitepublic/LPRBrowser.aspx
Oregon Product #22	http://oregon.gov/ODA/oda_licenses.shtml
Osteopathic Physician/Surgeon #29	http://egov.oregon.gov/BME/liccred.shtml
Permanent Color Technician #7	https://elite.hlo.state.or.us/elitepublic/LPRBrowser.aspx
Pesticide Applicator/Trainee #24	http://oregon.gov/ODA/oda_licenses.shtml
Pesticide Dealer/Consultant #24	http://oregon.gov/ODA/oda_licenses.shtml
Pesticide Product #24	http://oregon.gov/ODA/oda_licenses.shtml
Physical Therapist/Assistant #45	www.ptboard.state.or.us
Physician #29	http://egov.oregon.gov/BME/liccred.shtml
Physician Assistant #29	http://egov.oregon.gov/BME/liccred.shtml
Plans Examiner #19	www.oregonbcd.org/licensesearch.html
Plumber #19	www.oregonbcd.org/licensesearch.html
Podiatrist #29	http://egov.oregon.gov/BME/liccred.shtml
Pressure Vessel Installer #19	www.oregonbcd.org/licensesearch.html
Psychologist #16	http://mscfprod1.iservices.state.or.us/obpe/search/obpe_lookup.cfm
Psychologist Associate #16	http://mscfprod1.iservices.state.or.us/obpe/search/obpe_lookup.cfm
Public Accountant-CPA / Firm #5	http://boahost.com/egovlicsearch.lasso
Pump Installation Contr., Limited #21	www.cbs.state.or.us/external/imd/database/bcd/licensing/index.html
Radiologic Technologist Ltd Permit #39	www.obrt.state.or.us
Radiologic Therapy Technologist #39	www.obrt.state.or.us
Real Estate Appraiser #4	http://oregonaclb.org/index.php?option=com_content&task=view&id=20&Itemid=112
Refrigerated Plant #23	http://oregon.gov/ODA/oda_licenses.shtml
Respiratory Care Practitioner #32	https://elite.hlo.state.or.us/elitepublic/LPRBrowser.aspx
Respiratory Care Therapist #49	https://elite.hlo.state.or.us/elitepublic/LPRBrowser.aspx
Sanitarian #49	https://elite.hlo.state.or.us/elitepublic/LPRBrowser.aspx
Shellfish-related Industry #23	http://oregon.gov/ODA/oda_licenses.shtml
Sign Contractor, Limited #21	www.cbs.state.or.us/external/imd/database/bcd/licensing/index.html
Sign Journeyman, Electrical #19	www.oregonbcd.org/licensesearch.html
Slaughterhouse #23	http://oregon.gov/ODA/oda_licenses.shtml
Speech Language Pathologist #33	www.bspa.state.or.us/directory/ALPHA.htm
Stage Journeyman, Electrical #19	www.oregonbcd.org/licensesearch.html
Steamfitter #19	www.oregonbcd.org/licensesearch.html
Surveyor, Land #10	www.osbeels.org

Tattoo Artist #49	https://elite.hlo.state.or.us/elitepublic/LPRBrowser.aspx
Teacher #53	www.tspc.state.or.us/lookup_query.asp
Transaction Verification #20	http://oda.state.or.us/dbs/search.lasso#msd
Veterinarian #54	www.ovmeb.state.or.us/directory/default.htm
Veterinary Clinic, Livestock #22	http://oregon.gov/ODA/oda_licenses.shtml
Veterinary Product, Livestock #22	http://oregon.gov/ODA/oda_licenses.shtml
Waste Water System Operator #1	www.deq.state.or.us/wq/OpCert/opcert.htm
Water Heater Installer, Limited #19	www.oregonbcd.org/licensesearch.html
Water Rights Examiner #10	www.osbeels.org
Water Treatment Installer #19	www.oregonbcd.org/licensesearch.html
Weighing Devices #20	http://oda.state.or.us/dbs/search.lasso#msd

Oregon Licensing Quick Finder

Acupuncturist #29	503-229-5770
Aircraft Registration #3	503-378-4880
Airport/Aircraft Landing Area #3	503-378-4880
Amusement Ride Inspector #19	503-378-4133
Animal Euthanasia Technician #54	503-731-4051
Animal Feed (Livestock) #22	503-986-4691
Animal Food Processor #22	503-986-4680
Animal Health Technician #54	503-731-4051
Architect #6	503-378-4270
Architectural Firm #6	503-378-4270
Athletic Trainer #49	503-378-8667
Attorney #43	503-620-0222
Audiologist #33	971-673-0220
Auditor, Municipal #5	503-378-4181
Bakery #23	503-986-4720
Bank #26	503-378-4140
Bank Registered Agent #26	503-378-4140
Barber #7	503-378-8667
Body Piercer #7	503-378-8667
Boiler Welder #19	503-373-1268
Boilermaker #19	503-373-1268
Boxer #44	503-378-8739
Brand (Livestock) #22	503-986-4681
Brand Inspector #22	503-986-4681
Brewery #41	503-872-5124
Building Official #19	503-373-1248
Building Service Mechanic #19	503-373-1268
Cemetery #52	503-731-4040 x26
Check & Money Order Seller #26	503-378-4140
Chiropractor/Chiropractic Assistant #8	503-378-5816
Christmas Tree Grower #25	503-986-4644
Collection Agency #26	503-378-4140
Construction Contractor/Subcontractor #21	503-378-4621 x4900
Consumer Finance Company #26	503-378-4140
Corrections Officer #18	503-378-2100
Cosmetologist #7	503-378-8667
Counselor, Professional #28	503-378-5499
Court Reporter #31	503-986-5500
Credit Service Organization #26	503-378-4140
Credit Union #26	503-378-4140
Crematorium #52	503-731-4040 x26
Dairy Establishment #23	503-986-4720
Debt Consolidating Agency #26	503-378-4140
Dental Hygienist #51	503-229-5520
Dental Specialist #51	503-229-5520
Dentist #51	503-229-5520
Denture Technologist #49	503-378-8667
Denturist #9	503-378-8667
Diagnostic Radiologic Technolog't #39	971-673-0215
Diagnostic/Therapeutic Tech. #39	971-673-0215
Dietitian #11	971-673-0190
Digital Signature Authority #26	503-378-4140
Dog Racing Occupation #42	503-731-4052
Drug Manufacturer/Wholesaler #15	971-673-0001
Drug Outlet, Over-the-Counter #15	971-673-0001
Egg Handler/Breaker #23	503-986-4720
Electrical Installation #19	503-373-1268
Electrician #19	503-373-1268
Electrician, Maintenance #19	503-373-1268
Electrologist #7	503-378-8667
Electrology Instructor/School #7	503-378-8667
Elevator Journeyman, Limited #19	503-373-1268
Embalmer/Embalmer Apprentice #52	503-731-4040 x26
EMD #18	503-378-2100
Endowment Care #26	503-378-4140
Energy Technician, Limited/Restricted #19	503-373-1268
Engineer #10	503-362-2666
Escrow Agent/Agency #46	503-378-4170
Facial Technician/Technologist #7	503-378-8667
Farm Labor Contractor #21	503-731-4200
Fertilizer/Mineral/Lime Registrant #24	503-986-4600
Firefighter #18	503-378-2100
Florist #25	503-986-4644
Food Establishment, Retail #23	503-986-4720
Food Exporter/Processing Facility #23	503-986-4720
Food Producer/Distributor #23	503-986-4720
Food Storage Facility #23	503-986-4720
Forest Labor Contractor #21	503-731-4200
Frozen Desert-related Industry #23	503-986-4720
Funeral Establishment #52	503-731-4040 x26
Funeral Plan, Prearranged #26	503-378-4140
Funeral Pre-Need Salesperson #52	503-731-4040 x26
Funeral Service Practitioner/Apprentice #52	503-731-4040 x26
Geologist #12	503-566-2837
Geologist, Engineering #12	503-566-2837
Greenhouse Grower of Herbaceous Plants #25	503-986-4644
Hair Salon #7	503-378-8667
Hair Stylist #7	503-378-8667
Hairdresser #7	503-378-8667
Hearing Aid Dealer/Dispenser #2	503-378-8667
Heliport #3	503-378-4880
Home Inspector #21	503-378-4621 x4900
Horse Racing Occupation #42	503-731-4052
Immediate Disposition Comp. #52	503-731-4040 x26
Inspector, Building Code #19	503-373-1248
Inspector, Structural/Mechanical #19	503-373-1248
Insurance Adjuster #27	503-947-7980
Insurance Agency #27	503-947-7980
Insurance Agent #27	503-947-7980
Insurance Company #27	503-947-7980
Insurance Consultant #27	503-947-7980
Interpreter, Legal #31	503-986-5695
Investment Advisor #26	503-378-4140
Landscape Architect #50	503-589-0093
Landscape Business #21	503-378-4621
Landscaper #25	503-986-4644
Liquor Control #41	503-872-5000
Liquor Salesman/Agent #41	503-872-5123
Liquor, Wide Shipper #41	503-872-5124
Livestock-Related Business #22	503-986-4680
Lobbyist #40	503-378-5105
Manicurist/Nail Technician #7	503-378-8667
Manufactured Housing Constr. #19	503-373-1248
Marriage & Family Therapist #28	503-378-5499
Massage Therapist #38	503-365-8657
Measuring Devices #20	503-986-4550
Medical Doctor/Surgeon #29	503-229-5770
Medical Examiner #51	503-280-6061
Midwife #49	503-378-8667
Milk Hauler/Milk Stabilization/Handler #23	503-986-4720
Money Transmitter #26	503-378-4140
Mortgage Banker/Broker/Lender #26	503-378-4140
Motor Fuel Quality #20	503-986-4550
Naturopathic Physician #34	971-673-0193
Non-Alcoholic Beverage Plant #23	503-986-4720
Notary Public #37	503-986-2593
Nurse #13	971-673-0685
Nurse-LPN #13	971-673-0685
Nursery Dealer #25	503-986-4644
Nursery Stock/Native Plants Collector #25	503-986-4644
Nursing Assistant #13	971-673-0685
Nursing Home Administrator #35	971-673-0196
Occupational Therapist #36	971-673-0198
Occupational Therapy Assistant #36	971-673-0198
Oil Module #19	503-373-1268
Optometrist #14	(503)399-0662
Oral Pathology Endorsement #9	503-378-8667
Oregon Product #22	503-986-4680
Osteopathic Physician/Surgeon #29	503-229-5770
Parole/Probation Officer #18	503-378-2100
Pawnbroker #26	503-378-4140
Permanent Color Technician #7	503-378-8667
Pesticide Applicator/Trainee #24	503-986-4600
Pesticide Dealer/Consultant #24	503-986-4600
Pesticide Product #24	503-986-4600
Pharmacist / Pharmacy #15	971-673-0001
Physical Therapist/Assistant #45	971-673-0200
Physician #29	503-229-5770
Physician Assistant #29	503-229-5770
Pilot #3	503-378-4880
Plans Examiner #19	503-373-1248
Plumber #19	503-373-1268
Podiatrist #29	503-229-5770
Police Chief #18	503-378-2100
Police Officer #18	503-378-2100
Polygraph Examiner #18	503-378-2100
Pre-Need Salesperson #52	503-731-4040 x26
Pressure Vessel Installer #19	503-373-1268
Private Security Officer #18	503-378-2100
Property Manager #46	503-378-4170
Psychologist #16	503-378-4154
Psychologist Associate #16	503-378-4154
Public Accountant-CPA #5	503-378-4181
Public Accounting Firm #5	503-378-4181
Pump Installation Contr., Limited #21	503-731-4072
Radiologic Technologist Ltd Permit #39	971-673-0215
Radiologic Therapy Technologist #39	971-673-0215
Real Estate Agent/Sales #46	503-378-4170
Real Estate Appraiser #4	503-485-2555
Real Estate Branch Office #46	503-378-4170

Real Estate Broker #46 503-378-4170
Refrigerated Plant #23.........................503-986-4720
Respiratory Care Practitioner #32503-378-8667x4330
Respiratory Care Therapist #49 503-378-8667
Sanitarian #47.....................................503-378-8667
Sanitarian #49.....................................503-378-8667
Savings & Loan Association #26...........503-378-4140
School Counselor/Supervisor #53........503-378-6813
School Superintendent/Admin. #53.......503-378-6813
Securities Broker/Dealer/Seller #26.....503-378-4140
Shellfish-related Industry #23...............503-986-4720
Sign Contractor, Limited #21...............503-731-4072
Sign Journeyman, Electrical #19..........503-373-1268
Slaughterhouse #23 503-986-4720

Social Worker, Clinical #48 503-378-5735
Special Qualifications Corporation #26.503-378-4140
Speech Language Pathologist #33 971-673-0220
Speech-Language Pathology Assistant #33
                              971-673-0220
Stage Journeyman, Electrical #19 503-373-1268
Steamfitter #19 503-373-1268
Surveyor, Land #10 503-362-2666
Tattoo Artist #49 503-378-8667
Tax Consultant/Preparer #17 503-378-4034
Teacher #53 503-378-6813
Telecommunicator #18.........................503-378-2100
Transaction Verification #20.................503-986-4550
Travel Agent #26 503-378-4140

Trust Company #26.............................503-378-4140
Veterinarian #54 503-731-4051
Veterinary Clinic, Livestock #22 503-986-4680
Veterinary Product, Livestock #22 503-986-4680
Veterinary Technician #54 503-731-4051
Waste Water Treatment System Operator #1
                              503-229-5622
Water Heater Installer, Limited #19 503-373-1268
Water Rights Examiner #10 503-362-2666
Water Treatment Installer #19 503-373-1268
Water Well Constructor #30 503-378-8455
Weighing Devices #20 503-986-4550
Winery #41 503-872-5124
Wrestler #44 503-378-8739

Oregon Licensing Agency Information

1 Department of Environmental Quality, Operator Certification Program, Water Quality Division, 811 SW 6th Ave, Portland, OR 97204; 503-229-5696, Fax: 503-229-6037.
www.deq.state.or.us/

2 Advisory Council on Hearing Aids, 700 Summer St, #320, Salem, OR 97301-1287; 503-378-8667, Fax: 503-370-9004.
www.oregon.gov/HLO/HAS/index.shtml
Email: hdlp.mail@state.or.us

3 Department of Aviation, Aeronautics Section, 3040 25th S SE, Salem, OR 97302; 503-378-4880, Fax: 503-373-1688. www.aviation.state.or.us

4 Appraiser Certification & Licensure Board, 1860 Hawthorne Avenue NE #200, Salem, OR 97303; 503-485-2555, Fax: 503-485-2559.
http://oregonaclb.org/
Email: jan@oregonaclb.org
Search data http://oregonaclb.org/index.php?option=com_content&task=view&id=20&Itemid=112

5 Board of Accountancy, 3218 Pringle Rd SE, #110, Salem, OR 97302-6307; 503-378-4181, Fax: 503-378-3575.
http://egov.oregon.gov/BOA/about_us.shtml
Email: david.r.hunter@state.or.us

6 Board of Architect Examiners, 205 Liberty St. NE Suite A, Salem, OR 97301; 503-763-0662, Fax: 503-364-0510.
www.oregon.gov/ARCHITECT/index.shtml
Email: architect.board@state.or.us
Search Database at
http://new.orbae.com/index.php?option=com_obae

7 Health Licensing Office, Board of Barbers & Hairdressers, 700 Summer St NE #320, Salem, OR 97301-1287; 503-378-8667, Fax: 503-370-9004.
www.hlo.state.or.us
Email: hdlp.mail@state.or.us
Search Database at https://elite.hlo.state.or.us/elitepublic/LPRBrowser.aspx

8 Board of Chiropractic Examiners, 3218 Pringle Rd SE, #150, Salem, OR 97302-6311; 503-378-5816, Fax: 503-362-1260.
http://oregon.gov/OBCE/contact_us.shtml
Email: oregon.obce@state.or.us

9 Board of Denture Technology, 700 Summer St, #320, Salem, OR 97301-1287; 503-378-8667, Fax: 503-585-2114.
www.oregon.gov/HLO/DT/index.shtml
Email: hdlp.mail@state.or.us
Search Database at https://elite.hlo.state.or.us/elitepublic/LPRBrowser.aspx

10 Board of Examiners for Engineer & Land Surveyors, 728 Hawthorne Ave NE, Salem, OR 97301; 503-362-2666, Fax: 503-362-5454.
www.osbeels.org
Email: osbeels@osbeels.org
Search Database at www.osbeels.org

11 Board of Examiners of Licensed Dietitians, 800 NE Oregon St, #407, Portland, OR 97232; 971-673-0190, Fax: 971-673-0226.
www.bld.state.or.us
Email: doug.vanfleet@state.or.us
Search Database at http://bld.oregonlookups.com/
Note: They do sell/provide lists.

12 Oregon State Board of Geologist Examiners, Sunset Center South, 1193 Royvonne Ave. SE #24, Salem, OR 97302; 503-566-2837, Fax: 503-485-2947.
www.oregon.gov/OSBGE
Email: osbge@open.org
Search Database at
www.open.org/~osbge/registrants.htm

13 Board of Nursing, 800 NE Oregon St, #465, Portland, OR 97232-2162; 971-673-0685, Fax: 971-673-0684.
www.oregon.gov/OSBN/contact_us.shtml
Email: oregon.bn.info@state.or.us
Search Database at http://mscfprod1.iservices.state.or.us/nursinglu/LicenseLookup.cfm

14 Board of Optometry, 1900 Hines St., SE, Salem, OR 97309; (503)399-0662, Fax: 503-399-0705. www.oregonobo.org
Email: oregon.obo@state.or.us
Search Database at
www.oregonobo.org/doctorinfo.htm

15 Board of Pharmacy, 800 NE Oregon St, State Office Bldg, Rm 425, Portland, OR 97232; 971-673-0001, Fax: 971-673-0002.
www.pharmacy.state.or.us
Email: pharmacy.board@state.or.us Note: Verifications are free at this time. Lists are $80.00, contact Michael regarding lists at x227.

16 Board of Psychologist Examiners, 3218 Pringle Road, #130, Salem, OR 97301-6309; 503-378-4154, Fax: 503-378-3575.
www.obpe.state.or.us
Search Database at http://mscfprod1.iservices.state.or.us/obpe/search/obpe_lookup.cfm

17 Board of Tax Practitioners, 3218 Pringle Road, #120, Salem, OR 97302; 503-378-4034, Fax: 503-378-3575.
www.oregon.gov/OTPB
Email: tax.bd@state.or.us

18 Department of Public Safety Standards & Training, 550 N Monmouth Ave, Monmouth, OR 97361; 503-378-42100, Fax: 503-378-3306.
www.dpsst.state.or.us

19 Department of Consumer & Business Svcs, Building Codes Division, PO Box 14470, Salem, OR 97309-0404; 503-378-4100, Fax: 503-378-2322. www.oregonbcd.org
Email: bcd.webmaster@state.or.us
Search Database at www.cbs.state.or.us/imd/database/bcd/licensing/indiv/index.html

20 Department of Agriculture, Measurements Standards Division, 635 Capitol St NE, Salem, OR 97301-2532; 503-986-4550, Fax: 503-986-4747.
http://oregon.gov/ODA
Email: msd-support@oda.state.or.us
Search Database at
http://oda.state.or.us/dbs/search.lasso#msd

21 Construction & Landscape Contractors Boards, 700 Summer St NE #300 PO Box 14140,, Salem, OR 97309-5052; 503-378-4621 x4900, Fax: 503-373-2007.
www.ccb.state.or.us/New_Web/new_contact_us.htm
Email: ccbinfo@ccb.state.or.us Note: 24-hour Contractor Inquiry Line - 503-378-4610 or 888-366-5635.

22 Department of Agriculture, Animal Health & Identification Division (State Vet.), 635 Capitol St NE, Salem, OR 97310-0110; 503-986-4680, Fax: 503-986-4734.
http://egov.oregon.gov/ODA/AHID/contact_us.shtml
Email: tberg@oda.state.or.us
Search Database at
http://oregon.gov/ODA/oda_licenses.shtml

23 Department of Agriculture, Food Safety Division, 635 Capitol St NE, Salem, OR 97301-2523; 503-986-4720, Fax: 503-986-4729.
http://egov.oregon.gov/ODA/FSD/index.shtml
Email: rmckay@oda.state.or.us
Search Database at
hhttp://oregon.gov/ODA/oda_licenses.shtml
Note: Updated weekly. Mailing labels available (database formatted ASCII files).

24 Department of Agriculture, Pesticides Division, 635 Capitol St NE, Salem, OR 97310-2523; 503-986-4635, Fax: 503-986-4735.
http://oregon.gov/ODA/PEST/index.shtml
Email: pestx@oda.state.or.us
Search Database at
http://oregon.gov/ODA/oda_licenses.shtml

25 Department of Agriculture, Plant Division, 635 Capitol St NE, Salem, OR 97310-0110; 503-986-4644, Fax: 503-986-4786.
http://oregon.gov/ODA/PEST/index.shtml
Search Database at www.oda.state.or.us/dbs/licenses/search.lasso?&division=nursery

26 Department of Consumer & Business Svcs, Division of Finance and Corporate Securities, 350 Winter St, Labor & Industries Bldg, Rm 410, Salem, OR 97301-3881; 503-378-4140, Fax: 503-947-7862.
www.oregon.gov/DCBS/index.shtml
Search Database at
www.cbs.state.or.us/imd/index_databases.html

27 Department of Consumer and Business Svcs, Insurance Division, PO Box 14480 (350 Winter St NE, Rm 440), Salem, OR 97309-0405; 503-947-7980, Fax: 503-378-4351.
www.cbs.state.or.us/external/ins/
Email: dcbs.insmail@state.or.us
Search Database at
http://www4.cbs.state.or.us/ex/ins/inslic/agent/

28 Licensed Professional Counselors & Therapists, 3218 Pringle Rd SE, #250, Salem, OR 97302-6312; 503-378-5499.
www.oblpct.state.or.us
Email: lpc.lmft@state.or.us
Search Database at
www.oblpct.state.or.us/OBLPCT/type.shtml
Note: They provide downloadable labels and lists of professionals. They provide a $6.00 disk for labels or a $6.00 annual directory.

29 Board of Medical Examiners, 1500 SW 1st Ave #620, Portland, OR 97201; 503-229-5770, Fax: 503-229-6543.
http://egov.oregon.gov/BME/
Email: bme.info@state.or.us
Search Database at
http://egov.oregon.gov/BME/liccred.shtml

30 Department of Water Resources, 725 Summer St. NE, Ste A, Salem, OR 97301-1271; 503-986-0900, Fax: 503-986-0903.
www.wrd.state.or.us

31 Judicial Department, Office of the State Court Administrator, 1163 State St, Salem, OR 97301-2563; 503-986-5500, Fax: 503-986-5503.
www.ojd.state.or.us/

32 Respiratory Therapist Licensing Board, 700 Summer St NE #320, Salem, OR 97310-1287; 503-378-8667 x4330, Fax: 503-370-9114.
www.oregon.gov/HLO/RT/contact_us.shtml
Email: hdlp.mail@state.or.us
Search Database at https://elite.hlo.state.or.us/elitepublic/LPRBrowser.aspx

33 Board of Examiners for Speech-Language Pathology & Audiology, 800 NE Oregon St #21, State Office Bldg, Portland, OR 97232; 971-673-0220, Fax: 503-731-4207.
http://egov.oregon.gov/BSPA/
Email: brenda.felber@state.or.us
Search Database at
www.bspa.state.or.us/directory/ALPHA.htm

34 Naturopathic Board of Examiners, 800 NE Oregon, #407, Portland, OR 97232; 971-673-0193, Fax: 971-673-0226.
www.obne.state.or.us   Email: obne.info@state.or.us
Search Database at
www.obne.state.or.us/OBNE/FindADoctor.shtml
Note: Mailing list form is at
www.obne.state.or.us/forms.htm

35 Nursing Home Board, 800 NE Oregon, #407, Portland, OR 97232; 971-673-0196, Fax: 971-673-0226.
www.oregon.gov/NHABD/index.shtml
Email: janet.bartel@state.or.us
Search Database at
www.nhabd.state.or.us/directory/index.htm

36 Occupational Therapy Licensing, 800 NE Oregon, #407, Portland, OR 97232; 971-673-0198, Fax: 971-673-0226.
www.otlb.state.or.us
Email: otlb.info@state.or.us
Search Database at
www.otlb.state.or.us/OTLB/Licensees.shtml

37 Office of Secretary of State, 255 Capitol St NE, #151, Salem, OR 97310-1327; 503-986-2593, Fax: 503-986-2300.
www.filinginoregon.com/notary/index.htm
Email: oregon.notary@state.or.us

38 Board of Massage Technicians, 748 Hawthorne Ave NE, Salem, OR 97301-4675; 503-365-8657, Fax: 503-385-4465.
www.oregonmassage.org
Email: shel@oregonmassage.org
Search Database at
www.oregonmassage.org/liclookup.php

39 Board of Radiologic Technology, 800 NE Oregon, #407, Portland, OR 97232; 971-673-0215, Fax: 971-673-0218.
www.obrt.state.or.us
Email: info.orbt@state.or.us

40 Government Standards & Pracrices Commission, 100 High St SE, #220, Salem, OR 97310; 503-378-5105, Fax: 503-373-1456.
www.gspc.state.or.us
Email: gspc.mail@state.or.us

41 Liquor Control Commission, 9079 SE McLoughlin Blvd, Milwaukie, OR 97222-7355; 503-872-5000, Fax: 503-872-5018.
www.olcc.state.or.us
Email: Shannon.KILEY@state.or.us

42 Racing Commission, 800 NE Oregon, #11, Portland, OR 97232; 503-731-4052, Fax: 503-731-4053.
http://racing.oregon.gov/
Email: sbarham@OregonVOS.net
Search Database at http://licenseinfo.oregon.gov/

43 State Bar Association, 5200 SW Meadows Rd, Lake Oswego, OR 97035; 503-620-0222, Fax: 503-684-1366.   www.osbar.org
Email: info@osbar.org
Search Database at
www.osbcle.org/members/start.asp

44 Boxing & Wrestling Commission, 3400 State St #G750, Salem, OR 97301; 503-378-8739, Fax: 503-304-9157.
Email: jim.cassidy@state.or.us

45 Physical Therapist Licensing Board, 800 NE Oregon St, #407, Portland, OR 97232-2162; 971-673-0200, Fax: 971-673-0226.
www.ptboard.state.or.us
Email: ptboard.info@state.or.us
Search Database at www.ptboard.state.or.us

46 Real Estate Agency, 1177 Center St NE, Salem, OR 97310-2503; 503-378-4170, Fax: 503-378-2491.
www.rea.state.or.us

47 Sanitarians Registration Board, 700 Summer St NE, #320, Salem, OR 97301-1287; 503-378-8667, Fax: 503-370-9004.
http://egov.oregon.gov/HLO/EHS/contact_us.shtml
Email: hdlp.mail@state.or.us

48 Board of Clinical Social Workers, 3218 Pringle Rd SE, #240, Salem, OR 97302-6310; 503-378-5735, Fax: 503-373-1427.
www.oregon.gov/BCSW/contact_us.shtml
Email: bcsw@state.or.us

49 Health Licensing Office, Admin Svcs Division Manager, 700 Summer St NE #320, Salem, OR 97310-1287; 503-378-8667, Fax: 503-585-9114.
www.hlo.state.or.us
Email: hlo.mail@state.or.us
Search Database at https://elite.hlo.state.or.us/elitepublic/LPRBrowser.aspx

50 Landscape Architect Board, 1193 Royvonne Ave SE #19, Salem, OR 97302; 503-589-0093, Fax: 503-589-0545.
www.oregon.gov/LANDARCH/contact_us.shtml
Email: oslab@uswest.net

51 Board of Dentistry, 1600 SW 4th Ave., Portland, OR 97201; 503-229-5520, Fax: 503-229-6606.
http://egov.oregon.gov/Dentistry/
Search Database at http://egov.oregon.gov/Dentistry/licensee_lookup.shtml

52 Mortuary & Cemetery Board, 800 NE Oregon, #430, Portland, OR 97232-2195; 503-731-4040 X26, Fax: 503-731-4494.
www.oregon.gov/MortCem/index.shtml
Email: mortuary.board@state.or.us
Search Database at http://licenseinfo.oregon.gov/

53 Teacher Standards & Practices Commission, 465 Commercial St. NE, Salem, OR 97301; 503-378-6813, Fax: 503-378-4448.
www.tspc.state.or.us/
Email: Matt.Garrett@state.or.us
Search Database at
www.tspc.state.or.us/lookup_query.asp

54 Veterinary Medical Board, 800 NE Oregon, #407, Portland, OR 97232; 503-731-4051, Fax: 503-731-4207.
Email: ovmeb@info@state.or.us
Search Database at
www.ovmeb.state.or.us/directory/default.htm

Oregon Federal Courts

The following list indicates the district and division name for each county in the state. If the bankruptcy court location is different from the district court, then the location of the bankruptcy court appears in parentheses.

Oregon County/Court Cross Reference

Baker	Portland	Lake	Medford (Eugene)
Benton	Eugene	Lane	Eugene
Clackamas	Portland	Lincoln	Eugene
Clatsop	Portland	Linn	Eugene
Columbia	Portland	Malheur	Portland
Coos	Eugene	Marion	Eugene
Crook	Portland	Morrow	Portland
Curry	Medford (Eugene)	Multnomah	Portland
Deschutes	Eugene (Portland)	Polk	Portland (Eugene)
Douglas	Eugene	Sherman	Portland
Gilliam	Portland	Tillamook	Portland
Grant	Portland	Umatilla	Portland
Harney	Portland	Union	Portland
Hood River	Portland	Wallowa	Portland
Jackson	Medford (Eugene)	Wasco	Portland
Jefferson	Portland	Washington	Portland
Josephine	Medford (Eugene)	Wheeler	Portland
Klamath	Medford (Eugene)	Yamhill	Portland

US District Court

Standards for Federal Courts: Search fee is $26.00 per item (one party name or case number). Copy fee is $.50 per page. Certification fee is $9.00 per document, double for exemplification, if available. All fees standard unless noted in profile. Mail Search: always enclose a stamped self addressed envelope unless otherwise noted. Most courts accept fax requests or will suggest a copying/search vendor. Before releasing records, all courts require prepayment, unless noted.

Open records are located at the court unless otherwise noted. District courts index by defendant and plaintiff as well as by case number. Bankruptcy courts usually index by debtor and case number. While most courts now have their indexes on computer, many may still maintain index card files as well.

Courts offering internet access via CM-ECF or older RACER, PACER, or Web-PACER systems charge $.08 per page fee unless noted as free. Where PACER is available, the universal sign-up number is 800-676-6856. Find PACER and the US Party/Case Index at http://pacer.psc.uscourts.gov.

Eugene Division Court Clerk, 100 Federal Bldg, 211 E 7th Ave, Eugene, OR 97401 (also use mail address for courier delivery), 541-465-6423, Fax-541-465-6344. Hours- 8:30AM-4:30PM. www.ord.uscourts.gov

Counties: Benton, Coos, Deschutes, Douglas, Lane, Lincoln, Linn, Marion.

Searches & Indexing: Results do not include SSN or DOB. Computer index maintained; criminal goes back to 1990, civil to 1988. See microfiche index for criminal records pre-1986. New cases in the index immediately after filing date. Records purged never. District-wide searches available here.

Fee & Payment: Pay by Visa/MC, money order, cashier's or personal check. Payee: Clerk, US District Court. Prepayment required.

Phone Search: Only docket information is available by phone.

Mail Search: SASE not required.

In Person Search: Fee charged if court performs your search. No self-serve copier available.

E-Services: ECF replaces PACER whose records did go back to 9/1988. ECF at https://ecf.ord.uscourts.gov. **Opinions Online:** www.ord.uscourts.gov/rulings/rulings.html. A few selected recent rulings only.

Medford Division Court Clerk, 201 James A Redden US Courthouse, 310 W 6th St, Medford, OR 97501 (also use mail address for courier delivery), 541-608-8777, Fax-541-608-8779. Hours- 8:30AM-4:30PM. www.ord.uscourts.gov

Counties: Curry, Jackson, Josephine, Klamath, Lake. Court set up in 4/1994; Cases prior to that time were tried in Eugene.

Searches & Indexing: Results do not include SSN or DOB. Computer index maintained. New cases in the index 1 day after filing date. Records purged never.

Fee & Payment: Pay by Visa/MC, money order, cashier's or personal check. Payee: Clerk, USDC. Prepayment required. Will fax docket listings no extra charge.

Phone Search: Only docket information is available by phone.

Mail Search: search usually completed- 2-5 days. SASE not required.

In Person Search: Fee charged if court performs your search. No self-serve copier available.

E-Services: ECF replaces PACER whose records did go back to 9/1988. ECF at https://ecf.ord.uscourts.gov **Opinions Online:** www.ord.uscourts.gov/rulings/rulings.html. A few selected recent rulings only.

Portland Division Clerk of Court, 740 US Courthouse, 1000 SW 3rd Ave, Portland, OR 97204-2902 (also use mail address for courier delivery), 503-326-8000, records rm- 503-326-8020, crim dockets- 503-326-8003, civil dockets-503-326-8008, Fax-503-326-8010. Hours- 8:30AM-4:30PM. www.ord.uscourts.gov

Counties: Baker, Clackamas, Clatsop, Columbia, Crook, Gilliam, Grant, Harney, Hood River, Jefferson, Malheur, Morrow, Multnomah, Polk, Sherman, Tillamook, Umatilla, Union, Wallowa, Wasco, Washington, Wheeler, Yamhill.

Searches & Indexing: Results do not include SSN or DOB. Computer index back to 1980; microfiche also maintained. New cases in the index 24 hours after filing date. Records purged never. District-wide searches available here; all civil cases after 8/88 and all criminal cases after 3/91 maintained.

Fee & Payment: Pay by Visa/MC, money order, cashier's or personal check. Payee: Clerk, USDC. Prepayment required.

Phone Search: If case number is provided by phone, docket information is released.

Mail Search: search usually completed- 2-5 days. SASE not required.

In Person Search: Fee charged if court performs your search. Self-serve copier - $.15 per page.

E-Services: ECF replaces PACER whose records did go back to 9/1988. ECF at https://ecf.ord.uscourts.gov **Opinions Online:** www.ord.uscourts.gov/rulings/rulings.html. A few selected recent rulings only.

US Bankruptcy Court

Eugene Division Court Clerk, PO Box 1335, Eugene, OR 97440 (courier address: 151 W 7th St, #300, Eugene, OR 97440), 541-465-6448. Hours-9AM-4:30PM. www.orb.uscourts.gov

Counties: Benton, Coos, Curry, Deschutes, Douglas, Jackson, Josephine, Klamath, Lake, Lane, Lincoln, Linn, Marion.

Searches & Indexing: Results include last 4 SSN digits or DOB; debtor may have chosen to release full SSN. Both computer and card indexes maintained. New cases in the index immediately after filing date. Records purged every 6 months.

Fee & Payment: Pay by money order, cashier's or personal check. Payee: Clerk, US Bankruptcy Court. Prepayment required.

Phone Search: Only docket information available by telephone. Voice Case Information Service available, call VCIS at 800-726-2227 or 503-326-2249.

Mail Search: SASE not required.

In Person Search: Fee charged if court performs your search. Self-serve copier - $.15 per page.

E-Services: PACER online at http://pacer.orb.uscourts.gov. PACER records go back to 1989. New records online after 1 day. ECF at https://ecf.orb.uscourts.gov **Opinions Online:** www.orb.uscourts.gov/opinion. **Other Online Access:** Access judges' calendars by judge name at www.orb.uscourts.gov/orb/cal.nsf/Judges'+Hearings+Calendars.

Portland Division Court Clerk, , 1001 SW 5th Ave, #700, Portland, OR 97204 (also use mail address for courier delivery), 503-326-2231. Hours- 9AM-4:30PM. www.orb.uscourts.gov

Counties: Baker, Clackamas, Clatsop, Columbia, Crook, Gilliam, Grant, Harney, Hood River, Jefferson, Malheur, Morrow, Multnomah, Polk, Sherman, Tillamook, Umatilla, Union, Wallowa, Wasco, Washington, Wheeler, Yamhill.

Searches & Indexing: Results include SSN. Both computer and card indexes maintained. New cases in the index immediately after filing date. Records purged every 6 months.

Fee & Payment: Pay by money order, cashier's or personal check. Payee: Clerk, US Bankruptcy Court. Prepayment required.

Phone Search: Only docket information is available by phone. Voice Case Information Service available, call VCIS at 800-726-2227 or 503-326-2249.

Mail Search: search usually completed- 1-2 days. Include SASE for return.

In Person Search: Fee charged if court performs your search. Self-serve copier - $.15 per page.

E-Services: PACER online at http://pacer.orb.uscourts.gov. PACER records go back to 1989. New records online after 1 day. ECF at https://ecf.orb.uscourts.gov **Opinions Online:** www.orb.uscourts.gov/opinion. **Other Online Access:** Access judges' calendars by judge name at www.orb.uscourts.gov/orb/cal.nsf/Judges'+Hearings+Calendars

Oregon County Courts

Court	Jurisdiction	No. of Courts	How Organized
Circuit Courts*	General	38	27 Districts
County Courts*	Probate	6	6 Counties
Justice Courts	Municipal	35	
Municipal Courts	Municipal	112	
Tax Court	Special	1	

* Profiled in this Sourcebook.

CIVIL									
Court	Tort	Contract	Real Estate	Min. Claim	Max. Claim	Small Claims	Estate	Eviction	Domestic Relations
Circuit Courts*	X	X	X	$0	No Max	$2500	X	X	X
County Courts*							X		X
Justice Courts	X	X	X	$200	$2500	$2500			
Municipal Courts									
Tax Court									

CRIMINAL					
Court	Felony	Misdemeanor	DWI/DUI	Preliminary Hearing	Juvenile
Circuit Courts*	X	X	X	X	X
County Courts*					X
Justice Courts		X	X	X	
Municipal Courts		X	X		
Tax Court					

ADMINISTRATION   Court Administrator, Supreme Court Building, 1163 State St, Salem, OR, 97301-2563; 503-986-5500, Fax: 503-986-5503. www.ojd.state.or.us

COURT STRUCTURE   Effective January 15, 1998, the District and Circuit Courts were combined into "Circuit Courts." At the same time, 3 new judicial districts were created by splitting existing ones.

ONLINE ACCESS   Online computer access is available through the Oregon Judicial Information Network (OJIN). OJIN Online includes almost all cases filed in the Oregon state courts. Generally, the OJIN database contains criminal, civil, small claims, probate, and some but not all juvenile records. However, it does not contain any records from municipal nor county courts. There is a one-time setup fee of $295.00, plus a monthly usage charge (minimum $10.00) based on transaction type, type of job, shift, and number of units/pages (which averages $10-13 per hour). For further information and/or a registration packet, write to: Oregon Judicial System, Information Systems Division, ATTN: Technical Support, 1163 State Street, Salem OR 97310, or call 800-858-9658, or visit www.ojd.state.or.us/ojin

Appellate opinions are found at www.publications.ojd.state.or.us/.

ADDITIONAL INFORMATION   Many Oregon courts indicated that in person searches would markedly improve request turnaround time as court offices are understaffed or spread very thin. Most Circuit Courts that have records on computer do have a public access terminal that will speed up in-person or retriever searches. Most records offices close from Noon to 1PM Oregon time for lunch. No staff is available during that period.

PROBATE COURTS   Probate is handled by the Circuit Court except in 6 counties (Gilliam, Grant, Harney, Malheur, Sherman, and Wheeler) where Probate in handled by County Courts.

Baker County

Circuit Court 1995 3rd St, #220, Baker City, OR 97814; phone: 541-523-6305; criminal fax: 541-523-9738; same fax for civil/probate; hours 8AM-N, 1-5PM (PST). *Felony, Misdemeanor, Civil, Probate.*
www.ojd.state.or.us/baker
Civil Records: Access: Phone, fax, mail, in person, online. Both court and visitors may perform in person searches. No search fee. Court makes copy: $.25 per page. Required to search: name, years to search. Civil cases indexed by defendant, plaintiff; on computer from 1987, archives back to 1865. Index remotely online on the statewide OJIN system, call 800-858-9658 for information. Mail turnaround time 10 days.
Criminal Records: Access: Phone, fax, mail, in person, online. Both court and visitors may perform in person searches. No search fee. Court makes copy: $.25 per page. Required to search: name, years to search. Criminal records on computer from 1987, archives back to 1865. Online access to criminal records is the same as civil. Mail turnaround time 10 days.
General Information: Public terminal goes back to 1987. No adoption, mental, juvenile or sealed records released. Fee to fax documents is $2.00 1st page; $1.00 each add'l. Certification fee: $5.00 per document. Payee: State of Oregon. Personal checks accepted. Prepayment and SASE required.

Benton County

Circuit Court Box 1870 (120 NW 4th St), Corvallis, OR 97339; phone: 541-766-6828; probate phone: 541-766-6825; fax: 541-766-6028; hours 8AM-N, 1-5PM (PST). *Felony, Misdemeanor, Civil, Eviction, Small Claims, Probate.*
www.ojd.state.or.us/benton
Civil Records: Access: Phone, mail, online, in person. Both court and visitors may perform in person searches. Search fee: Fee is court performs search. Court makes copy: $.25 per page. Required to search: name, years to search; also helpful: address. Civil cases indexed by defendant, plaintiff, case number. Civil records on computer from 1993, archives and microfiche back to the 1900s. Index remotely online on the statewide OJIN system, call 800-858-9658 for information. Mail turnaround time up to 1 week.
Criminal Records: Access: Phone, mail, online, in person. Both court and visitors may perform in person searches. Search fee: Fee if court performs search. Court makes copy: $.25 per page. Required to search: name, years to search, DOB, offense; also helpful: address, SSN, case number. Criminal records on computer from 1993, archives and microfiche back to the 1900s. Online access to criminal records is the same as civil. Mail turnaround time up to 1 week.
General Information: Public use terminal available. (Terminal located outside Rm 106.) No adoption, juvenile, sealed by judge, expunged, mental health records released. Will not fax documents. Certification fee: $5.00. Payee: State of Oregon. Personal checks accepted. Prepayment and SASE required.

Clackamas County

Circuit Court 807 Main St, Oregon City, OR 97045; phone: 503-655-8447; criminal phone: 503-655-8643; civil phone: 503-655-8447; probate phone: 503-655-8623; hours 10AM-5PM M-F (PST). *Felony, Misdemeanor, Civil, Eviction, Small Claims, Probate.*
Note: Records management: 503-650-3036.
Civil Records: Access: Mail, online, in person. Both court and visitors may perform in person searches. No search fee. Court makes copy: $.25 per page. Required to search: name, years to search. Civil cases indexed by defendant, plaintiff; on computer from 1986, index back to 1980. Index remotely online on

the statewide OJIN system, call 800-858-9658 for information. Mail turnaround time 4-6 weeks.
Criminal Records: Access: Mail, online, in person. Both court and visitors may perform in person searches. No search fee. Court makes copy: $.25 per page. Required to search: name, years to search, DOB. Criminal records on computer from 1986, index back to 1980. Online access to criminal records is the same as civil. Mail turnaround time 4-6 weeks.
General Information: Public terminal goes back to 1986. No adoption, juvenile, sealed by judge, expunged, mental health records released. Will not fax documents. Certification fee: $5.00 per document. Payee: State of Oregon. Personal checks accepted. Visa, MC accepted in person only. Prepayment and SASE required.

Clatsop County

Circuit Court Box 835, Astoria, OR 97103; phone: 503-325-8583; criminal phone: 503-325-8583; civil phone: 503-325-8555; probate phone: 503-325-5555; criminal fax: 503-325-8677; civil fax: 503-325-9300; probate fax: 503-325-9300; hours 8AM-N, 1-5PM (PST). *Felony, Misdemeanor, Civil, Eviction, Small Claims, Probate.*
www.ojd.state.or.us/clt/index.html
Civil Records: Access: Phone, mail, online, in person. Both court and visitors may perform in person searches. No search fee. Court makes copy: $.25 per page. Required to search: name, years to search. Civil cases indexed by defendant, plaintiff; on computer from 1987, archives back to 1900. Index remotely online on the statewide OJIN system, call 800-858-9658 for information. Mail turnaround time 2 weeks.
Criminal Records: Access: Phone, mail, online, in person. Both court and visitors may perform in person searches. No search fee. Court makes copy: $.25 per page. Required to search: name, years to search, DOB. Criminal records on computer from 1987, archives back to 1900. Online access to criminal records is the same as civil. Mail turnaround time 2 weeks.
General Information: Public terminal goes back to 1987. No adoption, juvenile, sealed by judge, expunged, or mental health records released. Fee top fax documents is $2.00 1st page plus $1.00 each add'l. Certification fee: $5.00 per certification. Payee: Clatsop County Circuit Court. Personal checks accepted. Prepayment and SASE required.

Columbia County

Circuit Court Columbia County Courthouse, 230 Strand St, St. Helens, OR 97051; phone: 503-397-2327; fax: 503-397-3226; hours 8AM-5PM (PST). *Felony, Misdemeanor, Civil, Eviction, Small Claims, Probate.*
www.ojd.state.or.us/col/
Civil Records: Access: Mail, fax, online, in person. Both court and visitors may perform in person searches. No search fee. Court makes copy: $.25 per page. Required to search: name, years to search; also helpful: SSN, DOB, address. Civil cases indexed by defendant, plaintiff; on computer from 9/1987, archives back to 1900. Index remotely online on the statewide OJIN system, call 800-858-9658 for information. Mail turnaround time 5-7 days.
Criminal Records: Access: Mail, fax, online, in person. Both court and visitors may perform in person searches. No search fee. Court makes copy: $.25 per page. Required to search: name, years to search, DOB; also helpful: address, SSN, signed release. Criminal records on computer from 9/1987, archives back to 1900. Online access to criminal records is the same as civil. Mail turnaround time 5-7 days.
General Information: Public terminal has criminal back to 1987 and civil back to 1987. No adoptions, juvenile, sealed by Judge, expunged, mental health records released. Will fax documents for $2.00 1st page, $1.00 each add'l. Certification fee: $5.00.

Payee: State of Oregon. Personal checks accepted. Prepayment and SASE required.

Coos County

Circuit Court Courthouse, Coquille, OR 97423; phone: 541-396-3121; criminal fax: X402; civil phone: X401; probate phone: 541-756-2020x556; fax: 541-396-3456; probate fax: 541-756-1727; hours 8AM-N,1-5PM M-F (PST). *Felony, Misdemeanor, Civil, Eviction, Small Claims, Probate.*
http://cooscurrycourts.org
Note: Eviction, Small Claims and Probate records are available at 541-756-2020 ext 556. Circuit Court Annex at 1975 McPherson, North Bend, OR 97459.
Civil Records: Access: Phone, mail, online, in person. Both court and visitors may perform in person searches. No search fee. Court makes copy: $.25 per page; same fee for self serve. Required to search: name, years to search; also helpful: address. Civil cases indexed by defendant, plaintiff; on computer from 1987, archives back to 1800. Index remotely online on the statewide OJIN system, call 800-858-9658 for information. Mail turnaround time 1-2 days.
Criminal Records: Access: Phone, mail, online, in person. Both court and visitors may perform in person searches. No search fee. Court makes copy: $.25 per page; same fee for self serve. Required to search: name, years to search, DOB; also helpful: address, SSN. Criminal records on computer from 1987, archives back to 1800. Online access to criminal records is the same as civil. Mail turnaround time 1-2 days.
General Information: Public terminal goes back to 1987. No adoptions, sealed by Judge, expunged, paternity or mental health records released. Will fax documents for a fee. Certification fee: $5.00. Payee: State Courts. Personal checks or Visa, MC accepted. Visa, MC. Not accepted for filing fees. Prepayment and SASE required.

Crook County

Circuit Court Crook County Courthouse, 300 NE 3rd St, Prineville, OR 97754; phone: 541-447-6541; fax: 541-447-5116; hours 8AM-5PM (PST). *Felony, Misdemeanor, Civil, Eviction, Small Claims, Probate.*
Civil Records: Access: Phone, fax, mail, in person, online. Both court and visitors may perform in person searches. No search fee. Court makes copy: $.25 per page. Required to search: name, years to search; also helpful: address. Civil cases indexed by defendant, plaintiff; on computer from 1986, microfiche from 1907, archives from 1907. Index remotely online on the statewide OJIN system, call 800-858-9658 for information. Mail turnaround time 2-4 days.
Criminal Records: Access: Phone, fax, mail, in person, online. Both court and visitors may perform in person searches. No search fee. Court makes copy: $.25 per page. Required to search: name, years to search, DOB; also helpful: address, SSN. Criminal records on computer from 1986, microfiche from 1907, archives from 1907. Online access to criminal records is the same as civil. Mail turnaround time 2-4 days.
General Information: No public access terminal. No adoptions, juvenile, sealed by Judge, expunged, paternity or mental health records released. Certification fee: $5.00 per doc. Payee: State of Oregon. Personal checks accepted. Prepayment and SASE required.

Curry County

Circuit Court PO Box 810, 29821 Ellensburg Ave, Gold Beach, OR 97444; phone: 541-247-4511; hours 8AM-N, 1-5PM MTWF; 8AM-N, 1:30-5PM Th (PST). *Felony, Misdemeanor, Civil, Eviction, Small Claims, Probate.*
www.cooscurrycourts.org

Civil Records: Access: Phone, mail, online, in person. Both court and visitors may perform in person searches. No search fee. Court makes copy: $.25 per page. Required to search: name, years to search; also helpful: address. Civil cases indexed by defendant, plaintiff; on computer from 1987, archives back to 1891. Index remotely online on the statewide OJIN system, call 800-858-9658 for information. Mail turnaround time 1-2 days.

Criminal Records: Access: Phone, mail, online, in person. Both court and visitors may perform in person searches. No search fee. Court makes copy: $.25 per page. Required to search: name, years to search, DOB; also helpful: address, SSN. Criminal records on computer from 1987, archives back to 1891. Online access to criminal records is the same as civil. Mail turnaround time 1-2 days.

General Information: Public terminal goes back to 1987. No adoptions, sealed by Judge, expunged, paternity or mental health records released. Certification fee: $5.00 per doc plus copy fee for add'l pages. Payee: State Courts. Personal checks or Visa, MC accepted. Prepayment and SASE required; add postage if SASE not enclosed.

Deschutes County

Deschutes County Courts 1100 NW Bond, Bend, OR 97701; phone: 541-388-5300; criminal phone: X2040; civil phone: X2090; probate phone: X2080; hours 8AM-5PM (PST). *Felony, Misdemeanor, Civil, Eviction, Small Claims, Probate.*

Civil Records: Access: Phone, mail, online, in person. Visitors must perform in person searches themselves. No search fee. Court makes copy: $.25 per page. Required to search: name, years to search. Civil cases indexed by defendant, plaintiff; on computer from 9/87, books from 1976, archived from 1916 on microfiche. Index remotely online on the statewide OJIN system, call 800-858-9658 for information. Also, current calendars are free at www.ojd.state.or.us/des/calendar.nsf/. Mail turnaround time 3-5 days.

Criminal Records: Access: Phone, mail, online, in person. Visitors must perform in person searches themselves. No search fee. Court makes copy: $.25 per page. Required to search: name, years to search, SSN. Criminal records on computer from 9/87, books from 1976, archived from 1916 on microfiche. Criminal Index available remotely online on the statewide OJIN system, call 800-858-9658. Records from 07/86 forward. Also, current calendars are free at www.ojd.state.or.us/des/calendar.nsf/. Mail turnaround time 3-5 days.

General Information: Public use terminal available. No adoptions, juvenile, sealed by Judge, expunged, mental health records released. Certification fee: $5.00. Payee: State of Oregon. Personal checks accepted. Prepayment and SASE required.

Douglas County

Circuit Court 1036 SE Douglas, Roseburg, OR 97470; phone: 541-957-2471; fax: 541-957-2462; hours 8AM-N, 1-5PM (PST). *Felony, Misdemeanor, Civil, Eviction, Small Claims, Probate.*
www.ojd.state.or.us/douglas

Civil Records: Access: Phone, mail, online, in person. Both court and visitors may perform in person searches. No search fee. Court makes copy: $.25 per page; same fee for self serve. Required to search: name, years to search. Civil cases indexed by defendant, plaintiff; on computer back to 10/1987, microfiche from 1974 (district) 1962 (circuit), archived from 1910. Index remotely online on the statewide OJIN system, call 800-858-9658 for information. Mail turnaround time at least two weeks.

Criminal Records: Access: Phone, mail, online, in person. Both court and visitors may perform in person searches. No search fee. Court makes copy: $.25 per page; same fee for self serve. Required to search: name, years to search, DOB. Criminal records

on computer back to 10/1987, microfiche from 1974 (district) 1962 (circuit), archived from 1910. Online access to criminal records is the same as civil. Mail turnaround time at least two weeks.

General Information: Public use terminal available. No adoptions, juvenile, sealed by Judge, expunged or mental health records released. Will scan written and send in "PDF" format to an email address at no cost. Certification fee: $5.00. Payee: Oregon Judicial Department. Personal checks accepted. Prepayment and SASE required.

Gilliam County

Circuit Court Box 622, Condon, OR 97823; phone: 541-384-3572; fax: 541-384-2170; hours 1-5PM (PST). *Felony, Misdemeanor, Civil.*
http://seventhdistrict.ojd.state.or.us

Civil Records: Access: Phone, mail, online, in person. Only the court performs in person searches; visitors may not. No search fee. Court makes copy: $.25 per page. Required to search: name, years to search. Civil cases indexed by defendant, plaintiff; on computer from 1989, index cards back to 1800s. Index remotely online on the statewide OJIN system, call 800-858-9658 for information. Mail turnaround time 1-2 days.

Criminal Records: Access: Phone, mail, online, in person. Only the court performs in person searches; visitors may not. No search fee. Court makes copy: $.25 per page. Required to search: name, years to search; also helpful: DOB. Criminal records on computer from 1989, index cards back to 1800s. Online access to criminal records is the same as civil. Mail turnaround time 1-2 days.

General Information: No public access terminal. No adoptions, juvenile, sealed by Judge, expunged, mental health records released. Will fax documents for an add'l fee. Additional postage may be required if copy weight exceeds 1 oz. Certification fee: $2.00 1st page, $1.00 each add'l page. Payee: Gilliam Circuit Court. Personal checks or Visa/MC accepted. Prepayment and SASE required.

County Court 221 S Oregon, PO Box 427, Condon, OR 97823; phone: 541-384-2311; fax: 541-384-2166; hours 8:30AM-N, 1-5PM (PST). *Probate.*

Grant County

Circuit Court PO Box 159, 201 S Humbolt St, Canyon City, OR 97820; phone: 541-575-1438; fax: 541-575-2165; hours 8AM-N, 1-5PM (PST). *Felony, Misdemeanor, Civil.*
www.ojd.state.or.us/grant

Civil Records: Access: Mail, online, in person. Only the court performs in person searches; visitors may not. No search fee. Court makes copy: $.25 per page. Required to search: name, years to search. Civil cases indexed by defendant, plaintiff; on computer from 1987, microfiche from 1950-1965, archives back to 1880. Index remotely online on the statewide OJIN system, call 800-858-9658 for information. Mail turnaround time 3-5 days.

Criminal Records: Access: Mail, online, in person. Only the court performs in person searches; visitors may not. No search fee. Court makes copy: $.25 per page. Required to search: name, years to search. Criminal records on computer from 1987, microfiche from 1950-1965, archives back to 1880. Online access to criminal records is the same as civil. Mail turnaround time 3-5 days.

General Information: No public access terminal. No adoptions, juvenile, sealed by Judge, expunged, mental health records released. Will not fax documents. Certification fee: $5.00 per document. Payee: Grant County Circuit Court. Personal checks accepted. Prepayment and SASE required.

County Court 201 Humbolt St, #290, Canyon City, OR 97820-6186; phone: 541-575-1675; fax: 541-575-2248; hours 8AM-5PM (PST). *Probate.*

Harney County

Circuit Court 450 N Buena Vista, Burns, OR 97720; phone: 541-573-5207; fax: 541-573-5715; hours 8AM-12PM; 1PM-5PM (PST). *Felony, Misdemeanor, Civil.*
www.ojd.state.or.us/harney

Civil Records: Access: Phone, fax, mail, online, in person. Both court and visitors may perform in person searches. Court makes copy: $.25 per page. Required to search: name, years to search. Civil cases indexed by defendant, plaintiff; on computer from 1988, microfiche from 1970-1979, archives back to 1880. Index remotely online on the statewide OJIN system, call 800-858-9658 for information. Mail turnaround time 5 days.

Criminal Records: Access: Phone, fax, mail, online, in person. Both court and visitors may perform in person searches. Court makes copy: $.25 per page. Required to search: name, years to search. Criminal records on computer from 1988, microfiche from 1970-1979, archives back to 1880. Online access to criminal records is the same as civil. Mail turnaround time 1-2 days.

General Information: Public use terminal available. No adoptions, juvenile, sealed by Judge, expunged, paternity or mental health records released. Will fax documents $2.00 1st page, $1.00 each add'l. Certification fee: $5.00. Payee: Harney Circuit Court. Personal checks accepted. Prepayment and SASE required.

County Court 450 N Buena Vista Ave, Burns, OR 97720-1518; phone: 541-573-6641; fax: 541-573-8370; hours 8:30AM-N, 1-5PM (PST). *Probate.*
www.co.harney.or.us/countycourt.htm

Hood River County

Circuit Court 309 State St, Hood River, OR 97031; phone: 541-386-1862; fax: 541-386-3465; hours 8AM-N, 1-5PM (PST). *Felony, Misdemeanor, Civil, Eviction, Small Claims, Probate.*
http://seventhdistrict.ojd.state.or.us

Civil Records: Access: Phone, fax, mail, online, in person. Both court and visitors may perform in person searches. No search fee. Court makes copy: $.25 per page. Required to search: name, years to search. Civil cases indexed by defendant, plaintiff; on computer from 1989, docket books from 1950. Index remotely online on the statewide OJIN system, call 800-858-9658 for information. Mail turnaround time 7 days.

Criminal Records: Access: Phone, fax, mail, online, in person. Both court and visitors may perform in person searches. No search fee. Court makes copy: $.25 per page. Required to search: name, years to search, DOB. Criminal records on computer from 1989, docket books from 1950. Online access to criminal records is the same as civil. Mail turnaround time 7 days.

General Information: Public terminal goes back to 1988. No adoptions, juvenile, sealed by Judge, expunged, paternity or mental health records released. Certification fee: $5.00 per doc. Payee: Hood River Trial Courts. Personal checks accepted. Credit cards accepted. Prepayment and SASE required.

Jackson County

Circuit Court 100 S Oakdale, Medford, OR 97501; phone: 541-776-7171; criminal phone: x583; civil phone: x582; probate phone: x130; criminal fax: 541-776-7057; same fax for civil/probate; hours 8:30AM-5PM (PST). *Felony, Misdemeanor, Civil Actions, Eviction, Small Claims, Probate.*
http://jackson-court.ojd.state.or.us

Civil Records: Access: Mail, online, in person. Visitors must perform in person searches themselves. No search fee. Court makes copy: $.25 per page. Required to search: name, years to search. Civil cases indexed by defendant, plaintiff; on computer from 1988, prior records on docket books and microfilm. Index remotely online on the statewide OJIN system, call 800-858-9658 for information. Mail turnaround time 1 week.

Criminal Records: Access: Mail, online, in person. Visitors must perform in person searches themselves. No search fee. Court makes copy: $.25 per page. Required to search: name, years to search, DOB. Criminal records on computer from 1988, prior records on docket books and microfilm. Online access to criminal records is the same as civil. Mail turnaround time 1 week.

General Information: Public terminal goes back to late 1980s. No adoptions, juvenile, sealed by Judge, expunged, mental health records released. Will fax documents; $2.00 for 1st page, $1.00 each add'l. Certification fee: $5.00 per document. Payee: Jackson County Courts. Personal checks accepted. Credit cards accepted. Prepayment and SASE required.

Jefferson County

Circuit Court 75 SE C St, #C, Madras, OR 97741-1750; phone: 541-475-3317; fax: 541-475-3421; hours 8AM-5PM (PST). *Felony, Misdemeanor, Civil, Eviction, Small Claims, Probate.*

Civil Records: Access: Mail, fax, online, in person. Both court and visitors may perform in person searches. No search fee. Court makes copy: $.25 per page; same fee for self serve. Required to search: name, years to search. Civil cases indexed by defendant, plaintiff; on computer from 10/1986, archives from 1916-1986. Index remotely online on the statewide OJIN system, call 800-858-9658 for information. Mail turnaround time 1-2 weeks.

Criminal Records: Access: Mail, fax, online, in person. Both court and visitors may perform in person searches. No search fee. Court makes copy: $.25 per page; same fee for self serve. Required to search: name, years to search, DOB. Criminal records on computer from 10/1986, archives from 1916-1986. Online access to criminal records is the same as civil. Mail turnaround time 1-2 weeks.

General Information: Public terminal goes back to 10/1986. No adoptions, juvenile, sealed by Judge, expunged, mental health records released. Certification fee: $5.00 per doc. Payee: State of Oregon. Personal checks and Visa/MC accepted. Prepayment and SASE required.

Josephine County

Circuit Court Josephine County Courthouse, Rm 254, 500 NW 6th St, Grants Pass, OR 97526; phone: 541-476-2309; fax: 541-471-2079; hours 8AM-4PM (PST). *Felony, Misdemeanor, Civil, Eviction, Small Claims, Probate.*

Civil Records: Access: Fax, mail, online, in person. Both court and visitors may perform in person searches. No search fee. Court makes copy: $.25 per page. Required to search: name, years to search. Civil cases indexed by defendant, plaintiff; on computer from 1987, microfilm prior to 1980, archives from 1920, index books. Index remotely online on statewide OJIN system, call 800-858-9658 for information. Mail turnaround time 5 days.

Criminal Records: Access: Fax, mail, online, in person. Both court and visitors may perform in person searches. No search fee. Court makes copy: $.25 per page. Required to search: name, years to search, DOB. Criminal records on computer from 1987, microfilm prior to 1980, archives from 1920, index books. Online access to criminal records is the same as civil. Mail turnaround time 5 days.

General Information: Public terminal goes back to 1987. (Terminal located on 2nd Fl by DA's office.) No adoptions, juvenile, sealed by Judge, expunged, mental health records released. No fee to fax back documents. Certification fee: $5.00 per doc. Payee: Josephine County Court. Personal checks or Visa, MC accepted. Prepayment and SASE required.

Klamath County

Circuit Court 316 Main St, Klamath Falls, OR 97601; phone: 541-883-5503; criminal phone: x232; civil phone: x222; probate phone: x222; fax: 541-882-6109; hours 8AM-5PM M-Th, 8:30AM-5:30PM Fri (PST). *Felony, Misdemeanor, Civil, Eviction, Small Claims, Probate.*

Civil Records: Access: Mail, fax, online, in person. Both court and visitors may perform in person searches. Search fee: $7.50 if requested by mail. Court makes copy: $.25 per page. Required to search: name, years to search. Civil cases indexed by defendant, plaintiff; on computer from 1988, microfiche from 1940-1980. Index remotely online on the statewide OJIN system, call 800-858-9658 for information. Mail turnaround time 2 weeks.

Criminal Records: Access: Mail, fax, online, in person. Both court and visitors may perform in person searches. Search fee: $7.50 if requested by mail. Court makes copy: $.25 per page. Required to search: name, years to search. Criminal records on computer from 1988, felony cases on microfiche from 1940-1980. Online access to criminal records is the same as civil. Mail turnaround time 2 weeks.

General Information: Public terminal goes back to 1989. No adoptions, juvenile, sealed by Judge, expunged, paternity or mental health records released. Fee to fax documents is $2.00 1st page and $1.00 each add'l page. Certification fee: $5.00 per doc. Payee: Klamath County Circuit Court. No personal checks accepted. Visa, MC accepted. Prepayment and SASE required.

Lake County

Circuit Court 513 Center St, Lakeview, OR 97630; phone: 541-947-6051; fax: 541-947-3724; probate fax: same; hours 8AM-N, 1-5PM (PST). *Felony, Misdemeanor, Civil, Eviction, Small Claims, Probate.*

Civil Records: Access: Mail, online, in person. Both court and visitors may perform in person searches. No search fee. Court makes copy: $.25 per page. Required to search: name, years to search. Civil cases indexed by defendant, plaintiff; on computer from 1988, index cards prior. Index remotely online on the statewide OJIN system, call 800-858-9658 for information. Mail turnaround time 2 weeks.

Criminal Records: Access: Mail, online, in person. Both court and visitors may perform in person searches. No search fee, pre 1988 $7.50. Court makes copy: $.25 per page. Required to search: name, years to search. Criminal records on computer from 1988, index cards prior. Online access to criminal records is the same as civil. Mail turnaround time 2 weeks.

General Information: Public terminal goes back to 1988. No adoptions, juvenile, sealed by Judge, expunged or mental health records released. Will fax only if local and prepaid; $2.00 1st page, $1.00 each add'l. Certification fee: $5.00. Payee: Lake County Circuit Court. Personal checks accepted. Prepayment and SASE required.

Lane County

Circuit Court 125 E 8th Ave, Eugene, OR 97401; phone: 541-682-4020; hours 8AM-5PM M-Th, closed Fri (PST). *Felony, Misdemeanor, Civil, Eviction, Small Claims, Probate.*

Civil Records: Access: Online, in person. Visitors must perform in person searches themselves. Court makes copy: $.25 per page. Required to search: name, years to search. Civil cases indexed by defendant, plaintiff; on computer from 1983, index books prior. Index remotely online on the statewide OJIN system, call 800-858-9658 for information.

Criminal Records: Access: Online, in person. Visitors must perform in person searches themselves. Court makes copy: $.25 per page. Required to search: name, years to search. Criminal records on computer from 1983, index books prior. Online access to criminal records is the same as civil.

General Information: Public terminal has criminal back to 1982 and civil back to 1983. No adoptions, juvenile, sealed by Judge, expunged, mental health records released. Certification fee: $5.00 per doc. Payee: Lane County Courts. Personal checks accepted. Credit cards accepted in person only on 2nd Fl. Prepayment required.

Lincoln County

Lincoln County Courts PO Box 100, 225 W Olive St, Newport, OR 97365; phone: 541-265-4236; fax: 541-265-7561; hours 8AM-5PM (PST). *Felony, Misdemeanor, Civil, Eviction, Small Claims, Probate.*

www.ojd.state.or.us/lincoln

Civil Records: Access: Mail, fax, online, in person. Both court and visitors may perform in person searches. No search fee. Court makes copy: $.25 per page. Required to search: name. Civil cases indexed by defendant, plaintiff; on computer from 2/88, archives back to 1893, prior to 1988, years to search must be specified. Index remotely online on the statewide OJIN system, call 800-858-9658 for information. Mail turnaround time 3 days.

Criminal Records: Access: Mail, fax, online, in person. Both court and visitors may perform in person searches. No search fee. Court makes copy: $.25 per page. Required to search: name, years to search. Criminal records on computer from 2/88, archives back to 1893, prior to 1988, years to search must be specified. Online access to criminal records is the same as civil. Mail turnaround time 1 week.

General Information: Public terminal goes back to 2/1988. No adoptions, sealed by Judge, expunged, or mental health records released. Will fax documents for $2.00 1st page and $1.00 each add'l. Certification fee: $5.00. Payee: State of Oregon. Personal checks accepted. Visa, MC accepted. $1.00 minimum cc charge. Prepayment and SASE required.

Linn County

Circuit Court PO Box 1749, 400 Fourth St, Albany, OR 97321; criminal phone: 541-967-3841; civil phone: 541-967-3845; probate phone: 541-967-3845; fax: 541-928-8725; hours 8AM-5PM (PST). *Felony, Misdemeanor, Civil, Eviction, Small Claims, Probate.*

www.ojd.state.or.us/linn-circuit

Civil Records: Access: Mail, online, in person. Both court and visitors may perform in person searches. No search fee. Court makes copy: $.25 per page. Required to search: name, years to search. Civil cases indexed by defendant, plaintiff; on computer from 6/1997, archives back to 1863. Index remotely online on the statewide OJIN system, call 800-858-9658 for information. Mail turnaround time 5-10 days.

Criminal Records: Access: Mail, online, in person. Both court and visitors may perform in person searches. No search fee. Court makes copy: $.25 per page. Required to search: name, years to search, DOB. Criminal records on computer from 6/1987, archives back to 1863. Online access to criminal records is the same as civil. Mail turnaround time 5-10 days.

General Information: Public terminal goes back to 6/1987. No adoptions, juvenile, sealed by judge, expunged, paternity or mental health records released. Will not fax documents. Certification fee: $5.00 per doc. Payee: State of Oregon. Personal checks or Visa, MC or debit card accepted. Prepayment and SASE required.

Malheur County

Circuit Court Oregon Judicial Department, 251 B St W, Vale, OR 97918; phone: 541-473-5171; fax: 541-473-2213; hours 8AM-5PM (MST). *Felony, Misdemeanor, Civil, Eviction, Small Claims.*

www.ojd.state.or.us/malheur

Civil Records: Access: Mail, online, in person. Both court and visitors may perform in person searches. Search fee: No fee, unless access needed to archived records then $15.00 per case. Court makes copy: $.25 per page; same fee for self serve. Required to search: name, years to search. Civil cases indexed by defendant, plaintiff; on computer from 7/1988, archived from 1887. Index remotely online on the statewide OJIN system, call 800-858-9658 for information. Mail turnaround time 2 weeks minimum.

Criminal Records: Access: Mail, online, in person. Both court and visitors may perform in person searches. Search fee: $15.00 per case, if case number known, then no fee. Court makes copy: $.25 per page. Required to search: name, years to search, DOB. Criminal records on computer from 7/1988, archived from 1887. Online access to criminal records is the same as civil. Mail turnaround time 2 weeks minimum.

General Information: Public terminal goes back to 1988. No adoptions, juvenile, sealed by Judge, expunged, mental health records released. Fee to fax documents is $2.50 1st page; $1.00 ea add'l. Incoming fax fee: $2.00 1st page, $1.00 2nd page. Certification fee: $5.00. Payee: Trial Court Administrator. Personal checks or Visa, MC accepted. Accepted for filing fees only. Prepayment required. SASE requested.

County Court 251 B St West #4, Vale, OR 97918; phone: 541-473-5124; probate phone: 541-473-5151; fax: 541-473-5523; hours 8:30AM-5:00PM (MST). *Probate.*

Marion County

Circuit Court PO Box 12869 (100 High St NE), Salem, OR 97309; phone: 503-588-5101; fax: 503-373-4360; hours 8AM-5PM (PST). *Felony, Misdemeanor, Civil, Eviction, Small Claims, Probate.*

http://marion-court.ojd.state.or.us
Civil Records: Access: Mail, online, in person. Both court and visitors may perform in person searches. No search fee. Court makes copy: $.25 per page. Required to search: name, years to search. Civil cases indexed by defendant, plaintiff; on computer from 10/1986, prior on microfiche/microfilm. Index remotely online on the statewide OJIN system, call 800-858-9658 for information. Mail turnaround time minimum 5 days.

Criminal Records: Access: Mail, online, in person. Both court and visitors may perform in person searches. No search fee. Court makes copy: $.25 per page. Required to search: name, years to search; also helpful: DOB, SSN. Criminal records on computer from 10/1986, prior on microfiche/microfilm. Online access to criminal records is the same as civil. Mail turnaround time minimum 5 days.

General Information: Public terminal goes back to 1986. No adoptions, juvenile, sealed by Judge, expunged, paternity or mental health records released. Will fax documents for $2.00 1st page; $1.00 each add'l page. Certification fee: $5.00. Payee: State of Oregon. Personal checks accepted. Prepayment and SASE required.

Morrow County

Circuit Court PO Box 609, Heppner, OR 97836; phone: 541-676-5264; fax: 541-676-9902; hours 8AM-N, 1-5PM (PST). *Felony, Misdemeanor, Civil, Eviction, Small Claims, Probate.*
www.ojd.state.or.us/morrow
Civil Records: Access: Phone, fax, mail, in person, online. Both court and visitors may perform in person searches. No search fee. Court makes copy: $.25 per page. Required to search: name, years to search. Civil cases indexed by defendant, plaintiff; on computer from 1987, archives back to 1940, index cards, docket books by case #. Index remotely online on the statewide OJIN system, call 800-858-9658 for information. Mail turnaround time 1-3 days.

Criminal Records: Access: Phone, fax, mail, online, in person. Both court and visitors may perform in person searches. No search fee. Court makes copy: $.25 per page. Required to search: name, years to

search, DOB. Criminal records on computer from 1987, archives back to 1940, index cards, docket books by case #. Online access to criminal records is the same as civil. Mail turnaround time 1-3 days.

General Information: No public access terminal. No adoptions, juvenile, sealed by Judge, expunged, paternity or mental health records released. No fee to fax documents. Certification fee: $5.00. Payee: Circuit Court. Personal checks accepted. Prepayment and SASE required.

Multnomah County

Circuit Court 1021 SW 4th Ave, Rm 131, Portland, OR 97204; phone: 503-988-3003; hours 8AM-5PM (Tele: 8:30-11AM; 1-3:30PM) (PST). *Felony, Misdemeanor, Civil Actions Over $10,000, Probate.*

Civil Records: Access: Mail, online, in person. Both court and visitors may perform in person searches. No search fee. Court makes copy: $.25 per page. Required to search: name, years to search. Civil cases indexed by defendant, plaintiff; on computer from 1988, microfiche, index books, docket books back to 1857. Index remotely online on the statewide OJIN system, call 800-858-9658 for information. Mail turnaround time 4-5 days.

Criminal Records: Access: Mail, online, in person. Both court and visitors may perform in person searches. No search fee. Court makes copy: $.25 per page. Required to search: name, years to search; also helpful: DOB. Criminal records on computer from 1988, microfiche, index books, docket books back to 1857. Online access to criminal records is the same as civil. Mail turnaround time 4-5 days.

General Information: Public terminal goes back to 1988. No adoptions, juvenile, sealed by Judge, expunged or mental health records released. Certification fee: $5.00. Payee: State of Oregon. Personal checks accepted. Prepayment and SASE required.

Circuit Court - Civil Division 1021 SW 4th Ave, Rm 210, Portland, OR 97204; phone: 503-988-3022; probate phone: 503-988-3016; hours 8:30AM-5PM (PST). *Civil Actions, Eviction, Small Claims.*
www.ojd.state.or.us/multnomah
Note: Record room is #131.
Civil Records: Access: Mail, online, in person. Both court and visitors may perform in person searches. No search fee. Court makes copy: $.25 per page. Required to search: name, years to search. Civil cases indexed by defendant, plaintiff; on computer from 1988, microfiche 1984-1988, docket cards by case and year. Index remotely online on the statewide OJIN system, call 800-858-9658 for information. Note: Some search limitations may apply. Mail turnaround time 5 days.

General Information: Public terminal has only civil records back to 1988. No adoptions, juvenile, sealed by Judge, expunged, paternity or mental health records released. Certification fee: $5.00 per document; exemplified-$10.00. Payee: State of Oregon. Personal checks and credit cards accepted. Prepayment and SASE required.

Polk County

Circuit Court Polk County Courthouse, Rm 301, 850 Main St, Dallas, OR 97338; phone: 503-623-3154; criminal phone: 503-831-1778; civil phone: 503-623-3154; probate phone: 503-623-3154; criminal fax: 503-831-1779; civil fax: 503-623-6614; hours 8AM-5PM (PST). *Felony, Misdemeanor, Civil, Eviction, Small Claims, Probate.*
www.ojd.state.or.us/plk/index.htm
Note: Probate is a separate index at this same address.
Civil Records: Access: Phone, fax, mail, online, in person. Both court and visitors may perform in person searches. No search fee. Court makes copy: $.25 per page; same fee for self serve. Required to search: name, years to search. Civil cases indexed by defendant, plaintiff; on computer from 1985, microfilm, archives from 1969 (District) back to

1800s (Circuit). Index remotely online on the statewide OJIN system, call 800-858-9658 for information. Mail turnaround time 2 weeks.

Criminal Records: Access: Phone, fax, mail, online, in person. Both court and visitors may perform in person searches. No search fee. Court makes copy: $.25 per page; same fee for self serve. Required to search: name, years to search, DOB; also helpful: SSN. Criminal records on computer from 1985, microfilm, archives from 1969 (District) back to 1800s (Circuit). Online access to criminal records is the same as civil. Mail turnaround time 2 weeks.

General Information: Public terminal goes back to 1985. No adoptions, juvenile, sealed by Judge, expunged, mental health records released. No fee to fax documents. Certification fee: $5.00. Payee: State of Oregon. Personal checks or Visa, MC accepted. Credit cards accepted in person and phone requests only. Prepayment and SASE required.

Sherman County

Circuit Court PO Box 402, Moro, OR 97039; phone: 541-565-3650; hours 1-5PM (PST). *Felony, Misdemeanor, Civil.*
Civil Records: Access: Phone, mail, online, in person. Both court and visitors may perform in person searches. No search fee. Court makes copy: $.25 per page; same fee for self serve. Required to search: name, years to search. Civil cases indexed by defendant, plaintiff; on computer from 1992, microfiche up to 1987, index books, judgment docket books. Index remotely online on the statewide OJIN system, call 800-858-9658 for information. Mail turnaround time 2-5 days.

Criminal Records: Access: Phone, mail, online, in person. Both court and visitors may perform in person searches. No search fee. Court makes copy: $.25 per page; same fee for self serve. Required to search: name, years to search, DOB. Criminal records on computer from 1992, microfiche up to 1987, index books, judgment docket books. Online access to criminal records is the same as civil. Mail turnaround time 2-5 days.

General Information: Public use terminal available. No adoptions, juvenile, sealed by Judge, expunged, paternity or mental health records released. Will fax documents for a fee of $2.00 1st.page, $1.00 per page. Certification fee: $5.00 per document. Payee: Sherman County Circuit Court. Personal checks accepted. Prepayment and SASE required.

County Court PO Box 365, 500 Court St, Moro, OR 97039; phone: 541-565-3606; fax: 541-565-3312; hours 8AM-5PM (PST). *Probate.*

Tillamook County

Circuit Court 201 Laurel Ave, Tillamook, OR 97141; phone: 503-842-8014; criminal fax: 503-842-2597; same fax for civil/probate; hours 8AM-N; 1PM-5PM (PST). *Felony, Misdemeanor, Civil, Eviction, Small Claims, Probate.*
Civil Records: Access: Mail, fax, online, in person. Both court and visitors may perform in person searches. No search fee, unless massive searching needed. Court makes copy: $.25 per page. Required to search: name, years to search. Civil cases indexed by defendant, plaintiff; on computer from 1987, prior on case files. Index remotely online on the statewide OJIN system, call 800-858-9658 for information. Mail turnaround time-call for estimate.

Criminal Records: Access: Mail, fax, online, in person. Both court and visitors may perform in person searches. No search fee, unless massive searching needed. Court makes copy: $.25 per page. Required to search: name, years to search. Criminal records on computer from 1987, prior on case files. Online access to criminal records is the same as civil. Mail turnaround time 2-3 days.

General Information: Public terminal goes back to 1987. No adoptions, juvenile, sealed by Judge, expunged, paternity or mental health records released. Will fax documents for $2.00 1st page; $1.00 each add'l. Certification fee: $5.00. Payee: Tillamook

Circuit Court. Personal checks accepted, Visa, MasterCard accepted with minimum payment of $3.00. Prepayment and SASE required.

Umatilla County

Circuit Court PO Box 1307, Pendleton, OR 97801; phone: 541-278-0341; fax: 541-276-9030; hours 8AM-N; 1PM-5PM (PST). *Felony, Misdemeanor, Civil, Eviction, Small Claims, Probate.*
www.ojd.state.or.us/umatilla
Civil Records: Access: Mail, online, in person. Both court and visitors may perform in person searches. Search fee: $12.65 per hour. Court makes copy: $.25 per page; same fee for self serve. Required to search: name, years to search. Civil cases indexed by defendant, plaintiff; on computer from 11/86, microfiche, index card, docket books. Index remotely online on the statewide OJIN system, call 800-858-9658 for information. Mail turnaround time 1-3 weeks.
Criminal Records: Access: Mail, online, in person. Both court and visitors may perform in person searches. Search fee: $12.65 per hour. Court makes copy: $.25 per page; same fee for self serve. Required to search: name, years to search. Criminal records on computer from 11/86, microfiche, index card, docket books. Online access to criminal records is the same as civil. Mail turnaround time 1-3 weeks.
General Information: Public terminal goes back to 11/1986. No adoptions, juvenile, sealed by Judge, expunged, paternity or mental health records released. Will not fax documents. Certification fee: $5.00 per document. Payee: Trial Court Administrator. Personal checks accepted. Credit cards accepted. Prepayment and SASE required.

Union County

Circuit Court 1008 K Ave, La Grande, OR 97850; phone: 541-962-9500; criminal fax: 541-963-3021; civil fax: 541-963-0444; probate fax: 541-963-0444; hours 8AM-N, 1-5PM (PST). *Felony, Misdemeanor, Civil, Eviction, Small Claims, Probate.*
www.ojd.state.or.us/union
Civil Records: Access: Mail, online, in person. Both court and visitors may perform in person searches. No search fee. Court makes copy: $.25 per page. Required to search: name, years to search. Civil cases indexed by defendant, plaintiff; on computer from 1986, archives back to 1800s, on ledger books/docket books. Index remotely online on the statewide OJIN system, call 800-858-9658 for information. Mail turnaround time 1-2 weeks.
Criminal Records: Access: Mail, fax, online, in person. Both court and visitors may perform in person searches. No search fee. Court makes copy: $.25 per page. Required to search: name, years to search, DOB. Criminal records on computer from 1986, archives back to 1800s, on ledger books/docket books. Online access to criminal records is the same as civil. Mail turnaround time 1-2 weeks.
General Information: Public terminal has criminal back to 1986 and civil back to 1986. No adoptions, juvenile, sealed by Judge, expunged, paternity or mental health records released. Certification fee: $5.00 per doc. Payee: Circuit Court. Personal checks or Visa, MC accepted. Prepayment and SASE required.

Wallowa County

Circuit Court 101 S River St, Rm 204, Enterprise, OR 97828; phone: 541-426-4991; fax: 541-426-4992; hours 8AM-N; 1-5PM (PST). *Felony, Misdemeanor, Civil, Eviction, Small Claims, Probate.*
www.ojd.state.or.us/wallowa
Civil Records: Access: Phone, mail, online, in person. Both court and visitors may perform in person searches. No search fee. Court makes copy: $.25 per page. Required to search: name, years to

search. Civil cases indexed by defendant, plaintiff; on computer from 1987, prior on docket books. Index remotely online on the statewide OJIN system, call 800-858-9658 for information. Mail turnaround time 1 week.
Criminal Records: Access: Phone, mail, online, in person. Both court and visitors may perform in person searches. No search fee. Court makes copy: $.25 per page. Required to search: name, years to search. Criminal records on computer from 1987, prior on docket books. Online access to criminal records is the same as civil. Mail turnaround time 1 week.
General Information: Public terminal goes back to 1987. No adoptions, juvenile, sealed by Judge, expunged, paternity or mental health records released. Will not fax documents. Certification fee: $5.00. Payee: Circuit Court. Personal checks accepted. Prepayment required. Copy fees may be billed. SASE required.

Wasco County

Circuit Court PO Box 1400, The Dalles, OR 97058-1400; phone: 541-506-2700; criminal phone: 541-506-2708; civil phone: 541-506-2704; probate phone: 541-506-2704; fax: 541-506-2711; hours 8AM-N,1-5PM (PST). *Felony, Misdemeanor, Civil, Eviction, Small Claims, Probate.*
http://seventhdistrict.ojd.state.or.us/html/wasco.html
Civil Records: Access: Phone, fax, mail, online, in person. Both court and visitors may perform in person searches. No search fee. Court makes copy: $.25 per page; same fee for self serve. Required to search: name, years to search. Civil cases indexed by defendant, plaintiff; on computer from 1989, prior records in docket books by case # and year back to 1900s. Index remotely online on the statewide OJIN system, call 800-858-9658 for information. Mail turnaround time 2-3 days.
Criminal Records: Access: Phone, fax, mail, online, in person. Both court and visitors may perform in person searches. No search fee. Court makes copy: $.25 per page; same fee for self serve. Required to search: name, years to search, DOB. Criminal records on computer from 1989, prior records in docket books by case # and year back to 1900s. Online access to criminal records is the same as civil. Mail turnaround time 2-3 days.
General Information: Public terminal goes back to 1989. No adoptions, juvenile, sealed by Judge, expunged, paternity or mental health records released. Fee to fax documents is $2.00 1st page, $1.00 ea add'l. Certification fee: $5.00. Payee: Trial Court Administrator. Personal checks or Visa, MC accepted. Prepayment and SASE required.

Washington County

Circuit Court 150 N 1st, Hillsboro, OR 97124; phone: 503-846-8888 x2302 (civ) x6060 (crim); probate phone: 503-846-2366; fax: 503-846-6087; probate fax: 503-846-8289; hours 8-11:30AM, 12:30-3PM (PST). *Felony, Misdemeanor, Civil, Eviction, Small Claims, Probate.*
www.ojd.state.or.us/wsh/default.htm
Civil Records: Access: Phone, mail, online, in person. Both court and visitors may perform in person searches. No search fee. Court makes copy: $.25 per page. Required to search: name, years to search. Civil cases indexed by defendant, plaintiff; on computer from 1982, prior on docket books. Index remotely online on the statewide OJIN system, call 800-858-9658 for information. Mail turnaround time 2-5 days.
Criminal Records: Access: Phone, mail, online, in person. Both court and visitors may perform in person searches. No search fee. Court makes copy: $.25 per page. Required to search: name, years to search, DOB. Criminal records on computer from 1982, prior on docket books. Online access to criminal records is the same as civil. Mail turnaround time 2-5 days.

General Information: Public terminal goes back to 1983. No adoptions, juvenile, sealed by Judge, expunged, paternity or mental health records released. Certification fee: $5.00. Payee: State of Oregon. Personal checks accepted. Prepayment required.

Wheeler County

Circuit Court PO Box 308, Fossil, OR 97830; phone: 541-763-2541; fax: 541-763-2543; hours 8:30AM-11:30AM (PST). *Felony, Misdemeanor, Civil.*
http://seventhdistrict.ojd.state.or.us
Civil Records: Access: Phone, mail, online, in person. Both court and visitors may perform in person searches. No search fee. Court makes copy: $.25 per page; same fee for self serve. Required to search: name, years to search. Civil cases indexed by defendant. Civil records on computer from 1989, docket books by case # and yr. Index remotely online on the statewide OJIN system, call 800-858-9658 for information. Mail turnaround time 1 week.
Criminal Records: Access: Phone, mail, online, in person. Only the court performs in person searches; visitors may not. No search fee. Court makes copy: $.25 per page; same fee for self serve. Required to search: name, years to search, DOB. Criminal records on computer from 1989, docket books by case # and yr. Online access to criminal records is the same as civil. Mail turnaround time 1 week.
General Information: No public access terminal. No adoptions, juvenile, sealed by Judge, expunged, paternity or mental health records released. Will fax documents to local or toll free line, otherwise extra fee incurred. If postage to return results is over $.37, then add'l postage fees will apply. Certification fee: $5.00 per certification. Payee: Wheeler Circuit Court. Personal checks accepted. MC/Visa accepted. Prepayment and SASE required.

County Court PO Box 327, 701 Adams, Rm 204, Fossil, OR 97830; phone: 541-763-2400; fax: 541-763-2026; hours 8:30AM-4PM (PST). *Probate.*
Note: Probate index available remotely online on the statewide OJIN system, call 800-858-9658 for information.

Yamhill County

Circuit Court 535 NE 5th, McMinnville, OR 97128; phone: 503-434-7530; probate phone: 502-434-7493; fax: 503-472-5805; hours 9AM-N, 1-5PM (PST). *Felony, Misdemeanor, Civil, Eviction, Small Claims, Probate.*
http://yamhill-court.ojd.state.or.us
Civil Records: Access: Mail, online, in person. Both court and visitors may perform in person searches. No search fee. Court makes copy: $.25 per page. Required to search: name, years to search. Civil cases indexed by defendant, plaintiff; on computer from 1987, microfiche (10 yrs Dist, unlimited Circuit), archives back to 1900s, docket books by case # and yr. Index remotely online on the statewide OJIN system, call 800-858-9658 for information. Mail turnaround time 1-7 days.
Criminal Records: Access: Mail, online, in person. Both court and visitors may perform in person searches. No search fee. Court makes copy: $.25 per page. Required to search: name, years to search, DOB. Criminal records on computer from 1987, microfiche (10 yrs Dist, unlimited Circuit), archives back to 1900s, docket books by case # and yr. Online access to criminal records is the same as civil. Mail turnaround time 1-7 days.
General Information: Public use terminal available. No adoptions, juvenile, sealed by Judge, expunged or mental health records released. Certification fee: $5.00. Payee: Trial Court. Two party, payroll checks not accepted. Visa, MC accepted. Prepayment required. SASE requested.

Oregon Recording Offices

ORGANIZATION: 36 counties, 36 recording offices. The recording officer is County Clerk. 35 counties are in the Pacific Time Zone (PST) and one is in the Mountain Time Zone (MST).

REAL ESTATE RECORDS: Some counties will not perform real estate searches. Search fees vary. Many counties will search all liens together for $12.50 per name. Copy fees are usually $.25 per page. Certification usually costs $3.75 per document. The Assessor keeps tax and ownership records.

UCC RECORDS: Financing statements are filed at the state level, except for real estate related collateral. Many county clerks will perform UCC searches, fees vary from $3.50 to $13.50, we suggest to call first.

TAX LIEN RECORDS: All federal and state tax liens on personal property are filed with the Secretary of State. Other federal and state tax liens are filed with the County Clerk. Most counties will perform tax lien searches and include both with a UCC search for an extra $7.50 per name. Search fees vary widely.

OTHER LIENS: County tax, public utility, construction, judgment, hospital.

ONLINE ACCESS: A few counties offer Internet access to assessor records. There is no statewide system available.

Baker County

County Clerk, 1995 Third St, #150, Baker, OR 97814-3398. 541-523-8207; fax-541-523-8240; hours: 8AM-5PM. www.bakercounty.org
Separate indices to search include deeds, mortgage, liens, county court. Records indexed on computer back to 1965. Only the public may search. Copy fee $.25 per page. Location fee $3.75 if recording number is not provided. Cert fee-$3.75 1st page, $.25 each add'l page plus copy fee. Payee- Baker County Clerk. **Online access to Property, Assessor records:** Access to the assessor property database is free at www.bakercounty.org/Assessor/Assessor_Search.html. Also for daily inmate listing go to www.bakersheriff.org/jaillist.htm. **Other phones:** Treasurer- 541-523-8221; Appraiser/Auditor- 541-523-8203; Elections- 541-523-8207; Vital Records- 541-731-4095. **Property tax/Assessor-** same address as above. 541-523-8203.

Benton County

County Clerk, 120 NW 4th St, Rm 4, Corvallis, OR 97330. 541-766-6831; fax-541-766-6675; hours: 8AM-5PM. www.co.benton.or.us
Separate indices to search include 1987 - present are computer based, all prior records are in index books. Office personnel or visitors may perform searches. Search fee $20.00 per hour in 25 min increments. Copy fee $.25 per page. Cert fee-$3.75 per record plus copy fee. Payee- Benton County Recorder. **Online access to Assessor, Surveys, Inmate, 30-day Released Inmate records:** The County is developing a Geographic Information System Internet site for viewing property information at http://gis.co.benton.or.us/v09_10/source/container.htm. Search fee is $3.75 per record found. Also, assessment and taxation database download is free at www.co.benton.or.us/assessor/data_extract.html. Search the sheriff's inmate list and 30-day release list at www.co.benton.or.us/sheriff/index.html. Also, sheriff's wanted "absconders" list at www.co.benton.or.us/sheriff/corrections/bccc/Abscond ers/. Also, a law enforcement case system may soon offer open case data. **Other phones:** Treasurer- 541-766-6808; Appraiser/Auditor- 541-766-6855; Elections- 541-766-6756; Vital Records- 503-731-4108. **Property tax/Assessor-** 541-766-6855.

Clackamas County

County Clerk, 2051 Kaen Rd, Oregon City, OR 97045. 503-650-5688, R/E recording phone-503-655-8551; hours: 8AM-5PM. www.co.clackamas.or.us/clerk
All records in one index. Only the public may search. Copy fee $.25; tax lien copy fee $4.00 1st page, $.25 each add'l. Cert fee- $3.75 per doc plus copy fee. Payee- Clackamas County Clerk. **Online access to Real Property, Most Wanted records:** Records on the County Metromap database are free at http://topaz.metro-region.org/metromap/metromap.cfm. No name searching. Also, search the sheriff's most wanted list at www.co.clackamas.or.us/sheriff/news/mostwanted.htm. **Other phones:** Treasurer- 503-655-8915; Elections- 503-655-8510; Vital Records- 503-731-4095. **Property tax/Assessor-** 168 Warner Milne Rd, Oregon City, OR 97045; 503-655-8671.

Clatsop County

County Clerk, PO Box 178, Astoria, OR 97103-0178. 503-325-8511; fax-503-325-9307; hours: 8:30AM-4PM. www.co.clatsop.or.us
Office personnel or visitors may perform searches. General index search fee $3.75 per document. Will not search tax liens. Copy fee $.25 per page. **Other phones:** Treasurer- 503-325-8565; Appraiser/Auditor- 503-325-8522; Elections- 503-325-8511; Vital Records- 503-325-8511. **Property tax/Assessor-** 503-325-8522.

Columbia County

County Clerk, 230 Strand St, Courthouse, St. Helens, OR 97051-2041. 503-397-3796; fax-503-397-7266; hours: Recording hours 9AM-4PM. www.co.columbia.or.us
Separate indices to search include deed, mortgage, misc. Search fee $3.75 per name, on computer index only. Copy fee $.25 per page. Cert fee-$3.75 per doc plus copy fee. Payee- Columbia County Clerk. **Other phones:** Treasurer- 503-397-7252; Appraiser/Auditor- 503-397-2240; Elections- 503-397-7214 & 3796; Vital Records- 503-397-3796. **Property tax/Assessor-** same address as above. 503-397-2240, assessor fax- 503-397-5153.

Coos County

County Clerk, 250 N Baxter; Courthouse, Coquille, OR 97423-1899. 541-396-3121 x228, 273, 407, 223, R/E recording phone-541-396-3121 x223; fax-541-396-6551; hours: 8:30AM-N, 1PM-4:30PM. www.co.coos.or.us
Records indexed on computer from 1990 to present, prior to 1990 in index books. Office suggests public do own search, but will search if submitted in writing with fees. Search fee $12.50 per name. Copy fee $4.00 1st page, $.25 each add'l if they locate; and copy. self serve $.25 per page. Cert fee- $3.75 per cert plus copy fee. Payee- Coos County Clerk. **Online access to Assessor, Property, Sale records:** Access to the assessor property and sales data is free at http://coos.gtrsoft.com. **Other phones:** Treasurer- 541-396-3121 x333; Appraiser/Auditor- 541-396-3121 x274; Elections- 541-

396-3121 x301. **Property tax/Assessor-** 541-396-3121 x274.

Crook County

County Clerk, 300 N E Third, Prineville, OR 97754. 541-447-6553; fax-541-416-2145; hours: 8AM-5PM. www.co.crook.or.us
Only the public may search. Copy fee $1.00 per page. Cert fee- $3.75 per cert plus copy fee. Payee- Crook County Clerk. **Other phones:** Treasurer- 541-447-6554; Elections- 541-447-6553. **Property tax/Assessor-** 541-447-4133.

Curry County

County Clerk, PO Box 746, Gold Beach, OR 97444. 541-247-3295; fax-541-247-6440; hours: 8:30AM-4PM. www.co.curry.or.us
All records in one index. Office personnel or visitors may perform searches. General index search fee $3.75 per book. Will search real estate records. Will not search UCC records. Tax lien search fee- $12.50 per debtor. Copy fee $.25 per page. Cert fee- $7.75 1st page, $.25 each add'l page. Payee- Curry County Clerk. **Other phones:** Treasurer- 541-247-3299; Appraiser/Auditor- 541-247-3294; Elections- 541-247-3297; Vital Records- 503-731-4095. **Property tax/Assessor-** PO Box 746, Gold Beach, OR 97444; 541-247-3294.

Deschutes County

County Clerk, 1300 NW Wall St. #200, Bend, OR 97701. 541-388-6549; fax-541-389-6830; hours: 8AM-4PM (recording hours). http://recordings.co.deschutes.or.us
All records in one index. Records indexed on a public use terminal back to 1985. Only the public may search. Copy fee $.25 per page plus $3.75 location fee. Cert fee- $3.75 per doc plus copy fee. Payee- Deschutes County Clerk. **Online access to Real Estate, Deed, Mortgage, Lien, Assessor, Property Tax records:** Access records on the county "Assessor Inquiry System" website at www.co.deschutes.or.us/dial.cfm. Access tax information, assessment, appraisal details, ownership, sales information, transaction histories, account histories, land use records, and lot numbers for no fee. Also, search real estate, deeds, mortgages, liens on the clerk's recording system web inquiry for free at http://recordings.co.deschutes.or.us. Free registration for username and password is required. **Other phones:** Treasurer- 541-388-6540; Elections- 541-388-6546; Vital Records- 503-731-4095. **Property tax/Assessor-** same address as above. 541-388-6508.

Douglas County

County Clerk, PO Box 10, Roseburg, OR 97470. 541-440-4322, R/E recording phone-541-440-4320; fax-541-440-4408; hours: 8AM-4PM.

All records in one index. Records indexed on computer. Office personnel or visitors may perform searches. Search fee $3.75. Copy fee $.50 per page; $2.50 minimum. Cert fee- $3.75 per doc plus copy fee.$4.25 by mail. Payee- Douglas County Clerk. **Online access to Assessor, Property records:** Access to the assessor property data is free at www.co.douglas.or.us/puboaa/cgi/oaasearch.pl. **Other phones:** Treasurer- 541-440-3311; Elections- 541-440-4252. **Property tax/Assessor-** 541-440-4222.

Gilliam County

County Clerk, PO Box 427, Condon, OR 97823. 541-384-2311; fax-541-384-2166; hours: 8:30AM-N, 1-5PM.

Office personnel or visitors may perform searches. General search fee $12.50 per name. Will not search real estate records. UCC search per debtor name-$5.00. Copy fee $.25 per page. Cert fee- $3.75 per cert plus copy fee. Payee- Gilliam County Clerk. **Other phones:** Treasurer- 541-384-6321; Appraiser/Auditor- 541-384-3781; Elections- 541-384-2311; Vital Records- 541-384-2311. **Property tax/Assessor-** 541-384-3781.

Grant County

County Clerk, 201 S. Humbolt, #290, Canyon City, OR 97820. 541-575-1675; fax-541-575-2248;

Office personnel or visitors may perform searches. Search fee $13.00 per name. Copy fee $3.75 per document. Cert fee- $3.75 per copy. Payee- County Clerk. **Other phones:** Treasurer- 541-575-1798; Appraiser/Auditor- 541-575-0107; Elections- 541-575-1675. **Property tax/Assessor-** 541-575-0107.

Harney County

County Clerk, 450 N. Buena Vista, Burns, OR 97720. 541-573-6641; fax-541-573-8370; hours: 8:30AM-5PM; closed 1 hr for lunch. www.co.harney.or.us

All records in one index. Records indexed on a public use terminal back to 1984. Only the public may search. Tax lien copy- $.50 per page. Cert fee- $3.75 per doc; $.50 per page plus copy fee. Payee- Harney County Clerk. **Other phones:** Treasurer- 541-573-6541; Appraiser/Auditor- 541-573-8368; Elections- 541-573-6641. **Property tax/Assessor-** same address as above. 541-573-8367.

Hood River County

County Clerk, 601 State St., Hood River, OR 97031-1871. 541-386-1442/or/6849, R/E recording phone-541-387-6849; fax-541-387-6864; hours: 8AM-5PM. www.co.hood-river.or.us

All records in one index. Only the public may search. Copy fee $3.75 1st page; $.25 each add'l. Cert fee- $7.75 per doc includes copies. Payee- Hood River County. **Other phones:** Treasurer- 541-386-1301; Elections- 541-386-1442. **Property tax/Assessor-** same address as above. 541-386-4522.

Jackson County

County Clerk, 10 S. Oakdale, Rm 216A, Medford, OR 97501. 541-774-6147, R/E recording phone-541-774-6152; fax-541-774-6714; hours: 8AM-4PM. www.jacksoncounty.org

All records in one index. Only the public may search. Copy fee $4.00 1st page; $.25 each add'l. Cert fee- $3.75 per cert plus copy fee. Payee-Jackson County Clerk. **Other phones:** Treasurer- 541-774-6541; Appraiser/Auditor- 541-774-6042; Elections- 541-774-6147; Vital Records- 502-731-4108. **Property tax/Assessor-** same address as above. 541-774-6059.

Jefferson County

County Clerk, 66 S.E. D St, #C, Madras, OR 97741. 541-475-4451; fax-541-325-5018;

Records indexed on computer back to 1985. Only the public may search. Copy fee $.50 for microfilm copy; $.25 for scanned image. Cert fee-$3.75. Payee- Jefferson County. **Other phones:** Treasurer- 541-325-5023; Appraiser/Auditor- 541-475-2443; Elections- 541-475-4451. **Property tax/Assessor-** 541-475-2443.

Josephine County

County Clerk, PO Box 69, Grants Pass, OR 97528. 541-474-5240; fax-541-476-5246; hours: 9AM-4PM.

All records in one index. Records indexed on a public use terminal back to 1981. Only the public may search. Copy fee $4.00 1st page; $.25 each add'l page per document. Cert fee- $3.75 per doc plus copy fee. Payee- Josephine-Co Clerk. **Other phones:** Treasurer- 541-474-5235; Appraiser/Auditor-541-474-5260; Elections- 541-474-5243. **Property tax/Assessor-** 500 NW 6th St, Grants Pass, OR 97526; 541-474-5260.

Klamath County

County Clerk, 305 Main St., Klamath Falls, OR 97601. 800-377-6094, 541-883-5134, R/E recording phone-541-883-5134; fax-541-885-6757; hours: 8AM-5PM www.co.klamath.or.us

All records in one index. Only the public may search. Copy fee $1.00 per page. Cert fee- $7.75 per doc, 2 pages included in copy fee. Payee- Klamath County Clerk. **Other phones:** Treasurer- 541-883-4297; Appraiser/Auditor- 541-883-5111; Elections- 541-883-5134. **Property tax/Assessor-** same address as above. 541-883-5111.

Lake County

County Clerk, 513 Center St, Lakeview, OR 97630-1539. 541-947-6006; fax-541-947-6015; hours: 8:30AM-5PM.

Office personnel or visitors may perform searches. UCC search per debtor name- $10.00. Tax liens included in UCC search if requested for $12.50 total fee. Separate federal/state combined tax lien search- $7.50 per debtor. General copy fee $4.00 1st page; $.25 each add'l. R/E record copy- $.25 per page. Cert fee- $3.75 per cert plus copy fee. Payee- Lake County Clerk. **Property tax/Assessor-** 541-947-6000.

Lane County

County Clerk, 275 W. 10th Ave., Eugene, OR 97401. 541-682-4234, R/E recording phone-541-682-3654; fax-541-682-2303; hours: 8AM-5PM; Recording 9AM-N, 1-4PM.

Only the public may search. General index search fee $3.75 per document by mail only. Will do real estate record searches and Federal/state combined tax lien search by mail only. Copy fee $.25 per page. Cert fee- $3.75 per cert plus copy fee. Payee- Lane County Clerk. **Online access to Assessor, Real Estate, Property records:** Property records on the County Tax Map site are free at www.co.lane.or.us/TaxStatement/Search.aspx. No name searching. Also, access to the Regional Land Information Database RLID is by subscription. Visit www.rlid.org or call Eric at 541-682-4338 for more information or signup. Initiation fee is $200; monthly access fee is $80.00. **Property tax/Assessor-** 541-687-4321.

Lincoln County

County Clerk, 225 W. Olive St; Rm 201, Newport, OR 97365-3869. 541-265-4131; fax-541-265-4950; hours: 8:30AM-5PM.

All records in one index. Records indexed on a public use terminal back to 1986. Only the public may search. Copy fee $3.75 plus $.25 per page. Cert fee- $7.50 per cert plus $.25 per page. Payee-Lincoln County Clerk. **Other phones:** Treasurer- 541-265-4139; Appraiser/Auditor- 541-265-4102;

Elections- 541-265-4131. **Property tax/Assessor-** same address as above. 541-265-4102.

Linn County

County Clerk, PO Box 100, Albany, OR 97321. 541-967-3829; fax-541-926-5109; hours: 8:30AM-5PM. www.co.linn.or.us

All records in one index. They will assist the public, but public do the searches. Will search UCC records. UCC search per debtor name- $4.00. Separate federal tax lien search- $5.00 per debtor. Copy fee $4.00 1st page, $.25 each add'l. Cert fee-$3.75 per doc. **Online access to Assessor, Real Estate, Property Sale records:** Records on the County Property Records database are free at www.co.linn.or.us/assessor/NewPropSearch.asp. Also, property sale data is free at www.co.linn.or.us/assessorshomep/sale_web.htm. **Other phones:** Treasurer- 541-967-3859; Elections- 541-967-3831; Vital Records- 503-731-4108; Records- 541-967-3829. **Property tax/Assessor-** same address as above. 541-967-3808.

Malheur County

County Clerk, 251 B St West, #4, Vale, OR 97918. 541-473-5151; fax-541-473-5523; hours: 8:30AM-5PM MST. www.malheurco.org

All records in one index. Records indexed on computer back to 1985. Office personnel or visitors may perform searches. Search fee $3.75 per name and per record. Copy fee $.25 per page. Cert fee- $3.75 per name + $.25 per copy. Payee-County Clerk. **Other phones:** Treasurer- 541-473-5165; Vital Records- 541-889-7279. **Property tax/Assessor-** 541-473-5117.

Marion County

County Clerk, PO Box 14500, Salem, OR 97309. 503-588-5225; fax-503-588-5237; hours: 8:30AM-5PM. http://clerk.co.marion.or.us/records

Only the public may search. Copy fee $.25 per page. Cert fee- $3.75. Payee- Marion County. **Online access to Jail Inmate, Sex Offender records:** Access to the sheriff's database of inmates and sex offenders is free at http://sheriff.co.marion.or.us. **Other phones:** Elections- 503-588-5041. **Property tax/Assessor-** 503-588-5236.

Morrow County

County Clerk, PO Box 338, Heppner, OR 97836. 541-676-9061, R/E recording phone-541-676-5604; fax-541-676-9876; hours: 8AM-N, 1-5PM. www.rootsweb.com/~ormorrow/MorrowCountyCourthouse.htm

Records indexed on computer back to 1984. Only the public may search. Copy fee $.25 per page. Cert fee- $3.75 per page plus copy fee. **Other phones:** Treasurer- 541-676-5630; Appraiser/Auditor-541-676-5607; Elections- 541-676-5607; Vital Records- 541-676-5603. **Property tax/Assessor-** PO Box 247, Heppner, OR 97836; 541-676-5607.

Multnomah County

County Clerk, PO Box 5007, Portland, OR 97208-5007. 503-988-3034; fax-503-988-3330; hours: 8AM-5PM; Phone hours: 9AM-4:30PM. www.co.multnomah.or.us/dss/at/index.html

Only the public may search. Copy fee $.25 per page; $4.00 minimum. Cert fee- $3.00 per cert plus copy fee. Payee- Multnomah County Recorder. **Online access to Real Property, Released Inmate, Restaurant Inspection records:** Records on the County Metromap database are free at http://topaz.metro-region.org/metromap/metromap.cfm. No name searching. The GIS-mapping site is very similar at http://gis.co.multnomah.or.us/sail/. Also, search the sheriff's release inmate list at www.inmatereleases.org/search.cfm. Search the Health Dept. restaurant inspections at www.mchealthinspect.org/inspections/index.html. **Other phones:** Appraiser/Auditor- 503-988-3367; Elections- 503-988-3720; Vital Records- 503-731-4095

(State); Tax information line- 503-988-3326. **Property tax/Assessor-** 503-988-3326.

Polk County

County Clerk, 850 Main St; Courthouse, Dallas, OR 97338-3179. 503-623-9217; fax-503-623-0717; hours: 8AM-5PM. www.co.polk.or.us
All records in one index. Only the public may search. Search fee $3.75. Copy fee $.25 per page. Cert fee- $3.75 plus copy fee. **Other phones:** Treasurer- 503-623-9264 (also Tax); Appraiser/Auditor- 503-623-8391; Elections- 503-623-9217; Vital Records- 503-623-8175. **Property tax/Assessor-** 503-623-8391.

Sherman County

Deputy Clerk, PO Box 365, Moro, OR 97039. 541-565-3606; fax-541-565-3312; hours: 8AM-5PM.
Office personnel or visitors may perform searches. Search fee $13.00 per name. Copy fee $.25 per page. Cert fee- $3.75 per cert. Payee- Sherman County. **Other phones:** Treasurer- 541-565-3553; Appraiser/Auditor- 541-565-3605; Elections- 541-565-3606. **Property tax/Assessor-** 541-565-3505.

Tillamook County

County Clerk, 201 Laurel Ave, Tillamook, OR 97141. 503-842-3402; fax-503-842-1599; 8AM-N, 1PM-5PM. www.co.tillamook.or.us/gov/clerk/default.htm
All records in one index. Records indexed on computer back to 8/1/1994. General index search fee $10.00 per 1/2 hour. Will do limited real estate searches. Will not search UCC records or tax liens. Copy fee $4.00 1st page, $.25 per add'l. Cert fee- $7.75 plus $.25 per add'l page, plus copy fee. Payee- Tillamook County Clerk. **Online access to Assessor, Property Tax, Recording, Deed, Lien, Judgment records:** Access recorded documents free at www.co.tillamook.or.us/recinq; use username "public" and password "inquiry." Assessment and taxation records on the County Property database are free at www.co.tillamook.or.us/Documents/Search/query.asp. Search by property ID number or by name in the general query. Also, search for property info on the GIS-mapping service site at http://gisweb.co.tillamook.or.us. **Other phones:** Treasurer- 503-842-3425; Appraiser/Auditor- 503-842-3400/3424; Elections- 503-842-3402; Vital Records- 503-731-4095. **Property tax/Assessor-** same address as above. 503-842-3400/3424.

Umatilla County

County Clerk, PO Box 1227, Pendleton, OR 97801-1227. 541-278-6236; fax-541-278-6345; 9AM-5PM.
All records in one index. Office personnel (if not too busy) or visitors may perform searches. Search fee $20.00 per name depending on length of search. Will do a federal tax lien search if requested; fee varies. Copy fee $.25 per page. Cert fee- $3.75 per doc, plus copy fee. Payee- Umatilla County Clerk. **Online access to Jail records:** Access to the sheriff's current jail roster is free at www.co.umatilla.or.us/deptwebs/jail/inmates/ICURRENT.HTM. **Other phones:** Treasurer- 541-278-6210; Elections- 541-278-6256; Vital Records- 541-278-6236. **Property tax/Assessor-** same address as above. 541-278-6219.

Union County

County Clerk, 1001 4th St, #D, La Grande, OR 97850. 541-963-1006; fax-541-963-1013; hours: 8:30AM-5PM M-TH; 9AM-4PM F. www.union-county.org
All records in one index. Records indexed on computer back to 1990. Only the public may search. Copy fee $.25 per page. Cert fee- $3.75 plus copy fee. Payee- Union County Clerk. **Online access to Property Tax, Assessor records:** Access property tax free at www.union-county.org/assessor_search.html. **Other phones:** Treasurer- 541-963-1018; Appraiser/Auditor- 541-963-1002; Elections- 541-963-1006; Vital Records- 541-963-1006. **Property tax/Assessor-** 1001 4th St, #A, La Grande, OR 97850; 541-963-1002.

Wallowa County

County Clerk, 101 S. River, Rm 100 Door 16, Enterprise, OR 97828. 541-426-4543 x15; fax-541-426-5901; hours: 8:30AM-5PM. www.co.wallowa.or.us/cc/
All records in one index. Recordings start in 1880s. Records indexed on a public use terminal back to 1990s. Office personnel or visitors may perform searches. General search fee $12.50 per name. UCC search per debtor name- $5.00. Copy fee $.25 per page; location fee $3.75. Cert fee- $3.75 per page plus copy fee. **Other phones:** Treasurer- 541-426-4543 x14; Appraiser/Auditor- 541-426-4543 x36; Elections- 541-426-4543 x15; Vital Records- 541-426-4543 x15; State- 503-731-4095. **Property tax/Assessor-** 101 S. River, Rm 103, Enterprise, OR 97828; 541-426-4543.

Wasco County

County Clerk, 511 Washington St.; Courthouse, The Dalles, OR 97058-2237. 541-506-2530; fax-541-506-2531; hours: 9AM-N, 1-4PM.
All records in one index. Records indexed on a public use terminal back to 1985. Only the public may search. Copy fee $3.75 plus $.25 per page. Cert fee- $3.75 per page plus copy fee. Payee- Wasco County Clerk. **Other phones:** Treasurer- 541-506-2772; Appraiser/Auditor- 541-506-2510; Elections- 541-506-2530; Vital Records- 503-731-4108. **Property tax/Assessor-** 511 Washington St.#208, The Dalles, OR 97058; 541-506-2510.

Washington County

County Clerk, 155 N. First Ave, Mail Stop 9, Hillsboro, OR 97124. 503-846-8752; fax-503-846-3909; hours: 8:30AM-4:30PM. www.co.washington.or.us
All records in one index from July, 1977 to present, direct & indirect separate prior to July, 1977. Office personnel or visitors may perform searches. General index search fee $39.00 per hour. Copy fee $4.00 1st page, $.25 each add'l page of same doc. Cert fee- $3.75 per cert, plus copy fee. Payee- Washington County Clerk. **Online access to Real Estate records:** Records on County GIS Intermap database are free at http://intratech.co.washington.or.us/intermap. General Recording Office information is at www.co.washington.or.us/deptmts/at/recordng/record.htm. Also, records on the County Metromap database are free online at http://topaz.metro-region.org/metromap/metromap.cfm. No name searching. **Other phones:** Appraiser/Auditor- 503-846-8826; Elections- 503-846-8670; Vital Records- 503-846-3538. **Property tax/Assessor-** 155 N 1st Ave, Mail Stop 8, Hillsboro, OR 97124; 503-846-8741.

Wheeler County

County Clerk, PO Box 327, Fossil, OR 97830-0327. 541-763-2400; fax-541-763-2026; 8:30AM-4PM.
Separate indices to search include Deeds and Mtgs. Record index not computerized. Office will perform a UCC search but public must search other records themselves. Search fee $3.75. Copy fee $.25 per page. Cert fee- $3.75 per doc, plus copy fee. Payee- Wheeler County Clerk. **Other phones:** Treasurer- 541-763-2078; Appraiser/Auditor- 541-763-4266; Elections- 541-763-2400; Vital Records- 541-763-2400. **Property tax/Assessor-** 541-763-4266.

Yamhill County

County Clerk, 535 NE 5th St, Rm 119, McMinnville, OR 97128-4593. 503-434-7518; fax-503-434-7520; hours: 9AM-5PM. www.co.yamhill.or.us/clerk
All records in one index. Office will perform a real estate search but public must search other records themselves. Search fee- hourly. Copy fee $.25 per page. Cert fee- $3.75 per cert plus copy fee. Payee- Yamhill County Clerk. **Online access to Property records:** Limited property information from the county surveyor is free at www.co.yamhill.or.us/surveyor/; no name searching. **Other phones:** Treasurer- 503-434-7533; Appraiser/Auditor- 503-434-7521; Elections- 503-434-7518; Vital Records- 503-434-7523. **Property tax/Assessor-** 535 NE 5th St, Rm 135, McMinnville, OR 97128; 503-434-7521.

Oregon County Locator

You will usually be able to find the city name in the City/County Cross Reference below. In that case, it is a simple matter to determine the county from the cross reference. However, only the official US Postal Service city names are included in this index. There are an additional 40,000 place names that people use in their addresses. Therefore, we have also included a ZIP/City Cross Reference immediately following the City/County Cross Reference.

If you know the ZIP Code but the city name does not appear in the City/County Cross Reference index, look up the ZIP Code in the ZIP/City Cross Reference, find the city name, then look up the city name in the City/County Cross Reference. For example, you want to know the county for an address of Menands, NY 12204. There is no "Menands" in the City/County Cross Reference. The ZIP/City Cross Reference shows that ZIP Codes 12201-12288 are for the city of Albany. Looking back in the City/County Cross Reference, Albany is in Albany County.

Oregon City/County Cross Reference

ADAMS Umatilla
ADEL Lake
ADRIAN Malheur
AGNESS Curry
ALBANY (97321) Linn(75), Benton(24)
ALBANY Linn
ALLEGANY Coos
ALSEA (97324) Benton(90), Lincoln(7), Lane(1)
ALVADORE Lane
AMITY (97101) Yamhill(84), Polk(15)
ANTELOPE Wasco
ARCH CAPE Clatsop
ARLINGTON Gilliam
AROCK Malheur
ASHLAND Jackson
ASHWOOD Jefferson
ASTORIA Clatsop
ATHENA Umatilla
AUMSVILLE Marion
AURORA (97002) Marion(76), Clackamas(23)
AZALEA Douglas
BAKER CITY (97814) Baker(95), Union(4)
BANDON Coos
BANKS Washington
BATES Grant
BAY CITY Tillamook
BEATTY Klamath
BEAVER Tillamook
BEAVERCREEK Clackamas
BEAVERTON Washington
BEND Deschutes
BLACHLY Lane
BLODGETT (97326) Lincoln(63), Benton(36)
BLUE RIVER Lane
BLY Klamath
BOARDMAN Morrow
BONANZA Klamath
BORING Clackamas
BRIDAL VEIL Multnomah
BRIDGEPORT Baker
BRIGHTWOOD Clackamas
BROADBENT Coos
BROGAN Malheur
BROOKINGS Curry
BROTHERS Deschutes
BROWNSVILLE Linn
BURNS Harney
BUTTE FALLS Jackson
BUXTON Washington
CAMAS VALLEY Douglas
CAMP SHERMAN Jefferson
CANBY Clackamas
CANNON BEACH Clatsop
CANYON CITY Grant
CANYONVILLE Douglas
CARLTON Yamhill
CASCADE LOCKS (97014) Multnomah(62), Hood River(37)
CASCADIA Linn
CAVE JUNCTION Josephine
CAYUSE Umatilla

CENTRAL POINT Jackson
CHEMULT (97731) Douglas(76), Klamath(23)
CHESHIRE Lane
CHILOQUIN Klamath
CHRISTMAS VALLEY Lake
CLACKAMAS Clackamas
CLATSKANIE (97016) Columbia(79), Clatsop(20)
CLOVERDALE Tillamook
COLTON Clackamas
COLUMBIA CITY Columbia
CONDON Gilliam
COOS BAY Coos
COQUILLE Coos
CORBETT (97019) Multnomah(95), Clackamas(4)
CORNELIUS Washington
CORVALLIS (97333) Benton(91), Linn(8)
CORVALLIS Benton
COTTAGE GROVE Lane
COVE Union
CRABTREE Linn
CRANE Harney
CRATER LAKE Klamath
CRAWFORDSVILLE Linn
CRESCENT Klamath
CRESCENT LAKE Klamath
CRESWELL Lane
CULP CREEK Lane
CULVER Jefferson
CURTIN Douglas
DAIRY Klamath
DALLAS Polk
DAYS CREEK Douglas
DAYTON Yamhill
DAYVILLE (97825) Grant(98), Wheeler(1)
DEADWOOD Lane
DEER ISLAND Columbia
DEPOE BAY Lincoln
DETROIT Marion
DEXTER Lane
DIAMOND Harney
DILLARD Douglas
DONALD Marion
DORENA Lane
DRAIN Douglas
DREWSEY Harney
DUFUR Wasco
DUNDEE Yamhill
DURKEE Baker
EAGLE CREEK Clackamas
EAGLE POINT Jackson
ECHO Umatilla
EDDYVILLE Lincoln
ELGIN Union
ELKTON Douglas
ELMIRA Lane
ENTERPRISE Wallowa
ESTACADA Clackamas
EUGENE Lane
FAIRVIEW Multnomah
FALL CREEK Lane
FALLS CITY Polk

FIELDS Harney
FLORENCE Lane
FOREST GROVE Washington
FORT KLAMATH Klamath
FORT ROCK Lake
FOSSIL Wheeler
FOSTER Linn
FOX Grant
FRENCHGLEN Harney
GALES CREEK Washington
GARDINER Douglas
GARIBALDI Tillamook
GASTON (97119) Washington(77), Yamhill(22)
GATES (97346) Marion(76), Linn(23)
GERVAIS Marion
GILCHRIST Klamath
GLADSTONE Clackamas
GLENDALE Douglas
GLENEDEN BEACH Lincoln
GLIDE Douglas
GOLD BEACH Curry
GOLD HILL Jackson
GOVERNMENT CAMP Clackamas
GRAND RONDE (97347) Polk(63), Yamhill(35), Tillamook(1)
GRANTS PASS (97527) Josephine(96), Jackson(3)
GRANTS PASS Josephine
GRASS VALLEY Sherman
GREENLEAF Lane
GRESHAM (97080) Multnomah(95), Clackamas(4)
GRESHAM Multnomah
HAINES Baker
HALFWAY Baker
HALSEY Linn
HAMMOND Clatsop
HARPER Malheur
HARRISBURG (97446) Linn(98), Lane(1)
HEBO Tillamook
HELIX Umatilla
HEPPNER Morrow
HEREFORD Baker
HERMISTON Umatilla
HILLSBORO (97123) Washington(96), Yamhill(3)
HILLSBORO Washington
HINES Harney
HOOD RIVER Hood River
HUBBARD (97032) Marion(84), Clackamas(15)
HUNTINGTON (97907) Malheur(66), Baker(33)
IDANHA (97350) Marion(75), Linn(25)
IDLEYLD PARK Douglas
IMBLER Union
IMNAHA Wallowa
INDEPENDENCE Polk
IONE Morrow
IRONSIDE Malheur
IRRIGON Morrow
JACKSONVILLE Jackson
JAMIESON Malheur

JEFFERSON (97352) Marion(97), Linn(2)
JOHN DAY Grant
JORDAN VALLEY Malheur
JOSEPH Wallowa
JUNCTION CITY (97448) Lane(98), Benton(1)
JUNTURA Malheur
KEIZER Marion
KENO Klamath
KENT Sherman
KERBY Josephine
KIMBERLY Grant
KLAMATH FALLS Klamath
LA GRANDE Union
LA PINE (97739) Deschutes(71), Klamath(27)
LAFAYETTE Yamhill
LAKE OSWEGO (97035) Clackamas(92), Multnomah(5), Washington(1)
LAKESIDE Coos
LAKEVIEW Lake
LANGLOIS Curry
LAWEN Harney
LEBANON Linn
LEXINGTON Morrow
LINCOLN CITY Lincoln
LOGSDEN Lincoln
LONG CREEK Grant
LORANE Lane
LOSTINE Wallowa
LOWELL Lane
LYONS (97358) Linn(68), Marion(31)
MADRAS Jefferson
MALIN Klamath
MANNING Washington
MANZANITA Tillamook
MAPLETON Lane
MARCOLA Lane
MARYLHURST Clackamas
MAUPIN Wasco
MCMINNVILLE Yamhill
MEACHAM Umatilla
MEDFORD Jackson
MEHAMA Marion
MERLIN Josephine
MERRILL Klamath
MIDLAND Klamath
MIKKALO Gilliam
MILL CITY (97360) Linn(71), Marion(28)
MILTON FREEWATER Umatilla
MITCHELL Wheeler
MOLALLA Clackamas
MONMOUTH (97361) Polk(97), Benton(2)
MONROE Benton
MONUMENT Grant
MORO Sherman
MOSIER Wasco
MOUNT ANGEL (97362) Marion(96), Clackamas(3)
MOUNT HOOD PARKDALE Hood River
MOUNT VERNON Grant
MULINO Clackamas
MURPHY Josephine
MYRTLE CREEK Douglas

MYRTLE POINT Coos
NEHALEM (97131) Tillamook(98), Clatsop(1)
NEOTSU Lincoln
NESKOWIN Tillamook
NETARTS Tillamook
NEW PINE CREEK (97635) Lake(71), Morrow(28)
NEWBERG (97132) Yamhill(98), Washington(1)
NEWPORT Lincoln
NORTH BEND Coos
NORTH PLAINS (97133) Washington(97), Multnomah(2)
NORTH POWDER (97867) Union(92), Baker(7)
NORWAY Coos
NOTI Lane
NYSSA Malheur
O BRIEN Josephine
OAKLAND Douglas
OAKRIDGE Lane
OCEANSIDE Tillamook
ODELL Hood River
ONTARIO Malheur
OPHIR Curry
OREGON CITY Clackamas
OTIS (97368) Lincoln(94), Tillamook(4), Baker(1)
OTTER ROCK Lincoln
OXBOW Baker
PACIFIC CITY Tillamook
PAULINA Crook
PENDLETON Umatilla
PHILOMATH Benton
PHOENIX Jackson
PILOT ROCK Umatilla
PLEASANT HILL Lane
PLUSH Lake
PORT ORFORD Curry
PORTLAND (97219) Multnomah(97), Clackamas(2)
PORTLAND (97231) Multnomah(90), Washington(6), Columbia(3)

PORTLAND (97266) Multnomah(74), Clackamas(25)
PORTLAND (97229) Washington(84), Multnomah(15)
PORTLAND Clackamas
PORTLAND Multnomah
PORTLAND Washington
POST Crook
POWELL BUTTE Crook
POWERS Coos
PRAIRIE CITY Grant
PRINCETON Harney
PRINEVILLE Crook
PROSPECT Jackson
RAINIER Columbia
REDMOND Deschutes
REEDSPORT Douglas
REMOTE Coos
RHODODENDRON Clackamas
RICHLAND Baker
RICKREALL Polk
RIDDLE Douglas
RILEY Harney
RITTER Grant
RIVERSIDE Malheur
ROCKAWAY BEACH Tillamook
ROGUE RIVER Jackson
ROSE LODGE Lincoln
ROSEBURG Douglas
RUFUS Sherman
SAGINAW Lane
SAINT BENEDICT Marion
SAINT HELENS Columbia
SAINT PAUL Marion
SALEM (97304) Polk(97), Yamhill(2)
SANDY Clackamas
SCAPPOOSE (97056) Columbia(98), Multnomah(1)
SCIO Linn
SCOTTS MILLS (97375) Marion(82), Clackamas(17)
SCOTTSBURG Douglas
SEAL ROCK Lincoln
SEASIDE Clatsop

SELMA Josephine
SENECA Grant
SHADY COVE Jackson
SHANIKO Wasco
SHEDD Linn
SHERIDAN (97378) Yamhill(84), Polk(15)
SHERWOOD (97140) Washington(89), Clackamas(8), Yamhill(1)
SILETZ Lincoln
SILVER LAKE Lake
SILVERTON Marion
SISTERS (97759) Deschutes(96), Jefferson(1), Linn(1)
SIXES Curry
SOUTH BEACH Lincoln
SPRAGUE RIVER Klamath
SPRAY Wheeler
SPRINGFIELD Lane
STANFIELD Umatilla
STAYTON (97383) Marion(96), Linn(3)
SUBLIMITY Marion
SUMMER LAKE Lake
SUMMERVILLE Union
SUMPTER (97877) Grant(82), Baker(18)
SUTHERLIN Douglas
SWEET HOME Linn
SWISSHOME Lane
TALENT Jackson
TANGENT Linn
TENMILE Douglas
TERREBONNE (97760) Jefferson(53), Deschutes(43), Crook(3)
THE DALLES Wasco
THURSTON Lane
TIDEWATER (97390) Lincoln(88), Lane(11)
TILLAMOOK Tillamook
TILLER Douglas
TIMBER Washington
TOLEDO Lincoln
TOLOVANA PARK Clatsop
TRAIL Jackson
TROUTDALE Multnomah
TUALATIN (97062) Washington(84), Clackamas(15)

TURNER Marion
TYGH VALLEY Wasco
UKIAH Umatilla
UMATILLA Umatilla
UMPQUA Douglas
UNITY Baker
VALE Malheur
VENETA Lane
VERNONIA Columbia
VIDA Lane
WALDPORT Lincoln
WALLOWA Wallowa
WALTERVILLE Lane
WALTON Lane
WARM SPRINGS Jefferson
WARREN Columbia
WARRENTON Clatsop
WASCO Sherman
WEDDERBURN Curry
WELCHES Clackamas
WEST LINN Clackamas
WESTFALL Malheur
WESTFIR Lane
WESTLAKE Lane
WESTON Umatilla
WHEELER Tillamook
WHITE CITY Jackson
WILBUR Douglas
WILDERVILLE Josephine
WILLAMINA (97396) Yamhill(53), Polk(46)
WILLIAMS Josephine
WILSONVILLE (97070) Clackamas(83), Washington(15)
WINCHESTER Douglas
WOLF CREEK Josephine
WOODBURN (97071) Marion(97), Clackamas(2)
YACHATS Lincoln
YAMHILL Yamhill
YONCALLA Douglas

Oregon ZIP/City Cross Reference

97001-97001	ANTELOPE
97002-97002	AURORA
97004-97004	BEAVERCREEK
97005-97008	BEAVERTON
97009-97009	BORING
97010-97010	BRIDAL VEIL
97011-97011	BRIGHTWOOD
97013-97013	CANBY
97014-97014	CASCADE LOCKS
97015-97015	CLACKAMAS
97016-97016	CLATSKANIE
97017-97017	COLTON
97018-97018	COLUMBIA CITY
97019-97019	CORBETT
97020-97020	DONALD
97021-97021	DUFUR
97022-97022	EAGLE CREEK
97023-97023	ESTACADA
97024-97024	FAIRVIEW
97026-97026	GERVAIS
97027-97027	GLADSTONE
97028-97028	GOVERNMENT CAMP
97029-97029	GRASS VALLEY
97030-97030	GRESHAM
97031-97031	HOOD RIVER
97032-97032	HUBBARD
97033-97033	KENT
97034-97035	LAKE OSWEGO
97036-97036	MARYLHURST
97037-97037	MAUPIN
97038-97038	MOLALLA
97039-97039	MORO
97040-97040	MOSIER
97041-97041	MOUNT HOOD PARKDALE
97042-97042	MULINO
97044-97044	ODELL
97045-97045	OREGON CITY
97048-97048	RAINIER
97049-97049	RHODODENDRON
97050-97050	RUFUS
97051-97051	SAINT HELENS
97053-97053	WARREN
97054-97054	DEER ISLAND
97055-97055	SANDY
97056-97056	SCAPPOOSE
97057-97057	SHANIKO
97058-97058	THE DALLES
97060-97060	TROUTDALE
97062-97062	TUALATIN
97063-97063	TYGH VALLEY
97064-97064	VERNONIA
97065-97065	WASCO
97067-97067	WELCHES
97068-97068	WEST LINN
97070-97070	WILSONVILLE
97071-97071	WOODBURN
97075-97078	BEAVERTON
97080-97080	GRESHAM
97101-97101	AMITY
97102-97102	ARCH CAPE
97103-97103	ASTORIA
97106-97106	BANKS
97107-97107	BAY CITY
97108-97108	BEAVER
97109-97109	BUXTON
97110-97110	CANNON BEACH
97111-97111	CARLTON
97112-97112	CLOVERDALE
97113-97113	CORNELIUS
97114-97114	DAYTON
97115-97115	DUNDEE
97116-97116	FOREST GROVE
97117-97117	GALES CREEK
97118-97118	GARIBALDI
97119-97119	GASTON
97121-97121	HAMMOND
97122-97122	HEBO
97123-97124	HILLSBORO
97125-97125	MANNING
97127-97127	LAFAYETTE
97128-97128	MCMINNVILLE
97130-97130	MANZANITA
97131-97131	NEHALEM
97132-97132	NEWBERG
97133-97133	NORTH PLAINS
97134-97134	OCEANSIDE
97135-97135	PACIFIC CITY
97136-97136	ROCKAWAY BEACH
97137-97137	SAINT PAUL
97138-97138	SEASIDE
97140-97140	SHERWOOD
97141-97141	TILLAMOOK
97143-97143	NETARTS
97144-97144	TIMBER
97145-97145	TOLOVANA PARK
97146-97146	WARRENTON
97147-97147	WHEELER
97148-97148	YAMHILL
97149-97149	NESKOWIN
97200-97299	PORTLAND
97301-97306	SALEM
97307-97307	KEIZER
97308-97314	SALEM
97321-97322	ALBANY
97324-97324	ALSEA
97325-97325	AUMSVILLE
97326-97326	BLODGETT
97327-97327	BROWNSVILLE
97329-97329	CASCADIA
97330-97333	CORVALLIS
97335-97335	CRABTREE
97336-97336	CRAWFORDSVILLE
97338-97338	DALLAS
97339-97339	CORVALLIS
97341-97341	DEPOE BAY
97342-97342	DETROIT
97343-97343	EDDYVILLE
97344-97344	FALLS CITY
97345-97345	FOSTER
97346-97346	GATES
97347-97347	GRAND RONDE
97348-97348	HALSEY
97350-97350	IDANHA
97351-97351	INDEPENDENCE
97352-97352	JEFFERSON
97355-97355	LEBANON
97357-97357	LOGSDEN
97358-97358	LYONS
97359-97359	MARION
97360-97360	MILL CITY
97361-97361	MONMOUTH
97362-97362	MOUNT ANGEL

97364-97364 NEOTSU	97446-97446 HARRISBURG	97537-97537 ROGUE RIVER	97820-97820 CANYON CITY
97365-97365 NEWPORT	97447-97447 IDLEYLD PARK	97538-97538 SELMA	97821-97821 CAYUSE
97366-97366 SOUTH BEACH	97448-97448 JUNCTION CITY	97539-97539 SHADY COVE	97823-97823 CONDON
97367-97367 LINCOLN CITY	97449-97449 LAKESIDE	97540-97540 TALENT	97824-97824 COVE
97368-97368 OTIS	97450-97450 LANGLOIS	97541-97541 TRAIL	97825-97825 DAYVILLE
97369-97369 OTTER ROCK	97451-97451 LORANE	97543-97543 WILDERVILLE	97826-97826 ECHO
97370-97370 PHILOMATH	97452-97452 LOWELL	97544-97544 WILLIAMS	97827-97827 ELGIN
97371-97371 RICKREALL	97453-97453 MAPLETON	97601-97603 KLAMATH FALLS	97828-97828 ENTERPRISE
97372-97372 ROSE LODGE	97454-97454 MARCOLA	97604-97604 CRATER LAKE	97830-97830 FOSSIL
97373-97373 SAINT BENEDICT	97455-97455 PLEASANT HILL	97620-97620 ADEL	97831-97831 FOX
97374-97374 SCIO	97456-97456 MONROE	97621-97621 BEATTY	97833-97833 HAINES
97375-97375 SCOTTS MILLS	97457-97457 MYRTLE CREEK	97622-97622 BLY	97834-97834 HALFWAY
97376-97376 SEAL ROCK	97458-97458 MYRTLE POINT	97623-97623 BONANZA	97835-97835 HELIX
97377-97377 SHEDD	97459-97459 NORTH BEND	97624-97624 CHILOQUIN	97836-97836 HEPPNER
97378-97378 SHERIDAN	97460-97460 NORWAY	97625-97625 DAIRY	97837-97837 HEREFORD
97380-97380 SILETZ	97461-97461 NOTI	97626-97626 FORT KLAMATH	97838-97838 HERMISTON
97381-97381 SILVERTON	97462-97462 OAKLAND	97627-97627 KENO	97839-97839 LEXINGTON
97383-97383 STAYTON	97463-97463 OAKRIDGE	97630-97630 LAKEVIEW	97840-97840 OXBOW
97384-97384 MEHAMA	97464-97464 OPHIR	97632-97632 MALIN	97841-97841 IMBLER
97385-97385 SUBLIMITY	97465-97465 PORT ORFORD	97633-97633 MERRILL	97842-97842 IMNAHA
97386-97386 SWEET HOME	97466-97466 POWERS	97634-97634 MIDLAND	97843-97843 IONE
97388-97388 GLENEDEN BEACH	97467-97467 REEDSPORT	97635-97635 NEW PINE CREEK	97844-97844 IRRIGON
97389-97389 TANGENT	97468-97468 REMOTE	97636-97636 PAISLEY	97845-97845 JOHN DAY
97390-97390 TIDEWATER	97469-97469 RIDDLE	97637-97637 PLUSH	97846-97846 JOSEPH
97391-97391 TOLEDO	97470-97470 ROSEBURG	97638-97638 SILVER LAKE	97848-97848 KIMBERLY
97392-97392 TURNER	97472-97472 SAGINAW	97639-97639 SPRAGUE RIVER	97850-97850 LA GRANDE
97394-97394 WALDPORT	97473-97473 SCOTTSBURG	97640-97640 SUMMER LAKE	97856-97856 LONG CREEK
97396-97396 WILLAMINA	97476-97476 SIXES	97641-97641 CHRISTMAS VALLEY	97857-97857 LOSTINE
97401-97405 EUGENE	97477-97478 SPRINGFIELD	97701-97709 BEND	97859-97859 MEACHAM
97406-97406 AGNESS	97479-97479 SUTHERLIN	97710-97710 FIELDS	97861-97861 MIKKALO
97407-97407 ALLEGANY	97480-97480 SWISSHOME	97711-97711 ASHWOOD	97862-97862 MILTON FREEWATER
97408-97408 EUGENE	97481-97481 TENMILE	97712-97712 BROTHERS	97864-97864 MONUMENT
97409-97409 ALVADORE	97482-97482 THURSTON	97720-97720 BURNS	97865-97865 MOUNT VERNON
97410-97410 AZALEA	97484-97484 TILLER	97721-97721 PRINCETON	97867-97867 NORTH POWDER
97411-97411 BANDON	97486-97486 UMPQUA	97722-97722 DIAMOND	97868-97868 PILOT ROCK
97412-97412 BLACHLY	97487-97487 VENETA	97730-97730 CAMP SHERMAN	97869-97869 PRAIRIE CITY
97413-97413 BLUE RIVER	97488-97488 VIDA	97731-97731 CHEMULT	97870-97870 RICHLAND
97414-97414 BROADBENT	97489-97489 WALTERVILLE	97732-97732 CRANE	97872-97872 RITTER
97415-97415 BROOKINGS	97490-97490 WALTON	97733-97733 CRESCENT	97873-97873 SENECA
97416-97416 CAMAS VALLEY	97491-97491 WEDDERBURN	97734-97734 CULVER	97874-97874 SPRAY
97417-97417 CANYONVILLE	97492-97492 WESTFIR	97735-97735 FORT ROCK	97875-97875 STANFIELD
97419-97419 CHESHIRE	97493-97493 WESTLAKE	97736-97736 FRENCHGLEN	97876-97876 SUMMERVILLE
97420-97420 COOS BAY	97494-97494 WILBUR	97737-97737 GILCHRIST	97877-97877 SUMPTER
97423-97423 COQUILLE	97495-97495 WINCHESTER	97738-97738 HINES	97880-97880 UKIAH
97424-97424 COTTAGE GROVE	97496-97496 WINSTON	97739-97739 LA PINE	97882-97882 UMATILLA
97425-97425 CRESCENT LAKE	97497-97497 WOLF CREEK	97740-97740 LAWEN	97883-97883 UNION
97426-97426 CRESWELL	97498-97498 YACHATS	97741-97741 MADRAS	97884-97884 UNITY
97427-97427 CULP CREEK	97499-97499 YONCALLA	97750-97750 MITCHELL	97885-97885 WALLOWA
97428-97428 CURTIN	97501-97501 MEDFORD	97751-97751 PAULINA	97886-97886 WESTON
97429-97429 DAYS CREEK	97502-97502 CENTRAL POINT	97752-97752 POST	97901-97901 ADRIAN
97430-97430 DEADWOOD	97503-97503 WHITE CITY	97753-97753 POWELL BUTTE	97902-97902 AROCK
97431-97431 DEXTER	97504-97504 MEDFORD	97754-97754 PRINEVILLE	97903-97903 BROGAN
97432-97432 DILLARD	97520-97520 ASHLAND	97756-97756 REDMOND	97904-97904 DREWSEY
97434-97434 DORENA	97522-97522 BUTTE FALLS	97758-97758 RILEY	97905-97905 DURKEE
97435-97435 DRAIN	97523-97523 CAVE JUNCTION	97759-97759 SISTERS	97906-97906 HARPER
97436-97436 ELKTON	97524-97524 EAGLE POINT	97760-97760 TERREBONNE	97907-97907 HUNTINGTON
97437-97437 ELMIRA	97525-97525 GOLD HILL	97761-97761 WARM SPRINGS	97908-97908 IRONSIDE
97438-97438 FALL CREEK	97526-97528 GRANTS PASS	97801-97801 PENDLETON	97909-97909 JAMIESON
97439-97439 FLORENCE	97530-97530 JACKSONVILLE	97810-97810 ADAMS	97910-97910 JORDAN VALLEY
97440-97440 EUGENE	97531-97531 KERBY	97812-97812 ARLINGTON	97911-97911 JUNTURA
97441-97441 GARDINER	97532-97532 MERLIN	97813-97813 ATHENA	97913-97913 NYSSA
97442-97442 GLENDALE	97533-97533 MURPHY	97814-97814 BAKER CITY	97914-97914 ONTARIO
97443-97443 GLIDE	97534-97534 O BRIEN	97817-97817 BATES	97917-97917 RIVERSIDE
97444-97444 GOLD BEACH	97535-97535 PHOENIX	97818-97818 BOARDMAN	97918-97918 VALE
97445-97445 GREENLEAF	97536-97536 PROSPECT	97819-97819 BRIDGEPORT	97920-97920 WESTFALL

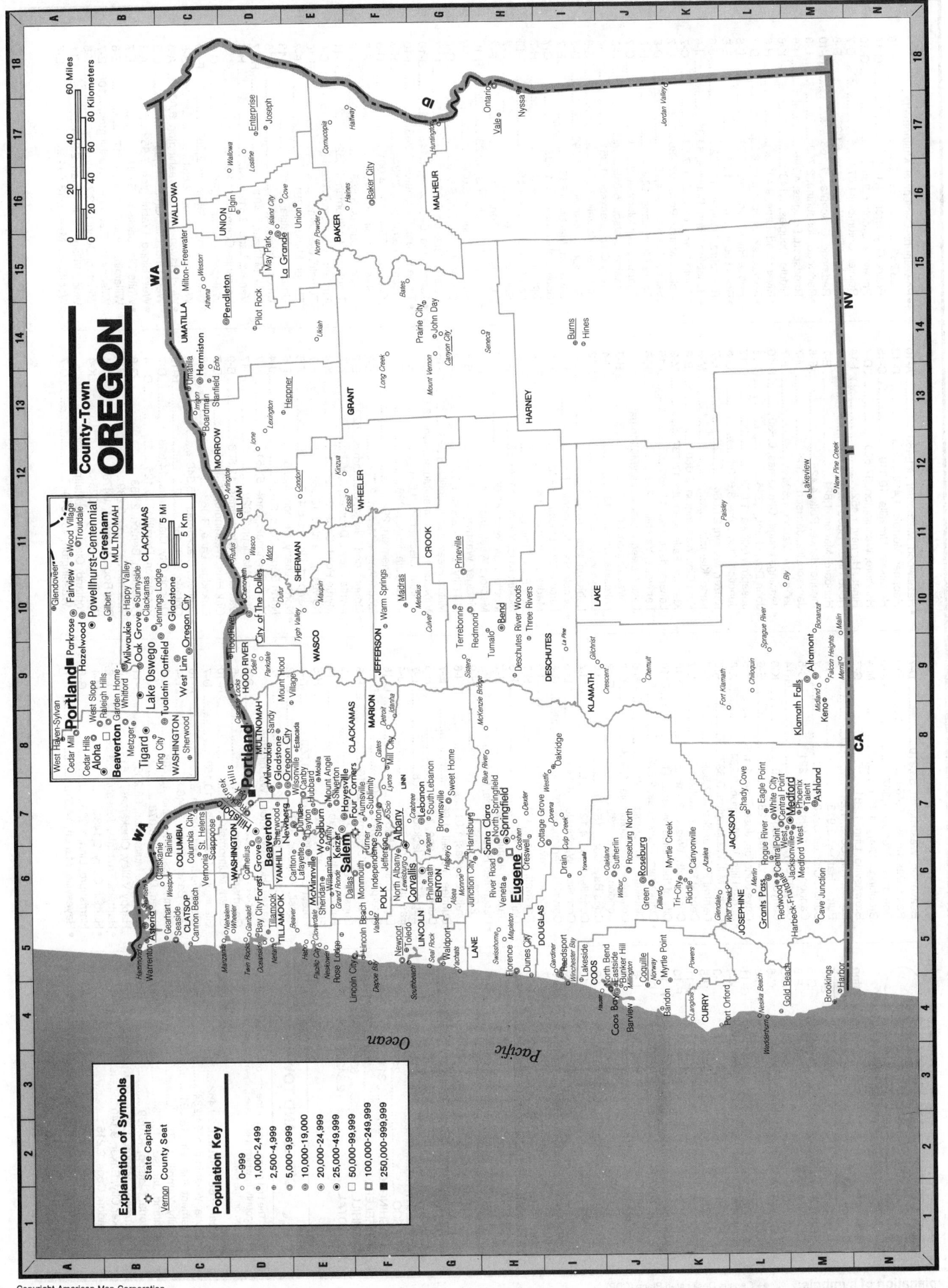

County-Town
OREGON

Explanation of Symbols

✪ State Capital

⊙ Vernon County Seat

Population Key

Symbol	Range
°	0-999
⊙	1,000-2,499
⊙	2,500-4,999
⊛	5,000-9,999
⊛	10,000-19,000
⊛	20,000-24,999
⊛	25,000-49,999
□	50,000-99,999
□	100,000-249,999
■	250,000-999,999

Beaverton, Washington, 53,310 ... D-7
Bend, Deschutes, 20,469 ... H-10
Boardman, Morrow, 1,387 ... C-13
Brookings, Curry, 4,400 ... M-4
Brownsville, Linn, 1,281 ... G-7
● Bunker Hill, Coos, 1,242 ... J-4
Burns, Harney, 2,913 ... I-14
Canby, Clackamas, 8,983 ... E-7
Cannon Beach, Clatsop, 1,221 ... C-5
Canyon City, Grant, 648 ... G-14
Canyonville, Douglas, 1,219 ... K-6
Carlton, Yamhill, 1,289 ... E-6
Cave Junction, Josephine, 1,126 ... M-5
● Cedar Hills, Washington, 9,294 ... A-8
● Cedar Mill, Washington, 9,697 ... A-8
Central Point, Jackson, 7,509 ... L-7
Central Point West, Jackson ... L-7
● Chenoweth, Wasco, 3,246 ... D-10
City of the Dalles, Wasco, 11,060 ... D-10
● Clackamas, Clackamas, 2,578 ... B-10
Clatskanie, Columbia, 1,629 ... B-6
Columbia City, Columbia, 1,003 ... C-7
Condon, Gilliam, 635 ... E-12
Coos Bay, Coos, 15,076 ... J-4
Coquille, Coos, 4,121 ... J-4
Cornelius, Washington, 6,148 ... D-6
Corvallis, Benton, 44,757 ... G-6
Cottage Grove, Lane, 7,402 ... I-6
Creswell, Lane, 2,431 ... H-7
Dallas, Polk, 9,422 ... F-6
Dayton, Yamhill, 1,526 ... E-7
Deschutes River Woods, Deschutes,
  2,373 ... H-9
Drain, Douglas, 1,011 ... I-6
Dundee, Yamhill, 1,663 ... E-7
Dunes City, Lane, 1,081 ... H-5
Eagle Point, Jackson, 3,008 ... L-7
Eastside, Coos ... J-4
Elgin, Union, 1,586 ... D-16
Enterprise, Wallowa, 1,905 ... D-17
Estacada, Clackamas, 2,016 ... E-8
Eugene, Lane, 112,669 ... H-6
Fairview, Multnomah, 2,391 ... A-11
Florence, Lane, 5,162 ... H-5
Forest Grove, Washington, 13,559 ... D-7
Fossil, Wheeler, 399 ... E-12
● Four Corners, Marion, 12,156 ... F-7
● Garden Home-Whitford, Washington,
  6,652 ... B-8
Gearhart, Clatsop, 1,027 ... B-5
Gilbert, Multnomah ... B-10
Gladstone, Clackamas, 10,152 ... D-7
Glendoveer, Multnomah ... A-10
Gold Beach, Curry, 1,546 ... L-4
Grants Pass, Josephine, 17,488 ... L-6
Green, Douglas, 5,076 ... J-6
Gresham, Multnomah, 68,235 ... B-11
Happy Valley, Clackamas, 1,519 ... B-10
● Harbeck-Fruitdale, Josephine, 3,982 ... L-6
Harbor, Curry, 2,143 ... M-4
Harrisburg, Linn, 1,939 ... G-6
Hayesville, Marion, 14,318 ... E-7

Hazelwood, Multnomah, 11,480 ... A-10
Heppner, Morrow, 1,412 ... D-13
Hermiston, Umatilla, 10,040 ... C-13
Hillsboro, Washington, 37,520 ... D-7
Hines, Harney, 1,452 ... I-14
Hood River, Hood River, 4,632 ... D-9
Hubbard, Marion, 1,881 ... E-7
Independence, Polk, 4,425 ... F-6
Jacksonville, Jackson, 1,896 ... M-7
Jefferson, Marion, 1,805 ... F-7
Jennings Lodge, Clackamas, 6,530 ... B-10
John Day, Grant, 1,836 ... G-14
Joseph, Wallowa, 1,073 ... D-17
Junction City, Lane, 3,670 ... G-6
Keizer, Marion, 21,884 ... E-7
Keno, Klamath ... M-9
King City, Washington, 2,060 ... B-8
Klamath Falls, Klamath, 17,737 ... M-9
La Grande, Union, 11,766 ... D-15
Lafayette, Yamhill, 1,292 ... E-6
Lake Oswego, Clackamas/Multnomah/
  Washington, 30,576 ... B-9
Lakeside, Coos, 1,437 ... I-4
Lakeview, Lake, 2,526 ... M-12
Lebanon, Linn, 10,950 ... G-7
Lincoln Beach, Lincoln, 1,507 ... F-5
Lincoln City, Lincoln, 5,892 ... F-5
Madras, Jefferson, 3,443 ... F-10
May Park, Union ... D-15
McMinnville, Yamhill, 17,894 ... E-6
Medford, Jackson, 46,951 ... M-7
Medford West, Jackson ... M-7
Metzger, Washington, 3,149 ... B-8
Mill City, Linn/Marion, 1,555 ... F-8
Milton-Freewater, Umatilla, 5,533 ... C-15
Milwaukie, Clackamas/Multnomah, 18,692 ... D-7
Molalla, Clackamas, 3,651 ... E-7
Monmouth, Polk, 6,288 ... F-6
Moro, Sherman, 292 ... D-11
Mount Angel, Marion, 2,778 ... E-7
Mount Hood Village, Clackamas, 2,234 ... E-8
Myrtle Creek, Douglas, 3,063 ... K-6
Myrtle Point, Coos, 2,712 ... K-4
Newberg, Yamhill, 13,086 ... E-7
Newport, Lincoln, 1,281 ... F-5
● North Albany, Benton, 4,325 ... F-6
North Bend, Coos, 9,614 ... J-4
North Springfield, Lane, 5,451 ... H-7
Nyssa, Malheur, 2,629 ... H-17
● Oak Grove, Clackamas, 12,576 ... B-9
Oak Hills, Washington, 6,450 ... I-8
Oakridge, Lane, 3,063 ... C-9
Oatfield, Clackamas, 15,348 ... C-9
Ontario, Malheur, 9,392 ... H-18
Oregon City, Clackamas, 14,698 ... D-7
Pendleton, Umatilla, 15,126 ... D-14
Philomath, Benton, 2,983 ... G-6
Phoenix, Jackson, 3,239 ... M-7
Pilot Rock, Umatilla, 1,478 ... D-14
Port Orford, Curry, 1,025 ... K-4
Portland, Clackamas/Multnomah/
  Washington, 437,319 ... D-7

● Powellhurst-Centennial, Multnomah,
  28,756 ... B-10
Prairie City, Grant, 1,117 ... G-14
Prineville, Crook, 5,355 ... G-10
Rainier, Columbia, 1,674 ... C-7
● Raleigh Hills, Washington, 6,066 ... B-8
Redmond, Deschutes, 7,163 ... G-10
Redwood, Josephine, 3,702 ... L-6
Reedsport, Douglas, 4,796 ... I-5
Riddle, Douglas, 1,143 ... K-6
● River Road, Lane, 9,443 ... H-6
Rockcreek, Washington, 8,282 ... D-7
Rogue River, Jackson, 1,759 ... L-6
Rose Lodge, Lincoln, 1,257 ... E-5
Roseburg, Douglas, 17,032 ... J-6
Roseburg North, Columbia, 7,535 ... C-7
Saint Helens, Columbia, 7,535 ... C-7
Salem, Marion/Polk, 107,786 ... E-7
Sandy, Clackamas, 4,152 ... D-8
Santa Clara, Lane, 12,834 ... H-6
● Scappoose, Columbia, 3,529 ... C-7
Seaside, Clatsop, 5,359 ... C-5
Shady Cove, Jackson, 1,351 ... L-7
Sheridan, Yamhill, 3,979 ... E-6
Sherwood, Washington, 3,093 ... D-7
Silverton, Marion, 5,635 ... E-7
South Lebanon, Linn, 1,203 ... G-7
Springfield, Lane, 44,683 ... H-7
Stanfield, Umatilla, 1,568 ... C-13
Stayton, Marion, 5,011 ... F-7
Sublimity, Marion, 1,491 ... F-7
Sunnyside, Clackamas, 4,423 ... B-10
Sutherlin, Douglas, 5,020 ... J-6
Sweet Home, Linn, 6,850 ... G-7
Talent, Jackson, 3,274 ... M-7
Terrebonne, Deschutes, 1,143 ... G-10
Three Rivers, Deschutes, 1,268 ... H-10
Tigard, Washington, 29,344 ... B-8
Tillamook, Tillamook, 4,001 ... D-5
Toledo, Lincoln, 3,174 ... F-5
Tri-City, Douglas, 3,585 ... K-6
Troutdale, Multnomah, 7,852 ... A-11
Tualatin, Clackamas/Washington, 15,013 ... C-8
Tumalo, Deschutes ... H-10
Turner, Marion, 1,281 ... F-7
Umatilla, Umatilla, 3,046 ... C-13
Union, Union, 1,847 ... E-16
Vale, Malheur, 1,491 ... H-17
Veneta, Lane, 2,519 ... H-6
Vernonia, Columbia, 1,808 ... C-6
Waldport, Lincoln, 1,595 ... G-5
● Warm Springs, Jefferson, 2,287 ... F-10
Warrenton, Clatsop, 2,681 ... B-5
West Haven-Sylvan, Washington, 6,009 ... A-8
West Linn, Clackamas, 16,367 ... C-9
● West Slope, Washington, 7,959 ... A-8
White City, Jackson, 5,891 ... L-7
Willamina, Polk/Yamhill, 1,717 ... E-6
Wilsonville, Clackamas/Washington, 7,106 ... E-7
Winston, Douglas, 3,773 ... J-6
Wood Village, Multnomah, 2,814 ... A-11
Woodburn, Marion, 13,404 ... E-7

Explanation of symbols: ● – Census Designated Place (CDP)

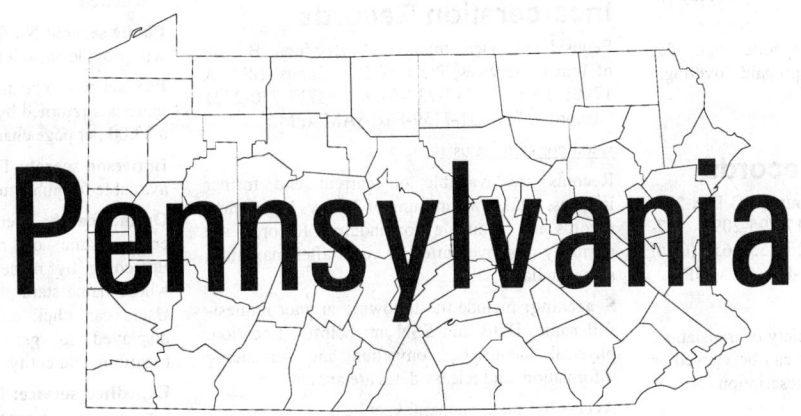

General Help Numbers:

Governor's Office
225 Main Capitol Bldg
Harrisburg, PA 17120
http://www.governor.state.pa.us/

717-787-2500
Fax 717-772-8284
9AM-4:30PM

Attorney General's Office
Strawberry Square, 16th Floor
Harrisburg, PA 17120
8242www.attorneygeneral.gov

717-787-3391
Fax 717-787-
8AM-5PM

Legislative Records
General Assembly, Legislative Reference Bureau
Main Capitol Bldg, Room 641
Harrisburg, PA 17120
www.legis.state.pa.us

717-787-2342

8:30AM-5PM

State Archives
Bureau of Archives & History
350 North St
Harrisburg, PA 17120
www.phmc.state.pa.us

717-783-3281
Fax 717-787-4822
9AM-4PM TU-F

State Specifics:

Capital:	Harrisburg Dauphin County
Time Zone:	EST
Number of Counties:	67
Population:	12,406,292
Web Site:	www.state.pa.us

State Agencies

Criminal Records

State Police, Central Repository -164, 1800 Elmerton Ave, Harrisburg, PA 17110-9758; 717-783-5494, 717-783-9973, 717-772-3681-Fax; 8:15AM-4:15PM.

www.psp.state.pa.us/psp/site/default.asp

Records are available from the 1920s. Records are available for all convictions. It takes 1 day before new records are available for inquiry. Records are indexed on fingerprint cards and inhouse computer. Records are normally destroyed after 3 years after individual is confirmed deceased by fingerprints. 60% of all arrests in database have

final dispositions recorded, 31% for those arrests within last 5 years.

Searching: Must make request on Request Form SP4-164 or the request will be returned. The form can be found on web page (help menu in PATCH section) or call for form. Include the following in your request-full name, date of birth, Social Security Number, sex, race, any aliases, all on proper form. A release is not required. The record database is 100% fingerprint-supported. Statutorily-required fingerprint searches include an FBI fingerprint search. Records include felony and misdemeanor convictions, also cases without dispositions less than 3 years old.

Access by: mail, online.

Fee & Payment: Fee is $10.00 per name search. Add $24.00 if for a statutorily-required FBI fingerprint check. Fee payee: Commonwealth of Pennsylvania. Prepayment required. No personal checks accepted. No credit cards accepted.

Mail search: Turnaround time: 2-3 weeks. Turnaround can be 6 weeks if a record has a hit. No self addressed stamped envelope is required.

Online search: Record checks are available for approved agencies through the Internet on the Pennsylvania Access to Criminal Histories (PATCH). Ongoing requesters may become registered users. This is a commercial system, the same $10.00 fee per name applies. PATCH accepts Visa, Discover, Master Card, AmEx cards.

Go to https://epatch.state.pa.us or call 717-705-1768 to register. Up to 10 records may be requested at one session.

Expedited service: Will expedite one day turnaround if you provide prepaid overnight shipping envelope.

Statewide Court Records

Administrative Office of PA Courts, PO Box 229, Mechanicsburg, PA 17055; 717-795-2097, 717-795-2062 (Communications), 717-255-1650 (Civil Appellate Cases), 717-795-2013-Fax; 9AM-5PM.

www.courts.state.pa.us

The website offers links to a variety of translation, terminology, and code files that can be viewed or downloaded, along with a brief description.

Access by: mail, online.

Mail search: One may request copies of records from the Appellate level courts - The Superior Court (criminal, family) and Commonwealth Court (civil). A Public Access Request Form is downloadable from the web page.

Online search: The Web Portal offers access to a variety of the Judiciary's Electronic Services (E-Services) such as Web Docket Sheets, DA Link, Superior Court's Web Docketing Statements, etc. Web Docket provides public access to view and print Case Docket Sheets from Pennsylvania's three Appellate Courts and Criminal Cases only from Courts of Common Pleas. Search by docket number, name or organization. Go to http://ujsportal.pacourts.us for details. Also, search Appellate Court dockets at http://pacmsdocketsheet.aopc.org/.

Sexual Offender Registry

State Police Central Repository, Megan's Law Unit, 1800 Elmerton Ave, Harrisburg, PA 17110-9758; 717-783-4363, 866-771-7130, 717-705-8839-Fax; 7AM-3PM.

www.pameganslaw.state.pa.us

Sexual offenders are required to register for either 10-years or for their lifetime. The length of time a sexual offender is required to register depends on the offense committed.

Records are available from April 21, 1996 forward. As of December 2004, there were over 7,100 active registered sex offenders in the state of Pennsylvania.

Searching: This office provides no searches except via the Internet or email.

Access by: online.

Online search: Limited information on all registered sex offenders can be viewed online from the webpage. Complete address information is listed only for sexually violent predators. Search by name, alias, city, county or ZIP. To make a specific request for information on Sexually Violent Predators, please email to ra-pspsvp@state.pa.us.

Incarceration Records

Pennsylvania Department of Corrections, Bureau of Inmate Services, PO Box 598, Camp Hill, PA 17001-0598; 717-737-6538, 717-730-2721 (Records), 717-731-7159-Fax; 8AM-4PM.

www.cor.state.pa.us

Records are available on current and former inmates. It takes a minimum of 30 days before new records are available for inquiry. Records are normally destroyed after 10 years after maximum sentence date.

Searching: Include the following in your request-full name. DOB and SSN are helpful. Location, physical identifiers, conviction and sentencing information, and release dates are available.

Access by: mail, phone, fax, online.

Fee & Payment: There is no fee.

Mail search: Turnaround time: 1 to 2 weeks. Turnaround time on archived records may be longer than 2 weeks. A SASE is requested.

Phone search: Includes historical information on released inmates.

Fax search: Can request via fax.

Online search: At the website, click on Inmate Locator for information about each inmate currently under the jurisdiction of the Department of Corrections. The site indicates where an inmate is housed, race, date of birth, marital status and other items. The Inmate Locator does not contain information on inmates not currently residing in a state correctional institution.

Corporation, Limited Partnership, Trademarks/Servicemarks, Fictitious Name, Assumed Name, Limited Liability Company, Limited Liability Partnerships

Corporation Bureau, Department of State, PO Box 8722, Harrisburg, PA 17105-8722 (Courier address: 206 North Office Bldg, Harrisburg, PA 17120); 717-787-1057, 717-783-2244-Fax; 8AM-5PM.

www.dos.state.pa.us/corps/site/default.asp

Records are available from 1700's on. Records are indexed on computer since the 1800's. It takes 4 to 7 days before new records are available for inquiry.

Searching: Include the following in your request-full name of business. Corporation records include: Articles of Incorporation, Officers, Directors, DBAs, Prior (merged) names, Withdrawn and Reserved (120 days) names. Annual Reports on for-profit corporations are not required by the Department of State.

Access by: mail, phone, fax, in person, online.

Fee & Payment: The search fee is $15.00. Request for copies is $15.00 plus $3.00 per page. Certification is $40.00 plus $3.00 per copy. Printouts from computer or microfilm is $3.00 a page. A Good Standing is $40.00. Fee payee: Department of State. Prepayment required. Ongoing requesters should open a customer deposit account. Personal checks accepted. No credit cards accepted.

Mail search: Turnaround time: 3 to 5 days. SASE is required.

Phone search: No fee for telephone request. They will provide basic information only.

Fax search: You must have an account to have materials returned by fax, same fees as above plus a $3.00 per page charge.

In person search: There are 2 computer terminals available for public use.

Online search: There is free general searching by entity name or number from the website. Searching by name provides a list of entities whose name starts with the search name entered. Users can click on any one entity in the list displayed to get more detailed information regarding that entity.

Expedited service: Expedited service is available for mail and phone searches. Add $70.00 per transaction. If ordered before 1 PM, the record will be available by 5 PM.

Uniform Commercial Code

UCC Division, Department of State, PO Box 8721, Harrisburg, PA 17105-8721 (Courier address: North Office Bldg, Rm 206, Harrisburg, PA 17120); 717-787-1057 x3, 717-783-2244-Fax; 8AM-5PM.

www.dos.state.pa.us/DOS/site/default.asp

Records are available from 1964 to present on microfiche and computer. It takes 2 to 3 days before new records are available for inquiry.

Searching: Use search request form UCC-11. All federal and state tax liens are filed at the Prothonotary of each county. Include the following in your request-debtor name. The agency will not expedite requests.

Access by: mail, fax, in person, online.

Fee & Payment: The search fee is $12.00 per debtor name, copies cost $3.00 per page. Certification is $28.00. Fee payee: Pennsylvania Department of State. Prepayment required. Deposit accounts are accepted. Personal checks accepted. No credit cards accepted for search requests.

Mail search: Turnaround time: 3 to 5 days.

Fax search: There is an additional $3.00 per page fee if returned by fax. A customer deposit account is required.

In person search: If the search is conducted by the customer, there is no $12.00 search fee.

Online search: The website allows a search of UCC-1 financing statements filed with the Corporation Bureau by debtor name or financing statement number; a list of financing statements is displayed. The site also allows a search of financing statement records filed with the Corporation Bureau by financing statement number.

Other access: Daily computer tapes and copies of microfilm are available. Call the number above for details.

Federal and State Tax Liens

Records not maintained by a state level agency.

All federal and state tax liens are filed at the Prothonotary of each county.

Sales Tax Registrations

Revenue Department, Sales Tax Registration Division, Dept 280905, Harrisburg, PA 17128-0905; 717-783-9360, 717-787-3708-Fax; 7:30AM-4:30PM.

www.revenue.state.pa.us

Businesses can register online at www.pa100.state.pa.us/.

Records are available from 1971 to present, easily searchable from 1995 to present. It takes 2 to 3 weeks before new records are available for inquiry.

Searching: This agency will only confirm that a business is registered. They will provide no other information unless a signed release is presented. Include the following in your request-EIN, tax permit number or business name. They will only search with a tax permit number.

Access by: mail, phone, fax.

Fee & Payment: There is no search fee.

Mail search: Turnaround time: 2 to 7 days. A SASE is requested.

Phone search: Records are available by phone.

Fax search: Same criteria as mail searches.

Birth Certificates

PA Department of Health, Division of Vital Records, PO Box 1528, New Castle, PA 16103-1528 (Courier address: 101 S Mercer St, Room 401, New Castle, PA 16101); 724-656-3100 (Message Phone), 724-652-8951-Fax; 8AM-4PM.

http://webserver.health.state.pa.us/health/cwp/view.asp?a=168&Q=229939

Records are available from 1906 to present.

Searching: Must have a signed release from person of record or immediate family member. Include the following in your request-full name, names of parents, mother's maiden name, date of birth, place of birth, relationship to person of record, reason for information request. Must include daytime phone number.

Access by: mail, fax, in person, online.

Fee & Payment: The fee is $10.00 per record. Fee payee: Vital Records. Prepayment required. Personal checks accepted. Credit cards accepted only by VitalChek.

Mail search: Turnaround time: 3 weeks. Credit cards not accepted for mail requests. A SASE is requested.

Fax search: See expedited services

In person search: Turnaround time is 1 hour.

Online search: Expedited service is available at www.vitalchek.com, a state designated vendor. Access to this site is also linked from the home page above.

Expedited service: Expedited service is available for fax requests. Use of the state form (downloadable from web site) is required. Turnaround time: 2 to 4 days. Add $7.00 for use of credit card, add fees for express delivery, if desired.

Death Records

Department of Health, Division of Vital Records, PO Box 1528, New Castle, PA 16103-1528 (Courier address: 101 S Mercer St, Room 401, New Castle, PA 16101); 724-656-3100 (Message Phone), 724-652-8951-Fax; 8AM-4:30PM.

www.dsf.health.state.pa.us/health/cwp/view.asp?a=168&Q=202275

Statewide records are available from this office. Records from 1994 forward are available from these cities (only for that particular city): Erie, Harrisburg, Philadelphia, Pittsburgh, and Scranton. Visit the website for address information.

Records are available from 1906 to present.

Searching: Must have a signed release from immediate family member, or give tangible evidence of need. Requester must be at least 18 years of age. Include the following in your request-full name, date of death, place of death, relationship to person of record, reason for information request. SSN helpful, if known. Include daytime phone number.

Access by: mail, fax, in person, online.

Fee & Payment: The fee is $9.00 per record. Fee payee: Vital Records. Prepayment required. Personal checks accepted. Credit cards accepted only by VitalChek.

Mail search: Turnaround time: 3 to 4 weeks. A SASE is requested.

Fax search: See Expedited Service.

In person search: Turnaround time 1 hour.

Online search: Expedited service is available at www.vitalchek.com, a state designated vendor. Access to this site is also linked from the home page above.

Expedited service: Expedited service is available for fax and online orders. Use of the state form (downloadable from web site) is required. Turnaround time: 2 to 4 days. Add $7.00 for use of credit card and cost of express delivery if desired.

Marriage Certificates, Divorce Records

Records not maintained by a state level agency.

Marriage and divorce records are found at county level at Prothonotary of issue.

Workers' Compensation Records

Bureau of Workers' Compensation, Physical Records Section, 1171 S Cameron St, Rm 103, Harrisburg, PA 17104-2501; 717-772-4447, 717-705-0940-Fax; 7:30AM-4PM.

www.dli.state.pa.us/landi/site/default.asp

Records are available for past 4 years. It takes 1 to 3 days before new records are available for inquiry. Records are indexed on inhouse computer. Records are normally destroyed after 4 years.

Searching: Only the party to the record is allowed full access without a subpoena or a signed release. The Agency will indicate if a record exists for a person, but will not give any other information to the public. Include the following in your request-claimant name, year, date of accident, Social Security Number. If not a party to claim, then include a signed release.

Access by: mail.

Fee & Payment: No fees involved for simple requests.

Mail search: Turnaround time: 14 days. No SASE is required.

Driver Records

Department of Transportation, Driver Record Services, PO Box 68695, Harrisburg, PA 17106-8695 (Courier address: 1101 S Front Street, 3rd Fl, Harrisburg, PA 17104); 717-391-6190, 800-932-4600 (In-state only), 7:30AM-4:30PM.

www.dmv.state.pa.us

Copies of tickets may be purchased from this location for a fee of $5.00 each.

Records are available for minimum of 3 calendar years for moving violations or departmental actions, minimum of 7 yrs for DWIs, and indefinite for suspensions. Accidents are reported on record as involvement only. Driver's address appears on the record. It takes 15 days from conviction receipt before new records are available for inquiry.

Searching: The agency must pre-authorize all customers of MVR vendor companies and of pre-employment screening firms. Include the following in your request-driver's license number, full name, date of birth. Casual requesters submit Form DL-503, which requires the signature of the subject or notarized signature of the requester. Large volume requesters must sign an agreement stating the individual authorizations are on file.

Access by: mail, in person, online.

Fee & Payment: The fee is $5.00 for each 3-year record or $10.00 for complete certified record. A 10 year employment record for commercial drivers is available for $5.00. Fee payee: Department of Transportation. Prepayment required. Personal checks not accepted. No credit cards accepted.

Mail search: Turnaround time: 7 to 10 days. No SASE is required.

In person search: The state will process one record request while you wait, additional requests are mailed back to the requester.

Online search: The online system is available to high volume requesters for three or ten-year records. Fee is $5.00 per record. Call 717-787-7154 for more information. The resale of records over the Internet is strictly forbidden. Drivers may order their own record from the web page.

Other access: Magnetic tape processing is available for batch requesters. There is a 500 record minimum order per day.

Vehicle Ownership Vehicle Identification

Department of Transportation, Vehicle Record Services, PO Box 68691, Harrisburg, PA 17106-8691 (Courier address: 1101 South Front St, Harrisburg, PA 17104); 717-391-6190, 800-932-6000 (In-state), 7:30AM-4:30PM.

www.dmv.state.pa.us

This agency also holds records for unattached mobile homes. Encumbrance/lien information is not considered public information and is only released per DPPA guidelines.

It takes 4 to 6 weeks before new records are available for inquiry. Records are normally destroyed after 10 years.

Searching: The requester must submit Form DL-135. The state does not authorize the bulk delivery or commercial use of ownership & vehicle information.

Access by: mail, in person.

Fee & Payment: The fee is $5.00 per transaction. Title history may have more than one transaction per vehicle. You can call first to determine the number. There is an additional $5.00 for certification. Fee payee: Department of Transportation. Prepayment required. Personal checks accepted. No credit cards accepted.

Mail search: Turnaround time: 7 to 10 days. You can order a record in person, but results will be mailed. No SASE is required.

In person search: Depending on the request, results given in person. basic info or lien data available over the counter. If microfilm needs to be pulled, results are mailed.

Other access: Bulk information is not sold for commercial purposes. Certain statistical type user requests will be honored.

Accident Reports

State Police Headquarters, Crash Reports Unit, 1800 Elmerton Ave, Harrisburg, PA 17110; 717-783-5516, 8AM-4PM.

www.psp.state.pa.us

Order form is available at the website.

Records are available for 10 years to present. It takes 60 days before new records are available for inquiry. Records are indexed on inhouse computer. Records are normally destroyed after 10 years.

Searching: Only those involved, their attorney or insurer may request a copy of the accident report. Include the following in your request-full name, date of accident, State Police incident number. The following data is not released: medical information or expunged records.

Access by: mail.

Fee & Payment: Reports are $8.00 per record. Fee payee: Commonwealth of Pennsylvania. Prepayment required. Personal checks accepted. No credit cards accepted.

Mail search: Turnaround time: 6 weeks or more.

Vessel Ownership
Vessel Registration

Access to Records is Restricted.

Fish and Boat Commission, Licensing & Registration Section, PO Box 68900, Harrisburg, PA 17106-8900; 717-705-7940, 717-705-7931-Fax; 8AM-4PM.

www.fish.state.pa.us

Boat registration and ownership information is not open to the public. Liens are filed at UCC filing locations. As of 1998, this agency issues certificates of title.

Voter Registration

Access to Records is Restricted.

Board of Commissions, Elections, & Leg., Elections, 210 N. Office Building, Harrisburg, PA 17120; 717-787-5280, 717-705-0721-Fax; 8AM-5PM.

www.dos.state.pa.us/bcel/site/default.asp

The state is in the process of implementing a statewide database (SURE Project). 80% of the counties now participate. Until 100% participation is available, it is suggested to do record searches at the county level. Records cannot be sold or re-sold for commercial purposes.

GED Certificates

Commonwealth Diploma Program, GED Testing, 333 Market St 12th Fl, Harrisburg, PA 17126-0333; 717-787-6747, 8:30AM-4:30PM.

www.paadulted.org/able/site/default.asp

It takes minutes before new records are available for inquiry.

Searching: They will only honor written requests. No verbal or fax verifications are given. For all requests the following is required: a signed release, name, approximate year of test, date of birth, SSN, city of test, and a phone number where you can be reached.

Access by: mail, in person.

Fee & Payment: Verifications and copies of transcripts are $3.00 each. The fee is non-refundable. Fee payee: Commonwealth of PA. Prepayment required. Cashier's checks and money orders are accepted. No credit cards or personal checks accepted.

Mail search: Turnaround time: 3 to 4 weeks. No SASE is required.

In person search: Counter service is available.

Hunting License

Access to Records is Restricted.

Game Commission, Hunting License Division, 2001 Elmerton Ave, Harrisburg, PA 17110-9797; 717-787-2084 (Hunting License Division), 717-705-1628-Fax; 7:45AM-4PM.

www.theoutdoorshop.state.pa.us/fbg

Hunting license information is not released to the public.

Fishing License

Access to Records is Restricted.

Fish & Boat Commission, Fishing License Division, PO Box 67000, Harrisburg, PA 17106 (Courier address: 1601 Elmerton, Harrisburg, PA 17110); 717-705-7930 (Fishing License Division), 717-787-4250 (PA Game Division), 717-705-7931-Fax; 8AM-4PM.

http://sites.state.pa.us/PA_Exec/Fish_Boat/mpag1.htm

Fishing license information is not released to the public.

Pennsylvania State Licensing Agencies

For details about the agency responsible for licensing/certifying/registering an item below or in the Agency Quick Finder section, match an item's number with the number of the agency in the *Licensing Agency Information* section.

Pennsylvania Licenses Searchable Online

Acupuncturist #20	http://licensepa.state.pa.us/default.asp
Amphetamine Program #20	http://licensepa.state.pa.us/default.asp
Anesthesia Permit, Dental #18	www.mylicense.state.pa.us
Animal Health Technician #20	http://licensepa.state.pa.us/default.asp
Appraiser, Residential #20	http://licensepa.state.pa.us/default.asp
Appraiser/Broker #20	http://licensepa.state.pa.us/default.asp
Architect #20	http://licensepa.state.pa.us/default.asp
Architectural Firm #20	http://licensepa.state.pa.us/default.asp
Athletic Agent #15	www.licensepa.state.pa.us/default.asp
Athletic Trainer #20	http://licensepa.state.pa.us/default.asp
Attorney #1	http://padisciplinaryboard.org/attsearchdc.php
Attorney, Disciplined #1	http://padisciplinaryboard.org/attsearchdcd.php
Auction House/Company #20	http://licensepa.state.pa.us/default.asp
Auctioneer #20	http://licensepa.state.pa.us/default.asp
Auctioneer, Real Estate #20	http://licensepa.state.pa.us/default.asp
Audiologist #20	http://licensepa.state.pa.us/default.asp
Bank #4	www.banking.state.pa.us/Banking/Banking/InstListQuery.asp
Barber/Barber Shop/Manager #20	http://licensepa.state.pa.us/default.asp
Barber School/Teacher #20	http://licensepa.state.pa.us/default.asp
Boxer #15	www.dos.state.pa.us/sac/cwp/view.asp?a=1090&q=436810&sacNav=|
Builder/Owner, Real Estate #20	http://licensepa.state.pa.us/default.asp
Campground Membership Seller #20	http://licensepa.state.pa.us/default.asp
Cemetery Broker/Seller/Regis. #20	http://licensepa.state.pa.us/default.asp
Check Casher #4	www.banking.state.pa.us/Banking/Banking/InstListQuery.asp
Chiropractor #20	http://licensepa.state.pa.us/default.asp
Consumer Discount Company #4	www.banking.state.pa.us/Banking/Banking/InstListQuery.asp
Continuing Edu. Provider, Financial #4	www.banking.state.pa.us/Banking/Banking/InstListQuery.asp
Cosmetologist/Cosmetician #20	http://licensepa.state.pa.us/default.asp
Cosmetology Teacher/School #20	http://licensepa.state.pa.us/default.asp
Cosmetology/Manicurist Shop #20	http://licensepa.state.pa.us/default.asp
Counselor, Professional #20	http://licensepa.state.pa.us/default.asp
Credit Services Loan Broker #4	www.banking.state.pa.us/Banking/Banking/InstListQuery.asp
Credit Union #4	www.banking.state.pa.us/Banking/Banking/InstListQuery.asp
Debt Collector #4	www.banking.state.pa.us/Banking/Banking/InstListQuery.asp
Dental Assist., Expanded Function #18	www.mylicense.state.pa.us
Dental Hygienist #18	www.mylicense.state.pa.us
Dentist #18	www.mylicense.state.pa.us
Dietitian/Nutritionist LDN #20	http://licensepa.state.pa.us/default.asp
Engineer #20	http://licensepa.state.pa.us/default.asp
Evaluator, Appraisal #20	http://licensepa.state.pa.us/default.asp
Financial Holding Company #4	www.banking.state.pa.us/Banking/Banking/InstListQuery.asp
Funeral Director/Supervisor/Establishment #20	http://licensepa.state.pa.us/default.asp
Geologist #20	http://licensepa.state.pa.us/default.asp
Hearing Examiners #20	http://licensepa.state.pa.us/default.asp
Installment Loan Seller #4	www.banking.state.pa.us/Banking/Banking/InstListQuery.asp
Insurance Agent #11	http://164.156.71.30/producer/ilist1.asp
Landscape Architect #20	http://licensepa.state.pa.us/default.asp
Loan Correspondent #4	www.banking.state.pa.us/Banking/Banking/InstListQuery.asp
Lobbyist #17	www.lobbyistnetwork.com/
Manicurist #20	http://licensepa.state.pa.us/default.asp
Marriage & Family Therapist #20	http://licensepa.state.pa.us/default.asp
Medical Doctor #20	http://licensepa.state.pa.us/default.asp
Midwife #20	http://licensepa.state.pa.us/default.asp
Money Transmitter #4	www.banking.state.pa.us/Banking/Banking/InstListQuery.asp
Mortgage (1st) Banker/Broker/Limited Broker #4	www.banking.state.pa.us/Banking/Banking/InstListQuery.asp
Mortgage (1st) Loan Correspondent #4	www.banking.state.pa.us/Banking/Banking/InstListQuery.asp
Mortgage (2nd) Lender/Broker/Agent #4	www.banking.state.pa.us/Banking/Banking/InstListQuery.asp

Mortgage (Accel'd) Paym't Provider #4 .... www.banking.state.pa.us/Banking/Banking/InstListQuery.asp
Nuclear Medicine Technologist #20 .... http://licensepa.state.pa.us/default.asp
Nurse #20 .... http://licensepa.state.pa.us/default.asp
Nursing Home Administrator #20 .... http://licensepa.state.pa.us/default.asp
Occupational Therapist/Assistant #20 .... http://licensepa.state.pa.us/default.asp
Optometrist #20 .... http://licensepa.state.pa.us/default.asp
Osteopathic Acupuncturist #20 .... http://licensepa.state.pa.us/default.asp
Osteopathic Physician Assistant #20 .... http://licensepa.state.pa.us/default.asp
Osteopathic Physician/Surgeon #20 .... http://licensepa.state.pa.us/default.asp
Osteopathic Respiratory Care #20 .... http://licensepa.state.pa.us/default.asp
Pawnbroker #4 .... www.banking.state.pa.us/Banking/Banking/InstListQuery.asp
Pharmacist/Pharmacy #20 .... http://licensepa.state.pa.us/default.asp
Physical Therapist/Assistant #20 .... http://licensepa.state.pa.us/default.asp
Physician Assistant #20 .... http://licensepa.state.pa.us/default.asp
Pilot, Navigational #20 .... http://licensepa.state.pa.us/default.asp
Podiatrist #20 .... http://licensepa.state.pa.us/default.asp
Psychologist #20 .... http://licensepa.state.pa.us/default.asp
Public Accountant-CPA #20 .... http://licensepa.state.pa.us/default.asp
Public Accounting Partnership #20 .... http://licensepa.state.pa.us/default.asp
Public Adjuster/ Solicitor #11 .... http://164.156.71.30/producer/ilist1.asp
Radiation Therapy Technician #20 .... http://licensepa.state.pa.us/default.asp
Radiologic Technologist #20 .... http://licensepa.state.pa.us/default.asp
Real Estate Agent/Broker/Sales/School #20 .... http://licensepa.state.pa.us/default.asp
Real Estate Appraiser #20 .... http://licensepa.state.pa.us/default.asp
Rental Listing Referral Agent #20 .... http://licensepa.state.pa.us/default.asp
Repossessor #4 .... www.banking.state.pa.us/Banking/Banking/InstListQuery.asp
Respiratory Care Practitioner #20 .... http://licensepa.state.pa.us/default.asp
Sales Finance Company #4 .... www.banking.state.pa.us/Banking/Banking/InstListQuery.asp
Savings Association #4 .... www.banking.state.pa.us/Banking/Banking/InstListQuery.asp
Social Worker #20 .... http://licensepa.state.pa.us/default.asp
Speech-Language Pathologist #20 .... http://licensepa.state.pa.us/default.asp
Surplus Lines Broker #11 .... http://164.156.71.30/producer/ilist1.asp
Surveyor, Land #20 .... http://licensepa.state.pa.us/default.asp
Table Funder, Wholesale #4 .... www.banking.state.pa.us/Banking/Banking/InstListQuery.asp
Teacher #6 .... https://www.tcs.ed.state.pa.us/validchk.asp
Therapist, Drugless #20 .... http://licensepa.state.pa.us/default.asp
Thrift Holding Company #4 .... www.banking.state.pa.us/Banking/Banking/InstListQuery.asp
Timeshare Salesperson #20 .... http://licensepa.state.pa.us/default.asp
Trust Company #4 .... www.banking.state.pa.us/Banking/Banking/InstListQuery.asp
Used Vehicle Lot #19 .... http://licensepa.state.pa.us/
Vehicle Auction #19 .... http://licensepa.state.pa.us/
Vehicle Dealer/Manufacturer/Dist. #19 .... http://licensepa.state.pa.us/
Vehicle Salesperson #19 .... http://licensepa.state.pa.us/
Veterinarian / Veterinary Technician #20 .... http://licensepa.state.pa.us/default.asp
Viatical Settlement Broker #11 .... http://164.156.71.30/producer/ilist1.asp

Pennsylvania Licensing Quick Finder

Acupuncturist #20 717-783-4858
Ambulance Service #8 717-787-8740
Amphetamine Program #20 717-787-2568
Anesthesia Permit, Dental #18 717-783-7162
Animal Health Technician #20 717-783-7134
Appraiser, Resi'l/Appraiser/Broker #20 . 717-783-4866
Architect #20 717-783-3397
Architectural Firm #20 717-783-3397
Athletic Agent #15 717-787-5720
Athletic Event Manager #15 717-787-5720
Athletic Event Ring Announcer/Timekeeper #15
    717-787-5720
Athletic Physician/Trainer #15 717-787-5720
Athletic Trainer #20 717-783-4858
Attorney #1 717-731-7073
Attorney, Disciplined #1 717-731-7073
Auction House/Company #20 717-783-3397
Auctioneer #20 717-783-3397
Auctioneer, Real Estate #20 717-783-3658
Audiologist #20 717-783-1389

Bank #4 717-787-3717
Barber/Barber Shop/Manager #20 717-783-3402
Barber School/Teacher #20 717-783-3402
Boat Registration #13 717-705-7940
Boxer #15 717-787-5720
Boxing Judge/Promoter/Second #15 717-787-5720
Builder/Owner, Real Estate #20 717-783-3658
Campground Membership Seller #20 .. 717-783-3658
Cemetery Broker/Seller/Regis. #20 717-783-3658
Check Casher #4 717-787-3717
Child Day Care Facility #12 717-787-8691
Chiropractor #20 717-783-7155
Consumer Discount Company #4 717-787-3717
Continuing Education Provider, Financial #4
    717-787-3717
Cosmetologist/Cosmetician #20 717-783-7130
Cosmetology Teacher/School #20 717-783-7130
Cosmetology/Manicurist Shop #20 717-783-7130
Counselor, Professional #20 717-783-1389
Credit Services Loan Broker #4 717-787-3717

Credit Union #4 717-787-3717
Debt Collector #4 717-787-3717
Dental Asst, Expanded Function #18 ... 717-783-7162
Dentist / Dental Hygienist #18 717-783-7162
Dietitian/Nutritionist LDN #20 717-783-7142
Education Specialist #6 717-787-3356
Emergency Health Professional #8 717-787-8740
Emergency Medical Technician #8 717-787-8740
Engineer #20 717-783-7049
Evaluator, Appraisal #20 717-783-4866
Financial Holding Company #4 717-787-3717
First Responder EMT #8 717-787-8740
Funeral Director/Supvr/Establ't #20 717-783-3397
Geologist #20 717-783-7049
Harness Racing #3 717-787-5789
Hearing Aid Dealer #7 717-783-1389
Hearing Aid Fitter/Fitter Apprentice #7 . 717-783-1389
Hearing Examiners #20 717-783-1389
Horse Racing #3 717-783-8726
Installment Loan Seller #4 717-787-3717

Insurance Agent #11 ... 717-787-3840, 877-336-7479	
Insurance Company #11	717-787-2735
Investment Adviser #16	717-783-4211
Kickboxer #15	717-787-5720
Laboratory, Medical #10	610-280-3464
Landscape Architect #20	717-772-8528
Liquor Distributor/Retailer/Whls #14	717-783-8250
Loan Correspondent #4	717-787-3717
Lobbyist #17	717-787-5920
Manicurist #20	717-783-7130
Marriage & Family Therapist #20	717-783-1389
Medical Doctor #20	717-787-2381
Medical School #20	717-783-1400
Midwife #20	717-783-1400
Money Transmitter #4	717-787-3717
Mortgage (1st) Banker/Broker #4	717-787-3717
Mortgage (1st) Loan Correspondent #4 717-787-3717	
Mortgage (2nd) Lender/Loan Broker/Agent #4	
	717-787-3717
Mortgage (Accelerated) Payment Provider #4	
	717-787-3717
Notary Public #5	717-787-5280
Nuclear Medicine Technologist #20	717-787-4858
Nurse #20	717-783-7142
Nursing Home #9	610-594-8041
Nursing Home Administrator #20	717-783-7155
Occupational Therapist/Assistant #20	717-783-1389
Optometrist #20	717-783-7155
Osteopathic Acupuncturist #20	717-783-4858
Osteopathic Physician Assistant #20	717-783-4858

Osteopathic Physician/Surgeon #20	717-783-4858
Osteopathic Respiratory Care #20	717-783-4858
Paramedic #8	717-787-8740
Pawnbroker #4	717-787-3717
Pest Management Consultant #2	717-787-5231 x2
Pesticide Applicator/Technician #2	717-787-5231 x2
Pesticide Dealer #2	717-787-5231 x2
Pharmacist/Pharmacy #20	717-783-7156
Physical Therapist/Assistant #20	717-783-7134
Physician Assistant #20	717-787-2381
Pilot, Navigational #20	717-787-6802
Podiatrist #20	717-783-4858
Pre-Hospital RN #8	717-787-8740
Private Investigator #15	717-255-2692
Private School Staff #6	717-783-3356
Professional Bondsman #11	
	717-787-3840, 877-336-7479
Psychologist #20	717-783-7134
Public Accountant-CPA, Individual/Corp. #20	
	717-783-1404
Public Accounting Partnership #20	717-783-1404
Public Adjuster/ Solicitor #11	
	717-787-3840, 877-336-7479
Radiation Therapy Technician #20	717-783-7155
Radiologic Auxiliary, Chiropractic #20	717-783-7155
Radiologic Technologist #20	717-783-4858
Real Estate Agent/Broker/Sales #20	717-783-3658
Real Estate Appraiser #20	717-783-4866
Real Estate School #20	717-783-3658
Referee #15	717-787-5720

Rental Listing Referral Agent #20	717-783-3658
Repossessor #4	717-787-3717
Respiratory Care Practitioner #20	717-783-4858
Sales Finance Company #4	717-787-3717
Savings Association #4	717-787-3717
School Administrator/Super. #6	717-783-3356
School Intermediate Unit Director #6	717-783-3356
School Supervisor #6	717-783-3356
Securities Agent #16	717-783-4212
Securities Broker/Dealer #16	717-783-4213
Social Worker #20	717-783-1389
Speech-Language Pathologist #20	717-783-1389
Surplus Lines Broker #11 717-787-3840, 877-336-7479	
Surveyor, Land #20	717-783-7049
Table Funder, Wholesale #4	717-787-3717
Teacher #6	717-787-3356
Therapist, Drugless #20	717-783-4858
Thrift Holding Company #4	717-787-3717
Timeshare Salesperson #20	717-783-3658
Title Insurance #11	717-787-3840, 877-336-7479
Trust Company #4	717-787-3717
Used Vehicle Lot #19	717-783-1697
Vehicle Auction #19	717-783-1697
Vehicle Dealer/Manufacturer/Dist. #19	717-783-1697
Vehicle Salesperson #19	717-783-1697
Veterinarian #20	717-783-7134
Veterinary Technician #20	717-783-7134
Viatical Settlement Broker #11	
	717-787-3840, 877-336-7479
Wrestling Promoter #15	717-787-5720

Pennsylvania Licensing Agency Information

1 Disciplinary Board of the Supreme Court, 2 Lemoyne Dr, First Fl, Lemoyne, PA 17055; 717-731-7073, Fax: 717-731-7080. www.padisciplinaryboard.org/ Search Database at www.padisciplinaryboard.org/disciplined_attorneys.html

2 Department of Agriculture, Bureau of Plant Industry, 2301 N Cameron St, Harrisburg, PA 17110-9408; 717-772-5231, Fax: 717-783-3275. www.agriculture.state.pa.us/ Email: dascott@state.pa.us

3 Department of Agriculture, Racing License Division, 2301 N Cameron St, Agriculture Office Bldg, Harrisburg, PA 17110-9408; 717-787-5196, Fax: 717-787-2271. www.pda.state.pa.us

4 Department of Banking, 333 Market St, 16th Fl, Harrisburg, PA 17111-2290; 717-214-8343, Fax: 717-787-8773. www.banking.state.pa.us/ Email: pabanking@banking.state.pa.us

5 Department of State, Elections & Legislation, 210 North Office Bldg, Rm 304, Harrisburg, PA 17120; 717-787-5280, Fax: 717-787-2854. www.dos.state.pa.us/bcel/site/default.asp Email: rcole@state.pa.us

6 Department of Education, Teacher Certification, 333 Market St, 3rd Fl, Harrisburg, PA 17126-0333; 717-787-3356, Fax: 717-783-6736. www.pde.state.pa.us Email: na-teachercert@state.pa.us Search Database at https://www.tcs.ed.state.pa.us/validchk.asp Note: Use a teacher's SSN to verify certifications.

7 Bureau of Profession and Occupational Affairs, Board of Examiners in Speech-Language and Hearing, PO Box 2649, Harrisburg, PA 17105; 717-783-1389, Fax: 717-787-7769. www.dos.state.pa.us/speech   *more*

Email: st-speech@state.pa.us Note: Direct list requests to Diane Miller at (717) 772-2244 or via email: diamiller@state.pa.us.

8 Department of Health, Emergency Medical Services, PO Box 90 (7th & Forster), Harrisburg, PA 17108; 717-787-8740, Fax: 717-772-0910. www.dsf.health.state.pa.us/health/site/

9 Department of Health, Long Term Care Division, 110 Pickering Way, Lionville, PA 19353; 610-594-8041, Fax: 610-436-3346. www.health.state.pa.us/qa/ltc

10 Department of Health, Bureau of Labs, PO Box 500, Exton, PA 19341-0500; 610-280-3464, Fax: 610-594-9763. www.health.state.pa.us/HPA/labinvst.htm

11 Department of Insurance, 1300 Strawberry Sq, Harrisburg, PA 17120; 717-787-2735, Fax: 717-787-8557. www.ins.state.pa.us/ins/site/default.asp

12 Department of Public Welfare, 1401 N 7th St., Harrisburg, PA 17105; 717-787-8691, Fax: 717-787-1529.

13 Fish & Boat Commission, 1601 Elmerton Ave, Harrisburg, PA 17110-9299; 717-705-7940, Fax: 717-705-7931. www.fish.state.pa.us

14 Liquor Control Board, PO Box 8940 (Capitol & Forester St), Harrisburg, PA 17105-8940; 717-783-8250, Fax: 717-772-2165. www.lcb.state.pa.us

15 Department of State, Athletic Commission, 2601 North 3rd Street, Harrisburg, PA 17110; 717-787-5720, Fax: 717-783-0824. www.dos.state.pa.us/sac/site/default.asp Email: ST-SAC@state.pa.us

16 Securities Commission, 1010 N 7th St, Eastgate-2nd Fl, Harrisburg, PA 17102-1410; 717-787-8061, Fax: 717-783-5122. www.psc.state.pa.us

17 State Ethics Commission, 309 Finance Bldg, PO Box 11470, Harrisburg, PA 17108-1470; 717-783-1610, Fax: 717-783-0806. www.ethics.state.pa.us Search Database at www.lobbyistnetwork.com/ Note: The PA Online Lobbyist Network can be searched free at www.lobbyistnetwork.com.

18 Department of State, Board of Dentistry, PO Box 2649 (124 Pine St), Harrisburg, PA 17105-2649; 717-783-7162, Fax: 717-787-7769. www.dos.state.pa.us/dent Email: st-dentistry@state.pa.us Search Database at www.mylicense.state.pa.us Note: Direct list requests to Diane Miller at (717) 772-2244 or via email: diamiller@state.pa.us.

19 Dept. of State, Professional & Occupational Affairs, Board of Vehicle Manufacturers, Dealers & Salespersons, Box 2649 (2601 Northfield St), Harrisburg, PA 17110; 717-783-1697, Fax: 717-787-0250. www.dos.state.pa.us/vehicle Email: ra-st-vehicle@state.pa.us Search Database at http://licensepa.state.pa.us/ Note: For verifications you may contact the Board via email at vehicle@pados.dos.state.pa.us. Direct list requests to Diane Miller at (717) 772-2244 or via email: diamiller@state.pa.us.

20 Department of State, Professional & Occupational Affairs, P.O. Box 2649 (124 Pine St), Harrisburg, PA 17105; 717-787-8503, Fax: 717-787-7769. www.dos.state.pa.us/bpoa/site/default.asp Email: RA-BPOA@state.pa.us Search Database at http://licensepa.state.pa.us/default.asp Direct list requests to Diane Miller at 717-772-2244 or via email: diamiller@state.pa.us.

Pennsylvania Federal Courts

The following list indicates the district and division name for each county in the state. If the bankruptcy court location is different from the district court, then the location of the bankruptcy court appears in parentheses.

Pennsylvania County/Court Cross Reference

County	District	Division
Adams	Middle	Harrisburg
Allegheny	Western	Pittsburgh
Armstrong	Western	Pittsburgh
Beaver	Western	Pittsburgh
Bedford	Western	Johnstown (Pittsburgh)
Berks	Eastern	Allentown/Reading (Reading)
Blair	Western	Johnstown (Pittsburgh)
Bradford	Middle	Scranton (Wilkes-Barre)
Bucks	Eastern	Philadelphia
Butler	Western	Pittsburgh
Cambria	Western	Johnstown (Pittsburgh)
Cameron	Middle	Williamsport (Wilkes-Barre)
Carbon	Middle	Scranton (Wilkes-Barre)
Centre	Middle	Williamsport (Harrisburg)
Chester	Eastern	Philadelphia
Clarion	Western	Pittsburgh (Erie)
Clearfield	Western	Johnstown (Pittsburgh)
Clinton	Middle	Williamsport (Wilkes-Barre)
Columbia	Middle	Williamsport (Wilkes-Barre)
Crawford	Western	Erie
Cumberland	Middle	Harrisburg
Dauphin	Middle	Harrisburg
Delaware	Eastern	Philadelphia
Elk	Western	Erie
Erie	Western	Erie
Fayette	Western	Pittsburgh
Forest	Western	Erie
Franklin	Middle	Harrisburg
Fulton	Middle	Harrisburg
Greene	Western	Pittsburgh
Huntingdon	Middle	Harrisburg
Indiana	Western	Pittsburgh
Jefferson	Western	Pittsburgh (Erie)
Juniata	Middle	Harrisburg
Lackawanna	Middle	Scranton (Wilkes-Barre)
Lancaster	Eastern	Allentown/Reading (Reading)
Lawrence	Western	Pittsburgh
Lebanon	Middle	Harrisburg
Lehigh	Eastern	Allentown/Reading (Reading)
Luzerne	Middle	Scranton (Wilkes-Barre)
Lycoming	Middle	Williamsport (Wilkes-Barre)
McKean	Western	Erie
Mercer	Western	Pittsburgh (Erie)
Mifflin	Middle	Harrisburg
Monroe	Middle	Scranton (Wilkes-Barre)
Montgomery	Eastern	Philadelphia
Montour	Middle	Williamsport (Harrisburg)
Northampton	Eastern	Allentown/Reading (Reading)
Northumberland	Middle	Williamsport (Harrisburg)
Perry	Middle	Williamsport (Harrisburg)
Philadelphia	Eastern	Philadelphia
Pike	Middle	Scranton (Wilkes-Barre)
Potter	Middle	Williamsport (Wilkes-Barre)
Schuylkill	Eastern	Allentown/Reading(Wilkes-Barre)
Snyder	Middle	Williamsport (Harrisburg)
Somerset	Western	Johnstown (Pittsburgh)
Sullivan	Middle	Williamsport (Wilkes-Barre)
Susquehanna	Middle	Scranton (Wilkes-Barre)
Tioga	Middle	Williamsport (Wilkes-Barre)
Union	Middle	Williamsport (Harrisburg)
Venango	Western	Erie
Warren	Western	Erie
Washington	Western	Pittsburgh
Wayne	Middle	Scranton (Wilkes-Barre)
Westmoreland	Western	Pittsburgh
Wyoming	Middle	Scranton (Wilkes-Barre)
York	Middle	Harrisburg

Standards for Federal Courts: Search fee is $26.00 per item (one party name or case number). Copy fee is $.50 per page. Certification fee is $9.00 per document, double for exemplification, if available. All fees standard unless noted in profile. Mail Search: always enclose a stamped self addressed envelope unless otherwise noted. Most courts accept fax requests or will suggest a copying/search vendor. Before releasing records, all courts require prepayment, unless noted.

Open records are located at the court unless otherwise noted. District courts index by defendant and plaintiff as well as by case number. Bankruptcy courts usually index by debtor and case number. While most courts now have their indexes on computer, many may still maintain index card files as well.

Courts offering internet access via CM-ECF or older RACER, PACER, or Web-PACER systems charge $.08 per page fee unless noted as free. Where PACER is available, the universal sign-up number is 800-676-6856. Find PACER and the US Party/Case Index at http://pacer.psc.uscourts.gov.

US District Court

Eastern District of Pennsylvania

Allentown/Reading Division Court Clerk, c/o Philadelphia Division, Rm 2609, US Courthouse, 601 Market St, Philadelphia, PA 19106-1797 (also use mail address for courier delivery), 215-597-7704, records rm- 267-597-7082, Fax-267-299-7135. Hours- 8:30AM-5PM. www.paed.uscourts.gov

Counties: Berks, Lancaster, Lehigh, Northampton, Schuylkill.

Searches & Indexing: Results do not include SSN or DOB. New cases in the index immediately after filing date. Records purged never. Open records located at Philadelphia Division.

Fee & Payment: Pay by money order, cashier's, business or personal check. Payee: Clerk, US District Court.

Phone Search: No searching by telephone.

Mail Search: Include SASE for return.

In Person Search: Fee charged if court performs your search. No self-serve copier available.

E-Services: PACER records go back to 7/1990. New records online after 1 day. ECF at https://ecf.paed.uscourts.gov. Criminal cases go back to 7/1992. **Opinions Online:** www.paed.uscourts.gov/us03006.asp. Opinions go back to 1997. **Other Online Access:** Online access is available free at www.paed.uscourts.gov/us04000.asp?19. No fee to search; select document type and enter name as search string.

Philadelphia Division Court Clerk, Rm 2609, US Courthouse, 601 Market St, Philadelphia, PA 19106-1797 (also use mail address for courier delivery), 215-597-7704, records rm- 267-299-7082, Fax-267-299-7135. Hours- 8:30AM-5PM. www.paed.uscourts.gov

Counties: Bucks, Chester, Delaware, Montgomery, Philadelphia.

Searches & Indexing: Results do not include SSN or DOB. Computer index back to 1990 maintained; also microfiche index. Indexes by judgment also available. New cases in the index immediately after filing date. Records purged never. District-wide searches available here.

Fee & Payment: Pay by Visa/MC, money order, cashier's, business or personal check. Payee: Clerk, US District Court. Will fax docket listings $.10 per page.

Phone Search: Docket information available via phone if case number is known.

Mail Search: search usually completed- up to 14 days. Include SASE for return.

In Person Search: Fee charged if court performs your search. No self-serve copier available.

E-Services: PACER records go back to 7/1990. New records online after 1 day. ECF at https://ecf.paed.uscourts.gov. Criminal cases go back to 7/1992. **Opinions Online:** www.paed.uscourts.gov/us03006.asp. Opinions go back to 1997. **Other Online Access:** Online access is free at www.paed.uscourts.gov/. No fee to search; select document type and enter name as search string.

US Bankruptcy Court

Eastern District of Pennsylvania

Philadelphia Division Court Clerk, 4th Fl, 900 Market St, Philadelphia, PA 19107 (also use mail address for courier delivery), 215-408-2800. Hours- 8:30AM-5PM. www.paeb.uscourts.gov

Counties: Bucks, Chester, Delaware, Montgomery, Philadelphia.

Searches & Indexing: Cases indexed by debtor, creditors, and case number. Results do not include SSN or DOB. Card and microfiche indexes maintained. New cases in the index 1 day after filing date. Records purged every 6 months.

Fee & Payment: Pay by Visa/MC, money order, cashier check, business check. No personal checks. Payee: Clerk, US Bankruptcy Court. Prepayment required.

Phone Search: Voice Case Information Service available, call VCIS at 215-597-2244.

Mail Search: search usually completed- 3 days. Include SASE for return.

In Person Search: Fee charged if court performs your search. In person searchers may not search the card index. Self-serve copier available - $.25 per page.

E-Services: PACER online at http://pacer.paeb.uscourts.gov. PACER records go back to 1988. New records online after 1 day. ECF at https://ecf.paeb.uscourts.gov **Other Online Access:** Click on "Published Opinions" at main website. Limited calendars are also available.

Reading Division Court Clerk, The Madison, 400 Washington St, Reading, PA 19601 (also use mail address for courier delivery), 610-320-5255. Hours- 8AM-4:30PM. www.paeb.uscourts.gov

Counties: Berks, Lancaster, Lehigh, Northampton.

Searches & Indexing: Results include last 4 SSN digits. Both computer and card indexes maintained. New cases in the index 1 day after filing date. Records purged every 6 months.

Fee & Payment: Pay by Visa/MC, money order, cashier check, business check. No personal checks. Payee: Clerk, US Bankruptcy Court. Prepayment required.

Phone Search: Only docket information is available by phone. Voice Case Information Service available, call VCIS at 215-597-2244.

Mail Search: search usually completed- 1-2 weeks. Include SASE for return.

In Person Search: Fee charged if court performs your search. No self-serve copier available.

E-Services: PACER online at http://pacer.paeb.uscourts.gov. PACER records go back to 1988. New records online after 1 day. ECF at https://ecf.paeb.uscourts.gov **Other Online Access:** Click on "Published Opinions" at main website. Limited calendars are also available.

US District Court

Middle District of Pennsylvania

Harrisburg Division Court Clerk, PO Box 983, Harrisburg, PA 17108-0983 (courier address: US Courthouse & Federal Bldg, 228 Walnut St, Harrisburg, PA 17108), 717-221-3920, records rm-717-221-3924, Fax-717-221-3959. Hours-8:30AM-5PM. www.pamd.uscourts.gov

Counties: Adams, Cumberland, Dauphin, Franklin, Fulton, Huntingdon, Juniata, Lebanon, Mifflin, York.

Searches & Indexing: Results do not include SSN or DOB. Both computer and card indexes maintained; computer back to 2003. New cases in the index immediately after filing date. Records purged never.

Fee & Payment: Pay by Visa, money order, cashier's or personal check. Payee: Clerk, US District Court. Prepayment required. Will fax documents $1.00 per page.

Phone Search: Only accession numbers for a specific case are available by phone.

Mail Search: search usually completed- 2-3 days. SASE not required.

In Person Search: Fee charged if court performs your search. No self-serve copier available.

E-Services: ECF replaces PACER whose records did go back to 5/1989. New records online after 1 day. ECF at https://ecf.pamd.uscourts.gov. Document images available. **Opinions Online:** www.pamd.uscourts.gov/opinions.htm.

Scranton Division Court Clerk, Clerk's Office, W J Nealon Federal Bldg & US Courthouse, PO Box 1148, Scranton, PA 18501 (courier address: 235 N Washington Ave, Rm 101, Scranton, PA 18503), 570-207-5680, Fax-717-207-5689 records rm fax- 717-207-5650; fax record requests to-717-207-5650. Hours- 8:30AM-5PM. www.pamd.uscourts.gov

Counties: Bradford, Carbon, Lackawanna, Luzerne, Monroe, Pike, Susquehanna, Wayne, Wyoming.

Searches & Indexing: Results do not include SSN or DOB. Computer index back to 1980 maintained; also microfiche index. New cases in the index 1 day after filing date. Records purged never. District-wide searches available here back to 1901.

Fee & Payment: Pay by Visa/MC, money order, cashier's or personal check. Payee: Clerk, US District Court. Prepayment required.

Phone Search: Only minimal docket information is released via phone.

Mail Search: search usually completed- 7 days. SASE not required.

In Person Search: Fee charged if court performs your search. No self-serve copier available.

E-Services: ECF replaces PACER whose records did go back to 5/1989. New records online after 1 day. ECF at https://ecf.pamd.uscourts.gov. Document images available. **Opinions Online:** www.pamd.uscourts.gov/opinions.htm.

Williamsport Division Court Clerk, Federal Bldg, Rm 218, 240 W 3rd St, Williamsport, PA 17701 (also use mail address for courier delivery), 570-323-6380, Fax-570-323-0636. Hours-8:30AM-5PM. www.pamd.uscourts.gov

Counties: Cameron, Centre, Clinton, Columbia, Lycoming, Montour, Northumberland, Perry, Potter, Snyder, Sullivan, Tioga, Union.

Searches & Indexing: Results do not include SSN or DOB. Computer index back to 1980 maintained. New cases in the index immediately after filing date. Records purged never.

Fee & Payment: Pay by Visa/MC, money order, cashier's or personal check. Payee: Clerk, US District Court. Prepayment required.

Phone Search: Only docket information is available by phone.

Mail Search: search usually completed- 1-2 days. Include SASE for return.

In Person Search: Fee charged if court performs your search. No self-serve copier available.

E-Services: ECF replaces PACER whose records did go back to 5/1989. New records online after 1 day. ECF at https://ecf.pamd.uscourts.gov. Document images available. **Opinions Online:** www.pamd.uscourts.gov/opinions.htm.

US Bankruptcy Court

Middle District of Pennsylvania

Harrisburg Division Court Clerk, PO Box 908, Harrisburg, PA 17108 (courier address: 228 Walnut St, 3rd Fl, Harrisburg, PA 17101), 717-901-2800, Fax-717-901-2822. Hours- 8AM-5PM. www.pamb.uscourts.gov

Counties: Adams, Centre, Cumberland, Dauphin, Franklin, Fulton, Huntingdon, Juniata, Lebanon, Mifflin, Montour, Northumberland, Perry, Schuylkill, Snyder, Union, York.

Searches & Indexing: Results include last 4 SSN digits. Computer index maintained. New cases in the index 1 day after filing date. Records purged never.

Fee & Payment: Pay by money order, cashier's or personal check. No debtor's checks accepted. Payee: Clerk, US Bankruptcy Court. Prepayment required.

Phone Search: Only docket information is available by phone. Voice Case Information Service available, call VCIS at 877-440-2699.

Mail Search: search usually completed- within 1 week. Include SASE for return.

In Person Search: Fee charged if court performs your search. Dukum's Copy Service 717-236-

0179, available 9AM-1PM. No self-serve copier available.

E-Services: PACER online at http://pacer.pamb.uscourts.gov. Document images available. PACER records go back to 8/1986. New records online after 1 day. ECF at https://ecf.pamb.uscourts.gov **Other Online Access:** Calendars free at www.pamb.uscourts.gov/calendars.htm.

Wilkes-Barre Division Clerk's Office, Max Rosen US Courthouse, 197 S Main St, Wilkes-Barre, PA 18701 (also use mail address for courier delivery), 570-826-6450, Fax-570-826-6401. Hours- 8AM-5PM. www.pamb.uscourts.gov

Counties: Bradford, Cameron, Carbon, Clinton, Columbia, Lackawanna, Luzerne, Lycoming, Monroe, Pike, Potter, Schuylkill, Sullivan, Susquehanna, Tioga, Wayne, Wyoming.

Searches & Indexing: Results include last 4 SSN digits only. Computer index maintained. New cases in the index 1-3 days after filing date.

Fee & Payment: Pay by money order, cashier's or personal check. No debtor's checks accepted. Payee: Clerk, US Bankruptcy Court.

Phone Search: Court conducts phone searches if name, SSN, or case number is provided; only docket information is released. Voice Case Information Service available, call VCIS at 877-440-2699.

Mail Search: search usually completed- 1-2 days. Include SASE for return.

In Person Search: permitted.

E-Services: PACER online at http://pacer.pamb.uscourts.gov. Document images available. PACER records go back to 1987. New records online after 1 day. ECF at https://ecf.pamb.uscourts.gov **Other Online Access:** Calendars free at www.pamb.uscourts.gov/calendars.htm.

US District Court

Western District of Pennsylvania

Erie Division Court Clerk, PO Box 1820, Erie, PA 16507 (courier address: 17 S Park Row, Erie, PA 16501), 814-464-9600. Hours- 8:30AM-4:30PM. www.pawd.uscourts.gov

Counties: Crawford, Elk, Erie, Forest, McKean, Venango, Warren.

Searches & Indexing: Court prefers that you perform searches at Pittsburgh Division. Results do not include SSN or DOB. Both computer and card indexes maintained. New cases in the index 1 day after filing date. Records purged never.

Fee & Payment: Pay by Visa/MC, money order, cashier's or personal check. Payee: Clerk, US District Court. Prepayment required.

Phone Search: Only case number, caption and attorneys' names released via phone.

Mail Search: search usually completed- 1-2 days. Include SASE for return.

In Person Search: Fee charged if court performs your search. No self-serve copier available.

E-Services: PACER online at http://pacer.pawd.uscourts.gov. PACER records go back to 1989. New records online after 1 day. ECF

at https://ecf.pawd.uscourts.gov **Opinions Online:** www.pawd.uscourts.gov/Pages/opinions.htm. Search opinions by judge name. **Other Online Access:** Access daily court calendar at www.pawd.uscourts.gov.

Johnstown Division Court Clerk, Penn Traffic Bldg, Rm 208, 319 Washington St, Johnstown, PA 15901 (also use mail address for courier delivery), 814-533-4504, Fax-814-533-4519. 8:30AM-4:30PM. www.pawd.uscourts.gov

Counties: Bedford, Blair, Cambria, Clearfield, Somerset.

Searches & Indexing: Results do not include SSN or DOB. Both computer and card indexes maintained; computer back to 6/1992. Card index from 1989 to 1992. New cases in the index 1 day after filing date. Records purged never.

Fee & Payment: Pay by Visa/MC, money order, cashier's or personal check. Payee: Clerk, US District Court. Prepayment required.

Phone Search: Only case number, caption and attorneys' names released via phone.

Mail Search: search usually completed- 1 day. SASE not required.

In Person Search: Fee charged if court performs your search. No self-serve copier available.

E-Services: PACER online at http://pacer.pawd.uscourts.gov. PACER records go back to 1989. New records online after 1 day. ECF at https://ecf.pawd.uscourts.gov **Opinions Online:** www.pawd.uscourts.gov/Pages/opinions.htm. Search opinions by judge name. **Other Online Access:** Access daily court calendar at www.pawd.uscourts.gov.

Pittsburgh Division Court Clerk, US Post Office & Courthouse, Rm 311, 700 Grant St, Pittsburgh, PA 15219 (also use mail address for courier delivery), 412-208-7500, records rm- 412-208-7507. Hours- 8:30AM-4:30PM. www.pawd.uscourts.gov

Counties: Allegheny, Armstrong, Beaver, Butler, Clarion, Fayette, Greene, Indiana, Jefferson, Lawrence, Mercer, Washington, Westmoreland.

Searches & Indexing: Erie and Johnstown Divisions send complete paper copies of case records to Pittsburgh, so all District case records are here. Results do not include SSN or DOB. Both computer and card indexes maintained; computer goes back to 1992. New cases in the index 2 days after filing date. Records purged never.

Fee & Payment: Pay by Visa/MC, money order, cashier's or personal check. Payee: Clerk, US District Court. Prepayment required.

Phone Search: Only docket information is available by phone.

Mail Search: search usually completed- 1 day. Include SASE for return.

In Person Search: Fee charged if court performs your search. No self-serve copier available.

E-Services: ECF replaces PACER whose records did go back to 1989. New records online after 1 day. ECF at https://ecf.pawd.uscourts.gov **Opinions Online:** www.pawd.uscourts.gov/Pages/opinions.htm. Search opinions by judge name. **Other Online Access:** Access daily court calendar at www.pawd.uscourts.gov.

US Bankruptcy Court

Western District of Pennsylvania

Erie Division Court Clerk, 17 S Park Row, Rm B160, Erie, PA 16501 (also use mail address for courier delivery), 814-464-9740. Hours- 9AM-4:30PM. www.pawb.uscourts.gov

Counties: Clarion, Crawford, Elk, Erie, Forest, Jefferson, McKean, Mercer, Venango, Warren.

Searches & Indexing: Computer index maintained. New cases in the index immediately after filing date. Records purged every 6 months.

Fee & Payment: Pay by money order, cashier's or personal check. No debtor's checks accepted. Payee: Clerk, US Bankruptcy Court. Prepayment required.

Phone Search: Docket information available by phone. Voice Case Information Service available, call VCIS at 412-355-3210.

Mail Search: search usually completed- 1-3 days. Include SASE for return.

In Person Search: Fee charged if court performs your search. No self-serve copier available.

E-Services: ECF replaces PACER whose records did go back to 1991. New records online after 1 day. ECF at https://ecf.pawb.uscourts.gov **Opinions Online:** www.pawb.uscourts.gov/opinions.htm. **Other Online Access:** Search calendars by judge's name free at www.pawb.uscourts.gov/calendar.htm.

Pittsburgh Division Court Clerk, 600 Grant St #5414, Pittsburgh, PA 15219-2801 (also use mail address for courier delivery), 412-644-2700. Hours- 9AM-4:30PM. www.pawb.uscourts.gov

Counties: Allegheny, Armstrong, Beaver, Bedford, Blair, Butler, Cambria, Clearfield, Fayette, Greene, Indiana, Lawrence, Somerset, Washington, Westmoreland.

Searches & Indexing: Results include last 4 SSN digits. Computer and microfiche indexes maintained. New cases in the index immediately after filing date. Records purged every 6 months. District-wide searches available here for cases back to 1986.

Fee & Payment: Pay by Visa/MC (in person only), money order, personal check. No debtor's checks accepted. Payee: Clerk, US Bankruptcy Court. Prepayment required.

Phone Search: Limited docket information available by phone. Voice Case Information Service available, call VCIS at 412-355-3210.

Mail Search: search usually completed- 1-2 days. Include SASE for return.

In Person Search: Fee charged if court performs your search. No self-serve copier available; you may use Mackey's copy service, 412-644-4874.

E-Services: ECF replaces PACER whose records did go back to 1991. New records online immediately. ECF at https://ecf.pawb.uscourts.gov **Opinions Online:** www.pawb.uscourts.gov/opinions.htm. **Other Online Access:** Search calendars by judge name free at www.pawb.uscourts.gov/calendar.htm

Pennsylvania County Courts

Court	Jurisdiction	No. of Courts	How Organized
Court of Common Pleas*	General	103	60 Districts
Philadelphia Municipal Court*	Municipal	1	1st District
Philadelphia Traffic Court	Municipal	1	1st District
Pittsburgh Magistrates Court	Municipal	1	Pittsburgh
Register of Wills*	Probate	67	
District Justice Courts	Limited	556	60 Districts

* Profiled in this Sourcebook.

Court	CIVIL								
	Tort	Contract	Real Estate	Min. Claim	Max. Claim	Small Claims	Estate	Eviction	Domestic Relations
Court of Common Pleas*	X	X	X	$0	No Max			X	X
Philadelphia Municipal Court*	X	X	X	$0	$10,000	$5000		X	X
Philadelphia Traffic Court									
Pittsburgh City Magistrates Court			X	$0	No Max				
Register of Wills*							X		
District Justice Courts	X	X	X	$0	$8000	$8000			

Court	CRIMINAL				
	Felony	Misdemeanor	DWI/DUI	Preliminary Hearing	Juvenile
Court of Common Pleas*	X	X	X	X	X
Philadelphia Municipal Court*	X	X	X	X	
Philadelphia Traffic Court					
Pittsburgh City Magistrates Court		X	X	X	
Register of Wills*					
District Justice Courts		X	X	X	

ADMINISTRATION   Administrative Office of Pennsylvania Courts, PO Box 229, Mechanicsburg, PA, 17055; 717-795-2097, Fax: 717-795-2013. www.courts.state.pa.us

COURT STRUCTURE   The Courts of Common Pleas are the general trial courts, with jurisdiction over both civil and criminal matters and appellate jurisdiction over matters disposed of by the special courts. The civil records clerk of the Court of Common Pleas is called the Prothonotary.

Small claims cases are, usually, handled by the District Justice Courts. These courts, which are designated as "special courts," also handle civil cases up to $8,000. However, all small claims and civil actions are recorded through the Prothonotary Section (civil) of the Court of Common Pleas, which then holds the records. It is not necessary to check with each Magisterial District Court, but rather to check with the Prothonotary for the county.

ONLINE ACCESS   The state's 556 District Justice Courts are served by a statewide, automated case management system; online access to the case management system is not available.

The Web Portal offers access to a variety of the Judiciary's Electronic Services (E-Services)

such as Web Docket Sheets, DA Link, Superior Court's Web Docketing Statements, etc. Web Docket provides public access to view and print Case Docket Sheets from Pennsylvania's three Appellate Courts and Criminal Cases only from Courts of Common Pleas. Search by docket number, name or organization. Go to http://ujsportal.pacourts.us for details. Also, search Appellate Court dockets at http://pacmsdocketsheet.aopc.org/.

The Infocon County Access System provides direct dial-up access to court record information for over 20 counties. Set up entails a $50.00 base set-up fee plus $25.00 per county. The monthly usage fee minimum is $25.00, plus time charges. For Information, call Infocon at 814-472-6066 or visit www.infoconcountyaccess.com.

ADDITIONAL INFORMATION

Fees vary widely among jurisdictions. Many courts will not conduct searches due to a lack of personnel or, if they do search, turnaround time may be excessively lengthy. Many courts have public access terminals for in-person searches.

PROBATE COURTS

Probate is handled by the Register of Wills.

Adams County

Court of Common Pleas - Civil 111-117 Baltimore St, Rm 103, Gettysburg, PA 17325; phone: 717-334-6781 X285; fax: 717-334-0532; hours 8AM-4:30PM (EST). *Civil, Eviction.*
Civil Records: Access: In person only. Visitors must perform in person searches themselves. Court makes copy: $.25 per page; same fee for self serve. Required to search: name, years to search. Civil cases indexed by defendant, plaintiff. Civil records on computer from 1988, some microfiche (dates unsure), on index from 1800s. Mail turnaround time 1-2 days.
General Information: Public terminal has only civil records back to 1988. No mental health, sealed records released. Certification fee: $4.75 per doc includes copies. Payee: Prothonotary. Personal checks accepted. Prepayment and SASE required.

Court of Common Pleas - Criminal 111-117 Baltimore St, Gettysburg, PA 17325; phone: 717-337-9806; fax: 717-334-9333; hours 8AM-4:30PM (EST). *Felony, Misdemeanor.*
Criminal Records: Access: Mail, in person, online. Both court and visitors may perform in person searches. No search fee, unless documentation required. Court makes copy: $.25 per page; same fee for self serve. Required to search: name, years to search, DOB. Criminal records on computer since 1986 on microfiche since 1974, previous records on microfilm to 1800s. Search dockets online free at http://ujsportal.pacourts.us/WebDocketSheets/OtherCriteria.aspx. Mail turnaround time 1 day.
General Information: Public terminal has only criminal records back to 1800s. No juvenile records released. Will fax documents for fee. Certification fee: $9.00 per certification. Payee: Clerk of Courts. Personal checks accepted; no third party checks. Prepayment and SASE required.

Register of Wills 111-117 Baltimore St Rm 102, Gettysburg, PA 17325; phone: 717-337-9826; fax: 717-334-1758; hours 8AM-4:30PM (EST). *Probate.*

Allegheny County

Court of Common Pleas - Civil City County Bldg, 414 Grant St, 1st Fl, Pittsburgh, PA 15219; phone: 412-350-4200; hours 8:30AM-4:30PM (EST). *Civil.*
www.alleghenycourts.us
Civil Records: Access: Mail, in person, online. Both court and visitors may perform in person searches. Search fee: $25.00 per name. Court makes copy: $.50 per page. Self serve copy fee: $.25 per page. Required to search: name, years to search. Civil cases indexed by defendant, plaintiff. Civil records archived from 1700s; on computer since 1/1/95. Online access to opinions at www.alleghenycourts.us/civil/search_opinions.asp. Also, search dockets online free at http://ujsportal.pacourts.us/WebDocketSheets/OtherCriteria.aspx. Mail turnaround time 10 days.
General Information: Public terminal has only civil records back to 1/1995. (Terminal also offers

Family Court records.) No juvenile records released. Will not fax documents. Certification fee: $8.00 per document. Payee: Prothonotary of Allegheny County. Business checks accepted. Prepayment required. Businesses may set up a draw down account. SASE required.

Court of Common Pleas - Criminal 220 Courthouse, 436 Grant St, Pittsburgh, PA 15219; phone: 412-350-5322; fax: 412-350-6154; hours 8:30AM-4:30PM (EST). *Felony, Misdemeanor.*
www.alleghenycourts.us/
Note: Pittsburgh Magistrate Court phone- 412-255-2700.
Criminal Records: Access: Mail, in person, online. Both court and visitors may perform in person searches. Search fee: $15.00 per name. Self serve copy fee: $.50 per page. Required to search: name, years to search, DOB; also helpful: SSN. Criminal records on files, microfilm back to 1800s; on computer since. Access to Common Pleas criminal records is free at https://www.alleghenycourts.us/cims/default.asp. Search by name, docket number or SSN. Also, as of 2/13/2006, search dockets online free by name at http://ujsportal.pacourts.us/WebDocketSheets/OtherCriteria.aspx. Mail turnaround time 2 days.
General Information: Public terminal has only criminal records back to 1988. All records public. Will fax back documents locally only, no add'l fee. Certification fee: $10.00 per doc includes copies. Payee: Clerk of Courts. Personal checks not accepted. Prepayment and SASE required.

Register of Wills 414 Grant St, City County Bldg, PIttsburgh, PA 15219; phone: 412-350-4183; fax: 412-350-3028; hours 8:30AM-4PM (EST). *Probate.*
www.county.allegheny.pa.us/regwills/index.asp

Armstrong County

Court of Common Pleas - Civil 500 E Market St, Kittanning, PA 16201; phone: 724-548-3251; probate phone: 724-548-3256; fax: 724-548-3236; hours 8AM-4:30PM (EST). *Civil, Eviction.*
www.geocities.com/acprothonotary
Civil Records: Access: Online, in person. Both court and visitors may perform in person searches. Search fee: $10.00. Court makes copy: $1.00 per page. Required to search: name, years to search. Civil cases indexed by defendant, plaintiff. Civil records on files, microfiche since 1930; on computer since 9/94. Online access is by subscription from private company - Infocon at www.infoconcountyaccess.com, 814-472-6066. See note at beginning of section.
General Information: Public terminal has only civil records back to 9/1994. No juvenile, civil commitment records released. Certification fee: $3.00. Payee: Prothonotary. Personal checks accepted. Prepayment required.

Court of Common Pleas - Criminal 500 Market St, Kittanning, PA 16201; phone: 724-548-3252; hours 8AM-4:30PM (EST). *Felony, Misdemeanor.*
www.co.armstrong.pa.us/courtindex.htm
Criminal Records: Access: Mail, online, in person. Both court and visitors may perform in person searches. Search fee: $10.00 per name. Court makes copy: $.50 per page, $1.00 if by mail. Self serve copy fee: $.50 per page. Required to search: name, years to search; also helpful: DOB, SSN. Criminal records in card file from early 1930; on computer since 1994. Search dockets online free at http://ujsportal.pacourts.us/WebDocketSheets/OtherCriteria.aspx. Also, see note at beginning of section. Mail turnaround time same day.
General Information: Public terminal has only criminal records back to 1994. No juvenile or mental health records released. Will not fax documents. Certification fee: $5.00 first page. Payee: Clerk of Courts. Personal checks accepted. Prepayment and SASE required.

Register of Wills 500 Market St, Armstrong County Courthouse, Kittanning, PA 16201; phone: 724-548-3256 X220; fax: 724-548-3236; hours 8AM-4:30PM (EST). *Probate.*
Note: Online access available by subscription from private company - Infocon - at www.infoconcountyaccess.com, 814-472-6066. See note at beginning of section.

Beaver County

Court of Common Pleas - Civil Beaver County Courthouse, 810 3rd St, Beaver, PA 15009; phone: 724-728-5700; hours 8:30AM-4:30PM (EST). *Civil, Eviction.*
www.co.beaver.pa.us/prothonotary/
Civil Records: Access: In person only. Both court and visitors may perform in person searches. No search fee. Court makes copy: $.25 per page. Required to search: name, years to search. Civil cases indexed by defendant, plaintiff. Civil records go back to 1800; on computer back to 1995. Mail turnaround time 1 week.
General Information: Public terminal has only civil records back to 1995. No sealed records released. Certification fee: $5.00 per cert includes copies. Payee: Prothonotary. Personal checks accepted. Prepayment required.

Court of Common Pleas - Criminal Beaver County Courthouse, 810 3rd St, Beaver, PA 15009; phone: 724-728-5700; fax: 724-728-8853; hours 8:30AM-4:30PM (EST). *Felony, Misdemeanor.*
www.co.beaver.pa.us
Criminal Records: Access: Fax, mail, in person, online. Both court and visitors may perform in person searches. Search fee: $17.50 per name. Court makes copy: $.25 per page. Required to search: name, years to search; also helpful: DOB, SSN. Criminal records on computer back to 1973, on microfiche since 1802. Search dockets online free at

http://ujsportal.pacourts.us/WebDocketSheets/Oth erCriteria.aspx. Mail turnaround time 1 week.

General Information: Public terminal has only criminal records. Records sealed by court order not released. Fee to fax documents is $1.00 per page. Certification fee: $8.75. Payee: Clerk of Courts Office. Personal checks accepted. Prepayment and SASE required.

Register of Wills Beaver County Courthouse, 810 3rd St, Beaver, PA 15009; phone: 724-728-5700 X11265, X11274; fax: 724-728-9810; hours 8:30AM-4:30PM (EST). *Probate.*

Bedford County

Court of Common Pleas - Criminal/Civil
Bedford County Courthouse, Bedford, PA 15522; phone: 814-623-4833; fax: 814-623-4831; hours 8:30AM-4:30PM (EST). *Felony, Misdemeanor, Civil, Eviction.*
Civil Records: Access: Mail, in person, online. Both court and visitors may perform in person searches. Search fee: $20.00 per name. Court makes copy: $.50 per page. Self serve copy fee: $.25 per page. Required to search: name, years to search. Civil cases indexed by defendant, plaintiff. Civil records on file from late 1700s. Online access is by subscription from private company - Infocon at www.infoconcountyaccess.com, 814-472-6066. See note at beginning of section. Mail turnaround time 2 weeks.
Criminal Records: Access: Mail, online, in person. Both court and visitors may perform in person searches. Search fee: $20.00 per name. Court makes copy: $.50 per page. Self serve copy fee: $.25 per page. Required to search: name, years to search, DOB. Criminal records on file from late 1700s. Online access to criminal records is the same as civil. Also, search dockets online free at http://ujsportal.pacourts.us/WebDocketSheets/Oth erCriteria.aspx. Mail turnaround time 2 weeks.
General Information: Public terminal goes back to 5/1998. No sex related or juvenile records released. Will fax documents to local or toll free line, if pre-paid. Certification fee: $4.50 includes copies. Payee: Prothonotary of Beford County. Personal checks not accepted. Prepayment and SASE required.

Register of Wills 200 S Juliana St, Bedford, PA 15522; phone: 814-623-4836; fax: 814-624-0488; hours 8:30AM-4:30PM (EST). *Probate, Misdemeanor.*
Note: Online access available by subscription from private company - Infocon at www.infoconcountyaccess.com, 814-472-6066. See note at beginning of section.

Berks County

Court of Common Pleas - Civil
Prothonotary, 633 Court St, 2nd Fl, Reading, PA 19601; phone: 610-478-6970; fax: 610-478-6969; hours 8AM-4PM (EST). *Civil, Eviction.*
Civil Records: Access: Mail, in person, online. Both court and visitors may perform in person searches. Court makes copy: $3.00 1st page; $1.00 each add'l page. Self serve copy fee: $.50 per page. Required to search: name, years to search. Civil cases indexed by defendant, plaintiff. Civil records partially on microfiche, on manual index files from 1750. Mail access limited to docket information only. The Register of Wills has a free searchable website at www.berksregofwills.com/search_page.htm including marriage, estate, birth and death records for the county. The estate and marriage records are current. Also, the Prothonatary has a remote system to access dockets from 2002 forward. Fee is $300 per year. For information, call 610-478-6967. Mail turnaround time 1-2 days.
General Information: Public terminal has only civil records. No mental, sealed records released. Will fax documents $5.00 1st page, $1.00 each add'l; for emergency only. Certification fee: $5.25. Payee: Prothonotary. Personal checks accepted. Prepayment and SASE required.

Court of Common Pleas - Criminal 4th Fl, 633 Court St, Reading, PA 19601; phone: 610-478-6550; fax: 610-478-6593; hours 8AM-5PM (EST). *Felony, Misdemeanor.*
Criminal Records: Access: Mail, in person, online. Visitors must perform in person searches themselves. No search fee. Court makes copy: $.25 per page first 10, then $1.00 per page. Required to search: name, years to search; also helpful: DOB, SSN. Criminal records on computer from 1985 in files from 1992, prior archived. Beginning 6/6/2005, search dockets online free at http://ujsportal.pacourts.us/WebDocketSheets/Oth erCriteria.aspx. Note: Will not do name lists by mail. Mail turnaround time 5 days.
General Information: Public terminal has only criminal records back to 1985. No juvenile records released. Certification fee: $8.00. Payee: Berks County Clerk of Courts. Only cashiers checks and money orders accepted. Credit cards accepted for payments on criminal cases only. Prepayment and SASE required.

Register of Wills 633 Court St, 2nd Fl, Reading, PA 19601; phone: 610-478-6600; fax: 610-478-6251; hours 8AM-5PM (EST). *Probate.*
www.berksregofwills.com
Note: The Registry of Wills has a free searchable website at www.berksregofwills.com including records both for the county and the City of Reading. The estate and marriage records are current.

Blair County

Court of Common Pleas - Criminal/Civil
423 Allegheny St, #144, Hollidaysburg, PA 16648; phone: 814-693-3080; criminal phone: 814-693-3084; hours 8AM-4PM (EST). *Felony, Misdemeanor, Civil, Eviction.*
Civil Records: Access: In person, online. Visitors must perform in person searches themselves. Court makes copy: $.50 per page; same fee for self serve. Required to search: name, years to search. Civil cases indexed by defendant, plaintiff. Civil records on computer from 1989, on index books from 1846 to 1989. Online access is by subscription from private company - Infocon at www.infoconcountyacces s.com, 814-472-6066. See note at beginning of section.
Criminal Records: Access: Mail, online, in person. Both court and visitors may perform in person searches. Search fee: $10.00 per name. Court makes copy: $.50 per page; same fee for self serve. Required to search: name, years to search, DOB; also helpful: SSN. Criminal records on computer from 1989, on index books from 1846 to 1989. Online access is the same as civil, see above. Also, beginning 9/19/2005, search criminal dockets online free at http://ujsportal.pacourts.us/WebDocketSheets/Oth erCriteria.aspx. Mail turnaround time 2 days.
General Information: Public terminal goes back to 1989. No adoption records released. Certification fee: $5.00. Payee: Blair County Prothonotary. Personal checks accepted. Prepayment and SASE required.

Register of Wills 423 Allegheny, #145, Hollidaysburg, PA 16648-2022; phone: 814-693-3092; fax: 814-693-3093; hours 8AM-4PM (EST). *Probate.*
Note: Online access available by subscription from private company - Infocon at www.infoconcountyacces s.com, 814-472-6066. See note at beginning of section.

Bradford County

Court of Common Pleas - Criminal/Civil
Courthouse, 301 Main St, Towanda, PA 18848; phone: 570-265-1705; fax: 570-265-1735; hours 9AM-5PM (EST). *Felony, Misdemeanor, Civil, Eviction.*
Civil Records: Access: Mail, in person. Both court and visitors may perform in person searches. Search fee: $8.00 per name. Court makes copy: $.25 per page; same fee for self serve. Required to search:

name, years to search. Civil cases indexed by defendant, plaintiff. Civil records on computer from 1986, on microfiche from mid 1800s, archived from mid-1940s. Mail turnaround time 1-2 days.
Criminal Records: Access: Mail, in person, online. Both court and visitors may perform in person searches. Search fee: $8.00 per name. Court makes copy: $.25 per page; same fee for self serve. Required to search: name, years to search, DOB. Criminal records on computer from 1986, on microfiche from mid 1800s, archived from mid-1940s. As of 7/5/2005, search dockets online free at http://ujsportal.pacourts.us/WebDocketSheets/Oth erCriteria.aspx. Mail turnaround time 1-2 days.
General Information: Public terminal goes back to 1986. Will fax documents to local or toll free line. Certification fee: $4.00 Civil. $8.00 for criminal records. Payee: Prothonotary. Personal checks accepted. Prepayment and SASE required.

Register of Wills 301 Main St, Towanda, PA 18848; phone: 570-265-1702; fax: 570-265-1721; hours 9AM-5PM (EST). *Probate.*

Bucks County

Court of Common Pleas - Civil 55 E Court St, Doylestown, PA 18901; phone: 215-348-6191; probate phone: 215-348-6265; fax: 215-348-6184; hours 8:15AM-4:15PM (EST). *Civil, Eviction.*
www.buckscounty.org/courts/
Civil Records: Access: Online, in person. Visitors must perform in person searches themselves. Court makes copy: $1.50 per page. Self serve copy fee: $.25 per page. Required to search: name, years to search. Civil cases indexed by defendant, plaintiff. Civil records on computer back to 1980, prior on dockets. For a limited time, access is free at www.buckscounty.org/departments/public_access. Register of Wills is also included.

General Information: Public terminal has only civil records. No mental, sealed records released. Certification fee: $4.75 plus $1.50 each add'l page. Payee: Prothonotary. Personal checks accepted. Prepayment required.

Court of Common Pleas - Criminal Bucks County Courthouse, 55 E Court St, Doylestown, PA 18901; phone: 215-348-6389; civil phone: 215-348-6191; probate: 215-348-6265; fax: 215-348-6740; hours 8AM-4:30PM (EST). *Felony, Misdemeanor.*
www.buckscounty.org/courts/
Criminal Records: Access: Mail, online, in person. Both court and visitors may perform in person searches. Search fee: $10.00 per name. Court makes copy: $.25 per page; same fee for self serve. Required to search: name, years to search, DOB. Criminal records on computer from 1980, some records on microfiche, on card index from 1932 to 1979. For a limited time, access is free at www.buckscounty.org/departments/public_access. Also, as of 1/2/2006, search dockets online free at http://ujsportal.pacourts.us/WebDocketSheets/Oth erCriteria.aspx. Mail turnaround time 5 days or less.
General Information: Public terminal has only criminal records back to 1980. No sealed, juvenile or mental records released. Fee to fax documents is $1.50 per page. Certification fee: $8.00. Payee: Clerk of Courts Criminal Division. Personal checks accepted. Prepayment and SASE required.

Register of Wills Bucks County Courthouse, 55 E Court St, Doylestown, PA 18901; phone: 215-348-6265; fax: 215-348-6156; hours 8AM-4:30PM (EST). *Probate.*
www.buckscounty.org
Note: For a limited time, access is free at www.buckscounty.org/departments/public_access.

Butler County

Court of Common Pleas - Civil Butler County Courthouse, PO Box 1208, Butler, PA 16001-1208; phone: 724-284-5214; hours 8:30AM-4:30PM (EST). *Civil, Eviction.*
Civil Records: Access: Phone, mail, online, in person. Visitors must perform in person searches themselves. Court makes copy: $.50 per page; $1.00 for film copies. Required to search: name, years to search. Civil cases indexed by defendant, plaintiff. Civil records on computer from 4/1/93, prior on docket books back to 1800. Online access is by subscription from private company - Infocon at www.infoconcountyaccess.com, 814-472-6066. See note at beginning of section.
General Information: Public terminal has only civil records. No mental records released. Certification fee: $4.00 per document. Payee: Prothonotary. Personal checks accepted. Prepayment required.

Court of Common Pleas - Criminal PO Box 1208, 124 W Diamond St, County Courthouse, Butler, PA 16003-1208; phone: 724-284-5233; civil phone: 724-284-5214; probate phone: 724-284-5348; fax: 724-284-5244; hours 8:30AM-4:30PM (EST). *Felony, Misdemeanor.*
Criminal Records: Access: Mail, online, in person. Both court and visitors may perform in person searches. Search fee: $16.00 per name. Court makes copy: $.50 per page; $1.00 for computer printout. Required to search: name, DOB; also helpful: years to search, SSN. Original records in office for 10 years. Computerized from 1988 to present, prior in Russell Index. Search dockets online free at http://ujsportal.pacourts.us/WebDocketSheets/OtherCriteria.aspx. Mail turnaround time 1-2 days.
General Information: Public terminal has only criminal records back to 1987. No mental, sealed, juvenile (16 & under) victim records released. Will fax documents only for government. Certification fee: $8.00 per page. Payee: Clerk of Courts. Personal checks accepted. Prepayment and SASE required.

Register of Wills Butler County Courthouse, PO Box 1208, Butler, PA 16003-1208; phone: 724-284-5348; fax: 724-284-5278; hours 8:30AM-4:30PM (EST). *Probate.*
Note: Online access available by subscription from private company - Infocon at www.infoconcountyaccess.com, 814-472-6066. See note at beginning of section. Also, search free at http://66.117.197.22/index.cfm?page=home. Click on "lookup" type at bottom of webpage

Cambria County

Court of Common Pleas - Civil 200 S Center St, Ebensburg, PA 15931; phone: 814-472-1636; fax: 814-472-5632; hours 9AM-4PM (EST). *Civil, Eviction.*
Note: Small claims cases are handled by district judges.
Civil Records: Access: Phone, mail, fax, in person. Both court and visitors may perform in person searches. No search fee. Court makes copy: $.25 per page; same fee for self serve. Required to search: name, years to search. Civil cases indexed by defendant, plaintiff. Civil records on computer from 1/1/94, prior on dockets from 1800s. Mail turnaround time usually 1 day.
General Information: Public terminal has only civil records back to 1/1994. No divorce or mental records released. Fee to fax documents is $1.00 per page. Certification fee: $3.00 includes copies. Payee: Prothonotary. Personal checks accepted. Prepayment required. SASE requested.

Court of Common Pleas - Criminal Cambria County Courthouse, S Center St, Ebensburg, PA 15931; phone: 814-472-1540; hours 9AM-4PM (EST). *Felony, Misdemeanor.*
Criminal Records: Access: Mail, in person, online. Only the court performs in person searches; visitors may not. Search fee: $4.40 per name. Court makes copy: $.50 per single page; $.75 two-sided page. Required to search: name, years to search, DOB; also helpful: SSN. Criminal conviction records are computerized, indexed from 1800s. Search dockets online free at http://ujsportal.pacourts.us/WebDocketSheets/OtherCriteria.aspx. Mail turnaround time 5-7 days.
General Information: No public access terminal. No sealed or child victim records released. Will fax documents to a local or toll free number; search fee must be paid. Certification fee: $8.80 per doc includes copies. Payee: Clerk of Court. Third party checks not accepted. Prepayment required.

Register of Wills 200 S Center St, Ebensburg, PA 15931; phone: 814-472-1440; probate phone: 814-472-1438; fax: 814-472-0762; hours 9AM-4PM (EST). *Probate.*
www.co.cambria.pa.us

Cameron County

Court of Common Pleas - Civil Cameron County Courthouse, 20 E 5th St, Emporium, PA 15834; phone: 814-486-9329; fax: 814-468-0464; hours 8:30AM-4PM (EST). *Civil, Eviction.*
Civil Records: Access: Phone, fax, mail, in person. Both court and visitors may perform in person searches. No search fee. Court makes copy: $.50 per page. Required to search: name, years to search. Civil cases indexed by defendant, plaintiff. Civil records on computer from 1988, archived from 1860 to present. Mail turnaround time same day.
General Information: Public terminal has only civil records back to 1985. No adoption, military discharge records released. Will not fax documents. Certification fee: $10.00 per doc includes copies. Payee: Prothonotary. Personal checks accepted. Credit cards not accepted. Prepayment required. Will bill fees with prior permission from clerk. SASE required.

Court of Common Pleas - Criminal 20 E 5th St, Emporium, PA 15834; phone: 814-486-9330; fax: 814-486-0464; hours 8:30AM-4PM (EST). *Felony, Misdemeanor.*
Criminal Records: Access: Phone, fax, mail, in person, online. Both court and visitors may perform in person searches. No search fee. Court makes copy: $10.00 per file. Self serve copy fee: $.50 per page. Required to search: name, years to search; also helpful: address, DOB, SSN. Criminal records archived from 1860. Search dockets online free at http://ujsportal.pacourts.us/WebDocketSheets/OtherCriteria.aspx. Mail turnaround time same day.
General Information: Public terminal has only criminal records back to 4/2004. No juvenile, mental health records released. Will not fax documents. Certification fee: $10.00. Cert fee includes copies. Payee: Clerk of Court. Personal checks accepted. Credit cards not accepted. Prepayment and SASE required.

Register of Wills Cameron County Courthouse, 20 E 5th St, Emporium, PA 15834; phone: 814-486-3355; fax: 814-486-0464; hours 8:30AM-4PM (EST). *Probate.*

Carbon County

Court of Common Pleas - Civil PO Box 130, Courthouse, Jim Thorpe, PA 18229; phone: 570-325-2481; fax: 570-325-8047; hours 8:30AM-4:30PM (EST). *Civil, Eviction.*
www.carboncourts.com
Note: Small Claims can be reached at 570-325-2751.
Civil Records: Access: In person, online. Visitors must perform in person searches themselves. Court makes copy: $1.00 per page. Self serve copy fee: $.25 per page. Required to search: name. Civil cases indexed by defendant, plaintiff. Civil records on computer from 1/84, financing statements from 1/87, on microfiche from 1/84, prior archived. Online access to clerk of courts docket records is free at www.carboncourts.com/pubacc.htm. Registration required.

General Information: Public terminal has only civil records back to 1984. No abuse, mental health records released. Certification fee: $8.15 per cert. Payee: Prothonotary of Carbon County. Personal checks accepted. Prepayment required.

Court of Common Pleas - Criminal County Courthouse, Jim Thorpe, PA 18229; phone: 570-325-3637; fax: 570-325-5705; hours 8:30AM-4PM (EST). *Felony, Misdemeanor.*
www.carboncourts.com
Criminal Records: Access: Phone, mail, in person, online. Only the court performs in person searches; visitors may not. No search fee. No copy fee. Required to search: name, years to search, DOB; also helpful: SSN. Criminal records on computer from 1973, on microfiche from 1800. Online access to the clerk of courts docket records is free at www.carboncourts.com/pubacc.htm. Registration required. Also, as of 8/22/2005, search dockets online free at http://ujsportal.pacourts.us/WebDocketSheets/OtherCriteria.aspx. Mail turnaround time 1 day.
General Information: No public access terminal. No juvenile, mental health records released. Will not fax documents. No certification fee . Payee: Clerk of Courts Carbon County. Personal checks accepted. Prepayment and SASE required.

Register of Wills PO Box 286, 2 Broadway, Jim Thorpe, PA 18229; phone: 570-325-2261; fax: 570-325-5098; hours 8:30AM-4:30PM (EST). *Probate.*
Note: Docket information is available free online at www.carboncourts.com/pubacc.htm. Registration required.

Centre County

Court of Common Pleas - Criminal/Civil Centre County Courthouse, Bellefonte, PA 16823; phone: 814-355-6796; hours 8:30AM-5PM (EST). *Felony, Misdemeanor, Civil, Eviction.*
www.co.centre.pa.us/271.asp
Civil Records: Access: In person only. Visitors must perform in person searches themselves. Court makes copy: $.50 per page; same fee for self serve. Required to search: name, years to search, DOB. Civil cases indexed by defendant, plaintiff. Civil records on computer from 7-1-94, on docket books from 1986, on microfiche and archived from 1800 to 1986.
Criminal Records: Access: Mail, in person, online. Both court and visitors may perform in person searches. Search fee: $7.00 per name. Court makes copy: $.50 per page; same fee for self serve. Required to search: name, years to search, DOB. Criminal records on computer from 7-1-94, on card files and docket books from 1986, on microfiche and archived from 1800 to 1986. Search dockets online free at http://ujsportal.pacourts.us/WebDocketSheets/OtherCriteria.aspx. Mail turnaround time 3-5 days.
General Information: Public terminal goes back to 7/1994. No sex related, juvenile, mental records released. Will not fax documents. Certification fee: $4.00 1st page, $.50 ea add'l. Payee: Clerk of Court. Personal checks accepted. Prepayment and SASE required.

Register of Wills Willowbank Office Bldg, 414 Holmes Ave, #2, Bellefonte, PA 16823; phone: 814-355-6724, 355-6760; fax: 814-355-8685; hours 8:30AM-5PM (EST). *Probate.*
www.co.centre.pa.us/courts.htm

Chester County

Court of Common Pleas - Civil 2 N High St, #130, West Chester, PA 19380; phone: 610-344-6300; criminal phone: 610-344-6135; hours 8:30AM-4:30PM (EST). *Civil, Eviction.*
http://dsf.chesco.org
Civil Records: Access: Online, in person. Visitors must perform in person searches themselves. Court makes copy: $1.15 1st page; $.55 each add'l. Required to search: name, years to search. Civil cases indexed by defendant, plaintiff. Civil records on dockets from 1985 to present, on microfiche from

1981 to 1984, archived from 1700s. Internet access to county records including court records requires a sign-up and credit card payment. Application fee: $50. There is a $10.00 per month minimum (no charge for no activity); and $.10 each transaction beyond 100. Sign-up and/or logon at http://epin.chesco.org. Also, a court case list is free at http://dsf.chesco.org/courts/site/default.asp; click on "Miscellaneous List."

General Information: Public terminal has only civil records back to 1990. No sealed records released. Certification fee: $5.00. Payee: Prothonotary. Business checks accepted. Prepayment required. SASE helpful.

Court of Common Pleas - Criminal 2 N High St, #160, West Chester, PA 19380; phone: 610-344-6135; fax: 610-344-6605; hours 8:30AM-4:30PM (EST). *Felony, Misdemeanor.*

www.chesco.org

Criminal Records: Access: Mail, online, in person. Both court and visitors may perform in person searches. Search fee: $15.00 per name. Court makes copy: $1.00 per page; same fee for self serve. Required to search: name, years to search; also helpful: DOB. Criminal records on computer and microfiche from mid-70s, archived from the 1700s. Internet access to county records including criminal records requires a sign-up and credit card payment. Application fee: $50. There is a $10.00 per month minimum (no charge for no activity); and $.10 each transaction beyond 100. Sign-up and/or logon at http://epin.chesco.org. Also, as of 2/13/2006, search dockets online free at http://ujsportal.pacourts.us/WebDocketSheets/OtherCriteria.aspx. Mail turnaround time 1 day.

General Information: Public terminal has only criminal records. No juvenile records released. Certification fee: $5.00. Payee: Clerk of Courts. Business checks accepted. Prepayment required.

Register of Wills 2 N High St, #109, West Chester, PA 19380-3073; phone: 610-344-6335; fax: 610-344-6218; hours 8:30AM-4:30PM (EST). *Probate.*

Note: Internet access to probate records requires a sign-up and payment. Sign-up and/or logon at http://epin.chesco.org.

Clarion County

Court of Common Pleas - Civil Clarion County Courthouse, 421 Main St, Clarion, PA 16214; phone: 814-226-1119; fax: 814-227-2501; hours 8:30AM-4:30PM (EST). *Civil, Eviction.*

Civil Records: Access: Phone, fax, mail, online, in person. Both court and visitors may perform in person searches. Search fee: $10.00 per name. Court makes copy: $.50 per page. Required to search: name, years to search. Civil cases indexed by defendant, plaintiff. Civil records on computer from mid-1990s, on dockets from 1800s. Online access is by subscription from private company - Infocon at www.infoconcountyaccess.com, 814-472-6066. See note at beginning of section. Mail turnaround time 2-3 days.

General Information: Public terminal has only civil records back to 1990. No juvenile, mental health records released. No fee to fax documents. Certification fee: $7.50. Payee: Prothonotary. Personal checks accepted. Prepayment and SASE required.

Court of Common Pleas - Criminal Clarion County Courthouse, Main St, Clarion, PA 16214; phone: 814-226-1119; fax: 814-227-2501; hours 8AM-4:30PM (EST). *Felony, Misdemeanor.*

Criminal Records: Access: Fax, mail, online, in person. Both court and visitors may perform in person searches. Search fee: $10.00 per name. Court makes copy: $.50 per page. Required to search: name, years to search, DOB. Criminal records on computer from 1990, microfiche 1976-1985, on docket books from 1800s. Internet access to court records is by subscription from a private company - Infocon at www.ic-access.com, 814-472-6066. See note at beginning of section. Also, search dockets free at

http://ujsportal.pacourts.us/WebDocketSheets/OtherCriteria.aspx. Mail turnaround time same day.

General Information: Public terminal has only criminal records back to 6/1990. No juvenile, mental health records released. No fee to fax documents. Certification fee: $7.50 per cert. Payee: Clerk of Court. Personal checks accepted. Prepayment required.

Register of Wills Clarion County Courthouse, 421 Main St, Clarion, PA 16214; phone: 814-226-4000 X2500; fax: 814-226-1117; hours 8:30AM-4:30PM (EST). *Probate.*

Note: Online access available by subscription from private company - Infocon at www.infoconcountyaccess.com, 814-472-6066. See note at beginning of section.

Clearfield County

Court of Common Pleas - Criminal/Civil PO Box 549, 1 N 2nd St, Clearfield, PA 16830; phone: 814-765-2641; criminal phone: x5980; civil phone: x5988; fax: 814-765-7659; hours 8:30AM-4PM (EST). *Felony, Misdemeanor, Civil, Eviction.*

www.clearfieldco.org

Civil Records: Access: Mail, in person. Both court and visitors may perform in person searches. Search fee: $7.00 per name, 5-years search. Court makes copy: $.25 per page; $1.00 minimum. Self serve copy fee: $.25 per page. Required to search: name, years to search; also helpful: address. Civil cases indexed by defendant, plaintiff. Civil records indexed (Russell System) on dockets from 1820s; on computer back to 11/00. Mail turnaround time same day.

Criminal Records: Access: Mail, in person, online. Both court and visitors may perform in person searches. Search fee: $7.00 per name, 5-year search. Court makes copy: $.25 per page; $1.00 minimum. Self serve copy fee: $.25 per page. Required to search: name, years to search, address, DOB, SSN, signed release. Criminal records indexed (Russell System) on dockets from 1820s; on computer back to 1/95. As of 11/7/2005, search dockets online free at http://ujsportal.pacourts.us/WebDocketSheets/OtherCriteria.aspx. Mail turnaround time 2 days.

General Information: Public terminal has criminal back to 10 years and civil back to 11/2000. No juvenile, sealed or mental health records released. Will not fax documents. Certification fee: $1.50. Payee: Prothonotary. Personal checks accepted. Prepayment and SASE required.

Register of Wills & Clerk of Orphans Court PO Box 361, Clearfield, PA 16830; phone: 814-765-2641 X1352; fax: 814-765-6089; hours 8:30AM-4PM (EST). *Probate.*

Note: Search records 1990 to present by name at www.landex.com; registration and fees required.

Clinton County

Court of Common Pleas - Criminal/Civil 230 E Water St, Lock Haven, PA 17745; phone: 570-893-4007; fax: 570-893-4288; hours 8AM-5PM M, T, Th, F; 8AM-12:30PM Wed (EST). *Felony, Misdemeanor, Civil, Eviction.*

www.clintoncountypa.com/courts.htm

Civil Records: Access: Online, in person. Visitors must perform in person searches themselves. Court makes copy: $.50 per page. Required to search: name, years to search. Civil cases indexed by defendant, plaintiff. Civil records on computer from 1992, on files from 1839. Online access is by subscription from private company - Infocon at www.infoconcountyaccess.com, 814-472-6066. See note at beginning of section.

Criminal Records: Access: Online, in person. Visitors must perform in person searches themselves. Court makes copy: $.50 per page. Required to search: name, years to search, DOB, SSN, signed release. Criminal records on computer from 1992, on files from 1839. Internet access to court records is by subscription from a private company - Infocon at www.ic-access.com, 814-

472-6066. See note at beginning of section. Also, as of 8/1/2005, search dockets online free at http://ujsportal.pacourts.us/WebDocketSheets/OtherCriteria.aspx.

General Information: Public terminal goes back to 1992. No sealed, mental health or minor victim abuse cases records released. Will not fax documents. Certification fee: Civil is $4.50 first page, $1.50 ea add'l. Criminal is $5.00 first page. $1.50 ea add'l. Payee: Clerk of Court or Prothonotary. Personal checks accepted. Prepayment required.

Register of Wills PO Box 943, Lock Haven, PA 17745; phone: 570-893-4010; fax: 570-893-4273; hours 8:30AM-5PM M,T,Th,F; 8AM-12:30PM Wed (EST). *Probate.*

www.clintoncountypa.com

Online access available by subscription from private company - Infocon at www.infoconcountyaccess.com, 814-472-6066. See note at beginning of section.

Columbia County

Court of Common Pleas - Criminal/Civil PO Box 380, Bloomsburg, PA 17815; phone: 570-389-5614; fax: 570-389-5620; hours 8AM-4:30PM (EST). *Felony, Misdemeanor, Civil, Eviction.*

http://columbiapa.org/county/courts/index.html

Note: Opinions for civil and criminal cases are listed at the website. Fax to "Attention Barb."

Civil Records: Access: In person only. Both court and visitors may perform in person searches. No search fee. Court makes copy: $.50 per page; same fee for self serve. Required to search: name, years to search. Civil cases indexed by defendant, plaintiff. Civil records on computer to 1992, on microfiche from 1814 to present, on dockets from 1814. Mail turnaround time same or next day.

Criminal Records: Access: Mail, in person, online. Both court and visitors may perform in person searches. Search fee: $20.00 per name. Court makes copy: $.50 per page; same fee for self serve. Required to search: name, years to search; also helpful: DOB. Criminal records on computer to 1992, on microfiche from 1814 to present, on dockets from 1814. As of 8/15/2005, search dockets online free at http://ujsportal.pacourts.us/WebDocketSheets/OtherCriteria.aspx. Mail turnaround same or next day.

General Information: Public terminal goes back to 1992. No juvenile, adoption, mental health petition or OAPSA records released. Certification fee: $4.00. Payee: Prothonotary or Clerk of Court. Personal checks accepted. Prepayment and SASE required.

Register of Wills 35 W Main St, PO Box 380, Bloomsburg, PA 17815; phone: 570-389-5635/32; fax: 570-389-5636; hours 8AM-4:30PM (EST). *Probate.*

Crawford County

Court of Common Pleas - Civil Crawford County Courthouse, 903 Diamond Pk, Meadville, PA 16335; phone: 814-333-7324; criminal phone: 814-333-7442; hours 8:30AM-4:30PM (EST). *Civil, Eviction.*

Civil Records: Access: Mail, in person. Both court and visitors may perform in person searches. Search fee: $7.50 per name. Court makes copy: $.75 per page. Docket copy $1.50 per page. Required to search: name, years to search. Civil cases indexed by defendant, plaintiff. Civil records on dockets from 1800s. Mail turnaround time 3 days.

General Information: Public terminal has only civil records. No mental health, sealed records released. Certification fee: $1.50. Payee: Prothonotary Crawford County. Personal checks accepted with ID. Prepayment and SASE required.

Court of Common Pleas - Criminal Crawford County Courthouse, 903 Diamond Pk, Meadville, PA 16335; phone: 814-333-7442; fax: 814-337-7349; hours 8:30AM-4:30PM (EST). *Felony, Misdemeanor.*

http://co.crawford.pa.us/clerk_of_courts/clerk_of_courts_home.htm
Criminal Records: Access: Mail, in person, online. Both court and visitors may perform in person searches. Search fee: $10.00 to search, up to 5 names per $10.00. Court makes copy: $1.00 per page. Required to search: name, years to search, signed release; also helpful: DOB & SSN. Criminal records computerized since 2000, on microfiche from 1974, on dockets from 1914, archived from 1880s. Search dockets online free at http://ujsportal.pacourts.us/WebDocketSheets/OtherCriteria.aspx. Mail turnaround time 10-14 days.
General Information: Public terminal has only criminal records back to 2000. No juvenile records released. Certification fee: $5.00 per document. Payee: Clerk of Courts. Personal checks accepted. Prepayment and SASE required.

Register of Wills 903 Diamond Pk, Meadville, PA 16335; phone: 814-373-2537; fax: 814-337-5296; hours 8:30AM-4:30PM (EST). *Probate.*

Cumberland County

Court of Common Pleas - Civil Cumberland County Courthouse, Rm 100, One Courthouse Sq, Carlisle, PA 17013-3387; phone: 717-240-6195; fax: 717-240-6573; hours 8AM-4:30PM (EST). *Civil, Eviction.*

Civil Records: Access: In person only. Visitors must perform in person searches themselves. Court makes copy: $.50 per page. Required to search: name, years to search; also helpful: address. Civil cases indexed by defendant, plaintiff. Civil records on computer from 1994, on microfiche from 1966-1988, on dockets from 1800s. Judges opinions and court documents are free online, but searchable only by judge name, then year.

General Information: Public terminal has only civil records. No mental health records released. Will not fax specific case file. No certification fee . Payee: Office of Prothonotary. No personal checks accepted. Prepayment required.

Court of Common Pleas - Criminal Cumberland County Courthouse, East Wing, 1 Courthouse Sq, Carlisle, PA 17013-3387; phone: 717-240-6250; fax: 717-240-6571; hours 8AM-4:30PM (EST). *Felony, Misdemeanor.*
www.ccpa.net
Criminal Records: Access: Mail, in person, online. Both court and visitors may perform in person searches. Search fee: $17.00 per name. Court makes copy: $.50 per page. Required to search: name, years to search, DOB or SSN. Criminal records on computer from 1994, on files from 1976, archived from 1800s. Search dockets online free at http://ujsportal.pacourts.us/WebDocketSheets/OtherCriteria.aspx. Mail turnaround time same day.
General Information: Public terminal has only criminal records back to 1993. No juvenile records released (Including any case with a juvenile as the victim). No certification fee . Payee: Clerk of Courts. Personal checks accepted. Prepayment and SASE required.

Register of Wills Cumberland County Courthouse, Rm 102, 1 Courthouse Sq, Carlisle, PA 17013; phone: 717-240-6345; fax: 717-240-7797; hours 8AM-4:30PM (EST). *Probate.*
www.ccpa.net/cumberland/cwp/view.asp?a=1750&Q=473616

Dauphin County

Court of Common Pleas - Civil PO Box 945, Harrisburg, PA 17108; criminal phone: 717-780-6530; civil phone: 717-780-6520; hours 8AM-4:30PM (EST). *Civil, Eviction.*
http://dsf.pacounties.org/dauphin/site/default.asp
Civil Records: Access: Phone, mail, in person. Both court and visitors may perform in person searches. Search fee: $7.75 per name. Fee is per 5 years searched. Court makes copy: $.75 per page. Required

to search: name, years to search. Civil cases indexed by defendant, plaintiff. Civil records on microfilm and dockets from 1970s, archived from 1700s; on computer back to 11/2001. Mail turnaround time 1 day.
General Information: Public terminal has only civil records back to 1983. No mental health released. Certification fee: $5.00 1st pg; $1.50 each add'l. Payee: Dauphin County Prothonotary. Business checks accepted. Prepayment and SASE required.

Court of Common Pleas - Criminal Front & Market St, Harrisburg, PA 17101; phone: 717-255-2692; hours 8AM-4:30PM (EST). *Felony, Misdemeanor.*
http://dsf.pacounties.org/dauphin/site/default.asp
Criminal Records: Access: Mail, in person, online. Both court and visitors may perform in person searches. Search fee: $21.50 per name. Court makes copy: $.50 per page. Required to search: name, years to search; also helpful: DOB, SSN. Criminal records on dockets and computer from 1950, archived from 1700s. As of 10/10/2005, search dockets online free at http://ujsportal.pacourts.us/WebDocketSheets/OtherCriteria.aspx. Mail turnaround time 1 week.
General Information: Public terminal has only criminal records back to 2002. No juvenile, mental records released. Certification fee: $9.00 per cert includes copies. Payee: Clerk of Court. Business checks accepted. Prepayment required.

Register of Wills Front & Market Sts, Rm 103, Harrisburg, PA 17101; phone: 717-780-6500; fax: 717-780-6474; hours 8AM-4:30PM (EST). *Probate.*
www.dauphincounty.org

Delaware County

Court of Common Pleas - Criminal/Civil 201 W Front St, Media, PA 19063; phone: 610-891-4370; fax: 610-891-7257; hours 8:30AM-4:30PM (EST). *Felony, Misdemeanor, Civil, Eviction.*
www.co.delaware.pa.us
Civil Records: Access: Online, in person. Visitors must perform in person searches themselves. Court makes copy: $1.00 per page. Required to search: name, years to search. Civil cases indexed by defendant, plaintiff. Civil records on computer from early 1990, on card file from 1920s, archived from 1800s. Online access to court civil records free (may begin charging at any time) at www2.co.delaware.pa.us/pa/default.htm. For more information, call 610-891-4675. Search online by document type, document number, etc.
Criminal Records: Access: Mail, in person, online. Both court and visitors may perform in person searches. No search fee. Court makes copy: $1.00 per page. Required to search: name, years to search; also helpful: DOB, SSN. Criminal records on computer from late 1970s, prior on files. As of 12/19/2005, search dockets online free at http://ujsportal.pacourts.us/WebDocketSheets/OtherCriteria.aspx. Mail turnaround time 1-3 days.
General Information: Public terminal has only civil records back to 1990. No juvenile, mental health records released. Certification fee: $4.50 per doc. Payee: Office of Judicial Support. Business checks accepted. Prepayment and SASE required.

Register of Wills Delaware County Courthouse, 201 W Front St, Media, PA 19063; phone: 610-891-4400; fax: 610-891-4812; hours 8:30AM-4:30PM (EST). *Probate.*

Elk County

Court of Common Pleas - Criminal/Civil PO Box 237, Ridgway, PA 15853; phone: 814-776-5344; fax: 814-776-5303; hours 8:30AM-4PM (EST). *Felony, Misdemeanor, Civil, Eviction.*
www.co.elk.pa.us/Courthouse.htm
Civil Records: Access: Phone, fax, mail, in person. Both court and visitors may perform in person searches. Search fee: $8.00 per name. Court makes copy: $.50 per page. Required to search: name, years

to search. Civil cases indexed by defendant, plaintiff. Civil records on dockets from 1843, on computer back to 1998. Mail turnaround time 1 day.
Criminal Records: Access: Phone, fax, mail, in person, online. Both court and visitors may perform in person searches. Search fee: $10.00 per name. Court makes copy: $.50 per page. Required to search: name, years to search, DOB. Criminal records on dockets from 1843, on computer back to 1998. Search dockets online free at http://ujsportal.pacourts.us/WebDocketSheets/OtherCriteria.aspx. Mail turnaround time 1 day.
General Information: Public terminal goes back to 1998. No mental health or juvenile records released. Certification fee: $4.75 for civil; $8.50 for criminal. Payee: Elk County Prothonotary. Personal checks accepted. Prepayment required. SASE requested.

Register of Wills PO Box 314, Ridgway, PA 15853; phone: 814-776-5349; fax: 814-776-5382; hours 8:30AM-4PM (EST). *Probate.*

Erie County

Court of Common Pleas - Civil Erie County Courthouse, 140 W 6th St, Erie, PA 16501; phone: 814-451-6250; criminal phone: 814-451-6221; probate phone: 814-451-6260; hours 8:30AM-4:30PM (EST). *Civil, Eviction.*
Civil Records: Access: Mail, online, in person. Both court and visitors may perform in person searches. Search fee: $10.00. Court makes copy: $.50 per page. Computer page $1.00 per page. Required to search: name, years to search. Civil cases indexed by defendant, plaintiff. Civil records on computer from 1992, on dockets from 1971, on microfilm/microfiche from 1800s. Online access is by subscription from private company - Infocon at www.infoconcountyaccess.com, 814-472-6066. See note at beginning of section. Mail turnaround time same day.
General Information: Public terminal has only civil records back to 1992. No sealed records released. Will fax documents to local or toll free line. Certification fee: $5.00. Payee: Prothonotary. Personal checks accepted. Prepayment and SASE required.

Court of Common Pleas - Criminal Erie County Courthouse, 140 W 6th St, Erie, PA 16501; phone: 814-451-6229; fax: 814-451-6420; hours 8:30AM-4:30PM (EST). *Felony, Misdemeanor.*
www.eriecountygov.org/default.aspx?id=courts
Criminal Records: Access: Mail, online, in person. Both court and visitors may perform in person searches. Search fee: $10.00 per name. Court makes copy: $.10 per page. Required to search: name, years to search, DOB. Criminal records go back to 1960; records computerized back to 1992. Internet access to court records is by subscription from a private company - Infocon at www.ic-access.com, 814-472-6066. See note at beginning of section. Also, as of 8/1/2005, search dockets online free at http://ujsportal.pacourts.us/WebDocketSheets/OtherCriteria.aspx. Mail turnaround time 1 week.
General Information: Public terminal has only criminal records back to 1992. No juvenile or ARD records released. Will fax documents to local or toll free line. No certification fee . Payee: Clerk of Courts. Personal checks accepted. Prepayment required.

Register of Wills Erie County Courthouse, 140 W 6th St, Erie, PA 16501; phone: 814-451-6260; fax: 814-451-7010; hours 8:30AM-4:30PM (EST). *Probate.*

https://secure.eriepa.us/default.aspx?id=clerk
Note: Online access available by subscription from - Infocon at www.infoconcountyaccess.com, 814-472-6066. See note at beginning of section.

Fayette County

Court of Common Pleas - Civil 61 E Main St, Uniontown, PA 15401; phone: 724-430-1272; fax: 724-430-4555; hours 8AM-4:30PM (EST). *Civil, Eviction.*

Civil Records: Access: Mail, in person. Both court and visitors may perform in person searches. Search fee: $5.00 per name. Court makes copy: $.50 per page; same fee for self serve. Required to search: name, years to search. Civil cases indexed by defendant, plaintiff. Civil records on computer from 1999, archived from 1700s. Mail turnaround time 2 weeks.

General Information: Public terminal has only civil records back to 1999. No mental records released. Will not fax documents. Certification fee: $10.00 per document includes copy fee. Payee: Prothonotary. Personal checks accepted. Prepayment required.

Court of Common Pleas - Criminal 61 E Main St, Uniontown, PA 15401; phone: 724-430-1253; fax: 724-438-8410; hours 8AM-4:30PM (EST). *Felony, Misdemeanor.*

Criminal Records: Access: Fax, mail, in person, online. Both court and visitors may perform in person searches. Search fee: $15.00 for 5-year search; $30.00 for 5-yr. plus. Court makes copy: $.50 per page. Required to search: name, years to search, DOB; also helpful: SSN. Criminal records on computer from 1993, on files from 1800s. Search dockets online free at http://ujsportal.pacourts.us/WebDocketSheets/OtherCriteria.aspx. Mail turnaround time 3-5 days.

General Information: Public terminal has only criminal records. No sex related or juvenile records released. Will fax documents $3.00 per doc. Certification fee: $16.50. Payee: Clerk of Courts. Personal checks accepted. Prepayment required.

Register of Wills 61 E Main St, Uniontown, PA 15401; phone: 724-430-1206; fax: 724-430-1275; hours 8AM-N, 1-4:30PM (EST). *Probate.*

Forest County

Court of Common Pleas 526 Elm St, #2, Forest County Courthouse, Tionesta, PA 16353; phone: 814-755-3526; criminal fax: 814-755-8837; same fax for civil/probate; hours 9AM-4PM (EST). *Felony, Misdemeanor, Civil, Eviction, Probate.*

Note: Computerized records includes the Register of Wills. Probate records are separate index at same address.

Civil Records: Access: Mail, fax, in person. Both court and visitors may perform in person searches. No search fee. Court makes copy: $2.00 per docket. Self serve copy fee: $.25 per page. Required to search: name, years to search. Civil cases indexed by defendant, plaintiff. Computerized records from 2002, civil records on dockets since 1995, archived from 1857. Mail turnaround time same day.

Criminal Records: Access: Mail, fax, in person, online. Both court and visitors may perform in person searches. Search fee: $10.00 per name. Court makes copy: $2.00 per docket. Self serve copy fee: $.25 per page. Required to search: name, years to search; also helpful: DOB, SSN. Computerized records from 1995, archived from 1857. Search dockets online free at http://ujsportal.pacourts.us/WebDocketSheets/OtherCriteria.aspx. Mail turnaround time same day.

General Information: Public terminal has criminal back to 1995 and civil back to 2002. No adoption records released. Will fax documents for $4.00 per document. Certification fee: $2.00. Payee: Clerk of Courts. Personal checks accepted. Prepayment and SASE required.

Franklin County

Court of Common Pleas - Civil 157 Lincoln Way E, Chambersburg, PA 17201; phone: 717-261-3858; fax: 717-264-6772; hours 8:30AM-4:30PM (EST). *Civil, Eviction.*

Civil Records: Access: In person, online. Visitors must perform in person searches themselves. Court makes copy: $.50 per page; same fee for self serve. Required to search: name, years to search. Civil cases indexed by defendant, plaintiff. Civil records on file from 1985; on computer back to 4/1/1999. Online access is by subscription from private company - Infocon at www.infoconcountyaccess.com, 814-472-6066. See note at beginning of section.

General Information: Public terminal has only civil records back to 11/1998. (Terminal also offers access to liens, division records, custody, protection from abuse and Judgment histories from 1981-1990.) No mental records released. Will fax specific case file requests for $1.00 per page. Certification fee: $5.00 per document plus copy fee for add'l pages. Payee: Prothonotary. Personal checks accepted. Prepayment required.

Court of Common Pleas - Criminal 157 Lincoln Way E, Chambersburg, PA 17201; phone: 717-261-3805; fax: 717-261-3896; hours 8:30AM-4:30PM (EST). *Felony, Misdemeanor.*

Criminal Records: Access: Mail, in person, online. Both court and visitors may perform in person searches. Search fee: $10.00 per name. Court makes copy: $.25 per page; same fee for self serve. Required to search: name, years to search, DOB. Computerized back to 1995; criminal records on files for 50 years, archived from 1800s. As of 10/3/2005, search dockets online free at http://ujsportal.pacourts.us/WebDocketSheets/OtherCriteria.aspx. Mail turnaround time same day.

General Information: Public terminal has only criminal records back to 1995. No juvenile records released. Will fax documents. Certification fee: $5.00 per document. Payee: Clerk of Courts. Personal checks accepted. Prepayment required. SASE requested.

Register of Wills 157 Lincoln Way E, Chambersburg, PA 17201; phone: 717-261-3872; fax: 717-263-5717; hours 8:30AM-4:30PM (EST). *Probate.*

Note: Online access available by subscription from private company - Infocon at www.infoconcountyaccess.com, 814-472-6066. See note at beginning of section.

Fulton County

Court of Common Pleas - Criminal/Civil Fulton County Courthouse, 201 N 2nd St, McConnellsburg, PA 17233; phone: 717-485-4212; fax: 717-485-5568; hours 8:30AM-4:30PM (EST). *Felony, Misdemeanor, Civil, Eviction.*

Note: Send faxes to Attention-Court of Common Pleas.

Civil Records: Access: In person only. Visitors must perform in person searches themselves. Court makes copy: $.25 per page. Required to search: name, years to search. Civil cases indexed by defendant, plaintiff. Civil records on docket index from 1850s; on computer back to 1999.

Criminal Records: Access: Mail, in person, online. Both court and visitors may perform in person searches. Search fee: $5.00 per name. Court makes copy: $.50 per page; computer printout- $1.00 per page. Required to search: name, years to search. Criminal records on docket index from 1850s; on computer back to 1994. As of 9/6/2005, search dockets online free at http://ujsportal.pacourts.us/WebDocketSheets/OtherCriteria.aspx. Mail turnaround time 3-5 days.

General Information: Public terminal has criminal back to 1996 and civil back to 1999. No juvenile, adoption records released. Will fax documents $5.00 per doc. Certification fee: $5.00 per doc includes copy

fee. Payee: Prothonotary. Personal checks accepted. Prepayment and SASE required.

Register of Wills 201 N 2nd St, McConnellsburg, PA 17233; phone: 717-485-4212; fax: 717-485-5568; hours 8:30AM-4:30PM (EST). *Probate.*

Greene County

Court of Common Pleas - Civil Greene County Courthouse, Rm 105, Waynesburg, PA 15370; phone: 724-852-5282; civil phone: 724-852-5289; probate phone: 724-852-5283; hours 8:30AM-4:30PM (EST). *Civil, Eviction.*

Civil Records: Access: Mail, in person. Visitors must perform in person searches themselves. No search fee. Court makes copy: $.50 per page; same fee for self serve. Required to search: name, years to search. Civil cases indexed by defendant, plaintiff. Civil records go back to 1797; on computer back to 1996. Mail turnaround time 1 week.

General Information: Public terminal has only civil records back to 1797. No mental health records released. Will not fax documents. Certification fee: $8.00 per record. Payee: Prothonotary. Personal checks accepted. Prepayment and SASE required.

Court of Common Pleas - Criminal Greene County Courthouse, 10 E High St, Waynesburg, PA 15370; phone: 724-852-5281; fax: 724-852-5316; hours 8:30AM-4:30PM (EST). *Felony, Misdemeanor.*

Criminal Records: Access: Mail, in person, online. Both court and visitors may perform in person searches. Search fee: $10.00 per name. Court makes copy: $.50 per page. Required to search: name, years to search, DOB, signed release; also helpful: SSN. Criminal records on index books from 1940s, on computer since 1996. Search dockets online free at http://ujsportal.pacourts.us/WebDocketSheets/OtherCriteria.aspx. Mail turnaround time same day.

General Information: Public terminal has only criminal records back to 1996. (Limited number of cases only.) No juvenile, adoption records released. Fee to fax documents is $2.00 1st page; $1.00 each add'l page. Certification fee: $8.00 per document. Payee: Clerk of Courts. Personal checks accepted. Prepayment and SASE required.

Register of Wills Greene County Courthouse, 10 E High St, Waynesburg, PA 15370; phone: 724-852-5283; hours 8:30AM-4PM (EST). *Probate.*

Huntingdon County

Court of Common Pleas - Criminal/Civil PO Box 39, Courthouse, Huntingdon, PA 16652; phone: 814-643-1610; fax: 814-643-4271; hours 8:30AM-4:30PM (EST). *Felony, Misdemeanor, Civil, Eviction.*

Civil Records: Access: In person, online. Visitors must perform in person searches themselves. Court makes copy: $.25 per page. Required to search: name, years to search; also helpful: address. Civil cases indexed by defendant, plaintiff. Civil records on computer from 8/03/92, on dockets from 1788. Online access is by subscription from private company - Infocon at www.infoconcountyaccess.com, 814-472-6066. See note at beginning of section.

Criminal Records: Access: In person, online. Visitors must perform in person searches themselves. No search fee. Court makes copy: $.25 per page. Required to search: name, years to search; also helpful: DOB, SSN. Criminal records on computer from 8/03/92, on dockets from 1788. Internet access to court records is by subscription from a private company - Infocon at www.ic-access.com, 814-472-6066. See note at beginning of section. Also, as of 10/24/2005, search dockets online free at http://ujsportal.pacourts.us/WebDocketSheets/OtherCriteria.aspx.

General Information: Public terminal goes back to 8/1992. No juvenile records released. Certification fee: $4.50 per cert includes copies. Payee:

Prothonotary. Personal checks accepted. Prepayment required.

Register of Wills Courthouse, 223 Penn St, Huntingdon, PA 16652; phone: 814-643-2740; hours 8:30AM-4:30PM (EST). *Probate*.

Note: Online access available by subscription from private company - Infocon at www.infoconcountyaccess.com, 814-472-6066. See note at beginning of section.

Indiana County

Court of Common Pleas - Criminal/Civil
County Courthouse, 825 Philadelphia St, Indiana, PA 15701; phone: 724-465-3855/3858; fax: 724-465-3968; hours 8AM-4PM (EST). *Felony, Misdemeanor, Civil, Eviction.*

Civil Records: Access: Mail, in person. Both court and visitors may perform in person searches. Search fee: $10.00 per name. Will not conduct judgment searches. Court makes copy: $.25 per page. Required to search: name, years to search. Civil cases indexed by defendant, plaintiff. Civil records on computer from 1994, prior on index files to1806. Mail turnaround time same day.

Criminal Records: Access: Mail, in person, online. Both court and visitors may perform in person searches. Search fee: $10.75 per name. Court makes copy: $.25 per page. Required to search: name, years to search, DOB, signed release. Criminal records on computer from 1994, prior on index files to 1806. Search dockets online free at http://ujsportal.pacourts.us/WebDocketSheets/OtherCriteria.aspx. Mail turnaround time same day.

General Information: Public terminal goes back to 1994. No juvenile, commitment records released. Will fax documents $.25 per page. Certification fee: $3.00. Payee: Clerk of Court or Prothonotary. Personal checks accepted. Prepayment required.

Register of Wills County Courthouse, 825 Philadelphia St, Indiana, PA 15701; phone: 724-465-3860; fax: 724-465-3863; hours 8AM-4PM (EST). *Probate.*

Jefferson County

Court of Common Pleas - Criminal/Civil
Courthouse, 200 Main St, Brookville, PA 15825; phone: 814-849-1606 X225; fax: 814-849-1625; hours 8:30AM-4:30PM (EST). *Felony, Misdemeanor, Civil, Eviction.*

Civil Records: Access: Mail, in person. Both court and visitors may perform in person searches. Search fee: $5.00 per name. Court makes copy: $.50 per page. Required to search: name, years to search. Civil cases indexed by defendant, plaintiff. Civil records on computer back to 1987; all incoming records microfilmed, records since 1823 on microfilm. Mail turnaround time 2 days.

Criminal Records: Access: Mail, in person, online. Both court and visitors may perform in person searches. Search fee: $5.00 per name. Court makes copy: $.50 per page. Required to search: name, years to search, DOB; also helpful: SSN. Criminal records on computer back to 1987; all incoming records microfilmed, records since 1947 on microfilm. Search dockets online free at http://ujsportal.pacourts.us/WebDocketSheets/OtherCriteria.aspx. Mail turnaround time 2 days.

General Information: Public use terminal available. No juvenile, mental health, records released, including criminal cases with a minor as a victim. Will fax documents for $3.00 1st page; $1.00 for every page thereafter. Certification fee: $1.50 per page. Payee: Clerk of Courts. Personal checks accepted. Prepayment and SASE required.

Register of Wills Jefferson County Courthouse, 200 Main St, Brookville, PA 15825; phone: 814-849-1610; fax: 814-849-1677; hours 8:30AM-4:30PM (EST). *Probate.*

Note: $10.00 search fee; $1.00 per page copy fee.

Juniata County

Court of Common Pleas - Criminal/Civil
Juniata County Courthouse, Mifflintown, PA 17059; phone: 717-436-7715; fax: 717-436-7734; hours 8AM-4:30PM (EST). *Felony, Misdemeanor, Civil, Eviction.*

Civil Records: Access: Mail, in person. Both court and visitors may perform in person searches. Search fee: $5.00 per name. Court makes copy: $.50 per page. Required to search: name, years to search. Civil cases indexed by defendant, plaintiff. Civil records on computer go back to 1993, on dockets from 1836. Mail turnaround time 1 week.

Criminal Records: Access: In person, online. Both court and visitors may perform in person searches. Court makes copy: $.50 per page. Required to search: name, years to search, DOB, SSN, signed release. Criminal records on computer go back to 1993, on dockets from 1894. Search dockets online free at http://ujsportal.pacourts.us/WebDocketSheets/OtherCriteria.aspx.

General Information: Public terminal goes back to 1993. No juvenile records released. Certification fee: $1.00 per page. Payee: Prothonotary or Clerk of Courts. Personal checks accepted. Prepayment and SASE required.

Register of Wills Juniata County Courthouse, PO Box 68, Mifflintown, PA 17059; phone: 717-436-7709; fax: 717-436-7756; hours 8AM-4:30PM M-F, 8AM-12PM Wed (June-Sept) (EST). *Probate.*

Note: Online access available by subscription from private company - Infocon at www.infoconcountyaccess.com, 814-472-6066. See note at beginning of section.

Lackawanna County

Court of Common Pleas - Civil
Clerk of Judicial Records, 200 N Washington Ave, Scranton, PA 18503-1551; phone: 570-963-6724; civil phone: 717-963-6723; hours 9AM-4PM (EST). *Civil, Eviction.*

Civil Records: Access: In person only. Visitors must perform in person searches themselves. Search fee: No civil searches performed by court - but exceptions are made. Court makes copy: $.50 per copy; $1.00 for mail requesters first copy, $.50 each add'l. Self serve copy fee: $.25 per page. Required to search: name, years to search. Civil cases indexed by defendant, plaintiff. Civil records computerized since 9/95, dockets from 1920s, archived from 1800s. Case number is required.

General Information: Public terminal has only civil records. No juvenile records released. Certification fee: $4.75. Payee: Clerk of Judicial Records. Business checks accepted. Prepayment required.

Court of Common Pleas - Criminal
Lackawanna County Courthouse, Scranton, PA 18503; phone: 570-963-6759; fax: 570-963-6459; hours 9AM-4PM (EST). *Felony, Misdemeanor.*

Criminal Records: Access: Mail, in person, online. Both court and visitors may perform in person searches. Search fee: $10.00 per name. Court makes copy: $.50 per page. Required to search: name, years to search, DOB, SSN. Criminal records computerized since 10/95, on dockets from 1983, archived from 1941, indexed by defendant only. Search dockets online free at http://ujsportal.pacourts.us/WebDocketSheets/OtherCriteria.aspx. Mail turnaround time 1-2 days.

General Information: Public terminal has only criminal records back to 1995. No juvenile records released. Will fax documents to local or toll free line. Certification fee: $8.00 per doc includes copies. Payee: Clerk of Judicial Records. Business checks accepted. Prepayment and SASE required.

Lackawanna County (continued)

Register of Wills Register of Wills, County Courthouse, 200 N Washington Ave, Scranton, PA 18503; phone: 570-963-6702; fax: 570-963-6377; hours 9AM-4PM (EST). *Probate.*

Lancaster County

Court of Common Pleas - Civil
50 N Duke St, PO Box 83480, Lancaster, PA 17608-3480; phone: 717-299-8282; fax: 717-293-7210; hours 8:30AM-5PM (EST). *Civil, Eviction.*
www.co.lancaster.pa.us/courts/site/default.asp

Civil Records: Access: Online, in person. Visitors must perform in person searches themselves. Court makes copy: $.50 per page. Required to search: name, years to search; also helpful: address. Civil cases indexed by defendant, plaintiff. Civil records on computer from 7/87, in files from 1987, judgments on dockets from 1800s, others archived from 1800s. Access Prothonotary's judgment records free at www.co.lancaster.pa.us/scripts/bannerweb.dll.
Also, historical court case schedules are free at www.co.lancaster.pa.us, click on "Court Schedules" Includes Register, Treasurer, and other courthouse record data. Search by name or case number. Call Kathy Harris at 717-299-8252 for more information.

General Information: Public terminal has only civil records back to 7/1987. No naturalization records released. Will fax documents $2.00 1st page, $1.00 each add'l. Fee higher for out of state faxing. Certification fee: $5.00 per document. Payee: Prothonotary. No personal or business checks accepted except from attorneys. Prepayment and SASE required.

Court of Common Pleas - Criminal
Clerk of Courts, 50 N Duke St, Lancaster, PA 17602; phone: 717-299-8275; fax: 717-295-3686; hours 8:30AM-5PM (EST). *Felony, Misdemeanor.*
www.co.lancaster.pa.us/courts/site/default.asp

Criminal Records: Access: Mail, in person, online. Both court and visitors may perform in person searches. Search fee: $20.00 per name. Court makes copy: $1.00 per copy or $1.00 per docket page including disposition; no copy fee if court does the search. Self serve copy fee: $1.00 per page. Required to search: name, years to search, SSN or DOB. Criminal records on computer from 1988, paper back to 1983, archived from 1901, indexes to 1729. Search dockets online free at http://ujsportal.pacourts.us/WebDocketSheets/OtherCriteria.aspx. Mail turnaround time 2 days.

General Information: Public terminal has only criminal records back to 1988. No juvenile records released. Will not fax documents. Certification fee: $8.00 per document. Payee: Clerk of Courts. Only cashiers checks and money orders accepted. Prepayment and SASE required.

Register of Wills 50 N Duke St, Lancaster, PA 17602; phone: 717-299-8243; fax: 717-295-5914; hours 8:30AM-4:30PM (EST). *Probate.*
www.co.lancaster.pa.us

Lawrence County

Court of Common Pleas - Criminal/Civil
430 Court St, New Castle, PA 16101-3593; phone: 724-656-2143; criminal phone: 724-656-2188; civil phone: 724-656-1960; fax: 724-656-1988; hours 8AM-4PM (EST). *Felony, Misdemeanor, Civil, Eviction.*
www.co.lawrence.pa.us

Civil Records: Access: Fax, mail, online, in person. Both court and visitors may perform in person searches. Search fee: $15.50 per name. Court makes copy: $.50 per page. Required to search: name, years to search. Civil cases indexed by defendant, plaintiff. Civil records on computer from 1994, on Russell Index from 1885. Online access is by subscription from private company - Infocon at www.infoconcountyaccess.com, 814-472-6066. See note at beginning of section. Mail turnaround time ASAP.

Criminal Records: Access: Fax, mail, online, in person. Both court and visitors may perform in person searches. Search fee: $16.00 per name. Court makes copy: $.80 per page. Required to search: name, years to search, signed release; also helpful: DOB, SSN. Criminal records on computer from 1994, on Russell Index from 1885. Internet access to court records is by subscription from a private company - Infocon at www.ic-access.com, 814-472-6066. See note at beginning of section. Also, search dockets online free at http://ujsportal.pacourts.us/WebDocketSheets/OtherCriteria.aspx. Mail turnaround time ASAP.

General Information: Public use terminal available. No adoption, juvenile, impounded, or juvenile sex crime victim records released. Will fax documents: local $1.00 plus $.50 per pg; long distance $3.00 plus $.50 per pg. Certification fee: $4.50 first certification, $1.50 ea add'l. Payee: Prothonotary. Business checks accepted. Prepayment required. SASE requested.

Register of Wills 430 Court St, New Castle, PA 16101-3593; phone: 724-656-2159; fax: 724-656-1966; hours 8AM-4PM (EST). *Probate.*

Note: Online access available by subscription from private company - Infocon at www.infoconcountyaccess.com, 814-472-6066. See note at beginning of section.

Lebanon County

Court of Common Pleas - Civil Municipal Bldg, Rm 104, 400 S 8th St, Lebanon, PA 17042; phone: 717-274-2801 X2120; hours 8:30AM-4:30PM (EST). *Civil, Eviction.*

Civil Records: Access: Mail, in person. Visitors must perform in person searches themselves. Court makes copy: $.50 per page. Required to search: name, years to search; also helpful: address. Civil cases indexed by defendant, plaintiff. Civil records on computer from 1985, on files from 1883. Mail turnaround time same day.

General Information: Public terminal has only civil records back to 1985. No mental health records released. Certification fee: $9.00 per cert. Payee: Prothonotary. Personal checks accepted. Prepayment and SASE required.

Court of Common Pleas - Criminal Municipal Bldg, Rm 102, 400 S 8th St, Lebanon, PA 17042; phone: 717-274-2801 X2118; hours 8:30AM-4:30PM (EST). *Felony, Misdemeanor.*

Criminal Records: Access: Mail, in person, online. Both court and visitors may perform in person searches. Search fee: $18.00 per name. Court makes copy: $.50 per page. Required to search: name, years to search. Criminal records on computer from 1986, indexed from 1800s. Search dockets online free at http://ujsportal.pacourts.us/WebDocketSheets/OtherCriteria.aspx. Note: Action number required for phone access. Mail turnaround time varies.

General Information: Public terminal has only criminal records back to 1986. No juvenile records released. Certification fee: $9.00 per doc. Payee: Clerk of Court. Personal checks accepted. Prepayment and SASE required.

Register of Wills Municipal Bldg, Rm 105, 400 S 8th St, Lebanon, PA 17042; phone: 717-274-2801 X2217; probate phone: x2217/2218; fax: 717-228-4467; hours 8:30AM-4:30PM (EST). *Probate.*

Note: Search fee is $5.00 per name.

Lehigh County

Court of Common Pleas - Civil 455 W Hamilton St, Allentown, PA 18101-1614; phone: 610-782-3148; probate phone: 610-782-3170; fax: 610-770-3840; probate fax: 610-782-3932; hours 8:30AM-4:30PM (EST). *Civil, Eviction.*

www.lccpa.org

Civil Records: Access: Mail, online, in person. Both court and visitors may perform in person searches. No search fee. Court makes copy: $.50 per page. Self serve copy fee: $.25 per page. Required to search: name, years to search, DOB. Civil cases indexed by defendant, plaintiff. Civil records on computer since 1985, on microfilm from 1812, some in books. Access to the county online system requires monthly usage fee. Search by name or case number. Call Lehigh Cty Fiscal Office at 610-782-3112 for more information. Mail turnaround time 2 days.

General Information: Public terminal has criminal back to 1990 and civil back to 1985. No sealed, confidential, or impounded records released. Certification fee: $4.75. Payee: Clerk of Courts-Civil. Personal checks accepted. Prepayment required.

Court of Common Pleas - Criminal Clerk of Courts, 455 W Hamilton St, Allentown, PA 18101-1614; phone: 610-782-3077; criminal phone: 610-782-3077; civil phone: 610-782-3148; fax: 610-770-6797; hours 8:30AM-4:30PM (EST). *Felony, Misdemeanor.*

www.lccpa.org

Criminal Records: Access: Mail, online, in person. Both court and visitors may perform in person searches. Search fee: $20.90 per name. Fee includes copy of certified docket. Court makes copy: $.50. Docket printout mailed $3.15. Self serve copy fee: $.25 per page. Required to search: name, years to search, DOB; SSN helpful. Criminal records on computer from 1990, on alpha index from 1962 to 1990, on microfilm from 1812. Access to the countywide online system requires monthly usage fee. Search by name or case number. Call Lehigh Cty Computer Svcs Dept at 610-782-3286 for more information. Also, as of 7/25/2005, search dockets online free at http://ujsportal.pacourts.us/WebDocketSheets/OtherCriteria.aspx. Note: Also, free online access is under development; currently calendars and bench warrants are online at www.lehighcountycourt.org under "Calendars & Schedules." Mail turnaround time 1 week.

General Information: Public terminal has only criminal records back to 1812. No juvenile or impounded records released. Certification fee: $8.45. Payee: Clerk of Courts-Criminal. Personal checks accepted. Prepayment and SASE required.

Register of Wills 455 W Hamilton, Allentown, PA 18101-1614; phone: 610-782-3170; fax: 610-782-3932; hours 8AM-4PM (EST). *Probate.*

Note: Online access to Wills: call Lehigh Cty Computer Svcs Dept at 610-782-3286 for info.

Luzerne County

Court of Common Pleas - Civil 200 N River St, Wilkes Barre, PA 18711-1001; phone: 570-825-1745; fax: 570-825-1757; hours 9AM-4:30PM (EST). *Civil, Eviction.*

Civil Records: Access: Phone, mail, in person. Both court and visitors may perform in person searches. Search fee: $17.00 per name for 5 years, $2.00 each add'l year. Court makes copy: $2.00 per page. Self serve copy fee: $.25 per page. Required to search: name, years to search, address. Civil cases indexed by defendant, plaintiff. Civil records partially on microfiche and archives, on dockets from 1935. Mail turnaround time 5 days.

General Information: No public access terminal. No mental, sealed records released. Fee to fax documents is $2.00 per page. Certification fee: $5.50. Payee: Prothonotary. Personal checks accepted. Visa, MC, AmEx accepted but not over the phone. Prepayment and SASE required.

Court of Common Pleas - Criminal 200 N River St, Wilkes Barre, PA 18711; phone: 570-825-1585; fax: 570-825-1843; hours 8AM-4:30PM (EST). *Felony, Misdemeanor.*

Criminal Records: Access: Fax, mail, in person, online. Only the court performs in person searches; visitors may not. Search fee: $15.00 per name. Court makes copy: $.35 per page. Required to search: name, years to search, DOB or SSN. Criminal records on computer, microfiche and archived from 1989, on files from 1972. Records from 1933 to 1959 destroyed in flood. Index starts in 1918. As of 12/5/2005, search dockets online free at http://ujsportal.pacourts.us/WebDocketSheets/OtherCriteria.aspx. Mail turnaround time 1-2 days.

General Information: No public access terminal. No "M" number (confidential custody case) records released. No fee to fax documents. Certification fee: $7.00. Payee: Clerk of Courts. Personal checks or Visa, MC, Discover accepted. Prepayment required.

Register of Wills 20 N Pennsylvania Ave, #231, Penn Place, Wilkes Barre, PA 18701; phone: 570-825-1668, 570-825-8241; fax: 570-826-0869; hours 9AM-4:30PM (EST). *Probate.*

Lycoming County

Court of Common Pleas - Criminal/Civil 48 W 3rd St, Williamsport, PA 17701; phone: 570-327-2251; fax: 570-327-2505; hours 8:30AM-5PM (EST). *Felony, Misdemeanor, Civil, Eviction.*

Civil Records: Access: In person only. Visitors must perform in person searches themselves. Court makes copy: $.50 per page. Required to search: name, years to search; also helpful: address. Civil cases indexed by defendant, plaintiff. Civil records on computer from 1983, on dockets from 1795.

Criminal Records: Access: Mail, in person, online. Both court and visitors may perform in person searches. Search fee: $10.00 per name. Court makes copy: $.50 per page. Required to search: name, years to search, DOB; also helpful: address. Criminal records on computer from 1910. Search dockets online free at http://ujsportal.pacourts.us/WebDocketSheets/OtherCriteria.aspx. Mail turnaround time same day.

General Information: Public terminal has criminal back to 1950s and civil back to 1983. No juvenile, cases involving minors, mental records released. Certification fee: $5.00 per cert includes copies. Payee: Prothonotary. Personal checks accepted. Prepayment and SASE required.

Register of Wills Lycoming Co Courthouse, 48 W 3rd St, Williamsport, PA 17701; phone: 570-327-2263, 327-2258; fax: 570-327-6790; hours 8:30AM-5PM (EST). *Probate.*

McKean County

Court of Common Pleas - Criminal/Civil PO Box 273, Smethport, PA 16749; phone: 814-887-3270; fax: 814-887-3219; hours 8:30AM-4:30PM (EST). *Felony, Misdemeanor, Civil, Eviction.*

Civil Records: Access: Phone, fax, mail, in person. Both court and visitors may perform in person searches. Search fee: $15.00 per name. Court makes copy: $.50 per page. Computer search copy fee: $1.00 per page. Required to search: name, years to search. Civil cases indexed by defendant, plaintiff. Civil records on computer since 1994, on microfiche from 1952 to 1962, on dockets from 1872. Mail turnaround time same day.

Criminal Records: Access: Mail, in person, online. Both court and visitors may perform in person searches. Search fee: $15.00 per name. Court makes copy: $.50 per page. Computer search copy fee $1.00 per page. Required to search: name, years to search, DOB. Criminal records on computer since 1994, on dockets from 1872. Search dockets online free at http://ujsportal.pacourts.us/WebDocketSheets/OtherCriteria.aspx. Mail turnaround time same day.

General Information: Public use terminal available. No sex related, juvenile, mental health records released. Will fax documents for $2.00 per page. Certification fee: $10.00. Payee: Prothonotary or Clerk of Courts. Personal checks accepted. Prepayment and SASE required.

Register of Wills PO Box 202, Smethport, PA 16749-0202; phone: 814-887-3260; fax: 814-887-2242; hours 8:30AM-4:30PM (EST). *Probate.*

Mercer County

Court of Common Pleas - Civil 105 Mercer County Courthouse, Mercer, PA 16137; phone: 724-662-3800; hours 8:30AM-4:30PM (EST). *Civil, Eviction.*

Civil Records: Access: In person, online. Visitors must perform in person searches themselves. Court makes copy: $1.00 per page. Required to search: name, years to search. Civil cases indexed by defendant, plaintiff. Civil records on computer since 1994; prior records on dockets from 1930s, archived from 1700s. Include SSN and DOB in your search. Online access is by subscription from private company - Infocon at www.infoconcountyaccess.com, 814-472-6066. See note at beginning of section. Mail turnaround time 1-2 days.

General Information: Public terminal has only civil records back to 1994. No mental, sealed records released. Certification fee: $4.50 per cert. Payee: Prothonotary or Clerk of Courts. Business checks accepted. Prepayment and SASE required.

Court of Common Pleas - Criminal 112 Mercer County Courthouse, Mercer, PA 16137; phone: 724-662-3800 X2248; fax: 724-662-1604; hours 8:30AM-4:30PM (EST). *Felony, Misdemeanor.*

Criminal Records: Access: Mail, in person, online. Both court and visitors may perform in person searches. Search fee: $10.00 per name. Court makes copy: $.50 per page. Required to search: name, years to search; also helpful: DOB, SSN. Criminal records on computer since 1993, indexed since 1920, on files from 1980. Search dockets online free at http://ujsportal.pacourts.us/WebDocketSheets/OtherCriteria.aspx. Mail turnaround time 2-4 days.

General Information: Public terminal has only criminal records. No juvenile records released. Fee to fax documents is $1.00 per page. Certification fee: $5.00. Payee: Clerk of Courts. Personal checks accepted. Prepayment and SASE required.

Register of Wills 112 Mercer County Courthouse, Mercer, PA 16137; phone: 724-662-3800 X2253; fax: 724-662-1604; hours 8:30AM-4:30PM (EST). *Probate.*

Mifflin County

Court of Common Pleas - Criminal/Civil 20 N Wayne St, Lewistown, PA 17044; phone: 717-248-8146; fax: 717-248-5275; hours 8AM-4:30PM (EST). *Felony, Misdemeanor, Civil, Eviction.* www.co.mifflin.pa.us

Civil Records: Access: In person, online. Visitors must perform in person searches themselves. Court makes copy: $.50 per page; same fee for self serve. Required to search: name, years to search. Civil cases indexed by defendant, plaintiff. Civil records on computer from 1993, on microfiche from 1971-1990 prior on books. The court calendar is at the website. Internet access to court records is by subscription from a private company - Infocon at www.ic-access.com, 814-472-6066. See note at beginning of section.

Criminal Records: Access: In person, online. Visitors must perform in person searches themselves. Court makes copy: $.50 per page; same fee for self serve. Required to search: name, years to search. Criminal records on computer from 1993, on microfiche from 1971-1990prior on books. The court calendar is at the website. Internet access to court records is by subscription from a private company - Infocon at www.ic-access.com, 814-472-6066. See note at beginning of section. Also, search dockets online free at http://ujsportal.pacourts.us/WebDocketSheets/OtherCriteria.aspx.

General Information: Public terminal goes back to 1971. No juvenile, mental health records released. Certification fee: $4.50. Payee: Clerk of Courts. Personal checks accepted. Prepayment required.

Register of Wills 20 N Wayne St, Lewistown, PA 17044; phone: 717-242-1449; fax: 717-248-2503; hours 8AM-4:30PM M-F (EST). *Probate.*

Note: Online access available by subscription from private company - Infocon at www.infoconcountyaccess.com, 814-472-6066.

Monroe County

Court of Common Pleas - Civil Monroe County Courthouse - Prothonotary, 7th & Monroe St, Stroudsburg, PA 18360; phone: 570-517-3988; fax: 570-420-3865; hours 8:30AM-4:30PM (EST). *Civil, Eviction.*

Note: Passport info 570-517-3370.

Civil Records: Access: Mail, in person. Both court and visitors may perform in person searches. Search fee: $5.00. Court makes copy: $1.00 per page. Required to search: name, years to search; also helpful: DOB, SSN, signed release. Civil cases indexed by defendant, plaintiff. Civil records indexed on computer 1995 to present, prior in dockets, books. Mail turnaround time 1 day.

General Information: Public terminal has only civil records. No juvenile records released. Certification fee: $3.00. Payee: Monroe County Prothonotary. Only cashiers checks and money orders accepted. Prepayment required.

Court of Common Pleas - Criminal Monroe County Courthouse, Rm 312, Stroudsburg, PA 18360-2190; phone: 570-517-3385; criminal phone: 570-517-3339; fax: 570-420-2582; hours 8:30AM-4:30PM (EST). *Felony, Misdemeanor.*

Criminal Records: Access: Mail, in person, online. Both court and visitors may perform in person searches. Search fee: $5.00 per name. Court makes copy: $1.00 per page. Self serve copy fee: $.25 per page. Required to search: name, years to search; also helpful: address, DOB, SSN. Criminal records on computer since 1995; prior on dockets. Search dockets online free at http://ujsportal.pacourts.us/WebDocketSheets/OtherCriteria.aspx. Mail turnaround time 1 day.

General Information: Public terminal has only criminal records back to 1995. No sex related, juvenile, adoption records released. Certification fee: $5.00 per document. Payee: Clerk of Court. Only cashiers checks and money orders accepted. Prepayment and SASE required.

Register of Wills Monroe County Courthouse, 7th and Monroe, Stroudsburg, PA 18360; phone: 570-517-3359; fax: 570-517-3873; hours 8:30AM-4PM (EST). *Probate.*

Note: Access wills records online at www.landex.com/remote/. Fee is $.20 per minute and $.50 per fax page. Wills go back to 11/1836.

Montgomery County

Court of Common Pleas - Civil PO Box 311, Airy & Swede St, Norristown, PA 19404-0311; phone: 610-278-3360; fax: 610-278-5994; hours 8:30AM-4:15PM (EST). *Civil, Eviction.* www.montcopa.org

Civil Records: Access: Online, in person. Visitors must perform in person searches themselves. Court makes copy: $1.00 for 1st 4 pages; $.50 each add'l. Required to search: name, years to search. Civil cases indexed by defendant, plaintiff. Civil records on computer from 4/82, on microfilm from 1800s. Court and other records are free online at www.montcopa.org/mway/index.html. This includes active and purged civil cases, also active probate cases. Mail turnaround time 2 days.

General Information: Public terminal has only civil records back to 1992. No mental health, divorce, sealed records released. Will fax documents for $1.00 1st page, $.50 each add'l. Certification fee: $4.50 per cert includes copies. Payee: Prothonotary. Personal checks accepted. Prepayment required.

Court of Common Pleas - Criminal PO Box 311, Main & Swede St, Norristown, PA 19404-0311; phone: 610-278-3346; fax: 610-278-5183; hours 8:30AM-4:15PM (EST). *Felony, Misdemeanor.* www.montcopa.org

Criminal Records: Access: Mail, online, in person. Both court and visitors may perform in person searches. Search fee: $16.50 per name. Court makes copy: $1.00 per page. Required to search: name, years to search, DOB, signed release. Criminal records on computer from 10/84, prior archived and on microfiche. Search dockets online free at http://ujsportal.pacourts.us/WebDocketSheets/OtherCriteria.aspx. Mail turnaround time 5 days.

General Information: Public terminal goes back to 1980. No impounded, sealed records released. Certification fee: $7.50 per cert. Payee: Clerk of Courts. Business checks or Visa, MC, Discover accepted. Accepted in person only. Prepayment and SASE required.

Register of Wills Airy & Swede St, PO Box 311, Norristown, PA 19404; phone: 610-278-3400; fax: 610-278-3240; hours 8:30AM-3PM (EST). *Probate.* www.montcopa.org

Note: Search active probate cases at www.montcopa.org/mway/index.html.

Montour County

Court of Common Pleas - Criminal/Civil Montour County Courthouse, 29 Mill St, Danville, PA 17821; phone: 570-271-3010; fax: 570-271-3089; hours 9AM-4PM (EST). *Felony, Misdemeanor, Civil, Eviction.* www.montourco.org

Civil Records: Access: Phone, fax, mail, in person, online. Both court and visitors may perform in person searches. Search fee: $10.00 per name. Court makes copy: $.50 per page. Required to search: name, years to search. Civil cases indexed by defendant, plaintiff. Civil records on books since 1991, on microfiche since 1939, on computer back to 1995. Actual files kept for 20 years. Online access is by subscription from private company - Infocon at www.infoconcountyaccess.com, 814-472-6066. See note at beginning of section. Mail turnaround time 1-2 days.

Criminal Records: Access: Phone, fax, mail, in person, online. Both court and visitors may perform in person searches. Search fee: $10.00 per name. Court makes copy: $.50 per page. Required to search: name, years to search, DOB. Criminal records on books since 1991, on microfiche since 1939, on computer back to 1995. Actual files kept for 20 years. Internet access to court records is by subscription from a private company - Infocon at www.ic-access.com, 814-472-6066. See note at beginning of section. Also, as of 8/29/2005, search dockets online free at http://ujsportal.pacourts.us/WebDocketSheets/OtherCriteria.aspx. Mail turnaround time 1-2 days.

General Information: Public terminal goes back to 1996. No sex related, juvenile or adoption records released. Will fax documents for $5.00 fax fee. Certification fee: $4.00. Payee: Prothonotary. Personal checks accepted. Prepayment and SASE required.

Register of Wills 29 Mill St, Danville, PA 17821; phone: 570-271-3012; fax: 570-271-3071; hours 9AM-4PM (EST). *Probate.*

Note: Online access available by subscription from private company - Infocon at www.infoconcountyaccess.com, 814-472-6066. See note at beginning of section.

Northampton County

Court of Common Pleas - Civil Gov't Center, 669 Washington St, Rm 207, Easton, PA 18042-7498; phone: 610-559-3060; hours 8:30AM-4:30PM (EST). *Civil, Eviction.* www.nccpa.org

Civil Records: Access: In person only. Visitors must perform in person searches themselves. Court

makes copy: $1.00 per page. Self serve copy fee: $.25 per page. Required to search: name, years to search; also helpful: address. Civil cases indexed by defendant, plaintiff. Civil records on computer since 1/85 (Civil) and 2/90 (Judgments). Search calendars and schedules for free online at www.nccpa.org/schedule.html.

General Information: Public terminal has only civil records back to 1985. No impounded or PFA abuse records released. Certification fee: $4.75. Payee: Clerk of Court-Civil or Prothonotary's Office. Business or certified checks accepted; no personal checks. Prepayment required.

Court of Common Pleas - Criminal 669 Washington St, Easton, PA 18042-7494; phone: 610-559-3000 X3046; fax: 610-252-4391; hours 8:30AM-4:30PM (EST). *Felony, Misdemeanor.* www.nccpa.org

Criminal Records: Access: Mail, in person, online. Both court and visitors may perform in person searches. Search fee: $10.00 per name. Court makes copy: $.50 per page. Required to search: name, years to search, DOB; also helpful: SSN. Criminal records on computer from 1984, on files from 1800s. Search calendars and schedules for free online at www.nccpa.org/schedule.html. Also, as of 10/17/2005, search dockets online free at http://ujsportal.pacourts.us/WebDocketSheets/OtherCriteria.aspx. Mail turnaround time same day.

General Information: Public terminal has only criminal records. No juvenile, expunged records released. Will fax documents to local or toll free line. Certification fee: $8.00. Payee: Criminal Division. Business checks or Visa, MC accepted. Prepayment required.

Register of Wills Governmment Ctr, 669 Washington St, Easton, PA 18042; phone: 610-559-3094; fax: 610-559-3735; hours 8:30AM-4:30PM (EST). *Probate.*

Northumberland County

Court of Common Pleas - Civil County Courthouse, 201 Market St, Rm #7, Sunbury, PA 17801-3468; phone: 570-988-4151; hours 9AM-5PM M; 9AM-4:30PM T-F (EST). *Civil, Eviction.*

Civil Records: Access: Phone, mail, in person. Both court and visitors may perform in person searches. Search fee: $7.00 per name. Court makes copy: $1.00 via mail; $.25 if in person. Required to search: name, years to search. Civil cases indexed by defendant, plaintiff. Civil records on file from 1772; on computer back to 1998. Mail turnaround time 1-2 days.

General Information: Public terminal has only civil records back to 1998. No adult abuse, involuntary treatment records released. Certification fee: $4.25 plus $1.25 each add'l page. Payee: Northumberland Prothonotary. Business checks accepted. Prepayment and SASE required.

Court of Common Pleas - Criminal County Courthouse, 201 Market St, Rm 7, Sunbury, PA 17801-3468; phone: 570-988-4148; criminal phone: 570-988-4148; hours 9AM-5PM M; 9AM-4:30PM T-F (EST). *Felony, Misdemeanor.*

Criminal Records: Access: Mail, in person, online. Both court and visitors may perform in person searches. Search fee: $10.00 per name. Court makes copy: $1.00 for first page, $.25 each add'l. Self serve copy fee: $.25 per page. Required to search: name, years to search, DOB; also helpful: SSN. Criminal records indexed in office from 1945, on dockets from 1776, archived from 1776 to 1945, on computer back to 1998. As of 7/25/2005, search dockets online free at http://ujsportal.pacourts.us/WebDocketSheets/OtherCriteria.aspx. Mail turnaround time 1-2 days.

General Information: Public terminal has only criminal records back to 1945. No juvenile records released. Will not fax documents. Certification fee: $4.00 per doc plus copy fee each add'l page. Payee: Clerk of Courts Office. Personal checks accepted. Prepayment and SASE required.

Register of Wills 201 Market St, County Courthouse, Sunbury, PA 17801; phone: 570-988-4143 and 570-988-4140; fax: 570-988-4141; hours 9AM-4:30PM (EST). *Probate.*

Perry County

Court of Common Pleas - Criminal/Civil PO Box 223 (1 Courthouse Sq), New Bloomfield, PA 17068; phone: 717-582-2131; criminal phone: 717-582-2131 X2241; civil phone: 717-582-2131 X2240; hours 8AM-4PM (EST). *Felony, Misdemeanor, Civil, Eviction.*

Civil Records: Access: In person only. Visitors must perform in person searches themselves. Court makes copy: $.40 per page; same fee for self serve. Required to search: name, years to search. Civil cases indexed by defendant, plaintiff. Civil records on dockets from 1800s.

Criminal Records: Access: Phone, fax, mail, in person, online. Both court and visitors may perform in person searches. Search fee: $10.00 per name. Court makes copy: $.40 per page; same fee for self serve. Required to search: name, years to search; also helpful: DOB, SSN. Criminal records on dockets from 1950. Search dockets online free at http://ujsportal.pacourts.us/WebDocketSheets/OtherCriteria.aspx. Mail turnaround time 1 week; phone turnaround is immediate.

General Information: Public use terminal available. No juvenile records released. No fee to fax documents. Certification fee: $5.00 per document includes copy fee. Payee: Prothonotary or Clerk of Courts. Personal checks accepted. Prepayment required. Will bill to attorneys and abstract companies upon approval. SASE required.

Register of Wills PO Box 223, New Bloomfield, PA 17068; phone: 717-582-2131; fax: 717-582-5149; hours 8AM-4PM (EST). *Probate.*

Philadelphia County

Court of Common Pleas - Civil First Judicial District of PA, Rm 284, City Hall, Philadelphia, PA 19107; phone: 215-686-6656; fax: 215-567-7380; hours 9AM-5PM (EST). *Civil.* http://courts.phila.gov

Note: Has separate search unit (215-868-6656), record unit (215-686-6661), and cert unit (215-686-6656 or 6663). Get case number from web or search unit (Rm 262), then get case files from record unit (Record Rm), then cert at Rm 269.

Civil Records: Access: Mail, online, in person. Both court and visitors may perform in person searches. No search fee. Court makes copy: $.50 per page. Required to search: name, years to search. Civil cases indexed by defendant, plaintiff. Civil records on computer from 1/82 to present, archived on files from 1700s to 1982. Access to 1st Judicial District Civil Trial records is free at http://fjdwebserver.phila.gov. Search by name, judgment and docket information. There is also a civil docket access name search at http://courts.phila.gov. Mail turnaround time 1-5 days.

General Information: Public terminal has only civil records back to 1982. No mental health, divorce, abuse, adoption records released. Certification fee: $30.00 per doc. Payee: Prothonotary. Business checks accepted. Prepayment and SASE required.

Clerk of Quarter Session 1301 Filbert St, #310, Philadelphia, PA 19107; phone: 215-683-7706, 7707; fax: 215-683-7713; hours 9AM-4PM (EST). *Felony, Misdemeanor.* http://courts.phila.gov

Criminal Records: Access: Mail, in person. Both court and visitors may perform in person searches. Search fee: $10.00 per name. Court makes copy: $.25 per page. Required to search: name, years to search, DOB, signed release; also helpful: address, race, sex. Criminal records on computer and microfiche from 1969, archived from 1800s; has case records back to late 1980s. Mail turnaround time 2-3 weeks.

General Information: Public terminal has only criminal records back to 1980. No sealed, grand jury, mental records released. Certification fee: $12.50 per doc. Payee: Clerk of Quarter Sessions. Business checks accepted. Prepayment and SASE required.

Municipal Court - Civil 34 S 11th St, Judgments & Petitions, Philadelphia, PA 19107; phone: 215-686-7989, 7950; hours 9AM-5PM (EST). *Civil Actions Under $10,000, Eviction.* http://fjd.phila.gov

Civil Records: Access: Phone, mail, in person, online. Only the court performs in person searches; visitors may not. No search fee. Court makes copy: $.50 per page. Required to search: name, years to search; also helpful- address. Civil cases indexed by defendant, plaintiff. Civil records on computer from 1969. Access muni court dockets online free at http://claims.courtapps.com/phmuni/cms/search2.do. Mail turnaround time 1-2 days.

General Information: Certification fee: $5.00 per doc. Payee: Municipal Court. Only cashiers checks and money orders accepted. Prepayment and SASE required.

Municipal Court - Misdemeanor 1301 Filbert St, #208 Criminal Justice Ctr, Philadelphia, PA; phone: 215-686-7000; criminal phone: 215-683-7706; hours 9AM-4PM (EST). *Felony Hearings, Misdemeanor (less than 5 years).*

http://courts.phila.gov./municipal/criminal/
Note: Court has jurisdiction over certain criminal offenses with jail terms up to five years. Closed cases held by Clerk of Quarter Session (see separate listing); open Misdemeanor cases at this Muni Court Clerk; 215-683-7290.

Criminal Records: Access: in person, online. Only the court performs in person searches; visitors may not. Court makes copy: $.50 per page. Required to search: name, years to search, address, DOB, signed release. Criminal records on computer from 1969. Online access free to docket info at http://claims.courtapps.com/phmuni/publicLogin.jsp. Note: Access disposed cases at Clerk of Quarter Sessions.

General Information: Public terminal has only criminal records back to - open cases only. (Terminal located at 2nd Fl Information Counter.) Certification fee: $5.00. Only cashiers checks and money orders accepted. Prepayment and SASE required.

Register of Wills City Hall, Rm 180, Philadelphia, PA 19107; phone: 215-686-6250/6282; fax: 215-686-6293; hours 8:30AM-4:30PM (EST). *Probate.*

Pike County

Court of Common Pleas 412 Broad St, Milford, PA 18337; phone: 570-296-7231; hours 8:30AM-4:30PM (EST). *Felony, Misdemeanor, Civil, Eviction.*

Civil Records: Access: Phone, mail, online, in person. Both court and visitors may perform in person searches. Court makes copy: $.25 per page; $5.00 for docket entries. Self serve copy fee: $.25 per page. Required to search: name, years to search. Civil cases indexed by defendant, plaintiff. Civil records on files for 100 yrs, computerized since 1995. Online access is by subscription from private company - Infocon at www.infoconcountyaccess.com, 814-472-6066. See note at beginning of section. Note: The court will only do searches from 01/95 forward. Mail turnaround time varies.

Criminal Records: Access: Phone, mail, online, in person. Both court and visitors may perform in person searches. Search fee: $10.00 per name. Court makes copy: $.25 per page; $5.00 for docket entries. Self serve copy fee: $.25 per page. Required to search: name, years to search. Criminal records on files for 100 yrs, computerized since 1995. Internet access to court records is by subscription from a private company - Infocon at www.ic-access.com, 814-472-6066. See note at beginning of section. Also, as of 9/19/2005, search dockets online free at http://ujsportal.pacourts.us/WebDocketSheets/OtherCriteria.aspx. Note: The court will only do searches from 01/95 forward. Mail turnaround time varies.

General Information: Public terminal goes back to 1995. No juvenile, adoption, sealed records released. Certification fee: $2.50 per page. Payee: Prothonotary. Personal checks not exceeding $25.00 accepted. Prepayment and SASE required.

Register of Wills 506 Broad St, Milford, PA 18337; phone: 570-296-3508; fax: 570-296-3514; hours 8:30AM-4:30PM (EST). *Probate.*

Note: Online access available by subscription from private company - Infocon at www.infoconcountyaccess.com, 814-472-6066. See note at beginning of section.

Potter County

Court of Common Pleas 1 E 2nd St, Rm 23, Coudersport, PA 16915; phone: 814-274-9740; fax: 814-274-3361; hours 8:30AM-4:30PM (EST). *Felony, Misdemeanor, Civil, Eviction.*

Civil Records: Access: Phone, fax, mail, in person, online. Both court and visitors may perform in person searches. No search fee. Court makes copy: $.25 per page. Required to search: name, years to search. Civil cases indexed by defendant, plaintiff. Civil records on dockets from early 1833 to 11/97; on computer since 11/97. Online access is by subscription from private company - Infocon at www.infoconcountyaccess.com, 814-472-6066. See note at beginning of section. Mail turnaround time 2 weeks, phone turnaround immediate unless a lengthy search.

Criminal Records: Access: Phone, fax, mail, in person, online. Both court and visitors may perform in person searches. No search fee. Court makes copy: $.25 per page. Required to search: name, years to search, DOB. Criminal records on card index from 1983 to 6/27/97; on computer since 6/27/97; archived since 1839. as of 5/23/2005, search dockets online free at http://ujsportal.pacourts.us/WebDocketSheets/OtherCriteria.aspx. See note at beginning of section. Mail turnaround time 2 weeks, phone turnaround immediate unless a lengthy search.

General Information: Public terminal has criminal back to 6/27/1997 and civil back to 11/1997. No juvenile records released. No fee to fax documents if limited. Certification fee: $5.00. Payee: Prothonotary & Clerk of Courts. Personal checks accepted. Prepayment and SASE required.

Register of Wills 1 E 2nd St, Courthouse, Rm 20, Coudersport, PA 16915; phone: 814-274-8370; fax: 814-274-3360; hours 8:30AM-4:30PM (EST). *Probate.*

Note: Online access available by subscription from private company - Infocon at www.infoconcountyaccess.com, 814-472-6066. See note at beginning of section.

Schuylkill County

Court of Common Pleas - Civil 401 N 2nd St, Pottsville, PA 17901-2528; phone: 570-628-1270; fax: 570-628-1261; hours 8:30AM-4:30PM (EST). *Civil, Eviction.*

www.co.schuylkill.pa.us

Civil Records: Access: Mail, in person, online. Both court and visitors may perform in person searches. Search fee: $5.00 per name. Court makes copy: $.25 per page; same fee for self serve. Required to search: name, years to search. Civil cases indexed by defendant, plaintiff. Civil records (suits) on computer from 1989, judgments on computer from 199 and on dockets from 1800s. Access civil court records and judgments free at www.co.schuylkill.pa.us/info/Civil/Inquiry/Search.csp. Mail turnaround time 1 day.

General Information: Public terminal has only civil records back to 1989. (Judgments go back to 1999.) No master reports or sealed records released.

Certification fee: $4.00 per page. Payee: Prothonotary. Personal checks accepted. Prepayment required. Will bill copy fees. SASE requested.

Court of Common Pleas - Criminal 410 N 2nd St, Pottsville, PA 17901; phone: 570-622-5570 X1141; civil phone: 570-628-1270; probate phone: 570-628-1377; fax: 570-628-1143; hours 8:30AM-4:30PM (EST). *Felony, Misdemeanor.*

www.co.schuylkill.pa.us

Criminal Records: Access: Fax, mail, in person, online. Both court and visitors may perform in person searches. Search fee: $11.50 per name. Court makes copy: $.25 per page. Required to search: name, years to search, DOB; also helpful: SSN. Criminal records on computer from 4/88, on dockets from 1800s. Search dockets online free at http://ujsportal.pacourts.us/WebDocketSheets/OtherCriteria.aspx. Mail turnaround time same day.

General Information: Public terminal has only criminal records back to 1988. No juvenile records released. No fee to fax documents. Certification fee: $8.75 per doc. Payee: Clerk of Courts. Business checks accepted. Prepayment required.

Register of Wills Courthouse 401 N 2nd St, Pottsville, PA 17901-2520; phone: 570-628-1377; fax: 570-628-1384; hours 8:30AM-4:30PM (EST). *Probate.*

Snyder County

Court of Common Pleas - Criminal/Civil Snyder County Courthouse, PO Box 217, Middleburg, PA 17842; phone: 570-837-4202; hours 8:30AM-4PM (EST). *Felony, Misdemeanor, Civil, Eviction.*

www.seda-cog.org/snyder/ical/calendar.asp

Civil Records: Access: Mail, in person. Both court and visitors may perform in person searches. Search fee: $10.00 per 5 years searched. Court makes copy: $.35 per page. Required to search: name, years to search. Civil cases indexed by defendant, plaintiff. Civil records on dockets from 1855, some on microfilm, computerized since 2001. Mail turnaround time 2 days.

Criminal Records: Access: Mail, in person, online. Both court and visitors may perform in person searches. Search fee: $16.00 per name per 10 years. Court makes copy: $.35 per page. Required to search: name, years to search. Criminal records on dockets from 1855, some on microfilm, computerized since 2001. As of 6/6/2005, search dockets online free at http://ujsportal.pacourts.us/WebDocketSheets/OtherCriteria.aspx. Mail turnaround time 2 days.

General Information: Public terminal goes back to 5/2001. No juvenile records released. Certification fee: $4.50 per cert. Payee: Prothonotary or Clerk of Courts. No personal checks. Prepayment and SASE required.

Register of Wills County Courthouse, 9 W Market St, PO Box 217, Middleburg, PA 17842; phone: 570-837-4224; fax: 570-837-4299; hours 8:30AM-4PM (EST). *Probate.*

www.seda-cog.org/snyder/ical/calendar.asp

Somerset County

Court of Common Pleas - Civil 111 E Union St, #190, Somerset, PA 15501; phone: 814-445-1428; fax: 814-444-9270; hours 8:30AM-4PM (EST). *Civil, Eviction.*

www.co.somerset.pa.us

Civil Records: Access: In person only. Both court and visitors may perform in person searches. No search fee. Court makes copy: $.50 per page; same fee for self serve. Required to search: name, years to search. Civil cases indexed by defendant, plaintiff. Civil records on computer from 1/92, on microfiche from 1920 to 1972, on dockets (Russell System for all other years prior to 1992). Mail turnaround time 2-3 days.

General Information: Public terminal has only civil records back to 1992. No commitment records released. No certification fee . Payee: Prothonotary of

Somerset Co. Business checks accepted. Prepayment and SASE required.

Court of Common Pleas - Criminal 111 E Union St, #180, Somerset, PA 15501; phone: 814-445-1435; civil phone: 814-445-1428; probate phone: 814-445-1548; hours 8:30AM-4PM (EST). *Felony, Misdemeanor.*

www.co.somerset.pa.us

Criminal Records: Access: Phone, mail, in person, online. Both court and visitors may perform in person searches. Search fee: $5.00 per name. Court makes copy: $.50 per page; same fee for self serve. Required to search: name, years to search, DOB; also helpful: SSN. Criminal records on microfilm from 1920, archive dates uncertain, computerized since 1996. As of 9/6/2005, search dockets online free at http://ujsportal.pacourts.us/WebDocketSheets/OtherCriteria.aspx. Mail turnaround time same day; phone turnaround is immediate.

General Information: Public terminal has only criminal records back to 1996. No impounded records released. Certification fee: $1.00. Payee: Clerk of Courts. Personal checks accepted. Will bill copy fees.

Register of Wills 111 E Union St, #170, Somerset, PA 15501-1416; phone: 814-445-1548; hours 8:30AM-4PM (EST). *Probate.*

www.co.somerset.pa.us/RegWills.htm

Sullivan County

Court of Common Pleas - Criminal/Civil Main St, Laporte, PA 18626; phone: 570-946-7351; probate phone: 570-946-7351; hours 8:30AM-4PM (EST). *Felony, Misdemeanor, Civil, Eviction, Probate.*

Note: Includes the Register of Wills.

Civil Records: Access: In person only. Visitors must perform in person searches themselves. Court makes copy: $2.00 per page. Required to search: name, years to search. Civil cases indexed by defendant, plaintiff. Civil records on dockets from 1847 to present and on computer from 8/2000.

Criminal Records: Access: In person, online. Visitors must perform in person searches themselves. Court makes copy: $2.00 per page. Required to search: name, years to search; also helpful: SSN. Criminal records on dockets from 1847 to present and on computer from 8/2000. As of 5/23/2005, search dockets online free at http://ujsportal.pacourts.us/WebDocketSheets/OtherCriteria.aspx.

General Information: Public terminal goes back to 8/7/2000. No juvenile records released. Certification fee: $3.00 per page. Payee: Prothonotary or Clerk of Courts. Personal checks accepted. Prepayment required.

Susquehanna County

Court of Common Pleas - Civil Susquehanna Courthouse, PO Box 218, Montrose, PA 18801; phone: 570-278-4600 x120; hours 9AM-4:30PM (EST). *Civil, Eviction.*

Civil Records: Access: Mail, in person, online. Both court and visitors may perform in person searches. Search fee: $7.50 per name. Court makes copy: $.25 per page; same fee for self serve. Required to search: name, years to search. Civil cases indexed by defendant, plaintiff. Civil records on dockets from 1800s. Online access is by subscription from private company - Infocon at www.infoconcountyaccess.com, 814-472-6066. See note at beginning of section. Mail turnaround time usually same day.

General Information: Public terminal has only civil records back to 8/1996. No juvenile records released. Certification fee: $4.50 per cert. Payee: Prothonotary. Personal checks accepted. Prepayment and SASE required.

Court of Common Pleas - Criminal PO Box 218, 11 Maple St, Susquehanna Courthouse, Montrose, PA 18801; phone: 570-278-4600 x321, x320, x323; fax: 570-278-4191; hours 8:30AM-4:30PM (EST). *Felony, Misdemeanor.*
Criminal Records: Access: Mail, in person, online. Both court and visitors may perform in person searches. Search fee: $5.00 per name per 5 years. Court makes copy: $.25 per page. Self serve copy fee: $1.00 per page. Required to search: name, years to search, DOB, SSN. Criminal records on dockets from 1800s, archived from 1971, computerized since 8/96. Internet access to court records is by subscription from a private company - Infocon at www.ic-access.com, 814-472-6066. See note at beginning of section. Also, as of 11/14/2005, search dockets online free at http://ujsportal.pacourts.us/WebDocketSheets/OtherCriteria.aspx. Mail turnaround time same day.
General Information: Public terminal has only criminal records back to 1996. No juvenile records released. Will fax documents. Certification fee: $3.00. Payee: Clerk of Courts. Personal checks accepted. Prepayment and SASE required.

Register of Wills PO Box 218. Susquehanna County Courthouse, 11 Maple St, Montrose, PA 18801; phone: 570-278-4600 X113; fax: 570-278-2963; hours 8:30AM-4:30PM (EST). *Probate.*

Tioga County

Court of Common Pleas - Criminal/Civil 116 Main St, Wellsboro, PA 16901; phone: 570-724-9281; hours 9AM-4:30PM (EST). *Felony, Misdemeanor, Civil, Eviction.*
Civil Records: Access: In person only. Visitors must perform in person searches themselves. Court makes copy: $.25 per page; same fee for self serve. Required to search: name. Civil cases indexed by defendant. Civil records on dockets from 1827; computerized records since 1997.
Criminal Records: Access: Mail, in person, online. Both court and visitors may perform in person searches. Search fee: $5.00 per name per year. Court makes copy: $.25 per page; same fee for self serve. Required to search: name, years to search, signed release. Criminal records on dockets from 1827; computerized records since 1965. Search dockets online free at http://ujsportal.pacourts.us/WebDocketSheets/OtherCriteria.aspx. Mail turnaround time same day when possible.
General Information: No public access terminal. No mental health, juvenile, abuse (14 or younger) records released. Certification fee: $4.50. Payee: Tioga County Prothonotary. Personal checks accepted. Prepayment and SASE required.

Register of Wills 116 Main St, Wellsboro, PA 16901; phone: 570-724-9260; hours 9AM-4:30PM (EST). *Probate.*
Note: Online access to wills is available through a private company at www.landex.com/remote/. Fee is $.20 per minute and $.50 per fax page. Images and wills go back to 2/1999.

Union County

Court of Common Pleas - Criminal/Civil 103 S 2nd St, Lewisburg, PA 17837; phone: 570-524-8751; fax: 570-524-8628; hours 8:30AM-4:30PM (EST). *Felony, Misdemeanor, Civil, Eviction.*
www.unionco.org
Civil Records: Access: Phone, mail, in person, online. Both court and visitors may perform in person searches. No search fee. Court makes copy: $.25 per page; same fee for self serve. Required to search: name, years to search. Civil cases indexed by defendant, plaintiff. Civil records on computer from 1988, on microfiche (orphans court 1813 to 1988, marriage 1885 to 2001), on dockets from 1800s to 1988. Access judgment records for no fee at a private company site at www.courthouseonline.com/JudgSearch.asp?State=PA&County=Union&Abbrev=Un&Office=PO.

Password required. Mail turnaround time same day schedule permitting.
Criminal Records: Access: Phone, mail, in person, online. Both court and visitors may perform in person searches. No search fee. Court makes copy: $.25 per page; same fee for self serve. Required to search: name, years to search. Criminal records on computer from 1988, on dockets from 1800s to 1988. Search dockets online free at http://ujsportal.pacourts.us/WebDocketSheets/OtherCriteria.aspx. Mail turnaround time same day schedule permitting.
General Information: Public terminal goes back to 1988. No juvenile records released. Will not fax documents. Certification fee: $5.00. Payee: Prothonotary or Clerk of Courts. Personal checks accepted. Prepayment and SASE required.

Register of Wills 103 S 2nd St, Lewisburg, PA 17837-1996; phone: 570-524-8761; hours 8:30AM-4:30PM (EST). *Probate.*
Note: Search wills online at www.courthouseonline.com/WillsSearch.asp?State=PA&County=Union&Abbrev=Un&Office=RW

Venango County

Court of Common Pleas - Criminal/Civil Venango County Courthouse, 1168 Liberty St, Franklin, PA 16323; phone: 814-432-9577; criminal phone: 814-432-9574; civil phone: 814-432-9577; fax: 814-432-9579; hours 8:30AM-4:30PM (EST). *Felony, Misdemeanor, Civil, Eviction.*
www.co.venango.pa.us
Civil Records: Access: Mail, in person. Both court and visitors may perform in person searches. Search fee: $7.00 per name. Court makes copy: $.50 per page; same fee for self serve. Required to search: name, years to search. Civil cases indexed by defendant, plaintiff. Civil records on computer from 1993, on dockets from 1800s. Mail turnaround time same day.
Criminal Records: Access: Mail, in person, online. Both court and visitors may perform in person searches. Search fee: $7.00 per name. Court makes copy: $.50 per page; same fee for self serve. Required to search: name, years to search, DOB; also helpful: SSN. Criminal records on computer from 1993, on dockets from 1800s. Search dockets online free at http://ujsportal.pacourts.us/WebDocketSheets/OtherCriteria.aspx. Mail turnaround time same day.
General Information: Public terminal goes back to 1993. No juvenile records released. Fee to fax documents is $1.00 per page. Certification fee: $7.00 per case. Payee: Clerk of Courts. Personal checks accepted. Prepayment and SASE required.

Register of Wills/Recorder of Deeds PO Box 831, 1168 Liberty St, Franklin, PA 16323; phone: 814-432-9534; probate phone: 814-432-9539; fax: 814-432-9569; hours 8:30AM-4:30PM (EST). *Probate.*

Warren County

Court of Common Pleas - Criminal/Civil 4th & Market St, Warren, PA 16365; phone: 814-728-3440; fax: 814-728-3459; hours 8:30AM-4:30PM (EST). *Felony, Misdemeanor, Civil, Eviction.*
Civil Records: Access: Fax, mail, in person. Both court and visitors may perform in person searches. Search fee: $20.00 per name. Court makes copy: $.25 per page. Required to search: name, years to search. Civil cases indexed by defendant, plaintiff. Civil records on computer from 2000, on dockets from 1800s. Mail turnaround time 2 days.
Criminal Records: Access: Fax, mail, in person, online. Both court and visitors may perform in person searches. Search fee: $20.00 per name. Court makes copy: $.25 per page. Required to search: name, years to search; also helpful: DOB. Criminal records on computer from 2000, on dockets from 1800s. Search dockets online free at http://ujsportal.pacourts.us/WebDocketSheets/OtherCriteria.aspx. Mail turnaround time 2 days.

General Information: Public terminal goes back to 2000. No juvenile records released. No fee to fax documents. Certification fee: $6.50 per cert. Payee: Prothonotary or Clerk of Courts. Business checks accepted. Prepayment and SASE required.

Register of Wills Courthouse, 204 4th Ave, Warren, PA 16365; phone: 814-728-3430; fax: 814-728-3476; hours 8:30AM-4:30PM (EST). *Probate.*

Washington County

Court of Common Pleas - Civil 1 S Main St, #1001, Washington, PA 15301; phone: 724-228-6770; fax: 724-229-5913; hours 9AM-4:30PM (EST). *Civil, Eviction.*
www.co.washington.pa.us
Civil Records: Access: In person only. Visitors must perform in person searches themselves. Court makes copy: $1.50 per page. Required to search: name, years to search. Civil cases indexed by defendant, plaintiff. Civil records on computer from 1987, prior on dockets to 1800s.

General Information: Public terminal has only civil records back to 1987. Certification fee: $4.50. Payee: Prothonotary. Only cashiers checks and money orders accepted. Checks from attorneys accepted. Prepayment required.

Court of Common Pleas - Criminal Courthouse, #1005, 1 S Main St, Washington, PA 15301; phone: 724-228-6787; fax: 724-228-6890; hours 9AM-4:30PM (EST). *Felony, Misdemeanor.*
www.co.washington.pa.us
Criminal Records: Access: Mail, in person, online. Both court and visitors may perform in person searches. Search fee: $10.00 per name. Court makes copy: $.25 per page; same fee for self serve. Required to search: name, years to search, DOB; also helpful: address, SSN. Criminal records on computer since 10/87, prior on dockets, archived from 1785. As of 6/20/2005, search dockets online free at http://ujsportal.pacourts.us/WebDocketSheets/OtherCriteria.aspx. Mail turnaround time over 1 week.
General Information: Public terminal has only criminal records back to 1987. No juvenile records released. Will not fax documents. Certification fee: $10.00. Payee: Clerk of Courts. Personal checks accepted. Prepayment and SASE required.

Register of Wills Courthouse, 1 S Main St, #1002, Washington, PA 15301; phone: 724-228-6775; hours 9AM-4:30PM (EST). *Probate.*

Wayne County

Court of Common Pleas - Criminal/Civil 925 Court St, Honesdale, PA 18431; phone: 570-253-5970 X200; fax: 570-253-0687; hours 8:30AM-4:30PM (EST). *Felony, Misdemeanor, Civil, Eviction.*
Civil Records: Access: In person only. Visitors must perform in person searches themselves. Court makes copy: $.50 per page; same fee for self serve. Required to search: name, years to search. Civil cases indexed by defendant, plaintiff. Civil records on daily docket entries, computerized since 1996.
Criminal Records: Access: In person, online. Visitors must perform in person searches themselves. No search fee. Court makes copy: $.50 per page; same fee for self serve. Required to search: name, years to search. Criminal records on daily docket entries, computerized since 1996. As of 6/20/2005, search dockets online free at http://ujsportal.pacourts.us/WebDocketSheets/OtherCriteria.aspx.
General Information: Public terminal goes back to 1996. Juvenile records not released. Will not fax documents. No certification fee . Personal checks accepted. Prepayment required.

Register of Wills 925 Court St, Honesdale, PA 18431; phone: 570-253-5970 X212; probate phone: x213; hours 8:30AM-4:30PM (EST). *Probate.*

Westmoreland County

Court of Common Pleas - Civil Courthouse Sq, Rm 501, PO Box 1630, Greensburg, PA 15601-1168; phone: 724-830-3502; fax: 724-830-3517; hours 8:30AM-4PM (EST). *Civil, Eviction.*
www.co.westmoreland.pa.us
Civil Records: Access: Online, in person. Visitors must perform in person searches themselves. Court makes copy: $.50 per page. Computer print out: $1.00 per page. Required to search: name, years to search. Civil cases indexed by defendant, plaintiff. Civil records on computer from 9/85, on dockets from 1700s. Access civil court dockets back to 1985 free at http://westmorelandweb400.us:8088/EGSPublicAccess.htm. Also, search Register of Wills and marriages free back to 1986. Access to full remote online system has $100 setup (no set-up if accessed via Internet) plus $20 monthly minimum. System includes civil, criminal, prothonotary indexes and recorder data. For info, call 724-830-3874, or click on "e-services" at website.

General Information: Public terminal has only civil records back to 1985. No mental health records released. Certification fee: $5.35 per cert. Payee: Prothonotary. Business checks accepted. Prepayment required.

Court of Common Pleas - Criminal Criminal Division, 203 Courthouse Square, Greensburg, PA 15601-1168; phone: 724-830-3734; fax: 724-830-3979; hours 8:30AM-4PM (EST). *Felony, Misdemeanor.*
www.co.westmoreland.pa.us
Criminal Records: Access: Fax, mail, online, in person. Both court and visitors may perform in person searches. Search fee: $17.80 per name. Court makes copy: $.50 per page. Computer copy $.50 per page; same fee for self serve. Required to search: name, years to search, signed release; also helpful: DOB, SSN. Criminal records on computer from 1941, on microfiche from 1793 to 1950, archived from 1773. Access to the commercial setup plus monthly minimum fee. For info, call 724-830-3734 or click on "e-services" at www.co.westmoreland.pa.us. Also, search dockets online free at http://ujsportal.pacourts.us/WebDocketSheets/OtherCriteria.aspx. Mail turnaround time 3 to 5 days.

General Information: Public terminal has only criminal records back to 1941. No juvenile records released. Will fax documents $10.00 per doc. Certification fee: $5.00. Payee: Clerk of Courts. Personal checks accepted. Attorney's checks accepted. Prepayment required.

Register of Wills 2 N Main St, #301, Greensburg, PA 15601; phone: 724-830-3177; fax: 724-850-3976; hours 8:30AM-4PM (EST). *Probate.*
Note: Search Register of Wills estate and marriage indices free back to 1986 at http://westmorelandweb400.us:8088/EGSPublicAccess.htm; fuller data requires registration and fees.

Wyoming County

Court of Common Pleas - Criminal/Civil Wyoming County Courthouse, Tunkhannock, PA 18657; phone: 570-836-3200 X232-234; fax: 570-836-4781; hours 8:30AM-4PM (EST). *Felony, Misdemeanor, Civil, Eviction.*
Civil Records: Access: In person only. Visitors must perform in person searches themselves. Court makes copy: $.25 per page; same fee for self serve. Required to search: name, years to search. Civil cases indexed by defendant, plaintiff. Civil records on dockets from 1800s.
Criminal Records: Access: In person, online. Visitors must perform in person searches themselves. Court makes copy: $.25 per page; same fee for self serve. Required to search: name, years to search; also helpful: DOB. Criminal records on dockets from 1800s. Search dockets online free at http://ujsportal.pacourts.us/WebDocketSheets/OtherCriteria.aspx.
General Information: Public terminal goes back to 1996. No juvenile records released. Certification fee: $7.00. Payee: Prothonotary or Clerk of Courts. Personal checks accepted. Prepayment required.

Register of Wills Wyoming County Courthouse, 1 Courthouse Sq, Tunkhannock, PA 18657; phone: 570-836-3200 X2235; fax: 570-996-5053; hours 8:30AM-4PM (EST). *Probate.*

York County

Court of Common Pleas - Civil York County Courthouse, 45 N George St, York, PA 17401; phone: 717-771-9611; criminal phone: 717-771-9612; hours 8:30AM-4:30PM (EST). *Civil.*
www.york-county.org/departments/courts/crtf1.htm
Civil Records: Access: Mail, online, in person. Visitors must perform in person searches themselves. Search fee: $1.00 per page. Court makes copy: $1.00 per page. Self serve copy fee: $.25 per page. Required to search: name, years to search. Civil cases indexed by defendant, plaintiff. Civil records on computer from mid-1988, on dockets from 1800s, archived from mid-1700s. Access to the remote online system is set-up through Information Services. For more information, call 717-771-9235. Mail turnaround time 1 day.
General Information: Public terminal has only civil records back to mid-1988. No mental health records released. Will not fax documents. Certification fee: $5.00 per page. Payee: Prothonotary. Only cashiers checks and money orders accepted. Prepayment and SASE required.

Court of Common Pleas - Criminal 45 N George St, York County Courthouse, York, PA 17401; phone: 717-771-9612; fax: 717-771-9096; hours 8:15AM-4:30PM (EST). *Felony, Misdemeanor.*
www.york-county.org/clerkofcourts.html
Criminal Records: Access: Fax, mail, online, in person. Both court and visitors may perform in person searches. No search fee. Court makes copy: $.50 per page. Required to search: name, approximate date to search. Criminal records on computer from 1986, on dockets from 1942, archived from 1700s. Search dockets online free at http://ujsportal.pacourts.us/WebDocketSheets/OtherCriteria.aspx. Mail turnaround time 1-2 weeks.
General Information: Public terminal has only criminal records back to 1986. (Several terminals available.) No sex crime, juvenile records released. No fee to fax documents. Certification fee: $9.00 per document includes copies. Will certify any add'l pages for $.50 per page copy fee. Payee: Clerk of Courts. Personal checks accepted. Prepayment and SASE required.

Register of Wills York County Judicial Center, 45 N George St, York, PA 17401; phone: 717-771-9263; fax: 717-771-4678; hours 8:00AM-4:15PM (EST). *Probate.*
Note: Online access to wills is available through a private company at www.landex.com/remote/. Fee is $.20 per minute and $.50 per fax page. Images and wills go back to 2/1999.

Pennsylvania Recording Offices

ORGANIZATION: 67 counties, 67 recording offices and 134 UCC filing offices. Each county has two different recording offices: the Prothonotary - their term for "Clerk" - accepted UCC and tax lien filings until 07/01/2001, and the Recorder of Deeds maintains real estate records. The entire state is in the Eastern Time Zone (EST).

REAL ESTATE RECORDS: County Recorders of Deeds will not perform real estate searches. Copy & certification fees vary.

UCC RECORDS: This was a dual filing state. Until 07/1/2001, Financing statements were filed both at the state level and with the Prothonotary, except for real estate related collateral, which were filed with the Recorder of Deeds. Now, only real estate related collateral is filed locally. Some county offices will not perform UCC searches. Use search request form UCC-11. Search fees are usually $59.00 per debtor name. Copies usually cost $.50-$2.00 per page. Counties also charge $5.00 per financing statement found on a search.

TAX LIEN RECORDS: All federal and state tax liens on personal property and on real property are filed with the Prothonotary. Usually, tax liens on personal property are filed in the judgment index of the Prothonotary. Some Prothonotaries will perform tax lien searches. Search fees are usually $5.00 per name.

OTHER LIENS: Judgment, municipal, mechanics.

ONLINE ACCESS: A number of counties provide web access to assessor data. The Infocon County Access System provides Internet and direct dial-up access to recorded record information for over 20 Pennsylvania counties. For information, call Infocon at 814-472-6066 or visit www.infoconcountyaccess.com

Adams County Prothonotary

County Prothonotary, 111-117 Baltimore St, Gettysburg, PA 17325. 717-334-6781; fax-717-334-0532; hours: 8AM-4:30PM.
Only the public may search. Copy fee $.25 per page. Cert fee- $4.75. Payee- County Prothonotary.

Adams County Recorder

County Recorder of Deeds, 111-117 Baltimore St; County Courthouse, Rm 102, Gettysburg, PA 17325. 717-337-9826; fax-717-334-1758; 8AM-4:30PM.
No tax liens filed here. Index: Misc. Records indexed on a public use terminal back to 1937. Only the public may search. UCC copy fee $2.00 per page. R/E record copy- $.25 per page. Cert fee- $2.00 per doc, plus copy fee. Payee- Adams County Recorder of Deeds. **Other phones:** Treasurer- 717-334-6781 x221. **Property tax/Assessor-** 717-337-9837.

Allegheny County Prothonotary

County Prothonotary, 414 Grant St; City County Bldg, Pittsburgh, PA 15219. 412-350-4200, R/E recording - 412-355-4226; fax-412-350-5260; 8:30AM-4:30PM.
http://prothonotary.county.allegheny.pa.us
Records indexed on a public use terminal back to 1/1/1995. Office personnel or visitors may perform searches. Search fee $25.00 per name. See Recorder for real estate records. UCC information or copy request per debtor name- $59.00. Copy fee $2.00, if tax lien $1.00 per page. Cert fee- $8.00 per cert plus copy fee. Payee- Allegheny County Prothonotary. **Online access to Civil Court, UCC, Tax Lien, Real Estate, Assessor records:** Access to Common Pleas Civil records is free at http://prothonotary.county.allegheny.pa.us/allegheny/welcome.htm. Registration is required. UCC records are pre-7-1-2001. Online access to the certified values database is free at the website. Also, online access to Allegheny County real estate database is free at http://www2.county.allegheny.pa.us/realestate/Search.asp.

Allegheny County Recorder

County Recorder of Deeds, 542 Forbes Ave; 101 County Office Bldg., Pittsburgh, PA 15219-2947. 412-350-4226; fax-412-350-6877; hours: 8:30AM-4:30PM. www.county.allegheny.pa.us

No tax liens filed here. Index: Books and computer. Records indexed on a public use terminal back to 1986. Office will perform a UCC search but public must search other records themselves. General index search fee $40.00. Copy fee $1.00 per page. Cert fee- $5.00 includes 1st 4 pages. Payee- Allegheny County Recorder of Deeds. **Online access to Recorder, Deed, Mortgage, Real Estate records:** Access Recorder's Index free at https://www.recorder.county.allegheny.pa.us/palr/pa003/index.jsp. Index goes back to 1986; images to 2002. Fee for doc is $1.00 per page, max fee 10 pages; Commercial draw down account copy fee is $.50 per page. Also, Land & A/R Inquiries found at www.county.allegheny.pa.us/dcs/dcsland.asp. **Other phones:** Treasurer- 412-355-4100. **Property tax/Assessor-** 412-350-4625.

Armstrong County Prothonotary

County Prothonotary, 500 E Market St; County Courthouse, Kittanning, PA 16201. 724-543-2500, R/E recording phone-724-548-3280, UCC recording phone-724-548-3251; fax-724-548-3351; hours: 8AM-4:30PM. www.geocities.com/acprothonotary
Separate indices to search. Records indexed on a public use terminal back to 1991. Office will perform a UCC search but public must search other records themselves. Search fee $5.00 per name. See Recorder for real estate records. Copy fee $1.00 per page. Cert fee- $1.50 per cert plus copy fee. Payee- Armstrong County Prothonotary.

Armstrong County Recorder

County Recorder of Deeds, 500 Market St; County Courthouse, Kittanning, PA 16201-1495. 724-548-3256, R/E recording phone-724-548-3280; fax-724-548-3236; hours: 8AM-4:30PM.
No tax liens filed here. Separate indices to search include computer, books. Records indexed on a public use terminal back to 1942, images being added. Only the public may search, but office can do a name lookup on computer. General copy fee $.50 per page; $1.00 per page if mailed. R/E record copy- $1.00 per page. Cert fee- $1.50 per page plus copy fee. **Online access to Real Estate, Recording, Marriage, Probate, Orphans Court records:** Access is through a private company. For info, call Infocon at 814-472-6066 or www.infoconcountyaccess.com. Includes Orphan

Court, Recorder of Deeds, Register of Wills images. **Other phones:** Treasurer- 724-548-3260; Appraiser/Auditor- 724-548-3489; Elections- 724-548-3222; Vital Records- 724-548-3100. **Property tax/Assessor-** 450 E. Market St, Kittanning, PA 16201; 724-548-3487.

Beaver County Prothonotary

County Prothonotary, 810 Third St; County Courthouse, Beaver, PA 15009. 724-728-3934 x11279; fax-724-728-3360; hours: 8:30AM-4:30PM. http://co.beaver.pa.us/prothonotary
Only the public may search. Tax lien copy- $1.00 per page. Cert fee- $5.00 per request. Payee- Beaver County Prothonotary.

Beaver County Recorder

County Recorder of Deeds, 810 3rd St; County Courthouse, Beaver, PA 15009. 724-728-5700; fax-724-728-8479; hours: 8:30AM-4:30PM. www.co.beaver.pa.us
No tax liens filed here. All records in one index. Will not search real estate records. Will not search UCC records, but only real estate related UCC filed here. Copy fee $1.00 per page. Cert fee- $1.50 per cert plus copy fee. Payee- Beaver County Recorder of Deeds. **Online access to Real Estate, Deed, Mortgage, Assessor records:** Access to the Recorder's database index is free at http://co.beaver.pa.us/Recorder/disclaimer.htm. Access the Assessment office at www.co.beaver.pa.us/AssessmentPublic/. **Other phones:** Treasurer- 724-728-5700; Elections- 724-728-5700; 724-728-5700- Switchboard. **Property tax/Assessor-** 724-728-5700.

Bedford County Prothonotary

County Prothonotary, County Courthouse; Corner of Penn & Julliana, Bedford, PA 15522. 814-623-4833; fax-814-623-4831; hours: 8:30AM-4:30PM.
All records in one index. Office personnel or visitors may perform searches. Search fee $20.00 per name. See Recorder for real estate records. Will search UCC records; search includes tax liens if requested. Information or copy request per debtor name- $59.00. Copy fee $5.00 per page. Cert fee- $4.50 per cert plus copy fee. Payee- Bedford County Prothonotary.

Bedford County Recorder

County Recorder, 200 S. Juliana St; County Courthouse, Bedford, PA 15522. 814-623-4836; fax-814-624-0488; hours: 8:30AM-4:30PM. www.bedford.net/regrec/home.html
No tax liens filed here. All records in one index. Only the public may search. Copy fee $.25 per page. Cert fee- $1.00 per doc plus copy fee. Payee-Recorder of Deeds. **Online access to Real Estate, Recorder, Assessor, Probate, Marriage, RE Assessor, Tax Claim records:** Access is via a private company; call Infocon at 814-472-6066 or www.infoconcountyaccess.com. Includes Recorder of Deeds and Register of Wills images. **Other phones:** Treasurer- 814-623-4846; Elections- 814-623-4807; Vital Records- 814-623-4833. **Property tax/Assessor-** 814-623-4842.

Berks County Prothonotary

County Prothonotary, 633 Court St., Reading, PA 19601. 610-478-6970, R/E recording phone-610-478-3380; fax-610-478-6969; hours: 8AM-4PM. www.co.berks.pa.us/berks/cwp/view.asp?a=1150&q=444559
All records in one index. Records indexed on a public use terminal. Only the public may search. See Recorder for real estate records. Copy fee $.50 per page; if requested by mail- $3.00 1st page, $1.00 each add'l. Cert fee- $5.25 per document plus copy fee. **Online access to Judgment, Lien, UCC, Civil Court records:** Prothonotary offers internet access to above info back to 1/1996. Fee is $300. For info, call 610-478-6967.

Berks County Recorder

Recorder of Deeds, 633 Court St, 3rd Fl, Reading, PA 19601. 610-478-3380; fax-610-478-3359; hours: 8AM-5PM. www.berksrecofdeeds.com
No tax liens filed here. Separate indices to search. Records indexed on a public use terminal back to 1980. Office personnel or visitors may perform searches. Search fee $12.00 per name. Will not search real estate records. Copy fee $1.00 per page. Cert fee- $1.50 per cert plus copy fee. **Online access to Vital Statistic, Probate, DR Warrant records:** Access to the Registry of Wills' databases are free at www.berksregofwills.com/search_page.htm including county marriage, estate, birth and death records. Estate and marriage records are current. Also, search the domestic relations warrants list at www.drs.berks.pa.us/dro_warrant_list.htm. **Other phones:** Treasurer- 610-478-6640; Elections- 610-478-6490. **Property tax/Assessor-** 610-478-6262.

Blair County Prothonotary

County Prothonotary, 423 Allegheny St #144, Hollidaysburg, PA 16648. 814-693-3080, R/E recording phone-814-693-3095; hours: 8AM-4PM.
All records in one index. Records indexed on a public use terminal back to 1989. Only the public may search. See Recorder for real estate records. Copy fee $.50 per page. Cert fee- $5.00 per doc includes copy fee. Payee- Blair County Prothonotary.

Blair County Recorder

County Recorder of Deeds, 423 Allegheny St, #145, Hollidaysburg, PA 16648. 814-693-3095; fax-814-693-3093; hours: 8AM-4PM. www.blairco.org
All records in one index. Only the public may search. Copy fee $.25 per page. Cert fee- $2.00 per doc, plus copy fee. Payee- Blair County Recorder of Deeds. **Online access to Real Estate, Recording, Assessor, Marriage, Probate, Orphans Court, Tax Claim records:** Access is via a private company; call Infocon at 814-472-6066 or www.infoconcountyaccess.com. Indexes from 1998. **Other phones:** Treasurer- 814-693-3120; Appraiser/Auditor- 814-693-3110; Elections- 814-693-3150. **Property tax/Assessor-** 814-695-5541 x223.

Bradford County Prothonotary

County Prothonotary, 301 Main St; Courthouse, Towanda, PA 18848. 570-265-1705, R/E recording phone-570-265-1702; fax-570-265-1735; hours: 9AM-5PM.
All records in one index. Records indexed on a public use terminal back to 1986. Office will perform a UCC search but public must search other records themselves. Search fee $59.50 plus $5.00 each add'l judgment. See Recorder for real estate records. Copy fee $.25 per page. Cert fee- $4.00 per doc plus copy fee. Payee- Bradford County Prothonotary.

Bradford County Recorder

County Recorder of Deeds, 301 Main St; Courthouse, Towanda, PA 18848. 570-265-1702; fax-570-265-1721; hours: 9AM-5PM.
No tax liens filed here. Separate indices to search include grantor/grantee, mortgagor/mortgagee, lesser/lessee since 1985. Records indexed on a public use terminal back to 1997. Only the public may search. Copy fee $.50 per page. Cert fee- $2.00 per cert plus copy fee. Payee- Recorder of Deeds. **Online access to Real Estate, Deed, Mortgage, Will records:** Access to Recorder of Deeds and Wills and Orphans Court is by subscription at www.landex.com/remote/. Fee is $.20 per minute, $.50 per fax page. Recorder data goes back to 1971. Images go back to 1997, also 1985-89. Wills and orphan court goes back to 1997. **Other phones:** Treasurer- 570-265-1700; Appraiser/Auditor- 570-265-1714; Elections- 570-265-1717. **Property tax/Assessor-** 570-265-1714.

Bucks County Prothonotary

County Prothonotary, 55 E. Court St.; Courthouse, Doylestown, PA 18901. 215-348-6191, R/E recording phone-215-348-6209; fax-215-348-6184; hours: 8AM-4:15PM. www.buckscounty.org/courts/
All records in one index. Records indexed on a public use terminal back to 1980. Only the public may search. See Recorder for real estate records. Copy fee $1.50 per page; self serve $.25. Cert fee- $4.75 per doc with a SASE. Payee- Bucks County Prothonotary. **Online access to Property, Tax Lien, Probate, Court, Will, Tax Claim, Vital Statistic records:** Temporarily free records at www.buckscounty.org/departments/public_access/ go back to 1980. Includes lending agency, Register of Wills, liens, sheriff sales, voter registration, courts, prothonotary as well as assessor and recorder of deeds records. For information on the new fee system, contact Jack Morris at 215-348-6579 or view details at the website. Access to Vital Records at www.vitalchek.com.

Bucks County Recorder

County Recorder of Deeds, 55 E. Court St.; Courthouse, Doylestown, PA 18901-4367. 215-348-6209; fax-215-340-8157; hours: 8:15AM-4:15PM (Recording Hours 8:15AM-4PM). www.buckscounty.org/departments/recorder_of_deeds/index.html
No tax liens filed here. All records in one index. Records indexed on a public use terminal from 1/1/1980 to 8/31/2004. Only the public may search. Copy fee $1.00 per page. Cert fee- $1.50 per cert plus copy fee. Payee- Bucks County Recorder of Deeds. **Online access to Assessor, Recorder, Real Estate, Tax Lien, Probate, Court, Will, Voter Registration, Sheriff Sales, Tax Claim records:** Temporarily free records at www.buckscounty.org/departments/public_access/ go back to 1980. Includes lending agency, Register of Wills, liens, sheriff sales, voter registration, courts, prothonotary as well as assessor and recorder of deeds records. For information on the new fee system, contact Jack Morris at 215-348-6579 or view details at the website. **Other phones:** Treasurer- 215-348-6244; Vital Records- 724-656-3100. Elections- 215-348-6163. **Property tax/Assessor-** 215-348-6219.

Butler County Prothonotary

County Prothonotary, PO Box 1208, Butler, PA 16003-1208. 724-284-5214; hours: 8:30AM-4:30PM. www.co.butler.pa.us
Separate indices to search include judgment, ejection & miscellaneous, federal lien. Records indexed on computer back to 4/1/1993. Only the public may search. Copy fee $.50 per page; $1.00 per microfilm copy. Cert fee- $.50 per cert plus copy fee. Payee- Butler County Prothonotary. **Online access to Judgment, Fed Lien, Divorce, Civil Court records:** Private company offers online access to most of the recorded records. Call Infocon at 814-472-6066, www.infoconcountyaccess.com.

Butler County Recorder

County Recorder of Deeds, PO Box 1208, Butler, PA 16003-1208. 724-284-5340; fax-724-285-9099; hours: 8:30AM-4:30PM. www.co.butler.pa.us
No tax liens filed here. Separate indices to search include mortgages from 1800-1984 (mortgagee/or indexes). Records indexed on a public use terminal back to 1985. Office personnel or visitors may perform searches. Search fee $4.00 per name. Copy fee $1.00 per page. Cert fee- $1.50 per page plus copy fee. **Online access to Marriage, Probate, Orphans Court, Guardianship records:** Access marriage, probate, and prothonotary records via a private company; call Infocon at 814-472-6066, www.infoconcountyaccess.com. Images available. Also access probate court estate and guardianship records free at http://66.117.197.22/index.cfm?page=home. Click on the "llokup" type at bottom of webpage. **Other phones:** Treasurer- 724-284-5149; Elections- 724-284-5310. **Property tax/Assessor-** 724-284-5316.

Cambria County Prothonotary

County Prothonotary, 200 S. Center St., Ebensburg, PA 15931. 814-472-1637, R/E recording phone-814-472-1473, UCC recording phone-814-472-1636; fax-814-472-5632; 9AM-4PM. www.co.cambria.pa.us
Separate indices to search include judgments, misc. Only the public may search. See Recorder for real estate records. Copy fee $.25 per page. Cert fee- $3.00 per cert includes copies. Payee- Cambria County Prothonotary. **Online access to Lien, Civil, Judgment, Divorce records:** Access prothonotary records via a private company. Subscription required. For info, call Infocon at 814-472-6066, www.infoconcountyaccess.com.

Cambria County Recorder

Recorder of Deeds, Cambria County Courthouse; 200 S. Center St., Ebensburg, PA 15931. 814-472-1473; fax-814-472-1412; hours: 9AM-4PM. www.co.cambria.pa.us/cambria
No tax liens filed here. Index: Index on computer 1986-present with separate UCC index with recent filings; manual Russell indices from 1804-1985; Military discharges unsearchable. Records indexed on a public use terminal back to 1/1986. Only the public may search. Copy fee $.50 per page. Cert fee- $1.50 per document plus copy fee. Payee- Recorder of Deeds. **Online access to Property, Assessor, Marriage, Probate, Tax Claim, Orphans Court, Tax Claim records:** Access county records via a private company. Subscription required; images available. For info, call Infocon at 814-472-6066, www.infoconcountyaccess.com. **Other phones:** Treasurer- 814-472-1643; Elections- 814-472-1460; Register of Wills- 814-472-1440. **Property tax/Assessor-** 814-472-5440 x450.

Cameron County Prothonotary

County Prothonotary, 20 E. 5th St, Emporium, PA 15834. 814-486-3349; fax-814-486-0464; hours: 8:30AM-4PM.
All records in one index. Only the public may search. Copy fee $.50 per page. Cert fee- $10.00 per cert includes copy fee. Payee- Cameron County Prothonotary.

Cameron County Recorder

County Recorder of Deeds, 20 E. 5th St, Emporium, PA 15834. 814-486-3349; fax-814-486-0464; hours: 8:30AM-4PM.
No tax liens filed here. All records in one index. Only the public may search. Copy fee $.50 per page. Cert fee- $10.00 per copy. Payee- Recorder of Deeds. **Other phones:** Treasurer- 814-486-3348. **Property tax/Assessor-** 814-486-0723.

Carbon County Prothonotary

County Prothonotary, PO Box 130, Jim Thorpe, PA 18229-0127. 570-325-2481, R/E recording phone-570-325-2651 (Recorder of Deeds), UCC recording phone-570-325-2481 (Prothonotary); fax-570-325-8047; hours: 8:30AM-4:30PM.
All records in one index. Records indexed on a public use terminal back to 1984. Only the public may search. See Recorder for real estate records. Copy fee $1.00 per page. Cert fee- $9.20 per cert plus copy fee. Payee- Carbon County Prothonotary. **Online access to Tax Lien, Judgment, UCC, Probate, Civil Court, Will records:** Access to county prothonotary, Register of Wills, and Clerk of Courts remote public access dial-up database is free; 570-325-3288; instructions/ registration at www.carboncourts.com/pubacc.htm.

Carbon County Recorder

County Recorder of Deeds, PO Box 89, Jim Thorpe, PA 18229. 570-325-2651; fax-570-325-2726; hours: 8:30AM-4:30PM.
www.carboncounty.com/deeds.htm
No tax liens filed here. Separate indices to search include computer-1988 to present, Russell index-1843-1988. Records indexed on a public use terminal back to 1988. Only the public may search. Copy fee $.50 per page. Cert fee- $1.50 per cert plus copy fee. Payee- Carbon County Recorder of Deeds. **Online access to Property, Assessor records:** Access assessor property data free at www.carboncounty.com/records.htm. **Other phones:** Treasurer- 570-325-2251; Elections- 570-325-4801. **Property tax/Assessor-** 570-325-5254.

Centre County Prothonotary

County Prothonotary, Allegheny & High; County Courthouse, Bellefonte, PA 16823. 814-355-6796, R/E recording phone-814-355-6801; hours: 8:30AM-5PM. www.co.centre.pa.us/223.htm
Separate indices to search include civil, criminal, UCC. Office will perform a UCC search but public must search other records themselves. See Recorder for real estate records. UCC Information or copy request per debtor name- $59.00. Copy fee $.50 per page. Cert fee- $4.00 per page plus copy fee. Payee- Centre County Prothonotary. **Online access to Fed Lien, Judgment, Marriage, Court, Personal Property records:** Access Prothonotary data and more at http://epin.chesco.org; registration and fees required.

Centre County Recorder

County Recorder of Deeds, 414 Holmes Ave. #1, Bellefonte, PA 16823. 814-355-6801, R/E recording phone-814-355-6701; hours: 8:30AM-5PM. www.co.centre.pa.us/133.htm
No tax liens filed here. All records in one index. Only the public may search. Copy fee $.50 per page. Cert fee- $1.50 per doc plus copy fee. Payee- Recorder of Deeds. **Online access to Real Estate, Recorder, Deed, Domestic Relations Warrant, Tax Assessment, Naturalization, Slave records:** Access Recorder data by online subscription; fee is $250 set-up plus $.10 per click or other per click plan. This replaces the old dial-up system. Also, access pre-1929 naturalization and slave records free at http://county.centreconnect.org/hrip/index.htm. Also, access to the county list of bench warrants for child support non-payment is free at http://county.centreconnect.org/drs/default.asp. **Other phones:** Treasurer- 814-355-6810; Elections- 814-355-6703. **Property tax/Assessor-** 420 Holmes St,

Bellefonte PA 16823-1488; 814-355-6721, assessor fax- 814-355-6747.

Chester County Prothonotary

County Prothonotary, PO Box 2748, West Chester, PA 19380-0991. 610-344-6301, R/E recording phone-610-344-6330, UCC recording phone-717-772-2149; fax-610-344-5903; hours: 8:30AM-4:30PM. www.chesco.org/prothy.html
All records in one index. Records indexed on a public use terminal back to 1990. Only the public may search. See Recorder for real estate records. Copy fee $1.15 1st page; $.55 each add'l. Cert fee- $5.00 1st 4 pages plus copy fee. Payee- Prothonotary. **Online access to Court Docket, Property Tax, Warrant, Lien, Assessor records:** Access the prothonotary database at www.chesco.org/prothy.html.http://dsf.chesco.org/courts/cwp/view.asp?a=1518&q=606511. Click on "SEARCH:~." $50 set up fee and $10 each month of use (if over 100 transaction per/mo, add $.10 per document). Registration/password at 610-344-6884. Prothonotary records go back to 1990.

Chester County Recorder

County Recorder of Deeds, PO Box 2748, West Chester, PA 19380-0991. 610-344-6330; fax-610-344-6408; hours: 8:30AM-4:30PM
http://dsf.chesco.org/recorder/site/default.asp
No tax liens filed here. All records in one index. Records indexed on a public use terminal back to 1920. Only the public may search. Copy fee $5.00 per page; self serve $.50. Cert fee- $1.50. Fee to fax results is $5.00 per doc plus copy fee. Payee- Chester County Recorder of Deeds. **Online access to Real Estate, Recording, Deed, Court, Vital Statistic, Archive records:** Searching countywide records including court records requires a sign-up and credit card payment. Application fee is $50. with $10.00 per month minimum -no charge for no activity; and $.10 each transaction beyond 100. Sign-up and/or logon at http://epin.chesco.org. Also purchase county data as reports, labels, magnetic tape, and diskette. Also, genealogical and older vital statistics are free at www.chesco.org/archives. Also, search Recorder of Deeds records free at http://rod.chesco.org/icris/splash.jsp. **Other phones:** Treasurer- 610-344-6370; BLR (Bureau of Land Records-for help with UPI #)- 610-344-5968; Appraiser/Auditor- 610-344-6105; Elections- 610-344-6410; **Property tax/Assessor-** same address as above. 610-344-6105.

Clarion County Prothonotary

County Prothonotary, Main St; Courthouse, Clarion, PA 16214-1092. 814-226-4000; fax-814-226-8069; hours: 8:30AM-4:30PM.
Records indexed on computer back to 1990. Only the public may search. Copy fee $.50 per page.

Clarion County Recorder

County Recorder of Deeds, Courthouse; Corner of 5th Ave. & Main St., Clarion, PA 16214. 814-226-4000 x2500, R/E recording phone-814-226-4000 x2501; fax-814-226-1117; hours: 8:30AM-4:30PM.
No tax liens filed here. All records in one index. Records indexed on computer back to 1975. Only the public may search. Copy fee $.50 per page; $1.00 per page if mailed back. Cert fee- $4.00 per page includes copy fee for 1st 4 pages. **Online access to Real Estate, Recording, Assessor, OCC/PC, Marriage, Voter Registration, Orphans Court, Probate, Tax Claim records:** Access is through a private company. For info, call Infocon at 814-472-6066 or www.infoconcountyaccess.com. Includes images for Recorder, Register of Wills, and Orphans court. **Other phones:** Treasurer- 814-226-4000 x2861. **Property tax/Assessor-** 814-226-4000 x2301.

Clearfield County Prothonotary

County Prothonotary, PO Box 549, Clearfield, PA 16830. 814-765-2641, R/E recording phone-814-765-

2641 x1350, UCC recording phone-814-765-2641 x1330; fax-814-765-7659; hours: 8:30AM-4PM. www.clearfieldco.org
Records indexed on computer from 11/00 to present, index books prior to 11/00. Office personnel will make a computer check (4 years) or visitors may perform searches. Search fee $7.00 per name. Copy fee $.25 per page. Cert fee- $1.50 per doc includes copy fee. Payee- Prothonotary.

Clearfield County Recorder

County Recorder of Deeds, PO Box 361, Clearfield, PA 16830. 814-765-2641 x1350; fax-814-765-6089; hours: 8:30AM-4PM. www.clearfieldco.org
Only federal tax liens from 1963-1969 filed here. Only the public may search. Copy fee $.50 per page. Cert fee- $1.00 per document plus copy fee. **Online access to Real Estate, Deed, Mortgage, Probate, Orphans Court records:** Access to Recorder of Deeds and Wills and Orphans Court is by subscription at www.landex.com/remote/. Fee is $.20 per minute, $.50 per fax page. Recorder data goes back to 1986. Images go back to 1997. Wills and orphan court records go back to 1990. Also, assessors county tax sale list is updated weekly at www.clearfieldco.org/tax_sale_list. **Other phones:** Treasurer- 814-765-2641 x5985; Elections- 814-765-2641 x5996; Vital Records- 724-656-3100. **Property tax/Assessor-** 230 E Market St #117, Clearfield, PA 16830; 814-765-2641 x5997.

Clinton County Prothonotary

County Prothonotary, 230 E. Water St.; Courthouse, Lock Haven, PA 17745. 570-893-4007, R/E recording phone-570-893-4010, UCC recording phone-570-893-4007; fax-570-893-4288; hours: 8AM-5PM M,T,Th,F; 8AM-12:30PM W
www.clintoncountypa.com
Index: Many indices. Records indexed on a public use terminal back to 1992. Only the public may search. Copy fee $.50 per page. Cert fee- $5.00 per cert plus copy fee. Payee- Clinton County Prothonotary. **Online access to Tax Lien, Judgment records:** Online access via a private company, see Recorder of Deeds. Images available. **Other phones:** Treasurer- 570-893-4005; Appraiser/Auditor- 570-893-4030; Elections- 570-893-4000; Vital Records- 570-893-4010. **Property tax/Assessor-** 570-893-4033.

Clinton County Recorder

County Recorder of Deeds, PO Box 943, Lock Haven, PA 17745. 570-893-4010; fax-570-893-4273; hours: 8:30AM-5PM.
www.clintoncountypa.com/register_&_recorder.htm
No tax liens filed here. Separate indices to search include computer and books. Records indexed on computer. Only the public may search. Copy fee $.50 per page. Cert fee- $1.50 per cert plus copy fee. Payee- Clinton County Recorder of Deeds. **Online access to Real Estate, Recorder, Assessor, Probate, Orphan Court, Property, Tax Claim records:** Access to limited property data is free at www.clintoncountypa.com; click on "Parcel Query by Name." Site may be down. Also, access available via a private company. For info call Infocom at 814-472-6066 or www.infoconcountyaccess.com. Includes images for Recorder, Register of Wills, Orphans Court, prothonotary. **Other phones:** Treasurer- 570-893-4004. **Property tax/Assessor-** 230 E Water St, Lock Have, PA 17745; 570-893-4034.

Columbia County Prothonotary

County Prothonotary, PO Box 380, Bloomsburg, PA 17815. 570-389-5614, R/E recording phone-570-389-5635, UCC recording phone-570-389-5617; hours: 8AM-4:30PM.
All records in one index. See Recorder for real estate records. Will not search UCC records or tax liens. Copy fee $1.00 per page. Cert fee- $4.00 per page includes copy fee. Payee- Columbia County Prothonotary.

Columbia County Recorder

County Recorder of Deeds, PO Box 380, Bloomsburg, PA 17815. 570-389-5632; fax-570-389-5636; hours: 8AM-4:30PM.
www.columbiapa.org/county/reg_rec/index.html
No tax liens filed here. Separate indices to search include all land records from 1974 to 10/99 by book & page, from 10/99 to present-by instrument number. Only the public may search. General copy fee $1.00 per page. R/E record fee- $.50 per page. Cert fee- $1.50 per cert plus copy fee. Payee-Columbia County Recorder of Deeds. **Online access to Real Estate, Deed, Lien, Judgment, Recording, UCC records:** Access is via a private company at www.landex.com/remote/. Fee is $.20 per minute. Recorders index goes back to 1974; wills index back to 1995; UCCs to 1992; images go back to 1/1974; wills and UCCs to 10/1999. **Other phones:** Treasurer-570-389-5626; Appraiser/Auditor- 570-389-5645; Elections- 570-389-5640. **Property tax/Assessor-**same address as above. 570-389-5645.

Crawford County Prothonotary

County Prothonotary, 903 Diamond Park; County Courthouse, Meadville, PA 16335. 814-333-7324, R/E recording phone-814-373-2537, UCC recording phone-814-333-7324; fax-814-337-5416; hours: 8:30AM-4:30PM.
All records in one index. Records indexed on a public use terminal back to 2000. Office personnel or visitors may perform searches. Search fee $59.00. Copy fee $.75 per page.

Crawford County Recorder

County Recorder of Deeds, 903 Diamond Park; Courthouse, Meadville, PA 16335. 814-373-2537; fax-814-337-5296; hours: 8:30AM-4:30PM
www.co.crawford.pa.us
No tax liens filed here. All records in one index up back to 1987. Only the public may search, but will assist genealogical records. Copy fee $1.00 per page. Cert fee- $1.50 per doc, does not include copy fee. Payee- Crawford County Recorder of Deeds. **Other phones:** Treasurer- 814-333-7332; Elections- 814-333-7307. **Property tax/Assessor-** 814-333-7302.

Cumberland County Prothonotary

County Prothonotary, 1 Courthouse Sq; County Courthouse, Carlisle, PA 17013-3387. 717-240-6195; fax-717-240-6573; hours: 8AM-4:30PM.
Separate indices to search include electronically from 1994 to present, 2001 to present are digitally recorded. Records indexed on a public use terminal back to 1994. Only the public may search. See Recorder for real estate records. Copy fee $.50 per page. Cert fee- No fee for certification. Payee-Cumberland County Prothonotary. **Online access to Civil Court, Judgment, Tax Lien records:** Online access; see Cumberland recorder.

Cumberland County Recorder

County Recorder of Deeds, 1 Courthouse Sq; County Courthouse, Carlisle, PA 17013. 717-240-6370, UCC recording phone-717-240-5370; fax-717-240-7851; hours: 8AM-4:30PM.
No tax liens filed here. All records in one index after 12/1993, before separate index for deeds, mortgages, misc documents. Records indexed on a public use terminal back to 12/1993. Only the public may search. Copy fee $.50 per page. Cert fee- $10.00 per cert by mail includes copy fee. Payee- Cumberland County Recorder of Deeds. **Online access to Property Tax, Assessor, Real Estate, Recording, Marriage, Orphans Court, Probate, Tax Claim, Cemetery records:** Access to the property assessment data is free at www.ccpa.net/cumberland/cwp/view.asp?A=1137&Q=479825. No name searching. Also, access available via a private company. For info call Infocom at 814-472-6066 or www.infoconcountyaccess.com. Includes images for Recorder of Deeds records. Also, search cemetery records free on a private company site at

www.rootsweb.com/~usgenweb/pa/cumberland/cemet.htm. **Other phones:** Treasurer- 717-240-6380; Elections- 717-240-6385. **Property tax/Assessor-**same address as above. 717-240-6350.

Dauphin County Prothonotary

County Prothonotary, PO Box 945, Harrisburg, PA 17108. 717-780-6520; fax-none; hours: 8AM-4:30PM.
www.dauphincounty.org/dauphin/site/default.asp
Separate indices to search include UCC, miscellaneous, ejection. Records indexed on a public use terminal back to 1983. Search fee $8.75 unless otherwise indicated. See Recorder for real estate records. Tax liens not included in UCC search. UCC Information or copy request per debtor name- $57.50. Copy fee $.75 per page. Cert fee-$5.00 per case includes copy fee. Payee- Dauphin County Prothonotary.

Dauphin County Recorder

County Recorder of Deeds, PO Box 12000, Harrisburg, PA 17108. 717-780-6560; fax-717-780-6482; hours: 8AM-4:30PM.
No tax liens filed here. All records in one index. Records indexed on a public use terminal back to 1979. Only the public may search. Copy fee $.50 per page. Cert fee- $2.00 per page plus copy fee. **Online access to Property, Assessor, Property Sale records:** Access to county property data is free at www.dauphinpropertyinfo.org/propertymax/rover30.asp. To search free, create a limited guest account. Full access fee is $50.00 per month. If you wish to include property sales data, there is an add'l fee of $20.00. **Other phones:** Treasurer- 717-780-6550; Elections-717-780-6360. **PropertyAssessor-** 717-780-6101.

Delaware County Prothonotary

County Prothonotary, 201 W. Front St, Rm 127; Delaware County Gov't Ctr Bldg, Media, PA 19063. 610-891-5009; fax-610-891-7257; hours: 8:30AM-4:30PM. www.co.delaware.pa.us
All records in one index. Records indexed on a public use terminal back to 1970. Only the public may search. See Recorder for real estate records. Copy fee $1.00 per page. Cert fee- $4.50 per cert plus copy fee. Payee- Office of Judicial Support.

Delaware County Recorder

County Recorder of Deeds, 201 W. Front St, Rm 107; Government Ctr. Bldg., Media, PA 19063. 610-891-4148, R/E recording phone-610-891-4152; hours: 8:30AM-4:30PM.
http://www2.co.delaware.pa.us/pa/default.htm
No tax liens filed here. All records in one index. Only the public may search. Copy fee $1.00 per page. Cert fee- $7.00 for 1st 4 pages; $1.00 each add'l. Payee- Delaware County Recorder of Deeds. **Online access to Assessor, Deed, Real Estate, Judgment, Court records:** Access to the public access system is free - temporarily - at http://www2.co.delaware.pa.us/pa/publicaccess.asp. Records go back to 1982. No name searching. Also, property tax records are free on the Internet at http://taxrecords.com. **Other phones:** Treasurer- 610-891-4272; Elections- 610-891-4938. **Property tax/Assessor-** 610-891-4880/4891.

Elk County Prothonotary

County Prothonotary, PO Box 237, Ridgway, PA 15853-0237. 814-776-5344, R/E recording phone-814-776-5349; fax-814-776-5303; hours: 8:30AM-4PM.
All records in one index. Records indexed on computer back to 1998. Office personnel or visitors may perform searches. See Recorder for real estate records. Will search UCC records, tax liens not included in UCC search. Information or copy request per debtor name- $57.00. Separate tax lien search-$8.00 per debtor plus $1.50 for each lien found. Copy fee $.50 per page. Cert fee- $8.00 per search plus copy fee. Payee- Elk County Prothonotary. -814-776-5337.

Elk County Recorder

County Recorder of Deeds, PO Box 314, Ridgway, PA 15853-0314. 814-776-5349; fax-814-776-5382; hours: 8:30AM-4PM. www.co.elk.pa.us/regrecorder/
All records in one index. Records indexed on a public use terminal back to 1987. Only the public may search, but office may do limited real estate searches. Copy fee $.50 per page. Cert fee- $1.50 per instrument plus copy fee. Payee- Elk County Recorder of Deeds. **Other phones:** Treasurer- 814-776-5322; Elections- 814-776-5337. **Property tax/Assessor-** PO Box 488, 250 Main St, Ridgway, PA 15853; 814-776-5340, fax- 814-776-5305.

Erie County Prothonotary

County Prothonotary, 140 W. 6th St; Rm 120, Erie, PA 16501-1080. 814-451-6078; fax-814-451-7400; hours: 8:30AM-4:30PM. www.eriecountygov.org
All records in one index. See Recorder for real estate records. Will search UCC records and copy, including tax liens. Information or copy request per debtor name- $59.00. Copy fee $.50 per page. Cert fee-$5.00 per doc, plus copy fee. Payee- Erie County Prothonotary.

Erie County Recorder

County Recorder of Deeds, PO Box 1849, Erie, PA 16507-0849. 814-451-6246; fax-814-451-6213; hours: 8:30AM-4:30PM.
No tax liens filed here. Only the public may search. Copy fee $.50 per page. Cert fee- $1.00 per doc plus copy fee. Payee- Erie County Recorder of Deeds. **Online access to Real Estate, Sale, Recorder, Marriage, Probate, Orphan Court records:** Recorder access is through a private company. Includes images, courts, and prothonotary; call Infocon at 814-472-6066 or www.infoconcountyaccess.com. Also, access property records data free at www.eriepa.us/Assessment/Property/Search.aspx, no name searching. **Other phones:** Treasurer- 814-451-6080. **Property tax/Assessor-** 140 W 6th St, Erie, PA 16501; 814-451-6225.

Fayette County Prothonotary

County Prothonotary, 61 E. Main St; Courthouse, Uniontown, PA 15401. 724-430-1272, R/E recording phone-724-430-1238, UCC recording phone-724-430-1272; hours: 8AM-4:30PM.
All records in one index. See Recorder for real estate records. Will not search UCC records or tax liens. Copy fee $.50 per page. Payee- Fayette County Prothonotary. **Online access to Marriage, Lien, Judgment records:** Access prothonotary index by subscription; call Infocom at 814-472-6066 or www.infoconcountyaccess.com.

Fayette County Recorder

County Recorder of Deeds, 61 E. Main St; Courthouse, Uniontown, PA 15401-3389. 724-430-1238, UCC recording phone-724-430-1272; fax-724-430-1238; hours: 8AM-4:30PM.
No tax liens filed here. All records in one index. Records indexed on a public use terminal back to 1976. Only the public may search. Will not search real estate records. Copy fee $.50 per page. Cert fee-$3.00 per doc plus copy fee. Payee- Fayette County Recorder. **Online access to Property, Assessor, Marriage, Will, Probate, Orphans Court records:** Access to property assessments is free at www.fayetteproperty.org/assessor. Also, search marriages, orphan court, and Register of Wills data from a private company; for info call Infocom at 814-472-6066 or www.infoconcountyaccess.com. **Other phones:** Treasurer- 724-430-1256; Elections- 724-430-1289; Vital Records- 724-430-1206. **Property tax/Assessor-** 724-430-1350.

Forest County Prothonotary

County Prothonotary, 526 Elm St #2, Tionesta, PA 16353. 814-755-3526; fax-814-755-8837; hours: 9AM-4PM. www.co.forest.pa.us

Only the public may search. See Recorder for real estate records. Copy fee $.25 per page. Cert fee-$2.00 per cert plus copy fee. Payee- Recorder of Deeds.

Forest County Recorder

County Recorder of Deeds, 526 Elm St #2, Tionesta, PA 16353. 814-755-3526; fax-814-755-8837; hours: 9AM-4PM. www.co.forest.pa.us
All records in one index. Only the public may search. Copy fee $.25 per page. Cert fee- $2.00 per doc, plus copy fee. Copy fee is $25. per page. Payee- Recorder of Deeds. **Other phones:** Treasurer- 814-755-3536. **Property tax/Assessor-** 526 Elm St #1, Tionesta, PA 16353; 814-755-3532.

Franklin County Prothonotary

County Prothonotary, 157 Lincoln Way East; County Court House, Chambersburg, PA 17201. 717-261-3860, R/E recording phone-717-261-3872; fax-717-264-6772; hours: 8:30AM-5PM.
All records in one index. Records indexed on a public use terminal from 11/98 to present. Only the public may search. Copy fee $.50 per page. Cert fee- $5.00 1st page, $1.00 each add'l page.

Franklin County Recorder

County Recorder of Deeds, 157 Lincoln Way East, Chambersburg, PA 17201. 717-261-3872; fax-717-263-5717; 8:30AM-4:30PM. http://co.franklin.pa.us
No tax liens filed here. All records in one index. Records indexed on a public use terminal back to 1986. Only the public may search. Copy fee $.50 per page. Cert fee- $1.50 per page plus copy fee. Payee- County Recorder of Deeds. **Online access to Real Estate, Recorder, Probate records:** Access is via a private company; call Infocon at 814-472-6066 or www.infoconcountyaccess.com. **Other phones:** Treasurer- 717-261-3119; Elections- 717-261-3886; UCC/Personal Property- 717-261-3858. **Property tax/Assessor-** 717-261-3801.

Fulton County Prothonotary

County Prothonotary, 201 N. Second St; Fulton County Courthouse, McConnellsburg, PA 17233-1198. 717-485-4212; hours: 8:30AM-4:30PM.
All records in one index. Only the public may search. See Recorder for real estate records. Copy fee $1.00 per page. R/E or tax lien copy- $.50 per page. Cert fee- $5.00 per cert plus copy fee. Payee- Fulton County Prothonotary.

Fulton County Recorder

County Recorder of Deeds, 201 N. Second St; Fulton County Courthouse, McConnellsburg, PA 17233-1198. 717-485-4212; hours: 8:30AM-4:30PM.
Public computer system in office. All records in one index. Only the public may search. Copy fee $1.00 per page. R/E record copy- $.50 per page. Cert fee- $5.00 per doc, no page cost, includes copies. Payee- Fulton County Recorder of Deeds. **Other phones:** Treasurer- 717-485-4454; Elections- 717-485-3691. **Property tax/Assessor-** 717-485-3208.

Greene County Prothonotary

County Prothonotary, 10 E. High St, Rm 105, Waynesburg, PA 15370. 724-852-5289, R/E recording phone-724-852-5283; hours: 8:30AM-4:30PM.
Separate indices to search. Only the public may search. See Recorder for real estate records. Copy fee $1.00 per page. Tax lien copy- $.50 per page. Cert fee- $6.00 per cert plus copy fee. Payee- Greene County Prothonotary.

Greene County Recorder

County Recorder of Deeds, 10 E High St, Courthouse, Waynesburg, PA 15370. 724-852-5283, UCC recording phone-724-852-5289; fax-n/a; hours: 8:30AM-4:30PM. http://county.greenepa.net
No tax liens filed here. All records in one index. Office will perform a UCC search but public must search other records themselves. Information or copy request per debtor name- $63.00. Copy fee

$.50 per page; UCC copy $1.00. Cert fee- $5.00 per doc plus copy fee. Payee- Greene County Recorder of Deeds. **Online to Property, Real Estate, Deed records:** Property records by subscription, at www.county.greenepa.net/secured/gc/depts/cc/asses/prop-records.htm or call 877-795-3564. Fee is $700 per year; includes Property Record Card System. Also, real estate deed records by subscription at http://205.244.106.228/login.asp. Contact Recorder office for sign-up details. Real estate deed records also available on microfilm. **Other phones:** Treasurer- 724-852-5225; Elections- 724-852-5230. **Property tax/Assessor-** 93 E High St, Waynesburg, PA 15370; 724-852-5211.

Huntingdon County Prothonotary

County Prothonotary, PO Box 39, Huntingdon, PA 16652-1486. 814-643-1610, R/E recording phone-814-643-2740, UCC recording phone-814-643-1610; fax-814-643-4271; hours: 8:30AM-4:30PM.
All records in one index. Only the public may search. Copy fee $.25 per page. Cert fee- $4.50 per page includes copy fee. Payee- Prothonotary.

Huntingdon County Recorder

County Recorder of Deeds, 223 Penn St; Courthouse, Huntingdon, PA 16652. 814-643-2740; fax-814-643-8152; 8:30AM-4:30PM. http://huntingdoncounty.net
No tax liens filed here. All records in one index. Only the public may search. Copy fee $1.00 per page, depending on format. Cert fee- $1.50 per cert, copies not included. Payee- Huntingdon County Recorder of Deeds. **Online access to Real Estate, Recorder, Marriage, Probate, Orphans Court records:** Access is via a private company; see Infocon at www.infoconcountyaccess.com. **Other phones:** Treasurer- 814-643-3523; Elections- 814-643-3091. **Property tax/Assessor-** 814-643-1000.

Indiana County Prothonotary

Prothonotary & Clerk of Courts, 825 Philadelphia St; Courthouse, 1st Fl, Indiana, PA 15701-3934. 724-465-3855, R/E recording phone-724-465-3860, UCC recording phone-724-465-3855; fax-724-465-3968; hours: 8AM-4PM. www.countyofindiana.org
See Recorder for real estate records. Will search UCC records, but not tax liens. Information or copy request per debtor name- $59.00. Copy fee $.25 per page. Cert fee- None.

Indiana County Recorder

County Recorder of Deeds, 825 Philadelphia St; Courthouse, Indiana, PA 15701. 724-465-3860; fax-724-465-3863; hours: 8AM-4PM.
No tax liens filed here. All records in one index. Records indexed on a public use terminal back to 1969. Only the public may search. Copy fee $.25 per page. Cert fee- $3.00 for every 4 pages. Payee- Recorder of Deeds. **Other phones:** Treasurer- 724-465-3845; Elections- 724-465-3852; Vital Records- 724-656-3100. **Property Assessor-** 724-465-3812.

Jefferson County

Prothonotary & Clerk of Courts, 200 Main St; Court House, Rm 102, Brookville, PA 15825. 814-849-1606, R/E recording phone-814-849-1610; fax-814-849-1625; hours: 8:30AM-4:30PM.
Separate indices to search. Records indexed on a public use terminal back to 1987. Only the public may search. Copy fee $.50 per page. Cert fee- $1.50 per page includes copy fee. Payee- Jefferson County Prothonotary.

Jefferson County Recorder

County Recorder of Deeds, 200 Main St; Courthouse, Brookville, PA 15825. 814-849-1610; fax-814-849-1677; hours: 8:30AM-4:30PM.
No tax liens filed here. Only the public may search. Copy fee $1.00 per page. Cert fee- $1.50 per certification, copies not included. Payee- Recorder of Deeds. **Other phones:** Treasurer- 814-849-1609; Elections- 814-849-1603. **Property tax/Assessor-** 200 Main St, Brookville, PA 15825; 814-849-1643.

Juniata County Prothonotary

County Prothonotary, Courthouse, Mifflintown, PA 17059. 717-436-7715, R/E recording phone-717-436-7709, UCC recording phone-717-436-7715; fax-717-436-7734; hours: 8AM-4:30PM.
Separate indices to search include computer since 1993, docket books prior to 1993. Records indexed on a public use terminal back to 1993. Only the public may search. See Recorder for real estate records. Copy fee $1.00 per page. Cert fee- $4.50 per doc plus copy fee. Payee- Juniata County Prothonotary.

Juniata County Recorder

County Recorder of Deeds, PO Box 68, Mifflintown, PA 17059. 717-436-7709; fax-717-436-7756; hours: 8AM-4:30PM.
No tax liens filed here. Separate indices to search include books up to 1991, computer. Records indexed on a public use terminal back to 1993. Only the public may search. Copy fee $1.00 per page. Cert fee- $5.00 per doc. Payee- Juniata County Recorder of Deeds. **Online access to Real Estate, Marriage, Probate, Orphans Court records:** Access is via a private company; call Infocon at 814-472-6066 or www.infoconcountyaccess.com. Includes Recorder of Deeds record images. **Other phones:** Treasurer- 717-436-7742; Elections- 717-436-7706. **Property tax/Assessor-** PO Box 68, Mifflintown, PA 17059; 717-436-7740.

Lackawanna County Prothonotary

County Clerk of Judicial Records, 200 N. Washington Ave, Scranton, PA 18503. 570-963-6723; fax-none; hours: 9AM-4PM.
Only the public may search. See Recorder for real estate records. Cert fee- $4.50. Payee- Lackawanna County Clerk of Judicial Records.

Lackawanna County Recorder

County Recorder of Deeds, 200 N. Washington; Courthouse, Scranton, PA 18503. 570-963-6775; fax-570-963-6390; hours: 9AM-4PM www.lackawannacounty.org
No tax liens filed here. All records in one index. Records indexed on a public use terminal back to 1980. Only the public may search. Copy fee $.35 per page. Cert fee- $2.00 per doc plus copy fee. Payee- Lackawanna County Recorder of Deeds. **Online to Assessor, Property records:** Access data free at http://ao.lackawannacounty.org/agreed.php. **Other phones:** Treasurer- 570-963-6731. **Property tax/Assessor-** 100 Jefferson Ave, Scranton, PA 18503; 570-963-6728.

Lancaster County Prothonotary

County Prothonotary, PO Box 83480, Lancaster, PA 17608-3480. 717-299-8282, R/E recording phone-717-299-8238; fax-717-293-7210; hours: 8:30AM-5PM. www.co.lancaster.pa.us
Office will perform a UCC search but public must search other records themselves. See Recorder for real estate records. Information or copy request per debtor name- $57.00. Copy fee $.50 per page. Cert fee- $5.00 per page plus copy fee. Payee- Lancaster County Prothonotary.

Lancaster County Recorder

County Recorder of Deeds, PO Box 83480, Lancaster, PA 17608. 717-299-8238; fax-717-299-8393; hours: 8:30AM-4:30PM (recording); 8:30AM-5PM (for public). www.lancasterdeeds.com
No tax liens filed here. Office will perform a UCC search (only real estate related UCC filed here), but public must search other records themselves. Copy fee $.50 per page. Cert fee- $1.50 per cert plus copy fee. Payee- Lancaster County Recorder of Deeds. **Online access to Assessor, Real Estate, Recording, Tax Lien, UCC records:** Access to deeds, UCCs and other recordings is free at http://icris.lancasterdeeds.com/splash.jsp. Also, access to property data is free on the GIS-mapping site at

www.co.lancaster.pa.us/gis/site/default.asp?. Click on GIS-Property Search, then choose Query to search by owner name. **Other phones:** Treasurer- 717-299-8222. Elections- 717-299-8293. **Property tax/Assessor-** 717-299-8381.

Lawrence County Prothonotary

County Prothonotary, 430 Court St; Government Ctr, New Castle, PA 16101-3593. 724-656-1943, R/E recording phone-724-656-2128; fax-724-656-1988; hours: 8AM-4PM. www.co.lawrence.pa.us
All records in one index. Records indexed on computer. Only the public may search. Copy fee $2.00 per page. Cert fee- $1.25 per page plus copy fee. Payee- Lawrence County Prothonotary.

Lawrence County Recorder

County Recorder of Deeds, 430 Court St; Government Ctr, New Castle, PA 16101. 724-656-2127; fax-724-656-1966; 8AM-4PM; www.co.lawrence.pa.us
No tax liens filed here. All records in one index. Records indexed on a public use terminal back to 1979. Only the public may search. Copy fee $.50 per page. Cert fee- $1.50 per doc, plus copy fee. Payee- Recorder of Deeds. **Online access to Real Estate, Recording, Deed, Marriage, Probate, Orphans Court, Assessor, Property Tax records:** Access is via a private company; document images included; call Infocon at 814-472-6066 or www.infoconcountyaccess.com. Also, search assessments pdf pages by ward, borough or town at www.co.lawrence.pa.us/Preliminary_Assessment/Preli minary_Assessment.html. **Other phones:** Treasurer- 724-656-2183; Elections- 724-656-2161; Vital Records- 724-656-3100. **Property tax/Assessor-** 724-656-2191.

Lebanon County Prothonotary

County Prothonotary, 400 S. 8th St, Rm 104, Lebanon, PA 17042. 717-274-2801; hours: 8:30AM-4:30PM. www.lebcounty.org
All records in one index. Records indexed on a public use terminal back to 1985. Only the public may search. Copy fee $2.00, if tax lien or real estate $.50 per page. Cert fee- $9.00 per doc plus copy fee. Payee- Lebanon County Prothonotary.

Lebanon County Recorder

County Recorder of Deeds, 400 S. 8th St; Rm 107, Lebanon, PA 17042. 717-274-2801; R/E recording phone-717-274-2801 x2224, UCC recording phone-717-274-2801 x2225; fax-717-228-4456; hours: Recording hours 8:30AM-4PM. www.lebcounty.org
No tax liens filed here. Separate indices to search are in books. Records indexed on a public use terminal back to 2/2002. Only the public may search. General copy fee $1.00, UCCs $2.00 per page. Cert fee- $2.00 per cert plus copy fee. Payee- Lebanon County Recorder of Deeds. **Online access to Real Estate, Deed, Lien, Judgment, Recording, Assessor records:** Access to Recorder of Deeds official records is by subscription at www.landex.com/remote/. For info call OSS at 717-274-5890. Deed and mortgage index back to 1933; Misc index back to 1972; Deed images back to 1996; Mortgage images back to 2000; Miscellaneous images back to 2001. Also, access property data by subscription at www.courthouseonline.com. Sub fee $9.95 3-days, up to $275 per year. A free view available if you have control number and password from tax notice. **Other phones:** Treasurer- 717-274-2801; Appraiser/Auditor- 717-274-2801; Elections- 717-274-2801; Vital Records- 717-274-2801. **Property tax/Assessor-** 400 S 8th St, Rm 118, Lebanon, PA 17042; 717-274-2801.

Lehigh County Prothonotary

County Prothonotary, 455 W. Hamilton St., Rm 132, Allentown, PA 18101-1614. 610-782-3148, R/E recording phone-610-782-3162; fax-610-770-3840; hours: 8:30AM-4:30PM.

City of Bethlehem is in both Northampton and Lehigh counties. Separate indices to search include case file, judgments, ejectments. Only the public may search. Copy fee $2.00 per page. Cert fee- $4.75 per doc, plus copy fee. Payee- Lehigh County Clerk of Courts-Civil Division. **Online access to Judgment, Assessor, Property, Tax Sale, Delinquent Taxes, County Grants records:** County's full-access internet pay system initial cost was $300.00 a year but that fee is being reduced since the database is now smaller; a per minute usage fee may apply. For signup info, call the Fiscal Office at 610-782-3112. Also, at www.lehighcounty.org, the County Grants database free registration is required. Search assessments at www.lehighcounty.org/Assessment/Puba.cfm but no name searching. Search tax sale data by community free at www.lehighcounty.org/Fiscal/taxsale.cfm.

Lehigh County Recorder

County Recorder of Deeds, 17 S 7th St; Rm 350, Allentown, PA 18101. 610-782-3162, R/E recording phone-610-820-3162; fax-610-782-3116; hours: 8AM-4PM. www.lehighcounty.org
No tax liens filed here. Separate indices to search include computerized index from 1984-present; Russell index book form and computerized from 1812-1983 (grantee/grantor, mortgages). Records indexed on a public use terminal. Only the public may search. Copy fee $1.00 per page; $.25 self serve. Cert fee- $1.50 per doc plus copy fee. Payee- Recorder of Deeds. **Online access to Assessor, Property, Tax Lien, Delinquent Taxes, Game License, Judgment records:** County's full-access internet pay system initial cost was $300.00 a year but that fee is being reduced since the database is now smaller; a per minute usage fee may apply. Call Lehigh County Svcs Dept at 610-782-3286 for more information. **Other phones:** Treasurer- 610-820-3113; Elections- 610-820-3194; **Property tax/Assessor-** 610-782-3038.

Luzerne County Prothonotary

County Prothonotary, 200 N. River St; County Court House, Wilkes-Barre, PA 18711-1001. 570-825-1745; fax-570-825-1757; hours: 9AM-4:30PM.
Will search general civil records, will not search judgments. Separate indices to search. Records indexed on a public use terminal starting 3/1/2005. Office personnel or visitors may perform searches. Search fee $17.00 per name. Copy fee $2.00 per page. Cert fee- $5.50 per doc, add'l $2.00 for each cert of same page or doc plus copy fee. Payee- Prothonotary.

Luzerne County Recorder

County Recorder of Deeds, 200 N. River St; Courthouse, Wilkes-Barre, PA 18711. 570-825-1641; fax-570-970-4580; hours: 9AM-4:30PM. www.luzernecounty.org
Mortgages & Real Estate related UCCs only found in this office. Separate indices to search include records from 2001 forward in one index, prior to 2001, deeds, mortgages, commissions, power of attorney and charters separate. Only the public may search. Copy fee $2.00 per page; $.25 self serve. Cert fee- $2.00 per page, $1.00 per certification plus copy fee. Payee- Luzerne County Recorder of Deeds. **Online access to Recorder, Deed, Land, Property Assessment records:** Access is through a private company at www.landex.com/remote/. Fee is $.20 per minute and $.50 per fax page. Index goes back to 1/1993; images go back to 9/1993. Also at www.wbtimesleader.com/cgi-bin/authenticate.cgi are county property assessment database. **Other phones:** Treasurer- 570-825-1780; Elections- 570-825-1715. **Property tax/Assessor-** 570-825-1525.

Lycoming County Prothonotary

County Prothonotary, 48 W. Third St, Williamsport, PA 17701. 570-327-2251, R/E recording phone-570-327-2263; fax-570-327-2505; hours: 8:30AM-5PM.

All records in one index. Records indexed on a public use terminal back to 1983. Only the public may search. See Recorder for real estate records. Copy fee $.50 per page. Cert fee- $5.00 per doc includes copy fee. Payee- Lycoming County Prothonotary.

Lycoming County Recorder

County Recorder of Deeds, 48 W. Third St, Williamsport, PA 17701. 570-327-2263; fax-570-327-2511; hours: 8:30AM-5PM.
No tax liens filed here. All records in one index. Records indexed on computer back to 1957. Only the public may search. General copy fee $1.00 per page. R/E record copy- $.50 per page. Cert fee- $1.50 per cert plus copy fee. Payee- Lycoming County Recorder of Deeds. **Online to Property, Assessor records:** Access property data by subscription at www.courthouseonline.com. Sub fee $9.95 3-days, up to $275 per year. A free view available with control number and password from tax notice. **Other phones:** Treasurer- 570-327-2248; Elections- 570-327-2267. **Property/Assessor-** 570-327-2301.

McKean County Prothonotary

County Prothonotary, PO Box 273, Smethport, PA 16749. 814-887-3271, R/E recording phone-814-887-3253, UCC recording phone-814-887-3271; fax-814-887-3219; hours: 8:30AM-4:30PM.
Search fee $15.00 tax lien; $59.00 UCCs. See Recorder for real estate records. Copy fee $.50 per page. Cert fee- $10.00.

McKean County Recorder

Recorder of Deeds, 500 W. Main St., Smethport, PA 16749. 814-888-3250 x262,259,260, R/E recording phone-814-887-3250; fax-814-887-3255; hours: 8:30AM-4:30PM.
No tax liens filed here. All records in one index. Only the public may search. Copy fee $1.00 per page mailed. Cert fee- $1.50 per doc plus copy fee. Payee- Anne Bosworth-Recorder of Deeds. **Other phones:** Treasurer- 814-887-3220; Elections- 814-887-3203; Vital Records- 814-887-3260. **Property tax/Assessor-** 814-887-3215.

Mercer County Prothonotary

County Prothonotary, 105 Mercer County Courthouse, Mercer, PA 16137-0066. 724-662-3800 x2261; fax-none; hours: 8:30AM-4:30PM.
Only the public may search. See Recorder for real estate records. Copy fee $1.00 per page. Payee- Mercer County Prothonotary.

Mercer County Recorder

County Recorder of Deeds, 109 Courthouse, Mercer, PA 16137-1293. 724-662-3800, R/E recording phone-724-662-3800 x2277; fax-724-662-2096; hours: 8:30AM-4:30PM. www.mcc.co.mercer.pa.us
No tax liens filed here. All records in one index. Records indexed on a public use terminal back to 1972. Only the public may search. Copy fee $1.00 per page. Cert fee- $2.00 per page plus copy fee. Payee- Recorder. **Online access to Property, Assessor, Occ/PC, Tax Claim records:** Access to recorded records is available at http://141.151.130.246/resolution/. Also, access to index is via a private company. For info, call Infocon at 814-472-6066 or www.infoconcountyaccess.com. **Other phones:** Treasurer- 724-662-7508; Elections- 724-962-5711. **Property tax/Assessor-** 724-662-7551.

Mifflin County Prothonotary

County Prothonotary, 20 N. Wayne St, Lewistown, PA 17044. 717-248-8146; fax-717-248-5275; hours: 8AM-4:30PM.
All records in one index. Only the public may search. See Recorder for real estate records. Copy fee $.50 per page. Cert fee- $4.50 per page.

Mifflin County Recorder

County Recorder of Deeds, 20 N. Wayne St, Lewistown, PA 17044. 717-242-1449; fax-717-248-2503; hours: 8AM-4:30PM

www.co.mifflin.pa.us/mifflin
No tax liens filed here. Records indexed on computer from 1/93, hard copy-1990-1992, 1981-1989, 1789-1980. Only the public may search. Copy fee $.50 per page. $1.00 for ledgers. Cert fee- $1.50 per cert plus copy fee. Payee- Mifflin County Recorder of Deeds. **Online access to Real Estate, Recorder, Assessor, Probate, GIS Mapping, Orphans Court, Marriage, Tax Claim records:** Access is via a private company; call Infocon at 814-472-6066 or www.infoconcountyaccess.com; images soon to be available for Recorder records, indexes for others. Also, property data is free at www.co.mifflin.pa.us. Use the new free Web Mapping Parcel Application to name search for property data. **Other phones:** Treasurer- 717-248-8439. **Property tax/Assessor-** same address as above. 717-248-5783.

Monroe County Prothonotary

County Prothonotary, N. 7th & Monroe St; Courthouse, Rm 303, Stroudsburg, PA 18360-2190. 570-517-3988; fax-570-517-3865; hours: 8:30AM-4:30PM.
All records in one index. Records indexed on a public use terminal back to 1995. Office will perform a UCC search but public must search other records themselves. Search fee $5.00. See Recorder for real estate records. Copy fee $1.00 per page. Cert fee- $3.00 per page plus copy fee. Payee- Monroe County Prothonotary. **Online access to Tax Lien, Judgment, Marriage records:** Access is via a private company; call Infocon at 814-472-6066 or www.infoconcountyaccess.com.

Monroe County Recorder

County Recorder of Deeds, 7th & Monroe St; Courthouse, Stroudsburg, PA 18360-2185. 570-420-3530, R/E recording phone-570-420-3400; fax-570-517-3873; hours: 8:30AM-4:30PM.
No tax liens filed here. All records in one index. Records indexed on a public use terminal back to 1979. Only the public may search. Copy fee $.25 per page. Cert fee- $1.50 per doc plus copy fee. Payee- Recorder of Deeds. **Online access to Real Estate, Deed, Will, Mortgage records:** Access is through a private company at www.landex.com/remote/. Fee is $.20 per minute and $.50 per fax page. Land Index goes back to 1/1979; wills go back to 11/1836; images go back to 8/1997. **Other phones:** Treasurer- 570-517-3180; Elections- 570-517-3165. **Property tax/Assessor-** 1 Quaker Plaza, Stroudsburg, PA 18360; 570-517-3133.

Montgomery County Prothonotary

County Prothonotary, PO Box 311, Norristown, PA 19404. 610-278-3360; fax-610-278-5994; hours: 8:30AM-4:15PM. www.montcopa.org
All records in one index. Records indexed on a public use terminal back to 1980. Only the public may search. See Recorder for real estate records. Copy fee $.50 per page, $1.00 minimum. Cert fee- $4.50 per page plus copy fee. Payee- Montgomery County Prothonotary.

Montgomery County Recorder

County Recorder of Deeds, PO Box 311, Norristown, PA 19404-0311. 610-278-3289, R/E recording phone-610-278-3868; fax-610-278-3869; hours: 8:30AM-4:15PM. www.montcopa.org
No tax liens filed here. Records indexed on a public use terminal back to 1874. Office will perform a UCC search but public must search other records themselves. Copy fee $.50 per page. Cert fee- $1.50 per cert plus copy fee. Payee- Montgomery County Recorder of Deeds. **Online access to Assessor, Real Estate, Recording, Deed, Tax Lien, Owner Name, Estate, Tax Claim Property records:** Recorder of Deeds records are free at www.montcopa.org/MWAY/index.html. Records on the County PIR database are free at www.montcopa.org/reassessment/boahome0.htm. Records date back to 1990. Also, search estate names for free at www.montcopa.org/MWAY/estate.html.

Search BOA owner names at www.montcopa.org/MWAY/owner.html Also, search tax claim properties list at www.montcopa.org/taxclaim/repoproperties.asp. **Other phones:** Treasurer- 610-278-3066; Elections- 610-278-3075. **Property tax/Assessor-** 610-278-3761.

Montour County Prothonotary

County Prothonotary, 29 Mill St; Courthouse, Danville, PA 17821. 570-271-3010, R/E recording phone-570-271-3012; fax-570-271-3089; hours: 9AM-4PM. www.montourco.org/montour
See Recorder for real estate records. Information or copy request per debtor name- $57.00. Federal/state combined tax lien search- $10.00 per debtor. Copy fee $.50 per page. UCC copy $1.00 per page. Cert fee- $5.00 per doc plus copy fee. Payee- Montour County Prothonotary.

Montour County Recorder

Register & Recorder, 29 Mill St; Courthouse, Danville, PA 17821. 570-271-3012; fax-570-271-3071; www.montourco.org/montour
All records in one index. Records indexed on a public use terminal back to 1/1/1987. Office personnel or visitors may perform searches. Search fee $25.00. Copy fee $.50 per page. Cert fee- $.50 per page + $1.50. Payee- Register & Recorder. **Online access to Real Estate, Recorder, Deed, Probate, Marriage, Orphans Court records:** Access to Recorder of Deeds data is by subscription from a private company, visit www.infoconcountyaccess.com. Also includes Prothonotary, Clerk of Courts. Will index 1850 to present is free at www.montour.org, click on Register & Recorder, then Will Index, or try www.montourco.org/montour/cwp/view.asp?a=770&Q=417826&montourNav=|8473|. **Other phones:** Treasurer- 570-271-3016; Appraiser/Auditor- 570-271-3006; Elections- 570-271-3000. **Property tax/Assessor-** 570-271-3006.

Northampton County Prothonotary

County Prothonotary, 669 Washington St.; 2nd Fl, Rm 207, Easton, PA 18042-7498. 610-559-3060; hours: 8:30AM-4:30PM. www.northamptoncounty.org
City of Bethlehem is in both Northampton and Lehigh counties. All records in one index. Records indexed on a public use terminal back to 1985. Only the public may search. See Recorder for real estate records. Copy fee $.25 per page. Cert fee- $4.75 per page Payee- Northampton County Prothonotary.

Northampton County Recorder

County Recorder of Deeds, 669 Washington St; Government Ctr, Easton, PA 18042. 610-559-3077; fax-610-559-3103; hours: 8:30AM-4:30PM. http://northamptoncounty.org
The City of Bethlehem is in both Northampton and Lehigh counties. Separate indices to search include grantor/grantee, mortgagor/mortgagee, power of attorney, map index. Records indexed on a public use terminal back to 11/1985. Only the public may search. Copy fee $.25 per page. Map copies $1.00 per page. Cert fee- $2.50 per certification plus copy fee. Payee- Northampton County Recorder of Deeds. **Online access to Real Estate, Deed, Mortgage, Misc. Recording, Property, Assessor records:** Two sources available. One is a private company at www.landex.com/remote/. Fee is $.20 per minute and $.50 per fax page. Deeds data goes back to 11/85; mortgages to 2/86; faxable images go back to 11/85. Also, online access to assessor's property records data is free at www.ncpub.org. **Other phones:** Treasurer- 610-559-3102; Elections- 610-559-3055; Orphan's Court- 610-559-3095; Register of Wills -610-559-3092. **Property tax/Assessor-** 610-559-3160.

Northumberland County Prothonotary

County Prothonotary, 201 Market St; Courthouse, Rm 7, Sunbury, PA 17801-3468. 570-988-4151, R/E

recording phone-570-988-4143; hours: 9AM-4:30PM (Mon open until 5PM).
Records indexed on a public use terminal back to 1998. Office personnel or visitors may perform searches. Search fee $7.00 per name plus $1.00 for each record found. See Recorder for real estate records. Will not search tax liens. Copy fee $1.00 1st page through the mail, $.25 each add'l. Cert fee- $4.00 per 1st page, $1.00 each add'l page plus copy fee. Payee- Northumberland County Prothonotary.

Northumberland County Recorder

County Recorder of Deeds, 201 Market St; Court House, Sunbury, PA 17801. 570-988-4140; 9AM-4:30PM.
No tax liens filed here. All records in one index. Records indexed on a public use terminal back to 1974. Only the public may search. Copy fee $.50 per page. Cert fee- None. Payee- Northumberland County Recorder of Deeds. **Other phones:** Treasurer- 570-988-4160. **Property tax/Assessor-** 570-988-4312.

Perry County Prothonotary

County Prothonotary, PO Box 325, New Bloomfield, PA 17068-0325. 717-582-2131; hours: 8AM-4PM.
Records indexed on a public use terminal back to 1976. Only the public may search. Copy fee $.40 per page. Cert fee- $5.00 per cert plus copy fee. Payee- Perry County Prothonotary. **Online access to Property, Assessor records:** Access property data by subscription at www.courthouseonline.com. Sub fee $9.95 3-days, up to $275 per year. A free view available with control number and password from tax notice.

Perry County Recorder

County Recorder of Deeds, PO Box 223, New Bloomfield, PA 17068. 717-582-2131; fax-717-582-5149; hours: 8AM-4PM.
No tax liens filed here. All records in one index. Records indexed on a public use terminal back to 1958. Only the public may search. Copy fee $.40 per page. Cert fee- $2.00 per cert plus copy fee. Payee- Perry County Recorder of Deeds. **Online access to Real Estate, Deed records:** Access to Recorder of Deeds is by subscription at www.landex.com/remote/. Fee is $.20 per minute, $.50 per fax page. Recorder data goes back to 1973; images to 1820. **Other phones:** Treasurer- 717-582-8984 x4. **Property tax/Assessor-** 717-582-8984 x3.

Philadelphia County Prothonotary

County Prothonotary, Broad & Market Sts; City Hall, Rm 268, Philadelphia, PA 19107. 215-686-6670; hours: 9AM-3PM.
Separate indices to search include liens, judgments, older records. Lien records indexed on a public use terminal back to 1980. Agency or visitors may perform searches. See Recorder for real estate records. UCCS (if available) and tax liens are 2 separate searches; note phone numbers to each dept. UCC Information or copy request per debtor name- $59.00. Tax lien search- $35.00 per debtor. Copy fee $.50 per page. Cert fee- $30.00 per lien doc includes copy fee. Payee- Philadelphia County Prothonotary. **Online access to Judgment, Lien, Civil Court records:** Assess to records is free at http://fjdweb2.phila.gov/fjd1/repl1/zk_fjd_public_qry_00.zp_main_idx.html. Also, includes judgments and liens on behalf of governmental entities. Also, BRT property tax records free at http://brtweb.phila.gov/index.aspx. No name searching.

Philadelphia County Recorder

County Recorder of Deeds, Broad & Market Sts; City Hall, Rm 153, Philadelphia, PA 19107. 215-686-2260, R/E recording phone-215-686-2291; hours: 8AM-2PM. http://philadox.phila.gov
No tax liens filed here. All records in one index. Office will perform a UCC search but public must search other records themselves. Only real estate related UCC filed here. Copy fee $2.00 per page.

Cert fee- $2.00 per doc plus copy fee. Payee-Philadelphia County Recorder of Deeds. **Online access to Property, Assessor, Death, Recording, Deed, UCC records:** Search property assessment data for free at http://brtweb.phila.gov/index.aspx. No name searching. Also, name search recorder data for a fee at http://philadox.phila.gov/; registration required; fee is $125.00 per month or $15.00 per hour. Or, $750 per year or $60.00 per week. Images go back to 1976, index to 1957. Also, name searching is by subscription from a private company at http://currentstatus.com; call 800-477-8288 for info. Also, search Philadelphia area obituaries for free at www.legacy.com/philly/LegacyHome.asp. **Other phones:** Lien Dept- 215-686-8859; Older records -215-686-6669. **Property tax/Assessor**- 34 S 11th St, Muni Court Bldg, Philadelphia, PA 19107; 215-686-4334.

Pike County Prothonotary

County Prothonotary, 412 Broad St, Milford, PA 18337. 570-296-7231; fax-none; hours: 8:30AM-4:30PM.
All records in one index. Only the public may search. See Recorder for real estate records. Copy fee $.25 per page. Cert fee- $5.00 per doc plus copy fee. Payee- Pike County Prothonotary.

Pike County Recorder

County Recorder of Deeds, 506 Broad St, Milford, PA 18337. 570-296-3508; fax-570-296-3514; hours: 8:30AM-4:30PM. www.pikepa.org/recorder.htm
No tax liens filed here. Only the public may search. Copy fee $.50 per page; $2.00 per page if mailed. Cert fee- $2.00 per page plus copy fee. Payee-Pike County Recorder of Deeds. **Online access to Property, Assessor, Probate, Marriage, Orphans Court records:** Access property data free at www.pikegis.org/pike/viewer.htm. Also, access is through a private company. For info, call Infocon at 814-472-6066 or www.infoconcountyaccess.com. **Other phones:** Treasurer- 570-296-3441. **Property tax/Assessor**- 570-296-3417.

Potter County Prothonotary

County Prothonotary, 1 E. 2nd St, Rm 23; Courthouse, Coudersport, PA 16915. 814-274-9740, R/E recording phone-814-274-8370, UCC recording phone-814-274-9740; fax-814-274-3361; hours: 8:30AM-4:30PM. www.pottercountypa.net
Records indexed on a public use terminal back to 11/1997. Office will perform a UCC search but public must search other records themselves. Search fee $59.00. Copy fee $.25 per page.

Potter County Recorder

County Recorder of Deeds, Courthouse, Rm 20, Coudersport, PA 16915. 814-274-8370; fax-814-274-3360; hours: 8:30AM-4:30PM.
No tax liens filed here. Will not search real estate records. Will not name search UCC records. Information or copy request per debtor name- $57.00. Copy fee $1.00 per page. Cert fee- $1.50 per cert plus copy fee. Payee- Potter County Recorder of Deeds. **Online access to Real Estate, Assessor, Probate, Marriage, Orphans Court, Tax Claim records:** Access is via a private company; visit www.infoconcountyaccess.com. **Other phones:** Treasurer- 814-274-9775; Elections- 814-274-8467; Vital Records- 814-274-9740. **Property tax/Assessor**- 814-274-0488.

Schuylkill County Prothonotary

County Prothonotary, 401 N. Second St., Pottsville, PA 17901-2520. 570-628-1270, R/E recording phone-570-628-1480, UCC recording phone-570-628-1270; fax-570-628-1261; hours: 8:30AM-4:30PM. www.schuylkill.pa.us
All records in one index. Records indexed on a public use terminal back to 1999. Office personnel or visitors may perform searches. Search fee $5.00 per name. Copy fee $.25 per page. Cert fee- $4.00 per page includes copy fee. Payee- Schuylkill

County Prothonotary. **Online access to Marriage, Civil Court records:** Search marriage dockets 1885-1969 and 1989-present free at www.co.schuylkill.pa.us/info/Offices/Archives/MarriageDockets.csp. Also, judgments on civil court files at www.co.schuylkill.pa.us/info/Civil/Inquiry/Search.csp.

Schuylkill County Recorder

County Recorder of Deeds, 401 N. Second St., Pottsville, PA 17901. 570-628-1480; hours: 8:30AM-4:30PM. www.co.schuylkill.pa.us
No tax liens filed here. Will not search real estate records. Will not search UCC records. Copy fee $8.00 per document. Cert fee- $1.50 per cert plus copy fee. Payee- Schuylkill County Recorder of Deeds. **Online to Sheriff Sale:** Access sheriff sale free at www.co.schuylkill.pa.us/Offices/Sheriff/Sale.asp. **Other phones:** Treasurer- 570-628-1433; Elections- 570-628-3040. **Property tax/Assessor**- 570-628-1025.

Snyder County Prothonotary

County Prothonotary, PO Box 217, Middleburg, PA 17842-0217. 570-837-4202; fax-570-837-4275; hours: 8:30AM-4PM.
Only the public may search. See Recorder for real estate records. Copy fee $.35 per page. Cert fee- $4.50. Payee- Snyder County Prothonotary.

Snyder County Recorder

County Recorder of Deeds, PO Box 217, Middleburg, PA 17842-0217. 570-837-4225; fax-570-837-4299; hours: 8:30AM-4PM.
No tax liens filed here. All records in one index. Record index not computerized. Only the public may search. R/E record copy- $1.00 per page. Cert fee- $1.50 per cert plus copy fee. Payee- Snyder County Recorder of Deeds. **Other phones:** Treasurer- 570-837-4221. **Property tax/Assessor**- 570-837-4218.

Somerset County Prothonotary

County Prothonotary, 111 E. Union St, #190, Somerset, PA 15501. 814-445-1428, R/E recording 814-445-1547, UCC recording 814-445-1428; fax-814-444-9270; 8:30AM-4PM. www.co.somerset.pa.us
Index: All indices up to 1991 are separate; after 1991 all indices on computer. Records indexed on a public use terminal back to 1992. Office will perform a UCC search but public must search other records themselves. See Recorder for real estate records. UCC Information or copy request per debtor name- $59.00. Copy fee $.50 per page. Payee- Somerset County Prothonotary. **Online access to Property, Assessor, Maps records:** Access property records by monthly subscription; $35.00 start-up fee plus $10.00 per month. For info or signup, call Cindy or John at 814-445-1536. Provide your email, company info and check. System will eventually provide images and comparable sales.

Somerset County Recorder

County Recorder of Deeds, 300 N Center Ave, #400, Somerset, PA 15501. 814-445-1547; fax-814-445-1563; 8:30AM-4PM. www.co.somerset.pa.us
No tax liens filed here. Index: Records prior to 1985 are indexed by Russell index. Only the public may search. UCC copy fee $2.00 per page. R/E record copy- $.50 per page. Cert fee- $2.00 per page plus copy fee. Payee- Somerset County Recorder of Deeds. **Online access to Real Estate, Deed, Lien, Judgment, Recording records:** Access is through a private company at www.landex.com/remote/. Fee is $.20 per minute and $.50 per fax page. Recorders index and images go back to 1/1985. **Other phones:** Treasurer- 814-445-1482; Elections- 814-445-1549. **Property tax/Assessor**- 300 N Center Ave, #440, Somerset, PA 15501; 814-445-1536.

Sullivan County Prothonotary

County Prothonotary, Main St; Courthouse, Laporte, PA 18626. 570-946-7351; fax-570-946-7105; hours: 8:30AM-4PM.

Records indexed on computer and books. Only the public may search. See Recorder for real estate records. Copy fee $.25 per page. Cert fee- $3.00 plus copy fee. Payee- Sullivan County Prothonotary.

Sullivan County Recorder

County Recorder of Deeds, Main St; Courthouse, Laporte, PA 18626. 570-946-7351; fax-570-946-7105; hours: 8:30AM-4PM.
No tax liens filed here. Records indexed on computer and old book indexes. Only the public may search. Copy fee $1.00 per financing statement. R/E record copy- $.25 per page. Cert fee- $3.00 per cert plus copy fee. Payee- Sullivan County Recorder of Deeds. **Other phones:** Treasurer- 570-946-7331; Elections- 570-946-5201. **Property tax/Assessor**- 570-946-5061.

Susquehanna County Prothonotary

County Prothonotary, PO Box 218, Montrose, PA 18801-0218. 570-278-4600 x121, R/E recording phone-570-278-4600 x112, UCC recording phone-570-278-4600 x120; fax-570-278-4191; hours: 8:30AM-4:30PM.
All records in one index. Records indexed on a public use terminal back to 1996. Only the public may search. See Recorder for real estate records. Copy fee $.25; tax lien copy fee $2.35 per page. Cert fee- $4.50 per name plus copy fee. Payee- Prothonotary. **Online access to Tax Lien, Judgment, Civil Court records:** Access is via a private company; call Infocon at 814-472-6066 or www.infoconcountyaccess.com.

Susquehanna County Recorder

Recorder of Deeds, PO Box 218, Montrose, PA 18801. 570-278-4600 x112/3, R/E recording phone-570-278-4600 x112; fax-570-278-2963; 8:30AM-4:30PM. www.susqco.com/subsites/gov/pages/govhome.htm
No tax liens filed here. All records in one index. Only the public may search. General copy fee $1.00 1st page, $.25 add'l per page. R/E record copy- $2.00 per deed. Cert fee- $1.50 per doc plus copy fee. Payee- Recorder of Deeds. **Online access to Property, Assessor records:** Access property data by subscription at www.courthouseonline.com. Sub fee $9.95 3-days, up to $275 per year. A free view available with control number and password from tax notice. **Other phones:** Treasurer- 570-278-4600 x130; Elections- 570-278-4600 x220; Vital Records- 570-278-4600 x112. **Property tax/Assessor**- 570-278-4600 x150.

Tioga County Prothonotary

County Prothonotary, 116 Main St; Courthouse, Wellsboro, PA 16901. 570-724-9281, R/E recording phone-570-724-9260; hours: 9AM-4:30PM.
All records in one index. Only the public may search. See Recorder for real estate records. Copy fee $.25 per page. Cert fee- $5.00 per cert plus copy fee. Payee- Tioga County Prothonotary.

Tioga County Recorder

County Recorder of Deeds, 116 Main St; Courthouse, Wellsboro, PA 16901. 570-724-9260, R/E recording phone-570-724-1906; hours: 9AM-4:30PM.
No tax liens filed here. Only the public may search. Copy fee $1.00 per page. Cert fee- $1.50 per cert plus copy fee. Payee- Tioga County Recorder of Deeds. **Online access to Real Estate, Deed, Will, Property, Assessor records:** Access is through a private company at www.landex.com/remote/. Fee is $.20 per minute and $.50 per fax page. Recorders data goes back to 1977; images and wills go back to 2/1999. Also, access property data by subscription at www.courthouseonline.com. Sub fee $9.95 3-days, up to $275 per year. A free view available if you have control number and password from tax notice. **Other phones:** Treasurer- 570-724-9213; Elections- 570-723-8230. **Property tax/Assessor**- 118 Main St, Wellsboro, PA 16901; 570-724-9117.

Union County Prothonotary

County Prothonotary, 103 S. 2nd St; Courthouse, Lewisburg, PA 17837. 570-524-8751, R/E recording phone-570-524-8761; fax-570-524-1628; hours: 8:30AM-4:30PM. www.unionco.org
All records in one index. Records indexed on a public use terminal back to 1988. Only the public may search. Copy fee $2.00, if tax lien $.25 per page. Cert fee- $5.00 per doc, plus copy fee. Payee- Union County Prothonotary.

Union County Recorder

County Recorder of Deeds, 103 S. 2nd St; Courthouse, Lewisburg, PA 17837-1996. 570-524-8761; hours: 8:30AM-4:15PM. www.unionco.org
No tax liens filed here. All records in one index, current -1981. Only the public may search. Copy fee $1.00 per page. Cert fee- $1.50 per cert and $.25 per page plus copy fee. Payee- Union County Recorder of Deeds. **Online to Property, Assessor records:** Access property data by subscription at www.courthouseonline.com. Sub fee $9.95 3-days, up to $275 per year. Free view available with control number and password from tax notice. **Other phones:** Treasurer- 570-524-8781; Elections- 570-524-8603. **Property tax/Assessor-** 570-524-8611.

Venango County Prothonotary

County Prothonotary, Courthouse; PO Box 831, Franklin, PA 16323. 814-432-9534, R/E recording phone-814-432-9534; fax-814-432-9579; hours: 8:30AM-4:30PM. www.co.venango.pa.us
All records in one index. Records indexed on a public use terminal back to 1993. Office personnel or visitors may perform searches. Real estate record search fee- $7.50 per name. See Recorder for real estate records. Will search UCC records; search includes tax liens if requested. Information or copy request per debtor name- $59.00. Separate federal/state combined tax lien search- $7.00 per debtor. Copy fee $1.00 per page. Cert fee- $7.50 per name. Payee- Venango County Prothonotary.

Venango County Recorder

County Recorder of Deeds, PO Box 831, Franklin, PA 16323. 814-432-9539, R/E recording phone-814-432-9535; fax-814-432-9569; hours: 8:30AM-4:30PM. www.co.venango.pa.us/Directory/index.htm
No tax liens filed here. All records in one index. Records indexed on a public use terminal back to 1989. Only the public may search. Copy fee $1.00 per page. Cert fee- $1.50 per page. Payee- Recorder of Deeds. **Online access to Property, Assessor records:** Access property data by subscription at www.courthouseonline.com. Sub fee $9.95 3-days, up to $275 per year. A free view available if you have control number and password from tax notice. **Other phones:** Treasurer- 814-432-9525; Elections- 814-432-9514; Vital Records- 814-432-9535/1893/1905. **Property tax/Assessor-** same address as above. 814-432-9516.

Warren County Prothonotary

County Prothonotary, 4th & Market Sts; Courthouse, Warren, PA 16365. 814-723-7550; fax-814-728-3476; hours: 8:30AM-4:30PM.
All records in one index. Records indexed on a public use terminal back to 1985. Office will perform a UCC search but public must search other records themselves. See Recorder for real estate records. UCC search per debtor name- $5.00. Copy fee $.25 per page. Cert fee- $5.00 per cert includes copy fee. Payee- Warren County Prothonotary.

Warren County Recorder

County Recorder of Deeds, 204 Fourth Ave; Courthouse, Warren, PA 16365. 814-728-3430, R/E recording phone-814-723-3430; fax-814-728-3476; hours: 8:30AM-4:30PM.

No tax liens filed here. All records in one index. Records indexed on a public use terminal back to 1985. Only the public may search. Search fee $5.00 per name if the office assists. Copy fee $.25 per page. R/E record copy- $5.00 per document by mail. Cert fee- $5.00 per cert includes copies. Payee- Warren County Recorder of Deeds. **Other phones:** Treasurer- 814-723-7550. **Property tax/Assessor-** 814-723-7550.

Washington County Prothonotary

County Prothonotary, 1 S. Main St, #1001; Courthouse, Washington, PA 15301. 724-228-6770, R/E recording phone-724-228-6806; fax-724-229-5913; hours: 9AM-4:30PM.
Separate indices to search include judgments, miscellaneous. See Recorder for real estate records. Will search UCC records, but not tax liens. UCC information or copy request per debtor name- $59.00. Copy fee $1.50 per page. Cert fee- $4.50 per seal includes copy fee. Payee- Washington County Prothonotary.

Washington County Recorder

Recorder of Deeds, 1 S. Main St, Rm 1006; Washington County Courthouse, Washington, PA 15301. 724-228-6806; fax-724-228-6737; hours: 9AM-4:30PM. www.co.washington.pa.us
No tax liens filed here. All records in one index. Records indexed on a public use terminal back to 1952. Only the public may search. Copy fee $.50 per page. By mail-$10.00 per document. Cert fee- $10.00 per cert includes copy fee up to 25 pages. After 25 pages, add $10.00. Payee- Recorder of Deeds. **Other phones:** Treasurer- 724-228-6780; Elections- 724-228-6750. **Property tax/Assessor-** 100 W Bean St, Washington, PA 15301; 724-228-6850.

Wayne County Prothonotary

County Prothonotary, 925 Court St; Courthouse, Honesdale, PA 18431-1996. 570-253-5970 x200/3, R/E recording phone-570-253-5970 x212, UCC recording phone-570-253-5970 x200; fax-570-253-0687; hours: 8:30AM-4:30PM.
All records in one index. Office will perform a UCC search but public must search other records themselves. See Recorder for real estate records. Information or copy request per debtor name- $59.00. Copy fee $.50 per page. Cert fee- $.50 per page. Payee- Wayne County Prothonotary.

Wayne County Recorder

County Recorder of Deeds, 925 Court St, Honesdale, PA 18431-1996. 570-253-5970 x212; fax-n/a; hours: 8:30AM-4:30PM.
www.co.wayne.pa.us/?pageid=10
No tax liens filed here. Only the public may search. Copy fee $.50 per page. Cert fee- $1.50 per doc, plus copy fee. Payee- Wayne County Recorder of Deeds. **Online to Assessor, Property, records:** Search assessor property data free after registering at http://taxpub.co.wayne.pa.us/Main.asp. **Other phones:** Treasurer- 570-253-5970 x125; Elections- 570-253-5970 x165. **Property/Assessor-** 570-253-5970 x216.

Westmoreland County Prothonotary

County Prothonotary, PO Box 1630, Greensburg, PA 15601. 724-830-3516; fax-724-830-3517; hours: 8:30AM-4PM.
All records in one index. Records indexed on a public use terminal back to 1985. Only the public may search. Copy fee $.50 per page. Cert fee- $5.35 per cert plus copy fee. Payee- Westmoreland County Prothonotary.

Westmoreland County Recorder

County Recorder of Deeds, 2 N Main St #203, Greensburg, PA 15601. 724-830-3734, R/E recording

phone-724-830-3518; fax-724-850-3979; hours: 8:30AM-4;00PM
www.co.westmoreland.pa.us
No tax liens filed here. Office will perform a UCC search but public must search other records themselves. Search fee $17.50 per name. Copy fee $.50 per page. Cert fee- $8.90 per page plus copy fee. Payee- Westmoreland County Recorder. **Online access to Real Estate, Tax Lien, Mortgage, UCC, Deed records:** The Register's fee-based system has been replaced by a free, searchable site at www.wcdeeds.us/dts/default.asp. Choose simple, advanced, or instrument search. **Other phones:** Treasurer- 724-830-3173; Elections- 724-830-3150. **Property tax/Assessor-** 724-830-3490.

Wyoming County Prothonotary

County Prothonotary, 1 Courthouse Sq; Wyoming County Courthouse, Tunkhannock, PA 18657-1219. 717-836-3200, R/E recording phone-717-836-3200 x235, UCC recording phone-717-836-3200; hours: 8:30AM-4PM.
All records in one index. Records indexed on a public use terminal. Only the public may search. Copy fee $.25 per copy. Cert fee- $7.00 per cert plus copy fee. Payee- Wyoming County Prothonotary.

Wyoming County Recorder

County Recorder of Deeds, 1 Courthouse Sq, Tunkhannock, PA 18657. 570-996-2361, R/E recording phone-717-836-3200; hours: 8:30AM-4PM.
No tax liens filed here. Records indexed on a public use terminal back to 9/1975. Only the public may search. Copy fee $.25 per page. Cert fee- $5.00 per cert includes up to 8 copies. Payee- Wyoming County Recorder of Deeds. **Other phones:** Treasurer- 717-836-3200 x287. **Property tax/Assessor-** 717-836-3200 x261.

York County Prothonotary

County Prothonotary, 45 N George St, York, PA 17401. 717-771-9611, R/E recording phone-717-771-9806, UCC recording phone-717-771-9608; fax-717-771-4629; hours: 8:30AM-4:30PM. www.york-county.org
Separate indices to search include new on enact, old on lightspeed. Only the public may search. See Recorder for real estate records. Copy fee $1.00 per page. Cert fee- $5.25 per 1st page, $1.75 each add'l page plus copy fee.

York County Recorder

Recorder of Deeds, 100 W Market St, York, PA 17401. 717-771-9295; fax-717-771-9582; 8AM-4:30PM. www.york-county.org/departments/deeds/deeds.htm
No tax liens filed here. Separate indices to search include Grantor/Grantee, Mtgor/Mtgee. Records indexed on a public use terminal back to 1990. Only the public may search. General index search fee $5.00 per search. Copy fee $.50 per page. Cert fee- $1.50 per page plus copy fee. **Online access to Assessor, Real Estate, Deed, Death, Naturalization records:** Two sources are available. Online access to the assessors database is free through the GIS data at http://207.140.67.68/york. Also, access is by subscription from Landex at www.landex.com/remote. Base fee is $.20 per minute, $.50 per fax page. Records go back to 1990; images to 1990. Search inmate list at www.york-county.org/departments/prison/prison.htm. View sheriff's most wanteds at http://ycwebserver.york-county.org/sheriff/MostWanted.htm Parcel numbers at www.york-county.org/departments/assessment/tx_asmnt.htm. Search the death index prior to 1959 at www.york-county.org/cgi-bin/Affdeath.cgi; naturalizations at www.york-county.org/cgi-bin/natural.cgi. **Other phones:** Treasurer- 717-771-9603; Appraiser/Auditor- 717-771-9232; Elections- 717-771-9604. **Property tax/Assessor-** 717-771-92320.

Pennsylvania County Locator

You will usually be able to find the city name in the City/County Cross Reference below. In that case, it is a simple matter to determine the county from the cross reference. However, only the official US Postal Service city names are included in this index. There are an additional 40,000 place names that people use in their addresses. Therefore, we have also included a ZIP/City Cross Reference immediately following the City/County Cross Reference.

If you know the ZIP Code but the city name does not appear in the City/County Cross Reference index, look up the ZIP Code in the ZIP/City Cross Reference, find the city name, then look up the city name in the City/County Cross Reference. For example, you want to know the county for an address of Menands, NY 12204. There is no "Menands" in the City/County Cross Reference. The ZIP/City Cross Reference shows that ZIP Codes 12201-12288 are for the city of Albany. Looking back in the City/County Cross Reference, Albany is in Albany County.

Pennsylvania City/County Cross Reference

AARONSBURG Centre
ABBOTTSTOWN (17301) Adams(97), York(2)
ABINGTON Montgomery
ACKERMANVILLE Northampton
ACME (15610) Westmoreland(96), Fayette(3)
ACOSTA Somerset
ADAH Fayette
ADAMSBURG Westmoreland
ADAMSTOWN Lancaster
ADAMSVILLE (16110) Crawford(90), Mercer(9)
ADDISON Somerset
ADRIAN Armstrong
AIRVILLE York
AKRON Lancaster
ALBA Bradford
ALBION (16401) Erie(91), Crawford(8)
ALBION Erie
ALBRIGHTSVILLE (18210) Carbon(90), Monroe(9)
ALBURTIS (18011) Berks(61), Lehigh(38)
ALDENVILLE Wayne
ALEPPO Greene
ALEXANDRIA Huntingdon
ALIQUIPPA Beaver
ALLENPORT Washington
ALLENSVILLE (17002) Mifflin(87), Huntingdon(12)
ALLENTOWN (18109) Lehigh(97), Northampton(2)
ALLENTOWN Lehigh
ALLENWOOD (17810) Lycoming(63), Union(36)
ALLISON Fayette
ALLISON PARK Allegheny
ALLPORT Clearfield
ALTOONA Blair
ALUM BANK Bedford
ALVERDA Indiana
ALVERTON Westmoreland
AMBERSON Franklin
AMBLER Montgomery
AMBRIDGE (15003) Beaver(95), Allegheny(4)
AMITY Washington
ANALOMINK Monroe
ANDREAS (18211) Schuylkill(84), Carbon(15)
ANITA Jefferson
ANNVILLE Lebanon
ANTES FORT Lycoming
APOLLO (15613) Westmoreland(50), Armstrong(49)
AQUASHICOLA Carbon
ARCADIA Indiana
ARCHBALD Lackawanna
ARCOLA Montgomery
ARDARA Westmoreland
ARDMORE (19003) Montgomery(62), Delaware(37)
ARENDTSVILLE Adams

ARISTES Columbia
ARMAGH Indiana
ARMBRUST Westmoreland
ARNOT Tioga
ARONA Westmoreland
ARTEMAS Bedford
ASHFIELD Carbon
ASHLAND Schuylkill
ASHVILLE (16613) Cambria(98), Blair(1)
ASPERS Adams
ASTON Delaware
ATGLEN (19310) Chester(98), Lancaster(1)
ATHENS Bradford
ATLANTIC Crawford
ATLASBURG Washington
AUBURN Schuylkill
AUDUBON Montgomery
AULTMAN Indiana
AUSTIN (16720) Potter(58), Cameron(36), McKean(5)
AVELLA Washington
AVIS Clinton
AVONDALE Chester
AVONMORE Westmoreland
BADEN (15005) Beaver(87), Allegheny(12)
BAINBRIDGE Lancaster
BAIRDFORD Allegheny
BAKERS SUMMIT Bedford
BAKERSTOWN Allegheny
BALA CYNWYD Montgomery
BALLY Berks
BANGOR Northampton
BARNESBORO (15714) Cambria(79), Indiana(20)
BARNESVILLE Schuylkill
BART Lancaster
BARTO (19504) Berks(67), Montgomery(32)
BARTONSVILLE Monroe
BATH Northampton
BAUSMAN Lancaster
BEACH HAVEN Luzerne
BEACH LAKE (18405) Wayne(96), Pike(3)
BEALLSVILLE Washington
BEAR CREEK Luzerne
BEAR LAKE Warren
BEAVER FALLS Beaver
BEAVER MEADOWS (18216) Luzerne(69), Carbon(30)
BEAVER SPRINGS Snyder
BEAVERDALE Cambria
BEAVERTOWN Snyder
BECCARIA Clearfield
BECHTELSVILLE (19505) Berks(94), Montgomery(5)
BEDFORD Bedford
BEDMINSTER Bucks
BEECH CREEK (16822) Clinton(91), Centre(8)
BELLE VERNON (15012) Fayette(56), Westmoreland(41), Washington(1)
BELLEFONTE Centre

BELLEVILLE Mifflin
BELLWOOD Blair
BELSANO Cambria
BENDERSVILLE Adams
BENEZETT Elk
BENSALEM Bucks
BENTLEYVILLE Washington
BENTON (17814) Columbia(62), Luzerne(29), Lycoming(4), Sullivan(3)
BERLIN Somerset
BERNVILLE Berks
BERRYSBURG Dauphin
BERWICK (18603) Columbia(79), Luzerne(20)
BERWYN Chester
BESSEMER Lawrence
BETHEL Berks
BETHEL PARK Allegheny
BETHLEHEM (18018) Lehigh(52), Northampton(47)
BETHLEHEM (18017) Northampton(94), Lehigh(5)
BETHLEHEM Lehigh
BETHLEHEM Northampton
BEYER Indiana
BIG COVE TANNERY Fulton
BIG RUN Jefferson
BIGLER Clearfield
BIGLERVILLE (17307) Adams(98), Cumberland(1)
BIRCHRUNVILLE Chester
BIRD IN HAND Lancaster
BIRDSBORO Berks
BLACK LICK Indiana
BLAIN Perry
BLAIRS MILLS Huntingdon
BLAIRSVILLE (15717) Indiana(88), Westmoreland(11)
BLAKESLEE (18610) Monroe(98), Luzerne(1)
BLANCHARD Centre
BLANDBURG Cambria
BLANDON Berks
BLOOMING GLEN Bucks
BLOOMSBURG Columbia
BLOSSBURG Tioga
BLUE BALL Lancaster
BLUE BELL Montgomery
BLUE RIDGE SUMMIT Franklin
BOALSBURG Centre
BOBTOWN Greene
BODINES Lycoming
BOILING SPRINGS Cumberland
BOLIVAR Westmoreland
BOSWELL Somerset
BOVARD Westmoreland
BOWERS Berks
BOWMANSDALE Cumberland
BOWMANSTOWN Carbon
BOWMANSVILLE Lancaster
BOYERS Butler
BOYERTOWN (19512) Berks(95), Montgomery(4)

BOYNTON Somerset
BRACKENRIDGE Allegheny
BRACKNEY Susquehanna
BRADDOCK Allegheny
BRADENVILLE Westmoreland
BRADFORD McKean
BRADFORDWOODS Allegheny
BRANCHDALE Schuylkill
BRANCHTON Butler
BRANDAMORE Chester
BRANDY CAMP Elk
BRAVE Greene
BREEZEWOOD (15533) Bedford(94), Fulton(5)
BREINIGSVILLE Lehigh
BRIDGEPORT Montgomery
BRIDGEVILLE (15017) Allegheny(97), Washington(2)
BRIER HILL Fayette
BRISBIN Clearfield
BRISTOL Bucks
BROAD TOP Huntingdon
BROCKPORT (15823) Elk(81), Jefferson(18)
BROCKTON Schuylkill
BROCKWAY (15824) Jefferson(97), Clearfield(2)
BRODHEADSVILLE Monroe
BROGUE York
BROOKHAVEN Delaware
BROOKLYN Susquehanna
BROOKVILLE Jefferson
BROOMALL Delaware
BROWNFIELD Fayette
BROWNSTOWN Lancaster
BROWNSVILLE (15417) Fayette(62), Washington(37)
BRUIN Butler
BRUSH VALLEY Indiana
BRYN ATHYN Montgomery
BRYN MAWR (19010) Delaware(53), Montgomery(46)
BUCK HILL FALLS Monroe
BUCKINGHAM Bucks
BUENA VISTA Allegheny
BUFFALO MILLS (15534) Bedford(98), Somerset(1)
BULGER Washington
BUNOLA Allegheny
BURGETTSTOWN Washington
BURLINGTON Bradford
BURNHAM Mifflin
BURNSIDE Clearfield
BURNT CABINS (17215) Fulton(82), Huntingdon(17)
BUSHKILL Pike
BUTLER Butler
BYRNEDALE Elk
CABOT Butler
CADOGAN Armstrong
CAIRNBROOK Somerset
CALIFORNIA Washington
CALLENSBURG Clarion

CALLERY Butler
CALUMET Westmoreland
CALVIN Huntingdon
CAMBRA Luzerne
CAMBRIDGE SPRINGS (16403) Crawford(93), Erie(6)
CAMP HILL (17011) Cumberland(98), York(1)
CAMP HILL Cumberland
CAMP HILL Lebanon
CAMPBELLTOWN Lebanon
CAMPTOWN Bradford
CANADENSIS (18325) Monroe(63), Pike(36)
CANONSBURG Washington
CANTON (17724) Bradford(82), Tioga(7), Sullivan(7), Lycoming(3)
CARBONDALE Lackawanna
CARDALE Fayette
CARLISLE Cumberland
CARLTON (16311) Mercer(87), Venango(12)
CARMICHAELS Greene
CARNEGIE Allegheny
CARROLLTOWN Cambria
CARVERSVILLE Bucks
CASHTOWN Adams
CASSANDRA Cambria
CASSVILLE Huntingdon
CASTANEA Clinton
CATASAUQUA (18032) Lehigh(68), Northampton(31)
CATAWISSA (17820) Columbia(96), Montour(3)
CECIL Washington
CEDAR RUN Lycoming
CEDARS Montgomery
CENTER VALLEY Lehigh
CENTERPORT Berks
CENTERVILLE Crawford
CENTRAL CITY Somerset
CENTRALIA Columbia
CENTRE HALL Centre
CHADDS FORD (19317) Delaware(63), Chester(36)
CHALFONT Bucks
CHALK HILL Fayette
CHALKHILL Fayette
CHAMBERSBURG Franklin
CHAMBERSVILLE Indiana
CHAMPION (15622) Westmoreland(84), Fayette(8), Somerset(7)
CHANDLERS VALLEY Warren
CHARLEROI Washington
CHATHAM Chester
CHELTENHAM Montgomery
CHERRY TREE (15724) Indiana(66), Clearfield(26), Cambria(7)
CHERRYVILLE Northampton
CHEST SPRINGS Cambria
CHESTER Delaware
CHESTER HEIGHTS Delaware
CHESTER SPRINGS Chester
CHESTNUT RIDGE Fayette
CHESWICK Allegheny
CHEYNEY (19319) Delaware(97), Chester(2)
CHICORA (16025) Butler(81), Armstrong(18)
CHINCHILLA Lackawanna
CHRISTIANA Lancaster
CLAIRTON Allegheny
CLARENCE Centre
CLARENDON Warren
CLARIDGE Westmoreland
CLARINGTON (15828) Jefferson(92), Forest(5), Elk(2)
CLARION Clarion
CLARK Mercer
CLARKS MILLS Mercer
CLARKS SUMMIT Lackawanna
CLARKSBURG Indiana

CLARKSVILLE (15322) Washington(56), Greene(43)
CLAYSBURG (16625) Bedford(75), Blair(24)
CLAYSVILLE Washington
CLEARFIELD Clearfield
CLEARVILLE Bedford
CLIFFORD Susquehanna
CLIFTON HEIGHTS Delaware
CLIMAX Armstrong
CLINTON (15026) Beaver(78), Allegheny(15), Washington(6)
CLINTONVILLE Venango
CLUNE Indiana
CLYMER Indiana
COAL CENTER Washington
COAL TOWNSHIP Northumberland
COALDALE Schuylkill
COALPORT (16627) Clearfield(93), Cambria(6)
COATESVILLE Chester
COBURN Centre
COCHRANTON (16314) Crawford(90), Mercer(6), Venango(3)
COCHRANVILLE Chester
COCOLAMUS Juniata
CODORUS York
COGAN STATION Lycoming
COKEBURG Washington
COLEBROOK Lebanon
COLLEGEVILLE Montgomery
COLMAR Montgomery
COLUMBIA Lancaster
COLUMBIA CROSS ROADS (16914) Bradford(93), Tioga(6)
COLUMBUS Warren
COLVER Cambria
COMMODORE Indiana
CONCORD Franklin
CONCORDVILLE Delaware
CONESTOGA Lancaster
CONFLUENCE (15424) Somerset(77), Fayette(22)
CONNEAUT LAKE Crawford
CONNEAUTVILLE Crawford
CONNELLSVILLE Fayette
CONNOQUENESSING Butler
CONSHOHOCKEN Montgomery
CONWAY Beaver
CONYNGHAM Luzerne
COOKSBURG (16217) Clarion(91), Forest(8)
COOLSPRING Jefferson
COOPERSBURG (18036) Lehigh(88), Bucks(11)
COOPERSTOWN (16317) Venango(93), Crawford(6)
COPLAY Lehigh
CORAL Indiana
CORAOPOLIS Allegheny
CORNWALL Lebanon
CORRY (16407) Erie(87), Warren(7), Crawford(5)
CORSICA (15829) Jefferson(74), Clarion(25)
COUDERSPORT Potter
COULTERS Allegheny
COUPON Cambria
COURTNEY Washington
COVINGTON Tioga
COWANESQUE Tioga
COWANSVILLE Armstrong
CRABTREE Westmoreland
CRALEY York
CRANBERRY (16319) Venango(60), Clarion(39)
CRANBERRY TWP Butler
CRANESVILLE Erie
CREAMERY Montgomery
CREEKSIDE (15732) Indiana(92), Armstrong(4), Allegheny(2)
CREIGHTON Allegheny

CRESCENT Allegheny
CRESCO (18326) Monroe(98), Pike(1)
CRESSON Cambria
CRESSONA Schuylkill
CROSBY McKean
CROSS FORK (17729) Clinton(59), Potter(40)
CROWN Clarion
CROYDON Bucks
CRUCIBLE Greene
CRUM LYNNE Delaware
CRYSTAL SPRING Fulton
CUDDY Allegheny
CUMBOLA Schuylkill
CURLLSVILLE Clarion
CURRYVILLE Blair
CURTISVILLE Allegheny
CURWENSVILLE Clearfield
CUSTER CITY McKean
CYCLONE McKean
DAGUS MINES Elk
DAISYTOWN Washington
DALLAS (18612) Luzerne(97), Wyoming(2)
DALLAS Luzerne
DALLASTOWN York
DALMATIA (17017) Northumberland(64), Dauphin(35)
DALTON (18414) Lackawanna(78), Wyoming(21)
DAMASCUS Wayne
DANBORO Bucks
DANIELSVILLE Northampton
DANVILLE (17821) Montour(82), Northumberland(16), Columbia(1)
DANVILLE Montour
DARBY Delaware
DARLINGTON Beaver
DARRAGH Westmoreland
DAUBERVILLE Berks
DAUPHIN Dauphin
DAVIDSVILLE Somerset
DAWSON Fayette
DAYTON (16222) Armstrong(66), Jefferson(16), Indiana(16)
DE LANCEY Jefferson
DE YOUNG Elk
DEFIANCE Bedford
DELANO Schuylkill
DELAWARE WATER GAP Monroe
DELMONT Westmoreland
DELTA York
DENBO Washington
DENVER Lancaster
DERRICK CITY McKean
DERRY Westmoreland
DEVAULT Chester
DEVON Chester
DEWART Northumberland
DICKERSON RUN Fayette
DICKINSON Cumberland
DICKSON CITY Lackawanna
DILLINER Greene
DILLSBURG York
DILLTOWN Indiana
DIMOCK Susquehanna
DINGMANS FERRY Pike
DISTANT Armstrong
DIXONVILLE Indiana
DONEGAL Westmoreland
DONORA Washington
DORNSIFE (17823) Northumberland(98), Schuylkill(1)
DOUGLASSVILLE Berks
DOVER York
DOWNINGTOWN Chester
DOYLESBURG Franklin
DOYLESTOWN Bucks
DRAVOSBURG Allegheny
DRESHER Montgomery
DREXEL HILL Delaware
DRIFTING Clearfield
DRIFTON Luzerne

DRIFTWOOD (15832) Cameron(85), Elk(14)
DRUMORE Lancaster
DRUMS Luzerne
DRY RUN Franklin
DU BOIS Clearfield
DUBLIN Bucks
DUDLEY Huntingdon
DUKE CENTER McKean
DUNBAR Fayette
DUNCANNON Perry
DUNCANSVILLE Blair
DUNLEVY Washington
DUNLO Cambria
DUQUESNE Allegheny
DURHAM Bucks
DURYEA Luzerne
DUSHORE (18614) Sullivan(94), Wyoming(3), Bradford(1)
DYSART (16636) Cambria(90), Blair(9)
EAGLES MERE Sullivan
EAGLEVILLE Montgomery
EARLINGTON Montgomery
EARLVILLE Berks
EAST BERLIN (17316) Adams(81), York(18)
EAST BRADY (16028) Clarion(84), Armstrong(15)
EAST BUTLER Butler
EAST EARL Lancaster
EAST FREEDOM Blair
EAST GREENVILLE (18041) Montgomery(70), Lehigh(23), Bucks(3), Berks(2)
EAST HICKORY Forest
EAST MC KEESPORT Allegheny
EAST MILLSBORO Fayette
EAST PETERSBURG Lancaster
EAST PITTSBURGH Allegheny
EAST PROSPECT York
EAST SMETHPORT McKean
EAST SMITHFIELD Bradford
EAST SPRINGFIELD Erie
EAST STROUDSBURG Monroe
EAST TEXAS Lehigh
EAST VANDERGRIFT Westmoreland
EAST WATERFORD (17021) Juniata(87), Huntingdon(6), Franklin(3), Perry(2)
EASTON Northampton
EAU CLAIRE Butler
EBENSBURG Cambria
EBERVALE Luzerne
EDGEMONT Delaware
EDINBORO (16412) Erie(76), Crawford(23)
EDINBORO Erie
EDINBURG Lawrence
EDMON Armstrong
EFFORT Monroe
EIGHTY FOUR Washington
ELCO Washington
ELDERSVILLE Washington
ELDERTON Armstrong
ELDRED McKean
ELGIN Erie
ELIZABETH Allegheny
ELIZABETHTOWN (17022) Lancaster(90), Dauphin(9)
ELIZABETHVILLE Dauphin
ELKINS PARK Montgomery
ELKLAND Tioga
ELLIOTTSBURG Perry
ELLSWORTH Washington
ELLWOOD CITY (16117) Lawrence(67), Beaver(32)
ELM Lancaster
ELMHURST Lackawanna
ELMORA Cambria
ELRAMA Washington
ELTON Cambria
ELVERSON (19520) Chester(69), Berks(30)

ELYSBURG (17824) Northumberland(81), Columbia(17), Montour(1)
EMEIGH Cambria
EMIGSVILLE York
EMLENTON (16373) Venango(49), Clarion(47), Butler(3)
EMMAUS Lehigh
EMPORIUM (15834) Cameron(97), Elk(1)
ENDEAVOR Forest
ENOLA Cumberland
ENON VALLEY (16120) Lawrence(94), Beaver(5)
ENTRIKEN Huntingdon
EPHRATA Lancaster
EQUINUNK Wayne
ERIE Erie
ERNEST Indiana
ERWINNA Bucks
ESSINGTON Delaware
ETTERS York
EVANS CITY Butler
EVERETT Bedford
EVERSON Fayette
EXCELSIOR Northumberland
EXPORT Westmoreland
EXTON Chester
FACTORYVILLE (18419) Wyoming(79), Lackawanna(20)
FAIRBANK Fayette
FAIRCHANCE Fayette
FAIRFIELD Adams
FAIRHOPE Somerset
FAIRLESS HILLS Bucks
FAIRMOUNT CITY Clarion
FAIRVIEW Erie
FAIRVIEW VILLAGE Montgomery
FALLENTIMBER (16639) Cambria(83), Clearfield(16)
FALLS (18615) Wyoming(90), Luzerne(7), Lackawanna(2)
FALLS CREEK (15840) Jefferson(96), Clearfield(3)
FANNETTSBURG Franklin
FARMINGTON Fayette
FARRANDSVILLE Clinton
FARRELL Mercer
FAWN GROVE York
FAYETTE CITY Fayette
FAYETTEVILLE (17222) Franklin(94), Adams(5)
FEASTERVILLE TREVOSE Bucks
FELTON York
FENELTON Butler
FERNDALE Bucks
FINLEYVILLE (15332) Washington(92), Allegheny(7)
FIRST NAT BANK Erie
FISHER Clarion
FISHERTOWN Bedford
FLEETVILLE Lackawanna
FLEETWOOD Berks
FLEMING Centre
FLICKSVILLE Northampton
FLINTON Cambria
FLOURTOWN Montgomery
FOGELSVILLE Lehigh
FOLCROFT Delaware
FOLSOM Delaware
FOMBELL (16123) Beaver(69), Lawrence(30)
FORBES ROAD Westmoreland
FORCE Elk
FORD CITY Armstrong
FORD CLIFF Armstrong
FOREST CITY (18421) Susquehanna(47), Wayne(31), Lackawanna(20)
FOREST GROVE Bucks
FORESTVILLE Butler
FORKSVILLE Sullivan
FORT HILL Somerset
FORT LITTLETON Fulton
FORT LOUDON Franklin

FORT WASHINGTON Bucks
FORT WASHINGTON Montgomery
FOUNTAINVILLE Bucks
FOXBURG Clarion
FRACKVILLE Schuylkill
FRANCONIA Montgomery
FRANKLIN Venango
FRANKLINTOWN York
FREDERICK Montgomery
FREDERICKSBURG (17026) Lebanon(90), Berks(9)
FREDERICKTOWN Washington
FREDONIA Mercer
FREEBURG Snyder
FREEDOM Beaver
FREELAND Luzerne
FREEPORT (16229) Armstrong(64), Butler(23), Westmoreland(10), Allegheny(1)
FRENCHVILLE Clearfield
FRIEDENS Somerset
FRIEDENSBURG Schuylkill
FRIENDSVILLE Susquehanna
FROSTBURG Jefferson
FRYBURG Clarion
FURLONG Bucks
GAINES (16921) Tioga(96), Potter(3)
GALETON Potter
GALLITZIN (16641) Cambria(96), Blair(3)
GANS Fayette
GAP (17527) Lancaster(91), Chester(8)
GARARDS FORT Greene
GARDENVILLE Bucks
GARDNERS (17324) Adams(66), Cumberland(33)
GARLAND Warren
GARRETT Somerset
GASTONVILLE Washington
GEIGERTOWN Berks
GENESEE Potter
GEORGETOWN Beaver
GERMANSVILLE Lehigh
GETTYSBURG Adams
GIBBON GLADE Fayette
GIBSON Susquehanna
GIBSONIA (15044) Allegheny(95), Butler(4)
GIFFORD McKean
GILBERT Monroe
GILBERTON Schuylkill
GILBERTSVILLE Montgomery
GILLETT Bradford
GIPSY Indiana
GIRARD Erie
GIRARDVILLE Schuylkill
GLADWYNE Montgomery
GLASGOW Cambria
GLASSPORT Allegheny
GLEN CAMPBELL (15742) Indiana(91), Clearfield(8)
GLEN HOPE Clearfield
GLEN LYON Luzerne
GLEN MILLS (19342) Delaware(98), Chester(1)
GLEN RICHEY Clearfield
GLEN RIDDLE LIMA Delaware
GLEN ROCK York
GLENMOORE Chester
GLENOLDEN Delaware
GLENSHAW Allegheny
GLENSIDE Montgomery
GLENVILLE York
GLENWILLARD Allegheny
GOODVILLE Lancaster
GORDON Schuylkill
GORDONVILLE Lancaster
GOULDSBORO (18424) Wayne(54), Lackawanna(38), Luzerne(3), Monroe(2)
GOWEN CITY Northumberland
GRADYVILLE Delaware
GRAMPIAN Clearfield
GRAND VALLEY (16420) Warren(81), Crawford(17), Jefferson(1)

GRANTHAM Cumberland
GRANTVILLE (17028) Dauphin(80), Lebanon(19)
GRANVILLE Mifflin
GRANVILLE SUMMIT Bradford
GRAPEVILLE Westmoreland
GRASSFLAT Clearfield
GRATZ Dauphin
GRAY Somerset
GRAYSVILLE Greene
GREAT BEND Susquehanna
GREELEY Pike
GREEN LANE (18054) Montgomery(83), Bucks(16)
GREEN PARK Perry
GREENCASTLE Franklin
GREENOCK Allegheny
GREENSBURG Westmoreland
GREENTOWN Pike
GREENVILLE (16125) Mercer(95), Crawford(4)
GRINDSTONE Fayette
GROVE CITY (16127) Mercer(93), Venango(5)
GROVER Bradford
GUYS MILLS Crawford
GWYNEDD Montgomery
GWYNEDD VALLEY Montgomery
HADLEY Mercer
HALIFAX Dauphin
HALLSTEAD Susquehanna
HAMBURG Berks
HAMILTON Jefferson
HAMLIN Wayne
HANNASTOWN Westmoreland
HANOVER (17331) York(83), Adams(16)
HANOVER York
HARBORCREEK Erie
HARFORD Susquehanna
HARLEIGH Luzerne
HARLEYSVILLE Montgomery
HARMONSBURG Crawford
HARMONY (16037) Butler(82), Lawrence(13), Beaver(3)
HARRISBURG Dauphin
HARRISON CITY Westmoreland
HARRISON VALLEY Potter
HARRISONVILLE Fulton
HARRISVILLE (16038) Venango(53), Butler(46)
HARTLETON Union
HARTSTOWN Crawford
HARVEYS LAKE (18618) Luzerne(86), Wyoming(13)
HARWICK Allegheny
HASTINGS (16646) Cambria(95), Clearfield(4)
HATBORO (19040) Montgomery(96), Bucks(3)
HATFIELD (19440) Montgomery(91), Bucks(8)
HAVERFORD (19041) Montgomery(73), Delaware(26)
HAVERTOWN Delaware
HAWK RUN Clearfield
HAWLEY (18428) Wayne(64), Pike(35)
HAWTHORN Clarion
HAZEL HURST McKean
HAZLETON Luzerne
HEGINS Schuylkill
HEILWOOD Indiana
HELFENSTEIN Schuylkill
HELLERTOWN (18055) Northampton(97), Bucks(2)
HENDERSONVILLE Washington
HENRYVILLE Monroe
HEREFORD Berks
HERMAN Butler
HERMINIE Westmoreland
HERMITAGE Mercer
HERNDON (17830) Northumberland(98), Dauphin(1)

HERRICK CENTER Susquehanna
HERSHEY (17033) Dauphin(96), Lebanon(3)
HESSTON Huntingdon
HIBBS Fayette
HICKORY Washington
HIDDEN VALLEY Somerset
HIGHSPIRE Dauphin
HILLER Fayette
HILLIARDS Butler
HILLSDALE Indiana
HILLSGROVE (18619) Sullivan(81), Lycoming(18)
HILLSVILLE Lawrence
HILLTOWN Bucks
HOLBROOK Greene
HOLICONG Bucks
HOLLIDAYSBURG Blair
HOLLSOPPLE Somerset
HOLMES Delaware
HOLTWOOD Lancaster
HOME Indiana
HOMER CITY Indiana
HOMESTEAD Allegheny
HONESDALE Wayne
HONEY BROOK (19344) Chester(89), Lancaster(10)
HONEY GROVE (17035) Juniata(98), Perry(1)
HOOKSTOWN Beaver
HOOVERSVILLE Somerset
HOP BOTTOM Susquehanna
HOPELAND Lancaster
HOPEWELL Bedford
HOPWOOD Fayette
HORSHAM Montgomery
HOSTETTER Westmoreland
HOUSTON Washington
HOUTZDALE Clearfield
HOWARD Centre
HUGHESVILLE Lycoming
HUMMELS WHARF Snyder
HUMMELSTOWN Dauphin
HUNKER Westmoreland
HUNLOCK CREEK Luzerne
HUNTINGDON Huntingdon
HUNTINGDON VALLEY (19006) Montgomery(91), Bucks(8)
HUNTINGTON MILLS Luzerne
HUSTONTOWN (17229) Fulton(93), Huntingdon(6)
HUTCHINSON Westmoreland
HYDE Clearfield
HYDE PARK Westmoreland
HYDETOWN Crawford
HYNDMAN (15545) Bedford(77), Somerset(22)
HYNER Clinton
ICKESBURG Perry
IDAVILLE Adams
IMLER (16655) Bedford(98), Blair(1)
IMMACULATA Chester
IMPERIAL Allegheny
INDIAN HEAD Fayette
INDIANA Indiana
INDIANOLA Allegheny
INDUSTRY Beaver
INGOMAR Allegheny
INTERCOURSE Lancaster
IRVINE Warren
IRVONA Clearfield
IRWIN Westmoreland
ISABELLA Fayette
JACKSON Susquehanna
JACKSON CENTER Mercer
JACOBS CREEK Westmoreland
JAMES CITY Elk
JAMES CREEK (16657) Huntingdon(98), Bedford(1)
JAMESTOWN (16134) Crawford(90), Mercer(9)
JAMISON Bucks

JEANNETTE Westmoreland
JENKINTOWN Montgomery
JENNERS Somerset
JENNERSTOWN Somerset
JERMYN Lackawanna
JEROME Somerset
JERSEY MILLS Lycoming
JERSEY SHORE (17740) Lycoming(86),
     Clinton(13)
JERSEY SHORE Lycoming
JESSUP Lackawanna
JIM THORPE Carbon
JOFFRE Washington
JOHNSONBURG Elk
JOHNSTOWN (15905) Cambria(89),
     Somerset(10)
JOHNSTOWN Cambria
JONES MILLS Westmoreland
JONESTOWN Lebanon
JOSEPHINE Indiana
JULIAN Centre
JUNEAU Indiana
JUNEDALE Carbon
KANE (16735) McKean(71), Elk(28)
KANTNER Somerset
KARNS CITY (16041) Butler(54),
     Armstrong(45)
KARTHAUS (16845) Clearfield(70),
     Centre(29)
KEISTERVILLE Fayette
KELAYRES Schuylkill
KELTON Chester
KEMBLESVILLE Chester
KEMPTON (19529) Berks(51), Lehigh(48)
KENNERDELL Venango
KENNETT SQUARE Chester
KENT Indiana
KERSEY Elk
KIMBERTON Chester
KING OF PRUSSIA Chester
KING OF PRUSSIA Montgomery
KINGSLEY Susquehanna
KINGSTON Luzerne
KINTNERSVILLE Bucks
KINZERS Lancaster
KIRKWOOD Lancaster
KITTANNING Armstrong
KLEINFELTERSVILLE Lebanon
KLINGERSTOWN (17941) Schuylkill(84),
     Northumberland(15)
KNOX Clarion
KNOX DALE Jefferson
KNOXVILLE Tioga
KOPPEL Beaver
KOSSUTH Clarion
KREAMER Snyder
KRESGEVILLE Monroe
KULPMONT Northumberland
KULPSVILLE Montgomery
KUNKLETOWN (18058) Monroe(70),
     Carbon(29)
KUTZTOWN (19530) Berks(90), Lehigh(9)
KYLERTOWN Clearfield
LA BELLE Fayette
LA JOSE Clearfield
LA PLUME Lackawanna
LACEYVILLE (18623) Wyoming(46),
     Bradford(38), Susquehanna(15)
LACKAWAXEN Pike
LAFAYETTE HILL Montgomery
LAHASKA Bucks
LAIRDSVILLE Lycoming
LAKE ARIEL (18436) Wayne(67),
     Lackawanna(32)
LAKE CITY Erie
LAKE COMO Wayne
LAKE HARMONY Carbon
LAKE LYNN Fayette
LAKE WINOLA Wyoming
LAKEVILLE Wayne
LAKEWOOD Wayne
LAMAR Clinton

LAMARTINE Clarion
LAMPETER Lancaster
LANCASTER Lancaster
LANDENBERG Chester
LANDINGVILLE Schuylkill
LANDISBURG Perry
LANDISVILLE Lancaster
LANESBORO Susquehanna
LANGELOTH Washington
LANGHORNE Bucks
LANSDALE Montgomery
LANSDOWNE Delaware
LANSE Clearfield
LANSFORD Carbon
LAPORTE Sullivan
LARIMER Westmoreland
LATROBE Westmoreland
LATTIMER MINES Luzerne
LAUGHLINTOWN Westmoreland
LAURELTON Union
LAURYS STATION Lehigh
LAVELLE Schuylkill
LAWN Lebanon
LAWRENCE Washington
LAWRENCEVILLE Tioga
LAWTON Susquehanna
LE RAYSVILLE (18829) Bradford(95),
     Susquehanna(4)
LEBANON Lebanon
LECK KILL (17836) Northumberland(78),
     Schuylkill(21)
LECKRONE Fayette
LECONTES MILLS Clearfield
LEDERACH Montgomery
LEECHBURG (15656) Armstrong(51),
     Westmoreland(48)
LEEPER Clarion
LEESPORT Berks
LEETSDALE Allegheny
LEHIGH VALLEY Northampton
LEHIGHTON Carbon
LEHMAN Luzerne
LEISENRING Fayette
LEMASTERS Franklin
LEMONT Centre
LEMONT FURNACE Fayette
LEMOYNE Cumberland
LENHARTSVILLE Berks
LENNI Delaware
LENOXVILLE Susquehanna
LEOLA Lancaster
LEROY Bradford
LEVITTOWN Bucks
LEWIS RUN McKean
LEWISBERRY York
LEWISBURG Union
LEWISTOWN Mifflin
LEWISVILLE Chester
LIBERTY (16930) Tioga(73), Lycoming(26)
LIBRARY Allegheny
LICKINGVILLE Clarion
LIGHT STREET Columbia
LIGONIER Westmoreland
LILLY Cambria
LIMEKILN Berks
LIMEPORT Lehigh
LIMESTONE Clarion
LINCOLN UNIVERSITY Chester
LINDEN Lycoming
LINE LEXINGTON (18932) Bucks(93),
     Montgomery(6)
LINESVILLE Crawford
LIONVILLE Chester
LISTIE Somerset
LITITZ Lancaster
LITTLE MEADOWS (18830)
     Susquehanna(91), Bradford(8)
LITTLESTOWN Adams
LIVERPOOL (17045) Perry(71),
     Juniata(23), Snyder(4)
LLEWELLYN Schuylkill

LOCK HAVEN (17745) Clinton(98),
     Lycoming(1)
LOCUST GAP Northumberland
LOCUSTDALE Schuylkill
LOGANTON Clinton
LOGANVILLE York
LONG POND Monroe
LOPEZ Sullivan
LORETTO Cambria
LOST CREEK Schuylkill
LOWBER Westmoreland
LOYALHANNA Westmoreland
LOYSBURG Bedford
LOYSVILLE Perry
LUCERNEMINES Indiana
LUCINDA Clarion
LUDLOW McKean
LUMBERVILLE Bucks
LURGAN Franklin
LUTHERSBURG Clearfield
LUXOR Westmoreland
LUZERNE Luzerne
LYKENS Dauphin
LYNDELL Chester
LYNDORA Butler
LYON STATION Berks
MACKEYVILLE Clinton
MACUNGIE (18062) Lehigh(89), Berks(10)
MADERA Clearfield
MADISON Westmoreland
MADISONBURG Centre
MAHAFFEY (15757) Clearfield(98),
     Indiana(1)
MAHANOY CITY Schuylkill
MAHANOY PLANE Schuylkill
MAINESBURG (16932) Tioga(98),
     Bradford(1)
MAINLAND Montgomery
MALVERN Chester
MAMMOTH Westmoreland
MANCHESTER York
MANHEIM (17545) Lancaster(98),
     Lebanon(1)
MANNS CHOICE Bedford
MANOR Westmoreland
MANORVILLE Armstrong
MANSFIELD Tioga
MAPLETON DEPOT Huntingdon
MAR LIN Schuylkill
MARBLE Clarion
MARCHAND Indiana
MARCUS HOOK Delaware
MARIANNA Washington
MARIENVILLE (16239) Forest(62),
     Clarion(37)
MARIETTA Lancaster
MARION Franklin
MARION CENTER Indiana
MARION HEIGHTS Northumberland
MARKLETON Somerset
MARKLEYSBURG Fayette
MARS (16046) Butler(86), Allegheny(13)
MARSHALLS CREEK Monroe
MARSTELLER Cambria
MARTIN Fayette
MARTINDALE Lancaster
MARTINS CREEK Northampton
MARTINSBURG (16662) Blair(69),
     Bedford(30)
MARY D Schuylkill
MARYSVILLE (17053) Perry(97),
     Cumberland(2)
MASONTOWN Fayette
MATAMORAS Pike
MATHER Greene
MATTAWANA Mifflin
MAXATAWNY Berks
MAYPORT (16240) Jefferson(55),
     Clarion(40), Armstrong(3)
MAYTOWN Lancaster
MC ALISTERVILLE Juniata
MC CLELLANDTOWN Fayette

MC CLURE (17841) Mifflin(85), Snyder(14)
MC CONNELLSBURG Fulton
MC CONNELLSTOWN Huntingdon
MC DONALD (15057) Washington(81),
     Allegheny(18)
MC ELHATTAN Clinton
MC EWENSVILLE Northumberland
MC GRANN Armstrong
MC INTYRE Indiana
MC KEAN Erie
MC KEES ROCKS Allegheny
MC KEESPORT (15131) Allegheny(95),
     Westmoreland(4)
MC KEESPORT Allegheny
MC KNIGHTSTOWN Adams
MC SHERRYSTOWN Adams
MC VEYTOWN Mifflin
MCADOO (18237) Schuylkill(98),
     Carbon(1)
MEADOW LANDS Washington
MEADVILLE Crawford
MECHANICSBURG (17055)
     Cumberland(98), York(1)
MECHANICSBURG Cumberland
MECHANICSVILLE Bucks
MEDIA Delaware
MEHOOPANY Wyoming
MELCROFT Fayette
MENDENHALL Chester
MENGES MILLS York
MENTCLE Indiana
MERCERSBURG (17236) Franklin(92),
     Fulton(7)
MERION STATION Montgomery
MERRITTSTOWN Fayette
MERTZTOWN (19539) Berks(87),
     Lehigh(12)
MESHOPPEN (18630) Susquehanna(50),
     Wyoming(50)
MEXICO Juniata
MEYERSDALE Somerset
MIDDLEBURG Snyder
MIDDLEBURY CENTER Tioga
MIDDLEPORT Schuylkill
MIDDLETOWN Dauphin
MIDLAND Beaver
MIDWAY Washington
MIFFLIN Juniata
MIFFLINBURG Union
MIFFLINTOWN Juniata
MIFFLINVILLE Columbia
MILAN Bradford
MILANVILLE Wayne
MILDRED Sullivan
MILESBURG Centre
MILFORD Pike
MILFORD SQUARE Bucks
MILL CREEK (17060) Huntingdon(88),
     Mifflin(11)
MILL HALL Clinton
MILL RUN Fayette
MILL VILLAGE Erie
MILLERSBURG Dauphin
MILLERSTOWN (17062) Perry(90),
     Juniata(9)
MILLERSVILLE Lancaster
MILLERTON (16936) Tioga(87),
     Bradford(12)
MILLHEIM Centre
MILLMONT Union
MILLRIFT Pike
MILLS Potter
MILLSBORO Washington
MILLVILLE Columbia
MILNESVILLE Luzerne
MILROY Mifflin
MILTON (17847) Northumberland(94),
     Montour(5)
MINERAL POINT Cambria
MINERAL SPRINGS Clearfield
MINERSVILLE Schuylkill
MINGOVILLE Centre

MINISINK HILLS Monroe
MIQUON Montgomery
MODENA Chester
MOHNTON (19540) Berks(94), Lancaster(5)
MOHRSVILLE Berks
MONACA Beaver
MONESSEN Westmoreland
MONOCACY STATION Berks
MONONGAHELA (15063) Washington(95), Allegheny(3)
MONROETON Bradford
MONROEVILLE Allegheny
MONT ALTO Franklin
MONT CLARE Montgomery
MONTANDON Northumberland
MONTGOMERY Lycoming
MONTGOMERYVILLE Montgomery
MONTOURSVILLE Lycoming
MONTROSE Susquehanna
MOOSIC (18507) Lackawanna(98), Luzerne(1)
MORANN Clearfield
MORGAN Allegheny
MORGANTOWN (19543) Berks(78), Lancaster(17), Chester(3)
MORRIS (16938) Tioga(67), Lycoming(32)
MORRIS RUN Tioga
MORRISDALE Clearfield
MORRISVILLE Bucks
MORTON Delaware
MOSCOW (18444) Lackawanna(93), Wayne(6)
MOSHANNON Centre
MOUNT AETNA Berks
MOUNT BETHEL Northampton
MOUNT BRADDOCK Fayette
MOUNT CARMEL Northumberland
MOUNT GRETNA Lebanon
MOUNT HOLLY SPRINGS Cumberland
MOUNT JEWETT McKean
MOUNT JOY Lancaster
MOUNT MORRIS Greene
MOUNT PLEASANT (15666) Westmoreland(83), Fayette(16)
MOUNT PLEASANT MILLS (17853) Snyder(86), Juniata(13)
MOUNT POCONO Monroe
MOUNT UNION (17066) Huntingdon(70), Mifflin(29)
MOUNT WOLF York
MOUNTAIN TOP Luzerne
MOUNTAINHOME Monroe
MOUNTVILLE Lancaster
MUIR Schuylkill
MUNCY (17756) Lycoming(89), Northumberland(8), Montour(1)
MUNCY VALLEY (17758) Sullivan(65), Lycoming(34)
MUNSON (16860) Clearfield(76), Centre(23)
MURRYSVILLE (15668) Westmoreland(97), Allegheny(2)
MUSE Washington
MYERSTOWN (17067) Lebanon(81), Berks(18)
NANTICOKE Luzerne
NANTY GLO Cambria
NARBERTH Montgomery
NARVON (17555) Lancaster(96), Berks(2), Chester(1)
NATRONA HEIGHTS Allegheny
NAZARETH Northampton
NEEDMORE Fulton
NEELYTON Huntingdon
NEFFS Lehigh
NELSON Tioga
NEMACOLIN Greene
NESCOPECK (18635) Luzerne(74), Columbia(25)
NESQUEHONING (18240) Carbon(85), Schuylkill(14)

NEW ALBANY (18833) Bradford(89), Sullivan(10)
NEW ALEXANDRIA Westmoreland
NEW BALTIMORE Somerset
NEW BEDFORD Lawrence
NEW BERLIN Union
NEW BERLINVILLE Berks
NEW BETHLEHEM (16242) Clarion(92), Armstrong(7)
NEW BLOOMFIELD Perry
NEW BRIGHTON Beaver
NEW BUFFALO Perry
NEW CASTLE Lawrence
NEW COLUMBIA Union
NEW CUMBERLAND (17070) Cumberland(55), York(44)
NEW DERRY Westmoreland
NEW EAGLE Washington
NEW ENTERPRISE Bedford
NEW FLORENCE (15944) Indiana(63), Westmoreland(36)
NEW FREEDOM York
NEW FREEPORT Greene
NEW GALILEE (16141) Lawrence(70), Beaver(29)
NEW GENEVA Fayette
NEW GERMANTOWN Perry
NEW HOLLAND Lancaster
NEW HOPE Bucks
NEW KENSINGTON (15068) Westmoreland(91), Allegheny(8)
NEW KENSINGTON Westmoreland
NEW KINGSTOWN Cumberland
NEW LONDON Chester
NEW MILFORD Susquehanna
NEW MILLPORT Clearfield
NEW OXFORD Adams
NEW PARIS Bedford
NEW PARK York
NEW PHILADELPHIA Schuylkill
NEW PROVIDENCE Lancaster
NEW RINGGOLD Schuylkill
NEW SALEM Fayette
NEW STANTON Westmoreland
NEW TRIPOLI Lehigh
NEW WILMINGTON (16142) Lawrence(69), Mercer(30)
NEW WILMINGTON Lawrence
NEWBURG (17240) Cumberland(68), Franklin(31)
NEWELL Fayette
NEWFOUNDLAND (18445) Wayne(81), Pike(18)
NEWMANSTOWN (17073) Lebanon(93), Lancaster(6)
NEWPORT Perry
NEWRY Blair
NEWTON HAMILTON Mifflin
NEWTOWN Bucks
NEWTOWN SQUARE (19073) Delaware(97), Chester(2)
NEWVILLE Cumberland
NICHOLSON (18446) Wyoming(54), Susquehanna(42), Lackawanna(2)
NICKTOWN Cambria
NINEVEH Greene
NISBET Lycoming
NORMALVILLE Fayette
NORRISTOWN Chester
NORRISTOWN Montgomery
NORTH APOLLO Armstrong
NORTH BEND Clinton
NORTH EAST Erie
NORTH SPRINGFIELD Erie
NORTH VERSAILLES Allegheny
NORTH WALES (19454) Montgomery(81), Bucks(18)
NORTH WALES Montgomery
NORTH WASHINGTON Butler
NORTHAMPTON Northampton
NORTHPOINT Indiana
NORTHUMBERLAND Northumberland

NORVELT Westmoreland
NORWOOD Delaware
NOTTINGHAM (19362) Chester(98), Lancaster(1)
NOXEN (18636) Wyoming(84), Luzerne(15)
NU MINE Armstrong
NUANGOLA Luzerne
NUMIDIA Columbia
NUREMBERG (18241) Luzerne(56), Schuylkill(43)
OAK RIDGE Armstrong
OAKDALE Allegheny
OAKLAND MILLS Juniata
OAKMONT Allegheny
OAKS Montgomery
OHIOPYLE Fayette
OIL CITY Venango
OLANTA Clearfield
OLD FORGE Lackawanna
OLD ZIONSVILLE Lehigh
OLEY Berks
OLIVEBURG Jefferson
OLIVER Fayette
OLYPHANT Lackawanna
ONEIDA Schuylkill
ONO Lebanon
ORANGEVILLE Columbia
ORBISONIA (17243) Huntingdon(98), Juniata(1)
OREFIELD Lehigh
ORELAND Montgomery
ORRSTOWN Franklin
ORRTANNA Adams
ORSON Wayne
ORVISTON Centre
ORWIGSBURG Schuylkill
OSCEOLA Tioga
OSCEOLA MILLS (16666) Clearfield(91), Centre(7), Blair(1)
OSTERBURG Bedford
OTTSVILLE Bucks
OXFORD (19363) Chester(93), Lancaster(6)
PALM (18070) Berks(54), Montgomery(45)
PALMERTON (18071) Carbon(98), Monroe(1)
PALMYRA (17078) Lebanon(94), Dauphin(5)
PAOLI Chester
PARADISE Lancaster
PARDEESVILLE Luzerne
PARKER (16049) Clarion(75), Butler(12), Armstrong(11)
PARKER FORD Chester
PARKESBURG Chester
PARKHILL Cambria
PARRYVILLE Carbon
PATTON Cambria
PAUPACK Pike
PAXINOS Northumberland
PAXTONVILLE Snyder
PEACH BOTTOM Lancaster
PEACH GLEN Adams
PECKVILLE Lackawanna
PEN ARGYL Northampton
PENFIELD Clearfield
PENN Westmoreland
PENN RUN Indiana
PENNS CREEK Snyder
PENNS PARK Bucks
PENNSBURG (18073) Montgomery(91), Bucks(8)
PENNSYLVANIA FURNACE (16865) Centre(88), Huntingdon(11)
PENRYN Lancaster
PEQUEA Lancaster
PERKASIE Bucks
PERKIOMENVILLE Montgomery
PERRYOPOLIS Fayette
PETERSBURG Huntingdon
PETROLIA Butler

PHILADELPHIA Bucks
PHILADELPHIA Delaware
PHILADELPHIA Montgomery
PHILADELPHIA Philadelphia
PHILIPSBURG (16866) Centre(60), Clearfield(39)
PHOENIXVILLE (19460) Chester(98), Montgomery(1)
PICTURE ROCKS Lycoming
PILLOW Dauphin
PINE BANK Greene
PINE FORGE Berks
PINE GROVE Schuylkill
PINE GROVE MILLS Centre
PINEVILLE Bucks
PIPERSVILLE Bucks
PITCAIRN Allegheny
PITMAN (17964) Schuylkill(94), Northumberland(5)
PITTSBURGH (15241) Allegheny(98), Washington(1)
PITTSBURGH Allegheny
PITTSFIELD Warren
PITTSTON (18641) Luzerne(93), Lackawanna(6)
PITTSTON Luzerne
PLAINFIELD Cumberland
PLEASANT HALL Franklin
PLEASANT MOUNT Wayne
PLEASANT UNITY Westmoreland
PLEASANTVILLE (16341) Venango(92), Forest(7)
PLUMSTEADVILLE Bucks
PLUMVILLE Indiana
PLYMOUTH Luzerne
PLYMOUTH MEETING Montgomery
POCONO LAKE Monroe
POCONO LAKE PRESERVE Monroe
POCONO MANOR Monroe
POCONO PINES Monroe
POCONO SUMMIT Monroe
POCOPSON Chester
POINT MARION Fayette
POINT PLEASANT Bucks
POLK (16342) Venango(97), Mercer(2)
POMEROY Chester
PORT ALLEGANY (16743) McKean(95), Potter(4)
PORT CARBON Schuylkill
PORT CLINTON Schuylkill
PORT MATILDA Centre
PORT ROYAL Juniata
PORT TREVORTON Snyder
PORTAGE (15946) Cambria(94), Blair(2), Bedford(2)
PORTERS SIDELING York
PORTERSVILLE (16051) Butler(81), Lawrence(18)
PORTLAND Northampton
POTTERSDALE (16871) Clearfield(87), Clinton(12)
POTTS GROVE Northumberland
POTTSTOWN Chester
POTTSTOWN Montgomery
POTTSVILLE Schuylkill
POYNTELLE Wayne
PRESTO Allegheny
PRESTON PARK Wayne
PRICEDALE Westmoreland
PROMPTON Wayne
PROSPECT Butler
PROSPECT PARK Delaware
PROSPERITY (15329) Washington(88), Greene(11)
PULASKI (16143) Lawrence(89), Mercer(10)
PUNXSUTAWNEY (15767) Jefferson(91), Indiana(7), Clearfield(1)
QUAKAKE Schuylkill
QUAKERTOWN Bucks
QUARRYVILLE Lancaster
QUECREEK Somerset

QUEEN Bedford
QUENTIN Lebanon
QUINCY Franklin
RAILROAD York
RALSTON Lycoming
RAMEY Clearfield
RANSOM Lackawanna
RAVINE Schuylkill
REA Washington
READING Berks
REAMSTOWN Lancaster
REBERSBURG Centre
REBUCK Northumberland
RECTOR Westmoreland
RED HILL Montgomery
RED LION York
REEDERS Monroe
REEDSVILLE Mifflin
REFTON Lancaster
REHRERSBURG Berks
REINHOLDS (17569) Lancaster(80),
   Berks(19)
RENFREW Butler
RENO Venango
RENOVO Clinton
REPUBLIC Fayette
REVERE Bucks
REVLOC Cambria
REW McKean
REXMONT Lebanon
REYNOLDSVILLE Jefferson
RHEEMS Lancaster
RICES LANDING Greene
RICEVILLE Crawford
RICHBORO Bucks
RICHEYVILLE Washington
RICHFIELD (17086) Juniata(60),
   Snyder(39)
RICHLAND (17087) Lebanon(54),
   Berks(45)
RICHLANDTOWN Bucks
RIDDLESBURG Bedford
RIDGWAY (15853) Elk(96), Jefferson(3)
RIDLEY PARK Delaware
RIEGELSVILLE (18077) Bucks(90),
   Northampton(9)
RILLTON Westmoreland
RIMERSBURG Clarion
RINGGOLD Jefferson
RINGTOWN Schuylkill
RIVERSIDE Northumberland
RIXFORD McKean
ROARING BRANCH (17765) Tioga(57),
   Lycoming(41)
ROARING SPRING (16673) Blair(68),
   Bedford(31)
ROBERTSDALE (16674) Huntingdon(98),
   Fulton(1)
ROBESONIA (19551) Berks(93),
   Lebanon(4), Lancaster(2)
ROBINSON Indiana
ROCHESTER Beaver
ROCHESTER MILLS Indiana
ROCK GLEN Luzerne
ROCKHILL FURNACE Huntingdon
ROCKTON Clearfield
ROCKWOOD Somerset
ROGERSVILLE Greene
ROME Bradford
RONCO Fayette
RONKS Lancaster
ROSCOE Washington
ROSSITER (15772) Indiana(98),
   Jefferson(1)
ROSSVILLE York
ROULETTE Potter
ROUSEVILLE Venango
ROUZERVILLE Franklin
ROWLAND Pike
ROXBURY Franklin
ROYERSFORD Montgomery
RUFFS DALE Westmoreland

RURAL RIDGE Allegheny
RURAL VALLEY Armstrong
RUSHLAND Bucks
RUSHVILLE Susquehanna
RUSSELL Warren
RUSSELLTON Allegheny
SABINSVILLE (16943) Potter(56),
   Tioga(43)
SACRAMENTO Schuylkill
SADSBURYVILLE Chester
SAEGERTOWN Crawford
SAGAMORE Armstrong
SAINT BENEDICT Cambria
SAINT BONIFACE Cambria
SAINT CLAIR Schuylkill
SAINT JOHNS Luzerne
SAINT MARYS Elk
SAINT MICHAEL Cambria
SAINT PETERS Chester
SAINT PETERSBURG Clarion
SAINT THOMAS Franklin
SALFORD Montgomery
SALFORDVILLE Montgomery
SALINA Westmoreland
SALISBURY Somerset
SALIX Cambria
SALONA Clinton
SALTILLO Huntingdon
SALTSBURG (15681) Indiana(70),
   Westmoreland(29)
SANDY LAKE Mercer
SANDY RIDGE Centre
SARVER (16055) Butler(94), Armstrong(4)
SASSAMANSVILLE Montgomery
SAXONBURG Butler
SAXTON (16678) Bedford(94),
   Huntingdon(5)
SAYLORSBURG Monroe
SAYRE Bradford
SCENERY HILL Washington
SCHAEFFERSTOWN Lebanon
SCHELLSBURG Bedford
SCHENLEY Armstrong
SCHNECKSVILLE Lehigh
SCHUYLKILL HAVEN Schuylkill
SCHWENKSVILLE Montgomery
SCIOTA Monroe
SCOTLAND Franklin
SCOTRUN Monroe
SCOTTDALE (15683) Westmoreland(88),
   Fayette(11)
SCRANTON Lackawanna
SEANOR Somerset
SELINSGROVE (17870) Snyder(97),
   Union(2)
SELLERSVILLE Bucks
SELTZER Schuylkill
SEMINOLE Armstrong
SENECA Venango
SEVEN VALLEYS York
SEWARD (15954) Indiana(72),
   Westmoreland(27)
SEWICKLEY (15143) Allegheny(94),
   Beaver(5)
SEWICKLEY Allegheny
SHADE GAP Huntingdon
SHADY GROVE Franklin
SHAMOKIN Northumberland
SHAMOKIN DAM Snyder
SHANKSVILLE Somerset
SHARON Mercer
SHARON HILL Delaware
SHARPSVILLE Mercer
SHARTLESVILLE Berks
SHAVERTOWN Luzerne
SHAWANESE Luzerne
SHAWNEE ON DELAWARE Monroe
SHAWVILLE Clearfield
SHEAKLEYVILLE Mercer
SHEFFIELD (16347) Warren(84),
   Forest(15)

SHELOCTA (15774) Indiana(51),
   Armstrong(48)
SHENANDOAH Schuylkill
SHEPPTON Schuylkill
SHERMANS DALE (17090) Perry(98),
   Cumberland(1)
SHICKSHINNY (18655) Luzerne(92),
   Columbia(7)
SHINGLEHOUSE (16748) McKean(56),
   Potter(43)
SHIPPENSBURG (17257)
   Cumberland(62), Franklin(37)
SHIPPENVILLE Clarion
SHIPPINGPORT Beaver
SHIRLEYSBURG Huntingdon
SHOEMAKERSVILLE Berks
SHOHOLA Pike
SHREWSBURY York
SHUNK Sullivan
SIDMAN Cambria
SIGEL (15860) Jefferson(65), Elk(30),
   Clarion(3)
SILVER SPRING Lancaster
SILVERDALE Bucks
SINNAMAHONING Cameron
SIPESVILLE Somerset
SIX MILE RUN Bedford
SKIPPACK Montgomery
SKYTOP Monroe
SLATE RUN Lycoming
SLATEDALE Lehigh
SLATINGTON Lehigh
SLICKVILLE Westmoreland
SLIGO Clarion
SLIPPERY ROCK (16057) Butler(78),
   Lawrence(19), Mercer(2)
SLOVAN Washington
SMETHPORT McKean
SMICKSBURG (16256) Indiana(98),
   Jefferson(1)
SMITHFIELD Fayette
SMITHMILL Clearfield
SMITHTON Westmoreland
SMOCK Fayette
SMOKERUN Clearfield
SMOKETOWN Lancaster
SNOW SHOE Centre
SNYDERSBURG Clarion
SNYDERTOWN Northumberland
SOLEBURY Bucks
SONESTOWN Sullivan
SOUDERSBURG Lancaster
SOUDERTON (18964) Montgomery(95),
   Bucks(4)
SOUTH CANAAN Wayne
SOUTH FORK Cambria
SOUTH GIBSON Susquehanna
SOUTH HEIGHTS Beaver
SOUTH MONTROSE Susquehanna
SOUTH MOUNTAIN Franklin
SOUTH PARK Allegheny
SOUTH STERLING Wayne
SOUTHAMPTON Bucks
SOUTHEASTERN Chester
SOUTHVIEW Washington
SOUTHWEST Westmoreland
SPANGLER Cambria
SPARTANSBURG (16434) Crawford(96),
   Warren(3)
SPINNERSTOWN Bucks
SPRAGGS Greene
SPRANKLE MILLS Jefferson
SPRING CHURCH Armstrong
SPRING CITY Chester
SPRING CREEK Warren
SPRING GLEN (17978) Schuylkill(98),
   Dauphin(1)
SPRING GROVE York
SPRING HOUSE Montgomery
SPRING MILLS Centre
SPRING MOUNT Montgomery
SPRING RUN Franklin

SPRINGBORO Crawford
SPRINGDALE Allegheny
SPRINGFIELD Delaware
SPRINGS Somerset
SPRINGTOWN Bucks
SPRINGVILLE (18844) Susquehanna(98),
   Wyoming(1)
SPROUL Blair
SPRUCE CREEK Huntingdon
STAHLSTOWN Westmoreland
STAR JUNCTION Fayette
STARFORD Indiana
STARLIGHT Wayne
STARRUCCA (18462) Wayne(97),
   Susquehanna(2)
STATE COLLEGE Centre
STATE LINE Franklin
STEELVILLE Chester
STERLING (18463) Pike(63), Wayne(36)
STEVENS Lancaster
STEVENSVILLE Bradford
STEWARTSTOWN York
STILLWATER (17878) Columbia(74),
   Luzerne(25)
STOCKDALE Washington
STOCKERTOWN Northampton
STONEBORO (16153) Mercer(88),
   Venango(11)
STONY RUN Berks
STOYSTOWN Somerset
STRABANE Washington
STRASBURG Lancaster
STRATTANVILLE Clarion
STRAUSSTOWN Berks
STRONGSTOWN (15957) Indiana(60),
   Cambria(40)
STROUDSBURG Monroe
STUMP CREEK Jefferson
STURGEON Allegheny
SUGAR GROVE Warren
SUGAR RUN Bradford
SUGARLOAF Luzerne
SUMMERDALE Cumberland
SUMMERHILL Cambria
SUMMERVILLE (15864) Jefferson(64),
   Clarion(35)
SUMMIT HILL Carbon
SUMMIT STATION Schuylkill
SUMNEYTOWN Montgomery
SUNBURY Northumberland
SUPLEE Chester
SUSQUEHANNA (18847)
   Susquehanna(97), Wayne(2)
SUTERSVILLE Westmoreland
SWARTHMORE Delaware
SWEET VALLEY Luzerne
SWENGEL Union
SWIFTWATER Monroe
SYBERTSVILLE Luzerne
SYCAMORE Greene
SYKESVILLE (15865) Jefferson(94),
   Clearfield(5)
SYLVANIA Bradford
TAFTON Pike
TALMAGE Lancaster
TAMAQUA Schuylkill
TAMIMENT Pike
TANNERSVILLE Monroe
TARENTUM Allegheny
TARRS Westmoreland
TATAMY Northampton
TAYLOR Lackawanna
TAYLORSTOWN Washington
TELFORD (18969) Montgomery(60),
   Bucks(39)
TEMPLE Berks
TEMPLETON Armstrong
TERRE HILL Lancaster
THOMASVILLE York
THOMPSON (18465) Susquehanna(86),
   Wayne(13)
THOMPSONTOWN Juniata

THORNDALE Chester
THORNTON Delaware
THREE SPRINGS (17264) Huntingdon(96), Fulton(3)
TIDIOUTE (16351) Warren(95), Forest(4)
TIMBLIN Jefferson
TIOGA Tioga
TIONA Warren
TIONESTA (16353) Clarion(72), Forest(15), Venango(11)
TIPTON Blair
TIRE HILL Somerset
TITUSVILLE (16354) Crawford(64), Venango(34)
TOBYHANNA Monroe
TODD Huntingdon
TOPTON Berks
TORRANCE Westmoreland
TOUGHKENAMON Chester
TOWANDA Bradford
TOWER CITY Schuylkill
TOWNVILLE Crawford
TRAFFORD (15085) Westmoreland(98), Allegheny(1)
TRANSFER Mercer
TREICHLERS Northampton
TREMONT Schuylkill
TRESCKOW Carbon
TREVORTON Northumberland
TREXLERTOWN Lehigh
TROUT RUN Lycoming
TROUTVILLE Clearfield
TROXELVILLE Snyder
TROY (16947) Bradford(92), Tioga(7)
TRUMBAUERSVILLE Bucks
TUNKHANNOCK Wyoming
TURBOTVILLE (17772) Northumberland(55), Montour(44)
TURKEY CITY Clarion
TURTLE CREEK Allegheny
TURTLEPOINT McKean
TUSCARORA Schuylkill
TWIN ROCKS Cambria
TYLER HILL Wayne
TYLERSBURG Clarion
TYLERSPORT Montgomery
TYLERSVILLE Clinton
TYRONE (16686) Blair(73), Huntingdon(20), Centre(6)
ULEDI Fayette
ULSTER Bradford
ULYSSES Potter
UNION CITY (16438) Crawford(55), Erie(44)
UNION DALE (18470) Susquehanna(92), Wayne(7)
UNIONTOWN Fayette
UNIONVILLE Chester
UNITED Westmoreland
UNITY HOUSE Pike
UNITYVILLE (17774) Lycoming(98), Columbia(1)

UNIVERSITY PARK Centre
UPPER BLACK EDDY Bucks
UPPER DARBY Delaware
UPPERSTRASBURG Franklin
URSINA Somerset
UTICA (16362) Venango(86), Mercer(11), Crawford(1)
UWCHLAND Chester
VALENCIA (16059) Butler(92), Allegheny(7)
VALIER Jefferson
VALLEY FORGE Chester
VALLEY FORGE Montgomery
VALLEY VIEW Schuylkill
VAN VOORHIS Washington
VANDERBILT Fayette
VANDERGRIFT (15690) Westmoreland(55), Armstrong(44)
VENANGO Crawford
VENETIA Washington
VENUS (16364) Venango(69), Clarion(30)
VERONA Allegheny
VESTABURG Washington
VICKSBURG Union
VILLA MARIA Lawrence
VILLANOVA (19085) Delaware(56), Montgomery(43)
VINTONDALE (15961) Indiana(90), Cambria(9)
VIRGINVILLE Berks
VOLANT (16156) Lawrence(88), Mercer(11)
VOWINCKEL (16260) Clarion(95), Forest(4)
WAGONTOWN Chester
WALLACETON Clearfield
WALLINGFORD Delaware
WALNUT BOTTOM Cumberland
WALNUTPORT Northampton
WALSTON Jefferson
WALTERSBURG Fayette
WAMPUM (16157) Lawrence(92), Beaver(7)
WAPWALLOPEN Luzerne
WARFORDSBURG Fulton
WARMINSTER Bucks
WARREN Warren
WARREN CENTER Bradford
WARRENDALE Allegheny
WARRINGTON Bucks
WARRIORS MARK (16877) Huntingdon(50), Centre(49)
WASHINGTON BORO Lancaster
WASHINGTON CROSSING Bucks
WASHINGTONVILLE Montour
WATERFALL Fulton
WATERFORD (16441) Erie(95), Crawford(4)
WATERVILLE Lycoming
WATSONTOWN (17777) Northumberland(98), Montour(1)
WATTSBURG Erie

WAVERLY Lackawanna
WAYMART Wayne
WAYNE (19087) Delaware(49), Chester(40), Montgomery(9)
WAYNE Delaware
WAYNESBORO Franklin
WAYNESBURG Greene
WEATHERLY (18255) Carbon(96), Luzerne(3)
WEBSTER Westmoreland
WEEDVILLE Elk
WEIKERT Union
WELLERSBURG Somerset
WELLS TANNERY Fulton
WELLSBORO Tioga
WELLSVILLE York
WENDEL Westmoreland
WERNERSVILLE Berks
WEST ALEXANDER Washington
WEST CHESTER Chester
WEST DECATUR Clearfield
WEST ELIZABETH Allegheny
WEST FINLEY (15377) Washington(90), Greene(9)
WEST GROVE Chester
WEST HICKORY Forest
WEST LEBANON Indiana
WEST LEISENRING Fayette
WEST MIDDLESEX (16159) Mercer(80), Lawrence(19)
WEST MIDDLETOWN Washington
WEST MIFFLIN Allegheny
WEST MILTON Union
WEST NEWTON (15089) Westmoreland(97), Allegheny(2)
WEST PITTSBURG Lawrence
WEST POINT Montgomery
WEST SALISBURY Somerset
WEST SPRINGFIELD Erie
WEST SUNBURY Butler
WEST WILLOW Lancaster
WESTFIELD Tioga
WESTLAND Washington
WESTLINE McKean
WESTMORELAND CITY Westmoreland
WESTON Luzerne
WESTOVER Clearfield
WESTPORT Clinton
WESTTOWN Chester
WEXFORD Allegheny
WHEATLAND Mercer
WHITE Fayette
WHITE DEER Union
WHITE HAVEN (18661) Luzerne(91), Carbon(8)
WHITE MILLS Wayne
WHITEHALL Lehigh
WHITNEY Westmoreland
WICKHAVEN Fayette
WICONISCO Dauphin
WIDNOON Armstrong
WILBURTON Columbia

WILCOX (15870) Elk(94), McKean(5)
WILDWOOD Allegheny
WILKES BARRE Luzerne
WILLIAMSBURG (16693) Blair(93), Huntingdon(6)
WILLIAMSON Franklin
WILLIAMSPORT Lycoming
WILLIAMSTOWN Dauphin
WILLOW GROVE Montgomery
WILLOW HILL Franklin
WILLOW STREET Lancaster
WILMERDING Allegheny
WILMORE Cambria
WINBURNE Clearfield
WIND GAP Northampton
WIND RIDGE Greene
WINDBER (15963) Somerset(85), Cambria(14)
WINDSOR York
WINFIELD (17889) Union(82), Snyder(17)
WITMER Lancaster
WOMELSDORF Berks
WOOD Bedford
WOODBURY Bedford
WOODLAND Clearfield
WOODLYN Delaware
WOODWARD Centre
WOOLRICH Clinton
WORCESTER Montgomery
WORTHINGTON Armstrong
WORTHVILLE Jefferson
WOXALL Montgomery
WRIGHTSVILLE York
WYALUSING Bradford
WYANO Westmoreland
WYCOMBE Bucks
WYNCOTE Montgomery
WYNNEWOOD (19096) Montgomery(95), Delaware(4)
WYOMING Luzerne
WYSOX Bradford
YATESBORO Armstrong
YEAGERTOWN Mifflin
YORK HAVEN York
YORK NEW SALEM York
YORK SPRINGS (17372) Adams(96), York(2)
YOUNGSTOWN Westmoreland
YOUNGSVILLE Warren
YOUNGWOOD Westmoreland
YUKON Westmoreland
ZELIENOPLE (16063) Butler(83), Beaver(16)
ZIEGLERVILLE Montgomery
ZION GROVE (17985) Schuylkill(97), Columbia(2)
ZIONHILL Bucks
ZIONSVILLE (18092) Lehigh(94), Berks(5)
ZULLINGER Franklin

Pennsylvania ZIP/City Cross Reference

ZIP	City	ZIP	City	ZIP	City	ZIP	City
15001-15001	ALIQUIPPA	15104-15104	BRADDOCK	15370-15370	WAYNESBURG	15492-15492	WICKHAVEN
15003-15003	AMBRIDGE	15106-15106	CARNEGIE	15376-15376	WEST ALEXANDER	15501-15501	SOMERSET
15004-15004	ATLASBURG	15108-15108	CORAOPOLIS	15377-15377	WEST FINLEY	15502-15502	HIDDEN VALLEY
15005-15005	BADEN	15110-15110	DUQUESNE	15378-15378	WESTLAND	15510-15510	SOMERSET
15006-15006	BAIRDFORD	15112-15112	EAST PITTSBURGH	15379-15379	WEST MIDDLETOWN	15520-15520	ACOSTA
15007-15007	BAKERSTOWN	15116-15116	GLENSHAW	15380-15380	WIND RIDGE	15521-15521	ALUM BANK
15009-15009	BEAVER	15120-15120	HOMESTEAD	15401-15401	UNIONTOWN	15522-15522	BEDFORD
15010-15010	BEAVER FALLS	15122-15123	WEST MIFFLIN	15410-15410	ADAH	15530-15530	BERLIN
15012-15012	BELLE VERNON	15126-15126	IMPERIAL	15411-15411	ADDISON	15531-15531	BOSWELL
15014-15014	BRACKENRIDGE	15127-15127	INGOMAR	15412-15412	ALLENPORT	15532-15532	BOYNTON
15015-15015	BRADFORDWOODS	15129-15129	LIBRARY	15413-15413	ALLISON	15533-15533	BREEZEWOOD
15017-15017	BRIDGEVILLE	15129-15129	SOUTH PARK	15415-15415	BRIER HILL	15534-15534	BUFFALO MILLS
15018-15018	BUENA VISTA	15130-15135	MC KEESPORT	15416-15416	BROWNFIELD	15535-15535	CLEARVILLE
15019-15019	BULGER	15136-15136	MC KEES ROCKS	15417-15417	BROWNSVILLE	15536-15536	CRYSTAL SPRING
15020-15020	BUNOLA	15137-15137	NORTH VERSAILLES	15419-15419	CALIFORNIA	15537-15537	EVERETT
15021-15021	BURGETTSTOWN	15139-15139	OAKMONT	15420-15420	CARDALE	15538-15538	FAIRHOPE
15022-15022	CHARLEROI	15140-15140	PITCAIRN	15421-15421	CHALKHILL	15539-15539	FISHERTOWN
15024-15024	CHESWICK	15142-15142	PRESTO	15421-15421	CHALK HILL	15540-15540	FORT HILL
15025-15025	CLAIRTON	15143-15143	SEWICKLEY	15422-15422	CHESTNUT RIDGE	15541-15541	FRIEDENS
15026-15026	CLINTON	15144-15144	SPRINGDALE	15423-15423	COAL CENTER	15542-15542	GARRETT
15027-15027	CONWAY	15145-15145	TURTLE CREEK	15424-15424	CONFLUENCE	15544-15544	GRAY
15028-15028	COULTERS	15146-15146	MONROEVILLE	15425-15425	CONNELLSVILLE	15545-15545	HYNDMAN
15029-15029	COURTNEY	15147-15147	VERONA	15427-15427	DAISYTOWN	15546-15546	JENNERS
15030-15030	CREIGHTON	15148-15148	WILMERDING	15428-15428	DAWSON	15547-15547	JENNERSTOWN
15031-15031	CUDDY	15189-15189	SEWICKLEY	15429-15429	DENBO	15548-15548	KANTNER
15032-15032	CURTISVILLE	15200-15295	PITTSBURGH	15430-15430	DICKERSON RUN	15549-15549	LISTIE
15033-15033	DONORA	15301-15301	WASHINGTON	15431-15431	DUNBAR	15550-15550	MANNS CHOICE
15034-15034	DRAVOSBURG	15310-15310	ALEPPO	15432-15432	DUNLEVY	15551-15551	MARKLETON
15035-15035	EAST MC KEESPORT	15311-15311	AMITY	15433-15433	EAST MILLSBORO	15552-15552	MEYERSDALE
15036-15036	ELDERSVILLE	15312-15312	AVELLA	15434-15434	ELCO	15553-15553	NEW BALTIMORE
15037-15037	ELIZABETH	15313-15313	BEALLSVILLE	15435-15435	FAIRBANK	15554-15554	NEW PARIS
15038-15038	ELRAMA	15314-15314	BENTLEYVILLE	15436-15436	FAIRCHANCE	15555-15555	QUECREEK
15042-15042	FREEDOM	15315-15315	BOBTOWN	15437-15437	FARMINGTON	15557-15557	ROCKWOOD
15043-15043	GEORGETOWN	15316-15316	BRAVE	15438-15438	FAYETTE CITY	15558-15558	SALISBURY
15044-15044	GIBSONIA	15317-15317	CANONSBURG	15439-15439	GANS	15559-15559	SCHELLSBURG
15045-15045	GLASSPORT	15320-15320	CARMICHAELS	15440-15440	GIBBON GLADE	15560-15560	SHANKSVILLE
15046-15046	GLENWILLARD	15321-15321	CECIL	15442-15442	GRINDSTONE	15561-15561	SIPESVILLE
15046-15046	CRESCENT	15322-15322	CLARKSVILLE	15443-15443	HIBBS	15562-15562	SPRINGS
15047-15047	GREENOCK	15323-15323	CLAYSVILLE	15444-15444	HILLER	15563-15563	STOYSTOWN
15049-15049	HARWICK	15324-15324	COKEBURG	15445-15445	HOPWOOD	15564-15564	WELLERSBURG
15050-15050	HOOKSTOWN	15325-15325	CRUCIBLE	15446-15446	INDIAN HEAD	15565-15565	WEST SALISBURY
15051-15051	INDIANOLA	15327-15327	DILLINER	15447-15447	ISABELLA	15601-15606	GREENSBURG
15052-15052	INDUSTRY	15329-15329	PROSPERITY	15448-15448	JACOBS CREEK	15610-15610	ACME
15053-15053	JOFFRE	15330-15330	EIGHTY FOUR	15449-15449	KEISTERVILLE	15611-15611	ADAMSBURG
15054-15054	LANGELOTH	15331-15331	ELLSWORTH	15450-15450	LA BELLE	15612-15612	ALVERTON
15055-15055	LAWRENCE	15332-15332	FINLEYVILLE	15451-15451	LAKE LYNN	15613-15613	APOLLO
15056-15056	LEETSDALE	15333-15333	FREDERICKTOWN	15454-15454	LECKRONE	15615-15615	ARDARA
15057-15057	MC DONALD	15334-15334	GARARDS FORT	15455-15455	LEISENRING	15616-15616	ARMBRUST
15059-15059	MIDLAND	15336-15336	GASTONVILLE	15456-15456	LEMONT FURNACE	15617-15617	ARONA
15060-15060	MIDWAY	15337-15337	GRAYSVILLE	15458-15458	MC CLELLANDTOWN	15618-15618	AVONMORE
15061-15061	MONACA	15338-15338	GREENSBORO	15459-15459	MARKLEYSBURG	15619-15619	BOVARD
15062-15062	MONESSEN	15339-15339	HENDERSONVILLE	15460-15460	MARTIN	15620-15620	BRADENVILLE
15063-15063	MONONGAHELA	15340-15340	HICKORY	15461-15461	MASONTOWN	15621-15621	CALUMET
15064-15064	MORGAN	15341-15341	HOLBROOK	15462-15462	MELCROFT	15622-15622	CHAMPION
15065-15065	NATRONA HEIGHTS	15342-15342	HOUSTON	15463-15463	MERRITTSTOWN	15623-15623	CLARIDGE
15066-15066	NEW BRIGHTON	15344-15344	JEFFERSON	15464-15464	MILL RUN	15624-15624	CRABTREE
15067-15067	NEW EAGLE	15345-15345	MARIANNA	15465-15465	MOUNT BRADDOCK	15625-15625	DARRAGH
15068-15069	NEW KENSINGTON	15346-15346	MATHER	15466-15466	NEWELL	15626-15626	DELMONT
15071-15071	OAKDALE	15347-15347	MEADOW LANDS	15467-15467	NEW GENEVA	15627-15627	DERRY
15072-15072	PRICEDALE	15348-15348	MILLSBORO	15468-15468	NEW SALEM	15628-15628	DONEGAL
15074-15074	ROCHESTER	15349-15349	MOUNT MORRIS	15469-15469	NORMALVILLE	15629-15629	EAST VANDERGRIFT
15075-15075	RURAL RIDGE	15350-15350	MUSE	15470-15470	OHIOPYLE	15630-15630	EDMON
15076-15076	RUSSELLTON	15351-15351	NEMACOLIN	15472-15472	OLIVER	15631-15631	EVERSON
15077-15077	SHIPPINGPORT	15352-15352	NEW FREEPORT	15473-15473	PERRYOPOLIS	15632-15632	EXPORT
15078-15078	SLOVAN	15353-15353	NINEVEH	15474-15474	POINT MARION	15633-15633	FORBES ROAD
15081-15081	SOUTH HEIGHTS	15354-15354	PINE BANK	15475-15475	REPUBLIC	15634-15634	GRAPEVILLE
15082-15082	STURGEON	15356-15356	REA	15476-15476	RONCO	15635-15635	HANNASTOWN
15083-15083	SUTERSVILLE	15357-15357	RICES LANDING	15477-15477	ROSCOE	15636-15636	HARRISON CITY
15084-15084	TARENTUM	15358-15358	RICHEYVILLE	15478-15478	SMITHFIELD	15637-15637	HERMINIE
15085-15085	TRAFFORD	15359-15359	ROGERSVILLE	15479-15479	SMITHTON	15638-15638	HOSTETTER
15086-15086	WARRENDALE	15360-15360	SCENERY HILL	15480-15480	SMOCK	15639-15639	HUNKER
15087-15087	WEBSTER	15361-15361	SOUTHVIEW	15482-15482	STAR JUNCTION	15640-15640	HUTCHINSON
15088-15088	WEST ELIZABETH	15362-15362	SPRAGGS	15483-15483	STOCKDALE	15641-15641	HYDE PARK
15089-15089	WEST NEWTON	15363-15363	STRABANE	15484-15484	ULEDI	15642-15642	IRWIN
15090-15090	WEXFORD	15364-15364	SYCAMORE	15485-15485	URSINA	15644-15644	JEANNETTE
15091-15091	WILDWOOD	15365-15365	TAYLORSTOWN	15486-15486	VANDERBILT	15646-15646	JONES MILLS
15095-15096	WARRENDALE	15366-15366	VAN VOORHIS	15488-15488	WALTERSBURG	15647-15647	LARIMER
15101-15101	ALLISON PARK	15367-15367	VENETIA	15489-15489	WEST LEISENRING	15650-15650	LATROBE
15102-15102	BETHEL PARK	15368-15368	VESTABURG	15490-15490	WHITE	15655-15655	LAUGHLINTOWN

15656-15656 LEECHBURG	15760-15760 MARSTELLER	15955-15955 SIDMAN	16159-16159 WEST MIDDLESEX
15658-15658 LIGONIER	15761-15761 MENTCLE	15956-15956 SOUTH FORK	16160-16160 WEST PITTSBURG
15660-15660 LOWBER	15762-15762 NICKTOWN	15957-15957 STRONGSTOWN	16161-16161 WHEATLAND
15661-15661 LOYALHANNA	15763-15763 NORTHPOINT	15958-15958 SUMMERHILL	16172-16172 NEW WILMINGTON
15662-15662 LUXOR	15764-15764 OLIVEBURG	15959-15959 TIRE HILL	16201-16201 KITTANNING
15663-15663 MADISON	15765-15765 PENN RUN	15960-15960 TWIN ROCKS	16210-16210 ADRIAN
15664-15664 MAMMOTH	15767-15767 PUNXSUTAWNEY	15961-15961 VINTONDALE	16211-16211 BEYER
15665-15665 MANOR	15770-15770 RINGGOLD	15962-15962 WILMORE	16212-16212 CADOGAN
15666-15666 MOUNT PLEASANT	15771-15771 ROCHESTER MILLS	15963-15963 WINDBER	16213-16213 CALLENSBURG
15668-15668 MURRYSVILLE	15772-15772 ROSSITER	16001-16003 BUTLER	16214-16214 CLARION
15670-15670 NEW ALEXANDRIA	15773-15773 SAINT BENEDICT	16016-16020 BOYERS	16215-16215 KITTANNING
15671-15671 NEW DERRY	15774-15774 SHELOCTA	16021-16021 BRANCHTON	16216-16216 CLIMAX
15672-15672 NEW STANTON	15775-15775 SPANGLER	16022-16022 BRUIN	16217-16217 COOKSBURG
15673-15673 NORTH APOLLO	15776-15776 SPRANKLE MILLS	16023-16023 CABOT	16218-16218 COWANSVILLE
15674-15674 NORVELT	15777-15777 STARFORD	16024-16024 CALLERY	16220-16220 CROWN
15675-15675 PENN	15778-15778 TIMBLIN	16025-16025 CHICORA	16221-16221 CURLLSVILLE
15676-15676 PLEASANT UNITY	15779-15779 TORRANCE	16027-16027 CONNOQUENESSING	16222-16222 DAYTON
15677-15677 RECTOR	15780-15780 VALIER	16028-16028 EAST BRADY	16223-16223 DISTANT
15678-15678 RILLTON	15781-15781 WALSTON	16029-16029 EAST BUTLER	16224-16224 FAIRMOUNT CITY
15679-15679 RUFFS DALE	15783-15783 WEST LEBANON	16030-16030 EAU CLAIRE	16225-16225 FISHER
15680-15680 SALINA	15784-15784 WORTHVILLE	16033-16033 EVANS CITY	16226-16226 FORD CITY
15681-15681 SALTSBURG	15801-15801 DU BOIS	16034-16034 FENELTON	16228-16228 FORD CLIFF
15682-15682 SCHENLEY	15821-15821 BENEZETT	16035-16035 FORESTVILLE	16229-16229 FREEPORT
15683-15683 SCOTTDALE	15822-15822 BRANDY CAMP	16036-16036 FOXBURG	16230-16230 HAWTHORN
15684-15684 SLICKVILLE	15823-15823 BROCKPORT	16037-16037 HARMONY	16232-16232 KNOX
15685-15685 SOUTHWEST	15824-15824 BROCKWAY	16038-16038 HARRISVILLE	16233-16233 LEEPER
15686-15686 SPRING CHURCH	15825-15825 BROOKVILLE	16039-16039 HERMAN	16234-16234 LIMESTONE
15687-15687 STAHLSTOWN	15827-15827 BYRNEDALE	16040-16040 HILLIARDS	16235-16235 LUCINDA
15688-15688 TARRS	15828-15828 CLARINGTON	16041-16041 KARNS CITY	16236-16236 MC GRANN
15689-15689 UNITED	15829-15829 CORSICA	16045-16045 LYNDORA	16238-16238 MANORVILLE
15690-15690 VANDERGRIFT	15831-15831 DAGUS MINES	16046-16046 MARS	16239-16239 MARIENVILLE
15691-15691 WENDEL	15832-15832 DRIFTWOOD	16048-16048 NORTH WASHINGTON	16240-16240 MAYPORT
15692-15692 WESTMORELAND CITY	15834-15834 EMPORIUM	16049-16049 PARKER	16242-16242 NEW BETHLEHEM
15693-15693 WHITNEY	15840-15840 FALLS CREEK	16050-16050 PETROLIA	16244-16244 NU MINE
15695-15695 WYANO	15841-15841 FORCE	16051-16051 PORTERSVILLE	16245-16245 OAK RIDGE
15696-15696 YOUNGSTOWN	15845-15845 JOHNSONBURG	16052-16052 PROSPECT	16246-16246 PLUMVILLE
15697-15697 YOUNGWOOD	15846-15846 KERSEY	16053-16053 RENFREW	16248-16248 RIMERSBURG
15698-15698 YUKON	15847-15847 KNOX DALE	16054-16054 SAINT PETERSBURG	16249-16249 RURAL VALLEY
15701-15705 INDIANA	15848-15848 LUTHERSBURG	16055-16055 SARVER	16250-16250 SAGAMORE
15710-15710 ALVERDA	15849-15849 PENFIELD	16056-16056 SAXONBURG	16253-16253 SEMINOLE
15711-15711 ANITA	15851-15851 REYNOLDSVILLE	16057-16057 SLIPPERY ROCK	16254-16254 SHIPPENVILLE
15712-15712 ARCADIA	15853-15853 RIDGWAY	16058-16058 TURKEY CITY	16255-16255 SLIGO
15713-15713 AULTMAN	15856-15856 ROCKTON	16059-16059 VALENCIA	16256-16256 SMICKSBURG
15714-15714 BARNESBORO	15857-15857 SAINT MARYS	16061-16061 WEST SUNBURY	16257-16257 SNYDERSBURG
15715-15715 BIG RUN	15860-15860 SIGEL	16063-16063 ZELIENOPLE	16258-16258 STRATTANVILLE
15716-15716 BLACK LICK	15861-15861 SINNAMAHONING	16066-16066 CRANBERRY TWP	16259-16259 TEMPLETON
15717-15717 BLAIRSVILLE	15863-15863 STUMP CREEK	16101-16108 NEW CASTLE	16260-16260 VOWINCKEL
15720-15720 BRUSH VALLEY	15864-15864 SUMMERVILLE	16110-16110 ADAMSVILLE	16261-16261 WIDNOON
15721-15721 BURNSIDE	15865-15865 SYKESVILLE	16111-16111 ATLANTIC	16262-16262 WORTHINGTON
15722-15722 CARROLLTOWN	15866-15866 TROUTVILLE	16112-16112 BESSEMER	16263-16263 YATESBORO
15723-15723 CHAMBERSVILLE	15868-15868 WEEDVILLE	16113-16113 CLARK	16301-16301 OIL CITY
15724-15724 CHERRY TREE	15870-15870 WILCOX	16114-16114 CLARKS MILLS	16311-16311 CARLTON
15725-15725 CLARKSBURG	15901-15915 JOHNSTOWN	16115-16115 DARLINGTON	16312-16312 CHANDLERS VALLEY
15727-15727 CLUNE	15920-15920 ARMAGH	16116-16116 EDINBURG	16313-16313 CLARENDON
15728-15728 CLYMER	15921-15921 BEAVERDALE	16117-16117 ELLWOOD CITY	16314-16314 COCHRANTON
15729-15729 COMMODORE	15922-15922 BELSANO	16120-16120 ENON VALLEY	16316-16316 CONNEAUT LAKE
15730-15730 COOLSPRING	15923-15923 BOLIVAR	16121-16121 FARRELL	16317-16317 COOPERSTOWN
15731-15731 CORAL	15924-15924 CAIRNBROOK	16123-16123 FOMBELL	16319-16319 CRANBERRY
15732-15732 CREEKSIDE	15925-15925 CASSANDRA	16124-16124 FREDONIA	16321-16321 EAST HICKORY
15733-15733 DE LANCEY	15926-15926 CENTRAL CITY	16125-16125 GREENVILLE	16322-16322 ENDEAVOR
15734-15734 DIXONVILLE	15927-15927 COLVER	16127-16127 GROVE CITY	16323-16323 FRANKLIN
15736-15736 ELDERTON	15928-15928 DAVIDSVILLE	16130-16130 HADLEY	16326-16326 FRYBURG
15737-15737 ELMORA	15929-15929 DILLTOWN	16131-16131 HARTSTOWN	16327-16327 GUYS MILLS
15738-15738 EMEIGH	15930-15930 DUNLO	16132-16132 HILLSVILLE	16328-16328 HYDETOWN
15739-15739 ERNEST	15931-15931 EBENSBURG	16133-16133 JACKSON CENTER	16329-16329 IRVINE
15740-15740 FROSTBURG	15934-15934 ELTON	16134-16134 JAMESTOWN	16331-16331 KOSSUTH
15741-15741 GIPSY	15935-15935 HOLLSOPPLE	16136-16136 KOPPEL	16332-16332 LICKINGVILLE
15742-15742 GLEN CAMPBELL	15936-15936 HOOVERSVILLE	16137-16137 MERCER	16333-16333 LUDLOW
15744-15744 HAMILTON	15937-15937 JEROME	16140-16140 NEW BEDFORD	16334-16334 MARBLE
15745-15745 HEILWOOD	15938-15938 LILLY	16141-16141 NEW GALILEE	16335-16335 MEADVILLE
15746-15746 HILLSDALE	15940-15940 LORETTO	16142-16142 NEW WILMINGTON	16340-16340 PITTSFIELD
15747-15747 HOME	15942-15942 MINERAL POINT	16143-16143 PULASKI	16341-16341 PLEASANTVILLE
15748-15748 HOMER CITY	15943-15943 NANTY GLO	16145-16145 SANDY LAKE	16342-16342 POLK
15750-15750 JOSEPHINE	15944-15944 NEW FLORENCE	16146-16146 SHARON	16343-16343 RENO
15751-15751 JUNEAU	15945-15945 PARKHILL	16148-16148 HERMITAGE	16344-16344 ROUSEVILLE
15752-15752 KENT	15946-15946 PORTAGE	16150-16150 SHARPSVILLE	16345-16345 RUSSELL
15753-15753 LA JOSE	15948-15948 REVLOC	16151-16151 SHEAKLEYVILLE	16346-16346 SENECA
15754-15754 LUCERNEMINES	15949-15949 ROBINSON	16153-16153 STONEBORO	16347-16347 SHEFFIELD
15756-15756 MC INTYRE	15951-15951 SAINT MICHAEL	16154-16154 TRANSFER	16350-16350 SUGAR GROVE
15757-15757 MAHAFFEY	15952-15952 SALIX	16155-16155 VILLA MARIA	16351-16351 TIDIOUTE
15758-15758 MARCHAND	15953-15953 SEANOR	16156-16156 VOLANT	16352-16352 TIONA
15759-15759 MARION CENTER	15954-15954 SEWARD	16157-16157 WAMPUM	16353-16353 TIONESTA

Zip	City	Zip	City	Zip	City	Zip	City
16354-16354	TITUSVILLE	16646-16646	HASTINGS	16833-16833	CURWENSVILLE	17005-17005	BERRYSBURG
16360-16360	TOWNVILLE	16647-16647	HESSTON	16834-16834	DRIFTING	17006-17006	BLAIN
16361-16361	TYLERSBURG	16648-16648	HOLLIDAYSBURG	16835-16835	FLEMING	17007-17007	BOILING SPRINGS
16362-16362	UTICA	16650-16650	HOPEWELL	16836-16836	FRENCHVILLE	17008-17008	BOWMANSDALE
16364-16364	VENUS	16651-16651	HOUTZDALE	16837-16837	GLEN RICHEY	17009-17009	BURNHAM
16365-16367	WARREN	16652-16654	HUNTINGDON	16838-16838	GRAMPIAN	17010-17010	CAMPBELLTOWN
16368-16368	IRVINE	16655-16655	IMLER	16839-16839	GRASSFLAT	17011-17012	CAMP HILL
16368-16368	WARREN	16656-16656	IRVONA	16840-16840	HAWK RUN	17013-17013	CARLISLE
16369-16369	IRVINE	16657-16657	JAMES CREEK	16841-16841	HOWARD	17014-17014	COCOLAMUS
16369-16369	WARREN	16659-16659	LOYSBURG	16843-16843	HYDE	17015-17015	COLEBROOK
16370-16370	WEST HICKORY	16660-16660	MC CONNELLSTOWN	16844-16844	JULIAN	17016-17016	CORNWALL
16371-16371	YOUNGSVILLE	16661-16661	MADERA	16845-16845	KARTHAUS	17017-17017	DALMATIA
16372-16372	CLINTONVILLE	16662-16662	MARTINSBURG	16847-16847	KYLERTOWN	17018-17018	DAUPHIN
16373-16373	EMLENTON	16663-16663	MORANN	16848-16848	LAMAR	17019-17019	DILLSBURG
16374-16374	KENNERDELL	16664-16664	NEW ENTERPRISE	16849-16849	LANSE	17020-17020	DUNCANNON
16375-16375	LAMARTINE	16665-16665	NEWRY	16850-16850	LECONTES MILLS	17021-17021	EAST WATERFORD
16388-16388	MEADVILLE	16666-16666	OSCEOLA MILLS	16851-16851	LEMONT	17022-17022	ELIZABETHTOWN
16401-16401	ALBION	16667-16667	OSTERBURG	16852-16852	MADISONBURG	17023-17023	ELIZABETHVILLE
16402-16402	BEAR LAKE	16668-16668	PATTON	16853-16853	MILESBURG	17024-17024	ELLIOTTSBURG
16403-16403	CAMBRIDGE SPRINGS	16669-16669	PETERSBURG	16854-16854	MILLHEIM	17025-17025	ENOLA
16404-16404	CENTERVILLE	16670-16670	QUEEN	16855-16855	MINERAL SPRINGS	17026-17026	FREDERICKSBURG
16405-16405	COLUMBUS	16671-16671	RAMEY	16856-16856	MINGOVILLE	17027-17027	GRANTHAM
16406-16406	CONNEAUTVILLE	16672-16672	RIDDLESBURG	16858-16858	MORRISDALE	17028-17028	GRANTVILLE
16407-16407	CORRY	16673-16673	ROARING SPRING	16859-16859	MOSHANNON	17029-17029	GRANVILLE
16410-16410	CRANESVILLE	16674-16674	ROBERTSDALE	16860-16860	MUNSON	17030-17030	GRATZ
16411-16411	EAST SPRINGFIELD	16675-16675	SAINT BONIFACE	16861-16861	NEW MILLPORT	17031-17031	GREEN PARK
16412-16412	EDINBORO	16677-16677	SANDY RIDGE	16863-16863	OLANTA	17032-17032	HALIFAX
16413-16413	ELGIN	16678-16678	SAXTON	16864-16864	ORVISTON	17033-17033	HERSHEY
16415-16415	FAIRVIEW	16679-16679	SIX MILE RUN	16865-16865	PENNSYLVANIA FURNACE	17034-17034	HIGHSPIRE
16416-16416	GARLAND	16680-16680	SMITHMILL	16866-16866	PHILIPSBURG	17035-17035	HONEY GROVE
16417-16417	GIRARD	16681-16681	SMOKERUN	16868-16868	PINE GROVE MILLS	17036-17036	HUMMELSTOWN
16420-16420	GRAND VALLEY	16682-16682	SPROUL	16870-16870	PORT MATILDA	17037-17037	ICKESBURG
16421-16421	HARBORCREEK	16683-16683	SPRUCE CREEK	16871-16871	POTTERSDALE	17038-17038	JONESTOWN
16422-16422	HARMONSBURG	16684-16684	TIPTON	16872-16872	REBERSBURG	17039-17039	KLEINFELTERSVILLE
16423-16423	LAKE CITY	16685-16685	TODD	16873-16873	SHAWVILLE	17040-17040	LANDISBURG
16424-16424	LINESVILLE	16686-16686	TYRONE	16874-16874	SNOW SHOE	17041-17041	LAWN
16426-16426	MC KEAN	16689-16689	WATERFALL	16875-16875	SPRING MILLS	17042-17042	LEBANON
16427-16427	MILL VILLAGE	16691-16691	WELLS TANNERY	16876-16876	WALLACETON	17043-17043	LEMOYNE
16428-16428	NORTH EAST	16692-16692	WESTOVER	16877-16877	WARRIORS MARK	17044-17044	LEWISTOWN
16430-16430	NORTH SPRINGFIELD	16693-16693	WILLIAMSBURG	16878-16878	WEST DECATUR	17045-17045	LIVERPOOL
16432-16432	RICEVILLE	16694-16694	WOOD	16879-16879	WINBURNE	17046-17046	LEBANON
16433-16433	SAEGERTOWN	16695-16695	WOODBURY	16880-16880	BELLEFONTE	17047-17047	LOYSVILLE
16434-16434	SPARTANSBURG	16698-16698	HOUTZDALE	16881-16881	WOODLAND	17048-17048	LYKENS
16435-16435	SPRINGBORO	16699-16699	CRESSON	16882-16882	WOODWARD	17049-17049	MC ALISTERVILLE
16436-16436	SPRING CREEK	16701-16701	BRADFORD	16901-16901	WELLSBORO	17050-17050	MECHANICSBURG
16438-16438	UNION CITY	16720-16720	AUSTIN	16910-16910	ALBA	17051-17051	MC VEYTOWN
16440-16440	VENANGO	16724-16724	CROSBY	16911-16911	ARNOT	17052-17052	MAPLETON DEPOT
16441-16441	WATERFORD	16725-16725	CUSTER CITY	16912-16912	BLOSSBURG	17053-17053	MARYSVILLE
16442-16442	WATTSBURG	16726-16726	CYCLONE	16914-16914	COLUMBIA CROSS ROADS	17054-17054	MATTAWANA
16443-16443	WEST SPRINGFIELD	16727-16727	DERRICK CITY	16915-16915	COUDERSPORT	17055-17055	MECHANICSBURG
16444-16444	EDINBORO	16728-16728	DE YOUNG	16917-16917	COVINGTON	17056-17056	MEXICO
16475-16475	ALBION	16729-16729	DUKE CENTER	16918-16918	COWANESQUE	17057-17057	MIDDLETOWN
16500-16565	ERIE	16730-16730	EAST SMETHPORT	16920-16920	ELKLAND	17058-17058	MIFFLIN
16566-16566	FIRST NAT BANK	16731-16731	ELDRED	16921-16921	GAINES	17059-17059	MIFFLINTOWN
16601-16603	ALTOONA	16732-16732	GIFFORD	16922-16922	GALETON	17060-17060	MILL CREEK
16611-16611	ALEXANDRIA	16733-16733	HAZEL HURST	16923-16923	GENESEE	17061-17061	MILLERSBURG
16613-16613	ASHVILLE	16734-16734	JAMES CITY	16925-16925	GILLETT	17062-17062	MILLERSTOWN
16614-16614	BAKERS SUMMIT	16735-16735	KANE	16926-16926	GRANVILLE SUMMIT	17063-17063	MILROY
16616-16616	BECCARIA	16738-16738	LEWIS RUN	16927-16927	HARRISON VALLEY	17064-17064	MOUNT GRETNA
16617-16617	BELLWOOD	16740-16740	MOUNT JEWETT	16928-16928	KNOXVILLE	17065-17065	MOUNT HOLLY SPRINGS
16619-16619	BLANDBURG	16743-16743	PORT ALLEGANY	16929-16929	LAWRENCEVILLE	17066-17066	MOUNT UNION
16620-16620	BRISBIN	16744-16744	REW	16930-16930	LIBERTY	17067-17067	MYERSTOWN
16621-16621	BROAD TOP	16745-16745	RIXFORD	16932-16932	MAINESBURG	17068-17068	NEW BLOOMFIELD
16622-16622	CALVIN	16746-16746	ROULETTE	16933-16933	MANSFIELD	17069-17069	NEW BUFFALO
16623-16623	CASSVILLE	16748-16748	SHINGLEHOUSE	16935-16935	MIDDLEBURY CENTER	17070-17070	NEW CUMBERLAND
16624-16624	CHEST SPRINGS	16749-16749	SMETHPORT	16936-16936	MILLERTON	17071-17071	NEW GERMANTOWN
16625-16625	CLAYSBURG	16750-16750	TURTLEPOINT	16937-16937	MILLS	17072-17072	NEW KINGSTOWN
16627-16627	COALPORT	16751-16751	WESTLINE	16938-16938	MORRIS	17073-17073	NEWMANSTOWN
16629-16629	COUPON	16801-16801	STATE COLLEGE	16939-16939	MORRIS RUN	17074-17074	NEWPORT
16630-16630	CRESSON	16802-16802	UNIVERSITY PARK	16940-16940	NELSON	17075-17075	NEWTON HAMILTON
16631-16631	CURRYVILLE	16803-16805	STATE COLLEGE	16941-16941	GENESEE	17076-17076	OAKLAND MILLS
16633-16633	DEFIANCE	16820-16820	AARONSBURG	16942-16942	OSCEOLA	17077-17077	ONO
16634-16634	DUDLEY	16821-16821	ALLPORT	16943-16943	SABINSVILLE	17078-17078	PALMYRA
16635-16635	DUNCANSVILLE	16822-16822	BEECH CREEK	16945-16945	SYLVANIA	17080-17080	PILLOW
16636-16636	DYSART	16823-16823	BELLEFONTE	16946-16946	TIOGA	17081-17081	PLAINFIELD
16637-16637	EAST FREEDOM	16825-16825	BIGLER	16947-16947	TROY	17082-17082	PORT ROYAL
16638-16638	ENTRIKEN	16826-16826	BLANCHARD	16948-16948	ULYSSES	17083-17083	QUENTIN
16639-16639	FALLENTIMBER	16827-16827	BOALSBURG	16950-16950	WESTFIELD	17084-17084	REEDSVILLE
16640-16640	FLINTON	16828-16828	CENTRE HALL	17001-17001	CAMP HILL	17085-17085	REXMONT
16641-16641	GALLITZIN	16829-16829	CLARENCE	17002-17002	ALLENSVILLE	17086-17086	RICHFIELD
16644-16644	GLASGOW	16830-16830	CLEARFIELD	17003-17003	ANNVILLE	17087-17087	RICHLAND
16645-16645	GLEN HOPE	16832-16832	COBURN	17004-17004	BELLEVILLE	17088-17088	SCHAEFFERSTOWN

17089-17089 CAMP HILL
17090-17090 SHERMANS DALE
17091-17091 CAMP HILL
17091-17091 LEBANON
17093-17093 SUMMERDALE
17094-17094 THOMPSONTOWN
17097-17097 WICONISCO
17098-17098 WILLIAMSTOWN
17099-17099 YEAGERTOWN
17100-17177 HARRISBURG
17201-17201 CHAMBERSBURG
17210-17210 AMBERSON
17211-17211 ARTEMAS
17212-17212 BIG COVE TANNERY
17213-17213 BLAIRS MILLS
17214-17214 BLUE RIDGE SUMMIT
17215-17215 BURNT CABINS
17217-17217 CONCORD
17218-17218 DICKINSON
17219-17219 DOYLESBURG
17220-17220 DRY RUN
17221-17221 FANNETTSBURG
17222-17222 FAYETTEVILLE
17223-17223 FORT LITTLETON
17224-17224 FORT LOUDON
17225-17225 GREENCASTLE
17228-17228 HARRISONVILLE
17229-17229 HUSTONTOWN
17231-17231 LEMASTERS
17232-17232 LURGAN
17233-17233 MC CONNELLSBURG
17235-17235 MARION
17236-17236 MERCERSBURG
17237-17237 MONT ALTO
17238-17238 NEEDMORE
17239-17239 NEELYTON
17240-17240 NEWBURG
17241-17241 NEWVILLE
17243-17243 ORBISONIA
17244-17244 ORRSTOWN
17246-17246 PLEASANT HALL
17247-17247 QUINCY
17249-17249 ROCKHILL FURNACE
17250-17250 ROUZERVILLE
17251-17251 ROXBURY
17252-17252 SAINT THOMAS
17253-17253 SALTILLO
17254-17254 SCOTLAND
17255-17255 SHADE GAP
17256-17256 SHADY GROVE
17257-17257 SHIPPENSBURG
17260-17260 SHIRLEYSBURG
17261-17261 SOUTH MOUNTAIN
17262-17262 SPRING RUN
17263-17263 STATE LINE
17264-17264 THREE SPRINGS
17265-17265 UPPERSTRASBURG
17266-17266 WALNUT BOTTOM
17267-17267 WARFORDSBURG
17268-17268 WAYNESBORO
17270-17270 WILLIAMSON
17271-17271 WILLOW HILL
17272-17272 ZULLINGER
17294-17294 BLUE RIDGE SUMMIT
17301-17301 ABBOTTSTOWN
17302-17302 AIRVILLE
17303-17303 ARENDTSVILLE
17304-17304 ASPERS
17306-17306 BENDERSVILLE
17307-17307 BIGLERVILLE
17309-17309 BROGUE
17310-17310 CASHTOWN
17311-17311 CODORUS
17312-17312 CRALEY
17313-17313 DALLASTOWN
17314-17314 DELTA
17315-17315 DOVER
17316-17316 EAST BERLIN
17317-17317 EAST PROSPECT
17318-17318 EMIGSVILLE
17319-17319 ETTERS
17320-17320 FAIRFIELD

17321-17321 FAWN GROVE
17322-17322 FELTON
17323-17323 FRANKLINTOWN
17324-17324 GARDNERS
17325-17326 GETTYSBURG
17327-17327 GLEN ROCK
17329-17329 GLENVILLE
17331-17334 HANOVER
17337-17337 IDAVILLE
17339-17339 LEWISBERRY
17340-17340 LITTLESTOWN
17342-17342 LOGANVILLE
17343-17343 MC KNIGHTSTOWN
17344-17344 MC SHERRYSTOWN
17345-17345 MANCHESTER
17346-17346 MENGES MILLS
17347-17347 MOUNT WOLF
17349-17349 NEW FREEDOM
17350-17350 NEW OXFORD
17352-17352 NEW PARK
17353-17353 ORRTANNA
17354-17354 PORTERS SIDELING
17355-17355 RAILROAD
17356-17356 RED LION
17358-17358 ROSSVILLE
17360-17360 SEVEN VALLEYS
17361-17361 SHREWSBURY
17362-17362 SPRING GROVE
17363-17363 STEWARTSTOWN
17364-17364 THOMASVILLE
17365-17365 WELLSVILLE
17366-17366 WINDSOR
17368-17368 WRIGHTSVILLE
17370-17370 YORK HAVEN
17371-17371 YORK NEW SALEM
17372-17372 YORK SPRINGS
17375-17375 PEACH GLEN
17400-17415 YORK
17501-17501 AKRON
17502-17502 BAINBRIDGE
17503-17503 BART
17504-17504 BAUSMAN
17505-17505 BIRD IN HAND
17506-17506 BLUE BALL
17507-17507 BOWMANSVILLE
17508-17508 BROWNSTOWN
17509-17509 CHRISTIANA
17512-17512 COLUMBIA
17516-17516 CONESTOGA
17517-17517 DENVER
17518-17518 DRUMORE
17519-17519 EAST EARL
17520-17520 EAST PETERSBURG
17521-17521 ELM
17522-17522 EPHRATA
17527-17527 GAP
17528-17528 GOODVILLE
17529-17529 GORDONVILLE
17532-17532 HOLTWOOD
17533-17533 HOPELAND
17534-17534 INTERCOURSE
17535-17535 KINZERS
17536-17536 KIRKWOOD
17537-17537 LAMPETER
17538-17538 LANDISVILLE
17540-17540 LEOLA
17543-17543 LITITZ
17545-17545 MANHEIM
17547-17547 MARIETTA
17549-17549 MARTINDALE
17550-17550 MAYTOWN
17551-17551 MILLERSVILLE
17552-17552 MOUNT JOY
17554-17554 MOUNTVILLE
17555-17555 NARVON
17557-17557 NEW HOLLAND
17560-17560 NEW PROVIDENCE
17562-17562 PARADISE
17563-17563 PEACH BOTTOM
17564-17564 PENRYN
17565-17565 PEQUEA
17566-17566 QUARRYVILLE

17567-17567 REAMSTOWN
17568-17568 REFTON
17569-17569 REINHOLDS
17570-17570 RHEEMS
17572-17573 RONKS
17575-17575 SILVER SPRING
17576-17576 SMOKETOWN
17577-17577 SOUDERSBURG
17578-17578 STEVENS
17579-17579 STRASBURG
17580-17580 TALMAGE
17581-17581 TERRE HILL
17582-17582 WASHINGTON BORO
17583-17583 WEST WILLOW
17584-17584 WILLOW STREET
17585-17585 WITMER
17600-17699 LANCASTER
17701-17705 WILLIAMSPORT
17720-17720 ANTES FORT
17721-17721 AVIS
17722-17722 BODINES
17723-17723 JERSEY SHORE
17724-17724 CANTON
17726-17726 CASTANEA
17727-17727 CEDAR RUN
17728-17728 COGAN STATION
17729-17729 CROSS FORK
17730-17730 DEWART
17731-17731 EAGLES MERE
17734-17734 FARRANDSVILLE
17735-17735 GROVER
17737-17737 HUGHESVILLE
17738-17738 HYNER
17739-17739 JERSEY MILLS
17740-17740 JERSEY SHORE
17742-17742 LAIRDSVILLE
17743-17743 LEROY
17744-17744 LINDEN
17745-17745 LOCK HAVEN
17747-17747 LOGANTON
17748-17748 MC ELHATTAN
17749-17749 MC EWENSVILLE
17750-17750 MACKEYVILLE
17751-17751 MILL HALL
17752-17752 MONTGOMERY
17754-17754 MONTOURSVILLE
17756-17756 MUNCY
17758-17758 MUNCY VALLEY
17759-17759 NISBET
17760-17760 NORTH BEND
17762-17762 PICTURE ROCKS
17763-17763 RALSTON
17764-17764 RENOVO
17765-17765 ROARING BRANCH
17767-17767 SALONA
17768-17768 SHUNK
17769-17769 SLATE RUN
17770-17770 SONESTOWN
17771-17771 TROUT RUN
17772-17772 TURBOTVILLE
17773-17773 TYLERSVILLE
17774-17774 UNITYVILLE
17776-17776 WATERVILLE
17777-17777 WATSONTOWN
17778-17778 WESTPORT
17779-17779 WOOLRICH
17801-17801 SUNBURY
17810-17810 ALLENWOOD
17812-17812 BEAVER SPRINGS
17813-17813 BEAVERTOWN
17814-17814 BENTON
17815-17815 BLOOMSBURG
17820-17820 CATAWISSA
17821-17822 DANVILLE
17823-17823 DORNSIFE
17824-17824 ELYSBURG
17825-17825 EXCELSIOR
17827-17827 FREEBURG
17828-17828 GOWEN CITY
17829-17829 HARTLETON
17830-17830 HERNDON
17831-17831 HUMMELS WHARF

17832-17832 MARION HEIGHTS
17833-17833 KREAMER
17834-17834 KULPMONT
17835-17835 LAURELTON
17836-17836 LECK KILL
17837-17837 LEWISBURG
17839-17839 LIGHT STREET
17840-17840 LOCUST GAP
17841-17841 MC CLURE
17842-17842 MIDDLEBURG
17843-17843 BEAVER SPRINGS
17844-17844 MIFFLINBURG
17845-17845 MILLMONT
17846-17846 MILLVILLE
17847-17847 MILTON
17850-17850 MONTANDON
17851-17851 MOUNT CARMEL
17853-17853 MOUNT PLEASANT MILLS
17855-17855 NEW BERLIN
17856-17856 NEW COLUMBIA
17857-17857 NORTHUMBERLAND
17858-17858 NUMIDIA
17859-17859 ORANGEVILLE
17860-17860 PAXINOS
17861-17861 PAXTONVILLE
17862-17862 PENNS CREEK
17864-17864 PORT TREVORTON
17865-17865 POTTS GROVE
17866-17866 COAL TOWNSHIP
17867-17867 REBUCK
17868-17868 RIVERSIDE
17870-17870 SELINSGROVE
17872-17872 SHAMOKIN
17876-17876 SHAMOKIN DAM
17877-17877 SNYDERTOWN
17878-17878 STILLWATER
17880-17880 SWENGEL
17881-17881 TREVORTON
17882-17882 TROXELVILLE
17883-17883 VICKSBURG
17884-17884 WASHINGTONVILLE
17885-17885 WEIKERT
17886-17886 WEST MILTON
17887-17887 WHITE DEER
17888-17888 WILBURTON
17889-17889 WINFIELD
17901-17901 POTTSVILLE
17920-17920 ARISTES
17921-17921 ASHLAND
17922-17922 AUBURN
17923-17923 BRANCHDALE
17925-17925 BROCKTON
17927-17927 CENTRALIA
17929-17929 CRESSONA
17930-17930 CUMBOLA
17931-17932 FRACKVILLE
17933-17933 FRIEDENSBURG
17934-17934 GILBERTON
17935-17935 GIRARDVILLE
17936-17936 GORDON
17938-17938 HEGINS
17939-17939 HELFENSTEIN
17941-17941 KLINGERSTOWN
17942-17942 LANDINGVILLE
17943-17943 LAVELLE
17944-17944 LLEWELLYN
17945-17945 LOCUSTDALE
17946-17946 LOST CREEK
17948-17948 MAHANOY CITY
17949-17949 MAHANOY PLANE
17951-17951 MAR LIN
17952-17952 MARY D
17953-17953 MIDDLEPORT
17954-17954 MINERSVILLE
17957-17957 MUIR
17959-17959 NEW PHILADELPHIA
17960-17960 NEW RINGGOLD
17961-17961 ORWIGSBURG
17963-17963 PINE GROVE
17964-17964 PITMAN
17965-17965 PORT CARBON
17966-17966 RAVINE

17967-17967	RINGTOWN
17968-17968	SACRAMENTO
17970-17970	SAINT CLAIR
17972-17972	SCHUYLKILL HAVEN
17974-17974	SELTZER
17976-17976	SHENANDOAH
17978-17978	SPRING GLEN
17979-17979	SUMMIT STATION
17980-17980	TOWER CITY
17981-17981	TREMONT
17982-17982	TUSCARORA
17983-17983	VALLEY VIEW
17985-17985	ZION GROVE
18001-18003	LEHIGH VALLEY
18010-18010	ACKERMANVILLE
18011-18011	ALBURTIS
18012-18012	AQUASHICOLA
18013-18013	BANGOR
18014-18014	BATH
18015-18025	BETHLEHEM
18030-18030	BOWMANSTOWN
18031-18031	BREINIGSVILLE
18032-18032	CATASAUQUA
18034-18034	CENTER VALLEY
18035-18035	CHERRYVILLE
18036-18036	COOPERSBURG
18037-18037	COPLAY
18038-18038	DANIELSVILLE
18039-18039	DURHAM
18040-18040	EASTON
18041-18041	EAST GREENVILLE
18042-18045	EASTON
18046-18046	EAST TEXAS
18049-18049	EMMAUS
18050-18050	FLICKSVILLE
18051-18051	FOGELSVILLE
18052-18052	WHITEHALL
18053-18053	GERMANSVILLE
18054-18054	GREEN LANE
18055-18055	HELLERTOWN
18056-18056	HEREFORD
18058-18058	KUNKLETOWN
18059-18059	LAURYS STATION
18060-18060	LIMEPORT
18062-18062	MACUNGIE
18063-18063	MARTINS CREEK
18064-18064	NAZARETH
18065-18065	NEFFS
18066-18066	NEW TRIPOLI
18067-18067	NORTHAMPTON
18068-18068	OLD ZIONSVILLE
18069-18069	OREFIELD
18070-18070	PALM
18071-18071	PALMERTON
18072-18072	PEN ARGYL
18073-18073	PENNSBURG
18074-18074	PERKIOMENVILLE
18076-18076	RED HILL
18077-18077	RIEGELSVILLE
18078-18078	SCHNECKSVILLE
18079-18079	SLATEDALE
18080-18080	SLATINGTON
18081-18081	SPRINGTOWN
18083-18083	STOCKERTOWN
18084-18084	SUMNEYTOWN
18085-18085	TATAMY
18086-18086	TREICHLERS
18087-18087	TREXLERTOWN
18088-18088	WALNUTPORT
18091-18091	WIND GAP
18092-18092	ZIONSVILLE
18098-18099	EMMAUS
18100-18195	ALLENTOWN
18201-18202	HAZLETON
18210-18210	ALBRIGHTSVILLE
18211-18211	ANDREAS
18212-18212	ASHFIELD
18214-18214	BARNESVILLE
18216-18216	BEAVER MEADOWS
18218-18218	COALDALE
18219-18219	CONYNGHAM
18220-18220	DELANO
18221-18221	DRIFTON
18222-18222	DRUMS
18223-18223	EBERVALE
18224-18224	FREELAND
18225-18225	HARLEIGH
18229-18229	JIM THORPE
18230-18230	JUNEDALE
18231-18231	KELAYRES
18232-18232	LANSFORD
18234-18234	LATTIMER MINES
18235-18235	LEHIGHTON
18237-18237	MCADOO
18239-18239	MILNESVILLE
18240-18240	NESQUEHONING
18241-18241	NUREMBERG
18242-18242	ONEIDA
18243-18243	PARDEESVILLE
18244-18244	PARRYVILLE
18245-18245	QUAKAKE
18246-18246	ROCK GLEN
18247-18247	SAINT JOHNS
18248-18248	SHEPPTON
18249-18249	SUGARLOAF
18250-18250	SUMMIT HILL
18251-18251	SYBERTSVILLE
18252-18252	TAMAQUA
18254-18254	TRESCKOW
18255-18255	WEATHERLY
18256-18256	WESTON
18301-18301	EAST STROUDSBURG
18320-18320	ANALOMINK
18321-18321	BARTONSVILLE
18322-18322	BRODHEADSVILLE
18323-18323	BUCK HILL FALLS
18324-18324	BUSHKILL
18325-18325	CANADENSIS
18326-18326	CRESCO
18327-18327	DELAWARE WATER GAP
18328-18328	DINGMANS FERRY
18330-18330	EFFORT
18331-18331	GILBERT
18332-18332	HENRYVILLE
18333-18333	KRESGEVILLE
18334-18334	LONG POND
18335-18335	MARSHALLS CREEK
18336-18336	MATAMORAS
18337-18337	MILFORD
18340-18340	MILLRIFT
18341-18341	MINISINK HILLS
18342-18342	MOUNTAINHOME
18343-18343	MOUNT BETHEL
18344-18344	MOUNT POCONO
18346-18346	POCONO SUMMIT
18347-18347	POCONO LAKE
18348-18348	POCONO LAKE PRESERVE
18349-18349	POCONO MANOR
18350-18350	POCONO PINES
18351-18351	PORTLAND
18352-18352	REEDERS
18353-18353	SAYLORSBURG
18354-18354	SCIOTA
18355-18355	SCOTRUN
18356-18356	SHAWNEE ON DELAWARE
18357-18357	SKYTOP
18360-18360	STROUDSBURG
18370-18370	SWIFTWATER
18371-18371	TAMIMENT
18372-18372	TANNERSVILLE
18373-18373	UNITY HOUSE
18401-18401	ALDENVILLE
18403-18403	ARCHBALD
18405-18405	BEACH LAKE
18407-18407	CARBONDALE
18410-18410	CHINCHILLA
18411-18411	CLARKS SUMMIT
18413-18413	CLIFFORD
18414-18414	DALTON
18415-18415	DAMASCUS
18416-18416	ELMHURST
18417-18417	EQUINUNK
18419-18419	FACTORYVILLE
18420-18420	FLEETVILLE
18421-18421	FOREST CITY
18424-18424	GOULDSBORO
18425-18425	GREELEY
18426-18426	GREENTOWN
18427-18427	HAMLIN
18428-18428	HAWLEY
18430-18430	HERRICK CENTER
18431-18431	HONESDALE
18433-18433	JERMYN
18434-18434	JESSUP
18435-18435	LACKAWAXEN
18436-18436	LAKE ARIEL
18437-18437	LAKE COMO
18438-18438	LAKEVILLE
18439-18439	LAKEWOOD
18440-18440	LA PLUME
18441-18441	LENOXVILLE
18443-18443	MILANVILLE
18444-18444	MOSCOW
18445-18445	NEWFOUNDLAND
18446-18446	NICHOLSON
18447-18448	OLYPHANT
18449-18449	ORSON
18451-18451	PAUPACK
18452-18452	PECKVILLE
18453-18453	PLEASANT MOUNT
18454-18454	POYNTELLE
18455-18455	PRESTON PARK
18456-18456	PROMPTON
18457-18457	ROWLAND
18458-18458	SHOHOLA
18459-18459	SOUTH CANAAN
18460-18460	SOUTH STERLING
18461-18461	STARLIGHT
18462-18462	STARRUCCA
18463-18463	STERLING
18464-18464	TAFTON
18465-18465	THOMPSON
18466-18466	TOBYHANNA
18469-18469	TYLER HILL
18470-18470	UNION DALE
18471-18471	WAVERLY
18472-18472	WAYMART
18473-18473	WHITE MILLS
18500-18505	SCRANTON
18507-18507	MOOSIC
18508-18515	SCRANTON
18517-18517	TAYLOR
18518-18518	OLD FORGE
18519-18519	DICKSON CITY
18522-18577	SCRANTON
18601-18601	BEACH HAVEN
18602-18602	BEAR CREEK
18603-18603	BERWICK
18610-18610	BLAKESLEE
18611-18611	CAMBRA
18612-18612	DALLAS
18614-18614	DUSHORE
18615-18615	FALLS
18616-18616	FORKSVILLE
18617-18617	GLEN LYON
18618-18618	HARVEYS LAKE
18619-18619	HILLSGROVE
18621-18621	HUNLOCK CREEK
18622-18622	HUNTINGTON MILLS
18623-18623	LACEYVILLE
18624-18624	LAKE HARMONY
18625-18625	LAKE WINOLA
18626-18626	LAPORTE
18627-18627	LEHMAN
18628-18628	LOPEZ
18629-18629	MEHOOPANY
18630-18630	MESHOPPEN
18631-18631	MIFFLINVILLE
18632-18632	MILDRED
18634-18634	NANTICOKE
18635-18635	NESCOPECK
18636-18636	NOXEN
18637-18637	NUANGOLA
18640-18641	PITTSTON
18642-18642	DURYEA
18643-18643	PITTSTON
18644-18644	WYOMING
18651-18651	PLYMOUTH
18653-18653	RANSOM
18654-18654	SHAWANESE
18655-18655	SHICKSHINNY
18656-18656	SWEET VALLEY
18657-18657	TUNKHANNOCK
18660-18660	WAPWALLOPEN
18661-18661	WHITE HAVEN
18690-18690	DALLAS
18700-18703	WILKES BARRE
18704-18704	KINGSTON
18705-18706	WILKES BARRE
18707-18707	MOUNTAIN TOP
18708-18708	SHAVERTOWN
18709-18709	LUZERNE
18710-18774	WILKES BARRE
18801-18801	MONTROSE
18810-18810	ATHENS
18812-18812	BRACKNEY
18813-18813	BROOKLYN
18814-18814	BURLINGTON
18815-18815	CAMPTOWN
18816-18816	DIMOCK
18817-18817	EAST SMITHFIELD
18818-18818	FRIENDSVILLE
18820-18820	GIBSON
18821-18821	GREAT BEND
18822-18822	HALLSTEAD
18823-18823	HARFORD
18824-18824	HOP BOTTOM
18825-18825	JACKSON
18826-18826	KINGSLEY
18827-18827	LANESBORO
18828-18828	LAWTON
18829-18829	LE RAYSVILLE
18830-18830	LITTLE MEADOWS
18831-18831	MILAN
18832-18832	MONROETON
18833-18833	NEW ALBANY
18834-18834	NEW MILFORD
18837-18837	ROME
18839-18839	RUSHVILLE
18840-18840	SAYRE
18842-18842	SOUTH GIBSON
18843-18843	SOUTH MONTROSE
18844-18844	SPRINGVILLE
18845-18845	STEVENSVILLE
18846-18846	SUGAR RUN
18847-18847	SUSQUEHANNA
18848-18848	TOWANDA
18850-18850	ULSTER
18851-18851	WARREN CENTER
18853-18853	WYALUSING
18854-18854	WYSOX
18901-18901	DOYLESTOWN
18910-18910	BEDMINSTER
18911-18911	BLOOMING GLEN
18912-18912	BUCKINGHAM
18913-18913	CARVERSVILLE
18914-18914	CHALFONT
18915-18915	COLMAR
18916-18916	DANBORO
18917-18917	DUBLIN
18918-18918	EARLINGTON
18920-18920	ERWINNA
18921-18921	FERNDALE
18922-18922	FOREST GROVE
18923-18923	FOUNTAINVILLE
18924-18924	FRANCONIA
18925-18925	FURLONG
18926-18926	GARDENVILLE
18927-18927	HILLTOWN
18928-18928	HOLICONG
18929-18929	JAMISON
18930-18930	KINTNERSVILLE
18931-18931	LAHASKA
18932-18932	LINE LEXINGTON
18933-18933	LUMBERVILLE
18934-18934	MECHANICSVILLE
18935-18935	MILFORD SQUARE
18936-18936	MONTGOMERYVILLE

18938-18938 NEW HOPE	19037-19037 GLEN RIDDLE LIMA	19347-19347 KEMBLESVILLE	19470-19470 SAINT PETERS
18940-18940 NEWTOWN	19038-19038 GLENSIDE	19348-19348 KENNETT SQUARE	19472-19472 SASSAMANSVILLE
18942-18942 OTTSVILLE	19039-19039 GRADYVILLE	19350-19350 LANDENBERG	19473-19473 SCHWENKSVILLE
18943-18943 PENNS PARK	19040-19040 HATBORO	19351-19351 LEWISVILLE	19474-19474 SKIPPACK
18944-18944 PERKASIE	19041-19041 HAVERFORD	19352-19352 LINCOLN UNIVERSITY	19475-19475 SPRING CITY
18946-18946 PINEVILLE	19043-19043 HOLMES	19353-19353 LIONVILLE	19477-19477 SPRING HOUSE
18947-18947 PIPERSVILLE	19044-19044 HORSHAM	19354-19354 LYNDELL	19478-19478 SPRING MOUNT
18949-18949 PLUMSTEADVILLE	19046-19046 JENKINTOWN	19355-19355 MALVERN	19480-19480 UWCHLAND
18950-18950 POINT PLEASANT	19047-19048 LANGHORNE	19357-19357 MENDENHALL	19481-19485 VALLEY FORGE
18951-18951 QUAKERTOWN	19048-19048 FORT WASHINGTON	19358-19358 MODENA	19486-19486 WEST POINT
18953-18953 REVERE	19049-19049 LANGHORNE	19360-19360 NEW LONDON	19487-19487 KING OF PRUSSIA
18954-18954 RICHBORO	19049-19049 FORT WASHINGTON	19362-19362 NOTTINGHAM	19488-19489 NORRISTOWN
18955-18955 RICHLANDTOWN	19050-19050 LANSDOWNE	19363-19363 OXFORD	19490-19490 WORCESTER
18956-18956 RUSHLAND	19052-19052 LENNI	19365-19365 PARKESBURG	19492-19492 ZIEGLERVILLE
18957-18957 SALFORD	19053-19053 FEASTERVILLE TREVOSE	19366-19366 POCOPSON	19493-19496 VALLEY FORGE
18958-18958 SALFORDVILLE	19054-19059 LEVITTOWN	19367-19367 POMEROY	19501-19501 ADAMSTOWN
18960-18960 SELLERSVILLE	19059-19059 PHILADELPHIA	19369-19369 SADSBURYVILLE	19503-19503 BALLY
18962-18962 SILVERDALE	19061-19061 MARCUS HOOK	19370-19370 STEELVILLE	19504-19504 BARTO
18963-18963 SOLEBURY	19063-19063 MEDIA	19371-19371 SUPLEE	19505-19505 BECHTELSVILLE
18964-18964 SOUDERTON	19064-19064 SPRINGFIELD	19372-19372 THORNDALE	19506-19506 BERNVILLE
18966-18966 SOUTHAMPTON	19065-19065 MEDIA	19373-19373 THORNTON	19507-19507 BETHEL
18968-18968 SPINNERSTOWN	19066-19066 MERION STATION	19374-19374 TOUGHKENAMON	19508-19508 BIRDSBORO
18969-18969 TELFORD	19067-19067 MORRISVILLE	19375-19375 UNIONVILLE	19510-19510 BLANDON
18970-18970 TRUMBAUERSVILLE	19070-19070 MORTON	19376-19376 WAGONTOWN	19511-19511 BOWERS
18971-18971 TYLERSPORT	19072-19072 NARBERTH	19380-19383 WEST CHESTER	19512-19512 BOYERTOWN
18972-18972 UPPER BLACK EDDY	19073-19073 NEWTOWN SQUARE	19390-19390 WEST GROVE	19516-19516 CENTERPORT
18974-18974 WARMINSTER	19074-19074 NORWOOD	19395-19395 WESTTOWN	19517-19517 DAUBERVILLE
18976-18976 WARRINGTON	19075-19075 ORELAND	19397-19399 SOUTHEASTERN	19518-19518 DOUGLASSVILLE
18977-18977 WASHINGTON CROSSING	19076-19076 PROSPECT PARK	19401-19404 NORRISTOWN	19519-19519 EARLVILLE
18979-18979 WOXALL	19078-19078 RIDLEY PARK	19405-19405 BRIDGEPORT	19520-19520 ELVERSON
18980-18980 WYCOMBE	19079-19079 SHARON HILL	19406-19406 KING OF PRUSSIA	19522-19522 FLEETWOOD
18981-18981 ZIONHILL	19080-19080 WAYNE	19407-19407 AUDUBON	19523-19523 GEIGERTOWN
18991-18991 WARMINSTER	19081-19081 SWARTHMORE	19408-19408 EAGLEVILLE	19525-19525 GILBERTSVILLE
19001-19001 ABINGTON	19082-19082 UPPER DARBY	19409-19409 FAIRVIEW VILLAGE	19526-19526 HAMBURG
19002-19002 AMBLER	19083-19083 HAVERTOWN	19415-19415 EAGLEVILLE	19529-19529 KEMPTON
19003-19003 ARDMORE	19085-19085 VILLANOVA	19420-19420 ARCOLA	19530-19530 KUTZTOWN
19004-19004 BALA CYNWYD	19086-19086 WALLINGFORD	19421-19421 BIRCHRUNVILLE	19533-19533 LEESPORT
19006-19006 HUNTINGDON VALLEY	19087-19089 WAYNE	19422-19422 BLUE BELL	19534-19534 LENHARTSVILLE
19007-19007 BRISTOL	19090-19090 WILLOW GROVE	19423-19423 CEDARS	19535-19535 LIMEKILN
19008-19008 BROOMALL	19091-19091 MEDIA	19424-19424 BLUE BELL	19536-19536 LYON STATION
19009-19009 BRYN ATHYN	19092-19093 PHILADELPHIA	19425-19425 CHESTER SPRINGS	19538-19538 MAXATAWNY
19010-19010 BRYN MAWR	19094-19094 WOODLYN	19426-19426 COLLEGEVILLE	19539-19539 MERTZTOWN
19012-19012 CHELTENHAM	19095-19095 WYNCOTE	19428-19429 CONSHOHOCKEN	19540-19540 MOHNTON
19013-19013 CHESTER	19096-19096 WYNNEWOOD	19430-19430 CREAMERY	19541-19541 MOHRSVILLE
19014-19014 ASTON	19098-19098 HOLMES	19432-19432 DEVAULT	19542-19542 MONOCACY STATION
19015-19015 BROOKHAVEN	19099-19255 PHILADELPHIA	19435-19435 FREDERICK	19543-19543 MORGANTOWN
19016-19016 CHESTER	19301-19301 PAOLI	19436-19436 GWYNEDD	19544-19544 MOUNT AETNA
19017-19017 CHESTER HEIGHTS	19310-19310 ATGLEN	19437-19437 GWYNEDD VALLEY	19545-19545 NEW BERLINVILLE
19018-19018 CLIFTON HEIGHTS	19311-19311 AVONDALE	19438-19438 HARLEYSVILLE	19547-19547 OLEY
19019-19019 PHILADELPHIA	19312-19312 BERWYN	19440-19440 HATFIELD	19548-19548 PINE FORGE
19020-19020 BENSALEM	19316-19316 BRANDAMORE	19441-19441 HARLEYSVILLE	19549-19549 PORT CLINTON
19021-19021 CROYDON	19317-19317 CHADDS FORD	19442-19442 KIMBERTON	19550-19550 REHRERSBURG
19022-19022 CRUM LYNNE	19318-19318 CHATHAM	19443-19443 KULPSVILLE	19551-19551 ROBESONIA
19023-19023 DARBY	19319-19319 CHEYNEY	19444-19444 LAFAYETTE HILL	19554-19554 SHARTLESVILLE
19025-19025 DRESHER	19320-19320 COATESVILLE	19446-19446 LANSDALE	19555-19555 SHOEMAKERSVILLE
19026-19026 DREXEL HILL	19330-19330 COCHRANVILLE	19450-19450 LEDERACH	19557-19557 STONY RUN
19027-19027 ELKINS PARK	19331-19331 CONCORDVILLE	19451-19451 MAINLAND	19559-19559 STRAUSSTOWN
19028-19028 EDGEMONT	19333-19333 DEVON	19452-19452 MIQUON	19560-19560 TEMPLE
19029-19029 ESSINGTON	19335-19335 DOWNINGTOWN	19453-19453 MONT CLARE	19562-19562 TOPTON
19030-19030 FAIRLESS HILLS	19339-19340 CONCORDVILLE	19454-19455 NORTH WALES	19564-19564 VIRGINVILLE
19031-19031 FLOURTOWN	19341-19341 EXTON	19456-19456 OAKS	19565-19565 WERNERSVILLE
19032-19032 FOLCROFT	19342-19342 GLEN MILLS	19457-19457 PARKER FORD	19567-19567 WOMELSDORF
19033-19033 FOLSOM	19343-19343 GLENMOORE	19460-19460 PHOENIXVILLE	19600-19640 READING
19034-19034 FORT WASHINGTON	19344-19344 HONEY BROOK	19462-19462 PLYMOUTH MEETING	
19035-19035 GLADWYNE	19345-19345 IMMACULATA	19464-19465 POTTSTOWN	
19036-19036 GLENOLDEN	19346-19346 KELTON	19468-19468 ROYERSFORD	

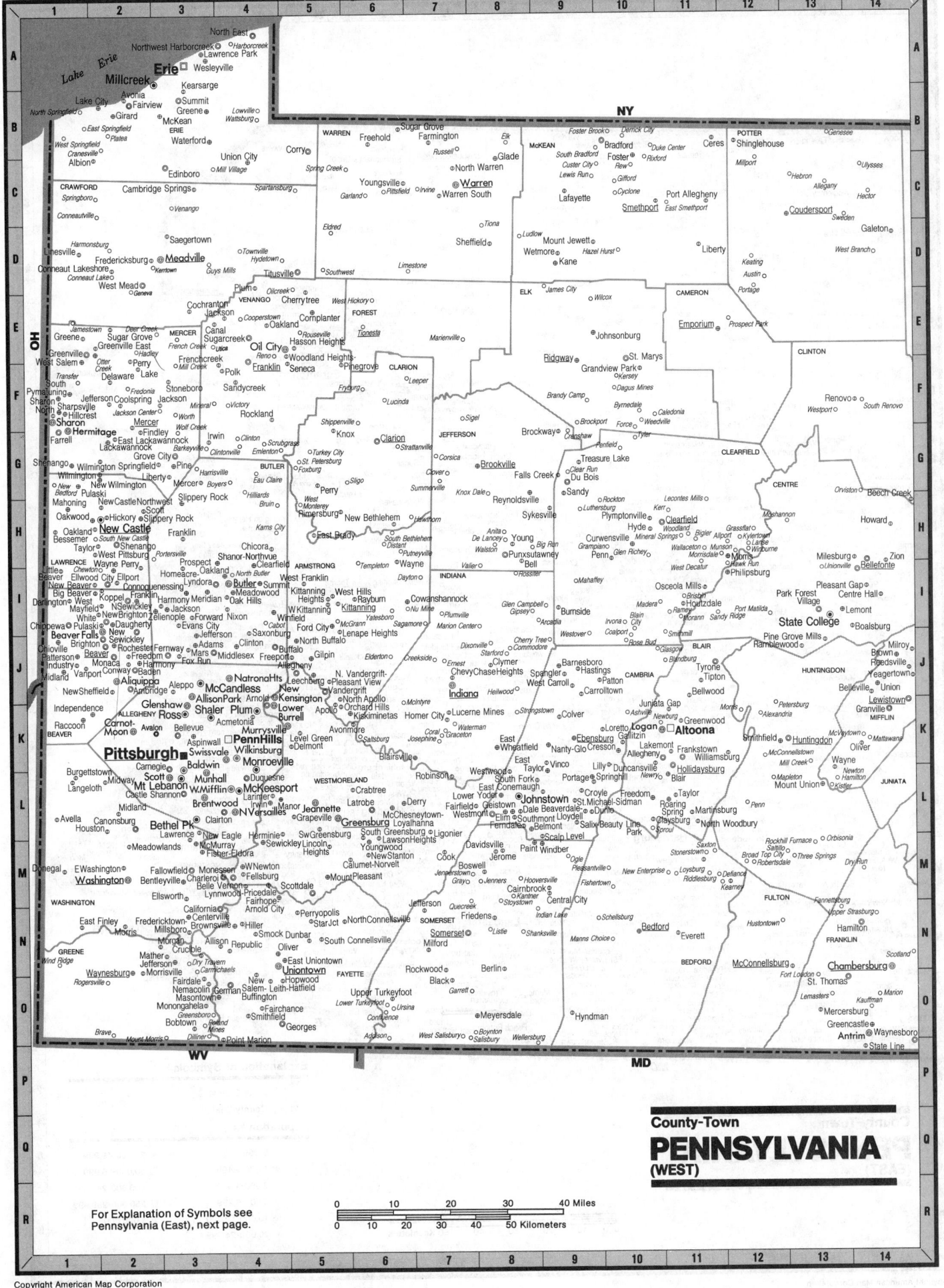

County-Town

PENNSYLVANIA
(WEST)

For Explanation of Symbols see
Pennsylvania (East), next page.

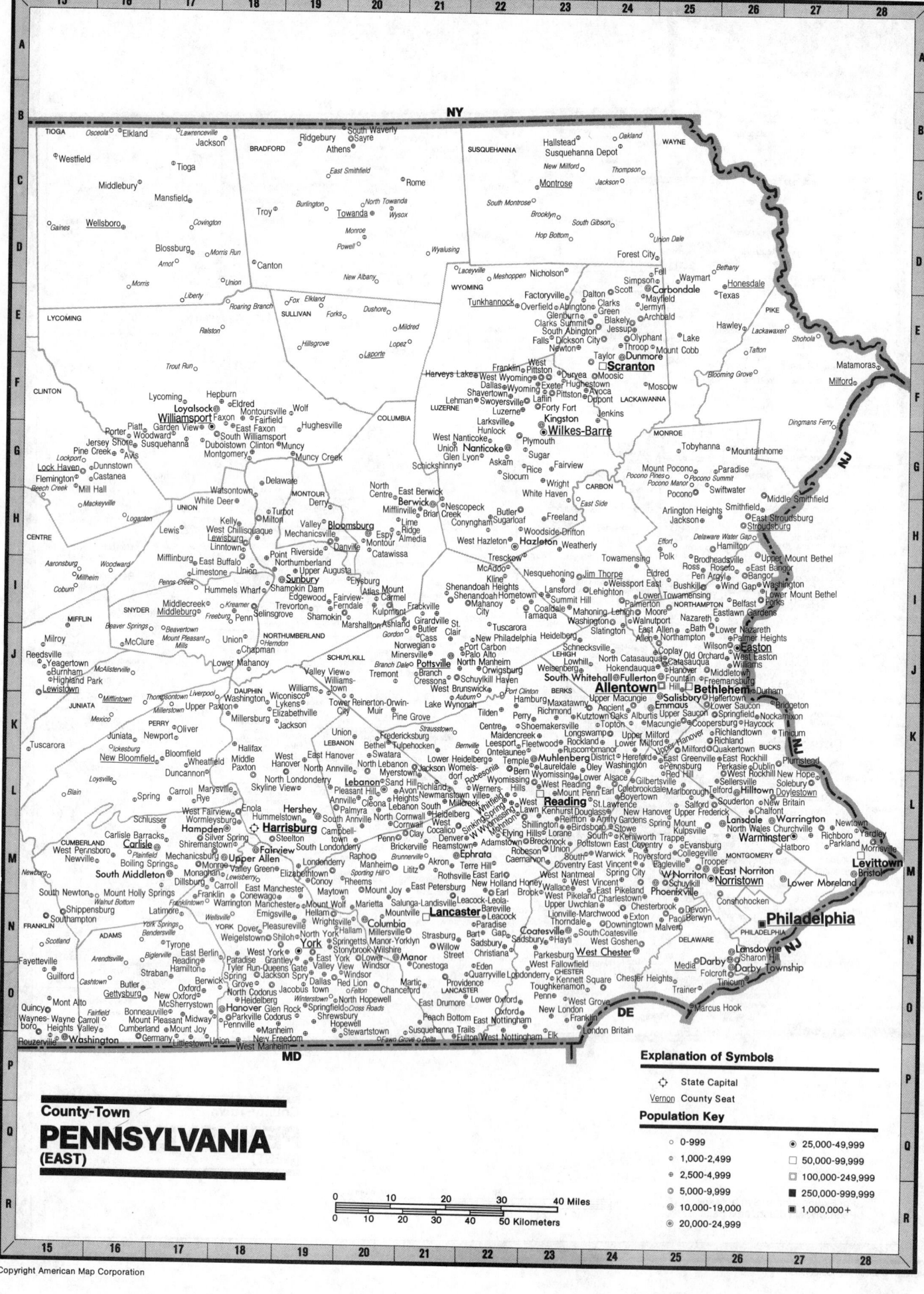

County-Town
PENNSYLVANIA
(EAST)

Explanation of Symbols

State Capital
Vernon County Seat

Population Key

○ 0-999	⊛ 25,000-49,999
⊕ 1,000-2,499	☐ 50,000-99,999
⊙ 2,500-4,999	☐ 100,000-249,999
⊚ 5,000-9,999	■ 250,000-999,999
⊛ 10,000-19,000	■ 1,000,000+
⊛ 20,000-24,999	

0   10   20   30   40 Miles
0   10   20   30   40   50 Kilometers

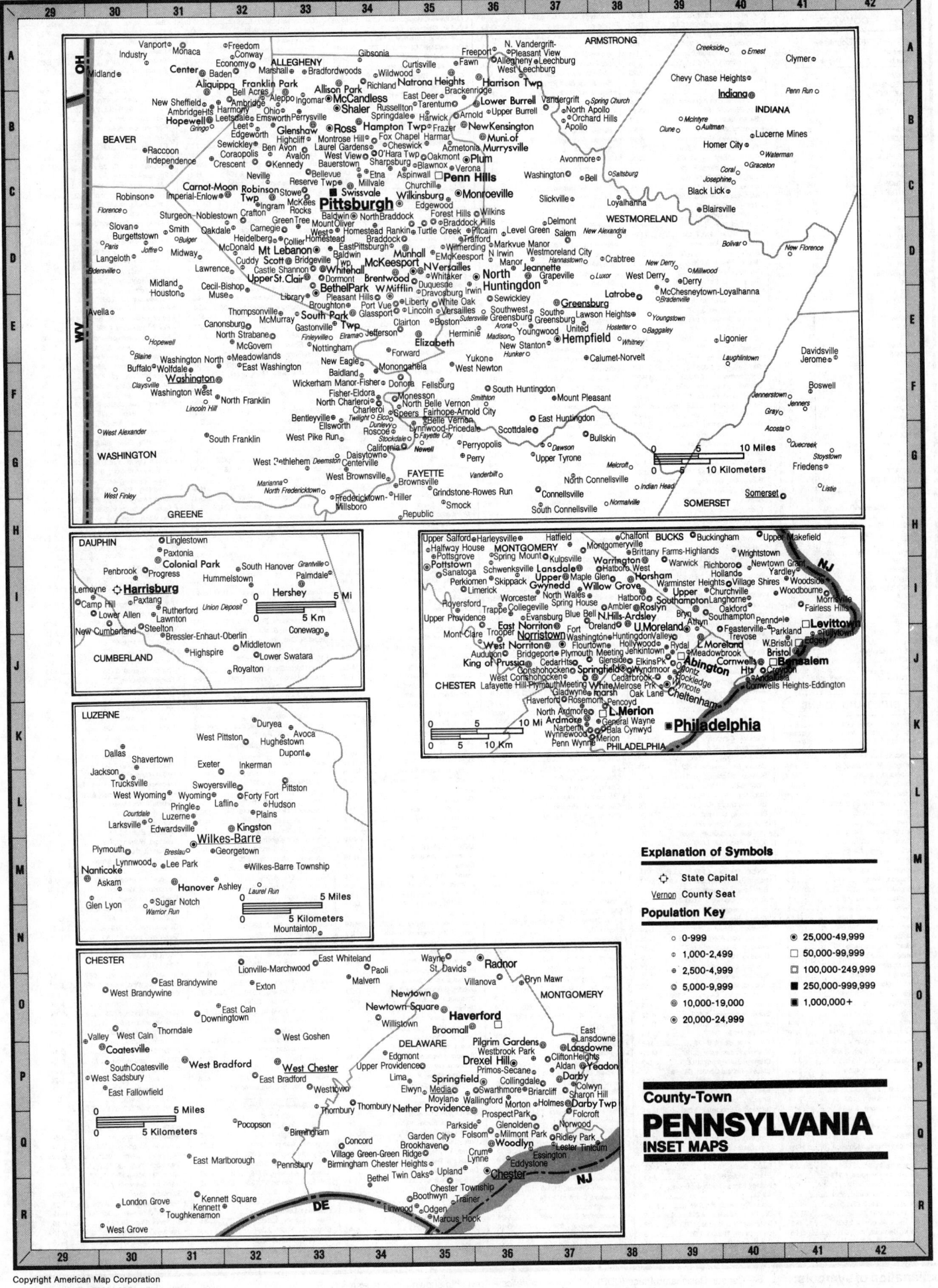

County-Town
PENNSYLVANIA
INSET MAPS

Explanation of Symbols

✧ State Capital
Vernon County Seat

Population Key

○ 0-999	◉ 25,000-49,999
◦ 1,000-2,499	□ 50,000-99,999
⊕ 2,500-4,999	▣ 100,000-249,999
◍ 5,000-9,999	■ 250,000-999,999
◉ 10,000-19,000	■ 1,000,000+
◉ 20,000-24,999	

CITIES AND TOWNS

Note: The first name is that of the city or town, second, that of the county in which it is located, then the population and location on the map.

Explanation of symbols: • – Census Designated Place (CDP)   ▲ italics – Townships (shown on the map)   • italics – Township shown which is also a CDP   italics – Townships (not shown on the map)

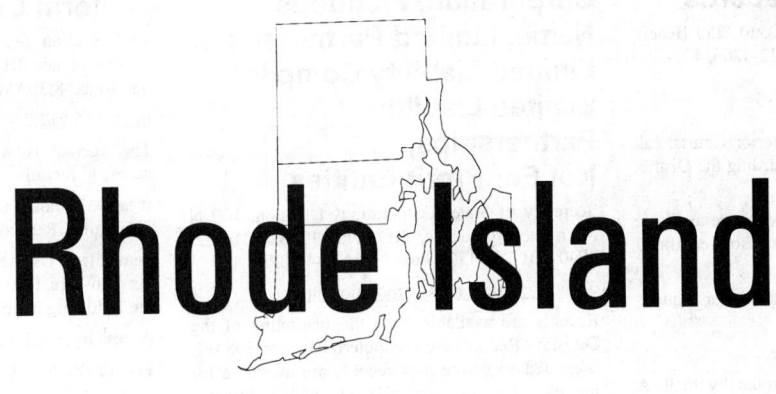

Rhode Island

General Help Numbers:

Governor's Office
State House Rm 115   401-222-2080
Providence, RI 02903   Fax 401-222-8096
www.governor.state.ri.us   8:30AM-4:30PM

Attorney General's Office
150 S Main St   401-274-4400
Providence, RI 02903   Fax 401-222-1331
www.riag.ri.gov/   8:30AM-4:30PM

Legislative Records
Secretary of State
Public Information Center   401-222-3983
State House, Room 38   Fax 401-222-1404
Providence, RI 02903   8:30AM-4:30PM
www.rilin.state.ri.us

State Archives
State Archives & Public Records Admin.   401-222-2353
337 Westminster St   Fax 401-222-3199
Providence, RI 02903   8:30AM-4:30PM M-SA
www.state.ri.us/archives

State Specifics:

Capital:	Providence Providence County
Time Zone:	EST
Number of Counties:	5
Population:	1,080,632
Web Site:	**www.state.ri.us**

State Agencies

Criminal Records

Department of Attorney General, Bureau of Criminal Identification, 150 S Main Street, Providence, RI 02903; 401-274-4400 x2232, 401-222-1331-Fax; 8:30AM-4:30PM.

www.riag.ri.gov

It takes 1-7 days before new records are available for inquiry. Records are normally destroyed after court order or expungment. 60% of all arrests in database have final dispositions recorded.

Searching: Criminal records are only released to law enforcement agencies, the subject, or to those with a signed notarized authorization from the subject. Include the following in your request-signed notarized release from subject, DOB, picture ID and DOB of the requester. Fingerprints and SSN are optional. They will call the Notary on the authorization for verification. 100% of the records are fingerprint-supported. All arrests and convictions are reported.

Access by: mail, in person.

Fee & Payment: The fee is $5.00 per name. If required, the FBI fingerprint search is an additional $24.00. Fee payee: Department of Attorney General. Prepayment required. Personal checks accepted. No credit cards or cash accepted.

Mail search: Turnaround time: up to 2 weeks. A SASE is required.

In person search: Turnaround time is while you wait.

Other access: This agency does not offer online access, but the state court system does offer an information site that should not be substituted as an official search. See that profile for details.

Statewide Court Records

Court Administrator, Supreme Court, 250 Benefit St, Providence, RI 02903; 401-222-3266, 401-222-4224-Fax; 8:30AM-4:30PM.

www.courts.state.ri.us

For questions regarding the Superior Courts, call 401-222-2622. For questions regarding the District Courts, call 401-458-5400.

It takes 24 hours before new records are available for inquiry. Records are normally destroyed after 3 to 50 years, depending on case.

Searching: Include the following in your request-names involved or case number.

Access by: mail, in person, online.

Mail search: Requests are accepted by mail. A SASE is required.

In person search: Limited in-person searching of District, Superior, and Family court cases are available. Most records are in the period from the mid 1980's through the mid 1990's. Go to the 8th floor Library.

Online search: The Rhode Island Judiciary offers free Internet access to court criminal records statewide at http://courtconnect.courts.state.ri.us. A word of caution, this website is provided as an informational service only and should not be relied upon as an official record of the court. Supreme Court opinions are available from the website.

Other access: Bulk data is available, call for details.

Sexual Offender Registry

Access to Records is Restricted.

Department of Attorney General, BCI Unit, 150 S Main Street, Providence, RI 02903; 401-274-4400, 8:30AM-4:30PM.

www.riag.state.ri.us

The state's Sexual Offender Registry is not available to the public. Searching must be done at the local level.

Incarceration Records

Rhode Island Department of Corrections, Records, PO Box 8249, (Courier address: 40 Howard Avenue, Cranston, RI 02920); 401-462-3900, 401-462-2630-Fax; 8AM-4:30PM.

www.doc.state.ri.us

Records are available on current and former inmates. It takes 1 to 3 days before new records are available for inquiry.

Searching: Include the following in your request-full name; DOB helpful. Location, physical identifiers, conviction and sentencing information, and release dates are provided.

Access by: mail, phone, fax, online.

Fee & Payment: There is no fee.

Mail search: Turnaround time: 30 days. No SASE is required.

Phone search: Limited name searching available by phone.

Fax search: Records are available by fax.

Online search: There is no access to inmate records through the agency, however the agency refers requesters to a private company offers free web access to DOC records at www.vinelink.com/index.jsp.

Corporation, Fictitious Name, Limited Partnerships, Limited Liability Companies, Limited Liability Partnerships, Not For Profit Entities

Secretary of State, Corporations Division, 100 N Main St, Providence, RI 02903-1335; 401-222-3040, 401-222-1309-Fax; 8:30AM-4:30PM.

www.corps.state.ri.us/corporations.htm

Records are available from the beginning of the Division. Records are computerized since 1984. It takes 5 days before new records are available for inquiry. Records are indexed on an inhouse computer.

Searching: Include the following in your request-full name of business.

Access by: mail, phone, in person, online.

Fee & Payment: The copy fee is $.15 per page. Certification costs $10.00 per document plus copy fees. There is no search fee. Fee payee: Secretary of State. Personal checks accepted. No credit cards accepted.

Mail search: Turnaround time: variable. A SASE helpful.

Phone search: They will give date of incorporation, registered agent, one officer, status, and whether domestic or foreign. Certified copies and documents can be ordered by phone, but must be picked up in person, takes 48 hours.

In person search: Certified copies and certifications may not be available same day.

Online search: At the web, search filings for active and inactive Rhode Island and foreign business corporations, non-profit corporations, limited partnerships, limited liability companies, and limited liability partnerships. Weekly listings of new corporations are also available. There is no fee.

Other access: The corporation database may be purchased on CD.

Trademarks/Servicemarks

Secretary of State, Trademark Section, 100 N Main St, Providence, RI 02903-1335; 401-222-1487, 401-222-3879-Fax; 8:30AM-4:30PM.

www.corps.state.ri.us/trademarks.htm

Records are available from the beginning of the Division. It takes less than one week before new records are available for inquiry.

Searching: All records are open to the public. Include the following in your request-trademark/servicemark name, registration number and applicant name, if known.

Access by: mail, phone, in person.

Fee & Payment: There is no search fee. The copy fee is $.15 per page. Fee payee: Secretary of State

Mail search: Turnaround time: 3 to 5 days. No SASE is required.

Phone search: Limited verification information available.

In person search: Counter service is available.

Uniform Commercial Code

UCC Section, Secretary of State, 100 North Main St, Providence, RI 02903; 401-222-3040, 401-222-3879-Fax; 8:30AM-4:30PM.

http://155.212.254.78/corporations.htm

The agency is working towards having online access to records within the year.

It takes 24 hours before new records are available for inquiry. Records are indexed on hard copy.

Searching: Use search request form UCC-11. All tax liens are filed at the city/town level. Include the following in your request-debtor name.

Access by: mail, in person.

Fee & Payment: The search fee is $5.00 per name, copies are $.15 each. Add $5.00 for certification. Fee payee: Secretary of State. Prepayment required. Personal checks accepted. No credit cards accepted.

Mail search: Turnaround time: 1 to 2 working days. SASE recommended.

In person search: If you do the search yourself, there is no search fee. Records may be viewed only.

Federal and State Tax Liens

Records not maintained by a state level agency.

All records are located at the county level.

Sales Tax Registrations

Taxation Division, Sales & Use Tax Office, One Capitol Hill, Providence, RI 02908-5800; 401-222-2937, 401-222-6288-Fax; 8:30AM-4PM.

www.tax.state.ri.us

Records are available from the 1960's. All current permits are on the computer, all inactive records are kept on microfiche. New records are available for inquiry immediately. Records are normally destroyed after 7 years.

Searching: This agency will only confirm that a business is registered. They will provide no other information. Include the following in your request-business name or tax permit number.

Access by: mail, phone, fax, in person.

Fee & Payment: There is no search fee nor a copy fee, unless extensive documents are requested.

Mail search: Turnaround time: 7 to 10 days. A SASE is requested.

Phone search: It will take 24 hours for a response.

Fax search: Same criteria as mail searching.

In person search: It will take 24 hours for a response.

Birth Certificates

State Department of Health, Division of Vital Records, 3 Capitol Hill, Room 101, Providence, RI 02908-5097; 401-222-2812, 401-222-2811, 8:30AM-4:30PM.

www.healthri.org/chic/vital/index.php

If the record is less than 100 years old, it can also be obtained from the city or town where birth occurred.

Records are available from 1902 to present. New records are available for inquiry immediately.

Records are indexed on microfiche, inhouse computer.

Searching: Investigative searches must have a signed release from person of record or immediate family member. Include the following in your request-full name, names of parents, mother's maiden name, date of birth, place of birth. Vital records are confidential. Therefore, only those individuals who have what is called a "Direct and Tangible Interest" in the records may have access to records.

Access by: mail, phone, in person.

Fee & Payment: The fee is $15.00 per record. There is a $.50 search fee for each additional year searched after 2 years. Fee payee: General Treasurer, State of Rhode Island. Prepayment required. Credit cards for emergencies only. Personal checks accepted. Major credit cards accepted.

Mail search: Turnaround time: 6 to 8 weeks. For 2-week service, add an additional $5.00 and mark "rush" on outside of envelope. A SASE is requested. Include photo copy of requester's ID (DL, passport, etc).

Phone search: This is for emergency, expedited needs only.

In person search: Turnaround time while you wait.

Expedited service: Expedited service is available for mail and phone searches. Add $5.00 for 2-week mail processing. Add $23.00 for Courier address service and use of a credit card for 3-5 day service.

Death Records

State Department of Health, Division of Vital Records, 3 Capitol Hill, Room 101, Providence, RI 02908-5097; 401-222-2812, 401-222-2811, 8:30AM-4:30PM.

www.healthri.org/chic/vital/index.php

Records less than 50 years old can be obtained at the town or city where death took place.

Records are available from 1952 to present. For records from 1853 to 1951, contact RI Archives at 401-222-2353. New records are available for inquiry immediately. Records are indexed on microfiche, inhouse computer.

Searching: Investigative searches must have a signed release from immediate family member. Include the following in your request-full name, date of death, place of death, names of parents, mother's maiden name. Vital records are confidential. Therefore, only those individuals who have what is called a "Direct and Tangible Interest" in the records may have access to records.

Access by: mail, phone, in person.

Fee & Payment: The fee is $15.00 per record. There is a $.50 search fee for each additional year searched after 2 years. Fee payee: General Treasurer, State of Rhode Island. Prepayment required. Credit cards are for emergency use only. Personal checks accepted. Major credit cards accepted.

Mail search: Turnaround time: 6 to 8 weeks. For 2-week service, add an additional $5.00 and mark "rush" on outside of envelope. A SASE is requested. Include photo copy of requester's ID (DL, passport, etc).

Phone search: See expedited services.

In person search: Simple requests may be processed while you wait.

Expedited service: Expedited service is available for mail and phone searches. Add $5.00 for 2-week mail processing. Add $23.00 for Courier address service and use of a credit card for 3-5 day service.

Marriage Certificates

State Department of Health, Division of Vital Records, 3 Capitol Hill, Room 101, Providence, RI 02908-5097; 401-222-2812, 401-222-2811, 8:30AM-4:30PM M-F.

www.healthri.org/chic/vital/index.php

The record may be obtained from the town or city where the marriage took place, if the record is less than 100 years old.

Records are available from 1902 to present. New records are available for inquiry immediately. Records are indexed on microfiche, inhouse computer.

Searching: Investigative searches must have a signed release from persons of record or immediate family member. Include the following in your request-names of husband and wife, date of marriage, place or county of marriage, wife's maiden name. Vital records are confidential. Therefore, only those individuals who have what is called a "Direct and Tangible Interest" in the records may have access to records.

Access by: mail, phone, in person.

Fee & Payment: The fee is $15.00 per record. There is a $.50 search fee for each additional year searched after 2 years. Fee payee: General Treasurer, State of Rhode Island. Prepayment required. Credit card use is for expedited service only. Personal checks accepted. Major credit cards accepted.

Mail search: Turnaround time: 6 to 8 weeks. For 2-week service, add an additional $5.00 and mark "rush" on outside of envelope. A SASE is requested. Include photo copy of requester's ID (DL, passport, etc).

Phone search: See expedited services.

In person search: Simple requests may be processed while you wait.

Expedited service: Expedited service is available for mail and phone searches. Add $5.00 for 2-week mail processing. Add $23.00 for Courier address service and use of a credit card for 3-5 day service.

Divorce Records

Records not maintained by a state level agency.

Divorce records are found at one of the 4 county Family Courts.

Workers' Compensation Records

Department of Labor & Training, Division of Workers' Compensation, PO Box 20190, Cranston, RI 02920 (Courier address: 1511 Pontiac Ave, Cranston, RI 02920); 401-462-8100, 401-462-8105-Fax; 8:30AM-4PM.

www.dlt.state.ri.us

Records are available from 1970s. New records are available for inquiry immediately. Records are indexed on inhouse computer. Records are normally destroyed after 30 years.

Searching: Records are not available for employment screening. A first report of injury is not public, by law. Records are released to claimant, attorneys, employer and insurer only if connected to case. Include the following in your request-claimant name, Social Security Number, file number (if known), reason for information request, specific records that you need copies of. Records of insurance carrier coverage only are available for no charge by phone or mail. The following data is not released: medical records.

Access by: mail, fax, in person.

Fee & Payment: The search fee is $15.00 per hour. Copies are $.15 per page. There is a $.40 per page fee for return by fax. Fee payee: Department of Labor & Training. Prepayment is required for first time requesters. Personal checks accepted. No credit cards accepted.

Mail search: Turnaround time: 1 to 2 weeks. A SASE is requested.

Fax search: You may request records by fax.

In person search: Proof of identity is required.

Driver Records

Division of Motor Vehicles, Driving Record Clerk, Operator Control, 286 Main Street, Pawtucket, RI 02860; 401-721-2650, 8:30AM-4:30PM.

www.dmv.state.ri.us

The agency follows DPPA. Ongoing requesters should be approved and have an account. Casual requesters must have consent of subject or no record is given.

Records are available for 3 years for accidents and moving violations, 5 years for alcohol-related violations or suspensions, 3 years after reinstatement for suspensions. Surrendered licenses are purged 3 years after expiration. It takes 20 days after received from courts before new records are available for inquiry.

Searching: Information is not made available for the purpose of commercial solicitation or trade. A description of proposed use must be submitted in advance for departmental approval of high volume requesters. Include the following in your request-driver's license number, full name, date of birth. Use of a state form is suggested, but not required. Copies of tickets may be obtained without fee by writing to the Traffic Tribunal at 345 Harris Ave, Providence 02908. The following data is not released: Social Security Numbers.

Access by: mail, in person, online.

Fee & Payment: The fee is $16.00 per record request, $18.00 if online. This is the highest fee in the nation for an online driving record. Fee payee: Division of Motor Vehicles. Prepayment required. Personal checks accepted. No credit cards accepted.

Mail search: Turnaround time: 7-10 days. A SASE is requested.

In person search: Although you may request a record in person, results must be picked up 3-4 days later or are mailed.

Online search: Driving records are available online for permissible users from the state's web portal. The fee is $18.00 per record. All users must be approved by the DMV's Administrator's Office. For details, please call Ms. Elaine Phillips at 401-588-3003.

Vehicle Ownership
Vehicle Identification

Registry of Motor Vehicles, Vehicle Records, 100 Main Street, Pawtucket, RI 02860; 401-722-4131, 401-721-2697-Fax; 8:30AM-3:30PM.

www.dmv.state.ri.us

Records are available for 3 years for title information, for 10 years for registration information. It takes 1 week before new records are available for inquiry. Records are normally destroyed after 3 years after titled vehicle is 10 years old (title records). Registration records available for 10 years.

Searching: Request must be in writing and the purpose stated. Records will not be released for commercial or solicitation purposes. Casual requesters cannot obtain records unless written consent of subject is given. Include the following in your request-for title: reason for request, VIN, year, make, owner name/address, your signature. For registration: VIN, plate, owner name/address, your name/adr. For DR: DR#, name, address. In all record requests, the agency would like to know the reason for request.

Access by: mail, in person.

Fee & Payment: The fee is $10.00 per record request for registration and license data, and $25.00 for title information. The state will release lien information. There is a full charge for a no record found request. Fee payee: Registry of Motor Vehicles. Prepayment required. Personal checks accepted. No credit cards accepted.

Mail search: Turnaround time: 1 week. A self addressed stamped envelope is requested. Title information turnaround is 4-6 weeks.

In person search: Title information can be obtained in person. Registration records are not released in person, but are mailed.

Other access: Bulk retrieval of vehicle and ownership information is limited to statistical purposes.

Accident Reports

Rhode Island State Police, Accident Records, 311 Danielson Pike, North Scituate, RI 02857-1907; 401-444-1143, 401-444-1133-Fax; 10AM-4PM M,T,F; till 6:30PM on Wed.

www.risp.state.ri.us

Records are available for the past 2 years plus the current year. Accidents before that are stored in archives. Hard copy files are indexed. It takes 3-5 days before new records are available for inquiry. Records are normally destroyed after 5 years.

Searching: Include the following in your request-reason for information request, full name, date of accident, location of accident.

Access by: mail, phone, in person.

Fee & Payment: The fee is $10.00 per record. Fee payee: Rhode Island State Police Prepayment required. Personal checks accepted. No credit cards accepted.

Mail search: Turnaround time: 1 week. A SASE is requested.

Phone search: No fee for telephone request. The office will let a requester know if a report is available, but information will not be given over the phone.

In person search: Same day processing is available, provided report has been received.

Vessel Ownership
Vessel Registration

Dept of Environmental Management, Boat Registration & Licensing, 235 Promenade, Rm 360, Providence, RI 02908; 401-222-6647, 401-222-1181-Fax; 8:30AM-3:30PM M-F.

www.state.ri.us/dem

Records are available from the late 1970s to the present. Records are computer indexed for the last 3 years. This is a title state, lien information shows on the title record. All boats over 14 ft must be titled and registered.

Searching: All requests must be in writing on the agency's request form. Call or write for the form. Records cannot be purchased for solicitation or commercial purposes. This agency complies with DPPA. Include the following in your request-name or registration number or RI number.

Access by: mail, fax, in person.

Fee & Payment: There is no fee, unless extensive searching is involved which is a $15.00 per hour charge.

Mail search: Turnaround time: 1 to 2 weeks. No SASE is required.

Fax search: Will accept fax requests if on agency Form.

In person search: Turnaround time depending on staff availability.

Voter Registration

Access to Records is Restricted.

Secretary of State, Elections Division, 100 North Main Street 2nd Floor, Providence, RI 02904; 401-624-7650, 401-287-6545-Fax; 8:30AM-4:30PM.

www.maine.gov/sos/cec/elec

The State Central Voter Register is maintained by the Elections Division. This register is updated on a quarterly basis with information obtained from each of the 39 local boards of canvassers. A new system will be in place by 2006. The Local Board of Canvassers keeps records at the town and city level. Although records are open, they may not be purchased for commercial purposes.

GED Certificates

Department of Education, GED Testing, 255 Westminster, Providence, RI 02908; 401-222-7463, 401-222-2537-Fax; 8AM-3:30PM.

www.ridoe.net

Searching: Include the following in your request-Social Security Number, date of birth, year of testing name at time of test. A signed release is also required for a verification or transcript copy.

Access by: mail, phone, in person.

Fee & Payment: The fee for a transcript is $5.00 or duplicate diploma. There is no fee for a verification. Fee payee: General Treasurer, State of Rhode Island. Prepayment required. Personal checks accepted. No credit cards accepted.

Mail search: Turnaround time: 1 week or less. No SASE is required.

Phone search: Limited data is available.

In person search: Simple requests may be processed while you wait.

Hunting and Fishing License Information

Boat Registration & Licensing, Licensing, 235 Promenade St, Rm 360, Providence, RI 02908; 401-222-3576, 401-222-1181-Fax; 8:30AM-3:30PM.

www.state.ri.us/dem

Recreational license information is kept on paper (forwarded to this office by vendors), and is not computerized.

Records are available for several years. It takes 10 days before new records are available for inquiry.

Searching: Although all records are considered open, commercial use of the records is not permitted. Include the following in your request-date of application, date of birth, address. Also, include where purchased. Requests must be in writing.

Access by: mail, phone, fax, in person.

Fee & Payment: There is no fee for a short search or confirmation. Otherwise, for extensive searches the rate $15.00 per hour. Fee payee: RI DEM. Prepayment required. Personal checks accepted. No credit cards accepted.

Mail search: Turnaround time: 1 week to 10 days.

Phone search: They will confirm only.

Fax search: Same criteria as mail searches.

In person search: But, they will return by mail.

Rhode Island State Licensing Agencies

For details about the agency responsible for licensing/certifying/registering an item below or in the Agency Quick Finder section, match an item's number with the number of the agency in the *Licensing Agency Information* section.

Rhode Island Licenses Searchable Online

Acupuncturist #13	http://health.ri.mylicense.com
Ambulatory Care Facility #13	http://health.ri.mylicense.com
Asbestos Abatement Worker #13	http://health.ri.mylicense.com
Assisted Living Facility #13	http://health.ri.mylicense.com
Athletic Trainer #13	http://health.ri.mylicense.com
Audiologist #13	http://health.ri.mylicense.com
Automobile Body Shop #11	www.dbr.state.ri.us/pdf_forms/clr/Auto%20Body%20Shop%20-%20Licensee%20List.pdf
Automobile Glass Installer #11	www.dbr.state.ri.us/pdf_forms/clr/Auto%20Glass%20-%20Licensee%20List.pdf
Automobile Wrecker #11	www.dbr.state.ri.us/pdf_forms/clr/Auto%20Wrecking%20-%20Licensee%20List.pdf
Barber/Barber Shop/Barber Instructor #13	http://health.ri.mylicense.com
Birth Center #13	http://health.ri.mylicense.com
Blood Test Screener #13	http://health.ri.mylicense.com
Cable Installer #4	www.crb.state.ri.us/search.php
Charter School #16	www.ridoe.net/charterschools/list.htm
Check Casher #5	www.dbr.state.ri.us/pdf_forms/bank/List%20of%20Licensees%202001-28-04.pdf
Chimney Sweep #4	www.crb.state.ri.us/search.php
Chiropractor #13	http://health.ri.mylicense.com
Clinical Lab Scientist/Technician #7	http://health.ri.mylicense.com/
Contractor, Resid'l Building #4	www.crb.state.ri.us/search.php
Contractor, Watch List #4	www.crb.state.ri.us/watchlist.php
Controlled Substance Wholesaler #3	http://health.ri.mylicense.com/
Cosmetologist/Cosmetology Instr. #13	http://health.ri.mylicense.com
CPA #1	www.dbr.state.ri.us/pdf_forms/ba/Licensed%20CPAs%20and%20PAs.pdf
Cytotechnologist #7	http://health.ri.mylicense.com/
Debt Pooler #5	www.dbr.state.ri.us/pdf_forms/bank/List%20of%20Licensees%202001-28-04.pdf
Dental Hygienist #13	http://health.ri.mylicense.com
Dentist #13	http://health.ri.mylicense.com
Dietitian/Nutritionist #13	http://health.ri.mylicense.com
Electrologist #13	http://health.ri.mylicense.com
Electron Microscopy, Lab Scientist #7	http://health.ri.mylicense.com/
Embalmer #13	http://health.ri.mylicense.com
Emergency Care Facility #13	http://health.ri.mylicense.com
Emergency Medical Tech/Services #13	http://health.ri.mylicense.com
Esthetician #13	http://health.ri.mylicense.com
Financial Institution #5	www.dbr.state.ri.us/pdf_forms/bank/List%20of%20Licensees%202001-28-04.pdf
Funeral Director #13	http://health.ri.mylicense.com
Group Home #13	http://health.ri.mylicense.com
Hairdresser/Hairdresser Instructor #13	http://health.ri.mylicense.com
Hazardous Waste Transporter #9	www.state.ri.us/dem/programs/benviron/waste/transpor/index.htm
Hearing Aid Dispenser #13	http://health.ri.mylicense.com
Histologic Technician, Clinical #7	http://health.ri.mylicense.com/
Home Care Provider #13	http://health.ri.mylicense.com
Home Nursing Care #13	http://health.ri.mylicense.com
Hospice Provider #13	http://health.ri.mylicense.com
Hospital #13	http://health.ri.mylicense.com/
Hypodermic Dispenser #3	http://health.ri.mylicense.com
Insurance Broker/Producer/Agent #5	www.dbr.state.ri.us/lic_search.php
Interpreter for the Deaf #13	http://health.ri.mylicense.com
Laboratory, Medical #13	http://health.ri.mylicense.com
Lender/Loan Broker #5	www.dbr.state.ri.us/pdf_forms/bank/List%20of%20Licensees%202001-28-04.pdf
Lobbyist #14	www.corps.state.ri.us/lobby/default.asp
Manicurist/Manicurist Shop #13	http://health.ri.mylicense.com
Marriage & Family Therapist #13	http://health.ri.mylicense.com
Massage Therapist #13	http://health.ri.mylicense.com
Medical Doctor #13	http://health.ri.mylicense.com
Medical Waste Transporter #9	www.state.ri.us/dem/programs/benviron/waste/transpor/index.htm
Mental Health Counselor #13	http://health.ri.mylicense.com
Midwife #13	http://health.ri.mylicense.com
Money Broker / Money Transferer #5	www.dbr.state.ri.us/pdf_forms/bank/List%20of%20Licensees%202001-28-04.pdf
Mortgage Broker #5	www.dbr.state.ri.us/pdf_forms/bank/List%20of%20Licensees%202001-28-04.pdf

Notary Public #15 .... www.corps.state.ri.us/notaries/notaries.htm#data
Nuclear Medicine Technologist #13 .... http://health.ri.mylicense.com
Nurse/Nursing Assistant/Nursing Service #13 ..... http://health.ri.mylicense.com
Nursing Home Administrator #13 .... http://health.ri.mylicense.com
Occupational Therapist #13 .... http://health.ri.mylicense.com
Office Operatories (Medical) #13 .... http://health.ri.mylicense.com
Optician #13 .... http://health.ri.mylicense.com
Optometrist #13 .... http://health.ri.mylicense.com
Osteopathic Physician #13 .... www.docboard.org/ri/df/search.htm
Outpatient Rehabilitation #13 .... http://health.ri.mylicense.com
Pharmacist/Pharmacy Technician/Pharmacy #3 .... http://health.ri.mylicense.com
Phlebotomy Station #13 .... http://health.ri.mylicense.com
Physical Therapist /Therapist Assistant #13 .... http://health.ri.mylicense.com
Physician / Physician Assistant #13 .... http://health.ri.mylicense.com
Physicians Controlled Substance #3 .... http://health.ri.mylicense.com
Podiatrist #13 .... http://health.ri.mylicense.com
Prosthetist #13 .... http://health.ri.mylicense.com
Psychologist #13 .... http://health.ri.mylicense.com
Public Accountant-CPA #1 .... www.dbr.state.ri.us/pdf_forms/ba/Licensed%20CPAs%20and%20PAs.pdf
Public Accounting Firm #1 .... www.dbr.state.ri.us/pdf_forms/ba/Licensed%20Public%20Accounting%20Firms.pdf
Radiation Therapist #13 .... http://health.ri.mylicense.com
Radiographer #13 .... http://health.ri.mylicense.com
Real Estate Agent/Sales #5 .... www.dbr.state.ri.us/pdf_forms/RE-Real%20Estate%20Salespersons.pdf
Real Estate Appraiser #5 .... www.dbr.state.ri.us/pdf_forms/RE-Real%20Estate%20Appraisers.pdf
Real Estate Broker #5 .... www.dbr.state.ri.us/pdf_forms/RE-Real%20Estate%20Brokers.pdf
Residential Care Facility #13 .... http://health.ri.mylicense.com
Residential Facility #22 .... www.dcyf.ri.gov
Respiratory Care Practitioner #13 .... http://health.ri.mylicense.com
Roofer, Commercial #4 .... www.crb.state.ri.us/search.php
Salvage Yard #11 .... www.dbr.state.ri.us/pdf_forms/clr/Auto%20Salvage%20-%20Licensee%20List.pdf
Sanitarian #13 .... http://health.ri.mylicense.com
Security Alarm Installer #4 .... www.crb.state.ri.us/search.php
Septic Transporter #9 .... www.state.ri.us/dem/programs/benviron/waste/transpor/index.htm
Social Worker #13 .... http://health.ri.mylicense.com
Speech/Language Pathologist #13 .... http://health.ri.mylicense.com
Surgery Center, Freestanding #13 .... http://health.ri.mylicense.com
Tanning Facility #13 .... http://health.ri.mylicense.com
Tattoo Artist #13 .... http://health.ri.mylicense.com
Underground Sprinkler Installer #4 .... www.crb.state.ri.us/search.php
Veterinarian #13 .... http://health.ri.mylicense.com
X-ray Facility/Portable #13 .... http://health.ri.mylicense.com

Rhode Island Licensing Quick Finder

Acupuncturist #13 401-222-2827
Alarm Agent/Company #11 401-222-3857
Ambulatory Care Facility #13 401-222-2827
Arborist #10 401-647-3367
Architect #5 401-222-2565
Asbestos Abatement Worker #13 401-222-3601
Assisted Living Facility #13 401-222-2827
Athletic Trainer #13 401-222-5888
Attorney #21 401-222-4233
Auctioneer #11 401-222-3857
Audiologist #13 401-222-2827
Automobile Body Shop / Wrecker #11 . 401-222-3857
Automobile Glass Installer #11 401-222-3857
Bank #5 401-222-2405
Bank Holding Company #5 401-222-2405
Barber/Barber Instructor/Shop #13 ... 401-222-2827
Beekeeper #9 .... 401-222-2781 x4519
Birth Center #13 401-222-2827
Blaster #19 401-294-0861
Blood Test Screener #13 401-222-2827
Bondsman #18 401-222-3212
Boxer #5 401-222-6541
Cable Installer #4 401-222-1268
Cattle Dealer #9 .... 401-222-2781 x4503
Charter School #16 401-222-4600
Check Casher #5 401-222-2405
Chemical Dependency Prof./Advanced or Clinic #6
.... 401-233-2215

Chimney Sweep #4 401-222-1268
Chiropractor #13 401-222-2827
Clinical Lab Scientist/Technician #7 401-222-2877
Clinical Supervisor, Recognized #6 401-233-2215
Contractor, Resid'l Building #4 401-222-1268
Contractor, Watch List #4 401-222-1268
Controlled Substance Wholesaler #3 ... 401-222-1374
Cosmetologist/Cosmetology Instr. #13 401-222-2827
Court Reporter #2 401-222-3215
CPA #1 401-222-3185
Credit Union #5 401-222-2405
Cytotechnologist #7 401-222-2827
Day Care, Children #22 401-528-3624
Debt Pooler #5 401-222-2405
Dental Hygienist #13 401-222-2151
Dentist #13 401-222-2151
Dietitian/Nutritionist #13 401-222-5888
Electrician #8 401-462-8571
Electrologist #13 401-222-2827
Electron Microscopy, Clinical Lab Scientist #7
.... 401-222-2827
Elevator Inspector/Mechanic #8 401-462-8579
Embalmer #13 401-222-2827
Emergency Care Facility #13 401-222-2827
Emergency Medical Tech/Services #13 401-222-2401
Engineer #2 401-222-2038
Esthetician #13 401-222-2827
Family/Group Day Care Home Provider #22

.... 401-528-3624
Financial Institution #5 401-222-2405
Fire Alarm Installer #19 401-294-0861
Fire Extinguisher Installer/Service #19 401-294-0861
Fireworks Shooter #19 401-294-0861
Fisher, Commercial #9 401-222-6647
Foster Care/Home #22 401-528-3606
Fur Buyer #9 401-222-6647
Funeral Director #13 401-222-2827
Fur Buyer #9 401-222-6647
Group Home #13 401-222-2827
Hairdresser/Hairdresser Instructor #13 401-222-2827
Hazardous Waste Transporter #9 401-222-4700 x7517
Health Club #11 401-222-3857
Hearing Aid Dispenser #13 401-222-2827
Histologic Technician, Clinical #7 401-222-2827
Hoisting Engineer #8 401-462-8554
Home Care Provider #13 401-222-2827
Home Nursing Care #13 401-222-2827
Hospice Provider #13 401-222-2827
Hospital #13 401-222-2827
Hypodermic Dispenser #3 401-222-1374
Insurance Adjuster #5 401-222-2223
Insurance Appraiser / Solicitor #5 401-222-2223
Insurance Broker/Producer/Agent #5 ... 401-222-2223
Interpreter for the Deaf #13 401-222-2827
Investment Advisor #5 401-222-3048
Laboratory, Medical #13 401-222-2827
Land Surveyor Firm #2 401-222-2038

Landscape Architect #2	401-222-2038
Landscaper #5	401-222-2565
Lender/Loan Broker #5	401-222-2405
Lifeguard #12	401-222-2632
Liquor Control #5	401-222-2562
Lobbyist #14	401-222-6616
Manicurist / Manicurist Shop #13	401-222-2827
Marriage & Family Therapist #13	401-222-2827
Massage Therapist #13	401-222-2827
Medical Doctor #13	401-222-2827
Medical Waste Transporter #9	401-222-4700 x7517
Mental Health Counselor #13	401-222-2827
Midwife #13	401-222-5700
Mobile Home Park #11	401-222-3857
Mobile/Mfg'd Home Mfg./Dealer #11	401-222-3857
Money Broker #5	401-222-2405
Money Transferer #5	401-222-2405
Mortgage Broker #5	401-222-2405
Notary Public #15	401-222-1487
Nuclear Medicine Technologist #13	401-222-5700
Nurse #13	401-222-5700
Nurse-LPN #13	401-222-5700
Nurseryman #9	401-222-2781 x4516
Nursing Assistant #13	401-222-5888
Nursing Home Administrator #13	401-222-5888
Nursing Service #13	401-222-2827
Occupational Therapist #13	401-222-2827
Office Operatories (Medical) #13	401-222-2827
Optician #13	401-222-2827
Optometrist #13	401-222-2827
Osteopathic Physician #13	401-222-3855
Outpatient Rehabilitation #13	401-222-2827
Park Ranger #12	401-222-2632
Pesticide Applicator #9	401-222-2781 x4510
Pharmacist/Pharm Tech/Pharmacy #3	401-222-1374
Phlebotomy Station #13	401-222-2827
Physical Therapist / Assistant #13	401-222-2827
Physician #13	401-222-2827
Physician Assistant #13	401-222-2827
Physicians Controlled Substance #3	401-222-1374
Pilot, Ship #20	401-783-5551
Pipefitter #8	401-462-8535
Plumber/Master Plumber/Journeyman #8	401-462-8525
Podiatrist #13	401-222-2827
Prevention Specialist/Spvr./Adv'd #6	401-233-2215
Prosthetist #13	401-222-2827
Psychologist #13	401-222-2827
Public Accountant-CPA / Firm #1	401-222-3185
Pyrotechnic Operator #19	401-294-0861
Radiation Therapist #13	401-222-2827
Radiographer #13	401-222-2827
Reading Specialist #16	401-222-2675
Real Estate Agent/Sales/Broker #5	401-222-2255
Real Estate Appraiser #5	401-222-2255
Refrigeration Technician #8	401-462-8535
Residential Care Facility #13	401-222-2827
Residential Facility #22	401-528-3623
Respiratory Care Practitioner #13	401-222-2827
Roofer, Commercial #4	401-222-1268
Salvage Yard #11	401-222-3857
Sanitarian #13	401-222-2827
School Coach #16	401-222-2675
School Guidance Counselor #16	401-222-2675
School Principal/Superintendent/Supervisor #16	401-222-2675
School Psychologist/Social Worker #16	401-222-2675
Securities Broker/Dealer #5	401-222-3048
Securities Broker/Dealer Sales Rep. #5	401-222-3048
Security Alarm Installer #4	401-222-1268
Septic Transporter #9	401-222-4700 x7517
Sewage Disposal System Installer #9	401-222-6820
Sheet Metal Technician/Worker #8	401-462-8535
Social Worker #13	401-222-2827
Speech/Language Pathologist #13	401-222-2827
Surgery Center, Freestanding #13	401-222-2827
Surveyor, Land #5	401-222-2565
Tanning Facility #13	401-222-2827
Tattoo Artist #13	401-222-2827
Teacher #16	401-222-2675
Telecommunications Technician #8	401-462-8533
Trapper #9	401-222-6647
Travel Agent #11	401-222-3857
Underground Sprinkler Installer #4	401-222-1268
Upholstery/Bedding Mfg. #11	401-222-3857
Vendor Employee #5	401-222-2405
Veterinarian #13	401-222-2827
Waste Water Treatment Plant Op. #9	401-222-6820
Wildlife Propagator #9	401-222-6647
Wildlife Rehabilitator #17	401-789-0281
Woods Operator #10	401-647-3367
Wrestler #5	401-222-6541
X-ray Facility / X-ray, Portable #13	401-222-2827

Rhode Island Licensing Agency Information

1 Department of Business Regulation, Board of Accountancy, 233 Richmond St, Providence, RI 02903-4236; 401-222-3185, Fax: 401-222-6654. www.dbr.state.ri.us/account.html
Search Database at www.dbr.state.ri.us/pdf_forms/ba/Licensed%20CPAs%20and%20PAs.pdf

2 Court Administrator Office, 250 Benefit St, #506, Providence, RI 02903; 401-222-3215, Fax: 401-222-8749.

3 Board of Pharmacy, 3 Capitol Hill, Rm 205, Providence, RI 02908; 401-222-1374, Fax: 401-222-2158. www.health.state.ri.us
Search Database at http://health.ri.mylicense.com/

4 Contractors' Registration Board, 1 Capitol Hill, 2nd Fl, Providence, RI 02908; 401-222-1268, Fax: 401-222-2599. www.crb.state.ri.us
Email: gwhalen@doa.state.ri.us
Search Database at www.crb.state.ri.us/search.php

5 Business Regulation Department, Division of Commercial Licensing & Regulation, 233 Richmond St, Providence, RI 02903-4232; 401-222-2246. www.dbr.state.ri.us

6 Certification of Chemical Dependency Professionals, 345 Waterman Ave, Smithfield, RI 02917; 401-233-2215, Fax: 401-233-0690.
Email: ricert@msn.com

7 Clinical Laboratory Advisory Board, 3 Capitol Hill, Rm 104, Providence, RI 02908; 401-222-2827, Fax: 401-222-1272.
www.health.state.ri.us
Search Database at http://health.ri.mylicense.com/

8 Department of Labor & Training, Division of Professional Regulation - Bldg #70, PO Box 20247 (1511 Pontiac Av), Providence, RI 02920-0943; 401-462-8527, Fax: 401-462-8528.
www.dlt.state.ri.us

9 Department of Environmental Management, Bureau of Natural Resources, 235 Promenade St, #260, Providence, RI 02908-5767; 401-222-4700, Fax: 401-222-6802.
www.state.ri.us/dem/programs/index.htm

10 Department of Environmental Management, Division of Forest Environment, 1037 Hartford Pike, North Scituate, RI 02857; 401-647-3367, Fax: 401-647-3590. www.state.ri.us/dem/programs/bnatres/forest/index.htm
Email: riforestry@edgenet.net

11 Division of Licensing & Consumer Protection, Commercial Licensing, 233 Richmond St, Providence, RI 02903; 401-222-3857, Fax: 401-222-6654. www.dbr.state.ri.us

12 Division of Parks & Recreation, 2321 Hartford Ave, Johnston, RI 02919; 401-222-2632, Fax: 401-934-0610. www.riparks.com/index.htm
Email: riparks@earthlink.net

13 Health Department, Professional Regulation Division, 3 Capitol Hill, Rm 205, Providence, RI 02908-5097; 401-222-2827, Fax: 401-222-1272.
www.health.state.ri.us
Email: library@health.state.ri.us
Search Database at http://health.ri.mylicense.com
Note: Also, search medical doctors and osteopaths at www.docboard.org/ri/df/search.htm.

14 Office of Secretary of State, Lobbyist Registration, State House, Smith St, Rm 38, Providence, RI 02903; 401-222-6616, Fax: 401-222-1404. www.state.ri.us/
Note: To search, there are separate buttons for the Notary Public Section or Lobbyist.

15 Office of Secretary of State, Notary Public Section, 100 N Main St, Providence, RI 02903; 401-222-1487, Fax: 401-222-3879.
http://www3.sec.state.ri.us/ *more*

Email: notaries@sec.state.ri.us Search Database at www.corps.state.ri.us/notaries/notaries.htm#data
Note: To search, there are separate buttons for the Notary Public Section or Lobbyist.

16 Department of Education, Office of Teacher Certification, 255 Westminster St, Providence, RI 02903; 401-222-4600, Fax: 401-222-2048.
www.ridoe.net

17 Department of Environmental Management, Division of Fish & Wildlife, Box 218, West Kingston, RI 02892; 401-789-0281, Fax: 401-783-7490.
www.state.ri.us/dem Email: lgibson@

18 Superior Court, Bondsman Registration, 250 Benefit St, Rm 533, Providence, RI 02903; 401-222-3212, Fax: 401-272-4645. Note: Direct written requests to Judge Jos. F. Rodgers, Jr.

19 State Fire Marshall's Office, 24 Conway Ave, Quansit-Davisville Industrial Park, Davisville/North Kingston, RI 02852; 401-294-0861, Fax: 401-294-1171.

20 Pilotage Commission, 301 Great Island Rd, Galilee, RI 02882; 401-783-5551, Fax: 401-783-7285.

21 Supreme Court, Board of Bar Examiners, 250 Benefit St, Providence, RI 02903; 401-222-4233, Fax: 401-222-3599. www.courts.state.ri.us/supreme/bar/barexaminers.htm
Email: kcacchiotti@courts.state.ri.us

22 Department of Children, Youth & Famillies, 101 Friendship St #101, Providence, RI 02903; 401-528-3624. www.dcyf.state.ri.us
Search Database at www.dcyf.state.ri.us/cgi-bin/dcyf.cgi.

Rhode Island Federal Courts

The following list indicates the district and division name for each county in the state.

Rhode Island County/Court Cross Reference

Bristol..Providence

Kent..Providence

Newport...Providence

Providence...Providence

Washington..Providence

US District Court

Providence Division Clerk's Office, One Exchange Terrace, Federal Bldg, Providence, RI 02903 (also use mail address for courier delivery), 401-752-7200, Fax-401-752-7247. Hours- 9AM-4:30PM. www.rid.uscourts.gov

Counties: All counties in Rhode Island.

Searches & Indexing: Results do not include SSN or DOB. Both computer and card indexes maintained; computer goes back to 1992. New cases in the index 1-2 days after filing date. Records purged never. District-wide searches available here.

Fee & Payment: Pay by money order, cashier's or personal check. Payee: Clerk, US District Court. Prepayment required.

Phone Search: Only case number or name released via phone.

Mail Search: search usually completed- 1-2 days. Include SASE for return.

In Person Search: Fee charged if court performs your search. Self-serve copier available - $.25 per page.

E-Services: ECF replaces PACER whose records did go back to 12/1988. New records online after 1 day. ECF at https://ecf.rid.uscourts.gov **Opinions Online:** www.rid.uscourts.gov/Judges%20Opinions.asp. **Other Online Access:** Court calendars can be found at www.rid.uscourts.gov/calendars.asp.

US Bankruptcy Court

Providence Bankruptcy Division Court Clerk, 6th Fl, 380 Westminster St, Providence, RI 02903 (also use mail address for courier delivery), 401-528-4477, records rm- 401-528-4477, Fax-401-528-4470. Hours- 9AM-4PM. www.rib.uscourts.gov

Counties: All counties in Rhode Island.

Searches & Indexing: Results include last 4 SSN digits. Computer index maintained. New cases in the index same day after filing date.

Fee & Payment: Pay by Visa/MC, money order, cashier's or personal check. No debtor's checks accepted. Payee: Clerk, US Bankruptcy Court. Prepayment required. Will email or fax back documents no charge.

Phone Search: Only docket information is available by phone. Voice Case Information Service available, call VCIS at 800-843-2841 or 401-528-4476.

Mail Search: search usually completed- same day. Include SASE for return.

In Person Search: Fee charged if court performs your search. Self-serve copier available - $.10 per page.

E-Services: ECF replaces PACER. Document images available. PACER records go back to 1990. New records online immediately. ECF at https://ecf.rib.uscourts.gov **Opinions Online:** www.rib.uscourts.gov/CourtResources/Opinions/opinions.htm

Standards for Federal Courts: Search fee is $26.00 per item (one party name or case number). Copy fee is $.50 per page. Certification fee is $9.00 per document, double for exemplification, if available. All fees standard unless noted in profile. Mail Search: always enclose a stamped self addressed envelope unless otherwise noted. Most courts accept fax requests or will suggest a copying/search vendor. Before releasing records, all courts require prepayment, unless noted.

Open records are located at the court unless otherwise noted. District courts index by defendant and plaintiff as well as by case number. Bankruptcy courts usually index by debtor and case number. While most courts now have their indexes on computer, many may still maintain index card files as well.

Courts offering internet access via CM-ECF or older RACER, PACER, or Web-PACER systems charge $.08 per page fee unless noted as free. Where PACER is available, the universal sign-up number is 800-676-6856. Find PACER and the US Party/Case Index at http://pacer.psc.uscourts.gov.

Rhode Island County Courts

Court	Jurisdiction	No. of Courts	How Organized
Superior Courts*	General	4	4 Divisions
District Courts*	Limited	4	6 Divisions
Municipal Courts	Municipal	16	
Probate Courts*	Probate	39	39 Cities/ Towns
Family Courts	Special	4	4 Divisions
Workers' Compensation Court	Special	1	

* Profiled in this Sourcebook.

Court	CIVIL								
	Tort	Contract	Real Estate	Min. Claim	Max. Claim	Small Claims	Estate	Eviction	Domestic Relations
Superior Courts*	X	X	X	$5000	No Max				
District Courts*	X	X	X	$1500	$10,000	$1500		X	
Municipal Courts									
Probate Courts*							X		
Family Courts									X
Workers' CompCourt									

Court	CRIMINAL				
	Felony	Misdemeanor	DWI/DUI	Preliminary Hearing	Juvenile
Superior Courts*	X				
District Courts*		X	X	X	
Municipal Courts					
Probate Courts*					
Family Courts					X
Workers' Comp Court					

ADMINISTRATION   Court Administrator, Supreme Court, 250 Benefit St, Providence, RI, 02903; 401-222-3266, Fax: 401-222-4224. www.courts.state.ri.us

COURT STRUCTURE   Rhode Island has five counties, but only four Superior/District Court Locations (2nd-Newport, 3rd-Kent, 4th-Washignton, and 6th-Providence/Bristol Districts). Bristol and Providence counties are completely merged at the Providence location. Civil claims between $5000 and $10,000 may be filed in either Superior or District Court at the discretion of the filer. For questions regarding the Superior Courts, call 401-222-2622. For questions regarding the District Courts, call 401-458-3156.

ONLINE ACCESS   The Rhode Island Judiciary offers free Internet access to court criminal records statewide at http://courtconnect.courts.state.ri.us. A word of caution, this website is provided as an informational service only and should not be relied upon as an official record of the court. Superior (civil, family) and Appellate courts are online internally for court personnel only.

PROBATE COURTS   Probate is handled by the Town Clerk at the 39 cities and towns across Rhode Island.

Bristol County

Superior & District Courts c/o Bristol Town Hall, 10 Court St, Bristol, RI 02809; phone: 401-253-7000; fax: 401-253-1570; hours 8:30-4PM (EST). *Probate Only.*
Note: Do not send criminal or civil (except probate) record requests here. All civil and criminal cases are handled by the Providence County courts.

Barrington Town Hall 283 County Road, Barrington, RI 02806; phone: 401-247-1900 x4; fax: 401-247-3765; hours 8:30AM-4:30PM (EST). *Probate.*

Bristol Town Hall 10 Court St, Bristol, RI 02809; phone: 401-253-7000 x21; fax: 401-253-1570; hours 8:30AM-4PM (EST). *Probate.*

Warren Town Hall 514 Main St, Warren, RI 02885; phone: 401-245-7340; fax: 401-245-7421; hours 9AM-4PM (EST). *Probate.*

Kent County

Superior Court 222 Quaker Ln, Warwick, RI 02886; phone: 401-822-1311; civil phone: 401-822-1310; hours 8:30AM-4:00PM (EST). *Felony, Civil Actions Over $10,000.*
www.courts.state.ri.us
Civil Records: Access: In person only. Visitors must perform in person searches themselves. Court makes copy: $.15 per page. Self serve copy fee: $.15 per page. Required to search: name, years to search. Civil cases indexed by defendant, plaintiff. Civil records on computer from 1987.
Criminal Records: Access: In person, online. Visitors must perform in person searches themselves. Court makes copy: $.15 per page. Self serve copy fee: $.15 per page. Required to search: name, years to search, signed release; also helpful: DOB. Criminal records on computer from 1987. Access criminal records free at http://courtconnect.courts.state.ri.us as an informational service only; should not be relied upon as official court record.
General Information: Public terminal has criminal back to 1987 and civil back to 1997. No adoption, confidential or sealed records released. Certification fee: $3.00 per page. Exemplified copies: $9.00 each plus cert fee. Payee: Clerk of Superior Court. Personal checks accepted. Prepayment required.

3rd Division District Court 222 Quaker Ln, Warwick, RI 02886-0107; phone: 401-822-1771; hours 8:30AM-4:30PM (EST). *Misdemeanor, Civil Actions Under $10,000, Eviction, Small Claims.*
Civil Records: Access: In person only. Visitors must perform in person searches themselves. Court makes copy: $1.00 per page. Required to search: name, years to search. Civil cases indexed by defendant, plaintiff. Civil records for 1995-1997 on index cards. Archives stored at Rhode Island Judicial Records Center, 1 Hill St, Pawtucket, RI 02860, 401-277-3249. Records destroyed after 10 years, but remain in docket books.
Criminal Records: Access: In person, online. Visitors must perform in person searches themselves. Court makes copy: $1.00 per page. Required to search: name, years to search, DOB, signed release. Criminal records for 1995-1997 on index cards. Archives stored at Rhode Island Judicial Records Center. Records destroyed after 10 years, but remain in docket books. Free internet access at http://courtconnect.courts.state.ri.us as an informational service only; should not be relied upon as official court record.
General Information: No public access terminal. No mental or sealed records released. Certification fee: $1.00 per page. Payee: 3rd District Court. Personal checks accepted. Visa, AmEx accepted. Prepayment required.

Coventry Town Hall 1670 Flat River Rd, Coventry, RI 02816; phone: 401-822-9174; fax: 401-822-9132; hours 8:30AM-4:30PM (EST). *Probate.*

East Greenwich Town Hall PO Box 111, 125 Main St, East Greenwich, RI 02818; phone: 401-886-8607; 8604; fax: 401-886-8625; hours 8:30AM-4:30PM (EST). *Probate.*

Warwick City Hall 3275 Post Rd, Warwick, RI 02886; phone: 401-738-2000 (x6213); fax: 401-738-6639; hours 8:30AM-4:30PM (EST). *Probate.*

West Greenwich Town Hall 280 Victory Hwy, West Greenwich, RI 02817; phone: 401-392-3800; fax: 401-392-3805; hours 9AM-4PM M,T,Th,F; 9AM-4PM, 7-9PM W (EST). *Probate.*

West Warwick Town Hall 1170 Main St, West Warwick, RI 02893-4829; phone: 401-822-9201; fax: 401-822-9266; hours 8:30AM-4:30PM; 8:30AM-4PM June 1st-Labor Day (EST). *Probate.*

Newport County

Superior Court Florence K Murray Judicial Complex, 45 Washington Sq, Newport, RI 02840; phone: 401-841-8330; fax: 401-846-1673; hours 8:30AM-4:30PM (July and August till 4PM) (EST). *Felony, Civil Actions Over $10,000.*
Civil Records: Access: Mail, fax, in person. Both court and visitors may perform in person searches. Search fee: $15.00 per hour for search and review. Court makes copy: $.15 per page. Required to search: name, years to search. Civil cases indexed by defendant, plaintiff. Civil records on computer from 1989. Prior records archived at Rhode Island Records Center. Mail turnaround time 1 day.
Criminal Records: Access: Mail, fax, in person, online. Both court and visitors may perform in person searches. Search fee: $15.00 per hour for search and review. Court makes copy: $.15 per page. Required to search: name, years to search, DOB. Criminal records on computer from 1983, index from 1968. Prior records archived at Records Center. Access criminal records free at http://courtconnect.courts.state.ri.us as an informational service only; should not be relied upon as official court record. Mail turnaround time 1 day.
General Information: Public use terminal available. No child molestation or sexual assault records released. Certification fee: $3.00 per page. Payee: Clerk Superior Court. Personal checks accepted. Prepayment and SASE required.

2nd District Court 45 Washington Square, Newport, RI 02840; phone: 401-841-8350; hours 8:30AM-4:30PM (4PM-summer hours) (EST). *Misdemeanor, Civil Actions Under $10,000, Eviction, Small Claims.*
Civil Records: Access: In person only. Visitors must perform in person searches themselves. Court makes copy: $.15 per page. Required to search: name, years to search. Civil cases indexed by defendant, plaintiff. Civil records on index cards for past 3 years, prior archived at Pawtucket Judicial Records Center.
Criminal Records: Access: In person, online. Visitors must perform in person searches themselves. Court makes copy: $.15 per page. Required to search: name. Overall records from 1999-2002. Computerized records from 1999-2004. Free internet access at http://courtconnect.courts.state.ri.us as an informational service only; should not be relied upon as official court record.
General Information: Public terminal has only criminal records back to 1999. No juvenile, family court, sealed, expunged or ordered by judge or adoption records released. Certification fee: $1.00. Payee: 2nd District Court. No personal checks accepted. Prepayment required.

Jamestown Town Hall 93 Narragansett Ave, Jamestown, RI 02835; phone: 401-423-7200; fax: 401-423-7230; hours 8AM-4:30PM (EST). *Probate.*
Note: Probate Court held at 26 North Rd on first Wed. of every month at 2PM.

Little Compton Town Hall 40 Commons, PO Box 226, Little Compton, RI 02837; phone: 401-635-4400; fax: 401-635-2470; hours 8AM-4PM (EST). *Probate.*

Middletown Town Hall 350 E Main Rd, Middletown, RI 02842; phone: 401-847-0009; fax: 401-845-0406; hours 8AM-5PM (EST). *Probate.*

Newport City Hall 43 Broadway, Newport, RI 02840; phone: 401-846-9600 x1; fax: 401-849-8757; hours 8:30AM-4:30PM (EST). *Probate.*

Portsmouth Town Hall 2200 E Main Rd, Portsmouth, RI 02871; phone: 401-683-2101; hours 9AM-4PM (EST). *Probate.*

Tiverton Town Hall 343 Highland Rd, Tiverton, RI 02878; phone: 401-625-6700; fax: 401-625-6705; hours 8:30AM-4PM (EST). *Probate.*

Providence County

Providence/Bristol Superior Court 250 Benefit St, Providence, RI 02903; phone: 401-222-3250; hours 8:30AM-4PM (EST). *Felony, Civil Actions Over $10,000.*

www.courts.state.ri.us
Note: All civil and criminal cases are handled by the Providence County court & Bristol County court.
Civil Records: Access: Phone, mail, in person. Visitors must perform in person searches themselves. Court makes copy: $.15 per page. Required to search: name, years to search. Civil cases indexed by defendant, plaintiff. Civil records on computer since 1983.
Criminal Records: Access: In person, online. Visitors must perform in person searches themselves. Court makes copy: $.15 per page. Required to search: name, years to search, DOB. Criminal records on computer since 1983. Access criminal records free at http://courtconnect.courts.state.ri.us as an informational service only; should not be relied upon as official court record.
General Information: Public terminal goes back to 1992. No adoption, confidential or sealed records released. Certification fee: $3.00. Payee: Providence Superior Court. Personal checks accepted. Prepayment required.

6th Division District Court 1 Dorrance Plaza, 2nd Fl, Providence, RI 02903; phone: 401-458-5400; hours 8:30AM-4PM (EST). *Misdemeanor, Civil Actions Under $10,000, Eviction, Small Claims.*
Civil Records: Access: Mail, phone, in person. Both court and visitors may perform in person searches. No search fee. Court makes copy: $.10 per page. Required to search: name, years to search. Civil cases indexed by defendant, plaintiff. Civil records on card files to present. Note: Phone access limited to one name. Mail turnaround time varies.
Criminal Records: Access: Mail, phone, in person, online. Both court and visitors may perform in person searches. No search fee. Court makes copy: $.10 per page. Required to search: name, years to search. Criminal records for misdemeanor on computer from 1989; records at court only 2 years. Access criminal records free at http://courtconnect.courts.state.ri.us as an informational service only; should not be relied upon as official court record. Note: Phone requests limited to one name. Mail turnaround time varies.
General Information: Public terminal has only criminal records back to 1992. No adoption, confidential or sealed records released. Certification fee: $1.50. Payee: 6th Division District Court. Personal checks accepted. Prepayment and SASE required.

Burrillville Town Hall 105 Harrisville Main St, Harrisville, RI 02830; phone: 401-568-4300 x114 or x110; fax: 401-568-0490; hours 8:30AM-4:30PM M-W; 8:30AM-7:00PM Th; 8:30AM-12:30PM F (EST). *Probate.*
www.burrillville.org/Public_Documents/BurrillvilleRI_Clerk/probate

Central Falls City Hall City Clerk's Office, 580 Broad St, Central Falls, RI 02863; phone: 401-727-7400; fax: 401-727-7406; hours 8:30AM-4:30PM (EST). *Probate.*
www.centralfallsri.us

Cranston City Hall 869 Park Ave, Cranston, RI 02910; phone: 401-461-1000 X3197; probate phone: 401-780-3197; fax: 401-780-3165; hours 8:30AM-4:30PM (EST). *Probate.*

Cumberland Town Hall PO Box 7, 45 Broad St, Cumberland, RI 02864; phone: 401-728-2400; civil phone: x154; probate phone: x137; fax: 401-724-1103; hours 8:30AM-4:30PM (EST). *Probate, Misdemeanor Traffic.*

East Providence City Hall 145 Taunton Ave, East Providence, RI 02914; phone: 401-435-7595; fax: 401-435-4630; hours 8AM-4PM (EST). *Probate.*

Foster Town Hall 181 Howard Hill Rd, Foster, RI 02825; phone: 401-392-9200; fax: 401-392-9201; hours 9AM-4PM (EST). *Probate.*

Glocester Town Hall PO Box B, 1145 Putnam Pike, Chepachet, RI 02814; phone: 401-568-6206; fax: 401-568-5850; hours 8AM-4:30PM (EST). *Probate.*
www.glocesterri.org

Johnston Town Hall 1385 Hartford Ave, Johnston, RI 02919; phone: 401-351-8832; fax: 401-553-8835; hours 8:30AM-4:30PM (EST). *Probate.*

Lincoln Town Hall PO Box 100, 100 Old River Rd, Lincoln, RI 02865; phone: 401-333-8450, 333-8451; fax: 401-333-3648; hours 9AM-4:30PM (EST). *Probate.*
www.lincolnri.org/clerksoffice.shtml
Note: Court meets fourth Monday at 9 AM.

North Providence Town Hall 2000 Smith St, North Providence, RI 02911; phone: 401-232-0900; fax: 401-233-1409; hours 8:30AM-4:30PM (EST). *Probate.*

North Smithfield Town Hall Municipal Annex, 575 Smithfield Rd, North Smithfield, RI 02896; phone: 401-767-2200 x216; probate phone: 401-767-2200 x220, 221; fax: 401-356-4057; hours 8AM-4PM M, T, W; 8AM-7PM Th; 8AM-N F (EST). *Probate.*

Pawtucket City Hall 137 Roosevelt Ave, Pawtucket, RI 02860; phone: 401-728-0500 x259 or x223; fax: 401-728-8932; hours 8:30AM-4:30PM (EST). *Probate.*

Providence Probate Court 25 Dorrance St, Providence, RI 02903; phone: 401-421-7740; fax: 401-861-6208; hours 8:30AM-4:00PM (EST). *Probate.*
Note: All civil and criminal cases are handled by the Providence County courts.

Scituate Town Hall 195 Danielson Pike, PO Box 328, North Scituate, RI 02857; phone: 401-647-2822; fax: 401-647-7220; hours 8:30AM-4PM (EST). *Probate.*

Smithfield Town Hall 64 Farnum Pike, Smithfield, RI 02917; phone: 401-233-1000 x111; probate phone: 401-233-1000 X114; fax: 401-232-7244; hours 8:30AM-4:30PM (EST). *Probate.*

Woonsocket City Hall 169 Main St, Woonsocket, RI 02895; phone: 401-762-6400; probate phone: 401-767-9248; fax: 401-765-0022; hours 8:30AM-4PM (EST). *Probate.*

Washington County

Superior Court 4800 Towerhill Rd, Wakefield, RI 02879; phone: 401-782-4121; hours 8:30AM-4:30PM (Sept-June) 8:30AM-4PM (July & Aug) (EST). *Felony, Civil Actions Over $10,000.*
Civil Records: Access: Phone, mail, in person. Both court and visitors may perform in person searches. No search fee. Court makes copy: $.15 per page. Required to search: name, years to search. Civil cases indexed by defendant, plaintiff. Civil records on computer from 1984, on index prior to 1984. Archived at Record Center, 401-277-3249. Phone requests taken only after 3PM. Mail turnaround time 1 week.
Criminal Records: Access: Mail, in person, online. Both court and visitors may perform in person searches. No search fee. Court makes copy: $.15 per page. Required to search: name, years to search; also helpful: DOB. Criminal records on computer from 1984, on index prior to 1984. Archived at Record Center, 401-277-3249. Access criminal records free at http://courtconnect.courts.state.ri.us as an informational service only; should not be relied upon as official court record. Mail turnaround time 1 week.
General Information: Public terminal goes back to 1984. No confidential or sealed records released. Will fax documents to local or toll free line. Certification fee: $3.00. Payee: Washington Superior Court. Personal checks accepted. Prepayment and SASE required.

4th District Court 4800 Towerhill Rd, Wakefield, RI 02879; phone: 401-782-4131; hours 8:30AM-4:30PM (EST). *Misdemeanor, Civil Actions Under $10,000, Eviction, Small Claims.*
Civil Records: Access: In person only. Visitors must perform in person searches themselves. Court makes copy: $.15 per page. Required to search: name, years to search. Civil cases indexed by defendant, plaintiff. Civil records on index cards, small claims indexed by plaintiff only.
Criminal Records: Access: In person, online. Visitors must perform in person searches themselves. Court makes copy: $.15 per page. Required to search: name, years to search, DOB. Criminal records available on computer beginning in 1996. Free internet access at http://courtconnect.courts.state.ri.us as an informational service only; should not be relied upon as official court record.
General Information: Public terminal has only criminal records back to 1996. No family court records released. Certification fee: $3.00. Payee:

Court Clerk. Visa/MC, money orders accepted. Personal checks not accepted. Prepayment required.

Charlestown Town Hall 4540 S County Tr, Charlestown, RI 02813; phone: 401-364-1200; fax: 401-364-1238; hours 8:30AM-4:30PM (EST). *Probate.*
Note: Nothing done on county level. Each city/town has their own Probate Court. Court first Tuesday of the month at 9:30AM.

Exeter Town Hall 675 Ten Rod Rd, Exeter, RI 02822; phone: 401-294-3891 (295-7500); fax: 401-295-1248; hours 9AM-4PM (EST). *Probate.*
Note: Probate Court held fourth Monday monthly at 2:00 PM.

Hopkinton Town Hall 1 Town House Rd, Hopkinton, RI 02833; phone: 401-377-7777; fax: 401-377-7788; hours 8:30AM-4:30PM or by appointment (EST). *Probate.*
Note: Civil cases etc heard in County Courthouse, not Town.

Narragansett Town Hall 25 5th Ave, Narragansett, RI 02882; phone: 401-782-0621; 401-789-1044 X621; fax: 401-783-9637; hours 8:30AM-4:30PM (EST). *Probate.*

New Shoreham Town Hall 16 Old Town Rd, PO Drawer 220, Block Island, RI 02807; phone: 401-466-3200; fax: 401-466-3219; hours 9AM-3PM (EST). *Probate.*

North Kingstown Town Hall 80 Boston Neck Rd, North Kingstown, RI 02852-5762; phone: 401-294-3331; probate phone: 401-294-3331 x122; fax: 401-294-2437; hours 8:30AM-4:30PM (EST). *Probate.*
www.northkingstown.org

Richmond Town Hall 5 Richmond Townhouse Rd, Wyoming, RI 02898; phone: 401-539-9000 x9; fax: 401-539-1089; hours 8:30AM-4PM (EST). *Probate.*

South Kingstown Town Hall 180 High St, Wakefield, RI 02879; phone: 401-789-9331; fax: 401-789-5280; hours 8:30AM-4:30PM (EST). *Probate.*

Westerly Town Hall 45 Broad St, Westerly, RI 02891; phone: 401-348-2500; fax: 401-348-2571; hours 8:30AM-4:30PM (EST). *Probate.*
Note: This court also handles ordinance violations.

Rhode Island Recording Offices

ORGANIZATION: 5 counties and 39 towns, 39 recording offices. The recording officer is Town/City Clerk (Recorder of Deeds). The Town/City Clerk usually also serves as the Recorder of Deeds. There is no county administration in Rhode Island that handles recording. The entire state is in the Eastern Time Zone (EST). Be aware that the recordings in the counties of Bristol, Newport, and Providence can relate to property located in other cities/ towns even though each of these three cities bears the same name as the county.

Towns will not perform real estate searches. Copy fees are usually $1.50 per page. Certification usually costs $3.00 per document.

REAL ESTATE RECORDS: Towns will not perform real estate searches. Copy fees are usually $1.50 per page. Certification usually costs $3.00 per document.

UCC RECORDS: Financing statements are filed at the state level, except for farm related and real estate related collateral, which are filed with the Town/City Clerk. Most recording offices will not perform UCC searches. Use search request form UCC-11. Copy fees are usually $1.50 per page. Certification usually costs $3.00 per document.

TAX LIEN RECORDS: All federal and state tax liens on personal property and on real property are filed with the Recorder of Deeds. Towns will not perform tax lien searches.

OTHER LIENS: Mechanics, municipal, lis pendens.

ONLINE ACCESS: A private vendor has placed on the Internet the assessor records from a number of towns. Visit http://www.visionappraisal.com/databases/ri/index.htm

Barrington Town

Town Clerk, 283 County Rd; Town Hall, Barrington, RI 02806. 401-247-1900; fax-401-247-3765; hours: 8:30AM-4:30PM.
All records in one index. Records indexed on computer back to 1/1984. Only the public may search. Copy fee $1.50 per page. Cert fee- $3.00 per cert plus copy fee. Payee- Town of Barrington. **Other phones:** Treasurer- x2; Appraiser/Auditor- 401-247-1900; Elections- x4; Vital Records- x4. **Property tax/Assessor-** same address as above. 401-247-1900 x3.

Bristol Town

Recorder of Deeds, 10 Court St; Town Hall, Bristol, RI 02809. 401-253-7000, R/E recording phone-401-253-7000 x136; fax-401-253-3080; hours: 8:30AM-4PM.
All records in one index. Records indexed on a public use terminal back to 1991. Only the public may search. Copy fee $1.50 per page. Cert fee- $3.00 per cert includes copy fee. Payee- Town of Bristol. **Other phones:** Treasurer- 401-253-7000 x116; Elections- 401-253-7000 x135; Vital Records- 401-253-7000 x121. **Property tax/Assessor-** same address as above. 401-253-7000 x138.

Burrillville Town

Town Clerk, 105 Harrisville Main St; Town Hall, Harrisville, RI 02830-1499. 401-568-4300, R/E recording phone-401-568-4300 x113; fax-401-568-0490; hours: 8:30AM-4:30PM M-W; 8:30AM-7PM Th; 8:30AM-12:30PM F. www.burrillville.org
Only the public may search. Copy fee $1.50 per page. Cert fee- $3.00 per cert plus copy fee. Payee- Burrillville Town Clerk. **Online access to Property, Tax Assessor records:** Access to property records is free at www.opaldata.com/crcdb/burrillville.htm. **Other phones:** Treasurer- 401-568-4300; Appraiser/Auditor- 401-568-4300; Elections- 401-568-4300; Vital Records- 401-568-4300 x111. **Property tax/Assessor-** 401-568-4300.

Central Falls City

City Clerk, 580 Broad St; City Hall, Central Falls, RI 02863. 401-727-7400; fax-401-727-7406; hours: 8:30AM-4:30PM. www.centralfallsri.us
All records in one index. Records indexed on computer back to 1988. Only the public may search. Copy fee $1.00 per page. Cert fee- $3.00 per page plus copy fee. Payee- City of Central Falls. **Online access to Property, Assessor records:** Access to city property data is free at http://data.visionappraisal.com/CentralFallsRI/. Does not require a username & password. Simply click on link. **Other phones:** Treasurer- 401-727-7470; Elections- 401-727-7450; Vital Records- 401-727-7400. **Property tax/Assessor-** 401-727-7430.

Charlestown Town

Town Clerk, 4540 South County Trail, Charlestown, RI 02813. 401-364-1200; fax-401-364-1238; hours: 8:30AM-4:30PM. www.charlestownri.org
All records in one index. Records indexed on a public use terminal back to 1945. Only the public may search. Copy fee $1.50 per page. Cert fee- $3.00 per doc, plus copy fee. Payee- Town of Charlestown. **Online access to Assessor records:** Search town assessor database at http://data.visionappraisal.com/CharlestownRI/. Does not require a username & password. Simply click on link. **Other phones:** Treasurer- 401-364-1235; Elections- 401-364-1200; Vital Records- 401-364-1200. **Property tax/Assessor-** same address as above. 401-364-1233.

Coventry Town

Town Clerk, 1670 Flat River Rd; Town Hall, Coventry, RI 02816-8911. 401-822-9174; fax-401-822-9132;
All records in one index. Record index not computerized. Only the public may search. Copy fee $1.00 per page. Cert fee- $3.00 per doc plus $1.50 per page. **Other phones:** Treasurer- 401-822-9155; Elections- 401-822-9150; Vital Records- 401-822-9170. **Property tax/Assessor-** 401-822-9163.

Cranston City

City Clerk, 869 Park Ave; City Hall, Cranston, RI 02910. 401-461-1000 x3130, R/E recording phone-401-780-3130; fax-401-780-3165; hours: 8:30AM-4:30PM. www.cranstonri.com/
All records in one index. Records indexed on a public use terminal back to 1986. Office will perform a UCC search but public must search other records themselves. UCC search per debtor name- $5.00. Copy fee $1.50 per page. Cert fee- $3.00 per cert plus copy fee. Payee- City of Cranston. **Online access to Assessor, Property records:** Records on the city assessor database are online at http://data.visionappraisal.com/CranstonRI/. Free registration is required for full data. **Other phones:** Treasurer- 401-780-3143; Elections- 401-780-3126; Vital Records- 401-780-3238. **Property tax/Assessor-** same address as above. 401-461-1000 x3181.

Cumberland Town

Town Clerk, PO Box 7, Cumberland, RI 02864-0808. 401-728-2400, R/E recording phone-401-728-2400 x35; fax-401-724-1103; hours: 8:30AM-4:30PM. www.cumberlandri.org
Only the public may search. Copy fee $1.00 per page. Cert fee- $3.00 per cert plus copy fee. Payee- Town of Cumberland. **Online access to Property, Assessor records:** Access to property data is free at www.opaldata.com/crcdb/cumberland.htm. **Other phones:** Treasurer- 401-728-2400 x20; Appraiser/Auditor- 401-728-2400 x15; Elections- 401-728-2400 x31; Vital Records- 401-728-2400 x33. **Property tax/Assessor-** 401-728-2400 x13.

East Greenwich Town

Town Clerk, PO Box 111, East Greenwich, RI 02818. 401-886-8603, R/E recording phone-401-886-8602; fax-401-886-8625; hours: 8:30AM-4:30PM. www.eastgreenwichri.com
All records in one index. Records indexed on computer back to 1969. Only the public may search. Copy fee $1.50 per page. Cert fee- $3.00 per doc plus copy fee. Payee- East Greenwich Town Clerk/Recorder of Deeds. **Online access to Property records:** Limited Finance Dept. property sales information is listed at www.eastgreenwichri.com/finance.htm. See bottom of web page. **Other phones:** Treasurer- 401-886-8608; Elections- 401-886-8603; Vital Records- 401-886-

8602. **Property tax/Assessor-** same address as above. 401-886-8614.

East Providence City

City Clerk, 145 Taunton Ave; City Hall, East Providence, RI 02914. 401-435-7500, R/E recording phone-401-435-7594; fax-401-435-4630; hours: 8AM-3:30PM.
www.eastprovidenceri.net/citygov/cityclerk.php
All records in one index. Records indexed on a public use terminal back to 1981. Only the public may search. Copy fee $1.00 per page. Cert fee- $3.00 per doc plus copy fee. Payee- City of East Providence. **Online access to Assessor, Property records:** Assess to Town property data is free at http://data.visionappraisal.com/EastProvidenceRI/. Does not require a username & password. Simply click on link. **Other phones:** Treasurer- 401-435-7560; Elections- 401-435-7503; Vital Records- 401-435-7596. **Property tax/Assessor-** same address as above. 401-435-7574.

Exeter Town

Deputy Town Clerk, 675 Ten Rod Rd; Town Hall, Exeter, RI 02822. 401-294-3891; fax-401-295-1248; hours: 9AM-4PM. www.town.exeter.ri.us
All records in one index. Only the public may search. Copy fee $1.50 per page. Cert fee- $3.00 per page plus copy fee. **Online access to Assessor, Property records:** Access may be available from a private company at www.opaldata.com/crcdb/exeter.htm. **Other phones:** Treasurer- 401-267-1024; Appraiser/Auditor- 401-294-5734; Elections- 401-294-2287; Vital Records- 401-294-3891. **Property tax/Assessor-** same address as above. 401-294-5734.

Foster Town

Town Clerk, 181 Howard Hill Rd; Town Hall, Foster, RI 02825-1227. 401-392-9200; fax-401-392-9201; hours: 9AM-3:30PM.
Separate indices to search include IHTL. Record index not computerized. Only the public may search. Copy fee $1.50 per page. Cert fee- $3.00 per cert plus copy fee. Payee- Town of Foster. **Other phones:** Treasurer- 401-392-9207; Elections- 401-392-9200; Vital Records- 401-392-9200. **Property tax/Assessor-** same address as above. 401-392-9202.

Glocester Town

Town Clerk, PO Drawer B, Glocester/ Chepachet, RI 02814-0702. 401-568-6206, R/E recording phone-401-568-6206x1; fax-401-568-5850; hours: 8AM-4:30PM. www.glocesterri.org/townclerk.htm
All records in one index. Records indexed on computer. Only the public may search. Copy fee $1.50 per page. Cert fee- $3.00 per doc, plus copy fee. Payee- Town of Glocester. **Other phones:** Treasurer- 401-568-6206x5; Elections- 401-568-6206x1; Vital Records- 401-568-6206x1; Tax Collector- 401-568-6206x4. **Property tax/Assessor-** same address as above. 401-568-6206x3.

Hopkinton Town

Town Clerk, 1 Town House Rd; Town Hall, Hopkinton, RI 02833. 401-377-7777; fax-401-377-7788; hours: 8:30AM-4:30PM. www.hopkintonri.org
Separate indices to search include plat maps. Records indexed on a public use terminal from to January 1, 1990 to present. Only the public may search. Copy fee $1.50 per page. Cert fee- $3.00 per cert plus $1.50 per page. Payee- Town of Hopkinton. **Online access to Property, Assessor records:** Access to town property data is free at www.opaldata.com/crcdb/hopkinton.htm. **Other phones:** Treasurer- 401-377-7766; Elections- 401-377-7777; Vital Records- 401-377-7777. **Property tax/Assessor-** same address as above. 401-377-7780.

Jamestown Town

Town Clerk, 93 Narragansett Ave; Town Hall, Jamestown, RI 02835. 401-423-7200; fax-401-423-7230; hours: 8AM-4:30PM. www.jamestownri.net
All records in one index. Records indexed on a public use terminal back to 1967. Only the public may search. Copy fee $1.50 per page; self serve $.50. Cert fee- $3.00 per page plus clerk's copy fee. **Other phones:** Treasurer- 401-423-7220; Appraiser/Auditor- 401-423-7200; Elections- 401-423-7200; Vital Records- 401-423-7200. **Property tax/Assessor-** same address as above. 401-423-7200.

Johnston Town

Town Clerk, 1385 Hartford Ave; Town Hall, Johnston, RI 02919. 401-351-6618; fax-401-553-8835; hours: 8:30AM-4:30PM. www.johnston-ri.com
All records in one index. Records indexed on a public use terminal back to 1984. Office personnel or visitors may perform searches. Search fee varies. Will not search real estate records. Copy fee $1.00 per page. Cert fee- $3.00 per doc plus copy fee. Payee- Town of Johnston. **Online access to Assessor, Property records:** Assess to Town property data is free at http://data.visionappraisal.com/JohnstonRI/. Free registration for full data. **Other phones:** Treasurer- 401-351-6618; Appraiser/Auditor- 401-351-6618; Elections- 401-351-6618; Vital Records- 401-351-6618. **Property tax/Assessor-** same address as above. 401-351-6618.

Lincoln Town

Town Clerk, 100 Old River Rd; PO Box 100, Lincoln, RI 02865. 401-333-1100, R/E recording phone-401-333-8452; fax-401-333-3648; hours: 9AM-4:30PM. www.lincolnri.net
Only the public may search. Copy fee $1.50 per page. Cert fee- $3.00 per instrument. Payee- Town of Lincoln. **Online access to Assessor records:** Access to town property data is available free at www.opaldata.com/crcdb/lincoln.htm. **Other phones:** Treasurer- 401-333-8441; Appraiser/Auditor- 401-333-1100; Elections- 401-333-1140; Vital Records- 401-333-8452. **Property tax/Assessor-** same address as above. 401-333-8449.

Little Compton Town

Town Clerk, PO Box 226, Little Compton, RI 02837-0226. 401-635-4400; fax-401-635-2470; hours: 8AM-4PM.
Separate indices to search include liens, attachments. Record index not computerized. Only the public may search. Copy fee $1.50 per page. Cert fee- $3.00 per instrument plus copy fee. Payee- Town of Little Compton. **Other phones:** Treasurer- 401-635-4219; Elections- 401-635-4400; Vital Records- 401-635-4400. **Property tax/Assessor-** same address as above. 401-635-4509.

Middletown Town

Town Clerk, 350 E. Main Rd; Town Hall, Middletown, RI 02842. 401-847-0009; fax-401-848-0500; hours: 8AM-5PM. www.ci.middletown.ri.us
All records in one index. Records indexed on a public use terminal back to 7/1/1984. Only the public may search. Copy fee $1.50 per page. Cert fee- $3.00 per doc + $1.50 per pages of doc. Payee- Town of Middletown. **Online access to Assessor, Property records:** Records on the town assessor database are online at http://data.visionappraisal.com/MiddletownRI/. Free registration for full data. **Other phones:** Treasurer- 401-846-4473; Elections- 401-849-5540; Vital Records- 401-847-0009. **Property tax/Assessor-** same address as above. 401-847-7300.

Narragansett Town

Town Clerk, 25 Fifth Ave; Town Hall, Narragansett, RI 02882. 401-789-1044, R/E recording phone-401-789-1044 x623; fax-401-783-9637; hours: 8:30AM-4:30PM. www.narragansettri.com

Separate indices to search include books. Records indexed on a public use terminal back to 1985. Only the public may search. Copy fee $1.00 per page. R/E record copy- $1.50 per page. Cert fee- $3.00 per cert plus copy fee. Payee- Town of Narragansett. **Online access to Assessor, Property, Sex Offender records:** Records on the town assessor database are online at http://data.visionappraisal.com/NarragansettRI/. Free registration is required for full data. Also, sex offender site at www.paroleboard.ri.gov/L3_offenders/listings.htm. **Other phones:** Treasurer- 401-782-0601; Elections- 401-782-0625; Vital Records- 401-782-0624. **Property tax/Assessor-** same address as above. 401-789-1044 x236.

New Shoreham Town

Town Clerk, PO Drawer 220, Block Island, RI 02807. 401-466-3200; fax-401-466-3219; hours: 9AM-3PM.
All records in one index. Only the public may search. Copy fee $1.50 per page. Cert fee- $3.00 plus copy fee. Payee- Town of New Shoreham. **Online access to Assessor, Property records:** Assess to Town property data is free at http://data.visionappraisal.com/NewShorehamRI/. Does not require username & password. Simply click on link. **Other phones:** Treasurer- 401-466-3208; Appraiser/Auditor- 401-466-3208; Elections- 401-466-3200; Vital Records- 401-466-3200. **Property tax/Assessor-** PO Box 220, Block Island, RI 02807; 401-466-3217.

Newport City

Recorder of Deeds, 43 Broadway; City Hall, Newport, RI 02840-2798. 401-845-5334; fax-401-849-8757; hours: 8:30AM-4:30PM (Recording Hours 8:30AM-3:30PM). www.cityofnewport.com
All records in one index. Records indexed on a public use terminal back to 1981. Only the public may search. Copy fee $1.50 per page. Cert fee- $3.00 per cert plus copy fee. Payee- City of Newport. **Online access to Assessor, Property records:** Access is via a private company at http://data.visionappraisal.com/NewportRI/. Free registration is required for full data. **Other phones:** Elections- 401-845-5385 or 5383 or 5384 or 5386; Vital Records- 401-845-5342 or 5340 or 5341 or 5351 or 5349; Timeshare Request:- 401-845-5338. **Property tax/Assessor-** 401-845-5365 or 5364.

North Kingstown Town

Town Clerk, 80 Boston Neck Rd; Town Hall, North Kingstown, RI 02852. 401-294-3331, R/E recording phone-401-294-3331 x125; hours: 8:30AM - 4:30PM. www.northkingstown.org
Separate indices to search include grantor/grantee. Only the public may search. Copy fee $1.50 per page. Cert fee- $3.00 per doc plus copy fee. Payee- Town of N Kingstown. **Online access to Assessor, Property records:** Access is via a private company at http://data.visionappraisal.com/NorthkingstownRI/. Free registration is required for full data. **Other phones:** Treasurer- 401-294-3331 x148; Elections- 401-294-3331 x129; Vital Records- 401-294-3331 x122. **Property tax/Assessor-** same address as above. 401-294-3331 x110.

North Providence Town

Town Clerk, 2000 Smith St; Town Hall, North Providence, RI 02911. 401-232-0900, R/E recording phone-401-232-0900 x213-214; fax-401-233-1409; hours: 8:30AM-4:30PM (Summer hours 8:30 AM-4PM).
Only the public may search. Copy fee $2.00, if tax lien or real estate $1.00 per page. Cert fee- $3.00 per cert plus copy fee. Payee- Town of North Providence. **Other phones:** Treasurer- 401-232-0900 x218; Elections- 401-232-0900 x241-235; Vital Records- 401-232-0900 x213-214. **Property tax/Assessor-** 401-232-0900 x209.

North Smithfield Town

Town Clerk, 575 Smithfield Rd; Town Hall, North Smithfield, RI 02896. 401-767-2200, R/E recording phone-401-767-2200 x1; fax-401-356-4057; hours: 8AM-4PM M-W; 8AM-7PM Th; 8AM-N Fri.
All records in one index. Only the public may search. Copy fee $1.50 per page. Cert fee- $3.00 per doc plus copy fee. Payee- Town of North Smithfield. **Online access to Assessor, Property records:** Access is via a private company at http://data.visionappraisal.com/NorthsmithfieldRI/. Free registration is required to view full data. **Other phones:** Treasurer- 401-767-2202; Elections- 401-767-2200 x216; Vital Records- 401-767-2200 x216. **Property tax/Assessor-** same address as above. 401-767-2200.

Pawtucket City

City Clerk, 137 Roosevelt Ave; City Hall, Pawtucket, RI 02860. 401-728-0500, R/E recording phone-401-728-0500 x262; fax-401-728-8932; hours: 8:30AM-3:30PM. www.pawtucketri.com
All records in one index. Only the public may search. Copy fee $1.50 per page. Cert fee- $3.00 per doc includes copies. Payee- City of Pawtucket. **Online access to Recording, Deed, Real Estate records:** Access real estate data free at http://209.113.149.21/alis/ww400r.pgm. Online indices go back to 1970. **Other phones:** Treasurer- 401-728-0500 x244; Elections- 401-728-0500 x207; Vital Records- 401-728-0500 x224. **Property tax/Assessor-** same address as above. 401-728-0500 x338.

Portsmouth Town

Town Clerk, 2200 East main St, Portsmouth, RI 02871. 401-683-2101; hours: Recording hours 9AM-3:45PM. www.portsmouthri.com/frames.htm
Separate indices to search. Records indexed 1950 to 1985 on cards, computerized since. Will not search real estate records. Will not search UCC records or tax liens. Copy fee $1.50 per page. Cert fee- $3.00 per certification. Payee- Town of Portsmouth. **Online access to Assessor, Property records:** Search town assessor database at http://data.visionappraisal.com/PortsmouthRI/. Free registration for full data. **Other phones:** Treasurer- 401-683-9118; Appraiser/Auditor- 401-683-1536; Elections- 401-683-3157; Vital Records- 401-683-2101. **Property tax/Assessor-** 401-683-1536.

Providence City

City Clerk, 25 Dorrance St; City Hall, Providence, RI 02903. 401-421-7740 x312; hours: 8:30AM-3:30PM. Separate indices to search include grantor/grantee, UCC. Records indexed on computer. Only the public may search. They will give limited information by phone. Copy fee $2.00, if tax lien or real estate $1.50 per page. Cert fee- $3.00 per cert plus copy fee. Payee- Providence City Recorder of Deeds. **Property tax/Assessor-** City Hall, Rm 208, Providence, RI 02903; 401-421-5900.

Richmond Town

Town Clerk, 5 Richmond Townhouse Rd.; Town Hall, Wyoming, RI 02898. 401-539-9000 x9; fax-401-539-1089; hours: 9AM-4PM. www.richmondri.com
All records in one index. Records indexed on a public use terminal back to 1985. Only the public may search. Copy fee $1.50 per page. Cert fee- $3.00 per doc plus copy fee. Payee- Town of Richmond. **Online access to Assessor records:** Search town assessor database at http://data.visionappraisal.com/RichmondRI/. Does not require a username & password. Simply click on link. **Other phones:** Treasurer- 401-539-9000 x8; Elections- 401-539-9000 x9; Vital Records- 401-539-9000 x9. **Property tax/Assessor-** same address as above. 401-539-9000 x7.

Scituate Town

Town Clerk, PO Box 328, North Scituate, RI 02857-0328. 401-647-2822; fax-401-647-7220; hours: 8:30AM-4PM. www.scituateri.org/townhall.htm
All records in one index. Records indexed on a public use terminal back to 1981. Only the public may search. Copy fee $1.50 per page. Cert fee- $3.00 1st pg, $1.50 each add'l. Payee- Town of Scituate. **Online access to Property, Assessor records:** Access to town property data is free at www.opaldata.com/crcdb/scituate.htm. **Other phones:** Treasurer- 401-647-2547. **Property tax/Assessor-** same address as above. 401-647-2919.

Smithfield Town

Town Clerk, 64 Farnum Pike; Town Hall, Esmond, RI 02917. 401-233-1000; fax-401-232-7244; hours: 8:30-4:30PM. www.smithfieldri.com
Index: Indices separated by year. Records indexed on a public use terminal back to 2004. Only the public may search. Copy fee $1.50 1st page, $1.00 per add'l. Cert fee- $3.00 per instrument plus copy fee. Payee- Town of Smithfield. **Online access to Property, Assessor records:** Access to town property data is free at http://data.visionappraisal.com/SmithfieldRI/. Free registration for full data. **Other phones:** Treasurer- 401-233-1005; Elections- 401-233-1000; Vital Records- 401-233-1000. **Property tax/Assessor-** same address as above. 401-233-1014.

South Kingstown Town

Town Clerk, PO Box 31, Wakefield, RI 02880. 401-789-9331, R/E recording phone-401-789-9331 x234; fax-401-788-9792; hours: 8:30AM-4:30PM, recording to 4PM. www.southkingstownri.com
All records in one index. Records indexed on a public use terminal back to 1980. Only the public may search. Copy fee $1.50 per page. Cert fee- $3.00 per cert plus copy fee. Payee- Town of South Kingstown. **Online access to Real Estate, Assessor records:** Access to the property values database is free at www.southkingstownri.com/code/propvalues_search.cfm. Also, assess to Town property data is free online at http://data.visionappraisal.com/SouthKingstownRI/. Does not require a username & password. Simply click on link. **Other phones:** Treasurer- 401-789-9331 x209; Elections- 401-789-9331 x231; Vital Records- 401-789-9331 x230. **Property tax/Assessor-** same address as above. 401-789-9331 x220.

Tiverton Town

Town Clerk, 343 Highland Rd; Town Hall, Tiverton, RI 02878. 401-625-6700, R/E recording phone-401-625-6703; fax-401-625-6705; hours: 8:30AM-4PM. Separate indices to search. Records indexed on a public use terminal back to 1984. Only the public may search. Copy fee $1.50 per page. Cert fee- $3.00 per cert plus copy fee. Payee- Town of Tiverton. **Other phones:** Treasurer- 401-625-5323; Elections- 401-625-6703; Vital Records- 401-625-6703. **Property tax/Assessor-** same address as above. 401-625-5609.

Warren Town

Town Clerk, 514 Main St; Town Hall, Warren, RI 02885. 401-245-7340; fax-401-245-7421; hours: 9AM-4PM.
Records indexed on a public use terminal back to 1984. Only the public may search. Copy fee $.15 per page. R/E or tax lien copy- $1.50 per page. Cert fee- $3.00 per doc plus copy fee. Payee- Town of Warren. **Other phones:** Treasurer- 401-245-7341; Appraiser/Auditor- 401-245-7342; Elections- 401-245-7340; Vital Records- 401-245-7340; Town Manager- 401-245-7554. **Property tax/Assessor-** same address as above. 401-245-7342.

Warwick City

City Clerk, 3275 Post Rd, Warwick, RI 02886. 401-738-2000, R/E recording phone-401-738-2000 x6218; fax-401-738-6639; hours: 8:30AM-4PM. www.warwickri.com
All records in one index. Records indexed on a public use terminal back to 1/1983. Office will perform a UCC search but public must search other records themselves. Search fee $5.00 per request. Copy fee $1.50 per page. Cert fee- $3.00 per cert + $1.50 per page. **Online access to Tax Assessor records:** Access found at www.warwickri.gov. **Other phones:** Treasurer- 401-738-2000 x6228; Elections- 401-738-2000 x6223; Vital Records- 401-738-2000 x6215. **Property tax/Assessor-** same address as above. 401-738-2000 x6016.

West Greenwich Town

Town Clerk, 280 Victory Highway; Town Hall, West Greenwich, RI 02817. 401-397-5016; fax-401-392-3805; hours: 9AM-4PM M-F; 7-9PM M.
Only the public may search. Cert fee- $4.50. Payee- West Greenwich Town Clerk. **Property tax/Assessor-** 401-397-5016 x3.

West Warwick Town

Town Clerk, 1170 Main St; Town Hall, West Warwick, RI 02893-4829. 401-822-9201; fax-401-822-9266; hours: 8:30AM-4:30PM. www.westwarwickri.org
All records in one index. Records indexed on computer back to 1967. Only the public may search. Copy fee $.15 per page. R/E or tax lien copy- $1.50 per page. Cert fee- $3.00 per doc plus copy fee. Payee- Town of West Warwick. **Other phones:** Treasurer- 401-822-9216; Elections- 401-822-9201; Vital Records- 401-822-9201. **Property tax/Assessor-** same address as above. 401-822-9208.

Westerly Town

Town Clerk, 45 Broad St; Town Hall, Westerly, RI 02891. 401-348-2500; fax-401-348-2571; hours: 8:30AM-4:30PM M-F.
All records in one index. Only the public may search. Copy fee $1.50 per page. Cert fee- $3.00 per doc plus copy fee. Payee- Westerly Town Clerk. **Other phones:** Treasurer- 401-348-2500; Appraiser/Auditor- 401-348-2500; Elections- 401-348-2500; Vital Records- 401-348-2500. **Property tax/Assessor-** 45 Broad St, Westerly, RI 02891; 401-348-2500.

Woonsocket City

Town Clerk, 169 Main St; City Hall, Woonsocket, RI 02895. 401-762-6400, R/E recording phone-401-767-9248; fax-401-765-4569; hours: 8:30AM-4PM. www.ci.woonsocket.ri.us/
All records in one index. Record index not computerized. Only the public may search. Copy fee $1.50 per page. Cert fee- $3.00 per doc plus copy fee. Payee- City Clerks Office. **Online access to Wanted Person records:** Access wanted persons list free at www.woonsocketpolice.com/wanted.htm. **Other phones:** Treasurer- 401-767-9280; Elections- 401-767-9224; Vital Records- 401-767-8875. **Property tax/Assessor-** same address as above. 401-762-6400 x272.

Rhode Island County Locator

You will usually be able to find the city name in the City/County Cross Reference below. In that case, it is a simple matter to determine the county from the cross reference. However, only the official US Postal Service city names are included in this index. There are an additional 40,000 place names that people use in their addresses. Therefore, we have also included a ZIP/City Cross Reference immediately following the City/County Cross Reference.

If you know the ZIP Code but the city name does not appear in the City/County Cross Reference index, look up the ZIP Code in the ZIP/City Cross Reference, find the city name, then look up the city name in the City/County Cross Reference. For example, you want to know the county for an address of Menands, NY 12204. There is no "Menands" in the City/County Cross Reference. The ZIP/City Cross Reference shows that ZIP Codes 12201-12288 are for the city of Albany. Looking back in the City/County Cross Reference, Albany is in Albany County.

Rhode Island City/County Cross Reference

ADAMSVILLE Newport
ALBION Providence
ASHAWAY Washington
BARRINGTON Bristol
BLOCK ISLAND Washington
BRADFORD Washington
BRISTOL Bristol
CAROLINA Washington
CENTRAL FALLS Providence
CHARLESTOWN Washington
CHEPACHET Providence
CLAYVILLE Providence
COVENTRY Kent
CRANSTON Providence
CUMBERLAND Providence
EAST GREENWICH Kent
EAST PROVIDENCE Providence
ESCOHEAG Washington

EXETER Washington
FISKEVILLE Providence
FORESTDALE Providence
FOSTER Providence
GLENDALE Providence
GREENE Kent
GREENVILLE Providence
HARMONY Providence
HARRISVILLE Providence
HOPE Providence
HOPE VALLEY Washington
HOPKINTON Washington
JAMESTOWN Newport
JOHNSTON Providence
KENYON Washington
KINGSTON Washington
LINCOLN Providence
LITTLE COMPTON Newport

MANVILLE Providence
MAPLEVILLE Providence
MIDDLETOWN Newport
NARRAGANSETT Washington
NEWPORT Newport
NORTH KINGSTOWN Washington
NORTH PROVIDENCE Providence
NORTH SCITUATE Providence
NORTH SMITHFIELD Providence
OAKLAND Providence
PASCOAG Providence
PAWTUCKET Providence
PEACE DALE Washington
PORTSMOUTH Newport
PROVIDENCE Providence
PRUDENCE ISLAND Bristol
RIVERSIDE Providence
ROCKVILLE Washington

RUMFORD Providence
SAUNDERSTOWN Washington
SHANNOCK Washington
SLATERSVILLE Providence
SLOCUM Washington
SMITHFIELD Providence
TIVERTON Newport
WAKEFIELD Washington
WARREN Bristol
WARWICK Kent
WEST GREENWICH Kent
WEST KINGSTON Washington
WEST WARWICK Kent
WESTERLY Washington
WOOD RIVER JUNCTION Washington
WOONSOCKET Providence
WYOMING Washington

Rhode Island ZIP/City Cross Reference

02801-02801 ADAMSVILLE
02802-02802 ALBION
02804-02804 ASHAWAY
02806-02806 BARRINGTON
02807-02807 BLOCK ISLAND
02808-02808 BRADFORD
02809-02809 BRISTOL
02812-02812 CAROLINA
02813-02813 CHARLESTOWN
02814-02814 CHEPACHET
02815-02815 CLAYVILLE
02816-02816 COVENTRY
02817-02817 WEST GREENWICH
02818-02818 EAST GREENWICH
02821-02821 ESCOHEAG
02822-02822 EXETER
02823-02823 FISKEVILLE
02824-02824 FORESTDALE
02825-02825 FOSTER
02826-02826 GLENDALE
02827-02827 GREENE
02828-02828 GREENVILLE
02829-02829 HARMONY
02830-02830 HARRISVILLE
02831-02831 HOPE
02832-02832 HOPE VALLEY
02833-02833 HOPKINTON
02835-02835 JAMESTOWN
02836-02836 KENYON
02837-02837 LITTLE COMPTON
02838-02838 MANVILLE
02839-02839 MAPLEVILLE
02840-02841 NEWPORT
02842-02842 MIDDLETOWN
02852-02854 NORTH KINGSTOWN
02857-02857 NORTH SCITUATE
02858-02858 OAKLAND
02859-02859 PASCOAG

02860-02862 PAWTUCKET
02863-02863 CENTRAL FALLS
02864-02864 CUMBERLAND
02865-02865 LINCOLN
02871-02871 PORTSMOUTH
02872-02872 PRUDENCE ISLAND
02873-02873 ROCKVILLE
02874-02874 SAUNDERSTOWN
02875-02875 SHANNOCK
02876-02876 SLATERSVILLE
02877-02877 SLOCUM
02878-02878 TIVERTON
02879-02880 WAKEFIELD
02881-02881 KINGSTON
02882-02882 NARRAGANSETT
02883-02883 PEACE DALE
02885-02885 WARREN
02886-02889 WARWICK
02891-02891 WESTERLY
02892-02892 WEST KINGSTON
02893-02893 WEST WARWICK
02894-02894 WOOD RIVER JUNCTION
02895-02895 WOONSOCKET
02896-02896 NORTH SMITHFIELD
02898-02898 WYOMING
02900-02909 PROVIDENCE
02910-02910 CRANSTON
02911-02911 NORTH PROVIDENCE
02912-02912 PROVIDENCE
02914-02914 EAST PROVIDENCE
02915-02915 RIVERSIDE
02916-02916 RUMFORD
02917-02917 SMITHFIELD
02918-02918 PROVIDENCE
02919-02919 JOHNSTON
02920-02921 CRANSTON
02940-02940 PROVIDENCE

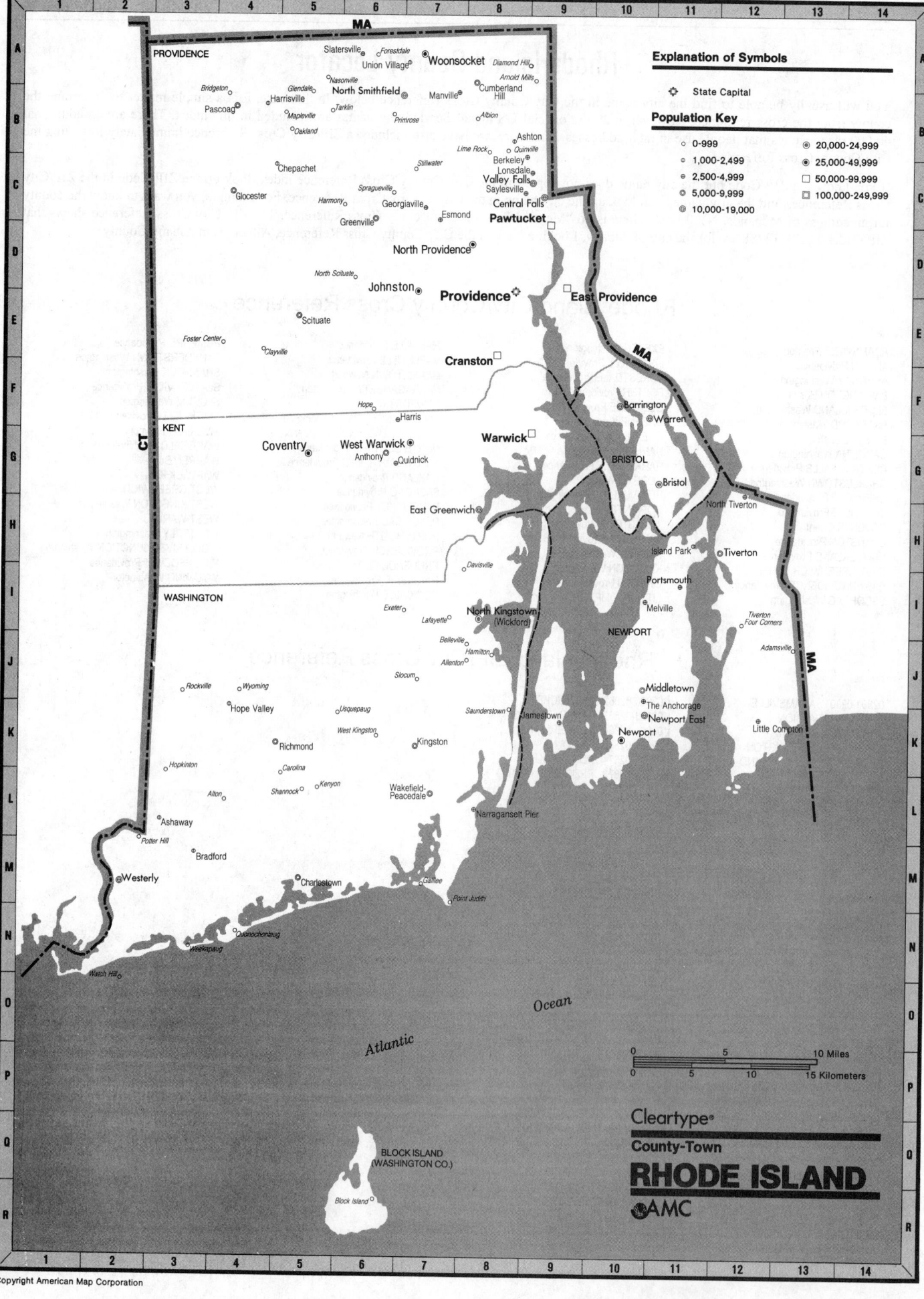

COUNTIES

(5 Counties)

Name of County	Population	Location on Map
BRISTOL	48,859	G-10
KENT	161,135	G-3
NEWPORT	87,194	I-10
PROVIDENCE	596,270	A-2
WASHINGTON	110,006	I-3
TOTAL	1,003,464	

CITIES AND TOWNS

Note: The first name is that of the city or town, second, that of the county in which it is located, then the population and location on the map.

Anthony, Kent G-6
• Ashaway, Washington, 1,584 .... L-3
Ashton, Providence B-8
• *Barrington, Bristol, 15,849* F-10
Berkeley, Providence B-8
• Bradford, Washington, 1,604 .... M-3
• *Bristol, Bristol, 21,625* G-11
Burrillville, Providence, 16,230 .... B-5
Central Falls, Providence, 17,637 .... C-9
▲ *Charlestown, Washington, 6,478* M-5
Chepachet, Providence C-4
▲ *Coventry, Kent, 31,083* G-4
Cranston, Providence, 76,060 .... E-8
Cumberland, Providence, 29,038 .... A-8
• Cumberland Hill, Providence, 6,379 .... A-8
▲ *East Greenwich, Kent, 11,865* H-7
East Providence, Providence, 50,380 ..... D-9
Esmond, Providence C-7
Exeter, Washington, 5,461 .... I-6
Foster, Providence, 4,316 .... E-3
Georgiaville, Providence C-7
▲ *Glocester, Providence, 9,227* C-4
• Greenville, Providence, 8,303 .... C-6
• Harrisville, Providence, 1,654 .... B-4
Harris, Kent F-6
• Hope Valley, Washington, 1,446 .... K-4
Hopkinton, Washington, 6,873 .... K-3
Island Park, Newport H-11
▲ *Jamestown, Newport, 4,999* J-9
▲ *Johnston, Providence, 26,542* D-7
• Kingston, Washington, 6,504 .... K-7
▲ *Lincoln, Providence, 18,045* C-8
▲ *Little Compton, Newport, 3,339* K-12
Lonsdale, Providence C-8
Manville, Providence B-7
• Melville, Newport, 4,426 .... I-10
Middletown, Newport J-10
Middletown, Newport, 19,460 .... K-11
Narragansett, Washington, 14,985 .... M-7
• Narragansett Pier, Washington, 3,721 ..... L-8
Newport, Newport, 28,227 .... K-10
• Newport East, Newport, 11,080 .... K-10
▲ *North Kingstown, Washington, 23,786* I-8
• *North Providence, Providence, 32,090* ... D-8
▲ *North Smithfield, Providence, 10,497* A-6
North Tiverton, Newport H-11
• Pascoag, Providence, 5,011 .... B-4
Pawtucket, Providence, 72,644 .... C-9
Portsmouth, Newport I-11
Portsmouth, Newport, 16,857 .... I-11
Providence, Providence, 160,728 .... D-8
Quidnick, Kent G-6
▲ *Richmond, Washington, 5,351* K-5
Saylesville, Providence C-8
▲ *Scituate, Providence, 9,796* E-6
Slatersville, Providence A-6
Smithfield, Providence, 19,163 .... C-7

South Kingstown, Washington, 24,631 .... K-6
The Anchorage, Newport J-10
Tiverton, Newport, 14,312 .... I-12
• Tiverton, Newport, 7,259 .... H-12
Union Village, Providence A-7
• Valley Falls, Providence, 11,175 .... C-9
• Wakefield-Peacedale, Washington,
  7,134 .... L-7
▲ *Warren, Bristol, 11,385* F-10
Warwick, Kent, 85,427 .... G-8
West Greenwich, Kent, 3,492 .... H-4
• *West Warwick, Kent, 29,268* G-7
• *Westerly, Washington, 16,477* M-2
Westerly, Washington, 21,605 .... N-2
Woonsocket, Providence, 43,877 .... A-7

Explanation of symbols: • – Census Designated Place (CDP)   • *italics* – Township shown which is also a CDP   *italics* – Townships (not shown on the map)
▲ *italics* – Townships (shown on the map)

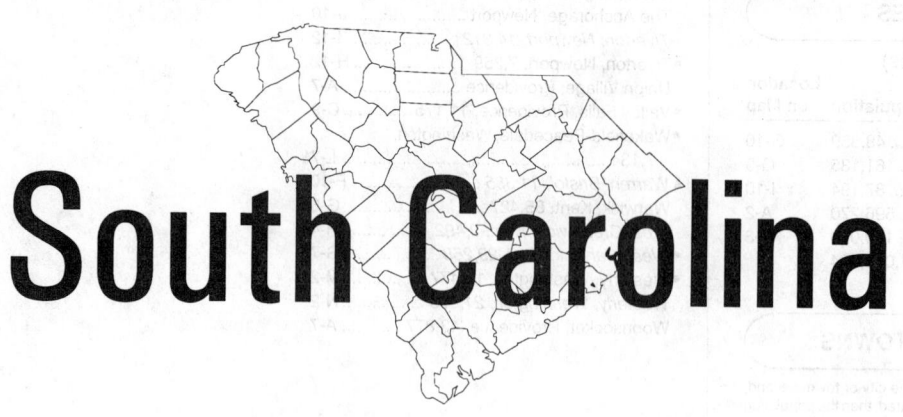

South Carolina

General Help Numbers:

Governor's Office
PO Box 12267
Columbia, SC 29211
www.state.sc.us/governor

803-734-2100
Fax 803-734-5167
8AM-6PM

Attorney General's Office
PO Box 11549
Columbia, SC 29211
www.scattorneygeneral.org

803-734-3970
Fax 803-734-4323
8:30AM-5:30PM

Legislative Records
1105 Pendleton St. Blatt Bldg. Rm 223
Columbia, SC 29201
www.scstatehouse.net

803-734-3179

9AM-5PM M-F

State Archives
8301 Parklane Rd
Columbia, SC 29223
www.state.sc.us/scdah

803-896-6100
Fax 803-896-6198
8:30AM-5PM M-F

State Specifics:

Capital:	**Columbia** **Richland County**
Time Zone:	**EST**
Number of Counties:	**46**
Population:	**4,198,068**
Web Site:	**Www.myscgov.com**

State Agencies

Criminal Records

South Carolina Law Enforcement Division (SLED), Criminal Records Section, PO Box 21398, Columbia, SC 29221 (Courier address: 4400 Broad River Rd, Columbia, SC 29210); 803-896-7043, 803-896-7022-Fax; 8:30AM-5PM.

www.sled.state.sc.us

Records are available from the 1960s. It takes 1 to 12 days before new records are available for inquiry. Records are indexed on inhouse computer. Records are normally destroyed after expunged, otherwise maintained indefinitely. 72% of all arrests in database have final dispositions recorded, 85% for those arrests within last 5 years.

Searching: Criminal records are open without restrictions. Include the following in your request—full name, any aliases, sex, race, and DOB. The SSN is helpful. 100% of the records are fingerprint supported. However, this agency will not do fingerprint searches. All records are released, including those without dispositions.

Access by: mail, in person, online.

Fee & Payment: The search fee is $25.00 per individual. The fee is $8.00 for non-profit organizations, pre-approval is required. Fee payee: SLED. Prepayment required. Business and company checks are accepted, personal checks are not. No credit cards accepted, except online.

Mail search: Turnaround time: 5 to 7 days. They will return by overnight delivery service if prepaid and materials provided. A SASE is requested.

In person search: Turnaround time is within minutes for three names or less.

Online search: SLED offers commercial access to criminal record history from 1960 forward on the website. Fees are $25.00 per screening or $8.00 if for a charitable organization. Credit card ordering accepted. Visit the website or call 803-896-7219 for details.

Statewide Court Records

Court Administration, 1015 Sumter St, 2nd Floor, Columbia, SC 29201; 803-734-1800, 803-734-1355-Fax; 8:30AM-5PM M-F.

www.sccourts.org

All trial court record access must be done at the local level.

Access by: online.

Online search: Appellate and Supreme Court opinions and calendars are available from www.sccourts.org/opinions/index.cfm. There is no online access to statewide trial court records.

Sexual Offender Registry

Sex Offender Registry, c/o SLED, PO Box 21398, Columbia, SC 29221 (Courier address: 4400 Broad River Rd, Columbia, SC 29210); 803-896-7043, 803-896-7022-Fax; 8:30AM-5PM.

www.sled.state.sc.us

Records are available from 1994 to present. It takes one hour or less before new records are available for inquiry. Records are normally destroyed after court order.

Searching: Include the following in your request-proper form. All requests are screened as to the age of the offender. Therefore, all requests must be on a state form, which can be downloaded from the Internet. The following data is not released: registrants under 17 unless as required by law.

Access by: mail, phone, online.

Fee & Payment: There is no fee unless ordered by a business then fee is $17.00. Fee payee: SLED Personal Checks are not accepted.

Mail search: Turnaround time: 5 to 7 days. They will return by overnight delivery service if prepaid and materials provided. A SASE is requested.

Phone search: Searching by telephone available.

Online search: Access is available from the website. Click on Sexual Offender Registry. Search by name or ZIP Code, county or city.

Incarceration Records

Department of Corrections, Inmate Records Branch, 4444 Broad River Rd, Columbia, SC 29221-1787; 803-896-8531, 877-846-3472 (Automated Information), 803-896-1217-Fax; 8AM-5PM.

www.state.sc.us/scdc

Records are available on current and former inmates. It takes 1 to 2 days before new records are available for inquiry.

Searching: Include the following in your request-provide full name, DOB, SSN. The SCDC number is helpful. Location, SCDC number, physical identifiers, conviction and sentencing information, FBI number, and release dates are provided.

Access by: mail, phone, online.

Fee & Payment: There is no search fee, but there is a copy fee of $.25 per page.

Mail search: Turnaround time: 1-2 weeks. A SASE is requested.

Phone search: Name searching available by phone.

Online search: The Inmate Search is found at http://sword.doc.state.sc.us/incarceratedInmateSearch/index.jsp or click on Inmate search at the main website.

Corporation, Trademarks/Servicemarks, Limited Partnerships, Limited Liability Companies, Limited Liability Partnerships

Corporation Division, Capitol Complex, PO Box 11350, Columbia, SC 29211 (Courier address: Edgar A. Brown Bldg, Room 525, 1205 Pendleton Street, Columbia, SC 29201); 803-734-2158, 803-734-1614-Fax; 8:30PM-5PM.

www.scsos.com

This office also handles not-for-profit entity records. Trademarks and service marks are not on the computer but are in this department.

Records are available from 1800's on. In house computer records are from 1985 on. Older records are stored at the State Archives. New records are available for inquiry immediately. Records are indexed on microfilm, inhouse computer.

Searching: This office will not release annual reports, officer names or director names. For that information, call the Dept of Revenue at 803-898-5769. Include the following in your request-full name of business. In addition to the articles of incorporation, corporation records include the following information: Prior (merged) names, Inactive and Reserved names. This agency will invoice SC lawyers, otherwise prepayment required.

Access by: mail, phone, in person, online.

Fee & Payment: No search fee, copy fee is $1.00 per page for the first page and $.50 per page for each additional. If record is to be certified, the fee is an additional $2.00. A Good Standing is $10.00. Fee payee: Secretary of State. Personal checks accepted. No credit cards accepted.

Mail search: Turnaround time: 1 to 2 days. A SASE is requested.

Phone search: No fee for telephone request. They will provide basic information only.

In person search: Information requests are available.

Online search: This free web-based program is called the Online Business Filings, the search page is at www.scsos.com/corp_search.htm. The database provides access to basic filing information about any entity filed with the office. Registered agents' names and addresses, dates of business filings and types of filings are all available. The database is updated every 48 hours.

Fictitious Name, Assumed Name, Trade Names

Records not maintained by a state level agency.

Records are found at the county level.

Annual Reports, Directors and Officers

Department of Revenue, Office Services/Records, Photocopy Section, Columbia, SC 29214; 803-898-5769, 803-898-5888-Fax; 8:30AM-5PM.

www.sctax.org/DOR/default.htm

Records are available from 1990 on. Current year records are kept in this office, previous record years are in storage. Records are indexed on inhouse computer, hard copy.

Searching: Information on partnerships and on taxes is not public. Include the following in your request-full name of business. They will give officers and registered agent information only if it appears on the annual report. Request forms can be downloaded from the website.

Access by: mail, fax, in person.

Fee & Payment: The fee is $2.63 which is on a per year basis for the annual reports. The annul report gives the director and officer names. Fee payee: South Carolina Department of Revenue. Prepayment required. Personal checks accepted. No credit cards accepted.

Mail search: Turnaround time: 1 week. A SASE is requested.

Fax search: Turnaround is usually in 1 day.

In person search: You may request information in person, but will not receive copies the same day.

Uniform Commercial Code

UCC Division, Secretary of State, PO Box 11350, Columbia, SC 29211 (Courier address: Edgar Brown Bldg, 1205 Pendelton St #525, Columbia, SC 29201); 803-734-1961, 803-734-1610-Fax; 8:30AM-5PM.

www.scsos.com/Uniform_Commercial_Code.htm

Effective March 1, 2004, all UCC filings received after October 27, 2003 are not available through Direct Access (online). Records must be requested directly from the UCC Search Division via mail, fax or email.

Records are available from 1968. Records are computerized since 1985.

Searching: The agency prefers UCC-11 forms (download form from web), but will still accept UCC-4 for in-state requests. All tax liens are filed at the county level. Include the following in your request-debtor name.

Access by: mail, fax, in person, online.

Fee & Payment: The search fee is $5.00. Copies are $2.00 for the first page, plus $1.00 for each page of attachments. Certification is $2.00 per copy. Fee payee: Secretary of State. Prepayment required. Personal checks accepted. No credit cards accepted.

Mail search: Turnaround time: 3 to 5 days. A SASE is requested.

Fax search: There is an additional $5.00 fee for faxing in and $10.00 fee for faxing out.

In person search: You can use their PC to look up records, but copies requested are still mailed days later.

Online search: Access index of records filed before 10/27/03 at www.scsos.com/uccsearch.htm. No. fee. Search by debtor name or number. Information on filings after that date must be obtained by mail or email at SCUCC@INFOAVE.NET.

Federal and State Tax Liens

Records not maintained by a state level agency.

Tax lien data is found at the county level.

Sales Tax Registrations

Revenue Dept, Sales Tax Registration Records, PO Box 125, Columbia, SC 29214 (Courier address: 301 Gervais St, Columbia, SC 29201); 803-898-5872, 8:30AM-4:45PM.

www.sctax.org/default.htm

Records are available for 4 to 5 years, then are archived on hard copy. Records are indexed on inhouse computer.

Searching: This agency will only confirm that a business is registered. They will provide no other information. Include the following in your request-business name. They can also search by tax permit number, owner name, business name, or Federal ID.

Access by: mail, phone.

Mail search: Turnaround time: 7 days. A SASE is requested. No fee for mail request.

Phone search: No fee for telephone request.

Birth Certificates

South Carolina DHEC, Vital Records, 2600 Bull St, Columbia, SC 29201-1797; 803-898-3630, 803-898-3631 (Order Line), 877-284-1008 (Expedite), 803-898-3761-Fax; 8:30AM-4:30PM.

www.scdhec.net/vr/index.htm

A "short form" wallet size birth certificate can be obtained from any SC county. This form will not show parent names.

Records are available from January 1, 1915 to present. It takes 2 months before new records are available for inquiry. Records are indexed on microfiche, inhouse computer.

Searching: Records will only be released to the registrant (if 18 or older), parents named on certificate,, guardian or legal representative. Include the following in your request-full name, full names of father, mother's full maiden name, date of birth, place of birth. Two types of certificates are issued: wallet-size; photocopy certification (actual birth certificate).

Access by: mail, phone, fax, in person, online.

Fee & Payment: The fee is $12.00 per name. Add $3.00 per copy for additional copies of same certificate. Add $9.95 for use of credit card. Fee payee: DHEC. Prepayment required. Credit cards accepted for phone and fax requests only. Personal checks not accepted. MasterCard, Visa, Discover accepted.

Mail search: Turnaround time: 7 to 8 weeks. No SASE is required.

Phone search: Phone requests are accepted, using a credit card. See expedited service from Vitalchek.

Fax search: Same criteria as phone searches. Is considered expedited.

In person search: Turnaround time is within 1 hour.

Online search: Order from state-designated vendor - www.vitalchek.com. See expedited services.

Expedited service: Expedited service is available for mail requests for an additional $5.00 from this agency. To have search "expedited" by phone, online or fax from www.vitalchek.com, add $17.95; add $13.50 for FedEx delivery.

Death Records

South Carolina DHEC, Vital Records, 2600 Bull St, Columbia, SC 29201-1797; 803-898-3630, 803-898-3631 (Order Line), 803-799-0301-Fax; 8:30AM-4:30PM.

www.scdhec.net/vr/index.htm

Records are available from January 1, 1915 to date. New records are available for inquiry immediately. Records are indexed on microfiche, inhouse computer.

Searching: Copies are available to those who show a direct, tangible interest in a determination of a personal or property right. If less than 5 years, records are at county also. Include the following in your request-full name, date of death, place of death.

Access by: mail, phone, fax, in person, online.

Fee & Payment: The search fee is $12.00 per name. Add $3.00 per copy for additional copies. Add $9.95 for use of credit card. Fee payee: DHEC. Prepayment required. Credit cards accepted for phone and fax requests only. Personal checks accepted. Major credit cards accepted.

Mail search: Turnaround time: 7 to 8 weeks. No SASE is required.

Phone search: Phone requests are accepted, using a credit card. See expedited service from Vitalchek.

Fax search: See expedited service.

In person search: Turnaround time within 1 hour.

Online search: Order from state-designated vendor - www.vitalchek.com. See expedited services.

Expedited service: Expedited service is available for mail requests for an additional $5.00 from this agency. To have search "expedited" by phone, online or fax from www.vitalchek.com, add $17.95; add $13.50 for FedEx delivery.

Marriage Certificates

South Carolina DHEC, Vital Records, 2600 Bull St, Columbia, SC 29201-1797; 803-898-3630, 803-898-3631 (Order Line), 803-799-0301-Fax; 8:30AM-4:30PM.

www.scdhec.net/vr/index.htm

Copies may also be obtained from the Probate Judge in the county where license was issued.

Records are available from July 1, 1950 to present. New records are available for inquiry immediately. Records are indexed on microfiche, inhouse computer.

Searching: Records are released only to the subjects, their adult children, former or present spouses and legal representatives. Others may obtain a statement of marriage date and place. Include the following in your request-names of husband and wife, date of marriage, place or county where marriage license issued.

Access by: mail, phone, fax, in person, online.

Fee & Payment: The search fee is $12.00 per name, add $3.00 for each additional copy. Use of credit card is additional $9.95. Fee payee: DHEC. Prepayment required. Credit cards accepted for phone and fax searches only. Personal checks accepted. Major credit cards accepted.

Mail search: Turnaround time: 7 weeks. No SASE is required.

Phone search: Phone requests are accepted, using a credit card. See expedited service from Vitalchek.

Fax search: See expedited service.

In person search: Turnaround time within 1 hour.

Online search: Order from state-designated vendor - www.vitalchek.com. See expedited services.

Expedited service: Expedited service is available for mail requests for an additional $5.00 from this agency. To have search "expedited" by phone, online or fax from www.vitalchek.com, add $17.95; add $13.50 for FedEx delivery.

Divorce Records

South Carolina DHEC, Vital Records, 2600 Bull St, Columbia, SC 29201-1797; 803-898-3630, 803-898-3631 (Order Line), 803-799-0301-Fax; 8:30AM-4:30PM.

www.scdhec.net/vr/index.htm

Records are available from July 1, 1962 to present. New records are available for inquiry immediately. Records are indexed on microfiche, inhouse computer.

Searching: Records are available only to the parties, their adult children, a present or former spouse, and their legal representatives. Others may obtain a statement of the date and county of the event. Include the following in your request-names of husband and wife, date of divorce, place of divorce.

Access by: mail, phone, fax, in person, online.

Fee & Payment: The fee is $12.00 per name. Add $3.00 per copy for additional copies. Use of credit card is $9.95. Fee payee: DHEC. Prepayment required. Credit cards accepted for phone and fax requests only. Personal checks accepted. Major credit cards accepted.

Mail search: Turnaround time: 7 weeks. No SASE is required.

Phone search: Phone requests are accepted, using a credit card. See expedited service from Vitalchek.

Fax search: See expedited service.

In person search: Turnaround time within 1 hour.

Online search: Order from state-designated vendor - www.vitalchek.com. See expedited services.

Expedited service: Expedited service is available for mail requests for an additional $5.00 from this agency. To have search "expedited" by phone, online or fax from www.vitalchek.com, add $17.95; add $13.50 for FedEx delivery.

Workers' Compensation Records

Workers Compensation Commission, PO Box 1715, Columbia, SC 29202 (Courier address: 1612 Marion St, Columbia, SC 29201); 803-737-5700, 803-737-5768-Fax; 8:30AM-5PM.

www.sclrc.org/GED.htm

Records are available from 1983 on the computer. Some of the older records are at this office and the rest are at the State Archives. Call office first for location of records. New records are available for inquiry immediately. Records are indexed on inhouse computer, books (volumes). Records are normally destroyed after 5 years after closing.

Searching: Must have a signed release from claimant and you must specify what records you want. Include the following in your request-claimant name, Social Security Number, date of accident.

Access by: mail, fax, in person.

Fee & Payment: The search fee is $10.00 per record and includes a computer printout. File copies cost $20.00 for the first up to 20 pages and $.50 for each additional page. Fee payee: SC Workers Compensation Commission. Prepayment required. Personal checks accepted. No credit cards accepted.

Mail search: Turnaround time: 1 week. A SASE is requested.

Fax search: You can request by fax, but reply is sent by mail, same turnaround time.

In person search: Records are still returned by mail.

Driver License Information, Driver Records

Department of Motor Vehicles, Driver Records Section, PO Box 1498, Blythewood, SC 29016-0028; 803-896-5000, 803-737-1077-Fax; 8:30AM-5PM.

www.scdmvonline.com

Copies of tickets are available from this department for a fee of $6.00 per record.

Records are available for up to 10 years for moving violations, DWIs and suspensions. Records provided to the public are limited to 3 or 10 years. The state will show moving violations regardless of whether the fine was not paid and license suspended. It takes 1 to 4 weeks before new records are available for inquiry. Records are normally destroyed after 10 years.

Searching: Driving records and Identification card information is confidential by statute. Requests must fall within the guidelines of DPPA. Casual requesters must submit consent of subject if personal information is to be released. Include the following in your request-Form MV-70 which requires driver's license number or full name and DOB. Consent of driver needed if requester not DPPA approved. The following data is not released: Social Security Numbers or personal information (height, weight, sex, eye color, etc.).

Access by: mail, phone, fax, in person, online.

Fee & Payment: The fee is $6.00 per record request. Fee payee: Department of Motor Vehicles Prepayment required. Personal checks accepted. Credit cards only accepted for call center and online.

Mail search: Turnaround time: 5 days. Fee and return address must be submitted with each request. No SASE is required.

Phone search: Phone searching is only available for account holders.

Fax search: Fax requesting is only available for account holders.

In person search: Most DMV Branch offices in the state will process up to 10 records while you wait.

Online search: The online system offers basic driver data, for a 3 year or a 10 year record. This is a single inquiry process. Network charges will be incurred as well as initial set-up and a security deposit. The system is up between 8 AM and 7 PM. Fee is $6.00 per record. Access is through the AAMVAnet (IBMIN), which requesters much "join." Call Wanda DeLeon at 803-896-9092 for further information.

Other access: Magnetic tape and cassette batch processing is available.

Vehicle Ownership
Vehicle Identification

Division of Motor Vehicles, Title and Registration Records Section, PO Box 1498, Blythewood, SC 29016; 803-896-5000, 803-896-6685-Fax; 8:30AM-5PM.

www.scdmvonline.com

Records are available for 10 years for titles, 3 years for registration. The index to the records is computerized since 1984. It takes one day before new records are available for inquiry.

Searching: Information regarding the name, address and telephone number will not be released to the public, unless the requester completes form provided by department. Information is not provided to casual requesters. Requesters must be in compliance with DPPA.

Access by: mail, phone, fax, in person.

Fee & Payment: The fee is $6.00 per record request for all records, including lien information. Fee payee: SC Department of Motor Vehicles. Prepayment required. A deposit account is available for ongoing requesters by mail or phone. Personal checks accepted. No credit cards accepted.

Mail search: Turnaround time: 3 days. No SASE is required.

Phone search: Telephone searching is available for pre-approved, ongoing requesters. A deposit is required.

Fax search: See expedited service. This is only available to pre-approved, ongoing requesters. A deposit is required.

In person search: You may search in person.

Other access: South Carolina offers a variety of bulk retrieval programs where permitted by law. There is a minimum charge of $1,000.00. For more information, call customer service department for automated searches.

Expedited service: Expedited service is available for fax searches for approved, ongoing accounts. Turnaround time: 1 to 2 days.

Accident Reports

Accident Reports, Financial Responsibility Office, PO Box 1498, Blythewood, SC 29016-0050; 803-896-5000, 8:30AM-5PM.

www.scdmvonline.com

Records are available for 10 years to present. The records are indexed on computer. It takes one week after receipt from enforcement agency before new records are available for inquiry. Records are indexed on inhouse computer.

Searching: Must have full name of all the drivers involved in the accident. Include the following in your request-full name, date of accident, driver's license number, county.

Access by: mail, in person.

Fee & Payment: The fee is $6.00 for an accident research or insurance research. You may call to find out if record is on file. Fee payee: Department of Motor Vehicles Ongoing requesters may open an account with a $100.00 deposit and then will be billed monthly. Personal checks accepted. No credit cards accepted now, but may the near future.

Mail search: Turnaround time: 7 to 10 days. Information requests are available. A SASE is requested.

In person search: Records will be processed while you wait, but only at a field office on Shep Road.

Expedited service: Expedited service is available for $20.00 per report. Turnaround time: 3 days or less.

Vessel Ownership
Vessel Registration

Dept of Natural Resources, Registration & Titles, PO Box 167, Columbia, SC 29202 (Courier address: 1000 Assembly St, Room 104, Columbia, SC 29201); 803-734-3857, 803-734-4138-Fax; 8:30AM-5PM.

www.dnr.state.sc.us

Boats are registered and titled. Motors are titled. Thus, to search for a boat with a motor, two record checks are required.

Records are available from mid 80's to present. Inactive records are put on microfiche seven years after becoming inactive. It takes 30 days before new records are available for inquiry. Records are indexed on computer, older records on microfiche.

Searching: State law prohibits the release of records for commercial solicitation. All motorized boats must be titled and registered. All sailboats must be titled, and if used with propulsion then registered. To search, one of the following is required: name and address, hull ID #, title #, or SC (serial) #. The following data is not released: Social Security Numbers.

Access by: mail, in person.

Fee & Payment: The search fee for all types of searches is $10.00 per record request. If search both if no motor, and $20.00 per record for the motor registration. Fee payee: SC Dept of Natural Resources. Prepayment required. Personal checks accepted. No credit cards accepted.

Mail search: Turnaround time: 7 to 20 days. No SASE is required.

In person search: Turnaround time is usually same day.

Voter Registration

State Election Commission, Records, PO Box 5987, Columbia, SC 29250; 803-734-9060, 803-734-9366-Fax; 8:30AM-5PM.

www.state.sc.us/scsec

Records are available for all active records. It takes one day or less before new records are available for inquiry.

Searching: Records are open to the public. To search, provide the name with the county, or DOB and/or SSN. The following data is not released: Social Security Numbers.

Access by: mail, phone, fax, in person.

Fee & Payment: There is no search fee unless extensive time involved. Copies are $.20 each. Requester must pre-pay if Courier address service desired. Fee payee: State Election Commission. Prepayment required. Personal checks accepted. No credit cards accepted.

Mail search: Turnaround time: 1 to 2 days. SASE requested.

Phone search: Records are available by phone.

Fax search: Same criteria as mail searching. There is a $.20 fee per page to return by fax.

In person search: Simple requests may be processed while you wait.

Other access: Lists, labels, diskettes, and magnetic tapes are available with a variety of sort features. The minimum charge varies from $75 to $160 depending on the media.

GED Certificates

GED Testing Office, 1429 Senate St, #402, Columbia, SC 29201; 803-734-8347 x5, 803-734-8336-Fax; 8:30AM-5PM M-F.

www.sde.state.sc.us

It takes 6 weeks before new records are available for inquiry.

Searching: To search, all of the following is required: a signed release, name, SSN, and approximate date and city. Specify if for civilian or military use.

Access by: mail, fax, in person.

Fee & Payment: There is no fee for a verification. There is a $5.00 fee for a copy of a transcript by mail, $3.00 if by fax. Fee payee: SC Dept of Education. Prepayment required. Cash and money orders are accepted. No credit cards accepted.

Mail search: Turnaround time is 3-5 days. No SASE is required.

Fax search: After sending fax, call back in 15 minutes for verification.

In person search: Records may be requested in person. Requester must present state-issued ID.

Hunting and Fishing License Information

Access to Records is Restricted.

SC Department of Natural Resources, Licensing Division, PO Box 11710, Columbia, SC 29211-1710; 803-734-3833, 8:30AM-5PM.

www.dnr.state.sc.us

The agency is in the process of creating a centralized database. Most licenses are kept on file within the License Division by the county and agent where the license was sold, however the records are not open to the public.

South Carolina State Licensing Agencies

For details about the agency responsible for licensing/certifying/registering an item below or in the Agency Quick Finder section, match an item's number with the number of the agency in the *Licensing Agency Information* section.

South Carolina Licenses Searchable Online

Accounting Practitioner-AP #2	https://verify.llronline.com/LicLookup/
Acupuncturist #39	http://verify.llronline.com/LicLookup/Med/Med.aspx?div=16
Airport Contact #35	www.scaeronautics.com/directorySearch.asp
Animal Health Technician #43	https://verify.llronline.com/LicLookup/
Architect #3	https://verify.llronline.com/LicLookup/
Architectural Partners/Corp #3	https://verify.llronline.com/LicLookup/
Attorney #48	www.scbar.org/member/directory.asp
Auction Company #50	https://verify.llronline.com/LicLookup/
Auctioneer/Auctioneer Apprentice #50	https://verify.llronline.com/LicLookup/
Audiologist #22	https://verify.llronline.com/LicLookup/
Aviation Facility #35	www.scaeronautics.com/AirportSearch.asp
Barber Instructor/School #47	https://verify.llronline.com/LicLookup/
Barber/Barber Apprentice #47	https://verify.llronline.com/LicLookup/
Bodywork Therapist #47	https://verify.llronline.com/LicLookup/
Building Inspector/Official #21	https://verify.llronline.com/LicLookup/
Burglar Alarm Contractor #24	https://verify.llronline.com/LicLookup/
Chiropractor #4	https://verify.llronline.com/LicLookup/
Contractor, General & Mechanical #24	https://verify.llronline.com/LicLookup/
Contractor, Specialty Resid'l #45	https://verify.llronline.com/LicLookup/
Cosmetologist #5	https://verify.llronline.com/LicLookup/
Cosmetology Instructor/School #5	https://verify.llronline.com/LicLookup/
Counselor, Professional #8	https://verify.llronline.com/LicLookup/
Dental Hygienist #6	https://verify.llronline.com/LicLookup/
Dental Specialist/Technician #6	https://verify.llronline.com/LicLookup/
Dentist #6	https://verify.llronline.com/LicLookup/
Embalmer #11	https://verify.llronline.com/LicLookup/
Emergency Med. Svc. (Ambulance) #27	www.scems.com/emsassn/members.html
Engineer #7	https://verify.llronline.com/LicLookup/
Esthetician #5	https://verify.llronline.com/LicLookup/
Ethics Debtors #37	www.state.sc.us/ethics/Debtors%20page%20Lead.htm
Forester #38	http://verify.llronline.com/LicLookup/Forestry/Foresters.asp?div=30
Funeral Director #11	https://verify.llronline.com/LicLookup/
Funeral Home #11	https://verify.llronline.com/LicLookup/
Geologist #20	https://verify.llronline.com/LicLookup/
Hair Care Master Specialist #47	https://verify.llronline.com/LicLookup/
Home Builder, Residential #45	https://verify.llronline.com/LicLookup/
Housing Inspector #21	https://verify.llronline.com/LicLookup/
Inspector, Mech./Elec./Plumb./Prov. #21	https://verify.llronline.com/LicLookup/
Insurance Agency/Company/Filing #31	https://www.doi.state.sc.us/Eng/Public/Static/DBSearch.aspx
Insurance Agent #31	https://www.doi.state.sc.us/Eng/Public/Static/DBSearch.aspx
Landscape Architect #40	www.dnr.state.sc.us/water/envaff/prolicense/prolicense.html
Lobbyist #37	www.scstatehouse.net/reports/ethrpt.htm
Lobbyist Principal #37	www.scstatehouse.net/reports/ethrpt.htm
Manicure Assistant #47	https://verify.llronline.com/LicLookup/
Manicurist #5	https://verify.llronline.com/LicLookup/
Manufact'd House Mfg/Dealer/Rep #41	https://verify.llronline.com/LicLookup/
Manu'd House Sales/Install/Repair #41	https://verify.llronline.com/LicLookup/
Marriage & Family Therapist #8	https://verify.llronline.com/LicLookup/
Massage Therapist #47	https://verify.llronline.com/LicLookup/
Medical Doctor #39	http://verify.llronline.com/LicLookup/Med/Med.aspx?div=16
Nail Technician #5	https://verify.llronline.com/LicLookup/
Nurses, RN / LPN #12	https://verify.llronline.com/LicLookup/
Nursing Home Administrator #32	https://verify.llronline.com/LicLookup/
Occupational Therapist/Assistant #13	https://verify.llronline.com/LicLookup/
Optometrist #9	https://verify.llronline.com/LicLookup/
Osteopathic Physician #39	http://verify.llronline.com/LicLookup/Med/Med.aspx?div=16
Percolation Test Technician #36	https://verify.llronline.com/LicLookup/

Pharmacist/Pharmacy Technician #15 .... https://verify.llronline.com/LicLookup/
Pharmacy/Drug Outlet #15 .... https://verify.llronline.com/LicLookup/
Physical Therapist/Therapist Asst #16 .... https://verify.llronline.com/LicLookup/
Physician Assistant #39 .... http://verify.llronline.com/LicLookup/Med/Med.aspx?div=16
Pilot #35 .... www.scaeronautics.com/AirportSearch.asp
Plans Examiner #21 .... https://verify.llronline.com/LicLookup/
Podiatrist #17 .... https://verify.llronline.com/LicLookup/
Produce Whlse Dealer #25 .... www.scda.state.sc.us/buyscproducts/wholesalers/wholesalers.htm
Psycho-Educational Specialist #8 .... https://verify.llronline.com/LicLookup/
Psychologist #18 .... https://verify.llronline.com/LicLookup/
Public Accountant-CPA #2 .... https://verify.llronline.com/LicLookup/
Real Estate Appraiser #44 .... http://verify.llronline.com/LicLookup/Rea/Rea.aspx?div=25
Residential Care, Community #32 .... https://verify.llronline.com/LicLookup/
Respiratory Care Practitioner #39 .... http://verify.llronline.com/LicLookup/Med/Med.aspx?div=16
Shampoo Assistant #47 .... https://verify.llronline.com/LicLookup/
Social Worker #18 .... https://verify.llronline.com/LicLookup/
Soil Classifier #40 .... www.dnr.state.sc.us/water/envaff/prolicense/prolicense.html
Solid Waste Landfill #30 .... www.scdhec.net/lwm/html/min.html
Speech-Language Pathologist #22 .... https://verify.llronline.com/LicLookup/
Sprinkler Systems Contr. #24 .... https://verify.llronline.com/LicLookup/
Surveyor, Land #7 .... https://verify.llronline.com/LicLookup/
Swimming Pool/Spa Operator #36 .... https://verify.llronline.com/LicLookup/
Veterinarian #43 .... https://verify.llronline.com/LicLookup/
Waste Water Plant Operator #36 .... https://verify.llronline.com/LicLookup/
Water Treatment Registration #36 .... https://verify.llronline.com/LicLookup/
Well Driller #36 .... https://verify.llronline.com/LicLookup/
Wholesaler/Shipper (Food) #25 .... www.scda.state.sc.us/buyscproducts/shippers/shippers.htm

South Carolina Licensing Quick Finder

Accounting Practitioner-AP #2 803-896-4770
Acupuncturist #39 803-896-4500
Agricultural Dealer/Handler #25 803-734-2182
Airport Contact #35 803-896-6260
Alcoholic Bev. Vendor/Mfg./Whlse. #34 803-898-5864
Alcoholic Beverage Sunday Sales #34 . 803-898-5880
Amusement Ride #46 803-734-9711
Animal Health Technician #43 803-896-4598
Architect #3 803-896-4408
Architectural Partners/Corp #3 803-896-4408
Athletic Contest #49 803-896-4571
Athletic Trainer #49 803-896-4571
Attorney #48 803-799-6653
Auction Company #50 803-896-4853
Auctioneer/Auctioneer Apprentice #50.. 803-896-4853
Audiologist #22 803-896-4650
Aviation Facility #35 803-896-6260
Bank #10 803-734-2001
Barber Instructor/School #47 803-896-4588
Barber Shop #47 803-896-4588
Barber/Barber Apprentice #47 803-896-4588
Bodywork Therapist #47 803-896-4498
Boxer/Boxing Professional #49 803-896-4571
Building Inspector/Official #21 803-896-4688
Burglar Alarm Contractor #24 803-896-4686
Butterfat Tester #25 803-737-9700
Chiropractor #4 803-896-4587
Constable #29 803-896-7014
Contact Lens License #14 803-896-4681
Contractor, General & Mechanical #24 . 803-896-4686
Contractor, Specialty Resid'l #45 803-896-4696
Cosmetologist/Instructor/School #5 803-896-4494
Counselor, Professional #8 803-896-4658
Dental Hygienist #6 803-896-4599
Dental Specialist/Technician #6 803-896-4599
Dentist #6 803-896-4599
Electrician #42 803-933-1209
Elevator Service #46 803-734-9711
Embalmer #11 803-896-4497
Emergency Medical Svc. (Ambulance Co) #27
.... 803-545-4202

Emergency Medical Technician #27 803-545-4204
Engineer #7 803-896-4422
Esthetician #5 803-896-4494
Ethics Debtors #37 803-253-4192
Feed Manufacturer/Product #25 803-737-9700
Financial Institution #10 803-734-2001
Forester #38 803-896-4675
Funeral Director #11 803-896-4497
Funeral Home #11 803-896-4497
Geologist #20 803-896-4498
Hair Care Master Specialist #47 803-896-4588
Hearing Aid Dispenser/Fitter #22 803-896-4650
Heating & Air/Gas Fitting #42 803-933-1209
Home Builder, Residential #45 803-896-4696
Housing Inspector #21 803-896-4688
Inspect'r, Mech./Elec./Plumb./Prov #21 803-896-4688
Insurance Agency/Company/Filing #31 803-737-6221
Insurance Agent #31 803-737-6095
Investment Advisor #1 803-734-9916
Landscape Architect #40 803-734-9131
Liquor Permit, Special Event #34 803-898-5864
Lobbyist #37 803-253-4192
Lobbyist Principal #37 803-253-4192
Manicure Assistant #47 803-896-4588
Manicurist #5 803-896-4494
Manufac'd House Mfg/Dealer/Rep #41 . 803-896-4682
Manufactured House Sales/Install/Repair #41
.... 803-896-4682
Marriage & Family Therapist #8 803-896-4658
Massage Therapist #47 803-896-4498
Medical Doctor #39 803-896-4500
Mine Site #30 803-896-4000
Nail Technician #5 803-896-4494
Notary Public #23 803-734-2512
Nurses, RN / LPN #12 803-896-4550
Nursing Home Administrator #32 803-896-4544
Occupational Therapist/Assistant #13.. 803-896-4683
Optician #14 803-896-4681
Optician Apprentice #14 803-896-4681
Optometrist #9 803-869-4679
Osteopathic Physician #39 803-896-4500

Percolation Test Technician #36 803-896-4430
Pesticide Applicator/Dealer #33 803-646-2155
Pharmacist/Pharmacy Technician #15 . 803-896-4700
Pharmacy/Drug Outlet #15 803-896-4700
Physical Therapist/Therapist Asst #16. 803-896-4655
Physician Assistant #39 803-896-4500
Pilot #35 803-896-6260
Pipefitter #42 803-933-1209
Plans Examiner #21 803-896-4688
Plumbing #42 803-933-1209
Podiatrist #17 803-896-4685
Polygraph Examiner #29 803-896-7292
Private Detective #29 803-896-7014
Produce Whlse Dealer #25 803-737-9700
Property Manager #44 803-896-4400
Psycho-Educational Specialist #8 803-896-4658
Psychologist #18 803-896-4664
Public Accountant-CPA #2 803-896-4770
Pyrotechnic Technician #19 803-896-9807
Pyrotechnic Wholesaler/Facility/Jobber #19
.... 803-896-4420
Real Estate Appraiser #44 803-896-4400
Real Estate Broker #44 803-896-4400
Residential Care, Community #32 803-896-4544
Respiratory Care Practitioner #39 803-896-4500
Sanitarian #28 803-896-0646
School Guidance Counselor #26 803-734-8466
School Media Communications Specialist #26
.... 803-734-8466
School Principal/Supervisor/Superintendent #26
.... 803-734-8466
Securities Agent/Broker/Dealer #1 803-734-9916
Security Guard/Security Company #29 803-896-7014
Seed Salesperson #25 803-737-9690
Shampoo Assistant #47 803-896-4588
Sheet Metal #42 803-933-1209
Social Worker #18 803-896-4665
Soil Classifier #40 803-734-9131
Solid Waste Landfill / Operator #30 803-896-4148
Speech-Language Pathologist #22 803-896-4650
Sprinkler Systems Contractor #24 803-896-4686

Surveyor, Land #7 803-896-4422
Swimming Pool/Spa Operator #36 803-896-4430
Teacher #26.. 803-734-8466
Timeshare/Land Salesperson #44 803-896-4400

Veterinarian #43 803-896-4598
Waste Water Treatment Plant Operator #36
.... 803-896-4430
Water Treatment Registration #36 803-896-4430

Weighman/Weighmaster #25 803-737-9696
Well Driller #36 803-896-4430
Wholesaler/Shipper (Food) #25 803-737-9700
Wrestler/Wrestling Professional #49.... 803-896-4571

South Carolina Licensing Agency Information

1 Attorney Generals Office, Securities Division, PO Box 11549 (1000 Assembly St, Rembert C. Dennis Building), Columbia, SC 29211-1549; 803-734-9916, Fax: 803-734-0032.

2 Department of Labor, Licensing & Regulation, Board of Accountancy, PO Box 11329 (110 Centerview Dr.), Columbia, SC 29211; 803-896-4770, Fax: 803-896-4554.
www.llr.state.sc.us/pol.asp
Email: mcwhortm@mail.llr.state.sc
Search Database at
https://verify.llronline.com/LicLookup/

3 Department of Labor, Licensing & Regulation, Board of Architectural Examiners, PO Box 11419 (110 Centerview Dr, #201), Columbia, SC 29211; 803-896-4408, Fax: 803-734-4410.
www.llr.state.sc.us/pol.asp
Search Database at
https://verify.llronline.com/LicLookup/

4 Department of Labor, Licensing & Regulation, Division of Chiropractic Examiners, PO Box 11329 (110 Centerview Dr, #306), Columbia, SC 29211-1329; 803-896-4587, Fax: 803-896-4719.
www.llr.state.sc.us/pol.asp
Email: denninsonp@ur.sc.gov
Search Database at
https://verify.llronline.com/LicLookup/

5 Department of Labor, Licensing & Regulation, Board of Cosmetology, PO Box 11329 (110 Centerview Dr), Columbia, SC 29211-1329; 803-896-4494, Fax: 803-896-4484.
www.llr.state.sc.us/pol.asp
Search Database at
https://verify.llronline.com/LicLookup/ Note: See also Board of Barber examiners for Shampoo Assistant and Master Hair Care Specialist.

6 Department of Labor, Licensing & Regulation, Board of Dentistry, PO Box 11329 (110 Centerview Dr, Ste 306), Columbia, SC 29211-1329; 803-896-4599, Fax: 803-896-4596.
www.llr.state.sc.us/pol/dentistry
Email: joness@mail.llr.state.sc.us
Search Database at
https://verify.llronline.com/LicLookup/

7 Department of Labor, Licensing & Regulation, Board of Prof. Engineers & Land Surveyors, PO Box 11597 (110 Centerview Dr, #201), Columbia, SC 29211-1597; 803-896-4422, Fax: 803-896-4427. www.llr.state.sc.us/pol.asp
Search Database at
https://verify.llronline.com/LicLookup/

8 Department of Labor, Licensing & Regulation, Board of Examiners of Prof. Counselors / Family Therapists, PO Box 11329 (110 Centerview, #306), Columbia, SC 29211; 803-896-4658, Fax: 803-896-4719.
www.llr.state.sc.us/pol.asp
Email: harringtons@mail.llr.state.sc.us
Search Database at
https://verify.llronline.com/LicLookup/ Note: List are availibe through email or on diskette for fee of $30.00.

9 Department of Labor, Licensing & Regulation, Board of Examiners in Optometry, PO Box 11329 (110 Centerview Dr.), Columbia, SC 29211-1329; 803-896-4679, Fax: 803-896-4719.
www.llr.state.sc.us/pol.asp
Email: combsa@mail.llr.state.sc.us
Search Database at
https://verify.llronline.com/LicLookup/ Note: Online disciplinary records only go back to 1994.

10 Board of Financial Institutions, PO Box 12549 (1015 Sumter St, Rm 309), Columbia, SC 29201; 803-734-2001, Fax: 803-734-2013.

11 Department of Labor, Licensing & Regulation, Board of Funeral Service, PO Box 11329 (110 Centerview Dr, #104), Columbia, SC 29211-1329; 803-896-4497, Fax: 803-896-4484/4554.
www.llr.state.sc.us/pol.asp
Search Database at
https://verify.llronline.com/LicLookup/

12 Department of Labor, Licensing & Regulation, Board of Nursing, PO Box 12367 (110 Centerview Dr, #202), Columbia, SC 29211-2367; 803-896-4550, Fax: 803-896-4525.
www.llr.state.sc.us/pol/nursing/
Email: hurseboard@llr.sc.gov
Search Database at
https://verify.llronline.com/LicLookup/

13 Department of Labor, Licensing & Regulation, Board of Occupational Therapy, PO Box 11329 (110 Centerview Dr, #306), Columbia, SC 29211; 803-896-4683, Fax: 803-896-4719.
www.llr.state.sc.us/pol.asp
Email: cokk@mail.llr.state.sc.us
Search Database at
https://verify.llronline.com/LicLookup/ Note: Online records only go back to 1994.

14 Department of Labor, Licensing & Regulation, Board of Examiners in Optometry, PO Box 11329 (110 Centerview Dr.), Columbia, SC 29211-1329; 803-896-4681, Fax: 803-896-4719.
www.llr.state.sc.us/pol.asp
Email: combsa@mail.llr.state.sc.us
Search Database at
https://verify.llronline.com/LicLookup/ Note: Online records only go back to 1994.

15 Department of Labor, Licensing & Regulation, Board of Pharmacy, 110 Centerview Dr, Kingstree Bldg, #306, Columbia, SC 29211-1927; 803-896-4700, Fax: 803-896-4596.
www.llr.state.sc.us/pol.asp
Email: funderbm@mail.llr.state.sc.us
Search Database at
https://verify.llronline.com/LicLookup/

16 Department of Labor, Licensing & Regulation, Board of Physical Therapy Examiners, PO Box 11329 (110 Centerview Dr,), Columbia, SC 29211; 803-896-4655, Fax: 803-896-4719.
www.llr.state.sc.us/pol/physicaltherapy
Email: reynoldsv@llr.sc.gov
Search Database at
https://verify.llronline.com/LicLookup/

17 Department of Labor, Licensing & Regulation, Board of Podiatry Examiners, PO Box 11289 (110 Centerview Dr, #202), Columbia, SC 29211-1289; 803-896-4685, Fax: 803-896-4515.
www.llr.state.sc.us/pol/podiatry
Email: podiatry@mail.llr.state.sc.us
Search Database at
https://verify.llronline.com/LicLookup/

18 Department of Labor, Licensing & Regulation, Board of Examiners in Psychology/Social Work Examiners, PO Box 11329 (110 Centerview Dr), Columbia, SC 29211-1329; 803-896-4664, Fax: 803-896-4687.
www.llr.state.sc.us/pol.asp
Email: glennp@llk.sc.gov
Search Database at
https://verify.llronline.com/LicLookup/ Note: Online psychologist records only go bck to 1994.

19 Department of Labor, Licensing & Regulation, Board of Pyrotechnic Safety, PO Box 11847 (110 Centerview Dr, #201), Columbia, SC 29211-1329; 803-896-4400, Fax: 803-896-4404.
www.llr.state.sc.us/POL/Pyrotechnic

20 Department of Labor, Licensing & Regulation, Board of Registration for Geologists, PO Box 11329 (110 Centerview Dr, #104), Columbia, SC 29211-1329; 803-896-4498, Fax: 803-896-4484.
www.llr.state.sc.us/pol.asp
Email: pyattl@mail.llr.state.sc.us
Search Database at
https://verify.llronline.com/LicLookup/

21 Department of Labor, Licensing & Regulation, Building Codes Council, PO Box 11329 (110 Centerview Dr, #102), Columbia, SC 29211-1329; 803-896-4636, Fax: 803-896-4814.
www.llr.state.sc.us/pol.asp
Email: reynoldsv@mail.llr.state.sc.us
Search Database at
https://verify.llronline.com/LicLookup/

22 Department of Labor, Licensing & Regulation, Board of Examiners for Speech-Language Pathology & Audiology, PO Box 11329 (110 Centerview Dr, #306), Columbia, SC 29211-1329; 803-896-4650, Fax: 803-896-4719.
www.llr.state.sc.us/pol/speech
Email: reynoldsv@mail.llr.state.sc.us
Search Database at
https://verify.llronline.com/LicLookup/

23 Secretary of State, Notaries & Apostilles Office, PO Box 11350 (1205 Pendleton St #525), Columbia, SC 29211; 803-734-2512.
www.scsos.com/notariesbc.htm
Email: pathamby@infoave.net

24 Department of Labor, Licensing & Regulation, Contractor's Licensing Board, PO Box 11329 (110 Centerview Dr, #201), Columbia, SC 29211-1329; 803-896-4686, Fax: 803-896-4364.
www.llr.state.sc.us/pol.asp
Search Database at
https://verify.llronline.com/LicLookup/

25 Department of Agriculture, PO Box 11280, Columbia, SC 29211; 803-734-2210, Fax: 803-734-2192.
www.scda.state.sc.us
Email: bwalton@scda.sc.gov
Search Database at www.scda.state.sc.us/

26 Department of Education, Division of Teacher Quality, 3700 Forest Drive, Suite500, Columbia, SC 29204; 803-734-8466, Fax: 803-734-2873.
Email: certification@scteachers.org

27 Department of Health & Environmental Control, EMS Department, 2600 Bull St, Columbia, SC 29201; 803-545-4204, Fax: 803-545-4212. www.scemsa.com

28 Department of Health & Environmental Control, Department of Licensing - Sanitarians, 2600 Bull St, Columbia, SC 29201; 803-896-0646, Fax: 803-896-0645.
www.scdhec.net   Email: macphadt@dhec.sc.gov

29 Law Enforcement Division, Regulatory Department, 4400 Broad River Rd, Columbia, SC 29210; 803-737-9000, Fax: 803-896-7041.
www.sled.state.sc.us

30 Department of Health & Environmental Control, Bureau of Land and Waste Management, 2600 Bull St, Columbia, SC 29201; 803-896-4000, Fax: 803-896-4001.
www.scdhec.net   Search Database at www.scdhec.net/lwm/html/min.html   Note: For Landfill Operators, search by county.

31 Department of Insurance, PO Box 100105 (300 Arbor Lake Dr., #1200), Columbia, SC 29202-3105; 803-737-6095, Fax: 803-737-6100.
www.doi.state.sc.us
Email: AgntMail@doi.state.sc.us
Search Database at https://www.doi.state.sc.us/Eng/Public/Static/DBSearch.aspx

32 Department of Labor, Licensing & Regulation, Board of Long Term Care Administrators, PO Box 11329, Columbia, SC 29211; 803-896-4544, Fax: 803-896-4555.
www.llr.state.sc.us/pol.asp
Email: welbornd@mail.llr.state.sc.us
Search Database at https://verify.llronline.com/LicLookup/

33 Department of Pesticide Regulation, 511 Westinghouse Rd, Pendelton, SC 29670; 864-646-2150, Fax: 864-646-2179.
http://dpr.clemson.edu

34 Department of Revenue & Taxation, Alcoholic Beverage Section, PO Box 125, Columbia, SC 29214; 803-898-5864, Fax: 803-898-5899. Note: The state list of Sunday Sales permits for alcoholic beverages is temporarily unavailable.

35 Division of Aeronautics, PO Box 280068 (2553 Airport Blvd, West Columbia), Columbia, SC 29228-0068; 803-896-6260, Fax: 803-896-6277. www.scaeronautics.com/
Email: pwerts@aeronautics.state.sc.us

36 Department of Labor, Licensing & Regulation, Environmental Certification Board, PO Box 11409, Columbia, SC 29211; 803-896-4430, Fax: 803-896-4424.
www.llr.state.sc.us/pol/environmental
Search Database at https://verify.llronline.com/LicLookup/

37 Ethics Commission, 5000 Thurmond Mall #250, Columbia, SC 29201; 803-253-4192, Fax: 803-253-7539.
www.state.sc.us/ethics/
Search Database at www.scstatehouse.net/reports/ethrpt.htm

38 Department of Labor, Licensing & Regulation, Board of Registration for Foresters, PO Box 11329, Columbia, SC 29211-1329; 803-896-4498, Fax: 803-896-4484.
www.llr.state.sc.us/pol.asp
Email: pyattl@mail.llr.state.sc.us
Search Database at http://verify.llronline.com/LicLookup/Forestry/Foresters.asp?div=30

39 Department of Labor, Licensing & Regulation, Board of Medical Examiners, PO Box 11289 (110 Centerview Dr, #202), Columbia, SC 29211-1289; 803-896-4500, Fax: 803-896-4515.
www.llr.state.sc.us/POL/Medical/
Email: medboard@mail.llr.state.sc.us
Search Database at http://verify.llronline.com/LicLookup/Med/Med.aspx?div=16

40 Department of Natural Resources, Land, Water & Conservation Div., Licensing Program, 1000 Assembly St. (PO Box 167), Columbia, SC 29201; 803-734-9131, Fax: 803-734-9200.
www.dnr.state.sc.us
Email: moorer@dnr.
Search Database at www.dnr.state.sc.us/water/envaff/prolicense/prolicense.html

41 Department of Labor, Licensing & Regulation, Manufactured Housing Board, PO Box 11329 (110 Centerview Dr, #102), Columbia, SC 29211-1329; 803-896-4682, Fax: 803-896-4814.
www.llr.state.sc.us/pol.asp
Email: bennettd@mail.llr.state.sc.us
Search Database at https://verify.llronline.com/LicLookup/

42 Municipal Association of South Carolina, Trades Certification Program, PO Box 12109 (1411 Gervais St), Columbia, SC 29211; 803-779-9574, Fax: 803-933-1299.
www.masc.sc/trades/trades.htm   Note: Will verify by phone.

43 Department of Labor, Licensing & Regulation, Board of Veterinary Medical Examiners, PO Box 11329, Columbia, SC 29211-1329; 803-896-4598, Fax: 803-896-4719.
www.llr.state.sc.us/pol.asp
Email: motonm@llr.sc.gov
Search Database at https://verify.llronline.com/LicLookup/

44 Real Estate Commission, PO Box 11847 (110 Centerview Dr #201), Columbia, SC 29211-1847; 803-896-4400, Fax: 803-896-4404.
www.llr.state.sc.us/pol.asp
Email: selmanr@mail.llr.state.sc.us

45 Department of Labor, Licensing & Regulation, Residential Home Builders Commission, PO Box 11329 (110 Centerview Dr, #201), Columbia, SC 29211-1329; 803-896-4696, Fax: 803-896-4656.
www.llr.state.sc.us/pol.asp
Email: driverc@mail.llr.state.sc.us
Search Database at https://verify.llronline.com/LicLookup/

46 Department of Labor, Licensing & Regulation, Office of Elevators & Amusement Rides, PO Box 11329, Columbia, SC 29211-1329; 803-734-9711, Fax: 803-737-9119.
www.llr.state.sc.us

47 Department of Labor, Licensing & Regulation, Board of Barber Examiners, Massage/Bodywork Therapy, PO Box 11329 (110 Centerview Dr, #104), Columbia, SC 29211-1329; 803-896-4491, Fax: 803-896-4484.
www.llr.state.sc.us/POL/Barber/
Email: jonese@mail.llr.state.sc.us
Search Database at https://verify.llronline.com/LicLookup/

48 Supreme Court, 950 Taylor St, Columbia, SC 29202; 803-799-6653, Fax: 803-799-4118.
www.scbar.org
Email: scbar-info@scbar.org
Search Database at www.scbar.org/member/directory.asp

49 Department of Labor, Licensing & Regulation, Athletic Commission, PO Box 11329 (110 Centerview Dr), Columbia, SC 29211; 803-896-4571, Fax: 803-896-4595.
www.llr.state.sc.us/pol.asp
Email: halll@mail.llr.state.sc.us

50 Department of Labor, Licensing & Regulation, Auctioneer's Commission, PO Box 11329 (110 Centerview Dr, #104), Columbia, SC 29211-1329; 803-896-4853, Fax: 803-896-4484.
www.llr.state.sc.us/pol.asp
Email: pyatt@mail.llr.state.sc.us
Search Database at https://verify.llronline.com/LicLookup/

South Carolina Federal Courts

The following list indicates the district and division name for each county in the state. If the bankruptcy court location is different from the district court, then the location of the bankruptcy court appears in parentheses.

South Carolina County/Court Cross Reference

Abbeville	Greenwood (Columbia)	Greenwood	Greenwood (Columbia)
Aiken	Greenwood (Columbia)	Hampton	Beaufort (Columbia)
Allendale	Greenwood (Columbia)	Horry	Florence (Columbia)
Anderson	Anderson (Columbia)	Jasper	Beaufort (Columbia)
Bamberg	Greenwood (Columbia)	Kershaw	Columbia
Barnwell	Greenwood (Columbia)	Lancaster	Greenwood (Columbia)
Beaufort	Beaufort (Columbia)	Laurens	Greenville (Columbia)
Berkeley	Charleston (Columbia)	Lee	Columbia
Calhoun	Greenwood (Columbia)	Lexington	Columbia
Charleston	Charleston (Columbia)	Marion	Florence (Columbia)
Cherokee	Spartanburg (Columbia)	Marlboro	Florence (Columbia)
Chester	Spartanburg (Columbia)	McCormick	Greenwood (Columbia)
Chesterfield	Florence (Columbia)	Newberry	Greenwood (Columbia)
Clarendon	Charleston (Columbia)	Oconee	Anderson (Columbia)
Colleton	Charleston (Columbia)	Orangeburg	Greenwood (Columbia)
Darlington	Florence (Columbia)	Pickens	Anderson (Columbia)
Dillon	Florence (Columbia)	Richland	Columbia
Dorchester	Charleston (Columbia)	Saluda	Greenwood (Columbia)
Edgefield	Greenwood (Columbia)	Spartanburg	Spartanburg (Columbia)
Fairfield	Greenwood (Columbia)	Sumter	Columbia
Florence	Florence (Columbia)	Union	Spartanburg (Columbia)
Georgetown	Charleston (Columbia)	Williamsburg	Florence (Columbia)
Greenville	Greenville (Columbia)	York	Spartanburg (Columbia)

Standards for Federal Courts: Search fee is $26.00 per item (one party name or case number). Copy fee is $.50 per page. Certification fee is $9.00 per document, double for exemplification, if available. All fees standard unless noted in profile. Mail Search: always enclose a stamped self addressed envelope unless otherwise noted. Most courts accept fax requests or will suggest a copying/search vendor. Before releasing records, all courts require prepayment, unless noted.

Open records are located at the court unless otherwise noted. District courts index by defendant and plaintiff as well as by case number. Bankruptcy courts usually index by debtor and case number. While most courts now have their indexes on computer, many may still maintain index card files as well.

Courts offering internet access via CM-ECF or older RACER, PACER, or Web-PACER systems charge $.08 per page fee unless noted as free. Where PACER is available, the universal sign-up number is 800-676-6856. Find PACER and the US Party/Case Index at http://pacer.psc.uscourts.gov.

US District Court

District of South Carolina

Anderson Division c/o Greenville Division, PO Box 10768, Greenville, SC 29603 (courier address: 300 E Washington St, Greenville, SC 29601), 864-241-2700, Fax-864-241-2711. Hours-8:30AM-4:30PM. www.scd.uscourts.gov

Counties: Anderson, Oconee, Pickens.

Searches & Indexing: Cases indexed by and case number. Results do not include SSN or DOB. Open records located at Greenville Division.

Fee & Payment: Pay by Visa/MC/AmEx, no business or personal checks accepted.

Phone Search: No searching by telephone.

Mail Search: SASE required.

In Person Search: permitted. A copy service can make copies for $.09 per page. No self-serve copier available.

E-Services: ECF replaces PACER whose records did go back to 1990. New records online after 1 day. ECF at http://ecf.scd.uscourts.gov **Opinions Online:** www.law.sc.edu/dsc/dsc.htm.

Beaufort Division c/o Charleston Division, PO Box 835, Charleston, SC 29402 (courier address: 85 Broad St, Hollings Judicial Center, Charleston, SC 29401), 843-579-1401, Fax-803-579-1402. Hours- 9AM-4:30PM. www.scd.uscourts.gov

Counties: Beaufort, Hampton, Jasper.

Searches & Indexing: Cases indexed by and case number. Results do not include SSN or DOB. Index on computer back to 1991. Records purged after 1 year for civil. Open records located at Charleston Division. Civil records sent to Federal Records Center 1 year after case closed; criminal records after 5 years.

Fee & Payment: Pay by Visa/MC, money order, cashier's or personal check. No business checks accepted.

Phone Search: No searching by telephone.

Mail Search: Include SASE for return.

In Person Search: No self-serve copier available.

E-Services: ECF replaces PACER whose records did go back to 1990. New records online after 1 day. ECF at http://ecf.scd.uscourts.gov **Opinions Online:** www.law.sc.edu/dsc/dsc.htm.

Charleston Division Court Clerk, PO Box 835, Charleston, SC 29402 (courier address: 85 Broad St, Hollings Judicial Center, Charleston, SC 29401), 843-579-1401, Fax-803-579-1402. Hours-9AM-4:30PM. www.scd.uscourts.gov

Counties: Berkeley, Charleston, Clarendon, Colleton, Dorchester, Georgetown.

Searches & Indexing: Results do not include SSN or DOB. Computer index back to 1991 maintained. Older records indexed on cards and microfiche. New cases in the index 1-2 days after filing date. Records purged never. District-wide searches available for cases back to 1980.

Fee & Payment: Pay by money order, cashier's or personal check. Credit cards accepted. Payee: US District Court. Prepayment required.

Phone Search: No searching by telephone.

Mail Search: search usually completed- 1-2 days. Include SASE for return.

In Person Search: Fee charged if court performs your search. No self-serve copier available.

E-Services: ECF replaces PACER whose records did go back to 1990. New records online after 1 day. ECF at http://ecf.scd.uscourts.gov. Document images available. **Opinions Online:** www.law.sc.edu/dsc/dsc.htm.

Columbia Division Court Clerk, 1845 Assembly St, Columbia, SC 29201 (also use mail address for courier delivery), 803-765-5816. Hours- 8:30AM-4:30PM. www.scd.uscourts.gov

Counties: Kershaw, Lee, Lexington, Richland, Sumter.

Searches & Indexing: Results do not include SSN or DOB. Computer index maintained; civil back to 1990, criminal to 1992. Older records indexed on microfiche. New cases in the index 1 month after filing date. Records purged never. District-wide searches available here.

Fee & Payment: Pay by money order, cashier's or personal check. Credit cards accepted. Payee: Clerk, US District Court. Prepayment required.

Phone Search: No searching by telephone. If case number, caption and judge are provided, court gives docket information via phone. Court will not search case numbers or captions via phone.

Mail Search: search usually completed- 2-3 days. SASE not required.

In Person Search: Fee charged if court performs your search. No self-serve copier available.

E-Services: ECF replaces PACER whose records did go back to 1990. New records online after 1 day. ECF at http://ecf.scd.uscourts.gov. Document images available. **Opinions Online:** www.law.sc.edu/dsc/dsc.htm.

Florence Division Court Clerk, PO Box 2317, Florence, SC 29503 (courier address: 401 W Evans St, McMillan Federal Bldg, Rm 361, Florence, SC 29501), 843-676-3820, Fax-843-676-3831. 8:30AM-4:30PM. www.scd.uscourts.gov

Counties: Chesterfield, Darlington, Dillon, Florence, Horry, Marion, Marlboro, Williamsburg.

Searches & Indexing: Results do not include SSN or DOB. Computer and card indexes maintained; computer back to 1995. Microfiche index goes back to 1982. New cases in the index 24-48 hours after filing date. Records purged never. District-wide searches available here.

Fee & Payment: Pay by Personal or business check accepted. Payee: Clerk, US District Court. Prepayment required. No credit cards.

Phone Search: No searching by telephone.

Mail Search: search usually completed- 2-3 days. Include SASE for return.

In Person Search: Fee charged if court performs your search. No self-serve copier available.

E-Services: ECF replaces PACER whose records did go back to 1990. New records online after 1 day. ECF at http://ecf.scd.uscourts.gov. Document images available. **Opinions Online:** www.law.sc.edu/dsc/dsc.htm.

Greenville Division Court Clerk, PO Box 10768, Greenville, SC 29603 (courier address: 300 E Washington St, Greenville, SC 29601), 864-241-2700, Fax-864-241-2711. Hours- 8:30AM-4:30PM. www.scd.uscourts.gov

Counties: Greenville, Laurens.

Searches & Indexing: No identifiers on civil records since 2002; none on criminal starting 2005. Computer index back to 1991 maintained. Older records indexed on microfiche. New cases in the index 24 hours after filing date. Records purged never.

Fee & Payment: Pay by Visa/MC/AmEx, money order, cashier's or personal check. Payee: Clerk, US District Court. Prepayment required.

Phone Search: Only case number, parties and attorneys' names is released via phone.

Mail Search: search usually completed- 1 day. SASE required.

In Person Search: Fee charged if court performs your search. An authorized contract copy service can make copies for $.09 each. No self-serve copier available.

E-Services: ECF replaces PACER whose records did go back to 1990. New records online after 1 day. ECF at http://ecf.scd.uscourts.gov. Document images available. **Opinions Online:** www.law.sc.edu/dsc/dsc.htm.

Greenwood Division c/o Greenville Division, PO Box 10768, Greenville, SC 29603 (courier address: 300 E Washington St, Greenville, SC 29601), 864-241-2700, Fax-864-241-2711. Hours- 8:30AM-4:30PM. www.scd.uscourts.gov

Counties: Abbeville, Aiken, Allendale, Bamberg, Barnwell, Calhoun, Edgefield, Fairfield, Greenwood, Lancaster, McCormick, Newberry, Orangeburg, Saluda.

Searches & Indexing: Cases indexed by and case number. Results do not include SSN or DOB. Records purged never. Open records located at Greenville Division.

Fee & Payment: Pay by Visa/MC/AmEx, no business or personal checks accepted.

Phone Search: No searching by telephone.

Mail Search: SASE required.

In Person Search: permitted. A copy service can make copies for $.09 per page. No self-serve copier available.

E-Services: ECF replaces PACER whose records did go back to 1990. New records online after 1 day. ECF at http://ecf.scd.uscourts.gov **Opinions Online:** www.law.sc.edu/dsc/dsc.htm.

Spartanburg Division c/o Greenville Division, PO Box 10768, Greenville, SC 29603 (courier address: 300 E Washington St, Greenville, SC 29601), 864-241-2700, Fax-864-241-2711. Hours- 8:30AM-4:30PM. www.scd.uscourts.gov

Counties: Cherokee, Chester, Spartanburg, Union, York.

Searches & Indexing: Cases indexed by and case number. Results do not include SSN or DOB. Open records located at Greenville Division.

Fee & Payment: Pay by Visa/MC/AmEx, no business or personal checks accepted.

Phone Search: No searching by telephone.

Mail Search: SASE required.

In Person Search: permitted. A copy service can make copies for $.09 per page. No self-serve copier available.

E-Services: ECF replaces PACER whose records did go back to 1990. New records online after 1 day. ECF at http://ecf.scd.uscourts.gov **Opinions Online:** www.law.sc.edu/dsc/dsc.htm.

US Bankruptcy Court

District of South Carolina

Columbia Division Court Clerk, 1100 Laurel St, Columbia, SC 29201 (also use mail address for courier delivery), 803-765-5436. Hours- 9AM-4:30PM. www.scb.uscourts.gov

Counties: All counties in South Carolina.

Searches & Indexing: Results include last 4 SSN digits. Both computer and card indexes maintained. New cases in the index immediately after filing date. Records purged never.

Fee & Payment: Pay by money order, cashier's or personal check. No debtor's checks accepted. Payee: Clerk, US Bankruptcy Court. Prepayment required.

Phone Search: No searching by telephone. , call VCIS at 800-669-8767 or 803-765-5211.

Mail Search: search usually completed- 1 week. Include SASE for return.

In Person Search: Fee charged if court performs your search. Copying and searching available for fee via the court's copy service, West Coast Copy, 803-255-0166. No self-serve copier available.

E-Services: ECF replaces PACER. Document images and crditor lists available. PACER records go back to 11/1988. New records online immediately. ECF at https://ecf.scb.uscourts.gov **Opinions Online:** www.scb.uscourts.gov/opinions.html. **Other Online Access:** Calendars free at www.scb.uscourts.gov/calendars/calendars.htm

South Carolina County Courts

Court	Jurisdiction	No. of Courts	How Organized
Circuit Courts*	General	46	16 Circuits
Magistrate Courts*	Limited	182	
Municipal Courts	Municipal	160	
Probate Courts*	Probate	46	
Family Courts	Special	46	16 Circuits

* Profiled in this Sourcebook.

Court	CIVIL								
	Tort	Contract	Real Estate	Min. Claim	Max. Claim	Small Claims	Estate	Eviction	Domestic Relations
Circuit Courts*	X	X	X	$5000	No Max	$7500			
Magistrate Courts	X		X	$0	$7500	$7500		X	
Municipal Courts									
Probate Courts*							X		
Family Courts									X

Court	CRIMINAL				
	Felony	Misdemeanor	DWI/DUI	Preliminary Hearing	Juvenile
Circuit Courts*	X	X	X		
Magistrate Courts*		X	X	X	
Municipal Courts		X	X	X	
Probate Courts*					
Family Courts					X

ADMINISTRATION
Court Administration, 1015 Sumter St, 2nd Floor, Columbia, SC, 29201; 803-734-1800, Fax: 803-734-1355. www.sccourts.org

COURT STRUCTURE
The 46 SC counties are divided among sixteen judicial circuits. The circuit courts are in operation at the county level and consist of a court of general sessions (criminal) and a court of common pleas (civil). A family court is also in operation at the county level. The over 300 Magistrate and Municipal Courts (often referred to as "Summary Courts") only handle misdemeanor cases involving a $500.00 fine and/or 30 days or less jail time.

The maximum civil claim monetary amount for the Magistrate Courts increased from $2,500 to $5,000 as of January 1, 1996. In 2001, this civil limit was raised to $7,500.

ONLINE ACCESS
Appellate and Supreme Court opinions are available from the web site. There is no access to statewide trial court records, but several counties offer online access.

ADDITIONAL INFORMATION
If requesting a record in writing, it is recommended that the words "request that General Session, Common Pleas, and Family Court records be searched" be included in the request.

Most South Carolina courts will not conduct searches. However, if a name and case number are provided, many will pull and copy the record. Search fees vary widely as they are set by each county individually.

Abbeville County

Circuit Court PO Box 99, 103 Court Sq, Rm 102, Abbeville, SC 29620; phone: 864-366-5074; hours 8AM-5PM (EST). *Felony, Misdemeanor, Civil Actions Over $7,500.*

Civil Records: Access: In person only. Visitors must perform in person searches themselves. Court makes copy: $.50 per page. Required to search: name, years to search. Civil cases indexed by defendant, plaintiff; on card index from 1870.

Criminal Records: Access: In person only. Visitors must perform in person searches themselves. Court makes copy: $.50 per page. Required to search: name, years to search; SSN helpful. Criminal records on card index from 1870.

General Information: No public access terminal. No adoption, juvenile, sealed or expunged records released. Certification fee: $1.00 per page. Payee: Clerk of Court. Personal checks accepted. Prepayment required.

Probate Court PO Box 70, Abbeville, SC 29620; phone: 864-459-4626; hours 9AM-5PM (EST). *Probate.*

Aiken County

Circuit Court PO Box 583, Aiken, SC 29802; phone: 803-642-1715; hours 8:30AM-5PM (EST). *Felony, Misdemeanor, Civil Actions Over $7,500.* http:www.aikencountysc.gov

Civil Records: Access: In person only. Both court and visitors may perform in person searches. Court makes copy: $.25 per page; same fee for self serve. Required to search: name, years to search. Civil cases indexed by defendant, plaintiff; on computer from 1988; on microfiche, archives and card index from 1800s.

Criminal Records: Access: In person only. Both court and visitors may perform in person searches. Search fee: Court may charge a search fee. Court makes copy: $.25 per page; same fee for self serve. Required to search: name, years to search, DOB; SSN helpful. Criminal records on computer from 1990; on microfiche, archives and card index from 1800s.

General Information: Public use terminal available. No adoption, juvenile, sealed or expunged records released. Will not fax specific case file. Certification fee: $1.00. Payee: Clerk of Court. Only cashiers checks and money orders accepted. Prepayment required.

Aiken Magistrate Court 1680 Richland Ave W, #70, Aiken, SC 29801; phone: 803-642-1744/1747; fax: 803-642-1749; hours 9AM-5PM (EST). *Misdemeanor, Civil Actions Under $7,500, Eviction, Small Claims.*

Graniteville Magistrate Court 50 Canal St, #14, Graniteville, SC 29829; phone: 803-663-6634; fax: 803-663-6635; hours 9AM-5PM (EST). *Civil Actions Under $7,500, Misdemeanor, Eviction, Small Claims.*

Note: Misdemeanor records accessed same as civil.

Langley Magistrate Court PO Box 769, 129 Langley Dam Rd, Langley, SC 29834; phone: 803-593-5171/5172; fax: 803-593-8402; hours 9AM-5PM (EST). *Misdemeanor, Civil Actions Under $7,500, Eviction, Small Claims.*

Monetta Magistrate Court 5697 Columbia Hwy N, PO Box 190, Monetta, SC 29105; phone: 803-685-7125; fax: 803-685-7988; hours 8:30AM-12:30PM;1:30-4:30PM (EST). *Misdemeanor, Civil Actions Under $7,500, Eviction, Small Claims.*

New Ellenton Magistrate Court PO Box 40, 327 Main St, New Ellenton, SC 29809; phone: 803-652-3609; fax: 803-652-2653; hours 9-5:00PM (EST). *Misdemeanor, Civil Actions Under $7,500, Eviction, Small Claims.*

North Augusta Magistrate Court PO Box 6493, North Augusta, SC 29861; phone: 803-202-3580/3581; fax: 803-202-3583; hours 9AM-5PM

(EST). *Misdemeanor, Civil Actions Under $7,500, Eviction, Small Claims.*

Probate Court PO Box 1576, 109 Park Ave, Aiken, SC 29802; phone: 803-642-2002; fax: 803-642-2007; hours 8:30AM-5PM (EST). *Probate.*

Allendale County

Circuit Court PO Box 126, 292 Barnwell Hwy, Allendale, SC 29810; phone: 803-584-2737; fax: 803-584-7046; hours 9AM-5PM (EST). *Felony, Misdemeanor, Civil Actions Over $7,500.*

Civil Records: Access: Phone, fax, mail, in person. Both court and visitors may perform in person searches. Search fee: $5.00 per name. Court makes copy: $.50 per page. Required to search: name, years to search. Civil cases indexed by defendant, plaintiff; on computer 1988, card index from 1919. Mail turnaround time 2 days.

Criminal Records: Access: Phone, fax, mail, in person. Both court and visitors may perform in person searches. Search fee: $5.00 per name. Court makes copy: $.50 per page. Required to search: name, years to search, DOB, signed release; also helpful: SSN. Criminal records kept on computer for 3 years. Mail turnaround time 2 days.

General Information: Public terminal goes back to 1987. No adoption, juvenile, sealed or expunged records released. Certification fee: $2.00. Payee: Clerk of Court. Personal checks accepted. Prepayment and SASE required.

Allendale Magistrate Court 160 Law Enforcement Court, Fairfax, SC 29827; phone: 803-584-3755; fax: 803-584-7980; hours 9AM-5PM (EST). *Misdemeanor, Civil Actions Under $7,500, Eviction, Small Claims.*

Note: Now combined with Fairfax Court; address and phone given above.

Fairfax Magistrate Court 160 Law Enforcement Court, PO Box 516, Fairfax, SC 29827; phone: 803-584-3755; fax: 803-584-7980; hours 9-5PM (EST). *Misdemeanor, Civil Actions Under $7,500, Eviction, Small Claims, Traffic.*

Probate Court PO Box 603, Courthouse Complex, Allendale, SC 29810; phone: 803-584-3157; hours 9AM-5PM (EST). *Probate.*

Anderson County

Circuit Court PO Box 8002, Anderson, SC 29622; phone: 864-260-4053; fax: 864-260-4715; hours 8:30AM-5PM (EST). *Felony, Misdemeanor, Civil Actions Over $7,500.*

Civil Records: Access: In person, online. Visitors must perform in person searches themselves. Court makes copy: $.50 per page. Required to search: name, years to search. Civil cases indexed by defendant, plaintiff; on computer back to 1994, prior on cards. Access to Circuit Court records is free at http://acpass.andersoncountysc.org/coc_main.htm. Includes Family Court records.

Criminal Records: Access: In person, online. Visitors must perform in person searches themselves. Court makes copy: $.50 per page. Required to search: name, years to search, DOB, SSN, signed release. Criminal records on computer back to 1994, prior on cards. Access to criminal records is the same as civil.

General Information: Public terminal goes back to 1993. No adoption, juvenile, sealed or expunged records released. No certification fee. Payee: Clerk of Court. Personal checks accepted. Prepayment required.

Anderson Magistrate Court PO Box 8002, 107 S Main St, Anderson, SC 29622; phone: 864-260-4156/4055; fax: 864-260-4144; hours 8:30AM-5PM (EST). *Misdemeanor, Civil Actions Under $7,500, Eviction, Small Claims.* www.andersoncountysc.org

Honea Path Magistrate Court PO Box 505,

Honea Path, SC 29654; phone: 864-369-0015; fax: 864-369-0015; hours 8:30AM-2PM M, T, Th; 8:30AM-N W (EST). *Misdemeanor, Civil Actions Under $7,500, Eviction, Small Claims.*

Iva Magistrate Court

Court closed 2004; records at Starr Magistrate Court.

Pelzer Magistrate Court PO Box 824, 26 Main St, Pelzer, SC 29669; phone: 864-947-5225; fax: Same; hours 9AM-4PM M, T, 11AM-3PM W, 9AM-1PM Th, Closed Fri (EST). *Civil Actions Under $7,500, Eviction, Small Claims, Misdemeanor.*

Pendleton Magistrate Court 100 E Queen, Pendleton, SC 29670; phone: 864-646-6701; fax: 864-646-6704; hours 8AM-4PM T W; 8AM-2PM Th (EST). *Misdemeanor, Civil Actions Under $7,500, Eviction, Small Claims.*

Piedmont Magistrate Court PO Box 51312, 104 Annex Way, Piedmont, SC 29642; phone: 864-295-2651; fax: 864-295-5962; hours 8:30AM-5PM (EST). *Misdemeanor, Civil Actions Under $7,500, Eviction, Small Claims.*

Starr Magistrate Court PO Box 247, 7627 Hwy 81 S, Starr, SC 29684; phone: 864-352-3157; fax: 864-352-3157; hours 7AM-N M-Th (EST). *Misdemeanor, Civil Actions Under $7,500, Eviction, Small Claims.*

Note: Also holds records for Iva Magistrate Court which has been closed.

Williamston Magistrate Court 12 W Main St, PO Box 125, Williamston, SC 29697; phone: 864-847-8580; hours 9AM-N; 1PM-5PM T, W, Th (EST). *Misdemeanor, Civil Actions Under $7,500, Eviction, Small Claims.*

Probate Court PO Box 8002, 100 S Main St, Anderson, SC 29622; phone: 864-260-4049; fax: 864-260-4811; hours 8:30AM-3;45PM (EST). *Probate.*

Note: Access to the county probate court, marriage, estate, and guardian/conservatorship records is available free at http://acpass.andersoncountysc.org/Probate_Main.htm

Bamberg County

Circuit Court PO Box 150, Bamberg, SC 29003; phone: 803-245-3025; fax: 803-245-3088; hours 9AM-5PM (EST). *Felony, Misdemeanor, Civil Actions Over $7,500.*

Civil Records: Access: Mail, in person fax. Both court and visitors may perform in person searches. Search fee: $5.00 per name. Court makes copy: $.25 per page; same fee for self serve. Required to search: name, years to search. Civil cases indexed by defendant, plaintiff; on index books, files back to 1890. Mail turnaround time 1-2 days.

Criminal Records: Access: Mail, in person, fax. Both court and visitors may perform in person searches. Search fee: $5.00 per name. Court makes copy: $.25 per page; same fee for self serve. Required to search: name, years to search, DOB; also helpful: SSN. Criminal records on index books, files back to 1890. Mail turnaround time 1-2 days.

General Information: No public access terminal. No adoption, juvenile, sealed or expunged records released. Certification fee: $1.00 per cert. Payee: Clerk of Court. Personal checks accepted. Prepayment and SASE required.

Bamberg Magistrate Court PO Box 187, 2873 Main Hwy, Bamberg, SC 29003; phone: 803-245-3016; fax: 803-245-3085; hours 9AM-5PM M-F (EST). *Misdemeanor, Civil Actions Under $7,500, Eviction, Small Claims.*

Probate Court PO Box 180, 2959 Main Hwy, Bamberg, SC 29003; phone: 803-245-3008; fax: 803-245-3008; hours 9AM-5PM (EST). *Probate.*

Barnwell County

Circuit Court PO Box 723, Barnwell, SC 29812; phone: 803-541-1020; fax: 803-541-1025; hours 9AM-5PM (EST). *Felony, Misdemeanor, Civil Actions Over $7,500.*
Note: Records location is; 141 Main St, Barnwell, SC, 29812.
Civil Records: Access: In person only. Visitors must perform in person searches themselves. Court makes copy: $.50 per page. Required to search: name, years to search. Civil cases indexed by defendant. Civil records on computer from 1988.
Criminal Records: Access: In person only. Visitors must perform in person searches themselves. Court makes copy: $.50 per page. Required to search: name, years to search, DOB, SSN. Criminal records on computer from 1988.
General Information: No adoption, juvenile, sealed or expunged records released. Certification fee: $1.00. Payee: Clerk of Court. Personal checks accepted. Prepayment required.

Barnwell Magistrate Court PO Box 1205, 130 Calhoun St, Barnwell, SC 29812; phone: 803-541-1035; fax: 803-541-1055; hours 9AM-N, 1-5PM (EST). *Misdemeanor, Civil Actions Under $7,500, Eviction, Small Claims.*

Blackville Magistrate Court 5997 Lartique St, Blackville, SC 29817; phone: 803-284-2765; fax: 803--284-9107; hours 8AM-5PM M,T,Th,F; 8AM-N Wed (EST). *Misdemeanor, Civil Actions Under $7,500, Eviction, Small Claims.*

Williston Magistrate Court PO Box 485, 12445 Main St, Williston, SC 29853; phone: 803-266-3700; fax: 803-266-5496; hours 9AM-5PM (EST). *Misdemeanor, Civil Actions Under $7,500, Eviction, Small Claims.*

Probate Court Rm 108, County Courthouse, 57 Wall St, Barnwell, SC 29812; phone: 803-541-1032; fax: 803-541-1012; hours 9AM-5PM (EST). *Probate.*

Beaufort County

Circuit Court PO Drawer 1128, 102 Ribaut Rd, Rm 208, Beaufort, SC 29901; phone: 843-470-5218; fax: 843-470-5248; hours 8AM-5PM (EST). *Felony, Misdemeanor, Civil Actions Over $7,500.*
www.bcgov.org/Clerk_Court/clerk_court.htm
Civil Records: Access: Mail, in person. Both court and visitors may perform in person searches. Search fee: $10.00 per name. Court makes copy: $.25 per page. Required to search: name, years to search. Civil cases indexed by defendant, plaintiff; on computer back to 1985; prior in index books.
Criminal Records: Access: Mail, in person. Both court and visitors may perform in person searches. Search fee: $10.00 per name. Court makes copy: $.25 per page. Required to search: name, years to search, DOB; also helpful: SSN. Criminal records on computer back to 1985; prior in index books.
General Information: Public terminal has criminal back to 1985 and civil back to 1997. No adoption, juvenile, sealed or expunged records released. Certification fee: $1.00. Payee: Clerk of Court. Personal checks accepted. Prepayment required.

Beaufort Magistrate Court PO Box 2207, 100 Ribaut St, Beaufort, SC 29901-2207; phone: 843-470-5201/5210; criminal phone: 843-470-5202; civil phone: 843-470-5210; criminal fax: 843-470-5206; civil fax: 843-470-5208; hours 8AM-4PM M-Th, 8AM-N F
8AM-4PM M-Th (EST). *Misdemeanor, Civil Actions Under $7,500, Eviction, Small Claims, Traffic.*

Bluffton Magistrate Court PO Box 840, 59 Ulmer Rd, Bluffton, SC 29910; phone: 843-757-1500; fax: 843-757-1527; hours 8AM-5PM (EST). *Misdemeanor, Civil Actions Under $7,500, Eviction, Small Claims.*

Hilton Head Magistrate Court PO Box 22895, Hilton Head, SC 29925; phone: 843-842-4260; fax: 843-842-4261. *Misdemeanor, Civil Actions Under $7,500, Eviction, Small Claims.*

Lobeco Magistrate Court PO Box 845, Lobeco, SC 29931-0845; phone: 843-846-3902; hours 5:30PM-7:30P M, W (EST). *Misdemeanor, Civil Actions Under $7,500, Eviction, Small Claims.*

St Helena Island Magistrate Court PO Box 1271, St Helena Island, SC 29920; phone: 843-838-3212; hours 1PM-5PM (EST). *Misdemeanor, Civil Actions Under $7,500, Eviction, Small Claims.*

Probate Court PO Box 1083, 102 Ribaut Rd, Beaufort, SC 29901-1083; phone: 843-470-5319; fax: 843-470-5324; hours 8AM-5PM (EST). *Probate.*

Berkeley County

Circuit Court PO Box 219, Moncks Corner, SC 29461; phone: 843-719-4400; hours 9AM-5PM (EST). *Felony, Misdemeanor, Civil Actions Over $7,500.*
Civil Records: Access: In person only. Visitors must perform in person searches themselves. Court makes copy: $.35 per page. Required to search: name, years to search. Civil cases indexed by defendant, plaintiff; on computer from early 1980s, prior on books.
Criminal Records: Access: In person only. Visitors must perform in person searches themselves. Court makes copy: $.35 per page. Required to search: name, years to search, DOB, SSN. Criminal records on computer from early 1980s, prior on books. Court personnel will not perform name searches for criminal record information.
General Information: Public terminal has criminal back to 1990 and civil back to 1984. No adoption, juvenile, sealed or expunged records released. Certification fee: 1st cert free; $1.00 per doc each add'l.

Central Summary Court 103 Gulledge St, Moncks Corner, SC 29461; phone: 843-719-4050 or 723-3800 X4050; fax: 843-719-4534; hours 9AM-5PM (EST). *Misdemeanor, Civil Actions Under $7,500, Eviction, Small Claims.*
www.co.berkeley.sc.us
Note: Formerly Moncks Corner Magistrate Court.

Goose Creek Magistrate Court 538 Redbank Rd, Goose Creek, SC 29445; phone: 843-553-7080; fax: 843-553-7074; hours 9AM-5PM (EST). *Misdemeanor, Civil Actions Under $7,500, Eviction, Small Claims.*
Note: The former Summervile Magistrate Court merged with this court. Note there is also a Summerville Magistrate Court in Dorchester county.

St Stephen Magistrate Court 1158 S Main St, St Stephen, SC 29479; phone: 843-567-7400; fax: 843-567-3106; hours 9AM-5PM (EST). *Misdemeanor, Civil Actions Under $7,500, Eviction.*

Probate Court 300 B California Ave, Moncks Corner, SC 29461; phone: 843-719-4519; fax: 843-719-4527; hours 9AM-5PM (EST). *Probate.*

Calhoun County

Circuit Court PO Box 709, St Matthews, SC 29135-0709; phone: 803-874-3524; fax: 803-874-1942; hours 9AM-5PM (EST). *Felony, Misdemeanor, Civil Actions Over $7,500.*
Civil Records: Access: In person only. Visitors must perform in person searches themselves. Self serve copy fee: $.25 per page. Required to search: name, years to search. Civil cases indexed by defendant, plaintiff; on computer from 1984, prior on index books from 1908.
Criminal Records: Access: In person only. Both court and visitors may perform in person searches. No search fee. Self serve copy fee: $.25 per page. Required to search: name, years to search, DOB.

Criminal records on computer from 1984, prior on index books from 1908.
General Information: Public use terminal available. No adoption, juvenile, sealed or expunged records released. Will not fax specific case file. No certification fee. Payee: Clerk of Court. Personal checks accepted. Prepayment required.

Cameron Magistrate Court PO Box 663, 204 Boyce Lawton Dr, Cameron, SC 29030; phone: 803-823-2266; fax: 803-823-2288; hours 1PM-5PM T,Th (EST). *Misdemeanor, Civil Actions Under $7,500, Eviction, Small Claims.*

Cameron Magistrate Court Cameron Town Hall, PO Box 663, Cameron, SC 29030; phone: 803-823-2266; fax: 803-823-2288; hours 1PM-5PM T, Th (EST). *Misdemeanor, Civil Actions Under $7,500, Eviction, Small Claims.*
Note: This court is also a Municipal Court.

St Matthews Magistrate Court 1623 Bridge St W, PO Box 191, St Matthews, SC 29135; phone: 803-874-1112; fax: 803-874-1111; hours 8:30AM-4PM (EST). *Misdemeanor, Civil Actions Under $7,500, Eviction, Small Claims.*

Probate Court 902 Huff Dr, St Matthews, SC 29135; phone: 803-874-3514; fax: 803-874-1942; hours 9AM-5PM (EST). *Probate.*

Charleston County

Circuit Court 100 Broad St, #106, Charleston, SC 29401-2210; phone: 843-958-5000; fax: 843-958-5020; hours 8:30AM-5PM (EST). *Felony, Misdemeanor, Civil Actions Over $7,500.*
http://www3.charlestoncounty.org
Civil Records: Access: Online, in person. Visitors must perform in person searches themselves. Court makes copy: $.25 per page; same fee for self serve. Required to search: name, years to search. Civil cases indexed by defendant, plaintiff; on computer from 1988, microfiche and archives from mid 1853. Access to civil records 1988 forward, also judgments and lis pendens are free at http://www3.charlestoncounty.org/connect. Online document images go back to 1/1/1999.
Criminal Records: Access: Online, in person. Both court and visitors may perform in person searches. Court makes copy: $.25 per page; same fee for self serve. Required to search: name, years to search, DOB; also helpful: SSN. Criminal records on computer from 4/92, prior on books and microfilm from 1918. Access to records from 04/92 forward free at http://www3.charlestoncounty.org/connect. Search by name or case number.
General Information: Public terminal goes back to 1975. No adoption, juvenile, sealed or expunged records released. No fee to fax documents. Certification fee: $1.00 per cert. Payee: Clerk of Court. Business checks accepted. Prepayment required.

Charleston Magistrate Court 4045 Bridgeview Dr, PO Box 60037, Charleston, SC 29419; phone: 843-202-6600; criminal phone: 843-554-2462; fax: 843-202-6620; hours 8:30AM-4:30PM (EST). *Civil Actions Under $7,500, Misdemeanor, Eviction, Small Claims.*
www.charlestoncounty.org
Note: County magistrate requests for background checks forwarded to Sheriff's Office-843-202-6610.
Civil Records: Access: In person, online. Court makes copy: $.25 per page. Civil records from 1998 forward can be access via http://www3.charlestoncounty.org/connect.
Criminal Records: Access: In person, online. Court makes copy: $.25 per page for disposition. Access criminal and traffic records from 1993 forward free at http://www3.charlestoncounty.org/connect. Requests for background checks forwarded to Sheriff's Office, except if military personnel.
General Information: Certification fee: $7.00 per doc. Payee: County Treasurer. Prepayment required.

Charleston Magistrate Court 995 Morrison Dr, PO Box 941, Charleston, SC 29402; phone: 843-724-6720; fax: 843-724-6785; hours 8:30AM-5PM M-Th; 8:30AM-1PM F (EST). *Small Claims.*
Note: Access civil records from 1998 forward free at http://www3.charlestoncounty.org/connect.

Charleston Magistrate Court 995 Morrison Dr, PO Box 941, Charleston, SC 29402; phone: 843-724-6719; hours 8:30AM-5PM M-Th; 8:30AM-1PM F (EST). *Evictions.*
Note: Access civil records from 1998 forward free at http://www3.charlestoncounty.org/connect.

East Cooper Magistrate Court 1189 Iron Bridge Rd, #300, PO Box 584, Mt Pleasant, SC 29466; phone: 843-856-1205; fax: 843-856-1188; hours 8AM-4;30PM (EST). *Misdemeanor, Civil Actions Under $7,500, Eviction.*
http://www3.charlestoncounty.org/docs/CoC/index.html
Note: Access civil records from 1998 forward free at http://www3.charlestoncounty.org/connect.

Edisto Island Magistrate Court 8070 Indigo Hill Rd, PO Box 159, Edisto Island, SC 29438; phone: 843-869-2909; fax: 843-869-4460; hours 4:00PM-6PM M, W (EST). *Misdemeanor, Civil Actions Under $7,500, Eviction, Traffic.*
Note: Access civil records from 1998 forward free at http://www3.charlestoncounty.org/connect.

James Island Magistrate Court PO Box 12226, James Island, SC 29422; phone: 843-795-1140; fax: 843-406-2753; hours 8:30AM-12;30, 1;30-4;30PM M-Th; 8AM-N F (EST). *Misdemeanor, Civil Actions Under $7,500, Eviction.*
Note: Access civil records from 1998 forward free at http://www3.charlestoncounty.org/connect.

Johns Island Magistrate Court 1527 Main Rd, Johns Island, SC 29455; phone: 843-559-1218; fax: 843-559-2378; hours 9AM-5PM T,Th; 9AM-6;30PM M,W,F (EST). *Misdemeanor, Civil Actions Under $7,500, Eviction.*
Note: Access civil records from 1998 forward free at http://www3.charlestoncounty.org/connect.

McClellanville Magistrate Court PO Box 7, 10009 Hwy 17 N, McClellanville, SC 29458; phone: 843-887-3334; fax: 843-887-3901; hours 9AM-N, 1-4PM M-Th (EST). *Misdemeanor, Civil Actions Under $7,500, Eviction, Small Claims.*
Note: Access civil records from 1998 forward free at http://www3.charlestoncounty.org/connect.

North Charleston Magistrate Court 4045 Bridge View Dr, #B146, PO Box 70235, North Charleston, SC 29405; phone: 843-202-6650; fax: 843-202-6652; hours 8:30AM-4:30PM (EST). *Misdemeanor, Civil Actions Under $7,500, Small Claims.*
Note: Access civil records from 1998 forward free at http://www3.charlestoncounty.org/connect.

North Charleston Magistrate Court 7272 Cross County Rd, North Charleston, SC 29419; phone: 843-767-2743; fax: 843-760-6887; hours 8:30AM-4:30PM (EST). *Misdemeanor, Civil Actions Under $7,500, Eviction.*
Note: Access civil records from 1998 forward free at http://www3.charlestoncounty.org/connect.

North Charleston Magistrate Court 2036 Cherokee St, PO Box 71316, North Charleston, SC 29416; phone: 843-745-2215; fax: 843-745-2334; hours 8:30AM-1, 2-4:30PM (EST). *Misdemeanor, Civil Actions Under $7,500, Eviction, Small Claims.*
Note: Access civil records from 1998 forward free at http://www3.charlestoncounty.org/connect.

Ravenel Magistrate Court 5962 Hwy 165, #200, Ravenel, SC 29470; phone: 843-889-8332; fax: 843-889-9202; hours 8:30AM-4:30PM (EST). *Misdemeanor, Civil Actions Under $7,500, Eviction, Small Claims.*
Note: Access civil records from 1998 forward free at http://www3.charlestoncounty.org/connect.

West Ashley Magistrate Court 1720 Sam Rittenberg Blvd, Unit 11, PO Box 31861, Charleston, SC 29417; phone: 843-766-6531; fax: 843-571-4751; hours 8:30AM-4:30 PM M-Th; 8AM-1PM F (EST). *Civil Actions Under $7,500, Eviction.*
www.charlestoncounty.org
Note: Access civil records from 1998 forward free at http://www3.charlestoncounty.org/connect.

Probate Court 84 Broad St, North Charleston, SC 29401-2284; phone: 843-958-5030; fax: 843-958-5044; hours 8:30AM-5PM (EST). *Probate.*
Note: Access to Estate and Wills records is free at http://www3.charlestoncounty.org/connect/LU_GRO UP_2?ref=Conserv.

Cherokee County

Circuit Court PO Drawer 2289, Gaffney, SC 29342; phone: 864-487-2571; civil phone: 864-487-2533; probate phone: 864-487-2588; fax: 864-487-2754; hours 8:30AM-5PM (EST). *Felony, Misdemeanor, Civil Actions Over $7,500.*
Civil Records: Access: In person only. Visitors must perform in person searches themselves. Court makes copy: $.50 per page; same fee for self serve. Required to search: name, years to search. Civil cases indexed by defendant, plaintiff. Civil records go back to 1897; computerized records go back to 1994.
Criminal Records: Access: In person only. Visitors must perform in person searches themselves. Court makes copy: $.50 per page; same fee for self serve. Required to search: name, years to search. Criminal records on computer from 1994, prior on books.
General Information: Public terminal goes back to 1989. No adoption, juvenile, sealed or expunged records released. Certification fee: $1.00. Payee: Clerk of Court. Business checks accepted. Prepayment required.

Blacksburg Magistrate Court 101 S John St #A, PO Box 427, Blacksburg, SC 29702; phone: 864-839-2492; fax: 864-839-3415; hours 8:30AM-5PM (EST). *Misdemeanor, Civil Actions Under $7,500, Eviction, Small Claims.*

Cherokee County Magistrate Court PO Box 336, 312 E Frederick St, Gaffney, SC 29342-0336; phone: 864-487-2533/2501; criminal phone: 864-487-2533; civil phone: 864-487-2502; fax: 864-902-8425; hours 8:30AM-5PM (EST). *Misdemeanors, Civil Actions Under $7,500, Eviction, Small Claims.*
www.cherokeemagistrate.com
Note: Civil Action minimum was increased to $7,500 on January 1, 2001.

Probate Court PO Box 22, 1434 N Limestone St, Peachtree Ctr, Gaffney, SC 29342; phone: 864-487-2583; fax: 864-902-8426; hours 9AM-4:30PM (EST). *Probate.*
www.cherokeecountyprobate.com
Note: Marriage license phone-864-487-2589.

Chester County

Circuit Court PO Drawer 580, Chester, SC 29706; phone: 803-385-2605; fax: 803-581-7975; hours 8:30AM-5PM (EST). *Felony, Misdemeanor, Civil Actions Over $7,500.*
Civil Records: Access: In person only. Visitors must perform in person searches themselves. Court makes copy: $.50 per legal page; $.25 per letter page; same fee for self serve. Required to search: name, years to search, address. Civil cases indexed by defendant, plaintiff; on computer from 1989, microfiche from 1927.
Criminal Records: Access: In person. Visitors must perform in person searches themselves. Court makes copy: $.50 per legal page; $.25 per letter page; same fee for self serve. Required to search: name, years to search, DOB, signed release; also helpful: SSN. Criminal records on computer from 1994, docket books prior.
General Information: Public terminal has only civil records back to 1992. No adoption, juvenile, sealed or expunged records released. Certification fee:

$1.00. Payee: Clerk of Court. Personal checks accepted. Prepayment required.

Chester Magistrate Court 2740 Dawson Dr, PO Box 727, Chester, SC 29706; phone: 803-581-5136; 581-3040; fax: 803-581-3033; hours 8;30AM-5PM (EST). *Misdemeanor, Civil Actions Under $7,500, Eviction, Small Claims.*

Probate Court PO Drawer 580, 140 Main St, Chester, SC 29706; phone: 803-385-2604; fax: 803-581-5180; hours 8:30AM-5PM (EST). *Probate.*
Note: Records go back to late 1780s.

Chesterfield County

Circuit Court PO Box 529, Chesterfield, SC 29709; phone: 843-623-2574; probate phone: 843-623-2376; fax: 843-623-6944; hours 8:30AM-5PM (EST). *Felony, Misdemeanor, Civil Actions Over $7,500.*
Civil Records: Access: Mail, in person. Both court and visitors may perform in person searches. Search fee: $5.00 per name. Court makes copy: $2.00 per document and $.25 per page after 1st 4 pages. Self serve copy fee: $.25 per page. Required to search: name, years to search. Civil cases indexed by defendant, plaintiff; on computer back to 1986, prior on docket books. Mail turnaround time 3 days.
Criminal Records: Access: Mail, in person. Both court and visitors may perform in person searches. Search fee: $5.00 per name. Court makes copy: $2.00 per document and $.25 per page after 1st 4 pages. Self serve copy fee: $.25 per page. Required to search: name, years to search, DOB, SSN. Criminal records on computer back to 1986, prior on docket books. Mail turnaround time 3 days.
General Information: No adoption, juvenile, sealed or expunged records released. Will fax documents free to toll-free number; $5.00 fee if to non-toll-free number. No certification fee. Payee: Clerk of Court. Personal checks accepted. Prepayment and SASE required.

Cheraw Magistrate Court 1486 Hinson Hill Rd, Cheraw, SC 29520; phone: 843-623-2955; hours 11AM-5PM M,T,W; 12-3PM Thur (EST). *Misdemeanor, Civil Actions Under $7,500, Eviction, Small Claims.*

Cheraw Magistrate Court 563 Hwy 52 N, PO Box 364, Cheraw, SC 29520; phone: 843-537-3323; fax: 843-537-3883; hours 8AM-6PM (EST). *Misdemeanor, Civil Actions Under $7,500, Eviction, Small Claims.*

Cheraw Magistrate Court 1515 Jackson Rd, Chesterfield, SC 29709; phone: 843-623-7829. *Misdemeanor, Civil Actions Under $7,500, Eviction, Small Claims.*
Note: Magistrate has retired; court records now at Chesterfield, address and phone given above.

Chesterfield Magistrate Court 1515 E Jackson Rd, Chesterfield, SC 29709; phone: 843-623-7829; hours 9AM-4PM M-Th (EST). *Misdemeanor, Civil Actions Under $7,500, Eviction, Small Claims.*
Note: Now holds records for Cheraw magistrate Court, which has closed.

McBee Magistrate Court Box 576, McBee, SC 29101; phone: 843-335-5030; hours 9AM-4PM M, 9AM-3PM T,W, Th, Closed Fri (EST). *Misdemeanor, Civil Actions Under $7,500, Eviction, Small Claims.*

Pageland Magistrate Court 310 W McGregor St, PO Box 133, Pageland, SC 29728; phone: 843-672-5685; hours 10AM-3PM (EST). *Misdemeanor, Civil Actions Under $7,500, Eviction, Small Claims.*

Patrick Magistrate Court 10292 Hwy 102, Patrick, SC 29584; phone: 843-498-6398; hours 1PM-5PM M-Th (EST). *Misdemeanor, Civil Actions Under $7,500, Eviction, Small Claims.*

Ruby Magistrate Court 408 Deaton St, PO Box 131, Ruby, SC 29741; phone: 843-634-6597; hours 10AM-3PM, closed Wed (EST). *Misdemeanor, Civil Actions Under $7,500, Eviction, Small Claims.*

Probate Court County Courthouse, 200 W Main St, Chesterfield, SC 29709; phone: 843-623-2376; fax: 843-623-9886; hours 8:30AM-5PM (EST). *Probate.*

Clarendon County

Circuit Court PO Box 136, Manning, SC 29102; phone: 803-435-4444; criminal phone: 803-435-4210x309; civil phone: 803-435-4443; fax: 803-435-4844; hours 8:30AM-5PM (EST). *Felony, Misdemeanor, Civil Actions Over $7,500.*
Civil Records: Access: Mail, in person. Both court and visitors may perform in person searches. Search fee: $10.00. Includes all copy fees. Court makes copy: $.25 per page. Required to search: name, years to search. Civil cases indexed by defendant, plaintiff; on computer from 1988, index books from 1865. Mail turnaround time 5 days.
Criminal Records: Access: Mail, in person. Both court and visitors may perform in person searches. Search fee: $10.50. Includes copy fees. Court makes copy: $.25 per page. Required to search: name, years to search. Criminal records on computer from 1983, index books from 1865. Mail turnaround 5 days.
General Information: Public terminal goes back to 1985. No adoption, juvenile, sealed or expunged records released. Certification fee: $2.00. Payee: Clerk of Court. Personal checks accepted. Prepayment and SASE required.

Manning Magistrate Court 102 S Mill St, PO Box 371, Manning, SC 29102; phone: 803-435-2670/8925; fax: 803-435-0885; hours 8:30AM-5PM (EST). *Misdemeanor, Civil Actions Under $7,500, Eviction, Small Claims.*

Summerton Magistrate Court 10 W Main St, PO Box 279, Summerton, SC 29148; phone: 803-485-2525 x14; fax: 803-485-2914; hours 9AM-5PM (EST). *Misdemeanor, Civil Actions Under $7,500, Eviction, Small Claims.*

Probate Court PO Box 307, Manning, SC 29102; phone: 803-435-8774; fax: 803-435-8698; hours 8:30AM-5PM (EST). *Probate.*

Colleton County

Circuit Court PO Box 620, Walterboro, SC 29488; phone: 843-549-5791; fax: 843-549-2875; hours 8:00AM-5PM (EST). *Felony, Misdemeanor, Civil Actions Over $7,500.*
www.colletoncounty.org/legalcourt/index.html
Civil Records: Access: Phone, fax, mail, in person. Both court and visitors may perform in person searches. Search fee: $10.00 per name. Court makes copy: $.50 per page; same fee for self serve. Required to search: name, years to search. Civil cases indexed by defendant, plaintiff; on computer from 1986, on index books from 1865. Mail turnaround 2 days.
Criminal Records: Access: Phone, fax, mail, in person. Both court and visitors may perform in person searches. Search fee: $10.00 per name. Court makes copy: $.50 per page; same fee for self serve. Required to search: name, years to search; also helpful: SSN, DOB. Criminal records on computer from 1986, on index books from 1865. Mail turnaround time 2 days.
General Information: Public terminal has criminal back to 1985-6 and civil back to 1998. No adoption, juvenile, PTI, sealed or expunged records released. Extra $2.00 fee to receive and fax documents. Certification fee: $1.00. Payee: Clerk of Court. Business checks accepted. Prepayment and SASE required.

Green Pond Magistrate Court 8464 Ace Basin Pky, Green Pond, SC 29446; phone: 843-844-8486; fax: 843-844-8835; hours 9AM-4:30PM (EST). *Misdemeanor, Civil Actions Under $7,500, Eviction, Small Claims.*

Walterboro Magistrate Court 40-B Klein St, PO Box 1732, Walterboro, SC 29488; phone: 843-549-1122; fax: 843-549-9010; hours 8AM-5PM (EST). *Misdemeanor, Civil Actions Under $7,500, Eviction, Small Claims.*

Walterboro Magistrate Court 149 Magistrate Ln, Walterboro, SC 29488; phone: 843-538-3637/3903; fax: 843-538-5173; hours 8AM-5PM (EST). *Misdemeanor, Civil Actions Under $7,500, Eviction, Small Claims.*

Probate Court PO Box 1036, 200 E Washington St, Walterboro, SC 29488-0031; phone: 843-549-7216; fax: 843-549-5571; hours 8:00AM-5PM (EST). *Probate.*

Darlington County

Circuit Court PO Box 1177, Darlington, SC 29540; phone: 843-398-4339; fax: 843-398-4172; hours 8:30AM-5PM (EST). *Felony, Misdemeanor, Civil Actions Over $7,500.*
Civil Records: Access: In person only. Visitors must perform in person searches themselves. Court makes copy: $.10 per page; same fee for self serve. Required to search: name, years to search. Civil cases indexed by defendant, plaintiff; on computer from 1989, on index books from 1805.
Criminal Records: Access: In person only. Visitors must perform in person searches themselves. Court makes copy: $.10 per page; same fee for self serve. Required to search: name, years to search; also helpful: DOB, SSN. Criminal records on computer from 1989, on index books from 1805. Will give disposition & sentence over phone if case number given.
General Information: Public terminal goes back to 1989. No adoption, juvenile, sealed or expunged records released. Will fax documents to local or toll free line. No certification fee. Payee: Clerk of Court. Business checks accepted. Prepayment required.

Darlington Magistrate Court PO Box 782 (115 Camp Rd), Darlington, SC 29532; phone: 843-398-4340; fax: 843-398-4458; hours 8:30AM-5PM (EST). *Misdemeanor, Civil Actions Under $7,500, Eviction, Small Claims.*

Hartsville Magistrate Court 404 S 4th St, PO Box 1765, Hartsville, SC 29550; phone: 843-332-9661; fax: 843-332-7212; hours 8:30AM-5PM (EST). *Misdemeanor, Civil Actions Under $7,500, Eviction, Small Claims.*

Lamar Magistrate Court 103 Warren Ave, PO Box 38, Lamar, SC 29069; phone: 843-326-5441; fax: 843-326-1543; hours 8AM-6PM T, W, Th (EST). *Misdemeanor, Civil Actions Under $7,500, Eviction, Small Claims.*

Probate Court #1 Public Sq, Courthouse, Rm 208, Darlington, SC 29532; phone: 843-398-4310; fax: 843-398-4076; hours 8:30AM-5PM (EST). *Probate.*

Dillon County

Circuit Court PO Drawer 1220, 301 W Main St, Dillon, SC 29536; phone: 843-774-1425; hours 8:30AM-5PM (EST). *Felony, Misdemeanor, Civil Actions Over $7,500.*
Civil Records: Access: Mail, in person. Both court and visitors may perform in person searches. Search fee: $10.00 per name. Court makes copy: $.50 per page; same fee for self serve. Required to search: name, years to search. Civil cases indexed by defendant, plaintiff; on computer from 1990, on docket books prior. Public can search index books for free. Mail turnaround time 1 day.
Criminal Records: Access: Mail, in person. Both court and visitors may perform in person searches. Search fee: $10.00 per name. Court makes copy: $.50 per page for self serve. Required to search: name, years to search; also helpful: DOB, SSN. Criminal records on computer from 1990, on docket books prior. Public can search index books for free. Mail turnaround time 1 day.

General Information: No adoption, juvenile, sealed or expunged records released. Will fax documents to local or toll free line. No certification fee. Payee: Clerk of Court. Personal checks accepted. Prepayment and SASE required.

Dillon Magistrate Court 200 S 5th Ave, PO Box 1016, Dillon, SC 29536; phone: 843-774-1406; fax: 843-774-1453; hours 8:30AM-5PM (EST). *Misdemeanor, Civil Actions Under $7,500, Eviction, Small Claims.*

Dillon Magistrate Court 200 S 5th Ave, PO Box 1016, Dillon, SC 29536; phone: 843-774-1407; fax: 843-774-1453; hours 8:30AM-5PM (EST). *Misdemeanor, Civil Actions Under $7,500, Eviction, Small Claims.*

Lake View Magistrate Court PO Box 824, 205 N Main St, Lake View, SC 29563; phone: 843-759-2861; fax: 843-759-0177; hours 1PM, T (EST). *Misdemeanor, Civil Actions Under $7,500, Eviction, Small Claims.*

Probate Court PO Box 189, Dillon, SC 29536; phone: 843-774-1423; fax: 843-841-3732; hours 8:30AM-4;30PM (EST). *Probate.*

Dorchester County

Circuit Court 101 Ridge St, St George, SC 29477; phone: 843-563-0160; criminal phone: 843-563-0121; civil phone: 843-563-0113; fax: 843-563-0178; hours 8:30AM-5PM (EST). *Felony, Misdemeanor, Civil Actions Over $7,500.*
Civil Records: Access: In person only. Visitors must perform in person searches themselves. Court makes copy: $.50 per page; same fee for self serve. Required to search: name, years to search. Civil cases indexed by defendant, plaintiff; on index books back to 1950s, on computer since 1994.
Criminal Records: Access: In person only. Visitors must perform in person searches themselves. Court makes copy: $.50 per page; same fee for self serve. Required to search: name, years to search, DOB, signed release; SSN helpful. Criminal records on index books back to 1950s, on computer since 1994.
General Information: Public use terminal available. No adoption, juvenile, sealed or expunged records released. Will not fax specific case file. No certification fee. Payee: Clerk of Court. Personal checks accepted. Prepayment required.

Dorchester County Court 101 Ridge St, St George, SC 29477; phone: 843-563-0164; fax: 843-563-0123; hours 8AM-5PM (EST). *Civil Actions Under $7,500, Eviction, Small Claims.*
Civil Records: Access: Mail. Search fee: none, no certification fee either. Court makes copy: $1.00 per page; same fee for self serve. Records computerized since 1994. Mail turnaround time 5-7 days.
General Information: Public terminal has only civil records back to 1994.

St George Magistrate Court 101 Ridge St, St. George, SC 29477; phone: 843-832-0130; fax: 843-563-0123; hours 8:30AM-5PM (EST). *Misdemeanor, Civil Actions Under $7,500, Eviction, Small Claims.*

Summerville Magistrate Court 212 Deming Way, Box 10, Summerville, SC 29483; phone: 843-832-0370; fax: 843-832-0371; hours 8:30AM-5PM (EST). *Misdemeanor, Civil Actions Under $7,500, Eviction, Small Claims.*

Probate Court 101 Ridge St, County Courthouse, St George, SC 29477; phone: 843-563-0105; fax: 843-563-0245; hours 8:30AM-5PM (EST). *Probate.*

Edgefield County

Circuit Court PO Box 34, Edgefield, SC 29824; phone: 803-637-4082; fax: 803-637-4117; hours 8:30AM-5PM (EST). *Felony, Misdemeanor, Civil Actions Over $7,500.*
Civil Records: Access: Mail, in person. Both court and visitors may perform in person searches. Search fee: $2.00 per name. Court makes copy: $.50

per page; same fee for self serve. Required to search: name, years to search. Civil cases indexed by defendant, plaintiff. Civil records archived from 1839; on computer back to 1987. Mail turnaround time 1 day.

Criminal Records: Access: Mail, in person. Both court and visitors may perform in person searches. Search fee: $200 per name. Court makes copy: $.50 per page; same fee for self serve. Required to search: name, years to search, DOB; also helpful: SSN. Criminal records archived from 1839; on computer back to 1987. Mail turnaround time 1 day.

General Information: Public use terminal available. No adoption, juvenile, sealed or expunged records released. Certification fee: $1.00. Payee: Clerk of Court. Business checks accepted. Prepayment and SASE required.

Edgefield Magistrate Court 215 Jeter St, PO Box 664, Edgefield, SC 29824; criminal phone: 803-637-4052; civil phone: 803-637-4090; fax: 803-637-4101; hours 8:30AM-4:30PM (EST). *Misdemeanor, Civil Actions Under $7,500, Eviction, Small Claims.*

Probate Court 129 Courthouse Square, #212, Edgefield, SC 29824; phone: 803-637-4076; fax: 803-637-7157; hours 8:30AM-5PM (EST). *Probate.*

Fairfield County

Circuit Court PO Drawer 299, Winnsboro, SC 29180; phone: 803-712-6526; hours 9AM-5PM (EST). *Felony, Misdemeanor, Civil Actions Over $7,500.*

Civil Records: Access: In person only. Visitors must perform in person searches themselves. Court makes copy: $.30 per page. Required to search: name, years to search. Civil cases indexed by defendant, plaintiff; on docket books. The court provides an index, but will not do record searching.

Criminal Records: Access: In person only. Visitors must perform in person searches themselves. Court makes copy: $.30 per page. Required to search: name, years to search, DOB; SSN helpful. Criminal records on docket books.

General Information: No adoption, juvenile, sealed or expunged records released. Certification fee: $1.00. Payee: Clerk of Court. No personal checks accepted. Prepayment required.

Winnsboro Magistrate Court 115-B S Congress St, Winnsboro, SC 29180; phone: 803-635-4525; fax: 803-635-5717; hours 9AM-4:30PM (EST). *Misdemeanor, Civil Actions Under $7,500, Eviction, Small Claims.*

Probate Court PO Box 385, Courthouse, Congress St, Winnsboro, SC 29180; phone: 803-712-6519; fax: 803-712-6939; hours 9AM-5PM (EST). *Probate.*
www.sccourts.org/trial/probate/probatejudges.cfm?co untyno=20

Florence County

Circuit Court Drawer E, City County Complex, 180 N Irby St, City County Complex, Florence, SC 29501; phone: 843-665-3031; hours 8:30AM-5PM (EST). *Felony, Misdemeanor, Civil Actions Over $7,500.*
www.florenceco.org/index.html
Civil Records: Access: In person, online. Both court and visitors may perform in person searches. Search fee: $5.00 per name. Court makes copy: $.50. Required to search: name, years to search. Civil cases indexed by defendant, plaintiff; on computer from 1984, on microfiche and docket books from 1900s. Search judgments, liens, deeds, recorded documents back to 1994 at http://web.florenceco.org/cgi-bin/coc/coc.cgi.
Criminal Records: Access: Online, in person. Visitors must perform in person searches themselves. No copy fee. Required to search: name, years to search, DOB; also helpful: SSN. Criminal records on computer from 1984, on microfiche and docket books from 1898. Access criminal record

from 1995 forward free at http://web.florenceco.org/cgi-bin/warrants/war.cgi. **General Information:** Public terminal goes back to 1998. No adoption, juvenile, sealed or expunged records released. Certification fee: $1.00. Payee: Clerk of Court. Personal checks accepted. Prepayment required.

Florence Magistrate Court 180 N Irby St, MSC-W, 120 Courthouse Sq, Florence, SC 29501; phone: 843-665-0031; fax: 843-661-7800; hours 8:30AM-4;30PM (EST). *Misdemeanor, Civil Actions Under $7,500, Eviction, Small Claims.*

Johnsonville Magistrate Court 117 W Broadway, PO Box 904, Johnsonville, SC 29555; phone: 843-380-9211; fax: 843-380-9411; hours 8:30AM-4;30PM M,T,W (EST). *Misdemeanor, Civil Actions Under $7,500, Eviction, Small Claims.*
www.florenceco.org

Lake City Magistrate Court PO Box 39, Lake City, SC 29560; phone: 843-394-5461; fax: 843-394-3865; hours 8:30AM-5PM (EST). *Misdemeanor, Civil Actions Under $7,500, Eviction, Small Claims.*

Olanta Magistrate Court PO Box 362, 220 E Main St, Olanta, SC 29114; phone: 843-396-9056; hours 8:30AM-N, 1-5PM T, W, Th (EST). *Misdemeanor, Civil Actions Under $7,500, Eviction, Small Claims.*

Pamplico Magistrate Court 124 3rd Ave E, PO Box 367, Pamplico, SC 29583; phone: 843-493-0072; fax: 843-493-5391; hours 8:30AM-4:30PM T W Th; 8:30AM-2:30PM M (EST). *Civil Actions Under $7,500, Misdemeanor, Eviction, Small Claims, Traffic.*

Timmonsville Magistrate Court 307 Smith St, PO Box 190, Timmonsville, SC 29161; phone: 843-346-7472; fax: 843-346-0660; hours 8:30-5PM (EST). *Misdemeanor, Civil Actions Under $7,500, Eviction, Small Claims.*

Probate Court 180 N Irby, MSC-L, Florence, SC 29501; phone: 843-665-3085; fax: 843-665-3068; hours 8:30AM-5PM (EST). *Probate.*

Georgetown County

Circuit Court PO Box 421270, 715 Prince St, Georgetown, SC 29442; phone: 843-546-3215; criminal phone: 843-545-3053; civil phone: 843-545-3041; hours 8:30AM-5PM (EST). *Felony, Misdemeanor, Civil Actions Over $7,500.*
Civil Records: Access: In person only. Visitors must perform in person searches themselves. Court makes copy: $.50 per page. Self serve copy fee: $.25 per page. Required to search: name, years to search. Civil cases indexed by defendant, plaintiff; on index from 1926.
Criminal Records: Access: In person only. Visitors must perform in person searches themselves. Court makes copy: $.50 per page. Self serve copy fee: $.25 per page. Required to search: name, years to search, DOB; SSN helpful. Criminal records on index from 1926, computerized since 2001.
General Information: Public terminal goes back to 2000. No adoption, juvenile, sealed or expunged records released. Certification fee: $1.00 per page. Payee: Clerk of Court. Business checks accepted. Prepayment required.

Andrews Magistrate Court 110 N Morgan Ave, Andrews, SC 29510; phone: 843-264-8811; fax: 843-264-5177; hours 8:30AM-4:30PM (EST). *Misdemeanor, Civil Actions Under $7,500, Eviction, Small Claims.*

Georgetown Magistrate Court 333 Cleland St, Georgetown, SC 29442; phone: 843-545-3381; criminal phone: 843-545-3380; civil phone: 843-545-3391; probate phone: 843-546-9798; fax: 843-545-3394; hours 8:30AM-5PM (EST). *Misdemeanor, Civil Actions Under $7,500, Eviction, Small Claims.*

Georgetown Magistrate Court 1277 N Frasier St, PO Box 1838, Georgetown, SC 29442. *Traffic Only.*
Note: This court now handles only traffic offenses.

Murrells Inlet Magistrate Court 4450 Murrells Inlet Rd, PO Box 859, Murrells Inlet, SC 29576; phone: 843-651-6292; fax: 843-651-6685; hours 8AM-4:30PM (EST). *Misdemeanor, Civil Actions Under $7,500, Eviction, Small Claims.*

Pawleys Island Magistrate Court 291 Parkersville Rd, PO Box 1830, Pawleys Island, SC 29585; phone: 843-237-8995; fax: 843-237-3244; hours 8;30AM-4:30PM (EST). *Misdemeanor, Civil Actions Under $7,500, Eviction, Small Claims.*

Plesant Hill Magistrate Court 9174 Pleasant Hill Dr, Hemingway, SC 29554; phone: 843-558-9711; fax: 843-558-5827; hours 8:30AM-Noon,1PM-4:30 (EST). *Misdemeanor, Civil Actions Under $7,500, Eviction, Small Claims.*

Probate Court PO Box 421270, 715 Prince St, Georgetown, SC 29442; phone: 843-545-3274; fax: 843-545-3292; hours 8:30AM-5PM (EST). *Probate.*

Greenville County

Circuit Court 305 E North St, Rm 227, Greenville, SC 29601; phone: 864-467-8551; fax: 864-467-8513; hours 8:30AM-5PM (EST). *Felony, Misdemeanor, Civil Actions Over $7,500.*
www.greenvillecounty.org
Civil Records: Access: In person, online. Visitors must perform in person searches themselves. Court makes copy: $.25 per page. Required to search: name, years to search. Civil cases indexed by defendant, plaintiff; on computer from 1985, on docket books from 1900s. Online access same as criminal, see below.
Criminal Records: Access: In person, online. Visitors must perform in person searches themselves. Court makes copy: $.25 per page. Required to search: name, years to search, DOB, SSN, signed release. Criminal records on computer from 1985, on docket books from 1900s. Access court records free at www.upstatepublicindex.org. Click on Greenville. Records go back to 1983.
General Information: Public terminal goes back to 1982. No adoption, juvenile, sealed or expunged records released. Certification fee: $1.00. Payee: Clerk of Court. Only cashiers checks and money orders accepted. Prepayment required.

Gantt Magistrate Court 1103 White Horse Rd, Greenville, SC 29605; criminal phone: 864-277-4429; civil phone: 864-277-0856; fax: 864-277-4376; hours 8:30AM-5PM (EST). *Misdemeanor, Civil Actions Under $7,500, Eviction, Small Claims.*
www.greenvillecounty.org/Magistrate_Courts/
Note: Access court records free at www.upstatepublicindex.org. Click on Greenville. Records go back to 1988.

Greenville Magistrate Courts #1 & #2 4 McGhee St, LEC Rm 116A, Greenville, SC 29601; phone: 864-467-5312 (City #1), 864-467-5302 (City #2); fax: 864-467-5105; hours 8:30AM4;30PM (EST). *Misdemeanor, Civil Actions Under $7,500, Eviction, Small Claims.*
www.greenvillecounty.org/Magistrate_Courts/
Note: Access court records free at www.upstatepublicindex.org. Click on Greenville. Records go back to 1988.

Piedmont Magistrate Court 8150 Augusta Rd, Piedmont, SC 29673; phone: 864-277-9555; fax: 864-277-8345; hours 8:30AM-5PM (EST). *Misdemeanor, Civil Actions Under $7,500, Eviction, Small Claims.*
www.greenvillecounty.org/Magistrate_Courts/
Note: Access court records free at www.upstatepublicindex.org. Click on Greenville. Records go back to 1988.

Simpsonville Magistrate Court 3725 Grandview Dr #5, Simpsonville, SC 29680; phone: 864-963-3457; fax: 864-963-0029; hours 8:30AM-5:00PM (EST). *Misdemeanor, Civil Actions Under $7,500, Eviction, Small Claims.*
www.greenvillecounty.org/Magistrate_Courts/
Note: Access court records free at www.upstatepublicindex.org. Click on Greenville. Records go back to 1988.

Taylors Magistrate Court 2801 Wade Hampton Blvd, Taylors, SC 29687; phone: 864-244-2922; fax: 864-268-1333; hours 8:30AM-5PM (EST). *Misdemeanor, Civil Actions Under $7,500, Eviction, Small Claims.*
www.greenvillecounty.org/Magistrate_Courts/
Note: Access court records free at www.upstatepublicindex.org. Click on Greenville. Records go back to 1988.

Travelers Rest Magistrate Court 114 N Poinsett Hwy, Travelers Rest, SC 29690; phone: 864-834-6910; fax: 864-834-6911; hours 9AM-5PM (EST). *Misdemeanor, Civil Actions Under $7,500, Eviction, Small Claims.*
www.greenvillecounty.org/Magistrate_Courts/
Note: Access court records free at www.upstatepublicindex.org. Click on Greenville. Records go back to 1988.

West Greenville Magistrate Court 6247 White Horse Rd, Greenville, SC 29611; phone: 864-294-4810; fax: 864-294-4801; hours 8:30AM-5PM (EST). *Misdemeanor, Civil Actions Under $7,500, Eviction, Small Claims.*
www.greenvillecounty.org/Magistrate_Courts/
Note: Access court records free at www.upstatepublicindex.org. Click on Greenville. Records go back to 1988.

Probate Court 301 University Ridge, #1200, Greenville, SC 29601; phone: 864-467-7170; fax: 864-467-7198; hours 8:30AM-5PM (EST). *Probate.*
www.greenvillecounty.org/Probate_Court/
Note: Access court records free at www.upstatepublicindex.org. Click on Greenville. Records go back to 1988.

Greenwood County

Circuit Court Courthouse, Rm 114, 528 Monument St, Greenwood, SC 29646; phone: 864-942-8089; criminal phone: 864-942-8612; civil phone: 864-942-8089; fax: 864-942-8693; hours 8:30AM-5PM (EST). *Felony, Misdemeanor, Civil Actions Over $7,500.*
Civil Records: Access: Mail, in person. Visitors must perform in person searches themselves. Search fee: $2.00 per name. Court makes copy: $.25 per page; same fee for self serve. Required to search: name, years to search. Civil cases indexed by defendant, plaintiff; on docket books from 1897; on computer back to 2000. Mail turnaround time 1-2 days.
Criminal Records: Access: Mail, in person. Visitors must perform in person searches themselves. Search fee: $2.00 per name. Court makes copy: $.25 per page; same fee for self serve. Required to search: name, years to search, DOB; also helpful: SSN. Criminal records on alpha index from 1897; on computer back to 2000. The court will not perform party name searches for in-person requesters. Mail turnaround time 1-2 days.
General Information: Public use terminal available. No adoption, juvenile, sealed or expunged records released. Will not fax documents. Certification fee: $2.00. Payee: Clerk of Court. Business checks accepted. Prepayment and SASE required.

Greenwood Magistrate Court Greenood County Courthouse, Rm 100, 528 Monument St, Greenwood, SC 29646; phone: 864-942-8655; fax: 864-942-8663; hours 8:30AM-5PM (EST). *Misdemeanor, Civil Actions Under $7,500, Eviction, Small Claims.*

Probate Court PO Box 1210, 528 Monument St, Greenwood, SC 29648; phone: 864-942-8625; fax: 864-942-8620; hours 8:30AM-5PM (EST). *Probate.*

Hampton County

Circuit Court PO Box 7, 1 Elm St, Courthouse Sq, Hampton, SC 29924; phone: 803-943-7510; fax: 803-943-7596; hours 8AM-5PM (EST). *Felony, Civil Actions Over $7,500.*
Civil Records: Access: Fax, mail, in person. Visitors must perform in person searches themselves. Search fee: $2.00 per name. Court makes copy: $.50 per page. Required to search: name, years to search. Civil cases indexed by defendant, plaintiff; on docket books, archived from 1878.
Criminal Records: Access: Fax, mail, in person. Visitors must perform in person searches themselves. Search fee: $2.00 per name. Court makes copy: $.50 per page. Required to search: name, years to search, DOB; also helpful: SSN. Criminal records on docket books, archived from 1878.
General Information: No adoption, juvenile, sealed or expunged records released. Certification fee: $1.00 per cert. Payee: Clerk of Court. Personal checks accepted. Prepayment required.

Estill Magistrate Court PO Box 969, 125 Railroad St. SE, Estill, SC 29918; phone: 803-625-3232; fax: 803-625-2148; hours 2PM-5PM (EST). *Misdemeanor, Civil Actions Under $7,500, Eviction, Small Claims.*

Varnville Magistrate Court Law Enforcement Ctr, 411 Cemetery Rd, PO Box 1299, Varnville, SC 29944; phone: 803-943-7511; fax: 803-943-7557; hours 8:30AM-4:30PM (EST). *Misdemeanor, Civil Actions Under $7,500, Eviction, Small Claims.*

Probate Court PO Box 601, 1 M St West, Courthouse Sq, Hampton, SC 29924; phone: 803-943-7512; fax: 803-943-7540; hours 8AM-5PM (EST). *Probate.*

Horry County

Circuit Court PO Box 677, Conway, SC 29526; phone: 843-915-5080; criminal phone: 843-915-6082; civil phone: 843-915-6081; fax: 843-915-6031; hours 8AM-5PM (EST). *Felony, Misdemeanor, Civil Actions Over $7,500.*
Civil Records: Access: Phone, mail, in person. Both court and visitors may perform in person searches. Search fee: $3.00 per name. Court makes copy: $.25 per page; same fee for self serve. Required to search: name, years to search. Civil cases indexed by defendant, plaintiff; on computer from 1987, on alpha index from 1920s. Mail turnaround time 2 days.
Criminal Records: Access: Phone, mail, in person. Both court and visitors may perform in person searches. Search fee: $3.00 per name. Court makes copy: $.25 per page; same fee for self serve. Required to search: name, years to search, DOB, SSN, signed release. Criminal records on computer from 1987, on alpha index from 1920s. Mail turnaround time 2 days.
General Information: No adoptions, juvenile, sealed or expunged records released. Certification fee: $1.00 per page. Payee: Clerk of Court. Business checks accepted. Prepayment required. SASE helpful.

Little River Magistrate Court 107 Highway 57 N, Little River, SC 29566; phone: 843-399-5543; fax: 843-399-6792; hours 8AM-5PM (EST). *Civil Actions Under $7,500, Eviction, Small Claims, Misdemeanors.*

Aynor Magistrate Court PO Box 115, 640 6th Ave, Aynor, SC 29511; phone: 843-358-5508; fax: 843-358-0704; hours 8AM-5PM (EST). *Misdemeanor, Civil Actions Under $7,500, Eviction, Small Claims.*

Conway Magistrate Court 1201 3rd Ave, 2nd Fl, Conway, SC 29526; phone: 843-915-5290; fax: 843-915-6290; hours 8AM-5PM (EST). *Misdemeanor, Civil Actions Under $7,500, Eviction, Small Claims.*

Conway Magistrate Court 1201 3rd Ave, PO Box 1236, Conway, SC 29528; phone: 843-915-5290; fax: 843-915-6290; hours 8AM-5PM (EST). *Misdemeanor, Civil Actions Under $7,500, Eviction, Small Claims.*

Green Sea Magistrate Court 5527 Hwy #9, PO Box 153, Green Sea, SC 29545; phone: 843-392-1219; fax: 843-392-1834; hours 8AM-5PM (EST). *Misdemeanor, Civil Actions Under $7,500, Eviction, Small Claims.*

Loris Magistrate Court 3817 Walnut St, Loris, SC 29569; phone: 843-756-7918/6674; fax: 843-756-1355; hours 8AM-5PM (EST). *Misdemeanor, Civil Actions Under $7,500, Eviction, Small Claims.*

Myrtle Beach Magistrate Court 1201 21st Ave N, Myrtle Beach, SC 29577; phone: 843-444-6127; fax: 843-444-6131; hours 8AM-5PM (EST). *Misdemeanor, Civil Actions Under $7,500, Eviction, Small Claims.*

South Strand Magistrate Court 9630 Scipio Ln, Myrtle Beach, SC 29588-7568; phone: 843-915-5291; fax: 843-203-6291; hours 8AM-5PM (EST). *Misdemeanor, Civil Actions Under $7,500, Eviction, Small Claims.*

Probate Court PO Box 288, Conway, SC 29528; phone: 843-915-5370; fax: 843-915-6370/1; hours 8AM-5PM (EST). *Probate.*
www.horrycounty.org/

Jasper County

Circuit Court PO Box 248, Ridgeland, SC 29936; phone: 843-726-7710; fax: 843-726-7782; hours 8:30AM-5PM (EST). *Felony, Misdemeanor, Civil Actions Over $7,500.*
Civil Records: Access: In person only. Visitors must perform in person searches themselves. Court makes copy: $1.00 per page; same fee for self serve. Required to search: name, years to search. Civil cases indexed by defendant, plaintiff; on computer back to 1999; prior on books to 1912.
Criminal Records: Access: In person only. Both court and visitors may perform in person searches. Search fee: $5.00 per name. Court makes copy: $1.00 per page; same fee for self serve. Required to search: name, years to search, DOB; SSN helpful, signed release. Criminal records on computer back to 1999; prior on books to 1912.
General Information: Public terminal goes back to 1993. No adoption, juvenile, sealed or expunged records released. Fee to fax specific case file is $2.00 per page. Certification fee: $1.00. Payee: Clerk of Court. Personal checks not accepted. Prepayment required.

Hardeeville Magistrate Court 21 Martin St, PO Box 1169, Hardeeville, SC 29927; phone: 843-784-2628; fax: 843-784-3245; hours 9AM-5PM (EST). *Misdemeanor, Civil Actions Under $7,500, Eviction, Small Claims.*

Pineland Magistrate Court
Note: Pineland Magistrate Court is closed, case at the nearby Ridgeland Magistrate Court.

Ridgeland Magistrate Court 111 W Adams St, PO Box 665, Ridgeland, SC 29936; phone: 843-726-7933; fax: 843-726-7745; hours 9AM-N; 1-5PM (EST). *Misdemeanor, Civil Actions Under $7,500, Eviction, Small Claims.*

Probate Court PO Box 1028, 305 Russell St, Ridgeland, SC 29936; phone: 843-726-7719; fax: 843-726-5173; hours 9AM-5PM (EST). *Probate.*

Kershaw County

Circuit Court County Courthouse, Rm 313, PO Box 1557, Camden, SC 29020; phone: 803-425-1500 x5623; fax: 803-425-1505; hours 8:30AM-5PM (EST). *Felony, Misdemeanor, Civil Actions Over $7,500.*
Civil Records: Access: Mail, in person. Visitors must perform in person searches themselves.

Search fee: $20.00. Court makes copy: $.50 per page; same fee for self serve. Required to search: name, years to search. Civil cases indexed by defendant, plaintiff. Civil records archived from 1797, computerized records from 1994. Mail turnaround time 1 day.

Criminal Records: Access: Mail, in person. Visitors must perform in person searches themselves. Search fee: $20.00. Court makes copy: $.50 per page; same fee for self serve. Required to search: name, years to search, DOB; also helpful: SSN. Criminal records archived from 1890, computerized records from 1994. Mail turnaround time 1 day.

General Information: Public terminal goes back to 1994. No adoption, juvenile, sealed or expunged records released. Will not fax documents. Certification fee: $1.00 per document. Payee: Clerk of Court. Personal checks accepted. Prepayment required.

Bethune Magistrate Court 202 N Main St, PO Box 215, Bethune, SC 29009; phone: 843-334-8460; hours 9AM-5PM (EST). *Misdemeanor, Civil Actions Under $7,500, Eviction, Small Claims.*

Camden Magistrate Court County Courthouse, #202, 1121 Broad St, PO Box 1528, Camden, SC 29020; phone: 803-425-1500 X386; fax: 803-425-6044; hours 8AM-5PM (EST). *Misdemeanor, Civil Actions Under $7,500, Eviction, Small Claims.*

Probate Court 1121 Broad St, Rm 225, Courthouse, Camden, SC 29020; phone: 803-425-1500 x5351; fax: 803-425-1526; hours 8:30AM-5PM (EST). *Probate.*

Lancaster County

Circuit Court PO Box 1809, Lancaster, SC 29721; phone: 803-285-1581; fax: 803-416-9388; hours 8:30AM-5PM (EST). *Felony, Misdemeanor, Civil Actions Over $7,500.*

Civil Records: Access: In person only. Both court and visitors may perform in person searches. No search fee. Court makes copy: $.25 per page; same fee for self serve. Required to search: name, years to search. Civil cases indexed by defendant, plaintiff; on computer from 1987, microfiche from 1937, alpha index from 1764.

Criminal Records: Access: In person only. Both court and visitors may perform in person searches. No search fee. Court makes copy: $.25 per page; same fee for self serve. Required to search: name, years to search, DOB; SSN helpful. Criminal records on computer from 1987.

General Information: Public use terminal available. No adoption, juvenile, sealed or expunged records released. Certification fee: $2.50. Payee: Clerk of Court. Personal checks accepted. Prepayment required.

Lancaster Magistrate Court 101 S Wylie St, Lancaster, SC 29720; phone: 803-283-3983; fax: 803-416-9407; hours 8:30AM-5PM (EST). *Misdemeanor, Civil Actions Under $7,500, Eviction, Small Claims.*

Probate Court PO Box 1809, 101 N Main St, Lancaster, SC 29721; phone: 803-283-3379; fax: 803-283-3370; hours 8:30AM-5PM (EST). *Probate.* www.lancastercountysc.net/ProbateCourt/

Laurens County

Circuit Court PO Box 287, Laurens, SC 29360; phone: 864-984-3538; fax: 864-984-7023; hours 9AM-5PM (EST). *Felony, Misdemeanor, Civil Actions Over $7,500.*

Civil Records: Access: Mail, in person. Both court and visitors may perform in person searches. Search fee: $5.00 per name. Court makes copy: $.50 per page. Required to search: name, years to search. Civil cases indexed by defendant, plaintiff; on index books back to 1800s; on computer back to 1980. Mail turnaround time 2-3 days.

Criminal Records: Access: Mail, in person. Both court and visitors may perform in person searches. Search fee: $5.00 per name. Court makes copy: $.50 per page. Required to search: name, years to search, DOB; also helpful: SSN. Criminal records on index books back to 1950s; on computer back to 1980. Mail turnaround time 2-3 days

General Information: No adoption, juvenile, sealed or expunged records released. Certification fee: $1.00 per page. Payee: Clerk of Court. Personal checks accepted. Prepayment and SASE required.

Clinton Magistrate Court 203 W Pitts St, Clinton, SC 29325; phone: 864-833-5879; fax: 864-833-7502; hours 8AM-5PM M, T; 8AM-N W; 8AM-10AM F (EST). *Misdemeanor, Civil Actions Under $7,500, Eviction, Small Claims.*

Gray Court Magistrate Court 329 Main St, Town Hall, PO Box 438, Gray Court, SC 29645; phone: 864-876-4390; hours 9AM-5PM,M,T,W; 9AM-2PM Th (EST). *Misdemeanor, Civil Actions Under $7,500, Eviction, Small Claims.*

Laurens Magistrate Court PO Box 925, 154 Templeton Rd, Laurens, SC 29360; phone: 864-683-4485; hours 9AM-5PM (EST). *Misdemeanor, Civil Actions Under $7,500, Eviction, Small Claims.*

Probate Court PO Box 194, 100 Hillcrest Sq #A, Laurens, SC 29360; phone: 864-984-7315; probate phone: 864-984-7731; fax: 864-984-3779; hours 9AM-5PM (EST). *Probate.* www.sccourts.org/trial/probate/probatejudges.cfm?countyno=30

Lee County

Circuit Court PO Box 387, Bishopville, SC 29010; phone: 803-484-5341; fax: 803-484-1632; hours 9AM-5PM (EST). *Felony, Misdemeanor, Civil Actions Over $7,500.*

Civil Records: Access: Mail, in person. Both court and visitors may perform in person searches. Search fee: $5.00 per name. Court makes copy: $.25 per page. $1.00 minimum. Self serve copy fee: $.25 per page. Required to search: name, years to search. Civil cases indexed by defendant, plaintiff; on computer from 1991, on archives from 1900s. Mail turnaround time 2 days.

Criminal Records: Access: Mail, in person. Both court and visitors may perform in person searches. Search fee: $2.00 per name. Court makes copy: $.25 per page. $1.00 minimum. Self serve copy fee: $.25 per page. Required to search: name, years to search, DOB; also helpful: SSN. Criminal records on computer from 1991, on archives from 1900s. Mail turnaround time 2 days.

General Information: Public terminal goes back to 1985. No adoption, juvenile, sealed or expunged records released. Will not fax documents. Certification fee: $1.00 per page includes copy fee. Payee: Clerk of Court. Business checks accepted. Prepayment and SASE required.

Bishopville Magistrate Court 115 Gregg St, PO Box 2, Bishopsville, SC 29010; phone: 803-484-6463; fax: 803-484-5163; hours 9AM-5-PM (EST). *Misdemeanor, Civil Actions Under $7,500, Eviction, Small Claims.*

Probate Court PO Box 24, Bishopville, SC 29010; phone: 803-484-5341 X338, X339, X361; fax: 803-484-6881; 9AM-5PM (EST). *Probate.*

Lexington County

Circuit Court Lexington County Judicial Ctr, Rm 107, 205 E Main St, Lexington, SC 29072; phone: 803-785-8212; criminal phone: 803-785-8223; civil phone: 803-785-8252; probate phone: 803-785-8324; fax: 803-785-8314; hours 8AM-5PM (EST). *Felony, Misdemeanor, Civil Actions Over $7,500.*

Civil Records: Access: Mail, in person. Both court and visitors may perform in person searches. Search fee: $3.00 per name. Court makes copy: $.25 per page; included in search fee. Self serve copy fee: $.25 per page. Required to search: name, years to

search. Civil cases indexed by defendant, plaintiff; on index from 1936. Mail turnaround time 3 days.

Criminal Records: Access: Fax, mail, in person. Both court and visitors may perform in person searches. Search fee: $3.00 per name. Court makes copy: $.25 per page; included in search fee. Self serve copy fee: $.25 per page. Required to search: name, years to search, DOB, SSN. Criminal records on computer since 1983. Mail turnaround time 3 days.

General Information: Public terminal goes back to 1984. No adoption, juvenile, sealed or expunged records released. Certification fee: $1.00 per cert. Payee: County of Lexington. Personal checks accepted. Prepayment and SASE required.

Batesburg Leesville Magistrate Court 231 W Church St, Batesburg, SC 29006; phone: 803-359-8330; criminal phone: 803-359-8330; civil phone: 803-359-0204; fax: 803-332-0357; hours 8:AM-4:30PM (EST). *Misdemeanor, Civil Actions Under $7,500, Eviction, Small Claims.*

Cayce Magistrate Court 650 Knox Abbott Dr, Cayce, SC 29033; phone: 803-796-7100; fax: 803-796-7635; hours 8AM-4:30PM (EST). *Misdemeanor, Civil Actions Under $7,500, Eviction, Small Claims.*

Columbia Magistrate Court 111 Lin Creek, Columbia, SC 29212; phone: 803-781-7584/7585; fax: 803-749-4050; hours 8AM-4;30PM (EST). *Misdemeanor, Civil Actions Under $7,500, Eviction, Small Claims.*

Lexington Magistrate Court 605 W Main St, #100, Magistrate's Office, Lexington, SC 29072; phone: 803-785-8221; fax: 803-785-8155; hours 8:30AM-4:30PM (EST). *Misdemeanor, Civil Actions Under $7,500, Eviction, Small Claims.*

Swansea Magistrate Court 500 Charlie Rast Rd, PO Box 457, Swansea, SC 29160; phone: 803-568-3616; fax: 803-785-4078; hours 8:30AM-4:30PM (EST). *Misdemeanor, Civil Actions Under $7,500, Eviction, Small Claims.*

Probate Court County Courthouse, Rm 110, 205 E Main St #134, Lexington, SC 29072-3488; phone: 803-785-8324; hours 8AM-5PM (EST). *Probate.*

Marion County

Circuit Court PO Box 295, 100 W Court St, Marion, SC 29571; phone: 843-423-8240; hours 8:30AM-5PM (EST). *Felony, Misdemeanor, Civil Actions Over $7,500.*

Civil Records: Access: In person only. Visitors must perform in person searches themselves. Court makes copy: $.25 per page. Required to search: name, years to search. Civil cases indexed by defendant, plaintiff; on computer since 1988; prior records on index cards from 1800s.

Criminal Records: Access: In person only. Visitors must perform in person searches themselves. Court makes copy: $.25 per page. Required to search: name, years to search, DOB; SSN helpful. Criminal records on computer since 1988; prior records on index cards from 1800s.

General Information: No adoption, juvenile, sealed or expunged records released. Certification fee: $1.00 per cert. Payee: Circuit Court Clerk.

Gresham Magistrate Court 2715 Hwy 76 E, #B, Mullins, SC 25974; hours 8:30AM-5PM (EST). *Misdemeanor, Civil Actions Under $7,500, Eviction, Small Claims.*
Note: For records, call 843-423-8208.

Marion Magistrate Court 2715 E Hwy 76, #B, Mullins, SC 29574-6015; phone: 843-423-8208; fax: 843-423-8394; hours 8:30AM-5PM (EST). *Misdemeanor, Civil Actions Under $7,500, Eviction, Small Claims.*

Mullins Magistrate Court 2715 US Hwy 76, #B, Mullins, SC 29574; phone: 843-423-8208 X231; fax: 843-423-8394; hours 8:30AM-5PM (EST). *Misdemeanor, Civil Actions Under $7,500, Eviction, Small Claims.*

Probate Court PO Box 583, 201 Court St, Marion, SC 29571; phone: 843-423-8244; fax: 843-431-5026; hours 8:30AM-5PM (EST). *Probate.*

Marlboro County

Circuit Court PO Drawer 996, 105 Main St, Bennettsville, SC 29512; phone: 843-479-5613; fax: 843-479-5640; hours 8:30AM-5PM (EST). *Felony, Misdemeanor, Civil Actions Over $7,500.*
Civil Records: Access: Mail, in person. Visitors must perform in person searches themselves. Search fee: $5.00 per name. Court makes copy: $.25 per page. Self serve copy fee: $.10 per page. Required to search: name, years to search. Civil cases indexed by defendant, plaintiff; on computer from 1981, on index from 1786. Mail turnaround time 1 day.
Criminal Records: Access: Mail, in person. Visitors must perform in person searches themselves. Search fee: $5.00 per name. Court makes copy: $.25 per page. Self serve copy fee: $.10 per page. Required to search: name, years to search, DOB; also helpful: SSN. Criminal records on computer from 1985, on index from 1786. Mail turnaround time 1 day.
General Information: Public terminal has only civil records back to 1981. No adoption, juvenile, sealed or expunged records released. Certification fee: $2.00. Payee: Clerk of Court. Personal checks accepted. Prepayment and SASE required.

Bennettsville Magistrate Court 211 N Marlboro St, PO Box 418, Bennettsville, SC 29512; phone: 843-479-5620; fax: 843-479-5646; hours 8:30AM-4:30PM M-Th; Civil 4-5PM (EST). *Misdemeanor, Civil Actions Under $7,500, Eviction, Small Claims.*
Note: Court is again active.

Marlboro County Summary Court PO Box 418, 105 Main St, Bennettsville, SC 29512; phone: 843-479-5620/5613; fax: 843-479-5646; hours 8:30AM-4:30PM (EST). *Civil Actions Under $7,500, Eviction, Small Claims.*
Note: Same searching and fees as at Circuit Court.

Probate Court PO Box 455, Main St, Bennettsville, SC 29512; phone: 843-479-5610; fax: 843-479-5668; hours 8:30AM-5PM (EST). *Probate.*

McCormick County

Circuit Court 133 S Mine St, McCormick, SC 29835; phone: 864-465-2195; probate phone: 864-465-2428; fax: 864-465-0071; hours 9AM-5PM (EST). *Felony, Misdemeanor, Civil Actions Over $7,500.*
Civil Records: Access: In person only. Visitors must perform in person searches themselves. Self serve copy fee: $.35 per page. Required to search: name, years to search. Civil cases indexed by defendant, plaintiff; on index books from 1916.
Criminal Records: Access: In person only. Visitors must perform in person searches themselves. Court makes copy: $.35 per page. Self serve copy fee: $.35 per page. Required to search: name, years to search, DOB; SSN helpful. Criminal records on index books from 1916.
General Information: No adoption, juvenile, sealed or expunged records released. Will not fax specific case file. Certification fee: $1.00 per page. Payee: Clerk of Court. Prepayment required.

McCormick Magistrate Court 211 W Augusta Ext., PO Box 1116, McCormick, SC 29835; phone: 864-465-2316; fax: 864-465-2582; hours 9AM-5PM (EST). *Misdemeanor, Civil Actions Under $7,500, Eviction, Small Claims.*

Probate Court 133 S Mine St, #101, McCormick, SC 29835; phone: 864-465-2630; fax: 864-465-0071; hours 9AM-5PM (EST). *Probate.*

Newberry County

Circuit Court PO Box 278, 1226 College St, Newberry, SC 29108; phone: 803-321-2110; fax: 803-321-2111; hours 8:30AM-5PM (EST). *Felony, Misdemeanor, Civil Actions Over $7,500.*
www.newberrycounty.net
Civil Records: Access: In person only. Both court and visitors may perform in person searches. Court makes copy: $.20 per page. Required to search: name, years to search. Civil cases indexed by defendant, plaintiff; on computer from 1983, docket books from 1776.
Criminal Records: Access: In person only. Visitors must perform in person searches themselves. Court makes copy: $.20 per page. Required to search: name, years to search, DOB; SSN helpful. Criminal records on computer from 1983, docket books from 1776.
General Information: Public terminal goes back to 1989. No adoption, juvenile, sealed, PTI or expunged records released. Certification fee: $1.00 per page. Payee: Clerk of Court. Only cashiers checks and money orders accepted. Prepayment required.

Little Mountain Magistrate Court 824 Main St, PO Box 95, Little Mountain, SC 29075; phone: 803-345-1040; fax: 803-945-7222; hours 2PM-5PM T, W (EST). *Misdemeanor, Civil Actions Under $7,500, Eviction, Small Claims.*

Newberry Magistrate Court 3239 Louis Rich Rd, Newberry, SC 29108; criminal phone: 803-321-2144; civil phone: 803-321-2145; probate phone: 803-321-2118; criminal fax: 803-321-2172; same fax for civil/probate; hours 8:30-5PM (EST). *Misdemeanor, Civil Actions Under $7,500, Eviction, Small Claims, Traffic.*

Whitmire Magistrate Court 313 Main St, PO Box 62, Whitmire, SC 29178; phone: 803-694-5756; fax: 803-694-5756; hours 1:30PM-6PM M; 1:30PM-6PM W (EST). *Misdemeanor, Civil Actions Under $7,500, Eviction, Small Claims.*

Probate Court PO Box 442, 1309 College St, Newberry, SC 29108; phone: 803-321-2118; fax: 803-321-2119; hours 8:30AM-5PM (EST). *Probate.*
www.newberrycounty.net/

Oconee County

Circuit Court PO Box 678, 205 W Main St, Walhalla, SC 29691; phone: 864-638-4280; fax: 864-638-4282; hours 8:30AM-5PM (EST). *Felony, Misdemeanor, Civil Actions Over $7,500.*
Civil Records: Access: In person only. Visitors must perform in person searches themselves. Court makes copy: $1.00 for first page, $.50 each add'l. Self serve copy fee: $.50 per page. Required to search: name, years to search. Civil cases indexed by defendant, plaintiff; on index cards from 1868; on computer back to 1994.
Criminal Records: Access: In person only. Visitors must perform in person searches themselves. Court makes copy: $1.00 per page. Self serve copy fee: $.50 per page. Required to search: name, years to search; also helpful: DOB, SSN, signed release. Criminal records on index cards from 1868; on computer back to 1994.
General Information: Public terminal goes back to 1996. No adoption, juvenile, sealed or expunged records released. No certification fee. Payee: Clerk of Court. Personal checks accepted. Prepayment required.

County Summary Court 208 Booker Dr, Walhalla, SC 29691; phone: 864-638-4127; fax: 864-638-4229; hours 8:30AM-5PM (EST). *Civil Actions Under $7,500, Eviction, Small Claims.*
Note: No fees are charged for record access or copies.
Civil Records: Access: Mail. Only the court performs in person searches; visitors may not. Required to search: name. Indexed by defendant. Small claims and civil in same index. Evictions destroyed annually; complaints after 10 years; claim/delivery records after 3 years. Mail turnaround time 5-7 days.

General Information: Will not fax documents. Payee: Oconee County Summary Court.

Walhalla Magistrate Court 208 Booker Dr, Walhalla, SC 29691; criminal phone: 864-638-4125; civil phone: 864-638-4127; fax: 864-638-4229; hours 8:30AM-5PM (EST). *Misdemeanor, Civil Actions Under $7,500, Eviction, Small Claims.*

Probate Court PO Box 471, 415 S Pine St, Walhalla, SC 29691; phone: 864-638-4275; fax: 864-638-4278; hours 8:30AM-5PM (EST). *Probate.*

Orangeburg County

Circuit Court PO Box 9000, Orangeburg, SC 29116; phone: 803-533-6260; fax: 803-534-3848; hours 8:30AM-5PM (EST). *Felony, Misdemeanor, Civil Actions Over $7,500.*
Civil Records: Access: In person only. Visitors must perform in person searches themselves. Court makes copy: $.50 per page. Required to search: name, years to search. Civil cases indexed by defendant, plaintiff; on index cards from 1924.
Criminal Records: Access: In person only. Visitors must perform in person searches themselves. Court makes copy: $.50 per page. Required to search: name, years to search, DOB; SSN helpful. Criminal records on index cards from 1924.
General Information: No adoption, juvenile, sealed or expunged records released. Certification fee: $1.00. Payee: Clerk of Court. Personal checks accepted. Prepayment required.

Bowman Magistrate Court 6803 Charleston Hwy, PO Box 365, Bowman, SC 29018; phone: 803-829-2831; hours 1-4PM, M, F (EST). *Misdemeanor, Civil Actions Under $7,500, Eviction, Small Claims.*

Branchville Magistrate Court 7644 Freedom Rd, PO Box 85, Branchville, SC 29432; phone: 803-274-8820; fax: 803-274-8760; hours 4PM-7PM M & W (EST). *Misdemeanor, Civil Actions Under $7,500, Eviction, Small Claims.*

Elloree Magistrate Court 2614 Cleveland St, PO Box 436, Elloree, SC 29047; phone: 803-897-4626; hours M,W 5PM-8PM (EST). *Misdemeanor, Civil Actions Under $7,500, Eviction, Small Claims.*
www.orangeburgcounty.org/

Eutawville Magistrate Court 220 Porcher Ave, PO Box 188, Eutawville, SC 29048; phone: 803-492-3374; fax: 803-496-5850; hours 5;30-7PM, W, Th (EST). *Misdemeanor, Civil Actions Under $7,500, Eviction, Small Claims.*

Holly Hill Magistrate Court 7324 Old State Rd, Hwy 176, PO Box 154, Holly Hill, SC 29059; phone: 803-496-9533; fax: 803-496-9533; hours 11AM-4PM T & Th (EST). *Misdemeanor, Civil Actions Under $7,500, Eviction, Small Claims.*

North Magistrate Court 9305 North Rd, PO Box 399, North, SC 29112; phone: 803-247-2101; fax: 803-247-3045; hours 8:30AM-4:30PM M-Th; 8:30AM-3PM F (EST). *Misdemeanor, Civil Actions Under $7,500, Eviction, Small Claims.*

Norway Magistrate Court 8413 Savannah Hwy, PO Box 67, Norway, SC 29113; phone: 803-263-4100; hours 9AM-N M,W (EST). *Misdemeanor, Civil Actions Under $7,500, Eviction, Small Claims.*

Orangeburg County Magistrate Court 1540 Ellis Ave NE, PO Box 9000, Orangeburg, SC 29116; phone: 803-533-5880/5879; fax: 803-516-4011; hours 8:30AM-5PM (EST). *Misdemeanor, Civil Actions Under $7,500, Eviction, Small Claims.*

Orangeburg Magistrate Court PO Box 9000, 1540 Ellis Ave, Orangeburg, SC 29116; phone: 803-533-5843; fax: 803-533-5929; hours 8:30-5PM (EST). *Misdemeanor, Civil Actions Under $7,500, Eviction, Small Claims.*

Springfield Magistrate Court 7304 Festival Trail Rd, PO Box 125, Springfield, SC 29146; phone: 803-258-1002; fax: 803-258-1006; hours 9AM-

5PM Monday only (EST). *Misdemeanor, Civil Actions Under $7,500, Eviction, Small Claims.*

Probate Court PO Drawer 9000, 190 Gibson St, Orangeburg, SC 29116-9000; phone: 803-533-6280; fax: 803-533-6279; 8:30AM-5PM (EST). *Probate.* www.sccourts.org/probate/index.cfm?countyno=38

Pickens County

Circuit Court PO Box 215, Pickens, SC 29671; phone: 864-898-5857; fax: 864-898-5863; hours 8:30AM-5PM (EST). *Felony, Misdemeanor, Civil Actions Over $7,500.*
www.co.pickens.sc.us/
Civil Records: Access: In person, online. Both court and visitors may perform in person searches. Court makes copy: $.25 per page. Required to search: name, years to search. Civil cases indexed by defendant, plaintiff; on computer from 1990, on index from 1970. Online access same as criminal, see below.
Criminal Records: Access: In person, online. Both court and visitors may perform in person searches. No search fee. Court makes copy: $.25 per page. Required to search: name, years to search, DOB; also helpful: SSN. Criminal records on computer from 1990, on index from 1970. Access to court records free at www.upstatepublicindex.org. Click on Pickens.
General Information: Public use terminal available. No adoption, juvenile, sealed or expunged records released. Certification fee: $1.00. Payee: Clerk of Court. Personal checks accepted. Prepayment required.

Clemson Magistrate Court 115-B Commons Way, Central, SC 29630; phone: 864-639-8084; fax: 864-639-0701; hours 8:30AM-4:30PM (EST). *Misdemeanor, Civil Actions Under $7,500, Eviction, Small Claims.*
Note: Access to court records free at www.upstatepublicindex.org. Click on Pickens.

Easley Magistrate Court 135 Folger Ave, Easley, SC 29640; phone: 864-850-7076; fax: 864-850-7075; hours 8:30AM-4;30PM (EST). *Misdemeanor, Civil Actions Under $7,500, Eviction, Small Claims.*
Note: Access to court records free at www.upstatepublicindex.org. Click on Pickens.

Liberty Magistrate Court #147-B Kay Holcombe Rd, Liberty, SC 29657; phone: 864-843-5821; criminal phone: 854-843-5833; fax: 864-843-5824; hours 8:30AM-5PM (EST). *Misdemeanor, Civil Actions Under $7,500, Eviction, Small Claims.*
Note: Access to court records free at www.upstatepublicindex.org. Click on Pickens.

Pickens Magistrate Court 216-A, Law Enforcement Ctr Rd, Pickens, SC 29671; phone: 864-898-5551/5552; fax: 864-898-5546; hours 8:30AM-4;30PM (EST). *Misdemeanor, Civil Actions Under $7,500, Eviction, Small Claims.*
Note: Access to court records free at www.upstatepublicindex.org. Click on Pickens.

Probate Court 222 McDaniel Ave, #B-16, Pickens, SC 29671; phone: 864-898-5903; fax: 864-898-5924; hours 8:00AM-5PM (EST). *Probate.*

Richland County

Circuit Court PO Box 2766, Columbia, SC 29202; phone: 803-576-1999; criminal fax: 803-576-1925; civil fax: 803-748-5039; hours 8:30AM-5PM (EST). *Felony, Misdemeanor, Civil Actions Over $7,500.*
Note: Preliminary hearings lists are online at www.richlandonline.com/departments/solicitor/hearings.asp. Limited daily trial dockets are online at www.richlandonline.com/departments/solicitor/trialdockets.asp.
Civil Records: Access: Mail, in person, online. Both court and visitors may perform in person searches. Search fee: $2.00 per name. Court makes copy: $.50 for 1st page, $.15 each add'l. Self serve copy fee: $.15 per page. Required to search: name, years to search.

Civil cases indexed by defendant, plaintiff; on computer from 1987. Many prior records indexed to 1920's. Limited court rosters online at www.richlandonline.com/departments/clerkofcourt/courtroster.asp; search by date.
Criminal Records: Access: In person, online. Visitors must perform in person searches themselves. No search fee. Court makes copy: $.50 for first page, $.15 each add'l. Self serve copy fee: $.15 per page. Required to search: name, years to search; also helpful: DOB, SSN. Criminal records on index to 1920's, computerized since 1987. Limited court rosters online at www.richlandonline.com/departments/clerkofcourt/courtroster.asp; search by date. Mail turnaround time 1 day.
General Information: Public terminal goes back to 1987. No adoption, juvenile, sealed or expunged records released. Will fax to gov't agencies only. No certification fee. Payee: Richland County Clerk. Personal checks accepted. Prepayment and SASE required.

Note: Online access to all Richland County Summary/Magistrate Courts is free at www.richlandonline.com/departments/magistrate/index.asp.

Central Magistrate Court Richland Central Court, 1400 Huger St, PO Box 192, Columbia, SC 29202; phone: 803-576-2300; fax: 803-576-2325; hours 8:30AM-5PM M-F (EST). *Misdemeanor (Criminal Domestic Violence), Civil Actions Under 7,500, Traffic.*

Columbia Magistrate Court 1731 Laurel St, PO Box 192, Columbia, SC 29202; phone: 803-576-2510; fax: 803-576-2519; hours 8:30AM-5PM (EST). *Misdemeanor, Civil Actions Under $7,500, Eviction, Small Claims.*

Dentsville Magistrate Court 2500 Decker Blvd, #B-1, Columbia, SC 29206; phone: 803-576-2560; fax: 803-576-2569; hours 8:30AM-5PM (EST). *Misdemeanor, Civil Actions Under $7,500, Eviction, Small Claims.*

Dutch Fork Magistrate Court 1400 Eugie St, Columbia, SC 29210; phone: 803-576-2540; fax: 803-576-2545; hours 8:30AM-5PM (EST). *Misdemeanor, Civil Actions Under $7,500, Eviction, Small Claims.*

Hopkins Magistrate Court PO Box 70, 6108 Cabin Creek Rd, Hopkins, SC 29061; phone: 803-576-2530; fax: 803-576-2535; hours 8:30AM-5PM (EST). *Misdemeanor, Civil Actions Under $7,500, Eviction, Small Claims.*

Lykesland Magistrate Court 1403 Caroline Rd, PO Box 9523, Columbia, SC 29290; phone: 803-576-2500; fax: 803-576-2504; hours 8:30AM-5PM (EST). *Misdemeanor, Civil Actions Under $7,500, Eviction, Small Claims.*

Olympia Magistrate Court 1601 B Shop Rd, PO Box 9305, Columbia, SC 29201; phone: 803-576-2550; fax: 803-576-2555; hours 8:30AM-5PM (EST). *Misdemeanor, Civil Actions Under $7,500, Eviction, Small Claims.*
www.richlandonline.com/departments/magistrate/index.asp

Pontiac Magistrate Court 10509 Two Notch Rd, #D, Elgin, SC 29045; phone: 803-576-2520; fax: 803-576-2522; hours 8:30AM-5PM (EST). *Misdemeanor, Civil Actions Under $7,500, Eviction, Small Claims.*

Upper Township Magistrate Court 4919 Rhett St, Columbia, SC 29203; phone: 803-576-2570; fax: 803-576-2579; hours 8:30AM-5PM (EST). *Misdemeanor, Civil Actions Under $7,500, Eviction, Small Claims.*

Waverly Magistrate Court 2712 Middleburg Dr, #106, Columbia, SC 29204; phone: 803-576-2590; fax: 803-576-2599; hours 8:30AM-5PM

(EST). *Misdemeanor, Civil Actions Under $7,500, Eviction, Small Claims.*

Probate Court PO Box 192 (1701 Main St, #207), Columbia, SC 29202; phone: 803-576-1961; fax: 803-576-1993; hours 8:30AM-5PM (EST). *Probate.* www.richlandonline.com/probate.htm

Saluda County

Circuit Court County Courthouse, 100 E Church St, #6, Saluda, SC 29138; phone: 864-445-4500; fax: 864-445-3772; hours 8:30AM-5PM (EST). *Felony, Misdemeanor, Civil Actions Over $7,500.*
Civil Records: Access: In person. Both court and visitors may perform in person searches. No search fee. Court makes copy: $.25 per page; same fee for self serve. Required to search: name, years to search, address. Civil cases indexed by defendant, plaintiff; on computer from 1995, on index from 1897.
Criminal Records: Access: In person. Both court and visitors may perform in person searches. No search fee. Court makes copy: $.25 per page; same fee for self serve. Required to search: name, years to search, address, DOB, signed release; also helpful: SSN. Criminal records on computer from 1995, on index from 1897. Request must be in writing.
General Information: Public terminal goes back to 1995. No adoption, juvenile, sealed or expunged records released. Certification fee: $1.00. Payee: Clerk of Court. Personal checks accepted. Prepayment required.

Saluda Magistrate Court 108 S Rudolph St, Courthouse Annex, Saluda, SC 29138; phone: 864-445-4500; criminal phone: x2236; civil phone: x2239; fax: 864-445-3684; hours 8AM-5PM (EST). *Misdemeanor, Civil Actions Under $7,500, Eviction, Small Claims.*

Probate Court 100 E Church St, Saluda, SC 29138; phone: 864-445-7110x1; fax: 864-445-9726; hours 8:30AM-5PM (EST). *Probate.*

Spartanburg County

Circuit Court County Courthouse, 180 Magnolia St, Spartanburg, SC 29306; phone: 864-596-2591; fax: 864-596-2239; hours 8:30AM-5PM (EST). *Felony, Misdemeanor, Civil Actions Over $7,500.*
www.spartanburgcounty.org/govt/depts/coc/index.htm
Civil Records: Access: In person only. Visitors must perform in person searches themselves. Court makes copy: $1.00 per page. Required to search: name, years to search. Civil cases indexed by defendant, plaintiff; on computer from 1975, on microfiche from 1960, on alpha index from 1800s.
Criminal Records: Access: In person only. Visitors must perform in person searches themselves. Court makes copy: $1.00 per page. Required to search: name, years to search, DOB, SSN, signed release. Criminal records on computer from 1975, on microfiche from 1960, on alpha index from 1800s. The public may search the index.
General Information: Public terminal has only civil records back to 1970. No adoption, juvenile, sealed or expunged records released. Certification fee: $1.00 per cert. Payee: Clerk of Court. Personal checks accepted. Prepayment required.

Chesnee Magistrate Court 201 Cherokee St, Chesnee, SC 29323; phone: 864-461-3402; fax: 864-596-3622. *Misdemeanor, Civil Actions Under $7,500, Eviction, Small Claims.*

Inman Magistrate Court 7 Mill St, Inman, SC 29349; phone: 864-472-4447/6247; fax: 864-596-3622; hours 9AM-8PM M; 8AM-N T (EST). *Misdemeanor, Civil Actions Under $7,500, Eviction, Small Claims.*

Landrum Magistrate Court 137-B N Howard Ave, PO Box 744, Landrum, SC 29356; phone: 864-457-7245; fax: 864-596-3622; hours Open Tues-8Am-7PM, and Th (EST). *Misdemeanor, Civil Actions Under $7,500, Eviction, Small Claims.*

Pacolet Magistrate Court 980 Sunny Acres Rd, PO Box 416, Pacolet Mills, SC 29373; phone: 864-474-0344/3391; fax: 864-474-4744; hours 6PM-10PM M & W; 6PM-9PM Th (EST). *Misdemeanor, Civil Actions Under $7,500, Eviction, Small Claims.*

Reidville Magistrate Court 162 Leonard Rd, PO Box 124, Reidville, SC 29375; phone: 864-433-9223; hours 10AM-5:30PM T; 9AM-2PM Th (EST). *Misdemeanor, Civil Actions Under $7,500, Eviction, Small Claims.*

Spartanburg Magistrate Court County Courthouse, Rm 105, 180 Magnolia St, Spartanburg, SC 29306; phone: 864-596-2564; fax: 864-596-3622; hours 8:30AM-5PM (EST). *Misdemeanor, Civil Actions Under $7,500, Eviction, Small Claims.*

Probate Court 180 Magnolia St, Rm 302, Spartanburg, SC 29306-2392; phone: 864-596-2556; fax: 864-596-2011; hours 8:30AM-5PM (EST). *Probate.*

Sumter County

Circuit Court 141 N Main, Sumter, SC 29150; phone: 803-436-2227; criminal phone: 803-436-2264/65; civil phone: 803-436-2231; fax: 803-436-2223; hours 8:30AM-5PM (EST). *Felony, Misdemeanor, Civil Actions Over $7,500.*
www.sumtercountysc.org
Civil Records: Access: Mail, in person, online. Both court and visitors may perform in person searches. Search fee: $10.00 per name. Court makes copy: $.25 per page; same fee for self serve. Required to search: name, years to search; also helpful: address. Civil cases indexed by defendant, plaintiff; on computer from 1987, microfiche and books from 1900s. Family court records are online at the website. Mail turnaround time 2 days.
Criminal Records: Access: Mail, in person. Both court and visitors may perform in person searches. Search fee: $5.00 per name. Court makes copy: $.25 per page; same fee for self serve. Required to search: name, years to search, DOB, SSN, signed release; also helpful: address. Criminal records in books. Mail turnaround time 2 days.
General Information: No adoption, juvenile, sealed or expunged records released. Will not fax documents. Certification fee: $5.00. Payee: Sumter County Treasurer. Business checks accepted. Prepayment and SASE required.

Mayesville Magistrate Court PO Box 236, Town Hall, Mayesville, SC 29104; phone: 803-436-9372; hours Thur Evening Court (EST). *Misdemeanor, Civil Actions Under $7,500, Small Claims.*

Sumter Magistrate Court 115 N Harvin St, PO Box 1428, Sumter, SC 29151; phone: 803-436-2280; fax: 803-436-2789; hours 8:30AM-5PM (EST). *Misdemeanor, Civil Actions Under $7,500, Eviction, Small Claims.*

Probate Court 141 N Main, Rm 111, Sumter, SC 29150; phone: 803-436-2166; fax: 803-436-2407; hours 8:30AM-5PM (EST). *Probate.*

Union County

Circuit Court PO Box 703 (210 W Main St), Union, SC 29379; phone: 864-429-1630; fax: 864-429-1715; hours 9AM-5PM (EST). *Felony, Misdemeanor, Civil Actions Over $7,500.*
www.countyofunion.com/Clerk.html
Note: The court will mail or fax specific case documents, if case number provided. Fees involved.
Civil Records: Access: In person only. Visitors must perform in person searches themselves. Court makes copy: $.50 per page; same fee for self serve. Required to search: name, years to search. Civil cases indexed by defendant, plaintiff. All records on computer.
Criminal Records: Access: In person only. Visitors must perform in person searches themselves. Court makes copy: $.50 per page; same fee for self serve. Required to search: name, years to search; SSN helpful, DOB. Criminal records on computer.
General Information: Public terminal goes back to 1981. No adoption, juvenile, sealed or expunged records released. Certification fee: $1.00 per page. Payee: Clerk of Court. Personal checks accepted. Prepayment required.

Union Magistrate Court 210 W Main St, Union, SC 29379; phone: 864-429-1648; fax: 864-429-1685; hours 9AM-5PM (EST). *Misdemeanor, Civil Actions Under $7,500, Eviction, Small Claims.*
Note: This is the only Magistrate court bldg in county. There are 3 part-time magistrates who work out of jails or other county offices at night when required.

Probate Court PO Box 447, 210 W Main St, Union, SC 29379; phone: 864-429-1625; fax: 864-427-1198; hours 9AM-5PM (EST). *Probate.*

Williamsburg County

Circuit Court 125 W Main St, Kingstree, SC 29556; phone: 843-355-9321 X552; hours 8AM-5PM (EST). *Felony, Misdemeanor, Civil Actions Over $7,500.*
Civil Records: Access: In person. Both court and visitors may perform in person searches. Search fee: $5.00 per name. Court makes copy: $.25 per page. Required to search: name, years to search. Civil cases indexed by defendant, plaintiff; on books, archived from 1980-1989, indexed from 1806; computerized records since 1993.
Criminal Records: Access: In person. Both court and visitors may perform in person searches. No search fee. Court makes copy: $.25 per page. Required to search: name, years to search, DOB; also helpful: SSN. Criminal records on books, archived from 1980-1989, indexed from 1806; computerized records since 1993.
General Information: No adoption, juvenile, sealed or expunged records released. No certification fee. Payee: Clerk of Court. Personal checks accepted. Prepayment required.

Hemingway Magistrate Court 206 E Broad St, PO Box 416, Hemingway, SC 29554; phone: 843-558-2116; hours 6PM-9PM, T,Th (EST). *Misdemeanor, Civil Actions Under $7,500, Eviction, Small Claims.*

Kingstree Magistrate Court 10 Courthouse Sq, Kingstree, SC 29556; phone: 843-355-9321 x179; fax: 843-355-6444; hours 8:00AM-5PM (EST). *Misdemeanor, Civil Actions Under $7,500, Eviction, Small Claims.*

Nesmith Magistrate Court 10 Courthouse Sq, PO Box 673, Kingstree, SC 29556; phone: 843-355-9321 x179; fax: 843-355-6444; hours 8AM-5PM (EST). *Misdemeanor, Civil Actions Under $7,500, Eviction, Small Claims.*

Probate Court PO Box 1005, 125 W Main, Kingstree, SC 29556; phone: 843-355-9321 x558; fax: 843-355-9305; hours 8:00AM-5PM (EST). *Probate.*

York County

Circuit Court PO Box 649, 1675 - 1G York Hwy, York, SC 29745; phone: 803-684-8506; criminal phone: 803-628-3036; civil phone: 803-684-8507; probate phone: 803-684-8513; hours 8AM-5PM (EST). *Felony, Misdemeanor, Civil Actions Over $7,500.*
Note: Civil court located at 2 S Congress St.
Civil Records: Access: Mail, in person. Both court and visitors may perform in person searches. Search fee: $5.00 per name. Court makes copy: $.40 per page. Required to search: name, years to search. Civil cases indexed by defendant, plaintiff; on computer from 1982, in books from 1932. Mail turnaround time 1 day.
Criminal Records: Access: Mail, in person. Both court and visitors may perform in person searches. Search fee: $5.00 per name. Court makes copy: $.40 per page. Required to search: name, years to search, DOB; also helpful: SSN. Criminal records on computer from 1982, in books from 1932. Mail turnaround time 1 day.
General Information: No adoption, juvenile, sealed or expunged records released. Will fax documents $5.00 per doc. Certification fee: $1.00. Payee: Clerk of Court. No personal checks accepted. Prepayment and SASE required.

Clover Magistrate Court 201 S Main St, Clover, SC 29710; phone: 803-222-9404; fax: 803-222-3653; hours 8AM-5PM (EST). *Misdemeanor, Civil Actions Under $7,500, Eviction, Small Claims.*

Fort Mill Magistrate Court 114 Springs St, Fort Mill, SC 29715; phone: 803-547-5572/5573; fax: 803-547-6344; hours 8AM-5PM (EST). *Misdemeanor, Civil Actions Under $7,500, Eviction, Small Claims.*

Hickory Grove Magistrate Court PO Box 37, Hickory Grove, SC 29717; phone: 803-925-2815; hours 9AM-N, T,3-5PM W, Th, Fri (EST). *Misdemeanor, Civil Actions Under $7,500, Eviction, Small Claims.*

Rock Hill Magistrate Court 529 S Cherry, Rock Hill, SC 29730; phone: 803-909-7600; fax: 803-909-7606. *Misdemeanor, Civil Actions Under $7,500, Eviction, Small Claims.*

York Magistrate Court 1675 York Hwy, York, SC 29745; phone: 803-628-3029; fax: 803-628-3225; hours 8AM-5PM (EST). *Misdemeanor, Civil Actions Under $7,500, Eviction, Small Claims.*

Probate Court PO Box 219, 1 E Liberty St, York, SC 29745; phone: 803-684-8513 X8630; fax: 803-684-8536; hours 8AM-5PM (EST). *Probate.*

South Carolina Recording Offices

ORGANIZATION: 46 counties, 46 recording offices. The recording officer is. Register of Mesne Conveyances or Clerk of Court (This varies by county). The entire state is in the Eastern Time Zone (EST).

REAL ESTATE RECORDS: Most counties will not perform real estate searches. Copy and certification fees vary. The Assessor keeps tax records.

UCC RECORDS: Financing statements are filed at the state level, except for real estate related collateral, which are filed with the Register. However, prior to 07/2001, consumer goods and farm collateral were also filed at the Register and these older records can be searched there. As a general rule, all recording offices will perform UCC searches. Search fees are usually $5.00 per debtor name. Copy fees are usually $1.00 per page.

TAX LIEN RECORDS: All federal and state tax liens on personal property and on real property are filed with the Register of Mesne Conveyances (Clerk of Court). Few counties will perform tax lien searches.

ONLINE ACCESS: There is no statewide system, buy several counties have placed free record data on their web sites.

Abbeville County

Clerk of Court, PO Box 99, Abbeville, SC 29620. 864-366-5312 x201, R/E recording phone-864-366-5074; fax-864-366-9188; hours: 8:30AM-5PM.
Separate indices to search. Record index not computerized. Only the public may search. Copy fee $.25 per page. Payee- Abbeville Clerk of Court. **Other phones:** Treasurer- 864-366-5074; Appraiser/Auditor- 864-366-5074; Elections- 864-366-5074. **Property tax/Assessor-** 864-366-5074.

Aiken County

County Register of Mesne Conveyances, PO Box 537, Aiken, SC 29802-0537. 803-642-2072, UCC recording phone-803-642-2075; hours: 8:30AM-5PM.
All records in one index. Records indexed on a public use terminal back to 1982. Office will perform a UCC search but public must search other records themselves. Search fee $5.00 per name. Will not search tax lien records. Copy fee $.50 per page; self serve $.25. Cert fee- $1.00 per cert plus copy fee. Payee- Aiken County Register of Mesne Conveyances. **Online access to Land, Property, Assessor, Recorder, Deed records:** Access to property and deeds indexes and images is via a private company at www.titlesearcher.com. Fee/registration required. **Other phones:** Treasurer- 803-642-2055; Appraiser/Auditor- 803-642-1576; Elections- 803-642-2028. **Property tax/Assessor-** same address as above. 803-642-1576.

Allendale County

Clerk of Court, PO Box 126, Allendale, SC 29810. 803-584-2737; fax-803-584-7046; hours: 9AM-5PM.
All records in one index. Records indexed on computer back to 1987. Only the office personnel may search. Search fee $5.00 per name. Will not search real estate records. Copy fee $.50 per page; real estate $.25 per page. Cert fee- $2.00 per page includes copy fee. Payee- Allendale Clerk of Court. **Other phones:** Treasurer- 803-584-3876. **Property tax/Assessor-** 803-584-2572.

Anderson County

Register of Deeds, PO Box 8002, Anderson, SC 29622. 864-260-4054; fax-864-260-4443; hours: 8:30AM-5PM. www.andersoncountysc.org
Only the public may search. Cert fee- $1.00 per doc plus copy fee. **Online access to Real Estate, Property Tax, Sale, Assessor, Marriage, Estate, Guardianship, Vehicle, Permit, Court records:** Access to the county ACPASS super search site is free at http://acpass.andersoncountysc.org/courts.htm. **Other phones:** Treasurer- 864-260-4033; Anderson County Operator- 864-260-4444. **Property tax/Assessor-** 864-260-4028.

Bamberg County

Clerk of Court, PO Box 150, Bamberg, SC 29003. 803-245-3025; fax-803-245-3088; hours: 9AM-5PM.

Separate indices to search include deeds, mortgages, Lis Pendens, judgments, fed tax and other liens. Record index not computerized. Only the public may search. Separate federal tax lien search- $5.00 per debtor. Copy fee $.25 per page. Cert fee- $5.00 per doc plus copy fee. Payee- Clerk of Court. **Other phones:** Treasurer- 803-245-3003; Appraiser/Auditor- 803-245-3010; Elections- 803-245-3028; Probate Court- 803-245-3008; Auditor - 803-245-3006. **Property tax/Assessor-** PO Box 511, Bamberg, SC 29003; 803-245-3010.

Barnwell County

Clerk of Court, PO Box 723, Barnwell, SC 29812-0723. 803-541-1020; fax-803-541-1025; 9AM-5PM.
All records in one index. Records indexed on a public use terminal back to 1980. Only the public may search. Copy fee $.50 per page. Cert fee- $1.00 per page plus copy fee. **Other phones:** Treasurer- 803-541-1050. **Property tax/Assessor-** same address as above. 803-541-1011.

Beaufort County

Clerk of Court, PO Box 1128, Beaufort, SC 29901. 843-470-5218, R/E recording phone-843-470-2700, UCC recording phone-843-470-2715; fax-843-470-5248; www.co.beaufort.sc.us
Will search UCC records. UCC search per debtor name- $5.00. UCC search request using non-standard form (per name)- $8.00. **Online access to Assessor, Property records:** Access to the public records search database is free online at http://rodweb.co.beaufort.sc.us. Also, search assessor data at www.co.beaufort.sc.us/assessor/frameset.asp. A fuller records subscription service requiring registration, fees, and logon is under development. **Other phones:** Treasurer- 843-470-2766; Elections- 843-470-3753. **Property tax/Assessor-** 843-470-2513.

Berkeley County

Clerk of Court, 223 N. Live Oak Drive, Moncks Corner, SC 29461. 843-719-4084; fax-843-719-4851; hours: 8AM-5PM. www.co.berkeley.sc.us
Only the public may search. Copy fee $.35 per page. Cert fee- $2.00. Payee- Berkeley County Clerk of Court. **Online access to Property, Assessor, Personal Property, Vehicle Tax, Property Sale, Real Estate, Recording, UCC records:** Access real estate data is at www.co.berkeley.sc.us/e_services/index.php. Also, search the clerks document database for free at www.landaccess.com. Click on SC-Berkeley. Records go back to 1/2/1997. **Other phones:** Treasurer- 843-761-3800. **Assessor-** 843-761-6900 x4061.

Calhoun County

Clerk of Court, 902 F.R. Huff Drive, St. Matthews, SC 29135. 803-874-3524; fax-803-874-1942; 9AM-5PM.
Only the public may search. Copy fee $.25 per page. Cert fee- $.25 per page. Payee- Calhoun County Treasurer. **Online access to Land, Property, Assessor, Recorder, Deed records:** Access to property and deeds indexes and images is via a private

company at www.titlesearcher.com. Fee/registration required. **Other phones:** Treasurer- 803-874-3519. **Property tax/Assessor-** 803-874-3613.

Charleston County

R.M.C., PO Box 726, Charleston, SC 29402. 843-958-4800; fax-843-958-4803; hours: 8:30AM-5PM. www.charlestoncounty.org
Separate indices to search include day book (same day recording), deed, mortgage, misc. Records indexed on a public use terminal back to 1978. Only the public may search. Copy fee $.25 per page. Cert fee- $5.00 per cert plus copy. **Online access to Real Estate, Deed, Mortgage, Property Tax, Judgment, Marriage, Will/Estate, Guardianship, Conservatorship records:** Access to the county's GIS mapping database of property records is free at http://gisweb.charlestoncounty.org. Also, online access the auditor & treasurer's tax system database is free at http://taxweb.charlestoncounty.org. Also, search the court records for judgments at http://www3.charlestoncounty.org/connect?ref=MIE. Also, search all records including marriages, estates/wills, and guardianships at www.charlestoncounty.org/index2.asp?p=/publicrecords.htm. **Other phones:** Treasurer- 843-958-4360; Elections- 843-745-2226; Vital Records- 843-740-0801. **Property tax/Assessor-** 843-958-4100.

Cherokee County

Clerk of Court, PO Drawer 2289, Gaffney, SC 29342. 864-487-2571; fax-864-487-2754; hours: 8:30AM-5PM. www.cherokeecountysc.com
All records in one index. Only the public may search. Copy fee $.50 per page. Cert fee- $1.00 per cert plus copy fee. Payee- Cherokee Clerk of Court. **Other phones:** Treasurer- 864-487-2551; Elections- 864-487-2563; Vital Records- 864-487-2571. **Property tax/Assessor-** 864-487-2552.

Chester County

Clerk of Court, PO Drawer 580, Chester, SC 29706. 803-385-2605; fax-803-581-7975;
Office will perform a UCC search but public must search other records themselves. UCC search per debtor name- $5.00. Copy fee $.25 per page. **Other phones:** Treasurer- 803-385-2608. **Property tax/Assessor-** 803-377-4177.

Chesterfield County

Clerk of Court, PO Box 529, Chesterfield, SC 29709. 843-623-2574, UCC recording phone-843-623-7853; fax-843-623-6944; hours: 8:30AM-5PM.
Index: Tax liens, Mental health liens, Common Pleas, Mech Liens, Lis Pends, Judgments, General Sessions. Records indexed on a public use terminal back to 1996. Only the public may search. Copy fee $2.00 per document. Cert fee- None. Payee- Clerk of Court. **Other phones:** Treasurer- 843-623-2563; Appraiser/Auditor- 843-623-7362; Elections- 843-623-2265; Vital Records- 843-623-2117. **Property tax/Assessor-** 843-623-7362.

Clarendon County

Clerk of Court-Register of Deeds, PO Box 136, Manning, SC 29102. 803-435-4443, R/E recording 803-435-4444; fax-803-435-8258; hours: 8:30AM-5PM.
Records indexed on a public use terminal back to 1988. Only the public may search. Copy fee $.25 per page. Cert fee- $2.00 per 4 pages; $.25 each add'l page; all copies must be certified. **Property tax/Assessor**- 803-435-4423.

Colleton County

Register of Deeds, PO Box 620, Walterboro, SC 29488-0028. 843-542-2745; fax-843-542-2749; hours: 8AM-5PM. www.colletoncounty.org
Separate indices to search include land, UCC's, specials indexes. Records indexed on a public use terminal back to 1986 for lands; July, 1995 for specials; July 1, 1994 thru August 31, 2001 for UCC's. Only the public may search. Copy fee $1.50 1st page; $.50 each add'l page if to mail, $.25 in person. Cert fee- $1.00 per doc plus copy fee. Payee- Clerk of Court. **Other phones:** Treasurer- 843-549-2233; Elections- 843-549-2842; Vital Records- 843-549-1516. **Property tax/Assessor**-843-549-1213.

Darlington County

Clerk of Court, PO Box 1177, Darlington, SC 29540. 843-398-4330; fax-843-393-6871; hours: 8:30AM-5PM. www.darcosc.com
Only the public may search. Copy fee $1.00 per page. **Online access to Property, Assessor records:** Access property records free at www.darcosc.com/assessor/search.asp. **Other phones:** Treasurer- 843-398-4160. **Property tax/Assessor**-843-398-4180.

Dillon County

Clerk of Court, PO Drawer 1220, Dillon, SC 29536. 843-774-1425; fax-843-841-3706; hours: 8:30AM-5PM.
Index: More than one index. Record index not computerized. Office will perform a UCC search but public must search other records themselves. Search fee $10.00. Copy fee $.50 per page. Cert fee- None. Payee- Dillon Clerk of Court. **Other phones:** Treasurer- 843-774-1416; Appraiser/Auditor-843-774-1412; Elections- 843-774-1403; Vital Records- 843-774-5611; Auditor- 843-774-1418; Probate -8437741423. **Property tax/Assessor**- 843-774-1412.

Dorchester County

Clerk of Court, PO Box 38, St. George, SC 29477. 843-563-0106, R/E recording phone-843-832-0153; fax-843-563-0182; hours: 8:30AM-5PM.
Only the public may search. Copy fee $.50 per page. Cert fee- $2.00. Payee- Dorchester County Clerk of Court. **Other phones:** Treasurer- 843-563-0165; Appraiser/Auditor- 843-563-0156; Elections-843-563-0132; Vital Records- 843-563-0107. **Property tax/Assessor**- 843-563-0156.

Edgefield County

Clerk of Court, PO Box 34, Edgefield, SC 29824. 803-637-4080, R/E recording phone-803-637-4049; fax-803-637-4117; hours: 8:30AM-5PM.
Only the public may search. Copy fee $1.00 per page. Cert fee- $1.00 per Document. Payee-Registrar of Deeds. **Other phones:** Treasurer- 803-637-4069; Appraiser/Auditor- 803-637-4057; Elections- 803-637-4072. **Property tax/Assessor**- 803-637-4066.

Fairfield County

Clerk of Court, PO Drawer 299, Winnsboro, SC 29180. 803-712-6526; hours: 9AM-5PM.
Only the public may search. Copy fee $.25 per page. Cert fee- $1.00 per cert plus copy fee. Payee-Fairfield Clerk of Court. **Other phones:** Treasurer-803-635-1411. **Property/Assessor**- 803-635-1411.

Florence County

Clerk of Court, MSC-E City/County Complex, Florence, SC 29501. 843-665-3031; fax-843-665-3097; hours: 8:30AM-5PM. http://web.florenceco.org
Only the public may search. Copy fee $1.00 per page. Cert fee- None. Payee- Florence County. **Online access to Recorder, Grantor/Grantee, Deed, Lien, Judgment, Property, Assessor, Vehicle records:** Access recorder data free at http://web.florenceco.org/cgi-bin/coc/coc.cgi. Also, access property tax records free at http://web.florenceco.org/cgi-bin/ta/tax-inq.cgi. Access vehicle tax records free at http://web.florenceco.org/cgi-bin/ta/vehing.cgi. **Other phones:** Treasurer- 843-665-3041; Elections- 843-665-2351. **Property tax/Assessor**- 180 N Irby St, MSC-A, Florence, SC 29501; 843-665-3056.

Georgetown County

Register of Deeds, PO Box 421270, Georgetown, SC 29442. 843-545-3088; hours: 8:30AM-5PM. www.georgetowncountysc.org
Separate indices to search include deeds, mortgages, tax liens, plats, misc liens. Only the public may search. Copy fee $.50 per page. Cert fee- $1.00 per cert plus copy fee. Payee-Georgetown County Register of Deeds. **Online access to Property, GIS, Recording, Real Estate, Deed, UCC records:** Access to property data on the GIS-mapping site is free at http://gismap.georgetowncountysc.org/viewer.htm. Click on the binoculars to get to the neame search feature. Also, access the clerks database free at www.landaccess.com. Click on SC-Georgetown. Index goes back to 1/1977 for deeds, 7/1986 for mortgages, 1/1989 for UCC and 7/1989 for tax liens. **Other phones:** Treasurer- 843-545-3098; Elections- 843-545-3339; Vital Records- 843-546-0174. **Property tax/Assessor** 843-545-3014.

Greenville County

Register of Deeds, 301 University Ridge, #1300; County Sq #1300, Greenville, SC 29601-3655. 864-467-7240, UCC recording phone-864-467-7180; fax-864-467-7107; hours: 8:30AM-5PM. www.greenvillecounty.org
Only the public may search. Copy fee $.25 per page. Cert fee- $1.00 per doc, plus copy fee. Payee- Register of Deeds. **Online access to Real Property, Deed, Vehicle, Property Tax, Most Wanted, Missing Person records:** Search the Register of Deeds database free online at www.greenvillecounty.org. Click on Register of Deeds Search. Also, search the property tax and vehicles data at www.greenvillecounty.org/voTaxQry/wcmain.asp. Also, search the real estate information data at www.greenvillecounty.org/vrealpr24/clrealprop.asp. No name searching. Also, search the sheriff's most wanted and missing persons lists at www.gcso.org. **Other phones:** Treasurer- 864-467-7210. **Property tax/Assessor**- 864-467-7300.

Greenwood County

Clerk of Court, 528 Monument St.; Courthouse, Greenwood, SC 29646. 864-942-8551, UCC recording phone-864-942-8613; fax-864-942-8693; hours: 8:30AM-5PM. www.co.greenwood.sc.us
Separate indices to search include Computer and Hard Copy. Only the public may search. Copy fee $.25 per page. Cert fee- $2.00 per cert plus copy fee. Payee- Greenwood Clerk of Court. **Online access to Assessor, Property records:** Records on the County Parcel Search database are free at http://165.166.39.5/giswebsite/default.htm. Click on search and choose to search by owner name. An interactive map is included. **Other phones:** Treasurer-864-942-8528; Appraiser/Auditor- 864-942-8534; Elections- 864-942-8521. **Property tax/Assessor**- 864-942-8536.

Hampton County

Clerk of Court, PO Box 7, Hampton, SC 29924. 803-943-7510; fax-803-943-7596; hours: 8AM-5PM.

Separate indices to search include deeds, mortgages, liens, miscellaneous, plats. Records indexed on a public use terminal back to 2000. Only the public may search. Copy fee $5.00 per instrument. Cert fee- $1.00 per instrument includes copy fee. Payee- Clerk of Court. **Other phones:** Treasurer- 803-943-7509; Appraiser/Auditor- 803-943-7507; Vital Records- 803-943-3878. **Property tax/Assessor**- 803-943-7507.

Horry County

Register of Deeds, PO Box 470, Conway, SC 29528. 843-915-5000, R/E recording phone-843-915-5430; fax-843-915-6430; hours: 8AM-5PM. www.horrycounty.org
Separate indices to search include deeds, mortgages, tax liens, condo liens, mechanic liens. Records indexed on computer back to 1984. Only the public may search. Copy fee $8.00 for 1-4 pages, $1.00 each add'l; $1.00 per page self serve. Cert fee- $2.00 per cert plus copy fee. Payee- Register of Deeds. **Online to Recorder, Deed, Lien, Real Property records:** Recorders database is free at www.horrycounty.org/gateway/disclaimer/idx_rod.html Also, search the real property database at www.horrycounty.org/gateway/disclaimer/idx_real.html. **Other phones:** Treasurer- 843-915-5430; Appraiser/Auditor- 843-915-5050; Elections- 843-915-5440; Vital Records- 843-248-3958; Register of Deeds Main Switchboard- 843-915-5430. **Property tax/Assessor**- 843-915-5000.

Jasper County

Clerk of Court, PO Box 248, Ridgeland, SC 29936. 843-726-7710; fax-843-726-7782; hours: 9AM-5PM. All records in one index. Records indexed on a public use terminal. Only the public may search. Copy fee $1.00 per page. **Other phones:** Treasurer-843-726-7722; Appraiser/Auditor- 843-726-7725; Elections- 843-726-7709; Vital Records- 843-726-7790. **Property tax/Assessor**- 843-726-7725.

Kershaw County

Register of Deeds, 515 Walnut St #180, Camden, SC 29020. 803-425-1500, R/E recording phone-803-425-1500 x5365/5367/5434, UCC recording phone-803-425-1500 x5367/5365/5434; fax-803-425-7673; hours: 8:30AM-5PM.
Separate indices to search include Grantor/Grantee, mortgagor/mortgagee, plats-owner, UCC's-debtor/lender, specials-state & federal tax liens-name. Only the public may search. Copy fee $.50 per page. Cert fee- $1.00 per doc plus copy fee. Payee- Kershaw Register of Deeds. **Other phones:** Treasurer- 803-425-1500 x5314; Appraiser/Auditor- 803-425-1500 x5327; Elections- 803-424-4016/ 424-4017; Vital Records- 803-425-6012. **Property tax/Assessor**- 515 Walnut St, Camden, SC 29020; 803-425-1500 x5332.

Lancaster County

Clerk of Court, 101 N Main St, Lancaster, SC 29720. 803-285-1581, R/E recording phone-803-416-9440; fax-803-416-9388; www.lancastercountysc.net
Separate indices to search include Lis Pendens, judgments. Records indexed on computer back to 1980s. Only the public may search. Copy fee $.25 per page. Cert fee- $2.00 per page plus copy fee. Payee- Clerk of Court. **Online access to Property, Assessor records:** Access property data free at www.lancastercountysc.net/onlinetaxes/. **Other phones:** Treasurer- 803-285-7939; Elections- 803-285-2969; Vital Records- 803-286-9948. **Property tax/Assessor**- same address as above. 803-285-6964.

Laurens County

Clerk of Court, PO Box 287, Laurens, SC 29360. 864-984-3538; fax-864-984-7023; hours: 9AM-5PM.
Only the public may search. Copy fee $1.00 per page. R/E record copy- $.50 per page. Cert fee- $1.00 per cert plus copy fee. Payee- Laurens Clerk of Court. **Property tax/Assessor**- 864-984-6546.

Lee County

Register of Deeds, PO Box 387, Bishopville, SC 29010. 803-484-5341, R/E recording phone-803-484-5341 x333, UCC recording phone-803-484-5341 x378; fax-803-484-1632; hours: 9AM-5PM.
Separate indices to search. Records indexed on a public use terminal back to 1994. Only the public may search. Copy fee $.25 per page. Cert fee-$1.00 per doc plus $1.00 for copy fee. Payee-Register of Deeds. **Other phones:** Treasurer- 803-484-5341 x327. **Property tax/Assessor-** same address as above. 803-484-5341 x362.

Lexington County

Register of Deeds, 212 S Lake Dr, Lexington, SC 29072. 803-785-8168, UCC recording phone-803-785-8470; fax-803-785-8189; hours: 8AM-5PM. www.lex-co.com/Departments/RegisterOfDeeds/Index.html
Only the public may search. Copy fee $.35 per page. Cert fee- $1.00 per doc, plus copy fee. Payee- County of Lexington. **Online access to Assessor, Property, Real Property records:** Access to county Re-assessment Information is free at www.myscgov.com/cgi/hsrun/Distributed2/LCDAE/LCDAE.hjx;start=LCDAE.Hsmaster.run. Register of Deeds records are found at www.lex-co.com/Departments/RegisterOfDeeds/OnlineServices.html. **Other phones:** Treasurer- 803-785-8217. **Property tax/Assessor-** 803-785-8190.

Marion County

Clerk of Court, PO Box 295, Marion, SC 29571. 843-423-8240; fax-843-423-8306; hours: 8:30AM-5PM.
Separate indices to search include real estate and tax liens. Records indexed on a public use terminal back to 1/98. Only the public may search. Copy fee $1.00 per page. R/E record copy- $3.00 1st 4 pages, $.25 each add'l. Tax lien copy- $2.00 per lien. Cert fee- $1.00 per page plus copy fee. Payee-Marion Clerk of Court. **Other phones:** Treasurer- 843-423-8230. **Property tax/Assessor-** 843-423-8225.

Marlboro County

Clerk of Court, PO Drawer 996, Bennettsville, SC 29512. 843-479-5613; fax-843-479-5640; hours: 8:30AM-5PM.
Records indexed on a public use terminal back to 1985. Only the public may search. Copy fee $1.00 per page. R/E record copy- $.20 per page. Cert fee-$2.00 per cert plus copy fee. Payee- Marlboro Clerk of Court.

McCormick County

Clerk of Court, 133 S. Mine St Rm102; Courthouse, Rm 102, McCormick, SC 29835. 864-465-2195; fax-864-465-0071; hours: 9AM-5PM.
Separate indices to search include Grantor/Grantee, Mtgr/Mtge, Judgmnts, Lis Pendens, St &Fed liens, Misc. Record index not computerized. Only the public may search. Copy fee $.35 per page. Cert fee- $1.00 per cert plus copy fee. Payee- Clerk of Court. **Other phones:** Treasurer- 864-465-2332; Appraiser/Auditor- 864-465-2107; Elections- 864-465-2089; Property Appraiser-864-465-2931. **Property tax/Assessor-** PO Box 836, McCormick, SC 29835; 864-465-2931.

Newberry County

Court Clerk, PO Drawer 10, Newberry, SC 29108. 803-321-2110; fax-803-321-2111; hours: 8:30AM-5PM.
Separate indices to search. Records indexed on a public use terminal back to 1990. Office will perform a UCC search but public must search other records themselves. UCC search per debtor name- $5.00. Copy fee $.20 per page. Cert fee-$1.20. Payee- Newberry County Clerk. **Online to Assessor, Real Estate, Auditor, Property Tax, Treasurer records:** Assessor data is free at http://209.213.28.38/vpn/assessor2.htm. Property tax

data at www.newberrycounty.net/auditor/Index.html. Also, the treasurer database is free at http://209.213.28.38/vpn/treasurer.htm. **Other phones:** Treasurer- 803-321-2130. **Property tax/Assessor-** same address as above. 803-321-2125.

Oconee County

Register of Deeds, 415 S Pine St, Walhalla, SC 29691. 864-638-4285; 8:30AM-5PM. www.oconeesc.com
Separate indices to search include deeds, mortgages, tax liens, mechanics liens, assessments. Only the public may search. General copy fee $5.00 for 4 pages; $.50 each add'l. R/E record copy- $.50 per page. Cert fee- $1.00. Payee-Register of Deeds. **Online to Land, Deed, Mortgage, Plat records:** Access records free at www.oconeesc.com/resolution/default.asp. **Other phones:** Treasurer- 864-638-4162. **Property tax/Assessor-** 415 S Pine St, Walhalla, SC 29691; 864-638-4150.

Orangeburg County

Register of Deeds, Box 9000, Orangeburg, SC 29116-9000. 803-533-6236; fax-803-535-2354; hours: 8:30AM-5PM. www.orangeburgscrod.org
Separate indices to search include deed, mortgage, plat. Records indexed on computer back to 1989. Only the public may search. Copy fee $.50 per page. Cert fee- No fee for certification. Payee-Register of Deeds. **Online to Assessor, Property records:** Access to county property tax records is free at www.orangeburgcounty.org/Assessor/main.asp. **Other phones:** Treasurer- 803-533-6130; Appraiser/Auditor- 803-533-6229; Elections- 803-533-6213; Vital Records- 803-533-6239. **Property tax/Assessor-** 803-533-6220.

Pickens County

Register of Deeds, 222 McDaniel Ave. B-5, Pickens, SC 29671. 864-898-5868; fax-864-898-5924; hours: 8AM-5PM. www.co.pickens.sc.us/regofdeeds/
Separate indices to search include grantor/grantee, mortgagor/mortgagee, plat, liens. Records indexed on a public use terminal back to 1986. Only the public may search. Copy fee $.75 for microfilm, $.50 for 8 1/2 x 11 or 14, $1.00 for 11 x 17 per page. Cert fee- $1.00 per doc includes copy fee. Payee- Register of Deeds. **Online access to Property, Assessor, Most Wanted, Property Tax records:** Search property tax records at www.co.pickens.sc.us/onlinetaxes/. Also, search assessor property records free online at http://67.32.48.35/assessor/disclaim.asp. View the sheriff's most wanted list online at www.pickenscosheriff.org/most_wanted.htm. **Other phones:** Treasurer- 864-898-5883; Appraiser/Auditor-864-898-5878; Elections- 864-898-5848; Vital Records- 864-898-5965. **Property tax/Assessor-** 222 McDaniel Ave #B-8, Pickens, SC 29671; 864-898-5871.

Richland County

Register of Deeds, PO Box 192, Columbia, SC 29202. 803-576-1910; fax-803-576-1922; 8:30AM-5PM.
Separate indices to search. Records indexed on a public use terminal back to 1985. Only the public may search. Copy fee $.50 per page. Cert fee-$1.00 per doc plus copy fee. Payee- Richland County Register of Deeds. **Online to Assessor, Property, Register of Deeds, Real Estate, Marriage, Inmate, Lost Pet records:** Access to county property information is free at www.richlandmaps.com. Click on "Property Info" however, no name searching. Search www.richlandonline.com/services/assessorsearch/assessorsearch.asp for assessments,no name searching. Also, search register of deeds free online at www.richlandonline.com/services/rodsearch.asp; no name searching. Also, search marriages, inmates, and lost pet databases free online at www.richlandonline.com/services/onlineservices.asp.

Property tax/Assessor- 2020 Hampton, Columbia, SC 29202; 803-748-5038.

Saluda County

Clerk of Court, Courthouse, Saluda, SC 29138. 864-445-4500, R/E recording phone-864-445-3303; fax-864-445-3772; hours: 8:30AM-5PM.
Records indexed on a public use terminal. Only the public may search. Copy fee $1.00 per page. Tax lien copy- $.25 per page. Cert fee- $1.00 per cert plus copy fee. Payee- Saluda County Clerk of Court. **Other phones:** Treasurer- 864-445-2875. **Property tax/Assessor-** 864-445-8121.

Spartanburg County

County Register of Mesne Conveyances, 366 N. Church St; County Admin. Offices, Spartanburg, SC 29303. 864-596-2514; hours: 8:30AM-5PM.
Only the public may search. Copy fee $.50 per page. Cert fee- $2.00 per cert plus copy fee. Payee-Spartanburg County Register of Mesne Conveyances. **Other phones:** Treasurer- 864-596-2603. **Property tax/Assessor-** 864-596-2544.

Sumter County

Register of Deeds, 141 N. Main St.; Courthouse, Rm 202, Sumter, SC 29150. 803-436-2177, UCC recording phone-803-436-2179; hours: 8:30AM-5PM. www.sumtercountysc.org
Only the public may search. Copy fee $.50 per page. Cert fee- $2.00 1st pg, $.50 each. Payee-Sumter County Register of Deeds. **Online access to Real Estate, Recording, Deed, Property Tax records:** Search county e-gov data free at www.sumtercountysc.org/disclaim.htm. **Other phones:** Treasurer- 803-436-2213; Appraiser/Auditor- 803-436-2112; Elections- 803-436-2310. **Property tax/Assessor-** 803-436-2112.

Union County

Clerk of Court, PO Box 703, Union, SC 29379. 864-429-1630; fax-864-429-1715; hours: 9AM-5PM. www.judicial.state.sc.us/clerks/union
Separate indices to search. Records indexed on a public use terminal back to 1998. Only the public may search. Copy fee $.50 per page. Cert fee-$1.00 per UCC plus copy fee. Payee- Union Clerk of Court. **Other phones:** Treasurer- 864-429-1606; Elections- 864-429-1616; Vital Records- 864-429-1690. **Property tax/Assessor-** 864-429-1650.

Williamsburg County

Clerk of Court, 125 W. Main St, Kingstree, SC 29556. 843-355-9321 ext552; fax-843-355-7821; 8AM-5PM.
All records in one index. Records indexed on a public use terminal. Only the public may search. Copy fee $1.00 per page. Tax lien copy- $.25. Cert fee- $3.00 per page. Payee- Williamsburg County Clerk of Court. **Property tax/Assessor-** 843-354-7059.

York County

Clerk of Court, PO Box 649, York, SC 29745. 803-684-8510; hours: 8AM-5PM.
Office will perform a tax lien search but public must search other records themselves. Federal/state combined tax lien search- $5.00 per debtor. Copy fee $1.00 per page. R/E or tax lien copy- $.40 per page. Cert fee- $1.00 per doc plus copy fee. Payee- York Clerk of Court. **Online to Property, GIS, Recorder, Real Estate, Deed, UCC records:** Access to the county GIS and property data is free at http://maps.yorkcountygov.com/gisonline/. Click on "GIS Online" and name search at the main map page. Also, access to the clerk's records database is free at www.landaccess.com. Click on SC-York. Index goes back to 7/1982. **Other phones:** Treasurer- 803-684-8528; Elections- 803-684-1242; Vital Records- 803-909-7300. **Property tax/Assessor-** 803-684-8526.

South Carolina County Locator

You will usually be able to find the city name in the City/County Cross Reference below. We have also included a ZIP/City Cross Reference following the City/County Cross Reference.

South Carolina City/County Cross Reference

ABBEVILLE Abbeville
ADAMS RUN (29426) Charleston(78), Dorchester(21)
AIKEN Aiken
ALCOLU (29001) Clarendon(93), Sumter(6)
ALLENDALE Allendale
ANDERSON Anderson
ANDREWS (29510) Georgetown(58), Williamsburg(41)
ARCADIA Spartanburg
AWENDAW Charleston
AYNOR Horry
BALLENTINE Richland
BAMBERG Bamberg
BARNWELL Barnwell
BATESBURG (29006) Lexington(51), Saluda(30), Aiken(17)
BATH Aiken
BEAUFORT Beaufort
BEECH ISLAND Aiken
BELTON (29627) Anderson(93), Greenville(5)
BENNETTSVILLE Marlboro
BETHERA Berkeley
BETHUNE (29009) Kershaw(83), Chesterfield(9), Lee(7)
BISHOPVILLE Lee
BLACKSBURG (29702) Cherokee(96), York(3)
BLACKSTOCK (29014) Chester(58), Fairfield(41)
BLACKVILLE (29817) Barnwell(79), Bamberg(20)
BLAIR Fairfield
BLENHEIM Marlboro
BLUFFTON Beaufort
BLYTHEWOOD (29016) Richland(91), Fairfield(8)
BONNEAU Berkeley
BORDEN Sumter
BOWLING GREEN York
BOWMAN (29018) Orangeburg(93), Dorchester(6)
BRADLEY (29819) Greenwood(80), Abbeville(17), McCormick(1)
BRANCHVILLE (29432) Orangeburg(72), Bamberg(23), Dorchester(4)
BRUNSON Hampton
BUFFALO Union
CADES (29518) Williamsburg(96), Clarendon(3)
CALHOUN FALLS (29628) Abbeville(97), McCormick(2)
CAMDEN (29020) Kershaw(94), Lee(5)
CAMERON (29030) Calhoun(72), Orangeburg(27)
CAMPOBELLO (29322) Spartanburg(98), Greenville(1)
CANADYS Colleton
CARLISLE (29031) Union(47), Chester(34), Fairfield(18)
CASSATT (29032) Kershaw(72), Lee(27)
CATAWBA York
CAYCE Lexington
CENTENARY Marion
CENTRAL (29630) Pickens(93), Anderson(6)
CHAPIN (29036) Lexington(72), Richland(21), Newberry(6)
CHAPPELLS (29037) Newberry(68), Saluda(28), Laurens(3)
CHARLESTON (29406) Charleston(76), Berkeley(23)

CHARLESTON (29418) Charleston(78), Dorchester(21)
CHARLESTON (29420) Dorchester(63), Charleston(36)
CHARLESTON Berkeley
CHARLESTON Charleston
CHARLESTON AFB Charleston
CHERAW Chesterfield
CHEROKEE FALLS Cherokee
CHESNEE (29323) Spartanburg(87), Cherokee(12)
CHESTER Chester
CHESTERFIELD Chesterfield
CLARKS HILL (29821) Edgefield(51), McCormick(48)
CLEARWATER Aiken
CLEMSON Pickens
CLEVELAND (29635) Greenville(73), Pickens(26)
CLIFTON Spartanburg
CLINTON Laurens
CLIO (29525) Marlboro(97), Dillon(2)
CLOVER York
COLUMBIA (29212) Lexington(78), Richland(21)
COLUMBIA (29210) Richland(69), Lexington(30)
COLUMBIA Lexington
COLUMBIA Richland
CONESTEE Greenville
CONVERSE Spartanburg
CONWAY Horry
COOSAWATCHIE Jasper
COPE Orangeburg
CORDESVILLE Berkeley
CORDOVA Orangeburg
COTTAGEVILLE Colleton
COWARD Florence
COWPENS (29330) Spartanburg(64), Cherokee(35)
CROCKETVILLE Hampton
CROSS (29436) Berkeley(94), Orangeburg(5)
CROSS ANCHOR Spartanburg
CROSS HILL (29332) Laurens(90), Newberry(9)
DALE Beaufort
DALZELL (29040) Sumter(81), Lee(18)
DARLINGTON Darlington
DAUFUSKIE ISLAND Beaufort
DAVIS STATION Clarendon
DENMARK Bamberg
DILLON Dillon
DONALDS (29638) Abbeville(86), Greenwood(13)
DORCHESTER Dorchester
DRAYTON Spartanburg
DUE WEST Abbeville
DUNCAN Spartanburg
EARLY BRANCH (29916) Hampton(57), Jasper(42)
EASLEY (29642) Pickens(69), Anderson(30)
EASLEY Pickens
EASTOVER Richland
EDGEFIELD Edgefield
EDGEMOOR Chester
EDISTO ISLAND (29438) Colleton(58), Charleston(41)
EFFINGHAM Florence
EHRHARDT (29081) Bamberg(92), Colleton(7)
ELGIN (29045) Kershaw(56), Richland(39), Fairfield(3)

ELKO Barnwell
ELLIOTT Lee
ELLOREE (29047) Orangeburg(50), Calhoun(49)
ENOREE (29335) Spartanburg(70), Laurens(25), Union(4)
ESTILL Hampton
EUTAWVILLE Orangeburg
FAIR PLAY (29643) Oconee(80), Anderson(19)
FAIRFAX (29827) Allendale(98), Hampton(1)
FAIRFOREST Spartanburg
FINGERVILLE Spartanburg
FLORENCE (29501) Florence(92), Darlington(7)
FLORENCE Florence
FLOYD DALE Dillon
FOLLY BEACH Charleston
FORK Dillon
FORT LAWN Chester
FORT MILL (29715) York(69), Lancaster(30)
FORT MILL York
FOUNTAIN INN (29644) Laurens(60), Greenville(39)
FURMAN Hampton
GABLE (29051) Clarendon(53), Sumter(46)
GADSDEN Richland
GAFFNEY Cherokee
GALIVANTS FERRY Horry
GARNETT (29922) Hampton(69), Jasper(30)
GASTON (29053) Lexington(81), Calhoun(18)
GEORGETOWN Georgetown
GIFFORD Hampton
GILBERT Lexington
GLENDALE Spartanburg
GLOVERVILLE Aiken
GOOSE CREEK Berkeley
GRAMLING Spartanburg
GRANITEVILLE Aiken
GRAY COURT Laurens
GREAT FALLS (29055) Chester(65), Fairfield(34)
GREELEYVILLE (29056) Williamsburg(88), Clarendon(11)
GREEN POND Colleton
GREEN SEA Horry
GREENVILLE (29611) Greenville(93), Anderson(3), Pickens(2)
GREENVILLE Greenville
GREENWOOD Greenwood
GREER (29651) Greenville(54), Spartanburg(45)
GREER Greenville
GRESHAM Marion
GROVER Dorchester
HAMER Dillon
HAMPTON Hampton
HARDEEVILLE Jasper
HARLEYVILLE Dorchester
HARTSVILLE (29550) Darlington(84), Chesterfield(13), Lee(1)
HARTSVILLE Darlington
HEATH SPRINGS (29058) Lancaster(94), Kershaw(5)
HEMINGWAY (29554) Georgetown(52), Williamsburg(44), Florence(2)
HICKORY GROVE York
HILDA Barnwell
HILTON HEAD ISLAND Beaufort

HODGES (29653) Greenwood(93), Abbeville(6)
HODGES Greenwood
HOLLY HILL (29059) Orangeburg(96), Berkeley(3)
HOLLYWOOD Charleston
HONEA PATH (29654) Anderson(59), Abbeville(21), Laurens(11), Greenville(7)
HOPKINS Richland
HORATIO Sumter
HUGER (29450) Berkeley(98), Charleston(1)
INMAN Spartanburg
IRMO (29063) Richland(91), Lexington(8)
ISLANDTON Colleton
ISLE OF PALMS Charleston
IVA (29655) Anderson(58), Abbeville(41)
JACKSON Aiken
JACKSONBORO Colleton
JAMESTOWN Berkeley
JEFFERSON Chesterfield
JENKINSVILLE Fairfield
JOANNA Laurens
JOHNS ISLAND Charleston
JOHNSONVILLE (29555) Florence(93), Williamsburg(6)
JOHNSTON (29832) Edgefield(72), Saluda(27)
JONESVILLE Union
KERSHAW (29067) Lancaster(73), Kershaw(26)
KINARDS (29355) Newberry(54), Laurens(45)
KINGS CREEK Cherokee
KINGSTREE Williamsburg
KLINE Barnwell
LA FRANCE Anderson
LADSON (29456) Dorchester(41), Berkeley(40), Charleston(18)
LADYS ISLAND Beaufort
LAKE CITY (29560) Florence(73), Williamsburg(14), Clarendon(12)
LAKE VIEW Dillon
LAMAR (29069) Darlington(87), Lee(12)
LANDO Chester
LANDRUM (29356) Spartanburg(58), Greenville(41)
LANE Williamsburg
LANGLEY Aiken
LATTA (29565) Dillon(87), Marion(10), Marlboro(2)
LAURENS Laurens
LEESVILLE (29070) Lexington(74), Saluda(25)
LEXINGTON Lexington
LIBERTY (29657) Pickens(86), Anderson(13)
LIBERTY HILL Kershaw
LITTLE MOUNTAIN (29075) Newberry(81), Richland(13), Lexington(5)
LITTLE RIVER Horry
LITTLE ROCK Dillon
LIVINGSTON Orangeburg
LOBECO Beaufort
LOCKHART Union
LODGE (29082) Colleton(92), Bamberg(7)
LONE STAR Calhoun
LONG CREEK Oconee
LONGS Horry
LORIS Horry
LOWNDESVILLE Abbeville
LUGOFF (29078) Kershaw(96), Richland(3)
LURAY (29932) Allendale(56), Hampton(43)

LYDIA Darlington
LYMAN Spartanburg
LYNCHBURG (29080) Lee(50), Sumter(49)
MANNING Clarendon
MARIETTA (29661) Greenville(76), Pickens(23)
MARTIN (29836) Allendale(94), Barnwell(5)
MAULDIN Greenville
MAYESVILLE (29104) Lee(50), Sumter(49)
MAYO Spartanburg
MC BEE (29101) Chesterfield(83), Darlington(16)
MC CLELLANVILLE Charleston
MC COLL Marlboro
MC CONNELLS York
MC CORMICK (29835) McCormick(93), Edgefield(6)
MC CORMICK McCormick
MILEY Hampton
MINTURN Dillon
MODOC (29838) Edgefield(62), McCormick(36), Fairfield(1)
MONCKS CORNER Berkeley
MONETTA (29105) Aiken(66), Saluda(33)
MONTICELLO Fairfield
MONTMORENCI Aiken
MOORE Spartanburg
MOUNT CARMEL McCormick
MOUNT CROGHAN Chesterfield
MOUNT PLEASANT Charleston
MOUNTAIN REST Oconee
MOUNTVILLE Laurens
MULLINS Marion
MURRELLS INLET (29576) Horry(56), Georgetown(43)
MYRTLE BEACH Horry
NEESES Orangeburg
NESMITH Williamsburg
NEW ELLENTON Aiken
NEW ZION (29111) Clarendon(92), Williamsburg(7)
NEWBERRY Newberry
NEWRY Oconee
NICHOLS (29581) Horry(81), Marion(10), Dillon(8)
NINETY SIX (29666) Greenwood(95), Saluda(4)
NORRIS Pickens
NORTH (29112) Orangeburg(91), Calhoun(6), Lexington(2)
NORTH AUGUSTA (29841) Aiken(98), Edgefield(1)
NORTH AUGUSTA (29860) Edgefield(65), Aiken(34)
NORTH AUGUSTA Aiken
NORTH CHARLESTON Berkeley
NORTH CHARLESTON Charleston
NORTH MYRTLE BEACH Horry

NORWAY Orangeburg
OKATIE Beaufort
OLANTA (29114) Florence(59), Sumter(39)
OLAR (29843) Bamberg(90), Barnwell(9)
ORANGEBURG (29118) Orangeburg(94), Calhoun(5)
ORANGEBURG Orangeburg
PACOLET (29372) Spartanburg(69), Union(15), Cherokee(14)
PACOLET MILLS Spartanburg
PAGELAND Chesterfield
PAMPLICO Florence
PARKSVILLE McCormick
PATRICK Chesterfield
PAULINE (29374) Spartanburg(94), Union(6)
PAWLEYS ISLAND Georgetown
PEAK Newberry
PELION Lexington
PELZER (29669) Anderson(65), Greenville(34)
PENDLETON (29670) Anderson(98), Pickens(1)
PERRY Aiken
PICKENS Pickens
PIEDMONT (29673) Anderson(50), Greenville(49)
PINELAND (29934) Jasper(83), Hampton(16)
PINEVILLE Berkeley
PINEWOOD (29125) Clarendon(54), Sumter(45)
PINOPOLIS Berkeley
PLUM BRANCH (29845) McCormick(94), Edgefield(5)
POMARIA Newberry
PORT ROYAL Beaufort
POSTON Horry
PROSPERITY (29127) Newberry(95), Saluda(4)
RAINS Marion
RAVENEL (29470) Charleston(87), Dorchester(12)
REEVESVILLE (29471) Dorchester(96), Orangeburg(3)
REIDVILLE Spartanburg
REMBERT (29128) Sumter(77), Lee(15), Kershaw(7)
RICHBURG Chester
RICHLAND Oconee
RIDGE SPRING (29129) Aiken(47), Saluda(44), Edgefield(8)
RIDGELAND (29936) Jasper(97), Beaufort(2)
RIDGEVILLE (29472) Dorchester(62), Colleton(20), Berkeley(16)
RIDGEWAY (29130) Fairfield(86), Kershaw(11), Richland(1)

RIMINI (29131) Sumter(65), Clarendon(34)
RION Fairfield
ROCK HILL York
ROEBUCK Spartanburg
ROUND O Colleton
ROWESVILLE Orangeburg
RUBY Chesterfield
RUFFIN Colleton
RUSSELLVILLE Berkeley
SAINT GEORGE Dorchester
SAINT HELENA ISLAND Beaufort
SAINT MATTHEWS (29135) Calhoun(97), Orangeburg(2)
SAINT STEPHEN Berkeley
SALEM Oconee
SALLEY (29137) Aiken(85), Orangeburg(14)
SALTERS Williamsburg
SALUDA (29138) Saluda(97), Greenwood(2)
SANDY SPRINGS Anderson
SANTEE Orangeburg
SARDINIA Clarendon
SCOTIA Hampton
SCRANTON Florence
SEABROOK Beaufort
SELLERS (29592) Dillon(70), Marion(29)
SENECA Oconee
SHARON York
SHAW A F B Sumter
SHELDON Beaufort
SILVERSTREET Newberry
SIMPSONVILLE Greenville
SIX MILE Pickens
SLATER Greenville
SMOAKS (29481) Colleton(85), Bamberg(14)
SMYRNA York
SOCIETY HILL (29593) Darlington(53), Chesterfield(46)
SPARTANBURG (29307) Spartanburg(97), Cherokee(2)
SPARTANBURG Spartanburg
SPRINGFIELD (29146) Orangeburg(73), Aiken(26)
STARR Anderson
STARTEX Spartanburg
STATE PARK Richland
SULLIVANS ISLAND Charleston
SUMMERTON Clarendon
SUMMERVILLE (29483) Dorchester(70), Berkeley(29)
SUMMERVILLE (29485) Dorchester(89), Charleston(10)
SUMMERVILLE Dorchester
SUMTER Sumter
SUNSET Pickens
SWANSEA (29160) Lexi'n(52),Calhoun(47)

SYCAMORE Allendale
TAMASSEE Oconee
TATUM Marlboro
TAYLORS Greenville
TIGERVILLE Greenville
TILLMAN Jasper
TIMMONSVILLE (29161) Florence(80), Darlington(19)
TOWNVILLE (29689) Anderson(89), Oconee(10)
TRAVELERS REST Greenville
TRENTON (29847) Edgefield(65), Aiken(34)
TRIO Williamsburg
TROY (29848) Greenwood(85), McCormick(10), Saluda(2), Edgefield(1)
TURBEVILLE (29162) Clarendon(97), Sumter(2)
ULMER Allendale
UNA Spartanburg
VAN WYCK Lancaster
VANCE Orangeburg
VARNVILLE (29944) Hampton(89), Jasper(10)
VAUCLUSE Aiken
WADMALAW ISLAND Charleston
WAGENER Aiken
WALHALLA Oconee
WALLACE Marlboro
WALTERBORO Colleton
WARD Saluda
WARE SHOALS (29692) Laurens(66), Greenwood(24), Abbeville(9)
WARRENVILLE Aiken
WATERLOO Laurens
WEDGEFIELD Sumter
WELLFORD Spartanburg
WEST COLUMBIA Lexington
WEST UNION Oconee
WESTMINSTER Oconee
WESTVILLE Kershaw
WHITE OAK Fairfield
WHITE ROCK Richland
WHITE STONE Spartanburg
WHITMIRE (29178) Newberry(78), Union(16), Laurens(5)
WILLIAMS Colleton
WILLIAMSTON Anderson
WILLISTON (29853) Barnwell(65), Aiken(34)
WINDSOR Aiken
WINNSBORO (29180) Fairfield(97), Richland(2)
WISACKY Lee
WOODRUFF (29388) Spartanburg(93), Laurens(6)
YEMASSEE (29945) Colleton(30), Hampton(29), Jasper(28), Beaufort(11)

South Carolina ZIP/City Cross Reference

29153-29154	SUMTER
29160-29160	SWANSEA
29161-29161	TIMMONSVILLE
29162-29162	TURBEVILLE
29163-29163	VANCE
29164-29164	WAGENER
29166-29166	WARD
29168-29168	WEDGEFIELD
29169-29172	WEST COLUMBIA
29175-29175	WESTVILLE
29176-29176	WHITE OAK
29177-29177	WHITE ROCK
29178-29178	WHITMIRE
29180-29180	WINNSBORO
29183-29183	WISACKY
29200-29292	COLUMBIA
29301-29319	SPARTANBURG
29320-29320	ARCADIA
29321-29321	BUFFALO
29322-29322	CAMPOBELLO
29323-29323	CHESNEE
29324-29324	CLIFTON
29325-29325	CLINTON
29329-29329	CONVERSE
29330-29330	COWPENS
29331-29331	CROSS ANCHOR
29332-29332	CROSS HILL
29333-29333	DRAYTON
29334-29334	DUNCAN
29335-29335	ENOREE
29336-29336	FAIRFOREST
29338-29338	FINGERVILLE
29340-29342	GAFFNEY
29346-29346	GLENDALE
29348-29348	GRAMLING
29349-29349	INMAN
29351-29351	JOANNA
29353-29353	JONESVILLE
29355-29355	KINARDS
29356-29356	LANDRUM
29360-29360	LAURENS
29364-29364	LOCKHART
29365-29365	LYMAN
29368-29368	MAYO
29369-29369	MOORE
29370-29370	MOUNTVILLE
29372-29372	PACOLET
29373-29373	PACOLET MILLS
29374-29374	PAULINE
29375-29375	REIDVILLE
29376-29376	ROEBUCK
29377-29377	STARTEX
29378-29378	UNA
29379-29379	UNION
29384-29384	WATERLOO
29385-29385	WELLFORD
29386-29386	WHITE STONE
29388-29388	WOODRUFF
29390-29391	DUNCAN
29395-29395	JONESVILLE
29401-29403	CHARLESTON
29404-29404	CHARLESTON AFB
29405-29410	CHARLESTON
29410-29410	NORTH CHARLESTON
29411-29415	CHARLESTON
29415-29415	NORTH CHARLESTON
29416-29425	CHARLESTON
29426-29426	ADAMS RUN
29429-29429	AWENDAW
29430-29430	BETHERA
29431-29431	BONNEAU
29432-29432	BRANCHVILLE
29433-29433	CANADYS
29434-29434	CORDESVILLE
29435-29435	COTTAGEVILLE
29436-29436	CROSS
29437-29437	DORCHESTER
29438-29438	EDISTO ISLAND
29439-29439	FOLLY BEACH
29440-29442	GEORGETOWN
29445-29445	GOOSE CREEK
29446-29446	GREEN POND
29447-29447	GROVER
29448-29448	HARLEYVILLE
29449-29449	HOLLYWOOD
29450-29450	HUGER
29451-29451	ISLE OF PALMS
29452-29452	JACKSONBORO
29453-29453	JAMESTOWN
29455-29455	JOHNS ISLAND
29456-29456	LADSON
29457-29457	JOHNS ISLAND
29458-29458	MC CLELLANVILLE
29461-29461	MONCKS CORNER
29464-29466	MOUNT PLEASANT
29468-29468	PINEVILLE
29469-29469	PINOPOLIS
29470-29470	RAVENEL
29471-29471	REEVESVILLE
29472-29472	RIDGEVILLE
29474-29474	ROUND O
29475-29475	RUFFIN
29476-29476	RUSSELLVILLE
29477-29477	SAINT GEORGE
29479-29479	SAINT STEPHEN
29481-29481	SMOAKS
29482-29482	SULLIVANS ISLAND
29483-29485	SUMMERVILLE
29487-29487	WADMALAW ISLAND
29488-29488	WALTERBORO
29492-29492	CHARLESTON
29493-29493	WILLIAMS
29501-29506	FLORENCE
29510-29510	ANDREWS
29511-29511	AYNOR
29512-29512	BENNETTSVILLE
29516-29516	BLENHEIM
29518-29518	CADES
29519-29519	CENTENARY
29520-29520	CHERAW
29525-29525	CLIO
29526-29528	CONWAY
29530-29530	COWARD
29532-29532	DARLINGTON
29536-29536	DILLON
29540-29540	DARLINGTON
29541-29541	EFFINGHAM
29542-29542	FLOYD DALE
29543-29543	FORK
29544-29544	GALIVANTS FERRY
29545-29545	GREEN SEA
29546-29546	GRESHAM
29547-29547	HAMER
29550-29551	HARTSVILLE
29554-29554	HEMINGWAY
29555-29555	JOHNSONVILLE
29556-29556	KINGSTREE
29560-29560	LAKE CITY
29563-29563	LAKE VIEW
29564-29564	LANE
29565-29565	LATTA
29566-29566	LITTLE RIVER
29567-29567	LITTLE ROCK
29568-29568	LONGS
29569-29569	LORIS
29570-29570	MC COLL
29571-29571	MARION
29572-29572	MYRTLE BEACH
29573-29573	MINTURN
29574-29574	MULLINS
29575-29575	MYRTLE BEACH
29576-29576	MURRELLS INLET
29577-29579	MYRTLE BEACH
29580-29580	NESMITH
29581-29581	NICHOLS
29582-29582	NORTH MYRTLE BEACH
29583-29583	PAMPLICO
29584-29584	PATRICK
29585-29585	PAWLEYS ISLAND
29587-29587	MYRTLE BEACH
29588-29588	POSTON
29588-29588	MYRTLE BEACH
29589-29589	RAINS
29590-29590	SALTERS
29591-29591	SCRANTON
29592-29592	SELLERS
29593-29593	SOCIETY HILL
29594-29594	TATUM
29595-29595	TRIO
29596-29596	WALLACE
29597-29598	NORTH MYRTLE BEACH
29601-29617	GREENVILLE
29620-29620	ABBEVILLE
29621-29626	ANDERSON
29627-29627	BELTON
29628-29628	CALHOUN FALLS
29630-29630	CENTRAL
29631-29634	CLEMSON
29635-29635	CLEVELAND
29636-29636	CONESTEE
29638-29638	DONALDS
29639-29639	DUE WEST
29640-29642	EASLEY
29643-29643	FAIR PLAY
29644-29644	FOUNTAIN INN
29645-29645	GRAY COURT
29646-29649	GREENWOOD
29650-29652	GREER
29653-29653	HODGES
29654-29654	HONEA PATH
29655-29655	IVA
29656-29656	LA FRANCE
29657-29657	LIBERTY
29658-29658	LONG CREEK
29659-29659	LOWNDESVILLE
29661-29661	MARIETTA
29662-29662	MAULDIN
29664-29664	MOUNTAIN REST
29665-29665	NEWRY
29666-29666	NINETY SIX
29667-29667	NORRIS
29669-29669	PELZER
29670-29670	PENDLETON
29671-29671	PICKENS
29672-29672	SENECA
29673-29673	PIEDMONT
29675-29675	RICHLAND
29676-29676	SALEM
29677-29677	SANDY SPRINGS
29678-29679	SENECA
29680-29681	SIMPSONVILLE
29682-29682	SIX MILE
29683-29683	SLATER
29684-29684	STARR
29685-29685	SUNSET
29686-29686	TAMASSEE
29687-29687	TAYLORS
29688-29688	TIGERVILLE
29689-29689	TOWNVILLE
29690-29690	TRAVELERS REST
29691-29691	WALHALLA
29692-29692	WARE SHOALS
29693-29693	WESTMINSTER
29695-29695	HODGES
29696-29696	WEST UNION
29697-29697	WILLIAMSTON
29698-29698	GREENVILLE
29702-29702	BLACKSBURG
29703-29703	BOWLING GREEN
29704-29704	CATAWBA
29705-29705	CHEROKEE FALLS
29706-29706	CHESTER
29708-29708	FORT MILL
29709-29709	CHESTERFIELD
29710-29710	CLOVER
29712-29712	EDGEMOOR
29714-29714	FORT LAWN
29715-29716	FORT MILL
29717-29717	HICKORY GROVE
29718-29718	JEFFERSON
29719-29719	KINGS CREEK
29720-29722	LANCASTER
29724-29724	LANDO
29726-29726	MC CONNELLS
29727-29727	MOUNT CROGHAN
29728-29728	PAGELAND
29729-29729	RICHBURG
29730-29734	ROCK HILL
29741-29741	RUBY
29742-29742	SHARON
29743-29743	SMYRNA
29744-29744	VAN WYCK
29745-29745	YORK
29801-29808	AIKEN
29809-29809	NEW ELLENTON
29810-29810	ALLENDALE
29812-29812	BARNWELL
29813-29813	HILDA
29814-29814	KLINE
29816-29816	BATH
29817-29817	BLACKVILLE
29819-29819	BRADLEY
29821-29821	CLARKS HILL
29822-29822	CLEARWATER
29824-29824	EDGEFIELD
29826-29826	ELKO
29827-29827	FAIRFAX
29828-29828	GLOVERVILLE
29829-29829	GRANITEVILLE
29831-29831	JACKSON
29832-29832	JOHNSTON
29834-29834	LANGLEY
29835-29835	MC CORMICK
29836-29836	MARTIN
29838-29838	MODOC
29839-29839	MONTMORENCI
29840-29840	MOUNT CARMEL
29841-29841	NORTH AUGUSTA
29842-29842	BEECH ISLAND
29843-29843	OLAR
29844-29844	PARKSVILLE
29845-29845	PLUM BRANCH
29846-29846	SYCAMORE
29847-29847	TRENTON
29848-29848	TROY
29849-29849	ULMER
29850-29850	VAUCLUSE
29851-29851	WARRENVILLE
29853-29853	WILLISTON
29856-29856	WINDSOR
29860-29861	NORTH AUGUSTA
29899-29899	MC CORMICK
29901-29906	BEAUFORT
29907-29907	LADYS ISLAND
29909-29909	OKATIE
29910-29910	BLUFFTON
29911-29911	BRUNSON
29912-29912	COOSAWATCHIE
29913-29913	CROCKETVILLE
29914-29914	DALE
29915-29915	DAUFUSKIE ISLAND
29916-29916	EARLY BRANCH
29918-29918	ESTILL
29920-29920	SAINT HELENA ISLAND
29921-29921	FURMAN
29922-29922	GARNETT
29923-29923	GIFFORD
29924-29924	HAMPTON
29925-29926	HILTON HEAD ISLAND
29927-29927	HARDEEVILLE
29928-29928	HILTON HEAD ISLAND
29929-29929	ISLANDTON
29931-29931	LOBECO
29932-29932	LURAY
29933-29933	MILEY
29934-29934	PINELAND
29935-29935	PORT ROYAL
29936-29936	RIDGELAND
29938-29938	HILTON HEAD ISLAND
29939-29939	SCOTIA
29940-29940	SEABROOK
29941-29941	SHELDON
29943-29943	TILLMAN
29944-29944	VARNVILLE
29945-29945	YEMASSEE
29948-29948	HILTON HEAD ISLAND

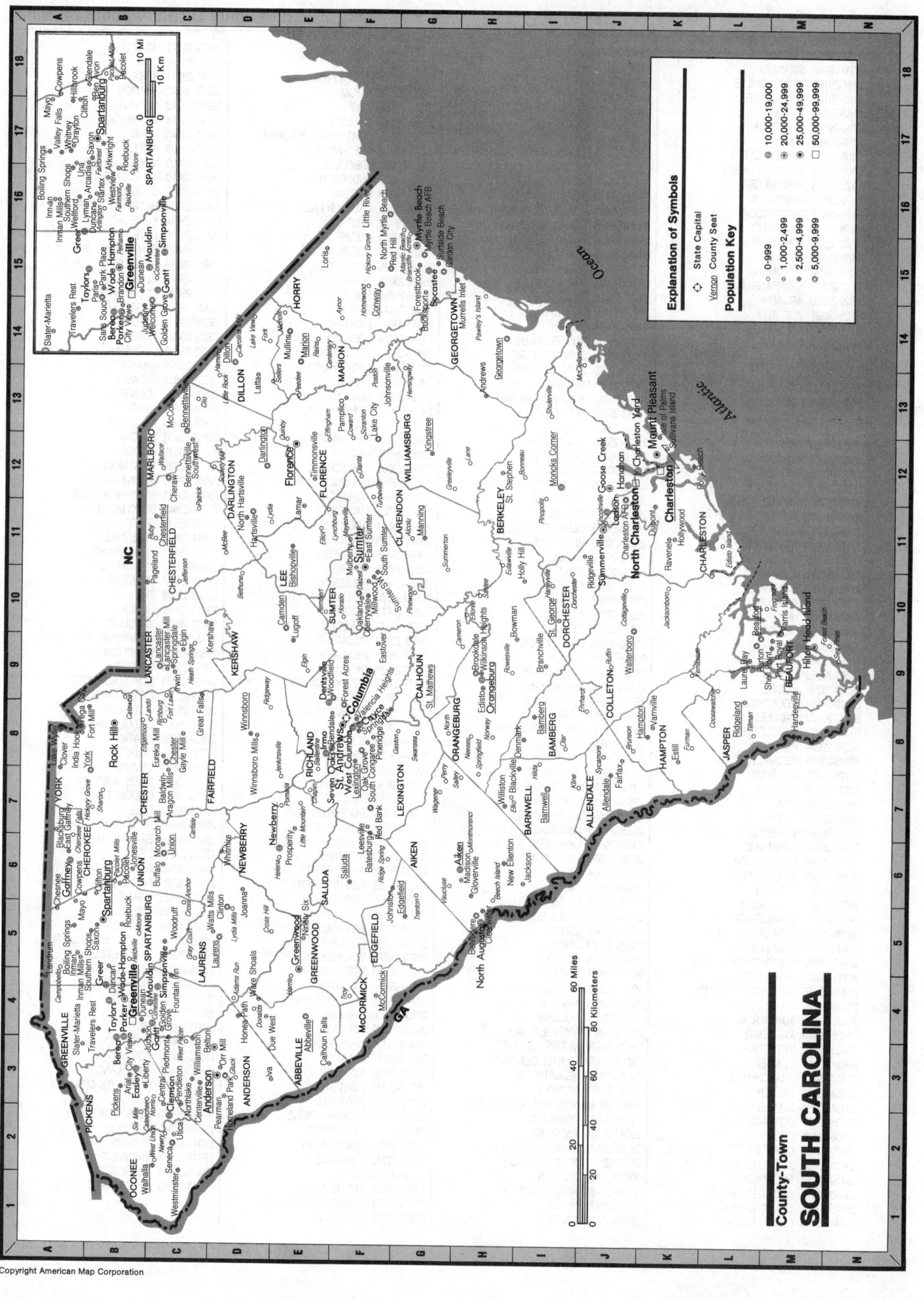

Copyright American Map Corporation

Explanation of Symbols

⊕ State Capital
<u>Vernon</u> County Seat

Population Key
○ 0-999
⊙ 1,000-2,499
◉ 2,500-4,999
● 5,000-9,999
◉ 10,000-19,000
◎ 20,000-24,999
◉ 25,000-49,999
□ 50,000-99,999

County-Town
SOUTH CAROLINA

COUNTIES

(46 Counties)

Name of County	Population	Location on Map
ABBEVILLE	23,862	E-3
AIKEN	120,940	G-6
ALLENDALE	11,722	J-7
ANDERSON	145,196	C-2
BAMBERG	16,902	I-8
BARNWELL	20,293	I-7
BEAUFORT	86,425	L-9
BERKELEY	128,776	I-11
CALHOUN	12,753	G-9
CHARLESTON	295,039	K-11
CHEROKEE	44,506	A-6
CHESTER	32,170	C-8
CHESTERFIELD	38,577	C-11
CLARENDON	28,450	G-11
COLLETON	34,377	J-10
DARLINGTON	61,851	D-12
DILLON	29,114	D-13
DORCHESTER	83,060	I-10
EDGEFIELD	18,375	G-5
FAIRFIELD	22,295	E-8
FLORENCE	114,344	E-12
GEORGETOWN	46,302	H-14
GREENVILLE	320,167	B-4
GREENWOOD	59,567	E-5
HAMPTON	18,191	K-8
HORRY	144,053	F-15
JASPER	15,487	L-8
KERSHAW	43,599	E-10
LANCASTER	54,516	C-9
LAURENS	58,092	D-5
LEE	18,437	E-11
LEXINGTON	167,611	F-8
MARION	33,899	E-14
MARLBORO	29,361	C-12
MCCORMICK	8,868	F-4
NEWBERRY	33,172	E-6
OCONEE	57,494	C-1
ORANGEBURG	84,803	H-9
PICKENS	93,894	B-2
RICHLAND	285,720	F-9
SALUDA	16,357	F-6
SPARTANBURG	226,800	B-5
SUMTER	102,637	F-10
UNION	30,337	C-6
WILLIAMSBURG	36,815	G-12
YORK	131,497	B-7
TOTAL	3,486,703	

CITIES AND TOWNS

Note: The first name is that of the city or town, second, that of the county in which it is located, then the population and location on the map.

Abbeville, Abbeville, 5,778 ... E-4
Aiken, Aiken, 19,872 ... H-6
Allendale, Allendale, 4,410 ... J-7
Anderson, Anderson, 26,184 ... D-3
Andrews, Georgetown/Williamsburg, 3,050 ... H-13
•Arial, Pickens, 2,604 ... B-3
Baldwin-Aragon Mills, Chester ... C-7
Bamberg, Bamberg, 3,843 ... I-8
Barnwell, Barnwell, 5,255 ... I-7
Batesburg, Lexington/Saluda, 4,082 ... F-7
Beaufort, Beaufort, 9,576 ... L-10
Belton, Anderson, 4,646 ... D-3
Belvedere, Aiken, 6,133 ... H-5
Bendale, Richland ... E-8
Bennettsville, Marlboro, 9,345 ... C-13
Bennettsville Southwest, Marlboro ... C-12
•Berea, Greenville, 13,535 ... B-3
Bishopville, Lee, 3,560 ... E-11
Blacksburg, Cherokee, 1,907 ... A-7
Blackville, Barnwell, 2,688 ... I-8
•Boiling Springs, Spartanburg, 3,522 ... A-5
Bowman, Orangeburg, 1,063 ... H-9
Branchville, Orangeburg, 1,107 ... I-9
Brandon, Greenville ... B-15
•Brookdale, Orangeburg, 5,339 ... H-9
Bucksport, Horry, 1,022 ... G-15
Buffalo, Union, 1,569 ... C-6
•Burton, Beaufort, 6,917 ... L-9
Calhoun Falls, Abbeville, 2,328 ... E-3
Camden, Kershaw, 6,696 ... E-10
Cayce, Lexington, 11,163 ... F-8
•Centerville, Anderson, 4,866 ... C-3
Central, Pickens, 2,438 ... C-2
Charleston, Charleston, 80,414 ... K-12
Charleston Base, Charleston ... J-12
Charleston Yard, Charleston ... J-12
Cherryvale, Sumter, 5,505 ... F-10
Chesnee, Cherokee/Spartanburg, 1,280 ... A-5
Chester, Chester, 7,158 ... C-8
Chesterfield, Chesterfield, 1,373 ... C-11
City View, Greenville, 1,490 ... B-3
Clearwater, Aiken, 4,731 ... H-5
Clemson, Anderson/Pickens, 11,096 ... C-2
Clifton, Spartanburg ... A-17
Clinton, Laurens, 7,987 ... D-5
Clover, York, 3,422 ... B-8
Columbia, Richland, 98,052 ... F-8
Conway, Horry, 9,819 ... F-15
Cowpens, Spartanburg, 2,176 ... A-6
Darlington, Darlington, 7,311 ... D-12
Denmark, Bamberg, 3,762 ... I-8
Dentsville, Richland, 11,839 ... E-9
Dillon, Dillon, 6,829 ... D-14
Due West, Abbeville, 1,220 ... D-4
Duncan, Spartanburg, 2,152 ... B-5
Dunean, Greenville, 4,637 ... B-4
Dupont, Charleston ... K-11
Easley, Pickens, 15,195 ... B-3
•East Gaffney, Cherokee, 3,278 ... A-6
•East Sumter, Sumter, 1,590 ... F-11
Eastover, Richland, 1,044 ... F-9
Edgefield, Edgefield, 2,563 ... G-5
•Edisto, Orangeburg, 2,815 ... H-9
•Elgin, Lancaster, 2,196 ... C-9
Estill, Hampton, 2,387 ... K-8
•Eureka Mill, Chester, 1,738 ... C-8
Fairfax, Allendale/Hampton, 2,317 ... J-8
Florence, Florence, 29,813 ... E-12
Folly Beach, Charleston, 1,398 ... K-12
Forest Acres, Richland, 7,197 ... F-8
•Forestbrook, Horry, 2,502 ... G-15
Fort Mill, York, 4,930 ... B-8
Fountain Inn, Greenville/Laurens, 4,388 ... C-4
Gaffney, Cherokee, 13,145 ... A-6
•Gantt, Greenville, 13,891 ... C-4
Garden City, Horry, 6,305 ... G-15
Gayle Mill, Chester, 1,037 ... C-8
Georgetown, Georgetown, 9,517 ... H-14
Glendale, Spartanburg ... A-18
•Gloverville, Aiken, 2,753 ... H-6
•Golden Grove, Greenville, 2,055 ... C-4
Goose Creek, Berkeley/Charleston, 24,692 ... J-12
Great Falls, Chester, 2,307 ... C-9
Greenville, Greenville, 58,282 ... B-4
Greenwood, Greenwood, 20,807 ... E-5
Greer, Greenville/Spartanburg, 10,322 ... B-4
Hampton, Hampton, 2,997 ... K-8
Hanahan, Berkeley, 13,176 ... J-12
Hardeeville, Jasper, 1,583 ... M-8
Hartsville, Darlington, 8,372 ... D-11
Hillbrook, Spartanburg ... A-17
Hilton Head Island, Beaufort, 23,694 ... M-9
Holly Hill, Orangeburg, 1,478 ... I-10
Hollywood, Charleston, 2,094 ... K-11
•Homeland Park, Anderson, 6,569 ... D-3
Honea Path, Abbeville/Anderson, 3,841 ... D-4
•India Hook, York, 1,506 ... A-8
Inman, Spartanburg, 1,742 ... A-5
Inman Mills, Spartanburg, 1,571 ... A-5
Irmo, Lexington/Richland, 11,280 ... E-8
•Irwin, Lancaster, 1,296 ... C-9
Isle of Palms, Charleston, 3,680 ... K-13
Iva, Anderson, 1,174 ... D-3
Jackson, Aiken, 1,681 ... I-6
•Joanna, Laurens, 1,735 ... D-6
Johnsonville, Florence, 1,415 ... F-13
Johnston, Edgefield, 2,688 ... G-6
Jonesville, Union, 1,205 ... B-6
•Judson, Greenville, 2,859 ... B-4
Kershaw, Lancaster, 1,814 ... D-10
Kingstree, Williamsburg, 3,858 ... G-12
•Ladson, Berkeley/Charleston, 13,540 ... J-11
Lake City, Florence, 7,153 ... F-12
Lake Wylie, York, 2,599 ... A-8
Lamar, Darlington, 1,125 ... E-11
Lancaster, Lancaster, 8,914 ... C-9
•Lancaster Mill, Lancaster, 2,373 ... C-9
Landrum, Spartanburg, 2,347 ... A-4
Latta, Dillon, 1,565 ... D-13
Laurel Bay, Beaufort, 4,972 ... L-9
Laurens, Laurens, 9,694 ... D-5
Leesville, Lexington, 2,025 ... F-7
Lexington, Lexington, 3,289 ... F-8
•Little River, Horry, 3,470 ... F-16
Loris, Horry, 2,067 ... E-15
Lugoff, Kershaw, 3,211 ... E-10
Lyman, Spartanburg, 2,271 ... A-16
Manning, Clarendon, 4,428 ... G-11
Marion, Marion, 7,658 ... E-14
Mauldin, Greenville, 11,587 ... C-4
•Mayo, Spartanburg, 1,569 ... B-5
McColl, Marlboro, 2,685 ... C-13
McCormick, McCormick, 1,659 ... F-4
Millwood, Sumter, 1,070 ... F-10
•Monarch Mill, Union, 1,214 ... C-6
Moncks Corner, Berkeley, 5,607 ... I-12
Mount Pleasant, Charleston, 30,108 ... K-12
•Mulberry, Sumter, 1,097 ... F-11
Mullins, Marion, 5,910 ... E-14
•Murrells Inlet, Georgetown, 3,334 ... G-15
Myrtle Beach, Horry, 24,848 ... G-15
Myrtle Beach Base, Horry ... G-15
New Ellenton, Aiken, 2,515 ... H-6
Newberry, Newberry, 10,542 ... E-6
Ninety Six, Greenwood, 2,099 ... E-5
North Augusta, Aiken/Edgefield, 15,351 ... H-5
North Charleston, Berkeley/Charleston/Dorchester, 70,218 ... J-12
•North Hartsville, Darlington, 2,906 ... D-11
North Myrtle Beach, Horry, 8,636 ... F-16
•Northlake, Anderson, 3,162 ... C-3
•Oak Grove, Lexington, 7,173 ... F-8
Oakland, Sumter, 1,298 ... F-10
Orangeburg, Orangeburg, 13,739 ... H-9
Pacolet, Spartanburg, 1,736 ... B-6
Pageland, Chesterfield, 2,666 ... B-10
Pamplico, Florence, 1,314 ... F-13
Paris, Greenville ... B-15
Park Place, Greenville ... B-15
•Parker, Greenville, 11,072 ... B-3
Parris Island, Beaufort, 7,172 ... M-10
Pendleton, Anderson, 3,314 ... C-3
•Piedmont, Anderson/Greenville, 4,143 ... C-3
Pineridge, Lexington, 1,731 ... F-8
Port Royal, Beaufort, 2,985 ... M-9
Prosperity, Newberry, 1,116 ... E-7
Ravenel, Charleston, 2,165 ... K-11
•Red Bank, Lexington, 5,950 ... F-7
Red Hill, Horry, 6,112 ... F-15
Ridgeland, Jasper, 1,071 ... L-8
Ridgeville, Dorchester, 1,625 ... I-11
Rock Hill, York, 41,643 ... B-8
•Roebuck, Spartanburg, 1,966 ... B-5
Saint Andrews, Richland, 25,692 ... F-8
Saint George, Dorchester, 2,077 ... I-10
Saint Matthews, Calhoun, 2,345 ... G-9
Saint Stephen, Berkeley, 1,697 ... H-12
Saluda, Saluda, 2,798 ... F-6
Sans Souci, Greenville, 7,612 ... B-14
•Saxon, Spartanburg, 4,002 ... B-5
Seneca, Oconee, 7,726 ... C-2
Seven Oaks, Lexington, 15,722 ... E-8
Shannontown, Sumter ... F-11
Shell Point, Beaufort, 2,885 ... M-9
Simpsonville, Greenville, 11,708 ... C-4
•Slater-Marietta, Greenville, 2,245 ... A-3
•Socastee, Horry, 10,426 ... G-15
South Congaree, Lexington, 2,406 ... F-8
South Sumter, Sumter, 4,371 ... F-10
•Southern Shops, Spartanburg, 3,378 ... B-5
•Springdale, Lancaster, 2,643 ... C-9
Springdale, Lexington, 3,226 ... F-8
•Startex, Spartanburg, 1,162 ... B-16
•Taylors, Greenville, 19,619 ... B-4
•Tega Cay, York, 3,016 ... A-8
Timmonsville, Florence, 2,182 ... E-12
Travelers Rest, Greenville, 3,069 ... B-4
Union, Union, 9,836 ... C-6
•Utica, Oconee, 1,478 ... C-2
•Valencia Heights, Richland, 4,122 ... F-8
Valley Falls, Spartanburg, 3,504 ... A-17
Varnville, Hampton, 1,970 ... K-8
•Wade Hampton, Greenville, 20,014 ... B-4
Walhalla, Oconee, 3,755 ... C-2
Walterboro, Colleton, 5,492 ... J-10
Ware Shoals, Abbeville/Greenwood/Laurens, 2,497 ... D-4
•Watts Mills, Laurens, 1,535 ... D-5
•Welcome, Greenville, 6,560 ... B-14
Wellford, Spartanburg, 2,511 ... A-16
West Columbia, Lexington, 10,588 ... F-8
Westminster, Oconee, 3,120 ... C-1
Whitmire, Newberry, 1,702 ... D-6
•Wilkinson Heights, Orangeburg, 3,394 ... H-9
Williamston, Anderson, 3,876 ... C-3
Williston, Barnwell, 3,099 ... H-7
Winnsboro, Fairfield, 3,475 ... D-8
•Winnsboro Mills, Fairfield, 2,275 ... D-8
Woodfield, Richland, 8,862 ... F-9
Woodruff, Spartanburg, 4,365 ... C-5
York, York, 6,709 ... B-7

Explanation of symbols: • – Census Designated Place (CDP)

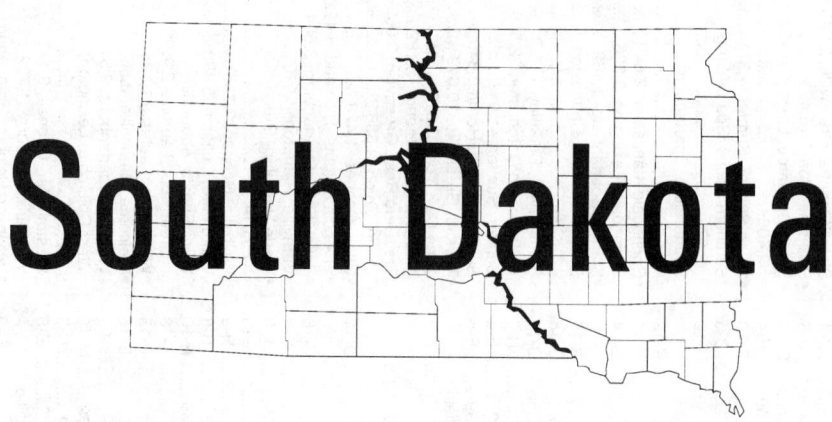

General Help Numbers:

Governor's Office

State Capitol, 500 E Capitol Ave   605-773-3212
Pierre, SD 57501-5070   Fax 605-773-4711
www.state.sd.us/governor/   8AM-5PM

Attorney General's Office

State Capitol, 500 E Capitol Ave   605-773-3215
Pierre, SD 57501-5070   Fax 605-773-4106
www.state.sd.us/attorney/index.htm   8AM-5PM

Legislative Records

South Dakota Legislature, Capitol Bldg
Legislative Research Council   605-773-3251
500 E Capitol Ave   Fax 605-773-4576
Pierre, SD 57501   8AM-5PM
http://legis.state.sd.us

State Archives

Cultural Heritage Center/State Archives   605-773-3804
900 Governors Dr   Fax 605-773-6041
Pierre, SD 57501-2217   9AM-4:30PM
http://www.sdhistory.org/

State Specifics:

Capital:

Pierre
Hughes County

Time Zone:

CST*

* South Dakota's eighteen western-most counties are MST: They are: Bennett, Butte, Corson, Custer, Dewey, Fall River, Haakon, Harding, Jackson, Lawrence, Meade, Mellette, Pennington, Perkins, Shannon, Stanley, Todd, Ziebach,

Number of Counties:

66

Population:

770,883

Web Site:

www.state.sd.us

State Agencies

Criminal Records

Division of Criminal Investigation, Identification Section, 500 E Capitol, Pierre, SD 57501-5070; 605-773-3331, 605-773-4629-Fax; 8AM-5PM.

http://dci.sd.gov

Records are available for 10 years for misdemeanors and lifetime for felonies. It takes 1 day before new records are available for inquiry. Records are indexed on inhouse computer (90+%); only older records not computerized. 100% of arrest records are fingerprint supported. Records are normally destroyed after 10 years if a misdemeanor, generally. 98% of all arrests in database have final dispositions recorded.

Searching: Include the following in your request-date of birth, full name, set of fingerprints, signed release form. The form requires identifying information: color of hair and eyes, height, weight, date of birth, SSN. The following data is not released: juvenile records, minor traffic violations or out-of-state or federal charges. All open records without dispositions are released.

Access by: mail.

Fee & Payment: The fee is $15.00 per name. Statutorily-required fingerprint checks will include an FBI fingerprint check for an additional $24.00. Fee payee: Division of Criminal Investigation. Prepayment required. Personal checks accepted. No credit cards accepted.

Mail search: Turnaround time: 5 to 10 working days. Upon receipt of those requirements, they will conduct a search of their files and supply a copy of any criminal history that is found or a statement that there is no criminal history. A SASE is helpful.

Other access: The State Court Administrator's Office has a statewide database of criminal record information from the state's circuit courts. For more information about setting up a commercial account, contact Jill Gusso at 605-773-3474.

Statewide Court Records

State Court Administrator, State Capitol Bldg, 500 E Capitol Ave, Pierre, SD 57501-5059; 605-773-3474, 605-773-5627-Fax; 8AM-5PM.

www.sdjudicial.com

The Supreme Court calendar, opinions, live and archived oral arguments may be searched from the website, along with many other court-related service information.

Records are available for criminal records from July 1, 1989 forward. This agency is in the process of developing a statewide civil database also.

Searching: South Dakota has a statewide criminal record search database administrated by this office. Requesters then may mail requests to one of the addresses listed below for statewide searching. Requesters may to set up a commercial account by faxing a written requests to Jill Gusso, Unified Court System at 605-773-4874 or email jill.gusso@ujs.state.sd.us. Accounts are billed monthly.

Access by: mail, fax.

Fee & Payment: The search fee is $15.00 per record. State authorized commercial accounts may order and receive records by fax, there is an additional $5.00 fee unless a non-toll free line is used.

Mail search: Turnaround time: is usually 1-3 days. Mail requests should be addressed to the Minor County Clerk of Court, PO Box 265, Howard SD 57349 or to Aurora County Clerk of Court, PO Box 366, Plankton, SD 57368-0366. Providing an SASE is suggested.

Fax search: If authorized.

Sexual Offender Registry

Division of Criminal Investigation, Identification Section - SOR Unit, 500 E Capitol, Pierre, SD 57501-5070 (Courier address: 3444 East Highway 34, Pierre, SD 57501); 605-773-3331, 605-773-4614, 605-773-2596-Fax; 8AM-5PM.

http://dci.sd.gov/administration/id/sexoffender/index.asp

State law prohibits this agency from releasing data to the public from a statewide repository. However, online access (see below) is available by county. This agency urges the public to visit local law enforcement offices for access to lists.

Records are available from at least 1994. 1994 was the star-up date, but records are retroactive. It takes 7 days before new records are available for inquiry. Records are normally destroyed after court order, moved, or deceased.

Access by: online.

Online search: Searching is available from the website. Note that there is no statewide search, all searches are done on a county basis.

Incarceration Records

SD Department of Corrections, Central Records Office, PO Box 5911, Pierre, SD 57117; 605-367-5140, 605-367-5584-Fax; 8AM-4PM.

www.state.sd.us/corrections/corrections.html

Records are available on current and former inmates. It takes up to 3 days before new records are available for inquiry. Records are normally destroyed after five years from final discharge.

Searching: The computerized records system does not track records back further than those inmates who were discharged in 1985. Include the following in your request-name and DOB or SSN. Location, conviction and sentencing information are available. The following data is not released: medical, treatment, and disciplinary records.

Access by: phone.

Phone search: For phone search, call the number above or the Department's Office of Community Relations at 302-739-5601 x246.

Other access: View the Most Wanted List at www.state.sd.us/corrections/most_wanted.htm.

Corporation, Limited Partnerships, Limited Liability Company, Trademarks/Servicemarks

Corporation Division, Secretary of State, 500 E Capitol Ave, Suite B-05, Pierre, SD 57501-5070; 605-773-4845, 605-773-3539 (Trademarks), 605-773-4550-Fax; 8AM-5PM.

www.sdsos.gov/corporations

Trademarks are in a different Division, call 605-773-3539.

Records are available from the founding of the state. New records are available for inquiry immediately. Records are indexed on microfiche, inhouse computer.

Searching: Include the following in your request-full name of business. In addition to the articles of incorporation, corporation records include the following information: Annual Reports, Officers, Directors, Registered Agent, Prior (merged) names, Inactive and Reserved names.

Access by: mail, phone, fax, in person, online.

Fee & Payment: There is no fee for a general search. A Certificate of Good Standing is available for a fee of $15.00. Copies are $1.00 per page, add $10.00 for certification. Fee payee: Secretary of State. Prepayment required. Personal checks accepted. Major credit cards accepted.

Mail search: Turnaround time: 1 to 3 days. A SASE is requested.

Phone search: They will provide basic information only.

Fax search: Records can be returned by fax for $1.00 per page plus a $5.00 fax fee.

In person search: Turnaround time is immediate.

Online search: Search the Secretary of State Corporations Div. Database free at www.state.sd.us/applications/st02corplook/corpfile.asp. Trademark searches may be requested via e-mail at anissa.grambihler@state.sd.us.

Other access: The corporate database may be purchased on CD for $1,000 with $500 monthly updates.

Expedited service: Expedited service is available for an additional $20.00 per request.

Fictitious Name Assumed Name

Records not maintained by a state level agency.

Records are located at the county level.

Uniform Commercial Code, Federal Tax Liens

UCC Division, Secretary of State, 500 East Capitol, Pierre, SD 57501-5077; 605-773-4422, 605-773-4550-Fax; 8AM-5PM.

www.sdsos.gov/ucc

Federal tax liens on business filed here, if on individuals then filed at county level.

Records are available for all active records. It takes less than 1 day before new records are available for inquiry. Records are indexed on computer. Records are normally destroyed after one year after lapse.

Searching: Use search request form UCC-11. The search includes federal tax liens on businesses. Include the following in your request-debtor name.

Access by: mail, phone, fax, in person, online.

Fee & Payment: The fee is $20.00 per debtor name, ($15.00 if online). Copies are $1.00 per page. There is an additional $10.00 if certification of document desired. Fee payee: Secretary of State. Prepayment required. Personal checks accepted. Major credit cards accepted, except Amex.

Mail search: Turnaround time: 1 to 2 days. A SASE is requested.

Phone search: Limited information is given over the phone. Reports can be ordered.

Fax search: Use of a credit card is required or prepay. Fee is additional $5.00 to fax back.

In person search: Simple requests may be processed while you wait.

Online search: Dakota Fast File is the filing and searching service available from the website. This is a commercial service that requires registration and a $120-360 fee per year. A certified search is also available.

Other access: FTP downloads are available for purchase.

Expedited service: Expedited service is available for mail, phone and fax searches. Turnaround time: 1 day. Add $20.00 per debtor name.

State and Federal Tax Liens

Records not maintained by a state level agency.

All state tax liens and federal tax liens on individuals are filed at the county level.

Sales Tax Registrations

Department of Revenue and Regulation, Business Tax Division, 445 E Capitol, Pierre, SD 57501-3100; 605-773-3311, 605-773-6729-Fax; 8AM-5PM.

www.state.sd.us/drr2/revenue.html

Searching: This agency will only confirm if a business is registered and licensed. They will provide no other information. Include the following in your request-business name. Also search by tax permit number or owner name.

Access by: mail, phone, fax, in person.

Mail search: Turnaround time: 2 to 3 weeks. A SASE is requested. No fee for mail request.

Phone search: No fee for telephone request.

Fax search: There is no fee, turnaround time is 2-3 weeks.

In person search: No fee for request. Usually requests can be processed while you wait.

Birth Certificates

South Dakota Department of Health, Vital Records, 600 E Capitol, Pierre, SD 57501-2536; 605-773-4961, 605-773-5683-Fax; 8AM-5PM.

www.state.sd.us/doh/VitalRec/index.htm

Records are available from 1906 to present. New records are available for inquiry immediately.

Searching: Include the following in your request- full name, names of parents, mother's maiden name, date of birth, place of birth. Any county Register of Deeds can provide a computer generated birth certificate for the same fee. The following data is not released: sealed records.

Access by: mail, phone, in person, online.

Fee & Payment: The search fee is $10.00. Fee payee: South Dakota Department of Health. Prepayment required. Personal checks accepted. Major credit cards accepted.

Mail search: Turnaround time: 4 to 5 days. No SASE is required.

Phone search: You must use a credit card, considered expedited service.

In person search: Turnaround time 30 minutes.

Online search: You can search free at the website for birth records over 100 years old. You can order recent (less than 100 years) birth records at the website, for a fee.

Expedited service: Expedited service is available for web and phone searches. Turnaround time: overnight delivery. Add $5.00 expedite fee and delivery fee.

Death Records

South Dakota Department of Health, Vital Records, 600 E Capitol, Pierre, SD 57501-2536; 605-773-4961, 605-773-5683-Fax; 8AM-5PM.

www.state.sd.us/doh/VitalRec/index.htm

Records are available from 1905 to present. New records are available for inquiry immediately.

Searching: Include the following in your request- full name, date of death, place of death. The following data is not released: sealed records.

Access by: mail, phone, in person, online.

Fee & Payment: The fee is $10.00 per record. Fee payee: South Dakota Department of Health. Prepayment required. Personal checks accepted. Major credit cards accepted.

Mail search: Turnaround time: 4 to 5 days. No SASE is required.

Phone search: You must use a credit card.

In person search: Turnaround time is 30 minutes.

Online search: Records may be ordered online at the web site.

Expedited service: Expedited service is available for Internet and phone searches. Turnaround time: overnight delivery. Add $5.00 expedite fee and delivery fee.

Marriage Certificates

South Dakota Department of Health, Vital Records, 600 E Capitol, Pierre, SD 57501-2536; 605-773-4961, 605-773-5683-Fax; 8AM-5PM.

www.state.sd.us/doh/VitalRec/index.htm

Records are available from 1905 to present. New records are available for inquiry immediately.

Searching: Include the following in your request- names of husband and wife, date of marriage, place or county of marriage. Also include wife's maiden name.

Access by: mail, phone, in person, online.

Fee & Payment: The fee is $10.00 per record. Fee payee: South Dakota Department of Health. Prepayment required. Personal checks accepted. Major credit cards accepted.

Mail search: Turnaround time: 4 to 5 days. No SASE is required.

Phone search: You must use a credit card.

In person search: Turnaround time is 30 minutes.

Online search: Records may be ordered online at the web site.

Expedited service: Expedited service is available for Internet and phone searches. Turnaround time: overnight delivery. Add $5.00 expedite fee and delivery fee.

Divorce Records

South Dakota Department of Health, Vital Records, 600 E Capitol, Pierre, SD 57501-2536; 605-773-4961, 605-773-5683-Fax; 8AM-5PM.

www.state.sd.us/doh/VitalRec/index.htm

Records are available from 1905 to present. New records are available for inquiry immediately.

Searching: Include the following in your request- names of husband and wife, date of divorce, place of divorce. The following data is not released: sealed records.

Access by: mail, phone, in person, online.

Fee & Payment: The fee is $10.00 per record. Fee payee: South Dakota Department of Health. Prepayment required. Personal checks accepted. Major credit cards accepted.

Mail search: Turnaround time: 4 to 5 days. No SASE is required.

Phone search: You must use a credit card.

In person search: Turnaround time 30 minutes.

Online search: Records may be ordered at the web site.

Expedited service: Expedited service is available for Internet and phone searches. Turnaround time: overnight delivery. Add $5.00 expedite fee and delivery fee.

Workers' Compensation Records

Labor Department, Workers Compensation Division, 700 Governors Dr, Pierre, SD 57501; 605-773-3681, 605-773-4211-Fax; 8AM-5PM.

www.state.sd.us/dol/dlm/dlm-home.htm

Records are available from 1973. New records are available for inquiry immediately. Records are indexed on inhouse computer.

Searching: Must have a signed release from the claimant. Must also specify which records you are requesting. A computer search will only go back to July 1989. Fraud reports and sealed files are not released. Include the following in your request- claimant name, Social Security Number, date of accident, body part injured.

Access by: mail.

Fee & Payment: Search fee is $20.00 per file or date of injury, copies are included. Fee payee: Division of Labor Management. Prepayment required. Personal checks accepted. No credit cards accepted.

Mail search: Turnaround time: 1 week.

Driver Records

Dept of Public Safety, Office of Driver Licensing, 118 W Capitol, Pierre, SD 57501; 605-773-6883, 605-773-3018-Fax; 8AM-5PM.

www.state.sd.us/dps/dl

Ticket information is maintained at the local courts, not at the state.

Records are available for 3 years for moving violations and DWIs. Speeding violations less than 10 mph over and out-of-state speeding violations (except for commercial drivers), suspensions and revocations are not listed on the record. It takes 1 to 3 weeks before new records are available for inquiry.

Searching: Casual requesters can only obtain records with the written permission of the subject. All other requesters must certify for what reason they are obtaining the information and comply with DPPA policies. Request forms can be downloaded from website. Include the following in your request-full name, date of birth. If for a non-permissible (DPPA) use, then notarized signature of driver needed. A secondary search will be done with the license number if no record is found on the name search. Suggest employers and insurance companies use MVR Request Form 2. The following data is not released: Social Security Numbers.

Access by: mail, phone, in person, online.

Fee & Payment: The fee is $4.00 per record. The agency charges sales tax, if record request comes from a South Dakota address. Fee payee: Dept of Public Safety Prepayment required. Personal checks accepted. No credit cards accepted.

Mail search: Turnaround time: 48 hours. The DL#, name, and DOB are all needed when requesting records via mail.

Phone search: Pre-approved accounts may order via the telephone. This is a very limited access.

In person search: Turnaround time while you wait at this location and at the Sioux Falls Driver Exam Station.

Online search: The system is open for batch requests 24 hours a day. There is a minimum of 250 requests daily. It generally takes 10 minutes to process a batch. The current fee is $4.00 per record and there are some start-up costs. For more information, call 605-773-6883.

Other access: Lists are available to the insurance industry.

Vehicle Ownership
Vehicle Identification
Vessel Ownership
Vessel Registration

Division of Motor Vehicles, Information Section, 445 E Capitol Ave, Pierre, SD 57501-3185; 605-773-3541, 605-773-2550-Fax; 8AM-5PM.

www.state.sd.us/drr2/motorvehicle/index.htm

The DMV took over the registration and title process for boats in 1992. All boats (except canoes, inflatables, kayaks, sailboards) over 12 ft in length, and motorized boats must be titled and registered.

Records are available for 20 years to present. It takes 2 weeks before new records are available for inquiry.

Searching: The agency requires all requests for vehicle related records be on the Division DPPA Form. Casual requesters (individuals) can only obtain information with written permission of the subject. Include the following in your request-DPPA Form. All requests must be in writing.

Access by: mail, in person.

Fee & Payment: The fee for VIN, plate, owner, title, or lien searches is $2.00 per record. A complete title history from microfilm is $5.00. Fee payee: Division of Motor Vehicles. Prepayment required. Personal checks accepted. No credit cards accepted.

Mail search: Turnaround time: 1 day to 1 week. Must provide DPPA request form. A SASE is requested.

In person search: You may request records in person, but the request must be in writing on the Division DPPA Form.

Accident Reports

Department of Public Safety, Accident Records, 118 W Capitol Ave, Pierre, SD 57501-2000; 605-773-3868, 605-773-6893-Fax; 8AM-5PM.

Records are available for 10 years to present. It takes 2 weeks from receipt from law enforcement agency before new records are available for inquiry.

Searching: Include the following in your request-full name, date of accident, location of accident.

Access by: mail, in person.

Fee & Payment: The fee is $4.00 per record. Fee payee: Accident Records. Prepayment required. Personal checks accepted. No credit cards accepted.

Mail search: Turnaround time: 5 days. A self addressed envelope is requested.

In person search: Normal turnaround time is immediate if the record is on file.

Expedited service: Will return report via fax once record fee is paid.

Voter Registration

Secretary of State, Elections Division, 500 E Capitol #204, Pierre, SD 57501; 605-773-3537, 605-773-6580-Fax; 8AM-5PM.

www.sdsos.gov/Elections

The Secretary of State and County Auditors throughout the state have compiled a statewide voter registration file of the official voter registration files in each county auditor's office. County auditors update the statewide file on a daily basis.

It takes 24 hours before new records are available for inquiry.

Searching: Name searching should be done at the county level. Data files or paper lists of the file or portions of the file may be purchased from the Secretary of State. Information obtained from the statewide file may not be used or sold for any commercial purpose and may not be placed on the internet.

Access by: mail, in person.

Fee & Payment: Only fees involved are for bulk list purchase.

Mail search: Records are available by mail.

In person search: Records may be searched in person.

Other access: The webpage has a list of various files available for purchase on CD or paper. For example, statewide CD is $2,500, statewide printed list is $5,500. Data may be purchased by county or legislative district.

GED Certificates

SD Department of Labor, AEL/GED/Literacy, 700 Governors Drive, Pierre, SD 57501-2291; 605-773-3101, 605-773-6184-Fax; 8AM-5PM.

www.state.sd.us/dol/GED/index.html

You may e-mail requests to marcia.hess@state.sd.us.

Records are available from 1942 to present. It takes 3-4 weeks before new records are available for inquiry. Records are normally destroyed after 2 years for partial test scores.

Searching: Include the following in your request-name at time of test, DOB, SSN and a signed release is required for either a verification or a copy of a transcript.

Access by: mail, fax, in person.

Fee & Payment: The fee for verifications or for a copy of a transcript is $5.00. Fee payee: SD Dept of Labor Prepayment required. Personal checks not accepted.

Mail search: Turnaround time: 1 to 3 days. No SASE is required. No fee for mail request.

Fax search: Results available in 1 day, but will only send transcript after $5.00 fee received.

In person search: You can wait for results.

Hunting and Fishing License Information

Game, Fish & Parks Department, License Division, 412 W Missouri, Pierre, SD 57501; 605-773-3926, 606-773-3485, 605-773-5842-Fax; 8AM-5PM.

www.state.sd.us/gfp

Records are available for current and previous years only.

Searching: Requests must be in writing. They will release address data. The DOB and address are helpful.

Access by: in person.

Fee & Payment: The fee is case dependent per the extent of the names and the search.

In person search: There is no fee, if the search request is simple.

Other access: Mailing lists are available for purchase. They have records for big game licensees.

South Dakota State Licensing Agencies

For details about the agency responsible for licensing/certifying/registering an item below or in the Agency Quick Finder section, match an item's number with the number of the agency in the *Licensing Agency Information* section.

South Dakota Licenses Searchable Online

Abstractor Business #1	www.state.sd.us/drr/reg/abstracters/roster.htm
Ambulance Service #20	www.state.sd.us/dps/ems/
Animal Remedy (drug for animals) #19	www.state.sd.us/doa/das/hp-af-ar.htm
Architect #23	www.state.sd.us/dol/boards/engineer/Roster/roster.htm
Athletic Trainer #10	www.state.sd.us/doh/medical/
Auctioneer #28	www.state.sd.us/drr2/reg/realestate/roster_licensees/roster.htm
Audiologist #30	www.state.sd.us/doh/audiology/roster.htm
Bail Bond Agent #37	www.state.sd.us/drr2/reg/insurance/producers/bailbonds.xls
Bank #2	www.state.sd.us/drr2/reg/bank/licensees/state_banks.doc
Barber #4	www.state.sd.us/dol/boards/barber/barbers.htm
Barber Shop #4	www.state.sd.us/dol/boards/barber/shops.htm
Beauty Shop/Salon #18	www.state.sd.us/applications/LD19Cosmet/license.asp
Cosmetologist / Instructor / Salon #18	www.state.sd.us/applications/LD19Cosmet/license.asp
Counselor #6	www.state.sd.us/dhs/boards/counselor/roster.htm
Crematory #29	www.state.sd.us/doh/funeral/roster.htm
Dietitian/Nutritionist #10	www.state.sd.us/doh/medical/
Driller, Oil and Gas #17	www.state.sd.us/denr/DES/Mining/Oil&Gas/NewPermit.htm
Embalmer #29	www.state.sd.us/doh/funeral/roster.htm
Engineer #23	www.state.sd.us/dol/boards/engineer/Roster/roster.htm
Engineer, Petroleum Environmental #23	www.state.sd.us/dol/boards/engineer/Roster/roster.htm
Esthetician #18	www.state.sd.us/applications/LD19Cosmet/license.asp
Fertilizer #19	www.state.sd.us/doa/das/hp-fert.htm
Funeral Director/Embalmer/Establism't/Service #29	www.state.sd.us/doh/funeral/roster.htm
Hearing Aid Dispenser #30	www.state.sd.us/doh/audiology/roster.htm
Home Inspector #28	www.state.sd.us/drr2/reg/realestate/roster_licensees/roster.htm
Insurance Company #37	www.state.sd.us/drr2/reg/insurance/CompareStatmt/Address.htm
Landscape Architect #23	www.state.sd.us/dol/boards/engineer/landsurveynumbers.htm
Lobbyist #27	www.sdsos.gov/lobbyist/
Manicurist/Nail Technician #18	www.state.sd.us/applications/LD19Cosmet/license.asp
Marriage & Family Therapist #6	www.state.sd.us/dhs/boards/counselor/roster.htm
Medical Assistant #10	www.state.sd.us/doh/medical/
Medical Doctor #10	www.state.sd.us/doh/medical/
Money Lender #2	www.state.sd.us/drr2/reg/bank/licensees/moneylender.doc
Money Order Business #2	www.state.sd.us/drr2/reg/bank/licensees/moneyorder.doc
Mortgage Broker/Lender #2	www.state.sd.us/drr2/reg/bank/licensees/mortgagebroker.doc
Nail Salon #18	www.state.sd.us/applications/LD19Cosmet/license.asp
Notary Public #27	www.sdsos.gov/notaries/
Nursing Home Administrator #8	www.state.sd.us/doh/nursingfacility/roster.htm
Occupational Therapist/Assistant #10	www.state.sd.us/doh/medical/
Oil & Gas Driller #17	www.state.sd.us/denr/DES/Mining/Oil&Gas/NewPermit.htm
Optometrist #9	www.arbo.org/index.php?action=findanoptometrist
Osteopathic Physician #10	www.state.sd.us/doh/medical/
Pesticide Applicator/Dealer #19	www.state.sd.us/doa/das/
Pet Health Insurer #37	www.state.sd.us/drr2/reg/insurance/CompareStatmt/PetInsurers.htm
Petro. Release Assessor/Remediator #23	www.state.sd.us/dol/boards/engineer/Roster/roster.htm
Physical Therapist/Assistant #10	www.state.sd.us/doh/medical/
Physician / Medical Assistant #10	www.state.sd.us/doh/medical/
Podiatrist #14	www.state.sd.us/doh/podiatry/roster.htm
Property Manager #28	www.state.sd.us/drr2/reg/realestate/roster_licensees/roster.htm
Psychologist #15	www.state.sd.us/dhs/boards/psychologists/roster.htm
Public Accountant-CPA #3	www.state.sd.us/dol/boards/accountancy/Annual%20Register%20-%20Jan05.pdf
Real Estate Agent/Sales/Broker #28	www.state.sd.us/drr2/reg/realestate/roster_licensees/roster.htm
Re-insurer, Accredited/Qualified #37	www.state.sd.us/drr2/reg/insurance/Financial/AQReinsurers.pdf
Respiratory Care Practitioner #10	www.state.sd.us/doh/medical/
Social Worker #15	www.state.sd.us/dhs/boards/socialwork/roster.htm
Surveyor, Land #23	www.state.sd.us/dol/boards/engineer/Roster/roster.htm
Timeshare Real Estate #28	www.state.sd.us/drr2/reg/realestate/roster_licensees/roster.htm
Waste Water System Operator / Plant Operator #12	www.state.sd.us/denr/databases/operator/index.cfm
Water Distributor #12	www.state.sd.us/denr/databases/operator/index.cfm
Water Treatment Operator / Plant Operator #12	www.state.sd.us/denr/databases/operator/index.cfm
Weapon, Concealed #27	www.sdsos.gov/firearms/

South Dakota Licensing Quick Finder

9-1-1 Telecommunicator #25 605-773-3584
Abstractor / Abstractor Business #1 605-869-2269
Acupuncturist #5 605-668-9017
Alcoholic Beverage Distributor #21 605-773-3311
Ambulance Service #20............................ 605-773-4031
Animal Feed Seller/Producer #19 605-773-4432
Animal Remedy (medicine/drug for animals) #19
.... 605-773-4432
Appliance Contractor/Journeyman/Apprentice #34
.... 605-773-3429
Architect #23 605-394-2510
Asbestos Abatement Worker #36......... 605-773-3153
Asbestos Service Company #36 605-773-3153
Athletic Trainer #10............................... 605-336-1965
Attorney #32 605-224-7554
Auctioneer #28....................................... 605-773-3600
Audiologist #30 605-642-1600
Bail Bond Agent #37 605-773-3513
Bank #2... 605-773-3421
Barber / Barber Shop #4 605-642-1600
Beauty Shop/Salon #18.......................... 605-773-6193
Brokerage Firm #31................................ 605-773-4823
Business Opportunities Broker #31 605-773-4823
Canine Team #25 605-773-3584
Chiropractor #5....................................... 605-668-9017
Cigarette Wholesaler #21 605-773-3311
Clinical Nurse Specialist #11 605-362-2760
Cosmetologist / Salon#18...................... 605-773-6193
Cosmetology Instructor #18.................. 605-773-6193
Counselor #6 605-331-2927
Court/Shorthand Reporter #38 605-773-3474
Crematory #29.. 605-642-1600
Dental Assistant #7................................ 605-224-1282
Dental Hygienist #7................................ 605-224-1282
Dentist #7.. 605-224-1282
Dietitian/Nutritionist #10....................... 605-336-1965
Driller, Oil and Gas #17 605-394-2229
Drug Wholesaler #13.............................. 605-362-2737
Electrical Inspector #33 605-773-3573
Electrician #33 605-773-3573
Embalmer #29 605-642-1600
Emergency Medical Technician #20 605-773-4031
Engineer #23 605-394-2510
Engineer, Petroleum Environmen'l #23. 605-394-2510
Environmental Site Assessor #36 605-773-3296
Esthetician #18....................................... 605-773-6193

Fertilizer #19... 605-773-4432
Franchise Sales #31............................... 605-773-4823
Funeral Director/Embalmer #29 605-642-1600
Funeral Establishment #29.................... 605-642-1600
Funeral Service #29............................... 605-642-1600
Gaming #24 605-773-6050
Hazardous Waste #36............................ 605-773-3153
Hearing Aid Dispenser #30 605-642-1600
Home Inspector #28............................... 605-773-3600
Insurance Agent #37.............................. 605-773-3513
Insurance Company #37 605-773-3563
Investment Advisor #31......................... 605-773-4823
Landfill #36... 605-773-3153
Landscape Architect #23........................ 605-394-2510
Laundromat #21 605-773-3311
Law Enforcement Officer #25................ 605-773-3584
Livestock Dealer #16.............................. 605-773-3321
Loan Production #2................................. 605-773-3421
Lobbyist #27 605-773-3539
Manicurist/Nail Technician #18 605-773-6193
Marriage & Family Therapist #6 605-331-2927
Medical Assistant #10 605-336-1965
Medical Doctor #10................................ 605-336-1965
Midwife Nurse #11................................. 605-362-2760
Milk Grader/Hauler/Tester/Sampler #19 605-773-4294
Mobile Home Contractor #34 605-773-3429
Money Lender #2.................................... 605-773-3421
Money Order Business #2...................... 605-773-3421
Mortgage Broker/Lender #2 605-773-3421
Nail Salon #18.. 605-773-6193
Notary Public #27.................................. 605-773-3539
Nurse #11.. 605-362-2760
Nurse Aide Certified #11 605-362-2760
Nurse Anesthetist #11........................... 605-362-2760
Nurse Practitioner, Certified #11 605-362-2760
Nurses Aide / Aide Applicant #35......... 605-362-2762
Nursing Home Administrator #8 605-331-5040
Occupational Therapist/Assistant #10.. 605-336-1965
Oil & Gas Driller #17............................. 605-394-2229
Optometrist #9 605-347-2136
Osteopathic Physician #10.................... 605-336-1965
Paramedic #20 605-773-4031
Pesticide Applicator/Dealer #19 605-773-4432
Pet Health Insurer #37 605-773-3563
Petroleum Release Assessor/Remediator #23
.... 605-394-2510

Pharmacist/Pharmacy #13 605-362-2737
Physical Therapist/Assistant #10 605-336-1965
Physician/Medical Assistant #10.......... 605-336-1965
Plumber #34 605-773-3429
Podiatrist #14 605-642-1600
Polygraph Examiner #25........................ 605-773-3584
Property Manager #28 605-773-3600
Psychologist #15.................................... 605-642-1600
Public Accountant-CPA #3.................... 605-367-5770
Racing #24 605-773-6050
Radiologist (Chiropractic) #5................. 605-668-9017
Radiology (Dental) #7 605-224-1282
Real Estate Agent/Sales/Broker #28 ... 605-773-3600
Real Estate Broker #28.......................... 605-773-3600
Recycler #36 605-773-3153
Recycler, Specialty #36.......................... 605-773-3153
Re-insurer, Accredited/Qualified #37 ... 605-773-3563
Respiratory Care Practitioner #10........ 605-336-1965
School Counselor #22............................ 605-773-3553
School Principal/Superintendent #22... 605-773-3553
Scrap Tire Company #36 605-773-3153
Securities Agent/Broker/Dealer #31..... 605-773-4823
Sewage & Water Installation Contractor/Installer #34
.... 605-773-3429
Social Worker #15.................................. 605-642-1600
Spill Clean-up Company #36 605-773-3296
StorageTank,Above/Below Ground #36 605-773-3296
Surveyor, Land #23................................. 605-394-2510
Tank Remover #36.................................. 605-773-3296
Teacher #22 605-773-3553
Testing Lab, Environmental #36 605-773-3296
Timeshare Real Estate #28.................... 605-773-3600
Veterinarian/Veterinary Technician #16 605-773-3321
Veterinary Corporation #16................... 605-773-3321
Waste Water Collection System Operator #12
.... 605-773-3151
Waste Water Treatment Plant Operator #12
.... 605-773-3151
Water Conditioning Plumbing Installer #34
.... 605-773-3429
Water Distributor #12............................. 605-773-3151
Water Treatment Operator #26............ 605-773-4208
Water Treatment Plant Operator #12... 605-773-3151
Weapon, Concealed #27........................ 605-773-3537
Well Driller #36....................................... 605-773-3352

South Dakota Licensing Agency Information

1 Abstractors Board of Examiners, PO Box 187, Kennebec, SD 57544-0187; 605-869-2269, Fax: 605-869-2269.
www.state.sd.us/drr/reg/abstracters/abst-hom.htm
Email: lctc@wcenet.com   Search Database at www.state.sd.us/drr2/reg/abstracters/abst-hom.htm

2 Department of Revenue & Regulation, Division of Banking, 217 1/2 W Missouri, Pierre, SD 57501-4590; 605-773-3421, Fax: 605-773-5367.
www.state.sd.us/banking
Email: cassandra.nagel@state.sd.us
Search Database at
www.state.sd.us/drr2/reg/bank/licensee.htm

3 Board of Accountancy, 301 E 14th St, #200, Sioux Falls, SD 57104-5022; 605-367-5770, Fax: 605-367-5773.
www.state.sd.us/dol/boards/accountancy/acc-home.htm   Email: sdbdact@dtgnet.com
Search Database at www.state.sd.us/dol/boards/accountancy/Annual%20Register%20-%20Jan05.pdf   Note: To search, scroll down through the alphabetical listings.

4 Board of Barber Examiners, c/o Carol Tellinghuisen, Executive Secretary, 135 E Illinois #214, Spearfish, SD 57783; 605-642-1600, Fax: 605-642-1756.
www.state.sd.us/dol/boards/barber/
Email: proflic@rushmore.com
Search Database at
www.state.sd.us/dol/boards/barber/roster.htm

5 Board of Chiropractic Examiners, 2603 Ella Lane, Yankton, SD 57078; 605-668-9017, Fax: 605-668-9017.
www.state.sd.us/doh/chiropractic/
Email: sdbce@mchsi.com

6 Board of Counselor Examiners, PO Box 1822, Sioux Falls, SD 57101-1822; 605-331-2927, Fax: 605-331-2043.
www.state.sd.us
Email: sdbce.msp@midconetwork.com
Search Database at
www.state.sd.us/dhs/boards/counselor/roster.htm

7 Board of Dentistry, PO Box 1037, Pierre, SD 57501-1037; 605-224-1282, Fax: 605-224-7426.
www.state.sd.us/doh/dentistry/

8 Board of Examiners for Nursing Home Administrators, PO Box 632, Sioux Falls, SD 57101-0632; 605-331-5040, Fax: 605-331-2043.
www.state.sd.us/doh/nursingfacility/index.htm

9 Board of Examiners in Optometry, PO Box 628, Sturgis, SD 57785-0370; 605-347-2136, Fax: 605-347-5823.
www.state.sd.us/doh/optometry/
Email: sdoptbd_99@yahoo.com
Search Database at www.arbo.org/index.php?action=findanoptometrist

10 Board of Medical & Osteopathic Examiners, 1323 S Minnesota Ave, Sioux Falls, SD 57105-0685; 605-336-1965, Fax: 605-336-0270.
www.state.sd.us/doh/medical/
Email: jphalen@sdsma.org

11 Board of Nursing, 4305 S Louise Ave, #201, Sioux Falls, SD 57106-3124; 605-362-2760, Fax: 605-362-2768.
www.state.sd.us/doh/nursing/
Email: jean.mcguire@state.sd.us Note: Online searching/verification system is being updated; check main website.

12 Board of Operator Certification, 523 E Capitol Ave, Foss Bldg, Pierre, SD 57501; 605-773-3151, Fax: 605-773-6035.
www.state.sd.us/denr/denr.html
Email: rob.kittay@state.sd.us
Search Database at www.state.sd.us/denr/databases/operator/index.cfm

13 Board of Pharmacy, 4305 S Louise Ave, #104, Sioux Falls, SD 57106-3115; 605-362-2737, Fax: 605-362-2738.
www.state.sd.us/doh/pharmacy/index.htm
Email: dennis.jones@state.sd.us

14 Board of Podiatry Examiners, 135 E Illinois, #214, Spearfish, SD 57783; 605-642-1600, Fax: 605-642-1756.
www.state.sd.us/doh/podiatry/index.htm
Email: proflic@rushmore.com
Search Database at www.state.sd.us/doh/podiatry/roster.htm

15 Board of Social Work Examiners/Psychologist Examiners, 135 E Illinois, #214, Spearfish, SD 57783; 605-642-1600, Fax: 605-642-1756.
www.state.sd.us/dhs/boards/socialwork/soc-hom.htm
Email: proflic@rushmore.com
Search Database at www.state.sd.us/dhs/boards/socialwork/roster.htm

16 Board of Veterinary Medical Examiners, 411 S Fort St, Pierre, SD 57501-4503; 605-773-3321, Fax: 605-773-5459.
www.state.sd.us/doa/veterinary/
Email: dr.holland@state.sd.us

17 Department of Environment & Natural Resources, Oil & Gas Section, Minerals & Mining Program, 2050 W. Main, #1, Rapid City, SD 57701; 605-394-2229.
www.state.sd.us/denr/DES/Mining/Oil&Gas/O&G home.htm
Search Database at www.state.sd.us/denr/DES/Mining/Oil&Gas/NewPermit.htm Note: Permit records go back five years.

18 Cosmetology Commission, 500 E Capitol, Pierre, SD 57501-5070; 605-773-6193, Fax: 605-773-7175.
www.state.sd.us/dol/boards/cos/
Email: sdcosmo@sd.cybernex.net
Search Database at www.state.sd.us/applications/LD19Cosmet/license.asp

19 Department of Agriculture, Division of Ag Services, 523 E Capitol, Foss Bldg, Pierre, SD 57501-3182; 605-773-3724, Fax: 605-773-3481.
www.state.sd.us/doa/das/

20 Department Public Safety, Emergency Medical Services, 118 W. Capitol, Pierre, SD 57501; 605-773-4031, Fax: 605-773-6631.
www.state.sd.us/dps/ems
Email: bob.graff@state.sd.us Note: Search license lists for air ambulance and instate/out-of-state ground ambulance services.

21 Department of Revenue & Regulation, Property & Special Taxes - Special Tax Division, 445 E Capitol Ave, Pierre, SD 57501-3185; 605-773-3311, Fax: 605-773-5129.
www.state.sd.us/drr2/revenue.html
Email: specialT@rev.state.sd.us

22 Education & Cultural Affairs Department, Office of Policy & Accountability, 700 Governors Dr, Pierre, SD 57501-2291; 605-773-3553, Fax: 605-773-6139.
www.state.sd.us/deca/
Email: janelle.toman@state.sd.us

23 Department of Labor, Board of Technical Professions, 2040 W Main St, #304, Rapid City, SD 57702-2447; 605-394-2510, Fax: 605-395-2509.
www.state.sd.us/dcr/engineer
Email: ann.whipple@state.sd.us
Search Database at www.state.sd.us/dol/boards/engineer/Roster/roster.htm Note: Roster available for $25.00 by print, disk, or email.

24 Gaming Commission, 221 W Capitol Ave (c/o 1320 E Sioux Ave), Pierre, SD 57501-5070; 605-773-6050, Fax: 605-773-6053.
www.state.sd.us/dcr/gaming/gam-hom.htm

25 Law Enforcement Standards & Training Commission, Division of Criminal Justice Training Center, Pierre, SD 57501; 605-773-3584, Fax: 605-773-7203.
www.state.sd.us
Email: bryan.gortmaker@state.sd.us

26 Department of Environment & Natural Resources, Division of Environmental Svcs, Drinking Water Program, 523 E Capitol Ave, Pierre, SD 57501; 605-773-4208.
www.state.sd.us/denr/enviro

27 Office of Secretary of State, Lobbyist Coordinator, Notaries, 500 E Capitol Ave, State Capitol Bldg, #204, Pierre, SD 57501-5070; 605-773-3537, Fax: 605-773-6580.
http://sdsos.gov/
Email: anissa.grambihler@state.sd.us
Search Database at http://sdsos.gov/

28 Real Estate Commission, 221 W Capitol St 101, Pierre, SD 57501; 605-773-3600, Fax: 605-773-4356.
www.state.sd.us/drr/reg/realestate/index.htm
Email: norma.schilling@state.sd.us
Search Database at www.state.sd.us/drr2/reg/realestate/roster_licensees/roster.htm

29 Board of Funeral Services, 135 E Illinois, #214, Spearfish, SD 57783; 605-642-1600, Fax: 605-642-1756.
www.state.sd.us/doh/funeral/
Email: proflic@rushmore.com
Search Database at www.state.sd.us/doh/funeral/roster.htm

30 Board of Hearing Aid Dispensers and Audiologists, 135 E Illinois # 214, Spearfish, SD 57783-0654; 605-642-1600, Fax: 605-642-1756.
www.state.sd.us/doh/audiology/
Email: proflic@rushmore.com
Search Database at www.state.sd.us/doh/audiology/roster.htm

31 Dept of Revenue & Regulation, Division of Securities, 445 E Capitol Ave, Pierre, SD 57501-3185; 605-773-4823, Fax: 605-773-5953.
www.state.sd.us/drr2/reg/securities/broker.htm
Email: melita.hauge@state.sd.us

32 State Bar, 222 E Capitol Ave, Pierre, SD 57501-2596; 605-224-7554, Fax: 605-224-0282.
www.sdbar.org
Email: tbarnett@sdbar.org

33 Electrical Commission, 308 S. Pierre St., Pierre, SD 57501-5070; 605-773-3573, Fax: 605-773-6213.
www.state.sd.us/dcr/electrical/ELEC_HOM.htm

34 Plumbing Commission, 308 S. Pierce St. %1320 E Sioux Ave., Pierre, SD 57501; 605-773-3429, Fax: 605-773-5405.
www.state.sd.us/dcr/plumbing
Email: mike.richards@state.sd.us

35 Healthcare Administration, Nurses Aide Testing, 804 N Western Av, Souix Falls, SD 57104-2098; 605-362-2762, Fax: 605-339-1354.
www.sdhca.org
Email: sdhca@worldnet.att.net

36 Department of Environment & Natural Resources, Division of Environmental Svcs, 523 E Capitol Ave, Pierre, SD 57501-3182; 605-773-3153, Fax: 605-773-6035.
www.state.sd.us/denr/denr.html
Search Database at www.state.sd.us/denr/DES/WasteMgn/WMPpage1.htm

37 Department of Commerce & Regulation, Division of Insurance, 445 E Capitol, Pierre, SD 57501; 605-773-3563, Fax: 605-773-5369.
www.state.sd.us/dcr/insurance

38 Supreme Court, Unified Judicial Court Administrators Office, Capitol Bldg, 500 E Capitol, Pierre, SD 57501; 605-773-3474, Fax: 605-773-5627.
www.sdjudicial.com/
Email: jill.gusso@ujs.state.sd.us

South Dakota Federal Courts

The following list indicates the district and division name for each county in the state. If the bankruptcy court location is different from the district court, then the location of the bankruptcy court appears in parentheses.

South Dakota County/Court Cross Reference

Aurora	Sioux Falls	Hyde	Pierre
Beadle	Sioux Falls	Jackson	Pierre
Bennett	Rapid City (Pierre)	Jerauld	Pierre
Bon Homme	Sioux Falls	Jones	Pierre
Brookings	Sioux Falls	Kingsbury	Sioux Falls
Brown	Aberdeen (Pierre)	Lake	Sioux Falls
Brule	Sioux Falls	Lawrence	Rapid City (Pierre)
Buffalo	Pierre	Lincoln	Sioux Falls
Butte	Aberdeen (Pierre)	Lyman	Pierre
Campbell	Aberdeen (Pierre)	Marshall	Aberdeen (Pierre)
Charles Mix	Sioux Falls	McCook	Sioux Falls
Clark	Aberdeen (Pierre)	McPherson	Aberdeen (Pierre)
Clay	Sioux Falls	Meade	Rapid City (Pierre)
Codington	Aberdeen (Pierre)	Mellette	Pierre
Corson	Aberdeen (Pierre)	Miner	Sioux Falls
Custer	Rapid City (Pierre)	Minnehaha	Sioux Falls
Davison	Sioux Falls	Moody	Sioux Falls
Day	Aberdeen (Pierre)	Pennington	Rapid City (Pierre)
Deuel	Aberdeen (Pierre)	Perkins	Rapid City (Pierre)
Dewey	Pierre	Potter	Pierre
Douglas	Sioux Falls	Roberts	Aberdeen (Pierre)
Edmunds	Aberdeen (Pierre)	Sanborn	Sioux Falls
Fall River	Rapid City (Pierre)	Shannon	Rapid City (Pierre)
Faulk	Pierre	Spink	Aberdeen (Pierre)
Grant	Aberdeen (Pierre)	Stanley	Pierre
Gregory	Pierre	Sully	Pierre
Haakon	Pierre	Todd	Pierre
Hamlin	Aberdeen (Pierre)	Tripp	Pierre
Hand	Pierre	Turner	Sioux Falls
Hanson	Sioux Falls	Union	Sioux Falls
Harding	Rapid City (Pierre)	Walworth	Aberdeen (Pierre)
Hughes	Pierre	Yankton	Sioux Falls
Hutchinson	Sioux Falls	Ziebach	Pierre

Standards for Federal Courts: Search fee is $26.00 per item (one party name or case number). Copy fee is $.50 per page. Certification fee is $9.00 per document, double for exemplification, if available. All fees standard unless noted in profile. Mail Search: always enclose a stamped self addressed envelope unless otherwise noted. Most courts accept fax requests or will suggest a copying/search vendor. Before releasing records, all courts require prepayment, unless noted.

Open records are located at the court unless otherwise noted. District courts index by defendant and plaintiff as well as by case number. Bankruptcy courts usually index by debtor and case number. While most courts now have their indexes on computer, many may still maintain index card files as well.

Courts offering internet access via CM-ECF or older RACER, PACER, or Web-PACER systems charge $.08 per page fee unless noted as free. Where PACER is available, the universal sign-up number is 800-676-6856. Find PACER and the US Party/Case Index at http://pacer.psc.uscourts.gov.

US District Court

District of South Dakota

Aberdeen Division c/o Pierre Division, Federal Bldg & Courthouse, 225 S Pierre St, Rm 405, Pierre, SD 57501 (also use mail address for courier delivery), 605-224-5849, Fax-605-224-0806. Hours- 8AM-5PM. www.sdd.uscourts.gov

Counties: Brown, Campbell, Clark, Codington, Corson, Day, Deuel, Edmunds, Grant, Hamlin, McPherson, Marshall, Roberts, Spink, Walworth. Judge Battey's closed case records are located at the Rapid City Division.

Searches & Indexing: Cases indexed by and case number. Results do not include SSN or DOB. Records purged every 6 months. Open records located at Pierre Division.

Fee & Payment: Pay by Visa/MC//AmEx/Discover, money order, cashier's or personal check. No business checks accepted.

Phone Search: No searching by telephone.

Mail Search: Include SASE for return.

In Person Search: permitted. No self-serve copier available.

E-Services: ECF replaces PACER whose records did go back to 1991. New records online after 1 day. ECF at https://ecf.sdd.uscourts.gov. Access written opinions free via PACER at www.sdd.uscourts.gov/writop.htm. **Other Online Access:** Access to very limited court calendar at www.sdd.uscourts.gov.

Pierre Division Court Clerk, Federal Bldg & Courthouse, Rm 405, 225 S Pierre St, Pierre, SD 57501 (also use mail address for courier delivery), 605-224-5849, Fax-605-224-0806. Hours- 8AM-5PM. www.sdd.uscourts.gov

Counties: Buffalo, Dewey, Faulk, Gregory, Haakon, Hand, Hughes, Hyde, Jackson, Jerauld, Jones, Lyman, Mellette, Potter, Stanley, Sully, Todd, Tripp, Ziebach.

Searches & Indexing: Results do not include SSN or DOB. Both computer and card indexes maintained; computer goes back to 1992. New cases in the index 1 day after filing date. Records purged every 6 months.

Fee & Payment: Pay by Visa/MC, money order, cashier's or personal check. Payee: Clerk, US District Court. Prepayment required.

Phone Search: Only docket information is available by phone.

Mail Search: search usually completed- 1-2 days. Include SASE for return.

In Person Search: Fee charged if court performs your search. No self-serve copier available.

E-Services: ECF replaces PACER whose records did go back to 1991. New records online after 1 day. ECF at https://ecf.sdd.uscourts.gov. Access written opinions free via PACER at www.sdd.uscourts.gov/writop.htm. **Other Online Access:** Access to very limited court calendar can be found at www.sdd.uscourts.gov.

Rapid City Division Clerk's Office, Rm 302, 515 9th St, Rapid City, SD 57701 (also use mail address for courier delivery), 605-342-3066, Fax-605-343-4367. Hours- 7:30AM-5PM. www.sdd.uscourts.gov

Counties: Bennett, Butte, Custer, Fall River, Harding, Lawrence, Meade, Pennington, Perkins, Shannon. Judge Battey's closed cases are located here.

Searches & Indexing: Results do not include SSN or DOB. Both computer and card indexes maintained; computer goes back to 1985. New cases in the index 24 hours after filing date. Records purged every 6 months.

Fee & Payment: Pay by Visa/MC, money order, cashier's, business or personal check. Payee: Clerk, US District Court. Prepayment required. Will fax documents $1.50 per page, prepaid.

Phone Search: Only docket information available by telephone.

Mail Search: search usually completed- 1-2 days. SASE not required.

In Person Search: Fee charged if court performs your search. No self-serve copier available.

E-Services: ECF replaces PACER whose records did go back to 1991. New records online after 1 day. ECF at https://ecf.sdd.uscourts.gov. Access written opinions free via PACER at www.sdd.uscourts.gov/writop.htm. **Other Online Access:** Access to very limited court calendar can be found at www.sdd.uscourts.gov.

Sioux Falls Division Court Clerk, PO Box 5060, Sioux Falls, SD 57117-5060 (courier address: Rm 128, US Courthouse, 400 S Phillips Ave, Sioux Falls, SD 57104), 605-330-4447, Fax-605-330-4312. Hours- 8AM-5PM. www.sdd.uscourts.gov

Counties: Aurora, Beadle, Bon Homme, Brookings, Brule, Charles Mix, Clay, Davison, Douglas, Hanson, Hutchinson, Kingsbury, Lake, Lincoln, McCook, Miner, Minnehaha, Moody, Sanborn, Turner, Union, Yankton.

Searches & Indexing: Results do not include SSN or DOB. Both computer and card indexes maintained, computer back to 1970. New cases in the index 1 day after filing date. Records purged every 6 months.

Fee & Payment: Pay by Visa/MC, money order, cashier's or personal check. Payee: Clerk, US District Court. Prepayment required. Will fax documents $1.50 per page.

Phone Search: Only docket information for civil cases is released via phone.

Mail Search: search usually completed- same day if possible. Include SASE for return.

In Person Search: Fee charged if court performs your search. No self-serve copier available.

E-Services: ECF replaces PACER whose records did go back to 1991. New records online after 1 day. ECF at https://ecf.sdd.uscourts.gov. Access written opinions free via PACER at www.sdd.uscourts.gov/writop.htm. **Other Online Access:** Access to very limited court calendar can be found at www.sdd.uscourts.gov.

US Bankruptcy Court
District of South Dakota

Pierre Division Clerk of Court, Rm 203, Federal Bldg, 225 S Pierre St, Pierre, SD 57501 (also use mail address for courier delivery), 605-224-0560, Fax-605-224-9020 records rm fax- 605-224-9808; fax record requests to-605-224-9808. www.sdb.uscourts.gov

Counties: Bennett, Brown, Buffalo, Butte, Campbell, Clark, Codington, Corson, Custer, Day, Deuel, Dewey, Edmunds, Fall River, Faulk, Grant, Gregory, Haakon, Hamlin, Hand, Harding, Hughes, Hyde, Jackson, Jerauld, Jones, Lawrence, Lyman, Marshall, McPherson, Meade, Mellette, Pennington, Perkins, Potter, Roberts, Shannon, Spink, Stanley, Sully, Todd, Tripp, Walworth, Ziebach.

Searches & Indexing: Cases indexed by debtor, creditors, and case number. Computer index

maintained. New cases in the index immediately after filing date. Records purged never. District-wide searches available here back to 10/1/91.

Fee & Payment: Pay by money order, cashier check, in-state business check. No personal checks. Payee: Clerk, US Bankruptcy Court. Prepayment required. Will fax docket listings no extra charge.

Phone Search: Only docket information is available by phone. Voice Case Information Service available, call VCIS at 800-768-6218 or 605-330-4559.

Mail Search: search usually completed- 1 day. Include SASE for return.

In Person Search: permitted. No self-serve copier available.

E-Services: ECF replaces PACER. Document images available. PACER records go back to 10/1991. ECF at https://ecf.sdb.uscourts.gov **Opinions Online:** www.sdb.uscourts.gov/Decisions.htm.

Sioux Falls Division Clerk of Court, PO Box 5060, Sioux Falls, SD 57117-5060 (courier address: Rm 117, 400 S Phillips Ave, Sioux Falls, SD 57102), 605-330-4544, Fax-605-330-4560. Hours- 8AM-4PM. www.sdb.uscourts.gov

Counties: Aurora, Beadle, Bon Homme, Brookings, Brule, Charles Mix, Clay, Davison, Douglas, Hanson, Hutchinson, Kingsbury, Lake, Lincoln, McCook, Miner, Minnehaha, Moody, Sanborn, Turner, Union, Yankton.

Searches & Indexing: Cases indexed by debtor, creditors, and case number. Computer index maintained. New cases in the index 1 day after filing date. Records purged never. District-wide searches available here back to 10/1/91.

Fee & Payment: Pay by money order, cashier check, in-state business check. No personal checks. Payee: Clerk, US Bankruptcy Court. Prepayment required. Will fax docket listings no extra charge.

Phone Search: Only docket information is available by phone. Voice Case Information Service available, call VCIS at 800-768-6218 or 605-330-4559.

Mail Search: search usually completed- 1 day. Include SASE for return.

In Person Search: permitted. No self-serve copier available.

E-Services: ECF replaces PACER. Document images available. PACER records go back to 10/1991. ECF at https://ecf.sdb.uscourts.gov **Opinions Online:** www.sdb.uscourts.gov/Decisions.htm

South Dakota County Courts

Court	Jurisdiction	No. of Courts	How Organized
Circuit Courts*	General	66	7 Circuits
Magistrate Courts		66	

* Profiled in this Sourcebook.

Court	CIVIL								
	Tort	Contract	Real Estate	Min. Claim	Max. Claim	Small Claims	Estate	Eviction	Domestic Relations
Circuit Courts*	X	X	X	$0	No Max	$8000	X	X	X
Magistrate Courts				$0	$10,000	$8000	X	X	X

Court	CRIMINAL				
	Felony	Misdemeanor	DWI/DUI	Preliminary Hearing	Juvenile
Circuit Courts*	X	X	X	X	X
Magistrate Courts		X	X	X	

ADMINISTRATION State Court Administrator, State Capitol Building, 500 E Capitol Av, Pierre, SD, 57501; 605-773-3474, Fax: 605-773-5627. www.sdjudicial.com

COURT STRUCTURE The state re-aligned their circuits from 8 to 7 effective June, 2000.

South Dakota has a statewide criminal record search database, administrated by the State Court Administrator's Office in Pierre. All criminal record information from July 1, 1989 forward, statewide, is contained in the database. Requesters with accounts may mail requests to one of the addresses listed below for statewide searching. Requesters may set up a commercial account by faxing a written request to Jill Gusso, Unified Court System at 605-773-4874 or email jill.gusso@ujs.state.sd.us. Accounts are billed monthly. The search fee is $15.00 per record. State authorized commercial accounts may order and receive records by fax, there is an additional $5.00 fee unless a non-toll free line is used.

Mail requests should be addressed to the Minor County Clerk of Court, PO Box 265, Howard SD 57349 or to Aurora County Clerk of Court, PO Box 366, Plankton, SD 57368-0366. Providing an SASE is suggested.

ONLINE ACCESS There is no statewide online access computer system currently available for trial court records. The Supreme Court calendar, opinions, and 2nd oral arguments may be searched from the website.

ADDITIONAL INFORMATION Most South Dakota courts do not allow the public to perform searches, but rather require the court clerk to do them for a fee of $15.00 per name. A special Record Search Request Form must be used. Searches will be returned with a disclaimer stating that the clerk is not responsible for the completeness of the search. Clerks are not required to respond to telephone or fax requests, but many courts will return records via fax to ongoing commercial accounts. Many courts are not open all day so they prefer written requests.

Aurora County

Circuit Court PO Box 366, 401 N Main St, Plankinton, SD 57368-0366; phone: 605-942-7165; fax: 605-942-7170; hours 8AM-N, 1-5PM (CST). *Felony, Misdemeanor, Civil, Eviction, Small Claims, Probate.*
Civil Records: Access: Fax, mail, in person. Both court and visitors may perform in person searches. Search fee: $15.00 per name. Court makes copy: $.20 per page. Required to search: name, years to search; also helpful: address. Civil cases indexed by defendant, plaintiff. Civil records on manual index since 1879, some computerized since 1988. Mail turnaround time 1 day.
Criminal Records: Access: Fax, mail, in person. Only the court performs in person searches; visitors may not. Search fee: $15.00 per name. Court makes copy: $.20 per page. Required to search: name, years to search, signed release; also helpful: address,

DOB, SSN. Criminal records are computerized since 7/89 on a statewide system. Mail turnaround time 1 day.
General Information: No juvenile, sealed, dismissed, adoption or mental health records released. Will fax documents for $1.00 per page; $5.00 minimum. Certification fee: $2.00 per page. Payee: Aurora County Clerk of Court. Business and personal checks accepted. Prepayment and SASE required.

Beadle County

Circuit Court PO Box 1358, Huron, SD 57350-1358; phone: 605-353-7165; criminal fax: 605-353-0118; same fax for civil/probate; hours 8AM-5PM (CST). *Felony, Misdemeanor, Civil, Eviction, Small Claims, Probate.*
www.sdjudicial.com/circuit_courts/index.asp?circuit=3
Note: Searching party must complete form requesting examination of file; clerk will redact any data of a confidential or personal nature.

Civil Records: Access: Mail, in person. Only the court performs in person searches; visitors may not. Search fee: $15.00 per name. Court makes copy: $.20 per page. Required to search: name, years to search. Civil cases indexed by defendant, plaintiff. Civil records on computer from 1990 (limited), cards from 1900. Not for public use. Mail turnaround time up to 2 weeks.
Criminal Records: Access: Mail, in person. Only the court performs in person searches; visitors may not. Search fee: $15.00 per name. Court makes copy: $.20 per page. Required to search: name, years to search, DOB; also helpful: SSN. Criminal records are computerized since 7/89 on a statewide system. Mail requests are forwarded to Hand County for processing. Mail turnaround time up to 2 weeks.
General Information: No juvenile, sealed, dismissed, adoption, or mental health records released. Will fax documents for $5.00 per transmission. Certification fee: $2.00 per cert. Payee:

Beadle County Clerk of Court. Personal checks accepted. Out of state checks not accepted. Prepayment required.

Bennett County

Circuit Court PO Box 281, Martin, SD 57551-0281; phone: 605-685-6969; fax: 605-685-1075; hours 8AM-4:30PM (MST). *Felony, Misdemeanor, Civil, Eviction, Small Claims, Probate.*
Note: Probate a separate index at this same address.
Civil Records: Access: Mail, in person. Only the court performs in person searches; visitors may not. Search fee: $15.00 per name. Court makes copy: $.20 per page. Required to search: name, years to search; also helpful: address. Civil cases indexed by defendant, plaintiff. Civil records on index from 1912. Mail turnaround time 48 hours.
Criminal Records: Access: Mail, in person. Only the court performs in person searches; visitors may not. Search fee: $15.00 per name. Court makes copy: $.20 per page. Required to search: name, years to search, DOB; also helpful: address. Request form available. Criminal records are computerized since 7/89 on a statewide system, searchable since 1912. All mail requests are forwarded to Potter County for processing. Mail turnaround time 48 hours.
General Information: No juvenile, sealed, dismissed, or mental health records released. Will only fax documents to ongoing requesters who have an account. Certification fee: $2.00 includes copy. Payee: Bennett County Clerk of Courts. Business checks accepted. Prepayment and SASE required.

Bon Homme County

Circuit Court PO Box 6, Tyndall, SD 57066; phone: 605-589-4215; fax: 605-589-4245; hours 8AM-4:30PM (CST). *Felony, Misdemeanor, Civil, Eviction, Small Claims, Probate.*
Civil Records: Access: Fax, mail, in person. Both court and visitors may perform in person searches. Search fee: $15.00 per name. Court makes copy: $.25 per page. Self serve copy fee: $.10 per page. Required to search: name, years to search; also helpful: address. Civil cases indexed by defendant, plaintiff. Civil records on alpha index books from 1877. Requests should be in writing. Mail turnaround time 3 days to 1 week.
Criminal Records: Access: Mail, in person. Only the court performs in person searches; visitors may not. Search fee: $15.00 per name. Court makes copy: $.25 per page. Self serve copy fee: $.10 per page. Required to search: name, years to search, DOB, signed release; also helpful: address, SSN. Criminal records are computerized since 7/89 on a statewide system. All mail requests are forwarded to Douglas County for processing. Mail turnaround time 3 days to 1 week.
General Information: No juvenile, sealed, dismissed, or mental health records released. Will fax documents $1.00 per page, $5.00 minimum, no fee if local or toll free. Certification fee: $2.00 per cert. Cert fee includes copies. Payee: Bon Homme County Clerk of Court. Personal checks accepted. Prepayment and SASE required.

Brookings County

Circuit Court 314 6th Ave, Brookings, SD 57006; phone: 605-688-4200; fax: 605-688-4952; hours 8AM-5PM (CST). *Felony, Misdemeanor, Civil, Eviction, Small Claims, Probate.*
www.sdjudicial.com/circuit_courts/index.asp?circuit=3
Civil Records: Access: Mail, in person. Only the court performs in person searches; visitors may not. Search fee: $15.00 per name. Court makes copy: $.20 per page; same fee for self serve. Required to search: name, years to search; also helpful: address. Civil cases indexed by defendant, plaintiff. Civil records on alpha index books from 1900s. Mail turnaround time 3 days.
Criminal Records: Access: Mail, in person. Only the court performs in person searches; visitors may

not. Search fee: $15.00 per name. Court makes copy: $.20 per page; same fee for self serve. Required to search: name, years to search, DOB; also helpful: address, SSN. Criminal records on computer since 7/1989 on a statewide system. All mail requests are forwarded to Hand County for processing. Mail turnaround time 3 days.
General Information: No juvenile, sealed, dismissed, or mental health records released. Fee to fax documents is $1.00 per page; $5.00 minimum. Certification fee: $2.00 per cert. Payee: Brookings County Clerk of Court. Only cashiers checks and money orders accepted. Prepayment and SASE required.

Brown County

Circuit Court 101 1st Ave SE, Aberdeen, SD 57401; phone: 605-626-2451; fax: 605-626-2491; hours 8AM-5PM (CST). *Felony, Misdemeanor, Civil, Eviction, Small Claims, Probate.*
Civil Records: Access: Mail, in person. Both court and visitors may perform in person searches. Search fee: $15.00 per name. Court makes copy: $.20 per page. Required to search: name, years to search; also helpful: address. Civil cases indexed by defendant, plaintiff. Civil records on registers from 1975 (misdemeanor), registers from 1900s (civil). Mail turnaround time 1-3 days.
Criminal Records: Access: Mail, in person. Only the court performs in person searches; visitors may not. Search fee: $15.00 per name. Court makes copy: $.20 per page. Required to search: name, years to search, DOB; also helpful: address, signed release, SSN. Criminal records on computer since 7/1989 on a statewide system. All mail requests are forwarded to Edmunds County for processing. Mail turnaround time 1-3 days.
General Information: No juvenile, sealed, dismissed, or mental health records released. Will fax documents to local or toll free line. Certification fee: $2.00 per cert. Payee: Brown County Clerk of Court. Personal checks accepted. Prepayment and SASE required.

Brule County

Circuit Court 300 S Courtland, #111, Chamberlain, SD 57325-1599; phone: 605-734-4580; fax: 605-734-4582; hours 8AM-N, 1-5PM (CST). *Felony, Misdemeanor, Civil, Eviction, Small Claims, Probate.*
Civil Records: Access: Fax, mail, in person. Both court and visitors may perform in person searches. Search fee: $15.00 per name. Court makes copy: $.20 per page. Required to search: name, years to search; also helpful: address. Civil cases indexed by defendant, plaintiff. Civil records on index books or docket books from 1875. Mail turnaround time 3-5 days.
Criminal Records: Access: Fax, mail, in person. Only the court performs in person searches; visitors may not. Search fee: $15.00 per name. Court makes copy: $.20 per page. Required to search: name, years to search, DOB; also helpful: address, SSN. Criminal records on computer since 7/1989 on a statewide system. All mail requests are forwarded to Miner County for processing. Fax requests accepted for commercial accounts only and are forwarded as well. Mail turnaround time 3-5 days.
General Information: No juvenile, sealed, dismissed, or mental health records released. Will fax documents $1.00 per page, $5.00 minimum. Certification fee: $2.00 per doc. Payee: Brule County Clerk of Court. Personal checks accepted. Prepayment and SASE required.

Buffalo County

Circuit Court PO Box 148, Gann Valley, SD 57341; phone: 605-293-3234; fax: 605-293-3240; hours 9AM-N (CST). *Felony, Misdemeanor, Civil, Eviction, Small Claims, Probate.*
Note: Only records prior to 2000 are at Gann Valley. Records after 2000 are at the Brule Circuit Court

Clerk, 300 S Courtland, #111, Chamberlin, SD 57325, 605-734-4586. Records at 605-734-4580

Butte County

Circuit Court PO Box 237, Belle Fourche, SD 57717-0237; phone: 605-892-2516; fax: 605-892-2836; hours 8AM-N, 1-5PM (MST). *Felony, Misdemeanor, Civil, Eviction, Small Claims, Probate.*
Civil Records: Access: Mail, in person. Only the court performs in person searches; visitors may not. Search fee: $15.00 per name. Court makes copy: $.20 per page. Required to search: name, years to search; also helpful: DOB, address. Civil cases indexed by defendant, plaintiff. All data on alpha index from 1900s. Mail turnaround time varies.
Criminal Records: Access: Mail, in person. Only the court performs in person searches; visitors may not. Search fee: $15.00 per name. Court makes copy: $.20 per page. Required to search: name, years to search; also helpful: DOB, address. Criminal records on computer since 7/89 on a statewide system. Mail turnaround time varies.
General Information: No juvenile, sealed, dismissed, or mental health records released. Will fax documents to local or toll free line. Certification fee: $2.00 per cert. Payee: Butte County Clerk of Court. Personal checks accepted. Prepayment and SASE required.

Campbell County

Circuit Court PO Box 146, Mound City, SD 57646; phone: 605-955-3536; fax: 605-955-5303; hours 8AM-N T-W-F (CST). *Felony, Misdemeanor, Civil, Small Claims, Probate.*
Civil Records: Access: Mail, in person. Both court and visitors may perform in person searches. Search fee: $15.00 per name. Court makes copy: $.20 per page. Required to search: name, years to search; also helpful: address. Civil cases indexed by defendant, plaintiff. All data on alpha index from 1800s. Mail turnaround time varies.
Criminal Records: Access: Mail, in person. Only the court performs in person searches; visitors may not. Search fee: $15.00 per name. Court makes copy: $.20 per page. Required to search: name, years to search, DOB; also helpful: address, SSN. Although records are computerized at the state level, this office has records and indices on paper. All mail requests are forwarded to Edmunds County for processing. Mail turnaround time varies.
General Information: No juvenile, sealed, dismissed, or mental health records released. Will fax documents to local or toll free line. Certification fee: $2.00 per cert. Payee: Campbell County Clerk of Court. Only cashiers checks and money orders accepted. Prepayment and SASE required.

Charles Mix County

Circuit Court PO Box 640, Main St, Lake Andes, SD 57356; phone: 605-487-7511; fax: 605-487-7547; hours 8AM-4:30PM (CST). *Felony, Misdemeanor, Civil, Eviction, Small Claims, Probate.*
Civil Records: Access: Mail, in person. Both court and visitors may perform in person searches. Search fee: $15.00 per name. Court makes copy: $.20 per page. Required to search: name, years to search; also helpful: address. Civil cases indexed by defendant, plaintiff. Civil records on alpha index books from 1917. Mail turnaround time 2-5 days.
Criminal Records: Access: Mail, in person. Only the court performs in person searches; visitors may not. Search fee: $15.00 per name. Court makes copy: $.20 per page. Required to search: name, years to search, DOB; also helpful: address, SSN. Criminal records on computer since 7/89 on a statewide system located in Douglas County. All mail and fax requests are forwarded to Douglas County for processing. Mail turnaround time 2-5 days.
General Information: No juvenile, sealed, dismissed, or mental health records released. Will fax

documents $1.00 per page, $5.00 minimum. Certification fee: $2.00 per doc. Payee: Charles Mix County Clerk of Court. Personal check accepted with SSN or DL#. Prepayment and SASE required.

Clark County

Circuit Court PO Box 294, Clark, SD 57225; phone: 605-532-5851; hours 8AM-N, 1-5PM (CST). *Felony, Misdemeanor, Civil, Eviction, Small Claims, Probate.*
www.sdjudicial.com/circuit_courts/index.asp?circuit=3

Civil Records: Access: Mail, in person. Only the court performs in person searches; visitors may not. Search fee: $15.00 per name. Court makes copy: $.20 per page. Required to search: name, years to search; also helpful: address. Civil cases indexed by defendant, plaintiff. Civil records on alpha index cards from 1969. Mail turnaround time 1-4 days.

Criminal Records: Access: Mail, in person. Only the court performs in person searches; visitors may not. Search fee: $15.00 per name. Court makes copy: $.20 per page. Required to search: name, years to search, DOB; also helpful: address, SSN. Criminal records on computer since 1986 on a statewide system. All mail requests are forwarded to Hand County for processing, PO Box 122, Miller, SD 57362-0122. Mail turnaround time 1-4 days.

General Information: No juvenile, sealed, dismissed, or mental health records released. Certification fee: $2.00 per cert. Payee: Clark County Clerk of Court. Personal checks accepted. Prepayment and SASE required.

Clay County

Circuit Court PO Box 377, Vermillion, SD 57069; phone: 605-677-6755/6; fax: 605-677-8885; hours 8AM-5PM (CST). *Felony, Misdemeanor, Civil, Eviction, Small Claims, Probate.*

Civil Records: Access: Mail, in person. Both court and visitors may perform in person searches. Search fee: $15.00 per name. Court makes copy: $.20 per page; same fee for self serve. Required to search: name, years to search; also helpful: address. Civil cases indexed by defendant, plaintiff. Civil records on computer from 1993, in books to 1920, and archived from 1800s. Mail turnaround time 2-4 days.

Criminal Records: Access: Mail, in person. Only the court performs in person searches; visitors may not. Search fee: $15.00 per name. Court makes copy: $.20 per page; same fee for self serve. Required to search: name, years to search, DOB; also helpful: address, SSN. Criminal records on computer from 1989, in books to 1920, and archived from 1800s. All mail requests are forwarded to Aurora or Hanson County for processing. Mail turnaround time 2-4 days.

General Information: No juvenile, sealed, dismissed, or mental health records released. Will fax documents to local or toll free line. Certification fee: $2.00 per doc. Payee: Clay County Clerk of Court. Personal checks accepted. Prepayment and SASE required.

Codington County

Circuit Court Clerk of Court, PO Box 1054, Watertown, SD 57201; phone: 605-882-5095; hours 8AM-5PM (CST). *Felony, Misdemeanor, Civil, Eviction, Small Claims, Probate.*
www.sdjudicial.com/circuit_courts/index.asp?circuit=3

Civil Records: Access: Mail, in person. Only the court performs in person searches; visitors may not. Search fee: $15.00 per name (includes copies, unless copying entire file). Court makes copy: $.20 per page. Required to search: name, DOB, years to search. Civil cases indexed by defendant, plaintiff. Civil records on computer from 1991 and alpha index cards back to 1890. Mail turnaround time 2 days.

Criminal Records: Access: Mail, in person. Only the court performs in person searches; visitors may not. Search fee: $15.00 per name (includes copies, unless copying entire file). Court makes copy: $.20 per page. Required to search: name, years to search, DOB. Criminal records on computer since 7/89 on a statewide system. Mail turnaround time 2 days.

General Information: No juvenile, sealed, or mental health records released. Fax fee of $10.00 in and $5.00 out. Certification fee: $2.00 per cert. Payee: Codington County Clerk of Court. Business checks accepted. Prepayment and SASE required.

Corson County

Circuit Court PO Box 175, McIntosh, SD 57641; phone: 605-273-4201; criminal fax: 605-273-4597; same fax for civil/probate; hours 9:30AM-2:30PM (MST). *Felony, Misdemeanor, Civil, Eviction, Small Claims, Probate.*
Note: Probate is a separate index at this same address.

Civil Records: Access: Mail, fax. Only the court performs in person searches; visitors may not. Search fee: $15.00 per name. Court makes copy: $.20 per page; same fee for self serve. Required to search: name, years to search; also helpful: address. Civil cases indexed by defendant, plaintiff. All data on alpha index from 1940s. Mail turnaround time 1 day.

Criminal Records: Access: Mail, in person. Only the court performs in person searches; visitors may not. Search fee: $15.00 per name. Court makes copy: $.20 per page; same fee for self serve. Required to search: name, years to search, DOB; also helpful: address, SSN. Criminal records on computer back to 1989. All phone requests are forwarded to Lawrence County for processing. Mail turnaround time 1 day.

General Information: No juvenile, sealed, dismissed, adoption or mental health records released. Will fax documents if you have account with UJS. Set up account with Court Admin Office in Pierre, call 605-773-4873. Certification fee: $2.00 per cert. Payee: Corson County Clerk of Court. Personal checks accepted. Prepayment required.

Custer County

Circuit Court 420 Mt Rushmore Rd, Custer, SD 57730; phone: 605-673-4816; fax: 605-673-3416; hours 8AM-5PM (MST). *Felony, Misdemeanor, Civil, Eviction, Small Claims, Probate.*

Civil Records: Access: Mail, in person. Only the court performs in person searches; visitors may not. Search fee: $15.00 per name. Court makes copy: $.25 per page. Required to search: name, years to search, SSN; also helpful: address. Civil cases indexed by defendant, plaintiff. Probate on microfiche from 1915, all other data on docket books and index cards from 1960s. Mail turnaround time 2 days.

Criminal Records: Access: Mail, in person. Only the court performs in person searches; visitors may not. Search fee: $15.00 per name. Court makes copy: $.25 per page. Required to search: name, years to search, DOB, SSN, signed release; also helpful: address. Criminal records on computer since 7/89 on a statewide system. Criminal searches are performed through the Search Center at Harding County Clerk, PO Box 534, Buffalo, SD 57720. Mail turnaround time 2 days.

General Information: No juvenile, sealed, dismissed, or mental health records released. Certification fee: $2.00 per doc. Payee: Custer County Clerk of Court. Personal checks accepted. Prepayment and SASE required.

Davison County

Circuit Court PO Box 927, 200 E Fourth Ave, Mitchell, SD 57301; phone: 605-995-8105; hours 8AM-5PM (CST). *Felony, Misdemeanor, Civil, Eviction, Small Claims, Probate.*

Civil Records: Access: Mail, in person. Both court and visitors may perform in person searches. Search fee: $15.00 per name. Court makes copy: $.20 per page. Required to search: name, years to search; also helpful: address. Civil cases indexed by defendant. All data on alpha index from 1900s. Mail turnaround time 1 week.

Criminal Records: Access: Mail, in person. Only the court performs in person searches; visitors may not. Search fee: $15.00 per name. Court makes copy: $.20 per page. Required to search: name, years to search, DOB; also helpful: address, SSN. Criminal records are computerized since 7/89 on a statewide system. All mail requests are forwarded to Miner County for processing. Mail turnaround time 1 week.

General Information: No juvenile, sealed, dismissed, or mental health records released. Certification fee: $2.00 per doc. Payee: Davison County Clerk of Court. Personal checks accepted. Out of state checks not accepted. Prepayment and SASE required.

Day County

Circuit Court 711 W 1st St, Webster, SD 57274; phone: 605-345-3771; fax: 605-345-3818; hours 8AM-5PM (CST). *Felony, Misdemeanor, Civil, Small Claims, Probate.*
Note: Mail requests managed by the Edmonds County Clerk of Courts

Civil Records: Access: In person only. Only the court performs in person searches; visitors may not. Search fee: $15.00 per name. Court makes copy: $.20 per page. Required to search: name, years to search; also helpful: address. Civil cases indexed by defendant. Civil records on docket books from 1800s. Mail turnaround time 1 week.

Criminal Records: Access: In person only. Only the court performs in person searches; visitors may not. Search fee: $15.00 per name. Court makes copy: $.20 per page. Required to search: name, years to search, DOB; also helpful: address, SSN. Criminal records on computer since 1982 on a statewide system. All mail requests are forwarded to Edmunds County for processing.

General Information: No juvenile, sealed, dismissed, or mental health records released. Certification fee: $2.00 per doc. Payee: Day County Clerk of Court. Prepayment required.

Deuel County

Circuit Court PO Box 308, Clear Lake, SD 57226; phone: 605-874-2120; hours 8AM-5PM (CST). *Felony, Misdemeanor, Civil, Eviction, Small Claims, Probate.*
www.sdjudicial.com/circuit_courts/index.asp?circuit=3

Civil Records: Access: Mail, in person. Only the court performs in person searches; visitors may not. Search fee: $15.00 per name. Court makes copy: $.20 per page; same fee for self serve. Required to search: name, years to search; also helpful: address. Civil cases indexed by defendant, plaintiff. Civil records on docket books. Mail turnaround time 1-2 days.

Criminal Records: Access: Mail, in person. Only the court performs in person searches; visitors may not. Search fee: $15.00 per name. Court makes copy: $.20 per page; same fee for self serve. Required to search: name, years to search, DOB; also helpful-signed release. Criminal records on computer since 7/89 on a statewide system. Best to forward criminal record searches to the Criminal Search Center in Hand County. Mail turnaround time 1-2 days.

General Information: No juvenile, sealed, dismissed, or mental health records released. Will not fax documents. Certification fee: $2.00 per doc. Payee: Deuel County Clerk of Court. Personal checks accepted. Prepayment and SASE required.

Dewey County

Circuit Court PO Box 96, C St, County Courthouse, Timber Lake, SD 57656; phone: 605-865-3566; hours 9:30AM-N, 1-2:30PM (MST). *Felony, Misdemeanor, Civil, Eviction, Small Claims, Probate.*

Civil Records: Access: Mail, in person. Both court and visitors may perform in person searches. Search fee: $15.00 per name. Court makes copy: $.25 per page. Required to search: name, years to search; also helpful: address. Civil cases indexed by defendant, plaintiff. All data on alpha index and docket books from 1900s; computerized back to 1999. Mail turnaround time 2 days to 1 week.

Criminal Records: Access: Mail, in person. Only the court performs in person searches; visitors may not. Search fee: $15.00 per name. Court makes copy: $.25 per page. Required to search: name, years to search, DOB; also helpful: address, SSN, signed release. Criminal records data on alpha index and docket books from 1900s; computerized back to 1999. All mail requests are forwarded to Lawrence County for processing. Mail turnaround time 2 days to 1 week.

General Information: No juvenile, adoption, sealed, dismissed, or mental health records released. Fee to fax documents is $1.00 per page; $5.00 per document. Certification fee: $2.00 per doc. Payee: Dewey County Clerk of Court. Personal checks accepted. Prepayment and SASE required.

Douglas County

Circuit Court Clerk of Court, PO Box 36, Armour, SD 57313; phone: 605-724-2585; hours 8:30AM-1:30PM M-Th (CST). *Felony, Misdemeanor, Civil, Eviction, Small Claims, Probate.*

Civil Records: Access: Mail, in person. Both court and visitors may perform in person searches. Search fee: $15.00 per name. Court makes copy: $.25 per page; same fee for self serve. Required to search: name, years to search; also helpful: address. Civil cases indexed by defendant. Civil records on docket books from late 1800s. Mail turnaround time 1 week.

Criminal Records: Access: Fax, mail, in person. Only the court performs in person searches; visitors may not. Search fee: $15.00 per name. Court makes copy: $.25 per page; same fee for self serve. Required to search: name, years to search, DOB, signed release; also helpful: address, SSN. Criminal records are computerized since 7/89 on a statewide system. Mail turnaround time 1 week.

General Information: No juvenile, sealed, or mental health records released. Will fax documents to local or toll free line. Certification fee: $2.00 per cert. Payee: Douglas County Clerk of Court. Personal checks accepted. Prepayment and SASE required.

Edmunds County

Circuit Court PO Box 384, Ipswich, SD 57451; phone: 605-426-6671; criminal fax: 605-426-6323; same fax for civil/probate; hours 8AM-N, 1-5PM (CST). *Felony, Misdemeanor, Civil, Eviction, Small Claims, Probate.*

Civil Records: Access: Fax, mail, in person. Both court and visitors may perform in person searches. Search fee: $15.00 per name. Court makes copy: $.25 per page; same fee for self serve. Required to search: name, years to search; also helpful: address. Civil cases indexed by defendant, plaintiff. Civil records on docket books from late 1800s. Mail turnaround time 1 day to 1 week.

Criminal Records: Access: Fax, mail, in person. Only the court performs in person searches; visitors may not. Search fee: $15.00 per name. Court makes copy: $.25 per page; same fee for self serve. Required to search: name, years to search, DOB; also helpful: DR#, signed release. Criminal records on computer since 7/89; prior records on docket books. Fax requests are for commercial accounts only.

Results are statewide. Mail turnaround time 24-48 hours.

General Information: No juvenile, sealed or mental health records released. Will fax documents to local or toll free line. Certification fee: $2.00 per cert. Payee: Edmunds County Clerk of Court. Personal checks accepted. Prepayment and SASE required.

Fall River County

Circuit Court 906 N River St, Hot Springs, SD 57747; phone: 605-745-5131; hours 8AM-5PM (MST). *Felony, Misdemeanor, Civil, Eviction, Small Claims, Probate.*

Note: Also handles cases for Shannon County. Specify which county in any search request.

Civil Records: Access: Mail, in person. Only the court performs in person searches; visitors may not. Search fee: $15.00 per name. Court makes copy: $.25 per page. Required to search: name, years to search; also helpful: DOB. Civil cases indexed by defendant, plaintiff. Civil records on computer from 1992, files from 1889 archived off site. Mail turnaround time 1-2 weeks.

Criminal Records: Access: Mail, in person. Only the court performs in person searches; visitors may not. Search fee: $15.00 per name. Court makes copy: $.25 per page. Required to search: name, years to search, DOB; also helpful: address, SSN. Criminal records on computer since 7/89 on a statewide system. Mail turnaround time 1 week.

General Information: No juvenile, sealed, adoption, or mental health records released. Will fax documents to local or toll free line. Certification fee: $2.00 per doc. Payee: Clerk of Court. Personal checks accepted. Prepayment and SASE required.

Faulk County

Circuit Court PO Box 357, Faulkton, SD 57438; phone: 605-598-6223; fax: 605-598-6252; hours 1:00PM-5:00PM (CST). *Felony, Misdemeanor, Civil, Eviction, Small Claims, Probate.*

Civil Records: Access: Mail, in person. Both court and visitors may perform in person searches. Search fee: $15.00 per name. Court makes copy: $.20 per page. Required to search: name, years to search; also helpful: address. Civil cases indexed by defendant. Civil records on docket books from 1900s. Mail turnaround time 1-2 days.

Criminal Records: Access: Mail, in person. Only the court performs in person searches; visitors may not. Search fee: $15.00 per name. Court makes copy: $.20 per page. Required to search: name, years to search, DOB; also helpful: address, SSN. Criminal records are computerized since 7/89 on a statewide system. Mail turnaround time 1-2 days.

General Information: No juvenile, sealed, dismissed, adoption, or mental health records released. Will fax documents for $1.00 per page with $5.00 minimum. Certification fee: $2.00 per cert. Payee: Faulk County Clerk of Court. Personal checks accepted. Prepayment and SASE required.

Grant County

Circuit Court PO Box 509, Milbank, SD 57252; phone: 605-432-5482; hours 8AM-N, 1-5PM (CST). *Felony, Misdemeanor, Civil, Eviction, Small Claims, Probate.*

www.sdjudicial.com/circuit_courts/index.asp?circuit=3

Civil Records: Access: Mail, in person. Only the court performs in person searches; visitors may not. Search fee: $15.00 per name. Court makes copy: $.25 per page. Required to search: name, years to search; also helpful: address. Civil cases indexed by defendant, plaintiff. Civil records on computer from 1995, docket books from 1800s. Mail turnaround time 1 week by mail; immediate by phone if on computer.

Criminal Records: Access: Mail, in person. Only the court performs in person searches; visitors may not. Search fee: $15.00 per name. Court makes copy: $.25 per page. Required to search: name, years to

search, DOB; also helpful: address, SSN. Criminal records on computer since 7/89 on a statewide system. All mail requests are forwarded to and processed by Hand County. Mail turnaround time 1 week by mail; immediate by phone if on computer.

General Information: No juvenile, sealed, dismissed, or mental health records released. Certification fee: $2.00 per doc. Payee: Grant County Clerk of Court. Prepayment and SASE required.

Gregory County

Circuit Court PO Box 430, Burke, SD 57523; phone: 605-775-2665; hours 8AM-N, 1-5PM (CST). *Felony, Misdemeanor, Civil, Eviction, Small Claims, Probate.*

Note: Probate is a separate index at this same address.

Civil Records: Access: Mail, in person. Only the court performs in person searches; visitors may not. Search fee: $15.00 per name. Court makes copy: $.20 per page. Required to search: name, years to search; also helpful: address. Civil cases indexed by defendant, plaintiff. Civil records on docket books from late 1800s, computerized since 1999. Mail turnaround time 1 week.

Criminal Records: Access: Mail, in person. Only the court performs in person searches; visitors may not. Search fee: $15.00 per name. Court makes copy: $.20 per page. Required to search: name, years to search, DOB, signed release; also helpful: address, SSN. Criminal records on computer back to 7/89 on a statewide system. All mail requests are forwarded to Potter County for processing. Mail turnaround time 1 week.

General Information: No juvenile, sealed, dismissed, or mental health records released. Will fax documents for a fee. Certification fee: $2.00. Payee: Gregory County Clerk of Court. Only cashiers checks and money orders accepted. Prepayment and SASE required.

Haakon County

Circuit Court PO Box 70, Philip, SD 57567; phone: 605-859-2627; criminal fax: 605-859-2257; same fax for civil/probate; hours 8AM-N (MST). *Felony, Misdemeanor, Civil, Eviction, Small Claims, Probate.*

Civil Records: Access: Mail, in person. Only the court performs in person searches; visitors may not. Search fee: $15.00 per name. Court makes copy: $.20 per page. Required to search: name, years to search; also helpful: address. Civil cases indexed by defendant, plaintiff. Civil records on register from 1915. Mail turnaround time 1 day.

Criminal Records: Access: Mail, in person. Only the court performs in person searches; visitors may not. Search fee: $15.00 per name. Court makes copy: $.20 per page. Required to search: name, years to search, DOB; also helpful: address, SSN. Criminal records are computerized since 7/89 on a statewide system. All mail requests are forwarded to Potter County for processing. Mail turnaround time 1 day.

General Information: No juvenile, sealed, dismissed, or mental health records released. Fee to fax documents is $1.00 per page; $5.00 minimum. Certification fee: $2.00 includes copy fee. Payee: Haakon County Clerk of Court. Local checks accepted only. Prepayment and SASE required.

Hamlin County

Circuit Court PO Box 256, Hayti, SD 57241; phone: 605-783-3751; criminal fax: 605-783-2157; same fax for civil/probate; hours 8:30AM-N, 12:30-4:30PM (CST). *Felony, Misdemeanor, Civil, Eviction, Small Claims, Probate.*

www.sdjudicial.com/circuit_courts/index.asp?circuit=3

Civil Records: Access: Mail, in person. Only the court performs in person searches; visitors may not. Search fee: $15.00 per name. Court makes copy: $.15 per page; same fee for self serve. Required to search: name, years to search; also helpful: address.

Civil cases indexed by defendant, plaintiff. Civil records on docket books from 1800s. Mail turnaround time 1 day.

Criminal Records: Access: Mail, in person. Only the court performs in person searches; visitors may not. Search fee: $15.00 per name. Court makes copy: $.15 per page; same fee for self search. Required to search: name, years to search, DOB; also helpful: address, SSN. Criminal records on computer since 7/89 on a statewide system. Mail turnaround 1 day.

General Information: No juvenile, sealed, dismissed, or mental health records released. Will fax documents for $5.00. Certification fee: $2.00 per cert. Payee: Hamlin County Clerk of Court. Personal checks accepted. Prepayment and SASE required.

Hand County

Circuit Court PO Box 122, Miller, SD 57362; phone: 605-853-3337; criminal fax: 605-853-3779; same fax for civil/probate; hours 8AM-5PM (CST). *Felony, Misdemeanor, Civil, Small Claims, Probate.* www.sdjudicial.com/circuit_courts/index.asp?circuit=3

Civil Records: Access: Mail, in person. Only the court performs in person searches; visitors may not. Search fee: $15.00 per name. Court makes copy: $.20 per page. Required to search: name, years to search; also helpful: address. Civil cases indexed by defendant. All data on alpha index and docket books from late 1800s. Mail turnaround time 1 day.

Criminal Records: Access: Fax, mail, in person. Only the court performs in person searches; visitors may not. Search fee: $15.00 per name. Court makes copy: $.20 per page. Required to search: name, years to search, DOB; also helpful: address, SSN. Criminal records on computer since 7/89 on a statewide system. Fax requesting for commercial accounts only. Mail turnaround time 1 day.

General Information: No juvenile, sealed, dismissed, or mental health records released. Will fax documents; fee is $5.00 per doc if non-toll free number; no charge if to toll-free number. Certification fee: $2.00. Payee: Hand County Clerk of Court. Business checks accepted. Prepayment and SASE required.

Hanson County

Circuit Court PO Box 127, Alexandria, SD 57311; phone: 605-239-4446; criminal fax: 605-239-9446; same fax for civil/probate; hours 8AM-5PM; Closed from 12:00-1:00 (CST). *Felony, Misdemeanor, Civil, Small Claims, Probate.*

Civil Records: Access: Fax, mail, in person. Only the court performs in person searches; visitors may not. Search fee: $15.00 per name. Court makes copy: $.20 per page; same fee for self serve. Required to search: name, years to search; also helpful: address. Civil cases indexed by defendant, plaintiff. Civil records on docket books from 1902; on computer back to 2000. Mail turnaround time varies.

Criminal Records: Access: Mail, in person. Only the court performs in person searches; visitors may not. Search fee: $15.00 per name. Court makes copy: $.20 per page; same fee for self serve. Required to search: name, years to search, DOB; also helpful: address, SSN. Criminal records computerized since 7/89 on a statewide system. Mail turnaround time varies.

General Information: No juvenile, sealed, dismissed, adoption or mental health records released. Will fax documents for $5.00 per document. $1.00 per page after 5 pages. Certification fee: $2.00 includes copy fee. Payee: Hanson County Clerk of Court. Personal checks accepted. Prepayment and SASE required.

Harding County

Circuit Court PO Box 534, Buffalo, SD 57720; phone: 605-375-3351; fax: 605-375-3432; hours 9:30AM-N, 1-2:30PM (MST). *Felony, Misdemeanor, Civil, Eviction, Small Claims, Probate.*

Note: For eviction information the court says to contact Harding County Sheriff, PO Box 293, Buffalo SD 57720.

Civil Records: Access: Mail, in person. Both court and visitors may perform in person searches. Search fee: $15.00 per name. Court makes copy: $.20 per page. Required to search: name, years to search, DOB; also helpful: address. Civil cases indexed by defendant. Civil records in archives from 1909 to 1920, index books from 1920. Mail turnaround time 1 week.

Criminal Records: Access: Fax, mail, in person. Only the court performs in person searches; visitors may not. Search fee: $15.00 per name. Court makes copy: $.20 per page. Required to search: name, years to search, DOB; also helpful: address, SSN. Criminal records are computerized since 7/89 on a statewide system. Fax requests for commercial accounts only. Mail turnaround time 1 week.

General Information: No juvenile, sealed, dismissed, or mental health records released. Will fax documents $1.00 per page, $5.00 minimum, no fee if local or toll free. Certification fee: $2.00. Payee: Harding County Clerk of Court. Personal checks accepted. Prepayment and SASE required.

Hughes County

Circuit Court 104 E Capital, Pierre, SD 57501; phone: 605-773-3713; hours 8AM-5PM (CST). *Felony, Misdemeanor, Civil, Eviction, Small Claims, Probate.*

Civil Records: Access: Mail, in person. Only the court performs in person searches; visitors may not. Search fee: $15.00 per name. Court makes copy: $.20 per page. Required to search: name, years to search; also helpful: address. Civil cases indexed by defendant, plaintiff. Civil records on microfiche from 1948 to 1973. From 1974 forward have hard copy file, starting 1991 index and docketing on computer. Mail turnaround time approx. 2 days.

Criminal Records: Access: Mail, in person. Only the court performs in person searches; visitors may not. Search fee: $15.00 per name. Court makes copy: $.20 per page. Required to search: name, years to search, DOB; also helpful: address. Criminal records on computer since 1988 on a statewide system. All mail requests are forwarded to Potter County for processing. Mail turnaround time approx. 2 days.

General Information: No juvenile, adoption, any record sealed by the Court or mental health records released. Certification fee: $2.00 per cert. Payee: Hughes County Clerk of Court. Personal checks accepted. Prepayment and SASE required.

Hutchinson County

Circuit Court 140 Euclid, Rm 36, Olivet, SD 57052-2103; phone: 605-387-4215; fax: 605-387-4208; hours 8AM-N, 1-5PM (CST). *Felony, Misdemeanor, Civil, Eviction, Small Claims, Probate.*

Civil Records: Access: Fax, mail, in person. Only the court performs in person searches; visitors may not. Search fee: $15.00 per name. Court makes copy: $.10 per page. Required to search: name, years to search; also helpful: address. Civil cases indexed by defendant, plaintiff. Civil records on docket books and index cards from 1800s, on computer since 1994. Mail turnaround time 1 day.

Criminal Records: Access: Fax, mail, in person. Only the court performs in person searches; visitors may not. Search fee: $15.00 per name. Court makes copy: $.10 per page. Required to search: name, years to search, DOB; also helpful: address, SSN. Older records on docket books and index cards, records since 7/89 are computerized on a statewide system. All fax and mail requests are forwarded to Douglas County for processing. Mail turnaround time 1 day.

General Information: No juvenile, sealed, dismissed, adoption or mental health records released. Will fax documents $5.00 per doc; no fee to toll free number; must be a commercial account. Certification

fee: $2.00 per cert. Payee: Hutchinson County Clerk of Court. Business checks accepted. Prepayment and SASE required.

Hyde County

Circuit Court PO Box 306, Highmore, SD 57345; phone: 605-852-2512; criminal fax: 605-852-2767; same fax for civil/probate; hours 8AM-12PM (CST). *Felony, Misdemeanor, Civil, Eviction, Small Claims, Probate.*

Civil Records: Access: Fax, mail, in person. Only the court performs in person searches; visitors may not. Search fee: $15.00 per name. Court makes copy: $.25 per page; same fee for self serve. Required to search: name, years to search; also helpful: address. Civil cases indexed by defendant, plaintiff. Civil records on docket books from 1920s, computerized from 2000. Mail turnaround time 1-3 days.

Criminal Records: Access: Fax, mail, in person. Only the court performs in person searches; visitors may not. Search fee: $15.00 per name. Court makes copy: $.25 per page; same fee for self serve. Required to search: name, years to search, DOB, signed release; also helpful: address, SSN. Criminal records are computerized since 7/89 on a statewide system. All fax and mail requests are forwarded to Potter County for processing. Mail turnaround time 1-3 days.

General Information: No juvenile, sealed, dismissed, or mental health records released. Will fax documents $5.00 per doc; no fee to local or toll free number. Certification fee: $2.00 per cert includes copies. Payee: Hyde County Clerk of Courts. Personal checks accepted. Prepayment and SASE required.

Jackson County

Circuit Court PO Box 128, Kadoka, SD 57543; phone: 605-837-2122; hours 8AM-N, 1-5PM (MST). *Felony, Misdemeanor, Civil, Eviction, Small Claims, Probate.*

Civil Records: Access: Mail, in person. Only the court performs in person searches; visitors may not. Search fee: $15.00 per name. Court makes copy: $.20 per page; same fee for self serve. Required to search: name, years to search; also helpful: address. Civil cases indexed by defendant. Civil records on "Register of Action" from 1915; on computer back to 1993. Mail turnaround time 1-2 days.

Criminal Records: Access: Mail, in person. Only the court performs in person searches; visitors may not. Search fee: $15.00 per name. Court makes copy: $.20 per page; same fee for self serve. Required to search: name, years to search, DOB; also helpful: address, SSN. Criminal records on computer back to 7/89 on a statewide system; other records go back to 1920. All mail requests are forwarded to Potter County for processing. Mail turnaround time 1-2 days.

General Information: No juvenile, sealed, dismissed, or mental health records released. Will fax documents to local or toll free line. Certification fee: $2.00 per cert. Payee: Jackson County Clerk of Court. Personal checks accepted. Prepayment and SASE required.

Jerauld County

Circuit Court PO Box 435, 203 S Wallace St, Wessington Springs, SD 57382; phone: 605-539-1202; fax: 605-539-1203; hours 8AM-5PM (CST). *Felony, Misdemeanor, Civil, Eviction, Small Claims, Probate.* www.sdjudicial.com/circuit_courts/index.asp?circuit=3

Civil Records: Access: Mail, in person. Only the court performs in person searches; visitors may not. Search fee: $15.00 per name. Court makes copy: $.25 per page. Required to search: name, years to search; also helpful: address. Civil cases indexed by defendant. Civil records on docket books from 1900s. Mail turnaround time 2 days.

Criminal Records: Access: Mail, in person. Only the court performs in person searches; visitors may not. Search fee: $15.00 per name. Court makes copy:

$.25 per page. Required to search: name, years to search, DOB; also helpful: address, SSN. Criminal records are computerized since 1989 on a statewide system. Fax requesting for commercial accounts only. Mail turnaround time 2 days.

General Information: No juvenile, sealed, dismissed, or mental health records released. Will fax documents $5.00 per page. Certification fee: $2.00 per doc. Payee: Jerauld County Clerk of Court. Personal checks accepted. Prepayment and SASE required.

Jones County

Circuit Court PO Box 448, 310 Main St, Murdo, SD 57559; phone: 605-669-2361; fax: 605-669-2641; hours 8AM-N, 1-5PM (CST). *Felony, Misdemeanor, Civil, Eviction, Small Claims, Probate.*

Note: Criminal cases and records at Potter County.

Civil Records: Access: Mail, in person. Only the court performs in person searches; visitors may not. Search fee: $15.00 per name. Court makes copy: $.20 per page. Required to search: name, years to search; also helpful: address. Civil cases indexed by defendant, plaintiff. Civil records on docket books from 1900s. Mail turnaround time 3 days to 1 week.

Criminal Records: Access: Mail, in person. Only the court performs in person searches; visitors may not. Search fee: $15.00 per name. Court makes copy: $.20 per page. Required to search: name, years to search, DOB, SSN; also helpful: address. Criminal records are computerized since 7/89 on a statewide system. Records on books go back to 1917. All requests are forwarded to Potter County for processing. Mail turnaround time 3 days to 1 week.

General Information: No juvenile, sealed, dismissed, or mental health records released. Fee to fax back is $1.00 per page; minimum $5.00. Certification fee: $2.00 per doc. Payee: Jones County Clerk of Court (civil cases); Potter County Clerk of Court (criminal cases). Business checks accepted. Prepayment and SASE required.

Kingsbury County

Circuit Court PO Box 176, De Smet, SD 57231-0176; phone: 605-854-3811; criminal fax: 605-854-9080; same fax for civil/probate; hours 8AM-N, 1-5PM (CST). *Felony, Misdemeanor, Civil, Eviction, Small Claims, Probate.*
www.sdjudicial.com/circuit_courts/index.asp?circuit=3

Note: Probate is a separate index at this same address.

Civil Records: Access: Mail, in person. Both court and visitors may perform in person searches. Search fee: $15.00 per name. Court makes copy: $.20 per page. Required to search: name, years to search; also helpful: address plus DOB. Civil cases indexed by defendant, plaintiff. Civil records on computer printed index from 1978 and bound books from 1890. Mail turnaround time same day.

Criminal Records: Access: Mail, in person. Only the court performs in person searches; visitors may not. Search fee: $15.00 per name. Court makes copy: $.20 per page. Required to search: name, years to search, DOB; also helpful: address, SSN. Criminal records on computer since 7/89 on a statewide system. All mail requests are forwarded to Hand County for processing. Mail turnaround time same day.

General Information: No juvenile, sealed, dismissed, adoption or mental health records released. Will fax documents for $1.00 per page, $5.00 minimum. Certification fee: $2.00 per cert includes copy fee. Payee: Kingsbury County Clerk of Court. Personal checks accepted. Prepayment and SASE required.

Lake County

Circuit Court 200 E Center St, Madison, SD 57042; phone: 605-256-5644; hours 8AM-N, 1-5PM (CST). *Felony, Misdemeanor, Civil, Eviction, Small Claims, Probate.*
www.sdjudicial.com/circuit_courts/index.asp?circuit=3

Civil Records: Access: Mail, in person. Only the court performs in person searches; visitors may not. Search fee: $15.00 per name. Court makes copy: $.20 per page. Required to search: name, years to search; also helpful: address. Civil cases indexed by defendant. Civil records on computer from 1985, docket books from 1800s. Mail turnaround time 1 day.

Criminal Records: Access: Mail, in person. Only the court performs in person searches; visitors may not. Search fee: $15.00 per name. Court makes copy: $.20 per page. Required to search: name, years to search, DOB, signed release; also helpful: address, SSN. Criminal records on computer since 1989 on a statewide system; prior records on docket books since 1800s. All mail requests are forwarded to Miner County for processing. Mail turnaround time 1 day.

General Information: No juvenile, sealed, dismissed, or mental health records released. Certification fee: $2.00 per doc. Payee: Lake County Clerk of Court. Personal checks accepted. Prepayment and SASE required.

Lawrence County

Circuit Court PO Box 626, Deadwood, SD 57732; phone: 605-578-2040; hours 8AM-5PM (MST). *Felony, Misdemeanor, Civil, Eviction, Small Claims, Probate.*

Civil Records: Access: Mail, in person. Only the court performs in person searches; visitors may not. Search fee: $15.00 per name. Court makes copy: $.20 per page. Required to search: name, years to search; also helpful: address. Civil cases indexed by defendant, plaintiff. Civil records on computer from 1989 and index books from 1800s. Mail turnaround time 2 weeks.

Criminal Records: Access: Mail, in person. Only the court performs in person searches; visitors may not. Search fee: $15.00 per name. Court makes copy: $.20 per page. Required to search: name, years to search, DOB; also helpful: address, SSN. Criminal records on computer since 7/89 on a statewide system. Mail turnaround time 2 weeks.

General Information: No juvenile, sealed, dismissed, or mental health records released. Will fax documents $5.00 per doc; no fee to local or toll free number. Certification fee: $2.00 per doc. Payee: Lawrence County Clerk of Court. Personal checks accepted. Prepayment and SASE required.

Lincoln County

Circuit Court Clerk of Courts, 100 E 5th St, Canton, SD 57013; phone: 605-987-5891; hours 8AM-5PM (CST). *Felony, Misdemeanor, Civil, Eviction, Small Claims, Probate.*

Civil Records: Access: Mail, in person. Both court and visitors may perform in person searches. Search fee: $15.00 per name. Court makes copy: $.20 per page. Required to search: name, years to search; also helpful: address. Civil cases indexed by defendant, plaintiff. Civil records on docket books from 1900s. Visitor may search written index pre-1993; only the court searches computer records 1994 forward. Mail turnaround time 3 days, longer for probate.

Criminal Records: Access: Mail, in person. Both court and visitors may perform in person searches. Search fee: $15.00 per name. Court makes copy: $.20 per page. Required to search: name, years to search, DOB; also helpful: address, SSN. Criminal records on computer since 7/89 on a statewide system. All mail requests are forwarded to Douglas County. Mail turnaround time 3 days, longer for probate.

General Information: Public terminal has criminal back to 1989 and civil back to 1996. No juvenile,

sealed, dismissed, adoption or mental health records released. Certification fee: $2.00 per doc. Payee: Lincoln County Clerk of Court. Personal checks accepted. Prepayment and SASE required.

Lyman County

Circuit Court PO Box 235, Kennebec, SD 57544; phone: 605-869-2277; hours 8AM-5PM (CST). *Felony, Misdemeanor, Civil, Eviction, Small Claims, Probate.*

Civil Records: Access: Mail, in person. Both court and visitors may perform in person searches. Search fee: $15.00 per name. Court makes copy: $.25 per page. Required to search: name, years to search; also helpful: address. Civil cases indexed by defendant, plaintiff. Civil records on docket books from 1900s; on computer back one year. Mail turnaround time 1 week.

Criminal Records: Access: Mail, in person. Only the court performs in person searches; visitors may not. Search fee: $15.00 per name. Court makes copy: $.25 per page. Required to search: name, years to search, DOB; also helpful: address, SSN. Criminal records on computer since 7/89 on a statewide system. All mail requests forwarded to Potter county for processing. Mail turnaround time 1 week.

General Information: No juvenile, sealed, dismissed, or mental health records released. Fee to fax documents is $1.00 per page. Certification fee: $2.00 per cert. Payee: Lyman County Clerk of Court. Personal checks accepted. Prepayment and SASE required.

Marshall County

Circuit Court PO Box 130, Britton, SD 57430; phone: 605-448-5213; hours 8AM-N, 1-5PM M-Th (CST). *Felony, Misdemeanor, Civil, Eviction, Small Claims, Probate.*

Civil Records: Access: Mail, in person. Only the court performs in person searches; visitors may not. Search fee: $15.00 per name. Court makes copy: $.20 per page. Required to search: name, years to search; also helpful: address. Civil cases indexed by defendant, plaintiff. Civil records on docket books from 1800s. Mail turnaround time 1 week.

Criminal Records: Access: Mail, in person. Only the court performs in person searches; visitors may not. Search fee: $15.00 per name. Court makes copy: $.20 per page. Required to search: name, years to search, DOB; also helpful: address, SSN. Criminal records are computerized since 7/89 on a statewide system. All mail requests forwarded to Edmunds County Search Center for processing. (605-426-6671) Mail turnaround time 1 week.

General Information: No juvenile, sealed, dismissed, or mental health records released. Will fax documents to local or toll free line. Certification fee: $2.00 per cert. Payee: Marshall County Clerk of Court. Personal checks accepted. Prepayment and SASE required.

McCook County

Circuit Court PO Box 504, Salem, SD 57058; phone: 605-425-2781; fax: 605-425-3144; hours 8AM-12:30; 1-4:30PM (CST). *Felony, Misdemeanor, Civil, Eviction, Small Claims, Probate.*

Civil Records: Access: Mail, in person. Both court and visitors may perform in person searches. Search fee: $15.00 per name. Court makes copy: $.20 per page. Required to search: name, years to search; also helpful: address. Civil cases indexed by defendant, plaintiff. Civil records in index and docket books from late 1800s. Mail turnaround time 1 day.

Criminal Records: Access: Mail, in person. Only the court performs in person searches; visitors may not. Search fee: $15.00 per name. Court makes copy: $.20 per page. Required to search: name, years to search, DOB, signed release; also helpful: address, SSN. Criminal records are computerized since 7/89 on a statewide system. All mail requests are forwarded to Miner County for processing. In person requests must be written. Mail turnaround time 1 day.

General Information: No juvenile, sealed, dismissed, or mental health records released. Certification fee: $2.00 per cert. Payee: McCook County Clerk of Court. Personal checks accepted. Prepayment and SASE required.

McPherson County

Circuit Court PO Box 248, Leola, SD 57456; phone: 605-439-3361; fax: 605-439-3394; hours 8AM-N (CST). *Felony, Misdemeanor, Civil, Eviction, Small Claims, Probate.*

Civil Records: Access: Mail, in person. Both court and visitors may perform in person searches. Search fee: $15.00 per name. Court makes copy: $.25 per page; same fee for self serve. Required to search: name, years to search; also helpful: address. Civil cases indexed by defendant, plaintiff. Civil records on register of action from 1910, records are not computerized. There is no fee if case number is known for in person searchers. Mail turnaround time 1 day to 1 week.

Criminal Records: Access: Mail, in person. Only the court performs in person searches; visitors may not. Search fee: $15.00 per name. Court makes copy: $.25 per page; same fee for self serve. Required to search: name, years to search, DOB, signed release; also helpful: address, SSN. Criminal records on register of action from 1910, records are not computerized. All mail requests are forwarded to Edmunds County for processing. Ph#-605-426-6671. Mail turnaround time 1 day to 1 week.

General Information: No juvenile, sealed, dismissed, adoption or mental health records released. Will fax documents to local or toll free line. Certification fee: $2.00 per cert. Payee: McPherson County Clerk of Court. Personal checks accepted. Prepayment and SASE required.

Meade County

Circuit Court PO Box 939, Sturgis, SD 57785; phone: 605-347-4411; fax: 605-347-3526; hours 8AM-N, 1-5PM (MST). *Felony, Misdemeanor, Civil, Eviction, Small Claims, Probate.*

Civil Records: Access: Mail, in person. Both court and visitors may perform in person searches. Search fee: $15.00 per name. Court makes copy: $.20 per page. Required to search: name, years to search; also helpful: address. Civil cases indexed by defendant, plaintiff. Civil records on index cards and docket books from 1800s. Mail turnaround time 1 day to 2 weeks.

Criminal Records: Access: Mail, in person. Only the court performs in person searches; visitors may not. Search fee: $15.00 per name. Court makes copy: $.20 per page. Required to search: name, DOB, signed release; also helpful: address, SSN. Criminal records on computer since 7/89 on a statewide system. All mail requests are forwarded to Lawrence County for processing. Mail turnaround time 1 day to 2 weeks.

General Information: No juvenile, sealed, dismissed, or mental health records released. Certification fee: $2.00 per doc. Payee: Meade County Clerk of Courts. Personal checks accepted. Prepayment and SASE required.

Mellette County

Circuit Court PO Box 257, White River, SD 57579; phone: 605-259-3230; fax: 605-259-3194; hours 8AM-N (CST). *Felony, Misdemeanor, Civil, Eviction, Small Claims, Probate.*

Civil Records: Access: Phone, mail, in person. Both court and visitors may perform in person searches. Search fee: $15.00 per name. Court makes copy: $.20 per page. Required to search: name, years to search; also helpful: address. Civil cases indexed by defendant. Civil records on index cards and docket books from 1900s. Mail turnaround time 3 days; probate up to 1 month.

Criminal Records: Access: Mail, in person. Only the court performs in person searches; visitors may not. Search fee: $15.00 per name. Court makes copy: $.20 per page. Required to search: name, years to search, DOB, signed release; also helpful: address, SSN. Criminal records are computerized since 7/89 on a statewide system. All mail requests are forwarded to Potter County for processing. Mail turnaround time 3 days; probate up to 1 month.

General Information: No juvenile, sealed, dismissed, or mental health records released. Will fax documents to local or toll free line. Certification fee: $2.00 per cert. Payee: Mellette County Clerk of Court. Personal checks accepted. Prepayment and SASE required.

Miner County

Circuit Court PO Box 265, Howard, SD 57349; phone: 605-772-4612; criminal fax: 605-772-4412; same fax for civil/probate; hours 8AM-N; 1-5PM (CST). *Felony, Misdemeanor, Civil, Eviction, Small Claims, Probate.*
www.sdjudicial.com/circuit_courts/index.asp?circuit=3

Civil Records: Access: Mail, in person. Both court and visitors may perform in person searches. Search fee: $15.00 per name. Court makes copy: $.25 per page. Required to search: name, years to search. Civil cases indexed by defendant, plaintiff. Civil records on docket books from 1900's. Mail turnaround time 2 days.

Criminal Records: Access: Fax, mail, in person. Only the court performs in person searches; visitors may not. Search fee: $15.00 per name. Court makes copy: $.25 per page. Required to search: name, years to search, DOB; also helpful: SSN. Criminal records are computerized since 1989. This is a statewide search. Mail turnaround time 2 days.

General Information: No juvenile, sealed, dismissed or mental health records released. Will fax documents $5.00 per doc; no fee to local or toll free number. Certification fee: $2.00 per page. Cert fee includes copies. Payee: Miner County Clerk of Court. Personal checks accepted. Prepayment and SASE required.

Minnehaha County

Circuit Court 425 N Dakota Ave, Sioux Falls, SD 57104; phone: 605-367-5900; fax: 605-367-5916; hours 8AM-5PM (CST). *Felony, Misdemeanor, Civil, Eviction, Small Claims, Probate.*
Note: Please use their request form when requesting search.

Civil Records: Access: Mail, in person. Only the court performs in person searches; visitors may not. Search fee: $15.00 per name. Court makes copy: $.20 per page. Required to search: name, years to search; also helpful: address. Civil cases indexed by defendant, plaintiff. Civil records on computer from 1989, docket books from 1800s. Mail turnaround time 2 weeks.

Criminal Records: Access: Mail, in person. Only the court performs in person searches; visitors may not. Search fee: $15.00 per name. Court makes copy: $.20 per page. Required to search: name, years to search, DOB, signed release; also helpful: address, SSN. Criminal records on computer since 7/89. All mail requests are forwarded to either Jerauld or Sanborn counties for processing, which uses the statewide system. Mail turnaround time 2 weeks.

General Information: No juvenile, sealed, dismissed or mental health records released. Certification fee: $2.00 per doc. Payee: Minnehaha County Clerk of Court. Personal checks accepted. Prepayment and SASE required.

Moody County

Circuit Court 101 E Pipestone, Flandreau, SD 57028; phone: 605-997-3181; criminal fax: 605-997-3861; same fax for civil/probate; hours 8AM-5PM (CST). *Felony, Misdemeanor, Civil, Eviction, Small Claims, Probate.*
www.sdjudicial.com/circuit_courts/index.asp?circuit=3

Note: Probate records are in a separate index at this address.

Civil Records: Access: Mail, in person. Only the court performs in person searches; visitors may not. Search fee: $15.00 per name. Court makes copy: $.25 per page. Required to search: name, years to search; also helpful: address. Civil cases indexed by defendant, plaintiff. Civil records on computer from 1992 and docket books from 1800s. Mail turnaround time 2-3 days.

Criminal Records: Access: Mail, in person. Only the court performs in person searches; visitors may not. Search fee: $15.00 per name. Court makes copy: $.25 per page. Required to search: name, years to search, DOB; also helpful: address, SSN. Criminal records on computer since 7/89 on a statewide index. All mail requests are forwarded to Miner County of processing. Mail turnaround time 2-3 days.

General Information: No juvenile, sealed, dismissed, adoption or mental health records released. Will fax documents for $1.00 per page. Certification fee: $2.00 per page includes copy fee. Payee: Moody County Clerk of Court. Personal checks accepted. Prepayment and SASE required.

Pennington County

Circuit Court PO Box 230, Rapid City, SD 57709; criminal phone: 605-394-2570; civil phone: 605-394-2575; probate phone: 605-394-2575; hours 8AM-5PM (MST). *Felony, Misdemeanor, Civil, Eviction, Small Claims, Probate.*

Civil Records: Access: Mail, in person. Only the court performs in person searches; visitors may not. Court makes copy: $.25 per page. Required to search: name, years to search; also helpful: address. Civil records on computer from 1991, cards and docket books from 1900s. Mail turnaround time 2 weeks.

Criminal Records: Access: Mail, in person. Search fee: $15.00. Court makes copy: $.25 per page. Required to search: DOB, years to search. Note: If prior to 1989, mail requests should be sent to Pennington County Clerk - arrest date and charge is required to conduct search. If 1989 to present, mail to Harding County Clerk, POB 534, Buffalo, SD 57720, 605-375-3351. Mail turnaround time 2 weeks.

General Information: No juvenile, sealed, or mental health records released. Certification fee: $2.00 per cert. Prepayment and SASE required.

Perkins County

Circuit Court PO Box 426, Bison, SD 57620-0426; phone: 605-244-5626; fax: 605-244-7110; hours 8AM-N, 1-5PM (MST). *Felony, Misdemeanor, Civil, Eviction, Small Claims, Probate.*

Civil Records: Access: Fax, mail, in person. Both court and visitors may perform in person searches. Search fee: $15.00 per name. Court makes copy: $.25 per page; same fee for self serve. Required to search: name, years to search. Civil cases indexed by defendant, plaintiff. Civil records on docket books from 1908; on computer back to 1999. Mail turnaround time varies.

Criminal Records: Access: Fax, mail, in person. Only the court performs in person searches; visitors may not. Search fee: $15.00 per name. Court makes copy: $.25 per page; same fee for self serve. Required to search: name, years to search, DOB, signed release. Criminal records are computerized back to 7/89 on a statewide system. All fax and mail requests are forwarded to Lawrence County for processing. Mail turnaround time varies.

General Information: No juvenile, sealed or mental health records released. Will fax documents $1.00 per page, $5.00 minimum; no fee if toll free call. Certification fee: $2.00 per cert. Payee: Perkins County Clerk of Courts. Only cashiers checks and money orders accepted. Prepayment required. SASE requested.

Potter County

Circuit Court PO Box 67, 201 S Exene St, Gettysburg, SD 57442; phone: 605-765-9472; fax: 605-765-9670; hours 8AM-N, 1-5PM (CST). *Felony, Misdemeanor, Civil, Eviction, Small Claims, Probate.*

Civil Records: Access: Mail, in person. Only the court performs in person searches; visitors may not. Search fee: $15.00 per name. Court makes copy: $.20 per page. Required to search: name, years to search; also helpful: address. Civil cases indexed by defendant, plaintiff. Civil records on index cards and docket books from 1889. Request must be in writing. Mail turnaround time 1-2 days.

Criminal Records: Access: Fax, mail, in person. Only the court performs in person searches; visitors may not. Search fee: $15.00 per name. Court makes copy: $.20 per page. Required to search: name, years to search, DOB, signed release; also helpful: address, SSN. Criminal records are indexed on computer since 7/89 on a statewide system. Requests must be in writing. Mail turnaround time 1-2 days.

General Information: No juvenile, sealed, dismissed, adoption or mental health records released. Will fax documents $5.00 per doc; no fee to toll free number; must be a commercial account. Certification fee: $2.00 per doc. Payee: Potter County Clerk of Court. Personal checks accepted. Prepayment and SASE required.

Roberts County

Circuit Court 411 2nd Ave E, Sisseton, SD 57262; phone: 605-698-3395; fax: 605-698-7894; hours 8AM-5PM (CST). *Felony, Misdemeanor, Civil, Eviction, Small Claims, Probate.*

Civil Records: Access: Mail, in person. Only the court performs in person searches; visitors may not. Search fee: $15.00 per name. Court makes copy: $.20 per page. Required to search: name, years to search; also helpful: address. Civil cases indexed by defendant, plaintiff. Civil records on computer from 1992, microfilm from 1920 to 1985 and original files from 1986. Mail turnaround time 2-3 days.

Criminal Records: Access: Mail, in person. Only the court performs in person searches; visitors may not. Search fee: $15.00 per name. Court makes copy: $.20 per page. Required to search: name, years to search, DOB; also helpful: address, SSN. Criminal records on computer since 1988 on a state wide system. Criminal search requests should be sent to Edmunds County (PO Box 384, Ipswich SD 57451; 605-426-6323 fax) for processing. Mail turnaround time 2-3 days.

General Information: No juvenile, sealed, dismissed, adoption or mental health records released. Will fax documents to local or toll free line. Certification fee: $2.00 includes copy fee. Payee: Roberts County Clerk of Court (or, Edmunds City Clerk, if a criminal search. Personal checks accepted. Prepayment and SASE required.

Sanborn County

Circuit Court PO Box 56, Woonsocket, SD 57385; phone: 605-796-4515; fax: 605-796-4502; hours 8AM-5PM (CST). *Felony, Misdemeanor, Civil, Eviction, Small Claims, Probate.*
www.sdjudicial.com/circuit_courts/index.asp?circuit=3

Civil Records: Access: Mail, in person. Only the court performs in person searches; visitors may not. Search fee: $15.00 per name. Court makes copy: $.25 per page. Required to search: name, years to search; also helpful: address. Civil cases indexed by defendant, plaintiff. Civil records on docket books from 1890s. Mail turnaround time 1 week.

Criminal Records: Access: Fax, mail, in person. Only the court performs in person searches; visitors may not. Search fee: $15.00 per name. Court makes copy: $.25 per page. Required to search: name, years to search, DOB; also helpful: address, SSN. Criminal records are computerized since 1989 on a statewide system. Mail turnaround time 1 week.

General Information: No juvenile, sealed, dismissed, or mental health records released. Will fax documents $1.00 per page, $5.00 minimum; no fee if toll free call. Certification fee: $2.00 per cert. Payee: Sanborn County Clerk of Courts. Personal checks accepted; no two party checks. Prepayment and SASE required.

Shannon County

Circuit Court 906 N River St, Hot Springs, SD 57747; phone: 605-745-5131; hours 8AM-5PM (MST). *Felony, Misdemeanor, Civil, Eviction, Small Claims, Probate.*
Note: Also handles cases for Fall River County. Specify which county in your search request.

Civil Records: Access: Mail, in person. Only the court performs in person searches; visitors may not. Search fee: $15.00 per name. Court makes copy: $.25 per page. Required to search: name, years to search; also helpful: address, DOB, SSN. Civil cases indexed by defendant, plaintiff. Civil records on computer from 1992, older files archived off site to 1889. Mail turnaround time 1-2 weeks.

Criminal Records: Access: Mail, in person. Only the court performs in person searches; visitors may not. Search fee: $15.00 per name. Court makes copy: $.25 per page. Required to search: name, years to search, DOB; also helpful: address, SSN. Criminal records on computer since 7/89 on a statewide system. Mail turnaround time 1 week.

General Information: No juvenile, sealed, adoption, or mental health records released. Will fax documents to local or toll free line. Certification fee: $2.00 per doc. Payee: Shannon County Clerk of Court. Personal checks accepted. Prepayment and SASE required.

Spink County

Circuit Court 210 E 7th Ave, Redfield, SD 57469; phone: 605-472-4535; criminal fax: 605-472-4352; same fax for civil/probate; hours 8AM-5PM (CST). *Felony, Misdemeanor, Civil, Eviction, Small Claims, Probate.*

Civil Records: Access: Phone, fax, mail, in person. Only the court performs in person searches; visitors may not. Search fee: $15.00 per name. Court makes copy: $.20 per page. Required to search: name, years to search; also helpful: address. Civil cases indexed by defendant, plaintiff. Civil records on docket books from 1882. Mail turnaround time 1 day.

Criminal Records: Access: Phone, fax, mail, in person. Only the court performs in person searches; visitors may not. Search fee: $15.00 per name. Court makes copy: $.20 per page. Required to search: name, years to search, DOB; also helpful: address, SSN. Criminal records on computer since 1988 on a statewide system. All fax and mail requests are forwarded to Edmunds County for processing. Mail turnaround time 1 day.

General Information: No juvenile, sealed, dismissed, or mental health records released. Will fax documents $5.00 per doc; no fee to toll free number; must be a commercial account. Certification fee: $2.00 per doc includes copy fee. Payee: Spink County Clerk of Court. Personal checks accepted. Prepayment and SASE required.

Stanley County

Circuit Court PO Box 758, Fort Pierre, SD 57532; phone: 605-223-7735; fax: 605-223-7738; hours 8AM-5PM (CST). *Felony, Misdemeanor, Civil, Eviction, Small Claims, Probate.*

Civil Records: Access: Fax, mail, in person. Both court and visitors may perform in person searches. Search fee: $15.00 per name. Court makes copy: $.20 per page. Required to search: name, years to search; also helpful: address. Civil cases indexed by defendant, plaintiff. Civil records on docket books from 1973. Requests must be in writing. Mail turnaround time 1-2 days.

Criminal Records: Access: Fax, mail, in person. Only the court performs in person searches;

Sully County

Circuit Court PO Box 188, Onida, SD 57564; phone: 605-258-2535; fax: 605-258-2270; hours 8AM-N (CST). *Felony, Misdemeanor, Civil, Eviction, Small Claims, Probate.*

Civil Records: Access: Mail, in person. Only the court performs in person searches; visitors may not. Search fee: $15.00 per name. Court makes copy: $.25 per page plus tax ($.02); same fee for self serve. Required to search: name, years to search; also helpful: address. Civil cases indexed by defendant, plaintiff. Civil records on docket books from 1900s. Mail turnaround time 1-2 days.

Criminal Records: Access: Mail, in person. Only the court performs in person searches; visitors may not. Search fee: $15.00 per name. Court makes copy: $.25 per page plus tax ($.02); same fee for self serve. Required to search: name, years to search; also helpful: address. Criminal records on computer since 7/89 on statewide system; local computer back to 2000. All mail requests are forwarded to Potter County for processing. Mail turnaround time 1-2 days.

General Information: Public terminal has only civil records back to 2000. No juvenile, sealed, dismissed, or mental health records released. Will fax documents for fee. Certification fee: $2.00 per cert. Payee: Sully County Clerk of Court. No personal checks accepted. Prepayment and SASE required.

Todd County

Circuit Court 200 E 3rd St, PO Box 311, Winner, SD 57580; phone: 605-842-2266; fax: 605-842-2267; hours 8AM-5PM (MST). *Felony, Misdemeanor, Civil, Eviction, Small Claims, Probate.*

Civil Records: Access: Mail, in person. Only the court performs in person searches; visitors may not. Search fee: $15.00 per name. Court makes copy: $.25 per page. Required to search: name, years to search; also helpful: address. Civil cases indexed by defendant, plaintiff. Civil records on docket books from 1920s. Mail turnaround time 2 days.

Criminal Records: Access: Mail, in person. Only the court performs in person searches; visitors may not. Search fee: $15.00 per name. Court makes copy: $.25 per page. Required to search: name, years to search, DOB, signed release; also helpful: address, SSN. Criminal records on computer since 7/89 on statewide system. All mail requests are forwarded to Potter County for processing. Mail turnaround time 2 days.

General Information: No juvenile, sealed, dismissed, or mental health records released. Certification fee: $2.00 per doc. Payee: Todd County Clerk of Court. Personal checks accepted. Prepayment and SASE required.

Tripp County

Circuit Court PO Box 311, 200 E 3rd St, Winner, SD 57580; phone: 605-842-2266; fax: 605-842-2267; hours 8AM-5PM (CST). *Felony, Misdemeanor, Civil, Eviction, Small Claims, Probate.*

Civil Records: Access: Mail, in person. Only the court performs in person searches; visitors may not. Search fee: $15.00 per name. Court makes copy: $.20 per page. Required to search: name, years to search; also helpful: address. Civil cases indexed by defendant, plaintiff. Civil records on docket books from 1920s. All requests must be in writing. Mail turnaround time 2 days.

Criminal Records: Access: Mail, in person. Only the court performs in person searches; visitors may not. Search fee: $15.00 per name. Court makes copy: $.25 per page. Required to search: name, years to search, DOB, signed release; also helpful: address, SSN. Criminal records on computer since 1989 on statewide system. All mail requests are forwarded to Potter County for processing. Mail turnaround time 2 days.

General Information: No juvenile, sealed, dismissed, or mental health records released. Certification fee: $2.00 per doc. Payee: Tripp County Clerk of Court. Personal checks accepted. Prepayment and SASE required.

Turner County

Circuit Court PO Box 446, Parker, SD 57053; phone: 605-297-3115; fax: 605-297-2115; hours 8:30AM-5PM (CST). *Felony, Misdemeanor, Civil, Eviction, Small Claims, Probate.*

Civil Records: Access: Mail, in person. Only the court performs in person searches; visitors may not. Search fee: $15.00 per name. Court makes copy: $.25 per page. Required to search: name, years to search; also helpful: address, DOB, and drivers license number. Civil cases indexed by defendant, plaintiff. Civil records on index cards and docket books from 1900s. Mail turnaround time 2 days.

Criminal Records: Access: Mail, in person. Only the court performs in person searches; visitors may not. Search fee: $15.00 per name. Court makes copy: $.25 per page. Required to search: name, years to search, DOB, signed release; also helpful: address, drivers license number. Criminal records on computer since 7/89 on a statewide system. All mail requests are forwarded to Douglas County for processing. Mail turnaround time 2 days.

General Information: No juvenile, sealed, dismissed, or mental health records released. Fee to fax documents is $1.00 per page; $5.00 minimum. Certification fee: $2.00. Payee: Turner County Clerk of Courts. Prepayment and SASE required.

Union County

Circuit Court 209 E Main St #230, Elk Point, SD 57025; phone: 605-356-2132; fax: 605-356-3687; hours 8:30AM-5PM (CST). *Felony, Misdemeanor, Civil, Eviction, Small Claims, Probate.*

Civil Records: Access: Fax, mail, in person. Only the court performs in person searches; visitors may not. Search fee: $15.00 per name. Court makes copy: $.20 per page. Required to search: name, years to search; also helpful: address. Civil cases indexed by

defendant, plaintiff. Civil records on computer from 1990, docket books from 1900s. Mail turnaround time 1-2 days.

Criminal Records: Access: Fax, mail, in person. Only the court performs in person searches; visitors may not. Search fee: $15.00 per name. Court makes copy: $.20 per page. Required to search: name, years to search, DOB; also helpful: address, SSN. Criminal records on computer since 1988 on a statewide system, on docket books from 1900s. All mail requests for years 1988 to present are forwarded to Douglas County for processing. Mail turnaround time 1-2 days.

General Information: No juvenile, sealed, dismissed, or mental health records released. Fee to fax documents is $5.00 or $1.00 per page, whichever is greater. Certification fee: $2.00 per cert. Payee: Union County Clerk of Court. Personal checks accepted. Prepayment and SASE required.

Walworth County

Circuit Court PO Box 328, Selby, SD 57472; phone: 605-649-7311; fax: 605-649-7624; hours 8AM-5PM (CST). *Felony, Misdemeanor, Civil, Eviction, Small Claims, Probate.*

Civil Records: Access: Fax, mail, in person. Only the court performs in person searches; visitors may not. Search fee: $15.00 per name. Court makes copy: $.20 per page. Required to search: name, years to search; also helpful: address. Civil cases indexed by defendant, plaintiff. Civil records on index cards and docket books from 1900s. Mail turnaround time 1-2 days.

Criminal Records: Access: Fax, mail, in person. Only the court performs in person searches; visitors may not. Search fee: $15.00 per name. Court makes copy: $.20 per page. Required to search: name, years to search, DOB, signed release; also helpful: address, SSN. Criminal records on computer since 7/89 in a statewide system. All mail requests are forwarded to Edmunds County for processing. Mail turnaround time 1-2 days.

General Information: No juvenile, sealed, dismissed, or mental health records released. Certification fee: $2.00 per doc. Payee: Walworth County Clerk of Court. Personal checks accepted. Prepayment and SASE required.

Yankton County

Circuit Court Clerk of Courts, PO Box 155, Yankton, SD 57078; phone: 605-668-3080; criminal fax: 605-668-5411; same fax for civil/probate; hours 8AM-5PM (CST). *Felony, Misdemeanor, Civil, Small Claims, Eviction, Probate.*

Note: Probate is a separate index at this same address.

Civil Records: Access: Mail, in person. Both court and visitors may perform in person searches. Search fee: $15.00 per name. Court makes copy: $.20 per page. Required to search: name, years to search; also helpful: address, DOB, SSN. Civil cases indexed by defendant, plaintiff. Civil records on computer from 1991, docket books from 1900s. Visitors only have access to the book index. Mail turnaround time 1 week.

Criminal Records: Access: Mail, in person. Both court and visitors may perform in person searches. Search fee: $15.00 per name. Must be a state authorized account. Court makes copy: $.20 per page. Required to search: name, years to search; also helpful: address, SSN. Criminal records on computer since 7/89 on a statewide system, Class II offenses not accessible on computer to public. Visitors only have access to the book index. All mail requests are forwarded to Douglas County for processing. Mail turnaround time 1 week.

General Information: No juvenile, sealed, dismissed, or mental health records released. Will fax documents to toll-free number for $1 per page, $5 minimum. Certification fee: $2.00 per doc. Payee: Yankton County Clerk of Court. Personal checks accepted. Prepayment and SASE required.

Ziebach County

Circuit Court PO Box 306, Dupree, SD 57623; phone: 605-365-5159; hours 9:30AM-N, 1-2:30PM (MST). *Felony, Misdemeanor, Civil, Eviction, Small Claims, Probate.*

Note: Probate is a separate index at this same address.

Civil Records: Access: Mail, in person. Only the court performs in person searches; visitors may not. Search fee: $15.00 per name. Court makes copy: $.10 per page. Required to search: name, years to search; also helpful: address. Civil cases indexed by defendant. Civil records on index books from 1900s. Mail turnaround time 2-3 days.

Criminal Records: Access: Mail, in person. Only the court performs in person searches; visitors may not. Search fee: $15.00 per name. Court makes copy: $.10 per page. Required to search: name, years to search, DOB; also helpful: address, SSN. Criminal records on index books from 1900s. All mail requests are forwarded to Lawrence County for processing. Mail turnaround time 2-3 days.

General Information: No juvenile, sealed, dismissed, adoption or mental health records released. Will fax documents to local or toll free line, otherwise $1.00 per page, $5.00 minimum. Certification fee: $2.00 per doc includes copies. Payee: Ziebach County Clerk of Court. Personal checks accepted. Prepayment and SASE required.

South Dakota Recording Offices

ORGANIZATION: 66 counties, 66 recording offices. The recording officer is. Register of Deeds. 48 counties are in the Central Time Zone (CST) and 18 are in the Mountain Time Zone (MST).

REAL ESTATE RECORDS: Many counties will perform real estate searches. Search fees and copy fees vary. Certification usually costs $1.00 per document.

UCC RECORDS: Financing statements are filed at the state level, except for real estate related collateral, which are filed with the Register of Deeds. All recording offices will perform UCC searches. All counties have access to a statewide database of UCC filings. Use search request form UCC-11. Searches fees are usually $12.00 to $20.00 per debtor name, $10.00 if online. Copy fees are usually $1.00 per page. Certification is $2.00 or $5.00.

TAX LIEN RECORDS: Federal and state tax liens on personal property of businesses are filed with the Secretary of State. Other federal and state tax liens are filed with the county Register of Deeds. Most counties will perform tax lien searches. Search fees and copy fees vary.

OTHER LIENS: Mechanics, motor vehicle, materials.

ONLINE ACCESS: Access to UCC records are available online through the SOS's Fast File Internet Access System at http://www.sdsos.gov/ucc/. Registration and annual fee is required. A certified search is also available. A new system named "Expa" is soon to be available for the occasional user.

Aurora County

Register of Deeds, PO Box 397, Plankinton, SD 57368. 605-942-7161; fax-605-942-7751; hours: 8AM-N, 1-5PM.
Office will perform a UCC search but public must search other records themselves. Search fee $20.00. General copy fee $1.00 per page. R/E or tax lien copy- $1.00 per document. Cert fee- $2.00 per doc plus copy fee. Payee- Register of Deeds. **Other phones:** Treasurer- 605-942-7162; Vital Records- 605-942-7161. **Property tax/Assessor-** 605-942-7164.

Beadle County

Register of Deeds, PO Box 55, Huron, SD 57350-0055. 605-353-8412; fax-605-353-8402; hours: 8AM-5PM.
All records in one index. Records indexed on a public use terminal back to 1993. Office will perform a UCC search but public must search other records themselves. Search fee $5.00 per name. UCC search per debtor name- $10.00. Copy fee $1.00 per page. Tax lien copy- $.50 per page. Cert fee- $2.00 per doc plus copy fee. Payee- Register of Deeds. **Other phones:** Treasurer- 605-353-8405; Appraiser/Auditor- 605-353-8408; Elections- 605-353-8400; Vital Records- 605-353-8412. **Property tax/Assessor-** PO Box 328, Huron, SD 57350; 605-353-8408.

Bennett County

Register of Deeds, PO Box 433, Martin, SD 57551-0433. 605-685-6054; fax-605-685-6311; hours: 8AM-N, 12:30-4:30AM.
All records in one index. Office will perform a UCC search but public must search other records themselves. UCC search per debtor name- $15.00 per person. Copy fee $1.00 per document. Cert fee- $2.00 per doc includes copy fee. Payee-Register of Deeds. **Other phones:** Treasurer- 605-685-6092; Vital Records- 605-685-6054. **Property tax/Assessor-** PO Box 426, Martin, SD 57551; 605-685-6991.

Bon Homme County

Register of Deeds, PO Box 3, Tyndall, SD 57066. 605-589-4217, R/E recording phone-605-589-3302; fax-605-589-4202; hours: 8AM-4:30PM.
Office personnel or visitors may perform searches. Search fee $15.00 per name. Will not search real estate records. Copy fee $1.00 per page. Cert fee- $2.00 per cert plus copy fee. Payee- Bon Homme

County Register of Deeds. **Property tax/Assessor-** 605-589-3462.

Brookings County

Register of Deeds, 314 6th Ave; Courthouse, Brookings, SD 57006-2084. 605-696-8240; fax-605-696-8245; hours: 8AM-5PM.
Record index not computerized. Office will perform a UCC search but public must search other records themselves. Search fee $20.00. Copy fee $1.00 per page. Cert fee- $2.00 per cert plus copy fee. Payee- Brookings County Register of Deeds. **Other phones:** Treasurer- 605-696-8250; Appraiser/Auditor- 605-696-8301; Elections- 605-696-8220; Vital Records- 605-696-8240. **Property tax/Assessor-** 605-696-8220.

Brown County

Register of Deeds, PO Box 1307, Aberdeen, SD 57402-1307. 605-626-7140; fax-605-626-4010; hours: 8AM-5PM.
Records indexed on computer back to 1990 (deeds only). Office will perform a UCC search but public must search other records themselves. UCC search per debtor name- $20.00. Copy fee $1.00 per page. Cert fee- $2.00 up to 5 pages, $.20 after includes copy fee. **Other phones:** Treasurer- 605-626-7133; Elections- 605-626-7110; Vital Records- 605-626-7140. **Property tax/Assessor-** same address as above. 605-622-7133.

Brule County

Register of Deeds, 300 S. Courtland; #110, Chamberlain, SD 57325. 605-734-4434; fax-605-734-6610; hours: 8AM-N,1-5PM.
Office personnel or visitors may perform searches. Search fee $4.00 per name. Will not search real estate records. UCC search per debtor name- $12.00. Copy fee $1.00 per page. Cert fee- $5.00 per doc plus copy fee. Payee- Brule County Register of Deeds. **Other phones:** Treasurer- 605-734-4436; Elections- 605-734-4430; Vital Records- 605-734-4434. **Property tax/Assessor-** 605-734-4432.

Buffalo County

Register of Deeds, PO Box 174, Gann Valley, SD 57341. 605-293-3239; fax-605-293-3240; hours: 9AM-5PM.
Separate indices to search include deeds, misc in deed index, mortgages, UCC in mortgage index. Record index not computerized. Office personnel or visitors may perform searches. UCC search per

debtor name- $12.00. UCC search request using non-standard form (per name)- $13.00. Separate federal tax lien search- $5.00. Separate federal & state combined tax lien search- $10.00. Copy fee $.25; tax lien $1.00 per page. Cert fee- $1.00 per cert plus copy fee. Payee- Register of Deeds. **Other phones:** Treasurer- 605-293-3236. **Property tax/Assessor-** PO Box 165, Gann Valley, SD 57341; 605-293-3236.

Butte County

Register of Deeds, 839 Fifth Ave, Belle Fourche, SD 57717. 605-892-2912; fax-605-829-4525; hours: 8AM-5PM.
Separate indices to search include mtgs, Deeds. Records indexed on a public use terminal back to 1996. Office will perform a UCC and tax lien search but public must search other records themselves. Search fee $20.00. Copy fee $1.00 1st 5 pages, $.20 add'l per page. Cert fee- $2.00 per doc, plus $.20 copy fee per page. Payee- Butte County Register of Deeds. **Other phones:** Treasurer- 605-892-4456; Appraiser/Auditor- 605-892-3950; Elections- 605-892-4485; Vital Records- 605-892-2912. **Property tax/Assessor-** same address as above. 605-892-3950.

Campbell County

Register of Deeds, PO Box 148, Mound City, SD 57646-0148. 605-955-3505; fax-605-955-3308; hours: 8AM-N; 1-5PM.
Separate indices to search include Deeds and Mtgs. Record index not computerized. Office personnel or visitors may perform searches. Search fee $20.00. General copy fee $1.00 per doc, over 5 pgs, $.20 per add'l page. R/E record copy- $1.00 1st 5 pages; $.20 per page thereafter. Cert fee- $2.00 per page plus copy fee. Payee- Campbell County Register of Deeds. **Other phones:** Treasurer- 605-955-3388; Appraiser/Auditor- 605-955-3577; Elections- 605-955-3366; Vital Records- 605-955-3505. **Property tax/Assessor-** 605-955-3577.

Charles Mix County

Register of Deeds, PO Box 206, Lake Andes, SD 57356-0206. 605-487-7141; fax-605-487-7221; hours: 8AM-4:30PM.
Separate indices to search include alpha index, legal description. Records indexed on computer back to 1995. Office will perform a UCC search but public must search other records themselves. UCC search per debtor name- $12.00. Copy fee $1.00 per instrument. Cert fee- $2.00 per cert

includes copy fee. Payee- Charles Mix County Register of Deeds. **Other phones:** Treasurer- 605-487-7542; Elections- 605-487-7131; Vital Records- 605-487-7141. **Property tax/Assessor-** 605-487-7382.

Clark County

Register of Deeds, PO Box 294, Clark, SD 57225-0294. 605-532-5363; R/E recording phone-605-632-5363; fax-605-532-5931; hours: 8AM-5PM.
All records in one index. Records indexed on computer back to 1995. Office personnel or visitors may perform searches. General index search fee $10.00. Copy fee $1.00 per instrument. Tax lien copy- $.50 per page. Cert fee- $2.00 per cert plus copy fee. Payee- Register of Deeds. **Other phones:** Treasurer- 605-532-5911; Elections-605-532-5921; Vital Records- 605-632-5363. **Property tax/Assessor-** 605-532-3751.

Clay County

Register of Deeds, 211 W. Main St, #202, Vermillion, SD 57069. 605-677-7130; hours: 8AM-5PM.
Office will perform a UCC search but public must search other records themselves. Search fee $5.00 per page. UCC search per debtor name- $20.00. Copy fee $1.00 per page. Cert fee- $2.00 per cert plus copy fee. Payee- Clay County Register of Deeds. **Other phones:** Treasurer- 605-677-7123; Elections- 605-677-7120; Vital Records- 605-677-7130. **Property tax/Assessor-** 211 W. Main St, #1, Vermillion, SD 57069; 605-677-7140.

Codington County

Register of Deeds, 14 1st Ave S.E., Watertown, SD 57201-3695. 605-882-6278; fax-602-882-5230; hours: 8AM-5PM.
www.codington.org/Register%20of%20Deeds.htm
Separate indices to search include Deeds and Mtgs. Records indexed on computer to 2000. Office will perform a UCC and Tax lien search but public must search other records themselves. Search fee $20.00. Copy fee $1.00 per document. Cert fee- $2.00 per doc plus copy fee. Payee- Register of Deeds. **Other phones:** Treasurer- 605-886-6285; Appraiser/Auditor- 605-886-6274; Elections- 605-882-6297; Vital Records- 605-882-6278. **Property tax/Assessor-** same address as above. 605-886-6274.

Corson County

Register of Deeds, PO Box 256, McIntosh, SD 57641-0256. 605-273-4395; fax-605-273-4233; hours: 8AM-N, 1-5PM.
Office personnel or visitors may perform searches. Search fee $10.00 per name. Will not search real estate records. Copy fee $1.00 per page. Cert fee- $2.00 per cert. Payee- Register of Deeds. **Other phones:** Treasurer- 605-273-4552. **Property tax/Assessor-** 605-273-4354.

Custer County

Register of Deeds, 420 Mount Rushmore Rd, Custer, SD 57730-1934. 605-673-8171; fax-605-673-8148; hours: 8AM-5PM M-Th.
All records in one index. Only the public may search. Copy fee $1.00 for up to 4 pages, $.25 each add'l. Cert fee- $2.00 per page plus copy fee. **Other phones:** Treasurer- 605-673-8172; Appraiser/Auditor- 605-673-8970; Elections- 605-673-8173; Vital Records- 605-673-8171. **Property tax/Assessor-** same address as above. 605-673-8170.

Davison County

Register of Deeds, 200 E. 4th; Courthouse, Mitchell, SD 57301-2692. 605-995-8616; fax-605-995-8648; hours: 8AM-5PM.
www.davisoncounty.org/registerofdeeds.html
Will not search real estate records. Will search UCC records. Tax lien search available. UCC search per debtor name- $20.00. Tax lien search fee- $20.00 per debtor name (in writing, $15.00 for verbal).

Copy fee $1.00 per page. Cert fee- $1.00 per doc plus copy fee. **Other phones:** Treasurer- 605-995-8617; Appraiser/Auditor- 605-995-8613; Elections-605-995-8608; Vital Records- 605-995-8616; Court Clerk- 605-995-8105. **Property tax/Assessor-** 605-995-8613.

Day County

Register of Deeds, 711 W. First St, Webster, SD 57274-1396. 605-345-9506; fax-605-345-9507; 8AM-N, 1-5PM.
All records in one index. Records indexed on computer back to 1999. Office will perform a UCC and tax lien search but public must search other records themselves. Search fee $12.00 UCCs; tax liens $20.00. Copy fee $1.00 per page. Cert fee- $2.00 per cert plus copy fee. Payee- Day County Register of Deeds. **Other phones:** Treasurer-605-345-9510; Elections- 605-345-9500; Vital Records- 605-345-9506. **Property tax/Assessor-** 605-345-9502.

Deuel County

Register of Deeds, PO Box 307, Clear Lake, SD 57226. 605-874-2268; fax-605-874-1306; hours: 8AM-5PM.
Separate indices to search include deeds, mortgages, state & federal tax liens, UCC's. Record index not computerized. Office personnel or visitors may perform searches. Search fee $5.00 per name. UCC search per debtor name- $12.00. Copy fee $1.00 per page. Cert fee- $2.00 per recorded instrument. Payee- Register of Deeds. **Other phones:** Treasurer- 605-874-2483; Elections-605-874-2312; Vital Records- 605-874-2268. **Property tax/Assessor-** 605-874-2229.

Dewey County

Register of Deeds, PO Box 117, Timber Lake, SD 57656-0117. 605-865-3661; fax-605-865-3691; hours: 8AM-N, 1-5PM.
Office personnel or visitors may perform searches. Search fee $8.00 per name. UCC search per debtor name- $10.00. Copy fee $1.00 per page. Cert fee-$2.00 per cert. Payee- Dewey County Clerk. **Other phones:** Treasurer- 605-865-3501; Appraiser/Auditor- 605-865-3730; Elections- 605-865-3672; Vital Records- 605-865-3661. **Property tax/Assessor-** 605-865-3573.

Douglas County

Register of Deeds, PO Box 267, Armour, SD 57313-0267. 605-724-2204; fax-605-724-2204; hours: 8AM-12, 1PM-5PM.
Separate indices to search include grantor/grantee, legal description. Record index not computerized. Only the office personnel may search. Search fee $10.00 per name. Copy fee $1.00 per page. Cert fee- $2.00 per doc plus copy fee. Payee- Register of Deeds. **Other phones:** Treasurer- 605-724-2318; Appraiser/Auditor- 605-724-2688; Elections- 605-724-2423; Vital Records- 605-724-2204. **Property tax/Assessor-** 605-724-2688.

Edmunds County

Register of Deeds, PO Box 386, Ipswich, SD 57451-0386. 605-426-6431; fax-605-426-6257; hours: 8AM-N,1-5PM.
Record index not computerized. Only the public may search. Copy fee $1.00 per page. Cert fee-$2.00 per cert plus copy fee. Payee- Edmunds County Register of Deeds. **Other phones:** Treasurer-605-426-6801; Appraiser/Auditor- 605-426-6841; Elections- 605-426-6762; Vital Records- 605-426-6431. **Property tax/Assessor-** 605-426-6841.

Fall River County

Register of Deeds, 906 N. River St, Hot Springs, SD 57747. 605-745-5139; fax-605-745-6835; hours: 8AM-5PM.
All records in one index. Record index not computerized. Only the public may search. Copy fee $1.00 per doc up to 5 pages, $.20 per add'l page. Fax back- $3.00 fee. Cert fee- $2.00 per doc

plus copy fee. **Other phones:** Treasurer- 605-745-5145; Elections- 605-745-5130; Vital Records- 605-745-5139. **Property tax/Assessor-** 605-745-5136.

Faulk County

Register of Deeds, PO Box 309, Faulkton, SD 57438. 605-598-6228; fax-605-598-6680; 8AM-N,1-5PM.
Separate indices to search. Record index not computerized. Only the public may search. Copy fee $1.00 per page. Cert fee- $2.00 per cert includes copy fee. Payee- Faulk County Register of Deeds. **Other phones:** Treasurer- 605-598-6232; Vital Records- 605-598-6228. **Property tax/Assessor-** same address as above. 605-598-6225.

Grant County

Register of Deeds, PO Box 587, Milbank, SD 57252. 605-432-4752; fax-605-432-9004; hours: 8AM-5PM.
Separate indices to search include town, rural, and all. Search fee $10.00 unless otherwise indicated. Will search real estate records as time permits. UCC search per debtor name- $20.00. Copy fee $1.00 per page. Cert fee- $2.00 per cert plus copy fee. Payee- Grant County Register of Deeds. **Other phones:** Treasurer- 605-432-5651; Appraiser/Auditor-605-432-6532; Elections- 605-432-6711; Vital Records- 605-432-4752. **Property tax/Assessor-** 210 E 5th Ave, Milbank, SD 57252; 605-432-6532.

Gregory County

Register of Deeds, PO Box 437, Burke, SD 57523. 605-775-2624; fax-605-775-2596; hours: 8AM-N,1-5PM.
Office will perform a UCC search but public must search other records themselves. UCC search per debtor name- $10.00. Copy fee $1.00 per page. Tax lien copy- $.50. Cert fee- $3.00 per cert. Payee- Gregory County Register of Deeds. **Other phones:** Treasurer- 605-775-2605. **Property tax/Assessor-** 605-775-2673.

Haakon County

Register of Deeds, PO Box 100, Philip, SD 57567-0100. 605-859-2785; hours: 8AM-N,1-5PM.
Separate indices to search include deeds, mortgages, misc. Office will perform a UCC search but public must search other records themselves. UCC search per debtor name- $12.00. Copy fee $1.00 per page. Cert fee- $2.00 per cert plus copy fee. Payee- Haakon County Register of Deeds. **Other phones:** Treasurer- 605-859-2612; Appraiser/Auditor- 605-859-2800. **Property tax/Assessor-** 605-859-2824.

Hamlin County

Register of Deeds, PO Box 56, Hayti, SD 57241. 605-783-3206; hours: 8AM-N, 1-5PM.
Separate indices to search include deeds, misc, mortgage. Record index not computerized. Only the public may search. Copy fee $1.00 per page. Cert fee- $2.00 per instrument. Payee- Hamlin County Register of Deeds. **Other phones:** Treasurer-605-783-3441. **Property tax/Assessor-** 605-783-3331.

Hand County

Register of Deeds, 415 W. 1st Ave, Miller, SD 57362-1346. 605-853-3512; fax-605-853-2769; 8AM-5PM.
Separate indices to search include mortgages and deeds (misc), have separate indexes by land. Only the public may search. Copy fee $1.00 per page. Cert fee- $2.00 per copy plus copy fee. Payee- Register of Deeds. **Other phones:** Treasurer- 605-853-2136; Appraiser/Auditor- 605-853-2182; Vital Records- 605-853-3512. **Property tax/Assessor-** 415 W 1st Ave, Miller, SD 57362; 605-853-2115.

Hanson County

Register of Deeds, PO Box 500, Alexandria, SD 57311-0500. 605-239-4512; fax-605-239-4296; hours: 8AM-N; 1-5PM.
Records indexed on a public use terminal back to 1990. Office will perform a UCC and Tax lien search but public must search other records

themselves. Search fee $20.00. Copy fee $1.00 per page. Cert fee- $2.00 per doc; $.20 each page after 5 pages. Payee- Register of Deeds. **Other phones:** Treasurer- 605-239-4723; Appraiser/Auditor- 605-239-4445; Elections- 605-239-4714; Vital Records- 605-239-4512. **Property tax/Assessor-** same address as above. 605-239-4445.

Harding County

Register of Deeds, PO Box 101, Buffalo, SD 57720. 605-375-3321; fax-605-375-3310; 8AM-N, 1-5PM. Index: Deeds, Oil & Gas, Miscellaneous. Record index not computerized. Office will perform a UCC search but public must search other records themselves. Search fee $15.00. Copy fee $1.00 per page. Cert fee- $5.00. Payee- Harding County Register of Deeds. **Other phones:** Treasurer- 605-375-3542. **Property tax/Assessor-** 605-375-3234.

Hughes County

Register of Deeds, 104 E. Capital, Pierre, SD 57501. 605-773-7495; fax-605-773-7479; hours: 8AM-5PM. www.sdcounties.org Separate indices to search include Deeds and Mtgs. Visitors may perform searches. Office personal perform limited searches. Search fee $20.00 per name; verbal search $15.00. Copy fee $1.00 per page. Cert fee- $2.00 for 1st 5 pages, $.20 extra thereafter. Payee- Hughes County. **Other phones:** Treasurer- 605-773-7491; Appraiser/Auditor- 605-773-7483; Elections- 605-773-7451; Vital Records- 605-773-7495. **Property tax/Assessor-** 605-773-7483.

Hutchinson County

Register of Deeds, 140 Euclid St, Rm 37, Olivet, SD 57052-2103. 605-387-4217; R/E recording phone-605-387-2838, UCC recording phone-605-387-4217; fax-605-387-4209; hours: 8AM-4;30PM. Index: More than 1 index. Records indexed on computer. Office will perform a UCC search but public must search other records themselves. UCC search per debtor name- $20.00. Copy fee $1.00 per page 1st 5 pgs; $.20 each add'l page. Cert fee- $2.00 per cert. **Other phones:** Treasurer- 605-387-4213; Appraiser/Auditor- 605-387-4210; Elections- 605-387-4212. **Property tax/Assessor-** 605-387-4210.

Hyde County

Register of Deeds, PO Box 342, Highmore, SD 57345. 605-852-2517; fax-605-852-3178; hours: 8AM-N, 1-5PM. Office personnel or visitors may perform searches. Search fee $10.00 per name. Will not search real estate records. Copy fee $1.00 per page. Cert fee- $2.00 per doc plus copy fee. Payee- Hyde County Register of Deeds. **Other phones:** Treasurer- 605-852-2510. **Property tax/Assessor-** 605-852-2570.

Jackson County

Register of Deeds, PO Box 248, Kadoka, SD 57453. 605-837-2420; hours: 8AM-5PM. Separate indices to search include deeds and mortgages. Will not search real estate records. Will search UCC records; search includes tax liens if requested. UCC search per debtor name- $10.00. Separate federal tax lien search- $4.00 per debtor. Separate state tax lien search- $4.00 per debtor. Copy fee $1.00 per page. Cert fee- $2.00 per cert, does not include copies. Payee- Jackson County Register of Deeds. **Other phones:** Treasurer- 605-837-2423. **Property tax/Assessor-** 605-837-2424.

Jerauld County

Register of Deeds, PO Box 452, Wessington Springs, SD 57382-0452. 605-539-1221; 8AM-12, 1PM-5PM. Index: In Books. Office personnel or visitors may perform searches. Search fee $10.00. Copy fee $1.00 per page. Cert fee- $2.00 per cert plus copy fee. Payee- Jerauld County Register of Deeds. **Other phones:** Treasurer- 605-539-1241. **Property tax/Assessor-** 605-539-9701.

Jones County

Register of Deeds, PO Box 446, Murdo, SD 57559. 605-669-7104; fax-605-669-7120; hours: 8AM-5PM. Office personnel or visitors may perform searches. Search fee $10.00 per name. Will not search real estate records. Copy fee $1.00 per page. Cert fee- $2.00 1st 5 pg, $.20 each addl. Payee- Jones County Register of Deeds. **Other phones:** Treasurer- 605-669-2122. **Property tax/Assessor-** 605-669-2122.

Kingsbury County

Register of Deeds, PO Box 146, De Smet, SD 57231-0146. 605-854-3591; fax-605-854-3833; hours: 8AM-N, 1PM-5PM. Office personnel or visitors may perform searches. Search fee $5.00 per name. Will not search real estate records. UCC search per debtor name- $20.00. Copy fee $1.00 per page. Cert fee- $2.00 per cert. Payee- Kingsbury County Register of Deeds. **Other phones:** Treasurer- 605-854-3411; Elections- 605-854-3832. **Property tax/Assessor-** 605-854-3593.

Lake County

Register of Deeds, PO Box 266, Madison, SD 57042. 605-256-7614; fax-605-256-7622; hours: 8AM-5PM. All records in one index. Records indexed on computer back to 1/1/2000. Office personnel or visitors may perform searches. Search fee $10.00 per name. Copy fee $1.00 per page. Cert fee- $2.00 per instrument plus copy fee. Payee-Register of Deeds. **Other phones:** Treasurer- 605-256-7618; Vital Records- 605-256-7614. **Property tax/Assessor-** address above. 605-256-7605.

Lawrence County

Register of Deeds, PO Box 565, Deadwood, SD 57732. 605-578-3930; fax-605-722-6221; hours: 8AM-5PM. Office personnel or visitors may perform searches. Search fee $5.00 per name. UCC search per debtor name- $20.00. Copy fee $1.00 per page. Cert fee- $2.00 1st 5 pg, $.20 each addl. Payee- Lawrence County Register of Deeds. **Property tax/Assessor-** 605-578-3680.

Lincoln County

Register of Deeds, 100 E. 5th, Canton, SD 57013-1789. 605-764-5661; fax-605-764-5932; hours: 8AM-5PM. Separate indices to search include land records by legal descriptions. Records indexed on a public use terminal. Office personnel or visitors may perform searches. Search fee $20.00 per name. Copy fee $1.00 per page up to 5 pages, $.20 per page after 5 pages. Cert fee- $2.00 per cert plus copy fee. Payee- Lincoln County Register of Deeds. **Other phones:** Treasurer- 605-764-5701; Elections- 605-764-2581; Vital Records- 605-764-5661. **Property tax/Assessor-** address above. 605-764-2571.

Lyman County

Register of Deeds, PO Box 98, Kennebec, SD 57544-0098. 605-869-2297; fax-605-869-2203; hours: 8AM-N, 1-5PM. Office personnel or visitors may perform searches. Search fee $5.00 per name. Will not search UCC records. Copy fee $1.00 per page. Tax lien copy- $.50 per page. Cert fee- $2.00 per page. Payee- Lyman Co. Registrar of Deeds. **Other phones:** Treasurer- 605-869-2295; Appraiser/Auditor- 605-869-2206; Elections- 605-869-2247; Vital Records- 605-869-2297. **Property tax/Assessor-** 605-869-2206.

Marshall County

Register of Deeds, PO Box 130, Britton, SD 57430. 605-448-2352; fax-605-448-2116; hours: 8AM-5PM. Separate indices to search include deeds, satisfactions, mortgages, miscellaneous. Office personnel or visitors may perform searches, includes real estate records only if provided with legal description. Search fee $20.00 per debtor name. Copy fee $1.00 per page. Cert fee- $2.00

per doc plus copy fee. Payee- Marshall County Register of Deeds. **Other phones:** Treasurer- 605-448-2451; Appraiser/Auditor- 605-448-2822; Elections- 605-448-2401; Vital Records- 605-448-2352. **Property tax/Assessor-** same address as above. 605-448-5291.

McCook County

Register of Deeds, PO Box 338, Salem, SD 57058-0338. 605-425-2701; fax-605-425-2534; hours: 8:30AM-4:30PM. Office personnel or visitors may perform searches. Search fee $5.00 per name. UCC search per debtor name- $12.00. Copy fee $1.00 per page. Cert fee- $2.00 per cert plus copy fee. Payee- McCook County Register of Deeds. **Other phones:** Treasurer- 605-425-2721; Elections- 605-425-2791; Vital Records- 605-425-2701. **Property tax/Assessor-** 605-425-2681.

McPherson County

Register of Deeds, PO Box 129, Leola, SD 57456. 605-439-3151; fax-605-439-3394; hours: 8AM-5PM. Separate indices to search include deeds, mortgages, misc, easements, sat. Office will perform a UCC search but public must search other records themselves. UCC search per debtor name- $20.00. Federal/state combined tax lien -no charge. Copy fee $1.00 per page. Cert fee- $2.00 per cert plus copy fee. Payee- Register of Deeds. **Other phones:** Treasurer- 605-439-3544. **Property tax/Assessor-** 605-439-3663.

Meade County

Register of Deeds, 1425 Sherman St, Sturgis, SD 57785. 605-347-2356; fax-605-347-5925; hours: 8AM-5PM. www.meadecounty.org Separate indices to search include satisfactions, mortgage, deed, misc. Record index not computerized. Office will perform a UCC search but public must search other records themselves. Search fee $10.00 per name. Copy fee $1.00 per document after 5 pages. Add'l fee-$.25 per page. Cert fee- $2.00 per doc plus copy fee. **Other phones:** Treasurer- 605-347-5871; Elections- 605-347-2360; Vital Records- 605-347-3356. **Property tax/Assessor-** 1425 Sherman St, Sturgis, SD 57785; 605-347-3818.

Mellette County

Register of Deeds, PO Box 183, White River, SD 57579-0183. 605-259-3371; fax-605-259-3194; hours: 8AM-N,1-5PM. All records in one index. Records index not computerized. Office personnel or visitors may perform searches. Search fee $10.00 per name. Copy fee $1.00 per page. Cert fee- $2.00 per cert plus copy fee. Payee- Mellette County Register of Deeds. **Other phones:** Treasurer- 605-259-3151. **Property tax/Assessor-** PO Box 198, White River, SD 57579; 605-259-3150.

Miner County

Register of Deeds, PO Box 546, Howard, SD 57349. 605-772-5621; fax-605-772-4148; 8AM-N, 1-5PM. All records in one index. Records indexed on computer back to 2005. Only the public may search. Copy fee $1.00 per instrument up to 5 pgs. R/E record copy- $1.00 per instrument up to 5 pages. Cert fee- $2.00 per page includes copy fee. Payee- Miner County Register of Deeds. **Other phones:** Treasurer- 605-772-4652; Appraiser/Auditor- 605-772-4671. **Property tax/Assessor-** PO Box 577, Howard, SD 57349; 605-772-4241.

Minnehaha County

Register of Deeds, 415 N Dakota Ave, Sioux Falls, SD 57104-2465. 605-367-4223; fax-605-367-8314; hours: 8AM-5PM. www.minnehahacounty.org/depts/register_deeds/register_deeds.asp Office personnel or visitors may perform searches. Search fee $4.00 per name. Will not search real estate records. UCC search per debtor name- $20.00. Copy fee $1.00 per page. Cert fee- $2.00 1st 5 pg, $.20 each addl. Payee- Minnehaha County Register of Deeds. **Online access to Property Tax records:** The county property tax database is free at www.minnehahacounty.org/property_tax/Index.asp. No name searching at this time. **Other phones:** Treasurer- 605-367-4212; Appraiser/Auditor- 605-367-4228; Elections- 605-367-4220; Vital Records- 605-367-4223. **Property tax/Assessor**- 605-367-4228.

Moody County

Register of Deeds, PO Box 247, Flandreau, SD 57028-0247. 605-997-3151; fax-605-997-9996; 8AM-5PM. All records in one index. Office will perform a UCC search but public must search other records themselves. UCC search per debtor name- $20.00. Copy fee $1.00 per page. Cert fee- $2.00 per cert; $.20 per page after 5 pages. Payee- Moody County Register of Deeds. **Other phones:** Treasurer- 605-997-3171; Appraiser/Auditor- 605-997-3161; Vital Records- 605-997-3151. **Property tax/Assessor**-605-997-3101.

Pennington County

Register of Deeds, 315 St. Joe St, Rapid City, SD 57701. 605-394-2177; hours: 8AM-5PM. www.co.pennington.sd.us
Separate indices to search include Deeds and Mtgs. Office will perform a UCC search but public must search other records themselves. Search fee $20.00. Copy fee $1.00 per page. R/E record copy- $1.00 1st 5 pages; $.20 each add'l page. Cert fee- $1.00 per page plus copy fee. Payee- Pennington County Register of Deeds. **Online access to Property Tax, Assessor records:** Access to the county property tax database is free at www.co.pennington.sd.us/doe/look%20up%20options.htm. **Other phones:** Treasurer- 605-394-2161; Elections- 605-394-2153; Vital Records- 605-394-2177. **Property tax/Assessor**- same address as above. 605-394-2175.

Perkins County

Register of Deeds, PO Box 127, Bison, SD 57620. 605-244-5620; fax-605-244-7289; hours: 8AM-5PM.
Separate indices to search include grantor/grantee/ mortgages, deed, miscellaneous. Records indexed on computer back to 1996. Office will perform a UCC search but public must search other records themselves. UCC search per debtor name- $20.00. Copy fee $1.00 per page. Cert fee- $2.00 per instrument plus copy fee. Payee- Perkins Co. Registrar of Deeds. **Other phones:** Treasurer- 605-244-5613; Elections- 605-244-5624; Vital Records- 605-773-4961. **Property tax/Assessor**- PO Box 6, Bison, SD 57620; 605-244-5623.

Potter County

Register of Deeds, 201 S. Exene, Gettysburg, SD 57442. 605-765-9467; fax-605-765-2836; hours: 8AM-5PM.
Office will perform a UCC search but public must search other records themselves. UCC search per debtor name- $10.00. Copy fee $1.00 per page. Cert fee- $2.00 per cert. Payee- Potter County Register of Deeds. **Other phones:** Treasurer- 605-765-9403; Elections- 605-765-9408; Vital Records- 605-765-9467. **Property tax/Assessor**- 605-765-2481.

Roberts County

Register of Deeds, 411 E. 2nd Ave, Sisseton, SD 57262. 605-698-7152; fax-605-698-4277; 8AM-5PM. Office personnel or visitors may perform searches. UCC search per debtor name- $20.00. Copy fee $1.00 per page. Cert fee- $10.00 per cert plus copy fee. Payee- Roberts County Register of Deeds. **Other phones:** Treasurer- 605-698-7245. **Property tax/Assessor**-605-698-3205.

Sanborn County

Register of Deeds, PO Box 295, Woonsocket, SD 57385. 605-796-4516; fax-605-796-4509; 8AM-5PM. Separate indices to search include deeds, mortgage. Records indexed on computer back to 2004. Only the public may search. General copy fee $1.00 1st 5 pages, $.20 each add'l. Tax lien copy- $.50 per page. Cert fee- $2.00 per doc plus copy fee. Payee- Register of Deeds. **Other phones:** Treasurer- 605-796-4512; Vital Records- 605-796-4516. **Property tax/Assessor**- PO Box 416, Woonsocket, SC 57385; 605-796-4514.

Shannon County

Register of Deeds, 906 N. River St, Hot Springs, SD 57747. 605-745-5139; fax-605-745-6835; hours: 8AM-5PM.
All records in one index. Only the public may search. Copy fee $1.00 per page. $.20 each after 1st 5 pages. Payee- Shannon County Register of Deeds. **Other phones:** Treasurer- 605-745-5145. **Property tax/Assessor**- 605-745-5141.

Spink County

Register of Deeds, 210 E. 7th Ave, Redfield, SD 57469-0266. 605-472-0150, R/E recording phone-605-472-4588; fax-605-472-2410; hours: 8AM-5PM.
Separate indices to search include Deeds and Mtgs. Record index not computerized. Office personnel or visitors may perform searches. Search fee $13.00 UCCs, $5.00 tax liens. No real estate records. Copy fee $1.00 per page. Tax lien copy- $.50 per page. Cert fee- $2.00 per page includes copy fee. **Other phones:** Treasurer- 605-472-4583; Elections- 605-472-1825; Vital Records- 605-472-4588. **Property tax/Assessor**- 605-472-4585.

Stanley County

Register of Deeds, PO Box 596, Fort Pierre, SD 57532. 605-223-7786; fax-605-223-7788; 8AM-N,1-5PM.
Separate indices to search include deeds, mortgages. Record index not computerized. Office personnel or visitors may perform searches. UCC search per debtor name- $20.00. Separate federal tax lien search- $5.00. Copy fee $1.00 per page. Cert fee- $2.00 1st 5 pg, $.20 each addl page, plus copy fee. Payee- Stanley County Register of Deeds. **Other phones:** Treasurer- 605-223-7783; Elections- 605-223-7780; Vital Records- 605-223-7786. **Property tax/Assessor**- 605-223-7780.

Sully County

Register of Deeds, PO Box 265, Onida, SD 57564. 605-258-2331; fax-605-258-2884;
Office will perform a UCC search but public must search other records themselves. UCC search per debtor name- $10.00. **Other phones:** Treasurer- 605-258-2444; Appraiser/Auditor- 605-258-2522; Elections- 605-258-2541; Vital Records- 605-258-2331. **Property tax/Assessor**- 605-258-2522.

Todd County

Register of Deeds, 200 E 3rd St, Winner, SD 57580-1806. 605-842-2208; fax-605-842-1116; hours: 8AM-5PM.
Separate indices to search. Records indexed on a public use terminal. Only the public may search. Copy fee $1.00 per page. Fax back fee- $3.00. Cert fee- $5.00 per cert. Payee- Todd County Registrar of Deeds. **Other phones:** Treasurer- 605-842-1700. **Property tax/Assessor**- 605-856-4633.

Tripp County

Register of Deeds, 200 E 3rd St, Courthouse, Winner, SD 57580-1806. 605-842-2208; fax-605-842-3621; hours: 8AM-5PM.
Separate indices to search include land records, federal and tax lien books. Records indexed on a public use terminal. Only the public may search. Copy fee $1.00 per page. Fax fee $3.00 per page. Cert fee- $5.00 per cert plus copy fee. Payee- Tripp County Register of Deeds. **Other phones:**

Treasurer- 605-842-1700. **Property tax/Assessor**-605-842-2300.

Turner County

Register of Deeds, PO Box 485, Parker, SD 57053-0485. 605-297-3443; fax-605-297-5556;
Office personnel or visitors may perform searches. Search fee $5.00 per name. Will not search real estate records. UCC search per debtor name- $10.00. Tax lien copy- $.50 per page. **Other phones:** Treasurer- 605-297-4425. **Property tax/Assessor**- 605-297-4420.

Union County

Register of Deeds, 209 E Main St #210, Elk Point, SD 57025. 605-356-2191, R/E recording phone-605-356-2041, UCC recording phone-605-356-2191; fax-605-356-3047; hours: 8:30AM-5PM.
Separate indices to search include books, computer, microfiche. Records indexed on a public use terminal back to 1993; more being added. Office personnel or visitors may perform searches. Office will search real estate records on computer no fee. UCC or state tax lien search per debtor name- $10.00. Separate federal tax lien search- $20.00 per search. Copy fee $1.00 per 1st 4 pages. Cert fee- $2.00 5 pages, $.20 per add'l page. Payee- Register of Deeds. **Online access to Property records:** Access to data is from a private company at www.publicbuzz.com; registration is required and free for one county only. Register and select Union, SD as your free county; purchase more counties for $5 per month. **Other phones:** Treasurer- 605-356-2391; Elections- 605-356-2101; Vital Records- 605-356-2191. **Property tax/Assessor**- 209 E Main St #130, Elk Point, SD 57025; 605-356-2252, assessor fax-605-356-3074.

Walworth County

Register of Deeds, PO Box 159, Selby, SD 57472-0159. 605-649-7057, R/E recording phone-605-649-7311; fax-605-649-7867; hours: 8AM-N,1-5PM.
Office personnel or visitors may perform searches. General search fee $5.00 per name. UCC search per debtor name- $12.00. UCC search request using non-standard form (per name)- $13.00. Copy fee $1.00 per page. Tax lien copy- $.50. Cert fee- $2.00 1st 5 pg, $.20 each addl. Payee- Walworth County Register of Deeds. **Other phones:** Treasurer- 605-649-7737. **Property tax/Assessor**- 605-649-7737.

Yankton County

Register of Deeds, PO Box 694, Yankton, SD 57078. 605-260-4400 x5; fax-605-668-9682; hours: 9AM-5PM. www.co.yankton.sd.us
Office personnel or visitors may perform searches. Search fee $10.00 per name. Will not search real estate records. Copy fee $1.00 per page. Cert fee- $2.00 per cert plus copy fee. Payee- Yankton County Register of Deeds. **Other phones:** Treasurer- 605-260-4400 x7. **Property tax/Assessor**- 605-260-4400 x3.

Ziebach County

Register of Deeds, PO Box 68, Dupree, SD 57623. 605-365-5165; fax-605-365-5204; hours: 8AM-5PM.
Office will perform a UCC search but public must search other records themselves. UCC search per debtor name- $10.00. Copy fee $1.00 per page. Cert fee- $2.00 per cert plus copy fee. Payee- Ziebach County Register of Deeds. **Other phones:** Treasurer- 605-365-5173. **Property tax/Assessor**- 605-365-5129.

South Dakota County Locator

You will usually be able to find the city name in the City/County Cross Reference below. In that case, it is a simple matter to determine the county from the cross reference. However, only the official US Postal Service city names are included in this index. We have also included a ZIP/City Cross Reference immediately following the City/County Cross Reference. If you know the ZIP Code but the city name does not appear in the City/County Cross Reference index, look up the ZIP Code in the ZIP/City Cross Reference, find the city name, then look up the city name in the City/County Cross Reference.

South Dakota City/County Cross Reference

ABERDEEN Brown
AGAR Sully
AKASKA Walworth
ALCESTER (57001) Union(94), Lincoln(5)
ALEXANDRIA (57311) Hanson(97), Hutchinson(1)
ALLEN (57714) Bennett(93), Jackson(6)
ALPENA (57312) Jerauld(58), Beadle(39), Sanborn(1)
AMHERST (57421) Marshall(91), Brown(8)
ANDOVER (57422) Day(95), Brown(4)
ARDMORE Fall River
ARLINGTON (57212) Kingsbury(70), Brookings(22), Hamlin(6)
ARMOUR (57313) Douglas(80), Charles Mix(19)
ARTESIAN Sanborn
ASHTON (57424) Spink(93), Faulk(6)
ASTORIA (57213) Deuel(75), Brookings(24)
AURORA (57002) Brookings(97), Moody(2)
AVON (57315) Bon Homme(98), Charles Mix(1)
BADGER Kingsbury
BALTIC Minnehaha
BANCROFT Kingsbury
BARNARD Brown
BATESLAND (57716) Shannon(86), Bennett(13)
BATH Brown
BEAVER CREEK Tripp
BELLE FOURCHE (57717) Butte(96), Lawrence(2)
BELVIDERE (57521) Jackson(78), Mellette(21)
BERESFORD (57004) Union(62), Lincoln(29), Clay(8)
BETHLEHEM Meade
BIG STONE CITY (57216) Grant(76), Roberts(23)
BISON Perkins
BLACK HAWK (57718) Meade(98), Pennington(1)
BLUNT (57522) Hughes(90), Sully(9)
BONESTEEL Gregory
BOWDLE (57428) Edmunds(79), Walworth(19)
BOX ELDER (57719) Pennington(89), Meade(10)
BRADLEY Clark
BRANDON Minnehaha
BRANDT Deuel
BRENTFORD Spink
BRIDGEWATER (57319) McCook(72), Turner(13), Hutchinson(13)
BRISTOL Day
BRITTON Marshall
BROOKINGS (57006) Brookings(97), Moody(2)
BROOKINGS Brookings
BRUCE Brookings
BRYANT (57221) Hamlin(86), Clark(10), Kingsbury(2)
BUFFALO Harding
BUFFALO GAP (57722) Custer(69), Fall River(22), Shannon(7)
BUFFALO RIDGE Minnehaha
BULLHEAD Corson
BURBANK (57010) Clay(73), Union(26)
BURKE Gregory

CAMP CROOK Harding
CANISTOTA McCook
CANOVA (57321) Hanson(46), Miner(43), McCook(9)
CANTON Lincoln
CAPUTA Pennington
CARPENTER (57322) Beadle(41), Clark(39), Spink(19)
CARTER (57526) Tripp(75), Todd(18), Mellette(5)
CARTHAGE (57323) Miner(90), Kingsbury(8)
CASTLEWOOD (57223) Hamlin(97), Deuel(2)
CAVOUR Beadle
CEDARBUTTE Mellette
CENTERVILLE (57014) Turner(72), Clay(13), Lincoln(13)
CHAMBERLAIN (57325) Brule(98), Buffalo(1)
CHAMBERLAIN Brule
CHANCELLOR (57015) Turner(96), Minnehaha(3)
CHERRY CREEK Ziebach
CHESTER (57016) Lake(89), Minnehaha(10)
CLAIRE CITY Roberts
CLAREMONT (57432) Brown(83), Marshall(16)
CLARK (57225) Clark(90), Deuel(9)
CLEAR LAKE (57226) Deuel(97), Hamlin(2)
COLMAN (57017) Moody(95), Lake(4)
COLOME Tripp
COLTON (57018) Minnehaha(96), Lake(3)
COLUMBIA Brown
CONDE (57434) Spink(67), Brown(16), Day(8), Clark(6)
CORONA (57227) Roberts(97), Grant(2)
CORSICA Douglas
CORSON Minnehaha
CREIGHTON Pennington
CRESBARD (57435) Faulk(90), Edmunds(9)
CROCKER Clark
CROOKS Minnehaha
CUSTER (57730) Custer(97), Pennington(2)
DALLAS (57529) Gregory(69), Tripp(30)
DANTE Charles Mix
DAVIS (57021) Turner(98), Lincoln(1)
DE SMET Kingsbury
DEADWOOD Lawrence
DELL RAPIDS (57022) Minnehaha(88), Moody(11)
DELMONT (57330) Douglas(73), Charles Mix(18), Hutchinson(8)
DIMOCK (57331) Hutchinson(67), Douglas(17), Davison(14)
DOLAND Spink
DRAPER (57531) Jones(98), Lyman(1)
DUPREE (57623) Ziebach(91), Dewey(8)
EAGLE BUTTE Dewey
EDEN (57232) Marshall(97), Day(2)
EDGEMONT (57735) Custer(62), Fall River(37)
EGAN Moody
ELK POINT Union
ELKTON (57026) Brookings(82), Moody(17)

ELLSWORTH AFB Meade
ELM SPRINGS Meade
EMERY (57332) Hutchinson(48), Hanson(38), McCook(12)
ENNING Meade
ERWIN (57233) Kingsbury(96), Hamlin(3)
ESTELLINE (57234) Hamlin(67), Deuel(30), Brookings(2)
ETHAN (57334) Davison(65), Hanson(25), Hutchinson(9)
EUREKA (57437) McPherson(75), Campbell(24)
FAIRBURN Custer
FAIRFAX Gregory
FAIRVIEW Lincoln
FAITH (57626) Meade(52), Perkins(42), Ziebach(5)
FAULKTON Faulk
FEDORA (57337) Miner(94), Sanborn(5)
FERNEY Brown
FIRESTEEL (57628) Corson(50), Dewey(50)
FLANDREAU Moody
FLORENCE (57235) Codington(93), Day(6)
FORT MEADE Meade
FORT PIERRE (57532) Stanley(98), Lyman(1)
FORT THOMPSON Buffalo
FRANKFORT Spink
FREDERICK Brown
FREEMAN (57029) Hutchinson(76), Turner(23)
FRUITDALE Butte
FULTON (57340) Hanson(90), Miner(9)
GANN VALLEY (57341) Buffalo(96), Brule(3)
GARDEN CITY Clark
GARRETSON Minnehaha
GARY Deuel
GAYVILLE (57031) Yankton(81), Clay(18)
GEDDES (57342) Charles Mix(98), Douglas(1)
GETTYSBURG (57442) Potter(96), Dewey(2), Sully(1)
GLAD VALLEY Ziebach
GLENCROSS (57630) Dewey(91), Corson(8)
GLENHAM (57631) Walworth(91), Campbell(9)
GOODWIN (57238) Deuel(72), Codington(23), Hamlin(3), Grant(1)
GREGORY (57533) Gregory(88), Lyman(6), Tripp(5)
GRENVILLE Day
GROTON Brown
HAMILL (57534) Tripp(85), Lyman(14)
HARRISBURG Lincoln
HARRISON Douglas
HARROLD (57536) Hughes(84), Sully(11), Hyde(3)
HARTFORD Minnehaha
HAYES (57537) Stanley(88), Haakon(12)
HAYTI Hamlin
HAZEL (57242) Hamlin(78), Codington(21)
HECLA Brown
HENRY (57243) Codington(95), Clark(4)
HERMOSA (57744) Custer(53), Pennington(45), Shannon(1)
HERREID Campbell
HERRICK Gregory

HETLAND Kingsbury
HIGHMORE (57345) Hyde(90), Faulk(9)
HILL CITY Pennington
HITCHCOCK (57348) Beadle(65), Spink(34)
HOLABIRD Hyde
HOSMER (57448) Edmunds(77), McPherson(22)
HOT SPRINGS (57747) Fall River(97), Custer(2)
HOUGHTON Brown
HOVEN (57450) Potter(61), Walworth(38)
HOWARD Miner
HOWES (57748) Meade(98), Buffalo(1)
HUDSON (57034) Lincoln(93), Union(6)
HUMBOLDT (57035) Minnehaha(97), McCook(2)
HURLEY Turner
HURON Beadle
IDEAL Tripp
INTERIOR (57750) Jackson(96), Pennington(3)
IONA (57542) Lyman(98), Gregory(1)
IPSWICH (57451) Edmunds(95), Brown(4)
IRENE (57037) Yankton(63), Clay(19), Turner(17)
IROQUOIS (57353) Kingsbury(65), Beadle(32), Clark(1)
ISABEL (57633) Dewey(62), Corson(32), Ziebach(5)
JAVA (57452) Walworth(74), Campbell(26)
JEFFERSON Union
KADOKA (57543) Jackson(98), Haakon(1)
KAYLOR Hutchinson
KELDRON Corson
KENNEBEC (57544) Lyman(98), Tripp(1)
KEYSTONE Pennington
KIMBALL (57355) Jerauld(55), Brule(42), Buffalo(2)
KRANZBURG Codington
KYLE (57752) Shannon(80), Jackson(20)
LABOLT Grant
LAKE ANDES Charles Mix
LAKE CITY Marshall
LAKE NORDEN (57248) Hamlin(86), Kingsbury(13)
LAKE PRESTON Kingsbury
LANE Jerauld
LANGFORD (57454) Marshall(79), Day(20)
LANTRY Dewey
LEAD Lawrence
LEBANON Potter
LEMMON (57638) Perkins(96), Corson(3)
LENNOX (57039) Lincoln(94), Turner(5)
LEOLA (57456) McPherson(98), Edmunds(1)
LESTERVILLE (57040) Yankton(95), Bon Homme(4)
LETCHER (57359) Sanborn(76), Aurora(11), Davison(10), Jerauld(1)
LINN (57483) Hand(48), Faulk(35), Spink(16)
LITTLE EAGLE Corson
LODGEPOLE Perkins
LONG VALLEY Jackson
LONGLAKE McPherson
LOWER BRULE Lyman
LUDLOW Harding
LYONS Minnehaha
MAHTO Corson

MANDERSON Shannon
MANSFIELD (57460) Brown(62), Spink(18), Faulk(9), Edmunds(9)
MARCUS Meade
MARION (57043) Turner(94), McCook(3), Hutchinson(1)
MARTIN Bennett
MARTY Charles Mix
MARVIN (57251) Grant(91), Roberts(8)
MC INTOSH Corson
MC LAUGHLIN Corson
MEADOW (57644) Perkins(75), Corson(14), Ziebach(10)
MECKLING Clay
MELLETTE (57461) Spink(98), Brown(1)
MENNO (57045) Hutchinson(86), Yankton(12), Turner(1)
MIDLAND (57552) Haakon(52), Stanley(32), Jackson(9), Mellette(3)
MILBANK (57252) Grant(98), Roberts(1)
MILBANK Grant
MILESVILLE Haakon
MILLER (57362) Hand(98), Buffalo(1)
MINA (57462) Edmunds(86), Brown(13)
MISSION Todd
MISSION HILL Yankton
MISSION RIDGE Stanley
MITCHELL (57301) Davison(98), Hanson(1)
MOBRIDGE Walworth
MONROE (57047) McCook(61), Turner(38)
MONTROSE (57048) McCook(90), Minnehaha(8)
MORRISTOWN Corson
MOUND CITY Campbell
MOUNT VERNON (57363) Davison(91), Aurora(4), Sanborn(3)
MUD BUTTE (57758) Meade(78), Perkins(17), Butte(3)
MURDO (57559) Jones(95), Mellette(4)
NEMO Lawrence
NEW EFFINGTON Roberts
NEW HOLLAND Douglas
NEW UNDERWOOD (57761) Pennington(62), Meade(37)
NEWELL (57760) Butte(80), Meade(17), Harding(1)
NISLAND Butte
NORRIS (57560) Mellette(53), Bennett(28), Jackson(18)
NORTH SIOUX CITY Union
NORTHVILLE (57465) Spink(62), Faulk(38)
NUNDA Lake
OACOMA Lyman
OELRICHS Fall River
OGLALA Shannon
OKATON Jones
OKREEK Todd
OLDHAM (57051) Kingsbury(92), Miner(5), Lake(1)

OLIVET Hutchinson
ONAKA (57466) Faulk(78), Edmunds(19), Potter(1)
ONIDA (57564) Sully(97), Hyde(2)
OPAL Meade
ORAL Fall River
ORIENT (57467) Hand(69), Faulk(30)
ORTLEY (57256) Grant(55), Roberts(33), Day(6), Codington(5)
OWANKA (57767) Pennington(64), Meade(36)
PARADE Dewey
PARKER (57053) Turner(95), McCook(3), Minnehaha(1)
PARKSTON (57366) Hutchinson(94), Douglas(4)
PARMELEE (57566) Todd(82), Mellette(17)
PEEVER Roberts
PHILIP (57567) Haakon(79), Jackson(12), Gregory(7)
PICKSTOWN Charles Mix
PIEDMONT Meade
PIERPONT Day
PIERRE (57501) Hughes(97), Sully(2)
PINE RIDGE Shannon
PLANKINTON Aurora
PLATTE (57369) Charles Mix(95), Aurora(2), Douglas(1)
POLLOCK Campbell
PORCUPINE Shannon
PRAIRIE CITY (57649) Perkins(89), Harding(10)
PRESHO Lyman
PRINGLE Custer
PROVO Fall River
PUKWANA (57370) Brule(83), Buffalo(16)
QUINN (57775) Pennington(56), Haakon(25), Jackson(18)
RALPH Harding
RAMONA (57054) Lake(97), Kingsbury(1), Miner(1)
RAPID CITY (57702) Pennington(98), Meade(1)
RAPID CITY Pennington
RAVINIA Charles Mix
RAYMOND (57258) Clark(87), Spink(12)
RED OWL Meade
REDFIELD (57469) Spink(96), Hand(3)
REDIG Harding
REE HEIGHTS (57371) Hand(96), Hyde(2), Buffalo(1)
RELIANCE Lyman
RENNER Minnehaha
REVA (57651) Harding(66), Perkins(33)
REVILLO (57259) Grant(68), Deuel(31)
RIDGEVIEW Dewey
ROCHFORD Pennington
ROCKHAM (57470) Faulk(54), Hand(45)
ROSCOE Edmunds
ROSEBUD Todd

ROSHOLT Roberts
ROSLYN (57261) Day(98), Marshall(1)
ROWENA Minnehaha
RUTLAND (57057) Lake(97), Moody(2)
SAINT CHARLES Gregory
SAINT FRANCIS Todd
SAINT LAWRENCE Hand
SAINT ONGE (57779) Lawrence(93), Butte(6)
SALEM (57058) McCook(93), Miner(6)
SCENIC (57780) Pennington(94), Shannon(5)
SCOTLAND (57059) Bon Homme(89), Hutchinson(10)
SELBY Walworth
SENECA (57473) Faulk(80), Potter(19)
SHADEHILL Perkins
SHERMAN Minnehaha
SINAI Brookings
SIOUX FALLS (57108) Lincoln(76), Minnehaha(23)
SIOUX FALLS (57106) Minnehaha(92), Lincoln(7)
SIOUX FALLS Minnehaha
SISSETON (57262) Roberts(96), Marshall(3)
SMITHWICK Fall River
SOUTH SHORE (57263) Codington(81), Grant(18)
SPEARFISH Lawrence
SPENCER (57374) Hanson(53), McCook(46)
SPRINGFIELD Bon Homme
STEPHAN Hyde
STICKNEY (57375) Aurora(97), Davison(2)
STOCKHOLM (57264) Grant(98), Codington(1)
STRANDBURG (57265) Grant(70), Deuel(25), Codington(3)
STRATFORD (57474) Brown(94), Spink(5)
STURGIS (57785) Meade(98), Lawrence(1)
SUMMIT (57266) Roberts(55), Grant(44)
TABOR (57063) Bon Homme(84), Yankton(15)
TEA (57064) Lincoln(94), Turner(5)
TIMBER LAKE Dewey
TOLSTOY (57475) Potter(59), Edmunds(38), Walworth(1)
TORONTO (57268) Deuel(76), Brookings(23)
TRAIL CITY (57657) Corson(90), Dewey(9)
TRENT Moody
TRIPP (57376) Hutchinson(86), Bon Homme(12), Charles Mix(1)
TULARE (57476) Spink(86), Hand(13)
TURTON Spink
TUTHILL Bennett
TWIN BROOKS Grant
TYNDALL Bon Homme
UNION CENTER Meade

UTICA Yankton
VALE (57788) Meade(52), Butte(47)
VALLEY SPRINGS Minnehaha
VEBLEN (57270) Marshall(86), Roberts(13)
VERMILLION Clay
VIBORG (57070) Turner(93), Yankton(6)
VIENNA (57271) Clark(76), Hamlin(23)
VIRGIL (57379) Beadle(80), Jerauld(19)
VIVIAN (57576) Lyman(92), Jones(8)
VOLGA (57071) Brookings(95), Lake(3), Moody(1)
VOLIN (57072) Yankton(78), Clay(21)
WAGNER Charles Mix
WAKONDA (57073) Clay(94), Turner(5)
WAKPALA Corson
WALKER Corson
WALL Pennington
WALLACE (57272) Codington(87), Clark(10), Day(2)
WANBLEE (57577) Jackson(98), Bennett(1)
WARD Moody
WARNER Brown
WASTA (57791) Pennington(50), Meade(49)
WATAUGA Corson
WATERTOWN Codington
WAUBAY (57273) Day(88), Roberts(11)
WAVERLY Codington
WEBSTER (57274) Day(98), Clark(1)
WENTWORTH (57075) Lake(98), Moody(1)
WESSINGTON (57381) Beadle(59), Hand(40)
WESSINGTON SPRINGS (57382) Jerauld(94), Aurora(3), Beadle(1)
WESTPORT (57481) Brown(59), McPherson(30), Edmunds(10)
WEWELA Tripp
WHITE Brookings
WHITE LAKE (57383) Aurora(98), Brule(1)
WHITE OWL Meade
WHITE RIVER Mellette
WHITEHORSE Dewey
WHITEWOOD (57793) Lawrence(84), Meade(13), Butte(2)
WILLOW LAKE Clark
WILMOT Roberts
WINFRED (57076) Miner(53), Lake(46)
WINNER (57580) Tripp(98), Todd(1)
WITTEN Tripp
WOLSEY Beadle
WOOD Mellette
WOONSOCKET (57385) Sanborn(83), Jerauld(14), Aurora(1)
WORTHING Lincoln
WOUNDED KNEE Shannon
YALE Beadle
YANKTON Yankton
ZEONA (57795) Perkins(66), Butte(33)

South Dakota ZIP/City Cross Reference

ZIP	City
57001-57001	ALCESTER
57002-57002	AURORA
57003-57003	BALTIC
57004-57004	BERESFORD
57005-57005	BRANDON
57006-57007	BROOKINGS
57010-57010	BURBANK
57012-57012	CANISTOTA
57013-57013	CANTON
57014-57014	CENTERVILLE
57015-57015	CHANCELLOR
57016-57016	CHESTER
57017-57017	COLMAN
57018-57018	COLTON
57019-57019	CORSON
57020-57020	CROOKS
57021-57021	DAVIS
57022-57022	DELL RAPIDS
57024-57024	EGAN
57025-57025	ELK POINT
57026-57026	ELKTON
57027-57027	FAIRVIEW
57028-57028	FLANDREAU
57029-57029	FREEMAN
57030-57030	GARRETSON
57031-57031	GAYVILLE
57032-57032	HARRISBURG
57033-57033	HARTFORD
57034-57034	HUDSON
57035-57035	HUMBOLDT
57036-57036	HURLEY
57037-57037	IRENE
57038-57038	JEFFERSON
57039-57039	LENNOX
57040-57040	LESTERVILLE
57041-57041	LYONS
57042-57042	MADISON
57043-57043	MARION
57044-57044	MECKLING
57045-57045	MENNO
57046-57046	MISSION HILL
57047-57047	MONROE
57048-57048	MONTROSE
57049-57049	NORTH SIOUX CITY
57050-57050	NUNDA
57051-57051	OLDHAM
57052-57052	OLIVET
57053-57053	PARKER
57054-57054	RAMONA
57055-57055	RENNER
57056-57056	ROWENA
57057-57057	RUTLAND
57058-57058	SALEM
57059-57059	SCOTLAND
57060-57060	SHERMAN
57061-57061	SINAI
57062-57062	SPRINGFIELD
57063-57063	TABOR
57064-57064	TEA
57065-57065	TRENT
57066-57066	TYNDALL
57067-57067	UTICA
57068-57068	VALLEY SPRINGS
57069-57069	VERMILLION
57070-57070	VIBORG
57071-57071	VOLGA
57072-57072	VOLIN
57073-57073	WAKONDA
57074-57074	WARD
57075-57075	WENTWORTH
57076-57076	WINFRED
57077-57077	WORTHING
57078-57079	YANKTON
57100-57110	SIOUX FALLS
57115-57115	BUFFALO RIDGE
57116-57198	SIOUX FALLS

57201-57201 WATERTOWN	57340-57340 FULTON	57472-57472 SELBY	57647-57647 PARADE
57202-57202 WAVERLY	57341-57341 GANN VALLEY	57473-57473 SENECA	57648-57648 POLLOCK
57212-57212 ARLINGTON	57342-57342 GEDDES	57474-57474 STRATFORD	57649-57649 PRAIRIE CITY
57213-57213 ASTORIA	57344-57344 HARRISON	57475-57475 TOLSTOY	57650-57650 RALPH
57214-57214 BADGER	57345-57345 HIGHMORE	57476-57476 TULARE	57651-57651 REVA
57216-57216 BIG STONE CITY	57346-57346 STEPHAN	57477-57477 TURTON	57652-57652 RIDGEVIEW
57217-57217 BRADLEY	57348-57348 HITCHCOCK	57479-57479 WARNER	57653-57653 SHADEHILL
57218-57218 BRANDT	57349-57349 HOWARD	57481-57481 WESTPORT	57656-57656 TIMBER LAKE
57219-57219 BRISTOL	57350-57350 HURON	57483-57483 LINN	57657-57657 TRAIL CITY
57220-57220 BRUCE	57353-57353 IROQUOIS	57501-57501 PIERRE	57658-57658 WAKPALA
57221-57221 BRYANT	57354-57354 KAYLOR	57520-57520 AGAR	57659-57659 WALKER
57223-57223 CASTLEWOOD	57355-57355 KIMBALL	57521-57521 BELVIDERE	57660-57660 WATAUGA
57224-57224 CLAIRE CITY	57356-57356 LAKE ANDES	57522-57522 BLUNT	57661-57661 WHITEHORSE
57225-57225 CLARK	57357-57357 RAVINIA	57523-57523 BURKE	57701-57703 RAPID CITY
57226-57226 CLEAR LAKE	57358-57358 LANE	57526-57526 CARTER	57706-57706 ELLSWORTH AFB
57227-57227 CORONA	57359-57359 LETCHER	57527-57527 CEDARBUTTE	57708-57708 BETHLEHEM
57229-57229 CROCKER	57361-57361 MARTY	57528-57528 COLOME	57709-57709 RAPID CITY
57231-57231 DE SMET	57362-57362 MILLER	57529-57529 DALLAS	57714-57714 ALLEN
57232-57232 EDEN	57363-57363 MOUNT VERNON	57531-57531 DRAPER	57715-57715 ARDMORE
57233-57233 ERWIN	57364-57364 NEW HOLLAND	57532-57532 FORT PIERRE	57716-57716 BATESLAND
57234-57234 ESTELLINE	57365-57365 OACOMA	57533-57533 GREGORY	57717-57717 BELLE FOURCHE
57235-57235 FLORENCE	57366-57366 PARKSTON	57534-57534 HAMILL	57718-57718 BLACK HAWK
57236-57236 GARDEN CITY	57367-57367 PICKSTOWN	57536-57536 HARROLD	57719-57719 BOX ELDER
57237-57237 GARY	57368-57368 PLANKINTON	57537-57537 HAYES	57720-57720 BUFFALO
57238-57238 GOODWIN	57369-57369 PLATTE	57538-57538 HERRICK	57722-57722 BUFFALO GAP
57239-57239 GRENVILLE	57370-57370 PUKWANA	57540-57540 HOLABIRD	57724-57724 CAMP CROOK
57241-57241 HAYTI	57371-57371 REE HEIGHTS	57541-57541 IDEAL	57725-57725 CAPUTA
57242-57242 HAZEL	57373-57373 SAINT LAWRENCE	57542-57542 IONA	57729-57729 CREIGHTON
57243-57243 HENRY	57374-57374 SPENCER	57543-57543 KADOKA	57730-57730 CUSTER
57244-57244 HETLAND	57375-57375 STICKNEY	57544-57544 KENNEBEC	57732-57732 DEADWOOD
57245-57245 KRANZBURG	57376-57376 TRIPP	57545-57545 BEAVER CREEK	57735-57735 EDGEMONT
57246-57246 LABOLT	57379-57379 VIRGIL	57547-57547 LONG VALLEY	57736-57736 ELM SPRINGS
57247-57247 LAKE CITY	57380-57380 WAGNER	57548-57548 LOWER BRULE	57737-57737 ENNING
57248-57248 LAKE NORDEN	57381-57381 WESSINGTON	57551-57551 MARTIN	57738-57738 FAIRBURN
57249-57249 LAKE PRESTON	57382-57382 WESSINGTON SPRINGS	57552-57552 MIDLAND	57741-57741 FORT MEADE
57251-57251 MARVIN	57383-57383 WHITE LAKE	57553-57553 MILESVILLE	57742-57742 FRUITDALE
57252-57253 MILBANK	57384-57384 WOLSEY	57555-57555 MISSION	57744-57744 HERMOSA
57255-57255 NEW EFFINGTON	57385-57385 WOONSOCKET	57557-57557 MISSION RIDGE	57745-57745 HILL CITY
57256-57256 ORTLEY	57386-57386 YALE	57559-57559 MURDO	57747-57747 HOT SPRINGS
57257-57257 PEEVER	57399-57399 HURON	57560-57560 NORRIS	57748-57748 HOWES
57258-57258 RAYMOND	57401-57402 ABERDEEN	57562-57562 OKATON	57750-57750 INTERIOR
57259-57259 REVILLO	57420-57420 AKASKA	57563-57563 OKREEK	57751-57751 KEYSTONE
57260-57260 ROSHOLT	57421-57421 AMHERST	57564-57564 ONIDA	57752-57752 KYLE
57261-57261 ROSLYN	57422-57422 ANDOVER	57566-57566 PARMELEE	57754-57754 LEAD
57262-57262 SISSETON	57424-57424 ASHTON	57567-57567 PHILIP	57755-57755 LUDLOW
57263-57263 SOUTH SHORE	57426-57426 BARNARD	57568-57568 PRESHO	57756-57756 MANDERSON
57264-57264 STOCKHOLM	57427-57427 BATH	57569-57569 RELIANCE	57757-57757 MARCUS
57265-57265 STRANDBURG	57428-57428 BOWDLE	57570-57570 ROSEBUD	57758-57758 MUD BUTTE
57266-57266 SUMMIT	57429-57429 BRENTFORD	57571-57571 SAINT CHARLES	57759-57759 NEMO
57268-57268 TORONTO	57430-57430 BRITTON	57572-57572 SAINT FRANCIS	57760-57760 NEWELL
57269-57269 TWIN BROOKS	57432-57432 CLAREMONT	57574-57574 TUTHILL	57761-57761 NEW UNDERWOOD
57270-57270 VEBLEN	57433-57433 COLUMBIA	57576-57576 VIVIAN	57762-57762 NISLAND
57271-57271 VIENNA	57434-57434 CONDE	57577-57577 WANBLEE	57763-57763 OELRICHS
57272-57272 WALLACE	57435-57435 CRESBARD	57578-57578 WEWELA	57764-57764 OGLALA
57273-57273 WAUBAY	57436-57436 DOLAND	57579-57579 WHITE RIVER	57765-57765 OPAL
57274-57274 WEBSTER	57437-57437 EUREKA	57580-57580 WINNER	57766-57766 ORAL
57276-57276 WHITE	57438-57438 FAULKTON	57584-57584 WITTEN	57767-57767 OWANKA
57278-57278 WILLOW LAKE	57439-57439 FERNEY	57585-57585 WOOD	57769-57769 PIEDMONT
57279-57279 WILMOT	57440-57440 FRANKFORT	57601-57601 MOBRIDGE	57770-57770 PINE RIDGE
57301-57301 MITCHELL	57441-57441 FREDERICK	57620-57620 BISON	57772-57772 PORCUPINE
57311-57311 ALEXANDRIA	57442-57442 GETTYSBURG	57621-57621 BULLHEAD	57773-57773 PRINGLE
57312-57312 ALPENA	57445-57445 GROTON	57622-57622 CHERRY CREEK	57774-57774 PROVO
57313-57313 ARMOUR	57446-57446 HECLA	57623-57623 DUPREE	57775-57775 QUINN
57314-57314 ARTESIAN	57448-57448 HOSMER	57625-57625 EAGLE BUTTE	57776-57776 REDIG
57315-57315 AVON	57449-57449 HOUGHTON	57626-57626 FAITH	57777-57777 RED OWL
57316-57316 BANCROFT	57450-57450 HOVEN	57628-57628 FIRESTEEL	57778-57778 ROCHFORD
57317-57317 BONESTEEL	57451-57451 IPSWICH	57629-57629 GLAD VALLEY	57779-57779 SAINT ONGE
57319-57319 BRIDGEWATER	57452-57452 JAVA	57630-57630 GLENCROSS	57780-57780 SCENIC
57321-57321 CANOVA	57454-57454 LANGFORD	57631-57631 GLENHAM	57782-57782 SMITHWICK
57322-57322 CARPENTER	57455-57455 LEBANON	57632-57632 HERREID	57783-57783 SPEARFISH
57323-57323 CARTHAGE	57456-57456 LEOLA	57633-57633 ISABEL	57785-57785 STURGIS
57324-57324 CAVOUR	57457-57457 LONGLAKE	57634-57634 KELDRON	57787-57787 UNION CENTER
57325-57326 CHAMBERLAIN	57460-57460 MANSFIELD	57636-57636 LANTRY	57788-57788 VALE
57328-57328 CORSICA	57461-57461 MELLETTE	57638-57638 LEMMON	57790-57790 WALL
57329-57329 DANTE	57462-57462 MINA	57639-57639 LITTLE EAGLE	57791-57791 WASTA
57330-57330 DELMONT	57465-57465 NORTHVILLE	57640-57640 LODGEPOLE	57792-57792 WHITE OWL
57331-57331 DIMOCK	57466-57466 ONAKA	57641-57641 MC INTOSH	57793-57793 WHITEWOOD
57332-57332 EMERY	57467-57467 ORIENT	57642-57642 MC LAUGHLIN	57794-57794 WOUNDED KNEE
57334-57334 ETHAN	57468-57468 PIERPONT	57643-57643 MAHTO	57795-57795 ZEONA
57335-57335 FAIRFAX	57469-57469 REDFIELD	57644-57644 MEADOW	57799-57799 SPEARFISH
57337-57337 FEDORA	57470-57470 ROCKHAM	57645-57645 MORRISTOWN	
57339-57339 FORT THOMPSON	57471-57471 ROSCOE	57646-57646 MOUND CITY	

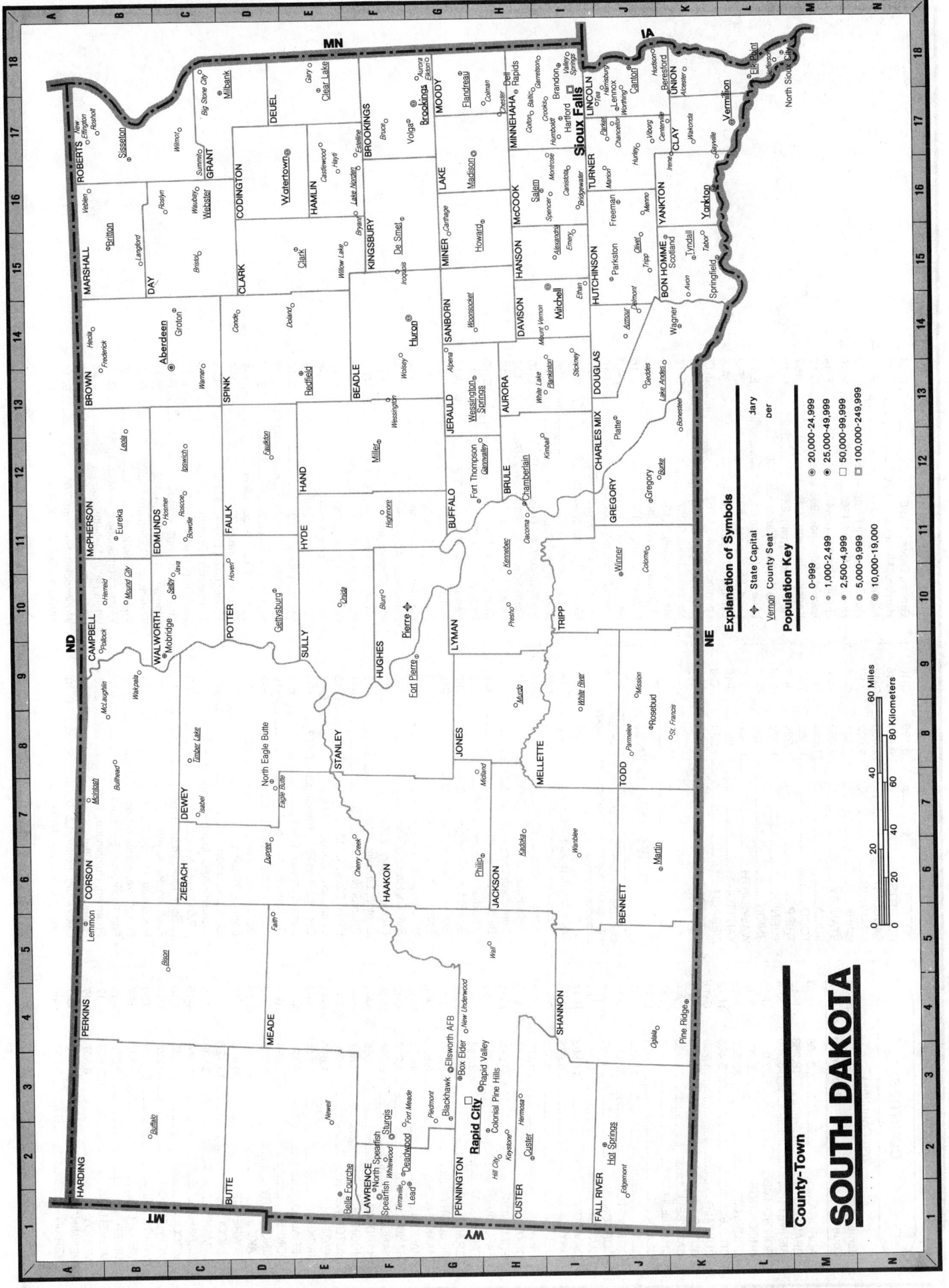

County-Town

SOUTH DAKOTA

COUNTIES

(66 Counties)

Name of County	Population	Location on Map
AURORA	3,135	H-13
BEADLE	18,253	F-13
BENNETT	3,206	J-5
BON HOMME	7,089	J-14
BROOKINGS	25,207	F-17
BROWN	35,580	A-13
BRULE	5,485	H-12
BUFFALO	1,759	G-11
BUTTE	7,914	C-1
CAMPBELL	1,965	A-9
CHARLES MIX	9,131	J-12
CLARK	4,403	D-15
CLAY	13,186	K-17
CODINGTON	22,698	D-16
CORSON	4,195	A-6
CUSTER	6,179	I-1
DAVISON	17,503	H-14
DAY	6,978	B-15
DEUEL	4,522	D-17
DEWEY	5,523	C-7
DOUGLAS	3,746	I-13
EDMUNDS	4,356	B-11
FALL RIVER	7,353	I-1
FAULK	2,744	C-11
GRANT	8,372	C-16
GREGORY	5,359	J-11
HAAKON	2,624	F-6
HAMLIN	4,974	E-16
HAND	4,272	E-12
HANSON	2,994	H-15
HARDING	1,669	A-1
HUGHES	14,817	F-9
HUTCHINSON	8,262	I-14
HYDE	1,696	E-11
JACKSON	2,811	H-6
JERAULD	2,425	G-13
JONES	1,324	G-8
KINGSBURY	5,925	F-15
LAKE	10,550	G-16
LAWRENCE	20,655	F-1
LINCOLN	15,427	I-17
LYMAN	3,638	G-9
MARSHALL	4,844	A-15
MCCOOK	5,688	H-16
MCPHERSON	3,228	A-11
MEADE	21,878	D-4
MELLETTE	2,137	H-7
MINER	3,272	G-15
MINNEHAHA	123,809	H-17
MOODY	6,507	G-17
PENNINGTON	81,343	G-1
PERKINS	3,932	A-4
POTTER	3,190	C-10
ROBERTS	9,914	A-16
SANBORN	2,833	G-14
SHANNON	9,902	I-4
SPINK	7,981	C-13
STANLEY	2,453	E-8
SULLY	1,589	E-9
TODD	8,352	J-7
TRIPP	6,924	I-10
TURNER	8,576	I-16
UNION	10,189	K-17
WALWORTH	6,087	B-9
YANKTON	19,252	J-16
ZIEBACH	2,220	C-6
TOTAL	**696,004**	

CITIES AND TOWNS

Note: The first name is that of the city or town, second, that of the county in which it is located, then the population and location on the map.

Aberdeen, Brown, 24,927 .... C-14
Alexandria, Hanson, 518 .... I-15
Armour, Douglas, 854 .... J-14
Belle Fourche, Butte, 4,335 .... E-1
Beresford, Lincoln/Union, 1,849 .... K-17
Bison, Perkins, 451 .... B-5
• Blackhawk, Meade, 1,995 .... G-2
Box Elder, Pennington, 2,680 .... G-3
Brandon, Minnehaha, 3,543 .... I-18
Britton, Marshall, 1,394 .... B-15
Brookings, Brookings, 16,270 .... F-17
Buffalo, Harding, 488 .... B-2
Burke, Gregory, 756 .... J-12
Canton, Lincoln, 2,787 .... J-18
Chamberlain, Brule, 2,347 .... H-11
Clark, Clark, 1,292 .... E-15
Clear Lake, Deuel, 1,247 .... E-17
• Colonial Pine Hills, Pennington, 1,553 .... H-2
Custer, Custer, 1,741 .... H-2
De Smet, Kingsbury, 1,172 .... F-16
Deadwood, Lawrence, 1,830 .... F-2
Dell Rapids, Minnehaha, 2,484 .... H-18
Dupree, Ziebach, 484 .... D-7
Elk Point, Union, 1,423 .... L-18
• Ellsworth AFB, Meade/Pennington, 7,017 .... G-3
Eureka, McPherson, 1,197 .... B-11
Faulkton, Faulk, 809 .... D-12
Flandreau, Moody, 2,311 .... G-18
Fort Pierre, Stanley, 1,854 .... F-9
• Fort Thompson, Buffalo, 1,088 .... G-11
Freeman, Hutchinson, 1,293 .... J-16
Gannvalley, Buffalo G-12
Gettysburg, Potter, 1,510 .... D-10
Gregory, Gregory, 1,384 .... J-11

Groton, Brown, 1,196 .... C-14
Hartford, Minnehaha, 1,262 .... I-17
Highmore, Hyde, 835 .... F-11
Hot Springs, Fall River, 4,325 .... I-2
Howard, Miner, 1,156 .... H-16
Huron, Beadle, 12,448 .... F-14
Ipswich, Edmunds, 965 .... C-12
Kadoka, Jackson, 736 .... H-7
Kennebec, Lyman, 284 .... H-10
Lake Andes, Charles Mix, 846 .... J-13
Lake Norden, Hamlin, 427 .... E-16
Lead, Lawrence, 3,632 .... F-2
Lemmon, Perkins, 1,614 .... A-5
Lennox, Lincoln, 1,767 .... J-17
Leola, McPherson, 521 .... B-13
Madison, Lake, 6,257 .... G-17
Martin, Bennett, 1,151 .... J-6
McIntosh, Corson, 302 .... A-7
Milbank, Grant, 3,879 .... C-18
Miller, Hand, 1,678 .... F-12
Mitchell, Davison, 13,798 .... I-15
Mobridge, Walworth, 3,768 .... B-9
Mound City, Campbell, 89 .... B-10
Murdo, Jones, 679 .... H-9
• North Eagle Butte, Dewey, 1,423 .... D-7
North Sioux City, Union, 2,019 .... L-18
• North Spearfish, Lawrence, 2,274 .... F-2
Olivet, Hutchinson, 74 .... J-15
Onida, Sully, 761 .... E-10
Parker, Turner, 984 .... J-17
Parkston, Hutchinson, 1,572 .... J-15
Philip, Haakon, 1,077 .... G-6
Pierre, Hughes, 12,906 .... F-9
Pine Ridge, Shannon, 2,596 .... K-4
Plankinton, Aurora, 604 .... I-14
Platte, Charles Mix, 1,311 .... J-13
Rapid City, Pennington, 54,523 .... G-3
• Rapid Valley, Pennington, 5,968 .... G-3
Redfield, Spink, 2,770 .... E-13
• Rosebud, Todd, 1,538 .... J-8
Salem, McCook, 1,289 .... C-10
Selby, Walworth, 707 .... H-16
Sioux Falls, Lincoln/Minnehaha, 100,814 .... I-17
Sisseton, Roberts, 2,181 .... B-17
Spearfish, Lawrence, 6,966 .... F-1
Sturgis, Meade, 5,330 .... F-2
Timber Lake, Dewey, 517 .... C-8
Tyndall, Bon Homme, 1,201 .... K-15
Vermillion, Clay, 10,034 .... L-17
Volga, Brookings, 1,263 .... F-17
Wagner, Charles Mix, 1,462 .... K-14
Watertown, Codington, 17,592 .... D-17
Webster, Day, 2,017 .... C-16
Wessington Springs, Jerauld, 1,083 .... G-13
White River, Mellette, 595 .... I-8
Winner, Tripp, 3,354 .... J-10
Woonsocket, Sanborn, 766 .... G-14
Yankton, Yankton, 12,703 .... K-16

Explanation of symbols: •– Census Designated Place (CDP)

General Help Numbers:

Governor's Office

State Capitol, 1st Floor
Nashville, TN 37243-0001
www.state.tn.us/governor

615-741-2001
Fax 615-532-9711
8AM-5PM

Attorney General's Office

PO Box 20207
Nashville, TN 37202-0207
www.attorneygeneral.state.tn.us

615-741-3491
Fax 615-741-2009
8AM-4:30PM

Legislative Records

Office of Legislative Information Services
Rachel Jackson Bldg, 1st Floor
Nashville, TN 37243
www.legislature.state.tn.us

615-741-3511
615-741-0927
8AM-4:30PM

State Archives

State Library & Archives Division
403 7th Ave N
Nashville, TN 37243-0312
www.state.tn.us/sos/statelib/tslahome.htm

615-741-7996
Fax 615-532-2472
8AM-6PM M-SA

State Specifics:

Capital:

Nashville
Davidson County

Time Zone:

CST*

* Tennessee's twenty-nine eastern-most counties are EST: They are: Anderson, Blount, Bradley, Campbell, Carter, Claiborne, Cocke, Grainger, Greene, Hamilton, Hancock, Hawkins, Jefferson, Johnson, Knox, Loudon, McMinn, Meigs, Monroe, Morgan, Polk, Rhea, Roane, Scott, Sevier, Sullivan, Unicoi, Union, Washington.

Number of Counties:

95

Population:

5,841,748

Web Site:

www.state.tn.us

State Agencies

Criminal Records

Tennessee Bureau of Investigation, TN Open Records Information Srvs, 901 R S Gass Blvd, Nashville, TN 37216; 615-744-4000 x1, 615-744-4651-Fax; 24 hours daily.

www.tbi.state.tn.us

Records available to general public. Per statute, fingerprint-based background checks be conducted for paid or volunteer employment or licensing such as such as child care, teachers, security and armed guards, security system contractors, etc.

It takes 12 to 24 hours before new records are available for inquiry. Records are indexed on inhouse computer and fingerprint cards. Records maintained for 80 years. 100% of arrest records are fingerprint supported. All records are fingerprint based, as submitted by the arresting agencies.

Searching: The agency maintains a website at www.ticic.state.tn.us for searching of sexual offenders, missing children, and people placed on parole who reside in TN. Include the following in your request-name, DOB, AKA's. Sex, race and current address are helpful. The search system is called TORIS (Tennessee Open Records Information Service). A request form can be downloaded from the webpage. The agency suggests that ongoing requester be registered with an account. All records are released to those entitled, including those without dispositions.

Access by: mail, fax.

Fee & Payment: The fee is $29.00 per record check, which includes alias name checks. Fee payee: Tennessee Bureau of Investigation Unless a registered account, prepayment required. Business checks accepted, personal checks are not. VISA, MasterCard, Discover accepted.

Mail search: Turnaround time: 2-5 days. SASE not required.

Fax search: Use of credit card is required unless received from a registered customer.

Statewide Court Records

Administrative Office of the Courts, Nashville City Center, 511 Union St, Suite 600, Nashville, TN 37219; 615-741-2687, 615-741-6285-Fax; 8AM-4:30PM.

www.tsc.state.tn.us

Except for certain online research capabilities, all court record access must be done at the local level.

Access by: online.

Online search: Appellate Court opinions are at www.tsc.state.tn.us/geninfo/Courts/AppellateCourt

s.htm. Several counties offer online access to court records, but there is no statewide access system.

Sexual Offender Registry

Tennessee Bureau of Investigation, Sexual Offender Registry, 901 R S Gass Blvd., Nashville, TN 37216; 888-837-4170 (SOR Hotline), 615-744-4655 (Fax).

www.ticic.state.tn.us

Offender records are not available to the public for viewing. TN Code Ann 40-39-206 specifies that only information released to public on TBI website is for offenders whose offense occurred on or after 07/01/97. Otherwise, records are confidential.

Records are available from 07/01/97 forward. It takes 12 to 84 hours before new records are available for inquiry.

Searching: The public should contact local law enforcement agencies to make inquires on confidential offenders. Include the following in your request-name, DOB; SSN is helpful. The following data is not released: expunged records

Access by: phone, online.

Phone search: Inquiry by name available by name at TBI SOR Hotline.

Online search: Search sexual offenders at website by last name, ccity ounty or ZIP Code. One may also search for missing children, and people placed on parole who reside in Tennessee.

Incarceration Records

Tennessee Department of Corrections, Rachel Jackson Building, Ground Fl, 320 6th Avenue, N., Nashville, TN 37243-0465; 615-741-1000, 615-532-1497-Fax; 8AM-5PM.

www.state.tn.us/correction

Records are available on current and former inmates. It takes 7 days before new records are available for inquiry. Records are normally destroyed after 100 years.

Searching: Location, conviction and sentencing information are provided. Include the following in your request-first and last name. The SSN and DOB are helpful. The following data is not released: medical information and SSNs.

Access by: mail, phone, fax, online.

Fee & Payment: Fees apply when hard copies are needed: $10.00 for search, $.20 per page Fee payee: State of Tennessee

Mail search: Turnaround time: 10 - 15 working days. Also, historical archived inmate information is available from Operational Support Services; generally, there is a $10.00 archive search fee and $.20 per page copy fee.

Phone search: Limited phone searching is available.

Fax search: Fax requesting available.

Online search: Extensive search capabilities are offered from the website. Click on FOIL - Inmate Search.

Other access: A CD-Rom is available with only public information from current offender database; nominal fee; contact the Planning & Research Division.

Expedited service: Will expedite for law enforcement or subpoena emergency (3 days), but only if shipping is paid in advance.

Corporation, Limited Partnership, Fictitious Name, Assumed Name, Limited Liability Company Records

TN Sec of State: Corporations, William R Snodgrass Tower, 312 Eighth Ave. N, 6th Fl, Nashville, TN 37243; 615-741-2286, 615-741-6488 (Copies), 615-741-7310-Fax; 8AM-4:30PM.

www.state.tn.us/sos/bus_svc/index.htm

Records are available from 1875 to present. Records are computerized and are on microfilm from 1979. It takes 2 to 3 days before new records are available for inquiry. Records are indexed on inhouse computer.

Searching: All information is considered public record. Include the following in your request-full name of business. In addition to the articles of incorporation, corporation records include the following information: Annual Reports, Officers, Directors, DBAs (assumed names only), Prior (merged) names, Inactive and Reserved names.

Access by: mail, phone, in person, online.

Fee & Payment: Each set of documents per business is $20.00 per entity, which includes certification. Fee payee: Secretary of State. Prepayment required. Personal checks accepted. No credit cards accepted.

Mail search: Turnaround time: 1 to 3 days. Certificates are usually processed in 1 day.

Phone search: Limited information is given over the phone. Requests for certificates must be in writing.

In person search: Turnaround time is immediate unless certified documents are ordered which are ready the next day.

Online search: There is a free online search at www.tennesseeanytime.org/sosname/ for name availability and at www.tennesseeanytime.org/soscorp/ for business records. This gives online access to over 4,000,000 records relating to corporations, limited liability companies, limited partnerships and limited liability partnerships formed or registered in Tennessee.

Other access: Some data can be purchased in bulk or list format. Call 615-532-9007 for more details.

Trademarks/Servicemarks, Trade Names

Secretary of State, Trademarks/Tradenames Division, 312 8th Ave North, 6th Fl, Nashville, TN 37243-0306; 615-741-0531, 615-741-7310-Fax; 8AM-4:30PM.

www.state.tn.us/sos/bus_svc/trademarks.htm

Records are available from the 1950s to present. It takes 2 to 3 days before new records are available for inquiry. Records are indexed on microfilm.

Searching: Include the following in your request-trademark/servicemark name, name of owner, date of application.

Access by: mail, phone, in person, online.

Fee & Payment: There is $20.00 search fee, add $2.00 for certification. Fee payee: Secretary of State. Personal checks accepted. No credit cards accepted.

Mail search: Turnaround time: 1 to 3 days. A SASE is requested.

Phone search: No fee for telephone request.

In person search: Turnaround time is while you wait.

Online search: A record search of TN Trademarks (newest records are 3 days old) is at www.ja.state.tn.us/sos/iets2/ietm/PgTrademarkSearch.jsp.

Other access: The agency will provide a file update every three months for $1.00 per page. Requests must be in writing.

Uniform Commercial Code

TN Sec of State - UCC Records, William R Snodgrass Tower, 312 Eighth Ave N, 6th Fl, Nashville, TN 37243; 615-741-3276, 615-741-7310-Fax; 8AM-4:30PM.

www.state.tn.us/sos

State and federal tax liens are filed at the county level with the Register of Deeds where the lienee or its property is located.

Records are available from 1964. Records are computerized from 03/01/96. It takes 2-3 days before new records are available for inquiry.

Searching: Use search request form UCC-11. Include the following in your request-debtor name.

Access by: mail, in person, online.

Fee & Payment: The fee is $15.00 per debtor or debtor address, copies are $1.00 per page. Fee payee: Secretary of State. Prepayment required. Personal checks accepted. No credit cards accepted.

Mail search: Turnaround time: 2-3 days.

In person search: The results are mailed in 2-3 days.

Online search: Free access to general data at www.ja.state.tn.us/sos/iets3/ieuc/PgUCCSearch.jsp. Search by debtor name or file number. Images are not available.

Federal and State Tax Liens

Records not maintained by a state level agency.

State and federal tax liens are filed at the county level with the Register of Deeds where the lienee or its property is located.

Sales Tax Registrations

Access to Records is Restricted.

Revenue Department, Sales Tax Registration, Andrew Jackson Bldg, 500 Deaderick St, Nashville, TN 37242-0100; 615-741-3580, 615-253-0600, 615-253-6299-Fax; 8AM-4:30PM.

www.state.tn.us/revenue

This agency refuses to make any information about registrants available.

Birth Certificates

Tennessee Department of Health, Office of Vital Records, 421 5th Ave North, 1st floor, Nashville, TN 37247; 615-741-1763, 615-741-0778 (Credit card order), 615-741-9860-Fax; 8AM-4PM.

http://www2.state.tn.us/health/vr/index.htm

Records are available for 100 years to present. For birth records prior, contact the State Library and Archives at 615-741-2764. Short forms are only available since 1949. New records are available for inquiry immediately. Records are indexed on inhouse computer.

Searching: Must have a signed release from person of record or immediate family member for certified copy. Medical and health information is not released. Include the following in your request-full name, names of parents, mother's maiden name, date of birth, place of birth, relationship to person of record. Daytime phone helpful.

Access by: mail, phone, fax, in person, online.

Fee & Payment: $12.00 for the long (copy of actual certificate) form; $7.00 for the short computerized form. Add $4.00 per name per copy for additional copies. Fee payee: Tennessee Vital Records. Prepayment required. Personal checks accepted. Major credit cards accepted.

Mail search: Turnaround time: 2 to 3 weeks.

Phone search: You must use credit cards with fax or phone requests. There is an additional $10.00 fee. Phone service is available from 8AM to 4PM.

Fax search: Same criteria as phone searching. Use 615-726-2559.

In person search: Wait time is 15 minutes.

Online search: Records may be ordered from the web site, but are returned by mail. Go to https://health.state.tn.us/vrocs/vr.aspx. There is an additional $9.00 fee involved to use this service.

Expedited service: Expedited service is available for phone, fax or online searches. Turnaround time: 2 to 3 days. Phone and fax records ordered by credit card, for $10.00 extra, can be returned overnight for an additional fee of $14.00.

Death Records

Tennessee Department of Health, Office of Vital Records, 421 5th Ave North, 1st floor, Nashville, TN 37247; 615-741-1763, 615-741-0778 (Credit card order), 615-741-9860-Fax; 8AM-4PM.

http://www2.state.tn.us/health/vr/index.htm

Records are available for 50 years. Previous records are at the State Archives at 615-726-2559. It takes 3 months or less before new records are available for inquiry. Records are indexed on inhouse computer.

Searching: Must have a signed release from immediate family member. Cause of death is restricted to immediate family members or their representatives and must be specifically requested. Include the following in your request-full name, names of parents, mother's maiden name, date of death, place of death, reason for information request, relationship to person of record. Daytime phone helpful.

Access by: mail, phone, fax, in person, online.

Fee & Payment: The fee is $7.00 per name. Fee payee: Tennessee Vital Records. Prepayment required. Personal checks accepted. Major credit cards accepted.

Mail search: Turnaround time: 2 to 3 weeks.

Phone search: Credit card for an additional fee of $10.00. Turnaround time is one day.

Fax search: Same criteria as phone searching. Use 615-726-2559.

In person search: Wait is 15 minutes.

Online search: Records may be ordered online at the web site, but are returned by mail. Go to https://health.state.tn.us/vrocs/vr.aspx. There is an additional $9.00 fee involved to use this service. The Cleveland (Tennessee) Public Library staff and volunteers have published the 1914-1925 death records of thirty-three counties at www.tennessee.gov/tsla/history/vital/death.htm. It should be noted that the records of children under two years of age have been omitted from this project.

Expedited service: Expedited service is available for phone, fax or online searches. Turnaround time: 2 to 3 days. Phone and fax records ordered by credit card, for $10.00 extra, can be returned overnight for an additional fee of $14.00.

Marriage Certificates

Tennessee Department of Health, Office of Vital Records, 421 5th Ave North, 1st floor, Nashville, TN 37237; 615-741-1763, 615-741-0778 (Credit card order), 615-741-9860-Fax; 8AM-4PM.

http://www2.state.tn.us/health/vr/index.htm

Records are available for 50 years. Older records are at the state archives. It takes 1 month before new records are available for inquiry. Records are indexed on inhouse computer.

Searching: Must have a signed release from persons of record or immediate family member for certified copy. Information on race or previous marriages is only released for statistical purposes. Include the following in your request-names of husband and wife, date of marriage, place or county of marriage.

Access by: mail, phone, fax, in person, online.

Fee & Payment: The search fee is $12.00. Add $4.00 for each additional copy. Fee payee: Tennessee Vital Records. Prepayment required. Personal checks accepted. Major credit cards accepted.

Mail search: Turnaround time: 2 to 3 weeks.

Phone search: You must use a credit card for an additional $10.00 fee. Records are processed in 24 hours.

Fax search: Same criteria as phone searching. Use 615-726-2559.

In person search: Wait time is about 15 minutes.

Online search: Records may be ordered from the web site, but are returned by mail. Go to https://health.state.tn.us/vrocs/vr.aspx. There is an additional $9.00 fee involved to use this service.

Expedited service: Expedited service is available for phone, fax or online searches. Turnaround time: 2 to 3 days. Phone and fax records ordered by credit card, for $10.00 extra, can be returned overnight for an additional fee of $14.00.

Divorce Records

Tennessee Department of Health, Office of Vital Records, 421 5th Ave North, 1st floor, Nashville, TN 37247; 615-741-1763, 615-741-0778 (Credit card order), 615-741-9860-Fax; 8AM-4PM.

http://www2.state.tn.us/health/vr/index.htm

Records are available for 50 years. Older records are at the state archives. It takes 2 weeks to 2 months before new records are available for inquiry. Records are indexed on inhouse computer.

Searching: Must have a signed release from person of record or immediate family member. Information on previous marriages and education

is released for statistical use only. Include the following in your request-names of husband and wife, date of divorce, place of divorce.

Access by: mail, phone, fax, in person, online.

Fee & Payment: The search fee is $12.00, $4.00 charge for an extra copy. Fee payee: Tennessee Vital Records. Prepayment required. Personal checks aand major credit cards accepted.

Mail search: Turnaround time: 2 to 3 weeks.

Phone search: You must use a credit card and there is an additional fee of $10.00. Records are processed in one day.

Fax search: Same criteria as phone searching. Use 615-726-2559.

In person search: Wait time is about 15 minutes.

Online search: Records may be ordered online, but are returned by mail. Go to https://health.state.tn.us/vrocs/vr.aspx. There is an additional $9.00 fee involved to use this service.

Expedited service: Expedited service is available for phone, fax or online searches. Turnaround time: 2 to 3 days. Phone and fax records ordered by credit card, for $10.00 extra, can be returned overnight for an additional fee of $14.00.

Workers' Compensation Records

Tennessee Department of Labor, Workers Compensation Division, 710 James Robertson Pkwy, 2nd Floor, Nashville, TN 37243-0661; 615-253-1842, 615-532-1942-Fax; 8AM-4:30PM.

www.state.tn.us/labor-wfd/wcomp.html

Records are available from 09/91 on computer, from 1987 to present on microfiche. Prior records are maintained on index cards. It takes 90 days before new records are available for inquiry.

Searching: Unless you have a signed authorization from the injured party or are an attorney representing the injured party, a court order is required to obtain records. This information is not considered public record; however, they'll tell if a claim is on file. The SSN, company name, and date of injury is required for searching records after 1987, prior record searching requires the name of the company.

Access by: mail, fax, in person.

Fee & Payment: The search fee is $10.00, copy fee is $.25 per page, add cost of postage also. Fee payee: State of Tennessee Treasurer. Personal checks accepted. No credit cards accepted.

Mail search: Turnaround time: 1 week. They will invoice you for copies and postage.

Fax search: This will not effect turnaround time.

In person search: Records are still returned in 2 weeks, but you can pick them up.

Driver Records

Dept. of Safety, Financial Responsibility Section, Attn: Driving Records, 1150 Foster Ave, Nashville, TN 37210; 615-741-3954, 615-253-2093-Fax; 8AM-4:30PM.

www.tennessee.gov/safety

Tickets are available from this office for a $5.00 fee per record.

Records are available for past 3 years for convictions, if valid; 7 years if the license is suspended, restricted, or revoked. It takes 30 days or more before new records are available for inquiry. Records are normally destroyed after when records are destroyed depends on the type of violation.

Searching: Tennessee passed legislation similar to DPPA. Casual requesters must have written notarized authorization to receive record information with address data. Include the following in your request-license number and last name or DOB.

Access by: mail, in person, online.

Fee & Payment: The fee is $5.00 per record, $7.00 if online. Fee payee: Tennessee Department of Safety. Prepayment required. Certified checks or money orders are preferred. No personal checks accepted. MasterCard/Visa accepted in person only.

Mail search: Turnaround time: 2 weeks.

In person search: Up to 10 requests will be processed while you wait at this location or at offices in Nashville, Memphis, Knoxville, Chattanooga, and various Driver License Testing Centers.

Online search: Driving records are available to subscribers, signup at www.tennesseeanytime.org. There is a $75 registration fee. Records are available 24 hours daily on an interactive basis. Records are $7.00 each. Suggested only for ongoing users. Call 1-866-886-3468 for more information.

Other access: Magnetic tape retrieval is available for high volume users. Purchase of the DL file is available for approved requesters.

Vehicle Ownership
Vehicle Identification

Title and Registration Division, Information Unit, 44 Vantage Way #160, Nashville, TN 37243-8050; 615-741-3101 (Titles), 888-871-3171, 615-253-4259-Fax; 8AM-4:30PM.

www.tennessee.gov/safety/titleandregistration.htm

Records are available for 5 years to present. Microfilm records go back to 1964. It takes 12 weeks before new records are available for inquiry.

Searching: The agency follows the DPPA guidelines for permissible requesters. Records are not released to casual requesters without consent. The state recommends use of their form-SF1255. Include the following in your request-purpose of request, copy of requester's photo ID, and requester's signature.

Access by: mail, in person, online.

Fee & Payment: The fee is $1.00 for general inquiry, $5.00 for current title data, and $15.00 for a complete title history. Fee payee: Titling and Registration. Prepayment required. Personal checks accepted. No credit cards accepted.

Mail search: Turnaround time: 2 to 4 weeks. A SASE is requested.

In person search: Turnaround time is while you wait, unless photocopy of actual document is required. The office closes at 4PM for walk-in customers. Photo ID required.

Online search: Onlines access is available for approved subscribers at www.tennesseeanytime.org/ivtr. IVTR allows

subscribers to retrieve vehicle, title, and registration information for vehicles registered in Tennessee. Search with license plate or VIN. The fee is $2.00 per search. All subscribers must be approved per DPPA.

Accident Reports

Financial Responsibility Section, Records Unit, 1150 Foster Avenue, Nashville, TN 37210; 615-741-3954, 615-253-2093-Fax; 8AM-4:30PM.

www.tennessee.gov/safety

Also, you can obtain accident reports from the investigating agency.

Records are available from 1992 to present. It takes 30 days before new records are available for inquiry. Records are normally destroyed after 10 years.

Searching: Include the following in your request-full name, date of accident, location of accident. Also, include the county of the accident and DL of driver(s).

Access by: mail, in person.

Fee & Payment: The fee is $4.00 per record copy. Fee payee: Tennessee Department of Safety. Prepayment required. Agency prefers money orders and certified checks. Personal checks not accepted. MasterCard & Visa accepted for in person only.

Mail search: Turnaround time: 2 weeks.

In person search: Turnaround time is generally while you wait.

Vessel Ownership
Vessel Registration

Wildlife Resources Agency, Boating Division, PO Box 40747, Nashville, TN 37204; 615-781-6585, 615-741-4606-Fax; 8AM-4:30PM.

www.state.tn.us/twra

All liens are filed with the Secretary of State.

Records are available for the past 3 years. Records are indexed on computer. The state does not issue titles. All motorized boats and all sailboats must be registered. It takes 30 days before new records are available for inquiry. Records are normally destroyed after 5 years.

Searching: Search via email to darren.rider@state.tn.us To search, one of the following is required: Tennessee ID #, hull id #, name, or SSN.

Access by: mail, phone, fax, in person.

Fee & Payment: There is no fee to do 1 or 2 searches; however, large lists may incur a charge.

Mail search: Turnaround time: 2 days.

Phone search: Whether a phone search will be performed depends on how busy the personnel is at the time of the call. Phone searches are only verbal verifications and require a Tennessee ID # to search.

Fax search: Turnaround time is 2 days. Results will be sent by mail.

In person search: Turnaround time is usually immediate, when staff available.

Voter Registration
Access to Records is Restricted.

Secretary of State, Division of Elections, 312 Eighth Avenue North, 9th Fl, Nashville, TN 37243; 615-741-7956, 615-741-1278-Fax; 8AM-4:30PM.

www.state.tn.us/sos/election.htm

The statewide database cannot be accessed. However, records are held by the Administrator of Elections at the county level. Records can only be purchased for politically-related purposes. A CD is $2500. Email questions to tennessee.elections@state.tn.us.

GED Certificates

Department of Labor & Workforce Development, GED Records - Davy Crockett Tower, 500 James Robertson Parkway, 11th Fl, Nashville, TN 37245; 615-741-7054, 615-532-4899-Fax; 8AM-4:30PM.

www.state.tn.us/labor-wfd/AE/aeged.htm

It takes 2 weeks before new records are available for inquiry. Records are normally destroyed after a minimum of 25 years.

Searching: Include the following in your request-date of birth, Social Security Number, signed release. Include your daytime telephone number. Year diploma issued also helpful.

Access by: mail, fax, in person.

Fee & Payment: There is no fee for a verification.

Mail search: Turnaround time: 7 to 10 days.

Fax search: Turnaround time is generally in 3 days.

In person search: Simple requests may be processed while you wait.

Hunting and Fishing License Information

Wildlife Resources Agency, Revenue Division, PO Box 40747, Nashville, TN 37204; 615-781-6585, 615-781-5277-Fax; 8AM-4:30PM.

www.state.tn.us/twra

There is a central database of hunting or fishing licenses

Records are available since 1999.

Searching: Include the following in your request-reason for request.

Access by: mail, phone, fax, in person.

Fee & Payment: There is no search fee, the copy fee is $1.00 per copy. Special requests projects are billed at $23.50 per hour, one hour minimum.

Mail search: Turnaround time: 1 week.

Phone search: Verification only.

Fax search: Search requests accepted by fax.

In person search: Turnaround time while you wait, time permitting.

Tennessee State Licensing Agencies

For details about the agency responsible for licensing/certifying/registering an item below or in the Agency Quick Finder section, match an item's number with the number of the agency in the *Licensing Agency Information* section.

Tennessee Licenses Searchable Online

Accounting Firm #3	www.state.tn.us/cgi-bin/commerce/roster3.pl
Alarm Contractor #3	www.state.tn.us/cgi-bin/commerce/roster3.pl
Animal Euthanasia Technician #7	http://www2.state.tn.us/health/licensure/index.htm
Architect #3	www.state.tn.us/cgi-bin/commerce/roster3.pl
Athletic Trainer #7	http://www2.state.tn.us/health/licensure/index.htm
Auctioneer / Auction Company #3	www.state.tn.us/cgi-bin/commerce/roster3.pl
Audiologist #7	http://www2.state.tn.us/health/licensure/index.htm
Barber School/Barber Shop #3	www.state.tn.us/cgi-bin/commerce/roster3.pl
Barber/Barber Technician #3	www.state.tn.us/cgi-bin/commerce/roster3.pl
Boxing/Racing Personnel #3	www.state.tn.us/cgi-bin/commerce/roster3.pl
Chiropractor/Chiropractic Therapy Assist. #7	http://www2.state.tn.us/health/licensure/index.htm
Clinical Lab Technician/Personnel #6	http://www2.state.tn.us/health/licensure/index.htm
Collection Agent/Manager #3	www.state.tn.us/cgi-bin/commerce/roster3.pl
Contractor #3	www.state.tn.us/cgi-bin/commerce/roster3.pl
Cosmetologist #3	www.state.tn.us/cgi-bin/commerce/roster3.pl
Cosmetology Shop/School #3	www.state.tn.us/cgi-bin/commerce/roster3.pl
Counselor, Alcohol & Drug Abuse #7	http://www2.state.tn.us/health/licensure/index.htm
Counselor, Associate/Professional #7	http://www2.state.tn.us/health/licensure/index.htm
Dental Hygienist #7	http://www2.state.tn.us/health/licensure/index.htm
Dentist/Dental Assistant #7	http://www2.state.tn.us/health/licensure/index.htm
Dietitian/Nutritionist #7	http://www2.state.tn.us/health/licensure/index.htm
Electrologist / Electrology Instructor/School #7	http://www2.state.tn.us/health/licensure/index.htm
Embalmer #3	www.state.tn.us/cgi-bin/commerce/roster3.pl
Emer. Medical Personnel/Dispatcher #7	http://www2.state.tn.us/health/licensure/index.htm
Emergency Medical Service #7	http://www2.state.tn.us/health/licensure/index.htm
Engineer #3	www.state.tn.us/cgi-bin/commerce/roster3.pl
First Responder EMS #7	http://www2.state.tn.us/health/licensure/index.htm
Funeral & Burial Director/Apprentice #3	www.state.tn.us/cgi-bin/commerce/roster3.pl
Funeral & Burial Est./Cemetery #3	www.state.tn.us/cgi-bin/commerce/roster3.pl
Geologist #3	www.state.tn.us/cgi-bin/commerce/roster3.pl
Hearing Aid Dispenser #7	http://www2.state.tn.us/health/licensure/index.htm
Home Improvement #3	www.state.tn.us/cgi-bin/commerce/roster3.pl
Insurance Agent / Insurance Firm #3	www.state.tn.us/cgi-bin/commerce/roster3.pl
Interior Designer #3	www.state.tn.us/cgi-bin/commerce/roster3.pl
Laboratory Personnel, Medical #6	http://www2.state.tn.us/health/licensure/index.htm
Landscape Architect/Architect Firm #3	www.state.tn.us/cgi-bin/commerce/roster3.pl
Lobbyist #10	www.state.tn.us/tref/lobbyists/lobbyists.htm
Manicurist #3	www.state.tn.us/cgi-bin/commerce/roster3.pl
Marriage & Family Therapist #7	http://www2.state.tn.us/health/licensure/index.htm
Massage Therapist/Establishment #7	http://www2.state.tn.us/health/licensure/index.htm
Medical Disciplinary Tracking #6	http://www2.state.tn.us/health/abuseregistry/index.html
Medical Doctor #6	http://www2.state.tn.us/health/licensure/index.htm
Midwife #7	http://www2.state.tn.us/health/licensure/index.htm
Motor Vehicle Auction #3	www.state.tn.us/cgi-bin/commerce/roster3.pl
Motor Vehicle Dealer/Salesperson #3	www.state.tn.us/cgi-bin/commerce/roster3.pl
Nurse-RN/LPN #6	http://www2.state.tn.us/health/licensure/index.htm
Nurses' Aide #6	http://www2.state.tn.us/health/licensure/index.htm
Nursing Home Administrator #7	http://www2.state.tn.us/health/licensure/index.htm
Occupational Therapist/Assistant #7	http://www2.state.tn.us/health/licensure/index.htm
Optician, Dispensing #7	http://www2.state.tn.us/health/licensure/index.htm
Optometrist #7	http://www2.state.tn.us/health/licensure/index.htm
Orthopedic Physician Assistant #6	http://www2.state.tn.us/health/licensure/index.htm
Osteopathic Physician #6	http://www2.state.tn.us/health/licensure/index.htm

Pastoral Therapist, Clinical #7 .... http://www2.state.tn.us/health/licensure/index.htm
Personnel Leasing #3 .... www.state.tn.us/cgi-bin/commerce/roster3.pl
Pest Control Operator #11 .... http://www2.state.tn.us/agriculture/onlineinfo/
Pharmacist / Pharmacy / Pharmacy Researcher #3 .... www.state.tn.us/cgi-bin/commerce/roster3.pl
Physical Therapist/Assistant #6 .... http://www2.state.tn.us/health/licensure/index.htm
Physician Assistant #6 .... http://www2.state.tn.us/health/licensure/index.htm
Podiatrist #7 .... http://www2.state.tn.us/health/licensure/index.htm
Polygraph Examiner #3 .... www.state.tn.us/cgi-bin/commerce/roster3.pl
Private Investigative / PI Company #3 .... www.state.tn.us/cgi-bin/commerce/roster3.pl
Private Security Guard #3 .... www.state.tn.us/cgi-bin/commerce/roster3.pl
Psychological Examiner #7 .... http://www2.state.tn.us/health/licensure/index.htm
Psychologist #7 .... http://www2.state.tn.us/health/licensure/index.htm
Public Accountant-CPA #3 .... www.state.tn.us/cgi-bin/commerce/roster3.pl
Racetrack #3 .... www.state.tn.us/cgi-bin/commerce/roster3.pl
Radiologic Technologist #6 .... http://www2.state.tn.us/health/licensure/index.htm
Real Estate Agent/Broker/Sales/Firm #3 .... www.state.tn.us/cgi-bin/commerce/roster3.pl
Real Estate Appraiser #3 .... www.state.tn.us/cgi-bin/commerce/roster3.pl
Respiratory Care Therapist/Assist. #6 .... http://www2.state.tn.us/health/licensure/index.htm
School Administrator #5 .... www.k-12.state.tn.us/tcertinf
School Counselor / Librarian / Psychologist #5 .... www.k-12.state.tn.us/tcertinf
School Food Service Supervisor #5 .... www.k-12.state.tn.us/tcertinf
School Reading Specialist #5 .... www.k-12.state.tn.us/tcertinf
School Vocational Endorsement #5 .... www.k-12.state.tn.us/tcertinf
Security Company / Security Guard #3 .... www.state.tn.us/cgi-bin/commerce/roster3.pl
Security Trainer #3 .... www.state.tn.us/cgi-bin/commerce/roster3.pl
Shampoo Technician #3 .... www.state.tn.us/cgi-bin/commerce/roster3.pl
Social Worker, Master/Clinical #7 .... http://www2.state.tn.us/health/licensure/index.htm
Speech Pathologist #7 .... http://www2.state.tn.us/health/licensure/index.htm
Surveyor, Land #3 .... www.state.tn.us/cgi-bin/commerce/roster3.pl
Teacher #5 .... www.k-12.state.tn.us/tcertinf
Timeshare Agent #3 .... www.state.tn.us/cgi-bin/commerce/roster3.pl
Veterinarian #7 .... http://www2.state.tn.us/health/licensure/index.htm
X-ray Operator #6 .... http://www2.state.tn.us/health/licensure/index.htm
X-ray Technologist, Podiatry #6 .... http://www2.state.tn.us/health/licensure/index.htm

Tennessee Licensing Quick Finder

Accounting Firm #3 615-741-2550	Counselor, Associate/Professional #7 . 615-532-3202	Insurance Education Provider #3 615-741-2693
Alarm Contractor #3 615-741-9771	Court Reporter/Stenographer #2 423-756-0221	Insurance Firm #3 615-741-2693
Alcohol Package Store #1 615-741-1602	Dental Hygienist #7 615-532-3202	Interior Designer #3 615-741-3221
Alcohol Server #1 615-741-1602	Dentist/Dental Assistant #7 615-532-3202	Investment Advisor #3 615-741-2947
American Reg. Rad. Tech. #6 .. 615-687-0048	Dietitian/Nutritionist #7 615-532-3202	Laboratory Personnel, Medical #6 615-532-5128
Animal Euthanasia Technician #7 .. 615-532-3202	Electrologist #7 615-532-3202	Landscape Architect/Architect Firm #3 615-741-3221
Animal/Livestock Dealer #11 .. 615-837-5241	Electrology Instructor/School #7 615-532-3202	Liquor Sale/Permit #1 615-741-1602
Architect #3 615-741-3221	Elevator Inspector #2 615-741-2123	Livestock Brand #11 615-837-5241
Athletic Trainer #7 615-532-3202	Embalmer #3 615-741-5062	Lobbyist #10 615-741-7959
Attorney #12 .... 615-361-7500, 800-486-5714	Emergency Medical Personnel/Dispatcher #7	Manicurist #3 615-741-2515
Auctioneer / Auction Company #3 615-741-3600	 615-532-3202	Marriage & Family Therapist #7 615-532-3202
Audiologist #7 615-532-3202	Emergency Medical Service #7 615-532-3202	Massage Therapist/Establishment #7 .. 615-532-5083
Barber School/Barber Shop #3 615-741-2294	Engineer #3 615-741-3221	Medical Disciplinary Tracking #6 615-532-3421
Barber/Barber Technician #3 615-741-2294	Environmentalist #7 615-532-3202	Medical Doctor #6 615-532-4384
Bed & Breakfast #4 615-741-7206	Fire Protection Sprinkler System Contractor #3	Midwife #7 615-532-3202
Boiler Operator #8 901-379-4200	 615-741-1322	Milk Tester/Sampler #11 615-837-5151
Boxing/Racing Personnel #3 615-741-6837	First Responder EMS #7 615-532-3202	Motor Vehicle Auction #3 615-741-2711
Camp #4 615-741-7206	Food Service Establishment #4 615-741-7206	Motor Vehicle Dealer/Salesperson #3 . 615-741-2711
Chiropractor/Chiropractic Therapy Assist. #7	Funeral & Burial Director/Apprentice #3 615-741-5062	Notary Public #9 615-741-3699
.... 615-532-3202	Funeral & Burial Est./Cemetery #3 615-741-5062	Nurse-RN/LPN #6 615-532-5166
Clinical Lab Technician/Personnel #6 .. 615-532-5128	Geologist #3 615-741-3611	Nursery #11 615-837-5512
Collection Agent/Manager #3 615-741-1741	Health Care Facility #6 615-741-7221	Nursery Plant Dealer #11 615-837-5512
Contractor #3 615-741-8307	Hearing Aid Dispenser #7 615-532-3202	Nurses' Aide #6 615-741-7670
Cosmetologist #3 615-741-2515	Home Improvement #3 615-741-8307	Nursing Home Administrator #7 615-532-3202
Cosmetology Shop/School #3 615-741-2515	Hotel #4 615-741-7206	Occupational Therapist/Assistant #7 ... 615-532-3202
Counselor, Alcohol & Drug Abuse #7 .. 615-532-5097	Insurance Agent #3 615-741-2693	Optician, Dispensing #7 615-532-3202

Optometrist #7 615-532-3202	Racetrack #3 615-741-2384	Shampoo Technician #3 615-741-2515
Orthopedic Physician Assistant #6 615-532-4384	Radiologic Technologist #6 615-532-3202	Shorthand Reporter #2 423-756-0221
Osteopathic Physician #6 615-532-4384	Real Estate Agent/Broker/Sales #3 615-741-2273	Social Worker, Master/Clinical #7 615-532-3202
Pastoral Therapist, Clinical #7 615-532-3202	Real Estate Appraiser #3 615-741-1831	Speech Pathologist #7 615-532-3202
Personnel Leasing #3 615-741-3449	Real Estate Firm #3 615-741-2273	Surveyor, Land #3 615-741-3611
Pest Control Operator #11 615-837-5138	Refrigeration Installer/Contractor #8 901-379-4200	Swimming Pool #4 615-741-7206
Pharmacist / Pharmacy #3 615-741-2718	Respiratory Care Therapist/Tech./Assist. #6	Tattoo Artist/Apprentice #4 615-741-7206
Pharmacy Researcher #3 615-741-2718	 615-532-5096	Teacher #5 615-532-4885
Physical Therapist/Assistant #6 615-532-5135	School Administrative Administrator #5 615-532-4885	Timeshare Agent #3 615-741-2273
Physician Assistant #6 615-532-4384	School Counselor #5 615-532-4885	Veterinarian #7 615-532-3202
Plumber/Plumbing Company #8 901-379-4200	School Food Service Supervisor #5 615-532-4885	Water Treatment Plant Operator #13 ... 615-898-8090
Podiatrist #7 615-532-3202	School Librarian / Psychologist #5 615-532-4885	Weigh Scales Service Technician #11. 615-837-5109
Polygraph Examiner #3 615-741-4827	School Reading Specialist #5 615-532-4885	Weigher, Public (Bulk Products, Aggregates) #11
Private Investigative Company #3 615-741-4827	School Vocational Endorsement #5 615-532-4885	 615-837-5109
Private Investigator #3 615-741-4827	Securities Agent #3 615-741-2947	Weighmaster #11 615-837-5109
Private Security Guard #3 615-741-6382	Securities Broker/Dealer #3 615-741-2947	Wine Production/Sale/Transport #1 615-741-1602
Psychological Examiner #7 615-532-3202	Security Company #3 615-741-9771	X-ray Operator #6 615-532-4384
Psychologist #7 615-532-3202	Security Guard #3 615-741-9771	X-ray Technologist, Podiatry #6 615-532-5157
Public Accountant-CPA #3 615-741-2550	Security Trainer #3 615-741-9771	

Tennessee Licensing Agency Information

1 Alcoholic Beverage Commission, 226 Capitol Blvd Bldg, #300, Nashville, TN 37243-0755; 615-741-1602, Fax: 615-741-0847.
www.state.tn.us/abc/
Email: stallman@mail.state.tn.us

2 Department of Labor, Boiler & Elevator Division, Board of Boiler Rules, 710 James Robertson Pky, Andrew Johnson Tower 3rd Fl, Nashville, TN 37243; 615-741-2123, Fax: 615-532-1469.
www.state.tn.us/labor-wfd/bediv.html

3 Department of Commerce & Insurance, 500 James Robertson Pky, 2nd Fl, Nashville, TN 37243; 615-741-2241, Fax: 615-532-2965.
www.state.tn.us/commerce/index.html
Email: dci@mail.state.tn.us
Search Database at www.state.tn.us/cgi-bin/commerce/roster3.pl Note: Additional toll-free phone number for insurance-related professional licensing is 888-416-0868 .

4 Department of Health, Division of General Environmental Health, 425 5th Ave N, Cordell Hull Bldg 6th Fl, Nashville, TN 37247-3901; 615-741-7206, Fax: 615-741-8510.
www.state.tn.us/health

5 Department of Education, Office of Teacher Licensing, 710 James Robertson Pky, Andrew Johnson Tower, 5th Fl, Nashville, TN 37243-0377; 615-532-4885, Fax: 615-532-1448.
www.state.tn.us/education/lic/
Email: Sandy.willis@state.tn.us
Search Database at www.k-12.state.tn.us/tcertinf
Note: Teacher certification search may be available at the website.

6 Department of Health, Medical Professions, 425 5th Ave N, Cordell Hull Bldg, 1st Fl, Nashville, TN 37247-1010; 615-532-3202.
http://www2.state.tn.us/health
Search Database at
http://www2.state.tn.us/health/licensure/index.htm

7 Department of Health, Allied Health Professions - Licensing, 425 5th Ave N, Cordell Hull Bldg, 1st Fl, Nashville, TN 37247-1010; 615-532-3202.
http://www2.state.tn.us/health
Search Database at
http://www2.state.tn.us/health/licensure/index.htm

8 Mechanical Licensing Board, (Shelby County/Western Tennesee), 6465 Mullins Station Rd, Memphis, TN 38134; 901-379-4200, Fax: 901-379-4202.

9 Office of Secretary of State, 312 8th Av N, 6th Fl, W R Snodgrass Tower, Nashville, TN 37243-0306; 615-741-3699, Fax: 615-741-7310.

10 Registry of Election Finance, 404 James Robertson Pky, #1614, Nashville, TN 37243; 615-741-7959, Fax: 615-532-8902/8905.
www.state.tn.us/tref
Email: registry.info@state.tn.us
Search Database at
www.state.tn.us/tref/lobbyists/lobbyists.htm

11 Department of Agriculture, Melrose Station, PO Box 40627, Nashville, TN 37204; 615-837-5120, Fax: 615-837-5335.
www.state.tn.us/agriculture

12 Supreme Court of Tennessee, Board of Professional Responsibility, 1101 Kermit Dr., #730, Nashville, TN 37217; 615-361-7500, 800-486-5714, Fax: 615-367-2480.
Email: ethics@tbpr.org

13 Water & Wastewater Certification Program, 2022 Blanton Dr, Fleming Training Ctr, Murfreesboro, TN 37129; 615-898-8090, Fax: 615-818-8064.

Tennessee Federal Courts

The following list indicates the district and division name for each county in the state. If the bankruptcy court location is different from the district court, then the location of the bankruptcy court appears in parentheses.

Tennessee County/Court Cross Reference

County	District	Division
Anderson	Eastern	Knoxville
Bedford	Eastern	Winchester (Chattanooga)
Benton	Western	Jackson
Bledsoe	Eastern	Chattanooga
Blount	Eastern	Knoxville
Bradley	Eastern	Chattanooga
Campbell	Eastern	Knoxville
Cannon	Middle	Nashville
Carroll	Western	Jackson
Carter	Eastern	Greeneville
Cheatham	Middle	Nashville
Chester	Western	Jackson
Claiborne	Eastern	Knoxville
Clay	Middle	Cookeville (Nashville)
Cocke	Eastern	Greeneville
Coffee	Eastern	Winchester (Chattanooga)
Crockett	Western	Jackson
Cumberland	Middle	Cookeville (Nashville)
Davidson	Middle	Nashville
De Kalb	Middle	Cookeville (Nashville)
Decatur	Western	Jackson
Dickson	Middle	Nashville
Dyer	Western	Memphis
Fayette	Western	Memphis
Fentress	Middle	Cookeville (Nashville)
Franklin	Eastern	Winchester (Chattanooga)
Gibson	Western	Jackson
Giles	Middle	Columbia (Nashville)
Grainger	Eastern	Knoxville
Greene	Eastern	Greeneville
Grundy	Eastern	Winchester (Chattanooga)
Hamblen	Eastern	Greeneville
Hamilton	Eastern	Chattanooga
Hancock	Eastern	Greeneville
Hardeman	Western	Jackson
Hardin	Western	Jackson
Hawkins	Eastern	Greeneville
Haywood	Western	Jackson
Henderson	Western	Jackson
Henry	Western	Jackson
Hickman	Middle	Columbia (Nashville)
Houston	Middle	Nashville
Humphreys	Middle	Nashville
Jackson	Middle	Cookeville (Nashville)
Jefferson	Eastern	Knoxville
Johnson	Eastern	Greeneville
Knox	Eastern	Knoxville
Lake	Western	Jackson
Lauderdale	Western	Memphis
Lawrence	Middle	Columbia (Nashville)
Lewis	Middle	Columbia (Nashville)
Lincoln	Eastern	Winchester (Chattanooga)
Loudon	Eastern	Knoxville
Macon	Middle	Cookeville (Nashville)
Madison	Western	Jackson
Marion	Eastern	Chattanooga
Marshall	Middle	Columbia (Nashville)
Maury	Middle	Columbia (Nashville)
McMinn	Eastern	Chattanooga
McNairy	Western	Jackson
Meigs	Eastern	Chattanooga
Monroe	Eastern	Knoxville
Montgomery	Middle	Nashville
Moore	Eastern	Winchester (Chattanooga)
Morgan	Eastern	Knoxville
Obion	Western	Jackson
Overton	Middle	Cookeville (Nashville)
Perry	Western	Jackson
Pickett	Middle	Cookeville (Nashville)
Polk	Eastern	Chattanooga
Putnam	Middle	Cookeville (Nashville)
Rhea	Eastern	Chattanooga
Roane	Eastern	Knoxville
Robertson	Middle	Nashville
Rutherford	Middle	Nashville
Scott	Eastern	Knoxville
Sequatchie	Eastern	Chattanooga
Sevier	Eastern	Knoxville
Shelby	Western	Memphis
Smith	Middle	Cookeville (Nashville)
Stewart	Middle	Nashville
Sullivan	Eastern	Greeneville
Sumner	Middle	Nashville
Tipton	Western	Memphis
Trousdale	Middle	Nashville
Unicoi	Eastern	Greeneville
Union	Eastern	Knoxville
Van Buren	Eastern	Winchester (Chattanooga)
Warren	Eastern	Winchester (Chattanooga)
Washington	Eastern	Greeneville
Wayne	Middle	Columbia (Nashville)
Weakley	Western	Jackson
White	Middle	Cookeville (Nashville)
Williamson	Middle	Nashville
Wilson	Middle	Nashville

Standards for Federal Courts: Search fee is $26.00 per item (one party name or case number). Copy fee is $.50 per page. Certification fee is $9.00 per document, double for exemplification, if available. All fees standard unless noted in profile. Mail Search: always enclose a stamped self addressed envelope unless otherwise noted. Most courts accept fax requests or will suggest a copying/search vendor. Before releasing records, all courts require prepayment, unless noted. Open records are located at the court unless otherwise noted. District courts index by defendant and plaintiff as well as by case number. Bankruptcy courts usually index by debtor and case number. While most courts now have their indexes on computer many may still maintain index card files.

Courts offering internet access via CM-ECF or older RACER, PACER, or Web-PACER systems charge $.08 per page fee unless noted as free. Where PACER is available, the universal sign-up number is 800-676-6856. Find PACER and the US Party/Case Index at http://pacer.psc.uscourts.gov.

US District Court

Eastern District of Tennessee

Chattanooga Division Clerk's Office, PO Box 591, Chattanooga, TN 37401 (courier address: Rm 309, 900 Georgia Ave, Chattanooga, TN 37402), 423-752-5200, Fax-423-752-5205. Hours-8AM-4PM. www.tned.uscourts.gov

Counties: Bledsoe, Bradley, Hamilton, McMinn, Marion, Meigs, Polk, Rhea, Sequatchie.

Searches & Indexing: Results do not include SSN or DOB. Both computer and card indexes maintained; computer goes back to 1992. New cases in the index 1-2 days after filing date. Records purged never. **Fee & Payment:** Pay by money order, cashier's or personal check. Payee: Clerk, US District Court. Prepayment required. **Phone Search:** Only docket information available by telephone. **Mail Search:** search usually completed- 1-2 days. Include SASE for return. **In Person Search:** Fee charged if court performs your search. Obtain copying from a copy service, Legal Impressions. No self-serve copier available.

E-Services: ECF replaces PACER whose records did go back to 1994. ECF at https://ecf.tned.uscourts.gov **Opinions Online:** www.tned.uscourts.gov/opinions/search.html.

Greeneville Division US District Court Clerk, 220 W Depot St, Ste 200, Greeneville, TN 37743 (also use mail address for courier delivery), 423-639-3105, Fax-423-639-7134. Hours- 8AM-4PM. www.tned.uscourts.gov **Counties:** Carter, Cocke, Greene, Hamblen, Hancock, Hawkins, Johnson, Sullivan, Unicoi, Washington.

Searches & Indexing: Results do not include SSN or DOB. Both computer and card indexes maintained; criminal index back to 1994, civil to 1992. New cases in the index immediately after filing date. Records purged never.

Fee & Payment: Pay by money order, cashier's or personal check. Payee: Clerk, US District Court. Prepayment required.

Phone Search: Only docket information is available by phone. **Mail Search:** search usually completed- 1 day. SASE not required. **In Person Search:** Fee charged if court performs your search. You may only use the computer terminal to search cases back to 10/1992. No self-serve copier.

E-Services: ECF replaces PACER whose records did go back to 1994. ECF at https://ecf.tned.uscourts.gov **Opinions Online:** www.tned.uscourts.gov/opinions/search.html.

Knoxville Division Clerk's Office, 800 Market St Ste 130, Knoxville, TN 37902 (use mail address for courier delivery), 865-545-4228, Fax-865-545-4247. 8am-4pm. www.tned.uscourts.gov **Counties:** Anderson, Blount, Campbell, Claiborne, Grainger, Jefferson, Knox, Loudon, Monroe, Morgan, Roane, Scott, Sevier, Union.

Searches & Indexing: Results do not include SSN or DOB. Both computer and card indexes maintained. Computer civil index back to 6/1992, criminal to 1993; index cards prior. New cases in index 1-2 days after filing. Records purged never.

Fee & Payment: Pay by money order, cashier's or personal check. Payee: Clerk, US District Court. Prepayment required.

Phone Search: Only docket information is available by phone. **Mail Search:** search usually completed- 7 days. SASE not required. **In Person**

Search: Fee charged if court performs your search. No self-serve copier available.

E-Services: ECF replaces PACER whose records did go back to 1994. ECF at https://ecf.tned.uscourts.gov **Opinions Online:** www.tned.uscourts.gov/opinions/search.html.

Winchester Division Court Clerk, PO Box 459, Winchester, TN 37398 (courier address: 200 S Jefferson St, Rm 201, Winchester, TN 37397), 931-967-1444, Fax-931-967-9693. Hours- 8AM-12, 1-4PM. www.tned.uscourts.gov

Counties: Bedford, Coffee, Franklin, Grundy, Lincoln, Moore, Van Buren, Warren.

Searches & Indexing: Results do not include SSN or DOB. Office began maintaining records in 1997. Computer index back to 1992 maintained. New cases in the index 1-2 days after filing date. Records purged never.

Fee & Payment: Pay by money order, cashier's or personal check. Payee: Clerk, US District Court. Prepayment required.

Phone Search: Only docket information available by phone. **Mail Search:** search usually completed-1 day. Include SASE for return. **In Person Search:** Fee charged if court performs your search. No self-serve copier available.

E-Services: ECF replaces PACER whose records did go back to 1994. ECF at https://ecf.tned.uscourts.gov **Opinions Online:** www.tned.uscourts.gov/opinions/search.html.

US Bankruptcy Court

Eastern District of Tennessee

Northeastern Division Court Clerk, 220 W Depot St #218, Greeneville, TN 37743 (also use mail address for courier delivery), 423-787-0113. Hours- 8AM-4:30PM. www.tneb.uscourts.gov

Carter, Cocke, Greene, Hamblen, Hancock, Hawkins, Johnson, Sullivan, Unicoi, Washington.

Searches & Indexing: Results include last 4 SSN digits only. Both computer and card indexes maintained. New cases in the index 2-3 days after filing date. Records purged as deemed necessary. District-wide searches available here for limited information back to 1/86

Fee & Payment: Pay by money order, cashier's or personal check. Payee: Clerk, US Bankruptcy Court. Prepayment required. **Phone Search:** Voice Case Information Service available, call 800-767-1512 or 423-752-5272. **Mail Search:** search usually completed- 1-2 days. Include SASE for return. **In Person Search:** Fee charged if court performs your search. No self-serve copier.

E-Services: ECF replaces PACER whose records did go back to 1/1986. New records online after 1 day. ECF- https://ecf.tneb.uscourts.gov **Opinions:** www.tneb.uscourts.gov/html/selopinions.htm.

Northern Division Court Clerk, 800 Market St #330, Howard H Baker Jr US Courthouse, Knoxville, TN 37902 (also use mail address for courier delivery), 865-545-4279. 8AM-4PM. www.tneb.uscourts.gov **Counties:** Anderson, Blount, Campbell, Claiborne, Grainger, Jefferson, Knox, Loudon, Monroe, Morgan, Roane, Scott, Sevier, Sullivan, Unicoi, Union, Washington.

Searches & Indexing: Results include last 4 SSN digits only. Both computer and card indexes maintained. New cases in the index 2-3 days after

filing date. Records purged as deemed necessary. District-wide searches available here for limited data back to 1/86 **Fee & Payment:** Pay by money order, cashier's or personal check. Payee: Clerk, US Bankruptcy Court. Prepayment required.

Phone Search: By phone, court only confirms debtor name, SSN, address, attorney, trustee, chapter filed, date of filing, date of discharge/dismissal, date case closed, in addition to limited data regarding motions, hearings, etc. Voice Case Information Service available, call 800-767-1512 or 423-752-5272. **Mail Search:** search usually completed- 1-2 days. Include SASE for return. **In Person Search:** Fee charged if court performs your search. No self-serve copier.

E-Services: ECF replaces PACER whose records did go back to 1/1986. New records online after 1 day. ECF- https://ecf.tneb.uscourts.gov **Opinions:** www.tneb.uscourts.gov/html/selopinions.htm.

Southern Division Court Clerk, Historic US Courthouse, 31 E 11th St, Chattanooga, TN 37402 (also use mail address for courier delivery), 423-752-5163. 8AM-4:30PM. www.tneb.uscourts.gov

Counties: Bedford*, Bledsoe, Bradley, Coffee*, Franklin*, Grundy*, Hamilton, Lincoln*, Marion, McMinn, Meigs, Moore*, Polk, Rhea, Sequatchie, Van Buren*, Warren*. This court also holds records for the Winchester Division, which is not a staffed office. Winchester Division counties are marked with an asterisk (*).

Searches & Indexing: To obtain positive identification, a social security number or address is needed. Results include last 4 SSN digits only. Computer index maintained. New cases in the index immediately after filing date. Records purged as deemed necessary.

Fee & Payment: Pay by money order, cashier check, business check. No personal checks. Payee: Bankruptcy Court. Will invoice for copy fees only.

Phone Search: Court will confirm bankruptcy filings via phone and only honor up to 3 requests per phone call per day. Voice Case Information Service available, call VCIS at 800-767-1512 or 423-752-5272. **Mail Search:** search usually completed- 24 hours. SASE not required. **In Person Search:** Fee charged if court performs your search. No self-serve copier available.

E-Services: ECF replaces PACER whose records did go back to 1/1986. New records online after 1 day. ECF- https://ecf.tneb.uscourts.gov **Opinions:** www.tneb.uscourts.gov/html/selopinions.htm.

US District Court

Middle District of Tennessee

Columbia Division c/o Nashville Division, 800 US Courthouse, 801 Broadway, Nashville, TN 37203 (also use mail address for courier delivery), 615-736-5498, Fax-615-736-7488. 8AM-5PM. www.tnmd.uscourts.gov **counties:** Giles, Hickman, Lawrence, Lewis, Marshall, Maury, Wayne.

Searches & Indexing: Results do not include SSN or DOB. Index on computer back to 1991. New cases in the index immediately after filing date. Records purged yearly. Open records located at Nashville Division. **Fee & Payment:** Pay by money order, cashier's or personal check. No credit cards. Payee: Clerk, US District Court. Prepayment required.

Phone Search: No searching by telephone. **Mail Search:** Email requests accepted-copyrequest@tnmd.uscourts.gov. No SASE required. **In Person Search:** No self-serve copier.

E-Services: ECF replaces PACER whose records did go back 3 years. New records online after 1 day. ECF at https://ecf.tnmd.uscourts.gov. Opinions and dockets available on ECF; registration required.

Cookeville Division c/o Nashville Division, 800 US Courthouse, 801 Broadway, Nashville, TN 37203 (also use mail address for courier delivery), 615-736-5498, Fax-615-736-7488. 8AM-5PM. www.tnmd.uscourts.gov **Counties:** Clay, Cumberland, De Kalb, Fentress, Jackson, Macon, Overton, Pickett, Putnam, Smith, White.

Searches & Indexing: Results do not include SSN or DOB. Computer index maintained, civil back to 1991, criminal to 1993. Records also indexed on microfiche. New cases in the index immediately after filing date. Records purged yearly. Open records located at Nashville Division.

Fee & Payment: Pay by money order, cashier's, business or personal check. No credit cards. Payee: Clerk, US District Court. Prepayment required.

Phone Search: Only docket information is available by phone. **Mail Search:** search usually completed- 3 days. Email requests accepted-copyrequest@tnmd.uscourts.gov. Include SASE for return. **In Person Search:** Fee charged if court performs your search. No self-serve copier.

E-Services: ECF replaces PACER whose records did go back 3 years. New records online after 1 day. ECF at https://ecf.tnmd.uscourts.gov. Opinions and dockets available on ECF.

Nashville Division Court Clerk, 800 US Courthouse, 801 Broadway, Nashville, TN 37203 (also use mail address for courier delivery), 615-736-5498, records rm- 615-736-5498, crim dockets- 615-736-7396, civil dockets- 615-736-7178, Fax-615-736-7488. Hours- 8AM-5PM. www.tnmd.uscourts.gov **Counties:** Cannon, Cheatham, Davidson, Dickson, Houston, Humphreys, Montgomery, Robertson, Rutherford, Stewart, Sumner, Trousdale, Williamson, Wilson.

Searches & Indexing: Results do not include SSN or DOB. Computer index back to 1991 maintained; also on microfiche. New cases in the index immediately after filing date. Records purged yearly. **Fee & Payment:** Pay by money order, cashier's or personal check. No credit cards. Payee: Clerk, US District Court. Prepayment required. **Phone Search:** Only docket information is available by phone. **Mail Search:** search usually completed- 2-3 days. Email requests accepted-copyrequest@tnmd.uscourts.gov. SASE not required. **In Person Search:** Fee charged if court performs your search. No self-serve copier.

E-Services: ECF replaces PACER whose records did go back 3 years. New records online after 1 day. ECF at https://ecf.tnmd.uscourts.gov. Opinions and dockets available on ECF.

US Bankruptcy Court

Middle District of Tennessee

Nashville Division Court Clerk, PO Box 24890, Nashville, TN 37202-4890 (courier address: Customs House, Rm 200, 701 Broadway, Nashville, TN 37203), 615-736-5584. Hours-8AM-4PM. www.tnmb.uscourts.gov

Counties: Cannon, Cheatham, Clay, Cumberland, Davidson, De Kalb, Dickson, Fentress, Giles, Hickman, Houston, Humphreys, Jackson, Lawrence, Lewis, Macon, Marshall, Maury, Montgomery, Overton, Pickett, Putnam, Robertson, Rutherford, Smith, Stewart, Sumner, Trousdale, Wayne, White, Williamson, Wilson. Nashville holds records for the Columbia and Cookeville Divisions.

Searches & Indexing: Results include last 4 SSN digits. Both computer and card indexes maintained. New cases in the index 24 hours after filing date. Records purged never.

Fee & Payment: Pay by money order, cashier check, business check. No personal checks. Payee: Clerk, Bankruptcy Court. Prepayment required.

Phone Search: Only docket information is available by phone. Voice Case Information Service available, call 615-736-5584 x0. **Mail Search:** search usually completed- 24-48 hours. Include SASE for return. **In Person Search:** Fee charged if court performs your search. Forms are available to request access to files. No self-serve copier available.

E-Services: ECF replaces PACER whose records did go back to 9/1989. New records online immediately. ECF at https://ecf.tnmb.uscourts.gov **Other Online Access:** A court docket query is free at www.tnmb.uscourts.gov/courtdocket.html. Court now participate in the US party case index.

US District Court

Western District of Tennessee

Jackson Division Court Clerk, US Courthouse 262, 111 S Highland, Jackson, TN 38301 (also use mail address for courier delivery), 731-421-9200, Fax-731-421-9210. Hours-8:30AM-4:30PM. www.tnwd.uscourts.gov

Counties: Benton, Carroll, Chester, Crockett, Decatur, Gibson, Hardeman, Hardin, Haywood, Henderson, Henry, Lake, McNairy, Madison, Obion, Perry, Weakley. **Searches & Indexing:** Computer index maintained. New cases in the index 1-2 days after filing date. Records purged as deemed necessary.

Fee & Payment: Pay by Visa/MC, money order, cashier's or personal check. Payee: Clerk, US District Court. Prepayment required.

Phone Search: Only docket information is available by phone. **Mail Search:** search usually completed- 1-2 days. Include SASE for return. **In Person Search:** Fee charged if court performs your search. No self-serve copier available.

E-Services: ECF replaces PACER. Document images available. PACER records go back to 1993. New records online after 1 day. ECF at https://ecf.tnwd.uscourts.gov

Memphis Division Court Clerk, Federal Bldg, Rm 242, 167 N Main, Memphis, TN 38103 (also use mail address for courier delivery), 901-495-1200, records rm- 901-495-1206, Fax-901-495-1250. 8:30AM-4:30PM. www.tnwd.uscourts.gov

Counties: Dyer, Fayette, Lauderdale, Shelby, Tipton. **Searches & Indexing:** Results do not include SSN or DOB. Computer index back to 1992 maintained. New cases in the index 1-2 days after filing date. Records purged as deemed necessary. **Fee & Payment:** Pay by Visa/MC, money order, cashier's or personal check. Payee:

Clerk, US District Court. Prepayment required. Will fax docket listings $.50 per page.

Phone Search: Only docket information is available by phone. **Mail Search:** search usually completed- 1-2 days. Include SASE for return. **In Person Search:** Fee charged if court performs your search. No self-serve copier available.

E-Services: ECF replaces PACER. Document images available. PACER records go back to 1993. New records online after 1 day. ECF at https://ecf.tnwd.uscourts.gov

US Bankruptcy Court

Western District of Tennessee

Eastern Division Court Clerk, Rm 107, 111 S Highland Ave, Jackson, TN 38301 (also use mail address for courier delivery), 731-421-9300. Hours- 8:30AM-4:30PM. www.tnwb.uscourts.gov

Counties: Benton, Carroll, Chester, Crockett, Decatur, Gibson, Hardeman, Hardin, Haywood, Henderson, Henry, Lake, Madison, McNairy, Obion, Perry, Weakley.

Searches & Indexing: Results include last 4 SSN digits only. Computer index maintained. New cases in the index immediately after filing date. Records purged never.

Fee & Payment: Pay by money order, cashier check, business check. No personal checks. Payee: US Bankruptcy Court. Prepayment required. A search fee is charged only when certification of the search is issued. **Phone Search:** Only docket information is available by phone. Voice Case Information Service available, call 888-381-4961 or 901-328-3509. **Mail Search:** search usually completed- 1-2 days. SASE not required. **In Person Search:** Fee charged if court performs your search. No self-serve copier available.

E-Services: PACER online at http://pacer.tnwb.uscourts.gov. PACER records go back to 1989. New records online after 1 day. ECF at https://ecf.tnwb.uscourts.gov **Opinions Online:** www.tnwb.uscourts.gov/Opinions/search.asp. **Other Access:** Calendars at www.tnwb.uscourts.gov/vCal/Cal3.asp. Also, case closings located at www.tnwb.uscourts.gov/CaseInfo/CaseInfo.asp.

Western Division Court Clerk, Suite 413, 200 Jefferson Ave, Memphis, TN 38103 (also use mail address for courier delivery), 901-328-3500, Fax-901-328-3500. Hours- 8:30AM-4:30PM. www.tnwb.uscourts.gov **Counties:** Dyer, Fayette, Lauderdale, Shelby, Tipton.

Searches & Indexing: Results include last 4 SSN digits only. Computer index maintained. New cases in the index 2 days after filing date.

Fee & Payment: Pay by money order, cashier check, business check. No personal checks. Payee: Clerk, US Bankruptcy Court. Prepayment required. In general, if cost of copies exceeds the amount paid, court will bill for the excess by mail.

Phone Search: Only docket information is available by phone. Voice Case Information Service available, call 888-381-4961. **Mail Search:** search usually completed- 3-4 working days. SASE not required. **In Person Search:** permitted. No self-serve copier available.

E-Services: same as Eastern Division; see above.

Tennessee County Courts

Court	Jurisdiction	No. of Courts	How Organized
Circuit Courts*	General	15	31 Districts
Chancery Courts*	General	87	31 Districts
General Sessions Courts*	Limited	16	By County
Combined Circuit/ General Sessions*		87	By County
Municipal Courts	Municipal	300	
Probate/County Courts*	Probate	25	By County
Juvenile Courts	Special	17	By County

* Profiled in this Sourcebook.

Court	CIVIL								
	Tort	Contract	Real Estate	Min. Claim	Max. Claim	Small Claims	Estate	Eviction	Domestic Relations
Circuit Courts*	X	X	X	$0	No Max				X
Chancery Court*	X	X	X	$0	No Max		X		X
General Sessions *	X	X	X	$0	$15,000	X	X		X
Municipal Courts									
Probate/County Courts*							X		
Juvenile Courts									X

Court	CRIMINAL				
	Felony	Misdemeanor	DWI/DUI	Preliminary Hearing	Juvenile
Circuit Courts*	X	X	X		
Criminal Courts*	X	X	X		
Chancery Court*					
General Sessions *		X	X	X	X
Municipal Courts		X	X		
Probate Courts*					
Juvenile Courts					X

ADMINISTRATION Administrative Office of the Courts, 511 Union St (Nashville City Center) #600, Nashville, TN, 37219; 615-741-2687, Fax: 615-741-6285. www.tsc.state.tn.us

COURT STRUCTURE Criminal cases are handled by the Circuit Courts and General Sessions Courts. Generally, misdemeanor cases are heard by General Sessions, but in Circuit Court if connected to a felony. All General Sessions Courts have raised the maximum civil case limit to $15,000 from $10,000. The Chancery Courts, in addition to handling probate, also hear certain types of equitable civil cases. Combined courts vary by county, and the counties of Davidson, Hamilton, Knox, and Shelby have separate Criminal Courts.

ONLINE ACCESS The Administrative Office of Courts provides access to Appellate Court opinions at the web site www.tsc.state.tn.us. Several counties offer online access to court records.

PROBATE COURTS Probate is handled in the Chancery or County Courts, except in several counties where it is handled by the Probate Court.

Anderson County

7th District Circuit & General Sessions Court 100 N Main St, Clinton, TN 37716; phone: 865-457-5400; criminal phone: 865-463-6822; civil phone: 865-463-6821; fax: 865-259-2345; hours 8AM-4:30PM (EST). *Felony, Misdemeanor, Civil, Eviction, Small Claims.*

Civil Records: Access: In person only. Visitors must perform in person searches themselves. Court makes copy: $1.00 per page. Self serve copy fee: $.25 per page. Required to search: name, years to search. Civil cases indexed by defendant, plaintiff; on computer from 1988, archived from 1947.

Criminal Records: Access: In person only. Visitors must perform in person searches themselves. Court makes copy: $1.00 per page. Self serve copy fee: $.25 per page. Required to search: name, years to search, DOB, SSN. Criminal records on computer from 1988, archived from 1947.

General Information: Public terminal goes back to 1992. No juvenile records released. Will not fax specific case file. Certification fee: $2.00 per page. Payee: Circuit Court Clerk or General Sessions Clerk. Personal checks accepted. Prepayment required.

Chancery Court Anderson County Courthouse, PO Box 501, Clinton, TN 37717; phone: 865-457-5400; probate phone: 865-457-6207; fax: 865-457-6267; hours 8:30AM-4:30PM (EST). *Civil, Probate.*

Civil Records: Access: Phone, mail, in person. Both court and visitors may perform in person searches. Court makes copy: $2.00 for first page, $1.00 each add'l. Required to search: name, years to search. Civil cases indexed by defendant, plaintiff; on computer 1992 to present, prior records on another system. Mail turnaround time 2 days.

General Information: No adoption or mental health records released. Certification fee: $4.00. Payee: Clerk and Master. Personal checks accepted. Prepayment required.

Bedford County

17th District Circuit & General Sessions Court 1 Public Sq, #200, Shelbyville, TN 37160; phone: 931-684-3223; fax: 931-684-4141; hours 8AM-4PM (CST). *Felony, Misdemeanor, Civil, Eviction, Small Claims.*

Civil Records: Access: In person only. Visitors must perform in person searches themselves. Court makes copy: $1.00 per page; same fee for self serve. Required to search: name, years to search. Civil cases indexed by defendant, plaintiff; on archives and books from 1934; computerized records since 1994.

Criminal Records: Access: In person only. Visitors must perform in person searches themselves. Court makes copy: $1.00 per page; same fee for self serve. Required to search: name, years to search, DOB; SSN helpful. Criminal records on archives and books from 1934; computerized records since 1994.

General Information: Public terminal goes back to 1994. No juvenile, adoptions, mental health, expunged or sealed records released. Certification fee: $2.00. Payee: Thomas Smith, Clerk. Personal checks accepted. Prepayment required.

Chancery Court Chancery Court, 1 Public Sq, #302, Shelbyville, TN 37160; phone: 931-684-1672; fax: 931-680-0144; hours 8AM-4PM M-Th, 8AM-5PM Fri (CST). *Civil, Probate.*

Civil Records: Access: In person only. Visitors must perform in person searches themselves. Court makes copy: $.50 per page. Required to search: name, years to search. Civil cases indexed by defendant, plaintiff; on books from 9/82 (probate), prior records back to 1800s filed in county clerk's office.

General Information: No adoption records released. Certification fee: $5.00. Payee: Clerk and Master. Personal checks accepted. Prepayment required.

Benton County

24th District Circuit & General Sessions Court 1 E Court Sq, Rm 207, Camden, TN 38320; phone: 731-584-6711; fax: 731-584-2081; hours 8AM-4PM M-Th; 8AM-5PM F (CST). *Felony, Misdemeanor, Civil, Eviction, Small Claims.*

Civil Records: Access: In person only. Both court and visitors may perform in person searches. No search fee. Court makes copy: $1.00 per page. Required to search: name, years to search. Civil cases indexed by defendant, plaintiff. Civil records computerized since 1995. Public can only use docket books to search, older records archived to 1800s.

Criminal Records: Access: In person only. Both court and visitors may perform in person searches. No search fee. Court makes copy: $1.00 per page. Required to search: name, years to search. Criminal records computerized since 1995. Public can only use docket books to search, older records archived to 1800s.

General Information: No juvenile records released without judge approval. Will not fax specific case file. Certification fee: $5.00 per doc. Payee: Circuit Court Clerk or General Session. Business checks accepted. Prepayment required.

Chancery Court 1 E Court Sq, Courthouse Rm 206, Camden, TN 38320; phone: 731-584-4435; fax: 731-584-1407; hours 8AM-4PM M-Th; 8AM-5PM F (CST). *Civil, Probate.*

Civil Records: Access: In person only. Only the court performs in person searches; visitors may not. Court makes copy: $1.00 per page. Required to search: name, years to search. Civil cases indexed by defendant, plaintiff; on computer back to 1994; in books since 1880.

General Information: No adoption or sealed records released. Certification fee: $6.00 per document. Payee: Clerk & Master. Personal checks accepted. Prepayment required.

Bledsoe County

12th District Circuit & General Sessions Court PO Box 455, Pikeville, TN 37367; phone: 423-447-6488; fax: 423-447-2534; hours 8AM-4PM (CST). *Felony, Misdemeanor, Civil, Eviction, Small Claims.*

Civil Records: Access: In person only. Visitors must perform in person searches themselves. Court makes copy: $.50 per page; same fee for self serve. Required to search: name, years to search. Civil cases indexed by plaintiff. Civil records archived from 1920 in books. Books available for public to search.

Criminal Records: Access: In person only. Visitors must perform in person searches themselves. Court makes copy: $.50 per page; same fee for self serve. Required to search: name, years to search, DOB. Criminal records archived from 1920 in books. Books available for public to search.

General Information: Public terminal has only criminal records. No juvenile records released. Certification fee: $3.00. Prepayment required.

Chancery Court PO Box 389, Pikeville, TN 37367; phone: 423-447-2484; fax: 423-447-6856; hours 8AM-4PM M,T,W,F; 8AM-N Sat (CST). *Civil, Probate.*

Civil Records: Access: Fax, mail, in person. Both court and visitors may perform in person searches. No search fee. Court makes copy: $1.00 per page. Self serve copy fee: $.25 per page. Required to search: name, years to search. Civil cases indexed by defendant, plaintiff; on books since 1856. Mail turnaround time 3 days.

General Information: No juvenile or adoption records released. Will fax documents for $2.00 per page. Certification fee: $2.00 per page. Payee: Bledsoe County Clerk and Master. Personal checks accepted. Prepayment required.

Blount County

5th District General Sessions Court 926 E Lamar Alexander Pky, Maryville, TN 37804-6201; phone: 865-273-5450; criminal/civil phone: 865-273-5400; fax: 865-273-5411; hours 8AM-4:30PM (EST). *Misdemeanor, Civil, Eviction, Small Claims.* www.blounttn.org/circuit/

Civil Records: Access: Mail, in person. Both court and visitors may perform in person searches. Search fee: $15.00 per name. Court makes copy: $1.00 per page; same fee for self serve. Required to search: name, years to search. Civil cases indexed by defendant, plaintiff. Civil records archived in books back to 1991; on computer back to 1996. Mail turnaround time 6-10 days.

Criminal Records: Access: Mail, in person. Both court and visitors may perform in person searches. Search fee: $15.00 per name. Court makes copy: $1.00 per page; same fee for self serve. Required to search: name, years to search. Criminal records archived in books back to 1991; on computer back to 1996. Mail turnaround time 6-10 days.

General Information: Public terminal goes back to 1997. No juvenile records released. Will fax documents. Certification fee: $5.00 per document. Payee: Circuit Court Clerk or General Session. Business checks accepted. Prepayment required.

Circuit Court 926 E Lamar Alexander Pky, 1st Fl, Maryville, TN 37804; phone: 865-273-5400; probate phone: 865-273-5800; fax: 865-273-5411; hours 8AM-4:30PM (EST). *Felony, Misdemeanor, Civil.*

Civil Records: Access: Mail, in person. Both court and visitors may perform in person searches. Search fee: $15.00 per name. Court makes copy: $1.00 per page; same fee for self serve. Required to search: name, years to search. Civil cases indexed by defendant. Civil records on books.

Criminal Records: Access: Mail, in person. Visitors must perform in person searches themselves. Search fee: $15.00 per name. Court makes copy: $1.00 per page; same fee for self serve. Required to search: name, years to search. Criminal records on books.

General Information: Public terminal goes back to 8 years. No juvenile records released. Will fax documents for $1.00 per page. Certification fee: $5.00 per cert. Payee: Circuit Court Clerk. Only cashiers checks and money orders accepted. Prepayment required.

County Clerk 345 Court St, Old Courthouse, Maryville, TN 37804; phone: 865-273-5800; fax: 865-273-5815; hours 8AM-4:30PM (EST). *Probate.*

Bradley County

10th District Circuit & General Sessions Court Courthouse, Rm 205, 155 N Ocoee St, Cleveland, TN 37311-5068; criminal phone: 423-728-7263; civil phone: 423-728-7052; fax: 423-476-0488; hours 8:30AM-4:30PM M-Th, 8:30AM-5PM Fri (EST). *Felony, Misdemeanor, Civil, Eviction, Small Claims.*

Civil Records: Access: Mail, in person. Both court and visitors may perform in person searches. Search fee: $25.00 per name. Court makes copy: $1.00 per page. Required to search: name, years to search. Civil cases indexed by defendant, plaintiff. Civil records archived from 1990, on computer from 1990. Mail turnaround time 10 days.

Criminal Records: Access: Mail, in person. Both court and visitors may perform in person searches. Search fee: $25.00 per name plus $2.00 data charge. Court makes copy: $1.00 per page. Required to search: name, years to search, signed release. Criminal records archived from 1990, on computer from 1990. Mail turnaround time 10 days.

General Information: Public terminal goes back to 1990. No juvenile records released. Fee to fax documents is $1.00 per page. Certification fee: $5.00 per doc. Payee: Circuit Court Clerk or General Session. Personal checks accepted. Prepayment required.

Chancery Court 55 N Ocoee St, Rm 203, Cleveland, TN 37311; phone: 423-728-7205; probate phone: 423-728-7207; fax: 423-339-0723; hours 8:30AM-4:30PM M-Th, 8:30AM-5PM Fri (EST). *Civil, Probate.*

Civil Records: Access: Phone, in person. Both court and visitors may perform in person searches. Search fee: Search fee based on request submitted. Court makes copy: $1.00 per page. Self serve copy fee: $.30 per page. Required to search: name, years to search. Civil cases indexed by defendant, plaintiff. Civil records filed in books back to 1861. Mail turnaround time same day.

General Information: Public terminal has only civil records back to 2004. No adoption records released. Will fax documents if requested. Certification fee: $10.00. Payee: Clerk and Master. Personal checks accepted. Prepayment required.

Campbell County

8th District Circuit & General Sessions Court PO Box 26, Jacksboro, TN 37757; phone: 423-562-2624; fax: 423-563-0342; hours 8AM-4:30PM (EST). *Felony, Misdemeanor, Civil, Eviction, Small Claims.*

Civil Records: Access: Mail, in person. Both court and visitors may perform in person searches. No search fee. Court makes copy: $.25 per page. Required to search: name, years to search. Civil cases indexed by defendant, plaintiff; on computer since 1991. On microfiche from 1987 and archived since court started located at La Follette Library, La Follette, TN 37766. Mail turnaround time depends on type of search.

Criminal Records: Access: Mail, in person. Both court and visitors may perform in person searches. No search fee. Court makes copy: $.25 per page. Required to search: name, years to search, DOB, SSN. Criminal records on computer since 1991. On microfiche from 1987 and archived since court started located at La Follette Library, La Follette, TN 37766. Mail turnaround time depends on type of search.

General Information: Public terminal goes back to 1991. No juvenile, adoption and judicial hospitalization records released. Certification fee: $3.00. Payee: Circuit Court Clerk or General Session. Business checks accepted. Prepayment required.

Chancery Court PO Box 182 (570 Main St, #110), Jacksboro, TN 37757; phone: 423-562-3496; fax: 423-562-9732; hours 8AM-4:30PM (EST). *Civil, Probate.*

Civil Records: Access: In person, mail. Visitors must perform in person searches themselves. Court makes copy: $1.00 per page. Required to search: name, years to search. Civil cases indexed by defendant, plaintiff. Civil records filed in books, microfiche available at LaFollette Library since 1842. Mail turnaround time 1-2 days.

General Information: No adoption records released. Fee to fax documents is $1.00 per page and $.50 per document. Certification fee: $4.00. Payee: Clerk and Master. Business checks accepted. Prepayment required. SASE preferred.

Cannon County

16th District Circuit & General Sessions Court County Courthouse Public Sq, Woodbury, TN 37190; phone: 615-563-4461; fax: 615-563-6391; hours 8AM-4PM M,T,Th,F; 8AM-N W (CST). *Felony, Misdemeanor, Civil, Eviction, Small Claims.*

Civil Records: Access: In person only. Visitors must perform in person searches themselves. Court makes copy: $1.00 per page; same fee for self serve. Required to search: name, years to search. Civil cases indexed by defendant, plaintiff. Civil records archived on books from 1980s, computerized since 10/2003.

Criminal Records: Access: In person only. Visitors must perform in person searches themselves. Court makes copy: $1.00 per page; same fee for self serve. Required to search: name, years to search, DOB. Criminal records archived on books from 1980s, computerized since 10/2003.

General Information: Public terminal goes back to 10/2003. No juvenile records released. Certification fee: $4.00. Payee: Circuit Court Clerk or General Session. Personal checks accepted. Prepayment required.

County Court 1 County Courthouse Public Square, Woodbury, TN 37190; phone: 615-563-4278/5936; fax: 615-563-1289; hours 8AM-4PM M,T,Th,F; 8AM-N Sat (CST). *Probate.*

Carroll County

24th District Circuit & General Sessions Court 99 Court Sq, #103, Huntingdon, TN 38344; criminal phone: 731-986-1927; civil phone: 731-986-1929 (Circuit), 731-986-1926 (Gen Sess); hours 8AM-4PM (CST). *Felony, Misdemeanor, Civil, Eviction, Small Claims.*

Civil Records: Access: In person only. Only the court performs in person searches; visitors may not. Search fee: $5.00 per name. Court makes copy: $.50 per page. No copies by mail; same fee for self serve. Required to search: name, years to search. Civil cases indexed by defendant, plaintiff. Civil records archived from 1924; on computer from 1989. Mail turnaround time approx. 2 days.

Criminal Records: Access: In person only. Only the court performs in person searches; visitors may not. Search fee: $5.00 per name. Court makes copy: $.50 per page. No copies by mail; same fee for self serve. Required to search: name, years to search, DOB. Criminal records archived from 1925; on computer from 1989.

General Information: Will not fax specific case file. Certification fee: $4.00 per record. Payee: Circuit Court Clerk or General Session. Only cashiers checks and money orders accepted. Prepayment required.

Chancery Court 99 Court Sq, #105, Huntingdon, TN 38344; phone: 731-986-1920; fax: 731-986-6051; hours 8AM-4PM M-F (CST). *Civil, Probate.*

Civil Records: Access: Mail, in person. Both court and visitors may perform in person searches. Search fee: $10.00. Court makes copy: $1.00 per page. Required to search: name, years to search. Civil cases indexed by defendant, plaintiff; on computer since 6/88, records go back to 1822. Mail turnaround time 5-10 days.

General Information: No adoption or sealed documents released. Will fax documents for $2.00 per page. Certification fee: $6.00 per document. Payee: Clerk and Master. Checks, money orders and cashiers checks accepted. Prepayment required. SASE or $.52 postage required.

Carter County

1st District Circuit & General Sessions Court Carter County Justice Ctr, 900 E Elk Ave, Elizabethton, TN 37643; phone: 423-542-1835; civil phone: 423-542-1825; fax: 423-542-3742; hours 8AM-5PM (EST). *Felony, Misdemeanor, Civil, Eviction, Small Claims.*

Civil Records: Access: In person only. Visitors must perform in person searches themselves. Court makes copy: $1.00 per page; same fee for self serve. Required to search: name, years to search. Civil cases indexed by defendant, plaintiff. Civil records archived from 1800s (partial lost in fire), on computer from 2/92.

Criminal Records: Access: In person only. Visitors must perform in person searches themselves. Court makes copy: $1.00 per page; same fee for self serve. Required to search: name, years to search. Criminal records archived from 1800s (partial lost in fire), on computer from 4-92.

General Information: Public terminal goes back to 1992. No juvenile, psychiatric or expunged records released. Certification fee: $7.00 plus $1.00 per page after the first. Payee: Circuit Court Clerk or General Session. Personal checks accepted. Prepayment required.

County Court 801 E Elk Ave, Elizabethton, TN 37643; phone: 423-542-1814; fax: 423-547-1502; hours 8AM-4:30PM (EST). *Probate.*

Cheatham County

23rd District Circuit Court 100 Public Sq, Rm 225, Ashland City, TN 37015; phone: 615-792-3272; fax: 615-792-3203; hours 8AM-4PM (CST). *Felony, Civil Actions over $15,000, Misdemeanors.*

Note: Circuit Court is Rm 225, General Sessions is Rm 223 (615-792-4866); they must be searched separately. Circuit court handles felony, civil actions over $15,000, some misdemeanors; General Sessions handles misdemeanors, small claims, civil under $15,000.

Civil Records: Access: Mail, in person. Both court and visitors may perform in person searches. Search fee: $5.00 per name. Court makes copy: $2.50 per document or $1.00 per pg. Required to search: name, years to search. Civil cases indexed by defendant, plaintiff. Civil records archived on books from 1946 in office, since court started in storage and on computer from 1990. Mail turnaround time 2-3 days.

Criminal Records: Access: Mail, in person. Both court and visitors may perform in person searches. Search fee: $5.00 per name. Court makes copy: $2.50 per document or $1.00 per page. Required to search: name, years to search. Criminal records archived on books from 1946 in office, since court started in storage and on computer from 1990. Mail turnaround time 2-3 days.

General Information: No juvenile records released. Certification fee: $5.00. Payee: Circuit Court Clerk. Prepayment and SASE required.

General Sessions 100 Public Sq, Rm 223, Ashland City, TN 37015; phone: 615-792-4866; fax: 615-792-3203; hours 8AM-4PM (CST). *Misdemeanor, Civil under $15,000, Eviction, Small Claims.*

Civil Records: Access: Mail, in person. Both court and visitors may perform in person searches. Search fee: $5.00 per name. Court makes copy: $1.00 per page; same fee for self serve. Required to search: name, years to search. Civil cases indexed by defendant, plaintiff. Civil records archived on books from 1946 in office, since court started in storage and on computer from 1990. Mail turnaround time 2-3 days.

Criminal Records: Access: Mail, in person. Both court and visitors may perform in person searches. Search fee: $5.00 per name. Court makes copy: $1.00 per page; same fee for self serve. Required to search: name, years to search. Criminal records archived on books from 1946 in office, since court started in storage and on computer from 1990. Mail turnaround time 2-3 days.

General Information: No juvenile records released. Certification fee: $5.00. Payee: General Sessions Clerk. Prepayment and SASE required.

Chancery Court Clerk & Master, #106, Ashland City, TN 37015; phone: 615-792-4620; fax: 615-792-6059; hours 8AM-4PM (CST). *Civil, Probate.*

Civil Records: Access: In person only. Visitors must perform in person searches themselves. Court makes copy: $1.00 per page. Required to search: name, years to search. Civil cases indexed by defendant, plaintiff; on computer.

General Information: No adoption records released. Certification fee: $2.00. Payee: Chancery Court. Personal checks accepted. Prepayment and SASE required.

Chester County

26th District Circuit & General Sessions Court PO Box 133, Henderson, TN 38340; phone: 731-989-2454; fax: 731-989-9184; hours 8AM-4PM (CST). *Felony, Misdemeanor, Civil, Eviction, Small Claims.*

Civil Records: Access: Mail, in person. Both court and visitors may perform in person searches.

Search fee: $20.00. Court makes copy: $1.00 per page. Required to search: name, years to search. Civil cases indexed by defendant, plaintiff; in books and archived from 1892. Mail turnaround time 2 days.
Criminal Records: Access: Mail, in person. Both court and visitors may perform in person searches. Search fee: $20.00 per name. Court makes copy: $1.00 per page. Required to search: name, years to search, DOB. Criminal records in books and archived from 1892. Mail turnaround time 2 days.
General Information: No juvenile records released. Certification fee: $5.00. Payee: Circuit Court, or General Sessions Clerk. Prepayment required.

Chancery Court Clerk & Master, PO Box 262, Henderson, TN 38340; phone: 731-989-7171; fax: 731-989-7176; hours 8AM-4PM (CST). *Civil, Probate.*
Civil Records: Access: Mail, in person. Visitors must perform in person searches themselves. Search fee: $5.00. Court makes copy: $1.00 per page. Required to search: name, years to search. Civil cases indexed by defendant, plaintiff; on books. Mail turnaround time 2 days.
General Information: No adoption or sealed records released. Will fax for fee of $5.00 per certified copy. Certification fee: $3.00. Payee: Clerk and Master. Personal checks accepted. Prepayment required.

Claiborne County

8th District Criminal, Circuit & General Sessions Court 1740 Main St, #201, Tazewell, TN 37879; criminal phone: 423-626-8181; civil phone: 423-626-3334; fax: 423-626-5631; hours 8:30AM-4PM M-F, 9AM-N Sat (EST). *Felony, Misdemeanor, Civil, Eviction, Small Claims.*
Civil Records: Access: Mail, fax, in person. Both court and visitors may perform in person searches. Search fee: $10.00 per name. Court makes copy: included in search fee. Self serve copy fee: $.25 per page. Required to search: name, years to search. Civil cases indexed by defendant, plaintiff. Civil records archived since 1932; on computer back to 1986. Mail turnaround time 2-3 days.
Criminal Records: Access: Mail, fax, in person. Both court and visitors may perform in person searches. Search fee: $10.00 per name. Court makes copy: Included in $10.00 search fee. Self serve copy fee: $.25 per page. Required to search: name, years to search. Criminal records archived since 1932; on computer back to 1986. Mail turnaround time 2-3 days.
General Information: Public use terminal available. No adoption records released. Fee to fax documents is $.25 per page. Certification fee: $5.00. Payee: Circuit Court Clerk or General Sessions. Business checks or in state personal checks accepted. Prepayment and SASE required.

Chancery Court PO Box 180, Tazewell, TN 37879; phone: 423-626-3284; fax: 423-626-3604; hours 8:30AM-N, 1-4PM (EST). *Civil, Probate.*
Civil Records: Access: Mail, in person. Both court and visitors may perform in person searches. No search fee. Court makes copy: $.25 per page. Required to search: name, years to search. Civil cases indexed by defendant, plaintiff. Civil records kept on books back to 1932; recent on computer. Mail turnaround time 1-2 days.
General Information: Public terminal has only civil records back to 1976. No adoption records released. Certification fee: $5.00 per document. Payee: Clerk and Master. Personal checks accepted. Prepayment required.

Clay County

13th District Circuit & General Sessions Court PO Box 749, Celina, TN 38551; phone: 931-243-2557; fax: 931-243-2961; hours 8AM-5PM (CST). *Felony, Misdemeanor, Civil, Eviction, Small Claims.*
Civil Records: Access: In person only. Visitors must perform in person searches themselves. Court

makes copy: $.25 per page; same fee for self serve. Required to search: name, years to search. Civil cases indexed by plaintiff, defendant. Civil records archived from early 1900s, on microfiche from 1986.
Criminal Records: Access: In person only. Visitors must perform in person searches themselves. Court makes copy: $.25 per page; same fee for self serve. Required to search: name, years to search; SSN helpful. Criminal records archived from early 1900s, on microfiche from 1986.
General Information: Public terminal goes back to 2000. No juvenile records released. No certification fee. Payee: Circuit Court, or General Sessions Clerk. Personal checks accepted. Prepayment required.

Chancery Court PO Box 332, Celina, TN 38551; phone: 931-243-3145; fax: 931-243-3157; hours 8AM-4PM M,T,Th,F; 8AM-N Wed (CST). *Civil, Probate.*
Civil Records: Access: Mail, in person. Both court and visitors may perform in person searches. No search fee. Court makes copy: $.50 per page. Required to search: name, years to search. Civil cases indexed by defendant, plaintiff; on books. Mail turnaround time 1 week.
General Information: No juvenile records released. Certification fee: $5.00 per doc.

Cocke County

4th District Circuit Court 111 Court Ave, Rm 201, Newport, TN 37821; phone: 423-623-6124; fax: 423-625-3889; hours 8:30AM-5PM (EST). *Felony, Misdemeanor, Civil Actions Over $15,000.*
Civil Records: Access: Mail, in person. Both court and visitors may perform in person searches. Search fee: $3.00 per name. Court makes copy: $.25 per page. Required to search: name, years to search. Civil cases indexed by defendant, plaintiff. Civil records archived from late 1800s. Mail turnaround time ASAP.
Criminal Records: Access: Mail, in person. Both court and visitors may perform in person searches. Search fee: $3.00 per name. Court makes copy: $.25 per page. Required to search: name, years to search, DOB. Criminal records archived from late 1800s. Mail turnaround time ASAP.
General Information: No divorce or sealed records released. Will fax documents to local or toll free line. Certification fee: $5.00. Payee: Circuit Court. Personal checks accepted. Prepayment and SASE required.

General Sessions Court 111 Court Ave, Newport, TN 37821; phone: 423-623-8619; fax: 423-623-9808; hours 8AM-4PM (EST). *Misdemeanor, Civil Actions Under $15,000, Eviction, Small Claims.*
Civil Records: Access: Phone, mail, in person. Both court and visitors may perform in person searches. Search fee: $3.00 per name. Court makes copy: $3.00 per document. Required to search: name, years to search. Civil cases indexed by defendant, plaintiff; on books at least 10 years. Mail turnaround time varies.
Criminal Records: Access: Phone, mail, in person. Both court and visitors may perform in person searches. Search fee: $3.00 per name. Court makes copy: $3.00 per document. Self serve copy fee: $3.00 per page. Required to search: name, years to search. DOB, SSN. Criminal records on books at least 10 years. Mail turnaround time varies.
General Information: Public terminal has criminal back to 2001 and civil back to 2000. Will fax documents, if prepaid. Certification fee: $3.00. Payee: General Sessions Court. Business checks accepted. Prepayment and SASE required.

Chancery Court Courthouse Annex, 360 E Main St, #103, Newport, TN 37821; phone: 423-623-3321; criminal phone: 423-623-6124; fax: 423-625-3642; hours 8AM-4:30PM (EST). *Civil, Probate.*
Civil Records: Access: Phone, mail, in person. Only the court performs in person searches; visitors may not. No search fee. Court makes copy: $.25 per page; same fee for self serve. Required to search: name,

years to search. Civil cases indexed by defendant, plaintiff; on computer since 1984, on books from 1930. Mail turnaround time 1 week.
General Information: No sealed records released. Will fax documents to local or toll free line. Certification fee: $3.00. Payee: Chancery Court, Clerk and Master. Personal checks accepted. Prepayment and SASE required.

Coffee County

14th District Circuit & General Sessions Court PO Box 629, Manchester, TN 37349; phone: 931-723-5110; fax: 931-723-5116; hours 8AM-4:30PM (CST). *Felony, Misdemeanor, Civil, Eviction, Small Claims.*
Civil Records: Access: Mail, in person. Both court and visitors may perform in person searches. Search fee: $15.00 per case/defendant from 1991 to present; $50.00 if prior. Court makes copy: $.50 per page add'l $.25. Self serve copy fee: none. Required to search: name, years to search. Civil cases indexed by defendant, plaintiff. Civil records archived from late 1800s, indexed chronologically by court date. Mail turnaround time 1 week.
Criminal Records: Access: Mail, in person. Both court and visitors may perform in person searches. Search fee: Same fees as civil. Court makes copy: $.50 per page, $.25 ea add'l. Self serve copy fee: none. Required to search: name, years to search, DOB; also helpful: SSN. Criminal records archived from late 1800s, indexed chronologically by court date. Mail turnaround time 1 week.
General Information: Public terminal has criminal back to 1995 and civil back to 1996. No juvenile record released. Certification fee: $3.50. Payee: General Sessions Clerk. Personal checks accepted. Prepayment and SASE required.

Chancery Court 300 Hillsboro Blvd, Rm 102, Manchester, TN 37355; phone: 931-723-5132; criminal phone: 931-723-5132; fax: 931-723-5116; hours 8AM-4:30PM (CST). *Civil, Probate.*
Civil Records: Access: Mail, in person. Both court and visitors may perform in person searches. No search fee. Court makes copy: $.50 per page. Self serve copy fee: none. Required to search: name, years to search. Civil cases indexed by defendant, plaintiff; on books after 1980, before 1980 filed in County Clerk's Office. Mail turnaround time 1-2 days.
General Information: Public terminal has only civil records. No juvenile or adoption records released. Certification fee: $3.50. Payee: Chancery Court. Personal checks accepted. Prepayment required. SASE helpful.

Crockett County

Circuit & General Sessions Court 1 S Bell St, #6, Courthouse, Alamo, TN 38001; phone: 731-696-5462; fax: 731-696-2605; hours 8AM-4PM (CST). *Felony, Misdemeanor, Civil, Eviction, Small Claims.*
Civil Records: Access: Mail, fax, in person. Both court and visitors may perform in person searches. Search fee: $10.00 per name. Court makes copy: $1.00 per page; same fee for self serve. Required to search: name, years to search. Civil cases indexed by defendant, plaintiff. Civil records archived since court started, records prior to 1986 on docket books. All requests must be in writing. Mail turnaround time 1-2 days.
Criminal Records: Access: Mail, fax, in person. Both court and visitors may perform in person searches. Search fee: $10.00 per name. Court makes copy: $1.00 per page; same fee for self serve. Required to search: name, years to search, DOB; also helpful: SSN, sex. Criminal records on docket books, on computer from 1993. All requests must be in writing. Mail turnaround time 1-2 days.
General Information: Public terminal goes back to 1994. No adoption or mental records released. Certification fee: $6.00 per document. Payee: Circuit Court, or General Sessions Clerk. Business checks accepted. Prepayment required. SASE requested.

Chancery Court 1 S Bell St, #5, Alamo, TN 38001; phone: 731-696-5458; fax: 731-696-3028; hours 8AM-4PM (CST). *Civil, Probate.*

Civil Records: Access: Mail, in person. Both court and visitors may perform in person searches. Court makes copy: $1.00 per page. Required to search: name, years to search. Civil cases indexed by defendant, plaintiff; on books back to 1872. Mail turnaround time 1-3 days.

General Information: No adoption records released. Will fax documents for $1.00 per page. Certification fee: $6.00 for cert and seal. Payee: Chancery Court Clerk. Personal checks accepted. Prepayment and SASE required.

Cumberland County

13th District Circuit & General Sessions Court 2 N Main St, #302, Crossville, TN 38555; phone: 931-484-6647; fax: 931-456-5013; hours 8AM-4PM (CST). *Felony, Misdemeanor, Civil, Eviction, Small Claims.*

Note: Above phone number is for General Sessions; Circuit can be reached at 931-484-5852.

Civil Records: Access: In person only. Visitors must perform in person searches themselves. No copy fee. Required to search: name, years to search. Civil cases indexed by defendant, plaintiff. Civil records archived on books from 1940s approx.; on computer back to 1996.

Criminal Records: Access: In person only. Visitors must perform in person searches themselves. No copy fee. Required to search: name, years to search, DOB; SSN helpful. Criminal records archived on books from 1940s approx.; on computer back to 1996.

General Information: Public terminal goes back to 1996. No sealed records released. No certification fee. Prepayment required.

Chancery Court 2 N Main St, #101, Crossville, TN 38555-4583; phone: 931-484-4731; criminal phone: 931-484-5852; fax: 931-456-5013; hours 8AM-4PM (CST). *Civil, Probate.*

Civil Records: Access: Mail, in person. Both court and visitors may perform in person searches. No search fee. Court makes copy: $.50 per page. Required to search: name, years to search. Civil cases indexed by defendant, plaintiff; on computer since 1991, on books since 1900s. Mail turnaround time 2 days.

General Information: No juvenile, adoption records released. Certification fee: $5.00 per doc. Payee: Clerk and Master. Only cashiers checks and money orders accepted. Prepayment required. SASE requested.

Davidson County

20th District Criminal Court Metro Courthouse, Rm 309, 601 Mainstream Dr, Nashville, TN 37201; phone: 615-862-5601; fax: 615-862-5164; hours 8AM-4PM (CST). *Felony, Misdemeanor.*

www.nashville.gov/ccc/index.htm

Criminal Records: Access: Mail, online, in person. Both court and visitors may perform in person searches. Search fee: $15.00 per name. Court makes copy: $.25 per page. Required to search: name, years to search, DOB, signed release; also helpful: SSN, race. Access Metropolitan Nashville and Davidson County Criminal Court database free at www.jis.nashville.org/ccc/CaseSearch.asp. Search by name, warrant, or case number. Also, the City of Nashville sponsors an Internet site at www.police.nashville.org/justice/default.asp. Mail turnaround time 2-3 days.

General Information: No records unauthorized by statutes released. Certification fee: $6.00 per document. Payee: Criminal Court Clerk. Personal checks accepted, but not for record checks. Visa, MC, Discover. Prepayment and SASE required.

Circuit Court 506 Metro Courthouse, Nashville, TN 37201; phone: 615-862-5181; fax: 615-862-5191; hours 8AM-4:30PM (CST). *Civil.*

www.nashville.gov/circuit

Note: Physical address is 523 Mainstream Dr, #200, Nashville.

Civil Records: Access: Mail, in person, online. Both court and visitors may perform in person searches. No search fee. Court makes copy: $.50 per page. Required to search: name, years to search. Civil cases indexed by defendant, plaintiff. Domestic records go back to 1947. Civil records archived on books from 1800s, on computer from 1975. Access filed cases online on CaseLink at www.nashville.gov/circuit/caselink/; $20.00 per month fee required plus username, password. Email Caselink@Nashville.Gov for signup or add'l info. Intended to be free searching, soon. Mail turnaround time 2-3 days.

General Information: Public terminal has only civil records. No juvenile or adoption records released. Will not fax documents. Certification fee: $2.00 per doc plus $2.00 per page, includes copies. Payee: Circuit Court Clerk. Prepayment required.

General Sessions Court 501 Great Circle Rd, Nashville, TN 37228; phone: 615-862-5195; fax: 615-862-5924; hours 8AM-4:30PM (CST). *Civil Actions Under $15,000, Eviction, Small Claims.*

www.nashville.gov/circuit/sessions/

Note: There is no "Small Claims" court, these type of cases are handled by the General Sessions Civil Division.

Civil Records: Access: Mail, in person, online. Visitors must perform in person searches themselves. Search fee: $6.00 for an abstract of judgment. Court makes copy: $.50 per page. Required to search: name, years to search. Records indexed on computer since 1990. Access filed cases online on CaseLink at www.nashville.gov/circuit/caselink/; $20.00 per month fee required, plus username and password. Email Caselink@Nashville.Gov for signup or add'l info. Intended to be free searching, soon.

General Information: Public terminal has only civil records back to 1990. No juvenile records released. Certification fee: $3.00 per page. Payee: General Sessions Court Clerk. Prepayment required.

Probate Court 601 Mainstream Dr (temporary address), Nashville, TN 37201; phone: 615-862-5980; fax: 615-862-5987; hours 8AM-4:30 (CST). *Probate.*

Note: Regular address is; 105 Metro Courthouse; temporarily away. See Circuit or General Sessions Court for web access to filed cases.

De Kalb County

13th District Circuit & General Sessions Court 1 Public Sq, Rm 303, Smithville, TN 37166; phone: 615-597-5711; fax: 615-597-9919; hours 8AM-4:30PM (8AM-5PM Fri) (CST). *Felony, Misdemeanor, Civil, Eviction, Small Claims.*

Civil Records: Access: In person only. Both court and visitors may perform in person searches. Court makes copy: $1.00 per page. Required to search: name, years to search. Civil cases indexed by defendant, plaintiff. Civil records archived in office last 10 years. Prior to 1982, records are not very accurate because of fire. Dist Court records on computer back to 2001; General Sessions to mid-2000.

Criminal Records: Access: In person only. Visitors must perform in person searches themselves. Court makes copy: $1.00 per page. Required to search: name, years to search, DOB; SSN helpful. Criminal records archived in office last 10 years. Prior to 1982, records are not very accurate because of fire. Dist Court records on computer back to 2001; General Sessions to mid-2000.

General Information: Public use terminal available. No juvenile records released. Will fax specific case file for $1.00 per page. Certification fee: $6.00. Payee:

Circuit Court, or General Sessions Clerk. Personal checks accepted. Prepayment required.

Chancery Court 1 Public Square, Rm 302, Smithville, TN 37166; phone: 615-597-4360; hours 8AM-4PM (CST). *Civil, Probate.*

Civil Records: Access: In person only. Visitors must perform in person searches themselves. Court makes copy: $1.00 per page; same fee for self serve. Required to search: name, years to search. Civil cases indexed by defendant, plaintiff; on books, computerized as of 6/00.

General Information: Public terminal has only civil records back to 6/2000. No adoption, juvenile records released. Certification fee: $6.00. Payee: Clerk and Master. Personal checks accepted. Prepayment required.

Decatur County

24th District Circuit & General Sessions Court PO Box 488, Decaturville, TN 38329; phone: 731-852-3125; fax: 731-852-2130; hours 8AM-4PM M,T,Th,F; 8AM-N W & S (CST). *Felony, Misdemeanor, Civil, Eviction, Small Claims.*

Civil Records: Access: In person only. Visitors must perform in person searches themselves. Court makes copy: $1.00 per page. Required to search: name, years to search. Civil cases indexed by defendant, plaintiff. Civil records archived on books from 1927; computerized records since 1996.

Criminal Records: Access: In person only. Visitors must perform in person searches themselves. Court makes copy: $1.00 per page. Required to search: name, years to search, DOB, SSN, signed release. Criminal records archived on books from 1927; computerized records since 1996.

General Information: Public terminal goes back to 8/1996. No adoption records released. Certification fee: $2.00 per page. Payee: Circuit Court. Business checks accepted. Prepayment required.

Chancery Court Clerk & Master, Decaturville, TN 38329; phone: 731-852-3422; fax: 731-852-2130; hours 9M-4PM M,T,Th,F; 9AM-N Wed (CST). *Civil, Probate.*

Civil Records: Access: In person only. Visitors must perform in person searches themselves. Court makes copy: $.25 per page. Required to search: name, years to search. Civil cases indexed by plaintiff. Probate records in books since 1869 for probate, civil records in books since 1958.

General Information: No adoption records released. Certification fee: $2.00. Payee: Elizabeth Carpenter, Clerk and Master. Personal checks accepted. Prepayment required.

Dickson County

23rd District Circuit Court Court Square, PO Box 70, Charlotte, TN 37036; phone: 615-789-7010; fax: 615-789-7018; hours 8AM-4PM (CST). *Felony, Misdemeanor, Civil Actions Over $15,000.*

Civil Records: Access: Phone, fax, mail, in person. Both court and visitors may perform in person searches. Search fee: $6.00 per name. Court makes copy: $.75 per page. Self serve copy fee: $.50 per page. Required to search: name, years to search. Civil cases indexed by defendant, plaintiff. Civil records archived from 1800s, on computer from 1986, some records back to 1974. Mail turnaround time 1 day.

Criminal Records: Access: Phone, fax, mail, in person. Both court and visitors may perform in person searches. Search fee: $6.00 per name. Court makes copy: $.75 per page. Self serve copy fee: $.50 per page. Required to search: name, years to search; also helpful: DOB. Criminal records archived from 1800s, on computer from 1986, some records back to 1974. Mail turnaround time 1 day.

General Information: No adoption records released. Will fax documents $6.00 per document. Certification fee: $2.00. Payee: Circuit Court Clerk. Personal checks accepted. Prepayment and SASE required.

General Sessions PO Box 217, Charlotte, TN 37036; phone: 615-789-5414; fax: 615-789-3456; hours 8AM-4PM (CST). *Civil Actions Under $15,000, Eviction, Small Claims.*

Civil Records: Access: Phone, mail, in person. Both court and visitors may perform in person searches. Search fee: $6.00. Court makes copy: $.50 per page. Required to search: name, years to search. Civil cases indexed by defendant. Civil records archived since court began, on computer from 8/1991. Mail turnaround time 2-3 days.

General Information: Public terminal has only civil records back to 1991. (Includes DUIs.) No sealed or expunged records released. Certification fee: $3.00. Payee: General Sessions. Personal checks accepted. Prepayment and SASE required.

County Court Court Square, 4000 Hwy 48 N, #1, Charlotte, TN 37036; phone: 615-789-0250; fax: 615-789-0295; hours 8AM-4PM (CST). *Probate.*

Dyer County

29th District Circuit & General Sessions Court PO Box 1360, Dyersburg, TN 38025; phone: 731-286-7809; fax: 731-288-7728; hours 8:30AM-4:30PM (CST). *Felony, Misdemeanor, Civil, Eviction, Small Claims.*

Note: Public may search books.

Civil Records: Access: Mail, in person. Both court and visitors may perform in person searches. Search fee: $25.00 per name. Court makes copy: $.50 per page. Required to search: name, years to search. Civil cases indexed by defendant, plaintiff. Civil records archived since 1992. Mail turnaround time 2 weeks.

Criminal Records: Access: Mail, in person. Both court and visitors may perform in person searches. Search fee: $25.00 per name. Court makes copy: $.50 per page; same fee for self serve. Required to search: name, years to search, DOB, SSN. Criminal records archived since 1992. Mail turnaround time 2 weeks.

General Information: Public terminal goes back to 1992. No juvenile records released. No certification fee. Payee: Circuit Court, or General Sessions Clerk. Personal checks not accepted. Prepayment and SASE required.

Chancery Court PO Box 1360, Dyersburg, TN 38024; phone: 731-286-7818; fax: 731-288-7706; hours 8:30AM-4:30PM (CST). *Civil, Probate.*

Civil Records: Access: Mail, in person. Both court and visitors may perform in person searches. No search fee. Court makes copy: $.50 per page. Required to search: name, years to search. Civil cases indexed by defendant, plaintiff; on books. Mail turnaround time 1 week.

General Information: No adoption, juvenile records released. Certification fee: $1.00. Payee: Chancery Court Clerk. Personal checks accepted. Prepayment required. SASE requested.

Fayette County

25th District Circuit & General Sessions Court PO Box 670, Somerville, TN 38068; phone: 901-465-5205; fax: 901-465-5215; hours 9AM-5PM (CST). *Felony, Misdemeanor, Civil, Eviction, Small Claims.*

Civil Records: Access: In person only. Visitors must perform in person searches themselves. Court makes copy: $.50 per page. Required to search: name, years to search. Civil cases indexed by defendant, plaintiff; on computer since 1991, prior records archived since court began, some older records destroyed by fire.

Criminal Records: Access: In person only. Visitors must perform in person searches themselves. Court makes copy: $.50 per page. Required to search: name, years to search, DOB, SSN. Criminal records on computer since 1991, prior records archived since court began, some older records destroyed by fire.

General Information: Public terminal goes back to 1990. No adoption or sealed records released. Certification fee: $6.00 per doc. Payee: Circuit Court,

or General Sessions Clerk. Personal checks accepted. Prepayment required.

Chancery Court PO Drawer 220, Somerville, TN 38068; phone: 901-465-5220; fax: 901-465-5217; hours 9AM-5PM (CST). *Civil, Probate.*

Civil Records: Access: In person only. Visitors must perform in person searches themselves. Court makes copy: $1.00 per page. Required to search: name, years to search. Civil cases indexed by defendant, plaintiff; on computer since 10/92; on books.

General Information: Public terminal has only civil records back to 1992. No adoption records released. Will fax specific case file copies. Certification fee: $4.00 for 1st page, $2.00 each add'l. Payee: Clerk and Master. Personal checks accepted. Prepayment required.

Fentress County

8th District Circuit & General Sessions Court PO Box 699, Jamestown, TN 38556; phone: 931-879-7919; fax: 931-879-3014; hours 8AM-4PM M-F; 8AM-N Sat (CST). *Felony, Misdemeanor, Civil, Eviction, Small Claims.*

Civil Records: Access: Mail, in person. Both court and visitors may perform in person searches. Search fee: $25.00 per name. Court makes copy: $.10 per page. Required to search: name, years to search. Civil cases indexed by defendant, plaintiff. Civil records archived from 1800s, readily available for 20 years. Mail turnaround time 5 days.

Criminal Records: Access: Mail, in person, fax. Both court and visitors may perform in person searches. Search fee: $25.00 per name. Court makes copy: $.10 per page. Required to search: name, years to search, DOB, SSN. Criminal records archived from 1800s, readily available for 20 years. Mail turnaround time 5 days.

General Information: No juvenile records released. Certification fee: none reported. Payee: Circuit Court Clerk or General Session. Personal checks accepted. Prepayment and SASE required.

Chancery Court PO Box 66, Jamestown, TN 38556; phone: 931-879-8615; fax: 931-879-4236; hours 9AM-5PM M,T,Th,F; 9AM-N Wed (CST). *Civil, Probate.*

Civil Records: Access: Mail, in person. Both court and visitors may perform in person searches. No search fee. Court makes copy: $.50 per page; same fee for self serve. Required to search: name, years to search. Civil cases indexed by defendant, plaintiff; in books. Mail turnaround time 1-5 days.

General Information: No sealed or adoption records released. Certification fee: $4.00. Payee: Clerk and Master. Personal checks accepted. Prepayment required.

Franklin County

12th District Circuit Court & General Sessions 1 S Jefferson St, Winchester, TN 37398; phone: 931-967-2923; fax: 931-962-1479; hours 8AM-4:30PM (CST). *Felony, Misdemeanor, Civil, Eviction, Small Claims.*

Civil Records: Access: Mail, in person. Both court and visitors may perform in person searches. Search fee: $10.00 per name. Court makes copy: $.25 per page. Required to search: name, years to search. Civil cases indexed by defendant, plaintiff. Civil records archived on docket books from 1940s, on computer since mid 1991. Mail turnaround time 1 week.

Criminal Records: Access: Mail, in person. Both court and visitors may perform in person searches. Search fee: $10.00 per name. Court makes copy: $.25 per page. Required to search: name, years to search, DOB; also helpful: SSN. Criminal records archived on docket books from 1940s, on computer since mid 1991. Mail turnaround time 1 week.

General Information: Public terminal goes back to mid-1991. No juvenile records released. Will fax documents. Certification fee: $4.00 per cert includes

copy fee. Payee: Circuit Court Clerk or General Session. Business checks accepted. Prepayment required.

County Court 1 S Jefferson St, Winchester, TN 37398; phone: 931-962-1485; fax: 931-962-3394; hours 8AM-4:30PM (CST). *Probate.*

Gibson County

28th District Circuit & General Sessions Court 295 N College, PO Box 147, Trenton, TN 38382; phone: 731-855-7615; fax: 731-855-7676; hours 8AM-4:30PM (CST). *Felony, Misdemeanor, Civil, Eviction, Small Claims.*

Civil Records: Access: Fax, mail, in person. Both court and visitors may perform in person searches. Search fee: $5.00 per name. Court makes copy: $.25 per page; same fee for self serve. Required to search: name, years to search; also helpful: address. Civil cases indexed by defendant, plaintiff. Civil records archived in vault mid 1800s, in office since 1982. On computer since 1990. Mail turnaround time 1-3 days.

Criminal Records: Access: Fax, mail, in person. Both court and visitors may perform in person searches. Search fee: $5.00 per name. Court makes copy: $.25 per page; same fee for self serve. Required to search: name, years to search; also helpful: address, DOB, SSN. Criminal records archived in vault mid 1800s, in office since 1982. On computer since 1990. Mail turnaround time 1-3 days.

General Information: Public terminal goes back to 1992. No adoption or expunged records released. $5.00 fee to fax documents. Certification fee: $5.00. Payee: Circuit Court Clerk. Business checks accepted. In-state checks accepted. Prepayment required. SASE requested.

Chancery Court Clerk & Master, PO Box 290, Trenton, TN 38382; phone: 731-855-7639; fax: 731-855-7655; hours 8AM-4:30PM (CST). *Civil, Probate.*

Civil Records: Access: In person only. Visitors must perform in person searches themselves. Court makes copy: $1.00 per page. Required to search: name, years to search. Civil cases indexed by defendant, plaintiff. Probate records in this office since 9/82, prior records filed in County Clerk's office, computerized records go back to 1967.

General Information: Public terminal has only civil records back to 1958. No adoption, commitment records released. Will fax documents $10.00 per doc. Certification fee: $6.00 per document. Payee: Clerk & Master. No personal checks accepted. Prepayment required.

Giles County

22nd District Circuit & General Sessions Court PO Box 678, Pulaski, TN 38478; phone: 931-363-5311; fax: 931-424-4790; hours 8AM-4PM (CST). *Felony, Misdemeanor, Civil, Eviction, Small Claims.*

Civil Records: Access: mail, fax, in-person. Both court and visitors may perform in person searches. Search fee: $20.00 per name. Court makes copy: $1.00 per page. Self serve copy fee: $1.00 per page. Required to search: name, years to search. Civil cases indexed by defendant, plaintiff; on computer from 1/90, remaining records filed in docket books. Mail turnaround time 1 week.

Criminal Records: Access: Phone, mail, fax, in person. Both court and visitors may perform in person searches. Search fee: $20.00 per name. Court makes copy: $1.00 per page. Self serve copy fee: $1.00 per page. Required to search: name, years to search, DOB; also helpful: SSN. Criminal records on computer from 1/90, remaining records filed in docket books. Mail turnaround time 1 week.

General Information: Public terminal goes back to 1/1990. No juvenile records released without signed release. Certification fee: $6.00. Payee: Circuit Court Clerk. Prepayment and SASE required.

Chancery Court PO Box 678, Pulaski, TN 38478-0678; phone: 931-363-2620; fax: 931-363-2106; hours 8AM-4PM M-F (CST). *Probate.*

Grainger County

4th District Circuit & General Sessions
Court PO Box 157, Rutledge, TN 37861; phone: 865-828-3605; fax: 865-828-3339; hours 8:30AM-4:30PM M,T,TH,F (Wed and Sat 8:30AM-12) (EST). *Felony, Misdemeanor, Civil, Eviction, Small Claims.*
Civil Records: Access: In person only. Visitors must perform in person searches themselves. Court makes copy: $.50 per page. Self serve copy fee: $.50 per page. Required to search: name, years to search. Civil cases indexed by defendant, plaintiff. Civil records archived from 1977 in office.
Criminal Records: Access: In person only. Visitors must perform in person searches themselves. Court makes copy: $.50 per page. Self serve copy fee: $.50 per page. Required to search: name, years to search, DOB, SSN. Records archived from 1977 in office.
General Information: Public terminal goes back to 11/2001. No sealed records released. Certification fee: $4.00. Payee: Circuit Court Clerk. Business checks accepted. Prepayment required.

Chancery Court Clerk & Master, PO Box 160, Rutledge, TN 37861; phone: 865-828-4436; fax: 865-828-8714; hours 8:30AM-4:30PM M,T,Th,F, 8:30AM-N Wed (EST). *Civil, Probate.*
Civil Records: Access: Phone, fax, mail, in person. Both court and visitors may perform in person searches. No search fee. Court makes copy: $1.00 per page; same fee for self serve. Required to search: name, years. Civil cases indexed by defendant, plaintiff; on books. Mail turnaround varies.
General Information: No adoption records released. Will fax documents to local or toll free line. Certification fee: $4.00. Payee: Clerk & Master. Personal checks accepted. Prepayment required. SASE requested.

Greene County

3rd District Circuit & General Sessions
Court 101 S Main, Geene County Courthouse, Greeneville, TN 37743; phone: 423-798-1760; hours 8AM-4:30PM (EST). *Felony, Misdemeanor, Civil, Eviction, Small Claims.*
Civil Records: Access: In person only. Visitors must perform in person searches themselves. Court makes copy: $1.00 per page. Required to search: name, years to search. Civil cases indexed by defendant, plaintiff. Civil records archived since court started, on computer from end of 1990.
Criminal Records: Access: In person only. Visitors must perform in person searches themselves. Court makes copy: $1.00 per page. Required to search: name, years to search. Criminal records archived since court started, on computer from end of 1990.
General Information: Public use terminal available. No adoption records released. Certification fee: $3.00. Payee: Circuit Court Clerk. Personal checks accepted. Prepayment required.

County Court 204 N Cutler St, #200, County Courthouse Annex, Greeneville, TN 37745; phone: 423-798-1708, 798-1709; fax: 423-798-1822; hours 8AM-4:30PM (EST). *Probate.*

Grundy County

12th District Circuit & General Sessions
Court PO Box 161, Altamont, TN 37301; phone: 931-692-3368; fax: 931-692-2414; hours 8AM-4PM M-Th; 8AM-5PM F (CST). *Felony, Misdemeanor, Civil, Eviction, Small Claims.*
Civil Records: Access: Mail, fax, in person. Both court and visitors may perform in person searches. Search fee: $10.00 per name. Fee is per court. Court makes copy: $1.00 per page. Required to search: name, years to search. Civil cases indexed by defendant, plaintiff; on computer since 1993, prior records in books to 1990. Before 1990 on microfiche since 1868. Mail turnaround time 5 days.

Criminal Records: Access: Mail, fax, in person. Both court and visitors may perform in person searches. Search fee: $10.00 per name. Fee is per court. Court makes copy: $1.00 per page. Required to search: name, years to search, DOB; also helpful: SSN. Criminal records on computer since 1993, prior records in books to 1990. Before 1990 on microfiche since 1868. Mail turnaround time 5 days.
General Information: No juvenile records released. Fee to fax documents is $4.00 per document. Certification fee: $5.00. Payee: Circuit Court Clerk. Prepayment required.

Chancery Court PO Box 174, Altamont, TN 37301; phone: 931-692-3455; fax: 931-692-4125; hours 8AM-4PM M-Th; 8AM-5PM F (CST). *Civil, Probate.*
Civil Records: Access: Phone, mail, in person. Both court and visitors may perform in person searches. Search fee: $5.00 per name. Court makes copy: $.25 per page. Required to search: name, years to search. Civil cases indexed by defendant, plaintiff; on computer since 1993, on books back to 1990. Mail turnaround time 5 days.
General Information: No adoption records released. Will fax documents to local or toll free line. Certification fee: $2.00. Payee: Clerk & Master. Personal checks accepted. Prepayment required. SASE requested.

Hamblen County

3rd District Circuit & General Sessions
Court 510 Allison St, Morristown, TN 37814; phone: 423-586-5640; fax: 423-585-2764; hours 8AM-4PM (CST). *Felony, Misdemeanor, Civil, Eviction, Small Claims.*
Civil Records: Access: Mail, in person. Both court and visitors may perform in person searches. Search fee: $5.00 per name. Court makes copy: $.50 per page; same fee for self serve. Required to search: name, years to search. Civil cases indexed by defendant, plaintiff. Civil records archived from early 1900s, on computer from 1989. Mail turnaround time 1 day.
Criminal Records: Access: Mail, in person. Both court and visitors may perform in person searches. Search fee: $5.00 per name. Court makes copy: $.50 per page; same fee for self serve. Required to search: name, years to search, DOB; also helpful: SSN. Criminal records archived from early 1900s, on computer from 1989. Mail turnaround time 1 day.
General Information: Public terminal goes back to 1989. No adoption records released. Certification fee: $4.00. Payee: Circuit Court Clerk or General Sessions. No personal checks accepted. Prepayment and SASE required.

Chancery Court 511 W 2nd North St, Morristown, TN 37814; phone: 423-586-9112; fax: 423-318-2510; hours 8AM-4PM M-Th; 8AM-4:30PM F (EST). *Civil.*
Civil Records: Access: Phone, fax, mail, in person. Both court and visitors may perform in person searches. No search fee. Court makes copy: $.50 per page; same fee for self serve. Required to search: name, years to search. Civil cases indexed by defendant, plaintiff; on computer from 1979; prior on books back to 1870's. Mail turnaround time 3-5 days.
General Information: Public terminal has only civil records back to 1979. No adoption records released. Will fax documents $1.00 per page. Certification fee: $2.00 plus $1.00 per page. Payee: Clerk & Master. Personal checks accepted. Prepayment required.

Hamilton County

11th District Civil Court
Rm 500, Courthouse, 625 Georgia Ave, Chattanooga, TN 37402; phone: 423-209-6700; fax: 423-209-6701; hours 8AM-4PM (EST). *Civil Actions Over $15,000.*
www.hamiltontn.gov/courts/

Civil Records: Access: Phone, fax, mail, in person, online. Both court and visitors may perform in person searches. No search fee. Court makes copy: first 1-5 pages $1.00, 6-10 $2.00, then $.25 ea add'l. Required to search: name, years to search. Civil cases indexed by defendant, plaintiff. Civil records archived from 1921, on computer back to 7/89. Court minutes are on microfiche thru 1997, from 1997 forward on digital images. Online access to current court dockets are free at www.hamiltontn.gov/courts/CircuitClerk/dockets/default.htm. Mail turnaround time 1 week.
General Information: Public terminal has only civil records back to 1989. No adoptions or judicial hospitalization records released. Will fax documents to local numbers only. Certification fee: $4.00. Payee: Circuit Court Clerk. Personal checks accepted. Prepayment required.

11th District General Sessions Court
Civil Division, 600 Market St, Rm 111, Chattanooga, TN 37402; phone: 423-209-7630; fax: 423-209-7631; hours 8AM-4PM (EST). *Civil Actions Under $15,000, Eviction, Small Claims.*
www.hamiltontn.gov/courts/sessions/default.htm
Civil Records: Access: Phone, mail, in person, online. Both court and visitors may perform in person searches. No search fee. Court makes copy: $1.00 per page. Self serve copy fee: $1.00 per page. Required to search: name, years to search. Civil cases indexed by defendant, plaintiff. Civil records archived on docket books, on computer from 6/1985. Online access to current court dockets is free at www.hamiltontn.gov/Courts/Sessions/dockets/default.htm Mail turnaround time 3-4 days.
General Information: Public terminal has only civil records back to 1985. No mental health records released. Certification fee: $4.00. Payee: Sessions Court Clerk. Personal checks accepted. Prepayment required.

11th District Criminal Court
600 Market St, Rm 102, Chattanooga, TN 37402; phone: 423-209-7500; fax: 423-209-7501; hours 8AM-4PM (EST). *Felony, Misdemeanor.*
www.hamiltontn.gov/courts/
Criminal Records: Access: Mail, in person, online. Both court and visitors may perform in person searches. Search fee: $10.00 per name. Court makes copy: $1.00 per page. Required to search: name, years to search, DOB, signed release; also helpful: SSN. Criminal records on computer since 1990, prior records in books. Online access to current court dockets is free at www.hamiltontn.gov/Courts/CriminalClerk/dockets/default.htm. Mail turnaround time 1 week.
General Information: Public terminal has only criminal records back to 1990. No juvenile records released. No certification fee. Payee: Criminal Court Clerk. Only cashiers checks and money orders accepted. Prepayment required. SASE helpful.

Chancery Court Chancery Court, Clerk & Master, 201 E 7th St, Rm 300, Chattanooga, TN 37402; phone: 423-209-6600; fax: 423-209-6601; hours 8AM-4PM (EST). *Civil, Probate.*
www.hamiltontn.gov/Courts/ClerkMaster/default.htm
Civil Records: Access: Phone, mail, in person, online. Both court and visitors may perform in person searches. No search fee. Court makes copy: $1.00 per page 1-5 pages; $2.00 each 5-10 pages; $.25 over 10. Required to search: name, years to search. Civil cases indexed by defendant, plaintiff; on index cards from 1919, on dockets from 6/56, microfilm: wills since 1862, inventories since 1911, settlements since 1869, bonds and letters since 1878. Chancery motions/dockets are online at www.hamiltontn.gov/Courts/Chancery/dockets/default.htm. Mail turnaround time 2-3 days.
General Information: Public terminal has only civil records. No mental health, adoption records released. $1.00 fax fee to fax documents (1-5 pages). Certification fee: $4.00 ($10 if Act of Congress) plus $2.00 per page. Payee: Hamilton County Clerk and

Master. Personal checks accepted. Prepayment and SASE required.

Hancock County

3rd District Circuit & General Sessions
Court PO Box 347, Sneedville, TN 37869; phone: 423-733-2954; fax: 423-733-2119; hours 8AM-4PM, W Sat 8-12:00 (EST). *Felony, Misdemeanor, Civil, Eviction, Small Claims.*
Note: Note that some records were destroyed by fire and are not available.
Civil Records: Access: Mail, in person. Both court and visitors may perform in person searches. Search fee: $4.00 per name. Court makes copy: $.50 per page; same fee for self serve. Required to search: name, years to search. Civil cases indexed by plaintiff. Civil records archived on books from 1934. Mail turnaround time 3-4 days.
Criminal Records: Access: Mail, in person. Both court and visitors may perform in person searches. Search fee: $4.00 per name. Court makes copy: $.50 per page; same fee for self serve. Required to search: name, years to search, DOB; also helpful: SSN. Criminal records archived on books from 1934. Mail turnaround time 3-4 days.
General Information: Public terminal has criminal back to 20 years and civil back to 7 years. No juvenile records released. Will fax documents. No certification fee. Payee: Circuit Court Clerk. Personal checks accepted. Prepayment required.

Chancery Court PO Box 277, Sneedville, TN 37869; phone: 423-733-4524; fax: 423-733-2762; hours 8AM-4PM (EST). *Civil, Probate.*
Civil Records: Access: Mail, in person. Both court and visitors may perform in person searches. No search fee. Court makes copy: $1.00 per page; same fee for self serve. Required to search: name, years to search. Civil cases indexed by defendant, plaintiff; on books. Mail turnaround time 2 days.
General Information: Public terminal has only civil records. No adoption records released. Certification fee: $1.00. Payee: Clerk & Master. Personal checks accepted. Prepayment required. SASE requested.

Hardeman County

25th District Circuit & General Sessions
Court Courthouse, 100 N Main, Bolivar, TN 38008; phone: 731-658-6524; criminal fax: 731-658-4584; same fax for civil/probate; hours 8:30AM-4:30PM M-Th, 8AM-5PM Fri (CST). *Felony, Misdemeanor, Civil, Eviction, Small Claims.*
Civil Records: Access: In person only. Visitors must perform in person searches themselves. Court makes copy: $1.00 per page. Required to search: name, years to search. Civil cases indexed by defendant, plaintiff; on computer since 12/92, archived General Sessions from 1960 and Circuit from 1800s.
Criminal Records: Access: In person only. Visitors must perform in person searches themselves. Court makes copy: $1.00 per page. Required to search: name, years to search, DOB, SSN, signed release. Criminal records on computer since 12/92, archived General Sessions from 1960 and Circuit from 1800s.
General Information: Public use terminal available. No juvenile records released. Will not fax specific case file. Certification fee: $4.00 per document includes copies. Payee: Circuit Court Clerk. Only cashiers checks and money orders accepted. Hardeman county personal checks accepted. Prepayment required.

Chancery Court PO Box 45, Bolivar, TN 38008; phone: 731-658-3142; fax: 731-658-4580; hours 8:30AM-4:30PM M-Th, 8:30AM-5PM F (CST). *Civil, Probate.*
Civil Records: Access: Phone, mail, fax, in person. Both court and visitors may perform in person searches. No search fee. Court makes copy: $.50 per page. Add'l fee for postage. Required to search: name, years to search. Civil cases indexed by defendant,

plaintiff; on books back to 1825; computerized back to 1975. Mail turnaround time 1 day.
General Information: Public terminal has only civil records back to 1975. No mental health, adoption records released. Fee to fax documents is $1.00 per page. Certification fee: $2.00 per page. Payee: Chancery Court Clerk. Business checks accepted. Prepayment required. SASE requested.

Hardin County

24th District Circuit & General Sessions
Court 601 Main St, Savannah, TN 38372; phone: 731-925-3583; hours 8AM-4:30PM M,T,Th,F; 8AM-N W (CST). *Felony, Misdemeanor, Civil, Eviction, Small Claims.*
Civil Records: Access: In person only. Visitors must perform in person searches themselves. Court makes copy: $.50 per page. Required to search: name, years to search. Civil cases indexed by defendant, plaintiff. Civil records archived on books and on microfiche from 1800s, on computer from 1996.
Criminal Records: Access: In person only. Visitors must perform in person searches themselves. Court makes copy: $.50 per page. Required to search: name, years to search. Criminal records archived on books and on microfiche from 1800s, on computer from 1996.
General Information: Public terminal goes back to 1996. No juvenile records released. Certification fee: $5.00. Payee: Circuit Court Clerk. Hardin county personal checks accepted. Prepayment required.

Clerk and Master Office 465 Main St, Savannah, TN 38372; phone: 731-925-8166; fax: 731-925-0255; hours 8AM-4:30PM M,T,Th,F; 8AM-N Wed (CST). *Probate.*
Note: Clerk and Master became managers of probate records in 2004; formerly, records were with County Court clerk.

Hawkins County

3rd District Circuit & General Sessions
Court 100 E Main St, Rogersville, TN 37857; phone: 423-272-3397; fax: 423-272-9646; hours 8AM-4PM (EST). *Felony, Misdemeanor, Civil, Eviction, Small Claims.*
Note: Records prior to 1950 are kept off-site and are monitored by a genealogical group.
Civil Records: Access: In person only. Visitors must perform in person searches themselves. Court makes copy: $1.00 per page. Required to search: name, years to search. Civil cases indexed by defendant, plaintiff. Civil records archived on books from 1800s.
Criminal Records: Access: In person only. Visitors must perform in person searches themselves. Court makes copy: $1.00 per page. Required to search: name, years to search. Criminal records archived on books from 1800s.
General Information: Public terminal goes back to 1995. No juvenile records released. Certification fee: $4.00 ($6 if Acts of Congress) plus $2.00 per page. Payee: Circuit Court Clerk. No personal checks accepted.

Chancery Court PO Box 908, Rogersville, TN 37857; phone: 423-272-8150; fax: 423-272-7347; hours 8AM-4PM (EST). *Civil, Probate.*
Civil Records: Access: In person, mail. Visitors must perform in person searches themselves. Search fee: No fee, except for genealogy. Court makes copy: $1.00 per page. Required to search: name, years to search. Civil cases indexed by defendant, plaintiff; on index books from 1927 to present.
General Information: No adoption records released. Certification fee: $2.00 per page. Payee: Hawkins County Clerk and Master. Personal checks accepted. Prepayment required.

Haywood County

28th District Circuit & General Sessions
Court 1 N Washington Ave, Brownsville, TN 38012; phone: 731-772-1112; fax: 731-772-8139; hours 8:30AM-5PM (CST). *Felony, Misdemeanor, Civil, Eviction, Small Claims.*
Civil Records: Access: Phone, mail, in person. Both court and visitors may perform in person searches. No search fee. Court makes copy: $1.00 per page; same fee for self serve. Required to search: name, years to search. Civil cases indexed by defendant, plaintiff; on computer since 8/1991. General Sessions archived since 1960's; Circuit Court archived since 1800s. Mail turnaround time dependent upon search.
Criminal Records: Access: Phone, mail, in person. Both court and visitors may perform in person searches. No search fee. Court makes copy: $1.00 per page; same fee for self serve. Required to search: name, years to search, DOB; also helpful: SSN. Criminal records on computer since 8/1991. General Sessions archived since 1960's; Circuit Court archived since 1800s. Mail turnaround time dependent upon search.
General Information: Public terminal goes back to 8/1991. No juvenile records released. Certification fee: $3.50. Payee: Circuit Court Clerk. No personal checks accepted. Prepayment required.

Chancery Court 1 N Washington, PO Box 356, Brownsville, TN 38012; phone: 731-772-0122; fax: 731-772-3197; hours 8:30AM-5PM (CST). *Civil, Probate.*
Civil Records: Access: In person only. Visitors must perform in person searches themselves. Court makes copy: $1.00 per page; same fee for self serve. Required to search: name, years to search. Civil cases indexed by defendant, plaintiff. Probate records on books since 9/82; other records go back to 1800s.
General Information: No adoption or sealed records released. Certification fee: $5.00. Payee: Chancery Court. Personal checks accepted. Prepayment required.

Henderson County

26th District Circuit & General Sessions
Court 17 Monroe Ave #9, Henderson County Courthouse, Lexington, TN 38351; phone: 731-968-2031; fax: 731-967-9441; hours 8AM-4:30PM; closed Wed (CST). *Felony, Misdemeanor, Civil, Eviction, Small Claims.*
Civil Records: Access: Mail, in person. Both court and visitors may perform in person searches. Search fee: $6.00 per name. Court makes copy: $1.00 per page; same fee for self serve. Required to search: name, years to search. Civil cases indexed by defendant, plaintiff; on cards or books, archived from 1800s; on computer back 5 years. Mail turnaround time 1-2 weeks.
Criminal Records: Access: Mail, in person. Both court and visitors may perform in person searches. Search fee: $6.00 per name. Court makes copy: $1.00 per page; same fee for self serve. Required to search: name, years to search, DOB; also helpful- SSN. Criminal records on cards or books, archived from 1800s; on computer back 5 years. Mail turnaround time 1-2 weeks.
General Information: Public terminal goes back to 1994. No sealed indictment records released. Will fax documents for $10.00 per document. Certification fee: $4.00. Payee: General Sessions Court Clerk. No personal checks accepted. Prepayment and SASE required.

Chancery Court 17 Monroe, Rm 2, 2nd Fl, Lexington, TN 38351; phone: 731-968-2801; fax: 731-967-5380; hours 8AM-4:30PM (CST). *Civil, Probate.*
Civil Records: Access: Phone, mail, fax, in person. Both court and visitors may perform in person searches. No search fee. Court makes copy: $2.00 per page. Required to search: name, years to search. Civil cases indexed by defendant, plaintiff; on computer

back to 6/2000; prior in books to 1895. Mail turnaround time dependent on search length.

General Information: No confidential adoption records released. Fee to fax documents is $2.00 per page. Certification fee: $2.00. Payee: Chancery Court. Only cashiers checks and money orders accepted. Prepayment and SASE required.

Henry County

24th District Circuit & General Sessions Court
PO Box 429, Paris, TN 38242; phone: 731-642-0461; fax: 731-642-1244; hours 8AM-4:30PM (CST). *Felony, Misdemeanor, Civil, Eviction, Small Claims.*

Note: The General Sessions Court records date to 1962, when court was created.

Civil Records: Access: Fax, mail, in person. Both court and visitors may perform in person searches. Search fee: $5.00. Court makes copy: $.25 per page; same fee for self serve. Required to search: name, years to search. Civil cases indexed by defendant, plaintiff. Civil records archived from 1820s (you search) or 1900s (they search); General Sessions on computer from 1991. Mail turnaround time 1-2 weeks.

Criminal Records: Access: Fax, mail, in person. Both court and visitors may perform in person searches. Search fee: $5.00. Court makes copy: $.25 per page; same fee for self serve. Required to search: name, years to search; also helpful: SSN, DOB. Criminal records archived from 1820s to 1939, (you search) or 1940 present (they search); General Sessions on computer from 1991. Mail turnaround time 1-2 weeks.

General Information: Public terminal goes back to 1991 for General Sessions; 2002 for Circuit. No juvenile records released. Will fax documents only of account is set up before hand. Certification fee: $2.00 per cert. Payee: Circuit Court Clerk or General Sessions Court Clerk. Personal checks accepted. Prepayment required.

County Court PO Box 24, 101 W Washington St, Paris, TN 38242; phone: 731-642-2412; fax: 731-644-0947; hours 8AM-4:30PM (CST). *Probate.*

Hickman County

21st District Circuit & General Sessions Court
104 College Ave, #204, Centerville, TN 37033; phone: 931-729-2211; probate phone: 931-729-2522; fax: 931-729-6141; hours 8AM-4PM (CST). *Felony, Misdemeanor, Civil, Eviction, Small Claims.*

Civil Records: Access: Mail, fax, in person. Both court and visitors may perform in person searches. Search fee: $10.00 per name. Court makes copy: $1.00 per page. Required to search: name, years to search. Civil cases indexed by defendant, plaintiff; on computer since 1993, prior records on books to 1849.

Criminal Records: Access: Mail, fax, in person. Both court and visitors may perform in person searches. Search fee: $10.00 per name. Court makes copy: $1.00 per page. Required to search: name, years to search. Criminal records on computer since 1993, prior records on books to 1849.

General Information: No juvenile records released. Will fax documents if copy of check also faxed. Certification fee: $5.00. Payee: Circuit Court Clerk. No personal checks accepted. Prepayment required.

Chancery Court 104 College Ave, #202, Centerville, TN 37033; phone: 931-729-2522; fax: 931-729-3726; hours 8AM-4PM (CST). *Civil, Probate.*

Civil Records: Access: Mail, in person. Both court and visitors may perform in person searches. Court makes copy: $1.00 per page (will be $.50 after 01/06). Required to search: name, years to search. Civil cases indexed by defendant, plaintiff; on books since 1865; computerized records since 2001. Mail turnaround time 1 week.

General Information: No confidential or adoption records released. Will fax documents for $2.00 per

page. Certification fee: $3.00. Payee: Clerk & Master. Personal checks accepted. Prepayment required. SASE requested.

Houston County

23rd District Circuit & General Sessions Court
PO Box 414, Erin, TN 37061; phone: 931-289-4673; fax: 931-289-5182; hours 8AM-4:30PM (CST). *Felony, Misdemeanor, Civil, Eviction, Small Claims.*

Civil Records: Access: In person only. Visitors must perform in person searches themselves. Court makes copy: $.25 per page. Required to search: name, years to search. Civil cases indexed by defendant, plaintiff. Civil records archived from 1930s in books. This office does not do record searches anymore.

Criminal Records: Access: In person only. Visitors must perform in person searches themselves. Court makes copy: $.25 per page. Required to search: name, years to search, DOB; SSN helpful. Criminal records archived from 1930s in books. This office does not do record searches.

General Information: No juvenile records released. Certification fee: $3.50. Payee: Circuit Court Clerk. Personal checks accepted. Prepayment required.

Chancery Court PO Box 332, Erin, TN 37061; phone: 931-289-3870; fax: 931-289-5679; hours 8AM-4PM (CST). *Civil, Probate.*

Civil Records: Access: Mail, in person. Both court and visitors may perform in person searches. No search fee. Court makes copy: $.25 per page; same fee for self serve. Required to search: name, years to search. Civil cases indexed by defendant, plaintiff; on books. All requests must be in writing. Mail turnaround time 2 days.

General Information: No adoption records released. Certification fee: $3.50. Payee: Clerk & Master. Personal checks accepted. Prepayment required.

Humphreys County

23rd District Circuit & General Sessions Court
Courthouse, Rm 106, Waverly, TN 37185; phone: 931-296-2461; fax: 931-296-1651; hours 8AM-4:30PM (CST). *Felony, Misdemeanor, Civil, Eviction, Small Claims.*

Civil Records: Access: Fax, mail, in person. Only the court performs in person searches; visitors may not. Search fee: $1.00 per name per year minimum 7 years. If more than 15 years, the fee is a flat $25.00. Court makes copy: $1.00 per page. Required to search: name, years to search. Civil cases indexed by defendant, plaintiff; on computer back to 1989. Mail turnaround time 10 days.

Criminal Records: Access: Fax, mail, in person. Only the court performs in person searches; visitors may not. Search fee: $1.00 per name per year minimum 7 years. If more than 15 years, the fee is a flat $25.00. Court makes copy: $1.00 per page. Required to search: name, years to search, DOB, SSN, signed release. Criminal records on computer back to 1989. Mail turnaround time 10 days.

General Information: No expunged records released. Certification fee: $1.00 per page. Payee: Circuit Court Rm 106 Waverly TN. Business checks accepted. Prepayment and SASE required.

County Court Clerk, Rm 2 Courthouse Annex, Waverly, TN 37185; phone: 931-296-7671, 931-296-6503; fax: 931-296-0823; hours 8AM-4:30PM (CST). *Probate.*

Jackson County

15th District Circuit & General Sessions Court
PO Box 205, Gainesboro, TN 38562; phone: 931-268-9314; fax: 931-268-4555; hours 8AM-4PM M,T,Th,F; 8AM-3PM W; 8AM-N Sat (CST). *Felony, Misdemeanor, Civil, Eviction, Small Claims.*

Civil Records: Access: Fax, mail, in person. Both court and visitors may perform in person searches. Search fee: $5.00 per name. Court makes copy: $.50 per page; first 24 are free. Required to search: name, years to search. Civil cases indexed by defendant,

plaintiff. Civil records archived from 1900s in books, computerized since 2000. Mail turnaround time 1 week.

Criminal Records: Access: Fax, mail, in person. Both court and visitors may perform in person searches. Search fee: $5.00 per name. Court makes copy: $.50 per page; first 24 are free. Required to search: name, years to search, DOB; also helpful: SSN. Criminal records archived from 1900s in books, computerized since 2000. Mail turnaround time 1 week.

General Information: Public terminal goes back to 2000. No juvenile records released. Certification fee: $5.00 per doc. Payee: Circuit Court Clerk. Business checks accepted. Prepayment and SASE required.

Chancery Court PO Box 733, Gainesboro, TN 38562-0733; phone: 931-268-9516; fax: 931-268-9512; hours 8AM-4PM M,T,Th,F; 8AM-3PM Wed (CST). *Probate.*
www.jacksonco.com

Jefferson County

4th District Circuit & General Sessions Court
PO Box 671, Dandridge, TN 37725; phone: 865-397-2786; hours 8AM-4PM M-F (EST). *Felony, Misdemeanor, Civil, Eviction, Small Claims.*

Civil Records: Access: Mail, in person. Visitors must perform in person searches themselves. No search fee. Court makes copy: $.25 per page. Required to search: name, years to search. Civil cases indexed by defendant, plaintiff. Civil records archived from early 1900s on books. Mail turnaround time 1 week.

Criminal Records: Access: Mail, in person. Both court and visitors may perform in person searches. Search fee: none; 5-yr felony search. Court makes copy: $.25 per page. Required to search: name, years to search, DOB, SSN, signed release. Criminal records archived from early 1900s on books. Searches done by the court are for only 5 years of records. Mail turnaround time 1 week.

General Information: No adoption or juvenile records released. Certification fee: $3.00. Cert fee includes copies. Payee: Circuit Court Clerk. Only cashiers checks and money orders accepted. Prepayment and SASE required.

County Court PO Box 710, 214 W Main St, Dandridge, TN 37725; phone: 865-397-2935; fax: 865-397-3839; hours 8AM-4;30PM M-F, 8AM-11PM Sat (EST). *Probate.*

Johnson County

1st District Circuit & General Sessions Court
PO Box 73, 222 W Main St, Mountain City, TN 37683; phone: 423-727-9012; fax: 423-727-7047; hours 8:30AM-5PM (EST). *Felony, Misdemeanor, Civil, Eviction, Small Claims.*

Civil Records: Access: Phone, mail, in person. Both court and visitors may perform in person searches. Search fee: $5.00 per name. No copy fee. Required to search: name, years to search. Civil cases indexed by defendant, plaintiff; in docket books, sessions 1976, criminal & circuit 1800s. Mail turnaround time 2-3 days.

Criminal Records: Access: Phone, mail, in person. Both court and visitors may perform in person searches. Search fee: $5.00 per name. No copy fee. Required to search: name, years to search, DOB. Criminal records in docket books, sessions 1976, criminal & circuit 1800s. Mail turnaround time 2-3 days.

General Information: Public terminal goes back to 2000. No adoption, expunged or juvenile records released. Certification fee: None, but $2.00 if done by the Clerk and Master's Office. Payee: Circuit Court Clerk. Only cashiers checks and money orders accepted. Prepayment and SASE required.

Chancery Court PO Box 196, Mountain City, TN 37683; phone: 423-727-7853; fax: 423-727-7047; hours 8:30AM-Noon;1-5PM (EST). *Civil, Probate.*

Civil Records: Access: Mail, in person. Both court and visitors may perform in person searches. No search fee. Court makes copy: $1.00 per page. Required to search: name, years to search. Civil cases indexed by defendant, plaintiff; on books and files. Mail turnaround time same day.

General Information: No adoption records released. Certification fee: $2.00 plus $2.00 per page. Payee: Clerk & Master. Only cashiers checks and money orders accepted. Prepayment and SASE required.

Knox County

6th District Criminal Court 400 W Main St, Rm 149, Knoxville, TN 37902; phone: 865-215-2492; fax: 865-215-4291; hours 8AM-4:30PM (EST). *Felony, Misdemeanor.*

www.knoxcounty.org

Criminal Records: Access: Fax, mail, in person. Only the court performs in person searches; visitors may not. Search fee: $5.00 per name. Court makes copy: $2.00 per page. Required to search: name, years to search, DOB; also helpful: address, SSN, signed release. Criminal records on computer back to 1980; on books from 1962. Mail turnaround time 48 hours.

General Information: Public terminal has only criminal records back to 1980. No sealed records released. Certification fee: $2.00 per page. Payee: Criminal Court Clerk. Personal checks accepted. Prepayment required.

Circuit Court 400 Main Ave, Rm M-30, PO Box 379, Knoxville, TN 37901; phone: 865-215-2400; fax: 865-215-4251; hours 8AM-4:30 PM (EST). *Civil Actions Over $15,000.*

www.knoxcounty.org

Civil Records: Access: Phone, fax, mail, in person. Both court and visitors may perform in person searches. Search fee: $5.00. Court makes copy: $1.00 per page. Required to search: name, years to search. Civil cases indexed by defendant, plaintiff; on computer from 1986, prior records archived and on microfilm. Mail turnaround time 2-3 days.

General Information: Public terminal has only civil records. No adoption or sealed records released. Certification fee: $3.50. Payee: Circuit Court Clerk. Personal checks or Visa, MC accepted. Prepayment required.

General Sessions Court 300 Main Ave, Rm 318, PO Box 379, Knoxville, TN 37901; phone: 865-215-2518; fax: 865-215-4296; hours 8AM-4:30PM (EST). *Civil Actions Under $15,000, Eviction, Small Claims.*

www.knoxcounty.org

Civil Records: Access: Mail, in person. Both court and visitors may perform in person searches. Search fee: $5.00. Court makes copy: $1.50 per page. Required to search: name, years to search. Civil cases indexed by defendant, plaintiff; on books and computer. Mail turnaround time 1 week.

General Information: Public terminal has only civil records back to 2000. No juvenile or adoption records released. Certification fee: $3.50. Payee: General Sessions Court. Personal checks or Visa, MC accepted. Prepayment required.

Chancery Court 400 W Main St, Rm 125, Knoxville, TN 37902; phone: 865-215-2555 (Chancery); criminal phone: 865-215-2492; probate phone: 865-215-2389; fax: 865-215-2920; hours 8AM-4:30PM (EST). *Civil, Probate.*

www.knoxcounty.org

Civil Records: Access: Phone, fax, mail, in person. Visitors must perform in person searches themselves. Search fee: $5.00. Court makes copy: $2.00 per page. Required to search: name, years to search. Civil cases indexed by defendant, plaintiff; on computer since 1978, prior records on books. Mail turnaround time 1-2 days.

General Information: Public terminal has only civil records back to 1978. No commitment or adoption records released. Will fax documents $1.00 per page. Certification fee: $4.00. Payee: Chancery or

Probate Court. Personal checks accepted. Prepayment required. SASE requested.

Lake County

29th District Circuit & General Sessions Court 229 Church St, PO Box 11, Tiptonville, TN 38079; phone: 731-253-7137; fax: 731-253-8930; hours 8AM-4PM (CST). *Felony, Misdemeanor, Civil, Eviction, Small Claims.*

Civil Records: Access: In person only. Visitors must perform in person searches themselves. Court makes copy: $1.00 per page. Required to search: name, years to search. Civil cases indexed by defendant, plaintiff. Civil records archived on books in office up to 30 yrs, vault records before 1960; General Sessions computer records go back to 1997.

Criminal Records: Access: In person only. Visitors must perform in person searches themselves. Court makes copy: $1.00 per page. Required to search: name, years to search, DOB; SSN helpful. Criminal records archived on books in office up to 30 yrs, vault records before 1960.

General Information: No sealed records released. Certification fee: $3.00. Payee: Circuit Court Clerk. Personal checks accepted. Prepayment required.

Chancery Court 229 Church Lake County Courthouse, Box 12, Tiptonville, TN 38079; phone: 731-253-8926; fax: 731-253-9815; hours 9AM-4PM (CST). *Probate.*

Lauderdale County

25th District Circuit Court Lauderdale County Justice Ctr, 675 Hwy 51 S, PO Box 509, Ripley, TN 38063; phone: 731-635-0101; criminal phone: 731-635-2572; civil phone: 731-635-2572; fax: 731-221-8663; hours 8AM-4:30PM (CST). *Felony, Misdemeanor, Civil Actions Over $15,000.*

Civil Records: Access: Phone, mail, in person. Both court and visitors may perform in person searches. Search fee: $10.00 per name. Court makes copy: $1.00 per page; same fee for self serve. Required to search: name, years to search. Civil cases indexed by defendant, plaintiff. Civil records archived on books from 1800s; on computer back to 1992. Mail turnaround time 2-3 days.

Criminal Records: Access: Mail, in person. Both court and visitors may perform in person searches. Search fee: $10.00 per name. Court makes copy: $1.00 per page; same fee for self serve. Required to search: name, years to search; also helpful: DOB, SSN. Criminal records archived on books from 1800s; on computer back to 1992. Mail turnaround time 2-3 days.

General Information: Public terminal goes back to 12 years. No sealed or adoption records released. Will fax documents for $1.00 per page. Certification fee: $5.00 per page. Payee: Circuit Court Clerk. Personal checks accepted in county. Prepayment and SASE required.

General Sessions Court PO Box 509, Ripley, TN 38063; phone: 731-635-2572; fax: 731-221-8663; hours 8AM-4:30PM (till noon on Wed) (CST). *Civil Actions Under $15,000, Eviction, Small Claims.*

Civil Records: Access: Mail, in person. Both court and visitors may perform in person searches. Search fee: $10.00 per name. Court makes copy: $1.00 per page. Self serve copy fee: $.50 per page. Required to search: name, years to search. Civil cases indexed by defendant, plaintiff; on computer since 1992, records prior to 1984 on docket books. Mail turnaround time 2-3 days.

General Information: Public terminal has only civil records back to 1992. No confidential records released. Certification fee: $10.00. Payee: General Sessions. Business checks accepted. Prepayment and SASE required.

County Court Courthouse, 100 Court Sq, Ripley, TN 38063; phone: 731-635-2561; fax: 731-635-9682; hours 8AM-4:30PM M,T,Th,F; 8AM-N W (CST). *Probate.*

Lawrence County

22nd District Circuit & General Sessions Court NBU #12, 240 W Gaines, Lawrenceburg, TN 38464; phone: 931-762-4398; criminal phone: 931-762-4898; civil phone: 931-766-4152; fax: 931-766-4471; hours 8AM-4:30PM (CST). *Felony, Misdemeanor, Civil, Eviction, Small Claims, Probate.*

Civil Records: Access: In person only. Visitors must perform in person searches themselves. Court makes copy: $1.00 per page. Required to search: name, years to search. Civil cases indexed by defendant, plaintiff. Civil records archived on books since court started in 1940s.

Criminal Records: Access: In person only. Visitors must perform in person searches themselves. Court makes copy: $1.00 per page. Required to search: name, years to search, DOB, SSN. Criminal records archived on books since court started in 1940s.

General Information: Public terminal goes back to 1994. No expunged records released. Will fax specific case file for $1.00 per page. Certification fee: $5.00. Payee: Circuit Court Clerk. Only cashiers checks and money orders accepted. Prepayment required.

Lewis County

21st District Circuit & General Sessions Court Courthouse, 110 Park Ave N, Rm 201, Hohenwald, TN 38462; phone: 931-796-3724; fax: 931-796-6021; hours 8AM-4:30PM (CST). *Felony, Misdemeanor, Civil, Eviction, Small Claims.*

Civil Records: Access: In person only. Visitors must perform in person searches themselves. Court makes copy: $1.00 per page; same fee for self serve. Required to search: name, years to search. Civil cases indexed by defendant, plaintiff. Civil records archived 15 years in office, 1800s in vault.

Criminal Records: Access: In person only. Visitors must perform in person searches themselves. Court makes copy: $1.00 per page; same fee for self serve. Required to search: name, years to search; SSN helpful. Criminal records archived 15 years in office, 1800s in vault.

General Information: No juvenile, adoption records released. Will not fax specific case file. Certification fee: $4.00 per document. Payee: Circuit Court Clerk. Personal checks accepted. Prepayment required.

Chancery Court Lewis County Courthouse, 110 Park Ave N, Rm 208, Hohenwald, TN 38462; phone: 931-796-3734; fax: 931-796-6017; hours 8AM-4:30PM (CST). *Civil, Probate.*

Civil Records: Access: In person only. Visitors must perform in person searches themselves. Court makes copy: $1.00 per page. Required to search: name, years to search. Civil cases indexed by defendant, plaintiff; on computer since 10/94, prior records indexed on computer by name or case number.

General Information: No adoption records released. Certification fee: $2.00. Payee: Clerk & Master. Personal checks accepted. Prepayment required.

Lincoln County

17th District Circuit & General Sessions Court 112 Main Ave S, Rm 203, Fayetteville, TN 37334; phone: 931-433-2334; fax: 931-438-1577; hours 8AM-4PM (CST). *Felony, Misdemeanor, Civil, Eviction, Small Claims.*

Civil Records: Access: Phone, fax, mail, in person. Both court and visitors may perform in person searches. Search fee: $10.00 per name. Fee is for 5 years. Add $1.00 for each add'l year. Court makes copy: $1.00 per page. Required to search: name, years to search. Civil cases indexed by defendant, plaintiff. Civil records archived on books since court started; files go back 10 years; on computer back to 1995. Mail turnaround time 1-2 days.

Criminal Records: Access: Phone, fax, mail, in person. Both court and visitors may perform in person searches. Search fee: $10.00 per name. Fee is for 5 years. Add $1.00 for each add'l year. Court makes copy: $1.00 per page. Required to search: name, years to search, DOB, SSN, signed release. Criminal records archived on books since court started; files go back 10 years; on computer back to 1995. Mail turnaround time 1-2 days.

General Information: No probation records released. Will fax documents $2.00 per page. Certification fee: $4.00. Payee: Circuit Court Clerk. Business checks accepted. Prepayment and SASE required.

Chancery Court 112 Main Ave, Rm B109, Fayetteville, TN 37334; phone: 931-433-1482; fax: 931-433-9313; hours 8AM-4PM (CST). *Civil, Probate.*

Civil Records: Access: In person only. Visitors must perform in person searches themselves. Court makes copy: $1.00 per page. Required to search: name, years to search. Civil cases indexed by defendant, plaintiff. Civil records archived on books.

General Information: No adoption, divorce records released. Fee to fax documents is $1.00 per page. Certification fee: $4.00 plus $2.00 per page. Payee: Clerk & Master. Personal checks accepted. Prepayment required.

Loudon County

9th District Criminal & Circuit Court PO Box 280, Loudon, TN 37774; phone: 865-458-2042; fax: 865-458-2043; hours 8AM-4:30PM (EST). *Felony, Civil.*

www.loudoncounty.com/ccc.htm

Civil Records: Access: Phone, fax, mail, in person. Both court and visitors may perform in person searches. Search fee: $5.00 per name. Court makes copy: $1.00 per page. Required to search: name, years to search. Civil cases indexed by defendant, plaintiff. Civil records archived from 1870 on books, on computer from 8/1990. Mail turnaround time 2-4 days.

Criminal Records: Access: Phone, fax, mail, in person. Both court and visitors may perform in person searches. Search fee: $5.00 per name. Court makes copy: $1.00 per page. Required to search: name, years to search. Criminal records archived from 1800s on books, on computer from 8/1990. Mail turnaround time 2-4 days.

General Information: No juvenile, adoption records released. Will fax documents for no fee. Certification fee: $2.00 per document. Payee: Circuit Court. Personal checks accepted. Prepayment required. SASE requested.

General Sessions Court 12680 Hwy 11 W, #3, Lenoir City, TN 37771; phone: 865-986-3505; fax: 865-986-7355; hours 8AM-5PM (EST). *Misdemeanor, Eviction, Small Claims.*

www.loudoncounty.com/ccc.htm

Civil Records: Access: Phone, fax, mail, in person. Both court and visitors may perform in person searches. Search fee: $5.00 per name. Court makes copy: $1.00 per page. Required to search: name, years to search. Civil cases indexed by defendant, plaintiff. Civil records archived from 1960 on books, on computer from 1995. Mail turnaround time 2-4 days.

Criminal Records: Access: Phone, fax, mail, in person. Both court and visitors may perform in person searches. Search fee: $5.00 per name. Court makes copy: $1.00 per page. Required to search: name, years to search. Criminal records archived from 1960 on books, on computer from 1995. Mail turnaround time 2-4 days.

General Information: No juvenile, adoption records released. Certification fee: $2.00. Payee: General Sessions Court. Personal checks accepted. Prepayment required. SASE requested.

County Court 101 Mulberry St, #200, Loudon, TN 37774; phone: 865-458-2726; fax: 865-458-9891; hours 8AM-4:30PM (EST). *Probate.*

Macon County

15th District Circuit & General Sessions Court Court Clerk, 904 Hwy 52 Bypass, Lafayette, TN 37083; phone: 615-666-2354; probate phone: 615-666-2000; fax: 615-666-3001; probate fax: 615-666-8943; hours 8AM-4:30PM M-Th; 8AM-5PM F (CST). *Felony, Misdemeanor, Civil, Eviction, Small Claims, Probate.*

Note: Probate located at same address, separate office; hours are 8AM-4PM.

Civil Records: Access: In person only. Visitors must perform in person searches themselves. Court makes copy: $1.00 per page; same fee for self serve. Required to search: name, years to search. Civil cases indexed by defendant, plaintiff. Civil records archived in office from 1975, rest in records room from 1960; on computer since 1997.

Criminal Records: Access: In person only. Visitors must perform in person searches themselves. Court makes copy: $1.00 per page; same fee for self serve. Required to search: name, years to search, DOB; SSN helpful. Criminal records archived in office from 1975, rest in records room from 1960, on computer since 1997.

General Information: Public terminal goes back to 1997. No juvenile or adoption records released. Will not fax specific case file. Certification fee: $5.00 per certification. Payee: Circuit Court Clerk. Personal checks accepted only if from this county. Prepayment required.

Madison County

26th District Circuit Court 515 S Liberty St, Jackson, TN 38301; phone: 731-423-6035 x1049; fax: 731-988-3007; hours 8AM-4PM (CST). *Felony, Misdemeanor, Civil Actions Over $15,000.*

www.co.madison.tn.us

Note: Misdemeanor cases here are usually accompanied by felonies.

Civil Records: Access: In person only. Visitors must perform in person searches themselves. Court makes copy: $.25 per page. If searcher brings own paper $.10 charged per page. Required to search: name, years to search. Civil cases indexed by defendant, plaintiff. Civil records archived on books in office from 1963; on computer back to 1995.

Criminal Records: Access: In person only. Visitors must perform in person searches themselves. Court makes copy: $.25 per page. If searcher supplies paper $.10 each page. Required to search: name, years to search; also helpful: DOB, SSN. Criminal records computerized since 1995, on books from 1965.

General Information: Public terminal goes back to 1995. No sealed records released. Will not fax specific case file. Certification fee: $5.00 per document. Payee: Circuit Court Clerk. Cashiers checks and money orders accepted. Prepayment required.

General Sessions Court 515 S Liberty St, Jackson, TN 38301; criminal phone: 731-423-6128; civil phone: 731-423-6018; fax: 731-265-5398; hours 8AM-4PM (CST). *Misdemeanor, Civil Actions Under $15,000, Eviction, Small Claims.*

Civil Records: Access: Mail, in person. Visitors must perform in person searches themselves. No search fee. Court makes copy: $1.50 per page. Required to search: name, years to search. Civil cases indexed by defendant, plaintiff. Civil records computerized since 1/98, archived on books in office from 1982, rest stored elsewhere from 1950s.

Criminal Records: Access: In person only. Visitors must perform in person searches themselves. Court makes copy: $1.50 per page. Required to search: name. Records stored since 1950s, computerized since 1/98.

General Information: Public terminal goes back to 1994. Certification fee: $4.00 for civil, $5.00 for criminal. Payee: General Sessions Court. Only cashiers checks and money orders accepted. Prepayment required.

Probate Division - General Sessions Division II 110 Irby St, #102, Jackson, TN 38302; phone: 731-988-3025; fax: 731-988-3807; hours 8:30-12, 1-4:30PM (CST). *Probate.*

Marion County

12th District Circuit & General Sessions Court PO Box 789, Courthouse Sq, Jasper, TN 37347; phone: 423-942-2134; fax: 423-942-4160; hours 8AM-4PM (CST). *Felony, Misdemeanor, Civil, Eviction, Small Claims.*

Civil Records: Access: Phone, mail, in person. Both court and visitors may perform in person searches. Search fee: $3.00 per name. Court makes copy: $.50 per page. Self serve copy fee: $.50 per page. Required to search: name, years to search. Civil cases indexed by defendant, plaintiff; on computer from 1988, prior records archived on books and microfiche since 1922. Mail turnaround time 1 week.

Criminal Records: Access: Phone, mail, in person. Both court and visitors may perform in person searches. Search fee: $3.00 per name. Court makes copy: $.50 per page. Self serve copy fee: $.50 per page. Required to search: name, years to search, DOB; also helpful: SSN. Criminal records on computer from 1988, prior records archived on books and microfiche since 1922. Mail turnaround time 1 week.

General Information: No adoption records released. Will fax documents to local or toll free line. Certification fee: $3.00. Payee: Circuit Court Clerk. Personal checks accepted. Prepayment required.

Chancery Court PO Box 789, Jasper, TN 37347; phone: 423-942-2601; fax: 423-942-0291; hours 8AM-4PM (CST). *Civil, Probate.*

Civil Records: Access: Mail, in person. Both court and visitors may perform in person searches. No search fee. Court makes copy: $.50 per page. Required to search: name, years to search. Civil cases indexed by defendant, plaintiff; on computer since 3/94, prior records on books. Mail turnaround time 1 day.

General Information: Public terminal has only civil records. No adoption records released. Will not fax documents. Certification fee: $3.00. Payee: Clerk and Master. Personal checks accepted. Prepayment required. SASE requested.

Marshall County

17th District Circuit & General Sessions Court Courthouse, Lewisburg, TN 37091; phone: 931-359-0536; criminal fax: 931-359-0543; same fax for civil/probate; hours 8AM-4PM (CST). *Felony, Misdemeanor, Civil, Eviction, Small Claims.*

Civil Records: Access: In person only. Visitors must perform in person searches themselves. Court makes copy: $1.00 per page; same fee for self serve. Required to search: name, years to search. Civil cases indexed by plaintiff. Civil records archived on books; also on computer back to 2000.

Criminal Records: Access: In person only. Visitors must perform in person searches themselves. Court makes copy: $1.00 per page; same fee for self serve. Required to search: name, years to search; also helpful: DOB, SSN. Criminal records go back to 1987; on computer back to 2000.

General Information: Public terminal goes back to 2000. No adoption records released. Will fax specific document to local or toll-free number. Certification fee: $5.00 per document. Payee: Circuit Court Clerk. No personal checks accepted. Prepayment required.

Chancery Court 201 Marshall County Courthouse, Lewisburg, TN 37091; phone: 931-359-2181; fax: 931-359-0524; hours 8AM-4PM (CST). *Probate.*

Note: Probate is handled by the Clerk & Master.

Maury County

Circuit & General Sessions Court Maury County Courthouse, 41 Public Square, Columbia, TN 38401; phone: 931-375-1110; criminal phone: 931-375-1105/1108; civil phone: 931-375-1109/1110; fax: 931-375-1114; hours 8AM-4PM (CST). *Felony, Misdemeanor, Civil, Eviction, Small Claims.*

Civil Records: Access: Fax, mail, in person. Visitors must perform in person searches themselves. No search fee. Court makes copy: $1.00 per page; same fee for self serve. Required to search: name, years to search. Civil cases indexed by defendant, plaintiff; on books since 1984; on computer back to 1989.

Criminal Records: Access: In person only. Visitors must perform in person searches themselves. Court makes copy: $1.00 per page; same fee for self serve. Required to search: name, years to search; also helpful: DOB, SSN. Criminal records on computer back to 1989; others go back to early 1900s.

General Information: Public terminal goes back to 1989. No juvenile records released. Will fax documents for $1.00 per page. Certification fee: $6.00. Payee: Circuit Court Clerk. No personal checks accepted; use money order or cashiers check. Prepayment required.

Probate Court Maury County Courthouse, Clerk & Masters Office, 41 Public Square, Columbia, TN 38401; phone: 931-375-1306; fax: 931-375-1319; hours 8AM-4PM (CST). *Probate.*

Note: Records on computer go back to 1991.

McMinn County

10th District Circuit & General Sessions Court PO Box 506, Athens, TN 37303; phone: 423-745-1923; criminal phone: 423-745-1924; civil phone: 423-745-1924; probate phone: 423-745-1281; fax: 423-744-1642; hours 8:30AM-4PM (EST). *Felony, Misdemeanor, Civil, Eviction, Small Claims, Probate.*

Civil Records: Access: Phone, fax, mail, in person. Both court and visitors may perform in person searches. Search fee: $6.00 per name. Court makes copy: $1.00 per page; same fee for self serve. Required to search: name, years to search; also helpful: address. Civil cases indexed by defendant, plaintiff. Civil records archived approximately 20 years; computerized back to 1996. Phone access is limited to three names. Mail turnaround time 24-48 hours.

Criminal Records: Access: Phone, fax, mail, in person. Both court and visitors may perform in person searches. Search fee: $6.00. Court makes copy: $1.00 per page; same fee for self serve. Required to search: name, years to search, DOB, SSN; also helpful: address. Criminal records archived approximately 20 years; computerized back to 1996. Mail turnaround time 24-48 hours.

General Information: No juvenile, adoption records released. Fee to fax documents is $2.00 per page. Certification fee: $4.00 per cert plus $2.00 per page. Payee: Circuit Court Clerk. Business checks accepted. Prepayment required.

McNairy County

25th District Circuit & General Sessions Court 300 Industrial Dr, Selmer, TN 38375; phone: 731-645-1015; fax: 731-645-1003; hours 8AM-4:30PM M-F; 8AM-N Sat (CST). *Felony, Misdemeanor, Civil, Eviction, Small Claims.*

Civil Records: Access: Mail, in person. Both court and visitors may perform in person searches. Search fee: $20.00 per name. Court makes copy: $.25 per page; same fee for self serve. Required to search: name, years to search. Civil cases indexed by defendant, plaintiff. Civil records archived on docket books since 1966; computerized records since 2/95. Mail turnaround time 1-2 days.

Criminal Records: Access: Mail, in person. Both court and visitors may perform in person searches. Search fee: $20.00 per name. Court makes copy: $.25 per page; same fee for self serve. Required to search:

name, years to search, DOB, SSN. Criminal records archived on docket books since 1966; computerized records since 2/95. Mail turnaround time 1-2 days.

General Information: Public terminal goes back to 1995. No juvenile records released. Certification fee: $6.00 per cert. Payee: Circuit Court Clerk. Personal checks accepted. Prepayment required.

Chancery Court Chancery Court, Clerk & Master, Courthouse, Rm 205, Selmer, TN 38375; phone: 731-645-5446; fax: 731-646-1165; hours 8AM-4PM (Closed Wed) (CST). *Civil, Probate.*

Civil Records: Access: In person only. Visitors must perform in person searches themselves. Court makes copy: $.50. Required to search: name, years to search. Civil cases indexed by defendant, plaintiff; on books.

General Information: No adoption records released. Will not fax documents. Certification fee: $5.00. Payee: Clerk & Master. Personal checks accepted. Prepayment required.

Meigs County

9th District Circuit & General Sessions Court PO Box 205, Decatur, TN 37322; phone: 423-334-5821; fax: 423-334-4819; hours 8:30AM-4;30PM till noon on Wed (EST). *Felony, Misdemeanor, Civil, Eviction, Small Claims.*

Civil Records: Access: Mail, in person. Both court and visitors may perform in person searches. No search fee. Court makes copy: $.25 per page. Required to search: name, years to search. Civil cases indexed by defendant, plaintiff. Civil records archived in office from 1930s, records in storage go further. They refer all name searches to an outside agency.

Criminal Records: Access: In person only. Both court and visitors may perform in person searches. No search fee. Court makes copy: $.25 per page. Required to search: name, years to search. Criminal records archived in office from 1930s, records in storage go further. They refer all name searches to an outside agency.

General Information: No juvenile records released. Certification fee: $10.00. Payee: Circuit Court Clerk. Personal checks accepted. Prepayment required.

Chancery Court PO Box 5, Decatur, TN 37322; phone: 423-334-5243; hours 8AM-5PM M,T,Th,F; 8:30AM-N Wed (EST). *Civil, Probate.*

Civil Records: Access: In person only. Visitors must perform in person searches themselves. Court makes copy: $.25 per page. Required to search: name, years to search. Civil cases indexed by defendant, plaintiff; on dockets since 1940.

General Information: No adoption records released. Will fax documents for $.25 per page for 3 pages or less. Certification fee: $5.50. Cert fee includes copies. Payee: Meigs County Chancery Court. Personal checks accepted. Prepayment required.

Monroe County

10th District Circuit I Courts 105 College St, Madisonville, TN 37354; phone: 423-442-2396; fax: 423-442-9538; hours 8AM-4:30PM (EST). *Felony, Misdemeanor, Civil over $10,000.*

Note: This court does record searches for the General Sessions Court.

Civil Records: Access: Mail, in person. Both court and visitors may perform in person searches. Search fee: $10.00 per name. Court makes copy: $1.00 per page. Required to search: name, years to search. Civil cases indexed by defendant, plaintiff; on computer since 1991, records on books in office for 10 years, unspecified prior to then. Mail turnaround time 2 days.

Criminal Records: Access: Mail, in person. Both court and visitors may perform in person searches. Search fee: $10.00 per name. Court makes copy: $1.00 per page. Required to search: name, years to search. Criminal records on computer since 1991, records on books in office for 10 years, unspecified prior to then. Mail turnaround time 2 days.

General Information: Public terminal goes back to 1991. (Terminal also holds records for General Sessions Court.) No juvenile records released. Will fax documents for $2.00 per page. Certification fee: $4.00. Payee: Circuit Court Clerk. Personal checks accepted. Prepayment required.

General Sessions Court 300 Tellico St, Madisonville, TN 37354; phone: 423-442-9537; fax: 423-420-9091; hours 8AM-4:30PM (EST). *Civil under $15,000, Eviction, Small Claims.*

Civil Records: Access: Mail, in person. Both court and visitors may perform in person searches. Search fee: $10.00 per name. Court makes copy: $1.00 per page; same fee for self serve. Required to search: name, years to search. Civil cases indexed by defendant, plaintiff; on computer since 1991, records on books in this office for 3 years, otherwise in offsite storage. All name searches must be performed at the Circuit Clerk's office. They have a public access terminal there. All mail requests are also forwarded to the Circuit Clerks Office. Mail turnaround time 2 days.

General Information: Public terminal has only civil records back to 1991. (Terminal located at Circuit Clerk's office.) No juvenile records released. Will fax documents for $2.00 per page. Certification fee: $5.00. Payee: Circuit Court Clerk. No personal checks accepted. Prepayment required.

Chancery Court 105 College St, #2, Madisonville, TN 37354; phone: 423-442-2644; probate phone: 423-442-4573; fax: 423-420-0048; hours 8:30AM-4:30PM (4PM on W) (EST). *Civil, Probate.*

Civil Records: Access: Mail, in person. Both court and visitors may perform in person searches. No search fee. Court makes copy: $2.00 per page. Required to search: name, years to search. Civil cases indexed by plaintiff and defendant. Civil records on computer since 1993, prior records on books. Mail turnaround time 2-3 days.

General Information: No adoption, sealed records released. Will fax documents to local or toll free line. Certification fee: $4.00. Payee: Chancery Court. Personal checks accepted. Prepayment required. SASE requested.

Montgomery County

Montgomery County Circuit & General Sessions Court 2 Millennium Plaza, #115, Clarksville, TN 37040; phone: 931-648-5700; fax: 931-920-1820; hours 8AM-4:30PM (CST). *Felony, Misdemeanor, Civil, Evictions, Small Claims.*

Note: Call before faxing to confirm fax number.

Civil Records: Access: Mail, in person. Both court and visitors may perform in person searches. Search fee: $10.00 per name. Court makes copy: $.50 per page. Required to search: name, years to search. Civil cases indexed by defendant, plaintiff; on computer back to 11/1999, archived on books in office from 1970s, on microfiche from 1950s.

Criminal Records: Access: Mail, in person. Both court and visitors may perform in person searches. Search fee: $10.00 per name. Court makes copy: $.50 per page. Required to search: name, years to search, DOB; also helpful-signed release, SSN. Criminal records on computer back to 1985; prior records archived on books from 1970s, on microfiche from 1950s.

General Information: Public use terminal available. No juvenile records released. Will fax documents to local or toll free line. Certification fee: $6.00 per doc. Payee: Circuit Court (Criminal or General Sessions Court (civil). Business checks accepted. Prepayment and SASE required.

Chancery Court Chancery Court, Clerk & Master, County Court Center, 2 Millenium Plaza, #101, Clarksville, TN 37040; phone: 931-648-5703; fax: 931-648-5759; hours 8AM-4:15PM (CST). *Civil, Probate.*

Civil Records: Access: In person only. Visitors must perform in person searches themselves. Court

makes copy: $1.00 per page. Required to search: name, years to search. Civil cases indexed by defendant, plaintiff. Criminal records on books, microfilm, or computer.
General Information: Public terminal has only civil records back to 1999. No adoption or sealed records released. Certification fee: $2.00 per page. Payee: Clerk & Master. Business checks accepted. Prepayment required.

Moore County

17th District Circuit & General Sessions Court
Courthouse, PO Box 206, Lynchburg, TN 37352; phone: 931-759-7208; hours 8AM-4:30PM MTWF; 8AM-N Sat (CST). *Felony, Misdemeanor, Civil, Eviction, Small Claims.*
Civil Records: Access: Mail, in person. Both court and visitors may perform in person searches. Search fee: $5.00 per name. Court makes copy: $2.00 per page. Required to search: name, years to search. Civil cases indexed by defendant, plaintiff. Civil records archived to 1862, on docket books and microfiche from 1862 to 1980s. Mail turnaround time 7-10 days.
Criminal Records: Access: Mail, in person. Both court and visitors may perform in person searches. Search fee: $5.00 per name. Court makes copy: $2.00 per page. Required to search: name, years to search. Criminal records archived to 1862, on docket books and microfiche from 1862 to 1980s. Mail turnaround time 7-10 days.
General Information: No juvenile records released. Will fax documents to local or toll-free number. Certification fee: $2.00 per page. Payee: Circuit Court Clerk. Only cashiers checks and money orders accepted. Prepayment and SASE required.

Chancery Court
PO Box 206, Lynchburg, TN 37352; phone: 931-759-7028; fax: 931-759-5610; hours 8AM-4:30PM M-W,F; 8AM-N Sat (CST). *Civil, Probate.*
Civil Records: Access: In person only. Visitors must perform in person searches themselves. Court makes copy: $1.00 per page; same fee for self serve. Required to search: name, years to search. Civil cases indexed by plaintiff. Civil records on books.
General Information: No adoption or sealed records released. Certification fee: $5.00 per document. Payee: Clerk and Master. Only cashiers checks and money orders accepted. Prepayment required.

Morgan County

9th District Circuit & General Sessions Court
PO Box 163, Wartburg, TN 37887; phone: 423-346-3503; fax: 423-346-5947; hours 8AM-4PM (EST). *Felony, Misdemeanor, Civil, Eviction, Small Claims.*
Civil Records: Access: In person only. Visitors must perform in person searches themselves. Court makes copy: $2.00 first page, $.50 each add'l. Required to search: name, years to search. Civil cases indexed by defendant, plaintiff. Civil records archived on books from 1855.
Criminal Records: Access: In person only. Visitors must perform in person searches themselves. Court makes copy: $2.00 first page, $.50 each add'l. Required to search: name, years to search; also helpful: DOB, SSN. Criminal records archived on books from 1855; computerized since 2/01.
General Information: No sealed records released. Certification fee: $6.00. Payee: Circuit Court Clerk. Only cashiers checks and money orders accepted. Prepayment required.

Chancery Court
PO Box 789, Wartburg, TN 37887; phone: 423-346-3881; fax: 423-346-4217; probate fax: same; hours 8AM-4PM (EST). *Civil, Probate.*
Note: Probate is separate index at same address.
Civil Records: Access: Phone, mail, in person. Both court and visitors may perform in person searches. No search fee. Court makes copy: $.50 per page. Required to search: name, years to search. Civil cases

indexed by defendant, plaintiff; in books since 1883, on microfiche since 1939 at state archives. Mail turnaround time 1-8 days.
General Information: No adoption or conservatorship records released. Will fax documents to local or toll free line. Certification fee: $10.00 per document includes copies. Payee: Clerk & Master. Personal checks accepted. Prepayment and SASE required.

Obion County

27th District Circuit Court
7 Bill Burnett Cir, Union City, TN 38261; phone: 731-885-1372; fax: 731-885-7922; hours 8:30AM-4:30PM (CST). *Felony, Misdemeanor, Civil Actions Over $10,000.*
Civil Records: Access: Mail, in person. Both court and visitors may perform in person searches. Search fee: $5.00 per name. Court makes copy: $1.00 per page. Required to search: name, years to search. Civil cases indexed by defendant, plaintiff. Civil records for criminal archived on books from 1969, civil on books from 1974, rest are located elsewhere. Mail turnaround time 2 days.
Criminal Records: Access: Mail, in person. Both court and visitors may perform in person searches. Search fee: $5.00. Misdemeanor records are $5.00 per year. Court makes copy: $1.00 per page. Required to search: name, years to search, DOB, SSN. Criminal records for criminal archived on books from 1969, civil on books from 1974, rest are located elsewhere. Mail turnaround time 2 days.
General Information: No adoption records released. Will fax documents to local or toll-free number. Certification fee: $3.00 includes copy fee. Payee: Circuit Court. Business checks accepted. Prepayment and SASE required.

General Sessions Court
9 Bill Burnett Cir, Union City, TN 38281-0236; phone: 731-885-1811; fax: 731-885-7515; hours 8:30AM-4:30PM (CST). *Civil Actions Under $15,000, Eviction, Small Claims.*
Civil Records: Access: Mail, in person. Both court and visitors may perform in person searches. Search fee: $5.00 per name, 5 years or less; $10.00 over 5 years. Court makes copy: $1.00 per page. Required to search: name. Civil cases indexed by defendant, plaintiff. Civil records kept in office for last 10 years, computerized since 1994. Mail turnaround time 2 days.
General Information: Public terminal has only civil records back to 1994. No juvenile or adoption records released. Certification fee: $3.00. Payee: Circuit Court Clerk. Personal checks accepted. Prepayment and SASE required.

Chancery Court
PO Box 187, Union City, TN 38281; phone: 731-885-2562; fax: 731-885-7922; hours 8:30AM-4:30PM (CST). *Civil, Probate.*
Civil Records: Access: Phone, mail, in person. Both court and visitors may perform in person searches. Search fee: $5.00 per name. Court makes copy: $1.00 per page. Required to search: name, years to search. Civil cases indexed by defendant, plaintiff. Civil records (probate) from 9/82 on books in Chancery office, prior records on index books in County Clerk's office. Mail turnaround time 2 days.
General Information: No adoption or sealed records released. Will fax documents for $5.00 per document. Certification fee: $4.00. Payee: Clerk and Master. Personal checks accepted. Prepayment required.

Overton County

13th District Circuit & General Sessions Court
Overton County Courthouse, 100 John Tom Poindexter Dr, Livingston, TN 38570; phone: 931-823-2312; fax: 931-823-9728; hours 8AM-4:30PM M,T,Th, F; 8AM-N Wed & Sat (CST). *Felony, Misdemeanor, Civil, Eviction, Small Claims.*
Civil Records: Access: Mail, in person. Both court and visitors may perform in person searches. No search fee. Court makes copy: $.50 per page. Required to search: name, years to search. Civil cases

indexed by defendant, plaintiff. Civil records archived on books from late 1800s; computerized records since 1996. Mail turnaround time 3-5 days.
Criminal Records: Access: Mail, in person. Both court and visitors may perform in person searches. No search fee. Court makes copy: $.50 per page. Required to search: name, years to search, DOB, SSN, signed release. Criminal records archived on books from late 1800s; computerized records since 1996. Mail turnaround time 3-5 days.
General Information: No juvenile records released. Certification fee: $5.00 per page. Payee: Circuit Court Clerk. Business checks accepted. Prepayment and SASE required.

County Court
100 Court Sq,Courthouse Annex, University St, PO Box 127, Livingston, TN 38570; phone: 931-823-2536; fax: 931-823-7631; hours 8AM-4PM (CST). *Probate.*

Perry County

21st District Circuit & General Sessions Court
PO Box 91, Linden, TN 37096; phone: 931-589-2218; fax: 931-589-2350; hours 8AM-4PM (CST). *Felony, Misdemeanor, Civil, Eviction, Small Claims.*
Civil Records: Access: Mail, in person, phone. Both court and visitors may perform in person searches. No search fee. Court makes copy: $1.50 per page. Self serve copy fee: $1.00 per page. Required to search: name, years to search. Civil cases indexed by defendant, plaintiff. Civil records archived on books from 1941, on microfiche (limited) at library. Mail turnaround time 2-3 days.
Criminal Records: Access: Mail, in person, phone. Both court and visitors may perform in person searches. No search fee. Court makes copy: $1.50 per page. Self serve copy fee: $1.00 per page. Required to search: name, years to search, DOB, SSN. Criminal records archived on books from 1941, on microfiche (limited) at library. Mail turnaround time 2-3 days.
General Information: No adoption records released. No certification fee. Payee: Circuit Court Clerk. Personal checks accepted. Prepayment and SASE required.

Chancery Court
PO Box 251, Linden, TN 37096; phone: 931-589-2217; fax: 931-589-2350; hours 8AM-4PM (CST). *Civil, Probate.*
Civil Records: Access: In person only. Visitors must perform in person searches themselves. Court makes copy: $1.00 per page; same fee for self serve. Required to search: name, years to search. Civil cases indexed by defendant, plaintiff. Civil records (probate) on books from 1982, prior records in County Clerks office.
General Information: No adoption records released. Certification fee: $5.00. Payee: Clerk and Master. Local checks accepted. Prepayment required.

Pickett County

13th District Circuit & General Sessions Court
PO Box 188, Byrdstown, TN 38549; phone: 931-864-3958; fax: 931-864-6885; hours 8AM-4PM (CST). *Felony, Misdemeanor, Civil, Eviction, Small Claims.*
Civil Records: Access: Mail, in person. Both court and visitors may perform in person searches. Search fee: $10.00 per name. No copy fee. Required to search: name, years to search. Civil cases indexed by defendant. Civil records archived on books but not specific. Mail turnaround time 3-4 days.
Criminal Records: Access: Mail, in person. Both court and visitors may perform in person searches. Search fee: $10.00 per name. No copy fee. Required to search: name, years to search; also helpful: SSN. Criminal records not computerized, all on books. Mail turnaround time 3-4 days.
General Information: No adoption or juvenile records released. No certification fee. Payee: Circuit Court Clerk. Personal checks accepted. Prepayment required.

County Court Courthouse Square #2, Byrdstown, TN 38549; phone: 931-864-3879; fax: 931-864-7087; hours 8AM-4PM M T Th F, 8-11AM W & S (CST). *Probate.*

Polk County

10th District Circuit & General Sessions Court PO Box 256, Benton, TN 37307; phone: 423-338-4524; fax: 423-338-8611; hours 8:30AM-4:30PM M-F (EST). *Felony, Misdemeanor, Civil, Eviction, Small Claims.*

Civil Records: Access: Mail, fax, in person. Both court and visitors may perform in person searches. Search fee: $5.00 per name. Court makes copy: $5.00 per document. Self serve copy fee: $.50 per page. Required to search: name, years to search. Civil cases indexed by defendant, plaintiff. Civil records archived from 1936, computerized since 2000. Mail turnaround time 1 day.

Criminal Records: Access: Mail, fax, in person. Both court and visitors may perform in person searches. Search fee: $5.00 per name. Court makes copy: $5.00 per document. Self serve copy fee: $.50 per page. Required to search: name, years to search, DOB, SSN. Criminal records archived from 1936, computerized since 2000. Mail turnaround time 3 days.

General Information: Public terminal goes back to 2000. No juvenile records released. Will fax documents for $5.00 per name. Certification fee: $7.50 per document. Payee: Circuit Court Clerk. Personal checks accepted. Prepayment required. SASE requested.

Chancery Court PO Drawer L, Benton, TN 37307; phone: 423-338-4522; fax: 423-338-4553; hours 8:30AM-4:30PM (EST). *Civil, Probate.*

Civil Records: Access: Mail, in person. Both court and visitors may perform in person searches. Search fee: $5.00 per name. Fee varies by document. Court makes copy: $1.00 per page. Required to search: name, years to search. Civil cases indexed by defendant, plaintiff; on books up to 1800s, computerized since 10/00. Mail turnaround time 3 days.

General Information: No adoption records released. Will fax documents to local or toll free line. Certification fee: $2.00 per certificate and $2.00 per page. Payee: Chancery Court. Personal checks accepted. Prepayment required.

Putnam County

13th District Circuit & General Sessions Court 421 E Spring St, 1C-49A, Cookeville, TN 38501; phone: 931-528-1508; fax: 931-526-2004; hours 8AM-4PM (CST). *Felony, Misdemeanor, Civil, Eviction, Small Claims.*

www.dockets.putnamco.org
Current docket information available at the web site.

Civil Records: Access: In person only. Visitors must perform in person searches themselves. Court makes copy: $.25 per page; same fee for self serve. Required to search: name, years to search. Civil cases indexed by defendant, plaintiff. Civil records archived in office from 1980s, unknown before then; computerized records since 1995.

Criminal Records: Access: In person. Visitors must perform in person searches themselves. Court makes copy: $.25 per page; same fee for self serve. Required to search: name, years to search; also helpful: SSN. Romputerized since 1995.

General Information: Public terminal goes back to 1995. No juvenile or adoption records released. Certification fee: $4.50. Payee: Circuit Court Clerk. Business checks accepted. Prepayment required.

Probate & Juvenile Court PO Box 220, Cookeville, TN 38503-0220; phone: 931-526-7106; fax: 931-372-8201; hours 8AM-4:00PM (CST). *Probate, Juvenile.*

Rhea County

12th District Circuit & General Sessions Court 1475 Market St, Rm 200, Dayton, TN 37321; phone: 423-775-7805; criminal phone: 423-775-7818; civil phone: 423-775-7895; probate phone: 423-775-7806; fax: 423-775-7895; probate fax: 423-775-4046; hours 8AM-4:30PM (EST). *Felony, Misdemeanor, Civil, Eviction, Small Claims, Probate.*

Note: Probate located at the Rhea County Clerk and Master's Office.

Civil Records: Access: In person only. Visitors must perform in person searches themselves. Court makes copy: $.50 per page. Required to search: name, years to search. Civil cases indexed by defendant, plaintiff; in docket books.

Criminal Records: Access: Mail, fax, in person. Both court and visitors may perform in person searches. No search fee. Court makes copy: $.50 per page. Required to search: name, years to search; also helpful: DOB, SSN. Criminal records in docket books. Note: Court will only do name searches if current or within past year.

General Information: No adoption records released. Certification fee: $5.00 per doc. Payee: Circuit Court Clerk. Local personal checks accepted; no out of state checks. Prepayment required.

Roane County

9th District Circuit & General Sessions Court PO Box 73, Kingston, TN 37763; phone: 865-376-2390; fax: 865-717-4141; hours 8:30AM-6PM Mon; 8:30AM-4:30PM T-F (EST). *Felony, Misdemeanor, Civil, Eviction, Small Claims.*

Note: General Sessions phone is 865-376-5584, their records are separate from Circuit Court records.

Civil Records: Access: Mail, fax, in person. Both court and visitors may perform in person searches. Search fee: $5.00 per name. Court makes copy: $.50 per page; same fee for self serve. Required to search: name, years to search. Civil cases indexed by defendant, plaintiff. Civil records archived since court started, General Sessions and Circuit are on computer since 1991. Mail turnaround time 2-3 days.

Criminal Records: Access: Mail, fax, in person. Both court and visitors may perform in person searches. Search fee: $5.00 per name. Court makes copy: $.50 per page; same fee for self serve. Required to search: name, years to search, DOB; also helpful, SSN, signed release. Criminal records archived since court started, General Sessions and Circuit are on computer since 1991. Mail turnaround time 2-3 days.

General Information: Public terminal goes back to 1990. No adoption, expunged records released. Will fax documents. Certification fee: $5.00. Payee: Circuit Court Clerk. Business checks accepted. Prepayment and SASE required.

Chancery Court PO Box 402, Kingston, TN 37763; phone: 865-376-2487; fax: 865-376-1228; hours 8:30AM-6PM M, 8:30AM-4:30PM T-F (EST). *Civil, Probate.*

Civil Records: Access: Phone, mail, in person. Both court and visitors may perform in person searches. Search fee: $5.00. Court makes copy: $.50 per page. Required to search: name, years to search. Civil cases indexed by defendant, plaintiff; on books; on computer since 7/95. Tax records on computer since 1982. Mail turnaround time same day.

General Information: No adoption records released. Fee to fax documents is $1.00 per page. Certification fee: $2.00 per page. Payee: Clerk and Master. Personal checks accepted. Prepayment required.

Robertson County

19th District Circuit Court Robertson County Courthouse, Rm 200, Springfield, TN 37172; phone: 615-384-7864; fax: 615-384-0246; hours 8AM-4:30PM (CST). *Felony, Misdemeanor.*

Civil Records: Access: Phone, fax, mail, in person. Both court and visitors may perform in person

searches. Search fee: $5.00 per name. Court makes copy: $.50 per page; same fee for self serve. Required to search: name, years to search. Civil cases indexed by defendant, plaintiff. Civil records archived in office from 2003, archived from 1800s located elsewhere. Mail turnaround time 15 days.

Criminal Records: Access: Phone, fax, mail, in person. Both court and visitors may perform in person searches. Search fee: $5.00 per name. Court makes copy: $.50 per page; same fee for self serve. Required to search: name, years to search; also helpful: DOB, SSN. Criminal records archived in office from 2003, archived from 1800s located elsewhere. No long distance outgoing faxing. Mail turnaround time 15 days.

General Information: Public terminal goes back to 1994. No sealed records released. Certification fee: $2.00 plus $1.00 per page. Payee: Circuit Court Clerk. Personal checks not accepted. Prepayment and SASE required.

General Sessions Court 529 S Brown St, Springfield, TN 37172-2941; phone: 615-382-2324; fax: 615-382-3113; hours 8AM-4:30PM (CST). *Misdemeanor, Civil Actions under $15,000, Eviction, Small Claims, Traffic.*

Civil Records: Access: Fax, mail, in person. Both court and visitors may perform in person searches. Search fee: $5.00 per name. Court makes copy: $.50 per page; same fee for self serve. Required to search: name, years to search. Civil cases indexed by defendant, plaintiff. Civil records archived in office from 2000, archived from 1800s located elsewhere. Mail turnaround time 7 days.

Criminal Records: Access: Fax, mail, in person. Both court and visitors may perform in person searches. Search fee: $5.00 per name. Court makes copy: $.50 per page; same fee for self serve. Required to search: name, years to search; also helpful: DOB, SSN. Criminal records archived in office from 2000, archived from 1800s located elsewhere. No long distance outgoing faxing. Mail turnaround time 7 days.

General Information: Public terminal goes back to 1994. No sealed records released. Certification fee: $2.00 plus $1.00 per page. Payee: General Sessions Court Clerk. Personal checks not accepted. Prepayment and SASE required.

Chancery Court 501 Main St - 101 Robertson, County Courthouse, Springfield, TN 37172; phone: 615-384-5650; fax: 615-382-3128; hours 8AM-4:30PM (CST). *Civil, Probate.*

Civil Records: Access: Mail, in person. Both court and visitors may perform in person searches. Search fee: $2.00. Court makes copy: $1.00 per page. Required to search: name, years to search. Civil cases indexed by defendant, plaintiff; in books since 1982, computerized from 9/94 to present, all chancery records on books. Mail turnaround time 1-2 days.

General Information: No adoption records released. Will fax documents for $2.00 per name. Certification fee: $2.00. Payee: Clerk & Master. Personal checks accepted. Prepayment and SASE required.

Rutherford County

16th District Circuit Court Judicial Bldg, Rm 201, Murfreesboro, TN 37130; criminal phone: 615-898-7812; civil phone: 615-898-7820; fax: 615-217-7118; hours 8AM-4:15PM (CST). *Felony, Misdemeanor, Civil Actions Over $15,000.*

Civil Records: Access: In person only. Visitors must perform in person searches themselves. Court makes copy: $1.00 per page. Required to search: name, years to search. Civil cases indexed by defendant, plaintiff. Civil on computer since 1986.

Criminal Records: Access: In person only. Visitors must perform in person searches themselves. Court makes copy: $1.00 per page. Required to search: name, years to search, DOB, signed release; SSN helpful. Criminal on computer since 1990.

General Information: Public terminal has criminal back to 1990 and civil back to 1986. No expunged, sealed criminal records released. Certification fee:

$2.00 per page. Payee: Circuit Court Clerk. Personal checks accepted.

General Sessions Court Judicial Bldg, Rm 101, Murfreesboro, TN 37130; phone: 615-898-7831; fax: 615-898-7835; hours 8AM-4:15PM (CST). *Civil Actions Under $15,000, Eviction, Small Claims.*

Civil Records: Access: In person only. Visitors must perform in person searches themselves. Court makes copy: $1.00 per page. Required to search: name, years to search, DOB, SSN. Civil cases indexed by defendant, plaintiff. Civil records go back to 1948; on computer from 1986.

General Information: Public terminal has only civil records back to 1986. No juvenile records released. Certification fee: $4.00. Payee: General Sessions Court. No personal checks accepted. Prepayment required.

County Court 319 N Maple St, Murfreesboro, TN 37130; phone: 615-898-7798; fax: 615-217-6597; 8AM-4PM M-Th; 8AM-5PM F (CST). *Probate.*

Scott County

8th District Circuit & General Sessions Court PO Box 330, Huntsville, TN 37756; phone: 423-663-2440; criminal fax: 423-663-2595; same fax for civil/probate; hours 8AM-4:30PM (EST). *Felony, Misdemeanor, Civil, Eviction, Small Claims, Probate.*

Note: Probate is a separate index at this same address.

Civil Records: Access: Phone, mail, in person. Both court and visitors may perform in person searches. Search fee: $10.00 per name per year. Court makes copy: $.50 per page; same fee for self serve. Required to search: name, years to search. Civil cases indexed by defendant, plaintiff. Civil records archived in docket books but not specified, on computer from 1991. Mail turnaround time same week.

Criminal Records: Access: Phone, mail, in person. Both court and visitors may perform in person searches. Search fee: $10.00 per name per year. Fee varies according to info requested. Court makes copy: $.50 per page; same fee for self serve. Required to search: name, years to search, DOB; also helpful: SSN. Criminal records archived in docket books but not specified, on computer from 1991. Mail turnaround time same week.

General Information: No juvenile records released. Will fax documents to local or toll free line. Certification fee: $2.00 per seal. Payee: Circuit Court Clerk. Personal checks accepted. Prepayment and SASE required.

Sequatchie County

12th District Circuit & General Sessions Court PO Box 551, Dunlap, TN 37327; phone: 423-949-2618; fax: 423-949-2902; hours 8AM-4PM (CST). *Felony, Misdemeanor, Civil, Eviction, Small Claims.*

Civil Records: Access: Phone, fax, mail, in person. Both court and visitors may perform in person searches. No search fee. Court makes copy: $1.00 per page. Required to search: name, years to search. Civil cases indexed by defendant, plaintiff. Civil records archived on books but not specified. Mail turnaround time 1 week.

Criminal Records: Access: Phone, fax, mail, in person. Both court and visitors may perform in person searches. No search fee. Court makes copy: $1.00 per page. Required to search: name, years to search, DOB; also helpful: SSN. Criminal records not computerized. Mail turnaround time 1 week.

General Information: No adoption records released. Will fax documents for $1.00 per page. Certification fee: $4.00. Payee: Circuit Court Clerk. Personal checks accepted. Prepayment required.

Chancery Court PO Box 1651, Dunlap, TN 37327; phone: 423-949-3670; fax: 423-949-2570; hours 8AM-4PM (CST). *Civil, Probate.*

Civil Records: Access: Fax, mail, in person. Both court and visitors may perform in person searches.

No search fee. Court makes copy: $1.00 per page. Required to search: name, years to search. Civil cases indexed by defendant, plaintiff; on books. Mail turnaround time 1 week.

General Information: No sealed or adoption records released. Will fax documents $1.00 per page. Certification fee: $2.00 per page. Payee: Clerk and Master. Personal checks accepted. Prepayment required.

Sevier County

4th District Circuit Court 125 Court Ave, #204E, Sevierville, TN 37862; criminal phone: 865-774-3731; civil phone: 865-453-5536; fax: 865-774-9792; hours 8AM-4:30PM M-Th, 8AM-6PM F (EST). *Felony, Misdemeanor, Civil Actions over $15,000.*

Civil Records: Access: Fax, mail, in person. Both court and visitors may perform in person searches. Search fee: $10.00. Court makes copy: $1.00 per page. Self serve copy fee: $.50 per page. Required to search: name, years to search. Civil cases indexed by defendant, plaintiff. Civil records computerized back to 1993. Records before 1980s difficult to locate. Mail turnaround time 1 week.

Criminal Records: Access: Fax, mail, in person. Both court and visitors may perform in person searches. Search fee: $10.00. Court makes copy: $1.00 per page. Self serve copy fee: $.50 per page. Required to search: name, years to search; also helpful: SSN. Criminal records computerized back to 1993. Mail turnaround time 1 week.

General Information: Public terminal goes back to 1993. No expunged records released. Will fax documents $1.00 per page. Certification fee: $4.00. Payee: Circuit Court or General Sessions Clerk. Personal checks accepted. Prepayment and SASE required.

General Sessions Court 125 Court Ave, #107E, Sevierville, TN 37862; phone: 865-453-6116; criminal phone: 865-453-6116; civil phone: 865-429-5671; fax: 865-774-3842; hours 8AM-4:30PM M-Th, 8AM-6PM F (EST). *Misdemeanor, Civil Actions Under $25,000, Eviction, Small Claims.*

Civil Records: Access: Phone, fax, mail, in person. Both court and visitors may perform in person searches. Search fee: $15.00 per name. Court makes copy: $1.00 per page; same fee for self serve. Required to search: name, years to search. Civil cases indexed by defendant, plaintiff. Civil records computerized back to 1995. Records before 1980s difficult to locate. Mail turnaround time 1 week.

Criminal Records: Access: Fax, mail, in person. Both court and visitors may perform in person searches. Search fee: $15.00 per name. Court makes copy: $1.00 per page; same fee for self serve. Required to search: name, years to search; also helpful: SSN, date of arrest. Criminal records computerized back to 1995; index back to 1973. Mail turnaround time 1 week.

General Information: Public terminal goes back to 1995. No expunged records released. Will fax documents $1.00 per page. Certification fee: $5.00. Payee: Circuit Court or General Sessions Clerk. Personal checks not accepted. Prepayment required.

County Court 125 Court Ave, #202 East, Sevierville, TN 37862; phone: 865-453-5502; fax: 865-453-6830; hours 8AM-4:30PM (EST). *Probate.*

Shelby County

Circuit Court 140 Adams Ave, Rm 224, Memphis, TN 38103; phone: 901-545-4006; fax: 901-545-3952; hours 8AM-4:30PM (CST). *Civil Actions Over $25,000.*

www.circuitcourt.co.shelby.tn.us/

Note: A second office is located at 942 Mt. Moriah, phone 901-685-9992.

Civil Records: Access: Fax, mail, in person, online. Both court and visitors may perform in person searches. Search fee: $5.00 per name. Court makes

copy: $.50 per page; same fee for self serve. Required to search: name; also helpful: years to search. Civil cases indexed by defendant, plaintiff. Civil records archived from early 1900s, on computer from 1991, on microfiche from 1980. Search the clerk's circuit court records for free at the website or at http://circuitdata.co.shelby.tn.us/crwebplsql/ck_public_qry_main.cp_main_idx%20. Mail turnaround time 5-8 days.

General Information: Public terminal has only civil records back to 1994. No juvenile or adoption records released. Will fax documents $1.00 per page. Certification fee: $5.00 instate, $8.00 out-of-state. Payee: Circuit Court Clerk. Personal checks accepted. Prepayment required.

30th District Criminal Court Office of the Criminal Court, 201 Poplar, Rm 4-01, Memphis, TN 38103; phone: 901-545-5040; fax: 901-545-3679; hours 8AM-4:30PM (CST). *Felony.*

http://co4.shelbycountytn.gov/court_clerks/criminal_court/index.html

Criminal Records: Access: Fax, mail, in person, online. Both court and visitors may perform in person searches. Search fee: $5.00 per name. There is no fee if you do the search yourself. Court makes copy: $2.00 per page. Required to search: name, years to search, DOB, SSN. Criminal records on computer as far back as 1989, prior records archived. Search the criminal court records for free at http://jssi.co.shelby.tn.us/. Mail turnaround 3 days.

General Information: Public terminal has only criminal records back to 1989 but may not be complete. No expunged or sealed records released. Fee to fax documents is $4.00 per document if out of town, $3.00 is in-town. Certification fee: $6.00 per doc. Payee: Criminal Court Clerk. Business checks accepted. Visa, MC accepted in person only. Prepayment required.

Chancery Court 140 Adams, Rm 308, Memphis, TN 38103; phone: 901-545-4002; fax: 901-545-3309; hours 8AM-4:30PM (CST). *Civil Actions Under $25,000, Equity Cases (also, lower Circuit Court Civil issues).*

http://chancerycourt.co.shelby.tn.us

Civil Records: Access: Mail, fax, in person, online. Only the court performs in person searches; visitors may not. Search fee: $5.00 per name. Court makes copy: $1.00 per page. Required to search: name, years to search. Civil cases indexed by defendant, plaintiff. Search index free at http://chancerydata.co.shelby.tn.us/chwebplsql/ck_public_qry_main.cp_main_idx. Mail turnaround time 1 week.

General Information: No juvenile or adoption records released. Certification fee: $10.00 per document. Payee: Chancery Court Clerk. Prepayment required. SASE requested.

General Sessions - Civil 140 Adams, Rm 106, Memphis, TN 38103; phone: 901-545-4031; fax: 901-545-4515; hours 8AM-4:30PM (CST). *Civil Actions Under $25,000, Eviction, Small Claims.*

http://generalsessionscourt.co.shelby.tn.us

Note: Also an East Division office at 942-A Mt. Moriah Rd, ph 901-685-9992, fax 901-685-9856.

Civil Records: Access: In person, online. Visitors must perform in person searches themselves. Court makes copy: $1.50 per page. Required to search: name, years to search. Civil cases indexed by defendant, plaintiff. Civil records archived 10 years in office, some microfiche and on computer from 1982. Search the court records for free at http://circuitdata.co.shelby.tn.us/gnwebplsql/ck_public_qry_main.cp_main_idx.

General Information: Public terminal has only civil records. No mental commitment records released. Certification fee: $6.00 per doc. Payee: General Sessions Court Clerk. Personal checks accepted. Prepayment required.

General Sessions - Criminal 201 Poplar, Rm 81, Memphis, TN 38103; phone: 901-545-5100; fax: 901-545-3655; hours 8AM-4:30PM (CST). *Misdemeanor.*

http://generalsessionscourt.co.shelby.tn.us

Criminal Records: Access: Mail, in person, online. Both court and visitors may perform in person searches. Search fee: $10.00 per name. Use of terminal is $10.00 each 20 minutes. Court makes copy: $1.50 per page. Required to search: name, years to search, DOB; also helpful: SSN. Criminal records on computer since 1982, prior records archived since court started. Search the criminal court records for free at http://jssi.co.shelby.tn.us/. Mail turnaround time 2-5 days.

General Information: No mental records released. No certification fee. Payee: General Sessions Court. Personal checks accepted. Prepayment required.

Probate Court 140 Adams, Rm 124, Memphis, TN 38103; phone: 901-545-4040; fax: 901-545-4746; hours 8AM-4:30PM (CST). *Probate.*

www.shelbyprobate.com

Note: Probate court records and dockets are free at www.probatedata.co.shelby.tn.us/default2.htm. Search online by name or case number.

Smith County

15th District Circuit & General Sessions Court 211 Main St, Carthage, TN 37030; phone: 615-735-0500 (Gen Sess.); 615-735-8260 (Circuit Ct); fax: 615-735-8261; hours 8AM-4PM M-F (CST). *Felony, Misdemeanor, Civil, Eviction, Small Claims.*

Civil Records: Access: Mail, in person. Visitors must perform in person searches themselves. No search fee. Court makes copy: $.25 per page. Required to search: name, years to search. Civil cases indexed by defendant, plaintiff; on computer from 3/92, prior records archived on books, questionable to dates. Mail turnaround time 1-2 days.

Criminal Records: Access: Phone, mail, in person. Visitors must perform in person searches themselves. No search fee. Court makes copy: $.25 per page. Required to search: name, years to search. Criminal records on computer from 3/92, prior records archived on books, questionable to dates. Mail turnaround time 1-2 days.

General Information: No juvenile records released. Will not fax documents. Certification fee: $6.00. Payee: Circuit Court Clerk. Only cashiers checks and money orders accepted. Prepayment required.

Chancery Court 211 N Main St, Carthage, TN 37030; phone: 615-735-2092; fax: 615-735-8261; hours 8AM-4PM (CST). *Civil, Probate.*

Civil Records: Access: Fax, mail, in person. Only the court performs in person searches; visitors may not. No search fee. Court makes copy: $.50 per page if mailed, $.25 if in person. Required to search: name, years to search. Civil cases indexed by defendant, plaintiff; on books back to 1825. Mail turnaround time 1 day.

General Information: No adoption records released. Fee to fax documents is $1.00 per page. Certification fee: $4.00. Payee: Clerk and Master. Personal checks accepted. Prepayment required. SASE requested.

Stewart County

23rd District Circuit & General Sessions Court PO Box 193, Dover, TN 37058; phone: 931-232-7042; fax: 931-232-3111; hours 8AM-4:30PM (CST). *Felony, Misdemeanor, Civil, Eviction, Small Claims.*

Civil Records: Access: Mail, in person. Visitors must perform in person searches themselves. No search fee. Required to search: name, years to search. Civil cases indexed by plaintiff. Civil records archived on books from 1800s, on computer through 8/1993. Mail turnaround time 1-10 days.

Criminal Records: Access: Mail, in person. Visitors must perform in person searches themselves. No search fee. Required to search: name, years to search.

Criminal records archived on books from 1800s, on computer through 8/1993. Mail turnaround time 1-10 days.

General Information: No expunged records released. Will fax documents to local or toll free line. No certification fee.

Chancery Court PO Box 102, Dover, TN 37058; phone: 931-232-5665; fax: 931-232-0049; hours 8AM-4:30PM (CST). *Civil, Probate.*

Civil Records: Access: Mail, in person. Only the court performs in person searches; visitors may not. No search fee. Court makes copy: $.50 per page. Required to search: name, years to search. Civil cases indexed by defendant, plaintiff; on books to 1865; computerized since 1994. Mail turnaround time 1 week.

General Information: No adoption records released. Certification fee: $4.00. Payee: Clerk and Master. Personal checks accepted. Prepayment and SASE required.

Sullivan County

Bristol Circuit Court - Civil Division Courthouse, Rm 131, 801 Anderson St, Bristol, TN 37620; phone: 423-989-4354; hours 8AM-5PM (EST). *Civil.*

www.bridgeweb.org

Civil Records: Access: In person only. Visitors must perform in person searches themselves. Court makes copy: $1.00 per page. Civil cases indexed by defendant, plaintiff. Civil records archived from 1930s (minute books, unsure of docket books), on computer from 1986.

General Information: Public terminal has only civil records back to 1986. No adoption or sealed records released. Will not fax documents. Certification fee: $6.00 for seal. Payee: Circuit Court Clerk. Personal checks accepted.

Kingsport Circuit Court - Civil Division 225 W Center St, Kingsport, TN 37660; phone: 423-224-1724; hours 8AM-5PM (EST). *Civil Actions Over $15,000.*

Civil Records: Access: Phone, mail, in person. Both court and visitors may perform in person searches. No search fee. Court makes copy: $1.00 per page. Required to search: name, years to search. Civil cases indexed by defendant, plaintiff. Civil records archived from 1920s, on computer from 1985. Mail turnaround time 2-3 days.

General Information: Public terminal has only civil records back to 1985. No juvenile, adoption records released. Will not fax documents. Certification fee: $6.00. Payee: Circuit Court Clerk. Personal checks accepted. Prepayment required. SASE requested.

2nd District Circuit Court 140 Blockville ByPass, PO Box 585, Blountville, TN 37617; phone: 423-323-5158; fax: 423-279-3258; hours 8AM-5PM (EST). *Felony, Misdemeanor.*

Criminal Records: Access: In person only. Visitors must perform in person searches themselves. Court makes copy: $1.00 per page. Required to search: name, years to search, DOB; SSN helpful. Criminal records on computer since 12/83; prior records archived since the 1800s.

General Information: Public terminal has only criminal records back to 1984. No juvenile records released. Certification fee: $9.00 per page. Payee: Circuit Court Clerk. Personal checks accepted.

Chancery Court PO Box 327, Blountville, TN 37617; phone: 423-323-6483; fax: 423-279-3280; hours 8AM-5PM (EST). *Civil, Probate.*

Civil Records: Access: Mail, in person. Both court and visitors may perform in person searches. No search fee. Court makes copy: $1.00 per page; same fee for self serve. Required to search: name, years to search. Civil cases indexed by defendant, plaintiff; on books back to 1867; computerized records go back to 1996.

General Information: Public terminal has only civil records. No adoption records released.

Certification fee: $5.00. Payee: Chancery Court. Personal checks accepted. Prepayment required.

Bristol General Sessions Court Courthouse, 801 Anderson St, Rm 131, Bristol, TN 37620; phone: 423-989-4352; hours 8AM-5PM (EST). *Misdemeanor, Civil Actions Under $15,000, Eviction, Small Claims.*

www.bridgeweb.org/docketts.htm

Civil Records: Access: In person, online. Visitors must perform in person searches themselves. Required to search: name, years to search. Civil cases indexed by defendant, plaintiff. Civil records archived since court started (stored in Blountville), on computer from 1986. Access to dockets and rules is free at www.bridgeweb.org/docketts.htm.

Criminal Records: Access: In person, online. Visitors must perform in person searches themselves. Required to search: name, years to search. Criminal records archived since court started (stored in Blountville), on computer from 1986. Access to dockets and rules is free online at www.bridgeweb.org/docketts.htm.

General Information: Public terminal goes back to 1987. No juvenile records released. Certification fee: $8.00. Payee: Circuit Court Clerk. Personal checks accepted. Prepayment required.

Kingsport General Sessions 200 Shelby St, Kingsport, TN 37660; phone: 423-224-1711; hours 8AM-5PM (EST). *Misdemeanor, Civil Actions Under $15,000, Eviction, Small Claims.*

Civil Records: Access: In person only. Visitors must perform in person searches themselves. Court makes copy: $1.00 per page. Required to search: name, years to search. Civil cases indexed by defendant, plaintiff. Civil records archived in office from 1973, on computer from 1981.

Criminal Records: Access: In person only. Visitors must perform in person searches themselves. Court makes copy: $1.00 per page. Required to search: name, years to search; SSN helpful. Criminal records archived in office from 1973, on computer from 1981.

General Information: Public terminal goes back to 1981. No juvenile records released. Certification fee: $8.00 per page. Payee: General Sessions Clerk. Personal checks accepted. Prepayment required.

Sumner County

18th District Circuit & General Sessions Court Public Sq, PO Box 549, Gallatin, TN 37066; phone: 615-452-4367; fax: 615-451-6027; hours 8AM-4:30PM (CST). *Felony, Misdemeanor, Civil, Eviction, Small Claims.*

Civil Records: Access: In person only. Visitors must perform in person searches themselves. Court makes copy: $1.00 per page; after 1/1/06- $.50 per page. Required to search: name, years to search. Civil cases indexed by defendant, plaintiff. Civil records archived on books in office from 1981.

Criminal Records: Access: In person only. Visitors must perform in person searches themselves. Court makes copy: $1.00 per page; after 1/1/06- $.50 per page. Required to search: name, years to search. Criminal records archived on index books in office from 1958; computerized back to 1997.

General Information: Public terminal has only criminal records back to 1997. No juvenile, adoption records released. Certification fee: $4.00. Payee: Circuit Court Clerk. Only cashiers checks and money orders accepted. Prepayment required.

Chancery Court Rm 400, Sumner County Courthouse, Gallatin, TN 37066; phone: 615-452-4282; fax: 615-451-6031; hours 8AM-4:30PM (CST). *Civil, Probate.*

Civil Records: Access: Phone, fax, mail, in person. Both court and visitors may perform in person searches. Search fee: $5.00. Court makes copy: $1.00 per page. Required to search: name, years to search. Civil cases indexed by defendant, plaintiff. Civil records go back to 1981. Mail turnaround 1-2 days.

General Information: No juvenile or adoption records released. Will fax documents for $1.00 per page. Certification fee: $4.00 plus $2.00 per page. Payee: Clerk and Master. Only money orders, cash, or business checks accepted. Prepayment required.

Tipton County

25th District Circuit & General Sessions
Court 1801 S College, Rm 102, Covington, TN 38019; phone: 901-475-3310; fax: 901-475-3318; hours 8AM-5PM (CST). *Felony, Misdemeanor, Civil, Eviction, Small Claims.*
Civil Records: Access: Mail, in person. Both court and visitors may perform in person searches. Search fee: $10.00 per name per court. $25.00 for computer info before 7/91. Court makes copy: $.50 per page. Required to search: name, years to search. Civil cases indexed by defendant, plaintiff; on computer from 7/1991, prior records on docket books. Mail turnaround time 1 week.
Criminal Records: Access: Mail, in person. Both court and visitors may perform in person searches. Search fee: $10.00 per name per court. Court makes copy: $.50 per page. Required to search: name, years to search, DOB; also helpful: SSN. Criminal records on computer from 7/1992, prior records on docket books. Mail turnaround time 1 week.
General Information: Public use terminal available. No juvenile or adoption records released. Certification fee: $5.00. Payee: Circuit Court Clerk or General Sessions. Personal checks accepted. Prepayment required. SASE requested.

Chancery Court Tipton County Justice Ctr, 1801 S College, #110, Covington, TN 38019; phone: 901-476-0209; fax: 901-476-0246; hours 8AM-5PM (CST). *Civil, Probate.*
Civil Records: Access: Phone, fax, mail, in person. Both court and visitors may perform in person searches. No search fee. Court makes copy: $.50 per page. Self serve copy fee: $.25 per page. Required to search: name, years to search. Civil cases indexed by defendant, plaintiff; on books since 1800s, on computer since 1991. Mail turnaround time ASAP.
General Information: Public terminal has only civil records. No adoption records released. Certification fee: $4.00 plus $2.00 per page. Payee: Tipton County Chancery Court. Personal checks accepted. Prepayment and SASE required.

Trousdale County

15th District Circuit & General Sessions
Court 200 E Main St, Rm 5, Hartsville, TN 37074; phone: 615-374-3411; fax: 615-374-1100; hours 8AM-4:30PM (CST). *Felony, Misdemeanor, Civil, Eviction, Small Claims.*
Civil Records: Access: In person only. Visitors must perform in person searches themselves. Court makes copy: $.75 per page. Required to search: name, years to search. Civil cases indexed by defendant, plaintiff. Civil records on books since 1927.
Criminal Records: Access: In person only. Visitors must perform in person searches themselves. Court makes copy: $.75 per page. Required to search: name, years to search. Criminal records archived on books since 1940.
General Information: No juvenile or adoption records released. Will fax specific case file for fee. Certification fee: $3.00. Payee: Circuit Court Clerk. Only cashiers checks and money orders accepted. Prepayment required.

Chancery Court Courthouse Rm 1, 200 E Main St, Hartsville, TN 37074; phone: 615-374-2996; fax: 615-374-1100; 8AM-4:30PM (CST). *Civil, Probate.*
Civil Records: Access: In person only. Visitors must perform in person searches themselves. Court makes copy: $1.00 per page. Required to search: name, years to search. Civil cases indexed by defendant, plaintiff; on book since 9/80, prior records in County Clerks office.
General Information: No adoption or sealed records released. Will fax documents. Certification fee: $3.00 plus $.50 per page. Payee: Clerk and Master. Personal checks accepted. Prepayment required.

Unicoi County

1st District Circuit & General Sessions
Court PO Box 2000, Erwin, TN 37650; phone: 423-743-3541; fax: 423-743-1118; hours 9AM-5PM (EST). *Felony, Misdemeanor, Civil, Eviction, Small Claims.*
Civil Records: Access: Mail, in person. Both court and visitors may perform in person searches. Search fee: $10.00 per name. Court makes copy: $.25 per page. Required to search: name, years to search. Civil cases indexed by defendant, plaintiff. Civil records archived on books from 1932 (felonies) and 1961 (misdemeanors); only general sessions is on computer back to late 1996. Mail turnaround time 2 days.
Criminal Records: Access: Mail, in person. Both court and visitors may perform in person searches. Search fee: $10.00 per name. Court makes copy: $.25 per page. Required to search: name, years to search, DOB. Criminal records archived on books from 1932 (felonies) and 1961 (misdemeanors); only general sessions is on computer back to late 1996. Mail turnaround time 2 days.
General Information: Public terminal goes back to 1996. No adoption records released. Will fax documents to local or toll free line. Certification fee: $4.50 per document plus $.50 per page. Payee: Circuit Court Clerk. Personal checks accepted. Prepayment required.

Probate Court PO Box 2000, Erwin, TN 37650; phone: 423-743-3541; fax: 423-743-1118; hours 9AM-5PM M-F, 9AM-N Sat (EST). *Probate.*

Union County

8th District Circuit & General Sessions
Court 901 E Main St, #220, Maynardville, TN 37807; phone: 865-992-5493; fax: 865-992-8099; hours 8AM-4PM Mon-Fri; 8AM-N Sat (EST). *Felony, Misdemeanor, Civil, Eviction, Small Claims.*
Civil Records: Access: Mail, in person. Both court and visitors may perform in person searches. Search fee: $10.00 per name. Court makes copy: $.25 per page; same fee for self serve. Required to search: name, years to search. Civil cases indexed by defendant, plaintiff. Civil records archived on books from 1969. Mail turnaround time 1 week.
Criminal Records: Access: Mail, in person. Both court and visitors may perform in person searches. Search fee: $10.00 per name. Court makes copy: $.25 per page; same fee for self serve. Required to search: name, years to search, DOB, SSN. Criminal records archived on books from 1969. Mail turnaround time 1 week.
General Information: Public terminal has criminal back to 1994; General Sessions criminal back to 1994 and civil back to 1987 civil; Circuit civil back to 2000. No sealed records released. Will fax documents. Certification fee: $4.00 includes copy fee. Payee: Circuit Court Clerk. Personal checks accepted. Prepayment required.

Chancery Court 901 Main St, #215, Maynardville, TN 37807-3510; phone: 865-992-5942; fax: 865-992-9338; hours 8AM-4PM (6PM F) (EST). *Civil, Probate.*
Note: Probate is a separate index at this same address.
Civil Records: Access: Phone, mail, in person. Both court and visitors may perform in person searches. No search fee. Court makes copy: $.25 per page; same fee for self serve. Required to search: name, years to search. Civil cases indexed by plaintiff. Civil records on books back to 1969. Mail turnaround 1 week.
General Information: No adoption records released. Fee to fax documents is $1.00 per page. Certification fee: $4.00 per document includes copies. Payee: Union County Clerk and Master. Personal checks accepted. Prepayment required.

Van Buren County

31st District Circuit & General Sessions
Court PO Box 126, Spencer, TN 38585; phone: 931-946-2153; fax: 931-946-7572; hours 8AM-5PM (CST). *Felony, Misdemeanor, Civil, Eviction, Small Claims.*
Civil Records: Access: Mail, in person. Both court and visitors may perform in person searches. Search fee: $10.00 per name. Court makes copy: $.50 per page. Required to search: name, years to search. Civil cases indexed by defendant. Civil records archived on books, date unspecified. Mail turnaround time 2 weeks.
Criminal Records: Access: Mail, in person. Both court and visitors may perform in person searches. Search fee: $10.00 per name. Court makes copy: $.50 per page. Required to search: name, years to search, DOB; also helpful: SSN. Criminal records archived on books, date unspecified. Mail turnaround time 2 weeks.
General Information: No juvenile records released. Will fax documents to local or toll free line. Certification fee: $3.00. Payee: Circuit Court Clerk. Only cashiers checks and money orders accepted. Prepayment required.

County Court PO Box 153, 179 Veterans Sq, Spencer, TN 38585; phone: 931-946-7175; fax: 931-946-7572; hours 8AM-4PM (CST). *Probate.*

Warren County

31st District Circuit & General Sessions
Court 111 Court Sq, PO Box 639, McMinnville, TN 37111; phone: 931-473-2373; probate phone: 931-473-2364; fax: 931-473-3726; hours 8AM-4:30PM M-Th, 8AM-5PM F (CST). *Felony, Misdemeanor, Civil, Eviction, Small Claims.*
Civil Records: Access: Mail, in person. Both court and visitors may perform in person searches. Search fee: $5.00 per name. Court makes copy: $1.00 per page. Required to search: name, years. Civil cases indexed by defendant, plaintiff; on computer since 1988 (Gen. Sessions), archived in office from 1939 (Circuit). Mail turnaround 1-2 days.
Criminal Records: Access: Mail, in person. Both court and visitors may perform in person searches. Search fee: $5.00 per name. Court makes copy: $1.00 per page. Required to search: name, years to search, DOB, SSN, offense, date of offense. Criminal records on computer since 1988 (General Sessions), archived in office from 1939 (Circuit). Mail turnaround time 1-2 days.
General Information: Public terminal goes back to 1996. No adoption or juvenile records released. Will fax documents for an add'l $5.00 fee. Certification fee: $2.00. Payee: Circuit Court Clerk. Personal checks accepted. Prepayment required.

Chancery Court PO Box 639, McMinnville, TN 37111; phone: 931-473-2364; fax: 931-473-3232; hours 8AM-4:30PM M-Th, 8AM-5PM F (CST). *Civil, Probate.*
Civil Records: Access: Mail, in person. Both court and visitors may perform in person searches. No search fee. Court makes copy: $1.00 per page. Required to search: name, years to search. Civil cases indexed by defendant, plaintiff; on books. Mail turnaround time 1 week.
General Information: No adoption records released. Certification fee: $4.00 for first page. Payee: Clerk and Master. Personal checks accepted. Prepayment and SASE required.

Washington County

1st District Circuit & General Sessions
Court PO Box 356, Jonesborough, TN 37659; phone: 423-753-1611; fax: 423-926-4862; hours 8AM-5PM (EST). *Felony, Misdemeanor, Civil, Eviction, Small Claims.*
Civil Records: Access: In person only. Both court and visitors may perform in person searches. Search fee: $5.00 per name. Court makes copy: $2.00 per page. Required to search: name, years to search.

Civil cases indexed by defendant, plaintiff. Civil records archived from 1800s, on computer from 1989. **Criminal Records:** Access: In person only. Both court and visitors may perform in person searches. Search fee: $5.00 per name. Court makes copy: $2.00 per page. Required to search: name, years to search, DOB, SSN. Criminal records archived from 1800s, on computer from 1989.

General Information: Public terminal goes back to 1989. No sealed, juvenile, adoption records released. Certification fee: $4.00. Payee: Circuit Court Clerk. Personal checks accepted. Prepayment required.

General Sessions 101 E Market St, Johnson City, TN 37604; phone: 423-461-1412; fax: 423-926-4862; hours 8AM-5PM (EST). *Civil Actions Under $15,000, Eviction, Small Claims.*

Civil Records: Access: Mail, in person. Both court and visitors may perform in person searches. Search fee: $5.00 per name. Court makes copy: $.50 per page; same fee for self serve. Required to search: name, years to search. Civil cases indexed by defendant, plaintiff. Civil records archived since court started, computerized since 1990. Mail turnaround time 1-2 weeks.

General Information: Public terminal has only civil records back to 1990. No sealed records released. Certification fee: $8.00. Payee: Circuit Court Clerk. In state checks accepted. Prepayment required. SASE requested.

Johnson City Law Court - Civil 101 E Market St, Johnson City, TN 37604; phone: 423-461-1475; fax: 423-926-4862; hours 8AM-5PM (EST). *Civil Actions Over $15,000.*

Civil Records: Access: Mail, in person. Both court and visitors may perform in person searches. Search fee: $5.00 per name. Court makes copy: $2.00 per page. Required to search: name, years to search. Civil cases indexed by defendant, plaintiff; on computer from 1988. Mail turnaround time 1 week.

General Information: Public terminal has only civil records back to 1988. No sealed records released. Certification fee: $4.00. Payee: Circuit Court Clerk. Personal checks accepted. Out of state checks not accepted. Prepayment required. SASE requested.

Probate Court PO Box 218, 100 Main St, Jonesborough, TN 37659; phone: 423-753-1623; fax: 423-753-4716; hours 8AM-5PM (EST). *Probate.*

Wayne County

22nd District Circuit & General Sessions Court PO Box 869, 100 Court Circle #302, Waynesboro, TN 38485; phone: 931-722-5519; fax: 931-722-9949; hours 8AM-4PM M,T,Th,F; 8AM-N Wed & Sat (CST). *Felony, Misdemeanor, Civil, Eviction, Small Claims.*

Civil Records: Access: Phone, mail, in person. Both court and visitors may perform in person searches. No search fee. Court makes copy: $.25 per page. Required to search: name, years to search. Civil cases indexed by defendant, plaintiff. Civil records archived on books from 1900s. Mail turnaround 7-10 days.

Criminal Records: Access: Mail, in person. Both court and visitors may perform in person searches. Search fee: $5.00 per name. Court makes copy: $.25 per page. Required to search: name, years to search, DOB, SSN. Criminal records archived on books from 1900s. Mail turnaround time 7-10 days.

General Information: No juvenile or adoption records released. No certification fee. Payee: Circuit Court Clerk. Personal checks accepted. Prepayment required.

Chancery Court PO Box 101, Waynesboro, TN 38485; phone: 931-722-5517; fax: 931-722-5517; hours 8AM-4PM (CST). *Civil, Probate.*

Civil Records: Access: Mail, in person. Both court and visitors may perform in person searches. No search fee. Court makes copy: $1.00 per page. Required to search: name, years to search. Civil cases

indexed by defendant, plaintiff; on books; computerized since 12/92. Mail turnaround 2 days.

General Information: No adoption records released. Will fax documents to local or toll free line. Certification fee: $3.00 minimum or $1.00 per page. Payee: Clerk and Master. Personal checks accepted. Prepayment required. SASE requested.

Weakley County

27th District Circuit & General Sessions Court PO Box 28, Dresden, TN 38225; phone: 731-364-3455; fax: 731-364-6765; hours 8AM-4:30PM (CST). *Felony, Misdemeanor, Civil, Eviction, Small Claims.*

www.weakleycountytn.gov/circuitcourtclerk.html

Civil Records: Access: In person only. Visitors must perform in person searches themselves. Court makes copy: $.50 per page; same fee for self serve. Required to search: name, years to search. Civil cases indexed by defendant, plaintiff. Civil records archived on since court started, on books; computerized since 1997.

Criminal Records: Access: In person only. Visitors must perform in person searches themselves. Court makes copy: $.50 per page; same fee for self serve. Required to search: name, years to search, DOB; SSN helpful. Criminal records archived on since court started, on books; computerized since 1997.

General Information: Public terminal goes back to 1960s. No adoption or sealed records released. Certification fee: $6.00. Payee: Circuit Court Clerk. No personal checks accepted. Prepayment required.

Chancery Court PO Box 197, Dresden, TN 38225; phone: 731-364-3454; fax: 731-364-5247; hours 8AM-4:30PM (CST). *Civil, Probate.*

Note: Court will not do searches for genealogy.

Civil Records: Access: Mail, in person. Both court and visitors may perform in person searches. Court makes copy: $.50 per page. Required to search: name, years to search. Civil cases indexed by defendant, plaintiff; on computer since 1982, prior records indexed from 1927; Probate to 1800s. Mail turnaround time 1 week.

General Information: No adoption or sealed records released. Will fax documents for $1.00 per page. Fee must be prepaid. Certification fee: $4.00. Payee: Clerk and Master. Personal checks accepted. Prepayment required.

White County

13th District Circuit & General Sessions Court 111 Depot St, #1, Sparta, TN 38583; phone: 931-836-3205; fax: 931-836-3526; hours 8AM-5PM (CST). *Felony, Misdemeanor, Civil, Eviction, Small Claims.*

Civil Records: Access: In person only. Visitors must perform in person searches themselves. Court makes copy: $.50. Required to search: name, years to search. Civil cases indexed by defendant, plaintiff. Civil records archived since court started, computerized since 1996.

Criminal Records: Access: In person only. Visitors must perform in person searches themselves. Court makes copy: $.50. Required to search: name, years to search, DOB; SSN helpful. Criminal records archived since court started; computerized records since 19996.

General Information: Public use terminal available. No juvenile, adoption records released. Will not fax specific case file. Certification fee: $3.50 per certification includes copies. Payee: Circuit Court Clerk. No personal checks accepted. Prepayment required.

Chancery Court White County Courthouse, Rm 303, Sparta, TN 38583; phone: 931-836-3787; fax: 931-836-2124; hours 8AM-4PMn (CST). *Civil, Probate.*

Civil Records: Access: Phone, in person. Visitors must perform in person searches themselves. Court makes copy: $2.00 per instrument; same fee for self serve. Required to search: name, years to search. Civil

cases indexed by defendant, plaintiff. Overall records go back to 1842.

General Information: No adoption records released. Will not fax documents. Certification fee: $2.00. Payee: Clerk and Master. Personal checks accepted. Prepayment required.

Williamson County

21st District Circuit & General Sessions Court 135 4th Ave, Rm 203, Franklin, TN 37064; phone: 615-790-5454; fax: 615-790-5626; hours 8AM-4:30PM (CST). *Felony, Misdemeanor, Civil, Eviction, Small Claims.*

Civil Records: Access: In person only. Visitors must perform in person searches themselves. Court makes copy: $1.00 per page; same fee for self serve. Required to search: name, years to search. Civil cases indexed by defendant, plaintiff. Civil records archived on books from 1810, on computer from 1992.

Criminal Records: Access: In person only. Visitors must perform in person searches themselves. Court makes copy: $1.00 per page; same fee for self serve. Required to search: name, years to search; also helpful: DOB, SSN. Criminal records archived on books from 1810, on computer from 1992.

General Information: Public terminal goes back to 1992. Certification fee: $4.00. Payee: Circuit Court Clerk. Personal checks accepted. Prepayment required.

Chancery Court Clerk & Master, PO Box 1666, Franklin, TN 37064; phone: 615-790-5428; fax: 615-790-5626; hours 8AM-4:30PM (CST). *Civil, Probate.*

Civil Records: Access: Phone, mail, in person. Both court and visitors may perform in person searches. No search fee. Court makes copy: $1.00 per page. Required to search: name, years to search. Civil cases indexed by defendant, plaintiff; on computer since 1991, prior records on books since 1800s (no probate on computer).

General Information: Public terminal has civil records back to 1991. No adoption, sealed records released. Certification fee: $2.00 per document. Payee: Clerk and Master. Local checks accepted. Prepayment required. SASE requested.

Wilson County

15th District Circuit & General Sessions Court PO Box 518, Lebanon, TN 37088-0518; phone: 615-444-2042; hours 8AM-4PM M-Th, 8AM-5PM F (CST). *Felony, Misdemeanor, Civil, Eviction, Small Claims.*

Civil Records: Access: In person only. Visitors must perform in person searches themselves. Court makes copy: $1.00 per page. Required to search: name, years to search. Civil cases indexed by defendant, plaintiff. Civil records archived in office from 1982, on computer from 1990, on microfiche from 1940s.

Criminal Records: Access: In person only. Visitors must perform in person searches themselves. Court makes copy: $1.00 per page. Required to search: name, years to search, DOB, SSN. Criminal records archived in office from 1982, on computer from 1990, on microfiche from 1940s.

General Information: Public terminal goes back to 1990. No adoption, juvenile records released. Certification fee: $6.00 plus $2.00 each add'l page. Payee: Circuit Court Clerk. Business checks accepted. Prepayment required.

Probate Court PO Box 1557, Lebanon, TN 37088; phone: 615-444-2835; fax: 615-443-6191; hours 8AM-4PM (CST). *Probate.*

Note: Probate is now Clerk & Master

Tennessee Recording Offices

ORGANIZATION:	95 counties, 96 recording offices. The recording officer is. Register of Deeds. Sullivan County has two offices. 66 counties are in the Central Time Zone (CST) and 29 are in the Eastern Time Zone (EST).
REAL ESTATE RECORDS:	Counties will not perform real estate searches. Certified copies usually cost $1.00 per page. Tax records are kept at the Assessor's Office.
UCC RECORDS:	Financing statements are filed at the state level, except for real estate related collateral, which are filed with the Register of Deeds. However, prior to 07/2001, consumer goods and farm collateral were also filed at the Register of Deeds and these older records can be searched there. Many recording offices will not perform UCC searches. Use search request form UCC-11. Search fee is usually $12-15, the copy fee is $1.00.
TAX LIEN RECORDS:	All federal tax liens are filed with the county Register of Deeds. State tax liens are filed with the Secretary of State or the Register of Deeds. Counties will not perform tax lien searches.
OTHER LIENS:	Judgment, materialman, mechanics, trustee.
ONLINE ACCESS:	The State Comptroller of the Treasury Real Estate Assessment Database can be searched free at http://170.142.31.248/. Select a county then search by name for real property information. Counties not on the system are Davidson, Hamilton, Knox, Shelby, and Unicoi.

Online access to a number of county' property and deeds indexes and images is available via a private company at www.titlesearcher.com or email support@TitleSearcher.com. Registration, login, and monthly $35 fee per county required, plus $20.00 set up. A $5 per day plan is also available.

Also, online access to a large group of county property, deeds, judgment, liens, and UCCs is available via a private company at www.ustitlesearch.com or call 615-223-5420. Registration, login, and monthly $25 fee required, plus $50 set up. Use DEMO username to try system.

Finally, www.tnrealestate.com offers free and fee services for real estate information from all counties.

Anderson County

Register of Deeds, 100 N Main St; Courthouse, Rm 205, Clinton, TN 37716-3688. 865-457-5400; fax-865-457-1638; hours: 8:30AM-4:30PM.
All records in one index. Records indexed on a public use terminal back to 1990. Only the public may search. No copy fee. Cert fee- $1.00 per page. Payee- Anderson County Register of Deeds. **Online access to Land, Property Assessor, Recorder, Deed records:** Assessment data on the state comptroller system is free at http://170.142.31.248/. Access property and deeds indexes/images at www.titlesearcher.com; fee/registration required. Also, see state introduction. **Property tax/Assessor-** 865-457-5400 x225.

Bedford County

Register of Deeds, 108 Northside Sq, Shelbyville, TN 37160. 931-684-5719; fax-931-685-2086; hours: 8AM-4PM.
Records indexed on a public use terminal back to April, 1996. Only the public may search. Copy fee $.25 per page. Cert fee- $1.00 per page. Payee- Bedford County Register of Deeds. **Online access to Land, Property Assessor, Recorder, Deed records:** Assessment data on the state comptroller system is free at http://170.142.31.248/. Access property and deeds indexes/images at www.titlesearcher.com; fee/registration required. Also, see state introduction. **Other phones:** Treasurer- 931-684-4303; Appraiser/Auditor- 931-684-4303; Elections- 931-684-0531. **Property tax/Assessor-** 931-684-6390.

Benton County

Register of Deeds, 1 E. Court Sq, #105, Camden, TN 38320-2070. 731-584-6661; hours: 8AM-4PM; 8AM-5PM F.
Only the public may search. Copy fee $1.00 per page. R/E record copy- $.75 per page. Cert fee- $1.00 per cert plus copy fee. Payee- Benton County Register of Deeds. **Online access to Real Estate, Deed, Judgment, Lien, UCC, Property Assessor records:** Assessment data on the state comptroller system is free at http://170.142.31.248/. Access real estate records at www.ustitlesearch.net, registration/fee required; also see state introduction. **Property tax/Assessor-** 731-584-7615.

Bledsoe County

Register of Deeds, PO Box 385, Pikeville, TN 37367. 423-447-2020; fax-423-447-6856; hours: 8AM-4PM.
All records in one index. Records indexed on computer back to 2001. Only the public may search. Copy fee $.25 per page. Cert fee- $1.00 per page. Payee- Register of Deeds. **Online access to Land, Property Assessor, Deed, Recording records:** Assessment data on the state comptroller system is free at http://170.142.31.248/. Access property and deeds indexes/images at www.titlesearcher.com; fee/registration required. Also, see state introduction. **Other phones:** Treasurer- 423-447-2369; Appraiser/Auditor- 423-447-6548; Elections- 423-447-2776. **Property tax/Assessor-** PO Box 345, Pikeville, TN 37367; 423-447-6548.

Blount County

Register of Deeds, 349 Court St, Maryville, TN 37804-5906. 865-273-5880; fax-865-273-5890; hours: 8AM-4:30PM.
Only the public may search. Copy fee $.50 per page. Cert fee- $1.00. Payee- Blount County Register of Deeds. **Online access to Property Assessor records:** Assessment data on the state comptroller system is free at http://170.142.31.248/. **Property tax/Assessor-** 865-982-5130.

Bradley County

Register of Deeds, PO Box 579, Cleveland, TN 37364-0579. 423-728-7240, R/E recording phone-423-476-0513; fax-423-478-8888; hours: 8:30AM-4:30PM.
All records in one index. Records indexed on computer back to 12/16/98. Only the public may search. Copy fee $1.00 per page. Cert fee- $1.00 per page plus copy fee. **Online access to Land, Property Assessor, Deed, Recording records:** Assessment data on the state comptroller system is free at http://170.142.31.248/. Access property and deeds indexes/images at www.titlesearcher.com; fee/registration required. Also, see state introduction. **Property tax/Assessor-** 423-476-0505.

Campbell County

Register of Deeds, PO Box 85, Jacksboro, TN 37757. 423-562-3864, UCC recording phone-423-562-8195; fax-423-562-9833; hours: 8AM-4:30PM.

Separate indices to search. Records indexed on computer back to 1965. Only the public may search. Copy fee $1.00 per page. R/E or tax lien copy-$.25 per copy. Cert fee- $1.00 per page includes copy fee. Payee- Campbell County Register of Deeds. **Online access to Land, Deed, Property Assessor, Deed, Recording records:** Assessment data on the state comptroller system is free at http://170.142.31.248/. Access real estate records at www.ustitlesearch.net, registration/fee required, images go back to 6/2003. Also, access property and deeds indexes/images for fee at www.titlesearcher.com. **Other phones:** Treasurer- 423-562-5185; Appraiser/Auditor- 423-562-3201. **Property tax/Assessor-** 423-562-3201.

Cannon County

Register of Deeds, Courthouse, Woodbury, TN 37190. 615-563-2041; fax-615-563-5696; hours: 8AM-4PM.
Records indexed on a public use terminal back to 1999. Only the public may search. Copy fee $.50 per page. Cert fee- $1.00 per page. **Online access to Real Estate, Deed, Judgment, Lien, UCC, Property Assessor records:** Assessment data on the state comptroller system is free at http://170.142.31.248/. Access real estate records at www.ustitlesearch.net, registration/fee required; also see state introduction. **Property tax/Assessor-** 615-563-5437.

Carroll County

Register of Deeds, 625 High St, #104; Carroll County Office Complex, Huntingdon, TN 38344. 731-986-1952; fax-731-986-1955; hours: 8AM-4PM.
Separate indices to search include Warranty Deed index, Trust Deed index. Only the public may search. Copy fee $.25 per page. Cert fee- $1.50 plus copy fee. Payee- Carroll County Register of Deeds. **Online access to Real Estate, Deed, Judgment, Lien, UCC, Property Assessor records:** Assessment data on the state comptroller system is free at http://170.142.31.248/. Access real estate indexes and images at www.ustitlesearch.net. Registration/monthly fee required. Also see state introduction. **Property tax/Assessor-** 731-986-1975.

Carter County

Register of Deeds, 801 E. Elk Ave, Elizabethton, TN 37643. 423-542-1830; hours: 8:30AM-4:30PM. www.carterdeeds.com
Records indexed on computer back to 1997. Only the public may search. Copy fee $.50 per page. Cert fee- $1.00 per page plus copy fee. Payee- Carter County Register of Deeds. **Online access to Land, Property Assessor, Deed, Recording records:** Assessment data on the state comptroller system is free at http://170.142.31.248/. Access property and deeds indexes/images at www.titlesearcher.com; fee/registration required. Also, see state introduction. **Property tax/Assessor**- 423-542-1806.

Cheatham County

Register of Deeds, PO Box 453, Ashland City, TN 37015. 615-792-4317; fax-615-792-2039; hours: 8AM-4PM.
Only the public may search. Copy fee $.25 per page. Cert fee- $1.00. Payee- Register of Deeds. **Online access to Real Estate, Deed, Judgment, Lien, UCC, Property Assessor records:** Assessment data on the state comptroller system is free at http://170.142.31.248/. Access real estate indexes/images at www.ustitlesearch.net; registration/monthly fee required. Also see state introduction. **Other phones:** Treasurer- 615-792-4298. **Property tax/Assessor**- 615-792-5371.

Chester County

Register of Deeds, PO Box 292, Henderson, TN 38340. 731-989-4991; hours: 8AM-4PM.
All records in one index. Only the public may search. Copy fee $5.00 per doc if mailed. Cert fee- $1.00 per page includes copy fee. Payee- Chester County Register of Deeds. **Online access to Real Estate, Deed, Judgment, Lien, UCC, Property Assessor records:** Assessment data on the state comptroller system is free at http://170.142.31.248/. Access real estate indexes/images at www.ustitlesearch.net; registration/monthly fee required. Also see state introduction. **Other phones:** Treasurer- 731-989-3993. **Property tax/Assessor**- 159 E Main St, Henderson, TN 38340; 731-989-4882.

Claiborne County

Register of Deeds, PO Box 117, Tazewell, TN 37879. 423-626-3325; fax-423-626-5631; hours: 8:30AM-4PM.
Only the public may search. Copy fee $.25 per page. Cert fee- $4.00 per cert plus copy fee. Payee- Claiborne County Register of Deeds. **Online access to Land, Property Assessor, Deed, Recording records:** Assessment data on the state comptroller system is free at http://170.142.31.248/. Access property and deeds indexes/images at www.titlesearcher.com; fee/registration required. Also, see state introduction. **Other phones:** Treasurer- 423-626-3275. **Property tax/Assessor**- 423-626-3276.

Clay County

Register of Deeds, PO Box 430, Celina, TN 38551. 931-243-3298; fax-931-243-6723; hours: 8AM-4PM M,T,Th,F; 8AM-N Sat.
All records in one index. Records indexed on computer back to 2001. Only the public may search. Copy fee $.25 per page. Cert fee- $1.00 per page plus copy fee. Payee- Clay County Register of Deeds. **Online access to Land, Property Assessor, Deed, Recording records:** Assessment data on the state comptroller system is free at http://170.142.31.248/. Access property and deeds indexes/images at www.titlesearcher.com; fee/registration required. Also, see state introduction. **Other phones:** Treasurer- 931-243-2310. **Property tax/Assessor**- 931-243-2599.

Cocke County

Register of Deeds, 111 Court Ave, Rm 102; Courthouse, Newport, TN 37821-3102. 423-623-7540; hours: 8AM-4:30PM M,T,Th,F; 8AM-N W,Sat.

Only the public may search. Copy fee $.25 per page. Cert fee- None. Payee- Cocke County Register of Deeds. **Online access to Land, Property Assessor, Deed, Recording records:** Assessment data on the state comptroller system is free at http://170.142.31.248/. Access property and deeds indexes/images at www.titlesearcher.com; fee/registration required. Also, see state introduction. **Other phones:** ; Trustee- 423-623-3037. **Property tax/Assessor**- 423-623-7024.

Coffee County

Register of Deeds, PO Box 178, Manchester, TN 37349. 931-723-5130; fax-931-723-8232;
Separate indices to search include deeds, trust deeds and liens. Only the public may search. Copy fee $1.00 per page. R/E or tax lien copy- $.50 per page. Cert fee- $1.00 per page includes copy fee. Payee- Register of Deeds. **Online access to Land, Property Assessor, Deed, Recording records:** Assessment data on the state comptroller system is free at http://170.142.31.248/. Access property and deeds indexes/images at www.titlesearcher.com; fee/registration required. Also, see state introduction. **Property tax/Assessor**- 931-723-5126.

Crockett County

Register of Deeds, 1 S Bells St #2; County Courthouse, Alamo, TN 38001. 731-696-5455; fax-731-696-3028; hours: 8AM-4PM.
Index: Trust Deeds, Liens, Property Deeds. Records indexed on a public use terminal back to 9/2001. Only the public may search. Copy fee $.25 per page. Cert fee- $1.00 per page. Payee- Crockett County Register of Deeds. **Online access to Real Estate, Deed, Judgment, Lien, UCC, Property Assessor records:** Assessment data on the state comptroller system is free at http://170.142.31.248/. Access real estate indexes/images at www.ustitlesearch.net; registration/monthly fee required. Also see state introduction. **Other phones:** Treasurer- 731-696-5454. **Property tax/Assessor**- same address as above. 731-696-5456.

Cumberland County

Register of Deeds, 2 N. Main St, #204, Crossville, TN 38555-4583. 931-484-5559; hours: 8AM-4PM.
All records in one index. Records indexed on a public use terminal back to 1992. Only the public may search. Copy fee $1.00 per page. R/E or tax lien copy- $5.00 up to 10 pages; $.50 each add'l page. Cert fee- $2.00 1st pg, $1.00 each add'l plus copy fee. Payee- Cumberland County Register of Deeds. **Online access to Land, Property Assessor, Deed, Recording records:** Assessment data on the state comptroller system is free at http://170.142.31.248/. Access property and deeds indexes/images at www.titlesearcher.com; fee/registration required. Also, see state introduction. **Other phones:** Elections- 931-484-4919; Trustee- 931-484-5730. **Property tax/Assessor**- 2 S Main #101, Crossville, TN 38555; 931-484-5745.

Davidson County

Register of Deeds, 103 Metro Courthouse, Nashville, TN 37201-5028. 615-862-6790; fax-615-880-2039; hours: 8AM-4:30PM. www.nashville.gov/ROD/
All records in one index. Records indexed on a public use terminal. Only the public may search. Copy fee $.50 per page. Cert fee- $1.00 per page plus copy fee. Payee- Register of Deeds. **Online access to Property, Inmate, Recording, Deed, Judgment, Lien records:** Property records on the Metro Planning Commission Nashville City database are free at http://www3.nashville.org. Click on "text only search." Search county assessments free at http://hobsvtxie01.nashville.org/Default.asp?br=exp&vr=6. Also, Register of Deeds offers records access by subscription; monthly fees vary, a set-up fee is $25.00. For info, call 615-862-6790. Includes books A thru 3784. Also, a commercial online service allows subscribers to download data via an FTP site. To subscribe fill out application and send $25.00 check.

Also, search inmate info on private company website at www.vinelink.com/pickplat.jsp?stateCode=TN. **Property tax/Assessor**- 615-862-6080.

De Kalb County

Register of Deeds, One Public Sq, Rm 201, Smithville, TN 37166. 615-597-4153; fax-615-597-7420; hours: 8AM-4:30PM.
Only the public may search. Copy fee $.25 per page. Cert fee- $1.00. Payee- De Kalb County Register of Deeds. **Online access to Property Assessor records:** Assessment data on the state comptroller system is free at http://170.142.31.248/. **Other phones:** ; Trustee- 615-597-5176. **Property tax/Assessor**- 615-597-5925.

Decatur County

Register of Deeds, PO Box 488, Decaturville, TN 38329. 731-852-3712; hours: 8AM-4PM M,T,Th,F; 8AM-N W,Sat.
Records indexed on computer back to January, 1998. Only the public may search. Copy fee $1.00 per page. Cert fee- $1.00 per page. Payee- Decatur County Register of Deeds. **Online access to Land, Property Assessor, Deed, Recording records:** Assessment data on the state comptroller system is free at http://170.142.31.248/. Access property and deeds indexes/images at www.titlesearcher.com; fee/registration required. Also, see state introduction. **Other phones:** Treasurer- 731-852-3723. **Property tax/Assessor**- 731-852-3117.

Dickson County

Register of Deeds, PO Box 130, Charlotte, TN 37036. 615-789-5123; fax-615-789-3893; hours: 8AM-4PM.
All records in one index. Records indexed on computer back to 10/1996. Only the public may search. Copy fee $1.00 per page. Tax lien copy- $.25. Cert fee- $1.00. Payee- Dickson County Register of Deeds. **Online access to Real Estate, Deed, Judgment, Lien, UCC, Property Assessor records:** Assessment data on the state comptroller system is free at http://170.142.31.248/. Access real estate indexes/images at www.ustitlesearch.net, or a 2nd company at www.titlesearcher.com; registration/monthly fee required. Also see state introduction. **Other phones:** Treasurer- 615-789-7006; Elections- 615-789-6021. **Property tax/Assessor**- 615-789-7015.

Dyer County

Register of Deeds, PO Box 1360, Dyersburg, TN 38025-1360. 731-286-7806; fax-731-288-7724; hours: 8:30AM-4:30PM. www.co.dyer.tn.us
Records indexed on a public use terminal. Only the public may search. Copy fee $.50 per page. Cert fee- $1.00 per instrument plus copy fee. Payee- Dyer County Register. **Online access to Real Estate, Deed, Judgment, Lien, UCC, Property Tax records:** Assessment data on the state comptroller system is free at http://170.142.31.248/. Access real estate indexes/images at www.ustitlesearch.net; registration/monthly fee required. Also see state introduction. **Other phones:** Treasurer- 731-286-7802; Elections- 731-286-4268; Vital Records- 731-286-7814. **Property tax/Assessor**- same address as above. 731-286-7805.

Fayette County

Register of Deeds, PO Box 99, Somerville, TN 38068-0099. 901-465-5251; hours: 9AM-5PM.
Only the public may search. Copy fee $1.00 per page. Cert fee- $1.00 per cert + $1.00 per page. Payee- Fayette County Register of Deeds. **Online access to Land, Property Assessor, Deed, Recording records:** Assessment data on state comptroller system is free at http://170.142.31.248/. Access property and deeds indexes/images at www.titlesearcher.com; fee/registration required. Also, see state introduction. **Other phones:** Treasurer- 901-465-5224; Elections- 901-465-5223. **Property/Assessor**- 901-465-5226.

Fentress County

Register of Deeds, PO Box 341, Jamestown, TN 38556. 931-879-7818; fax-931-879-4502; hours: 8AM-4PM. All records in one index. Only the public may search. Copy fee $1.00 per page. R/E or tax lien copy- $.25 per page. Cert fee- $1.00 per page plus copy fee. Payee- Register of Deeds. **Online access to Land, Property Assessor, Deed, Recording records:** Assessment data on the state comptroller system is free at http://170.142.31.248/. Access property and deeds indexes/images at www.titlesearcher.com; fee/registration required. Also, see state introduction. **Other phones:** Treasurer- 931-879-7717; Appraiser/Auditor- 931-879-8294; Elections- 931-879-7162; Vital Records- 931-879-8014; County Executive- 931-879-7713. **Property tax/Assessor-** 931-879-9194.

Franklin County

Register of Deeds, 1 S Jefferson St, Rm #6; Franklin County Courthouse, Winchester, TN 37398-0101. 931-967-2840; hours: 8AM-4:30PM; 8AM-N Sat. Separate indices to search include trust and deed indexes. Only the public may search. Copy fee $1.00 per page. R/E or tax lien copy- $.50 per page. Cert fee- $1.00 per page, includes copy fee. Faxed pages $2.00 per page. Payee- Franklin County Register of Deeds. **Online access to Land, Property Assessor, Deed, Recorder records:** Assessment data on the state comptroller system is free at http://170.142.31.248/. Access property and deeds indexes/images at www.titlesearcher.com; fee/registration required. Also, see state introduction. **Other phones:** Treasurer- 931-967-2962. **Property tax/Assessor-** 931-967-3869.

Gibson County

Register of Deeds, 1 Court Sq; Courthouse, Trenton, TN 38382. 731-855-7628; fax-731-855-7650; hours: 8AM-4:30PM M-F; 8AM-N Sat. Only the public may search. Copy fee $.50 per page. **Online access to Real Estate, Deed, Judgment, Lien, UCC, Property Assessor records:** Assessment data on the state comptroller system is free at http://170.142.31.248/. Access real estate indexes/images at www.ustitlesearch.net; registration/monthly fee required. Also see state introduction. **Other phones:** Elections- 731-855-7669. **Property tax/Assessor-** 731-855-7634.

Giles County

Register of Deeds, PO Box 678, Pulaski, TN 38478. 931-363-5137; fax-931-424-4797; hours: 8AM-4PM. Separate indices to search include deeds, deeds of trust, releases, greenbelts, liens, NOC, federal liens. Only the public may search. Copy fee $1.00 per page. Cert fee- $1.00 per page included copy fee. Payee- Giles County Register of Deeds. **Online access to Land, Property Assessor, Deed, Recording records:** Assessment data on the state comptroller system is free at http://170.142.31.248/. Access property and deeds indexes/images at www.titlesearcher.com; fee/registration required. Also, see state introduction. **Other phones:** Treasurer- 931-363-1676; Appraiser/Auditor- 931-363-2166; Elections- 931-363-2424; Trustee- 931-363-1676. **Property tax/Assessor-** 931-363-2166.

Grainger County

Register of Deeds, PO Box 174, Rutledge, TN 37861. 865-828-3511; fax-865-828-4300; hours: 8:30-4:30PM. All records in one index. Records indexed on computer back to June, 2000. Only the public may search. Copy fee $1.00 per page. Cert fee- $5.00 per cert includes copy fee. Payee- Grainger County Register of Deeds. **Online access to Land, Property Assessor, Deed, Recording records:** Assessment data on the state comptroller system is free at http://170.142.31.248/. Access property and deeds indexes/images at www.titlesearcher.com; fee/registration required. Also, see state introduction. **Other phones:** Vital Records- 615-741-1763; Trustee-

865-828-3514. **Property tax/Assessor-** 865-828-5858.

Greene County

Register of Deeds, 101 S. Main St. #201; Courthouse, Greeneville, TN 37743. 423-798-1726, R/E recording phone-423-639-1726; hours: 8AM-4:30PM. Only the public may search. Copy fee $1.00 per page. Cert fee- $1.00 per page. Payee- Greene County Register of Deeds. **Online access to Land, Property Assessor, Deed, Recording records:** Assessment data on the state comptroller system is free at http://170.142.31.248/. Access property and deeds indexes/images at www.titlesearcher.com; fee/registration required. Also, see state introduction. **Other phones:** Treasurer- 423-639-1705. **Property tax/Assessor-** 423-638-1738.

Grundy County

Register of Deeds, PO Box 35, Altamont, TN 37301-0035. 931-692-3621; fax-931-692-3627; hours: 8AM-4PM M-Th, 8AM-5PM F. www.tngenweb.org/grundy/ All records in one index. Records indexed on a public use terminal back to 1/1/1990. Only the public may search. Copy fee $.25 per page. Cert fee- $1.00 per page plus copy fee. **Online access to Real Estate, Deed, Judgment, Lien, UCC, Property Assessor records:** Assessment data on the state comptroller system is free at http://170.142.31.248/. Access property and deeds indexes/images at www.titlesearcher.com; fee/registration required. Also, see state introduction. **Property tax/Assessor-** 931-692-3596.

Hamblen County

Register of Deeds, 511 W. 2nd North St, Morristown, TN 37814. 423-586-6551; fax-423-381-2505; hours: 8AM-4PM M-F. Office personnel or visitors may perform searches. Search fee $1.00 per doc + $.25 per page to mail. Will not search real estate records. UCC search per debtor name- $15.00. Copy fee $1.00 per page. R/E record copy- $1.00 per document + $.25 per page to mail. Cert fee- $1.00 per page. Payee- Register of Deeds. **Online access to Land, Property Assessor, Deed, Recording records:** Assessment data on the state comptroller system is free at http://170.142.31.248/. Access property and deeds indexes/images at www.titlesearcher.com; fee/registration required. Also, see state introduction.

Hamilton County

Register of Deeds, PO Box 1639, Chattanooga, TN 37401-1639. 423-209-6560; fax-423-209-6561; hours: 7:30AM-5PM. www.hamiltontn.gov/register Records indexed on a public use terminal back to 7/1/1969. Only the public may search. Copy fee $.50 per page. Cert fee- $1.00 per page. Payee- Hamilton County Register of Deeds. **Online access to Real Estate, Recording, Deed, Property Assessor, Delinquent Tax records:** The County Register of Deeds subscription service is $50 per month and $1.00 per fax page. Search by name, address, or book & page. For info, call 423-209-6560; or visit www.hamiltontn.gov/Register/default.htm. Credit cards accepted. Also, property assessor and register of deeds records are free at www.hamiltontn.gov/DataServices/default.htm. Click on "Assessor of Property Inquiry." Also, search here for court records. Also back tax lists are at www.hamiltontn.gov/Trustee/delinquent%20taxes.htm. Also, search City of Chattanooga property tax database at http://propertytax.chattanooga.gov. **Other phones:** Treasurer- 423-209-7270. **Property tax/Assessor-** 423-209-7300.

Hancock County

Register of Deeds, PO Box 347, Sneedville, TN 37869. 423-733-4545; 8:30AM-4PM; 8:30AM-N W,Sat. Index: Deeds are in a general index; other documents are indexed in the front of each book. Records indexed on computer back to 1/21/2003.

Only the public may search. Copy fee $.25 per page. Cert fee- $5.00 per doc plus copy fee. Payee- Hancock County Register of Deeds. **Online access to Real Estate, Deed, Judgment, Lien, UCC, Property Assessor records:** Assessment data on the state comptroller system is free at http://170.142.31.248/. Access real estate indexes/images at www.ustitlesearch.net; registration/monthly fee required. Also see state introduction. **Other phones:** Treasurer- 423-733-2939; Elections- 423-733-4549; Clerk & Master- 423-733-4524. **Property tax/Assessor-** 423-733-2332.

Hardeman County

Register of Deeds, Courthouse, 100 N Main St., Bolivar, TN 38008. 731-658-3476; fax-731-658-3075; hours: 8:30AM-4:30PM; 8:30AM-5PM F. Separate indices to search include Deeds, Trust deeds, Liens, Military Discharges. Records indexed on a public use terminal back to 1997. Only the public may search. Copy fee $1.00 per page. R/E or tax lien copy- $.50 per page. Cert fee- $1.00 per page. Payee- Hardeman County Register of Deeds. **Online access to Real Estate, Deed, Judgment, Lien, UCC, Property Assessor records:** Assessment data on the state comptroller system is free at http://170.142.31.248/. Access real estate indexes/images at www.ustitlesearch.net; registration/monthly fee required. Also see state introduction. **Other phones:** Treasurer- 731-658-5541; Appraiser/Auditor- 731-658-6522; Elections- 731-658-4751. **Property tax/Assessor-** 731-658-6522.

Hardin County

Register of Deeds, Courthouse, Savannah, TN 38372. 731-925-4936; hours: 8AM-4:30PM M,T,Th,F; 8AM-N W. Only the public may search. Copy fee $1.00 per page. Tax lien copy- $.25 per page. Cert fee- $1.00 per cert plus copy fee. Payee- Hardin County Register of Deeds. **Online access to Real Estate, Deed, Judgment, Lien, UCC, Property Assessor records:** Assessment data on the state comptroller system is free at http://170.142.31.248/. Access real estate indexes/images at www.ustitlesearch.net; registration/monthly fee required. Also see state introduction. **Other phones:** Treasurer- 731-925-8180. **Property tax/Assessor-** 731-925-9031.

Hawkins County

Register of Deeds, PO Box 235, Rogersville, TN 37857. 423-272-8304; fax-423-921-3170; hours: 8AM-4PM; W & Sat 8AM-N. All records in one index. Only the public may search. Copy fee $1.00 per page. Cert fee- $1.00 per page includes copy. Payee- Register of Deeds. **Online access to Land, Property Assessor, Deed, Recording records:** Assessment data on the state comptroller system is free at http://170.142.31.248/. Access property and deeds indexes/images at www.titlesearcher.com; fee/registration required. Also, see state introduction. **Other phones:** Treasurer- 423-272-7022 Trustee; Elections- 423-272-8061. **Property tax/Assessor-** 110 E Main St, Rm 201, Rogersville, TN 37857; 423-272-8505.

Haywood County

Register of Deeds, 1 N. Washington; Courthouse, Brownsville, TN 38012. 731-772-1432; hours: 8:30AM-5PM. Only the public may search. Copy fee $1.00 per page. Tax lien copy- $.25 per page. Payee- Haywood County Register of Deeds. **Online access to Property Assessor, Real Estate records:** Assessment data on the state comptroller system is free at http://170.142.31.248/. Access real estate indexes/images at www.ustitlesearch.net; registration/monthly fee required. Also see state introduction. **Other phones:** Treasurer- 731-772-1722. **Property tax/Assessor-** 731-772-0432.

Henderson County

Register of Deeds, 17 Monroe Ave #5, Lexington, TN 38351. 731-968-2941; hours: 8AM-4:30PM.
Separate indices to search include direct, reverse index books, trust book, deed book and misc book. Only the public may search. Copy fee $.25 per copy. Cert fee- $1.00 per page plus copy fee. Payee- Henderson County Register of Deeds. **Online access to Real Estate, Deed, Judgment, Lien, UCC, Property Assessor records:** Assessment data on the state comptroller system is free at http://170.142.31.248/. Access real estate indexes/images at www.ustitlesearch.net; registration/monthly fee required. Also see state introduction. **Other phones:** Treasurer- 731-968-2246. **Property tax/Assessor-** 731-968-6881.

Henry County

Register of Deeds, PO Box 44, Paris, TN 38242. 731-642-4081; fax-731-642-2123; 8:30AM-4:30PM.
Index: Pre-1991 records in separate indices. Records indexed on a public use terminal back to 7/1999. Only the public may search. Copy fee $.50 per page. Cert fee- $1.00 per page plus copy fee. **Online access to Real Estate, Deed, Judgment, Lien, UCC, Property Assessor records:** Assessment data on the state comptroller system is free at http://170.142.31.248/. Access real estate indexes/images at www.ustitlesearch.net; registration/monthly fee required. Also see state introduction. **Other phones:** Elections- 731-642-0411; Trustee- 731-642-6633. **Property tax/Assessor-** 731-642-0162.

Hickman County

Register of Deeds, #1 Courthouse, Centerville, TN 37033-1639. 931-729-4882; fax-931-729-6113; hours: 7:30AM-4PM.
Office will perform a UCC search but public must search other records themselves. UCC search per debtor name- $15.00. Copy fee $1.00 per page. Cert fee- $1.00 per page. Payee- Hickman County Register of Deeds. **Online access to Land, Property Assessor, Deed, Recording records:** Assessment data on the state comptroller system is free at http://170.142.31.248/. Access property and deeds indexes/images at www.titlesearcher.com; fee/registration required. Also, see state introduction. **Property tax/Assessor-** 931-729-2169.

Houston County

Register of Deeds, PO Box 388, Erin, TN 37061. 931-289-3141; fax-931-289-4240;
Record index not computerized. Only the public may search. **Online access to Real Estate, Deed, Judgment, Lien, UCC, Property Assessor records:** Assessment data on the state comptroller system is free at http://170.142.31.248/. Access real estate indexes/images at www.ustitlesearch.net; registration/monthly fee required. Also see state introduction. **Other phones:** Vital Records- 615-726-2559. **Property tax/Assessor-** 931-289-3929.

Humphreys County

Register of Deeds, 102 Thompson St; Courthouse Annex, Rm 3, Waverly, TN 37185. 931-296-7681; hours: 8AM-4:30PM.
Separate indices to search include warranty deed, trust deeds, UCC, liens, releases. Only the public may search. Copy fee $.50 per page; $.25 self serve; $1.00 if mailed. Cert fee- $1.00 per page. Payee- Humphreys County Register of Deeds. **Online access to Land, Property Assessor, Deed, Recording records:** Assessment data on the state comptroller system is free at http://170.142.31.248/. Access property and deeds indexes/images at www.titlesearcher.com; fee/registration required. Also, see state introduction. **Other phones:** Treasurer- 931-296-2414. **Property tax/Assessor-** 931-296-2919.

Jackson County

Register of Deeds, PO Box 301, Gainesboro, TN 38562. 931-268-9012; hours: 8AM-4PM M,T,Th,F; 8AM-2PM W; 8AM-N Sat.
Records indexed on a public use terminal back to 9/26/2000. Only the public may search. Copy fee $1.00 per page. R/E or tax lien copy- $.25 per page. Cert fee- $1.00 per doc includes copy fee. Payee- Jackson County Register of Deeds. **Online access to Land, Property Assessor, Deed, Recording records:** Assessment data on the state comptroller system is free at http://170.142.31.248/. Access property and deeds indexes/images at www.titlesearcher.com; fee/registration required. Also, see state introduction. **Other phones:** Treasurer- 931-268-9417; Elections- 931-268-9284. **Property/Assessor-** 931-268-0246.

Jefferson County

Register of Deeds, PO Box 58, Dandridge, TN 37725. 865-397-2918; hours: 8AM-4PM.
Records indexed on a public use terminal from 9/1/1998 to present. Only the public may search. Copy fee $1.00 per page. Cert fee- $1.00 per page. Payee- Jefferson County Register of Deeds. **Online access to Land, Property Assessor, Deed, Recording records:** Assessment data on the state comptroller system is free at http://170.142.31.248/. Access property and deeds indexes/images at www.titlesearcher.com; fee/registration required. Also, see state introduction. **Other phones:** Treasurer- 865-397-2101. **Property tax/Assessor-** 865-397-3326.

Johnson County

Register of Deeds, 222 W Main St, Mountain City, TN 37683. 423-727-7841; fax-423-727-7047; hours: 8:30AM-5PM.
Records indexed on a public use terminal back to 2003. Only the public may search. Copy fee $1.00 per page. Cert fee- $1.00 per cert includes copy fee. Payee- Register of Deeds. **Online to Land, Property Assessor, Deed, Recording records:** Assessment data is free at http://170.142.31.248/. Property and deeds indexes/images at www.titlesearcher.com; fee/registration required. Also, see state introduction. **Other phones:** Treasurer- 423-727-9062; Elections- 423-727-8592. **Property tax/Assessor-** 423-727-7692.

Knox County

Register of Deeds, 400 W. Main Ave; Rm 225, Knoxville, TN 37902. 865-215-2330; fax-865-215-2332; hours: 8AM-4:30PM. www.knoxcounty.org/register/
Only the public may search. Will not search tax liens. Copy fee $1.00 per page. R/E or tax lien copy- $.50 per page. Cert fee- $1.00 per page. Payee- Knox County Register of Deeds. **Online access to Real Estate, Assessor, Property Tax records:** Search the property tax rolls for free at www.knoxcounty.org/trustee/taxsearch-site.php. Also, the GIS Dept offers a property map and details report at www.kgis.org/PropertyMapByAddress.asp. Address searching only. **Other phones:** Treasurer- 865-521-2305. **Property tax/Assessor-** 865-521-2360.

Lake County

Register of Deeds, 229 Church St, Box 5; Courthouse, Tiptonville, TN 38079. 731-253-7462; fax-731-253-9815; hours: 8AM-4PM.
Separate indices to search include deed index and mortgage index. Records indexed on a public use terminal back to 3/2001. Only the public may search. Copy fee $.50 per page. Cert fee- $1.00 per page include copy fee. Payee- Register of Deeds. **Online access to Real Estate, Deed, Judgment, Lien, UCC, Property Assessor records:** Assessment data on the state comptroller system is free at http://170.142.31.248/. Access real estate indexes/images at www.ustitlesearch.net; registration/monthly fee required. Also see state introduction. **Other phones:** ; Trustee- 731-253-7502. **Property tax/Assessor-** 229 Church St, Box 10, Tiptonville, TN 38079; 731-253-7200.

Lauderdale County

Register of Deeds, Courthouse, Ripley, TN 38063. 731-635-2171; fax-731-635-9682; hours: 8AM-4:30PM.
Records indexed on computer back to May, 1989. Only the public may search. Copy fee $.25 per page; $1.00 to fax back. Cert fee- $1.00 per page plus copy fee. **Online access to Real Estate, Deed, Judgment, Lien, UCC, Property Assessor records:** Assessment data on the state comptroller system is free at http://170.142.31.248/. Access real estate indexes/images at www.ustitlesearch.net; registration/monthly fee required. Also see state introduction. **Other phones:** Treasurer- 731-635-0712; Elections- 615-741-7956. **Property tax/Assessor-** 731-635-9561.

Lawrence County

Register of Deeds, 240 W. Gaines St; N.B.U. #18, Lawrenceburg, TN 38464. 931-766-4100; fax-931-766-5602; hours: 8AM-4:30PM. www.co.lawrence.tn.us/
Separate indices to search include trust indexes, warranty indexes and lien indexes. Records indexed on a public use terminal back to 1999. Office will perform a UCC search but public must search other records themselves. Copy fee $.25 per page. Cert fee- $1.00 per page includes copy fee. Payee- Teresa Dunkin, Register of Deeds. **Online access to Land, Property Assessor, Deed, Recording records:** Assessment data on the state comptroller system is free at http://170.142.31.248/. Access property and deeds indexes/images at www.titlesearcher.com; fee/registration required; Also see state introduction. **Other phones:** Treasurer- 931-766-4110; Appraiser/Auditor- 931-766-4104; Elections- 931-766-4130; Vital Records- 615-741-1763. **Property tax/Assessor-** 931-766-4104.

Lewis County

Register of Deeds, 110 N Park Ave; Courthouse, Rm 104, Hohenwald, TN 38462. 931-796-2255; hours: 8AM-4:30PM.
All records in one index. Records indexed on a public use terminal back to 7/1/2000. Only the public may search. Copy fee $1.00 per page. R/E or tax lien copy- $.25 per page. Cert fee- $1.00 per doc plus copy fee. Payee- Lewis County Register of Deeds. **Online access to Real Estate, Deed, Judgment, Lien, UCC, Property Assessor records:** Assessment data on the state comptroller system is free at http://170.142.31.248/. Access real estate indexes/images at www.ustitlesearch.net; registration/monthly fee required. Also see state introduction. **Other phones:** Treasurer- 931-796-2226; Elections- 931-796-3662. **Property tax/Assessor-** same address as above. 931-796-5848.

Lincoln County

Register of Deeds, 112 Main Ave S, Rm 104, Fayetteville, TN 37334. 931-433-5366; fax-931-433-9312; hours: 8AM-4PM.
All records in one index. Records indexed on a public use terminal back to 3/1999. Only the public may search. Copy fee $.25 per page. Cert fee- $1.00 per sheet. Payee- Lincoln County Register of Deeds. **Online to Land, Property Assessor, Deed, Recording records:** Assessment data is free at http://170.142.31.248/. Access property and deeds indexes/images at www.titlesearcher.com; fee/registration required. Also, see state introduction. **Other phones:** Treasurer- 931-433-1371; Elections- 931-433-6220. **Property tax/Assessor-** 931-433-5409.

Loudon County

Register of Deeds, PO Box 395, Loudon, TN 37774. 865-458-2605; fax-865-458-9028; 8AM-4:30PM.
All records in one index. Records indexed on a public use terminal back to 10/1997. Only the public may search. Copy fee $.25 per page. Cert fee- $1.00 per page includes copy fee. Payee- Loudon County Register of Deeds. **Online to Land, Property Assessor, Deed, Recording records:**

Assessment data is free at http://170.142.31.248/. Access property and deeds indexes/images at www.titlesearcher.com; fee/registration required. Also, see state introduction. **Other phones:** Treasurer- 865-458-3103; Elections- 865-458-2560. **Property tax/Assessor-** 865-458-2050.

Macon County

Register of Deeds, Courthouse; Rm 102, Public Sq, Lafayette, TN 37083. 615-666-2353; fax-615-666-2691; 8AM-Noon-1PM-4:30PM (til 4PM TH). www.maconcountytn.com/register_of_deeds.htm
Separate indices to search include direct, reverse, mortgage, debtor, charter, lien, POA, release, misc indexes, discharge records, bonds, subdivision, financing statements. Only the public may search. Copy fee $.25 per page. Cert fee- $1.00 per page plus copy fee. Payee- Macon County Register of Deeds. **Online access to Land, Property Assessor, Deed, Recording records:** Access to records must go through Business Information Systems (BIS) at 866-604-3673 who maintain their records. Assessment data on the state comptroller system is free at http://170.142.31.248/. Access property and deeds indexes/images at www.titlesearcher.com; fee/registration required. Also, see state introduction. **Other phones:** Elections- 615-666-2199; Trustee- 615-666-3624. **Property/Assessor-** Courthouse, Rm 103, Public Sq, Lafayette, TN 37083. 615-666-3688.

Madison County

Register of Deeds, 100 Main St; Courthouse, Rm 109, Jackson, TN 38301. 731-423-6028; fax-731-422-1171; Records indexed on a public use terminal back to 1985. Only the public may search. Copy fee $1.00 per page if mailed. Cert fee- $1.00 per page. Payee- Register of Deeds. **Online access to Land, Property Assessor, Deed, Recording records:** Assessment data on the state comptroller system is free at http://170.142.31.248/. Access property and deeds indexes/images at www.titlesearcher.com; fee/registration required. Also, see state introduction. **Other phones:** Treasurer- 731-423-6027. **Property tax/Assessor-** 731-423-6100.

Marion County

Register of Deeds, PO Box 789, Jasper, TN 37347. 423-942-2573; hours: 8AM-4PM M-F.
All records in one index. Only the public may search. Copy fee $.50 per page. Cert fee- $1.00 per page, plus copy fee. Payee- Marion County Register of Deeds. **Online access to Land, Property Assessor, Deed, Recording records:** Assessment data on the state comptroller system is free at http://170.142.31.248/. Access property and deeds indexes/images at www.titlesearcher.com; fee/registration required. Also, see state introduction. **Other phones:** Trustee- 423-942-2681. **Property tax/Assessor-** 423-942-3494.

Marshall County

Register of Deeds, 1103 Courthouse Annex, Lewisburg, TN 37091. 931-359-4933; fax-931-359-0559; hours: 8AM-4PM.
All records in one index. Records indexed on a public use terminal back to 1993. Only the public may search. Copy fee $1.00 per page. Cert fee- $1.00 per page includes copy fee. Payee- Marshall County Register of Deeds. **Online access to Real Estate, Deed, Judgment, Lien, UCC, Property Assessor records:** Assessment data on the state comptroller system is free at http://170.142.31.248/. Access real estate indexes/images at www.ustitlesearch.net or a 2nd private company at www.titlesearcher.com; registration/monthly fee required. Also see state introduction. **Property tax/Assessor-** 3330 Courthouse Annex, Lewisburg, TN 37091; 931-359-3238.

Maury County

Register of Deeds, PO Box 769, Columbia, TN 38402-0769. 931-381-3690 x358; fax-931-375-2119; hours: 8AM-4PM.

Separate indices to search include liens, notices of completion, greenbelts, charters. Records indexed on a public use terminal back to 8/11/1998. Only the public may search. Copy fee $.50 per page. Cert fee- $1.00 per cert includes copy fee. Payee- Maury County Register of Deeds. **Online access to Land, Property Assessor, Deed, Recording, Sexual Offender Registry records:** Assessment data on the state comptroller system is free at http://170.142.31.248/. Access property and deeds indexes/images at www.titlesearcher.com; fee/registration required. Also, see state introduction. Also, Sexual offender registry found at www.ticic.state.tn.us/SEX_ofndr/search_short.asp.
Other phones: Elections- 931-381-4691. **Property tax/Assessor-** 931-381-3690 x253.

McMinn County

Register of Deeds, PO Box 1074, Athens, TN 37371-1074. 423-745-1232; fax-423-745-0095; 8:30-4 M-F.
Office will perform a UCC search but public must search other records themselves. UCC search per debtor name- $15.00. Copy fee $.25 per page. Cert fee- $1.00 per page. Payee- Register of Deeds. **Online access to Real Estate, Deed, Judgment, Lien, UCC, Property Assessor records:** Assessment data on the state comptroller system is free at http://170.142.31.248/. Access real estate indexes/images back to 9/1999 at www.ustitlesearch.net; registration/monthly fee required. Also see state introduction. **Other phones:** Treasurer- 423-745-4103; Elections- 423-745-0843; Trustee- 423-745-1291; Circuit Court Clerk -423-745-1923. **Property tax/Assessor-** 423-745-2743.

McNairy County

Register of Deeds, PO Box 158, Selmer, TN 38375. 731-645-3656; fax-731-645-3656; hours: 8AM-4:30PM M,T,Th,F; 8AM-N Sat.
Office personnel or visitors may perform searches. Search fee $25.00 per name. UCC search per debtor name- $12.00. Cert fee- $2.00 per doc plus copy fee. Payee- McNairy County Register of Deeds. **Online access to Real Estate, Deed, Judgment, Lien, UCC, Property Assessor records:** Assessment data on the state comptroller system is free at http://170.142.31.248/. Access real estate indexes/images at www.ustitlesearch.net; registration/monthly fee required. Also see state introduction. **Other phones:** Vital Records- 731-645-3511. **Property tax/Assessor-** 731-645-5146.

Meigs County

Register of Deeds, PO Box 245, Decatur, TN 37322. 423-334-5228; fax-423-334-5228; hours: 8AM-5PM M,T,Th,F; 8AM-N Sat.
Only the public may search. Cert fee- $2.00 per page. Payee- Meigs County Register of Deeds. **Online access to Property Assessor, Real Estate records:** Assessment data on the state comptroller system is free at http://170.142.31.248/. Access real estate indexes/images at www.ustitlesearch.net; registration/monthly fee required. Also see state introduction. **Other phones:** ; Trustee- 423-334-5119. **Property tax/Assessor-** 423-334-5231.

Monroe County

Register of Deeds, 103 College St - #4, Madisonville, TN 37354. 423-442-2440; hours: 8:30AM-4:30PM M,T,Th,F; 8:30AM-N W & Sat.
Index: Prior to 1998, separate indices to search include grantor and grantee. Records indexed on a public use terminal back to 1/1998. Office will perform a pre-1998 UCC search but public must search other records themselves. Copy fee $1.00 per page. Tax lien copy- $.50 per page. Cert fee- $1.00 per page. Payee- Monroe County Register of Deeds. **Online access to Land, Property Assessor, Deed, Recording records:** Assessment data on the state comptroller system is free at http://170.142.31.248/. Access property and deeds indexes/images at www.titlesearcher.com; fee/registration required. Also, see state introduction.

Other phones: Treasurer- 423-442-2920; Appraiser/Auditor- 423-442-3637; Elections- 423-442-2461. **Property tax/Assessor-** 103 College St, Madisonville, TN 37354; 423-442-3637.

Montgomery County

Register of Deeds, PO Box 1124, Clarksville, TN 37041. 931-648-5713; fax-931-553-5157; hours: 8AM-4:30PM.
Only the public may search. Copy fee $.25 per page. Cert fee- $1.00. Payee- Register of Deeds. **Online access to Real Estate, Deed, Judgment, Lien, UCC, Property Assessor records:** Assessment data on the state comptroller system is free at http://170.142.31.248/. Access real estate indexes/images at www.ustitlesearch.net; registration/monthly fee required. Also see state introduction. **Other phones:** ; Trustee- 931-648-5710. **Property tax/Assessor-** 931-648-5709.

Moore County

Register of Deeds, PO Box 206, Lynchburg, TN 37352. 931-759-7913; fax-931-759-6394; hours: 8AM-4:30PM; Closed Th; 8AM-N Sat.
Records indexed on a public use terminal back to 2002. Only the public may search. Copy fee $1.00 per page. R/E record copy- $.50 per page. Cert fee- $1.00 per cert plus copy fee. Payee- Moore County Register of Deeds. **Online access to Property Assessor, Real Estate records:** Assessment data on the state comptroller system is free at http://170.142.31.248/. Access property and deeds indexes/images at www.titlesearcher.com; fee/registration required. Also, see state introduction. **Property tax/Assessor-** 931-759-7044.

Morgan County

Register of Deeds, PO Box 311, Wartburg, TN 37887. 423-346-3105; hours: 8AM-4PM.
All records in one index. Records indexed on a public use terminal back to 7/2003. Only the public may search. Copy fee $.50 per page. $1.00 per page for fax. Cert fee- $1.00 per page includes copy fee. Payee- Morgan County Register of Deeds. **Online access to Real Estate, Deed, Judgment, Lien, UCC, Property Assessor records:** Assessment data on the state comptroller system is free at http://170.142.31.248/. Access real estate indexes/images at www.ustitlesearch.net; registration/monthly fee required. Also see state introduction. **Other phones:** Appraiser/Auditor- 423-346-3130. **Property tax/Assessor-** 423-346-3130.

Obion County

Register of Deeds, PO Box 514, Union City, TN 38261. 731-885-9351; fax-731-885-7515; 8:AM-4:30PM.
Separate indices to search include warranty deed, trust deed, Lien, and Misc. index. Only the public may search. Copy fee $.50 per page. Cert fee- $1.00 per page. Payee- Register of Deeds. **Online access to Property Assessor records:** Assessment data on the state comptroller system is free at http://170.142.31.248/. **Other phones:** Elections- 731-885-1901. **Property tax/Assessor-** 731-885-2931.

Overton County

Register of Deeds, 317 E. University St, Rm 150, Livingston, TN 38570. 931-823-4011; hours: 8AM-4:30PM.
All records in one index. Record index not computerized. Only the public may search. Copy fee $1.00 per page. R/E or tax lien copy- $.25 per page. Cert fee- $1.00 per page plus copy fee. Payee- Overton County Register of Deeds. **Online access to Property Assessor, Real Estate records:** Assessment data on the state comptroller system is free at http://170.142.31.248/. Access real estate indexes/images at www.ustitlesearch.net; registration/monthly fee required. Also see state introduction. **Other phones:** Treasurer- 931-832-6220; Elections- 931-823-5985; Tax Assessor- 931-823-1651. **Property tax/Assessor-** same address as above.

Perry County

Register of Deeds, PO Box 62, Linden, TN 37096-0062. 931-589-2210; fax-931-589-2215; 8AM-4PM.
All records in one index. Records indexed on a public use terminal back to 8/2000. Only the public may search. Copy fee $1.00 per page. Tax lien copy- $.25 per page. Cert fee- $5.00 per doc plus copy fee. Payee- Perry County Register of Deeds. **Online access to Land, Property Assessor, Deed, Recording records:** Assessment data on the state comptroller system is free at http://170.142.31.248/. Access property and deeds indexes/images at www.titlesearcher.com; fee/registration required. Also, see state introduction. **Other phones:** Treasurer- 931-589-2313. **Property tax/Assessor-** 931-589-2277.

Pickett County

Register of Deeds, PO Box 5, Byrdstown, TN 38549. 931-864-3316; fax-931-864-6615; hours: 8-11AM, Noon-4PM.
Only the public may search. Copy fee $.25 per page. Cert fee- $3.00. Payee- Register of Deeds. **Online access to Property Assessor records:** Assessment data on the state comptroller system is free at http://170.142.31.248/. **Property tax/Assessor-** 931-864-3114.

Polk County

Register of Deeds, PO Box 293, Benton, TN 37307. 423-338-4537; hours: 8:30AM-4:30PM.
Separate indices to search include grantor/grantee. Will not search real estate records. Will not search UCC records or tax liens. Copy fee $1.00 per page. Cert fee- $1.00 per page. Payee- Polk County Register of Deeds. **Online access to Land, Property Assessor, Deed, Recording records:** Assessment data on the state comptroller system is free at http://170.142.31.248/. Access property and deeds indexes/images at www.titlesearcher.com; fee/registration required. Also, see state introduction. **Other phones:** ; Trustee- 423-338-4545. **Property tax/Assessor-** 423-338-4505.

Putnam County

Register of Deeds, PO Box 487, Cookeville, TN 38503-0487. 931-526-7101; hours: 8AM-4PM.
Office will perform a UCC search but public must search other records themselves. UCC search per debtor name- $15.00. Copy fee $1.00 per page. Tax lien copy- $.25 per page. Cert fee- $1.00 per page. Payee- Putnam County Register of Deeds. **Online access to Real Estate, Deed, Judgment, Lien, UCC, Property Assessor records:** Assessment data on the state comptroller system is free at http://170.142.31.248/. Access real estate indexes/images at www.ustitlesearch.net; registration/monthly fee required. Also see state introduction. **Other phones:** Treasurer- 931-528-8845. **Property tax/Assessor-** 931-528-8428.

Rhea County

Register of Deeds, 375 Church St #106, Dayton, TN 37321. 423-775-7841; hours: 8AM-4:30PM.
Only the public may search. Copy fee $.25 per page. Cert fee- $1.00 per page plus copy fee. Payee- Rhea County Register of Deeds. **Online access to Land, Property Assessor records:** Assessment data on the state comptroller system is free at http://170.142.31.248/. Access property and deeds indexes/images at www.titlesearcher.com; fee/registration required. Images go back to 5/28/03. Also, see state introduction. **Other phones:** Treasurer- 423-775-7810; County Clerk- 423-775-7808. **Property tax/Assessor-** 375 Church St #100, Dayton, TN 37321; 423-775-7840.

Roane County

Register of Deeds, PO Box 181, Kingston, TN 37763. 865-376-4673; hours: 8:30AM-6PM M; 8:30AM-4:30PM T-F.

Index: Pre-1999 records in 2 indices- warranty deeds and trust deeds/miscellaneous. Records indexed on computer back to 10/1999. Only the public may search. Copy fee $1.00 per page. Cert fee- $1.00 per page includes copy fee. Payee- Roane County Register of Deeds. **Online access to Land, Property Assessor, Deed, Recording records:** Assessment data on the state comptroller system is free at http://170.142.31.248/. Access property and deeds indexes/images at www.titlesearcher.com; fee/registration required, images go back to 6/5/03. Also, see state introduction. **Other phones:** ; Trustee- 865-376-4938. **Assessor-** 865-376-4362.

Robertson County

Register of Deeds, 525 S. Brown St., Springfield, TN 37172. 615-384-3772; hours: 8AM-4:30PM.
Records indexed on a public use terminal back to 1998. Only the public may search. Cert fee- $1.00 per page plus copy fee. Payee- Robertson County Register of Deeds. **Online access to Real Estate, Deed, Judgment, Lien, UCC, Property Assessor records:** Assessment data on the state comptroller system is free at http://170.142.31.248/. Access real estate indexes/images at www.ustitlesearch.net; registration/monthly fee required. Also see state introduction. **Other phones:** Elections- 615-384-5592. **Property tax/Assessor-** 615-384-4311.

Rutherford County

Register of Deeds, PO Box 5050, Murfreesboro, TN 37133-5050. 615-898-7870; fax-615-898-7987; hours: 8AM-4PM.
Only the public may search. Copy fee $.50 per page. Cert fee- $1.00. Payee- Rutherford County Register of Deeds. **Online access to Real Estate, Deed, Judgment, Lien, UCC, Property Assessor records:** Assessment data on the state comptroller system is free at http://170.142.31.248/. Access real estate indexes/images at www.ustitlesearch.net; registration/monthly fee required. Also see state introduction. **Property tax/Assessor-** 615-898-7750.

Scott County

Register of Deeds, PO Box 61, Huntsville, TN 37756. 423-663-2417; fax-423-663-8281; 8AM-4:30PM.
Separate indices to search include direct index book alpha and a reverse index. Only the public may search. Copy fee $.50 per page; $1.00 per page if UCC. Cert fee- $1.00 per page plus copy fee. Payee- Scott County Register of Deeds. **Online access to Property Assessor records:** Assessment data on the state comptroller system is free at http://170.142.31.248/. **Other phones:** Treasurer- 423-663-2598. **Property tax/Assessor-** 423-663-2420.

Sequatchie County

Register of Deeds, PO Box 174, Dunlap, TN 37327. 423-949-2512; fax-423-949-6554; hours: 8AM-5PM.
All records in one index. Records indexed on a public use terminal back to 7/10/01. Only the public may search. Copy fee $.25 per page; fax back $1.00 per page. Cert fee- $1.00 per page plus copy fee. Payee- Sequatchie County Register of Deeds. **Online access to Land, Property Assessor, Deed, Recording records:** Assessment data on the state comptroller system is free at http://170.142.31.248/. Access property and deeds indexes/images at www.titlesearcher.com; fee/registration required. Also, see state introduction. **Property tax/Assessor-** 423-949-3534.

Sevier County

Register of Deeds, 125 Court Ave; Courthouse #209W, Sevierville, TN 37862. 865-453-2758; hours: 8AM-4:30PM M-Th; 8AM-6PM F.
Only the public may search. General copy fee $1.00; tax lien $.20 per page. R/E record copy- $1.00 up to 4 pages. Cert fee- $1.00 per page. Payee- Sevier County Register of Deeds. **Online access to Land, Property Assessor, Deed, Recording records:** Assessment data on the state comptroller system is free at http://170.142.31.248/. Access property

and deeds indexes/images at www.titlesearcher.com; fee/registration required. Also, see state introduction. **Other phones:** Appraiser/Auditor- 865-453-3242; Elections- 865-453-6985; Trustee- 865-453-2767. **Property tax/Assessor-** 865-453-3242.

Shelby County

Register of Deeds, 160 N. Main St, Rm 519, Memphis, TN 38103. 901-545-4366; fax-901-545-3837; hours: 8AM-4:30PM. http://register.shelby.tn.us
All records in one index. Records indexed on a public use terminal full from 12/01 to present, partial back to 1986. Only the public may search. Copy fee $.10 per page. Plat copies-$1.50 per page. Cert fee- $1.00 per doc includes copy fee. Payee- Shelby County Retister. **Online access to Real Estate, Lien, Recording, Judgment, Lien, Property Assessor records:** Access the register of deeds database free at http://register.shelby.tn.us/menu.php. Partial indexes and images go back to 1986; full to 12/2001. Also, access property assessor data free at www.assessor.shelby.tn.us/content.aspx. Also, access property and deeds indexes/images at www.titlesearcher.com; fee/registration required. Also see state introduction. **Other phones:** ; Tax Assessor- 901-379-7333. **Property tax/Assessor-** 1075 Mullins Station Rd, Memphis, TN 38134; not known.

Smith County

Register of Deeds, 122 Turner High Circle, #113, Carthage, TN 37030. 615-735-1760; fax-615-735-8263; hours: 8AM-4PM.
Separate indices to search include before 6/28/99 they have different index books. Records indexed on a public use terminal back to 6/28/1999. Only the public may search. Copy fee $.25 per page. Cert fee- $1.00 plus $2.00 processing includes copy fee. Payee- Smith County Register of Deeds. **Online access to Land, Property Assessor, Deed, Recording records:** Assessment data on the state comptroller system is free at http://170.142.31.248/. Access property and deeds indexes/images at www.titlesearcher.com; fee/registration required. Also, see state introduction. **Property tax/Assessor-** 615-735-1750.

Stewart County

Register of Deeds, PO Box 57, Dover, TN 37058. 931-232-5990; fax-931-232-5990; hours: 8AM-4:30PM.
All records in one index from 2001 forward. Records indexed on computer since 2001. Only the public may search. Copy fee $.25 per page. Cert fee- $1.00 per page. Payee- Stewart County Register of Deeds. **Online access to Real Estate, Deed, Judgment, Lien, UCC, Property Assessor records:** Assessment data on the state comptroller system is free at http://170.142.31.248/. Access real estate indexes/images at www.ustitlesearch.net; registration/monthly fee required. Also see state introduction. **Other phones:** ; Trustee- 931-232-7026. **Property tax/Assessor-** 931-232-5252.

Sullivan County (Blountville Office)

Register of Deeds, 3411 Hwy 126, #101, Blountville, TN 37617. 423-323-6420; fax-423-279-2771; hours: 8AM-5PM.
Only the public may search. Copy fee $2.00 per page. Cert fee- $1.00. Payee- Sullivan County Register of Deeds. **Online access to Property Assessor records:** Assessment data on the state comptroller system is free at http://170.142.31.248/. **Other phones:** Appraiser/Auditor- 423-323-6455; Elections- 423-323-6444; Vital Records- 423-279-2777; Trustee- 423-323-6464. **Property tax/Assessor-** 423-323-6455.

Sullivan County (Bristol Office)

Register of Deeds, 801 Anderson St Rm 102, Bristol, TN 37620. 423-989-4370; hours: 8AM-5PM.
All records in one index. Only the public may search. Copy fee $2.00, if tax lien or real estate

$1.00 per page. Cert fee- $1.00 per page plus copy fee. Payee- Sullivan County Register of Deeds. **Online access to Property Assessor records:** Assessment data on the state comptroller system is free at http://170.142.31.248/. **Other phones:** Treasurer- 423-323-6464; Appraiser/Auditor- 423-323-6455; Elections- 423-323-6444; Vital Records- 423-279-2777. **Property tax/Assessor-** 3411 Hwy 126, Blountville, TN 37617; 423-323-6455.

Sumner County

Register of Deeds, PO Box 299, Gallatin, TN 37066-0299. 615-452-3892; hours: 8AM-4:30PM. www.deeds.sumnercounty.org
All records in one index. Only the public may search. Copy fee $1.00 per page. Cert fee- $1.00 per page include copy fee. Payee- Sumner County Register of Deeds. **Online access to Real Estate, Recording, Deed, Property Tax, Assessor records:** Assessment data on the state comptroller system is free at http://170.142.31.248/. Also, access real estate indexes/images back to 10/22/1989 at www.ustitlesearch.net; registration/monthly fee required. Also, search property data free on the GIS site at http://tn.sumner.geopowered.com. At the map, click on "search for property" then name search. Also see state introduction. **Other phones:** ; Trustee- 615-452-1260. **Property tax/Assessor-** 355 N. Belvedere Dr., Gallatin, TN 37066; 615-452-2412.

Tipton County

Register of Deeds, PO Box 626, Covington, TN 38019-0644. 901-476-0204; fax-901-476-0227; hours: 8AM-5PM.
All records in one index. Records indexed on a public use terminal back to 10/2000. Only the public may search. Copy fee $1.00 per page. Cert fee- $1.00 per page includes copy fee. Payee-Tipton County Register of Deeds. **Online access to Real Estate, Deed, Judgment, Lien, UCC, Property Assessor records:** Assessment data on the state comptroller system is free at http://170.142.31.248/. Access real estate indexes/images back to 10/22/1989 at www.ustitlesearch.net; registration/monthly fee required. Also see state introduction. **Other phones:** Treasurer- 901-476-0211; Elections- 901-476-0223. **Property tax/Assessor-** 901-476-0213.

Trousdale County

Register of Deeds, 200 E. Main St. #8, Hartsville, TN 37074-1706. 615-374-2921; fax-615-374-1100; hours: 8AM-4:30PM.
All records in one index. Records indexed on a public use terminal back to 3/1/2003. Only the public may search. Copy fee $.25 per page. Cert fee- $3.00 per page plus copy fee. Payee-Trousdale County Register of Deeds. **Online access to Real Estate, Deed, Judgment, Lien, UCC, Property Assessor records:** Assessment data is free at http://170.142.31.248/. Access real estate indexes/images back to 10/22/1989 at www.ustitlesearch.net; registration/monthly fee required. Also see state introduction. **Property tax/Assessor-** 615-374-2553.

Unicoi County

Register of Deeds, PO Box 305, Erwin, TN 37650-0305. 423-743-6104; fax-423-743-6278; hours: 9AM-5PM; 9AM-N Sat.
All records in one index. Only the public may search. Copy fee $1.00 per page. Cert fee- $1.00 per page plus copy fee. Payee- Unicoi County Register of Deeds. **Online access to Land, Deed, Recording records:** Access property and deeds indexes/images is via a private company at www.titlesearcher.com. Fee/registration required; images go back to 1/997. Also see state introduction. **Other phones:** Treasurer- 423-743-3011; Elections- 423-743-6521. **Property tax/Assessor-** PO Box 257, Erwin, TN 37650; 423-743-3801.

Union County

Register of Deeds, 901 Main St #108, Maynardville, TN 37807. 865-992-8024; fax-865-992-8024; hours: 8AM-4PMM,T,W,Th; 8AM-6PM F.
All records in one index. Records indexed on a public use terminal back to 12/14/2000. Only the public may search. Copy fee $.25 per page. Cert fee- $1.00 per page plus copy fee. Payee- Union County Register of Deeds. **Online access to Land, Lien, Will, Deed, Judgment, Recorder, Property Assessor records:** Access assessment data on the state comptroller system free at http://170.142.31.248/. Access property and deeds indexes/images at www.titlesearcher.com; fee/registration required. Also, see state introduction. **Other phones:** Treasurer- 865-992-5943; Elections- 865-992-3471; Vital Records- 865-992-3867; Trustee- 865-992-5943. **Property tax/Assessor-** 865-992-3211.

Van Buren County

Register of Deeds, PO Box 9, Spencer, TN 38585. 931-946-7363; fax-931-946-7363; 8AM-4PM (5PM F)
Records indexed on a public use terminal back to 2001. Only the public may search. Copy fee $.50 per page. Cert fee- $3.00 per page plus copy fee. **Online access to Land, Property Assessor, Deed, Recording records:** Assessment data on the state comptroller system is free at http://170.142.31.248/. Access property and deeds indexes/images at www.titlesearcher.com; fee/registration required. **Property tax/Assessor-** 931-946-2451.

Warren County

Register of Deeds, PO Box 128, McMinnville, TN 37111. 931-473-2926, UCC recording phone-931-473-8663; fax-931-474-2114; 8AM-4:30PM (5PM F)
All records in one index. Records indexed on a public use terminal back to 1998. Only the public may search. Copy fee $1.00 per page. Cert fee-$2.00 per page plus copy fee. Payee- Warren County Register of Deeds. **Online access to Real Estate, Deed, Judgment, Lien, UCC, Property Assessor records:** Assessment data on the state comptroller system is free at http://170.142.31.248/. Access real estate indexes/images at www.ustitlesearch.net; registration/monthly fee required. Also see state introduction. **Property tax/Assessor-** 201 Locust St #1P, McMinnville, TN 37110; 931-473-3450.

Washington County

Register of Deeds, PO Box 69, Jonesboro, TN 37659. 423-753-1644, R/E recording phone-423-753-1645, UCC recording phone-423-753-1648; fax-423-753-1743; hours: 8AM-5PM.
All records in one index. Only the public may search. Copy fee $.50 per page. Cert fee- None. Payee- Washington County Register of Deeds. **Online access to Real Estate, Deed, Judgment, Lien, UCC, Property Assessor records:** Assessment data on the state comptroller system is free at http://170.142.31.248/. Access property and deeds indexes/images at www.titlesearcher.com; fee/registration required. Also, see state introduction. **Other phones:** Treasurer- 423-753-1610; Appraiser/Auditor- 423-753-1670; Elections- 423-753-1688; Vital Records- 423-753-1621. **Property tax/Assessor-** 423-753-1670.

Wayne County

Register of Deeds, PO Box 465, Waynesboro, TN 38485. 931-722-5518; fax-931-722-5518; hours: 8AM-4PM M T TH F; 8AM-N W & Sat.
Records indexed on a public use terminal back to 30 yrs. Only the public may search. Copy fee $.50 per page, $1.00 per page for faxing. Cert fee- $1.00 per cert + $.25 per page. Payee- Wayne County Register. **Online access to Land, Property Assessor, Deed, Recording records:** Assessment data on the state comptroller system is free at http://170.142.31.248/. Access real estate indexes/images at www.ustitlesearch.net or at a 2nd

company at www.titlesearcher.com; registration/monthly fee required. Also see state introduction. **Other phones:** Treasurer- 931-722-3269; Appraiser/Auditor- 931-722-5282; Elections- 931-722-3517. **Property tax/Assessor-** PO Box 466, Waynesboro, TN 38485; 931-722-5282.

Weakley County

Register of Deeds, PO Box 45, Dresden, TN 38225-0045. 731-364-3646; fax-731-364-5284; hours: 8:30AM-4:30PM.
Only the public may search. Copy fee $.25 per page. Cert fee- $1.00. Payee- Register of Deeds. **Online access to Land, Property Assessor, Deed, Recording records:** Assessment data on the state comptroller system is free at http://170.142.31.248/. Access property and deeds indexes/images at www.titlesearcher.com; fee/registration required. Also see state introduction. **Other phones:** ; Trustee- 731-364-3643. **Property tax/Assessor-** 731-364-3677.

White County

Register of Deeds, PO Box 86, Sparta, TN 38583-0086. 931-836-2817; fax-931-836-8418; hours: 8AM-5PM. www.sparta-chamber.net/main.htm
Separate indices to search prior to 1990. Only the public may search. Copy fee $1.00 per page faxed or mailed, $5.00 minimum. Cert fee- $1.00 per page plus copy fee. **Online access to Deed, Property Assessor, Recording records:** Assessment data is free at http://170.142.31.248/. Access property and deeds indexes/images at www.titlesearcher.com; fee/registration required. **Other phones:** Elections- 615-741-7956. **Property tax/Assessor-** 931-836-3480.

Williamson County

Register of Deeds, PO Box 808, Franklin, TN 37065-0808. 615-790-5706; fax-615-790-5459; hours: 8AM-4:30PM.
All records in one index. Records indexed on computer back to 1980. Only the public may search. Copy fee $1.00 per page. Cert fee- $1.00 per page plus copy fee. Payee- Williamson County Register of Deeds. **Online access to Deed, Property, Tax Assessor, Recording records:** Access to the Professional Access database by subscription is a $50 per month fee. Information and sign-up at http://williamson-tn.org/co_gov/profacc.htm. Also, assessment data on the state comptroller system is free at http://170.142.31.248/. Also, access property and deeds indexes/images back to 11/1992 at www.titlesearcher.com; fee/registration required. Also see state introduction. **Other phones:** Treasurer- 615-790-5709; Appraiser/Auditor- 615-790-5708; Elections- 615-790-5711. **Property tax/Assessor-** 1320 W Main St, 3rd Fl, Franklin, TN 37064; 615-790-5708.

Wilson County

Register of Deeds, PO Box 176, Lebanon, TN 37087-0176. 615-443-2611; fax-615-443-3288; hours: 8AM-4PM. www.wilsondeeds.com
Separate indices to search include 1992 back direct & reverse. Records indexed on a public use terminal back to January, 1992. Only the public may search. Copy fee $.25 per page. Cert fee- $1.00 per page plus copy fee. Payee- Wilson Register. **Online access to Real Estate, Lien, Recording, Property Assessor records:** Access to the Register of Deeds database requires a $10 registration fee and $25.00 per month usage fee at www.wilsondeeds.com. Includes indices back to 1993; images back to 1996. Also, assessment data on the state comptroller system is free at http://170.142.31.248/. Also, online access to property and deeds indexes and images is via a private company at www.titlesearcher.com. A per day only fee/registration required. Also see state introduction. **Other phones:** Treasurer- 615-444-0894; Appraiser/Auditor- 615-444-8661; Elections- 615-444-0216. **Property tax/Assessor-** 615-444-8661.

Tennessee County Locator

You will usually be able to find the city name in the City/County Cross Reference below. In that case, it is a simple matter to determine the county from the cross reference. However, only the official US Postal Service city names are included in this index. There are an additional 40,000 place names that people use in their addresses. Therefore, we have also included a ZIP/City Cross Reference immediately following the City/County Cross Reference.

If you know the ZIP Code but the city name does not appear in the City/County Cross Reference index, look up the ZIP Code in the ZIP/City Cross Reference, find the city name, then look up the city name in the City/County Cross Reference. For example, you want to know the county for an address of Menands, NY 12204. There is no "Menands" in the City/County Cross Reference. The ZIP/City Cross Reference shows that ZIP Codes 12201-12288 are for the city of Albany. Looking back in the City/County Cross Reference, Albany is in Albany County.

Tennessee City/County Cross Reference

ADAMS (37010) Robertson(58), Montgomery(41)
ADAMSVILLE (38310) McNairy(56), Hardin(43)
AFTON Greene
ALAMO Crockett
ALCOA Blount
ALEXANDRIA (37012) De Kalb(78), Wilson(11), Smith(10)
ALLARDT Fentress
ALLONS (38541) Overton(66), Clay(33)
ALLRED Overton
ALPINE (38543) Overton(81), Pickett(18)
ALTAMONT Grundy
ANDERSONVILLE (37705) Anderson(68), Union(31)
ANTIOCH Davidson
APISON Hamilton
ARDMORE (38449) Giles(68), Lincoln(31)
ARLINGTON (38002) Shelby(90), Fayette(9)
ARNOLD AFB Coffee
ARRINGTON (37014) Williamson(58), Rutherford(41)
ARTHUR Claiborne
ASHLAND CITY (37015) Cheatham(95), Davidson(3)
ATHENS McMinn
ATOKA (38004) Tipton(94), Shelby(5)
ATWOOD (38220) Carroll(94), Gibson(5)
AUBURNTOWN (37016) Cannon(73), Wilson(26)
BAKEWELL Hamilton
BATH SPRINGS Decatur
BAXTER (38544) Putnam(91), De Kalb(8)
BEAN STATION Grainger
BEECH BLUFF (38313) Madison(51), Henderson(25), Chester(23)
BEECHGROVE (37018) Coffee(97), Bedford(2)
BEERSHEBA SPRINGS Grundy
BELFAST Marshall
BELL BUCKLE (37020) Bedford(79), Rutherford(20)
BELLS (38006) Crockett(78), Haywood(15), Madison(5)
BELVIDERE Franklin
BENTON Polk
BETHEL SPRINGS (38315) McNairy(84), Chester(15)
BETHPAGE (37022) Sumner(73), Trousdale(24), Macon(1)
BIG ROCK Stewart
BIG SANDY Benton
BIRCHWOOD (37308) Hamilton(65), Meigs(34)
BLAINE (37709) Grainger(83), Union(14), Knox(2)
BLOOMINGTON SPRINGS (38545) Jackson(61), Putnam(38)
BLOUNTVILLE Sullivan
BLUFF CITY Sullivan
BOGOTA Dyer
BOLIVAR Hardeman

BON AQUA (37025) Hickman(80), Dickson(17), Williamson(2)
BRADEN Fayette
BRADFORD Gibson
BRADYVILLE (37026) Cannon(90), Coffee(9)
BRENTWOOD (37027) Williamson(82), Davidson(17)
BRENTWOOD Williamson
BRICEVILLE Anderson
BRIGHTON (38011) Tipton(97), Shelby(2)
BRISTOL Sullivan
BROWNSVILLE Haywood
BRUCETON (38317) Carroll(94), Benton(5)
BRUNSWICK Shelby
BRUSH CREEK Smith
BUCHANAN Henry
BUENA VISTA (38318) Carroll(97), Benton(2)
BUFFALO VALLEY (38548) Putnam(76), Smith(23)
BULLS GAP (37711) Greene(60), Hawkins(35), Hamblen(3)
BUMPUS MILLS Stewart
BURLISON Tipton
BURNS Dickson
BUTLER (37640) Johnson(66), Carter(33)
BYBEE Cocke
BYRDSTOWN (38549) Pickett(98), Fentress(1)
CALHOUN (37309) McMinn(87), Polk(12)
CAMDEN Benton
CAMPAIGN Warren
CARTHAGE Smith
CARYVILLE Campbell
CASTALIAN SPRINGS (37031) Sumner(59), Trousdale(40)
CEDAR GROVE Carroll
CEDAR HILL (37032) Robertson(94), Cheatham(4)
CELINA (38551) Clay(98), Jackson(1)
CENTERVILLE Hickman
CHAPEL HILL (37034) Marshall(83), Bedford(16)
CHAPMANSBORO (37035) Cheatham(98), Montgomery(1)
CHARLESTON Bradley
CHARLOTTE (37036) Dickson(93), Cheatham(6)
CHATTANOOGA (37419) Hamilton(87), Marion(12)
CHATTANOOGA Hamilton
CHESTNUT MOUND Smith
CHEWALLA McNairy
CHRISTIANA Rutherford
CHUCKEY (37641) Greene(89), Washington(10)
CHURCH HILL Hawkins
CLAIRFIELD (37715) Claiborne(83), Campbell(16)
CLARKRANGE Fentress
CLARKSBURG Carroll
CLARKSVILLE Montgomery
CLEVELAND Bradley

CLIFTON (38425) Wayne(94), Perry(5)
CLINTON Anderson
COALFIELD Morgan
COALMONT Grundy
COKERCREEK Monroe
COLLEGE GROVE (37046) Williamson(85), Rutherford(12), Marshall(1)
COLLEGEDALE Hamilton
COLLIERVILLE (38017) Shelby(82), Fayette(17)
COLLIERVILLE Shelby
COLLINWOOD Wayne
COLUMBIA Maury
COMO Henry
CONASAUGA Polk
COOKEVILLE (38501) Putnam(92), Jackson(6)
COOKEVILLE (38506) Putnam(82), Overton(12), White(5)
COOKEVILLE Putnam
COPPERHILL Polk
CORDOVA Shelby
CORNERSVILLE (37047) Marshall(79), Giles(19), Lincoln(1)
CORRYTON (37721) Knox(79), Union(20)
COSBY (37722) Cocke(82), Sevier(17)
COTTAGE GROVE (38224) Henry(94), Weakley(5)
COTTONTOWN (37048) Sumner(91), Robertson(8)
COUNCE Hardin
COVINGTON Tipton
COWAN Franklin
CRAB ORCHARD Cumberland
CRAWFORD Overton
CROCKETT MILLS Crockett
CROSS PLAINS Robertson
CROSSVILLE Cumberland
CRUMP Hardin
CULLEOKA (38451) Maury(87), Marshall(12)
CUMBERLAND CITY (37050) Stewart(80), Montgomery(13), Houston(6)
CUMBERLAND FURNACE (37051) Dickson(66), Montgomery(33)
CUMBERLAND GAP Claiborne
CUNNINGHAM (37052) Montgomery(97), Dickson(2)
CYPRESS INN Wayne
DANDRIDGE (37725) Jefferson(98), Sevier(1)
DARDEN (38328) Henderson(76), Decatur(23)
DAYTON (37321) Rhea(98), Bledsoe(1)
DECATUR (37322) Meigs(96), McMinn(3)
DECATURVILLE (38329) Decatur(94), Henderson(5)
DECHERD (37324) Franklin(97), Grundy(2)
DEER LODGE (37726) Morgan(85), Fentress(14)
DEL RIO Cocke
DELANO (37325) Polk(79), McMinn(20)
DELLROSE Lincoln

DENMARK Madison
DENVER Humphreys
DICKSON (37055) Dickson(98), Hickman(1)
DICKSON Dickson
DIXON SPRINGS (37057) Trousdale(48), Macon(29), Smith(21)
DOVER Stewart
DOWELLTOWN De Kalb
DOYLE (38559) White(74), Van Buren(25)
DRESDEN Weakley
DRUMMONDS Tipton
DUCK RIVER Hickman
DUCKTOWN Polk
DUFF Campbell
DUKEDOM Weakley
DUNLAP (37327) Sequatchie(90), Bledsoe(9)
DYER Gibson
DYERSBURG Dyer
EADS (38028) Fayette(56), Shelby(43)
EAGAN Claiborne
EAGLEVILLE (37060) Rutherford(85), Bedford(9), Williamson(4)
EATON Gibson
EIDSON (37731) Hawkins(65), Hancock(34)
ELBRIDGE Obion
ELGIN Scott
ELIZABETHTON Carter
ELKTON Giles
ELLENDALE Shelby
ELMWOOD Smith
ELORA (37328) Lincoln(80), Franklin(19)
ENGLEWOOD (37329) McMinn(93), Monroe(6)
ENVILLE (38332) Chester(89), McNairy(10)
ERIN (37061) Houston(96), Humphreys(3)
ERWIN (37650) Unicoi(95), Washington(4)
ESTILL SPRINGS (37330) Franklin(94), Coffee(5)
ETHRIDGE (38456) Lawrence(77), Giles(22)
ETOWAH McMinn
EVA Benton
EVENSVILLE (37332) Rhea(98), Bledsoe(1)
FAIRVIEW (37062) Williamson(98), Dickson(1)
FALL BRANCH (37656) Greene(49), Washington(43), Sullivan(7)
FARNER Polk
FAYETTEVILLE Lincoln
FINGER (38334) McNairy(80), Chester(19)
FINLEY Dyer
FIVE POINTS Lawrence
FLAG POND Unicoi
FLINTVILLE (37335) Lincoln(96), Franklin(3)
FOSTERVILLE Rutherford
FOWLKES Dyer
FRANKEWING (38459) Giles(56), Lincoln(43)
FRANKLIN Williamson

FRIENDSHIP (38034) Crockett(80), Dyer(19)
FRIENDSVILLE (37737) Blount(92), Loudon(7)
FRUITVALE Crockett
GADSDEN Crockett
GAINESBORO Jackson
GALLATIN Sumner
GALLAWAY Fayette
GATES (38037) Lauderdale(68), Haywood(31)
GATLINBURG Sevier
GEORGETOWN (37336) Meigs(40), Bradley(40), Hamilton(19)
GERMANTOWN Shelby
GIBSON Gibson
GLADEVILLE Wilson
GLEASON (38229) Weakley(98), Henry(1)
GOODLETTSVILLE (37072) Davidson(59), Sumner(32), Robertson(8)
GOODLETTSVILLE Davidson
GOODSPRING Giles
GORDONSVILLE Smith
GRAND JUNCTION (38039) Hardeman(72), Fayette(27)
GRANDVIEW (37337) Cumberland(52), Rhea(47)
GRANVILLE (38564) Jackson(90), Putnam(9)
GRAYSVILLE (37338) Rhea(63), Bledsoe(23), Sequatchie(11), Hamilton(1)
GREENBACK (37742) Loudon(73), Blount(26)
GREENBRIER Robertson
GREENEVILLE Greene
GREENFIELD Weakley
GRIMSLEY Fentress
GRUETLI LAAGER Grundy
GUILD Marion
GUYS McNairy
HALLS (38040) Lauderdale(83), Crockett(11), Dyer(4)
HAMPSHIRE (38461) Maury(93), Lewis(6)
HAMPTON Carter
HARRIMAN (37748) Roane(89), Morgan(10)
HARROGATE Claiborne
HARTFORD Cocke
HARTSVILLE (37074) Trousdale(86), Macon(13)
HEISKELL (37754) Anderson(53), Knox(40), Union(5)
HELENWOOD Scott
HENDERSON (38340) Chester(91), Hardeman(8)
HENDERSONVILLE Sumner
HENNING Lauderdale
HENRY Henry
HERMITAGE (37076) Davidson(95), Wilson(4)
HICKMAN (38567) Smith(95), De Kalb(4)
HICKORY VALLEY (38042) Hardeman(98), Fayette(1)
HICKORY WITHE Fayette
HILHAM (38568) Overton(58), Clay(26), Jackson(14)
HILLSBORO Coffee
HIXSON Hamilton
HOHENWALD Lewis
HOLLADAY (38341) Benton(82), Decatur(13), Henderson(3)
HOLLOW ROCK Carroll
HORNBEAK Obion
HORNSBY (38044) Hardeman(91), McNairy(5), Chester(3)
HUMBOLDT (38343) Gibson(76), Crockett(15), Madison(7)
HUNTINGDON Carroll
HUNTLAND Franklin
HUNTSVILLE Scott
HURON Henderson

HURRICANE MILLS Humphreys
IDLEWILD Gibson
INDIAN MOUND (37079) Stewart(80), Montgomery(19)
IRON CITY (38463) Lawrence(63), Wayne(36)
ISABELLA Polk
JACKS CREEK Chester
JACKSBORO Campbell
JACKSON Madison
JAMESTOWN Fentress
JASPER Marion
JELLICO Campbell
JOELTON (37080) Davidson(51), Cheatham(48)
JOHNSON CITY (37601) Washington(76), Carter(22), Unicoi(1)
JOHNSON CITY Washington
JONESBOROUGH Washington
KELSO Lincoln
KENTON (38233) Gibson(68), Obion(31)
KINGSPORT (37660) Sullivan(95), Hawkins(4)
KINGSPORT (37663) Sullivan(97), Washington(2)
KINGSPORT Sullivan
KINGSTON Roane
KINGSTON SPRINGS Cheatham
KNOXVILLE (37931) Knox(98), Anderson(1)
KODAK (37764) Sevier(89), Knox(9)
KYLES FORD Hancock
LA FOLLETTE Campbell
LA GRANGE Fayette
LA VERGNE (37086) Rutherford(98), Davidson(1)
LA VERGNE Rutherford
LACONIA Fayette
LAFAYETTE Macon
LAKE CITY (37769) Anderson(78), Campbell(21)
LANCASTER (38569) Smith(77), De Kalb(22)
LANCING Morgan
LASCASSAS (37085) Rutherford(79), Wilson(20)
LAUREL BLOOMERY Johnson
LAVINIA Carroll
LAWRENCEBURG (38464) Lawrence(94), Giles(3), Wayne(2)
LEBANON (37087) Wilson(96), Trousdale(2)
LEBANON (37090) Wilson(97), Smith(2)
LEBANON Wilson
LENOIR CITY (37771) Loudon(92), Roane(7)
LENOIR CITY Loudon
LENOX Dyer
LEOMA (38468) Lawrence(90), Giles(9)
LEWISBURG (37091) Marshall(96), Bedford(3)
LEXINGTON Henderson
LIBERTY (37095) De Kalb(76), Cannon(19), Wilson(3)
LIMESTONE (37681) Greene(55), Washington(44)
LINDEN (37096) Perry(88), Wayne(10)
LIVINGSTON Overton
LOBELVILLE (37097) Perry(98), Humphreys(1)
LONE MOUNTAIN Claiborne
LOOKOUT MOUNTAIN Hamilton
LORETTO Lawrence
LOUDON (37774) Loudon(94), Roane(4)
LOUISVILLE Blount
LOWLAND Hamblen
LUPTON CITY Hamilton
LURAY Chester
LUTTRELL (37779) Union(92), Knox(5), Grainger(1)
LUTTS Wayne
LYLES Hickman

LYNCHBURG Moore
LYNNVILLE (38472) Giles(92), Marshall(7)
MACON Fayette
MADISON Davidson
MADISONVILLE (37354) Monroe(98), McMinn(1)
MANCHESTER Coffee
MANSFIELD Henry
MARTIN Weakley
MARYVILLE (37801) Blount(94), Monroe(5)
MARYVILLE Blount
MASCOT (37806) Knox(91), Grainger(8)
MASON (38049) Fayette(78), Tipton(21)
MAURY CITY Crockett
MAYNARDVILLE (37807) Union(98), Knox(1)
MC DONALD (37353) Bradley(88), Hamilton(11)
MC EWEN (37101) Humphreys(89), Houston(5), Hickman(5)
MC KENZIE (38201) Carroll(75), Weakley(14), Henry(10)
MC LEMORESVILLE Carroll
MC MINNVILLE (37110) Warren(97), Grundy(1), Cannon(1)
MC MINNVILLE Warren
MEDINA (38355) Gibson(57), Madison(42)
MEDON (38356) Madison(54), Hardeman(33), Chester(11)
MEMPHIS Shelby
MERCER (38392) Madison(66), Hardeman(33)
MICHIE (38357) McNairy(80), Hardin(19)
MIDDLETON Hardeman
MIDWAY Greene
MILAN Gibson
MILLEDGEVILLE (38359) Chester(77), McNairy(19), Hardin(2)
MILLIGAN COLLEGE Carter
MILLINGTON (38053) Shelby(83), Tipton(16)
MILLINGTON Shelby
MILTON (37118) Rutherford(66), Wilson(24), Cannon(9)
MINOR HILL Giles
MISTON Dyer
MITCHELLVILLE Sumner
MOHAWK Greene
MONROE (38573) Overton(64), Pickett(35)
MONTEAGLE (37356) Marion(83), Grundy(16)
MONTEREY (38574) Putnam(65), Overton(15), Cumberland(14), Fentress(4)
MOORESBURG (37811) Hawkins(95), Grainger(4)
MORLEY Campbell
MORRIS CHAPEL (38361) Hardin(89), McNairy(10)
MORRISON (37357) Warren(58), Coffee(30), Cannon(9), Grundy(1)
MORRISTOWN Hamblen
MOSCOW Fayette
MOSHEIM Greene
MOSS Clay
MOUNT CARMEL Hawkins
MOUNT JULIET (37122) Wilson(96), Rutherford(3)
MOUNT JULIET Wilson
MOUNT PLEASANT (38474) Maury(94), Lewis(3), Giles(1), Lawrence(1)
MOUNT VERNON Monroe
MOUNTAIN CITY Johnson
MOUNTAIN HOME Washington
MULBERRY (37359) Moore(53), Lincoln(46)
MUNFORD Tipton
MURFREESBORO Rutherford
NASHVILLE (37221) Davidson(96), Williamson(3)
NASHVILLE Davidson
NEW JOHNSONVILLE Humphreys

NEW MARKET Jefferson
NEW TAZEWELL (37825) Claiborne(96), Union(3)
NEW TAZEWELL Claiborne
NEWBERN Dyer
NEWCOMB Campbell
NEWPORT Cocke
NIOTA (37826) McMinn(94), Meigs(6)
NOLENSVILLE (37135) Williamson(78), Rutherford(15), Davidson(6)
NORENE Wilson
NORMANDY (37360) Coffee(46), Bedford(38), Moore(14)
NORRIS Anderson
NUNNELLY Hickman
OAK RIDGE (37830) Anderson(93), Roane(5), Knox(1)
OAK RIDGE Anderson
OAKDALE Morgan
OAKFIELD Madison
OAKLAND Fayette
OBION (38240) Obion(93), Dyer(6)
OCOEE Polk
OLD HICKORY (37138) Davidson(68), Wilson(31)
OLDFORT (37362) Bradley(87), Polk(12)
OLIVEHILL (38475) Hardin(86), Wayne(13)
OLIVER SPRINGS (37840) Roane(35), Morgan(32), Anderson(32)
ONEIDA Scott
ONLY Hickman
OOLTEWAH Hamilton
ORLINDA Robertson
OZONE Cumberland
PALL MALL (38577) Fentress(50), Pickett(49)
PALMER (37365) Grundy(90), Sequatchie(7), Marion(1)
PALMERSVILLE Weakley
PALMYRA Montgomery
PARIS (38242) Henry(98), Weakley(1)
PARROTTSVILLE Cocke
PARSONS Decatur
PEGRAM (37143) Cheatham(86), Davidson(13)
PELHAM Grundy
PETERSBURG (37144) Lincoln(56), Marshall(32), Bedford(7), Moore(1)
PETROS Morgan
PHILADELPHIA (37846) Loudon(59), Roane(23), Monroe(15), McMinn(1)
PICKWICK DAM Hardin
PIGEON FORGE Sevier
PIKEVILLE (37367) Bledsoe(84), Cumberland(9), Van Buren(6)
PINEY FLATS Sullivan
PINSON (38366) Chester(52), Madison(47)
PIONEER (37847) Scott(63), Campbell(36)
PLEASANT HILL Cumberland
PLEASANT SHADE (37145) Smith(73), Macon(15), Jackson(11)
PLEASANT VIEW (37146) Cheatham(71), Robertson(28)
PLEASANTVILLE Hickman
POCAHONTAS (38061) Hardeman(63), McNairy(36)
PORTLAND (37148) Sumner(94), Robertson(5)
POWDER SPRINGS (37848) Union(66), Grainger(33)
POWELL (37849) Knox(82), Anderson(17)
PRIMM SPRINGS (38476) Williamson(36), Hickman(35), Maury(27)
PROSPECT Giles
PRUDEN Claiborne
PULASKI Giles
PURYEAR Henry
QUEBECK White
RAMER McNairy
READYVILLE (37149) Rutherford(64), Cannon(35)

REAGAN (38368) Henderson(76), Chester(23)
RED BOILING SPRINGS (37150) Macon(75), Clay(23)
RELIANCE (37369) Polk(81), Monroe(18)
RICEVILLE McMinn
RICKMAN Overton
RIDDLETON Smith
RIDGELY (38080) Lake(62), Dyer(33), Obion(3)
RIDGETOP Robertson
RIPLEY (38063) Lauderdale(94), Haywood(5)
RIVES Obion
ROAN MOUNTAIN Carter
ROBBINS (37852) Scott(90), Morgan(9)
ROCK ISLAND (38581) Warren(77), Van Buren(21)
ROCKFORD (37853) Blount(94), Knox(5)
ROCKVALE (37153) Rutherford(91), Bedford(8)
ROCKWOOD (37854) Roane(76), Cumberland(15), Morgan(7)
ROGERSVILLE Hawkins
ROSSVILLE Fayette
RUGBY Morgan
RUSSELLVILLE Hamblen
RUTHERFORD Gibson
RUTLEDGE Grainger
SAINT ANDREWS Franklin
SAINT BETHLEHEM Montgomery
SAINT JOSEPH Lawrence
SALE CREEK Hamilton
SALTILLO (38370) Hardin(96), Henderson(3)
SAMBURG Obion
SANTA FE Maury
SARDIS (38371) Hardin(59), Henderson(40)
SAULSBURY Hardeman
SAVANNAH Hardin
SCOTTS HILL (38374) Decatur(98), Henderson(1)
SELMER McNairy
SEQUATCHIE Marion
SEVIERVILLE (37876) Sevier(97), Jefferson(2)
SEVIERVILLE Sevier
SEWANEE Franklin
SEYMOUR (37865) Sevier(80), Blount(19)

SHADY VALLEY Johnson
SHARON Weakley
SHARPS CHAPEL Union
SHAWANEE Claiborne
SHELBYVILLE (37160) Bedford(97), Moore(2)
SHELBYVILLE Bedford
SHERWOOD Franklin
SHILOH (38376) Hardin(80), McNairy(19)
SIGNAL MOUNTAIN (37377) Hamilton(88), Sequatchie(11)
SILERTON Hardeman
SILVER POINT (38582) Putnam(71), De Kalb(28)
SLAYDEN Dickson
SMARTT Warren
SMITHVILLE (37166) De Kalb(89), Warren(9), Cannon(1)
SMYRNA Rutherford
SNEEDVILLE (37869) Hancock(65), Hawkins(27), Claiborne(7)
SODDY DAISY (37379) Hamilton(94), Sequatchie(4)
SODDY DAISY Hamilton
SOMERVILLE Fayette
SOUTH FULTON (38257) Obion(94), Weakley(5)
SOUTH PITTSBURG Marion
SOUTHSIDE Montgomery
SPARTA (38583) White(86), De Kalb(6), Cumberland(3), Putnam(2)
SPEEDWELL (37870) Claiborne(76), Campbell(12), Union(10)
SPENCER Van Buren
SPRING CITY (37381) Rhea(95), Bledsoe(4)
SPRING CREEK Madison
SPRING HILL (37174) Maury(56), Williamson(42)
SPRINGFIELD Robertson
SPRINGVILLE Henry
STANTON (38069) Haywood(83), Tipton(8), Fayette(8)
STANTONVILLE McNairy
STEWART (37175) Houston(79), Stewart(20)
STRAWBERRY PLAINS (37871) Knox(44), Jefferson(40), Sevier(15)
SUGAR TREE (38380) Decatur(67), Benton(32)

SUMMERTOWN (38483) Lawrence(76), Lewis(19), Giles(2), Maury(1)
SUMMITVILLE Coffee
SUNBRIGHT (37872) Morgan(95), Scott(4)
SURGOINSVILLE Hawkins
SWEETWATER (37874) Monroe(87), McMinn(6), Loudon(5)
TAFT Lincoln
TALBOTT (37877) Hamblen(61), Jefferson(38)
TALLASSEE Blount
TAZEWELL (37879) Claiborne(95), Hancock(4)
TELFORD Washington
TELLICO PLAINS Monroe
TEN MILE (37880) Roane(58), Meigs(40)
TENNESSEE RIDGE (37178) Houston(86), Stewart(13)
THOMPSONS STATION Williamson
THORN HILL (37881) Grainger(64), Hancock(34)
TIGRETT Dyer
TIPTONVILLE Lake
TOONE Hardeman
TOWNSEND Blount
TRACY CITY (37387) Marion(66), Grundy(33)
TRADE Johnson
TREADWAY Hancock
TRENTON Gibson
TREZEVANT Carroll
TRIMBLE (38259) Dyer(86), Obion(8), Gibson(4)
TROY Obion
TULLAHOMA (37388) Coffee(72), Franklin(18), Moore(8)
TURTLETOWN Polk
UNICOI Unicoi
UNION CITY Obion
UNIONVILLE (37180) Bedford(94), Rutherford(5)
VANLEER (37181) Dickson(98), Houston(1)
VIOLA Warren
VONORE (37885) Monroe(97), Loudon(2)
WALLAND Blount
WALLING White
WARTBURG Morgan
WARTRACE (37183) Bedford(72), Coffee(18), Moore(8)

WASHBURN (37888) Grainger(90), Union(9)
WATAUGA (37694) Carter(76), Sullivan(18), Washington(5)
WATERTOWN (37184) Wilson(96), Smith(3)
WATTS BAR DAM Rhea
WAVERLY Humphreys
WAYNESBORO (38485) Wayne(98), Lewis(1)
WESTMORELAND (37186) Sumner(58), Macon(41)
WESTPOINT (38486) Lawrence(84), Wayne(15)
WESTPORT (38387) Carroll(90), Benton(9)
WHITE BLUFF (37187) Dickson(93), Cheatham(6)
WHITE HOUSE (37188) Robertson(60), Sumner(39)
WHITE PINE (37890) Jefferson(93), Hamblen(6)
WHITES CREEK Davidson
WHITESBURG (37891) Hamblen(68), Hawkins(31)
WHITESIDE Marion
WHITEVILLE (38075) Hardeman(70), Fayette(15), Haywood(14)
WHITLEYVILLE (38588) Jackson(75), Clay(19), Macon(5)
WHITWELL (37397) Marion(95), Sequatchie(4)
WILDER (38589) Overton(54), Fentress(45)
WILDERSVILLE Henderson
WILLIAMSPORT (38487) Maury(94), Hickman(5)
WILLISTON Fayette
WINCHESTER (37398) Franklin(98), Moore(1)
WINFIELD Scott
WINONA Scott
WOODBURY (37190) Cannon(98), Warren(1)
WOODLAND MILLS Obion
WOODLAWN Montgomery
WYNNBURG Lake
YORKVILLE Gibson
YUMA (38390) Carroll(80), Henderson(19)

Tennessee ZIP/City Cross Reference

37010-37010 ADAMS	37046-37046 COLLEGE GROVE	37078-37078 HURRICANE MILLS	37140-37140 ONLY
37011-37011 ANTIOCH	37047-37047 CORNERSVILLE	37079-37079 INDIAN MOUND	37141-37141 ORLINDA
37012-37012 ALEXANDRIA	37048-37048 COTTONTOWN	37080-37080 JOELTON	37142-37142 PALMYRA
37013-37013 ANTIOCH	37049-37049 CROSS PLAINS	37082-37082 KINGSTON SPRINGS	37143-37143 PEGRAM
37014-37014 ARRINGTON	37050-37050 CUMBERLAND CITY	37083-37083 LAFAYETTE	37144-37144 PETERSBURG
37015-37015 ASHLAND CITY	37051-37051 CUMBERLAND FURNACE	37085-37085 LASCASSAS	37145-37145 PLEASANT SHADE
37016-37016 AUBURNTOWN	37052-37052 CUNNINGHAM	37086-37086 LA VERGNE	37146-37146 PLEASANT VIEW
37018-37018 BEECHGROVE	37054-37054 DENVER	37087-37088 LEBANON	37147-37147 PLEASANTVILLE
37019-37019 BELFAST	37055-37056 DICKSON	37089-37089 LA VERGNE	37148-37148 PORTLAND
37020-37020 BELL BUCKLE	37057-37057 DIXON SPRINGS	37090-37090 LEBANON	37149-37149 READYVILLE
37022-37022 BETHPAGE	37058-37058 DOVER	37091-37091 LEWISBURG	37150-37150 RED BOILING SPRINGS
37023-37023 BIG ROCK	37059-37059 DOWELLTOWN	37095-37095 LIBERTY	37151-37151 RIDDLETON
37024-37024 BRENTWOOD	37060-37060 EAGLEVILLE	37096-37096 LINDEN	37152-37152 RIDGETOP
37025-37025 BON AQUA	37061-37061 ERIN	37097-37097 LOBELVILLE	37153-37153 ROCKVALE
37026-37026 BRADYVILLE	37062-37062 FAIRVIEW	37098-37098 LYLES	37155-37155 SAINT BETHLEHEM
37027-37027 BRENTWOOD	37063-37063 FOSTERVILLE	37101-37101 MC EWEN	37160-37162 SHELBYVILLE
37028-37028 BUMPUS MILLS	37064-37065 FRANKLIN	37110-37111 MC MINNVILLE	37165-37166 SLAYDEN
37029-37029 BURNS	37066-37066 GALLATIN	37115-37116 MADISON	37166-37166 SMITHVILLE
37030-37030 CARTHAGE	37067-37069 FRANKLIN	37118-37118 MILTON	37167-37167 SMYRNA
37031-37031 CASTALIAN SPRINGS	37070-37070 GOODLETTSVILLE	37119-37119 MITCHELLVILLE	37171-37171 SOUTHSIDE
37032-37032 CEDAR HILL	37071-37071 GLADEVILLE	37121-37122 MOUNT JULIET	37172-37172 SPRINGFIELD
37033-37033 CENTERVILLE	37072-37072 GOODLETTSVILLE	37127-37133 MURFREESBORO	37174-37174 SPRING HILL
37034-37034 CHAPEL HILL	37073-37073 GREENBRIER	37134-37134 NEW JOHNSONVILLE	37175-37175 STEWART
37035-37035 CHAPMANSBORO	37074-37074 HARTSVILLE	37135-37135 NOLENSVILLE	37178-37178 TENNESSEE RIDGE
37036-37036 CHARLOTTE	37075-37075 HENDERSONVILLE	37136-37136 NORENE	37179-37179 THOMPSONS STATION
37037-37037 CHRISTIANA	37076-37076 HERMITAGE	37137-37137 NUNNELLY	37180-37180 UNIONVILLE
37040-37044 CLARKSVILLE	37077-37077 HENDERSONVILLE	37138-37138 OLD HICKORY	37181-37181 VANLEER

37183-37183 WARTRACE	37377-37377 SIGNAL MOUNTAIN	37756-37756 HUNTSVILLE	38006-38006 BELLS
37184-37184 WATERTOWN	37378-37378 SMARTT	37757-37757 JACKSBORO	38007-38007 BOGOTA
37185-37185 WAVERLY	37379-37379 SODDY DAISY	37760-37760 JEFFERSON CITY	38008-38008 BOLIVAR
37186-37186 WESTMORELAND	37380-37380 SOUTH PITTSBURG	37762-37762 JELLICO	38010-38010 BRADEN
37187-37187 WHITE BLUFF	37381-37381 SPRING CITY	37763-37763 KINGSTON	38011-38011 BRIGHTON
37188-37188 WHITE HOUSE	37382-37382 SUMMITVILLE	37764-37764 KODAK	38012-38012 BROWNSVILLE
37189-37189 WHITES CREEK	37383-37383 SEWANEE	37765-37765 KYLES FORD	38014-38014 BRUNSWICK
37190-37190 WOODBURY	37384-37384 SODDY DAISY	37766-37766 LA FOLLETTE	38015-38015 BURLISON
37191-37191 WOODLAWN	37385-37385 TELLICO PLAINS	37769-37769 LAKE CITY	38016-38016 CORDOVA
37200-37250 NASHVILLE	37387-37387 TRACY CITY	37770-37770 LANCING	38017-38017 COLLIERVILLE
37301-37301 ALTAMONT	37388-37388 TULLAHOMA	37771-37772 LENOIR CITY	38018-38018 CORDOVA
37302-37302 APISON	37389-37389 ARNOLD AFB	37773-37773 LONE MOUNTAIN	38019-38019 COVINGTON
37303-37303 ATHENS	37391-37391 TURTLETOWN	37774-37774 LOUDON	38021-38021 CROCKETT MILLS
37304-37304 BAKEWELL	37394-37394 VIOLA	37777-37777 LOUISVILLE	38023-38023 DRUMMONDS
37305-37305 BEERSHEBA SPRINGS	37395-37395 WATTS BAR DAM	37778-37778 LOWLAND	38024-38025 DYERSBURG
37306-37306 BELVIDERE	37396-37396 WHITESIDE	37779-37779 LUTTRELL	38027-38027 COLLIERVILLE
37307-37307 BENTON	37397-37397 WHITWELL	37801-37804 MARYVILLE	38028-38028 EADS
37308-37308 BIRCHWOOD	37398-37398 WINCHESTER	37806-37806 MASCOT	38029-38029 ELLENDALE
37309-37309 CALHOUN	37400-37499 CHATTANOOGA	37807-37807 MAYNARDVILLE	38030-38030 FINLEY
37310-37310 CHARLESTON	37501-37544 MEMPHIS	37809-37809 MIDWAY	38033-38033 FOWLKES
37311-37312 CLEVELAND	37601-37615 JOHNSON CITY	37810-37810 MOHAWK	38034-38034 FRIENDSHIP
37313-37313 COALMONT	37616-37616 AFTON	37811-37811 MOORESBURG	38036-38036 GALLAWAY
37314-37314 COKERCREEK	37617-37617 BLOUNTVILLE	37812-37812 MORLEY	38037-38037 GATES
37315-37315 COLLEGEDALE	37618-37618 BLUFF CITY	37813-37816 MORRISTOWN	38039-38039 GRAND JUNCTION
37316-37316 CONASAUGA	37620-37625 BRISTOL	37818-37818 MOSHEIM	38040-38040 HALLS
37317-37317 COPPERHILL	37640-37640 BUTLER	37819-37819 NEWCOMB	38041-38041 HENNING
37318-37318 COWAN	37641-37641 CHUCKEY	37820-37820 NEW MARKET	38042-38042 HICKORY VALLEY
37320-37320 CLEVELAND	37642-37642 CHURCH HILL	37821-37822 NEWPORT	38043-38043 HICKORY WITHE
37321-37321 DAYTON	37643-37644 ELIZABETHTON	37824-37825 NEW TAZEWELL	38044-38044 HORNSBY
37322-37322 DECATUR	37645-37645 MOUNT CARMEL	37826-37826 NIOTA	38045-38045 LACONIA
37323-37323 CLEVELAND	37650-37650 ERWIN	37828-37828 NORRIS	38046-38046 LA GRANGE
37324-37324 DECHERD	37656-37656 FALL BRANCH	37829-37829 OAKDALE	38047-38047 LENOX
37325-37325 DELANO	37657-37657 FLAG POND	37830-37831 OAK RIDGE	38048-38048 MACON
37326-37326 DUCKTOWN	37658-37658 HAMPTON	37840-37840 OLIVER SPRINGS	38049-38049 MASON
37327-37327 DUNLAP	37659-37659 JONESBOROUGH	37841-37841 ONEIDA	38050-38050 MAURY CITY
37328-37328 ELORA	37660-37669 KINGSPORT	37842-37842 OZONE	38052-38052 MIDDLETON
37329-37329 ENGLEWOOD	37680-37680 LAUREL BLOOMERY	37843-37843 PARROTTSVILLE	38053-38055 MILLINGTON
37330-37330 ESTILL SPRINGS	37681-37681 LIMESTONE	37845-37845 PETROS	38056-38056 MISTON
37331-37331 ETOWAH	37682-37682 MILLIGAN COLLEGE	37846-37846 PHILADELPHIA	38057-38057 MOSCOW
37332-37332 EVENSVILLE	37683-37683 MOUNTAIN CITY	37847-37847 PIONEER	38058-38058 MUNFORD
37333-37333 FARNER	37684-37684 MOUNTAIN HOME	37848-37848 POWDER SPRINGS	38059-38059 NEWBERN
37334-37334 FAYETTEVILLE	37686-37686 PINEY FLATS	37849-37849 POWELL	38060-38060 OAKLAND
37335-37335 FLINTVILLE	37687-37687 ROAN MOUNTAIN	37851-37851 PRUDEN	38061-38061 POCAHONTAS
37336-37336 GEORGETOWN	37688-37688 SHADY VALLEY	37852-37852 ROBBINS	38063-38063 RIPLEY
37337-37337 GRANDVIEW	37690-37690 TELFORD	37853-37853 ROCKFORD	38066-38066 ROSSVILLE
37338-37338 GRAYSVILLE	37691-37691 TRADE	37854-37854 ROCKWOOD	38067-38067 SAULSBURY
37339-37339 GRUETLI LAAGER	37692-37692 UNICOI	37857-37857 ROGERSVILLE	38068-38068 SOMERVILLE
37340-37340 GUILD	37694-37694 WATAUGA	37860-37860 RUSSELLVILLE	38069-38069 STANTON
37341-37341 HARRISON	37699-37699 PINEY FLATS	37861-37861 RUTLEDGE	38070-38070 TIGRETT
37342-37342 HILLSBORO	37701-37701 ALCOA	37862-37862 SEVIERVILLE	38071-38071 TIPTON
37343-37343 HIXSON	37705-37705 ANDERSONVILLE	37863-37863 PIGEON FORGE	38074-38074 BOLIVAR
37345-37345 HUNTLAND	37707-37707 ARTHUR	37864-37864 SEVIERVILLE	38075-38075 WHITEVILLE
37346-37346 ISABELLA	37708-37708 BEAN STATION	37865-37865 SEYMOUR	38076-38076 WILLISTON
37347-37347 JASPER	37709-37709 BLAINE	37866-37866 SHARPS CHAPEL	38077-38077 WYNNBURG
37348-37348 KELSO	37710-37710 BRICEVILLE	37867-37867 SHAWANEE	38079-38079 TIPTONVILLE
37349-37349 MANCHESTER	37711-37711 BULLS GAP	37868-37868 PIGEON FORGE	38080-38080 RIDGELY
37350-37350 LOOKOUT MOUNTAIN	37713-37713 BYBEE	37869-37869 SNEEDVILLE	38083-38083 MILLINGTON
37351-37351 LUPTON CITY	37714-37714 CARYVILLE	37870-37870 SPEEDWELL	38088-38088 CORDOVA
37352-37352 LYNCHBURG	37715-37715 CLAIRFIELD	37871-37871 STRAWBERRY PLAINS	38100-38137 MEMPHIS
37353-37353 MC DONALD	37716-37717 CLINTON	37872-37872 SUNBRIGHT	38138-38139 GERMANTOWN
37354-37354 MADISONVILLE	37719-37719 COALFIELD	37873-37873 SURGOINSVILLE	38140-38182 MEMPHIS
37355-37355 MANCHESTER	37721-37721 CORRYTON	37874-37874 SWEETWATER	38183-38183 GERMANTOWN
37356-37356 MONTEAGLE	37722-37722 COSBY	37876-37876 SEVIERVILLE	38184-38197 MEMPHIS
37357-37357 MORRISON	37723-37723 CRAB ORCHARD	37877-37877 TALBOTT	38201-38201 MC KENZIE
37358-37358 MOUNT VERNON	37724-37724 CUMBERLAND GAP	37878-37878 TALLASSEE	38220-38220 ATWOOD
37359-37359 MULBERRY	37725-37725 DANDRIDGE	37879-37879 TAZEWELL	38221-38221 BIG SANDY
37360-37360 NORMANDY	37726-37726 DEER LODGE	37880-37880 TEN MILE	38222-38222 BUCHANAN
37361-37361 OCOEE	37727-37727 DEL RIO	37881-37881 THORN HILL	38223-38223 COMO
37362-37362 OLDFORT	37729-37729 DUFF	37882-37882 TOWNSEND	38224-38224 COTTAGE GROVE
37363-37363 OOLTEWAH	37730-37730 EAGAN	37883-37883 TREADWAY	38225-38225 DRESDEN
37364-37364 CLEVELAND	37731-37731 EIDSON	37885-37885 VONORE	38226-38226 DUKEDOM
37365-37365 PALMER	37732-37732 ELGIN	37886-37886 WALLAND	38227-38227 ELBRIDGE
37366-37366 PELHAM	37733-37733 RUGBY	37887-37887 WARTBURG	38229-38229 GLEASON
37367-37367 PIKEVILLE	37737-37737 FRIENDSVILLE	37888-37888 WASHBURN	38230-38230 GREENFIELD
37369-37369 RELIANCE	37738-37738 GATLINBURG	37890-37890 WHITE PINE	38231-38231 HENRY
37370-37370 RICEVILLE	37742-37742 GREENBACK	37891-37891 WHITESBURG	38232-38232 HORNBEAK
37371-37371 ATHENS	37743-37745 GREENEVILLE	37892-37892 WINFIELD	38233-38233 KENTON
37372-37372 SAINT ANDREWS	37748-37748 HARRIMAN	37893-37893 WINONA	38235-38235 MC LEMORESVILLE
37373-37373 SALE CREEK	37752-37752 HARROGATE	37900-37999 KNOXVILLE	38236-38236 MANSFIELD
37374-37374 SEQUATCHIE	37753-37753 HARTFORD	38001-38001 ALAMO	38237-38238 MARTIN
37375-37375 SEWANEE	37754-37754 HEISKELL	38002-38002 ARLINGTON	38240-38240 OBION
37376-37376 SHERWOOD	37755-37755 HELENWOOD	38004-38004 ATOKA	38241-38241 PALMERSVILLE

38242-38242 PARIS	38253-38253 RIVES	38255-38255 SHARON
38251-38251 PURYEAR	38254-38254 SAMBURG	38256-38256 SPRINGVILLE
38259-38259 TRIMBLE	38348-38348 LAVINIA	38450-38450 COLLINWOOD
38260-38260 TROY	38351-38351 LEXINGTON	38451-38451 CULLEOKA
38261-38261 UNION CITY	38352-38352 LURAY	38452-38452 CYPRESS INN
38271-38271 WOODLAND MILLS	38355-38355 MEDINA	38453-38453 DELLROSE
38281-38281 UNION CITY	38356-38356 MEDON	38454-38454 DUCK RIVER
38301-38308 JACKSON	38357-38357 MICHIE	38455-38455 ELKTON
38310-38310 ADAMSVILLE	38358-38358 MILAN	38456-38456 ETHRIDGE
38311-38311 BATH SPRINGS	38359-38359 MILLEDGEVILLE	38457-38457 FIVE POINTS
38313-38313 BEECH BLUFF	38361-38361 MORRIS CHAPEL	38459-38459 FRANKEWING
38314-38314 JACKSON	38362-38362 OAKFIELD	38460-38460 GOODSPRING
38315-38315 BETHEL SPRINGS	38363-38363 PARSONS	38461-38461 HAMPSHIRE
38316-38316 BRADFORD	38365-38365 PICKWICK DAM	38462-38462 HOHENWALD
38317-38317 BRUCETON	38366-38366 PINSON	38463-38463 IRON CITY
38318-38318 BUENA VISTA	38367-38367 RAMER	38464-38464 LAWRENCEBURG
38320-38320 CAMDEN	38368-38368 REAGAN	38468-38468 LEOMA
38321-38321 CEDAR GROVE	38369-38369 RUTHERFORD	38469-38469 LORETTO
38324-38324 CLARKSBURG	38370-38370 SALTILLO	38471-38471 LUTTS
38326-38326 COUNCE	38371-38371 SARDIS	38472-38472 LYNNVILLE
38327-38327 CRUMP	38372-38372 SAVANNAH	38473-38473 MINOR HILL
38328-38328 DARDEN	38374-38374 SCOTTS HILL	38474-38474 MOUNT PLEASANT
38329-38329 DECATURVILLE	38375-38375 SELMER	38475-38475 OLIVEHILL
38330-38330 DYER	38376-38376 SHILOH	38476-38476 PRIMM SPRINGS
38331-38331 EATON	38377-38377 SILERTON	38477-38477 PROSPECT
38332-38332 ENVILLE	38378-38378 SPRING CREEK	38478-38478 PULASKI
38333-38333 EVA	38379-38379 STANTONVILLE	38481-38481 SAINT JOSEPH
38334-38334 FINGER	38380-38380 SUGAR TREE	38482-38482 SANTA FE
38336-38336 FRUITVALE	38381-38381 TOONE	38483-38483 SUMMERTOWN
38337-38337 GADSDEN	38382-38382 TRENTON	38485-38485 WAYNESBORO
38338-38338 GIBSON	38387-38387 WESTPORT	38486-38486 WESTPOINT
38339-38339 GUYS	38388-38388 WILDERSVILLE	38487-38487 WILLIAMSPORT
38340-38340 HENDERSON	38389-38389 YORKVILLE	38488-38488 TAFT
38341-38341 HOLLADAY	38390-38390 YUMA	38501-38503 COOKEVILLE
38342-38342 HOLLOW ROCK	38391-38391 DENMARK	38504-38504 ALLARDT
38343-38343 HUMBOLDT	38392-38392 MERCER	38505-38506 COOKEVILLE
38344-38344 HUNTINGDON	38393-38393 CHEWALLA	38541-38541 ALLONS
38345-38345 HURON	38401-38402 COLUMBIA	38542-38542 ALLRED
38346-38346 IDLEWILD	38425-38425 CLIFTON	38543-38543 ALPINE
38347-38347 JACKS CREEK	38449-38449 ARDMORE	38544-38544 BAXTER

38257-38257 SOUTH FULTON
38258-38258 TREZEVANT
38545-38545 BLOOMINGTON SPRINGS
38547-38547 BRUSH CREEK
38548-38548 BUFFALO VALLEY
38549-38549 BYRDSTOWN
38550-38550 CAMPAIGN
38551-38551 CELINA
38552-38552 CHESTNUT MOUND
38553-38553 CLARKRANGE
38554-38554 CRAWFORD
38555-38555 CROSSVILLE
38556-38556 JAMESTOWN
38557-38558 CROSSVILLE
38559-38559 DOYLE
38560-38560 ELMWOOD
38562-38562 GAINESBORO
38563-38563 GORDONSVILLE
38564-38564 GRANVILLE
38565-38565 GRIMSLEY
38567-38567 HICKMAN
38568-38568 HILHAM
38569-38569 LANCASTER
38570-38570 LIVINGSTON
38571-38572 CROSSVILLE
38573-38573 MONROE
38574-38574 MONTEREY
38575-38575 MOSS
38577-38577 PALL MALL
38578-38578 PLEASANT HILL
38579-38579 QUEBECK
38580-38580 RICKMAN
38581-38581 ROCK ISLAND
38582-38582 SILVER POINT
38583-38583 SPARTA
38585-38585 SPENCER
38587-38587 WALLING
38588-38588 WHITLEYVILLE
38589-38589 WILDER

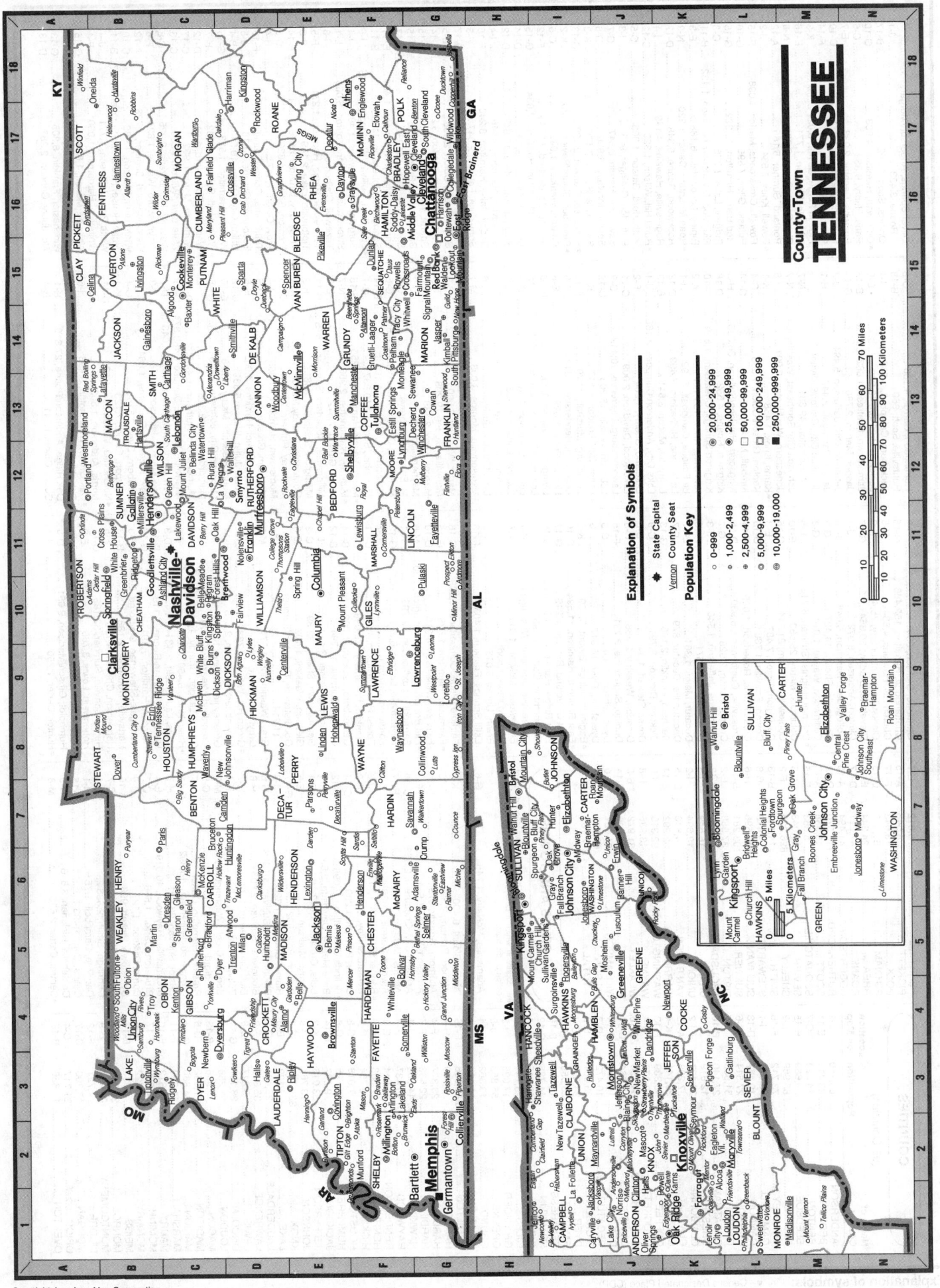

County-Town
TENNESSEE

Explanation of Symbols

✚ State Capital

<u>Vernon</u> County Seat

Population Key

○ 0-999	◉ 20,000-24,999	
◦ 1,000-2,499	⊙ 25,000-49,999	
⊚ 2,500-4,999	▢ 50,000-99,999	
⊛ 5,000-9,999	⬚ 100,000-249,999	
⊜ 10,000-19,000	■ 250,000-999,999	

COUNTIES

Name of County	Population	Location on Map
	(95 Counties)	
ANDERSON	68,250	J-1
BEDFORD	30,411	E-11
BENTON	14,524	C-7
BLEDSOE	9,669	E-15
BLOUNT	85,969	L-2
BRADLEY	73,712	F-16
CAMPBELL	35,079	I-1
CANNON	10,467	D-13
CARROLL	27,514	C-6
CARTER	51,505	I-7
CHEATHAM	27,140	C-10
CHESTER	12,819	F-5
CLAIBORNE	26,137	I-2
CLAY	7,238	A-15
COCKE	29,141	K-4
COFFEE	40,339	F-13
CROCKETT	13,378	D-4
CUMBERLAND	34,736	C-16
DAVIDSON	510,784	C-11
DEKALB	14,360	D-14
DECATUR	10,472	D-7
DICKSON	35,061	D-9
DYER	34,854	C-3
FAYETTE	25,559	F-3
FENTRESS	14,669	B-16
FRANKLIN	34,725	F-13
GIBSON	46,315	C-5
GILES	25,741	F-10
GRAINGER	17,095	I-3
GREENE	55,853	J-5
GRUNDY	13,362	F-14
HAMBLEN	50,480	I-4
HAMILTON	285,536	F-16
HANCOCK	6,739	H-4
HARDEMAN	23,377	F-4
HARDIN	22,633	F-7
HAWKINS	44,565	I-4
HAYWOOD	19,437	E-3
HENDERSON	21,844	E-6
HENRY	27,888	B-6
HICKMAN	16,754	D-9
HOUSTON	7,018	B-8
HUMPHREYS	15,795	C-8
JACKSON	9,297	B-14
JEFFERSON	33,016	K-3
JOHNSON	13,766	H-8
KNOX	335,749	J-2
LAKE	7,129	B-3
LAUDERDALE	23,491	D-9
LAWRENCE	35,303	F-9
LEWIS	9,247	E-8
LINCOLN	28,157	G-11
LOUDON	31,255	L-1
MACON	15,906	B-13
MADISON	77,982	D-5
MARION	24,860	G-14
MARSHALL	21,539	F-11
MAURY	54,812	E-10
MCMINN	42,383	F-17
MCNAIRY	22,422	F-6
MEIGS	8,033	E-17
MONROE	30,541	L-1
MONTGOMERY	100,498	B-9
MOORE	4,721	F-12
MORGAN	17,300	C-17
OBION	31,717	C-4
OVERTON	17,636	B-15
PERRY	6,612	E-7
PICKETT	4,548	A-15
POLK	13,643	F-17
PUTNAM	51,373	C-15
RHEA	24,344	E-16
ROANE	47,227	D-17
ROBERTSON	41,494	A-10
RUTHERFORD	118,570	D-12
SCOTT	18,358	A-17
SEQUATCHIE	8,863	F-15
SEVIER	51,043	L-3
SHELBY	826,330	B-13
SMITH	14,143	B-13
STEWART	9,479	B-8
SULLIVAN	143,596	H-6
SUMNER	103,281	B-11
TIPTON	37,568	B-13
TROUSDALE	5,920	B-12
UNICOI	16,549	I-6
UNION	13,694	I-2
VAN BUREN	4,846	E-15
WARREN	32,992	E-14
WASHINGTON	92,315	I-6
WAYNE	13,935	F-8
WEAKLEY	31,972	B-5
WHITE	20,090	C-14
WILLIAMSON	81,021	D-10
WILSON	67,675	C-12
TOTAL	**4,877,185**	

CITIES AND TOWNS

Note: The first name is that of the city or town, second, that of the county in which it is located, then the population and location on the map.

Adamsville, McNairy, 1,745 — G-6
Alamo, Crockett, 2,426 — D-4
Alcoa, Blount, 6,400 — K-2
Algood, Putnam, 2,399 — C-15
Altamont, Grundy, 679 — F-14
Arlington, Shelby, 1,541 — F-2
Ashland City, Cheatham, 2,552 — C-10
Athens, McMinn, 12,054 — F-17
Atwood, Carroll, 1,066 — E-6
•Banner Hill, Unicoi, 1,717 — I-6
Bartlett, Shelby, 26,989 — F-2
Baxter, Putnam, 1,289 — C-14
Belle Meade, Davidson, 2,839 — C-11
Bells, Crockett, 1,643 — E-4
Bemis, Madison — E-5
Benton, Polk, 992 — G-17
Blaine, Grainger, 1,326 — J-3
•Bloomingdale, Sullivan, 10,953 — H-6
Blountville, Sullivan, 2,605 — H-6
Bluff City, Sullivan, 1,390 — H-7
Bolivar, Hardeman, 5,969 — F-4
Boones Creek, Washington — M-7
Bradford, Gibson, 1,154 — C-5
Braemar-Hampton, Carter — N-7
Brentwood, Williamson, 16,392 — D-11
Bristol, Sullivan, 23,421 — H-7
Brownsville, Haywood, 10,019 — E-4
Bruceton, Carroll, 1,586 — C-7
Burns, Dickson, 1,127 — D-9
Byrdstown, Pickett, 998 — A-16
Camden, Benton, 3,643 — C-7
Carthage, Smith, 2,386 — C-13
Caryville, Campbell, 1,751 — I-1
Celina, Clay, 1,493 — A-15
Centerville, Hickman, 3,616 — D-9
Central, Carter, 2,635 — N-7

Charlotte, Dickson, 854 — D-9
Chattanooga, Hamilton, 152,466 — G-15
Church Hill, Hawkins, 4,834 — H-5
Clarksville, Montgomery, 75,494 — B-9
Cleveland, Bradley, 30,354 — G-17
Clinton, Anderson, 8,972 — J-1
Collegedale, Hamilton, 5,048 — G-16
Collierville, Shelby, 14,427 — G-3
Collinwood, Wayne, 1,014 — G-8
•Colonial Heights, Sullivan, 6,716 — L-6
Columbia, Maury, 28,583 — E-10
Cookeville, Putnam, 21,744 — C-15
Covington, Tipton, 7,487 — E-3
Cowan, Franklin, 1,738 — G-13
Cross Plains, Robertson, 1,025 — B-11
Crossville, Cumberland, 6,930 — D-16
Crump, Hardin, 2,028 — G-7
Dandridge, Jefferson, 1,540 — J-3
Dayton, Rhea, 5,671 — F-16
Decatur, Meigs, 1,361 — E-17
Decaturville, Decatur, 879 — E-7
Decherd, Franklin, 2,196 — G-13
Dickson, Dickson, 8,791 — C-9
Dover, Stewart, 1,341 — B-8
Dresden, Weakley, 2,488 — C-5
Dunlap, Sequatchie, 3,731 — F-15
Dyer, Gibson, 2,204 — C-5
Dyersburg, Dyer, 16,317 — C-3
•Eagleton Village, Blount, 5,169 — K-2
•East Brainerd, Hamilton, 11,594 — G-16
East Cleveland, Bradley, 1,249 — G-17
East Ridge, Hamilton, 21,101 — G-16
Elizabethton, Carter, 11,931 — I-7
Embreeville Junction, Washington — N-7
Englewood, McMinn, 1,611 — M-7
Erin, Houston, 1,586 — B-8
Erwin, Unicoi, 5,015 — I-6
Estill Springs, Franklin, 1,408 — F-13
Etowah, McMinn, 3,815 — F-18
•Fairfield Glade, Cumberland, 2,209 — C-16
Fairmount, Hamilton, 1,578 — G-15
Fairview, Williamson, 4,210 — D-10
Fall Branch, Greene/Washington, 1,203 — M-6
Farragut, Knox/Loudon, 12,793 — K-1
Fayetteville, Lincoln, 6,921 — F-17
Fordtown, Sullivan — L-7
Forest Hills, Davidson, 4,231 — J-6
Franklin, Williamson, 20,098 — F-2
Gainesboro, Jackson, 1,002 — C-14
Gallatin, Sumner, 18,794 — B-12
Gatlinburg, Sevier, 3,417 — L-3
Germantown, Shelby, 32,893 — E-4
Gleason, Weakley, 1,402 — E-5
Goodlettsville, Davidson/Sumner, 11,219 — B-11
Gray, Washington, 1,071 — M-7
Graysville, Rhea, 1,301 — F-16
•Green Hill, Wilson, 6,763 — C-11
Greenbrier, Robertson, 2,873 — B-11
Greeneville, Greene, 13,532 — J-5
Greenfield, Weakley, 2,105 — C-5
Gruetli-Laager, Grundy, 1,810 — F-14
Halls, Lauderdale, 2,431 — D-3
Harriman, Morgan/Roane, 7,119 — D-17
Harrison, Hamilton, 7,191 — H-7
•Harrogate-Shawanee, Claiborne, 2,657 — H-3
Hartsville, Trousdale, 2,769 — B-13
Henderson, Chester, 4,760 — F-5
Hendersonville, Sumner, 32,188 — C-11
Hohenwald, Lewis, 3,760 — E-9
•Hopewell, Bradley, 2,569 — G-16
•Hunter, Carter, 1,250 — M-8

Huntingdon, Carroll, 4,180 — D-6
Huntsville, Scott, 660 — B-18
Jacksboro, Campbell, 1,568 — I-1
Jackson, Madison, 48,949 — E-5
Jamestown, Fentress, 1,862 — B-16
Jasper, Marion, 2,780 — G-14
Jefferson City, Jefferson, 5,494 — J-3
Jellico, Campbell, 2,447 — H-1
Johnson City, Carter/Sullivan/Washington, 49,381 — N-7
Johnson City Southeast, Washington — N-7
Jonesboro, Washington, 3,091 — I-6
Karns, Knox, 1,458 — K-1
Kenton, Gibson/Obion, 1,366 — C-4
Kimball, Marion, 1,243 — G-14
Kingsport, Hawkins/Sullivan, 36,365 — H-6
Kingston, Roane, 4,552 — D-18
Kingston Springs, Cheatham, 1,529 — C-10
Knoxville, Knox, 165,121 — K-2
La Follette, Campbell, 7,192 — I-1
La Vergne, Rutherford, 7,499 — D-12
Lafayette, Macon, 3,641 — B-13
Lake City, Anderson/Campbell, 2,166 — J-1
Lakeland, Shelby, 1,204 — F-2
Lakewood, Davidson, 2,009 — C-11
Lawrenceburg, Lawrence, 10,412 — G-9
Lebanon, Wilson, 15,208 — C-12
Lenoir City, Loudon, 6,147 — K-1
Lewisburg, Marshall, 9,879 — E-11
Lexington, Henderson, 5,810 — E-6
Linden, Perry, 1,099 — E-8
Livingston, Overton, 3,809 — B-15
Lookout Mountain, Hamilton, 1,901 — G-15
Loretto, Lawrence, 1,515 — G-9
Loudon, Loudon, 4,026 — L-1
Lynchburg, Moore, 4,721 — F-12
Lynn Garden, Sullivan — L-6
Madisonville, Monroe, 3,033 — M-1
Manchester, Coffee, 7,709 — F-13
Martin, Weakley, 8,600 — B-5
Maryville, Blount, 19,208 — K-2
•Mascot, Knox, 2,138 — J-2
Maynardville, Union, 1,298 — J-2
McEwen, Humphreys, 1,442 — C-8
McKenzie, Carroll/Henry/Weakley, 5,168 — C-6
McMinnville, Warren, 11,194 — E-14
Memphis, Shelby, 610,337 — G-1
•Middle Valley, Hamilton, 12,255 — G-15
Midway, Washington, 2,953 — N-7
Milan, Gibson, 7,512 — D-5
Millersville, Robertson/Sumner, 2,575 — B-11
Millington, Shelby, 17,866 — F-2
Monteagle, Grundy/Marion, 1,138 — G-14
Monterey, Putnam, 2,559 — C-15
Morristown, Hamblen, 21,385 — J-4
Mosheim, Greene, 1,451 — J-5
Mount Carmel, Hawkins, 4,082 — H-5
Mount Juliet, Wilson, 5,389 — C-11
Mount Pleasant, Maury, 4,278 — E-10
Mountain City, Johnson, 2,169 — H-8
Munford, Tipton, 2,326 — F-2
Murfreesboro, Rutherford, 44,922 — D-12
Nashville-Davidson, Davidson, 488,374 — C-11
New Johnsonville, Humphreys, 1,643 — D-7
New Market, Jefferson, 1,086 — J-3
New Tazewell, Claiborne, 1,864 — H-3
Newbern, Dyer, 2,515 — C-4
Newport, Cocke, 7,123 — K-4
•Nolensville, Williamson, 1,570 — D-11
Norris, Anderson, 1,303 — J-1
•Oak Grove, Washington, 3,498 — I-6
Oak Hill, Davidson, 4,301 — C-11
Oak Ridge, Anderson/Roane, 27,310 — K-1
Obion, Obion, 1,241 — B-4

Oliver Springs, Anderson/Morgan/Roane, 3,433 — J-1
Oneida, Scott, 3,502 — B-17
•Ooltewah, Hamilton, 4,903 — G-16
Paris, Henry, 9,332 — C-6
Parsons, Decatur, 2,033 — E-7
Pegram, Cheatham, 1,371 — C-10
Pelham, Grundy — F-14
Pigeon Forge, Sevier, 3,027 — K-3
Pikeville, Bledsoe, 1,771 — E-16
•Pine Crest, Carter, 3,821 — N-8
Portland, Sumner, 5,165 — A-12
Powell, Knox, 7,534 — J-2
Powells Crossroads, Marion, 1,098 — F-15
Pulaski, Giles, 7,895 — G-10
Red Bank, Hamilton, 12,322 — G-15
Ridgely, Lake, 1,775 — C-3
Ridgetop, Davidson/Robertson, 1,132 — B-11
Ripley, Lauderdale, 6,188 — E-3
Roan Mountain, Carter, 1,220 — N-9
Rockwood, Roane, 5,348 — D-17
Rogersville, Hawkins, 4,149 — I-4
Rural Hill, Wilson, 1,329 — C-12
Rutherford, Gibson, 1,303 — C-5
Rutledge, Grainger, 903 — I-3
Savannah, Hardin, 6,547 — G-7
Selmer, McNairy, 3,838 — G-6
Sevierville, Sevier, 7,178 — K-3
•Sewanee, Franklin, 2,128 — G-13
Seymour, Blount/Sevier, 7,026 — K-2
Sharon, Weakley, 1,047 — C-5
Shelbyville, Bedford, 14,049 — F-12
Signal Mountain, Hamilton, 7,034 — G-15
Smithville, DeKalb, 3,791 — D-14
Smyrna, Rutherford, 13,647 — D-12
Sneedville, Hancock, 1,446 — I-4
Soddy-Daisy, Hamilton, 8,240 — F-16
Somerville, Fayette, 2,047 — F-3
South Cleveland, Bradley, 5,372 — G-17
South Fulton, Obion, 2,688 — B-5
South Pittsburg, Marion, 3,295 — G-14
Sparta, White, 4,681 — D-15
Spencer, Van Buren, 1,125 — E-15
Spring City, Rhea, 2,199 — E-17
Spring Hill, Maury/Williamson, 1,464 — E-11
Springfield, Robertson, 11,227 — B-11
•Spurgeon, Sullivan/Washington, 3,149 — I-6
Surgoinsville, Hawkins, 1,499 — I-4
Sweetwater, McMinn/Monroe, 5,066 — L-1
Tazewell, Claiborne, 2,150 — I-3
Tennessee Ridge, Houston, 1,271 — B-8
Tiptonville, Lake, 2,149 — B-3
Tracy City, Grundy, 1,556 — F-14
Trenton, Gibson, 4,836 — D-5
Troy, Obion, 1,047 — B-4
Tullahoma, Coffee/Franklin, 16,761 — F-13
Tusculum, Greene, 1,918 — J-5
Union City, Obion, 10,513 — B-4
Walden, Hamilton, 1,523 — G-15
Walnut Hill, Sullivan, 3,332 — H-7
Walterhill, Rutherford, 1,043 — D-12
Wartburg, Morgan, 932 — F-2
Watertown, Wilson, 1,250 — C-13
Waverly, Humphreys, 3,925 — C-8
Waynesboro, Wayne, 1,824 — F-8
Westmoreland, Sumner, 1,726 — A-12
White Bluff, Dickson, 1,988 — C-10
White House, Robertson/Sumner, 2,987 — B-11
White Pine, Jefferson, 1,771 — J-4
Whiteville, Hardeman, 1,050 — F-4
Whitwell, Marion, 1,622 — G-15
•Wildwood Lake, Bradley, 2,680 — G-17
Winchester, Franklin, 6,305 — G-13
Woodbury, Cannon, 2,287 — D-13

Explanation of symbols: •– Census Designated Place (CDP)

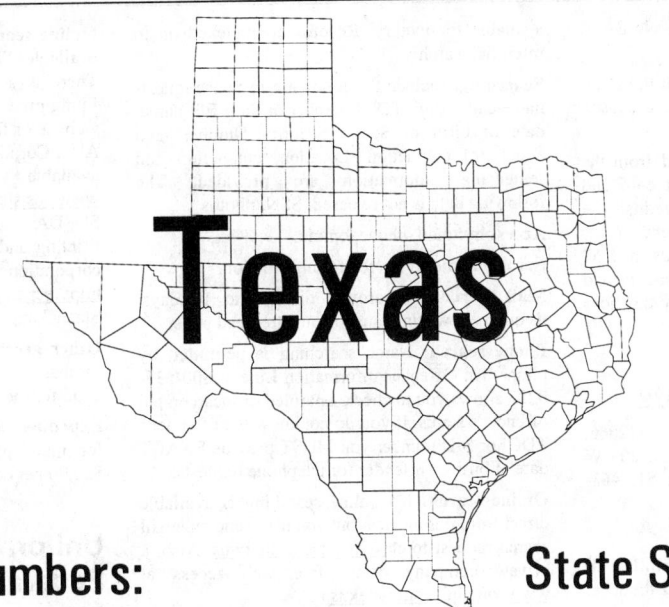

Texas

General Help Numbers:

Governor's Office
PO Box 12428
Austin, TX 78711-2428
www.governor.state.tx.us

512-463-2000
Fax 512-463-1849
7:30AM-5:30PM

Attorney General's Office
PO Box 12548
Austin, TX 78711-2548
www.oag.state.tx.us

512-463-2100
Fax 512-463-2063
7:30AM-5:30PM

Legislative Records
Legislative Reference Library
PO Box 12488
Austin, TX 78711-2488
www.lrl.state.tx.us

512-463-2182
Fax 512-475-4626
8AM-5PM

State Archives
PO Box 12927
Austin, TX 78711-2927
www.tsl.state.tx.us

512-463-5455
Fax 512-463-5430
8AM-5PM
Genealogy 8-5 TU-SA

State Specifics:

Capital: Austin
Travis County

Time Zone: CST*
* Texas' two western-most counties are MST:
They are: El Paso and Hudspeth,

Number of Counties: 254

Population: 22,490,022

Web Site: www.state.tx.us

State Agencies

Criminal Records

Dept of Public Safety, Correspondence Section, Crime Records Service, PO Box 15999, Austin, TX 78761-5999; 512-424-2474, 512-424-5011-Fax; 8AM-5PM.

http://records.txdps.state.tx.us

The database has many gaps, especially critical is Dallas County. A 2002 report from the Texas DPS states that overall only 69% of the all criminal records are recorded in the database.

Records are available from 1930 to present. It takes 1 day before new records are available for inquiry. Records are indexed on inhouse computer. 100% of arrest records are fingerprint supported.

61% of all arrests in database have final dispositions recorded.

Searching: To obtain ALL arrest information (conviction and non-conviction), must have a signed release and full set of fingerprints from the person of record. Include the following in your request-fingerprint card (with full name, DOB, sex, race, SSN), reason for request, signed release, full name and address of requester. To obtain conviction and deferred adjudication data only, submit full name, sex, race, and DOB. The SSN is helpful, but not required. No letter of authorization is needed for the conviction only report. The following data is not released: juvenile records. Fingerprint searches show complete record; name

search is conviction only and deferred adjudications. Since 1/1/93, records should include complete information regarding charge, disposition, date of conviction, and county. Data prior to this date may not be complete.

Access by: mail, in person, online.

Fee & Payment: The fee is $15.00 for the full search using fingerprints, and $10.00 for a name-based search. If approved, the FBI fingerprint check is an additional $24.00. Fee payee: Texas Department of Public Safety. Prepayment required. Credit cards are accepted for online searches only. Personal checks accepted. Credit cards accepted: MasterCard, Visa.

Mail search: Turnaround time: 7 days. No SASE is required.

In person search: Records requested at the Dept. of Public Safety Crime Records Service in Austin usually takes 1 business day.

Online search: Records can be pulled from the website. Requesters may use a credit card and establish an account to pre-purchase credits. The fee established by the Department (Sec. 411.135(b)) is $3.15 per request plus a $.57 handling fee. These checks are instantaneous and provide convictions and deferred adjudications only.

Statewide Court Records

Office of Court Administration, PO Box 12066, Austin, TX 78711-2066 (Courier address: 205 W 14th St, Ste. 600, Austin, TX 78711); 512-463-1625, 512-463-1648-Fax; 8AM-5PM.

www.courts.state.tx.us/oca

Except for certain online research capabilities, all trial court record access must be done at the local level.

Searching: Trial court records are maintained by each county.

Access by: online.

Online search: Case records of the Supreme Court can be searched at www.supreme.courts.state.tx.us. Court of Criminal Appeals opinions at www.cca.courts.state.tx.us. All Appellate Court case records at www.courts.state.tx.us/appcourt.asp.

Sexual Offender Registry

Dept of Public Safety, Sex Offender Registration, PO Box 4143, Austin, TX 78765-4143; 512-424-2800, 512-424-5666-Fax; 8AM-5PM.

http://records.txdps.state.tx.us

It takes 1 day before new records are available for inquiry.

Searching: A sex offender's home telephone number, SSN, drivers license number will not be released.

Access by: mail, online.

Fee & Payment: A $10.00 fee is charged for mail searches only. Fee payee: Texas Department of Public Safety. Prepayment required. Personal checks accepted.

Mail search: Turnaround time: 1-2 weeks. There is a $10.00 fee. No SASE is required.

Online search: Sex offender data is available at http://records.txdps.state.tx.us/soSearch/soSearch.cfm. There is no charge for a sex offender search. To see which organizations have purchased the sexual offender database, go to http://records.txdps.state.tx.us/forsale.cfm.

Incarceration Records

Texas Department of Criminal Justice, Bureau of Classification and Records, PO Box 99, Huntsville, TX 77342 (Courier address: 861 IH 45 North, Huntsville, TX 77320); 936-295-6371 (Offender Locator), 800-535-0283 (In State Parole Status line), 8AM-5PM.

www.tdcj.state.tx.us

Records are available on current and former inmates. It takes 1-3 days before new records are available for inquiry. Records are indexed on in microfiche archive.

Searching: Include the following in your request-name and 7-digit TDCJ number or their full name, date of birth or Social Security Number, and county of conviction. Location, conviction and sentencing information are provided. The following data is not released: SSN, photos

Access by: mail, phone, online.

Fee & Payment: No fee for information.

Mail search: Turnaround time: 7 to 10 days. Requests in writing must be on letterhead paper.

Phone search: Name searching is permitted by phone. An Offender Information Line at 800-535-0283 allows you to check a paroled or incarcerated offender's status. If you do not know the offender's TDCJ or SID number you MUST provide EXACT date of birth of offender for telephone requests.

Online search: No online searching is available direct from this agency, but you may send an email search request to classify@tdcj.state.tx.us. Also, a private company offers free web access at www.vinelink.com/index.jsp.

Corporation, Fictitious Name, Limited Partnership, Limited Liability Company, Assumed Name, Trademarks/Servicemarks

Secretary of State, Corporation Section, PO Box 13697, Austin, TX 78711-3697 (Courier address: J Earl Rudder Bldg, 1019 Brazos, B-13, Austin, TX 78701); 512-463-5555 (Information), 512-463-5578 (Copies), 512-463-5709-Fax; 8AM-5PM.

www.sos.state.tx.us

Ongoing requesters are encouraged to set-up a Client Account.

Records are available from the 1800s. Records are indexed on inhouse computer, online.

Searching: New records are available immediately on the computer, but it takes 10 days before new records are available to be copied. Requests may be ordered via e-mail from the website. Include the following in your request-full name of business, corporation file number. In addition to the articles of incorporation, corporation records include the following information: Public Information Reports (extracted information from the database only), Officers, Directors, DBAs, Prior (merged) names, Inactive and Reserved names.

Access by: mail, phone, fax, in person, online.

Fee & Payment: Certification is $10.00 plus $1.00 per document page. Long form is $25.00. Uncertified copies are $.10 per page, if over 50 copies then $.15 per page. If credit card used, add 2.1%. Fee payee: Secretary of State. Frequent requesters may set up a pre-paid billing account. Personal checks and MasterCard, Visa, Discover accepted.

Mail search: Turnaround time: 3 to 5 days. No SASE is required.

Phone search: No fee for telephone request.

Fax search: Fax requests cost an additional $2.00 per page plus expedited fees.

In person search: Public access terminals are available for walk-in requesters.

Online search: There are several online methods available. Web access is available 24 hours daily. There is a $1.00 fee for each record searched. Filing procedures and forms are available from the website or from 900-263-0060 ($1.00 per minute). Also, Corporate and other TX Sec of State data is available via SOSDirect on the Web; visit www.sos.state.tx.us/corp/sosda/index.shtml. SOSDA accounts are converted to SOSDirect. Printing and certifying capabilities. Also, general corporation information is available at no fee at http://ecpa.cpa.state.tx.us/coa/Index.html from the State Comptroller office.

Other access: The agency makes portions of its database available for purchase. Call 512-475-2755 for more information.

Expedited service: Expedited service is available for mail, phone and in person searches. Add $10.00 per document.

Uniform Commercial Code, Federal Tax Liens

UCC Section, Secretary of State, PO Box 13193, Austin, TX 78711-3193 (Courier address: 1019 Brazos St, Rm B-13, Austin, TX 78701); 512-475-2703, 512-463-1425-Fax; 8AM-5PM.

www.sos.state.tx.us/ucc/index.shtml

Records are available from 1966; imaged and stored in the BEST System. It takes 3 to 5 days before new records are available for inquiry. Records are indexed on microfilm, microfiche and inhouse computer. Records are normally destroyed after (purged) 1 year past lapse date.

Searching: Use search request form UCC-11. The search includes all federal liens on businesses. Federal liens on individuals and all state tax liens are filed at the county level. Include the following in your request-debtor name.

Access by: mail, phone, fax, in person, online.

Fee & Payment: Using the approved form - $15.00 per name; other forms - $30.00 per name; copies - $1.00 per page. Effective 5/9/01, a version of the UCC-11 was designated as the standard form. Fee payee: Secretary of State. Prepayment required. Personal checks and MasterCard, Visa, Discover and LegalEase cards accepted.

Mail search: Turnaround time: 1 to 2 weeks. No SASE is required.

Phone search: Debtor names will be released. Collateral is listed on imaged documents only.

Fax search: There is an additional fee of $15.00.

In person search: You may request information in person.

Online search: UCC and other Texas Secretary of State data is available via SOSDirect on the Web at www.sos.state.tx.us/corp/sosda/index.shtml. UCC records are $1.00 per search, with printing ($1.00 per page) and certifying ($10.00), also. General information and forms can also be found at the website.

Other access: This agency offers the database for sale, contact the Information Services Dept at 512-463-5609 for further details.

Expedited service: Expedited service is available for mail, in-person and phone searches. Turnaround time: 24 hours. Add $15.00 per form. Expedited mail service is offered. Also, you can include your delivery service account number for fastest return.

State Tax Liens

Records not maintained by a state level agency.

Records are located at the county level.

Sales Tax Registrations

Comptroller of Public Accounts, Sales Tax Permits, PO Box 13528, Austin, TX 78711-3528 (Courier address: LBJ Office Bldg, 111 E 17th St, Austin, TX 78774); 800-531-5441 x66013, 800-252-1386 (Other Business Searches), 512-475-1610-Fax; 8AM-5PM.

www.window.state.tx.us/taxinfo/sales

Records are available from 1985 to present. It takes 6 weeks before new records are available for inquiry. Records are normally destroyed after 20 years.

Searching: This agency will provide the following business information: business name, address, phone number, tax permit number, a list of officers & directors, and the registered agent for a corporation. Audit results are not released. Include the following in your request-business name. They will also search by tax payer number.

Access by: mail, phone, fax, in person, online.

Fee & Payment: There is no search fee. Fee payee: Comptroller of Public Accounts. Prepayment required. Personal checks accepted. No credit cards accepted.

Mail search: Turnaround time: 10 working days. If more than 3 businesses are requested, the agency prefers that you request by mail. No fee for mail request.

Phone search: No fee for telephone request. The agency will provide responses to 3 business names or less over the phone.

Fax search: Fax search requests accepted.

In person search: No fee for request. They will verify information or will mail a letter.

Online search: This office makes general corporation information available at http://ecpa.cpa.state.tx.us/vendor/tpsearch1.html. There is no fee. Go to http://aixtcp.cpa.state.tx.us/star/ to search 16,000+ documents by index or collection. Send email requests, send to open.records@cpa.state.tx.us.

Other access: Sales tax registration lists are available to download as ftp files.

Expedited service: Will expedite at customer expense.

Birth Certificates

Department of State Health Srvs, Bureau of Vital Statistics, PO Box 12040, Austin, TX 78711-2040 (Courier address: 1100 W 49th St, Austin, TX 78756-3191); 512-758-7366, 512-758-7711-Fax; 8AM-5PM.

www.dshs.state.tx.us/vs/default.shtm

Records are available from 1903 to present. It takes receipt from local registration officials before new records are available for inquiry. Records are indexed on microfiche, index cards, inhouse computer.

Searching: Must have a signed, notarized release from person of record or immediate family member and name and address of requester for records less than 75 years old. Otherwise a Verification of Birth is issued. Include the

following in your request-full name, names of parents, mother's maiden name, date of birth, place of birth, relationship to person of record, reason for information request. Must send a copy of requester's photo ID or show a photo ID for in-person searches. The following data is not released: Social Security Numbers.

Access by: mail, fax, in person.

Fee & Payment: The search fee is $11.00 per name. Fee payee: Bureau of Vital Statistics. Prepayment required. Credit cards accepted for fax requests only. Personal checks accepted. Credit cards accepted: MasterCard, Visa.

Mail search: Turnaround time: 6 to 8 weeks. No SASE is required.

Fax search: See expedited service.

In person search: Go directly to Local Registrar's office for births that occurred anywhere in Texas. Remote site will issue an abstract of birth facts (a legal birth certificate). Remote Site Access is not available at all county offices. Turnaround time 1-2 hours.

Other access: Birth Indexes from 1926-1995 are available on CD-Rom and microfiche.

Expedited service: Expedited service is available for fax searches at 512-458-7711. Turnaround time: 48 to 96 hours. Add $5.00 expedited service fee, and either $8.00 for UPS ground or $13.65 for US Express mail.

Death Records

Department of State Health Srvs, Bureau of Vital Statistics, PO Box 12040, Austin, TX 78711-2040 (Courier address: 1100 W 49th St, Austin, TX 78756-3191); 512-758-7366, 512-758-7711-Fax; 8AM-5PM.

www.dshs.state.tx.us/vs/default.shtm

Records are available from 1903 to present. It takes receipt from local registration officials before new records are available for inquiry. Records are indexed on microfiche, index cards, inhouse computer.

Searching: Must have a signed release from immediate family member and requester's name and current address for records less than 25 years old. Otherwise a Verification of Death is issued. Include the following in your request-full name, date of death, place of death, Social Security Number, relationship to person of record, reason for information request. You must include a copy of requesters' photo ID or show a photo ID for in person requests. The following data is not released: Social Security Numbers.

Access by: mail, fax, in person.

Fee & Payment: The search fee is $9.00 per name. Add $3.00 per name per copy for each additional copy. Fee payee: Bureau of Vital Statistics. Prepayment required. Credit cards accepted for fax requests only. Personal checks accepted. Credit cards accepted: MasterCard, Visa.

Mail search: Turnaround time: 6 to 8 weeks. No SASE is required.

Fax search: See expedited service.

In person search: Turnaround time 1-2 hours.

Other access: Death Indexes from 1964-1998 are available on CD-Rom and microfiche.

Expedited service: Expedited service is available for fax searches at 512-458-7711. Turnaround time: 48 to 96 hours. Add $5.00 expedited service

fee, and either $8.00 for UPS ground or $13.65 for US Express mail.

Marriage Certificates

Department of State Health Srvs, Bureau of Vital Statistics, PO Box 12040, Austin, TX 78711-2040 (Courier address: 1100 W 49th St, Austin, TX 78756-3191); 512-758-7366, 512-758-7711-Fax; 8AM-5PM.

www.dshs.state.tx.us/vs/default.shtm

Records are available from 1966 to present. It takes delivery from the county clerk before new records are available for inquiry. Records are indexed on microfiche, index cards, inhouse computer.

Searching: This agency will only supply a verification. They only have a copy of the application form and an index to the county record. The actual certificate must be obtained from the county recorder of record. Include the following in your request-names of husband and wife, date of marriage, place or county of marriage. The following data is not released: Social Security Numbers.

Access by: mail, fax, in person, online.

Fee & Payment: The search fee is $9.00 per record. Fee payee: Bureau of Vital Statistics. Prepayment required. Credit cards accepted for fax requests only. Personal checks accepted. Credit cards accepted: MasterCard, Visa.

Mail search: Turnaround time: 6 to 10 weeks. No SASE is required.

Fax search: See expedited service.

In person search: Turnaround time while you wait.

Online search: Marriage records for 1966 to 2001 are available through a private company website at www.genlookups.com/texas_marriages/.

Expedited service: Expedited service is available for fax searches. Turnaround time: 48 to 96 hours. Add $5.00 expedited service fee, and either $8.00 for UPS ground or $13.65 for US Express mail.

Divorce Records

Department of State Health Srvs, Bureau of Vital Statistics, PO Box 12040, Austin, TX 78711-2040 (Courier address: 1100 W 49th St, Austin, TX 78756-3191); 512-758-7366, 512-758-7711-Fax; 8AM-5PM.

www.dshs.state.tx.us/vs/default.shtm

Records are available from 1968 to present. It takes delivery from the county district clerk before new records are available for inquiry. Records are indexed on microfiche, inhouse computer.

Searching: This agency will only supply a verification. They only have the report of divorce form and an index that directs you to the county district court of record. A copy of the actual record must be obtained at the county level. Include the following in your request-names of husband and wife, date of divorce, year divorce case began, case number (if known).

Access by: mail, fax, in person, online.

Fee & Payment: The search fee is $9.00 per name. Fee payee: Bureau of Vital Statistics. Prepayment required. Credit cards accepted for fax requests only. Personal checks accepted. Credit cards accepted: MasterCard, Visa.

Mail search: Turnaround time: 6 to 12 weeks. No SASE is required.

Fax search: See expedited service.

In person search: Turnaround time 1-2 hours.

Online search: Divorce indexes can be downloaded and searched by year at www.dshs.state.tx.us/vs/marriagedivorce/dindex.s htm. A second private company website at www.genlookups.com/texas_divorces/ offers records from 1968 to 2001.

Expedited service: Expedited service is available for fax searches at 512-458-7711. Turnaround time: 48 to 96 hours. Add $5.00 expedited service fee, and either $8.00 for UPS ground or $13.65 for US Express mail.

Workers' Compensation Records

Texas Workers' Compensation Commission, 7551 Metro Center Dr, #100, MS-92B, Austin, TX 78744; 512-804-4000, 512-804-4990 (Reprographics Department), 512-804-4993-Fax; 8AM-5PM.

www.twcc.state.tx.us

General information about previous work related injuries will only be provided to employers if the applicant has had two or more injuries in the last five years and the employer has made a conditional offer of employment.

Records are available from 1962. Records are indexed on inhouse computer. Records are normally destroyed after 50 years.

Searching: A signed, notarized release is required to obtain file copies. Use Form TWCC-153 for claim file or medical records or hearing record. Include the following in your request-claimant name, Social Security Number, date of accident. Use of TWCC 153 Form is required. The file number is required to receive copies. If you don't know the file number or date of accident, you must submit Form TWCC-155. Claim file records are confidential; only parties to claim have access.

Access by: mail, fax, online.

Fee & Payment: The fees for TWCC-153 are $1.00 for the first page and $.30 each additional page and $1.00 for certification. The fees for TWCC-155 are $15.00 search fee and $1.00 for certification. Fee payee: Texas Workers' Compensation Commission. Prepayment required. An invoice will be sent when using TWCC 153 Form. Copies are held until payment received. Personal checks accepted. No credit cards accepted.

Mail search: Turnaround time: 4 to 6 weeks. No SASE is required.

Fax search: See expedited service.

Online search: The website gives administrative decisions for cases back to 1991 and also permits searching for employers with coverage.

Expedited service: Expedited service is available for mail or fax service, using the TWCC 153 form. Fee foe expedited copy service is additional $25.00.

Driver Records

Department of Public Safety, Driver Records Section, PO Box 149246, Austin, TX 78714-9246 (Courier address: 5805 N Lamar Blvd, Austin, TX 78752); 512-424-2032, 512-424-2600, 512-424-7285-Fax; 8AM-5PM.

www.txdps.state.tx.us

Tickets are only available from the court system.

Records are available for 5 years for moving violations and suspensions, indefinite for DWIs, 11 years for SR judgments. Non-moving violations do not appear on the record. It takes 30 days before new records are available for inquiry. Records are normally destroyed after 125 years, generally.

Searching: Requesters must use Form DR-1. This form contains space for written consent if personal information is requested by a casual user. The name and driver's license number or date of birth, are needed when ordering. The following data is not released: Social Security Numbers or medical records, class type listings

Access by: mail, in person, online.

Fee & Payment: Driving record fees of mail or walk-ins are $6.00 for a 3 year driving record, $10.00 if certified. Fee is $6.50-$7.50 for online access. A license statue including latest address is $4.00 per report. There is a full charge for a "no record found." Fee payee: Texas Department of Public Safety. Prepayment required. Personal checks accepted. No credit cards accepted.

Mail search: Turnaround time: 7 to 10 days. No SASE is required.

In person search: Eligible Texas Driver License holders may request their own individual Driver Record online. The printed record is postal mailed by DPS within 5 business days. Normal turnaround time is same day.

Online search: Access is limited to only high volume users who have a permissible use and sign an agreement. Records are $6.50 for the three year record (Type 2) or $7.50 for the complete record (Type 3). Both batch and interactive modes are available. Call 512-424-2600 to receive a copy of the license agreement.

Other access: Bulk data is available in electronic format for approved requesters. Weekly updates are available. The file does not include driver history data.

Vehicle Ownership
Vehicle Identification

Department of Transportation, Vehicle Titles and Registration Division,, Austin, TX 78779 (Courier address: 4000 Jackson Ave, Austin, TX 78731); 512-465-7611, 512-465-7736-Fax; 8AM-5PM.

www.dot.state.tx.us/vtr/vtrreginfo.htm

Submit a "Request for TX Motor Vehicle Information" Form VTR-275, including a signed statement certifying that information is requested for a lawful & legitimate purpose, to be used in accordance with 18 USC, Sec2721-2725 and the TX Trans Code, Ch#730.

Records are available as active files until there is no activity for 18 months, upon which records become inactive. After 5 years of inactivity, records are archived. Title history information is available on microfiche for 16 years to present. It takes 48 hours after entry into the system before new records are available for inquiry. Records are

indexed on microfilm and microfiche; current records indexed on computer. Motor Vehicle records are indexed by VIN, title number, plate number, and expiration year. Records are normally destroyed after 16 years (title history records).

Searching: For plate checks and title histories, include a signed/completed Request for Texas Motor Vehicle Information Form VTR-275 certifying your eligibility to receive information. The state does not provide name search capability. Use Form VTR-275 for ordering a vehicle history. Personal information is not released to casual requesters without attaching written consent of subject. The following data is not released: Social Security Numbers.

Access by: mail, phone, online.

Fee & Payment: The current fee for VIN and plate checks is $2.30 per record. The fee for a title search/history is $5.75. Add $1.00 for certification. Fee payee: Texas Department of Transportation. Prepayment required. Personal checks accepted. No credit cards accepted.

Mail search: Turnaround time: 7-10 days for plates. Turnaround time for title histories is 4 weeks. Use of the state form is required.

Phone search: The department accepts phone search requests for current records The telephone current record lookups contain no personal information.

Online search: Online access is available for pre-approved accounts by contract. A $200 deposit is required, there is a $23.00 charge per month and $.12 fee per inquiry. Searching by name is not permitted. For more information, contact Production Data Control.

Other access: The department offers tape cartridge retrieval for customized searches or based on the entire database, to eligible organizations under signed contract. Weekly updates and batch inquiries are available. Database contains about 28,000,000 records.

Expedited service: The department will overnight the information requested when the customer provides their account number and service provider.

Accident Reports

Texas Department of Public Safety, Crash Records Bureau, PO Box 15999, Austin, TX 78761-5999 (Courier address: 5805 N Lamar Blvd, Austin, TX 78752); 512-424-2600, 8AM-5PM.

www.txdps.state.tx.us

Records are available for 10 years to present. It takes 30 days before new records are available for inquiry.

Searching: Accident reports investigated by law enforcement agencies and driver reports are open to the public. Items required to search include two or more of following: full name of any person involved, specific city/county location, and date of incident.

Access by: mail, in person.

Fee & Payment: Fee is $6.00 per uncertified report and $8.00 per certified report. There is a $6.00 charge for a no record found search. Fee payee: Texas Department of Public Safety. Prepayment required. Personal checks accepted. No credit cards accepted.

Mail search: Turnaround time: 4 to 6 weeks.

In person search: Requests will be processed immediately, unless extensive lists presented.

Vessel Ownership
Vessel Registration

Parks & Wildlife Dept, 4200 Smith School Rd, Austin, TX 78744; 512-389-4828, 800-262-8755, 512-389-4900-Fax; 8AM-5PM.

www.tpwd.state.tx.us/fishboat/boat/owner

Record checks can be processed at any TPWD Boats Law Enforcement Field Office. All history requests must be submitted to the TPWD Headquarters in Austin.

Records are available from 1976 to present for all boats. Records indexed on computer. All motorized boats must be registered and titled. Sailboats 14 ft and over must be registered and titled. Lien data shows on reports. It takes less than 1 day before new records are available for inquiry. Records are indexed on computer. Records are normally destroyed after 10 years.

Searching: More detailed data is available for most recent 10-year period. The written request must be submitted on completed PWD763 Form (ownership, lien-holder information printout or ownership history request) along with applicable fee.

Access by: mail, in person.

Fee & Payment: There is a $2.00 fee for a record check and a $10.00 fee for a complete history from microfilm. Fee payee: TX Parks & Wildlife Dept. Prepayment required. Personal checks accepted. No credit cards accepted.

Mail search: Turnaround time: 2 to 3 weeks. Turnaround time is often longer in the summer. No SASE is required.

In person search: Histories are returned by mail.

Other access: Records are released in bulk format; however, requesters are screened for lawful purpose. The agency requires a copy of any item mailed or distributed as a result of purchase. Media includes tape, labels, and printed lists.

Voter Registration
Access to Records is Restricted.

Secretary of State, Elections Division, PO Box 12060, Austin, TX 78711-2060; 800-252-8683, 512-475-2811-Fax; 8AM-5PM.

www.sos.state.tx.us

To do individual look-ups, one must go to the Tax Assessor-Collector at the county level. Records are open. The state will sell the entire database, for non-commercial purposes, in a variety of media and sort formats.

GED Certificates

Texas Education Agency, GED Unit CC:350, PO Box 13817, Austin, TX 78711 (Courier address: 1701 N Congress Ave, Austin, TX 78701-1494); 512-463-9292, 512-305-9493-Fax; 8AM-5PM.

www.tea.state.tx.us/ged

Records are available from 1944 to present. It takes 2 weeks before new records are available for inquiry. Records are indexed on mainframe computer.

Searching: Include the following in your request- name, and DOB or SSN. A signed release is needed for transcript, but not for verification only .

Access by: mail, phone, fax, in person.

Fee & Payment: There is no fee for verification, but $5.00 fee for a record of transcripts. Also, if the subject did not pay the GED fees and the record is prior to 1994, a fee may be charged to the requester. Fee payee: TEA-GED

Mail search: Turnaround time: 1 to 2 days. No SASE is required.

Phone search: If a SSN or DOB is presented, this agency will verify if a person has a GED.

Fax search: Verifications can be done by fax. To receive copy of grades fax requests require a signed release.

In person search: Over-the-counter service available.

Hunting and Fishing License Information

TX Parks & Wildlife Department, License Section, 4200 Smith School Rd, Austin, TX 78744; 512-389-4820, 512-389-4330-Fax; 8AM-5PM.

www.tpwd.state.tx.us

Records are available from 09/01/92 forward and are computerized. Records between 09/01/96 to 0/31/02 cane provided, but a fee may be required; also, records may be incomplete. It takes seconds before new records are available for inquiry.

Searching: All requests must be in writing on their official Form, unless request is for self. They will release address, status, and date of issue. Include the following in your request-driver's DL#, SSN and DOB, or by first and last name with DOB.

Access by: mail, fax, in person.

Fee & Payment: There is no fee, unless for licenses issued between 09/01/96 and 08/31/02.

Mail search: Turnaround time: 10 days. TWPD abides by Open Records Law. Up to 5 names can be requested by mail.

Fax search: Up to 5 names can be requested by fax. Results are mailed or can be faxed.

In person search: Over-the-counter service available only for license holder or signed consent

Texas State Licensing Agencies

For details about the agency responsible for licensing/certifying/registering an item below or in the Agency Quick Finder section, match an item's number with the number of the agency in the *Licensing Agency Information* section.

Texas Licenses Searchable Online

Acupuncturist #30	http://reg.tsbme.state.tx.us/onlineverif/phys_noticeverif.asp?
Air Conditioning/Refrigeration Contr. #14	www.license.state.tx.us/LicenseSearch/
Alarm Installer/Company/Sales #35	www.tcps.state.tx.us/individual/individual_search.aspx
Alarm/Security Instructor #35	www.tcps.state.tx.us/individual/individual_search.aspx
Alcoholic Bev. Dist./Mfg./Retailer #46	www.tabc.state.tx.us/pubinfo/rosters/default.htm
Alcoholic Beverage Permit #46	www.tabc.state.tx.us/pubinfo/rosters/default.htm
Architect #61	www.tbae.state.tx.us/PublicInfo/FindProfessional_Arch.shtml
Architectural Barrier #14	www.license.state.tx.us/LicenseSearch/
Athletic Trainer #21	www.dshs.state.tx.us/at/at_roster.shtm
Attorney #40	www.texasbar.com
Auctioneer #14	www.license.state.tx.us/LicenseSearch/
Audiologist #22	www.dshs.state.tx.us/plc/default.shtm
Audiology Assistant #22	www.dshs.state.tx.us/plc/default.shtm
Bank Agency, Foreign #1	www.banking.state.tx.us/asp/fba/lookup.asp
Bank, State Chartered #1	www.banking.state.tx.us/asp/bank/lookup.asp
Barber #2	www.tsbbe.state.tx.us
Barber School #2	www.tsbbe.state.tx.us/webpages/schoolr.htm
Barber Shop / Barber Student #2	www.tsbbe.state.tx.us
Boiler Inspector/Installer #14	www.license.state.tx.us/LicenseSearch/
Boxing/Combative Sports Event #14	www.license.state.tx.us/LicenseSearch/
Career Counselor #14	www.license.state.tx.us/LicenseSearch/
Check Seller #1	www.banking.state.tx.us/asp/soc/lookup.asp
Child Support Agency, Private #1	www.banking.state.tx.us/pcsea/licensed.htm
Counselor, Professional #41	www.dshs.state.tx.us/counselor/lpc_rosters.shtm
Courier Company #35	www.tcps.state.tx.us/individual/individual_search.aspx
CPA Individual/Firm/Sponsor #43	www.tsbpa.state.tx.us/srcmain.htm
Currency Exchange #1	www.banking.state.tx.us/asp/cex/lookup.asp
Dentists / Dental Hygienist / Dental Laboratory #23	www.tsbde.state.tx.us/dbsearch/
Dietitian #22	www.dshs.state.tx.us/plc/default.shtm
ECA #27	http://160.42.108.3/ems_web/blh_html_page1.htm
Elevator/Escalator #14	www.license.state.tx.us/LicenseSearch/
Emergency Medical Technician #27	http://160.42.108.3/ems_web/blh_html_page1.htm
Engineer #5	www.tbpe.state.tx.us/downloads.htm
Engineering Firm #5	www.tbpe.state.tx.us/downloads.htm
Fire Alarm System Contr. #53	www.tdi.state.tx.us/fire/fmli.html
Fire Extinguisher Contractor #53	www.tdi.state.tx.us/fire/fmli.html
Fire Inspector/Investigator #56	www.tcfp.state.tx.us
Fire Protection Sprinkler Contractor #53	www.tdi.state.tx.us/fire/fmli.html
Fire Suppression Specialist #56	www.tcfp.state.tx.us
Firearm Instructor #35	www.tcps.state.tx.us/individual/individual_search.aspx
Firefighter #56	www.tcfp.state.tx.us
Fireworks Display #53	www.tdi.state.tx.us/fire/fmli.html
Funeral Prepaid Permit Holder #1	www.banking.state.tx.us/asp/pfc/lookup.asp
Guard Dog Company #35	www.tcps.state.tx.us/individual/individual_search.aspx
Hearing Instrument Dispenser/Fitter #22	www.dshs.state.tx.us/plc/default.shtm
Independent Instructor #28	www.dshs.state.tx.us/massage/default.shtm
Industrialized Housing #14	www.license.state.tx.us/LicenseSearch/
Insurance Adjuster #48	www.texasonline.state.tx.us/NASApp/tdi/TdiARManager
Insurance Agency/Agent/Company #48	www.texasonline.state.tx.us/NASApp/tdi/TdiARManager
Interior Designer #61	www.tbae.state.tx.us/PublicInfo/FindProfessional_IntDes.shtml
Landscape Architect #61	www.tbae.state.tx.us/PublicInfo/FindProfessional_LandArch.shtml
Lead Abatement Project Designer #55	www.tdh.state.tx.us/beh/lead/default.htm
Lead Risk Assessor/Inspector/Lead Firm #55	www.tdh.state.tx.us/beh/lead/default.htm
Lead Training Program Provider #55	www.tdh.state.tx.us/beh/lead/default.htm
Lobbyist #50	www.ethics.state.tx.us/php/index.html
Manicurist/Manicurist Shop #2	www.tsbbe.state.tx.us

Marriage & Family Therapist #31 .... www.dshs.state.tx.us/mft/mft_contact.shtm
Massage Therapist / Instructor #28 .... www.dshs.state.tx.us/massage/default.shtm
Massage Therapy Establish't/School #28 .... www.dshs.state.tx.us/massage/default.shtm
Medical Doctor/Physician #30 .... http://reg.tsbme.state.tx.us/onlineverif/phys_noticeverif.asp?
Medical Specialty (Doctor) #30 .... http://reg.tsbme.state.tx.us/onlineverif/phys_noticeverif.asp?
Nurse, Advanced Practice #63 .... https://www.bne.state.tx.us/olv/apninq.htm
Nurse, Vocational #63 .... https://www.bne.state.tx.us/olv/vninq.htm
Nurse/RN #63 .... https://www.bne.state.tx.us/olv/rninq.htm
Occupational Therapist/Assistant #17 .... www.ecptote.state.tx.us/license/otverif.php
Occ'l/Physical Therapy Facility #17 .... www.ecptote.state.tx.us/license/ftverif.php
Optometrist #51 .... www.tob.state.tx.us/tob%20verifications.htm
Orthotics & Prosthetics Facility #26 .... www.dshs.state.tx.us/plc/default.shtm
Orthotist/Prosthetist #26 .... www.dshs.state.tx.us/plc/default.shtm
Paramedic #27 .... http://160.42.108.3/ems_web/blh_html_page1.htm
Perfusionist #26 .... www.dshs.state.tx.us/plc/default.shtm
Perpetual Care Cemetery #1 .... www.banking.state.tx.us/asp/pcc/lookup.asp
Personal Employment Service #14 .... www.license.state.tx.us/LicenseSearch/
Pharmacist / Pharmacist Intern #24 .... www.tsbp.state.tx.us/dbsearch/Default.htm
Pharmacy / Pharmacy Technician #24 .... www.tsbp.state.tx.us/dbsearch/Default.htm
Physical Therapist/Assistant #17 .... www.ecptote.state.tx.us/license/ptverif.php
Physician Assistant #30 .... http://reg.tsbme.state.tx.us/onlineverif/phys_noticeverif.asp?
Physicist, Medical #26 .... www.dshs.state.tx.us/plc/default.shtm
Podiatrist #20 .... www.foot.state.tx.us/verifications.htm
Political Action Committee List #50 .... www.ethics.state.tx.us/dfs/paclists.htm
Political Contributor #50 .... www.ethics.state.tx.us/php/cesearch.html
Polygraph Examiner Sex Offenders #26 .... www.dshs.state.tx.us/plc/default.shtm
Private Business Letter of Authority #35 .... www.tcps.state.tx.us/individual/individual_search.aspx
Private Investigator #35 .... www.tcps.state.tx.us/individual/individual_search.aspx
Property Tax Consultant #14 .... www.license.state.tx.us/LicenseSearch/
Psychological Associate #19 .... www.tsbep.state.tx.us/
Psychologist / Psychologist, Provisional #19 .... www.tsbep.state.tx.us/
Public Accountant-CPA / CPA Firm #43 .... www.tsbpa.state.tx.us/srcmain.htm
Public Accountant Educ'r/Sponsor #43 .... www.tsbpa.state.tx.us/srcmain.htm
Radiology Technician #16 .... www.dshs.state.tx.us/mrt/mrt_roster.shtm
Real Estate Agent/Broker/Sales/Inspector #52 .... www.trec.state.tx.us/licenseeLookup/search.aspx
Real Estate Appraiser #47 .... www.talcb.state.tx.us/appraisers/Appraiser_Search.asp
Representative Ofc. (Foreign Bank) #1 .... www.banking.state.tx.us/asp/rep/lookup.asp
Respiratory Care Practitioner #29 .... www.dshs.state.tx.us/respiratory/rc_roster.shtm
Sanitarian #22 .... www.dshs.state.tx.us/plc/default.shtm
School Psychology Specialist #19 .... www.tsbep.state.tx.us/
Security Agency, Private #35 .... www.tcps.state.tx.us/individual/individual_search.aspx
Security Agent/Service/Sales #35 .... www.tcps.state.tx.us/individual/individual_search.aspx
Service Contract Provider #14 .... www.license.state.tx.us/LicenseSearch/
Sex Offender Treatment Provider #26 .... www.dshs.state.tx.us/plc/default.shtm
Social Worker #26 .... www.dshs.state.tx.us/plc/default.shtm
Speech-Language Pathologist #22 .... www.dshs.state.tx.us/plc/default.shtm
Staff Leasing #14 .... www.license.state.tx.us/LicenseSearch/
STAP Vendor #6 .... www.puc.state.tx.us/relay/stapc/vendors.cfm
Surveyor, Land #4 .... http://txls.state.tx.us/sect03/rosters.html
Surveyor, Out-of-Texas #4 .... http://txls.state.tx.us/sect03/rosters.html
Surveyor, State Land #4 .... http://txls.state.tx.us/sect03/rosters.html
Talent Agency #14 .... www.license.state.tx.us/LicenseSearch/
Tax Appraisal Professional #59 .... www.txbtpe.state.tx.us
Teacher #42 .... https://secure.sbec.state.tx.us/SBECONLINE/virtcert.asp
Temporary Common Worker #14 .... www.license.state.tx.us/LicenseSearch/
Transportation Service Provider #54 .... www.license.state.tx.us/LicenseSearch/
Trust Company #1 .... www.banking.state.tx.us/asp/trustco/lookup.asp
Undergr'd Storage Tank Installer #60 .... www.tceq.state.tx.us/compliance/compliance_support/licensing/ust_lic.html
Vehicle Protection Provider #14 .... www.license.state.tx.us/LicenseSearch/
Veterinarian #18 .... www.tbvme.state.tx.us/verify.htm
Water Well & Pump Installer #14 .... www.license.state.tx.us/LicenseSearch/
Weather Modification Service #14 .... www.license.state.tx.us/LicenseSearch/

Texas Licensing Quick Finder

Acupuncturist #30	512-305-7067
Agricultural Specialties, Perishable #11	512-463-7476
Air Conditioning/Refrig.Contr. #14	512-463-6599
Alarm Installer/Company/Sales #35	512-424-7710
Alarm/Security Instructor #35	512-424-7710
Alcoholic Bev. Dist./Mfg./Retailer #46	512-206-3360
Alcoholic Beverage Permit #46	512-206-3360
Architect #61	512-305-9000
Architectural Barrier #14	512-463-6599
Asbestos Abatement Contr. #12	512-834-6600 x2789
Asbestos Air Monitor Tech. #12	512-834-6600x2789
Asbestos Consult/Inspector #12	512-834-6600 x2789
Asbestos Mgmt Planner #12	512-834-6600 x2789
Asbestos Worker #12	512-834-6600 x2789
Athletic Agent #38	512-475-1769
Athletic Trainer #21	512-834-6615
Attorney #40	512-463-1463
Auctioneer #14	512-463-6599
Audiologist #22	512-834-6627
Audiology Assistant #22	512-834-6627
Automobile Club #38	512-475-1769
Bank Agency, Foreign #1	512-475-1300
Bank, State Chartered #1	512-475-1300
Barber #2	512-936-6333
Barber School / Shop / Student #2	512-936-6333
Beauty Shop/Salon #8	512-380-7659
Boiler Inspector/Installer #14	800-722-7843
Boxing/Combative Sports Event #14	512-463-5101
Business Opportunity #38	512-475-1769
Career Counselor #14	512-463-6599
Check Seller #1	512-475-1290
Child Care Facility/Administrator #49	512-438-3269
Child Support Enforcement Agency, Private #1	512-475-1300
Chiropractic Facility #25	512-305-6700
Chiropractic Radiologic Tech. #25	512-305-6700
Chiropractor #25	512-305-6700
Contact Lens Dispenser #26	512-834-4515
Cosmetologist #8	512-380-7659
Counselor, Professional #41	512-834-6658
Counselor,Profession'l Supervisor #41	512-834-6658
County Librarian #44	512-463-5466
Courier Company #35	512-424-7710
Court Reporter #9	512-463-1630
Court Reporting Firm #9	512-463-1630
CPA Individual/Firm/Sponsor #43	512-305-7853
Credit Service Organization #38	512-463-6906
Currency Exchange #1	512-475-1290
Day Care Center #49	512-438-3269
Day Care, Residential #49	512-438-3269
Dental Assistant #23	512-463-6400
Dental Hygienist #23	512-463-6400
Dental Laboratory #23	512-463-6400
Dentist #23	512-463-6400
Dietitian #22	512-834-6601
Dog Racing/Dog Racing Professional #36	512-833-6697
ECA #27	512-834-6700
Egg License #11	512-463-7476
Elevator/Escalator #14	512-463-6599
Emergency Medical Technician #27	512-834-6700
Engineer #5	512-440-7723
Engineering Firm #5	512-440-7723
Family Home Day Care #49	512-438-3269
Farm/Agricultural Service Co. #11	512-463-7476
Fire Alarm System Contr. #53	512-305-7935
Fire Extinguisher Contractor #53	512-305-7934
Fire Inspector/Investigator #56	512-239-4911
Fire Protection Sprinkler Contr. #53	512-305-7933
Fire Suppression Specialist #56	512-239-4911
Firearm Instructor #35	512-424-7710
Firefighter #56	512-239-4911
Fireworks Display #53	512-305-7930
Fish Farmer #11	512-463-7476
Fishing Guide #45	512-389-4818
Funeral Director #15	512-936-2474
Funeral Establ./Pre-Need Funeral Home #15	512-936-2474
Funeral Prepaid Permit Holder #1	512-475-1290
Grain Warehouser #11	512-463-7476
Guard Dog Company #35	512-424-7710
Health Related Registry #22	512-834-6602
Health Spa #38	512-463-6906
Hearing Instrum't Dispenser/Fitter #22	512-834-6784
Home Equity & Secondary Mortgage Lenders #7	512-936-7600
Home Health Agency #26	512-834-6646
Horse Racing/Horse Racing Prof. #36	512-833-6697
Independent Instructor #28	512-834-6616
Industrialized Housing #14	512-463-7353
Insurance Adjuster #48	512-322-3503
Insurance Agency/Agent #48	512-322-3503
Insurance Company #48	512-322-3507
Interior Designer #61	512-305-9000
Interpreter for the Deaf #6	512-407-3250
Investment Advisor #39	512-305-8332
Irrigator #57	512-239-6719
Landscape Architect #61	512-305-9000
Law Enforcement Officer #58	512-936-7700
Lead Abatement Project Designer #55	512-834-6612
Lead Abatement Worker/Super. #55	512-834-6612
Lead Firm #55	512-834-6612
Lead Risk Assessor/Inspector #55	512-834-6612
Lead Training Program Provider #55	512-834-6612
Loan Company #7	512-936-7600
Loan Officer #37	512-475-1350
Lobbyist #50	512-463-5800
LPG-Liquef'd Petroleum Gas Tech #11	512-462-1441
Mammography System #16	512-834-6688 x2037
Manicurist/Manicurist Shop #2	512-936-6333
Marriage & Family Therapist #31	512-834-6657
Massage Therapist #28	512-834-6616
Massage Therapist, Temporary #28	512-834-6616
Massage Therapy Establishment/School #28	512-834-6616
Massage Therapy School #28	512-834-6616
Massage Therapy School Instruct'r #28	512-834-6616
Medical Doctor/Physician #30	512-305-7030
Medical Laboratory Practitioner #22	512-834-6602
Medical Specialty (Doctor) #30	512-305-7030
Medication Aide #13	512-438-3011
Membership Camping Resort #38	512-463-6906
Mortgage Banker #37	512-475-1350
Mortgage Broker #37	512-475-1350
Motor Vehicle Sales Finance Co. #7	512-936-7600
Notary Public #33	512-463-5705
Notary Public #38	512-475-5705
Nurse, Advanced Practice #63	512-305-6809
Nurse, Vocational #63	512-305-6809
Nurse/RN #63	512-305-6809
Nursery/Floral #11	512-463-7476
Nurses' Aide #13	800-452-3934, 512-438-3811
Nursing Home Administrat'/Facility#13	512-438-3011
Occupational Therapist/Assistant #17	512-305-6900
Occupational/Physical Therapy Facility #17	512-305-6900
Optician #26	512-834-6661
Optometrist #51	512-305-8500
Organic Grower #11	512-463-7476
Orthotics & Prosthetics Facility #26	512-834-4520
Orthotist/Prosthetist #26	512-834-4520
Paramedic #27	512-834-6700
Pawn Shop #7	512-936-7600
Perfusionist #26	512-834-6751
Perpetual Care Cemetery #1	512-475-1290
Personal Employment Service #14	512-463-6599
Pesticide Applicator/Dealer #10	512-475-1639
Pharmacist #24	512-305-8012
Pharmacist Intern #24	512-305-8011
Pharmacy / Pharmacy Technician #24	512-305-8031
Physical Therapist/Assistant #17	512-305-6900
Physician Assistant #30	512-305-7030
Physicist, Medical #26	512-834-6655
Plumber Master/Journeyman #3	512-458-2145 x227
Plumbing Inspector #3	512-458-2145 x227
Podiatrist #20	512-305-7000
Political Action Committee List #50	512-463-5800
Political Contributor #50	512-463-5800
Polygraph Examiner #34	512-424-2058
Polygraph Examiner of Sex Offenders #26	512-834-6655
Private Business Letter of Auth. #35	512-424-7710
Private Investigator #35	512-424-7710
Property Rights #38	512-475-1769
Property Tax Consultant #14	512-463-6599
Psychological Associate #19	512-305-7700
Psychologist #19	512-305-7700
Psychologist, Provisional #19	512-305-7700
Public Accountant-CPA #43	512-305-7853
Public Accountant-CPA Educator/Sponsor #43	512-305-7853
Public Accountant-CPA Firm #43	512-305-7853
Public Safety Organization, Promoter #38	512-475-0775
Radiology Technician #16	512-834-6617
Real Estate Agent/Broker/Sales #52	512-459-6544
Real Estate Appraiser #47	512-465-3950
Real Estate Inspector #52	512-459-6544
Representative Offices (Foreign Banks) #1	512-475-1300
Respiratory Care Practitioner #29	512-834-6632
Sanitarian #22	512-834-4517
Sanitation Code Enforcement Officer #22	512-834-6635
Savings & Loan Association #37	512-475-1350
Savings Bank #37	512-475-1350
School Psychology Specialist #19	512-305-7700
Securities Agent/Salesperson #39	512-305-8332
Securities Broker/Dealer #39	512-305-8332
Security Agency, Private #35	512-424-7710
Security Agent/Service/Sales #35	512-424-7710
Seed Dealer #11	512-463-7476
Service Contract Provider #14	512-463-6599
Sex Offender Treatment Provider #26	512-834-4530
Shorthand Reporter #9	512-463-1630
Social Worker #26	512-719-3521
Speech-Language Pathologist #22	512-834-6627
Staff Leasing #14	512-475-2896
STAP Vendor #6	512-407-3250
Surveyor, Land #4	512-452-9427
Surveyor, Out-of-Texas #4	512-452-9427
Surveyor, State Land #4	512-452-9427
Talent Agency #14	512-463-6599
Tax Appraisal Professional #59	512-305-7300
Teacher #42	512-936-8400
Telephone Solicitation #38	512-475-0775
Temporary Common Worker #14	512-463-6599
Third Part Debt Collector #38	512-463-6906
Transportation Service Provider #54	512-465-3500
Trust Company #1	512-475-1300
Underground Storage Tank Install #60	512-239-2191
Vehicle Protection Provider #14	512-463-6599
Veterans Organization Solicitation #38	512-475-0775
Veterinarian #18	512-305-7555
Water Well & Pump Installer #14	512-463-7880
Weather Modification Service #14	512-463-6599
Weigher, Public #11	512-463-7607
Weights/Measures Service #11	512-463-7607
Wig Specialist #2	512-936-6333
Wrestling Promoter #38	512-463-6906
X-ray Machine #16	512-834-6688 x2202

Texas Licensing Agency Information

1 Banking Department, 2601 N Lamar Blvd, Austin, TX 78705-4294; 512-475-1300, Fax: 512-475-1313.
www.banking.state.tx.us
Search Database at
www.banking.state.tx.us/itds.htm

2 Board of Barber Examiners, 5717 Balcones Dr. #217, Austin, TX 78731; 512-936-6333, Fax: 512-458-4901.
www.tsbbe.state.tx.us
Email: glenn.parker@tsbbe.state.tx.us
Search Database at
www.tsbbe.state.tx.us/index.html   Note: Online search of individuals requires license number. Cost of bulk record request is estimated based on amount of information requested. Also see cosmetology board for add'l manicurist licenses.

3 Board of Plumbing Examiners, PO Box 4200, Austin, TX 78765-4200; 512-458-2145, Fax: 512-450-0637.
www.tsbpe.state.tx.us
Email: info@tsbpe.state.tx.us

4 Board of Professional Land Surveying, 7701 N Lamar, #400, Austin, TX 78752; 512-452-9427, Fax: 512-452-7711.
www.txls.state.tx.us
Email: lois.coleman@mail.capnet.state.tx.us
Search Database at
http://txls.state.tx.us/sect03/rosters.html

5 Board of Registration for Professional Engineers, 1917 IH35 S (78760), Austin, TX 78741; 512-440-7723, Fax: 512-442-1414.
www.tbpe.state.tx.us
Email: peboard@tbpe.state.tx.us
Search Database at
www.tbpe.state.tx.us/downloads.htm   Note: Licensing data available as pdf downloads; lists updated twice monthly.

6 Commission for the Deaf & Hard of Hearing, PO Box 12904, Austin, TX 78711; 512-407-3250 Voice; 512-407-3251 TTY, Fax: 512-451-9316.
www.dars.state.tx.us/dhhs/index.shtml
Email: angelab@tcdhh.tx.us

7 Office of Consumer Credit Commissioner, 2601 N Lamar Blvd, Austin, TX 78705-4207; 512-936-7600, Fax: 512-936-7610.
www.occc.state.tx.us
Email: info@occc.state.tx.us

8 Cosmetology Commission, 5717 Balcones Dr, Austin, TX 78755; 512-380-7659, Fax: 512-419-9885.
www.txcc.state.tx.us
Email: licensing@txcc.state.tx.us

9 Court Reporter Certification Board, PO Box 13131, Austin, TX 78711-3131; 512-463-1630, Fax: 512-463-1117.
www.crcb.state.tx.us
Email: info@crcb.state.tx.us   Note: Interested parties may submit an open records request for a list. Refer to our website link "Making requests from CRCB".

10 Department of Agriculture, Pesticide Program, P.O. Box 12847 (1700 Congress Ave), Austin, TX 78711; 512-475-1639, Fax: 512-475-1618.
www.agr.state.tx.us/pesticide/index.htm
Email: contact@agr.state.tx.us

11 Department of Agriculture, Regulatory Programs, PO Box 12847 (1700 N Congress, Stephen F Austin Bldg), Austin, TX 78711; 512-463-7476, 800-835-5832, Fax: 512-463-1104.
www.agr.state.tx.us
Email: contact@agr.state.tx.us

12 Department of Health, Toxic Substances Control Division, Asbestos Programs Branch, 1100 W 49th St, Austin, TX 78756; 512-834-6600 x2789, Fax: 512-834-6644.
www.tdh.state.tx.us/beh/asbestos/
Email: todd.wingler@tdh.state.tx.us   Note: Make in person requests at 8407 Wall St, #N320, Austin.

13 Aging and Dissability Services, Long Term Care Regulatory Credentialing Dept, PO Box 149030, Mail Code Y979 (701 W. 51st St), Austin, TX 78714-9030; 512-438-3011, Fax: 512-834-6764.
www.dads.state.tx.us/services/index.html
Email: ltcr@dhs.state.tx.us

14 Department of Licensing & Regulation, PO Box 12157 (920 Colorado), Austin, TX 78711-2157; 512-463-6599, Fax: 512-475-2854.
www.license.state.tx.us
Search Database at
www.license.state.tx.us/LicenseSearch

15 Funeral Service Commission, PO Box 12217 (510 S Congress Ave, #206), Austin, TX 78704-1718; 512-936-2474, Fax: 512-479-5064.

www.tfsc.state.tx.us   Email: info@tfsc.state.tx.us

16 Department of Health, Bureau of Radiation Control, 1100 West 49th St, Austin, TX 78756-3189; 512-834-6688, Fax: 512-834-6690.
www.tdh.state.tx.us/radiation/ir.htm

17 Executive Council on Physical Therapy & Occupational Therapy Examiners, 333 Guadalupe St, Tower 2, #510, Austin, TX 78701; 512-305-6900, Fax: 512-305-6951.
www.ecptote.state.tx.us
Email: ecptote@mail.capnet.state.tx.us
Search data at www.ecptote.state.tx.us/license/otve rif.php   Note: Will sell mailing lists for licensees.

18 Health Department, State Veterinary Board, 333 Guadalupe, Tower 3, #810, Austin, TX 78701-3998; 512-305-7555, Fax: 512-305-7556.
www.texasonline.state.tx.us/tbvme
Email: Vet.Board@tbvme.state.tx.us

19 Board of Examiners of Psychologists, 333 Guadalupe, #2-450, Austin, TX 78701; 512-305-7700, Fax: 512-305-7701.
www.tsbep.state.tx.us
Email: brenda.skiff@tsbep.state.tx.us

20 Board of Podiatric Medical Examiners, 333 Guadalupe, #2-320, Austin, TX 78701; 512-305-7000, Fax: 512-305-7003.
www.foot.state.tx.us
Email: hemant.makan@foot.state.tx.us
Search Database at
www.foot.state.tx.us/verifications.htm

21 Health Department, Advisory Board of Athletic Trainers, 1100 W 49th St, Austin, TX 78756; 512-834-6615, Fax: 512-834-6677.
www.dshs.state.tx.us/at/   Email: at@tdh.state.tx.us
Search Database at
www.dshs.state.tx.us/at/at_roster.shtm

22 Texas State Health Services, Professional Licensing & Certification - Medical, 1100 W 49th St, Austin, TX 78756-3183; 512-834-6635, Fax: 512-834-6707.
www.dshs.state.tx.us/plc/default.shtm
Email: registry@licc.tdh.state.tx.us

23 Health Department, Dental Board, 333 Guadalupe, Tower 3, #800, Austin, TX 78701; 512-463-6400, Fax: 512-463-7452.
www.tsbde.state.tx.us
Email: webmaster@tsbde.state.tx.us
Search Database at www.tsbde.state.tx.us/dbsearch

24 Health Department, Board of Pharmacy, 333 Guadalupe, Box 21, Tower 3, #600, Austin, TX 78701-3942; 512-305-8000, Fax: 512-305-8082.
www.tsbp.state.tx.us
Email: openrec@tsbp.state.tx.us
Search Database at
www.tsbp.state.tx.us/dbsearch/Default.htm

25 Texas Board of Chiropractic Examiners, 333 Guadalupe, Tower 3, #825, Austin, TX 78701; 512-505-6700, Fax: 512-305-6705.
www.tbce.state.tx.us
Email: tbce@tbce.state.tx.us
Search Database at www.texasonline.com

26 Department of Health, Professional Licensing & Certification Div, 1100 W 49th St, Austin, TX 78756-3180; 512-834-6658, Fax: 512-834-6789.
www.dshs.state.tx.us/plc/default.shtm
Email: lpc@licc.tdh.state.tx.us

27 Health Department, Bureau of Emergency Management, 1100 W 49th St, Austin, TX 78756; 512-834-6700, Fax: 512-834-6736.
www.tdh.state.tx.us/hcqs/ems/emshome.htm
Email: emscert@ems.tdh.state.tx.us
Search Database at
http://160.42.108.3/ems_web/blh_html_page1.htm

28 Health Department, Professional Licensure & Certification, Massage Therapy Registration Program, 1100 W 49th St, Austin, TX 78756; 512-834-6616, Fax: 512-834-6677.
www.dshs.state.tx.us/plc/default.shtm
Email: massage@dshs

29 Health Department, Professional Licensure & Certification, Respiratory Care Division, 1100 W 49th St, Austin, TX 78756; 512-834-6632, Fax: 512-834-4518.
www.dshs.state.tx.us/respiratory/
Email: resp@tdh.state.tx.us
Search Database at
www.dshs.state.tx.us/respiratory/rc_roster.shtm

30 Medical Board, MC 240, PO Box 2018, Austin, TX 78768-2018; 512-305-7010, Fax: 512-463-9416. www.tsbme.state.tx.us
Email: verifcic@tsbme.state.tx.us
Search data at http://reg.tsbme.state.tx.us/onlineve rif/phys_noticeverif.asp?   Note: Also search physician on private national website at www.docboard.org/tx/df/txsearch.htm.

31 Health Department, Professional Licensure & Certification, Marriage & Family Therapists, 1100 W 49th St, Austin, TX 78756; 512-834-6657, Fax: 512-834-6677.
www.dshs.state.tx.us/mft/mft_contact.shtm
Email: mft@licc.tdh.state.tx.us
Search Database at
www.dshs.state.tx.us/mft/mft_contact.shtm

33 Office of Secretary of State, Notary Public Unit, PO Box 13375 (1019 Brazos, Rm 214), Austin, TX 78711; 512-463-5705. www.sos.state.tx.us/statdoc/index.shtml Email: ckramer@sos.state.tx.us

34 Polygraph Examiner Board, PO Box 4087, Austin, TX 78773-4087; 512-424-2058, Fax: 512-424-5739. www.tpeb.state.tx.us Email: polygraph.board@mail.capnet.state.tx.us Note: There is a polygraph examiners association that posts its member list; http://polygraph.org/states/tape/members_roster.htm. However, this list is not generated by the official state board.

35 Private Security Bureau, PO Box 4087, Austin, TX 78773; 512-424-7710, Fax: 512-424-7729. www.txdps.state.tx.us/psb/ Search Database at www.tcps.state.tx.us/individual/individual_search.aspx

36 Racing Commission, 8505 Cross Park Dr, #110, Austin, TX 78754; 512-833-6699, Fax: 512-833-6907.

37 Savings & Loan Department, 2601 N Lamar Blvd, #201, Austin, TX 78705-4241; 512-475-1350, Fax: 512-475-1360. www.tsld.state.tx.us Email: tsld@tsld.state.tx.us

38 Secretary of State, Statutory Documents Section, PO Box 12887 (1019 Bravos), Austin, TX 78711-2887; 512-475-1769, Fax: 512-475-2815. www.sos.state.tx.us

39 Securities Board, 208 E 10th St, 5th Fl, Austin, TX 78701; 512-305-8300, Fax: 512-305-8310. www.ssb.state.tx.us Email: webmaster@ssb.state.tx.us

40 State Bar of Texas, 1414 Colorado, #300, Austin, TX 78701-1627; 512-463-1463 x1383, Fax: 512-462-1475. www.texasbar.com Search Database at www.texasbar.com Note: You may also search attorneys by name at a private website at www.texaslegaldirectories.com/find.html.

41 Board of Examiners for Professional Counselors, 1100 W 49th St, Austin, TX 78756; 512-834-6658, Fax: 512-834-6789. www.dshs.state.tx.us/counselor Email: lpc@tdh.state.tx.us Search Database at www.dshs.state.tx.us/counselor/lpc_rosters.shtm

42 Board for Educator Certification, PO Box 12728, Austin, TX 78711-2728; 512-936-8275, Fax: 512-936-8277. www.sbec.state.tx.us Email: sbec@sbec.state.tx.us Search Database at https://secure.sbec.state.tx.us/SBECONLINE/virtcert.asp

43 Board of Public Accountancy, 333 Guadalupe St, Tower III, #900, Austin, TX 78701-3900; 512-305-7800, Fax: 512-505-7875. www.tsbpa.state.tx.us Search Database at www.tsbpa.state.tx.us/srcmain.htm

44 Library & Archives Commission, P.O. Box 12927, Austin, TX 78711-2927; 512-463-5466, Fax: 512-463-8800. www.tsl.state.tx.us Email: ld@tsl.state.tx.su

45 State Parks & Wildlife Department, 4200 Smith School Rd, Austin, TX 78744; 512-389-4800, Fax: 512-389-4349. www.tpwd.state.tx.us

46 Alcoholic Beverage Commission, PO Box 13127 (5806 Mesa Dr), Austin, TX 78711; 512-206-3333, Fax: 512-451-0240. www.tabc.state.tx.us Note: Information regarding licenses/permits to the public in various formats such as 8 1/2" X 11" printouts, PC disks, mailing labels and 3480 tapes for a fee.

47 Appraisers Licensing & Certification Board, 1101 Camino La Costa, Austin, TX 78752; 512-465-3950, Fax: 512-465-3953. www.talcb.state.tx.us Search Database at www.talcb.state.tx.us/appraisers/Appraiser_Search.asp

48 Department of Insurance, 333 Guadalupe, Austin, TX 78701; 512-463-6169, Fax: 512-475-2025. www.tdi.state.tx.us Email: consumer_protection@tdi.state.tx.us Search Database at www.texasonline.state.tx.us/NASApp/tdi/TdiARManager Note: Company downloads are at www.tdi.state.tx.us/general/forms/colists.html; agents downloads at www.tdi.state.tx.us/general/forms/agentlists.html.

49 Department of Protective & Regulatory Services, Child Care Licensing Division, 701 W 51st St, #E-550, Austin, TX 78751; 512-438-4800, Fax: 512-438-3848. www.tdprs.state.tx.us

50 Ethics Commission, PO Box 12070, Austin, TX 78711-2070; 512-463-5800, Fax: 512-463-5777. www.ethics.state.tx.us Email: disclosure@ethics.state.tx.us Search Database at www.ethics.state.tx.us/dfs/dfs.htm

51 Optometry Board, 333 Guadalupe St, #2-420, Austin, TX 78701-3942; 512-305-8500, Fax: 512-305-8501. www.tob.state.tx.us Email: Chris.Kloeris@mail.capnet.state.tx.us Search Database at www.tob.state.tx.us/tob%20verifications.htm Note: Also, you may search licensees at the national website at www.arbo.org/odfinder/LicSearch.asp.

52 Real Estate Commission, PO Box 12188, (1101 Camino La Costa), Austin, TX 78711-2188; 512-459-6544, Fax: 512-465-3913. www.trec.state.tx.us Email: glen.bridge@trec.state.tx.us Search Database at www.trec.state.tx.us/publicinfo

53 State Fire Marshal, 333 Guadalupe, Austin, TX 78701; 512-305-7910, Fax: 512-305-7922. www.tdi.state.tx.us/fire/fmli.html

54 Department of Transportation, Transportation Service Licensing Dept., 4203 Bull Creek, Austin, TX 78731; 512-465-3500, Fax: 512-465-3535. www.dot.state.tx.us

55 Department of Health, Toxic Substances Control Division, Environmental Lead Program, 1100 W 49th St, Austin, TX 78756-3199; 512-834-6612, Fax: 512-834-6644. www.tdh.state.tx.us/beh/lead/default.htm Email: peter.tadin@tdh.state.tx.us

56 Commission on Fire Protection, 12015 Park 35 Circle #570 , PO Box 2286, Austin, TX 78768-2286; 512-239-4911, Fax: 512-239-4917. www.tcfp.state.tx.us Email: info@tcfp.state.tx.us

57 Commission on Environmental Quality MC178, PO Box 13087, Austin, TX 78711-3087; 512-239-6719, Fax: 512-239-0533. www.tceq.state.tx.us/ Email: irrclerk@tnrcc.state.tx.us Search Database at http://www.tceq.state.tx.us/nav/data/licensed_data.html

58 Commission on Law Enforcement Officer, 6330 U.S. 290 East #200, Austin, TX 78723; 512-936-7700, Fax: 512-936-7714. www.tcleose.state.tx.us/ Email: kris.faldyn@mail.capnet.state.tx.us

59 Board of Tax Professional Examiners, 333 Guadalupe St, Tower II #520, Austin, TX 78701; 512-305-7300, Fax: 512-305-7304. www.txbtpe.state.tx.us Email: btpe@mail.compact.state.tx.us Search Database at www.txbtpe.state.tx.us Note: To search online, the board member number is required.

60 Texas Commission on Environmental Quality, PO Box 13087, Austin, TX 78711-3087; 512-239-2191, Fax: 512-239-0533. www.tceq.state.tx.us/nav/permits/ Email: wkurio@tnrcc.state.tx.us Search Database at www.tceq.state.tx.us/compliance/compliance_support/licensing/ust_lic.html

61 Board of Architectural Examiners, 333 Guadalupe,Suite 2-350, Austin, TX 78701; 512-305-9000, Fax: 512-305-8900. www.tbae.state.tx.us Search Database at www.tbae.state.tx.us/PublicInfo/FindProfessional.shtml

63 Board of Nurse Examiners, 333 Guadalupe #3-460, Austin, TX 78701; 512-305-7400, Fax: 512-305-7401. https://www.bne.state.tx.us/ Search Database at https://www.bne.state.tx.us/olv/rning.htm

Texas Federal Courts

The following list indicates the district and division name for each county in the state. If the bankruptcy court location is different from the district court, then the location of the bankruptcy court appears in parentheses.

Texas County/Court Cross Reference

County	District	Division
Anderson	Eastern	Tyler
Andrews	Western	Midland (Midland/Odessa)
Angelina	Eastern	Texarkana (Beaumont)
Aransas	Southern	Corpus Christi
Archer	Northern	Wichita Falls
Armstrong	Northern	Amarillo
Atascosa	Western	San Antonio
Austin	Southern	Houston
Bailey	Northern	Lubbock
Bandera	Western	San Antonio
Bastrop	Western	Austin
Baylor	Northern	Wichita Falls
Bee	Southern	Corpus Christi
Bell	Western	Waco
Bexar	Western	San Antonio
Blanco	Western	Austin
Borden	Northern	Lubbock
Bosque	Western	Waco
Bowie	Eastern	Texarkana
Brazoria	Southern	Galveston (Houston)
Brazos	Southern	Houston
Brewster	Western	Pecos (Midland/Odessa)
Briscoe	Northern	Amarillo
Brooks	Southern	Corpus Christi
Brown	Northern	San Angelo (Lubbock)
Burleson	Western	Austin
Burnet	Western	Austin
Caldwell	Western	Austin
Calhoun	Southern	Victoria (Corpus Christi)
Callahan	Northern	Abilene (Lubbock)
Cameron	Southern	Brownsville (Corpus Christi)
Camp	Eastern	Marshall
Carson	Northern	Amarillo
Cass	Eastern	Marshall
Castro	Northern	Amarillo
Chambers	Southern	Galveston (Houston)
Cherokee	Eastern	Tyler
Childress	Northern	Amarillo
Clay	Northern	Wichita Falls
Cochran	Northern	Lubbock
Coke	Northern	San Angelo (Lubbock)
Coleman	Northern	San Angelo (Lubbock)
Collin	Eastern	Sherman (Plano)
Collingsworth	Northern	Amarillo
Colorado	Southern	Houston
Comal	Western	San Antonio
Comanche	Northern	Fort Worth
Concho	Northern	San Angelo (Lubbock)
Cooke	Eastern	Sherman (Plano)
Coryell	Western	Waco
Cottle	Northern	Wichita Falls
Crane	Western	Midland (Midland/Odessa)
Crockett	Northern	San Angelo (Lubbock)
Crosby	Northern	Lubbock
Culberson	Western	Pecos (Midland/Odessa)
Dallam	Northern	Amarillo
Dallas	Northern	Dallas
Dawson	Northern	Lubbock
De Witt	Southern	Victoria (Houston)
Deaf Smith	Northern	Amarillo
Delta	Eastern	Sherman (Plano)
Denton	Eastern	Sherman (Plano)
Dickens	Northern	Lubbock
Dimmit	Western	San Antonio
Donley	Northern	Amarillo
Duval	Southern	Corpus Christi
Eastland	Northern	Abilene (Lubbock)
Ector	Western	Midland (Midland/Odessa)
Edwards	Western	Del Rio (San Antonio)
El Paso	Western	El Paso
Ellis	Northern	Dallas
Erath	Northern	Fort Worth
Falls	Western	Waco
Fannin	Eastern	Sherman (Plano)
Fayette	Southern	Houston
Fisher	Northern	Abilene (Lubbock)
Floyd	Northern	Lubbock
Foard	Northern	Wichita Falls
Fort Bend	Southern	Houston
Franklin	Eastern	Texarkana
Freestone	Western	Waco
Frio	Western	San Antonio
Gaines	Northern	Lubbock
Galveston	Southern	Galveston (Houston)
Garza	Northern	Lubbock
Gillespie	Western	Austin
Glasscock	Northern	San Angelo (Lubbock)
Goliad	Southern	Victoria (Corpus Christi)
Gonzales	Western	San Antonio
Gray	Northern	Amarillo
Grayson	Eastern	Sherman (Plano)
Gregg	Eastern	Tyler
Grimes	Southern	Houston
Guadalupe	Western	San Antonio
Hale	Northern	Lubbock
Hall	Northern	Amarillo
Hamilton	Western	Waco
Hansford	Northern	Amarillo
Hardeman	Northern	Wichita Falls
Hardin	Eastern	Beaumont
Harris	Southern	Houston
Harrison	Eastern	Marshall
Hartley	Northern	Amarillo
Haskell	Northern	Abilene (Lubbock)
Hays	Western	Austin
Hemphill	Northern	Amarillo
Henderson	Eastern	Tyler
Hidalgo	Southern	McAllen (Corpus Christi)
Hill	Western	Waco
Hockley	Northern	Lubbock
Hood	Northern	Fort Worth
Hopkins	Eastern	Sherman (Plano)
Houston	Eastern	Texarkana (Beaumont)
Howard	Northern	Abilene (Lubbock)
Hudspeth	Western	Pecos (Midland/Odessa)
Hunt	Northern	Dallas

County	District	City
Hutchinson	Northern	Amarillo
Irion	Northern	San Angelo (Lubbock)
Jack	Northern	Fort Worth
Jackson	Southern	Victoria (Corpus Christi)
Jasper	Eastern	Beaumont
Jeff Davis	Western	Pecos (Midland/Odessa)
Jefferson	Eastern	Beaumont
Jim Hogg	Southern	Laredo (Houston)
Jim Wells	Southern	Corpus Christi
Johnson	Northern	Dallas
Jones	Northern	Abilene (Lubbock)
Karnes	Western	San Antonio
Kaufman	Northern	Dallas
Kendall	Western	San Antonio
Kenedy	Southern	Corpus Christi
Kent	Northern	Lubbock
Kerr	Western	San Antonio
Kimble	Western	Austin
King	Northern	Wichita Falls
Kinney	Western	Del Rio (San Antonio)
Kleberg	Southern	Corpus Christi
Knox	Northern	Wichita Falls
La Salle	Southern	Laredo (Corpus Christi)
Lamar	Eastern	Sherman (Plano)
Lamb	Northern	Lubbock
Lampasas	Western	Austin
Lavaca	Southern	Victoria (Houston)
Lee	Western	Austin
Leon	Western	Waco
Liberty	Eastern	Beaumont
Limestone	Western	Waco
Lipscomb	Northern	Amarillo
Live Oak	Southern	Corpus Christi
Llano	Western	Austin
Loving	Western	Pecos (Midland/Odessa)
Lubbock	Northern	Lubbock
Lynn	Northern	Lubbock
Madison	Southern	Houston
Marion	Eastern	Marshall
Martin	Western	Midland (Midland/Odessa)
Mason	Western	Austin
Matagorda	Southern	Galveston (Houston)
Maverick	Western	Del Rio (San Antonio)
McCulloch	Western	Austin
McLennan	Western	Waco
McMullen	Southern	Laredo (Houston)
Medina	Western	San Antonio
Menard	Northern	San Angelo (Lubbock)
Midland	Western	Midland (Midland/Odessa)
Milam	Western	Waco
Mills	Northern	San Angelo (Lubbock)
Mitchell	Northern	Abilene (Lubbock)
Montague	Northern	Wichita Falls
Montgomery	Southern	Houston
Moore	Northern	Amarillo
Morris	Eastern	Marshall
Motley	Northern	Lubbock
Nacogdoches	Eastern	Texarkana (Beaumont)
Navarro	Northern	Dallas
Newton	Eastern	Beaumont
Nolan	Northern	Abilene (Lubbock)
Nueces	Southern	Corpus Christi
Ochiltree	Northern	Amarillo
Oldham	Northern	Amarillo
Orange	Eastern	Beaumont
Palo Pinto	Northern	Fort Worth
Panola	Eastern	Tyler
Parker	Northern	Fort Worth
Parmer	Northern	Amarillo
Pecos	Western	Pecos (Midland/Odessa)
Polk	Eastern	Texarkana (Beaumont)
Potter	Northern	Amarillo
Presidio	Western	Pecos (Midland/Odessa)
Rains	Eastern	Tyler
Randall	Northern	Amarillo
Reagan	Northern	San Angelo (Lubbock)
Real	Western	San Antonio
Red River	Eastern	Sherman (Plano)
Reeves	Western	Pecos (Midland/Odessa)
Refugio	Southern	Victoria (Corpus Christi)
Roberts	Northern	Amarillo
Robertson	Western	Waco
Rockwall	Northern	Dallas
Runnels	Northern	San Angelo (Lubbock)
Rusk	Eastern	Tyler
Sabine	Eastern	Texarkana (Beaumont)
San Augustine	Eastern	Texarkana (Beaumont)
San Jacinto	Southern	Houston
San Patricio	Southern	Corpus Christi
San Saba	Western	Austin
Schleicher	Northern	San Angelo (Lubbock)
Scurry	Northern	Lubbock
Shackelford	Northern	Abilene (Lubbock)
Shelby	Eastern	Texarkana (Beaumont)
Sherman	Northern	Amarillo
Smith	Eastern	Tyler
Somervell	Western	Waco
Starr	Southern	McAllen (Corpus Christi)
Stephens	Northern	Abilene (Lubbock)
Sterling	Northern	San Angelo (Lubbock)
Stonewall	Northern	Abilene (Lubbock)
Sutton	Northern	San Angelo (Lubbock)
Swisher	Northern	Amarillo
Tarrant	Northern	Fort Worth
Taylor	Northern	Abilene (Lubbock)
Terrell	Western	Del Rio (San Antonio)
Terry	Northern	Lubbock
Throckmorton	Northern	Abilene (Lubbock)
Titus	Eastern	Texarkana
Tom Green	Northern	San Angelo (Lubbock)
Travis	Western	Austin
Trinity	Eastern	Texarkana (Beaumont)
Tyler	Eastern	Texarkana (Beaumont)
Upshur	Eastern	Marshall
Upton	Western	Midland (Midland/Odessa)
Uvalde	Western	Del Rio (San Antonio)
Val Verde	Western	Del Rio (San Antonio)
Van Zandt	Eastern	Tyler
Victoria	Southern	Victoria (Corpus Christi)
Walker	Southern	Houston
Waller	Southern	Houston
Ward	Western	Pecos (Midland/Odessa)
Washington	Western	Austin
Webb	Southern	Laredo (Houston)
Wharton	Southern	Houston
Wheeler	Northern	Amarillo
Wichita	Northern	Wichita Falls
Wilbarger	Northern	Wichita Falls
Willacy	Southern	Brownsville (Corpus Christi)
Williamson	Western	Austin
Wilson	Western	San Antonio
Winkler	Western	Pecos (Midland/Odessa)
Wise	Northern	Fort Worth
Wood	Eastern	Tyler
Yoakum	Northern	Lubbock
Young	Northern	Wichita Falls
Zapata	Southern	Laredo (Houston)
Zavala	Western	Del Rio (San Antonio)

Standards for Federal Courts: Search fee is $26.00 per item (one party name or case number). Copy fee is $.50 per page. Certification fee is $9.00 per document, double for exemplification, if available. All fees standard unless noted in profile. Mail Search: always enclose a stamped self addressed envelope unless otherwise noted. Most courts accept fax requests or will suggest a copying/search vendor. Before releasing records, all courts require prepayment, unless noted.

Open records are located at the court unless otherwise noted. District courts index by defendant and plaintiff as well as by case number. Bankruptcy courts usually index by debtor and case number. While most courts now have their indexes on computer, many may still maintain index card files as well.

Courts offering internet access via CM-ECF or older RACER, PACER, or Web-PACER systems charge $.08 per page fee unless noted as free. Where PACER is available, the universal sign-up number is 800-676-6856. Find PACER and the US Party/Case Index at http://pacer.psc.uscourts.gov.

US District Court

Eastern District of Texas

Beaumont Division Court Clerk, PO Box 3507, Beaumont, TX 77704 (courier address: Rm 104, 300 Willow, Beaumont, TX 77701), 409-654-7000, Fax-409-654-7080. Hours- 8AM-5PM. www.txed.uscourts.gov

Counties: Delta*, Fannin*, Hardin, Hopkins*, Jasper, Jefferson, Lamar*, Liberty, Newton, Orange, Red River. Counties marked with an asterisk are the old Paris Division, whose case records are maintained here. New records are at Sherman Div.

Searches & Indexing: Beaumont also maintains records for Paris Division. Results do not include SSN or DOB. Computer and microfiche indexes maintained. New cases in the index immediately after filing date. Records purged once yearly. District-wide searches available back to 3/86.

Fee & Payment: Pay by Visa/MC, money order, cashier's or personal check. Payee: Clerk, US District Court. Prepayment required.

Phone Search: Only docket information is available by phone. **Mail Search:** search usually completed- 1 week. SASE not required. **In Person Search:** Fee charged if court performs your search. Self-serve copier - $.25 per page.

E-Services: ECF replaces PACER whose records did go back to 1992. New records online after 1 day. ECF at https://ecf.txed.uscourts.gov **Other Online Access:** View Frequently Requested Cases free at www.txed.uscourts.gov.

Lufkin Division Court Clerk, 104 N Third St, Lufkin, TX 75901 (also use mail address for courier delivery), 936-632-2739. Hours- 8AM-5PM. www.txed.uscourts.gov

Counties: Angelina, Houston, Nacogdoches, Polk, Sabine, San Augustine, Shelby, Trinity, Tyler.

Searches & Indexing: Results do not include SSN or DOB. Computer and microfiche indexes maintained. New cases in the index immediately after filing date.

Fee & Payment: Pay by Visa/MC, money order, cashier's or personal check. Payee: US District Court. Prepayment required.

Phone Search: Only docket information is available by phone.

Mail Search: search usually completed- 1 week. Include SASE for return and a fee may be charged.

In Person Search: Fee charged if court performs your search. Self-serve copier - $.50 per page.

E-Services: ECF replaces PACER. New records online after 1 day. ECF at https://ecf.txed.uscourts.gov **Other Online Access:** View Frequently Requested Cases free at www.txed.uscourts.gov.

Marshall Division Court Clerk, 100 E Houston, Rm 125, Marshall, TX 75670 (also use mail address for courier delivery), 903-935-2912, records rm- 903-935-2912, crim dockets- 903-794-8561, Fax-903-938-2651. Hours- 8AM-5PM. www.txed.uscourts.gov

Counties: Camp, Cass, Harrison, Marion, Morris, Upshur.

Searches & Indexing: Results do not include SSN or DOB. All records on computer. New cases in the index 1 day after filing date.

Fee & Payment: Pay by money order, cashier's or personal check. Payee: US District Court. Prepayment required.

Phone Search: Only docket information is available by phone. **Mail Search:** search usually completed- 1 month. Include SASE for return.

In Person Search: Fee charged if court performs your search. Self-serve copier - $.50 per page.

E-Services: ECF replaces PACER whose records did go back to 1992. New records online after 1 day. ECF at https://ecf.txed.uscourts.gov **Other Online Access:** View Frequently Requested Cases free at www.txed.uscourts.gov.

Sherman Division Court Clerk, 101 E Pecan St, Rm112, Sherman, TX 75090 (also use mail address for courier delivery), 903-892-2921. Hours- 8AM-5PM. www.txed.uscourts.gov

Counties: Collin, Cooke, Delta*, Denton, Fannin*, Grayson, Hopkins*, Lamar*. Counties marked with an asterisk were part of the old Paris Division; these old records are at Beaumont. New records are at Sherman.

Searches & Indexing: Results do not include SSN or DOB. Computer index maintained. New cases in the index 1 day after filing date. Records purged once yearly. District-wide searches available here.

Fee & Payment: Pay by money order, cashier's or personal check. Payee: Clerk, US District Court. Prepayment required.

Phone Search: Docket info available via phone.

Mail Search: search usually completed- 1 week. Include SASE for return.

In Person Search: Fee charged if court performs your search. No self-serve copier available.

E-Services: ECF replaces PACER whose records did go back to 1992. New records online after 1 day. ECF at https://ecf.txed.uscourts.gov **Other Online Access:** View Frequently Requested Cases free at www.txed.uscourts.gov.

Texarkana Division Clerk's Office, 500 State Line Ave, Rm 301, Texarkana, TX 75501 (also use mail address for courier delivery), 903-794-8561, Fax-903-794-0600. Hours- 8AM-5PM. www.txed.uscourts.gov

Counties: Bowie, Franklin, Titus.

Searches & Indexing: Results do not include SSN or DOB. Computer, microfiche and card indexes maintained. New cases in the index 1-2 days after filing date. No set time when cases sent to Fort Worth Records Center.

Fee & Payment: Pay by money order, cashier's or personal check. Payee: Clerk, US District Court. Prepayment required.

Mail Search: search usually completed- 2-3 days. Include SASE for return.

In Person Search: Fee charged if court performs your search. No Self-serve copier - $.50 per page.

E-Services: ECF replaces PACER whose records did go back to 1992. New records online after 1 day. ECF at https://ecf.txed.uscourts.gov **Other Online Access:** View Frequently Requested Cases free at www.txed.uscourts.gov.

Tyler Division Clerk of Court, Rm 106, 211 W Ferguson, Tyler, TX 75702 (also use mail address for courier delivery), 903-590-1000, Fax-903-590-1015. Hours- 8AM-5PM. www.txed.uscourts.gov

Counties: Anderson, Cherokee, Gregg, Henderson, Panola, Rains, Rusk, Smith, Van Zandt, Wood.

Searches & Indexing: Results include last 4 SSN digits, also birth year. Computer, microfiche and card indexes maintained. New cases in the index 1-2 days after filing date. Records purged as deemed necessary.

Fee & Payment: Pay by money order, cashier's or personal check. Payee: Clerk, US District Court. Prepayment required.

Phone Search: Only docket information is available by phone.

Mail Search: search usually completed- 1 week. SASE not required.

In Person Search: Fee charged if court performs your search. Self-serve copier - $.25 per page.

E-Services: ECF replaces PACER whose records did go back to 1992. New records online after 1 day. ECF at https://ecf.txed.uscourts.gov **Other Online Access:** View Frequently Requested Cases free at www.txed.uscourts.gov.

US Bankruptcy Court

Eastern District of Texas

Beaumont Division Court Clerk, 300 Willow St, #100, Beaumont, TX 77701 (also use mail address for courier delivery), 409-839-2617. Hours- 8AM-4PM. www.txeb.uscourts.gov

Counties: Angelina, Hardin, Houston, Jasper, Jefferson, Liberty, Nacogdoches, Newton, Orange, Polk, Sabine, San Augustine, Shelby, Trinity, Tyler.

Searches & Indexing: Results do not include SSN or DOB. Computer index maintained. New cases in the index immediately after filing date. Records purged every 6 months.

Fee & Payment: Pay by money order, cashier's or personal check, credit card. Payee: Clerk, US Bankruptcy Court. Prepayment required.

Phone Search: Only docket information is available by phone. Voice Case Information Service available, call VCIS at 800-466-1694 or 903-590-3251.

Mail Search: search usually completed- 1 week. Include SASE for return.

In Person Search: permitted. Searchers must fill out a card with their phone number, date, and the case number. Self-serve copier - $.25 per page.

E-Services: ECF replaces PACER whose records did go back to 1989. ECF at https://ecf.txeb.uscourts.gov. Document images available. **Opinions Online:** www.txeb.uscourts.gov/reports.asp. Click on Chapter 7 Asset Case Trustee's Final Reports. **Other Online Access:** Calendars at www.txeb.uscourts.gov/judges.asp.

Marshall Division Court Clerk, c/o Tyler Division, 110 N College Ave, Tyler, TX 75702 (also use mail address for courier delivery), 903-590-3200, Fax-903-590-1226. Hours- 8AM-4PM. www.txeb.uscourts.gov

Counties: Camp, Cass, Harrison, Marion, Morris, Upshur.

Searches & Indexing: Cases indexed by and case number. Results include last 4 SSN digits. Computer index maintained. Records purged every 6 months. Open records located at Tyler Division.

Fee & Payment: Pay by money order, cashier check only.

Phone Search: Voice Case Information Service available, call 800-466-1694 or 903-590-3251.

Mail Search: search usually completed- 2-3 days. SASE not required.

In Person Search: permitted. Self-serve copier - $.25 per page.

E-Services: ECF replaces PACER whose records did go back to 1989. ECF at https://ecf.txeb.uscourts.gov. Document images available. **Opinions Online:** www.txeb.uscourts.gov/reports.asp. Click on Chapter 7 Asset Case Trustee's Final Reports. **Other Online Access:** Calendars at www.txeb.uscourts.gov/judges.asp.

Plano Division Court Clerk, Suite 300B, 660 N Central Expressway, Plano, TX 75074 (also use mail address for courier delivery), 972-509-1240, Fax-972-509-1245. Hours- 8AM-4PM. www.txeb.uscourts.gov

Counties: Collin, Cooke, Delta, Denton, Fannin, Grayson, Hopkins, Lamar, Red River.

Searches & Indexing: Cases indexed by debtor, creditors, and case number. Results include last 4 SSN digits. Computer index maintained. New cases in the index 24 hours after filing date. Records purged every 6 months.

Fee & Payment: Pay by money order, cashier's or personal check. Payee: Clerk, US Bankruptcy Court. Prepayment required.

Phone Search: Only docket information is available by phone. Voice Case Information Service available, call VCIS at 800-466-1694 or 903-590-5251.

Mail Search: search usually completed- same day if possible. Include SASE for return.

In Person Search: Fee charged if court performs your search. Self-serve copier - $.25 per page.

E-Services: ECF replaces PACER - records did go back to 1989. ECF at https://ecf.txeb.uscourts.gov.

Document images available. **Opinions Online:** www.txeb.us courts.gov/reports.asp. Click on Chapter 7 Asset Case Trustee's Final Reports. **Other Access:** Calendars at www.txeb.uscourts.gov/judges.asp.

Texarkana Division Court Clerk, c/o Plano Division, Suite 300B, 660 N Central Expressway, Plano, TX 75074 (also use mail address for courier delivery), 972-509-1240, Fax-972-509-1245. Hours- 8AM-4PM. www.txeb.uscourts.gov

Counties: Bowie, Franklin, Titus.

Searches & Indexing: Results include last 4 SSN digits. Computer index maintained. New cases in the index 24 hours after filing date. Records purged every 6 months. Open records located at Plano Division.

Fee & Payment: Pay by money order, cashier's or personal check. Payee: Clerk, US Bankruptcy Court. Prepayment required.

Phone Search: Voice Case Information Service available, call 800-466-1694 or 903-590-3251.

Mail Search: search usually completed- same day. Include SASE for return.

In Person Search: permitted. No self-serve copier available.

E-Services: ECF replaces PACER whose records did go back to 1989. ECF at https://ecf.txeb.uscourts.gov. Document images available. **Opinions Online:** www.txeb.us courts.gov/reports.asp. Click on Chapter 7 Asset Case Trustee's Final Reports. **Other Access:** Calendars at www.txeb.uscourts.gov/judges.asp.

Tyler Division Court Clerk, 110 N College Ave, 9th Fl, Tyler, TX 75702 (use mail address for courier delivery), 903-590-3200, Fax-903-590-1226. Hours- 8AM-4PM. www.txeb.uscourts.gov

Counties: Anderson, Cherokee, Gregg, Henderson, Panola, Rains, Rusk, Smith, Van Zandt, Wood.

Searches & Indexing: Results include last 4 SSN digits. Computer, microfiche and card indexes maintained. Card index for cases prior to 10/1987 only. New cases in the index 1 day after filing date. Records purged every 6 months. District-wide searches available back to 10/87. Court maintains automated case records and finance records for entire Eastern district.

Fee & Payment: Pay by money order, cashier's or personal check. Payee: Clerk, US Bankruptcy Court. Prepayment required.

Phone Search: This court will answer questions pertaining to information not available from VCIS. Voice Case Information Service available, call VCIS at 800-466-1694 or 903-590-3251.

Mail Search: search usually completed- 2-3 days. SASE not required.

In Person Search: permitted. Self-serve copier - $.25 per page.

E-Services: ECF replaces PACER whose records did go back to 1989. ECF at https://ecf.txeb.uscourts.gov. Document images available. **Opinions Online:** www.txeb.us courts.gov/reports.asp. Click on Chapter 7 Asset Case Trustee's Final Reports. **Other Access:** Calendars at www.txeb.uscourts.gov/judges.asp.

US District Court
Northern District of Texas

Abilene Division Court Clerk, PO Box 1218, Abilene, TX 79604 (courier address: Rm 2008, 341 Pine St, Abilene, TX 79601), 325-677-6311. 8:30AM-N, 1-4:30PM. www.txnd.uscourts.gov

Counties: Callahan, Eastland, Fisher, Haskell, Howard, Jones, Mitchell, Nolan, Shackelford, Stephens, Stonewall, Taylor, Throckmorton.

Searches & Indexing: Results do not include SSN or DOB. Both computer and card indexes maintained, computer back to 1992. New cases in the index 2 days after filing date. Records purged once yearly. District-wide searches available here back to 1983.

Fee & Payment: Pay by money order, cashier's or personal check. Payee: Clerk, US District Court. Prepayment required.

Phone Search: Only a name or case number is released via phone. **Mail Search:** search usually completed- 2 days. SASE not required. **In Person Search:** Fee charged if court performs your search. No self-serve copier available.

E-Services: ECF replaces PACER. Document images available. PACER records go back to 6/1991. New records online after 1 day. ECF at https://ecf.txnd.uscourts.gov **Opinions Online:** www.txnd.uscourts.gov/judges/.

Amarillo Division Court Clerk, 205 E 5th St, Amarillo, TX 79101 (also use mail address for courier delivery), 806-324-2352. Hours- 8:30AM-N, 1-4:30PM. www.txnd.uscourts.gov

Counties: Armstrong, Briscoe, Carson, Castro, Childress, Collingsworth, Dallam, Deaf Smith, Donley, Gray, Hall, Hansford, Hartley, Hemphill, Hutchinson, Lipscomb, Moore, Ochiltree, Oldham, Parmer, Potter, Randall, Roberts, Sherman, Swisher, Wheeler.

Searches & Indexing: Results do not include SSN or DOB. Computer, microfiche and card indexes maintained; computer goes back to 1996. New cases in the index immediately after filing date. Records purged once yearly.

Fee & Payment: Pay by Visa/MC, money order, cashier's or personal check. Payee: Clerk, US District Court. Prepayment required.

Phone Search: No party information is released via phone. Only pleadings are released via phone. **Mail Search:** search usually completed- 1-2 days. SASE not required. **In Person Search:** Fee charged if court performs your search. No self-serve copier available.

E-Services: ECF replaces PACER. Document images available. PACER records go back to 6/1991. New records online after 1 day. ECF at https://ecf.txnd.uscourts.gov **Opinions Online:** www.txnd.uscourts.gov/judges/.

Dallas Division Court Clerk, Rm 1452, 1100 Commerce St, Dallas, TX 75242 (also use mail address for courier delivery), 214-753-2200, records rm- 214-753-2196. Hours- 9AM-4PM. www.txnd.uscourts.gov

Counties: Dallas, Ellis, Hunt, Johnson, Kaufman, Navarro, Rockwall.

Searches & Indexing: Results do not include SSN or DOB. Computer index maintained back to 1992. Computer index goes back to 1990; entire district included. Records also indexed on microfiche since 1957. New cases in the index 2 days after filing date. Records purged once yearly. District-wide searches available back to 1957.

Fee & Payment: Pay by Visa/MC, money order, cashier's or personal check. Payee: Clerk, US District Court. Prepayment required.

Phone Search: Only computerized docket information is released via phone.

Mail Search: search usually completed- 2 days. Include SASE for return.

In Person Search: Fee charged if court performs your search. Self-serve copier - $.25 per page.

E-Services: ECF replaces PACER. Document images available. PACER records go back to 6/1991. New records online after 1 day. ECF at https://ecf.txnd.uscourts.gov **Opinions Online:** www.txnd.uscourts.gov/judges/.

Fort Worth Division
Clerk's Office, 501 W Tenth St, Rm 310, Fort Worth, TX 76102 (also use mail address for courier delivery), 817-850-6600, Fax-817-850-6633. Hours- 9AM-4PM. www.txnd.uscourts.gov

Counties: Comanche, Erath, Hood, Jack, Palo Pinto, Parker, Tarrant, Wise.

Searches & Indexing: Results do not include SSN or DOB. Computer index maintained. Computer records go back to 1990 for civil cases; 1993 for criminal. Records also indexed on microfiche. New cases in the index 1 day after filing date. Records purged once yearly. District-wide searches from 1957 forward available.

Fee & Payment: Pay by Visa/MC, money order, cashier's or personal check. Payee: Clerk, US District Court. Prepayment required.

Phone Search: If provided a case number via phone, this court will only release minimal case information. Court will not search for case numbers via phone.

Mail Search: search usually completed- 1 week. SASE not required.

In Person Search: Fee charged if court performs your search. Self-serve copier - $.25 per page.

E-Services: ECF replaces PACER. Document images available. PACER records go back to 6/1991. New records online after 1 day. ECF at https://ecf.txnd.uscourts.gov **Opinions Online:** www.txnd.uscourts.gov/judges/.

Lubbock Division
Clerk of Court, Rm 209, 1205 Texas Ave, Lubbock, TX 79401 (also use mail address for courier delivery), 806-472-7624, Fax-806-472-7639. Hours- 8:30AM-N, 1-4:30PM. www.txnd.uscourts.gov

Counties: Bailey, Borden, Cochran, Crosby, Dawson, Dickens, Floyd, Gaines, Garza, Hale, Hockley, Kent, Lamb, Lubbock, Lynn, Motley, Scurry, Terry, Yoakum.

Searches & Indexing: Results do not include SSN or DOB. Computer, microfiche and card indexes maintained; computer goes back to 1980. New cases in the index 1 day after filing date. Records purged once yearly. No cases may have been sent to Federal Records Center.

Fee & Payment: Pay by Visa/MC, money order, cashier's or personal check. Payee: Clerk, US District Court. Prepayment required.

Mail Search: search usually completed- 2-3 days. Include SASE for return.

In Person Search: Fee charged if court performs your search. An in person request must be made in writing. No self-serve copier available.

E-Services: ECF replaces PACER. Document images available. PACER records go back to 6/1991. New records online after 1 day. ECF at https://ecf.txnd.uscourts.gov **Opinions Online:** www.txnd.uscourts.gov/judges/.

San Angelo Division
Clerk's Office, Rm 202, 33 E Twohig, San Angelo, TX 76903 (also use mail address for courier delivery), 325-655-4506, Fax-325-658-6826. Hours- 8:30AM-N,1:00-4:30PM. www.txnd.uscourts.gov

Counties: Brown, Coke, Coleman, Concho, Crockett, Glasscock, Irion, Menard, Mills, Reagan, Runnels, Schleicher, Sterling, Sutton, Tom Green.

Searches & Indexing: Results do not include SSN or DOB. Card and microfiche indexes maintained. New cases in the index immediately after filing date. Records purged yearly. Civil records retained 3 years; criminal records 7 to 8 years.

Fee & Payment: Pay by money order, cashier's or personal check. Payee: Clerk, US District Court. Prepayment required.

Phone Search: Only docket information available by telephone.

Mail Search: search usually completed- 1-2 days. Include SASE for return.

In Person Search: Fee charged if court performs your search. No self-serve copier available.

E-Services: ECF replaces PACER. Document images available. PACER records go back to 6/1991. New records online after 1 day. ECF at https://ecf.txnd.uscourts.gov **Opinions Online:** www.txnd.uscourts.gov/judges/.

Wichita Falls Division
Court Clerk, PO Box 1234, Wichita Falls, TX 76307 (courier address: Rm 203, 1000 Lamar, Wichita Falls, TX 76301), 940-767-1902, Fax-940-767-2526. Hours- 8:30AM-N, 1-4:30PM. www.txnd.uscourts.gov

Counties: Archer, Baylor, Clay, Cottle, Foard, Hardeman, King, Knox, Montague, Wichita, Wilbarger, Young.

Searches & Indexing: Results do not include SSN or DOB. A card index is maintained. Old records also indexed on microfiche. New cases in the index immediately after filing date. Records purged once yearly.

Fee & Payment: Pay by money order, cashier's or personal check. Payee: Clerk, US District Court. Prepayment required.

Phone Search: Only docket information is available by phone.

Mail Search: search usually completed- 2 days. Include SASE for return.

In Person Search: Fee charged if court performs your search. No self-serve copier available.

E-Services: ECF replaces PACER. Document images available. PACER records go back to 6/1991. New records online after 1 day. ECF at https://ecf.txnd.uscourts.gov **Opinions Online:** www.txnd.uscourts.gov/judges/.

US Bankruptcy Court
Northern District of Texas

Amarillo Division
Court Clerk, 624 S Polk St #100, Amarillo, TX 79101-2320 (also use mail address for courier delivery), 806-324-2302. Hours- 8AM-4PM. www.txnb.uscourts.gov

Counties: Armstrong, Briscoe, Carson, Castro, Childress, Collingsworth, Dallam, Deaf Smith, Donley, Gray, Hall, Hansford, Hartley, Hemphill, Hutchinson, Lipscomb, Moore, Ochiltree, Oldham, Parmer, Potter, Randall, Roberts, Sherman, Swisher, Wheeler.

Searches & Indexing: Results include last 4 SSN digits. Both computer and card indexes maintained. Card index available prior to 6/1988. New cases in the index immediately after filing date. Records purged every 6 months.

Fee & Payment: Pay by money order, cashier check, business check. No personal checks. Payee: Clerk, Bankruptcy Court. Prepayment required.

Phone Search: Only docket information is available by phone. Voice Case Information Service available, call VCIS at 800-886-9008 or 214-753-2128.

Mail Search: search usually completed- 1-2 days. Include SASE for return.

In Person Search: permitted. Search fee required should the court have to pull a file and count pages. Court does not charge to do in person name searches. Self-serve copier - $.50 per page.

E-Services: ECF replaces PACER whose records did go back to 1994. New records online after 1 day. ECF at https://ecf.txnb.uscourts.gov. Document images go back to 2/03. **Opinions Online:** www.txnb.uscourts.gov/opinions/. **Other Online Access:** Calendars free at www.txnb.uscourts.gov/judges/.

Dallas Division
Court Clerk, 1100 Commerce St, Suite 1254, Dallas, TX 75242-1496 (also use mail address for courier delivery), 214-753-2000, Fax-214-753-2038. Hours- 8:30AM-4:30PM. www.txnb.uscourts.gov

Counties: Dallas, Ellis, Hunt, Johnson, Kaufman, Navarro, Rockwall. This court maintains records for the Wichita Falls Division.

Searches & Indexing: Cases indexed by debtor, creditors, and case number. Results include last 4 SSN digits. Only a computer index maintained. New cases in the index 1-2 days after filing date. Records purged every 6 months. District-wide searches available back to 8/92.

Fee & Payment: Pay by no business or personal checks accepted. Payee: Clerk, US Bankruptcy Court. Prepayment required.

Phone Search: Only docket information is available by phone. Voice Case Information Service available, call VCIS at 800-886-9008 or 214-753-2128.

Mail Search: search usually completed- 2-3 days. Include SASE for return.

In Person Search: Fee charged if court performs your search. No search fee for searching docket sheets or claims registers in person No self-serve copier available.

E-Services: ECF replaces PACER whose records did go back to 1994. New records online after 1 day. ECF at https://ecf.txnb.uscourts.gov. Document images go back to 2/03. **Opinions**

Online: www.txnb.uscourts.gov/opinions/. **Other Online Access:** Calendars free at www.txnb.uscourts.gov/judges/.

Fort Worth Division Court Clerk, 501 W 10th, Suite 147, Fort Worth, TX 76102 (also use mail address for courier delivery), 817-333-6000, Fax-817-333-6001. Hours- 8:30AM-4:30PM. www.txnb.uscourts.gov

Counties: Comanche, Erath, Hood, Jack, Palo Pinto, Parker, Tarrant, Wise.

Searches & Indexing: Results include last 4 SSN digits. Both computer and card indexes maintained. Computer records go back to 8/1992; 1987 to 8/1992 records indexed manually; records up to 1986 on index cards. New cases in the index 1-2 days after filing date. Records purged every 6 months. Closed cases held in-house as space permits; sent at year end to Fort Worth Records Center.

Fee & Payment: Pay by money order, cashier's or personal check. No debtor's checks accepted. Payee: Clerk, US Bankruptcy Court. Prepayment required.

Phone Search: Only docket information is available by phone; court will search by debtor's name for records back to 1987. Voice Case Information Service available, call VCIS at 800-886-9008 or 214-753-2128.

Mail Search: search usually completed- 1-2 days. Include SASE for return.

In Person Search: Fee charged if court performs your search. Self-serve copier - $.25 per page.

E-Services: ECF replaces PACER whose records did go back to 1994. New records online after 1 day. ECF at https://ecf.txnb.uscourts.gov. Document images go back to 2/03. **Opinions Online:** www.txnb.uscourts.gov/opinions/. **Other Online Access:** Calendars free at www.txnb.uscourts.gov/judges/.

Lubbock Division Court Clerk, 306 Federal Bldg, 1205 Texas Ave, Lubbock, TX 79401-4002 (also use mail address for courier delivery), 806-472-5000. Hours- 8AM-4PM. www.txnb.uscourts.gov

Counties: Bailey, Borden, Brown, Callahan, Cochran, Cooke, Coleman, Concho, Crockett, Crosby, Dawson, Dickens, Eastland, Fisher, Floyd, Gaines, Garza, Glasscock, Hale, Haskell, Hockley, Howard, Irion, Jones, Kent, Lamb, Lubbock, Lynn, Menard, Mills, Mitchell, Motley, Nolan, Reagan, Runnels, Schleicher, Scurry, Shackelford, Stephens, Sterling, Stonewall, Sutton, Taylor, Terry, Throckmorton, Tom Green, Yoakum.

Searches & Indexing: Results include last 4 SSN digits. All records back to 2/03 maintained on computer. New cases in the index immediately after filing date. Records purged every 6 months. Paper records of open cases located at this court.

Fee & Payment: Pay by Visa/MC (but not from debtor), money order, cashier check, business check. No personal checks. Payee: Clerk, US Bankruptcy Court. Prepayment required.

Phone Search: Only basic case info from 1987 to present available by phone. Voice Case Information Service available, call VCIS at 800-886-9008 or 214-753-2128.

Mail Search: search usually completed- 3 days. Include SASE for return.

In Person Search: permitted. No self-serve copier available.

E-Services: ECF replaces PACER whose records did go back to 1994. New records online immediately. ECF at https://ecf.txnb.uscourts.gov. Document images go back to 2/03. **Opinions Online:** www.txnb.uscourts.gov/opinions/. **Other Online Access:** Calendars free at www.txnb.uscourts.gov/judges/.

Wichita Falls Division c/o Dallas Division, Rm 1254, 1100 Commerce St, Dallas, TX 75242-1496 (also use mail address for courier delivery), 214-753-2000, records rm- 214-767-0814. Hours- 8:30AM-4:30PM. www.txnb.uscourts.gov

Counties: Archer, Baylor, Clay, Cottle, Foard, Hardeman, King, Knox, Montague, Wichita, Wilbarger, Young.

Searches & Indexing: Cases indexed by and case number. Results include last 4 SSN digits. Records purged every 6 months. Paper records located at Dallas Division.

Fee & Payment: Pay by no business or personal checks accepted. Payee: Clerk, U.S. Bankruptcy Court.

Phone Search: Voice Case Information Service available, call 800-886-9008 or 214-753-2128.

Mail Search: Include SASE for return.

In Person Search: permitted. No self-serve copier available.

E-Services: ECF replaces PACER whose records did go back to 1994. New records online after 1 day. ECF at https://ecf.txnb.uscourts.gov. Document images go back to 2/03. **Opinions Online:** www.txnb.uscourts.gov/opinions/. **Other Online Access:** Calendars free at www.txnb.uscourts.gov/judges/.

US District Court

Southern District of Texas

Brownsville Division Court Clerk, 600 E Harrison St, Rm 101, Brownsville, TX 78520-7114 (also use mail address for courier delivery), 956-548-2500, Fax-956-548-2598. Hours- 8AM-5PM. www.txsd.uscourts.gov

Counties: Cameron, Willacy. Also holds bankruptcy court records here. You may search entire Southern District electronically at any of the seven courthouse locations.

Searches & Indexing: Results do not include SSN or DOB. Computer, microfiche and card indexes maintained; computer goes back to 1995. New cases in the index 2 days after filing date. Records purged every 6 months.

Fee & Payment: Pay by money order, cashier's or personal check. Payee: Clerk, US District Court. Prepayment required.

Phone Search: Only docket information is available by phone.

Mail Search: search usually completed- 1 week. Include SASE for return.

In Person Search: Fee charged if court performs your search. No self-serve copier available.

E-Services: ECF replaces PACER whose records did go back to 6/1990. New records online after 1 day. ECF at https://ecf.txsd.uscourts.gov. Document images available. **Opinions Online:** www.txsd.uscourts.gov/opinions/dcdisclaimer.htm

Corpus Christi Division Clerk's Office, 1133 N Shoreline Blvd, #208, Corpus Christi, TX 78401 (also use mail address for courier delivery), 361-888-3142. Hours- 8:30AM-4:30PM. www.txsd.uscourts.gov

Counties: Aransas, Bee, Brooks, Duval, Jim Wells, Kenedy, Kleberg, Live Oak, Nueces, San Patricio.

Searches & Indexing: Results do not include SSN or DOB. Computer and microfiche indexes maintained. New cases in the index 3 to 5 days after filing date. Records purged every 6 months.

Fee & Payment: Pay by money order, cashier's or personal check. Payee: Clerk, US District Court. Prepayment required.

Phone Search: No searching by telephone.

Mail Search: search usually completed- 24 hours. Include SASE for return.

In Person Search: permitted. Court will assist in searches. Request for copies taken and filled as personnel are available. No self-serve copier available.

E-Services: ECF replaces PACER whose records did go back to 6/1990. New records online after 1 day. ECF at https://ecf.txsd.uscourts.gov. Document images available. **Opinions Online:** www.txsd.uscourts.gov/opinions/dcdisclaimer.htm

Galveston Division Clerk's Office, PO Box 2300, Galveston, TX 77553 (courier address: 601 Rosenberg, Rm 411, Galveston, TX 77550), 409-766-3530. Hours- 9AM-4:30PM. www.txsd.uscourts.gov

Counties: Brazoria, Chambers, Galveston, Matagorda. Also holds bankruptcy court records here. You may search entire Southern District electronically at any of the seven courthouse locations.

Searches & Indexing: Results do not include SSN or DOB. Computer, microfiche and card indexes maintained; computer goes back to 1990. New cases in the index 1 day after filing date. Records purged every 6 months.

Fee & Payment: Pay by money order, cashier's, business or personal check. Payee: Clerk, US District Court. Prepayment required.

Phone Search: Only case status and trial settings are released via phone.

Mail Search: search usually completed- 1-2 days. Include SASE for return.

In Person Search: Fee charged if court performs your search. Self-serve copier - $.50 per page.

E-Services: ECF replaces PACER whose records did go back to 6/1990. New records online after 1 day. ECF at https://ecf.txsd.uscourts.gov. Document images available. **Opinions Online:** www.txsd.uscourts.gov/opinions/dcdisclaimer.htm

Houston Division Court Clerk, PO Box 61010, Houston, TX 77208 (courier address: Rm 1217, 515 Rusk, Houston, TX 77002), 713-250-5500, records rm- 713-250-5543, crim dockets- 713-250-5786, civil dockets- 713-250-5786. Hours- 9AM-4:30PM. www.txsd.uscourts.gov

Counties: Austin, Brazos, Colorado, Fayette, Fort Bend, Grimes, Harris, Madison, Montgomery, San Jacinto, Walker, Waller, Wharton.

Searches & Indexing: Criminal docketing for the district is performed in Houston. Results include last 4 SSN digits. Computer, microfiche and card indexes maintained. New cases in the index 1 day or same day after filing date. Records purged every 6 months. District-wide searches available here back to 1979.

Fee & Payment: Pay by money order, cashier's or personal check. Payee: Clerk, US District Court. Prepayment required.

Phone Search: No searching by telephone.

Mail Search: search usually completed- ASAP. Also mail search using the court's copy service, LDR; call 713-222-6444. SASE not required.

In Person Search: Fee charged if court performs your search. Court personnel will assist searchers. A copy service is available, call 713-236-0903. No self-serve copier available.

E-Services: ECF replaces PACER whose records did go back to 6/1990. New records online after 1 day. ECF at https://ecf.txsd.uscourts.gov. Document images available. **Opinions Online:** www.txsd.uscourts.gov/opinions/dcdisclaimer.htm

Laredo Division Court Clerk, 1300 Victoria St #1131, Laredo, TX 78040 (also use mail address for courier delivery), 956-723-3542. Hours- 9AM-4PM. www.txsd.uscourts.gov

Counties: Jim Hogg, La Salle, McMullen, Webb, Zapata. Also holds bankruptcy court records here. You may search entire Southern District electronically at any of the 7 courthouse locations.

Searches & Indexing: Style of case is needed to search. Computer index maintained. New cases in the index immediately after filing date. Records purged every 6 months.

Fee & Payment: Pay by cashier check. Business checks are not accepted. No personal or business checks accepted. Payee: Clerk, US District Court. Prepayment required.

Phone Search: No searching by telephone.

Mail Search: search usually completed- 1-2 days. SASE not required.

In Person Search: Fee charged if court performs your search. No self-serve copier available.

E-Services: ECF replaces PACER whose records did go back to 6/1990. New records online after 1 day. ECF at https://ecf.txsd.uscourts.gov. Document images available. **Opinions Online:** www.txsd.uscourts.gov/opinions/dcdisclaimer.htm

McAllen Division Court Clerk, Suite 1011, 1701 W Business Hwy 83, McAllen, TX 78501 (use mail address for courier delivery), 956-618-8065. Hours- 8AM-5PM. www.txsd.uscourts.gov

Counties: Hidalgo, Starr. Also holds bankruptcy court records here. You may search entire Southern District electronically at any of the seven courthouse locations.

Searches & Indexing: Court in operation less than 10 years. Results do not include SSN or DOB. Both computer and card indexes maintained; computer goes back to 1988. New cases in the index 1 day after filing date. Records purged every 6 months.

Fee & Payment: Pay by money order, cashier check, business check. No personal checks. Payee: Clerk, US District Court. Prepayment required.

Phone Search: Only docket information available by phone.

Mail Search: search usually completed- week-10 days. Include SASE for return.

In Person Search: Fee charged if court performs your search. No self-serve copier available.

E-Services: ECF replaces PACER whose records did go back to 6/1990. New records online after 1 day. ECF at https://ecf.txsd.uscourts.gov. Document images available. **Opinions Online:** www.txsd.uscourts.gov/opinions/dcdisclaimer.htm

Victoria Division Clerk US District Court, PO Box 1638, Victoria, TX 77902 (courier address: Rm 406, 312 S Main, Victoria, TX 77901), 361-788-5000. Hours- 8:30AM-4:30PM. www.txsd.uscourts.gov

Counties: Calhoun, De Witt, Goliad, Jackson, Lavaca, Refugio, Victoria. Also holds bankruptcy court records here. You may search entire Southern District electronically at any of the seven courthouse locations.

Searches & Indexing: Results do not include SSN or DOB. Both computer and card indexes maintained; computer goes back to 1996. New cases in the index 2 days after filing date. Records purged every 6 months.

Fee & Payment: Pay by money order, cashier's or personal check. Payee: Clerk, US District Court. Prepayment required.

Phone Search: Only docket information is available by phone.

Mail Search: search usually completed- 2-3 days. Include SASE for return.

In Person Search: permitted. Self-serve copier - $.50 per page.

E-Services: ECF replaces PACER whose records did go back to 6/1990. New records online after 1 day. ECF at https://ecf.txsd.uscourts.gov. Document images available. **Opinions Online:** www.txsd.uscourts.gov/opinions/dcdisclaimer.htm

US Bankruptcy Court
Southern District of Texas

Corpus Christi Division Court Clerk, 1133 N Shoreline Blvd - 2rd Fl, Corpus Christi, TX 78401 (also use mail address for courier delivery), 361-888-3484. Hours- 9AM - 4:30PM. www.txsd.uscourts.gov

Counties: Aransas, Bee, Brooks, Cameron*, Duval, Hidalgo**, Jim Wells, Kenedy, Kleberg, Live Oak, Nueces, San Patricio, Starr**, Willacy*. Files from Brownsville, Corpus Christi, and McAllen are maintained here. You may search entire Southern District electronically at any of the seven courthouse locations. Open case records for counties marked with a single asterisk (*) are at Galveston Division (see US Dist Court). Open case records for counties marked with a double asterisk (**) are at McAllen Division (see US Dist Court).

Searches & Indexing: Houston office also holds old Victoria Division records. Results include last 4 SSN digits only. Computer and microfiche indexes maintained. New cases in the index 1-2 days after filing date.

Fee & Payment: Pay by money order, cashier's or personal check. Payee: Clerk, US Bankruptcy Court. Prepayment required.

Phone Search: Voice Case Information Service available, call 800-745-4459 or 713-250-5049.

Mail Search: search usually completed- 1-2 days. Include SASE for return.

In Person Search: Fee charged if court performs your search. A copy page printed off the computer is $.10 each. Self-serve copier - $.25 per page.

E-Services: PACER online at http://pacer.txs.uscourts.gov. Document images available. PACER records go back to 6/1991. New records online after 1 day. ECF at https://ecf.txsb.uscourts.gov **Opinions Online:** www.txsd.uscourts.gov/opinions/dcdisclaimer.htm . Search bankruptcy orders by year back to 2001 free. **Other Online Access:** Court calendars at www.txsd.uscourts.gov/judges/judgeban.htm.

Houston Division Court Clerk, Rm 1217, 515 Rusk Ave, Houston, TX 77002 (also use mail address for courier delivery), 713-250-5500. Hours- 9AM-4:30PM. www.txs.uscourts.gov

Counties: Austin, Brazoria**, Brazos, Calhoun***, Chambers**, Colorado, De Witt***, Fayette, Fort Bend, Galveston**, Goliad***, Grimes, Harris, Jackson***, Jim Hogg*, La Salle*, Lavaca***, Madison, Matagorda**, McMullen*, Montgomery, Refugio***, San Jacinto, Victoria***, Walker, Waller, Wharton, Webb* Zapata*. Open case records for counties with a single asterisk (*) are at Laredo Division (see US Dist Court). Open case records for counties with double asterisk (**) are at Galveston Div. (see US Dist Court). Open case records for counties with 3 asterisks (***) are at Victoria Div (see US Dist Court). Search entire Southern District electronically at any of the 7 courthouse locations.

Searches & Indexing: Earliest case files from 1987. Results include last 4 SSN digits. Computer, microfiche and card indexes maintained. New cases in the index usually same day after filing date. Records purged every 6 months.

Fee & Payment: Pay by money order, cashier's or personal check. Payee: Clerk, US District Court. Prepayment required.

Phone Search: Only docket information available by phone. Voice Case Information Service available, call VCIS at 800-745-4459.

Mail Search: search usually completed- 2-3 weeks. Include SASE for return.

In Person Search: Fee charged if court performs your search. There is an on-site copy service. No self-serve copier available.

E-Services: PACER online at http://pacer.txs.uscourts.gov. Document images available. PACER records go back to 6/1991. New records online after 1 day. ECF at https://ecf.txsb.uscourts.gov **Opinions Online:** www.txsd.uscourts.gov/bkgenord/bkgenord.htm. Search bankruptcy orders by year back to 2001 free. **Other Online Access:** Court calendars at www.txsd.uscourts.gov/judges/judgeban.htm.

US District Court
Western District of Texas

Austin Division Court Clerk, Rm 130, 200 W 8th St, Austin, TX 78701 (also use mail address for courier delivery), 512-916-5896, Fax-512-916-5894. Hours- 8AM-5PM. www.txwd.uscourts.gov

Counties: Bastrop, Blanco, Burleson, Burnet, Caldwell, Gillespie, Hays, Kimble, Lampasas, Lee, Llano, McCulloch, Mason, San Saba, Travis, Washington, Williamson.

Searches & Indexing: Results do not include SSN or DOB. Computer and microfiche indexes maintained. New cases in the index 1 day after filing date. Records purged every 6 months.

Fee & Payment: Pay by money order, cashier's or personal check. Payee: Clerk, US District Court. Prepayment required.

Phone Search: Only docket information is available by phone.

Mail Search: search usually completed- 7-10 days. Include SASE for return.

In Person Search: Fee charged if court performs your search. Self-serve copier - $.35 per page.

E-Services: PACER online at http://pacer.txwd.uscourts.gov. PACER records go back to 1994. New records online after 1 day. ECF at https://ecf.txwd.uscourts.gov. ECF may still be under development. **Opinions Online:** www.nysd.uscourts.gov/courtweb/public.htm. **Other Online Access:** Access judges' calendars at www.txwd.uscourts.gov/calendar/default.asp.

Del Rio Division Court Clerk, Rm 100, 111 E Broadway, Del Rio, TX 78840 (also use mail address for courier delivery), 830-703-2054. Hours- 8AM-5PM. www.txwd.uscourts.gov

Counties: Edwards, Kinney, Maverick, Terrell, Uvalde, Val Verde, Zavala.

Searches & Indexing: Results do not include SSN or DOB. Computer index maintained. New cases in the index 1 month after filing date. Records purged every 6 months.

Fee & Payment: Pay by money order, cashier's or personal check. Payee: Clerk, US District Court. Prepayment required.

Phone Search: Only docket information is available by phone.

Mail Search: search usually completed- 1-2 days. Include SASE for return.

In Person Search: Fee charged if court performs your search. No self-serve copier available.

E-Services: PACER online at http://pacer.txwd.uscourts.gov. PACER records go back to 1994. New records online after 1 day. ECF at https://ecf.txwd.uscourts.gov. ECF may still be under development. **Opinions Online:** www.nysd.uscourts.gov/courtweb/public.htm. **Other Online Access:** Access judges' calendars at www.txwd.uscourts.gov/calendar/default.asp.

El Paso Division US District Clerk Office, Rm 350, 511 E San Antonio, El Paso, TX 79901 (also use mail address for courier delivery), 915-534-6725. 8AM-5PM. www.txwd.uscourts.gov

Counties: El Paso.

Searches & Indexing: Results do not include SSN or DOB. Computer, microfiche and card indexes maintained. New cases in the index 1-2 days after filing date. Records purged every 6 months.

Fee & Payment: Pay by money order, cashier's or personal check. Payee: Clerk, US District Court. Prepayment required.

Phone Search: Only docket information is available by phone.

Mail Search: search usually completed- 7-10 days. Include SASE for return.

In Person Search: Fee charged if court performs your search. Self-serve copier - $.25 per page.

E-Services: PACER online at http://pacer.txwd.uscourts.gov. PACER records go

back to 1994. New records online after 1 day. ECF at https://ecf.txwd.uscourts.gov. ECF may still be under development. **Opinions Online:** www.nysd.uscourts.gov/courtweb/public.htm. **Other Online Access:** Access judges' calendars at www.txwd.uscourts.gov/calendar/default.asp.

Midland Division Clerk, US District Court, 200 E Wall St, Rm 107, Midland, TX 79701 (also use mail address for courier delivery), 432-686-4001. Hours- 8AM-5PM. www.txwd.uscourts.gov

Counties: Andrews, Crane, Ector, Martin, Midland, Upton.

Searches & Indexing: Results do not include SSN or DOB. Computer, microfiche and card indexes maintained; computer goes back to 1985. New cases in the index immediately after filing date. Records purged every 6 months.

Fee & Payment: Pay by money order, cashier's or personal check. Payee: Clerk, US District Court. Prepayment required.

Phone Search: Most information is released via phone.

Mail Search: search usually completed- 1-2 days. Include SASE for return.

In Person Search: Fee charged if court performs your search. For self-serve copies, bring your own change or else. Self-serve copier - $.25 per page.

E-Services: PACER online at http://pacer.txwd.uscourts.gov. PACER records go back to 1994. New records online after 1 day. ECF at https://ecf.txwd.uscourts.gov. ECF may still be under development. **Opinions Online:** www.nysd.uscourts.gov/courtweb/public.htm. **Other Online Access:** Access judges' calendars at www.txwd.uscourts.gov/calendar/default.asp.

Pecos Division Court Clerk, 410 S Cedar St, US Courthouse, Pecos, TX 79772 (also use mail address for courier delivery), 432-445-4228, Fax-432-445-9859. Hours- 8AM-5PM. www.txwd.uscourts.gov

Counties: Brewster, Culberson, Hudspeth, Jeff Davis, Loving, Pecos, Presidio, Reeves, Ward, Winkler.

Searches & Indexing: Results do not include SSN or DOB. Computer and card indexes maintained; computer index back to 1991. New cases in the index immediately after filing date. Records purged every 6 months.

Fee & Payment: Pay by money order, cashier's or personal check. No debtor's checks accepted. Payee: Clerk, District Court. Prepayment required.

Mail Search: search usually completed- 2-3 days. Include SASE for return.

In Person Search: Fee charged if court performs your search. Self-serve copier - $.25 per page.

E-Services: PACER online at http://pacer.txwd.uscourts.gov. PACER records go back to 1994. New records online after 1 day. ECF at https://ecf.txwd.uscourts.gov. ECF may still be under development. **Opinions Online:** www.nysd.uscourts.gov/courtweb/public.htm. **Other Online Access:** Access judges' calendars at www.txwd.uscourts.gov/calendar/default.asp.

San Antonio Division US Clerk's Office, 655 E Durango Blvd, Suite G-65, San Antonio, TX 78206 (also use mail address for courier delivery), 210-472-6550, Fax-210-472-6573. Hours- 8AM-5PM. www.txwd.uscourts.gov

Counties: Atascosa, Bandera, Bexar, Comal, Dimmit, Frio, Gonzales, Guadalupe, Karnes, Kendall, Kerr, Medina, Real, Wilson.

Searches & Indexing: Results include last 4 SSN digits, also birth year. Computer and microfiche indexes maintained. New cases in index 1-2 days after filing date. Records purged every 6 months.

Fee & Payment: Pay by money order, cashier's or personal check. Payee: Clerk, US District Court. Prepayment required.

Mail Search: search usually completed- soon as work load permits. Include SASE for return.

In Person Search: Fee charged if court performs your search. Self-serve copier - $.35 per page.

E-Services: PACER online at http://pacer.txwd.uscourts.gov. PACER records go back to 1994. New records online after 1 day. ECF at https://ecf.txwd.uscourts.gov. ECF may still be under development. **Opinions Online:** www.nysd.uscourts.gov/courtweb/public.htm. **Other Online Access:** Access judges' calendars at www.txwd.uscourts.gov/calendar/default.asp.

Waco Division Clerk of Court, Rm 380, 800 Franklin, Waco, TX 76701 (also use mail address for courier delivery), 254-750-1501. Hours- 8AM-5PM. www.txwd.uscourts.gov

Counties: Bell, Bosque, Coryell, Falls, Freestone, Hamilton, Hill, Leon, Limestone, McLennan, Milam, Robertson, Somervell.

Searches & Indexing: Results do not include SSN or DOB. A card index is maintained. New cases in the index 1-2 days after filing date. Records purged every 6 months.

Fee & Payment: Pay by money order, cashier's or personal check. Payee: Clerk, US District Court. Prepayment required.

Phone Search: Only docket information is available by phone.

Mail Search: search usually completed- 1-2 days. Include SASE for return.

In Person Search: Fee charged if court performs your search. Self-serve copier - $.15 per page.

E-Services: PACER online at http://pacer.txwd.uscourts.gov. PACER records go back to 1994. New records online after 1 day. ECF at https://ecf.txwd.uscourts.gov. ECF may still be under development. **Opinions Online:** www.nysd.uscourts.gov/courtweb/public.htm. **Other Online Access:** Access judges' calendars at www.txwd.uscourts.gov/calendar/default.asp.

US Bankruptcy Court
Western District of Texas

Austin Division Court Clerk, Homer Thornberry Judicial Bldg, 903 San Jacinto, # 322, Austin, TX 78701 (also use mail address for courier delivery), 512-916-5237, Fax-512-916-5278. Hours- 8AM-4PM. www.txwb.uscourts.gov

Counties: Bastrop, Blanco, Burleson, Burnet, Caldwell, Gillespie, Hays, Kimble, Lampasas, Lee, Llano, Mason, McCulloch, San Saba, Travis, Washington, Williamson.

Searches & Indexing: Cases indexed by debtor, creditors, and case number. Results include last 4 SSN digits. Computer and microfiche indexes maintained. New cases in the index 24 hours after filing date. Records purged every 6-8 months.

Fee & Payment: Pay by Visa/MC (in person only), money order, cashier's or personal check. No debtor's checks accepted. Payee: US Bankruptcy Court. Prepayment required.

Phone Search: Only docket information is available by phone. Voice Case Information Service available, call VCIS at 888-436-7477 or 210-472-4023.

Mail Search: search usually completed- 3 days. Include SASE for return.

In Person Search: Fee charged if court performs your search. Self-serve copier in the lobby - $.25 per page.

E-Services: ECF replaces PACER whose records did go back to 5/1987. New records online after 1 day. ECF at https://ecf.txwb.uscourts.gov **Opinions Online:** www.txwb.uscourts.gov/opinions/judges.php. **Other Online Access:** Calendars at www.txwb.uscourts.gov/information/calendars/calendar_index.htm.

El Paso Division Court Clerk, PO Box 971040, El Paso, TX 79925 (courier address: 8515 Lockheed, El Paso, TX 79997), 915-779-7362, Fax-915-779-5693. Hours- 8AM-4PM. www.txwb.uscourts.gov

Counties: El Paso.

Searches & Indexing: Results include last 4 SSN digits only. Computer index back to 1987 maintained. Card index to 1987 and microfiche up to 1980. New cases in the index 24 hours after filing date. Records purged every 6-8 months.

Fee & Payment: Pay by money order, cashier check only. Payee: Clerk, US Bankruptcy Court. Prepayment required.

Phone Search: Only docket information is available by phone. Voice Case Information Service available, call VCIS at 888-436-7477 or 210-472-4023.

Mail Search: search usually completed- 10 days. Include SASE for return.

In Person Search: Fee charged if court performs your search. Self-serve copier - $.25 per page.

E-Services: ECF replaces PACER whose records did go back to 5/1987. New records online after 1 day. ECF at https://ecf.txwb.uscourts.gov **Opinions Online:** www.txwb.uscourts.gov/opinions/judges.php. **Other Access:** Calendars at www.txwb.uscourts.gov/information/calendars/calendar_index.htm.

Midland/Odessa Division Court Clerk, US Post Office Annex, Rm P-163, 100 E Wall St, Midland, TX 79701 (also use mail address for courier delivery), 432-683-1650. Hours- 8AM-N, 1-4PM. www.txwb.uscourts.gov

Counties: Andrews, Brewster, Crane, Culberson, Ector, Hudspeth, Jeff Davis, Loving, Martin, Midland, Pecos, Presidio, Reeves, Upton, Ward, Winkler.

Searches & Indexing: Records from the Pecos Division, which closed, were transferred here. Results do not include SSN or DOB; clerk will verify if your SSN is correct. Computer, microfiche and card indexes maintained. New cases in the index immediately after filing date.

Fee & Payment: Pay by money order, cashier's or personal check. No debtor's checks accepted. Payee: Clerk, US Bankruptcy Court. Prepayment required.

Phone Search: Only docket information is available by phone. Voice Case Information Service available, call VCIS at 888-436-7477 or 210-472-4023.

Mail Search: search usually completed- same day if possible. Include SASE for return.

In Person Search: Fee charged if court performs your search. For self-serve copies, bring your own change or else. Self-serve copier - $.25 per page.

E-Services: ECF replaces PACER whose records did go back to 5/1987. New records online after 1 day. ECF at https://ecf.txwb.uscourts.gov **Opinions Online:** www.txwb.uscourts.gov/opinions/judges.php. **Other Access:** Calendars free at www.txwb.uscourts.gov/information/calendars/calendar_index.htm.

San Antonio Division Court Clerk, PO Box 1439, San Antonio, TX 78295 (courier address: 615 E Houston St, Rm 147, San Antonio, TX 78205), 210-472-6720, Fax-210-472-5916. Hours- 8AM-4PM. www.txwd.uscourts.gov

Counties: Atascosa, Bandera, Bexar, Comal, Dimmit, Edwards, Frio, Gonzales, Guadalupe, Karnes, Kendall, Kerr, Kinney, Maverick, Medina, Real, Terrell, Uvalde, Val Verde, Wilson, Zavala.

Searches & Indexing: Cases indexed by debtor name and case number. Results include full SSN. Computer index maintained. New cases in the index 24 hours after filing date. Records purged every 6-8 months. District-wide searches available here back 10 years.

Fee & Payment: Pay by Visa/MC/AmEx, money order, cashier check. No personal or business checks accepted.

Phone Search: Voice Case Information Service available, call 888-436-7477 or 210-472-4023.

Mail Search: search usually completed- 1 week. Include SASE for return.

In Person Search: permitted. There is a copy service on site. Self-serve copier - $.35 per page.

E-Services: PACER online at http://pacer.txwb.uscourts.gov. PACER records go back to 5/1987. New records online after 1 day. ECF at https://ecf.txwb.uscourts.gov **Opinions Online:** www.nysd.uscourts.gov/courtweb/public.htm. **Other Access:** Access judges' calendars at www.txwd.uscourts.gov/calendar/default.asp.

Waco Division Court Clerk, 800 Franklin Ave #140, Waco, TX 76701 (also use mail address for courier delivery), 254-750-1513, Fax-254-750-1529. Hours- 8AM-4PM. www.txwb.uscourts.gov

Counties: Bell, Bosque, Coryell, Falls, Freestone, Hamilton, Hill, Leon, Limestone, McLennan, Milam, Robertson, Somervell.

Searches & Indexing: Results include SSN. Computer index maintained. New cases in the index same day after filing date. Records purged every 6-8 months.

Fee & Payment: Pay by money order, cashier's or personal check. Payee: Clerk, US Bankruptcy Court. Prepayment required.

Phone Search: Only docket information is available by phone. Voice Case Information Service available, call VCIS at 888-436-7477 or 210-472-4023.

Mail Search: search usually completed- 3 days. Include SASE for return.

In Person Search: Fee charged if court performs your search. Self-serve copier - $.10 per page.

E-Services: ECF replaces PACER whose records did go back to 5/1987. New records online after 1 day. ECF at https://ecf.txwb.uscourts.gov **Opinions Online:** www.txwb.uscourts.gov/opinions/judges.php. **Other Access:** Calendars free at www.txwb.uscourts.gov/information/calendars/calendar_index.htm

Texas County Courts

Court	Jurisdiction	No. of Courts	How Organized
District Courts*	General	172	420 Districts
County Constitutional Courts*	Limited	254	254 Counties
County Courts at Law Courts*	Limited	81	81 Counties
Justice of the Peace Courts	By Precinct	835	
Municipal Courts	Municipal	882	
Probate Courts*	Probate	17	10 Counties

* Profiled in this Sourcebook.

Court	CIVIL								
	Tort	Contract	Real Estate	Min. Claim	Max. Claim	Small Claims	Estate	Eviction	Domestic Relations
District Courts*	X	X	X	$200	No Max				X
County Courts*	X	X	X	$200	Varies		X		X
Justice of the Peace Courts	X	X		$0	$5000	$5000		X	
Municipal Courts									
Probate Courts*							X		

Court	CRIMINAL				
	Felony	Misdemeanor	DWI/DUI	Preliminary Hearing	Juvenile
District Courts*	X				X
County Courts*		X	X		X
Justice of the Peace Courts		X		X	
Municipal Courts		X			
Probate Courts*					

ADMINISTRATION   Office of Court Administration, PO Box 12066, Austin, TX, 78711; 512-463-1625, Fax: 512-463-1648. www.courts.state.tx.us

COURT STRUCTURE   The legal court structure for Texas is explained extensively in the "Texas Judicial Annual Report." Generally, Texas District Courts have general civil jurisdiction and exclusive felony jurisdiction, along with typical variations such as contested probate and divorce. As of 01/15/04, four additional District Courts were implemented.

The County Court structure consists of two forms of courts - "Constitutional" and "at Law. " The Constitutional upper cliam limit is $100,000 while the At Law upper limit is $5,000. For civil matters up to $5000, we recommend searchers start at the Constitutional County Court as they, generally, offer a shorter waiting time for cases in urban areas. In some counties the District Court or County Court handles evictions. District Courts handle felonies. County Courts handle misdemeanors and general civil cases.

We have indicated when a record search is automatically combined for two courts, for example a District and County court or both county courts.

ONLINE ACCESS   Appellate court case information is searchable for free on the Internet from the web site of each appellate court, reached from the web site mentioned above. Court of Criminal Appeals opinions are found at www.cca.courts.state.tx.us. A number of local county courts offer online access to their records, but there is no statewide system of local level court records.

PROBATE COURTS   Probate is handled in Probate Court in the 10 largest counties and in District Courts or County Courts at Law elsewhere. However, the County Clerk is responsible for the records in every county.

Anderson County

District Court PO Box 1159, Palestine, TX 75802-1159; phone: 903-723-7412; hours 8AM-N, 1-5PM (CST). *Felony, Civil.*
www.co.anderson.tx.us
Note: The court also holds family Cases.
Civil Records: Access: Phone, mail, in person. Both court and visitors may perform in person searches. Search fee: $5.00 per name. Court makes copy: $1.00 per page. Required to search: name, years to search. Civil cases indexed by defendant, plaintiff; on computer from 1984; prior on card index back to 1946. Mail turnaround time 2 days.
Criminal Records: Access: Mail, in person. Both court and visitors may perform in person searches. Search fee: $5.00 per name. Court makes copy: $1.99 per page. Required to search: name, years to search, DOB, SSN. Criminal records on computer from 1984; prior on index. Mail turnaround time 2 days.
General Information: Public terminal goes back to 1984. No juvenile or adoption records released. Will not fax documents. Certification fee: $1.00 per page. Payee: Anderson County District Clerk. Personal checks accepted. Prepayment and SASE required.

County Court 500 N Church, Palestine, TX 75801; phone: 903-723-7432; probate phone: 903-723-7430; probate fax: same; hours 8AM-5PM (CST). *Misdemeanor, Civil, Probate.*
Civil Records: Access: Mail, in person. Both court and visitors may perform in person searches. Search fee: $5.00 per name. Court makes copy: $1.00 per page. Required to search: name, years to search. Civil cases indexed by defendant, plaintiff; on computer from 1982, land cases from 1983. Mail turnaround time 1 week.
Criminal Records: Access: Mail, in person. Both court and visitors may perform in person searches. Search fee: $5.00 per name. Court makes copy: $1.00 per page. Required to search: name, years to search, DOB. Criminal records on computer from 1969. Mail turnaround time 1 week.
General Information: Public terminal has criminal back to 1969 and civil back to 1982. Certification fee: $5.00. Payee: County Clerk. Personal checks accepted. Prepayment and SASE required.

Andrews County

District Court PO Box 328, Andrews, TX 79714; phone: 432-524-1417; hours 8AM-5PM (CST). *Felony, Civil.*
Civil Records: Access: Mail, in person. Only the court performs in person searches; visitors may not. Search fee: $5.00 per name. Court makes copy: $1.00 for first page, $.25 each add'l. Required to search: name, years to search. Civil cases indexed by defendant, plaintiff. Civil records computerized since 1975. Mail turnaround time 1 day.
Criminal Records: Access: Mail, in person. Only the court performs in person searches; visitors may not. Search fee: $5.00 per name. Court makes copy: $1.00 for first page, $.25 each add'l. Required to search: name, years to search, DOB; also helpful: SSN. Criminal records computerized since 1975; prior to 1910. Mail turnaround time 1 day.
General Information: No juvenile, mental, sealed, terminations or adoption records released. Will not fax documents. Certification fee: $2.00. Payee: District Clerk. Personal checks accepted. Prepayment and SASE required.

County Court PO Box 727, Andrews, TX 79714; phone: 432-524-1426; hours 8AM-5PM (CST). *Misdemeanor, Civil, Probate.*
Note: Probate in a separate index at this same address.
Civil Records: Access: Phone, mail, in person. Both court and visitors may perform in person searches. Search fee: $10.00 per name. Court makes copy: $1.00 per page. Required to search: name, years to search. Civil cases indexed by defendant, plaintiff; on computer since 1980; prior records in manual index. Mail turnaround time 1 day.

Criminal Records: Access: Phone, mail, in person. Both court and visitors may perform in person searches. Search fee: $10.00 per name. Court makes copy: $1.00 per page. Required to search: name, years to search, DOB or SSN; also helpful: sex. Criminal records on computer since 1985; prior records in manual index. Mail turnaround time 1 day.
General Information: No juvenile, mental, sealed, or adoption records released. Will not fax documents. Certification fee: $5.00 per document. Payee: F. Wm. Hoermann County Clerk. Personal checks accepted if in state. Prepayment required.

Angelina County

District Court PO Box 908, Lufkin, TX 75902; phone: 936-634-4312; fax: 936-634-5915; hours 8AM-5PM (CST). *Felony, Civil.*
Civil Records: Access: Mail, in person. Both court and visitors may perform in person searches. Search fee: $5.00 per name. Court makes copy: $1.00 per page. Required to search: name, years to search. Civil cases indexed by defendant, plaintiff; on computer from 1986, on index books from 1800s. Must state whether search is on plaintiff or defendant. Mail turnaround time 2-3 days.
Criminal Records: Access: Mail, in person. Both court and visitors may perform in person searches. Search fee: $5.00 per name. Court makes copy: $1.00 per page. Required to search: name, years to search, DOB; also helpful: SSN. Criminal records on computer from 1984, on index books from 1800s. Mail turnaround time 2-3 days.
General Information: Public terminal goes back to 1996. No juvenile, mental, sealed, or adoption records released. Will fax documents for a $5.00 fee. Certification fee: $2.00. Payee: District Clerk. Personal checks not accepted. Prepayment and SASE required.

County Court PO Box 908 (215 E Lufkin Ave), Lufkin, TX 75902; phone: 936-634-8339; fax: 936-634-8460; hours 8AM-5PM (CST). *Misdemeanor, Civil, Probate.*
www.angelinacounty.net
Civil Records: Access: Mail, in person. Both court and visitors may perform in person searches. Search fee: $5.00 per name plus 10-year period. Court makes copy: $1.00 per page. Required to search: name, years to search. Civil cases indexed by defendant, plaintiff. Civil records go back to 1893; computerized records go back to 8/1995. Mail turnaround time 1-2 days.
Criminal Records: Access: Mail, in person. Both court and visitors may perform in person searches. Search fee: $5.00 per name plus 10-year period. Will search back to 1984. Court makes copy: $1.00 per page. Required to search: name, years to search; also helpful: DOB. Criminal records go back to 1893; computerized records go back to 1983. Mail turnaround time 1-2 days.
General Information: No mental or sealed records released. These records are not filed in our office. Will not fax documents. Certification fee: $5.00. Payee: County Clerk. Business checks accepted. Prepayment and SASE required.

Aransas County

District Court 301 N Live Oak, Rockport, TX 78382; phone: 361-790-0128; fax: 361-790-5211; hours 8AM-5PM (CST). *Felony, Civil.*
Civil Records: Access: Mail, in person. Both court and visitors may perform in person searches. Search fee: $5.00 per name. Court makes copy: $1.00 per page; same fee for self serve. Required to search: name, years to search. Civil cases indexed by defendant, plaintiff; in index books from 1800s, computerized since 1999. Mail turnaround time 1-2 days.
Criminal Records: Access: Mail, in person. Both court and visitors may perform in person searches. Search fee: $5.00 per name. Court makes copy: $1.00 per page; same fee for self serve. Required to search: name, years to search. Criminal records in index

books from 1800s, computerized since 1999. Mail turnaround time 1-2 days.
General Information: Public terminal has criminal back to 1965 and civil back to 2000. No juvenile, mental, sealed, or adoption records released. Will not fax documents. Certification fee: $1.00 per document. Payee: District Clerk. Personal checks accepted. Prepayment and SASE required.

County Court 301 N Live Oak, Rockport, TX 78382; phone: 361-790-0122; fax: 360-790-0119; hours 8AM-4:30PM (CST). *Misdemeanor, Civil, Probate.*
Civil Records: Access: Mail, in person. Both court and visitors may perform in person searches. Search fee: $5.00 per name. Court makes copy: $1.00 per page; same fee for self serve. Required to search: name, years to search. Civil cases indexed by defendant, plaintiff; in index books from 1947, computerized records go back to 1998. Mail turnaround time 2 days.
Criminal Records: Access: Mail, in person. Both court and visitors may perform in person searches. Search fee: $5.00 per name. Court makes copy: $1.00 per page; same fee for self serve. Required to search: name, years to search, DOB. Criminal records in index books from 1947; computerized records go back to 1995. Mail turnaround time 2 days.
General Information: Public terminal has criminal back to 1992 and civil back to 1995. No mental or sealed records released; we do not have juvenile or adoption records in our office. Will fax documents to local or toll free line. Certification fee: $5.00. Payee: County Clerk. Personal checks accepted. Prepayment and SASE required.

Archer County

District Court PO Box 815, Archer City, TX 76351; phone: 940-574-4615; fax: 940-574-2432; hours 8:30AM-5PM (CST). *Felony, Civil.*
Civil Records: Access: Mail, in person. Both court and visitors may perform in person searches. Search fee: $5.00 per name. Fee is per index searched. Court makes copy: $1.00 per page; same fee for self serve. Required to search: name, years to search. Civil cases indexed by defendant, plaintiff; in index books from 1900s. Mail turnaround time 2-3 days.
Criminal Records: Access: Mail, in person. Both court and visitors may perform in person searches. Search fee: $5.00 per name. Fee is per index searched. Court makes copy: $1.00 per page; same fee for self serve. Required to search: name, years to search. Criminal records in index books from 1900s. Mail turnaround time 2-3 days.
General Information: No juvenile, mental, sealed, or adoption records released. Will fax documents after search fee is received. Certification fee: $1.00 per page. Payee: District Clerk. Personal checks accepted. Prepayment and SASE required.

County Court PO Box 427, Archer City, TX 76351; phone: 940-574-4302; criminal fax: 940-574-4625; same fax for civil/probate; hours 8:30AM-5PM (CST). *Misdemeanor, Civil, Probate.*
Note: Probate is a separate index at this same address.
Civil Records: Access: Phone, mail, in person. Both court and visitors may perform in person searches. Search fee: $5.00 per name. Fee is per index searched. Court makes copy: $1.00 per page; same fee for self serve. Required to search: name, years to search. Civil cases indexed by defendant, plaintiff; in index books from 1900s. Mail turnaround time 1 day.
Criminal Records: Access: Phone, mail, in person. Both court and visitors may perform in person searches. Search fee: $5.00 per name. Fee is per index searched. Court makes copy: $1.00 per page; same fee for self serve. Required to search: name, years to search. Criminal records in index books from 1900s. Mail turnaround time 1 day.
General Information: No juvenile, mental, sealed, or adoption records released. Will fax documents for $1.00 per page. Certification fee: $5.00 per document includes copy fee. Payee: County Clerk. Personal checks accepted. Prepayment and SASE required.

Armstrong County

District & County Court PO Box 309, 100 Trice St, Claude, TX 79019; phone: 806-226-2081; criminal fax: 806-226-5301; same fax for civil/probate; hours 8AM-N, 1-5PM (CST). *Felony, Misdemeanor, Civil, Probate.*
Note: Probate is a separate index at this same address.
Civil Records: Access: Mail, in person. Both court and visitors may perform in person searches. Search fee: $5.00 per name. Court makes copy: $1.00 per page; same fee for self serve. Required to search: name, years to search. Civil cases indexed by defendant, plaintiff; in index books from 1800s. Mail turnaround time 1-2 days.
Criminal Records: Access: Mail, in person. Both court and visitors may perform in person searches. Search fee: $5.00 per name. Court makes copy: $1.00 per page; same fee for self serve. Required to search: name, years to search. Criminal records in index books from 1800s; computerized back to 1992. Mail turnaround time 1-2 days.
General Information: No juvenile, mental, sealed, or adoption records released. Will fax documents for $1.00 per fax. Certification fee: $5.00 per cert. Payee: County Clerk. Personal checks accepted. Prepayment and SASE required.

Atascosa County

District Court Courthouse Circle, #4-B, Jourdanton, TX 78026; phone: 830-769-3011; fax: 830-769-1332; hours 8AM-N, 1-5PM (CST). *Felony, Civil.*
Civil Records: Access: Mail, in person. Both court and visitors may perform in person searches. Search fee: $5.00 per name. Court makes copy: $1.00 per page; same fee for self serve. Required to search: name, years to search; also helpful: address. Civil cases indexed by defendant, plaintiff; in index books from 1857. Mail turnaround time not known.
Criminal Records: Access: Mail, in person. Both court and visitors may perform in person searches. Search fee: $5.00 per name. Court makes copy: $1.00 per page; same fee for self serve. Required to search: name, years to search; also helpful: DOB, SSN. Criminal records in index books from 1857. Mail turnaround time not known.
General Information: No juvenile, mental, sealed, or adoption records released. Fee to fax documents is $2.00 per page. Certification fee: $1.00. Payee: District Clerk. Personal checks accepted. Prepayment and SASE required.

County Court #1 Courthouse Cirlce, #102, Jourdanton, TX 78026; phone: 830-767-2511; fax: 830-769-1021; hours 8AM-5PM (CST). *Misdemeanor, Civil, Probate.*
Civil Records: Access: Mail, in person. Both court and visitors may perform in person searches. Court makes copy: $1.00 per page. Required to search: name, years to search. Civil cases indexed by defendant, plaintiff; in index books from 1900s; on computer back to 2000.
Criminal Records: Access: In person only. Visitors must perform in person searches themselves. Court makes copy: $1.00 per page. Required to search: name, years to search. Criminal records in index books from 1900s; on computer back to 2000.
General Information: No juvenile, mental, sealed, or adoption records released. Will fax documents for $1.50 per page. Certification fee: $5.00. Payee: County Clerk. Personal checks accepted. Prepayment and SASE required.

Austin County

District Court 1 E Main, Bellville, TX 77418-1598; phone: 979-865-5911 x121; hours 8AM-N, 1-5PM (CST). *Felony, Civil.*
www.austincounty.com/dclerk.html
Note: The 155 District website is www.cvtv.net/~tx155district/. Daily dockets available.

Civil Records: Access: Mail, in person. Both court and visitors may perform in person searches. Search fee: $5.00 per name. Court makes copy: $1.00 per page; same fee for self serve. Required to search: name, years to search. Civil cases indexed by defendant, plaintiff; in index books from 1843; on computer back to 1995.
Criminal Records: Access: Mail, in person. Both court and visitors may perform in person searches. Search fee: $5.00 per name. Court makes copy: $1.00 per page; same fee for self serve. Required to search: name, years to search; also helpful: DOB, SSN. Criminal records in index books from 1843; on computer back to 1996.
General Information: Public terminal has criminal back to 1996 and civil back to 1995. No juvenile, mental, sealed, or adoption records released. Fee to fax documents is $2.00 per document. Certification fee: Included in copy fee; will certify only if document is complete. Payee: District Clerk. Personal checks accepted. Prepayment and SASE required.

County Court at Law 1 E Main, Bellville, TX 77418; phone: 979-865-5911; criminal phone: x190; civil phone: x191; probate phone: x191; criminal fax: 979-865-0336; same fax for civil/probate; hours 8AM-5PM (CST). *Misdemeanor, Civil, Probate.*
Civil Records: Access: Mail, in person. Both court and visitors may perform in person searches. Search fee: $5.00 per name. Court makes copy: $1.00 per page; same fee for self serve. Required to search: name, years to search. Civil cases indexed by defendant, plaintiff; on computer from 6/95, index books from 1843. Mail turnaround time 2 days.
Criminal Records: Access: Mail, in person. Both court and visitors may perform in person searches. Search fee: $5.00 per name. Court makes copy: $1.00 per page; same fee for self serve. Required to search: name, years to search, DOB; also helpful: SSN. Criminal records on computer from 5/95, index books from 1876. Mail turnaround time 2 days.
General Information: Public terminal has criminal back to 1995 and civil back to 1983. No juvenile, mental, sealed, or adoption records released. Will fax documents for $2.00 per document. Certification fee: $5.00 per document. Payee: Carrie Gregor, County Clerk. Prepayment and SASE required.

Bailey County

District Court 300 S 1st St, Muleshoe, TX 79347; phone: 806-272-3165; fax: 806-272-3124; hours 8AM-5PM (CST). *Felony, Civil.*
Civil Records: Access: Phone, mail, fax, in person, online. Both court and visitors may perform in person searches. Search fee: $5.00 per name. Court makes copy: $1.00 per page; same fee for self serve. Required to search: name, years to search. Civil cases indexed by defendant, plaintiff; in index books, archived from 1925, computerized back to 1995. Online access is through www.idocket.com; registration and password required. Records go back to 12/31/1995. Mail turnaround time 1 day.
Criminal Records: Access: Phone, mail, in person, online. Both court and visitors may perform in person searches. Search fee: $5.00 per name. Court makes copy: $1.00 per page; same fee for self serve. Required to search: name, years to search. Criminal records in index books, archived from 1925, computerized back to 1995. Online access is through www.idocket.com; registration and password required. Records go back to 12/31/1995. Mail turnaround time 1 day.
General Information: No juvenile, mental, sealed, or adoption records released. Will fax documents for $1.00 per page. Certification fee: $1.00 per page. Payee: District Clerk. Personal checks accepted. Prepayment and SASE required.

County Court 300 S 1st St, Muleshoe, TX 79347; phone: 806-272-3044; criminal fax: 806-272-3538; same fax for civil/probate; hours 8:30AM-N, 1-5PM (CST). *Misdemeanor, Civil, Probate.*
Note: Probate has a separate index.

Civil Records: Access: Mail, in person, online. Both court and visitors may perform in person searches. Search fee: $10.00 per name. Court makes copy: $1.00 per page; same fee for self serve. Required to search: name, years to search. Civil cases indexed by defendant, plaintiff; in index books, archived from 1925. Online access is through www.idocket.com; registration and password required. Civil records go back to 12/31/1995 and 13/31/96 for probate. Mail turnaround time 10 days.
Criminal Records: Access: Mail, in person, online. Both court and visitors may perform in person searches. Search fee: $10.00 per name. Court makes copy: $1.00 per page; same fee for self serve. Required to search: name, years to search. Criminal records in index books, archived from 1925. Online access is through www.idocket.com; registration and password required. Records go back to 12/31/1996. Mail turnaround time 10 days.
General Information: No juvenile, mental, sealed, or adoption records released. Will fax documents. Certification fee: $5.00 per document. Payee: County Clerk. Personal checks accepted. Prepayment and SASE required.

Bandera County

District Court PO Box 2688 (500 Main St), Bandera, TX 78003; phone: 830-796-4606; fax: 830-796-8499; hours 7:30AM-4:30PM (CST). *Felony, Civil, Probate.*
www.banderacounty.org/departments/district_clerk.htm
Civil Records: Access: Phone, fax, mail, in person, online. Both court and visitors may perform in person searches. Search fee: $5.00 per name. Court makes copy: $1.00 per page certified; non-certified is $1.00 1st pg, $.25 each add'l. Required to search: name, years to search; also helpful: address. Civil cases indexed by defendant, plaintiff; on computer back to 1988, index books from 1857. Civil case information is free at www.idocket.com. Registration and password required. Free searching is limited. Records go back to 12/31/1990. Mail turnaround time 2 days.
Criminal Records: Access: Fax, mail, in person, online. Both court and visitors may perform in person searches. Search fee: $5.00 per name. Court makes copy: $1.00 per page certified; non-certified is $1.00 1st pg, $.25 each add'l. Required to search: name, years to search, signed release; also helpful: address, DOB, SSN. Criminal records on computer back to 1988, index books from 1857. Felony records access is through www.idocket.com; registration and password required. Records go back to 12/31/1990. Mail turnaround time 2 days.
General Information: Public terminal goes back to 1990. No juvenile, mental or sealed records released. Fee to fax documents is $2.00 for 1st page, $1.00 each add'l. Certification fee: $5.00. Payee: Bandera County District Clerk. Personal checks accepted. Prepayment and SASE required.

County Court PO Box 823 (500 Main St), Bandera, TX 78003; phone: 830-796-3332; criminal fax: 830-796-8323; same fax for civil/probate; hours 8AM-N, 1-4:30PM (CST). *Misdemeanor, Civil, Eviction, Probate.*
Note: Probate is a separate index at this same address.
Civil Records: Access: Fax, mail, in person. Both court and visitors may perform in person searches. Search fee: $5.00 per name. Court makes copy: $1.00 per page. Required to search: name, years to search; also helpful: address. Civil cases indexed by defendant, plaintiff; on computer from 1988, index books from 1857. Mail turnaround time 2 days.
Criminal Records: Access: Fax, mail, in person. Both court and visitors may perform in person searches. Search fee: $5.00 per name. Court makes copy: $1.00 per page. Required to search: name, years to search, signed release; also helpful: address, DOB, SSN. Criminal records on computer from 1988, index books from 1857. Mail turnaround time 2 days.

General Information: No juvenile, mental or sealed records released. Fee to fax documents is $2.00 for 1st page, $1.00 each add'l. Certification fee: $5.00 per document. Payee: Bandera County Court Clerk. Personal checks accepted. Prepayment and SASE required.

Bastrop County

District Court PO Box 770, Bastrop, TX 78602; phone: 512-332-7244; fax: 512-332-7249; hours 8AM-5PM (CST). *Felony, Civil.*
Civil Records: Access: Mail, in person,fax. Both court and visitors may perform in person searches. Search fee: $5.00 per name. Court makes copy: $.50 per page; same fee for self serve. Required to search: name, years to search. Civil cases indexed by defendant, plaintiff; on microfilm from 1986, archived from early 1800s. Mail turnaround time 1 day.
Criminal Records: Access: Mail, in person, fax. Both court and visitors may perform in person searches. Search fee: $5.00 per name. Court makes copy: $.50 per page; same fee for self serve. Required to search: name, years to search, signed release. Criminal records on computer since 1989; prior on microfilm from 1986, archived from early 1800s. Mail turnaround time 1 day.
General Information: Public terminal has criminal back to 1995 and civil back to 1989. No juvenile, mental, sealed, or adoption records released. Certification fee: $1.00. Payee: District Clerk. Personal checks accepted. Prepayment and SASE required.

County Court PO Box 577, Bastrop, TX 78602; phone: 512-332-7234; fax: 512-332-7241; hours 8AM-5:PM (CST). *Misdemeanor, Probate.*
Criminal Records: Access: Phone, mail, in person. Both court and visitors may perform in person searches. Search fee: $5.00 per name. Court makes copy: $1.00 per page; same fee for self serve. Required to search: name, years to search, DOB, SSN. Criminal records on computer since 1986, prior on index books. Mail turnaround time 1-2 days.
General Information: No juvenile, mental, sealed, or adoption records released. Fee to fax documents is $5.00. Certification fee: $5.00. Payee: Bastrop County Clerk. Personal checks accepted. Prepayment and SASE required.

Baylor County

District & County Court PO Box 689, Seymour, TX 76380; phone: 940-889-3322; hours 8:30AM-5PM (CST). *Felony, Misdemeanor, Civil, Probate.*
Civil Records: Access: Phone, mail, in person. Both court and visitors may perform in person searches. Search fee: $10.00 per name. Court makes copy: $1.00 per page. Required to search: name, years to search. Civil cases indexed by defendant, plaintiff; in books from 1900s. Mail turnaround time 1-2 days.
Criminal Records: Access: Phone, mail, in person. Both court and visitors may perform in person searches. Search fee: $10.00 per name. Court makes copy: $1.00 per page. Required to search: name, years to search. Criminal records in books from 1900s. Mail turnaround time 1-2 days.
General Information: No juvenile, mental, sealed, or adoption records released. Will not fax documents. Certification fee: $3.00 felony, $6.00 misdemeanor County Court certification. Payee: Baylor County Clerk. Personal checks accepted. Prepayment and SASE required.

Bee County

District Court PO Box 666, Beeville, TX 78104-0666; phone: 361-362-3242; fax: 361-362-3282; hours 8AM-5PM (CST). *Felony, Civil.*
Civil Records: Access: Mail, in person, online. Both court and visitors may perform in person searches. Search fee: $5.00 per name. Court makes copy: $1.00 per page. Required to search: name, years to search. Civil cases indexed by defendant, plaintiff; on index books from 1856, computerized since 2000. Online

access is at www.idocket.com; registration and password required. This is a fee service, unless only one name searched a day. Records may go back to 12/31/1987. Mail turnaround time 1-3 days.
Criminal Records: Access: Mail, in person, online. Both court and visitors may perform in person searches. Search fee: $5.00 per name. Court makes copy: $1.00 per page. Required to search: name, years to search, signed release. Criminal records on index books from 1856, computerized since 2000. Felony record access is at www.idocket.com; registration and password required. This is a fee service, unless only one name searched a day. Records may go back to 12/31/1987. Mail turnaround time 1-3 days.
General Information: Public terminal has only civil records back to 2000. No juvenile, mental, sealed, or adoption records released. Certification fee: $2.00. Payee: District Clerk. Personal checks accepted. Prepayment and SASE required.

County Court 105 W Corpus Christi St, Rm 103, Beeville, TX 78102; phone: 361-362-3245; criminal fax: 361-362-3247; same fax for civil/probate; hours 8AM-N, 1-5PM (CST). *Misdemeanor, Civil, Probate.*
Civil Records: Access: Phone, fax, mail, in person. Both court and visitors may perform in person searches. Search fee: $5.00 per name. Court makes copy: $1.00 per page. Required to search: name, years to search. Civil cases indexed by defendant, plaintiff; on index books from 1900; computerized since 1995. Mail turnaround time 1 day.
Criminal Records: Access: Phone, fax, mail, in person. Both court and visitors may perform in person searches. Search fee: $6.00 per name. Add $5.00 for certificate. Court makes copy: $1.00 per page. Required to search: name, years to search, DOB; also helpful: SSN. Criminal records on index books from 1900; computerized since 1995. Mail turnaround time 1 day.
General Information: Public use terminal available. No juvenile, mental, sealed, or adoption records released. Fee to fax documents is $2.00 per page. Certification fee: $2.00 per page includes copy fee. Payee: County Clerk. Personal checks accepted. Prepayment and SASE required.

Bell County

District Court 104 S Main St, PO Box 909, Belton, TX 76513; phone: 254-933-5197; criminal phone: 254-933-5957; civil phone: 254-933-5195; fax: 254-933-5199; hours 8AM-5PM (CST). *Felony, Civil.*
www.bellcountytx.com/districtclerk/index.htm
Civil Records: Access: Mail, in person. Both court and visitors may perform in person searches. Search fee: $5.00 per name. Court makes copy: $.50 per page; same fee for self serve. Required to search: name, years to search. Civil cases indexed by defendant, plaintiff; on computer back to 1987, alpha index from 1982, chrono from 1800. Mail turnaround time 1-2 days.
Criminal Records: Access: Mail, in person. Both court and visitors may perform in person searches. Search fee: $5.00 per name. Court makes copy: $.50 per page; same fee for self serve. Required to search: name, years to search, DOB; also helpful, SSN, signed release, cause number. Criminal records on computer back to 1987, alpha index from 1982, chrono from 1800. Mail turnaround time 1-2 days.
General Information: Public terminal goes back to 1987. No juvenile, mental, sealed, or adoption records released. Will fax documents. Certification fee: $1.00 per page. Payee: District Clerk, Bell County. Only cashiers checks and money orders accepted. Prepayment and SASE required.

County Court Bell County Clerk's Office, PO Box 480, Belton, TX 76513; phone: 254-933-5165; criminal: 254-933-5170; civil: 254-933-5174; probate: 254-993-5167; fax: 254-933-5176; hours 8AM-5PM (CST). *Misdemeanor, Civil, Probate.*

Civil Records: Access: Mail, in person. Both court and visitors may perform in person searches. Search fee: $5.00 per name. Court makes copy: $1.00 per page; same fee for self serve. Required to search: name, years to search. Civil cases indexed by defendant, plaintiff; on computer since 9/1989. Mail turnaround time 5 days.
Criminal Records: Access: Mail, in person. Both court and visitors may perform in person searches. Search fee: $5.00 per name. Court makes copy: $1.00 per page; same fee for self serve. Required to search: name, years to search, DOB, SSN. Criminal records on computer since 1986. In person searching closed for lunch hour. Mail turnaround time 5 days.
General Information: Public terminal has criminal back to 1986 and civil back to 1989. No juvenile, mental, sealed, or adoption records released. Certification fee: $1.00. Payee: County Clerk. Local checks only. Prepayment required.

Bexar County

District Court - Central Records 100 Dolorosa, County Courthouse, Chief Court Clerk/Records, San Antonio, TX 78205; phone: 210-335-2113; criminal phone: 210-335-2591; civil phone: 210-335-2661; hours 8AM-5PM (CST). *Felony, Civil.*
www.co.bexar.tx.us/dclerk
Note: There is a separate court clerk for civil and criminal, and fee for searching in each, though records are centralized.
Civil Records: Access: Mail, fax, online, in person. Both court and visitors may perform in person searches. Search fee: $5.00 per name. Court makes copy: $1.00 per page. Self serve copy fee: $.50 per page. Required to search: name, years to search. Civil cases indexed by defendant, plaintiff; on computer from 1982-present, chrono index from 1909. Access to the remote online system requires $100 setup fee, plus a $25 monthly fee, plus inquiry fees. Call Jennifer Mann at 210-335-0212 for more information. Also, free online access to records at www.co.bexar.tx.us/webapps/html/dkliting01.asp. Note: For fax requests, call court to request form, then submit form with payment with Discover Card. Mail turnaround time up to 10 days.
Criminal Records: Access: Mail, fax, online, in person. Both court and visitors may perform in person searches. Search fee: $5.00 per name. Court makes copy: $1.00 per page. Self serve copy fee: $.50 per page. Required to search: name, years to search, signed release, DOB. Criminal records on computer back to 1974, chrono index from 1909. Online access to criminal records is the same as civil. Note: For fax requests, call court to request form, then submit form with payment with Discover Card. Mail turnaround time up to 10 days.
General Information: Public terminal has criminal back to 1974 and civil back to 1982. No juvenile, mental, sealed, or adoption records released. Fee to fax documents is $.50 per page. Certification fee: $1.00 per page. Cert fee includes copy fee. Payee: District Clerk. Only cashiers checks and money orders accepted. Prepayment and SASE required.

County Court - Civil Central Filing Department 100 Dolorosa, San Antonio, TX 78205-3083; phone: 210-335-2231; criminal phone: 210-335-2238; fax: 210-35-2097; hours 8AM-5PM (CST). *Civil.*
Note: There are twelve hearing locations in this county where open cases are held. All closed cases are forwarded here.
Civil Records: Access: Mail, in person. Both court and visitors may perform in person searches. Search fee: $5.00 per name. Fee is for 10 year search. Court makes copy: $1.00 per page. Required to search: name, years to search. Civil cases indexed by defendant, plaintiff; on computer go back 10 years, index books prior. Open and closed records maintained. Mail turnaround time 5-7 days.
General Information: Public terminal has only civil records. No mental, sealed records released.

Will not fax documents. Certification fee: $5.00. Payee: County Clerk. Personal checks accepted. Prepayment and SASE required.

County Court - Criminal 300 Dolorosa, #4101, San Antonio, TX 78205; phone: 210-335-2238; criminal phone: 210-335-2238; civil phone: 210-335-2231; probate phone: 210-335-2241; fax: 210-335-3938; hours 8AM-5PM (CST). *Misdemeanor.*
www.co.bexar.tx.us/dclerk

Criminal Records: Access: Mail, online, in person. Both court and visitors may perform in person searches. Search fee: $6.00 per name. Fee is per ten year period. $1.00 for each add'l year. Court makes copy: $1.00 per page. Required to search: name, years to search, DOB, signed release; also helpful: SSN. Criminal records on computer since 1983, alpha index since 1983, on card index from 1909, records go back to 1899. Access to the criminal online system requires $100 setup fee, plus a $25 monthly fee, plus inquiry fees. Call Jennifer Mann at 210-335-0212 for more information. Mail turnaround time 2-3 days.

General Information: Public terminal has only criminal records back to 1983. No sealed records released. Will fax documents $1.00 per page fax fee. Certification fee: $5.00 per document. Payee: County Clerk. Personal checks must be in state. Prepayment required. SASE requested.

Probate Court #2 100 Dolorosa St, Rm 204, San Antonio, TX 78205; phone: 210-335-2241; fax: 210-335-2199; hours 8AM-5PM (CST). *Probate.*
www.co.bexar.tx.us/pcourt/probatecourts.htm

Blanco County

County Court PO Box 65, Johnson City, TX 78636; phone: 830-868-7357; fax: 830-868-4158; hours 8AM-4:30PM (CST). *Misdemeanor, Civil, Probate.*
Note: Probate is separate index at this same address.

Civil Records: Access: Mail, in person. Both court and visitors may perform in person searches. Search fee: $5.00 per name. Court makes copy: $1.00 per page; same fee for self serve. Required to search: name, years to search. Civil cases indexed by defendant, plaintiff; on computer from 1994, index books back to 1876. Mail turnaround time 2 days.

Criminal Records: Access: Mail, in person. Both court and visitors may perform in person searches. Search fee: $5.00 per name. Court makes copy: $1.00 per page; same fee for self serve. Required to search: name, years to search, DOB, SSN. Criminal records on computer from 1994, index books back to 1876. Mail turnaround time 1 day.

General Information: Public terminal goes back to 1994. No juvenile, mental, sealed, or adoption records released. Will fax search documents. Certification fee: $5.00 per document. Payee: County Clerk. Personal checks accepted. Prepayment and SASE required.

District Court PO Box 382, Johnson City, TX 78636; phone: 830-868-0973; criminal fax: 830-868-2084; same fax for civil/probate; hours 8AM-4:30PM (CST). *Felony, Civil, Probate.*
www.courts.state.tx.us/district/33rd/index.htm

Civil Records: Access: Mail, in person. Both court and visitors may perform in person searches. Search fee: $5.00 per name. Court makes copy: $1.00 for first per page; $.25 each add'l page. Required to search: name, years to search. Civil cases indexed by defendant, plaintiff; on computer from 1994, index books back to 1876. Mail turnaround time 1 day.

Criminal Records: Access: Mail, in person. Both court and visitors may perform in person searches. Search fee: $5.00 per name. Court makes copy: $1.00 for first page; $.25 per page add'l. Required to search: name, years to search, DOB, SSN. Criminal records on computer from 1994, index books back to 1876. Mail turnaround time 1 day.

General Information: Public use terminal available. (.) No juvenile, mental, sealed, or adoption records released. Certification fee: $1.00 per page includes

copy fee. Payee: District Clerk. Personal checks accepted. Prepayment and SASE required.

Borden County

District & County Court PO Box 124, Gail, TX 79738; phone: 806-756-4312; criminal fax: 806-756-4405; same fax for civil/probate; hours 8AM-5PM (CST). *Felony, Misdemeanor, Civil, Probate.*

Civil Records: Access: Mail, in person. Both court and visitors may perform in person searches. Search fee: $5.00 per name. Court makes copy: $1.00 per page. Required to search: name, years to search. Civil cases indexed by defendant, plaintiff; in index books, archived from 1900. Mail turnaround time 1 week.

Criminal Records: Access: Mail, in person. Both court and visitors may perform in person searches. Search fee: $5.00 per name. Court makes copy: $1.00 per page. Required to search: name, years to search. Criminal records in index books, archived from 1900. Mail turnaround time 1 week.

General Information: No juvenile, mental, sealed, or adoption records released. Fee to fax documents is $1.00 per page. Certification fee: $5.00 per cert. Payee: District Clerk. Personal checks accepted. Prepayment and SASE required.

Bosque County

District Court Main & Morgan St, PO Box 674, Meridian, TX 76665; phone: 254-435-2334; hours 8AM-5PM (CST). *Felony, Civil.*

Civil Records: Access: Mail, in person. Both court and visitors may perform in person searches. Search fee: $5.00 per name. Court makes copy: $1.00 per page; same fee for self serve. Required to search: name, years to search. Civil cases indexed by defendant, plaintiff; on computer from 1984, files/books from 1870s. Mail turnaround time 1 day.

Criminal Records: Access: Mail, in person. Both court and visitors may perform in person searches. Search fee: $5.00 per name. Court makes copy: $1.00 per page; same fee for self serve. Required to search: name, years to search, DOB or SSN. Computerized from 1984, criminal records on books/files from 1856. Mail turnaround time 1 day.

General Information: Public terminal goes back to 1994. No juvenile, mental, sealed, or adoption records released. Certification fee: $1.00. Payee: District Clerk. Personal checks accepted. Prepayment and SASE required.

County Court PO Box 617, Meridian, TX 76665; phone: 254-435-2201; fax: 254-435-2152; hours 8AM-5PM (CST). *Misdemeanor, Civil, Probate.*

Civil Records: Access: Mail, in person. Both court and visitors may perform in person searches. Search fee: $5.00 per name. Court makes copy: $1.00 per page. Required to search: name, years to search. Civil cases indexed by defendant, plaintiff; in index books from 1854; on computer back to 1997. Mail turnaround time 1-2 days.

Criminal Records: Access: Mail, in person. Both court and visitors may perform in person searches. Search fee: $5.00 per name. Court makes copy: $1.00 per page. Required to search: name, years to search, DOB, SSN. Criminal records in index books from 1854; on computer back to 1997. Mail turnaround time 1-2 days.

General Information: Public terminal has only civil records. No juvenile, mental, sealed, or adoption records released. Certification fee: $5.00. Payee: County Clerk. In state personal checks accepted. Prepayment and SASE required.

Bowie County

District & County Court at Law 710 James Bowie Dr, PO Box 248, New Boston, TX 75570; phone: 903-628-6835; probate phone: 903-628-6740; fax: 903-628-2217; hours 8AM-5PM (CST). *Felony, Misdemeanor, Civil, Probate.*
www.co.bowie.tx.us/

Note: Probate records are at this address in the County Clerk's office.

Civil Records: Access: Mail, in person. Both court and visitors may perform in person searches. Search fee: $5.00 per name. Court makes copy: $1.00 per page. Required to search: name, years to search. Civil cases indexed by defendant, plaintiff; on computer from 1978, on microfiche from 1900s, chrono index from 1800s. Mail turnaround time 1 day.

Criminal Records: Access: Mail, in person. Both court and visitors may perform in person searches. Search fee: $5.00 per name. Court makes copy: $1.00 per page. Required to search: name, years to search, DOB. Criminal records on computer from 1978, on microfiche from 1900s, chrono index from 1800s. Mail turnaround time 1 day.

General Information: No juvenile, mental, sealed, or adoption records released. Will fax documents for $5.00 per doc. Certification fee: $1.00. Payee: District Clerk. Personal checks accepted. Prepayment and SASE required.

Brazoria County

District Court 111 E Locus, #500, Angleton, TX 77515-4678; phone: 979-864-1316; hours 8AM-5PM (CST). *Felony, Civil.*
www.brazoria-county.com/dclerk/

Civil Records: Access: Phone, mail, in person. Both court and visitors may perform in person searches. Search fee: $5.00 per name. Fee is per 10 year period. Court makes copy: $1.00 per page; same fee for self serve. Required to search: name, years to search. Civil cases indexed by defendant, plaintiff; on computer from 1987, index chrono from 1900, prior alpha. Mail turnaround time 1-2 days.

Criminal Records: Access: Phone, mail, in person. Both court and visitors may perform in person searches. Search fee: $5.00 per name. Fee is per 10 year period. Court makes copy: $1.00 per page; same fee for self serve. Required to search: name, years to search, DOB, signed release; also helpful: SSN. Criminal records on computer from 1986, index chrono from 1900, prior alpha. Mail turnaround time 1-2 days.

General Information: Public terminal goes back to 1987. No juvenile, mental, sealed, or adoption records released. Will fax documents for $10.00 per document. Certification fee: $1.00. Payee: District Clerk. Only cashiers checks and money orders accepted. Prepayment and SASE required.

County Court 111 E Locust, #200, Angleton, TX 77515; criminal phone: 979-864-1380; civil phone: 979-864-1385; fax: 979-864-1020; hours 8AM-4:30PM (CST). *Misdemeanor, Civil.*
www.brazoria-county.com

Civil Records: Access: Fax, mail, in person, online. Both court and visitors may perform in person searches. Search fee: $5.00 per name. Court makes copy: $1.00 per page. Required to search: name, years to search. Civil cases indexed by defendant, plaintiff; on computer from 1984; prior on books or microfiche back to 1800s. Fee must be prepaid before faxing search request. Access civil records free at http://records.brazoria-county.com. Mail turnaround time 2 days.

Criminal Records: Access: Fax, mail, in person, online. Both court and visitors may perform in person searches. Search fee: $5.00 per name. Court makes copy: $1.00 per page. Required to search: name, years to search, DOB. Criminal records on computer from 1984; prior on books or microfiche back to 1800s. Access criminal records and county inmates and bonds free at http://records.brazoria-county.com. Mail turnaround time 2 days.

General Information: Public use terminal available. No juvenile, mental, sealed records released. Certification fee: $5.00 per document. Payee: Joyce Hudman, County Clerk. Personal checks accepted. Prepayment and SASE required.

Probate Court 111 E Locust, #200, Angleton, TX 77515; phone: 979-864-1367; fax: 979-864-1031; hours 8AM-4:30PM (CST). *Probate.*
Access probate records free at http://records.brazoria-county.com.

Brazos County

District Court PO Box 2208, 300 E 26th St, #216, Bryan, TX 77806; phone: 979-361-4230; fax: 979-361-0197; hours 8AM-5PM (CST). *Felony, Civil.* www.co.brazos.tx.us/courts/
Civil Records: Access: Mail, in person. Both court and visitors may perform in person searches. Search fee: $5.00 per name. Court makes copy: $.50 per page. Required to search: name, years to search. Civil cases indexed by defendant, plaintiff; on computer, index chrono from 1800s. Mail turnaround time 1-2 days.
Criminal Records: Access: Mail, in person. Both court and visitors may perform in person searches. Search fee: $5.00 per name. Court makes copy: $.50 per page. Required to search: name, years to search; also helpful: DOB, SSN. Criminal records on computer, index chrono from 1800s. Mail turnaround time 1-2 days.
General Information: No juvenile, mental, sealed, or adoption records released. Will fax documents to toll free number. Certification fee: $1.00 per page. Payee: District Clerk. Personal checks accepted. Prepayment and SASE required.

County Court 300 E 26th St, #120, Bryan, TX 77803; phone: 979-361-4128; criminal phone: 979-361-4125; hours 8AM-5PM (CST). *Misdemeanor, Civil under $500, Probate.*
Note: County Clerk holds misdemeanor records prior to 1986 only. Newer cases are filed at the District Clerks Office.
Civil Records: Access: Mail, in person. Both court and visitors may perform in person searches. Search fee: $5.00 per name. Court makes copy: $1.00 per page. Required to search: name, years to search. Civil cases indexed by defendant, plaintiff; on computer from 1986, index chrono from 1958. Access civils records free at http://records.brazoria-county.com. Mail turnaround time 2-3 days.
Criminal Records: Access: Mail, in person. Both court and visitors may perform in person searches. Search fee: $5.00 per name. Court makes copy: $1.00 per page. Required to search: name, years to search, DOB. Criminal records on computer from 1986, index chrono from 1958. Mail turnaround time 2-3 days.
General Information: Public terminal goes back to 1986. No juvenile, mental, sealed, or adoption records released. Certification fee: $5.00. Payee: County Clerk or District Clerk. Only cashiers checks and money orders accepted. Prepayment and SASE required.

Brewster County

District Court PO Box 1024, Alpine, TX 79831; phone: 432-837-6216; fax: 432-837-6217; hours 9AM-12, 1-5PM (CST). *Felony, Civil.*
Civil Records: Access: Phone, fax, mail, in person. Both court and visitors may perform in person searches. Search fee: $8.00. Court makes copy: $1.00 per page. Required to search: name; also helpful: years to search. Civil cases indexed by defendant, plaintiff. Civil records are computerized since 1994, indexed from 1899. Mail turnaround time 2-3 days.
Criminal Records: Access: Phone, fax, mail, in person. Both court and visitors may perform in person searches. Search fee: $8.00. Court makes copy: $1.00 per page. Required to search: name, DOB; also helpful: years to search. Criminal records are computerized since 1994, indexed from 1899. Mail turnaround time 2-3 days.
General Information: No fee to fax documents to local number. Certification fee: $1.00 per page. Payee: District Clerk. Personal checks accepted. Prepayment required.

County Court PO Box 119 (201 W Ave. E), Alpine, TX 79831; phone: 432-837-3366; fax: 432-837-6217; hours 9AM-5PM (CST). *Misdemeanor, Civil Probate.*
Civil Records: Access: Mail, fax, in person. Both court and visitors may perform in person searches. Search fee: $10.00 per name. No copy fee. Self serve copy fee: $1.00 per page. Required to search: name, years to search. Civil cases indexed by defendant, plaintiff; in index books from 1950s; computerized since 1995. Mail turnaround time 1 week.
Criminal Records: Access: Mail, fax, in person. Both court and visitors may perform in person searches. Search fee: $10.00 per name. No copy fee. Self serve copy fee: $1.00 per page. Required to search: name, years to search, DOB, signed release; also helpful: SSN. Criminal records in index books from 1920s, computerized since 1994. Mail turnaround time 1 week.
General Information: Public terminal goes back to 1994. No juvenile, mental, sealed, or adoption records released. Fee to fax documents is $2.00 per page. Certification fee: $5.00. Payee: County Clerk. Personal checks accepted. Prepayment and SASE required.

Briscoe County

District & County Court PO Box 555, Silverton, TX 79257; phone: 806-823-2134; fax: 806-823-2359; hours 8AM-5PM (CST). *Felony, Misdemeanor, Civil, Probate.*
Civil Records: Access: Fax, mail, in person. Both court and visitors may perform in person searches. Search fee: $5.00 per name. Court makes copy: $1.00 per page. Required to search: name, years to search. Civil cases indexed by defendant, plaintiff; in index books from 1892. Mail turnaround time 1 day.
Criminal Records: Access: Fax, mail, in person. Both court and visitors may perform in person searches. Search fee: $5.00 per name. Court makes copy: $1.00 per page. Required to search: name, years to search, DOB. Criminal records in index books from 1892. Mail turnaround time 1 day.
General Information: No juvenile, mental, sealed, or adoption records released. Will fax documents for $5.00 per name, if copy of check faxed first. Certification fee: $5.00. Payee: District or County Clerk. Personal checks accepted. Prepayment and SASE required.

Brooks County

District Court PO Box 534, Falfurrias, TX 78355; phone: 361-325-5604; criminal phone: x239; civil phone: x237; fax: 361-325-5679; hours 8AM-5PM (CST). *Felony, Civil.*
Civil Records: Access: Phone, fax, mail, online, in person. Both court and visitors may perform in person searches. Search fee: $5.00 per name. Court makes copy: $1.00 per page. Self serve copy fee: $.25 per page. Required to search: name, years to search; also helpful: address. Civil cases indexed by defendant, plaintiff; on computer back to 1992, index books since 1920. Civil case information is online at www.idocket.com. Free searching is limited. Records go back to 12/31/1993. Mail turnaround time 1 week.
Criminal Records: Access: Phone, fax, mail, online, in person. Both court and visitors may perform in person searches. Search fee: $5.00 per name. Court makes copy: $1.00 per page. Self serve copy fee: $.25 per page. Required to search: name, years to search, DOB, SSN; also helpful: address. Criminal records on computer back to 1992, index books since 1920, microfiche since 1939. Criminal records access is through www.idocket.com; registration and password required. Records go back to 12/31/1993. Mail turnaround time 1 week.
General Information: No juvenile, mental, sealed, or adoption records released. Fee to fax documents is $1.00 per page. Certification fee: $2.00 per document. Payee: District Clerk. Business checks accepted. Prepayment and SASE required.

County Court PO Box 427, Falfurrias, TX 78355; phone: 361-325-5604; criminal phone: EXT 229, 245; civil phone: ext 247,245; fax: 361-325-4944; hours 8AM-5PM (CST). *Misdemeanor, Civil, Probate.*
Civil Records: Access: Phone, fax, mail, in person. Both court and visitors may perform in person searches. Search fee: $10.00 per name. Court makes copy: $1.00 per page. Required to search: name, years to search. Civil cases indexed by plaintiff. Civil records in index books since 1911. Mail turnaround time 1-2 days.
Criminal Records: Access: Phone, fax, mail, in person. Both court and visitors may perform in person searches. Search fee: $10.00 per name. Court makes copy: $1.00 per page. Required to search: name, years to search, DOB. Criminal records in index books since 1911. Mail turnaround time 1-2 days.
General Information: No juvenile, mental, sealed, or adoption records released. Will fax documents $5.00 1st page, $2.00 each add'l. Certification fee: $5.00. Payee: County Clerk. Personal checks accepted. Prepayment and SASE required.

Brown County

District Court 200 S Broadway, Brownwood, TX 76801; phone: 325-646-5514; hours 8AM-5PM (CST). *Felony, Civil.*
Civil Records: Access: Mail, in person. Both court and visitors may perform in person searches. Search fee: $5.00 per name. Court makes copy: $1.00 per page. Self serve copy fee: $.50 per page. Required to search: name, years to search. Civil cases indexed by defendant, plaintiff; on computer since 1995; prior records on books to 1930s. Mail turnaround time 2-3 days.
Criminal Records: Access: Mail, in person, phone. Both court and visitors may perform in person searches. Search fee: $5.00 per name. Court makes copy: $1.00 per page. Self serve copy fee: $.50 per page. Required to search: name, years to search. Criminal records on computer since 1995; prior records on books to 1930s. Mail turnaround time 2-3 days.
General Information: Public terminal goes back to 1995. No juvenile, mental, sealed, or adoption records released. Will not fax documents. Certification fee: $1.00 per page. Payee: District Clerk. Business checks accepted. Prepayment and SASE required.

County Court 200 S Broadway, Brownwood, TX 76801; phone: 325-643-2594; hours 8:30AM-5PM (CST). *Misdemeanor, Civil, Probate.*
Civil Records: Access: Mail, in person. Both court and visitors may perform in person searches. Search fee: $5.00 per name. Court makes copy: $1.00 per page. Self serve copy fee: $.25 per page. Required to search: name, years to search. Civil cases indexed by defendant, plaintiff; on computer from 1988 on microfiche from 1900s. Mail turnaround time 1-2 days.
Criminal Records: Access: Mail, in person. Both court and visitors may perform in person searches. Search fee: $5.00 per name. Court makes copy: $1.00 per page. Self serve copy fee: $.25 per page. Required to search: name, years to search; also helpful: DOB, SSN. Criminal records on computer from 1988, on microfiche from 1900s. Mail turnaround time 1-2 days.
General Information: Public terminal goes back to 1987. No juvenile, mental, sealed records released. Certification fee: $5.00. Payee: Brown County Clerk. Personal checks accepted. Prepayment and SASE required.

Burleson County

District Court 100 W Buck, #303, Caldwell, TX 77836; phone: 979-567-2336; hours 8AM-12, 1-5PM (CST). *Felony, Civil.*
Civil Records: Access: Mail, in person. Both court and visitors may perform in person searches. Search fee: $5.00 per name. Court makes copy: $1.00

per page. Required to search: name, years to search. Civil cases indexed by defendant, plaintiff; on microfilm from 1980, index books prior. Mail turnaround time 1-2 days.

Criminal Records: Access: Mail, in person. Both court and visitors may perform in person searches. Search fee: $5.00 per name. Court makes copy: $1.00 per page. Required to search: name, years to search. Criminal records on microfilm from 1980, index books prior. Mail turnaround time 1-2 days.

General Information: No juvenile, mental, sealed, or adoption records released. Will fax to toll-free number. Certification fee: $1.00 per page. Payee: District Clerk. Personal checks accepted. Prepayment required. SASE or toll-free phone number required.

County Court 100 W Buck, #203, Caldwell, TX 77836; phone: 979-567-2329; fax: 979-567-2376; hours 8AM-5PM (CST). *Misdemeanor, Civil, Probate.*

Civil Records: Access: Phone, mail, fax, in person. Both court and visitors may perform in person searches. Search fee: $10.00. Court makes copy: $1.00 per page; same fee for self serve. Required to search: name, years to search. Civil cases indexed by defendant, plaintiff; indexed to 1900, records archived to 1900s. Mail turnaround time 2-4 days.

Criminal Records: Access: Mail, fax, in person. Visitors must perform in person searches themselves. Search fee: $10.00. Court makes copy: $1.00 per page; same fee for self serve. Required to search: name, years to search, DOB, SSN. Criminal records indexed to 1990, records archived to 1900s. Mail turnaround time 2-4 days.

General Information: No juvenile, mental, or sealed records released. Fee to fax documents is $1.00 per page. Certification fee: $5.00. Payee: County Clerk. Personal checks accepted. Prepayment and SASE required.

Burnet County

District Court 1701 E Polk St, #90, Burnet, TX 78611; phone: 512-756-5450; hours 8AM-5PM (CST). *Felony, Civil.*
www.courts.state.tx.us/district/33rd/index.htm
Civil Records: Access: Mail, in person. Both court and visitors may perform in person searches. Search fee: $5.00 per name. Court makes copy: $1.00 per page. Required to search: name, years to search. Civil cases indexed by defendant, plaintiff; on computer from 1991, index books from 1856. Mail turnaround time 2 days.

Criminal Records: Access: Mail, in person. Both court and visitors may perform in person searches. Search fee: $5.00 per name. Court makes copy: $1.00 per page. Required to search: name, years to search; also helpful: DOB, SSN. Criminal records on computer from 1988, index book from 1856. Mail turnaround time 2 days.

General Information: Public terminal goes back to 1990. No juvenile, mental, sealed, or adoption records released. Will fax documents for $2.00 per page. Certification fee: $1.00 per page. Certification included in copy fee. Payee: District Clerk. Personal checks accepted. Prepayment and SASE required.

County Court 220 S Pierce, Burnet, TX 78611; phone: 512-756-5403; criminal phone: 512-756-5407; civil phone: 512-756-5481; probate phone: 512-756-5408; criminal fax: 512-756-5410; same fax for civil/probate; hours 8AM-5PM (CST). *Misdemeanor, Civil, Probate.*
Civil Records: Access: Fax, mail, in person. Both court and visitors may perform in person searches. Search fee: $10.00 per name. Court makes copy: $1.00 per page. Required to search: name, years to search. Civil cases indexed by defendant, plaintiff; on computer from 1989, on microfiche from 1852. Mail turnaround time 2 days.

Criminal Records: Access: Fax, mail, in person. Both court and visitors may perform in person searches. Search fee: $10.00 per name. Court makes copy: $1.00 per page. Required to search: name, years to search, offense, date of offense. Criminal records

on computer from 1989, on microfiche from 1852. Mail turnaround time 2 days.

General Information: Public terminal goes back to 1989. No juvenile, mental, sealed, or adoption records released. Will fax documents $3.00 per page. Certification fee: $5.00 per document. Payee: County Clerk. Personal checks accepted. Prepayment and SASE required.

Caldwell County

District Court 201 E San Antonio St, Lockhart, TX 78644; phone: 512-398-1806; criminal phone: 512-398-1805; hours 8:30AM-N, 1-5PM (CST). *Felony, Civil.*

Civil Records: Access: Phone, fax, mail, in person. Both court and visitors may perform in person searches. Search fee: $5.00 per name. Court makes copy: $.50 per page. Required to search: name, years to search. Civil cases indexed by defendant, plaintiff; on computer since 1988, index books from 1846. Mail turnaround time 1-3 days.

Criminal Records: Access: Phone, fax, mail, in person. Both court and visitors may perform in person searches. Search fee: $5.00 per name. Court makes copy: $.50 per page. Required to search: name, years to search; also helpful: DOB, SSN. Criminal records on computer since 1988, index books from 1846. Mail turnaround time 1-3 days.

General Information: Public terminal goes back to 1988. No juvenile, mental, sealed, or adoption records released. Will fax documents to local or toll free line. Certification fee: $1.00. Payee: District Clerk. Personal checks accepted. Prepayment and SASE required.

County Court PO Box 906, Lockhart, TX 78644; phone: 512-398-1804; hours 8:30AM-N, 1-5PM (CST). *Misdemeanor, Civil, Probate.*
Note: Probate is a separate index at this same address.
Civil Records: Access: Mail, in person. Both court and visitors may perform in person searches. Search fee: $5.00 per name. Court makes copy: $1.00 per page. Required to search: name, years to search. Civil cases indexed by defendant, plaintiff; in index books since 1967. Mail turnaround time 2-4 days.

Criminal Records: Access: Mail, in person. Both court and visitors may perform in person searches. Search fee: $5.00 per name. Court makes copy: $1.00 per page. Required to search: name, years to search, DOB, offense, date of offense. Criminal records in index books since 1967. Mail turnaround time 2-4 days.

General Information: No juvenile, mental, sealed, or adoption records released. Will not fax documents. Certification fee: $5.00 per document. Payee: Caldwell County Clerk. Personal checks accepted. Prepayment required.

Calhoun County

District Court PO Box 658 (c/o District Clerk), Port Lavaca, TX 77979; phone: 361-553-8698; hours 8AM-5PM (CST). *Felony, Civil.*
Civil Records: Access: Mail, in person. Both court and visitors may perform in person searches. Search fee: $5.00 per name. Court makes copy: $1.00 per page. Required to search: name, years to search. Civil cases indexed by defendant, plaintiff; in index books from 1852. Mail turnaround time 2 days.

Criminal Records: Access: Mail, in person. Both court and visitors may perform in person searches. Search fee: $5.00 per name. Court makes copy: $1.00 per page. Required to search: name, years to search, signed release; also helpful: DOB. Criminal records in index books from 1852. Mail turnaround time 2 days.

General Information: No mental, sealed, or adoption records released. Will not fax documents. Certification fee: $1.00 per page. Payee: District Clerk. Personal checks accepted. Prepayment and SASE required.

County Court 211 S Ann, Port Lavaca, TX 77979; phone: 361-553-4411; criminal phone: 361-553-4414; civil phone: 361-553-4415; probate phone: 361-553-4413; fax: 361-553-4420; hours 8AM-5PM (CST). *Misdemeanor, Civil, Probate.*
Note: Established 11/1986.
Civil Records: Access: Phone, mail, in person. Both court and visitors may perform in person searches. Search fee: $5.00 per name. Court makes copy: $1.00 per page. Required to search: name, years to search. Civil cases indexed by defendant, plaintiff; in index books from 11/1986; indexed on computer back to 2000. Mail turnaround time 1-2 days.

Criminal Records: Access: Phone, mail, in person. Both court and visitors may perform in person searches. Search fee: $5.00 per name. Court makes copy: $1.00 per page. Required to search: name, years to search. Criminal records in index books from 11/1986; indexed on computer back to 1993. Mail turnaround time 1-2 days.

General Information: Public use terminal available. No juvenile, mental, sealed, or adoption records released. Will fax documents for $2.00 IF ONLY ONE PAGE. Certification fee: $5.00. Payee: County Clerk. Personal checks accepted. Prepayment and SASE required.

Callahan County

District Court 100 W 4th St, #300, Baird, TX 79504-5396; phone: 325-854-1800; fax: 325-854-2919; hours 8AM-5PM (CST). *Felony, Civil.*
Civil Records: Access: Mail, in person. Both court and visitors may perform in person searches. Search fee: $5.00 per name. Court makes copy: $1.00 per page. Required to search: name, years to search. Civil cases indexed by defendant, plaintiff; in index books since 1879. Mail turnaround time 1-2 days.

Criminal Records: Access: Mail, in person. Both court and visitors may perform in person searches. Search fee: $5.00 per name. Court makes copy: $1.00 per page. Required to search: name, years to search. Criminal records in index books since 1879. Mail turnaround time 1-2 days.

General Information: No juvenile, mental, sealed, or adoption records released. Certification fee: $1.00. Payee: District Clerk. Personal checks accepted. Prepayment and SASE required.

County Court 100 W 4th St, #104, Baird, TX 79504-5300; phone: 325-854-1217; fax: 325-854-1227; hours 8AM-5PM (CST). *Misdemeanor, Civil, Probate.*
Civil Records: Access: Mail, in person. Both court and visitors may perform in person searches. Search fee: $6.00 per name. Court makes copy: $1.00 per page; same fee for self serve. Required to search: name, years to search. Civil cases indexed by defendant, plaintiff. Civil records go back to 1877; computerized records go back to 1992. Mail turnaround time 1-2 days.

Criminal Records: Access: Phone, fax, mail, in person. Both court and visitors may perform in person searches. Search fee: $6.00 per name. Court makes copy: $1.00 per page; same fee for self serve. Required to search: name, years to search. Criminal records go back to 1877; computerized records go to 1992. Mail turnaround time 1-2 days.

General Information: No juvenile, mental, sealed, or adoption records released. Fee to fax documents is $1.50 per page. Certification fee: $5.00 per document. Payee: Jeanie Bohannon, County Clerk. Personal checks accepted. Prepayment and SASE required.

Cameron County

District Court 974 E Harrison St, Brownsville, TX 78520; phone: 956-544-0839; hours 8Am-5PM (CST). *Felony, Civil.*
Civil Records: Access: Mail, online, in person. Both court and visitors may perform in person searches. Search fee: $5.00 per name. Court makes copy: $1.00 per page. Required to search: name, years to search. Civil cases indexed by defendant, plaintiff; on computer from 1989. Online access is at

www.idocket.com; registration and password required. This is a fee service, unless only one name search a day. Records may go back to 12/31/1988. Mail turnaround time 1 week. On cases prior to 1990 turnaround can be more than 1 week.

Criminal Records: Access: Mail, in person, online. Only the court performs in person searches; visitors may not. Search fee: $5.00 per name. Court makes copy: $1.00 per page. Required to search: name, years to search, DOB, SSN, signed release, offense. Criminal records on computer since 1987. Felony records access is at www.idocket.com; registration and password required. This is a fee service, unless only one name search a day. Records may go back to 12/31/1988. Mail turnaround time 1 week. On cases prior to 1990 turnaround can be more than 1 week.

General Information: Public terminal has only civil records back to 1989. No juvenile, mental, sealed, or adoption records released. No certification fee. Payee: Cameron County District Clerk. Personal checks accepted. Prepayment and SASE required.

County Court No. 1, 2 & 3 PO Box 2178, Brownsville, TX 78522-2178; criminal phone: 956-544-0848; civil phone: 956-544-0867; probate phone: 956-544-0867; criminal fax: 956-544-0894; same fax for civil/probate; hours 8AM-5PM (CST). *Misdemeanor, Civil, Probate.*
www.co.cameron.tx.us
Civil Records: Access: Mail, in person. Both court and visitors may perform in person searches. Search fee: $5.00 per name. Court makes copy: $1.00 per page. Required to search: name, years to search. Civil cases indexed by defendant, plaintiff; on optical imaging since 1994, on computer from 1987, index books from 1912. Mail turnaround time 1-2 days.
Criminal Records: Access: Mail, in person. Both court and visitors may perform in person searches. Search fee: $5.00 per name. Court makes copy: $1.00 per page. Required to search: name, years to search, DOB. Criminal records on optical imaging since 1994, on computer from 1987, index books from 1912. Mail turnaround time 1-2 days.
General Information: Public use terminal available. No juvenile, mental, sealed, or adoption records released. Will fax documents $4.25 1st page, $2.25 each add'l. Certification fee: $5.00 per document. Payee: Joe G Rivera, County Clerk. Personal checks not accepted. Prepayment and SASE required.

Camp County

District Court 126 Church St, Rm 204, Pittsburg, TX 75686; phone: 903-856-3221; fax: 903-856-0560; hours 8AM-5PM (CST). *Felony, Civil.*
Civil Records: Access: Mail, fax, in person. Both court and visitors may perform in person searches. Search fee: $5.00 per name. Court makes copy: $.50 per page; same fee for self serve. Required to search: name, years to search. Civil cases indexed by defendant, plaintiff; in index books from 1874; computerized since 1995. Mail turnaround time 1 week.
Criminal Records: Access: Mail, in person. Both court and visitors may perform in person searches. Search fee: $5.00 per name. Court makes copy: $.50 per page; same fee for self serve. Required to search: name, years to search, signed release. Criminal records in index books from 1874; computerized since 1993. Mail turnaround time 1 week.
General Information: No juvenile, mental, sealed, or adoption records released. Fee to fax documents is $.25 per page. Certification fee: $2.00 first page; $.25 each add'l. Payee: District Clerk. Personal checks accepted. Prepayment and SASE required.

County Court 126 Church St, Rm 102, Pittsburg, TX 75686; phone: 903-856-2731; probate phone: 903-856-2731; fax: 903-856-6112; hours 8AM-N, 1-5PM (CST). *Misdemeanor, Civil, Probate.*
Civil Records: Access: Fax, mail, in person. Both court and visitors may perform in person searches. Search fee: $10.00 per name. Court makes copy:

$1.00 per page; same fee for self serve. Required to search: name, years to search. Civil cases indexed by defendant, plaintiff; in index books from 1960; computerized since 1999. Fax access is only allowed with prepayment of fees. Mail turnaround time 1 day.
Criminal Records: Access: Fax, mail, in person. Both court and visitors may perform in person searches. Search fee: $10.00 per name. Court makes copy: $1.00 per page; same fee for self serve. Required to search: name, years to search, signed release, offense. Criminal records in index books from 1960; computerized since 1999. Mail turnaround time 1 day.
General Information: No juvenile, mental, sealed, or adoption records released. Certification fee: $5.00. Payee: Camp County Clerk. Personal checks accepted. Prepayment and SASE required.

Carson County

District & County Court PO Box 487, Panhandle, TX 79068; phone: 806-537-3873; criminal fax: 806-537-3623; same fax for civil/probate; hours 8AM-N, 1-5PM (CST). *Felony, Misdemeanor, Civil, Probate.*
Note: Probate is a separate index at this same address.
Civil Records: Access: Mail, fax, in person. Both court and visitors may perform in person searches. Search fee: $5.00 per name. Court makes copy: $1.00 per page. Required to search: name, years to search. Civil cases indexed by defendant, plaintiff; on computer from 1981, index books from 1800s. Mail turnaround time 1 day or less.
Criminal Records: Access: Mail, fax, in person. Visitors must perform in person searches themselves. Search fee: $5.00 per name. Court makes copy: $1.00 per page. Required to search: name, years to search. Criminal records are not computerized. Mail turnaround time 1 day.
General Information: No juvenile, mental, sealed, or adoption records released. Will fax documents if fees have been paid. Certification fee: $5.00 per document. Payee: Carson County Clerk. Personal checks accepted. Prepayment and SASE required.

Cass County

District Court PO Box 510, Linden, TX 75563; phone: 903-756-7514; fax: 903-756-5253; hours 8AM-5PM (CST). *Felony, Civil.*
Civil Records: Access: Mail, in person. Both court and visitors may perform in person searches. Search fee: $5.00 per name. Court makes copy: $1.00 per page. Required to search: name, years to search. Civil cases indexed by defendant, plaintiff; on computer from 1968, index books from 1900s. Mail turnaround time 1 day.
Criminal Records: Access: Mail, in person. Both court and visitors may perform in person searches. Search fee: $5.00 per name. Court makes copy: $1.00 per page. Required to search: name, years to search. Criminal records on computer from 1968, index books from 1900s. Mail turnaround time 1 day.
General Information: Public terminal has criminal back to 1988 and civil back to 1962. No juvenile, mental, sealed, or adoption records released. Fee to fax documents is $.25 per minute; minimum $3.00. Certification fee: $2.00 per document includes copy fee. Payee: District Clerk. Personal checks accepted. Prepayment and SASE required.

County Court PO Box 449, Linden, TX 75563; phone: 903-756-5071; fax: 903-756-5071; probate fax: same; hours 8AM-5PM (CST). *Misdemeanor, Probate.*
Note: Probate is a separate index at same address.
Criminal Records: Access: Mail, in person. Both court and visitors may perform in person searches. Search fee: $10.00 per name. Court makes copy: $1.00 per page. Required to search: name, years to search. Criminal records in index books from 1983, computerized since 1999. Mail turnaround time 1 day.

General Information: No juvenile, mental, sealed, or adoption records released. Will fax documents for $3.00 fax fee. Certification fee: $5.00 per document. Payee: County Clerk. Money order or cashiers check accepted. Prepayment and SASE required.

Castro County

District & County Court 100 E Bedford, Rm 101, Dimmitt, TX 79027; phone: 806-647-3338; fax: 806-647-5438; hours 8AM-5PM (CST). *Felony, Misdemeanor, Civil, Probate.*
www.242ndcourt.com
Civil Records: Access: Mail, in person. Both court and visitors may perform in person searches. Search fee: $5.00 per name. Court makes copy: $1.00 per page; same fee for self serve. Required to search: name, years to search. Civil cases indexed by defendant, plaintiff; in index books. Mail turnaround time 1 day.
Criminal Records: Access: Mail, in person. Both court and visitors may perform in person searches. Search fee: $5.00 per name. Court makes copy: $1.00 per page; same fee for self serve. Required to search: name, years to search; also helpful: DOB, SSN. Criminal records in index books; computerized records since 2000. Mail turnaround time 1 day.
General Information: No juvenile, mental, sealed, or adoption records released. Will fax documents for $2.00 plus $1.00 per page. Certification fee: $5.00 per doc in county court, $1.00 in district per page. Payee: County or District Court Clerk. Personal checks accepted. Prepayment and SASE required.

Chambers County

District Clerk Drawer NN, Anahuac, TX 77514; phone: 409-267-8276; hours 8AM-N, 1-5PM (CST). *Felony, Civil.*
Civil Records: Access: Mail, in person. Both court and visitors may perform in person searches. Search fee: $5.00 per name. Court makes copy: $1.00 per page; same fee for self serve. Required to search: name, years to search. Civil cases indexed by defendant, plaintiff; on computer back to 1800s. Mail turnaround time 1 day.
Criminal Records: Access: Mail, in person. Both court and visitors may perform in person searches. Search fee: $5.00 per name. Court makes copy: $1.00 per page; same fee for self serve. Required to search: name, years to search, DOB, SNN. Criminal records on computer back to 1940s. Mail turnaround time 1 day.
General Information: Public use terminal available. No juvenile, mental, sealed, or adoption records released. Certification fee: $5.00. Payee: R B Scherer Jr, District Clerk. Personal checks accepted. Prepayment and SASE required.

County Court PO Box 728, Anahuac, TX 77514; phone: 409-267-8315; criminal phone: 409-267-8313; civil phone: 409-267-8309; probate phone: 409-267-8309; criminal fax: 409-267-8315; same fax for civil/probate; hours 8AM-5PM (CST). *Misdemeanor, Civil, Probate.*
www.co.chambers.tx.us
Note: Probate is s separate office at this same address.

Civil Records: Access: Mail, in person. Both court and visitors may perform in person searches. Search fee: $5.00 per name. Court makes copy: $1.00 per page. Required to search: name, years to search; also helpful: address. Civil cases indexed by defendant, plaintiff; on computer from 2000, index books in office from 1905. Mail turnaround time 2-3 days.
Criminal Records: Access: Mail, in person. Both court and visitors may perform in person searches. Search fee: $5.00 per name. Court makes copy: $1.00 per page. Required to search: name, years to search, DOB, offense; also helpful: address. Criminal records on computer from 2000, index books in office from 1905. Mail turnaround time 2-3 days.
General Information: No juvenile or mental records released. Will fax documents for $1.00 per page plus

copy charge -local; fee of $1.50 per page -long distance plus copy charge. Certification fee: $5.00 per document. Payee: Chambers County Clerk. Personal checks accepted. Prepayment required.

Cherokee County

District Court Drawer C, Rusk, TX 75785; phone: 903-683-6908 clerk; criminal phone: 903-683-4533; civil phone: 903-683-5945/5883; fax: 903-683-2971; hours 8AM-N, 1-5PM (CST). *Felony, Civil.*

Civil Records: Access: Mail, fax, in person. Both court and visitors may perform in person searches. Search fee: $5.00 per name. Court makes copy: $.50 per page. Required to search: name, years to search. Civil cases indexed by defendant, plaintiff; on computer from 1992, index books from 1848. Mail turnaround time 1-2 days.

Criminal Records: Access: Mail, fax, in person. Both court and visitors may perform in person searches. Search fee: $5.00 per name. Court makes copy: $.50 per page. Required to search: name, years to search. Criminal records on computer from 1992, index books from 1848. Mail turnaround time 1-2 days.

General Information: Public use terminal available. No juvenile, mental, sealed, or adoption records released. Will not fax documents. Certification fee: $1.00 per page. Payee: District Clerk. Personal checks accepted. Prepayment and SASE required.

County Court Cherokee County Clerk, PO Box 420, Rusk, TX 75785; phone: 903-683-2350; criminal fax: 903-683-5931; same fax for civil/probate; hours 8AM-5PM (CST). *Misdemeanor, Civil, Probate.*

Civil Records: Access: Mail, in person. Both court and visitors may perform in person searches. Search fee: $5.00 per name. Court makes copy: $1.00 per page. Required to search: name, years to search. Civil cases indexed by defendant, plaintiff; on computer back to 1987, index books from 1846. Mail turnaround time 2-4 days.

Criminal Records: Access: Mail, in person. Both court and visitors may perform in person searches. Search fee: $10.00 per name. Court makes copy: $1.00 per page. Required to search: name, years to search. Criminal records on computer back to 1987, index books from 1920s. Mail turnaround time 2-4 days.

General Information: No juvenile, mental, sealed, or adoption records released. Certification fee: $5.00 per document. Payee: County Clerk. Personal checks accepted. Prepayment and SASE required.

Childress County

District & County Court Courthouse, Box 4, Childress, TX 79201; phone: 940-937-6143; criminal fax: 940-937-3708; same fax for civil/probate; hours 8:30AM-N, 1-5PM (CST). *Felony, Misdemeanor, Civil, Probate.*

Civil Records: Access: Mail, in person. Both court and visitors may perform in person searches. Search fee: $5.00 per name. Court makes copy: $1.00 per page; same fee for self serve. Required to search: name, years to search. Civil cases indexed by defendant, plaintiff; on computer from 1995, index books from 1920. Mail turnaround time 1 day.

Criminal Records: Access: Mail, in person. Both court and visitors may perform in person searches. Search fee: $5.00 per name. Court makes copy: $1.00 per page; same fee for self serve. Required to search: name, years to search, DOB. Criminal records on computer from 1995, index books from 1920. Mail turnaround time 1 day.

General Information: No juvenile, mental, sealed, or adoption records released. Will fax documents. Certification fee: $1.00 per cert. County Court cert fee is $5.00 per document. Payee: District or County Clerk. Personal checks accepted. Prepayment required.

Clay County

District Clerk PO Box 568, Henrietta, TX 76365; phone: 940-538-4561; fax: 940-538-4431; hours 8AM-N, 1-5PM (CST). *Felony, Civil.*

Civil Records: Access: Mail, in person. Both court and visitors may perform in person searches. Search fee: $5.00 per name. Court makes copy: $1.00 per page. Self serve copy fee: $.25 per page. Required to search: name, years to search. Civil cases indexed by defendant, plaintiff; in index books from 1873. Mail turnaround time 1-2 days.

Criminal Records: Access: Mail, in person. Both court and visitors may perform in person searches. Search fee: $5.00 per name. Court makes copy: $1.00 per page. Self serve copy fee: $.25 per page. Required to search: name, years to search. Criminal records in index books from 1873. Mail turnaround 1-2 days.

General Information: No juvenile, mental, sealed, or adoption records released. Will fax documents to local or toll-free number. Certification fee: $1.00 per page includes copy fee. Payee: District Clerk. Personal checks accepted. Prepayment and SASE required.

County Court PO Box 548, Henrietta, TX 76365; phone: 940-538-4631; hours 8AM-5PM (CST). *Misdemeanor, Civil, Probate.*

Note: Probate is a separate index at this same address.

Civil Records: Access: Mail, in person. Both court and visitors may perform in person searches. Search fee: $5.00 per name. Court makes copy: $1.00 per page; same fee for self serve. Required to search: name, years to search. Civil cases indexed by defendant, plaintiff; in index books from 1873, records go back to 1910; no computerized records. Mail turnaround time 2-4 days.

Criminal Records: Access: Mail, in person. Both court and visitors may perform in person searches. Search fee: $5.00 per name. Court makes copy: $1.00 per page; same fee for self serve. Required to search: name, years to search. Criminal records in index books from 1873, records go back to 1910; no computerized records. Mail turnaround 2-4 days.

General Information: No juvenile, mental, sealed, or adoption records released. Certification fee: $5.00 per document. Payee: County Clerk. Personal checks accepted. Prepayment and SASE required.

Cochran County

District & County Court County Courthouse, Rm 102, Morton, TX 79346; phone: 806-266-5450; criminal fax: 806-266-9027; same fax for civil/probate; hours 8AM-5PM (CST). *Felony, Misdemeanor, Civil, Probate.*

Civil Records: Access: Phone, fax, mail, in person, online. Both court and visitors may perform in person searches. Search fee: $5.00 per name. Court makes copy: $1.00 per page. Required to search: name, years to search. Civil cases indexed by defendant, plaintiff; in index books go back to 1925. Email address for search requests is cclerk@door.net. Mail turnaround time 1 day.

Criminal Records: Access: Fax, mail, in person, online. Both court and visitors may perform in person searches. Search fee: $5.00 per name. Court makes copy: $1.00 per page. Required to search: name, years to search, DOB; also helpful: sex. Criminal records in index books go back to 1925. Email address for search requests is cclerk@door.net. Mail turnaround time 1 day.

General Information: No juvenile, mental, sealed, or adoption records released. Will fax documents to 800 number free; otherwise fee to fax is $5.00. Certification fee: $5.00 per document. Payee: District or County Clerk. Personal checks accepted. Prepayment and SASE required.

Coke County

District & County Court PO Box 150, Robert Lee, TX 76945; phone: 325-453-2631; criminal fax: 325-453-2650; same fax for civil/probate; hours 8AM-5PM (CST). *Felony, Misdemeanor, Civil, Probate.*

Civil Records: Access: Mail, in person. Both court and visitors may perform in person searches. Search fee: $5.00 per name. Court makes copy: $1.00 per page; same fee for self serve. Required to search: name, years to search. Civil cases indexed by defendant, plaintiff; in index books since 1889, computerized since 1993. Mail turnaround 2 days.

Criminal Records: Access: Mail, in person. Both court and visitors may perform in person searches. Search fee: $5.00 per name. Court makes copy: $1.00 per page; same fee for self serve. Required to search: name, years to search. Criminal records in index books since 1889. Mail turnaround time 2 days.

General Information: No juvenile, mental, sealed, or adoption records released. Will fax documents $2.00 per page. Certification fee: $5.00. Payee: Coke County Clerk. Personal checks accepted. Prepayment required.

Coleman County

District Court PO Box 512, Coleman, TX 76834; phone: 325-625-2568; hours 8AM-4:30PM (CST). *Felony, Civil.*

Civil Records: Access: Mail, in person. Both court and visitors may perform in person searches. Search fee: $5.00 per name. Court makes copy: $1.00 per page. Required to search: name, years to search. Civil cases indexed by defendant, plaintiff; in index books since 1934; earlier records not indexed. Mail turnaround time up to 5 days.

Criminal Records: Access: Mail, in person. Both court and visitors may perform in person searches. Search fee: $5.00 per name. Court makes copy: $1.00 per page. Required to search: name, years to search; also helpful are DOB, SSN. Criminal records in index books since 1931; earlier records not indexed. Mail turnaround time up to 5 days.

General Information: No juvenile, mental, sealed, or adoption records released. Will not fax documents. Certification fee: $1.00. Payee: District Clerk. Personal checks accepted. Prepayment and SASE required.

County Court PO Box 591, Coleman, TX 76834; phone: 325-625-2889; hours 8AM-5PM (CST). *Misdemeanor, Civil, Probate.*

Civil Records: Access: Mail, in person. Both court and visitors may perform in person searches. Search fee: $5.00 per name. Court makes copy: $1.00 per page. Required to search: name, years to search. Civil cases indexed by defendant, plaintiff; in index books from 1971. Mail turnaround time 1-2 days.

Criminal Records: Access: Mail, in person. Both court and visitors may perform in person searches. Search fee: $5.00 per name. Court makes copy: $1.00 per page. Required to search: name, years to search. Criminal records in index books from 1977, archived from 1900s. Mail turnaround time 1-2 days.

General Information: No juvenile, mental, sealed, or adoption records released. Certification fee: $5.00. Payee: County Clerk. Personal checks accepted. Prepayment and SASE required.

Collin County

District Clerk PO Box 578, McKinney, TX 75070; criminal phone: 972-548-4430; civil phone: 972-548-4320; criminal fax: 972-548-4764; civil fax: 972-548-4697; hours 8AM-4:30PM (CST). *Felony, Civil.*

www.co.collin.tx.us/district_courts/index.jsp

Civil Records: Access: Mail, fax, online, in person. Both court and visitors may perform in person searches. Search fee: $5.00 per name. Court makes copy: $1.00 per page. Required to search: name, years to search. Civil cases indexed by defendant, plaintiff; on computer and microfiche from 1986 (some records are on computer through the 1970s), index books from 1846. name and case look up is at www.co.collin.tx.us/rsp-bin/pbkr125.pgm. Search case schedules for free at www.co.collin.tx.us/ShowScheduleSearchServlet. There is also a commercial system- see county courts. Call Patty Ostrom at 972-548-4503 for subscription info. Note: Fax service only to ongoing subscriber. Mail turnaround time 2-3 days.

Criminal Records: Access: Mail, fax, online, in person. Both court and visitors may perform in person searches. Search fee: $5.00 per name. Court makes copy: $1.00 per page. Required to search: name, years to search, DOB. Criminal records on computer and microfiche from 1986 (some records are on computer through the 1970s), index books from 1846. Online access to criminal records is the same as civil. Note: Fax service only to ongoing subscriber. Mail turnaround time 2-3 days.

General Information: Public terminal goes back to 1986. No juvenile, mental, sealed, or adoption records released. Will return by fax, if subscriber. No certification fee. Payee: District Clerk. Personal checks accepted. Prepayment and SASE required.

County Court At Law 1800 N Graves, #110, McKinney, TX 75069; phone: 972-548-6420; probate phone: 972-548-6465; fax: 972-548-6433; hours 8AM-4:30PM (CST). *Misdemeanor, Civil, Probate.*
www.co.collin.tx.us/county_court_law/index.jsp
Probate is in #115; Probate fax is 972-548-6468.

Civil Records: Access: Mail, online, in person. Both court and visitors may perform in person searches. Search fee: $5.00 per name. Court makes copy: $1.00 per page; same fee for self serve. Required to search: name, years to search. Civil cases indexed by defendant, plaintiff; on computer and microfiche from 1975. Online access is free at www.co.collin.tx.us/ShowCaseLookupServlet?district_or_county_court=county. Mail turnaround time 2-4 days.

Criminal Records: Access: Mail, online, in person. Both court and visitors may perform in person searches. Search fee: $5.00 per name. Court makes copy: $1.00 per page; same fee for self serve. Required to search: name, DOB. Criminal records computerized since early 1970s. Online access to misdemeanor records is the same as civil. Mail turnaround time 2-4 days.

General Information: Public terminal goes back to 1970s. No juvenile, mental, sealed, or adoption records released. Will not fax documents. Certification fee: $5.00. Payee: County Clerk. Personal checks accepted. Prepayment required.

Collingsworth County

District & County Court County Courthouse, Rm 3, 800 W Ave, Box 10, Wellington, TX 79095; phone: 806-447-2408; fax: 806-447-2409; hours 9AM-5PM (CST). *Felony, Misdemeanor, Civil, Probate.*

Civil Records: Access: Phone, fax, mail, in person. Both court and visitors may perform in person searches. Search fee: $10.00 per name. Court makes copy: $1.00 per page; same fee for self serve. Required to search: name, years to search. Civil cases indexed by defendant, plaintiff; on index books from 1800s. Mail turnaround time 2 days.

Criminal Records: Access: Mail, in person. Both court and visitors may perform in person searches. Search fee: $10.00 per name. Court makes copy: $1.00 per page; same fee for self serve. Required to search: name, years to search, DOB. Criminal records on index books from 1800s. Mail turnaround time 2 days.

General Information: No juvenile, mental health, sealed, or adoption records released. Will fax documents for $1.50 per page. Certification fee: $5.00. Payee: Collingsworth County Clerk. Personal checks accepted. Prepayment and SASE required.

Colorado County

District Court County Courthouse, Rm 210E, 400 Spring St, Columbus, TX 78934; phone: 979-732-2536; hours 8AM-N, 1-5PM (CST). *Felony, Civil.*

Civil Records: Access: Mail, in person. Both court and visitors may perform in person searches. Search fee: $5.00 per name. Court makes copy: $1.00 per page; same fee for self serve. Required to search: name, years to search. Civil cases indexed by plaintiff; in index books from 1837. Mail turnaround time 1 day.

Criminal Records: Access: Mail, in person. Both court and visitors may perform in person searches. Search fee: $5.00 per name. Court makes copy: $1.00 per page; same fee for self serve. Required to search: name, years to search. Criminal records in index books from 1837. Mail turnaround time 1 day.

General Information: No juvenile, mental, sealed, or adoption records released. Certification fee: $2.00. Payee: District Clerk. Personal checks accepted. Prepayment and SASE required.

County Court 400 Spring St #103, County Courthouse, Columbus, TX 78934; phone: 979-732-2155; fax: 979-732-8852; hours 8AM-5PM (CST). *Misdemeanor, Civil, Probate.*

Civil Records: Access: Mail, in person. Both court and visitors may perform in person searches. Search fee: $10.00 per name. Court makes copy: $1.00 per page. Required to search: name, years to search. Civil cases indexed by defendant, plaintiff; in index books from 1850, computerized since 1996. Mail turnaround time 1-2 days.

Criminal Records: Access: Mail, in person. Both court and visitors may perform in person searches. Search fee: $10.00 per name. Court makes copy: $1.00 per page. Required to search: name, years to search. Criminal records in index books from 1850, computerized since 1996. Mail turnaround time 1-2 days.

General Information: No juvenile, mental, sealed, or adoption records released. Certification fee: $5.00. Payee: County Clerk. Personal checks accepted. Prepayment and SASE required.

Comal County

District Court 150 N Seguin, #304, New Braunfels, TX 78130-5161; phone: 830-620-5574; fax: 830-608-2006; hours 8AM-4:30PM (CST). *Felony, Civil.*
www.co.comal.tx.us

Civil Records: Access: Fax, mail, in person, online. Both court and visitors may perform in person searches. Search fee: $5.00 per name. Court makes copy: $1.00 for first page, $.25 each add'l. Required to search: name, years to search. Civil cases indexed by defendant, plaintiff; on computer from 1984, index books from 1846. Online access to county judicial records is free at www.co.comal.tx.us/recordsearch.htm. Search by either party name. Mail turnaround time 3 days.

Criminal Records: Access: Fax, mail, in person, online. Both court and visitors may perform in person searches. Search fee: $5.00 per name. Court makes copy: $1.00 for first page, $.25 each add'l. Required to search: name, years to search, DOB; also helpful: SSN, sex. Criminal records on computer from 1984, index books from 1846. Online access to county criminal judicial records is at www.co.comal.tx.us/recordsearch.htm. Search by defendant name. Mail turnaround time 3 days.

General Information: Public terminal goes back to 1985. No juvenile, sealed, or adoption records released. Will fax documents $5.00 per page. Fee is for incoming and outgoing faxes. Certification fee: $1.00 per page. Cert fee includes copies. Payee: District Clerk. Personal checks accepted. Prepayment and SASE required.

County Court at Law 100 Main Plaza, #303, New Braunfels, TX 78130; phone: 830-608-8615; criminal phone: 830-620-5582; civil phone: 830-620-5586; probate phone: 830-620-5539; fax: 830-608-2021; hours 8AM-4:30PM (CST). *Misdemeanor, Civil, Probate.*
www.comalcounty.net

Civil Records: Access: Phone, fax, mail, in person, online. Both court and visitors may perform in person searches. Search fee: $5.00 per name. Court makes copy: $1.00 per page; same fee for self serve. Required to search: name, years to search. Civil cases indexed by defendant, plaintiff; on computer since

1977. Online access to county judicial records is free at www.co.comal.tx.us/recordsearch.htm. Search by either party name. Mail turnaround time 1 week.

Criminal Records: Access: Phone, fax, mail, in person. Both court and visitors may perform in person searches. Search fee: $5.00 per name. Court makes copy: $1.00 per page; same fee for self serve. Required to search: name, years to search; also helpful: address, DOB. Criminal records on computer since 1977. Online access to county criminal judicial records is free at www.co.comal.tx.us/recordsearch.htm. Search by defendant name. Mail turnaround time 1 week.

General Information: Public use terminal available. No juvenile, mental, sealed or adoption records released. Will fax documents $1.00 per page. Certification fee: $5.00. Payee: County Court at Law. Only cashiers checks and money orders accepted. Credit cards accepted. Prepayment required.

Comanche County

District Court County Courthouse, Box 206, Comanche, TX 76442; phone: 325-356-2342; fax: 325-356-2150; hours 8:30AM-N, 1-5PM (CST). *Felony, Civil.*

Civil Records: Access: Mail, in person. Only the court performs in person searches; visitors may not. Search fee: $5.00 per name. Court makes copy: $1.00 per page. Required to search: name, years to search. Civil cases indexed by defendant, plaintiff; on computer back 1 year, index books from 1876. Mail turnaround time 1 day.

Criminal Records: Access: Mail, in person. Only the court performs in person searches; visitors may not. Search fee: $5.00 per name. Court makes copy: $1.00 per page. Required to search: name, years to search. Criminal records on computer from 1990, index books from 1876. Mail turnaround time 1 day.

General Information: No juvenile, mental, sealed, or adoption records released. Will not fax documents. Certification fee: $2.00. Payee: District Clerk. Personal checks accepted. Prepayment and SASE required.

County Court County Courthouse, Comanche, TX 76442; phone: 325-356-2655; fax: 325-356-5764; hours 8:30AM-5PM (CST). *Misdemeanor, Civil, Probate.*

Civil Records: Access: Mail, in person. Both court and visitors may perform in person searches. Search fee: $5.00 per name. Court makes copy: $1.00 per page. Required to search: name, years to search. Civil cases indexed by defendant, plaintiff; in index books from 1856. Mail turnaround time 1 day.

Criminal Records: Access: Mail, in person. Both court and visitors may perform in person searches. Search fee: $5.00 per name. Court makes copy: $1.00 per page. Required to search: name, years to search. Criminal records in index books from 1856. Mail turnaround time 1 day.

General Information: No juvenile, mental, sealed, or adoption records released. Will fax documents for $1.50 per fax. Certification fee: $5.00. Payee: County Clerk. Personal checks accepted. Prepayment and SASE required.

Concho County

District & County Court PO Box 98, Paint Rock, TX 76866; phone: 325-732-4322; criminal fax: 325-732-2040; same fax for civil/probate; hours 8:30AM-5PM (CST). *Felony, Misdemeanor, Civil, Probate.*
Note: Probate is in a separate index at this address.

Civil Records: Access: Mail, in person. Both court and visitors may perform in person searches. Search fee: $5.00 per name. Court makes copy: $1.00 per page. Required to search: name, years to search. Civil cases indexed by defendant, plaintiff; in index books from 1879; computerized back to 1994. Mail turnaround time 1 day.

Criminal Records: Access: Mail, in person. Only the court performs in person searches; visitors may not. Search fee: $5.00 per name. Court makes copy: $1.00 per page. Required to search: name, years to search, DOB; also helpful: SSN. Criminal records in index books from 1879; computerized back to 1994. Mail turnaround time 1 day.

General Information: No juvenile, mental, sealed, or adoption records released. Will not fax documents. Certification fee: $5.00 for County Court; $1.00 for District. Payee: District or County Clerk. Personal checks accepted. Prepayment and SASE required.

Cooke County

District Court County Courthouse, 100 S Dixon, Gainesville, TX 76240; phone: 940-668-5450; fax: 940-668-5476; hours 8AM-5PM (CST). *Felony, Civil.*

Civil Records: Access: Mail, in person. Both court and visitors may perform in person searches. Search fee: $5.00 per name. Court makes copy: $.50 per page; same fee for self serve. Required to search: name, years to search. Civil cases indexed by defendant, plaintiff; on microfiche from late 1900s, index books from 1800s. Must request specifically if you wish to go back more than 10 years. Mail turnaround time varies.

Criminal Records: Access: Mail, in person. Both court and visitors may perform in person searches. Search fee: $5.00 per name. Court makes copy: $.50 per page; same fee for self serve. Required to search: name, years to search. Criminal records on microfiche from late 1900,s, index books from 1800s. Mail turnaround time varies.

General Information: No juvenile, mental, sealed, or adoption records released. Will fax documents. Certification fee: $1.00 per page includes copy fee. Payee: District Clerk. Only cashiers checks and money orders accepted. Prepayment and SASE required.

County Court County Courthouse, Gainesville, TX 76240; phone: 940-668-5422; fax: 940-668-5486; hours 8AM-5PM (CST). *Misdemeanor, Civil, Probate.*

Civil Records: Access: Mail, in person. Both court and visitors may perform in person searches. Search fee: $5.00 per name. Court makes copy: $1.00 per page; same fee for self serve. Required to search: name, years to search. Civil cases indexed by defendant, plaintiff; in index books and original papers from late 1850s. Mail turnaround time 1 day.

Criminal Records: Access: Mail, in person. Both court and visitors may perform in person searches. Search fee: $5.00 per name. Court makes copy: $1.00 per page. Required to search: name, years to search, DOB. Criminal records go back to 1969. Mail turnaround time 1 day.

General Information: No juvenile, mental, sealed, or adoption records released. Will fax documents of search to toll free lines or when pre-paid. Certification fee: $5.00 per instrument. Payee: Cooke County Clerk. Personal checks accepted. Prepayment required.

Coryell County

District Court PO Box 4, Gatesville, TX 76528; phone: 254-865-5911; fax: 254-865-5064; hours 8AM-5PM (CST). *Felony, Civil.*

Civil Records: Access: Fax, mail, in person. Both court and visitors may perform in person searches. Search fee: $5.00 per name. Court makes copy: $1.00 per page. Self serve copy fee: $.50 per page. Required to search: name, years to search. Civil cases indexed by defendant, plaintiff; in index books from 1854; computerized back to 2000. Mail turnaround time 1 day.

Criminal Records: Access: Fax, mail, in person. Both court and visitors may perform in person searches. Search fee: $5.00 per name. Court makes copy: $1.00 per page. Self serve copy fee: $.50 per page. Required to search: name, years to search, DOB, SSN. Criminal records in index books from 1854; computerized back to 2000. Mail turnaround time 1 day.

General Information: Public terminal goes back to 1999. No juvenile, sealed, or adoption records released. Fee to fax documents is $1.00 per page. No certification fee. Payee: District Clerk. Personal checks accepted from Coryell County residents only. Money order, cashiers check or credit card accepted for others. Prepayment and SASE required.

County Court PO Box 237, Gatesville, TX 76528; phone: 254-865-5911 x235; fax: 254-865-8631; hours 8AM-N, 1-5PM (CST). *Misdemeanor, Civil, Probate.*

Civil Records: Access: Mail, in person. Visitors must perform in person searches themselves. Search fee: $10.00 per name per 10 years, when court does mail search. Court makes copy: $1.00 per page; same fee for self serve. Required to search: name, years to search. Civil cases indexed by defendant, plaintiff; on computer back to 1993, index books from 1846. Mail turnaround time 1-5 days.

Criminal Records: Access: Mail, in person. Visitors must perform in person searches themselves. Search fee: $10.00 per name per 10 years, when court does mail search. Court makes copy: $1.00 per page; same fee for self serve. Required to search: name, years to search, DOB, SSN. Criminal records on computer back to 1993; index books from 1846. Mail turnaround time 1-5 days.

General Information: Public terminal goes back to 1993. No juvenile, mental, sealed, or adoption records released. Will fax documents $1.00 per page. Fax fee for out of county request is $5.00 plus $1.00 per page. Certification fee: $5.00 first page and $1.00 ea add'l. Payee: County Clerk. Business checks accepted. Personal checks must be in county. Prepayment and SASE required.

Cottle County

District & County Court PO Box 717, Paducah, TX 79248; phone: 806-492-3823; fax: 806-492-2625; hours 9AM-N, 1-5PM (CST). *Felony, Misdemeanor, Civil, Probate.*

Civil Records: Access: Mail, in person. Both court and visitors may perform in person searches. Search fee: $5.00 per name. Court makes copy: $1.00 per page. Required to search: name, years to search. Civil cases indexed by defendant, plaintiff; in index books from 1892. Mail turnaround time 2-3 days.

Criminal Records: Access: Mail, in person. Both court and visitors may perform in person searches. Search fee: $5.00 per name. Court makes copy: $1.00 per page. Required to search: name, years to search. Criminal records in index books from 1892. Mail turnaround time 2-3 days.

General Information: No juvenile, mental, sealed, or adoption records released. Certification fee: $1.00 in District Court; $5.00 for County Court. Payee: Cottle County Clerk. Personal checks accepted. Prepayment and SASE required.

Crane County

District & County Court PO Box 578, Crane, TX 79731; phone: 432-558-3581; fax: 432-558-1148; hours 9AM-12 1-5PM (CST). *Felony, Misdemeanor, Civil, Probate.*

Note: Probate is a separate index at this same address.

Civil Records: Access: Mail, in person. Visitors must perform in person searches themselves. Search fee: $5.00 per name per 10 years searched. Court makes copy: $1.00 per page. Required to search: name, years to search. Civil cases indexed by defendant, plaintiff. Limited civil records on computer from 1990; index books from 1927. Mail turnaround time 2-5 days.

Criminal Records: Access: Mail, in person. Both court and visitors may perform in person searches. Search fee: $5.00 per name per ten years searched. Court makes copy: $1.00 per page. Required to search: name, years to search, offense. Limited criminal records on computer from 1990; index books from 1927. Mail turnaround time 2-5 days.

General Information: Public terminal goes back to 1990. No juvenile, mental, sealed or adoption records

released. Certification fee: $5.00 per doc County Court; $1.00 per doc in Dist Court. Payee: District or County Clerk. Only cashiers checks and money orders accepted. Prepayment required. SASE requested.

Crockett County

District & County Court PO Drawer C, Ozona, TX 76943; phone: 325-392-2022; fax: 325-392-3472; hours 8AM-5PM (CST). *Felony, Misdemeanor, Civil, Probate.*

Civil Records: Access: Mail, in person. Both court and visitors may perform in person searches. Search fee: $10.00 per name. Court makes copy: $1.00 per page; same fee for self serve. Required to search: name, years to search. Civil cases indexed by defendant, plaintiff; on computer from 1982, index books from 1800s. Mail turnaround time 1 week.

Criminal Records: Access: Mail, in person. Both court and visitors may perform in person searches. Search fee: $10.00 per name. Court makes copy: $1.00 per page; same fee for self serve. Required to search: name, years to search, DOB, SSN, signed release. Criminal records on computer from 1982, index books from 1800s. Mail turnaround time 1 week.

General Information: No juvenile, mental, sealed, or adoption records released. Fee to fax documents is $2.00 per page. Certification fee: $5.00 per document. Payee: District or County Clerk. Personal checks accepted. Prepayment required.

Crosby County

District Court 201 W Aspen St, #207, Crosbyton, TX 79322-2500; phone: 806-675-2071; fax: 806-675-2433; hours 8AM-N, 1-5PM (CST). *Felony, Civil.*

Civil Records: Access: Phone, fax, mail, in person. Both court and visitors may perform in person searches. Search fee: $5.00 per name. Court makes copy: $1.00 per page. Required to search: name, years to search. Civil cases indexed by defendant, plaintiff; in index books from 1896. Mail turnaround time 1 day.

Criminal Records: Access: Phone, fax, mail, in person. Both court and visitors may perform in person searches. Search fee: $5.00 per name. Court makes copy: $1.00 per page. Required to search: name, years to search. Criminal records in index books from 1896. Mail turnaround time 1 day.

General Information: No juvenile, mental, sealed, or adoption records released. No fee to fax documents. Only for local or toll free calls. Certification fee: $1.00. Payee: District Clerk. Personal checks accepted. Prepayment and SASE required.

County Court 201 W Aspen St, #102, Crosbyton, TX 79322-2500; phone: 806-675-2334; hours 8AM-N, 1:00PM-5PM (CST). *Misdemeanor, Civil, Probate.*

Note: Probate is a separate index at this same address.

Civil Records: Access: Mail, in person. Both court and visitors may perform in person searches. Search fee: $5.00 per name. Court makes copy: $1.00 per page; same fee for self serve. Required to search: name, years to search. Civil cases indexed by defendant, plaintiff; on microfiche from 1990, index books from 1886. Mail turnaround time 1 day.

Criminal Records: Access: Mail, in person. Both court and visitors may perform in person searches. Search fee: $5.00 per name. Court makes copy: $1.00 per page; same fee for self serve. Required to search: name, years to search. Criminal records on microfiche from 1990, index books from 1886. Mail turnaround time 1 day.

General Information: No juvenile, mental, sealed, or adoption records released. Will fax documents for $1.00 per page. Certification fee: $5.00 per document. Payee: County Clerk. Personal checks accepted. Prepayment required.

Culberson County

District & County Court PO Box 158, Van Horn, TX 79855; phone: 432-283-2058; hours 8AM-N; 1PM-5PM (CST). *Felony, Misdemeanor, Civil, Probate.*

Civil Records: Access: Phone, mail, fax, in person. Both court and visitors may perform in person searches. Search fee: $5.00 per name. Court makes copy: $1.00 per page. Required to search: name, years to search. Civil cases indexed by defendant, plaintiff; in index books since 1911. Mail turnaround time 2 days.

Criminal Records: Access: Phone, mail, fax, in person. Both court and visitors may perform in person searches. Search fee: $5.00 per name. Court makes copy: $1.00 per page. Required to search: name, years to search, signed release. Criminal records in index books since 1911. Mail turnaround time 2 days.

General Information: No juvenile, mental, sealed, or adoption records released. Fee to fax documents is $1.00 per page. Certification fee: $5.00. Payee: District or County Clerk. Personal checks accepted. Prepayment and SASE required.

Dallam County

District & County Court PO Box 1352, Dalhart, TX 79022; phone: 806-244-4751; fax: 806-244-3751; hours 9AM-5PM (CST). *Felony, Misdemeanor, Civil, Probate.*

Civil Records: Access: Fax, mail, in person. Both court and visitors may perform in person searches. Search fee: $5.00 per name. Court makes copy: $1.00 per page. Required to search: name, years to search. Civil cases indexed by defendant, plaintiff; in index books from 1800s; computerized since 1991. Mail turnaround time 1 day.

Criminal Records: Access: Fax, mail, in person. Both court and visitors may perform in person searches. Search fee: $5.00 per name. Court makes copy: $1.00 per page. Required to search: name, years to search. Criminal records in index books from 1800s; computerized since 1991. Mail turnaround time 1 day.

General Information: No juvenile, mental, sealed, or adoption records released. Fee to fax documents is $5.00 1st page, $1.00 each add'l. Certification fee: $5.00. Payee: Dallam County Clerk. Personal checks accepted. Prepayment and SASE required.

Dallas County

District Court - Civil 600 Commerce St, Dallas, TX 75202-4606; phone: 214-653-7421; hours 8AM-6:00PM (CST). *Civil.*
www.dallascounty.org
Civil Records: Access: Mail, in person. Both court and visitors may perform in person searches. Search fee: $5.00 per name. Court makes copy: $1.00 per page. Required to search: name, years to search, DOB. Civil cases indexed by defendant, plaintiff; on computer since 1967; on dockets back to 1940; records prior to 1940 are maintained by Texas Historical Div. of the Dallas Public Library. As per Commissioners Court Order 2005-1162, Family and District Court information via the Dallas County Public Access Dial In System is no longer unavailable effective August 26, 2005.
General Information: Public terminal has only civil records. No sealed records released. Fee to fax documents is $1.00 per page. Certification fee: $5.00. Payee: District Clerk. Only cashiers checks and money orders accepted. Prepayment required.

District Court - Criminal 133 N Industrial Blvd, LB12, Attn: District Clerk, Dallas, TX 75207-4313; phone: 214-653-5950; fax: 214-653-5986; hours 8AM-4:30PM (CST). *Felony.*
www.dallascounty.org
Criminal Records: Access: Mail, online, in person. Both court and visitors may perform in person searches. Search fee: $5.00 per name. Court makes copy: $1.00 per page. Required to search: name, years

to search, DOB. Criminal records on computer from 1972, on microfiche from 1979. Two electronic sources available. Public Access System allows remote access at $1.00 per minute to this court and other court/public records. Dial-in access number is 900-263-INFO. ProComm Plus is recommended. Search by name or case number. Call the Public Access Administrator at 214-653-7717 for more info and order $2.00 set-up CD-rom. Also, name search at www.dallascounty.org/applications/english/record-search/intro.html; index includes DOB. $5.50 fee per search, use credit card. Note: Save by becoming a subscriber for $75 per year. Includes civil, criminal, probate, marriages, UCC, and soon, real estate. Call 972-866-3911 for info. Mail turnaround time 1-2 days.
General Information: Public terminal has only criminal records back to 1972. No juvenile, mental, sealed, or adoption records released. Certification fee: $1.00 per page. Payee: District Clerk. Only cashiers checks and money orders accepted. Prepayment and SASE required.

County Court - Misdemeanor 133 N Industrial Blvd, #LB43, Dallas, TX 75207-4313; phone: 214-653-5740; hours 8AM-4PM (CST). *Misdemeanor.*
www.dallascounty.org
Criminal Records: Access: Mail, online, in person. Both court and visitors may perform in person searches. Search fee: $5.00 per name. Court makes copy: $1.00 per page. Required to search: name, years to search, DOB. Criminal records on computer from 1972. For older searches call 214-653-5763. Two electronic sources are available. Public Access System allows remote access at $1.00 per minute to these and other court/public records. Dial-in access number is 900-263-INFO. ProComm Plus is recommended. Searching is by name or case number. Call the Public Access Administrator at 214-653-7717 for more info and order $2.00 set-up CD-rom. Also, name search for free at www.dallascounty.org/applications/english/record-search/intro.html; index includes DOB. $5.50 fee per record using credit card. Mail turnaround time 2-3 weeks.
General Information: Public terminal has only criminal records. No juvenile, mental, sealed, or adoption records released. Certification fee: $5.00. Payee: County Clerk. Only cashiers checks and money orders accepted or cash if in person. Prepayment and SASE required.

County Court - Civil 509 W Main, 3rd Fl, Dallas, TX 75202; phone: 214-653-7131; criminal phone: 214-653-5740; civil phone: 214-653-7441; fax: 214-653-7176; hours 8AM-4:30PM (CST). *Civil.*
www.dallascounty.org
Note: No civil claims limit as of 05/23/97.
Civil Records: Access: Phone, mail, in person. Both court and visitors may perform in person searches. Search fee: $5.00 per name per 10 years. Court makes copy: $1.00 per page. Required to search: name, years to search. Civil cases indexed by defendant, plaintiff; on computer from 1964, index books from 1800s as per Commissioners Court Order 2005-1162, Family and District Court information via the Dallas County Public Access Dial In System is no longer unavailable effective August 26, 2005. Mail turnaround time 1 day.
General Information: Public terminal has only civil records back to 1964. No juvenile, mental, sealed, or adoption records released. Will not fax documents. Certification fee: $5.00. Payee: County Clerk. Personal checks accepted. Prepayment and SASE required.

Probate Court #3 509 Main St, Records Bldg, 2nd Fl, Dallas, TX 75202; phone: 214-653-7243; fax: 214-653-7695; hours 8AM-4:30PM (CST). *Probate.*
Note: The remote access system for civil and criminal records in this county also includes probate records.

You may also name search for free at www.dallascounty.org/applications/english/record-search/intro.html; there is a fee for documents.

Dawson County

District Court Drawer 1268, Lamesa, TX 79331; phone: 806-872-7373; fax: 806-872-9513; hours 8:30AM-5PM (CST). *Felony, Civil.*
Civil Records: Access: Mail, in person. Both court and visitors may perform in person searches. Search fee: $5.00 per name. Court makes copy: $1.00 per page. Required to search: name, years to search. Civil cases indexed by defendant, plaintiff; in index books/files from 1900; computerized records since 1995. Mail turnaround time 1 day.
Criminal Records: Access: Mail, in person. Both court and visitors may perform in person searches. Search fee: $5.00 per name. Court makes copy: $1.00 per page. Required to search: name, years to search, signed release. Criminal records in index books/files from 1900s; computerized records since 1995. Mail turnaround time 1 day.
General Information: No juvenile, mental, sealed, or adoption records released. Will fax documents $1.00 per page. Certification fee: $1.00 per page. Payee: Dawson County District Clerk. Personal checks accepted. Prepayment required.

County Court Drawer 1268, Lamesa, TX 79331; phone: 806-872-3778; civil phone: 806-872-6191; civil phone: 806-872-6191; probate phone: 806-872-7685; criminal fax: 806-872-2473; same fax for civil/probate; hours 8:30AM-1200-15PM (CST). *Misdemeanor, Civil, Probate.*
Civil Records: Access: Fax, mail, in person. Both court and visitors may perform in person searches. Search fee: $5.00 per name. Court makes copy: $1.00 per page; same fee for self serve. Required to search: name, years to search. Civil cases indexed by defendant, plaintiff; in index files since 1906, on computer back to 1992. Fees must be prepaid before fax access is allowed. Mail turnaround time 1 day.
Criminal Records: Access: Mail, in person. Both court and visitors may perform in person searches. Search fee: $5.00 per name. Court makes copy: $1.00 per page; same fee for self serve. Required to search: name, years to search, DOB; also helpful-signed release, offense, date of offense. Criminal records in index files since 1906; on computer back to 1986. Fees must be prepaid before fax access is allowed. Mail turnaround time 1 day.
General Information: No juvenile, mental or sealed records released. Fee to fax documents is $5.00 per document and $1.00 per page. Certification fee: $5.00 per document. Payee: County Clerk. No personal checks accepted. Prepayment required.

De Witt County

County Court 307 N Gonzales, Cuero, TX 77954; phone: 361-275-3724; criminal fax: 361-275-8994; same fax for civil/probate; hours 8AM-5PM (CST). *Misdemeanor, Probate.*
Note: Probate is in a separate index at this same address.
Civil Records: Access: Phone, fax, mail, in person. Both court and visitors may perform in person searches. Search fee: $5.00 per name. Court makes copy: $1.00 per page; same fee for self serve. Required to search: name, years to search. Civil cases indexed by defendant, plaintiff. Civil records go back to 1960s; on computer back to 1998.
Criminal Records: Access: Mail, in person. Both court and visitors may perform in person searches. Search fee: $5.00 per name. Court makes copy: $1.00 per page; same fee for self serve. Required to search: name, years to search; also helpful: DOB, SSN. Criminal records go back to 1960s; on computer back to 1998.
General Information: No juvenile, mental, sealed, or adoption records released. Fee to fax documents is $1.00 per page. Certification fee: $5.00 per document. Payee: DeWitt County Clerk. Personal checks accepted. Prepayment and SASE required.

District Court PO Box 845, Cuero, TX 77954; phone: 361-275-2221; hours 8AM-5PM (CST). *Felony, Civil.*

Civil Records: Access: Mail, in person. Both court and visitors may perform in person searches. Search fee: $5.00 per name. Court makes copy: $1.00 per page. Required to search: name, years to search. Civil cases indexed by defendant, plaintiff. Mail turnaround time 1 week.

Criminal Records: Access: Mail, in person. Both court and visitors may perform in person searches. Search fee: $5.00 per name. Court makes copy: $1.00 per page. Required to search: name, years to search, DOB, SSN, signed release. Criminal records maintained on books. Mail turnaround time 1 week.

General Information: No juvenile, mental, sealed, or adoption records released. Certification fee: $1.00. Payee: DeWitt County District Clerk. Personal checks accepted. Prepayment and SASE required.

Deaf Smith County

District Court 235 E 3rd St, Rm 304, Hereford, TX 79045; phone: 806-364-3901; fax: 806-363-7007; hours 8AM-5PM (CST). *Felony, Civil.*

Civil Records: Access: Fax, mail, in person. Both court and visitors may perform in person searches. Search fee: $5.00 per name. Court makes copy: $1.00 per page. Required to search: name, years to search, DOB, SSN. Civil cases indexed by defendant, plaintiff; on computer from 2/1993; prior on microfiche from 5/15/1981. Mail turnaround time 1 day.

Criminal Records: Access: Fax, mail, in person. Both court and visitors may perform in person searches. Search fee: $5.00 per name. Court makes copy: $1.00 per page. Required to search: name, years to search; also helpful: DOB, SSN, case number. Criminal records on computer from 2/1993; prior on microfiche from 5/15/1981. Mail turnaround time 1 day.

General Information: Public terminal goes back to 2/1993. No juvenile, mental, sealed, or adoption records released. Fee to fax documents is $2.00 per page. Certification fee: $1.00. Payee: District Clerk. Personal checks accepted. Prepayment and SASE required.

County Court Deaf Smith Courthouse, 235 E 3rd, Rm 203, Hereford, TX 79045; phone: 806-363-7077; fax: 806-363-7023; hours 8AM-5PM (CST). *Misdemeanor, Civil, Probate.*

Civil Records: Access: Mail, in person. Both court and visitors may perform in person searches. Search fee: $5.00 per name. Court makes copy: $1.00 per page; same fee for self serve. Required to search: name, years to search. Civil cases indexed by defendant, plaintiff; on computer from 1989, microfiche from 1981, index books from early 1900s. Mail turnaround time 1 day.

Criminal Records: Access: Mail, in person. Both court and visitors may perform in person searches. Search fee: $5.00 per name. Court makes copy: $1.00 per page; same fee for self serve. Required to search: name, years to search. Criminal records on computer from 1993, microfiche from 1981, index books from early 1900s. Mail turnaround time 1 day, usually.

General Information: Public terminal has criminal back to 1993 and civil back to 1989. No juvenile, mental, sealed, or adoption records released. Will fax documents for the $1.00 copy fee for each page faxed. Copies for ongoing criminal investigations/prosecutions are no charge. Certification fee: $5.00 per document. Payee: County Clerk. Personal checks accepted. Prepayment required.

Delta County

District & County Court PO Box 455, Cooper, TX 75432; phone: 903-395-4400 x223; criminal phone: 903-395-4400; civil phone: 903-395-4400; probate phone: 903-395-4400; criminal fax: 903-395-4260; same fax for civil/probate; hours 8AM-5PM (CST). *Felony, Misdemeanor, Civil, Probate.*

Note: Probate is a separate index at this same address.

Civil Records: Access: Phone, mail, in person. Both court and visitors may perform in person searches. Search fee: $5.00 per name. Court makes copy: $1.00 per page; same fee for self serve. Required to search: name, years to search. Civil cases indexed by defendant, plaintiff; in index books from late 1800s. Phone searches must be pre-paid. Mail turnaround time 1 day.

Criminal Records: Access: Phone, mail, in person. Both court and visitors may perform in person searches. Search fee: $5.00 per name. Court makes copy: $1.00 per page; same fee for self serve. Required to search: name, years to search, DOB. Criminal records in index books from late 1800s. Phone searches must be prepaid. Mail turnaround time 1 day.

General Information: Public terminal has only civil records back to - record index is not complete. No juvenile, mental, sealed, or adoption records released. Fee to fax documents is $2.50 per page plus $1.00 per document. Certification fee: $5.00 per doc. Payee: County or District Clerk. Personal checks accepted. Prepayment and SASE required.

Denton County

District Court PO Box 2146, Denton, TX 76202; phone: 940-349-2200; criminal phone: 940-349-2210; civil phone: 940-349-2205; criminal fax: 940-349-2211; civil fax: 940-349-2201; hours 8AM-4:30PM (CST). *Felony, Civil.*

http://dentoncounty.com/dept/main.asp?Dept=26

Civil Records: Access: Phone, mail, fax, online, in person. Both court and visitors may perform in person searches. Search fee: $5.00 per name. Court makes copy: $1.00 per page. Self serve copy fee: $.25 per page. Required to search: name, years to search. Civil cases indexed by defendant, plaintiff; on computer from 1990, archived from 1936. Civil searches at http://justice.dentoncounty.com at no charge. Search by name or cause number. Mail turnaround time 1-2 weeks.

Criminal Records: Access: Mail, fax, online, in person. Both court and visitors may perform in person searches. Search fee: $5.00 per name. Court makes copy: $1.00 per page. Self serve copy fee: $.25 per page. Required to search: name, years to search, DOB. Criminal records on computer from 1990, archived from 1936. Criminal searches are at http://justice.dentoncounty.com at no charge. Records go back to 1994 forward. Access also includes sheriff bond and jail records. Mail turnaround time 1-2 weeks.

General Information: Public terminal goes back to 1990. No juvenile, mental, sealed, expunctions or adoption records released. Fee to fax documents is $1.00 per page. Certification fee: $1.00 per document. Payee: District Clerk. Personal checks or Visa, MC accepted. Use of credit card requires a 5% surcharge. Prepayment and SASE required.

County Court Attn: County Clerk, PO Box 2187, Denton, TX 76202-2187; phone: 940-349-2012; civil phone: 940-349-2016; probate phone: 940-349-2036; fax: 940-349-2013; hours 8AM-5PM (CST). *Misdemeanor, Civil, Probate.*

http://dentoncounty.com/deptall.asp

Civil Records: Access: Mail, in person, online. Both court and visitors may perform in person searches. Search fee: $5.00 per name. Add $1.00 per year prior to 1989. Court makes copy: $1.00 per page. Required to search: name, years to search. Civil cases indexed by defendant, plaintiff; on computer from 1989, microfiche from 1968. Online access to civil court records is free at http://justice.dentoncounty.com/CivilSearch/civfrmd.htm. Mail turnaround time 1-2 weeks.

Criminal Records: Access: Mail, in person, online. Both court and visitors may perform in person searches. Search fee: $5.00 per name. Add $1.00 per year over first 5. Court makes copy: $1.00 per page. Required to search: name, years to search, DOB. Criminal records on computer from 1989, microfiche from 1968. Online access to county criminal records is free at http://justice.dentoncounty.com/CrimSearch/crimfrmd.htm. Jail, bond, and parole records are also available at http://justice.dentoncounty.com. Search for registered sex offenders by ZIP Code at http://sheriff.dentoncounty.com/sex_offenders/default.htm. Mail turnaround time 1-2 weeks.

General Information: Public terminal goes back to 1989. No juvenile, mental, sealed, or adoption records released. Will not fax documents. Certification fee: $5.00 per doc. Payee: Denton County Clerk. Only cashiers checks and money orders accepted. Prepayment and SASE required.

Dickens County

District & County Court PO Box 120, Dickens, TX 79229; phone: 806-623-5531; fax: 806-623-5319; hours 8AM-5PM (CST). *Felony, Misdemeanor, Civil, Probate.*

Civil Records: Access: Mail, fax, phone, in person. Both court and visitors may perform in person searches. Search fee: $5.00 per name. Court makes copy: $1.00 per page; same fee for self serve. Required to search: name, years to search, DOB, SSN and signed release. Civil cases indexed by defendant, plaintiff; in index books since late 1891. Mail turnaround time 1-2 days.

Criminal Records: Access: Mail, fax, phone, in person. Both court and visitors may perform in person searches. Search fee: $5.00 per name. Court makes copy: $1.00 per page; same fee for self serve. Required to search: name, years to search; also helpful: DOB, SSN and signed release. Criminal records in index books since late 1891. Mail turnaround time 1-2 days.

General Information: No juvenile, mental, sealed or adoption records released. Will fax documents for $1.00 per page. Certification fee: $5.00. Payee: District Court. Personal checks accepted. Prepayment and SASE required.

Dimmit County

District Court 103 N 5th St, Carrizo Springs, TX 78834; phone: 830-876-4243; fax: 830-876-4200; hours 8AM-N; 1PM-5PM (CST). *Felony, Civil.*

Note: Probate is in the county clerk office.

Civil Records: Access: Mail, in person. Both court and visitors may perform in person searches. Search fee: $5.00 per name. Court makes copy: $1.00 per page; same fee for self serve. Required to search: name, years to search; also helpful: address. Civil cases indexed by defendant, plaintiff; in index books, archived from 1936. Mail turnaround time 2-3 days.

Criminal Records: Access: Mail, in person. Both court and visitors may perform in person searches. Search fee: $5.00 per name. Court makes copy: $1.00 per page; same fee for self serve. Required to search: name, years to search; also helpful: DOB, SSN. Criminal records in index books, archived from 1936. Mail turnaround time 2-3 days.

General Information: No juvenile, mental, sealed, or adoption records released. Certification fee: $1.00 per page. Payee: District Clerk. Personal checks accepted. Prepayment and SASE required.

County Court 103 N 5th, Carrizo Springs, TX 78834; phone: 830-876-4238; criminal fax: 830-876-4205; same fax for civil/probate; hours 8AM-5PM (CST). *Misdemeanor, Civil, Probate.*

Note: Probate is a separate index.

Civil Records: Access: Fax, mail, in person. Both court and visitors may perform in person searches. Search fee: $10.00 per name. Court makes copy: $1.00 per page; same fee for self serve. Required to search: name, years to search. Civil cases indexed by defendant, plaintiff; on microfiche from 1992, index books prior. Mail turnaround time 1 day.

Criminal Records: Access: Fax, mail, in person. Both court and visitors may perform in person searches. Search fee: $10.00 per name. Court makes copy: $1.00 per page; same fee for self serve. Required to search: name, years to search, signed release, DOB; also helpful: sex, SSN. Criminal records on microfiche from 1992, computerized since 1996. Mail turnaround time 1 day.

General Information: No juvenile, mental, sealed, or adoption records released. Fee to fax documents is $2.00 1st page; $1.00 each add'l. Certification fee: $5.00 per certification. Payee: County Clerk. Personal checks accepted. Prepayment and SASE required.

Donley County

District & County Court PO Drawer U, Clarendon, TX 79226; phone: 806-874-3436; fax: 806-874-3351; hours 8AM-N, 1-5PM (CST). *Felony, Misdemeanor, Civil, Probate.*

Civil Records: Access: Mail, in person. Both court and visitors may perform in person searches. Search fee: $5.00 per name. Court makes copy: $1.00 per page; same fee for self serve. Required to search: name, years to search. Civil cases indexed by defendant, plaintiff; on computer from 1991, index books from 1890s. Mail turnaround time 1 day.

Criminal Records: Access: Mail, in person. Both court and visitors may perform in person searches. Search fee: $5.00 per name. Court makes copy: $1.00 per page; same fee for self serve. Required to search: name, years to search, DOB, signed release, aliases; also helpful: SSN. Records on computer from 1991, index books from 1890s. Mail turnaround 1 day.

General Information: Public terminal goes back to 1994. No juvenile, mental, sealed, or adoption records released. Certification fee: $1.00. Payee: County Clerk. Personal checks accepted. Prepayment and SASE required.

Duval County

District Court PO Drawer 428, San Diego, TX 78384; phone: 361-279-3322 x239; hours 8AM-5PM (CST). *Felony, Civil.*

Civil Records: Access: Mail, in person. Both court and visitors may perform in person searches. Search fee: $15.00 per name. Fee is for large cases. Court makes copy: $1.00 per page. Required to search: name, years to search. Civil cases indexed by defendant, plaintiff; on index books from 1900s. Mail turnaround time 1-2 days.

Criminal Records: Access: Phone, mail, in person. Both court and visitors may perform in person searches. Search fee: $15.00 per name. Fee is for large cases. Court makes copy: $1.00 per page. Required to search: name, years to search. Criminal records not computerized, indexed in books since 1900's. Mail turnaround time 1-2 days.

General Information: No sealed, or adoption records released. Certification fee: $5.00. Payee: District Clerk. Personal checks accepted. Prepayment and SASE required.

County Court PO Box 248, San Diego, TX 78384; phone: 361-279-3322; fax: 361-279-3159; hours 8AM-N, 1-5PM (CST). *Misdemeanor, Civil, Probate.*

Civil Records: Access: Mail, in person. Both court and visitors may perform in person searches. Search fee: $10.00 per name. Court makes copy: $1.00 per page. Required to search: name, years to search. Civil cases indexed by defendant, plaintiff; in index books from 1800s, records go back to the early 1900's. Mail turnaround time 2 days.

Criminal Records: Access: Mail, in person. Both court and visitors may perform in person searches. Search fee: $10.00 per name. Court makes copy: $1.00 per page. Required to search: name, years to search, offense, date of offense. Criminal records in index books from 1800s. Mail turnaround 2 days.

General Information: No juvenile, mental, sealed, or adoption records released. Certification fee: $5.00. Payee: County Clerk. Personal checks accepted. Prepayment and SASE required.

Eastland County

District Court 100 W Main St, #206, Eastland, TX 76448; phone: 254-629-2664; fax: 254-629-6070; hours 8AM-5PM (CST). *Felony, Civil.*

Civil Records: Access: Phone, fax, mail, in person. Both court and visitors may perform in person searches. Search fee: $5.00. Court makes copy: $1.00 per page. Required to search: name, years to search. Civil cases indexed by defendant, plaintiff; on computer from 1930. Mail turnaround time 1 day.

Criminal Records: Access: Phone, fax, mail, in person. Both court and visitors may perform in person searches. Search fee: $5.00. Court makes copy: $1.00 per page. Required to search: name, years to search. Criminal records on computer from 1976, archived from 1875. Mail turnaround time 1 day.

General Information: No juvenile, mental, sealed, or adoption records released. Will fax documents to toll free line. Certification fee: $5.00 per document. Payee: District Clerk. Personal checks accepted. Prepayment and SASE required.

County Court PO Box 110, Eastland, TX 76448; phone: 254-629-1583; fax: 254-629-8125; hours 8AM-5PM (CST). *Misdemeanor, Probate.*

Note: No civil records after 1977; criminal and probate records only thereafter. Probate is in a separate index at this same address.

Criminal Records: Access: Mail, in person. Both court and visitors may perform in person searches. Search fee: $5.00 per name. Court makes copy: $1.00 per page. Required to search: name, years to search, DOB; also helpful: SSN. Signed release required if subject is a minor. Criminal records in index books from 1873. Name searches only. Mail turnaround time 1-2 days.

General Information: No juvenile, mental, sealed, or adoption records released. Will fax documents for $5.00 fee. Certification fee: $5.00 per cert. Payee: Eastland County Clerk. Personal checks accepted. Checks must have phone number & DL number on check. Prepayment required.

Ector County

District Court County Courthouse, 300 N Grant, Rm 301, Odessa, TX 79761; phone: 432-498-4290; fax: 432-498-4292; hours 8AM-5PM (CST). *Felony, Civil.*

Civil Records: Access: Phone, fax, mail, in person. Both court and visitors may perform in person searches. Search fee: $5.00 per name. Court makes copy: $.25 per page. Required to search: name, years to search. Civil cases indexed by defendant, plaintiff; on computer from 1989, index books from 1880. Mail turnaround time 2 weeks.

Criminal Records: Access: Phone, mail, in person. Both court and visitors may perform in person searches. Search fee: $5.00 per name. Court makes copy: $.25 per page. Required to search: name, years to search. Criminal records on computer from 1989, index books from 1880. Mail turnaround time 2 weeks.

General Information: Public terminal goes back to 1989. No juvenile, mental, sealed, or adoption records released. Will fax documents $2.00 per page. Certification fee: $1.00 per page includes copy fee. Payee: Ector County District Clerk. Business checks accepted. Prepayment and SASE required.

County Court PO Box 707, Odessa, TX 79760; phone: 432-498-4130; fax: 432-498-4177; hours 8AM-4:30PM (CST). *Misdemeanor, Civil, Probate.*

Civil Records: Access: Mail, in person. Both court and visitors may perform in person searches. Search fee: $5.00 per name per ten years. Court makes copy: $1.00 per page. Required to search: name, years to search. Civil cases indexed by defendant, plaintiff; on computer from 1992, index books from 1900s. Mail turnaround time 2 days.

Criminal Records: Access: Mail, in person. Both court and visitors may perform in person searches. Search fee: $5.00 per name per ten years. Court makes copy: $1.00 per page. Required to search: name, years to search; also helpful: DOB, SSN. Criminal records on computer from 1989, index books from 1900s. Mail turnaround time 2 days.

General Information: Public terminal has criminal back to 1989 and civil back to 1992. No juvenile,

mental, sealed, or adoption records released. Fee to fax documents is $2.00 per document. Certification fee: $5.00 per doc. Payee: County Clerk. Personal checks accepted. Prepayment and SASE required.

Edwards County

District & County Court PO Box 184, Rocksprings, TX 78880; phone: 830-683-2235; fax: 830-683-5376; hours 8AM-N, 1-5PM (CST). *Felony, Misdemeanor, Civil, Probate.*

Civil Records: Access: Phone, fax, mail, in person. Both court and visitors may perform in person searches. Search fee: $10.00 per name. Court makes copy: $1.00 per page. Required to search: name, years to search. Civil cases indexed by defendant, plaintiff; on computer from 1991, Real Property on computer from 1960, index books from 1885. Mail turnaround time 1 day or less.

Criminal Records: Access: Phone, fax, mail, in person. Both court and visitors may perform in person searches. Search fee: $10.00 per name. Court makes copy: $1.00 per page. Required to search: name, years to search. Criminal records on computer from 1991, index books from 1960. Mail turnaround time 1 day.

General Information: No juvenile, mental, sealed, or adoption records released. Fee to fax documents is $2.50 1st page, $.50 per page thereafter. Certification fee: $5.00. Payee: Edwards County Clerk. Personal checks accepted. Prepayment and SASE required.

El Paso County

District Court 500 E San Antonio, Rm 103, El Paso, TX 79901; phone: 915-546-2021; criminal phone: 915-834-8255; civil phone: 915-834-8256; fax: 915-546-8139; hours 8AM-4:45PM (MST). *Felony, Civil.*

www.co.el-paso.tx.us/districtclerk/

Civil Records: Access: Mail, in person, online. Both court and visitors may perform in person searches. Search fee: $6.00 per name. Fee is per 10 year period. Court makes copy: $.25 per page. Required to search: name, years to search. Civil cases indexed by defendant, plaintiff; on computer from 1976, microfiche from 1971, index books from 1800s. Online access to civil court records is free at www.epcounty.com/search.htm. Also, access is at www.idocket.com; registration and password required; online civil records go back to 12/31/2000. Mail turnaround time 1-3 days.

Criminal Records: Access: Mail, in person, online. Both court and visitors may perform in person searches. Search fee: $6.00 per name. Fee is per 10 year period. Court makes copy: $.25 per page. Required to search: name, years to search, DOB, signed release; also helpful: sex. Criminal records on computer from 1986, microfiche from 1971, index books from 1800s. Online access to criminal court records is free at www.epcounty.com/search.htm. Also, online access is at www.idocket.com; registration and password required; online records go back to 6/1/2001. Mail turnaround time 1-3 days.

General Information: Public terminal has criminal back to - not known and civil back to 2002. No juvenile, mental, sealed, or adoption records released. Certification fee: $1.00. Payee: District Clerk. Business checks accepted. Visa/MC accepted, but only by mail or phone. Prepayment and SASE required.

County Court 500 E San Antonio St, Rm 105, El Paso, TX 79901; phone: 915-546-2072; hours 8AM-4:45PM (MST). *Misdemeanor, Civil.*

www.co.el-paso.tx.us

Civil Records: Access: Mail, fax, in person, online. Both court and visitors may perform in person searches. Search fee: $5.00 per name. Court makes copy: $1.00 per page. Required to search: name, years to search. Civil cases indexed by defendant, plaintiff; on computer from 1989, on microfiche and archived from 1952. Online access to civil court records is free at www.co.el-paso.tx.us/search.htm. Also, search vital records and recordings. Also, access is through www.idocket.com; registration and password required. Civil and probate records go back to 12/31/1986. Mail turnaround time up to 1 week.

Criminal Records: Access: Phone, mail, fax, in person, online. Both court and visitors may perform in person searches. Search fee: $5.00 per name. Court makes copy: $1.00 per page. Required to search: name, years to search, DOB, SSN. Criminal records computerized since 1989. Online access to misdemeanor criminal records is the same as civil. Mail turnaround time up to 1 week.

General Information: Public terminal goes back to 1989. No juvenile, mental, sealed, or adoption records released. Certification fee: $5.00 per document. Payee: County Clerk. Personal checks or credit cards accepted. Prepayment and SASE required.

Probate Court 500 E San Antonio, Rm 703, County Courthouse, El Paso, TX 79901; phone: 915-546-2163; fax: 915-533-4448; hours 8AM-Noon,1-5PM (MST). *Probate.*

Note: Access probate records at through www.idocket.com; registration and password required. Records go back to 12/31/1986.

Ellis County

District Court 305 E Franklin, Waxahachie, TX 75165; phone: 972-825-5091; fax: 972-825-5010; hours 8AM-5PM (CST). *Felony, Civil.*

Civil Records: Access: Mail, in person. Both court and visitors may perform in person searches. Search fee: $5.00 per name. Court makes copy: $.50 per page. Required to search: name, years to search. Civil cases indexed by defendant, plaintiff; on computer from 1992, index books from 1800s. Mail turnaround time 1 week.

Criminal Records: Access: Mail, in person. Both court and visitors may perform in person searches. Search fee: $5.00 per name. Court makes copy: $.50 per page. Required to search: name, years to search, DOB, offense. Criminal records on computer from 1992, index books from 1800s. Mail turnaround time 1 week.

General Information: Public terminal goes back to 1992. No juvenile, mental, sealed, or adoption records released. Certification fee: $1.00 per page. Payee: District Clerk's Office. Only cashiers checks and money orders accepted. Prepayment and SASE required.

County Court PO Box 250, Waxahachie, TX 75168; phone: 972-923-5070; criminal phone: 972-923-5078; civil phone: 972-923-5083; probate phone: 972-923-5083; criminal fax: 972-923-5075; same fax for civil/probate; hours 8AM-4:30PM (CST). *Misdemeanor, Civil, Probate.*

www.co.ellis.tx.us

Civil Records: Access: Mail, in person. Both court and visitors may perform in person searches. Search fee: $5.00 per name. Fee is per 5 year period. Court makes copy: $1.00 per page; same fee for self serve. Required to search: name, years to search. Civil cases indexed by defendant, plaintiff; on computer go back to 1995. Prior to computer records go back to 1969. Mail turnaround time 1-5 days.

Criminal Records: Access: Mail, in person. Both court and visitors may perform in person searches. Search fee: $5.00 per name. Fee is per 5 year period. Court makes copy: $1.00 per page; same fee for self serve. Required to search: name, years to search, DOB, SSN. Criminal records on computer since 1992, index books from 1959. Mail turnaround time 1-5 days.

General Information: Public terminal goes back to 1992. No juvenile, mental, sealed, or adoption records released. Will not fax documents. Certification fee: $5.00 per document. Payee: Ellis County Clerk. Personal checks accepted. Prepayment and SASE required.

Erath County

District Court 112 W College, Courthouse Annex, Stephenville, TX 76401; phone: 254-965-1486; fax: 254-965-7156; hours 8AM-5PM (CST). *Felony, Civil.*

Note: District Court Phone # is 254-965-1485; Fax is 254-965-4287

Civil Records: Access: Mail, fax, in person. Both court and visitors may perform in person searches. Search fee: $5.00 per name. Fee is per name per search. Court makes copy: $1.00 per page. Required to search: name, years to search. Civil cases indexed by defendant, plaintiff. Limited civil records on computer last 10 years, in person must be done using docket books. Mail turnaround time 1-2 days.

Criminal Records: Access: Mail, fax, in person. Both court and visitors may perform in person searches. Search fee: $5.00 per name. Court makes copy: $1.00 per page. Required to search: name, years to search, DOB; also helpful: SSN. Limited criminal records on computer last 10 years, in person must be done using docket books. Mail turnaround time 1-2 days.

General Information: Public terminal goes back to 5 years. No juvenile, mental, sealed, or adoption records released. Fee to fax documents is $1.00 per page. Certification fee: $5.00. Payee: District Clerk. Personal checks accepted. Prepayment and SASE required.

County Court Erath County Courthouse, Stephenville, TX 76401; phone: 254-965-1482; criminal phone: 254-965-1407; civil phone: 254-965-1428; probate phone: 254-965-1428; criminal fax: 254-965-5732; same fax for civil/probate; hours 8AM-4PM (CST). *Misdemeanor, Civil, Probate.*

Note: Probate is a separate index at this same address.

Civil Records: Access: Mail, in person. Both court and visitors may perform in person searches. Search fee: $5.00 per name. Court makes copy: $1.00 per page; same fee for self serve. Required to search: name, years to search. Civil cases indexed by defendant, plaintiff; on computer back to 1993, index books since 1970. Mail turnaround time 1 week.

Criminal Records: Access: Mail, in person. Both court and visitors may perform in person searches. Search fee: $10.00 per name. Court makes copy: $1.00 per page; same fee for self serve. Required to search: name, years to search, DOB. Criminal records on computer back to 1993, index books from 1960. Mail turnaround time 1 week.

General Information: Public terminal goes back to 1993. No juvenile, mental, sealed, or adoption records released. Certification fee: $5.00 per document. Payee: County Clerk. Personal checks accepted. Prepayment and SASE required.

Falls County

District Court PO Box 75, 125 Bridge St, Rm 301, Marlin, TX 76661; phone: 254-883-1419; hours 8AM-N, 1-4:30PM (CST). *Felony, Civil.*

Note: Mail requests to PO Box 229. In care of the District Clerk.

Civil Records: Access: Mail, in person. Both court and visitors may perform in person searches. Search fee: $5.00 per name. Court makes copy: $1.00 per page. Required to search: name, years to search. Civil cases indexed by defendant, plaintiff. Overall records go back to 1850's. Computerized records go back to 1998. Mail turnaround time 1-5 days.

Criminal Records: Access: Mail, in person. Both court and visitors may perform in person searches. Search fee: $5.00 per name. Court makes copy: $1.00 per page. Required to search: name, years to search; also helpful: DOB. Criminal records in index books. Mail turnaround time 1-5 days.

General Information: Public terminal has only civil records back to 1998. No juvenile, mental, sealed, child support or adoption records released. No certification fee. Payee: District Clerk. Personal checks accepted. Prepayment and SASE required.

County Court PO Box 458, Marlin, TX 76661; phone: 254-883-1408; fax: 254-883-1406; hours 8AM-5PM (CST). *Misdemeanor, Civil, Probate.*

Civil Records: Access: Phone, mail, in person. Both court and visitors may perform in person searches. Search fee: $5.00 per name. Court makes copy: $1.00 per page. Required to search: name, years to search. Civil cases indexed by defendant, plaintiff; in index books from 1985. Phone search only if fee prepaid. Mail turnaround time 1 day.

Criminal Records: Access: Phone, mail, in person. Both court and visitors may perform in person searches. Search fee: $5.00 per name. Court makes copy: $1.00 per page. Required to search: name, years to search, DOB, SSN. Criminal records in index books from 1985. Phone search only if fee is prepaid. Mail turnaround time 1 day.

General Information: No juvenile, mental, sealed, or adoption records released. Certification fee: $5.00 per instrument. Payee: County Clerk. Local personal and business checks accepted. Prepayment and SASE required.

Fannin County

District Court Fannin County Courthouse, #201, Bonham, TX 75418; phone: 903-583-7459; fax: 903-640-1826; hours 9AM-N, 1-4PM (CST). *Felony, Civil.*

Civil Records: Access: Fax, mail, in person. Both court and visitors may perform in person searches. Search fee: $5.00 per name. Court makes copy: $1.00 per page. Required to search: name, years to search. Civil cases indexed by defendant, plaintiff; in index books, archived from 1865. Mail turnaround time 2 days.

Criminal Records: Access: Fax, mail, in person. Both court and visitors may perform in person searches. Search fee: $5.00 per name. Fee is for felonies only. Court makes copy: $1.00 per page. Required to search: name, years to search, address, DOB, SSN. Criminal records on computer from 1985, books from 1975, archived from 1865. Mail turnaround time 2 days.

General Information: No juvenile, mental, sealed, or adoption records released. No fee to fax documents. Fax available to 800 numbers only. Certification fee: $2.00. Payee: District Clerk, Fannin County. Personal checks accepted. Prepayment and SASE required.

County Court County Courthouse, 101 E Sam Rayburn, Bonham, TX 75418; phone: 903-583-7486; criminal phone: 903-583-7488; civil phone: 903-640-2008; probate phone: 903-640-2008; hours 8AM-5PM (CST). *Misdemeanor, Civil, Probate.*

Note: Address to Ste 103 for criminal and Ste 106 for civil or probate.

Civil Records: Access: Mail, in person. Both court and visitors may perform in person searches. Search fee: $5.00 per name. Court makes copy: $1.00 per page. Required to search: name, years to search. Civil cases indexed by defendant, plaintiff; in index books. Mail turnaround time 1 day.

Criminal Records: Access: Mail, in person. Both court and visitors may perform in person searches. Search fee: $5.00 per name. Court makes copy: $1.00 per page. Required to search: name, years to search, DOB; also helpful-SSN. Criminal records on computer back to 1979; prior on index books. Mail turnaround time 1 day.

General Information: No juvenile, mental, sealed, or adoption records released. Certification fee: $5.00. Payee: County Clerk. Personal checks accepted if local. Prepayment and SASE required.

Fayette County

District Court Fayette County Courthouse, 151 N Washington, La Grange, TX 78945; phone: 979-968-3548; fax: 979-968-2618; hours 8AM-5PM (CST). *Felony, Civil.*

www.cvtv.net/~tx155district/

Civil Records: Access: Mail, in person. Both court and visitors may perform in person searches. Search fee: $5.00 per name. Court makes copy: $1.00

per page. Required to search: name, years to search. Civil cases indexed by defendant, plaintiff; in index books, on computer since 1992. Mail turnaround time 2-3 days.

Criminal Records: Access: Mail, in person. Both court and visitors may perform in person searches. Search fee: $5.00 per name. Court makes copy: $1.00 per page. Required to search: name, years to search. Criminal records in index books, on computer since 1990. Mail turnaround time 2-3 days.

General Information: Public terminal has criminal back to 1987 and civil back to 1990. No juvenile, mental, sealed, or adoption records released. Will fax documents for $5.00 per page. Certification fee: $2.00. Payee: Fayette County District Clerk. Personal checks accepted. Prepayment and SASE required.

County Court PO Box 59, La Grange, TX 78945; phone: 979-968-3251; fax: 979-968-8531; hours 8AM-5PM (CST). *Misdemeanor, Civil, Probate.*

Civil Records: Access: Mail, in person. Both court and visitors may perform in person searches. Search fee: $5.00 per name. Court makes copy: $1.00 per page. Required to search: name, years to search. Civil cases indexed by defendant, plaintiff; in index books, archived from 1970. Mail turnaround time 1 day.

Criminal Records: Access: Mail, in person. Both court and visitors may perform in person searches. Search fee: $5.00 per name. Court makes copy: $1.00 per page. Required to search: name, years to search. Criminal records on computer from 1980, index books prior. Mail turnaround time 1 day.

General Information: No juvenile, mental, sealed, or adoption records released. Will fax documents for double the fee, paid in advance. Certification fee: $5.00. Payee: County Clerk. Personal checks accepted. Prepayment and SASE required.

Fisher County

32nd District Court PO Box 88, Roby, TX 79543; phone: 325-776-2279; fax: 325-776-3253; hours 8AM-5PM (CST). *Felony, Civil.*

Civil Records: Access: Mail, fax, in person. Both court and visitors may perform in person searches. Search fee: $5.00 per name. Court makes copy: $.50 per page; same fee for self serve. Required to search: name, years to search; also helpful: address. Civil cases indexed by defendant, plaintiff; in index books from 1886. Mail turnaround time 1-2 days.

Criminal Records: Access: Mail, fax, in person. Both court and visitors may perform in person searches. Search fee: $5.00 per name. Court makes copy: $.50 per page; same fee for self serve. Required to search: name, years to search, signed release; also helpful: address, DOB. Criminal records in index books from 1886. Mail turnaround time 1-2 days.

General Information: No juvenile, mental, sealed, or adoption records released. Fee to fax documents is $1.00 per page. Certification fee: $1.00 per page. Payee: District Clerk. Business checks accepted. Prepayment and SASE required.

County Court Box 368, Roby, TX 79543-0368; phone: 325-776-2401; fax: 325-776-3274; hours 8AM-N, 1-5PM (CST). *Misdemeanor, Civil, Probate.*

Civil Records: Access: Mail, in person. Both court and visitors may perform in person searches. Search fee: $5.00 per name. Self serve copy fee: $1.00 per page. Required to search: name, years to search. Civil cases indexed by defendant, plaintiff; on computer from 1994 index books from 1880. Mail turnaround time 1 day.

Criminal Records: Access: Mail, in person. Both court and visitors may perform in person searches. Search fee: $5.00 per name. Self serve copy fee: $1.00 per page. Required to search: name, years to search, signed release. Records on computer from 1994, index books from 1886. Mail turnaround time 1 day.

General Information: No juvenile, mental, sealed, or adoption records released. Will not fax documents. Certification fee: $5.00 per document. Payee: Fisher County Clerk. Personal checks accepted. Prepayment and SASE required.

Floyd County

District Court PO Box 67, Floydada, TX 79235; phone: 806-983-4923; fax: 806-983-4983; hours 8:30AM-N, 1-4:45PM (CST). *Felony, Civil.*

Civil Records: Access: Phone, mail, in person. Both court and visitors may perform in person searches. Search fee: $5.00 per name. Court makes copy: $1.00 1st page, $.25 each addl. Required to search: name, years to search. Civil cases indexed by defendant, plaintiff; in index books from early 1891. Mail turnaround time 1 day.

Criminal Records: Access: Mail, in person. Both court and visitors may perform in person searches. Search fee: $5.00 per name. Court makes copy: $1.00 1st page, $.25 each addl. Required to search: name, years to search. Criminal records in index books from early 1891. Mail turnaround time 1 day.

General Information: No juvenile, mental, sealed, or adoption records released. Certification fee: $1.00. Payee: District Clerk. Personal checks accepted. Prepayment and SASE required.

County Court Courthouse, Rm 101, Main St, Floydada, TX 79235; phone: 806-983-4900; fax: 806-983-4926; hours 8:30AM-N, 1-5PM (CST). *Misdemeanor, Civil, Probate.*

Civil Records: Access: Phone, mail, in person. Both court and visitors may perform in person searches. Search fee: $10.00 per name. Court makes copy: $1.00 per page; same fee for self serve. Required to search: name, years to search. Civil cases indexed by defendant, plaintiff; in index books from 1890. Mail turnaround time 2-4 days.

Criminal Records: Access: Phone, mail, in person. Both court and visitors may perform in person searches. Search fee: $10.00 per name. Court makes copy: $1.00 per page; same fee for self serve. Required to search: name, years to search, DOB. Criminal records in index books from 1890. Mail turnaround time 1-5 days.

General Information: No juvenile, mental, sealed, or adoption records released. Will fax documents for $1.00 per page. Certification fee: $5.00. Payee: County Clerk. Personal checks accepted. Prepayment required.

Foard County

District & County Court PO Box 539, Crowell, TX 79227; phone: 940-684-1365; fax: 940-684-1918; hours 9AM-4:30PM (CST). *Felony, Misdemeanor, Civil, Probate.*

Civil Records: Access: Mail, in person. Both court and visitors may perform in person searches. Search fee: $10.00 per name. Court makes copy: $1.00 per page; same fee for self serve. Required to search: name, years to search. Civil cases indexed by defendant, plaintiff. Civil records go back to 1908, civil records in index books from 1910; on computer from 1989. Mail turnaround time varies.

Criminal Records: Access: Mail, in person. Both court and visitors may perform in person searches. Search fee: $10.00 per name. Court makes copy: $1.00 per page; same fee for self serve. Required to search: name, years to search, DOB. Criminal records go back to 1908, in index books from 1910; on computer from 1989. Mail turnaround varies.

General Information: No juvenile, mental, sealed, or adoption records released. Fee to fax documents is $2.50 1st page, $.25 per page each add'l. Certification fee: $5.00. Payee: District or County Clerk. Personal checks accepted. Prepayment and SASE required.

Fort Bend County

District Court 301 Jackson, Richmond, TX 77469; phone: 281-341-4515; criminal phone: 281-341-4542; civil phone: 281-341-4562; fax: 281-341-4519; hours 8AM-5PM (CST). *Felony, Civil.* www.co.fort-bend.tx.us/

Note: Physical court location is 401 Jackson.

Civil Records: Access: Phone, mail, online, in person. Both court and visitors may perform in person searches. Search fee: $5.00 per name. Court makes copy: $.50 per page. Include $1.00 for postage. Fee for microfilm copies $.50 per page. Self serve copy fee: $.50 per page. Required to search: name, years to search. Civil cases indexed by defendant, plaintiff; on computer from 1991, index books from early 1900s. Search for free at http://courtcn.co.fort-bend.tx.us/. Records go back to 9/2000; no DOBs. Mail turnaround time 7 to 14 days.

Criminal Records: Access: Mail, online, in person. Both court and visitors may perform in person searches. Search fee: $5.00 per name. Court makes copy: $.50 per page. Include $1.00 for postage. Fee for microfilm copies $.50 per page. Self serve copy fee: $.50 per page. Required to search: name, years to search, DOB, SSN. Criminal records on computer from 1981, index books from early 1900s. Criminal records are on the same system as civil records. Mail turnaround time 2-3 weeks.

General Information: Public terminal has criminal back to 1982 and civil back to 1991. (Terminal located at 401 Jackson, Rm 100, Richmond.) No juvenile, mental, sealed, termination or adoption records released. Certification fee: $.50 per page. Certification included in copy fee. Payee: District Clerk. No out of state personal checks accepted. For legal ease account info call 281-341-4508. Prepayment and SASE required.

County Court Attn: Clerk, 301 Jackson St, #101, Richmond, TX 77469; phone: 281-341-8685; criminal fax: 281-341-8681; civil fax: 281-341-4520; probate fax: 281-341-4520; hours 8AM-4PM (CST). *Misdemeanor, Civil, Probate, Juvenile.* www.co.fort-bend.tx.us

Civil Records: Access: Mail, online, in person. Both court and visitors may perform in person searches. Search fee: $10.00 per name. Search fee is for each type record to be searched. Court makes copy: $1.00 per page. Required to search: name, years to search. Civil cases indexed by defendant, plaintiff; on computer from 1984, also 1984-present optical imaged. Online access to the civil records index free at www.co.fort-bend.tx.us/Admin_of_Justice/County_Clerk/index _info_research.htm. Includes Probate records index online. Mail turnaround time 1-2 days.

Criminal Records: Access: Mail, online, in person. Both court and visitors may perform in person searches. Search fee: $10.00 per name. A search fee for each type record to be searched required. Court makes copy: $1.00 per page. Required to search: name, years to search, DOB. Criminal records on computer from 1983, also 1983 to present optical imaged. Online access to the criminal index is the same as civil. Mail turnaround time 1-2 days.

General Information: Public terminal has only civil records back to 1/1998. No juvenile, mental, sealed, or adoption records released. Fee to fax documents is $1.00 per page. Certification fee: $5.00 per document. Payee: Ft Bend County Clerk. Personal checks or Visa, MC accepted. Prepayment required.

Franklin County

District Court PO Box 750, Mount Vernon, TX 75457; phone: 903-537-4786; fax: 903-537-4786; hours 8AM-5PM (CST). *Felony, Civil.*

Civil Records: Access: Mail, in person. Both court and visitors may perform in person searches. Search fee: $5.00 per name. Court makes copy: $1.00 per page; same fee for self serve. Required to search: name, years to search. Civil cases indexed by defendant, plaintiff; on computer from 1987, on microfiche from 1986, index books from 1800s. Mail turnaround time 1 day.

Criminal Records: Access: Mail, in person. Both court and visitors may perform in person searches. Search fee: $5.00 per name. Court makes copy: $1.00 per page; same fee for self serve. Required to search: name, years to search; also helpful: DOB, SSN. Criminal records on computer from 1987, on microfiche from 1986, index books from 1800s. Mail turnaround time 1 day.

General Information: No juvenile, mental, sealed, or adoption records released: Will fax documents for $1.00 per page. Certification fee: $5.00. Payee: District Clerk. Personal checks accepted. Prepayment and SASE required.

County Court PO Box 68, Mount Vernon, TX 75457; phone: 903-537-4252 x6; criminal fax: 903-537-4252; same fax for civil/probate; hours 8AM-5PM (CST). *Misdemeanor, Civil, Probate.*

Civil Records: Access: Mail, fax, in person. Both court and visitors may perform in person searches. Search fee: $5.00 per name. Court makes copy: $1.00 per page; same fee for self serve. Required to search: name, years to search. Civil cases indexed by defendant, plaintiff; on computer from 1993, index books from 1847. Mail turnaround time 1 week.

Criminal Records: Access: Mail, fax, in person. Both court and visitors may perform in person searches. Search fee: $5.00 per name. Court makes copy: $1.00 per page; same fee for self serve. Required to search: name, years to search, DOB and SSN. Criminal records on computer from 1993, index books from 1847. Mail turnaround time 1 week.

General Information: Public terminal goes back to 1993. No juvenile, mental, sealed, or adoption records released. Fee to fax documents is $1.00 per page. Certification fee: $5.00 per document. Payee: County Clerk. Personal checks accepted if from Texas only. Prepayment and SASE required.

Freestone County

District Court PO Box 722, Fairfield, TX 75840; phone: 903-389-2534; hours 8AM-5PM (CST). *Felony, Civil.*

Civil Records: Access: Phone, mail, in person. Both court and visitors may perform in person searches. Search fee: $5.00 per name. Court makes copy: $1.00 per page. Required to search: name, years to search. Civil cases indexed by defendant, plaintiff; in index books from 1830s. Mail turnaround time 1 day.

Criminal Records: Access: Phone, mail, in person. Both court and visitors may perform in person searches. Search fee: $5.00 per name. Court makes copy: $1.00 per page. Required to search: name, years to search. Criminal records in index books from 1830s. Mail turnaround time 1 day.

General Information: No juvenile, mental, sealed, or adoption records released. Certification fee: $1.00 per page. Payee: District Clerk. Personal checks accepted. Prepayment and SASE required.

County Court PO Box 1010, Fairfield, TX 75840; phone: 903-389-2635; hours 8AM-5PM (CST). *Misdemeanor, Civil, Probate.*

Civil Records: Access: In person only. Visitors must perform in person searches themselves. Court makes copy: $1.00 per page. Required to search: name, years to search. Civil cases indexed by defendant, plaintiff; in index books from 1967.

Criminal Records: Access: Mail, in person. Both court and visitors may perform in person searches. Search fee: $5.00 per name. Court makes copy: $1.00 per page. Required to search: name, years to search. Criminal records in index books from 1967. Mail turnaround time 2 days.

General Information: No juvenile, mental, sealed, or adoption records released. Certification fee: $5.00 per document. Payee: Freestone County Clerk. Personal checks accepted. Prepayment and SASE required.

Frio County

District Court 500 E San Antonio, Box 8, Pearsall, TX 78061; phone: 830-334-8073; fax: 830-334-0047; hours 8AM-5PM (CST). *Felony, Civil.*

Civil Records: Access: Mail, in person. Both court and visitors may perform in person searches. Search fee: $10.00 per name. Court makes copy: $1.00 per page; same fee for self serve. Required to search: name, years to search; also helpful: address. Civil cases indexed by defendant, plaintiff; in index books from 1948. Mail turnaround time 2-3 days.

Criminal Records: Access: Mail, in person. Both court and visitors may perform in person searches. Search fee: $10.00 per name. Court makes copy: $1.00 per page; same fee for self serve. Required to search: name, years to search, DOB; also helpful: address. Criminal records in index books from 1950. Mail turnaround time 2-3 days.

General Information: No juvenile, mental, sealed, or adoption records released. Fee to fax documents is $2.00 per page. Certification fee: $1.00 per page includes copy fee. Payee: District Clerk. Business checks accepted. Prepayment and SASE required.

County Court 500 E San Antonio St, #6, Pearsall, TX 78061; phone: 830-334-2214; criminal fax: 830-334-0021; same fax for civil/probate; hours 8AM-5PM (CST). *Misdemeanor, Civil, Probate.*

Civil Records: Access: Fax, mail, in person. Both court and visitors may perform in person searches. Search fee: $10.00 per name. Court makes copy: $1.00 per page; same fee for self serve. Required to search: name, years to search. Civil cases indexed by defendant, plaintiff. Civil records go back to 1800s, civil records in index books from 1876, no computerized records. Mail turnaround time 2-4 days.

Criminal Records: Access: Fax, mail, in person. Both court and visitors may perform in person searches. Search fee: $10.00 per name. Court makes copy: $1.00 per page; same fee for self serve. Required to search: name, years to search. Criminal records go back to 1800s, criminal records in index books from 1876; no computerized records. Mail turnaround time 2-4 days.

General Information: No juvenile, mental, sealed, or adoption records released. Will fax documents $2.00 per page. Certification fee: $5.00 per certificate. Payee: County Clerk. Personal checks accepted. Prepayment and SASE required.

Gaines County

District Court 101 S Main, Rm 213, Seminole, TX 79360; phone: 432-758-4013; fax: 432-758-4036; hours 8AM-N, 1-5PM (CST). *Felony, Civil.*

Civil Records: Access: Phone, mail, in person. Only the court performs in person searches; visitors may not. Search fee: $5.00 per name. Court makes copy: $1.00 per page; same fee for self serve. Required to search: name, years to search. Civil cases indexed by defendant, plaintiff; on computer from 1980, index books from 1900s. Mail turnaround time 1 day.

Criminal Records: Access: Phone, mail, in person. Only the court performs in person searches; visitors may not. Search fee: $5.00 per name. Court makes copy: $1.00 per page; same fee for self serve. Required to search: name, years to search. Criminal records on computer from 1980, index books from 1900s. Mail turnaround time 1 day.

General Information: No juvenile, mental, sealed, or adoption records released. Will fax documents to local or toll free line. Certification fee: $5.00 per certification. Payee: District Clerk. Personal checks accepted. Prepayment and SASE required.

County Court 101 S Main, Rm 107, Seminole, TX 79360; phone: 432-758-4003; fax: 432-758-1442; hours 8AM-5PM (CST). *Misdemeanor, Civil, Probate.*

Civil Records: Access: Mail, in person. Both court and visitors may perform in person searches. No search fee. Court makes copy: $1.00 per page; same fee for self serve. Required to search: name, years to search. Civil cases indexed by defendant, plaintiff. Civil records available from 1800s, computerized since 1991. Mail turnaround time 1 day.

Criminal Records: Access: Mail, in person. Both court and visitors may perform in person searches. No search fee. Court makes copy: $1.00 per page; same fee for self serve. Required to search: name, years to search. Criminal records available from 1800s, computerized since 1991. Probate records may be accessed with same criteria as civil records. Mail turnaround time 1 day.

General Information: Public terminal goes back to 1991. No juvenile, mental, sealed, or adoption records released. Will fax documents for $1.00 per page plus $2.00 call. Certification fee: $5.00. Payee: County Clerk. Personal checks accepted. Prepayment and SASE required.

Galveston County

District Court 722 Moody St, Rm 404, Galveston, TX 77550; phone: 409-766-2424; fax: 409-766-2292; hours 8AM-5PM (CST). *Felony, Civil.*
www.co.galveston.tx.us/District_Courts/default.htm

Civil Records: Access: Fax, mail, in person. Search fee: $5.00 per name. Court makes copy: $1.00 per page; over 15 pages is $.25 each add'l. Required to search: name, years to search. Civil cases indexed by defendant, plaintiff; on computer from 1984, on microfiche from 1982, archived from 1849. Online access to Judge's daily calendars is free at the website. Note: Fax access is only allowed with prepaid accounts. Mail turnaround time 2-5 days.

Criminal Records: Access: Fax, mail, in person. Both court and visitors may perform in person searches. Search fee: $5.00 per name. Court makes copy: $1.00 per page; over 15 pages is $.25 each add'l. Required to search: name, years to search, DOB. Criminal records on computer from 1984, on microfiche from 1982, archived from 1849. Online access to Judge's daily calendars is free at the website. Note: There is a $1.50 per page for incoming faxes. Mail turnaround time 2-5 days.

General Information: Public use terminal available. No juvenile, mental, sealed, or adoption records released. Will fax documents long distance for $5.00 fax fee plus $1.50 per page. Local fax is simply $1.50 per page. Certification fee: $2.00 for an affidavit. Payee: District Clerk. Personal checks accepted. Prepayment and SASE required.

County Court PO Box 2450, Galveston, TX 77553-2450; phone: 409-766-2200; criminal phone: 409-770-5112; civil phone: 409-766-2203; probate phone: 409-766-2202; hours 8AM-5PM (CST). *Misdemeanor, Civil, Probate.*
www.co.galveston.tx.us/County_Courts/

Civil Records: Access: Mail, in person, online. Both court and visitors may perform in person searches. Search fee: $5.00 per name. Court makes copy: $1.00 per page. Required to search: name, years to search; DOB or SSN helpful. Civil cases indexed by defendant, plaintiff; on computer from 1984, index books from 1947. Online access is at http://ccweb.co.galveston.tx.us. Index search if free; records go back to 1983 generally. Probate records go back to 1987. Access to the GCNET remote online service has been suspended. Mail turnaround time 1-2 days.

Criminal Records: Access: Mail, in person, online. Both court and visitors may perform in person searches. Search fee: $5.00 per name. Court makes copy: $1.00 per page. Required to search: name, years to search, DOB; also helpful: SSN. Criminal records on computer from 1984, index books from 1947. Online access is at http://ccweb.co.galveston.tx.us. Index search if free; records go back to 1983 generally. Mail turnaround time 1-2 days.

General Information: Public terminal goes back to 1983. No juvenile, mental, sealed, or adoption records released. Certification fee: $5.00 per document. Payee: County Clerk. Prepayment and SASE required.

Garza County

District & County Court PO Box 366, Post, TX 79356; phone: 806-495-4430; fax: 806-495-4431; hours 8AM-N,1-5PM (CST). *Felony, Misdemeanor, Civil, Probate.*

Civil Records: Access: Mail, in person. Both court and visitors may perform in person searches. Search fee: $5.00 per name. Court makes copy: $1.00 per page. Required to search: name, years to search. Civil cases indexed by defendant, plaintiff; on index books. Mail turnaround time 2-3 days.

Criminal Records: Access: Mail, in person. Both court and visitors may perform in person searches. Search fee: $5.00 per name. Court makes copy: $1.00 per page. Required to search: name, years to search, DOB. Criminal records on index books. Mail turnaround time 2-3 days.

General Information: Fee to fax documents is $4.00 per document. Certification fee: $5.00. Payee: District or County Clerk. Personal checks accepted. Prepayment required.

Gillespie County

District Court 101 W Main, Rm 204, Fredericksburg, TX 78624; phone: 830-997-6517; hours Public hours 8AM-5PM (CST). *Felony, Civil.*

Civil Records: Access: Mail, in person. Both court and visitors may perform in person searches. Search fee: $5.00 per name. Court makes copy: $1.00 for 1st page, $.25 each add'l. Required to search: name, years to search. Civil cases indexed by defendant, plaintiff; in index books from 1800s. Index #1 from 1800s-1927, Index #2 from 1927-1988, Index #3 from 1989-present. Mail turnaround time 1-2 days.

Criminal Records: Access: Mail, in person. Both court and visitors may perform in person searches. Search fee: $5.00 per name. Court makes copy: $1.00 for 1st page, $.25 each add'l. Required to search: name, years to search; also helpful: DOB, SSN. Criminal records in index books from 1800s. Index #1 from 1800s-1927, Index #2 from 1927-1988, Index #3 from 1989-present. Mail turnaround time 1-2 days.

General Information: No juvenile, mental, sealed, or adoption records released. Will fax documents. Certification fee: $1.00 per page includes copy fee. Payee: Gillespie County District Clerk. Personal checks accepted. Prepayment and SASE required.

County Court 101 W Main, #13, Fredericksburg, TX 78624; phone: 830-997-6515; criminal fax: 830-997-9958; same fax for civil/probate; hours 8AM-4PM (CST). *Misdemeanor, Civil, Probate.*

Civil Records: Access: Mail, in person. Both court and visitors may perform in person searches. Search fee: $5.00 per name. Court makes copy: $1.00 per page. Required to search: name, years to search; also helpful: address. Civil cases indexed by defendant, plaintiff; on computer from 1988, on microfiche from 1990, index books from 1900s. Mail turnaround time 1-2 days.

Criminal Records: Access: Mail, in person. Both court and visitors may perform in person searches. Search fee: $5.00 per name. Court makes copy: $1.00 per page. Required to search: name, years to search, aliases; also helpful: DOB, SSN. Criminal records on computer from 1987, on microfiche from 1990, index books from 1900s. Mail turnaround time 1-2 days.

General Information: Public terminal goes back to 1989. No juvenile, mental, sealed, or adoption record released. Will fax documents for no add'l fee. Certification fee: $10.00 per document includes copies. Payee: Mary Lynn Rusche County Clerk. No out-of-town personal checks accepted. Prepayment and SASE required.

Glasscock County

District & County Court PO Box 190, 117 E Currie, Garden City, TX 79739; phone: 432-354-2371; fax: 432-354-2616; hours 8AM-4PM (CST). *Felony, Misdemeanor, Civil, Probate.*

Civil Records: Access: Mail, in person. Both court and visitors may perform in person searches. Search fee: $10.00 per name. Court makes copy: $1.00 per page. Required to search: name, years to search. Civil cases indexed by defendant, plaintiff; in index books from 1893. Mail turnaround time 2 days.

Criminal Records: Access: Mail, in person. Both court and visitors may perform in person searches. Search fee: $10.00 per name. Court makes copy: $1.00 per page. Required to search: name, years to search, DOB. Criminal records in index books from 1893. Mail turnaround time 2 days.

General Information: No juvenile, mental, or adoption records released. Will fax documents for $2.00 per page. Certification fee: $5.00 per document. Payee: District or County Clerk. Personal checks accepted. Prepayment and SASE required.

Goliad County

District & County Court PO Box 50 (127 N Courthouse Sq), Goliad, TX 77963; phone: 361-645-3294; criminal fax: 361-645-3858; same fax for civil/probate; hours 8AM-5PM, closed 1 hour at noon (CST). *Felony, Misdemeanor, Civil, Probate.*

Civil Records: Access: Mail, in person. Both court and visitors may perform in person searches. Search fee: $10.00 per name. Fee is per court. Court makes copy: $1.00 per page. Required to search: name, years to search; also helpful: address. Civil cases indexed by defendant, plaintiff; on computer since 1983 (real property only), on microfiche and index books from 1870. Mail turnaround time 1-2 days.

Criminal Records: Access: Mail, in person. Both court and visitors may perform in person searches. Search fee: $10.00 per name. Fee is per court. Court makes copy: $1.00 per page. Required to search: name, years to search; also helpful: address, DOB, SSN, offense. Criminal records in index books and folders from 1870. Mail turnaround time 1-2 days.

General Information: No juvenile, mental, sealed, or adoption records released. Fee to fax documents is $2.00 per page includes copy fee. Certification fee: $5.00 for County Court; $1.00 per page in District Court. Payee: Goliad County/District Clerk. Personal checks accepted. Prepayment required.

Gonzales County

District Court 414 St Joseph #300, Gonzales, TX 78629; phone: 830-672-2326; fax: 830-672-9313; hours 8AM-N 1-5PM (CST). *Felony, Civil.*

Civil Records: Access: Phone, fax, mail, in person. Both court and visitors may perform in person searches. Search fee: $5.00 per name. Court makes copy: $1.00 per page; same fee for self serve. Required to search: name, years to search; also helpful: address. Civil cases indexed by defendant, plaintiff; on computer from 1991, index books from 1800s. Mail turnaround time 1-2 days.

Criminal Records: Access: Phone, fax, mail, in person. Both court and visitors may perform in person searches. Search fee: $5.00 per name. Court makes copy: $1.00 per page; same fee for self serve. Required to search: name, years to search; also helpful: address, DOB, SSN. Criminal records on computer from 1991, index books from 1800s. Mail turnaround time 1-2 days.

General Information: No juvenile, mental, sealed, or adoption records released. Fee to fax documents is $1.00 per page. No certification fee. Payee: District Clerk. Personal checks accepted. Prepayment and SASE required.

County Court PO Box 77, Gonzales, TX 78629; phone: 830-672-2801; criminal fax: 830-672-2636; same fax for civil/probate; hours 8AM-5PM (CST). *Misdemeanor, Civil, Probate.*

Civil Records: Access: Fax, mail, in person. Both court and visitors may perform in person searches. Search fee: $5.00 per name. Court makes copy: $1.00 per page; same fee for self serve. Required to search: name, years to search. Civil cases indexed by defendant, plaintiff; on computer since 1993, original jackets since 1975, index books from 1900s. Mail turnaround time 1-2 days.

Criminal Records: Access: Mail, in person. Both court and visitors may perform in person searches. Search fee: $5.00 per name. Court makes copy: $1.00 per page; same fee for self serve. Required to search: name, years to search, offense, date of offense. Criminal records on computer since 1993, original jackets, index books from 1900s. Mail turnaround time 1-2 days.

General Information: No mental or drug dependant commitment records released. Fee to fax documents is

$5.00. Certification fee: $5.00 per instrument. Payee: County Clerk. Personal checks accepted. Prepayment and SASE required.

Gray County

District Court PO Box 1139, Pampa, TX 79066-1139; phone: 806-669-8010; fax: 806-669-8053; hours 8:30AM-5PM (CST). *Felony, Civil.*

Civil Records: Access: Fax, mail, in person. Both court and visitors may perform in person searches. Search fee: $5.00 per name. Court makes copy: $.50 per page. Required to search: name, years to search, DOB. Civil cases indexed by defendant, plaintiff; on computer from 1940, index books from 1910. All requests must be in writing. Mail turnaround time 1-2 days.

Criminal Records: Access: Fax, mail, in person. Both court and visitors may perform in person searches. Search fee: $5.00 per name. Court makes copy: $.50 per page. Required to search: name, years to search; also helpful: DOB. Criminal records go back to 1930; criminal records on computer from 1965. All requests must be in writing. Mail turnaround time 1-2 days.

General Information: No juvenile, mental, sealed, or adoption records released. Will fax documents $1.00 per page. Certification fee: $1.00 per page. Payee: District Clerk. Personal checks accepted. Prepayment and SASE required.

County & Probate Court PO Box 1902, Pampa, TX 79066-1902; phone: 806-669-8004; fax: 806-669-8054; hours 8:30AM-5PM (CST). *Misdemeanor, Civil, Probate.*

Civil Records: Access: Phone, fax, mail, in person. Both court and visitors may perform in person searches. Search fee: $10.00 per name. Fee is per index. Court makes copy: $1.00 per page; same fee for self serve. Required to search: name, years to search. Civil cases indexed by defendant, plaintiff; on type written indices from 1900s. Mail turnaround time 1-2 days.

Criminal Records: Access: Phone, fax, mail, in person. Both court and visitors may perform in person searches. Search fee: $10.00 per name. Fee is per index. Court makes copy: $1.00 per page; same fee for self serve. Required to search: name, years to search, DOB. Criminal records on type written indices from 1900s. Mail turnaround time 1-2 days.

General Information: Public terminal has criminal back to 1983 and civil back to 4/19/02. No juvenile, mental, sealed, or adoption records released. They will not release any records with the SSN on it. Will fax documents $2.50 1st page, $1.00 each add'l. Certification fee: $5.00. Payee: Susan Winborne, County Clerk. Personal checks accepted. Prepayment and SASE required.

Grayson County

District Court 200 S Crockett, Rm 120-A, Sherman, TX 75090; phone: 903-813-4352; fax: 903-870-0609; hours 8AM-5PM (CST). *Felony, Civil, Family.*

www.co.grayson.tx.us

Civil Records: Access: Mail, in person. Both court and visitors may perform in person searches. Search fee: $5.00 per name. Court makes copy: $1.00 per page. Self serve copy fee: $.25 per page. Required to search: name, years to search. Civil cases indexed by defendant, plaintiff; on computer from 1988, microfilm since 1939, index books since 1900s. Mail turnaround time 1-2 days.

Criminal Records: Access: Mail, in person. Both court and visitors may perform in person searches. Search fee: $5.00 per name. Court makes copy: $1.00 per page. Self serve copy fee: $.25 per page. Required to search: name, years to search, DOB; also helpful: SSN. Criminal records on computer since 1988, microfilm since 1939, index books since 1900s. Mail turnaround time 1-2 days.

General Information: Public terminal has criminal back to 1983 and civil back to 1989. No juvenile, mental, sealed, expunction or adoption records released. Will not fax documents. Certification fee: $1.00. Payee: District Clerk. Personal checks accepted. Prepayment and SASE required.

County Court 200 S Crockett, Sherman, TX 75090; phone: 903-813-4336; civil phone: 903-813-4335; probate phone: 903-813-4241; fax: 903-892-8300; hours 8AM-5PM (CST). *Misdemeanor, Civil, Probate.*

www.co.grayson.tx.us

Civil Records: Access: Mail, in person, online. Both court and visitors may perform in person searches. Search fee: $5.00 per name. Court makes copy: $1.00 per page. Required to search: name, years to search. Civil cases indexed by defendant, plaintiff; on computer since 1992, index books since 1952. Online access to civil records free at www.co.grayson.tx.us:3004/judsrch.asp. Also includes sheriffs' bail, and sheriff's jail searching. Mail turnaround time 1-2 days.

Criminal Records: Access: Mail, in person, online. Both court and visitors may perform in person searches. Search fee: $5.00 per name. Court makes copy: $1.00 per page. Required to search: name, years to search, also helpful: DOB, SSN. Criminal records on computer from 1982. Online access to criminal records is the same as civil. Mail turnaround time 1-2 days.

General Information: Public use terminal available. No juvenile, mental, sealed, or adoption records released. Will fax documents if prepaid. Certification fee: $5.00. Payee: County Clerk. Personal checks accepted. Prepayment and SASE required.

Gregg County

District Court PO Box 711, Longview, TX 75606; criminal phone: 903-237-8459; civil phone: 903-237-2663; fax: 903-236-8474; hours 8AM-5PM (CST). *Felony, Civil.*

www.co.gregg.tx.us/government/courts.asp

Civil Records: Access: Phone, fax, mail, in person, online. Both court and visitors may perform in person searches. Search fee: $5.00 per name. Court makes copy: $1.00 per page. Required to search: name, years to search. Civil cases indexed by defendant, plaintiff; on computer back to 1981, index books from 1873. Online access to county judicial records is free at www.co.gregg.tx.us/judsrch.htm. Search by name, cause number, status. Mail turnaround time 1-2 days.

Criminal Records: Access: Phone, fax, mail, in person, online. Both court and visitors may perform in person searches. Search fee: $5.00 per name. Court makes copy: $1.00 per page. Required to search: name, years to search. Criminal records on computer back to 1977, index books from 1873. Online access to criminal records is the same as civil. Also includes jail and bond search. Mail turnaround time 1-2 days.

General Information: Public use terminal available. No juvenile, mental, sealed, or adoption records released. Will fax documents $1.00 per page. Certification fee: $1.00 per page. Payee: District Clerk. Only cashiers checks and money orders accepted. Prepayment and SASE required.

County Court 101 E Methvin, #200, Longview, TX 75606; phone: 903-236-8430; fax: 903-237-2574; hours 8AM-5PM (CST). *Misdemeanor, Civil, Probate.*

www.co.gregg.tx.us/government/commissionersCourt/county_judge.asp

Civil Records: Access: Mail, in person, online. Both court and visitors may perform in person searches. Search fee: $5.00 per name. Court makes copy: $1.00 per page. Required to search: name, years to search. Civil cases indexed by defendant, plaintiff; on computer from 1983, index books after 1962. Online access to county judicial records is free at www.co.gregg.tx.us/judsrch.htm. Search by name, cause number, or status. Mail turnaround time 1 week.

Criminal Records: Access: Mail, in person, online. Both court and visitors may perform in person

searches. Search fee: $5.00 per name. Court makes copy: $1.00 per page. Required to search: name, years to search, DOB or SSN. Criminal records on computer from 1983, index books after 1932. Online access to criminal records is the same as civil. Jail and bond search also available. Mail turnaround time 1 week.

General Information: Public terminal has criminal back to 1983 and civil back to 1983. (Probate index goes back to 1908.) No juvenile, mental, sealed, or adoption records released. Fee to fax documents is $1.00 per page. Certification fee: $5.00. Payee: Gregg County Clerk. Only in state personal checks accepted. Prepayment and SASE required.

Grimes County

District Court PO Box 234, Anderson, TX 77830; phone: 936-873-2111 x240; fax: 936-873-2514; hours 8AM-5PM, closed 1 hour at noon (CST). *Felony, Civil.*

Civil Records: Access: Phone, fax, mail, in person. Both court and visitors may perform in person searches. Search fee: $5.00 per name. Court makes copy: $1.00 per page. Required to search: name, years to search. Civil cases indexed by defendant, plaintiff; on computer from 1990, index books from 1800s. Mail turnaround time 1-2 days.

Criminal Records: Access: Phone, fax, mail, in person. Both court and visitors may perform in person searches. Search fee: $5.00 per name. Court makes copy: $1.00 per page. Required to search: name, years to search, DOB, SSN. Criminal records on computer from 1990, index books from 1800s. Mail turnaround time 1-2 days.

General Information: No juvenile, mental, sealed, or adoption records released. Will fax documents for $1.00 per page. Certification fee: $1.00. Payee: District Clerk. Personal checks accepted. Prepayment required.

County Court PO Box 209, Anderson, TX 77830; phone: 936-873-2606 X251; fax: 936-873-3308; hours 8AM-4:45PM (CST). *Misdemeanor, Civil, Probate.*

Civil Records: Access: Mail, in person. Only the court performs in person searches; visitors may not. Search fee: $5.00 per name. Court makes copy: $1.00 per page. Required to search: name, years to search. Civil cases indexed by defendant, plaintiff; in index books from 1850. Mail turnaround time 1-2 days.

Criminal Records: Access: Mail, in person. Only the court performs in person searches; visitors may not. Search fee: $5.00 per name. Court makes copy: $1.00 per page. Required to search: name, years to search, offense, date of offense. Criminal records in index books from 1850. Mail turnaround time 1-2 days.

General Information: No juvenile, mental, sealed, or adoption records released. Will not fax documents. Certification fee: $5.00. Payee: County Clerk. Personal checks accepted. Prepayment and SASE required.

Guadalupe County

District Court 101 E Court St, Seguin, TX 78155; phone: 830-303-4188; criminal phone: x276; civil phone: x262; fax: 830-379-1943; hours 8AM-5PM (CST). *Felony, Civil.*

www.co.guadalupe.tx.us/

Civil Records: Access: In person, online. Visitors must perform in person searches themselves. Court makes copy: $.25 per page. Required to search: name, years to search. Civil cases indexed by defendant, plaintiff; on computer from 1987, index books from 1846. Online access is at www.idocket.com; one free search per day; subscription required for more. Online records go back to 1/1/1987 Mail turnaround time 1 day.

Criminal Records: Access: In person, online. Visitors must perform in person searches themselves. Court makes copy: $.25 per page. Required to search: name, years to search, DOB; also

helpful: SSN. Criminal records on computer from 1985, index books from 1846. Felony records access is through www.idocket.com; registration and password required. Records go back to 12/31/1991.

General Information: Public terminal has criminal back to 1985 and civil back to 1987. No juvenile, mental, sealed, or adoption records released. Will fax specific case file requests for $5.00 fee. Certification fee: $1.00 per page and includes copy fee. Payee: District Clerk. Personal checks or Visa, MC, AmEx accepted. Prepayment required.

County Court 101 E Court St, Seguin, TX 78155; phone: 830-303-4188 x266,234,232; fax: 830-372-1206; hours 8AM-4:30PM (CST). *Misdemeanor, Civil, Probate.*

Civil Records: Access: Mail, in person. Both court and visitors may perform in person searches. Search fee: $10.00 per name. Court makes copy: $1.00 per page. Required to search: name, years to search. Civil cases indexed by defendant, plaintiff; on computer from 1988, index books from 1968. Mail turnaround time 5 days.

Criminal Records: Access: Mail, in person. Both court and visitors may perform in person searches. Search fee: $10.00 per name. Court makes copy: $1.00 per page. Required to search: name, years to search, DOB; also helpful: SSN. Criminal records on computer from 1988, index books from 1968. Mail turnaround time 5 days.

General Information: Public terminal goes back to 1988. No juvenile, mental, sealed, or adoption records released. Certification fee: $5.00 per doc. Payee: County Clerk. Personal checks accepted. Checks accepted for civil fees. Prepayment and SASE required.

Hale County

District Court 500 Broadway, #200, Plainview, TX 79072-8050; phone: 806-291-5226; fax: 806-291-5206; hours 8AM-N; 1-5PM (CST). *Felony, Civil.*

www.242ndcourt.com/

Civil Records: Access: Phone, fax, mail, in person. Both court and visitors may perform in person searches. Search fee: $5.00 per name. Court makes copy: $1.00 per page; same fee for self serve. Required to search: name, years to search. Civil cases indexed by defendant, plaintiff; on computer back to 1990; index cards from 1975; prior back to 1897. Mail turnaround time 1-2 days.

Criminal Records: Access: Phone, fax, mail, in person. Both court and visitors may perform in person searches. Search fee: $5.00 per name. Court makes copy: $1.00 per page; same fee for self serve. Required to search: name, years to search, SSN; also helpful: DOB. Criminal records on computer back to 1990, index cards from 1975; prior back to 1897. Mail turnaround time 1-2 days.

General Information: Public terminal goes back to 1990. No juvenile, mental, sealed, or adoption records released. Will fax documents for $2.00 per document. Certification fee: $1.00 each. Payee: District Clerk. Personal checks and credit cards accepted. Prepayment and SASE required.

County Court 500 Broadway, #140, Plainview, TX 79072-8030; phone: 806-291-5261; criminal phone: 806-291-5219; civil phone: 806-291-5261; probate phone: 806-291-5261; criminal fax: 806-291-9810; same fax for civil/probate; hours 8AM-N, 1-5PM (CST). *Misdemeanor, Civil, Probate.* Note: Probate records are in a separate index.

Civil Records: Access: Mail, fax, in person. Both court and visitors may perform in person searches. Search fee: $5.00 per name. Court makes copy: $1.00 per page; same fee for self serve. Required to search: name, years to search, address. Civil cases indexed by defendant, plaintiff; in index books from 1928; on computer back to 1995. Mail turnaround time-same day if before 3PM.

Criminal Records: Access: Mail, fax, in person. Both court and visitors may perform in person searches. Search fee: $5.00 per name. Court makes copy: $1.00 per page; same fee for self serve. Required to search: name, years to search, DOB. Criminal records in index books from 1928; on computer back to 1995, limited records back to 1990. Mail turnaround time 1-2 days.

General Information: Public terminal goes back to 1995. (Clerk guarantees accuracy of computer records.) No juvenile, mental, sealed, or adoption records released. Will fax documents for copy fee plus $1.00 for long distance call. Certification fee: $5.00 per document. Payee: County Clerk. Personal checks accepted. Prepayment and SASE required.

Hall County

District & County Court County Courthouse, 512 Main St, #8, Memphis, TX 79245; phone: 806-259-2627; fax: 806-259-5078; hours 8:30AM-N; 1-5PM (CST). *Felony, Misdemeanor, Civil, Probate.*
Civil Records: Access: Mail, in person. Both court and visitors may perform in person searches. Search fee: $5.00 per name. Court makes copy: $1.00 per page. Required to search: name, years to search. Civil cases indexed by defendant, plaintiff; on computer from 1992, index books from 1890. Mail turnaround time 1-2 days.
Criminal Records: Access: Mail, in person. Both court and visitors may perform in person searches. Search fee: $5.00 per name. Court makes copy: $1.00 per page. Required to search: name, years to search, offense. Criminal records on computer from 1992, index books from 1890. Mail turnaround time 1-2 days.
General Information: No juvenile, mental, sealed, or adoption records released. Will fax documents to local or toll free line. Certification fee: $5.00. Payee: Hall County Clerk. Personal checks accepted. Prepayment and SASE required.

Hamilton County

District Court County Courthouse, Hamilton, TX 76531; phone: 254-386-3417; fax: 254-386-8610; hours 8AM-5PM M-Th; 8AM-4:30PM F (CST). *Felony, Civil.*
Civil Records: Access: Fax, mail, in person. Both court and visitors may perform in person searches. Search fee: $5.00 per name. Court makes copy: $1.00 per page; same fee for self serve. Required to search: name, years to search. Civil cases indexed by defendant, plaintiff. Civil records since 1985 in index books, computerized since 1999. Mail turnaround time 2-4 days.
Criminal Records: Access: Fax, mail, in person. Both court and visitors may perform in person searches. Search fee: $5.00 per name. Court makes copy: $1.00 per page; same fee for self serve. Required to search: name, years to search. Criminal records in index books since 1985, computerized since 1999. Mail turnaround time 2-4 days.
General Information: No juvenile, mental, sealed, or adoption records released. No fee to fax documents. Certification fee: $2.00 per document. Payee: District Clerk. Personal checks accepted. Prepayment and SASE required.

County Court County Courthouse, Hamilton, TX 76531; phone: 254-386-3518; criminal fax: 254-386-8727; same fax for civil/probate; hours 8AM-5PM (CST). *Misdemeanor, Civil, Probate.*
Civil Records: Access: Mail, fax, in person. Both court and visitors may perform in person searches. Search fee: $5.00 per name. Court makes copy: $1.00 per page; same fee for self serve. Required to search: name, years to search. Civil cases indexed by defendant, plaintiff; in index books; on computer since. Mail turnaround time 1-2 days.
Criminal Records: Access: Mail, fax, in person. Both court and visitors may perform in person searches. Search fee: $5.00 per name. Court makes copy: $1.00 per page; same fee for self serve. Required to search: name, years to search, DOB or SSN. Criminal records in index books; on computer since. Mail turnaround time 1-2 days.

General Information: No juvenile, mental, sealed, or adoption records released. Will fax documents for fee. Certification fee: $1.00 per page. Payee: County Clerk. Personal checks accepted. Prepayment and SASE required.

Hansford County

District & County Court 15 NW Court, Spearman, TX 79081; phone: 806-659-4110; fax: 806-659-4168; hours 8:00AM-5PM (CST). *Felony, Misdemeanor, Civil, Probate.*
Civil Records: Access: Phone, fax, mail, in person. Both court and visitors may perform in person searches. Search fee: $5.00 per name. Court makes copy: $1.00 per page. Required to search: name, years to search. Civil cases indexed by defendant, plaintiff; on computer from 1/92, index books from 1900s. Mail turnaround time ASAP.
Criminal Records: Access: Phone, fax, mail, in person. Both court and visitors may perform in person searches. Search fee: $5.00 per name. Court makes copy: $1.00 per page. Required to search: name, years to search; also helpful: DOB, SSN. Criminal records on computer since 6/92, archived from 1900s. Mail turnaround time 1-2 days.
General Information: Public terminal goes back to 1992. No juvenile, mental, sealed, or adoption records released. Will fax documents for $3.00. Certification fee: $2.00 in District Court; $5.00 in County Court. Payee: District/County Clerk. Personal checks accepted. Prepayment and SASE required.

Hardeman County

District & County Court PO Box 30, Quanah, TX 79252; phone: 940-663-2901; probate fax: 940-663-5161; hours 8:30AM-5PM (CST). *Felony, Misdemeanor, Civil, Probate.*
Note: Probate is separate index at this same address.
Civil Records: Access: Mail, in person. Both court and visitors may perform in person searches. Search fee: $10.00 per name. Court makes copy: $1.00 per page; same fee for self serve. Required to search: name, years to search. Civil cases indexed by defendant, plaintiff; in index books from 1900s. Mail turnaround time 1-2 days.
Criminal Records: Access: Mail, in person. Both court and visitors may perform in person searches. Search fee: $10.00 per name. Court makes copy: $1.00 per page; same fee for self serve. Required to search: name, years to search. Criminal records in index books from 1920. Mail turnaround time 1-2 days.
General Information: No juvenile, mental, sealed, or adoption records released. Will not fax documents. Certification fee: $5.00 per cert. Payee: District Clerk. Personal checks accepted. Prepayment and SASE required.

Hardin County

District Court PO Box 2997, 300 Monroe, Kountze, TX 77625; phone: 409-246-5150; hours 8AM-4PM (CST). *Felony, Civil.*
Civil Records: Access: Mail, in person. Both court and visitors may perform in person searches. Search fee: $5.00 per name. Court makes copy: $1.00 per page. Self serve copy fee: $.50 per page. Required to search: name, years to search. Civil cases indexed by defendant, plaintiff; in index books since 1920, computerized since 1997. Mail turnaround time 1-2 days.
Criminal Records: Access: Mail, in person. Both court and visitors may perform in person searches. Search fee: $5.00 per name. Court makes copy: $1.00 per page. Self serve copy fee: $.50 per page. Required to search: name, years to search, DOB; also helpful: SSN, sex. Criminal records in index books since 1920, computerized since 1997. Mail turnaround time 1-2 days.
General Information: No juvenile, mental, sealed, or adoption records released. Fee to fax documents is $1.00 per page. Certification fee: $2.00 per doc.

Payee: District Clerk. Business checks accepted. Prepayment and SASE required.

County Court PO Box 38, Kountze, TX 77625; phone: 409-246-5185; hours 8AM-5PM (CST). *Misdemeanor, Civil, Probate.*
Civil Records: Access: Mail, in person, phone. Both court and visitors may perform in person searches. Search fee: $5.00 per name. Court makes copy: $1.00 per page; same fee for self serve. Required to search: name, years to search. Civil cases indexed by defendant, plaintiff; in index books since 1850; on computer back to 1999. Mail turnaround time 1-2 days.
Criminal Records: Access: Mail, in person, phone. Both court and visitors may perform in person searches. Search fee: $5.00 per name. Court makes copy: $1.00 per page; same fee for self serve. Required to search: name, years to search. Criminal records on computer since 1992, index books from 1850. Mail turnaround time 1-2 days.
General Information: No juvenile, mental, sealed, or adoption records released. Certification fee: $6.00 per doc. Payee: Hardin County Clerk. Personal checks accepted. Prepayment required.

Harris County

District Court District Clerk, PO Box 4651, Houston, TX 77210-4651; phone: 713-755-5734, 888-545-5577; criminal phone: 713-755-7801; civil phone: 713-755-5711 x2; criminal fax: 713-755-5480; civil fax: 713-755-5751; hours 8AM-6PM (CST). *Felony, Misdemeanor, Civil Over $100,000.*
www.hcdistrictclerk.com
Note: Criminal at 1201 Franklin #3138; Civil at 301 Fannin St #105B.
Civil Records: Access: Fax, online, in person. Both court and visitors may perform in person searches. Search fee: $5.00 per name. Court makes copy: $1.00 per page. Required to search: name, years to search. Civil cases indexed by defendant, plaintiff; on computer from 1969. First, an online case lookup service is free at www.hcdistrictclerk.com/CFTS/CaseLocationSearch.asp. Online records go back to 10/1989. Second, register for free-to-view e-docs service at https://e-docs.hcdistrictclerk.com/eDocs.Web/Login.aspx and pay $1 per page (credit cards accepted) for civil documents. Note: Also, access to records is to qualified JIMs subscribers at www.jims.hctx.net.
Criminal Records: Access: Mail, online, in person. Both court and visitors may perform in person searches. Search fee: $5.00 per name. Court makes copy: $1.00 per page. Required to search: name, years to search, DOB. Criminal records on computer since 1976. Online access to criminal records is same as civil.
General Information: Public terminal has criminal back to 1985 and civil back to 1978. No juvenile or sealed records released. Fax-service requires credit card pre-payment. Certification fee: $1.00 criminal, $2.00 civil. Payee: District Clerk. Court: business check accepted from attorney with TX Bar Card, corporate or company check with Harris Co. address. Prepayment required.

County Court PO Box 1525, 301 Fannin, Civil Courts Bldg, Rm 101, Houston, TX 77251-1525; phone: 713-755-6421; hours 8AM-4:30PM (CST). *Civil Under $100,000.*
www.cclerk.hctx.net
Note: The Information Department (for record information) telephone is 713-755-6405, located at County Admin Bldg, 1001 Preston, 4th Fl. Small claims and evictions are handled by county Justice of Peace Courts; usually there are two per precinct.
Civil Records: Access: Phone, mail, online, in person. Both court and visitors may perform in person searches. Search fee: $5.00 for mail requests. Court makes copy: $1.00 per page. Required to search: name, years to search. Civil cases indexed by defendant, plaintiff; on computer and microfiche from 1963. Online access is free at www.cclerk.hctx.net.

System includes civil data search and county civil settings inquiry and other county clerk functions. For further information, visit the website or call 713-755-6421. Note: Also, online access is at www.idocket.com; registration and password required. This is a fee service, unless only one name search a day. Records go back to 1998. Mail turnaround time 24-48 hours.

General Information: Public terminal has only civil records. (Public terminal also includes Probate records.) Certification fee: $5.00. Payee: Harris County Clerk. Business checks or Visa, MC, Discover, AmEx accepted. Prepayment and SASE required.

Probate Court 1115 Congress, 5th Fl, Houston, TX 77002; phone: 713-755-6425; fax: 713-755-5468; hours 8AM-4:30PM (CST). *Probate.*
Note: Probate dockets are available through the Harris County online system. Call 713-755-7815 for information. Dockets are available free at www.cclerk.hctx.net/coolice/default.asp?Category=ProbateCourt&Service=pc_inquiry. Records go back to 1837.

Harrison County

71st District Court PO Box 1119, 200 W Houston St #143, Marshall, TX 75671-1119; phone: 903-935-8409; hours 8AM-5PM (CST). *Felony, Civil.*
www.co.harrison.tx.us
Civil Records: Access: Mail, in person. Both court and visitors may perform in person searches. Search fee: $5.00 per name. Court makes copy: $1.00 per page. Required to search: name, years to search; also helpful: address. Civil cases indexed by defendant, plaintiff; on computer from 1988, index books from 1845. Mail turnaround time 1-2 days.
Criminal Records: Access: Mail, in person. Both court and visitors may perform in person searches. Search fee: $5.00 per name. Court makes copy: $1.00 per page. Required to search: name, years to search, DOB; also helpful: address, SSN. Criminal records on computer from 1988, index books from 1845. Mail turnaround time 1-2 days.
General Information: Public terminal goes back to 1988. No juvenile, mental, sealed, or adoption records released. No certification fee. Payee: Harrison County District Clerk. Personal checks accepted. Prepayment and SASE required.

County Court PO Box 1365, Marshall, TX 75671; phone: 903-935-8403; fax: 903-935-4877; hours 8AM-5PM (CST). *Misdemeanor, Civil, Probate.*
Note: Probate is a separate index at this same address.
Civil Records: Access: Mail, in person. Both court and visitors may perform in person searches. Search fee: $5.00 per name. Court makes copy: $1.00 per page; same fee for self serve. Required to search: name, years to search. Civil cases indexed by defendant, plaintiff; in docket books from 1800; on computer back to 2001. Mail turnaround time 10 days.
Criminal Records: Access: Mail, in person. Both court and visitors may perform in person searches. Search fee: $5.00 per name. Court makes copy: $1.00 per page; same fee for self serve. Required to search: name, years to search, DOB. Criminal records in docket books from 1800; on computer back to 2001. Mail turnaround time 10 days.
General Information: No juvenile, mental, sealed, birth, death or adoption records released. Fee to fax documents is $4.00. Certification fee: $5.00 per document. Payee: County Clerk. No personal checks accepted. Prepayment required.

Hartley County

District & County Court PO Box Q, Channing, TX 79018; phone: 806-235-3582; fax: 806-235-2316; hours 8:30AM-N, 1-5PM (CST). *Felony, Misdemeanor, Civil, Probate.*
Note: Probate is a separate index at this same address

Civil Records: Access: Mail, in person. Both court and visitors may perform in person searches. Search fee: $5.00 per name. Charge is for each book searched. Court makes copy: $1.00 per page County Ct; $.25 per page in district court. Required to search: name, years to search. Civil cases indexed by defendant, plaintiff; on computer from 1994, index books from 1890. Mail turnaround time 1-2 days.
Criminal Records: Access: Mail, in person. Both court and visitors may perform in person searches. Search fee: $5.00 per name, per book searched (misdemeanor or felony). Court makes copy: $1.00 per page County Ct; $.25 per page in district court. Required to search: name, years to search, DOB. Criminal records on computer from 1994, index books from 1890. Mail turnaround time 1-2 days.
General Information: Public use terminal available. No juvenile, mental, sealed, or adoption records released. Will fax documents if prepaid. Certification fee: $5.00 per cert in County Ct; $1.00 per page plus copies in District Ct. Payee: Hartley County Clerk. Personal checks accepted. Prepayment and SASE required.

Haskell County

District Court PO Box 27, Haskell, TX 79521; phone: 940-864-2030; hours 8:30AM-N, 1-5PM M-Th; 8:30AM-4:30PM F (CST). *Felony, Civil.*
Civil Records: Access: Mail, in person. Both court and visitors may perform in person searches. Search fee: $5.00 per name. Court makes copy: $1.00 per page. Required to search: name, years to search. Civil cases indexed by defendant, plaintiff; on computer from 1992, index books from 1896. Mail turnaround time 1-2 days.
Criminal Records: Access: Mail, in person. Both court and visitors may perform in person searches. Search fee: $5.00 per name. Court makes copy: $1.00 per page. Required to search: name, years to search, signed release. Criminal records on computer from 1992, index books from 1896. Mail turnaround time 1-2 days.
General Information: No juvenile, mental, sealed, or adoption records released. Certification fee: $1.00. Payee: District Clerk. Business checks accepted. In-state checks accepted. Prepayment and SASE required.

County Court PO Box 725, Haskell, TX 79521; phone: 940-864-2451; fax: 940-864-6164; hours 8AM-N, 1-5PM (CST). *Misdemeanor, Civil, Probate.*
Civil Records: Access: Phone, fax, mail, in person. Both court and visitors may perform in person searches. Search fee: $5.00 per name. Court makes copy: $1.00 per page; same fee for self serve. Required to search: name, years to search. Civil cases indexed by defendant, plaintiff; in index books from 1903; computerized records since 1994. Mail turnaround time 1-2 days.
Criminal Records: Access: Fax, mail, in person. Both court and visitors may perform in person searches. Search fee: $5.00 per name. Court makes copy: $1.00 per page; same fee for self serve. Required to search: name, years to search. Criminal records in index books from 19; computerized records since 1994. Mail turnaround time 1-2 days.
General Information: No juvenile, mental, sealed, or adoption records released. Will fax documents $2.00 per page. Certification fee: $5.00. Payee: County Clerk. Personal checks accepted. Prepayment required. SASE helpful.

Hays County

District Court 110 E Martin Luther King, #123, San Marcos, TX 78666; phone: 512-393-7660; fax: 512-393-7674; hours 8AM-5PM (CST). *Felony, Civil.*
www.co.hays.tx.us
Civil Records: Access: Phone, mail, in person, online. Both court and visitors may perform in person searches. Search fee: $5.00 per name. Court makes copy: $.50 per page. Required to search: name,

years to search. Civil cases indexed by defendant, plaintiff; on computer from 1987, index books from 1890s. Online access is through www.idocket.com; registration and password required. Records go back to 12/31/1986. Mail turnaround time 1-5 days.
Criminal Records: Access: Phone, mail, in person, online. Both court and visitors may perform in person searches. Search fee: $5.00 per name. Court makes copy: $.50 per page. Required to search: name, years to search; also helpful: DOB, SSN. Criminal records on computer from 1987, index books from 1890s. Online access is through www.idocket.com; registration and password required. Records go back to 12/31/1986. Mail turnaround time 1-5 days.
General Information: Public terminal goes back to 1989. No sealed or adoption records released. Certification fee: $1.00 per page. Payee: District Clerk. Personal checks accepted. Prepayment and SASE required.

County Court Justice Center, 110 E Martin L King Dr, San Marcos, TX 78666; phone: 512-393-7738; criminal phone: 512-393-7738; civil phone: 512-393-7739; probate phone: 512-393-7734; criminal fax: 512-393-7735; same fax for civil/probate; hours 8AM-5PM (CST). *Misdemeanor, Civil, Probate.*
www.co.hays.tx.us
Civil Records: Access: Mail, in person, online. Both court and visitors may perform in person searches. Search fee: $5.00 per name. Court makes copy: $1.00 per page; same fee for self serve. Required to search: name, years to search. Civil cases indexed by defendant, plaintiff; on computer from 1988, index books from 1848. Online access is through www.idocket.com; registration and password required. Includes probate, Records from 01/88. Mail turnaround time 1-2 weeks.
Criminal Records: Access: Mail, in person, online. Both court and visitors may perform in person searches. Search fee: $5.00 per name. Court makes copy: $1.00 per page; same fee for self serve. Required to search: name, years to search, DOB. Criminal records on computer from 1988, index books from 1848. Misdemeanor records access is through www.idocket.com; registration and password required. Records go back to 12/31/1987. Mail turnaround time 1-2 weeks.
General Information: Public terminal goes back to 1987. No juvenile, mental, sealed, or adoption records released. Will fax documents if other fees paid. Certification fee: $5.00 per document. Payee: Hays County Clerk. Personal checks accepted. Prepayment required.

Hemphill County

District & County Court PO Box 867, Canadian, TX 79014; phone: 806-323-6212; hours 8AM-5PM (CST). *Felony, Misdemeanor, Civil, Probate.*
Note: Probate is a separate index at this same address.
Civil Records: Access: Phone, mail, in person. Both court and visitors may perform in person searches. Search fee: $5.00 per name. Court makes copy: $1.00 per page. Self serve copy fee: $.50 per page. Required to search: name, years to search. Civil cases indexed by defendant, plaintiff; indexed from 1890s, in storage. Mail turnaround time 1-2 weeks.
Criminal Records: Access: Phone, mail, in person. Both court and visitors may perform in person searches. Search fee: $5.00 per name. Court makes copy: $1.00 per page. Self serve copy fee: $.50 per page. Required to search: name, years to search, DOB. Criminal records indexed from 1890s, in storage. Mail turnaround time 1-2 weeks.
General Information: No juvenile, mental, sealed, or adoption records released. Will not fax documents. Certification fee: $5.00 per page. Payee: Hemphill County Clerk. Personal checks accepted. Prepayment and SASE required.

Henderson County

District Court District Clerk Henderson County, 100 E Tyler, Rm 203, Athens, TX 75751; phone: 903-675-6115; fax: 903-677-7274; hours 8AM-5PM (CST). *Felony, Civil.*
Note: This office accepts no fax over 5 pages.
Civil Records: Access: Mail, in person, phone, fax. Both court and visitors may perform in person searches. Search fee: $5.00 per name. Court makes copy: $1.00 per page. Required to search: name, years to search. Civil cases indexed by defendant, plaintiff; on computer from 1987, index books from 1849. Mail turnaround time 1-2 days.
Criminal Records: Access: Mail, in person. Both court and visitors may perform in person searches. Search fee: $5.00 per name. Court makes copy: $1.00 per page. Required to search: name, years to search, DOB; also helpful: SSN. Criminal records on computer from 1987, index books from 1849. Mail turnaround time 1-2 days.
General Information: Public use terminal available. No juvenile, mental, sealed, or adoption records released. No certification fee. Payee: District Clerk. Personal checks accepted. Prepayment and SASE required.

County Court PO Box 632, Athens, TX 75751; phone: 903-675-6140; criminal phone: 903-677-7205; civil phone: 903-675-6144; probate phone: 903-677-7206; fax: 903-675-6105; hours 8AM-5PM (CST). *Misdemeanor, Civil, Probate.*
Civil Records: Access: Phone, mail, fax, in person. Both court and visitors may perform in person searches. Search fee: $5.00 per name. Court makes copy: $1.00 per page; same fee for self serve. Required to search: name, years to search. Civil cases indexed by defendant, plaintiff; on computer back to 1984, index books from 1960s. Mail turnaround time 1-2 weeks.
Criminal Records: Access: Mail, fax, in person. Both court and visitors may perform in person searches. Search fee: $5.00 per name. Court makes copy: $1.00 per page; same fee for self serve. Required to search: name, years to search, DOB, SSN. Criminal records on computer back to 1984, index books from 1960s. Mail turnaround time 1-2 weeks.
General Information: Public terminal goes back to 1984. No juvenile, mental, sealed, or adoption records released. Fee to fax documents is $2.00 per page. Certification fee: $1.00 per document. Payee: County Clerk. Personal checks accepted. Prepayment and SASE required.

Hidalgo County

District Court 100 N Closner, Box 87, Edinburg, TX 78540; phone: 956-318-2200; hours 8AM-5PM (CST). *Felony, Civil.*
Civil Records: Access: Mail, in person, online. Only the court performs in person searches; visitors may not. Search fee: $5.00 per name. Court makes copy: $.25 per page. Required to search: name, years to search. Civil cases indexed by defendant, plaintiff; on computer from 1987. Online access is through www.idocket.com; registration and password required. Records go back to 12/31/1986. Mail turnaround time 1-2 days.
Criminal Records: Access: Mail, in person, online. Only the court performs in person searches; visitors may not. Search fee: $5.00 per name. Court makes copy: $.25 per page. Required to search: name, years to search, DOB. Criminal records on computer from 1987. Online access is through www.idocket.com; registration and password required. Records go back to 12/31/1986. Mail turnaround time 1-2 days.
General Information: No juvenile, mental, sealed, or adoption records released. Will not fax documents. Certification fee: $1.00 per page. Payee: District Clerk. Business checks accepted. Prepayment and SASE required.

County Court PO Box 58, Edinburg, TX 78540; phone: 956-318-2100; hours 7:30AM-5:00PM (CST). *Misdemeanor, Civil, Probate.*
Civil Records: Access: Mail, in person, online. Both court and visitors may perform in person searches. Search fee: $5.00 per name. Court makes copy: $1.00 per page. Self serve copy fee: $1.00 per page. Required to search: name, years to search. Civil cases indexed by defendant, plaintiff; on computer from 1985, index books before 1985. Online access is through www.idocket.com; registration and password required. Civil and probate records go back to 12/31/1986. Mail turnaround time 1-2 days.
Criminal Records: Access: Mail, in person, online. Both court and visitors may perform in person searches. Search fee: $5.00 per name. Court makes copy: $1.00 per page. Self serve copy fee: $1.00 per page. Required to search: name, years to search. Criminal records on computer from 1985, index books before 1985. Misdemeanor records access is through www.idocket.com; registration and password required. Records go back to 12/31/1991. Mail turnaround time 1-2 days.
General Information: Public terminal goes back to 1982. No juvenile, mental, sealed, or adoption records released. Certification fee: $5.00 per doc. Payee: County Clerk. Business checks accepted. Prepayment and SASE required.

Hill County

District Court PO Box 634, Hillsboro, TX 76645; phone: 254-582-4042; fax: 254-582-4035; hours 8AM-5PM (CST). *Felony, Misdemeanor, Civil.*
Civil Records: Access: Mail, in person, online. Both court and visitors may perform in person searches. Search fee: $5.00 per name. Court makes copy: $1.00 per page. Required to search: name, years to search. Civil cases indexed by defendant, plaintiff; on optical imaging from 9/1993, on computer from 1991, microfilm from 1930s to 1950s, index books from 1900s. Online access to court records is through www.idocket.com. One search a day is free; subscription required for more. Records go back to 12/31/1990. Mail turnaround time 1-2 days.
Criminal Records: Access: Mail, in person, online. Both court and visitors may perform in person searches. Search fee: $5.00 per name. Court makes copy: $1.00 per page. Required to search: name, years to search; also helpful: DOB, SSN. Criminal records on optical imaging from 9/1993, on computer from 1989, microfilm from 1930s to 1950s, index books from 1900s. Criminal records access is through www.idocket.com; registration and password required. Records go back to 12/31/1990. Mail turnaround time 1-2 days.
General Information: Public terminal goes back to 1990. No juvenile, mental, sealed, or adoption records released. Will fax documents for $1.50 per page. Certification fee: $1.00. Payee: District Clerk. Personal checks accepted in person. Prepayment and SASE required.

County Court PO Box 398, 1 Courthouse Sq, Hillsboro, TX 76645; phone: 254-582-4012; probate phone: 254-582-4030; fax: 254-582-4003; hours 8AM-5PM (CST). *Probate.*

Hockley County

District Court 802 Houston St, #316, Levelland, TX 79336; phone: 806-894-8527; fax: 806-894-3891; hours 9AM-5PM (CST). *Felony, Civil.*
Civil Records: Access: Phone, mail, in person. Both court and visitors may perform in person searches. Search fee: $5.00 per name. Court makes copy: $1.00 per page. Required to search: name, years to search. Civil cases indexed by defendant, plaintiff; on computer from 1990, archived from 1922. Mail turnaround time 1-2 days.
Criminal Records: Access: Phone, mail, in person. Both court and visitors may perform in person searches. Search fee: $5.00 per name. Court makes copy: $1.00 per page. Required to search: name, years

to search. Criminal records on computer from 1990, archived from 1922. Mail turnaround time 1-2 days.
General Information: Public terminal goes back to 1990. No juvenile, mental, sealed, or adoption records released. Certification fee: $2.00. Payee: District Clerk. Only cashiers checks and money orders accepted. Prepayment and SASE required.

County Court County Courthouse, 802 Houston St, #213, Levelland, TX 79336; phone: 806-894-3185; hours 9AM-5PM (CST). *Misdemeanor, Civil, Probate.*
Civil Records: Access: Mail, in person. Both court and visitors may perform in person searches. No search fee. Court makes copy: $1.00 per page. Required to search: name, years to search. Civil cases indexed by defendant, plaintiff; on computer from 1990, index books from 1960. Mail turnaround time 1-2 days.
Criminal Records: Access: Mail, in person. Both court and visitors may perform in person searches. Search fee: $5.00 per name. Court makes copy: $1.00 per page. Required to search: name, years to search; also helpful: DOB. Criminal records on computer from 1990, index books from 1960. Mail turnaround time 1-2 days.
General Information: Public use terminal available. No juvenile, mental, sealed, or adoption records released. Certification fee: $5.00 per document. Payee: Hockley County Clerk. Only cashiers checks and money orders accepted. Prepayment and SASE required.

Hood County

District Court County Courthouse, 100 E Pearl, #21, Granbury, TX 76048; phone: 817-579-3236; fax: 817-579-3239; hours 8AM-5PM (CST). *Felony, Civil.*
Civil Records: Access: Mail, in person. Both court and visitors may perform in person searches. Search fee: $5.00 per name. Court makes copy: $1.00 1st page; $.25 each add'l. Required to search: name, years to search. Civil cases indexed by defendant, plaintiff; on computer and microfiche from 1983, index books before 1983. Mail turnaround time 1-2 days.
Criminal Records: Access: Mail, in person. Both court and visitors may perform in person searches. Search fee: $5.00 per name. Court makes copy: $1.00 1st page; $.25 each add'l. Required to search: name, years to search, DOB, SSN, signed release. Criminal records on computer and microfiche from 1983, index books before 1983. Mail turnaround time 1-2 days.
General Information: No juvenile, mental, sealed, or adoption records released. Certification fee: $1.00 per page includes copy fee. Payee: District Clerk. Personal checks accepted. Prepayment and SASE required.

County Court PO Box 339, Granbury, TX 76048; phone: 817-579-3222; fax: 817-579-3227; hours 8AM-5PM (CST). *Misdemeanor, Civil, Probate.*
Civil Records: Access: Mail, in person. Both court and visitors may perform in person searches. Search fee: $5.00 per name. Court makes copy: $1.00 per page; same fee for self serve. Required to search: name, years to search. Civil cases indexed by defendant, plaintiff; in index books. Mail turnaround time 1 day.
Criminal Records: Access: Mail, in person. Both court and visitors may perform in person searches. Search fee: $5.00 per name. Court makes copy: $1.00 per page; same fee for self serve. Required to search: name, years to search; also helpful: DOB. Criminal records on computer and microfiche from 1982, index books before 1982. Mail turnaround time 1 day.
General Information: No juvenile, mental, sealed, or adoption records released. Will fax documents if prepaid. Certification fee: $5.00. Payee: Hood County Clerk. Personal checks accepted. Prepayment and SASE required.

Hopkins County

District Court 118 Church St, Sulphur Springs, TX 75483; phone: 903-438-4081; criminal phone: 903-438-4083; civil phone: 903-438-4084; hours 8AM-5PM (CST). *Felony, Civil.*
Civil Records: Access: Mail, in person. Both court and visitors may perform in person searches. Search fee: $5.00 per name. Court makes copy: $1.00 per page. Required to search: name, years to search. Civil cases indexed by defendant, plaintiff; on computer from 1987, index books from 1840. Mail turnaround time 2 days.
Criminal Records: Access: Mail, in person. Both court and visitors may perform in person searches. Search fee: $5.00 per name. Court makes copy: $1.00 per page. Required to search: name, years to search. Criminal records on computer from 1987, index books from 1840, archived from 1890. Mail turnaround time 2 days.
General Information: Public use terminal available. No juvenile, mental, sealed, or adoption records released. Will fax documents. Certification fee: $2.00. Payee: District Clerk. Personal checks accepted. Prepayment and SASE required.

County Court PO Box 288, Sulphur Springs, TX 75483; phone: 903-438-4074; probate phone: 903-438-4074; criminal fax: 903-438-4110; same fax for civil/probate; hours 8AM-5PM (CST). *Misdemeanor, Civil, Probate.*
www.hopkinscountytx.org/departments.htm
Note: Probate Court at 411 College St. but index is here.
Civil Records: Access: Mail, in person. Both court and visitors may perform in person searches. Search fee: $5.00 per name. Court makes copy: $1.00 per page. Self serve copy fee: $1.00 per page. Required to search: name, years to search. Civil cases indexed by defendant, plaintiff; on computer since 1992, index books from 1846. Mail turnaround time 1-2 days.
Criminal Records: Access: Mail, in person. Both court and visitors may perform in person searches. Search fee: $5.00 per name. Court makes copy: $1.00 per page. Self serve copy fee: $1.00 per page. Required to search: name, years to search; also helpful-DOB, SSN, signed release. Criminal records on computer from 1985, index books from 1846. Mail turnaround time 1-2 days.
General Information: Public terminal has criminal back to 1985 and civil back to 1992. No juvenile, mental, or sealed records released. Will fax documents for $1.00 per page. Certification fee: $5.00 per document. Payee: County Clerk. Personal checks accepted. Will accept credit cards. Prepayment and SASE required.

Houston County

District Court Houston County Courthouse, 401 E Houston, PO Box 1186, Crockett, TX 75835; phone: 936-544-3255 x222; fax: 936-544-9523; hours 8AM-4:30PM (CST). *Felony, Civil.*
Civil Records: Access: Fax, mail, in person. Both court and visitors may perform in person searches. Search fee: $5.00 per name. Court makes copy: $1.00 per page. Required to search: name, years to search. Civil cases indexed by plaintiff. Civil records on computer from 10/99, index books since 1800s. Mail turnaround time 2-5 days.
Criminal Records: Access: Fax, mail, in person. Both court and visitors may perform in person searches. Search fee: $5.00 per name. Court makes copy: $1.00 per page. Required to search: name, years to search, signed release; also helpful: DOB, SSN. Criminal records on computer since 10/99, index books since 1800s. Mail turnaround time 1-2 days.
General Information: Public terminal goes back to 1800s. No juvenile, mental, sealed, or adoption records released. Will fax documents $3.50 1st page, $.50 each add'l. No certification fee. Payee: District Clerk. Personal checks accepted. Prepayment and SASE required.

County Court PO Box 370, Crockett, TX 75835; phone: 936-544-3255; criminal phone: x241; civil phone: x239; probate phone: x239 or x241; criminal fax: 936-544-1954; same fax for civil/probate; hours 8AM-4:30 (CST). *Misdemeanor, Civil, Probate.*
Civil Records: Access: Mail, in person. Both court and visitors may perform in person searches. Search fee: $5.00 per name. Court makes copy: $1.00 per page; same fee for self serve. Required to search: name, years to search. Civil cases indexed by defendant, plaintiff; on computer since 2000, microfiche since 1983, index books since 1881 (probate). Mail turnaround time 1-2 days.
Criminal Records: Access: Mail, in person. Both court and visitors may perform in person searches. Search fee: $5.00 per name. Court makes copy: $1.00 per page; same fee for self serve. Required to search: name, years to search. Criminal records on computer since 2000, index books since 1881. Mail turnaround time 1-2 days.
General Information: Public terminal goes back to 1999. No juvenile, mental, sealed, or adoption records released. Will fax documents to local or toll-free number for $1.00 per page. Certification fee: $5.00 per document. Payee: County Clerk. Personal checks accepted. Prepayment required.

Howard County

District Court PO Box 2138, Big Spring, TX 79721; phone: 432-264-2223; fax: 432-264-2256; hours 8AM-5PM (CST). *Felony, Civil.*
Civil Records: Access: Mail, in person. Both court and visitors may perform in person searches. Search fee: $5.00 per name. Court makes copy: $1.00 per page. Required to search: name, years to search. Civil cases indexed by defendant, plaintiff; on computer from 1990, index books from 1881. Mail turnaround time 1-2 days.
Criminal Records: Access: Mail, in person. Both court and visitors may perform in person searches. Search fee: $5.00 per name. Court makes copy: $1.00 per page. Required to search: name, years to search. Criminal records on computer from 1990, index books from 1881. Mail turnaround time 1-2 days.
General Information: No juvenile, mental, sealed or adoption records released. Fee to fax documents is $1.00 per page. Certification fee: $1.00 per page. Payee: District Clerk. Personal checks accepted. Prepayment and SASE required.

County Court PO Box 1468, Big Spring, TX 79721; phone: 432-264-2213; fax: 432-264-2215; hours 8AM-5PM (CST). *Misdemeanor, Civil, Probate.*
Civil Records: Access: Phone, mail, in person. Both court and visitors may perform in person searches. Search fee: $5.00 per name. Court makes copy: $1.00 per page. Required to search: name, years to search. Civil cases indexed by defendant, plaintiff; in index books since 1881. Mail turnaround time 1-2 days.
Criminal Records: Access: Phone, mail, in person. Both court and visitors may perform in person searches. Search fee: $5.00 per name. Court makes copy: $1.00 per page. Required to search: name, years to search. Criminal records in index books since 1881. Mail turnaround time 1-2 days.
General Information: No juvenile, mental, sealed, or adoption records released. Will fax documents $5.00 per doc. Certification fee: $5.00. Payee: County Clerk. Business checks accepted. Prepayment required.

Hudspeth County

District & County Court PO Drawer 58, Sierra Blanca, TX 79851; phone: 915-369-2301; fax: 915-369-3055; hours 8AM-5PM (MST). *Felony, Misdemeanor, Civil, Probate.*
Civil Records: Access: Phone, fax, mail, in person. Both court and visitors may perform in person searches. Search fee: $5.00 per name. Court makes copy: $1.00 per page; same fee for self serve. Required to search: name, years to search. Civil cases indexed by defendant, plaintiff; in index books from 1900s; on computer since 1988. Mail turnaround time 1-2 days.
Criminal Records: Access: Phone, fax, mail, in person. Both court and visitors may perform in person searches. Search fee: $5.00 per name. Court makes copy: $1.00 per page; same fee for self serve. Required to search: name, years to search, DOB. Criminal records in index books from 1900s; on computer since 1998. Mail turnaround time 1-2 days.
General Information: Public terminal goes back to 10 years. No juvenile, mental, sealed, or adoption records released. Will fax documents $1.00 per page. Certification fee: $5.00. Payee: District/County Clerk. Personal checks accepted. Prepayment and SASE required.

Hunt County

District Court Court Clerk, PO Box 1437, Greenville, TX 75403; phone: 903-408-4172; hours 8AM-5PM (CST). *Felony, Civil.*
Civil Records: Access: Mail, in person. Both court and visitors may perform in person searches. Search fee: $5.00 per name. Court makes copy: $1.00 per page; same fee for self serve. Required to search: name, years to search. Civil cases indexed by defendant, plaintiff; on computer from 1992, microfiche from 1973, index books from 1900s. Mail turnaround time 1-2 days.
Criminal Records: Access: Mail, in person. Both court and visitors may perform in person searches. Search fee: $5.00 per name. Court makes copy: $1.00 per page; same fee for self serve. Required to search: name, years to search, DOB. Criminal records on computer from 1992, microfilm from 1973, index books from 1900s. Mail turnaround time 1-2 days.
General Information: No juvenile, sealed, or adoption records released. Certification fee: $1.00. Payee: District Clerk. Personal checks accepted. Prepayment and SASE required.

County Court PO Box 1316, Greenville, TX 75403-1316; phone: 903-408-4130; criminal phone: 903-408-4129; civil phone: 903-408-4260; probate phone: 903-408-4136; hours 8AM-5PM (CST). *Misdemeanor, Civil, Probate.*
Civil Records: Access: Mail, in person. Both court and visitors may perform in person searches. Search fee: $5.00 per name. Court makes copy: $1.00 per page; same fee for self serve. Required to search: name, years to search. Civil cases indexed by defendant, plaintiff; on computer since 1986, index books prior to 1986. Mail turnaround time 1-2 days.
Criminal Records: Access: Mail, in person. Both court and visitors may perform in person searches. Search fee: $5.00 per name. Court makes copy: $1.00 per page; same fee for self serve. Required to search: name, years to search, DOB. Criminal records on computer since 1986, index books from 1940; on microfilm prior to 1986. Mail turnaround time 1-2 days.
General Information: Public use terminal available. No juvenile, mental, sealed, or adoption records released. No fax documents available. Certification fee: $5.00. Payee: County Clerk. Personal checks accepted. Prepayment and SASE required.

Hutchinson County

District Court PO Box 580, Stinnett, TX 79083; phone: 806-878-4017; fax: 806-878-4042; hours 9AM-5PM (CST). *Felony, Civil.*
Civil Records: Access: Mail, in person. Both court and visitors may perform in person searches. Search fee: $5.00 per name. Court makes copy: $.25 per page. $1.00 minimum. Required to search: name, years to search. Civil cases indexed by defendant, plaintiff; on computer from 1989, docket books from 1920. Mail turnaround time 3 to 5 days.
Criminal Records: Access: Mail, in person. Both court and visitors may perform in person searches. Search fee: $5.00 per name. Court makes copy: $.25 per page. $1.00 minimum. Required to search: name,

years to search, signed release; also helpful: DOB, SSN. Criminal records on computer from 1989, docket books from 1920. Mail turnaround time 2 days.

General Information: Public terminal goes back to 1989. No juvenile, mental, sealed, or adoption records released. Fee to fax documents is $1.00 per page. Certification fee: $1.00 per page. Payee: District Clerk. Personal checks accepted. Prepayment and SASE required.

County Court PO Box 1186, Hutchinson County Clerk, Stinnett, TX 79083; phone: 806-878-4002; fax: 806-878-3497; hours 9AM-5PM (CST). *Misdemeanor, Civil, Probate.*

Civil Records: Access: Mail, in person. Both court and visitors may perform in person searches. Search fee: $5.00 per name. Court makes copy: $1.00 per page. Required to search: name, years to search. Civil cases indexed by defendant, plaintiff; in index books from 1900s. Mail turnaround time 2 days.

Criminal Records: Access: Mail, in person. Both court and visitors may perform in person searches. Search fee: $5.00 per name. Court makes copy: $1.00 per page. Required to search: name, years to search, signed release, DOB or SSN. Criminal records on computer since 1990, index books from 1900s. Mail turnaround time 2 days.

General Information: No juvenile, mental, sealed, or adoption records released. Certification fee: $5.00. Payee: Hutchinson County Clerk. Business checks accepted. Prepayment required.

Irion County

District & County Court PO Box 736, Mertzon, TX 76941-0736; phone: 325-835-2421; fax: 325-835-2008; hours 8AM-5PM, closed at noon 1 hr (CST). *Felony, Misdemeanor, Civil, Probate.*

Note: Office is closed at noon for one hour.

Civil Records: Access: Mail, fax, in person. Both court and visitors may perform in person searches. Search fee: $5.00 per name. Fee is per court. Court makes copy: $1.00 per page. Required to search: name, years to search. Civil cases indexed by defendant, plaintiff; in index books from 1886. This is a two-person office and some days shuts down at 1PM. It is best to call first if visiting in person. Mail turnaround time 5-20 days.

Criminal Records: Access: Mail, fax, in person. Both court and visitors may perform in person searches. Search fee: $5.00 per name. Fee is per court. Court makes copy: $1.00 per page. Required to search: name, years to search; also helpful: DOB, SSN, DL. Criminal records on index books from 1886. Mail turnaround time 5-20 days.

General Information: No juvenile, mental, or sealed records released. Will fax documents $1.00 per page if long distance, $.50 per page if local. Certification fee: $1.00. County Court cert fee $5.00. Payee: District/County Clerk. Personal checks accepted. Prepayment and SASE required.

Jack County

District Court 100 Main, County Courthouse, Jacksboro, TX 76458; phone: 940-567-2141; fax: 940-567-2696; hours 8AM-5PM (CST). *Felony, Civil.*

Civil Records: Access: Mail, in person. Both court and visitors may perform in person searches. Search fee: $10.00 per name. Court makes copy: $.50 per page; same fee for self serve. Required to search: name, years to search. Civil cases indexed by defendant, plaintiff; in index books from 1857. Mail turnaround time 2 days.

Criminal Records: Access: Mail, in person. Both court and visitors may perform in person searches. Search fee: $10.00 per name. Court makes copy: $.50 per page; same fee for self serve. Required to search: name, years to search. Criminal records in index books from 1857. Mail turnaround time 2 days.

General Information: No juvenile, mental, sealed, or adoption records released. Certification fee: $10.00.

Payee: Jack County District Clerk. Personal checks accepted. Prepayment and SASE required.

County Court 100 Main, Jacksboro, TX 76458; phone: 940-567-2111; fax: 940-567-6441; hours 8AM-5PM (CST). *Misdemeanor, Civil, Probate.*

Civil Records: Access: Mail, in person. Both court and visitors may perform in person searches. Search fee: $5.00 per name. Court makes copy: $1.00 per page; same fee for self serve. Required to search: name, years to search. Civil cases indexed by defendant, plaintiff; in index books from 1856, computerized since 1999. Mail turnaround time 1-2 days.

Criminal Records: Access: Phone, mail, in person. Both court and visitors may perform in person searches. Search fee: $5.00 per name. Court makes copy: $1.00 per page; same fee for self serve. Required to search: name, years to search. Criminal records in index books from 1856, computerized since 1999. Mail turnaround time 1-2 days.

General Information: No juvenile, mental, sealed, or adoption records released. Will fax documents for $1.00 per page. Certification fee: $5.00. Payee: Jack County Clerk. Personal checks accepted. Prepayment and SASE required.

Jackson County

District Court 115 W Main, Rm 203, Edna, TX 77957; phone: 361-782-3812; fax: 361-782-3056; hours 8AM-5PM (CST). *Felony, Civil.*

Civil Records: Access: Phone, mail, in person. Both court and visitors may perform in person searches. Search fee: $5.00 per name. Court makes copy: $1.00 per page; same fee for self serve. Required to search: name, years to search. Civil cases indexed by defendant, plaintiff; in index books from 1850. Mail turnaround time 1 day.

Criminal Records: Access: Mail, in person. Both court and visitors may perform in person searches. Search fee: $5.00 per name. Court makes copy: $1.00 per page; same fee for self serve. Required to search: name, years to search. Criminal records on microfiche from 1981, index books from 1850. Mail turnaround time 1-2 days.

General Information: No sealed, or adoption records released. Will fax documents. Certification fee: $1.00. Payee: District Clerk. Personal checks accepted. Prepayment and SASE required.

County Court 115 W Main, Rm 101, Edna, TX 77957; phone: 361-782-3563; fax: 361-782-3132; hours 8AM-N, 1-4PM (CST). *Misdemeanor, Civil, Probate.*

Note: Probate is separate index at this same address.

Civil Records: Access: Mail, in person. Both court and visitors may perform in person searches. Search fee: $5.00 per name. Court makes copy: $1.00 per page. Required to search: name, years to search. Civil cases indexed by defendant, plaintiff; in index books from 1900s; computerized back to 1993.

Criminal Records: Access: Main, in person. Both court and visitors may perform in person searches. Search fee: $5.00 per name. Court makes copy: $1.00 per page. Required to search: name, years to search, DOB, offense, date of offense. Criminal records in index books from 1900s. Mail turnaround time 1-2 days.

General Information: No juvenile, mental, sealed, or adoption records released. Fee to fax documents is $4.25 for the 1st page and $2.25 per page thereafter. Certification fee: $5.00 per document. Payee: County Clerk. Personal checks accepted. Prepayment required.

Jasper County

District Court County Courthouse, #202, PO Box 2088, Jasper, TX 75951; phone: 409-384-2721; fax: 409-383-7501; hours 8AM-4:30PM (CST). *Felony, Civil.*

Civil Records: Access: Mail, in person. Both court and visitors may perform in person searches. Search fee: $5.00 per name. Court makes copy: $1.00

per page; same fee for self serve. Required to search: name, years to search. Civil cases indexed by defendant, plaintiff; on computer since 1991, index books and microfilm since 1850s. Mail turnaround time 1-2 days.

Criminal Records: Access: Mail, in person. Only the court performs in person searches; visitors may not. Search fee: $5.00 per name. Court makes copy: $1.00 per page; same fee for self serve. Required to search: name, years to search. Criminal records on computer since 12/96; index books and microfilm since 1850s. Mail turnaround time 1-2 days.

General Information: Public terminal has only civil records back to 1990. No juvenile, mental, sealed, or adoption records released. No certification fee. Payee: District Clerk/Court. Personal checks accepted. Prepayment and SASE required.

County Court Rm 103, Courthouse, Main at Lamar, PO Box 2070, Jasper, TX 75951; phone: 409-384-2632; criminal phone: 409-384-5078; civil phone: 409-384-2632; probate phone: 409-384-2632; criminal fax: 409-384-7198; same fax for civil/probate; hours 8AM-4:30PM (CST). *Misdemeanor, Civil, Probate.*

Civil Records: Access: Phone, mail, fax, in person. Both court and visitors may perform in person searches. Search fee: $10.00 per name. There is no fee if you do the search yourself. Court makes copy: $1.00 per page. Required to search: name, years to search. Civil cases indexed by defendant, plaintiff; in index books; on computer back to 1987. Mail turnaround time 1 day.

Criminal Records: Access: Phone, mail, fax, in person. Both court and visitors may perform in person searches. Search fee: $10.00 per name. There is no fee if you do the search yourself. Court makes copy: $1.00 per page. Required to search: name, years to search, DOB; also helpful: SSN. Criminal records in index books; on computer back to 1987. Mail turnaround time 1 day.

General Information: Public terminal has criminal back to 1990 and civil back to 1991. No juvenile, mental, sealed, or adoption records released. Fee to fax documents is $3.00 per page. Certification fee: $5.00 per document. Payee: Debbie Newman County Clerk. Personal checks require drivers license. Prepayment required.

Jeff Davis County

District & County Court PO Box 398, Fort Davis, TX 79734; phone: 432-426-3251; criminal fax: 432-426-3760; same fax for civil/probate; hours 9AM-N, 1-5PM (CST). *Felony, Misdemeanor, Civil, Probate.*

Civil Records: Access: Mail, in person. Both court and visitors may perform in person searches. Search fee: $5.00 per name. Court makes copy: $1.00 per page. Required to search: name, years to search. Civil cases indexed by defendant, plaintiff; in index books. Mail turnaround time 2 days.

Criminal Records: Access: Mail, in person, fax. Both court and visitors may perform in person searches. Search fee: $5.00 per name. Court makes copy: $1.00 per page. Required to search: name, years to search. Criminal records in index books. Mail turnaround time 2 days.

General Information: No juvenile, mental, sealed, or adoption records released. Will fax documents to local or toll free line. Certification fee: $5.00 per certification. Payee: County Clerk. Personal checks accepted. Prepayment required. SASE helpful.

Jefferson County

District Court PO Box 3707, Pearl St Courthouse, Beaumont, TX 77704; phone: 409-835-8580; criminal phone: 409-835-8583; civil phone: 409-835-8580; fax: 409-835-8527; hours 8AM-5PM (CST). *Felony, Civil.*

www.co.jefferson.tx.us

Civil Records: Access: Mail, online, in person. Both court and visitors may perform in person searches. Search fee: $10.00 per name. Court makes copy:

$1.00 per page; same fee for self serve. Required to search: name, years to search. Civil cases indexed by defendant, plaintiff; on computer and index books since 1940s. Online access to the civil records index at www.co.jefferson.tx.us/dclerk/civil_index/main.htm. Search by year by defendant or plaintiff by year 1985 to present. Also, you may name search at http://jeffersontxclerk.hartic.com/search.asp?cabinet=civil. Index goes back to 1995; images back to 12/1998. Note: Search results are not certified unless done by the court itself. Mail turnaround time 2-4 days.

Criminal Records: Access: Mail, online, in person. Both court and visitors may perform in person searches. Search fee: $10.00 per name. Court makes copy: $1.00 per page; same fee for self serve. Required to search: name, years to search; also helpful: DOB, SSN. Criminal records on computer and index books since 1940s. Online access to the criminal records index is at www.co.jefferson.tx.us/dclerk/criminal_index/main.htm. Search by name by year 1981 to present. Also, felony records are free at http://jeffersontxclerk.hartic.com/search.asp?cabinet=criminal. Add'l criminal records are being added. Mail turnaround time 2-4 days.

General Information: Public terminal has criminal back to 1936 and civil back to 1945. (Civil, Family, and E-file on selected cases.) No juvenile, mental, sealed, or adoption records released. Will fax documents local for $3.00 1st page, $1.00 each add'l. Long distance 1st page is $5.00. There is also a similar fax fee to send to them. Certification fee: $5.00 per instrument. Payee: District Clerk. Only cashiers checks and money orders accepted. Prepayment and SASE required.

County Court PO Box 1151, Beaumont, TX 77704; phone: 409-835-8479; probate phone: 409-835-8483; criminal fax: 409-839-2394; same fax for civil/probate; hours 8AM-5PM (CST). *Misdemeanor, Civil, Probate.*

http://jeffersontxclerk.hartintercivic.com
Note: Search probate records back to 1988 free at http://jeffersontxclerk.hartintercivic.com/search.asp?cabinet=probate. Images go back to 1998. Probate records in a separate index.

Civil Records: Access: Mail, in person and online. Both court and visitors may perform in person searches. Search fee: $10.00 per name. Court makes copy: $1.00 per page. Required to search: name, years to search. Civil cases indexed by defendant, plaintiff; on computer since 11/1/95, index books to 1836. Search the county clerk's civil database free at http://jeffersontxclerk.hartintercivic.com/search.asp?cabinet=civil. Index goes back to 1995; images back to 12/1998. Mail turnaround time 1 day.

Criminal Records: Access: Mail, in person, online. Both court and visitors may perform in person searches. Search fee: $10.00 per name. Court makes copy: $1.00 per page. Required to search: name, years to search, DOB. Criminal records on computer since 1-1-82, index books to 1836. Access to Class A&B and C Misdemeanor that are appealed records back to 1982 are free at http://jeffersontxclerk.hartintercivic.com/search.asp?cabinet=criminal. Add'l criminal records are being added. Mail turnaround time 1 day.

General Information: Public terminal has criminal back to 1/1983 for index; 12/14/1998 for images and civil back to 11/1/1995 for index; 12/14/1998 for images. (Probate index goes back to 10/1988.) No juvenile, mental, sealed, or adoption records released. Will fax documents for $2.50 1st page, $.25 each add'l. Certification fee: $5.00 per cause number. Payee: County Clerk. Personal checks accepted. Credit cards accepted. Prepayment required.

Jim Hogg County

District & County Court PO Box 878, Hebbronville, TX 78361; phone: 361-527-4031; criminal fax: 361-527-5843; same fax for civil/probate; hours 9AM-5PM (CST). *Felony, Misdemeanor, Civil, Probate.*
Note: Probate records are in a separate index.
Civil Records: Access: Mail, fax, in person. Both court and visitors may perform in person searches. Search fee: $15.00 per name. Court makes copy: $1.00 per page; same fee for self serve. Required to search: name, years to search. Civil cases indexed by defendant, plaintiff; in index books.
Criminal Records: Access: In person only. Only the court performs in person searches; visitors may not. Search fee: $15.00 per name. Court makes copy: $1.00 per page; same fee for self serve. Required to search: name, years to search. Criminal records in index books. Mail turnaround time 2-4 days.
General Information: No juvenile, mental, sealed, or adoption records released. Fee to fax documents is $3.00 per page. Certification fee: $5.00 per document. Payee: District Clerk. Personal checks accepted. Prepayment and SASE required.

Jim Wells County

79th District Court PO Drawer 2219, Alice, TX 78333; phone: 361-668-5717; hours 8AM-N, 1-5PM (CST). *Felony, Civil.*
Civil Records: Access: Mail, in person. Both court and visitors may perform in person searches. Search fee: $5.00 per name. Court makes copy: $1.00 per page. Required to search: name, years to search. Civil cases indexed by defendant, plaintiff; on computer since 1992, index books since 1912. Mail turnaround time 2 days.
Criminal Records: Access: Mail, in person. Both court and visitors may perform in person searches. Search fee: $5.00 per name. Court makes copy: $1.00 per page. Required to search: name, years to search; also helpful: SSN. Criminal records on computer since 1992, index books since 1912. Mail turnaround time 2 days.
General Information: No juvenile, mental, sealed, or adoption records released. Certification fee: $2.00. Payee: District Clerk. Personal checks accepted. Prepayment and SASE required.

County Court PO Box 1459, 200 N Almond, Alice, TX 78333; phone: 361-668-5702; hours 8:00AM-N, 1-5PM (CST). *Misdemeanor, Civil, Probate.*
Civil Records: Access: Mail, in person. Both court and visitors may perform in person searches. Search fee: $10.00 per name. Court makes copy: $1.00 per page; same fee for self serve. Required to search: name, years to search. Civil cases indexed by defendant, plaintiff; in index books from 1911. Mail turnaround time 1 day.
Criminal Records: Access: Phone, mail, in person. Both court and visitors may perform in person searches. Search fee: $10.00 per name. Court makes copy: $1.00 per page; same fee for self serve. Required to search: name, years to search, address, DOB. Criminal records on computer since 1992, index books from 1911. Mail turnaround time 1 day.
General Information: No juvenile, mental, sealed, or adoption records released. Will not fax documents. Certification fee: $5.00 per document. Payee: County Clerk. Personal checks accepted. Prepayment required.

Johnson County

District Court PO Box 495, Cleburne, TX 76033-0495; phone: 817-556-6839; fax: 817-556-6120; hours 8AM-5PM (CST). *Felony, Civil.*
www.johnsoncountytx.org
Civil Records: Access: Fax, mail, in person. Both court and visitors may perform in person searches. Search fee: $5.00 per name. Court makes copy: $1.00 per page; same fee for self serve. Required to search: name; also helpful: years to search. Civil cases

indexed by defendant, plaintiff; on computer from mid-1989, index books back to 1800s. Mail turnaround time 2-4 days.
Criminal Records: Access: Fax, mail, in person. Both court and visitors may perform in person searches. Search fee: $5.00 per name. Court makes copy: $.50 per page; same fee for self serve. Required to search: name; also helpful: years to search, aliases. Criminal records on computer from mid-1989, index books back to 1800s. Mail turnaround time 2-4 days.
General Information: Public terminal goes back to mid-1989. No juvenile, mental, sealed, or adoption records released. Fee to fax documents is $2.00 per page. Certification fee: $1.00 per page include copy fee. Payee: District Clerk. Business checks accepted. Prepayment and SASE required.

County Court Guinn Justice Center, 204 S Buffalo Ave #407, Cleburne, TX 76033-0662; phone: 817-556-6323; criminal phone: ext 1326; civil phone: ext 1311; probate phone: ext 1308; hours 8AM-N, 1-4:30PM (CST). *Misdemeanor, Civil, Probate.*
www.johnsoncountytx.org/
Civil Records: Access: Mail, in person, online. Both court and visitors may perform in person searches. Search fee: $5.00 per name. Court makes copy: $1.00 per page. Required to search: name, years to search. Civil cases indexed by defendant, plaintiff; on computer since 1988, index books from 1985. Online access via http://idocket.com/homepage2.htm. Registration required. Civil records back to 12/31/85, probate to 12/31/88. Mail turnaround time 2-3 days.
Criminal Records: Access: Mail, in person, online. Both court and visitors may perform in person searches. Search fee: $5.00 per name. Court makes copy: $1.00 per page. Required to search: name, years to search, and DOB or SSN. Rcords on computer since 1988, index books from 1985. Access via http://idocket.com/homepage2.htm. Registration required. Misdemeanor (no felony) records back to 12/31/85. Mail turnaround 1-2 days.
General Information: Public terminal has criminal back to 1988 and civil back to 1985. No juvenile, mental, sealed, or adoption records released. Certification fee: $3.00. Payee: County Clerk. Business checks accepted. Prepayment and SASE required.

Jones County

District Court PO Box 308, Anson, TX 79501; phone: 325-823-3731; fax: 325-823-4200; hours 8AM-5PM (CST). *Felony, Misdemeanor, Civil.*
Civil Records: Access: Mail, in person. Both court and visitors may perform in person searches. Search fee: $5.00 per name. Court makes copy: $1.00 per page; same fee for self serve. Required to search: name, years to search. Civil cases indexed by defendant, plaintiff; on computer since 1990, index books since 1881. Mail turnaround time same day.
Criminal Records: Access: Mail, in person. Both court and visitors may perform in person searches. Search fee: $5.00 per name. Court makes copy: $1.00 per page; same fee for self serve. Required to search: name, years to search, DOB. Criminal records on computer since 1986, index books since 1881. Mail turnaround time same day.
General Information: No juvenile, mental, sealed, or adoption records released. Will fax documents to local or toll free line. Certification fee: $2.00. Payee: Nona Carter, District Clerk. Personal checks accepted. Can set up deposit account. Prepayment and SASE required.

Karnes County

District Court County Courthouse, 101 N Panna Maria Ave, Karnes City, TX 78118-2930; phone: 830-780-2562; fax: 830-780-3227; hours 8AM-N, 1-5PM (CST). *Felony, Civil.*
Civil Records: Access: Mail, in person, fax. Both court and visitors may perform in person searches.

Search fee: $5.00 per name. Court makes copy: $1.00 per page. Required to search: name, years to search. Civil cases indexed by defendant, plaintiff; in index books from 1858. Mail turnaround time 1-2 days.

Criminal Records: Access: Mail, in person. Both court and visitors may perform in person searches. Search fee: $5.00 per name. Court makes copy: $1.00 per page. Required to search: name, years to search. Criminal records in index books from 1906. Mail turnaround time 1-2 days.

General Information: No juvenile, mental, sealed, or adoption records released. Will fax documents for $.25 per page. Certification fee: $2.00. Payee: District Clerk. Personal checks accepted. Prepayment and SASE required.

County Court 101 N Panna Maria Ave, #9 Courthouse, Karnes City, TX 78118-2929; phone: 830-780-3938; criminal fax: 830-780-4576; same fax for civil/probate; hours 8AM-5PM (CST). *Misdemeanor, Civil, Probate.*

Civil Records: Access: Mail, in person. Both court and visitors may perform in person searches. Search fee: $10.00 per name. Court makes copy: $1.00 per page; same fee for self serve. Required to search: name, years to search. Civil cases indexed by defendant, plaintiff; in index books from 1920, no computerization. Mail turnaround time 2 days.

Criminal Records: Access: Mail, in person. Both court and visitors may perform in person searches. Search fee: $10.00 per name. Court makes copy: $1.00 per page; same fee for self serve. Required to search: name, years to search. Criminal records in index books from 1900, computerized since 1991. Mail turnaround time 2 days.

General Information: No juvenile, mental, sealed, or adoption records released. Fee to fax documents is $2.00 per page. Certification fee: $5.00 per doc. Payee: Alva Jonas, County Clerk. Personal checks accepted. Prepayment and SASE required.

Kaufman County

District Court County Courthouse, 100 W Mulberry St, Kaufman, TX 75142; phone: 972-932-4331 X214; hours 8AM-5PM (CST). *Felony, Civil.*

Civil Records: Access: Mail, in person. Both court and visitors may perform in person searches. Search fee: $10.00 per name. Court makes copy: $1.00 per page. Required to search: name, years to search. Civil cases indexed by defendant, plaintiff; on computer or books from 1849. Mail turnaround time up to 1 week.

Criminal Records: Access: Mail, in person. Both court and visitors may perform in person searches. Search fee: $10.00 per name. Court makes copy: $1.00 per page. Required to search: name, years to search. Criminal records on computer or books from 1849. Mail turnaround time up to 1 week.

General Information: Public use terminal available. No sealed, or adoption records released. Certification fee: $1.00. Payee: Kaufman Distric Clerk. Personal checks accepted. Prepayment and SASE required.

County Court County Courthouse, Kaufman, TX 75142; phone: 972-932-4331 x1218; criminal fax: 972-932-4086; civil fax: 972-932-0659; probate fax: 972-932-0659; hours 8AM-4:30PM (CST). *Misdemeanor, Civil, Probate.*

http:www.kaufmancounty.net

Civil Records: Access: Mail, in person. Both court and visitors may perform in person searches. Search fee: $5.00 per name; probate is $10.00 per name. Court makes copy: $1.00 per page; same fee for self serve. Required to search: name, years to search. Civil cases indexed by defendant, plaintiff; on computer from 1985, index books to 1959. Mail turnaround time 10 days.

Criminal Records: Access: Mail, in person. Both court and visitors may perform in person searches. Search fee: $5.00 per name. Court makes copy: $1.00 per page; same fee for self serve. Required to search: name, years to search. Criminal records on computer from 1985, index books to 1870. Mail turnaround time 10 days.

General Information: Public terminal goes back to 1985. No juvenile, mental, sealed, or adoption records released. Will fax documents for $3.00 per document. Certification fee: $5.00 first page; $1.00 each add'l page,. Payee: County Clerk. Personal checks accepted. Prepayment and SASE required.

Kendall County

District Court 201 E. San Antonio, #201, Boerne, TX 78006; phone: 830-249-9343; hours 8AM-N, 1-5PM (CST). *Felony, Civil.*

Civil Records: Access: Mail, in person. Both court and visitors may perform in person searches. Search fee: $5.00 per name. Court makes copy: $.50 per page. Required to search: name, years. Civil cases indexed by defendant, plaintiff; in index books back to early 1900s. Mail turnaround 1-2 days.

Criminal Records: Access: Mail, in person. Both court and visitors may perform in person searches. Search fee: $5.00 per name. Court makes copy: $.50 per page. Required to search: name, DOB, years to search, signed release; also helpful: SSN. Criminal records in index books back to early 1900s. Mail turnaround time 2-4 days.

General Information: No juvenile, mental, sealed, or adoption records released. Will not fax documents. Certification fee: $1.00 per page. Payee: District Clerk. Personal checks accepted. Prepayment and SASE required.

County Court 201 E San Antonio, #127, Boerne, TX 78006; phone: 830-249-9343; fax: 830-249-3472; hours 8AM-5PM (CST). *Misdemeanor, Probate.*

Civil Records: Access: Mail, in person. Both court and visitors may perform in person searches. Search fee: $10.00 per name. Court makes copy: $1.00 per page; same fee for self serve. Required to search: name, years to search. Civil cases indexed by defendant, plaintiff; in index books from 1860s. Mail turnaround time 2-4 days.

Criminal Records: Access: Mail, in person. Both court and visitors may perform in person searches. Search fee: $5.00 per name. Court makes copy: $1.00 per page; same fee for self serve. Required to search: name, years to search. Criminal records in index books from 1860s. Mail turnaround time 2-4 days.

General Information: No juvenile, mental, sealed, or adoption records released. No fee to fax documents. Certification fee: $5.00. Payee: County Clerk. Personal checks accepted. Prepayment and SASE required.

Kenedy County

District & County Court PO Box 227, Sarita, TX 78385; phone: 361-294-5220; fax: 361-294-5218; hours 8:30AM-N, 1PM-4:30PM (CST). *Felony, Misdemeanor, Civil, Probate.*

Civil Records: Access: Phone, fax, mail, in person. Both court and visitors may perform in person searches. Search fee: $5.00 per name. Court makes copy: $1.00 per page. Required to search: name, years to search. Civil cases indexed by defendant, plaintiff; on microfilm since 1991, minute books since 1921. Mail turnaround time 5 days.

Criminal Records: Access: Phone, fax, mail, in person. Both court and visitors may perform in person searches. Search fee: $5.00 per name. Court makes copy: $1.00 per page. Required to search: name, years to search. Criminal records on microfilm since 1991, minute books since 1921. Mail turnaround time 5 days.

General Information: No juvenile, mental, sealed, or adoption records released. Certification fee: $5.00 per doc. Payee: District/County Clerk. Personal checks accepted. Prepayment required.

Kent County

District & County Court PO Box 9, Jayton, TX 79528; phone: 806-237-3881; criminal fax: 806-237-2632; same fax for civil/probate; hours 8:30AM-N, 1-5PM (CST). *Felony, Misdemeanor, Civil, Probate.*

Civil Records: Access: Mail, in person. Both court and visitors may perform in person searches. Search fee: $5.00 per name. Court makes copy: $1.00 per page; same fee for self serve. Required to search: name, years to search. Civil cases indexed by defendant, plaintiff; in index books. Mail turnaround time ASAP.

Criminal Records: Access: Mail, in person. Both court and visitors may perform in person searches. Search fee: $5.00 per name. Court makes copy: $1.00 per page; same fee for self serve. Required to search: name, years to search. Criminal records in index books. Mail turnaround time ASAP.

General Information: No juvenile, mental, sealed, or adoption records released. Will not fax documents. Certification fee: $5.00 per document. Payee: County Clerk. Only cashiers checks and money orders accepted. Prepayment and SASE required.

Kerr County

District Court 700 Main, County Courthouse, Kerrville, TX 78028; phone: 830-792-2281; fax: 830-792-2289; hours 8AM-5PM (CST). *Felony, Civil.*

Civil Records: Access: Mail, in person. Both court and visitors may perform in person searches. Search fee: $5.00 per name. Court makes copy: $1.00 1st page; $.25 each add'l; same fee for self serve. Required to search: name, years to search. Civil cases indexed by defendant, plaintiff; on computer from late 1991, index books prior to 1991. Mail turnaround time 2-4 days.

Criminal Records: Access: Mail, in person. Both court and visitors may perform in person searches. Search fee: $5.00 per name. Court makes copy: $1.00 1st page; $.25 each add'l; same fee for self serve. Required to search: name, years to search, DOB, SSN. Criminal records on computer from late 1990, index books prior. Mail turnaround time 2-4 days.

General Information: Public terminal goes back to early 1990s. No juvenile, mental, sealed, or adoption records released. Fee to fax documents is $1.00 per page. Certification fee: $1.00 per page includes copy. Payee: District Clerk. Personal checks accepted. Prepayment and SASE required.

County Court & County Court at Law 700 Main St, #122, Kerrville, TX 78028-5389; phone: 830-792-2262; probate phone: 830-792-2298; criminal fax: 830-792-2274; same fax for civil/probate; hours 8AM-5PM (CST). *Misdemeanor, Civil, Probate.*

www.kerrcounty.org/

Civil Records: Access: Phone, mail, fax, in person. Both court and visitors may perform in person searches. Search fee: $5.00 per name. Court makes copy: $1.00 per page; same fee for self serve. Required to search: name, years to search. Civil cases indexed by defendant, plaintiff; on computer since 1988, microfiche since 1985, index books prior to 1985. Mail turnaround time 3 days.

Criminal Records: Access: Phone, mail, fax, in person. Both court and visitors may perform in person searches. Search fee: $5.00 per name. Court makes copy: $1.00 per page; same fee for self serve. Required to search: name, years to search, DOB; also helpful: SSN. Criminal records on computer since 1985, index books prior to 1918. Mail turnaround time 3 days.

General Information: Public terminal goes back to 1986. No juvenile, mental, sealed, or adoption records released. Fee to fax documents is $1.00 per page. Certification fee: $5.00 per document. Payee: Kerr County Clerk. Only cashiers checks and money orders accepted. Prepayment required.

Kimble County

District & County Court 501 Main St, Junction, TX 76849; phone: 325-446-3353; criminal fax: 325-446-2986; same fax for civil/probate; hours 8AM-N, 1-5PM (CST). *Felony, Misdemeanor, Civil, Probate.*

Note: Probate records are in a separate index.

Civil Records: Access: In person only. Visitors must perform in person searches themselves. Court makes copy: $1.00 per page. Required to search: name, years to search. Civil cases indexed by defendant, plaintiff; in index books (records are micro-filmed for security only).

Criminal Records: Access: Mail, in person. Both court and visitors may perform in person searches. Search fee: $5.00 per name. Court makes copy: $1.00 per page. Required to search: name, years to search, DOB. Criminal records in index books (records are micro-filmed for security only). The clerk will search back 7 years. Request for criminal search must be in writing and can be faxed if you have prearranged for payment. Mail turnaround time 3-4 days.

General Information: No juvenile, mental, sealed, or adoption records released. Will fax documents to local or toll free line. Certification fee: $5.00. Payee: Kimble County/District Clerk. Personal checks accepted. Prepayment and SASE required.

King County

District & County Court PO Box 135, Guthrie, TX 79236; phone: 806-596-4412; criminal phone: 806-596-4412; civil phone: 806-596-4412; probate phone: 806-596-4412; fax: 806-596-4664; hours 9AM-N, 1-5PM (CST). *Felony, Misdemeanor, Civil, Probate.*

Civil Records: Access: Mail, in person. Both court and visitors may perform in person searches. Search fee: $5.00 per name. Court makes copy: $1.00 per page; same fee for self serve. Required to search: name, years to search. Civil cases indexed by defendant, plaintiff; in index books. Mail turnaround time 2-4 days.

Criminal Records: Access: Mail, in person. Both court and visitors may perform in person searches. Search fee: $5.00 per name. Court makes copy: $1.00 per page; same fee for self serve. Required to search: name, years to search, DOB. Criminal records in index books. Mail turnaround time 2-4 days.

General Information: No juvenile, mental, sealed, or adoption records released. Will fax documents for $1.00 per page. Certification fee: $5.00. Payee: District Clerk. Personal checks accepted. Prepayment and SASE required.

Kinney County

District & County Court PO Drawer 9, 501 S "N" St, Brackettville, TX 78832; phone: 830-563-2521; fax: 830-563-2644; hours 8AM-5PM (CST). *Felony, Misdemeanor, Civil, Probate.*

Civil Records: Access: Phone, fax, mail, in person. Both court and visitors may perform in person searches. Search fee: $10.00 per name. Court makes copy: $1.00 per page; same fee for self serve. Required to search: name, years to search. Civil cases indexed by defendant, plaintiff; in index books from late 1800s; computerized back to 1996. Mail turnaround time 1 week.

Criminal Records: Access: Phone, fax, mail, in person. Both court and visitors may perform in person searches. Search fee: $10.00 per name. Court makes copy: $1.00 per page; same fee for self serve. Required to search: name, years to search, DOB. Criminal records in index books from late 1800s; computerized records back to 1996. Mail turnaround time 1 week.

General Information: No juvenile, mental, sealed, or adoption records released. Will fax documents for $3.00 for 1st page; $2.00 each add'l. Certification fee: $5.00 in County court; $1.00 in District. Payee: County & District Clerk. Personal checks accepted. Prepayment and SASE required.

Kleberg County

District & County Court at Law PO Box 312, Kingsville, TX 78364-0312; phone: 361-595-8561; fax: 361-595-8525; hours 8AM-N, 1-5 PM (CST). *Felony, Civil.*

Civil Records: Access: Phone, fax, mail, in person, online. Both court and visitors may perform in person searches. Search fee: $5.00 per name. Court makes copy: $1.00 1st page, $.25 each add'l. Self serve copy fee: $1.00 per page. Required to search: name, years to search. Civil cases indexed by defendant, plaintiff; in index books since 1916. Computerized records go back to 1992. Online access is at www.idocket.com; registration and password required. There is a fee service, unless only one name search is done a day. Records go back to 12/31/1991. Mail turnaround time 1-2 days.

Criminal Records: Access: Phone, fax, mail, in person, online. Both court and visitors may perform in person searches. Search fee: $5.00 per name. Court makes copy: $1.00 1st page, $.25 each add'l. Self serve copy fee: $1.00 per page. Required to search: name, years to search; also helpful: DOB, SSN. Criminal records in index books since 1916. Computerized records go to 1992. Online access is at www.idocket.com; registration and password required. This is a $$ fee service, unless only one name search is done a day. Records go back to 12/31/1995. Mail turnaround time 1-2 days.

General Information: Public terminal goes back to 1992. No sealed or adoption records released. Will fax documents $5.00 per doc; incoming fax fee $1.00. Certification fee: $1.00. Payee: District Clerk. Local personal checks accepted. Prepayment and SASE required.

County Court - Criminal PO Box 1327, Kingsville, TX 78364; phone: 361-595-8548; fax: 361-593-1355; hours 8AM-5PM (CST). *Misdemeanor, Probate.*
www.co.kleberg.tx.us/courtatlaw.html
Note: Court also handles civil cases dealing with occupational licenses and bond forfeitures.

Criminal Records: Access: Phone, mail, in person. Both court and visitors may perform in person searches. Search fee: $10.00 per name per 10 years. Court makes copy: $1.00 per page. Required to search: name, years to search, DOB. Criminal records on computer since 1989, index books since 1913. Mail turnaround time 3 to 5 days.

General Information: Public terminal has only criminal records. No juvenile or mental records released. Certification fee: $5.00. Payee: Kleberg County Clerk. Business checks accepted. Prepayment required. SASE requested.

Knox County

District & County Court PO Box 196, Benjamin, TX 79505; phone: 940-459-2441; criminal fax: 940-459-2005; same fax for civil/probate; hours 8AM-5PM (CST). *Felony, Misdemeanor, Civil, Probate.*
Note: Probate is separate index at this same address.

Civil Records: Access: Mail, in person. Both court and visitors may perform in person searches. Search fee: $5.00 per name. Court makes copy: $1.00 per page; same fee for self serve. Required to search: name, years to search. Civil cases indexed by defendant, plaintiff; in index books. Mail turnaround time same day.

Criminal Records: Access: Mail, in person. Both court and visitors may perform in person searches. Search fee: $5.00 for a misdemeanor search; $5.00 for a felony search. Court makes copy: $1.00 per page; same fee for self serve. Required to search: name, years to search, DOB, SSN, signed release. Criminal records in index books back to 1885. Mail turnaround time 1 day.

General Information: No juvenile, mental, sealed, or adoption records released. Fee to fax documents is $1.00 per page. Certification fee: $5.00 per document. Payee: District/County Clerk. Personal checks accepted. Prepayment and SASE required.

La Salle County

District Court Courthouse Square, #107, Cotulla, TX 78014; phone: 830-879-4432; fax: 830-879-2933; hours 8AM-5PM (CST). *Felony, Civil.*

Civil Records: Access: Phone, mail, in person. Both court and visitors may perform in person searches. Search fee: $5.00 per name. Court makes copy: $1.00 per page; same fee for self serve. Required to search: name, years to search. Civil cases indexed by defendant, plaintiff; on computer back to 1990, prior in index books. Mail turnaround time 1-2 days.

Criminal Records: Access: Mail, in person. Both court and visitors may perform in person searches. Search fee: $5.00 per name. Court makes copy: $1.00 per page; same fee for self serve. Required to search: name, years to search. Criminal records on computer back to 1990, prior in index books. Mail turnaround time 1-2 days.

General Information: No juvenile, mental, sealed, or adoption records released. Will fax documents for $1.00 per page. Certification fee: $5.00. Payee: District Clerk. Personal checks accepted. Prepayment and SASE required.

District & County Courts PO Box 340, Cotulla, TX 78014; phone: 830-879-4432; criminal fax: 830-879-2933; same fax for civil/probate; hours 8AM-5PM (CST). *Misdemeanor, Civil, Probate.*

Civil Records: Access: Mail, in person. Both court and visitors may perform in person searches. Search fee: $5.00 per name. Court makes copy: $1.00 per page. Required to search: name, years to search. Civil cases indexed by defendant, plaintiff; on computer since 1994, prior on index books. Mail turnaround time 1-2 days.

Criminal Records: Access: Mail, in person. Both court and visitors may perform in person searches. Search fee: $5.00 per name. Court makes copy: $1.00 per page. Required to search: name, years to search. Criminal records on computer since 1994, prior on index books to 1988. Mail turnaround time 1-2 days.

General Information: No juvenile, mental, sealed, or adoption records released. Will fax documents for $1.00 per page. Certification fee: $5.00 per document. Payee: County Clerk. Personal checks accepted. Prepayment and SASE required.

Lamar County

District Court 119 N Main, Rm 306, Paris, TX 75460; phone: 903-737-2427; hours 8AM-5PM (CST). *Felony, Civil.*
www.co.lamar.tx.us/

Civil Records: Access: Mail, in person, online. Both court and visitors may perform in person searches. Search fee: $5.00 per name. Court makes copy: $1.00 per page; same fee for self serve. Required to search: name, years to search. Civil cases indexed by defendant, plaintiff; on computer since 1/1994, index books prior to 1994. Access to county judicial records is free at www.co.lamar.tx.us/. Search by either party name. Mail turnaround time 1-2 days.

Criminal Records: Access: Mail, in person, online. Both court and visitors may perform in person searches. Search fee: $5.00 per name. Court makes copy: $1.00 per page; same fee for self serve. Required to search: name, years to search. Criminal records on computer since 1/1994, index books prior to 1994. Access to county judicial records is free online at www.co.lamar.tx.us. Search by defendant name. Mail turnaround time 1-2 days.

General Information: Public terminal has criminal back to 1987 and civil back to 1994. No juvenile, mental, sealed, or adoption records released. No certification fee. Payee: District Clerk. Personal checks accepted. Prepayment and SASE required.

County Court 119 N Main, Paris, TX 75460; phone: 903-737-2420; hours 8AM-5PM (CST). *Misdemeanor, Civil, Probate.*
www.co.lamar.tx.us

Civil Records: Access: Phone, fax, mail, in person, online. Both court and visitors may perform in person searches. Search fee: $5.00 per name. Court makes copy: $1.00 per page. Required to search: name, years to search. Civil cases indexed by defendant, plaintiff; in index books since 1913; on computer back to 1998. Access to county judicial records is free at http://68.89.102.225/. Search by either party name. Mail turnaround time 2-3 days.

Criminal Records: Access: Phone, fax, mail, in person, online. Both court and visitors may perform in person searches. Search fee: $5.00 per name. Court makes copy: $1.00 per page. Required to search: name, years to search, DOB; SSN or drivers license number also required. Criminal records on computer back to 1988, index books since 1913. Access to county judicial records is free online at www.co.lamar.tx.us. Search by defendant name. Mail turnaround time 2-3 days.

General Information: No juvenile, mental, sealed, or adoption records released. Will not fax documents. Certification fee: $5.00 per document. Payee: County Clerk. Business checks accepted. Personal checks must be local. Prepayment required.

Lamb County

District Court 100 6th, Rm 212, Courthouse, Littlefield, TX 79339; phone: 806-385-4222; fax: 806-385-3554; hours 8AM-N, 1-5PM (CST). *Felony, Civil.*

Civil Records: Access: Mail, in person. Both court and visitors may perform in person searches. Search fee: $5.00 per name. Court makes copy: $1.00 per page; same fee for self serve. Required to search: name, years to search. Civil cases indexed by defendant, plaintiff; on computer since 1987; on index books back to 1940. Mail turnaround time 2-3 days.

Criminal Records: Access: Mail, in person. Both court and visitors may perform in person searches. Search fee: $5.00 per name. Court makes copy: $1.00 per page; same fee for self serve. Required to search: name, years to search; also helpful: DOB, SSN. Criminal records in index books to 1940s; on computer since 1987. Mail turnaround time 2-3 days.

General Information: No juvenile, mental, sealed, or adoption records released. Will fax documents to local or toll free line. Certification fee: $5.00 per document. Payee: District Court. Personal checks accepted. Prepayment and SASE required.

County Court County Courthouse, Rm 103, Box 3, Littlefield, TX 79339-3366; phone: 806-385-4222 X214; fax: 806-385-6485; hours 8:30AM-Noon1-5PM (CST). *Misdemeanor, Civil, Probate.*

Civil Records: Access: Mail, in person. Both court and visitors may perform in person searches. Search fee: $5.00 per name. Court makes copy: $1.00 per page. Required to search: name, years to search. Civil cases indexed by defendant, plaintiff; in index books. Mail turnaround time 1-2 days.

Criminal Records: Access: Mail, in person. Both court and visitors may perform in person searches. Search fee: $5.00 per name. Court makes copy: $1.00 per page. Required to search: name, years to search; also helpful: DOB, SSN. Criminal records in index books. Mail turnaround time 1-2 days.

General Information: No juvenile, mental, sealed, or adoption records released. Certification fee: $5.00 per document. Payee: Lamb County Clerk. Personal checks accepted. Prepayment and SASE required.

Lampasas County

District Court PO Box 327, Lampasas, TX 76550; phone: 512-556-8271 X240; fax: 512-556-9463; hours 8AM-5PM (CST). *Felony, Civil.*

Civil Records: Access: Mail, in person. Both court and visitors may perform in person searches. Search fee: $5.00 per name. Court makes copy: $1.00 per page. Required to search: name, years to search. Civil cases indexed by defendant, plaintiff; in index books, computerized since 1997. Mail turnaround time 2-4 days.

Criminal Records: Access: Mail, in person. Both court and visitors may perform in person searches. Search fee: $5.00 per name. Court makes copy: $1.00 per page. Required to search: name, years to search. Criminal records in index books; on computer for 5 years. Mail turnaround time 2-4 days.

General Information: No juvenile, mental, sealed, or adoption records released. Fee to fax documents is $1.00 per page. Certification fee: $2.00 per document. Payee: District Clerk. Business checks accepted. Prepayment and SASE required.

County Court PO Box 347, Lampasas, TX 76550; phone: 512-556-8271 x202; hours 8AM-5PM (CST). *Misdemeanor, Civil, Probate.*

Note: Probate is separate index at this same address.

Civil Records: Access: Mail, in person. Both court and visitors may perform in person searches. Search fee: $5.00 per name. Court makes copy: $1.00 per page; same fee for self serve. Required to search: name, years to search. Civil cases indexed by defendant, plaintiff; in index books. Mail turnaround time 1-2 days.

Criminal Records: Access: Mail, in person. Both court and visitors may perform in person searches. Search fee: $5.00 per name. Court makes copy: $1.00 per page; same fee for self serve. Required to search: name, years to search; also helpful: DOB, SSN. Criminal records in index books. Mail turnaround time 1-2 days.

General Information: No juvenile, mental, sealed, or adoption records released. Will not fax documents. Certification fee: $5.00 per document. Payee: County Clerk. Personal checks must be in state. Prepayment required. SASE requested.

Lavaca County

District Court PO Box 306, Hallettsville, TX 77964; phone: 361-798-2351; fax: 361-798-5674; hours 8AM-N, 1-5PM (CST). *Felony, Civil.*

Civil Records: Access: Phone, mail, in person. Both court and visitors may perform in person searches. Search fee: $5.00 per name. Court makes copy: $1.00 per page; same fee for self serve. Required to search: name, years to search. Civil cases indexed by defendant, plaintiff; in index books from 1847. Information released to attorneys only. Mail turnaround time same day.

Criminal Records: Access: Mail, in person. Both court and visitors may perform in person searches. Search fee: $5.00 per name. Court makes copy: $1.00 per page; same fee for self serve. Required to search: name, years to search. Criminal records in index books from 1847. Information released to law enforcement only. Mail turnaround time same day.

General Information: No juvenile, Department of Human Services, adoptions and expunction records released. Will fax documents to local or toll free line. Certification fee: $2.00. Payee: Lavaca County District Clerk. Personal checks accepted. Prepayment and SASE required.

County Court PO Box 326, Hallettsville, TX 77964; phone: 361-798-3612; hours 8AM-5PM (CST). *Misdemeanor, Civil, Probate.*

Civil Records: Access: Mail, in person. Both court and visitors may perform in person searches. Search fee: $5.00 per name per 10 years. Court makes copy: $1.00 per page; same fee for self serve. Required to search: name, years to search, DOB; also helpful: address, SSN, DL#. Civil cases indexed by defendant, plaintiff; on computer go back to late 1993; earlier in index books. Mail turnaround time same day as received.

Criminal Records: Access: Mail, in person. Both court and visitors may perform in person searches. Search fee: $5.00 per name per 5 years. Court makes copy: $1.00 per page; same fee for self serve. Required to search: name, years to search; also helpful: address, DOB, DL#, SSN. Records on computer go back to late 1993; earlier in index books. Mail turnaround time same day as received.

General Information: Public use terminal available. No mental health or sealed records released.

Certification fee: $5.00 per document. Payee: County Clerk. Personal checks accepted. Prepayment required.

Lee County

District Court PO Box 176, Giddings, TX 78942; phone: 979-542-2947; fax: 979-542-2444; hours 8AM-N, 1-5PM (CST). *Felony, Civil.*

Civil Records: Access: Mail, in person. Both court and visitors may perform in person searches. Search fee: $5.00 per name. Court makes copy: $1.00 per page; same fee for self serve. Required to search: name, years to search. Civil cases indexed by defendant, plaintiff; on index books from 1800s. Mail turnaround time 1-2 days.

Criminal Records: Access: Mail, in person. Both court and visitors may perform in person searches. Search fee: $5.00 per name. Court makes copy: $1.00 per page; same fee for self serve. Required to search: name, years to search; also helpful: DOB, SSN. Criminal records on computer since 1989. Mail turnaround time 1-2 days.

General Information: No juvenile or adoption records released. Will fax documents to local or toll free line. Certification fee: $2.00 per cert. Payee: District Clerk, Lee County. Personal checks accepted. Prepayment required.

County Court PO Box 419, Giddings, TX 78942; phone: 979-542-3684; criminal fax: 979-542-2623; same fax for civil/probate; hours 8AM-5PM (CST). *Misdemeanor, Civil, Probate.*

Civil Records: Access: Mail, in person. Both court and visitors may perform in person searches. Search fee: $5.00 per name. Court makes copy: $1.00 per page. Required to search: name, years to search. Civil cases indexed by defendant, plaintiff; in index books since 1874 (beginning 1995 on computer). Mail turnaround time 1-3 days.

Criminal Records: Access: Mail, in person. Both court and visitors may perform in person searches. Search fee: $5.00 per name. Court makes copy: $1.00 per page. Required to search: name, years to search. Criminal records on computer since 1992, index books since 1874. Mail turnaround time 1-3 days.

General Information: No juvenile, mental, sealed or adoption records released. Will fax documents to local or toll free line. Certification fee: $5.00. Payee: County Clerk. Personal checks accepted. Prepayment and SASE required.

Leon County

District Court PO Box 39, 139 E Main St, Centerville, TX 75833; phone: 903-536-2227; hours 8AM-5PM (CST). *Felony, Civil.*

Civil Records: Access: Mail, in person. Both court and visitors may perform in person searches. Search fee: $5.00 per name. Court makes copy: $1.00 per page; same fee for self serve. Required to search: name, years to search. Civil cases indexed by defendant, plaintiff; in index books. Mail turnaround time 2-4 days.

Criminal Records: Access: Mail, in person. Only the court performs in person searches; visitors may not. Search fee: $5.00 per name. Court makes copy: $1.00 per page; same fee for self serve. Required to search: name, years to search. Criminal records in index books. Mail turnaround time 2-4 days.

General Information: No juvenile, mental, sealed, or adoption records released. Certification fee: $2.00. Payee: Leon County District Clerk. Personal checks accepted. Prepayment and SASE required.

County Court PO Box 98, 204 E St Mary St, Centerville, TX 75833; phone: 903-536-2352; hours 8AM-5PM (CST). *Misdemeanor, Civil, Probate.*

Civil Records: Access: Mail, in person. Both court and visitors may perform in person searches. Search fee: $5.00 per name. Court makes copy: $1.00 per page. Required to search: name, years to search. Civil cases indexed by defendant, plaintiff; in index books. Mail turnaround time 1-3 days.

Criminal Records: Access: Mail, in person. Both court and visitors may perform in person searches. Search fee: $5.00 per name. Court makes copy: $1.00 per page. Required to search: name, years to search, signed release. Criminal records in index books. Mail turnaround time 1-3 days.

General Information: No juvenile, mental, sealed, or adoption records released. Certification fee: $5.00 per doc. Payee: Leon County Clerk. Business checks accepted. Personal checks accepted in person only. Prepayment and SASE required.

Liberty County

District Court 1923 Sam Houston, Rm 303, Liberty, TX 77575; phone: 936-336-4600; hours 8AM-N, 1-5PM (CST). *Felony, Civil.*
Civil Records: Access: Mail, in person. Both court and visitors may perform in person searches. Search fee: $5.00 per name. Court makes copy: $1.00 per page. Required to search: name, years to search. Civil cases indexed by defendant, plaintiff; on computer since 1993, index books prior. Mail turnaround time 2-4 days.
Criminal Records: Access: Mail, in person. Both court and visitors may perform in person searches. Search fee: $5.00 per name. Court makes copy: $1.00 per page. Required to search: name, years to search. Criminal records on computer since 1993, index books prior. Mail turnaround time 2-4 days.
General Information: Public terminal has criminal back to 1894 and civil back to 1875. No juvenile, mental, sealed, or adoption records released. Payee: District Clerk. Personal checks accepted. Prepayment and SASE required.

County Court PO Box 369, 1923 Sam Houston #208, Liberty, TX 77575; phone: 936-336-4670; hours 8AM-5PM (CST). *Misdemeanor, Civil, Probate.*
Civil Records: Access: Mail, in person. Both court and visitors may perform in person searches. Search fee: $5.00 per name. Court makes copy: $1.00 per page. Required to search: name, years to search. Civil cases indexed by defendant, plaintiff; in index books; later on computer. Mail turnaround time 2-4 days.
Criminal Records: Access: Mail, in person. Both court and visitors may perform in person searches. Search fee: $5.00 per name. Court makes copy: $1.00 per page. Required to search: name, years to search, DOB, SSN, signed release. Criminal records in index books; later on computer. Mail turnaround time 2-4 days.
General Information: Public terminal goes back to 1995. No juvenile, mental, sealed, or adoption records released. Will not fax documents. Certification fee: $5.00 per doc. Payee: County Clerk. Business checks accepted. Personal checks accepted in person only. Prepayment and SASE required.

Limestone County

District Court PO Box 230, Groesbeck, TX 76642; phone: 254-729-3206; fax: 254-729-2960; hours 8AM-5PM (CST). *Felony, Civil.*
Note: Ext. 256 for criminal, 288 for civil.
Civil Records: Access: Phone, fax, mail, in person. Both court and visitors may perform in person searches. Search fee: $5.00 per name. Court makes copy: $1.00 per page. Self serve copy fee: $.50 per page. Required to search: name, years to search. Civil cases indexed by defendant, plaintiff; on computer since 9/1990, index books since 1883. Mail turnaround time 1 week.
Criminal Records: Access: Phone, fax, mail, in person. Both court and visitors may perform in person searches. Search fee: $5.00 per name. Court makes copy: $1.00 per page. Self serve copy fee: $.50 per page. Required to search: name, years to search, DOB; also helpful: SSN. Criminal records on computer since 9/1990, index books since 1911. Mail turnaround time 1 week.
General Information: Public terminal goes back to 1991. No juvenile, mental, sealed, or adoption records

released. Will fax documents for $1.00 1st page, $.25 each add'l. Certification fee: $2.00 per cert. Payee: District Clerk. Personal checks accepted. Prepayment required.

County Court PO Box 350, Groesbeck, TX 76642; phone: 254-729-5504; fax: 254-729-2951; hours 8AM-5PM (CST). *Misdemeanor, Civil, Probate.*
Civil Records: Access: Mail, in person. Both court and visitors may perform in person searches. Search fee: $5.00 per name. Court makes copy: $1.00 per page. Required to search: name, years to search. Civil cases indexed by defendant, plaintiff; in index books to early 1900s, computerized since 1985. Mail turnaround time 2 days.
Criminal Records: Access: Mail, in person. Both court and visitors may perform in person searches. Search fee: $5.00 per name. Court makes copy: $1.00 per page. Required to search: name, years to search; also helpful: DOB, SSN, signed release. Criminal records in index books to 1900s, computerized since 1985. Mail turnaround time 2 days.
General Information: Public use terminal available. No juvenile, mental, sealed, or adoption records released. Fee to fax documents is $2.00 per page. Certification fee: $5.00. Payee: Limestone County Clerk. Personal checks accepted. Prepayment required.

Lipscomb County

District & County Court PO Box 70, Lipscomb, TX 79056; phone: 806-862-3091; fax: 806-862-3004; hours 8:30AM-N, 1-5PM (CST). *Felony, Misdemeanor, Civil, Probate.*
Civil Records: Access: Fax, mail, in person. Both court and visitors may perform in person searches. Search fee: $10.00 per name. Court makes copy: $1.00 per page. Required to search: name. Civil cases indexed by defendant, plaintiff; in index books since 1887; on computer back to 1999. Mail turnaround time 2 days.
Criminal Records: Access: Fax, mail, in person. Both court and visitors may perform in person searches. Search fee: $5.00 per name. Court makes copy: $1.00 per page. Required to search: name; also helpful: DOB. Criminal records in index books since 1887; on computer back to 1999. Mail turnaround time 2 days.
General Information: No juvenile, mental, sealed, or adoption records released. Will fax documents $1.00 1st page, $.50 each add'l. Certification fee: $5.00 in County Court; $1.00 in District. Payee: County Clerk. Personal checks accepted. Prepayment required.

Live Oak County

District Court PO Drawer 440, George West, TX 78022; phone: 361-449-2733 X105; hours 8AM-5PM (CST). *Felony, Civil.*
Civil Records: Access: Phone, fax, mail, in person. Both court and visitors may perform in person searches. Search fee: $10.00 per name. Court makes copy: $1.00 per page; same fee for self serve. Required to search: name, years to search. Civil cases indexed by defendant, plaintiff; in index books and microfiche since 1850s. Mail turnaround time 1-2 days.
Criminal Records: Access: Phone, fax, mail, in person. Both court and visitors may perform in person searches. Search fee: $10.00 per name. Court makes copy: $1.00 per page; same fee for self serve. Required to search: name, years to search, DOB; also helpful: SSN. Criminal records in index books and microfiche since 1850s. Mail turnaround time 1-2 days.
General Information: No juvenile, mental, sealed, or adoption records released. Will fax documents for $1.00 per page. Certification fee: $1.00. Payee: District Clerk. Personal checks accepted. Prepayment and SASE required.

County Court PO Box 280, George West, TX 78022; phone: 361-449-2733 X3; criminal phone: X129; civil phone: X103; probate phone: X103; hours 9AM-4PM (CST). *Misdemeanor, Civil, Probate.*
Civil Records: Access: Mail, in person. Both court and visitors may perform in person searches. Search fee: $10.00 per name. Court makes copy: $1.00 per page. Required to search: name, years to search. Civil cases indexed by defendant, plaintiff; in index books. Mail turnaround time 1-2 days.
Criminal Records: Access: Mail, in person. Both court and visitors may perform in person searches. Search fee: $10.00 per name. Court makes copy: $1.00 per page. Required to search: name, years to search. Criminal records in index books. Mail turnaround time 1-2 days.
General Information: No juvenile, mental, sealed, or adoption records released. No fax machine. Certification fee: $5.00. Payee: County Clerk. Personal checks accepted. Prepayment and SASE required.

Llano County

District Clerk PO Box 877, Llano, TX 78643-0877; phone: 325-247-5036; fax: 325-248-0492; hours 8AM-4:30PM (CST). *Felony, Civil.*
www.courts.state.tx.us/district/33rd/index.htm
Civil Records: Access: Mail, in person. Both court and visitors may perform in person searches. Search fee: $5.00 per name. Fee is per 5 year period. Court makes copy: $1.00 per page; same fee for self serve. Required to search: name, years to search. Civil cases indexed by defendant, plaintiff; in index books back to 1900, computerized back to 1995. Mail turnaround time 1-3 days.
Criminal Records: Access: Mail, in person. Both court and visitors may perform in person searches. Search fee: $5.00 per name. Fee is per 5 year period. Court makes copy: $1.00 per page; same fee for self serve. Required to search: name, years to search. Criminal records in index books back to 1900, computerized back to 1995. Mail turnaround time 1-3 days.
General Information: Public terminal goes back to 1995. No juvenile, mental, sealed, or adoption records released. Will fax documents to local or toll free line. Certification fee: $1.00 per page. Payee: Llano County District Clerk. Personal checks accepted. Prepayment and SASE required.

County Court PO Box 40, Llano, TX 78643-0040; phone: 325-247-4455; fax: 325-247-2406; hours 8AM-4:30PM (CST). *Misdemeanor, Civil, Probate.*
Civil Records: Access: Phone, mail, in person. Both court and visitors may perform in person searches. Search fee: $5.00 per name. Court makes copy: $1.00 per page; same fee for self serve. Required to search: name, years to search. Civil cases indexed by defendant, plaintiff; on computer since 1985, index books prior. Mail turnaround time 2-4 days.
Criminal Records: Access: Phone, mail, in person. Both court and visitors may perform in person searches. Search fee: $5.00 per name. Court makes copy: $1.00 per page; same fee for self serve. Required to search: name, years to search; also helpful: DOB. Criminal records on computer since 1985, index books prior. Mail turnaround time 2-4 days.
General Information: Public use terminal available. No juvenile, mental, sealed, or adoption records released. Will fax documents to local or toll free line. Certification fee: $5.00. Payee: County Clerk. Personal checks accepted. Prepayment required.

Loving County

District & County Court PO Box 194, Mentone, TX 79754; phone: 432-377-2441; fax: 432-377-2701; hours 9AM-N, 1-5PM (CST). *Felony, Misdemeanor, Civil, Probate.*
Civil Records: Access: Phone, fax, mail, in person. Both court and visitors may perform in person searches. Search fee: $5.00 per name. Court makes

copy: $1.00 per page. Required to search: name, years to search. Civil cases indexed by defendant, plaintiff; in index books from 1935; computerized back to 1987. Mail turnaround time 2 days.

Criminal Records: Access: Phone, fax, mail, in person. Both court and visitors may perform in person searches. Search fee: $5.00 per name. Court makes copy: $1.00 per page. Required to search: name, years to search. Criminal records in index books from 1935; computerized back to 1987. Mail turnaround time 2 days.

General Information: No juvenile, mental, sealed, or adoption records released. Fee to fax documents is $1.50 per page. Certification fee: $5.00. Payee: Loving County Clerk. Personal checks accepted. Prepayment and SASE required.

Lubbock County

District Court PO Box 10536 (904 Broadway #105), Lubbock, TX 79408-3536; phone: 806-775-1623; probate phone: 806-775-1051; fax: 806-775-1382; hours 8AM-5PM (CST). *Felony, Civil.*
www.co.lubbock.tx.us/DClerk/d_clerk.htm
Civil Records: Access: Fax, mail, in person. Both court and visitors may perform in person searches. Search fee: $5.00 per name. Court makes copy: $1.00 per page; same fee for self serve. Required to search: name, years to search. Civil cases indexed by defendant, plaintiff; on computer back to 1983, in index books to 1908. Mail turnaround time 2 buisness days.
Criminal Records: Access: Fax, mail, in person. Both court and visitors may perform in person searches. Search fee: $5.00 per name. Court makes copy: $1.00 per page; same fee for self serve. Required to search: name, years to search, DOB; also helpful: SSN, signed release. Criminal records on computer back to 1983, in index books to 1908. Mail turnaround time 2 business days.
General Information: Public use terminal available. No juvenile, mental, sealed, or adoption records released. Will fax documents for $5.00 per document plus $1.00 per page copy fee. Certification fee: $1.00. Payee: District Clerk. Visa/MC accepted, also money order and cashier's check. Prepayment and SASE required.

County Courts Courthouse, Rm 207, PO Box 10536, Lubbock, TX 79408; criminal phone: 806-775-1044; civil phone: 806-775-1051; probate phone: 806-775-1048; hours 8:30AM-5PM (CST). *Misdemeanor, Civil, Probate.*
www.co.lubbock.tx.us/CCourt/c_courts.htm
Civil Records: Access: Mail, in person. Both court and visitors may perform in person searches. Search fee: $10.00 per name. Fee is for each 10 year period. Court makes copy: $1.00 per page. Required to search: name, years to search. Civil cases indexed by defendant, plaintiff; on computer back to 1986, index books prior. Mail turnaround time 3-5 days.
Criminal Records: Access: Mail, in person. Both court and visitors may perform in person searches. Search fee: $10.00 per name. Court makes copy: $1.00 per page. Required to search: name, years to search. Criminal records on computer back to 1986, index books prior. Mail turnaround time 3-5 days.
General Information: Public terminal goes back to 1987. No juvenile, mental, sealed, or adoption records released. Certification fee: $5.00 per doc. Payee: County Clerk. Personal checks accepted. Prepayment and SASE required.

Lynn County

District Court PO Box 939, Tahoka, TX 79373; phone: 806-561-4274; fax: 806-561-4151; hours 8:30AM-5PM (CST). *Felony, Civil.*
Civil Records: Access: Fax, mail, in person. Both court and visitors may perform in person searches. Search fee: $5.00 per name. Court makes copy: $1.00 per page. Required to search: name, years to search. Civil cases indexed by defendant, plaintiff; on computer from 1997, index books from 1916. Mail turnaround time 2 days.

Criminal Records: Access: Fax, mail, in person. Both court and visitors may perform in person searches. Search fee: $5.00 per name. Court makes copy: $1.00 per page. Required to search: name, years to search. Criminal records on computer from 1997, index books from 1916. Mail turnaround time 2 days.
General Information: No juvenile, mental, sealed, or adoption records released. Will fax documents $2.00 per page. Certification fee: $1.00 per page. Payee: District Clerk. Personal checks accepted. Prepayment and SASE required.

County Court PO Box 937, Tahoka, TX 79373; phone: 806-561-4750; fax: 806-561-4988; hours 8:30AM-5PM (CST). *Misdemeanor, Civil, Probate.*
Civil Records: Access: Mail, in person. Both court and visitors may perform in person searches. Search fee: $5.00. Court makes copy: $1.00 per page. Required to search: name, years to search. Civil cases indexed by defendant, plaintiff; in index books from 1903; on computer back to 1997. Mail turnaround time same day.
Criminal Records: Access: Mail, in person. Both court and visitors may perform in person searches. Search fee: $5.00. Court makes copy: $1.00 per page. Required to search: name, years to search. Criminal records in index books from 1903; on computer back to 1997. Mail turnaround time 2-4 days.
General Information: Public terminal goes back to 1997. No juvenile, mental, sealed, or adoption records released. Fee to fax documents is $2.00 per page. Certification fee: $5.00. Payee: Lynn County Clerk. Personal checks accepted. Prepayment and SASE required.

Madison County

District Court 101 W Main, Rm 226, Madisonville, TX 77864; phone: 936-348-9203; hours 8AM-N, 1-5PM (CST). *Felony, Civil.*
Civil Records: Access: Mail, in person. Both court and visitors may perform in person searches. Search fee: $5.00 per name. Court makes copy: $1.00 per page; same fee for self serve. Required to search: name, years to search. Civil cases indexed by defendant, plaintiff; in index books to 1935. Mail turnaround time 1 day.
Criminal Records: Access: Mail, in person. Both court and visitors may perform in person searches. Search fee: $5.00 per name. Court makes copy: $1.00 per page; same fee for self serve. Required to search: name, years to search. Criminal records in index books to 1835. Mail turnaround time 1 day.
General Information: No juvenile, mental, sealed, or adoption records released. No certification fee. Payee: District Clerk. Personal checks accepted. Prepayment and SASE required.

County Court 101 W Main, Rm 102, Madisonville, TX 77864; phone: 936-348-2638; criminal fax: 936-348-5858; same fax for civil/probate; hours 8AM-4:30PM (CST). *A & B Misdemeanors, Civil, Probate.*
www.co.madison.tx.us/coclerk.html
Civil Records: Access: Mail, in person, fax. Both court and visitors may perform in person searches. Search fee: $10.00 per name. Court makes copy: $1.00 per page. Required to search: name, years to search. Civil cases indexed by defendant. Civil records on computer from 1/00; index books back to 1970. Mail turnaround time as soon as fees are paid.
Criminal Records: Access: Mail, in person. Only the court performs in person searches; visitors may not. Search fee: $10.00 per name. Court makes copy: $1.00 per page. Required to search: name, years to search, DOB. Criminal records on computer from 1982; records go back to early 1900's (not indexed). Mail turnaround time as soon as fees are paid.
General Information: No juvenile, mental, sealed, or adoption records released. Fee to fax documents is $1.00 per page. Certification fee: $5.00 per document. Payee: Madison County Clerk. Personal checks accepted. Prepayment and SASE required.

Marion County

District Court PO Box 628, Jefferson, TX 75657; phone: 903-665-2441/2013; hours 8AM-5PM (CST). *Felony, Civil.*
Civil Records: Access: Mail, in person. Both court and visitors may perform in person searches. Search fee: $5.00 per name. Court makes copy: $1.00 per page; same fee for self serve. Required to search: name, years to search. Civil cases indexed by defendant, plaintiff; on computer from 1997, index books up to 1986. Mail turnaround time 1 week.
Criminal Records: Access: Mail, in person. Both court and visitors may perform in person searches. Search fee: $5.00 per name. Court makes copy: $1.00 per page; same fee for self serve. Required to search: name, years to search. Criminal records on computer from 1997, index books up to 1986. Mail turnaround time 1 week.
General Information: No juvenile, mental, sealed, or adoption records released. Certification fee: $1.00. Payee: District Clerk. Personal checks accepted. Prepayment and SASE required.

County Court PO Box 763, Jefferson, TX 75657; phone: 903-665-3971; hours 8AM-N, 1-5PM (CST). *Misdemeanor, Probate.*
Criminal Records: Access: Phone, mail, in person. Both court and visitors may perform in person searches. No search fee. Court makes copy: $1.00 per page; same fee for self serve. Required to search: name, years to search. Criminal records in index books from 1966; computerized back to 1997. Mail turnaround time 2-4 days.
General Information: No juvenile, mental, sealed, or adoption records released. Certification fee: $5.00. Payee: County Clerk. Personal checks accepted. Prepayment and SASE required.

Martin County

District & County Court PO Box 906, Stanton, TX 79782; phone: 432-756-3412; fax: 432-607-2212; hours 8AM-N, 1-5PM (CST). *Felony, Misdemeanor, Civil, Probate.*
Civil Records: Access: Mail, in person. Both court and visitors may perform in person searches. Search fee: $5.00 per name. Court makes copy: $1.00 per page. Required to search: name, years to search. Civil cases indexed by defendant, plaintiff; in index books to 1900. Mail turnaround time 2-4 days.
Criminal Records: Access: Mail, in person. Both court and visitors may perform in person searches. Search fee: $5.00 per name. Court makes copy: $1.00 per page. Required to search: name, years to search. Criminal records in index books to 1900, computerized since 1980. Mail turnaround time 2-4 days.
General Information: No juvenile, mental, sealed, or adoption records released. Fee to fax documents is $1.00 per page. Certification fee: $5.00. Payee: County/District Clerk. Personal checks accepted. Prepayment and SASE required.

Mason County

District & County Court PO Box 702, Mason, TX 76856; phone: 325-347-5253; criminal fax: 325-347-6868; same fax for civil/probate; hours 8AM-N, 1-4PM (CST). *Felony, Misdemeanor, Civil, Probate.*
Note: Search fee includes both county and district courts.
Civil Records: Access: Mail, in person. Both court and visitors may perform in person searches. Search fee: $10.00 per name. Court makes copy: $1.00 per page; same fee for self serve. Required to search: name, years to search. Civil cases indexed by defendant, plaintiff; in index books to 1858; on computer back to 1993. Mail turnaround time 2 days.
Criminal Records: Access: Mail, in person. Both court and visitors may perform in person searches. Search fee: $10.00 per name. Court makes copy: $1.00 per page; same fee for self serve. Required to

search: name, years to search; also helpful: DOB, SSN. Criminal records go back to 1877; on computer back to 1993. Mail turnaround time 2 days.
General Information: Public use terminal available. No juvenile, mental, sealed, or adoption records released. Will fax documents for no add'l fee. Certification fee: $5.00 per document. Payee: County/District Clerk. Personal checks accepted. Prepayment and SASE required.

Matagorda County

District Court 1700 7th St, Rm 307, Bay City, TX 77414-5092; phone: 979-244-7621; hours 8AM-N, 1-5PM (CST). *Felony, Civil.*
www.co.matagorda.tx.us/
Civil Records: Access: Mail, in person. Both court and visitors may perform in person searches. Search fee: $5.00 per name. Court makes copy: $1.00 per page. Required to search: name, years to search. Civil cases indexed by defendant, plaintiff; in index books and card files back to 1910; computerized back to 1994. Mail turnaround time 1-2 days.
Criminal Records: Access: Mail, in person. Both court and visitors may perform in person searches. Search fee: $5.00 per name. Court makes copy: $1.00 per page. Required to search: name, years to search, DOB. Criminal records in index books back to 1910; computerized back to 1994. Mail turnaround time 1-2 days.
General Information: No juvenile, sealed, or adoption records released. Will not fax documents. Certification fee: $2.00. Payee: District Clerk. Personal checks accepted. Prepayment and SASE required.

County Court 1700 7th St, Rm 202, Bay City, TX 77414-5094; phone: 979-244-7680; criminal phone: 979-244-7680; civil phone: 979-244-7683; probate phone: 979-244-7685; criminal fax: 979-244-7688; same fax for civil/probate; hours 8AM-5PM (CST). *Misdemeanor, Civil, Probate.*
Note: Probate is a separate index at this address.
Civil Records: Access: Mail, in person. Both court and visitors may perform in person searches. Search fee: $5.00 per name. Court makes copy: $1.00 per page; same fee for self serve. Required to search: name, years to search. Civil cases indexed by defendant, plaintiff; on computer from 1994, index books prior. Mail turnaround time 1-2 days.
Criminal Records: Access: Mail, in person. Both court and visitors may perform in person searches. Search fee: $5.00 per name. Court makes copy: $1.00 per page; same fee for self serve. Required to search: name, years to search, DOB, SSN. Criminal records on computer from 1994, index books prior. Mail turnaround time 1-2 days.
General Information: Public terminal goes back to 1987. No juvenile, mental, sealed, or adoption records released. Fee to fax documents is $2.00 per page. Certification fee: $5.00 per document. Payee: County Clerk. Provide ID then personal checks accepted. Visa, MC accepted. Prepayment and SASE required.

Maverick County

District Court 500 Quarry St, #5, Eagle Pass, TX 78853; phone: 830-773-2629; fax: 830-773-4439; hours 8AM-5PM (CST). *Felony, Civil.*
Civil Records: Access: Mail, in person. Both court and visitors may perform in person searches. Search fee: $5.00 per name. Court makes copy: $1.00 per page; same fee for self serve. Required to search: name, years to search. Civil cases indexed by defendant, plaintiff; in index books; recent records computerized. Mail turnaround time 1 week.
Criminal Records: Access: Mail, in person. Both court and visitors may perform in person searches. Search fee: $5.00 per name. Court makes copy: $1.00 per page; same fee for self serve. Required to search: name, years to search. Criminal records in index books; recent records computerized. Mail turnaround time 2-4 days.
General Information: No juvenile, mental, sealed, or adoption records released. Fee to fax documents is

$1.00 per page. Certification fee: $5.00. Payee: District Clerk. Personal checks not accepted. Prepayment and SASE required.

County Court 500 Quarry St, #2, Eagle Pass, TX 78853; phone: 830-773-2829 x228; fax: 830-752-4479; hours 8AM-5PM (CST). *Misdemeanor, Civil, Probate.*
Civil Records: Access: Mail, in person. Both court and visitors may perform in person searches. Search fee: $10.00 per name. Court makes copy: $1.00 per page. Required to search: name, years to search. Civil cases indexed by defendant, plaintiff; on index books. Mail turnaround time 1-2 days.
Criminal Records: Access: Mail, in person. Both court and visitors may perform in person searches. Search fee: $5.00 per name. Court makes copy: $1.00 per page. Required to search: name, years to search, DOB, SSN. Criminal records on index books. Mail turnaround time 1-2 days.
General Information: No juvenile, mental, sealed, or adoption records released. Fee to fax documents is 1.00 per page. Certification fee: $5.00 per cert includes copy fee. Payee: County Clerk. Personal checks accepted. Prepayment and SASE required.

McCulloch County

District Court County Courthouse, Rm 205, Brady, TX 76825; phone: 325-597-0733; fax: 325-597-0606; hours 8:30AM-5PM (CST). *Felony, Civil.*
Civil Records: Access: Mail, fax, in person, online. Both court and visitors may perform in person searches. Search fee: $5.00 per name. Court makes copy: $1.00 per page. Required to search: name, years to search. Civil cases indexed by defendant, plaintiff; in index books back to 1900s. Civil case information is free at www.idocket.com. Free searching is limited. Records go back to 12/31/1995. Mail turnaround time 2-4 days.
Criminal Records: Access: Mail, fax, in person, online. Both court and visitors may perform in person searches. Search fee: $5.00 per name. Court makes copy: $1.00 per page. Required to search: name, years to search; also helpful: DOB, SSN. Criminal records in index books back to 1990; on computer back to 1995. Criminal records access is through www.idocket.com; registration and password required. Records go back to 12/31/1995. Mail turnaround time 2-4 days.
General Information: Public terminal goes back to 1995. No juvenile, mental, sealed, or adoption records released. Will fax documents for $5.00 per page. Certification fee: $2.00. Payee: District Clerk. Personal checks accepted. Prepayment and SASE required.

County Court County Courthouse, Brady, TX 76825; phone: 325-597-0733; hours 8AM-Noon; 1-5PM (CST). *Misdemeanor, Civil, Probate.*
Civil Records: Access: Mail, in person, online. Both court and visitors may perform in person searches. Search fee: $5.00 per name. Court makes copy: $1.00 per page. Required to search: name, years to search. Civil cases indexed by defendant, plaintiff; in index books since early 1900's, computerized since 10/95. Online access is through www.idocket.com; registration and password required. Records go back to 12/31/1996; includes probate records. Mail turnaround time 7 days.
Criminal Records: Access: Mail, in person, online. Both court and visitors may perform in person searches. Search fee: $5.00 per name. Court makes copy: $1.00 per page. Required to search: name, years to search. Criminal records in index books since 1900's, computerized since 10/95. Criminal records access is through www.idocket.com; registration and password required. Records go back to 12/31/1996. Mail turnaround time 7 days.
General Information: No juvenile, mental, sealed, or adoption records released. Certification fee: $1.00 per page. Payee: County Clerk. Personal checks accepted. Prepayment and SASE required.

McLennan County

District Court PO Box 2451, 219 N 6th St #300, Waco, TX 76703; criminal phone: 254-757-5054; civil phone: 254-757-5057; civil fax: 254-757-5060; hours 8AM-5PM (CST). *Felony, Civil.*
www.co.mclennan.tx.us/
Civil Records: Access: Fax, mail, in person. Both court and visitors may perform in person searches. Search fee: $5.00 per name. Court makes copy: $1.00 per page. Required to search: name, years to search. Civil cases indexed by defendant, plaintiff; on computer since 1986, index books from 1850. Mail turnaround time 2 days.
Criminal Records: Access: Mail, in person. Both court and visitors may perform in person searches. Search fee: $5.00 per name. Court makes copy: $1.00 per page. Required to search: name, years to search. Criminal records on computer since 1959, index books from 1850. Mail turnaround time 2 days.
General Information: Public terminal goes back to 1959. No juvenile, mental, sealed, or adoption records released. No certification fee. Payee: Joe Johnson, District Clerk. Personal checks accepted. Prepayment and SASE required.

County Clerk's Office PO Box 1727, Waco, TX 76703; criminal phone: 254-757-5140/5185; civil phone: 254-757-5189; probate phone: 254-757-5186; fax: 254-757-5146; hours 8AM-5PM (CST). *Misdemeanor, Civil, Probate.*
Civil Records: Access: Mail, in person. Both court and visitors may perform in person searches. Search fee: $5.00 per name. Court makes copy: $1.00 per page. Required to search: name, years to search. Civil cases indexed by defendant, plaintiff; in index books back to 1876 computerized since 2000. Probate to 1850, computerized since 1967. Mail turnaround time 1-3 days.
Criminal Records: Access: Mail, in person. Both court and visitors may perform in person searches. Search fee: $5.00 per name. Court makes copy: $1.00 per page. Required to search: name, years to search; also helpful: DOB, SSN. Criminal records on computer since 1993; in index books to 1935. Mail turnaround time 2-4 days.
General Information: Public terminal has criminal back to 1993 and civil back to 2000. No mental or sealed records released. Certification fee: $5.00. Payee: County Clerk. Business checks accepted. Prepayment and SASE required.

McMullen County

District & County Court PO Box 235, Tilden, TX 78072; phone: 361-274-3215; fax: 361-274-3858; hours 8AM-4PM (CST). *Felony, Misdemeanor, Civil, Probate.*
Civil Records: Access: Mail, in person. Both court and visitors may perform in person searches. Search fee: $5.00 per name. Court makes copy: $1.00 per page. Required to search: name, years to search. Civil cases indexed by defendant, plaintiff; in index books from 1918. Mail turnaround time 2-4 days.
Criminal Records: Access: Mail, in person. Both court and visitors may perform in person searches. Search fee: $10.00 per name. Court makes copy: $1.00 per page. Required to search: name, years to search. Criminal records in index books from 1918. Mail turnaround time 2-4 days.
General Information: No juvenile, mental, sealed, or adoption records released. Will fax documents for a fee of $ 3.00 1st page $1.00 add'l. Certification fee: $5.00. Payee: County Clerk. Personal checks accepted. Prepayment and SASE required.

Medina County

District Court County Courthouse, Rm 209, 1100 16th St, Hondo, TX 78861; phone: 830-741-6070; hours 8AM-5PM (CST). *Felony, Civil.*
Civil Records: Access: Phone, mail, in person. Both court and visitors may perform in person searches. Search fee: $5.00 per name. Court makes copy: $1.00 first page; $.50 each add'l. Required to search: name,

years to search. Civil cases indexed by defendant, plaintiff; on computer since 1990, index books since 1849. Mail turnaround time 10 days.

Criminal Records: Access: Mail, in person. Both court and visitors may perform in person searches. Search fee: $5.00 per name. Court makes copy: $1.00 first page; $.50 each add'l. Required to search: name, years to search, DOB, SSN. Criminal records on computer since 1990, index books since 1849. Mail turnaround time 10 days.

General Information: Public terminal goes back to 1990. No juvenile, mental, sealed, or adoption records released. Certification fee: $1.00 per page. Payee: Medina County District Clerk. Out-of-state checks not accepted. Prepayment and SASE required.

County Court at Law 1100 16th St, Rm 203, Hondo, TX 78861; phone: 830-741-6040; hours 8AM-N, 1-5PM (CST). *Misdemeanor, Civil, Probate.*

Civil Records: Access: Phone, mail, in person. Both court and visitors may perform in person searches. Search fee: $5.00 per name. Court makes copy: $1.00 per page; same fee for self serve. Required to search: name, years to search. Civil cases indexed by defendant, plaintiff; on computer since late 1993, index books prior to 1881. Mail turnaround time 1-2 days.

Criminal Records: Access: Phone, mail, in person. Both court and visitors may perform in person searches. Search fee: $5.00 per name. Court makes copy: $1.00 per page; same fee for self serve. Required to search: name, years to search; also helpful: address, DOB, SSN. Criminal records on computer since late 1993, index books prior to 1953. Mail turnaround time 1-2 days.

General Information: No juvenile, mental, sealed, or sealed records released. Will fax documents for $3.00 1st page +$1.00 Add'l. Certification fee: $5.00. Payee: County Clerk. Personal checks accepted. Prepayment and SASE required.

Menard County

District & County Court PO Box 1038, 213 E San Saba Ave, Menard, TX 76859; phone: 325-396-4682; fax: 325-396-2047; hours 8AM-N, 1-5PM (CST). *Felony, Misdemeanor, Civil, Probate.*

Civil Records: Access: Fax, mail, in person. Both court and visitors may perform in person searches. Search fee: $10.00 per name. Court makes copy: $1.00 per page. Required to search: name, years to search. Civil cases indexed by defendant, plaintiff; in index books. Mail turnaround time 2-4 days.

Criminal Records: Access: Mail, in person. Both court and visitors may perform in person searches. Search fee: $10.00 per name. Court makes copy: $1.00 per page. Required to search: name, years to search. Criminal records in index books. Mail turnaround time 2-4 days.

General Information: No juvenile, mental, sealed, or adoption records released. Will fax documents for $1.00 per page. Certification fee: $5.00 per doc. Payee: District/County Clerk. Personal checks accepted. Prepayment and SASE required.

Midland County

District Court 200 W Wall, #301, Midland, TX 79701; phone: 432-688-4500; hours 8AM-5PM (CST). *Felony, Civil.*
www.co.midland.tx.us/DC/default.asp

Civil Records: Access: Mail, in person, online. Both court and visitors may perform in person searches. Search fee: $5.00 per name. Court makes copy: $1.00 per page; same fee for self serve. Required to search: name, years to search. Civil cases indexed by defendant, plaintiff; on computer back to 1965, index books prior. Access to the district Clerk database is at www.co.midland.tx.us/DC/Database/search.asp. Registration and password required; contact the clerk for access restrictions. Mail turnaround time 2 days.

Criminal Records: Access: Mail, in person, online. Both court and visitors may perform in person

searches. Search fee: $5.00 per name. Court makes copy: $1.00 per page; same fee for self serve. Required to search: name, years to search. Criminal records on computer back to 1940, index books prior. Online access to criminal records is the same as civil. Mail turnaround time 2 days.

General Information: Public terminal has criminal back to 1940 and civil back to 1965. No juvenile, mental, sealed, or adoption records released. Fee to fax documents is $1.00 per page. No certification fee. Payee: District Clerk. Business checks accepted. Prepayment and SASE required.

County Court PO Box 211, Midland, TX 79702; phone: 432-688-4402; civil phone: 432-688-4405; probate phone: 432-688-4480; criminal fax: 432-688-4926; same fax for civil/probate; hours 8AM-5PM (CST). *Misdemeanor, Civil, Probate.*
www.co.midland.tx.us/CC/default.asp

Civil Records: Access: Mail, in person, online. Both court and visitors may perform in person searches. Search fee: $5.00 per name. Court makes copy: $1.00 per page. Required to search: name; also helpful: years to search, address. Civil cases indexed by defendant, plaintiff; on computer since 1987, index books since 1885. Probate records on computer since 1887. Online access to the County Clerk database is free at www.co.midland.tx.us/CC/Database/default.asp. Mail turnaround time 1-2 days.

Criminal Records: Access: Mail, in person, online. Both court and visitors may perform in person searches. Search fee: $5.00 per name. Court makes copy: $1.00 per page. Required to search: name; also helpful: years to search, address, DOB, SSN. Criminal records on computer since 1978, index books since 1885. Online access to criminal records is the same as civil. Mail turnaround time 1-2 days.

General Information: Public terminal has criminal back to 1978 and civil back to 1985. No juvenile, mental, sealed, or adoption records released. Will fax documents for $2.00. Certification fee: $5.00 per cert. Payee: County Clerk. Only cashiers checks and money orders accepted. Prepayment required.

Milam County

District Court 102 S Fannin Ave #5, Cameron, TX 76520; phone: 254-697-7052; hours 8AM-5PM (CST). *Felony, Civil.*

Civil Records: Access: Mail, in person. Both court and visitors may perform in person searches. Search fee: $5.00 per name. Court makes copy: $1.00 per page. Required to search: name, years to search. Civil cases indexed by defendant, plaintiff; on microfilm and index books. Mail turnaround time same day.

Criminal Records: Access: Mail, in person. Both court and visitors may perform in person searches. Search fee: $5.00 per name. Court makes copy: $1.00 per page. Required to search: name, years to search. Criminal records on microfilm and index books. Mail turnaround time same day.

General Information: No juvenile, mental, sealed, or adoption records released. Certification fee: $1.00. Payee: District Clerk. Only cashiers checks and money orders accepted. Prepayment and SASE required.

County Court 107 W Main St, Cameron, TX 76520; phone: 254-697-7049; criminal fax: 254-697-7055; same fax for civil/probate; hours 8AM-5PM (CST). *Misdemeanor, Civil, Probate.*

Civil Records: Access: Mail, in person. Both court and visitors may perform in person searches. Search fee: $5.00 per name. Court makes copy: $1.00 per page; same fee for self serve. Required to search: name, years to search. Civil cases indexed by defendant, plaintiff; in books go back to 1874, computerized since 1992. Mail turnaround time same day.

Criminal Records: Access: Mail, in person. Both court and visitors may perform in person searches. Search fee: $5.00 per name. Court makes copy: $1.00 per page; same fee for self serve. Required to search:

name, years to search, signed release, SSN. Criminal records in books go back to 1874, computerized since 1992. Mail turnaround time 1-2 days.

General Information: Public terminal goes back to 1992. No juvenile, mental, sealed, or adoption records released. Fee to fax documents is $2.00 plus $1.00 per page. Certification fee: $5.00 per document. Payee: Milam County Clerk. Personal checks accepted. Prepayment and SASE required.

Mills County

District & County Court PO Box 646, Goldthwaite, TX 76844; phone: 325-648-2711; criminal fax: 325-648-3251; same fax for civil/probate; hours 8AM-N, 1-5PM (CST). *Felony, Misdemeanor, Civil, Probate.*

Civil Records: Access: Fax, mail, in person. Both court and visitors may perform in person searches. Search fee: $5.00 per name. Court makes copy: $1.00 per page; same fee for self serve. Required to search: name, years to search; also helpful: cause number. Civil cases indexed by defendant, plaintiff; in index books since 1887; no computerized records. Mail turnaround time 1-2 days.

Criminal Records: Access: Mail, fax, in person. Both court and visitors may perform in person searches. Search fee: $5.00 per name. Court makes copy: $1.00 per page; same fee for self serve. Required to search: name, years to search, DOB, signed release; also helpful: cause number. Criminal records in index books since 1887; no computerized records. Mail turnaround time 1-2 days.

General Information: No juvenile, mental, sealed, or adoption records released. Will not fax documents. Certification fee: $5.00 per cert. Payee: County-District Clerk. Personal checks accepted. Prepayment required. SASE requested.

Mitchell County

District Court County Courthouse, Colorado City, TX 79512; phone: 325-728-5918; hours 9AM-4PM (CST). *Felony, Civil.*

Civil Records: Access: Mail, in person. Both court and visitors may perform in person searches. Search fee: $5.00 per name. Court makes copy: $.35 per page. Required to search: name, years to search. Civil cases indexed by defendant, plaintiff; in index books. Mail turnaround time 1 day.

Criminal Records: Access: Mail, in person. Only the court performs in person searches; visitors may not. Search fee: $5.00 per name. Court makes copy: $.35 per page. Required to search: name, years to search. Criminal records in index books. Mail turnaround time 1 day.

General Information: No juvenile, mental, sealed, or adoption records released. Certification fee: $1.00 per document. Payee: District Clerk. Personal checks accepted. Prepayment and SASE required.

County Court 349 Oak St, Rm 103, Colorado City, TX 79512; phone: 325-728-3481; criminal fax: 325-728-5322; same fax for civil/probate; hours 8AM-N, 1-5PM (CST). *Misdemeanor, Civil, Probate.*

Civil Records: Access: Fax, mail, in person. Both court and visitors may perform in person searches. Search fee: $5.00 per name. Court makes copy: $1.00 per page; same fee for self serve. Required to search: name, years to search. Civil cases indexed by defendant, plaintiff; in index books back to 1882, on computer from 9-1-1998 to present. Mail turnaround time 2-4 days.

Criminal Records: Access: Mail, in person. Both court and visitors may perform in person searches. Search fee: $5.00 per name. Court makes copy: $1.00 per page; same fee for self serve. Required to search: name, years to search; also helpful: DOB. Criminal records in index books back to 1948, on computer from 9-1-1998 to present. Mail turnaround time 2-4 days.

General Information: Public terminal goes back to 9/1998. No juvenile, mental, sealed, or adoption, commitment records released. Will fax documents long distance for $3.00 for 1st page, $1.00 per add'l page. Will fax documents to local or toll-free number for $2.00 for 1st page and $1.00 per add'l page. Certification fee: $5.00 per document. Payee: Mitchell County Clerk. No out of state personal checks. Money orders accepted. Credit Cards accepted (4% flat fee). Prepayment required.

Montague County

District Clerk PO Box 155, Montague, TX 76251; phone: 940-894-2571; hours 8AM-5PM (CST). *Felony, Civil.*

Civil Records: Access: Mail, in person. Both court and visitors may perform in person searches. Search fee: $5.00 per name. Court makes copy: $1.00 per page; same fee for self serve. Required to search: name, years to search. Civil cases indexed by defendant, plaintiff; on computer and index books. Mail turnaround time 2-4 days.

Criminal Records: Access: Mail, in person. Both court and visitors may perform in person searches. Search fee: $5.00 per name. Court makes copy: $1.00 per page; same fee for self serve. Required to search: name, years to search. Criminal records on computer and index books. Mail turnaround time 2-4 days.

General Information: No juvenile, mental, sealed, or adoption records released. No certification fee. Payee: District Clerk. Personal checks not accepted. Prepayment and SASE required.

County Court PO Box 77, Montague, TX 76251; phone: 940-894-2461; fax: 940-894-6601; hours 8AM-5PM (CST). *Misdemeanor, Civil, Probate.*

Civil Records: Access: Mail, in person. Both court and visitors may perform in person searches. Search fee: $10.00 per 10 years per name. Court makes copy: $1.00 per page; same fee for self serve. Required to search: name, years to search. Civil cases indexed by defendant, plaintiff; on computer since 1993, index books prior. Mail turnaround 1-2 days.

Criminal Records: Access: Mail, in person. Both court and visitors may perform in person searches. Search fee: $5.00 per 10 years per name. Court makes copy: $1.00 per page; same fee for self serve. Required to search: name, years to search, DOB. Criminal records on computer since 1993, index books prior. Mail turnaround time 1-2 days.

General Information: No juvenile, mental, sealed, or adoption records released. Will fax documents for $2.75 1st page, $.75 each add'l page. Certification fee: $5.00. Payee: County Clerk. Personal checks and credit cards accepted. Prepayment and SASE required.

Montgomery County

District Court PO Box 2985, Conroe, TX 77305; phone: 936-539-7855; criminal fax: 936-539-7829; civil fax: 936-538-8138; hours 8AM-4PM; 8AM-4PM 1st Wed of month (CST). *Felony, Civil.*
www.co.montgomery.tx.us/dcourts/index.shtml
Note: Probate is a separate index at this same courthouse.

Civil Records: Access: Mail, in person. Both court and visitors may perform in person searches. Search fee: $5.00 per name. Court makes copy: $1.00 per page; same fee for self serve. Required to search: name, years to search. Civil cases indexed by defendant, plaintiff; in index books since 1900, on computer since 1990. Mail turnaround time 3-6 days.

Criminal Records: Access: Mail, in person. Both court and visitors may perform in person searches. Search fee: $5.00 per name. Court makes copy: $1.00 per page; same fee for self serve. Required to search: name, years to search. Criminal records in index books since 1900, on computer since 1990. Mail turnaround time 3-6 days.

General Information: Public terminal goes back to 1990. No juvenile, mental, sealed, or adoption records released. Will not fax documents. No certification fee. Payee: Barbara Adamick, District Clerk. Personal checks not accepted. Prepayment required. SASE is required.

County Court PO Box 959, Conroe, TX 77305; phone: 936-539-7885; probate phone: 936-539-7892; fax: 936-760-6990; hours 8AM-5PM (CST). *Misdemeanor, Civil, Probate.*
www.co.montgomery.tx.us

Civil Records: Access: Mail, in person. Both court and visitors may perform in person searches. Search fee: $5.00 per name. Court makes copy: $1.00 per page. Required to search: name, years to search, DOB and SSN. Civil cases indexed by defendant, plaintiff; on computer since 1971, and index books. Mail turnaround time 2-5 days.

Criminal Records: Access: Mail, in person. Both court and visitors may perform in person searches. Search fee: $5.00 per name. Court makes copy: $1.00 per page. Required to search: name, years to search, DOB and SSN. Criminal records on computer since 1985, and index books. Mail turnaround time 2-5 days.

General Information: Public terminal has criminal back to 1985 and civil back to 1971. No mental or sealed records released. Fee to fax documents is $2.00 per page. Certification fee: $5.00. Cert fee includes copy fee. Payee: County Clerk. Personal checks accepted. Prepayment and SASE required.

Moore County

District Court 715 Dumas Ave, #109, Dumas, TX 79029; phone: 806-935-4218; fax: 806-935-6325; hours 8:30AM-5PM (CST). *Felony, Civil.*

Civil Records: Access: Mail, in person. Both court and visitors may perform in person searches. Search fee: $5.00 per name. Court makes copy: $1.00 per page. Required to search: name, years to search. Civil cases indexed by defendant, plaintiff; on computer back to 1990; docket books and original files thru 1999. Mail turnaround time 1 day.

Criminal Records: Access: Mail, in person. Both court and visitors may perform in person searches. Search fee: $5.00 per name. Court makes copy: $1.00 per page. Required to search: name, years to search, DOB; also helpful: SSN. Criminal records on computer back to 1990; docket books and original file thru 1999. Mail turnaround time 1 day.

General Information: Public terminal goes back to 1999. No juvenile, mental, sealed, or adoption records released. Will fax documents to a toll free number. Certification fee: $1.00. Payee: District Clerk. Personal checks accepted. Prepayment and SASE required.

County Court 715 Dumas Ave, Rm 105, Dumas, TX 79029; phone: 806-935-6164/2009; fax: 806-935-9004; hours 8:30AM-5PM (CST). *Misdemeanor, Civil, Probate.*

Civil Records: Access: Mail, in person. Both court and visitors may perform in person searches. Search fee: $5.00 per name. Court makes copy: $1.00 per page. Required to search: name, years to search. Civil cases indexed by defendant, plaintiff; on computer back to 1996, in index books prior. Mail turnaround time 24 hours.

Criminal Records: Access: Mail, fax, in person. Both court and visitors may perform in person searches. Search fee: $5.00 per name. Court makes copy: $1.00 per page; same fee for self serve. Required to search: name, years to search, signed release, DOB or SSN. Criminal records on computer back to 1987, in index books prior. Mail turnaround time 24 hours.

General Information: Public terminal goes back to 1986. No juvenile, mental, sealed, or adoption records released. Fee to fax documents is $5.00 plus $1.00 per page. Certification fee: $5.00. Payee: Moore County Clerk. Business checks accepted. Prepayment and SASE required.

Morris County

District Court 500 Broadnax, Daingerfield, TX 75638; phone: 903-645-2321; fax: 903-645-5729; hours 8AM-5PM (CST). *Felony, Civil.*

Civil Records: Access: Mail, in person. Both court and visitors may perform in person searches.

Search fee: $5.00 per name. Court makes copy: $1.00 per page. Required to search: name, years to search. Civil cases indexed by defendant, plaintiff; in index books and file folders from 1930s, computerized since 2000. Mail turnaround time 1 day.

Criminal Records: Access: Mail, in person. Both court and visitors may perform in person searches. Search fee: $5.00 per name. Court makes copy: $1.00 per page. Required to search: name, years to search, DOB. Criminal records in index books and file folders from 1930s, computerized since 2000. Mail turnaround time 1 day.

General Information: No juvenile, mental, sealed, or adoption records released. No certification fee. Payee: Morris County District Clerk. Personal checks accepted. Prepayment and SASE required.

County Court 500 Broadnax, Daingerfield, TX 75638; phone: 903-645-3911; probate phone: 903-645-3911; fax: 903-645-4026; probate fax: same; hours 8AM-5PM (CST). *Misdemeanor, Probate.*

Criminal Records: Access: Mail, in person. Both court and visitors may perform in person searches. Search fee: $5.00 per name. Court makes copy: $1.00 per page. Required to search: name, DOB, years to search. Criminal record on index books, computerized since 1999. Mail turnaround time 1 day.

General Information: No juvenile, mental, sealed, or adoption records released. Certification fee: $5.00. Payee: County Clerk. Personal checks accepted. Prepayment required. SASE requested.

Motley County

District & County Court PO Box 660, Matador, TX 79244; phone: 806-347-2621; fax: 806-347-2220; hours 9AM-N, 1-5PM (CST). *Felony, Misdemeanor, Civil, Probate.*

Civil Records: Access: Mail, fax, in person. Both court and visitors may perform in person searches. Search fee: $10.00 per name. Court makes copy: $1.00 per page. Required to search: name, years to search, address. Civil cases indexed by defendant, plaintiff; in docket books, archived from 1891. Mail turnaround time 1-2 days.

Criminal Records: Access: Mail, fax, in person. Only the court performs in person searches; visitors may not. Search fee: $10.00 per name. Court makes copy: $1.00 per page. Required to search: name, years to search, DOB. Criminal records in docket books, archived from 1891. Mail turnaround time 1-2 days.

General Information: No juvenile, mental, sealed or adoption records released. Will fax documents to local or toll free number. Certification fee: $5.00 per instrument. Payee: Motley County Clerk. Personal checks accepted. Prepayment and SASE required.

Nacogdoches County

District Court 101 W Main, #215, Nacogdoches, TX 75961; phone: 936-560-7730; criminal phone: 936-560-7740; civil phone: 936-560-7729; fax: 936-560-7839; hours 8AM-5PM (CST). *Felony, Civil.*

Civil Records: Access: Mail, in person, online. Both court and visitors may perform in person searches. Search fee: $5.00 per name. Court makes copy: $1.00 per page. Required to search: name, years to search. Civil cases indexed by defendant, plaintiff; on computer from 1987, index books prior. Online access is available by subscription at www.idocket.com including civil and family back to 12/31/1986. Mail turnaround time 5-6 days.

Criminal Records: Access: Mail, in person, online. Both court and visitors may perform in person searches. Search fee: $5.00 per name. Court makes copy: $1.00 per page. Required to search: name, years to search, signed release. Criminal records on computer from 1987, index books prior. Online access is available by subscription at www.idocket.com; online records go back to 12/31/1986. Mail turnaround time 5-6 days.

General Information: Public terminal goes back to 1987. No juvenile, mental, sealed, or adoption records released. Will fax documents to local or toll free line.

No certification fee. Payee: Nacogdoches County. Business checks accepted. Prepayment and SASE required.

County Court County Clerk, 101 W Main, Rm 205, Nacogdoches, TX 75961; phone: 936-560-7733; fax: 936-559-5926; hours 8AM-5PM (CST). *Misdemeanor, Civil, Probate.*
www.co.nacogdoches.tx.us/
Note: The County Clerk is the Clerk for County Court at Law, except for Juvenile, Family Law, including Divorce & Adoption (for these cases see the District Clerk).
Civil Records: Access: Mail, in person, online. Both court and visitors may perform in person searches. Search fee: $5.00 per name. Court makes copy: $1.00 per page; same fee for self serve. Required to search: name, years to search. Civil cases indexed by defendant, plaintiff; on computer since 6/1986, index books prior. Online access is available by subscription at www.idocket.com including civil and probate back to 12/31/1986. Mail turnaround time 2-4 days.
Criminal Records: Access: Mail, in person, online. Both court and visitors may perform in person searches. Search fee: $5.00 per name. Court makes copy: $1.00 per page; same fee for self serve. Required to search: name, years to search. Criminal records on computer since 1986, index books prior. Online access is available by subscription at www.idocket.com; online records go back to 12/31/1986. Mail turnaround time 2-4 days.
General Information: Public terminal goes back to 1986. No sealed released. Will fax documents to local or toll free line. Certification fee: $5.00. Payee: County Clerk. Personal checks accepted. Prepayment and SASE required.

Navarro County

District Court PO Box 1439, Corsicana, TX 75151; phone: 903-654-3040; fax: 903-654-3088; hours 8AM-5PM (CST). *Felony, Civil.*
www.navarrocounty.org/
Civil Records: Access: Phone, fax, mail, online, in person. Both court and visitors may perform in person searches. Search fee: $5.00 per name. Court makes copy: $1.00 for first page, $.25 each add'l. Required to search: name, years to search. Civil cases indexed by defendant, plaintiff; on computer since 1990, index books and microfiche since 1900s. Civil case information is online at www.idocket.com. Free searching is limited. Records go back to 12/31/1990. Mail turnaround time 1-2 days.
Criminal Records: Access: Phone, fax, mail, in person, online. Both court and visitors may perform in person searches. Search fee: $5.00 per name. Court makes copy: $1.00 for first page, $.25 each add'l. Required to search: name, years to search. Criminal records on computer since 1990, index books and microfiche since 1900s. Criminal records access is through www.idocket.com; registration and password required. Records go back to 12/31/1990. Mail turnaround time 1-2 days.
General Information: Public terminal goes back to 1990. No juvenile, sealed, or adoption records released. Will fax documents $5.00 1st page, $1.00 each add'l. Certification fee: $1.00 per page. Payee: District Clerk. Personal checks accepted. Prepayment and SASE required.

County Court PO Box 423, Corsicana, TX 75151; phone: 903-654-3035; hours 8AM-4:45PM (CST). *Misdemeanor, Civil, Probate.*
Civil Records: Access: Mail, in person. Both court and visitors may perform in person searches. Search fee: $5.00 per name. Fee is for 10 year period. Court makes copy: $1.00 per page; same fee for self serve. Required to search: name, years to search. Civil cases indexed by defendant, plaintiff; in index books to 1960's; on computer back to 1999. Mail turnaround time 2-4 days.
Criminal Records: Access: Mail, in person. Both court and visitors may perform in person searches. Search fee: $5.00 per name. Fee is for 10 year period.

Court makes copy: $1.00 per page; same fee for self serve. Required to search: name, years to search, DOB or SSN. Criminal records in index books to 1930's; on computer back to 1999. Mail turnaround time 2-4 days.
General Information: Public terminal has criminal back to 1999 and civil back to - as per District Clerk's office. No juvenile, mental, sealed, or adoption records released. Certification fee: $5.00. Payee: County Clerk. Personal checks accepted. Prepayment and SASE required.

Newton County

District Court PO Box 535, Newton, TX 75966; phone: 409-379-3951; fax: 409-799-9087; hours 8AM-4:30PM (CST). *Felony, Civil.*
Civil Records: Access: Mail, in person. Both court and visitors may perform in person searches. Search fee: $5.00 per name. Court makes copy: $1.00 per page. Required to search: name, years to search. Civil cases indexed by defendant, plaintiff; in index books. Mail turnaround time same day.
Criminal Records: Access: Mail, in person. Both court and visitors may perform in person searches. Search fee: $5.00 per name. Court makes copy: $1.00 per page. Required to search: name, years to search. Criminal records in index books. Mail turnaround time same day.
General Information: No juvenile, mental, sealed, or adoption records released. Will fax documents for $2.00 per page. Certification fee: $2.00. Payee: District Clerk. Personal checks accepted. Prepayment and SASE required.

County Court PO Box 484, Newton, TX 75966; phone: 409-379-5341; fax: 409-379-9049; hours 8AM-4:30PM (CST). *Misdemeanor, Civil, Probate.*
Civil Records: Access: Mail, in person. Both court and visitors may perform in person searches. Search fee: $5.00 per name. Court makes copy: $1.00 per page. Required to search: name, years to search. Civil cases indexed by defendant, plaintiff; on index books from 1953. Mail turnaround time 1-2 days.
Criminal Records: Access: Mail, in person. Both court and visitors may perform in person searches. Search fee: $5.00 per name. Court makes copy: $1.00 per page. Required to search: name, years to search. Criminal records on index books from 1953. Mail turnaround time 1-2 days.
General Information: No juvenile, mental, sealed, or adoption records released. Fee to fax documents is $.50 per page. Certification fee: $5.00. Payee: County Clerk. Personal checks accepted. Prepayment required.

Nolan County

District Court 100 E 3rd, #200A, Sweetwater, TX 79556; phone: 325-235-2111; hours 8:30AM-N, 1-5PM (CST). *Felony, Civil.*
Civil Records: Access: Mail, in person. Both court and visitors may perform in person searches. Search fee: $5.00 per name. Court makes copy: $1.00 for first page, $.50 each add'l. Self serve copy fee: $.25 per page. Required to search: name, years to search. Civil cases indexed by defendant, plaintiff; in index books, records are not computerized. Mail turnaround time same day.
Criminal Records: Access: Mail, in person. Only the court performs in person searches; visitors may not. Search fee: $5.00 per name. Court makes copy: $1.00 for first page, $.50 each add'l. Self serve copy fee: $.25 per page. Required to search: name, years to search. Criminal records in index books, records are not computerized. Include which years to search. If requester provides a toll-free number, the court will call with results if asked. Mail turnaround time same day.
General Information: No juvenile, mental, sealed, or adoption records released. Certification fee: $1.00 per page. Payee: District Clerk. Personal checks accepted. Prepayment and SASE required.

County Court 100 E 3rd St, #108, Sweetwater, TX 79556-4546; phone: 325-235-2462; fax: 325-236-9416; hours 8:30AM-5PM (CST). *Misdemeanor, Civil, Probate.*
Civil Records: Access: Mail, in person. Both court and visitors may perform in person searches. Search fee: $5.00 per name. Court makes copy: $1.00 per page. Required to search: name, years to search. Civil cases indexed by defendant, plaintiff; in index books, computerized since 1999. Mail turnaround time same day.
Criminal Records: Access: Mail, in person. Both court and visitors may perform in person searches. Search fee: $5.00 per name. Court makes copy: $1.00 per page. Required to search: name, years to search. Criminal records in index books, computerized since 1999. Mail turnaround time same day.
General Information: Public terminal goes back to 1999. No juvenile, mental, sealed, or adoption records released. Certification fee: $5.00. Payee: County Clerk. Personal checks accepted. Prepayment and SASE required.

Nueces County

District & County Court PO Box 2987, Corpus Christi, TX 78403-2987; phone: 361-888-0450; criminal phone: 361-888-0495; fax: 361-888-0571; hours 8AM-5PM (CST). *Felony, Misdemeanor, Civil, Probate.*
www.co.nueces.tx.us/districtclerk/
Note: Records are combined at this location.

Civil Records: Access: Mail, in person, online. Both court and visitors may perform in person searches. Search fee: $5.00 per name. Court makes copy: $1.00 per page; same fee for self serve. Required to search: name, years to search. Civil cases indexed by defendant, plaintiff; on computer since 1980, index books prior. Online access to civil District & County Court records are free at www.co.nueces.tx.us/districtclerk/. Click on Civil/Criminal Case Search, register, then search by name, company, or cause number. Mail turnaround time 2-4 days.
Criminal Records: Access: Mail, in person, online. Both court and visitors may perform in person searches. Search fee: $5.00 per name. Court makes copy: $1.00 per page; same fee for self serve. Required to search: name, years to search. Criminal records on computer since 1980, index books prior. Online access to criminal District & County Court records are free at www.co.nueces.tx.us/districtclerk/. Click on Civil/Criminal Case Search, register, then search by name, SID number, or cause number. Mail turnaround time 2-4 days.
General Information: Public terminal goes back to 1980. No juvenile, mental, sealed, or adoption records released. Certification fee: $1.00. Payee: District Clerk. Personal checks accepted. Prepayment and SASE required.

Ochiltree County

District Court 511 S Main, Perryton, TX 79070; phone: 806-435-8054; fax: 806-435-8058; hours 8:30AM-5PM (CST). *Felony, Civil.*
Civil Records: Access: Fax, mail, in person. Both court and visitors may perform in person searches. Search fee: $5.00 per name. Court makes copy: $1.00 per page. Required to search: name, years to search. Civil cases indexed by defendant, plaintiff; in index books; on computer back to 1995. Mail turnaround time 7 days.
Criminal Records: Access: Fax, mail, in person. Only the court performs in person searches; visitors may not. Search fee: $5.00 per name. Court makes copy: $1.00 per page. Required to search: name, years to search. Criminal records in index books; on computer back to 1995. Mail turnaround time 7 days.
General Information: No juvenile, mental, sealed, or adoption records released. No fee to fax documents.

No certification fee. Payee: District Clerk. Personal checks accepted. Prepayment and SASE required.

County Court 511 S Main St, Perryton, TX 79070; phone: 806-435-8039; criminal fax: 806-435-2081; same fax for civil/probate; hours 8:30AM-N, 1-5PM (CST). *Misdemeanor, Civil, Probate.*
Civil Records: Access: Fax, mail, in person. Both court and visitors may perform in person searches. Search fee: $5.00 per name. Court makes copy: $1.00 per page. Required to search: name, years to search. Civil cases indexed by defendant, plaintiff; in index books. Mail turnaround time same day.
Criminal Records: Access: Fax, mail, in person. Both court and visitors may perform in person searches. Search fee: $5.00 per name. Court makes copy: $1.00 per page. Required to search: name, years to search. Criminal records in index books. Mail turnaround time usually mailed out same day of receipt.
General Information: No juvenile, mental, sealed, or adoption records released. Will fax documents for $2.00 1st page, $1.00 each add'l. Certification fee: $5.00 per cert. Payee: Ochiltree County Clerk. Personal checks accepted. Prepayment required. SASE requested.

Oldham County

District & County Court PO Box 360, Vega, TX 79092; phone: 806-267-2667; hours 8:30AM-N, 1-5PM (CST). *Felony, Misdemeanor, Civil, Probate.*
Civil Records: Access: Mail, in person. Both court and visitors may perform in person searches. Search fee: $5.00 per name. Court makes copy: $1.00 per page. Required to search: name, years to search. Civil cases indexed by defendant, plaintiff; in index books. Mail turnaround time 2-4 days.
Criminal Records: Access: Mail, in person. Both court and visitors may perform in person searches. Search fee: $5.00 per name. Court makes copy: $1.00 per page. Required to search: name, years to search. Criminal records in index books. Mail turnaround time 2-4 days.
General Information: No juvenile, mental, sealed, or adoption records released. Certification fee: $5.00 in county court, $1.00 in district. Payee: Oldham County/District Clerk. Personal checks accepted. Prepayment and SASE required.

Orange County

District Court 801 W Division Ave, Orange, TX 77630; phone: 409-883-7740; hours 8AM-5PM (CST). *Felony, Civil.*
Civil Records: Access: Mail, in person. Both court and visitors may perform in person searches. Search fee: $5.00 per name. Court makes copy: $1.00 per page. Self serve copy fee: $.50 per page. Required to search: name, years to search. Civil cases indexed by defendant, plaintiff; on computer since 1985, index books prior. Mail turnaround time 2-4 days.
Criminal Records: Access: Mail, in person, fax. Both court and visitors may perform in person searches. Search fee: $5.00 per name. Court makes copy: $1.00 per page. Self serve copy fee: $.50 per page. Required to search: name, years to search. Criminal records computerized since 1989. Mail turnaround time 2-4 days.
General Information: Public terminal goes back to 1986. No juvenile, mental, sealed, or adoption records released. Certification fee: $1.00. Payee: District Clerk. Only cashiers checks and money orders accepted. Prepayment and SASE required.

County Court 123 S 6th St, Orange, TX 77630; phone: 409-882-7055; fax: 409-882-7012; hours 8AM-5PM (CST). *Misdemeanor, Civil, Probate.*
www.co.orange.tx.us
Civil Records: Access: Phone, fax, mail, in person. Both court and visitors may perform in person searches. No search fee. Court makes copy: $1.00 per page. Required to search: name, years to search. Civil cases indexed by defendant, plaintiff. Civil records

back to 1852; on computer back to 1982. Mail turnaround time 7-10 days.
Criminal Records: Access: Phone, fax, mail, in person. Both court and visitors may perform in person searches. No search fee. Court makes copy: $1.00 per page. Required to search: name, years to search. Criminal records back to 1897, on computer back to 1897. Mail turnaround time 7-10 days.
General Information: Public terminal has criminal back to 1897 and civil back to 1982. No juvenile, mental, sealed. Fee to fax documents is $1.00 per page. Certification fee: $5.00. Payee: Karen Jo Vance, County Clerk. Personal checks accepted. Prepayment required.

Palo Pinto County

District Court PO Box 189, Palo Pinto, TX 76484-0189; phone: 940-659-1279; hours 8AM-4:30PM (CST). *Felony, Civil.*
Civil Records: Access: Mail, in person. Both court and visitors may perform in person searches. Search fee: $5.00 per name. Court makes copy: $1.00 per page. Required to search: name, years to search. Civil cases indexed by defendant, plaintiff; on computer since 1993, index books prior. Mail turnaround time 1-2 days.
Criminal Records: Access: Mail, in person. Both court and visitors may perform in person searches. Search fee: $5.00 per name. Court makes copy: $1.00 per page. Required to search: name, years to search. Criminal records on computer since 1993, index books prior. Mail turnaround time 1-2 days.
General Information: Public use terminal available. No juvenile, mental, sealed, or adoption records released. Certification fee: $1.00. Payee: District Clerk. Personal checks accepted. Prepayment and SASE required.

County Court PO Box 219, Palo Pinto, TX 76484; phone: 940-659-1277; criminal phone: 940-659-1218; civil phone: 940-659-1220; probate phone: 940-659-1220; criminal fax: 940-659-2590; same fax for civil/probate; hours 8:30AM-4:30PM (CST). *Misdemeanor, Civil, Probate.*
Note: Probate in separate index at this same address.
Civil Records: Access: Mail, in person, phone. Both court and visitors may perform in person searches. Search fee: $5.00 per name. Court makes copy: $1.00 per page; same fee for self serve. Required to search: name, years to search. Civil cases indexed by defendant, plaintiff; on computer back to 1998 index books from 1857. Mail turnaround time next day.
Criminal Records: Access: Mail, in person. Both court and visitors may perform in person searches. Search fee: $5.00 per name. Court makes copy: $1.00 per page; same fee for self serve. Required to search: name, years to search, DOB; also helpful: SSN. Criminal records on computer back to 1986; index books from 1857. Mail turnaround time next day.
General Information: No juvenile, mental, sealed records released. Will not fax documents. Certification fee: $5.00 per instrument. Payee: County Clerk. Personal checks accepted in person, not by mail. Prepayment required.

Panola County

District Court County Courthouse, Rm 227, Carthage, TX 75633; phone: 903-693-0306; fax: 903-693-6914; hours 8AM-5PM (CST). *Felony, Civil.*
Civil Records: Access: Mail, in person. Both court and visitors may perform in person searches. Search fee: $5.00 per name. Court makes copy: $1.00 per page; same fee for self serve. Required to search: name, years to search. Civil cases indexed by defendant, plaintiff; in index books from 1865; computerized back to 1994. Mail turnaround time 3 days.
Criminal Records: Access: Mail, in person. Both court and visitors may perform in person searches. Search fee: $5.00 per name. Court makes copy: $1.00 per page; same fee for self serve. Required to search: name, years to search, DOB. Criminal records in

index books from 1900's; computerized back to 1994. Mail turnaround time 3 days.
General Information: Public terminal goes back to 1994. No sealed, or adoption records released. Fee to fax documents is $1.00 per page. Certification fee: $1.00 per page includes copy fee. Payee: District Clerk. Personal checks accepted. Prepayment and SASE required.

County Court County Courthouse, Rm 201, Carthage, TX 75633; phone: 903-693-0302; hours 8AM-5PM (CST). *Misdemeanor, Civil, Probate.*
Note: Probate is a separate index at this same address.
Civil Records: Access: Mail, in person. Both court and visitors may perform in person searches. Search fee: $5.00 per name. Court makes copy: $1.00 per page; same fee for self serve. Required to search: name, years to search. Civil cases indexed by defendant, plaintiff; in index books; computerized since 1996. Mail turnaround time 2-4 days.
Criminal Records: Access: Mail, in person, fax. Both court and visitors may perform in person searches. Search fee: $5.00 per name. Court makes copy: $1.00 per page; same fee for self serve. Required to search: name, years to search, DOB. Criminal records in index books; computerized since 1996. Mail turnaround time 2-4 days.
General Information: No juvenile, mental, sealed, or adoption records released. Will fax documents for $1.00 per 10 pages. Certification fee: $5.00 per document. Payee: County Clerk. Personal checks require ID. Prepayment required.

Parker County

District Court PO Box 2050, 117 Ft. Worth Ave, Weatherford, TX 76086; phone: 817-598-6194; criminal phone: 817-598-6194 or x6200/x6214; civil phone: 817-598-6114; fax: 817-598-6131; hours 8AM-5PM (CST). *Felony, Civil.*
www.parkercountytx.com
Note: All civil cases filed with District Clerk.
Civil Records: Access: Mail, in person, online. Both court and visitors may perform in person searches. Search fee: $5.00 per name. Court makes copy: $1.00 per page. Required to search: name, years to search, and/or cause number. Civil cases indexed by defendant, plaintiff; in index books. Access to court records is free at www.parkercountytx.com. Mail turnaround time same day.
Criminal Records: Access: Mail, in person, online. Both court and visitors may perform in person searches. Search fee: $5.00 per name. Court makes copy: $1.00 per page. Required to search: name, years to search, DOB, and/or cause number; also helpful: SSN. Criminal records in index books; on computer back to 7/1988. Access to criminal records and sheriff inmates and bonds searching is free at www.parkercountytx.com. Online court records go back to 7/88. Mail turnaround time same day.
General Information: No juvenile, mental, sealed, or adoption records released. Will not fax documents. Certification fee: $1.00 per page copy fee only. Payee: District Clerk. Personal checks accepted with valid DR number. Prepayment and SASE required.

County Court Parker County Clerk - Court Division, PO Box 819, Weatherford, TX 76086-0819; phone: 817-594-1632; hours 8AM-N, 1-4PM (CST). *Misdemeanor.*
Note: There are two District Courts (43rd & 415th) and two County Courts-at-Law at this location. Records are co-mingled.
Civil Records: Access: Phone, mail, in person, online. Both court and visitors may perform in person searches. Search fee: $5.00 per name. Court makes copy: $1.00 per page. Required to search: name, years to search. Civil cases indexed by defendant, plaintiff; in index books; on computer since 8/1985. Online access to civil is same as criminal, see below. Mail turnaround time 1-2 days.
Criminal Records: Access: Phone, mail, in person, online. Both court and visitors may perform in person searches. Search fee: $5.00 per name. Court

makes copy: $1.00 per page. Required to search: name, years to search, DOB; signed release. Criminal records on computer since 8/1985, index books and archived since 1900s. Online access is free at www.parkercountytx.com. Search the sheriff bond and jail lists here also. Mail turnaround time 1-2 days.

General Information: Public use terminal available. No juvenile, mental, sealed, or adoption records released. Certification fee: $5.00. Payee: County Clerk. Personal checks accepted. Prepayment and SASE required.

Probate Court 1112 Santa Fe Dr, Weatherford, TX 76086; phone: 817-594-7461; fax: 817-594-9540; hours 8AM-5PM (CST). *Probate.*

Parmer County

District Court PO Box 195, Farwell, TX 79325-0195; phone: 806-481-3419; fax: 806-481-9416; hours 8:30AM-N, 1-5PM (CST). *Felony, Civil.*

Civil Records: Access: Fax, mail, in person, online. Both court and visitors may perform in person searches. Search fee: $5.00 per name. Court makes copy: $1.00 per page. Required to search: name, years to search. Civil cases indexed by defendant, plaintiff; in index books since 1917. Online access is through www.idocket.com; registration and password required. Records go back to 12/31/1995. Mail turnaround time 1 day.

Criminal Records: Access: Fax, mail, in person, online. Both court and visitors may perform in person searches. Search fee: $5.00 per name. Court makes copy: $1.00 per page. Required to search: name, years to search. Criminal records in index books since 1917. Online access is through www.idocket.com; registration and password required. Records go back to 12/31/1995. Mail turnaround time 1 day.

General Information: No juvenile, mental, sealed, or adoption records released. Will fax documents $1.00 per page. No certification fee. Payee: District Clerk. Personal checks accepted. Prepayment and SASE required.

County Court PO Box 356, Farwell, TX 79325; phone: 806-481-3691; fax: 806-481-9154; probate fax: same; hours 8:30AM-N; 1-5PM (CST). *Misdemeanor, Civil, Probate.*

Civil Records: Access: Mail, in person. Both court and visitors may perform in person searches. Search fee: $5.00 per name. Court makes copy: $1.00 per page. Self serve copy fee: $.25 per page. Required to search: name, years to search. Civil cases indexed by defendant, plaintiff; in index books to 1924, computerized since 1996. Mail turnaround time 2-4 days.

Criminal Records: Access: Mail, in person. Both court and visitors may perform in person searches. Search fee: $5.00 per name. Court makes copy: $1.00 per page. Self serve copy fee: $.25 per page. Required to search: name, years to search. Criminal records in index books to 1920, computerized since 1996. Mail turnaround time 2-4 days.

General Information: Public use terminal available. No juvenile, mental, sealed, or adoption records released. Will fax documents for $1.50 per page. Certification fee: $5.00. Payee: County Clerk. Personal checks accepted. Prepayment and SASE required.

Pecos County

District Court 400 S Nelson, Fort Stockton, TX 79735; phone: 432-336-3503; fax: 432-336-6437; hours 8AM-5PM (CST). *Felony, Civil.*

Civil Records: Access: Fax, mail, in person. Both court and visitors may perform in person searches. Search fee: $5.00 per name. There is a $10.00 fee per year, when going back further than 7 years. Court makes copy: $1.00 per page; same fee for self serve. Required to search: name, years to search, SSN. Civil cases indexed by defendant; on computer since 1996, index books prior to the 1920's. A seven

year search is performed. Mail turnaround time 2-4 days.

Criminal Records: Access: Fax, mail, in person. Both court and visitors may perform in person searches. Search fee: $5.00 per name. There is a $10.00 fee per year, when going back further than 7 years. Court makes copy: $1.00 per page; same fee for self serve. Required to search: name, years to search, DOB, signed release; also helpful-address, SSN. Criminal records on computer since 1996, index books prior to 1924. Mail turnaround time 2-4 days.

General Information: No juvenile, mental, sealed, or adoption records released. Fee to fax documents is $1.00 per page. No certification fee. Payee: District Clerk. Personal checks accepted. Prepayment and SASE required.

County Court 103 W Callaghan, Fort Stockton, TX 79735; phone: 432-336-7555; fax: 432-336-7557; hours 8AM-5PM (CST). *Misdemeanor, Civil, Probate.*

Civil Records: Access: Mail, in person. Both court and visitors may perform in person searches. Search fee: $5.00 per name. Court makes copy: $1.00 per page. Required to search: name, years to search. Civil cases indexed by defendant, plaintiff; on computer and index books to 1955. Mail turnaround time same day.

Criminal Records: Access: Mail, in person. Both court and visitors may perform in person searches. Search fee: $5.00 per name. Court makes copy: $1.00 per page. Required to search: name, years to search. Criminal records on computer and index books to 1955. Mail turnaround time same day.

General Information: No juvenile, mental, sealed, or adoption records released. Fee to fax documents is $1.00 per page. Certification fee: $5.00. Payee: County Clerk. Personal checks accepted. Prepayment and SASE required.

Polk County

District Court 101 W Church, #205, Livingston, TX 77351; phone: 936-327-6814; fax: 936-327-6851; hours 8AM-5PM (CST). *Felony, Civil.*

Civil Records: Access: Fax, mail, in person. Both court and visitors may perform in person searches. Search fee: $5.00 per name. Fee is per 10 year period. Court makes copy: $1.00 per page. Required to search: name, years to search. Civil cases indexed by defendant, plaintiff; in index books, computerized since 1996. Mail turnaround time 2-4 days.

Criminal Records: Access: Fax, mail, in person. Both court and visitors may perform in person searches. Search fee: $5.00 per name. Fee is per 10 year period. Court makes copy: $1.00 per page. Required to search: name, years to search; also helpful: DOB. Criminal records in index books, computerized since 1996. Mail turnaround time 2-4 days.

General Information: Public terminal goes back to 1995. No juvenile, mental, sealed, or adoption records released. Certification fee: $2.00 per doc. Payee: District Clerk. Personal checks accepted. Prepayment and SASE required.

County Court PO Drawer 2119, Livingston, TX 77351; phone: 936-327-6804; criminal phone: 936-327-6805; civil phone: 936-327-6804; probate phone: 936-327-6804; criminal fax: 936-327-6874; same fax for civil/probate; hours 8AM-5PM (CST). *Misdemeanor, Civil, Probate.*

Note: Probate is a separate index at this same address.

Civil Records: Access: Mail, in person. Both court and visitors may perform in person searches. Search fee: $5.00 per name. Court makes copy: $1.00 per page; same fee for self serve. Required to search: name, years to search. Civil cases indexed by defendant, plaintiff; in index books, on computer since 1988, available since 1846. Mail turnaround time 2-4 days.

Criminal Records: Access: Mail, in person. Only the court performs in person searches; visitors may not. Search fee: $5.00 per name. Court makes copy: $1.00 per page; same fee for self serve. Required to

search: name, years to search; also helpful: DOB, SSN. Criminal records in index books; on computer back to 1982. Mail turnaround time 2-4 days.

General Information: Public terminal has criminal back to 1987 and civil back to 1846. No mental records released. Certification fee is $2.00 per document and $1.00 per page. Certification fee: $5.00 per document. Payee: County Clerk. Personal checks accepted for civil only. Prepayment and SASE required.

Potter County

District Court PO Box 9570, Amarillo, TX 79105-9570; phone: 806-379-2300; criminal phone: 806-379-2311; civil phone: 806-379-2307; fax: 806-372-5061; hours 7:30AM-5:30PM (CST). *Felony, Civil.*

www.co.potter.tx.us/districtclerk

Civil Records: Access: Phone, fax, mail, online, in person. Both court and visitors may perform in person searches. Search fee: $5.00 per name. Court makes copy: $.50 per page; same fee for self serve. Required to search: name, years to search. Civil cases indexed by defendant, plaintiff; on computer since 9/87, index books prior. Civil case information from 1988 forward is online at www.idocket.com. Free case searching is limited Mail turnaround time less than 10 days.

Criminal Records: Access: Fax, mail, online, in person. Both court and visitors may perform in person searches. Search fee: $5.00 per name. Court makes copy: $.50 per page; same fee for self serve. Required to search: name, years to search. Criminal records on computer since 9/87, index books prior. Online access to criminal records is the same as civil. Mail turnaround time 2-4 days.

General Information: Public terminal goes back to 1988. No juvenile, mental, sealed, or adoption records released. Will fax documents $1.00 per page. Certification fee: $1.00 per page. Payee: District Clerk. Business checks or Visa, MC accepted. Add 5% of transaction total for credit card use fee. Prepayment and SASE required.

County Court & County Courts at Law 1 & 2 PO Box 9638, Amarillo, TX 79105; phone: 806-379-2285; criminal phone: 806-379-2283; civil phone: 806-379-2280; probate phone: 806-379-2285; fax: 806-379-2296; hours 8AM-5PM (CST). *Misdemeanor, Civil, Probate.*

www.co.potter.tx.us/countyclerk/index.html

Civil Records: Access: Mail, in person. Both court and visitors may perform in person searches. Search fee: none, but must pay the certification fee. Court makes copy: $1.00 per page; same fee for self serve. Required to search: exact name, years to search. Civil cases indexed by defendant, plaintiff; on computer since 1990, index books and microfiche since 1889. Probate records available since 1800s. Mail turnaround time 1-2 days.

Criminal Records: Access: Mail, in person. Both court and visitors may perform in person searches. Search fee: none, but must pay the certification fee. Court makes copy: $1.00 per page; same fee for self serve. Required to search: exact name, years to search, DOB. Criminal records on computer since 1990, index books and microfiche since 1889. Mail turnaround time 1-2 days.

General Information: Public terminal has only criminal records back to 1898. No juvenile, mental or sealed records released. Will fax documents for fee. Certification fee: $5.00 for Certification of Fact. Payee: Potter County Clerk. Personal checks or Visa, MC accepted. Prepayment and SASE required.

Presidio County

District & County Court PO Box 789, Marfa, TX 79843; phone: 432-729-4812; Dist.-729-3857; criminal fax: 432-729-4313; same fax for civil/probate; hours 8AM-N, 1-4PM (CST). *Felony, Misdemeanor, Civil, Probate.*

Note: Probate is a separate index as this same address

Civil Records: Access: Mail, in person. Both court and visitors may perform in person searches. Search fee: $6.00 per name. Court makes copy: $1.00 per page; same fee for self serve. Required to search: name, years to search. Civil cases indexed by defendant, plaintiff; in index books. Requests must be in writing. Mail turnaround time 2-4 days.
Criminal Records: Access: Mail, in person. Both court and visitors may perform in person searches. Search fee: $6.00 per name. Court makes copy: $1.00 per page; same fee for self serve. Required to search: name, years to search. Criminal records in index books. Requests must be in writing. Mail turnaround time 2-4 days.
General Information: No juvenile, mental, sealed, or adoption records released. Will fax documents for $3.00 per document. Certification fee: $5.00 per document. Payee: District Clerk. Personal checks accepted. Prepayment and SASE required.

Rains County

District & County Court PO Box 187, Emory, TX 75440; phone: 903-474-9999; probate phone: 903-474–9999 x17; fax: 903-473-0163; probate fax: 903-474-9390; hours 8AM-5PM (CST). *Felony, Misdemeanor, Civil, Probate.*
Note: Fax for County Clerk is 903-474-9390.
Civil Records: Access: Mail, fax, in person. Both court and visitors may perform in person searches. Search fee: $5.00 per name. Court makes copy: $1.00 per page. Required to search: name. Civil cases indexed by defendant, plaintiff; on computer back to 1989, index books prior to 1903. Mail turnaround time same day.
Criminal Records: Access: Mail, fax, in person. Both court and visitors may perform in person searches. Search fee: $5.00 per name. Court makes copy: $1.00 per page. Required to search: name; also helpful: DOB. Criminal records on computer back to 1989, index books prior to 1880. Mail turnaround time same day.
General Information: No juvenile, mental, sealed, or adoption records released. Certification fee: $5.00. Payee: Linda Wallace County Clerk or Deborah Traylor, District Clerk. Personal checks accepted. Prepayment and SASE required.

Randall County

District Courts PO Box 1096, 501 16th St #301, Canyon, TX 79015; phone: 806-468-5600; fax: 806-468-5604; hours 8AM-5PM (CST). *Felony, Civil.*
www.randallcounty.org
Civil Records: Access: Fax, mail, online, in person. Both court and visitors may perform in person searches. Search fee: $5.00 per name. Court makes copy: $.50 per page. Required to search: name, years to search. Civil cases indexed by defendant, plaintiff; on computer since 1984. Civil case information is free at www.idocket.com. Free searching is limited. Records from 12/31/84. Mail turnaround time 1-2 days.
Criminal Records: Access: Fax, mail, online, in person. Both court and visitors may perform in person searches. Search fee: $5.00 per name. Court makes copy: $.50 per page. Required to search: name, years to search. Criminal records on computer since 1985; prior in docket books. Online access to criminal records is the same as civil. Mail turnaround time 1-2 days.
General Information: Public terminal has criminal back to 1985 and civil back to 1983. No juvenile, mental, sealed, or adoption records released. Fee to fax documents is $5.00 1st pg; $1.00 each add'l. Certification fee: $1.00 per page includes copy fee. Payee: District Clerk. Personal checks or Visa, MC accepted. Prepayment required.

County Court PO Box 660, Canyon, TX 79015; phone: 806-468-5505; fax: 806-468-5509; hours 8AM-5PM (CST). *Misdemeanor, Civil, Probate.*
www.randallcounty.org/cclerk/default.htm
Note: Probate is separate index at this same address.

Civil Records: Access: Mail, fax, in person, email. Both court and visitors may perform in person searches. Search fee: $10.00 per name. Court makes copy: $1.00 per page; same fee for self serve. Required to search: name, years to search, SASE. Civil cases indexed by defendant, plaintiff; in index books 1900 to present. Civil case information is online from idocket at http://idocket.com/counties.htm. Free searching is limited. Records go back to 12/31/1999; probate back to 12/31/1969. Mail turnaround time 2-4 days.
Criminal Records: Access: Mail, fax, in person, online, email. Both court and visitors may perform in person searches. Search fee: $10.00 per name. Court makes copy: $1.00 per page; same fee for self serve. Required to search: name, years to search; also helpful: DOB. Criminal records on computer since 1984; prior records in index books. Criminal case information is online from idocket at http://idocket.com/counties.htm. Online records go back to 12/31/1991. Mail turnaround time 2-4 days.
General Information: Public terminal has criminal back to 1991 and civil back to 1999. No juvenile, mental, sealed, or adoption records released. Fee to fax documents is $1.00 per page, $5.00 fee add'l if call is long distance. Certification fee: $5.00 per document. Payee: Randall County Clerk. Personal checks accepted. Prepayment and SASE required.

Reagan County

District & County Court PO Box 100, 3rd St at Plaza, Big Lake, TX 76932; phone: 325-884-2442; fax: 325-884-1503; hours 8:30AM-5PM (CST). *Felony, Misdemeanor, Civil, Probate.*
Civil Records: Access: Mail, in person. Both court and visitors may perform in person searches. Search fee: $5.00 per name. Court makes copy: $1.00 per page. Required to search: name, years to search. Civil cases indexed by defendant, plaintiff; in index books to 1903. Mail turnaround time same day.
Criminal Records: Access: Mail, in person. Both court and visitors may perform in person searches. Search fee: $5.00 per name. Court makes copy: $1.00 per page. Required to search: name, years to search. Criminal records in index books to 1903. Mail turnaround time same day.
General Information: No juvenile, mental, sealed, or adoption records released. Will fax documents $5.00 per doc; no fee to toll-free number. Certification fee: $5.00 per doc. Payee: County/District Clerk. Personal checks not accepted if out-of-state. Prepayment and SASE required.

Real County

District & County Court PO Box 750, Leakey, TX 78873; phone: 830-232-5202; fax: 830-232-6888; hours 8AM-5PM (CST). *Felony, Misdemeanor, Civil, Probate.*
Civil Records: Access: In person only. Visitors must perform in person searches themselves. Court makes copy: $1.00 per page. Required to search: name, years to search. Civil cases indexed by defendant, plaintiff; in index books.
Criminal Records: Access: In person only. Visitors must perform in person searches themselves. Court makes copy: $1.00 per page. Required to search: name, years to search, DOB. Criminal records in index books.
General Information: No juvenile, mental, sealed, or adoption records released. Certification fee: $5.00 per document. Payee: District/County Court. Personal checks accepted. Prepayment required.

Red River County

District Court 400 N Walnut, Clarksville, TX 75426; phone: 903-427-3761; fax: 903-427-1201; hours 8:30AM-N, 1-5PM (CST). *Felony, Civil.*
Civil Records: Access: Mail, in person. Both court and visitors may perform in person searches. Search fee: $5.00 per name. Court makes copy: $1.00

per page. Required to search: name, years to search. Civil cases indexed by defendant, plaintiff; in index books and on microfilm to 1800s. Mail turnaround time same day.
Criminal Records: Access: Mail, in person. Both court and visitors may perform in person searches. Search fee: $5.00 per name. Court makes copy: $1.00 per page. Required to search: name, years to search. Criminal records in index books and on microfilm to 1800s. Mail turnaround time same day.
General Information: Public terminal goes back to 3 years. No juvenile, mental, sealed, or adoption records released. Will fax documents to local or toll free line. Certification fee: $1.00 per page includes copies. Payee: District Clerk. Personal checks accepted. Prepayment and SASE required.

County Court 200 N Walnut, Clarksville, TX 75426; phone: 903-427-2401; hours 8:30AM-5PM (CST). *Misdemeanor, Probate.*
Civil Records: Access: Mail, in person. Both court and visitors may perform in person searches. Search fee: $5.00 per name. Court makes copy: $1.00 per page; same fee for self serve. Required to search: name, years to search, SSN. Criminal records on computer (name only) since 1980, in index books since 1960s. Mail turnaround time 1-2 days.
General Information: Public terminal has only criminal records back to 1980. No mental, sealed, or adoption records released. Certification fee: $5.00. Payee: County Clerk. Personal checks accepted. Prepayment and SASE required.

Reeves County

District Court PO Box 848, Pecos, TX 79772; phone: 432-445-2714; probate phone: 432-445-5467; fax: 432-445-7455; hours 8AM-N, 1-5PM (CST). *Felony, Civil.*
Note: Probate records handled by County Clerk.
Civil Records: Access: Phone, mail, in person. Both court and visitors may perform in person searches. Search fee: $5.00 per name. Court makes copy: $.25 per page; same fee for self serve. Required to search: name, years to search. Civil cases indexed by defendant, plaintiff; on computer since 1/91, index books prior. Mail turnaround time 2 days.
Criminal Records: Access: Mail, in person. Both court and visitors may perform in person searches. Search fee: $5.00 per name. Court makes copy: $.25 per page; same fee for self serve. Required to search: name, years to search. Criminal records on computer back to 1/90, index books prior. Mail turnaround time 2-4 days.
General Information: No juvenile, mental, sealed, or adoption records released. Certification fee: $1.00 per page. Payee: District Clerk Reeves County. Personal checks accepted. Prepayment and SASE required.

County Court PO Box 867, Pecos, TX 79772; phone: 432-445-5467; criminal fax: 432-445-3997; same fax for civil/probate; hours 8AM-5PM (CST). *Misdemeanor, Civil, Probate.*
Note: Probate is a separate index at this same address.
Civil Records: Access: Mail, in person. Both court and visitors may perform in person searches. Search fee: $10.00 per name. Court makes copy: $1.00 per page. Required to search: name, years to search; also helpful: address. Civil cases indexed by defendant, plaintiff; on computer go back 10 years, index books prior. Mail turnaround time 1-3 days.
Criminal Records: Access: Mail, in person. Both court and visitors may perform in person searches. Search fee: $10.00 per name. Court makes copy: $1.00 per page. Required to search: name, years to search, DOB; also helpful: address. Criminal records on computer go back 10 years; index books prior. Mail turnaround time 5 days.
General Information: No juvenile, mental, sealed, or adoption records released. Will fax documents $.50 per page. Certification fee: $5.00 per cert includes copy fee. Payee: Reeves County Clerk. Personal checks accepted. Prepayment and SASE required.

Refugio County

District Court PO Box 736, Refugio, TX 78377; phone: 361-526-2721; hours 8AM-N, 1-5PM (CST). *Felony, Civil.*
Civil Records: Access: Mail, in person. Both court and visitors may perform in person searches. Search fee: $5.00 per name. Court makes copy: $1.00 per page. Required to search: name, years to search. Civil cases indexed by defendant, plaintiff; on computer back to 1992, index books back to 1879. Mail turnaround time 2-4 days.
Criminal Records: Access: Mail, in person. Both court and visitors may perform in person searches. Search fee: $5.00 per name. Court makes copy: $1.00 per page. Required to search: name, years to search, date of birth; also helpful-SSN, signed release. Criminal records on computer back to 1992, index books back to 1879. Mail turnaround time 2-4 days.
General Information: No juvenile, mental, sealed, or adoption records released. Certification fee: $1.00 per seal. Payee: District Clerk. Personal checks accepted. Prepayment and SASE required.

County Court PO Box 704, Refugio, TX 78377; phone: 361-526-2233; fax: 361-526-1325; hours 8AM-5PM (CST). *Misdemeanor, Civil, Probate.*
Civil Records: Access: Mail, in person. Both court and visitors may perform in person searches. Search fee: $5.00 per name. Court makes copy: $1.00 per page. Required to search: name, years to search. Civil cases indexed by defendant, plaintiff; in index books, began computerization in 2003. Mail turnaround time 5-10 days.
Criminal Records: Access: Mail, in person. Both court and visitors may perform in person searches. Search fee: $5.00 per name. Court makes copy: $1.00 per page. Required to search: name, years to search. Criminal records on computer since 1992, index books prior. Mail turnaround time 5-10 days.
General Information: No juvenile, mental, sealed, or adoption records released. Will not fax documents. Certification fee: $5.00 per document. Payee: Ruby Garcia, County Clerk. Personal checks accepted. Prepayment required.

Roberts County

District & County Court PO Box 477, Miami, TX 79059; phone: 806-868-2341; hours 8AM-N, 1-5PM (CST). *Felony, Misdemeanor, Civil, Probate.*
Civil Records: Access: Mail, in person. Both court and visitors may perform in person searches. Search fee: $5.00 per name. Court makes copy: $1.00 per page. Include postage with copy fee. Required to search: name, years to search. Civil cases indexed by defendant, plaintiff; in index books. Mail turnaround time 2-4 days.
Criminal Records: Access: Mail, in person. Both court and visitors may perform in person searches. Search fee: $5.00 per name. Court makes copy: $1.00 per page. Include postage with copy fee. Required to search: name, years to search, DOB, SSN. Criminal records in index books. Mail turnaround time 2-4 days.
General Information: No juvenile, mental, sealed, or adoption records released. Will fax documents $3.00 first pg; $1.00 each add'l. Certification fee: $5.00 per doc in County Court; $1.00 per page in District Court. Payee: Roberts County. Personal checks accepted. Prepayment and SASE required.

Robertson County

District Court PO Box 250, Franklin, TX 77856; phone: 979-828-3636; hours 8AM-5PM (CST). *Felony, Civil.*
www.robertsoncountycourthouse.com/
Civil Records: Access: Mail, in person. Both court and visitors may perform in person searches. Search fee: $5.00 per name. Court makes copy: $1.00 per page; same fee for self serve. Required to search: name, years to search, SSN. Civil cases indexed by defendant, plaintiff; on computer since 1987 and index books. Mail turnaround time 1-2 days.

Criminal Records: Access: Mail, in person. Both court and visitors may perform in person searches. Search fee: $5.00 per name. Court makes copy: $1.00 per page; same fee for self serve. Required to search: name, years to search, DOB; also helpful: SSN. Criminal records on computer since 1987 and index books. Mail turnaround time 1-2 days.
General Information: No juvenile, sealed, or adoption records released. Certification fee: $1.00 per page. Payee: Robertson County District Clerk. Personal checks accepted. Prepayment and SASE required.

County Court PO Box 1029, Franklin, TX 77856; phone: 979-828-4130; fax: 979-828-1260; hours 8AM-5PM (CST). *Misdemeanor, Civil, Probate.*
Civil Records: Access: Mail, fax, in person. Both court and visitors may perform in person searches. Search fee: $5.00 per name. Court makes copy: $1.00 per page; same fee for self serve. Required to search: name, years to search. Civil cases indexed by defendant, plaintiff; on computer back from 1990 to present, index books from 1985 to present. Mail turnaround time same day.
Criminal Records: Access: Mail, fax, in person. Both court and visitors may perform in person searches. Search fee: $5.00 per name. Court makes copy: $1.00 per page; same fee for self serve. Required to search: name, years to search, DOB. Criminal records on computer back to 1986 to present, index books from 1918. Mail turnaround time same day.
General Information: No juvenile, mental, sealed, or adoption records released. Certification fee: $5.00. Payee: Robertson County Clerk. Personal checks accepted. Prepayment required.

Rockwall County

District Court 1101 Ridge Rd, #209, Rockwall, TX 75087; phone: 972-882-0260; fax: 972-882-0268; hours 8AM-5PM (CST). *Felony, Civil.*
www.rockwallcountytexas.com
Civil Records: Access: Mail, in person, online. Both court and visitors may perform in person searches. Search fee: $5.00 per name. Fee is per 5 year period. Court makes copy: $1.00 per page. Required to search: name, years to search. Civil cases indexed by defendant, plaintiff; on computer back to 1994, index books prior. Online access is same as criminal, see below. Mail turnaround time 2-4 days.
Criminal Records: Access: Mail, in person, online. Both court and visitors may perform in person searches. Search fee: $5.00 per name. Court makes copy: $1.00 per page. Required to search: name, years to search, DOB. Criminal records on computer back to 1980, index books prior. Online access is free at www.rockwallcountytexas.com/judicialsearch/. Search sheriff bond and jail lists too. Mail turnaround time 2-4 days.
General Information: Public terminal has criminal back to 1981 and civil back to 1994. No juvenile, mental, sealed, or adoption records released. Will not fax documents. Certification fee: $1.00 per page. Payee: District Clerk. Personal checks accepted. Prepayment and SASE required.

County Court 1101 Ridge Rd, #101, Rockwall, TX 75087; phone: 972-882-0220; fax: 972-882-0229; hours 8AM-5PM (CST). *Misdemeanor, Civil, Probate.*
www.rockwallcountytexas.com
Civil Records: Access: Phone, mail, in person, online. Both court and visitors may perform in person searches. Search fee: $5.00 per name. Court makes copy: $1.00 per page; same fee for self serve. Required to search: name, years to search. Civil cases indexed by defendant, plaintiff; on computer back to 1985 and in index books from 1800s. Online access is same as criminal, see below. Mail turnaround time 2-4 days.
Criminal Records: Access: Phone, mail, in person, online. Both court and visitors may perform in person searches. Search fee: $5.00 per name. Court makes copy: $1.00 per page; same fee for self serve.

Required to search: name, years to search. Criminal records on computer back to 1987 and in index books from 1800s. Online access is free at www.rockwallcountytexas.com/judicialsearch/. Search sheriff bond and jail lists too. Mail turnaround time 2-4 days.
General Information: Public terminal goes back to 2000. No juvenile, mental, sealed, or adoption records released. Fee to fax documents is $5.00 per document. Certification fee: $5.00. Payee: County Clerk. Personal checks accepted. Prepayment and SASE required.

Runnels County

District Court PO Box 166, Ballinger, TX 76821; phone: 325-365-2638; fax: 325-365-9229; hours 8:30AM-5PM (CST). *Felony, Civil.*
Civil Records: Access: Phone, fax, mail, in person. Both court and visitors may perform in person searches. Search fee: $5.00 per name. Court makes copy: $1.00 per page; same fee for self serve. Required to search: name; also helpful: years to search. Civil cases indexed by defendant, plaintiff; in index books since 1882. Mail turnaround time 1-2 days.
Criminal Records: Access: Phone, fax, mail, in person. Both court and visitors may perform in person searches. Search fee: $5.00 per name. Court makes copy: $1.00 per page; same fee for self serve. Required to search: name; also helpful: years to search, DOB, SSN. Criminal records in index books since 1882. Mail turnaround time 1-2 days.
General Information: No juvenile, mental, sealed or adoption records released. Will fax documents $1.00 per page. Certification fee: $1.00 per cert. Payee: District Clerk. Personal checks accepted. Prepayment and SASE required.

County Court PO Box 189, Ballinger, TX 76821; phone: 325-365-2720; criminal fax: 325-365-3408; same fax for civil/probate; hours 8:30AM-N, 1-5PM (CST). *Misdemeanor, Civil, Probate.*
Civil Records: Access: Phone, mail, in person. Both court and visitors may perform in person searches. Search fee: $5.00. Court makes copy: $1.00 per page. Self serve copy fee: $.50 per page. Required to search: name, years to search. Civil cases indexed by defendant, plaintiff; in docket books with alphabetical index and file jacket by number; computerized since 1992. Mail turnaround time 1-2 days.
Criminal Records: Access: Phone, mail, in person. Both court and visitors may perform in person searches. Search fee: $5.00. Court makes copy: $1.00 per page. Self serve copy fee: $.50 per page. Required to search: name, years to search; also helpful: DOB. Criminal records in docket books with alphabetical index and file jacket by number; computerized since 1992. Mail turnaround time 1-2 days.
General Information: No juvenile or mental records released. Will fax documents to toll-free number. Certification fee: $5.00. Payee: County Clerk, Runnels County. Personal checks accepted. Prepayment required.

Rusk County

District Court PO Box 1687, 115 N Main St #301, Henderson, TX 75653; phone: 903-657-0353; fax: 903-657-1914; hours 8AM-5PM (CST). *Felony, Civil.*
Civil Records: Access: Mail, in person. Both court and visitors may perform in person searches. Search fee: $5.00 per name. Court makes copy: $1.00 per page. Required to search: name, years to search. Civil cases indexed by defendant, plaintiff; in index books; on computer back to 1973. Mail turnaround time 2-4 days.
Criminal Records: Access: Mail, in person. Both court and visitors may perform in person searches. Search fee: $5.00 per name. Court makes copy: $1.00 per page. Required to search: name, years to search, DOB, SSN, signed release. Criminal records in index books; on computer back to 1973. Mail turnaround time 2-4 days.

General Information: Public terminal goes back to 1985. No juvenile, mental, sealed, or adoption records released. Certification fee: $1.00 per page includes copy fee. Payee: District Clerk. Only cashiers checks and money orders accepted. Prepayment and SASE required.

County Court at Law PO Box 758, 115 N Main St #206, Henderson, TX 75653-; phone: 903-657-0330; fax: 903-657-0300; hours 8AM-5PM (CST). *Misdemeanor, Civil, Probate.*
Note: Misdemeanor & probate records are at County Clerk.
Civil Records: Access: Mail, in person. Both court and visitors may perform in person searches. Search fee: $5.00 per name. Court makes copy: $1.00 per page. Required to search: name, years to search. Civil cases indexed by defendant, plaintiff; in index books. Mail turnaround time 2-4 days.
Criminal Records: Access: Mail, in person. Both court and visitors may perform in person searches. Search fee: $5.00 per name. Court makes copy: $1.00 per page. Required to search: name, years to search, DOB, SSN. Criminal records are not computerized, are indexed in books. Mail turnaround time 2-4 days.
General Information: No juvenile, mental, sealed, or adoption records released. Certification fee: $5.00 per doc. Payee: District Clerk. Business checks accepted. Prepayment and SASE required.

Sabine County

District Court PO Box 850, Hemphill, TX 75948; phone: 409-787-2912; fax: 409-787-2623; hours 8AM-4:00PM (CST). *Felony, Civil.*
Civil Records: Access: Mail, in person. Both court and visitors may perform in person searches. Search fee: $10.00 per name. Court makes copy: $1.00 per page; same fee for self serve. Required to search: name, years to search. Civil cases indexed by defendant, plaintiff; on computer since 1992. Overall records go back to 1900. Mail turnaround time 1-2 days.
Criminal Records: Access: Mail, in person. Both court and visitors may perform in person searches. Search fee: $10.00 per name. Court makes copy: $1.00 per page; same fee for self serve. Required to search: name, years to search. Criminal records on computer since 1992. Overall records go back to 1900. Mail turnaround time 1-2 days.
General Information: No juvenile, mental, sealed, or adoption records released. Will not fax documents. No certification fee. Payee: District Clerk. Personal checks accepted. Prepayment and SASE required.

County Court PO Drawer 580, Hemphill, TX 75948-0580; phone: 409-787-2889; hours 8AM-4PM (CST). *Misdemeanor, Probate.*
Criminal Records: Access: Mail, in person. Both court and visitors may perform in person searches. Search fee: $10.00 per name. Court makes copy: $1.00 per page; same fee for self serve. Required to search: name, years to search. Criminal records on computer since 1992, index books prior. Mail turnaround time 2 days.
General Information: No juvenile, mental, sealed, or adoption records released. Will not fax documents. Certification fee: $5.00. Payee: Sabine County Clerk. Business checks accepted. Prepayment and SASE required.

San Augustine County

District Court County Courthouse, Rm 202, San Augustine, TX 75972; phone: 936-275-2231; fax: 936-275-2389; hours 8AM-4:15PM (CST). *Felony, Civil.*
Civil Records: Access: Phone, mail, in person. Both court and visitors may perform in person searches. Search fee: $5.00 per name. Court makes copy: $1.00 per page; same fee for self serve. Required to search: name, years to search. Civil cases indexed by plaintiff. Civil records in index books. Mail turnaround time 2-4 days.

Criminal Records: Access: Phone, mail, in person. Only the court performs in person searches; visitors may not. Search fee: $5.00 per name. Court makes copy: $1.00 per page; same fee for self serve. Required to search: name, years to search. Criminal records in index books. Mail turnaround time 2-4 days.
General Information: No juvenile, mental, sealed, or adoption records released. Will fax documents to local or toll free line. Certification fee: $1.00. Payee: District Clerk. Personal checks accepted. Prepayment and SASE required.

County Court 100 W Columbia, Rm 106, San Augustine, TX 75972; phone: 936-275-2452; fax: 936-275-9579; hours 8AM-4:30PM (CST). *Misdemeanor, Probate.*
Criminal Records: Access: Phone, mail, in person. Both court and visitors may perform in person searches. Search fee: $10.00 per name. Court makes copy: $1.00 per page; same fee for self serve. Required to search: name, years to search; also helpful: address, DOB, SSN. Criminal records go back to 1984; on computer since 1990. Copies must be paid for in advance. Will fax back if $5.00 paid in advance. Mail turnaround time 2-3 days.
General Information: No juvenile, mental, sealed, or adoption records released. Certification fee: $5.00. Payee: County Clerk. Personal checks accepted. Prepayment and SASE required.

San Jacinto County

District Court 1 State Hwy 150, Rm 4, Coldspring, TX 77331; phone: 936-653-2909; fax: 936-653-4659; hours 8AM-N, 1-5PM (CST). *Felony, Civil.*
Civil Records: Access: Mail, in person. Both court and visitors may perform in person searches. Search fee: $5.00 per name. Court makes copy: $1.00 per page. Required to search: name, years to search. Civil cases indexed by defendant, plaintiff; in index books. Mail turnaround time 2-4 days.
Criminal Records: Access: Mail, in person. Both court and visitors may perform in person searches. Search fee: $5.00 per name. Court makes copy: $1.00 per page. Required to search: name, years to search. Criminal records on computer since 1986. Mail turnaround time 2-4 days.
General Information: Public terminal goes back to 1999. No juvenile, mental, sealed, or adoption records released. Will fax documents for $1.00 per page. Certification fee: $5.00. Payee: District Clerk. Personal checks accepted. Prepayment and SASE required.

County Court 1 State Hwy 150, Rm 2, Coldspring, TX 77331; phone: 936-653-2324; fax: 936-653-8312; hours 8AM-4:30PM (CST). *Misdemeanor, Civil, Probate.*
www.co.san-jacinto.tx.us
Civil Records: Access: Mail, in person. Both court and visitors may perform in person searches. Search fee: $9.00 per name. Court makes copy: $1.00 per page. Required to search: name, years to search. Civil cases indexed by defendant, plaintiff; in index books. Mail turnaround time 2 weeks.
Criminal Records: Access: Mail, in person. Both court and visitors may perform in person searches. Search fee: $9.00 per name. Court makes copy: $1.00 per page. Required to search: name, years to search; also helpful: address, DOB, SSN. Criminal records in index books. Mail turnaround time 2 weeks.
General Information: Public terminal has only criminal records back to 1988. No juvenile, mental, sealed, or adoption records released. Will fax documents to toll free or local number. Certification fee: $5.00. Payee: County Clerk. Personal checks accepted. Only cashiers checks and money orders accepted for criminal searches. Prepayment and SASE required.

San Patricio County

District Court PO Box 1084, Sinton, TX 78387; phone: 361-364-6225; hours 8AM-5PM (CST). *Felony, Civil.*
Civil Records: Access: Mail, in person. Both court and visitors may perform in person searches. Search fee: $5.00 per name. Fee is per division. Court makes copy: $1.00 per page; same fee for self serve. Required to search: name, years to search. Civil cases indexed by defendant, plaintiff; in index books from 1800s; computerized back to 1993. Mail turnaround time 2-4 days.
Criminal Records: Access: Mail, in person. Both court and visitors may perform in person searches. Search fee: $5.00 per name. Fee is per division. Court makes copy: $1.00 per page; same fee for self serve. Required to search: name, years to search. Criminal records in index books from 1800s; computerized back to 1993. Mail turnaround time 2-4 days.
General Information: Public terminal goes back to 1994. No juvenile, mental, sealed, or adoption records released. Will fax documents. Certification fee: $1.00. Payee: District Clerk. Business checks accepted. Prepayment and SASE required.

County Court PO Box 578, Sinton, TX 78387; phone: 361-364-6290; fax: 361-364-6112; hours 8AM-5PM (CST). *Misdemeanor, Civil, Probate.*
Civil Records: Access: Phone, mail, in person. Both court and visitors may perform in person searches. Search fee: $5.00 per name. Court makes copy: $1.00 per page. Required to search: name, years to search; also helpful: address. Civil cases indexed by defendant, plaintiff; in index books and microfilm, some as far back as 1824; computerized back to 2002. Mail turnaround time 2-3 days.
Criminal Records: Access: Phone, mail, in person. Both court and visitors may perform in person searches. Search fee: $5.00 per name. Court makes copy: $1.00 per page. Required to search: name, years to search; also helpful: address, DOB, SSN, anything. Criminal records in index books and microfilm; computerized back to 2002. Mail turnaround time 2-3 days.
General Information: Public use terminal available. No juvenile, mental, or sealed records released. Certification fee: $5.00. Payee: County Clerk. Personal checks accepted. Prepayment and SASE required.

San Saba County

District & County Court County Courthouse, 500 E Wallace, #202, San Saba, TX 76877; phone: 325-372-3375; hours 8AM-N, 1-4:30PM (CST). *Felony, Misdemeanor, Civil, Probate.*
www.courts.state.tx.us/district/33rd/index.htm
Civil Records: Access: Phone, mail, in person. Both court and visitors may perform in person searches. Search fee: $10.00 per name. Court makes copy: $1.00 per page. Required to search: name, years to search. Civil cases indexed by defendant, plaintiff; in index books. Mail turnaround time 2-3 days.
Criminal Records: Access: Mail, in person. Both court and visitors may perform in person searches. Search fee: $10.00 per name. Court makes copy: $1.00 per page. Required to search: name, years to search; also helpful: DOB. Criminal records in index books. Mail turnaround time 2-3 days.
General Information: No juvenile, mental, sealed, or adoption records released. Certification fee: $5.00. Payee: District/County Clerk. Personal checks accepted. Prepayment and SASE required.

Schleicher County

District & County Court PO Drawer 580, Courthouse Sq, Eldorado, TX 76936; phone: 325-853-2833; fax: 325-853-2768; hours 9AM-N, 1-5PM (CST). *Felony, Misdemeanor, Civil, Probate.*
Civil Records: Access: Mail, in person. Both court and visitors may perform in person searches. Search fee: $10.00 per name. Court makes copy: $1.00 per page. Required to search: name, years to

search. Civil cases indexed by defendant, plaintiff; in index books. Mail turnaround time 2-3 days.

Criminal Records: Access: Mail, in person. Both court and visitors may perform in person searches. Search fee: $10.00 per name. Court makes copy: $1.00 per page. Required to search: name, years to search. Criminal records in index books. Mail turnaround time 2-3 days.

General Information: No juvenile, mental, sealed, or adoption records released. Will fax documents for $2.00 per page, must be paid before search. Certification fee: $5.00 per doc. Payee: District/County Clerk. Personal checks accepted. Prepayment and SASE required.

Scurry County

132nd District Court 1806 25th St, #402, Snyder, TX 79549; phone: 325-573-5641; hours 8AM-5PM (CST). *Felony, Civil.*

Civil Records: Access: Mail, in person. Both court and visitors may perform in person searches. Search fee: $5.00 per name. Court makes copy: $1.00 for first page, $.25 each add'l. Required to search: name, years to search. Civil cases indexed by defendant, plaintiff. Civil records go back to 1890; computerized records since 1994. All requests must be in writing. Mail turnaround time 2-3 days.

Criminal Records: Access: Mail, in person. Both court and visitors may perform in person searches. Search fee: $5.00 per name. Court makes copy: $1.00 for first page, $.25 each add'l. Required to search: name, years to search, address, DOB, SSN, sex. Criminal records go back to 1890; computerized records since 1994. All requests must be in writing. Mail turnaround time 2-3 days.

General Information: No juvenile, mental, sealed, or adoption records released. Fee to fax documents is $1.00 per page. Certification fee: $1.00 per page. Cert fee includes copies. Payee: District Clerk. Personal checks accepted. Prepayment and SASE required.

County Court County Courthouse, 1806 25th St, #300, Snyder, TX 79549; phone: 325-573-5332; fax: 325-573-7396; hours 8:30AM-5PM (CST). *Misdemeanor, Civil, Probate.*

Civil Records: Access: Mail, in person. Both court and visitors may perform in person searches. Search fee: $10.00 per name. Court makes copy: $1.00 per page. Required to search: name, years to search. Civil cases indexed by defendant, plaintiff; in index books since 1900s; on computer back to 1996. Mail turnaround time 1-2 days.

Criminal Records: Access: Mail, in person. Both court and visitors may perform in person searches. Search fee: $5.00 per name. Fee includes copies. Court makes copy: $1.00 per page. Required to search: name, years to search; also helpful: address, DOB, SSN. Criminal records in index books since 1900s; on computer back to 1996. Written request always required. Mail turnaround time 1-2 days.

General Information: Public terminal goes back to 1996. No mental or sealed records released. Fee to fax documents is $1.00 per page. Certification fee: $5.00. Payee: County Clerk Scurry County. Personal checks accepted. Prepayment and SASE required.

Shackelford County

District & County Court PO Box 247, Albany, TX 76430; phone: 325-762-2232 x100; fax: 325-762-2830; hours 8:30AM-N, 1-5PM (CST). *Felony, Misdemeanor, Civil, Probate.*

Civil Records: Access: Mail, in person. Both court and visitors may perform in person searches. Search fee: $5.00 per name. Fee is per court. Court makes copy: $1.00 per page; same fee for self serve. Required to search: name, years to search. Civil cases indexed by defendant, plaintiff; on computer since 1987, index books since 1867. Mail turnaround time 5 days after receipt.

Criminal Records: Access: Mail, in person. Both court and visitors may perform in person searches. Search fee: $5.00 per name. Fee is per court. Court makes copy: $1.00 per page; same fee for self serve.

Required to search: name, years to search. Criminal records since 1867. Mail turnaround time 5 days after receipt.

General Information: Public terminal goes back to 1987. No juvenile, mental, sealed, or adoption records released. Will fax documents; cannot fax certified pages. Certification fee: $5.00 per document District Ct; $1.00 if County Ct. Payee: Clerk, Shackelford County. Personal checks accepted. Prepayment and SASE required.

Shelby County

District Court PO Drawer 1953, 200 Sn Augustine St, Center, TX 75935; phone: 936-598-4164; hours 8AM-4:30PM (CST). *Felony, Civil.*

Civil Records: Access: Mail, in person. Both court and visitors may perform in person searches. Search fee: $5.00 per name. Court makes copy: $1.00 per page. Required to search: name, years to search. Civil cases indexed by defendant, plaintiff; in index books; on computer back to 2000. Mail turnaround time 2-3 days.

Criminal Records: Access: Mail, in person. Both court and visitors may perform in person searches. Search fee: $5.00 per name. Court makes copy: $1.00 per page. Required to search: name, years to search, signed release. Criminal records in index books; on computer back to 2000. Mail turnaround time 2-3 days.

General Information: No juvenile, mental, sealed, or adoption records released. Certification fee: $1.00 per doc. Payee: District Clerk. Will accept attorneys check. Prepayment and SASE required.

County Court PO Box 1987, Center, TX 75935; phone: 936-598-6361; criminal fax: 936-598-3701; same fax for civil/probate; hours 8AM-4:30PM (CST). *Misdemeanor, Civil, Probate.*

Note: Probate records in a separate index at this same address.

Civil Records: Access: Mail, in person. Both court and visitors may perform in person searches. Search fee: $10.00 per name. Court makes copy: $1.00 per page. Required to search: name, years to search. Civil cases indexed by defendant, plaintiff. Civil & probate records in index books back to 1882; on computer back to 1990. Mail turnaround time 1-2 days.

Criminal Records: Access: Mail, in person. Both court and visitors may perform in person searches. Search fee: $10.00 per name. Court makes copy: $1.00 per page. Required to search: name, years to search, SSN, DOB; also helpful: signed release. Criminal records in index books back to 1920; on computer back to 1990. All requests must be in writing. Mail turnaround time 1-2 days.

General Information: No juvenile, mental, sealed, or adoption records released. Will fax documents for $5.00 fee per document. Certification fee: $5.00 per certification. Payee: Shelby County Clerk. Personal checks accepted. Prepayment and SASE required.

Sherman County

District & County Court PO Box 270, 701 N 3rd St, Stratford, TX 79084; phone: 806-366-2371; criminal fax: 806-366-5670; same fax for civil/probate; hours 8AM-N, 1-5PM (CST). *Felony, Misdemeanor, Civil, Probate.*

Civil Records: Access: Mail, in person. Both court and visitors may perform in person searches. Search fee: $5.00 per name. Court makes copy: $1.00 per page. Self serve copy fee: $.25 per page. Required to search: name, years to search. Civil cases indexed by plaintiff. Civil records to 1930. Mail turnaround time 2-3 days.

Criminal Records: Access: Mail, in person. Both court and visitors may perform in person searches. Search fee: $5.00 per name. Court makes copy: $1.00 per page. Self serve copy fee: $.25 per page. Required to search: name, years to search. Criminal records to 1947. Mail turnaround time 2-3 days.

General Information: No juvenile, mental, sealed, or adoption records released. Will fax documents for

$5.00 1st page, plus $1.00 each add'l pg. Certification fee: $5.00 per document. Payee: Sherman County Clerk. Personal checks accepted. No credit cards. Prepayment and SASE required.

Smith County

District Court PO Box 1077, Tyler, TX 75710; phone: 903-535-0666; fax: 903-535-0683; hours 8AM-5PM (CST). *Felony, Civil.*
www.smith-county.com/dc_desc.htm

Civil Records: Access: Mail, in person. Both court and visitors may perform in person searches. Search fee: $5.00 per name. Court makes copy: $1.00 per page. Required to search: name, years to search. Civil cases indexed by defendant, plaintiff; in index books. Mail turnaround time 2-3 days.

Criminal Records: Access: Mail, in person. Both court and visitors may perform in person searches. Search fee: $5.00 per name. Court makes copy: $1.00 per page. Required to search: name, years to search. Criminal records in index books to 1846, computerized since 1/99. Mail turnaround time 2-3 days.

General Information: No juvenile, mental, sealed, or adoption records released. Will not fax documents. Certification fee: $1.00 per doc. Payee: District Clerk. Cashiers checks and money orders accepted. Prepayment and SASE required.

County Court at Law PO Box 1018, 200 E Ferguson, #300, Tyler, TX 75710; phone: 903-535-0630; criminal phone: 903-535-0645/46/47; civil phone: 903-535-0636/37/38; probate phone: 903-535-0634; fax: 903-535-0684; hours 8AM-5PM (CST). *Misdemeanor, Civil, Probate.*
www.smith-county.com/cs_county_court.htm
Note: There are three Courts at Law at this location.

Civil Records: Access: Mail, in person. Both court and visitors may perform in person searches. Search fee: $5.00 per name. Court makes copy: $1.00 per page. Required to search: name, years to search. Civil cases indexed by defendant, plaintiff; in index books. Mail turnaround time 2-4 days.

Criminal Records: Access: Mail, in person. Both court and visitors may perform in person searches. Search fee: $5.00 per name. Court makes copy: $1.00 per page. Required to search: name, years to search; also helpful: DOB, SSN. Criminal records in index books. Mail turnaround time 2-4 days.

General Information: Public terminal has criminal back to 1995 and civil back to 1997. (Probates records on terminal to 1992.) No juvenile, mental, sealed, or adoption records released. Will fax documents for $1.00 per page. Certification fee: $5.00 per certificate. Payee: Smith County Clerk. Personal checks accepted. Prepayment and SASE required.

Somervell County

District & County Court PO Box 1098, Glen Rose, TX 76043; phone: 254-897-4427; fax: 254-897-3233; hours 8AM-5PM (CST). *Felony, Misdemeanor, Civil, Probate.*

Note: Evictions are handled by Justice of the Peace, POB 237, Glen Rose, TX 76043, 254-897-2120.

Civil Records: Access: Mail, in person. Both court and visitors may perform in person searches. Search fee: $5.00 per name. Court makes copy: $1.00 per page; same fee for self serve. Required to search: name, years to search; also helpful: address. Civil cases indexed by defendant, plaintiff; on computer since 1991, microfilm since 1980, index books since 1875. Mail turnaround time same day.

Criminal Records: Access: Mail, in person. Both court and visitors may perform in person searches. Search fee: $5.00 per name. Court makes copy: $1.00 per page; same fee for self serve. Required to search: name, years to search, DOB, SSN, signed release; also helpful: address. Criminal records on computer since 1991, microfilm since 1980, index books since 1875. Mail turnaround time same day.

General Information: No juvenile, mental, sealed, or adoption records released. Fee to fax documents is

$1.00 per page. Certification fee: $5.00. Payee: County/District Clerk. Personal checks accepted. Prepayment required. SASE preferred.

Starr County

District & County Court Starr County Courthouse, Rm 304, Rio Grande City, TX 78582; phone: 956-487-8482 (Dist) 487-8485 (County); criminal phone: 956-487-8485; civil phone: 956-487-8482; probate phone: 956-487-8032; criminal fax: 956-487-8493; same fax for civil/probate; hours 8AM-5PM (CST). *Felony, Misdemeanor, Civil, Probate.*
Civil Records: Access: Phone, fax, mail, in person. Both court and visitors may perform in person searches. Search fee: $7.00 per name. Court makes copy: $1.00 per page. Required to search: name, years to search. Civil cases indexed by defendant, plaintiff; on index books from 1920s, computerized since 1992. Mail turnaround time 2 days.
Criminal Records: Access: Phone, fax, mail, in person. Only the court performs in person searches; visitors may not. Search fee: $7.00 per name. Court makes copy: $1.00 per page. Required to search: name, years to search, SSN; also helpful: DOB. Criminal records on computer since 1992; in docket books to 1800s. Mail turnaround time 2 days.
General Information: No adoption records released. Will fax documents $5.00 1st page; $1.00 each add'l. Certification fee: $5.00 per document. Payee: District Clerk. Personal checks accepted. Prepayment and SASE required.

County Court Starr County Courthouse, Rm 201, Rio Grande City, TX 78582; phone: 956-487-8032; fax: 956-487-8674; hours 8AM-5PM (CST). *Misdemeanor, Probate.*
Criminal Records: Access: Mail, in person, online. Both court and visitors may perform in person searches. Search fee: $10.00 per name. Court makes copy: $1.00 per page. Self serve copy fee: $1.00 per page. Required to search: name, years to search; also helpful: SSN, DOB. Criminal records on computer since 1997, in index books since 1984, archived prior. Online access is at www.idocket.com; registration and password required. This is fee service, unless only one name search is done a day. Records go back to 12/31/1996. Mail turnaround 2-4 days.
General Information: No juvenile, mental, sealed, or adoption records released. Fee to fax documents is $1.00 per page. Certification fee: $5.00. Payee: County Clerk. Personal checks accepted. Prepayment required. SASE requested.

Stephens County

District Court 200 W Walker, Breckenridge, TX 76424; phone: 254-559-3151; fax: 254-559-8127; hours 8:30AM-5PM (CST). *Felony, Civil, Misdemeanor.*
Civil Records: Access: Fax, mail, in person. Both court and visitors may perform in person searches. Search fee: $5.00 per name. Court makes copy: $1.00 per page. Required to search: name, years to search. Civil cases indexed by defendant, plaintiff; in index books, archived from 1900; on computer back to 1995. Mail turnaround time same day.
Criminal Records: Access: Fax, mail, in person. Both court and visitors may perform in person searches. Search fee: $5.00 per name. Court makes copy: $1.00 per page. Required to search: name, years to search, DOB. Criminal records in index books, archived from 1900; on computer back to 1995. Mail turnaround time same day.
General Information: No juvenile, mental, sealed, or adoption records released. Will fax documents $1.00 per page; to local and 800 numbers only. Certification fee: $1.00. Payee: District Clerk. Personal checks accepted. Prepayment and SASE required.

County Clerk 200 W Walker, Breckenridge, TX 76424; phone: 254-559-3700; hours 8:30AM-N, 1-5PM (CST). *Probate.*

Sterling County

District & County Court PO Box 55, Sterling City, TX 76951; phone: 325-378-5191; fax: 325-378-2266; hours 8:30AM-4PM M-Th; -1:30PM F (CST). *Felony, Misdemeanor, Civil, Probate.*
Note: Probate is a separate index at this same address.
Civil Records: Access: Mail, in person. Both court and visitors may perform in person searches. No search fee. Court makes copy: $1.00 per page. Required to search: name, years to search; also helpful: address. Civil cases indexed by defendant, plaintiff; in index books from 1900s. Mail turnaround time 1-2 days.
Criminal Records: Access: Mail, in person. Both court and visitors may perform in person searches. No search fee. Court makes copy: $1.00 per page. Required to search: name, years to search; also helpful: DOB, SSN. Criminal records in index books from 1900s. Mail turnaround time 1-2 days.
General Information: No juvenile, mental, sealed, or adoption records released. Fee to fax documents is $1.00 per page. Certification fee: $5.00 per document. Payee: Sterling County/District Clerk. Personal checks accepted. Prepayment and SASE required.

Stonewall County

District & County Court PO Drawer P, Aspermont, TX 79502; phone: 940-989-2272; fax: 940-989-2715; hours 8AM-N, 1-4:30PM (CST). *Felony, Misdemeanor, Civil, Probate.*
Civil Records: Access: Phone, mail, in person. Both court and visitors may perform in person searches. No search fee. Court makes copy: $1.00 per page; same fee for self serve. Required to search: name, years to search. Civil cases indexed by defendant, plaintiff; in index books to 1900's. Mail turnaround time 2 days.
Criminal Records: Access: Phone, mail, in person. Both court and visitors may perform in person searches. No search fee. Court makes copy: $1.00 per page; same fee for self serve. Required to search: name, years to search. Criminal records in index books to 1900's. Mail turnaround time 2 days.
General Information: No juvenile, mental, sealed, or adoption records released. Will fax documents for $2.00 per page. Certification fee: $5.00. Payee: County Clerk. Personal checks accepted. Prepayment and SASE required.

Sutton County

District & County Court 300 E Oak, #3, Sonora, TX 76950; phone: 325-387-3815; hours 8:30AM-4:30PM (CST). *Felony, Misdemeanor, Civil, Probate.*
Civil Records: Access: Phone, mail, in person. Both court and visitors may perform in person searches. Search fee: $10.00 per name. Court makes copy: $1.00 per page; same fee for self serve. Required to search: name, years to search. Civil cases indexed by defendant, plaintiff; on computer back to 1992, index books prior. Mail turnaround time 2-4 days.
Criminal Records: Access: Mail, in person. Both court and visitors may perform in person searches. Search fee: $10.00 per name. Court makes copy: $1.00 per page; same fee for self serve. Required to search: name, years to search. Criminal records on computer back to 1995, index books prior to 1890. Mail turnaround time 2-4 days.
General Information: No juvenile, mental, sealed, or adoption records released. Will fax documents to local or toll free line. Certification fee: $5.00. Payee: County Clerk. Personal checks accepted. Prepayment and SASE required.

Swisher County

District & County Court County Courthouse, 119 S Maxwell, Tulia, TX 79088; phone: 806-995-4396; criminal fax: 806-995-4121; same fax for civil/probate; hours 8AM-5PM (CST). *Felony, Misdemeanor, Civil, Probate.*
Note: Probate is a separate index at this same address.

Civil Records: Access: Mail, fax, in person, email. Both court and visitors may perform in person searches. Search fee: $5.00 per name. Court makes copy: $1.00 per page. Self serve copy fee: $.50 per page. Required to search: name, years to search. Civil cases indexed by defendant, plaintiff; on computer since 1992, index books prior. Mail turnaround time 1 day.
Criminal Records: Access: Mail, fax, in person, email. Both court and visitors may perform in person searches. Search fee: $5.00 per name. Court makes copy: $1.00 per page. Self serve copy fee: $.50 per page. Required to search: name, years to search, DOB and SSN. Criminal records on computer since 1992, index books prior to early 1900's. Mail turnaround time 1-2 days.
General Information: No juvenile, mental, sealed, or adoption records released. Fee to fax documents is $3.00 per page $1.00 each add'l page. Certification fee: $1.00 per page. Payee: County/District Clerk. Personal checks and credit cards accepted. Provide credit card info for email or fax requests. Prepayment required. SASE requested.

Tarrant County

District Court 401 W Belknap, County District Clerk's Office, Fort Worth, TX 76196-0402; phone: 817-884-1574 (884-1265 Family Division); criminal phone: 817-884-1342; civil phone: 817-884-1240; hours 8AM-5PM (CST). *Felony, Civil.*
www.tarrantcounty.com/ecourts/site/default.asp
Civil Records: Access: Mail, online, in person. Both court and visitors may perform in person searches. Search fee: $5.00 per name if the office does the search. Court makes copy: $.35 per page. Required to search: full name and DOB. Civil cases indexed by defendant, plaintiff; on computer since 1989, file jackets prior to 1989; records go back to 1800s. Access to the remote online system requires $50 setup that includes software and a monthly fee of $35 per month with add'l month prepaid; for 1 to 5 users; fees increase with more users. Call 817-884-1345 for info and signup. Index records are available for free at http://cc.co.tarrant.tx.us/CivilCourts/ccl/default.asp. Mail turnaround time 1-3 days.
Criminal Records: Access: Mail, online, in person. Both court and visitors may perform in person searches. Search fee: $5.00 per name if the office does the search. Court makes copy: $.35 per page. Required to search: full name, years to search, DOB; also helpful: SSN. Criminal records on computer back to 1975, microfilm since 1970, index books and case files since 1800s. Online access same as civil. Mail turnaround time 1-3 days.
General Information: Public terminal goes back to 1975. No juvenile, mental, sealed, or adoption records released. Certification fee: $1.00 per page. Payee: District Clerk. Business checks accepted. Prepayment required.

County Court - Criminal 401 W Belknap, County District Clerk's Office, Fort Worth, TX 76196-0402; phone: 817-884-1195; fax: 817-884-3295; hours 7:30AM-4:30PM (CST). *Misdemeanor.*
www.tarrantcounty.com/ecourts/site/default.asp
Note: Small Claims, Evictions, and low-level civil cases are handled by JP/Municipal Courts.
Criminal Records: Access: Mail, online, in person. Both court and visitors may perform in person searches. Search fee: $5.00 per name. Court makes copy: $1.00 per page. Required to search: name, years to search, DOB. Criminal records on computer back to 1974. Access to the remote online system requires $50 setup that includes software and a monthly fee of $35 per month with additional month prepaid to start. This is for 1 to 5 users. Fees increase with more users. The District Court records are on this system also. Call 817-884-3202 for more information. Mail turnaround time 1-3 days.
General Information: Public terminal has only criminal records. No juvenile, mental, sealed, or

adoption records released. Certification fee: $5.00 per case. Business checks accepted. Prepayment and SASE required.

Probate Court County Courthouse, 100 W Weatherford St, Probate Court #1 Rm 260A, Fort Worth, TX 76196; phone: 817-884-1200; probate phone: 817-884-1254; fax: 817-884-3178; hours 8AM-4:30PM (CST). *Probate.*
www.tarrantcounty.com/ecourts/site/default.asp
Search probate records by name or case number at http://cc.co.tarrant.tx.us/CivilCourts/Probate/default.asp.

Taylor County

District Court 300 Oak St, Abilene, TX 79602; phone: 325-674-1316; hours 8AM-N, 1-5PM (CST). *Felony, Civil.*
Civil Records: Access: Mail, in person. Both court and visitors may perform in person searches. Search fee: $5.00 per name. Court makes copy: $1.00 per page. Required to search: name, years to search. Civil cases indexed by defendant, plaintiff; on computer since 1996; prior records in index books to 1885. Mail turnaround time 5 days.
Criminal Records: Access: Mail, in person. Both court and visitors may perform in person searches. Search fee: $5.00 per name. Court makes copy: $1.00 per page. Required to search: name, years to search, DOB; also helpful: SSN. Criminal records on computer since 1982; prior records in index books to 1885. Mail turnaround time 5 days.
General Information: Public terminal has criminal back to 1982 and civil back to 1996. No juvenile, mental, sealed, or adoption records released. Certification fee: $1.00. Payee: Taylor County District Clerk. Business checks accepted. Prepayment and SASE required.

County Court PO Box 5497, Abilene, TX 79608; phone: 325-674-1202; fax: 325-674-1279; hours 8AM-5PM (CST). *Misdemeanor, Civil, Probate.*
www.taylorcountytexas.org
Civil Records: Access: Mail, in person. Both court and visitors may perform in person searches. Search fee: $5.00 per name per 10 years searched. Probate searches are $5.00, years not applicable. Court makes copy: $1.00 per page; same fee for self serve. Required to search: name, years to search. Civil cases indexed by defendant, plaintiff; on computer less than ten years, index books prior. Mail turnaround time 2-4 days.
Criminal Records: Access: Mail, in person. Both court and visitors may perform in person searches. Search fee: $5.00 per name per 10 years searched. Court makes copy: $1.00 per page; same fee for self serve. Required to search: name, years to search, DOB; also helpful: address, SSN. Criminal records on computer back to 1980; overall records go back to 1949. Mail turnaround time 2-4 days.
General Information: Public terminal goes back to 1981. (Probate back to 1888.) No juvenile, mental, sealed, or adoption records released. Fee to fax documents is $1.00 per page, $2.00 per doc. Certification fee: $5.00. Payee: County Clerk. Personal checks accepted. Prepayment and SASE required.

Terrell County

District & County Court PO Drawer 410, Sanderson, TX 79848; phone: 432-345-2391; fax: 432-345-2740; hours 9AM-N, 1-5PM (CST). *Felony, Misdemeanor, Civil, Probate.*
Civil Records: Access: Mail, in person. Both court and visitors may perform in person searches. Search fee: $5.00 per name. Court makes copy: $1.00 per page. Required to search: name, years to search. Civil cases indexed by defendant, plaintiff; in index books. All requests must be in writing. Mail turnaround time 2-4 days.
Criminal Records: Access: Mail, in person. Both court and visitors may perform in person searches. Search fee: $5.00 per name. Court makes copy: $1.00 per page. Required to search: name, years to search.

Criminal records in index books. All requests must be in writing. Mail turnaround time 2-4 days.
General Information: No juvenile, mental, sealed, or adoption records released. No certification fee. Payee: County Clerk. Personal checks accepted. Prepayment required.

Terry County

District Court 500 W Main, Rm 209E, Brownfield, TX 79316; phone: 806-637-4202; hours 8:30AM-5PM (CST). *Felony, Civil.*
Civil Records: Access: Mail, in person. Both court and visitors may perform in person searches. Search fee: $5.00 per name. Court makes copy: $1.00 per page. Required to search: name, years to search. Civil cases indexed by defendant, plaintiff; in index books and on computer. Mail turnaround time same day.
Criminal Records: Access: Mail, in person. Only the court performs in person searches; visitors may not. Search fee: $5.00 per name. Court makes copy: $1.00 per page. Required to search: name, years to search, DOB; also helpful: SSN. Criminal records in index books and on computer. Mail turnaround time same day.
General Information: No juvenile, mental, sealed, or adoption records released. Will fax documents to local or toll free line. Certification fee: $1.00 per document. Payee: District Clerk. Personal checks accepted. Prepayment and SASE required.

County Court 500 W Main, Rm 105, Brownfield, TX 79316-4398; phone: 806-637-8551; fax: 806-637-4871; hours 8:30AM-5PM (CST). *Misdemeanor, Civil, Probate.*
Civil Records: Access: Mail, in person. Both court and visitors may perform in person searches. Search fee: $10.00 per name. Court makes copy: $1.00 per page. Required to search: name, years to search. Civil cases indexed by defendant, plaintiff; in index books to 1904, computerized since 1981. Mail turnaround time 2-3 days.
Criminal Records: Access: Mail, in person. Both court and visitors may perform in person searches. Search fee: $10.00 per name. Court makes copy: $1.00 per page. Required to search: name, years to search; also helpful: address, DOB, SSN. Criminal records in index books back to 1904, computerized since 1981. Mail turnaround time 1-2 days.
General Information: No juvenile, mental, sealed, or adoption records released. Fee to fax documents is $1.00 per page. Certification fee: $5.00. Payee: County Clerk. Personal checks accepted. Prepayment and SASE required.

Throckmorton County

District & County Court PO Box 309, Throckmorton, TX 76483; phone: 940-849-2501; hours 8AM-N, 1-4:30PM M-Th; 8AM-N Friday (CST). *Felony, Misdemeanor, Civil, Probate.*
Civil Records: Access: Mail, in person. Both court and visitors may perform in person searches. Search fee: $10.00 per name. Court makes copy: $1.00 per page; same fee for self serve. Required to search: name, years to search; also helpful: address. Civil cases indexed by defendant, plaintiff; in index books; computerized records go back to 1990. Mail turnaround time 1 week.
Criminal Records: Access: Mail, in person. Both court and visitors may perform in person searches. Search fee: $10.00 per name. Court makes copy: $1.00 per page; same fee for self serve. Required to search: name, years to search. Criminal records in index books; computerized records go back to 1990. Mail turnaround time 2-4 days.
General Information: No juvenile, mental, sealed, or adoption records released. Certification fee: $5.00. Payee: County/District Clerk. Personal checks accepted. Prepayment and SASE required.

Titus County

District Court 105 W 1st St, PO Box 492, Mount Pleasant, TX 75455; phone: 903-577-6721; fax: 903-577-6719; hours 8AM-5PM (CST). *Felony, Civil.*
Civil Records: Access: Phone, mail, in person. Both court and visitors may perform in person searches. Search fee: $5.00 per name. Court makes copy: $1.00 per page; same fee for self serve. Required to search: name, years to search. Civil cases indexed by defendant, plaintiff; in index books from 1895; computerized back to 1992. Mail turnaround time 2-3 days.
Criminal Records: Access: Phone, mail, in person. Both court and visitors may perform in person searches. Search fee: $5.00 per name. Court makes copy: $1.00 per page; same fee for self serve. Required to search: name, years to search. Criminal records in index books from 1895; computerized back to 1992. Mail turnaround time 2-3 days.
General Information: Public terminal goes back to 10 years. No juvenile, mental, sealed, or adoption records released. Certification fee: $5.00. Payee: District Clerk. Personal checks accepted. Prepayment and SASE required.

County Court 100 W 1st St, #204, Mount Pleasant, TX 75455; phone: 903-577-6796; fax: 903-577-6793; hours 8AM-5PM (CST). *Misdemeanor, Civil, Probate.*
Civil Records: Access: Mail, in person. Both court and visitors may perform in person searches. Search fee: $10.00 per name. Court makes copy: $1.00 per page; same fee for self serve. Required to search: name, years to search; also helpful: address. Civil cases indexed by defendant, plaintiff; on computer since 1/1994, index books since 1895. Mail turnaround time 1 week to 10 days.
Criminal Records: Access: Mail, in person. Both court and visitors may perform in person searches. Search fee: $10.00 per name. Court makes copy: $1.00 per page; same fee for self serve. Required to search: name, years to search; also helpful: address, DOB, SSN. Criminal records on computer since 1/1994, index books since 1930. Mail turnaround time 1 week to 10 days.
General Information: No juvenile, mental, sealed, or adoption records released. Certification fee: $5.00. Payee: County Clerk. Business checks accepted. Prepayment and SASE required.

Tom Green County

District Court County Courthouse, 112 W Beauregard, San Angelo, TX 76903; phone: 325-659-6579; fax: 325-659-3241; hours 8AM-5PM (CST). *Felony, Civil.*
www.co.tom-green.tx.us/distclrk/
Civil Records: Access: Mail, in person, online. Both court and visitors may perform in person searches. Search fee: $5.00 per name per 5 years searched. Court makes copy: $1.00 per page. Required to search: name, years to search; also helpful. Civil cases indexed by defendant, plaintiff; in index books from 1900s; on computer back to 1993. Online access to civil case records back to 1994 is online at http://justice.co.tom-green.tx.us. Search by name, case number. Mail turnaround time 1 week.
Criminal Records: Access: Mail, in person, online. Both court and visitors may perform in person searches. Search fee: $5.00 per name per 5 years searched. Court makes copy: $1.00 per page. Required to search: name, years to search, DOB. Criminal records in index books from 1900s; on computer back to 1993. Online access to criminal records is the same as civil. Mail turnaround time 1 week.
General Information: Public terminal goes back to 1994. No juvenile, mental, sealed, or adoption records released. Fee to fax documents is $1.50 per page. No certification fee. Payee: District Clerk. Personal checks accepted. Prepayment and SASE required.

County Court 124 W Beauregard, San Angelo, TX 76903; phone: 325-659-6555; hours 8AM-4:30PM (CST). *Misdemeanor, Civil, Probate.* http://justice.co.tom-green.tx.us

Civil Records: Access: Mail, in person, online. Both court and visitors may perform in person searches. Search fee: $5.00 per name. Court makes copy: $1.00 per page; same fee for self serve. Required to search: name, years to search; also helpful: address. Civil cases indexed by defendant, plaintiff; on computer since 1994, index books prior. Online access to civil records back to 1994 is free at the website. Mail turnaround time same day.

Criminal Records: Access: Mail, in person, online. Both court and visitors may perform in person searches. Search fee: $5.00 per name. Court makes copy: $1.00 per page; same fee for self serve. Required to search: name, years to search, DOB; also helpful: address, SSN. Criminal records on computer since 1994, index books prior. Online access to criminal records is the same as civil. website also includes Sheriff jail and bond records. Mail turnaround time same day.

General Information: Public terminal goes back to 1994. No juvenile, mental, sealed, or adoption records released. Will fax documents to local or toll free line. Certification fee: $5.00. Payee: County Clerk. Prepayment and SASE required.

Travis County

District Court PO Box 1748, 1001 Guadalupe St #301, Austin, TX 78767; phone: 512-854-9420; criminal phone: 512-854-9457; civil phone: 512-854-9457; fax: 512-854-9549; hours 8AM-5PM (CST). *Felony, Civil.*

Civil Records: Access: Mail, in person. Both court and visitors may perform in person searches. Search fee: $5.00 per name. Add $2.00 per year prior to 1988. Court makes copy: $.50 per page. Required to search: name, years to search. Civil cases indexed by defendant, plaintiff; on computer since 1986, microfiche and index books. Mail turnaround time 2-3 days.

Criminal Records: Access: Fax, mail, in person. Both court and visitors may perform in person searches. Search fee: $5.00 per name. Add $2.00 per year prior to 1988. Court makes copy: $.50 per page. Required to search: name, years to search, DOB. Criminal records on computer since 1988, index books prior to 1988. Mail turnaround time 2-3 days, normally.

General Information: Public terminal has criminal back to 1988 and civil back to 1986. No juvenile, mental, sealed, or adoption records released (all felony cases are public record). Certification fee: $1.00 per page. Payee: District Clerk. Personal checks or Visa, MC, Discover accepted. Prepayment and SASE required.

County Court PO Box 1748, 5501 Airport Blvd #B100, Austin, TX 78767-1748; criminal phone: 512-854-9440 x7; civil phone: 512-854-9090; probate phone: 512-854-9595; fax: 512-854-4220; hours 8AM-5PM (CST). *Misdemeanor, Civil, Probate.* www.co.travis.tx.us

Note: Records include appeals from the Travis County JP Courts.

Civil Records: Access: Mail, in person, online. Both court and visitors may perform in person searches. Search fee: $5.00 per name. Fee applies to cases opened prior to June 1986. Court makes copy: $1.00 per page. Self serve copy fee: $.25 per page. Required to search: name, years to search. Civil cases indexed by defendant, plaintiff; on computer since 6/86, microfilm prior to 1845, probate from 1992 forward. Also, access to probate court records only is free at http://deed.co.travis.tx.us/search.aspx?cabinet=probate. Mail turnaround time 2-5 days.

Criminal Records: Access: Mail, in person. Both court and visitors may perform in person searches. Search fee: $5.00 per name. $10.00 per name for microfilm. Court makes copy: $1.00 per page. Self

serve copy fee: $.25 per page. Required to search: name, years to search; also helpful: address, DOB, SSN. Criminal misdemeanor records on computer since 1981; prior records on microfilm to 1845. Mail turnaround time 2-5 days.

General Information: Public terminal has criminal back to 1983 and civil back to 1986. No juvenile, mental, sealed, or adoption records released. Certification fee: $5.00 per doc. Payee: Travis County Clerk. Personal checks accepted. Prepayment required.

Trinity County

District Court PO Box 548, Groveton, TX 75845; phone: 936-642-1118; hours 8AM-5PM (CST). *Felony, Civil.*

Civil Records: Access: Mail, in person. Both court and visitors may perform in person searches. Search fee: $5.00 per name. Court makes copy: $1.00 per page; same fee for self serve. Required to search: name, years to search. Civil cases indexed by defendant, plaintiff; on computer since 1980, index books prior. Mail turnaround time 1 day.

Criminal Records: Access: Mail, in person. Both court and visitors may perform in person searches. Search fee: $5.00 per name. Court makes copy: $1.00 per page; same fee for self serve. Required to search: name, years to search. Criminal records on computer since 1980, index books prior. Mail turnaround time 1 day

General Information: No juvenile, mental, sealed, or adoption records released. Will not fax documents. Certification fee: $1.00 per page. Payee: District Clerk. Personal checks accepted. Prepayment required.

County Court PO Box 456, Groveton, TX 75845; phone: 936-642-1208; criminal fax: 936-642-3004; same fax for civil/probate; hours 8AM-5PM (CST). *Misdemeanor, Civil, Probate.*

Civil Records: Access: Mail, in person. Both court and visitors may perform in person searches. Search fee: $10.00 per name. Court makes copy: $1.00 per page; same fee for self serve. Required to search: name, years to search; also helpful: address. Civil cases indexed by defendant, plaintiff; in index books back to 1982. Date of birth helpful for searching. Mail turnaround time 1 day.

Criminal Records: Access: Mail, in person. Both court and visitors may perform in person searches. Search fee: $10.00 per name. Court makes copy: $1.00 per page; same fee for self serve. Required to search: name, years to search, SSN; also helpful: address, DOB, sex. Criminal records in index books back to 1982. Mail turnaround time 1 day.

General Information: No juvenile, mental, sealed, or adoption records released. Fee to fax documents is $1.00 per page. Certification fee: $5.00 per cert. Payee: County Clerk. Personal checks accepted. Prepayment and SASE required.

Tyler County

District Court 203 Courthouse, 100 W Bluff, Woodville, TX 75979; phone: 409-283-2162; hours 8AM-N, 1-4:30PM (CST). *Felony, Civil.*

Civil Records: Access: Mail, in person. Both court and visitors may perform in person searches. Search fee: $5.00 per name. Court makes copy: $1.00 per page; same fee for self serve. Required to search: name, years to search. Civil cases indexed by defendant, plaintiff; in index books. Mail turnaround time same day.

Criminal Records: Access: Mail, in person. Both court and visitors may perform in person searches. Search fee: $5.00. Court makes copy: $1.00 per page; same fee for self serve. Required to search: name, years to search. Criminal records in index books. Mail turnaround time same day.

General Information: No juvenile, mental, sealed, or adoption records released. Will not fax documents. Payee: District Clerk. Business checks accepted. Prepayment and SASE required.

County Court County Courthouse, Rm 110, 100 W Bluff, Woodville, TX 75979; phone: 409-283-2281; hours 8AM-4:30PM (CST). *Misdemeanor, Civil, Probate.*

Civil Records: Access: Phone, mail, in person. Both court and visitors may perform in person searches. Search fee: $5.00 per name. Court makes copy: $1.00 per page; same fee for self serve. Required to search: name, years to search. Civil cases indexed by defendant, plaintiff; on computer back to 1989, microfilm since 1973, index books from 1800s. Mail turnaround time 1 day.

Criminal Records: Access: Mail, in person. Both court and visitors may perform in person searches. Search fee: $5.00 per name. Court makes copy: $1.00 per page; same fee for self serve. Required to search: name, years to search; also helpful: address, DOB, SSN. Criminal records on computer back to 1989, microfilm since 1973, index books from 1800s. Mail turnaround time 1-2 days.

General Information: Public use terminal available. No juvenile, mental, sealed or adoption records released. Will fax documents for $3.00 per page. Certification fee: $5.00. Payee: County Clerk. Personal checks accepted. Prepayment required.

Upshur County

District Court PO Box 950, Gilmer, TX 75644; phone: 903-843-5031; fax: 903-843-3540; hours 8AM-5PM M-Th; 8AM-4:30PM Fri (CST). *Felony, Misdemeanor, Civil, Probate.* www.countyofupshur.com

Civil Records: Access: Mail, in person. Both court and visitors may perform in person searches. Search fee: $5.00 per name. Court makes copy: $1.00 per page. Required to search: name, years to search. Civil cases indexed by defendant, plaintiff; in index books to 1800s. Mail turnaround time same day.

Criminal Records: Access: Mail, in person. Both court and visitors may perform in person searches. Search fee: $5.00 per name. Court makes copy: $1.00 per page. Required to search: name, years to search. Criminal records in index books to 1800s. Note: In county court, only the court may search. Mail turnaround time same day.

General Information: Public use terminal available. No juvenile, mental, sealed or adoption records released. Will fax documents. Certification fee: $1.00 per document. Payee: District Clerk. No personal checks accepted. Prepayment and SASE required.

County Court PO Box 730, Courthouse Sq, Hwy 154 West, Gilmer, TX 75644; phone: 903-680-8126; fax: 903-843-5492; hours 8AM-5PM (CST). *Misdemeanor, Civil, Probate.*

Civil Records: Access: Mail, in person. Both court and visitors may perform in person searches. Search fee: $5.00 per name per 10 year period. Court makes copy: $1.00 per page. Required to search: name, years to search. Civil cases indexed by defendant, plaintiff; in index books to 1936; on computer back to 1979. Mail turnaround time same day.

Criminal Records: Access: Mail, in person. Both court and visitors may perform in person searches. Search fee: $5.00 per name per 10 year period. Court makes copy: $1.00 per page. Required to search: name, years to search, DOB, offense, signed release. Criminal records in index books to 1936; on computer back to 1979. Note: In county court, only the court may search. Mail turnaround time same day.

General Information: Public terminal goes back to 1982. No juvenile, mental, sealed or adoption records released. Will fax documents for $1.00 per page, prepaid. Certification fee: $5.00 per doc. Payee: County Clerk. Personal checks accepted. Prepayment and SASE required.

Upton County

District & County Court PO Box 465, Rankin, TX 79778; phone: 432-693-2861; criminal fax: 432-693-2129; same fax for civil/probate; hours 8AM-5PM (CST). *Felony, Misdemeanor, Civil, Probate.*

www.co.upton.tx.us

Civil Records: Access: Fax, mail, in person. Both court and visitors may perform in person searches. Search fee: $5.00 per name. Court makes copy: $1.00 per page. Required to search: name, years to search. Civil cases indexed by defendant, plaintiff; on computer back to 1987; in index books to 1910. Mail turnaround time 1-2 days.

Criminal Records: Access: Fax, mail, in person. Both court and visitors may perform in person searches. Search fee: $5.00 per name. Court makes copy: $1.00 per page. Required to search: name, years to search, signed release; also helpful: address, DOB. Criminal records on computer back to 1987; in index books to 1910. Mail turnaround time 1-2 days.

General Information: No juvenile, mental, sealed, or adoption records released. Fee to fax documents is $2.00 per page. Certification fee: $5.00 per document. Payee: District/County Clerk. Personal checks accepted. Prepayment and SASE required.

Uvalde County

District Court County Courthouse, #15, Uvalde, TX 78801; phone: 830-278-3918; hours 8AM-5PM (CST). *Felony, Civil.*

Civil Records: Access: Phone, mail, in person. Both court and visitors may perform in person searches. Search fee: $5.00 per name. Court makes copy: $.75 per page. Required to search: name, years to search. Civil cases indexed by defendant, plaintiff; in index books. Mail turnaround time 2-3 days.

Criminal Records: Access: Phone, mail, in person. Both court and visitors may perform in person searches. Search fee: $5.00 per name. Court makes copy: $.75 per page. Required to search: name, years to search, DOB, SSN. Criminal records in index books. Mail turnaround time 2-3 days.

General Information: No juvenile, mental, sealed, or adoption records released. Will not fax documents. Certification fee: $1.00 per page. Payee: District Clerk. No personal checks accepted. Prepayment and SASE required.

County Clerk PO Box 284, 100 Getty St, Uvalde, TX 78802; phone: 830-278-6614; hours 8AM-5PM (CST). *Misdemeanor, Civil, Probate.*

Civil Records: Access: Mail, in person. Both court and visitors may perform in person searches. Search fee: $10.00 per name. The fee covers a 10 year search. Court makes copy: $1.00 per page. Required to search: name, years to search. Civil cases indexed by defendant, plaintiff; in index books from 1856, computerized records from 1997. Mail turnaround time 1-2 days.

Criminal Records: Access: Mail, in person. Both court and visitors may perform in person searches. Search fee: $10.00 per name. The fee covers a 10 year search. Court makes copy: $1.00 per page. Required to search: name, years to search, DOB, SSN. Criminal records in index books from 1856, computerized records from 1997. Mail turnaround time 1-2 days.

General Information: Public terminal has criminal back to 6/1997 and civil back to 1997. No juvenile, mental, sealed, or adoption records released. Certification fee: $5.00 per page. Payee: Lucille C Hutcherson, Uvalde County Clerk. Personal checks accepted. Prepayment required.

Val Verde County

District Court PO Box 1544, 100 E Broadway, Del Rio, TX 78841; phone: 830-774-7538; criminal phone: 830-774-7539; civil phone: 830-774-7538; fax: 803-774-7643; hours 8AM-4:30PM (CST). *Felony, Civil.*

Civil Records: Access: Mail, in person. Both court and visitors may perform in person searches.

Search fee: $5.00 per name. Court makes copy: $.50 per page. Required to search: name, years to search. Civil cases indexed by defendant, plaintiff; on computer since 1990, index books prior. Mail turnaround time 2-5 days.

Criminal Records: Access: Mail, in person. Both court and visitors may perform in person searches. Search fee: $5.00 per name. Court makes copy: $.50 per page. Required to search: name, years to search. Criminal records on computer since 1990, index books prior. Mail turnaround time 2-5 days.

General Information: Public terminal has criminal back to 1993 and civil back to 1989. No juvenile, mental, sealed, or adoption records released. Will not fax documents. Certification fee: $1.00 per page includes copy fee. Payee: District Clerk. Business and local checks accepted. Prepayment and SASE required.

County Court PO Box 1267, Del Rio, TX 78841-1267; phone: 830-774-7564; hours 8AM-4:30PM (CST). *Misdemeanor, Civil, Probate.*

Civil Records: Access: Mail, in person. Both court and visitors may perform in person searches. Search fee: $5.00 per name. Court makes copy: $1.00 per page. Required to search: name, years to search. Civil cases indexed by defendant, plaintiff; in index books back to 1885, computerized since 1999. Mail turnaround time 1-2 days.

Criminal Records: Access: Mail, in person. Both court and visitors may perform in person searches. Search fee: $5.00 per name. Court makes copy: $1.00 per page. Required to search: name, years to search; also helpful: address, DOB, SSN. Criminal records in index books, computerized since 1999. Mail turnaround time 1-2 days.

General Information: No juvenile, mental, sealed, or adoption records released. Certification fee: $5.00 per cert. Payee: County Clerk. Personal checks accepted. Prepayment and SASE required.

Van Zandt County

District Court 121 E Dallas St, Rm 302, Canton, TX 75103; phone: 903-567-6576; fax: 903-567-1283; hours 8AM-5PM (CST). *Felony, Civil.*

Civil Records: Access: Phone, fax, mail, in person. Both court and visitors may perform in person searches. Search fee: $5.00 per name. Court makes copy: $1.00 per page. Required to search: name, years to search. Civil cases indexed by defendant, plaintiff; in index books back to 1800s; on computer back to 1980. Mail turnaround time 2-4 days.

Criminal Records: Access: Mail, fax, in person. Both court and visitors may perform in person searches. Search fee: $5.00 per name. Court makes copy: $1.00 per page. Required to search: name, years to search, DOB. Criminal records in index books back to 1800s; on computer back to 1980. Mail turnaround time 2-4 days.

General Information: Public terminal goes back to 1990. No juvenile, mental, sealed, or adoption records released. Will fax documents for $1.00 per page. Certification fee: $1.00. Payee: District Clerk. Personal checks accepted. Prepayment and SASE required.

County Court 121 E Dallas St, #202, Canton, TX 75103; phone: 903-567-6503; criminal fax: 903-567-6722; same fax for civil/probate; hours 8AM-5PM (CST). *Misdemeanor, Civil, Probate.*

Civil Records: Access: Mail, in person. Both court and visitors may perform in person searches. Search fee: $5.00 per name. Court makes copy: $1.00 per page. Self serve copy fee: $.50 per page. Required to search: name, years to search. Civil cases indexed by defendant, plaintiff; on computer back to 1993. Mail turnaround time 2-4 days.

Criminal Records: Access: Mail, in person. Both court and visitors may perform in person searches. Search fee: $5.00 per name. Court makes copy: $1.00 per page. Self serve copy fee: $.50 per page. Required to search: name, years to search; also helpful: address, DOB, SSN. Criminal records on computer back to 1987. Mail turnaround time 2-4 days.

General Information: Public terminal has criminal back to 1987 and civil back to 1993. No juvenile, mental, sealed, or adoption records released. Fee to fax documents is $3.00 per doc, plus $1 per page. Certification fee: $5.00 1st page; $1.00 each add'l,. Payee: County Clerk. Personal checks accepted. Prepayment and SASE required.

Victoria County

District Court PO Box 2238, Victoria, TX 77902; phone: 361-575-0581; criminal fax: 361-572-9549; civil fax: 361-572-5682; hours 8AM-5PM (CST). *Felony, Civil.*

Civil Records: Access: Mail, in person, online. Both court and visitors may perform in person searches. Search fee: $5.00 per name. Court makes copy: $1.00 per page. Required to search: name, years to search. Civil cases indexed by defendant, plaintiff; on computer since 1989, index books since 1838. Online access is through www.idocket.com; registration and password required. Records go back to 12/31/1993. Mail turnaround time 1-2 days.

Criminal Records: Access: Mail, in person, online. Both court and visitors may perform in person searches. Search fee: $5.00 per name. Court makes copy: $1.00 per page. Required to search: name, years to search, DOB. Criminal records on computer since 1989, index books since 1838s. Online access is through www.idocket.com; registration and password required. Records go back to 12/31/1993. Mail turnaround time 1-2 days.

General Information: Public terminal goes back to 1990. No juvenile, mental, sealed, or adoption records released. No fee for local fax; Long distance fax fee $5.00 plus $1.00 per pg. Certification fee: $1.00 per page. Payee: District Clerk. Personal checks accepted. Prepayment and SASE required.

County Court 115 N Bridge, Rm 103, Victoria, TX 77901; phone: 361-575-1478; criminal fax: 361-575-6276; same fax for civil/probate; hours 8AM-5PM (CST). *Misdemeanor, Civil, Probate.*

Civil Records: Access: Phone, mail, in person, online. Both court and visitors may perform in person searches. Search fee: $10.00 per name. Court makes copy: $1.00 per page; same fee for self serve. Required to search: name, years to search. Civil cases indexed by defendant, plaintiff; on Cox index back to 1836; on computer back to 1991. Online access is through www.idocket.com; registration and password required. Records go back to 12/31/1991. Mail turnaround time 1 day.

Criminal Records: Access: Phone, fax, mail, in person, online. Both court and visitors may perform in person searches. Search fee: $10.00 per name. Court makes copy: $1.00 per page; same fee for self serve. Required to search: name, years to search; also helpful: address, DOB, SSN. Criminal records on Cox index back to 1836; on computer back to 1989. Online access is through www.idocket.com; registration and password required. Records go back to 12/31/1989. Mail turnaround time 1 day.

General Information: Public terminal has criminal back to 1989 and civil back to 1991. No juvenile, mental, sealed, birth, death or adoption records released. Will fax documents $3.50 per doc, or $3.50 plus $1.50 per page to non toll-free number. Certification fee: $5.00 per document. Payee: Victoria County Clerk. Personal checks accepted. Prepayment and SASE required.

Walker County

District Court 1100 University Ave, Rm 209, Huntsville, TX 77340; phone: 936-436-4972; hours 8AM-N, 1-5PM (CST). *Felony, Civil.*

Civil Records: Access: Mail, in person. Both court and visitors may perform in person searches. Search fee: $5.00 per name. Court makes copy: $1.00 per page. Required to search: name, years to search. Civil cases indexed by defendant, plaintiff; on index books. Mail turnaround time 1-2 days.

Criminal Records: Access: Mail, in person. Both court and visitors may perform in person searches.

Search fee: $5.00 per name. Court makes copy: $1.00 per page. Required to search: name, years to search. Criminal records on index books. Mail turnaround time 1-2 days.

General Information: No juvenile, mental, sealed, abortion or adoption records released. Will fax documents to local or toll free line. No certification fee. Payee: District Clerk. Business checks accepted. Prepayment and SASE required.

County Court PO Box 210, Huntsville, TX 77342-0210; phone: 936-436-4922; criminal fax: 936-436-4962; civil fax: 936-436-4928; probate fax: 936-436-4928; hours 8AM-4:45PM (CST). *Misdemeanor, Civil, Probate.*

www.co.walker.tx.us/courts.htm

Note: Criminal fax # 936-436-4962.

Civil Records: Access: Mail, in person. Both court and visitors may perform in person searches. Search fee: $5.00 per name. Court makes copy: $1.00 per page. Required to search: name, years to search, DOB, SSN. Civil cases indexed by defendant, plaintiff; in index books. Mail turnaround time 2-3 days.

Criminal Records: Access: Mail, in person. Both court and visitors may perform in person searches. Search fee: $5.00 per name. Court makes copy: $1.00 per page. Required to search: name, years to search; also helpful: address, DOB, SSN. Criminal records in index books to 1977, computerized since 1998. Mail turnaround time 2-3 days.

General Information: Public terminal has only criminal records back to 1991; records back to 9/1/77 being added. No juvenile, mental, sealed, or adoption records released. Will not fax documents. Certification fee: $5.00 per document. Payee: County Clerk. Personal checks accepted. Prepayment and SASE required.

Waller County

District Court 836 Austin St, Rm 318, Hempstead, TX 77445; phone: 979-826-7735; fax: 979-826-7738; hours 8AM-N, 1-5PM (CST). *Felony, Civil.*

www.cvtv.net/~tx155district/

Civil Records: Access: Mail, in person. Both court and visitors may perform in person searches. Search fee: $5.00 per name. Court makes copy: $1.00 per page. Required to search: name, years to search, DOB, SSN. Civil cases indexed by defendant, plaintiff; on index books to 1866, computerized in 2002. Mail turnaround time 2 days.

Criminal Records: Access: Mail, in person. Both court and visitors may perform in person searches. Search fee: $5.00 per name. Court makes copy: $1.00 per page. Required to search: name, years to search, DOB, SSN. Criminal records on computer since 9/99, archived to early 1900s. Mail turnaround time 2 days.

General Information: Public terminal has only civil records back to 5/2000. No juvenile, mental, sealed, or adoption records released. Certification fee: $1.00. Payee: District Clerk. Personal checks accepted. Prepayment and SASE required.

County Court 836 Austin St, Rm 217, Hempstead, TX 77445; phone: 979-826-7711; hours 8AM-N, 1-5PM (CST). *Misdemeanor, Civil, Probate.*

Civil Records: Access: Mail, in person. Both court and visitors may perform in person searches. Search fee: $5.00 per name. Court makes copy: $1.00 per page. Required to search: name, years to search. Civil cases indexed by defendant, plaintiff; in index books; on computer back to 1994. Mail turnaround time same day if possible.

Criminal Records: Access: Mail, in person. Both court and visitors may perform in person searches. Search fee: $5.00 per name. Court makes copy: $1.00 per page. Required to search: name, years to search, signed release; also helpful: DOB, SSN. Criminal records in index books; on computer back to 1994. Mail turnaround time 2-3 days.

General Information: Public terminal goes back to 1994. No juvenile, mental, sealed, or adoption records released. Certification fee: $5.00. Payee: Waller County Clerk. No personal checks accepted for copies. Prepayment and SASE required.

Ward County

District Court PO Box 440, Monahans, TX 79756; phone: 432-943-2751; fax: 432-943-3810; hours 8AM-N-1-5PM (CST). *Felony, Civil.*

Civil Records: Access: Mail, in person. Both court and visitors may perform in person searches. Search fee: $5.00 per name. Court makes copy: $.50 per page. Required to search: name, years to search. Civil cases indexed by defendant, plaintiff; on computer since 1980, index books prior. Mail turnaround time 1-2 days.

Criminal Records: Access: Mail, in person. Both court and visitors may perform in person searches. Search fee: $5.00 per name. Court makes copy: $.50 per page. Required to search: name, years to search. Criminal records on books, computerized since 1980. Mail turnaround time 1-2 days.

General Information: No juvenile, mental, sealed, or adoption records released. Will fax documents for $2.00 per page. Only if prepaid. Certification fee: $1.00 per page. Payee: District Clerk. Business checks accepted. Prepayment and SASE required.

County Court County Courthouse, Monahans, TX 79756; phone: 432-943-3294; fax: 432-943-6054; hours 8AM-5PM (CST). *Misdemeanor, Civil, Probate.*

Civil Records: Access: Mail, in person. Both court and visitors may perform in person searches. Search fee: $5.00 per name. Court makes copy: $1.00 per page. Required to search: name, years to search. Civil cases indexed by defendant, plaintiff; in index books; computerized records go back 10 years. In person requests must be accompanied by written request. Mail turnaround time 1-2 days.

Criminal Records: Access: Mail, in person. Both court and visitors may perform in person searches. Search fee: $5.00 per name. Court makes copy: $1.00 per page. Required to search: name, years to search, DOB, signed release; also helpful: address, SSN. Criminal records in index books; computerized records go back 10 years. In person requests must be accompanied by a written request. Mail turnaround time 1-2 days.

General Information: No juvenile, mental, sealed, or adoption records released. Fee to fax documents is $3.00 per page. Certification fee: $5.00. Payee: County Clerk. Personal checks accepted. Prepayment and SASE required.

Washington County

District Court 100 E Main, #304, Brenham, TX 77833-3753; phone: 979-277-6200; hours 8AM-5PM (CST). *Felony, Civil.*

Civil Records: Access: Mail, in person, online. Both court and visitors may perform in person searches. Search fee: $5.00 per name. Court makes copy: $.50 per page; same fee for self serve. Required to search: name, years to search. Civil cases indexed by defendant, plaintiff; in index books since 1800s; on computer back to 1988. Online access to court records is through www.idocket.com. One search a day is free; subscription required for more. Mail turnaround time 1-2 days.

Criminal Records: Access: Mail, in person, online. Both court and visitors may perform in person searches. Search fee: $5.00 per name. Court makes copy: $.50 per page; same fee for self serve. Required to search: name, years to search; also helpful: DOB. Criminal records in index books since 1800s; on computer back to 1988. Online access to court records is through www.idocket.com. One search a day is free; subscription required for more. Mail turnaround time 1-2 days.

General Information: Public terminal goes back to 1988. No juvenile, mental, sealed, or adoption records released. Will fax documents to local or toll free line.

Certification fee: $1.00 per page. Payee: District Clerk. Personal checks accepted. Prepayment required.

County Court 100 E Main, #102, Brenham, TX 77833; phone: 979-277-6200; fax: 979-277-6278; hours 8AM-5PM (CST). *Misdemeanor, Civil, Probate.*

Civil Records: Access: Mail, in person. Both court and visitors may perform in person searches. Search fee: $5.00 per name. Court makes copy: $1.00 per page. Required to search: name, years to search. Civil cases indexed by defendant, plaintiff; in index books from 1868; computerized back to 1985. In person request must be accompanied by a written request. Mail turnaround time 1-2 days.

Criminal Records: Access: Mail, in person. Both court and visitors may perform in person searches. Search fee: $5.00 per name. Court makes copy: $1.00 per page. Required to search: name, years to search; also helpful: address, DOB, SSN. Criminal records in index books from 1870; computerized back to 1992. In person requests must be accompanied by a written request. Mail turnaround time 1-2 days.

General Information: Public terminal has criminal back to 1990 and civil back to 1985. No juvenile, mental, sealed, or adoption records released. Fee to fax documents is $1.00 per page and must be pre-paid. Certification fee: $5.00 per instrument. Payee: Washington County Clerk. Personal checks accepted. Prepayment and SASE required.

Webb County

District Court PO Box 667, 1110 Victoria #203, Laredo, TX 78042-0667; phone: 956-523-4268; fax: 956-523-5063; hours 8AM-5PM (CST). *Felony, Civil.*

www.webbcounty.com

Civil Records: Access: Phone, mail, fax, in person, online. Both court and visitors may perform in person searches. Search fee: $5.00 per name. Court makes copy: $1.00 per page. Required to search: name, years to search, address; also helpful: DOB, SSN. Civil cases indexed by defendant, plaintiff; on computer back to 11/1988, index books prior. Online access is through www.idocket.com; registration and password required. Records go back to 12/31/1988. Mail turnaround time 1 week.

Criminal Records: Access: Mail, fax, in person, online. Both court and visitors may perform in person searches. Search fee: $5.00 per name. Court makes copy: $1.00 per page. Required to search: name, years to search, DOB or SSN, signed release. Criminal records on computer back to 11/1988, index books prior. Online access is through www.idocket.com; registration and password required. Records go back to 12/31/1988. Mail turnaround time 1 week.

General Information: Public terminal goes back to 1988. No juvenile, mental, sealed, or adoption records released. Will fax documents for $5.00 plus add'l $1.00 per page. Certification fee: $1.00 per page includes copy fee. Payee: District Clerk. Personal checks accepted. Prepayment and SASE required.

County Court 1110 Victoria, #201, Laredo, TX 78040; phone: 956-523-4266; criminal phone: 956-523-4261; civil phone: 956-523-4262; probate phone: 956-523-4257; fax: 956-523-5035; hours 8AM-5PM (CST). *Misdemeanor, Civil Under $5,000, Probate.*

Civil Records: Access: Mail, in person, online. Both court and visitors may perform in person searches. Search fee: $5.00 per name. Court makes copy: $1.00 per page; same fee for self serve. Required to search: name, years to search. Civil cases indexed by defendant, plaintiff; on computer since 1988, index books prior. Online access is through www.idocket.com; registration and password required. Includes probate. Mail turnaround time 2-3 days.

Criminal Records: Access: Mail, in person, online. Both court and visitors may perform in person searches. Search fee: $5.00 per name. Court makes copy: $1.00 per page; same fee for self serve.

Required to search: name, years to search, DOB; also helpful: address, SSN. Criminal records on computer since 1988, index books prior to 10/75. Criminal records access is through www.idocket.com; registration and password required. Records go back to 12/31/1988. Mail turnaround time 2-3 days.

General Information: Public terminal goes back to 1988. No juvenile, mental, sealed, or adoption records released. Will fax documents $4.00 for 1st page; $.50 each add'l page; half that fee per page for incoming faxes. Certification fee: $5.00. Payee: County Clerk. Personal checks accepted. Prepayment and SASE required.

Wharton County

District Court PO Drawer 391, Wharton, TX 77488; phone: 979-532-5542; fax: 979-532-1299; hours 8AM-N, 1-4:30PM (CST). *Felony, Civil.*
Civil Records: Access: Mail, fax, in person. Both court and visitors may perform in person searches. Search fee: $5.00 per name. Court makes copy: $1.00 per page. Self serve copy fee: $.50 per page. Required to search: name, years to search. Civil cases indexed by defendant, plaintiff; on computer since 1989, index books prior to 1848. Mail turnaround time same day.
Criminal Records: Access: Mail, fax, in person. Both court and visitors may perform in person searches. Search fee: $5.00 per name. Court makes copy: $1.00 per page. Self serve copy fee: $.50 per page. Required to search: name, years to search. Criminal records on computer since 1989, index books prior to 1932. Mail turnaround time same day.
General Information: No juvenile, mental, sealed, or adoption records released. Will fax documents for $5.00 plus add'l $1.00 per page. Certification fee: $2.00 per document. Payee: District Clerk of Wharton. Personal checks accepted. Prepayment and SASE required.

County Court PO Box 69, Wharton, TX 77488; phone: 979-532-2381; hours 8AM-5PM (CST). *Misdemeanor, Civil, Probate.*
Civil Records: Access: Mail, in person. Both court and visitors may perform in person searches. Search fee: $5.00 per name per 10 years searched. Court makes copy: $1.00 per page; same fee for self serve. Required to search: name, years to search. Civil cases indexed by defendant, plaintiff; on computer since 1991, index books since 1978, prior indexes in storage to 1893. Mail turnaround time 1-2 days.
Criminal Records: Access: Mail, in person. Both court and visitors may perform in person searches. Search fee: $5.00 per name per 10 years searched. Court makes copy: $1.00 per page; same fee for self serve. Required to search: name, years to search, DOB, signed release; also helpful: address, SSN, copy of ID. Criminal records on computer since 1991, index books since 1978, prior indexes in storage to 1893. Mail turnaround time 1-2 days.
General Information: Public terminal goes back to 1991. No juvenile, mental, sealed, or adoption records released. Fee to fax documents is $2.00 plus $1.00 per page. Certification fee: $5.00. Payee: County Clerk. Business checks accepted; personal checks accepted only if local resident. Prepayment and SASE required.

Wheeler County

District Court PO Box 528, Wheeler, TX 79096; phone: 806-826-5931; fax: 806-826-5503; hours 8AM-5PM (CST). *Felony, Civil.*
Civil Records: Access: Phone, mail, in person. Both court and visitors may perform in person searches. Search fee: $5.00 per name. Court makes copy: $1.00 per page; same fee for self serve. Required to search: name, years to search. Civil cases indexed by defendant, plaintiff; in index books. Mail turnaround time 2-3 days.
Criminal Records: Access: Phone, mail, in person. Both court and visitors may perform in person searches. Search fee: $5.00 per name. Court makes

copy: $1.00 per page; same fee for self serve. Required to search: name, years to search. Criminal records in index books. Mail turnaround time 2-3 days.
General Information: No juvenile, mental, sealed, or adoption records released. Will fax documents for $1.00 per page, if prepaid. Certification fee: $1.00. Payee: District Clerk. Personal checks accepted. Prepayment required.

County Court PO Box 465, 401 Main St, Wheeler, TX 79096; phone: 806-826-5544; fax: 806-826-3282; hours 8AM-5PM (CST). *Misdemeanor, Civil, Probate.*
Civil Records: Access: Mail, in person. Both court and visitors may perform in person searches. Search fee: $10.00 per name. Court makes copy: $1.00 per page. Required to search: name, years to search. Civil cases indexed by defendant, plaintiff; in index books back to 1800s. Mail turnaround time 1 day.
Criminal Records: Access: Mail, in person. Both court and visitors may perform in person searches. Search fee: $10.00 per name. Court makes copy: $1.00 per page. Required to search: name, years to search; also helpful: DOB, SSN. Criminal records in index books. Mail turnaround time 1 day.
General Information: No juvenile, mental, sealed, or adoption records released. Will fax documents for $1.00 per page. Certification fee: $5.00 per doc. Payee: County Clerk. Business checks accepted. Prepayment and SASE required.

Wichita County

District Court PO Box 718, Wichita Falls, TX 76307; criminal phone: 940-766-8197; civil phone: 940-766-8190; hours 8AM-5PM (CST). *Felony, Civil.*
Civil Records: Access: Phone, mail, in person. Both court and visitors may perform in person searches. Search fee: $5.00 per name. Court makes copy: $1.00 per page; same fee for self serve. Required to search: name, years to search. Civil cases indexed by defendant, plaintiff; on computer since 1984, index books prior. Phone searches must be prepaid. Mail turnaround time 2-3 days.
Criminal Records: Access: Phone, mail, in person. Both court and visitors may perform in person searches. Search fee: $5.00 per name. Court makes copy: $1.00 per page; same fee for self serve. Required to search: name, years to search. Criminal records on computer since 1984, index books before. Phone searches must be prepaid. Mail turnaround time 2-3 days.
General Information: Public terminal goes back to 1800s. No juvenile, mental, sealed, or adoption records released. Will not fax documents. Certification fee: $1.00. Payee: District Clerk. Personal checks accepted. Prepayment and SASE required.

County Court PO Box 1679, Wichita Falls, TX 76307; phone: 940-766-8160; criminal phone: 940-766-8173; probate phone: 940-766-8172; fax: 940-716-8554; hours 8AM-5PM (CST). *Misdemeanor, Probate.*
Criminal Records: Access: Phone, mail, in person. Both court and visitors may perform in person searches. Search fee: $10.00 per name searched. Court makes copy: $1.00 per page. Required to search: name, years to search; also helpful: DOB, SSN. Criminal records on computer or printed index from 1980 to present. Mail turnaround time 1 week or less
General Information: Public terminal has only criminal records. No juvenile, mental, sealed, or adoption records released. Mental can be released with an order from the judge. Will fax to toll-free numbers only. Certification fee: $5.00 per document. Payee: Wichita County Clerk. No personal checks accepted. Prepayment and SASE required.

Wilbarger County

District Court 1700 Wilbarger, Rm 33, Vernon, TX 76384; phone: 940-553-3411; fax: 940-553-2316; hours 8AM-5PM (CST). *Felony, Civil.*
Civil Records: Access: Mail, in person. Both court and visitors may perform in person searches. Search fee: $5.00 per name. Court makes copy: $1.00 per page; same fee for self serve. Required to search: name, years to search. Civil cases indexed by defendant, plaintiff. Civil records go back to 1800s; computerized records go back 4 years. Mail turnaround time 2-3 days.
Criminal Records: Access: Mail, in person. Both court and visitors may perform in person searches. Search fee: $5.00 per name. Court makes copy: $1.00 per page; same fee for self serve. Required to search: name, years to search, DOB. Criminal records go back to 1800s; computerized records go back 4 years. Mail turnaround time 2-3 days.
General Information: No juvenile, mental, sealed, or adoption records released. Will return results by fax or phone if an 800 number is provided. Will fax documents to toll-free number. Certification fee: $5.00 per document. Payee: District Clerk. Business checks accepted. Prepayment and SASE required.

County Court 1700 Wilbarger, Rm 15, Vernon, TX 76384; phone: 940-552-5486; hours 8AM-5PM (CST). *Misdemeanor, Civil, Probate.*
Note: Probate is a separate index at this same address.
Civil Records: Access: Mail, in person. Both court and visitors may perform in person searches. Search fee: $10.00 per name. Court makes copy: $1.00 per page; same fee for self serve. Required to search: name, years to search. Civil cases indexed by defendant. Civil records go back to 1887; no computerized records. Mail turnaround time same day.
Criminal Records: Access: Mail, in person. Both court and visitors may perform in person searches. Search fee: $10.00 per name. Court makes copy: $1.00 per page; same fee for self serve. Required to search: name, years to search; also helpful: address, DOB, SSN. Criminal records go back to 1887; computerized records go back to 1999. Mail turnaround time same day.
General Information: No juvenile, mental, sealed, or adoption records released. Fee to fax documents is $1.00 per page. Certification fee: $5.00 per document. Payee: County Clerk. Personal checks accepted. Prepayment and SASE required.

Willacy County

District Court County Courthouse, Raymondville, TX 78580; phone: 956-689-2532; fax: 956-689-5713; hours 8AM-5PM (CST). *Felony, Civil.*
Civil Records: Access: Mail, in person, phone. Both court and visitors may perform in person searches. Search fee: $8.00 per name. Court makes copy: $1.00 per page; same fee for self serve. Required to search: name, years to search. Civil cases indexed by defendant, plaintiff; in index books. Mail turnaround time 2-3 days.
Criminal Records: Access: Mail, in person. Both court and visitors may perform in person searches. Search fee: $8.00 per name. Court makes copy: $1.00 per page; same fee for self serve. Required to search: name, years to search. Criminal records in index books. Mail turnaround time 2-3 days.
General Information: No juvenile, mental, sealed, or adoption records released. Will fax documents for $2.00 per page. No certification fee. Payee: District Clerk. Personal checks accepted. Prepayment and SASE required.

County Court 540 W Hidalgo, Raymondville, TX 78580; phone: 956-689-2710; fax: 956-689-9849; hours 8AM-N, 1-5PM (CST). *Misdemeanor, Civil, Probate.*
Civil Records: Access: Mail, fax, in person. Both court and visitors may perform in person searches. Search fee: $5.00 per name, ten year search only. Court makes copy: $1.00 per page; same fee for self

serve. Required to search: name, years to search; also helpful: address. Civil records go back to 1920's. Mail turnaround time 2-3 days.

Criminal Records: Access: Mail, in person. Both court and visitors may perform in person searches. Search fee: $5.00 per name. Court makes copy: $1.00 per page; same fee for self serve. Required to search: name, years to search; also helpful: address, DOB, SSN. Criminal records go back to 1921, computerized since 1990. Mail turnaround time 2-3 days.

General Information: No juvenile, mental, sealed, or adoption records released. Fee to fax documents is $2.00 per page. Certification fee: $5.00. Payee: County Clerk. Personal checks accepted. Prepayment and SASE required.

Williamson County

District Court PO Box 24, Georgetown, TX 78627; phone: 512-943-1212; fax: 512-943-1222; hours 8AM-5PM (CST). *Felony, Civil.*
www.williamson-county.org
Civil Records: Access: Mail, in person. Both court and visitors may perform in person searches. Search fee: $5.00 per name. Court makes copy: $1.00 1st page; $.25 each add'l. Required to search: name, years to search. Civil cases indexed by defendant, plaintiff; on computer since 1989, index books prior. Mail turnaround time 2-3 days.

Criminal Records: Access: Mail, in person. Both court and visitors may perform in person searches. Search fee: $5.00 per name. Court makes copy: $1.00 1st page; $.25 each add'l. Required to search: name, years to search, DOB, signed release; also helpful: SSN. Criminal records on computer since 1989, index books prior. Sheriff bond and inmate data is at http://judicialsearch.wilco.org. Mail turnaround time 2-3 days.

General Information: Public terminal goes back to 1989. No juvenile, mental, sealed, or adoption records released. Will not fax documents. Certification fee: Cert fee included in copy fee. Payee: District Clerk. Personal checks accepted. Prepayment and SASE required.

County Court 405 MLK St, Box 14, Georgetown, TX 78626; criminal phone: 512-943-1150; civil phone: 512-943-1140; probate phone: 512-943-1140; fax: 512-943-1445; hours 8AM-5PM (CST). *Misdemeanor, Civil, Probate.*
Note: Fax is for civil records only.
Civil Records: Access: Mail, in person, online. Both court and visitors may perform in person searches. Search fee: $10.00 per name. Court makes copy: $1.00 per page. Required to search: name, years to search. Civil cases indexed by defendant, plaintiff; on computer since 1985, index books since 1848.GA. Access to limited civil case records is free at http://judicialsearch.wilco.org. Mail turnaround time 2 days.

Criminal Records: Access: Mail, in person, online. Both court and visitors may perform in person searches. Search fee: $10.00 per name. Court makes copy: $1.00 per page. Required to search: name, years to search; also helpful: DOB, SSN. Criminal records on computer since 1983. Overall records go back to 1800. Access to a criminal case records from 1983 is free at http://judicialsearch.wilco.org. Sheriff bond and inmate data is also available. Mail turnaround time 2 days.

General Information: Public terminal has criminal back to 1983 and civil back to 1985. No juvenile, mental, sealed, or adoption records released. Fee to fax documents is $1.00 per page. Certification fee: $5.00. Payee: County Clerk. Personal checks accepted. Prepayment and SASE required.

Wilson County

District Court PO Box 812, Floresville, TX 78114; phone: 830-393-7322; fax: 830-393-7319; hours 8AM-N, 1-5PM (CST). *Felony, Civil.*
Note: Request must be in writing if court personnel are to do search.

Civil Records: Access: Fax, mail, in person. Both court and visitors may perform in person searches. Search fee: $5.00 per name. Court makes copy: $1.00 per page. Required to search: name, years to search. Civil cases indexed by defendant, plaintiff. Civil records go back to 1960. Mail turnaround time 2-3 days.

Criminal Records: Access: Fax, mail, in person. Both court and visitors may perform in person searches. Search fee: $5.00 per name. Court makes copy: $1.00 per page. Required to search: name, years to search; also helpful: DOB. Criminal records go back to 1975. Mail turnaround time 2 days.

General Information: No juvenile, mental, sealed, or adoption records released. Will fax documents to local or toll free line. Certification fee: $1.00. Payee: District Clerk. Personal checks accepted. Prepayment and SASE required.

County Court PO Box 27, Floresville, TX 78114; phone: 830-393-7308; fax: 830-393-7334; hours 8AM-5PM (CST). *Misdemeanor, Civil, Probate.*
Civil Records: Access: Phone, mail, fax, in person. Both court and visitors may perform in person searches. No search fee. Court makes copy: $1.00 per page; same fee for self serve. Required to search: name, years to search. Civil cases indexed by defendant, plaintiff. Civil records available from 1862. Mail turnaround time same day.

Criminal Records: Access: Phone, mail, fax, in person. Both court and visitors may perform in person searches. No search fee. Court makes copy: $1.00 per page; same fee for self serve. Required to search: name, years to search, DOB. Criminal records stored since 1917, computerized since 11/2002. Mail turnaround time same day.

General Information: Will not fax documents. Certification fee: $5.00. Payee: Eva S Martinez, County Clerk. Personal checks accepted. Prepayment and SASE required.

Winkler County

District Court PO Box 1065, Kermit, TX 79745; phone: 432-586-3359; hours 8AM-5PM (CST). *Felony, Civil.*
Civil Records: Access: Phone, mail, in person. Both court and visitors may perform in person searches. Search fee: $5.00 per name. Court makes copy: $1.00 per page. Required to search: name, years to search. Civil cases indexed by defendant, plaintiff; on computer since 1991 (child-support only), index books prior. Mail turnaround time 3-4 days.

Criminal Records: Access: Mail, in person. Both court and visitors may perform in person searches. Search fee: $5.00 per name. Court makes copy: $1.00 per page. Required to search: name, years to search, DOB, SSN. Criminal records on computer since 1991, index books prior. Mail turnaround time 3-4 days.

General Information: No juvenile, mental, sealed, or adoption records released. Payee: District Clerk. Personal checks accepted. Prepayment and SASE required.

County Court PO Box 1007, Kermit, TX 79745; phone: 432-586-3401; hours 8AM-5PM (CST). *Misdemeanor, Civil, Probate.*
Civil Records: Access: Mail, in person. Visitors must perform in person searches themselves. Search fee: $5.00 per name. Court makes copy: $1.00 per page. Required to search: name, years to search. Civil cases indexed by defendant, plaintiff. All civil records in index books. Mail turnaround time 2-3 days.

Criminal Records: Access: Mail, in person. Visitors must perform in person searches themselves. Search fee: $5.00 per name. Court makes copy: $1.00 per page. Required to search: name, years to search; also helpful: address, DOB, SSN. Criminal records on computer back to 1991; prior in index books. Mail turnaround time 2-3 days.

General Information: No juvenile, mental, sealed, or adoption records released. Certification fee: $5.00.

Payee: County Clerk. Business checks accepted. Prepayment and SASE required.

Wise County

District Court PO Box 308, Decatur, TX 76234; phone: 940-627-5535; fax: 940-627-0705; hours 8AM-5PM (CST). *Felony, Civil.*
Civil Records: Access: Mail, in person. Visitors must perform in person searches themselves. Search fee: $5.00 per name. Court makes copy: $1.00 per page. Required to search: name, years to search. Civil cases indexed by defendant, plaintiff; in index books since 1895, computerized since 1999. Mail turnaround time same day.

Criminal Records: Access: Mail, in person. Visitors must perform in person searches themselves. Search fee: $5.00 per name. Court makes copy: $1.00 per page. Required to search: name, years to search; also helpful-DOB, SSN. Criminal records in docket books to 1896, computerized since 1999. Mail turnaround time same day.

General Information: Public use terminal available. No juvenile, mental, sealed, or adoption records released. Will fax documents. Certification fee: $2.00. Payee: Wise County District Clerk. Personal checks accepted. Prepayment and SASE required.

County Court at Law PO Box 359, Decatur, TX 76234; phone: 940-627-3351; fax: 940-627-2138; hours 8AM-5PM (CST). *Misdemeanor, Civil, Probate.*
Civil Records: Access: Mail, in person. Both court and visitors may perform in person searches. Search fee: $10.00 per name. Court makes copy: $1.00 per page. Required to search: name, years to search. Civil cases indexed by defendant, plaintiff; in index books since sovereignty; on computer back to 1998. Mail turnaround time 1 day.

Criminal Records: Access: Mail, in person. Both court and visitors may perform in person searches. Search fee: $10.00 per name. Court makes copy: $1.00 per page. Required to search: name, years to search; also helpful: DOB, SSN. Criminal records in index books since sovereignty; on computer back to 1997. Mail turnaround time 1 day.

General Information: Public terminal has criminal back to 1997 and civil back to 1998. No mental health or sealed records released. Will fax documents for fee. Certification fee: $5.00. Payee: Wise County Clerk. Personal checks accepted. Prepayment and SASE required.

Wood County

District Court PO Box 1707, Quitman, TX 75783; phone: 903-763-2361; fax: 903-763-1511; hours 8AM-5PM (CST). *Felony, Civil.*
www.co.wood.tx.us/dclerk.html
Civil Records: Access: Mail, fax, in person. Both court and visitors may perform in person searches. Search fee: $5.00 per name. Court makes copy: $1.00 per page. Required to search: name, years to search. Civil cases indexed by defendant, plaintiff; on computer since 1990, microfilm since 1981, index books since 1890. Mail turnaround time 2-3 days.

Criminal Records: Access: Mail, fax, in person. Both court and visitors may perform in person searches. Search fee: $5.00 per name. Court makes copy: $1.00 per page. Required to search: name, years to search; also helpful: DOB, SSN. Criminal records on computer since 1990, microfilm since 1981, index books since 1890. Mail turnaround time 2-3 days.

General Information: Public terminal goes back to 1980. No juvenile, mental, sealed, or adoption records released. Will not fax documents. Certification fee: $1.00 per document. Payee: District Clerk. Personal checks accepted. Prepayment and SASE required.

County Court PO Box 1796, Quitman, TX 75783; phone: 903-763-2711; fax: 903-763-5641; hours 8AM-5PM (CST). *Misdemeanor, Civil, Probate.*
Note: Probate is a separate index at this same address.

Civil Records: Access: Mail, in person. Both court and visitors may perform in person searches. Search fee: $5.00 per name. Court makes copy: $1.00 per page. Required to search: name, years to search. Civil cases indexed by defendant, plaintiff; on computer since 1980; index books since early 1900s. Mail turnaround time same day.

Criminal Records: Access: Mail, in person. Both court and visitors may perform in person searches. Search fee: $5.00 per name. Court makes copy: $1.00 per page. Required to search: name, years to search; also helpful DOB, SSN, signed release, DL#. Criminal records on computer back to 1986; index books from 1965, archived to 1900. Mail turnaround time same day.

General Information: Public terminal goes back to 1980. No mental or sealed records released. Will fax documents for $2.00 per page. Certification fee: $5.00 per document. Payee: Wood County Clerk. Personal checks accepted. Prepayment and SASE required.

Yoakum County

District Court PO Box 899, Plains, TX 79355; phone: 806-456-7491 x297; fax: 806-456-8767; hours 8AM-5PM (CST). *Felony, Civil.*
Civil Records: Access: Fax, mail, in person. Both court and visitors may perform in person searches. Search fee: $5.00 per name. Court makes copy: $1.00 1st page, $.25 each add'l. Required to search: name, years to search. Civil cases indexed by defendant, plaintiff; on computer since 1980, index books since 1907. Mail turnaround time same day.
Criminal Records: Access: Fax, mail, in person. Both court and visitors may perform in person searches. Search fee: $5.00 per name. Court makes copy: $1.00 1st page, $.25 each add'l. Required to search: name, years to search, DOB; also helpful: SSN. Criminal records on computer since 1980, index books since 1930. Mail turnaround time same day.
General Information: Public terminal goes back to 1980. No juvenile, mental, sealed, or adoption records released. Will fax documents for no fee. Certification fee: $1.00 per page. Payee: District Clerk. Personal checks accepted. Prepayment and SASE required.

County Court PO Box 309, Plains, TX 79355; phone: 806-456-2721; fax: 806-456-2258; hours 8AM-5PM (CST). *Misdemeanor, Civil, Probate.*
Civil Records: Access: Phone, mail, in person. Both court and visitors may perform in person searches. Search fee: $5.00 per name. Court makes copy: $1.00 per page. Self serve copy fee: $1.00 per page. Required to search: name, years to search; also helpful: address. Civil cases indexed by defendant, plaintiff; in minutes books and microfilm since 9/1986; on computer back to 1/1986. Mail turnaround time same day.
Criminal Records: Access: Mail, in person. Both court and visitors may perform in person searches. Search fee: $5.00 per name. Court makes copy: $1.00 per page. Self serve copy fee: $1.00 per page. Required to search: name, years to search, DOB; also helpful: address, SSN. Criminal minutes books and microfilm since 9/1986; on computer back to 1/1986. Mail turnaround time same day.
General Information: Public terminal goes back to 9/1986. No juvenile or mental records released. Will fax documents for $2.00 per fax plus $1.00 per page. Certification fee: $5.00 per document. Payee: County Clerk, Yoakum County. Personal checks accepted. Prepayment required.

Young County

District Court 516 4th St, Rm 201, Courthouse, Graham, TX 76450; phone: 940-549-0029; fax: 940-549-4874; hours 8:30AM-N, 1-5PM (CST). *Felony, Civil.*
Civil Records: Access: Mail, in person. Both court and visitors may perform in person searches. Search fee: $5.00 per name. Court makes copy: $1.00 for first page, $.25 each add'l. Required to search: name, years to search. Civil cases indexed by defendant, plaintiff; on computer since 1988, index books prior. Search fee must be prepaid before fax access is allowed. Mail turnaround time 1-2 days.
Criminal Records: Access: Mail, in person. Both court and visitors may perform in person searches. Search fee: $5.00 per name. Court makes copy: $1.00 for first page, $.25 each add'l. Required to search: name, years to search; also helpful: DOB, SSN. Criminal records on computer since 1988, index books prior. Mail turnaround time 1-2 days.
General Information: No juvenile, mental, sealed, or adoption records released. No fee to fax documents. Certification fee: $1.00 per page. Payee: District Clerk. Personal checks accepted. Prepayment and SASE required.

County Court 516 4th St, Rm 104, Graham, TX 76450; phone: 940-549-8432; fax: 940-521-0305; hours 8:30AM-N, 1-5PM (CST). *Misdemeanor, Civil, Probate.*
Civil Records: Access: Mail, in person. Both court and visitors may perform in person searches. Search fee: $5.00 per name. Court makes copy: $1.00 per page; same fee for self serve. Required to search: name, years to search. Civil cases indexed by defendant, plaintiff; on computer since 1991, index books prior to 1800s. Mail turnaround time same day.
Criminal Records: Access: Mail, in person. Both court and visitors may perform in person searches. Search fee: $5.00 per name. Court makes copy: $1.00 per page; same fee for self serve. Required to search: name, years to search. Criminal records on computer since 1991, index books prior to 1800s. Mail turnaround time same day.
General Information: Public terminal goes back to 1991. No juvenile, mental, sealed, or adoption records released. Fee to fax documents is $1.00 per page. Certification fee: $5.00. Payee: County Clerk. Personal checks accepted. Prepayment required.

Zapata County

District Court PO Box 788, Clerk's Office, Zapata, TX 78076; phone: 956-765-9930; fax: 956-765-9931; hours 8AM-N, 1-5PM (CST). *Felony, Civil.*
Civil Records: Access: Mail, in person. Both court and visitors may perform in person searches. Search fee: $5.00 per name. Court makes copy: $1.00 per page. Required to search: name, years to search. Civil cases indexed by plaintiff. Civil records in index books. Mail turnaround time 1-3 days.
Criminal Records: Access: Mail, in person. Both court and visitors may perform in person searches. Search fee: $5.00 per name. Court makes copy: $1.00 per page. Required to search: name, years to search. Criminal records in index books. Mail turnaround time 1-3 days.
General Information: No juvenile, mental, sealed, or adoption records released. Will not fax documents. Certification fee: $5.00 per document. Payee: District Clerk/County Clerk. Personal checks accepted. Prepayment and SASE required.

County Court PO Box 789, Zapata, TX 78076; phone: 956-765-9915; criminal fax: 956-765-9933; same fax for civil/probate; hours 8AM-N, 1-5PM (CST). *Misdemeanor, Civil, Probate.*
Civil Records: Access: Mail, in person. Both court and visitors may perform in person searches. Search fee: $5.00 per name. Court makes copy: $1.00 per page; same fee for self serve. Required to search: name, years to search. Civil cases indexed by plaintiff only. Civil records in index books since 1800s, computerized records back to 1990. Mail turnaround time 1-2 days.
Criminal Records: Access: Mail, in person. Both court and visitors may perform in person searches. Search fee: $5.00 per name. Court makes copy: $1.00 per page; same fee for self serve. Required to search: name, years to search, DOB, SSN. Criminal records in index books since 1800s, computerized records back to 1930. Mail turnaround time 1-2 days.
General Information: No juvenile, mental, sealed, or adoption records released. Will fax documents $4.00 for 1st page, $1.00 each add'l. Certification fee: $5.00 per document. Payee: Consuelo R Villarreal, County Clerk. Personal checks accepted. Prepayment required.

Zavala County

District Court PO Box 704, Crystal City, TX 78839; phone: 830-374-3456; hours 8AM-N, 1-5PM (CST). *Felony, Civil.*
Civil Records: Access: Phone, mail, in person. Both court and visitors may perform in person searches. Search fee: $10.00 per name. Court makes copy: $1.00 per page; same fee for self serve. Required to search: name, years to search. Civil cases indexed by defendant, plaintiff; in index books from 1900s. Mail turnaround time 1-2 days.
Criminal Records: Access: Phone, mail, in person. Both court and visitors may perform in person searches. Search fee: $10.00 per name. Court makes copy: $1.00 per page; same fee for self serve. Required to search: name, years to search. Criminal records in index books from 1900s. Mail turnaround time 1-2 days.
General Information: No juvenile, mental, sealed, or adoption records released. Will fax documents for no fee. No certification fee. Payee: Zavala County District Clerk. Personal checks accepted. Prepayment and SASE required.

County Court Zavala County Courthouse, 200 E Uvalde, Crystal City, TX 78839; phone: 830-374-2331; fax: 830-374-5955; hours 8AM-5PM (CST). *Misdemeanor, Civil, Probate.*
Civil Records: Access: Mail, in person. Both court and visitors may perform in person searches. Search fee: $10.00 per name. Court makes copy: $1.00 per page. Required to search: name, years to search. Civil cases indexed by defendant, plaintiff; in index books from 1880s. Mail turnaround time 1-2 days.
Criminal Records: Access: Mail, in person. Both court and visitors may perform in person searches. Search fee: $10.00 per name. Court makes copy: $1.00 per page. Required to search: name, years to search, DOB. Criminal records in index books from 1880s. Mail turnaround time 1-2 days.
General Information: No juvenile, mental, sealed, or adoption records released. Certification fee: $1.00 per doc. Payee: Zavala County Clerk. Personal checks accepted. Prepayment and SASE required.

Texas Recording Offices

ORGANIZATION: 254 counties, 254 recording offices. The recording officer is County Clerk. 252 counties are in the Central Time Zone (CST) and 2 are in the Mountain Time Zone (MST).

REAL ESTATE RECORDS: Some counties will perform real estate searches. Copy fees are usually $1.00 per page. Certification usually costs $5.00 per document. Each county has an "Appraisal District" which is responsible for collecting taxes.

UCC RECORDS: Financing statements are filed at the state level, except for real estate related collateral, which are filed with the County Clerk. Most Texas recording offices will perform UCC searches. Searches fees are usually $10.00 per debtor name using the approved UCC-11 request form, but may be $15.00 for using a non-Texas form. Copy fees are usually $1.00-$2.00 per page.

TAX LIEN RECORDS: Federal tax liens on personal property of businesses are filed with the Secretary of State. Other federal and all state tax liens are filed with the County Clerk. All counties will perform tax lien searches. Search fees and copy fees can vary, but records are usually provided as part of the UCC search.

OTHER LIENS: Mechanics, judgment, hospital, labor, lis pendens.

ONLINE ACCESS: Numerous counties offer online access to assessor and recorded document data. A good place to link to county appraisal districts is www.texascad.com where you can click through to many county appraisers, many with free searching. Also, two private companies offer access to multiple counties' tax assessor data; www.taxnetusa.com and www.txcountydata.com. Many Texas counties may be accessed from multiple sites, some below.

www.txcountydata.com - Assessor and property information records for many Texas counties on the TXCOUNTYDATA site are available for no fee. At this site click on "County Search" then use the pull down menu in the county field to select the county to search. The County Info page for each county lists the Appraiser, mailing address, phone, fax, website, email. Generally, you can search any county account, owner name, address, or property ID number. Search allows you to access owner address, property address, legal description, taxing entities, exemptions, deed, account number, abstract/subdivision, neighborhood, valuation info, and more.

www.taxnetusa.com - TaxNetUSA offers appraisal district and property information records for a large number of Texas counties. They offer a free search as well as online subscriptions services using a sliding fee scale, or you may purchase data as downloads. Visit the website or call 877-652-2707 for more info To search free at the TaxNetUSA site, click on the "Coverage Area" and select a county. Generally, but in varying degrees from county to county, the basic search allows you to access general property information: name, address, valuation, etc., and you may search by parcel number, owner name, or address. Depending on the county, more "detailed" information may be available.

www.titlex.com offers recording office records in county grantor/grantee indices - including real estate, deeds, liens, judgments records and more - free many Texas counties.

www.texaslandrecords.com offers free land index searching at a group of 22 or more Texas counties, plus a deeper real estate subscription service which requires fees, registration, and password.

Anderson County

County Clerk, 500 N. Church St, Palestine, TX 75801. 903-723-7432, R/E recording phone-903-723-7484; fax-903-723-7801; hours: 8AM-5PM.

All records in one index. General index search fee $5.00 per name. Will search real estate records for the years of 1985 to present. Will search UCC records prior to 7/2001 and current fixture (land) files. Will search tax liens. UCC search per debtor name- $10.00. Copy fee $1.00 per page. Cert fee- $5.00 per doc, does not include copies. Payee- Anderson County Clerk. **Online access to Appraiser, Property Tax, Real Estate, Deed, Judgment, Lien, Grantor/Grantee records:** Access recording records free at www.titlex.com; select Anderson county. Records range is 6/1972 to 12/2003. Also, property tax inquiries can be made at www.txcountydata.com/county.asp?County=001.
Other phones: Treasurer- 903-723-7408; Appraiser/Auditor- 903-723-2949; Elections- 903-723-7438; Vital Records- 903-723-7490. **Property tax/Assessor-** 903-723-7438.

Andrews County

County Clerk, PO Box 727, Andrews, TX 79714. 432-524-1426; fax-432-524-1473; hours: 8AM-5PM. www.co.andrews.tx.us
All records in one index. Records indexed. Only the public may search. Copy fee $1.00 per page. Cert fee- $5.00 per doc plus copy fee. Payee- Andrews County Clerk. **Other phones:** Treasurer-

432-524-1410; Appraiser/Auditor- 432-523-9111; Elections- 432-524-1426; Vital Records- 432-524-1426. **Property tax/Assessor-** P O Box 18, Andrews, TX 79714; 432-524-1409.

Angelina County

County Clerk, PO Box 908, Lufkin, TX 75902-0908. 936-634-8339; fax-936-634-8460; hours: 8AM-4:30PM. www.angelinacounty.net/counclrk.html
All records in one index. Records indexed on a public use terminal back to 1962. Only the public may search. General index search fee $5.00 per name. Copy fee $1.00 per page. Cert fee- $5.00 per cert plus copy fee. Payee- Angelina County Clerk. **Online access to Appraiser, Property Tax, Probate, Judgment records:** Access appraisal district data free at www.angelinacad.org/Appraisal/PublicAccess/. Also see note at beginning of section. Access assessment records at www.texaslandrecords.com and at www.txcountydata.com. Also, search probate records and judgment records at http://idocket.com/countycourt.htm. **Other phones:** Appraiser/Auditor- 936-634-8456. **Property tax/Assessor-** 606 E Lufkin Ave, Lufkin, TX 75901; 936-634-8376.

Aransas County

County Clerk, 301 N. Live Oak, Rockport, TX 78382. 361-790-0122; fax-361-790-0119; hours: 8AM-4:30PM. www.aransascounty.org

Index: Pre-10/1984 has separate indices to search. Only the public may search. Copy fee $1.00 per page. Fed tax lien- $1.50 per page, $5.00 minimum. Cert fee- $5.00 per cert plus copy fee. Payee- Aransas County Clerk. **Online access to Real Estate, Deed, Lien, Judgment, Birth, Death, Appraiser, Property Tax records:** Access to recordings, land records, births, deaths is free at http://apolloplus.com then click on member counties to access Aransas Co. Also, dated appraiser and property tax information is at www.aransascad.org/Appraisal/PublicAccess/. Also see note at beginning of section. **Other phones:** Treasurer- 361-790-0132; Appraiser/Auditor- 361-729-9733; Elections- 361-729-7431; Vital Records- 361-790-0122. **Property tax/Assessor-** 361-790-0160.

Archer County

County Clerk, PO Box 427, Archer City, TX 76351. 940-574-4302; fax-940-574-4625; hours: 8:30AM-5PM.
Only the public may search. Copy fee $1.00 per page. Cert fee- $5.00 per cert plus copy fee. Payee- Archer County Clerk. **Online access to Appriaser, Property Tax records:** Access property records at www.taxnetusa.com. **Other phones:** Treasurer- 940-574-4822; Appraiser/Auditor- 940-574-2172; Elections- 940-574-4302; Vital Records- 940-574-4302. **Property tax/Assessor-** PO Box 700, Archer City, TX 76351; 940-574-4531.

Armstrong County

County Clerk, PO Box 309, Claude, TX 79019-0309. 806-226-2081; fax-806-226-5301; hours: 8AM-N, 1-5PM.
Separate indices to search include Probate, Civil, and Criminal. Records indexed on a public use terminal back to 1993. Only the public may search. Copy fee $1.00 per page. Cert fee- $5.00 per cert plus copy fee. Payee- Armstrong County Clerk. **Other phones:** Treasurer- 806-226-3651; Appraiser/Auditor- 806-226-4481; Elections- 806-226-2081; Vital Records- 806-226-2081. **Property tax/Assessor-** PO Box 835, Claude, TX 79019; 806-226-4481.

Atascosa County

County Clerk, #1 Courthouse Circle #102, Jourdanton, TX 78026. 830-767-2511; fax-830-769-1021; hours: 8AM-5PM.
Index: Various records for early records prior to 1995. Records indexed on a public use terminal back to 1995. Only the public may search. Copy fee $1.00 per page. Cert fee- $5.00 per cert plus copy fee. Payee- Atascosa County Clerk. **Online access to Real Estate, Grantor/Grantee, Judgment, Deed, Lien, Appraiser, Property Tax records:** Access recording records free at www.titlex.com; select Atascosa County. Also, see note at beginning of section. **Other phones:** Treasurer- 830-769-3024; Appraiser/Auditor- 830-742-3591; Elections- 830-769-1472; Vital Records- 830-767-2511. **Property tax/Assessor-** 1001 Oak St, Jourdanton, TX 78026; 830-769-3142.

Austin County

County Clerk, 1 E. Main, Bellville, TX 77418-1551. 979-865-5911; fax-979-865-0336; hours: 8AM-5PM.
All records in one index. Office will perform a UCC search but public must search other records themselves. Search fee $10.00 per name. Copy fee $1.00 per page. Cert fee- $5.00 per cert plus copy fee. Payee- Austin County Clerk. **Online access to Appraiser, Property Tax, Real Estate, Deed, Judgment, Lien, Grantor/Grantee records:** Access recording records free at www.titlex.com; select Austin county. Records range is 8/1997 to 8/2001. Also, search property tax records for free at www.austincad.org. Also, see note at beginning of section. **Other phones:** Treasurer- 979-865-5911; Appraiser/Auditor- 979-865-9124; Elections- 979-865-5911; Vital Records- 979-865-5911. **Property tax/Assessor-** 20 S Holland, Bellville, TX 77418; 979-865-8633.

Bailey County

County Clerk, 300 S. First, #200, Muleshoe, TX 79347. 806-272-3044; fax-806-272-3538; hours: 8:30AM-N 1-5PM.
Separate indices to search. Records indexed on computer back to 1995. Only the public may search. Copy fee $1.00 per page. Cert fee- $5.00 per cert and $1.00 per page. Payee- Bailey County Clerk. **Online access to Property, Appraiser, Probate, Judgment records:** Access to Appraisal District records is free at http://clientdb.trueautomation.com/clientdb/main.asp?id =3. Also, to search probate records and judgment records go to http://idocket.com/countycourt.htm. **Other phones:** Treasurer- 806-272-3239; Appraiser/Auditor- 806-272-5501; Elections- 806-272-3044; Vital Records- 806-272-3044. **Property tax/Assessor-** 806-272-3022.

Bandera County

County Clerk, PO Box 823, Bandera, TX 78003. 830-796-3332; fax-830-796-8323; hours: 8AM-Noon, 1PM-4:30PM.
All records in one index. Records indexed on a public use terminal back to 1983. Office personnel or visitors may perform searches. Search fee $5.00 per name. Copy fee $1.00 per page. Cert fee- $5.00 per cert plus copy fee. Payee- Bandera County Clerk. **Online access to Property, Personal Property, Appraiser, Probate, Judgment records:**

Access to Bandera County Appraisal Roll Search is free at http://hp3.quickaccess.com/bandera/. Also, See note at beginning of section Also, to search probate records and judgment records go to http://idocket.com/countycourt.htm. **Other phones:** Treasurer- 830-796-4573; Appraiser/Auditor- 830-796-3030; Elections- 830-796-3731; Vital Records- 512-458-7111. **Property tax/Assessor-** PO Box 368, Bandera, TX 78003; 830-796-3731.

Bastrop County

County Clerk, PO Box 577, Bastrop, TX 78602. 512-332-7234; fax-512-332-7241; hours: 8AM-5PM.
Separate indices to search include Computer and Paper-1920-1973, 1993-1973, 1994-1995. Records indexed on computer back to 1996. Only the public may search. Copy fee $1.00 per page, if tax lien or real estate $1.00 per page. Cert fee- $5.00 per cert plus copy fee. Payee- Bastrop County Clerk. **Online access to Appraiser, Property Tax, Real Estate, Judgment, Lien, Grantor/Grantee records:** Access recording records free at www.titlex.com; select Bastrop county. Record range is 3/2001 to 8/31/2001. Also, access to tax office records is free at www.bastroptac.com. Also, see note at beginning of section. **Other phones:** Treasurer- 512-332-7204; Appraiser/Auditor- 512-303-3536; Elections- 512-332-7234; Vital Records- 512-332-7234; Voter Registrar- 512-332-7261. **Property tax/Assessor-** PO Box 579, Bastrop, TX 78602; 512-581-7160.

Baylor County

County Clerk, PO Box 689, Seymour, TX 76380-0689. 940-889-3322; fax-940-889-4300; 8:30AM-5PM.
All records in one index. Record index not computerized. Office personnel or visitors may perform searches. Search fee $5.00 per name unless otherwise indicated. Real estate owner, mortgage, and property transfer searches available. Will search UCC records prior to 7/2001 and current fixture (land) files. UCC search includes tax liens if requested. UCC search per debtor name- $15.00. Separate federal and/or tax lien search- $15.00 per debtor. Copy fee $1.00 per page. Cert fee- $6.00 per cert (County records) plus copy fee. Payee- Baylor County Clerk. **Other phones:** Treasurer- 940-889-1846; Appraiser/Auditor- 940-888-5636; Elections- 940-889-3322; Vital Records- 940-889-3322. **Property tax/Assessor-** 211 N Washington, Seymour, TX 76380; 940-889-3169.

Bee County

County Clerk, 105 W. Corpus Christi St; Rm 103, Beeville, TX 78102. 361-362-3245; fax-361-362-3247; hours: 8AM-N, 1-5PM.
Separate indices to search include Official Public Records as of June, 1995, prior to June, 1995 each has own index. Office personnel or visitors may perform searches. General search fee $5.00 per book per name. Will search real estate records; written request required. UCC search per debtor name- $16.00. UCC search request using non-standard form (per name)- $31.00. Copy fee $1.00 per page. Cert fee- $5.00 per cert plus copy fee. Payee- Bee County Clerk. **Online access to Property Tax, Land, Probate, Judgment records:** Access land records online at www.texaslandrecords.com. Also, to search probate records and judgment records go to http://idocket.com/countycourt.htm. **Other phones:** Appraiser/Auditor- 361-358-0193; Elections- 361-362-3245; Vital Records- 361-362-3245. **Property tax/Assessor-** 361-362-3250.

Bell County

County Clerk, PO Box 480, Belton, TX 76513-0480. 254-933-5174, R/E recording phone-254-933-5171; fax-254-933-5176; hours: 8AM-5PM. www.bellcountytx.com/countyclerk/index.htm
All records in one index. Office will perform a UCC search but public must search other records themselves. Search fee $10.00. Copy fee $1.00 per page. Cert fee- $5.00 per cert plus copy fee. Payee-

Bell County Clerk. **Online to Property, Appraiser records:** Access to Appraisal District records is free at http://clientdb.trueautomation.com/clientdb/main.asp?id =21. **Other phones:** Treasurer- 817-933-5255; Appraiser/Auditor- 254-939-5841; Vital Records- 254-934-5165. **Property tax/Assessor-** 411 E Central, Belton, TX 76513; 254-934-5320.

Bexar County

County Clerk, 100 Dolorosa, Rm 108; Bexar County Courthouse, San Antonio, TX 78205-3083. 210-335-2581, 335-2273, 335-3041, R/E recording phone-210-335-2581; hours: 8AM-5PM. www.countyclerk.bexar.landata.com
Real estate search fee $1.00 per year. Real estate owner, mortgage, and property transfer searches available. Will search UCC records prior to 7/2001 and current fixture (land) files. Tax liens not included in UCC search. UCC search per debtor name- $1.00 per year. Separate federal tax lien search fee- $10.00 plus $1.50 per page. Separate federal/state combined tax lien search- $1.00 per debtor per year. Copy fee $1.00 per page. Cert fee- $5.00 per cert, does not include copies. Payee- Bexar County Clerk. **Online access to Real Estate, Grantor/Grantee, Marriage, UCC, Assumed Name, Recording, Property Tax, Appraiser, Probate records:** Access to the County Clerk database is free at www.countyclerk.bexar.landata.com. Includes land records, deeds, UCCs, assumed names and foreclosure notices. Probate is recently added. Images are to be added on a new subscription service. Also, online access to the county Central Appraisal District database is free at www.bcad.org/clientdb/main.asp?id=1. **Other phones:** Appraiser/Auditor- 210-224-8511; Elections- 210-335-8683; Vital Records- 210-335-2585. **Property tax/Assessor-** 233 N Pecos-LaTrinidad, San Antonio, TX 78205; 210-335-2251.

Blanco County

County Clerk, PO Box 65, Johnson City, TX 78636. 830-868-7357; fax-830-868-4158; 8AM-4:30PM.
All records in one index. Will not search UCC or Real Estate records, but will search tax liens. Tax lien search fee- $5.00 per debtor. Copy fee $1.00 per page. Cert fee- $5.00 per cert plus copy fee. Payee- Blanco County Clerk. **Online access to Appraiser, Property Tax records:** Access at ww.txcountydata.com, see note at beginning of section. **Other phones:** Treasurer- 830-868-4566; Appraiser/Auditor- 830-868-4624; Vital Records- 830-868-7357. **Property tax/Assessor-** PO Box 465, Johnson City, TX 78636; 830-868-7178.

Borden County

County Clerk, PO Box 124, Gail, TX 79738-0124. 806-756-4312; fax-806-756-4405; 8AM-N, 1-5PM.
All records in one index. Records indexed on computer back to. Office personnel or visitors may perform searches. Search fee $5.00 per name unless otherwise indicated. Will not search real estate records. UCC search per debtor name- $10.00. Copy fee $2.00, if tax lien or real estate $1.00 per page. Cert fee- $5.00 per cert plus copy fee. Payee- Borden County Clerk. **Other phones:** Treasurer- 806-756-4415; Appraiser/Auditor- 806-756-4484; Elections- 806-756-4312; Vital Records- 806-756-4312. **Property tax/Assessor-** PO Box 115, Gail, TX 79738-0115; 806-756-4391.

Bosque County

County Clerk, PO Box 617, Meridian, TX 76665. 254-435-2201; fax-254-435-2152; hours: 8AM-5PM.
Index: Pre-1997 records in paper index. Records indexed on computer back to 1997. Office personnel or visitors may perform searches. Search fee $5.00 per name. Real estate owner, mortgage, and property transfer searches available only. Copy fee $1.00 per page. Cert fee- $5.00 per cert plus copy fee. Payee- Bosque County Clerk. **Online access to Appraisal, Property records:** Access property records at www.txcountydata.com. **Other phones:** Treasurer- 254-435-2931; Appraiser/Auditor- 254-435-

2304; Elections- 254-435-2201; Vital Records- 254-435-2201; Appraisal District- 254-435-2304. **Property tax/Assessor**- PO Box 346, Meridian, TX 76665; 254-435-2301.

Bowie County

County Clerk, PO Box 248, New Boston, TX 75570. 903-628-6740; fax-903-628-6729; hours: 8AM-5PM. All records in one index. Only the office personnel may search. Search fee $10.00 per name. Will not search real estate records. Will search UCC records prior to 7/2001 and current fixture (land) files. Copy fee $1.00 per page. Cert fee- $2.00 per document plus copy fee. Payee- County Clerk. **Online access to Property Tax, Appraiser records:** Assess to Appraisal District's Appraisal Roll data is free at www.bowiecad.org/Search.htm. **Other phones:** Treasurer- 903-628-6722; Appraiser/Auditor- 903-628-6724; Elections- 903-628-6810; Vital Records- 903-628-6744; **Property tax/Assessor**- 903-628-6733.

Brazoria County

County Clerk, 111 E. Locust, #200, Angleton, TX 77515-4654. 979-849-5711, R/E recording phone-979-864-1355 x5, UCC recording phone-979-864-1355 x9; fax-979-864-1358; hours: 8AM-4:30PM. www.brazoria.tx.us.landata.com
All records in one index. Records indexed on a public use terminal back to 1/1/1900. Office personnel or visitors may perform searches. Search fee $5.00 per name. Copy fee $1.00 per page. Cert fee- $5.00 per cert plus copy fee. Payee- County Clerk. **Online access to Appraiser, Property Tax, Real Estate, Grantor/Grantee, Deed, Lien, Judgment, Bond, Inmate records:** Access to the county Central Appraisal District database is free at www.brazoriacad.org. Click on "appraisal roll." Access recording records free at www.titlex.com; select Brazoria county. Records range from 3/2001 to 1/2004. Also, see note at beginning of section. Also, access sheriff bond and inmate records free at http://records.brazoria-county.com. **Other phones:** Treasurer- 979-849-5711; Appraiser/Auditor- 979-849-7792; Elections- 979-864-1355 x8; Vital Records- 979-864-1355 x6. **Property tax/Assessor**- 111 E. Locust, #100, Angleton, TX 77515; 979-849-1320.

Brazos County

County Clerk, 300 E. 26th St; #120, Bryan, TX 77803. 979-361-4132; fax-979-361-4125; hours: 8AM-5PM. All records in one index. Records indexed on a public use terminal back to 1967. Office personnel or visitors may perform searches. General index search fee $5.00 per name. Will not search real estate records. Copy fee $1.00 per page. Cert fee- $5.00 per cert plus copy fee. Payee- Brazos County Clerk. **Online access to Appraiser, Property Tax, Land records:** Access to County Appraisal District data is free at www.brazoscad.org. Also, for land records search go to www.texaslandrecords.com. Also, see notes at beginning of section. **Other phones:** Treasurer- 979-361-4340; Appraiser/Auditor- 979-774-4100; Elections- 979-361-4124; Vital Records- 979-361-4528. **Property tax/Assessor**- 300 E William J Bryan Pky, Bryan, TX 77803; 979-361-7400.

Brewster County

County Clerk, PO Box 119, Alpine, TX 79831. 432-837-3366; fax-432-837-6217; hours: 8:30AM-5PM. All records in one index. Records indexed on computer from 9/98 to present. Office personnel or visitors may perform searches. Search fee $10.00 per name. Copy fee $1.00 per page. Cert fee- $5.00 per cert plus copy fee. **Online access to Property, Appraiser records:** Access property data by download from a private company; fees apply; add'l data includes minerals, ofc exports, delinquents; visit www.ptax.org/tax_office_data.htm or phone 201-571-0425. **Other phones:** Treasurer- 432-837-6200; Appraiser/Auditor- 432-837-2558; Elections- 432-837-6230; Vital Records- 432-837-3366. **Property tax/Assessor**- 107 W Ave E #1, Alpine, TX 79830; 432-837-2214.

Briscoe County

County Clerk, PO Box 555, Silverton, TX 79257. 806-823-2134; fax-806-823-2359; hours: 8AM-5PM. All records in one index. Record index not computerized. Office personnel or visitors may perform searches. General index search fee $5.00 per name. Will search UCC records prior to 7/2001 only. Tax liens not included in UCC search. UCC search per debtor name- $11.00. Copy fee $1.00 per page. Cert fee- $5.00 per doc plus copy fee. Payee- County Clerk. **Other phones:** Treasurer- 806-823-2133; Appraiser/Auditor- 806-823-2161; Elections- 806-823-2134; Vital Records- 806-823-2134. **Property tax/Assessor**- 806-823-2136.

Brooks County

County Clerk, PO Box 427, Falfurrias, TX 78355. 361-325-5604, R/E recording phone-361-325-5604 x1; fax-361-325-4944; hours: 8AM-N, 1-5PM. All records in one index. Records indexed on computer back to 1993. Only the office personnel may search. Search fee $10.00. Copy fee $1.00 per page. Cert fee- $5.00 per doc + $1.00 per page. Payee- Brooks County Clerk. **Online access to Real Estate Recording, Deed, Probate, Judgment records:** Access recording office land data at www.etitlesearch.com; registration required, fee based on usage. Also, to search probate records and judgment records go to http://idocket.com/countycourt.htm. **Other phones:** Treasurer- 361-325-5604 x229; Appraiser/Auditor- 361-325-5681. **Property tax/Assessor**- 361-325-5604 x226.

Brown County

County Clerk, 200 S. Broadway; Courthouse, Brownwood, TX 76801. 325-643-2594; hours: 8:30AM-5PM. All records in one index. Office will perform a UCC search but public must search other records themselves. Search fee $10.00. Copy fee $1.00 per page. Cert fee- $5.00 per doc, plus copy fee. Payee- Brown County Clerk. **Online access to Appraiser, Property Tax records:** Access to Appraisal District records is free at http://clientdb.trueautomation.com/clientdb/main.asp?id =30. Also, see note at beginning of section. **Other phones:** Treasurer- 325-646-6033; Appraiser/Auditor- 325-643-5676; Elections- 325-643-2594; Vital Records- 325-643-2594. **Property tax/Assessor**- 325-643-5676.

Burleson County

County Clerk, 100 W Buck St #203, Caldwell, TX 77836. 979-567-2329; fax-979-567-2376; hours: 8AM-5PM. Only the public may search. Copy fee $1.00 per page. Cert fee- $5.00 per cert plus copy fee. Payee- Burleson County Clerk. **Online access to Appraiser, Property Tax records:** See note at beginning of section; www.txcountydata.com. **Other phones:** Appraiser/Auditor- 979-567-2318; Elections- 979 567 2306. **Property tax/Assessor**- 979-567-2336.

Burnet County

County Clerk, 220 S. Pierce St, Burnet, TX 78611. 512-756-5406; fax-512-756-5410; hours: 8AM-5PM. All records in one index. Office personnel or visitors may perform searches. Search fee $10.00 per debtor. Will not search real estate records. Will search UCC records prior to 7/2001 and current fixture (land) files. Tax liens not included in UCC search. Copy fee $1.00 per page. Cert fee- $5.00 per cert plus copy fee. Payee- Burnet County Clerk. **Online access to Real Estate, Grantor/Grantee, Deed, Lien, Judgment, Appraiser, Property Tax records:** Access recording records free at www.titlex.com; select Burnett county. Records range from 1/1998 to 11/2001. Also, see note at beginning of section, www.tycountydata.com. **Other phones:** Treasurer- 512-756-5498; Appraiser/Auditor- 512-756-8291; Elections- 512-756-5406; Vital Records- 512-756-5406. **Property tax/Assessor**- 1701 E Polk, Burnet, TX 78611; 512-756-5420.

Caldwell County

County Clerk, PO Box 906, Lockhart, TX 78644-0906. 512-398-1804; hours: 8:30AM-N, 1-5PM. Office personnel or visitors may perform searches. Search fee $5.00. Real estate owner, mortgage, and property transfer searches available. Will search UCC records prior to 7/2001 only. Tax liens not included in UCC search. Copy fee $1.00 per page. Cert fee- $5.00 per cert plus copy fee. Payee- Caldwell County Clerk. **Online to Appraiser, Property Tax, Personal Property records:** The county Appraisal District database free at www.txcountydata.com. Also, access Appraisal District records free at http://clientdb.trueautomation.com/clientdb/main.asp?id =37. Also, see notes at beginning of section. **Other phones:** Treasurer- 512-398-1800; Appraiser/Auditor- 512-398-5550; Elections- 512-398-1830; Vital Records- 512-398-1804. **Property tax/Assessor**- 512-398-1830.

Calhoun County

County Clerk, 211 S. Ann, Port Lavaca, TX 77979. 361-553-4411; fax-361-553-4420; hours: 8AM-5PM. Separate indices to search include deed records, official records. Only the public may search. Copy fee $1.00 per page. Cert fee- $5.00 per cert + $1.00 per page. Payee- County Clerk. **Online access to Real Estate, Grantor/Grantee, Deed, Judgment, Lien, Property Tax, Appraiser records:** Access recording records free at www.titlex.com; select Calhoun county. Records range up to 9/2003. Also, access Appraisal District records free at http://clientdb.trueautomation.com/clientdb/main.asp?id =24. **Other phones:** Treasurer- 361-553-4620; Appraiser/Auditor- 361-552-8808; Elections- 361-553-4440; Vital Records- 361-553-4411. **Property tax/Assessor**- 361-553-4433.

Callahan County

County Clerk, 100 W. 4th, #104; Courthouse, Baird, TX 79504. 325-854-1217; fax-325-854-1227; hours: 8AM-5PM. Office will perform a UCC search but public must search other records themselves. UCC search per debtor name- $11.00. UCC search request using non-standard form (per name)- $26.00. Copy fee $1.00 per page. Cert fee- $5.00 per cert plus copy fee. Payee- Callahan County Clerk. **Other phones:** Treasurer- 325-854-1399; Appraiser/Auditor- 325-854-1165; Elections- 325-854-1217; Vital Records- 325-854-1217. **Property tax/Assessor**- same address as above. 915-854-1020.

Cameron County

County Clerk, PO Box 2178, Brownsville, TX 78520. 956-544-0815, UCC recording phone-956-550-1329; fax-956-544-0813; hours: 8AM-5PM. www.cameroncountyclerk.org
All records in one index. Records indexed on a public use terminal back to 1965. Office personnel or visitors may perform searches. Search fee $5.00 per name. UCC search per debtor name- $10.00. Copy fee $1.00 per page. Cert fee- $5.00 per doc plus copy fee. Payee- Cameron County Clerk. **Online to Appraiser, Property Tax, Probate, Judgment records:** Appraisal district property records free at www.cameroncad.org/search_namenew.htm. Access probate and judgment records free at http://idocket.com/countycourt.htm Also, see note at beginning of section. **Other phones:** Treasurer- 956-544-0819; Appraiser/Auditor- 956-399-9322 or 541-3365; Elections- 956-544-0809; Vital Records- 956-544-0817. **Property tax/Assessor**- 964 E Harrison, Brownsville, TX 78520; 956-544-0800.

Camp County

County Clerk, 126 Church St; Rm 102, Pittsburg, TX 75686. 903-856-2731; fax-903-856-2309; 8AM-5PM. All records in one index. Records indexed on computer back to 1997. Office will perform a UCC and Tax lien search but public must search other records themselves. Search fee $10.00. Copy fee $1.00 per page. Cert fee- $5.00 per page plus copy fee. Payee- Camp County Clerk. **Other phones:** Treasurer- 903-856-7862; Appraiser/Auditor- 903-856-6538; Elections- 903-856-2731; Vital Records- 903-856-2731. **Property tax/Assessor-** 115 North Ave, Pittsburg, TX 75686; 903-856-3391.

Carson County

County Clerk, PO Box 487, Panhandle, TX 79068. 806-537-3873; fax-806-537-3623; hours: 8AM-N, 1-5PM.
Records indexed on a public use terminal back to 5/1981. Only the public may search. Copy fee $1.00 per page. Cert fee- $5.00 per cert plus copy fee. Payee- Carson County Clerk. **Other phones:** Treasurer- 806-537-3753; Appraiser/Auditor- 806-537-3569; Elections- 806-537-3873; Vital Records- 806-537-3873. **Property tax/Assessor-** same address as above. 806-537-3412.

Cass County

County Clerk, PO Box 449, Linden, TX 75563. 903-756-5071; fax-903-756-8057; hours: 8AM-4;30PM.
All records in one index. Records indexed on a public use terminal back to 1846. Office will perform a UCC search but public must search other records themselves. Search fee $10.00. Copy fee $1.00 per page. Cert fee- $5.00 per page plus copy fee. Payee- Cass County Clerk. **Other phones:** Treasurer- 903-756-7626; Appraiser/Auditor- 903-756-7545; Elections- 903-756-5071; Vital Records- 903-756-5071. **Property tax/Assessor-** P O Box 870, Linden, TX 75563; 903-756-5313.

Castro County

County Clerk, 100 E. Bedford, Rm 101, Dimmitt, TX 79027-2643. 806-647-3338; hours: 8AM-5PM.
All records in one index. Office will perform a UCC search but public must search other records themselves. Search fee $16.00. Copy fee $1.00 per page. Cert fee- $5.00 per cert plus copy fee. Payee- Castro County Clerk. **Other phones:** Treasurer- 806-647-5534; Appraiser/Auditor- 806-647-5131; Elections- 806-647-3338; Vital Records- 806-647-3338. **Property tax/Assessor-** 806-647-5336.

Chambers County

County Clerk, PO Box 728, Anahuac, TX 77514. 409-267-8309; fax-409-267-8315; hours: 8AM-5PM.
Separate indices to search include official public records indexes; miscellaneous indexes contain marriage license, assumed name certificates, plats. Records indexed on computer back to 1990. Office personnel or visitors may perform searches. Search fee $5.00 each 10 year search. Must provide specific information. Will not search real estate records. Will not search UCC records. Copy fee $1.00 per page. Cert fee- $5.00 per cert plus copy fee. Payee- Chambers County Clerk. **Online access to Property Tax, Appraiser records:** Search the appraiser property tax database for free at www.chamberscad.org. Also, see note at beginning of section. **Other phones:** Treasurer- 409-267-8286; Appraiser/Auditor- 409-267-3795; Elections- 409-267-8309. **Property tax/Assessor-** PO Box 519, Anahuac, TX 77514; 409-267-8301.

Cherokee County

County Clerk, PO Box 420, Rusk, TX 75785. 903-683-2350; fax-903-683-5931; hours: 8AM-5PM.
All records in one index. Records indexed on a public use terminal back to 1976. Office personnel or visitors may perform searches. Search fee $10.00. Copy fee $1.00 per page. Cert fee- $5.00 per page plus copy fee. Payee- Cherokee County Clerk. **Online access to Real Estate, Grantor/Grantee, Deed, Judgment, Lien, Property Tax, Appraiser, Land, Probate records:** Access recording records free at www.titlex.com; select Cherokee county. Records range from 5/1973 to 2/2004. Also, see note at beginning of section. Also, search the Cherokee CAD database for free at http://clientdb.trueautomation.com/clientdb/main.asp?id=2. Also, for land records search go to

www.texaslandrecords.com. Also, to search probate records and judgment records go to http://idocket.com/countycourt.htm. **Other phones:** Treasurer- 903-683-4935; Appraiser/Auditor- 903-683-2296; Elections- 903-683-2350; Vital Records- 903-683-2350. **Property tax/Assessor-** same address as above. 903-683-5478.

Childress County

County Clerk, Courthouse Box 4, Childress, TX 79201. 940-937-6143; fax-940-937-3479; 8:30AM-5PM.
All records in one index. Record index not computerized. Only the public may search. Copy fee $1.00 per page. Cert fee- $5.00 per instrument. Payee- County Clerk, Zona Prince. **Other phones:** Treasurer- 940-937-6271; Appraiser/Auditor- 940-937-6062; Elections- 940-937-6143; Vital Records- 940-937-6143. **Property tax/Assessor-** 940-937-2232.

Clay County

County Clerk, PO Box 548, Henrietta, TX 76365. 940-538-4631; fax-none; hours: 8AM-5PM.
Separate indices to search include deed, deed of trust, tax lien, abstracts, judgments, mechanic liens. Record index not computerized. Office will perform a UCC search but public must search other records themselves. UCC search per debtor name- $10.00. Copy fee $1.00 per page. Cert fee- $5.00 per cert plus copy fee. Payee- Clay County Clerk. **Online access to Property Tax records:** See note at beginning of section. **Other phones:** Treasurer- 940-538-4631; Appraiser/Auditor- 940-538-4311; Elections- 940-538-4631; Vital Records- 940-538-4631. **Property tax/Assessor-** 100 N Bridge St, Henrietta, TX 76365; 940-538-4356.

Cochran County

County Clerk, 100 N. Main; Courthouse, Morton, TX 79346-2598. 806-266-5450; fax-806-266-9027; hours: 8AM-5PM.
All records in one index. Record index not computerized. Office personnel or visitors may perform searches. Search fee $5.00 per name. Copy fee $1.00 per page. Cert fee- $5.00 per cert plus copy fee. Payee- Cochran County Clerk. **Other phones:** Treasurer- 806-266-5161; Appraiser/Auditor- 806-266-5584; Elections- 806-266-5450; Vital Records- 806-266-5450. **Property tax/Assessor-** 806-266-5171.

Coke County

County Clerk, PO Box 150, Robert Lee, TX 76945. 325-453-2631; fax-325-453-2650; hours: 8AM-5PM.
All records in one index. Search fee $5.00 per name unless otherwise indicated. Will not search real estate records. UCC search per debtor name- $10.00. Federal/state combined tax lien search- $18.00 per debtor. Copy fee $1.00 per page. $2.00 per page for UCC. Cert fee- $5.00 per cert plus copy fee. Payee- Coke County Clerk. **Other phones:** Treasurer- 325-453-2713; Appraiser/Auditor- 325-453-4528; Elections- 325-453-2631; Vital Records- 325-453-2631. **Property tax/Assessor-** PO Box 169, Robert Lee, TX 76945; 325-453-2614.

Coleman County

County Clerk, PO Box 591, Coleman, TX 76834. 325-625-2889; hours: 8AM-5PM.
Separate indices to search include deed, deed of trust, mechanics lien, state tax lien, federal tax lien, abstract judgment. Office will perform a UCC search but public must search other records themselves. UCC search per debtor name- $10.00. Copy fee $1.00 per page. Cert fee- $5.00 per cert plus copy fee. Payee- Coleman County Clerk. **Online access to Appraiser, Property Tax records:** See note at beginning of section, www.txcountydata.com. **Other phones:** Treasurer- 325-625-4221; Appraiser/Auditor- 325-625-4155. **Property tax/Assessor-** 100 W Liveoat #104, Coleman, TX 76834; 325-625-2153.

Collin County

County Clerk, 200 S. McDonald; Annex "A", #120, McKinney, TX 75069. 972-548-4185; fax-972-547-5731; hours: 8AM-5PM (8AM-4PM land recording). www.co.collin.tx.us
Office will perform a UCC search but public must search other records themselves. Search fee $10.00. Copy fee $1.00 per page. Cert fee- $5.00 per cert plus copy fee. Payee- Collin County Clerk. **Online access to Appraiser, Property Tax, Business Personal Property, Deed, Lien, Judgment, Vital Statistic, Mortgage records:** Access to the county clerk Deeds database is free at www.collincountytexas.gov/DeedSearch. Also, search the Appraiser's property tax and business property database for free at www.collincad.org/search.php. Also, search the tax assessor and collector look up free at www.co.collin.tx.us/tax_assessor/taxstmt_search.jsp. Also, see note at beginning of section. **Other phones:** Treasurer- 972-548-4202; Appraiser/Auditor- 972-578-5200; Elections- 972-548-4185; Vital Records- 972-548-4134. **Property tax/Assessor-** 972-547-5020.

Collingsworth County

County Clerk, 800 West Ave; Box 10, Wellington, TX 79095. 806-447-2408; fax-806-447-2409; hours: 9AM-5PM.
All records in one index. Record index not computerized. Office personnel or visitors may perform searches. General index search fee $10.00 per search. Tax liens not included in UCC search. UCC search per debtor name- $16.00. UCC search request using non-standard form (per name)- $31.00. Copy fee $1.00 per page. Cert fee- $5.00 per cert plus copy fee. Payee- Collingsworth County Clerk. **Other phones:** Treasurer- 806-447-2616; Appraiser/Auditor- 806-447-5172; Elections- 806-447-2408; Vital Records- 806-447-2408. **Property tax/Assessor-** 800 West Ave Box 2, Wellington, TX 79095; 806-447-5606.

Colorado County

County Clerk, 400 Spring St Rm 103; Couthouse, Columbus, TX 78934. 979-732-2155, R/E recording phone-979-732-6561 or 2155; fax-979-732-8852; hours: 8AM-5PM.
www.rtis.com/reg/colorado-cty/gov.htm
Will search real estate records. Will not search UCC records or tax liens. Copy fee $1.00 per page. Cert fee- $5.00 per cert plus copy fee. Payee- Colorado County Clerk. **Online access to Real Estate, Grantor/Grantee, Deed, Judgment, Lien, Cemetery, Property Tax, Appraiser records:** Access recording records free at www.titlex.com; select Colorado county. Records range is 5/1997 to 9/2001. Also, vital statistics are free from an unofficial at www.rootsweb.com/~txcolora/vitalrecords.htm. Divorces go back to 1968; deaths back to 1964; marriages back to 1966. Also, access Appraisal District records free at http://clientdb.trueautomation.com/clientdb/main.asp?id=31. Also, see note at beginning of section. Also for property search go to www.coloradocad.org/ and click on property search. **Other phones:** Treasurer- 979-732-2865; Appraiser/Auditor- 979-732-8222; Vital Records- 979-732-6561 or 2155. **Property tax/Assessor-** 979-732-2710.

Comal County

County Clerk, 150 N Seguin, #101; #104, New Braunfels, TX 78130. 830-620-5513; fax-830-620-3410; hours: 8AM-4:30PM. www.co.comal.tx.us
All records in one index. Records indexed on a public use terminal back to 1995 to present. Office personnel or visitors may perform searches. General search fee $5.00 per name. UCC search per debtor name- $10.00. UCC search request using non-standard form (per name)- $25.00. Copy fee $1.00 per name. Cert fee- $5.00 per copy. **Online access to Property, Appraiser records:** Access Appraisal District records free at http://clientdb.trueautomation.com/clientdb/main.asp?id=35. Also search property at www.comalcad.org.

Other phones: Treasurer- 830-620-5506; Appraiser/Auditor- 830-625-8597; Elections- 830-620-5538; Vital Records- 830-620-5515. **Property tax/Assessor-** 830-620-5521.

Comanche County

County Clerk, Courthouse; 101 West Central Ave, Comanche, TX 76442. 325-356-2655; fax-325-356-5764; hours: 8:30-5PM.

Separate indices to search include deeds of trust, judgments, tax liens, lis pendens. Office personnel or visitors may perform searches. General search fee $5.00. Will not search real estate records. Will search UCC records prior to 7/2001 and current fixture (land) files. UCC search includes tax liens if requested. UCC search per debtor name- $10.00. UCC search request using non-standard form (per name)- $25.00. Copy fee $1.00 per page. Cert fee- $5.00 per cert plus copy fee. Payee- Comanche County Clerk. **Online access to Appraiser, Property Tax records:** Access Appraisal District records free at http://clientdb.trueautomation.com/clientdb/main.asp?id =12. Also, see note at beginning of section, www.txcountydata.com. **Other phones:** Treasurer- 325-356-2838; Appraiser/Auditor- 325-356-5253; Elections- 325-356-2655; Vital Records- 325-356-2655. **Property tax/Assessor-** 325-356-3101.

Concho County

County Clerk, PO Box 98, Paint Rock, TX 76866-0098. 325-732-4322; fax-325-732-2040; hours: 8:30AM-5PM.

Separate indices to search include misc, liens, land. Real estate record owner and mortgage searches available. UCC search (including tax liens) per debtor name- $10.00. Separate federal/state combined tax lien search- $5.00 per debtor. Copy fee $1.00 per page. Cert fee- $5.00 per cert plus copy fee. Payee- Concho County Clerk. **Other phones:** Treasurer- 325-732-4279; Appraiser/Auditor- 325-732-4389; Elections- 325-732-4322; Vital Records- 325-732-4322. **Property tax/Assessor-** PO Box 67, Paint Rock, TX 76866-0067; 325-732-4460.

Cooke County

County Clerk, Courthouse, Gainesville, TX 76240. 940-668-5420, UCC recording phone-940-668-5474; fax-940-668-5440; hours: 8AM-5PM.

Index: By years. Record index not computerized. Office will perform a UCC and Tax lien search but public must search other records themselves. Search fee $10.00. Copy fee $1.00 per page. Cert fee- $5.00 per cert plus copy fee. Payee- County Clerk. **Online access to Property, Appraiser records:** Access the Cooke CAD Live database free at http://clientdb.trueautomation.com/clientdb/main.asp?id =10. **Other phones:** Treasurer- 940-668-5423; Appraiser/Auditor- 940-665-7651; Elections- 940-668-5420; Vital Records- 940-668-5421. **Property tax/Assessor-** 100 S Dixon, Gainesville, TX 76240; 940-668-5425.

Coryell County

County Clerk, PO Box 237, Gatesville, TX 76528. 254-865-5911, R/E recording phone-254-865-5911 x235; fax-254-865-8631; hours: 8AM-N, 1-5PM. www.co.coryell.tx.us/

Office will perform a UCC search but public must search other records themselves. Search fee $10.00. Copy fee $1.00 per page. Cert fee- $5.00 per doc plus copy fee. **Online access to Property, Appraiser records:** Access Appraisal District property records free at http://clientdb.trueautomation.com/clientdb/main.asp?id =45. **Other phones:** Appraiser/Auditor- 254-865-6593. **Property tax/Assessor-** 254-865-6593.

Cottle County

County Clerk, PO Box 717, Paducah, TX 79248. 806-492-3823; fax-806-492-2625; hours: 9AM-12-1-5PM.

Index: Books. Records indexed on computer back to 10/1/2003. Office personnel or visitors may perform searches. Search fee $5.00. Copy fee $1.00 per page. Cert fee- $5.00 per cert plus copy fee. Payee- Cottle County Clerk. **Other phones:** Treasurer- 806-492-3738; Appraiser/Auditor- 806-492-3345. **Property tax/Assessor-** same address as above. 806-492-3345.

Crane County

County Clerk, PO Box 578, Crane, TX 79731. 432-558-3581; hours: 9AM-N, 1-5PM. www.co.crane.tx.us

All records in one index. Only the public may search. Copy fee $1.00 per page. Cert fee- $5.00 per cert plus copy fee. Payee- Crane County Clerk. **Other phones:** Treasurer- 432-558-3372; Appraiser/Auditor- 432-558-1021; Elections- 432-558-3581; Vital Records- 432-558-3581. **Property tax/Assessor-** PO Box 878, Crane, TX 79731; 432-558-2622.

Crockett County

County Clerk, PO Drawer C, Ozona, TX 76943. 325-392-2022; fax-325-392-3472; hours: 8AM-5PM, M-Th, 8AM-4PM, F.

Index: Books. Records indexed on a public use terminal back to 1980. Office personnel or visitors may perform searches. Search fee $10.00. Copy fee $1.00 per page. Cert fee- $5.00 per cert plus copy fee. Payee- Crockett County Clerk. **Other phones:** Treasurer- 325-392-3376; Appraiser/Auditor- 325-392-2674; Elections- 325-392-2022; Vital Records- 325-392-2022. **Property tax/Assessor-** same address as above. 325-392-2674.

Crosby County

County Clerk, 201 W Aspen St, Rm 102, Crosbyton, TX 79322. 806-675-2334; hours: 8AM-N, 1-5PM.

All records in one index. Only the public may search. Copy fee $1.00 per page. UCC copy $2.00 per page. Cert fee- $5.00 per cert plus copy fee. Payee- Crosby County Clerk. **Other phones:** Appraiser/Auditor- 806-675-2356. **Property tax/Assessor-** 806-675-2311.

Culberson County

County Clerk, PO Box 158, Van Horn, TX 79855. 432-283-2058; fax-432-283-9234; hours: 8AM-12, 1PM-5PM.

All records in one index. Record index not computerized. Office will perform a Tax lien search but public must search other records themselves. General index search fee $10.00 per document. Copy fee $1.00 per page. Cert fee- $5.00 per cert plus copy fee. Payee- County Clerk. **Other phones:** Treasurer- 432-283-2115; Appraiser/Auditor- 432-283-2977; Elections- 432-283-2058; Vital Records- 432-283-2058. **Property tax/Assessor-** PO Box 668, Van Horn, TX 79855; 432-283-2130.

Dallam County

County Clerk, PO Box 1352, Dalhart, TX 79022. 806-249-4751, R/E recording phone-806-244-4751; fax-806-249-2252; hours: 8AM-5PM M-Th, 8AM-1PM F.

All records in one index. Records indexed on computer back to 1995. Only the public may search. Copy fee $1.00 per page. Cert fee- $5.00 per doc plus copy fee. Payee- Dallam County District Clerk. **Other phones:** Appraiser/Auditor- 806-249-6767; Elections- 806-244-4751; Vital Records- 806-244-4751. **Property tax/Assessor-** 806-244-2801.

Dallas County

County Clerk, 509 Main St.; Records Bldg, 2nd Fl, Dallas, TX 75202-3502. 214-653-7275, UCC recording 214-653-7135; fax-214-653-7082; 8AM-4:30PM. www.dallascounty.org/html/citizen-serv/county-clerk/

Separate indices to search include Real property, Personal property, Assumed name indexes.

Records indexed on a public use terminal back to 1964. Office will perform a UCC and Tax lien search but public must search other records themselves. Search fees- tax lien $5.00; UCCs $13.00. Copy fee $1.00 minimum $5.00. Cert fee- $5.00 per cert plus copy fee. Payee- Dallas County Clerk. **Online access to Property Tax, Personal Property, Voter Registration, Marriage, UCC, Assumed Name, Probate records:** Name search indices of marriages, assumed names, UCCs, probate, court records (and soon, real estate) back to 1977 on the online records searches page at www.dallascounty.org/applications/english/record-search/intro.html. Indices include DOB. $6.00 fee to view and print documents; credit cards accepted. Purchase per item or subscribe for $75 annual fee. Also, access Central Appraisal District data free at www.dallascad.org/SearchOwner.aspx. Also, access County Voter Registration Records free at www.dalcoelections.org/voters.asp. Will show if registered and in what precinct. **Other phones:** Treasurer- 214-653-7321; Appraiser/Auditor- 214-631-0520; Elections- 214-819-6300; Vital Records- 314-653-7978. **Property tax/Assessor-** 214-653-0520.

Dawson County

County Clerk, PO Drawer 1268, Lamesa, TX 79331. 806-872-3778, R/E recording phone-806-872-3778/7685/6191; fax-806-872-2473; 8:30AM-5PM.

Separate indices to search. Records indexed on a public use terminal back to 1992. Only the public may search. Copy fee $1.00 per page. Cert fee- $5.00 per cert plus copy fee. Payee- Dawson County Clerk. **Other phones:** Treasurer- 806-872-7474; Appraiser/Auditor- 806-872-7060; Elections-806-872-3778; Vital Records- 806-872-3778. **Property tax/Assessor-** 806-872-7181.

De Witt County

County Clerk, 307 N. Gonzales; Courthouse, Cuero, TX 77954. 361-275-3724; fax-361-275-8994; hours: 8AM-N, 1-5PM.

All records in one index. Records indexed on Official Public Records since January, 1996. Office will perform a UCC search but public must search other records themselves. Search fee $10.00 per debtor. Will search UCC records prior to 7/2001 and current fixture (land) files. Tax liens not included in UCC search, must search each location. UCC search request per name- $25.00. Copy fee $1.00 per page. Cert fee- $5.00 per cert plus copy fee. Payee- De Witt County Clerk. **Other phones:** Appraiser/Auditor- 361-275-5753. **Property tax/Assessor-** PO Box 489, Cuero, TX 77954; 361-275-3410.

Deaf Smith County

County Clerk, 235 E. 3rd, Rm 203, Hereford, TX 79045-5542. 806-363-7077; fax-806-363-7023; hours: 8AM-5PM.

All records in one index. Office will perform a UCC search but public must search other records themselves. Search fee $5.00 per debtor. Will search UCC records prior to 7/2001 and current fixture (land) files. UCC search per debtor name- $10.00. UCC search request using non-standard form (per name)- $25.00. Copy fee $1.00 per page. Cert fee- $5.00 per cert plus copy fee. Payee- Deaf Smith County Clerk. **Other phones:** Treasurer- 806-363-7088; Appraiser/Auditor- 806-364-0625; Elections-806-363-7077; Vital Records- 806-363-7077. **Property tax/Assessor-** 136 E 3rd St, Herford, TX 79045; 806-363-7044.

Delta County

County Clerk, 200 W. Dallas Ave, Cooper, TX 75432. 903-395-4400, R/E recording phone-903-395-4400 x222; fax-903-395-2178; hours: 8AM-5PM.

All records in one index. Records indexed on a public use terminal back to 1/1/2003. Office personnel or visitors may perform searches. Search fee $10.00. Separate state/federal tax lien search fee- $5.00 per debtor. Copy fee $2.00, if tax lien or real estate $1.00 per page. Cert fee- $5.00 per cert plus copy fee. Payee- Delta County Clerk. **Online access to Property, Appraiser records:** Access Appraisal District records free at http://clientdb.trueautomation.com/clientdb/main.asp?id =39. **Other phones:** Treasurer- 903-395-4400 x225; Appraiser/Auditor- 903-395-4118; Elections- 903-395-4400 x222; Vital Records- 903-395-4400 x222. **Property tax/Assessor-** same address as above. 903-395-4400 x228.

Denton County

County Clerk, PO Box 2187, Denton, TX 76202-2187. 940-349-2010; fax-940-349-2019; 8AM-5PM (8AM-4:30 Wed). www.dentoncounty.com/dept/ccl.htm
Records indexed on a public use terminal back to 1974. Office personnel (mail only) or visitors may perform searches. General index search fee $5.00 per 5 years, per name. Will search UCC records prior to 7/2001 and current fixture (land) files. Tax liens not included in UCC search. UCC search per debtor name- $10.00. UCC search request using non-standard form (per name)- $25.00. Copy fee $1.00 per page. Cert fee- $5.00 per cert plus copy fee. Payee- Denton County Clerk, Cynthia Mitchell. **Online access to Real Estate, Recording, Voter Registration, Most Wanted, Parolee, Sex Offender, Bond, Jail, Conviction records:** Access county property database indices free for name/instrument No fee to view, but to print is $1.00 per page; isit https://www.texaslandrecords.com/txlr/TxlrApp/index.jsp. With a full subscription, you can search full indices and download images. Also, search the voter registration rolls for free at http://elections.dentoncounty.com/VRSearch/default.asp. Search the "justice" database free at http://justice.dentoncounty.com. Includes parolees, sex offenders, most wanted lists, bond, jail, convictions and court records databases. **Other phones:** Treasurer- 940-349-3150; Appraiser/Auditor- 940-349-3800; Elections- 940-349-3200; Vital Records- 940-349-2018; Admin- 940-349-2012. **Property tax/Assessor-** 300 E McKinney, (PO Box 90223, Denton 76202), Denton, TX 76201; 940-349-3500.

Dickens County

County Clerk, PO Box 120, Dickens, TX 79229. 806-623-5531; fax-806-623-5319; 8AM-N, 1-5PM.
All records in one index. Record index not computerized. Office personnel or visitors may perform searches. General index search fee $5.00. Copy fee $1.00 per page. Cert fee- $5.00 per cert plus copy fee. Payee- Dickens County Clerk. **Other phones:** Appraiser/Auditor- 806-623-5216; Elections- 806-623-5531. **Property tax/Assessor-** PO Box 119, Dickens, TX 79229; 806-623-5216.

Dimmit County

County Clerk, 103 N. 5th St, Carrizo Springs, TX 78834. 830-876-2323 x233, R/E recording phone-830-876-4238; fax-830-876-4205; hours: 8AM-5PM.
All records in one index as of 7/2003. Record index not computerized. Office personnel or visitors may perform searches. General index search fee $10.00 per 10 years. Copy fee $1.00 per page. Cert fee- $5.00 per doc includes copy fee. **Online access to Property, Appraiser records:** Access Appraisal District records free at http://clientdb.trueautomation.com/clientdb/main.asp?id =40. **Other phones:** Treasurer- 830-876-4246 x3; Appraiser/Auditor- 830-876-3420; Elections- 830-876-4238; Vital Records- 830-876-4238. **Property tax/Assessor-** 407 West Houston, Carrizo Springs, TX 78834; 830-876-4246 x1.

Donley County

County Clerk, PO Drawer U, Clarendon, TX 79226. 806-874-3436; fax-806-874-3351; hours: 8AM-N, 1-5PM.
All records in one index. Records indexed on a public use terminal back to 9/1994. Office personnel or visitors may perform searches. Search fee $5.00. UCC search $10.00. Copy fee $1.00 per page. Cert fee- $5.00 per page plus copy fee. Payee- Donley County District Clerk. **Online access to Property, Appraiser records:** Access property data by download from a private company; fees apply; add'l data includes minerals, ofc exports, delinquents; visit www.ptax.org/tax_office_data.htm or phone 201-571-0425. **Other phones:** Treasurer- 806-874-2328; Appraiser/Auditor- 806-874-2744; Elections- 806-874-3436; Vital Records- 806-874-3436. **Property tax/Assessor-** 806-874-2193.

Duval County

County Clerk, PO Box 248, San Diego, TX 78384. 361-279-3322 x727/274, R/E recording phone-361-279-3322 x272; fax-361-279-3159; 8AM-N, 1-5PM.
All records in one index. Office personnel or visitors may perform searches. General index search fee $10.00 per search. Will search real estate records. Will search UCC records prior to 7/2001 and current fixture (land) files. Tax liens not included in UCC search. UCC search per debtor name- $10.00. Tax lien search fee- $10.00 per debtor. Separate federal tax lien search- $10.00 per debtor. Separate state tax lien search- $10.00 per debtor. Copy fee $1.00 per page. Cert fee- $5.00 per cert plus copies. Payee- Duval County Clerk. **Other phones:** Treasurer- 361-279-6128; Appraiser/Auditor- 361-279-3305; Elections- 361-279-3322 x272; Vital Records- 361-279-3322 x272. **Property tax/Assessor-** PO Box 337, San Diego, TX 78384; 361-279-6138/6140.

Eastland County

County Clerk, PO Box 110, Eastland, TX 76448-0110. 254-629-1583; fax-254-629-8125; hours: 8AM-5PM.
All records in one index. Office personnel or visitors may perform searches. Will not search real estate records. Will search UCC records, tax liens not included in UCC search. UCC search per debtor name- $10.00. UCC search request using non-standard form (per name)- $25.00. Tax lien search fee- $5.00 per search. Copy fee $1.00 per page. Cert fee- $5.00 per cert plus copy fee. Payee- Eastland County Clerk. **Online access to Vital Statistic records:** Access to vital statistics from an unofficial source is free at http://ftp.rootsweb.com/pub/usgenweb/tx/eastland/vitals/. Births go back to 1926; deaths to 1964, Divorce to 1968, Marriages to 1966. **Other phones:** Treasurer- 254-629-2672; Appraiser/Auditor- 254-629-8597; Elections- 254-629-1583; Vital Records- 254-629-1583. **Property tax/Assessor-** 254-629-1564.

Ector County

County Clerk, PO Box 707, Odessa, TX 79760. 432-498-4130; fax-432-498-4177; hours: 8AM-4:30PM. www.texaslandrecords.com/txect/index.jsp
Records indexed on computer back to 1994. Office will perform a UCC or tax lien search but public must search other records themselves. Search fee $10.00 per debtor. Will search real estate records only if volume and page number is provided. Copy fee $1.00 per page. Cert fee- $5.00 per cert plus copy fee. Payee- Linda Haney, County Clerk. **Online access to Real Estate, Appraiser, Personal Property, Recording, Lien, UCC, Judgment records:** Search the appraisal district property data and personal property free at www.ectorcad.org. Search the recorder index free at www.texaslandrecords.com/txect/index.jsp. A subscription service is available here for full document viewing. **Other phones:** Treasurer- 432-498-4060; Appraiser/Auditor- 432-332-6834; Elections- 432-498-4030. **Property tax/Assessor-** 1010 W 8th, Odessa, TX 79761; 432-498-4050.

Edwards County

County Clerk, PO Box 184, Rocksprings, TX 78880-0184. 830-683-2235; fax-830-683-5376; 8AM-5PM.
All records in one index. Records indexed on computer back to 1885. Office personnel or visitors may perform searches. UCC search per debtor name- $10.00. Separate federal, state, or combined tax lien search- $10.00 per debtor. Copy fee $1.00 per page. Cert fee- $5.00 per cert plus copy fee. Payee- Edwards County Clerk. **Other phones:** Treasurer- 830-683-5116; Appraiser/Auditor- 830-683-4189. **Property tax/Assessor-** PO Box 378, Rocksprings, TX 78880; 830-683-2337.

El Paso County

County Clerk, 500 E. San Antonio; Rm 105, El Paso, TX 79901-2496. 915-546-2074, UCC recording phone-915-546-2071; fax-915-546-2012; 8AM-4:45PM.
All records in one index. Records indexed on a public use terminal back to 1981. Only the public may search. Copy fee $1.00 per page. Cert fee- $5.00 per cert plus copy fee. Payee- El Paso County Clerk. **Online access to Assumed Name, Property Tax, Real Estate, Vital Statistic, Probate, Judgment records:** Search vital statistics (birth, death, marriage), assumed names, and property records free at www.co.el-paso.tx.us/search.htm. Also, search property tax data free at www.elpasocad.org. Also, to search probate records and judgment records go to http://idocket.com/countycourt.htm Also, see note at beginning of section. **Other phones:** Appraiser/Auditor- 915-780-2000; Elections- 915-546-2154; Vital Records- 915-546-2071. **Property tax/Assessor-**915-541-4054.

Ellis County

County Clerk, PO Box 250, Waxahachie, TX 75168. 972-923-5070; fax-972-923-5075; 8AM-4:30PM.
All records in one index from 1992 forward. Office personnel or visitors may perform searches. General index search fee $5.00 per 5 years per name. Real estate owner, mortgage, and property transfer searches available. Will search UCC records prior to 7/2001 and current fixture (land) files. UCC search includes tax liens if requested. UCC search per debtor name- $10.00 per 5 years. Separate state/federal tax lien search fee- $10.00. Copy fee $1.00 per page. Cert fee- $5.00 per cert plus copy fee. Payee- Ellis County Clerk. **Online access to Appraiser, Property Tax records:** Search the property appraiser database for free at www.elliscad.org. Also, see note at beginning of section. **Other phones:** Treasurer- 972-825-5125; Appraiser/Auditor- 972-937-3552; Elections- 972-923-5195; Vital Records- 972-923-5070. **Property tax/Assessor-** 972-923-5150.

Erath County

County Clerk, 100 W. Washington St.; Courthouse, Stephenville, TX 76401. 254-965-1482; fax-254-965-5732; hours: 8AM-4PM.
All records in one index. Records indexed on a public use terminal back to 1988. Office will perform a UCC and Tax lien search but public must search other records themselves. Search fee $10.00. Copy fee $1.00 per page. Cert fee- $5.00 per cert plus copy Payee- Erath County Clerk. **Online to Property Tax, Appraiser records:** Access the county appraisal roll free at www.myswdata.com/swd_find.aspx. Also, see note at beginning of section. **Other phones:** Treasurer- 254-965-1483; Appraiser/Auditor- 254-965-1482; Elections- 254-965-1482; Vital Records- 254-965-1410. **Property/Assessor-** 320 W College St, Stephenville, TX 76401; 254-965-7301.

Falls County

County Clerk, PO Box 458, Marlin, TX 76661. 254-883-1408; fax-254-883-1406; 8AM-N, 1-5PM.
All records in one index. Office will perform a UCC search but public must search other records themselves. UCC search per debtor name- $10.00. Copy fee $1.00 per page. Cert fee- $5.00 per cert plus copy fee. Payee- Falls County Clerk. **Other phones:** Treasurer- 254-883-1433; Appraiser/Auditor- 254-883-2543; Elections- 254-883-1408; Vital Records- 254-883-1408. **Property tax/Assessor-** PO Box 59, Marlin, TX 76661; 254-883-1436.

Fannin County

County Clerk, 101 E. Sam Rayburn Dr.; Courthouse, #102, Bonham, TX 75418-4346. 903-583-7486; fax-903-583-9598; hours: 8AM-5PM.

Index: Indices have been combined all-in-one. Records indexed on a public use terminal back to 1968. Office will perform a UCC search but public must search other records themselves. Will not search real estate records. Will search UCC records prior to 7/2001 and current fixture (land) files. UCC search includes tax liens if requested. UCC search per debtor name- $5.00. Copy fee $1.00 per page. Cert fee- $5.00 per cert plus copy fee. Payee- Fannin County Clerk. **Online access to Appraiser, Property Tax records:** Access Appraisal District records free at http://clientdb.trueautomation.com/clientdb/main.asp?id =34. Also, see notes at beginning of section. **Other phones:** Appraiser/Auditor- 903-583-8701. **Property tax/Assessor-** 903-583-7493.

Fayette County

County Clerk, PO Box 59, La Grange, TX 78945. 979-968-3251, R/E recording phone-409-968-3251; fax-979-968-8531; hours: 8AM-N, 1-5PM. www.co.fayette.tx.us

Separate indices to search. Records indexed on computer back to 1993. Only the public may search. Copy fee $2.00, if real estate $1.00 per page. Cert fee- $5.00 per cert plus copy fee. Payee-Fayette County Clerk. **Online access to Real Estate, Grantor/Grantee, Deed, Lien, Judgment records:** Access recording records free at www.titlex.com; select Fayette county. **Other phones:** Treasurer- 979-968-3055; Appraiser/Auditor- 979-968-8383; Elections-979-968-3251; Vital Records- 979-968-3251. **Property tax/Assessor-** Courthouse, LaGrange, TX 78945; 979-968-3164.

Fisher County

County Clerk, PO Box 368, Roby, TX 79543-0368. 325-776-2401; fax-325-776-3274; hours: 8AM-5PM. All records in one index. General index search fee $5.00 per name. UCC search per debtor name-$10.00. Copy fee $1.00 per page. Cert fee- $5.00 per page. **Other phones:** Treasurer- 325-776-3257; Appraiser/Auditor- 325-776-2181; Elections- 325-776-2401; Vital Records- 325-776-2401. **Property tax/Assessor-** 325-776-2181.

Floyd County

County Clerk, 105 Main St; Courthouse, Rm 101, Floydada, TX 79235. 806-983-4900; fax-806-983-4909; hours: 8:30AM-12, 1-5PM.

All records in one index. Office personnel or visitors may perform searches. Search fee $10.00 per debtor. Copy fee $1.00 per page. Cert fee- $5.00 per cert plus copy fee. Payee- Floyd County Clerk. **Other phones:** Treasurer- 806-983-4910; Appraiser/Auditor- 806-983-5256; Elections- 806-983-4900; Vital Records- 806-983-4900. **Property tax/Assessor-** 100 Main St., Courthouse, Rm 116, Floydada, TX 79235; 806-983-4908.

Foard County

County Clerk, PO Box 539, Crowell, TX 79227. 940-684-1365; fax-940-684-1918; hours: 9AM-4:30PM. All records in one index. General index search fee $10.00 per name. Will search real estate records. Will search UCC records prior to 7/2001 and current fixture (land) files. Tax liens not included in UCC search. UCC search request using non-standard form (per name)- $25.00. Separate state tax lien search-$10.00 per debtor. Federal/state combined tax lien search- $10.00 per debtor. Copy fee $1.00 per page. Cert fee- $5.00 plus copy fees. Payee- Foard County Clerk. **Other phones:** Treasurer- 940-684-1818; Appraiser/Auditor- 940-684-1225; Elections-940-684-1365; Vital Records- 940-684-1365. **Property tax/Assessor-** 940-684-1501.

Fort Bend County

County Clerk, 301 Jackson, #101, Richmond, TX 77469. 281-341-8685; fax-281-341-8669; hours: 8AM-4PM. www.co.fort-bend.tx.us

Records indexed on a public use terminal back to 12/1973. Office will perform a Fed Tax lien search but public must search other records themselves. Search fee $10.00. Copy fee $1.50 per page, but not less that $5.00 per debtor per request. Cert fee- $5.00 per cert plus copy fee. Payee- Fort Bend County Clerk. Credit cards accepted (M/C or Visa). **Online to Real Estate, Grantor/Grantee, Deed, Lien, Judgment, Appraiser, UCC, Marriage, Death, Birth, Probate records:** Access to the county clerk database is free at www.co.fort-bend.tx.us/admin_of_justice/County_Clerk/index_info research.htm. Search the property index by name, or the plat index. And, search county probate and court records. For information, contact Diane Shepard at 281-341-8664. UCCs records can be searched for free at http://ccweb.co.fort-bend.tx.us/ucc/uccDefault.asp. Also, access recording records free at www.titlex.com; select Ft Bend county. Record range is 1/1974 to 11/2001. Also, see note at beginning of section for add'l fee service for tax records and recordings. **Other phones:** Treasurer- 281-341-3750; Appraiser/Auditor-281-344-8623; Elections- 281-341-8670; Vital Records- 281-341-8685. **Property tax/Assessor-** 281-341-3735.

Franklin County

County Clerk, 200 N Kaufman St, Mount Vernon, TX 75457-0068. 903-537-4252 x6, UCC recording phone-903-537-4252 ext 6; fax-903-537-2982; hours: 8AM-5PM. www.co.franklin.tx.us/

Office personnel or visitors may perform searches. General index search fee $5.00 per name. Copy fee $1.00 per page. Cert fee- $5.00 per cert plus copy fee. Payee- Franklin County Clerk. No out of state personal checks. **Online access to Property Tax records:** See note at beginning of section. **Other phones:** Treasurer- 903-537-2206 x8; Appraiser/Auditor- 903-537-2286; Elections- 903-537-4252 x3; Vital Records- 903-537-4252 ext 6. **Property tax/Assessor-** 903-537-2358.

Freestone County

County Clerk, PO Box 1010, Fairfield, TX 75840. 903-389-2635; hours: 8AM-5PM M-Th; 8AM-4:30PM F.

All records in one index. Records indexed on a public use terminal back to 1981. Only the public may search. Copy fee $1.00 per page. Cert fee- $5.00 per cert plus copy fee. Payee- Freestone County Clerk. **Online access to Appraiser records:** Search the Appraiser's property tax database for free at www.freestonecad.org/. **Other phones:** Treasurer- 903-389-2180; Appraiser/Auditor- 903-389-5510; Elections- 903-389-2635; Vital Records- 903-389-2635. **Property tax/Assessor-** PO Box 257, Fairfield, TX 75840; 903-389-2336.

Frio County

County Clerk, 500 E. San Antonio St, # 6, Pearsall, TX 78061. 830-334-2214; fax-830-334-0021; hours: 8AM-N; 1-5PM.

Separate indices to search. Only the public may search. General index search fee $10.00. Copy fee $1.00 per page. Cert fee- $5.00 per cert plus copy fee. Payee- Frio County Clerk. **Other phones:** Treasurer- 830-334-0040; Appraiser/Auditor- 830-334-4163; Elections- 830-334-2214; Vital Records- 830-334-2214. **Property tax/Assessor-** 830-334-2152.

Gaines County

County Clerk, 101 S. Main, Rm 107, Seminole, TX 79360. 432-758-4003, UCC recording phone-432-758-4033; fax-432-758-1442; hours: 8AM-5PM.

All records in one index. Will not search real estate records. Will search UCC records, tax liens not included in UCC search. UCC search per debtor name-$10.00. UCC search request using non-standard form (per name)- $20.00. Separate federal tax lien

search- $5.00 per debtor. Separate state tax lien search- $5.00 per debtor. Separate federal/state combined tax lien search-20.00 per debtor. Copy fee $1.00 per page. Cert fee- $5.00 per cert plus copy fee. Payee- Gaines County Clerk. **Online access to Property, Appraiser records:** Access Appraisal District records free at http://clientdb.trueautomation.com/clientdb/main.asp?id =47. **Other phones:** Treasurer- 432-758-4009; Appraiser/Auditor- 432-758-3263; Elections- 432-758-4033 or 758-4003; Vital Records- 432-758-4033. **Property tax/Assessor-** 101 S Main, Rm 108, Seminole, TX 79360; 432-758-4008.

Galveston County

County Clerk, PO Box 2450, Galveston, TX 77553-2450. 409-766-2200, R/E recording phone-409-766-2208; fax-409-770-5133; hours: 8AM-5PM. www.co.galveston.tx.us/County_Clerk/

All records in one index. Office will perform a UCC search records prior to 7/2001 which includes tax liens, but public must search other records themselves. Search fee $5.00 per debtor. Will not search real estate records. Copy fee $1.00 per page; $5.00 minimum. Cert fee- $5.00 per cert plus copy fee. Payee- Galveston County Clerk. **Online access to Real Estate, Grantor/Grantee, Deed, Lien, Judgment, Appraiser, Property Tax, Personal Property, Sheriff Sale, UCC, Vital Statistic, Court records:** Several sources exist. Access the county online official records index free at http://ccweb.co.galveston.tx.us/localization/menu.asp. Recording index records dates back to 1965; courts back to mid-'80s generally. Still in development. No images as yet. For info, call 409-766-5115. Also, search recorder records free at www.titlex.com. Also, Central Appraisal Dist. database is free at www.galvestoncad.org. Also, sheriff sales data free at http://www2.co.galveston.tx.us/sheriff/sheriff_sale.pdf. Also, a Grantor/Grantee index is at www.titlex.com; select Galveston County; records go back to 1/1965. Also, see note at beginning of section. **Other phones:** Treasurer- 409-770-5395; Appraiser/Auditor- 409-935-1980; Elections- 409-766-2207; Vital Records- 409-766-2207. **Property tax/Assessor-** PO Box 1169, Galveston, TX 77553-1169; 409-766-2280.

Garza County

County Clerk, PO Box 366, Post, TX 79356-0366. 806-495-4430; fax-806-495-4431; hours: 8AM-N, 1-5PM.

All records in one index. Office will perform a UCC search but public must search other records themselves. Search fee $5.00 per name. UCC search request using non-standard form (per name)- $25.00. Copy fee $2.00 per page. Cert fee- $5.00 per cert plus copy fee. Payee- Garza County Clerk. **Other phones:** Treasurer- 806-495-4423; Appraiser/Auditor- 806-495-3518; Elections- 806-495-4430; Vital Records- 806-495-4430. **Property tax/Assessor-** same address as above. 806-495-4448.

Gillespie County

County Clerk, 101 W. Main; Rm 109, Unit #13, Fredericksburg, TX 78624. 830-997-6515; fax-830-997-9958; hours: 8AM-4PM.

All records in one index. Only the public may search. Copy fee $1.00; tax lien or real estate $1.00 per page. Cert fee- $10.00 per cert plus copy fee. Payee- Gillespie County Clerk. **Online access to Appraiser, Property Tax records:** See note at beginning of section. **Other phones:** Treasurer- 830-997-6521; Appraiser/Auditor- 830-997-9807; Elections- 830-997-6515; Vital Records- 830-997-6515. **Property tax/Assessor-** 101 W. Main, Unit #2, Fredericksburg, TX 78624; 830-997-6519.

Glasscock County

County Clerk, PO Box 190, Garden City, TX 79739. 432-354-2371; fax-432-354-2348; hours: 8AM-4PM.

All records in one index. Office personnel or visitors may perform searches. General index search fee $10.00 per name. Will not search real estate records. Copy fee $1.00 per page. Cert fee- $5.00 per cert plus copy fee. Payee- Glasscock County Clerk. **Other phones:** Treasurer- 432-354-2415; Appraiser/Auditor- 432-354-2580; Elections- 432-354-2371; Vital Records- 432-354-2371. **Property tax/Assessor-** PO Box 89, Garden City, TX 79739; 432-354-2361.

Goliad County

County Clerk, PO Box 50, Goliad, TX 77963. 361-645-3294; fax-361-645-3858; hours: 8AM-N, 1PM-5PM. www.goliadcogovt.org
All records in one index. Office will perform a UCC search but public must search other records themselves. Search fee $10.00. Copy fee $1.00 per page. Cert fee- $5.00 per cert plus $1.00 per page. Payee- County Clerk. **Online access to Real estate, Grantor/Grantee, Deed, Lien, Judgment records:** Access recording records free at www.titlex.com; select Goliad county. Records range is 1/1950 to 12/2003. Also, see note at beginning of section. **Other phones:** Treasurer- 361-645-3551; Appraiser/Auditor- 361-645-2492; Elections- 361-645-3294; Vital Records- 361-645-3294. **Property tax/Assessor-** PO Box 800, Goliad, TX 77963; 361-645-3354 or 2541.

Gonzales County

County Clerk, PO Box 77, Gonzales, TX 78629. 830-672-2801; fax-830-672-2636; hours: 8AM-5PM.
Separate indices to search include prior to 1980, deed, deed of trust, oil & gas, cont sale, judgment, state & federal tax liens. Office will perform a UCC and tax liens search but public must search other records themselves. Search fee $5.00 per debtor. Will not search real estate records. Copy fee $1.00 per page. Cert fee- $5.00 per instrument plus copy fee. Payee- County Clerk. **Other phones:** Treasurer- 830-627-2621; Appraiser/Auditor- 830-672-2879; Vital Records- 830-672-2801. **Property tax/Assessor-** PO Box 677, Gonzales, TX 78629; 830-627-2841.

Gray County

County Clerk, PO Box 1902, Pampa, TX 79066-1902. 806-669-8004; fax-806-669-8054; 8:30AM-N, 1-5PM.
All records in one index. Records indexed on a public use terminal back to 1990. Office personnel or visitors may perform searches. Search fee $10.00 per name. Will not search real estate records. Copy fee $1.00 per page. Cert fee- $5.00 per cert plus copy fee. Payee- Gray County Clerk. **Other phones:** Treasurer- 806-669-8009; Appraiser/Auditor- 806-665-0791; Elections- 806-669-8004; Vital Records- 806-669-8004. **Property tax/Assessor-** same address as above. 806-669-8018.

Grayson County

County Clerk, 100 W. Houston #17, Sherman, TX 75090. 903-813-4243, R/E recording phone-903-813-4238, UCC recording phone-903-813-4239; fax-903-870-0829; hours: 8AM-5PM. www.co.grayson.tx.us/main.htm
All records in one index. Records indexed on a public use terminal back to 1968. Office will perform a UCC and Tax lien search but public must search other records themselves. General index search fee $10.00 per name per 10 years. Copy fee $2.00, if tax lien or real estate $1.00 per page. Cert fee- $5.00 per cert plus copy fee. Payee- Grayson County Clerk. **Online to Real Estate, Grantor/Grantee, Lien, Judgment, Appraiser, Property Tax, Bad Check, Sheriff Sale, Sheriff Bond, Jail, Vital Statistic records:** Search the CAD system for property, mortgage, and property data at http://clientdb.trueautomation.com/clientdb/main.asp?id=15. Also search Appraiser property data for free at www.graysoncad.org. Access recording records free at www.titlex.com. Also, sheriff sales data is at www.co.grayson.tx.us/Tax%20Office/ssale.pdf. Also, search the county attorney's hot check list at www.co.grayson.tx.us/Attorney/HC%20List.PDF.
Also, for land records search and vital records go to www.texaslandrecords.com. Search the sheriff bond records and jail data at http://co.grayson.tx.us:3004/judsrch.asp. Also, see note at beginning of section. **Other phones:** Treasurer- 903-813-4251; Appraiser/Auditor- 903-893-9673; Elections- 903-813-4260; Vital Records- 903-813-4243. **Property tax/Assessor-** 903-893-8683.

Gregg County

County Clerk, PO Box 3049, Longview, TX 75606. 903-236-8430, R/E recording phone-903-236-8430 x746, UCC recording phone-903-236-8430 X746 or 846; fax-903-237-2574; hours: 8AM-5PM. www.co.gregg.tx.us
All records in one index. Only the public may search. Copy fee $1.00 per page. Cert fee- $5.00 per cert plus copy fee. Payee- Gregg County Clerk. **Online access to Real Estate, Grantor/Grantee, Deed, Mortgage, Lien, Judgment, Assessor, Property Tax, Vital Statistic, UCC records:** Access to the County Clerk's recording database is free to view at www.co.gregg.tx.us/hartIAM/. Fee to get documents. Also, search property tax records for free at www.co.gregg.tx.us/tax/viking.asp. Also, access recording records free at www.titlex.com; select Gregg county.Records range is 4/1977 to 5/2005. Also, see note at beginning of section. **Other phones:** Treasurer- 903-236-8430 X853; Appraiser/Auditor- 903-238-8823; Elections- 903-236-8458; Vital Records- 903-236-8430 X637. **Property/Assessor-** 101 E. Methvin, #21, Longview, TX 75606; 903-237-2552.

Grimes County

County Clerk, PO Box 209, Anderson, TX 77830. 936-873-2111, UCC recording phone-936-873-2606 x252; fax-936-873-3308; hours: 8AM-N, 1-4:45PM.
All records in one index. Records indexed on a public use terminal back to 1967. Office will perform a UCC search but public must search other records themselves. Search fee $5.00 per name. Copy fee $2.00 per page, if tax lien or real estate $1.00 per page. Cert fee- $5.00 per cert plus copy fee. Payee- Grimes County Clerk. **Other phones:** Treasurer- 936-873-2606 x233; Appraiser/Auditor- 936-873-2163; Elections- 936-873-2606 x246; Vital Records- 936-873-2606 x250. **Property tax/Assessor-** PO Box 455, Anderson, TX 77830; 936-873-2606 x231.

Guadalupe County

County Clerk, PO Box 990, Seguin, TX 78156-0990. 830-303-4188 x236; fax-830-401-0300; hours: 8AM-4:30PM.
Separate indices to search include indexes back to the 1800's. Records indexed on a public use terminal back to 1974. Office will perform a federal & state tax lien searches, but public must search other records themselves. Search fee $10.00 per name. Copy fee $1.00 per page. Federal tax lien copy- $1.50 per page. Cert fee- $5.00 per cert plus copy fee. Payee- Guadalupe County Clerk. **Online to Property, Appraiser, Probate, Judgment records:** Access to Appraisal District records is free at http://clientdb.trueautomation.com/clientdb/main.asp?id=27. Also, to search probate records and judgment records go to http://idocket.com/countycourt.htm. **Other phones:** Treasurer- 830-303-4188 x338; Appraiser/Auditor- 830-372-2871 or 830-303-3313; Elections- 830-303-6363; Vital Records- 830-303-4188 x233. **Property tax/Assessor-** 307 W Court St, Seguin, TX 78155; 830-303-3421 x354.

Hale County

County Clerk, 500 Broadway #140, Plainview, TX 79072-8030. 806-291-5261; fax-806-291-9810; hours: 8AM-N,1-5PM.
Records indexed on computer from 1995 to present; 1994 and back in books. Only the public may search. Copy fee $1.00 per page. Cert fee- $5.00 per cert plus copy fee. Payee- Hale County Clerk. **Online access to Property, Appraiser records:** Access to property data is free at http://clientdb.trueautomation.com/clientdb/main.asp?id=8. **Other phones:** Treasurer- 806-291-5213; Appraiser/Auditor- 806-293-2547; Elections- 806-291-5261; Vital Records- 806-291-5219. **Property tax/Assessor-** 511 Broadway, Plainview, TX 79072; 806-291-5276.

Hall County

County Clerk, Courthouse, Box 8, Memphis, TX 79245. 806-259-2627; fax-806-259-5078; hours: 8:30AM-N, 1-5PM.
Index: Books, computer. Records indexed on a public use terminal back to 1992. Office personnel or visitors may perform searches. Search fee $10.00. Copy fee $1.00 per page. Cert fee- $5.00 per cert plus copy fee. Payee- Hall County Clerk. **Other phones:** Treasurer- 806-259-2421; Appraiser/Auditor- 806-259-2393. **Property tax/Assessor-** Courthouse, Box 14, Courthouse, Box 8; 806-259-2125.

Hamilton County

County Clerk, 101 E. Main St; Courthouse, Hamilton, TX 76531. 254-386-3518; fax-254-386-8727; hours: 8AM-5PM.
All records in one index. Record index not computerized. Office personnel or visitors may perform searches. UCC search per debtor name- $15.00. UCC search request using non-standard form (per name)- $30.00. Tax lien search fee- $5.00 per debtor. Separate federal tax lien search- $10.00 per debtor. Federal/state combined tax lien search- $10.00 per debtor. R/E or tax lien copy- $1.00 per page. Cert fee- $1.00 per doc plus copy fee. Payee- Hamilton County Clerk. **Other phones:** Treasurer- 254-386-5315; Appraiser/Auditor- 254-386-8945; Elections- 254-386-3518; Vital Records- 254-386-3518. **Property tax/Assessor-** 254-386-5114.

Hansford County

County Clerk, 15 N.W. Court, Spearman, TX 79081. 806-659-4110; fax-806-659-4168; hours: 8AM-5PM.
Records indexed on computer from 1980, prior in index books. Only the office personnel may search. Search fee $5.00. Will not search real estate records. Will search UCC records prior to 7/2001 and current fixture (land) files. Copy fee $1.00 per page. Cert fee- $5.00 per cert plus copy fee. **Online access to Property, Appraiser, Personal Property records:** Access to property data is free at www.ptax.org/offices/hansford/hansfordcad.htm. Also, access property data by download; fees apply; add'l data includes minerals, ofc exports, delinquents; visit www.ptax.org/tax_office_data.htm or phone 201-571-0425. **Other phones:** Treasurer- 806-659-4125; Appraiser/Auditor- 806-659-5575; Elections- 806-659-4110; Vital Records- 806-659-4110. **Property tax/Assessor-** 14 NW Court, Spearman, TX 79081; 806-659-4120.

Hardeman County

County Clerk, PO Box 30, Quanah, TX 79252-0030. 940-663-2901; fax-940-663-5161; 8:30AM-5PM.
All records in one index. Record index not computerized. Office personnel or visitors may perform searches. Search fee $10.00. Will not search real estate records. Copy fee $1.00 per page. Cert fee- $5.00 per cert plus copy fee. Payee- Hardeman County Clerk. **Other phones:** Treasurer- 940-663-5401; Appraiser/Auditor- 940-663-2532; Elections- 940-663-2901; Vital Records- 940-663-2901. **Property tax/Assessor-** 940-663-5221.

Hardin County

County Clerk, PO Box 38, Kountze, TX 77625. 409-246-5185; fax-409-246-3208; hours: 8AM-5PM.
All records in one index. Office personnel or visitors may perform searches. Search fee $5.00. Copy fee $1.00 per page. Cert fee- $6.00 per cert plus copy fee. Payee- Hardin County Clerk. **Other phones:** Treasurer- 409-246-5121; Appraiser/Auditor- 409-246-2507; Elections- 409-246-5185; Vital Records- 409-246-5185. **Property tax/Assessor-** PO Box 2260, Kountze, TX 77625; 409-246-5180.

Harris County

County Clerk, PO Box 1525, Houston, TX 77251-1525. 713-755-6405, UCC recording phone-713-755-6439; fax-713-755-4977; hours: 8AM-4:30PM. www.cclerk.hctx.net
Personal checks are not accepted for mail requests. Separate indices to search include real property, marriage license, assumed name, county civil courts at law, probate. Records indexed on computer back to 1961. Only the public may search. General copy fee $5.00 for 1-3 pages; $1.50 each add'l. R/E record copy- $1.00 per page. Cert fee- $5.00 per doc plus copy fee. Payee-Harris County Clerk. **Online access to Real Estate, Grantor/Grantee, Lien, Judgment, Appraiser, Voter, UCC, Assumed Name, Vital Statistic, Personal Property, Delinquent Tax, Probate records:** Access to Assumed Name records, UCC filings, vital statistic, and Real Property are at www.cclerk.hctx.net/coolice/default.asp?Category=RealProperty&Service=mastermenu. Appraiser records are at www.hcad.org/Records. County Court Civil, marriage and informal marriage records also available. Also, search tax assessor data free at www.tax.co.harris.tx.us/dbsearch/dbsearch.asp. Also, access recording records free at www.titlex.com; select Harris county. Also, to search probate records and judgment records go to http://idocket.com/countycourt.htm. **Other phones:** Treasurer- 713-755-5120; Appraiser/Auditor- 713-957-5291; Elections- 713-755-5792; Vital Records- 713-755-6438. **Property tax/Assessor-** 713-368-2200.

Harrison County

County Clerk, PO Box 1365, Marshall, TX 75671. 903-935-8403; fax-903-935-4877; hours: 8AM-5PM.
All records in one index. Office personnel or visitors may perform searches, (office personnel will not search for real estate titles). Will not search real estate records. Will search UCC records prior to 7/2001 and current fixture (land) files. UCC search includes tax liens if requested. UCC search per debtor name- $5.00. Separate federal tax lien search-$10.00 per debtor. Separate state tax lien search-$5.00 per debtor. Separate federal/state combined tax lien search- $15.00 per debtor. Copy fee $1.00 per page. Cert fee- $5.00 per cert plus copy fee. Payee- Harrison County Clerk. **Online access to Property Tax records:** Search the appraiser database for free at www.harrisoncad.org/swd_find.aspx. Also, see note at beginning of section. **Other phones:** Treasurer- 903-935-8404; Appraiser/Auditor- 903-935-1991; Elections- 903-935-4822; Vital Records- 903-935-8403. **Property tax/Assessor-** PO Box 967, Marshall, TX 75671; 903-935-8411.

Hartley County

County Clerk, PO Box Q, Channing, TX 79018. 806-235-3582; fax-806-235-2316; 8:30AM-N, 1-5PM.
All records in one index. Only the public may search. Copy fee $1.00 per page. Cert fee- $5.00 per doc plus $1.00 per page copy fee. Payee-Hartley County Clerk. **Online to Property, Appraiser, Personal Property records:** Property data free at www.ptax.org/offices/hartley/hartley01.html. Also by download; fees apply; add'l data includes minerals, ofc exports, delinquents; visit www.ptax.org/tax_office_data.htm or phone 201-571-0425. **Other phones:** Treasurer- 806-235-3572; Appraiser/Auditor- 806-365-4515; Elections- 806-235-3582; Vital Records- 806-235-3582; Judge- 806-235-3142. **Property tax/Assessor-** 806-365-4515.

Haskell County

County Clerk, PO Box 725, Haskell, TX 79521-0725. 940-864-2451; fax-940-864-6164; hours: 8AM-5PM.
All records in one index. Records indexed on computer back to 1994. Office personnel or visitors may perform searches. General index search fee $5.00 per name. UCC search per debtor name- $10.00. Separate tax lien search- $10.00 per debtor. Copy fee $1.00 per page. Cert fee- $5.00 per doc plus copy fee. Payee- Haskell County Clerk. **Other phones:** Treasurer- 940-864-3448; Appraiser/Auditor- 940-864-3805; Elections- 940-864-2451; Vital Records- 940-864-2451. **Property tax/Assessor-** 1 Ave. D, Courthouse, Haskell, TX 79521; 940-864-2181.

Hays County

County Clerk, 137 N. Guadalupe; Hays County Records Bldg., San Marcos, TX 78666. 512-393-7329; fax-512-393-7337; hours: 8AM-5PM. www.co.hays.tx.us
Records indexed on a public use terminal back to 1/1/1990. Office personnel or visitors may perform searches. General index search fee $10.00 per name per 10 years. Copy fee $1.00 per page. Cert fee- $5.00 per cert plus copy fee. Payee- Hays County Clerk. **Online access to Appraiser, Property Tax, Probate, Judgment records:** Access probate and judgment records free at http://idocket.com/countycourt.htm. Also, search land record index free at www.texaslandrecords.com. Also, see notes at beginning of section. **Other phones:** Treasurer- 512-393-2236; Appraiser/Auditor- 512-268-2522; Elections- 512-393-7310. **Property tax/Assessor-** 102 N LBJ, San Marcos, TX 78666; 512-393-5545.

Hemphill County

County Clerk, PO Box 867, Canadian, TX 79014. 806-323-6212; hours: 8AM-5PM.
All records in one index. General index search fee $5.00 per name. Copy fee $1.00 per page. Cert fee- $5.00 per cert plus copy fee. Payee- Hemphill County Clerk. **Other phones:** Treasurer- 806-323-6671; Appraiser/Auditor- 806-323-8022; Elections-806-323-6212; Vital Records- 806-323-6212. **Property tax/Assessor-** 400 Main St, Canadian, TX 79014; 806-323-6661.

Henderson County

County Clerk, PO Box 632, Athens, TX 75751-0632. 903-675-6140; fax-903-675-6105; hours: 8AM-5PM.
All records in one index. Records indexed on a public use terminal back to 1967. Office will perform a UCC and Tax lien search but public must search other records themselves. Search fee $5.00. Copy fee $1.00 per page. Cert fee- $5.00 per cert plus copy fee. Payee- Henderson County Clerk. **Online to Property, Appraiser records:** Access property data free at www.hendersoncad.org or at www.myswdata.com/swd_find.aspx. Also, see note at beginning of section. **Other phones:** Treasurer- 903-675-6119; Appraiser/Auditor- 903-675-9296; Elections- 903-675-6140; Vital Records- 903-675-6140. **Property tax/Assessor-** 101 E Tyler, Athens, TX 75751; 903-675-6149.

Hidalgo County

County Clerk, PO Box 58, Edinburg, TX 78540. 956-318-2100; fax-956-318-2105; hours: 7:30AM-5:30PM. www.hidalgo.tx.us.landata.com/
Index: Books, computer. Records indexed on a public use terminal back to 1980. Office personnel or visitors may perform searches. Search fee $11.00. Copy fee $2.00, if real estate $1.00 per page. Cert fee- $5.00 per cert plus copy fee. Payee-Hidalgo County Clerk. **Online access to Appraiser, Property Tax, Probate, Judgment records:** Access probate and judgment records free at http://idocket.com/countycourt.htm. Also, search land record index free at www.texas.landrecords.com. Also, see note at beginning of section. **Other phones:** Appraiser/Auditor- 956-782-2255; Elections- 956-318-2570. **Property tax/Assessor-** 956-318-2180.

Hill County

County Clerk, PO Box 398, Hillsboro, TX 76645. 254-582-4030, R/E recording phone-254-582-2161; fax-254-582-4003; hours: 8AM-5PM.
All records in one index. Records indexed on a public use terminal back to 1993. Office personnel or visitors may perform searches. Search fee $10.00. Copy fee $1.00 per page. Cert fee- $5.00 per cert plus copy fee. Payee- Hill County Clerk. **Online access to Property, Appraiser, Personal Property, Probate, Judgment records:** Access to Appraisal district property records is free at www.hillcad.org/in/reportshome.php. Also, access Appraisal District records free at http://clientdb.trueautomation.com/clientdb/main.asp?id=23. Also, to search probate records and judgment records go to http://idocket.com/countycourt.htm. Also, see note at beginning of section. **Other phones:** Treasurer- 254-582-2632; Appraiser/Auditor- 254-582-2508. **Property tax/Assessor-** PO Box 412, Hillsboro, TX 76645; 254-582-4000.

Hockley County

County Clerk, 800 Houston St, #213, Levelland, TX 79336. 806-894-3185; fax-none; hours: 9AM-5PM. www.co.hockley.tx.us/coclerk.html
Index: Indices arranged by year. Office will perform a UCC search but public must search other records themselves. UCC search per debtor name- $10.00. Federal/state combined tax lien search- $14.00 per debtor. Copy fee $1.00 per page. Cert fee- $5.00 per cert plus copy fee. Payee-Hockley County Clerk. **Online access to Appraiser, Property records:** Access to property records from the Appraisal District to be online 9/2005; call 806-894-9654 for info. **Other phones:** Treasurer- 806-894-3718; Appraiser/Auditor- 806-894-9654; Elections-806-894-3185; Vital Records- 806-894-3185. **Property tax/Assessor-** 802 Houston St, #106, Levelland, TX 79336; 806-894-4938.

Hood County

County Clerk, PO Box 339, Granbury, TX 76048-0339. 817-579-3222; fax-817-579-3227; hours: 8AM-5PM.
Separate indices to search include before 1996 recorded in deed records, after 1996 real records, deeds, leases, deed trust, assignments, etc. Records indexed on a public use terminal back to 1982. Office personnel or visitors may perform searches. General index search fee $5.00 per name. Copy fee $1.00 per page. Cert fee- $5.00 per cert plus copy fee. Payee- Hood County Clerk. **Online access to Appraiser, Property Tax records:** Search the county appraisal roll for free at www.hoodcad.org. Also, see note at beginning of section. **Other phones:** Treasurer- 817-579-3208; Appraiser/Auditor- 817-573-2471; Elections- 817-408-3455; Vital Records- 817-408-3455. **Property tax/Assessor-** 100 Gordon St, Granbury, TX 76048; 817-579-3295.

Hopkins County

County Clerk, PO Box 288, Sulphur Springs, TX 75483. 903-438-4074, R/E recording phone-903-885-4074, UCC recording phone-903-438-4074; fax-903-438-4110; hours: 8AM-5PM. www.hopkinscountytx.org
All records in one index. Only the public may search. Copy fee $2.00, if tax lien or real estate $1.00 per page. Cert fee- $5.00 per cert plus copy fee. Payee- Hopkins County Clerk. **Other phones:** Treasurer- 903-438-4003; Appraiser/Auditor- 903-885-2173; Elections- 903-438-4074; Vital Records- 903-438-4074; Voter Registrar- 903-438-4063. **Property tax/Assessor-** 903-438-4063.

Houston County

County Clerk, PO Box 370, Crockett, TX 75835-0370. 936-544-3255, R/E recording phone-936-544-3255 x241; fax-936-544-1954; hours: 8AM-4:30PM.
All records in one index. Office personnel or visitors may perform searches. Search fee $10.00 per name. Copy fee $1.00 per page. Cert fee- $5.00 per cert plus copy fee. Payee- Houston County Clerk. **Other phones:** Treasurer- 936-544-3255 x236; Appraiser/Auditor- 936-544-9655; Elections- 936-544-3255 x241; Vital Records- 936-544-3255 x241. **Property tax/Assessor-** 401 E Golird #101, Crockett, TX 75835; 936-544-2761.

Howard County

County Clerk, PO Box 1468, Big Spring, TX 79721-1468. 432-264-2213, UCC recording phone-432-264-2214; fax-432-264-2215; hours: 8AM-5PM. www.howard-county.net
All records in one index. Records indexed on a public use terminal back to 1983. Search fee $5.00 per name per instrument. Will do very limited searches of real estate records. UCC and tax lien searches are separate. Copy fee $1.00 per page; $5.00 minimum. Tax lien copy- $2.00 per name. Cert fee- $5.00 per cert plus copy fee. Payee- Howard County Clerk. **Other phones:** Treasurer-432-264-2218; Appraiser/Auditor- 432-263-8301; Elections- 432-264-2214; Vital Records- 432-264-2214. **Property tax/Assessor-** PO Box 1111, Big Springs,Tx 79721-1111; 432-264-2232.

Hudspeth County

County Clerk, PO Drawer 58, Sierra Blanca, TX 79851. 915-369-2301; fax-915-369-0055; 8AM-N, 1-5PM.
All records in one index. Records indexed on a public use terminal back to 1986. Office personnel or visitors may perform searches. Search fee $5.00 per name. Will search real estate records. Will search UCC records prior to 7/2001 and current fixture (land) files. UCC search per debtor name- $10.00. Federal/state combined tax lien search is available. Copy fee $1.00 per page. Cert fee- $5.00 per doc plus copy fee. Payee- County Clerk. **Other phones:** Treasurer- 915-369-3511; Appraiser/Auditor- 915-369-4118; Elections- 915-369-2301; Vital Records- 915-369-2301; Auditor- 915-369-4147. **Property tax/Assessor-** PO Box 158, Sierra Blanca, TX 79851; 915-369-2331.

Hunt County

County Clerk, PO Box 1316, Greenville, TX 75403-1316. 903-408-4130; fax-none; hours: 8AM-5PM. www.huntcounty.net
Office personnel or visitors may perform searches. Search fee $10.00 per name/debtor. Will not search real estate records. Copy fee $1.00 per page. Cert fee- $5.00 per cert plus copy fee. Payee- Hunt County Clerk. **Online access to Appraiser, Property Tax, Sheriff Sale records:** Access property tax data and sheriff sales data free at www.hctax.info/. Also, see notes at beginning of section. **Other phones:** Treasurer- 903-408-4171; Appraiser/Auditor- 903-408-3510; Elections- 903-454-5467; Vital Records- 903-408-4130. **Property tax/Assessor-** 2500 Stonewall St, Greenville, TX 75401; 903-408-4000.

Hutchinson County

County Clerk, PO Box 1186, Stinnett, TX 79083. 806-878-4002; fax-806-878-3497; hours: 9AM-5PM.
Only the public may search. Copy fee $1.00 per page. Cert fee- $5.00 per cert plus copy fee. Payee- Hutchinson County Clerk. **Other phones:** Treasurer- 806-878-4010; Appraiser/Auditor- 806-274-2294; Elections- 806-878-4002; Vital Records- 806-878-4002. **Property tax/Assessor-** PO Box 989, Stinnett, TX 79083; 806-878-4005.

Irion County

County Clerk, PO Box 736, Mertzon, TX 76941-0736. 325-835-2421; fax-325-835-2008; hours: 8AM-N; 1PM-5PM.
All records in one index. Record index not computerized. Office personnel (office searches names only), or visitors may perform searches. General index search fee $5.00 per name. Copy fee $1.00 per page. Cert fee- $5.00 per doc plus copy fee. Payee- Irion County Clerk. **Other phones:** Treasurer- 325-835-4111; Appraiser/Auditor- 325-835-3551; Elections- 325-835-2421; Vital Records- 325-835-2421. **Property tax/Assessor-** PO Box 859, Mertzon, TX 76941; 325-835-7771.

Jack County

County Clerk, 100 Main St, Jacksboro, TX 76458. 940-567-2111; hours: 8AM-5PM.
Search fee $5.00 per name. Will not search real estate records. Copy fee $1.00 per page; UCC copy $1.00 per page. Cert fee- $5.00 per cert plus copy fee. Payee- Jack County Clerk. **Other phones:** Treasurer- 940-567-2251; Appraiser/Auditor- 940-567-6301; Elections- 940-567-2111; Vital Records- 940-567-2111. **Property tax/Assessor-** same address as above. 940-567-2352.

Jackson County

County Clerk, 115 W. Main, Rm 101, Edna, TX 77957. 361-782-3563; fax-361-782-3132; 8AM-N, 1-4PM.
Separate indices to search include Grantor/Grantee back to 1/1993, also various year indexes back to 1918. Office will perform a UCC search but public must search other records themselves. UCC search per debtor name- $10.00. Will search liens for $5.00 per debtor name. Copy fee $1.00 per page. Cert fee- $5.00 per cert plus copy fee. Payee-Jackson County Clerk. **Online access to Real Estate, Grantor/Grantee, Deed, Lien, Judgment records:** Access recording records free at www.titlex.com; select Jackson county.Records range is 1/1993 to 9/2004. Also, see note at beginning of section. **Other phones:** Treasurer- 361-782-3402; Appraiser/Auditor- 361-782-7115; Elections- 361-782-3563; Vital Records- 361-782-3563. **Property tax/Assessor-** 361-782-3473.

Jasper County

County Clerk, PO Box 2070, Jasper, TX 75951. 409-384-2632; fax-409-384-7198; hours: 8AM-4:30PM.
All records in one index. Records indexed on a public use terminal back to 1987. Office personnel or visitors may perform searches. Search fee $10.00 per name. Copy fee $1.00 per page. Cert fee- $5.00. Payee- County Clerk. **Other phones:** Treasurer- 409-384-2461; Appraiser/Auditor- 409-384-2544; Elections- 409-384-3399; Vital Records- 409-384-2632. **Property tax/Assessor-** 409-384-6896.

Jeff Davis County

County Clerk, PO Box 398, Fort Davis, TX 79734. 432-426-3251; fax-432-426-3760; hours: 9AM-N, 1-5PM.
All records in one index. Office will perform a UCC or combined tax lien search but public must search other records themselves. UCC or tax lien search per debtor name- $10.00. Copy fee $1.00 per page. Cert fee- $5.00 per doc plus copy fee. Payee- County Clerk. **Other phones:** Treasurer- 432-426-3242; Appraiser/Auditor- 432-857-3333 or 426-3210. **Property tax/Assessor-** 432-426-3213.

Jefferson County

County Clerk, PO Box 1151, Beaumont, TX 77704-1151. 409-835-8475; fax-409-839-2394; hours: 8AM-5PM. www.co.jefferson.tx.us
Separate indices to search include Official Public Records, assumed names, marriages, criminal, misdemeanors, probate, civil, UCC's. Office will perform a UCC search but public must search other records themselves. Search fee $10.00 per name. UCC search request using non-standard form (per name)- $25.00. Will do a federal tax lien search if requested. Copy fee $1.00 per page. Cert fee- $5.00 per cert plus copy fee. Payee- Jefferson County Clerk. **Online access to Recording, Deed, Lien, Judgment, Property Tax, Marriage, UCC, Assumed Name records:** Access the recorder database free at http://jeffersontxclerk.hartintercivic.com. Recording index goes back to 1983; images to 1983. Marriages go back to 1995; UCCs to 7/2001. Also, access property tax records free at www.jcad.org/search/. Also, see note at beginning of section. **Other phones:** Treasurer- 409-835-8509; Appraiser/Auditor- 409-835-4611; Elections- 409-835-8760; Vital Records- 409-835-8475. **Property tax/Assessor-** 409-835-8516.

Jim Hogg County

County Clerk, PO Box 878, Hebbronville, TX 78361. 361-527-4031; fax-361-527-5843; hours: 9AM-5PM.
All records in one index. General index search fee $15.00 per search. Will search real estate records. Will search UCC records prior to 7/2001 and current fixture (land) files. Copy fee $1.00 per page. Cert fee- $5.00 per doc plus copy fee. Payee- Jim Hogg- County Clerk. **Online access to Real Estate Recording, Deed records:** Access recording office land data at www.etitlesearch.com; registration required, fee based on usage. **Other phones:** Treasurer- 361-527-3164; Appraiser/Auditor- 361-527-4033; Elections- 361-527-4031; Vital Records- 361-527-4031. **Property tax/Assessor-** 361-527-5847.

Jim Wells County

County Clerk, PO Box 1459, Alice, TX 78333. 361-668-5702; fax-361-668-8671; 8AM-N, 1-5PM.
All records in one index. Office personnel or visitors may perform searches. Search fee $10.00 per name. Will not search real estate records. Will search UCC records prior to 7/2001 and current fixture (land) files. Will search tax liens. Copy fee $1.00 per page. Cert fee- $5.00 per cert plus copy fee. Payee-Jim Wells County Clerk. **Online access to Real Estate Recording, Deed records:** Access recording office land data at www.etitlesearch.com; registration required, fee based on usage. **Other phones:** Treasurer- 361-668-5713; Appraiser/Auditor- 361-668-9656. **Property tax/Assessor-** 200 N Almond St, Alice, TX 78332; 361-668-5711.

Johnson County

County Clerk, PO Box 1056, Cleburne, TX 76033-0662. 817-556-6314, R/E recording phone-817-556-6313; fax-817-556-6326; hours: 8AM-N, 1-4:30PM. www.johnsoncountytx.org
All records in one index. Search fee $5.00 unless otherwise indicated. Will search UCC records prior to 7/2001 and current fixture (land) files. UCC search includes tax liens if requested. UCC search per debtor name- $10.00. Copy fee $1.00 per page. Cert fee- $5.00 per doc, copies not included. **Online access to Appraiser, Property Tax, Deed, Marriage, UCC, Probate, Judgment records:** Records from the County Appraiser are free at www.johnsoncountytaxoffice.org/vinelink Also, to search probate records and judgment records go to http://idocket.com/countycourt.htm. Also, see note at beginning of section. **Other phones:** Treasurer- 817-566-6340; Appraiser/Auditor- 817-558-8100; Elections- 817-556-6197; Vital Records- 817-556-6191. **Property tax/Assessor-** 817-556-6100.

Jones County

County Clerk, PO Box 552, Anson, TX 79501-0552. 325-823-3762; fax-325-823-4223; hours: 8AM-5PM.
Separate indices to search. Records indexed on a public use terminal back to 1991. Search fee $5.00 per name. Will not search real estate records. Copy fee $1.00 per page. Cert fee- $5.00 per doc. Payee- Jones County Clerk. **Other phones:** Treasurer- 325-823-3742; Appraiser/Auditor- 325-823-2422; Elections- 325-823-3762; Vital Records- 325-823-3762. **Property tax/Assessor-** 325-823-2437.

Karnes County

County Clerk, 101 N. Panna Maria Ave.; Courthouse - #9, Karnes City, TX 78118-2929. 830-780-3938; fax-830-780-4576; hours: 8AM-5PM.
Separate indices to search. Search fee $10.00 per name. Will not search real estate records. Will search UCC records prior to 7/2001 and current fixture (land) files. Tax liens not included in UCC search. Tax lien searches are available. UCC search request using non-standard form (per name)- $25.00. Copy fee $5.00 per doc. Cert fee- $1.00 per page plus copy fee. Payee- Karnes County Clerk. **Online access to Property, Appraiser records:** Access property data by download from a private company; fees apply; add'l data includes minerals, ofc exports, delinquents; visit www.ptax.org/tax_office_data.htm or phone 201-571-0425. **Other phones:** Treasurer- 830-780-2312; Appraiser/Auditor- 830-780-2433; Elections- 830-780-3938; Vital Records- 830-780-3938. **Property**

tax/Assessor- 200 E Culvert, Karnes City, TX 78118; 830-780-2431.

Kaufman County

County Clerk, Courthouse, Kaufman, TX 75142. 972-932-4331; fax-972-932-7628; hours: 8AM-5PM. www.kaufmancounty.net

Separate indices to search include computer, grantor, grantee, book. Records indexed on a public use terminal back to 1968. General index search fee $10.00 per name. Will search real estate records. Copy fee $1.00 per page. Cert fee- $6.00 1st page, $2.00 each add'l page, includes copy fee. Payee- Kaufman County Clerk. **Online access to Real Estate, Grantor/Grantee, Deed, Lien, Judgment, Appraiser, Property Tax records:** Access recording records free at www.titlex.com; select Kaufman county.Records range is 3/1/1969 to within a month of present. Also, see note at beginning of section. Also, search land records at www.texaslandrecords.com; a free search is allowed; later, signup or one-day pass is required. Also, search appraisal roll data free at www.kaufmancad.org and at http://clientdb.trueautomation.com/clientdb/main.asp?id =36. **Other phones:** Treasurer- 972-932-4331; Appraiser/Auditor- 972-932-6081; Elections- 972-932-4331; Vital Records- 972-932-4331. **Property tax/Assessor**- 972-932-4331.

Kendall County

County Clerk, 201 E. San Antonio, #127, Boerne, TX 78006. 830-249-9343; fax-830-249-3472; hours: 8AM-5PM.

All records in one index. Records indexed on a public use terminal back to 1983. Office personnel or visitors may perform searches. Search fee $5.00. Copy fee $1.00 per page. Cert fee- $5.00 per cert plus copy fee. Payee- Kendall County Clerk. **Online access to Real Estate, Grantor/Grantee, Deed, Lien, Judgment, Appraiser, Property Tax records:** Access recording records free at www.titlex.com; select Kendall county. Also see note at beginning of section. **Other phones:** Treasurer- 830-249-9343; Appraiser/Auditor- 830-249-8012; Elections- 830-249-9343; Vital Records- 830-249-9343. **Property tax/Assessor**- same address as above. 830-249-9343.

Kenedy County

County Clerk, PO Box 227, Sarita, TX 78385-0227. 361-294-5220; fax-361-294-5218; hours: 8:30AM-N, 1-4:30PM.

Separate indices to search include official records, liens, probate, courts. Record index not computerized. Search fee $5.00 per name. Copy fee $1.00 per page. Cert fee- $5.00 per cert plus copy fee. Payee- Kenedy County Clerk. **Other phones:** Treasurer- 361-294-5304; Appraiser/Auditor- 361-321-1695; Elections- 361-294-5220; Vital Records- 361-294-5220. **Property tax/Assessor**- PO Box 129, Sarita, TX 78385-0129; 361-294-5202.

Kent County

County Clerk, PO Box 9, Jayton, TX 79528-0009. 806-237-3881; fax-806-237-2632; hours: 8:30AM-N, 1-5PM. www.co.kent.tx.us

All records in one index. Records indexed on computer back to 1990. Office personnel or visitors may perform searches. General index search fee $5.00 per name per instrument. Copy fee $1.00 per page. Cert fee- $5.00 per cert plus copy fee. Payee- Kent County Clerk. **Other phones:** Treasurer- 806-237-3075; Appraiser/Auditor- 806-237-3036; Elections- 806-237-3881; Vital Records- 806-237-3881. **Property tax/Assessor**- 100 N Main St, Jayton, TX 79528; 806-237-3801.

Kerr County

County Clerk, 700 Main St; Courthouse, Rm 122, Kerrville, TX 78028-5389. 830-792-2255; fax-830-792-2274; hours: 8AM-5PM. www.co.kerr.tx.us/

All records in one index. Only the public may search. Copy fee $1.00 per page. Cert fee- $5.00

per doc plus copy fee. **Online access to Appraiser, Property Tax, Real Estate, Recorder records:** Access to recorder land data is to be available in 2005 at www.kerr.tx.us.landata.com. Search index after free registration; fee required for full benefits. Also, see note at beginning of section. **Other phones:** Treasurer- 830-792-2275; Appraiser/Auditor- 830-895-5223; Elections- 830-792-2255; Vital Records- 830-792-2255. **Property tax/Assessor**- 700 Main St, Courthouse, Kerrville, TX 78028; 830-792-2242.

Kimble County

County Clerk, 501 Main St, Junction, TX 76849. 325-446-3353; fax-325-446-2986; 8AM-N, 1-5PM.

Separate indices to search include Deed, DT, Abstract, Federal Lien, State Lien, Hospital Lien, Lis Penden, District Min., County Min, etc. Only the public may search. Copy fee $1.00 per page. Cert fee- $5.00 per cert plus copy fees. Payee- Kimble County Clerk. **Other phones:** Treasurer- 325-446-2847; Appraiser/Auditor- 325-446-3717; Elections- 325-446-3353; Vital Records- 325-446-3353. **Property tax/Assessor**- 325-446-3717.

King County

County Clerk, PO Box 135, Guthrie, TX 79236. 806-596-4412; fax-806-596-4664; 9AM-N, 1-5PM.

All records in one index. General index search fee $5.00 per book. Will search real estate records. Will search UCC records prior to 7/2001 and current fixture (land) files. Tax liens not included in UCC search. Copy fee $1.00 per page. Cert fee- $5.00 per cert plus copy fee. Payee- King County Clerk. **Other phones:** Treasurer- 806-596-4319; Appraiser/Auditor- 806-596-4588; Elections- 806-596-4412; Vital Records- 806-596-4412. **Property tax/Assessor**- 806-596-4318.

Kinney County

County Clerk, PO Drawer 9, Brackettville, TX 78832. 830-563-2521; fax-830-563-2644; 8AM-N; 1-5PM.

All records in one index. Records indexed on computer back to 1996. Office personnel or visitors may perform searches. Search fee $5.00 per name. Copy fee $1.00 per page. Cert fee- $5.00 per page plus copy fee. Payee- County Clerk. **Other phones:** Treasurer- 830-563-2777; Appraiser/Auditor- 830-563-2323; Elections- 830-563-2521; Vital Records- 830-563-2521. **Property tax/Assessor**- 830-563-2688.

Kleberg County

County Clerk, PO Box 1327, Kingsville, TX 78364-1327. 361-595-8548; fax-361-593-1355; hours: 8AM-5PM. www.klebergcad.org

All records in one index. Records indexed on a public use terminal back to 1994. Office will perform a UCC search but public must search other records themselves. Search fee $5.00. Copy fee $1.00 per page. Cert fee- $5.00 per cert plus copy fee. Payee- Kleberg County Clerk. **Online access to Appraisal, Property, Property Tax, Probate, Judgment records:** Access to county appraisal rolls and property data is free at www.klebergcad.org/search_appr.php. Also, to search probate records and judgment records go to http://idocket.com/countycourt.htm. Also, see note at beginning of section. **Other phones:** Treasurer- 361-595-8535; Appraiser/Auditor- 361-595-5775; Elections- 361-595-8548; Vital Records- 361-595-8548. **Property tax/Assessor**- PO Box 1457, Kingsville, TX 78363; 361-595-8542.

Knox County

County Clerk, PO Box 196, Benjamin, TX 79505. 940-454-2441, R/E recording phone-940-459-2441; fax-940-454-2005; hours: 8AM-12, 1-5PM.

All records in one index. Record index not computerized. Office personnel or visitors may perform searches. Search fee $5.00 per name. Will not search real estate records. Copy fee $1.00 per page. Cert fee- $5.00 per doc plus copy fee. Payee- Knox County Clerk. **Online access to Real Estate,**

Grantor/Grantee, Deed, Lien, Judgment records: Access recording records free at www.titlex.com; select Knox county. **Other phones:** Treasurer- 817-459-2251; Appraiser/Auditor- 940-459-3891; Elections- 940-459-2441; Vital Records- 940-459-2441. **Property tax/Assessor**- PO Box 47, Benjamin, TX 79505; 940-459-2411.

La Salle County

County Clerk, 101 Courthouse Squ #107, Cotulla, TX 78014. 830-879-4432; fax-830-879-2933; hours: 8AM-12; 1PM-5PM.

All records in one index. Only the office personnel may search. Search fee $5.00 unless otherwise indicated. Will not search real estate records. Will search UCC records prior to 7/2001 and current fixture (land) files. Copy fee $1.00 per page. Cert fee- $5.00 per cert, does not include copy fee. Payee- LaSalle Co Clerk. **Online access to Property, Appraiser, Real Estate Recording, Deed records:** Access property data by download from a private company; fees apply; add'l data includes minerals, ofc exports, delinquents; visit www.ptax.org/tax_office_data.htm or phone 201-571-0425. Also, access recording office land data at www.etitlesearch.com; registration required, fee based on usage. **Other phones:** Treasurer- 830-879-4440; Appraiser/Auditor- 830-879-2547; Elections- 830-879-4432; Vital Records- 830-879-4432. **Property tax/Assessor**- PO Box 737, Cotulla, TX 78014; 830-879-4437.

Lamar County

County Clerk, 119 N. Main #109; Courthouse, Paris, TX 75460. 903-737-2420; fax-903-782-1100; hours: 8AM-5PM.

Will not search real estate records. Will search UCC records prior to 7/2001 and current fixture (land) files. Tax liens not included in UCC search. UCC search per debtor name- $10.00. UCC search request using non-standard form (per name)- $25.00. Separate federal tax lien search- $10.00 per debtor. Separate state tax lien search- $10.00 per debtor. Federal/state combined tax lien search- $10.00 per search. Copy fee $1.00 per page. Cert fee- $5.00 per cert plus copy fee. Payee- Lamar County Clerk. **Online access to Property, Appraiser, Inmate, Sheriff Bond, Sex Offender, Death records:** Access Appraisal District records free at http://clientdb.trueautomation.com/clientdb/main.asp?id =7. Access to the sheriff's sex offender registry is free at www.lcsom.com/disclaimer.html. Cemetery records in Lamar County are free at http://userdb.rootsweb.com/cemeteries/TX/Lamar.

Also, State sex offender site is http://66.165.115.117/, also if you click on county judicial records search can search for criminal and civil records in Lamar county. **Other phones:** Treasurer- 903-737-2418; Appraiser/Auditor- 903-785-7822; Elections- 903-737-2420; Vital Records- 903-737-2420. **Property tax/Assessor**- 903-785-7822.

Lamb County

County Clerk, 100 6th Dr.; Rm 103 Box 3, Littlefield, TX 79339-3366. 806-385-4222 x210, R/E recording phone-806-385-4222; fax-806-385-6485; hours: 8:30AM-5PM.

All records in one index. Records indexed on computer back to 1989. Office will perform a UCC search but public must search other records themselves. UCC search per debtor name- $1.00. Federal tax lien search- $10.00; state lien-$5.00 per debtor. Copy fee $1.00 per page. Cert fee- $5.00 per cert plus copy fee. Payee- Lamb County Clerk. **Online access to Appraiser, Property Tax records:** Access Appraisal District records free at http://clientdb.trueautomation.com/clientdb/main.asp?id =44. Also see note at beginning of section. **Other phones:** Treasurer- 806-385-3770; Appraiser/Auditor- 806-385-6474; Elections- 806-385-4222; Vital Records- 806-385-4222. **Property tax/Assessor**- 100 6th Dr. #105, Littlefield, TX 79339; 806-385-4222.

Lampasas County

County Clerk, PO Box 347, Lampasas, TX 76550. 512-556-8271; hours: 8AM-5PM.
Record index not computerized. Office will perform a UCC and Tax lien search but public must search other records themselves. Search fee $5.00. Copy fee $1.00 per page. Cert fee- $5.00 per cert plus copy fee. Payee- Lampasas County Clerk. **Other phones:** Treasurer- 512-556-8058; Appraiser/Auditor- 512-556-8058. **Property tax/Assessor-** 512-556-8271.

Lavaca County

County Clerk, PO Box 326, Hallettsville, TX 77964-0326. 361-798-3612; fax-361-798-1610; hours: 8AM-5PM.
Separate indices to search. Only the public may search. Copy fee $1.00 per page. Cert fee- $5.00 per cert plus copy fee. Payee- Lavaca County Clerk. **Other phones:** Treasurer- 361-798-2181; Appraiser/Auditor- 361-798-4396; Elections- 361-798-3612; Vital Records- 361-798-3612. **Property tax/Assessor-** PO Box 293, Hallettsville, TX 77964; 361-798-3601.

Lee County

County Clerk, PO Box 419, Giddings, TX 78942. 979-542-3684; fax-979-542-2623; hours: 8AM-5PM.
All records in one index. Only the public may search. Copy fee $1.00 per page. Cert fee- $5.00 per cert plus copy fee. Payee- Lee County Clerk. **Online access to Property, Appraiser records:** Access Appraisal District records free at http://clientdb.trueautomation.com/clientdb/main.asp?id=9. **Other phones:** Treasurer- 979-542-2161; Appraiser/Auditor- 979-542-9618; Elections- 979-542-3684; Vital Records- 979-542-3684. **Property tax/Assessor-** 170 E Industry, Giddings, TX 78942; 979-542-2640.

Leon County

County Clerk, PO Box 98, Centerville, TX 75833. 903-536-2352; hours: 8AM-5PM.
All records in one index. Only the public may search. Copy fee $1.00 per page. Cert fee- $5.00. Payee- Leon County Clerk. **Online access to Property, Appraiser records:** Access property data by download from a private company; fees apply; add'l data includes minerals, ofc exports, delinquents; visit www.ptax.org/tax_office_data.htm or phone 201-571-0425. **Other phones:** Treasurer- 903-536-2915; Appraiser/Auditor- 903-536-2252; Elections- 903-536-2352; Vital Records- 903-536-2352. **Property tax/Assessor-** PO Box 37, Centerville, TX 75833; 903-536-2543.

Liberty County

County Clerk, PO Box 369, Liberty, TX 77575. 936-336-4670, R/E recording phone-409-336-4674; hours: 8AM-5PM.
Separate indices to search include all records from 1983 to present on computer, records prior to 1983 indexed alphabetically by year. Office personnel or visitors may perform searches. Search fee $10.00 per name. Copy fee $1.00 per page. Cert fee- $5.00 per cert plus copy fee. Payee- Liberty County Clerk. **Online access to Appraiser, Property Tax records:** See note at beginning of section. **Other phones:** Appraiser/Auditor- 409-336-5722. **Property tax/Assessor-** 936-336-4629.

Limestone County

County Clerk, PO Box 350, Groesbeck, TX 76642. 254-729-5504, R/E recording phone-254-729-3009; fax-254-729-2951; hours: 8AM-5PM.
Records indexed on a public use terminal back to 1985. Office personnel or visitors may perform searches. Search fee $10.00. Copy fee $1.00 per page. Cert fee- $5.00 per cert plus copy fee. Payee- Limestone County Clerk. **Online access to Appraiser, Property Tax records:** See notes at beginning of section. **Other phones:** Treasurer- 254-

729-3314; Appraiser/Auditor- 254-729-5504. **Property tax/Assessor-** 254-729-3405.

Lipscomb County

County Clerk, PO Box 70, Lipscomb, TX 79056. 806-862-3091; fax-806-862-3004; 8AM-12 1PM-5PM.
Records indexed on computer back to 1999. Office personnel or visitors may perform searches. General index search fee $10.00 per name. Copy fee $1.00 per page. Cert fee- $5.00 per page plus copy fee. Payee- Lipscomb County Clerk. **Online access to Property, Appraiser records:** Access property data by download from a private company; fees apply; add'l data includes minerals, ofc exports, delinquents; visit www.ptax.org/tax_office_data.htm or phone 201-571-0425. **Other phones:** Treasurer- 806-862-3821; Appraiser/Auditor- 806-624-2881. **Property tax/Assessor-** PO Box 147, Lipscomb, TX 79056; 806-862-2911.

Live Oak County

County Clerk, PO Box 280, George West, TX 78022. 361-449-2733 x3, R/E recording phone-361-449-2733, UCC recording phone-361-449-2733 x103 or 129; hours: 8AM-N, 1-5PM.
All records in one index. Records indexed on computer back to 3/4/2004. Office will perform a UCC and Tax lien search but public must search other records themselves. Search fee $10.00. Copy fee $1.00 per page. Cert fee- $5.00 per cert plus copy fee. Payee- Live Oak County Clerk. **Other phones:** Treasurer- 361-449-2641 x109; Appraiser/Auditor- 361-449-2641; Elections- 361-449-2733 x129 or 103; Vital Records- 361-449-2733 x129 or 103. **Property tax/Assessor-** PO Box 519, George West, TX 78022; 361-449-2733.

Llano County

County Clerk, PO Box 40, Llano, TX 78643-0040. 325-247-4455; fax-325-247-2406; hours: 8AM-5PM.
All records in one index. Records indexed on a public use terminal back to 1988. Office will perform a UCC search but public must search other records themselves. Will not search real estate records. UCC search per debtor name- $15.00. UCC search request using non-standard form (per name)- $25.00. Copy fee $1.00 per page. Cert fee- $5.00 per cert plus copy fee. Payee- Llano County Clerk. **Online access to Appraiser, Property Tax records:** See note at beginning of section. **Other phones:** Treasurer- 325-247-7743; Appraiser/Auditor- 325-247-3065. **Property tax/Assessor-** 325-247-4165.

Loving County

County Clerk, PO Box 194, Mentone, TX 79754. 432-377-2441; fax-432-377-2701; 9AM-N, 1-5PM.
All records in one index. Office will perform a UCC or tax lien search but public must search other records themselves. UCC search per debtor name- $15.00. Separate tax lien search fee-$2.00 per debtor. Copy fee $1.00 per page. Cert fee- $5.00 per doc plus copy fee. Payee- County Clerk. **Other phones:** Treasurer- 432-377-2311; Appraiser/Auditor- 432-377-2201; Elections- 432-377-2441; Vital Records- 432-377-2441. **Property tax/Assessor-** 432-377-2411.

Lubbock County

County Clerk, PO Box 10536, Lubbock, TX 79408-0536. 806-775-1060; fax-806-775-1660; hours: 8:30AM-5PM. www.co.lubbock.tx.us
Separate indices to search. Records indexed on a public use terminal back to 1974. Only the public may search except for Federal tax liens. Search fee $10.00 per name. Copy fee $1.00 per page. Cert fee- $5.00 per doc plus copy fee. Payee- Lubbock County Clerk. **Online access to Election, Appraiser, Property Tax records:** Access to the county clerks records is limited to election results at www.co.lubbock.tx.us/CClerk/county_clerk.htm. Also, search the property appraiser database for free at www.lubbockcad.org/Appraisal/PublicAccess/. **Other**

phones: Treasurer- 806-775-1018; Appraiser/Auditor- 806-762-5000; Elections- 806-775-1339; Vital Records- 806-775-2926 (birth/death), 806-775-1054(marriage); Tax Assessor- 806-775-1344; State Comtroller -806-762-5000. **Assessor-** 1715 26th St (PO Box 10568), Lubbock, TX 79408.

Lynn County

County Clerk, PO Box 937, Tahoka, TX 79373. 806-561-4750; fax-806-561-4988; hours: 8:30AM-5PM.
All records in one index. Office will perform a UCC search but public must search other records themselves. Search fee $10.00. Copy fee $1.00 per page. Cert fee- $5.00 per cert plus copy fee. Payee- Lynn County Clerk. **Other phones:** Treasurer- 806-561-4055; Appraiser/Auditor- 806-561-5477; Elections- 806-561-4750; Vital Records- 806-561-4750. **Property tax/Assessor-** PO Box 1205, Tahoka, TX 79373; 806-561-4112.

Madison County

County Clerk, 101 W. Main; Rm 102, Madisonville, TX 77864. 936-348-2638; fax-936-348-5858; hours: 8AM-4:30PM.
All records in one index. Records indexed on a public use terminal back to 1979. Office will perform a UCC and Tax lien search but public must search other records themselves. Search fee $10.00. Copy fee $1.00 per page. Cert fee- $5.00 per cert plus copy fee. Payee- Madison County Clerk. **Online access to Property records:** For a land records search go to www.texaslandrecords.com. **Other phones:** Treasurer- 936-348-5141; Appraiser/Auditor- 936-348-2783; Elections- 936-348-2638; Vital Records- 936-348-2638. **Property tax/Assessor-** PO Box 417, Madisonville, TX 77864; 936-348-2654.

Marion County

County Clerk, PO Box 763, Jefferson, TX 75657. 903-665-3971; fax-903-665-8732; 8AM-N, 1-5PM.
All records in one index. Office personnel or visitors may perform searches. Search fee $5.00 per name. Real estate owner, mortgage, and property transfer searches available if not busy. UCC search per debtor name- $16.00. Copy fee $1.00 per page. UCC copy $2.00 per page. Cert fee- $5.00 per cert plus copy fee. Payee- Marion County Clerk. **Online access to Real Estate, Grantor/Grantee, Deed, Lien, Judgment records:** Access recording records free at www.titlex.com; select Marion county. **Other phones:** Treasurer- 903-665-2472; Appraiser/Auditor- 903-665-2519; Elections- 903-665-3971; Vital Records- 903-665-3971. **Property tax/Assessor-** 114 W Austin #100, Jefferson, TX 75657; 903-665-3281.

Martin County

County Clerk, PO Box 906, Stanton, TX 79782. 432-756-3412; fax-432-607-2212; hours: 8AM-5PM.
Separate indices to search. Record index not computerized. Office will perform a UCC search but public must search other records themselves. UCC search includes tax liens if requested. UCC search per debtor name- $10.00. Separate tax lien search- $10.00 per debtor. Copy fee $1.00 per page. Cert fee- $5.00 per cert plus copy fee. Payee- Martin County Clerk. **Other phones:** Treasurer- 432-756-3631; Appraiser/Auditor- 432-756-2823; Elections- 432-756-3412; Vital Records- 432-756-3412. **Property tax/Assessor-** 432-756-3397.

Mason County

County Clerk, PO Box 702, Mason, TX 76856-0702. 325-347-5253; fax-325-347-6868; 8AM-N, 1-4PM.
Office personnel or visitors may perform searches. Search fee $10.00 per name. Will not search real estate records. Copy fee $2.00, if tax lien or real estate $1.00 per page. Cert fee- $5.00 per cert plus copy fee. Payee- Mason County Clerk. **Other phones:** Treasurer- 325-347-5251; Appraiser/Auditor- 325-347-5989; Elections- 325-347-5253; Vital Records- 325-347-5253. **Property tax/Assessor-** 325-347-6937.

Matagorda County

County Clerk, 1700 7th St, Rm 202, Bay City, TX 77414. 979-244-7680; fax-979-244-7688; hours: 8AM-5PM. www.co.matagorda.tx.us/
All records in one index. Records indexed on a public use terminal back to 1987. Office personnel or visitors may perform searches. Search fee $5.00 per name. Copy fee $1.00 per page. Cert fee-$5.00 per doc plus copy fee. Payee- County Clerk. **Online access to Property, Appraiser records:** Access to Appraisal District records is free at http://clientdb.trueautomation.com/clientdb/main.asp?id=25. **Other phones:** Treasurer- 979-244-7609; Appraiser/Auditor- 979-244-2031; Elections- 979-244-7680; Vital Records- 979-244-7680. **Property tax/Assessor-** 979-244-7670.

Maverick County

County Clerk, 500 Quarry St, #2, Eagle Pass, TX 78852. 830-773-2829; fax-830-752-4479; hours: 8AM-5PM. www.maverickcounty.org
All records in one index. Records indexed on a public use terminal back to 1992. Office personnel or visitors may perform searches. Search fee $10.00 per name. Will not search real estate records. Copy fee $2.00, if tax lien or real estate $1.00 per page. Cert fee- $5.00 per cert plus copy fee. Payee-Maverick County Clerk. **Online access to Appraiser, Property Tax records:** Access to county CAD property data is free at http://clientdb.trueautomation.com/clientdb/main.asp?id=19. Also, see note at beginning of section. **Other phones:** Treasurer- 830-773-2413; Appraiser/Auditor- 830-773-0255; Elections- 830-757-4175; Vital Records- 830-773-2829. **Property tax/Assessor-** 830-773-9273.

McCulloch County

County Clerk, Courthouse, Brady, TX 76825. 325-597-0733; fax-325-597-1731; 8AM-12; 1PM-5PM.
Records indexed on computer back to 1995. Only the public may search. Federal/state combined tax lien search- $5.00 per debtor. Copy fee $1.00 per page. Cert fee- $5.00 per instrument or $1.00 per page. Payee- McCulloch County Clerk. **Online access to Criminal Record, Misdemeanor Record, Felony Record, Probate, Judgment records:** Access criminal, misdemeanor and felony records at http://idocket.com/homepage2.htm. Also, to search probate records and judgment records go to http://idocket.com/countycourt.htm. **Other phones:** Treasurer- 325-597-0773 x116; Appraiser/Auditor- 325-597-1627; Elections- 325-597-8733x103; Vital Records- 325-597-0733; Voter Registrar- 325-597-7607. **Property tax/Assessor-** 325-597-7607.

McLennan County

County Clerk, PO Box 1727, Waco, TX 76703-1727. 254-757-5078; fax-254-757-5146; hours: 8AM-5PM.
Index: Pre-1996 indices include deed, D/T, M/L, judgment, lien, etc. Records indexed on computer back to 1996. Office personnel or visitors may perform searches. Search fee $10.00 per name. Office will not search real estate records. Copy fee $1.00 per page. Cert fee- $5.00 per cert plus copy fee. Payee- McLennan County Clerk. **Online access to Real Estate, Grantor/Grantee, Deed, Lien, Judgment, Appraiser, Property Tax records:** Access recording records free at www.titlex.com; select McLennan county. Records range from 1/1996 to 12/2002. Also, see note at beginning of section. Also, real estate appraisal records are at www.mclennancad.org and at http://clientdb.trueautomation.com/clientdb/main.asp?id=20. Also, access land records at http://etitlesearch.com. You can do a name search; choose from $50.00 monthly subscription or per-click account. Also, see note at beginning of section. **Other phones:** Appraiser/Auditor- 254-752-9864; Elections- 254-757-5043.

McMullen County

County Clerk, PO Box 235, Tilden, TX 78072-0235. 361-274-3215; fax-361-274-3858; hours: 8AM-4PM.
All records in one index. Record index not computerized. Office personnel or visitors may perform searches. Search fee $5.00 per name. Copy fee $2.00, if tax lien or real estate $1.00 per page. Cert fee- $5.00 per cert plus copy fee. Payee-McMullen County Clerk. **Other phones:** Treasurer- 361-274-3685; Appraiser/Auditor- 361-274-3233; Elections- 361-274-3215; Vital Records- 361-274-3215. **Property tax/Assessor-** PO Box 38, Tilden, TX 78072; 361-274-3233.

Medina County

County Clerk, Courthouse, Rm 109; 1100 16th St, Hondo, TX 78861. 830-741-6041; fax-830-741-6015; hours: 8AM-N, 1-5PM.
All records in one index. Records indexed on a public use terminal back to 1991. Office will perform a UCC search but public must search other records themselves. Separate federal tax lien search- $5.00 per debtor. Copy fee $1.00. Cert fee-$5.00 per page plus copy fee. **Other phones:** Treasurer- 830-741-6110; Appraiser/Auditor- 830-741-3035; Elections- 830-741-6040; Vital Records- 830-741-6041. **Property tax/Assessor-** 1102 15th St, Hondo, TX 78861; 830-741-6100.

Menard County

County Clerk, PO Box 1038, Menard, TX 76859. 325-396-4682; fax-325-396-2047; 8AM-noon; 1-5PM.
Office personnel or visitors may perform searches. Search fee $10.00 per name. Copy fee $1.00 per page. Cert fee- $5.00 per cert. Payee- Menard County Clerk. **Other phones:** Treasurer- 325-396-2748; Appraiser/Auditor- 325-396-4784; Elections- 325-396-4682; Vital Records- 325-396-4682. **Property tax/Assessor-** 325-396-4523.

Midland County

County Clerk, PO Box 211, Midland, TX 79702. 432-688-4401; fax-432-688-8914; hours: 8AM-5PM. www.co.midland.tx.us
All records in one index. Records indexed on a public use terminal back to 1981. Office will perform a UCC and Tax lien search but public must search other records themselves. Search fee $10.00. Copy fee $1.00 per page. Cert fee- $5.00 per cert and $1.00 per page. Payee- Midland County Clerk. **Online access to Real Estate, Grantor/Grantee, Deed, Lien, Judgment, Appraiser, Property Tax, Voter Registration records:** Access the property tax database free at www.co.midland.tx.us/Tax/Property/Database/search.asp or at www.myswdata.com/swd_find.aspx. Also, search property data on the mapping page at www.midcad.org/Search/index.htm. Access recording records free at www.titlex.com; select Midland county. Also, access voter registration data free at www.co.midland.tx.us/Elections/VoterDatabase/input.asp. Check names on warrant lists at www.co.midland.tx.us/Warrants/default.asp. **Other phones:** Treasurer- 432-688-4880; Appraiser/Auditor-432-699-4991; Elections- 432-688-4890; Vital Records- 432-688-4401. **Property tax/Assessor-** 2110 N A St, Midland, TX 79701; 432-688-4810.

Milam County

County Clerk, 107 W Main, Cameron, TX 76520. 254-697-7049/800-216-0490, R/E recording phone-254-697-7049; fax-254-697-7055; hours: 8AM-5PM.
Separate indices to search include deed, deed of trust, federal, state and release, abstract of judgment, assumed name, execution, etc prior to 1983. As of 1983 all records in Official Records. Office personnel or visitors may perform searches. Search fee $10.00 per name. Copy fee $1.00 per page. Cert fee- $5.00 per cert plus copy fee. Payee-Milam County Clerk. **Online access to Real Estate, Grantor/Grantee, Deed, Lien, Judgment, Appraiser, Property Tax records:** Access recording records free at www.titlex.com; select Milam county. Records range

is 5/2000 to 8/2001. Also, see note at beginning of section. Also, appraisal district data at www.txcountydata.com. Also see note at beginning of section. **Other phones:** Treasurer- 254-697-7032; Appraiser/Auditor- 254-697-6638; Elections- 254-697-7049; Vital Records- 254-697-7049. **Property tax/Assessor-** 101 S Fannin, PO Box 551, Cameron, TX 76520; 254-697-7017.

Mills County

County Clerk, PO Box 646, Goldthwaite, TX 76844-0646. 325-648-2711; fax-325-648-3251; hours: 8AM-N, 1-5PM.
Separate indices to search include Deeds, Civil, Probate. Office personnel or visitors may perform searches. Office personnel searches are very limited. Copy fee $1.00 per page. Cert fee- $5.00 per cert plus copy fee. Payee- Mills County Clerk. **Other phones:** Treasurer- 325-648-2636; Appraiser/Auditor- 325-648-2253; Elections- 325-648-2711; Vital Records- 325-648-2711. **Property tax/Assessor-** PO Box 56, Goldthwaite, TX 76844; 325-648-3879.

Mitchell County

County Clerk, 349 Oak St. #103, Colorado City, TX 79512-6213. 325-728-3481; fax-325-728-5322; hours: 8AM-N, 1-5PM.
Index: Indexes by document type. Search fee $5.00. Will not search real estate records. UCC search per debtor name- $21.00. Copy fee $1.00 per page; minimum $5.00. Cert fee- $5.00 per cert plus copy fee. Payee- Mitchell County Clerk. **Other phones:** Treasurer- 325-728-8356; Appraiser/Auditor- 325-728-2196; Elections- 325-728-2606; Vital Records- 325-728-3481. **Property tax/Assessor-** 440 E 2nd, Colorado City, TX 79512; 325-728-5028.

Montague County

County Clerk, PO Box 77, Montague, TX 76251-0077. 940-894-2461; fax-940-894-3110; hours: 8AM-5PM.
All records in one index. Office will perform a UCC or tax lien search but public must search other records themselves. UCC or tax lien search per 10 years per debtor name- $10.00. Copy fee $1.00 per page. Cert fee- $5.00 per doc plus copy fee. **Other phones:** Treasurer- 940-894-2161; Appraiser/Auditor- 940-894-2081. **Property tax/Assessor-** 940-894-3881.

Montgomery County

County Clerk, PO Box 959, Conroe, TX 77305. 936-539-7885; fax-936-760-6990; hours: 8:30AM-4:30PM. www.co.montgomery.tx.us
Records indexed on a public use terminal back to 1970. Office will perform a UCC and Tax lien search but public must search other records themselves. Search fee $10.00. Copy fee $1.00 per page. Cert fee- $5.00 per cert plus copy fee. Payee-Montgomery County Clerk. **Online access to Real Estate, Grantor/Grantee, Deed, Lien, Judgment, Probate records:** Access recording records free at www.titlex.com; select Montgomery county.Records go back to 1/1966. Also, search probate records and judgment records at http://idocket.com/countycourt.htm. **Other phones:** Treasurer- 936-759-7844; Appraiser/Auditor- 936-756-3354; Elections- 936-539-7843; Vital Records- 936-538-8114. **Property tax/Assessor-** 936-539-7897.

Moore County

County Clerk, 715 Dumas Ave, Rm 107, Dumas, TX 79029. 806-935-2009; fax-806-935-9004; hours: 8:30AM-5PM.
All records in one index. Search fee $5.00 unless otherwise indicated. Will not search real estate records. UCC search per debtor name- $15.00. Separate federal tax lien search- $10.00 per debtor. Copy fee $1.00 per page; UCC copy $2.00 per page. Cert fee- $5.00 per cert plus copy fee. Payee-Moore County Clerk. **Other phones:** Treasurer- 806-935-2019; Appraiser/Auditor- 806-935-4193;

Elections- 806-935-2009; Vital Records- 806-935-2009. **Property tax/Assessor-** 806-935-2008.

Morris County

County Clerk, 500 Broadnax St, Daingerfield, TX 75638. 903-645-3911; fax-903-645-4026; hours: 8AM-5PM.
All records in one index. Records indexed on a public use terminal back to 1965. Office will perform a UCC search but public must search other records themselves. Search fee $10.00 per name. Copy fee $1.00 per page. Cert fee- $5.00 per cert plus copy fee. Payee- Morris County Clerk. **Other phones:** Treasurer- 903-645-2916; Appraiser/Auditor- 903-645-5061; Elections- 903-645-3911; Vital Records- 903-645-3911. **Property tax/Assessor-** 500 Broadnax St, #1, Daingerfield, TX 75638; 903-645-2446.

Motley County

County Clerk, PO Box 660, Matador, TX 79244. 806-347-2621; fax-806-347-2220; hours: 8:30AM-5PM.
Separate indices to search. Search fee $10.00 per name. Copy fee $1.00 per page. Cert fee- $5.00 per cert plus copy fee. Payee- Motley County Clerk. **Other phones:** Treasurer- 806-347-2800; Appraiser/Auditor- 806-347-2273; Elections- 806-347-2621; Vital Records- 806-347-2621. **Property tax/Assessor-** PO Box 727, Matador, TX 79244; 806-347-2252.

Nacogdoches County

County Clerk, 101 W. Main, Rm 205, Nacogdoches, TX 75961. 936-560-7733; fax-936-559-5926; hours: 8AM-5PM. www.co.nacogdoches.tx.us
All records in one index. Office will perform a UCC search but public must search other records themselves. Search fee $10.00 per name. Copy fee $1.00 per page. Cert fee- $5.00 per cert plus copy fee. Payee- Nacogdoches County Clerk. **Online access to Real Estate, Lien, Judgment, Deed, Vital Statistic, Property Tax, Probate records:** Access to view and search the county Real Property (recorder) index is free at https://www.texaslandrecords.com/txlr/TxlrApp/index.jsp. Monthly subscription is recommended, but there is a pay as you go plan for $1 per document. Access to the county Central Appraisal District Appraisal Roll from TaxNetUSA MAY be at www.taxnetusa.com/nacogdoches/. Access to civil, criminal or misdemeanor records at www.idocket.com. Fees involved. **Other phones:** Treasurer- 936-560-7703; Appraiser/Auditor- 409-560-3447; Elections- 936-560-7825; Vital Records- 936-560-7733. **Property tax/Assessor-** 936-560-3447.

Navarro County

County Clerk, PO Box 423, Corsicana, TX 75151. 903-654-3035; hours: 8AM-5PM.
Records indexed on computer from 1995 to present; before 1995 manual indexes, UCC's and tax liens in different indexes. Office personnel or visitors may perform searches. General search fee $5.00 per 10 years. UCC search and tax lien searches- $10.00 per 10 years. Copy fee $1.00 per page. Cert fee- $5.00 per cert plus copy fee. Payee- Navarro County Clerk. **Online access to Appraiser, Property Tax, Probate, Judgment records:** Access probate and judgment records free at http://idocket.com/countycourt.htm Also, see note at beginning of section for "Advanced" fee service. **Other phones:** Treasurer- 903-654-3090; Appraiser/Auditor- 903-872-2476. **Property tax/Assessor-** 903-654-3080.

Newton County

County Clerk, PO Box 484, Newton, TX 75966-0484. 409-379-5341; fax-409-379-9049; 8AM-4:30PM.
All records in one index. Will not search real estate records. Will search UCC records prior to 7/2001 and current fixture (land) files. UCC search includes tax liens if requested. UCC search per debtor name- $10.00. UCC search request using non-standard

form (per name)- $25.00. Separate federal tax lien search- $10.00 per debtor. Separate state tax lien search- $10.00 per debtor. Copy fee $1.00 per page. Cert fee- $5.00 per cert plus copy fee. Payee- Newton County Clerk. **Online access to Appraiser, Property Tax, Death records:** For Appraiser/property tax: see note at beginning of section. Death records in this county may be accessed over the Internet at www.jas.net/jas.htm (site may be temporarily down). **Other phones:** Treasurer- 409-379-8127; Appraiser/Auditor- 409-379-3710; Vital Records- 409-379-5341. **Property tax/Assessor-** PO Box 456, Newton, TX 75966; 409-379-4241.

Nolan County

County Clerk, 100 E 3rd St #108, Sweetwater, TX 79556-0098. 325-235-2462, R/E recording phone-915-235-2462; fax-325-236-9416; 8:30AM-N, 1-5PM.
Separate indices to search include Grantor/Grantee. Records indexed on a public use terminal back to 1982. Office will perform a UCC search but public must search other records themselves. UCC search per debtor name- $16.00. UCC search request using non-standard form (per name)- $31.00. Copy fee $1.00 per page. Cert fee- $5.00 per cert plus copy fee. Payee- Nolan County Clerk. **Other phones:** Treasurer- 915-236-6932; Appraiser/Auditor- 915-235-8421; Elections- 915-235-2462; Vital Records- 915-235-2462. **Property tax/Assessor-** 100 E 3rd St #108, Sweetwater, TX 79556; 325-235-3331.

Nueces County

County Clerk, PO Box 2627, Corpus Christi, TX 78403. 361-888-0111, R/E recording phone-361-888-0611, UCC recording phone-361-888-0580; fax-361-888-0329; hours: 8AM-5PM. www.co.nueces.tx.us
Office personnel or visitors may perform searches. General search fee $5.00 per name. Will not search real estate records. UCC search per debtor name- $14.00. UCC search request using non-standard form (per name)- $29.00. Copy fee $1.00 per page. Cert fee- $5.00 per cert plus copy fee. Payee- Nueces County Clerk. **Online access to Real Estate, Grantor/Grantee, Deed, Judgment, Lien, Appraiser, Property Tax records:** Access to county clerk recording records is free at www.co.nueces.tx.us/countyclerk/records/; access is also free at www.titlex.com; select Nueces county. Also, access County Appraiser records free at www.nuecescad.net. Also, see notes at beginning of section. **Other phones:** Treasurer- 361-888-0515; Appraiser/Auditor- 361-881-8022; Elections- 361-888-0483; Vital Records- 361-888-0580. **Property tax/Assessor-** 361-888-0475.

Ochiltree County

County Clerk, 511 S. Main, Perryton, TX 79070. 806-435-8039; fax-806-435-2081; hours: 8:30AM-N, 1-5PM.
Separate indices to search include grantor, grantee, and numerical. Record index not computerized. Office will perform a UCC search but public must search other records themselves. UCC search per debtor name- $10.00. Copy fee $1.00 per page. Cert fee- $5.00 per cert plus copy fee. Payee- Ochiltree County Clerk. **Online access to Property, Appraiser records:** Access property data by download from a private company; fees apply; add'l data includes minerals, ofc export, delinquents; visit www.ptax.org/tax_office_data.htm or phone 201-571-0425. **Other phones:** Treasurer- 806-435-8046; Appraiser/Auditor- 806-435-9623; Elections- 806-435-8039; Vital Records- 806-435-8039. **Property tax/Assessor-** 806-435-8025.

Oldham County

County Clerk, PO Box 360, Vega, TX 79092. 806-267-2667; hours: 8:30AM-5PM.
All records in one index. Only the public may search. Copy fee $2.00, if real estate $1.00 per page. Cert fee- $5.00 per cert plus copy fee. Payee- Oldham County Clerk. **Other phones:** Treasurer-

806-267-2329; Appraiser/Auditor- 806-267-2442; Elections- 806-267-2667; Vital Records- 806-267-2667. **Property tax/Assessor-** 806-267-2280.

Orange County

County Clerk, 123 S Sixth St, Orange, TX 77630. 409-882-7055; fax-409-882-7012; hours: 8AM-5PM. www.co.orange.tx.us
All records in one index. Records indexed on a public use terminal back to 7/1985. Search fee none, unless otherwise indicated. UCC search per debtor name- $10.00. UCC search request using non-standard form (per name)- $25.00. Copy fee $1.00 per page. Cert fee- $5.00 per doc plus copy fee. Payee- County Clerk. **Online access to Property, Appraiser records:** Access to the county appraisal district records is free at www.orangecad.org. **Other phones:** Treasurer- 409-882-7991; Appraiser/Auditor- 409-745-4777; Elections- 409-882-7055; Vital Records- 409-882-7055. **Property tax/Assessor-** 123 S Sixth St, Orange, TX 77630; 409-882-7971.

Palo Pinto County

County Clerk, PO Box 219, Palo Pinto, TX 76484. 940-659-1277; fax-940-659-3628; 8:30AM-4:30PM.
Separate indices to search. Records indexed on a public use terminal back to 1986. Office will perform a tax lien search but public must search other records themselves. Tax lien search- federal $10.00 per debtor; state- $10.00. Copy fee $2.00, if tax lien or real estate $1.00 per page. Cert fee- $5.00 per cert plus copy fee. Payee- Palo Pinto County Clerk. **Other phones:** Treasurer- 940-659-1260; Appraiser/Auditor- 940-659-1281; Elections- 940-659-1277; Vital Records- 940-659-1277. **Property tax/Assessor-** PO Box 160, Palo Pinto, TX 76484; 940-659-1271.

Panola County

County Clerk, Sabine & Sycamore; Courthouse Bldg, Rm 201, Carthage, TX 75633. 903-693-0302; fax-903-693-2726; hours: 8AM-5PM.
All records in one index. Records indexed on a public use terminal. Office will perform a UCC and tax lien search but public must search other records themselves. Search fee $5.00. Copy fee $1.00 per page. Cert fee- $5.00 per cert plus copy fee. Payee- Panola County Clerk. **Online access to Real Estate, Grantor/Grantee, Deed, Lien, Judgment records:** Access recording records free at www.titlex.com; select Panola county. **Other phones:** Treasurer- 903-693-0325; Appraiser/Auditor- 903-693-2891; Elections- 903-693-0370; Vital Records- 903-693-0302. **Property tax/Assessor-** 903-693-0340.

Parker County

County Clerk, PO Box 819, Weatherford, TX 76086. 817-599-6185, R/E recording phone-817-599-6591; fax-817-598-6183; hours: 8AM-4PM.
Index: Indices are by year; on-site indices are in books. Record index not computerized. Search fee $5.00 per name. Will not search real estate records. Federal or state tax lien search fee- $10.00. Copy fee $1.00 per page. Cert fee- $5.00 per cert plus copy fee. Payee- Parker County Clerk. **Online access to Appraiser, Property Tax records:** See note at beginning of section for "Advanced" fee service. **Other phones:** Treasurer- 817-596-0078; Appraiser/Auditor- 817-596-0077; Elections- 817-599-6591; Vital Records- 817-599-6591. **Property tax/Assessor-** 1112 Santa Fe Drive, Weatherford, TX 76086; 817-599-7671.

Parmer County

County Clerk, PO Box 356, Farwell, TX 79325. 806-481-3691; fax-806-481-9154; hours: 8:30AM-5PM.
Records indexed on a public use terminal back to 1996. Office personnel or visitors may perform searches. Search fee $10.00. Will not search real estate records. Copy fee $1.00 per page. Cert fee- $5.00 per cert plus copy fee. Payee- Parmer County Clerk. **Online access to Probate, Judgment**

records: Access probate and judgment records free at http://idocket.com/countycourt.htm. **Other phones:** Treasurer- 806-481-9152; Appraiser/Auditor- 806-481-1405; Elections- 806-481-3691; Vital Records- 806-481-3691. **Property tax/Assessor-** same address as above. 806-481-3845.

Pecos County

County Clerk, 103 W. Callaghan St, Fort Stockton, TX 79735. 432-336-7555; fax-432-336-7557; hours: 8AM-5PM.
All records in one index. Records indexed on computer back to April, 1983. Only the public may search. Copy fee $1.00 per page. Cert fee- $5.00 per doc plus copy fee. **Other phones:** Treasurer- 432-336-3461; Appraiser/Auditor- 432-336-7587; Elections- 432-336-7555; Vital Records- 432-336-7555. **Property tax/Assessor-** 432-336-3386.

Polk County

County Clerk, PO Drawer 2119, Livingston, TX 77351. 936-327-6804; fax-936-327-6874; hours: 8AM-5PM.
All records in one index. Records indexed on a public use terminal back to 1846. Office personnel or visitors may perform searches. General index search fee $5.00 per name. Copy fee $1.00 per page. Cert fee- $5.00 per cert plus copy fee. Payee- Polk County Clerk. **Other phones:** Treasurer- 936-327-6816; Appraiser/Auditor- 936-327-6811; Elections- 936-327-6852; Vital Records- 936-327-6804; Court Clerk- 936-327-6805. **Property tax/Assessor-** 416 N Washington St, Livingston, TX 77351; 936-327-6801.

Potter County

County Clerk, PO Box 9638, Amarillo, TX 79105. 806-379-2275; fax-806-379-2296; hours: 8AM-5PM. www.prad.org
All records in one index. Records indexed on a public use terminal back to January, 1980. Office will perform a Federal tax lien search but public must search other records themselves. Search fee $10.00 per name. Copy fee $1.00 per page. Federal Tax lien copy- $1.50 per page. Cert fee- $5.00 per cert plus copy fee. Payee- Potter County Clerk. **Online access to Real Estate, Grantor/Grantee, Deed, Lien, Judgment, Appraiser, Property Tax, Probate records:** Records on the Potter-Randall Appraisal District database are free at www.prad.org. Records periodically updated; for current tax information call Potter-806-342-2600 or Randall- 806-665-6287. Also, access recording records free at www.titlex.com; select Potter county. Also, for land searches go to www.texaslandrecords.com. Also, to search probate records and judgment records go to http://idocket.com/countycourt.htm. Also, see note at beginning of section. **Other phones:** Treasurer- 806-349-4832; Appraiser/Auditor- 806-358-1601; Elections- 806-379-2299; Vital Records- 806-379-2290. **Property tax/Assessor-** PO Box 2289, Amarillo, TX 79105; 806-342-2600.

Presidio County

County Clerk, PO Box 789, Marfa, TX 79843. 432-729-4812; fax-432-729-4313; 8AM-N; 1-4PM.
All records in one index. Records indexed on a public use terminal back to 6/13/2002. Office personnel or visitors may perform searches. Office will only do small searches. Search fee $6.00 per name. Copy fee $1.00 per page. Cert fee- $5.00 per cert plus copy fee. Payee- Presidio County Clerk. **Other phones:** Treasurer- 432-729-4076; Appraiser/Auditor- 432-729-3431; Elections- 432-729-4812; Vital Records- 432-729-4812. **Property tax/Assessor-** 301 N Highland Ave, Marfa, TX 79843; 432-729-4081.

Rains County

County Clerk, PO Box 187, Emory, TX 75440. 903-474-9999; fax-903-474-9390; hours: 8AM-4:30PM.
Separate indices to search. Records indexed on a public use terminal back to 1992. Only the public may search. Copy fee $1.00 per page. Cert fee-

$5.00 per cert plus copy fee. Payee- Rains County Clerk. **Other phones:** Treasurer- 903-474-9999; Appraiser/Auditor- 903-473-2391; Elections- 903-474-9999; Vital Records- 903-474-9999. **Property tax/Assessor-** 903-474-9999.

Randall County

County Clerk, PO Box 660, Canyon, TX 79015. 806-468-5505; fax-806-656-6430; hours: 8AM-5PM. www.randallcounty.org
Separate indices to search include books, computer. Records indexed on a public use terminal back to 2000. Office personnel or visitors may perform searches. Search fee $10.00 per name. Will not search real estate records. UCC search per debtor name- $15.00. UCC search request using non-standard form (per name)- $30.00. Copy fee $1.00 per page. Cert fee- $5.00 per cert plus copy fee. Payee- Randall County Clerk. **Online access to Appraiser, Property Tax, Business Personal Property, Sheriff Sale, Real Estate, Recorder, Lien, Deed, Marriage, Probate, Judgment records:** Access Real Estate records from 2000 forward free at http://ccopr.randallcounty.org/, click on Official Public Records and then OPR search, or marriages, or Comm Court for Commissioner's Court data. Also, Criminal, Probate and Civil records found at www.idocket.com. Randall County appraisal, sheriff sales, and personal property records are combined online with Potter County; see Potter County for access information or www.prad.org. Also, see notes at beginning of section. **Other phones:** Treasurer- 806-468-5535; Appraiser/Auditor- 806-358-1601; Elections- 806-468-5510; Vital Records- 806-468-5505. **Property tax/Assessor-** 400 16th St, Canyon, TX 79015; 806-468-5540.

Reagan County

County Clerk, PO Box 100, Big Lake, TX 76932. 325-884-2442; fax-325-884-1503; hours: 8:30AM-5PM.
Office personnel or visitors may perform searches. Search fee $10.00 per name. Will not search real estate records. Copy fee $2.00, if tax lien or real estate $1.00 per page. Cert fee- $5.00 per cert plus copy fee. Payee- Reagan County Clerk. **Other phones:** Treasurer- 325-884-2090; Appraiser/Auditor- 325-884-3275; Elections- 325-884-2442; Vital Records- 325-884-2442. **Property tax/Assessor-** 325-884-2131.

Real County

County Clerk, PO Box 750, Leakey, TX 78873-0750. 830-232-5202; fax-830-232-6888; hours: 8AM-5PM. www.realcountytexas.com
All records in one index. Records indexed on computer back to 12/92. Only the public may search. Copy fee $1.00 per page. Cert fee- $5.00 per doc plus copy fee. Payee- Bella A. Rubio, County Clerk. **Other phones:** Treasurer- 830-232-6627; Appraiser/Auditor- 830-232-6248; Elections- 830-232-5202; Vital Records- 830-232-5202. **Property tax/Assessor-** 830-232-6210.

Red River County

County Clerk, 200 N. Walnut; Courthouse Annex, Clarksville, TX 75426-3075. 903-427-2401; fax-903-427-3589; hours: 8:30AM-5PM.
All records in one index. Records indexed on a public use terminal back to 1968 for deeds, other records back to 1984. Only the public may search. Copy fee $1.00 per page. Cert fee- $5.00 per cert plus copy fee. Payee- Red River County Clerk. **Online access to Appraiser records:** Access to county appraisal district records is free at www.redrivercad.org. **Other phones:** Treasurer- 903-427-3748; Appraiser/Auditor- 903-427-4181; Elections- 903-427-2401; Vital Records- 903-427-2401. **Property tax/Assessor-** same address as above. 903-427-3009.

Reeves County

County Clerk, PO Box 867, Pecos, TX 79772. 432-445-5467; fax-432-445-3997; hours: 8AM-5PM.

All records in one index. Records indexed on computer back to 1984. Search fee $10.00 per name. Will not search real estate records. Will search UCC records prior to 7/2001 and current fixture (land) files, and also search tax liens separately. Copy fee $1.00 per page. Cert fee- $5.00 per cert plus copy fee. Payee- Reeves County Clerk. **Other phones:** Treasurer- 432-445-2631; Appraiser/Auditor- 432-445-5122; Elections- 432-445-5467; Vital Records- 432-445-5467. **Property tax/Assessor-** PO Box 700, Pecos, TX 79772; 432-445-5473.

Refugio County

County Clerk, PO Box 704, Refugio, TX 78377. 361-526-2233; fax-361-526-1325; hours: 8AM-4PM.
All records in one index. Records indexed. Only the office personnel may search. Search fee $10.00. Real estate record owner and property searches available. Copy fee $1.00 per page. Cert fee- $5.00 per cert plus copy fee. Payee- Refugio County Clerk. **Online access to Marriage, Birth, Death, Divorce records:** Access to 19th & 20th century marriage, birth (1951 forward) and death records is free at www.rootsweb.com/~txrefugi/Marriageshome.htm. Additionally, you can search individual years for births (1926-1995), deaths (1964-1999), marriages (1966-2001), divorces (1968-2001) for free at www.rootsweb.com/~usgenweb/tx/refugio/refugtoc.htm. **Other phones:** Treasurer- 361-526-4223; Appraiser/Auditor- 361-526-5994; Vital Records- 361-526-2233. **Property tax/Assessor-** 361-526-2023.

Roberts County

County Clerk, PO Box 477, Miami, TX 79059-0477. 806-868-2341; fax-806-868-3381; 8AM-N; 1-5PM.
Separate indices to search include deed, lease, probate, judgment, liens, etc. Records indexed on computer back to 1996. Only the public may search. Copy fee $1.00 per page. Cert fee- $5.00 per doc plus copy fee. Payee- Pay fees to Robert Co Clerk. **Other phones:** Treasurer- 806-868-3201; Appraiser/Auditor- 806-868-5281; Vital Records- 806-868-2341. **Property tax/Assessor-** 806-868-3611.

Robertson County

County Clerk, PO Box 1029, Franklin, TX 77856. 979-828-4130; fax-979-828-1260; hours: 8AM-5PM.
Separate indices to search include Grantor or Grantee by years. Records indexed on a public use terminal back to 1/1/1983. Only the public may search. Copy fee $1.00 per page. Cert fee- $5.00 per cert plus copy fee. Payee- Robertson County Clerk. **Online access to Real Estate, Grantor/Grantee, Deed, Lien, Judgment records:** Access recording records free at www.titlex.com; select Robertson county. Also, access to land records is free or by subscription at www.texaslandrecords.com. **Other phones:** Treasurer- 979-828-3201; Appraiser/Auditor- 979-828-5800; Elections- 979-828-4130; Vital Records- 979-828-4130. **Property tax/Assessor-** PO Box 220, Franklin, TX 77856; 979-828-3337.

Rockwall County

County Clerk, 1101 Ridge Rd, S-101, Rockwall, TX 75087. 972-882-0220, UCC recording phone-972-882-0225; fax-972-882-0229; hours: 8AM-5PM.
All records in one index. Search fee $10.00. Will not search real estate records. Will search UCC records prior to 7/2001 and current fixture (land) files. UCC search includes tax liens if requested. UCC search per debtor name- $10.00. Copy fee $1.00 per page. Cert fee- $5.00 per cert plus copy fee. Payee- Rockwall County Clerk. **Online access to Real Estate, Deed, Appraiser, Property Tax records:** Access real estate records free at www.texaslandrecords.com. Also, access appraisal district property records free at www.rockwallcad.com. **Other phones:** Treasurer- 972-882-0290; Appraiser/Auditor- 972-771-2034; Elections- 972-882-0220; Vital Records- 972-882-0220. **Property tax/Assessor-** 101 S FanninSt, Rockwall, TX 75087; 972-882-0350.

Runnels County

County Clerk, PO Box 189, Ballinger, TX 76821-0189. 325-365-2720; fax-325-365-3408; 8:30AM-N, 1-5PM. Index: Indexes are separated by date. Records indexed on a public use terminal back to 1998. Office personnel or visitors may perform searches. Office will only do limited searching. Search fee $10.00 per name per document. Will search UCC records prior to 7/2001 and current fixture (land) files. Tax liens not included in UCC search. Copy fee $1.00 per page. Cert fee- $5.00 per cert plus copy fee. Payee- County Clerk, Runnels County. **Other phones:** Treasurer- 325-365-2428; Appraiser/Auditor- 325-365-3583; Elections- 325-365-2720; Vital Records- 325-365-2720. **Property/Assessor-** PO Box 517, Ballinger, TX 76821-0517; 325-365-2339.

Rusk County

County Clerk, PO Box 758, Henderson, TX 75653-0758. 903-657-0330; hours: 8AM-5PM.
Office personnel or visitors may perform searches. Search fee $5.00 per name. Will not search real estate records. Copy fee $1.00 per page. Cert fee- $5.00 per cert plus copy fee. Payee- Rusk County Clerk. **Online access to Real Estate, Grantor/Grantee, Deed, Judgment, Lien, Property Tax records:** Access recording records free at www.titlex.com; select Rusk county. Record range is 1/1979 to 11/2003. Also, see note at beginning of section. Also, access land records free at www.texaslandrecords.com. See www.taxnet.use.com for property tax records. **Other phones:** Treasurer- 903-657-0352; Appraiser/Auditor- 903-657-3578; Elections- 903-657-0301; Vital Records- 903-657-0301; 903-657-0327. **Property tax/Assessor-** 903-657-0321.

Sabine County

County Clerk, PO Drawer 580, Hemphill, TX 75948-0580. 409-787-3786; fax-409-787-2044; 8AM-4PM.
All records in one index. Records indexed on computer back to 1991. Office will perform a UCC search but public must search other records themselves. UCC search per debtor name- $10.00, for 10 years only. Copy fee $1.00 per page. Cert fee- $5.00 per cert plus copy fee. **Other phones:** Treasurer- 409-787-2210; Appraiser/Auditor- 409-787-2777; Elections- 409-787-3786; Vital Records- 409-787-3786. **Property tax/Assessor-** 409-787-2257.

San Augustine County

County Clerk, 100 W. Columbia; #106 Courthouse, San Augustine, TX 75972-1335. 936-275-2452; fax-936-275-9579; hours: 8AM-4:30PM.
All records in one index. Record index not computerized. Office will not perform RE, UCC or tax lien searches. Search fee $10.00 per name. Copy fee $1.00 per page but not less than $5.00 per debtor. Cert fee- $5.00 per cert plus copy fee. Payee- San Augustine County Clerk. **Other phones:** Treasurer- 936-275-9472; Appraiser/Auditor- 936-275-3496; Elections- 936-275-2452; Vital Records- 936-275-2452. **Property tax/Assessor-** 936-275-2300.

San Jacinto County

County Clerk, 1 State Hwy 150, #2, Coldspring, TX 77331. 936-653-2324; fax-936-653-8312; hours: 8AM-4:00PM.
All records in one index. Records indexed on a public use terminal back to 1996. Office personnel or visitors may perform searches. Search fee $10.00 per name. Will not search real estate records. UCC copy fee $1.00 per page. Cert fee- $5.00 per cert plus copy fee. Payee- San Jacinto County Clerk. **Online access to Appraiser, Property Tax records:** Access Appraisal District records free at http://clientdb.trueautomation.com/clientdb/main.asp?id=46. Also, see note at beginning of section. **Other phones:** Treasurer- 936-653-2353; Appraiser/Auditor- 936-653-4481; Elections- 936-653-2324; Vital Records- 936-653-2324. **Property tax/Assessor-** 1 State Hwy 150, Rm 3, Coldspring, TX 77331; 936-653-3292, assessor fax- 936-653-2533.

San Patricio County

County Clerk, PO Box 578, Sinton, TX 78387. 361-364-6290, R/E recording phone-361-364-6290 x241 or 242; fax-361-364-6112; hours: 8AM-4:30PM.
All records in one index. Will not search real estate records. Will search UCC records prior to 7/2001 and current fixture (land) files. Tax liens not included in UCC search. UCC search per debtor name- $10.00. Tax lien search fee- $10.00 per debtor per 10 years. Copy fee $1.00 per page. Cert fee- $5.00 per cert plus copy fee. Payee- San Patricio County Clerk. **Online access to Appraiser, Property Tax, Personal Property records:** Search the Appraiser database for free onlline at www.sanpatriciocad.org/sanpatsearch.html. Also see note at beginning of section. **Other phones:** Treasurer- 361-364-6228; Appraiser/Auditor- 361-364-5402; Elections- 361-364-6290 x236; Vital Records- 361-364-6290 x238. **Property tax/Assessor-** PO Box 280, Sinton, TX 78387; 361-364-6161.

San Saba County

County Clerk, 500 E. Wallace, San Saba, TX 76877. 325-372-3614; fax-325-372-5746; hours: 8AM-4:30PM. www.sansabacounty.org
All records in one index. Records indexed on computer back to 5/2001. Office will perform a UCC and Tax lien search but public must search other records themselves. Search fee $15.00. Copy fee $1.00 per page. Cert fee- $5.00 per doc, plus copy fee. Payee- Clerk. **Other phones:** Treasurer- 325-372-3337; Appraiser/Auditor- 325-372-5031; Elections- 325-372-3614; Vital Records- 325-372-3614. **Property tax/Assessor-** 325-372-5325.

Schleicher County

County Clerk, PO Drawer 580, Eldorado, TX 76936. 325-853-2833 ext 72, R/E recording phone-325-853-2833; fax-325-853-2768; hours: 9AM-N, 1-5PM.
All records in one index. Record index not computerized. Office personnel or visitors may perform searches. Search fee $10.00 per name. Copy fee $1.00 per page. Cert fee- $5.00 per cert plus copy fee. Payee- Schleicher County Clerk. **Other phones:** Appraiser/Auditor- 325-853-2671. **Property tax/Assessor-** 325-853-3066.

Scurry County

County Clerk, 1806 25th St; #300, Snyder, TX 79549-2530. 325-573-5332; fax-325-573-7396; 8:30-5PM.
All records in one index. Office will perform a UCC search but public must search other records themselves. Search fee $10.00. Copy fee $1.00 per page. Cert fee- $5.00 per doc plus copy fee. **Online access to Land records:** For land records search go to www.texaslandrecords.com. **Other phones:** Treasurer- 325-573-5382; Appraiser/Auditor- 325-573-8549. **Property tax/Assessor-** 325-573-9316.

Shackelford County

County Clerk, PO Box 247, Albany, TX 76430. 325-762-2232, R/E recording phone-325-762-2232 x100, UCC recording phone-x100; fax-325-762-2830; hours: 8:30AM-N, 1-5PM.
Records indexed on a public use terminal back to 1984. Office personnel or visitors may perform searches. General index search fee $5.00 per name. UCC search per debtor name- $10.00. Tax lien search fee- $5.00 per debtor. Copy fee $1.00 per page. Include SASE for mail return. Cert fee- $5.00 per cert plus copy fee. Payee- Shackelford County Clerk. **Other phones:** Treasurer- x121; Appraiser/Auditor- 325-762-2207; Elections- x100; Vital Records- x100. **Property tax/Assessor-** 325-762-2232 x107.

Shelby County

County Clerk, PO Box 1987, Center, TX 75935. 936-598-6361; fax-936-598-3701; hours: 8AM-4:30PM.
Only the public may search. Copy fee $1.00 per page. Cert fee- $5.00 per cert plus copy fee. Payee- Shelby County Clerk. **Other phones:** Treasurer- 936-598-3581; Appraiser/Auditor- 936-598-6171; Elections- 936-598-6361; Vital Records- 936-598-6361. **Property tax/Assessor-** 936-598-4441.

Sherman County

County Clerk, PO Box 270, Stratford, TX 79084. 806-366-2371; fax-806-366-5670; 8AM-N, 1-5PM.
Separate indices to search include Grantor/Grantee, Daily Register. Record index not computerized. Only the public may search. Copy fee $1.00 per page. Cert fee- $5.00 per page plus copy fee. Payee- Sherman County Clerk. **Other phones:** Treasurer- 806-396-5842; Appraiser/Auditor- 806-396-5566; Elections- 806-366-2371; Vital Records- 806-366-2371. **Property tax/Assessor-** 806-396-2150.

Smith County

County Clerk, PO Box 1018, Tyler, TX 75710. 903-535-0630, R/E recording phone-903-535-0652; fax-903-535-0684; hours: 8AM-5PM.
All records in one index. Records indexed on a public use terminal back to 9/1/1981. Office personnel or visitors may perform searches. Search fee $10.00 UCCs, $5.00 tax lien. Copy fee $1.00 per page. Cert fee- $5.00 per cert plus copy fee. Payee- Smith County Clerk. **Online access to Property, Appraiser records:** Access to county appraisal district records is free at www.smithcad.org. Also, for land records search go to www.texaslandrecords.com. Also, see note at beginning of section. **Other phones:** Treasurer- 903-535-0555; Appraiser/Auditor- 903-510-8600; Elections- 903-535-0657; Vital Records- 903-535-0650. **Property tax/Assessor-** 1517 W Front St, Tyler, TX 75702; 903-535-0835.

Somervell County

County/District Clerk, PO Box 1098, Glen Rose, TX 76043. 254-897-4427; fax-254-897-3233; 8AM-5PM.
All records in one index. Records indexed on computer back to 1997. Office will perform a UCC search but public must search other records themselves. Search fee $5.00. Copy fee $1.00 per page. Cert fee- $5.00 per cert plus copy fee. Payee- Somervell County Clerk. **Online to Appraiser, Property Tax records:** Appraisal District records free http://clientdb.trueautomation.com/clientdb/main.asp?id=29. Also see note at beginning of section. **Other phones:** Treasurer- 254-897-4814; Appraiser/Auditor- 254-897-4094; Elections- 254-897-4427; Vital Records- 254-897-4427. **Property tax/Assessor-** P O Box 305, Glen Rose, TX 76043; 254-897-2419.

Starr County

County Clerk, Courthouse, Rio Grande City, TX 78582. 956-487-8032; fax-956-487-8624; 8AM-5PM.
Records indexed on computer back to 1984. Office personnel or visitors may perform searches. General index search fee $10.00 per name. Copy fee $1.00 per page. Cert fee- $5.00 per cert plus copy fee. Payee- Starr County Clerk. **Online access to Probate, Judgment records:** Access probate and judgment records free at http://idocket.com/countycourt.htm. **Other phones:** Treasurer- 956-487-8106; Appraiser/Auditor- 956-487-5613; Vital Records- 956-487-8032. **Property tax/Assessor-** 956-487-8136.

Stephens County

County Clerk, Courthouse, Breckenridge, TX 76424. 254-559-3700; hours: 8:30AM-5PM.
Separate indices to search include books, computer. Office personnel or visitors may perform searches. Search fee $5.00 per name. Will not search real estate records. UCC search includes tax liens if requested. UCC search per debtor name- $10.00. Copy fee $1.00 per page. Cert fee- $5.00 per cert plus copy fee. Payee- Stephens County Clerk. **Other phones:** Treasurer- 254-559-3181; Appraiser/Auditor- 254-559-8233; Elections- 254-559-3700; Vital Records- 254-559-3700. **Property**

tax/Assessor- 200 W Walker, Breckenridge, TX 76424; 254-559-2732.

Sterling County

County Clerk, PO Box 55, Sterling City, TX 76951-0055. 325-378-5191; fax-325-378-2266; hours: 8AM-4PM M-Th; 8AM-1:30PM Fri
www.co.sterling.tx.us
Separate indices to search include official public records (1/1/1999 - present), grantor/grantee. Before 1999, separate indexes for deed, deed of trust, bill of sale, abstract of judgments, tax liens, mechanic liens, assumed name cert, patents, etc. Office will perform a UCC search but public must search other records themselves. UCC search per debtor name- $15.00. Copy fee $1.00 per page. Cert fee- $5.00 per cert plus copy fee. Payee-Sterling County Clerk. **Other phones:** Treasurer- 325-378-8511; Appraiser/Auditor- 325-378-7711; Elections- 325-378-5191; Vital Records- 325-378-5191. **Property tax/Assessor-** PO Box 888, Sterling City, TX 76951; 325-378-7711.

Stonewall County

County Clerk, PO Drawer P, Aspermont, TX 79502. 940-989-2272; fax-940-989-2715; 940-989-2032; hours: 8AM-4:30PM.
All records in one index. Search fee $5.00 unless otherwise indicated. UCC search per debtor name- $10.00. Copy fee $1.00 per page. Cert fee- $5.00 per cert plus copy fee. Payee- Stonewall County Clerk. **Other phones:** Treasurer- 940-989-3520; Appraiser/Auditor- 940-989-3363; Elections- 940-989-2272; Vital Records- 940-989-2272. **Property tax/Assessor-** 940-989-2633.

Sutton County

County Clerk, 300 E. Oak, #3; Sutton County Annex, Sonora, TX 76950. 325-387-3815; fax-325-387-6028; hours: 8:30AM-4:30PM.
All records in one index. Records indexed on computer back to 5/29/1992. Office personnel or visitors may perform searches. General index search fee $10.00 per name. Copy fee $1.00 per page. Cert fee- $5.00 per cert plus copy fee. Payee-Sutton County Clerk. **Other phones:** Treasurer- 325-387-2886; Appraiser- 325-387-2809; Auditor -325-387-5380. **Property tax/Assessor-** PO Box 858, Sonora, TX 76980; 325-387-2342.

Swisher County

County Clerk, 119 S. Maxwell; Courthouse, Tulia, TX 79088. 806-995-3294; fax-806-995-4121; 8AM-5PM.
All records in one index. Only the public may search. Separate federal tax lien search- $5.00 per debtor. Separate state tax lien search- $5.00 per debtor. Separate federal/state combined tax lien search- $5.00 per debtor, $5.00 each add'l name. Copy fee $1.00 per page. Cert fee- $5.00 per cert plus copy fee. Payee- Swisher County Clerk. **Online access to Appraiser, Property Tax records:** Search the appraisal tax rolls for free at www.txcountydata.com/county.asp?County=219. Also see notes at beginning of section. Will search Spouses names with no additional charge. **Other phones:** Treasurer- 806-995-2204; Appraiser/Auditor- 806-995-4118; Elections- 806-995-3294; Vital Records- 806-995-3294. **Property tax/Assessor-** 806-995-3513.

Tarrant County

County Clerk, 100 W. Weatherford; Courthouse, Rm 130, Ft. Worth, TX 76196. 817-884-1060; fax-817-884-3295; hours: 8AM-4:30PM
www.tarrantcounty.com/eCountyClerk
Office will perform a UCC search but public must search other records themselves. UCC search per debtor name- $16.00. UCC search request using non-standard form (per name)- $31.00. Copy fee $1.00 per page. Cert fee- $5.00 per cert plus copy fee. Payee- Tarrant County Clerk. **Online access to Property Tax, Appraiser, Real Estate, Grantor/Grantee, Lien, Judgment, Deed, Assumed Name, Marriage, UCC, Traffic, Court records:**

Access to the county Appraisal District Property data is free at www.tad.org/Datasearch/datasearch.htm. Also, search the county grantor/grantee index at http://ccanthem.co.tarrant.tx.us/search.aspx?cabinet=opr. Also, access a real estate and grantor/grantee index free at www.titlex.com where records range from 4/1997 to 11/2001 only; select Tarrant County. Also, assumed names, marriages, courts, UCCs, Traffic at www.tarrantcounty.com/ecountyclerk/cwp/view.asp?A=735&Q=427570. Also see note at beginning of section. **Other phones:** Appraiser/Auditor- 817-284-0024; Elections- 817-884-1115. **Property tax/Assessor-** 817-284-0024.

Taylor County

County Clerk, PO Box 5497, Abilene, TX 79608. 325-674-1202; fax-325-674-1279; hours: 8AM-5PM.
www.taylorcad.org
Office personnel or visitors may perform searches. Search fee $10.00 per name. Will not search real estate records. Copy fee $1.00 per page. Cert fee- $5.00 per cert plus copy fee. Payee- Taylor County Clerk. **Online access to Appraiser, Property Tax, Personal Property, Unclaimed Property records:** Access to the county Central Appraisal District database is free at www.taylorcad.org/tayname.html. Search is by name; other methods are at the website listed above. Search business personal property at www.taylorcad.org/tayppname.html. Also, search the treasurer's database of unclaimed property free at www.taylorcountytexas.org/unclaime.html. Also, for land records search go to www.texaslandrecords.com. Real Property records at www.taylorcountytexas.org. Also, access Appraisal District records free at http://clientdb.trueautomation.com/clientdb/main.asp?id=32. Also, see note at beginning of section. **Other phones:** Treasurer- 325-674-1231; Appraiser/Auditor- 325-676-9381; Elections- 325-674-1216; Vital Records- 325-674-1202. **Property tax/Assessor-** 325-672-4870.

Terrell County

County Clerk, PO Drawer 410, Sanderson, TX 79848. 432-345-2391; fax-432-345-2740; hours: 9AM-5PM.
All records in one index. Records indexed on computer back to 6/1/1994. Office personnel or visitors may perform searches. Search fee $5.00 per name. Copy fee $1.00 per page. Cert fee- $5.00 per cert plus copy fee. Payee- Terrell County Clerk. **Online access to Property, Appraiser records:** Access to Appraisal District records is free at http://clientdb.trueautomation.com/clientdb/main.asp?id=16. **Other phones:** Appraiser/Auditor- 432-345-2251. **Property tax/Assessor-** PO Box 747, Sanderson, TX 79848; 432-345-2525.

Terry County

County Clerk, 501 W. Main, Rm 105, Brownfield, TX 79316-4398. 806-637-8551; fax-806-637-4874; hours: 8:30AM-5PM.
All records in one index. Records indexed on computer back to 1981. Office personnel or visitors may perform searches. Search fee $10.00. Copy fee $1.00 per page. R/E record copy- $1.50 per page. Cert fee- $5.00 per doc plus copy fee. Payee- Terry County Clerk. **Other phones:** Treasurer- 806-637-3616; Appraiser/Auditor- 806-637-6966; Elections- 806-637-8551; Vital Records- 806-637-8551. **Property tax/Assessor-** 421 W Powell, Brownfield, TX 79316; 806-637-6966.

Throckmorton County

County Clerk, PO Box 309, Throckmorton, TX 76483. 940-849-2501; fax-940-849-3220; 8AM-N; 1-5PM.
All records in one index. Records indexed on a public use terminal back to 1990. Office personnel or visitors may perform searches. Search fee $10.00 per name. Copy fee $1.00 per page. Cert fee- $1.00 per page includes copy fee. Payee-County/ Disrtict Clerk. **Other phones:** Treasurer- 940-849-2921; Appraiser/Auditor- 940-849-5691; Elections- 940-849-2501; Vital Records- 940-849-

2501. **Property tax/Assessor-** PO Box 578, Throckmorton, TX 76483; 940-849-9421.

Titus County

County Clerk, 100 W. 1 St.; 2nd Fl, #204, Mount Pleasant, TX 75455. 903-577-6796; fax-903-572-5078; hours: 8AM-5PM.
Separate indices to search include grantor/grantee. Records indexed on computer from 1973 forward. Office will perform a tax lien search but public must search other records themselves. Search fee $10.00 per name. Copy fee $1.00 per page. Cert fee- $5.00 per cert plus copy fee. Payee- Titus County Clerk. **Online access to Property, Appraiser records:** Access property data by download from a private company; fees apply; add'l data includes minerals, ofc exports, delinquents; visit www.ptax.org/tax_office_data.htm or phone 201-571-0425. **Other phones:** Treasurer- 903-572-8723; Appraiser/Auditor- 903-577-7939; Vital Records- 903-577-6796. **Property tax/Assessor-** 903-572-6712.

Tom Green County

County Clerk, 124 W. Beauregard, San Angelo, TX 76903-5835. 325-659-6552, UCC recording phone- 325-659-3262; fax-325-659-3251; hours: 8AM-4:30PM.
Separate indices include Grantor and Grantee. General index search fee $5.00 per name; financing statements such as UCCs, Tax liens are $10.00. Copy fee $1.00 per page. UCC copy fee $1.50 per page. Cert fee- $5.00 per cert plus copy fee. Payee- Tom Green County Clerk. **Online access to Real Estate, Grantor/Grantee, Deed, Lien, Judgment records:** Access recording records free at www.titlex.com; select Tom Green county. **Other phones:** Appraiser/Auditor- 325-658-5575; Elections- 325-659-6541; Vital Records- 325-659-6556.

Travis County

County Clerk, PO Box 149325, Austin, TX 78714-9325. 512-854-9188, R/E recording phone-512-854-4526, UCC recording phone-512-854-9188; fax-512-854-4526; hours: 8AM-5PM. www.traviscad.org
For Recording, Elections, Accounting and Admin Div, courier address is: 5501 Airport Blvd, Austin, TX 78751. Office personnel or visitors may perform searches. Search fee $10.00 per debtor for 10 years. Copy fee $1.00 per page. Cert fee- $5.00 per cert plus copy fee. Payee- Travis County Clerk. **Online access to Appraiser, Property Tax, Business Property, Voter Registration, Grantor/Grantee, Recording, UCC, Marriage, Probate records:** Access to recorders official records is free at http://deed.co.travis.tx.us/search.aspx?cabinet=opr. Access to the Central Appraisal District database is free at www.traviscad.org/search.htm. Also, one may search the county tax payment system at www.texasonline.state.tx.us/NASApp/rap/BaseRap. Also, See note at beginning of section. **Other phones:** Treasurer- 512-854-9000; Appraiser/Auditor- 512-854-9317; Elections- 512-854-9075; Vital Records- 512-458-7111. **Property tax/Assessor-** 512-854-9473.

Trinity County

County Clerk, PO Box 456, Groveton, TX 75845. 936-642-1208; fax-936-642-3004; hours: 8AM-5PM.
All records in one index. Office personnel or visitors may perform searches. Search fee $10.00. Will search real estate records. Will search UCC records, tax liens not included in UCC search. Copy fee $1.00 per page. Cert fee- $5.00 per cert plus copy fee. Payee- Trinity County Clerk. **Other phones:** Treasurer- 936-642-1443; Appraiser/Auditor- 936-642-1502; Elections- 936-642-1208; Vital Records- 936-642-1208. **Property tax/Assessor-** PO Box 269, Groveton, TX 75845; 936-642-1637.

Tyler County

County Clerk, 110 W. Bluff, Rm 110, Woodville, TX 75979. 409-283-2281, R/E recording phone-409-283-2281 x10, UCC recording phone-409-283-2281 x13; hours: 8AM-4:30PM.

Searches are not guaranteed, they are only a computerized index print out. Real estate owner, mortgage, and property transfer searches available. Will search UCC records prior to 7/2001 and current fixture (land) files. Tax liens not included in UCC search. UCC search per debtor name- $10.00. UCC search request using non-standard form (per name)- $25.00. Tax lien search fee- $10.00 per debtor. Separate federal tax lien search- $10.00 per debtor. Separate state tax lien search- $10.00 per debtor. Copy fee $1.00 per page. Cert fee- $5.00 per cert, copies not included. Payee- Tyler County Clerk. **Online access to Property, Appraiser records:** Access to the county appraisal district records is free at www.tylercad.org. **Other phones:** Treasurer- 409-283-3054; Appraiser/Auditor- 409-283-3736; Elections- 409-283-2281 x10; Vital Records- 409-283-2281 x15. **Property tax/Assessor-** 1001 West Bluff, Woodville, TX 75979; 409-283-2734.

Upshur County

County Clerk, PO Box 730, Gilmer, TX 75644. 903-843-4014, R/E recording phone-903-680-8123, 8124, 8125, UCC recording phone-903-843-4015; fax-903-843-5492; hours: 8AM-5PM.
All records in one index. Records indexed on a public use terminal back to 8/1979. Only the public may search. Copy fee $1.00 per page. Cert fee- $5.00 per cert plus copy fee. Payee- Upshur County Clerk. **Online access to Real Estate, Grantor/Grantee, Deed, Lien, Judgment, Appraiser, Property Tax records:** Access recording records free at www.titlex.com. Records go back to 4/1978. Also, see note at beginning of section. **Other phones:** Treasurer- 903-680-8135, 8136, 8138; Appraiser/Auditor- 903-843-3041; Elections- 903-680-8126; Vital Records- 903-680-8123; Civil, Criminal & Probate- 903-680-8126, 8127. **Property tax/Assessor-** 903-843-3085.

Upton County

County Clerk, PO Box 465, Rankin, TX 79778. 432-693-2861; fax-432-693-2129; hours: 8AM-5PM. www.co.upton.tx.us
All records in one index. Office personnel or visitors may perform searches. General index search fee $5.00 per name per document. Will search real estate records with written request. Copy fee $1.00 per page. Cert fee- $5.00 per page plus copy fee. Payee- Upton County Clerk. **Other phones:** Treasurer- 432-693-2401; Appraiser/Auditor- 432-652-3221; Elections- 432-693-2861; Vital Records- 432-693-2861. **Property tax/Assessor-** 432-693-2572.

Uvalde County

County Clerk, PO Box 284, Uvalde, TX 78802-0284. 830-278-6614; hours: 8AM-5PM.
All records in one index. Records indexed on a public use terminal back to 1997. Only the public may search. Copy fee $1.00 per page. Cert fee- $5.00 per cert plus copy fee. Payee- Uvalde County Clerk. **Online to Property, Appraiser records:** The county appraisal district tax information is free at www.eztaxonline.com/uvalde/main.jsp. **Other phones:** Treasurer- 830-278-5821; Appraiser/Auditor- 830-278-1106; Elections- 830-278-3225; Vital Records- 830-278-6614. **Property tax/Assessor-** 830-278-3225.

Val Verde County

County Clerk, PO Box 1267, Del Rio, TX 78841-1267. 830-774-7564; hours: 8AM-4:30PM.
Separate indices to search include records from 1885-1992, official public records, 1992-present. Records indexed on computer. Only the public may search. Copy fee $1.00 per page. Cert fee- $5.00 per cert plus copy fee. Payee- Val Verde County Clerk. **Online access to Property, Appraiser, Probate, Judgment records:** Access Appraisal District records free online at http://clientdb.trueautomation.com/clientdb/main.asp?id =42. Also, to search probate records and judgment

records go to http://idocket.com/countycourt.htm. **Other phones:** Treasurer- 210-774-4602; Appraiser/Auditor- 830-774-4602. **Property tax/Assessor-** 830-774-7535.

Van Zandt County

County Clerk, 121 E. Dallas St; Courthouse - Rm 202, Canton, TX 75103. 903-567-6503; fax-903-567-6722; hours: 8AM-5PM. www.vanzandtcounty.org
Records indexed on computer back to 1971. Office will perform a tax lien search but public must search other records themselves. Tax lien search fee- $10.00 per debtor. Copy fee $1.00 per page. Cert fee- $6.00 1st page, $2.00 each add'l page, plus copy fee. Payee- Van Zandt County Clerk. **Online access to Real Estate, Grantor/Grantee, Deed, Judgment, Lien, Appraiser, Property Tax records:** Search the county appraisal rolls for free at www.vanzandtcad.org; includes plat maps online. Also, access recording records free at www.titlex.com; select Van Zandt county. Record range is 1/1971 to 9/2003. Also, see note at beginning of section. **Other phones:** Treasurer- 903-567-2551; Appraiser/Auditor- 903-567-6171; Elections- 903-567-6503; Vital Records- 903-567-6503. **Property tax/Assessor-** 121 E Dallas St #203, Canton, TX 75103; 903-567-6171.

Victoria County

County Clerk, PO Box 1968, Victoria, TX 77902. 361-575-1478; fax-361-575-6276; hours: 8AM-5PM.
All records in one index. Records indexed on computer. Only the public may search, but office will assist. Search fee $10.00. Will not search real estate records. Will search UCC records prior to 7/2001 and current fixture (land) files. Tax liens not included in UCC search. UCC search request using non-standard form (per name)- $25.00. Copy fee $1.00 per page. Cert fee- $5.00 per cert plus copy fee. Payee- Victoria County Clerk. **Online access to Real Estate, Grantor/Grantee, Deed, Judgment, Lien, Probate, Appraiser, Property Tax records:** Access recording records free at www.titlex.com; select Victoria county. Records range is 1/1964 to 5/26/2005 only. Also, access to appraisal district records is free at www.victoriacad.org, and at http://clientdb.trueautomation.com/clientdb/main.asp?id =33. Also, to search probate records and judgment records go to http://idocket.com/countycourt.htm. Also, see note at beginning of section. **Other phones:** Treasurer- 361-575-8588; Appraiser/Auditor- 361-576-3621; Elections- 361-576-0124; Vital Records- 361-575-1478 (county); Vital Records (city)- 361-485-3040. **Property tax/Assessor-** 361-576-3671.

Walker County

County Clerk, PO Box 210, Huntsville, TX 77342-0210. 936-436-4922; fax-936-436-4928; hours: 8AM-4:45PM. www.texaslandrecords.com
County web-site: www.co.walker.tx.us. Separate indices to search include numerous indexes from 1846 to present. Records indexed on computer from 1960 to present. Office personnel or visitors may perform searches. Will not do telephone searches. Search fee $5.00 per name for simple searches. UCC or tax lien search per debtor name- $10.00. Copy fee $1.00 per page. Cert fee- $5.00 per cert plus copy fee. Payee- James D. Patton, County Clerk. **Online to Property, Appraiser, Land records:** The county appraisal district records is free at http://clientdb.trueautomation.com/clientdb/main.asp?id =4. Also, for land records search go to www.texaslandrecords.com. Indexes from 1960-forward; images of the records from 1/1/2003 to current. **Other phones:** Treasurer- 936-436-4933; Appraiser/Auditor- 936-295-0402; Elections- 936-436-4950; Vital Records- 936-436-4922; Voter Registration- 936-436-4959. **Property tax/Assessor-** 1301 Sam Houston Ave, Huntsville, TX 77340; 936-436-4959.

Waller County

County Clerk, 836 Austin St; Rm 217, Hempstead, TX 77445. 979-826-7711; hours: 8AM-N, 1-5PM.

All records in one index. Only the public may search. Copy fee $1.00 per page. Cert fee- $5.00 per cert plus copy fee. Payee- Waller County Clerk. **Online access to Appraiser, Property Tax records:** See note at beginning of section. **Other phones:** Treasurer- 979-826-7707; Appraiser/Auditor- 409-396-6100; Elections- 979-826-7643; Vital Records- 979-826-7711. **Property tax/Assessor-** 979-826-7620.

Ward County

County Clerk, Corner of 4 & Allen, Monahans, TX 79756. 432-943-3294; fax-432-943-5064; 8AM-5PM. Only the public may search. Copy fee $1.00 per page. Cert fee- $5.00 plus $1.00 per page. Payee- Ward County Clerk. **Other phones:** Treasurer- 432-943-2841; Appraiser/Auditor- 432-943-3224; Elections- 432-943-3294; Vital Records- 432-943-3294. **Property tax/Assessor-** 432-943-2546.

Washington County

County Clerk, 100 E. Main; #102, Brenham, TX 77833. 979-277-6200; fax-979-277-6278; hours: 8AM-5PM. www.co.washington.tx.us/cclerk/index.html
Office personnel or visitors may perform searches. Search fee $5.00 per name. Copy fee $1.00 per page. Cert fee- $5.00 per doc plus copy fee. Payee- Washington County Clerk. **Online access to Real Estate, Grantor/Grantee, Deed, Judgment, Lien, Assessor, Property, Probate records:** Access recording records free at www.titlex.com; select Washignton county.Record range-1/1965 to 12/2003. Also, to search probate records and judgment records go to http://idocket.com/countycourt.htm. Also, see note at beginning of section. **Other phones:** Treasurer- 979-277-6200; Appraiser/Auditor- 979-277-6528; Elections- 979-277-6200; Vital Records- 979-277-6200. **Property tax/Assessor-** 979-277-6200.

Webb County

County Clerk, PO Box 29, Laredo, TX 78042. 956-523-4622, R/E recording phone-956-523-4266; fax-956-523-5035; 8AM-5PM. www.webbcounty.com
Records indexed on a public use terminal back to 1982. Office personnel or visitors may perform searches. Search fee $5.00. Copy fee $1.00 per page. Cert fee- $5.00 per cert plus copy fee. Payee- Webb County Clerk. **Online access to Appraiser, Property Tax, Real Estate Recording, Deed, Probate, Judgment records:** Search the county Central Appraisal District database at www.webbcad.org/search1.htm and online at http://clientdb.trueautomation.com/clientdb/main.asp?id =1. Also, access recording office land data at www.etitlesearch.com; registration required, fee based on usage. Also, to search probate records and judgment records go to http://idocket.com/countycourt.htm. Also, see note at beginning of section. **Other phones:** Treasurer- 956-523-4150; Appraiser/Auditor- 956-718-4091; Elections- 956-523-4050; Vital Records- 956-523-4266 (outside city limits); Vital Records (inside city limits)- 956-795-4929. **Property tax/Assessor-** 956-523-4200.

Wharton County

County Clerk, PO Box 69, Wharton, TX 77488. 979-532-2381; fax-979-532-8426; hours: 8AM-5PM.
Real property records indexed on computer from 1978 to present, criminal, civil and probate-1991 to present, 1978 and prior-separate, deed of trust, judgment, mechanic liens and tax liens. Office will perform a tax lien search but public must search other records themselves. Search fee $10.00 per name. Copy fee $1.00 per page. Cert fee- $5.00 per cert plus copy fee. Payee- Wharton County Clerk. **Online access to Real Estate, Grantor/Grantee, Deed, Lien, Judgment, Assessor, Property Tax records:** Access recording records free at www.titlex.com; select Wharton county. Records go up to 11/2003. **Other phones:** Treasurer- 979-532-2971; Appraiser/Auditor- 979-532-8931; Elections- 979-532-2381; Vital Records- 979-532-2381. **Property**

tax/Assessor- PO Box 189, Wharton, TX 77488; 979-532-3312.

Wheeler County

County Clerk, PO Box 465, Wheeler, TX 79096. 806-826-5544; fax-806-826-3282; hours: 8AM-5PM.
Office personnel or visitors may perform searches. Search fee $10.00 per name. Will not search real estate records. Copy fee $1.00 per page. Cert fee-$5.00 per cert plus copy fee. Payee- Wheeler County Clerk. **Other phones:** Treasurer- 806-826-3122; Appraiser/Auditor- 806-826-5900. **Property tax/Assessor-** 806-826-3131.

Wichita County

County Clerk, PO Box 1679, Wichita Falls, TX 76307-1679. 940-766-8144, R/E recording phone-940-766-8160; fax-940-716-8554; hours: 8AM-5PM.
All records in one index. Records indexed on a public use terminal. Only the public may search. Copy fee $1.00 per page. Cert fee- $5.00 per cert plus copy fee. Payee- Wichita County Clerk. **Online to Property, Appraisal, Land records:** Access to county appraisal district records is free at http://clientdb.trueautomation.com/clientdb/main.asp?id=43. Also, for land records search go to www.texaslandrecords.com. Also, see note at beginning of section. **Other phones:** Treasurer- 940-766-8245; Appraiser/Auditor- 940-322-2435; Elections- 940-766-8174; Vital Records- 940-766-8127. **Property tax/Assessor-** 940-322-2435.

Wilbarger County

County Clerk, 1700 Willbarger - #15; Courthouse, Vernon, TX 76384. 940-552-5486; fax-940-553-2320; hours: 8AM-5PM.
Only the public may search, except UCC and tax liens. Will not search real estate records. Will search UCC records prior to 7/2001 and current fixture (land) files. Tax liens not included in UCC search. UCC search per debtor name- $13.00. Separate federal or state tax lien search- $5.00 per search per 10 year period. Copy fee $1.00 per page. Cert fee-$5.00 per cert. Payee- Wilbarger County Clerk. **Online access to Property Tax, Personal Property records:** Search the appraisal rolls for free at www.taxnetusa.com/cfmsite/Wilbarger/default.html. Also see note at beginning of section. **Other phones:** Treasurer- 940-553-2302; Appraiser/Auditor- 940-553-1857; Elections- 940-552-5486; Vital Records- 940-552-5486. **Property tax/Assessor-** 1700 Willbarger - #17, Vernon, TX 76384; 940-552-9341.

Willacy County

County Clerk, 540 W. Hidalgo Ave; Courthouse Bldg, First Fl, Raymondville, TX 78580. 956-689-2710; fax-956-689-0937; hours: 8AM-N, 1-5PM.
Separate indices to search include Grantor/Grantee, by yrs. Record index not computerized. Office will perform a UCC search but public must search other records themselves. Search fee $5.00 per name for every 10 yrs. Copy fee $1.00 per page. Cert fee- $5.00 per cert plus copy fee. Payee- Willacy County Clerk. **Online access to Real Estate, Grantor/Grantee, Deed, Judgment, Lien, Appraiser, Property Tax records:** Access recording records free at www.titlex.com; select Willacy county.Record range is 8/1998 to 1/2004. Access Appraisal District records free at http://clientdb.trueautomation.com/clientdb/main.asp?id=14. **Other phones:** Treasurer- 956-689-2772; Appraiser/Auditor- 956-689-5979; Elections- 956-689-2710; Vital Records- 956-689-2710. **Property tax/Assessor-** 190 N 3rd St, Raymondville, TX 78580; 956-689-3621.

Williamson County

County Clerk, PO Box 18, Georgetown, TX 78627-0018. 512-943-1515, UCC recording phone-512-943-1514; fax-512-943-1616; hours: 8AM-5PM. www.wilco.org
Office personnel or visitors may perform searches. Search fee $10.00 per name. Will not search real estate records. Copy fee $1.00 if less than 5 copies. Cert fee- $5.00 per cert plus copy fee. Payee-Williamson County Clerk. **Online access to Real Estate, Appraiser, Property Tax, Tax Sale, Grantor/Grantee, Judgment, Lien, records:** Access recording records free at www.titlex.com; select Williamson county.Records go back to 5/1999. Access the appraiser database free at www.wcad.org. Also, access the monthly delinquent tax sale list at http://wcportals.wilco.org/tax%5Fassessor/. **Other phones:** Treasurer- 512-943-1587; Appraiser/Auditor- 512-930-3787; Elections- 512-943-1630; Vital Records- 512-943-1512. **Property tax/Assessor-** 512-943-1603.

Wilson County

County Clerk, PO Box 27, Floresville, TX 78114. 830-393-7308; fax-830-393-7334; hours: 8AM-5PM.
All records in one index. Records indexed on a public use terminal back to 1/1992. Only the public may search. Copy fee $1.00 per page. Cert fee- $5.00 per cert plus copy fee. Payee- Wilson County Clerk. **Online to Property Tax, Appraiser records:** Access to the county CAD records is free at http://clientdb.trueautomation.com/clientdb/main.asp?id=22. Also, see note at beginning of section. **Other phones:** Treasurer- 830-393-7310; Appraiser/Auditor- 830-393-3065; Elections- 830-393-7368; Vital Records- 830-393-7308. **Property tax/Assessor-** 2 Library Ln, Floresville, TX 78114; 830-393-7313.

Winkler County

County Clerk, PO Box 1007, Kermit, TX 79745. 432-586-3401; hours: 8AM-5PM.
All records in one index. Record index not computerized. Office will perform a UCC and Tax lien search but public must search other records themselves. Search fee $5.00. Copy fee $1.50 per page. Cert fee- $5.00 per cert plus copy fee. Payee-Winkler County Clerk. **Other phones:** Treasurer- 432-586-6604; Appraiser/Auditor- 432-586-2832. **Property tax/Assessor-** PO Drawer T, Kermit, TX 79745; 432-586-3465.

Wise County

County Clerk, PO Box 359, Decatur, TX 76234. 940-627-3351; fax-940-627-2138; hours: 8AM-5PM.
All records in one index. Records indexed on computer back to 1982. Search fee $10.00; will not search UCCs. Copy fee $1.00 per page. Cert fee-$5.00 per cert plus copy fee. Payee- Wise County Clerk. **Online access to Property, Appraiser, Land, Vital records:** Access to appraisal district records is free at www.wisecad.org or at www.myswdata.com/swd_find.aspx. Also, for land records search and vital records go to www.texaslandrecords.com. **Other phones:** Treasurer- 940-627-3540; Appraiser/Auditor- 940-627-3081; Elections- 940-627-3351; Vital Records- 940-627-3351. **Property tax/Assessor-** 404 W Walnut, Decatur, TX 76234; 940-627-3523.

Wood County

County Clerk, PO Box 1796, Quitman, TX 75783. 903-763-2711; fax-903-763-5641; hours: 8AM-5PM. www.co.wood.tx.us

Index: Indices by year. Only the public may search. Copy fee $1.00 per page; faxed back-$2.00 per page. Cert fee- $5.00 per cert plus copy fee. Payee- Wood County Clerk. **Online access to Real Estate, Grantor/Grantee, Deed, Lien, Judgment records:** Access recording records free at www.titlex.com; select Wood county. **Other phones:** Treasurer- 903-763-4186; Appraiser/Auditor- 903-763-4946; Elections- 903-763-2711; Vital Records- 903-763-2711. **Property tax/Assessor-** PO Box 1919, Quitman, TX 75783; 903-763-2261.

Yoakum County

County Clerk, PO Box 309, Plains, TX 79335. 806-456-2721, R/E recording phone-806-456-7491; fax-806-456-2258; hours: 8AM-5PM.
All records in one index. Records indexed on a public use terminal back to 1986. Office personnel or visitors may perform searches. Office personnel will only perform small searches. Search fee $5.00 per name plus $2.00 if faxed back. Copy fee $1.00 per page. Cert fee- $5.00 per cert plus copy fee. Payee- Yoakum County Clerk. **Other phones:** Treasurer- 806-456-7491; Appraiser/Auditor- 806-456-7491; Elections- 806-456-7491; Vital Records- 806-456-7491. **Property tax/Assessor-** 806-456-7491.

Young County

County Clerk, 516 Fourth St #104, Graham, TX 76450-3063. 940-549-8432, R/E recording phone-940-539-8432; fax-940-521-0305; hours: 8:30AM-5PM.
All records in one index. Records indexed on a public use terminal back to 1991. Only the public may search. Copy fee $2.00, if tax lien or real estate $1.00 per page. Cert fee- $5.00 per cert plus copy fee. Payee- Young County Clerk. **Online access to Property, Appraiser records:** Access property data by download from a private company; fees apply; add'l data includes minerals, ofc exports, delinquents; visit www.ptax.org/tax_office_data.htm **Other phones:** Treasurer- 940-549-2633; Appraiser/Auditor- 940-549-2392; Elections- 940-549-5132; Vital Records- 940-539-8432; 940-539-8433. **Property tax/Assessor-** 940-549-1393.

Zapata County

County Clerk, PO Box 789, Zapata, TX 78076. 956-765-9915; fax-956-765-9933; hours: 8AM-5PM.
Records indexed on a public use terminal back to 1994. Office personnel or visitors may perform searches. General index search fee $5.00 per name. UCCs $10.00. Copy fee $1.00 per page but not less than 5. Cert fee- $5.00 per cert plus copy fee. Payee- Zapata County Clerk. **Online access to Property, Appraiser, Real Estate Recording, Deed records:** Access to appraisal district records is free at http://clientdb.trueautomation.com/clientdb/main.asp?id=28. Also, access recording office land data at www.etitlesearch.com; registration required, fee based on usage. **Other phones:** Treasurer- 956-765-9925; Appraiser/Auditor- 956-765-9971. **Property tax/Assessor-** 956-765-9971.

Zavala County

County Clerk, Zavala Courthouse, Crystal City, TX 78839. 830-374-2331; fax-830-374-5955; hours: 8AM-5PM.
Office personnel or visitors may perform searches. Search fee $10.00 per name. Copy fee $1.00 per page. Cert fee- $1.00 per cert plus copy fee. Payee-Zavala County Clerk. **Other phones:** Treasurer- 830-374-2442; Appraiser/Auditor- 830-374-3476. **Property tax/Assessor-** 830-347-235

Texas County Locator

You will usually be able to find the city name in the City/County Cross Reference below. In that case, it is a simple matter to determine the county from the cross reference. However, only the official US Postal Service city names are included in this index. We have also included a ZIP/City Cross Reference immediately following the City/County Cross Reference. If you know the ZIP Code but the city name does not appear in the City/County Cross Reference index, look up the ZIP Code in the ZIP/City Cross Reference, find the city name, then look up the city name in the City/County Cross Reference.

Texas City/County Cross Reference

ABBOTT (76621) Hill(94), McLennan(5)
ABERNATHY (79311) Hale(68), Lubbock(31)
ABILENE (79601) Taylor(77), Jones(16), Callahan(3), Shackelford(2)
ABILENE (79602) Taylor(94), Callahan(5)
ABILENE Taylor
ACE Polk
ACKERLY (79713) Martin(38), Dawson(29), Howard(25), Borden(7)
ADDISON Dallas
ADKINS (78101) Bexar(82), Wilson(17)
ADRIAN (79001) Oldham(70), Deaf Smith(30)
AFTON Dickens
AGUA DULCE Nueces
AIKEN Floyd
ALAMO Hidalgo
ALANREED Gray
ALBA (75410) Wood(72), Rains(27)
ALBANY Shackelford
ALEDO (76008) Parker(84), Tarrant(15)
ALICE (78332) Jim Wells(98), Duval(1)
ALICE Jim Wells
ALIEF Harris
ALLEN Collin
ALLEYTON Colorado
ALLISON Wheeler
ALPINE Brewster
ALTAIR Colorado
ALTO Cherokee
ALVARADO Johnson
ALVIN (77511) Brazoria(93), Galveston(6)
ALVIN Brazoria
ALVORD Wise
AMARILLO (79124) Potter(93), Randall(6)
AMARILLO (79121) Randall(76), Potter(23)
AMARILLO Potter
AMARILLO Randall
AMHERST Lamb
ANAHUAC Chambers
ANDERSON Grimes
ANDREWS Andrews
ANGLETON Brazoria
ANNA Collin
ANNONA Red River
ANSON Jones
ANTHONY El Paso
ANTON (79313) Hockley(74), Lamb(17), Lubbock(5), Hale(1)
APPLE SPRINGS Trinity
AQUILLA (76622) Hill(92), McLennan(7)
ARANSAS PASS (78336) San Patricio(88), Aransas(11)
ARANSAS PASS San Patricio
ARCHER CITY Archer
ARGYLE Denton
ARLINGTON Tarrant
ARMSTRONG Kenedy
ARP Smith
ART Mason
ARTESIA WELLS La Salle
ARTHUR CITY Lamar
ASHERTON Dimmit
ASPERMONT Stonewall
ATASCOSA Bexar
ATHENS (75751) Henderson(98), Anderson(1)

ATHENS (75752) Henderson(93), Van Zandt(6)
ATLANTA Cass
AUBREY Denton
AUSTIN (78737) Hays(57), Travis(42)
AUSTIN (78728) Travis(94), Williamson(5)
AUSTIN (78736) Travis(97), Hays(2)
AUSTIN (78750) Travis(51), Williamson(48)
AUSTIN (78729) Williamson(92), Travis(7)
AUSTIN Travis
AUSTIN Williamson
AUSTWELL Refugio
AVALON Ellis
AVERY (75554) Red River(95), Bowie(4)
AVINGER (75630) Marion(55), Cass(44)
AXTELL (76624) McLennan(95), Limestone(4)
AZLE (76020) Tarrant(51), Parker(45), Wise(3)
AZLE Parker
BACLIFF Galveston
BAGWELL Red River
BAILEY Fannin
BAIRD Callahan
BALLINGER Runnels
BALMORHEA Reeves
BANDERA Bandera
BANGS (76823) Brown(88), Coleman(11)
BANQUETE Nueces
BARDWELL Ellis
BARKER Harris
BARKSDALE (78828) Edwards(68), Real(31)
BARNHART (76930) Irion(58), Crockett(41)
BARRY Navarro
BARSTOW Ward
BARTLETT (76511) Bell(53), Williamson(28), Milam(18)
BASTROP Bastrop
BATESVILLE Zavala
BATSON Hardin
BAY CITY Matagorda
BAYSIDE Refugio
BAYTOWN (77521) Harris(96), Chambers(3)
BAYTOWN Harris
BEASLEY Fort Bend
BEAUMONT Jefferson
BEBE Gonzales
BECKVILLE Panola
BEDFORD Tarrant
BEDIAS Grimes
BEEVILLE Bee
BELLAIRE Harris
BELLEVUE (76228) Clay(88), Montague(11)
BELLS Grayson
BELLVILLE Austin
BELMONT Gonzales
BELTON Bell
BEN ARNOLD Milam
BEN BOLT Jim Wells
BEN FRANKLIN Delta
BEN WHEELER Van Zandt
BENAVIDES Duval
BEND San Saba
BENJAMIN Knox
BERCLAIR Goliad
BERGHEIM Kendall

BERTRAM Burnet
BIG BEND NATIONAL PARK Brewster
BIG LAKE Reagan
BIG SANDY (75755) Upshur(52), Wood(47)
BIG SANDY Upshur
BIG SPRING (79720) Howard(98), Glasscock(1)
BIG SPRING Howard
BIG WELLS Dimmit
BIGFOOT Frio
BIROME Hill
BISHOP Nueces
BIVINS Cass
BLACKWELL (79506) Nolan(55), Coke(44)
BLANCO (78606) Blanco(90), Comal(7), Kendall(1)
BLANKET (76432) Brown(94), Comanche(5)
BLEDSOE Cochran
BLEIBLERVILLE Austin
BLESSING Matagorda
BLOOMBURG Cass
BLOOMING GROVE Navarro
BLOOMINGTON Victoria
BLOSSOM Lamar
BLUE RIDGE (75424) Collin(92), Fannin(7)
BLUEGROVE Clay
BLUFF DALE (76433) Erath(72), Hood(17), Somervell(9)
BLUFFTON Llano
BLUM Hill
BOERNE (78015) Bexar(64), Kendall(32), Comal(3)
BOERNE (78006) Kendall(82), Bexar(16), Comal(1)
BOGATA Red River
BOLING (77420) Wharton(92), Matagorda(6), Fort Bend(1)
BON WIER Newton
BONHAM Fannin
BOOKER (79005) Lipscomb(63), Ochiltree(36)
BORGER Hutchinson
BOVINA Parmer
BOWIE (76230) Montague(87), Jack(8), Clay(4)
BOYD (76023) Wise(96), Parker(3)
BOYS RANCH (79010) Oldham(83), Potter(16)
BRACKETTVILLE Kinney
BRADY (76825) McCulloch(98), Mason(1)
BRANDON Hill
BRASHEAR (75420) Hopkins(96), Rains(3)
BRAZORIA Brazoria
BRECKENRIDGE Stephens
BREMOND (76629) Robertson(95), Falls(4)
BRENHAM Washington
BRIDGE CITY Orange
BRIDGEPORT (76426) Wise(95), Jack(4)
BRIGGS Burnet
BRISCOE (79011) Hemphill(59), Wheeler(40)
BROADDUS San Augustine
BRONSON (75930) Sabine(72), San Augustine(27)
BRONTE (76933) Coke(61), Runnels(38)
BROOKELAND (75931) Sabine(82), Jasper(16)

BROOKESMITH (76827) Brown(98), Coleman(1)
BROOKSHIRE (77423) Waller(94), Fort Bend(5)
BROOKSTON Lamar
BROWNFIELD Terry
BROWNSBORO (75756) Henderson(94), Van Zandt(5)
BROWNSVILLE Cameron
BROWNWOOD Brown
BRUCEVILLE (76630) McLennan(97), Falls(2)
BRUNI (78344) Webb(91), Duval(8)
BRYAN (77808) Brazos(91), Robertson(8)
BRYAN Brazos
BRYSON Jack
BUCHANAN DAM Llano
BUCKHOLTS Milam
BUDA (78610) Hays(75), Travis(22), Caldwell(2)
BUFFALO (75831) Leon(96), Freestone(3)
BUFFALO GAP Taylor
BULA (79320) Bailey(81), Lamb(18)
BULLARD (75757) Smith(70), Cherokee(29)
BULVERDE Comal
BUNA Jasper
BURKBURNETT Wichita
BURKETT Coleman
BURKEVILLE Newton
BURLESON (76028) Johnson(77), Tarrant(22)
BURLESON Johnson
BURLINGTON (76519) Milam(50), Bell(37), Falls(11)
BURNET (78611) Burnet(96), Llano(3)
BURTON Washington
BUSHLAND Potter
BYERS Clay
BYNUM Hill
CACTUS Moore
CADDO Stephens
CADDO MILLS Hunt
CALDWELL Burleson
CALL (75933) Newton(71), Jasper(28)
CALLIHAM McMullen
CALVERT Robertson
CAMDEN Polk
CAMERON Milam
CAMP WOOD (78833) Real(84), Edwards(15)
CAMPBELL Hunt
CAMPBELLTON (78008) Atascosa(97), Live Oak(2)
CANADIAN (79014) Hemphill(93), Lipscomb(6)
CANTON Van Zandt
CANUTILLO El Paso
CANYON Randall
CANYON LAKE Comal
CARBON Eastland
CAREY Childress
CARLSBAD Tom Green
CARLTON (76436) Hamilton(61), Comanche(35), Erath(2)
CARMINE (78932) Fayette(95), Washington(4)
CARRIZO SPRINGS Dimmit

CARROLLTON (75007) Denton(90), Dallas(9)
CARROLLTON Dallas
CARROLLTON Denton
CARTHAGE Panola
CASON Morris
CASTELL (76831) Llano(65), Mason(35)
CASTROVILLE Medina
CAT SPRING (78933) Colorado(64), Austin(35)
CATARINA Dimmit
CAYUGA Anderson
CEDAR CREEK (78612) Bastrop(93), Travis(6)
CEDAR HILL Dallas
CEDAR LANE Matagorda
CEDAR PARK (78613) Williamson(85), Travis(14)
CEDAR PARK Williamson
CEE VEE Cottle
CELESTE (75423) Hunt(95), Fannin(4)
CELINA (75009) Collin(95), Denton(4)
CENTER (75935) Shelby(98), San Augustine(1)
CENTER POINT Kerr
CENTERVILLE Leon
CENTRALIA Trinity
CHALK Cottle
CHANDLER (75758) Henderson(88), Van Zandt(11)
CHANNELVIEW Harris
CHANNING (79018) Hartley(58), Moore(41)
CHAPMAN RANCH Nueces
CHAPPELL HILL (77426) Washington(90), Austin(9)
CHARLOTTE Atascosa
CHATFIELD Navarro
CHEROKEE San Saba
CHESTER (75936) Tyler(72), Polk(27)
CHICO (76431) Wise(96), Jack(3)
CHICOTA Lamar
CHILDRESS (79201) Childress(95), Cottle(2), Hall(2)
CHILLICOTHE (79225) Hardeman(93), Wilbarger(6)
CHILTON Falls
CHINA Jefferson
CHINA SPRING (76633) McLennan(91), Bosque(8)
CHIRENO Nacogdoches
CHRIESMAN Burleson
CHRISTINE Atascosa
CHRISTOVAL (76935) Tom Green(78), Schleicher(21)
CIBOLO (78108) Guadalupe(80), Bexar(17), Comal(1)
CISCO (76437) Eastland(92), Callahan(4), Stephens(3)
CLARENDON (79226) Donley(88), Armstrong(7), Hall(1), Briscoe(1)
CLARKSVILLE Red River
CLAUDE (79019) Armstrong(93), Randall(6)
CLAY Burleson
CLAYTON Panola
CLEBURNE (76033) Johnson(97), Somervell(2)
CLEBURNE Johnson
CLEVELAND (77328) Montgomery(40), San Jacinto(38), Liberty(20)
CLEVELAND Liberty
CLIFTON Bosque
CLINT El Paso
CLUTE Brazoria
CLYDE Callahan
COAHOMA (79511) Howard(76), Borden(23)
COLDSPRING San Jacinto
COLEMAN Coleman
COLLEGE STATION Brazos
COLLEGEPORT Matagorda

COLLEYVILLE Tarrant
COLLINSVILLE (76233) Grayson(75), Cooke(24)
COLMESNEIL Tyler
COLORADO CITY Mitchell
COLUMBUS Colorado
COMANCHE Comanche
COMBES Cameron
COMFORT (78013) Kendall(87), Kerr(12)
COMMERCE Hunt
COMO (75431) Hopkins(78), Wood(21)
COMSTOCK Val Verde
CONCAN Uvalde
CONCEPCION Duval
CONCORD Leon
CONE Crosby
CONROE Montgomery
CONVERSE Bexar
COOKVILLE Titus
COOLIDGE Limestone
COOPER Delta
COPEVILLE Collin
COPPELL Dallas
COPPERAS COVE (76522) Coryell(94), Lampasas(5)
CORPUS CHRISTI Nueces
CORRIGAN Polk
CORSICANA Navarro
COST Gonzales
COTTON CENTER Hale
COTULLA La Salle
COUPLAND (78615) Williamson(68), Travis(31)
COVINGTON Hill
COYANOSA Pecos
CRANDALL Kaufman
CRANE Crane
CRANFILLS GAP (76637) Bosque(98), Hamilton(1)
CRAWFORD McLennan
CRESSON (76035) Hood(56), Parker(33), Johnson(9)
CROCKETT Houston
CROSBY Harris
CROSBYTON Crosby
CROSS PLAINS (76443) Callahan(90), Brown(7), Coleman(2)
CROWELL (79227) Knox(59), Foard(40)
CROWLEY (76036) Tarrant(81), Johnson(18)
CRYSTAL CITY (78839) Zavala(98), Dimmit(1)
CUERO De Witt
CUMBY (75433) Hopkins(96), Hunt(3)
CUNEY Cherokee
CUNNINGHAM Lamar
CUSHING (75760) Nacogdoches(87), Rusk(12)
CYPRESS Harris
D HANIS Medina
DAINGERFIELD Morris
DAISETTA Liberty
DALE (78616) Caldwell(90), Bastrop(9)
DALHART (79022) Dallam(68), Hartley(30)
DALLARDSVILLE Polk
DALLAS (75252) Collin(97), Dallas(2)
DALLAS (75287) Collin(49), Denton(48), Dallas(2)
DALLAS Dallas
DAMON (77430) Fort Bend(53), Brazoria(46)
DANBURY Brazoria
DANCIGER Brazoria
DANEVANG Wharton
DARROUZETT Lipscomb
DAVILLA Milam
DAWN Deaf Smith
DAWSON Navarro
DAYTON (77535) Liberty(94), Chambers(5)
DE BERRY Panola
DE KALB Bowie
DE LEON Comanche

DEANVILLE Burleson
DECATUR (76234) Wise(98), Denton(1)
DEER PARK Harris
DEL RIO Edwards
DEL RIO Val Verde
DEL VALLE (78617) Travis(86), Bastrop(13)
DELL CITY Hudspeth
DELMITA (78536) Starr(86), Hidalgo(13)
DENISON Grayson
DENNIS Parker
DENTON Denton
DENVER CITY (79323) Yoakum(94), Gaines(5)
DEPORT (75435) Lamar(86), Red River(13)
DESDEMONA (76445) Eastland(82), Comanche(15), Erath(1)
DESOTO Dallas
DETROIT (75436) Red River(89), Lamar(10)
DEVERS Liberty
DEVINE Medina
DEWEYVILLE Newton
DIANA (75640) Upshur(67), Harrison(31), Marion(1)
DIBOLL Angelina
DICKENS Dickens
DICKINSON Galveston
DIKE Hopkins
DILLEY Frio
DIME BOX Lee
DIMMITT (79027) Castro(97), Lamb(1)
DINERO Live Oak
DOBBIN Montgomery
DODD CITY Fannin
DODGE Walker
DODSON (79230) Collingsworth(83), Childress(16)
DONIE (75838) Freestone(79), Limestone(20)
DONNA Hidalgo
DOOLE McCulloch
DOSS Gillespie
DOUCETTE Tyler
DOUGHERTY Floyd
DOUGLASS Nacogdoches
DOUGLASSVILLE Cass
DRIFTWOOD Hays
DRIPPING SPRINGS (78620) Hays(90), Travis(9)
DRISCOLL Nueces
DRYDEN Terrell
DUBLIN (76446) Erath(85), Comanche(14)
DUMAS Moore
DUMONT King
DUNCANVILLE Dallas
DUNN Scurry
DYESS AFB Taylor
EAGLE LAKE (77434) Colorado(98), Wharton(1)
EAGLE PASS Maverick
EARLY Brown
EARTH (79031) Lamb(77), Castro(18), Bailey(3)
EAST BERNARD (77435) Wharton(78), Fort Bend(20), Colorado(1)
EASTLAND Eastland
EASTON Gregg
ECLETO Karnes
ECTOR Fannin
EDCOUCH Hidalgo
EDDY (76524) McLennan(77), Falls(22)
EDEN Concho
EDGEWOOD Van Zandt
EDINBURG Hidalgo
EDMONSON Hale
EDNA Jackson
EDROY San Patricio
EGYPT Wharton
EL CAMPO Wharton
EL INDIO Maverick

EL PASO (79938) El Paso(97), Hudspeth(2)
EL PASO El Paso
ELBERT Throckmorton
ELDORADO Schleicher
ELECTRA (76360) Wichita(88), Wilbarger(11)
ELGIN (78621) Bastrop(77), Travis(13), Lee(5), Williamson(3)
ELIASVILLE Young
ELKHART Anderson
ELLINGER Fayette
ELM MOTT McLennan
ELMATON Matagorda
ELMENDORF (78112) Bexar(98), Wilson(1)
ELMO Kaufman
ELSA Hidalgo
ELYSIAN FIELDS Harrison
EMORY Rains
ENCINAL La Salle
ENCINO Brooks
ENERGY Comanche
ENLOE Delta
ENNIS (75119) Ellis(98), Navarro(1)
ENNIS Ellis
ENOCHS (79324) Bailey(93), Lamb(6)
EOLA (76937) Tom Green(69), Concho(30)
ERA Cooke
ESTELLINE Hall
ETOILE Nacogdoches
EULESS Tarrant
EUSTACE (75124) Henderson(77), Van Zandt(22)
EVADALE Jasper
EVANT (76525) Coryell(65), Hamilton(25), Lampasas(8)
FABENS El Paso
FAIRFIELD Freestone
FALCON HEIGHTS Starr
FALFURRIAS (78355) Brooks(95), Jim Wells(4)
FALLS CITY (78113) Wilson(41), Karnes(36), Atascosa(21)
FANNIN Goliad
FARMERSVILLE (75442) Collin(87), Hunt(12)
FARNSWORTH Ochiltree
FARWELL (79325) Parmer(92), Bailey(7)
FATE Rockwall
FAYETTEVILLE (78940) Fayette(86), Austin(12)
FENTRESS Caldwell
FERRIS (75125) Ellis(83), Dallas(16)
FIELDTON Lamb
FISCHER Comal
FLAT Coryell
FLATONIA (78941) Fayette(87), Bastrop(6), Gonzales(5)
FLINT Smith
FLOMOT (79234) Motley(85), Floyd(14)
FLORENCE (76527) Williamson(97), Bell(1), Burnet(1)
FLORESVILLE Wilson
FLOWER MOUND Denton
FLOYDADA (79235) Floyd(96), Crosby(3)
FLUVANNA (79517) Scurry(71), Borden(28)
FLYNN Leon
FOLLETT Lipscomb
FORESTBURG (76239) Montague(73), Cooke(26)
FORNEY (75126) Kaufman(97), Rockwall(2)
FORRESTON Ellis
FORSAN Howard
FORT DAVIS Jeff Davis
FORT HANCOCK Hudspeth
FORT MC KAVETT (76841) Menard(87), Kimble(8), Schleicher(3)
FORT STOCKTON Pecos

FORT WORTH (76126) Tarrant(87), Parker(12)
FORT WORTH (76178) Tarrant(96), Denton(3)
FORT WORTH Tarrant
FOWLERTON (78021) La Salle(80), Atascosa(10), McMullen(10)
FRANCITAS Jackson
FRANKLIN Robertson
FRANKSTON (75763) Anderson(52), Henderson(47)
FRED Tyler
FREDERICKSBURG (78624) Gillespie(86), Kendall(13)
FREDONIA (76842) Mason(54), San Saba(40), McCulloch(5)
FREEPORT Brazoria
FREER Duval
FRESNO Fort Bend
FRIENDSWOOD (77546) Galveston(68), Harris(31)
FRIENDSWOOD Galveston
FRIONA (79035) Parmer(94), Deaf Smith(4), Castro(1)
FRISCO (75034) Collin(55), Denton(44)
FRISCO Collin
FRITCH (79036) Hutchinson(94), Carson(5)
FROST Navarro
FRUITVALE Van Zandt
FULSHEAR Fort Bend
FULTON Aransas
GAIL Borden
GAINESVILLE Cooke
GALENA PARK Harris
GALLATIN Cherokee
GALVESTON Galveston
GANADO Jackson
GARCIASVILLE Starr
GARDEN CITY (79739) Glasscock(84), Reagan(15)
GARDENDALE Ector
GARLAND (75048) Dallas(80), Collin(19)
GARLAND Dallas
GARRISON (75946) Nacogdoches(53), Rusk(46)
GARWOOD Colorado
GARY (75643) Panola(94), Shelby(5)
GATESVILLE (76528) Coryell(97), Bell(2)
GATESVILLE Coryell
GAUSE Milam
GENEVA Sabine
GEORGE WEST Live Oak
GEORGETOWN Williamson
GERONIMO Guadalupe
GIDDINGS Lee
GILCHRIST Galveston
GILLETT Karnes
GILMER (75645) Upshur(98), Gregg(1)
GILMER Upshur
GIRARD Kent
GIRVIN Pecos
GLADEWATER (75647) Gregg(52), Upshur(37), Smith(9)
GLEN FLORA Wharton
GLEN ROSE Somervell
GLIDDEN Colorado
GOBER Fannin
GODLEY Johnson
GOLDEN Wood
GOLDSBORO (79519) Taylor(38), Coleman(33), Runnels(27)
GOLDSMITH Ector
GOLDTHWAITE Mills
GOLIAD Goliad
GONZALES Gonzales
GOODFELLOW AFB Tom Green
GOODRICH Polk
GORDON (76453) Palo Pinto(86), Erath(13)
GORDONVILLE Grayson

GOREE (76363) Knox(96), Haskell(2), Throckmorton(1)
GORMAN (76454) Eastland(73), Comanche(26)
GOULDBUSK Coleman
GRAFORD Palo Pinto
GRAHAM (76450) Young(93), Stephens(3), Palo Pinto(3)
GRANBURY (76048) Hood(98), Somervell(1)
GRANBURY (76049) Hood(96), Parker(2)
GRAND PRAIRIE (75052) Dallas(62), Tarrant(36)
GRAND PRAIRIE (75054) Tarrant(71), Dallas(28)
GRAND PRAIRIE Dallas
GRAND SALINE (75140) Van Zandt(98), Smith(1)
GRANDFALLS Ward
GRANDVIEW (76050) Johnson(90), Ellis(5), Hill(4)
GRANGER Williamson
GRAPELAND (75844) Houston(73), Anderson(26)
GRAPEVINE (76051) Tarrant(98), Dallas(1)
GRAPEVINE Tarrant
GREENVILLE Hunt
GREENWOOD Wise
GREGORY San Patricio
GROESBECK Limestone
GROOM (79039) Carson(64), Gray(33), Donley(1)
GROVES Jefferson
GROVETON Trinity
GRULLA Starr
GRUVER (79040) Hansford(60), Sherman(39)
GUERRA (78360) Jim Hogg(80), Starr(20)
GUNTER Grayson
GUSTINE Comanche
GUTHRIE King
GUY (77444) Fort Bend(75), Brazoria(24)
HALE CENTER (79041) Hale(97), Lamb(2)
HALLETTSVILLE Lavaca
HALLSVILLE Harrison
HALTOM CITY Tarrant
HAMILTON Hamilton
HAMLIN (79520) Jones(95), Fisher(4)
HAMSHIRE (77622) Jefferson(91), Chambers(8)
HANKAMER Chambers
HAPPY (79042) Randall(60), Swisher(19), Castro(12), Armstrong(7)
HARDIN Liberty
HARGILL Hidalgo
HARKER HEIGHTS Bell
HARLETON (75651) Harrison(95), Marion(4)
HARLINGEN Cameron
HARPER (78631) Gillespie(64), Kimble(26), Kerr(10)
HARROLD Wilbarger
HART (79043) Castro(76), Lamb(20), Hale(3)
HARTLEY Hartley
HARWOOD (78632) Gonzales(52), Caldwell(47)
HASKELL Haskell
HASLET (76052) Tarrant(88), Wise(6), Denton(5)
HASSE Comanche
HAWKINS Wood
HAWLEY Jones
HEARNE Robertson
HEBBRONVILLE Jim Hogg
HEDLEY Donley
HEIDENHEIMER Bell
HELOTES (78023) Bexar(91), Medina(8)
HEMPHILL Sabine
HEMPSTEAD Waller
HENDERSON Rusk
HENRIETTA (76365) Clay(98), Jack(1)

HEREFORD (79045) Deaf Smith(91), Castro(8)
HERMLEIGH (79526) Scurry(95), Fisher(3)
HEWITT McLennan
HEXT (76848) Menard(94), Mason(5)
HICO (76457) Hamilton(63), Erath(30), Bosque(5)
HIDALGO Hidalgo
HIGGINS (79046) Lipscomb(87), Hemphill(12)
HIGH ISLAND Galveston
HIGHLANDS Harris
HILLISTER Tyler
HILLSBORO Hill
HITCHCOCK Galveston
HOBSON Karnes
HOCHHEIM De Witt
HOCKLEY (77447) Harris(47), Waller(36), Montgomery(15)
HOLLAND Bell
HOLLIDAY Archer
HONDO Medina
HONEY GROVE (75446) Fannin(91), Lamar(8)
HOOKS Bowie
HOUSTON (77053) Fort Bend(56), Harris(43)
HOUSTON (77099) Harris(96), Fort Bend(3)
HOUSTON Harris
HOWE Grayson
HUBBARD (76648) Hill(91), Navarro(5), Limestone(2)
HUFFMAN Harris
HUFSMITH Harris
HUGHES SPRINGS (75656) Cass(89), Morris(10)
HULL Liberty
HUMBLE (77339) Harris(81), Montgomery(18)
HUMBLE Harris
HUNGERFORD Wharton
HUNT (78024) Kerr(96), Real(3)
HUNTINGTON Angelina
HUNTSVILLE (77320) Walker(91), San Jacinto(8)
HUNTSVILLE Walker
HURST Tarrant
HUTCHINS Dallas
HUTTO (78634) Williamson(98), Travis(1)
HYE Blanco
IDALOU Lubbock
IMPERIAL Pecos
INDUSTRY Austin
INEZ Victoria
INGLESIDE San Patricio
INGRAM Kerr
IOLA Grimes
IOWA PARK Wichita
IRA (79527) Scurry(81), Borden(18)
IRAAN Pecos
IREDELL (76649) Bosque(86), Erath(13)
IRENE Hill
IRVING Dallas
ITALY Ellis
ITASCA Hill
IVANHOE Fannin
JACKSBORO (76458) Jack(98), Wise(1)
JACKSONVILLE Cherokee
JARRELL Williamson
JASPER Jasper
JAYTON (79528) Kent(83), Stonewall(16)
JEFFERSON (75657) Marion(87), Cass(9), Harrison(2)
JERMYN (76459) Jack(95), Young(5)
JEWETT (75846) Leon(90), Limestone(9)
JOAQUIN (75954) Shelby(91), Panola(8)
JOHNSON CITY Blanco
JOINERVILLE Rusk
JONESBORO (76538) Hamilton(52), Coryell(47)

JONESVILLE (75659) Harrison(80), Rusk(20)
JOSEPHINE Collin
JOSHUA Johnson
JOURDANTON Atascosa
JUDSON Gregg
JUNCTION Kimble
JUSTICEBURG Garza
JUSTIN (76247) Denton(98), Wise(1)
KAMAY Wichita
KARNACK Harrison
KARNES CITY Karnes
KATY (77494) Fort Bend(90), Harris(8), Waller(1)
KATY (77450) Harris(69), Fort Bend(30)
KATY (77493) Harris(82), Waller(15), Fort Bend(1)
KATY Harris
KAUFMAN Kaufman
KEENE Johnson
KELLER Tarrant
KEMAH Galveston
KEMP (75143) Henderson(63), Kaufman(36)
KEMPNER (76539) Lampasas(82), Bell(8), Coryell(4), Burnet(3)
KENDALIA Kendall
KENDLETON Fort Bend
KENEDY Karnes
KENNARD (75847) Trinity(52), Houston(47)
KENNEDALE Tarrant
KENNEY Austin
KERENS Navarro
KERMIT Winkler
KERRICK Dallam
KERRVILLE (78028) Kerr(95), Gillespie(4)
KERRVILLE Kerr
KILDARE Cass
KILGORE (75662) Gregg(74), Rusk(24), Smith(1)
KILGORE Gregg
KILLEEN (76544) Bell(65), Coryell(34)
KILLEEN (76549) Bell(98), Burnet(1)
KILLEEN Bell
KINGSBURY Guadalupe
KINGSLAND (78639) Llano(87), Burnet(12)
KINGSVILLE Kleberg
KIRBYVILLE (75956) Jasper(98), Newton(1)
KIRKLAND Childress
KIRVIN Freestone
KLONDIKE Delta
KNICKERBOCKER Tom Green
KNIPPA Uvalde
KNOTT (79748) Howard(75), Martin(25)
KNOX CITY (79529) Knox(96), Haskell(3)
KOPPERL Bosque
KOSSE (76653) Limestone(87), Falls(10), Robertson(1)
KOUNTZE Hardin
KRESS (79052) Swisher(91), Hale(7), Castro(1)
KRUM Denton
KURTEN Brazos
KYLE (78640) Hays(98), Caldwell(1)
LA BLANCA Hidalgo
LA COSTE (78039) Medina(78), Bexar(21)
LA FERIA Cameron
LA JOYA Hidalgo
LA MARQUE Galveston
LA PORTE Harris
LA PRYOR Zavala
LA SALLE Jackson
LA VERNIA (78121) Wilson(76), Guadalupe(23)
LA VILLA Hidalgo
LA WARD Jackson
LADONIA (75449) Fannin(91), Hunt(8)
LAIRD HILL Rusk
LAKE CREEK Delta
LAKE DALLAS Denton

LAKE JACKSON Brazoria
LAKEVIEW Hall
LAMESA (79331) Dawson(97), Martin(1)
LAMPASAS Lampasas
LANCASTER Dallas
LANE CITY Wharton
LANEVILLE Rusk
LANGTRY Val Verde
LAREDO Webb
LARUE Henderson
LASARA Willacy
LATEXO Houston
LAUGHLIN A F B Val Verde
LAVON Collin
LAWN (79530) Taylor(93), Runnels(6)
LAZBUDDIE Parmer
LEAGUE CITY Galveston
LEAKEY Real
LEANDER (78641) Williamson(59),
  Travis(40)
LEANDER Travis
LEANDER Williamson
LEDBETTER (78946) Fayette(78),
  Washington(14), Lee(6)
LEESBURG (75451) Camp(89), Wood(6),
  Upshur(4)
LEESVILLE Gonzales
LEFORS Gray
LEGGETT Polk
LELIA LAKE Donley
LEMING Atascosa
LENORAH Martin
LEON JUNCTION Coryell
LEONA Leon
LEONARD (75452) Fannin(86), Hunt(7),
  Collin(6)
LEROY McLennan
LEVELLAND Hockley
LEWISVILLE Denton
LEXINGTON (78947) Lee(98), Milam(1)
LIBERTY Liberty
LIBERTY HILL (78642) Williamson(98),
  Burnet(1)
LILLIAN Johnson
LINCOLN Lee
LINDALE Smith
LINDEN Cass
LINDSAY Cooke
LINGLEVILLE Erath
LINN (78563) Hidalgo(94), Starr(5)
LIPAN (76462) Hood(45), Palo Pinto(20),
  Parker(16), Erath(12)
LIPSCOMB Lipscomb
LISSIE Wharton
LITTLE ELM Denton
LITTLE RIVER Bell
LITTLE RIVER ACADEMY Bell
LITTLEFIELD (79339) Lamb(92),
  Hockley(7)
LIVERPOOL Brazoria
LIVINGSTON Polk
LLANO Llano
LOCKHART Caldwell
LOCKNEY (79241) Floyd(97), Swisher(1)
LODI Marion
LOHN (76852) McCulloch(98), Concho(1)
LOLITA Jackson
LOMETA (76853) Lampasas(95), Mills(3)
LONDON (76854) Kimble(77), Menard(21)
LONE OAK (75453) Hunt(73), Rains(19),
  Hopkins(7)
LONE STAR (75668) Morris(86),
  Marion(11), Henderson(1)
LONG BRANCH (75669) Panola(98),
  Rusk(1)
LONG MOTT Calhoun
LONGVIEW (75602) Gregg(65),
  Harrison(34)
LONGVIEW (75603) Gregg(81), Rusk(18)
LONGVIEW (75604) Gregg(97), Upshur(2)
LONGVIEW (75605) Gregg(81),
  Harrison(17), Upshur(1)

LONGVIEW Gregg
LOOP Gaines
LOPENO Zapata
LORAINE (79532) Mitchell(94), Scurry(3),
  Nolan(2)
LORENA McLennan
LORENZO (79343) Crosby(71),
  Lubbock(28)
LOS EBANOS Hidalgo
LOS FRESNOS Cameron
LOS INDIOS Cameron
LOTT Falls
LOUISE (77455) Wharton(91), Jackson(8)
LOVELADY (75851) Houston(67),
  Trinity(32)
LOVING Young
LOWAKE Concho
LOZANO Cameron
LUBBOCK (79407) Lubbock(91),
  Hockley(8)
LUBBOCK Lubbock
LUEDERS (79533) Jones(58),
  Shackelford(37), Haskell(4)
LUFKIN Angelina
LULING (78648) Caldwell(91),
  Guadalupe(7), Gonzales(1)
LUMBERTON Hardin
LYFORD Willacy
LYONS Burleson
LYTLE (78052) Atascosa(79), Medina(13),
  Bexar(7)
MABANK (75156) Henderson(95),
  Kaufman(2), Van Zandt(1)
MABANK (75147) Kaufman(47), Van
  Zandt(46), Henderson(5)
MACDONA Bexar
MADISONVILLE Madison
MAGNOLIA (77355) Montgomery(98),
  Waller(1)
MAGNOLIA Montgomery
MAGNOLIA SPRINGS Bowie
MAGNOLIA SPRINGS Jasper
MALAKOFF Henderson
MALONE Hill
MANCHACA (78652) Travis(74), Hays(25)
MANOR Travis
MANSFIELD (76063) Tarrant(92),
  Johnson(7)
MANVEL Brazoria
MAPLE Bailey
MARATHON Brewster
MARBLE FALLS (78654) Burnet(95),
  Travis(4)
MARBLE FALLS (78657) Burnet(50),
  Llano(47), Blanco(1)
MARFA Presidio
MARIETTA Cass
MARION (78124) Guadalupe(93), Bexar(6)
MARKHAM Matagorda
MARLIN Falls
MARQUEZ Leon
MARSHALL Harrison
MART (76664) McLennan(83),
  Limestone(13), Falls(2)
MARTINDALE (78655) Caldwell(78),
  Guadalupe(21)
MARTINSVILLE Nacogdoches
MARYNEAL Nolan
MASON (76856) Mason(98), Menard(1)
MASTERSON (79058) Moore(58),
  Potter(41)
MATADOR Motley
MATAGORDA Matagorda
MATHIS (78368) San Patricio(94), Live
  Oak(5)
MAUD Bowie
MAURICEVILLE Orange
MAXWELL (78656) Caldwell(95), Hays(4)
MAY Brown
MAYDELLE Cherokee
MAYPEARL Ellis
MAYSFIELD Milam

MC CAMEY Upton
MC CAULLEY Fisher
MC COY Atascosa
MC DADE Bastrop
MC GREGOR (76657) McLennan(98),
  Coryell(1)
MC KINNEY Collin
MC LEOD Cass
MC NEIL Travis
MC QUEENEY Guadalupe
MCADOO (79243) Crosby(52), Dickens(47)
MCALLEN Hidalgo
MCFADDIN Victoria
MCLEAN (79057) Gray(70), Wheeler(20),
  Donley(9)
MEADOW (79345) Terry(86), Lynn(11),
  Taylor(1)
MEDINA Bandera
MEGARGEL Archer
MELISSA Collin
MELVIN (76858) McCulloch(60),
  Concho(39)
MEMPHIS (79245) Hall(97),
  Collingsworth(2)
MENARD (76859) Menard(78), Kimble(21)
MENTONE Loving
MERCEDES Hidalgo
MERETA Tom Green
MERIDIAN Bosque
MERIT Hunt
MERKEL (79536) Taylor(75), Jones(24)
MERTENS (76666) Hill(96), Navarro(3)
MERTZON Irion
MESQUITE Dallas
MEXIA (76667) Limestone(95),
  Freestone(4)
MEYERSVILLE (77974) De Witt(51),
  Victoria(48)
MIAMI (79059) Roberts(78), Gray(21)
MICO Medina
MIDFIELD Matagorda
MIDKIFF (79755) Upton(82), Midland(14),
  Reagan(2)
MIDLOTHIAN Ellis
MIDWAY (75852) Madison(97), Walker(1)
MILAM Sabine
MILANO (76556) Milam(98), Burleson(2)
MILES (76861) Tom Green(61),
  Runnels(36), Concho(1)
MILFORD (76670) Ellis(91), Navarro(7),
  Hill(1)
MILLERSVIEW Concho
MILLICAN Brazos
MILLSAP (76066) Parker(94), Palo Pinto(5)
MINDEN Rusk
MINEOLA (75773) Wood(91), Smith(7)
MINERAL Bee
MINERAL WELLS (76067) Palo Pinto(96),
  Parker(3)
MINERAL WELLS Palo Pinto
MINGUS (76463) Erath(75), Palo Pinto(23)
MIRANDO CITY Webb
MISSION Hidalgo
MISSOURI CITY (77489) Fort Bend(95),
  Harris(4)
MISSOURI CITY Fort Bend
MOBEETIE (79061) Wheeler(89), Gray(7),
  Hemphill(2)
MONAHANS Ward
MONT BELVIEU Chambers
MONTAGUE Montague
MONTALBA (75853) Anderson(98),
  Henderson(1)
MONTGOMERY (77356) Montgomery(98),
  Grimes(1)
MOODY (76557) McLennan(55), Bell(33),
  Coryell(10)
MOORE (78057) Medina(92), Frio(7)
MORAN (76464) Shackelford(81),
  Stephens(11), Callahan(6)
MORGAN Bosque
MORGAN MILL Erath

MORSE (79062) Hutchinson(87),
  Hansford(12)
MORTON (79346) Cochran(95), Bailey(4)
MOSCOW (75960) Polk(91), Tyler(8)
MOULTON Lavaca
MOUND Coryell
MOUNT CALM (76673) Hill(87),
  Limestone(9), McLennan(3)
MOUNT ENTERPRISE Rusk
MOUNT PLEASANT (75455) Titus(98),
  Franklin(1)
MOUNT PLEASANT Titus
MOUNT VERNON Franklin
MOUNTAIN HOME Kerr
MUENSTER Cooke
MULDOON Fayette
MULESHOE (79347) Bailey(83),
  Parmer(10), Lamb(4), Castro(1)
MULLIN Mills
MUMFORD Robertson
MUNDAY Knox
MURCHISON (75778) Henderson(65), Van
  Zandt(34)
MYRA Cooke
NACOGDOCHES Nacogdoches
NADA Colorado
NAPLES (75568) Morris(90), Cass(9)
NASH Bowie
NATALIA Medina
NAVAL AIR STATION/ JRB Tarrant
NAVASOTA Brazos
NAVASOTA Grimes
NAZARETH Castro
NECHES Anderson
NEDERLAND Jefferson
NEEDVILLE Fort Bend
NEMO (76070) Somervell(86), Johnson(13)
NEVADA Collin
NEW BADEN Robertson
NEW BOSTON Bowie
NEW BRAUNFELS (78130) Comal(83),
  Guadalupe(16)
NEW BRAUNFELS Comal
NEW CANEY Montgomery
NEW DEAL Lubbock
NEW HOME Lynn
NEW LONDON Rusk
NEW SUMMERFIELD Cherokee
NEW ULM (78950) Austin(64),
  Colorado(34)
NEW WAVERLY (77358) Walker(48), San
  Jacinto(39), Montgomery(12)
NEWARK (76071) Wise(96), Tarrant(3)
NEWCASTLE (76372) Young(78),
  Throckmorton(21)
NEWGULF Wharton
NEWPORT Clay
NEWTON (75966) Newton(95), Jasper(4)
NIXON (78140) Gonzales(88), Wilson(8),
  Guadalupe(3)
NOCONA Montague
NOLAN Nolan
NOLANVILLE Bell
NOME Jefferson
NORDHEIM (78141) De Witt(93),
  Karnes(6)
NORMANGEE (77871) Leon(59),
  Madison(40)
NORMANNA Bee
NORTH HOUSTON Harris
NORTH RICHLAND HILLS Tarrant
NORTH ZULCH Madison
NORTON Runnels
NOTREES Ector
NOVICE (79538) Coleman(51),
  Runnels(48)
NURSERY Victoria
O BRIEN Haskell
OAKHURST San Jacinto
OAKLAND Colorado
OAKVILLE Live Oak

OAKWOOD (75855) Leon(77), Freestone(22)
ODELL Hardeman
ODEM San Patricio
ODESSA (79766) Ector(89), Crane(6), Midland(3)
ODESSA (79765) Midland(52), Ector(47)
ODESSA Ector
ODONNELL (79351) Borden(40), Lynn(39), Dawson(19)
OGLESBY (76561) Coryell(90), McLennan(9)
OILTON Webb
OKLAUNION Wilbarger
OLD GLORY (79540) Stonewall(98), Haskell(1)
OLD OCEAN Brazoria
OLDEN Eastland
OLMITO Cameron
OLNEY (76374) Young(97), Archer(1), Throckmorton(1)
OLTON (79064) Lamb(79), Hale(20)
OMAHA Morris
ONALASKA Polk
ORANGE GROVE Jim Wells
ORANGEFIELD Orange
ORCHARD Fort Bend
ORE CITY (75683) Upshur(73), Marion(26)
ORLA Reeves
OTTINE Gonzales
OTTO Falls
OVALO (79541) Taylor(90), Callahan(9)
OVERTON (75684) Rusk(87), Smith(12)
OZONA (76943) Crockett(87), Val Verde(12)
PADUCAH (79248) Cottle(90), King(5), Foard(4)
PAIGE (78659) Bastrop(78), Lee(21)
PAINT ROCK Concho
PALACIOS (77465) Matagorda(73), Jackson(25)
PALESTINE (75803) Anderson(98), Henderson(1)
PALESTINE Anderson
PALMER Ellis
PALO PINTO Palo Pinto
PALUXY Hood
PAMPA (79065) Gray(97), Roberts(2)
PAMPA Gray
PANDORA Wilson
PANHANDLE (79068) Carson(97), Potter(1)
PANNA MARIA Karnes
PANOLA Panola
PARADISE Wise
PARIS Lamar
PASADENA Harris
PATTISON Waller
PATTONVILLE Lamar
PAWNEE Bee
PEACOCK Stonewall
PEAR VALLEY McCulloch
PEARLAND (77581) Brazoria(96), Harris(3)
PEARLAND Brazoria
PEARSALL Frio
PEASTER Parker
PECAN GAP (75469) Delta(91), Hunt(8)
PECOS Reeves
PEGGY Atascosa
PENDLETON Bell
PENELOPE Hill
PENITAS Hidalgo
PENNINGTON (75856) Trinity(68), Houston(31)
PENWELL Ector
PEP (79353) Hockley(96), Cochran(3)
PERRIN (76486) Jack(47), Palo Pinto(26), Parker(26)
PERRY Falls
PERRYTON Ochiltree
PETERSBURG (79250) Hale(48), Lubbock(22), Floyd(17), Crosby(11)

PETROLIA Clay
PETTUS Bee
PETTY Lamar
PFLUGERVILLE Travis
PHARR Hidalgo
PICKTON (75471) Hopkins(61), Wood(38)
PIERCE Wharton
PILOT POINT (76258) Denton(90), Grayson(9)
PINEHURST Montgomery
PINELAND Sabine
PIPE CREEK Bandera
PITTSBURG (75686) Camp(85), Upshur(7), Titus(5), Morris(1)
PLACEDO Victoria
PLAINS Yoakum
PLAINVIEW Hale
PLANO (75093) Collin(95), Denton(4)
PLANO Collin
PLANTERSVILLE (77363) Grimes(98), Waller(1)
PLEASANTON Atascosa
PLEDGER Matagorda
PLUM Fayette
POINT (75472) Rains(98), Hopkins(1)
POINT COMFORT Calhoun
POINTBLANK San Jacinto
POLLOK Angelina
PONDER Denton
PONTOTOC (76869) Llano(58), Mason(31), San Saba(9)
POOLVILLE (76487) Parker(68), Wise(22), Jack(8)
PORT ARANSAS Nueces
PORT ARTHUR Jefferson
PORT BOLIVAR Galveston
PORT ISABEL Cameron
PORT LAVACA Calhoun
PORT MANSFIELD Willacy
PORT NECHES Jefferson
PORT O CONNOR Calhoun
PORTER (77365) Montgomery(98), Harris(1)
PORTLAND San Patricio
POST (79356) Garza(91), Lynn(5), Crosby(2)
POTEET Atascosa
POTH Wilson
POTTSBORO Grayson
POTTSVILLE Hamilton
POWDERLY Lamar
POWELL Navarro
POYNOR Henderson
PRAIRIE HILL Limestone
PRAIRIE LEA Caldwell
PRAIRIE VIEW Waller
PREMONT Jim Wells
PRESIDIO Presidio
PRICE Rusk
PRIDDY Mills
PRINCETON Collin
PROCTOR Comanche
PROGRESO Hidalgo
PROSPER (75078) Collin(94), Denton(5)
PURDON Navarro
PURMELA (76566) Coryell(76), Hamilton(24)
PUTNAM Callahan
PYOTE Ward
QUAIL Collingsworth
QUANAH Hardeman
QUEEN CITY Cass
QUEMADO (78877) Maverick(98), Kinney(1)
QUINLAN (75474) Hunt(96), Kaufman(3)
QUITAQUE (79255) Briscoe(64), Motley(21), Floyd(13), Hall(1)
QUITMAN Wood
RAINBOW Somervell
RALLS Crosby
RANDOLPH Fannin

RANGER (76470) Eastland(85), Stephens(14)
RANKIN Upton
RANSOM CANYON Lubbock
RATCLIFF Houston
RAVENNA Fannin
RAYMONDVILLE Willacy
RAYWOOD Liberty
REAGAN Falls
REALITOS Duval
RED OAK (75154) Ellis(78), Dallas(21)
RED ROCK (78662) Bastrop(96), Caldwell(3)
REDFORD Presidio
REDWATER Bowie
REESE AIR FORCE BASE Lubbock
REFUGIO Refugio
REKLAW (75784) Cherokee(88), Rusk(11)
RHOME (76078) Wise(95), Denton(4)
RICE (75155) Navarro(94), Ellis(5)
RICHARDS (77873) Montgomery(54), Grimes(35), Walker(10)
RICHARDSON (75082) Collin(74), Dallas(25)
RICHARDSON (75080) Dallas(84), Collin(15)
RICHARDSON Dallas
RICHLAND Navarro
RICHLAND SPRINGS (76871) San Saba(95), Lampasas(3)
RICHMOND Fort Bend
RIESEL (76682) McLennan(96), Falls(3)
RINGGOLD (76261) Montague(92), Clay(8)
RIO FRIO Real
RIO GRANDE CITY Starr
RIO HONDO Cameron
RIO MEDINA Medina
RIO VISTA (76093) Johnson(92), Hill(7)
RISING STAR (76471) Eastland(79), Brown(16), Comanche(4)
RIVERSIDE Walker
RIVIERA Kleberg
ROANOKE (76262) Denton(63), Tarrant(36)
ROANOKE Denton
ROANS PRAIRIE Grimes
ROARING SPRINGS (79256) Motley(52), Dickens(47)
ROBERT LEE (76945) Coke(94), Tom Green(5)
ROBSTOWN Nueces
ROBY Fisher
ROCHELLE (76872) McCulloch(80), San Saba(19)
ROCHESTER Haskell
ROCK ISLAND Colorado
ROCKDALE (76567) Milam(94), Burleson(5)
ROCKLAND Tyler
ROCKPORT Aransas
ROCKSPRINGS Edwards
ROCKWALL (75087) Rockwall(97), Collin(2)
ROCKWALL Rockwall
ROCKWOOD Coleman
ROGERS (76569) Bell(86), Milam(13)
ROMA Starr
ROMAYOR Liberty
ROOSEVELT (76874) Sutton(66), Kimble(33)
ROPESVILLE (79358) Hockley(78), Lubbock(19), Terry(1)
ROSANKY (78953) Bastrop(53), Caldwell(46)
ROSCOE (79545) Nolan(93), Scurry(3), Fisher(3)
ROSEBUD (76570) Falls(85), Milam(13)
ROSENBERG Fort Bend
ROSHARON (77583) Brazoria(78), Fort Bend(21)
ROSS McLennan
ROSSER Kaufman

ROSSTON Cooke
ROTAN (79546) Fisher(95), Stonewall(3)
ROUND MOUNTAIN (78663) Blanco(88), Travis(8), Hays(3)
ROUND ROCK (78664) Williamson(95), Travis(4)
ROUND ROCK Williamson
ROUND TOP (78954) Fayette(97), Austin(2)
ROUND TOP Fayette
ROWENA (76875) Runnels(85), Concho(14)
ROWLETT (75089) Dallas(94), Rockwall(5)
ROWLETT Dallas
ROXTON Lamar
ROYALTY Ward
ROYSE CITY (75189) Rockwall(56), Hunt(26), Collin(16)
RULE (79547) Haskell(97), Stonewall(2)
RULE Haskell
RUNGE (78151) Karnes(94), De Witt(3), Goliad(1)
RUSK Cherokee
RYE Liberty
SABINAL Uvalde
SABINE PASS Jefferson
SACUL Nacogdoches
SADLER Grayson
SAINT HEDWIG Bexar
SAINT JO (76265) Montague(81), Cooke(18)
SALADO Bell
SALINENO Starr
SALT FLAT (79847) Hudspeth(74), Culberson(25)
SALTILLO (75478) Hopkins(87), Franklin(12)
SAMNORWOOD Collingsworth
SAN ANGELO Tom Green
SAN ANTONIO (78223) Bexar(98), Wilson(1)
SAN ANTONIO (78253) Bexar(89), Medina(10)
SAN ANTONIO (78264) Bexar(93), Atascosa(6)
SAN ANTONIO (78266) Comal(95), Bexar(4)
SAN ANTONIO Bexar
SAN AUGUSTINE San Augustine
SAN BENITO Cameron
SAN DIEGO (78384) Duval(94), Jim Wells(5)
SAN ELIZARIO El Paso
SAN FELIPE Austin
SAN ISIDRO Starr
SAN JUAN Hidalgo
SAN MARCOS (78666) Hays(92), Guadalupe(6), Caldwell(1)
SAN MARCOS Hays
SAN PERLITA Willacy
SAN SABA San Saba
SAN YGNACIO Zapata
SANDERSON Terrell
SANDIA (78383) Jim Wells(60), Nueces(35), Live Oak(4)
SANDY Blanco
SANFORD Hutchinson
SANGER Denton
SANTA ANNA Coleman
SANTA ELENA Starr
SANTA FE Galveston
SANTA MARIA Cameron
SANTA ROSA Cameron
SANTO Palo Pinto
SARAGOSA Reeves
SARATOGA Hardin
SARITA Kenedy
SATIN Falls
SAVOY Fannin
SCHERTZ (78154) Guadalupe(73), Bexar(23), Comal(2)

SCHULENBURG (78956) Fayette(89), Lavaca(10)
SCHWERTNER Williamson
SCOTLAND Archer
SCOTTSVILLE Harrison
SCROGGINS (75480) Franklin(95), Wood(4)
SCURRY Kaufman
SEABROOK Harris
SEADRIFT Calhoun
SEAGOVILLE (75159) Dallas(86), Kaufman(13)
SEAGRAVES (79359) Gaines(74), Terry(13), Yoakum(12)
SEALY Austin
SEBASTIAN Willacy
SEGUIN Guadalupe
SELMAN CITY Rusk
SEMINOLE Gaines
SEYMOUR (76380) Baylor(96), Knox(3)
SHAFTER Presidio
SHALLOWATER (79363) Lubbock(97), Hockley(1)
SHAMROCK (79079) Wheeler(90), Collingsworth(9)
SHAMROCK Wheeler
SHEFFIELD Pecos
SHEPHERD San Jacinto
SHEPPARD AFB Wichita
SHERIDAN Colorado
SHERMAN Grayson
SHINER (77984) Lavaca(91), Gonzales(8)
SHIRO Grimes
SIDNEY (76474) Comanche(98), Brown(1)
SIERRA BLANCA Hudspeth
SILSBEE Hardin
SILVER Coke
SILVERTON Briscoe
SIMMS Bowie
SIMONTON Fort Bend
SINTON (78387) San Patricio(92), Bee(7)
SKELLYTOWN (79080) Hutchinson(80), Carson(20)
SKIDMORE Bee
SLATON (79364) Lubbock(96), Lynn(3)
SLIDELL Wise
SMILEY Gonzales
SMITHVILLE (78957) Bastrop(98), Fayette(1)
SMYER Hockley
SNOOK Burleson
SNYDER Scurry
SOMERSET (78069) Atascosa(64), Bexar(35)
SOMERVILLE Burleson
SONORA Sutton
SOUR LAKE Hardin
SOUTH BEND Young
SOUTH HOUSTON Harris
SOUTH PADRE ISLAND Cameron
SOUTH PLAINS Floyd
SOUTHLAKE Tarrant
SOUTHLAND Garza
SOUTHMAYD Grayson
SPADE Lamb
SPEAKS Lavaca
SPEARMAN (79081) Hansford(92), Hutchinson(4), Ochiltree(3)
SPICEWOOD (78669) Travis(71), Burnet(26), Blanco(2)
SPLENDORA (77372) Montgomery(88), Liberty(11)
SPRING Harris
SPRING Montgomery
SPRING BRANCH Comal
SPRINGLAKE (79082) Lamb(84), Castro(15)
SPRINGTOWN (76082) Parker(78), Wise(21)
SPUR (79370) Dickens(89), Crosby(6), Kent(3)
SPURGER Tyler

STAFFORD (77477) Fort Bend(91), Harris(8)
STAFFORD Fort Bend
STAMFORD (79553) Jones(91), Haskell(8)
STANTON (79782) Martin(70), Glasscock(25), Midland(3)
STAPLES Guadalupe
STAR Mills
STEPHENVILLE Erath
STERLING CITY (76951) Sterling(98), Glasscock(1)
STINNETT (79083) Hutchinson(66), Moore(30), Hansford(2)
STOCKDALE Wilson
STONEWALL (78671) Gillespie(97), Blanco(2)
STOWELL Chambers
STRATFORD (79084) Sherman(95), Dallam(4)
STRAWN (76475) Eastland(76), Palo Pinto(23)
STREETMAN (75859) Freestone(65), Navarro(34)
SUBLIME Lavaca
SUDAN (79371) Lamb(62), Bailey(37)
SUGAR LAND Fort Bend
SULLIVAN CITY Hidalgo
SULPHUR BLUFF Hopkins
SULPHUR SPRINGS Hopkins
SUMMERFIELD (79085) Castro(85), Parmer(14)
SUMNER Lamar
SUNDOWN Hockley
SUNNYVALE Dallas
SUNRAY (79086) Moore(50), Sherman(48), Hansford(1)
SUNSET (76270) Montague(57), Wise(42)
SUTHERLAND SPRINGS Wilson
SWEENY (77480) Brazoria(95), Matagorda(4)
SWEET HOME Lavaca
SWEETWATER (79556) Nolan(95), Fisher(4)
SYLVESTER (79560) Fisher(89), Jones(10)
TAFT San Patricio
TAHOKA Lynn
TALCO (75487) Franklin(74), Titus(25)
TALPA (76882) Coleman(63), Runnels(36)
TARPLEY Bandera
TARZAN Martin
TATUM Rusk
TAYLOR Williamson
TEAGUE Freestone
TEHUACANA Limestone
TELEGRAPH (76883) Edwards(69), Kimble(30)
TELEPHONE Fannin
TELFERNER (77988) Lavaca(77), Victoria(22)
TELL (79259) Childress(56), Hall(43)
TEMPLE Bell
TENAHA (75974) Shelby(63), Panola(36)
TENNESSEE COLONY Anderson
TENNYSON Coke
TERLINGUA Brewster
TERRELL (75160) Kaufman(91), Hunt(8)
TERRELL Kaufman
TEXARKANA Bowie
TEXAS CITY Galveston
TEXLINE Dallam
THE COLONY Denton
THICKET Hardin
THOMASTON De Witt
THOMPSONS Fort Bend
THORNDALE (76577) Milam(95), Williamson(4)
THORNTON (76687) Limestone(73), Robertson(25)
THRALL (76578) Williamson(94), Milam(4), Lee(1)
THREE RIVERS Live Oak

THROCKMORTON Throckmorton
TILDEN McMullen
TIMPSON (75975) Shelby(97), Panola(1), Rusk(1)
TIOGA (76271) Grayson(88), Cooke(11)
TIVOLI (77990) Refugio(67), Calhoun(32)
TOKIO (79376) Yoakum(72), Terry(27)
TOLAR Hood
TOM BEAN Grayson
TOMBALL Harris
TORNILLO El Paso
TOW Llano
TOYAH Reeves
TOYAHVALE Reeves
TRENT (79561) Taylor(43), Nolan(36), Fisher(11), Jones(8)
TRENTON (75490) Fannin(97), Grayson(2)
TRINIDAD Henderson
TRINITY (75862) Trinity(95), Walker(4)
TROUP (75789) Smith(82), Cherokee(16), Rusk(1)
TROY (76579) Bell(95), Falls(4)
TRUSCOTT Knox
TULETA Bee
TULIA (79088) Swisher(96), Castro(1), Briscoe(1)
TURKEY (79261) Hall(92), Briscoe(7)
TUSCOLA Taylor
TYE Taylor
TYLER Smith
TYNAN Bee
UMBARGER Randall
UNIVERSAL CITY Bexar
UTOPIA Uvalde
UVALDE Uvalde
VALENTINE (79854) Presidio(57), Jeff Davis(42)
VALERA Coleman
VALLEY MILLS (76689) Bosque(59), McLennan(27), Coryell(13)
VALLEY SPRING Llano
VALLEY VIEW (76272) Cooke(98), Denton(1)
VAN (75790) Van Zandt(97), Smith(2)
VAN ALSTYNE (75495) Grayson(55), Collin(44)
VAN HORN Culberson
VAN VLECK Matagorda
VANCOURT (76955) Tom Green(51), Concho(48)
VANDERBILT Jackson
VANDERPOOL Bandera
VEGA (79092) Oldham(56), Deaf Smith(43)
VENUS (76084) Johnson(72), Ellis(27)
VERA (76383) Knox(91), Baylor(8)
VERIBEST Tom Green
VERNON Wilbarger
VICTORIA (77905) Victoria(91), Goliad(8)
VICTORIA Victoria
VIDOR Orange
VILLAGE MILLS Hardin
VOCA McCulloch
VON ORMY (78073) Bexar(89), Atascosa(10)
VOSS Coleman
VOTAW Hardin
VOTH Jefferson
WACO McLennan
WADSWORTH Matagorda
WAELDER (78959) Gonzales(70), Fayette(19), Bastrop(7), Caldwell(3)
WAKA Ochiltree
WALBURG Williamson
WALL Tom Green
WALLER (77484) Waller(73), Harris(21), Grimes(5)
WALLIS (77485) Austin(66), Fort Bend(32)
WALLISVILLE Chambers
WALNUT SPRINGS (76690) Bosque(75), Somervell(23), Erath(1)
WARDA Fayette
WARING Kendall

WARREN Tyler
WASKOM Harrison
WATER VALLEY Tom Green
WAXAHACHIE Ellis
WAYSIDE (79094) Armstrong(92), Swisher(7)
WEATHERFORD (76087) Parker(96), Hood(3)
WEATHERFORD Parker
WEBSTER Harris
WEESATCHE Goliad
WEIMAR (78962) Colorado(98), Fayette(1)
WEINERT Haskell
WEIR Williamson
WELCH (79377) Dawson(63), Terry(27), Gaines(9)
WELLBORN Brazos
WELLINGTON (79095) Collingsworth(94), Childress(5)
WELLMAN Terry
WELLS Cherokee
WESLACO Hidalgo
WEST McLennan
WEST COLUMBIA Brazoria
WEST POINT Fayette
WESTBROOK Mitchell
WESTHOFF De Witt
WESTMINSTER Collin
WESTON Collin
WHARTON Wharton
WHEELER Wheeler
WHEELOCK Robertson
WHITE DEER (79097) Carson(96), Gray(3)
WHITE OAK Gregg
WHITEFACE Cochran
WHITEHOUSE Smith
WHITESBORO (76273) Grayson(71), Cooke(28)
WHITEWRIGHT (75491) Grayson(73), Fannin(26)
WHITHARRAL Hockley
WHITNEY Hill
WHITSETT Live Oak
WHITT (76490) Parker(58), Palo Pinto(41)
WHON Coleman
WICHITA FALLS (76305) Wichita(62), Clay(37)
WICHITA FALLS (76310) Wichita(64), Archer(18), Clay(16)
WICHITA FALLS Wichita
WICKETT Ward
WIERGATE Newton
WILDORADO (79098) Deaf Smith(44), Randall(23), Oldham(22), Potter(9)
WILLIS (77378) Montgomery(81), San Jacinto(18)
WILLIS Montgomery
WILLOW CITY Gillespie
WILLS POINT (75169) Van Zandt(83), Hunt(9), Kaufman(6)
WILMER Dallas
WILSON Lynn
WIMBERLEY Hays
WINCHESTER Fayette
WINDOM Fannin
WINDTHORST (76389) Archer(61), Clay(29), Jack(8)
WINFIELD Titus
WINGATE (79566) Taylor(58), Runnels(34), Nolan(6)
WINK Winkler
WINNIE (77665) Chambers(98), Jefferson(1)
WINNSBORO (75494) Wood(72), Franklin(20), Hopkins(6)
WINONA Smith
WINTERS (79567) Runnels(97), Taylor(2)
WODEN Nacogdoches
WOLFE CITY (75496) Hunt(79), Fannin(20)
WOLFFORTH Lubbock
WOODLAKE Trinity
WOODLAWN Harrison

WOODSBORO Refugio
WOODSON (76491) Throckmorton(96), Stephens(3)
WOODVILLE Tyler
WOODWAY McLennan

WORTHAM (76693) Freestone(88), Navarro(7), Limestone(3)
WRIGHTSBORO Gonzales
WYLIE (75098) Collin(88), Dallas(9), Rockwall(1)

YANCEY Medina
YANTIS (75497) Wood(87), Hopkins(10), Rains(1)
YOAKUM (77995) Lavaca(51), De Witt(32), Victoria(16)

YORKTOWN De Witt
ZAPATA Zapata
ZAVALLA Angelina
ZEPHYR (76890) Brown(95), Mills(2), Comanche(1)

Texas ZIP/City Cross Reference

ZIP Range	City	ZIP Range	City	ZIP Range	City	ZIP Range	City
73301-73344	AUSTIN	75148-75148	MALAKOFF	75469-75469	PECAN GAP	75661-75661	KARNACK
75001-75001	ADDISON	75149-75150	MESQUITE	75470-75470	PETTY	75662-75663	KILGORE
75002-75002	ALLEN	75151-75151	CORSICANA	75471-75471	PICKTON	75666-75666	LAIRD HILL
75006-75008	CARROLLTON	75152-75152	PALMER	75472-75472	POINT	75667-75667	LANEVILLE
75009-75009	CELINA	75153-75153	POWELL	75473-75473	POWDERLY	75668-75668	LONE STAR
75010-75011	CARROLLTON	75154-75154	RED OAK	75474-75474	QUINLAN	75669-75669	LONG BRANCH
75013-75013	ALLEN	75155-75155	RICE	75475-75475	RANDOLPH	75670-75672	MARSHALL
75014-75017	IRVING	75156-75156	MABANK	75476-75476	RAVENNA	75680-75680	MINDEN
75019-75019	COPPELL	75157-75157	ROSSER	75477-75477	ROXTON	75681-75681	MOUNT ENTERPRISE
75020-75021	DENISON	75158-75158	SCURRY	75478-75478	SALTILLO	75682-75682	NEW LONDON
75022-75022	FLOWER MOUND	75159-75159	SEAGOVILLE	75479-75479	SAVOY	75683-75683	ORE CITY
75023-75026	PLANO	75160-75161	TERRELL	75480-75480	SCROGGINS	75684-75684	OVERTON
75027-75028	FLOWER MOUND	75163-75163	TRINIDAD	75481-75481	SULPHUR BLUFF	75685-75685	PANOLA
75029-75029	LEWISVILLE	75164-75164	JOSEPHINE	75482-75483	SULPHUR SPRINGS	75686-75686	PITTSBURG
75030-75030	ROWLETT	75165-75165	WAXAHACHIE	75485-75485	WESTMINSTER	75687-75687	PRICE
75032-75032	ROCKWALL	75166-75166	LAVON	75486-75486	SUMNER	75688-75688	SCOTTSVILLE
75034-75035	FRISCO	75167-75168	WAXAHACHIE	75487-75487	TALCO	75689-75689	SELMAN CITY
75037-75039	IRVING	75169-75169	WILLS POINT	75488-75488	TELEPHONE	75691-75691	TATUM
75040-75049	GARLAND	75172-75172	WILMER	75489-75489	TOM BEAN	75692-75692	WASKOM
75050-75054	GRAND PRAIRIE	75173-75173	NEVADA	75490-75490	TRENTON	75693-75693	WHITE OAK
75056-75056	THE COLONY	75180-75181	MESQUITE	75491-75491	WHITEWRIGHT	75694-75694	WOODLAWN
75057-75057	LEWISVILLE	75182-75182	SUNNYVALE	75492-75492	WINDOM	75701-75713	TYLER
75058-75058	GUNTER	75185-75187	MESQUITE	75493-75493	WINFIELD	75750-75750	ARP
75060-75063	IRVING	75189-75189	ROYSE CITY	75494-75494	WINNSBORO	75751-75752	ATHENS
75065-75065	LAKE DALLAS	75200-75398	DALLAS	75495-75495	VAN ALSTYNE	75754-75754	BEN WHEELER
75067-75067	LEWISVILLE	75401-75404	GREENVILLE	75496-75496	WOLFE CITY	75755-75755	BIG SANDY
75068-75068	LITTLE ELM	75407-75407	PRINCETON	75497-75497	YANTIS	75756-75756	BROWNSBORO
75069-75071	MC KINNEY	75409-75409	ANNA	75501-75507	TEXARKANA	75757-75757	BULLARD
75074-75075	PLANO	75410-75410	ALBA	75550-75550	ANNONA	75757-75758	CHANDLER
75076-75076	POTTSBORO	75411-75411	ARTHUR CITY	75551-75551	ATLANTA	75759-75759	CUNEY
75077-75077	LEWISVILLE	75412-75412	BAGWELL	75554-75554	AVERY	75760-75760	CUSHING
75078-75078	PROSPER	75413-75413	BAILEY	75555-75555	BIVINS	75762-75762	FLINT
75080-75083	RICHARDSON	75414-75414	BELLS	75556-75556	BLOOMBURG	75763-75763	FRANKSTON
75084-75084	IRVING	75415-75415	BEN FRANKLIN	75557-75557	MAGNOLIA SPRINGS	75764-75764	GALLATIN
75085-75085	RICHARDSON	75416-75416	BLOSSOM	75558-75558	COOKVILLE	75765-75765	HAWKINS
75086-75086	PLANO	75417-75417	BOGATA	75559-75559	DE KALB	75766-75766	JACKSONVILLE
75087-75087	ROCKWALL	75418-75418	BONHAM	75560-75560	DOUGLASSVILLE	75770-75770	LARUE
75088-75089	ROWLETT	75420-75420	BRASHEAR	75561-75561	HOOKS	75771-75771	LINDALE
75090-75092	SHERMAN	75421-75421	BROOKSTON	75562-75562	KILDARE	75772-75772	MAYDELLE
75093-75094	PLANO	75422-75422	CAMPBELL	75563-75563	LINDEN	75773-75773	MINEOLA
75097-75097	WESTON	75423-75423	CELESTE	75564-75564	LODI	75778-75778	MURCHISON
75098-75098	WYLIE	75424-75424	BLUE RIDGE	75565-75565	MC LEOD	75779-75779	NECHES
75099-75099	COPPELL	75425-75425	CHICOTA	75566-75566	MARIETTA	75780-75780	NEW SUMMERFIELD
75101-75101	BARDWELL	75426-75426	CLARKSVILLE	75567-75567	MAUD	75782-75782	POYNOR
75102-75102	BARRY	75428-75429	COMMERCE	75568-75568	NAPLES	75783-75783	QUITMAN
75103-75103	CANTON	75431-75431	COMO	75569-75569	NASH	75784-75784	REKLAW
75104-75104	CEDAR HILL	75432-75432	COOPER	75570-75570	NEW BOSTON	75785-75785	RUSK
75105-75105	CHATFIELD	75433-75433	CUMBY	75571-75571	OMAHA	75788-75788	SACUL
75106-75106	CEDAR HILL	75434-75434	CUNNINGHAM	75572-75572	QUEEN CITY	75789-75789	TROUP
75109-75110	CORSICANA	75435-75435	DEPORT	75573-75573	REDWATER	75790-75790	VAN
75114-75114	CRANDALL	75436-75436	DETROIT	75574-75574	SIMMS	75791-75791	WHITEHOUSE
75115-75115	DE SOTO	75437-75437	DIKE	75599-75599	TEXARKANA	75792-75792	WINONA
75116-75116	DUNCANVILLE	75438-75438	DODD CITY	75601-75615	LONGVIEW	75797-75797	BIG SANDY
75117-75117	EDGEWOOD	75439-75439	ECTOR	75630-75630	AVINGER	75798-75799	TYLER
75118-75118	ELMO	75440-75440	EMORY	75631-75631	BECKVILLE	75801-75803	PALESTINE
75119-75120	ENNIS	75441-75441	ENLOE	75633-75633	CARTHAGE	75831-75831	BUFFALO
75121-75121	COPEVILLE	75442-75442	FARMERSVILLE	75636-75636	CASON	75832-75832	CAYUGA
75123-75123	DE SOTO	75443-75443	GOBER	75637-75637	CLAYTON	75833-75833	CENTERVILLE
75123-75123	DESOTO	75444-75444	GOLDEN	75638-75638	DAINGERFIELD	75834-75834	CENTRALIA
75124-75124	EUSTACE	75446-75446	HONEY GROVE	75639-75639	DE BERRY	75835-75835	CROCKETT
75125-75125	FERRIS	75447-75447	IVANHOE	75640-75640	DIANA	75838-75838	DONIE
75126-75126	FORNEY	75448-75448	KLONDIKE	75641-75641	EASTON	75839-75839	ELKHART
75127-75127	FRUITVALE	75449-75449	LADONIA	75642-75642	ELYSIAN FIELDS	75840-75840	FAIRFIELD
75132-75132	FATE	75450-75450	LAKE CREEK	75643-75643	GARY	75844-75844	GRAPELAND
75134-75134	LANCASTER	75451-75451	LEESBURG	75644-75645	GILMER	75845-75845	GROVETON
75135-75135	CADDO MILLS	75452-75452	LEONARD	75647-75647	GLADEWATER	75846-75846	JEWETT
75137-75138	DUNCANVILLE	75453-75453	LONE OAK	75650-75650	HALLSVILLE	75847-75847	KENNARD
75140-75140	GRAND SALINE	75454-75454	MELISSA	75651-75651	HARLETON	75848-75848	KIRVIN
75141-75141	HUTCHINS	75455-75456	MOUNT PLEASANT	75652-75654	HENDERSON	75849-75849	LATEXO
75142-75142	KAUFMAN	75457-75457	MOUNT VERNON	75656-75656	HUGHES SPRINGS	75850-75850	LEONA
75143-75143	KEMP	75458-75458	MERIT	75657-75657	JEFFERSON	75851-75851	LOVELADY
75144-75144	KERENS	75459-75459	HOWE	75658-75658	JOINERVILLE	75852-75852	MIDWAY
75146-75146	LANCASTER	75460-75462	PARIS	75659-75659	JONESVILLE	75853-75853	MONTALBA
75147-75147	MABANK	75468-75468	PATTONVILLE	75660-75660	JUDSON	75855-75855	OAKWOOD

75856-75856 PENNINGTON	76064-76064 MAYPEARL	76371-76371 MUNDAY	76534-76534 HOLLAND
75858-75858 RATCLIFF	76065-76065 MIDLOTHIAN	76372-76372 NEWCASTLE	76537-76537 JARRELL
75859-75859 STREETMAN	76066-76066 MILLSAP	76373-76373 OKLAUNION	76538-76538 JONESBORO
75860-75860 TEAGUE	76067-76068 MINERAL WELLS	76374-76374 OLNEY	76539-76539 KEMPNER
75861-75861 TENNESSEE COLONY	76070-76070 NEMO	76377-76377 PETROLIA	76540-76547 KILLEEN
75862-75862 TRINITY	76071-76071 NEWARK	76379-76379 SCOTLAND	76548-76548 HARKER HEIGHTS
75865-75865 WOODLAKE	76073-76073 PARADISE	76380-76380 SEYMOUR	76549-76549 KILLEEN
75880-75880 TENNESSEE COLONY	76077-76077 RAINBOW	76383-76383 VERA	76550-76550 LAMPASAS
75882-75882 PALESTINE	76078-76078 RHOME	76384-76385 VERNON	76552-76552 LEON JUNCTION
75884-75886 TENNESSEE COLONY	76082-76082 SPRINGTOWN	76388-76388 WEINERT	76554-76554 LITTLE RIVER
75901-75915 LUFKIN	76084-76084 VENUS	76389-76389 WINDTHORST	76554-76554 LITTLE RIVER ACADEMY
75925-75925 ALTO	76085-76088 WEATHERFORD	76401-76402 STEPHENVILLE	76555-76555 MAYSFIELD
75926-75926 APPLE SPRINGS	76092-76092 SOUTHLAKE	76424-76424 BRECKENRIDGE	76556-76556 MILANO
75928-75928 BON WIER	76093-76093 RIO VISTA	76426-76426 BRIDGEPORT	76557-76557 MOODY
75929-75929 BROADDUS	76094-76094 ARLINGTON	76427-76427 BRYSON	76558-76558 MOUND
75930-75930 BRONSON	76095-76095 BEDFORD	76429-76429 CADDO	76559-76559 NOLANVILLE
75931-75931 BROOKELAND	76096-76096 ARLINGTON	76430-76430 ALBANY	76561-76561 OGLESBY
75932-75932 BURKEVILLE	76097-76097 BURLESON	76431-76431 CHICO	76564-76564 PENDLETON
75933-75933 CALL	76098-76098 AZLE	76432-76432 BLANKET	76565-76565 POTTSVILLE
75934-75934 CAMDEN	76099-76099 GRAPEVINE	76433-76433 BLUFF DALE	76566-76566 PURMELA
75935-75935 CENTER	76100-76116 FORT WORTH	76435-76435 CARBON	76567-76567 ROCKDALE
75936-75936 CHESTER	76117-76117 HALTOM CITY	76436-76436 CARLTON	76569-76569 ROGERS
75937-75937 CHIRENO	76118-76126 FORT WORTH	76437-76437 CISCO	76570-76570 ROSEBUD
75938-75938 COLMESNEIL	76127-76127 NAVAL AIR STATION/ JRB	76438-76438 ELIASVILLE	76571-76571 SALADO
75939-75939 CORRIGAN	76129-76179 FORT WORTH	76439-76439 DENNIS	76573-76573 SCHWERTNER
75941-75941 DIBOLL	76180-76180 NORTH RICHLAND HILLS	76442-76442 COMANCHE	76574-76574 TAYLOR
75942-75942 DOUCETTE	76181-76181 FORT WORTH	76443-76443 CROSS PLAINS	76576-76576 GATESVILLE
75943-75943 DOUGLASS	76182-76182 NORTH RICHLAND HILLS	76444-76444 DE LEON	76577-76577 THORNDALE
75944-75944 ETOILE	76185-76199 FORT WORTH	76445-76445 DESDEMONA	76578-76578 THRALL
75946-75946 GARRISON	76201-76210 DENTON	76446-76446 DUBLIN	76579-76579 TROY
75947-75947 GENEVA	76225-76225 ALVORD	76448-76448 EASTLAND	76596-76599 GATESVILLE
75948-75948 HEMPHILL	76226-76226 ARGYLE	76449-76449 GRAFORD	76621-76621 ABBOTT
75949-75949 HUNTINGTON	76227-76227 AUBREY	76450-76450 GRAHAM	76622-76622 AQUILLA
75951-75951 JASPER	76228-76228 BELLEVUE	76452-76452 ENERGY	76623-76623 AVALON
75954-75954 JOAQUIN	76230-76230 BOWIE	76453-76453 GORDON	76624-76624 AXTELL
75956-75956 KIRBYVILLE	76233-76233 COLLINSVILLE	76454-76454 GORMAN	76625-76625 BIROME
75957-75957 MAGNOLIA SPRINGS	76234-76234 DECATUR	76455-76455 GUSTINE	76626-76626 BLOOMING GROVE
75958-75958 MARTINSVILLE	76238-76238 ERA	76456-76456 HASSE	76627-76627 BLUM
75959-75959 MILAM	76239-76239 FORESTBURG	76457-76457 HICO	76628-76628 BRANDON
75960-75960 MOSCOW	76240-76241 GAINESVILLE	76458-76458 JACKSBORO	76629-76629 BREMOND
75961-75965 NACOGDOCHES	76244-76244 KELLER	76459-76459 JERMYN	76630-76630 BRUCEVILLE
75966-75966 NEWTON	76245-76245 GORDONVILLE	76460-76460 LOVING	76631-76631 BYNUM
75968-75968 PINELAND	76246-76246 GREENWOOD	76461-76461 LINGLEVILLE	76632-76632 CHILTON
75969-75969 POLLOK	76247-76247 JUSTIN	76462-76462 LIPAN	76633-76633 CHINA SPRING
75970-75970 ROCKLAND	76248-76248 KELLER	76463-76463 MINGUS	76634-76634 CLIFTON
75972-75972 SAN AUGUSTINE	76249-76249 KRUM	76464-76464 MORAN	76635-76635 COOLIDGE
75973-75973 SHELBYVILLE	76250-76250 LINDSAY	76465-76465 MORGAN MILL	76636-76636 COVINGTON
75974-75974 TENAHA	76251-76251 MONTAGUE	76466-76466 OLDEN	76637-76637 CRANFILLS GAP
75975-75975 TIMPSON	76252-76252 MUENSTER	76467-76467 PALUXY	76638-76638 CRAWFORD
75976-75976 WELLS	76253-76253 MYRA	76468-76468 PROCTOR	76639-76639 DAWSON
75977-75977 WIERGATE	76254-76254 NEWPORT	76469-76469 PUTNAM	76640-76640 ELM MOTT
75978-75978 WODEN	76255-76255 NOCONA	76470-76470 RANGER	76641-76641 FROST
75979-75979 WOODVILLE	76258-76258 PILOT POINT	76471-76471 RISING STAR	76642-76642 GROESBECK
75980-75980 ZAVALLA	76259-76259 PONDER	76472-76472 SANTO	76643-76643 HEWITT
75990-75990 WOODVILLE	76261-76261 RINGGOLD	76474-76474 SIDNEY	76644-76644 CLIFTON
76000-76007 ARLINGTON	76262-76262 ROANOKE	76475-76475 STRAWN	76645-76645 HILLSBORO
76008-76008 ALEDO	76263-76263 ROSSTON	76476-76476 TOLAR	76648-76648 HUBBARD
76009-76009 ALVARADO	76264-76264 SADLER	76481-76481 SOUTH BEND	76649-76649 IREDELL
76010-76019 ARLINGTON	76265-76265 SAINT JO	76483-76483 THROCKMORTON	76650-76650 IRENE
76020-76020 AZLE	76266-76266 SANGER	76484-76484 PALO PINTO	76651-76651 ITALY
76021-76022 BEDFORD	76267-76267 SLIDELL	76485-76485 PEASTER	76652-76652 KOPPERL
76023-76023 BOYD	76268-76268 SOUTHMAYD	76486-76486 PERRIN	76653-76653 KOSSE
76028-76028 BURLESON	76270-76270 SUNSET	76487-76487 POOLVILLE	76654-76654 LEROY
76031-76033 CLEBURNE	76271-76271 TIOGA	76490-76490 WHITT	76655-76655 LORENA
76034-76034 COLLEYVILLE	76272-76272 VALLEY VIEW	76491-76491 WOODSON	76656-76656 LOTT
76035-76035 CRESSON	76273-76273 WHITESBORO	76501-76508 TEMPLE	76657-76657 MC GREGOR
76036-76036 CROWLEY	76299-76299 ROANOKE	76511-76511 BARTLETT	76660-76660 MALONE
76039-76040 EULESS	76301-76310 WICHITA FALLS	76513-76513 BELTON	76661-76661 MARLIN
76041-76041 FORRESTON	76311-76311 SHEPPARD AFB	76517-76517 BEN ARNOLD	76664-76664 MART
76043-76043 GLEN ROSE	76351-76351 ARCHER CITY	76518-76518 BUCKHOLTS	76665-76665 MERIDIAN
76044-76044 GODLEY	76352-76352 BLUEGROVE	76519-76519 BURLINGTON	76666-76666 MERTENS
76048-76049 GRANBURY	76354-76354 BURKBURNETT	76520-76520 CAMERON	76667-76667 MEXIA
76050-76050 GRANDVIEW	76357-76357 BYERS	76522-76522 COPPERAS COVE	76670-76670 MILFORD
76051-76051 GRAPEVINE	76359-76359 ELBERT	76523-76523 DAVILLA	76671-76671 MORGAN
76052-76052 HASLET	76360-76360 ELECTRA	76524-76524 EDDY	76673-76673 MOUNT CALM
76053-76054 HURST	76363-76363 GOREE	76525-76525 EVANT	76675-76675 OTTO
76055-76055 ITASCA	76364-76364 HARROLD	76526-76526 FLAT	76676-76676 PENELOPE
76058-76058 JOSHUA	76365-76365 HENRIETTA	76527-76527 FLORENCE	76677-76677 PERRY
76059-76059 KEENE	76366-76366 HOLLIDAY	76528-76528 GATESVILLE	76678-76678 PRAIRIE HILL
76060-76060 KENNEDALE	76367-76367 IOWA PARK	76530-76530 GRANGER	76679-76679 PURDON
76061-76061 LILLIAN	76369-76369 KAMAY	76531-76531 HAMILTON	76680-76680 REAGAN
76063-76063 MANSFIELD	76370-76370 MEGARGEL	76533-76533 HEIDENHEIMER	76681-76681 RICHLAND

76682-76682 RIESEL	76949-76949 SILVER	77441-77441 FULSHEAR	77573-77574 LEAGUE CITY
76684-76684 ROSS	76950-76950 SONORA	77442-77442 GARWOOD	77575-77575 LIBERTY
76685-76685 SATIN	76951-76951 STERLING CITY	77443-77443 GLEN FLORA	77577-77577 LIVERPOOL
76686-76686 TEHUACANA	76953-76953 TENNYSON	77444-77444 GUY	77578-77578 MANVEL
76687-76687 THORNTON	76955-76955 VANCOURT	77445-77445 HEMPSTEAD	77580-77580 MONT BELVIEU
76689-76689 VALLEY MILLS	76957-76957 WALL	77446-77446 PRAIRIE VIEW	77581-77581 PEARLAND
76690-76690 WALNUT SPRINGS	76958-76958 WATER VALLEY	77447-77447 HOCKLEY	77582-77582 RAYWOOD
76691-76691 WEST	77000-77299 HOUSTON	77448-77448 HUNGERFORD	77583-77583 ROSHARON
76692-76692 WHITNEY	77301-77306 CONROE	77449-77450 KATY	77584-77584 PEARLAND
76693-76693 WORTHAM	77315-77315 NORTH HOUSTON	77451-77451 KENDLETON	77585-77585 SARATOGA
76700-76711 WACO	77316-77316 MONTGOMERY	77452-77452 KENNEY	77586-77586 SEABROOK
76712-76712 WOODWAY	77318-77318 WILLIS	77453-77453 LANE CITY	77587-77587 SOUTH HOUSTON
76714-76799 WACO	77320-77320 HUNTSVILLE	77454-77454 LISSIE	77588-77588 PEARLAND
76801-76801 BROWNWOOD	77325-77325 HUMBLE	77455-77455 LOUISE	77590-77592 TEXAS CITY
76802-76802 EARLY	77326-77326 ACE	77456-77456 MARKHAM	77597-77597 WALLISVILLE
76803-76804 BROWNWOOD	77327-77328 CLEVELAND	77457-77457 MATAGORDA	77598-77598 WEBSTER
76820-76820 ART	77331-77331 COLDSPRING	77458-77458 MIDFIELD	77611-77611 BRIDGE CITY
76821-76821 BALLINGER	77332-77332 DALLARDSVILLE	77459-77459 MISSOURI CITY	77612-77612 BUNA
76823-76823 BANGS	77333-77333 DOBBIN	77460-77460 NADA	77613-77613 CHINA
76824-76824 BEND	77334-77334 DODGE	77461-77461 NEEDVILLE	77614-77614 DEWEYVILLE
76825-76825 BRADY	77335-77335 GOODRICH	77462-77462 NEWGULF	77615-77615 EVADALE
76827-76827 BROOKESMITH	77336-77336 HUFFMAN	77463-77463 OLD OCEAN	77616-77616 FRED
76828-76828 BURKETT	77337-77337 HUFSMITH	77464-77464 ORCHARD	77617-77617 GILCHRIST
76831-76831 CASTELL	77338-77339 HUMBLE	77465-77465 PALACIOS	77619-77619 GROVES
76832-76832 CHEROKEE	77340-77344 HUNTSVILLE	77466-77466 PATTISON	77622-77622 HAMSHIRE
76834-76834 COLEMAN	77345-77347 HUMBLE	77467-77467 PIERCE	77623-77623 HIGH ISLAND
76836-76836 DOOLE	77348-77349 HUNTSVILLE	77468-77468 PLEDGER	77624-77624 HILLISTER
76837-76837 EDEN	77350-77350 LEGGETT	77469-77469 RICHMOND	77625-77625 KOUNTZE
76841-76841 FORT MC KAVETT	77351-77351 LIVINGSTON	77470-77470 ROCK ISLAND	77626-77626 MAURICEVILLE
76842-76842 FREDONIA	77353-77355 MAGNOLIA	77471-77471 ROSENBERG	77627-77627 NEDERLAND
76844-76844 GOLDTHWAITE	77356-77356 MONTGOMERY	77473-77473 SAN FELIPE	77629-77629 NOME
76845-76845 GOULDBUSK	77357-77357 NEW CANEY	77474-77474 SEALY	77630-77632 ORANGE
76848-76848 HEXT	77358-77358 NEW WAVERLY	77475-77475 SHERIDAN	77639-77639 ORANGEFIELD
76849-76849 JUNCTION	77359-77359 OAKHURST	77476-77476 SIMONTON	77640-77643 PORT ARTHUR
76852-76852 LOHN	77360-77360 ONALASKA	77477-77477 STAFFORD	77650-77650 PORT BOLIVAR
76853-76853 LOMETA	77362-77362 PINEHURST	77478-77479 SUGAR LAND	77651-77651 PORT NECHES
76854-76854 LONDON	77363-77363 PLANTERSVILLE	77480-77480 SWEENY	77655-77655 SABINE PASS
76855-76855 LOWAKE	77364-77364 POINTBLANK	77481-77481 THOMPSONS	77656-77656 SILSBEE
76856-76856 MASON	77365-77365 PORTER	77482-77482 VAN VLECK	77657-77657 LUMBERTON
76857-76857 MAY	77367-77367 RIVERSIDE	77483-77483 WADSWORTH	77659-77659 SOUR LAKE
76858-76858 MELVIN	77368-77368 ROMAYOR	77484-77484 WALLER	77660-77660 SPURGER
76859-76859 MENARD	77369-77369 RYE	77485-77485 WALLIS	77661-77661 STOWELL
76861-76861 MILES	77371-77371 SHEPHERD	77486-77486 WEST COLUMBIA	77662-77662 VIDOR
76862-76862 MILLERSVIEW	77372-77372 SPLENDORA	77487-77487 SUGAR LAND	77663-77663 VILLAGE MILLS
76864-76864 MULLIN	77373-77373 SPRING	77488-77488 WHARTON	77664-77664 WARREN
76865-76865 NORTON	77374-77374 THICKET	77489-77489 MISSOURI CITY	77665-77665 WINNIE
76866-76866 PAINT ROCK	77375-77375 TOMBALL	77491-77494 KATY	77670-77670 VIDOR
76867-76867 PEAR VALLEY	77376-77376 VOTAW	77496-77496 SUGAR LAND	77700-77708 BEAUMONT
76869-76869 PONTOTOC	77377-77377 TOMBALL	77497-77497 STAFFORD	77709-77709 VOTH
76870-76870 PRIDDY	77378-77378 WILLIS	77501-77508 PASADENA	77710-77710 BEAUMONT
76871-76871 RICHLAND SPRINGS	77379-77383 SPRING	77510-77510 SANTA FE	77711-77711 LUMBERTON
76872-76872 ROCHELLE	77384-77385 CONROE	77511-77512 ALVIN	77713-77726 BEAUMONT
76873-76873 ROCKWOOD	77386-77393 SPRING	77514-77514 ANAHUAC	77801-77808 BRYAN
76874-76874 ROOSEVELT	77396-77396 HUMBLE	77515-77516 ANGLETON	77830-77830 ANDERSON
76875-76875 ROWENA	77399-77399 LIVINGSTON	77517-77517 SANTA FE	77831-77831 BEDIAS
76877-76877 SAN SABA	77401-77402 BELLAIRE	77518-77518 BACLIFF	77833-77834 BRENHAM
76878-76878 SANTA ANNA	77404-77404 BAY CITY	77519-77519 BATSON	77835-77835 BURTON
76880-76880 STAR	77406-77406 RICHMOND	77520-77522 BAYTOWN	77836-77836 CALDWELL
76882-76882 TALPA	77410-77410 CYPRESS	77530-77530 CHANNELVIEW	77837-77837 CALVERT
76883-76883 TELEGRAPH	77411-77411 ALIEF	77531-77531 CLUTE	77838-77838 CHRIESMAN
76884-76884 VALERA	77412-77412 ALTAIR	77532-77532 CROSBY	77839-77839 CLAY
76885-76885 VALLEY SPRING	77413-77413 BARKER	77533-77533 DAISETTA	77840-77845 COLLEGE STATION
76886-76886 VERIBEST	77414-77414 BAY CITY	77534-77534 DANBURY	77850-77850 CONCORD
76887-76887 VOCA	77415-77415 CEDAR LANE	77535-77535 DAYTON	77852-77852 DEANVILLE
76888-76888 VOSS	77417-77417 BEASLEY	77536-77536 DEER PARK	77853-77853 DIME BOX
76889-76889 WHON	77418-77418 BELLVILLE	77538-77538 DEVERS	77855-77855 FLYNN
76890-76890 ZEPHYR	77419-77419 BLESSING	77539-77539 DICKINSON	77856-77856 FRANKLIN
76901-76906 SAN ANGELO	77420-77420 BOLING	77541-77542 FREEPORT	77857-77857 GAUSE
76908-76908 GOODFELLOW AFB	77422-77422 BRAZORIA	77545-77545 FRESNO	77859-77859 HEARNE
76909-76909 SAN ANGELO	77423-77423 BROOKSHIRE	77546-77546 FRIENDSWOOD	77861-77861 IOLA
76930-76930 BARNHART	77426-77426 CHAPPELL HILL	77547-77547 GALENA PARK	77862-77862 KURTEN
76932-76932 BIG LAKE	77428-77428 COLLEGEPORT	77549-77549 FRIENDSWOOD	77863-77863 LYONS
76933-76933 BRONTE	77429-77429 CYPRESS	77550-77555 GALVESTON	77864-77864 MADISONVILLE
76934-76934 CARLSBAD	77430-77430 DAMON	77560-77560 HANKAMER	77865-77865 MARQUEZ
76935-76935 CHRISTOVAL	77431-77431 DANCIGER	77561-77561 HARDIN	77866-77866 MILLICAN
76936-76936 ELDORADO	77432-77432 DANEVANG	77562-77562 HIGHLANDS	77867-77867 MUMFORD
76937-76937 EOLA	77433-77433 CYPRESS	77563-77563 HITCHCOCK	77868-77869 NAVASOTA
76939-76939 KNICKERBOCKER	77434-77434 EAGLE LAKE	77564-77564 HULL	77870-77870 NEW BADEN
76940-76940 MERETA	77435-77435 EAST BERNARD	77565-77565 KEMAH	77871-77871 NORMANGEE
76941-76941 MERTZON	77436-77436 EGYPT	77566-77566 LAKE JACKSON	77872-77872 NORTH ZULCH
76943-76943 OZONA	77437-77437 EL CAMPO	77568-77568 LA MARQUE	77873-77873 RICHARDS
76945-76945 ROBERT LEE	77440-77440 ELMATON	77571-77572 LA PORTE	77875-77875 ROANS PRAIRIE

Zip Range	City
77876-77876	SHIRO
77878-77878	SNOOK
77879-77879	SOMERVILLE
77880-77880	WASHINGTON
77881-77881	WELLBORN
77882-77882	WHEELOCK
77901-77905	VICTORIA
77950-77950	AUSTWELL
77951-77951	BLOOMINGTON
77954-77954	CUERO
77957-77957	EDNA
77960-77960	FANNIN
77961-77961	FRANCITAS
77962-77962	GANADO
77963-77963	GOLIAD
77964-77964	HALLETTSVILLE
77967-77967	HOCHHEIM
77968-77968	INEZ
77969-77969	LA SALLE
77970-77970	LA WARD
77971-77971	LOLITA
77972-77972	LONG MOTT
77973-77973	MCFADDIN
77974-77974	MEYERSVILLE
77975-77975	MOULTON
77976-77976	NURSERY
77977-77977	PLACEDO
77978-77978	POINT COMFORT
77979-77979	PORT LAVACA
77982-77982	PORT O CONNOR
77983-77983	SEADRIFT
77984-77984	SHINER
77985-77985	SPEAKS
77986-77986	SUBLIME
77987-77987	SWEET HOME
77988-77988	TELFERNER
77989-77989	THOMASTON
77990-77990	TIVOLI
77991-77991	VANDERBILT
77993-77993	WEESATCHE
77994-77994	WESTHOFF
77995-77995	YOAKUM
78001-78001	ARTESIA WELLS
78002-78002	ATASCOSA
78003-78003	BANDERA
78004-78004	BERGHEIM
78005-78005	BIGFOOT
78006-78006	BOERNE
78007-78007	CALLIHAM
78008-78008	CAMPBELLTON
78009-78009	CASTROVILLE
78010-78010	CENTER POINT
78011-78011	CHARLOTTE
78012-78012	CHRISTINE
78013-78013	COMFORT
78014-78014	COTULLA
78015-78015	BOERNE
78016-78016	DEVINE
78017-78017	DILLEY
78019-78019	ENCINAL
78021-78021	FOWLERTON
78022-78022	GEORGE WEST
78023-78023	HELOTES
78024-78024	HUNT
78025-78025	INGRAM
78026-78026	JOURDANTON
78027-78027	KENDALIA
78028-78029	KERRVILLE
78039-78039	LA COSTE
78040-78049	LAREDO
78050-78050	LEMING
78052-78052	LYTLE
78053-78053	MC COY
78054-78054	MACDONA
78055-78055	MEDINA
78056-78056	MICO
78057-78057	MOORE
78058-78058	MOUNTAIN HOME
78059-78059	NATALIA
78060-78060	OAKVILLE
78061-78061	PEARSALL
78062-78062	PEGGY
78063-78063	PIPE CREEK
78064-78064	PLEASANTON
78065-78065	POTEET
78066-78066	RIO MEDINA
78067-78067	SAN YGNACIO
78069-78069	SOMERSET
78070-78070	SPRING BRANCH
78071-78071	THREE RIVERS
78072-78072	TILDEN
78073-78073	VON ORMY
78074-78074	WARING
78075-78075	WHITSETT
78076-78076	ZAPATA
78101-78101	ADKINS
78102-78104	BEEVILLE
78107-78107	BERCLAIR
78108-78108	CIBOLO
78109-78109	CONVERSE
78111-78111	ECLETO
78112-78112	ELMENDORF
78113-78113	FALLS CITY
78114-78114	FLORESVILLE
78115-78115	GERONIMO
78116-78116	GILLETT
78117-78117	HOBSON
78118-78118	KARNES CITY
78119-78119	KENEDY
78121-78121	LA VERNIA
78122-78122	LEESVILLE
78123-78123	MC QUEENEY
78124-78124	MARION
78125-78125	MINERAL
78130-78132	NEW BRAUNFELS
78133-78133	CANYON LAKE
78135-78135	NEW BRAUNFELS
78140-78140	NIXON
78141-78141	NORDHEIM
78142-78142	NORMANNA
78143-78143	PANDORA
78144-78144	PANNA MARIA
78145-78145	PAWNEE
78146-78146	PETTUS
78147-78147	POTH
78148-78150	UNIVERSAL CITY
78151-78151	RUNGE
78152-78152	SAINT HEDWIG
78154-78154	SCHERTZ
78155-78156	SEGUIN
78159-78159	SMILEY
78160-78160	STOCKDALE
78161-78161	SUTHERLAND SPRINGS
78162-78162	TULETA
78163-78163	BULVERDE
78164-78164	YORKTOWN
78200-78299	SAN ANTONIO
78330-78330	AGUA DULCE
78332-78333	ALICE
78335-78336	ARANSAS PASS
78338-78338	ARMSTRONG
78339-78339	BANQUETE
78340-78340	BAYSIDE
78341-78341	BENAVIDES
78342-78342	BEN BOLT
78343-78343	BISHOP
78344-78344	BRUNI
78347-78347	CHAPMAN RANCH
78349-78349	CONCEPCION
78350-78350	DINERO
78351-78351	DRISCOLL
78352-78352	EDROY
78353-78353	ENCINO
78355-78355	FALFURRIAS
78357-78357	FREER
78358-78358	FULTON
78359-78359	GREGORY
78360-78360	GUERRA
78361-78361	HEBBRONVILLE
78362-78362	INGLESIDE
78363-78364	KINGSVILLE
78368-78368	MATHIS
78369-78369	MIRANDO CITY
78370-78370	ODEM
78371-78371	OILTON
78372-78372	ORANGE GROVE
78373-78373	PORT ARANSAS
78374-78374	PORTLAND
78375-78375	PREMONT
78376-78376	REALITOS
78377-78377	REFUGIO
78379-78379	RIVIERA
78380-78380	ROBSTOWN
78381-78382	ROCKPORT
78383-78383	SANDIA
78384-78384	SAN DIEGO
78385-78385	SARITA
78387-78387	SINTON
78389-78389	SKIDMORE
78390-78390	TAFT
78391-78391	TYNAN
78393-78393	WOODSBORO
78400-78480	CORPUS CHRISTI
78501-78505	MCALLEN
78516-78516	ALAMO
78520-78526	BROWNSVILLE
78535-78535	COMBES
78536-78536	DELMITA
78537-78537	DONNA
78538-78538	EDCOUCH
78539-78541	EDINBURG
78543-78543	ELSA
78545-78545	FALCON HEIGHTS
78547-78547	GARCIASVILLE
78548-78548	GRULLA
78549-78549	HARGILL
78550-78553	HARLINGEN
78557-78557	HIDALGO
78558-78558	LA BLANCA
78559-78559	LA FERIA
78560-78560	LA JOYA
78561-78561	LASARA
78562-78562	LA VILLA
78563-78563	LINN
78564-78564	LOPENO
78565-78565	LOS EBANOS
78566-78566	LOS FRESNOS
78567-78567	LOS INDIOS
78568-78568	LOZANO
78569-78569	LYFORD
78570-78570	MERCEDES
78572-78574	MISSION
78575-78575	OLMITO
78576-78576	PENITAS
78577-78577	PHARR
78578-78578	PORT ISABEL
78579-78579	PROGRESO
78580-78580	RAYMONDVILLE
78582-78582	RIO GRANDE CITY
78583-78583	RIO HONDO
78584-78584	ROMA
78585-78585	SALINENO
78586-78586	SAN BENITO
78588-78588	SAN ISIDRO
78589-78589	SAN JUAN
78590-78590	SAN PERLITA
78591-78591	SANTA ELENA
78592-78592	SANTA MARIA
78593-78593	SANTA ROSA
78594-78594	SEBASTIAN
78595-78595	SULLIVAN CITY
78596-78596	WESLACO
78597-78597	SOUTH PADRE ISLAND
78598-78598	PORT MANSFIELD
78599-78599	WESLACO
78602-78602	BASTROP
78603-78603	BEBE
78604-78604	BELMONT
78605-78605	BERTRAM
78606-78606	BLANCO
78607-78607	BLUFFTON
78608-78608	BRIGGS
78609-78609	BUCHANAN DAM
78610-78610	BUDA
78611-78611	BURNET
78612-78612	CEDAR CREEK
78613-78613	CEDAR PARK
78614-78614	COST
78615-78615	COUPLAND
78616-78616	DALE
78617-78617	DEL VALLE
78618-78618	DOSS
78619-78619	DRIFTWOOD
78620-78620	DRIPPING SPRINGS
78621-78621	ELGIN
78622-78622	FENTRESS
78623-78623	FISCHER
78624-78624	FREDERICKSBURG
78626-78628	GEORGETOWN
78629-78629	GONZALES
78630-78630	CEDAR PARK
78631-78631	HARPER
78632-78632	HARWOOD
78634-78634	HUTTO
78635-78635	HYE
78636-78636	JOHNSON CITY
78638-78638	KINGSBURY
78639-78639	KINGSLAND
78640-78640	KYLE
78641-78641	LEANDER
78642-78642	LIBERTY HILL
78643-78643	LLANO
78644-78644	LOCKHART
78645-78646	LEANDER
78648-78648	LULING
78650-78650	MC DADE
78651-78651	MC NEIL
78652-78652	MANCHACA
78653-78653	MANOR
78654-78654	MARBLE FALLS
78655-78655	MARTINDALE
78656-78656	MAXWELL
78657-78657	MARBLE FALLS
78658-78658	OTTINE
78659-78659	PAIGE
78660-78660	PFLUGERVILLE
78661-78661	PRAIRIE LEA
78662-78662	RED ROCK
78663-78663	ROUND MOUNTAIN
78664-78664	ROUND ROCK
78665-78665	SANDY
78666-78667	SAN MARCOS
78669-78669	SPICEWOOD
78670-78670	STAPLES
78671-78671	STONEWALL
78672-78672	TOW
78673-78673	WALBURG
78674-78674	WEIR
78675-78675	WILLOW CITY
78676-78676	WIMBERLEY
78677-78677	WRIGHTSBORO
78680-78683	ROUND ROCK
78691-78691	PFLUGERVILLE
78700-78799	AUSTIN
78801-78802	UVALDE
78827-78827	ASHERTON
78828-78828	BARKSDALE
78829-78829	BATESVILLE
78830-78830	BIG WELLS
78832-78832	BRACKETTVILLE
78833-78833	CAMP WOOD
78834-78834	CARRIZO SPRINGS
78835-78835	DEL RIO
78836-78836	CATARINA
78837-78837	COMSTOCK
78838-78838	CONCAN
78839-78839	CRYSTAL CITY
78840-78842	DEL RIO
78843-78843	LAUGHLIN A F B
78847-78847	DEL RIO
78850-78850	D HANIS
78851-78851	DRYDEN
78852-78853	EAGLE PASS
78860-78860	EL INDIO
78861-78861	HONDO
78870-78870	KNIPPA
78871-78871	LANGTRY
78872-78872	LA PRYOR

Zip Range	City
78873-78873	LEAKEY
78877-78877	QUEMADO
78879-78879	RIO FRIO
78880-78880	ROCKSPRINGS
78881-78881	SABINAL
78883-78883	TARPLEY
78884-78884	UTOPIA
78885-78885	VANDERPOOL
78886-78886	YANCEY
78931-78931	BLEIBLERVILLE
78932-78932	CARMINE
78933-78933	CAT SPRING
78934-78934	COLUMBUS
78935-78935	ALLEYTON
78938-78938	ELLINGER
78940-78940	FAYETTEVILLE
78941-78941	FLATONIA
78942-78942	GIDDINGS
78943-78943	GLIDDEN
78944-78944	INDUSTRY
78945-78945	LA GRANGE
78946-78946	LEDBETTER
78947-78947	LEXINGTON
78948-78948	LINCOLN
78949-78949	MULDOON
78950-78950	NEW ULM
78951-78951	OAKLAND
78952-78952	PLUM
78953-78953	ROSANKY
78954-78954	ROUND TOP
78956-78956	SCHULENBURG
78957-78957	SMITHVILLE
78959-78959	WAELDER
78960-78960	WARDA
78961-78961	ROUND TOP
78962-78962	WEIMAR
78963-78963	WEST POINT
78964-78964	WINCHESTER
79001-79001	ADRIAN
79002-79002	ALANREED
79003-79003	ALLISON
79005-79005	BOOKER
79007-79008	BORGER
79009-79009	BOVINA
79010-79010	BOYS RANCH
79011-79011	BRISCOE
79012-79012	BUSHLAND
79013-79013	CACTUS
79014-79014	CANADIAN
79015-79016	CANYON
79018-79018	CHANNING
79019-79019	CLAUDE
79021-79021	COTTON CENTER
79022-79022	DALHART
79024-79024	DARROUZETT
79025-79025	DAWN
79027-79027	DIMMITT
79029-79029	DUMAS
79031-79031	EARTH
79032-79032	EDMONSON
79033-79033	FARNSWORTH
79034-79034	FOLLETT
79035-79035	FRIONA
79036-79036	FRITCH
79039-79039	GROOM
79040-79040	GRUVER
79041-79041	HALE CENTER
79042-79042	HAPPY
79043-79043	HART
79044-79044	HARTLEY
79045-79045	HEREFORD
79046-79046	HIGGINS
79051-79051	KERRICK
79052-79052	KRESS
79053-79053	LAZBUDDIE
79054-79054	LEFORS
79056-79056	LIPSCOMB
79057-79057	MCLEAN
79058-79058	MASTERSON
79059-79059	MIAMI
79061-79061	MOBEETIE
79062-79062	MORSE
79063-79063	NAZARETH
79064-79064	OLTON
79065-79066	PAMPA
79068-79068	PANHANDLE
79070-79070	PERRYTON
79072-79073	PLAINVIEW
79077-79077	SAMNORWOOD
79078-79078	SANFORD
79079-79079	SHAMROCK
79080-79080	SKELLYTOWN
79081-79081	SPEARMAN
79082-79082	SPRINGLAKE
79083-79083	STINNETT
79084-79084	STRATFORD
79085-79085	SUMMERFIELD
79086-79086	SUNRAY
79087-79087	TEXLINE
79088-79088	TULIA
79090-79090	SHAMROCK
79091-79091	UMBARGER
79092-79092	VEGA
79093-79093	WAKA
79094-79094	WAYSIDE
79095-79095	WELLINGTON
79096-79096	WHEELER
79097-79097	WHITE DEER
79098-79098	WILDORADO
79100-79189	AMARILLO
79201-79201	CHILDRESS
79220-79220	AFTON
79221-79221	AIKEN
79222-79222	CAREY
79223-79223	CEE VEE
79224-79224	CHALK
79225-79225	CHILLICOTHE
79226-79226	CLARENDON
79227-79227	CROWELL
79229-79229	DICKENS
79230-79230	DODSON
79231-79231	DOUGHERTY
79232-79232	DUMONT
79233-79233	ESTELLINE
79234-79234	FLOMOT
79235-79235	FLOYDADA
79236-79236	GUTHRIE
79237-79237	HEDLEY
79238-79238	KIRKLAND
79239-79239	LAKEVIEW
79240-79240	LELIA LAKE
79241-79241	LOCKNEY
79243-79243	MCADOO
79244-79244	MATADOR
79245-79245	MEMPHIS
79247-79247	ODELL
79248-79248	PADUCAH
79250-79250	PETERSBURG
79251-79251	QUAIL
79252-79252	QUANAH
79255-79255	QUITAQUE
79256-79256	ROARING SPRINGS
79257-79257	SILVERTON
79258-79258	SOUTH PLAINS
79259-79259	TELL
79260-79260	TRUSCOTT
79261-79261	TURKEY
79311-79311	ABERNATHY
79312-79312	AMHERST
79313-79313	ANTON
79314-79314	BLEDSOE
79316-79316	BROWNFIELD
79320-79320	BULA
79321-79321	CONE
79322-79322	CROSBYTON
79323-79323	DENVER CITY
79324-79324	ENOCHS
79325-79325	FARWELL
79326-79326	FIELDTON
79329-79329	IDALOU
79330-79330	JUSTICEBURG
79331-79331	LAMESA
79336-79338	LEVELLAND
79339-79339	LITTLEFIELD
79342-79342	LOOP
79343-79343	LORENZO
79344-79344	MAPLE
79345-79345	MEADOW
79346-79346	MORTON
79347-79347	MULESHOE
79350-79350	NEW DEAL
79351-79351	ODONNELL
79353-79353	PEP
79355-79355	PLAINS
79356-79356	POST
79357-79357	RALLS
79358-79358	ROPESVILLE
79359-79359	SEAGRAVES
79360-79360	SEMINOLE
79363-79363	SHALLOWATER
79364-79364	SLATON
79366-79366	RANSOM CANYON
79367-79367	SMYER
79368-79368	SOUTHLAND
79369-79369	SPADE
79370-79370	SPUR
79371-79371	SUDAN
79372-79372	SUNDOWN
79373-79373	TAHOKA
79376-79376	TOKIO
79377-79377	WELCH
79378-79378	WELLMAN
79379-79379	WHITEFACE
79380-79380	WHITHARRAL
79381-79381	WILSON
79382-79382	WOLFFORTH
79383-79383	NEW HOME
79400-79464	LUBBOCK
79489-79489	REESE AIR FORCE BASE
79490-79499	LUBBOCK
79501-79501	ANSON
79502-79502	ASPERMONT
79503-79503	STAMFORD
79504-79504	BAIRD
79505-79505	BENJAMIN
79506-79506	BLACKWELL
79508-79508	BUFFALO GAP
79510-79510	CLYDE
79511-79511	COAHOMA
79512-79512	COLORADO CITY
79516-79516	DUNN
79517-79517	FLUVANNA
79518-79518	GIRARD
79519-79519	GOLDSBORO
79520-79520	HAMLIN
79521-79521	HASKELL
79525-79525	HAWLEY
79526-79526	HERMLEIGH
79527-79527	IRA
79528-79528	JAYTON
79529-79529	KNOX CITY
79530-79530	LAWN
79532-79532	LORAINE
79533-79533	LUEDERS
79534-79534	MC CAULLEY
79535-79535	MARYNEAL
79536-79536	MERKEL
79537-79537	NOLAN
79538-79538	NOVICE
79539-79539	O BRIEN
79540-79540	OLD GLORY
79541-79541	OVALO
79542-79542	PEACOCK
79543-79543	ROBY
79544-79544	ROCHESTER
79545-79545	ROSCOE
79546-79546	ROTAN
79547-79548	RULE
79549-79550	SNYDER
79553-79553	STAMFORD
79556-79556	SWEETWATER
79560-79560	SYLVESTER
79561-79561	TRENT
79562-79562	TUSCOLA
79563-79563	TYE
79565-79565	WESTBROOK
79566-79566	WINGATE
79567-79567	WINTERS
79600-79606	ABILENE
79607-79607	DYESS AFB
79608-79699	ABILENE
79701-79712	MIDLAND
79713-79713	ACKERLY
79714-79714	ANDREWS
79718-79718	BALMORHEA
79719-79719	BARSTOW
79720-79721	BIG SPRING
79730-79730	COYANOSA
79731-79731	CRANE
79733-79733	FORSAN
79734-79734	FORT DAVIS
79735-79735	FORT STOCKTON
79738-79738	GAIL
79739-79739	GARDEN CITY
79740-79740	GIRVIN
79741-79741	GOLDSMITH
79742-79742	GRANDFALLS
79743-79743	IMPERIAL
79744-79744	IRAAN
79745-79745	KERMIT
79748-79748	KNOTT
79749-79749	LENORAH
79752-79752	MC CAMEY
79754-79754	MENTONE
79755-79755	MIDKIFF
79756-79756	MONAHANS
79758-79758	GARDENDALE
79759-79759	NOTREES
79760-79769	ODESSA
79770-79770	ORLA
79772-79772	PECOS
79776-79776	PENWELL
79777-79777	PYOTE
79778-79778	RANKIN
79779-79779	ROYALTY
79780-79780	SARAGOSA
79781-79781	SHEFFIELD
79782-79782	STANTON
79783-79783	TARZAN
79785-79785	TOYAH
79786-79786	TOYAHVALE
79788-79788	WICKETT
79789-79789	WINK
79821-79821	ANTHONY
79830-79832	ALPINE
79834-79834	BIG BEND NATIONAL PARK
79835-79835	CANUTILLO
79836-79836	CLINT
79837-79837	DELL CITY
79838-79838	FABENS
79839-79839	FORT HANCOCK
79842-79842	MARATHON
79843-79843	MARFA
79845-79845	PRESIDIO
79846-79846	REDFORD
79847-79847	SALT FLAT
79848-79848	SANDERSON
79849-79849	SAN ELIZARIO
79850-79850	SHAFTER
79851-79851	SIERRA BLANCA
79852-79852	TERLINGUA
79853-79853	TORNILLO
79854-79854	VALENTINE
79855-79855	VAN HORN
79900-79999	EL PASO
88510-88595	EL PASO

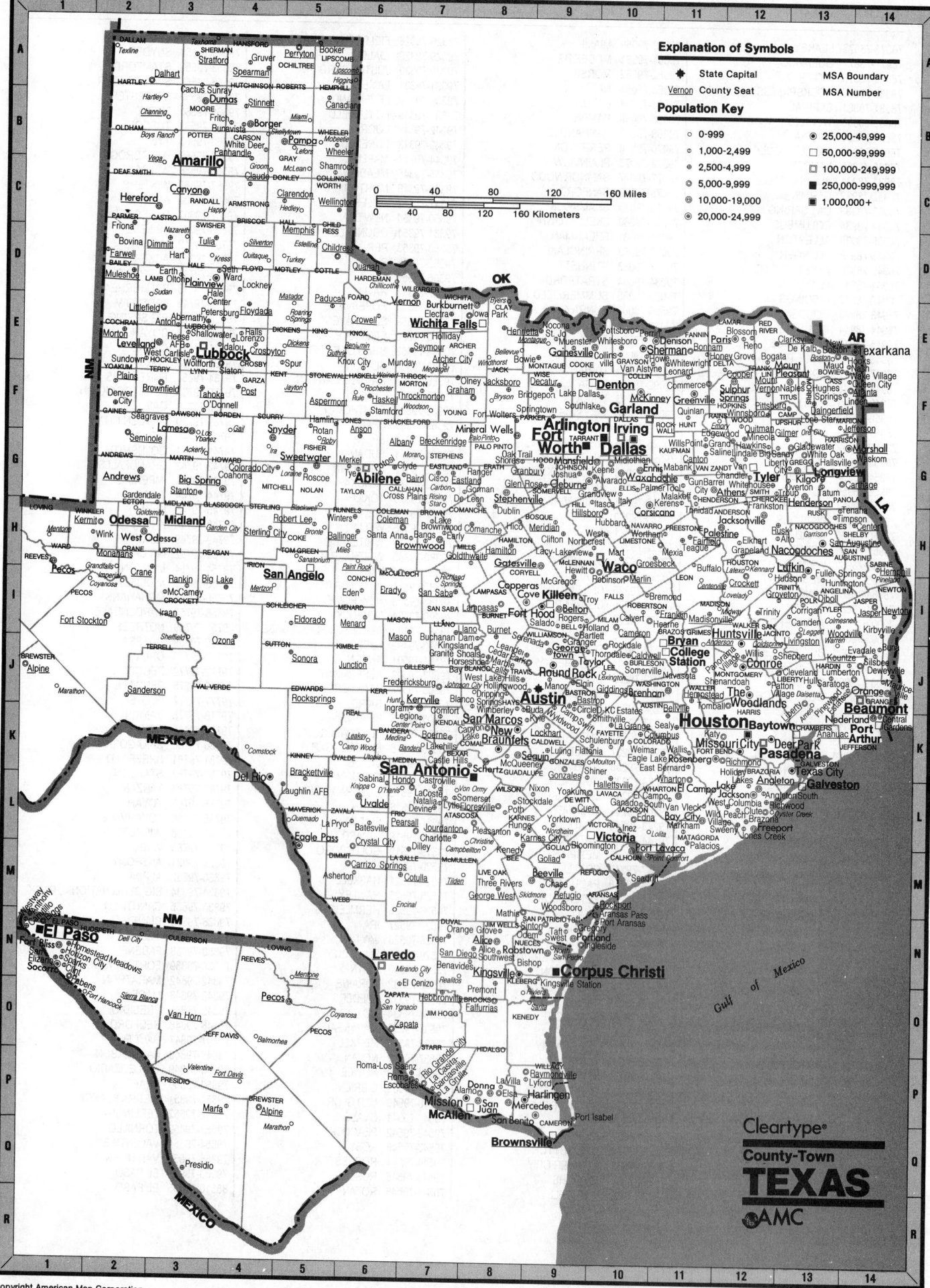

Cleartype®

County-Town

TEXAS

AMC

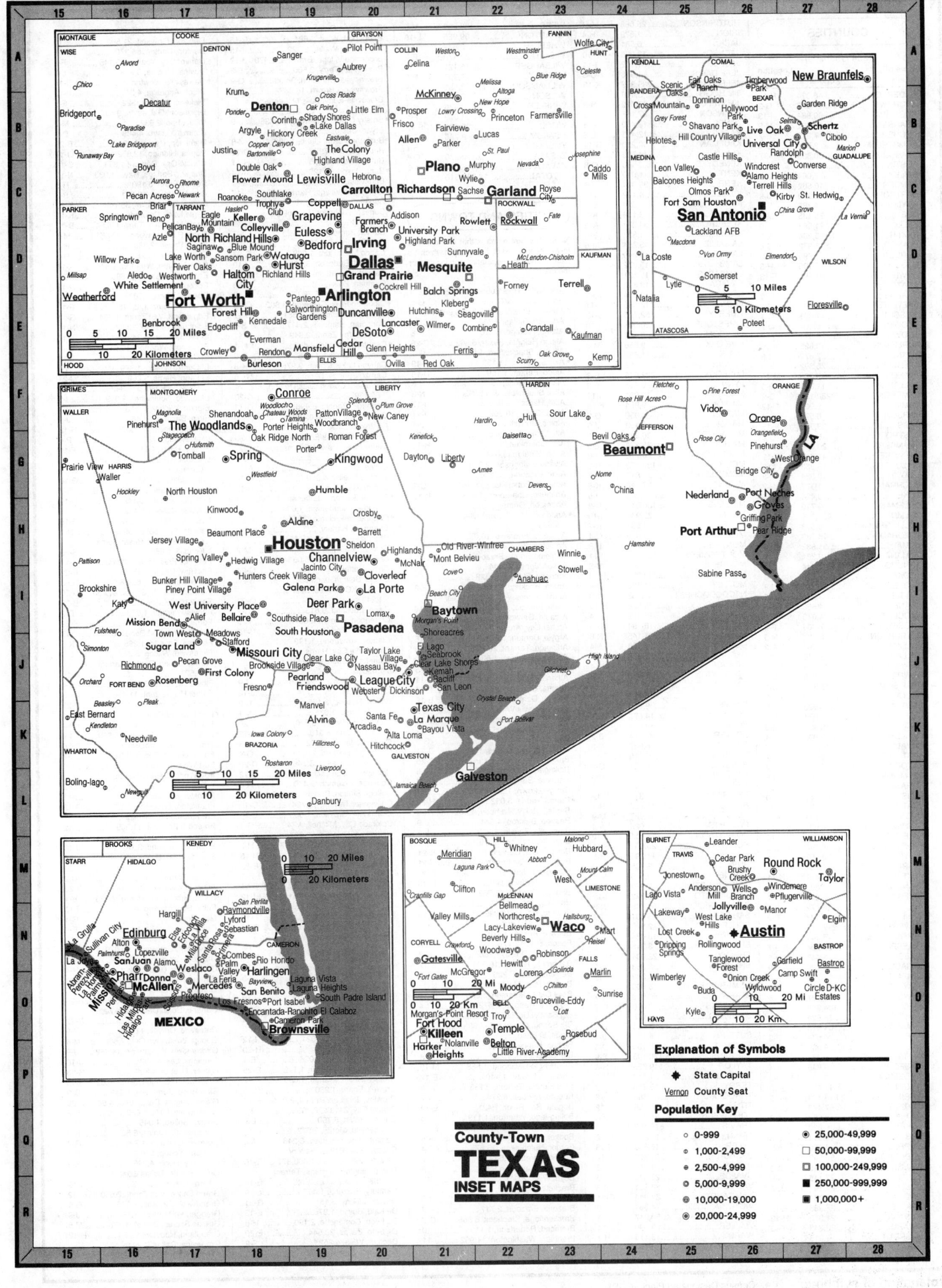

County-Town

TEXAS

INSET MAPS

Explanation of Symbols

✦ State Capital

Vernon County Seat

Population Key

○ 0-999	⊛ 25,000-49,999
⊚ 1,000-2,499	□ 50,000-99,999
⊙ 2,500-4,999	▫ 100,000-249,999
⊚ 5,000-9,999	■ 250,000-999,999
⊛ 10,000-19,000	■ 1,000,000+
⊛ 20,000-24,999	

COUNTIES

(254 Counties)

Name of County	Population	Location on Map
ANDERSON	48,024	H-11
ANDREWS	14,338	G-2
ANGELINA	69,884	I-13
ARANSAS	17,892	M-9
ARCHER	7,973	E-7
ARMSTRONG	2,021	C-4
ATASCOSA	30,533	L-7
AUSTIN	19,832	J-10
BAILEY	7,064	D-2
BANDERA	10,562	K-6
BASTROP	38,263	J-9
BAYLOR	4,385	E-6
BEE	25,135	M-8
BELL	191,088	I-9
BEXAR	1,185,394	K-7
BLANCO	5,972	J-8
BORDEN	799	F-3
BOSQUE	15,125	H-8
BOWIE	81,665	F-13
BRAZORIA	191,707	K-12
BRAZOS	121,862	I-11
BREWSTER	8,681	J-1
BRISCOE	1,971	C-4
BROOKS	8,204	O-8
BROWN	34,371	H-7
BURLESON	13,625	J-10
BURNET	22,677	I-8
CALDWELL	26,392	K-9
CALHOUN	19,053	M-10
CALLAHAN	11,859	G-6
CAMERON	260,120	Q-9
CAMP	9,904	F-12
CARSON	6,576	B-4
CASS	29,982	F-13
CASTRO	9,070	C-2
CHAMBERS	20,088	K-13
CHEROKEE	41,049	G-12
CHILDRESS	5,953	C-5
CLAY	10,024	E-8
COCHRAN	4,377	E-2
COKE	3,424	H-5
COLEMAN	9,710	H-6
COLLIN	264,036	F-10
COLLINGSWORTH	3,573	C-5
COLORADO	18,383	K-10
COMAL	51,832	K-8
COMANCHE	13,381	H-7
CONCHO	3,044	I-6
COOKE	30,777	F-9
CORYELL	64,213	I-8
COTTLE	2,247	D-5
CRANE	4,652	H-2
CROCKETT	4,078	I-3
CROSBY	7,304	F-4
CULBERSON	3,407	N-3
DALLAM	5,461	A-2
DALLAS	1,852,810	F-10
DAWSON	14,349	F-3
DEWITT	18,840	L-9
DEAF SMITH	19,153	C-2
DELTA	4,857	E-12
DENTON	273,525	F-9
DICKENS	2,571	E-4
DIMMIT	10,433	M-5
DONLEY	3,696	C-4
DUVAL	12,918	N-7
EASTLAND	18,488	G-7
ECTOR	118,934	H-2
EDWARDS	2,266	J-5
EL PASO	591,610	N-1
ELLIS	85,167	G-10
ERATH	27,991	G-8
FALLS	17,712	I-10
FANNIN	24,804	E-11
FAYETTE	20,095	J-10
FISHER	4,842	G-5
FLOYD	8,497	D-4
FOARD	1,794	E-6
FORT BEND	225,421	K-11
FRANKLIN	7,802	E-12
FREESTONE	15,818	H-11
FRIO	13,472	L-6
GAINES	14,123	F-2
GALVESTON	217,399	K-13
GARZA	5,143	F-4
GILLESPIE	17,204	J-7
GLASSCOCK	1,447	H-3
GOLIAD	5,980	L-9
GONZALES	17,205	K-9
GRAY	23,967	C-4
GRAYSON	95,021	E-10
GREGG	104,948	G-13
GRIMES	18,828	I-11
GUADALUPE	64,873	K-8
HALE	34,671	D-3
HALL	3,905	C-4
HAMILTON	7,733	H-8
HANSFORD	5,848	A-4
HARDEMAN	5,283	D-6
HARDIN	41,320	J-13
HARRIS	2,818,199	K-12
HARRISON	57,483	G-13
HARTLEY	3,634	A-2
HASKELL	6,820	F-6
HAYS	65,614	J-8
HEMPHILL	3,720	A-5
HENDERSON	58,543	G-11
HIDALGO	383,545	O-8
HILL	27,146	H-9
HOCKLEY	24,199	E-2
HOOD	28,981	G-8
HOPKINS	28,833	F-11
HOUSTON	21,375	H-12
HOWARD	32,343	G-3
HUDSPETH	2,915	N-1
HUNT	64,343	F-11
HUTCHINSON	25,689	A-4
IRION	1,629	H-4
JACK	6,981	F-8
JACKSON	13,039	L-10
JASPER	31,102	I-14
JEFF DAVIS	1,946	O-3
JEFFERSON	239,397	K-13
JIM HOGG	5,109	O-7
JIM WELLS	37,679	N-8
JOHNSON	97,165	G-9
JONES	16,490	F-6
KARNES	12,455	L-8
KAUFMAN	52,220	G-11
KENDALL	14,589	K-7
KENEDY	460	O-8
KENT	1,010	F-4
KERR	36,304	J-6
KIMBLE	4,122	J-5
KING	354	E-5
KINNEY	3,119	K-5
KLEBERG	30,274	N-8
KNOX	4,837	E-6
LA SALLE	5,254	M-6
LAMAR	43,949	E-11
LAMB	15,072	D-2
LAMPASAS	13,521	I-8
LAVACA	18,690	L-10
LEE	12,854	J-9
LEON	12,665	I-11
LIBERTY	52,726	J-13
LIMESTONE	20,946	H-10
LIPSCOMB	3,143	A-5
LIVE OAK	9,556	M-8
LLANO	11,631	I-7
LOVING	107	H-1
LUBBOCK	222,636	E-3
LYNN	6,758	F-3
MADISON	10,931	I-11
MARION	9,984	F-13
MARTIN	4,956	G-3
MASON	3,423	I-6
MATAGORDA	36,928	L-11
MAVERICK	36,378	L-5
MCCULLOCH	8,778	I-6
MCLENNAN	189,123	H-9
MCMULLEN	817	M-7
MEDINA	27,312	K-6
MENARD	2,252	I-5
MIDLAND	106,611	H-3
MILAM	22,946	I-10
MILLS	4,531	H-7
MITCHELL	8,016	G-4
MONTAGUE	17,274	E-8
MONTGOMERY	182,201	J-11
MOORE	17,865	B-3
MORRIS	13,200	F-13
MOTLEY	1,532	D-4
NACOGDOCHES	54,753	H-13
NAVARRO	39,926	H-10
NEWTON	13,569	I-14
NOLAN	16,594	G-5
NUECES	291,145	N-8
OCHILTREE	9,128	A-4
OLDHAM	2,278	B-2
ORANGE	80,509	J-14
PALO PINTO	25,055	G-8
PANOLA	22,035	G-13
PARKER	64,785	F-8
PARMER	9,863	C-2
PECOS	14,675	I-1
POLK	30,687	I-13
POTTER	97,874	B-3
PRESIDIO	6,637	P-3
RAINS	6,715	F-11
RANDALL	89,673	C-3
REAGAN	4,514	H-3
REAL	2,412	K-6
RED RIVER	14,317	E-12
REEVES	15,852	H-1
REFUGIO	7,967	M-9
ROBERTS	1,025	A-4
ROBERTSON	15,511	I-10
ROCKWALL	25,604	F-11
RUNNELS	11,294	H-5
RUSK	43,735	H-13
SABINE	9,586	H-14
SAN AUGUSTINE	7,999	H-13
SAN JACINTO	16,372	I-12
SAN PATRICIO	58,749	N-8
SAN SABA	5,401	I-7
SCHLEICHER	2,990	I-4
SCURRY	18,634	F-4
SHACKELFORD	3,316	F-6
SHELBY	22,034	H-13
SHERMAN	2,858	A-3
SMITH	151,309	G-12
SOMERVELL	5,360	G-9
STARR	40,518	O-7
STEPHENS	9,010	G-7
STERLING	1,438	H-4
STONEWALL	2,013	F-5
SUTTON	4,135	J-4
SWISHER	8,133	D-3
TARRANT	1,170,103	F-9
TAYLOR	119,655	G-6
TERRELL	1,410	J-2
TERRY	13,218	F-2
THROCKMORTON	1,880	F-6
TITUS	24,009	F-12
TOM GREEN	98,458	H-5
TRAVIS	576,407	J-8
TRINITY	11,445	I-12
TYLER	16,646	I-13
UPSHUR	31,370	F-12
UPTON	4,447	H-3
UVALDE	23,340	K-5
VAL VERDE	38,721	J-3
VAN ZANDT	37,944	G-11
VICTORIA	74,361	L-10
WALKER	50,917	I-11
WALLER	23,390	J-11
WARD	13,115	H-1
WASHINGTON	26,154	J-10
WEBB	133,239	M-5
WHARTON	39,955	L-10
WHEELER	5,879	B-5
WICHITA	122,378	E-7
WILBARGER	15,121	D-6
WILLACY	17,705	P-9
WILLIAMSON	139,551	I-9
WILSON	22,650	L-8
WINKLER	8,626	H-1
WISE	34,679	F-9
WOOD	29,380	F-12
YOAKUM	8,786	F-2
YOUNG	18,126	F-7
ZAPATA	9,279	O-6
ZAVALA	12,162	L-5
TOTAL	16,986,510	

CITIES AND TOWNS

Note: The first name is that of the city or town, second, that of the county in which it is located, then the population and location on the map.

Abernathy, Hale/Lubbock, 2,720 ...... E-3
Abilene, Jones/Taylor, 106,654 ...... G-6
• Abram-Perezville, Hidalgo, 3,999 . O-16
Addison, Dallas, 8,783 ...... C-20
Alamo, Hidalgo, 8,210 ...... P-8
Alamo Heights, Bexar, 6,502 ...... C-26
Albany, Shackelford, 1,962 ...... G-7
• Aldine, Harris, 11,133 ...... H-19
Aledo, Parker, 1,169 ...... D-16
Alice, Jim Wells, 19,788 ...... N-8
Alice Southwest, Jim Wells N-8
Alief, Harris I-17
Allen, Collin, 18,309 ...... B-21
Alpine, Brewster, 5,637 ...... J-1
Alta Loma, Galveston K-20
Alto, Cherokee, 1,027 ...... H-12
Alton, Hidalgo, 3,069 ...... N-16
Alvarado, Johnson, 2,918 ...... G-9
Alvin, Brazoria, 19,220 ...... K-19
Amarillo, Potter/Randall, 157,615 ... C-3
Anahuac, Chambers, 1,993 ...... K-13
Anderson, Grimes J-11
• Anderson Mill, Travis/Williamson, 9,468 ...... M-25
Andrews, Andrews, 10,678 ...... G-2
Angleton, Brazoria, 17,140 ...... L-12
Angleton South, Brazoria L-12
Anson, Jones, 2,644 ...... G-6
Anthony, El Paso, 3,328 ...... N-1
Anton, Hockley, 1,212 ...... E-3
Aransas Pass, Aransas/Nueces/ San Patricio, 7,180 ...... N-10
Arcadia, Galveston K-20
Archer City, Archer, 1,748 ...... E-8
Argyle, Denton, 1,575 ...... B-18
Arlington, Tarrant, 261,721 ...... G-10
Asherton, Dimmit, 1,608 ...... M-6
Aspermont, Stonewall, 1,214 ...... F-5
Athens, Henderson, 10,967 ...... G-11
Atlanta, Cass, 6,118 ...... F-14
Aubrey, Denton, 1,138 ...... B-19
Austin, Travis/Williamson, 465,622 .. J-9
Azle, Parker/Tarrant, 8,868 ...... D-17
• Bacliff, Galveston, 5,549 ...... J-21
Baird, Callahan, 1,658 ...... G-6
Balch Springs, Dallas, 17,406 ...... D-21
Balcones Heights, Bexar, 3,022 ...... C-25
Ballinger, Runnels, 3,975 ...... H-6
Bandera, Bandera, 877 ...... K-7
Bangs, Brown, 1,555 ...... H-7
• Barrett, Harris, 3,052 ...... H-20
Bartlett, Bell/Williamson, 1,439 ...... I-9
Bastrop, Bastrop, 4,044 ...... J-9
• Batesville, Zavala, 1,313 ...... L-6
Bay City, Matagorda, 18,170 ...... L-11
Bayou Vista, Galveston, 1,320 ...... K-21
Baytown, Chambers/Harris, 63,850 I-21
Beaumont, Jefferson, 114,323 ...... K-14
Beaumont Place, Harris H-18
Bedford, Tarrant, 43,762 ...... D-19
Beeville, Bee, 13,547 ...... M-9
Bellaire, Harris, 13,842 ...... I-18
Bellmead, McLennan, 8,336 ...... N-23
Bellville, Austin, 3,378 ...... K-11
Belton, Bell, 12,476 ...... I-9
Benavides, Duval, 1,788 ...... N-8
Benbrook, Tarrant, 19,564 ...... E-17
Benjamin, Knox, 225 ...... E-6
Beverly Hills, McLennan, 2,048 .... N-22
Bevil Oaks, Jefferson, 1,350 ...... G-24
Big Lake, Reagan, 3,672 ...... I-4
Big Sandy, Upshur, 1,185 ...... G-12
Big Spring, Howard, 23,093 ...... G-4
Biggs, El Paso N-1
Bishop, Nueces, 3,337 ...... N-9
Blanco, Blanco, 1,238 ...... J-8
• Bloomington, Victoria, 1,888 ...... M-10
Blossom, Lamar, 1,440 ...... E-12
Blue Mound, Tarrant, 2,133 ...... D-18
Boerne, Kendall, 4,274 ...... K-7
Bogata, Red River, 1,421 ...... E-12
• Boling-Iago, Wharton, 1,119 ...... L-16
Bonham, Fannin, 6,686 ...... E-11
Booker, Lipscomb/Ochiltree, 1,236 .. A-5
Borger, Hutchinson, 15,675 ...... B-4
Bovina, Parmer, 1,549 ...... D-2
Bowie, Montague, 4,990 ...... E-9
Boyd, Wise, 1,041 ...... C-17
Brackettville, Kinney, 1,740 ...... L-5
Brady, McCulloch, 5,946 ...... I-6
Brazoria, Brazoria, 2,717 ...... L-12
Breckenridge, Stephens, 5,665 ...... G-7
Bremond, Robertson, 1,110 ...... I-10
Brenham, Washington, 11,952 ...... J-11
• Briar, Parker/Tarrant/Wise, 3,899 . C-17
Bridge City, Orange, 8,034 ...... G-26
Bridgeport, Wise, 3,581 ...... B-16
Brookshire, Waller, 2,922 ...... I-15
Brookside Village, Brazoria, 1,470 . J-19
Brownfield, Terry, 9,560 ...... F-3
Brownsville, Cameron, 98,962 ...... Q-9
Brownwood, Brown, 18,387 ...... H-7
Bruceville-Eddy, Falls/McLennan, 1,075 ...... O-22
• Brushy Creek, Williamson, 5,833 ..... J-9
Bryan, Brazos, 55,002 ...... J-11
• Buchanan Dam, Llano, 1,099 ...... I-8
Buda, Hays, 1,795 ...... O-11
Buffalo, Leon, 1,555 ...... H-11
• Buna, Jasper, 2,127 ...... J-14
Bunavista, Hutchinson B-4
Bunker Hill Village, Harris, 3,391 .... I-17
Burkburnett, Wichita, 10,145 ...... E-8
Burleson, Johnson/Tarrant, 16,113 ...... E-18
Burnet, Burnet, 3,423 ...... I-8
Cactus, Moore, 1,529 ...... B-3
Caddo Mills, Hunt, 1,068 ...... C-23
Caldwell, Burleson, 3,181 ...... J-10
Calvert, Robertson, 1,536 ...... I-10
Camden, Polk I-13
Cameron, Milam, 5,580 ...... I-10
• Cameron Park, Cameron, 3,802 ... O-19
• Camp Swift, Bastrop, 2,681 ...... O-27
Canadian, Hemphill, 2,417 ...... B-5
Canton, Van Zandt, 2,949 ...... G-11
• Canutillo, El Paso, 4,442 ...... N-1
Canyon, Randall, 11,365 ...... C-3
• Canyon Lake, Comal, 9,975 ...... K-8
Carrizo Springs, Dimmit, 5,745 ...... M-6
Carrollton, Collin/Dallas/Denton, 82,169 ...... C-20
Carthage, Panola, 6,496 ...... G-13
Castle Hills, Bexar, 4,198 ...... K-8
Castroville, Medina, 2,159 ...... L-7
Cedar Hill, Dallas/Ellis, 19,976 ...... E-20
Cedar Park, Travis/Williamson, 5,161 ...... J-9
Celina, Collin, 1,737 ...... A-21
Center, Shelby, 4,950 ...... H-14
Centerville, Leon, 812 ...... I-11
• Central Gardens, Jefferson, 4,026 . K-14
Chandler, Henderson, 1,630 ...... G-12
• Channelview, Harris, 25,564 ...... H-20
Channing, Hartley, 277 ...... B-3
Charlotte, Atascosa, 1,475 ...... L-7
Chase, Bee M-9
Childress, Childress, 5,055 ...... D-5
China, Jefferson, 1,144 ...... G-24
Cibolo, Bexar/Guadalupe, 1,757 .... B-27
• Circle D-KC Estates, Bastrop, 1,247 ...... O-27
Cisco, Eastland, 3,813 ...... G-7
Clarendon, Donley, 2,067 ...... C-5
Clarksville, Red River, 4,311 ...... E-12
Claude, Armstrong, 1,199 ...... C-4
Clear Lake City, Harris J-20
Clear Lake Shores, Galveston, 1,096 ...... J-21
Cleburne, Johnson, 22,205 ...... G-9
Cleveland, Liberty, 7,124 ...... J-12
Clifton, Bosque, 3,195 ...... H-9
Clint, El Paso, 1,035 ...... N-1
• Cloverleaf, Harris, 18,230 ...... I-20
Clute, Brazoria, 8,910 ...... L-12
Clyde, Callahan, 3,002 ...... G-6
Coahoma, Howard, 1,133 ...... G-4
Cockrell Hill, Dallas, 3,746 ...... D-20
Coldspring, San Jacinto, 538 ...... J-12
Coleman, Coleman, 5,410 ...... H-6
College Station, Brazos, 52,456 ...... J-11
Colleyville, Tarrant, 12,724 ...... C-19
Collinsville, Grayson, 1,033 ...... E-10
Colorado City, Mitchell, 4,749 ...... G-4
Columbus, Colorado, 3,367 ...... K-10
Comanche, Comanche, 4,087 ...... H-8
Combes, Cameron, 2,042 ...... N-18
Combine, Dallas/Kaufman, 1,329 .. E-22
• Comfort, Kendall, 1,477 ...... K-7
Commerce, Hunt, 6,825 ...... F-11
Conroe, Montgomery, 27,610 ...... J-12
Converse, Bexar, 8,887 ...... C-27
Cooper, Delta, 2,153 ...... F-12
Coppell, Dallas/Denton, 16,881 ...... C-20
Copperas Cove, Coryell/ Lampasas, 24,079 ...... I-8
Corinth, Denton, 3,944 ...... B-19
Corpus Christi, Kleberg/Nueces/ San Patricio, 257,453 ...... N-9
Corrigan, Polk, 1,764 ...... I-13
Corsicana, Navarro, 22,911 ...... H-10
Cotulla, La Salle, 3,694 ...... M-7
Crandall, Kaufman, 1,652 ...... E-22
Crane, Crane, 3,533 ...... H-3
Crockett, Houston, 7,024 ...... I-12
• Crosby, Harris, 1,811 ...... H-20
Crosbyton, Crosby, 2,026 ...... E-4
• Cross Mountain, Bexar, 1,112 ...... B-25
Cross Plains, Callahan, 1,063 ...... H-7
Crowell, Foard, 1,230 ...... E-6
Crowley, Johnson/Tarrant, 6,974 ... E-18
Crystal City, Zavala, 8,263 ...... M-6
Cuero, DeWitt, 6,700 ...... L-9
Daingerfield, Morris, 2,572 ...... F-13
Dalhart, Dallam/Hartley, 6,246 ...... A-2
Dallas, Collin/Dallas/Denton/ Kaufman/Rockwall, 1,006,877 .... G-10
Dalworthington Gardens, Tarrant, 1,758 ...... E-19
Danbury, Brazoria, 1,447 ...... L-19
Dayton, Liberty, 5,151 ...... G-21
De Kalb, Bowie, 1,976 ...... E-13
De Leon, Comanche, 2,190 ...... H-8
De Soto, Dallas, 30,544 ...... E-20
Decatur, Wise, 4,252 ...... F-9
Deer Park, Harris, 27,652 ...... K-12
Del Rio, Val Verde, 30,705 ...... L-4
Denison, Grayson, 21,505 ...... E-10
Denton, Denton, 66,270 ...... F-9
Denver City, Yoakum, 5,145 ...... F-2
Devine, Medina, 3,928 ...... L-7
• Deweyville, Newton, 1,218 ...... J-14
Diboll, Angelina, 4,341 ...... I-13
Dickens, Dickens, 322 ...... E-5
Dickinson, Galveston, 9,497 ...... J-21
Dilley, Frio, 2,632 ...... M-7
Dimmitt, Castro, 4,408 ...... D-3
• Dominion, Bexar, 1,196 ...... B-26
Donna, Hidalgo, 12,652 ...... O-17
Double Oak, Denton, 1,664 ...... C-19
Dripping Springs, Hays, 1,033 ...... N-10
Dublin, Erath, 3,190 ...... H-8
Dumas, Moore, 12,871 ...... B-3
Duncanville, Dallas, 35,748 ...... E-20
Eagle Lake, Colorado, 3,551 ...... K-11
• Eagle Mountain, Tarrant, 5,847 ...... D-17
Eagle Pass, Maverick, 20,651 ...... M-5
Early, Brown, 2,380 ...... H-7
Earth, Lamb, 1,228 ...... D-3
• East Bernard, Wharton, 1,544 ...... K-11
Eastland, Eastland, 3,690 ...... G-7
Edcouch, Hidalgo, 2,878 ...... N-17
Eden, Concho, 1,567 ...... I-6
Edgecliff, Tarrant, 2,715 ...... E-18
Edgewood, Van Zandt, 1,284 ...... G-11
Edinburg, Hidalgo, 29,885 ...... N-16
Edna, Jackson, 5,343 ...... L-10
El Campo, Wharton, 10,511 ...... L-11
El Campo South, Wharton L-11
El Cenizo, Webb, 1,399 ...... N-7
El Lago, Harris, 3,269 ...... J-21
El Paso, El Paso, 515,342 ...... N-1
Eldorado, Schleicher, 2,019 ...... I-5
Electra, Wichita, 3,113 ...... E-7
Elgin, Bastrop, 4,846 ...... J-9
Elkhart, Anderson, 1,076 ...... H-12
Elsa, Hidalgo, 5,242 ...... P-8
Emory, Rains, 963 ...... F-11
• Encantada-Ranchito El Calaboz, Cameron, 1,143 ...... O-18
Ennis, Ellis, 13,883 ...... G-10
• Escobares, Starr, 1,705 ...... P-7
Euless, Tarrant, 38,149 ...... D-19
• Evadale, Jasper, 1,422 ...... J-14
Everman, Tarrant, 5,672 ...... E-18
• Fabens, El Paso, 5,599 ...... N-1
Fair Oaks Ranch, Bexar/Comal/ Kendall, 1,860 ...... B-25
Fairfield, Freestone, 3,234 ...... H-11
Fairview, Collin, 1,554 ...... B-22
Falfurrias, Brooks, 5,788 ...... O-8
Farmers Branch, Dallas, 24,250 .... D-20
Farmersville, Collin, 2,640 ...... B-23
Farwell, Parmer, 1,373 ...... D-2
Ferris, Ellis, 2,212 ...... E-22
• First Colony, Fort Bend, 18,327 ..... J-17
Flatonia, Fayette, 1,295 ...... K-9
Floresville, Wilson, 5,247 ...... L-8
Flower Mound, Denton/Tarrant, 15,527 ...... C-19
Floydada, Floyd, 3,896 ...... E-4
Forest Hill, Tarrant, 11,482 ...... E-18
Forney, Kaufman, 4,070 ...... D-22
• Fort Bliss, El Paso, 13,915 ...... N-1
Fort Davis, Jeff Davis P-4
• Fort Hood, Bell/Coryell, 35,580 ...... I-9
Fort Sam Houston, Bexar C-26
Fort Stockton, Pecos, 8,524 ...... I-2
Fort Wolters, Palo Pinto/Parker F-8
Fort Worth, Denton/Tarrant, 447,619 ...... G-9
Franklin, Robertson, 1,336 ...... I-11
Frankston, Anderson, 1,127 ...... G-12
Fredericksburg, Gillespie, 6,934 ...... J-7
Freeport, Brazoria, 11,389 ...... L-12
Freer, Duval, 3,271 ...... N-7
• Fresno, Fort Bend, 3,182 ...... J-18
Friendswood, Galveston/Harris, 22,814 ...... J-20
Friona, Parmer, 3,688 ...... D-2
Frisco, Collin/Denton, 6,141 ...... B-20
Fritch, Hutchinson/Moore, 2,335 ...... B-4
Fuller Springs, Angelina I-13
Gail, Borden G-4
Gainesville, Cooke, 14,256 ...... E-9
Galena Park, Harris, 10,033 ...... I-19
Galveston, Galveston, 59,070 ...... L-13
Ganado, Jackson, 1,701 ...... L-10
Garden City, Glasscock H-4
Garden Ridge, Comal, 1,450 ...... B-27
• Gardendale, Ector, 1,103 ...... H-3
• Garfield, Bastrop/Travis, 1,336 ...... N-26
Garland, Collin/Dallas/Rockwall, 180,650 ...... C-22
Gatesville, Coryell, 11,492 ...... H-9
George West, Live Oak, 2,586 ...... M-8
Georgetown, Williamson, 14,842 ...... J-9
Giddings, Lee, 4,093 ...... J-10
Gilmer, Upshur, 4,822 ...... G-13
Gladewater, Gregg/Upshur, 6,027 . G-13
Glen Rose, Somervell, 1,949 ...... G-9
Glenn Heights, Dallas/Ellis, 4,564 . E-20
Goldthwaite, Mills, 1,658 ...... H-8
Goliad, Goliad, 1,946 ...... M-9
Gonzales, Gonzales, 6,527 ...... K-9
Gorman, Eastland, 1,290 ...... G-7
Graham, Young, 8,986 ...... F-8
Granbury, Hood, 4,045 ...... G-9
Grand Prairie, Dallas/Ellis/ Tarrant, 99,616 ...... D-19
Grand Saline, Van Zandt, 2,630 .... G-12
Grandview, Johnson, 1,245 ...... G-9
Granger, Williamson, 1,190 ...... J-9
Granite Shoals, Burnet, 1,378 ...... J-8
Grapeland, Houston, 1,450 ...... H-12
Grapevine, Dallas/Denton/ Tarrant, 29,202 ...... C-19

Explanation of symbols: • – Census Designated Place (CDP)

Greenville, Hunt, 23,071 F-11
Gregory, San Patricio, 2,458 N-9
Griffing Park, Jefferson H-26
Groesbeck, Limestone, 3,185 H-10
Groves, Jefferson, 16,513 H-26
Groveton, Trinity, 1,071 I-12
Gruver, Hansford, 1,172 A-4
Gun Barrel City, Henderson, 3,526 G-11
Guthrie, King E-5
Hale Center, Hale, 2,067 E-3
Hallettsville, Lavaca, 2,718 L-10
Hallsville, Harrison, 2,288 G-13
Haltom City, Tarrant, 32,856 D-18
Hamilton, Hamilton, 2,937 H-8
Hamlin, Fisher/Jones, 2,791 F-5
Harker Heights, Bell, 12,841 P-21
Harlingen, Cameron, 48,735 N-18
Hart, Castro, 1,221 D-3
Haskell, Haskell, 3,362 F-6
Hawkins, Wood, 1,309 G-12
Hearne, Robertson, 5,132 I-10
Heath, Rockwall, 2,108 D-22
©Hebbronville, Jim Hogg, 4,465 O-7
Hebron, Denton, 1,128 C-20
Hedwig Village, Harris, 2,616 H-18
Helotes, Bexar, 1,535 B-25
Hemphill, Sabine, 1,182 H-14
Hempstead, Waller, 3,551 J-11
Henderson, Rusk, 11,139 G-13
Henrietta, Clay, 2,896 E-8
Hereford, Deaf Smith, 14,745 C-3
Hewitt, McLennan, 8,983 H-9
Hickory Creek, Denton, 1,893 B-19
Hico, Hamilton, 1,342 H-8
Hidalgo, Hidalgo, 3,292 O-16
Highland Park, Dallas, 8,739 D-20
Highland Village, Denton, 7,027 B-19
©Highlands, Harris, 6,632 H-20
Hill Country Village, Bexar, 1,038 B-26
Hillsboro, Hill, 7,072 H-10
Hitchcock, Galveston, 5,868 K-21
Holiday Lakes, Brazoria, 1,039 L-12
Holland, Bell, 1,118 I-9
Holliday, Archer, 1,475 E-7
Hollywood Park, Bexar, 2,841 B-26
©Homestead Meadows, El Paso, 4,978 N-1
Hondo, Medina, 6,018 L-7
Honey Grove, Fannin, 1,681 E-11
Hooks, Bowie, 2,684 E-13
Horizon City, El Paso, 2,308 N-1
©Horseshoe Bay, Burnet/Llano, 1,546 J-8
Houston, Fort Bend/Harris/Montgomery, 1,630,553 K-12
Howe, Grayson, 2,173 E-10
Hubbard, Hill, 1,589 H-10
Hudson, Angelina, 2,374 I-13
Hughes Springs, Cass/Morris, 1,938 F-13
Hull, Liberty J-13
Humble, Harris, 12,060 G-19
Hunters Creek Village, Harris, 3,954 I-18
Huntington, Angelina, 1,794 I-13
Huntsville, Walker, 27,925 I-12
Hurst, Tarrant, 33,574 D-18
Hutchins, Dallas, 2,719 E-21
Idalou, Lubbock, 2,074 E-4
©Inez, Victoria, 1,371 L-10
Ingleside, San Patricio, 5,696 N-9
Ingram, Kerr, 1,408 K-7
Iowa Park, Wichita, 6,072 E-7
Iraan, Pecos, 1,322 I-3
Irving, Dallas, 155,037 G-10
Italy, Ellis, 1,699 G-10
Itasca, Hill, 1,523 G-9
Jacinto City, Harris, 9,343 I-19
Jacksboro, Jack, 3,350 F-8
Jacksonville, Cherokee, 12,765 H-12
Jasper, Jasper, 6,959 I-14
Jayton, Kent, 608 F-5
Jefferson, Marion, 2,199 F-13
Jersey Village, Harris, 4,826 H-17
Johnson City, Blanco, 932 J-8
©Jollyville, Travis/Williamson, 15,206 N-26
Jonestown, Travis, 1,250 M-25
Jones Creek, Brazoria, 2,160 L-12
Joshua, Johnson, 3,828 G-9
Jourdanton, Atascosa, 3,220 L-8
Junction, Kimble, 2,654 J-6
Justin, Denton, 1,234 C-18
Karnes City, Karnes, 2,916 L-8
Katy, Fort Bend/Harris/Waller, 8,005 I-16
Kaufman, Kaufman, 5,238 E-23
Keene, Johnson, 3,944 G-9
Keller, Tarrant, 13,683 C-18
Kemah, Galveston, 1,094 J-21
Kemp, Kaufman, 1,184 F-23
Kenedy, Karnes, 3,763 L-8
Kennedale, Tarrant, 4,096 E-18
Kerens, Navarro, 1,702 G-11
Kermit, Winkler, 6,875 H-2
Kerrville, Kerr, 17,384 J-7
Kilgore, Gregg/Rusk, 11,066 G-13
Killeen, Bell, 63,535 P-21
©Kingsland, Llano, 2,725 J-8
Kingsville, Kleberg, 25,276 N-8
Kingsville Station, Kleberg N-9
©Kingwood, Harris/Montgomery, 37,397 G-19
Kinwood, Harris H-18
Kirby, Bexar, 8,326 C-26
Kirbyville, Jasper, 1,871 I-14
Kleberg, Dallas E-22
Knox City, Knox, 1,440 F-6
Kountze, Hardin, 2,056 J-14
Krum, Denton, 1,542 B-18

Kyle, Hays, 2,225 K-8
©La Casita-Garciasville, Starr, 1,186 P-7
La Coste, Medina, 1,021 L-7
La Feria, Cameron, 4,360 O-17
La Grange, Fayette, 3,951 K-10
La Grulla, Starr, 1,335 P-7
©La Homa, Hidalgo, 1,403 O-16
La Joya, Hidalgo, 2,604 N-15
La Marque, Galveston, 14,120 K-21
La Porte, Harris, 27,910 I-20
©La Pryor, Zavala, 1,343 L-6
La Villa, Hidalgo, 1,388 P-8
©Lackland AFB, Bexar, 9,352 D-25
Lacy-Lakeview, McLennan, 3,617 H-9
Lago Vista, Travis, 2,199 M-25
©Laguna Heights, Cameron, 1,671 O-19
Laguna Vista, Cameron, 1,166 O-19
©Lake Brownwood, Brown, 1,221 H-7
Lake Dallas, Denton, 3,656 F-10
Lake Jackson, Brazoria, 22,776 L-12
Lake Worth, Tarrant, 4,591 D-17
©Lakehills, Bandera, 2,147 K-7
Lakeway, Travis, 4,044 N-25
Lamesa, Dawson, 10,809 G-3
Lampasas, Lampasas, 6,382 I-8
Lancaster, Dallas, 22,117 E-21
Laredo, Webb, 122,899 N-6
©Laughlin AFB, Val Verde, 2,556 L-5
League City, Galveston/Harris, 30,159 J-20
Leakey, Real, 399 K-6
Leander, Travis/Williamson, 3,398 J-8
Legion, Kerr K-7
Leon Valley, Bexar, 9,581 C-25
Leonard, Fannin, 1,744 F-11
Levelland, Hockley, 13,986 E-3
Lewisville, Dallas/Denton, 46,521 C-19
Liberty, Liberty, 7,733 J-13
©Liberty City, Gregg, 1,607 G-13
Lindale, Smith, 2,428 G-12
Linden, Cass, 2,375 F-13
Lipscomb, Lipscomb A-5
Little Elm, Denton, 1,255 B-20
Little River-Academy, Bell, 1,390 P-22
Littlefield, Lamb, 6,489 E-3
Live Oak, Bexar, 10,023 B-27
Livingston, Polk, 5,019 I-13
Llano, Llano, 2,962 I-7
Lockhart, Caldwell, 9,205 K-9
Lockney, Floyd, 2,207 D-4
Lomax, Harris I-20
Lone Star, Morris, 1,615 F-13
Longview, Gregg/Harrison, 70,311 G-13
©Lopezville, Hidalgo, 2,827 N-16
Lorena, McLennan, 1,158 O-22
Lorenzo, Crosby, 1,208 E-4
Los Fresnos, Cameron, 2,473 O-18
©Lost Creek, Travis, 4,095 N-25
Lubbock, Lubbock, 186,206 E-3
Lucas, Collin, 2,205 B-22
Lufkin, Angelina, 30,206 H-13
Luling, Caldwell, 4,661 K-9
Lumberton, Hardin, 6,640 J-14
Lyford, Willacy, 1,674 P-9
Lytle, Atascosa/Bexar/Medina, 2,255 L-7
Mabank, Henderson/Kaufman, 1,739 G-11
Madisonville, Madison, 3,569 I-11
Malakoff, Henderson, 2,038 G-11
Manor, Travis, 1,041 J-9
Mansfield, Ellis/Johnson/Tarrant, 15,607 G-9
Manvel, Brazoria, 3,733 K-19
Marble Falls, Burnet, 4,007 J-8
Marfa, Presidio, 2,424 P-4
©Markham, Matagorda, 1,206 L-11
Marlin, Falls, 6,386 I-10
Marshall, Harrison, 23,682 G-13
Mart, McLennan, 2,004 H-10
Mason, Mason, 2,041 I-7
Matador, Motley, 790 E-5
Mathis, San Patricio, 5,423 M-8
Maud, Bowie, 1,049 F-13
©Mauriceville, Orange, 2,046 J-14
McAllen, Hidalgo, 84,021 P-8
McCamey, Upton, 2,493 I-3
McGregor, McLennan, 4,683 I-9
McKinney, Collin, 21,283 F-10
McNair, Harris H-20
©McQueeney, Guadalupe, 2,063 K-8
Meadows, Fort Bend, 4,606 J-17
Memphis, Hall, 2,465 C-5
Menard, Menard, 1,606 I-6
Mentone, Loving H-1
Mercedes, Hidalgo, 12,694 P-8
Meridian, Bosque, 1,390 H-9
Merkel, Taylor, 2,469 G-6
Mertzon, Irion, 778 I-4
Mesquite, Dallas, 101,484 D-22
Mexia, Limestone, 6,933 H-11
Miami, Roberts, 675 B-5
Midland, Bay/Midland, 89,443 H-3
Midlothian, Ellis, 5,141 G-10
©Mila Doce, Hidalgo, 2,089 M-17
Mineola, Wood, 4,321 G-12
Mineral Wells, Palo Pinto/Parker, 14,870 G-8
Mission, Hidalgo, 28,653 P-8
©Mission Bend, Fort Bend/Harris, 24,945 I-17
Missouri City, Fort Bend/Harris, 36,176 J-18
Monahans, Ward/Winkler, 8,101 H-2
Mont Belvieu, Chambers/Liberty, 1,323 H-21
Montague, Montague E-9
Moody, McLennan, 1,329 O-22
Morgan's Point Resort, Bell, 1,766 O-22
Morton, Cochran, 2,597 E-2

Mount Pleasant, Titus, 12,291 F-13
Mount Vernon, Franklin, 2,219 F-12
Muenster, Cooke, 1,387 E-9
Muleshoe, Bailey, 4,571 D-2
Munday, Knox, 1,600 F-6
Murphy, Collin, 1,547 C-22
Nacogdoches, Nacogdoches, 30,872 H-13
Naples, Morris, 1,508 F-13
Nash, Bowie, 2,162 E-13
Nassau Bay, Harris, 4,320 J-20
Natalia, Medina, 1,216 L-7
Navasota, Grimes, 6,296 J-11
Nederland, Jefferson, 16,192 K-14
Needville, Fort Bend, 2,199 K-16
New Boston, Bowie, 5,057 E-13
New Braunfels, Comal/Guadalupe, 27,334 K-8
New Caney, Montgomery F-20
Newton, Newton, 1,885 I-14
Nixon, Gonzales/Wilson, 1,995 L-9
Nocona, Montague, 2,870 E-9
Nolanville, Bell, 1,834 P-21
North Houston, Harris H-17
North Richland Hills, Tarrant, 45,895 D-18
Northcrest, McLennan, 1,725 H-9
Oak Ridge North, Montgomery, 2,454 G-18
©Oak Trail Shores, Hood, 1,750 G-8
Odem, San Patricio, 2,366 N-9
Odessa, Ector/Midland, 89,699 H-3
O'Donnell, Dawson/Lynn, 1,102 F-3
Old River-Winfree, Chambers, 1,233 H-21
Olmos Park, Bexar, 2,161 C-26
Olney, Young, 3,519 F-7
Olton, Lamb, 2,116 D-3
©Onion Creek, Travis, 1,544 O-26
Orange, Orange, 19,381 J-14
Orange Grove, Jim Wells, 1,175 N-8
Overton, Rusk/Smith, 2,105 G-13
Ovilla, Dallas/Ellis, 2,027 E-20
©Ozona, Crockett, 3,181 J-4
Paducah, Cottle, 1,788 E-5
Paint Rock, Concho, 227 H-6
Palacios, Matagorda, 4,418 L-11
Palestine, Anderson, 18,042 H-12
Palm Valley, Cameron, 1,199 O-18
Palmer, Ellis, 1,659 G-10
Palmview, Hidalgo, 1,818 O-16
Palo Pinto, Palo Pinto G-8
Pampa, Gray, 19,959 B-5
Panhandle, Carson, 2,353 C-4
Panorama Village, Montgomery, 1,556 J-12
Pantego, Tarrant, 2,371 E-19
Paris, Lamar, 24,699 E-12
Parker, Collin, 1,235 B-21
Pasadena, Harris, 119,363 K-12
Patton Village, Montgomery, 1,155 J-12
Pear Ridge, Jefferson H-26
Pearland, Brazoria/Harris, 18,697 J-19
Pearsall, Frio, 6,924 L-7
©Pecan Acres, Tarrant/Wise, 1,587 C-17
©Pecan Grove, Fort Bend, 9,502 J-17
Pecos, Reeves, 12,069 H-1
Pelican Bay, Tarrant, 1,271 D-17
©Penitas, Hidalgo, 1,077 O-16
Perrin, Grayson E-10
Perryton, Ochiltree, 7,607 A-5
Petersburg, Hale, 1,292 E-4
Pflugerville, Travis, 4,444 N-26
Pharr, Hidalgo, 32,921 N-16
Pilot Point, Denton, 2,538 A-20
©Pinehurst, Montgomery, 3,284 F-16
Pinehurst, Orange, 2,682 G-27
©Pinewood Estates, Hardin, 1,174 J-13
Piney Point Village, Harris, 3,197 I-18
Pittsburg, Camp, 4,007 F-13
Plains, Yoakum, 1,422 F-2
Plainview, Hale, 21,700 D-3
Plano, Collin/Denton, 128,713 C-21
Pleasanton, Atascosa, 7,678 L-8
Port Aransas, Nueces, 2,233 N-10
Port Arthur, Jefferson, 58,724 K-14
Port Isabel, Cameron, 4,467 O-19
Port Lavaca, Calhoun, 10,886 M-10
Port Neches, Jefferson, 12,974 H-26
Porter, Montgomery G-19
©Porter Heights, Montgomery, 1,448 G-19
Portland, Nueces/San Patricia, 12,224 N-9
Post, Garza, 3,768 F-4
Poteet, Atascosa, 3,206 E-26
Poth, Wilson, 1,642 L-8
©Potosi, Taylor, 1,441 G-6
Pottsboro, Grayson, 1,177 E-10
Prairie View, Waller, 4,004 G-15
Premont, Jim Wells, 2,914 O-8
Presidio, Presidio, 3,072 Q-3
Primera, Cameron, 2,030 N-17
Princeton, Collin, 2,321 B-22
©Progreso, Hidalgo, 1,951 O-17
Prosper, Collin, 1,018 B-21
Quanah, Hardeman, 3,413 D-6
Queen City, Cass, 1,748 F-13
Quinlan, Hunt, 1,360 F-11
Quitman, Wood, 1,684 F-12
Ralls, Crosby, 2,172 E-4
Randolph, Bexar B-27
Ranger, Eastland, 2,803 G-7
Rankin, Upton, 1,011 I-3
Raymondville, Willacy, 8,880 P-9
Red Oak, Ellis, 3,124 E-21
©Reese AFB, Lubbock, 1,263 E-3
Refugio, Refugio, 3,158 M-9
©Rendon, Tarrant, 7,658 E-18
Reno, Lamar, 1,784 E-12
Reno, Parker, 2,322 C-17

Richardson, Collin/Dallas, 74,840 C-21
Richland Hills, Tarrant, 7,978 D-18
Richmond, Fort Bend, 9,801 K-12
Richwood, Brazoria, 2,732 L-12
©Rio Grande City, Starr, 9,891 P-7
Rio Hondo, Cameron, 1,793 N-18
River Oaks, Tarrant, 6,580 D-17
Roanoke, Denton, 1,616 C-18
Robert Lee, Coke, 1,276 H-5
Robinson, McLennan, 7,111 H-10
Robstown, Nueces, 12,849 N-9
Roby, Fisher, 616 G-5
Rockdale, Milam, 5,235 J-10
Rockport, Aransas, 4,753 M-10
Rocksprings, Edwards, 1,339 K-5
Rockwall, Rockwall, 10,486 C-22
Rogers, Bell, 1,131 I-9
Rollingwood, Travis, 1,388 J-8
Roma, Starr, 8,059 P-7
Roman Forest, Montgomery, 1,033 F-20
Roscoe, Nolan, 1,446 G-5
Rosebud, Falls, 1,638 P-23
Rosenberg, Fort Bend, 20,183 K-11
Rotan, Fisher, 1,913 F-5
Round Rock, Travis/Williamson, 30,923 M-26
Rowlett, Dallas/Rockwall, 23,260 D-22
Royse City, Collin/Rockwall, 2,206 C-23
Runge, Karnes, 1,139 L-9
Rusk, Cherokee, 4,366 J-12
Sabinal, Uvalde, 1,584 L-6
Sabine Pass, Jefferson I-26
Sachse, Collin/Dallas, 5,346 C-21
Saginaw, Tarrant, 8,551 D-18
Saint Hedwig, Bexar, 1,443 C-28
Saint Jo, Montague, 1,048 E-9
©Salado, Bell, 1,216 I-9
San Angelo, Tom Green, 84,474 H-5
San Antonio, Bexar, 935,933 K-8
San Augustine, San Augustine, 2,337 H-14
San Benito, Cameron, 20,125 O-18
San Diego, Duval/Jim Wells, 4,983 N-8
©San Elizario, El Paso, 4,385 N-1
San Juan, Hidalgo, 10,815 P-8
©San Leon, Galveston, 3,328 J-21
San Marcos, Caldwell/Hays, 28,743 K-8
San Saba, San Saba, 2,626 I-7
©Sanderson, Terrell, 1,128 J-2
Sanger, Denton, 3,508 A-18
Sansom Park, Tarrant, 3,928 D-17
Santa Anna, Coleman, 1,249 H-7
Santa Fe, Galveston, 8,429 K-20
Santa Rosa, Cameron, 2,223 N-17
Saratoga, Hardin J-13
Sarita, Kenedy O-9
©Scenic Oaks, Bexar, 2,352 B-25
Schertz, Bexar/Comal/Guadalupe, 10,555 K-8
Schulenburg, Fayette, 2,455 K-10
©Scissors, Hidalgo, 1,513 O-17
Seabrook, Chambers/Galveston/Harris, 6,685 J-21
Seadrift, Calhoun, 1,277 M-10
Seagoville, Dallas/Kaufman, 8,969 E-22
Seagraves, Gaines, 2,398 F-2
Sealy, Austin, 4,541 K-11
©Sebastian, Willacy, 1,598 N-17
Seguin, Guadalupe, 18,853 K-8
Seminole, Gaines, 6,342 G-2
©Serenada, Williamson, 3,242 J-9
©Seth Ward, Hale, 1,402 D-4
Seymour, Baylor, 3,185 E-7
Shady Shores, Denton, 1,045 B-19
Shallowater, Lubbock, 1,708 E-3
Shamrock, Wheeler, 2,286 C-5
Shavano Park, Bexar, 1,708 B-26
©Sheldon, Harris, 1,653 H-19
Shenandoah, Montgomery, 1,718 J-12
Shepherd, San Jacinto, 1,812 J-12
Sherman, Grayson, 31,601 E-10
Shiner, Lavaca, 2,074 K-9
Shoreacres, Chambers/Harris, 1,316 J-21
Sierra Blanca, Hudspeth O-2
Silsbee, Hardin, 6,368 J-14
Silverton, Briscoe, 779 D-4
Sinton, San Patricio, 5,549 N-9
Slaton, Lubbock, 6,078 F-4
Smithville, Bastrop, 3,196 K-9
Snyder, Scurry, 12,195 G-4
Socorro, El Paso, 22,995 N-1
Somerset, Bexar, 1,144 L-7
Somerville, Burleson, 1,542 J-11
Sonora, Sutton, 2,751 J-5
Sour Lake, Hardin, 1,547 F-23
South Houston, Harris, 14,207 J-19
South Padre Island, Cameron, 1,677 O-19
Southlake, Denton/Tarrant, 7,065 F-10
Southside Place, Harris, 1,392 I-18
©Sparks, El Paso, 1,276 N-1
Spearman, Hansford, 3,197 A-4
©Spring, Harris, 33,111 G-18
Spring Valley, Harris, 3,392 H-18
Springtown, Parker, 1,740 F-9
Spur, Dickens, 1,300 F-5
Stafford, Fort Bend/Harris, 8,397 J-17
Stamford, Haskell/Jones, 3,817 F-6
Stanton, Martin, 2,576 G-3
Stephenville, Erath, 13,502 G-8
Sterling City, Sterling, 1,096 H-4
Stinnett, Hutchinson, 2,166 B-4
Stockdale, Wilson, 1,268 L-8
©Stowell, Chambers, 1,419 I-23
Stratford, Sherman, 1,781 A-3
Sugar Land, Fort Bend, 24,529 J-17

©Sullivan City, Hidalgo, 2,371 N-15
Sulphur Springs, Hopkins, 14,062 F-12
Sundown, Hockley, 1,759 E-2
Sunnyvale, Dallas, 2,228 D-22
Sunray, Moore, 1,729 A-3
Sunrise, Falls O-23
Sweeny, Brazoria, 3,297 L-12
Sweetwater, Nolan, 11,967 G-5
Taft, San Patricio, 3,222 N-9
©Taft Southwest, San Patricio, 2,012 N-9
Tahoka, Lynn, 2,868 F-3
©Tanglewood Forest, Travis, 2,941 O-25
Tatum, Panola/Rusk, 1,289 G-13
Taylor, Williamson, 11,472 J-9
Taylor Lake Village, Harris, 3,394 J-20
Teague, Freestone, 3,268 H-11
Temple, Bell, 46,109 O-22
Tenaha, Shelby, 1,072 H-13
Terrell, Kaufman, 12,490 D-23
Terrell Hills, Bexar, 4,592 C-26
Texarkana, Bowie, 31,656 E-14
Texas City, Galveston, 40,822 K-21
The Colony, Denton, 22,113 B-20
©The Woodlands, Montgomery, 29,205 J-12
Thorndale, Milam/Williamson, 1,092 J-9
Three Rivers, Live Oak, 1,889 M-8
Throckmorton, Throckmorton, 1,036 F-7
Tilden, McMullen M-7
©Timberwood Park, Bexar, 2,578 B-26
Timpson, Shelby, 1,029 H-13
Tomball, Harris/Montgomery, 6,370 G-17
Tool, Henderson, 1,712 G-11
©Town West, Fort Bend, 6,166 J-17
Trinidad, Henderson, 1,056 H-11
Trinity, Trinity, 2,648 I-12
Trophy Club, Denton/Tarrant, 3,922 C-18
Troup, Cherokee/Smith, 1,659 G-12
Troy, Bell, 1,395 I-9
Tulia, Swisher, 4,699 D-3
Tye, Taylor, 1,088 G-6
Tyler, Smith, 75,450 G-12
Universal City, Bexar, 13,057 B-27
University Park, Dallas, 22,259 D-20
Uvalde, Uvalde, 14,729 L-6
Valley Mills, Bosque/McLennan, 1,085 N-21
Van, Van Zandt, 1,854 G-12
Van Alstyne, Grayson, 2,090 E-10
Van Horn, Culberson, 2,930 O-3
©Van Vleck, Matagorda, 1,534 L-11
Vega, Oldham, 840 C-3
Vernon, Wilbarger, 12,001 E-7
Victoria, Victoria, 55,076 L-9
Vidor, Orange, 10,935 F-26
Waco, McLennan, 103,590 H-10
Wake Village, Bowie, 4,757 F-13
Waller, Harris/Waller, 1,493 G-16
Wallis, Austin, 1,001 K-11
Waskom, Harrison, 1,812 G-14
Watauga, Tarrant, 20,009 D-18
Waxahachie, Ellis, 18,168 G-10
Weatherford, Parker, 14,804 D-16
Webster, Harris, 4,678 J-20
Weimar, Colorado, 2,052 K-10
Wellington, Collingsworth, 2,456 C-5
©Wells Branch, Travis, 7,094 M-26
Weslaco, Hidalgo, 21,877 O-17
West, McLennan, 2,515 H-10
West Carlisle, Lubbock E-3
West Columbia, Brazoria, 4,372 L-12
West Lake Hills, Travis, 2,542 J-8
©West Odessa, Ector, 16,568 H-2
West Orange, Orange, 4,187 G-26
West University Place, Harris, 12,920 I-18
©Westway, El Paso, 2,381 N-1
Westworth, Tarrant, 2,350 D-17
Wharton, Wharton, 9,011 L-11
Wheeler, Wheeler, 1,393 B-5
White Deer, Carson, 1,125 B-4
White Oak, Gregg, 5,136 G-13
White Settlement, Tarrant, 15,472 D-17
Whitehouse, Smith, 4,032 G-12
Whitesboro, Grayson, 3,209 E-10
Whitewright, Fannin/Grayson, 1,713 E-11
Whitney, Hill, 1,626 M-22
Wichita Falls, Archer/Wichita, 96,259 E-8
©Wild Peach Village, Brazoria, 2,440 L-12
Willis, Montgomery, 2,764 J-12
Willow Park, Parker, 2,328 D-16
Wills Point, Van Zandt, 2,986 G-11
Wilmer, Dallas, 2,479 E-21
©Wimberley, Hays, 2,403 J-8
Windcrest, Bexar, 5,331 C-26
©Windemere, Travis, 3,207 M-26
Wink, Winkler, 1,189 H-2
©Winnie, Chambers, 2,238 H-23
Winnsboro, Franklin/Wood, 2,904 F-12
Winters, Runnels, 2,905 H-6
Wolfe City, Hunt, 1,505 A-24
Wolfforth, Lubbock, 1,941 E-3
Woodbranch, Montgomery, 1,312 F-20
Woodsboro, Refugio, 1,731 M-9
Woodville, Tyler, 2,636 I-13
Woodway, McLennan, 8,695 N-22
Wortham, Freestone, 1,020 H-11
©Wyldwood, Bastrop, 1,764 O-26
Wylie, Collin/Dallas/Rockwall, 8,716 C-22
Yoakum, DeWitt/Lavaca, 5,611 L-9
Yorktown, DeWitt, 2,207 L-9
©Zapata, Zapata, 7,119 O-6

Explanation of symbols: © - Census Designated Place (CDP)

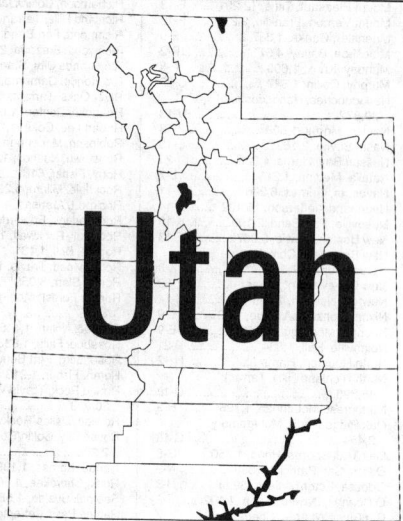

General Help Numbers:

Governor's Office
East Office Bldg. Suite220
Salt Lake City, UT 84114
www.governor.utah.gov

801-538-1000
Fax 801-538-1528
8AM-5PM

Attorney General's Office
East Office Bldg. Suite320220
Salt Lake City, UT 84114
http://attorneygeneral.utah.gov

801-538-9600
Fax 801-538-1121
8AM-5:30PM

State Court Administrator
Office of Legislative Research and General Counsel
W 210 State Capitol Complex
Salt Lake City, UT 84114
http://le.utah.gov

801-538-1588
Fax 801-538-1712
8AM-5PM

State Archives
PO Box 141021
Salt Lake City, UT 84114-1021
www.archives.state.ut.us

801-538-3848
Fax 801-538-3854
8AM-5PM M-F

State Specifics:

Capital: Salt Lake City
Salt Lake County

Time Zone: MST

Number of Counties: 29

Population: 2,389,039

Web Site: www.utah.gov/main/index

State Agencies

Criminal Records

Access to Records is Restricted.

Bureau of Criminal Identification, Records Supervisor, Box 148280, Salt Lake City, UT 84114-8280 (Courier address: 3888 West 5400 South, Salt Lake City, UT 84118); 801-965-4555, 801-965-4749-Fax; 8AM-5PM.

http://bci.utah.gov

Employers not identified by state statute cannot request records, even with notarized release from prospective employee. This agency recommends the subject state in request for the report to be sent directly to the employer or third party. Records are not open to the public nor to employers not

identified by statute signature. Those agencies authorized by law do not need to submit fingerprints, but still must have subject's notarized signature.

Statewide Court Records

Court Administrator, PO Box 140241, Salt Lake City, UT 84114-0241 (Courier address: 450 S State, Salt Lake City, UT 84114); 801-578-3800, 801-238-7832 (Search Request Info), 801-578-3859-Fax; 8AM-5PM. www.utcourts.gov

Records are available for many district court locations since late 1980's, smaller courts from

mid 1990's. Complete, consistent data is available for all district court locations since 1998.

Searching: Include the following in your request- full name, DOB, specific counties or geographic area to search. The SSN is optional. The following data is not released: juvenile records, and records from Justice Courts.

Access by: online.

Online search: Case information from all Utah District Court locations is available through XChange. Fees include $25.00 registration and $30.00 per month which includes 200 searches. Each additional search is billed at $.20 per search. Information about XChange and the subscription agreement can be found at www.utcourts.gov/records. One can search for supreme or appellate opinions at the website.

Sexual Offender Registry

Sex Offenders Registration Program, 14717 S Minuteman Dr, Draper, UT 84020; 801-545-5908, 801-545-5911-Fax; 8AM-5PM.

www.corrections.utah.gov

Utah Code § 77-27-21.5, requires the Utah Dept. of Corrections to operate, and maintain a registry of persons who have been convicted of certain sex offenses. The offenses are listed in subsection (1)(e)(i),(ii),(iii).

Records are available from 1987. It takes 60 days after sentencing before new records are available for inquiry.

Searching: Include the following in your request-name, DOB or SSN, requester name address and phone number.

Access by: mail, phone, in person, online.

Mail search: Turnaround time: 20 days. Records are searchable by petitioner submitting name and phone number, then search by ZIP Code, or by name and an identifier (such as DOB, SSN, etc.)

Phone search: Searches may be requested by phone, but results are mailed.

In person search: But they will respond by mail only.

Online search: The Registry may be searched from the web page. Records are searchable by name, ZIP Code, or name and ZIP Code. The information released includes photos, descriptions, addresses, vehicles, offenses, and targets. Also, requests nay be emailed to registry@utah.gov

Incarceration Records

Utah Department of Corrections, Records IDIO, PO Box 250, Draper, UT 84020 (Courier address: 14717 S Minuteman Dr, Draper, UT 84020); 801-576-7791, 877-884-8463 (Phone Service), 801-572-7794-Fax; 8AM-4PM.

www.cr.ex.state.ut.us

The Utah Most Wanted List is found at www.cr.ex.state.ut.us/community/mostwanted/index.html.

Records are available on current and former inmates. It takes 1 to 20 days before new records are available for inquiry.

Searching: Include the following in your request-full name and DOB. The SSN and inmate number are helpful. Location, conviction and sentencing information, and release dates are provided. The following data is not released: SSN, DOB and specific prison housing location.

Access by: mail, phone, fax.

Fee & Payment: There is a $.25 fee per copy. Fee payee: Utah State Prison

Mail search: Turnaround time: 7 to 10 days. A SASE is requested.

Phone search: The agency outsources to a private company; see toll free line listed above. This service provides custody status and release dates and offers notification if an inmate is released or moved.

Fax search: Searching by fax is permitted.

Other access: Records are released in bulk on tape or CD. Call 801-545-5625 for details.

Corporation, Limited Liability Company, Fictitious Name, Limited Partnership, Assumed Name, Trademarks/Servicemarks

Commerce Department, Corporate Division, PO Box 146705, Salt Lake City, UT 84114-6705 (Courier address: 160 E 300 S, 2nd fl, Salt Lake City, UT 84111); 801-530-4849 (Call Center), 801-530-6111-Fax; 8AM-5PM.

www.commerce.utah.gov

Records are available for active entities only. It takes 5-10 days before new records are available for inquiry. Records are indexed on inhouse computer and via the Internet.

Searching: Include the following in your request-full name of business. In addition to the articles of incorporation, corporation records include the following information: Annual Reports, Officers, Directors, DBAs, Prior (merged) names and Reserved names.

Access by: mail, phone, fax, in person, online.

Fee & Payment: Search fee is $12.00. Certification is $12.00. Copies are $.30 per page, no charge if under 10 copies. Fax transmittals are $5.00 for the first page and $1.00 each page after. Fee payee: State of Utah. Prepayment required. Personal checks accepted. Credit cards accepted: MasterCard, Visa.

Mail search: Turnaround time: 5-10 days. A SASE is requested.

Phone search: Copies cost $.30 per page. They will answer questions on name availability, status, agent and officer information.

Fax search: Turnaround time is 5-10 days. There is an additional fee of $5.00 for the first page and $1.00 for each add'l.

In person search: However, usually turnaround time is 5-10 days unless expedited fee paid.

Online search: A business entity/principle search is at www.utah.gov/services/business.html. Basic information (name, address, agent) is free. Detailed data is available for minimal fees, but registration is required. The website also offers an Unclaimed Property search page.

Other access: State allows e-mail access for orders of Certification of Existence at orders@br.state.ut.us.

Expedited service: Expedited service is available. Turnaround time: 24-48 hours. Add $75.00 per business name.

Uniform Commercial Code

Department of Commerce, UCC Division, Box 146705, Salt Lake City, UT 84114-6705 (Courier address: 160 E 300 South, Heber M Wells Bldg, 2nd Floor, Salt Lake City, UT 84111); 801-530-4849, 877-526-3994 (In State), 801-530-6438-Fax; 8AM-5PM.

www.commerce.utah.gov/cor/uccpage.htm

The phone number above is the "only way in" and caller can experience 30-60 minute waits. Suggest faxing or email questions to corpucc@utah.gov

Records are available from 1965. Records are computerized since 1995. It takes 24 hours or less before new records are available for inquiry.

Searching: Use search request form UCC-11 (can be downloaded from web). All tax liens are filed at the county level. Include the following in your request-file number(s) and/or debtor name(s), name and address of requesting party, and daytime phone number.

Access by: mail, fax, in person, online.

Fee & Payment: For a certified search, the fee is $12.00 per file number certified plus copies are $.30 per page. For uncertified searches, the fee is only $.30 per page. There is no fee if under 10 specified copies. Fee payee: State of Utah. They will bill for copy charges. Personal checks accepted. Credit cards accepted: MasterCard, Visa.

Mail search: Turnaround time: 10 working days. A SASE is requested.

Fax search: Same fees and turnaround time as mail search apply. They will invoice.

In person search: Counter service is available.

Online search: UCC uncertified records are available free online at https://secure.utah.gov/uccsearch/. Search by debtor individual name or organization, or by filing number. Certified searches may also be ordered for $12.00 per search. To receive certified searches, you must be a registered user. The website gives details. Note there is a $50 annual registration fee which includes 10 user logins. Email requests are accepted at orders@br.state.ut.us.

Other access: Records are available on CD-ROM. Suggest writing or faxing, as the phone number above can give 30-60 minute waits.

Expedited service: Expedited service is available for mail and phone searches. Add $75.00 per name. Turnaround time is 24 hours.

Federal and State Tax Liens

Records not maintained by a state level agency.

Records are found at the local level.

Sales Tax Registrations

Taxpayer Services, Technical Research, 210 N 1950 W, Salt Lake City, UT 84134; 801-297-2200, 801-297-7697-Fax; 8AM-5PM.

http://tax.utah.gov/sales/index.html

General forms and tax law information can be downloaded from the website.

Records are available for 15 years for business records, for 10 years for individual records.

Searching: Requester must have written consent. This agency will only confirm that a business is registered and active if a tax permit number is provided. They will provide no other information. Records are not accessible by the public; access is limited to the owner(s) of the account(s). You can show power of attorney to access, also. Requests must be in writing using Form TC880.

Access by: mail, in person.

Fee & Payment: Copies are $6.50 per record. Fee payee: Utah Tax Commission. Prepayment required. Personal checks accepted. No credit cards accepted.

Mail search: Turnaround time: 1 to 2 weeks. No SASE is required. Must use the required form.

In person search: Must use the required form. Turnaround time is 24 hours.

Birth Certificates

Department of Health, Office of Vital Records & Statistics, Box 141012, Salt Lake City, UT 84114-1012 (Courier address: 288 N 1460 W, Salt Lake City, UT 84114); 801-538-6105 (This Agency), 801-538-6380 (Vitalchek), 801-538-9467-Fax; 9AM-5PM (walk-in counter closes at 4:30 PM).

http://health.utah.gov/vitalrecords

Must have a signed release from person of record or immediate family member.

Records are available from 1905 on. Index computer files go back to 1978. Indexes are not available to the public. It takes 1-2 weeks before new records are available for inquiry.

Searching: At the website you can download an application or order online from the state. The Expedited Service described below is for faster service via a vendor; www.vitalchek.com. Include the following in your request-full name, names of parents, mother's maiden name, date of birth, place of birth, relationship to person of record, reason for information request. Be sure to sign the request and include a daytime phone number. You may phone, fax or email to request an application form. The following data is not released: medical records.

Access by: mail, fax, in person, online.

Fee & Payment: Search fee is $15.00. Fee is $50.00 if the entire index must be searched. Add $8.00 per name for second copies. Fee payee: Vital Records. Prepayment required. Personal checks accepted. Major credit cards accepted.

Mail search: Turnaround time: 2 to 3 weeks. No SASE is required.

Fax search: See expedited service.

In person search: Turnaround time 15 to 30 minutes.

Online search: Orders may be placed via www.vitalchek.com. See expedited service.

Expedited service: Expedited service is available for mail and fax searches. Turnaround time: overnight delivery. Expedite fee is $10.00, add $5.50 if going thru Vitalchek.com. You must use a credit card. Add fees for express mail for overnight service.

Death Records

Department of Health, Office of Vital Records & Statistics, Box 141012, Salt Lake City, UT 84114-1012 (Courier address: 288 N 1460 W, Salt Lake City, UT 84114); 801-538-6105 (This Agency), 801-538-6380 (Vitalchek), 801-538-9467-Fax; 9AM-5PM (walk-in counter closes at 4:30 PM).

http://health.utah.gov/vitalrecords

Certificates can be obtained by an immediate family member or with written permission from the immediate family.

Records are available from 1905 on. Index computer files go back since 1978. Indexes are not available to the public. It takes 1-2 weeks before new records are available for inquiry.

Searching: At the website you can download an application or order online from the state. The Expedited Service described below is for faster service via a vendor; www.vitalchek.com. Include the following in your request-full name, date of death, place of death, relationship to person of record, reason for information request. If you do not know the date of death, include last known

date alive. You may phone, fax or email to request an application form.

Access by: mail, fax, in person, online.

Fee & Payment: Search fee is $13.00, add $8.00 per name for second copies. Fee payee: Vital Records. Prepayment required. Personal checks accepted. Major credit cards accepted.

Mail search: Turnaround time: 2 weeks. No SASE is required.

Fax search: See expedited service.

In person search: Turnaround time 15 to 30 minutes.

Online search: Orders can be placed via a state designated vendor. Go to www.vitalcheck.com. Extra fees are involved.

Other access: Search the state Cemetery and Burials database for free at http://webapps.dced.state.ut.us/burials.

Expedited service: Expedited service is available for mail and fax searches. Turnaround time: overnight delivery. Expedite fee is $10.00, add $5.50 if going thru Vitalchek.com. You must use a credit card. Add fees for express mail for overnight service.

Marriage Certificates

Department of Health, Office of Vital Records & Statistics, Box 141012, Salt Lake City, UT 84114-1012 (Courier address: 288 N 1460 W, Salt Lake City, UT 84114); 801-535-6105 (This Agency), 801-538-6380 (Vitalchek), 801-538-9467-Fax; 9AM-5PM (walk-in counter closes at 4:30 PM).

http://health.utah.gov/vitalrecords

Certification of marriage occurring in Utah from 1978 through 2001 are issued in this office. Requests for certified copies of marriage prior to 1978 are issued by the county where the marriage occurred.

It takes 1-2 weeks before new records are available for inquiry.

Searching: Records are certification summaries and not copies of the original records. Download an application at the Forms link on the website navigation bar. Mail or bring the application to the Service Window in-person, or you may write a letter. Include the following in your request-date & place of occurrence, groom's name, bride's maiden name. You may phone, fax or email to request an application form.

Access by: mail, in person, online.

Fee & Payment: $9.00 is for the abstract certificate. Fee payee: Vital Records. Prepayment required Personal checks accepted Major credit cards accepted.

Mail search: Turnaround time: 2-3 weeks.

In person search: Turn in your order form for a certificate before 4:30 p.m., and wait while it is processed. Requests received at the counter after 4:30 p.m. are processed the following day.

Online search: Orders can be placed via a state designated vendor. Go to www.vitalcheck.com. Extra fees are involved.

Expedited service: Expedited service is available for mail and fax searches. Turnaround time: same day service. Expedite fee is $10.00, add $5.50 if going thru Vitalchek.com. You must use a credit card. Add fees for express mail for overnight service.

Divorce Records

Department of Health, Office of Vital Records & Statistics, Box 141012, Salt Lake City, UT 84114-1012 (Courier address: 288 N 1460 W, Salt Lake City, UT 84114); 801-538-6101 (This Agency), 801-538-6380 (Vitalchek), 801-538-9467-Fax; 9AM-5PM (walk-in counter closes at 4:30 PM).

http://health.utah.gov/vitalrecords

The offices releases certificates of abstract. Actual copies can only be obtained from the state by an immediate family member or with written permission from the immediate family.

Records are available from 1978 to present. Requests for certified copies of divorce prior to 1978 are issued by the county where the divorce occurred. It takes 1-2 weeks before new records are available for inquiry.

Searching: Records are certification summaries and not copies of the original records. Download an application at the Forms link on the website navigation bar. Mail or bring the application to the Service Window in-person, or you may write a letter. Include the following in your request-date and place of occurrence, date and place of marriage, husband's name, wife's name. You may phone or fax to request an application form.

Access by: mail, in person, online.

Fee & Payment: $8.00 for an abstract only. Fee payee: Vital Records. Prepayment required Personal checks accepted All major credit cards accepted.

Mail search: Turnaround time: 2-3 weeks.

In person search: Turn in your order form for a certificate before 4:30 p.m., and wait while it is processed the same day.

Online search: Orders can be placed via a state designated vendor. Go to www.vitalcheck.com. Extra fees are involved.

Expedited service: Expedited service is available for mail and fax searches. Turnaround time: 1-2 days. Expedite fee is $10.00, add $5.50 if going thru Vitalchek.com. You must use a credit card. Add fees for express mail for overnight service.

Workers' Compensation Records

Labor Commission, Division of Industrial Accidents, PO Box 146610, Salt Lake City, UT 84114-6610 (Courier address: 160 E 300 S, 3rd Floor, Salt Lake City, UT 84114); 801-530-6800, 801-530-6804-Fax; 8AM-5PM.

www.laborcommission.utah.gov

Records are available from 1970 to 1988 on microfiche, from 1989 to present on computer. It takes one week before new records are available for inquiry. Records are normally destroyed after 75 years.

Searching: Must have a notarized release from claimant (not over 90 days old). If a conditional job has been offered, then include a statement of such with employer's name and signature. Include the following in your request-Social Security Number, date of birth, as well as release form. Phone or fax to request form.

Access by: mail, fax, in person.

Fee & Payment: The search fee is $15.00 per name, copies are $.50 per page. Fee payee: Division of Industrial Accidents. Prepayment required. Personal checks accepted. No credit cards accepted.

Mail search: Turnaround time: 2 to 3 days. Include requester's telephone number so they can call with the total charge, which must be paid before records are released. No SASE is required.

Fax search: Prepayment is required.

In person search: Same criteria as mail requests.

Driver Records

Department of Public Safety, Driver License Division, Customer Service Section, PO Box 30560, Salt Lake City, UT 84130-0560 (Courier address: 4501 South 2700 West, 3rd Floor South, Salt Lake City, UT 84119); 801-965-4437, 801-965-4496-Fax; 8AM-5PM.

http://driverlicense.utah.gov

Copies of tickets are $5.00 per record.

Records are available for 3 years for moving violations, 10 years for DWIs and 3 years for suspensions (alcohol related suspensions are 10 years). Records on commercial drivers are kept for 10 years. It takes 2 weeks to 6 months before new records are available for inquiry. Records are normally destroyed after 10 years.

Searching: Interstate speeding convictions less than 10 mph over are not shown. Accidents are reported only if driver had citation. Addresses removed from report to comply with DPPA. Requests must comply with DPPA permissible uses. The driver's full name and DOB and/or license number are needed when ordering. Also helpful: SSN.

Access by: mail, fax, in person, online.

Fee & Payment: The fee is $4.25 per record, $7.25 if online. Fee payee: Department of Public Safety. Prepayment required. Personal checks accepted. Major credit cards accepted.

Mail search: Turnaround time: approx. 1 week. Will FedEx if requester has account or submits pre-paid envelope. A SASE is requested.

Fax search: Requests may be faxed, but results are returned by mail.

In person search: Up to 10 requests can be processed immediately; any additional requests are available the next day. Driving records can be obtained at any one of 17 branch offices throughout the state.

Online search: Driving records are available to eligible organizations through the eUtah. The system is available 24 hours daily. The fee per driving record is $7.25, there is an annual $50.00 subscription fee, also. For more information, visit the website at www.utah.gov/registration/ Utah drivers may order their own record at https://secure.utah.gov/recordrequest/. The fee is $4.25 per record.

Vehicle & Vessel Ownership
Vehicle Identification
Vessel Registration

State Tax Commission, Motor Vehicle Records Section, 210 North 1950 West, Salt Lake City, UT 84134; 801-297-3507, 801-297-3578-Fax; 8AM-5PM. http://dmv.utah.gov

Records are available for 15 years. All boats 1985 or newer must be titled. All motors over 25 HP

must be titled. All boats, except canoes, must be registered. It takes 2 weeks before new records are available for inquiry.

Searching: Access is not open to casual requesters without notarized consent of subject. Requesters should use Form TC-890. The name or the vehicle ID or registration number or hull ID is needed to search. The agency will not do a name check. The following data is not released: medical records or Social Security Numbers.

Access by: mail, phone, in person, online.

Fee & Payment: The current fee is $3.00 per record, $4.00 if by fax, and $6.50 for each microfilm record requested. State has established accounts for dealerships and financial institutions requesting lien-holder information. Fee payee: State Tax Commission. Prepayment required. Personal checks accepted. No credit cards accepted.

Mail search: Turnaround time: 5 - 7 days. Boat records can take as long as 1 week to process.

Phone search: Searching is available for pre-approved, established accounts.

In person search: Turnaround time while you wait for small amounts.

Online search: Motor Vehicle Dept. titles, liens, and registration searches are available at www.utah.gov/registration/. Registration and a $50.00 subscription fee is required plus $2.00 per record access.

Accident Reports

Driver's License Division, Accident Reports Section, PO Box 30560, Salt Lake City, UT 84130-0560 (Courier address: 4501 South 2700 West, 3rd Floor South, Salt Lake City, UT 84119); 801-965-4428, 801-964-4536-Fax; 8AM-5PM.

Records are available from 1994 to 2002 on microfilm and 2002 to present on optical imaging system. It takes 2 weeks or more before new records are available for inquiry. Records are indexed on 10 years. Records are normally destroyed after placed on microfilm.

Searching: Records are restricted only to those involved or with an interest. Members of the news media received limited information. Include the following in your request-full name, date of accident, location of accident, name of requestor and reason for request. Request must be in writing

Access by: mail, fax, in person.

Fee & Payment: The fee is $5.00 per record. Fee payee: Department of Public Safety. Prepayment required. The state will allow ongoing requesters to pre-pay with an account. Personal checks accepted. Credit cards accepted if in person.

Mail search: Turnaround time: 2 weeks or more.

Fax search: Money must be received up front before records can be returned by fax.

In person search: Records will be mailed, or can be picked up if pre-paid.

Voter Registration
Access to Records is Restricted.

Elections Office, Utah Capitol Complex, East Office Bldg - #E325, Salt Lake City, UT 84114-2325; 801-538-1041, 801-538-1133-Fax; 8AM-5PM.

http://elections.utah.gov

Individual record requests are referred to the county clerk offices. Records that have not been secured by the registrant are open to the public; however, the counties will not release the SSN or DL. The entire state voter registration database (current records only) can be purchased from this office for approximately $1,050. The website indicates some financial disclosures regarding political parties, action groups, lobbyists, and corporations.

GED Certificates

Utah State Office of Education, GED Testing Records, PO Box 144200, Salt Lake City, UT 84114-4200; 801-538-7921, 801-538-7868-Fax; 8AM-4PM.

www.usoe.k12.ut.us/adulted/ged/index.html

Records prior to 1990 may be at the testing sites in hard copy. Storage depends on the site. Testing sites may have fees to verify or release records.

Records are available from 1970 to present. It takes 3 to 5 days before new records are available for inquiry.

Searching: The agency would rather fax than mail responses. Include the following in your request-Social Security Number, signed release, DOB, name at time of testing, current name if different, name and phone number of the requester. The following information is not required to search, but is very helpful: date/year of test and city of test.

Access by: mail, fax, in person.

Fee & Payment: There is no fee for verification.

Mail search: Turnaround time: 3 to 5 days. No SASE is required.

Fax search: Same criteria as phone searching.

In person search: Searchers should call first.

Hunting and Fishing License Information

Utah Division of Wildlife Resources, PO Box 146301, Salt Lake City, UT 84114-6301 (Courier address: 1594 West North Temple, #2110, Salt Lake City, UT 84116); 801-538-4700, 877-592-5169, 801-538-4709-Fax; 8AM-5PM.

www.wildlife.utah.gov

Records are available for the current year plus the 3 previous years are kept on computer. Records are indexed on inhouse computer. Records are normally destroyed after 4 years.

Searching: Must use the official request form supplied by this agency. You must show a reasonable purpose in order to obtain information. Include the following in your request-name. DOB and SSN are helpful. The following data is not released: telephone numbers and other personal information.

Access by: mail, fax.

Fee & Payment: Fees are based upon actual cost of computer time, personnel time plus copy fee of $.25 per page. Fee payee: Utah Division of Wildlife Resources. Prepayment required. Personal checks accepted. No credit cards accepted.

Mail search: Turnaround time: 10 days. No SASE is required.

Fax search: Requests accepted by fax.

Other access: Draw lists are provided for a fee at the time of big game drawing.

Utah State Licensing Agencies

For details about the agency responsible for licensing/certifying/registering an item below or in the Agency Quick Finder section, match an item's number with the number of the agency in the *Licensing Agency Information* section.

Utah Licenses Searchable Online

Accounting Firm #5	https://secure.utah.gov/llv/llv
Acupuncturist #5	https://secure.utah.gov/llv/llv
Alarm Company/Alarm Co. Agent/Response Runner #5	https://secure.utah.gov/llv/llv
Animal Euthanasia Agency #5	https://secure.utah.gov/llv/llv
Arbitrator, Alt. Dispute Resolution #5	https://secure.utah.gov/llv/llv
Architect #5	https://secure.utah.gov/llv/llv
Athletic Event Promoter/Judge/Manager #5	https://secure.utah.gov/llv/llv
Attorney #9	www.utahbar.org/html/find_a_lawyer.html
Bank #10	www.dfi.utah.gov/Banks.htm
Barber/Barber School/Instructor #5	https://secure.utah.gov/llv/llv
Bedding/Upholstery Mfg/Whls/Dealer #3	http://ag.utah.gov/licenses/Cur_Lic.html
Beekeeper #3	http://ag.utah.gov/licenses/Cur_Lic.html
Boxer #5	https://secure.utah.gov/llv/llv
Brand Inspector #3	http://ag.utah.gov/licenses/Cur_Lic.html
Building Inspector/Trainee #5	https://secure.utah.gov/llv/llv
Building Trades, General #5	https://secure.utah.gov/llv/llv
Burglar Alarm Agent #5	https://secure.utah.gov/llv/llv
Check Cashier/Payday Lender #10	www.dfi.utah.gov/ckcash.htm
Chiropractor #5	https://secure.utah.gov/llv/llv
Consumer Lender #10	www.dfi.utah.gov/consumer.htm
Contractor #5	https://secure.utah.gov/llv/llv
Controlled Substance Precursor Dist. #5	https://secure.utah.gov/llv/llv
Cosmetologist/Cosmetology School/Instructor #5	https://secure.utah.gov/llv/llv
Counselor, Professional or Trainee #5	https://secure.utah.gov/llv/llv
Credit Union #10	www.dfi.utah.gov/CreditUn.htm
Deception Detection Examiner #5	https://secure.utah.gov/llv/llv
Dentist / Dental Hygienist #5	https://secure.utah.gov/llv/llv
Dental Hygienist/Local Anesthesia #5	https://secure.utah.gov/llv/llv
Dietitian #5	https://secure.utah.gov/llv/llv
Egg & Poultry Inspector #3	http://ag.utah.gov/licenses/Cur_Lic.html
Electrician #5	https://secure.utah.gov/llv/llv
Electrologist #5	https://secure.utah.gov/llv/llv
Employee Leasing Company #5	https://secure.utah.gov/llv/llv
Employment Provider, Profess'l #5	https://secure.utah.gov/llv/llv
Endowment Care/Cemetery #5	https://secure.utah.gov/llv/llv
Engineer / Engineer, Structural Professional #5	https://secure.utah.gov/llv/llv
Environmental Health Specialist #5	https://secure.utah.gov/llv/llv
Escrow Agent #10	www.dfi.utah.gov/escrow.htm
Feed #3	http://ag.utah.gov/licenses/Cur_Lic.html
Food & Dairy Inspector #3	http://ag.utah.gov/licenses/Cur_Lic.html
Funeral Svc Director/Apprentice/Establishment #5	https://secure.utah.gov/llv/llv
Genetic Counselor #5	https://secure.utah.gov/llv/llv
Geologist #7	https://secure.utah.gov/llv/llv
Grain & Seed #3	http://ag.utah.gov/licenses/Cur_Lic.html
Health Care Assistant #5	https://secure.utah.gov/llv/llv
Health Facility Administrator #5	https://secure.utah.gov/llv/llv
Hearing Aid Specialist #5	https://secure.utah.gov/llv/llv
Hearing Instrument Prof./Intern #5	https://secure.utah.gov/llv/llv
Holding Company #10	www.dfi.utah.gov/HCSList.htm
Industrial Banks #10	www.dfi.utah.gov/industbk.htm
Insurance Agent #8	www.insurance.state.ut.us/companies.html
Insurance Establishment #8	www.insurance.state.ut.us/companies.html
Interpreter for the Deaf #11	www.aslterps.utah.gov/cert_terp.php
Laboratory, Analytical #5	https://secure.utah.gov/llv/llv
Landscape Architect #5	https://secure.utah.gov/llv/llv
Lien Recovery Fund Member #5	https://secure.utah.gov/llv/llv
Manufac'd Housing Dealer/Seller #5	https://secure.utah.gov/llv/llv

Marriage & Family Therapist/Trainee #5	https://secure.utah.gov/llv/llv
Massage Technician/Apprentice #5	https://secure.utah.gov/llv/llv
Meat Inspector #3	http://ag.utah.gov/licenses/Cur_Lic.html
Mediator, Alt. Dispute Resolution #5	https://secure.utah.gov/llv/llv
Medical Doctor/Surgeon #5	https://secure.utah.gov/llv/llv
Midwife Nurse #5	https://secure.utah.gov/llv/llv
Mortgage Broker, Residential #2	www.commerce.state.ut.us/dre/database.html
Mortgage Loan Service #10	www.dfi.utah.gov/mortgage.htm
Naturopath #5	https://secure.utah.gov/llv/llv
Naturopathic Physician #5	https://secure.utah.gov/llv/llv
Negotiator, Alt. Dispute Resolution #5	https://secure.utah.gov/llv/llv
Nuclear Pharmacy #5	https://secure.utah.gov/llv/llv
Nurse #5	https://secure.utah.gov/llv/llv
Nurse-LPN #5	https://secure.utah.gov/llv/llv
Occupational Therapist/Assistant #5	https://secure.utah.gov/llv/llv
Optometrist #5	https://secure.utah.gov/llv/llv
Osteopathic Physician #5	https://secure.utah.gov/llv/llv
Pesticide Dealer/Applicator #3	http://ag.utah.gov/licenses/Cur_Lic.html
Pharmaceutical Admin. Facility #5	https://secure.utah.gov/llv/llv
Pharmaceutical Dog Trainer #5	https://secure.utah.gov/llv/llv
Pharmaceutical Researcher #5	https://secure.utah.gov/llv/llv
Pharmaceutical Teaching Org. #5	https://secure.utah.gov/llv/llv
Pharmaceutical Whse./Dist./Mfg. #5	https://secure.utah.gov/llv/llv
Pharmacist/Pharmacist Intern #5	https://secure.utah.gov/llv/llv
Pharmacy #5	https://secure.utah.gov/llv/llv
Pharmacy Retail/Branch/Institutional/Hospital #5	https://secure.utah.gov/llv/llv
Pharmacy Technician #5	https://secure.utah.gov/llv/llv
Physical Therapist #5	https://secure.utah.gov/llv/llv
Physician Assistant #5	https://secure.utah.gov/llv/llv
Plumber Apprentice/Journeyman #5	https://secure.utah.gov/llv/llv
Podiatrist #5	https://secure.utah.gov/llv/llv
Polygraph Examiner #5	https://secure.utah.gov/llv/llv
Pre-Need Provider/Sales Agent #5	https://secure.utah.gov/llv/llv
Probation Provider, Private #5	https://secure.utah.gov/llv/llv
Psychological Assistant #5	https://secure.utah.gov/llv/llv
Psychologist #5	https://secure.utah.gov/llv/llv
Public Accountant-CPA #5	https://secure.utah.gov/llv/llv
Radiology Practical Technician #5	https://secure.utah.gov/llv/llv
Radiology Technologist #5	https://secure.utah.gov/llv/llv
Real Estate Agent/Broker #2	www.commerce.state.ut.us/dre/database.html
Real Estate Appraiser #2	www.commerce.state.ut.us/dre/database.html
Real Estate Establishment #5	https://secure.utah.gov/llv/llv
Recreational Therapist #5	https://secure.utah.gov/llv/llv
Recreational Vehicle Dealer #5	https://secure.utah.gov/llv/llv
Referee #5	https://secure.utah.gov/llv/llv
Respiratory Care Practitioner #5	https://secure.utah.gov/llv/llv
Sanitarian #5	https://secure.utah.gov/llv/llv
Savings & Loan #10	www.dfi.utah.gov/sls.htm
Securities Broker/Dealer #5	https://secure.utah.gov/llv/llv
Security Company/Security Officer, Private #5	https://secure.utah.gov/llv/llv
Shorthand Reporter #5	https://secure.utah.gov/llv/llv
Social Svc Aide/Worker/Trainee #5	https://secure.utah.gov/llv/llv
Social Worker/Social Worker, Clinical #5	https://secure.utah.gov/llv/llv
Speech Pathologist/Audiologist #5	https://secure.utah.gov/llv/llv
Substance Abuse Counselor #5	https://secure.utah.gov/llv/llv
Surveyor, Land #5	https://secure.utah.gov/llv/llv
Third Party Payment Issuer #10	www.dfi.utah.gov/montrans.htm
Title Lender #10	www.dfi.utah.gov/titlelen.htm
Trade Instructor #5	https://secure.utah.gov/llv/llv
Trust Company #10	www.dfi.utah.gov/trslist.htm
Veterinarian/Veterinary Intern #5	https://secure.utah.gov/llv/llv
Veterinary Pharmaceut'l Outlet #5	https://secure.utah.gov/llv/llv
Weights & Measures #3	http://ag.utah.gov/licenses/Cur_Lic.html
Wine Store #1	www.alcbev.state.ut.us/Stores/wine_stores.html

Utah Licensing Quick Finder

Accounting Firm #5.............................801-530-6628
Acupuncturist #5.................................801-530-6628
Alarm Company Agent/Response Runner/Firm #5
....801-530-6628
Animal Euthanasia Agency #5 801-530-6628
Arbitrator, Alternate Dispute Resolution #5
....801-530-6628
Architect #5...801-530-6628
Athletic Event Promoter #5...................801-530-6628
Athletic Judge/Manager/Promoter #5...801-530-6628
Attorney #9..801-531-9077
Bank #10..801-538-8835
Barber/Barber School/Instructor #5......801-530-6628
Bedding/Upholstery Mfg/Whlse/Dealer #3
....801-538-7151
Beekeeper #3 801-538-7184
Boxer #5...801-530-6628
Brand Inspector #3 801-538-7137
Building Inspector/Trainee #5...............801-530-6628
Building Trades, General #5.................801-530-6628
Burglar Alarm Agent #5 801-530-6964
Check Cashier/Payday Lender #10......801-538-8842
Chiropractor #5 801-530-6628
Consumer Lender #10..........................801-538-8830
Contractor #5 801-530-6628
Control'd Substance Precursor Dist.#5.801-530-6964
Cosmetologist #5 801-530-6628
Cosmetology School/Instructor #5 801-530-6628
Counselor, Professional / Trainee #5...801-530-6628
Credit Union #10..................................801-538-8840
Deception Detection Examin'r/Intern #5 801-530-6628
Dentist / Dental Hygienist #5 801-530-6628
Dental Hygienist/Local Anesthesia #5..801-530-6628
Dietitian #5...801-530-6628
Egg & Poultry Inspector #3...................801-538-7124
Electrician, Apprentice/Journeyman/Master #5
....801-530-6628
Electrologist #5 801-530-6628
Employee Leasing Company #5 801-530-6628
Employment Provider, Professional #5 801-530-6628
Endowment Care/Cemetery #5 801-530-6628
Engineer #5 801-530-6628
Engineer, Structural Professional #5....801-530-6628
Environmental Health Specialist #5......801-530-6628
Escrow Agent #10.................................801-538-8842
Feed #3...801-538-7183

Food & Dairy Inspector #3....................801-538-7145
Funeral Service Director/Apprentice #5 801-530-6628
Funeral Service Establishment #5 801-530-6628
Genetic Counselor #5 801-530-6628
Geologist #7 801-537-6628
Grain & Seed #3 801-538-7183
Health Care Assistant #5......................801-530-6628
Health Facility Administrator #5 801-530-6628
Hearing Aid Specialist #5 801-530-6964
Hearing Instrument Prof./Intern #5.......801-530-6628
Holding Company #10...........................801-538-8842
Industrial Banks #10.............................801-538-8841
Insurance Agent / Establishment #8 801-538-3805
Interpreter for the Deaf #11 801-263-4860
Laboratory, Analytical #5......................801-530-6628
Landscape Architect #5........................801-530-6628
Lien Recovery Fund Member #5............801-530-6628
Liquor License #1.................................801-977-6800
Liquor Store (retail liquor license) #1 . 801-977-6800
Manufactured Housing Dealer/Salesman #5
....801-530-6628
Marriage & Family Therap't/Trainee #5. 801-530-6628
Massage Technician/Apprentice #5 801-530-6964
Meat Inspector #3.................................801-538-7161
Mediator, Alternate Dispute Resolution #5
....801-530-6628
Medical Doctor/Surgeon #5..................801-530-6628
Midwife Nurse #5..................................801-530-6628
Mortgage Broker, Residential #2..........801-530-6747
Mortgage Loan Service #10 801-538-8830
Naturopath #5.......................................801-530-6628
Naturopathic Physician #5....................801-530-6628
Negotiator, Alternate Dispute Resolution #5
....801-530-6628
Notary Public #4 801-530-6078
Nuclear Pharmacy #5...........................801-530-6628
Nurse-LPN #5.......................................801-530-6628
Occupational Therapist/Assistant #5....801-530-6628
Optometrist #5......................................801-530-6628
Osteopathic Physician #5.....................801-530-6628
Pesticide Dealer/Applicator #3 801-538-7188
Pharmaceutical Admin. Facility #5.......801-530-6628
Pharmaceutical Dog Trainer #5 801-530-6628
Pharmaceutical Researcher #5............801-530-6628
Pharmaceutical Teaching Org. #5........801-530-6628
Pharmaceutical Whse./Dist./Mfg. #5....801-530-6628

Pharmacist/Pharmacist Intern #5.........801-530-6628
Pharmacy Retail/Branch #5 801-530-6628
Pharmacy Technician #5.......................801-530-6628
Pharmacy, Institutional/Hospital #5......801-530-6628
Physical Therapist #5...........................801-530-6628
Physician Assistant #5 801-530-6628
Plumber Apprentice/Journeyman #5.....801-530-6628
Podiatrist #5 801-530-6628
Polygraph Examiner #5.........................801-530-6964
Pre-Need Provider/Sales Agent #5......801-530-6628
Probation Provider, Private #5 801-530-6628
Psychological Assistant #5....................801-530-6628
Psychologist #5 801-530-6628
Public Accountant-CPA #5....................801-530-6628
Radiology Practical Technician #5.........801-530-6628
Radiology Technologist #5.....................801-530-6628
Real Estate Agent/Broker #2................801-530-6747
Real Estate Appraiser #2 801-530-6747
Real Estate Establishment #5...............801-530-6628
Recreational Therapist #5 801-530-6628
Recreational Vehicle Dealer #5 801-530-6628
Referee #5...801-530-6628
Respiratory Care Practitioner #5...........801-530-6628
Sanitarian #5 801-530-6628
Savings & Loan #10 801-538-8842
School Administrator #6 801-538-7740
School Librarian #6 801-538-7740
Securities Broker/Dealer #5 801-530-6628
Security Company #5..............................801-530-6628
Security Officer, Armed/Unarmed Private #5
....801-530-6964
Shorthand Reporter #5...........................801-530-6964
Social Service Aide/Worker/Trainee #5 801-530-6628
Social Worker #5....................................801-530-6628
Speech Pathologist/Audiologist #5 801-530-6628
Substance Abuse Counselor #5 801-530-6628
Surveyor, Land #5..................................801-530-6628
Teacher #6 801-538-7740
Third Party Payment Issuer #10 801-538-8842
Title Lender #10 801-538-8842
Trade Instructor #5.................................801-530-6628
Trust Company #10.................................801-538-8842
Veterinarian/Veterinary Intern #5 801-530-6628
Veterinary Pharmaceutical Outlet #5 ... 801-530-6628
Weights & Measures #3 801-538-7158
Wine Store #1...801-977-6800

Utah Licensing Agency Information

1 Alcoholic Beverage Control Department, 1625 S 900 W, Salt Lake City, UT 84130; 801-977-6800, Fax: 801-977-6888. www.alcbev.state.ut.us Email: abcmain.hotline@state.ut.us

2 Commerce Department, Real Estate Division, PO Box 146711 (160 E 300 S, 2nd Fl, 84145), Salt Lake City, UT 84114-6711; 801-530-6747, Fax: 801-530-6749. www.commerce.utah.gov/dre Email: realest@br.state.ut.us Search Database at www.commerce.state.ut.us/dre/database.html

3 Department of Agriculture and Food, Regulatory Services, PO Box 146500 (350 North Redwood Rd), Salt Lake City, UT 84114-6500; 801-538-7100, Fax: 801-538-7126. http://ag.utah.gov/about.html Search Database at http://ag.utah.gov/licenses/Cur_Lic.html

4 Division of Cooperations & Commercial Code, State Office Building, Rm 1160, Salt Lake City, UT 84114-6705; 801-530-1040. www.commerce.state.ut.us/corporat/notarypublic.htm Email: kbachman@br.stateut.us

5 Department of Commerce, Division of Occupational & Professional Licensing, PO Box 146741 (160 E 300 S, Heber M Wells Bldg, 84111), Salt Lake City, UT 84114-6741; 801-530-6628, Fax: 801-530-6511. www.dopl.utah.gov Email: doplweb@utah.gov Search Database at https://secure.utah.gov/llv/llv

6 Educator Licensing, Office of Education, PO Box 144200 (250 E 500 S), Salt Lake City, UT 84114-4200; 801-538-7740, Fax: 801-538-7973. www.usoe.k12.ut.us Note: The CACTUS teacher information system at www.uen.org/training/free/cactus.cgi?c_id=11341 &a_id ... requires user name and password.

7 Division of Occupational and Professional Licensing, Geologist Licensing Board, PO Box 146741, Salt Lake City, UT 84114-6741; 801-530-6628, Fax: 801-530-6511. www.dopl.utah.gov Search Database at https://secure.utah.gov/llv/llv

8 Insurance Department, 3110 State Office Bldg, Salt Lake City, UT 84114-6901; 801-538-3805, Fax: 801-538-3829.

www.insurance.state.ut.us Search Database at www.insurance.state.ut.us/companies.html

9 State Bar Association, 645 S 200 E, Salt Lake City, UT 84111; 801-531-9077, Fax: 801-531-0660. www.utahbar.org Email: john.baldwin@utahbar.org Search Database at www.utahbar.org/html/find_a_lawyer.html

10 Department of Financial Institutions, 324 S State #201, PO Box 146800, Salt Lake City, UT 84114-6800; 801-538-8830, Fax: 801-538-8894. www.dfi.utah.gov Search Database at www.dfi.utah.gov

11 Division of Services for the Deaf & Hard of Hearing, Interpreter Program, 5709 S 1500 W, Salt Lake City, UT 84123; 801-263-4860, Fax: 801-263-4865. www.aslterps.utah.gov Email: mfjensen@utah.gov Search Database at www.aslterps.utah.gov/cert_terp.php

Utah Federal Courts

County/Court Cross Reference

All counties report to Salt Lake City.

Standards for Federal Courts: Search fee is $26.00 per item (one party name or case number). Copy fee is $.50 per page. Certification fee is $9.00 per document, double for exemplification, if available. All fees standard unless noted in profile. Mail Search: always enclose a stamped self addressed envelope unless otherwise noted. Most courts accept fax requests or will suggest a copying/search vendor. Before releasing records, all courts require prepayment, unless noted.

Open records are located at the court unless otherwise noted. District courts index by defendant and plaintiff as well as by case number. Bankruptcy courts usually index by debtor and case number. While most courts now have their indexes on computer, many may still maintain index card files as well.

Courts offering internet access via CM-ECF or older RACER, PACER, or Web-PACER systems charge $.08 per page fee unless noted as free. Where PACER is available, the universal sign-up number is 800-676-6856. Find PACER and the US Party/Case Index at http://pacer.psc.uscourts.gov.

US District Court

District of Utah

Salt Lake Division Clerk's Office, Rm 150, 350 S Main St, Salt Lake City, UT 84101-2180 (also use mail address for courier delivery), 801-524-6100, Fax-801-526-1175. Hours- 8:30AM-4:30PM. www.utd.uscourts.gov

Counties: All counties in Utah. Although all cases are heard here, the district is divided into Northern and Central Divisions. Northern Division includes the counties of Box Elder, Cache, Rich, Davis, Morgan and Weber; Central Division includes all other counties.

Searches & Indexing: Results do not include SSN or DOB. Computer index maintained. Older records on microfiche. New cases in the index 1 day after filing date. Records purged never.

Fee & Payment: Pay by Visa/MC, money order, cashier's or personal check. Payee: Clerk, US District Court. Prepayment required.

Phone Search: Limited information released via telephone.

Mail Search: search usually completed- 2-3 days. SASE not required.

In Person Search: Fee charged if court performs your search. Self-serve copier available - $.15 per page.

E-Services: ECF replaces PACER. Document images available. PACER records go back to 7/1989. New records online after 1 day. ECF at https://ecf.utd.uscourts.gov **Opinions Online:** www.utd.uscourts.gov/opinions/opinions.html. **Other Online Access:** Calendars at www.utd.uscourts.gov/reports/dt.pl.

US Bankruptcy Court

District of Utah

Salt Lake Division Clerk of Court, Frank E Moss Courthouse, 350 S Main St, Rm 301, Salt Lake City, UT 84101 (use mail address for courier delivery), 801-524-6687, Fax- 801-524-4409. Hours- 8AM-4:30PM. www.utb.uscourts.gov

Counties: All counties in Utah. Although all cases are handled here, the court divides itself into 2 divisions. Northern Division includes counties of Box Elder, Cache, Rich, Davis, Morgan and Weber, and the Central Division includes the remaining counties. Court is held 3 times per month in Ogden for northern cases and once a month in St. George for southern.

Searches & Indexing: Cases indexed by debtor, creditors, and case number. Results include last 4 SSN digits only. Computer index maintained. New cases in the index as soon as the workload permits after filing date. Records purged after 12 months.

Fee & Payment: Pay by money order, cashier's or personal check. No debtor's checks accepted. Payee: Clerk, US Bankruptcy Court. Prepayment required.

Phone Search: Only docket information is available by phone. Voice Case Information Service available, call VCIS at 800-733-6740 or 801-524-3107.

Mail Search: search usually completed- 1 week. Include SASE for return.

In Person Search: Fee charged if court performs your search. Imaged copies available. No self-serve copier available.

E-Services: ECF replaces PACER. Document images available. PACER records go back to 1/1985. ECF at https://ecf.utb.uscourts.gov. Recent case filings reports are free. **Opinions Online:** www.utb.uscourts.gov/LocalOpinions/opinions.htm. **Other Online Access:** Calendars free at www.utb.uscourts.gov/chamberaccess/chambers.htm

Utah County Courts

Court	Jurisdiction	No. of Courts	How Organized
District Courts*	General	41	8 Districts
Justice Courts	Limited	147	128 Cities/Counties
Juvenile Courts	Special		8 Juvenile Districts

* Profiled in this Sourcebook.

Court						CIVIL			
	Tort	Contract	Real Estate	Min. Claim	Max. Claim	Small Claims	Estate	Eviction	Domestic Relations
District Courts*	X	X	X	$20,000	No Max	$5000	X	X	X
Justice Courts	X	X		$0	$1000	$7500			
Juvenile Courts									

Court			CRIMINAL		
	Felony	Misdemeanor	DWI/DUI	Preliminary Hearing	Juvenile
District Courts*	X	X	X	X	
Justice Courts		X	X		
Juvenile Courts					X

ADMINISTRATION Court Administrator, 450 S State Street, Salt Lake City, UT, 84114; 801-578-3800, Fax: 801-578-3859. http://www.utcourts.gov/

COURT STRUCTURE 41 District Courts are arranged in eight judicial districts. Branch courts in larger counties, such as Salt Lake, which were formerly Circuit Courts and elevated to District Courts have full jurisdiction over felony as well as misdemeanor cases. Justice Courts are established by counties and municipalities and have the authority to deal with class B and C misdemeanors, violations of ordinances, small claims, and infractions committed within their territorial jurisdiction. The Justice Court shares jurisdiction with the Juvenile Court over minors 16 or 17 years old, who are charged with certain traffic offenses. Automobile homicide, alcohol or drug related traffic offenses, reckless driving, fleeing an officer, and driving on a suspended license are excepted. Those charges are handled through Juvenile Court.

ONLINE ACCESS Case information from all Utah District Court locations is available through XChange. Fees include $25.00 registration and $30.00 per month which includes 200 searches. Each additional search is billed at $.20. Records go back to at least 1998 for all District Courts. Information about XChange and the subscription agreement can be found at www.utcourts.gov/records/xchange.

One may search for supreme or appellate opinions at the main web site.

ADDITIONAL INFORMATION The Salt Lak Distrcit Court has an automated information phone line that provides court appearance look-up, outstanding fine balance look-up, and judgment/divorce decree lookup. Call 801-238-7830.

Beaver County

5th Judicial District Court PO Box 1683, 2160 S 600 W, Beaver, UT 84713; phone: 435-438-5309; fax: 435-438-5395; hours 8AM-5PM (MST). *Felony, Misdemeanor, Civil, Eviction, Probate.*
Civil Records: Access: Fax, mail, in person, online. Both court and visitors may perform in person searches. No search fee. Court makes copy: $.25 per page. Required to search: name, years to search. Civil cases indexed by defendant, plaintiff. Civil records archived from 1800s, are on computer back to 1997. Online access through Xchange, see www.utcourts.gov/records/. Also, see state introduction. Mail turnaround time 2-7 days.

Criminal Records: Access: Fax, mail, in person, online. Both court and visitors may perform in person searches. No search fee. Court makes copy: $.25 per page. Required to search: name, years to search, DOB. Criminal records archived from 1896, are on computer back to 1997. Online access through Xchange, see www.utcourts.gov/records/. Also, see state introduction. Mail turnaround time 2-7 days.
General Information: Public terminal goes back to 1997. No adoption, juvenile, sealed records released. Fee to fax documents is $.25 per page. Certification fee: $5.00 plus $.50 per page includes copies. Payee: 5th District Court. Personal checks, Visa/MC accepted. Prepayment and SASE required.

Box Elder County

1st District Court PO Box 873, 43 S Main St, Brigham City, UT 84302; phone: 435-734-4600; fax: 435-734-4610; hours 8AM-5PM (MST). *Felony, Misdemeanor, Civil, Eviction, Small Claims, Probate.*
Civil Records: Access: Phone, fax, mail, online, in person. Both court and visitors may perform in person searches. No search fee. Court makes copy: $.25 per page. Required to search: name, years to search. Civil cases indexed by defendant, plaintiff. Civil records on computer from 3/87, books, microfiche, archived from 1856. Online access through Xchange, see www.utcourts.gov/records/.

Also, see state introduction. Mail turnaround time 1 week.

Criminal Records: Access: Fax, mail, online, in person. Both court and visitors may perform in person searches. No search fee. Court makes copy: $.25 per page. Required to search: name, years to search; also helpful: DOB, SSN. Criminal records on computer from 3/87, books, microfiche, archived from 1856. Online access through Xchange, see www.utcourts.gov/records/. Also, see state introduction. Mail turnaround time 1 week.

General Information: Public terminal goes back to 3/1987. No adoptions, sealed records released. Fee to fax documents is $5.00 up to 10 pages, then $1.00 per add'l page. Certification fee: $4.00 plus $.50 per page. Payee: 1st District Court. Personal checks, Visa/MC accepted. Prepayment and SASE required.

Cache County

1st District Court 135 N 100 W, Logan, UT 84321; phone: 435-750-1300; fax: 435-750-1355; hours 8AM-5PM (MST). *Felony, Misdemeanor, Civil, Eviction, Small Claims, Probate.*

Civil Records: Access: Phone, mail, online, in person. Both court and visitors may perform in person searches. Search fee: $15.00 per hour. Court makes copy: $.25 per page. Required to search: name, years to search. Civil cases indexed by defendant, plaintiff. Civil records on computer from 11-87, archived from 1983, microfiche in Salt Lake City. Online access through Xchange, see www.utcourts.gov/records/. Also see state introduction. Mail turnaround time 10 days.

Criminal Records: Access: Phone, mail, online, in person. Both court and visitors may perform in person searches. Search fee: $15.00 per hour. Court makes copy: $.25 per page. Required to search: name, years to search; also helpful: DOB, SSN. Criminal records on computer from 11-87, archived from 1983, microfiche in Salt Lake City. Online access through Xchange, see www.utcourts.gov/records/. Also see state introduction. Mail turnaround time 2 weeks.

General Information: Public terminal goes back to 1987. No sealed records released. Fee to fax documents is $5.00 for up to 10 pages. Certification fee: $4.00 plus $.50 per page. Payee: 1st Judicial District. Personal checks or Visa, MC accepted. Prepayment and SASE required.

Carbon County

7th District Court 149 E 100 S, Price, UT 84501; phone: 435-636-3400; fax: 435-637-7349; hours 8AM-5PM (MST). *Felony, Misdemeanor, Civil, Eviction, Small Claims, Probate.*

Civil Records: Access: Phone, mail, online, in person. Both court and visitors may perform in person searches. No search fee. Court makes copy: $.25 per page. Required to search: name, years to search. Civil cases indexed by defendant, plaintiff. Civil records on computer from 1988, on microfiche from 1985, archived prior to 1988. Online access through Xchange, see www.utcourts.gov/records/. Also see state introduction. Mail turnaround time 48 hours.

Criminal Records: Access: Phone, mail, online, in person. Both court and visitors may perform in person searches. No search fee. Court makes copy: $.25 per page. Required to search: name, years to search, DOB; also helpful: SSN. Criminal records on computer from 1988, on microfiche from 1985, archived prior to 1988. Online access through Xchange, see www.utcourts.gov/records/. Also see state introduction. Mail turnaround time 48 hours.

General Information: Public terminal goes back to 1987. No sealed records released. Fee to fax documents is $5.00 1st page, $1.00 each add'l. Certification fee: $4.00 plus $.50 per page includes copies. Payee: 7th District Court. Personal checks, Visa/MC accepted. Prepayment required. Will bill fax fees. SASE required.

Daggett County

8th District Court PO Box 219, Manila, UT 84046; phone: 435-784-3154; fax: 435-784-3335; hours 8AM-N, 1-5PM (MST). *Felony, Misdemeanor, Civil, Eviction, Probate.*

Civil Records: Access: Phone, fax, mail, in person, online. Both court and visitors may perform in person searches. Search fee: $15.00 per hour, 1st 15 minutes no charge. Court makes copy: $.25 per page; same fee for self serve. Required to search: name, years to search. Civil cases indexed by defendant, plaintiff. Civil records archived from 1918. Online access through Xchange, see www.utcourts.gov/records/. Also see state introduction. Note: Fax access requires prior approval. Mail turnaround time 10 days.

Criminal Records: Access: Fax, mail, in person, online. Both court and visitors may perform in person searches. Search fee: $15.00 per hour, 1st 15 minutes no charge. Court makes copy: $.25 per page; same fee for self serve. Required to search: name, years to search, DOB; signature and record request form required. Criminal records archived from 1918. Online access through Xchange, see www.utcourts.gov/records/. Also see state introduction. Mail turnaround time 10 days.

General Information: No sealed records released. Fee to fax documents is $5.00 per document up to 10 pages plus $.50 per page add'l. Certification fee: $4.00 plus $.50 per page. Payee: Daggett County. Personal checks accepted. Prepayment and SASE required.

Davis County

2nd District Court PO Box 769, Farmington, UT 84025; phone: 801-447-3800; criminal fax: 801-447-3881; same fax for civil/probate; hours 8AM-5PM (MST). *Felony, Civil, Probate.*

Civil Records: Access: Phone, mail, online, in person. Both court and visitors may perform in person searches. Search fee: $15.00 per hour. First 15 minutes no charge. Court makes copy: $.25 per page; same fee for self serve. Required to search: name, years to search. Civil cases indexed by defendant, plaintiff. Civil records on computer back to 1982, prior on microfiche and archived to 1896. Online access through Xchange, see www.utcourts.gov/records/. Also see state introduction. Mail turnaround time 2-3 days.

Criminal Records: Access: Phone, mail, online, in person. Both court and visitors may perform in person searches. Search fee: $15.00 per hour. First 15 minutes no charge. Court makes copy: $.25 per page; same fee for self serve. Required to search: name, years to search, DOB; also helpful: SSN. Criminal records on computer back to 1989, prior on microfiche and archived to 1896. Online access through Xchange, see www.utcourts.gov/records/. Also see state introduction. Mail turnaround time 2-3 days.

General Information: Public terminal has criminal back to 1990 and civil back to 1982. No adoption, criminal pre-sentence investigation records released. Will fax documents; no fee indicated. Certification fee: $4.00 per document. Payee: 2nd District Court. Personal checks accepted. Prepayment and SASE required.

2nd District Court - Bountiful Department 805 S Main, Bountiful, UT 84010; criminal phone: 801-397-7008; civil phone: 801-397-7004; fax: 801-397-7010; hours 8AM-5PM (MST). *Felony, Misdemeanor, Civil, Eviction, Small Claims, Probate.*

Note: Small Claims at 397-7002 and Traffic at 397-7000.

Civil Records: Access: Phone, mail, online, in person. Both court and visitors may perform in person searches. No search fee. Court makes copy: $.25 per page. Required to search: name, years to search; also helpful: address. Civil cases indexed by defendant, plaintiff. Civil records on computer since 10/86. Online access through Xchange, see www.utcourts.gov/records/. Also see state introduction. Note: For in person searching, call ahead. Mail turnaround time 1 week.

Criminal Records: Access: Phone, mail, online, in person. Both court and visitors may perform in person searches. No search fee. Court makes copy: $.25 per page. Required to search: name, years to search, DOB, signed release. Criminal records on computer since 10/86. Online access through Xchange, see www.utcourts.gov/records/. Also see state introduction. Note: For in person searching, call ahead. Mail turnaround time 1 week.

General Information: Public use terminal available. Will fax documents for $5.00 for 1st 10 pages, then $.25 per page. Certification fee: $4.00 plus $.50 per page. Payee: Second District Court. Personal checks accepted. Prepayment and SASE required.

2nd District Court - Layton Department 425 Wasatch Dr, Layton, UT 84041; phone: 801-444-4300; hours 8AM-5PM (MST). *Felony, Misdemeanor, Civil, Eviction, Small Claims, Probate, Traffic.*

Civil Records: Access: Mail, online, in person. Visitors must perform in person searches themselves. Court makes copy: $.25 per page. Required to search: name, years to search. Civil cases indexed by defendant, plaintiff. Civil records on computer from 1988, archived from start of court. Computer index alpha and case number, archives by alpha from 1982, prior to 1982 not indexed. Online access through Xchange, see www.utcourts.gov/records/. Also see state introduction.

Criminal Records: Access: Mail, online, in person. Both court and visitors may perform in person searches. No search fee. Court makes copy: $.25 per page. Required to search: name, years to search; also helpful: DOB, SSN. Criminal records on computer from 1988, archived from start of court. Computer index alpha and case number, archives by alpha from 1982, prior to 1982 not indexed. Online access through Xchange, see www.utcourts.gov/records/. Also see state introduction. Mail turnaround time 1 day.

General Information: Public terminal goes back to 1988. No confidential records, probation reports, sealed records released. Will fax documents for $5.00 per page. Certification fee: $4.00 plus $.50 per add'l page includes copy fee. Payee: 2nd District Court. Personal checks, Visa/MC accepted. Prepayment required. SASE requested.

Duchesne County

8th District Court PO Box 990, Duchesne, UT 84021; phone: 435-738-2753; criminal fax: 435-738-2754; same fax for civil/probate; hours 8AM-5PM (MST). *Felony, Misdemeanor, Civil, Eviction, Small Claims, Probate.*

Civil Records: Access: Phone, mail, fax, online, in person. Both court and visitors may perform in person searches. Search fee: $15.00 per hour. First 15 minutes no charge. Court makes copy: $.25 per page. Required to search: name, years to search. Civil cases indexed by defendant, plaintiff. Civil records on computer back to 6/1993, civil on microfiche back to 1912. Online access through Xchange, see www.utcourts.gov/records/. Mail turnaround time 1-5 days.

Criminal Records: Access: Phone, mail, fax, online, in person. Both court and visitors may perform in person searches. Search fee: $15.00 per hour. First 15 minutes no charge. Court makes copy: $.25 per page. Required to search: name, years to search. Criminal records on computer back to 1993; index books back to 1912. Criminal records access through Xchange. For information contact Jolene Cox 578-3831. Also, see state introduction. Mail turnaround time 1-5 days.

General Information: Public terminal goes back to 6/1993. No confidential records released. Fee to fax documents is $5.00 for 10 pages or less; $.50 each add'l over 10 pages. Certification fee: $4.00 per doc plus $.50 per page. Payee: 8th District Court. Personal checks accepted. Accepts Visa/MC, money order. Prepayment and SASE required.

8th District Court - Roosevelt Department

PO Box 1286, 255 S State St, Roosevelt, UT 84066; phone: 435-722-0235; fax: 435-722-0236; hours 8AM-5PM (MST). *Felony, Misdemeanor, Civil, Eviction, Probate.*

Civil Records: Access: Mail, fax, online, in person. Both court and visitors may perform in person searches. Search fee: $15.00 per hour, first 15 minutes no charge. Court makes copy: $.25 per page. Required to search: name, years to search. Civil cases indexed by defendant, plaintiff. Civil records on computer since 1993. Online access through Xchange, see www.utcourts.gov/records/. Also see state introduction. Mail turnaround time 2-5 days.

Criminal Records: Access: Mail, fax, online, in person. Both court and visitors may perform in person searches. Search fee: $15.00 per hour, first 15 minutes no charge. Court makes copy: $.25 per page. Required to search: name, years to search; also helpful: DOB. Criminal records on computer since 1994. Online access through Xchange, see www.utcourts.gov/records/. Also see state introduction. Mail turnaround time 2-5 days.

General Information: Public terminal goes back to 1991. No confidential, sealed, expunged or juvenile records released. Will fax documents for $5.00 plus $.50 each add'l page. Certification fee: $4.00 plus $.50 per page includes copies. Personal checks, Visa/MC accepted. Prepayment required.

Emery County

7th District Court PO Box 635, 1850 N 560 W, Castle Dale, UT 84513; phone: 435-381-2619; fax: 435-381-5625; hours 8AM-5PM (MST). *Felony, Misdemeanor, Civil, Eviction, Probate.*

Note: Phone for hearing impaired is 800-992-0172.

Civil Records: Access: Phone, fax, mail, in person, online. Both court and visitors may perform in person searches. Search fee: $10.00 per hour; first 20 minutes no charge. Court makes copy: $.25 per page. Required to search: name, years to search. Civil cases indexed by defendant, plaintiff. Civil records on computer from 1997, older on microfilm and archived. Online access through Xchange, see www.utcourts.gov/records/. Also see state introduction. Mail turnaround time 1 week.

Criminal Records: Access: Phone, fax, mail, in person, online. Both court and visitors may perform in person searches. Search fee: $10.00 per hour; first 20 minutes no charge. Court makes copy: $.25 per page. Required to search: name, years to search, DOB. Criminal records on computer from 1997, older on microfilm and archived. Online access through Xchange, see www.utcourts.gov/records/. Also see state introduction. Mail turnaround time 1 week.

General Information: Public terminal goes back to 1997. No adoption, sealed records released. Will fax documents $5.00 1st page, $.50 each add'l. Certification fee: $4.00 plus $.50 per page includes copy fee. Payee: 7th District Court. Personal checks, Visa/MC accepted. Prepayment and SASE required.

Garfield County

6th District Court PO Box 77, Panguitch, UT 84759; phone: 435-676-8826 X104; fax: 435-676-8239; hours 9AM-5PM (MST). *Felony, Misdemeanor, Civil, Eviction, Small Claims, Probate.*

Civil Records: Access: Phone, fax, mail, in person, online. Only the court performs in person searches; visitors may not. Search fee: $15.00 per hour. Court makes copy: $.25 per page. Required to search: name, years to search. Civil cases indexed by defendant, plaintiff. Civil records archived for 100 years; on computer back to 2000. Online access through Xchange, see www.utcourts.gov/records/. Also see state introduction. Mail turnaround time 1 day.

Criminal Records: Access: Fax, mail, in person, online. Only the court performs in person searches;

visitors may not. Search fee: $15.00 per hour. Court makes copy: $.25 per page. Required to search: name, years to search. Criminal records archived for 100 years; on computer back to 2000. Online access through Xchange, see www.utcourts.gov/records/. Also see state introduction. Mail turnaround time 1 day.

General Information: No adoption records released. Fee to fax documents is $1.00 for 1st page, $.50 each add'l. Certification fee: $4.00 plus $.50 per page. Payee: 6th District Court. Personal checks accepted. Prepayment required.

Grand County

7th District Court 125 E Center, Moab, UT 84532; phone: 435-259-1349; fax: 435-259-4081; hours 8AM-5PM (MST). *Felony, Misdemeanor, Civil, Eviction, Probate.*

Civil Records: Access: Phone, mail, online, in person. Both court and visitors may perform in person searches. Search fee: none for 1st 20 minutes; $15.00 per hour thereafter. Court makes copy: $.25 per page; same fee for self serve. Required to search: name, years to search. Civil cases indexed by defendant, plaintiff. District records on computer from Spring 1990, Circuit from spring 1989, archived since court started. Online access through Xchange, see www.utcourts.gov/records/. Also see state introduction. Mail turnaround time 5 days.

Criminal Records: Access: Phone, mail, online, in person. Both court and visitors may perform in person searches. Search fee: none for 1st 20 minutes; $15.00 per hour thereafter. Court makes copy: $.25 per page; same fee for self serve. Required to search: name, years to search; also helpful: DOB, SSN. District records on computer from spring 1990, Circuit from spring 1989, archived since court started. Online access through Xchange, see www.utcourts.gov/records/. Also see state introduction. Mail turnaround time 1-5 days.

General Information: Public terminal goes back to 1990. No adoption, expunged records released. Will fax documents $5.00 flat rate for 1-10 pages, then $.50 each after 10. Certification fee: $4.00 plus $.50 per page. Payee: 7th District Court. Personal checks or Visa, MC accepted. Prepayment and SASE required.

Iron County

5th District Court 40 N 100 E, Cedar City, UT 84720; phone: 435-867-3250; criminal phone: 435-867-3243/44; civil phone: 435-867-3240/42; probate phone: 435-867-3244; criminal fax: 435-867-3212; same fax for civil/probate; hours 8AM-5PM (MST). *Felony, Misdemeanor, Civil, Eviction, Small Claims, Probate.*

Note: Hearing location also in Parawon, but records held here.

Civil Records: Access: Mail, phone, online, in person. Both court and visitors may perform in person searches. Search fee: varies. Court makes copy: $.25 per page. Required to search: name. Civil cases indexed by defendant, plaintiff. District records on computer from 4/89, former Circuit Court records on computer from 1987, archived from 1900. Online access through Xchange, see www.utcourts.gov/records/. Also see state introduction. Mail turnaround time 2-3 days.

Criminal Records: Access: Mail, phone, online, in person. Both court and visitors may perform in person searches. Search fee: varies. Court makes copy: $.25 per page. Required to search: name, years to search, DOB, SSN. District records on computer from 4/89, former Circuit Court records on computer from 1987, archived from 1900. Online access through Xchange, see www.utcourts.gov/records/. Also see state introduction. Mail turnaround time 2-3 days.

General Information: Public terminal goes back to 1987. No sealed records released. Will fax documents for $5.00 for up to 10 pages. Certification fee: $4.00 per document. Payee: 5th District Court. Personal checks accepted. Prepayment and SASE required.

Juab County

4th District Court 160 N. Main, PO Box 249, Nephi, UT 84648; phone: 435-623-0901; criminal fax: 435-623-0922; same fax for civil/probate; hours 8AM-5PM (MST). *Felony, Misdemeanor, Civil, Eviction, Probate.*

Civil Records: Access: Phone, mail, online, in person. Both court and visitors may perform in person searches. Search fee: $15.00 per hour. First 15 minutes are no charge. Court makes copy: $.25 per page. Required to search: name, years to search. Civil cases indexed by defendant, plaintiff. Civil records on computer from 11/94, archived since court started. Online access through Xchange, see www.utcourts.gov/records/. Also see state introduction. Mail turnaround time 1 week.

Criminal Records: Access: Phone, mail, online, in person. Both court and visitors may perform in person searches. Search fee: $15.00 per hour. First 15 minutes are no charge. Court makes copy: $.25 per page. Required to search: name, years to search. Criminal records on computer from 11/94, archived since court started. Online access through Xchange, see www.utcourts.gov/records/. Also see state introduction. Mail turnaround time 1 week.

General Information: Public terminal goes back to 11/1994. All records must be viewed in this office. Will not fax documents. Certification fee: $4.00 plus $.50 per page includes copies. Payee: 4th District Court. Personal checks accepted. Prepayment and SASE required.

Kane County

6th District Court 76 N Main, Kanab, UT 84741; phone: 435-644-2458; fax: 435-644-2052; hours 8AM-5PM (MST). *Felony, Misdemeanor, Civil, Eviction, Small Claims, Probate.*

Civil Records: Access: Phone, fax, mail, in person, online. Only the court performs in person searches; visitors may not. Search fee: First 15 minutes of search is free, thereafter $25.00 per hour. Court makes copy: $.25 per page; same fee for self serve. Required to search: name, years to search. Civil cases indexed by defendant, plaintiff. Civil records on computer from 1985, archived since court started. Online access through Xchange, see www.utcourts.gov/records/. Also see state introduction. Mail turnaround time 2-3 days.

Criminal Records: Access: Phone, fax, mail, in person, online. Only the court performs in person searches; visitors may not. Search fee: First 15 minutes of search is free, thereafter $25.00 per hour. Court makes copy: $.25 per page; same fee for self serve. Required to search: name, years to search. Criminal records on computer from 1985, archived since court started. Online access through Xchange, see www.utcourts.gov/records/. Also see state introduction. Mail turnaround time 2-3 days.

General Information: No sealed, expunged records released. Fee to fax documents is $.50 per page. Certification fee: $4.00 per page. Payee: Kane County. Personal checks accepted. Prepayment required. SASE requested.

Millard County

4th District Court 765 S Hwy 99, #6, Fillmore, UT 84631; phone: 435-743-6223; fax: 435-743-6923; hours 8AM-5PM (MST). *Felony, Misdemeanor, Civil, Eviction, Small Claims, Probate.*

Civil Records: Access: Phone, mail, online, in person. Both court and visitors may perform in person searches. Search fee: $10.00 per hour. Court makes copy: $.25 per page. Required to search: name, years to search. Civil cases indexed by defendant, plaintiff. Civil records on computer from 1988, archived from 1896. Online access through Xchange, see www.utcourts.gov/records/. Also see state introduction. Mail turnaround time 1 day.

Criminal Records: Access: Phone, mail, online, in person. Both court and visitors may perform in person searches. Search fee: $10.00 per hour. Court makes copy: $.25 per page. Required to search: name, years to search. Criminal records on computer from 1988, archived from 1896. Online access through Xchange, see www.utcourts.gov/records/. Also see state introduction. Mail turnaround time 1 day.

General Information: Public terminal goes back to 1988. No pre-sentence, expunged or sealed records released. Certification fee: $4.00 plus $.50 per page. Payee: 4th District Court. Business checks accepted. Prepayment and SASE required.

Morgan County

2nd District Court PO Box 886, Morgan, UT 84050; phone: 801-845-4020; fax: 801-829-6176; hours 8AM-5PM (MST). *Felony, Misdemeanor, Civil, Eviction, Small Claims, Probate.*

Civil Records: Access: Phone, fax, mail, online, in person. Both court and visitors may perform in person searches. Search fee: $25.00 per name, if extensive. Court makes copy: $.25 per page. Required to search: name, years to search. Civil cases indexed by defendant, plaintiff. Civil records on computer since 1992; on microfiche, books, archived from 1862. Online access through Xchange, see www.utcourts.gov/records/. Also see state introduction. Extensive (special) search requests must be in writing. Mail turnaround time several days.

Criminal Records: Access: Phone, fax, mail, online, in person. Both court and visitors may perform in person searches. Search fee: $25.00 per name, if extensive. Court makes copy: $.25 per page. Required to search: name, years to search, DOB; also helpful: SSN. Criminal records on computer since 1992, prior in books. Online access through Xchange, see www.utcourts.gov/records/. Also see state introduction. Extensive (special) search requests must be in writing. Mail turnaround time several days.

General Information: Public terminal goes back to 1992. No sealed records released. No fee to fax documents. Certification fee: $4.00 plus $.50 per page. Payee: Morgan District. Personal checks accepted. Prepayment required. SASE requested.

Piute County

6th District Court PO Box 99, 550 N Main St, Junction, UT 84740; phone: 435-577-2840; fax: 435-577-2433; hours 9AM-N, 1-5PM (MST). *Felony, Misdemeanor, Civil, Eviction, Small Claims, Probate.*

Civil Records: Access: Mail, in person, online. Both court and visitors may perform in person searches. No search fee. Court makes copy: $.25 per page. Required to search: name, years to search. Civil cases indexed by defendant, plaintiff. Civil records archived from 1889. Online access through Xchange, see www.utcourts.gov/records/. Also see state introduction. Mail turnaround time 2-3 days.

Criminal Records: Access: Mail, in person, online. Both court and visitors may perform in person searches. No search fee. Court makes copy: $.25 per page. Required to search: name, years to search. Criminal records archived from 1889. Online access through Xchange, see www.utcourts.gov/records/. Also see state introduction. Mail turnaround time 2-3 days.

General Information: No sealed records released. Will fax back documents in emergency for $.50 per page. Certification fee: $4.00 plus $.50 per page. Payee: Piute County District Court. Personal checks accepted. Search fees may be billed if prior arrangement made. SASE required.

Rich County

1st District Court PO Box 218, Randolph, UT 84064; phone: 435-793-2415; criminal fax: 435-793-2410; same fax for civil/probate; hours 9AM-5PM (MST). *Felony, Misdemeanor, Civil, Eviction, Probate.*

Civil Records: Access: Phone, fax, mail, in person, online. Both court and visitors may perform in

person searches. Search fee: $10.00 per hour. Court makes copy: $.25 per page; same fee for self serve. Required to search: name, years to search; also helpful: address. Civil cases indexed by defendant, plaintiff. Civil records ago back to 1896; computerized records since 1999. Online access through Xchange, see www.utcourts.gov/records/. Also see state introduction. Mail turnaround time 2-3 days.

Criminal Records: Access: Phone, fax, mail, in person, online. Both court and visitors may perform in person searches. Search fee: $10.00 per hour. Court makes copy: $.25 per page; same fee for self serve. Required to search: name, years to search; also helpful: address, DOB, SSN. Criminal records go back to 1896; computerized records since 1999. Online access through Xchange, see www.utcourts.gov/records/. Also see state introduction. Mail turnaround time 2-3 days.

General Information: No sealed records released. Will fax documents to local or toll free line. Certification fee: $4.00 per page. Payee: Rich County. Personal checks accepted. Prepayment and SASE required.

Salt Lake County

3rd District Court - Salt Lake Dept. 450 S State St, Salt Lake City, UT 84111; phone: 801-238-7300; probate phone: 801-238-7162; fax: 801-238-7396; probate fax: 801-238-7407; hours 8AM-5PM (MST). *Felony, Misdemeanor, Civil, Eviction, Small Claims, Probate.*

Civil Records: Access: Mail, online, in person. Both court and visitors may perform in person searches. Search fee: First 20 minutes no charge. Court makes copy: $.25 per page. Required to search: name, years to search. Civil cases indexed by defendant, plaintiff. Civil records on computer from 1985, archived after 1969. Online access through Xchange, see www.utcourts.gov/records/. Also see state introduction. An automated court information line allows phone access to court dates, fine balances, and judgment/divorce decrees (case or citation number required) at 801-238-7830. Mail turnaround time 2-3 days.

Criminal Records: Access: Mail, online, in person. Both court and visitors may perform in person searches. Search fee: First 20 minutes no charge. Court makes copy: $.25 per page. Required to search: name, years to search, DOB; also helpful: SSN. Criminal records on computer from 1986, archived after satisfaction or dismissal, destroyed prior to 1985. Online access through Xchange, see www.utcourts.gov/records/. Also see state introduction. Mail turnaround time 2-3 days.

General Information: Public terminal has criminal back to 1986 and civil back to 1985. No confidential records released. Will fax documents $5.00 up to 10 pages; $.50 per each add'l page. Certification fee: $4.00 per doc and $.50 per page. Payee: 3rd District Court. Business checks or Visa, MC accepted. Prepayment required.

3rd District Court - Sandy Department 8080 S Redwood Rd, West Jordan, UT 84088; phone: 801-233-9700; criminal fax: 801-233-9760; civil fax: 801-233-9761; hours 8AM-5PM (MST). *Felony, Misdemeanor, Civil, Eviction, Small Claims.* Note: Now combined with the old West Valley Dept. to form the new West Jordan Dept.

3rd District Court - West Jordan Department 8080 S Redwood Rd, West Valley, UT 84119; phone: 801-233-9700; criminal fax: 801-233-9760; civil fax: 801-233-9761; hours 8AM-5PM (MST). *Felony, Misdemeanor, Civil, Eviction.* Note: Now combined with old Sandy Division; formerly known as the West Valley Dept.

Civil Records: Access: Mail, online, in person. Both court and visitors may perform in person searches. Search fee: $15.00 per hour. Court makes copy: $.50 per page. Self serve copy fee: $.25 per page. Required to search: name, years to search. Civil cases indexed

by defendant, plaintiff. Civil records on computer since 1986, archived from 1983. Online access through Xchange, see www.utcourts.gov/records/. Also see state introduction. Mail turnaround time 1 week.

Criminal Records: Access: Mail, online, in person. Both court and visitors may perform in person searches. Search fee: $15.00 per hour. Court makes copy: $.50 per page. Self serve copy fee: $.25 per page. Required to search: name, years to search. Criminal records on computer since 1986, archived from 1983. Online access through Xchange, see www.utcourts.gov/records/. Also see state introduction. Mail turnaround time 1 week.

General Information: Public terminal goes back to 1986. No sealed records released. Certification fee: $4.00. Payee: 3rd District Court. Personal checks or Visa, MC accepted. Prepayment and SASE required.

San Juan County

7th District Court PO Box 68, Monticello, UT 84535; phone: 435-587-2122; fax: 435-587-2372; hours 8AM-5PM (MST). *Felony, Misdemeanor, Civil, Eviction, Probate.*

Civil Records: Access: Phone, mail, fax, online, in person. Both court and visitors may perform in person searches. Search fee: $15.00 per hour. Court makes copy: $.25 per page. Required to search: name, years to search. Civil cases indexed by defendant, plaintiff. Civil records on computer since 1991; on index books from 1919 to 1991. Online access through Xchange, see www.utcourts.gov/records/. Also see state introduction. Mail turnaround time 1 week.

Criminal Records: Access: Mail, fax, online, in person. Both court and visitors may perform in person searches. Search fee: $15.00 per hour. Court makes copy: $.25 per page. Required to search: name, years to search. Criminal records on computer since 1991; on index books from 1919 to 1991. Online access through Xchange, see www.utcourts.gov/records/. Also see state introduction. Mail turnaround time 1 week.

General Information: Public use terminal available. No juvenile records released. Fee to fax documents is $5.00 up to 10 pages; $.50 per each add'l page. Certification fee: $4.00 plus $.50 per page. Payee: 7th District Court. Personal checks or Visa, MC accepted. Visa, MC accepted in person and by phone. Prepayment and SASE required.

Sanpete County

6th District Court 160 N Main, Manti, UT 84642; phone: 435-835-2121; fax: 435-835-2135; hours 8AM-5PM (MST). *Felony, Misdemeanor, Civil, Eviction, Small Claims, Probate.*

Civil Records: Access: Phone, fax, mail, in person, online. Both court and visitors may perform in person searches. Search fee: $15.00 per hour after first 15 minutes free. Court makes copy: $.25 per page. Required to search: name, years to search. Civil cases indexed by defendant, plaintiff. Civil records on computer from 1998. Online access through Xchange, see www.utcourts.gov/records/. Also see state introduction. Mail turnaround time 10 days.

Criminal Records: Access: Phone, fax, mail, in person, online. Both court and visitors may perform in person searches. Search fee: $15.00 per hour. Court makes copy: $.25 per page. Required to search: name, years to search; also helpful: DOB. Criminal records on computer from 1998. Online access through Xchange, see www.utcourts.gov/records/. Also see state introduction. Mail turnaround time 10 days.

General Information: Public use terminal available. No criminal, expunged, or sealed records released. Will fax documents $.50 1st page. Certification fee: $4.00 plus $.50 per page. Payee: 6th District Court. Personal checks accepted. Prepayment required. SASE requested.

Sevier County

6th District Court 895 E 300 N, Richfield, UT 84701-2345; phone: 435-896-2700; fax: 435-896-8047; hours 8AM-5PM (MST). *Felony, Misdemeanor, Civil, Eviction, Probate.*

Civil Records: Access: Phone, fax, mail, in person. Both court and visitors may perform in person searches. Search fee: $15.00 per hour. For search requiring 15 minutes or less, no charge. Court makes copy: $.25 per page. Self serve copy fee: copies made off computer access terminal are $.05 each. Required to search: name, years to search. Civil cases indexed by defendant, plaintiff. Circuit records on computer from 1989, District on computer from 1991. Online access through Xchange, see www.utcourts.gov/records/. Also see state introduction. Mail turnaround time 2-3 days.

Criminal Records: Access: Fax, mail, online, in person. Both court and visitors may perform in person searches. Search fee: $15.00 per hour. For search requiring 15 minutes or less, no charge. Court makes copy: $.25 per page. Self serve copy fee: copies made off computer access terminal are $.05 each. Required to search: name, years to search, DOB, SSN. Circuit records on computer from 1989, District on computer from 1991. Online access through Xchange, see www.utcourts.gov/records/. Also see state introduction. Mail turnaround time 2-3 days.

General Information: Public terminal goes back to 1992. No sealed records released. Will fax documents $5.00 1st page, $.50 each add'l. Certification fee: $4.00 plus $.50 per page includes copies. Payee: 6th District Court. Personal checks, Visa/MC accepted. Prepayment required.

Summit County

3rd District Court 6300 N Silver Creek, Park City, UT 84098; phone: 435-615-4300. *Felony, Misdemeanor, Civil, Small Claims, Evictions, Probate.*

Civil Records: Access: Mail, online, in person. Both court and visitors may perform in person searches. Search fee: $10.00 per hour, first 20 minutes free. Court makes copy: $.25 per page. Required to search: name, years to search; also helpful: DOB. By plaintiff and defendant. All indexes on computer back to 1993, records archived back to 1900's. Online access through Xchange, see www.utcourts.gov/records/. Also see state introduction.

Criminal Records: Access: Mail, online, in person. Both court and visitors may perform in person searches. Search fee: $10.00 per hour. First 20 minutes no charge. Court makes copy: $.25 per page. Required to search: name, years to search; also helpful: DOB. Criminal records on computer since 1993. Online access through Xchange, see www.utcourts.gov/records/. Also see state introduction.

General Information: Public use terminal available. Certification fee: $4.00 plus $.50 per page.

3rd District Court PO Box 128, 60 N Main, Coalville, UT 84017; phone: 435-336-3205; fax: 435-336-3061; hours 8AM-5PM (MST). *Probate.* Note: The courts is open 2 to 3 days a week.

Tooele County

3rd District Court 47 S Main, Tooele, UT 84074; phone: 435-843-3210; fax: 435-882-8524; hours 8AM-5PM (MST). *Felony, Misdemeanor, Civil, Eviction, Small Claims, Probate.*

Civil Records: Access: Fax, mail, online, in person. Both court and visitors may perform in person searches. Search fee: $15.00 per hour. First 20 minutes no charge. Court makes copy: $.25 per page; same fee for self serve. Required to search: name, years to search. Civil cases indexed by defendant, plaintiff. Civil records on computer from 1982, archived since court started. Online access through Xchange, see www.utcourts.gov/records/. Also see state introduction. Mail turnaround time 2-3 days.

Criminal Records: Access: Fax, mail, online, in person. Both court and visitors may perform in person searches. Search fee: $15.00 per hour. First 20 minutes no charge. Court makes copy: $.25 per page; same fee for self serve. Required to search: name, years to search; also helpful: SSN. Criminal records on computer back to 1989, archived since court started. Online access through Xchange, see www.utcourts.gov/records/. Also see state introduction. Mail turnaround time 2-3 days.

General Information: Public terminal has criminal back to 1989 and civil back to 1982. No adoption records released. Will fax documents $5.00 for 10 pages; $.50 each add'l. Certification fee: $4.00 plus $.50 per page. Payee: 3rd District Court. Personal checks accepted. Prepayment and SASE required.

Uintah County

8th District Court 920 E Hwy 40, Vernal, UT 84078; phone: 435-781-9300; fax: 435-789-0564; hours 8AM-5PM (MST). *Felony, Misdemeanor, Civil, Eviction, Probate.*

Civil Records: Access: Mail, online, in person. Both court and visitors may perform in person searches. Search fee: $15.00 per hour. First 20 minutes no charge. Court makes copy: $.25 per page. Required to search: name, years to search. Civil cases indexed by defendant, plaintiff. Circuit records on computer from 1987, everything else from 1989, archived since court started. Online access through Xchange, see www.utcourts.gov/records/. Also see state introduction. Mail turnaround time 2-3 days.

Criminal Records: Access: Mail, online, in person. Both court and visitors may perform in person searches. Search fee: $15.00 per hour. First 20 minutes no charge. Court makes copy: $.25 per page. Required to search: name, years to search. Circuit records on computer from 1987, everything else from 1989, archived since court started. Online access through Xchange, see www.utcourts.gov/records/. Also see state introduction. Mail turnaround time 2-3 days.

General Information: Public terminal goes back to 1987. No sealed records released. Will fax documents to local or toll free line. Certification fee: $4.00 plus $.50 per page. Payee: 8th District Court. Personal checks accepted. Prepayment and SASE required.

Utah County

4th District Court 125 N 100 W, Provo, UT 84601; phone: 801-429-1000; criminal phone: 801-429-1171; civil phone: 801-429-1172; probate phone: 1-801-429-1172; fax: 801-429-1033; hours 8AM-5PM (MST). *Felony, Misdemeanor, Civil, Eviction, Small Claims, Probate.* www.utcourts.gov/

Civil Records: Access: Phone, mail, fax, in person, online. Both court and visitors may perform in person searches. Search fee: $15.00 per hour. Court makes copy: $.25 per page; same fee for self serve. Required to search: name, years to search. Civil cases indexed by defendant, plaintiff. Civil and probate on computer from 1986, judgments, tax liens, and divorce decrees on microfiche from 1900 to 1975, archived from 1900s. Online access through Xchange, see www.utcourts.gov/records/. Also see state introduction. Mail turnaround time 7-10 days.

Criminal Records: Access: Phone, mail, fax, in person, online. Both court and visitors may perform in person searches. Search fee: $15.00 per hour. Court makes copy: $.25 per page; same fee for self serve. Required to search: name, years to search, DOB. Felony on computer from 1989; archived from 1900s. Online access through Xchange, see www.utcourts.gov/records/. Also see state introduction. Mail turnaround time 7-10 days.

General Information: Public terminal has criminal back to 1989 and civil back to 1986. No sealed records released. Certification fee: $4.00 plus $.50 per page. Payee: 4th District Court. Personal checks or Visa, MC accepted. Accepted in person only. Prepayment and SASE required.

4th District Court - Orem Department 97 E Center, Orem, UT 84057; criminal phone: 801-764-5865; civil phone: 801-764-5864; fax: 801-226-5244; hours 8AM-5PM (MST). *Misdemeanor, Civil, Eviction, Small Claims.*

Civil Records: Access: Mail, online, in person. Both court and visitors may perform in person searches. Search fee: $15.00 per hour. First 20 minutes no charge. Court makes copy: $.25 per page. Required to search: name, years to search. Civil cases indexed by defendant, plaintiff. Civil records on computer since 1988. Online access through Xchange, see www.utcourts.gov/records/. Also see state introduction. Mail turnaround time 5-7 days.

Criminal Records: Access: Mail, online, in person. Both court and visitors may perform in person searches. Search fee: $15.00 per hour. First 20 minutes no charge. Court makes copy: $.25 per page. Required to search: name, years to search; also helpful: DOB. Criminal records on computer since 1988. Online access through Xchange, see www.utcourts.gov/records/. Also see state introduction. Mail turnaround time 5-7 days.

General Information: Public terminal goes back to 1988. No sealed, expunged or confidential records released. Will fax documents to local or toll-free number. Certification fee: $4.00 plus $.50 per page. Payee: 4th District Court. Personal checks or Visa, MC accepted. Prepayment required.

4th District Court - Spanish Forks Department 40 S Main St, Spanish Forks, UT 84660; phone: 801-798-8674; fax: 801-798-1377; hours 8AM-5PM (MST). *Misdemeanor, Civil, Eviction, Small Claims.*

Civil Records: Access: Phone, fax, mail, online, in person. Both court and visitors may perform in person searches. Search fee: $15.00 per hour. First 15 minutes no charge. Court makes copy: $.25 per page. Required to search: name, years to search. Civil cases indexed by defendant, plaintiff. Civil records stored from 1978, on computer since 1987. Online access through Xchange, see www.utcourts.gov/records/. Also see state introduction. Mail turnaround time 5-7 days.

Criminal Records: Access: Phone, fax, mail, online, in person. Both court and visitors may perform in person searches. Search fee: $15.00 per hour. First 15 minutes no charge. Court makes copy: $.25 per page. Required to search: name, years to search; also helpful: DOB. Criminal records stored from 1978, on computer since 1987. Online access through Xchange, see www.utcourts.gov/records/. Also see state introduction. Mail turnaround time 5-7 days.

General Information: Public use terminal available. No sealed, expunged or confidential records released. No fee to fax documents. Fax requires prior arrangement. Certification fee: $4.00 plus $.50 per page. Payee: 4th District Court. Personal checks or Visa, MC accepted. Prepayment required.

4th District Court - American Fork Department 75 E 80 N, #202, PO Box 986, American Fork, UT 84003-0986; phone: 801-756-9654; fax: 801-763-0153; hours 8AM-5PM (MST). *Misdemeanor, Civil, Eviction, Small Claims.*

Civil Records: Access: Mail, online, in person. Both court and visitors may perform in person searches. Search fee: $10.00 per hour. First 20 minutes no charge. Court makes copy: $.25 per page. Required to search: name, years to search. Civil cases indexed by defendant, plaintiff. Civil records on computer since 1988. Online access through Xchange, see www.utcourts.gov/records/. Also see state introduction. Mail turnaround time 5-7 days.

Criminal Records: Access: Mail, online, in person. Both court and visitors may perform in person searches. Search fee: $10.00 per hour. First 20 minutes no charge. Court makes copy: $.25 per page. Required to search: name, years to search; also helpful: DOB. Criminal records stored since 1988. Online access through Xchange, see www.utcourts.gov/records/. Also see state introduction. Mail turnaround time 5-7 days.

General Information: Public terminal goes back to 5/1988. No sealed, expunged or confidential records released. Will fax documents for $5.00 per fax. Certification fee: $4.00 plus $.50 per page. Payee: 4th District Court. Personal checks or Visa, MC accepted. Prepayment and SASE required.

Wasatch County

4th District Court 1361 S Hwy 40, PO Box 730, Heber City, UT 84032; phone: 435-654-4676; criminal fax: 435-654-5281; same fax for civil/probate; hours 8AM-5PM (MST). *Felony, Misdemeanor, Civil, Eviction, Probate.*

Note: Small claims are handled at one of two Justice Courts. Heber City Justice Court- 435-654-1662, Wasatch County Justice Court- 435-654-2679.

Civil Records: Access: Phone, fax, mail, online, in person. Both court and visitors may perform in person searches. No search fee. Court makes copy: $.25 per page. Required to search: name, years to search. Civil cases indexed by defendant, plaintiff. Civil records on computer since 1/95; records archived since court started. Online access through Xchange, see www.utcourts.gov/records/. Also see state introduction. Mail turnaround time 1-2 days.

Criminal Records: Access: Phone, fax, mail, online, in person. Both court and visitors may perform in person searches. No search fee. Court makes copy: $.25 per page. Required to search: name, years to search; also helpful: DOB, signed release. Criminal records on computer since 1/95; records archived since court started. Online access through Xchange, see www.utcourts.gov/records/. Also see state introduction. Mail turnaround time 1-2 days.

General Information: Public terminal goes back to 1/1995. No adoption records released. Fee to fax documents is $1.00 plus $.25 per page. Certification fee: $4.00 plus $.50 per page. Payee: 4th District Court. Personal checks accepted. Prepayment and SASE required.

Washington County

5th District Court 220 N 200 E, St. George, UT 84770; criminal phone: 435-986-5700; civil phone: 435-986-5701; fax: 435-986-5723; hours 8AM-5PM (MST). *Felony, Misdemeanor, Civil, Eviction, Small Claims, Probate.*

Civil Records: Access: Mail, online, in person, fax. Both court and visitors may perform in person searches. No search fee. Court makes copy: $.25 per page. Required to search: name. Civil cases indexed by defendant, plaintiff. District Court records on computer from 4/1990; Circuit Court on computer from 1987. Online access through Xchange, see www.utcourts.gov/records/. Also see state introduction. Mail turnaround time 2-3 days.

Criminal Records: Access: Mail, online, in person, fax. Both court and visitors may perform in person searches. No search fee. Court makes copy: $.25 per page. Required to search: name, years to search. District Court records on computer from 4/1990; Circuit Court on computer from 1987. Online access through Xchange, see www.utcourts.gov/records/. Also see state introduction. Mail turnaround time 2-3 days.

General Information: Public use terminal available. No mental health, adoption records released. Fee to fax documents is extra $.25 per page. (min $5.00 charge). Certification fee: $4.00 plus $.50 per page. Payee: 5th District Court. Personal checks or Visa, MC accepted. Prepayment and SASE required.

Wayne County

6th District Court PO Box 189, Loa, UT 84747; phone: 435-836-1301; fax: 435-836-2479; hours 9AM-5PM (MST). *Felony, Misdemeanor, Civil, Eviction, Small Claims, Probate.*

Civil Records: Access: Phone, mail, fax, in person, online. Both court and visitors may perform in person searches. Search fee: $15.00 per hour. Court makes copy: $.25 per page. Required to search: name, years to search. Civil cases indexed by defendant, plaintiff. Civil records archived since court started; computerized from 10/2000. Online access through Xchange, see www.utcourts.gov/records/. Also see state introduction. Mail turnaround time 2-3 days.

Criminal Records: Access: Phone, mail, fax, in person, online. Both court and visitors may perform in person searches. Search fee: $15.00 per hour. Court makes copy: $.25 per page. Required to search: name, years to search; also helpful: SSN. Criminal records archived since court started; computerized from 10/2000. Online access through Xchange, see www.utcourts.gov/records/. Also see state introduction. Mail turnaround time 2-3 days.

General Information: No sealed records released. Fee to fax documents is $1.00 per page. Certification fee: $4.00 plus $.50 per page. Payee: 6th District Court. Personal checks accepted. Prepayment and SASE required.

Weber County

2nd District Court 2525 Grant Ave, Ogden, UT 84401; phone: 801-395-1060; criminal phone: 801-395-1102; civil phone: 801-395-1091; probate phone: 801-395-1173; fax: 801-395-1182; hours 8AM-5PM (MST). *Felony, Misdemeanor, Civil, Eviction, Small Claims, Probate.*

Note: Until 12/02, there was a District Court also in Roy. However, this court is now a Justice Court.

Civil Records: Access: Phone, mail, online, in person. Both court and visitors may perform in person searches. Search fee: $15.00 per hour. First 15 minutes no charge. Court makes copy: $.25 per page. Required to search: name, years to search. Civil cases indexed by defendant, plaintiff. Civil records on computer the past 10 years, books prior to that. Online access through Xchange, see www.utcourts.gov/records/. Also see state introduction. An automated court information line allows phone access to court dates, fine balances, and judgment/divorce decrees (case or citation number required) at 801-395-1111. Mail turnaround time 2-9 days.

Criminal Records: Access: Phone, mail, online, in person. Both court and visitors may perform in person searches. Search fee: $15.00 per hour. First 15 minutes no charge. Court makes copy: $.25 per page. Required to search: name, years to search, DOB, SSN. Criminal records on computer the past 10 years, books prior to that. Online access through Xchange, see www.utcourts.gov/records/. Also see state introduction. Mail turnaround time 2-9 days.

General Information: Public use terminal available. No adoption, voluntary commitments, expunged criminal records released. Will fax documents $5.00 per page. Certification fee: $4.00 plus $.50 per page. Payee: Ogden District Court. Personal checks or Visa, MC accepted. Prepayment and SASE required.

Utah Recording Offices

ORGANIZATION: 29 counties 29 recording offices. The recording officers are County Recorder and Clerk of District Court (state tax liens). The entire state is in the Mountain Time Zone (MST).

REAL ESTATE RECORDS: County Recorders will not perform real estate searches. Copy fees vary, and certification fees are usually $2.00 per document.

UCC RECORDS: Financing statements are filed at the state level, except for real estate related collateral, which are filed with the Register of Deeds (and at the state level in certain cases). Many filing offices will not perform UCC searches. Copy fees vary, but is usually $1.00. Certification usually costs $5.00 per document.

TAX LIEN RECORDS: All federal tax liens are filed with the County Recorder. They do not perform searches. All state tax liens are filed with Clerk of District Court, many of which have online access. Refer to the County Court section for information about Utah District Courts.

ONLINE ACCESS: A number of counties offer online access, some are fee-based.

Beaver County

County Recorder, PO Box 431, Beaver, UT 84713. 435-438-6480; fax-435-438-6481; hours: 9AM-5PM. All records in one index. Office will perform a UCC search but public must search other records themselves. UCC search per debtor name- fee determined by length of search. Copy fee $1.00 per page. Cert fee- $5.00 per cert plus copy fee. Payee- Beaver County Recorder. **Other phones:** Treasurer- 435-438-6410; Appraiser/Auditor- 435-438-6460. **Property tax/Assessor-** PO Box 352, Beaver, UT 84713; 435-438-6400.

Box Elder County

County Recorder, 1 S. Main; Courthouse, Brigham City, UT 84302-2599. 435-734-3353, R/E recording phone-435-734-3391; fax-435-723-7562; hours: 8AM-5PM. www.boxeldercounty.org
All records in one index. Records indexed on computer back to 1986. Only the public may search. Copy fee $1.00 per document. Cert fee- $5.00 per doc plus $.25 per page. **Other phones:** Treasurer- 435-734-3333; Appraiser/Auditor- 435-734-3317; Elections- 435-734-3391. **Property tax/Assessor-** 435-734-3333.

Cache County

County Recorder, 179 N. Main St #101, Logan, UT 84321. 435-716-7180; fax-435-716-7187; hours: 8AM-5PM.
www.cachecounty.org/recorder/index.php
All records in one index. Records indexed on a public use terminal back to 1980. Only the public may search. Copy fee $1.00 per page. Cert fee- $5.00 per doc plus copy fee. Payee- Cache County Recorder. **Online access to Recording, Grantor/Grantee, Lien, Property records:** Access to recording records is via subscription at www.landlight.com. Choose from 3 subscription plans; short free trial is offered. Grantor/Grantee Index goes back to 10/1980; Abstracts to 7/1984; images to 12/1992. Call 435-787-9003 for more information regarding online access. **Other phones:** Treasurer- 435-716-8394; Appraiser/Auditor- 435-716-7123. **Property tax/Assessor-** 179 N. Main St #205, Logan, UT 84321; 435-716-7100.

Carbon County

County Recorder, 120 E Main; Courthouse Bldg., Price, UT 84501. 435-636-3244; fax-435-637-6757; hours: 8AM-5PM.
Only the public may search. Copy fee $.25 per page. Cert fee- $5.00. Payee- Carbon County Recorder. **Other phones:** Treasurer- 435-636-3258; Appraiser/Auditor- 435-636-3227; Elections- 435-636-3220. **Property tax/Assessor-** 435-636-3249.

Daggett County

County Recorder, PO Box 219, Manila, UT 84046-0219. 435-784-3210; fax-435-784-3335; hours: 9AM-N; 1-5PM.
Index: Books and Computer, by name and Legal description. Only the public may search. Copy fee $.25 per page. Cert fee- $5.00 per page. Payee- Dagget Co. Recorder. **Other phones:** Treasurer- 435-784-3154; Appraiser/Auditor- 435-784-3210; Elections- 435-784-3154. **Property tax/Assessor-** PO Box 387, Manila, UT 84046; 435-784-3222.

Davis County

County Recorder, PO Box 618, Farmington, UT 84025. 801-451-3225, R/E recording phone-385-451-3225, UCC recording phone-801-451-3225; fax-801-451-3141; hours: 8:30AM-5PM. www.co.davis.ut.us
Only the public may search. Copy fee $1.00 per page. Cert fee- $5.00 per doc, plus copy fee. Payee- Davis County Recorder. **Online access to Real Estate, Lien records:** Access to the county land records database requires written registration and $15.00 per month fee plus $.10 per transaction. Records go back to 1981. For information and sign-up, contact Janet at 801-451-3347. **Other phones:** Treasurer- 385-451-3243; Appraiser/Auditor- 385-451-3214; Elections- 385-451-3213; Vital Records- 801-451-3337. **Property tax/Assessor-** 385-451-3252.

Duchesne County

County Recorder, PO Box 916, Duchesne, UT 84021. 435-738-1160; fax-435-738-1220; 8:30AM-5PM.
Separate indices to search include surface and misc and mineral. Only the public may search. Copy fee $1.00 per copy. Cert fee- $5.00 plus copy fee. Payee- County Recorder. **Other phones:** Treasurer- 435-738-1193; Appraiser/Auditor- 435-738-1123; Elections- 435-738-1101. **Property tax/Assessor-** 435-738-1115.

Emery County

County Recorder, PO Box 698, Castle Dale, UT 84513-0698. 435-381-2414; fax-435-381-2614; hours: 8:30AM-5PM. www.emerycounty.com
All records in one index. Records indexed on computer back to 1986. Only the public may search. Copy fee $.25 per page. Cert fee- $5.00 per cert plus $.50 per page. Payee- Emery County Recorder. **Online access to Plat, Property records:** Access plat/property records free at www.emerycounty.com/recorder/needa_plat.htm. **Other phones:** Treasurer- 435-381-2510; Appraiser/Auditor- 435-381-2474; Elections- 435-381-5106. **Property tax/Assessor-** 435-381-2474.

Garfield County

County Recorder, PO Box 77, Panguitch, UT 84759. 435-676-1112 x112; fax-435-676-8239; hours: 9AM-N, 1-5PM.
Only the public may search. Copy fee $.50 per page. Cert fee- $5.00. Payee- Garfield County Recorder. **Other phones:** Treasurer- 435-676-1109; Appraiser/Auditor- 435-676-8826 x100. **Property tax/Assessor-** 435-676-1107.

Grand County

County Recorder & Deputies, 125 E. Center St., Moab, UT 84532. 435-259-1331; fax-435-259-1320; hours: 8AM-5PM.
Separate indices to search. Only the public may search. Copy fee $1.00 per page. Cert fee- $5.00 1st page; $1.00 each add'l page plus copy fee. Payee- Grand County Recorder. **Other phones:** Treasurer- 435-295-1337; Appraiser/Auditor- 435-259-1322. **Property tax/Assessor-** 125 E Center, Moab, UT 84532; 435-295-1329.

Iron County

County Recorder, PO Box 506, Parowan, UT 84761. 435-477-8350; fax-435-477-8847; 8:30AM-5PM.
Only the public may search. Copy fee $1.00 per page. Cert fee- $5.00 per cert, does not include copies. Payee- Iron County Recorder. **Other phones:** Treasurer- 435-477-8360; Appraiser/Auditor- 435-477-8331. **Property tax/Assessor-** 435-477-8311.

Juab County

County Recorder, 160 N. Main, Nephi, UT 84648. 435-623-3430; hours: 8:30AM-5PM.
Search fee $1.00 for a computer printout. Will not search real estate records. Will search UCC records. Will not do federal tax lien search. UCC search per debtor name- $10.00. Copy fee $1.00 per page. Cert fee- $5.00 per cert plus copy fee. Payee- Juab County Recorder. **Other phones:** Treasurer- 435-623-0096; Appraiser/Auditor- 435-623-3410. **Property tax/Assessor-** 435-623-3425.

Kane County

County Recorder, 76 N. Main St, Kanab, UT 84741-3209. 435-644-2360; hours: 8AM-N, 1-5PM.
Separate indices to search include grantor/grantee, mortgage, misc., Fed tax, judgment. Only the public may search. Copy fee $.50 per page. Cert fee- $5.00 per cert plus copy fee. Payee- Kane County Recorder. **Other phones:** Treasurer- 435-644-5659; Elections- 435-644-2458. **Property tax/Assessor-** 435-644-2649.

Millard County

County Recorder, 50 S. Main, Fillmore, UT 84631. 435-743-6210; fax-435-743-4221; hours: 8AM-5PM. Separate indices to search include alphabetical, abstract retrieval, parcel ownership retrieval. Records indexed on a public use terminal back to 1985. Only the public may search. Copy fee $1.00 per page. Cert fee- $5.00 1st page, $.50 each add'l page plus copy fee. Payee- Millard County Recorder. **Other phones:** Treasurer- 435-743-5322; Appraiser/Auditor- 435-743-5227. **Property tax/Assessor-** same address as above. 435-743-5719.

Morgan County

County Recorder, PO Box 886, Morgan, UT 84050. 801-829-3277; fax-801-845-4066; hours: 8AM-5PM. www.morgan-county.net
Separate indices to search include grantor, grantee, parcel abstract, UCC, Fed liens, judgments. Only the public may search. Copy fee $1.50 per page. Cert fee- $5.00 per doc plus copy fee. Payee- Morgan Co. Recorder. **Other phones:** Treasurer- 801-845-4030; Appraiser/Auditor- 801-845-4011. **Property tax/Assessor-** PO Box 420, Morgan, UT 84050; 801-845-4000.

Piute County

County Recorder, PO Box 116, Junction, UT 84740. 435-577-2505; fax-435-577-2433; hours: 9AM-5PM. Separate indices to search include deeds and mortgages. Records indexed on a public use terminal back to 1999. Office will perform a UCC search but public must search other records themselves. General index search fee $10.00 per search. Will not search real estate records as a practice. UCC search per debtor name- $10.00. Copy fee $1.00 per page. Cert fee- $4.50 plus copy fee. Payee- Piute County Recorder. **Other phones:** Treasurer- 435-577-2505; Appraiser/Auditor- 435-577-2840. **Property tax/Assessor-** 435-577-2988.

Rich County

County Recorder, PO Box 322, Randolph, UT 84064. 435-793-2005; fax-435-793-2007; 9AM-N,1-5PM. Records indexed on computer. Only the public may search. Copy fee $1.00 per page. Cert fee- $5.00 per cert plus copy fee. Payee- Rich County Recorder. **Other phones:** Treasurer- 435-793-5155; Appraiser/Auditor- 435-793-2415. **Property tax/Assessor-** 435-793-5215.

Salt Lake County

County Recorder, 2001 S. State St; Rm N-1600, Salt Lake City, UT 84190-1150. 801-468-3391; fax-801-468-3335; hours: 8AM-5PM. www.co.slc.ut.us
Office will perform a UCC search but public must search other records themselves. Copy fee $2.00 per page. Cert fee- $5.00 per cert plus copy fee. Payee- Salt Lake County Recorder. **Online access to Assessor, Property Tax, Land records:** Records on the county Truth-In-Tax Information website are free at www.slpropertyinfo.org. **Other phones:** Treasurer- 801-468-3140; Appraiser/Auditor- 801-468-3389. **Property tax/Assessor-** 801-468-2165.

San Juan County

County Recorder, PO Box 789, Monticello, UT 84535. 435-587-3228; fax-435-587-2425; hours: 8AM-5PM. www.sanjuancounty.org/recorder.htm
All records in one index. Only the public may search. Copy fee $1.00 per page; $.50 if computer print. R/E or tax lien copy- $.75 per page. Cert fee- $5.00 per doc, plus copy fee. Payee- San Juan County Recorder. **Other phones:** Treasurer- 435-547-3237; Appraiser/Auditor- 435-587-3223; Elections- 435-587-3223; Vital Records- 435-587-2021. **Property tax/Assessor-** 435-587-3221.

Sanpete County

County Recorder, PO Box 129, Manti, UT 84642. 435-835-2181; fax-435-835-2182; hours: 8:00AM-5PM. Separate indices to search include grantor/grantee, fee&entry, brief legal, ownership name. Only the public may search. Copy fee $1.00 per page. Cert fee- $5.00 per cert plus copy fee. Payee- Sanpete County Recorder. **Other phones:** Treasurer- 435-835-2101; Appraiser/Auditor- 435-835-2142; Elections- 435-835-2131. **Property tax/Assessor-** same address as above. 435-835-2111.

Sevier County

County Recorder, 250 N. Main, Richfield, UT 84701. 435-896-9262 x210; fax-435-896-8888; hours: 8AM-5PM. www.sevierutah.net
All records in one index. Only the public may search. Copy fee $.25 per page. Fax fee $2.00 per doc. Cert fee- $5.00 per doc plus copy fee. Payee- Sevier County Recorder. **Other phones:** Treasurer- 435-896-9262 x240; Appraiser/Auditor- 435-896-9262 x203; Elections- 435-896-9262 x201. **Property tax/Assessor-** 250 N. Main, Richfield, UT 84701; 435-896-9262 x230.

Summit County

County Recorder, PO Box 128, Coalville, UT 84017. 435-336-3238; fax-435-336-3055; hours: 8AM-5PM M-F. www.co.summit.ut.us
Only the public may search. Copy fee $.50 per page, $.25 self serve. Cert fee- $5.00 per page plus copy fee. Payee- Summit County Recorder. **Other phones:** Treasurer- 435-336-3266; Appraiser/Auditor- 435-336-3254. **Property tax/Assessor-** same address as above. 435-336-3248.

Tooele County

County Recorder, 47 S. Main St; Rm 213, Tooele, UT 84074-2194. 435-843-3180; fax-435-882-7317; hours: 8:30AM-5PM. www.co.tooele.ut.us
Office will perform a UCC search but public must search other records themselves. Copy fee $1.00 per page. Cert fee- $7.00 1st page, $2.00 each add'l page. **Online access to Property Tax records:** Access to the property information database may be operational at www.co.tooele.ut.us/taxinfo.html. **Other phones:** Treasurer- 435-843-3191; Appraiser/Auditor- 435-843-3130; Elections- 435-843-3140; Vital Records- 435-843-2300. **Property tax/Assessor-** 435-843-3101.

Uintah County

County Recorder, 147 E. Main St.; County Bldg., Vernal, UT 84078. 435-781-5461, R/E recording phone-435-781-5398; fax-435-781-5319; hours: 8AM-5PM. www.co.uintah.ut.us
Only the public may search. Copy fee $.50 per page. Cert fee- $2.00 per cert plus copy fee. Payee- Uintah County Recorder. **Other phones:** Treasurer- 435-781-5362; Appraiser/Auditor- 435-781-5360. **Property tax/Assessor-** 435-781-5349.

Utah County

County Recorder, PO Box 122, Provo, UT 84603. 801-851-8179; fax-801-951-8181; hours: 8:30AM-5PM. www.utahcountyonline.org
Separate indices to search include 22 categories. Records indexed on a public use terminal back to 1978. Only the public may search. Copy fee $1.00 per page. Cert fee- $5.00 per cert plus copy fee. Payee- Utah County Recorder. **Online access to Recorder, Deed, Real Estate, Lien, Assessor, Delinquent Tax, Property Tax, Treasurer records:** Access to the land records database and also map searching is free at www.utahcountyonline.org/Dept/Record/LandRecordsandMaps/WebAccess.asp.
Indexes go back to 1978; parcel indexes back to 1981. Document images go back to 1965. Building and GIS information is also online. Also, name search property data free at http://pbw.co.utah.ut.us/scripts/pbcgi70.exe/uc/u_functions/uof_namesearch. **Other phones:** Treasurer- 801-851-8259; Appraiser/Auditor- 801-851-8291; Elections- 801-951-8123; Vital Records- 801-851-4526. **Property tax/Assessor-** 801-951-8275.

Wasatch County

County Recorder, 25 N. Main, Heber, UT 84032. 435-657-3210; hours: 8AM-5PM. www.co.wasatch.ut.us/d/recorder.html
All records in one index. Only the public may search. Copy fee $.50 per page. Cert fee- $5.00 per cert plus copy fee. Payee- Wasatch County Recorder. **Online access to Real Property, Grantor/Grantee, Marriage records:** Access to a limited grantor/grantee index also maps and subdivisions are at www.co.wasatch.ut.us/web_access.htm. Only documents from 10/15/1998 to present are accessible. Grantor/Grantee can only be searched for data since 5/20/2002. Use "Advanced Search". Includes marriages. Also, the county GIS Dept. plans to have "metadata" property information free at its GIS mapping site at www.co.wasatch.ut.us/d/dpgis.html. **Other phones:** Treasurer- 435-657-3217; Appraiser/Auditor- 435-657-3221; Vital Records- 435-654-2700. **Property tax/Assessor-** 25 N. Main, Heber, UT 84032; 435-657-3221.

Washington County

County Recorder, 87 N 200 E, #101, St. George, UT 84770. 435-634-5709; fax-435-652-5895; hours: 8AM-5PM. www.washco.state.ut.us
All records in one index. Only the public may search. Copy fee $1.00 per page. Cert fee- $5.00 per cert + $1.00 per page. Payee- Washington County Recorder. **Online access to Property, Tax Roll records:** Access to the tax roll database is free at www.washco.state.ut.us/index.php?page=taxes&sub=taxsearch. **Other phones:** Treasurer- 435-652-5711; Appraiser/Auditor- 435-634-5703; Elections- 435-634-5712. **Property tax/Assessor-** 87 N 200 E #201, St. George, UT 84770; 435-634-5703.

Wayne County

County Recorder, PO Box 187, Loa, UT 84747-0187. 435-836-1303; fax-435-836-2479; hours: 9AM-5PM. www.waynecnty.com
Records indexed on computer back to 1998. Only the public may search. Copy fee $.50 per page. Cert fee- $3.00 per cert, $1.00 per page of doc. Payee- Wayne County Recorder. **Other phones:** Treasurer- 435-836-2765 x2; Clerk/Auditor- 435-836-2765. **Property tax/Assessor-** 435-836-2765.

Weber County

County Recorder, 2380 Washington Blvd, #370, Ogden, UT 84401. 801-399-8441; hours: 8AM-5PM. www.co.weber.ut.us
Records indexed on a public use terminal back to 1980. Only the public may search. Copy fee $1.00 per page. Cert fee- $5.00 per cert plus copy fee. Payee- Weber County Recorder. **Online access to Real Estate records:** Property records on the County Parcel Search site are free at www.co.weber.ut.us/gis/2002/psearch/. Also, Abstract Title Registration is found at http://otgweb.co.weber.ut.us/abstract/login.asp. **Other phones:** Treasurer- 801-399-8454; Appraiser/Auditor- 801-399-8400; Elections- 801-399-8400; Vital Records- 801-399-7130. **Property tax/Assessor-** 2380 Washington Blvd, #380, Ogden, UT 84401; 801-399-8572.

Utah County Locator

You will usually be able to find the city name in the City/County Cross Reference below. In that case, it is a simple matter to determine the county from the cross reference. However, only the official US Postal Service city names are included in this index. There are an additional 40,000 place names that people use in their addresses. Therefore, we have also included a ZIP/City Cross Reference immediately following the City/County Cross Reference.

If you know the ZIP Code but the city name does not appear in the City/County Cross Reference index, look up the ZIP Code in the ZIP/City Cross Reference, find the city name, then look up the city name in the City/County Cross Reference. For example, you want to know the county for an address of Menands, NY 12204. There is no "Menands" in the City/County Cross Reference. The ZIP/City Cross Reference shows that ZIP Codes 12201-12288 are for the city of Albany. Looking back in the City/County Cross Reference, Albany is in Albany County.

Utah City/County Cross Reference

ALPINE Utah
ALTAMONT Duchesne
ALTON Kane
ALTONAH Duchesne
AMERICAN FORK Utah
ANETH San Juan
ANNABELLA Sevier
ANTIMONY Garfield
AURORA Sevier
AXTELL Sanpete
BEAR RIVER CITY Box Elder
BERYL Iron
BICKNELL Wayne
BINGHAM CANYON Salt Lake
BLANDING San Juan
BLUEBELL Duchesne
BLUFF San Juan
BONANZA Uintah
BOULDER Garfield
BOUNTIFUL Davis
BRIAN HEAD Iron
BRIDGELAND Duchesne
BRIGHAM CITY Box Elder
BRYCE Garfield
BRYCE CANYON Garfield
CACHE JUNCTION Cache
CANNONVILLE Garfield
CASTLE DALE Emery
CEDAR CITY Iron
CEDAR VALLEY Utah
CENTERFIELD Sanpete
CENTERVILLE Davis
CENTRAL Washington
CHESTER Sanpete
CIRCLEVILLE Piute
CISCO Grand
CLARKSTON Cache
CLAWSON Emery
CLEARFIELD Davis
CLEVELAND Emery
COALVILLE Summit
COLLINSTON Box Elder
CORINNE Box Elder
CORNISH Cache
CROYDON Morgan
DAMMERON VALLEY Washington
DELTA Millard
DEWEYVILLE Box Elder
DRAPER Salt Lake
DUCHESNE Duchesne
DUCK CREEK VILLAGE Kane
DUGWAY Tooele
DUTCH JOHN Daggett
EAST CARBON Carbon
ECHO Summit
EDEN Weber
ELBERTA Utah
ELMO Emery
ELSINORE Sevier
EMERY Emery
ENTERPRISE Washington
EPHRAIM Sanpete
ESCALANTE Garfield

EUREKA Juab
FAIRVIEW Sanpete
FARMINGTON Davis
FAYETTE Sanpete
FERRON Emery
FIELDING Box Elder
FILLMORE Millard
FORT DUCHESNE Uintah
FOUNTAIN GREEN Sanpete
FRUITLAND Duchesne
GARDEN CITY Rich
GARLAND Box Elder
GARRISON Millard
GLENDALE Kane
GLENWOOD Sevier
GOSHEN Utah
GRANTSVILLE Tooele
GREEN RIVER Emery
GREENVILLE Beaver
GREENWICH Piute
GROUSE CREEK Box Elder
GUNLOCK Washington
GUNNISON Sanpete
GUSHER Uintah
HANKSVILLE Wayne
HANNA Duchesne
HATCH Garfield
HEBER CITY Wasatch
HELPER Carbon
HENEFER Summit
HENRIEVILLE Garfield
HIAWATHA Carbon
HILDALE Washington
HILL AFB Davis
HINCKLEY Millard
HOLDEN Millard
HONEYVILLE Box Elder
HOOPER (84315) Weber(92), Davis(7)
HOWELL Box Elder
HUNTINGTON Emery
HUNTSVILLE Weber
HURRICANE Washington
HYDE PARK Cache
HYRUM Cache
IBAPAH Tooele
IVINS Washington
JENSEN Uintah
JOSEPH Sevier
JUNCTION Piute
KAMAS (84036) Summit(86), Wasatch(13)
KANAB Kane
KANARRAVILLE Iron
KANOSH Millard
KAYSVILLE Davis
KENILWORTH Carbon
KINGSTON Piute
KOOSHAREM Sevier
LA SAL San Juan
LA VERKIN Washington
LAKE POWELL San Juan
LAKETOWN Rich
LAPOINT Uintah
LAYTON Davis

LEAMINGTON Millard
LEEDS Washington
LEHI Utah
LEVAN Juab
LEWISTON Cache
LINDON Utah
LOA Wayne
LOGAN Cache
LYMAN Wayne
LYNNDYL Millard
MAGNA Salt Lake
MANILA Daggett
MANTI Sanpete
MANTUA Box Elder
MAPLETON Utah
MARYSVALE Piute
MAYFIELD Sanpete
MEADOW Millard
MENDON Cache
MEXICAN HAT San Juan
MIDVALE Salt Lake
MIDWAY Wasatch
MILFORD Beaver
MILLVILLE Cache
MINERSVILLE Beaver
MOAB Grand
MODENA Iron
MONA Juab
MONROE Sevier
MONTEZUMA CREEK San Juan
MONTICELLO San Juan
MONUMENT VALLEY San Juan
MORGAN Morgan
MORONI Sanpete
MOUNT CARMEL Kane
MOUNT PLEASANT Sanpete
MOUNTAIN HOME Duchesne
MYTON (84052) Duchesne(75), Uintah(24)
NEOLA Duchesne
NEPHI Juab
NEW HARMONY Washington
NEWCASTLE Iron
NEWTON Cache
NORTH SALT LAKE Davis
OAK CITY Millard
OAKLEY Summit
OASIS Millard
OGDEN (84405) Weber(87), Davis(12)
OGDEN Weber
ORANGEVILLE Emery
ORDERVILLE Kane
OREM Utah
PANGUITCH Garfield
PARADISE Cache
PARAGONAH Iron
PARK CITY (84060) Summit(96), Wasatch(3)
PARK CITY Summit
PARK VALLEY Box Elder
PAROWAN Iron
PAYSON Utah
PEOA Summit
PINE VALLEY Washington

PLEASANT GROVE Utah
PLYMOUTH Box Elder
PORTAGE Box Elder
PRICE Carbon
PROVIDENCE Cache
PROVO Utah
RANDLETT Uintah
RANDOLPH Rich
REDMOND Sevier
RICHFIELD Sevier
RICHMOND Cache
RIVERSIDE Box Elder
RIVERTON Salt Lake
ROOSEVELT (84066) Duchesne(94), Uintah(5)
ROY Weber
RUSH VALLEY Tooele
SAINT GEORGE Washington
SALEM Utah
SALINA Sevier
SALT LAKE CITY Salt Lake
SANDY Salt Lake
SANTA CLARA Washington
SANTAQUIN Utah
SCIPIO Millard
SEVIER Sevier
SIGURD Sevier
SMITHFIELD Cache
SNOWVILLE Box Elder
SOUTH JORDAN Salt Lake
SPANISH FORK Utah
SPRING CITY Sanpete
SPRINGVILLE Utah
STERLING Sanpete
STOCKTON Tooele
SUMMIT Iron
SUNNYSIDE Carbon
SYRACUSE Davis
TABIONA Duchesne
TALMAGE Duchesne
TEASDALE Wayne
THOMPSON Grand
TOOELE Tooele
TOQUERVILLE Washington
TORREY Wayne
TREMONTON Box Elder
TRENTON Cache
TRIDELL Uintah
TROPIC Garfield
VERNAL Uintah
VERNON Tooele
VEYO Washington
VIRGIN Washington
WALES Sanpete
WALLSBURG Wasatch
WELLINGTON Carbon
WELLSVILLE Cache
WENDOVER Tooele
WEST JORDAN Salt Lake
WHITEROCKS Uintah
WILLARD Box Elder
WOODRUFF Rich
WOODS CROSS Davis

Utah ZIP/City Cross Reference

84001-84001	ALTAMONT
84002-84002	ALTONAH
84003-84003	AMERICAN FORK
84004-84004	ALPINE
84006-84006	BINGHAM CANYON
84007-84007	BLUEBELL
84008-84008	BONANZA
84010-84011	BOUNTIFUL
84012-84012	BRIDGELAND
84013-84013	CEDAR VALLEY
84014-84014	CENTERVILLE
84015-84016	CLEARFIELD
84017-84017	COALVILLE
84018-84018	CROYDON
84020-84020	DRAPER
84021-84021	DUCHESNE
84022-84022	DUGWAY
84023-84023	DUTCH JOHN
84024-84024	ECHO
84025-84025	FARMINGTON
84026-84026	FORT DUCHESNE
84027-84027	FRUITLAND
84028-84028	GARDEN CITY
84029-84029	GRANTSVILLE
84030-84030	GUSHER
84031-84031	HANNA
84032-84032	HEBER CITY
84033-84033	HENEFER
84034-84034	IBAPAH
84035-84035	JENSEN
84036-84036	KAMAS
84037-84037	KAYSVILLE
84038-84038	LAKETOWN
84039-84039	LAPOINT
84040-84041	LAYTON
84042-84042	LINDON
84043-84043	LEHI
84044-84044	MAGNA
84046-84046	MANILA
84047-84047	MIDVALE
84049-84049	MIDWAY
84050-84050	MORGAN
84051-84051	MOUNTAIN HOME
84052-84052	MYTON
84053-84053	NEOLA
84054-84054	NORTH SALT LAKE
84055-84055	OAKLEY
84056-84056	HILL AFB
84057-84059	OREM
84060-84060	PARK CITY
84061-84061	PEOA
84062-84062	PLEASANT GROVE
84063-84063	RANDLETT
84064-84064	RANDOLPH
84065-84065	RIVERTON
84066-84066	ROOSEVELT
84067-84067	ROY
84068-84068	PARK CITY
84069-84069	RUSH VALLEY
84070-84070	SANDY
84071-84071	STOCKTON
84072-84072	TABIONA
84073-84073	TALMAGE
84074-84074	TOOELE
84075-84075	SYRACUSE
84076-84076	TRIDELL

84078-84079	VERNAL
84080-84080	VERNON
84082-84082	WALLSBURG
84083-84083	WENDOVER
84084-84084	WEST JORDAN
84085-84085	WHITEROCKS
84086-84086	WOODRUFF
84087-84087	WOODS CROSS
84088-84088	WEST JORDAN
84089-84089	CLEARFIELD
84090-84094	SANDY
84095-84095	SOUTH JORDAN
84097-84097	OREM
84098-84098	PARK CITY
84100-84199	SALT LAKE CITY
84201-84244	OGDEN
84301-84301	BEAR RIVER CITY
84302-84302	BRIGHAM CITY
84304-84304	CACHE JUNCTION
84305-84305	CLARKSTON
84306-84306	COLLINSTON
84307-84307	CORINNE
84308-84308	CORNISH
84309-84309	DEWEYVILLE
84310-84310	EDEN
84311-84311	FIELDING
84312-84312	GARLAND
84313-84313	GROUSE CREEK
84314-84314	HONEYVILLE
84315-84315	HOOPER
84316-84316	HOWELL
84317-84317	HUNTSVILLE
84318-84318	HYDE PARK
84319-84319	HYRUM
84320-84320	LEWISTON
84321-84323	LOGAN
84324-84324	MANTUA
84325-84325	MENDON
84326-84326	MILLVILLE
84327-84327	NEWTON
84328-84328	PARADISE
84329-84329	PARK VALLEY
84330-84330	PLYMOUTH
84331-84331	PORTAGE
84332-84332	PROVIDENCE
84333-84333	RICHMOND
84334-84334	RIVERSIDE
84335-84335	SMITHFIELD
84336-84336	SNOWVILLE
84337-84337	TREMONTON
84338-84338	TRENTON
84339-84339	WELLSVILLE
84340-84340	WILLARD
84341-84341	LOGAN
84400-84415	OGDEN
84501-84501	PRICE
84510-84510	ANETH
84511-84511	BLANDING
84512-84512	BLUFF
84513-84513	CASTLE DALE
84515-84515	CISCO
84516-84516	CLAWSON
84518-84518	CLEVELAND
84520-84520	EAST CARBON
84521-84521	ELMO
84522-84522	EMERY

84523-84523	FERRON
84525-84525	GREEN RIVER
84526-84526	HELPER
84527-84527	HIAWATHA
84528-84528	HUNTINGTON
84529-84529	KENILWORTH
84530-84530	LA SAL
84531-84531	MEXICAN HAT
84532-84532	MOAB
84533-84533	LAKE POWELL
84534-84534	MONTEZUMA CREEK
84535-84535	MONTICELLO
84536-84536	MONUMENT VALLEY
84537-84537	ORANGEVILLE
84539-84539	SUNNYSIDE
84540-84540	THOMPSON
84542-84542	WELLINGTON
84601-84606	PROVO
84620-84620	AURORA
84621-84621	AXTELL
84622-84622	CENTERFIELD
84623-84623	CHESTER
84624-84624	DELTA
84626-84626	ELBERTA
84627-84627	EPHRAIM
84628-84628	EUREKA
84629-84629	FAIRVIEW
84630-84630	FAYETTE
84631-84631	FILLMORE
84632-84632	FOUNTAIN GREEN
84633-84633	GOSHEN
84634-84634	GUNNISON
84635-84635	HINCKLEY
84636-84636	HOLDEN
84637-84637	KANOSH
84638-84638	LEAMINGTON
84639-84639	LEVAN
84640-84640	LYNNDYL
84642-84642	MANTI
84643-84643	MAYFIELD
84644-84644	MEADOW
84645-84645	MONA
84646-84646	MORONI
84647-84647	MOUNT PLEASANT
84648-84648	NEPHI
84649-84649	OAK CITY
84650-84650	OASIS
84651-84651	PAYSON
84652-84652	REDMOND
84653-84653	SALEM
84654-84654	SALINA
84655-84655	SANTAQUIN
84656-84656	SCIPIO
84657-84657	SIGURD
84660-84660	SPANISH FORK
84662-84662	SPRING CITY
84663-84663	SPRINGVILLE
84664-84664	MAPLETON
84665-84665	STERLING
84667-84667	WALES
84701-84701	RICHFIELD
84710-84710	ALTON
84711-84711	ANNABELLA
84712-84712	ANTIMONY
84713-84713	BEAVER
84714-84714	BERYL

84715-84715	BICKNELL
84716-84716	BOULDER
84717-84717	BRYCE CANYON
84718-84718	CANNONVILLE
84719-84719	BRIAN HEAD
84720-84721	CEDAR CITY
84722-84722	CENTRAL
84723-84723	CIRCLEVILLE
84724-84724	ELSINORE
84725-84725	ENTERPRISE
84726-84726	ESCALANTE
84728-84728	GARRISON
84729-84729	GLENDALE
84730-84730	GLENWOOD
84731-84731	GREENVILLE
84732-84732	GREENWICH
84733-84733	GUNLOCK
84734-84734	HANKSVILLE
84735-84735	HATCH
84736-84736	HENRIEVILLE
84737-84737	HURRICANE
84738-84738	IVINS
84739-84739	JOSEPH
84740-84740	JUNCTION
84741-84741	KANAB
84742-84742	KANARRAVILLE
84743-84743	KINGSTON
84744-84744	KOOSHAREM
84745-84745	LA VERKIN
84746-84746	LEEDS
84747-84747	LOA
84749-84749	LYMAN
84750-84750	MARYSVALE
84751-84751	MILFORD
84752-84752	MINERSVILLE
84753-84753	MODENA
84754-84754	MONROE
84755-84755	MOUNT CARMEL
84756-84756	NEWCASTLE
84757-84757	NEW HARMONY
84758-84758	ORDERVILLE
84759-84759	PANGUITCH
84760-84760	PARAGONAH
84761-84761	PAROWAN
84762-84762	DUCK CREEK VILLAGE
84763-84763	ROCKVILLE
84764-84764	BRYCE
84765-84765	SANTA CLARA
84766-84766	SEVIER
84767-84767	SPRINGDALE
84770-84771	SAINT GEORGE
84772-84772	SUMMIT
84773-84773	TEASDALE
84774-84774	TOQUERVILLE
84775-84775	TORREY
84776-84776	TROPIC
84779-84779	VIRGIN
84780-84780	WASHINGTON
84781-84781	PINE VALLEY
84782-84782	VEYO
84783-84783	DAMMERON VALLEY
84784-84784	HILDALE
84790-84791	SAINT GEORGE

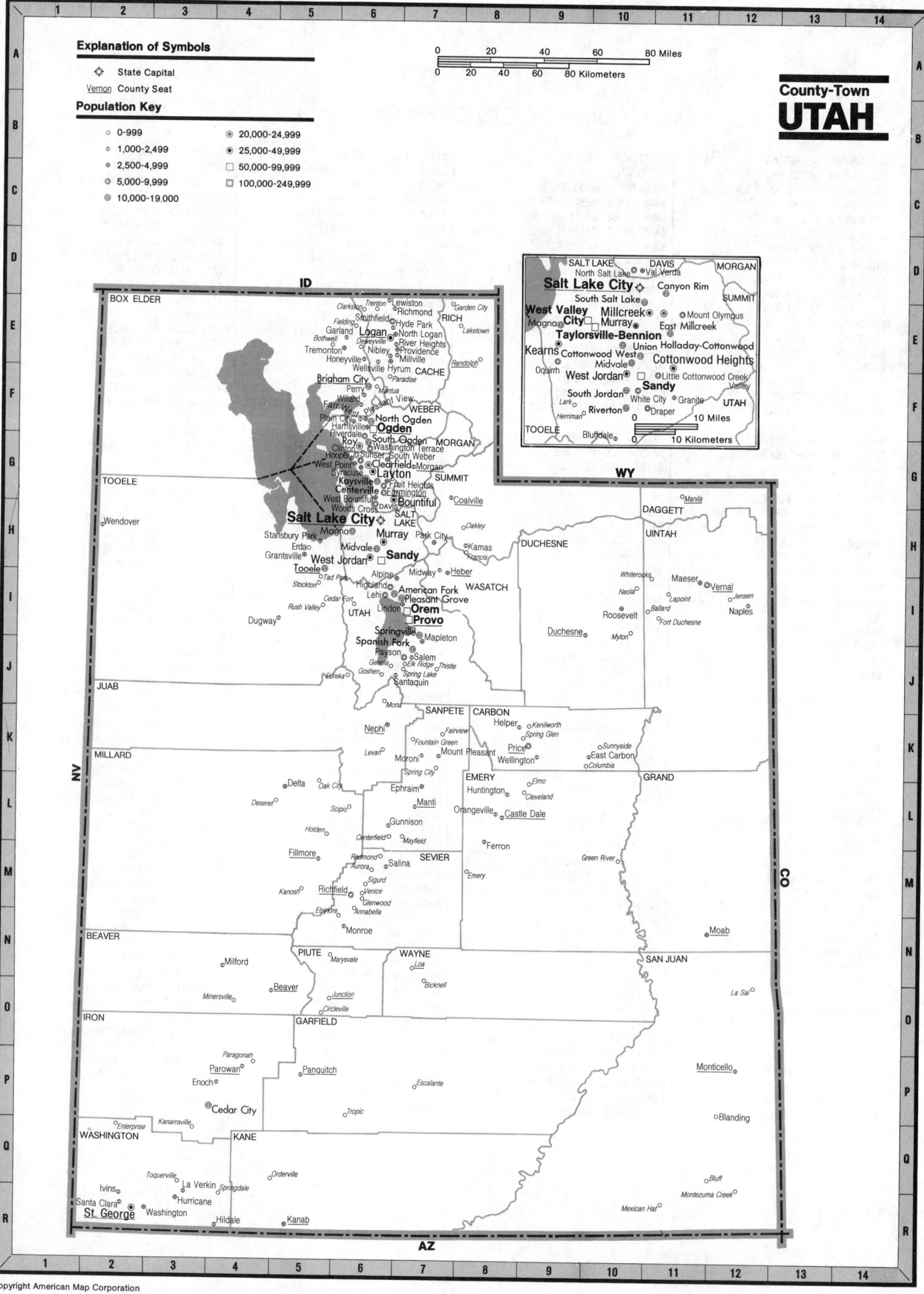

County-Town
UTAH

Explanation of Symbols

✧ State Capital
Vernon County Seat

Population Key

○ 0-999
◎ 1,000-2,499
◉ 2,500-4,999
◍ 5,000-9,999
◉ 10,000-19,000
◉ 20,000-24,999
◉ 25,000-49,999
□ 50,000-99,999
▢ 100,000-249,999

0 20 40 60 80 Miles
0 20 40 60 80 Kilometers

COUNTIES

(29 Counties)

Name of County	Population	Location on Map
BEAVER	4,765	N-2
BOX ELDER	36,485	E-2
CACHE	70,183	F-7
CARBON	20,228	K-8
DAGGETT	690	G-10
DAVIS	187,941	H-6
DUCHESNE	12,645	H-8
EMERY	10,332	L-8
GARFIELD	3,980	O-5
GRAND	6,620	K-10
IRON	20,789	O-2
JUAB	5,817	J-2
KANE	5,169	Q-4
MILLARD	11,333	K-2
MORGAN	5,528	G-7
PIUTE	1,277	N-5
RICH	1,725	E-7
SALT LAKE	725,956	H-6
SAN JUAN	12,621	N-11
SANPETE	16,259	K-7
SEVIER	15,431	M-7
SUMMIT	15,518	G-7
TOOELE	26,601	G-2
UINTAH	22,211	H-10
UTAH	263,590	I-6
WASATCH	10,089	I-8
WASHINGTON	48,560	Q-2
WAYNE	2,177	N-7
WEBER	158,330	F-7
TOTAL	1,722,850	

CITIES AND TOWNS

Note: The first name is that of the city or town, second, that of the county in which it is located, then the population and location on the map.

Alpine, Utah, 3,492 ..... I-6
American Fork, Utah, 15,696 ..... I-6
Beaver, Beaver, 1,998 ..... O-5
Blanding, San Juan, 3,162 ..... P-12
Bluffdale, Salt Lake, 2,152 ..... G-10
Bountiful, Davis, 36,659 ..... G-6
Brigham City, Box Elder, 15,644 ..... F-6
• Canyon Rim, Salt Lake, 10,527 ..... D-11
Castle Dale, Emery, 1,704 ..... L-8
Cedar City, Iron, 13,443 ..... P-4
Centerville, Davis, 11,500 ..... G-6
Clearfield, Davis, 21,435 ..... G-6
Clinton, Davis, 7,945 ..... G-6
Coalville, Summit, 1,065 ..... G-7
• Cottonwood Heights, Salt Lake, 28,766 ..... E-11
• Cottonwood West, Salt Lake, 17,476 .... E-10
Delta, Millard, 2,998 ..... L-5
Draper, Salt Lake/Utah, 7,257 ..... F-10
Duchesne, Duchesne, 1,308 ..... I-9
• Dugway, Tooele, 1,761 ..... I-5
East Carbon, Carbon, 1,270 ..... K-10
• East Millcreek, Salt Lake, 21,184 ..... E-11
Enoch, Iron, 1,947 ..... P-4
Ephraim, Sanpete, 3,363 ..... L-7
• Erda, Tooele, 1,113 ..... H-5
Farmington, Davis, 9,028 ..... G-6
Farr West, Weber, 2,178 ..... F-6
Ferron, Emery, 1,606 ..... L-8
Fillmore, Millard, 1,956 ..... M-5
Fruit Heights, Davis, 3,900 ..... G-6

Garland, Box Elder, 1,637 ..... E-6
• Granite, Salt Lake, 3,300 ..... E-10
Grantsville, Tooele, 4,500 ..... H-5
Gunnison, Sanpete, 1,298 ..... L-6
Harrisville, Weber, 3,004 ..... F-6
Heber, Wasatch, 4,782 ..... I-7
Helper, Carbon, 2,148 ..... K-8
Highland, Utah, 5,002 ..... I-6
Hildale, Washington, 1,325 ..... R-4
• Holladay-Cottonwood, Salt Lake, 14,095 ..... E-11
Honeyville, Box Elder, 1,112 ..... F-6
• Hooper, Weber, 3,468 ..... G-6
Huntington, Emery, 1,875 ..... L-8
Hurricane, Washington, 3,915 ..... R-3
Hyde Park, Cache, 2,190 ..... E-6
Hyrum, Cache, 4,829 ..... E-6
Ivins, Washington, 1,630 ..... R-2
Junction, Piute, 132 ..... O-5
Kamas, Summit, 1,061 ..... H-8
Kanab, Kane, 3,289 ..... R-5
Kaysville, Davis, 13,961 ..... G-6
• Kearns, Salt Lake, 28,374 ..... E-9
La Verkin, Washington, 1,771 ..... R-3
Layton, Davis, 41,784 ..... G-6
Lehi, Utah, 8,475 ..... I-6
Lewiston, Cache, 1,532 ..... E-6
Lindon, Utah, 3,818 ..... I-7
• Little Cottonwood Creek Valley, Salt Lake, 5,042 ..... E-10
Loa, Wayne, 444 ..... N-7
Logan, Cache, 32,762 ..... E-6
• Maeser, Uintah, 2,598 ..... I-11
• Magna, Salt Lake, 17,829 ..... E-9
Manila, Daggett, 207 ..... G-11
Manti, Sanpete, 2,268 ..... L-7
Mapleton, Utah, 3,572 ..... I-7
Midvale, Salt Lake, 11,886 ..... H-6
Midway, Wasatch, 1,554 ..... H-7
Milford, Beaver, 1,107 ..... N-4
• Millcreek, Salt Lake, 32,230 ..... E-11
Millville, Cache, 1,202 ..... F-6
Moab, Grand, 3,971 ..... N-11
Monroe, Sevier, 1,472 ..... N-6
Monticello, San Juan, 1,806 ..... P-12
Morgan, Morgan, 2,023 ..... G-7
Moroni, Sanpete, 1,115 ..... K-7
• Mount Olympus, Salt Lake, 7,413 ..... E-11
Mount Pleasant, Sanpete, 2,092 ..... K-7
Murray, Salt Lake, 31,282 ..... H-6
Naples, Uintah, 1,334 ..... I-12
Nephi, Juab, 3,515 ..... K-6
Nibley, Cache, 1,167 ..... E-6
North Logan, Cache, 3,768 ..... E-6
North Ogden, Weber, 11,668 ..... F-6
North Salt Lake, Davis, 6,474 ..... D-10
Ogden, Weber, 63,909 ..... F-6
• Oquirrh, Salt Lake, 7,593 ..... E-9
Orangeville, Emery, 1,459 ..... L-8
Orem, Utah, 67,561 ..... I-7
Panguitch, Garfield, 1,444 ..... P-5
Parowan, Iron, 1,873 ..... P-4
Park City, Summit/Wasatch, 4,468 ..... H-7
Payson, Utah, 9,510 ..... J-7
Perry, Box Elder, 1,211 ..... F-6
Plain City, Weber, 2,722 ..... F-6
Pleasant Grove, Utah, 13,476 ..... I-7
Pleasant View, Weber, 3,603 ..... F-6
Price, Carbon, 8,712 ..... K-9
Providence, Cache, 3,344 ..... E-6
Provo, Utah, 86,835 ..... I-7
Randolph, Rich, 488 ..... E-8
Richfield, Sevier, 5,593 ..... M-6
Richmond, Cache, 1,955 ..... E-6
River Heights, Cache, 1,274 ..... E-6
Riverdale, Weber, 6,419 ..... G-6

Riverton, Salt Lake, 11,261 ..... F-10
Roosevelt, Duchesne, 3,915 ..... I-10
Roy, Weber, 24,603 ..... G-6
Saint George, Washington, 28,502 ..... R-2
Salem, Utah, 2,284 ..... J-7
Salina, Sevier, 1,943 ..... M-6
Salt Lake City, Salt Lake, 159,936 ..... H-6
Sandy, Salt Lake, 75,058 ..... H-6
Santa Clara, Washington, 2,322 ..... R-2
Santaquin, Utah, 2,386 ..... J-6
Smithfield, Cache, 5,566 ..... E-6
South Jordan, Salt Lake, 12,220 ..... F-10
South Ogden, Weber, 12,105 ..... G-6
South Salt Lake, Salt Lake, 10,129 ..... E-10
South Weber, Davis, 2,863 ..... G-6
Spanish Fork, Utah, 11,272 ..... J-7
Springville, Utah, 13,950 ..... I-7
• Stansbury Park, Tooele, 1,049 ..... H-5
Sunset, Davis, 5,128 ..... G-6
Syracuse, Davis, 4,658 ..... G-6
• Taylorsville-Bennion, Salt Lake, 52,351 ..... E-10
Tooele, Tooele, 13,887 ..... H-5
Tremonton, Box Elder, 4,264 ..... E-6
• Union, Salt Lake, 13,684 ..... E-10
• Val Verda, Davis, 3,712 ..... D-10
Vernal, Uintah, 6,644 ..... I-11
Washington, Washington, 4,198 ..... R-3
Washington Terrace, Weber, 8,189 ..... G-6
Wellington, Carbon, 1,632 ..... K-9
Wellsville, Cache, 2,206 ..... E-6
Wendover, Tooele, 1,127 ..... H-2
West Bountiful, Davis, 4,477 ..... G-6
West Jordan, Salt Lake, 42,892 ..... H-6
West Point, Davis, 4,258 ..... G-6
West Valley City, Salt Lake, 86,976 ..... E-9
• White City, Salt Lake, 6,506 ..... F-10
Willard, Box Elder, 1,298 ..... F-6
Woods Cross, Davis, 5,384 ..... H-6

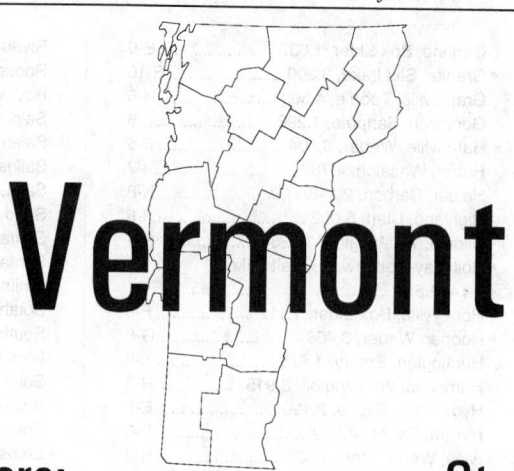

Vermont

General Help Numbers:

Governor's Office
Pavillion Office Bldg
109 State St
Montpelier, VT 05609-0101
www.vermont.gov/governor/

802-828-3333
Fax 802-828-3339
7:45AM-4:30PM

Attorney General's Office
109 State St
Montpelier, VT 05609-1001
www.atg.state.vt.us/

802-828-3171
Fax 802-828-2154
7:45AM-4:30PM

Legislative Records
State House-Legislative Council
115 State Street, Drawer 33
Montpelier, VT 05633
www.leg.state.vt.us

802-828-2231
Fax 802-828-2424
8AM-4:30PM

State Archives
State Archives Division
26 Terrace-Redstone Bldg
Montpelier, VT 05609-1103
http://vermont-archives.org

802-828-2308
Fax 802-828-1135
7:45AM-4:30PM

State Specifics:

Capital: Montpelier
Washington County

Time Zone: EST

Number of Counties: 14

Population: 621,394

Web Site: http://vermont.gov/

State Agencies

Criminal Records

Access to Records is Restricted.

State Repository, Vermont Criminal Information Center, 103 S. Main St., Waterbury, VT 05671-2101; 802-244-8727, 802-241-5552-Fax; 8AM-4:30PM.

www.dps.state.vt.us

Records are not publicly available and can only be accessed by those authorized by law and by subject for personal review. Those authorized include employers with employees working with children, elderly or disabled. Otherwise, search at the county level. 35% of records are fingerprint supported.

Statewide Court Records

Court Administrator, Administrative Office of Courts, 109 State St, Montpelier, VT 05609-0701; 802-828-3278, 802-828-3457-Fax; 7:45AM-4:30PM.

www.vermontjudiciary.org

Except for certain online research capabilities, all court record access must be done at the local level.

Searching: Include the following in your request-docket # or party name with DOB, if by mail.

Access by: mail, online.

Mail search:

Online search: Vermont Courts Online provides access to cases 12 of the counties' District, Family, and Superior Courts. It provides court calendar information for each court and detailed case

information for Superior Court. Not available for Chittenden and Franklin. Criminal records are not included. Go online to https://secure.vermont.gov/vtcdas/user. Records are in reat-time mode. There is a $10.00 registration fee plus a fee of $.50 per case for look-up. Supreme Court opinions are available from the main web site and are also maintained by the Vermont Department of Libraries at http://dol.state.vt.us.

Sexual Offender Registry

State Repository, Vermont Criminal Information Center, 103 S. Main St., Waterbury, VT 05671-2101; 802-244-8727, 802-241-5400, 802-241-5552-Fax; 8AM-4:30PM.

www.dps.state.vt.us/cjs/s_registry.htm

13 V.S.A. section 5401 et seq., requires the DPS to establish and maintain a registry of persons who are required to register as sex offenders and to post electronically information on sex offenders. The website contains only high-risk offenders.

Records are available from 1996. It takes 24 hours before new records are available for inquiry.

Searching: The complete record database is not publicly available and is accessible only by those authorized by law (employers with employees working with children, elderly, or disabled) or by the subject. Otherwise, requesters must search at local level. The website is searchable by the public.

Access by: phone, online.

Phone search: Telephone requests are accepted if search is not extensive.

Online search: The webpage gives access to the high-risk offendes only. Each requesters must register with his/her name and address. The requestor must also acknowledge a statement which specifies the conditions under which the registry information is being released.

Incarceration Records

Vermont Department of Corrections, Inmate Information Request, 103 S. Main Street, Waterbury, VT 05671-1001; 802-241-2276, 802-241-2565-Fax; 8AM-4:30PM.

www.doc.state.vt.us

Records are available on current and former inmates. It takes about 3 days before new records are available for inquiry. Records are normally destroyed after six years, depending on the DN.

Searching: Computerized records go back to 1988. Include the following in your request-first and last name. DOB and SSN are helpful. Location, conviction and sentencing information, and release dates are provided.

Access by: mail, phone, fax, online.

Fee & Payment: Requester may be asked to pay reproduction and research fees.

Mail search: Turnaround time: 5 to 7 days. Requests in writing must be specific about information requested. No SASE is required.

Phone search: Searching by telephone permitted if request also in writing.

Fax search: Searching by fax permitted.

Online search: The website provides an Incarcerated Offender Locator to ascertain where an inmate is located. Click at the top of main page, or go directly to www.doc.state.vt.us/offender. The search results gives name, DOB, location and case worker. This is not designed to provide complete inmate records nor is it a database of all inmates past and present in the system.

Corporation, Limited Liability Company, Limited Liability Partnerships, Limited Partnerships, Trademarks/Servicemarks

Secretary of State, Corporation Division, 81 River St, Montpelier, VT 05609-1104; 802-828-2386, 802-828-2853-Fax; 7:45AM-4:30PM.

www.sec.state.vt.us

Records are available from beginning of record keeping. Records are on computer if active. Inactive records are indexed by a card file.

Searching: Include the following in your request-full name of business.

Access by: mail, phone, fax, in person, online.

Fee & Payment: There is no search fee. The fee for certification is $20.00 plus $1.00 per page for copies. Fee payee: Secretary of State. Prepayment required. Personal checks accepted. No credit cards accepted.

Mail search: Turnaround time: 3 to 5 days. SASE requested.

Phone search: They will only confirm if business is active.

Fax search: Same criteria as mail searching. They will return a page or two by fax, if local number, otherwise results are mailed.

In person search: Simple requests may be processed while you wait.

Online search: Information on Corporate and trademark records can be accessed from the Internet for no fee. Tthe Corporation Name Finder, is at www.sec.state.vt.us/seek/database.htm#2. Many records, included corporation, UCC, trademark, tradename, and name look-ups are available. The Trade Name Finder is at www.sec.state.vt.us/seek/TRADSEEK.HTM.

Other access: There is an option on the Internet to download the entire corporation (and tradename) database.

Uniform Commercial Code

UCC Division, Secretary of State, 81 River St, Drawer 4, Montpelier, VT 05609-1101; 802-828-2386, 802-828-2853-Fax; 7:45AM-4:30PM.

www.sec.state.vt.us/corps/corpindex.htm

Records are available from 1967. All active records are computerized. It takes 3 to 5 days before new records are available for inquiry.

Searching: Use search request form UCC-11. All tax liens are filed at the town/city level. Include the following in your request-debtor name, business name.

Access by: mail, fax, in person, online.

Fee & Payment: Certified searches are $20.00 per name. Fee payee: Secretary of State. Prepayment required. Personal checks accepted. No credit cards accepted.

Mail search: Turnaround time: 4 days. A SASE is requested.

Fax search: Same criteria as mail searching, if account established.

In person search: Turnaround time depends on workload, may not be immediate.

Online search: Searches are available from the Internet site. You can search by debtor or business name, there is no fee.

Expedited service: Expedited service is available for account holders.

Federal and State Tax Liens

Records not maintained by a state level agency.

Records are found at the local town level.

Sales Tax Registrations

Administrative Agency/Tax Department, Taxpayers Services Division, 109 State St, Montpelier, VT 05609-1401; 802-828-2551, 802-828-5787-Fax; 7:45AM-4:30PM.

www.state.vt.us/tax

Records are available for 4 years on computer database, then records are archived. It takes 30 days before new records are available for inquiry.

Searching: This agency will only confirm that a business is registered. Taxpayer records are considered confidential, as provided by law. Include the following in your request-business name or tax permit number or owner name or federal tax ID.

Access by: mail, phone, fax.

Fee & Payment: There is no fee to confirm whether a business is registered to collect sales tax.

Mail search: Turnaround time: 7 to 10 days. A SASE is requested.

Phone search: No fee for telephone request.

Fax search: Requests may be faxed.

Birth Certificates

Reference & Research, Vital Records Section, US Rte 2, Drawer 33, Montpelier, VT 05633-7601; 802-828-3286, 802-828-3710-Fax; 8AM-4PM.

www.bgs.state.vt.us/gsc/pubrec/referen

For records for the past 5 years only, contact the Department of Health at 802-863-7300.

Records are available from 1760 to 1999. New records are available for inquiry immediately. Records are indexed on index cards, inhouse computer.

Searching: The records are open to the public. Include the following in your request-full name, names of parents, mother's maiden name, date of birth, place of birth.

Access by: mail, fax, in person.

Fee & Payment: The search fee is $9.50 per name. Fee payee: BGS State of VT Prepayment required. Personal checks accepted. Major credit cards accepted.

Mail search: Turnaround time: 3 to 5 days. A SASE is requested.

Fax search: See expedited service.

In person search: You may view the records for no charge.

Expedited service: Expedited service is available for fax searches. Turnaround time: 1 to 2 days. Add $6.00 for use of credit card and $23.50 for overnight shipping.

Death Records

Reference & Research, Vital Records, US Rte 2, Drawer 33, Montpelier, VT 05633-7601; 802-828-3286, 802-828-3710-Fax; 8AM-4PM.

www.bgs.state.vt.us/gsc/pubrec/referen

For records up to 5 years old, contact the Department of Health at 802-863-7300.

Records are available from 1760 to 1999. New records are available for inquiry immediately. Records are indexed on index cards, inhouse computer.

Searching: Records are open to the public. Include the following in your request-full name, date of death, place of death, names of parents.

Access by: mail, fax, in person.

Fee & Payment: The search fee is $9.50 per name. Fee payee: BGS State of VT Prepayment required. Credit cards accepted. Personal checks accepted.

Mail search: Turnaround time: 3 to 5 days. A SASE is requested.

Fax search: See expedited service.

In person search: You may view records at no charge.

Expedited service: Expedited service is available for fax searches. Turnaround time: 1 to 2 days. Add $6.00 for use of credit card and $23.50 for overnight shipping.

Marriage Certificates

Reference & Research, Vital Records Section, US Rte 2, Drawer 33, Montpelier, VT 05633-7601; 802-828-3286, 802-828-3710-Fax; 8AM-4PM.

www.bgs.state.vt.us/gsc/pubrec/referen

For records up to 5 years old, contact the VT Department of Health at 802-863-7300.

Records are available from 1760 to 1999. New records are available for inquiry immediately. Records are indexed on index cards, inhouse computer.

Searching: Records are open. Include the following in your request-names of husband and wife, date of marriage, place or county of marriage, names of parents.

Access by: mail, fax, in person.

Fee & Payment: The search fee is $9.50 per name. Fee payee: BGS State of VT Prepayment required. Personal checks accepted. Credit cards accepted.

Mail search: Turnaround time: 3 to 5 days. A SASE is requested.

Fax search: See expedited service.

In person search: Records may be viewed in person at no charge.

Expedited service: Available for fax requests. Turnaround time: 1-2 days. Add $6.00 for use of credit card and $23.50 for overnight delivery.

Divorce Records

Research & Reference, Vital Records Section, US Rte 2, Drawer 33, Montpelier, VT 05633-7601; 802-828-3286, 802-828-3710-Fax; 8AM-4PM.

www.bgs.state.vt.us/gsc/pubrec/referen

For records less than 5 years old, contact the VT Department of Health at 802-863-7300.

Records are available from 1760 to 1999. New records are available for inquiry immediately. Records are indexed on index cards, inhouse computer.

Searching: Records are open. Include the following in your request-names of husband and wife, date of divorce, place of divorce.

Access by: mail, fax, in person.

Fee & Payment: The search fee is $9.50 per name. Fee payee: BGS/Satte of VT Prepayment required. Personal checks and credit cards accepted.

Mail search: Turnaround time: 3 to 5 days. A SASE is requested.

Fax search: See expedited service.

In person search: There is no fee to view records.

Expedited service: Available for fax requests. Turnaround time: 1-2 days. Add $6.00 for use of credit card and $23.50 for overnight delivery.

Workers' Compensation Records

Labor and Industry, Workers Compensation Division, Drawer 20, Montpelier, VT 05620-3401 (Courier address: National Life Bldg, Montpelier, VT 05602); 802-828-2286, 802-828-2195-Fax; 7:45AM-4:30PM.

www.labor.vermont.gov/sections/wcsafety/index.html

Records are available on site and can be New records are available for inquiry immediately. Records are indexed on inhouse computer. Records are normally destroyed after last activity after 13 years.

Searching: Must be a party to the claim or have a signed release from the claimant. You also will get only the employer's first report of injury. Include the following in your request-claimant name, Social Security Number, place of employment at time of accident. The following data is not released: medical records.

Access by: mail, fax, in person.

Fee & Payment: No search fee, copy fee is $.04 per page. Fee payee: State of Vermont. Personal checks accepted. No credit cards accepted.

Mail search: Turnaround time: 2 weeks. A SASE is requested.

Fax search: Turnaround time is 2 weeks.

In person search: Turnaround time is while you wait if staff is available.

Driver Records
Driver License Information

Department of Motor Vehicles, DI - Records Unit, 120 State St, Montpelier, VT 05603-0001; 802-828-2050, 802-828-2098-Fax; 7:45AM-4:30PM.

www.aot.state.vt.us/dmv/dmvhp.htm

Ticket information is available from the Vermont Judicial Bureau, PO Box 607, White River Junction, VT 05001, 802-295-8869. There is no charge, but no information is given over the phone.

Records are available for convictions and accidents. Records are sold as 3 year records or as complete (8+ years) records. It takes 5-7 days normally before new records are available for inquiry.

Searching: Ongoing permissible users must use Form TA-VG-118. Otherwise, use TA-VG-116 for written authorization from the subject to release personal information to the requester. Include the following in your request-name, DOB, signed release, if necessary. Mail or walk-in requesters need the driver's full name and DOB; the license number is optional. Online requesters need only the license number, but the last name and DOB are helpful. The following data is not released: addresses, Social Security Numbers, medical information or personal information (height, weight, sex, eye color, etc.).

Access by: mail, in person, online.

Fee & Payment: The charge is $8.00 for 3 year record and $16.00 for the "complete" record. There is a full charge for a "no record found." Fee payee: Vermont Department of Motor Vehicles. Prepayment required. Personal checks accepted. No credit cards accepted.

Mail search: Turnaround time: 5 to 7 days. A SASE is requested.

In person search: Normal turnaround time is while you wait.

Online search: Online access costs $8.00 per 3 year record. The system is called "GovNet." Two methods are offered-single inquiry and batch mode. The system is open 24 hours a day, 7 days a week (except for file maintenance periods). Only the license number is needed when ordering, but it is suggested to submit the name and DOB also. For more information, call Driver Improvement at 802-828-2053.

Other access: This agency will sell its license file to approved requesters, but customization is not available.

Vehicle Ownership
Vehicle Identification
Vessel Ownership
Vessel Registration

Department of Motor Vehicles, Registration & License Information/Records, 120 State St, Montpelier, VT 05603; 802-828-2000, 802-828-2872-Fax; 7:45AM-4:30PM (on Wed only 1PM-4:30PM).

www.dmv.state.vt.us

Ongoing permissible users must be authorized first. Occasional requesters must use form TA-VG 116. If record use is not "permissible" per DPPA, written authorization is needed from subject. Otherwise, records with no personal data are released.

Records are available from 09/71 to present. Vessel records go back to the 1989 and are removed after 14 years of inactivity. All motorized boats must be registered. It takes 1 to 3 weeks before new records are available for inquiry. Records are normally destroyed after 2 years 1 month after expiration.

Searching: Potential lien-holders are provided a "yes or no" answer when asked about liens on a record. You must have name and DOB or plate # or VIN. To receive personal information, you must include signed release by individual, unless ongoing account. Use of Vermont DMV Record Request Form is advised. The following data is not released: Social Security Numbers, residence addresses, bulk information or lists for commercial purposes or medical information.

Access by: mail, in person.

Fee & Payment: $6.00 for each group (1-4) of registration records and $20.00 for an ownership (lien) search. Vessel fees are different: registration check is $6.00, title search is $7.00 or with lien is $13.00. Extensive research is $35.00 per hour. Fee payee: Vermont Department of Motor Vehicles. Prepayment required. Personal checks accepted. No credit cards accepted.

Mail search: Turnaround time: 7 to 10 days. A SASE is requested.

In person search: The turnaround time is generally 30 minutes for vehicle records. Vessel records are returned by mail.

Other access: High volume requesters can obtain records via magnetic tape. Bulk release of the database is not available except for statistical purposes. Apply to the Commissioner's Office.

Accident Reports

Department of Motor Vehicles, Accident Report Section, 120 State St, Montpelier, VT 05603; 802-828-2050, 7:45AM-4PM.

www.dmv.state.vt.us

Records are available for 5 years to present. Only records involving damage in excess of $1,000 or if injuries involved are reportable. It takes 45 days after the incident before new records are available for inquiry.

Searching: Include the following in your request- full name, date of accident, location of accident. If accident involves a criminal action it may take up to 3 months after accident date to get the report. The following data is not released: Social Security Numbers.

Access by: mail, in person.

Fee & Payment: The fee for certified copies are $15.00 for the police report, $10.00 for a copy of the individual's report, and $6.00 for insurance information of the accident. Fee payee: Vermont Department of Motor Vehicles. Prepayment required. Personal checks accepted. No credit cards accepted.

Mail search: Turnaround time: 15 days. A SASE is requested.

In person search: Simple requests may be processed while you wait.

Voter Registration
Access to Records is Restricted.

Secretary of State, Election Division, 26 Terrace St, Montpelier, VT 05609-1101; 802-828-2464, 802-828-5171-Fax; 7:45AM-4:30PM.

http://vermont-elections.org/soshome.htm

Currently all records are kept at the municipal level. However, the Federal Help America Vote Act of 2002 (HAVA) law requires implementation of a central, computerized, statewide voter registration system by 01/01/2006. The state will comply.

GED Certificates

Department of Education, GED Testing, 120 State Street, Montpelier, VT 05620; 802-828-5161, 802-828-3146-Fax; 8AM-4:30PM.

www.vermontcareers.org

Records are available from 1941 Records are indexed on computer since 1997. Older records must be looked up on paper file.

Searching: Include the following in your request- name, date of birth, Social Security Number, signed release.

Access by: mail, phone, fax, in person.

Fee & Payment: The fee is $3.00 for a transcript copy. There is no fee for a simple verification. Fee payee: Treasurer, State of Vermont. Prepayment required. Personal checks accepted. No credit cards accepted.

Mail search: Turnaround time: 1 week.

Phone search: The agency will give a verification over the phone.

Fax search: You may use the fax to verify a GED, but not for a transcript purchase unless money previously sent.

In person search: If staff available, requests will be processed while you wait.

Expedited service: Rush service is available for emergency situations.

Hunting and Fishing License Information
Access to Records is Restricted.

Fish & Wildlife Department, Licensing Division, 103 South Main Street - Bldg 10 South, Waterbury, VT 05671-0501; 802-241-3700, 802-241-3295-Fax; 7:45AM-4:30PM.

www.vtfishandwildlife.com

Although they maintain a central database on computer, the records are not open to the public. Vendors forward records on a yearly basis (July).

Vermont State Licensing Agencies

For details about the agency responsible for licensing/certifying/registering an item below or in the Agency Quick Finder section, match an item's number with the number of the agency in the *Licensing Agency Information* section.

Vermont Licenses Searchable Online

Accounting Firm #15 ....www.vtprofessionals.org
Acupuncturist #15 ....www.vtprofessionals.org
Alcohol & Drug Abuse Counselor #18 ....www.vtcertificationboard.org/counselors2.htm
Anesthesiologist Assistant #14 ....www.healthyvermonters.info/bmp/bmp.shtml#data
Architect #15...www.vtprofessionals.org
Armed Courier #15..www.vtprofessionals.org
Athletic Trainer #15...www.vtprofessionals.org
Auctioneer #15..www.vtprofessionals.org
Bank #5..www.bishca.state.vt.us/BankingDiv/banking_index.htm
Barber #15 ....www.vtprofessionals.org
Body Piercer #15 ....www.vtprofessionals.org
Boxing Manager/Promoter #15 ....www.vtprofessionals.org
Boxing Professional #15 ....www.vtprofessionals.org
Chemical Suppression TQP Cert #8..............www.state.vt.us/labind/weblic/cstqpcert.htm
Chimney Sweep #8..www.state.vt.us/labind/weblic/cswtqpcert.htm
Chiropractor #15 ....www.vtprofessionals.org
Cosmetologist #15 ....www.vtprofessionals.org
Credit Union #5 ....www.bishca.state.vt.us/BankingDiv/banking_index.htm
Crematory #15 ....www.vtprofessionals.org
Dentist / Dental Assistant #15.......................www.vtprofessionals.org
Dental Hygienist #15.......................................www.vtprofessionals.org
Dietitian #15..www.vtprofessionals.org
Electrician #8 ....www.state.vt.us/labind/weblic/elicenses.htm
Electrologist #15 ....www.vtprofessionals.org
Embalmer #15...www.vtprofessionals.org
Engineer #15...www.vtprofessionals.org
Esthetician #15 ....www.vtprofessionals.org
Fire Alarm System Installer/Dealer #8 ....www.state.vt.us/labind/weblic/fatqpcert.htm
Fire Sprinkler System Designer #8 ....www.state.vt.us/labind/weblic/slicenses.htm
Fire Sprinkler System Installer #8 ....www.state.vt.us/labind/weblic/sstqpcert.htm
Funeral Director #15 ....www.vtprofessionals.org
Hearing Aid Dispenser #15 ....www.vtprofessionals.org
LPG/Propane Installer #8................................www.state.vt.us/labind/weblic/gpicert.htm
Manicurist #15...www.vtprofessionals.org
Marriage & Family Therapist #15...................www.vtprofessionals.org
Medical Doctor/Surgeon #14 ....www.healthyvermonters.info/bmp/bmp.shtml#data
Mental Health Counselor, Clinical #15...........www.vtprofessionals.org
Midwife, Licensed #15 ....www.vtprofessionals.org
Natural Gas System Installer #8 ....www.state.vt.us/labind/weblic/gnicert.htm
Naturopathic Physician #15 ....www.vtprofessionals.org
Notary Public #15..www.vtprofessionals.org
Nurse/Nurse Practitioner/LNA #15.................www.vtprofessionals.org
Nursing Home Administrator #15 ....www.vtprofessionals.org
Occupational Therapist #15 ....www.vtprofessionals.org
Oil Burning Equipment Installer #8 ....www.state.vt.us/labind/weblic/oicert.htm
Optician #15..www.vtprofessionals.org
Optometrist #15 ....www.vtprofessionals.org
Osteopathic Physician #15 ....www.vtprofessionals.org
Pharmacist / Pharmacy #15...........................www.vtprofessionals.org
Photographer, Itinerant #15 ....www.vtprofessionals.org
Physical Therapist/Assistant #15 ....www.vtprofessionals.org
Physician Assistant #14 ....www.healthyvermonters.info/bmp/bmp.shtml#data
Plumber #8..www.state.vt.us/labind/weblic/plicenses.htm
Podiatrist #14 ....www.healthyvermonters.info/bmp/bmp.shtml#data

Private Investigator #15	www.vtprofessionals.org
Psychoanalyst #15	www.vtprofessionals.org
Psychologist/Psychotherapist #15	www.vtprofessionals.org
Public Accountant-CPA #15	www.vtprofessionals.org
Race Driver/Track Personnel #15	www.vtprofessionals.org
Racing Promoter #15	www.vtprofessionals.org
Radiologic Technologist #15	www.vtprofessionals.org
Real Estate Agent/Broker/Seller #12	www.vtprofessionals.org/
Real Estate Appraiser #12	www.vtprofessionals.org/
Security Guard #15	www.vtprofessionals.org
Social Worker, Clinical #15	www.vtprofessionals.org
Surveyor, Land #15	www.vtprofessionals.org
Tattoo Artist #15	www.vtprofessionals.org
Vendor, Itinerant #15	www.vtprofessionals.org
Veterinarian #15	www.vtprofessionals.org
Waste Water Plant Operator #1	www.anr.state.vt.us/dec/ww/opcert.htm

Vermont Licensing Quick Finder

Accounting Firm #15	802-828-2363
Acupuncturist #15	802-828-2363
Alcohol & Drug Abuse Counselor #18	802-878-7776
Anesthesiologist Assistant #14	802-657-4223
Architect #15	802-828-2363
Armed Courier #15	802-828-2363
Asbestos Abatement Contr/Worker #13	802-863-7231
Athletic Trainer #15	802-828-2363
Attorney #2	802-828-3281
Auctioneer #15	802-828-2363
Bank #5	802-828-3307
Barber #15	802-828-2363
Body Piercer #15	802-828-2363
Boiler & Pressure Vessel Inspector #9	802-879-2304
Boxing Manager/Promoter #15	802-828-2363
Boxing Professional #15	802-828-2363
Chemical Suppression TQP Cert #8	802-828-2107
Chimney Sweep #8	802-828-2107
Chiropractor #15	802-828-2363
Cosmetologist #15	802-828-2363
Credit Union #5	802-828-3307
Crematory #15	802-828-2363
Dealer/Repairer Weighing & Measuring Devices #4	802-244-4510
Dentist / Dental Assistant #15	802-828-2363
Dental Hygienist #15	802-828-2363
Dietitian #15	802-828-2363
Driver Training Instructor #11	802-828-2114
Driving Instructor/School, Commercial #11	802-828-2114
Electrician #8	802-828-2107
Electrologist #15	802-828-2363
Elevator Mechanic/Inspector #8	802-828-0743
Embalmer #15	802-828-2363
Emergency Care Attendant #7	802-863-7310
Emergency Medical Technician #7	802-863-7310
Engineer #15	802-828-2363
Esthetician #15	802-828-2363
Fire Alarm System Installer/Dealer #8	802-828-2107
Fire Sprinkler System Designer #8	802-828-2107
Fire Sprinkler System Installer #8	802-828-2107
Funeral Director #15	802-828-2363
Hearing Aid Dispenser #15	802-828-2363
Horse Racing Trainers/Owners/Professional #17	802-786-5050
Insurance Adjuster #5	802-828-3303
Insurance Agent/Consultant/Broker #5	802-828-3303
Insurance Appraiser #5	802-828-3303
Investment Advisor #5	802-828-3420
Issuer Agent #5	802-828-3420
Lead Abatement Contrac'r/Worker #13	802-863-7231
Lightning Rod Installer/Dealer #8	802-828-2107
Liquor, Retail/Wholesale #10	802-828-2339
Livestock Dealer #4	802-828-2421
Lottery Retailer #16	802-479-5686
LPG/Propane Installer #8	802-828-2107
Manicurist #15	802-828-2363
Marriage & Family Therapist #15	802-828-2363
Meat Inspection Laboratory #4	802-244-4510
Medical Doctor/Surgeon #14	802-657-4223
Mental Health Counselor, Clinical #15	802-828-2363
Midwife, Licensed #15	802-828-2363
Milk & Cream Tester #4	802-244-4510
Natural Gas System Installer #8	802-828-2107
Naturopathic Physician #15	802-828-2363
Notary Public #15	802-828-2363
Nurse/Nurse Practitioner/LNA #15	802-828-2363
Nursing Home Administrator #15	802-828-2363
Occupational Therapist #15	802-828-2363
Oil Burning Equipment Installer #8	802-828-2107
Optician #15	802-828-2363
Optometrist #15	802-828-2363
Osteopathic Physician #15	802-828-2363
Pari-Mutuel Seller #17	802-786-5050
Pesticide Applicator #4	802-828-3475
Pharmacist / Pharmacy #15	802-828-2363
Photographer, Itinerant #15	802-828-2363
Physical Therapist/Assistant #15	802-828-2363
Physician Assistant #14	802-657-4223
Plumber #8	802-828-2107
Podiatrist #14	802-657-4223
Polygraph Examiner #3	802-244-5354
Private Investigator #15	802-828-2363
Psychoanalyst #15	802-828-2363
Psychologist/Psychotherapist #15	802-828-2363
Public Accountant-CPA #15	802-828-2363
Public Adjuster #5	802-828-3303
Race Driver/Track Personnel #15	802-828-2363
Racing Promoter #15	802-828-2363
Radiologic Technologist #15	802-828-2363
Real Estate Agent/Broker/Sales #12	802-828-3228
Real Estate Appraiser #12	802-828-3228
School Guidance Counselor #6	802-828-2445
School Librarian/Media Specialist #6	802-828-2445
School Principal/Superintendent #6	802-828-2445
Securities Broker/Dealer #5	802-828-3420
Securities Sales Rep. #5	802-828-3420
Security Guard #15	802-828-2363
Social Worker, Clinical #15	802-828-2363
Surveyor, Land #15	802-828-2363
Tattoo Artist #15	802-828-2363
Teacher #6	802-828-2445
Vehicle Dealer #11	802-828-2038
Vendor, Itinerant #15	802-828-2363
Veterinarian #15	802-828-2363
Vocational Education Teacher #6	802-828-2445
Waste Water Treatment Plant Operator #1	802-241-3822

Vermont Licensing Agency Information

1 Agency of Natural Resources, Department of Environmental Conservation, 103 S Main St, The Sewing Bldg, Waterbury, VT 05671-0405; 802-241-3822, Fax: 802-241-2596. www.anr.state.vt.us

2 Board of Bar Examiners, 2418 Airport Rd, #2, Barre, VT 05641; 802-828-3281, Fax: 802-828-1695. www.vermontjudiciary.org Email: licensing@mail.crt.state.vt.us Note: They do not sell mailing lists.

3 Commission of Public Safety, 103 S Main St, Waterbury State Complex, Waterbury, VT 05671-2101; 802-244-8781, Fax: 802-241-5420. www.dps.state.vt.us/

4 Department of Agriculture, Consumer Assurance, 103 S Main St, Waterbury, VT 05671; 802-244-4510, Fax: 802-241-3008. www.vermontagriculture.com

5 Department of Banking, Securities, Insurance & Health Care Admin., 89 Main St, City Ctr, Drawer 20, Montpelier, VT 05620-3101; 802-828-3301, Fax: 802-828-3306. www.bishca.state.vt.us

6 Department of Education, Licening Professional Standards, 120 State St, Montpelier, VT 05620-2501; 802-828-2445, Fax: 802-828-5107. www.state.vt.us/educ/new/html/maincert.html Email: licensing@doe.state.vt.us

7 Department of Health, Emergency Medical Services Division, 108 Cherry St, (PO Box 70, 05402-0070), Burlington, VT 05402; 802-863-7310, Fax: 802-863-7577. www.vermontems.org

8 Department of Public Safety, Division of Fire Safety, 1311 US Route 302- Berlin #600, Barre, VT 05641-2351; 802-828-2106, Fax: 802-828-2195. www.state.vt.us/labind/fpindex.htm Email: fireinfo@labind.state.vt.us

9 Department of Labor & Industry, Fire Prevention Division - Boiler Inspector, 372 Hurricane Ln #102, Williston, VT 05495-2080; 802-879-2304, Fax: 802-879-2312. www.state.vt.us/labind/ Email: malcolm.wheel@labind.state.vt.us

10 Department of Liquor Control, PO Drawer 20, (13 Green Mountain Dr), Montpelier, VT 05620-4501; 802-828-2345, Fax: 802-828-2803. www.state.vt.us/dlc/

11 Department of Motor Vehicles, 120 State St, Montpelier, VT 05603; 802-828-2114, Fax: 802-828-2092. www.dmv.state.vt.us

12 Real Estate Commission, 81 Riverside St., Heritage Bldg, Montpelier, VT 05609-1106; 802-828-3228, Fax: 802-828-2368. www.sec.state.vt.us Email: real_estate@sec.state.vt.us Search Database at www.vtprofessionals.org/

13 Department of Health, Environmental Health, PO Box 70, (108 Cherry St), Burlington, VT 05402; 802-863-7200, Fax: 802-863-7754. www.state.vt.us/health

14 Board of Medical Practice, Department of Health, PO Box 70 (108 Cherry St), Burlington, VT 05402-0070; 802-657-4220 (800-745-7371 within Vermont), Fax: 802-657-4227. www.healthyvermonters.info/bmp/bmp.shtml Email: medicalboard@vdh.state.vt.us Search Database at www.healthyvermonters.info/bmp/bmp.shtml Note: Written verifications are available for $20 each; it is suggested to search files (dbf, delimited or excel) at the website, although seraching is also available from a private company at www.docboard.org/vt/df/vtsearch.htm.

15 Secretary of State, Office of Professional Regulation, 26 Terrace St, Drawer 09, Montpelier, VT 05609-1106; 802-828-2363, Fax: 802-828-2496. www.sec.state.vt.us Email: docketclerk@sec.state.vt.us Search Database at www.vtprofessionals.org

16 Lottery Commission, 1311 US Route 302-Berlin, Barre, VT 05641; 802-479-5686, Fax: 802-479-4294. www.vtlottery.com

17 Racing Commission, 88 Merchants Row #500, Rutland, VT 05701-3449; 802-786-5050, Fax: 802-786-5051.

18 Alcohol & Drug Abuse Certification Board, PO Box 135, St. Albans, VT 05478-0135; 802-878-7776, Fax: 802-879-6211. www.vtcertificationboard.org/ Email: vadacb@together.net Search Database at www.vtcertificationboard.org/counselors2.htm

Vermont Federal Courts

The following list indicates the district and division name for each county in the state. If the bankruptcy court location is different from the district court, then the location of the bankruptcy court appears in parentheses.

Vermont County/Court Cross Reference

Addison	Rutland	Lamoille	Burlington (Rutland)
Bennington	Rutland	Orange	Rutland
Caledonia	Burlington (Rutland)	Orleans	Burlington (Rutland)
Chittenden	Burlington (Rutland)	Rutland	Rutland
Essex	Burlington (Rutland)	Washington	Burlington (Rutland)
Franklin	Burlington (Rutland)	Windham	Rutland
Grand Isle	Burlington (Rutland)	Windsor	Rutland

Standards for Federal Courts: Search fee is $26.00 per item (one party name or case number). Copy fee is $.50 per page. Certification fee is $9.00 per document, double for exemplification, if available. All fees standard unless noted in profile. Mail Search: always enclose a stamped self addressed envelope unless otherwise noted. Most courts accept fax requests or will suggest a copying/search vendor. Before releasing records, all courts require prepayment, unless noted.

Open records are located at the court unless otherwise noted. District courts index by defendant and plaintiff as well as by case number. Bankruptcy courts usually index by debtor and case number. While most courts now have their indexes on computer, many may still maintain index card files as well.

Courts offering internet access via CM-ECF or older RACER, PACER, or Web-PACER systems charge $.08 per page fee unless noted as free. Where PACER is available, the universal sign-up number is 800-676-6856. Find PACER and the US Party/Case Index at http://pacer.psc.uscourts.gov.

US District Court

District of Vermont

Burlington Division Clerk's Office, PO Box 945, Burlington, VT 05402-0945 (courier address: Rm 506, 11 Elmwood Ave, Burlington, VT 05401), 802-951-6301. Hours- 8:30AM-5PM. www.vtd.uscourts.gov

Counties: Caledonia, Chittenden, Essex, Franklin, Grand Isle, Lamoille, Orleans, Washington. However, cases from all Vermont counties are randomly assigned to either Burlington or Rutland. Brattleboro is a hearing location only, not listed in this database.

Searches & Indexing: Both computer and card indexes maintained. New cases filed back to 1/1991 are on the automated in house system. Pre-1991 cases indexed on microfiche or microfilm. Effective 1/2005, court scans all documents into its electronic case file system; fully computerized

1/1/06. New cases in the index 1 working day after filing date. Open records only available on computer. District-wide computer searches available from both Division locations.

Fee & Payment: Pay by money order, cashier's or personal check. Payee: Clerk, US District Court. Prepayment required.

Phone Search: Only general information accessed by computer is released via phone.

Mail Search: search usually completed- 1 day. Include SASE for return.

In Person Search: Fee charged if court performs your search. Self-serve copier - $.50 per page.

E-Services: Login to RACER at https://pacer.login.uscourts.gov/cgi-bin/login.pl?court_id=r_vtdc. PACER records go back to 1/1991. New records online after 1 day. ECF at https://ecf.vtd.uscourts.gov **Opinions Online:** http://nysd.uscourts.gov/cwrulings.fwx?mode=rptform&cascode=D02VTXC. Filings of interest free at www.vtd.uscourts.gov/Decisions.html. **Other Online Access:** Search monthly court calendar at www.vtd.uscourts.gov/Calendars.htm.

Rutland Division Court Clerk, PO Box 607, Rutland, VT 05702-0607 (courier address: 151 West St, Rutland, VT 05701), 802-773-0245. Hours- 8:30AM-5:30PM. www.vtd.uscourts.gov

Counties: Addison, Bennington, Orange, Rutland, Windsor, Windham. However, cases from all Vermont counties are randomly assigned to either Burlington or Rutland. Brattleboro is a hearing location only, not listed in this database.

Searches & Indexing: Computer index maintained; criminal back to 2000, civil to 1995. New cases filed back to 1/1991 are on the automated in house system. Pre-1991 cases indexed on microfiche or microfilm. New cases in the index 1 day after filing date. Records purged never. District-wide computer searches available from both Division locations. No judge sits in Rutland itself, but one is in Brattleboro.

Fee & Payment: Pay by money order, cashier check, personal or business check. Payee: Clerk, US District Court. Prepayment required.

Phone Search: Only docket information available by phone.

Mail Search: search usually completed- 1-2 weeks. Include SASE for return.

In Person Search: Fee charged if court performs your search. Self-serve copier - $.50 per page.

E-Services: Login to PACER at https://pacer.login.uscourts.gov/cgi-bin/login.pl?court_id=r_vtdc. PACER records go back to 1/1991. New records online after 1 day. ECF at https://ecf.vtd.uscourts.gov **Opinions Online:** http://nysd.uscourts.gov/cwrulings.fwx?mode=rptform&cascode=D02VTXC. Filings of interest free at www.vtd.uscourts.gov/Decisions.html. **Other Online Access:** Search monthly court calendar at www.vtd.uscourts.gov/Calendars.htm.

US Bankruptcy Court

District of Vermont

Division Court Clerk, PO Box 6648, Rutland, VT 05702-6648 (courier address: 67 Merchants Row, Rutland, VT 05701), 802-776-2000, Fax-802-776-2020. Hours- 8AM-5PM. www.vtb.uscourts.gov

Counties: All counties in Vermont.

Searches & Indexing: Cases indexed by debtor, creditors, and case number. Results include last 4 SSN digits. Computer index maintained. New cases in the index immediately after filing date. Records purged never.

Fee & Payment: Pay by Visa/MC, money order, cashier's or personal check, cash. Payee: US Bankruptcy Court. Prepayment required. Copy fees apply to faxed dockets.

Phone Search: Basic docket data is available by phone. Voice Case Information Service available, call VCIS at 800-260-9956 or 802-776-2007.

Mail Search: search usually completed- 1-2 days. SASE not required.

In Person Search: Fee charged if court performs your search. No self-serve copier available.

E-Services: ECF replaces PACER. Document images available. PACER records go back to 1992; limited information prior. New records online after 1 day. ECF at https://ecf.vtb.uscourts.gov **Opinions Online:** www.vtb.uscourts.gov/opinions.html. **Other Online Access:** Calendars on main website.

Vermont County Courts

Court	Jurisdiction	No. of Courts	How Organized
Superior Courts*	General	11	14 Counties
District Courts*	Limited	11	3 Circuits
Combined Courts*		3	
Probate Courts*	Probate	18	
Family Courts	Special	14	14 Counties
Environmental Court	Special	1	

* Profiled in this Sourcebook.

Court	CIVIL								
	Tort	Contract	Real Estate	Min. Claim	Max. Claim	Small Claims	Estate	Eviction	Domestic Relations
Superior Courts*	X	X	X	$0	No Max	$3500		X	
District Courts*									
Probate Courts*							X		
Family Courts									X

Court	CRIMINAL				
	Felony	Misdemeanor	DWI/DUI	Preliminary Hearing	Juvenile
Superior Courts*					
District Courts*	X	X	X	X	
Family Courts					X

ADMINISTRATION Administrative Office of Courts, Court Administrator, 109 State St, Montpelier, VT, 05609-0701; 802-828-3278, Fax: 802-828-3457. www.vermontjudiciary.org

COURT STRUCTURE As of September, 1996, all small claims came under the jurisdiction of Superior Court, the court of general jurisdiction. All counties have a diversion program in which first offenders go through a process that includes a letter of apology, community service, etc. and, after 2 years, the record is expunged. These records are never released.

The Vermont Judicial Bureau has jurisdiction over Traffic, Municipal Ordinance, and Fish and Game, Minors in Possession, and hazing.

ONLINE ACCESS Vermont Courts Online provides access to cases 12 of the counties' District, Family, and Superior Courts. It provides court calendar information for each court and detailed case information for Superior Court. Not available for Chittenden and Franklin counties. Criminal records are not included. Go to https://secure.vermont.gov/vtcdas/user. Records are in reat-time mode. There is a $10.00 registration fee plus a fee of $.50 per case for look-up.

Supreme Court opinions are available from the main web site and are also maintained by the Vermont Department of Libraries at http://dol.state.vt.us.

ADDITIONAL INFORMATION There are statewide search, certification and copy fees, as follows: Search fee - $10.00 per name; Certification Fee - $5.00 per document plus copy fee; Copy Fee - $.25 per page with a $1.00 minimum.

Addison County

Superior Court 7 Mahady Ct, Middlebury, VT 05753; phone: 802-388-7741; fax: 802-388-4621; hours 8:30AM-4:30PM (EST). *Civil, Eviction, Small Claims.*
Civil Records: Access: Fax, mail, in person, online. Only the court performs in person searches; visitors may not. No search fee. Court makes copy: $.25 per page. Required to search: name, years to search. Civil cases indexed by defendant, plaintiff.

Civil records on index cards and recording books, computerized since 1995. Access by internet subscription, $10 activation plus $.50 per page; registration info at https://secure.vermont.gov/vtcdas/user. Mail turnaround time 2-3 days.
General Information: No sealed or unserved records released. Certification fee: $5.00 per doc. Payee: Addison Superior Court. Personal checks accepted. Prepayment required.

District Court 7 Mahady Ct, Middlebury, VT 05753; phone: 802-388-4237; hours 8AM-4:30PM (EST). *Felony, Misdemeanor.*
www.vermontjudiciary.org/courts/district/index.htm
Criminal Records: Access: Mail, in person. Only the court performs in person searches; visitors may not. Search fee: $10.00 per name. Court makes copy: $.25 per page, $1.00 minimum. Required to search: name, years to search, DOB. Criminal records on computer since mid 1991; prior on dockets and index

cards. Current calendars at website. Mail turnaround time up to 1 week.

General Information: No adoptions, juvenile, sealed, or expunged records released. Certification fee: $5.00 per doc. Payee: Addison District Court. Personal checks accepted. Prepayment required.

Probate Court 7 Mahady Ct, Middlebury, VT 05753; phone: 802-388-2612; hours 8AM-4:30PM (EST). *Probate.*

Bennington County

Superior Court 207 South St, PO Box 4157, Bennington, VT 05201; phone: 802-447-2700; criminal phone: 802-447-2727; fax: 802-447-2703; hours 8AM-4:30PM (EST). *Civil, Eviction, Small Claims.*

Civil Records: Access: Fax, phone, mail, in person, online. Both court and visitors may perform in person searches. No search fee. Court makes copy: $.25 per page. Required to search: name, years to search. Civil cases indexed by defendant, plaintiff. Civil records on computer from 1989, index from 1968. Access by internet subscription, $10 activation plus $.50 per page; registration info at https://secure.vermont.gov/vtcdas/user. Mail turnaround time 2-3 days.

General Information: No deposition, adoption, juvenile, sealed or expunged records released. Certification fee: $5.00 per doc. Payee: Bennington County. Personal checks accepted. Prepayment required.

District Court 200 Veterans Memorial Dr, #13, Bennington, VT 05201; phone: 802-447-2727; fax: 802-447-2750; hours 7:45AM-4:30PM (EST). *Felony, Misdemeanor.*
www.vermontjudiciary.org/courts/district/index.htm
Criminal Records: Access: Mail, in person. Both court and visitors may perform in person searches. Search fee: $10.00 per name. Court makes copy: $.25 per page. $1.00 minimum. Required to search: name, years to search, DOB. Criminal records on index cards, docket books, and computer. Current calendars at website. Mail turnaround time varies.

General Information: Public terminal has only criminal records. No sealed, diversion case records released. Will fax documents to toll free line. Certification fee: $5.00. Payee: Vermont District Court. Personal checks accepted. Prepayment required. SASE requested.

Probate Court - Bennington District 207 South St, PO Box 65, Bennington, VT 05201; phone: 802-447-2705; fax: 802-447-2703; hours 8AM-N, 1-4pm (EST). *Probate.*
Note: Fax to "Attention Probate Court."

Probate Court - Manchester District PO Box 446, 3588 Main St, Manchester, VT 05254; phone: 802-362-1410; hours 8AM-N, 1-4:20PM (EST). *Probate.*

Caledonia County

Superior Court 1126 Main St, #1, St Johnsbury, VT 05819; phone: 802-748-6600; fax: 802-748-6603; hours 8AM-4:30PM (EST). *Civil, Eviction, Small Claims.*

Civil Records: Access: Phone, mail, in person, online. Only the court performs in person searches; visitors may not. No search fee. Court makes copy: superior court $1.00 minimum; family court $.25 per page, $1.00 minimum. Required to search: name, years to search. Civil cases indexed by defendant, plaintiff. Civil records on computer from 1992, in archives before 1985, index from 1985, all other records on index cards. Access by internet subscription, $10 activation plus $.50 per page; registration info at https://secure.vermont.gov/vtcdas/user. Mail turnaround time 1 week.

General Information: No adoption, juvenile, sealed or expunged records released. Will fax documents $2.00 per page. Certification fee: $5.00 plus $.25 per page. Payee: Caledonia Superior Court. Personal

checks accepted. Prepayment required. SASE requested.

District Court 1126 Main St, #1, St Johnsbury, VT 05819; phone: 802-748-6600; fax: 802-748-6603; hours 8AM-4:30PM (EST). *Felony, Misdemeanor.*
www.vermontjudiciary.org/courts/district/index.htm
Criminal Records: Access: Fax, mail, in person. Both court and visitors may perform in person searches. Search fee: $10.00 per name. Court makes copy: $.25 per page; $1.00 minimum. Required to search: name, years to search; also helpful: DOB. Criminal records on computer since 1991, prior on index cards to 1950. Current calendars at website. Mail turnaround time less than 1 week.

General Information: No adoptions, juvenile, sealed or expunged records released. Will fax documents $2.00 per page. Certification fee: $5.00 per doc. Payee: Caledonia District Court. Personal checks accepted. Prepayment required.

Probate Court 1126 Main St, PO Box 406, St Johnsbury, VT 05819; phone: 802-748-6605; fax: 802-748-6603; hours 8AM-4:30PM (EST). *Probate.*

Chittenden County

Superior Court PO Box 187, 175 Main St, Burlington, VT 05402; phone: 802-863-3467; hours 8AM-4:30PM (EST). *Civil, Eviction, Small Claims.*
www.chittendensuperiorcourt.com/
Civil Records: Access: Phone, mail, in person, online. Only the court performs in person searches; visitors may not. No search fee. Court makes copy: $.25 per page. $1.00 minimum. Required to search: name, years to search. Civil cases indexed by defendant, plaintiff. Civil records on computer back to 1983, small claims since 1996, prior records on books from 1800s. The web page offers online access to court case information on cases filed in the last five years. Mail turnaround time 1 week.

General Information: No adoption, juvenile, sealed or expunged records released. Certification fee: $5.00. Payee: Chittenden County Superior Court. Personal checks accepted. Prepayment required.

District Court 32 Cherry St, #300, Burlington, VT 05401; phone: 802-651-1800; hours 8AM-4:30PM (EST). *Felony, Misdemeanor.*
Criminal Records: Access: Mail, in person. Both court and visitors may perform in person searches. Search fee: $10.00 per name. Court makes copy: $.25 per page, $1.00 minimum. Required to search: name, years to search; also helpful: DOB. Criminal records on new computer from 6/90, on old computer from 6/85 to 6/90, books by alpha name from 12/69 to 1980, on index cards from 1970. Mail turnaround time 1-2 days.

General Information: Public terminal has only criminal records back to 6/1990. No adoption, juvenile, sealed or expunged records released. Certification fee: $5.00. Payee: Vermont District Court. Personal checks accepted. Prepayment required.

Probate Court PO Box 511, 175 Main St, Burlington, VT 05402; phone: 802-651-1518; hours 8AM-4:30PM; till 4pm F (EST). *Probate.*

Essex County

District & Superior Court Box 75, Guildhall, VT 05905; phone: 802-676-3910; fax: 802-676-3463; hours 8AM-4:30PM (EST). *Felony, Misdemeanor, Civil, Eviction, Small Claims.*
www.vermontjudiciary.org/courts/district/index.htm
Civil Records: Access: Phone, fax, mail, in person. Only the court performs in person searches; visitors may not. No search fee. Court makes copy: $.25 per page. $1.00 minimum. Required to search: name, years to search. Civil cases indexed by defendant, plaintiff. Civil records indexed from 1974; on computer from 5/94. Calendar information on website. Will not accept phone requests for more than 2 names. Mail turnaround time 1 week.

Criminal Records: Access: Mail, in person. Only the court performs in person searches; visitors may not. Search fee: $10.00 per name. Court makes copy: $.25 per page. $1.00 minimum. Required to search: name, years to search, DOB. Criminal records indexed from 1974; on computer from 5/94. Current calendars at website. Mail turnaround time 1 week.

General Information: No adoptions, juvenile, sealed or expunged records released. Will fax documents $1.00 per page. Certification fee: $5.00. Payee: Depends on court (Superior or District). Only cashiers checks and money orders accepted. Prepayment and SASE required.

Probate Court PO Box 426, 49 Mill St Ext., Island Pond, VT 05846; phone: 802-723-4770; fax: 802-723-4770; hours 8:30AM-N, 1-3:30PM (EST). *Probate.*

Franklin County

Superior Court Box 808, Church St, St Albans, VT 05478; phone: 802-524-3863; fax: 802-524-7996; hours 8AM-4:30PM (EST). *Civil, Eviction, Small Claims.*
Civil Records: Access: Mail, in person. Only the court performs in person searches; visitors may not. No search fee. Court makes copy: $.25 per page. $1.00 minimum. Required to search: name, years to search; or by docket number. Civil cases indexed by defendant, plaintiff. Civil records on computer since 1996; prior on index cards from 1840. Mail turnaround time 1 week.

General Information: No adoption, juvenile, sealed or expunged records released. Certification fee: $5.00. Payee: Franklin Superior Court. Personal checks accepted. Prepayment and SASE required.

District Court 36 Lake St, St Albans, VT 05478; phone: 802-524-7997; fax: 802-524-7946; hours 8AM-4:30PM (EST). *Felony, Misdemeanor.*
www.vermontjudiciary.org/courts/district/index.htm
Criminal Records: Access: Mail, in person. Both court and visitors may perform in person searches. Search fee: $10.00 per name. Court makes copy: $.25 per page. Required to search: name, years to search; also helpful: DOB, SSN. Criminal records on computer since 1987. Current calendars at website. Note: Court will perform in person searches only if time permits. Mail turnaround time 7-10 days.

General Information: Public terminal has only criminal records back to 1990. No adoption, juvenile, sealed or expunged records released. Fee to fax documents is $1.00 per document and $.25 per page. Certification fee: $5.00 per doc. Payee: Vermont District Court. Personal checks accepted. Prepayment and SASE required.

Franklin Probate Court 17 Church St, St Albans, VT 05478; phone: 802-524-4112; fax: 802-524-7996; hours 8AM-N, 1-4:30PM (EST). *Probate.*

Grand Isle County

District & Superior Court PO Box 7, North Hero, VT 05474; phone: 802-372-8350; fax: 802-372-3221; hours 8AM-4:30PM (EST). *Felony, Misdemeanor, Civil, Eviction, Small Claims.*
www.vermontjudiciary.org/courts/district/index.htm
Civil Records: Access: Phone, fax, mail, in person. Both court and visitors may perform in person searches. No search fee. Court makes copy: $.25 per page. $1.00 minimum. Required to search: name, years to search. Civil cases indexed by defendant, plaintiff. Civil records on computer from 1990, on index 1940, in-house from 1970. Mail turnaround time 1-2 days.

Criminal Records: Access: Phone, fax, mail, in person. Both court and visitors may perform in person searches. Search fee: $10.00 per name. Court makes copy: $.25 per page. $1.00 minimum. Required to search: name, years to search; also helpful: DOB, SSN. Criminal records on computer from 1990, on index from 1940, in-house from 1979. Current calendars at website. Mail turnaround time 1-2 days.

General Information: No adoption, juvenile, sealed or expunged records released. Will not fax documents. Certification fee: $5.25. Payee: Grand Isle Superior or District Court. Personal checks accepted. Prepayment required.

Probate Court PO Box 7, 3677 US Route 2, North Hero, VT 05474; phone: 802-372-8350; fax: 802-372-3221; hours 8AM-4:30PM (EST). *Probate.*

Lamoille County

Superior Court Box 490, Hyde Park, VT 05655; phone: 802-888-2207; hours 8AM-Noon; 12:30-4:30PM (EST). *Civil, Eviction, Small Claims.*
Civil Records: Access: Mail, in person, online. Only the court performs in person searches; visitors may not. No search fee. Court makes copy: $.25 per page. Required to search: name, years to search. Civil cases indexed by defendant, plaintiff. Civil records on computer from 1989, index from 1970s. Access by internet subscription, $10 activation plus $.50 per page; registration information at https://secure.vermont.gov/vtcdas/user. Mail turnaround time 1 week.
General Information: No adoption, juvenile, sealed or expunged records released. Will not fax documents. Certification fee: $5.00 per doc. Payee: Lamoille Superior Court. Personal checks accepted. Prepayment and SASE required.

District Court PO Box 489, Hyde Park, VT 05655-0489; phone: 802-888-3887; civil phone: 802-888-2207; probate phone: 802-888-3306; fax: 802-888-2591; hours 8AM-4:30PM (EST). *Felony, Misdemeanor.*
www.vermontjudiciary.org/courts/district/index.htm
Criminal Records: Access: Mail, in person. Only the court performs in person searches; visitors may not. Search fee: $10.00 per name. Court makes copy: $.25 per page; $1.00 minimum. Required to search: name, DOB; also helpful: years to search. Criminal records on computer since 6/88; prior on index cards. Current calendars at website. Mail turnaround time 3 days if record on-site; 1 week if off-site.
General Information: No adoption, juvenile, sealed or expunged records released. Will fax documents to toll free or local lines only. Certification fee: $5.00 per document. Payee: Vermont District Court. Personal checks accepted. Prepayment and SASE required.

Probate Court PO Box 102, 154 Main St, Hyde Park, VT 05655-0102; phone: 802-888-3306; fax: 802-888-0669; hours 8AM-Noon, 12:30-4:30PM (EST). *Probate.*

Orange County

District & Superior Court 5 Court St, Chelsea, VT 05038-9746; phone: 802-685-4610; fax: 802-685-3173; hours 8AM-4:30PM (EST). *Felony, Misdemeanor, Civil, Eviction, Small Claims.*
www.vermontjudiciary.org/courts/district/index.htm
Civil Records: Access: Fax, mail, in person. Only the court performs in person searches; visitors may not. No search fee. Court makes copy: $.25 per page. $1.00 minimum. Required to search: name, years to search; also helpful: address. Civil cases indexed by defendant, plaintiff. Civil records on computer from 7/94, on index from 1967. Mail turnaround time 1 week.
Criminal Records: Access: Phone, fax, mail, in person. Only the court performs in person searches; visitors may not. Search fee: $10.00 per name. Court makes copy: $.25 per page. $1.00 minimum. Required to search: name, years to search, DOB; also helpful: address. Criminal records on computer from 1990, on index from 1967. Current calendars at website. Mail turnaround time 1 week.
General Information: No adoption, juvenile, sealed or expunged records released. Fee to fax documents is $1.00 per page. Certification fee: $5.00 per doc. Payee: District Court. Personal checks accepted. Prepayment required.

Probate Court 5 Court St, Chelsea, VT 05038-9746; phone: 802-685-4610; fax: 802-685-3246; hours 8AM-4:30PM (EST). *Probate.*
Note: The Bradford and Randolph Districts were consolidated into this one probate court as of June 1, 1994.

Orleans County

Superior Court 247 Main St, #1, Newport, VT 05855-1203; phone: 802-334-3344; fax: 802-334-3385; hours 8AM-4:30PM (EST). *Civil, Eviction, Small Claims.*
Civil Records: Access: Phone, fax, mail, in person, online. Only the court performs in person searches; visitors may not. No search fee. Court makes copy: $.25 per page. $1.00 minimum. Required to search: name; also helpful: years to search. Civil cases indexed by defendant, plaintiff. Civil records on computer since 1994; prior records on index from 1800s. Access by internet subscription, $10 activation plus $.50 per page; registration info at https://secure.vermont.gov/vtcdas/user. Mail turnaround time 1 week.
General Information: No juvenile records released. Certification fee: $5.00. Payee: Orleans Superior Court. Personal checks accepted. Prepayment and SASE required.

District Court 217 Main St, #4, Newport, VT 05855; phone: 802-334-3325; hours 8AM-4:30PM (EST). *Felony, Misdemeanor.*
www.vermontjudiciary.org/courts/district/index.htm
Criminal Records: Access: Mail. Only the court performs in person searches; visitors may not. Search fee: $10.00 per name. Court makes copy: $1.00 minimum; add $4.00 if copies retrieved from public records. Self serve copy fee: $.25 per page. Required to search: name, years to search, DOB. Criminal records on computer since 1/91; prior on index cards back to 1971. Current calendars at website. Mail turnaround time 1 week.
General Information: Public terminal has only criminal records back to 1971. No adoption, juvenile, sealed or expunged records released. Will fax documents to an "800" number. Above fees apply. Certification fee: $5.00. Payee: District Court of Vermont. Personal checks accepted. Prepayment and SASE required.

Probate Court 247 Main St, Newport, VT 05855; phone: 802-334-3366; fax: 802-334-3385; hours 8AM-N, 1-4PM (EST). *Probate.*

Rutland County

Superior Court 83 Center St, Rutland, VT 05701; phone: 802-775-4394; fax: 802-775-2291; 8AM-4:30PM (EST). *Civil, Eviction, Small Claims.*
Civil Records: Access: Mail, in person, online. Only the court performs in person searches; visitors may not. No search fee. Court makes copy: $.25 per page; $1.00 minimum. Self serve copy fee: $.25 per page. Required to search: name, years to search. Civil cases indexed by defendant, plaintiff. Civil records on computer from 1987, on index from late 1700s. Access by internet subscription, $10 activation plus $.50 per page; registration info at https://secure.vermont.gov/vtcdas/user. Mail turnaround time 1 week.
General Information: No adoption, juvenile, sealed or expunged records released. Will fax documents to local or toll free line. Certification fee: $5.00 per document. Payee: Rutland Superior Court. Personal checks accepted. Prepayment and SASE required.

District Court 9 Merchants Row, Rutland, VT 05701-2886; phone: 802-786-5880; hours 8AM-4:30PM (EST). *Felony, Misdemeanor.*
www.vermontjudiciary.org/courts/district/index.htm
Criminal Records: Access: Phone, mail, in person. Both court and visitors may perform in person searches. Search fee: $10.00 per name. Court makes copy: $.25 per page. $1.00 minimum. Required to search: name, years to search, DOB. Criminal records

on computer back to mid 1991. Current calendars at website. Mail turnaround time 1 week.
General Information: Public terminal has only criminal records. No sealed, expunged records released. Certification fee: $5.00. Payee: District Court of Vermont. Personal checks accepted. Prepayment and SASE required.

Probate Court - Fair Haven District 3 N Park Pl, Fair Haven, VT 05743; phone: 802-265-3380; fax: 802-265-3380; hours 8AM-4PM (EST). *Probate.*

Probate Court - Rutland District 83 Center St, Rutland, VT 05701; phone: 802-775-0114; hours 8AM-4:30PM (EST). *Probate.*

Washington County

Superior Court 65 State St, Montpelier, VT 05602-3594; phone: 802-828-2091; hours 8AM-4:30PM (EST). *Civil, Eviction, Small Claims #828-5551.*
Civil Records: Access: Phone, mail, in person, online. Only the court performs in person searches; visitors may not. No search fee. Court makes copy: $.25 per page. $1.00 minimum. Required to search: name, years to search; also helpful: address. Civil cases indexed by defendant, plaintiff. Civil records on computer from 1987, archives from 1900s. Access by internet subscription, $10 activation plus $.50 per page; registration info at https://secure.vermont.gov/vtcdas/user. Mail turnaround time 1-2 days.
General Information: No adoption, juvenile or expunged records released. Will fax documents for $1.00 per page. Certification fee: $5.00 per doc. Payee: Washington County Superior Court. Personal checks accepted. Prepayment required. SASE requested.

District Court 255 N Main, Barre, VT 05641; phone: 802-479-4252; hours 8AM-4:30PM (EST). *Felony, Misdemeanor.*
www.vermontjudiciary.org/courts/district/index.htm
Criminal Records: Access: Mail, in person. Only the court performs in person searches; visitors may not. Search fee: $10.00 per name. Court makes copy: $.25 per page. $1.00 minimum. Required to search: name, years to search; also helpful: DOB. Criminal records on computer since 1989; prior records in index from 1970s. Current calendars at website. Mail turnaround time 3-5 days.
General Information: No adoption, juvenile, sealed or expunged records released. Certification fee: $5.00. Payee: Washington District Court. Personal checks accepted. Prepayment required. SASE requested.

Probate Court 10 Elm St, #2, Montpelier, VT 05602; phone: 802-828-3405; hours 8AM-N, 1-4PM (EST). *Probate.*

Windham County

Superior Court Box 207, Newfane, VT 05345; phone: 802-365-7979; fax: 802-365-4360; hours 9AM-4PM (EST). *Civil, Eviction, Small Claims.*
Civil Records: Access: Phone, fax, mail, in person, online. Both court and visitors may perform in person searches. No search fee. Court makes copy: $.25 per page. $1.00 minimum. Required to search: name, years to search. Civil cases indexed by defendant, plaintiff. Civil records on computer from 1994, on index from 1919. Access by internet subscription, $10 activation plus $.50 per page; registration info at https://secure.vermont.gov/vtcdas/user. Note: Fax access available only in emergency. Mail turnaround time 1-2 days.
General Information: No adoption, juvenile, sealed or expunged records released. No fee to fax documents. Certification fee: $5.00. Payee: Windham Superior Court. Personal checks accepted. Prepayment and SASE required.

District Court 30 Putney Rd, #2, Brattleboro, VT 05301; phone: 802-257-2800; fax: 802-257-2853; hours 8AM-4:30PM (EST). *Felony, Misdemeanor, Civil Suspension.*

www.vermontjudiciary.org/courts/district/index.htm

Criminal Records: Access: Mail, in person. Both court and visitors may perform in person searches. Search fee: $10.00 per name. Court makes copy: $.25 per page, $1.00 minimum. Required to search: name, years to search; also helpful: address, DOB, SSN. Criminal record go back to 1969s; computer since 1990; prior on index cards and docket books. Current calendars at website. Mail turnaround time 5-7 days.

General Information: Public terminal has only criminal records back to 1991. No adoption, juvenile, sealed or expunged records released. Fee to fax documents is $.25 per page. Certification fee: $5.00 per page. Payee: Vermont District Court. Personal checks accepted. Prepayment required. SASE requested.

Probate Court - Marlboro District PO Box 523, 439 W River Rd, Brattleboro, VT 05302; phone: 802-257-2898; hours 8AM-N, 1-4:30PM (EST). *Probate.*

Probate Court - Westminster District PO Box 47, 39 Square, Bellows Falls, VT 05101-0047; phone: 802-463-3019; fax: 802-463-0144; hours 8AM-N,1-4:30PM (EST). *Probate.*

Windsor County

Superior Court Box 458, Woodstock, VT 05091; phone: 802-457-2121; fax: 802-457-3446; hours 8AM-4:30PM (EST). *Civil, Eviction, Small Claims.*

www.vermontjudiciary.org/courts/superior/index.htm

Civil Records: Access: Phone, mail, in person, online. Only the court performs in person searches; visitors may not. Search fee: Up to $10.00. Court makes copy: $.25 per page. $1.00 minimum. Required to search: name, years to search. Civil cases indexed by defendant, plaintiff. Civil records available since on computer 1990. Access by internet subscription, $10 activation plus $.50 per page; registration info at https://secure.vermont.gov/vtcdas/user. Mail turnaround time 48 hours.

General Information: No sealed or expunged records released. Certification fee: $5.00 per document. Payee: Windsor County Clerk or Windsor Superior Court. Personal checks accepted. Prepayment and SASE required.

District Court Windsor Circuit Unit 1, 82 Railroad Row, White River Junction, VT 05001-1962; phone: 802-295-8865; fax: 802-295-8897; hours 8AM-4:30PM (EST). *Felony, Misdemeanor.*

www.vermontjudiciary.org/courts/district/index.htm

Criminal Records: Access: Mail, in person. Only the court performs in person searches; visitors may not. Search fee: $10.00 per name. Court makes copy: $.25 per page. $1.00 minimum. Required to search: name, years to search; also helpful: DOB, SSN. Criminal records on computer from 1989, index from 1968. Current calendars at website. Note: Record request forms available, please use. Mail turnaround time 7 days.

General Information: No adoption, juvenile, sealed or expunged records released. Certification fee: $5.00. Payee: Vermont District Court. Personal checks accepted. Prepayment required. SASE requested.

Probate Court - Hartford District 62 Pleasant St, Woodstock, VT 05091; phone: 802-457-1503; fax: 802-457-5203; hours 8AM-N, 1-4:30PM (EST). *Probate.*

Probate Court - Windsor District PO Box 402, Rte 106, Cota Fuel Bldg, North Springfield, VT 05150; phone: 802-886-2284; fax: 802-886-2285; hours 8AM-N, 1-4:30PM (EST). *Probate.*

Vermont Recording Offices

ORGANIZATION: 14 counties and 246 towns/cities, 246 recording offices. The recording officer is Town/City Clerk. There is no county administration in Vermont. Many towns are so small that their mailing addresses are in different towns. Four towns/cities have the same name as counties - Barre, Newport, Rutland, and St. Albans. The entire state is in the Eastern Time Zone (EST).

Many towns are now charging a $2.00 per hour vault time fee for in person searchers.

REAL ESTATE RECORDS: Most towns/cities will not perform real estate searches. Copy fees and certification fees vary. Certified copies are generally $5.00 per page total. Deed copies usually cost $2.00 flat.

UCC RECORDS: This was a dual filing state until 12/31/94. From 01/01/95, only consumer goods and real estate related collateral were filed with Town/City Clerks. Starting 07/01/2001, only real estate collateral is filed at the local level. Most recording offices will perform UCC searches. Use search request form UCC-11. Search fees are usually $10.00 per name, more if non-standard form used, and copy fees vary.

TAX LIEN RECORDS: All federal and state tax liens on personal property and on real property are filed with the Town/City Clerk in the lien/attachment book and indexed in real estate records. Most towns/cities will not perform tax lien searches.

OTHER LIENS: Mechanics, local tax, judgment, foreclosure.

ONLINE ACCESS: While there is virtually no online access to county recorded documents, state recorded UCC data is available online from the Vermont Secretary of State.

Addison Town

Town Clerk, 7099 VT Rte 22A, Addison, VT 05491. 802-759-2020; fax-802-759-2233; hours: 8:30AM-N, 1PM-4:30PM.
All records in one index. Only the public may search. Copy fee $1.00 per page. Cert fee- $7.00 per page plus copy fee. Payee- Addison Town Clerk. **Property tax/Assessor-** same address as above. not known.

Albany Town

Town Clerk, PO Box 284, Albany, VT 05820-0284. 802-755-6100; hours: 9AM-4PM T,Th; 9AM-7PM W.
All records in one index. Office personnel or visitors may perform searches. Will not search real estate records. Will search UCC records, but not tax liens. UCC search per debtor name- $10.00. UCC search request using non-standard form (per name)- $15.00. Copy fee $1.00 per page. Cert fee- $7.00 per page. Payee- Albany Town Clerk. **Property tax/Assessor-** PO Box 284, Albany, VT 05820-0284; not known.

Alburg Town

Town Clerk, 1 N. Main St, Alburg, VT 05440-0346. 802-796-3468; fax-802-796-3939; hours: 9AM-N; 1-5PM.
Separate indices to search include liens and attachments, UCC's. Record index not computerized. Only the public may search. Copy fee $1.00 per 4 pages; copies sold in sets of 4. Cert fee- $2.00 per doc plus copy fee. Payee- Town of Alburg. **Other phones:** Treasurer- 802-796-3468; Elections-802-796-3468. **Property tax/Assessor-** 802-796-4061.

Andover Town

Town Clerk, 953 Weston-Andover Rd., Andover, VT 05143. 802-875-2765; fax-802-875-6647; hours: 9AM-1PM M,T,Th,F; Wed 11AM-3PM.
Separate indices to search include general index through 3/93, card index 03/03 to current. Record index not computerized. Office will perform a tax lien search but public must search other records themselves. Tax lien search fee-$2.00 per hour.

Copy fee $1.00 per page. Cert fee- $7.00 per doc plus copy fee. Payee- Town of Andover. **Property tax/Assessor-** 802-875-2765.

Arlington Town

Town Clerk, PO Box 304, Arlington, VT 05250. 802-375-2332; fax-802-375-2332; hours: 9AM-2PM.
All records in one index. Only the public may search. Copy fee $1.00 per page. Cert fee- $7.00 per doc includes copy fee. Payee- Arlington Town Clerk. **Other phones:** Treasurer- 802-375-1260. **Property tax/Assessor-** PO Box 268, Arlington, VT 05250; 802-375-9022.

Athens Town

Town Clerk, 56 Brookline Rd., Athens, VT 05143. 802-869-3370; fax-802-869-3370; hours: 9AM-1PM or by appointment.
All records in one index. Record index not computerized. Office will perform a UCC search but public must search other records themselves. Search fee $15.00. General copy fee $7.00 per doc in the index. R/E record copy- $2.00 per page. Cert fee- $5.00 per page plus copy fee. Payee- Athens Town Clerk. **Property tax/Assessor-** PO Box 651, Saxton River, VT 05143; 802-869-3995.

Bakersfield Town

Town Clerk, Box 203, Bakersfield, VT 05441. 802-827-4495; fax-802-527-3106;
Office will perform a UCC search but public must search other records themselves. Search fee $10.00. Copy fee $1.00 per page. Cert fee- $7.00 per page. Payee- Joyce-Town Clerk. **Other phones:** Treasurer- 802-827-4495; Appraiser/Auditor- 802-827-4495; Elections- 802-827-4495; Vital Records- 802-827-4495. **Property tax/Assessor-** 802-827-4495.

Baltimore Town

Town Clerk, 1210 Baltimore Rd., Baltimore, VT 05143. 802-263-5274; hours: 4PM-6PM W; 9AM-11AM TH. www.baltimorevt.org
Separate indices to search. Office personnel or visitors may perform searches. General index search fee $2.00 per hour. Copy fee $1.00 per page. Cert fee- $10.00 per doc plus copy fee. Payee- Town of Baltimore.

Barnard Town

Town Clerk, PO Box 274, Barnard, VT 05031-0274. 802-234-9211, R/E recording phone-802-243-9211; hours: 8AM-3:30PM M-W.
All records in one index. Records indexed. Only the public may search. Copy fee $1.00 per page. Cert fee- $7.00 per page plus copy fee. Payee- Town of Barnard. **Other phones:** Treasurer- 802-243-9050; Appraiser/Auditor- 802-243-9576; Elections- 802-243-9211; Vital Records- 802-243-9211. **Property tax/Assessor-** 802-243-9576.

Barnet Town

Town Clerk, Box 15, Barnet, VT 05821-0015. 802-633-2256; fax-802-633-4315; hours: 9AM-N, 1-4:30PM.
All records in one index. Office will perform a UCC search but public must search other records themselves. Search fee $10.00. Copy fee $1.00 per document. Cert fee- $7.00 per page plus copy fee. Payee- Town of Barnet.

Barre City

Town Clerk, Box 418, Barre, VT 05641. 802-476-0242; fax-802-476-0264; hours: 8AM-4PM.
Only the public may search. Copy fee $1.00 per page. Cert fee- $7.00 per page. Payee- Barre City. **Other phones:** Treasurer- 802-476-0242; Appraiser/Auditor- 802-476-0244; Elections- 802-476-0242; Vital Records- 802-476-0242. **Property tax/Assessor-** 802-476-0244.

Barre Town

Town Clerk, PO Box 124, Websterville, VT 05678-0124. 802-479-9391; fax-802-479-9332; hours: 8AM-4:30 M-F. www.barretown.org
Index: Books and computer. Only the public may search. Copy fee $1.00 per page. Cert fee- $7.00 per page plus copy fee. Payee- Town of Barre. **Other phones:** Treasurer- 802-479-9391; Appraiser/Auditor- 802-479-2595; Elections- 802-479-9391; Vital Records- 802-479-9391; Town Manager- 802-479-9331. **Property tax/Assessor-** PO Box 116, Websterville, VT 05678; 802-479-2595.

Barton Town

Town Clerk, PO Box 657, Barton, VT 05822-1386. 802-525-6222; fax-802-525-8856; hours: 7:30AM-4PM.
All records in one index. Record index not computerized. Office will perform a UCC search but public must search other records themselves. Copy fee $2.00 per UCC. Cert fee- $7.00. Payee- Barton Town Clerk. **Other phones:** Treasurer- 802-525-6222; Appraiser/Auditor- 802-525-6222; Elections- 802-525-6222; Vital Records- 802-525-6222. **Property tax/Assessor-** same address as above. 802-525-6222.

Belvidere Town

Town Clerk, 3996 Vermont Rt 109, Belvidere Center, VT 05492. 802-644-6621; fax-802-644-6621; hours: 8:30AM-3:30PM T W Th.
Separate indices to search include map surveys, UCCs. Only the public may search. Copy fee $7.00 per page. Cert fee- $6.00 per doc includes copy fee. Payee- Belvidere Town Clerk. **Other phones:** Tax Collector- 82-644-5427.

Bennington Town

Town Clerk, 205 South St, Bennington, VT 05201. 802-442-1043; fax-802-442-1068; hours: 8AM-5PM.
www.bennington.com/local.html
All records in one index. Record index not computerized. Office will perform a UCC search but public must search other records themselves. UCC search per debtor name- $10.00. UCC search request using non-standard form (per name)- $15.00. Copy fee $1.00 per page. Cert fee- $7.00 per page includes copy fee. Payee- Bennington Town Clerk. **Online access to Property, Assessor records:** Access to the Grand List search program is free at www.bennington.com/government/grandlist/index.html . No name searching at this time; site is under construction and data is incomplete. **Other phones:** Treasurer- 802-442-1041; Appraiser/Auditor- 802-442-1042; Elections- 802-442-1043; Vital Records- 802-442-1043. **Property tax/Assessor-** 205 South St, Bennington, VT 05201; 802-442-1042.

Benson Town

Town Clerk, PO Box 163, Benson, VT 05731-0163. 802-537-2611; fax-802-537-2612; 9AM-N, 1-5PM.
Record index not computerized. Only the public may search. Copy fee $1.00 per page. Cert fee- $7.00 per cert plus copy fee. Payee- Benson Town Clerk.

Berkshire Town

Town Clerk, RFD 1 Box 2560, Enosburg Falls, VT 05450. 802-933-2335; fax-802-933-5913; hours: 9AM-N, 1-4PM M,T,Th,F; 9AM-N W.
All records in one index. Only the public may search. Copy fee $1.00 per name. Cert fee- $6.00 per page plus copy fee. Payee- Berkshire Town Clerk. **Property tax/Assessor-** same address as above. not known.

Berlin Town

Town Clerk, 108 Shed Rd., Berlin, VT 05602. 802-229-9298; fax-802-229-9530; hours: 8:30AM 3:30 PM M-Th.
Office will perform a UCC search but public must search other records themselves. UCC search per debtor name- $10.00. Copy fee $.25 per page. Payee- Berlin Town Clerk. **Other phones:** Treasurer- 802-229-9380; Elections- 802-229-9298; Vital Records- 802-229-9298; Zoning Admin.- 802-229-2529. **Property tax/Assessor-** 802-229-4880.

Bethel Town

Town Clerk, PO Box 404, Bethel, VT 05032. 802-234-9722; fax-802-234-6840; hours: 8AM-4PM, M, TH; 8AM-Noon T, F.
All records in one index. Will not search real estate records. Will search UCC records, but not tax liens.

UCC search per debtor name- $10.00. UCC search request using non-standard form (per name)- $15.00. Copy fee $1.00 per page. **Other phones:** Treasurer- 802-234-9722; Elections- 802-234-9722; Vital Records- 802-234-9722. **Property tax/Assessor-** same address as above. 802-234-9722.

Bloomfield Town

Town Clerk, PO Box 336, No. Stratford, NH, VT 03590. 802-962-5191; fax-802-962-5191; hours: 9AM-3PM Tues & Thurs.
Record index not computerized. Only the public may search. Copy fee $1.00 per page. Cert fee- $7.00 per page. Payee- Town Clerk.

Bolton Town

Town Clerk, RD 1 Box 445, Waterbury, VT 05676. 802-434-3064; fax-802-434-6404; hours: 7AM-4PM M-TH.
Record index not computerized. Only the public may search. Copy fee $1.00 per page. Cert fee- $10.00 per page plus copy fee. Payee- Town of Bolton. **Other phones:** Treasurer- 802-434-5075; Appraiser/Auditor- 802-434-3064; Elections- 802-434-5075; Vital Records- 802-434-5075. **Property tax/Assessor-** 802-434-3064.

Bradford Town

Town Clerk, PO Box 339, Bradford, VT 05033-0339. 802-222-4727; fax-802-222-3520; hours: 8:30AM-4:30 M-TH; 9AM-Noon F.
Separate indices to search include general index and attachments. Record index not computerized. Only the public may search. Copy fee $1.00 per page. Cert fee- $7.00 per page includes copy fee. Payee- Town of Bradford. **Other phones:** Treasurer- 802-222-4727 x303; Appraiser/Auditor- 802-222-4727 x306; Elections- 802-222-4727; Vital Records- 802-222-4727. **Property tax/Assessor-** same address as above. 802-222-4727 x300.

Braintree Town

Town Clerk, 932 VT Route 12A, Braintree, VT 05060. 802-728-9787; fax-802-728-9787; hours: 7AM-N, 12;30-3;30, T, 8AM-N, 1-5PM, W, Th.
All records in one index. Record index not computerized. Only the public may search. Copy fee $2.00 per page. R/E or tax lien copy- $1.00 per page. Cert fee- $7.00 per page total. Payee- Braintree Town Clerk. **Property tax/Assessor-** 802-728-9787.

Brandon Town

Town Clerk, 49 Center St, Brandon, VT 05733. 802-247-5721; fax-802-247-5481; hours: 8AM-4PM.
www.town.brandon.vt.us
Separate indices to search include grantor and grantee by time periods. Records indexed on computer back to 1995. Only the public may search. Copy fee $20.00 per document. R/E record copy- $1.00 per page. Tax lien copy- $7.00 per page. Cert fee- $7.00 per page plus copy fee. Payee- Town of Brandon. **Other phones:** Treasurer- 802-247-5721; Appraiser/Auditor- 802-247-0226; Elections- 802-247-5721; Vital Records- 802-247-5721. **Property tax/Assessor-** same address as above. 802-247-0226.

Brattleboro Town

Town Clerk, 230 Main St #108, Brattleboro, VT 05301-2885. 802-254-4541, R/E recording phone-802-254-4541 x126; fax-802-257-2312; 8:30AM-5PM.
www.brattleboro.org
Will not search real estate records. Will search UCC records, but not tax liens. UCC search per debtor name- $10.00. Copy fee $1.00 per page; $2.00 minimum. Cert fee- $7.00 per page. Payee- Brattleboro Town Clerk. **Online access to Assessor, Property records:** Access the annual Grand List pdf file free at www.brattleboro.org/index.asp?. Click on Grand List here. **Other phones:** Treasurer- 802-254-4541 x123; Appraiser/Auditor- 802-254-4541 x119; Elections- 802-254-4541 x129; Vital Records- 802-

254-4541 x126. **Property tax/Assessor-** 802-254-4541 x119.

Bridgewater Town

Town Clerk, PO Box 14, Bridgewater, VT 05034. 802-672-3334; fax-802-672-5395; hours: 8AM-4PM M-Th.
All records in one index. Only the public may search. Copy fee $1.00 per page. Cert fee- $7.00 per page plus copy fee. Payee- Town of Bridgewater. **Other phones:** Treasurer- 802-672-3334; Appraiser/Auditor- 802-672-3334; Elections- 802-672-3334; Vital Records- 802-672-3334; Tax Collector- 802-672-3334. **Property tax/Assessor-** PO Box 50, Bridgewater, VT 05034; 802-672-3334.

Bridport Town

Town Clerk, Box 27, Bridport, VT 05734-0027. 802-758-2483; hours: 9AM-4PM M,T,F; 9AM-N 1-4PM Wed; 9AM-N Th.
All records in one index. Only the public may search, but town clerk may perform searches as a private contractor. Copy fee $.10 per page. Cert fee- $7.00 per doc plus copy fee. Payee- Bridport Town Clerk. **Other phones:** Treasurer- 802-758-2483. **Property tax/Assessor-** 802-758-2483.

Brighton Town

Town Clerk, PO Box 377, Island Pond, VT 05846. 802-723-4405; fax-802-723-4405; hours: 8AM-3:30PM
Only the public may search. Copy fee $.25; real estate $1.00 per page. Cert fee- $7.00 per doc plus copy fee. Payee- Brighton Town Clerk. **Other phones:** Treasurer- 802-723-4405; Appraiser/Auditor- 802-723-6672; Elections- 802-732-4405; Vital Records- 802-732-4405. **Property tax/Assessor-** 802-723-4405.

Bristol Town

Town Clerk, Box 249, Bristol, VT 05443. 802-453-2486; fax-802-453-5188; hours: 8AM-4:30PM.
All records in one index back to 1986, general index before that. Record index not computerized. Only the public may search. Search fee $2.00 per hour. Copy fee $1.00 per page. **Property tax/Assessor-** 802-453-2486.

Brookfield Town

Town Clerk, PO Box 463, Brookfield, VT 05036-0463. 802-276-3352; fax-802-276-3926; hours: 8:30AM-4:30PM M,T,F.
Separate indices to search include land records, permit files, lister cards, vital statistics, UCC's. Record index not computerized. Office will perform a UCC search but public must search other records themselves. Copy fee $1.00 each for land records, $.25 per page for others. Cert fee- $7.00 per page plus copy fee. Payee- Town of Brookfield.

Brookline Town

Town Clerk, PO Box 403, Brookline, VT 05345. 802-365-4648; fax-802-365-4648; hours: 9AM-2PM Wed.
All records in one index. Record index not computerized. Only the public may search. Copy fee $1.00 per page. Cert fee- $6.00 per page. Payee- Brookline Town Clerk.

Brownington Town

Town Clerk, 509 Dutton Brook Ln, Orleans, VT 05860. 802-754-8401; fax-802-754-8401; hours: 8:30-11AM M; 9AM-3:30PM W; 9AM-N Th.
All records in one index. Record index not computerized. Only the public may search. Copy fee $1.00 per page. Cert fee- $7.00 per page includes copies. Payee- Brownington Town Clerk. **Other phones:** Treasurer- 802-754-6559; Appraiser/Auditor- 802-754-8401.

Brunswick Town

Town Clerk, RFD 1, Box 470; 4495 Vermont Rte. 102, Brunswick, VT 05905. 802-962-5514; fax-802-962-5522; hours: 4PM-6PM, Th by app't.
Index: Books. Record index not computerized. Office will perform a UCC search but public must search other records themselves. Search fee $10.00. Copy fee $1.00 per page. Cert fee- $2.00 per page. Payee- Brunswick Town Clerk. **Other phones:** Treasurer- 802-962-5514; Elections- 802-962-5514; Vital Records- 802-962-5514. **Property tax/Assessor-** 994 VT Rte 102, Brunswick, VT 05905; 802-962-3450.

Burke Town

Town Clerk, 212 School St, West Burke, VT 05871. 802-467-3717; fax-802-467-8623; hours: 8AM-4PM. www.burkevt.org
All records in one index. Only the public may search. Copy fee $1.00 per page. Cert fee- $7.00 per page. **Other phones:** Treasurer- 802-467-3717. **Property tax/Assessor-** same address as above. 802-467-3717.

Burlington City

Town Clerk, 149 Church St; City Hall, Rm 20, Burlington, VT 05401. 802-865-7135, R/E recording phone-802-865-7133, UCC recording phone-802-865-7135; fax-802-865-7014; hours: 8AM-4:30PM. www.ci.burlington.vt.us
All records in one index. Records indexed on computer. Only the public may search. Copy fee $1.00 per page. Cert fee- $20.00 per page plus copy fee. Payee- Burlington City Clerk. **Online access to Property Tax, Assessor records:** Access to city property tax data is free at http://ci.burlingtontelecom.com/assessor/search/. **Other phones:** Treasurer- 802-865-7000; Appraiser/Auditor- 802-865-7114; Elections- 802-865-7137; Vital Records- 802-865-7000. **Property tax/Assessor-** 802-865-7114.

Cabot Town

Town Clerk, PO Box 36, Cabot, VT 05647-0036. 802-563-2279; fax-802-563-2423; hours: 9AM-5PM M-Th; 9AM-1PM F.
Record index not computerized. Only the public may search. Copy fee $2.00 per page. Cert fee- $7.00 per cert plus copy fee. **Other phones:** Treasurer- 802-563-2279; Appraiser/Auditor- 802-563-2279; Elections- 802-563-2279; Vital Records- 802-563-2279. **Property tax/Assessor-** 802-563-2279.

Calais Town

Town Clerk, 3120 perkin Brook Rd, Calais, VT 05650. 802-456-8720; 8AM-5PM M,T,Th; 8AM-N Sat.
Separate indices to search. Card file back to 1942, books prior. Will not search real estate records. Will search UCC records UCC search per debtor name- $10.00. UCC search request using non-standard form (per name)- $15.00. Copy fee $1.00 per page. Cert fee- $7.00 per page total includes copies. Payee- Calais Town Clerk. **Other phones:** All offices:- 802-223-5952.

Cambridge Town

Town Clerk, PO Box 127, Jeffersonville, VT 05464. 802-644-2251; fax-802-644-8348; hours: 8AM-4PM.
All records in one index. Record index not computerized. Only the public may search. Copy fee $.25 per page. Cert fee- $5.00 per cert plus copy fee. **Other phones:** Appraiser/Auditor- 802-644-2200; Vital Records- 802-644-2251. **Property tax/Assessor-** 802-644-2251.

Canaan Town

Town Clerk, PO Box 159, Canaan, VT 05903-0159. 802-266-3370; fax-802-266-7085; hours: 9AM-3PM.
All records in one index. Record index not computerized. Only the public may search. Copy fee $1.00 per page. Cert fee- $7.00 per page. Payee- Town of Canaan. **Other phones:** Treasurer-

802-266-3370; Appraiser/Auditor- 802-266-3370; Elections- 802-266-3370; Vital Records- 802-266-3370. **Property tax/Assessor-** 802-266-3370.

Castleton Town

Town Clerk, PO Box 727, Castleton, VT 05735. 802-468-2212, R/E recording phone-802-468-2212 x214, UCC recording phone-802-468-2212 x 214; fax-802-468-5482; hours: 8AM-N, 1-4PM.
Only the public may search. Cert fee- $7.00 per page. Payee- Town of Castleton. **Other phones:** Treasurer- 802-468-5319; Appraiser/Auditor- 802-468-2751; Elections- 802-468-2212 x214; Vital Records- 802-468-2212 x214.

Cavendish Town

Town Clerk, PO Box 126, Cavendish, VT 05142-0126. 802-226-7292; fax-802-226-7790; hours: 9AM-N, 1PM-4:30PM.
Only the public may search. Copy fee $1.00 per page. Cert fee- $5.00 per page. Payee- Cavendish Town Clerk. **Other phones:** Treasurer- 802-226-7292; Appraiser/Auditor- 802-226-7292; Elections- 802-226-7292; Vital Records- 802-226-7292. **Property tax/Assessor-** 802-226-7292.

Charleston Town

Town Clerk, 5063 Vermont Rt 105, West Charleston, VT 05872-7902. 802-895-2814; fax-802-895-2814; hours: 9AM-3PM (Closed Wed).
All records in one index. Only the public may search. Copy fee $1.00 per page. Deed copies $2.00 minimum. Cert fee- $7.00 per page plus copy fee. Payee- Town of Charleston. **Property tax/Assessor-** same address as above. not known.

Charlotte Town

Town Clerk, PO Box 119, Charlotte, VT 05445-0119. 802-425-3071; fax-802-425-4241; hours: 8AM-4PM. www.charlotte.govoffice2.com
All records in one index. Record index not computerized. Only the public may search. Copy fee $1.00 per page. Cert fee- $7.00 per page plus copy fee. Payee- Town of Charlotte. **Other phones:** Treasurer- 802-425-3071; Appraiser/Auditor- 802-425-3855; Elections- 802-425-3071; Vital Records- 802-425-3071; Planning & Zoning- 802-425-3533. **Property tax/Assessor-** same address as above. 802-425-3855.

Chelsea Town

Town Clerk, PO Box 266, Chelsea, VT 05038. 802-685-4460; fax-802-685-4460; hours: 8AM-N, 1-4PM.
Record index not computerized. Only the public may search. Copy fee $1.00 per page. Tax lien copy- $.25 per page. Cert fee- $7.00 per doc plus copy fee. Payee- Chelsea Town Clerk. **Property tax/Assessor-** 802-685-4460.

Chester Town

Town Clerk, PO Box 370, Chester, VT 05143. 802-875-2173; fax-802-875-2237; hours: 8AM-5PM.
All records in one index. Record index not computerized. Only the public may search. Copy fee $.50 per page. Cert fee- $7.00 per page plus copy fee. Payee- Town of Chester.

Chittenden Town

Town Clerk, PO Box 89, Chittenden, VT 05737. 802-483-6647; fax-802-438-2504; hours: 1:30-5PM (till 7PM W).
Chittenden is in Rutland County, not Chittenden County. Uninformed secured parties continue to attempt filings at the county level here even though there is no county filing in Vermont. Separate indices to search include liens and other recorded documents. Will not search real estate records. Will not search UCC records or tax liens. Copy fee $1.00 per page. Cert fee- $7.00 per page total. Payee- Chittenden Town Clerk. **Other phones:** Treasurer- 802-483-647.

Clarendon Town

Town Clerk, PO Box 30, North Clarendon, VT 05759-0030. 802-775-4274; fax-802-775-4274; hours: 10AM-4PM M-TH.
Separate indices to search include lien attachments books, mobile home transfer books, land records, UCC file. Only the public may search. Copy fee $2.00 per UCC. R/E or tax lien copy- $1.00 per page. Cert fee- $7.00 per page, includes copy fee. Payee- Town of Clarendon. **Other phones:** Treasurer- 802-775-1536; Appraiser/Auditor- 802-775-1536; Elections- 802-775-4274; Vital Records- 802-775-4274. **Property tax/Assessor-** same address as above. 802-775-1536.

Colchester Town

Town Clerk, PO Box 55, Colchester, VT 05446. 802-655-0812, R/E recording phone-802-654-0727, UCC recording phone-802-654-0700; fax-802-654-0757; hours: 8AM-4PM. www.town.colchester.vt.us
Records indexed on a public use terminal. Only the public may search. Copy fee $1.00 per page. Cert fee- $7.00 per page. Payee- Town of Colchester. **Other phones:** Treasurer- 802-655-0812; Appraiser/Auditor- 802-655-0863; Elections- 203-654-0727; Vital Records- 203-654-0727. **Property tax/Assessor-** 802-655-0863.

Concord Town

Town Clerk, PO Box 317, Concord, VT 05824-0317. 802-695-2220; fax-802-695-2220; hours: 7:30AM-3:30PM.
Records indexed on a public use terminal back to 1995. Only the public may search. Copy fee $1.00 per page. Cert fee- $7.00 per page plus copy fee. Payee- Town of Concord. **Other phones:** Treasurer- 802-695-2220; Appraiser/Auditor- 802-695-2220; Elections- 802-695-2220; Vital Records- 802-695-2220. **Property tax/Assessor-** 802-695-2220.

Corinth Town

Town Clerk, PO Box 461, Corinth, VT 05039. 802-439-5850; fax-802-439-5850;: M 8:30AM-3:30PM; Tu 11AM-3PM;Th 10AM-3PM;F 8:30-3PM.
Separate indices to search include books, computer. Records indexed on computer. Only the public may search. Copy fee $1.00 per page. Cert fee- $1.00 per page plus copy fee. Payee- Town of Corinth. **Other phones:** Treasurer- 802-439-5850; Elections- 802-439-5850; Vital Records- 802-439-5850. **Property tax/Assessor-** same address as above. 802-439-5098.

Cornwall Town

Town Clerk, 2629 Route 30, Cornwall, VT 05753-9299. 802-462-2775; fax-802-462-2606; hours: 8AM-4:30PM.
Record index not computerized. Only the public may search. Copy fee $1.00 per page. Cert fee- $7.00 per doc plus copy fee. **Property tax/Assessor-** 802-462-2855.

Coventry Town

Town Clerk, PO Box 104, Coventry, VT 05825. 802-754-2288; fax-802-754-6274; hours: 8AM-Noon M,T,Th, F; 7AM-4PM, W.
All records in one index. Record index not computerized. Only the public may search. Copy fee $1.00 per page. Cert fee- $7.00 per page. Payee- Coventry Town Clerk.

Craftsbury Town

Town Clerk, Box 55, Craftsbury, VT 05826. 802-586-2823; fax-802-586-2823; 8;30AM-4PM T, Th, F.
Records indexed on computer. Office personnel or visitors may perform searches. Search fee $10.00. Copy fee $1.00 per page. **Property tax/Assessor-** 802-586-2835.

Danby Town

Town Clerk, Box 231, Danby, VT 05739-0231. 802-293-5136; fax-802-293-5311; hours: 9AM-N, 1-4PM M-Th.
All records in one index. Only the public may search. Copy fee $1.00 per page. Cert fee- $7.00 per page. Payee- Town of Darby. **Other phones:** Treasurer- 802-293-5136; Appraiser- 802-293-5136; Elections- 802-293-5136; Vital Records- 802-293-5136. **Property tax/Assessor-** same address as above. 802-293-5136.

Danville Town

Town Clerk, PO Box 183, Danville, VT 05828. 802-684-3352; fax-802-684-9606; hours: 8AM-4PM.
All records in one index. Records indexed. Only the public may search. Copy fee $1.00 per page. Cert fee- $7.00 per page plus copy fee. Payee- Town of Danville.

Derby Town

Town Clerk, PO Box 25, Derby, VT 05829. 802-766-4906; fax-802-766-2027; hours: 8AM-4PM.
Separate indices to search include general index. Records indexed on computer back 40 years. Only the public may search. Copy fee $1.00 per page. Cert fee- $7.00 per cert plus copy fee. Payee-Derby Town Clerk. **Other phones:** Treasurer- 802-766-4906; Appraiser/Auditor- 802-766-2012; Elections- 802-766-4906; Vital Records- 802-766-4906; Zoning- 802-766-2017. **Property tax/Assessor-** 802-766-2012.

Dorset Town

Town Clerk, 112 Mad Tom Rd; Town Hall, East Dorset, VT 05253. 802-362-1178; fax-802-362-5156;
All records in one index. Office personnel or visitors may perform searches. Search fee $5.00 hour, not to exceed $25.00. Copy fee $1.00 per page. Cert fee- $7.00 per page plus copy fee. Payee- Dorset Town Clerk. **Property tax/Assessor-** 802-362-0162.

Dover Town

Town Clerk, PO Box 527, Dover, VT 05356-0527. 802-464-5100; fax-802-464-8721; hours: 9AM-5PM.
Index: Book 1793-1967, card file 1967 -present, computer. Records indexed on a public use terminal back to 1989. Only the public may search. Copy fee $1.00 per page. Cert fee- $7.00 per page plus copy fee. Payee- Dover Town Clerk. **Other phones:** Treasurer- 802-464-5100; Appraiser/Auditor- 802-464-8720; Elections- 802-464-5100; Vital Records- 802-464-5100. **Property tax/Assessor-** PO Box 428, Dover, VT 05356; 802-464-8720.

Dummerston Town

Town Clerk, 1523 Middle Rd., E. Dummerston, VT 05346. 802-257-1496; fax-802-257-4671; hours: 9AM-3PM M T TH F; Noon-3PM W.
All records in one index. Only the public may search. Copy fee $1.00 per page. Cert fee- $7.00 per page. Payee- Town of Dummerston. **Property tax/Assessor-** 1523 Middle Rd., E. Dummerston, VT 05346; not known.

Duxbury Town

Town Clerk, 3316 Crossett Hill Rd, Waterbury, VT 05676. 802-244-6660; fax-802-244-5442; hours: 8AM-4PM M-Th.
Only the public may search. Cert fee- $7.00 per page total. Payee- Town of Duxbury.

East Haven Town

Town Clerk, PO Box 10, East Haven, VT 05837-0010. 802-467-3772; hours: 1-6PM T; 8AM-1PM Th; and by appt.
Index: Pre-1984 indices in books. Only the public may search. Copy fee $1.00 per page. Cert fee- $7.00 per doc plus copy fee. Payee- East Haven Town Clerk. **Other phones:** Treasurer- 802-467-3772; Appraiser/Auditor- 802-467-3772; Elections-

802-467-3772; Vital Records- 802-467-3772. **Property tax/Assessor-** same address as above. 802-467-3772.

East Montpelier Town

Town Clerk, PO Box 157, East Montpelier, VT 05651-0157. 802-223-3313; fax-802-223-3314; hours: 9AM-5PM M-Th; 9AM-N Fri.
Separate indices to search include before July 1, 1988-indexed in land record index books 1-2-3, after July 1, 1988-card record index file. Beginning 11/30/2000-index done on computer. Records indexed on computer from 11/30/2000 to present. Only the public may search. Copy fee $2.00, if tax lien or real estate $1.00 per page. Cert fee- $7.00 per page plus copy fee. Payee- East Montpelier Town Clerk. **Other phones:** Treasurer- 802-223-3313; Appraiser/Auditor- 802-223-3313; Elections- 802-223-3313; Vital Records- 802-223-3313. **Property tax/Assessor-** 802-223-3313.

Eden Town

Town Clerk, 71 Old Schoolhouse Rd., Eden Mills, VT 05653. 802-635-2528; fax-802-635-1724; hours: 8AM-12:30-1:30-4PM,M-Th.
All records in one index. Only the public may search. Copy fee $1.00 per page. Cert fee- $7.00 per page plus copy fee. Payee- Eden Town Clerk. **Other phones:** Vital Records- 802-635-2528. **Property tax/Assessor-** same address as above. 802-635-2528.

Elmore Town

Town Clerk, PO Box 123, Lake Elmore, VT 05657. 802-888-2637; fax-802-888-2637; hours: 9AM-3PM T,W,Th.
Separate indices to search include grantor/grantee. Record index not computerized. Office personnel (limited searches) or visitors may perform searches. Copy fee $1.00 per page. Cert fee- $7.00 per page plus copy fee. Payee- Elmore Town Clerk. **Property tax/Assessor-** 802-888-2637.

Enosburgh Town

Town Clerk, PO Box 465, Enosburg Falls, VT 05450. 802-933-4421; fax-802-933-4832; hours: 8AM4PM (closed on Wednesdays).
All records in one index. Only the public may search. Copy fee $2.00 per doc. Cert fee- $7.00 per doc plus copy fee. **Other phones:** Treasurer- 802-933-4421; Appraiser/Auditor- 802-933-4421; Elections- 802-933-4421; Vital Records- 802-933-4421. **Property tax/Assessor-** same address as above. 802-933-4421.

Essex Town

Town Clerk, 81 Main St, Essex Junction, VT 05452. 802-879-0413; fax-802-878-1353; hours: 7:30AM-4:30PM. www.essex.org
All records in one index. Office will perform a UCC search but public must search other records themselves. UCC search per debtor name- $20.00. Copy fee $1.00 per page. Cert fee- $7.00 per page plus copy fee. Payee- Town of Essex. **Other phones:** Treasurer- 802-879-0413; Appraiser/Auditor- 802-878-1345; Elections- 802-879-0413; Vital Records- 802-879-0413. **Property tax/Assessor-** 802-878-1345.

Fair Haven Town

Town Clerk, 3 N. Park Pl, Fair Haven, VT 05743. 802-265-3610; fax-802-265-2158; hours: 8-4PM.
Separate indices to search include computer and books. Records indexed on a public use terminal back to 1959. Only the public may search. Copy fee $1.00 per page. Cert fee- $7.00 per cert includes copy fee. Payee- Town of Fair Haven. **Other phones:** Treasurer- 802-265-3010; Appraiser/Auditor- 802-265-3610; Elections- 802-265-3610; Vital Records- 802-265-3610. **Property tax/Assessor-** same address as above. 802-265-3610.

Fairfax Town

Town Clerk, PO Box 27, Fairfax, VT 05454. 802-849-6111; fax-802-849-6276; hours: 9AM-4PM, M-F.
Separate indices to search. Record index not computerized. Only the public may search. Copy fee $1.00 per page. Cert fee- $7.00 per page plus copy fee. Payee- Fairfax Town Office. **Other phones:** Treasurer- 802-849-6111; Vital Records- 802-849-6111. **Property tax/Assessor-** 802-849-6111.

Fairfield Town

Town Clerk, PO Box 5, Fairfield, VT 05455. 802-827-3261; hours: 9AM-3PM.
All records in one index. Only the public may search. Copy fee $1.00 per page, $2.00 minimum. Cert fee- $1.00 per page. Payee- Fairfield Town.

Fairlee Town

Town Clerk, PO Box 95, Fairlee, VT 05045-0095. 802-333-4363; fax-802-333-9214; hours: 8:30AM-3:30PM M-W; 9AM-1PM Th, or by app't.
Separate indices to search include general index, card file. Only the public may search. Copy fee $1.00 per page, $2.00 minimum. Cert fee- $6.00 per page plus copy fee. Payee- Fairlee Town Clerk. **Other phones:** Treasurer- 802-333-4363; Appraiser/Auditor- 802-333-9829; Elections- 802-333-4363; Vital Records- 802-333-4363; Zoning Admin- 802-333-4158. **Property tax/Assessor-** same address as above. 802-333-9829.

Fayston Town

Town Clerk, 866 N. Fayston Rd., No. Fayston, VT 05660. 802-496-2454 x21 or 23; fax-802-496-9850; 9AM-N, 12:30-3:30PM. www.central-vt.com
Only the public may search. Copy fee $1.00 per page. Cert fee- $7.00 per page plus copy fee. Payee- Town of Fayston. **Other phones:** Town Clerk/Tax Collector- 802-496-2454 x21. **Property tax/Assessor-** 802-496-2454 x24.

Ferrisburgh Town

Town Clerk, PO Box 6, Ferrisburgh, VT 05456-0006. 802-877-3429; fax-802-877-6757; hours: 8AM-4PM. www.twp.ferrisburgh.vt.us
Records indexed on computer from 3/2000 to present, card index from 1970 to 3/2000, general index from 1970-back. Only the public may search. Copy fee $1.00 per page. Cert fee- $7.00 per doc plus copy fee. Payee- Town of Ferrisburg.

Fletcher Town

Town Clerk, 215 Cambridge Rd, Cambridge, VT 05444. 802-849-6616; fax-802-849-2500; hours: 9AM-3:30PM M-Th; closed Fri.
All records in one index. Only the public may search. Copy fee $1.00 per page. Cert fee- $7.00 per page, includes copy fee. Payee- Town of Fletcher. **Other phones:** Treasurer- 802-849-6616; Appraiser/Auditor- 802-849-6616; Elections- 802-849-6616; Vital Records- 802-849-6616. **Property tax/Assessor-** address above. 802-849-6616.

Franklin Town

Town Clerk, PO Box 82, Franklin, VT 05457-0082. 802-285-2101; 9AM-4PM M,T,F; 9AM-7PM Th; 9AM-N Wed. www.franklinvermont.com
All records in one index. Office will perform a UCC search but public must search other records themselves. UCC search per debtor name- $10.00. Copy fee $2.00 per page; UCC copy $1.00 per page. Cert fee- $7.00 per cert includes copy fee. Payee- Town of Franklin. **Other phones:** Treasurer- 802-285-2101; Appraiser/Auditor- 802-285-2101; Elections- 802-285-2101; Vital Records- 802-285-2101. **Property tax/Assessor-** 802-285-2101.

Georgia Town

Town Clerk, 47 Town Common Rd North, St. Albans, VT 05478. 802-524-3524; fax-802-524-3543; hours: 8AM-5PM M-Th; 8AM-4PM Fri. www.townofgeorgia.com

Will charge in person searches for vault time-$2.00 per hour. Separate indices to search include general indexes to 1970, cards-1970-4 1 2001, computer 2001 to now. Only the public may search. Copy fee $1.00 per page. Cert fee- $7.00 per page plus copy fee. Payee- Town of Georgia. **Other phones:** Treasurer- 802-524-3524; Appraiser Auditor- 802-524-3543; Elections- 802-524-3524; Vital Records- 802-524-3524; Town Administrator- 802-524-9794. **Property tax/Assessor**- same address as above. 802-524-3543.

Glover Town

Town Clerk, 51 Bean Hill, Glover, VT 05839. 802-525-6227; fax-802-525-4115; hours: 8AM-4PM, M-F. All records in one index. Record index not computerized. Only the public may search. Copy fee $1.00 per page. Cert fee- $7.00 per page. Payee- Town of Glover. **Other phones:** Treasurer- 802-525-6227; Appraiser/Auditor- 802-525-6227; Elections- 802-525-6227; Vital Records- 802-525-6227. **Property tax/Assessor**- same address as above. 802-525-6227.

Goshen Town

Town Clerk, 50 Carlisle Hill Rd., Goshen, VT 05733. 802-247-6455; fax-none; hours: 9AM-1PM Tues. Separate indices, but agency in process of combining last 15 years into one index. Will not search real estate records. Will search UCC records and tax liens. UCC search per debtor name- $10.00. Copy fee $1.00 per page. Cert fee- $7.00 per page total, plus copy fee. Payee- Town Clerk. **Property tax/Assessor**- same address as above. 802-247-6455.

Grafton Town

Town Clerk, PO Box 180, Grafton, VT 05146. 802-843-2419; hours: 9AM-N, 1-4PM M,T,Th,F. Office personnel will only search if time; suggests visitors to perform searches. Search fee $5.00. Will not search real estate records. Will not search UCC records or tax liens. Copy fee $1.00 per page. Cert fee- $6.00 per page. Payee- Grafton Town Clerk.

Granby Town

Town Clerk, PO Box 56, Granby, VT 05840. 802-328-3611; fax-802-328-2200; hours: by appointment only. Office personnel or visitors may perform searches. General search fee $2.00 per name. UCC search per debtor name- $10.00. UCC search request using non-standard form (per name)- $15.00. Copy fee $1.00 per page. Cert fee- $7.00 per page. Payee- Town of Grandby. **Property tax/Assessor**- 802-328-2191.

Grand Isle Town Clerk

Town Clerk, PO Box 49, Grand Isle, VT 05458. 802-372-8830; fax-802-372-8815; 8:30AM-3:30PM. Only the public may search. Copy fee $7.00 per page. Cert fee- $7.00 per doc plus copy fee. Payee- Town of Grand Isle. **Other phones:** Treasurer- 802-372-8830; Appraiser/Auditor- 802-372-5233; Elections- 802-372-8830; Vital Records- 802-372-8830. **Property tax/Assessor**- 802-372-5233.

Granville Town

Town Clerk, PO Box 66, Granville, VT 05747-0066. 802-767-4403; fax-802-767-3968; hours: 9AM-3PM M-Th; closed Fri. All records in one index. Record index not computerized. Only the public may search. Copy fee $1.00 per page. Cert fee- $7.00 per page total. Payee- Granville Town Clerk. **Other phones:** Treasurer- 802-767-4403. **Property tax/Assessor**- same address as above. 802-767-4403.

Greensboro Town

Town Clerk, Box 119, Greensboro, VT 05841. 802-533-2911; hours: 9AM-Noon, 1PM-4:30PM T-TH; 10-Noon, 1PM-4:30PM F.

Separate indices to search include liens & attachments separate, zoning separate, deeds & mortgages. Only the public may search. Copy fee $1.00 per page. Cert fee- $7.00 per page includes copy fee. Payee- Greensboro Town Clerk.

Groton Town

Town Clerk, 314 Scott Highway, Groton, VT 05046. 802-584-3276; fax-802-584-3276; hours: 8:30AM-12:30, 1-5PM M T Th; 8:30AM-N W. www.grotonvt.com Record index not computerized. Only the public may search. Copy fee $1.00 per page. Cert fee- $7.00 per doc plus copy fee. Payee- Town of Groton. **Other phones:** Treasurer- 802-584-3276; Appraiser/Auditor- 802-584-3131; Elections- 802-584-3276; Vital Records- 802-584-3276. **Property tax/Assessor**- 802-584-3276/ 584-3131.

Guildhall Town

Town Clerk, PO Box 10, Guildhall, VT 05905. 802-676-3797; fax-802-676-3518; hours: 9AM-Noon T, Th or by appt. All records in one index. Record index not computerized. Only the public may search. Copy fee $1.50 per page from any records book, other $.50 per page. Cert fee- $7.00 per page plus copy fee. Payee- Town of Guildhall.

Guilford Town

Town Clerk, 236 School Rd., Guilford, VT 05301-8319. 802-254-6857; fax-802-257-5764; hours: 9AM-6PM M; 9AM-4PM T,Th,F; 9AM-N Wed. All records in one index. Office will perform a UCC search but public must search other records themselves. UCC search per debtor name- $10.00. Copy fee $1.00 per page. Cert fee- $7.00 per page plus copy fee. Payee- Town of Guilford. **Other phones:** Treasurer- 802-254-6857; Appraiser/Auditor- 802-254-6857; Elections- 802-254-6857; Vital Records- 802-254-6857. **Property tax/Assessor**- 802-254-6857.

Halifax Town

Town Clerk, PO Box 127, West Halifax, VT 05358. 802-368-7390; fax-802-368-7390; hours: 9AM-4PM M,T,F; 9AM-N Sat. Index: Card index and Books. Only the public may search. Copy fee $.25; R/E or tax lien $1.00 per copy. Cert fee- $7.00 per page plus copy fee. Payee- Halifax Town Clerk. **Other phones:** Treasurer- 802-368-7698; Appraiser/Auditor- 802-368-7390; Elections- 802-368-7390; Vital Records- 802-368-7390. **Property tax/Assessor**- same address as above. 802-368-7390.

Hancock Town

Town Clerk, PO Box 100, Hancock, VT 05748. 802-767-3660; fax-802-767-3660; hours: 9AM-3PM M-TH. Separate indices to search. Only the public may search. Copy fee $1.00 per page, $2.00 minimum. Cert fee- $7.00 per page plus copy fee. Payee- Town of Hancock. **Other phones:** Treasurer- 802-767-3660; Appraiser/Auditor- 802-767-3660; Elections- 802-767-3660; Vital Records- 802-767-3660. **Property tax/Assessor**- 802-767-3301.

Hardwick Town

Town Clerk, Box 523, Hardwick, VT 05843. 802-472-5971; fax-802-472-3793; hours: 9AM-4PM. All records in one index. Record index not computerized. Only the public may search. Copy fee $1.00 per page. Cert fee- $7.00 per page includes copy fee. Payee- Town of Hardwick. **Other phones:** Treasurer- 802-472-5971; Appraiser/Auditor- 802-472-5971; Elections- 802-472-5971; Vital Records- 802-472-5971. **Property tax/Assessor**- 802-472-5971.

Hartford Town

Town Clerk, 171 Bridge St, White River Junction, VT 05001-1920. 802-295-2785; hours: 8AM-N, 1-5PM. www.hartford-vt.org Separate indices to search include UCC. Will not search real estate records. Will search UCC records, but not tax liens. UCC search per debtor name- $10.00. UCC search request using non-standard form (per name)- $15.00. Copy fee $2.00 per page. R/E or tax lien copy- $1.00 per page. Cert fee- $7.00 per page includes copy fee. Payee- Town of Hartford. **Other phones:** Treasurer- 802-295-3002; Appraiser/Auditor- 802-295-3077; Elections- 802-295-2785; Vital Records- 802-295-2785. **Property tax/Assessor**- 171 Bridge St, White River Junction, VT 05001; 802-295-3077.

Hartland Town

Town Clerk, PO Box 349, Hartland, VT 05048-0349. 802-436-2444; fax-802-436-2464; hours: 8AM-4PM. Office personnel or visitors may perform searches. Search fee $10.00 per name. Will not search real estate records. Copy fee $1.00 per page. Cert fee- $7.00 per page. Payee- Town of Hartland. **Other phones:** Treasurer- 802-436-2464; Elections- 802-436-2444; Vital Records- 802-436-2444. **Property tax/Assessor**- 802-436-2464.

Highgate Town

Town Clerk, PO Box 67, Highgate Center, VT 05459. 802-868-4697; hours: 8:30AM-12, 1PM-4:30PM. Only the public may search. Payee- Town of Highgate. **Property tax/Assessor**- 802-868-2741.

Hinesburg Town

Town Clerk, PO Box 133, Hinesburg, VT 05461. 802-482-2281; fax-802-482-5404; hours: 8AM-4PM. All records in one index. Only the public may search. Copy fee $1.00 per page. Tax map- $.25 per copy. Cert fee- $7.00 per page includes copies. Payee- Town of Hinesburg. **Property tax/Assessor**- 802-482-3619.

Holland Town

Town Clerk, 120 School Rd., Holland/Derby Line, VT 05830. 802-895-4440; fax-802-895-4440; hours: 8AM-3PM M,T,Th; 8AM-N Fri; closed Wed. Separate indices to search include liens, UCCs. Only the public may search. Copy fee $1.00 per page. Cert fee- $7.00 per doc plus copy fee. Payee- Town of Holland. **Other phones:** Treasurer- 802-895-4440; Elections- 802-895-4440; Vital Records- 802-895-4440. **Property tax/Assessor**- same address as above. 802-895-4440.

Hubbardton Town

Town Clerk, 1831 Monument Hill Rd, Castleton, VT 05735. 802-273-2951; fax-802-273-3729; hours: 9AM-2PM M,W,F. All records in one index. Search fee $5.00 per hour. Real estate owner, mortgage, and property transfer searches available as time permits Copy fee $1.00 per page. Cert fee- $7.00 per doc plus copy fee. Payee- Hubbardton Town Clerk. **Property tax/Assessor**- same address as above. 802-273-2951.

Huntington Town

Town Clerk, 4930 Main Rd., Huntington, VT 05462. 802-434-2032; fax-802-434-4731; hours: 8AM-4PM M,W; 7AM-2PM Tu,F; 8AM-6PM Th. www.huntingtonvt.org All records in one index. Record index not computerized. Only the public may search. Copy fee $1.00 per page. Cert fee- $7.00 per page total includes copy fee. Payee- Town of Huntington. **Other phones:** Treasurer- 802-434-2032; Appraiser/Auditor- 802-434-5783; Elections- 802-434-2032; Vital Records- 802-434-2032; Administrator- 802-434-4779. **Property tax/Assessor**- same address as above. 802-434-5783.

Hyde Park Town

Town Clerk, PO Box 98, Hyde Park, VT 05655-0098. 802-888-2300; fax-802-888-6878; hours: 8AM-4PM. Separate indices to search include 1970 to present-cards, before 1970 general index. Record index not computerized. Only the public may search. Copy fee $1.00 per page. Cert fee- $7.00 per record plus copy fee. Payee- Town Clerk. **Other phones:** Treasurer- 802-888-2300; Appraiser/Auditor- 802-888-7786; Elections- 802-888-2300; Vital Records- 802-888-2300; Zoning/Health Officer- 802-888-7784. **Property tax/Assessor-** same address as above. 802-888-7786.

Ira Town

Town Clerk, 808 Route 133, West Rutland, VT 05777. 802-235-2745; hours: 9AM-2:30PM M; 2-7PM T. All records in one index. Record index not computerized. Only the public may search. Copy fee $1.00 per page. Cert fee- $7.00 per page plus copy fee. Payee- Ira Town Clerk. **Other phones:** Treasurer- 802-235-2745; Appraiser/Auditor- 802-235-2745; Elections- 802-235-2745; Vital Records- 802-235-2745. **Property tax/Assessor-** 802-235-2745.

Irasburg Town

Town Clerk, Box 51, Irasburg, VT 05845. 802-754-2242; fax-802-754-2242; hours: 9AM-3PM M,W,Th. All records in one index. Office personnel or visitors may perform searches. Will search real estate records. Will search UCC records and tax liens. UCC search per debtor name- $10.00. UCC search request using non-standard form (per name)- $15.00. Copy fee $1.00 per page. Cert fee- $2.00 per page plus copy fee. Payee- Irasburg Town Clerk. **Other phones:** Treasurer- 802-754-2242; Appraiser/Auditor- 802-754-2242; Elections- 802-754-2242; Vital Records- 802-754-2242. **Property tax/Assessor-** 802-754-2242.

Isle La Motte Town

Town Clerk, PO Box 250, Isle La Motte, VT 05463. 802-928-3434; fax-802-928-3002; hours: 8AM-3PM Tu,Th; 8AM-N Sat. All records in one index. Office will perform a UCC search but public must search other records themselves. UCC search per debtor name- $10.00. UCC search request using non-standard form (per name)- $15.00. Copy fee $1.00 per page. Cert fee- $7.00 per doc includes copy fee. Payee- Isle LaMotte Town Clerk. **Other phones:** Treasurer- 802-928-3434; Appraiser/Auditor- 802-928-3434; Elections- 802-928-3434; Vital Records- 802-928-3434. **Property tax/Assessor-** 204 Lakehurst Rd, Isle Lamotte, VT 05463; 802-928-3434.

Jamaica Town

Town Clerk, PO Box 173, Jamaica, VT 05343. 802-874-4681; hours: 9AM-N, 1-4PM T,W,Th,F. All records in one index. Record index not computerized. Only the public may search. Copy fee $1.00 per page, $2.00 minimum. Cert fee- $7.00 per page plus copy fee. Payee- Town of Jamaica. **Property tax/Assessor-** 802-874-4908.

Jay Town

Town Clerk, 1036 Vermont Rte. 242, Jay, VT 05859-9820. 802-988-2996; fax-802-988-2996; hours: 7AM-4PM (Closed M). Separate indices to search include zoning permits, UCC's and vital records. Record index not computerized. Office personnel or visitors may perform searches. Search fee $10.00 per name. Copy fee $1.00, $2.00 minimum. Cert fee- $7.00 per page. Payee- Town of Jay.

Jericho Town

Town Clerk, PO Box 67, Jericho, VT 05465. 802-899-4936; fax-802-899-5549; hours: 8AM-5PM M-TH, 8AM-3PM F. www.jerichovt.gov Separate indices to search include UCC's. Records indexed on computer back to 1999. Only the public may search. Copy fee $1.00 per page. Cert fee- $7.00 per page. Payee- Town of Jericho. **Other phones:** Treasurer- 802-899-4786; Appraiser/Auditor- 802-899-2640; Elections- 802-899-4936; Vital Records- 802-899-4936. **Property tax/Assessor-** 802-899-2640.

Johnson Town

Town Clerk, PO Box 383, Johnson, VT 05656. 802-635-2611; fax-802-635-9523; hours: 7:30AM-4PM. Only the public may search. Copy fee $1.00 per page. **Other phones:** Treasurer- 802-635-2611; Appraiser/Auditor- 802-635-2611; Elections- 802-635-2611; Vital Records- 802-635-2611. **Property tax/Assessor-** 802-635-2611.

Killington Town

Town Clerk, PO Box 429, Killington, VT 05751-0429. 802-422-3243; fax-802-422-3030; hours: 9AM-3PM. www.killingtontown.com Formerly known as the Town of Sherburne. Separate indices to search include land records, UCC, card index 1960-1980, Liens and attachments, maps, general index pre-1980. Only the public may search. Copy fee $1.00 per page. Cert fee- $7.00 per page includes copy fee. Payee- Killington Town Clerk. **Other phones:** Treasurer- 802-422-3241; Elections- 802-422-3243; Vital Records- 802-422-3243.

Kirby Town

Town Clerk, 346 Town Hall Rd.; Town of Kirby, Lyndonville, VT 05851-9802. 802-626-9386; fax-802-626-9386; hours: 8AM-3PM; T,TH. All records in one index. Record index not computerized. Only the public may search. Copy fee $1.00 per page. Cert fee- $2.00 per page plus copy fee. Payee- Town of Kirby. **Other phones:** Treasurer- 802-626-9386; Appraiser/Auditor- 802-626-9386; Elections- 802-626-9386; Vital Records- 802-626-9386. **Property tax/Assessor-** same address as above. 802-626-9386.

Landgrove Town

Town Clerk, Box 508, Londonderry, VT 05148. 802-824-3716; fax-802-824-3716; hours: 9AM-1PM. Separate indices to search include land records, UCCs, Liens. Record index not computerized. Office will perform a UCC and Tax lien search but public must search other records themselves. Search fee $10.00. Copy fee $7.00 per page. Cert fee- $7.00 per page. Payee- Landgrove Town Clerk. **Other phones:** Treasurer- 802-824-3716; Appraiser/Auditor- 802-824-3716; Elections- 802-824-3716; Vital Records- 802-824-3716. **Property tax/Assessor-** 15 Cody Rd, Londonderry, VT 05148; 802-824-3716.

Leicester Town

Town Clerk, 44 Schoolhouse Rd., Leicester, VT 05733. 802-247-5961; hours: 1-4PM M-W. All records in one index. No search fee but copy fees are similar to typical search fees. Will not search real estate records. Will not search UCC records or tax liens. Copy fee $7.00 per page; UCC copy $20.00 per page. Cert fee- $7.00 per page total. Payee- Leicester Town Clerk. **Other phones:** Treasurer- 802-247-5961; Appraiser/Auditor- 802-247-5961; Elections- 802-247-5961; Vital Records- 802-247-5961. **Property tax/Assessor-** 802-247-5961.

Lemington Town

Town Clerk, 2549 River Rd, VT 102, Lemington, VT 05903. 802-277-4814; hours: 10AM-1PM W. www.rootsweb.com/~vermont/TownLemington.html All records in one index. Records indexed on computer. Only the public may search. Copy fee $.50; $1.50 per page UCC. Cert fee- $6.00 per page includes copy fee. Payee- Town of Lemington.

Lincoln Town

Town Clerk, 62 Quaker St., Lincoln, VT 05443. 802-453-2980; fax-802-453-2975; hours: 9AM-N, 1PM-4PM T-F; 9AM-N Sat, Closed Monday. All records in one index. Only the public may search. Copy fee $1.00 per page.

Londonderry Town

Town Clerk, PO Box 118, South Londonderry, VT 05155-0118. 802-824-3356; hours: 9AM-3PM T-F; 9AM-12 Sat. Separate indices to search include card file drawers, old records in books. Only the public may search. Copy fee $1.00 per page. Cert fee- $7.00 per page plus copy fee. Payee- Londonderry Town Clerk.

Lowell Town

Town Clerk, 2170 VT Rt. 100, Lowell, VT 05847-0007. 802-744-6559; fax-802-744-2357; hours: 9AM-2:30PM Mon & Th. Record index not computerized. Only the public may search. Copy fee $1.00 per record. Cert fee- $7.00 per record plus copy fee. Payee- Lowell Town. **Other phones:** Treasurer- 802-744-6559; Appraiser/Auditor- 802-744-6559; Elections- 802-744-6559; Vital Records- 802-744-6559. **Property tax/Assessor-** same address as above. not known.

Ludlow Town

Town Clerk, PO Box 307, Ludlow, VT 05149. 802-228-3232; fax-802-228-8399; hours: 8:30AM-4:30PM. www.ludlow.vt.us All records in one index. Record index not computerized. Only the public may search. Copy fee $1.00 per page. Cert fee- $7.00 per page plus copy fee. Payee- Town of Ludlow. **Other phones:** Treasurer- 802-228-3232; Appraiser/Auditor- 802-228-7206; Elections- 802-228-3232; Vital Records- 802-228-3232. **Property tax/Assessor-** 802-228-7206.

Lunenburg Town

Town Clerk, PO Box 54, Lunenburg, VT 05906. 802-892-5959; fax-802-892-5100; hours: 8:30AM-N, 1PM-3PM. All records in one index. Office will perform a UCC search but public must search other records themselves. UCC search per debtor name- $10.00. UCC search request using non-standard form (per name)- $15.00. Copy fee $.50 per page. UCC copy $2.00 per page. Cert fee- $5.00 includes copy fee. Payee- Lunenburg Town Clerk. **Other phones:** Treasurer- 802-892-5959; Appraiser/Auditor- 802-892-1162; Elections- 802-892-5959; Vital Records- 802-892-5959. **Property tax/Assessor-** same address as above. 802-892-1162.

Lyndon Town

Town Clerk, PO Box 167, Lyndonville, VT 05851. 802-626-5785; fax-802-626-1265; 7:30AM-4:30PM. All records in one index. Records indexed on computer. Office will perform a UCC search but public must search other records themselves. Search fee $10.00. Copy fee $1.00 per page. Cert fee- $6.00 per page plus copy fee. Payee- Lyndon Town Clerk. **Other phones:** Treasurer- 802-626-5785; Appraiser/Auditor- 802-626-1270; Elections- 802-626-5785; Vital Records- 802-626-5785. **Property tax/Assessor-** same address as above. 802-626-1270.

Maidstone Town

Town Clerk, PO Box 118, Maidstone, VT 05905-0118. 802-676-3210; fax-802-676-3210; hours: 9AM-11AM M-TH. Separate indices to search include books and cards. Records index not computerized. Search fee $5.00 per hour. Will search real estate records. Will search UCC records, tax liens not included in UCC search. UCC search per debtor name- $10.00. Copy fee $1.00 per page; $2.00 minimum. Cert fee- $7.00 per doc plus copy fee. Payee- Maidstone Town

Clerk. **Other phones:** Treasurer- 802-676-3210; Elections- 802-676-3210; Vital Records- 802-676-3210. **Property tax/Assessor-** same address as above. 802-676-3210.

Manchester Town

Town Clerk, PO Box 830, Manchester Center, VT 05255. 802-362-1315; fax-802-362-1315; hours: 8:30AM-1PM, 2-4:30PM M-T-Th-F; 10AM-6PM W. www.town.manchester.vt.us
All records in one index. Only the public may search. General index search fee $5.00 per hour. Copy fee $1.00 per page. UCC copy fee $2.00 per page. Payee- Manchester Town Clerk. **Other phones:** Treasurer- 802-362-1197; Appraiser/Auditor- 802-362-1373; Elections- 802-362-1315; Vital Records- 802-362-1315; Town Manager- 802-362-1313; Planning/Zoning -802-362-4824. **Property tax/Assessor-** 6039 Main St, Manchester Center, VT 05255; 802-362-1373.

Marlboro Town

Town Clerk, PO Box E, Marlboro, VT 05344-0305. 802-254-2181; fax-802-257-2447; hours: 9AM-4PM M,W,Th.
All records in one index. Record index not computerized. Only the public may search. Minor checking search fee is $5.00 per name. Copy fee $1.00 per copy. Minimum $2.00. Cert fee- $7.00 per page plus copy fee. Payee- Town of Marlboro. **Other phones:** Treasurer- 802-254-2181; Appraiser/Auditor- 802-254-2181; Elections- 802-254-2181; Vital Records- 802-254-2181. **Property tax/Assessor-** same address as above. 802-254-2181.

Marshfield Town

Town Clerk, 122 School St, Rm 1, Marshfield, VT 05658. 802-426-3305; fax-802-426-3045; hours: 7:30AM-3:30PM.
Separate indices to search include surveys and UCC's. Only the public may search. Copy fee $1.00 per page; $2.00 minimum. Cert fee- $7.00 per page plus copy fee. Payee- Town of Marshfield. **Other phones:** Treasurer- 802-426-3305; Appraiser/Auditor- 802-426-3305; Elections- 802-426-3305; Vital Records- 802-426-3305; Delinquent Tax Collector- 802-426-3859. **Property tax/Assessor-** 802-426-3305.

Mendon Town

Town Clerk, 34 US Route 4, Mendon, VT 05701. 802-775-1662; fax-802-773-9682; hours: 8AM-3PM,M-W; 8AM-1PM,TH; CLOSED F.
Separate indices to search include land records and attachments on one index. Records indexed on computer back to 02/02. Only the public may search. Copy fee $1.00 per page. Cert fee- $7.00 per cert plus copy fee. Payee- Mendon Town Clerk. **Other phones:** Treasurer- 802-775-1662; Elections- 802-775-1662; Vital Records- 802-775-1662. **Property tax/Assessor-** same address as above. 802-496-9689.

Middlebury Town

Town Clerk, 94 Main St, Middlebury, VT 05753-1334. 802-388-4041 x222; fax-802-388-4261; hours: 8:30AM-4:30PM.
Separate indices to search include UCC's, maps. Records indexed on computer back to 1955. Only the public may search. Copy fee $1.00 per copy. Cert fee- $7.00 per page plus copy fee. Payee- Town of Middlebury. **Other phones:** Treasurer- 802-388-8101; Appraiser/Auditor- 802-388-4352; Elections- 802-388-8102 x240; Vital Records- 802-388-4041 x222. **Property tax/Assessor-** same address as above. 802-388-8108.

Middlesex Town

Town Clerk, 5 Church St., Middlesex, VT 05602. 802-223-5915; fax-802-223-0569; hours: M-Th 8:30-N, 1-4:30PM. www.middlesex-vt.org
All records in one index. Record index not computerized. Only the public may search. Copy fee $1.00 per page. Cert fee- $7.00 per cert plus copy fee. Payee- Town Clerk. **Other phones:** Treasurer- 802-223-5915; Appraiser/Auditor- 802-223-5915; Elections- 802-223-5915; Vital Records- 802-223-5915. **Property tax/Assessor-** 802-223-5915.

Middletown Springs Town

Town Clerk, PO Box 1232, Middletown Springs, VT 05757-1197. 802-235-2220; fax-802-235-2066; hours: 9AM-N, 1-4PM M, Tu; 1-4PM F; 9AM-N Sat. Office will perform a UCC search but public must search other records themselves. UCC search per debtor name- $10.00. UCC search request using non-standard form (per name)- $15.00. Copy fee $1.00 per page. Cert fee- $7.00 per page. Payee- Middletown Springs Town Clerk.

Milton Town

Town Clerk, PO Box 18, Milton, VT 05468. 802-893-4111; fax-802-893-1005; hours: 8AM-5PM. www.milton.govoffice2.com
All records in one index. Record index not computerized. Office will perform a UCC search but public must search other records themselves. UCC search per debtor name- $10.00. Copy fee $1.00 per page. Cert fee- $7.00 per page plus copy fee. Payee- Town of Milton. **Other phones:** Treasurer- 802-893-4111; Appraiser/Auditor- 802-893-4325; Elections- 802-893-4111; Vital Records- 802-893-4111. **Property tax/Assessor-** 43 Bombardier Rd., Milton, VT 05468; 802-893-4325.

Monkton Town

Town Clerk, 280 Yorkton Ridge, North Ferrisburg, VT 05473-9509. 802-453-3800; fax-802-453-5612; hours: 8AM-1PM M,T,Th,F; 8:30AM-N Sat.
Separate indices to search. Only the public may search. Copy fee $1.00 per page. Cert fee- $1.00 per page plus copy fee. Payee- Monkton Town Clerk. **Other phones:** Treasurer- 802-453-3800; Appraiser/Auditor- 802-453-3800; Elections- 802-453-3800; Vital Records- 802-453-3800. **Property tax/Assessor-** same address as above. 802-453-4515.

Montgomery Town

Town Clerk, PO Box 356, Montgomery Center, VT 05471-0356. 802-326-4719; fax-802-326-4939; hours: 8AM-N 1PM-4PM M,T,TH,F; 9AM-N W. www.vermont-towns.org/montgomery'
Separate indices to search include index cards 1994 to present, and general index back to 2002. Records indexed on computer back to 1/2/2003. Only the public may search. Copy fee $1.00 per page; $2.00 minimum. Cert fee- $6.00 per page plus copy fee. **Other phones:** Treasurer- 802-326-4719; Appraiser/Auditor- 802-326-4719; Elections- 802-326-4719; Vital Records- 802-326-4719. **Property tax/Assessor-** 802-326-4719.

Montpelier City

City Clerk, 39 Main St; City Hall, Montpelier, VT 05602. 802-223-9500; fax-802-223-9523; hours: 8AM-4:30PM.
Office will perform a UCC search but public must search other records themselves. UCC search per debtor name- $10.00. UCC search request using non-standard form (per name)- $15.00. Copy fee $2.00 per page. R/E record copy- $.50 per page. Cert fee- $7.00 per page. **Property tax/Assessor-** 802-223-9504.

Moretown Town

Town Clerk, PO Box 666, Moretown, VT 05660. 802-496-3645; hours: 9AM-noon, 1-4:30PM M-Th; 9AM-3:30PM F.
All records in one index. Only the public may search. Copy fee $1.00 per page. Cert fee- $7.00 per page plus copy fee. Payee- Moretown Town Clerk.

Morgan Town

Town Clerk, PO Box 45, Morgan, VT 05853-0045. 802-895-2927; fax-802-895-4204; hours: 8AM-2PM M, 7AM-2PM T-Th, 7AM-N Fri.
Index: All in on as of 2001. Only the public may search. Search fee- for self search $2.00 hour. R/E record copy- $1.00 per page, $2.00 minimum. Cert fee- $7.00 per page total. Payee- Morgan Town Clerk, Town of Morgan. **Other phones:** Treasurer- 802-895-2927; Appraiser/Auditor- 802-875-2858; Elections- 802-895-2927; Vital Records- 802-895-2927. **Property tax/Assessor-** 802-895-2858.

Morristown Town

Town Clerk, PO Box 748, Morrisville, VT 05661-0748. 802-888-6370; fax-802-888-6375; hours: 8:30AM-4:30PM, M,T,TH, F; 8:30AM-12:30PM, W. www.morristownvt.org
All records in one index. Office will perform a UCC search but public must search other records themselves. UCC search per debtor name- $5.00 per hour. UCC search request using non-standard form (per name)- $20.00. Copy fee $2.00 per page. R/E or tax lien copy- $1.00 per page. Cert fee- $7.00 per page includes copy fee. Payee- Town of Morristown. **Property tax/Assessor-** same address as above. 802-888-6371.

Mount Holly Town

Town Clerk, PO Box 248, Mount Holly, VT 05758. 802-259-2391; fax-802-259-2391; hours: 8:30AM-4PM M-TH.
Index: Liens in a separate book. Only the public may search. Copy fee $1.00 per page. Cert fee- $7.00 per page. Payee- Town Clerk. **Other phones:** Treasurer- 802-259-2391; Appraiser/Auditor- 802-259-2391; Elections- 802-259-2391; Vital Records- 802-259-2391. **Property tax/Assessor-** 802-259-2391.

Mount Tabor Town

Town Clerk, PO Box 245, Mt. Tabor, VT 05739. 802-293-5282; fax-802-293-5287; hours: Tues & Wed 9AM-Noon.
All records in one index. Office personnel or visitors may perform searches. Will search UCC records. UCC search per debtor name- $10.00. UCC search request using non-standard form (per name)- $15.00. Tax lien search fee- $10.00 per search. Separate federal tax lien search- $10.00 per search. Federal/state combined tax lien search- $10.00 per search. Copy fee $1.00 per page. Cert fee- $7.00 per copy includes copy fee. Payee- Mt. Tabor Town Clerk. **Other phones:** Treasurer- 802-293-5282; Appraiser/Auditor- 802-293-5282; Elections- 802-293-5282; Vital Records- 802-293-5282. **Property tax/Assessor-** 802-293-5282.

New Haven Town

Town Clerk, 78 North St., New Haven, VT 05472. 802-453-3516; fax-802-453-3516; hours: 9AM-3PM. www.newhavenvt.com
Only the public may search. Copy fee $2.00, if tax lien or real estate $1.00 per page. Cert fee- $7.00 per page total. Payee- Town of New Haven. **Property tax/Assessor-** same address as above. 802-453-3516.

Newark Town

Town Clerk, 1336 Newark St, Newark, VT 05871. 802-467-3336; hours: 9AM-4PM M,W,Th.
All records in one index. Record index not computerized. Only the public may search. Copy fee $1.00 per page. Cert fee- $7.00 per page total. Payee- Newark Town Clerk.

Newbury Town

Town Clerk, PO Box 126, Newbury, VT 05051. 802-866-5521; fax-802-866-5301; hours: 8:30AM-2:30PM, M-F; 2:30-6PM T. www.cohase.org
Record index not computerized. Only the public may search. Copy fee $1.00 per page. Cert fee- $7.00 per page includes copy fee. Payee- Newbury

Town Clerk. **Other phones:** Treasurer- 802-866-5521; Appraiser/Auditor- 802-866-5521; Elections-802-866-5521; Vital Records- 802-866-5521. **Property tax/Assessor**- same address as above. 802-866-5521.

Newfane Town

Town Clerk, PO Box 36, Newfane, VT 05345-0036. 802-365-7772; fax-802-365-7692; hours: 9AM-3PM. www.newfanevt.com
Index: Records are in 3 general indexes. Record index not computerized. Only the public may search. Copy fee $1.00 per page. Cert fee- $7.00 per page plus copy fee.

Newport City

Town Clerk, 222 Main St, Newport, VT 05855. 802-334-2112; fax-802-334-5632; 8:30AM-4:30PM.
Record index not computerized. Only the public may search. Search fee $25.00 per name. Will do a tax lien search. Copy fee $1.00 per page. Cert fee-$7.00 per page. Payee- City of Newport. **Online access to Assessor, Property records:** Access to Newport City assessor data is free at http://data.visionappraisal.com/newportvt/. **Other phones:** Treasurer- 802-334-2112; Appraiser/Auditor-802-334-6992; Elections- 802-334-2112; Vital Records- 802-334-2112. **Property tax/Assessor**- 802-334-6992.

Newport Town

Town Clerk, PO Box 85, Newport Center, VT 05857. 802-334-6442; fax-802-334-6442; hours: 7AM-4:30PM,M-Th, Closed F.
Only the public may search. Copy fee $1.00 per page. Cert fee- $7.00. Payee- Newport Town Clerk.

North Hero Town

Town Clerk, PO Box 38, North Hero, VT 05474-0038. 802-372-6926; fax-802-372-3806; hours: 9AM-4PM.
Records indexed on a public use terminal back to 12/15/2004. Only the public may search. Copy fee $1.00 per page. Cert fee- $7.00 per page. Payee-Town of North Hero+. **Other phones:** Treasurer-802-372-6926; Appraiser/Auditor- 802-372-6926; Elections- 802-372-6926; Vital Records- 802-372-6926. **Property tax/Assessor**- 802-372-6926.

Northfield Town

Town Clerk, 51 S. Main St, Northfield, VT 05663. 802-485-5421; fax-802-485-8426; www.northfield.vt.us
Will not search real estate records. Will search UCC records, but not tax liens. UCC search per debtor name- $20.00. Copy fee $1.00 per page. Cert fee-$7.00 per page, does not include copy fee. Payee-Town of Northfield. **Other phones:** Treasurer- 802-485-5421; Appraiser/Auditor- 802-485-6004; Elections- 802-485-5421; Vital Records- 802-485-5421. **Property tax/Assessor**- 51 S. Main St, Northfield, VT 05663; 802-485-6004.

Norton Town

Town Clerk, 12 VT Route 114E, Norton, VT 05907. 802-822-9935; fax-802-822-9935; hours: Appointment only.
All records in one index. Record index not computerized. Office personnel or visitors may perform searches. Search fee $5.00 per hour. Copy fee $2.00 per page. Cert fee- $7.00 per document plus copy fee. Payee- Norton Town Clerk. **Other phones:** Treasurer- 802-822-9935; Elections- 802-822-9935; Vital Records- 802-822-9935. **Property tax/Assessor**- same address as above. not known.

Norwich Town

Town Clerk, PO Box 376, Norwich, VT 05055. 802-649-1419; fax-802-649-0123; hours: 8:30-4:30 M,T,W,F, 8:30AM-7PM Th. www.norwich.vt.us
All records in one index. Record index not computerized. Office will perform a UCC search but public must search other records themselves. Copy fee $1.00 per page. Cert fee- $7.00 per cert plus copy fee. Payee- Norwich Town Clerk. **Other phones:** Treasurer- 802-649-0122; Elections- 802-649-1419; Vital Records- 802-649-1419. **Property tax/Assessor**- 802-649-1116.

Orange Town

Town Clerk, PO Box 233, East Barre, VT 05649. 802-479-2673; fax-802-479-2673; hours: 8AM-N, 1-4PM.
All records in one index. Record index not computerized. Only the public may search. Copy fee $1.00 per page. Cert fee- $7.00 per page. Payee- Town Clerk. **Property tax/Assessor**- same address as above. not known.

Orwell Town

Town Clerk, PO Box 32, Orwell, VT 05760-0032. 802-948-2032; hours: 9:30AM-N, 1-3:30PM M, T, Th, F.
Separate indices to search include general index books to 1997; cards 1997 to present. Only the public may search. General copy fee $1.00; UCC copy fee $2.00 per page; $5.00 if oversize. Cert fee- $7.00 per page plus copy fee. Payee- Town of Orwell. **Other phones:** Treasurer- 802-948-2811. **Property tax/Assessor**- same address as above. 802-948-2665.

Panton Town

Town Clerk, PO Box 174, Vergennes, VT 05491-0174. 802-475-2333; fax-802-475-2785; hours: 9AM-5PM M,Th; 9AM-2PM Tu, F; 4-7PM W. www.pantonvt.us/clerk.html
All records in one index. Records indexed not computerized. Office will perform a UCC search but public must search other records themselves. UCC search per debtor name- $10.00. Copy fee $7.00; tax liens $.25 per page. Cert fee- $7.00 per page total, includes copies. Payee- Panton Town Clerk. **Property tax/Assessor**- 802-496-9689.

Pawlet Town

Town Clerk, PO Box 128, Pawlet, VT 05761-0128. 802-325-3309, UCC recording phone-802-335-3309; fax-802-325-6109; 9AM-4PM T-TH; 9AM-N Fri.
All records in one index. Only the public may search. Copy fee $1.00 per page. Cert fee- $6.00 per page plus copy fee. Payee- Town of Pawlet. **Other phones:** Treasurer- 802-335-3309; Elections-802-335-3309; Vital Records- 802-335-3309. **Property tax/Assessor**- same address as above. 802-325-3309.

Peacham Town

Town Clerk, Box 244, Peacham, VT 05862. 802-592-3218; fax-802-592-3011; hours: 8:30AM-Noon T,W,Th,F; 3PM-7PM Wed. www.peacham.net
Office will perform a UCC search but public must search other records themselves. UCC search per debtor name- $10.00. UCC search request using non-standard form (per name)- $15.00. Copy fee $1.00 per page. Cert fee- $7.00 per page. Payee-Town of Peacham. **Other phones:** Appraiser/Auditor- 802-592-3011. **Property tax/Assessor**- 802-592-3011.

Peru Town

Town Clerk, Box 127, Peru, VT 05152. 802-824-3065; fax-802-824-3065; hours: 8:30AM-4PM T, Th.
Separate indices to search include 3 index books, separate lien & attachments. Record index not computerized. Only the public may search. Copy fee $1.00 per page. Cert fee- $7.00 per page. Payee- Town of Peru.

Pittsfield Town

Town Clerk, PO Box 556, Pittsfield, VT 05762-0556. 802-746-8170; fax-802-746-8170; hours: Noon-6PM T; 9AM-3PM W,Th.
Only the public may search. Copy fee $1.00 per page. Cert fee- $7.00 per page. Payee- Town of Pittsfield. **Other phones:** Treasurer- 802-746-8050. **Property tax/Assessor**- 802-746-8113.

Pittsford Town

Town Clerk, PO Box 10, Pittsford, VT 5763. 802-483-2931, R/E recording phone-802-483-6500 x12; fax-802-483-6612; hours: 8AM-4:30PM. www.town.pittsford.vt.us
All records in one index. Office personnel or visitors may perform searches. Will not search real estate records. UCC search per debtor name-$10.00. Federal/state combined tax lien search-$10.00 per search. Copy fee $1.00 per UCC. Cert fee- $7.00 per page. Payee- Town of Pittsford. **Other phones:** Treasurer- 802-483-6500 x12; Appraiser/Auditor- 802-483-6500 x12; Elections- 802-483-6500 x12; Vital Records- 802-483-6500 x12. **Property tax/Assessor**- same address as above. 802-483-6500 x15.

Plainfield Town

Town Clerk, PO Box 217, Plainfield, VT 5667. 802-454-8461; fax-802-454-8461; hours: 7:30AM-N, 12:30-4PM M,W,F.
All records in one index. Only the public may search. Records available for in person searching M/W/F 7:30AM-4PM. Will not search tax liens. Copy fee $1.00 per page. **Other phones:** Treasurer- 802-454-8461; Appraiser/Auditor- 802-454-8461; Elections- 802-454-8461. **Property tax/Assessor**- 802-454-8461.

Plymouth Town

Town Clerk, 68 Town Office Rd., Plymouth, VT 05056. 802-672-3655; fax-802-672-5466; hours: 8:30-11:30AM, 12:30-3:30PM.
Only the public may search. Copy fee $1.00 per page. Cert fee- $7.00. Payee- Plymouth Town Clerk. **Property tax/Assessor**- 802-672-3655.

Pomfret Town

Town Clerk, PO Box 64, South Pomfret, VT 05067. 802-457-3861; fax-none; 8:30AM-2:30PM M,W,F.
Only the public may search. Payee- Pomfret Town Clerk. **Other phones:** Elections- 802-457-3861. **Property tax/Assessor**- 802-457-3861.

Poultney Town

Town Clerk, 9 Main St, #2, Poultney, VT 05764. 802-287-5761; hours: 8:30AM-12:30, 1:30-4PM.
All records in one index. Office will perform a UCC search but public must search other records themselves. Husband and wife considered as one debtor for searching fee computation. Partnership name plus two partner names considered one name on filing for fee computation. UCC search per debtor name-$10.00. Copy fee $1.00 per page. UCC copy fee $2.00 per page. Cert fee- $7.00 per cert plus copy fee. Payee- Poultney Town Clerk. **Property tax/Assessor**- 802-287-5761.

Pownal Town

Town Clerk, PO Box 411, Pownal, VT 05261. 802-823-7757; fax-802-823-0116; hours: 9AM-2PM M W F; 9AM-4PM T and by appointment.
Record index not computerized. Office personnel or visitors may perform searches. Search fee $10.00 per name. Will not search real estate records. General copy fee $3.00 per page. Tax lien copy-$1.00. Cert fee- $7.00 per cert plus copy fee. Payee- Pownal Town Clerk. **Property tax/Assessor**- 802-823-5644.

Proctor Town

Town Clerk, 45 Main St, Proctor, VT 05765. 802-459-3333; fax-802-459-2356; hours: 8AM-4PM.
Only the public may search.

Putney Town

Town Clerk, PO Box 233, Putney, VT 05346. 802-387-5862 x14; hours: 9AM-2PM M, Th, F; 9AM-2PM, 7-9PM W; 9AM-N Sat.
Record index not computerized. Only the public may search. Copy fee $1.00 per page. Cert fee-

$7.00 per cert plus copy fee. Payee- Putney Town Clerk.

Randolph Town

Town Clerk, Drawer B, Randolph, VT 05060. 802-728-5682; fax-802-728-5818; hours: 8AM-N, 1-4:30PM. www.randolphvt.com
Separate indices to search include card index and general index. Record index not computerized. Office will perform a UCC search but public must search other records themselves. UCC search per debtor name- $20.00. Copy fee $2.00, if tax lien or real estate $1.00 per page. Cert fee- $7.00 per page plus copy fee. Payee- Town of Randolph. **Other phones:** Treasurer- 802-728-5682; Elections- 802-728-5682; Vital Records- 802-728-5682. **Property tax/Assessor-** same address as above. 802-728-5682.

Reading Town

Town Clerk, PO Box 72, Reading, VT 05062. 802-484-7250; fax-802-454-7250; hours: 8AM-4PM M-Th. www.readingvt.govoffice.com
All records in one index. Record index not computerized. Only the public may search. Copy fee $1.00 per page. Cert fee- $7.00 per page plus copy fee. Payee- Town of Reading. **Other phones:** Treasurer- 802-484-7250; Appraiser/Auditor- 802-484-7258; Elections- 802-484-7250; Vital Records- 802-484-7250. **Property tax/Assessor-** same address as above. 802-484-7258.

Readsboro Town

Town Clerk, PO Box 187, Readsboro, VT 05350. 802-423-5405; fax-802-423-5423; hours: 9AM-3PM M T TH F, 4PM-7PM 1st & 3rd W of the month.
Separate indices to search include A-Z, Frank Ross; A-Z readsboro, Volume 3; Computer print outs beginning with Volume 4. Records indexed on computer back to part of 1998. Only the public may search. General index search fee $5.00 per hour. Will search real estate records. Copy fee $1.00 per page. Cert fee- $7.00 per page plus copy fee. Payee- Town of Readsboro. **Other phones:** Treasurer- 802-423-5405; Elections- 802-423-5405; Vital Records- 802-423-5405. **Property tax/Assessor-** PO Box 247, Readsboro, VT 05350; 802-423-5405.

Richford Town

Town Clerk, PO Box 236, Richford, VT 05476-0236. 802-848-7751; fax-802-848-7752; hours: 8:30AM-4PM. www.richfordvt.com
All records in one index. Record index not computerized. Only the public may search. Copy fee $1.00 per page, $2.00 minimum. Cert fee- $7.00 per page plus copy fee. Payee- Town of Richford. **Other phones:** Treasurer- 802-848-7751; Appraiser/Auditor- 802-848-7751; Elections- 802-848-7751; Vital Records- 802-848-7751. **Property tax/Assessor-** same address as above. 802-848-7751.

Richmond Town

Town Clerk, PO Box 285, Richmond, VT 05477. 802-434-2221; hours: 8AM-6PM M; 8AM-4PM T-Th, 8AM-1PM F. www.richmondvt.com
All records in one index. Only the public may search. Copy fee $1.00 per page. Cert fee- $7.00 per doc plus copy fee. Payee- Town of Richmond. **Property tax/Assessor-** PO Box 285, Richmond, VT 05477; not known.

Ripton Town

Town Clerk, PO Box 10, Ripton, VT 05766-0010. 802-388-2266; fax-802-388-0012; hours: 2-6PM M; 9AM-1PM T,W,Th,F; closed Summer Fridays.
Separate indices to search include cards, books. Only the public may search. Copy fee $.25 per page. Cert fee- $5.00 per page includes copy fee. Payee- Town of Ripton. **Property tax/Assessor-** same address as above. 802-388-2266.

Rochester Town

Town Clerk, PO Box 238, Rochester, VT 05767-0238. 802-767-3631; fax-802-767-6028; hours: 9AM-N, 1PM-4PM.
Separate indices to search include vital records. Record index not computerized. Only the public may search. Copy fee $2.00 per page. R/E or tax lien copy- $7.00 per page. Cert fee- $7.00 per page plus copy fee. Payee- Town of Rochester. **Other phones:** Treasurer- 802-767-3631; Elections- 802-767-3631; Vital Records- 802-767-3631. **Property tax/Assessor-** 802-767-9872.

Rockingham Town

Town Clerk, PO Box 339, Bellows Falls, VT 05101-0339. 802-463-4336; fax-802-463-1228; hours: 8:30AM-4:30PM. www.rockbf.org
Separate indices to search include UCCs and everything else. Record index not computerized. Office will perform a UCC search but public must search other records themselves. UCC search per debtor name-$10.00 per search, tax liens not included. Copy fee $1.00 per page, $2.00 minimum. Cert fee- $7.00 per page total, plus copy fee. Payee- Town of Rockingham. **Other phones:** Treasurer- 802-463-3964; Elections- 802-463-4336; Vital Records- 802-463-4336; Health & Zoning- 802-463-3964. **Property tax/Assessor-** PO Box 370, Bellows Falls, VT 05101-0370; 802-463-1229.

Roxbury Town

Town Clerk, Box 53, Roxbury, VT 05669. 802-485-7840; fax-802-485-7860; hours: 9AM-N; 1PM-4PM T-F.
All records in one index. Record index not computerized. Only the public may search. Copy fee $1.00 per page. Cert fee- $7.00 per page plus copy fee. Payee- Town of Roxbury. **Other phones:** Treasurer- 802-485-7860; Appraiser/Auditor- 802-485-7840 or 485-7860; Elections- 802-485-7840; Vital Records- 802-485-7840. **Property tax/Assessor-** same address as above. 802-485-7840 or 485-7860.

Royalton Town

Town Clerk, PO Box 680, South Royalton, VT 05068-0680. 802-763-7207; fax-802-763-7307; hours: 8AM-3PM M-Th. www.royaltonvt.com
All records in one index. Record index not computerized. Only the public may search. Copy fee $1.00 per page. Cert fee- $2.00 per page plus copy fee. Payee- Town of Royalton. **Other phones:** Treasurer- 802-763-7207; Elections- 802-763-7207; Vital Records- 802-763-7207; Second phone- 802-763-7967. **Property tax/Assessor-** same address as above. 802-763-2202.

Rupert Town

Town Clerk, Box 140, West Rupert, VT 05776. 802-394-7728; fax-802-394-2524; hours: 2-7PM M; 12-5PM W; 10AM-3PM Th.
All records in one index. Office will perform a UCC search but public must search other records themselves. UCC search per debtor name- $10.00. UCC and tax lien copy fee $7.00; real estate is $1.00. per page. Cert fee- $7.00 per doc plus copy fee. Payee- Rupert Town Clerk. **Other phones:** Treasurer- 802-394-7728; Elections- 802-394-7728; Vital Records- 802-394-7728. **Property tax/Assessor-** PO Box 144, West Rupert, VT 05776; 802-394-7728.

Rutland City

City Clerk, PO Box 969, Rutland, VT 05702. 802-773-1801; hours: 9AM-4:45PM. www.rutlandcity.com
Separate indices to search. Will not search real estate records. Will not search UCC records or tax liens. Copy fee $1.00 per page. Cert fee- $7.00 per page total. Payee- Rutland City Clerk. **Other phones:** Treasurer- 802-773-1800; Appraiser/Auditor- 802-773-1800; Elections- 802-773-1801; Vital Records- 802-773-1801. **Property tax/Assessor-** PO Box 969, Rutland, VT 05701; 802-773-1800.

Rutland Town

Town Clerk, PO Box 225, Center Rutland, VT 05736. 802-773-2528; fax-802-773-7295; hours: 8AM-4:30PM.
All records in one index. Record index not computerized. Only the public may search. Copy fee $1.00 per page. Cert fee- $7.00 per page plus copy fee. Payee- Rutland Town Clerk. **Other phones:** Treasurer- 802-773-2528. **Property tax/Assessor-** 802-773-2528.

Ryegate Town

Town Clerk, PO Box 332, Ryegate, VT 05042. 802-584-3880; fax-802-584-3880; hours: 1-5PM M,T,W; 9AM-1PM F.
Index: Card File index. Only the public may search. Copy fee $1.00 per page. Cert fee- $10.00 per doc plus copy fee. Payee- Town of Ryegate. **Other phones:** Treasurer- 802-584-3880; Appraiser/Auditor- 802-584-3880; Elections- 802-584-3880; Vital Records- 802-584-3880. **Property tax/Assessor-** same address as above. 802-584-3880.

Salisbury Town

Town Clerk, PO Box 66, Salisbury, VT 05769-0066. 802-352-4228; fax-802-352-9832; hours: 12:30PM-4:30PM M W; 10AM-2PM T TH. www.salisburyvt.org
All records in one index. Office will perform a UCC search but public must search other records themselves. UCC search per debtor name- $10.00. Copy fee $1.00 per page. Cert fee- $7.00 per page. Payee- Town of Salisbury. **Other phones:** Listers- 802-352-9390. **Property tax/Assessor-** same address as above. not known.

Sandgate Town

Town Clerk, 3266 Sandgate Rd., Sandgate, VT 05250. 802-375-9075; fax-802-375-8350; 9AM-3PM T, W.
Index: Some Card Files, Original Handwritten index Book, Computer. Records indexed on computer back to 1962. Only the public may search. Copy fee $1.00 per page. Cert fee- $7.00 per doc, plus copy fee. Payee- Sandgate Town Clerk. **Other phones:** Treasurer- 802-375-9075; Appraiser/Auditor- 802-375-9075; Elections- 802-375-9075; Vital Records- 802-375-9075. **Property tax/Assessor-** same address as above. 802-375-9075.

Searsburg Town

Town Clerk, PO Box 157, Wilmington, VT 05363. 802-464-8081; fax-802-464-7610; hours: 8AM-4PM M; 8AM-Noon T F.
Office personnel or visitors may perform searches. Search fee $2.00 per name. Will not search real estate records. Copy fee $1.00 per page. Cert fee- $5.00 per page. Payee- Searsburg Town Clerk. **Other phones:** Treasurer- 802-464-8081; Elections- 802-464-8081; Vital Records- 802-464-8081. **Property tax/Assessor-** 802-464-8081.

Shaftsbury Town

Town Clerk, PO Box 409, Shaftsbury, VT 05262. 802-442-4038; fax-802-442-0955; hours: 9AM-5PM Mon; 9AM-3PM T-F. www.shaftsbury.net
All records in one index. Record index not computerized. Only the public may search. Copy fee $1.00 per page. Cert fee- $7.00 per cert plus copy fee. Payee- Shaftsbury Town Clerk. **Other phones:** Treasurer- 802-442-6242; Elections- 802-442-4038; Vital Records- 802-442-4038. **Property Assessor-** same address as above. 802-442-5740.

Sharon Town

Town Clerk, PO Box 250, Sharon, VT 05065. 802-763-8268; fax-802-763-7392; hours: 7AM-12PM M-Th. Record index not computerized. Only the public may search. Copy fee $1.00 per page. Cert fee- $7.00 per cert plus copy fee. Payee- Sharon Town Clerk.

Sheffield Town

Town Clerk, PO Box 165, Sheffield, VT 05866-0165. 802-626-8862; fax-802-626-8862; hours: 8AM-2PM,MWF, Closed T,Th.

Record index not computerized. Office will perform a UCC search but public must search other records themselves. UCC search per debtor name- $10.00. UCC search request using non-standard form (per name)- $15.00. Copy fee $1.00 per page. Tax lien copy- $.25 per page. Cert fee- $5.00 per page. Payee- Sheffield Town Clerk. **Property tax/Assessor**- 802-626-9273.

Shelburne Town

Town Clerk, PO Box 88, Shelburne, VT 05482. 802-985-5116; fax-802-985-9550; hours: 8:30AM-4:30PM. www.shelburneVT.org

Records indexed on a public use terminal back to 1992. Office will perform a UCC search but public must search other records themselves. Copy fee $1.00 per page. Cert fee- $7.00 per doc plus copy fee. **Other phones:** Treasurer- 802-985-5116; Appraiser/Auditor- 802-985-5115; Elections- 802-985-5116; Vital Records- 802-985-5116; 802-985-5117. **Property tax/Assessor**- same address as above. 802-985-5115.

Sheldon Town

Town Clerk, PO Box 66, Sheldon, VT 05483. 802-933-2524; fax-802-933-4951; hours: 8AM-3PM.

All records in one index. Office will perform a UCC search but public must search other records themselves. UCC search per debtor name- $10.00. UCC search request using non-standard form (per name)- $15.00. Copy fee $.25 per page. Cert fee- $5.00 per cert includes copy fee. Payee- Sheldon Town Clerk.

Shoreham Town

Town Clerk, 297 Main St., Shoreham, VT 05770-9759. 802-897-5841; fax-802-897-2545; hours: 9AM-4PM; closed Thurs.

Separate indices to search include land, UCC, maps, vital records. Office will perform a UCC search but public must search other records themselves. UCC search per debtor name- $10.00. UCC search request using non-standard form (per name)- $15.00. Copy fee $2.00 per document. R/E or tax lien copy- $1.00 per page. Cert fee- $7.00 per page includes one copy. Payee- Town of Shoreham. **Other phones:** Treasurer- 802-897-5841; Elections- 802-897-5841; Vital Records- 802-897-5841; Tax Collector- 802-897-7811; Zoning Admin - 802-453-3785. **Property tax/Assessor**- same address as above. 802-897-5841.

Shrewsbury Town

Town Clerk, 9823 Cold River Rd., Shrewsbury, VT 05738. 802-492-3511; fax-802-492-3511; hours: 10AM-3PM M-TH.

Index: Records in computer index since 1996; in separate books and indexes pre-1996. Only the public may search. Copy fee $1.00 per page. Cert fee- $7.00 per page. Payee- Anne Haley, Town Clerk. **Other phones:** Treasurer- 802-492-3558. **Property tax/Assessor**- same address as above. not known.

South Burlington City

Town Clerk, 575 Dorset St, South Burlington, VT 05403. 802-846-4105; hours: 8AM-4:30PM, M T TH F; 8AM-5:30PM, W. www.sburl.com

Only the public may search. Copy fee $1.00 per page. **Other phones:** Treasurer- 802-846-4119; Appraiser/Auditor- 802-846-4103; Elections- 802-846-4105; Vital Records- 802-846-4105; Taxes- 802-846-4109. **Property tax/Assessor**- 802-846-4103.

South Hero Town

Town Clerk, PO Box 175, South Hero, VT 05486. 802-372-5552; hours: 8:30AM-N, 1-4:30PM M-W; 8:30AM-N,1-5PM Th.

Only the public may search. Copy fee $1.00 per page. Cert fee- $7.00 per page plus copy fee. Payee- Town of South Hero. **Other phones:** Treasurer- 802-372-5552; Appraiser/Auditor- 802-372-5552; Elections- 802-372-5552; Vital Records- 802-372-5552. **Property tax/Assessor**- 333 Rt.2, South Hero, VT 05486; 802-372-5552.

Springfield Town

Town Clerk, 96 Main St, Springfield, VT 05156. 802-885-2104; fax-802-885-1617; hours: 8AM-4:30PM.

All records in one index. Office personnel or visitors may perform searches. Search fee $10.00 per hour. UCC search request using non-standard form (per name)- $15.00. Copy fee $2.00 per page. R/E or tax lien copy- $1.00 per page, $2.00 minimum. Cert fee- $7.00 per page includes copy fee. Payee- Town of Springfield. **Other phones:** Treasurer- 802-885-2104; Appraiser/Auditor- 802-885-2104; Elections- 802-885-2104; Vital Records- 802-885-2104. **Property tax/Assessor**- same address as above. 802-885-2104.

St. Albans City

City Clerk, PO Box 867, St. Albans, VT 05478-0867. 802-524-1501; hours: 7:30AM-4PM.

Index: UCCs indexed separately. Office will perform a UCC search but public must search other records themselves. UCC search per debtor name- $10.00. Copy fee $2.00 per page. Cert fee- $6.00 per page plus copy fee. Payee- St. Albans City. **Other phones:** Treasurer- 802-524-1501; Appraiser/Auditor- 802-524-1502; Elections- 802-524-1501; Vital Records- 802-524-1501; Water/Sewer- 802-524-1504; Accounting -802-524-1506. **Property tax/Assessor**- same address as above. 802-524-1502.

St. Albans Town

Town Clerk, PO Box 37, St. Albans Bay, VT 05481. 802-524-2415; fax-802-524-9609; hours: 8AM-4PM; closed to public on Wednesdays.

Separate indices to search include UCC's and trailers. Records indexed on a public use terminal back to May, 1999. Only the public may search. Copy fee $1.00 per page. Cert fee- $6.00 per page plus copy fee. Payee- Town of St. Albans. **Other phones:** Treasurer- 802-524-2415; Appraiser/Auditor- 802-524-2415; Elections- 802-524-2415; Vital Records- 802-524-2415. **Property tax/Assessor**- same address as above. 802-524-7589.

St. George Town

Town Clerk, 1 Barber Rd., St. George, VT 05495. 802-482-5272; fax-802-482-5548; hours: M-F 8-12PM.

All records in one index. Record index not computerized. Only the public may search. Copy fee $1.00 per copy. Cert fee- $1.00 per page plus copy fee. **Other phones:** Treasurer- 802-482-5272; Elections- 802-482-5272; Vital Records- 802-482-5272. **Property tax/Assessor**- P O Box 616, Wartsfield,Vt 05673; 802-496-9689.

St. Johnsbury Town

Town Clerk, 1187 Main St, #2, St. Johnsbury, VT 05819-2288. 802-748-4331; fax-802-748-1267; hours: 8AM-5PM; Summer Hrs. 7AM-4PM. www.town.st-johnsbury.vt.us

All records in one index. Record index not computerized. Office will perform a UCC search but public must search other records themselves. Search fee $10.00. Copy fee $2.00 per page. R/E or tax lien copy- $1.00 per page plus copy fee. Payee- Town of Johnsbury. **Other phones:** Treasurer- 802-748-1260; Appraiser/Auditor- 802-748-4272; Vital Records- 802-748-4331. **Property tax/Assessor**- same address as above. 802-748-4272.

Stamford Town

Town Clerk, 986 Main Rd., Stamford, VT 05352-9601. 802-694-1361; hours: 11AM-4PM T & W; Noon-4PM, 7-9PM Th; Noon-4PM F.

All records in one index. Only the public may search. Copy fee $2.00, if tax lien or real estate $1.00 per page. Cert fee- $7.00 per page plus copy fee. Payee- Town of Stamford. **Other phones:** Treasurer- 802-694-1361; Appraiser/Auditor- 802-694-1361; Elections- 802-694-1361; Vital Records- 802-694-1361. **Property tax/Assessor**- 986 Main Rd, Stamford, VT 05352-9601; 802-694-1361.

Stannard Town

Town Clerk, PO Box 94, Greensboro Bend, VT 05842-0094. 802-533-2577; hours: 8AM-Noon Wed.

All records in one index. Record index not computerized. Office personnel or visitors may perform searches. Search fee $2.00 per hour. Will not search real estate records. Will search UCC records, but not tax liens. UCC search per debtor name- $10.00. UCC search request using non-standard form (per name)- $15.00. Copy fee $1.00 per page. R/E record copy- $2.00 per page. Cert fee- $7.00 per page. Payee- Stannard Town Clerk.

Starksboro Town

Town Clerk, PO Box 91, Starksboro, VT 05487-0091. 802-453-2639; fax-802-453-7293; hours: 8:30AM-4:30PM M-Th.

All records in one index. Record index not computerized. Only the public may search. Copy fee $1.00 per page. Cert fee- $1.00 per page plus copy fee. Payee- Town of Starksboro. **Other phones:** Treasurer- 802-453-2639; Elections- 802-453-2639; Vital Records- 802-453-2639. **Property tax/Assessor**- same address as above. 802-453-6364.

Stockbridge Town

Town Clerk, PO Box 39, Stockbridge, VT 05772-0039. 802-746-8400; fax-802-746-8400; hours: 8AM-4:30PM T W TH; 8AM-N Fri.

All records in one index. Only the public may search. Copy fee $1.00 per page. Cert fee- $7.00 per page. Payee- Town of Stockbridge.

Stowe Town

Town Clerk, PO Box 248, Stowe, VT 05672. 802-253-6133; fax-802-253-6143; hours: 7:30AM-4:30PM.

All records in one index. Records indexed on a public use terminal back to 10/1/1986. Only the public may search. Copy fee $1.00 per page. Cert fee- $7.00 per page plus copy fee. Payee- Stowe Town Clerk. **Other phones:** Treasurer- 802-253-6133; Appraiser/Auditor- 802-253-6144; Elections- 802-253-6133; Vital Records- 802-253-6133. **Property tax/Assessor**- 802-253-6144.

Strafford Town

Town Clerk, PO Box 27, Strafford, VT 05072. 802-765-4411; fax-802-765-9621; hours: 8AM-5PM T,W; 8AM-7PM Th; 8AM-N Fri.

Only the public may search. Copy fee $1.00 per page. Cert fee- $7.00 per page plus copy fee. Payee- Town of Strafford. **Property tax/Assessor**- same address as above. 802-765-4411.

Stratton Town

Town Clerk, PO Box 166, West Wardsboro, VT 05360. 802-896-6184; fax-802-896-6630; hours: 9AM-3PM M-TH.

Separate indices to search include. Records indexed on cards back to 1987, index prior. Only the public may search. Copy fee $1.00 per page. Cert fee- $7.00 per page includes copy fee. Payee- Town of Stratton. **Other phones:** Treasurer- 802-896-6184; Appraiser/Auditor- 802-896-6184; Elections- 802-896-6184; Vital Records- 802-896-6184. **Property tax/Assessor**- same address as above. 802-896-6184.

Sudbury Town

Town Clerk, 36 Blacksmith Ln., Sudbury, VT 05733. 802-623-7296; fax-802-623-7296; hours: 9AM-4PM M; 7PM-9PM W; 9AM-3PM Fri.

Office personnel or visitors may perform searches. Search fee $5.00 per name. Will not search real estate records. Copy fee $1.00 per page. Cert fee- $7.00 per page. **Other phones:** Treasurer- 802-623-7296; Appraiser/Auditor- 802-623-7296; Elections- 802-623-7296; Vital Records- 802-623-7296. **Property tax/Assessor-** 802-623-7296.

Sunderland Town

Town Clerk, PO Box 295, East Arlington, VT 05252. 802-375-6106; hours: 8AM-2PM M,T,Th,; 8AM-N, 6-8PM W.
Only the public may search. Copy fee $1.00 per page. Cert fee- $7.00 per page total. Payee- Sunderland Town Clerk. **Property tax/Assessor-** 802-362-2284.

Sutton Town

Town Clerk, Box 106, Sutton, VT 05867. 802-467-3377; fax-802-467-1052; hours: 9AM-5PM,M,T,Th, F; 9AM-N Wed.
All records in one index. Record index not computerized. Only the public may search. Copy fee $1.00 per page. Cert fee- $7.00 plus copy fee. Payee- Sutton Town Clerk.

Swanton Town

Town Clerk, PO Box 711, Swanton, VT 05488. 802-868-4421; fax-802-868-4957; hours: 8AM-4PM.
Separate indices to search include land records, attachments by index and card file; UCC in separate card file. Only the public may search. Copy fee $1.00 per page, with a $2.00 minimum. Cert fee- $6.00 per page included copy fee. Payee- Town of Swanton. **Other phones:** Treasurer- 802-868-4421; Appraiser/Auditor- 802-868-4421; Elections- 802-868-4421; Vital Records- 802-868-4421. **Property tax/Assessor-** same address as above. 802-868-4421.

Thetford Town

Town Clerk, PO Box 126, Thetford Center, VT 05075-0126. 802-785-2922; fax-802-785-2031; hours: 8:30AM-3PM.
Separate indices to search include card file from 1967-2004; general index pre 1967 and 3/1/2004 forward. Records indexed on computer. Only the public may search. Copy fee $1.00 per page. Cert fee- $7.00 per page plus copy fee. Payee- Town of Thetford. **Other phones:** Treasurer- 802-785-2922 x19; Appraiser/Auditor- 802-785-2922 x15; Elections- 802-785-2922; Vital Records- 802-785-2922. **Property tax/Assessor-** 802-785-2922 x15.

Tinmouth Town

Town Clerk, 515 North End Rd., Tinmouth, VT 05773. 802-446-2498; fax-802-446-2498; hours: 8AM-12, 1-5PM M & Th & 8AM-N Sat Jan-May only.
All records in one index. Record index not computerized. Only the public may search. Copy fee $1.00 per page. Cert fee- $7.00 per page plus copy fee. **Other phones:** Treasurer- 802-446-2498; Appraiser/Auditor- 802-446-2498; Elections- 802-446-2498; Vital Records- 802-446-2498. **Property tax/Assessor-** same address as above. 802-446-2498.

Topsham Town

Town Clerk, PO Box 69, Topsham, VT 05076. 802-439-5505; fax-802-439-5505; hours: 1-6PM Mon.; 9AM-4PM T-F.
Separate indices to search include cards 1967-present, prior in general index. Record index not computerized. Only the public may search. Copy fee $1.00 per page. Cert fee- $7.00 per page. Payee- Topsham Town. **Other phones:** Treasurer- 802-439-5505; Appraiser/Auditor- 802-439-5505; Elections- 802-439-5505; Vital Records- 802-439-5505; Tax Collector- 802-439-5550. **Property tax/Assessor-** same address as above. 802-439-5505.

Townshend Town

Town Clerk, PO Box 223, Townshend, VT 05353-0223. 802-365-7300; fax-none; hours: 9AM-4PM M-W & F.
All records in one index. Only the public may search. Copy fee $.10 per page. R/E or tax lien copy- $1.00 per page. Cert fee- $7.00 per page plus copy fee. Payee- Town of Townshend. **Property tax/Assessor-** 802-365-7300.

Troy Town

Town Clerk, PO Box 80, North Troy, VT 05859. 802-988-2663; fax-802-988-4692; hours: 8AM-N, 1-4PM.
All records in one index. Office personnel or visitors may perform searches. Will not search real estate records. Will search UCC records; search includes tax liens if requested. UCC search per debtor name- $5.00. Separate federal/state combined tax lien search-no charge. Copy fee $1.00 per page; $2.00 minimum. Cert fee- $5.00 per cert plus copy fee. Payee- Troy Town Clerk.

Tunbridge Town

Town Clerk, PO Box 6, Tunbridge, VT 05077. 802-889-5521; fax-802-889-3744; hours: 8AM-N, 1-4PM M-Th.
Separate indices to search include card index 1974-current grantor/grantee cards. General index from beginning of time to 1974. Record index not computerized. Only the public may search. Copy fee $1.00 per page. Cert fee- $7.00 per page includes copy fee. Payee- Town of Tunbridge. **Other phones:** Treasurer- 802-889-5521; Appraiser/Auditor- 802-889-5521; Elections- 802-889-5521; Vital Records- 802-889-5521. **Property tax/Assessor-** same address as above. 802-889-5521.

Underhill Town

Town Clerk, PO Box 32, Underhill, VT 05490. 802-899-4434; fax-802-899-2137; hours: 8AM-4PM M T TH F; 8AM-6PM W. www.underhillvt.gov/
All records in one index. Record index not computerized. Only the public may search. Copy fee $1.00 per page. Cert fee- $7.00 per page plus copy fee. Payee- Underhill Town Clerk. **Other phones:** Treasurer- 802-899-4434; Appraiser/Auditor- 802-899-4797; Elections- 802-899-4434; Vital Records- 802-899-4434. **Property tax/Assessor-** same address as above. 802-899-4434.

Vergennes City

Town Clerk, PO Box 35, Vergennes, VT 05491-0035. 802-877-2841; fax-802-877-1160; hours: 8AM-4:30PM.
Separate indices to search include liens, maps, mobile homes, birth, deaths, marriage, land records, UCC's. Only the public may search. Copy fee $.15 to $.25 per page. R/E record copy-$1.00 per page. Cert fee- $7.00 per page plus copy fee. Payee- City Clerk. **Other phones:** Treasurer- 802-877-2841; Appraiser/Auditor- 802-877-2841; Elections- 802-877-2841; Vital Records- 802-877-2841. **Property tax/Assessor-** same address as above. 802-877-2841.

Vernon Town

Town Clerk, 567 Governor Hunt Rd., Vernon, VT 05354. 802-257-0292; fax-802-254-3561; hours: 8AM-4PM.
All records in one index. Records indexed on a public use terminal. Only the public may search. Copy fee $1.00 per page; $3.00 minimum. Cert fee- $7.00 per page. Payee- Town Clerk. **Other phones:** Treasurer- 802-257-0292; Appraiser/Auditor- 802-257-0292; Elections- 802-257-0292; Vital Records- 802-257-0292. **Property tax/Assessor-** same address as above. 802-257-0292.

Vershire Town

Town Clerk, 6894 Vermont Rte. 113, Vershire, VT 05079. 802-685-2227; hours: 8:30AM-3PM T-Th.
Separate indices to search include UCC, attachments, vital. Only the public may search. Copy fee $1.00 per page. Cert fee- $7.00 per page total. Payee- Vershire Town Clerk. **Other phones:** Treasurer- 802-685-2227. **Property tax/Assessor-** 802-685-2227.

Victory Town

Town Clerk, PO Box 609, North Concord, VT 05858. 802-328-2400; fax-802-328-2400; hours: 3PM-6PM T or by appointment.
Separate indices to search. Office personnel or visitors may perform searches. General copy fee $2.00 per page. Tax lien copy- $7.00 per page. Cert fee- $6.00 per page plus copy fee. Payee- Victory Town Clerk. **Other phones:** Treasurer- 802-328-2400.

Waitsfield Town

Town Clerk, 9 Bridge St, Waitsfield, VT 05673-0390. 802-496-2218; fax-802-496-9284; hours: 9AM-4PM.
Office will perform a UCC search but public must search other records themselves. UCC search per debtor name- $10.00. UCC search request using non-standard form (per name)- $15.00. Cert fee- $7.00 per page. Payee- Town of Waitsfield. **Other phones:** Treasurer- 802-496-2218; Elections- 802-496-2218; Vital Records- 802-496-2218. **Property tax/Assessor-** 802-496-9689.

Walden Town

Town Clerk, 12 Vt. Rte. 215, West Danville, VT 05873. 802-563-2220; fax-802-563-3008; hours: 9AM-3PM M-W; 9AM-5PM Th; closed Fri.
All records in one index. Office will perform a UCC search but public must search other records themselves. UCC search per debtor name- $10.00. Copy fee $1.00 per page. Cert fee- $7.00 per doc includes copies. Payee- Walden Town Clerk.

Wallingford Town

Town Clerk, PO Box 327, Wallingford, VT 05773. 802-446-2336; fax-802-446-3174; hours: 8AM-4:30PM M-Th; 8AM-N F. www.wallingfordvt.com
Only the public may search. Copy fee $2.00 per page. Cert fee- $7.00 per page. Payee- Wallingford Town Clerk. **Property tax/Assessor-** 802-446-2336.

Waltham Town

Town Clerk, PO Box 175, Vergennes, VT 05491. 802-877-3641; fax-802-877-3641; hours: 9AM-3PM T; 9AM-3PM F.
All records in one index. Only the public may search. Copy fee $1.00 per page. Cert fee- $1.00 per page plus copy fee. Payee- Waltham Town Clerk. **Other phones:** Zoning Admin- 802-877-6734. **Property tax/Assessor-** PO Box 175, Vergennes, VT 05491; not known.

Wardsboro Town

Town Clerk, PO Box 48, Wardsboro, VT 05355-0048. 802-896-6055; fax-802-896-1000; hours: 9AM-N, 1-4:30PM M-Th.
All records in one index. Record index not computerized. Only the public may search. Copy fee $1.00 per page. Cert fee- $7.00 per cert plus copy fee. Payee- Wardsboro Town Clerk. **Property tax/Assessor-** same address as above. 802-896-6055.

Warren Town

Town Clerk, PO Box 337, Warren, VT 05674. 802-496-2709, R/E recording phone-802-496-2709 x21; fax-802-496-2418; hours: 9AM-4:30PM.
Only the public may search. Copy fee $1.00 per page. Cert fee- $7.00 per page. Payee- Warren Town Clerk. **Other phones:** Treasurer- 802-496-2709 x25; Appraiser/Auditor- 802-496-2709 x26; Elections-

802-496-2709 x21; Vital Records- 802-496-2709 x21. **Property tax/Assessor-** 802-496-2709 x26.

Washington Town

Town Clerk, 2895 Rte. 110; Clerk's Office, Washington, VT 05675. 802-883-2218; fax-802-883-2218; hours: 8:30AM-2PM M,T.
All records in one index. Real estate record owner searches available. Will search UCC records; search includes tax liens if requested. UCC search per debtor name- $10.00. UCC search request using non-standard form (per name)- $15.00. Separate federal & state combined tax lien search- $5.00 per search. Copy fee $1.00 per page. Cert fee- $1.00 per page. Payee- Washington Town Clerk. **Other phones:** Treasurer- 802-883-2218; Elections- 802-883-2218; Vital Records- 802-883-2218. **Property tax/Assessor-** 802-883-2218.

Waterbury Town

Town Clerk, 51 S. Main St, Waterbury, VT 05676. 802-244-8447; fax-802-244-1014; hours: 8AM-4:30PM. www.waterburyvt.com
Separate indices to search include index card file. Only the public may search. Copy fee $1.00 per page. Cert fee- $7.00 per page plus copy fee. Payee- Town Clerk. **Other phones:** Treasurer- 802-244-8447; Appraiser/Auditor- 802-244-8447; Elections- 802-244-8447; Vital Records- 802-244-8447. **Property tax/Assessor-** same address as above. 802-244-1813.

Waterford Town

Town Clerk, PO Box 56, Lower Waterford, VT 05848. 802-748-2122; fax-802-748-8196; hours: 8:30AM-3:30PM, M, TH, F; Noon-6PM, T.
Separate indices to search include card file from book 44 to present, general index book for previous books. Only the public may search. Copy fee $1.00 per page. Cert fee- $7.00 per page. Payee- Town of Waterford. **Other phones:** Treasurer- 802-748-2122; Appraiser/Auditor- 802-748-2122; Elections- 802-748-2122; Vital Records- 802-748-2122. **Property tax/Assessor-** same address as above. 802-748-2122.

Waterville Town

Town Clerk, PO Box 31, Waterville, VT 05492. 802-644-8865; fax-802-644-8865; hours: 9AM-1:30PM M,T,Th; closed W,F.
All records in one index. Record index not computerized. Office will perform a UCC and Tax lien search but public must search other records themselves. Search fee $10.00. Copy fee $1.00 per page. Cert fee- $7.00 per doc plus copy fee. **Other phones:** Treasurer- 802-644-8865; Appraiser/Auditor- 802-644-8865; Elections- 802-644-8865; Vital Records- 802-644-8865. **Property tax/Assessor-** same address as above. 802-644-8865.

Weathersfield Town

Town Clerk, PO Box 550, Ascutney, VT 05030-0550. 802-674-9500; hours: 9AM-4PM M-T-W; 9AM-5PM Th.
Separate indices to search include UCC, surveys, older liens, zoning permits. Record index not computerized. Only the public may search. Copy fee $1.00 per page. Cert fee- $7.00 per doc plus copy fee. Payee- Weathersfield Town Clerk. **Other phones:** Elections- 802-674-9500; Vital Records- 802-674-9500. **Property tax/Assessor-** same address as above. 802-674-2626.

Wells Town

Town Clerk, PO Box 585, Wells, VT 05774. 802-645-0486; fax-802-645-0464; hours: 8:30AM-4PM.
All records in one index. Only the public may search. Copy fee $1.00 per page. Cert fee- $7.00 per page plus copy fee. Payee- Wells Town Clerk. **Other phones:** Treasurer- 802-645-0486; Lister- 802-645-0188. **Property tax/Assessor-** same address as above. not known.

West Fairlee Town

Town Clerk, Box 615, West Fairlee, VT 05083. 802-333-9696; fax-802-333-9611; hours: 8:30AM-2:30PM M,T,Th.
Index: Indices in front of books. Only the public may search. Copy fee $1.00 per page. Cert fee- $2.00 per page plus copy fee. Payee- Town of West Fairlee. **Other phones:** Treasurer- 802-333-9696; Elections- 802-333-9696; Vital Records- 802-333-9696. **Property tax/Assessor-** 802-333-9696.

West Haven Town

Town Clerk, 2919 Main Rd., West Haven, VT 05743-9610. 802-265-4880; fax-802-265-4880; hours: 1PM-3:30PM.
All records in one index. Record index not computerized. Office personnel or visitors may perform searches. Office will not search real estate records. Will search UCC records, search includes tax liens. UCC search per hour- $2.00. Separate federal tax lien search- $5.00 per hour. Separate state tax lien search- $3.00 per hour. Separate federal/state combined tax lien search- $5.00 per hour. Copy fee - $2.00 per hour. R/E record copy- $1.00 per page. Tax lien copy- $5.00 per page. Cert fee- $7.00 per doc plus copy fee. Payee- Town of West Haven. **Other phones:** Treasurer- 802-265-3675; Appraiser/Auditor- 802-265-7996; Elections- 802-265-4880; Vital Records- 802-265-4880. **Property tax/Assessor-** 2813 Main Rd, West Haven, VT 05743; 802-265-7996.

West Rutland Town

Town Clerk, 35 Marble St., West Rutland, VT 05777. 802-438-2204; fax-802-438-5133; hours: 9AM-4PM M-Th; Fri. by appointment. www.wrutland.net
Separate indices to search include written index, card index and computerized index. Records indexed on computer back to 2000. Office will perform a UCC search but public must search other records themselves. UCC search per debtor name- $20.00. Copy fee $2.00 per page, $5.00 per page if over 5" by 8". R/E or tax lien copy- $1.00 per page. Cert fee- $7.00 per page plus copy fee. Payee- Town of West Rutland. **Other phones:** Treasurer- 802-438-2263; Appraiser/Auditor- 802-438-2263; Elections- 802-438-2204; Vital Records- 802-438-2204. **Property tax/Assessor-** same address as above. 802-438-2263.

West Windsor Town

Town Clerk, Box 6, Brownsville, VT 05037. 802-484-7212; fax-802-484-3518; hours: 9AM-N, 1:30PM-4:30PM.
Separate indices to search include grantor/grantee. Office will perform a UCC search but public must search other records themselves. UCC search per debtor name- $10.00. UCC search request using non-standard form (per name)- $15.00. Copy fee $1.00 per page. Cert fee- $7.00 per page plus copy fee. Payee- Town of West Windsor. **Other phones:** Treasurer- 802-484-7212; Appraiser/Auditor- 802-484-7212. **Property tax/Assessor-** same address as above. 802-484-7212.

Westfield Town

Town Clerk, 1257 Vermont Rte. 100, Westfield, VT 05874. 802-744-2484; fax-802-744-2484; hours: 8AM-5PM M & W; 10AM-5PM Tu.
All records in one index. Record index not computerized. Only the public may search. Copy fee $1.00 per page. Cert fee- $7.00 per page total. Payee- Westfield Town Clerk. **Other phones:** Treasurer- 802-744-2484; Vital Records- 802-744-2484. **Property tax/Assessor-** same address as above. 802-744-2484.

Westford Town

Town Clerk, 1713 Vermont Route 128, Westford, VT 05494. 802-878-4587; fax-802-879-6503; hours: 8:30AM-4:30PM.
Separate indices to search include Land records (general index and card index), liens, UCC, surveys carded separately. Only the public may search. Copy fee $1.00 per page. Cert fee- $7.00 per page plus copy fee. Payee- Town of Westford. **Other phones:** Treasurer- 802-878-4587; Appraiser/Auditor- 802-878-4587; Elections- 802-878-4587; Vital Records- 802-878-4587. **Property tax/Assessor-** 802-878-4587.

Westminster Town

Town Clerk, PO Box 147, Westminster, VT 05158-0147. 802-722-4091; fax-802-722-9816; hours: 8:30AM-4PM. http://westminster.govoffice.com
All records in one index. Only the public may search. Copy fee $1.00 per page. Cert fee- $7.00 per page plus copy fee. Payee- Town of Westminster. **Other phones:** Treasurer- 802-722-4091; Appraiser/Auditor- 802-722-9516; Elections- 802-722-4091; Vital Records- 802-722-4091. **Property tax/Assessor-** 802-722-9516.

Westmore Town

Town Clerk, 54 Hinton Hill Rd., Orleans, VT 05860. 802-525-3007; fax-802-525-1131; hours: M 9AM-N;1-4PM, T&Th 9AM-N; 1-4PM, F 9AM-12PM.
Index: Card index. Record index not computerized. Only the public may search. Copy fee $1.00 per page. Cert fee- $7.00 per page plus copy fee. Payee- Town of Westmore.

Weston Town

Town Clerk, PO Box 98, Weston, VT 05161. 802-824-6645; fax-802-824-4121; hours: 9AM-1PM.
Separate indices to search include liens. Only the public may search. Copy fee $1.00 per page. Cert fee- $7.00 per page plus copy fee. Payee- Town Clerk. **Property tax/Assessor-** same address as above. not known.

Weybridge Town

Town Clerk, 1727 Quaker Village Rd., Weybridge, VT 05753. 802-545-2450; fax-802-545-2624; hours: 9AM-2PM M,T,TH,F.
All records in one index. Record index not computerized. Only the public may search. Copy fee $1.00 per page. Cert fee- $1.00 per page. Payee- Weybridge Town. **Other phones:** Treasurer- 802-545-2450; Appraiser/Auditor- 802-545-2450; Elections- 802-545-2450; Vital Records- 802-545-2450. **Property tax/Assessor-** 802-545-2450.

Wheelock Town

Town Clerk, PO Box 1328, Lyndonville, VT 05851-1328. 802-626-9094; fax-802-626-9094; hours: 8AM-4PM M-W, 10AM-6PM Th.
All records in one index. Only the public may search. Search fee $5.00 per hour. Real estate record owner searches available. Copy fee $1.00 per page. Cert fee- $7.00 per page plus copy fee. Payee- Wheelock Town Clerk. **Other phones:** Treasurer- 802-626-9094; Elections- 802-626-9094; Vital Records- 802-626-9094. **Property tax/Assessor-** same address as above. 802-626-9094.

Whiting Town

Town Clerk, 29 S. Main St., Whiting, VT 05778. 802-623-7813; hours: 9AM-Noon M,W,F and by App't.
Search fee $10.00 per name. UCC search request using non-standard form (per name)- $15.00. Copy fee $1.00 per page; UCC copy $.25 per page. Cert fee- $7.00 per page total. Payee- Whiting Town Clerk. **Other phones:** Treasurer- 802-623-7813. **Property tax/Assessor-** 802-623-7813.

Whitingham Town

Town Clerk, PO Box 529, Jacksonville, VT 05342. 802-368-7887; fax-802-368-7519; hours: 9AM-2PM (5-7PM W); 1st Sat of month 9AM-2PM.
All records in one index. Real estate owner, mortgage, and property transfer searches available. Will search UCC records; search includes tax liens if requested. UCC search per debtor name- $2.00 per

hour. Copy fee $1.00 per page. Cert fee- $7.00 per cert, does not include copies. Payee- Whitingham Town Clerk. **Other phones:** Treasurer- 802-368-7543; Appraiser/Auditor- 802-368-2838; Elections- 802-368-7887; Vital Records- 802-368-7887. **Property tax/Assessor-** PO BOX350, Jacksonville, VT 05342; 802-368-7887.

Williamstown Town

Town Clerk, PO Box 646, Williamstown, VT 05679. 802-433-5455; fax-802-433-2160; hours: 8AM-Noon 12:30PM-4:30PM. www.williamstownvt.org
Records indexed with card file and paper index after 10/01. Only the public may search. Copy fee $1.00 per page. Cert fee- $5.00 per cert includes copy fee. Payee- Williamstown Town Clerk. **Other phones:** Treasurer- 802-433-5455; Appraiser/Auditor- 802-433-5455; Elections- 802-433-5455; Vital Records- 802-433-5455. **Property tax/Assessor-** same address as above. 802-433-5455.

Williston Town

Town Clerk, 7900 Williston Rd., Williston, VT 05495. 802-878-5121; fax-802-764-1140; hours: 8AM-4:30PM. http://town.williston.vt.us
St. George is a separate town with a Williston mailing address. All records in one index. Record index not computerized. Only the public may search. Copy fee $1.00 per page. Cert fee- $7.00 per page plus copy fee. Payee- Town of Williston. **Other phones:** Treasurer- 802-878-5121; Appraiser/Auditor- 802-878-1091; Elections- 802-878-5121; Vital Records- 802-878-5121. **Property tax/Assessor-** 802-878-1091.

Wilmington Town

Town Clerk, PO Box 217; Town Hall, Wilmington, VT 05363-0217. 802-464-5836; fax-802-464-1238; hours: 8:30-N, 1-4PM M-W; 8:30AM-4PM Th; 8:30AM-6:30PM F. www.wilmingtonvermont.us
Index: Books; 1797-1965 (vol 1&2), 1965-2000 (card file), and computer, 1990-now. Records indexed on computer back to 1990. Only the office personnel may search. Copy fee $1.00 per page. Cert fee- $7.00 per page. Payee- Town of Wilmington. **Other phones:** Treasurer- 802-464-8591; Appraiser/Auditor- 802-464-8591; Elections- 802-464-5836; Vital Records- 802-464-5836. **Property tax/Assessor-** same address as above. 802-464-8591.

Windham Town

Town Clerk, 5976 Windham Hill Rd, Windham, VT 05039. 802-874-4211; fax-802-874-4144; hours: 10AM-3PM T,Th,F.

This office's jurisdiction includes ONLY Windham Town; do not confuse Windham Town with Windham County. Only the public may search. General copy fee $1.00 per page, $2.00 minimum on deeds. Cert fee- $7.00 per page plus copy fee. Payee- Windham Town Clerk.

Windsor Town

Town Clerk, PO Box 47, Windsor, VT 05089. 802-674-5610; fax-802-674-1017; hours: 8AM-4:30PM M,W,Th; 8AM-6PM Tues; 8AM-2PM F.
Index: UCCs in separate index. Record index not computerized. Only the public may search. Copy fee $1.00 per page. Cert fee- $7.00 per page. Payee- Town Clerk. **Other phones:** Treasurer- 802-674-6788; Appraiser/Auditor- 802-674-5414; Elections- 802-674-5610; Vital Records- 802-674-5610. **Property tax/Assessor-** 802-674-5414.

Winhall Town

Town Clerk, PO Box 389, Bondville, VT 05340. 802-297-2122; hours: 9AM-Noon (Closed Th).
Separate indices to search. Records indexed on cards, 3 indices prior to 1985. Only the public may search. Copy fee $.50 per page. Cert fee- $7.00 per page total. Payee- Winhall Town Clerk. **Other phones:** Treasurer- 802-297-1994; Appraiser/Auditor- 802-297-2151; Elections- 802-297-2122; Vital Records- 802-297-2122. **Property tax/Assessor-** 802-297-1994.

Winooski City

Town Clerk, 27 W. Allen St, Winooski, VT 05404. 802-655-6419; fax-802-655-6414; hours: 8-4PM.
Office will perform a UCC search but public must search other records themselves. UCC search per debtor name- $10.00. UCC search request using non-standard form (per name)- $15.00. Copy fee $1.00 per page. Cert fee- $7.00 per cert plus copy fee. Payee- Winooski City. **Property tax/Assessor-** same address as above. 802-655-6410.

Wolcott Town

Town Clerk, PO Box 100, Wolcott, VT 05680-0100. 802-888-2746; fax-802-888-2746; hours: 8AM-6PM T; 8AM-4PM W-F.
Separate indices to search include UCC's, zoning. Office personnel or visitors may perform searches. Search fee $5.00 per hour. Copy fee $1.00 per page. Cert fee- $7.00 per page plus copy fee. Payee- Town of Wolcott. **Other phones:** Treasurer- 802-888-2746; Appraiser/Auditor- 802-888-6858; Elections- 802-888-2746; Vital Records- 802-888-2746; Listers- 802-888-6858. **Property tax/Assessor-** same address as above. 802-888-2746.

Woodbury Town

Town Clerk, PO Box 123, Woodbury, VT 05681. 802-456-7051; fax-802-456-8834; hours: 8:30AM-1PM T-W-Th; 6-8PM Th evening.
Separate indices to search include card file. Office prefers public do their own research. Will not search real estate records. Will search UCC records, but not tax liens. UCC search per debtor name- $10.00. UCC search request using non-standard form (per name)- $15.00. R/E or tax lien copy- $1.00 per page, $2.00 minimum. Cert fee- $7.50 per page, plus copy fee. Payee- Woodbury Town Clerk. **Property tax/Assessor-** PO Box 10, Woodbury, VT 05681; 802-456-8836.

Woodford Town

Town Clerk, 1391 Vermont Rte. 9, Bennington, VT 05201. 802-442-4895; fax-802-442-4816; hours: 8:30AM-Noon M T W TH.
Above hours are for the Town Clerk office. Town office hours are 8:30AM-4PM, M-F. Separate indices to search include prior to 1963 records indexed in books, 1963 to present index cards used. Only the public may search. Copy fee $1.00 per page. Cert fee- $7.00 per page includes copy fee. Payee- Town Clerk. **Other phones:** Treasurer- 802-442-4895; Appraiser/Auditor- 802-442-4895; Elections- 802-442-4895; Vital Records- 802-442-4895. **Property tax/Assessor-** 802-442-4895.

Woodstock Town

Town Clerk, 31 The Green, Woodstock, VT 05091. 802-457-3611; fax-802-457-2329; hours: 8AM-N, 1-4:30PM. www.townofwoodstock.org
Separate indices to search include land, UCC, survey maps. Record index not computerized. Only the public may search. Copy fee $1.00 per page. Cert fee- $7.00 per page plus copy fee. Payee- Town of Woodstock. **Other phones:** Treasurer- 802-457-3456. **Property tax/Assessor-** PO Box 488, 31 The Green, Woodstock, VT 05091; 802-457-2607.

Worcester Town

Town Clerk, Drawer 161, Worcester, VT 05682-0161. 802-223-6942; fax-802-229-5216; hours: 8AM-4PM M,T,Th; 8AM-1PM F.
Index: Pre-2004 liens and attachments in separate books; Pre-1988 not indexed. Only the public may search. Copy fee $1.00 per page. Cert fee- $7.00 per page plus copy fee. Payee- Town of Worcester.

Vermont County Locator

You will usually be able to find the city name in the City/County Cross Reference below. In that case, it is a simple matter to determine the county from the cross reference. However, only the official US Postal Service city names are included in this index. We have also included a ZIP/City Cross Reference immediately following the City/County Cross Reference. If you know the ZIP Code but the city name does not appear in the City/County Cross Reference index, look up the ZIP Code in the ZIP/City Cross Reference, find the city name, then look up the city name in the City/County Cross Reference.

Vermont City/County Cross Reference

ADAMANT Washington
ALBANY Orleans
ALBURG Grand Isle
ARLINGTON Bennington
ASCUTNEY Windsor
AVERILL Essex
BAKERSFIELD Franklin
BARNARD Windsor
BARNET Caledonia
BARRE Washington
BARTON Orleans
BEEBE PLAIN Orleans
BEECHER FALLS Essex
BELLOWS FALLS Windham
BELMONT Rutland
BELVIDERE CENTER Lamoille
BENNINGTON Bennington
BENSON Rutland
BETHEL Windsor
BOMOSEEN Rutland
BONDVILLE Bennington
BRADFORD Orange
BRANDON (05733) Rutland(94), Addison(5)
BRATTLEBORO Windham
BRIDGEWATER Windsor
BRIDGEWATER CORNERS Windsor
BRIDPORT Addison
BRISTOL Addison
BROOKFIELD Orange
BROWNSVILLE Windsor
BURLINGTON Chittenden
CABOT (05647) Washington(98), Caledonia(1)
CAMBRIDGE (05444) Chittenden(94), Franklin(3), Lamoille(2)
CAMBRIDGEPORT Windham
CANAAN Essex
CASTLETON Rutland
CAVENDISH Windsor
CENTER RUTLAND Rutland
CHARLOTTE Chittenden
CHELSEA Orange
CHESTER Windsor
CHESTER DEPOT Windsor
CHITTENDEN Rutland
COLCHESTER Chittenden
CONCORD Essex
CORINTH Orange
COVENTRY Orleans
CRAFTSBURY Orleans
CRAFTSBURY COMMON Orleans
CUTTINGSVILLE Rutland
DANBY Rutland
DANVILLE Caledonia
DERBY Orleans
DERBY LINE Orleans
DORSET Bennington
EAST ARLINGTON Bennington
EAST BARRE (05649) Washington(93), Orange(6)
EAST BERKSHIRE Franklin
EAST BURKE Caledonia
EAST CALAIS Washington
EAST CHARLESTON Orleans
EAST CORINTH Orange
EAST DORSET (05253) Bennington(98), Rutland(1)
EAST DOVER Windham
EAST FAIRFIELD Franklin

EAST HARDWICK Caledonia
EAST HAVEN Essex
EAST MIDDLEBURY Addison
EAST MONTPELIER Washington
EAST POULTNEY Rutland
EAST RANDOLPH Orange
EAST RYEGATE Caledonia
EAST SAINT JOHNSBURY Caledonia
EAST THETFORD Orange
EAST WALLINGFORD Rutland
EDEN Lamoille
EDEN MILLS Lamoille
ELY Orange
ENOSBURG FALLS Franklin
ESSEX Chittenden
ESSEX JUNCTION Chittenden
FAIR HAVEN Rutland
FAIRFAX (05454) Chittenden(93), Franklin(6)
FAIRFIELD Franklin
FAIRLEE Orange
FERRISBURG Addison
FLORENCE Rutland
FOREST DALE Rutland
GAYSVILLE Windsor
GILMAN Essex
GLOVER Orleans
GRAFTON Windham
GRANBY Essex
GRAND ISLE Grand Isle
GRANITEVILLE (05654) Washington(88), Orange(11)
GRANVILLE Addison
GREENSBORO Orleans
GREENSBORO BEND Orleans
GROTON Caledonia
GUILDHALL Essex
HANCOCK Addison
HARDWICK Caledonia
HARTFORD Windsor
HARTLAND Windsor
HARTLAND FOUR CORNERS Windsor
HIGHGATE CENTER Franklin
HIGHGATE SPRINGS Franklin
HINESBURG Chittenden
HUNTINGTON Chittenden
HYDE PARK Lamoille
HYDEVILLE Rutland
IRASBURG Orleans
ISLAND POND Essex
ISLE LA MOTTE Grand Isle
JACKSONVILLE Windham
JAMAICA Windham
JEFFERSONVILLE Lamoille
JERICHO Chittenden
JOHNSON Lamoille
JONESVILLE Chittenden
KILLINGTON Rutland
LAKE ELMORE Lamoille
LONDONDERRY Windham
LOWELL Orleans
LOWER WATERFORD Caledonia
LUDLOW Windsor
LUNENBURG Essex
LYNDON Caledonia
LYNDON CENTER Caledonia
LYNDONVILLE Caledonia
MANCHESTER Bennington
MANCHESTER CENTER Bennington
MARLBORO Windham

MARSHFIELD Washington
MC INDOE FALLS Caledonia
MIDDLEBURY Addison
MIDDLETOWN SPRINGS Rutland
MILTON (05468) Chittenden(96), Franklin(3)
MONKTON Addison
MONTGOMERY Franklin
MONTGOMERY CENTER (05471) Franklin(97), Orleans(2)
MONTPELIER Washington
MORETOWN Washington
MORGAN Orleans
MORRISVILLE Lamoille
MOSCOW Lamoille
MOUNT HOLLY Rutland
NEW HAVEN Addison
NEWBURY Orange
NEWFANE Windham
NEWPORT Orleans
NEWPORT CENTER Orleans
NORTH BENNINGTON Bennington
NORTH CLARENDON Rutland
NORTH CONCORD Essex
NORTH FERRISBURG Addison
NORTH HARTLAND Windsor
NORTH HERO Grand Isle
NORTH HYDE PARK Lamoille
NORTH MONTPELIER Washington
NORTH POMFRET Windsor
NORTH POWNAL Bennington
NORTH SPRINGFIELD Windsor
NORTH THETFORD Orange
NORTH TROY Orleans
NORTHFIELD Washington
NORTHFIELD FALLS Washington
NORTON Essex
NORWICH Windsor
ORLEANS Orleans
ORWELL (05760) Addison(97), Rutland(2)
PASSUMPSIC Caledonia
PAWLET (05761) Rutland(98), Bennington(1)
PEACHAM Caledonia
PERKINSVILLE Windsor
PERU Bennington
PITTSFIELD (05762) Rutland(96), Windsor(3)
PITTSFORD Rutland
PLAINFIELD Washington
PLYMOUTH Windsor
POST MILLS Orange
POULTNEY Rutland
POWNAL Bennington
PROCTOR Rutland
PROCTORSVILLE Windsor
PUTNEY Windham
QUECHEE Windsor
RANDOLPH Orange
RANDOLPH CENTER Orange
READING Windsor
READSBORO Bennington
RICHFORD Franklin
RICHMOND Chittenden
RIPTON Addison
ROCHESTER (05767) Windsor(97), Addison(1)
ROXBURY (05669) Addison(91), Washington(7), Orange(1)
RUPERT Bennington

RUTLAND Rutland
SAINT ALBANS BAY Franklin
SAINT JOHNSBURY Caledonia
SAINT JOHNSBURY CENTER Caledonia
SALISBURY Addison
SAXTONS RIVER Windham
SHAFTSBURY Bennington
SHARON Windsor
SHEFFIELD Caledonia
SHELBURNE Chittenden
SHELDON Franklin
SHELDON SPRINGS Franklin
SHOREHAM Addison
SOUTH BARRE Washington
SOUTH BURLINGTON Chittenden
SOUTH HERO Grand Isle
SOUTH LONDONDERRY Windham
SOUTH NEWFANE Windham
SOUTH POMFRET Windsor
SOUTH ROYALTON Windsor
SOUTH RYEGATE Caledonia
SOUTH STRAFFORD Orange
SOUTH WOODSTOCK Windsor
SPRINGFIELD Windsor
STARKSBORO Addison
STOCKBRIDGE Windsor
STOWE Lamoille
STRAFFORD Orange
SUTTON Caledonia
SWANTON Franklin
TAFTSVILLE Windsor
THETFORD Orange
THETFORD CENTER Orange
TOWNSHEND Windham
TROY Orleans
TUNBRIDGE Orange
UNDERHILL Chittenden
UNDERHILL CENTER Chittenden
VERGENNES Addison
VERNON Windham
VERSHIRE Orange
WAITSFIELD Washington
WALLINGFORD Rutland
WARDSBORO Windham
WARREN Washington
WASHINGTON Orange
WATERBURY (05676) Washington(86), Chittenden(13)
WATERBURY Washington
WATERBURY CENTER Washington
WATERVILLE Lamoille
WEBSTERVILLE Washington
WELLS Rutland
WELLS RIVER Orange
WEST BURKE Caledonia
WEST CHARLESTON Orleans
WEST DANVILLE Caledonia
WEST DOVER Windham
WEST DUMMERSTON Windham
WEST FAIRLEE Orange
WEST GLOVER Orleans
WEST HALIFAX Windham
WEST HARTFORD Windsor
WEST NEWBURY Orange
WEST PAWLET (05775) Rutland(98), Bennington(2)
WEST RUPERT Bennington
WEST RUTLAND Rutland
WEST TOPSHAM Orange
WEST TOWNSHEND Windham

WEST WARDSBORO Windham
WESTFIELD Orleans
WESTFORD Chittenden
WESTMINSTER Windham
WESTMINSTER STATION Windham

WESTON Windsor
WHITE RIVER JUNCTION Windsor
WHITING (05778) Addison(96), Rutland(3)
WHITINGHAM Windham
WILDER Windsor

WILLIAMSTOWN Orange
WILLIAMSVILLE Windham
WILLISTON Chittenden
WILMINGTON Windham
WINDSOR Windsor

WINOOSKI Chittenden
WOLCOTT Lamoille
WOODBURY Washington
WOODSTOCK Windsor
WORCESTER Washington

Vermont ZIP/City Cross Reference

05001-05009	WHITE RIVER JUNCTION
05030-05030	ASCUTNEY
05031-05031	BARNARD
05032-05032	BETHEL
05033-05033	BRADFORD
05034-05034	BRIDGEWATER
05035-05035	BRIDGEWATER CORNERS
05036-05036	BROOKFIELD
05037-05037	BROWNSVILLE
05038-05038	CHELSEA
05039-05039	CORINTH
05040-05040	EAST CORINTH
05041-05041	EAST RANDOLPH
05042-05042	EAST RYEGATE
05043-05043	EAST THETFORD
05044-05044	ELY
05045-05045	FAIRLEE
05046-05046	GROTON
05047-05047	HARTFORD
05048-05048	HARTLAND
05049-05049	HARTLAND 4 CORNERS
05050-05050	MC INDOE FALLS
05051-05051	NEWBURY
05052-05052	NORTH HARTLAND
05053-05053	NORTH POMFRET
05054-05054	NORTH THETFORD
05055-05055	NORWICH
05056-05056	PLYMOUTH
05058-05058	POST MILLS
05059-05059	QUECHEE
05060-05060	RANDOLPH
05061-05061	RANDOLPH CENTER
05062-05062	READING
05065-05065	SHARON
05067-05067	SOUTH POMFRET
05068-05068	SOUTH ROYALTON
05069-05069	SOUTH RYEGATE
05070-05070	SOUTH STRAFFORD
05071-05071	SOUTH WOODSTOCK
05072-05072	STRAFFORD
05073-05073	TAFTSVILLE
05074-05074	THETFORD
05075-05075	THETFORD CENTER
05076-05076	EAST CORINTH
05077-05077	TUNBRIDGE
05079-05079	VERSHIRE
05081-05081	WELLS RIVER
05083-05083	WEST FAIRLEE
05084-05084	WEST HARTFORD
05085-05085	WEST NEWBURY
05086-05086	WEST TOPSHAM
05088-05088	WILDER
05089-05089	WINDSOR
05091-05091	WOODSTOCK
05101-05101	BELLOWS FALLS
05141-05141	CAMBRIDGEPORT
05142-05142	CAVENDISH
05143-05143	CHESTER
05144-05144	CHESTER DEPOT
05146-05146	GRAFTON
05148-05148	LONDONDERRY
05149-05149	LUDLOW
05150-05150	NORTH SPRINGFIELD
05151-05151	PERKINSVILLE
05152-05152	PERU
05153-05153	PROCTORSVILLE
05154-05154	SAXTONS RIVER
05155-05155	SOUTH LONDONDERRY
05156-05156	SPRINGFIELD
05158-05158	WESTMINSTER
05159-05159	WESTMINSTER STATION
05161-05161	WESTON
05201-05201	BENNINGTON
05250-05250	ARLINGTON
05251-05251	DORSET
05252-05252	EAST ARLINGTON
05253-05253	EAST DORSET
05254-05254	MANCHESTER
05255-05255	MANCHESTER CENTER
05257-05257	NORTH BENNINGTON
05260-05260	NORTH POWNAL
05261-05261	POWNAL
05262-05262	SHAFTSBURY
05301-05304	BRATTLEBORO
05340-05340	BONDVILLE
05341-05341	EAST DOVER
05342-05342	JACKSONVILLE
05343-05343	JAMAICA
05344-05344	MARLBORO
05345-05345	NEWFANE
05346-05346	PUTNEY
05350-05350	READSBORO
05351-05351	SOUTH NEWFANE
05352-05352	READSBORO
05353-05353	TOWNSHEND
05354-05354	VERNON
05355-05355	WARDSBORO
05356-05356	WEST DOVER
05357-05357	WEST DUMMERSTON
05358-05358	WEST HALIFAX
05359-05359	WEST TOWNSHEND
05360-05360	WEST WARDSBORO
05361-05361	WHITINGHAM
05362-05362	WILLIAMSVILLE
05363-05363	WILMINGTON
05401-05402	BURLINGTON
05403-05403	SOUTH BURLINGTON
05404-05404	WINOOSKI
05405-05406	BURLINGTON
05407-05407	SOUTH BURLINGTON
05439-05439	COLCHESTER
05440-05440	ALBURG
05441-05441	BAKERSFIELD
05442-05442	BELVIDERE CENTER
05443-05443	BRISTOL
05444-05444	CAMBRIDGE
05445-05445	CHARLOTTE
05446-05446	COLCHESTER
05447-05447	EAST BERKSHIRE
05448-05448	EAST FAIRFIELD
05449-05449	COLCHESTER
05450-05450	ENOSBURG FALLS
05451-05451	ESSEX
05452-05453	ESSEX JUNCTION
05454-05454	FAIRFAX
05455-05455	FAIRFIELD
05456-05456	FERRISBURG
05457-05457	FRANKLIN
05458-05458	GRAND ISLE
05459-05459	HIGHGATE CENTER
05460-05460	HIGHGATE SPRINGS
05461-05461	HINESBURG
05462-05462	HUNTINGTON
05463-05463	ISLE LA MOTTE
05464-05464	JEFFERSONVILLE
05465-05465	JERICHO
05466-05466	JONESVILLE
05468-05468	MILTON
05469-05469	MONKTON
05470-05470	MONTGOMERY
05471-05471	MONTGOMERY CENTER
05472-05472	NEW HAVEN
05473-05473	NORTH FERRISBURG
05474-05474	NORTH HERO
05476-05476	RICHFORD
05477-05477	RICHMOND
05478-05479	SAINT ALBANS
05481-05481	SAINT ALBANS BAY
05482-05482	SHELBURNE
05483-05483	SHELDON
05485-05485	SHELDON SPRINGS
05486-05486	SOUTH HERO
05487-05487	STARKSBORO
05488-05488	SWANTON
05489-05489	UNDERHILL
05490-05490	UNDERHILL CENTER
05491-05491	VERGENNES
05492-05492	WATERVILLE
05494-05494	WESTFORD
05495-05495	WILLISTON
05601-05633	MONTPELIER
05640-05640	ADAMANT
05641-05641	BARRE
05647-05647	CABOT
05648-05648	CALAIS
05649-05649	EAST BARRE
05650-05650	EAST CALAIS
05651-05651	EAST MONTPELIER
05652-05652	EDEN
05653-05653	EDEN MILLS
05654-05654	GRANITEVILLE
05655-05655	HYDE PARK
05656-05656	JOHNSON
05657-05657	LAKE ELMORE
05658-05658	MARSHFIELD
05660-05660	MORETOWN
05661-05661	MORRISVILLE
05662-05662	MOSCOW
05663-05663	NORTHFIELD
05664-05664	NORTHFIELD FALLS
05665-05665	NORTH HYDE PARK
05666-05666	NORTH MONTPELIER
05667-05667	PLAINFIELD
05669-05669	ROXBURY
05670-05670	SOUTH BARRE
05671-05671	WATERBURY
05672-05672	STOWE
05673-05673	WAITSFIELD
05674-05674	WARREN
05675-05675	WASHINGTON
05676-05676	WATERBURY
05677-05677	WATERBURY CENTER
05678-05678	WEBSTERVILLE
05679-05679	WILLIAMSTOWN
05680-05680	WOLCOTT
05681-05681	WOODBURY
05682-05682	WORCESTER
05701-05702	RUTLAND
05730-05730	BELMONT
05731-05731	BENSON
05732-05732	BOMOSEEN
05733-05733	BRANDON
05734-05734	BRIDPORT
05735-05735	CASTLETON
05736-05736	CENTER RUTLAND
05737-05737	CHITTENDEN
05738-05738	CUTTINGSVILLE
05739-05739	DANBY
05740-05740	EAST MIDDLEBURY
05741-05741	EAST POULTNEY
05742-05742	EAST WALLINGFORD
05743-05743	FAIR HAVEN
05744-05744	FLORENCE
05745-05745	FOREST DALE
05746-05746	GAYSVILLE
05747-05747	GRANVILLE
05748-05748	HANCOCK
05750-05750	HYDEVILLE
05751-05751	KILLINGTON
05753-05753	MIDDLEBURY
05757-05757	MIDDLETOWN SPRINGS
05758-05758	MOUNT HOLLY
05759-05759	NORTH CLARENDON
05760-05760	ORWELL
05761-05761	PAWLET
05762-05762	PITTSFIELD
05763-05763	PITTSFORD
05764-05764	POULTNEY
05765-05765	PROCTOR
05766-05766	MIDDLEBURY
05766-05766	RIPTON
05767-05767	ROCHESTER
05768-05768	RUPERT
05769-05769	SALISBURY
05770-05770	SHOREHAM
05772-05772	STOCKBRIDGE
05773-05773	WALLINGFORD
05774-05774	WELLS
05775-05775	WEST PAWLET
05776-05776	WEST RUPERT
05777-05777	WEST RUTLAND
05778-05778	WHITING
05819-05819	SAINT JOHNSBURY
05820-05820	ALBANY
05821-05821	BARNET
05822-05822	BARTON
05823-05823	BEEBE PLAIN
05824-05824	CONCORD
05825-05825	COVENTRY
05826-05826	CRAFTSBURY
05827-05827	CRAFTSBURY COMMON
05828-05828	DANVILLE
05829-05829	DERBY
05830-05830	DERBY LINE
05832-05832	EAST BURKE
05833-05833	EAST CHARLESTON
05836-05836	EAST HARDWICK
05837-05837	EAST HAVEN
05838-05838	EAST SAINT JOHNSBURY
05839-05839	GLOVER
05840-05840	GRANBY
05841-05841	GREENSBORO
05842-05842	GREENSBORO BEND
05843-05843	HARDWICK
05845-05845	IRASBURG
05846-05846	ISLAND POND
05847-05847	LOWELL
05848-05848	LOWER WATERFORD
05849-05849	LYNDON
05850-05850	LYNDON CENTER
05851-05851	LYNDONVILLE
05853-05853	MORGAN
05855-05855	NEWPORT
05857-05857	NEWPORT CENTER
05858-05858	NORTH CONCORD
05859-05859	NORTH TROY
05860-05860	ORLEANS
05861-05861	PASSUMPSIC
05862-05862	PEACHAM
05863-05863	SAINT JOHNSBURY CENTER
05866-05866	SHEFFIELD
05867-05867	SUTTON
05868-05868	TROY
05871-05871	WEST BURKE
05872-05872	WEST CHARLESTON
05873-05873	WEST DANVILLE
05874-05874	WESTFIELD
05875-05875	WEST GLOVER
05901-05901	AVERILL
05902-05902	BEECHER FALLS
05903-05903	CANAAN
05904-05904	GILMAN
05905-05905	GUILDHALL
05906-05906	LUNENBURG
05907-05907	NORTON

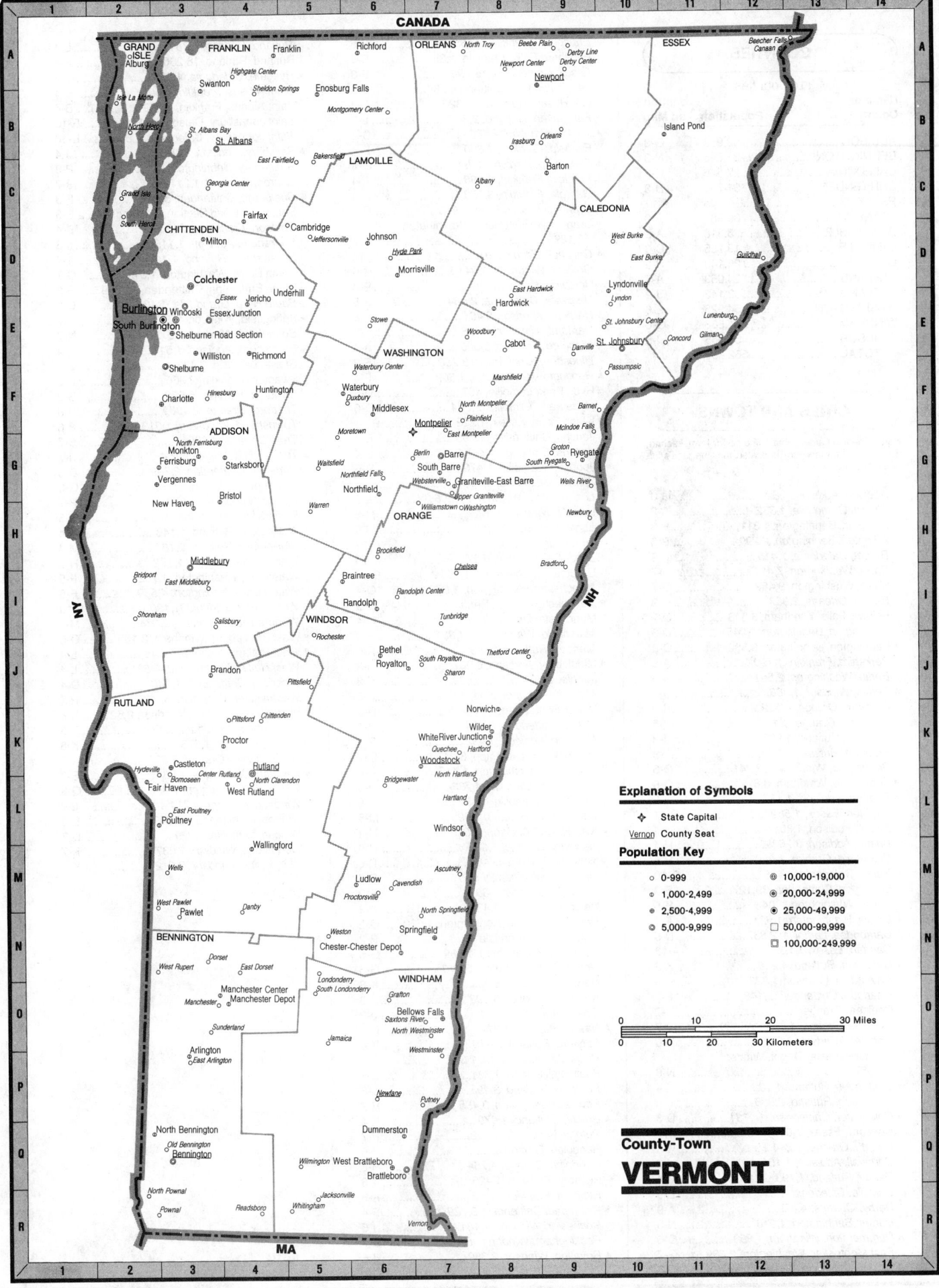

County-Town

VERMONT

Copyright American Map Corporation

COUNTIES

(14 Counties)

Name of County	Population	Location on Map
ADDISON	32,953	G-3
BENNINGTON	35,845	N-3
CALEDONIA	27,846	C-9
CHITTENDEN	131,761	D-3
ESSEX	6,405	A-11
FRANKLIN	39,980	A-3
GRAND ISLE	5,318	A-2
LAMOILLE	19,735	C-6
ORANGE	26,149	H-6
ORLEANS	24,053	A-7
RUTLAND	62,142	J-2
WASHINGTON	54,928	E-6
WINDHAM	41,588	O-6
WINDSOR	54,055	I-5
TOTAL	**562,758**	

CITIES AND TOWNS

Note: The first name is that of the city or town, second, that of the county in which it is located, then the population and location on the map.

Addison, Addison, 1,023 .... G-3
Alburg, Grand Isle, 1,362 .... A-2
Arlington, Bennington, 1,311 .... P-3
Arlington, Bennington, 2,299 .... P-3
Barnet, Caledonia, 1,415 .... F-9
Barre, Washington, 7,411 .... G-7
Barre, Washington, 9,482 .... G-7
Barton, Orleans, 2,967 .... C-9
Bellows Falls, Windham, 3,313 .... O-7
Bennington, Bennington, 16,451 .... Q-3
• Bennington, Bennington, 9,532 .... Q-3
Berkshire, Franklin, 1,190 .... A-5
Berlin, Washington, 2,561 .... G-6
▲ Bethel, Windsor, 1,866 .... J-6
Bradford, Orange, 2,522 .... I-9
▲ Braintree, Orange, 1,174 .... I-5
• Brandon, Rutland, 1,902 .... J-3
Brandon, Rutland, 4,223 .... J-3
Brattleboro, Windham, 12,241 .... Q-6
• Brattleboro, Windham, 8,612 .... Q-6
▲ Bridport, Addison, 1,137 .... I-2
Brighton, Essex, 1,562 .... B-11
Bristol, Addison, 1,801 .... H-4
Bristol, Addison, 3,762 .... H-4
▲ Brookfield, Orange, 1,089 .... H-6
Burke, Caledonia, 1,406 .... D-10
Burlington, Chittenden, 39,127 .... E-3
Cabot, Washington, 1,043 .... E-8
Calais, Washington, 1,521 .... F-7
Cambridge, Lamoille, 2,667 .... D-5
Canaan, Essex, 1,121 .... A-12
▲ Castleton, Rutland, 4,278 .... K-3
Cavendish, Windsor, 1,323 .... M-6
Charlotte, Chittenden, 3,148 .... F-3
Chelsea, Orange I-7
Chelsea, Orange, 1,166 .... I-7
Chester, Windsor, 2,832 .... N-6
• Chester-Chester Depot, Windsor,
 1,057 .... N-6
Chittenden, Rutland, 1,102 .... K-4
Clarendon, Rutland, 2,835 .... L-4
▲ Colchester, Chittenden, 14,731 .... D-3
Concord, Essex, 1,093 .... E-11
Corinth, Orange, 1,244 .... H-8
Cornwall, Addison, 1,101 .... I-3
Danby, Rutland, 1,193 .... M-4
Danville, Caledonia, 1,917 .... E-9
Derby, Orleans, 4,479 .... A-9
Dorset, Bennington, 1,918 .... N-3
▲ Dummerston, Windham, 1,863 .... Q-6
East Montpelier, Washington, 2,239 ..... G-7

Enosburg, Franklin, 2,535 .... B-5
Enosburg Falls, Franklin, 1,350 .... B-5
Essex, Chittenden, 16,498 .... E-3
Essex Junction, Chittenden, 8,396 .... E-3
• Fair Haven, Rutland, 2,432 .... L-2
Fair Haven, Rutland, 2,887 .... L-2
▲ Fairfax, Franklin, 2,486 .... C-4
Fairfield, Franklin, 1,680 .... B-4
▲ Ferrisburg, Addison, 2,317 .... G-3
Franklin, Franklin, 1,068 .... A-4
Georgia, Franklin, 3,753 .... C-3
Grand Isle, Grand Isle, 1,642 .... C-2
• Graniteville-East Barre, Washington,
 2,189 .... G-7
▲ Guildhall, Essex, 270 .... D-12
Guilford, Windham, 1,941 .... R-6
Hardwick, Caledonia E-8
Hardwick, Caledonia, 2,964 .... E-8
Hartford, Windsor, 9,404 .... K-8
Hartland, Windsor, 2,988 .... L-7
Highgate, Franklin, 3,020 .... A-4
Hinesburg, Chittenden, 3,780 .... F-3
▲ Huntington, Chittenden, 1,609 .... F-4
Hyde Park, Lamoille, 457 .... D-6
Hyde Park, Lamoille, 2,344 .... D-6
• Island Pond, Essex, 1,222 .... B-11
Jericho, Chittenden, 1,405 .... E-4
Jericho, Chittenden, 4,302 .... E-4
Johnson, Lamoille, 1,470 .... D-6
Johnson, Lamoille, 3,156 .... D-6
Londonderry, Windham, 1,506 .... L-5
Ludlow, Windsor, 1,123 .... M-6
Ludlow, Windsor, 2,302 .... M-6
Lunenburg, Essex, 1,176 .... E-12
Lyndon, Caledonia, 5,371 .... E-10
Lyndonville, Caledonia, 1,255 .... E-10
Manchester, Bennington, 3,622 .... O-4
• Manchester Center, Bennington, 1,574 ... O-3
Manchester Depot, Bennington O-4
Marshfield, Washington, 1,331 .... F-8
Mendon, Rutland, 1,049 .... K-5
• Middlebury, Addison, 6,007 .... I-3
Middlebury, Addison, 8,034 .... I-3
Middlesex, Washington, 1,514 .... F-6
Milton, Chittenden, 1,578 .... D-3
Milton, Chittenden, 8,404 .... D-3
▲ Monkton, Addison, 1,482 .... G-3
Montpelier, Washington, 8,247 .... G-7
Moretown, Washington, 1,415 .... F-6
Morristown, Lamoille, 4,733 .... D-6
Morrisville, Lamoille, 1,984 .... D-6
Mount Holly, Rutland, 1,093 .... M-5
▲ New Haven, Addison, 1,375 .... H-4
Newbury, Orange, 1,985 .... H-9
Newfane, Windham, 164 .... P-6
Newfane, Windham, 1,555 .... P-6
Newport, Orleans, 1,367 .... A-9
Newport, Orleans, 4,434 .... A-9
North Bennington, Bennington, 1,520 ..... Q-2
North Hero, Grand Isle B-2
Northfield, Washington, 1,889 .... G-6
Northfield, Washington, 5,610 .... G-6
Norwich, Windsor K-8
Norwich, Windsor, 3,093 .... K-8
Orwell, Addison, 1,114 .... J-2
▲ Pawlet, Rutland, 1,314 .... N-3
Pittsford, Rutland, 2,919 .... K-4
Plainfield, Washington, 1,302 .... F-7
Poultney, Rutland, 1,731 .... L-3
Poultney, Rutland, 3,498 .... L-3
Pownal, Bennington, 3,485 .... R-2
▲ Proctor, Rutland, 1,979 .... K-4
Putney, Windham, 2,352 .... P-7
Randolph, Orange I-6
Randolph, Orange, 4,764 .... I-6
Richford, Franklin, 1,425 .... A-6
Richford, Franklin, 2,178 .... A-6
▲ Richmond, Chittenden, 3,729 ..... F-4
Rochester, Windsor, 1,181 .... I-5
Rockingham, Windham, 5,484 ...... O-7
▲ Royalton, Windsor, 2,389 .... J-6

Rutland, Rutland, 3,781 .... L-4
Rutland, Rutland, 18,230 .... L-4
▲ Ryegate, Caledonia, 1,058 .... G-9
Saint Albans, Franklin, 4,606 .... B-4
Saint Albans, Franklin, 7,339 .... B-4
• Saint Johnsbury, Caledonia, 6,424 ...... E-10
Saint Johnsbury, Caledonia, 7,608 ...... E-10
▲ Salisbury, Addison, 1,024 .... I-4
Shaftsbury, Bennington, 3,368 .... P-3
Sharon, Windsor, 1,211 .... J-7
▲ Shelburne, Chittenden, 5,871 ..... F-3
Shelburne Road Section, Chittenden E-3
Sheldon, Franklin, 1,748 .... B-4
Shoreham, Addison, 1,115 .... I-3
Shrewsbury, Rutland, 1,107 .... L-4
• South Barre, Washington, 1,314 ... G-7
South Burlington, Chittenden, 12,809 ... E-3
South Hero, Grand Isle, 1,404 ...... C-2
• Springfield, Windsor, 4,207 .... N-7
Springfield, Windsor, 9,579 .... N-7
▲ Starksboro, Addison, 1,511 .... G-4
Stowe, Lamoille, 3,433 .... E-6
Swanton, Franklin, 2,360 .... B-3
Swanton, Franklin, 5,636 .... B-3
Thetford, Orange, 2,438 .... J-8
Townshend, Windham, 1,019 ...... P-6
Troy, Orleans, 1,609 .... B-7
▲ Tunbridge, Orange, 1,154 .... I-7
Underhill, Chittenden, 2,799 ...... D-5
Vergennes, Addison, 2,578 .... G-3
Vernon, Windham, 1,850 .... R-7
Waitsfield, Washington, 1,422 .... G-5
• Wallingford, Rutland, 1,148 ...... M-4
Wallingford, Rutland, 2,184 .... M-4
Warren, Washington, 1,172 .... H-5
Waterbury, Washington, 1,702 ... F-5
Waterbury, Washington, 4,589 ... F-5
Waterford, Caledonia, 1,190 ..... F-10
Weathersfield, Windsor, 2,674 ... M-7
• West Brattleboro, Windham, 3,135 ... Q-6
• West Rutland, Rutland, 2,246 ... L-4
West Rutland, Rutland, 2,448 .... L-4
Westford, Chittenden, 1,740 ..... D-4
Westminster, Windham, 3,026 ... P-7
• White River Junction, Windsor, 2,521 ... K-8
Whitingham, Windham, 1,177 .... R-5
• Wilder, Windsor, 1,576 .... K-8
Williamstown, Orange, 2,839 .... H-7
▲ Williston, Chittenden, 4,887 .... E-3
Wilmington, Windham, 1,968 .... Q-5
▲ Windsor, Windsor, 3,714 .... L-7
Winooski, Chittenden, 6,649 .... E-3
Wolcott, Lamoille, 1,229 .... D-7
Woodstock, Windsor, 1,037 ..... K-7
Woodstock, Windsor, 3,212 ..... K-7

Explanation of symbols: ● – Census Designated Place (CDP) • *italics* – Township shown which is also a CDP • *italics* – Townships (not shown on the map)
▲ *italics* – Townships (shown on the map)

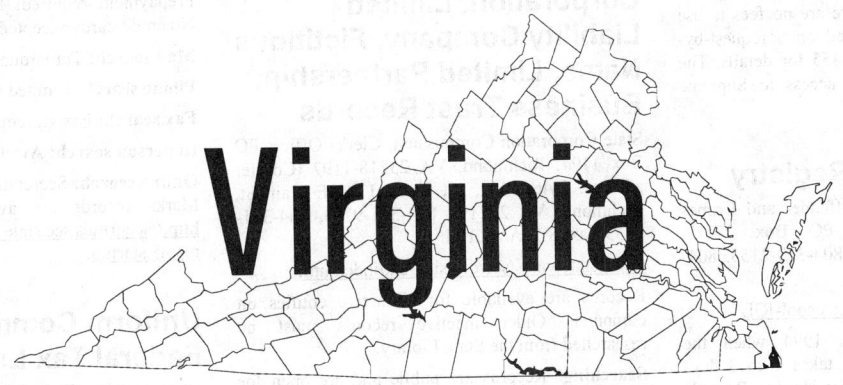

General Help Numbers:

Governor's Office
Capitol Bldg, 3rd Floor
Richmond, VA 23219
www.governor.virginia.gov

804-786-2211
Fax 804-371-6351
8:30AM-5:30PM

Attorney General's Office
900 E Main St
Richmond, VA 23219
www.oag.state.va.us

804-786-2071
Fax 804-786-1991
8:30AM-5PM

Legislative Records
Information & Public Relations
PO Box 406
Richmond, VA 23218
http://legis.state.va.us

804-698-1500
Fax 804-786-3215
8AM-5PM

State Archives
800 E. Broad St
Richmond, VA 23219-8000
www.lva.lib.va.us

804-692-3500
Fax 804-692-3556
9AM-5PM TU-SA

State Specifics:

Capital: Richmond
Richmond City County

Time Zone: EST

Number of Counties: 95

Population: 7,459,827

Web Site: www.myvirginia.org

State Agencies

Criminal Records

Virginia State Police, CCRE, PO Box C-85076, Richmond, VA 23261-5076, 804-323-2277, 804-323-0861-Fax; 8AM-5PM.

www.vsp.state.va.us

Records are available from 1966. It takes 1 to 3 days before new records are available for inquiry. 100% of arrest records are fingerprint supported. 83% of all arrests in database have final dispositions recorded.

Searching: Section 19.2-389 Code of Virginia outlines that non-criminal entities can receive conviction only records. Certain agencies may receive complete records. The website gives complete details. Include the following in your request-full name, date of birth, Social Security Number, sex, race. Turnaround time is 4-6 weeks. The general public and employers not covered by statute must have a signed release form from person of record, including notarized signatures for both subject and requester. These requesters must use form "SP-167" which is downloadable

from website. The following data is not released: dismissals, nolled pressed, whenever the disposition is missing, or if not guilty Certain agencies receive complete records; non-criminal justice entities receive conviction only records.

Access by: mail, online.

Fee & Payment: The fee is $15.00 per name; $20 if sex offender registry search included. When required, statutorily-required fingerprint check is $13; $37 if an FBI fingerprint check is also required. Fee payee: Virginia State Police. Prepayment required. Pay by certified check or money order. MasterCard/VISA are accepted.

Mail search: Turnaround time: 9 to 12 business days. General users must use the state form SP-167 which can be downloaded from the web at www.vsp.state.va.us/forms.htm. There is also a form SP-230 which you can use depending on your exempt status.

Online search: Certain entities, including screening companies, are can apply for online access via the NCJI System. The system is ONLY

available to IN-STATE accounts and allows you to submit requests faster. Fees are same as manual submission-$15.00 per record or $20.00 SOR record search. Username and password required. A a minimum usage requirement of 10 requests per month in use. Turnaround time is 24-72 hours.

Statewide Court Records

Administrative Office of Courts, 100 N 9th St, 3rd Floor, Richmond, VA 23219; 804-786-6455, 804-786-4542-Fax; 8AM-5PM.

www.courts.state.va.us

Access by: online.

Online search: There are 3 available systems. None are statewide; each county must be searched separately. Cases from 132 General District Courts may be searched free at http://208.210.219.132/courtinfo/vadistrict/select.jsp?court=. Search records of 90+ Circuit courts at http://208.210.219.132/courtinfo/vacircuit/select.jsp?court=. While these systems do not include

DOBs, SSNs and addresses, another access system known as LOPAS does. There are no fees to use LOPAS, but access is granted on a request-by-request basis. Call 804-786-6455 for details. The main webpage above offers access to Supreme Court and Appellate opinions.

Sexual Offender Registry

Virginia State Police, Sex Offender and Crimes Against Minors Registry, PO Box 27472, Richmond, VA 23261-7472; 804-323-2153, 804-323-0862-Fax; 8AM-5PM.

http://sex-offender.vsp.state.va.us/cool-ICE

Records are available from 1994 when the Registry was implemented. It takes 1 to 3 days before new records available for inquiry. Records normally destroyed after death of offender.

Searching: There are two searches. One is distinguished as a search for Crimes Against Minors (use form SP-266). The other is a Sex Offender Registry Name Request (use form SP-230 or SP-167). Include the following in your request-name, race, sex, DOB; also helpful-SSN, residence address. The following data is not released: DOB, SSN

Access by: mail, online.

Fee & Payment: $15.00 for mail searches, either type of search. No fee for the Internet search. No personal checks accepted. Visa/MC accepted.

Mail search: Turnaround time: 1 to 2 weeks, use one of the two forms described above.

Online search: Search by violent offenders from the website by name, city, county or ZIP Code.

Incarceration Records

Virginia Department of Corrections, Central Criminal Records Section, PO Box 26963, Richmond, VA 23261-6963 (Courier address: 6900 Atmore Drive, Richmond, VA 23225); 804-674-3131, 804-674-3598-Fax; 8AM-5PM.

www.vadoc.state.va.us

Requesters can email requests to clasrec@vadoc.state.va.us. Contact Virginia State Police to perform criminal background checks.

Records are available on current and former inmates (only current if request is online). It takes up to 10 days before new records are available for inquiry.

Searching: Computer records go back to 1986 Include the following in your request-full name; DOB and SSN helpful. Location, conviction and sentencing information, and release dates are provided.

Access by: mail, phone, online.

Fee & Payment: There is no fee.

Mail search: Turnaround time: 1 to 2 days.

Phone search: A phone search provides inmate location, address, and approximate release date.

Online search: At www.vipnet.org/cgi-bin/vadoc/doc.cgi is an Incarcerated Offender Locator to ascertain where an inmate is located. This is not designed to provide complete inmate records nor is it a database of all inmates past and present in the system. Also, a private company at www.vinelink.com/index.jsp offers free access at DOC records. DOC wanted/fugitives list is at www.vadoc.state.va.us/offenders/wanted/fugitives.htm.

Corporation, Limited Liability Company, Fictitious Name, Limited Partnership, Business Trust Records

State Corporation Commission, Clerks Office, PO Box 1197, Richmond, VA 23218-1197 (Courier address: Tyler Bldg, 1st Floor, 1300 E Main St, Richmond, VA 23219); 804-371-9733, 804-371-9133-Fax; 8:15AM-5PM.

www.state.va.us/scc/division/clk/index.htm

Records are available for all active entities on computer. Older inactive records must be researched from the State Library.

Searching: Records are public and are open for inspection. Original documents are microfilmed/imaged. Images are maintained permanently at the VA State Library. Include the following in your request-full name of business. In addition to the articles of incorporation, corporation records, the following information is available: Annual Reports, Officers, Directors, DBAs, Prior (merged) names, Inactive (back to 1976 on computer) and Reserved names, and Registered Agents.

Access by: mail, phone, fax, in person, online.

Fee & Payment: Plain copies cost $1.00 per page for the first two pages and $.50 for each additional page thereafter. Certification is $3.00. A good Standing is $6.00. Fee payee: Treasurer of Virginia. Prepayment required. Requesters with billing accounts are encouraged to fax orders. Personal checks accepted, no credit cards.

Mail search: Turnaround time: 3- 5 business days. Be sure to include your phone number and contact person with all written requests.

Phone search: No fee for telephone request. Agency will provide only limited information (screen data only) and name availability over the phone.

Fax search: Turnaround time is 3-5 business days.

In person search: Information is available via public access terminals and microfilm Certificates of Fact and Good Standing are generally available in 3 to 5 business days.

Online search: Their system is called Clerk's Information System and is available at www.state.va.us/scc/division/clk/diracc.htm. There are no fees.

Other access: The entire database is available.

Trademarks, Service Marks

State Corporation Commission, Virginia Securities Division, PO Box 1197 (1300 Main St, 9th Fl), Richmond, VA 23218 (Courier address: 1300 Main St, 9th Fl, Richmond, VA 23219); 804-371-9187, 804-371-9911-Fax; 8:15AM-5PM.

www.scc.virginia.gov/division.htm

Records are available from as early as the 1920s. Records are computerized since the 1970s. It takes less than 1 day before new records are available for inquiry. Records are normally destroyed after they have been inactive for 1 year.

Searching: Include the following in your request-name of mark or owner.

Access by: mail, phone, fax, in person, online.

Fee & Payment: There is no search fee. The copy fee is $2.00 for the first 2 pages and $.50 each additional page. Fee payee: Treasurer of Virginia.

Prepayment required. Personal checks accepted. No credit cards accepted.

Mail search: Turnaround time: 1 to 2 days.

Phone search: Limited to 1 or 2 searches per call.

Fax search: Fax searching available.

In person search: Available as time permits.

Online search: Searching Trademarks and Service Marks records are available on the web at http://securities.scc.state.va.us/pls/SERFIS/wbq_tmsm$.startup.

Uniform Commercial Code, Federal Tax Liens

UCC Division, State Corporation Commission, PO Box 1197, Richmond, VA 23218-1197 (Courier address: 1300 E Main St, 1st Floor, Richmond, VA 23219); 804-371-9733, 804-692-0681-Fax; 8:15AM-5PM.

www.state.va.us/scc/division/clk/index.htm

Records are available from the 1960s on microfiche and from mid 1992 on computer. New records are available for inquiry within 5 days.

Searching: Use search request form UCC-11. The search includes federal tax liens on businesses if specifically requested. Federal tax liens on individuals and all state tax liens are filed at the local level, which may be a county or independent city. Include the following in your request-debtor name. Turnaround time for copies of UCC searches is generally 5 days.

Access by: mail, phone, fax, in person, online.

Fee & Payment: Search request - $7.00; copies - $1.00 for each of the first 2 pages and $.50 for each additional page; certification - $1.00. Fee payee: State Corporation Commission. Prepayment required. Personal checks accepted. No credit cards accepted.

Mail search: Turnaround tme 5 days. SASE is requested.

Phone search: No fee for limited verification on a yes or no basis.

Fax search: Only available to those with billing accounts. Limit of 10 pages on return.

In person search: Counter service provides free access to microfilm records.

Online search: Their system is called Clerk's Information System and is available at www.state.va.us/scc/division/clk/diracc.htm. There are no fees. A wealth of information is available on this system.

State Tax Liens

Records not maintained by a state level agency.

All information is at the local city or county level.

Sales Tax Registrations

Taxation Department, Sales Tax Licenses, PO Box 1115, Richmond, VA 23218-1115; 804-367-8037, 804-367-2603-Fax; 8:30AM-4:30PM.

www.tax.virginia.gov

Registration information of businesses is available from the Corporation Commission.

Records are available for three years on computer, then put on microfilm for ten years, then purged.

Searching: This agency will provide no information without a written, signed, notarized authorization from the business itself; they will then provide the business name, address, phone, and tax permit number. Include the following in your request-business name, tax permit number. iFile is an Internet filing application offered by the Virginia Department of Taxation and the Virginia Employment Commission that allows businesses to file and pay taxes online via the Internet.

Access by: mail.

Mail search: Turnaround time: 1 week to 10 days. No fee for mail request.

Birth Certificates

State Health Department, Office of Vital Records, PO Box 1000, Richmond, VA 23218-1000 (Courier address: 1601 Willow Lawn Drive, #275, Richmond, VA 23220); 804-662-6200, 8AM-4:45PM, 8AM-12 Sat.

www.vdh.state.va.us/vitalrec

An application for certification may be downloaded from the website. Records are available from 1912 on. Records from 1853 to 1896 are located at the State Archives. New records are available for inquiry immediately. Records are indexed on microfiche and computer.

Searching: Recent vital records are available to immediate family members only. Birth records are public information 100 years after the date of the event. Include the following in your request-name at birth, date of birth, place of birth, mother's maiden name, father's name, relationship to the person on the certificate, photocopy ID of requester. Include your area code and daytime phone number, your return address, and be sure to sign your request and provide copy of ID.

Access by: mail, phone, fax, in person.

Fee & Payment: The fee is $12.00 per certificate. If certificate needs to be authorized, fee is additional an $12.00 per authentication. Fee payee: The State Health Department. Prepayment required. Personal checks accepted. Major credit cards accepted.

Mail search: Turnaround time is 4-6 weeks, unless birth occurred between 1940-1978, then time is 2-5 days.

Phone search: See Expedited Service. **Fax search:** See Expedited Service.

In person search: Turnaround time 15 minutes.

Expedited service: Expedited service is available from VitalChek Express Service. Use of credit card required. Phone 877-572-6333, select option #2. Check their website at www.vitalchek.com; e-mail to vitals.reply@vitalchek.com. Turnaround time: 2 - 5 days. Fee is $46.00.

Death Records

State Health Department, Office of Vital Records, PO Box 1000, Richmond, VA 23218-1000 (Courier address: 1601 Willow Lawn Drive, #275, Richmond, VA 23220); 804-662-6200, 8AM-4:45PM, 8AM-12 Sat.

www.vdh.state.va.us/vitalrec

An application for certification may be downloaded from website. Also, recent death records are available at the local health department where the death certificate was filed

Records are available from 1912 on. Records from 1853 to 1896 are located at the State Archives.

New records are available for inquiry immediately. Records are indexed on microfiche, computer.

Searching: Recent vital records are available to immediate family members only. Death records are public information 50 years after the date of the event. Include the following in your request-name of deceased, date of death, place of death, relationship to the deceased, reason for the certificate. Include your area code and daytime phone number, your return address, and be sure to sign your request and provide copy of ID.

Access by: mail, phone, fax, in person.

Fee & Payment: The fee is $12.00 per certificate. If certificate needs to be authorized, fee is additional an $12.00 per authentication. Fee payee: The State Health Department. Prepayment required. Personal checks accepted. Major credit cards accepted.

Mail search: Turnaround time: 4 to 6 weeks.

Phone search: See Expedited Service.

Fax search: See Expedited Service.

In person search: Turnaround time 15 minutes.

Expedited service: Expedited service is available from VitalChek Express Service. Use of credit card required. Phone 877-572-6333, select option #2. Check their website at www.vitalchek.com; e-mail to vitals.reply@vitalchek.com. Turnaround time: 2 - 5 days. Fee is $46.00.

Marriage Certificates

State Health Department, Office of Vital Records, PO Box 1000, Richmond, VA 23218-1000 (Courier address: 1601 Willow Lawn Drive, #275, Richmond, VA 23220); 804-662-6200, 8AM-4:45PM, 8AM-12 Sat.

www.vdh.state.va.us/vitalrec

An application for certification may be downloaded from website. Marriage and divorce records are available at the Circuit Court in which the event took place.

Records are available from 1853 to present. New records are available for inquiry immediately. Records are indexed on microfiche, inhouse computer.

Searching: Recent vital records are available to immediate family members only. Marriage records are public information 50 years after the date of the event. Include the following in your request-name, date of marriage, place of marriage, relationship to the person on the certificate, reason for the certificate. Include your area code and daytime phone number, your return address, and be sure to sign your request.

Access by: mail, phone, fax, in person.

Fee & Payment: The fee is $12.00 per certificate. If certificate needs to be authorized, fee is additional an $12.00 per authentication. Fee payee: The State Health Department. Prepayment required. Personal checks accepted. Major credit cards accepted.

Mail search: Turnaround time: 4 to 6 weeks.

Phone search: See Expedited Service.

Fax search: See Expedited Service.

In person search: Turnaround time 15 minutes.

Expedited service: Expedited service is available from VitalChek Express Service. Use of credit card required Phone 877-572-6333, select option #2 or visit www.vitalchek.com or e-mail to vitals.reply@vitalchek.com for fee information. Turnaround time: 2 - 5 days. Fee is $46.00.

Divorce Records

State Health Department, Office of Vital Records, PO Box 1000, Richmond, VA 23218-1000 (Courier address: 1601 Willow Lawn Drive, #275, Richmond, VA 23220); 804-662-6200, 8AM-4:45PM, 8AM-12 Sat.

www.vdh.state.va.us/vitalrec

An application for certification may be downloaded from website. Marriage and divorce records are available at the Circuit Court in which the event took place.

Records are available 1918 to present. New records are available for inquiry immediately. Records are indexed on microfiche, inhouse computer.

Searching: Recent vital records are available to immediate family members only. Divorce records are public information 50 years after the date of the event. Include the following in your request-name, date of divorce, place of divorce, relationship to the person on the certificate, reason for the certificate. Include your area code, daytime phone number, your return address, and be sure to sign your request and provide copy of ID.

Access by: mail, phone, fax, in person.

Fee & Payment: The fee is $12.00 per certificate. If certificate needs to be authorized, fee is additional an $12.00 per authentication. Fee payee: The State Health Department. Prepayment required. Personal checks accepted. Major credit cards accepted.

Mail search: Turnaround time: 4 to 6 weeks.

Phone search: See Expedited Service.

Fax search: See Expedited Service.

In person search: Turnaround time 15 minutes.

Expedited service: Expedited service is available from VitalChek Express Service. Use of credit card required Phone 877-572-6333, select option #2 or visit www.vitalchek.com or e-mail to vitals.reply@vitalchek.com for fee information. Turnaround time: 2 - 5 days. Fee is $46.00.

Workers' Compensation Records

Workers' Compensation Commission, 1000 DMV Dr, Richmond, VA 23220; 804-367-8633, 877-664-2566, 804-367-9740-Fax; 8:15AM-5PM.

www.vwc.state.va.us

Commission opinions are available at the website. Records are available from 1977 on. New records are available for inquiry immediately. Records are indexed on microfilm, inhouse computer.

Searching: To receive file copies, you must have a notarized release from the claimant. Awards issued are public information. Include the following in your request-claimant name, Social Security Number, claim number. All requests must be in writing. The following data is not released: sealed records.

Access by: mail, in person.

Fee & Payment: The search fee is $10.00. Copy fee $.50 per page for first 50 pages then $.25 ea add'l. $1.00 per page for imaged documents. Fee payee: Treasurer - State of Virginia. Prepayment required. Personal checks accepted. No credit cards accepted.

Mail search: Turnaround time: 1 to 4 days.

In person search: Request must be in writing.

Driver Records

Motorist Records Services, Attn: Records Request Work Center, PO Box 27412, Richmond, VA 23269; 804-367-0538, 8:30AM-5:30PM M-F; 8:30AM-12:30PM S.

www.dmv.state.va.us

Copies of tickets from non-computerized courts are available at this address for $8.00 per record only to driver or driver's authorized representative. Ticket information from computerized courts must be obtained from each court.

Records are available for 3 years for moving violations & misc convictions, 5 years for speeding & unauthorized use of a motor vehicle, 11 years for 3 reckless driving offenses and DWI, and 24 months from the complied date for suspensions. It takes 12 days from receipt before new records are available for inquiry. Records are indexed on inhouse computer.

Searching: Access to records follows DPPA guidelines. Casual requesters can only obtain records with consent using from CRD93 which can be downloaded from the web. Include the following in your request-full name, date of birth, sex. Insurance records display 5 years, employment records the last 7 years. Surrendered licenses are purged after 5 years.

Access by: mail, in person, online.

Fee & Payment: The current fee is $8.00 for mail or walk-in requests and $7.00 for online requests. Add $5.00 for certification. Fee payee: Department of Motor Vehicles. Prepayment required. Personal checks accepted. No credit cards accepted.

Mail search: Turnaround time: 5 days. The driver's name, DOB, and sex must "match" to get a record. Request must be on a DMV form or on letterhead. A SASE is requested.

In person search: Normal turnaround time is while you wait. There are 62 field offices where records can be requested.

Online search: Online service is provided by the Virginia Information Providers Network (VIPNet). Online reports are provided via the Internet on an interactive basis 24 hours daily. There is a $75 annual administrative fee and records are $7.00 each. Go to www.vipnet.org for more information (search "premium services") or call 804-786-4718.

Other access: The agency offers several monitoring programs for employers. Call 804-497-7155 for details.

Vehicle Ownership
Vehicle Identification

Department of Motor Vehicles, Vehicle Records Work Center, PO Box 27412, Richmond, VA 23269; 804-367-0538, 8:30AM-5:30PM M-F; 8:30AM-12:30PM S.

www.dmv.state.va.us

Lien information is only released to lending institutions, collection agencies, and businesses.

New records are available for inquiry in 12 days.

Searching: Casual requesters cannot obtain records without consent. High volume requesters must sign an agreement or contract and will be assigned a user number. Records cannot be purchased and resold for marketing purposes. Include the following in your request-Form CRD93. Private investigators who are registered as

compliance agents by the Department of Justice Services may obtain address information by submitting a license plate number.

Access by: mail, in person, online.

Fee & Payment: The fee is $8.00 for vehicle ownership and registration information or $8.00 per vehicle on a name search. There is a full charge for a "no record found." Add $5.00 for verification. Lien information is $8.00 to approved requesters. Fee payee: Department of Motor Vehicles. Prepayment required. Personal checks accepted. No credit cards accepted.

Mail search: Turnaround time: 7-10 days. A SASE is requested.

In person search: Turnaround time: while you wait, usually limited to five at one time.

Online search: The online system, managed by the Virginia Information Providers Network (VIPNet), is an interactive system open 24 hours daily. There is an annual $75.00 administration fee and records are $7.00 each. All accounts must be approved by both the DMV and VIPNet. Call 804-786-4718 to request an information use agreement application. The URL is www.vipnet.org.

Accident Reports

Department of Motor Vehicles, Driver Records Work Center, Rm 516, PO Box 27412, Richmond, VA 23269-0001; 804-367-0538, 866-368-5463, 804-367-0390-Fax; 8:30AM-5:30PM M-F; Till-12:30PM S.

www.dmv.state.va.us

Records are available for 40 months to present. Records are scanned into computer. It takes 25-30 days before new records are available for inquiry.

Searching: All requests must be in writing. Records are only released to those involved or with a tangible interest. Include the following in your request-full name of driver, date of accident, location of accident.

Access by: mail, fax, in person.

Fee & Payment: The fee is $8.00 per report. Prepayment is required, except for attorneys and insurance companies. Fee payee: Department of Motor Vehicles. Prepayment required. Personal checks accepted. Credit cards accepted: MasterCard, Visa.

Mail search: Turnaround time: 5 days.

Fax search: Must pay with a credit card and submit Fed tax ID#.

In person search: Turnaround time is while you wait, if personnel available.

Vessel Ownership,
Vessel Registration

Game & Inland Fisheries Dept, Boat Registration Dept, 4010 W Broad St, Richmond, VA 23230; 804-367-6135, 804-367-1064-Fax; 8:15AM-5PM.

www.dgif.virginia.gov

The records are open to the public: this agency does not follow DPPA.

Records are available from 1960 to the present. Records are indexed on computer from 1984 to the present. All motorized boats must be registered. All motorboats, or sailboats if over 18 ft are titled.

Lien information will show on record. It takes 24 hours before new records are available for inquiry.

Searching: One of the following is required for a search: name, SSN, title #, hull #.

Access by: mail, phone, in person, online.

Fee & Payment: If history or extensive research is required, there is a fee of $50.00 per boat. There is no fee for a simple name search or registration search. Fee payee: Game & Inland Fisheries Dept. Prepayment required. Personal checks and credit cards accepted.

Mail search: Turnaround time: 3 to 4 days.

Phone search: They will report the owner if a boat number is given, or if a lien exists, on a single request basis.

In person search: Turnaround time is immediate.

Online search: The VA boat registration database may be searched on the web at www.vipnet.org. There is both a free service and a more advanced pay service, but both require a subscription which is $75.00 a year.

Voter Registration

Access to Records is Restricted.

State Board of Elections, 200 N 9th Street, #101, Richmond, VA 23219; 804-786-6551, 804-371-0194-Fax; 8:30AM-5PM.

www.sbe.state.va.us

Individual searches must be done at the county or city level with the General Registrars. The state will sell all or portions of its statewide database (95 counties, 40 cities) to organizations promoting voter registration and participation.

GED Certificates

Virginia Dept of Education, GED Services, PO Box 2120, Richmond, VA 23218-2120; 804-786-4642, 804-225-3352-Fax; 8:15AM-5PM.

www.pen.k12.va.us

Records are available from 1942. It takes 4 weeks before new records are available for inquiry.

Searching: The records are not considered open to the public. To search, submit: a signed release, name, DOB, SSN, and year of test.

Access by: mail, in person.

Fee & Payment: There is a $5.00 fee for a verification or for a transcript. Add $5.00 for certification. Fee payee: VA Department of Education - GED Srvs. Prepayment required. Personal checks are accepted, no credit cards.

Mail search: Turnaround time: 3 to 4 weeks. A SASE is requested.

In person search: Turnaround time is typically immediate.

Hunting and Fishing License Information

Records not maintained by a state level agency.

They do not have a central database because there are hundreds of vendors throughout the state that sell licenses.

Virginia State Licensing Agencies

For details about the agency responsible for licensing/certifying/registering an item below or in the Agency Quick Finder section, match an item's number with the number of the agency in the *Licensing Agency Information* section.

Virginia Licenses Searchable Online

Acupuncturist #6	www.vipnet.org/dhp/cgi-bin/search_publicdb.cgi
Alcoholic Beverage Distributor #1	www.abc.state.va.us/proj/enft/enforcement/jsp/firstpage.jsp
Architect #10	www.dpor.state.va.us/regulantlookup/
Asbestos-related Occupation #10	www.dpor.state.va.us/regulantlookup/
Athletic Trainer #6	www.vipnet.org/dhp/cgi-bin/search_publicdb.cgi
Attorney/Attorney Associate #14	www.vsb.org/attorney/attSearch.asp?S=D
Auctioneer/Auction Company #10	www.dpor.state.va.us/regulantlookup/
Audiologist #6	www.vipnet.org/dhp/cgi-bin/search_publicdb.cgi
Barber/Barber School/Business #10	www.dpor.state.va.us/regulantlookup/
Boxer #10	www.dpor.state.va.us/regulantlookup/
Boxing/Wresting Occupation #10	www.dpor.state.va.us/regulantlookup/
Carpenter #10	www.dpor.state.va.us/regulantlookup/
Cemetery Company/Seller #10	www.dpor.state.va.us/regulantlookup/
Check Casher #7	www.state.va.us/scc/division/banking/chk_cash.htm
Chiropractor #6	www.vipnet.org/dhp/cgi-bin/search_publicdb.cgi
Clinical Nurse Specialist #6	www.vipnet.org/dhp/cgi-bin/search_publicdb.cgi
Contractor #10	www.dpor.state.va.us/regulantlookup/
Cosmetic Procedure Certification #6	www.vipnet.org/dhp/cgi-bin/search_publicdb.cgi
Cosmetologist/Cosmo School/Busi. #10	www.dpor.state.va.us/regulantlookup/
Counselor, Professional #6	www.vipnet.org/dhp/cgi-bin/search_publicdb.cgi
Crematory #6	www.vipnet.org/dhp/cgi-bin/search_publicdb.cgi
Dental Hygienist #6	www.vipnet.org/dhp/cgi-bin/search_publicdb.cgi
Dentist #6	www.vipnet.org/dhp/cgi-bin/search_publicdb.cgi
Embalmer #6	www.vipnet.org/dhp/cgi-bin/search_publicdb.cgi
Engineer #10	www.dpor.state.va.us/regulantlookup/
Fair Housing #10	www.dpor.state.va.us/regulantlookup/
Funeral Director/Establishment/Trainee #6	www.vipnet.org/dhp/cgi-bin/search_publicdb.cgi
Funeral Service Provider #6	www.vipnet.org/dhp/cgi-bin/search_publicdb.cgi
Gas Fitter #10	www.dpor.state.va.us/regulantlookup/
Geologist #10	www.dpor.state.va.us/regulantlookup/
Hair Braider #10	www.dpor.state.va.us/regulantlookup/
Hearing Aid Specialist #10	www.dpor.state.va.us/regulantlookup/
Home Inspector #10	www.dpor.state.va.us/regulantlookup/
Humane Society #6	www.vipnet.org/dhp/cgi-bin/search_publicdb.cgi
Interior Designer #10	www.dpor.state.va.us/regulantlookup/
Investment Advisor/Advisor Agency #12	http://securities.scc.state.va.us/pls/SERFIS/wbq_ai$.startup
Landscape Architect #10	www.dpor.state.va.us/regulantlookup/
Lead-Related Occupation #10	www.dpor.state.va.us/regulantlookup/
Lobbyist #11	www.commonwealth.virginia.gov/Lobbyist/database.cfm
Marriage & Family Therapist #6	www.vipnet.org/dhp/cgi-bin/search_publicdb.cgi
Massage Therapist #6	www.vipnet.org/dhp/cgi-bin/search_publicdb.cgi
Medical Doctor #6	www.vipnet.org/dhp/cgi-bin/search_publicdb.cgi
Medical Equipment Supplier #6	www.vipnet.org/dhp/cgi-bin/search_publicdb.cgi
Medical Wholesaler/Mfg #6	www.vipnet.org/dhp/cgi-bin/search_publicdb.cgi
Money Transmitter #7	www.state.va.us/scc/division/banking/moneytrans.htm
Mortgage Lender/Broker #7	www.state.va.us/scc/division/banking/vamortgagelist.htm
Nail Technician #10	www.dpor.state.va.us/regulantlookup/
Nurse/Nurse's Aide #6	www.vipnet.org/dhp/cgi-bin/search_publicdb.cgi
Nurse-LPN / RN #6	www.vipnet.org/dhp/cgi-bin/search_publicdb.cgi
Nursing Home Admin'r/Preceptor #6	www.vipnet.org/dhp/cgi-bin/search_publicdb.cgi
Occupational Therapist #6	www.vipnet.org/dhp/cgi-bin/search_publicdb.cgi
Optician #10	www.dpor.state.va.us/regulantlookup/
Optometrist #6	www.arbo.org/index.php?action=findanoptometrist

Oral/Maxillofacial Surgeon #6 ....www.vipnet.org/dhp/cgi-bin/search_publicdb.cgi
Osteopathic Physician #6 ....www.vipnet.org/dhp/cgi-bin/search_publicdb.cgi
Payday Lender #7 ....www.state.va.us/scc/division/banking/paydaylend.htm
Pharmacist/Pharmacy #6 ....www.vipnet.org/dhp/cgi-bin/search_publicdb.cgi
Physical Therapist #6 ....www.vipnet.org/dhp/cgi-bin/search_publicdb.cgi
Physician #6...www.vipnet.org/dhp/cgi-bin/search_publicdb.cgi
Physician Assistant #6 ....www.vipnet.org/dhp/cgi-bin/search_publicdb.cgi
Pilot, Branch #10...www.dpor.state.va.us/regulantlookup/
Podiatrist #6 ....www.vipnet.org/dhp/cgi-bin/search_publicdb.cgi
Polygraph Examiner #10 ....www.dpor.state.va.us/regulantlookup/
Prescriptive Authorization #6 ....www.vipnet.org/dhp/cgi-bin/search_publicdb.cgi
Property Association #10 ....www.dpor.state.va.us/regulantlookup/
Psychologist at School #6..................................www.vipnet.org/dhp/cgi-bin/search_publicdb.cgi
Psychologist, Clinical/Applied #6 ....www.vipnet.org/dhp/cgi-bin/search_publicdb.cgi
Psychology School #6 ....www.vipnet.org/dhp/cgi-bin/search_publicdb.cgi
Radiologic Technologist-limited #6 ....www.vipnet.org/dhp/cgi-bin/search_publicdb.cgi
Real Estate Agent/Business/School #10 ....www.dpor.state.va.us/regulantlookup/
Real Estate Appraiser/App'r Business #10 ....www.dpor.state.va.us/regulantlookup/
Rehabilitation Provider #6..................................www.vipnet.org/dhp/cgi-bin/search_publicdb.cgi
Respiratory Care Practitioner #6.....................www.vipnet.org/dhp/cgi-bin/search_publicdb.cgi
School Guidance Counselor #8 ....https://eb01.vak12ed.edu/tinfo
School Library Media Specialist #8..................https://eb01.vak12ed.edu/tinfo
School Principal/Superintendent #8.................https://eb01.vak12ed.edu/tinfo
Securities Broker/Dealer/Dealer Agent #12 ...http://securities.scc.state.va.us/pls/SERFIS/wbq_ai$.startup
Securities Brokerage #12.....................................http://securities.scc.state.va.us/pls/SERFIS/wbq_ai$.startup
Social Worker, Clinical/Registered #6...........www.vipnet.org/dhp/cgi-bin/search_publicdb.cgi
Soil Scientist #10 ....www.dpor.state.va.us/regulantlookup/
Speech Pathologist at School #6 ....www.vipnet.org/dhp/cgi-bin/search_publicdb.cgi
Speech Pathologist/Audiologist #6 ....www.vipnet.org/dhp/cgi-bin/search_publicdb.cgi
Substance Abuse Counselor #6 ....www.vipnet.org/dhp/cgi-bin/search_publicdb.cgi
Substance Abuse Treat't Practitioner #6 ....www.vipnet.org/dhp/cgi-bin/search_publicdb.cgi
Surveyor, Land #10...www.dpor.state.va.us/regulantlookup/
Tattoo Artist #10..www.dpor.state.va.us/regulantlookup/
Teacher #8 ....https://eb01.vak12ed.edu/tinfo
Tradesman #10...www.dpor.state.va.us/regulantlookup/
University Limited Medical License #6...........www.vipnet.org/dhp/cgi-bin/search_publicdb.cgi
Veterinarian/Veterinary Tech #6 ....www.vipnet.org/dhp/cgi-bin/search_publicdb.cgi
Warehouser, Medical #6 ....www.vipnet.org/dhp/cgi-bin/search_publicdb.cgi
Waste Mgm't Facility Operator #10...............www.dpor.state.va.us/regulantlookup/
Waste Water Treatment Operator #10..........www.dpor.state.va.us/regulantlookup/
Wax Technician #10 ....www.dpor.state.va.us/regulantlookup/
Wetlands Delineator #10.....................................www.dpor.state.va.us/regulantlookup/
Wrestler #10...www.dpor.state.va.us/regulantlookup/

Virginia Licensing Quick Finder

Acupuncturist #6 804-662-9908
Alcoholic Beverage Distributor #1 804-213-4400
Architect #10..804-367-8506
Asbestos-Related Occupation #10.......804-367-8595
Athletic Trainer #6................................804-662-9900
Attorney/Attorney Associate #14 804-775-0500
Auctioneer/Auction Company #10........804-367-8506
Audiologist #6 804-662-9900
Bank #7...804-371-9704
Barber/Barber School/Business #10 804-367-8509
Boxer #10..804-367-0186
Cardiac Technical Professional #15.....804-371-3500
Carpenter #10..804-367-8511
Cemetery Company/Seller #10 804-367-2039
Check Casher #7 ....804/371-9701
Chiropractor #6......................................804-662-9908
Clinical Nurse Specialist #6 804-662-9909
Contractor #10 804-367-8511

Cosmetic Procedure Certification #6...804-662-9900
Cosmetologist/Cosmetology School/Business #10
....804-367-8509
Counselor, Professional #6 804-662-9912
Credit Union #7......................................804-371-9267
Crematory #6 804-662-9900
Dental Hygienist #6 804-662-9906
Dentist #6 804-662-9906
Embalmer #6 804-662-9907
Emergency Medical Technician #15 804-371-3500
Engineer #10..804-367-8506
Funeral Director/Establ./Trainee #6 804-662-9907
Funeral Service Provider #6 804-662-9900
Gas Fitter #10 804-367-8511
Geologist #10 804-367-0524
Hair Braider #10 804-367-8509
Hearing Aid Specialist #10 804-367-8509
Home Inspector #10 804-367-8595

Horse Racing Professional #13 804-966-7400
Humane Society #6...............................804-662-9900
Insurance Agent/Agency #2.................804-371-9631
Interior Designer #10.............................804-367-8506
Investment Advisor/Advisor Agency#12 804-371-9686
Landscape Architect #10......................804-367-8506
Lead-Related Occupation #10 804-367-8595
Lobbyist #11 804-786-2441
Marriage & Family Therapist #6...........804-662-9912
Massage Therapist #6...........................804-662-9900
Medical Doctor #6 804-662-9908
Medical Equipment Supplier #6 804-662-9921
Medical Wholesaler/Mfg #6 804-662-9900
Money Transmitter #7 ....804/371-9701
Mortgage Lender/Broker #7 ....804/371-9701
Nail Technician #10...............................804-367-8509
Notary Public #9....................................804-786-2441
Nurse/Nurse's Aide #6 804-662-9909

Nurse-LPN / RN #6	804-662-9900
Nursing Home Administrator/Preceptor #6	804-662-7423
Occupational Therapist #6	804-662-9908
Optician #10	804-367-8509
Optometrist #6	804-662-9910
Oral/Maxillofacial Surgeon #6	804-662-9900
Osteopathic Physician #6	804-662-9908
Paramedic #15	804-371-3500
Payday Lender #7	804/371-9701
Personal Protection Specialist #5	804-786-0460
Pesticide Applicator (Private) #4	804-786-3798
Pesticide Applicator/Company (Commercial) #4	804-786-3798
Pharmacist/Pharmacy #6	804-662-9921
Physical Therapist #6	804-662-9908
Physician #6	804-662-9968
Physician Assistant #6	804-662-9900
Pilot, Branch #10	804-367-8514
Podiatrist #6	804-662-9908
Polygraph Examiner #10	804-367-6166

Prescriptive Authorization #6	804-662-9900
Private Investigator #5	804-786-0460
Property Association #10	804-367-8500
Psychologist at School #6	804-662-9900
Psychologist, Clinical/Applied #6	804-662-9913
Psychology School #6	804-662-9913
Radiologic Technologist-limited #6	804-662-9900
Real Estate Agent/Busi./School #10	804-367-8526
Real Estate Appraiser/Appraiser Business #10	804-367-2039
Rehabilitation Provider #6	804-662-9912
Respiratory Care Practitioner #6	804-662-9908
Savings Institution #7	804-371-9704
School Guidance Counselor #8	804-371-2522
School Library Media Specialist #8	804-371-2522
School Principal/Superintendent #8	804-371-2522
Securities Broker/Dealer/Dealer Agent #12	804-371-9686
Securities Brokerage #12	804-371-9187
Security Officer, Unarmed/Armed #5	804-786-0460
Security Tech. (Electronic Security) #5	804-786-0460

Shock/Trauma Professional #15	804-371-3500
Shorthand Reporter #3	703-768-8122
Social Worker, Clinical/Registered #6	804-662-9914
Soil Scientist #10	804-367-2785
Speech Pathologist at School #6	804-662-9900
Speech Pathologist/Audiologist #6	804-662-9111
Substance Abuse Counselor #6	804-662-9912
Substance Abuse Treatment Practitioner #6	804-662-9912
Surveyor, Land #10	804-367-8506
Teacher #8	804-371-2522
Tradesman #10	804-367-8511
University Limited Medical License #6	804-662-9900
Veterinarian/Veterinary Technician #6	804-662-9915
Veterinary Facility #6	804-662-9915
Warehouser, Medical #6	804-662-9900
Waste Management Facility Op. #10	804-367-8595
Waste Water Treatment Plant Op. 10	804-367-2176
Wax Technician #10	804-367-8509
Wrestler #10	804-367-0186

Virginia Licensing Agency Information

1 Alcoholic Beverage Control Board, 2901 Hermitage Rd, Richmond, VA 23220; 804-213-4577, Fax: 804-213-4586.
www.abc.state.va.us
Search Database at www.abc.state.va.us/proj/en ft/enforcement/jsp/firstpage.jsp

2 Bureau of Insurance, Financial Regulation-State Corporation Commission, PO Box 1157, (Tyler Building, 1300 E. Main St., Richmond, VA 23219), Richmond, VA 23218; 804-371-9631, Fax: 804-371-9349.
www.state.va.us/scc/division/boi/index.htm

3 CSR Contact Person, 2404 Belle Haven Meadows, Alexandria, VA 22306; 703-768-8122, Fax: 703-768-8921.

4 Department of Agriculture & Consumer Services, Office of Pesticide Services, PO Box 1163, Richmond, VA 23218; 804-786-3798, 371-6558, Fax: 804-371-8598 Admin ofc.; 786-9149 lic. app.   www.vdacs.state.va.us/pesticides/
Email: rgilliam@vdacs.state.va.us

5 Department of Criminal Justice, Private Security, 805 E Broad St, 10th Fl, Richmond, VA 23219; 804-786-4000, Fax: 804-786-6344.
www.dcjs.state.va.us

6 Department of Health Professions, 6603 W Broad St, 5th Fl, Richmond, VA 23230-1712; 804-662-9900 (DHP), Fax: 804-662-9943/9200.
www.dhp.virginia.gov/
Email: webmaster@dhp.virginia.gov
Search Database at www.vipnet.org/dhp/cgi-bin/search_publicdb.cgi   Note: A license and case

decision alert service allows you to track licensing status and disciplinary actions for health care professionals. Visit www.vipnet.org/dhp/demo/d hpserviceinfo.html to join. Licensee lists are also available. Credit cards accepted.

7 Corporation Commission, Bureau of Financial Institutions, PO Box 640 (1300 E. Main St #800), Richmond, VA 23218-0640; 804-371-9701, Fax: 804-371-9416.
www.state.va.us/scc/division/banking/index.htm
Email: bfiquestions@scc.state.va.us
Search Database at www.scc.virginia.gov/division/banking/licreg.htm

8 Department of Education, Division of Teacher Education & Licensure, PO Box 2120 (101 N 14th St, James Monroe Bldg.), Richmond, VA 23218-2120; 804-371-2522, Fax: 804-786-6759.
www.pen.k12.va.us
Email: ppitts@mail.vak12ed.edu
Search Database at https://eb01.vak12ed.edu/tinfo

9 Secretary of the Commonwealth, Notary Public Division, PO Box 1795, Richmond, VA 23218; 804-786-2441, Fax: 804-371-0017.
www.soc.state.va.us
Email: mford@gov.state.va.us

10 Department of Professional & Occupation Regulation, 3600 W Broad St, Richmond, VA 23230-4917; 804-367-8583, Fax: 804-367-2475.
www.state.va.us/dpor
Email: lexie.borkey@dpor.virginia.gov
Search Database at
www.dpor.state.va.us/regulantlookup/   Note: Board of Accountancy is Suite #696.

11 Secretary of the Commonwealth, 830 E Main Street, 14th Fl, Richmond, VA 23219; 804-781-2441, Fax: 804-371-0017.
www.soc.state.va.us
Email: lobbyist@gov.state.va.us
Search Database at www.commonwealth.virgin ia.gov/Lobbyist/database.cfm

12 Corporation Commission, Securities Division, PO Box 1197 (1300 E Main, 9th Fl), Richmond, VA 23218; 804-371-9187, Fax: 804-371-9911.
www.state.va.us/scc/division/srf
Search Database at http://securities.scc.state.va.u s/pls/SERFIS/wbq_ai$.startup

13 Virginia Racing Commission, 10700 Horsemans Road , PO Box 208, New Kent, VA 23124; 804-966-7400, Fax: 804-966-7418.
www.vrc.state.va.us
Email: shorland@vrc.state.va.us

14 State Bar Association, 707 E Main St, #1500, Richmond, VA 23219-2800; 804-775-0500, Fax: 804-775-0501.
www.vsb.org
Search Database at
www.vsb.org/attorney/attSearch.asp?S=D

15 Department of Health, Emergency Medical Services, 109 Governor St, Richmond, VA 23219; 804-864-7600, Fax: 804-864-7580.
www.vdh.state.va.us/oems

Virginia Federal Courts

The following list indicates the district and division name for each county in the state. If the bankruptcy court location is different from the district court, then the location of the bankruptcy court appears in parentheses.

Virginia County/Court Cross Reference

County	District	Division
Accomack	Eastern	Norfolk
Albemarle	Western	Charlottesville (Lynchburg)
Alexandria City	Eastern	Alexandria
Alleghany	Western	Roanoke (Harrisonburg)
Amelia	Eastern	Richmond
Amherst	Western	Lynchburg
Appomattox	Western	Lynchburg
Arlington	Eastern	Alexandria
Augusta	Western	Harrisonburg
Bath	Western	Harrisonburg
Bedford	Western	Lynchburg
Bedford City	Western	Lynchburg
Bland	Western	Roanoke
Botetourt	Western	Roanoke
Bristol City	Western	Abingdon (Roanoke)
Brunswick	Eastern	Richmond
Buchanan	Western	Abingdon (Roanoke)
Buckingham	Western	Lynchburg
Buena Vista City	Western	Lynchburg (Harrisonburg)
Campbell	Western	Lynchburg
Caroline	Eastern	Richmond
Carroll	Western	Roanoke
Charles City	Eastern	Richmond
Charlotte	Western	Danville (Lynchburg)
Charlottesville City	Western	Charlottesville (Lynchburg)
Chesapeake City	Eastern	Norfolk
Chesterfield	Eastern	Richmond
Clarke	Western	Harrisonburg
Clifton Forge City	Western	Roanoke (Harrisonburg)
Colonial Heights City	Eastern	Richmond
Covington City	Western	Roanoke (Harrisonburg)
Craig	Western	Roanoke
Culpeper	Western	Charlottesville (Lynchburg)
Cumberland	Western	Lynchburg
Danville City	Western	Danville (Lynchburg)
Dickenson	Western	Big Stone Gap (Roanoke)
Dinwiddie	Eastern	Richmond
Emporia City	Eastern	Richmond
Essex	Eastern	Richmond
Fairfax	Eastern	Alexandria
Fairfax City	Eastern	Alexandria
Falls Church City	Eastern	Alexandria
Fauquier	Eastern	Alexandria
Floyd	Western	Roanoke
Fluvanna	Western	Charlottesville (Lynchburg)
Franklin	Western	Roanoke
Franklin City	Eastern	Norfolk
Frederick	Western	Harrisonburg
Fredericksburg City	Eastern	Richmond
Galax City	Western	Roanoke
Giles	Western	Roanoke
Gloucester	Eastern	Newport News
Goochland	Eastern	Richmond
Grayson	Western	Roanoke
Greene	Western	Charlottesville (Lynchburg)
Greensville	Eastern	Richmond
Halifax	Western	Danville (Lynchburg)
Hampton City	Eastern	Newport News
Hanover	Eastern	Richmond
Harrisonburg City	Western	Harrisonburg
Henrico	Eastern	Richmond
Henry	Western	Danville (Lynchburg)
Highland	Western	Harrisonburg
Hopewell City	Eastern	Richmond
Isle of Wight	Eastern	Norfolk
James City	Eastern	Newport News
King George	Eastern	Richmond
King William	Eastern	Richmond
King and Queen	Eastern	Richmond
Lancaster	Eastern	Richmond
Lee	Western	Big Stone Gap (Roanoke)
Lexington City	Western	Lynchburg (Harrisonburg)
Loudoun	Eastern	Alexandria
Louisa	Western	Charlottesville (Lynchburg)
Lunenburg	Eastern	Richmond
Lynchburg City	Western	Lynchburg
Madison	Western	Charlottesville (Lynchburg)
Manassas City	Eastern	Alexandria
Manassas Park City	Eastern	Alexandria
Martinsville City	Western	Lynchburg
Mathews	Eastern	Newport News
Mecklenburg	Eastern	Richmond
Middlesex	Eastern	Richmond
Montgomery	Western	Roanoke
Nelson	Western	Charlottesville (Lynchburg)
New Kent	Eastern	Richmond
Newport News City	Eastern	Newport News
Norfolk City	Eastern	Norfolk
Northampton	Eastern	Norfolk
Northumberland	Eastern	Richmond
Norton City	Western	Big Stone Gap (Roanoke)
Nottoway	Eastern	Richmond
Orange	Western	Charlottesville (Lynchburg)
Page	Western	Harrisonburg
Patrick	Western	Danville (Lynchburg)
Petersburg City	Eastern	Richmond
Pittsylvania	Western	Danville (Lynchburg)
Poquoson City	Eastern	Newport News
Portsmouth City	Eastern	Norfolk
Powhatan	Eastern	Richmond
Prince Edward	Eastern	Richmond
Prince George	Eastern	Richmond
Prince William	Eastern	Alexandria
Pulaski	Western	Roanoke
Radford City	Western	Roanoke
Rappahannock	Western	Charlottesville (Harrisonburg)
Richmond	Eastern	Richmond
Richmond City	Eastern	Richmond
Roanoke	Western	Roanoke
Roanoke City	Western	Roanoke
Rockbridge	Western	Lynchburg (Harrisonburg)
Rockingham	Western	Harrisonburg
Russell	Western	Abingdon (Roanoke)
Salem City	Western	Roanoke
Scott	Western	Big Stone Gap (Roanoke)
Shenandoah	Western	Harrisonburg
Smyth	Western	Abingdon (Roanoke)
South Boston City	Western	Danville (Lynchburg)
Southampton	Eastern	Norfolk
Spotsylvania	Eastern	Richmond
Stafford	Eastern	Alexandria
Staunton City	Western	Harrisonburg
Suffolk City	Eastern	Norfolk
Surry	Eastern	Richmond
Sussex	Eastern	Richmond
Tazewell	Western	Abingdon (Roanoke)
Virginia Beach City	Eastern	Norfolk
Warren	Western	Harrisonburg
Washington	Western	Abingdon (Roanoke)
Waynesboro City	Western	Harrisonburg
Westmoreland	Eastern	Richmond
Williamsburg City	Eastern	Newport News
Winchester City	Western	Harrisonburg
Wise	Western	Big Stone Gap (Roanoke)
Wythe	Western	Roanoke
York	Eastern	Newport News

Standards for Federal Courts: Search fee is $26.00 per item (one party name or case number). Copy fee is $.50 per page. Certification fee is $9.00 per document, double for exemplification, if available. All fees standard unless noted in profile. Mail Search: always enclose a stamped self addressed envelope unless otherwise noted. Most courts accept fax requests or will suggest a copying/search vendor. Before releasing records, all courts require prepayment, unless noted.

Open records are located at the court unless otherwise noted. District courts index by defendant and plaintiff as well as by case number. Bankruptcy courts usually index by debtor and case number. While most courts now have their indexes on computer, many may still maintain index card files as well.

Courts offering internet access via CM-ECF or older RACER, PACER, or Web-PACER systems charge $.08 per page fee unless noted as free. Where PACER is available, the universal sign-up number is 800-676-6856. Find PACER and the US Party/Case Index at http://pacer.psc.uscourts.gov.

US District Court

Eastern District of Virginia

Alexandria Division Court Clerk, 401 Courthouse Square, Alexandria, VA 22314 (also use mail address for courier delivery), 703-299-2100, records rm- 703-299-2128, crim dockets- 703-299-2102, civil dockets- 703-299-2101. Hours- 8AM-5PM. www.vaed.uscourts.gov

Jurisdictions: Arlington, Fairfax, Fauquier, Loudoun, Prince William, Stafford, City of Alexandria, City of Fairfax, City of Falls Church, City of Manassas, City of Manassas Park.

Searches & Indexing: Results do not include SSN or DOB. Computer index maintained; civil back to 1995, criminal to 2000. Records indexed and stored in numerical order. New cases in the index 1 day after filing date. Records purged never.

Fee & Payment: Pay by money order, cashier's or personal check. No credit cards. Payee: Clerk, US District Court. Prepayment required.

Phone Search: Only docket information is available by phone.

Mail Search: search usually completed- 1 week. Include SASE for return.

In Person Search: Fee charged if court performs your search. A copy service is available. No self-serve copier available.

E-Services: ECF replaces PACER whose records did go back to 6/1990. ECF at https://ecf.vaed.uscourts.gov. Notable cases free at www.vaed.uscourts.gov/notablecases/index.html.

Newport News Division Clerk's Office, PO Box 494, Newport News, VA 23607 (courier address: US Post Office Bldg, Rm 201, 101 25th St, Newport News, VA 23607), 757-247-0784. Hours- 10AM-4PM. www.vaed.uscourts.gov

Jurisdictions: Gloucester, James City, Mathews, York, City of Hampton, City of Newport News, City of Poquoson, City of Williamsburg. This division houses misdemeanor records only. Please direct civil and felony record requests to Norfolk Division.

Searches & Indexing: Computer index maintained. New cases in index 1 day after filing date. Open records located at Norfolk Division.

Fee & Payment: Pay by money order or cashier's check.

Phone Search: No searching by telephone.

Mail Search: search usually completed- 2-3 days. Mail requests for civil and felony records are forwarded to Norfolk. Include SASE for return.

In Person Search: Fee charged if court performs search; no charge to use public access computer.

E-Services: ECF replaces PACER whose records did go back to 6/1990. New records online after 1 day. ECF at https://ecf.vaed.uscourts.gov. Notable cases - big cases - free at www.vaed.uscourts.gov/notablecases/index.html.

Norfolk Division Court Clerk, US Courthouse, Rm 193, 600 Granby St, Norfolk, VA 23510 (also use mail address for courier delivery), 757-222-7204, crim dockets- 757-222-7202, civil dockets- 757-222-7201. Hours- 10AM-4PM. www.vaed.uscourts.gov

Jurisdictions: Accomack, City of Chesapeake, City of Franklin, Isle of Wight, City of Norfolk, Northampton, City of Portsmouth, City of Suffolk, Southampton, City of Virginia Beach.

Searches & Indexing: Results do not include SSN or DOB. Computer, microfiche and card indexes maintained. Index on microfiche 1/1981 to 6/1991; prior to 1981 in card index. New cases in the index 1 day after filing date. Records purged irregularly.

Fee & Payment: Pay by business or personal check. Payee: Clerk, US District Court. Prepayment required. Credit cards accepted in person only.

Phone Search: Only docket information released via phone.

Mail Search: search usually completed- 1 week. Include SASE for return.

In Person Search: permitted. This court will only do searches if the public terminal is down. No self-serve copier available.

E-Services: ECF replaces PACER whose records did go back to 6/1990. New records online after 1 day. ECF at https://ecf.vaed.uscourts.gov. Notable cases - big cases - free at www.vaed.uscourts.gov/notablecases/index.html.

Richmond Division Court Clerk Office, 1000 E Main St, Rm 305, Lewis F Powell, Jr Courthouse Bldg, Richmond, VA 23219-3525 (also use mail address for courier delivery), 804-916-2200, crim dockets- 804-916-2230, civil dockets- 804-916-2220. Hours- 10AM-4PM. www.vaed.uscourts.gov

Jurisdictions: Amelia, Brunswick, Caroline, Charles City, Chesterfield, Dinwiddie, Essex, Goochland, Greensville, Hanover, Henrico, King and Queen, King George, King William, Lancaster, Lunenburg, Mecklenburg, Middlesex, New Kent, Northumberland, Nottoway, City of Petersburg, Powhatan, Prince Edward, Prince George, Richmond, City of Richmond, Spotsylvania, Surry, Sussex, Westmoreland, City of Colonial Heights, City of Emporia, City of Fredericksburg, City of Hopewell.

Searches & Indexing: Computer index maintained. Records indexed by case number. New cases in the index 1 day after filing date.

Fee & Payment: Pay by money order, cashier's or personal check. Payee: Clerk's Office, US District Court. Prepayment required.

Phone Search: Only docket information is available by phone. This court will not honor requests for lists of names via phone.

Mail Search: search usually completed- 1 week. SASE not required.

In Person Search: Fee charged if court performs your search. A copy service is available. No self-serve copier available.

E-Services: ECF replaces PACER whose records did go back to 6/1990. ECF at https://ecf.vaed.uscourts.gov. Notable cases free at www.vaed.uscourts.gov/notablecases/index.html. **Other Online Access:** Richmond court schedules at www.vaed.uscourts.gov/schedule/main.html.

US Bankruptcy Court

Eastern District of Virginia

Alexandria Division Court Clerk, 200 S Washington St #100, Alexandria, VA 22314 (also use mail address for courier delivery), 703-258-1200. Hours- 9AM-4PM. www.vaeb.uscourts.gov

Jurisdictions: City of Alexandria, Arlington, Fairfax, City of Fairfax, City of Falls Church, Fauquier, Loudoun, City of Manassas, City of Manassas Park, Prince William, Stafford.

Searches & Indexing: A creditor register is also kept for each case. Results include full SSN, DOB. Both computer and card indexes maintained. Cases prior to 12/1989 on index cards. New cases in the index 2 days after filing. Records purged never.

Fee & Payment: Pay by money order, cashier's or personal check. No debtor's checks accepted. Payee: Clerk, US Bankruptcy Court. Prepayment required.

Phone Search: Docket information available by phone. Voice Case Information Service available, call VCIS at 800-326-5879 or 804-771-2736.

Mail Search: search usually completed- 3 days. Include SASE for return.

In Person Search: permitted. Copying available from IKON Mgmt Svcs, 703-706-0494. No self-serve copier available.

E-Services: ECF replaces PACER whose records did go back to mid 1989. ECF at https://ecf.vaeb.uscourts.gov **Opinions Online:** www.vaeb.uscourts.gov/dtsearch.html. **Other Online Access:** Court calendars at www.vaeb.uscourts.gov/cal/calroot/judges.htm. Court now participates in the US party case index.

Newport News Division Bankruptcy Court Clerk, PO Box 1938, Norfolk, VA 23501-1938 (courier address: Walter E Hoffman US Courthouse, Rm 400, 600 Granby St, Norfolk, VA 23510), 757-222-7500. Hours- 9AM-4PM. www.vaeb.uscourts.gov

Jurisdictions: Newport News City. Records are at the Norfolk Bankruptcy Court.

Searches & Indexing: Results include last 4 SSN digits. Computer index maintained back to 1990. New cases in the index 2 days after filing date.

Fee & Payment: Pay by Visa/MC, money order, cashier's or personal check. No debtor's checks accepted. Payee: Clerk, US Bankruptcy Court. Prepayment required.

Phone Search: Call for name, case number, chapter, filing date, judge, attorney for debtor, trustee, date discharged. Voice Case Information Service available, call VCIS at 800-326-5879 or 804-771-2736.

Mail Search: search usually completed- within 2 days. Include SASE for return.

In Person Search: Fee charged if court performs your search. Copying available from Creative Assistant (757) 624-9998. No self-serve copier.

E-Services: ECF replaces PACER. ECF at http://ecf.vaeb.uscourts.gov **Opinions Online:** www.vaeb.uscourts.gov/dtsearch.html. **Other Online Access:** Court calendars at www.vaeb.uscourts.gov/cal/calroot/judges.htm. Court now participates in the US party case index.

Norfolk Division Court Clerk, PO Box 1938, Norfolk, VA 23501-1938 (courier address: Walter E Hoffman US Courthouse, Rm 400, 600 Granby St, Norfolk, VA 23510), 757-222-7500. Hours- 9AM-4PM. www.vaeb.uscourts.gov

Jurisdictions: Accomack, City of Cape Charles, City of Chesapeake, City of Franklin, Gloucester, City of Hampton, Isle of Wight, James City, Matthews, City of Norfolk, Northampton, City of Poquoson, City of Portsmouth, Southampton, City of Suffolk, City of Virginia Beach, City of Williamsburg, York.

Searches & Indexing: Results include last 4 SSN digits only. Computer index back to 1989 maintained. New cases in the index immediately after filing date. Records purged never.

Fee & Payment: Pay by Visa/MC/AmEx/Disc, money order, cashier's or personal check. No debtor's checks accepted. Payee: Clerk, US Bankruptcy Court. Prepayment required. Make search fee checks to court clerk.

Phone Search: Call for name, case number, chapter, filing date, judge, attorney for debtor, trustee, date discharged. Voice Case Information Service available, call VCIS at 800-326-5879 or 804-771-2736.

Mail Search: search usually completed- within 2 days. Include SASE for return.

In Person Search: Fee charged if court performs your search. Copying available from copy service or use Creative Assistant for copies, 757-624-9990; pay Creative Assistant separately. No self-serve copier available.

E-Services: ECF replaces PACER. ECF at https://ecf.vaeb.uscourts.gov **Opinions Online:** www.vaeb.uscourts.gov/dtsearch.html. **Other Online Access:** Court calendars at www.vaeb.uscourts.gov/cal/calroot/judges.htm. Court now participates in the US party case index.

Richmond Division Office of the Clerk, 1100 E Main St, Rm 310, Richmond, VA 23219-3515 (use mail address for courier delivery), 804-916-2400. Hours- 9AM-4PM. www.vaeb.uscourts.gov

Jurisdictions: Amelia, Brunswick, Caroline, Charles City, Chesterfield, City of Colonial Heights, Dinwiddie, City of Emporia, Essex, City of Fredericksburg, Goochland, Greensville, Hanover, Henrico, City of Hopewell, King and Queen, King George, King William, Lancaster, Lunenburg, Mecklenburg, Middlesex, New Kent, Northumberland, Nottoway, City of Petersburg, Powhatan, Prince Edward, Prince George, Richmond, City of Richmond, Spotsylvania, Surry, Sussex, Westmoreland.

Searches & Indexing: Results include last 4 SSN digits only. Computer index maintained. New cases in the index 1 day after filing date.

Fee & Payment: Pay by money order, cashier's or personal check. No debtor's checks accepted. Payee: Clerk, US Bankruptcy Court. Prepayment required.

Phone Search: Only docket information released via phone. Voice Case Information Service available, call VCIS at 800-326-5879.

Mail Search: search usually completed- 2 days. Include SASE for return.

In Person Search: Fee charged if court performs your search. Copying available from copy service. No self-serve copier available.

E-Services: ECF replaces PACER. ECF at https://ecf.vaeb.uscourts.gov **Opinions Online:** www.vaeb.uscourts.gov/dtsearch.html. **Other Online Access:** Court calendars at www.vaeb.uscourts.gov/cal/calroot/judges.htm. Court now participates in the US party case index.

US District Court

Western District of Virginia

Abingdon Division Clerk's Office, PO Box 398, Abingdon, VA 24212 (courier address: 180 W Main St, Abingdon, VA 24210), 276-628-5116, Fax-276-628-1028. Hours- 8:30AM-4:30PM. www.vawd.uscourts.gov

Jurisdictions: Buchanan, City of Bristol, Russell, Smyth, Tazewell, Washington.

Searches & Indexing: Results do not include SSN or DOB. Both computer and card indexes maintained; computer back to 1992. New cases in the index immediately after filing date. Records purged never.

Fee & Payment: Pay by Visa/MC/AmEx/Disc, money order, cashier's or personal check. Payee: Clerk, US District Court. Court will bill for searches and copies.

Phone Search: Docket information available via phone.

Mail Search: search usually completed- 2-3 days. SASE not required.

In Person Search: Fee charged if court performs your search. Self-serve copier - $.10 per page.

E-Services: ECF replaces PACER whose records did go back to mid 1990. ECF at https://ecf.vawd.uscourts.gov **Opinions Online:** www.vawd.uscourts.gov/opinion.asp. **Other Online Access:** Judges' calendars free at www.vawd.uscourts.gov/judgescal/default.asp.

Big Stone Gap Division Court Clerk, PO Box 490, Big Stone Gap, VA 24219 (courier address: 322 Wood Ave E, Rm 204, Big Stone Gap, VA 24219), 276-523-3557, records rm- 276-523-3557, Fax-276-523-6214. Hours- 8:30AM-4:30PM. www.vawd.uscourts.gov

Jurisdictions: Dickenson, Lee, Scott, Wise, City of Norton.

Searches & Indexing: Style of case is needed to conduct a search; civil action number very helpful. Results include last 4 SSN digits, also birth year. Computer index maintained; miicrofilm index maintained for older cases. New cases in the index immediately after filing. Records purged never.

Fee & Payment: Pay by money order, cashier's or personal check. Payee: Clerk, US District Court. Will fax docket listings.

Phone Search: Only docket information is available by phone.

Mail Search: search usually completed- 2 days. Include SASE for return.

In Person Search: Fee charged if court performs your search. No self-serve copier available.

E-Services: ECF replaces PACER whose records did go back to mid 1990. ECF at https://ecf.vawd.uscourts.gov **Opinions Online:** www.vawd.uscourts.gov/opinion.asp. **Other Online Access:** Judges' calendars free at www.vawd.uscourts.gov/judgescal/default.asp.

Charlottesville Division Court Clerk, Clerk, Rm 304, 255 W Main St, Charlottesville, VA 22902 (also use mail address for courier delivery), 434-296-9284, Fax-434-295-8909. Hours- 8:30AM-4:30PM. www.vawd.uscourts.gov

Jurisdictions: Albemarle, Culpeper, Fluvanna, Greene, Louisa, Madison, Nelson, Orange, Rappahannock, City of Charlottesville.

Searches & Indexing: Results do not include SSN or DOB. Computer, microfiche and card indexes maintained. Microfiche index 1981-1991; on cards prior. New cases in the index immediately after filing date. Records purged never. District-wide searches available here.

Fee & Payment: Pay by money order, cashier's or personal check. Payee: Clerk, US District Court. Prepayment required.

Phone Search: No searching by telephone.

Mail Search: search usually completed- 2-3 days. Include SASE for return.

In Person Search: Fee charged if court performs your search. Court only searches computer index. Visitors may search microfiche index. Self-serve copier available - $.50 per page.

E-Services: ECF replaces PACER whose records did go back to mid 1990. ECF at https://ecf.vawd.uscourts.gov **Opinions Online:** www.vawd.uscourts.gov/opinion.asp. **Other Online Access:** Judges' calendars free at www.vawd.uscourts.gov/judgescal/default.asp.

Danville Division Court Clerk, PO Box 1400, Danville, VA 24543-0053 (courier address: Dan Daniel Post Office Bldg, 700 Main St, Rm 202, Danville, VA 24541), 434-793-7147 x0, Fax-434-793-0284. Hours- 8:30AM-4:30PM. www.vawd.uscourts.gov

Jurisdictions: Charlotte, Halifax, Henry, Patrick, Pittsylvania, City of Danville, City of Martinsville, City of South Boston.

Searches & Indexing: Results include last 4 SSN digits. Both computer and card indexes maintained. New cases in the index immediately after filing date. Records purged never.

Fee & Payment: Pay by Visa/MC/AmEx/Disc, money order, cashier's or personal check. Payee: Clerk, US District Court. Prepayment required.

Phone Search: For expedited requests where fees are prepaid, this court will call to give information then follow with a written response.

Mail Search: search usually completed- 2-3 days. SASE not required.

In Person Search: Fee charged if court performs your search. No self-serve copier available.

E-Services: ECF replaces PACER whose records did go back to mid 1990. ECF at https://ecf.vawd.uscourts.gov **Opinions Online:** www.vawd.uscourts.gov/opinion.asp. **Other Online Access:** Judges' calendars free at www.vawd.uscourts.gov/judgescal/default.asp.

Harrisonburg Division Clerk of Court, 116 N Main St, Rm 314, Harrisonburg, VA 22802 (use mail address for courier delivery), 540-434-3181. Hours- 8:30AM-4:30PM. www.vawd.uscourts.gov

Jurisdictions: Augusta, Bath, Clarke, Frederick, Highland, Page, Rockingham, Shenandoah, Warren, City of Harrisonburg, City of Staunton, City of Waynesboro, City of Winchester.

Searches & Indexing: Results include last 4 SSN digits. Both computer and card indexes maintained. Computer has civil cases back to 1991, criminal to 1993. New cases in the index 1-2 days after filing date. Records purged never. District-wide searches available here, but court prefers searches be conducted where case is filed.

Fee & Payment: Pay by money order, cashier's or personal check. Payee: Clerk, US District Court. Prepayment required.

Phone Search: Limited information available by phone. **Mail Search:** search usually completed- 1-2 days. SASE not required. **In Person Search:** Fee charged if court performs your search. No self-serve copier available.

E-Services: ECF replaces PACER whose records did go back to mid 1990. ECF at https://ecf.vawd.uscourts.gov **Opinions Online:** www.vawd.uscourts.gov/opinion.asp. **Other Online Access:** Judges' calendars free at www.vawd.uscourts.gov/judgescal/default.asp.

Lynchburg Division Clerk of Court, PO Box 744, Lynchburg, VA 24505 (courier address: 1101 Court St #A66, Lynchburg, VA), 434-847-5722. Hours- 8:30AM-4:30PM. www.vawd.uscourts.gov

Jurisdictions: Amherst, Appomattox, Bedford, Buckingham, Campbell, Cumberland, Rockbridge, City of Bedford, City of Buena Vista, City of Lexington, City of Lynchburg.

Searches & Indexing: Results include last 4 SSN digits. Both computer and card indexes maintained, on computer back to 1989. New cases in the index immediately after filing date. Records purged never.

Fee & Payment: Pay by money order, cashier's or personal check. Payee: Clerk, US District Court. Prepayment required.

Phone Search: Only docket information is available by phone. **Mail Search:** search usually completed- 2 days. SASE not required. **In Person Search:** Fee charged if court performs your search. No self-serve copier available.

E-Services: ECF replaces PACER whose records did go back to mid 1990. ECF at https://ecf.vawd.uscourts.gov **Opinions Online:** www.vawd.uscourts.gov/opinion.asp. **Other Online Access:** Judges' calendars free at www.vawd.uscourts.gov/judgescal/default.asp.

Roanoke Division Clerk of Court, PO Box 1234, Roanoke, VA 24006 (courier address: 210 Franklin Rd SW, Roanoke, VA 24011), 540-857-5100, crim dockets- 540-857-5102, civil dockets- 540-857-5101, Fax-540-857-5110. Hours- 8:30AM-4:30PM. www.vawd.uscourts.gov

Jurisdictions: Alleghany, Bland, Botetourt, Carroll, Craig, Floyd, Franklin, Giles, Grayson, Montgomery, Pulaski, Roanoke, Wythe, City of Covington, City of Clifton Forge, City of Galax, City of Radford, City of Roanoke, City of Salem.

Searches & Indexing: Results include last 4 SSN digits. Computer, microfiche and card indexes maintained. Automated in-house records system goes back to 1991/1992. New cases in the index immediately after filing date. Records purged never. District-wide searches available for all records.

Fee & Payment: Pay by money order, cashier's or personal check. Payee: Clerk, US District Court. Prepayment required. Credit cards accepted in person only.

Phone Search: For expedited requests where fees are prepaid, this court will call to give information then follow with a written response.

Mail Search: search usually completed- 1 week. SASE not required.

In Person Search: Fee charged if court performs your search. No self-serve copier available.

E-Services: ECF replaces PACER whose records did go back to mid 1990. ECF at https://ecf.vawd.uscourts.gov **Opinions Online:** www.vawd.uscourts.gov/opinion.asp. **Other Online Access:** Judges' calendars free at www.vawd.uscourts.gov/judgescal/default.asp.

US Bankruptcy Court

Western District of Virginia

Harrisonburg Division Court Clerk, PO Box 1407, Harrisonburg, VA 22802 (courier address: 116 N Main St, Rm 223, Harrisonburg, VA 22802), 540-434-8327, Fax-540-434-9715. Hours- 8AM-4:30PM. www.vawb.uscourts.gov

Jurisdictions: Alleghany, Augusta, Bath, City of Buena Vista, Clarke, City of Clifton Forge, City of Covington, Frederick, City of Harrisonburg, Highland, City of Lexington, Page, Rappahannock, Rockbridge, Rockingham, Shenandoah, City of Staunton, Warren, City of Waynesboro, City of Winchester.

Searches & Indexing: Results include last 4 SSN digits. Both computer and card indexes maintained; computer goes back to 1986. Older cases on card index. New cases in the index immediately after filing date. Records purged never.

Fee & Payment: Pay by money order, cashier check, business check. No personal checks. Payee: Clerk, US Bankruptcy Court. Prepayment required.

Phone Search: Only docket information is available by phone and only if it is on computer.

Mail Search: search usually completed- 7-10 days. Include SASE for return.

In Person Search: Fee charged if court performs your search. No self-serve copier available.

E-Services: ECF replaces PACER whose records did go back to 3/1986. ECF at https://ecf.vawb.uscourts.gov **Opinions Online:** http://pacer.vawb.uscourts.gov/courtweb/enter1.html. **Other Access:** Calendars back to 1999 at http://pacer.vawb.uscourts.gov/Calendars/2005calendar.html. Court does not participate in the U.S. party case index.

Lynchburg Division Court Clerk, PO Box 6400, Lynchburg, VA 24505 (courier address: 1101 Court St, Rm 166, Lynchburg, VA 24504), 434-845-0317. Hours- 8AM-4:30PM. www.vawb.uscourts.gov

Jurisdictions: Albemarle, Amherst, Appomattox, Bedford, City of Bedford, Buckingham, Campbell, Charlotte, City of Charlottesville, Culpeper, Cumberland, City of Danville, Fluvanna, Greene, Halifax, Henry, Louisa, City of Lynchburg, Madison, City of Martinsville, Nelson, Orange, Patrick, Pittsylvania, City of South Boston.

Searches & Indexing: Results include last 4 SSN digits. Computer index back to 1986 maintained. New cases in the index 24 hours after filing date.

Fee & Payment: Pay by money order, cashier check, business check. No personal checks. Payee: Clerk, US Bankruptcy Court. Prepayment required.

Phone Search: Only name, date filed and chapter is released via phone.

Mail Search: search usually completed- 5 days. Include SASE for return.

In Person Search: Fee charged if court performs your search. No self-serve copier available.

E-Services: ECF replaces PACER whose records did go back to 1986. ECF at https://ecf.vawb.uscourts.gov **Opinions Online:** http://pacer.vawb.uscourts.gov/courtweb/enter1.html. **Other Access:** Calendars back to 1999 at http://pacer.vawb.uscourts.gov/Calendars/2005calendar.html. Court does not participate in the U.S. party case index.

Roanoke Division Court Clerk, PO Box 2390, Roanoke, VA 24010 (courier address: Commonwealth Bldg, 210 Church Ave, Roanoke, VA 24011), 540-857-2391, Fax-540-857-2873. Hours- 8AM-4:30PM. www.vawb.uscourts.gov

Jurisdictions: Bland, Botetourt, City of Bristol, Buchanan, Carroll, Craig, Dickenson, Floyd, Franklin, City of Galax, Giles, Grayson, Lee, Montgomery, City of Norton, Pulaski, City of Radford, Roanoke, City of Roanoke, Russell, City of Salem, Scott, Smyth, Tazewell, Washington, Wise, Wythe.

Searches & Indexing: Cases indexed by debtor, creditors, and case number. Results include last 4 SSN digits. Computer index maintained. Records indexed numerically; for example: 7-92-00123 = office number, year and 5 digit case number. New cases in the index same day if possible after filing date. Records purged never.

Fee & Payment: Pay by money order, cashier check, law firm check. No business or personal checks accepted. Payee: Clerk, US Bankruptcy Court. Prepayment required.

Phone Search: No searching by telephone. Only the number of pages of the requested items is given via phone. **Mail Search:** search usually completed- 2 days. Include SASE for return.

In Person Search: Fee charged if court performs your search. No self-serve copier available.

E-Services: ECF replaces PACER whose records did go back to 1988. ECF at https://ecf.vawb.uscourts.gov **Opinions Online:** http://pacer.vawb.uscourts.gov/courtweb/enter1.html. **Other Access:** Calendars back to 1999 at http://pacer.vawb.uscourts.gov/Calendars/2005calendar.html. Court does not participate in the U.S. party case index.

Virginia County Courts

Court	Jurisdiction	No. of Courts	How Organized
Circuit Courts*	General	117	31 Circuits
District Courts*	Limited	132	
Combined Courts*		11	

* Profiled in this Sourcebook.

	CIVIL								
Court	Tort	Contract	Real Estate	Min. Claim	Max. Claim	Small Claims	Estate	Eviction	Domestic Relations
Circuit Courts*	X	X	X	$3,000	No Max		X		X
District Courts*	X	X	X	$0	$15,000	$2,000		X	X

	CRIMINAL				
Court	Felony	Misdemeanor	DWI/DUI	Preliminary Hearing	Juvenile
Circuit Courts*	X				
District Courts*		X	X	X	X

ADMINISTRATION

Executive Secretary, Administrative Office of Courts, 100 N 9th Street, 3rd Fl, Supreme Court Building, Richmond, Virginia, 23219; 804-786-6455, Fax: 804-786-4542. www.courts.state.va.us

COURT STRUCTURE

The Circuit Courts in 31 districts are the courts of general jurisdiction. There are 132 District Courts of limited jurisdiction. Please note that a district can comprise a county or a city. Records of civil action from $3000 to $15,000 can be at either the Circuit or District Court as either can have jurisdiction. It is necessary to check both record locations as there is no concurrent database nor index.

ONLINE ACCESS

There are 3 available systems. None are statewide; each county must be searched separately.

132 General District Courts (many are combined courts) may be searched free at http://208.210.219.132/vadistrict/select.jsp. Here you can search both active and inactive cases.

Also, Virginia has the growing "Circuit Court Case Information Pilot Project" with free access to Circuit Court records. You may search records from over 90 courts at http://208.210.219.132/vacircuit/select.jsp

While these first 2 systems do not include DOBs, SSNs and addresses, the dialup system known as LOPAS does have birth month and day. There are no fees to use LOPAS, but access is granted on a request-by-request basis. Anyone wishing to establish an account or receive information on LOPAS must contact the Supreme Court of Virginia, 100 N 9th St, Richmond VA 23219 or by phone at 804-786-6455 or fax at 804-786-4542. LOPAS is a difficult system to "get on" as it is an old dial-up system and it is being gradually phased out.

The www.courts.state.va.us site offers access to Supreme Court and Appellate opinions.

ADDITIONAL INFORMATION

In many jurisdictions, the certification fee is $2.00 per document plus copy fee. The copy fee is $.50 per page.

📖📖📖📖📖📖📖

Accomack County

2nd Circuit Court PO Box 126, Accomac, VA 23301; phone: 757-787-5776; probate phone: 757-787-5776; fax: 757-787-1849; hours 9AM-5PM (EST). *Felony, Civil Actions Over $15,000, Probate.* www.courts.state.va.us/courts/circuit.html
Civil Records: Access: Fax, mail, online, in person. Both court and visitors may perform in person searches. No search fee. Court makes copy: $.50 per page; same fee for self serve. Required to search: name, years to search. Civil cases indexed by defendant, plaintiff; on microfiche and archived from 1663; on computer back to 1984. Remote online access to court case indexes is via LOPAS; call 804-786-5511 to apply. Mail turnaround time 1-2 days.
Criminal Records: Access: Fax, mail, online, in person. Both court and visitors may perform in person searches. No search fee. Court makes copy: $.50 per page; same fee for self serve. Required to search: name, years to search, DOB; also helpful: SSN. Criminal records on microfiche and archived from 1663; on computer back to 1984. Remote online access to court case indexes is via LOPAS; call 804-786-5511 to apply. Mail turnaround time 1-2 days.
General Information: Public terminal goes back to 1984. No juvenile, sealed, probate, tax return or adoption records released. Fee to fax documents is $2.00 1st page, $.50 each add'l. Certification fee: $2.00. Payee: Samuel H Cooper Jr, Clerk of Court. Personal checks accepted. Prepayment required.

2A General District Court PO Box 276, Accomac, VA 23301; phone: 757-787-0923; criminal phone: x117; civil phone: x123; hours 8:30AM-4:30PM (EST). *Misdemeanor, Civil Actions Under $15,000, Eviction, Small Claims.*
Civil Records: Access: Phone, mail, online, in person. Both court and visitors may perform in person searches. No search fee. Court makes copy: no fee if less than 10 pages. Required to search: name, years to search. Civil cases indexed by defendant.

Civil records retained ten years. Search at http://208.210.219.132/vadistrict/select.jsp. Also, online access case indexes is via LOPAS; call 804-786-5511 to apply. Mail turnaround time 1-3 days. **Criminal Records:** Access: Phone, mail, online, in person. Both court and visitors may perform in person searches. No search fee. Court makes copy: no fee if less than 10 pages. Required to search: name, years to search, DOB; also helpful: SSN. Criminal records retained ten years. Online access to criminal records is the same as civil. Mail turnaround time 1-3 days.

General Information: Public use terminal available. No juvenile, sealed, adoption records released. No certification fee. Payee: Accomack District Court. Personal checks or Visa, MC accepted. Prepayment and SASE required.

Albemarle County

16th Circuit & District Court 501 E Jefferson St, Charlottesville, VA 22902; phone: 434-972-4085; criminal phone: 424-972-4086; fax: 434-972-4071; hours 8:30AM-4:30PM (EST). *Felony, Misdemeanor, Civil, Eviction, Probate.*

www.courts.state.va.us/courts/circuit.html

Civil Records: Access: Mail, online, in person. Both court and visitors may perform in person searches. Search fee: $5.00 per name. Court makes copy: $.50 per page. Required to search: name, years to search. Civil records on microfiche from 1980 to present and archived from 1700s to 1990. Select and search Circuit Courts online at http://208.210.219.132/vacircuit/select.jsp. Search District courts at http://208.210.219.132/vadistrict/select.jsp. Also search via LOPAS; call 804-786-5511 to apply. Mail turnaround time 7-10 days.

Criminal Records: Access: Mail, online, in person. Both court and visitors may perform in person searches. Search fee: $5.00 per name. Court makes copy: $.50 per page. Required to search: name, years to search. Criminal records on microfiche from 1980 to present and archived from 1700s to 1990. Remote online access to court case indexes is via LOPAS; call 804-786-5511 to apply. Mail turnaround time 7-10 days.

General Information: No juvenile, sealed records released. Certification fee: $2.00. Payee: Albemarle Clerk of Court. Personal checks accepted. Prepayment required.

Alexandria City

18th Circuit Court 520 King St, #307, Alexandria, VA 22314; criminal phone: 703-838-4047; civil phone: 703-838-4044; probate phone: 703-838-4055; hours 9AM-5PM (EST). *Felony, Civil Actions Over $15,000, Probate.*

http://ci.alexandria.va.us/courts/courts_index.html

Civil Records: Access: In person only. Visitors must perform in person searches themselves. Court makes copy: $.50 per page; same fee for self serve. Required to search: name, years to search. Civil cases indexed by defendant, plaintiff; on computer from 1983 to present, microfiche from 1970s to present.

Criminal Records: Access: In person only. Visitors must perform in person searches themselves. Court makes copy: $.50 per page; same fee for self serve. Required to search: name, years to search; also helpful: DOB. Criminal records on computer since 7/87.

General Information: Public terminal has criminal back to 1987 and civil back to 1983. No juvenile, sealed, adoption or expunged records released. Certification fee: $2.00. Payee: Clerk of Court. Only cashiers checks and money orders accepted. Prepayment required.

18th District Court PO Box 20206, 520 King St, Alexandria, VA 22320; phone: 703-838-4041 (traffic); criminal phone: 703-838-4030; civil phone: 703-838-4021; hours 8AM-4PM (EST). *Misdemeanor, Civil Actions Under $15,000, Eviction, Small Claims.*

Note: Mail can go to PO Box 20206; ZIP-22320.

Civil Records: Access: Online, in person. Both court and visitors may perform in person searches. Court makes copy: $1.00 first 2 pages, $.50 each addl. Required to search: name, years to search. Civil cases indexed by defendant. Civil records on computer from 1993 to present, index cards prior to 1986. Search free at http://208.210.219.132/vadistrict/select.jsp.

Criminal Records: Access: Online, in person. Visitors must perform in person searches themselves. Court makes copy: $1.00 each first 2 pages, $.50 each add'l. Required to search: name. Criminal records on computer from 1993 to present. Online access to criminal records is the same as civil.

General Information: Will not fax back documents. No certification fee.

Alleghany County

25th Circuit Court PO Box 670, 266 W. Main St, Covington, VA 24426; phone: 540-965-1730; fax: 540-965-1732; probate hours 8:30AM-5PM M-F; 9AM-Noon Sat (EST). *Felony, Civil Actions Over $15,000, Probate.*

www.alleghanycountyclerk.com

Civil Records: Access: Online, in person. Visitors must perform in person searches themselves. Court makes copy: $.50 per page; same fee for self serve. Required to search: name. Civil cases indexed by plaintiff. Civil records available from 1822, all on microfilm. Search free at http://208.210.219.132/vacircuit/select.jsp.

Criminal Records: Access: Online, in person. Visitors must perform in person searches themselves. Court makes copy: $.50 per page; same fee for self serve. Required to search: name. Criminal records available from 1822, all on microfilm. Online access to criminal records is the same as civil.

General Information: No juvenile, adoption or sealed records released. Certification fee: $2.00 per doc. Payee: Michael D Wolfe, Clerk of Court. Personal checks discouraged. Prepayment required.

25th General District Court PO Box 139, Covington, VA 24426; phone: 540-965-1720; fax: 540-965-1722; hours 9AM-5PM (EST). *Misdemeanor, Civil Actions Under $15,000, Eviction, Small Claims.*

Civil Records: Access: Online, in person. Visitors must perform in person searches themselves. Court makes copy: $1.00 each for first 2 pages; $.50 each add'l. Required to search: name, years to search. Civil cases indexed by defendant, plaintiff; on computer from 1/90, prior on index cards. Search free at http://208.210.219.132/vadistrict/select.jsp. Also search via LOPAS; call 804-786-5511 to apply.

Criminal Records: Access: Online, in person. Visitors must perform in person searches themselves. Court makes copy: $1.00 each first 2 pages; $.50 each add'l. Required to search: name, years to search; also helpful: DOB, SSN. Criminal records on computer from 1/90, prior on index cards. Online access to criminal records is the same as civil.

General Information: No juvenile, sealed records released. No certification fee. Personal checks or Visa, MC accepted. Acepted for fines and cost only. Prepayment required.

Amelia County

11th Circuit Court PO Box 237 (1 E Main St, B-5), Amelia, VA 23068; phone: 804-561-2128; fax: 804-561-6364; hours 8:30AM-4:30PM (EST). *Felony, Civil Actions Over $15,000, Probate.*

Note: Will search on telephone request if not busy.

Civil Records: Access: Mail, online, in person. Both court and visitors may perform in person searches.

No search fee. Court makes copy: $.50 per page; same fee for self serve. Required to search: name, years to search. Civil cases indexed by defendant, plaintiff; on microfiche 1735 to present, indexed on books. Search free at http://208.210.219.132/vacircuit/select.jsp. Also search via LOPAS; call 804-786-5511 to apply. Mail turnaround time 3-5 days.

Criminal Records: Access: Mail, online, in person. Both court and visitors may perform in person searches. No search fee. Court makes copy: $.50 per page; same fee for self serve. Required to search: name, years to search, DOB; also helpful: SSN. Criminal records on microfiche 1735 to present, indexed on books. Online access to criminal records is the same as civil. Mail turnaround time 3-5 days.

General Information: Public terminal goes back to 6/7/2002. No juvenile, sealed records released. Will not fax documents. Certification fee: $2.00. Payee: Amelia County Circuit Court. Personal checks accepted. Prepayment and SASE required.

11th General District Court PO Box 24, Amelia, VA 23002; phone: 804-561-2456; fax: 804-561-6956; hours 8:30AM-4:30PM (EST). *Misdemeanor, Civil Actions Under $15,000, Eviction, Small Claims.*

Civil Records: Access: Online, in person. Visitors must perform in person searches themselves. Court makes copy: $1.00 for 1st two pages, $.50 each add'l page. Required to search: name, years to search. Civil cases indexed by defendant, plaintiff; on computer since 12/20/92. Search free at http://208.210.219.132/vadistrict/select.jsp. Also search via LOPAS; call 804-786-5511 to apply.

Criminal Records: Access: Online, in person. Visitors must perform in person searches themselves. Court makes copy: $1.00 for 1st two pages, $.50 each add'l. Required to search: name, years to search, DOB; also helpful: SSN. Criminal records on computer since 12/20/92. Online access to criminal records is the same as civil.

General Information: Public use terminal available. No juvenile, sealed records released. No certification fee. Payee: Amelia District Court. Personal checks accepted. Prepayment required.

Amherst County

24th Circuit Court PO Box 462, Amherst, VA 24521; phone: 434-946-9321; fax: 434-946-9323; hours 8AM-5PM (EST). *Felony, Civil Actions Over $15,000, Probate.*

www.courts.state.va.us/courts/circuit.html

Civil Records: Access: Online, in person. Visitors must perform in person searches themselves. Court makes copy: $.50 per page; same fee for self serve. Required to search: name, years to search. Civil cases indexed by defendant, plaintiff; on index books from 1761; on computer back to 1997. Remote online access to court case indexes is via LOPAS; call 804-786-5511 to apply.

Criminal Records: Access: Online, in person. Visitors must perform in person searches themselves. Court makes copy: $.50 per page; same fee for self serve. Required to search: name, years to search, date of offense. Criminal records on index books back to 1761; on computer back to 1997. Remote online access to court case indexes is via LOPAS; call 804-786-5511 to apply.

General Information: Public terminal goes back to 1998. No juvenile, sealed or adoption records released. Certification fee: $2.00. Payee: Clerk of Circuit Court. Personal checks accepted. Prepayment required.

24th General District Court PO Box 513, Amherst, VA 24521; phone: 434-946-9351; fax: 434-946-9359; hours 8AM-4PM (EST). *Misdemeanor, Civil Actions Under $15,000, Eviction, Small Claims.*

Note: Has handled misdemeanor cases since 1985.

Civil Records: Access: Mail, fax, online, in person. Both court and visitors may perform in person searches. Search fee: $10.00. Court makes copy: $1.00 per page. Required to search: name, years to search. Civil cases indexed by defendant, plaintiff; on computer 10 years prior. Search free at http://208.210.219.132/vadistrict/select.jsp. Also search via LOPAS; call 804-786-5511 to apply. Mail turnaround time 48 hours.

Criminal Records: Access: Mail, online, in person. Both court and visitors may perform in person searches. Search fee: $10.00. Court makes copy: $1.00 per page. Required to search: name, years to search, DOB, SSN. Criminal records on computer 10 years prior. Online access to criminal records is the same as civil. Mail turnaround time 48 hours.

General Information: Public terminal goes back to 10 years. No sealed records released. Will fax documents. No certification fee. Payee: Clerk of Court. Personal checks or Visa, MC accepted. Prepayment required.

Appomattox County

10th Circuit Court PO Box 672, 125 Court St, Appomattox, VA 24522; phone: 434-352-5275; fax: 434-352-2781; hours 8:30AM-4:30PM (EST). *Felony, Civil Actions Over $15,000, Probate.*
www.courts.state.va.us/courts/circuit.html
Civil Records: Access: Online, in person. Visitors must perform in person searches themselves. Court makes copy: $.50 per page. Required to search: name, years to search. Civil cases indexed by defendant, plaintiff; on books from 1892 to present; on computer since 1997. Search free at http://208.210.219.132/vacircuit/select.jsp. Also search via LOPAS; call 804-786-5511 to apply.
Criminal Records: Access: Online, in person. Visitors must perform in person searches themselves. Court makes copy: $.50 per page. Required to search: name, years to search. Criminal records on books from 1892 to present; on computer since 1997. Online access to criminal records is the same as civil.
General Information: Public terminal goes back to 7/1997. No juvenile, sealed records released. No certification fee. Payee: Clerk of Circuit Court. Personal checks accepted. Prepayment required.

10th General District Court PO Box 187, 121 Court St, Appomattox, VA 24522; phone: 434-352-5540; fax: 434-352-0717; hours 8:30AM-4:30PM (EST). *Misdemeanor, Civil Actions Under $15,000, Eviction, Small Claims.*
Civil Records: Access: Fax, mail, online, in person. Both court and visitors may perform in person searches. No search fee. Court makes copy: $1.00 1st page; $.50 each add'l. Required to search: name, years to search. Civil cases indexed by defendant, plaintiff; on card file from 1992 to present, prior in Circuit Court. Search free at http://208.210.219.132/vadistrict/select.jsp. Also search via LOPAS; call 804-786-5511 to apply. Mail turnaround time 1-5 days.
Criminal Records: Access: Fax, mail, online, in person. Both court and visitors may perform in person searches. No search fee. Court makes copy: $1.00 1st page; $.50 each add'l. Required to search: name, years to search; also helpful: SSN. Criminal records on card file from 1992 to present, prior in Circuit Court. Online access to criminal records is the same as civil. Mail turnaround time 1-5 days.
General Information: Public use terminal available. No juvenile, sealed records released. No fee to fax documents. No certification fee. Payee: General District Court. Personal checks or Visa, MC accepted.

Arlington County

17th Circuit Court 1425 N Courthouse Rd, Arlington, VA 22201; phone: 703-228-7010; criminal phone: 703-228-4399; civil phone: 703-228-7010; probate phone: 703-228-4376; hours 8AM-4PM (EST). *Felony, Civil Actions Over $15,000, Probate.*
http://158.59.15.115/arlington/
Civil Records: Access: Online, in person. Visitors must perform in person searches themselves. Court makes copy: $.50 per page. Required to search: name,

years to search. Civil cases indexed by defendant, plaintiff; on computer from 1987; prior on books from mid-1930 to present. Online access free at http://208.210.219.132/vacircuit/select.jsp. For information about the statewide online systems, see the state introduction.
Criminal Records: Access: Online, in person. Visitors must perform in person searches themselves. Court makes copy: $.50 per page. Required to search: name, years to search. Criminal records on computer from 1987; prior on books from mid-1930 to present. Online access to criminal records is the same as civil.
General Information: Public terminal goes back to 1987. No juvenile, adoption or sealed records released. Will not fax documents. Certification fee: $2.00. Payee: Clerk of Court. Personal checks accepted. Prepayment required.

17th General District Court 1425 N Courthouse Rd, Rm 2500, Arlington, VA 22201; phone: 703-228-7900; civil phone: 703-228-4485; hours 8AM-4PM (EST). *Misdemeanor, Civil Actions Under $15,000, Eviction, Small Claims.*
Note: Phone access limited to 4 requests.
Civil Records: Access: Phone, mail, online, in person. Both court and visitors may perform in person searches. No search fee. Court makes copy: $1.00 first 2 pages, $.25 each add'l. Required to search: name, years to search, case number. Civil cases indexed by defendant. Civil records on computer back to 1990, books from early 1970s. Search free at http://208.210.219.132/vadistrict/select.jsp. Also search via LOPAS; call 804-786-5511 to apply. Mail turnaround time 5 days.
Criminal Records: Access: Phone, mail, online, in person. Both court and visitors may perform in person searches. No search fee. Court makes copy: $1.00 each first 2 pages, $.25 each add'l. Required to search: name, years to search, DOB; also helpful-SSN. Criminal records on computer back to 1990. Online access to criminal records is the same as civil. Mail turnaround time 5 days.
General Information: Public use terminal available. No juvenile, sealed records released. Certification fee: $2.00. Payee: Clerk of Court. Personal checks accepted. Prepayment required.

Augusta County

25th Circuit Court PO Box 689, Staunton, VA 24402-0689; phone: 540-245-5321; fax: 540-245-5318; hours 8AM-5PM (EST). *Felony, Civil Actions Over $15,000, Probate.*
www.courts.state.va.us/courts/circuit.html
Note: Court prefers that searches be done in person. Mail access is limited; they will only search back to 1987. Phone available for very short search only.
Civil Records: Access: Mail, in person, online. Both court and visitors may perform in person searches. No search fee. Court makes copy: $.50 per page; same fee for self serve. Required to search: name, years to search. Civil cases indexed by defendant, plaintiff; on computer from 1987 to present, books from 1745 to 1986. Online access free at http://208.210.219.132/vacircuit/select.jsp. For information about the statewide online systems, see the state introduction. Mail turnaround time 1-2 days.
Criminal Records: Access: Mail, in person, online. Both court and visitors may perform in person searches. No search fee. Court makes copy: $.50 per page; same fee for self serve. Required to search: name, years to search; also helpful: DOB, SSN. Criminal records go back to 1987 felonies only. Online access to criminal records is the same as civil. Mail turnaround time 1-2 days.
General Information: Public terminal has criminal back to - not known and civil back to 1987. No juvenile, adoption or sealed records released. Certification fee: $2.00. Payee: Clerk, Augusta County Circuit Court. Personal checks accepted. Prepayment and SASE required.

25th General District Court 6 E Johnson St, 2nd Fl, Staunton, VA 24401; phone: 540-245-5300; fax: 540-245-5365; hours 8:30AM-4:30PM (EST). *Misdemeanor, Civil Actions Under $15,000, Eviction, Small Claims.*
www.courts.state.va.us/courts/gd/Augusta/home.html
Note: This court also handles traffic infractions.

Civil Records: Access: Mail, online, in person. Both court and visitors may perform in person searches. No search fee. Court makes copy: $.50 per page. Required to search: name, years to search. Civil cases indexed by defendant, plaintiff. Civil records kept for 10 years on computer. Search online free at http://208.210.219.132/vadistrict/select.jsp. Mail turnaround time 2-3 days.
Criminal Records: Access: Mail, online, in person. Both court and visitors may perform in person searches. No search fee. Court makes copy: $.50 per page. Required to search: name, years to search. Criminal records kept for 10 years on computer, then archived or destroyed. Search online free at http://208.210.219.132/vadistrict/select.jsp. Mail turnaround time 2-3 days.
General Information: Public terminal goes back to 10 years. Will not fax documents. No certification fee. Payee: Augusta General District Court. Personal checks or Visa, MC accepted. Prepayment required. SASE requested.

Bath County

25th Circuit Court PO Box 180, Warm Springs, VA 24484; phone: 540-839-7226; probate phone: 540-839-7226; fax: 540-839-7248; probate fax: 540-839-7248; hours 8:30AM-4:30PM (EST). *Felony, Civil Actions Over $15,000, Probate.*
www.courts.state.va.us/courts/circuit.html
Civil Records: Access: Mail, online, in person. Both court and visitors may perform in person searches. Court makes copy: $.50 per page. Required to search: name, years to search. Civil cases indexed by defendant, plaintiff; on books from 1791 to present. Remote online access to court case indexes is via LOPAS; call 804-786-5511 to apply.
Criminal Records: Access: Online, in person. Visitors must perform in person searches themselves. Court makes copy: $.50 per page. Required to search: name, years to search; also helpful: DOB, SSN. Criminal records on books from 1791 to present. Online access to criminal records is the same as civil.
General Information: Public terminal has criminal back to - not known and civil back to 1791. No juvenile, sealed or adoption records released. Certification fee: $2.00. Payee: Bath County Circuit Court. Personal checks accepted. Prepayment required.

25th General District Court PO Box 96, Warm Springs, VA 24484; phone: 540-839-7241; fax: 540-839-7242; hours 8:30AM-4:30PM (EST). *Misdemeanor, Civil Actions Under $15,000, Eviction, Small Claims.*
Civil Records: Access: Phone, fax, mail, online, in person. Both court and visitors may perform in person searches. No search fee. Court makes copy: $.50 per page. Required to search: name, years to search. Civil cases indexed by defendant, plaintiff; on files from 1985 to present, Prior records in Circuit Court. Search free at http://208.210.219.132/vadistrict/select.jsp. Also search via LOPAS; call 804-786-5511 to apply. Mail turnaround time 2 days; will give immediate response on phone if not an extensive search.
Criminal Records: Access: Phone, fax, mail, online, in person. Both court and visitors may perform in person searches. No search fee. Court makes copy: $.50 per page. Required to search: name, years to search, DOB; also helpful: SSN. Criminal records on files back 10 years, Prior records in Circuit Court. Online access to criminal records is the same as civil. Mail turnaround time 2 days; will give

immediate response on phone if not an extensive search.

General Information: No juvenile, sealed records released. No certification fee. Payee: Bath County Combined Court. Personal checks or Visa, MC accepted. Prepayment required. SASE requested.

Bedford County

County Circuit Court 123 E Main St, #201, Bedford, VA 24523; phone: 540-586-7632; fax: 540-586-6197; hours 8:30AM-5PM (EST). *Felony, Civil Actions Over $15,000, Probate.*
www.courts.state.va.us/courts/circuit.html
Civil Records: Access: Online, in person. Visitors must perform in person searches themselves. Court makes copy: $.50 per page. Required to search: name, years to search. Civil cases indexed by defendant, plaintiff; on computer from 1988, index books. Online access free at http://208.210.219.132/vacircuit/select.jsp. For information about the statewide online systems, see the state introduction.
Criminal Records: Access: Online, in person. Visitors must perform in person searches themselves. Court makes copy: $.50 per page. Required to search: name, years to search, DOB. Criminal records on computer from 1988, index books. Remote online access to court case indexes is via LOPAS; call 804-786-5511 to apply.
General Information: Public terminal goes back to 1988. No juvenile, sealed records released. Certification fee: $.50 per page. Payee: Bedford Clerk of Court. Personal checks accepted. Prepayment required.

24th General District Court 123 E Main St, #202, Bedford, VA 24523; phone: 540-586-7637; fax: 540-586-7684; hours 8AM-4PM (EST). *Misdemeanor, Civil Actions Under $15,000, Eviction, Small Claims, Traffic.*
Note: The court will not perform name searches.
Civil Records: Access: Mail, online, in person. Visitors must perform in person searches themselves. No search fee. Court makes copy: $1.00 1st 2 pages, $.50 each add'l. Required to search: name. Civil cases indexed by defendant. Civil records on computer for ten years. Search free at http://208.210.219.132/vadistrict/select.jsp. Also search via LOPAS; call 804-786-5511 to apply.
Criminal Records: Access: Mail, online, in person. Visitors must perform in person searches themselves. No search fee. Court makes copy: $1.00 1st 2 pages, $.50 each add'l. Required to search: name. Criminal records on computer for ten years. Online access to criminal records is the same as civil.
General Information: Public terminal goes back to 10 years. No sealed records released. No certification fee. Payee: Bedford General District Court. Personal checks or Visa, MC accepted. Prepayment and SASE required.

Bedford City

Circuit & District Courts
www.courts.state.va.us/courts/circuit.html
Note: See Bedford County.

Bland County

27th Circuit Court PO Box 295, Bland, VA 24315; phone: 276-688-4562; fax: 276-688-4562; hours 8AM-6PM (EST). *Felony, Civil Actions Over $15,000, Probate.*
www.courts.state.va.us/courts/circuit.html
Civil Records: Access: Phone, fax, mail, online, in person. Both court and visitors may perform in person searches. Search fee: $10.00 per name. Court makes copy: $.50 per page; same fee for self serve. Required to search: name, years to search. Civil cases indexed by defendant, plaintiff; on books from 1861 to present. Search free at http://208.210.219.132/vacircuit/select.jsp. Also

search via LOPAS; call 804-786-5511 to apply. Mail turnaround time 2 days.
Criminal Records: Access: Phone, fax, mail, online, in person. Both court and visitors may perform in person searches. Search fee: $10.00 per name. Court makes copy: $.50 per page; same fee for self serve. Required to search: name, years to search, signed release; also helpful: SSN. Criminal records on books from 1861 to present. Online access to criminal records is the same as civil. Mail turnaround time 2 days.
General Information: No juvenile, sealed or adoption records released. Will fax documents $1.00 per page. Certification fee: $2.00. Payee: Clerk of Court. Personal checks accepted. Prepayment required.

27th General District Court PO Box 157, Bland, VA 24315; phone: 276-688-4433; fax: 276-688-4789; hours 8AM-5PM (EST). *Misdemeanor, Civil Actions Under $15,000, Eviction, Small Claims.*
Civil Records: Access: Phone, fax, mail, online, in person. Both court and visitors may perform in person searches. No search fee. Court makes copy: $1.00 1st 2 pages, $.50 each add'l. Required to search: name, years to search. Civil cases indexed by defendant. Civil records on computer from 4/23/95. Search free at http://208.210.219.132/vadistrict/select.jsp. Also search via LOPAS; call 804-786-5511 to apply. Mail turnaround time 1-2 days.
Criminal Records: Access: Phone, fax, mail, online, in person. Both court and visitors may perform in person searches. No search fee. Court makes copy: $1.00 1st 2 pages, $.50 each add'l. Required to search: name, years to search; also helpful: DOB, SSN. Criminal records on computer from 4/23/92, card index back to 1985. Online access to criminal records is the same as civil. Note: Phone access limited to specific cases only. Mail turnaround time 1-2 days.
General Information: Public terminal has only civil records back to 1995. No juvenile, sealed or adoption records released. No certification fee. Payee: General District Court. Personal checks or Visa, MC accepted. SASE requested.

Botetourt County

25th Circuit Court PO Box 219, Fincastle, VA 24090; phone: 540-473-8274; fax: 540-473-8209; hours 8:30AM-4:30PM (EST). *Felony, Civil Actions Over $15,000, Probate.*
www.courts.state.va.us/courts/circuit.html
Civil Records: Access: Mail, online, in person. Both court and visitors may perform in person searches. No search fee. Court makes copy: $.50 per page. Required to search: name, years to search. Civil cases indexed by defendant, plaintiff; on computer 7/1/91 to present, books back to 1770. Search free at http://208.210.219.132/vacircuit/select.jsp. Also search via LOPAS; call 804-786-5511 to apply. Mail turnaround time same day.
Criminal Records: Access: Mail, online, in person. Both court and visitors may perform in person searches. No search fee. Court makes copy: $.50 per page. Required to search: name, years to search, DOB, SSN. Criminal records on computer 7/1/91 to present, books back to 1770. Online access to criminal records is the same as civil. Mail turnaround time same day.
General Information: No juvenile, sealed or adoption records released. Certification fee: $2.00. Payee: Clerk of Court. Personal checks accepted. Prepayment and SASE required.

25th General District Court PO Box 858, Fincastle, VA 24090-0858; phone: 540-473-8244; fax: 540-473-8344; hours 8AM-4PM (EST). *Misdemeanor, Civil Actions Under $15,000, Eviction, Small Claims.*
Civil Records: Access: Mail, online, in person. Both court and visitors may perform in person searches. No search fee. Court makes copy: $.50 per page.

Required to search: name, years to search. Civil cases indexed by defendant, plaintiff; on computer from 1995 to present. Civil records on files back to 1995. Search free at http://208.210.219.132/vadistrict/select.jsp. Also search via LOPAS; call 804-786-5511 to apply. Mail turnaround time 3-4 days.
Criminal Records: Access: Mail, online, in person. Both court and visitors may perform in person searches. No search fee. Court makes copy: $.50 per page. Required to search: name, years to search. Criminal records on computer from 1995 to present. Online access to criminal records is the same as civil. Mail turnaround time 3-4 days.
General Information: Public terminal goes back to 1995. No juvenile, sealed records released. No certification fee. Personal checks accepted. Checks that require verification calls not accepted. Visa, MC accepted. SASE requested.

Bristol City

28th Circuit Court 497 Cumberland St, Bristol, VA 24201; phone: 276-645-7321; fax: 276-821-6097; hours 9AM-5PM (EST). *Felony, Civil Actions Over $15,000, Probate.*
www.courts.state.va.us/courts/circuit.html
Civil Records: Access: Online, in person. Visitors must perform in person searches themselves. Court makes copy: $.50 per page. Required to search: name, years to search. Civil cases indexed by defendant, plaintiff. Civil records indexed from 1890 to present; on computer back to 1994. Search free at http://208.210.219.132/vacircuit/select.jsp. Also search via LOPAS; call 804-786-5511 to apply.
Criminal Records: Access: Online, in person. Visitors must perform in person searches themselves. Court makes copy: $.50 per page. Required to search: name, years to search. Criminal records indexed from 1890 to present; on computer back to 1994. Online access to criminal records is the same as civil.
General Information: Public terminal goes back to 1994. No juvenile, sealed or adoption records released. Certification fee: $1.00 per doc. Payee: Clerk of Circuit Court. Personal checks accepted. Prepayment required.

28th General District Court 497 Cumberland St, Bristol, VA 24201; phone: 276-645-7341; fax: 276-645-7342; hours 8:30AM-4PM (EST). *Misdemeanor, Civil Actions Under $15,000, Eviction, Small Claims.*
Civil Records: Access: Mail, fax, online, in person. Both court and visitors may perform in person searches. No search fee. Court makes copy: $.50 per page. Required to search: name, years to search. Civil cases indexed by defendant, plaintiff; on computer from 1989, card file 1983 to 1988. Search free at http://208.210.219.132/vadistrict/select.jsp. Also search via LOPAS; call 804-786-5511 to apply. Mail turnaround time 15 days.
Criminal Records: Access: Mail, fax, online, in person. Visitors must perform in person searches themselves. Court makes copy: $.50 per page. Required to search: name, years to search, DOB, SSN. Criminal records on computer from 1989, card file 1983 to 1988. Online access to criminal records is the same as civil. Mail turnaround time 15 days.
General Information: No juvenile, sealed records released. Certification fee: $2.00. Payee: General District Court. Personal checks or Visa, MC accepted. Prepayment required. SASE requested.

Brunswick County

6th Circuit Court 216 N Main St, Lawrenceville, VA 23868; phone: 434-848-2215; fax: 434-848-4307; hours 8:30AM-5PM (EST). *Felony, Civil, Probate.*
www.courts.state.va.us/courts/circuit.html
Civil Records: Access: In person, online. Visitors must perform in person searches themselves. Court makes copy: $.50 per page. Required to search: name, years to search. Civil cases indexed by defendant,

plaintiff. Civil records in books back to 1732; on computer since 1992 (office use only). Search free at http://208.210.219.132/vacircuit/select.jsp. Also search via LOPAS; call 804-786-5511 to apply. Also access record images via http://208.210.219.102/cgi-bin/p/rms.cgi; registration and password required.

Criminal Records: Access: In person, online. Visitors must perform in person searches themselves. Court makes copy: $.50 per page. Required to search: name, years to search. Criminal records in books back to 1732; on computer back to 1992 (office use only). Online access to criminal records is the same as civil.

General Information: No juvenile, sealed or adoption records released. Certification fee: $2.00. Payee: Clerk of Court. Personal checks accepted. Prepayment required.

6th General District Court 202 Main St, Lawrenceville, VA 23868-0066; phone: 434-848-2315; fax: 434-848-2550; hours 8AM-4PM (EST). *Misdemeanor, Civil Actions Under $15,000, Eviction, Small Claims.*

Civil Records: Access: Mail, in person, online. Both court and visitors may perform in person searches. No search fee. No copy fee. Required to search: name, years to search. Civil cases indexed by defendant, plaintiff. Civil records computerized since 1988, records go back to 1988. Search free at http://208.210.219.132/vadistrict/select.jsp. Also search via LOPAS; call 804-786-5511 to apply. Note: Court will search time permitting. Mail turnaround time 1-2 days.

Criminal Records: Access: Mail, in person, online. Both court and visitors may perform in person searches. No search fee. No copy fee. Required to search: name, years to search, DOB; also helpful: SSN, signed release. Criminal records computerized since 1991; records go back ten years. Online access to misdemeanor records is the same as civil. Note: Court will perform in person searches only if time permits. Mail turnaround time 1-2 days.

General Information: Public terminal goes back to 10 years. No juvenile, sealed records released. No certification fee. SASE required.

Buchanan County

29th Circuit Court PO Box 929, Grundy, VA 24614; phone: 276-935-6567; criminal phone: 276-935-6575; civil phone: 276-935-6575; fax: 276-935-7086; hours 8:30AM-5PM (EST). *Felony, Misdemeanor, Civil Actions Over $15,000, Probate.* www.courts.state.va.us/courts/circuit.html

Civil Records: Access: Phone, mail, online, in person. Both court and visitors may perform in person searches. No search fee. Court makes copy: $.50 per page; same fee for self serve. Required to search: name, years to search; also helpful: address. Civil cases indexed by defendant, plaintiff; on computer back to 1991, in books back to 1923. Remote online access to court case indexes is via LOPAS; call 804-786-5511 to apply.

Criminal Records: Access: Online, in person. Visitors must perform in person searches themselves. Court makes copy: $.50 per page; same fee for self serve. Required to search: name, years to search, DOB; also helpful: address, SSN. Criminal records on computer back to 1991; in books back to 1928. Remote online access to court case indexes is via LOPAS; call 804-786-5511 to apply.

General Information: Public use terminal available. No juvenile, sealed records released. Fee to fax documents is $3.00 per document. Certification fee: $.50. Payee: Clerk of Circuit Court. Personal checks accepted if in state.

29th Judicial District Court PO Box 654, Grundy, VA 24614; phone: 276-935-6526; fax: 276-935-5479; hours 8AM-4PM (EST). *Civil Actions Under $15,000, Eviction, Small Claims.*

Civil Records: Access: Fax, mail, in person, phone, online. Both court and visitors may perform in person searches. No search fee. No copy fee.

Required to search: name; also helpful: years to search. Civil cases indexed by defendant, plaintiff. Civil Records are indexed for 10 years, computerized back to 1993. Search free at http://208.210.219.132/vadistrict/select.jsp. Also search via LOPAS; call 804-786-5511 to apply. Mail turnaround time 1 week.

General Information: Public terminal has only civil records. Will fax to toll-free or local numbers only. No certification fee. Prepayment required.

Buckingham County

10th Circuit Court Rte 60, PO Box 107, Buckingham, VA 23921; phone: 434-969-4734; fax: 434-969-2043; hours 8:30AM-4:30PM (EST). *Felony, Civil Actions Over $15,000, Probate.* www.courts.state.va.us/courts/circuit.html

Civil Records: Access: Mail, online, in person. Both court and visitors may perform in person searches. No search fee. Court makes copy: $.50 per page. Required to search: name, years to search. Civil cases indexed by defendant, plaintiff; on books from 1869 to present, computerized since 2001. Remote online access to court case indexes is via LOPAS; call 804-786-5511 to apply.

Criminal Records: Access: In person, online. Only the court performs in person searches; visitors may not. Court makes copy: $.50 per page. Required to search: name, years to search; also helpful: DOB. Criminal records on books from 1869 to present. Remote online access to court case indexes is via LOPAS; call 804-786-5511 to apply.

General Information: Public terminal has only civil records. No juvenile, sealed or adoption records released. Certification fee: $2.00. Payee: Clerk of Court. Personal checks accepted.

Buckingham General District Court PO Box 127, Buckingham, VA 23921; phone: 434-969-4755; fax: 434-969-1762; hours 8:30AM-4:30PM (EST). *Misdemeanor, Civil Actions Under $15,000, Eviction, Small Claims.*

Civil Records: Access: Mail, online, in person, fax. Only the court performs in person searches; visitors may not. No search fee. No copy fee. Required to search: name, years to search. Civil cases indexed by defendant. Civil records on computer or hard copy from 1993, prior records on index cards. Search free at http://208.210.219.132/vadistrict/select.jsp. Also search via LOPAS; call 804-786-5511 to apply. Mail turnaround time 2 weeks.

Criminal Records: Access: Mail, online, in person, fax. Only the court performs in person searches; visitors may not. No search fee. No copy fee. Required to search: name, years to search, DOB, SSN, signed release. Criminal records on computer or hard copy from 1993, prior records on index cards. Online access to criminal records is the same as civil. Mail turnaround time 2 weeks.

General Information: No juvenile, sealed records released. No certification fee. Payee: Buckingham. Personal checks or Visa, MC accepted. Prepayment required.

Buena Vista City

25th Circuit & District Court 2039 Sycamore Ave, Buena Vista, VA 24416; phone: 540-261-8627 X626/627; criminal fax: 540-261-8625; same fax for civil/probate; hours 8:30AM-5PM (EST). *Felony, Misdemeanor, Civil, Eviction, Probate.* www.courts.state.va.us/courts/circuit.html

Civil Records: Access: Mail, online, in person. Both court and visitors may perform in person searches. No search fee. Court makes copy: $.50 per page; same fee for self serve. Required to search: name, years to search. Civil cases indexed by defendant, plaintiff; on manual records 1892 to present, computerized since 1996. Select and search Circuit Courts online at http://208.210.219.132/vacircuit/select.jsp. Search District courts at http://208.210.219.132/vadistrict/select.jsp. Also

search via LOPAS; call 804-786-5511 to apply. Mail turnaround time 1 day.

Criminal Records: Access: Mail, online, in person. Both court and visitors may perform in person searches. No search fee. Court makes copy: $.50 per page; same fee for self serve. Required to search: name, years to search. Criminal records on manual records 1892 to present, computerized since 1996. Online access to criminal records is the same as civil. Mail turnaround time 1 day.

General Information: Public use terminal available. No juvenile, sealed records released. Will not fax documents. Certification fee: $2.00 per cert. Payee: Buena Vista Circuit Court. Personal checks accepted. Prepayment and SASE required.

Campbell County

24th Circuit Court 732 Village Hwy, PO Box 7, Rustburg, VA 24588; phone: 434-592-9517; criminal phone: 434-592-9614; civil phone: 434-592-9610; probate phone: 434-592-9517; hours 8:30AM-4:30PM (EST). *Felony, Civil Actions Over $15,000, Probate.* www.courts.state.va.us/courts/circuit.html

Civil Records: Access: Mail, online, in person. Both court and visitors may perform in person searches. No search fee. Court makes copy: $.50 per page; same fee for self serve. Required to search: name, years to search. Civil cases indexed by defendant, plaintiff; on index books. Remote online access to court case indexes is via LOPAS; call 804-786-5511 to apply. Mail turnaround time 5 days.

Criminal Records: Access: Mail, online, in person. Both court and visitors may perform in person searches. No search fee. Court makes copy: $.50 per page; same fee for self serve. Required to search: name, years to search; also helpful: DOB. Criminal records on index books. Remote online access to court case indexes is via LOPAS; call 804-786-5511 to apply. Mail turnaround time 5 days.

General Information: Public terminal goes back to 1994-95. No juvenile, sealed or adoption records released. Will not fax documents. Certification fee: $2.00 per cert. Payee: Clerk of Court. Personal checks accepted. Prepayment and SASE required.

24th General District Court PO Box 97, New Courthouse Bldg, 1st Fl, Rustburg, VA 24588; phone: 434-332-9546; fax: 434-332-9694; hours 8AM-4PM (EST). *Misdemeanor, Civil Actions Under $15,000, Eviction, Small Claims.*

Civil Records: Access: Online, in person. Visitors must perform in person searches themselves. Court makes copy: $1.00 for 1st two pages, $.50 per add'l. Required to search: name, years to search. Civil cases indexed by defendant, plaintiff; on computer for 10 years. Search free at http://208.210.219.132/vadistrict/select.jsp. Also search via LOPAS; call 804-786-5511 to apply.

Criminal Records: Access: Online, in person, mail. Visitors must perform in person searches themselves. Court makes copy: $1.00 for 1st 2 pages, $.50 each add'l. Required to search: name, years to search. Criminal records on computer for 10 years. Online access to criminal records is the same as civil. Mail turnaround time 5 days.

General Information: No certification fee. Payee: Clerk of Court. Prepayment and SASE required.

Caroline County

15th Circuit Court Main St & Courthouse Ln, PO Box 309, Bowling Green, VA 22427-0309; phone: 804-633-5800; hours 8:30AM-4PM (EST). *Felony, Civil Actions Over $15,000, Probate.* www.courts.state.va.us/courts/circuit.html

Civil Records: Access: Online, in person. Visitors must perform in person searches themselves. Court makes copy: $.50 per page; same fee for self serve. Required to search: name, years to search. Civil cases indexed by defendant, plaintiff; on books from early 1900s to present. Remote online access to court case indexes is via LOPAS; call 804-786-5511 to apply.

Criminal Records: Access: Online, in person. Visitors must perform in person searches themselves. Court makes copy: $.50 per page; same fee for self serve. Required to search: name, years to search; also helpful: DOB. Criminal records on books from early 1900s to present, computerized since 1992. Remote online access to court case indexes is via LOPAS; call 804-786-5511 to apply.

General Information: Public use terminal available. No juvenile, sealed, adoption records released. Certification fee: $2.50. Payee: Clerk of Court. Personal checks accepted. Accepted for payment of fines & costs only. Not accepted over the phone. Prepayment required.

15th General District Court PO Box 511, 111 Ennis St, Bowling Green, VA 22427; phone: 804-633-5720; fax: 804-633-3033; hours 8AM-4PM (EST). *Misdemeanor, Civil Actions Under $15,000, Eviction, Small Claims.*

Civil Records: Access: Mail, online, fax, in person. Both court and visitors may perform in person searches. No search fee. No copy fee. Required to search: name, years to search. Civil cases indexed by defendant, plaintiff; on computer from 1/92. Search free at http://208.210.219.132/vadistrict/select.jsp. Also search via LOPAS; call 804-786-5511 to apply. Note: At the court's discretion, usually for high volume, you may have to fill out a research request form before they'll search. Mail turnaround time 5 days.

Criminal Records: Access: Mail, online, in person. Both court and visitors may perform in person searches. No search fee. No copy fee. Required to search: name, years to search, SSN. Criminal records on computer from 1/92. Online access to criminal records is the same as civil. Note: At the court's discretion, usually for high volume, you may have to fill out a research request form before they'll search. Mail turnaround time 5 days.

General Information: Public terminal has criminal back to 10 years and civil back to 1995. Will fax documents. No certification fee.

Carroll County

27th Circuit Court PO Box 218, Hillsville, VA 24343; phone: 276-728-3117; fax: 276-728-0255; hours 8AM-5PM (EST). *Felony, Civil Actions Over $15,000, Probate.*
www.courts.state.va.us/courts/circuit.html

Civil Records: Access: Online, mail, in person. Both court and visitors may perform in person searches. Search fee: $5.00 for five years searched. Court makes copy: $.50 per page. Required to search: name, years to search, also helpful: SSN. Civil cases indexed by defendant, plaintiff; on books from 1842 to present, on computer back to 1985. Search free at http://208.210.219.132/vacircuit/select.jsp. Also search via LOPAS; call 804-786-5511 to apply.

Criminal Records: Access: Online, in person. Both court and visitors may perform in person searches. Court makes copy: $.50 per page. Required to search: name, years to search; also helpful: SSN. Criminal records on books from 1842 to present; on computer back to 1985. Online access to criminal records is the same as civil.

General Information: Public terminal goes back to 1985. No juvenile, sealed, adoption records released. Certification fee: $2.00. Payee: Clerk of Court. Personal checks accepted. Prepayment required.

Carroll Combined District Court PO Box 698, Hillsville, VA 24343; phone: 276-728-7751; fax: 276-728-2582; hours 8AM-4:30PM (EST). *Misdemeanor, Civil Actions Under $15,000, Eviction, Small Claims.*

Civil Records: Access: In person, online. Visitors must perform in person searches themselves. No copy fee. Required to search: name, years to search. Civil cases indexed by defendant, plaintiff; on books from 1800s, on computer from 1988; no plaintiff index prior to computerization. Search free at http://208.210.219.132/vadistrict/select.jsp. Also search via LOPAS; call 804-786-5511 to apply.

Criminal Records: Access: In person, online. Visitors must perform in person searches themselves. No copy fee. Criminal records on books from 1800s, on computer 10 years. Online access to misdemeanor records is the same as civil.

General Information: Public use terminal available. No juvenile, sealed records released. No certification fee. Payee: General District Court. Personal checks or Visa, MC accepted. Prepayment required.

Charles City

9th Circuit Court 10702 Courthouse Rd, PO Box 86, Charles City, VA 23030-0086; phone: 804-829-9212; fax: 804-829-5647; hours 8:30AM-4:30PM (EST). *Felony, Civil Actions Over $15,000, Probate.*
www.courts.state.va.us/courts/circuit.html

Civil Records: Access: Mail, online, in person. Both court and visitors may perform in person searches. No search fee. Court makes copy: $.50 per page. Required to search: name, years to search. Civil cases indexed by defendant, plaintiff; on computer from 2000, on books from 1789-2000. Search free at http://208.210.219.132/vacircuit/select.jsp. Also search via LOPAS; call 804-786-5511 to apply. Mail turnaround time 2-5 days.

Criminal Records: Access: Mail, online, in person. Both court and visitors may perform in person searches. No search fee. Court makes copy: $.50 per page. Required to search: name, years to search, DOB, SSN, signed release. Criminal records on computer from 2000, on books from 1789-2000. Online access to criminal records is the same as civil. Mail turnaround time 2-5 days.

General Information: Public terminal goes back to 2000. No juvenile, sealed records released. Fee to fax documents is $.50 per page. Certification fee: $2.00. Payee: Clerk of Circuit Court. Personal checks accepted. Prepayment required.

9th General District Court PO Box 57, Charles City Courthouse, 10780m Courthouse Rd, Charles City, VA 23030; phone: 804-829-9224; fax: 804-829-6390; hours 8:30AM-4PM (EST). *Misdemeanor, Civil Actions Under $15,000, Eviction, Small Claims.*

Civil Records: Access: Mail, online, in person. Both court and visitors may perform in person searches. No search fee. No copy fee. Required to search: name, years to search. Civil cases indexed by defendant, plaintiff; on computer back to 1989; on books from 1700s. Search free at http://208.210.219.132/vadistrict/select.jsp. Also search via LOPAS; call 804-786-5511 to apply. Mail turnaround time 3 days.

Criminal Records: Access: Mail, online, in person. Both court and visitors may perform in person searches. No search fee. No copy fee. Required to search: name, years to search, DOB, SSN. Criminal records on computer back to 1989; on books from 1700s. Online access to criminal records is the same as civil. Mail turnaround time 3 days.

General Information: Public terminal goes back to 1989. No juvenile, sealed records released. No certification fee. Payee: Circuit Court. Personal checks accepted. Prepayment and SASE required.

Charlotte County

10th Circuit Court PO Box 38, Charlotte Courthouse, VA 23923; phone: 434-542-5147; fax: 434-542-4336; hours 8:30AM-4:30PM (EST). *Felony, Civil Actions Over $15,000, Probate.*
www.courts.state.va.us/courts/circuit.html

Civil Records: Access: In person, online. Visitors must perform in person searches themselves. Court makes copy: $.50 per page. Required to search: name, years to search. Civil cases indexed by defendant, plaintiff; on books from 1765, in folders by case number. Remote online access to court case indexes is via LOPAS; call 804-786-5511 to apply.

Criminal Records: Access: In person only. Visitors must perform in person searches themselves. Court makes copy: $.50 per page. Required to search: name, years to search, DOB. Criminal records on books from 1765, in folders by case number.

General Information: No juvenile, sealed records released. Certification fee: $3.00. Payee: Clerk of Circuit Court. Personal checks accepted. Prepayment required.

Charlotte General District Court PO Box 127, Charlotte Courthouse, VA 23923; phone: 434-542-5600; fax: 434-542-5902; hours 8:30AM-4:30PM (EST). *Misdemeanor, Civil Actions Under $15,000, Eviction, Small Claims.*

Civil Records: Access: Online, in person. Visitors must perform in person searches themselves. Court makes copy: $.50 per page; same fee for self serve. Required to search: name, years to search. Civil cases indexed by defendant, plaintiff; on computer back to 5/95. Search free at http://208.210.219.132/vadistrict/select.jsp. Also search via LOPAS; call 804-786-5511 to apply.

Criminal Records: Access: Online, in person. Visitors must perform in person searches themselves. Court makes copy: $.50 per page; same fee for self serve. Required to search: name, years to search, DOB; also helpful-SSN, signed release. Criminal records on computer back to 5/95. Online access to criminal records is the same as civil.

General Information: Public terminal goes back to 5/1995. No juvenile, sealed records released. No certification fee. Payee: Clerk of General District Court. Personal checks or Visa, MC accepted. Prepayment required.

Charlottesville City

16th Circuit Court 315 E High St, Charlottesville, VA 22902; phone: 434-295-3182; hours 8:30AM-4:30PM (EST). *Felony, Civil Actions Over $15,000, Probate.*
www.courts.state.va.us/courts/circuit/Charlottesville/home.html

Civil Records: Access: In person only. Visitors must perform in person searches themselves. Court makes copy: $.50 per page. Required to search: name, years to search. Civil cases indexed by defendant, plaintiff; on books from 1888 to present. Remote online access to court case indexes to LOPAS is not currently available; call 804-786-5511 for info.

Criminal Records: Access: In person only. Visitors must perform in person searches themselves. Court makes copy: $.50 per page. Required to search: name, years to search; also helpful: DOB. Criminal records on books from 1888 to present. Remote online access to court case indexes via LOPAS is not currently available; call 804-786-5511 for info.

General Information: No juvenile, sealed or adoption records released. Certification fee: $2.00. Payee: Charlottesville Circuit Court Clerk's Office. No out of state checks accepted. Prepayment required.

Charlottesville General District Court 606 E Market St, PO Box 2677, Charlottesville, VA 22902; phone: 434-970-3385; criminal phone: 434-970-3388; civil phone: 434-970-3392; fax: 434-970-3387; hours 8:30AM-4:30PM (EST). *Misdemeanor, Civil Actions Under $15,000, Eviction, Small Claims.*

Civil Records: Access: Mail, online, in person. Both court and visitors may perform in person searches. No search fee. Court makes copy: $1.00 for first page, $.50 each add'l. Self serve copy fee: $.50 per page. Required to search: name, years to search. Civil cases indexed by defendant, plaintiff. Civil records kept for 10 years. Search free at http://208.210.219.132/vadistrict/select.jsp. Also search via LOPAS; call 804-786-5511 to apply. Mail turnaround time 3 days.

Criminal Records: Access: Mail, online, in person. Both court and visitors may perform in person searches. No search fee. Court makes copy: $1.00 for first page, $.50 each add'l. Self serve copy fee: $.50 per page. Required to search: name, years to search; also helpful: DOB, SSN. Criminal records kept for 10 years. Online access to criminal records is the same as civil. Mail turnaround time 3 days.

General Information: Public terminal goes back to 10 years. No juvenile, sealed, confidential records released. Certification fee: Included in copy fee. Payee: General District Court. Personal checks accepted. Prepayment and SASE required.

Chesapeake City

1st Circuit Court 307 Albemarle Dr, #300A, Chesapeake, VA 23322-5579; phone: 757-382-3000; criminal fax: 757-382-3035; civil fax: 757-382-3034; hours 8:30AM-4PM (EST). *Felony, Civil Actions Over $15,000, Probate.*
www.courts.state.va.us/courts/circuit.html
Civil Records: Access: Mail, fax, online, in person. Visitors must perform in person searches themselves. Court makes copy: $.50 per page. Required to search: name, years to search. Civil cases indexed by defendant, plaintiff; on books from 1637, on computer from 1989. Online access free at http://208.210.219.132/vacircuit/select.jsp. For information about the statewide online systems, see the state introduction. Mail turnaround time 1 week.
Criminal Records: Access: Mail, fax, online, in person. Visitors must perform in person searches themselves. No search fee. Court makes copy: $.50 per page. Required to search: name, years to search, DOB; also helpful: SSN, sex, signed release. Criminal records on books from 1800s; on computer from 1989. Online access to criminal records is the same as civil. Mail turnaround time 1 week.
General Information: Public terminal goes back to 1989. No juvenile, sealed records released. Fee to fax documents is $.50 per page. Certification fee: $2.00. Payee: Clerk of Circuit Court. Personal checks accepted. Prepayment and SASE required.

1st General District Court 307 Albemarle Dr, #100, Chesapeake, VA 23322; criminal phone: 757-382-3134; civil phone: 757-382-3143; fax: 757-382-3171; hours 8AM-4PM (EST). *Misdemeanor, Civil Actions Under $15,000, Eviction, Small Claims.*
Note: Indicate division (civil, criminal or traffic) in address.
Civil Records: Access: Mail, online, in person. Both court and visitors may perform in person searches. No search fee. Court makes copy: $1.00 per page. Required to search: name, years to search. Civil cases indexed by defendant, plaintiff; on computer back to 1990; prior on books. Select and search District Courts at www.courts.state.va.us. For information about the statewide online systems, see the state introduction. Mail turnaround time 2-14 days.
Criminal Records: Access: Mail, online, in person. Both court and visitors may perform in person searches. No search fee. Court makes copy: $1.00 per page. Required to search: name, years to search, DOB; also helpful: SSN. Criminal records on computer back to 1990; prior on books. Online access to criminal records is the same as civil. Mail turnaround time 2-14 days.
General Information: Public use terminal available. No juvenile, sealed records released. Certification fee: $2.00. Payee: General District Court. Personal checks or Visa, MC accepted. Prepayment required.

Chesterfield County

12th Circuit Court 9500 Courthouse Rd, PO Box 125, Chesterfield, VA 23832; phone: 804-748-1241; fax: 804-796-5625; hours 8:30AM-5PM (EST). *Felony, Civil Actions Over $15,000, Probate.*
www.co.chesterfield.va.us/JusticeAdministration/CircuitCourtClerk/clerhome.asp
Note: The probate clerk will not search probate court records for you.
Civil Records: Access: Mail, in person, online. Both court and visitors may perform in person searches. No search fee. Court makes copy: $.50 per page. Required to search: name, years to search. Civil cases indexed by defendant, plaintiff; on computer go back to 1989; prior on index books. Remote online access to court case indexes is via LOPAS; call 804-786-5511 to apply. Mail turnaround time 1-2 days.

Criminal Records: Access: Mail, in person. Only the court performs in person searches; visitors may not. Court makes copy: $.50 per page. Required to search: name, years to search; also helpful: DOB, SSN, charge. Criminal records on computer go back to 1989, prior on index books.
General Information: Public terminal has only civil records back to 1989. No juvenile, adoption, sealed records released. Certification fee: $2.00. Payee: Chesterfield Circuit Court. Personal checks accepted. Prepayment and SASE required.

12th General District Court PO Box 144, Chesterfield, VA 23832; phone: 804-748-1231; fax: 804-748-1757; hours 8AM-4PM (EST). *Misdemeanor, Civil Actions Under $15,000, Eviction, Small Claims.*
www.courts.state.va.us/courts/gd/Chesterfield/home.html
Civil Records: Access: Mail, online, in person. Both court and visitors may perform in person searches. No search fee. Court makes copy: $.50 per page. Required to search: name, years to search. Civil cases indexed by defendant, plaintiff; on computer from 1986 to present, index books from 1975 to 1986. Search free at http://208.210.219.132/vadistrict/select.jsp. Also search via LOPAS; call 804-786-5511 to apply. Mail turnaround time 2 days.
Criminal Records: Access: Mail, online, in person. Both court and visitors may perform in person searches. No search fee. Court makes copy: $.50 per page. Required to search: name, years to search, DOB, SSN. Criminal records on computer from 1986 to present, index books from 1975 to 1986. Online access to criminal records is the same as civil. Mail turnaround time 2 days.
General Information: No sealed records released. Certification fee: $2.00. Personal checks or Visa, MC accepted.

Clarke County

26th Circuit Court PO Box 189, Berryville, VA 22611; phone: 540-955-5116; fax: 540-955-0284; hours 9AM-5PM (EST). *Felony, Civil Actions Over $15,000, Probate.*
www.courts.state.va.us/courts/circuit.html
Civil Records: Access: Phone, mail, fax, online, in person. Visitors must perform in person searches themselves. Court makes copy: $.50 per page; same fee for self serve. Required to search: name, years to search. Civil cases indexed by defendant, plaintiff; on books from 1920s. Remote online access to court case indexes is via LOPAS; call 804-786-5511 to apply.
Criminal Records: Access: Online, in person. Visitors must perform in person searches themselves. Court makes copy: $.50 per page; same fee for self serve. Required to search: name, years to search, signed release. Criminal records on books from 1920s. Remote online access to court case indexes is via LOPAS; call 804-786-5511 to apply.
General Information: No juvenile, sealed or adoption records released. No criminal records by mail. Fee to fax documents is $.50 per page. No certification fee. Payee: Clerk of Court. Personal checks accepted. Prepayment required. SASE requested.

General District Court PO Box 612, 104 N Church St, Berryville, VA 22611; phone: 540-955-5128; fax: 540-955-1195; hours 8:30AM-4:30PM (EST). *Misdemeanor, Civil Actions Under $15,000, Eviction, Small Claims.*
www.co.clarke.va.us
Civil Records: Access: Online, in person. Visitors must perform in person searches themselves. Court makes copy: $.50 per page; same fee for self serve. Required to search: name, years to search. Civil cases indexed by defendant, plaintiff; on computer from 1994, on index cards for 1991. Search free at http://208.210.219.132/vadistrict/select.jsp. Also search via LOPAS; call 804-786-5511 to apply.

Criminal Records: Access: Online, in person. Visitors must perform in person searches themselves. Court makes copy: $.50 per page; same fee for self serve. Required to search: name, years to search, DOB, SSN, date of conviction, charge; also helpful: docket number, defendant's name. Criminal records on computer from 1994. Online access to criminal records is the same as civil.
General Information: Public terminal has criminal back to 10 years and civil back to 20 years. Payee: Clarke County General District Court. Personal checks require name and address.

Clifton Forge City

25th Circuit Court *Felony, Civil Actions Over $15,000, Probate.*
www.courts.state.va.us/courts/circuit.html
Note: This court closed 7/1/01 and was combined with the Alleghany County Circuit Court.

25th General District Court PO Box 139, 266 W Main St, Covington, VA 24426; phone: 540-965-1720; fax: 540-965-1722; hours 9AM-5PM (EST). *Misdemeanor, Civil Actions Under $15,000, Eviction, Small Claims.*
Note: As of 7/1/2001, the Clifton Forge Court is combined with the Alleghany County District Court to form the 25th Combined District Court.

Colonial Heights City

12th Circuit Court 401 Temple Ave, PO Box 3401, Colonial Heights, VA 23834; phone: 804-520-9364; fax: 804-524-8726; hours 8:30AM-5PM (EST). *Felony, Civil Actions Over $15,000, Probate.*
www.courts.state.va.us/courts/circuit.html
Civil Records: Access: Mail, in person. Both court and visitors may perform in person searches. Search fee: $5.00 per name. Court makes copy: $.50 per page; same fee for self serve. Required to search: name, years to search. Civil cases indexed by defendant, plaintiff; on books from 1961, on computer from 1990. Mail turnaround time 2 days.
Criminal Records: Access: Mail, in person. Both court and visitors may perform in person searches. Search fee: $5.00 per name. Court makes copy: $.50 per page; same fee for self serve. Required to search: name, years to search; also helpful: DOB, SSN. Criminal records on books from 1961, on computer from 1990. Mail turnaround time 2 days.
General Information: No juvenile, sealed or adoption records released. Certification fee: $2.00 per document. Payee: Clerk of Circuit Court. Personal checks accepted. Prepayment and SASE required.

12th General District Court 401 Temple Ave, PO Box 279, Colonial Heights, VA 23834; phone: 804-520-9346 (Dial 0); fax: 804-520-9370; hours 8AM-4PM (EST). *Misdemeanor, Civil Actions Under $15,000, Eviction, Small Claims.*
Civil Records: Access: Mail, fax, online, in person. Both court and visitors may perform in person searches. No search fee. Court makes copy: $.50 per page. Required to search: name, years to search. Civil cases indexed by defendant, plaintiff; on computer from 1989 to present, index cards from 1985. Search free at http://208.210.219.132/vadistrict/select.jsp. Also search via LOPAS; call 804-786-5511 to apply. Mail turnaround time 1 week.
Criminal Records: Access: Mail, fax, online, in person. Both court and visitors may perform in person searches. No search fee. Court makes copy: $.50 per page. Required to search: name, years to search, DOB, SSN. Criminal records on computer from 1989 to present, index cards from 1985. Online access to criminal records is the same as civil. Mail turnaround time 1 week.
General Information: Public use terminal available. No juvenile, sealed records released. Certification fee: $.50. Payee: Colonial Heights Combined Court. Personal checks or Visa, MC accepted. Prepayment required. SASE requested.

Covington City

Circuit & District Courts
www.courts.state.va.us/courts/circuit.html
Note: See Alleghany County.

Craig County

25th Circuit Court PO Box 185, New Castle, VA 24127-0185; phone: 540-864-6141; hours 9AM-5PM (EST). *Felony, Civil Actions Over $15,000, Probate.*

www.courts.state.va.us/courts/circuit.html
Civil Records: Access: Online, in person. Visitors must perform in person searches themselves. Court makes copy: $.50 per page; same fee for self serve. Required to search: name, years to search. Civil cases indexed by defendant. Civil records on books from mid 1800s. Remote online access to court case indexes is via LOPAS; call 804-786-5511 to apply.
Criminal Records: Access: Online, in person. Visitors must perform in person searches themselves. Court makes copy: $.50 per page; same fee for self serve. Required to search: name, years to search; also helpful: SSN. Criminal records on books from mid 1800s. Online access to criminal records is the same as civil.
General Information: No juvenile, sealed or adoption records released. Certification fee: $2.00. Payee: Clerk of Court. Personal checks accepted. Prepayment required.

25th General District Court Craig County General District Court, PO Box 232, New Castle, VA 24127; phone: 540-864-5989; hours 8:15AM-4:45PM (EST). *Misdemeanor, Civil Actions Under $15,000, Eviction, Small Claims.*
Civil Records: Access: Mail, online, in person. Visitors must perform in person searches themselves. Court makes copy: $1.00 per page. Required to search: name, years to search. Civil cases indexed by defendant, plaintiff. Civil records in files 10 years back. Search free at http://208.210.219.132/vadistrict/select.jsp. Also search via LOPAS; call 804-786-5511 to apply.
Criminal Records: Access: Mail, online, in person. Visitors must perform in person searches themselves. Court makes copy: $1.00 per page. Required to search: name, years to search; also helpful: SSN. Criminal records in files 10 years back. Online access to criminal records is the same as civil. Note: Lengthy searches must be performed in person.
General Information: Public use terminal available. No juvenile, sealed records released. No certification fee. Payee: Craig County District Court. Personal checks or Visa, MC accepted. SASE required.

Culpeper County

16th Circuit Court 135 W Cameron St, Culpeper, VA 22701-3097; phone: 540-727-3438; hours 8:30AM-4:30PM (EST). *Felony, Civil Actions Over $15,000, Probate.*
www.courts.state.va.us/courts/circuit.html
Civil Records: Access: In person, online. Visitors must perform in person searches themselves. Court makes copy: $.50 per page. Required to search: name, years to search. Civil cases indexed by defendant, plaintiff; on computer from 1991, docket books from 1800s; records go back to 1950. Remote online access to court case indexes is via LOPAS; call 804-786-5511 to apply.
Criminal Records: Access: In person, online. Visitors must perform in person searches themselves. Court makes copy: $.50 per page. Required to search: name, years to search, signed release. Criminal records on computer from 1991, docket books from 1800s, records go back to 1950. Online access to criminal records is the same as civil.
General Information: Public use terminal available. No juvenile, sealed records released. Certification fee: $2.00. Payee: Clerk of Court. Personal checks not accepted. Prepayment required.

16th General District Court 135 W Cameron St, Culpeper, VA 22701; phone: 540-727-3417; fax: 540-727-3474; hours 8:30AM-4:30PM (EST). *Misdemeanor, Civil Actions Under $15,000, Eviction, Small Claims.*
Civil Records: Access: Mail, online, in person. Both court and visitors may perform in person searches. No search fee. Court makes copy: $1.00 for 1st two pages, $.50 each add'l page. Required to search: name, years to search. Civil cases indexed by defendant, plaintiff; on computer from 1987 to present, prior on index cards. Search free at http://208.210.219.132/vadistrict/select.jsp. Also search via LOPAS; call 804-786-5511 to apply. Mail turnaround time 1-5 days.
Criminal Records: Access: Mail, online, in person. Both court and visitors may perform in person searches. No search fee. Court makes copy: $1.00 for 1st two pages, $.50 each add'l. Required to search: name, years to search. Criminal records on computer from 1987 to present, prior on index cards. Online access to criminal records is the same as civil. Mail turnaround time 1-5 days.
General Information: Public terminal goes back to 1987. No juvenile, sealed records released. Certification fee: $1.00 per page. Payee: General District Court. Personal checks accepted. Prepayment and SASE required.

Cumberland County

10th Circuit Court PO Box 8, Cumberland, VA 23040; phone: 804-492-4442; hours 8:30AM-4:30PM (EST). *Felony, Civil Actions Over $15,000, Probate.*
www.courts.state.va.us/courts/circuit.html
Civil Records: Access: Online, in person. Visitors must perform in person searches themselves. Court makes copy: $.50 per page; same fee for self serve. Civil cases indexed by defendant, plaintiff. Civil records computerized from 1/2001. Search free at http://208.210.219.132/vacircuit/select.jsp. Also search via LOPAS; call 804-786-5511 to apply. Note: Phone access only for simple requests.
Criminal Records: Access: Online, in person. Visitors must perform in person searches themselves. Court makes copy: $.50 per page; same fee for self serve. Criminal records computerized from 1/2001. Online access to criminal records is the same as civil.
General Information: No juvenile, sealed records released. Certification fee: $.50 per page. Payee: Clerk of Circuit Court. Personal checks accepted. Prepayment required.

10th General District Court PO Box 24, Cumberland, VA 23040; phone: 804-492-4848; fax: 804-492-9455; hours 8:30AM-4:30PM (EST). *Misdemeanor, Civil Actions Under $15,000, Eviction, Small Claims.*
Civil Records: Access: Phone, fax, mail, online, in person. Only the court performs in person searches; visitors may not. No search fee. Court makes copy: $1.00 per page. Required to search: name, years to search. Civil cases indexed by defendant, plaintiff; on computer from 1993. Select and search District Courts at http://208.210.219.132/vadistrict/select.jsp. For information about the statewide online systems, see the state introduction. Mail turnaround time 2 days.
Criminal Records: Access: Phone, fax, mail, online, in person. Only the court performs in person searches; visitors may not. No search fee. Court makes copy: $1.00 per page. Required to search: name, years to search; also helpful: DOB, SSN, sex. Criminal records on computer from 1993. Online access to criminal records is the same as civil. Mail turnaround time 2 days.
General Information: No juvenile, sealed records released. Will not fax documents. No certification fee. Payee: Clerk of District Court. Personal checks or Visa, MC accepted. Prepayment and SASE required.

Danville City

22nd Circuit Court PO Box 3300 (401 Patton St), Danville, VA 24543; phone: 434-799-5168; fax: 434-799-6502; hours 9AM-4:30PM (EST). *Felony, Civil Actions Over $15,000, Probate.*
www.danville-va.gov/home.asp
Civil Records: Access: Online, in person. Visitors must perform in person searches themselves. Court makes copy: $.50 per page; same fee for self serve. Required to search: name, years to search. Civil cases indexed by defendant, plaintiff. Civil records in index books from 1841, judgments on computer since 1990. Online access free at http://208.210.219.132/vacircuit/select.jsp. For information about the statewide online systems, see the state introduction. Also, search daily docket from the web page.
Criminal Records: Access: Online, in person. Visitors must perform in person searches themselves. Court makes copy: $.50 per page; same fee for self serve. Required to search: name, years to search. Criminal records in index books from 1841. Criminal records on computer from 1988. Online access to criminal records is the same as civil.
General Information: Public use terminal available. No juvenile, sealed or adoption records released. Will not fax documents. Certification fee: $2.00. Payee: Gerald A Gibson, Clerk. Personal checks accepted. Prepayment required.

22nd General District Court PO Box 3300, Danville, VA 24543; phone: 434-799-5179; fax: 434-797-8814; hours 8:30AM-4:30PM (EST). *Misdemeanor, Civil Actions Under $15,000, Eviction, Small Claims.*
Civil Records: Access: Mail, online, in person. Both court and visitors may perform in person searches. No search fee. Court makes copy: $1.00 1st 2 pages, $.50 each add'l. Required to search: name, years to search. Civil cases indexed by defendant, plaintiff. Civil records go back 10 years; on computer back to 1994. Select and search District Courts at http://208.210.219.132/vadistrict/select.jsp. For information about the statewide online systems, see the state introduction. Mail turnaround time 2 days.
Criminal Records: Access: Mail, online, in person. Both court and visitors may perform in person searches. No search fee. Court makes copy: $1.00 1st 2 pages, $.50 each add'l. Required to search: name, years to search. Criminal records go back 10 years; on computer back to 1994. Select and search District Courts at http://208.210.219.132/vadistrict/select.jsp. Mail turnaround time 2 days.
General Information: Public terminal goes back to 10 years. No juvenile, sealed records released. No certification fee. Payee: General District Court. Personal checks or Visa, MC accepted. Prepayment required. SASE requested.

Dickenson County

29th Circuit Court PO Box 190, Clintwood, VA 24228; phone: 276-926-1616; fax: 276-926-6465; hours 8:30AM-4:30PM (EST). *Felony, Civil Actions Over $15,000, Probate.*
www.courts.state.va.us/courts/circuit.html
Civil Records: Access: Mail, online, in person. Both court and visitors may perform in person searches. No search fee. Court makes copy: $.50 per page; same fee for self serve. Required to search: name, years to search. Civil cases indexed by defendant, plaintiff; on computer from 1989, index book from 1880. Online access free at http://208.210.219.132/vacircuit/select.jsp. For information about the statewide online systems, see the state introduction. Mail turnaround time 1 week.
Criminal Records: Access: Mail, online, in person. Both court and visitors may perform in person searches. No search fee. Court makes copy: $.50 per page; same fee for self serve. Required to search: name, years to search, DOB; also helpful: SSN.

Criminal records on computer from 1989, index book from 1880. Online access to criminal records is the same as civil. Mail turnaround time 1 week.

General Information: Public terminal goes back to 1989. No juvenile, sealed, adoption, confidential records released. Will not fax documents. Certification fee: $2.50. Payee: Joe Tate, Clerk of Circuit Court. Personal checks not accepted. Prepayment required. SASE requested.

29th General District Court PO Box 128, Clintwood, VA 24228; phone: 276-926-1630; fax: 276-926-4815; hours 8:30AM-4:30PM (EST). *Misdemeanor, Civil Actions Under $15,000, Eviction, Small Claims.*

Civil Records: Access: Phone, mail, in person, online. Both court and visitors may perform in person searches. No search fee. Court makes copy: $.10 per page. Required to search: name, years to search. Civil cases indexed by defendant. Civil records on computer from 1/1/1995. Search free at http://208.210.219.132/vadistrict/select.jsp. Also search via LOPAS; call 804-786-5511 to apply. Mail turnaround time 1 week.

Criminal Records: Access: Phone, mail, in person, online. Both court and visitors may perform in person searches. No search fee. Court makes copy: $.10 per page. Required to search: name, years to search. Criminal records on computer from 1/1/1995. Online access to criminal records is the same as civil. Mail turnaround time 1 week.

General Information: Public terminal goes back to 1995. No juvenile, sealed records released. Will fax documents. No certification fee. Payee: Dickenson Combined Court or General District Court. Personal checks or Visa, MC accepted. Prepayment required. SASE requested.

Dinwiddie County

11th Circuit Court PO Box 63, Dinwiddie, VA 23841; phone: 804-469-4540; fax: 804-469-5386; hours 8:30AM-4:30PM (EST). *Felony, Civil Actions Over $15,000, Probate.*

www.courts.state.va.us/courts/circuit.html

Note: Probate is separate index at this same address.

Civil Records: Access: Mail, online, in person. Both court and visitors may perform in person searches. No search fee. Court makes copy: $.50 per page; same fee for self serve. Required to search: name, years to search; also helpful: address. Civil cases indexed by defendant, plaintiff; on index cards from 1833; deeds on computer since 1989. Search Circuit Courts at http://208.210.219.132/vadistrict/select.jsp. For information about the statewide online systems, see the state introduction. Mail turnaround 3 days.

Criminal Records: Access: Mail, online, in person. Both court and visitors may perform in person searches. No search fee. Court makes copy: $.50 per page; same fee for self serve. Required to search: name, years to search; also helpful: DOB, SSN. Criminal records on index cards from 1833; deeds on computer since 1989. Online access to criminal records is the same as civil. Mail turnaround time 3 days.

General Information: No juvenile, sealed or expunged records released. Will not fax documents. Certification fee: $2.00. Payee: Clerk of Court. Personal checks accepted. Prepayment required. SASE requested.

11th General District Court PO Box 280, Dinwiddie, VA 23841; phone: 804-469-4533; fax: 804-469-5383; hours 8:30AM-4:30PM (EST). *Misdemeanor, Civil Actions Under $15,000, Eviction, Small Claims, Traffic.*

Civil Records: Access: Mail, online, in person. Only the court performs in person searches; visitors may not. No search fee. Court makes copy: $.50 per page. Required to search: name, years to search. Civil cases indexed by defendant, plaintiff; on index cards from 1800s, on computer from 1989. Search free at http://208.210.219.132/vadistrict/select.jsp. Also search via LOPAS; call 804-786-5511 to apply. Mail turnaround time 3 days.

Criminal Records: Access: Mail, online, in person. Only the court performs in person searches; visitors may not. No search fee. Court makes copy: $.50 per page. Required to search: name, years to search. Criminal records on computer from 1989. Online access to criminal records is the same as civil. Mail turnaround time 3 days.

General Information: No juvenile, sealed records released. Certification fee: $2.00. Payee: District Court. Personal checks or Visa, MC accepted. Prepayment and SASE required.

Emporia City

Circuit Court

www.courts.state.va.us/courts/circuit.html

Note: See Greensville County

6th General District Court 315 S Main, Emporia, VA 23847; phone: 434-634-5400; fax: 434-634-0049; hours 8:30AM-4:30PM (EST). *Misdemeanor, Civil Actions Under $15,000, Eviction, Small Claims.*

Civil Records: Access: Online, in person. Visitors must perform in person searches themselves. Court makes copy: $1.00 plus $.25 each add'l page. Required to search: name, years to search. Civil cases indexed by defendant, plaintiff; on computer back to 1991. Search free at http://208.210.219.132/vadistrict/select.jsp. Also search via LOPAS; call 804-786-5511 to apply.

Criminal Records: Access: Online, in person. Visitors must perform in person searches themselves. Court makes copy: $1.00 per page; $.25 each add'l. Required to search: name, years to search. Criminal records on computer back to 1991. Online access to criminal records is the same as civil.

General Information: No juvenile records released. No certification fee.

Essex County

15th Circuit Court PO Box 445, 305 Prince St, Tappahannock, VA 22560; phone: 804-443-3541; hours 8:30AM-5PM (EST). *Felony, Civil Actions Over $15,000, Probate.*

www.courts.state.va.us/courts/circuit.html

Civil Records: Access: In person, online. Visitors must perform in person searches themselves. Court makes copy: $.50 per page; same fee for self serve. Required to search: name, years to search. Civil cases indexed by defendant, plaintiff; on books from 1656; deed index on computer back to 1977. Remote online access to court case indexes is via LOPAS; call 804-786-5511 to apply.

Criminal Records: Access: In person only. Visitors must perform in person searches themselves. Court makes copy: $.50 per page; same fee for self serve. Required to search: name, years to search. Criminal records on books from 1656. Online access to criminal records is the same as civil.

General Information: No juvenile, sealed records released. Certification fee: $2.00. Payee: Clerk of Court. Personal checks accepted. Prepayment required.

15th General District Court PO Box 66, Tappahannock, VA 22560; phone: 804-443-3744; fax: 804-443-4122; hours 8AM-12:30PM, 1-4:30PM (EST). *Misdemeanor, Civil Actions Under $15,000, Eviction, Small Claims.*

Civil Records: Access: Mail, online, in person. Both court and visitors may perform in person searches. No search fee. No copy fee. Required to search: name, years to search. Civil cases indexed by defendant, plaintiff; on computer from 5/92, prior on index cards. Search free at http://208.210.219.132/vadistrict/select.jsp. Also search via LOPAS; call 804-786-5511 to apply.

Criminal Records: Access: Online, in person. Visitors must perform in person searches themselves. No copy fee. Required to search: name, years to search, DOB, SSN. Criminal records on computer from 5/92, prior on index cards. Online access to criminal records is the same as civil.

General Information: Public terminal goes back to 5/1992. No juvenile, sealed records released. No certification fee. Prepayment required.

Fairfax County

19th Circuit Court 4110 Chain Bridge Rd, Fairfax, VA 22030; criminal phone: 703-246-2228; civil phone: 703-691-7320 x311; fax: 703-273-6564; hours 8AM-4PM (EST). *Felony, Civil Actions Over $15,000, Probate.*

www.fairfaxcounty.gov/courts/circuit

Civil Records: Access: In person, online. Visitors must perform in person searches themselves. Court makes copy: $.50 per page. Required to search: name, years to search. Civil cases indexed by defendant, plaintiff. Civil records computerized from 1979; index books for prior years; scanned back to 1700s. Remote online access to current court case indexes is via CPAN; call 703-246-2366 to apply. Fee is $25.00 per month per user.

Criminal Records: Access: In person, online. Visitors must perform in person searches themselves. Court makes copy: $.50 per page. Required to search: name, years to search, DOB; also helpful: SSN. Criminal records computerized from 1979. Online access to criminal records is same as civil, see above.

General Information: Public terminal goes back to 1979. No juvenile, sealed records released. Certification fee: $2.00. Payee: Fairfax Circuit Court. Personal checks not accepted. Visa/MC accepted only for criminal division. Prepayment required.

19th General District Court 4110 Chain Bridge Rd, Fairfax, VA 22030; phone: 703-246-2153; criminal phone: 703-691-7320; civil phone: 703-246-3012; fax: 703-591-2349; hours 8AM-4PM (EST). *Misdemeanor, Civil Actions under $15,000, Eviction, Small Claims.*

www.fairfaxcounty.gov/courts/gendist

Note: Traffic Division: 703-246-3764.

Civil Records: Access: Phone, in person, online. Visitors must perform in person searches themselves. Court makes copy: $.50 per page; same fee for self serve. Required to search: name, years to search. Civil cases indexed by defendant, plaintiff. Civil indexes for 10 years; onsite records held only 3 years before archiving; on computer back 10 years. Online access to civil records at http://208.210.219.132/vadistrict/select.jsp.

Criminal Records: Access: Phone, in person, online. Both court and visitors may perform in person searches. Court makes copy: $.50 per page; same fee for self serve. Required to search: name, years to search; also helpful: DOB, SSN. Criminal & traffic records on computer for 10 years; onsite records held only 3 years before archiving. Online access to criminal & traffic records at http://208.210.219.132/vadistrict/select.jsp. For information about the statewide online systems, see the state introduction.

General Information: Public terminal goes back to 10 years. No juvenile, sealed records released. Will not fax documents as a general rule. No certification fee. Payee: Fairfax General District Court. Personal checks accepted. Prepayment required.

Fairfax City

Circuit Court

www.courts.state.va.us/courts/circuit.html

Note: See Fairfax County.

19th General District Court 10455 Armstrong St, #304, Fairfax, VA 22030; phone: 703-385-7866; fax: 703-352-3195; hours 8:30AM-4:30PM (EST). *Misdemeanor, Traffic, Civil Under $15,000.*

www.courts.state.va.us/courts/gd/Fairfax_City/home.html

Note: Find Circuit Court cases and General District civil cases for this city in the Fairfax County listing

Civil Records: Access: Mail, in person, online. No search fee. Court makes copy: $1.00 for first 2 pages;

$.50 each add'l. Required to search: name, years to search. Search free at http://208.210.219.132/vadistrict/select.jsp. Mail turnaround time 1 day.

Criminal Records: Access: Mail, in person, online. Only the court performs in person searches; visitors may not. No search fee. Court makes copy: $1.00 for first 2 pages; $.50 each add'l. Required to search: name, years to search; also helpful: SSN. Criminal records on computer and index from 1985. Search free at http://208.210.219.132/vadistrict/select.jsp. Mail turnaround time same day.

General Information: No juvenile or sealed records released. Will not fax documents. No certification fee. Payee: General District Court. Personal checks or Visa, MC accepted. Prepayment required. SASE requested.

Falls Church City

Circuit Court
www.courts.state.va.us/courts/circuit.html
Note: See Arlington County.

17th District Courts Combined Falls Church District, 300 Park Ave, Falls Church, VA 22046-3305; phone: 703-248-5096 (GDC); civil phone: 703-248-5098; fax: 703-241-1407; hours 8AM-4PM (EST). *Misdemeanor, Civil Actions Under $15,000, Eviction, Small Claims.*
www.ci.falls-church.va.us
Note: Small claims phone is 703-248-5157; juvenile and domestic relations is 703-248-5099.

Civil Records: Access: Fax, online. Only the court performs in person searches; visitors may not. No search fee. Court makes copy: $1.00 1st page; $.50 each add'l page. Self serve copy fee: $.50 per page. Required to search: name, years to search. Civil cases indexed by defendant, plaintiff; on computer from 1994 to present and 1984-1985. Search free at http://208.210.219.132/vadistrict/select.jsp. Also search via LOPAS; call 804-786-5511 to apply.

Criminal Records: Access: Fax, online, in person. Only the court performs in person searches; visitors may not. No search fee. Court makes copy: $1.00 1st page; $.50 each add'l page. Self serve copy fee: $.50 per page. Required to search: name, years to search; also helpful: DOB, SSN. Criminal records on computer back to 1994. Online access to criminal records is the same as civil.

General Information: No juvenile or sealed records released. No fee to fax documents. No certification fee. Payee: Falls Church District Court. Personal checks or Visa, MC accepted. Prepayment required.

Fauquier County

Circuit Court 40 Culpeper St, Warrenton, VA 20186-3298; phone: 540-347-8610; criminal phone: 540-347-8605; civil phone: 540-347-8601; probate phone: 540-347-8606; hours 8AM-4:30PM (EST). *Felony, Civil Actions Over $15,000, Probate.*
www.fauquiercounty.gov/government/departments/circuitcourt
Note: Chancery court can be reached at 540-347-8607.

Civil Records: Access: Online, in person. Both court and visitors may perform in person searches. Court makes copy: $.50 per page. Required to search: name, years to search. Civil cases indexed by defendant, plaintiff; on computer back to 1988. Online access free at http://208.210.219.132/vacircuit/select.jsp. For information about the statewide online systems, see the state introduction.

Criminal Records: Access: Online, in person. Visitors must perform in person searches themselves. Court makes copy: $.50 per page. Required to search: name, years to search. Criminal records on computer back to 1988. Online access to criminal records is the same as civil. Note: Court recommends you contact the VA State Police.

General Information: Public terminal goes back to 1988. No juvenile, sealed, adoption records released.

Certification fee: $2.00. Payee: Clerk of Fauquier Circuit Court. Personal checks not accepted. Prepayment required.

20th General District Court 6 Court St, Warrenton, VA 20186; criminal phone: 540-347-8624; civil phone: 540-347-8676; fax: 540-347-5756; hours 8:30AM-4:30PM (EST). *Misdemeanor, Civil Actions Under $15,000, Eviction, Small Claims.*

Civil Records: Access: Online, in person. Visitors must perform in person searches themselves. Court makes copy: $1.00 1st 2 pages, $.50 each add'l. Required to search: name, years to search. Civil cases indexed by defendant, plaintiff; on computerized back 10 years. Search free at http://208.210.219.132/vadistrict/select.jsp. Also search via LOPAS; call 804-786-5511 to apply.

Criminal Records: Access: Online, in person. Visitors must perform in person searches themselves. Court makes copy: $1.00 1st 2 pages, $.50 each add'l. Required to search: name, years to search. Criminal records computerized back 10 years, criminal records only go back 10 years. Online access to criminal records is the same as civil.

General Information: Public use terminal available. No juvenile, sealed records released. No certification fee. Payee: General District Court. Personal checks accepted. Prepayment required.

Floyd County

27th Circuit Court 100 E Main St, #200, Floyd, VA 24091; phone: 540-745-9330; fax: 540-745-9303; hours 8:30AM-4:30PM M-F, 8:30AM-N Sat (EST). *Felony, Civil Actions Over $15,000, Probate.*
www.courts.state.va.us/courts/circuit.html
Note: Closed on Saturdays only if it is a holiday.

Civil Records: Access: Online, in person. Visitors must perform in person searches themselves. Court makes copy: $.50 per page. Required to search: name, years to search. Civil cases indexed by defendant, plaintiff; on files from 1831. Search free at http://208.210.219.132/vacircuit/select.jsp. Also search via LOPAS; call 804-786-5511 to apply.

Criminal Records: Access: Online, in person. Visitors must perform in person searches themselves. Court makes copy: $.50 per page. Required to search: name, years to search; also helpful: DOB, SSN. Criminal records on files from 1831. Online access to criminal records is the same as civil.

General Information: Public terminal goes back to 1996. No juvenile, sealed records released. Will not fax documents. Certification fee: $2.00. Payee: Clerk of Circuit Court. Personal checks accepted. Prepayment required.

27th General District Court 100 E Main St, Floyd, VA 24091-2101; phone: 540-745-9327; fax: 540-745-9329; hours 8AM-4:30PM (EST). *Misdemeanor, Civil Actions Under $15,000, Eviction, Small Claims.*

Civil Records: Access: Online, in person. Visitors must perform in person searches themselves. Court makes copy: $.50 per page. Required to search: name, years to search. Civil cases indexed by defendant, plaintiff. Civil records computerized since 1993. Select and search District Courts at http://208.210.219.132/vadistrict/select.jsp. Also, remote online access to court case indexes is via LOPAS; call 804-786-5511 to apply. Note: Phone search results may be of limited content.

Criminal Records: Access: Online, in person. Visitors must perform in person searches themselves. Court makes copy: $.50 per page. Required to search: name, years to search, DOB. Criminal records computerized since 1993. Online access to criminal records is the same as civil. Note: Phone search results may be of limited content.

General Information: Public use terminal available. No juvenile, sealed records released. No certification fee. Payee: Clerk of District Court. Prepayment required.

Fluvanna County

16th Circuit Court PO Box 550, Palmyra, VA 22963; phone: 434-591-1970; fax: 434-591-1971; hours 8:AM-4:30PM (EST). *Felony, Civil Actions Over $15,000, Probate.*
www.courts.state.va.us/courts/circuit.html

Civil Records: Access: Mail, in person, online. Both court and visitors may perform in person searches. Search fee: $5.00 per name. Court makes copy: $.50 per page. Required to search: name, years to search. Civil cases indexed by defendant, plaintiff; on index books from 1777; computerized back to 1985. Search free at http://208.210.219.132/vacircuit/select.jsp. Also search via LOPAS; call 804-786-5511 to apply. Mail turnaround time same 1-2 days.

Criminal Records: Access: Mail, in person, online. Both court and visitors may perform in person searches. Search fee: $5.00 per name. Court makes copy: $.50 per page. Required to search: name, years to search, DOB; also helpful: SSN. Criminal records on index books from 1777; computerized back to 1985. Online access to criminal records is the same as civil. Mail turnaround time 1-2 days.

General Information: No juvenile or sealed records released. Fee to fax documents is $2.00 per document. Certification fee: $2.00. Payee: Clerk of Circuit Court. Personal checks accepted. Prepayment and SASE required.

16th General District Court Fluvanna County Courthouse, PO Box 417, Palmyra, VA 22963; phone: 434-591-1980; fax: 434-591-1981; hours 8:30AM-4:30PM (EST). *Misdemeanor, Civil Actions Under $15,000, Eviction, Small Claims.*
Note: For fax, dial, wait for answer, then press 4.

Civil Records: Access: Online, in person. Visitors must perform in person searches themselves. Court makes copy: $.50 per page. Required to search: name, years to search. Civil cases indexed by defendant, plaintiff; on computer since 12/91, on books since 1984. Search free at http://208.210.219.132/vadistrict/select.jsp. Also search via LOPAS; call 804-786-5511 to apply.

Criminal Records: Access: Online, in person. Visitors must perform in person searches themselves. Court makes copy: $.50 per page. Required to search: name, years to search; also helpful: DOB, SSN. Criminal records on computer since 12/91, on books since 1984. Online access to criminal records is the same as civil.

General Information: Public terminal goes back to 1991. No juvenile records released. No certification fee. Payee: Fluvanna District Court. Personal checks accepted. Prepayment required.

Franklin County

22nd Judicial Circuit Court PO Box 567, 275 S Main St, #212, Rocky Mount, VA 24151; phone: 540-483-3065; fax: 540-483-3042; hours 8:30AM-5PM (EST). *Felony, Civil Actions Over $15,000, Probate.*
www.courts.state.va.us/courts/circuit/Franklin/home.html
Note: Note that Franklin City is not the same as Franklin County. Only Franklin County information is given here.

Civil Records: Access: In person, online. Visitors must perform in person searches themselves. Court makes copy: $.50 per page. Required to search: name. Civil cases indexed by defendant, plaintiff. Criminal records file on computer. Select and search Circuit Courts online at http://208.210.219.132/vacircuit/select.jsp. For information about the statewide online systems, see the state introduction.

Criminal Records: Access: In person, online. Visitors must perform in person searches themselves. Court makes copy: $.50 per page. Required to search: name, years to search. Criminal records file on computer. Online access to criminal records is the same as civil.

General Information: Public terminal goes back to 1986. No juvenile records released. Will fax documents for $.50 per page fee. Prepayment required.

22nd General District Court PO Box 569, 275 S Main St, #111, Rocky Mount, VA 24151; phone: 540-483-3060; fax: 540-483-3036; hours 8:30AM-4:30PM (EST). *Misdemeanor, Civil Actions Under $15,000, Eviction, Small Claims.*
www.courts.state.va.us/courts/combined/Franklin_City/home.html
Civil Records: Access: Online, in person. Visitors must perform in person searches themselves. Court makes copy: $.25 per page. Required to search: name, years to search. Civil cases indexed by defendant, plaintiff. Civil records file on computer from 1995. Search free at http://208.210.219.132/vadistrict/select.jsp. Also search via LOPAS; call 804-786-5511 to apply.
Criminal Records: Access: Online, in person. Visitors must perform in person searches themselves. Court makes copy: $.25 per page. Required to search: name, years to search. Criminal records file on computer from 1995. Online access to criminal records is the same as civil.
General Information: Public terminal goes back to 1995. Will not fax documents. No certification fee. Personal checks or Visa, MC accepted. Prepayment required.

Franklin-City

5th Judicial General District Combined 1020 Pretlow St, Franklin, VA 23851; phone: 757-562-8550; fax: 757-562-8561; hours 8AM-4PM (EST). *Misdemeanor, Civil Actions Under $15,000, Eviction, Traffic.*
www.courts.state.va.us/courts/combined/Franklin_City/home.html
Note: Southampton County serves as the Circuit Court for City of Franklin.
Civil Records: Access: Mail, online, in person. Both court and visitors may perform in person searches. No search fee. Court makes copy: $1.00 1st page; $.50 each add'l page. Required to search: name, years to search. Civil cases indexed by plaintiff. Civil records on computer since 1990. Select and search Circuit Courts online at http://208.210.219.132/vadistrict/select.jsp. For info on the statewide online systems, see the state introduction. Mail turnaround time 2-5 days.
Criminal Records: Access: Mail, online, in person. Both court and visitors may perform in person searches. No search fee. Court makes copy: $1.00 1st page; $.50 each add'l page. Required to search: name, years to search; also helpful: SSN. Criminal records on computer since 1990. Online access to criminal records is the same as civil. Mail turnaround time 2-5 days. Will expedite.
General Information: Public terminal goes back to 1990. No juvenile records released. No certification fee. Payee: Clerk of the District Court.

Frederick County

Circuit Court 5 N Kent St, Winchester, VA 22601; phone: 540-667-5770; probate phone: 540-665-5659; fax: 540-545-8711; hours 9AM-5PM (EST). *Felony, Misdemeanor, Civil, Probate.*
www.winfredclerk.com
Civil Records: Access: Mail, in person, online. Both court and visitors may perform in person searches. Court makes copy: $.50 per page. Required to search: name, years to search. Civil cases indexed by defendant, plaintiff; on books from 1970s. Search free at http://208.210.219.132/vacircuit/select.jsp. Also search via LOPAS; call 804-786-5511 to apply. Note: Mail access limited to simple requests.
Criminal Records: Access: In person, online. Visitors must perform in person searches themselves. Court makes copy: $.50 per page. Required to search: name, years to search. Criminal records on books from 1970s. Online access to

criminal records is the same as civil. Mail turnaround time 1-2 days.
General Information: Public terminal goes back to 1985. No juvenile, sealed or adoption records released. Certification fee: $3.00. Payee: Clerk of Circuit Court. Personal checks accepted. Prepayment required.

26th District Court 5 N Kent St, Winchester, VA 22601; phone: 540-722-7208; fax: 540-722-1063; hours 8AM-4PM (EST). *Misdemeanor, Civil Actions up to $15,000.*
Civil Records: Access: In person, online. Visitors must perform in person searches themselves. Court makes copy: $.50 per page. Required to search: name, years to search. Search free at http://208.210.219.132/vadistrict/select.jsp. Also search via LOPAS; call 804-786-5511 to apply.
Criminal Records: Access: In person, online. Visitors must perform in person searches themselves. Court makes copy: $.50 per page. Required to search: name, years to search. Online access to criminal records is the same as civil.
General Information: Public terminal goes back to 10 years. Certification fee: $.50 per page. Payee: Frederick District Court. Personal checks accepted. Prepayment required.

Fredericksburg City

15th Circuit Court 815 Princess Anne St, PO Box 359, Fredericksburg, VA 22404-0359; phone: 540-372-1066; hours 8AM-4PM (EST). *Felony, Civil Actions Over $15,000, Probate.*
www.courts.state.va.us/courts/circuit.html
Civil Records: Access: Online, in person. Visitors must perform in person searches themselves. Court makes copy: $.50 per page. Required to search: name, years to search. Civil cases indexed by defendant, plaintiff; on index books from 1765; computerized records since 1987. Online access free at www.courts.state.va.us/. For information about the statewide online systems, see the state introduction.
Criminal Records: Access: Online, in person. Visitors must perform in person searches themselves. Court makes copy: $.50 per page. Required to search: name, years to search, DOB; also helpful: SSN. Criminal records on index books from 1765; computerized records since 1987. Online access to criminal records is the same as civil.
General Information: Public terminal goes back to 1987. No juvenile, probate tax returns, sealed or adoption records released. Will not fax documents. Certification fee: $2.00. Payee: Clerk of Circuit Court. Personal checks accepted. Prepayment required.

15th General District Court PO Box 180, Fredericksburg, VA 22404; phone: 540-372-1044; criminal phone: 540-372-1043; civil phone: 540-372-1044; criminal fax: 540-372-1228; civil fax: 540-370-1729; hours 8AM-4PM (EST). *Misdemeanor, Civil Actions Under $15,000, Eviction, Small Claims.*
Civil Records: Access: Mail, online, in person. Both court and visitors may perform in person searches. No search fee. Court makes copy: $.50 per page. Required to search: name, years to search. Civil cases indexed by defendant, plaintiff; on computer the past 10 years, prior on index books. Search free at http://208.210.219.132/vadistrict/select.jsp. Also search via LOPAS; call 804-786-5511 to apply. Mail turnaround time 1-10 days.
Criminal Records: Access: Mail, online, in person. Both court and visitors may perform in person searches. No search fee. Court makes copy: $.50 per page. Required to search: name, years to search, DOB, SSN. Criminal records on computer the past 10 years, prior on index books. Online access to criminal records is the same as civil. Mail turnaround time 1-10 days.
General Information: Public use terminal available. No sealed records released. Certification fee: $2.00. Payee: Fredericksburg District Court. Personal checks accepted. Prepayment and SASE required.

Galax City

Circuit Court
www.courts.state.va.us/courts/circuit.html
Note: See Carroll County for Hillsville area and Grayson County for Independence area.

27th General District Court 353 N Main St, PO Box 214, Galax, VA 24333-0214; phone: 276-236-8731; fax: 276-236-2754; hours 8AM-4:30PM (EST). *Misdemeanor, Civil Actions Under $15,000, Eviction, Small Claims.*
Note: Circuit Court jurisdiction for this city can be in Carroll County or Grayson County depending on side of the city the offense occurred.
Civil Records: Access: Mail, fax, online, in person. Both court and visitors may perform in person searches. No search fee. Court makes copy: $.25 per page. Required to search: name, years to search. Civil cases indexed by defendant, plaintiff; on computer since 1990, prior on index books. Search free at http://208.210.219.132/vadistrict/select.jsp. Also search via LOPAS; call 804-786-5511 to apply. Mail turnaround time 1-5 days.
Criminal Records: Access: Mail, fax, online, in person. Both court and visitors may perform in person searches. No search fee. Court makes copy: $.25 per page. Required to search: name, years to search. Criminal records on computer since 1990, prior on index books. Online access to criminal records is the same as civil. Mail turnaround time 1-5 days.
General Information: Public use terminal available. No juvenile, sealed records released. No certification fee. Payee: Clerk of District Court Galax District. Personal checks or Visa, MC accepted. Prepayment required.

Giles County

27th Circuit Court 501 Wenonah Ave, PO Box 502, Pearisburg, VA 24134; phone: 540-921-1722; fax: 540-921-3825; hours 9AM-5PM (EST). *Felony, Civil Actions Over $15,000, Probate.*
www.courts.state.va.us/courts/circuit.html
Civil Records: Access: Mail, in person. Visitors must perform in person searches themselves. No search fee. Court makes copy: $.50 per page. Self serve copy fee: $.25 per page. Required to search: name, years to search. Civil cases indexed by defendant, plaintiff. Civil records (financial) on computer since 1994.
Criminal Records: Access: In person only. Visitors must perform in person searches themselves. Court makes copy: $.50 per page. Self serve copy fee: $.25 per page. Required to search: name, years to search, DOB; SSN helpful. Criminal records (financial) on computer since 1994. Mail turnaround time 1-2 days.
General Information: No juvenile, sealed records released. Certification fee: $3.00. Payee: Clerk of Circuit Court. Personal checks accepted. Prepayment required.

27th General District Court 120 N Main St, #1, Pearisburg, VA 24134; phone: 540-921-3533; fax: 540-921-3752; hours 8:30AM-4:30PM (EST). *Misdemeanor, Civil Actions Under $15,000, Eviction, Small Claims.*
www.courts.state.va.us/courts/combined/Giles/home.html
Civil Records: Access: Fax, mail, online, in person. Both court and visitors may perform in person searches. No search fee. Court makes copy: $1.00 for first page, $.50 each add'l. Required to search: name, years to search. Civil cases indexed by defendant, plaintiff; on computer since 1990. Search free at http://208.210.219.132/vadistrict/select.jsp. Also search via LOPAS; call 804-786-5511 to apply. Mail turnaround time 3-7 days.
Criminal Records: Access: Fax, mail, online, in person. Both court and visitors may perform in person searches. No search fee. Court makes copy: $1.00 for first page, $.50 each add'l. Required to search: name, years to search; also helpful: SSN.

Criminal records on computer since 1990. Online access to criminal records is the same as civil. Mail turnaround time 3-7 days.

General Information: Public use terminal available. No juvenile, sealed records released. Fee to fax documents is $1.00 per page. No certification fee. Payee: General District Court. Personal checks or Visa, MC accepted.

Gloucester County

9th Circuit Court PO Box 2118, Gloucester, VA 23061-0570; phone: 804-693-2502; fax: 804-693-2186; hours 8AM-4:30PM (EST). *Felony, Civil Actions Over $15,000, Probate.*

www.co.gloucester.va.us

Civil Records: Access: Fax, mail, online, in person. Both court and visitors may perform in person searches. No search fee. Court makes copy: $.50 per page. Required to search: name, years to search. Civil cases indexed by defendant, plaintiff; on index books from 1862; on computer since 1990. Online access free at http://208.210.219.132/vacircuit/select.jsp. For information about the statewide online systems, see the state introduction.

Criminal Records: Access: Online, in person. Visitors must perform in person searches themselves. Court makes copy: $.50 per page. Required to search: name, years to search, DOB. Criminal records on index books from 1862; on computer since 1990. Online access to criminal records is the same as civil.

General Information: Public terminal goes back to 1990. No juvenile, sealed or adoption records released. Certification fee: $2.00; $2.50 if judge's signature required. Payee: Clerk of Circuit Court. Personal checks accepted. Prepayment required. SASE requested.

9th General District Court PO Box 873, Gloucester, VA 23061; phone: 804-693-4860; fax: 804-693-6669; hours 8:30AM-4:30PM (EST). *Misdemeanor, Civil Actions Under $15,000, Eviction, Small Claims.*

Civil Records: Access: Fax, mail, online, in person. Both court and visitors may perform in person searches. No search fee. Court makes copy: $.50 per page. Required to search: name, years to search. Civil cases indexed by defendant, plaintiff; on index books from 1985; computerized back to 1992. Search free at http://208.210.219.132/vadistrict/select.jsp. Also search via LOPAS; call 804-786-5511 to apply. Mail turnaround time 1 week.

Criminal Records: Access: Fax, mail, online, in person. Both court and visitors may perform in person searches. No search fee. Court makes copy: $.50 per page. Required to search: name, years to search; also helpful: DOB, SSN. Criminal records on index books for 10 years; computerized back to 1992. Online access to criminal records is the same as civil. Mail turnaround time 1 week.

General Information: Public terminal goes back to 10 years. No juvenile, sealed records released. No fee to fax documents. No certification fee. Payee: Clerk of General District Court/Gloucester District Court. Personal checks or Visa, MC accepted. Prepayment required. SASE requested.

Goochland County

16th Circuit Court PO Box 196, Goochland, VA 23063; phone: 804-556-5353; fax: 804-556-4962; hours 8:30AM-4:15 PM (EST). *Felony, Civil Actions Over $15,000, Probate.*

www.courts.state.va.us/courts/circuit.html

Civil Records: Access: Online, in person. Visitors must perform in person searches themselves. Court makes copy: $.50 per page. Required to search: name, years to search. Civil cases indexed by defendant, plaintiff; on index books from 1850. Remote online access to court case indexes is via LOPAS; call 804-786-5511 to apply.

Criminal Records: Access: Online, in person. Visitors must perform in person searches themselves. Court makes copy: $.50 per page.

Required to search: name, years to search. Criminal records on index books from 1850. Remote online access to court case indexes is via LOPAS; call 804-786-5511 to apply. Also, may be free online at http://208.210.219.132/vacircuit/select.jsp?court=.

General Information: Public terminal has only civil records back to 2001. No juvenile, sealed or adoption records released. Certification fee: $1.00. Payee: Clerk of Circuit Court. Personal checks accepted. Prepayment required.

General District Court PO Box 47, Goochland, VA 23063; phone: 804-556-5309; hours 8:30AM-4:30PM (EST). *Misdemeanor, Civil Actions Under $15,000, Eviction, Small Claims.*

Civil Records: Access: Online, in person. Visitors must perform in person searches themselves. No copy fee. Required to search: name, years to search. Civil cases indexed by defendant, plaintiff; on index books and computer back to 1989. Search free at http://208.210.219.132/vadistrict/select.jsp. Also search via LOPAS; call 804-786-5511 to apply.

Criminal Records: Access: Online, in person. Visitors must perform in person searches themselves. No copy fee. Required to search: name, years to search, DOB. Criminal records on index books and computer back to 1989. Online access to criminal records is the same as civil.

General Information: Public terminal goes back to 1995. No juvenile records released. No certification fee. Prepayment required.

Grayson County

27th Circuit Court PO Box 130, Independence, VA 24348; phone: 276-773-2231; criminal fax: 276-773-3338; same fax for civil/probate; hours 8AM-5PM (EST). *Felony, Civil Actions Over $15,000, Probate.*

www.courts.state.va.us/courts/circuit.html

Note: Probate is a separate index at this address.

Civil Records: Access: Mail, online, in person. Both court and visitors may perform in person searches. No search fee. Court makes copy: $.50 per page; same fee for self serve. Required to search: name, years to search. Civil cases indexed by defendant, plaintiff; on index books since 1793. Select and search Circuit Courts online at http://208.210.219.132/vadistrict/select.jsp. For information about the statewide online systems, see the state introduction. Mail turnaround time 2-3 days.

Criminal Records: Access: Mail, online, in person. Visitors must perform in person searches themselves. No search fee. Court makes copy: $.50 per page; same fee for self serve. Required to search: name, years to search, DOB. Criminal records on index books since 1793. Online access to criminal records is the same as civil. Mail turnaround time 2-3 days.

General Information: Public use terminal available. No juvenile, sealed or adoption records released. Will fax documents for $.50 per page. Certification fee: $2.00 per instrument. Payee: Clerk of Circuit Court. Personal checks accepted. Prepayment required. SASE requested.

27th General District Court PO Box 280, Independence, VA 24348; phone: 276-773-2011; fax: 276-773-3174; hours 8AM-4:30PM (EST). *Misdemeanor, Civil Actions Under $15,000, Eviction, Small Claims.*

Civil Records: Access: Mail, online, in person. Both court and visitors may perform in person searches. No search fee. No copy fee. Required to search: name, years to search. Civil cases indexed by defendant. Civil records on index books from 1800s, on computer from 1989. Search free at http://208.210.219.132/vadistrict/select.jsp. Also search via LOPAS; call 804-786-5511 to apply. Mail turnaround time 1 week.

Criminal Records: Access: Mail, online, in person. Both court and visitors may perform in person searches. No search fee. No copy fee. Required to

search: name, years to search; also helpful: DOB, SSN. Criminal records on index books from 1800s, on computer from 1989. Online access to criminal records is the same as civil. Mail turnaround time 1 week.

General Information: Public terminal goes back to 1989. No juvenile, sealed records released. Will fax documents to local or toll free line. No certification fee.

Greene County

16th Circuit Court PO Box 386, Stanardsville, VA 22973; phone: 434-985-5208; criminal fax: 434-985-6723; same fax for civil/probate; hours 8:15AM-4:30PM (EST). *Felony, Civil Actions Over $15,000, Probate.*

www.courts.state.va.us/courts/circuit.html

Note: Probate is a separate index at this same address.

Civil Records: Access: Mail, in person, online. Both court and visitors may perform in person searches. No search fee. Court makes copy: $.50 per page; same fee for self serve. Required to search: name, years to search. Civil cases indexed by defendant, plaintiff; on index books from 1838. Remote online access to court case indexes is via LOPAS; call 804-786-5511 to apply. Mail turnaround time 7-10 days.

Criminal Records: Access: Mail, in person. Both court and visitors may perform in person searches. Search fee: $10.00 per name. Court makes copy: $.50 per page; same fee for self serve. Required to search: name, years to search. Criminal records on index books from 1838. Mail turnaround time 7-10 days.

General Information: No juvenile, sealed or adoption records released. Will not fax documents. Certification fee: $2.00 per instrument. Payee: Clerk of Circuit Court or Greene County Circuit. Personal checks accepted. Prepayment and SASE required.

16th General District Court PO Box 245, Greene County Courthouse, Stanardsville, VA 22973; phone: 434-985-5224; fax: 434-985-1448; hours 8:30AM-4PM (EST). *Misdemeanor, Civil Actions Under $15,000, Eviction, Small Claims.*

Civil Records: Access: Fax, mail, online, in person. Both court and visitors may perform in person searches. No search fee. Court makes copy: $.50 per page. Required to search: name, years to search. Civil cases indexed by defendant, plaintiff; on index books from 1838, on computer back to 10/93. Search free at http://208.210.219.132/vadistrict/select.jsp. Also search via LOPAS; call 804-786-5511 to apply.

Criminal Records: Access: In person, online. Visitors must perform in person searches themselves. Court makes copy: $.50 per page. Required to search: name, years to search, DOB; also helpful: SSN. Criminal records on computer back to 1/92, prior on cards, books. Online access to criminal records is the same as civil. Mail turnaround time 1 week.

General Information: Public terminal goes back to 1995. No juvenile, sealed records released. No fee to fax documents. No certification fee. Payee: Clerk of General District Court or Greene County Combined Court. Personal checks or Visa, MC accepted. Prepayment required.

Greensville County

6th Circuit Court PO Box 631, Emporia, VA 23847; phone: 434-348-4215; fax: 434-348-4020; hours 9AM-5PM (EST). *Felony, Civil Actions Over $15,000, Probate.*

www.courts.state.va.us/courts/circuit.html

Civil Records: Access: Online, in person. Visitors must perform in person searches themselves. Court makes copy: $.50 per page. Required to search: name, years to search. Civil cases indexed by defendant, plaintiff; on index books from 1781; on computer since 1989. Search free at http://208.210.219.132/vacircuit/select.jsp. Also search via LOPAS; call 804-786-5511 to apply.

Criminal Records: Access: Online, in person. Visitors must perform in person searches themselves. Court makes copy: $.50 per page. Required to search: name, years to search. Criminal records on index books from 1781; on computer since 1989. Online access to criminal records is the same as civil. Note: Court does not conduct criminal searches.

General Information: Public terminal goes back to 1989. No juvenile, sealed records released. Certification fee: $2.00. Payee: Clerk of Circuit Court. Business checks accepted. Prepayment required.

Greenville/Emporia Combined Court 315 S Main, Emporia, VA 23847; phone: 434-634-5460; fax: 434-634-0049; hours 8:30AM-4:30PM (EST). *Misdemeanor, Civil Actions Under $15,000, Eviction, Small Claims.*

Civil Records: Access: Online, in person. Visitors must perform in person searches themselves. Court makes copy: $.50 per page. Required to search: name, years to search. Civil cases indexed by defendant, plaintiff; on index books from 1800s; on computer back 10 years. Select and search District Courts at http://208.210.219.132/vadistrict/select.jsp. For information about the statewide online systems, see the state introduction.

Criminal Records: Access: Online, in person. Visitors must perform in person searches themselves. Court makes copy: $.50 per page. Required to search: name, years to search, DOB; also helpful: SSN. Criminal records on index books from 1800s; on computer back 10 years. Online access to criminal records is the same as civil.

General Information: Public use terminal available. No juvenile, sealed records released. No certification fee. Payee: Clerk of General District Court. Personal checks accepted.

Halifax County

10th Circuit Court PO Box 729, Halifax, VA 24558; phone: 434-476-6211; fax: 434-476-2890; hours 8:30AM-4:30PM (EST). *Felony, Civil Actions Over $15,000, Probate.*

www.courts.state.va.us/courts/circuit.html

Civil Records: Access: Online, in person. Visitors must perform in person searches themselves. Court makes copy: $.50 per page. Required to search: name, years to search. Civil cases indexed by defendant, plaintiff; on computer from 1988, on index books from 1752. Online access free at http://208.210.219.132/vacircuit/select.jsp. For information about the statewide online systems, see the state introduction.

Criminal Records: Access: Mail, online, in person. Only the court performs in person searches; visitors may not. Search fee: $5.00 per name. Court makes copy: $.50 per page. Required to search: name, years to search. Criminal records on computer from 1988, on index books from 1752. Online access free at http://208.210.219.132/vacircuit/select.jsp. For information about the statewide online systems, see the state introduction. Mail turnaround time 1-5 days.

General Information: Public use terminal available. No juvenile, sealed records released. Will fax documents for $.50 per page plus search fee per telephone call. Certification fee: $.50 per page. Payee: Circuit Court. Personal checks accepted. Prepayment and SASE required.

10th General District Court PO Box 458, Halifax County Courthouse, Halifax, VA 24558; phone: 434-476-3385; fax: 434-476-3387; hours 8:30AM-4:30PM (EST). *Misdemeanor, Civil Actions Under $15,000, Eviction, Small Claims.*

Civil Records: Access: Fax, mail, online, in person. Both court and visitors may perform in person searches. No search fee. Court makes copy: $.50 per page; same fee for self serve. Required to search: name, years to search, address. Civil cases indexed by defendant, plaintiff; on computer from 1993. Search free at http://208.210.219.132/vadistrict/select.jsp. Also search via LOPAS; call 804-786-5511 to apply. Mail turnaround time within 7 days.

Criminal Records: Access: Fax, mail, online, in person. Both court and visitors may perform in person searches. No search fee. Court makes copy: $.50 per page; same fee for self serve. Required to search: name. Criminal records on computer from 1993. Online access to criminal records is the same as civil. Mail turnaround time within 7 days.

General Information: Public use terminal available. (Available T, Th-F all day, also Wed. afternoons.) No juvenile, sealed records released. Fax fee only charged for large number of pages. No certification fee. Payee: General District Court. Personal checks accepted. Prepayment required.

Hampton City

8th Circuit Court 101 King's Way, PO Box 40, Hampton, VA 23669-0040; phone: 757-727-6105; hours 8:30AM-4PM (EST). *Felony, Civil Actions Over $15,000, Probate.*

www.courts.state.va.us/courts/circuit.html

Civil Records: Access: Phone, mail, fax, in person, online. Both court and visitors may perform in person searches. Search fee: $10.00 per name. Court makes copy: $.50 per page; same fee for self serve. Required to search: name, years to search. Civil cases indexed by defendant, plaintiff. Computerized records back to 1991, civil records on index books since 1834. Online access free at http://208.210.219.132/vacircuit/select.jsp. For information about the statewide online systems, see the state introduction. Mail turnaround time 5 to 10 days.

Criminal Records: Access: Mail, online, in person, online. Both court and visitors may perform in person searches. Search fee: $10.00 per name. Court makes copy: $.50 per page; same fee for self serve. Required to search: name, years to search. Computerized records back to 1991, criminal records on index books since1949. Online access to criminal records is the same as civil. Mail turnaround time 3 days.

General Information: Public terminal goes back to 1995. No pre-sentence, criminal correspondence, chancery, judges notes or medical records released. Will fax documents. Certification fee: $2.00. Payee: Clerk of Court. No out of state checks accepted. Prepayment and SASE required.

8th General District Court PO Box 70, Courthouse, Hampton, VA 23669-0070; criminal phone: 757-727-6260; civil phone: 757-727-6480; fax: 757-727-6035; hours 8AM-4PM (EST). *Misdemeanor, Civil Actions Under $15,000, Eviction, Small Claims.*

Civil Records: Access: Online, in person. Visitors must perform in person searches themselves. Court makes copy: $.50 each. Required to search: name, years to search. Civil cases indexed by defendant, plaintiff; on index books and computer for 10 years. Search free at http://208.210.219.132/vadistrict/select.jsp. Also search via LOPAS; call 804-786-5511 to apply. Note: Mail access limited to specific case and two names.

Criminal Records: Access: Online, in person. Visitors must perform in person searches themselves. Court makes copy: $.50 each. Required to search: name, years to search. Criminal records on index books and computer for 10 years. Online access to criminal records is the same as civil.

General Information: Public terminal goes back to 10 years. No sealed records released. Certification fee: $7.00. Payee: Hampton District Court. Personal checks accepted. Credit cards accepted. Accepted for fines only. Prepayment required.

Hanover County

15th Circuit Court 7507 Library Dr, PO Box 39, Hanover, VA 23069; phone: 804-365-6151; criminal phone: 804-365-6843; civil phone: 804-365-6143; probate phone: 804-365-6478; fax: 804-365-6278; hours 8:30AM-4:30PM (EST). *Felony, Civil Actions Over $15,000, Probate.*

www.co.hanover.va.us/circuitct/default.htm

Civil Records: Access: Online, in person. Visitors must perform in person searches themselves. Court makes copy: $.50 per page. Required to search: name, years to search; helpful- case number. Civil cases indexed by defendant, plaintiff. Civil records index in books, older records date from 1865. Remote online access to court case indexes is via LOPAS; call 804-786-5511 to apply.

Criminal Records: Access: Online, in person. Visitors must perform in person searches themselves. Court makes copy: $.50 per page. Required to search: name, years to search; helpful-case number. Criminal records index in books, older records date from 1850. Remote online access to court case indexes is via LOPAS; call 804-786-5511 to apply.

General Information: Public terminal goes back to 1990. No juvenile, sealed records released. Certification fee: $2.00 per cert. Payee: Clerk of Circuit Court. Personal checks accepted. Prepayment required.

15th General District Court PO Box 176, Hanover County Courthouse, Hanover, VA 23069; phone: 804-365-6191; civil phone: 804-365-6457; criminal fax: 804-365-6290; civil fax: 804-365-6436; hours 8AM-4PM (EST). *Misdemeanor, Civil Actions Under $15,000, Eviction, Small Claims.*

Civil Records: Access: Mail, online, in person. Visitors must perform in person searches themselves. Court makes copy: $1.00 per page for first 2 pages, $.50 each add'l page up to 10 pages; same fee for self serve. Required to search: name, years to search. Civil cases indexed by defendant, plaintiff; on computer back to 1994. Search free at http://208.210.219.132/vadistrict/select.jsp. Also search via LOPAS; call 804-786-5511 to apply. Mail turnaround time 7-10 business days.

Criminal Records: Access: Mail, online, in person. Visitors must perform in person searches themselves. Court makes copy: $1.00 per page for first 2 pages, $.50 each add'l page thereafter up to 10 pages; same fee for self serve. Required to search: name, years to search, DOB; also helpful: SSN. Criminal records on computer back 10 years. Online access to criminal records is the same as civil. Mail turnaround time 7-10 business days

General Information: Public terminal goes back to 10 years. No certification fee. Payee: Hanover General District Court. Personal checks or Visa, MC accepted.

Harrisonburg City

Circuit & District Courts

www.courts.state.va.us/courts/circuit.html

Note: See Rockingham County.

Henrico County

14th Circuit Court PO Box 27032, Richmond, VA 23273-7032; phone: 804-501-4202; criminal phone: 804-501-4758/5448; civil phone: 804-501-5422; probate phone: 804-501-4763; fax: 804-501-5214; hours 8AM-4:30PM (EST). *Felony, Civil Actions Over $15,000, Probate.*

www.co.henrico.va.us/clerk/

Civil Records: Access: Mail, online, in person. Visitors must perform in person searches themselves. Court makes copy: $.50 per page; same fee for self serve. Required to search: name, years to search. Civil cases indexed by defendant, plaintiff; on computer from 11/88, on index cards from 1850. Remote online access to court case indexes is via LOPAS; call 804-786-5511 to apply. Mail turnaround time 3-5 days.

Criminal Records: Access: Mail, online, in person. Visitors must perform in person searches themselves. Court makes copy: $.50 per page; same fee for self serve. Required to search: name, years to search. Criminal records on computer from 11/88, on index cards from 1850. Remote online access to court case indexes is via LOPAS; call 804-786-5511 to apply. Mail turnaround time 3-5 days.

General Information: Public terminal has criminal back to 1989 and civil back to 1960. No juvenile, judges notes, adoption sealed records released. Certification fee: $2.00 per document. Payee: Clerk of Circuit Court. Personal checks accepted. Prepayment and SASE required.

14th General District Court PO Box 27032, Richmond, VA 23273; criminal phone: 804-501-4723; civil phone: 804-501-4727; fax: 804-501-4141; hours 8AM-4PM (EST). *Misdemeanor, Civil Actions Under $15,000, Eviction, Small Claims.*

Civil Records: Access: Online, in person. Visitors must perform in person searches themselves. Court makes copy: $1.00 per page. Required to search: name, years to search. Civil cases indexed by defendant. Civil records on computer from 7/85. Search free at http://208.210.219.132/vadistrict/select.jsp. Also search via LOPAS; call 804-786-5511 to apply.

Criminal Records: Access: Online, in person, mail. Visitors must perform in person searches themselves. No search fee. Court makes copy: $1.00 minimum for 1st 2 pages, $.50 ea add'l. Required to search: name, years to search, DOB. Criminal records on computer from 1993. Online access to criminal records is the same as civil. Mail turnaround time 5 days.

General Information: Public use terminal available. No juvenile, sealed records released. No certification fee. Payee: Clerk of General District Court. Personal checks accepted. VISA and MC accepted. Not accepted over the phone. Prepayment and SASE required.

Henry County

21st Circuit Court 3160 Kings Mountain Rd, #B, Martinsville, VA 24112; phone: 276-634-4880 or 276-634-4884 (Law); criminal phone: 276-634-4889 or 276-634-4885; civil phone: 276-634-4886 (Chancery); probate phone: 276-634-4883; hours 9AM-5PM (EST). *Felony, Civil Actions Over $15,000, Probate.*
www.courts.state.va.us

Civil Records: Access: Online, in person. Visitors must perform in person searches themselves. Court makes copy: $.50 per page; same fee for self serve. Required to search: name, years to search. Civil cases indexed by defendant, plaintiff; on computer since 4/92, index back to 1777. Online access free at http://208.210.219.132/vacircuit/select.jsp. For information about the statewide online systems, see the state introduction.

Criminal Records: Access: Online, in person. Visitors must perform in person searches themselves. Court makes copy: $.50 per page; same fee for self serve. Required to search: name, years to search, DOB; also helpful: SSN. Criminal records computerized since 7/92, index back to 1777. Online access to criminal records is the same as civil.

General Information: Public terminal goes back to 1992. No juvenile, expungments, sealed or adoption records released. Certification fee: $2.00. Payee: Clerk of Circuit Court. Personal checks accepted. Prepayment required.

21st General District Court 3160 King's Mountain Rd #A, Martinsville, VA 24112; phone: 276-634-4815; fax: 276-634-4825; hours 9AM-5PM (EST). *Misdemeanor, Civil Actions Under $15,000, Eviction, Small Claims.*
www.courts.state.va.us

Civil Records: Access: Online, in person. Visitors must perform in person searches themselves. Court makes copy: $.50 per page. Required to search: name, years to search; also helpful: address. Civil cases indexed by defendant, plaintiff; on computer from 1995. Search free at http://208.210.219.132/vadistrict/select.jsp. Also search via LOPAS; call 804-786-5511 to apply.

Criminal Records: Access: Online, in person. Visitors must perform in person searches themselves. Court makes copy: $.50 per page. Required to search: name, years to search, DOB; also

helpful: address, SSN. Criminal records on computer from 1995. Online access to criminal records is the same as civil.

General Information: Public terminal goes back to 1995. No sealed records released. Will not fax documents. No certification fee. Payee: Henry County General District Court. Visa, MC cards accepted. Prepayment required.

Highland County

25th Circuit Court PO Box 190, Monterey, VA 24465; phone: 540-468-2447; fax: 540-468-3447; hours 8:45AM-4:30PM (EST). *Felony, Civil Actions Over $15,000, Probate.*
www.courts.state.va.us/courts/circuit.html

Civil Records: Access: Mail, online, in person. Both court and visitors may perform in person searches. No search fee. Court makes copy: $.50 per page; same fee for self serve. Required to search: name, years to search. Civil cases indexed by defendant, plaintiff; on index books from 1868. Remote online access to court case indexes is via LOPAS; call 804-786-5511 to apply. Mail turnaround time up to 1 week.

Criminal Records: Access: Mail, online, in person. Both court and visitors may perform in person searches. No search fee. Court makes copy: $.50 per page; same fee for self serve. Required to search: name, years to search. Criminal records on index books from 1868. Online access to criminal records is the same as civil. Mail turnaround time up to 1 week.

General Information: No juvenile, sealed records released. Will fax documents for $2.00 plus $.50 per page. Certification fee: $2.00. Payee: Clerk of Circuit Court. Personal checks accepted. Prepayment required.

25th General District Court Highland County Courthouse, PO Box 88, Monterey, VA 24465; phone: 540-468-2445; fax: 540-468-3449; hours 8:30AM-5:00PM (EST). *Misdemeanor, Civil Actions Under $15,000, Eviction, Small Claims.*

Civil Records: Access: Fax, mail, online, in person. Both court and visitors may perform in person searches. No search fee. Court makes copy: $1.00 for first 2 pages. $.50 each add'l page. Required to search: name, years to search. Civil cases indexed by defendant, plaintiff; on index books from 1991; computerized back to 1993. Search free at http://208.210.219.132/vadistrict/select.jsp. Also search via LOPAS; call 804-786-5511 to apply. Mail turnaround time 2-3 days.

Criminal Records: Access: Fax, mail, online, in person. Both court and visitors may perform in person searches. No search fee. Court makes copy: $1.00 for first 2 pages; $.50 per page add'l. Required to search: name, years to search; also helpful: DOB, SSN, signed release. Criminal records on index books from 1991; computerized back to 1993. Online access to criminal records is the same as civil. Mail turnaround time 2-3 days.

General Information: Public terminal goes back to 1993. No juvenile, sealed records released. Will fax documents. No certification fee. Payee: General District Court. Personal checks accepted. Prepayment required. SASE requested.

Hopewell City

6th Circuit Court 100 E Broadway, PO Box 310, 2nd Fl, Rm 251, Hopewell, VA 23860; phone: 804-541-2239; fax: 804-541-2438; hours 8:30AM-4PM (EST). *Felony, Civil Actions Over $15,000, Probate.*
www.courts.state.va.us/courts/circuit.html

Civil Records: Access: Mail, online, in person. Visitors must perform in person searches themselves. No search fee. Court makes copy: $.50 per page; same fee for self serve. Required to search: name, years to search. Civil cases indexed by defendant, plaintiff; on index books since 1916. Search free at http://208.210.219.132/vacircuit/select.jsp. Also search via LOPAS; call 804-786-5511 to apply.

Criminal Records: Access: Online, in person. Visitors must perform in person searches themselves. Court makes copy: $.50 per page; same fee for self serve. Required to search: name, years to search, DOB. Criminal records on index books since 1916. Online access to criminal records is the same as civil.

General Information: Public terminal goes back to 1990. No juvenile, sealed records released. Certification fee: $2.00. Payee: Clerk of Circuit Court. Personal checks not accepted. Prepayment and SASE required.

Hopewell District Court 100 E Broadway, Hopewell, VA 23860; phone: 804-541-2257; fax: 804-541-2364; hours 8:30AM-4:30PM (EST). *Misdemeanor, Civil Actions Under $15,000, Eviction, Small Claims.*

Civil Records: Access: Mail, online, in person. Both court and visitors may perform in person searches. No search fee. Court makes copy: $1.00 per page first 2 pages, then $.50 each. Required to search: name, years to search. Civil cases indexed by defendant, plaintiff; on computer from 1988, older case records archived. Search free at http://208.210.219.132/vadistrict/select.jsp. Also search via LOPAS; call 804-786-5511 to apply. Mail turnaround time 3-5 days.

Criminal Records: Access: Mail, online, in person. Both court and visitors may perform in person searches. No search fee. Court makes copy: $1.00 per page first 2 pages, then $.50 each. Required to search: name, years to search, DOB; also helpful: SSN. Criminal records on computer from 1988, older case records are archived. Online access to criminal records is the same as civil. Mail turnaround time 3-5 days.

General Information: Public use terminal available. No juvenile, sealed or domestic relations records released. No certification fee. Payee: Clerk of General District Court. Personal checks or Visa, MC accepted. Prepayment required. SASE requested.

Isle of Wight County

5th Circuit Court 17122 Monument Circle, PO Box 110, Isle of Wight, VA 23397; phone: 757-365-6233; hours 9AM-5PM (EST). *Felony, Civil Actions Over $15,000, Probate.*
www.courts.state.va.us/courts/circuit.html
Note: The Clerk can be reached at 757-365-6233.

Civil Records: Access: Online, in person. Visitors must perform in person searches themselves. Court makes copy: $.50 per page. Required to search: name, years to search. Civil cases indexed by defendant, plaintiff; on index books from 1800s; on computer back to 1988. Online access free at http://208.210.219.132/vacircuit/select.jsp. For information about the statewide online systems, see the state introduction.

Criminal Records: Access: Online, in person. Visitors must perform in person searches themselves. Court makes copy: $.50 per page. Required to search: name, years to search, DOB. Criminal records on index books from 1800s; on computer back to 1988. Online access to criminal records is the same as civil.

General Information: Public terminal goes back to 1988. No juvenile, sealed records released. Certification fee: $2.00. Payee: Clerk of Circuit Court. Personal checks accepted. Prepayment required.

5th General District Court Isle of Wight Courthouse, PO Box 122, Isle of Wight, VA 23397; phone: 757-365-6243; fax: 757-365-6246; hours 8AM-4PM (EST). *Misdemeanor, Civil Actions Under $15,000, Eviction, Small Claims.*
Note: The Clerk can be reached at 757-365-6244.

Civil Records: Access: Online, in person. Visitors must perform in person searches themselves. Court makes copy: $1.00 per page. Required to search: name, years to search. Civil cases indexed by defendant, plaintiff; on index books back to 1800s; on computer since 1994. Search free at

http://208.210.219.132/vadistrict/select.jsp.   Also search via LOPAS; call 804-786-5511 to apply.
Criminal Records: Access: Online, in person. Visitors must perform in person searches themselves. Court makes copy: $1.00 per page. Required to search: name, years to search. Criminal records on index books back to 1800s; on computer since 1994. Online access to criminal records is the same as civil.
General Information: Public terminal goes back to 10 years. Juvenile, sealed, adoption records not released. Certification fee: $1.00. Payee: Clerk of GDC. Personal checks or Visa, MC accepted. Prepayment required.

James City

Williamsburg-James City Circuit Court
5201 Monticello Ave #6, Williamsburg, VA 23188-8218; phone: 757-564-2242; fax: 757-564-2329; hours 8:30AM-4:30PM (EST). *Felony, Civil Actions Over $15,000, Probate.*
www.courts.state.va.us/courts/circuit.html
Civil Records: Access: Mail, online, in person. Both court and visitors may perform in person searches. Search fee: $10.00 per name. Court makes copy: $.50 per page. Required to search: name, years. Civil cases indexed by defendant, plaintiff; on computer since 1987, archived from 1970, prior in books. Access free at http://208.210.219.132/vacircuit/select.jsp. For information about the statewide online systems, see the state introduction. Mail turnaround time 1-2 days.
Criminal Records: Access: Mail, online, in person. Both court and visitors may perform in person searches. Search fee: $10.00 per name. Court makes copy: $.50 per page. Required to search: name, years to search, DOB; also helpful: SSN. Criminal records on computer since 1987, archived from 1970, prior on index books. Online access to criminal records is the same as civil. Mail turnaround time 1-2 days.
General Information: Public terminal goes back to 1987. No juvenile, sealed, adoption records released. Fee to fax documents is $1.00 per page. Certification fee: $2.00. Payee: Clerk of Circuit Court. Personal checks not accepted. Prepayment and SASE required.

9th General District Court James City County Courthouse, 5201 Monticello Ave, #2, Williamsburg, VA 23188-8218; phone: 757-564-2400; fax: 757-564-2410; hours 7:30AM-4PM (EST). *Misdemeanor, Civil Actions Under $15,000, Eviction, Small Claims.*
Civil Records: Access: Fax, mail, in person, online. Both court and visitors may perform in person searches. No search fee. Court makes copy: charge if extensive searching or copies needed. Required to search: name, years to search. Civil cases indexed by defendant, plaintiff; on index books from 1994, on computer from 1994. Search free at http://208.210.219.132/vadistrict/select.jsp.   Also search via LOPAS; call 804-786-5511 to apply. Mail turnaround time 10 days.
Criminal Records: Access: Fax, mail, in person, online. Both court and visitors may perform in person searches. No search fee. Court makes copy: will charge if extensive searching or copies needed. Required to search: name, years to search, DOB; also helpful: SSN. Criminal records on index books from 1994, on computer from 1994. Online access to criminal records is the same as civil. Mail turnaround time 10 days.
General Information: Public terminal goes back to 1994. No juvenile, sealed records released. No certification fee. Payee: General District Court. Personal checks or Visa, MC accepted. Prepayment required. SASE requested.

King and Queen County

9th Circuit Court PO Box 67, 234 Allen's Circle, King & Queen Court House, VA 23085; phone: 804-785-5984; fax: 804-785-5698; hours 9AM-5PM (EST). *Felony, Civil Actions Over $15,000, Probate.*
www.courts.state.va.us/courts/circuit.html

Civil Records: Access: Mail, in person, online. Visitors must perform in person searches themselves. Court makes copy: $.50 per page. Required to search: name, years to search. Civil cases indexed by plaintiff. Civil records archived from 1864, computerized since 1995. Remote online access to court case indexes is via LOPAS, call 804-786-5511 to apply.
Criminal Records: Access: Online, in person. Visitors must perform in person searches themselves. Court makes copy: $.50 per page. Required to search: name, years to search. Criminal records archived from 1864, computerized since 1995. Remote online access to court case indexes is via LOPAS, call 804-786-5511 to apply.
General Information: Public terminal goes back to 1995. No juvenile, sealed or adoption records released. Will fax documents for $1.00 per page. Certification fee: $2.00. Payee: Clerk of Circuit Court. Personal checks accepted. Prepayment required.

King & Queen General District Court PO Box 86, King & Queen Courthouse, VA 23085-0086; phone: 804-785-5982; fax: 804-785-5694; hours 8:30AM-4:30PM (EST). *Misdemeanor, Civil Actions Under $15,000, Eviction.*
www.kingandqueenco.net/html/Govt/gendist.html
Note: The General District Court also holds preliminary hearings in felony cases.
Civil Records: Access: Fax, mail, online, in person. Both court and visitors may perform in person searches. No search fee. Court makes copy: $1.00 for first page, $.50 each add'l. Required to search: name, years to search. Civil cases indexed by defendant, plaintiff; on computer back to 1991. Search free at http://208.210.219.132/vadistrict/select.jsp.   Also search via LOPAS; call 804-786-5511 to apply. Mail turnaround time 1-5 days.
Criminal Records: Access: Fax, mail, online, in person. Both court and visitors may perform in person searches. No search fee. Court makes copy: $1.00 for first page, $.50 each add'l. Required to search: name, years to search, DOB; also helpful: SSN, signed release. Criminal records on computer back to 1991. Online access to criminal records is the same as civil. Mail turnaround time 1-5 days.
General Information: Public terminal goes back to 1991. No fee to fax documents. No certification fee. Payee: General District Court. Personal checks accepted. Prepayment required.

King George County

15th Circuit Court 9483 Kings Highway, #3, King George, VA 22485; phone: 540-775-3322; hours 8:30AM-4:30PM (EST). *Felony, Civil Actions Over $15,000, Probate.*
www.courts.state.va.us/courts/circuit.html
Civil Records: Access: Mail, in person, online. Both court and visitors may perform in person searches. Search fee: $10.00 per name. Court makes copy: $.50 per page. Required to search: name, years to search. Civil cases indexed by defendant, plaintiff; on index books from 1800s; computerized records since 1990. Online access free at http://208.210.219.132/vacircuit/select.jsp.   For information about the statewide online systems, see the state introduction. Mail turnaround time 30 days.
Criminal Records: Access: Mail, in person, online. Both court and visitors may perform in person searches. Search fee: $10.00 per name. Court makes copy: $.50 per page. Required to search: name, years to search. Criminal records on index books from 1800s; computerized records since 1990. Online access is the same as civil. Mail turnaround time 30 days.
General Information: Public terminal goes back to 1990. No sealed records released. Certification fee: $2.00. Payee: Clerk of Circuit court. Personal checks accepted. Prepayment and SASE required.

15th Judicial District King George Combined Court PO Box 279, County Courthouse, King George, VA 22485; phone: 540-775-3573; hours 8AM-4:00PM (EST). *Misdemeanor, Civil Actions Under $15,000, Eviction, Small Claims.*
Civil Records: Access: Mail, in person, online. Both court and visitors may perform in person searches. No search fee. Court makes copy: $1.00 per page for the 1st two pages, $.50 each add'l page. Required to search: name, years to search. Civil cases indexed by defendant, plaintiff; on index books from early 1900s; computerized records since 1992. Online access is at http://208.210.219.132/vadistrict/select.jsp.   Mail turnaround time 1-5 days.
Criminal Records: Access: Mail, in person, online. Both court and visitors may perform in person searches. No search fee. Court makes copy: $1.00 per page 1st two pages, $.50 each add'l. Required to search: name, years to search, DOB; also helpful: SSN. Criminal records on index books from early 1900s; computerized records since 1992. Online access is at http://208.210.219.132/vadistrict/select.jsp.   Mail turnaround time 1-5 days.
General Information: Public terminal goes back to 1992. No juvenile, sealed records released. Certification fee: $2.00. Payee: Clerk of General District Court. Personal checks or Visa, MC accepted. Prepayment and SASE required.

King William County

9th Circuit Court 351 Courthouse Ln, PO Box 216, King William, VA 23086; phone: 804-769-4936; criminal phone: 804-769-4938; civil phone: 804-769-4936; probate phone: 804-769-4936; criminal fax: 804-769-4991; same fax for civil/probate; hours 8:30AM-4:30PM (EST). *Felony, Civil Actions Over $15,000, Probate.*
www.courts.state.va.us/courts/circuit.html
Civil Records: Access: Mail, in person, online. Both court and visitors may perform in person searches. No search fee. Court makes copy: $.50 per page; same fee for self serve. Required to search: name, years to search. Civil cases indexed by defendant, plaintiff; on index books from 1800s. Search free at http://208.210.219.132/vacircuit/select.jsp.   Also search via LOPAS; call 804-786-5511 to apply. Mail turnaround time 1 week.
Criminal Records: Access: Mail, in person, online. Both court and visitors may perform in person searches. No search fee. Court makes copy: $.50 per page; same fee for self serve. Required to search: name, years to search, DOB; also helpful: SSN. Criminal records on index books from 1800s, computerized records from 1999. Online access to criminal records is the same as civil. Mail turnaround time 1 week.
General Information: Public terminal goes back to 1999. No juvenile, sealed records released. Will fax documents to local or toll free line. Certification fee: $2.00 per instrument. Payee: Clerk of Circuit Court. Personal checks accepted. Prepayment and SASE required.

King William General District Court PO Box 5, 351 Courthouse Lane, King William, VA 23086; phone: 804-769-4948; fax: 804-769-4971; hours 8:30AM-4:30PM (EST). *Misdemeanor, Civil Actions Under $15,000, Eviction, Small Claims.*
Civil Records: Access: Fax, mail, online, in person. Both court and visitors may perform in person searches. No search fee. Court makes copy: $1.00 for first page, $.50 each add'l; same fee for self serve. Required to search: name, years to search. Civil cases indexed by defendant, plaintiff; on computer since 1992. Search free at http://208.210.219.132/vadistrict/select.jsp.   Also search via LOPAS; call 804-786-5511 to apply. Mail turnaround time 1-5 days.
Criminal Records: Access: Fax, mail, online, in person. Both court and visitors may perform in person searches. No search fee. Court makes copy:

$1.00 for first page, $.50 each add'l; same fee for self serve. Required to search: name, years to search, DOB; also helpful: signed release, SSN. Criminal records on computer back to 1992. Online access to criminal records is the same as civil. Mail turnaround time 1-5 days.

General Information: Public terminal goes back to 1992. No juvenile, sealed records released. No fee to fax documents. No certification fee. Payee: General District Court. Personal checks accepted. Prepayment required. SASE requested.

Lancaster County

15th Circuit Court Courthouse Bldg, PO Box 99, Lancaster, VA 22503; phone: 804-462-5611; fax: 804-462-9978; hours 8:30AM-4:30PM (EST). *Felony, Civil Actions Over $15,000, Probate.*
www.courts.state.va.us/courts/circuit.html

Civil Records: Access: Mail, online, in person. Both court and visitors may perform in person searches. No search fee. Court makes copy: $.50 per page. Required to search: name, years to search. Civil cases indexed by defendant, plaintiff; on index books from 1845. Search free at http://208.210.219.132/vacircuit/select.jsp. Also search via LOPAS; call 804-786-5511 to apply. Mail turnaround time same day.

Criminal Records: Access: Mail, online, in person. Both court and visitors may perform in person searches. No search fee. Court makes copy: $.50 per page. Required to search: name, years to search. Criminal records on index books from 1845. Online access to criminal records is the same as civil. Mail turnaround time same day.

General Information: Public use terminal available. No juvenile, sealed records released. Certification fee: $2.00. Payee: Clerk of Circuit Court. Personal checks accepted. Out of state checks not accepted. Prepayment required.

15th General District Court PO 129, Lancaster, VA 22503; phone: 804-462-0012; hours 8:AM-Noon; 1-4:30PM (EST). *Misdemeanor, Civil Actions Under $15,000, Eviction, Small Claims.*

Civil Records: Access: Mail, online, in person. Both court and visitors may perform in person searches. No search fee. Court makes copy: $1.00 for 1st page; $.50 each add'l; same fee for self serve. Required to search: name, years to search. Civil cases indexed by defendant. Civil records on computer from 11/93. Hard copies kept 10 years. Search free at http://208.210.219.132/vadistrict/select.jsp. Also search via LOPAS; call 804-786-5511 to apply. Mail turnaround time 1-2 days.

Criminal Records: Access: Mail, online, in person. Both court and visitors may perform in person searches. No search fee. Court makes copy: $1.00 1st page; $.50 each add'l; same fee for self serve. Required to search: name, years to search, DOB; also helpful: SSN. Criminal records on computer from 11/93. Hard copies kept 10 years. Online access to criminal records is the same as civil. Mail turnaround time 1-2 days.

General Information: Public terminal goes back to 11/93. No sealed records released. No certification fee. Payee: Clerk of General District Court. Personal checks accepted. Prepayment required. SASE helpful.

Lee County

30th Circuit Court PO Box 326, Jonesville, VA 24263; phone: 276-346-7763; fax: 276-346-3440; hours 8:30AM-5PM M-F; 9AM-N Sat (EST). *Felony, Civil Actions Over $15,000, Probate.*
www.courts.state.va.us/courts/circuit.html

Civil Records: Access: Phone, fax, mail, online, in person. Both court and visitors may perform in person searches. No search fee. Court makes copy: $.50 per page; same fee for self serve. Required to search: name, years to search. Civil cases indexed by defendant, plaintiff; on index books from 1800s. Select and search Circuit Courts online at http://208.210.219.132/vacircuit/select.jsp. For information about the statewide online systems,

see the state introduction. Phone & fax access limited to short searches. Mail turnaround time 1-3 days.

Criminal Records: Access: Phone, fax, mail, online, in person. Both court and visitors may perform in person searches. No search fee. Court makes copy: $.50 per page; same fee for self serve. Required to search: name, years to search, DOB; also helpful: SSN. Criminal records on index books from 1800s. Online access to criminal records is the same as civil. Mail turnaround time 1-3 days.

General Information: Public terminal goes back to 1988. No juvenile, sealed records released. Will fax documents to local or toll free line. Certification fee: $2.00. Payee: Clerk of Circuit Court. Personal checks accepted. Prepayment required.

30th General District Court Lee County Courthouse, PO Box 306, Jonesville, VA 24263; phone: 276-346-7729; fax: 276-346-7701; hours 8AM-4:30PM (EST). *Misdemeanor, Civil Actions Under $15,000, Eviction, Small Claims.*

Civil Records: Access: Mail, online, in person. Both court and visitors may perform in person searches. No search fee. Court makes copy: $1.00 for first page, $.50 each add'l. Required to search: name, years to search. Civil cases indexed by defendant, plaintiff; on index books from 1800s, on computer from 11/7/90. Search free at http://208.210.219.132/vadistrict/select.jsp. Also search via LOPAS; call 804-786-5511 to apply. Mail turnaround time 1-2 days.

Criminal Records: Access: Mail, online, in person, fax. Both court and visitors may perform in person searches. No search fee. Court makes copy: $1.00 for first page, $.50 each add'l. Required to search: name, years to search. Criminal records on index books from 1800s, on computer from 11/7/90. Online access to criminal records is the same as civil. Mail turnaround time 1-2 days.

General Information: Public terminal goes back to 1990. No juvenile, sealed records released. No certification fee. Payee: Clerk of General District Court. Personal checks accepted. Prepayment required. SASE helpful.

Lexington City County

Circuit & District Courts
www.courts.state.va.us/courts/circuit.html
Note: See Rockbridge County

Loudoun County

20th Circuit Court 18 E Market St, Leesburg, VA 20178; phone: 703-777-0270; probate phone: 703-777-0272; fax: 703-777-0530; probate fax: 703-737-8096; hours 8:30AM-4:30PM (EST). *Felony, Civil Actions Over $15,000, Probate.*
www.loudoun.gov/clerk/

Civil Records: Access: Phone, mail, online, in person. Both court and visitors may perform in person searches. No search fee. Court makes copy: $.50 per page; same fee for self serve. Required to search: name, years to search. Civil cases indexed by defendant, plaintiff; on computer since 1995; prior on index books from 1700s. Remote online access to court case indexes is via LOPAS; call 804-786-5511 to apply. Also, docket lists are free at http://inetdocs.loudoun.gov/clerk/docs/dockets_/index.htm. Note: Phone access limited to simple requests. Mail access for deeds and wills only.

Criminal Records: Access: Online, in person. Both court and visitors may perform in person searches. Court makes copy: $.50 per page; same fee for self serve. Required to search: name, years to search, DOB; also helpful: SSN. Criminal records on computer since 1995; prior on index books from 1700s. Remote online access to court case indexes is via LOPAS; call 804-786-5511 to apply. Also, docket lists are online free at http://inetdocs.loudoun.gov/clerk/docs/dockets_/index.htm.

General Information: Public terminal goes back to 1987. No juvenile, sealed or adoption records

released. Will not fax documents. Certification fee: $2.00. Payee: Clerk of Circuit Court. Business checks accepted. Personal checks accepted if in state. Prepayment required.

20th General District Court 18 E Market St, Leesburg, VA 20176; phone: 703-777-0312; fax: 703-777-0311; hours 8AM-4PM (EST). *Misdemeanor, Civil Actions Under $15,000, Eviction.*

Civil Records: Access: Mail, fax, online, in person. Both court and visitors may perform in person searches. No search fee. Court makes copy: $.50 per page. Required to search: name, years to search. Civil cases indexed by defendant, plaintiff; on computer back 10 years. Search free at http://208.210.219.132/vadistrict/select.jsp. Also search via LOPAS; call 804-786-5511 to apply. Mail turnaround time 5 days.

Criminal Records: Access: Mail, fax, online, in person. Both court and visitors may perform in person searches. No search fee. Court makes copy: $.50 per page. Required to search: name, years to search. Criminal records on computer back 10 years. Online access to criminal records is the same as civil. Mail turnaround time 5 days.

General Information: Public terminal goes back to 10 years. Certification fee: $.50. Payee: General District Court. Personal checks or Visa, MC accepted. Prepayment and SASE required.

Louisa County

16th Circuit Court Box 37, Louisa, VA 23093; phone: 540-967-5312; fax: 540-967-2705; hours 8:30AM-5PM (EST). *Felony, Civil Actions Over $15,000, Probate.*
www.courts.state.va.us/courts/circuit.html

Civil Records: Access: Online, in person. Visitors must perform in person searches themselves. Court makes copy: $.50 per page; same fee for self serve. Required to search: name, years to search. Civil cases indexed by defendant, plaintiff. Civil records archived from 1742; on computer back to 1989. Search free at http://208.210.219.132/vacircuit/select.jsp. Also search via LOPAS; call 804-786-5511 to apply.

Criminal Records: Access: Online, in person. Both court and visitors may perform in person searches. Court makes copy: $.50 per page; same fee for self serve. Required to search: name, years to search, DOB or SSN. Criminal records archived from 1742; on computer back to 1989. Online access to criminal records is the same as civil.

General Information: No juvenile, sealed records released. Certification fee: $2.00. Payee: Clerk of Circuit Court. Personal checks accepted. Prepayment required.

16th General District Court PO Box 452, Louisa, VA 23093; phone: 540-967-5330; fax: 540-967-2369; hours 8:30AM-4:30PM (EST). *Misdemeanor, Civil Actions Under $15,000, Eviction, Small Claims.*

Civil Records: Access: Online, in person. Visitors must perform in person searches themselves. Court makes copy: $1.00 for first page, $.50 each add'l. Required to search: name, years to search. Civil cases indexed by defendant, plaintiff; on computer from 1991. Search free at http://208.210.219.132/vadistrict/select.jsp. Also search via LOPAS; call 804-786-5511 to apply.

Criminal Records: Access: Online, in person. Visitors must perform in person searches themselves. Court makes copy: $1.00 for first page, $.50 each add'l. Required to search: name, years to search. Criminal records on computer from 1991. Online access to criminal records is the same as civil.

General Information: Public terminal goes back to 1995. No juvenile, sealed records released. Payee: Louisa District Court. Personal checks accepted. Prepayment required.

Lunenburg County

10th Circuit Court 11435 Courthouse Rd, Lunenburg, VA 23952; phone: 434-696-2230; fax: 434-696-3931; hours 8:30AM-4:30PM (EST). *Felony, Civil Actions Over $15,000, Probate.* www.courts.state.va.us/courts/circuit.html

Civil Records: Access: Online, in person. Visitors must perform in person searches themselves. Court makes copy: $.50 per page. Required to search: name, years to search. Civil cases indexed by defendant, plaintiff; on index books from 1700s; computerized records since 2002. Search free at http://208.210.219.132/vacircuit/select.jsp. Also search via LOPAS; call 804-786-5511 to apply.

Criminal Records: Access: In person, mail, online. Visitors must perform in person searches themselves. Search fee: Varies by numbers of yrs searched. Court makes copy: $.50 per page. Required to search: name, years to search. Criminal records on index books from 1700s; computerized records since 2002. Online access to criminal records is the same as civil. Mail turnaround time 1-2 days.

General Information: No juvenile, sealed records released. No fee to fax documents. Certification fee: $2.00 per page. Payee: Clerk of Circuit Court. Personal checks accepted. Prepayment required.

10th General District Court 11413 Courthouse Rd, Lunenburg, VA 23952; phone: 434-696-5508; fax: 434-696-3665; hours 8:30AM-4:30PM (EST). *Misdemeanor, Civil Actions Under $15,000, Eviction, Small Claims.*

Civil Records: Access: Mail, online, in person. Both court and visitors may perform in person searches. No search fee. Required to search: name, years to search. Civil cases indexed by defendant, plaintiff. Civil records computerized since 1995, on index books and cards from 1991, prior to 1985 at Circuit Court. Search free at http://208.210.219.132/vadistrict/select.jsp. Also search via LOPAS; call 804-786-5511 to apply. Mail turnaround time 3 days.

Criminal Records: Access: Mail, online, in person. Both court and visitors may perform in person searches. No search fee. Required to search: name, years to search, DBO, SSN. Criminal records computerized since 1995, on index books and cards from 1991, prior to 1985 at Circuit Court. Online access to criminal records is the same as civil. Mail turnaround time 3 days.

General Information: Public terminal goes back to 1995. No juvenile records released. No certification fee. SASE required.

Lynchburg City

24th Circuit Court 900 Court St, PO Box 4, Lynchburg, VA 24505-0004; phone: 434-847-1590; fax: 434-847-1864; hours 8:15AM-4:45PM (EST). *Felony, Civil Actions Over $15,000, Probate.* www.courts.state.va.us/courts/circuit.html

Civil Records: Access: Online, in person. Both court and visitors may perform in person searches. No search fee. Court makes copy: $.50 per page. Required to search: name, years to search. Civil cases indexed by defendant, plaintiff; on index books from 1800s, on computer since 1993. Search free at http://208.210.219.132/vacircuit/select.jsp. Also search via LOPAS; call 804-786-5511 to apply.

Criminal Records: Access: Online, in person. Both court and visitors may perform in person searches. Court makes copy: $.50 per page. Required to search: name, years to search; also helpful: DOB, SSN. Criminal records on index books from 1800s, on computer since 1993. Online access to criminal records is the same as civil.

General Information: Public terminal goes back to 2000. No juvenile, sealed records released. Certification fee: $2.00. Payee: Clerk of Circuit Court. Personal checks accepted. Prepayment required.

24th General District Court - Civil Division 905 Court St, Lynchburg, VA 24504; criminal phone: 434-455-2630; civil phone: 434-455-2640; fax: 434-847-1779; hours 8AM-4PM (EST). *Civil Actions Under $15,000, Eviction, Small Claims.*

Civil Records: Access: Mail, online, in person. Both court and visitors may perform in person searches. Court makes copy: $1.00 for first 2 pages, $.50 each add'l. Required to search: name, years to search; also helpful: address. Civil cases indexed by defendant, plaintiff. On computer since 1987. Search free at http://208.210.219.132/vadistrict/select.jsp. Also search via LOPAS; call 804-786-5511 to apply. Mail turnaround time 1-2 weeks.

General Information: Public terminal goes back to 10 years. (Terminal also has traffic cases.) No juvenile, sealed records released. No certification fee. Payee: Lynchburg General District Court. Personal checks accepted. Prepayment required.

24th General District Court - Criminal Division 905 Court St, Lynchburg, VA 24504; criminal phone: 434-455-2630; fax: 434-847-1779; hours 8AM-4PM (EST). *Misdemeanor.*

Criminal Records: Access: Online, in person. Visitors must perform in person searches themselves. Court makes copy: $1.00 for first 2 pages, $.50 each add'l. Required to search: name, years to search. Criminal records on index books and computer go back 10 years. For information about the statewide online systems, see the state introduction. Select and search General District Courts at http://208.210.219.132/vadistrict/select.jsp. Note: Mail access limited to specific cases only, not name searches.

General Information: Public terminal has only criminal records back to 10 years. No juvenile, sealed records released. No certification fee. Payee: Lynchburg General District Court. Personal checks accepted. Prepayment required.

Madison County

16th Circuit Court PO Box 220, 100 Court Sq,1 Main St, Madison, VA 22727; phone: 540-948-6888; fax: 540-948-3759; hours 8:30AM-4:30PM (EST). *Felony, Civil Actions Over $15,000, Probate.* www.courts.state.va.us/courts/circuit.html

Civil Records: Access: Mail, online, in person. Visitors must perform in person searches themselves. No search fee. Court makes copy: $.50 per page. Required to search: name, years to search. Civil cases indexed by defendant, plaintiff; on index books from 1792, on computer since 1989. Select and search Combined Courts online at http://208.210.219.132/vacircuit/select.jsp. For information about the statewide online systems, see the state introduction. Mail turnaround time 1 week.

Criminal Records: Access: Mail, online, in person. Visitors must perform in person searches themselves. No search fee. Court makes copy: $.50 per page. Required to search: name, years to search, DOB; also helpful: SSN. Criminal records on index books from 1792, on computer since 1989. Online access to criminal records is the same as civil. Mail turnaround time 1 week.

General Information: No juvenile, sealed records released. Certification fee: $2.00. Payee: Clerk of Circuit Court. Personal checks accepted. Prepayment and SASE required.

16th General District Court Madison County Courthouse, PO Box 470, Madison, VA 22727; phone: 540-948-4657; fax: 540-948-5649; hours 8:30AM-4:30PM (EST). *Misdemeanor, Civil Actions Under $15,000, Eviction, Small Claims.*

Civil Records: Access: Phone, fax, mail, online, in person. Only the court performs in person searches; visitors may not. No search fee. No copy fee. Required to search: name, years to search. Civil cases indexed by defendant, plaintiff; on index books and computer back to 1992. Search free at http://208.210.219.132/vadistrict/select.jsp. Also search via LOPAS; call 804-786-5511 to apply. Mail turnaround time 3-4 days.

Criminal Records: Access: Phone, fax, mail, online, in person. Only the court performs in person searches; visitors may not. No search fee. No copy fee. Required to search: name, years to search, DOB; also helpful: address, SSN. Criminal records on index books and computer back to 1992. Online access to criminal records is the same as civil. Mail turnaround time 3-4 days.

General Information: No juvenile, sealed or pre-trial records released. No fee to fax documents. No certification fee. SASE required.

Manassas City

Circuit & District Courts
www.courts.state.va.us/courts/circuit.html
Note: See Prince William County.

Manassas Park City

Circuit & District Courts
www.courts.state.va.us/courts/circuit.html
Note: See Prince William County.

Martinsville City

21st Circuit Court PO Box 1206, Martinsville, VA 24114-1206; phone: 276-403-5106; fax: 276-403-5232; hours 9AM-5PM (EST). *Felony, Civil Actions Over $15,000, Probate.* www.ci.martinsville.va.us/circuitclerk/

Civil Records: Access: Online, in person. Visitors must perform in person searches themselves. Court makes copy: $.50 per page; same fee for self serve. Required to search: name, years to search. Civil cases indexed by defendant, plaintiff; on computer since 1988, on index books from 1942. Online access free at http://208.210.219.132/vacircuit/select.jsp. For information about the statewide online systems, see the state introduction. Also, with password, access judgments at www.ci.martinsville.va.us/crms/.

Criminal Records: Access: Online, in person, mail, fax. Visitors must perform in person searches themselves. No search fee. Court makes copy: $.50 per page; same fee for self serve. Required to search: name, years to search; also helpful: DOB, SSN. Criminal records on computer since 1988, on index books from 1942. Online access to criminal records is the same as civil. Mail turnaround time 1-2 days.

General Information: Public terminal goes back to 2002. No juvenile, sealed records released. Certification fee: $2.00. Payee: Clerk of Circuit Court. Personal checks accepted. Prepayment required. SASE requested.

21st General District Court PO Box 1402, Martinsville, VA 24112; phone: 276-403-5125; fax: 276-403-5114; hours 9AM-5PM (EST). *Misdemeanor, Civil Actions Under $15,000, Eviction, Small Claims.* www.courts.state.va.us

Civil Records: Access: Online, in person. Visitors must perform in person searches themselves. Court makes copy: $.50 per page. Required to search: name, years to search. Civil cases indexed by defendant, plaintiff; on computer since 1993. Search free at http://208.210.219.132/vadistrict/select.jsp. Also search via LOPAS; call 804-786-5511 to apply.

Criminal Records: Access: Online, in person. Visitors must perform in person searches themselves. Court makes copy: $.50 per page. Required to search: name, years to search. Criminal records on computer since 1993. Online access to criminal records is the same as civil.

General Information: Public terminal has criminal back to 1995 and civil back to 1995. (Terminals available in County General District Court, 3160 Kings Mountain Rd, Martinsville) No sealed or expunged records released. No certification fee. Prepayment required.

Mathews County

9th Circuit Court PO Box 463, Mathews, VA 23109; phone: 804-725-2550; hours 8AM-4PM (EST). *Felony, Civil Actions Over $15,000, Probate.* www.courts.state.va.us/courts/circuit/Mathews/home. html

Civil Records: Access: In person only. Visitors must perform in person searches themselves. Court makes copy: $.50 per page. Required to search: name, years to search. Civil cases indexed by defendant, plaintiff; on index books from 1800s.

Criminal Records: Access: In person only. Visitors must perform in person searches themselves. Court makes copy: $.50 per page. Required to search: name, years to search; also helpful: DOB, SSN. Criminal records on index books from 1800s.

General Information: No juvenile, sealed records released. Certification fee: $2.00. Payee: Clerk of Circuit Court. Personal checks accepted. Prepayment required.

9th General District Court PO Box 169, Saluda, VA 23149; phone: 804-758-4312; hours 8:30AM-4:30PM (EST). *Misdemeanor, Civil Actions Under $15,000, Eviction, Small Claims.*

Civil Records: Access: Mail, online, in person. Both court and visitors may perform in person searches. No search fee. Court makes copy: $.50 per page. Required to search: name, years to search. Civil cases indexed by defendant. Civil records on computer 10 years back. Search free at http://208.210.219.132/vadistrict/select.jsp. Also search via LOPAS; call 804-786-5511 to apply. Mail turnaround time 7-10 days.

Criminal Records: Access: Mail, online, in person. Both court and visitors may perform in person searches. No search fee. Court makes copy: $.50 per page. Required to search: name, years to search, DOB, date of offense; also helpful: SSN. Criminal records on computer 10 years back. Online access to criminal records is the same as civil. Mail turnaround time 7-10 days.

General Information: Public terminal goes back to 10 years. No juvenile, sealed records released. No certification fee. Payee: Clerk of General District Court. Personal checks accepted. Prepayment and SASE required.

Mecklenburg County

10th Circuit Court PO Box 530, Boydton, VA 23917; phone: 434-738-6191 x4222; fax: 434-738-6861; hours 8:30AM-4:30PM (EST). *Felony, Civil Actions Over $15,000, Probate.* www.courts.state.va.us/courts/circuit.html

Civil Records: Access: Online, in person. Visitors must perform in person searches themselves. Court makes copy: $.50 per page. Required to search: name, years to search. Civil cases indexed by defendant, plaintiff; on index books from 1800s, on computer from 1987. Remote online access to court case indexes is via LOPAS; call 804-786-5511 to apply.

Criminal Records: Access: Online, in person. Visitors must perform in person searches themselves. Court makes copy: $.50 per page. Required to search: name, years to search. Criminal records on index books from 1800s, on computer from 1987. Remote online access to court case indexes is via LOPAS; call 804-786-5511 to apply.

General Information: Public terminal goes back to 1989. No juvenile, sealed or direct indictments (drug offenses) records released. Will fax specific case file data for $1.00 per page. Certification fee: $2.00. Payee: Clerk of Circuit Court. Personal checks accepted. Prepayment required.

10th General District Court PO Box 306, 911 Madison St, Boydton, VA 23917; phone: 434-738-6260; fax: 434-738-0761; hours 8:30AM-4:30PM (EST). *Misdemeanor, Civil Actions Under $15,000, Eviction, Small Claims.*

Civil Records: Access: Fax, mail, online, in person. Both court and visitors may perform in person searches. Search fee: $5.00. Court makes copy: $.50 per page. Required to search: name, years to search. Civil cases indexed by defendant, plaintiff; on computer since 1995. Search free at http://208.210.219.132/vadistrict/select.jsp. Also search via LOPAS; call 804-786-5511 to apply. Mail turnaround time 2 days.

Criminal Records: Access: Fax, mail, online, in person. Both court and visitors may perform in person searches. Search fee: $5.00. Court makes copy: $.50 per page. Required to search: name, years to search; also helpful: DOB, SSN. Criminal records on computer since 1995. Online access to criminal records is the same as civil. Mail turnaround time 2 days.

General Information: Public terminal goes back to 1995. Sealed, and adoption records not released. Will fax documents for $1.00 per page. No certification fee. Payee: Clerk of General District Court. Personal checks or Visa, MC accepted.

Middlesex County

9th Circuit Court PO Box 158, Saluda, VA 23149; phone: 804-758-5317; hours 8:30AM-4:30PM (EST). *Felony, Civil Actions Over $15,000, Probate.* www.courts.state.va.us/courts/circuit.html

Civil Records: Access: In person, online. Visitors must perform in person searches themselves. Court makes copy: $.50 per page; same fee for self serve. Required to search: name, years to search. Civil cases indexed by defendant, plaintiff; on index books from 1672; on computer back to 1992. Remote online access to court case indexes is via LOPAS; call 804-786-5511 to apply.

Criminal Records: Access: In person only. Visitors must perform in person searches themselves. Court makes copy: $.50 per page; same fee for self serve. Required to search: name, years to search, DOB, SSN. Criminal records on index books from 1674; on computer back to 1992.

General Information: No juvenile, sealed records released. Will not fax documents. Certification fee: $3.00. Payee: Clerk of Circuit Court. Personal checks accepted. Prepayment required.

9th General District Court PO Box 169, Saluda, VA 23149; phone: 804-758-4312; hours 8:30AM-4:30PM (EST). *Misdemeanor, Civil Actions Under $15,000, Eviction, Small Claims.*

Civil Records: Access: Mail, online, in person. Both court and visitors may perform in person searches. No search fee. Court makes copy: $.50 per page. Required to search: name, years to search. Civil cases indexed by defendant. Civil records held 10 years, computerized since 1997. Search free at http://208.210.219.132/vadistrict/select.jsp. Also search via LOPAS; call 804-786-5511 to apply. Mail turnaround time 2-3 days.

Criminal Records: Access: Mail, online, in person. Both court and visitors may perform in person searches. No search fee. Court makes copy: $.50 per page. Required to search: name, years to search. Criminal records held 10 years, computerized since 1997. Online access to criminal records is the same as civil. Mail turnaround time 2-3 days.

General Information: Public terminal goes back to 1997. No juvenile, sealed records released. No certification fee. Payee: Clerk of General District Court. Personal checks accepted. Prepayment and SASE required.

Montgomery County

27th Circuit Court PO Box 6309, Christiansburg, VA 24068; phone: 540-382-5760; fax: 540-382-6937; hours 8:30AM-4:30PM (EST). *Felony, Civil Actions Over $15,000, Probate.* www.courts.state.va.us/courts/circuit.html

Civil Records: Access: Phone, mail, online, in person. Both court and visitors may perform in person searches. Court makes copy: $.50 per page; same fee for self serve. Required to search: name, years to search. Civil cases indexed by defendant, plaintiff; on index books from 1800s, on computer

from 1/94. Online access free at http://208.210.219.132/vacircuit/select.jsp. For information about the statewide online systems, see the state introduction. Note: Phone & mail access limited to cases filed 7/93-present.

Criminal Records: Access: Online, in person. Visitors must perform in person searches themselves. Court makes copy: $.50 per page; same fee for self serve. Required to search: name, years to search; also helpful: DOB, SSN. Criminal records on computer since 9/93, prior in books. Online access to criminal records is the same as civil.

General Information: Public terminal has criminal back to - not known and civil back to 1994. No juvenile, sealed records released. Certification fee: $2.00. Payee: Clerk of Circuit Court. Personal checks accepted. Prepayment required.

27th General District Court Montgomery County Courthouse, 1 E Main St, #201, Christiansburg, VA 24073; phone: 540-382-5735; criminal phone: 540-394-2086; civil phone: 540-394-2085; fax: 540-382-6988; hours 8:30AM-4:30PM (EST). *Misdemeanor, Civil Actions Under $15,000, Eviction, Small Claims.*

Civil Records: Access: Online, in person. Visitors must perform in person searches themselves. Court makes copy: $.50 per page. Required to search: name, years to search. Civil cases indexed by defendant, plaintiff; on computerized records go back ten years. Search free at http://208.210.219.132/vadistrict/select.jsp. Also search via LOPAS; call 804-786-5511 to apply.

Criminal Records: Access: In person, online. Visitors must perform in person searches themselves. Court makes copy: $.50 per page. Required to search: name, years to search. Computerized records go back ten years. Online access to criminal records is the same as civil.

General Information: Public terminal goes back to 10 years. No juvenile records released. No certification fee. Payee: Clerk General District Court. Personal checks accepted. Prepayment required.

Nelson County

24th Circuit Court PO Box 10, Lovingston, VA 22949; phone: 434-263-7020; fax: 434-263-7027; hours 8AM-5PM (EST). *Felony, Civil Actions Over $15,000, Probate.* www.courts.state.va.us/courts/circuit.html

Civil Records: Access: Online, in person. Visitors must perform in person searches themselves. Court makes copy: $.50 per page. Required to search: name, years to search. Civil cases indexed by defendant, plaintiff; on index books from 1800s, deeds on computer from 7/93. Online access free at http://208.210.219.132/vacircuit/select.jsp. For information about the statewide online systems, see the state introduction.

Criminal Records: Access: Online, in person. Visitors must perform in person searches themselves. Court makes copy: $.50 per page. Required to search: name, years to search; also helpful- DOB, SSN. Criminal records on index books from 1800s, deeds on computer from 7/93. Online access to criminal records is the same as civil.

General Information: No juvenile, sealed records released. Certification fee: $2.00. Payee: Clerk of Circuit Court. Personal checks accepted. Prepayment required.

24th General District Court Nelson County Courthouse, 84 Courthouse Sq, PO Box 514, Lovingston, VA 22949; phone: 434-263-7040; fax: 434-263-7033; hours 8AM-4:30PM (EST). *Misdemeanor, Civil Actions Under $15,000, Eviction, Small Claims.*

Civil Records: Access: Fax, mail, online, in person. Both court and visitors may perform in person searches. No search fee. Court makes copy: $.50 per page. Required to search: name, years to search. Civil cases indexed by defendant, plaintiff; on computer for 10 years. Search free at http://208.210.219.132/vadistrict/select.jsp. Also search via LOPAS; call 804-786-5511 to apply. Mail turnaround time 3-4 days.

Criminal Records: Access: Fax, mail, online, in person. Both court and visitors may perform in person searches. No search fee. Court makes copy: $.50 per page. Required to search: name, years to search. Criminal records on computer for 10 years. Online access to criminal records is the same as civil. Mail turnaround time 3-4 days.

General Information: Public terminal goes back to 1994. No sealed records released. No fee to fax documents. No certification fee. Payee: Clerk of General District Court. Personal checks accepted. Prepayment and SASE required.

New Kent County

9th Circuit Court PO Box 98, 12001 Court House Circle, New Kent, VA 23124; phone: 804-966-9520; fax: 804-966-9528; hours 8:30AM-4:30PM (EST). *Felony, Civil Actions Over $15,000, Probate.*
www.courts.state.va.us/courts/circuit.html
Civil Records: Access: Online, in person. Visitors must perform in person searches themselves. Court makes copy: $.50 per page. Required to search: name, years to search. Civil cases indexed by defendant, plaintiff; on index books from 1865, some on cards; computerized back to 1992. Online access free at http://208.210.219.132/vacircuit/select.jsp. For information about the statewide online systems, see the state introduction.
Criminal Records: Access: Online, in person. Visitors must perform in person searches themselves. Court makes copy: $.50 per page. Required to search: name, years to search, DOB, SSN. Criminal records on index books from 1865, some on cards; computerized back to 1992. Online access to criminal records is the same as civil.
General Information: Public terminal goes back to 1992. No juvenile, sealed, adoption records released. Certification fee: $2.00. Payee: Circuit Court. Personal checks accepted. Prepayment required.

9th General District Court PO Box 127, New Kent, VA 23124; phone: 804-966-9530; fax: 804-966-9535; hours 8:30AM-4:30PM (EST). *Misdemeanor, Civil Actions Under $15,000, Eviction, Small Claims.*
Civil Records: Access: Mail, online, in person. Both court and visitors may perform in person searches. No search fee. Court makes copy: $1.00 per page. Required to search: name, years to search. Civil cases indexed by defendant, plaintiff. Civil records go back to 1992 and on computer since 1995. Search free at http://208.210.219.132/vadistrict/select.jsp. Also search via LOPAS; call 804-786-5511 to apply. Mail turnaround time 5 days.
Criminal Records: Access: Online, in person. Both court and visitors may perform in person searches. No search fee. Court makes copy: $1.00 per page. Required to search: name, years to search; also helpful: DOB and signed release. Criminal records go back to 1992 and on computer since 1995. Online access to criminal records is the same as civil. Note: The sheriff department or Commonwealth attorney are both alternative sources for criminal records. Mail turnaround time 5 days.
General Information: Public terminal goes back to 1995. No juvenile, sealed records released. No certification fee. Payee: General District Court. Personal checks or Visa, MC accepted. Prepayment and SASE required.

Newport News City

7th Circuit Court 2500 Washington Ave, Newport News, VA 23607; phone: 757-926-8561; fax: 757-926-8531; hours 8AM-4:45PM (EST). *Felony, Civil Actions Over $15,000, Probate.*
www.newport-news.va.us/court/index.htm
Civil Records: Access: Mail, online, in person. Both court and visitors may perform in person searches. Court makes copy: $.50 per page. Required to search: name, years to search. Civil cases indexed by defendant, plaintiff; on computer from 1987, prior on index books. Online access free at http://208.210.219.132/vacircuit/select.jsp. For information about the statewide online systems, see the state introduction. Note: Mail access only available for old records. Mail turnaround time 1-2 days.
Criminal Records: Access: Online, in person. Visitors must perform in person searches themselves. Court makes copy: $.50 per page. Required to search: name, years to search. Criminal records on computer from 1987, on index books from 1985 to 1987, prior on judgment books. Online access to criminal records is the same as civil.
General Information: Public use terminal available. No adoption, juvenile, sealed records released. Certification fee: $2.00. Payee: Clerk of Circuit Court. In state personal checks accepted. Prepayment required. SASE requested.

7th General District Court 2500 Washington Ave, Newport News, VA 23607; criminal phone: 757-926-8811; civil phone: 757-926-3520; fax: 757-926-8496; hours 7:30AM-4PM (EST). *Misdemeanor, Civil Actions Under $15,000, Eviction, Small Claims.*
Civil Records: Access: Phone, fax, mail, in person, online. Visitors must perform in person searches themselves. No search fee. Court makes copy: $.50 per page. Required to search: name, years to search. Civil records go back to 10 years. Search free at http://208.210.219.132/vadistrict/select.jsp. Also search via LOPAS; call 804-786-5511 to apply. Mail turnaround time varies.
Criminal Records: Access: Phone, fax, mail, online, in person. Both court and visitors may perform in person searches. No search fee. Court makes copy: $.50 per page. Required to search: name, years to search. Criminal records on computer back 10 years. Online access to criminal records is the same as civil. Mail turnaround time varies.
General Information: Public terminal goes back to 10 years. No juvenile, sealed records released. No certification fee. Payee: General District Court. Personal checks accepted. Credit cards accepted: Visa/MC for criminal records only. Prepayment required.

Norfolk City

4th Circuit Court 100 St Paul's Blvd, Norfolk, VA 23510; phone: 757-664-4380; criminal phone: 757-664-4384; civil phone: 757-664-4387; probate phone: 757-664-4385; fax: 757-664-4581; hours 8:45AM-4:45PM (EST). *Felony, Civil Actions Over $15,000, Probate.*
www.courts.state.va.us/courts/circuit.html
Civil Records: Access: Online, in person. Both court and visitors may perform in person searches. Search fee: $10.00 if years to search prior to 1996, none if later. Court makes copy: $.50 per page. Required to search: name, years to search. Civil cases indexed by defendant, plaintiff; on computer back to 1996, docket books back to 1800s. Online access free at http://208.210.219.132/vacircuit/select.jsp. For information about the statewide online systems, see the state introduction. Also access record images via http://208.210.219.102/cgi-bin/p/rms.cgi; registration and password required. Also, the Clerk of Circuit court subscription online system contains judgment records, wills, marriages, recorded documents etc at www.norfolk.gov/Circuit_Court/remoteaccess.asp. Fee is $50 per month. Judgments, Wills, Marriages, etc back to 1993.
Criminal Records: Access: Online, in person. Both court and visitors may perform in person searches. Search fee: $10.00 if years to search prior to 1996, none if later. Court makes copy: $.50 per page. Required to search: name, years to search, DOB, SSN, signed release. Criminal records go back to 1972; on computer back to 1996, docket books back to 1800s. Online access to dockets is free at http://208.210.219.132/vacircuit/select.jsp. Also access record images via http://208.210.219.102/cgi-bin/p/rms.cgi; registration and password required.
General Information: No juvenile, sealed records released. Certification fee: $2.00. Payee: Clerk of Circuit Court. Personal checks accepted. Prepayment required.

4th General District Court 811 E City Hall Ave, Norfolk, VA 23510; phone: 757-664-4910; criminal phone: 757-664-4915/6; civil phone: 757-664-4913/4; hours 8AM-4PM (EST). *Misdemeanor, Civil Actions Under $15,000, Eviction, Small Claims.*
Civil Records: Access: Mail, online, in person. Visitors must perform in person searches themselves. Search fee: $10.00 per name. Court makes copy: $1.00 per page. Required to search: name, years to search. Civil cases indexed by defendant, plaintiff. Civil records in files, on computer 10 years. Search free at http://208.210.219.132/vadistrict/select.jsp. Also search via LOPAS; call 804-786-5511 to apply. Mail turnaround time 1-2 weeks.
Criminal Records: Access: Mail, online, in person. Visitors must perform in person searches themselves. Search fee: $10.00. Court makes copy: $1.00 per page. Required to search: name, years to search. Criminal records in files, on computer 10 years. Online access to criminal records is the same as civil. Mail turnaround time 1-2 weeks.
General Information: Public use terminal available. No juvenile, sealed, or adoption records released. Certification fee: $1.00. Payee: Norfolk General District Court. Personal checks accepted. Prepayment required.

Northampton County

2nd Circuit Court PO Box 36 (16404 Courthouse Rd), Eastville, VA 23347-0036; phone: 757-678-0465; criminal fax: 757-678-5410; same fax for civil/probate; hours 9AM-4:30PM (EST). *Felony, Civil Actions Over $15,000, Probate.*
www.courts.state.va.us/courts/circuit.html
Note: Oldest continuous records in the USA.

Civil Records: Access: Phone, fax, mail, online, in person. Both court and visitors may perform in person searches. No search fee. Court makes copy: $.50 per page; same fee for self serve. Required to search: name, years to search. Civil cases indexed by defendant, plaintiff; on index books from 1632; on computer back to 1993. Search free at http://208.210.219.132/vacircuit/select.jsp. Also search via LOPAS; call 804-786-5511 to apply. Mail turnaround time 1 week.
Criminal Records: Access: Phone, mail, online, in person. Both court and visitors may perform in person searches. No search fee. Court makes copy: $.50 per page; same fee for self serve. Required to search: name, years to search, DOB. Criminal records on index books from 1632; on computer back to 1993, some previous. Online access to criminal index records is the same as civil. Mail turnaround time 1 week.
General Information: Public terminal goes back to 7/1997. No juvenile, sealed records released. Certification fee: $2.00 per instrument. Payee: Clerk of Circuit Court. Only local personal checks accepted. Prepayment and SASE required.

Northampton General District Court PO Box 1289, Eastville, VA 23347; phone: 757-678-0466; hours 8:30AM-4:30PM (EST). *Misdemeanor, Civil Actions Under $15,000, Eviction, Small Claims.*
Civil Records: Access: Mail, online, in person. Only the court performs in person searches; visitors may not. No search fee. Court makes copy: $.50 per page. Required to search: name, years to search. Civil cases indexed by defendant, plaintiff; on computer since 1990. Search free at http://208.210.219.132/vadistrict/select.jsp. Also

search via LOPAS; call 804-786-5511 to apply. Mail turnaround time 1-2 days.

Criminal Records: Access: Mail, online, in person. Only the court performs in person searches; visitors may not. No search fee. Court makes copy: $.50 per page. Required to search: name, years to search, DOB or SSN. Criminal records on computer since 1990. Online access to criminal records is the same as civil. Mail turnaround time 1-2 days.

General Information: No certification fee. Payee: General District Court. Personal checks accepted. SASE required.

Northumberland County

15th Circuit Court PO Box 217, Heathsville, VA 22473; phone: 804-580-3700; fax: 804-580-2261; hours 8:30AM-4:45PM (EST). *Felony, Civil Actions Over $15,000, Probate.*
www.courts.state.va.us/courts/circuit.html

Civil Records: Access: Mail, online, in person. Both court and visitors may perform in person searches. No search fee. Court makes copy: $.50 per page; same fee for self serve. Required to search: name, years to search. Civil cases indexed by defendant, plaintiff; on index books from 1650. Online access free at http://208.210.219.132/vacircuit/select.jsp. For information about the statewide online systems, see the state introduction. Mail turnaround time 1-2 days.

Criminal Records: Access: Mail, online, in person. Both court and visitors may perform in person searches. No search fee. Court makes copy: $.50 per page; same fee for self serve. Required to search: name, years to search, DOB. Criminal records on index books from 1650. Online access to criminal records is the same as civil. Mail turnaround time 1-2 days.

General Information: No juvenile, sealed records released. No certification fee. Payee: Clerk of Circuit Court. Personal checks accepted.

15th General District Court Northumberland Courthouse, PO Box 114, Heathsville, VA 22473; phone: 804-580-4323; fax: 804-580-6702; hours 8AM-4PM (EST). *Misdemeanor, Civil Actions Under $15,000, Eviction, Small Claims.*

Civil Records: Access: Online, in person. Visitors must perform in person searches themselves. Court makes copy: $.50 per page. Required to search: name, years to search. Civil cases indexed by defendant, plaintiff; on index books; on computer since 1994. Search free at http://208.210.219.132/vadistrict/select.jsp. Also search via LOPAS; call 804-786-5511 to apply.

Criminal Records: Access: Online, in person. Visitors must perform in person searches themselves. Court makes copy: $.50 per page. Required to search: name, years to search, DOB; also helpful: SSN. Criminal records on index books back to 1991; on computer since 1995. Online access to criminal records is the same as civil.

General Information: Public terminal goes back to 1995. No juvenile, sealed records released. No certification fee. Payee: Clerk of District Court. Personal checks or Visa, MC accepted. Prepayment required.

Norton City

Circuit & District Courts
www.courts.state.va.us/courts/circuit.html
Note: See Wise County.

Nottoway County

11th Circuit Court Courthouse, PO Box 25, Nottoway, VA 23955; phone: 434-645-9043; fax: 434-645-2201; hours 8:30AM-4:30PM (EST). *Felony, Civil Actions Over $15,000, Probate.*
www.courts.state.va.us/courts/circuit.html

Civil Records: Access: Mail, online, in person. Both court and visitors may perform in person searches. Search fee: $10.00 per hour. Court makes copy: $.50 per page; same fee for self serve. Required to search:

name, years to search. Civil cases indexed by defendant, plaintiff; on index books from late 1700s; on computer back to 2000. Search free at http://208.210.219.132/vacircuit/select.jsp. Also search via LOPAS; call 804-786-5511 to apply.

Criminal Records: Access: Online, in person. Visitors must perform in person searches themselves. Court makes copy: $.50 per page; same fee for self serve. Required to search: name, years to search; also helpful: DOB, SSN. Criminal records on index books from late 1700s; on computer back to 2000. Online access to criminal records is the same as civil.

General Information: Public terminal goes back to 2000. No juvenile, sealed records released. Fee to fax documents is $1.00 per document. Certification fee: $2.00. Payee: Clerk's Office. Personal checks accepted. Prepayment and SASE required.

11th General District Court PO Box 25, Nottoway, VA 23955; phone: 434-645-9312; fax: 434-645-8584; hours 8AM-4:15PM (EST). *Misdemeanor, Civil Actions Under $15,000, Eviction, Small Claims.*

Civil Records: Access: Mail, online, in person. Both court and visitors may perform in person searches. No search fee. Court makes copy: $1.00 for first page, $.50 each add'l. Required to search: name, years to search. Civil cases indexed by defendant, plaintiff; on index cards from 1986, on computer the past 10 years. Only court can search prior to 1989. Search free at http://208.210.219.132/vadistrict/select.jsp. Also search via LOPAS; call 804-786-5511 to apply. Mail turnaround time 2-3 days.

Criminal Records: Access: Mail, online, in person. Both court and visitors may perform in person searches. No search fee. Court makes copy: $1.00 for first page, $.50 each add'l. Required to search: name, years to search; also helpful: DOB, SSN. Criminal records on index cards from 1986, on computer the past 10 years Only court can search prior to 1989. Online access to criminal records is the same as civil. Mail turnaround time 2-3 days.

General Information: Public terminal goes back to 10 years. No juvenile records released. No certification fee. Payee: Nottoway District Court. Personal checks accepted. Prepayment and SASE required.

Orange County

16th Circuit Court PO Box 230, Orange, VA 22960; phone: 540-672-4030; criminal fax: 540-672-2939; same fax for civil/probate; hours 8:30AM-4:30PM (EST). *Felony, Civil Actions Over $15,000, Probate.*
www.courts.state.va.us/courts/circuit.html

Civil Records: Access: Online, in person. Both court and visitors may perform in person searches. No search fee. Court makes copy: $.50 per page; same fee for self serve. Required to search: name, years to search. Civil cases indexed by defendant, plaintiff; on computer since 1989, in index books from 1734 for deeds, from 1853 for births, from 1912 for marriages. Search free at http://208.210.219.132/vacircuit/select.jsp. Also search via LOPAS; call 804-786-5511 to apply.

Criminal Records: Access: Phone, fax, mail, online, in person. Both court and visitors may perform in person searches. No search fee. Court makes copy: $.50 per page; same fee for self serve. Required to search: name, years to search, DOB; also helpful: SSN. Criminal records on computer since 1989, in index books from 1734. Online access to criminal records is the same as civil. Mail turnaround time 1 week-10 days.

General Information: Public use terminal available. No juvenile, sealed records released. No fee to fax documents. No certification fee. Payee: Clerk of Circuit Court. Personal checks accepted. Prepayment required.

16th General District Court Orange County Courthouse, PO Box 821, Orange, VA 22960; phone: 540-672-3150; fax: 540-672-3150; hours 8:30AM-4:30PM (EST). *Misdemeanor, Civil Actions Under $15,000, Eviction, Small Claims.*

Civil Records: Access: Mail, online, in person. Only the court performs in person searches; visitors may not. No search fee. Court makes copy: $1.00 for first page, $.50 each add'l. Required to search: name, years to search. Civil cases indexed by defendant, plaintiff; on index books from 1800s, on computer from 1990. Search free at http://208.210.219.132/vadistrict/select.jsp. Also search via LOPAS; call 804-786-5511 to apply. Mail turnaround time 1-2 days.

Criminal Records: Access: Mail, online, in person. Only the court performs in person searches; visitors may not. No search fee. Court makes copy: $1.00 for first page, $.50 each add'l. Required to search: name, years to search, DOB; also helpful: SSN. Criminal records on index books from 1800s, on computer from 1990. Online access to criminal records is the same as civil. Mail turnaround time 1-2 days.

General Information: No juvenile, sealed records released. Certification fee: $1.00 for 1st page, $.50 each add'l. Payee: Clerk of District Court. In state checks or Visa, MasterCard accepted. Prepayment required.

Page County

26th Circuit Court 116 S Court St, #A, Luray, VA 22835; phone: 540-743-4064; fax: 540-743-2338; hours 9AM-5PM (EST). *Felony, Civil Actions Over $15,000, Probate.*
www.courts.state.va.us/courts/circuit.html

Civil Records: Access: Online, in person. Visitors must perform in person searches themselves. Court makes copy: $.50 per page; same fee for self serve. Required to search: name, years to search. Civil cases indexed by defendant, plaintiff; on index books from 1831. Computerized records go back to 1995. Online access free at http://208.210.219.132/vacircuit/select.jsp. For information about the statewide online systems, see the state introduction.

Criminal Records: Access: Online, in person. Visitors must perform in person searches themselves. Court makes copy: $.50 per page; same fee for self serve. Required to search: name, years to search, DOB; also helpful: SSN. Criminal records on index books from 1831. Computerized records go back to 1995. Online access to criminal records is the same as civil.

General Information: Public terminal goes back to 1995. No juvenile, sealed records released. Certification fee: $2.00. Payee: Ron Wilson, Clerk. No second party checks accepted. Prepayment required.

26th General District Court 116 S Court St, Luray, VA 22835; phone: 540-743-5705; fax: 540-743-5334; hours 8AM-4:30PM (EST). *Misdemeanor, Civil Actions Under $15,000, Eviction, Small Claims.*

Civil Records: Access: Mail, online, in person. Both court and visitors may perform in person searches. No search fee. Court makes copy: $.50 per page; same fee for self serve. Required to search: name, years to search. Civil cases indexed by defendant, plaintiff; on computer back to 1/90. Search free at http://208.210.219.132/vadistrict/select.jsp. Also search via LOPAS; call 804-786-5511 to apply. Mail turnaround time 7-10 days.

Criminal Records: Access: Mail, online, in person. Both court and visitors may perform in person searches. No search fee. Court makes copy: $.50 per page; same fee for self serve. Required to search: name, years to search; also helpful: DOB. Criminal records on computer back to 1/90. Online access to criminal records is the same as civil. Mail turnaround time 7-10 days.

General Information: Public use terminal available. No sealed records released. Certification fee: $1.00 per page. Payee: District Court. Personal checks accepted. SASE requested.

Patrick County

21st Circuit Court PO Box 148, Stuart, VA 24171; phone: 276-694-7213; fax: 276-694-6943; hours 9AM-5PM (on Wed to 3PM) (EST). *Felony, Civil Actions Over $15,000, Probate.*
www.courts.state.va.us/courts/circuit.html
Civil Records: Access: In person, online. Visitors must perform in person searches themselves. Court makes copy: $.50 per page; same fee for self serve. Required to search: name, years to search. Civil cases indexed by plaintiff. Civil records on index books from 1791. Search free at http://208.210.219.132/vacircuit/select.jsp. Also search via LOPAS; call 804-786-5511 to apply.
Criminal Records: Access: Online, in person. Visitors must perform in person searches themselves. Court makes copy: $.50 per page; same fee for self serve. Required to search: name, years to search; also helpful: DOB, SSN. Criminal records on index books from 1791. Online access to criminal records is the same as civil.
General Information: No juvenile, sealed records released. Certification fee: $2.00. Payee: Clerk of Circuit Court. Personal checks accepted. Prepayment required.

21st General District Court PO Box 149, Stuart, VA 24171; phone: 276-694-7258; fax: 276-694-5614; hours 8:30AM-5PM (EST). *Misdemeanor, Civil Actions Under $15,000, Eviction, Small Claims.*
Civil Records: Access: Mail, fax, online, in person. Both court and visitors may perform in person searches. No search fee. Required to search: name, years to search. Civil cases indexed by defendant, plaintiff. Civil records go back to 1992; on computer from 10/94. Search free at http://208.210.219.132/vadistrict/select.jsp. Also search via LOPAS; call 804-786-5511 to apply. Mail turnaround time 1 week.
Criminal Records: Access: Mail, online, in person. Both court and visitors may perform in person searches. No search fee. Required to search: name, years to search, DOB; also helpful: SSN. Criminal records go back to 1992; on computer from 10/94. Online access to criminal records is the same as civil. Mail turnaround time 1 week.
General Information: Public terminal goes back to 10/1994. No juvenile, sealed records released. No certification fee. SASE requested.

Petersburg City

11th Circuit Court 7 Courthouse Ave, Petersburg, VA 23803; phone: 804-733-2367; fax: 804-732-5548; hours 8AM-4PM (EST). *Felony, Civil Actions Over $15,000, Probate.*
www.courts.state.va.us/courts/circuit.html
Civil Records: Access: Online, in person. Visitors must perform in person searches themselves. Court makes copy: $.50 per page. Required to search: name, years to search. Civil cases indexed by defendant, plaintiff; on index books back to 1784; on computer back to 1988. Online access free at http://208.210.219.132/vacircuit/select.jsp. For information about the statewide online systems, see the state introduction.
Criminal Records: Access: Online, in person. Visitors must perform in person searches themselves. Court makes copy: $.50 per page. Required to search: name, years to search; also helpful: DOB, SSN. Criminal records go back to 1970; on computer back to 1996. Online access to criminal records is the same as civil.
General Information: No juvenile, sealed or adoption records released. Certification fee: $2.00. Payee: Petersburg Circuit Court Clerk. Personal checks accepted. Out of state checks not accepted. Prepayment required.

11th Judicial District Court 35 E Tabb St, Petersburg, VA 23803; phone: 804-733-2374; criminal phone: X4152; civil phone: X4153; fax: 804-733-2375; hours 8AM-4PM (EST). *Misdemeanor, Civil Actions Under $15,000, Eviction, Small Claims.*
www.courts.state.va.us/courts/gd/Petersburg/home.html
Note: When faxing, put to attention of civil or criminal.
Civil Records: Access: Fax, mail, online, in person. Both court and visitors may perform in person searches. No search fee. Court makes copy: $1.00 for first 2 pages. $.50 each add'l page. Required to search: name, years to search. Civil cases indexed by defendant, plaintiff; on index books back to 1983, computerized since 1992. Search free at http://208.210.219.132/vadistrict/select.jsp. Also search via LOPAS; call 804-786-5511 to apply. Mail turnaround time 1 week.
Criminal Records: Access: Fax, mail, online, in person. Both court and visitors may perform in person searches. No search fee. Court makes copy: $1.00 for first 2 pages. $.50 each add'l. Required to search: name, years to search, DOB; also helpful: SSN. Criminal records indexed on books for 11 years; on computer back to 1992. Online access to criminal records is the same as civil. Mail turnaround time 1 week.
General Information: Public terminal has criminal back to 10 years and civil back to 10 years. (Available M,W,TH,F after 1PM.) No sealed records released. Will not fax documents. No certification fee. Payee: General District Court. In state personal checks accepted. Prepayment required.

Pittsylvania County

22nd Circuit Court PO Drawer 31, Chatham, VA 24531; phone: 434-432-7887; probate phone: 434-432-7892; fax: 434-432-7892; hours 8:30AM-5PM (EST). *Felony, Civil Actions Over $15,000, Probate.*
www.courts.state.va.us/courts/circuit.html
Civil Records: Access: Online, in person. Visitors must perform in person searches themselves. Court makes copy: $.50 per page. Required to search: name, years to search. Civil cases indexed by defendant, plaintiff; on index books back to 1767; computerized records since 1995. Online access free at http://208.210.219.132/vacircuit/select.jsp. For information about the statewide online systems, see the state introduction. If documents mailed, add $.50 per page if SASE not included.
Criminal Records: Access: Online, in person. Visitors must perform in person searches themselves. Court makes copy: $.50 per page. Required to search: name, years to search, DOB, SSN. Criminal records on index books back to 1767; computerized records since 1995. Online access free at http://208.210.219.132/vacircuit/select.jsp. For information about the statewide online systems, see the state introduction. If documents mailed, add $.50 per page if SASE not included.
General Information: Public terminal has only criminal records back to 1995. No juvenile, sealed records released. Certification fee: $2.00. Payee: Clerk of Circuit Court. Personal checks accepted. Prepayment required.

22nd General District Court Pittsylvania Courthouse Annex 2nd Fl, PO Box 695, Chatham, VA 24531; phone: 434-432-7879; fax: 434-432-7915; hours 8:30AM-4:30PM (EST). *Misdemeanor, Civil Actions Under $15,000, Eviction, Small Claims.*
www.courts.state.va.us/courts/gd/Pittsylvania/home.html
Civil Records: Access: Online, in person. Visitors must perform in person searches themselves. Court makes copy: $.50 per page. Required to search: name, years to search. Civil cases indexed by defendant, plaintiff; on computer since 1994. Search free at http://208.210.219.132/vadistrict/select.jsp. Also search via LOPAS; call 804-786-5511 to apply.

Criminal Records: Access: Online, in person. Visitors must perform in person searches themselves. Court makes copy: $.50 per page. Required to search: name, years to search. Criminal records on computer since 1994. Online access to criminal records is the same as civil.
General Information: No juvenile, sealed records released. No certification fee. Payee: General District Court. Personal checks accepted.

Poquoson City

Circuit & District Courts
www.courts.state.va.us/courts/circuit.html
Note: See York County.

Portsmouth City

Circuit Court PO Drawer 1217, Portsmouth, VA 23705; phone: 757-393-8671; fax: 757-399-4826; hours 8:30AM-5:30PM (EST). *Felony, Civil Actions Over $15,000, Probate.*
www.courts.state.va.us/courts/circuit.html
Civil Records: Access: Mail, online, in person. Visitors must perform in person searches themselves. Search fee: $10.00 per name. Court makes copy: $.50 per page. Required to search: name, years to search. Civil cases indexed by defendant, plaintiff; on computer back to 6/1987, prior on index books back to 1858. Online access free at http://208.210.219.132/vacircuit/select.jsp. For information about the statewide online systems, see the state introduction. Note: Phone access limited to simple requests.
Criminal Records: Access: Mail, online, in person. Both court and visitors may perform in person searches. Search fee: $10.00 per name. Court makes copy: $.50 per page. Required to search: name, years to search, DOB; also helpful: SSN. Criminal records on computer back to 6/1987, prior indexed on books back to 1858. Online access to criminal records is the same as civil.
General Information: Public use terminal available. No juvenile, sealed records released. Certification fee: $2.00. Payee: Cynthia P Morrison, Clerk. Business checks accepted. No credit cards. Prepayment required.

General District Court PO Box 129, Portsmouth, VA 23705; criminal phone: 757-393-8681; civil phone: 757-393-8624; fax: 757-393-8634; hours 8:30AM-4:30PM (EST). *Misdemeanor, Civil Actions Under $15,000, Eviction, Small Claims.*
Note: Traffic Division: 757-393-8506.
Civil Records: Access: Online, in person. Visitors must perform in person searches themselves. No copy fee. Required to search: name, years to search. Civil cases indexed by defendant, plaintiff; on computer from 4/87, from 1983 to 4/87 paper files only. Search free at http://208.210.219.132/vadistrict/select.jsp. Also search via LOPAS; call 804-786-5511 to apply.
Criminal Records: Access: Mail, fax, online, in person. Both court and visitors may perform in person searches. Search fee: $7.00 per name. No copy fee. Required to search: name, years to search; also helpful: DOB, SSN. Criminal records on computer and case (paper files) maintained for 10 years. Online access to criminal records is the same as civil. Mail turnaround time within 14 days.
General Information: Public use terminal available. Juvenile, sealed records not released. No certification fee. Payee: Clerk of General District Court. Personal checks or Visa, MC accepted. SASE required.

Powhatan County

11th Circuit Court PO Box 37, Powhatan, VA 23139-0037; phone: 804-598-5660; criminal fax: 804-598-5608; same fax for civil/probate; hours 8:30AM-5PM (EST). *Felony, Civil Actions Over $15,000, Probate.*
www.courts.state.va.us/courts/circuit.html
Note: Probate records are in a separate index.

Civil Records: Access: In person, online. Visitors must perform in person searches themselves. Court makes copy: $.50 per page; same fee for self serve. Required to search: name, years to search. Civil cases indexed by defendant, plaintiff; on index books from 1777, on computer from 1993. Remote online access to court case indexes is via LOPAS; call 804-786-5511 to apply.

Criminal Records: Access: In person, online. Visitors must perform in person searches themselves. Court makes copy: $.50 per page; same fee for self serve. Required to search: name, years to search, signed release; also helpful: SSN. Criminal records on index books from 1777, on computer from 1993. Remote online access to court case indexes is via LOPAS; call 804-786-5511 to apply.

General Information: Public terminal goes back to 1993. No juvenile, sealed records released. Will not fax documents. Certification fee: $2.00 per document. Payee: Clerk of Court. Personal checks accepted. Prepayment required.

11th Judicial District Court Courthouse, 3880 Old Buckingham Rd, Powhatan, VA 23139; phone: 804-598-5665; fax: 804-598-5648; hours 8:30AM-5PM (EST). *Misdemeanor, Civil Actions Under $15,000, Eviction, Small Claims.*

Civil Records: Access: Phone, fax, mail, online, in person. Only the court performs in person searches; visitors may not. No search fee. Court makes copy: $.50 each for 1st two; $.25 each add'l. Required to search: name, years to search. Civil cases indexed by defendant. Civil records on index cards for 10 yrs, on computer from 1992. Search free at http://208.210.219.132/vadistrict/select.jsp. Also search via LOPAS; call 804-786-5511 to apply. Mail turnaround time 1 week.

Criminal Records: Access: Phone, fax, mail, online, in person. Only the court performs in person searches; visitors may not. No search fee. Court makes copy: $.50 each for 1st two; $.25 each add'l. Required to search: name, years to search, DOB; also helpful: SSN. Criminal records on index cards for 10 yrs, on computer from 1993. Online access to criminal records is the same as civil. Mail turnaround time 1 week.

General Information: No juvenile, sealed records released. No fee to fax documents. Local faxing only. No certification fee. Payee: Powhatan District Court. Personal checks accepted.

Prince Edward County

Circuit Court PO Box 304, 111 South St, Court House, Farmville, VA 23901-0304; phone: 434-392-5145; fax: 434-392-3913; hours 8:30AM-4:30PM (EST). *Felony, Civil Actions Over $15,000, Probate.*
www.courts.state.va.us/courts/circuit.html

Civil Records: Access: Online, in person. Visitors must perform in person searches themselves. Court makes copy: $.50 per page; court will charge for the time to make copies. Self serve copy fee: $.50 per page. Required to search: name, years to search. Civil cases indexed by defendant, plaintiff; on computer from 1990, books from 1930s. Remote online access to court case indexes is via LOPAS; call 804-786-5511 to apply.

Criminal Records: Access: Online, in person. Visitors must perform in person searches themselves. Court makes copy: $.50 per page; court will charge for the time to make copies. Self serve copy fee: $.50 per page. Required to search: name, years to search, DOB; also helpful: SSN. Criminal records on computer from 1990, books from 1930s. Online access to criminal records is the same as civil.

General Information: Public terminal goes back to 1990. (5 pub access terminals.) No juvenile, sealed records released. Certification fee: $2.00. Payee: Clerk of Circuit Court. Personal checks accepted. Prepayment required.

General District Court PO Box 41, Farmville, VA 23901-0041; phone: 434-392-4024; fax: 434-392-3800; hours 8:30AM-4:30PM (EST). *Misdemeanor, Civil Actions Under $15,000, Eviction, Small Claims.*

Civil Records: Access: Phone, mail, online, in person. Visitors must perform in person searches themselves. No search fee. Court makes copy: $1.00 per page; same fee for self serve. Required to search: name, years to search; also helpful: address. Civil cases indexed by defendant, plaintiff; on computer go back 10 years. Search free at http://208.210.219.132/vadistrict/select.jsp. Also search via LOPAS; call 804-786-5511 to apply. Mail turnaround time 1 week.

Criminal Records: Access: Mail, online, in person. Visitors must perform in person searches themselves. No search fee. Court makes copy: $1.00 per page; same fee for self serve. Required to search: name, years to search; also helpful: DOB, SSN. Criminal records on computer go back 10 years. Online access to criminal records is the same as civil. Mail turnaround time 1 week.

General Information: Public terminal goes back to 10 years. No juvenile, sealed records released. Will fax documents or specific for $1.00 per page. No certification fee. Payee: Clerk of District Court. Personal checks accepted. Prepayment and SASE required.

Prince George County

Circuit Court PO Box 98, Prince George, VA 23875; phone: 804-733-2640; fax: 804-861-5721; hours 8:30AM-5PM (EST). *Felony, Civil Actions Over $15,000, Probate.*
www.courts.state.va.us/courts/circuit.html

Civil Records: Access: Online, in person. Visitors must perform in person searches themselves. Court makes copy: $.50 per page. Required to search: name, years to search. Civil cases indexed by defendant, plaintiff; on index books since 1930s, computerized since 4/96. Search free at http://208.210.219.132/vacircuit/select.jsp. Also search via LOPAS; call 804-786-5511 to apply.

Criminal Records: Access: Online, in person. Visitors must perform in person searches themselves. Court makes copy: $.50 per page. Required to search: name, years to search, DOB; also helpful: SSN. Criminal records on index books since 1930s, computerized since 1/90. Online access to criminal records is the same as civil.

General Information: Public terminal has criminal back to 1990 and civil back to 1996. No juvenile or sealed records released. Certification fee: $2.00. Payee: Clerk of the Circuit Court. Personal checks accepted. Prepayment required.

6th General District Court P.C. Courthouse, PO Box 187, Prince George, VA 23875; phone: 804-733-2783; fax: 804-733-2678; hours 8:30AM-4:30PM (EST). *Misdemeanor, Civil Actions Under $15,000, Eviction, Small Claims.*

Civil Records: Access: Online, in person. Visitors must perform in person searches themselves. Court makes copy: $1.00 ea first 2 pages. $.50 ea add'l. Required to search: name, years to search. Civil cases indexed by defendant, plaintiff; on computer since 1991, prior on books since 1985. Search free at http://208.210.219.132/vadistrict/select.jsp. Also search via LOPAS; call 804-786-5511 to apply.

Criminal Records: Access: Online, in person. Visitors must perform in person searches themselves. Court makes copy: $1.00 ea first 2 pages. $.50 ea add'l. Required to search: name, years to search; also helpful: SSN. Criminal records on computer since 1991, prior on books since 1985. Online access to criminal records is the same as civil.

General Information: Public terminal goes back to 1991. No juvenile records released. No certification fee. Payee: Prince George Combined Court.

Prince William County

31st Circuit Court 9311 Lee Ave, Manassas, VA 20110; phone: 703-792-6015; criminal phone: 703-792-6031; civil phone: 703-792-6021; probate phone: 703-792-6085; criminal fax: 703-792-5746; civil fax: 702-792-7750; probate fax: 703-792-5899; hours 8:30AM-5PM (EST). *Felony, Civil Actions Over $15,000, Probate.*
www.pwcgov.org/default.aspx?topic=040017

Civil Records: Access: In person only. Visitors must perform in person searches themselves. Court makes copy: $.50 per page. Required to search: name, years to search. Civil cases indexed by defendant, plaintiff; on computer since 1989; prior on microfiche or books to 1939.

Criminal Records: Access: Mail, in person. Both court and visitors may perform in person searches. Search fee: $10.00 per name. Court makes copy: $.50 per page. Required to search: name, years to search, DOB; also helpful: SSN. Criminal records on computer since 1989; prior on microfiche or books to 1939. Mail turnaround time 1 week.

General Information: Public terminal goes back to 1989. No juvenile records released. Will not fax documents. Certification fee: $2.00 per document. Payee: Clerk of Circuit Court. Personal checks accepted. Prepayment required.

31st General District Court 9311 Lee Ave, Manassas, VA 20110; criminal phone: 703-792-6141; civil phone: 703-792-6149; fax: 703-792-6121; hours 8AM-4PM (EST). *Misdemeanor, Civil Actions Under $15,000, Eviction, Small Claims.*
www.courts.state.va.us/courts/gd/Prince_William/home.html

Civil Records: Access: Mail, fax, online, in person. Both court and visitors may perform in person searches. No search fee. Court makes copy: $1.00 for first 2 pages. $.50 each add'l page. Required to search: name, years to search. Civil cases indexed by defendant, plaintiff; on computer go back 10 years. Search free at http://208.210.219.132/vadistrict/select.jsp. Also search via LOPAS; call 804-786-5511 to apply. Mail turnaround time 10 days.

Criminal Records: Access: Mail, fax, online, in person. Both court and visitors may perform in person searches. No search fee. Court makes copy: $1.00 for first 2 pages. $.50 per page add'l. Required to search: name, years to search. Criminal records on computer go back 10 years. Online access to criminal records is the same as civil. Mail turnaround time 10 days.

General Information: Public terminal goes back to 10 years. No juvenile or sealed records released. No certification fee. Payee: Clerk G.D.C. Personal checks accepted. Prepayment and SASE required.

Pulaski County

Circuit Court 45 3rd St NW, #101, Pulaski, VA 24301; phone: 540-980-7825; fax: 540-980-7835; hours 8:30AM-4:30PM (EST). *Felony, Civil Actions Over $15,000, Probate.*
www.pulaskicircuitcourt.com

Civil Records: Access: Online, in person. Visitors must perform in person searches themselves. Court makes copy: $.50 per page. Required to search: name, years to search. Civil cases indexed by defendant, plaintiff; on index books from 1839, online since 1998. Online access to court records is $3000 annual fee http://records.pulaskicircuitcourt.com/splash.jsp. Registration required; search by name, document type or number. Also, access is free at http://208.210.219.132/vacircuit/select.jsp.

Criminal Records: Access: Online, in person. Visitors must perform in person searches themselves. Court makes copy: $.50 per page. Required to search: name, years to search, DOBV; also helpful: SSN. Criminal records on index books from 1839, online since 1998. Online access to criminal records is the same as civil. Note: This agency will perform no record checks and refer all requests to the State Police.

General Information: Public use terminal available. No juvenile, sealed records released. Certification fee: $1.00. Payee: Clerk of Court. Personal checks accepted. Prepayment required.

27th General District Court 45 3rd St NW, #102, Pulaski, VA 24301; phone: 540-980-7470; fax: 540-980-7792; hours 8:30AM-4:30PM (EST). *Misdemeanor, Civil Actions Under $15,000, Eviction, Small Claims.*

Civil Records: Access: Online, in person. Visitors must perform in person searches themselves. Court makes copy: $.50 per page. Required to search: name, years to search. Civil cases indexed by defendant, plaintiff; on computer since 1991. Search free at http://208.210.219.132/vadistrict/select.jsp. Also search via LOPAS; call 804-786-5511 to apply.

Criminal Records: Access: Online, in person. Visitors must perform in person searches themselves. Court makes copy: $.50 per page. Required to search: name, years to search, DOB; also helpful: SSN. Criminal records on computer since 1991. Online access to criminal records is the same as civil.

General Information: Public use terminal available. No juvenile, sealed records released. No certification fee. Payee: Clerk of General District Court. Personal checks or Visa, MC accepted. Prepayment required.

Radford City

27th Circuit Court 619 2nd St, Radford, VA 24141; phone: 540-731-3610; fax: 540-731-3612; hours 8:30AM-5PM (no machine receipts after 4:30PM) (EST). *Felony, Civil Actions Over $15,000, Probate.*

www.courts.state.va.us/courts/circuit.html

Civil Records: Access: Fax, mail, online, in person. Both court and visitors may perform in person searches. No search fee. Court makes copy: $.50 per page. Required to search: name, years to search. Civil cases indexed by defendant, plaintiff; on books from 1892; on computer back to 6/2000. Search free at http://208.210.219.132/vacircuit/select.jsp. Also search via LOPAS; call 804-786-5511 to apply. Mail turnaround time same day.

Criminal Records: Access: Fax, mail, online, in person. Both court and visitors may perform in person searches. No search fee. Court makes copy: $.50 per page. Required to search: name, years to search, DOB, signed release; also helpful: SSN. Criminal records on books from 1892; on computer back to 6/2000. Online access to criminal records is the same as civil. Mail turnaround time same day.

General Information: Public use terminal available. No juvenile, sealed or adoption records released. Will fax documents $.50 per page. Certification fee: $2.00. Payee: Radford Circuit Court. Personal checks accepted. Prepayment and SASE required.

27th General District Court 619 2nd St, Radford, VA 24141; phone: 540-731-3609; fax: 540-731-3692; hours 8:30AM-4:30PM (EST). *Misdemeanor, Civil Actions Under $15,000, Eviction, Small Claims.*

Civil Records: Access: Mail, online, in person. Both court and visitors may perform in person searches. Search fee: A search fee may be required. Court makes copy: $.50 per page; same fee for self serve. Required to search: name, years to search. Civil cases indexed by defendant, plaintiff. Search free at http://208.210.219.132/vadistrict/select.jsp. Also search via LOPAS; call 804-786-5511 to apply. Mail turnaround time 7 days or longer.

Criminal Records: Access: Fax, mail, online, in person. Both court and visitors may perform in person searches. Search fee: none, unless it is a lengthy search. Court makes copy: $.50 per page; same fee for self serve. Required to search: name, years to search, DOB, SSN, signed release. Criminal records on computer since 1989. Online access to criminal records is the same as civil. Mail turnaround time 7 days or longer.

General Information: Public terminal goes back to 10 years. No juvenile, sealed records released. Will fax documents $.50 per page. No certification fee. Payee: District Court. Personal checks accepted. Prepayment required.

Rappahannock County

20th Circuit Court PO Box 517, 238 Gay St, Washington, VA 22747; phone: 540-675-5350; hours 8:30AM-4:30PM (EST). *Felony, Civil Actions Over $15,000, Probate.*

www.courts.state.va.us/courts/circuit.html

Civil Records: Access: Mail, online, in person. Visitors must perform in person searches themselves. No search fee. Court makes copy: $.50 per page. Self serve copy fee: $.50 per page. Required to search: name, years to search. Civil cases indexed by defendant, plaintiff. Civil records computerized since 1995, on index cards from 1833, early records archived. Search free at http://208.210.219.132/vacircuit/select.jsp. Also search via LOPAS; call 804-786-5511 to apply. Note: Mail access limited to specific cases only. Court will only do searches as time permits. Mail turnaround time 1-2 days.

Criminal Records: Access: Mail, online, in person. Visitors must perform in person searches themselves. Search fee: Searches performed only as time permits. Court makes copy: $.50 per page. Self serve copy fee: $.50 per page. Required to search: name, years to search; also helpful: DOB, SSN. Criminal records computerized since 1995, on index cards from 1833, early records archived. Online access to criminal records is the same as civil. Note: Mail access limited to specific cases only. Mail turnaround time 1-2 days.

General Information: Public use terminal available. No juvenile, sealed records released. Certification fee: $2.50 per document. Payee: Clerk of the Circuit Court. Personal checks accepted. Prepayment and SASE required.

20th Combined District Court PO Box 206, Washington, VA 22747; phone: 540-675-5356; fax: 540-675-1431; hours 8:30AM-4:30PM (EST). *Misdemeanor, Civil Actions Under $15,000, Eviction, Small Claims.*

Civil Records: Access: Mail, online, in person. Both court and visitors may perform in person searches. No search fee. Court makes copy: $1.00 per page. Required to search: name, years to search. Civil cases indexed by defendant, plaintiff; on computer back to 1994, on index cards back to 1990, prior in Circuit Court. Search free at http://208.210.219.132/vadistrict/select.jsp. Also search via LOPAS; call 804-786-5511 to apply. Mail turnaround time up to 2 weeks.

Criminal Records: Access: Mail, online, in person. Both court and visitors may perform in person searches. No search fee. Court makes copy: $1.00 per page. Required to search: name, years to search, DOB; also helpful: SSN, signed release. Criminal records on computer back to 1994, index cards back to 1985, prior in Circuit Court. Online access to criminal records is the same as civil. Mail turnaround time up to 2 weeks.

General Information: No juvenile, sealed records released. No certification fee. Payee: Clerk of General District Court. Personal checks or Visa, MC accepted. Prepayment required. SASE requested.

Richmond County

15th Circuit Court 101 Court Cir, PO Box 1000, Warsaw, VA 22572; phone: 804-333-3781; criminal phone: same; civil phone: ss; criminal fax: 804-333-5396; same fax for civil/probate; hours 9AM-5PM (EST). *Felony, Civil Actions Over $15,000, Probate.*

www.courts.state.va.us/courts/circuit.html

Civil Records: Access: Phone, mail, in person, online. Both court and visitors may perform in person searches. No search fee. Court makes copy: $.50 per page; $1.00 per page if genealogy records. Self serve copy fee: $.50 per page. Required to search:

name, years to search; also helpful: address, SSN. Civil cases indexed by defendant, plaintiff. Civil records archived from 1692. Search free at http://208.210.219.132/vacircuit/select.jsp. Also search via LOPAS; call 804-786-5511 to apply. Mail turnaround time same day.

Criminal Records: Access: Mail, in person, online. Both court and visitors may perform in person searches. No search fee. Court makes copy: $.50 per page; same fee for self serve. Required to search: name, years to search, DOB; also helpful: address. Criminal records archived from 1692, computerized since 1994. Online access to criminal records is the same as civil. Mail turnaround time same day.

General Information: No juvenile, sealed records released. Will fax documents to local or toll free line. Certification fee: $2.00 per document. Payee: Clerk of Circuit Court. Personal checks accepted. Prepayment required. SASE requested.

15th Judicial District Court Richmond County Courthouse, PO Box 1000, Warsaw, VA 22572; phone: 804-333-4616; fax: 804-333-3741; hours 8AM-4:30PM (EST). *Misdemeanor, Civil Actions Under $15,000, Eviction, Small Claims.*

Civil Records: Access: Mail, online, in person. Both court and visitors may perform in person searches. No search fee. Required to search: name, years to search. Civil cases indexed by defendant, plaintiff. Civil records archived 10 years back; on computer from 1994. Search free at http://208.210.219.132/vadistrict/select.jsp. Also search via LOPAS; call 804-786-5511 to apply. Mail turnaround time 2 days.

Criminal Records: Access: Mail, online, in person. Both court and visitors may perform in person searches. No search fee. Required to search: name, years to search; also helpful: DOB, SSN. Criminal records archived 10 years back; on computer from 1994. Online access to criminal records is the same as civil. Mail turnaround time 2 days.

General Information: Public terminal goes back to 10 years. No juvenile, sealed records released. No certification fee. SASE requested.

Richmond City

13th Circuit Court - Division I John Marshall Courts Bldg, 400 N 9th St, Richmond, VA 23219; phone: 804-646-6505; criminal phone: 804-646-6553; civil phone: 804-646-6536; fax: 804-646-6562; hours 8:45AM-4:45PM (EST). *Felony, Civil Actions Over $15,000, Probate.*

www.courts.state.va.us/courts/circuit/Richmond/home.html

Note: Also search for felony records at the Manchester Courthouse location, 10th & Hull St.

Civil Records: Access: Mail, online, in person. Visitors must perform in person searches themselves. No search fee. Court makes copy: $.50 per page. Required to search: name, years to search. Civil cases indexed by defendant, plaintiff; on computer from 1987. On microfilm from 1980, on card index from 1970s, on index books from 1600s. Online access free at http://208.210.219.132/vacircuit/select.jsp. For information about the statewide online systems, see the state introduction.

Criminal Records: Access: Mail, online, in person. Visitors must perform in person searches themselves. No search fee. Court makes copy: $.50 per page. Required to search: name, years to search; also helpful: DOB, SSN. Criminal records on computer from 1987. On microfilm from 1980, on card index from 1970s, on index books from 1782. Online access to criminal records is the same as civil.

General Information: Public terminal goes back to 1987. No juvenile, sealed records released. Will not fax documents. Certification fee: $2.00. Payee: Bevill M Dean, Clerk. Personal checks accepted. Prepayment required.

13th General District Court - Civil Division 400 N 9th St, Rm 203, Richmond, VA 23219; phone: 804-646-6461; fax: 846-646-8758; hours 8AM-4PM (EST). *Civil Actions Under $15,000, Eviction, Small Claims.*
Civil Records: Access: Phone, mail, online, in person. Both court and visitors may perform in person searches. No search fee. Court makes copy: $.50 per page. Required to search: name, years to search. Civil cases indexed by defendant, plaintiff. Civil records computerized since 1994 in index books from 1973. Records destroyed after 20 years. Search free at http://208.210.219.132/vadistrict/select.jsp. Also search via LOPAS; call 804-786-5511 to apply. Mail turnaround time 1-2 days.
General Information: Public terminal has only civil records back to 1/1995. No juvenile, sealed records released. Will fax documents to toll free line, must be prepaid. No certification fee. Payee: Clerk of General District Court, Civil Division. Business checks accepted. Prepayment and SASE required.

13th Circuit Court Division II, Manchester Courthouse, 10th and Hull St, Richmond, VA 23224-4070; phone: 804-646-8470; fax: 804-646-8122; hours 8:45AM-4:45PM (EST). *Felony.*
www.vipnet.org/vipnet/clerks/richmondmanchester.html
Note: Also search for felony records at the John Marshall Courthouse (Division I) location.
Civil Records: Access: Mail, online, in person. Both court and visitors may perform in person searches. No search fee. Court makes copy: $.50 per page; same fee for self serve. Required to search: name, years to search. Civil cases indexed by defendant, plaintiff; on computer from 1989, on index cards from 1961 to 1988, prior archived in Richmond. Online access free at http://208.210.219.132/vacircuit/select.jsp. For information about the statewide online systems, see the state introduction. Mail turnaround time 1-2 days.
Criminal Records: Access: Mail, online, in person. Both court and visitors may perform in person searches. No search fee. Court makes copy: $.50 per page; same fee for self serve. Required to search: name, years to search. Criminal records on computer from 1989, on index cards from 1961 to 1988, prior archived in Richmond. Online access to criminal records is the same as civil. Mail turnaround time 1-2 days.

General Information: Public terminal goes back to 1989. No juvenile, sealed, adoption records released. Certification fee: $2.00. Payee: Clerk of Circuit Court. Business checks accepted. Prepayment and SASE required.

13th General District Court - Division II 905 Decatur St, Richmond, VA 23224; phone: 804-646-8990; fax: 804-646-0387; hours 8AM-4PM (EST). *Misdemeanor, Traffic.*
Criminal Records: Access: Mail, online, in person. Both court and visitors may perform in person searches. No search fee. Court makes copy: $1.00 per page. Required to search: name, years to search, DOB; also helpful: SSN. Criminal records on computer from 1986, records prior to 1980 destroyed. For information about the statewide online systems, see the state introduction. Select and search General District Courts at http://208.210.219.132/vadistrict/select.jsp. Mail turnaround time 1-5 days.
General Information: Public terminal has only criminal records back to 1986. No juvenile, sealed records released. Certification fee: $2.00. Payee: Clerk of General District Court. Personal checks accepted. Prepayment required.

Roanoke County

23rd Circuit Court PO Box 1126, Salem, VA 24153-1126; phone: 540-387-6205; fax: 540-387-6145; hours 8:30AM-4:30PM (EST). *Felony, Civil Actions Over $15,000, Probate.*
www.co.roanoke.va.us
Civil Records: Access: Online, in person. Visitors must perform in person searches themselves. Court makes copy: $.50 per page. Required to search: name, years to search. Civil cases indexed by defendant, plaintiff; on computer from 1986, on index books from 1838 to 1986, prior records to Botetourt County. Online access free at http://208.210.219.132/vacircuit/select.jsp. For information about the statewide online systems, see the state introduction.
Criminal Records: Access: Online, in person. Visitors must perform in person searches themselves. Court makes copy: $.50 per page. Required to search: name, years to search, DOB; also helpful: SSN. Criminal records on computer from 1986, on index books from 1838 to 1986, prior records to Botetourt County. Online access to criminal records is the same as civil.
General Information: Public terminal goes back to 1986. (Terminal at the City of Salem Courthouse.) No juvenile, sealed records released. Certification fee: $2.00. Payee: Clerk of Circuit Court. Personal checks accepted. Prepayment required.

23rd General District Court PO Box 997, Salem, VA 24153; phone: 540-387-6168; fax: 540-387-6066; hours 8:15AM-4:15PM (EST). *Misdemeanor, Civil Actions Under $15,000, Eviction, Small Claims.*
www.co.roanoke.va.us
Civil Records: Access: Mail, online, in person. Both court and visitors may perform in person searches. No search fee. Court makes copy: $.50 per page. Required to search: name, years to search. Civil cases indexed by defendant, plaintiff. Computerized records the past 10 years, on index cards from 1980. Prior at Circuit Court or Archives. Search free at http://208.210.219.132/vadistrict/select.jsp. Also search via LOPAS; call 804-786-5511 to apply. Mail turnaround time 5 days.
Criminal Records: Access: Mail, online, in person. Both court and visitors may perform in person searches. No search fee. Court makes copy: $.50 per page. Required to search: name, years to search, DOB; also helpful: SSN. Computerized records the past 10 years, on index cards from 1980. Prior at Circuit Court or Archives. Online access to criminal records is the same as civil. Mail turnaround time 5 days.
General Information: Public terminal goes back to 10 years. No sealed records released. Will fax documents to local numbers only. No certification fee. Payee: General. Personal checks or Visa, MC accepted. Not accepted for copy fees. Prepayment and SASE required.

Roanoke City

23rd Circuit Court PO Box 2610, Roanoke, VA 24010-2610; criminal phone: 540-853-6723; civil phone: 540-853-6702; probate phone: 540-853-6712; criminal fax: 540-853-2114; civil fax: 540-853-1024; hours 8:15AM-4:45PM (EST). *Felony, Civil Actions Over $15,000, Probate.*
www.roanokecountyva.gov/Departments/CircuitCourtClerksOffice/
Civil Records: Access: Mail, online, in person. Visitors must perform in person searches themselves. Court makes copy: $.50 per page; same fee for self serve. Required to search: name, years to search. Civil cases indexed by defendant, plaintiff; on computer from 1986, civil on microfiche from 1884, criminal on index books from 1800s, prior archived. Online access free at http://208.210.219.132/vacircuit/select.jsp. For information about the statewide online systems, see the state introduction.

Criminal Records: Access: Mail, online, in person. Visitors must perform in person searches themselves. Court makes copy: $.50 per page; same fee for self serve. Required to search: name, years to search, DOB; also helpful: SSN. Criminal records on computer from 1986, civil on microfiche from 1884, criminal on index books from 1800s, prior archived. Online access to criminal records is the same as civil.
General Information: Public terminal has criminal back to 1992 and civil back to late 1991. No juvenile, sealed records released. Will not fax documents. Certification fee: $2.00. Payee: Clerk of Circuit Court. Personal checks accepted. Prepayment required.

General District Court 315 W Church Ave, 2nd Fl, Roanoke, VA 24016-5007; criminal phone: 540-853-2361; civil phone: 540-853-2364; fax: 540-853-2364; hours 8AM-4PM (EST). *Misdemeanor, Civil Actions Under $15,000, Eviction, Small Claims.*
Note: Per state law, the court cannot release DOB and SSN.
Civil Records: Access: Mail, online, in person. Both court and visitors may perform in person searches. Search fee: $1.00 per name. Court makes copy: $1.00 per page. Required to search: name, years to search. Civil cases indexed by defendant, plaintiff; on computer from 1986, prior on index cards. Select and search District Courts at www.courts.state.va.us/. For information about the statewide online systems, see the state introduction. Mail turnaround time 1 week.
Criminal Records: Access: Online, in person. Visitors must perform in person searches themselves. Court makes copy: $1.00 per page. Required to search: name, years to search, DOB; also helpful: SSN. Criminal records on computer from 1986, prior on index cards. Online access to criminal records is the same as civil.
General Information: Public terminal goes back to 10 years. No juvenile records released. No certification fee. Payee: General District Court. Business checks accepted. Prepayment and SASE required.

Rockbridge County

25th Circuit Court Courthouse Sq, 2 S Main St, Lexington, VA 24450; phone: 540-463-2232; fax: 540-463-3850; hours 8:30AM-4:30PM (EST). *Felony, Civil Actions Over $15,000, Probate.*
www.courts.state.va.us/courts/circuit.html
Civil Records: Access: Online, in person. Visitors must perform in person searches themselves. Court makes copy: $.50 per page; same fee for self serve. Required to search: name, years to search. Civil cases indexed by defendant, plaintiff; on computer from 1985, on index books from 1778. Criminal records are easily obtained from the late 1960s. Prior records are not easily accessible. Search free at http://208.210.219.132/vacircuit/select.jsp. Also search via LOPAS; call 804-786-5511 to apply.
Criminal Records: Access: Online, in person. Visitors must perform in person searches themselves. Court makes copy: $.50 per page; same fee for self serve. Required to search: name, years to search, DOB. Criminal records on computer from 1985, on index books from 1778. Criminal records are easily obtained from the late 1960s. Prior records are not easily accessible. Online access to criminal records is the same as civil.
General Information: Public terminal goes back to 1985. No juvenile, sealed records released. Certification fee: $2.50. Payee: Clerk of Circuit Court. Personal checks accepted. Prepayment required.

District Court 150 S Main St, Lexington, VA 24450; phone: 540-463-3631; fax: 540-463-4213; hours 8:30AM-4:30PM (EST). *Misdemeanor, Civil Actions Under $15,000, Eviction, Small Claims.*
Note: Lexington-Rockbridge is a combined district court.

Civil Records: Access: Mail, online, in person. Both court and visitors may perform in person searches. No search fee. Court makes copy: $1.00 each 1st two pages; $.50 each add'l. Required to search: name, years to search. Civil cases indexed by defendant, plaintiff; on computer from 1989, on index cards from 1985 to 1989, prior to 1985 at Circuit Court. Records destroyed after 10 years. Search free at http://208.210.219.132/vadistrict/select.jsp. Also search via LOPAS; call 804-786-5511 to apply. Mail turnaround time 5-7 days.

Criminal Records: Access: Mail, online, in person. Both court and visitors may perform in person searches. No search fee. Court makes copy: $1.00 each first 2 pages; $.50 each add'l. Required to search: name, years to search, DOB; also helpful: SSN. Criminal records on computer from late 1989, on index cards from 1985 to 1989, prior to 1985 at Circuit Court. Online access to criminal records is the same as civil. Mail turnaround time 5-7 days.

General Information: Public terminal goes back to 1989. No juvenile, sealed records released. No certification fee. Payee: District Court. Prepayment and SASE required.

Rockingham County

26th Circuit Court Courthouse, Court Sq, Harrisonburg, VA 22801; criminal phone: 540-564-3118; civil phone: 540-564-3114; fax: 540-564-3127; hours 9AM-5PM (EST). *Felony, Civil Actions Over $15,000, Probate.*
www.courts.state.va.us/courts/circuit.html
Civil Records: Access: Online, in person. Visitors must perform in person searches themselves. Court makes copy: $.50 per page. Required to search: name, years to search. Civil cases indexed by defendant, plaintiff; on index cards from the beginning of the county. Online access free at http://208.210.219.132/vacircuit/select.jsp. For information about the statewide online systems, see the state introduction.
Criminal Records: Access: Online, in person. Visitors must perform in person searches themselves. Court makes copy: $.50 per page. Required to search: name, years to search. Criminal records on index cards from the beginning of the county. Online access to criminal records is the same as civil.
General Information: No juvenile, sealed records released. Certification fee: $2.00. Payee: Clerk of Circuit Court. Personal checks accepted. Prepayment required.

26th General District Court 53 Court Sq, Harrisonburg, VA 22801; criminal phone: 540-564-3130; civil phone: 540-564-3135; fax: 540-564-3096; hours 8AM-4PM (EST). *Misdemeanor, Civil Actions Under $15,000, Eviction, Small Claims.*
Civil Records: Access: Phone, mail, online, in person. Both court and visitors may perform in person searches. Search fee: $15.00 per hour. Court makes copy: $.50 per page. Required to search: name, years to search. Civil cases indexed by defendant, plaintiff; on computer the past 10 years, on index cards from 1978, prior at Circuit Court. Search free at http://208.210.219.132/vadistrict/select.jsp. Also search via LOPAS; call 804-786-5511 to apply. Mail turnaround time up to 1 week.
Criminal Records: Access: Phone, mail, online, in person. Both court and visitors may perform in person searches. Search fee: $15.00 per name. Court makes copy: $.50 per page. Required to search: name, years to search, DOB; also helpful: SSN. Criminal records on computer from the past 10 years, on index cards from 1985, prior at Circuit Court. Online access to criminal records is the same as civil. Mail turnaround time up to 1 week.
General Information: Public terminal goes back to 10 years. No juvenile, sealed, adoption records released. Certification fee: included in copy fee. Payee: General District Court. Personal checks or Visa, MC accepted. Prepayment and SASE required.

Russell County

29th Circuit Court PO Box 435, 121 E Main St, Lebanon, VA 24266; phone: 276-889-8023; criminal fax: 276-889-8003; same fax for civil/probate; hours 8AM-5PM (EST). *Felony, Civil Actions Over $15,000, Probate.*
www.courts.state.va.us/courts/circuit.html
Civil Records: Access: Mail, online, in person. Both court and visitors may perform in person searches. No search fee. Court makes copy: $.50 per page; same fee for self serve. Required to search: signed release, name, years to search. Civil cases indexed by defendant, plaintiff; on computer from 1990, archived from 1809. Search free at http://208.210.219.132/vacircuit/select.jsp. Also search via LOPAS; call 804-786-5511 to apply.
Criminal Records: Access: Mail, online, in person. Both court and visitors may perform in person searches. Court makes copy: $.50 per page; same fee for self serve. Required to search: signed release, name, years to search. Criminal records on computer from 1990, archived from 1809. Online access to criminal records is the same as civil.
General Information: Public terminal goes back to 2000. No juvenile, sealed records released. Will not fax documents. No certification fee. Payee: Clerk of Circuit Court. Personal checks accepted. Prepayment required.

29th General District Court Russell County Courthouse, PO Box 65, Lebanon, VA 24266; phone: 276-889-8051; fax: 276-889-8091; hours 8:30AM-4:30PM (EST). *Misdemeanor, Civil Actions Under $15,000, Eviction, Small Claims.*
Civil Records: Access: Phone, fax, mail, online, in person. Both court and visitors may perform in person searches. No search fee. No copy fee. Required to search: name. Civil cases indexed by defendant, plaintiff; on computer back to 1993. Search free at http://208.210.219.132/vadistrict/select.jsp. Also search via LOPAS; call 804-786-5511 to apply. Mail turnaround time 2-5 days.
Criminal Records: Access: Phone, fax, mail, online, in person. Both court and visitors may perform in person searches. No search fee. No copy fee. Required to search: name, DOB; also helpful: SSN. Criminal records on computer back to 1993; other records back to 1990. Online access to criminal records is the same as civil. Mail turnaround time 2-5 days.
General Information: Public terminal has criminal back to 1994 and civil back to 1993. No juvenile, sealed records released. No fee to fax documents. No certification fee.

Salem City

23rd Circuit Court 2 E Calhoun St, PO Box 891, Salem, VA 24153; phone: 540-375-3067; fax: 540-375-4039; hours 8:30AM-5PM (EST). *Felony, Civil Actions Over $15,000, Probate.*
www.courts.state.va.us/courts/circuit.html
Civil Records: Access: Online, in person. Both court and visitors may perform in person searches. Court makes copy: $.50 per page. Required to search: name, years to search. Civil cases indexed by defendant, plaintiff; on computer from 1985, on index books from 1968, prior at Roanoke Circuit Court. Search free at http://208.210.219.132/vacircuit/select.jsp. Also search via LOPAS; call 804-786-5511 to apply.
Criminal Records: Access: Online, in person. Visitors must perform in person searches themselves. Court makes copy: $.50 per page. Required to search: name, years to search, DOB; also helpful: SSN. Criminal records on computer from 1985, on index books from 1968, prior at Roanoke Circuit Court. Online access to criminal records is the same as civil.
General Information: Public terminal goes back to 1985. No juvenile, sealed or adoption records released. Certification fee: $2.00. Payee: Clerk of Circuit Court. Personal checks accepted. Prepayment required.

23rd General District Court 2 E Calhoun St, Salem, VA 24153; phone: 540-375-3044; fax: 540-375-4024; hours 8AM-4PM (EST). *Misdemeanor, Civil Actions Under $15,000, Eviction, Small Claims.*
Civil Records: Access: Online, in person. Visitors must perform in person searches themselves. Court makes copy: $1.00 per page. Required to search: name, years to search. Civil cases indexed by defendant, plaintiff; on computer for 10 years, prior records at City of Salem Circuit Court. Search free at http://208.210.219.132/vadistrict/select.jsp. Also search via LOPAS; call 804-786-5511 to apply.
Criminal Records: Access: Online, in person. Visitors must perform in person searches themselves. Court makes copy: $1.00 per page. Required to search: name, years to search, DOB, SSN. Criminal records on computer for 10 years, prior records at City of Salem Circuit Court. Online access to criminal records is the same as civil.
General Information: Public use terminal available. No juvenile, sealed records released. Certification fee: $1.00 per page. Payee: General District Court. Personal checks accepted. Prepayment required.

Scott County

Circuit Court 104 E Jackson St, #2, Gate City, VA 24251; phone: 276-386-3801; fax: 276-386-2430; hours 8:30AM-5PM (EST). *Felony, Civil Actions Over $15,000, Probate.*
www.courts.state.va.us/courts/circuit.html
Civil Records: Access: Phone, mail, online, in person. Both court and visitors may perform in person searches. No search fee. Court makes copy: $.50 per page; same fee for self serve. Required to search: name, years to search. Civil cases indexed by defendant, plaintiff; on index books back to 1815; on computer back to 1999. Search free at http://208.210.219.132/vacircuit/select.jsp. Also search via LOPAS; call 804-786-5511 to apply. Mail turnaround time 3-4 days.
Criminal Records: Access: Mail, online, in person. Both court and visitors may perform in person searches. No search fee. Court makes copy: $.50 per page; same fee for self serve. Required to search: name, years to search, DOB; also helpful: SSN. Criminal records on index books back to 1815; on computer back to 1999. Online access to criminal records is the same as civil. Mail turnaround time 3-4 days.
General Information: Public terminal has criminal back to 1815 and civil back to 1815. No juvenile, sealed records released. Fee to fax documents is $4.00 per page. Certification fee: $2.00. Payee: Mark A "Bo" Taylor, Clerk. Personal checks accepted. Prepayment and SASE required.

30th General District Court 104 E Jackson St, #9, Gate City, VA 24251; phone: 276-386-7341; fax: 276-386-2840; hours 8:15AM-4:45PM (EST). *Misdemeanor, Civil Actions Under $15,000, Eviction, Small Claims.*
Civil Records: Access: Mail, online, in person. Only the court performs in person searches; visitors may not. No search fee. Court makes copy: $1.00 per page. Required to search: name, years to search. Civil cases indexed by plaintiff. Civil records on index books, on computer from 1990. Search free at http://208.210.219.132/vadistrict/select.jsp. Also search via LOPAS; call 804-786-5511 to apply. Mail turnaround time up to 1-2 days.
Criminal Records: Access: Mail, online, in person. Only the court performs in person searches; visitors may not. No search fee. Court makes copy: $1.00 per page. Required to search: name, years to search, DOB; also helpful: SSN. Criminal records on index books, on computer from 1990. Online access to criminal records is the same as civil. Mail turnaround time up to 1-2 days.
General Information: No juvenile, sealed records released. No certification fee. Payee: General District

Court. Personal checks accepted. Prepayment and SASE required.

Shenandoah County

26th Circuit Court 112 S Main St, PO Box 406, Woodstock, VA 22664; phone: 540-459-6150; fax: 540-459-6155; hours 9AM-5PM (EST). *Felony, Civil Actions Over $15,000, Probate.*
www.courts.state.va.us/courts/circuit.html
Civil Records: Access: Mail, online, in person. Only the court performs in person searches; visitors may not. No search fee. Court makes copy: $.50 per page. Required to search: name, years to search. Civil cases indexed by defendant, plaintiff; on computer from 1996, on index cards from 1772. Search free at http://208.210.219.132/vacircuit/select.jsp. Also search via LOPAS; call 804-786-5511 to apply. Note: Mail access limited to specific cases only, or a single name search.
Criminal Records: Access: Online, in person. Visitors must perform in person searches themselves. Court makes copy: $.50 per page. Required to search: name, years to search, DOB; also helpful: SSN. Criminal records on computer from 1996, on index cards from 1772. Online access to criminal records is the same as civil.
General Information: No juvenile, sealed records released. Certification fee: $2.00 per doc. Payee: Clerk of Circuit Court. Personal checks accepted. Prepayment and SASE required.

26th General District Court 114 W Court St, Woodstock, VA 22664; phone: 540-459-6130; fax: 540-459-7279; hours 8:30AM-4:30PM (EST). *Misdemeanor, Civil Actions Under $15,000, Eviction, Small Claims.*
Civil Records: Access: Mail, online, in person. Visitors must perform in person searches themselves. Court makes copy: $1.00 minimum for first 2 pages, $.50 each add'l page. Required to search: name, years to search. Civil cases indexed by defendant, plaintiff; on computer from 1995, prior at Circuit Court. Search free at http://208.210.219.132/vadistrict/select.jsp. Also search via LOPAS; call 804-786-5511 to apply.
Criminal Records: Access: Online, mail, in person. Visitors must perform in person searches themselves. Court makes copy: $1.00 minimum for first 2 pages, $.50 each add'l. Required to search: name, years to search, DOB; also helpful: SSN. Criminal records on computer from 1995, prior at Circuit Court. Online access to criminal records is the same as civil. Note: This agency will not do criminal record checks and refer all requesters to the State Police or the online system.
General Information: Public terminal goes back to 1995. No sealed or adoption records relapsed. No certification fee. Payee: General District Court. Personal checks and Visa/MC credit cards accepted. Accepted for criminal fines and on online system only. Prepayment required.

Smyth County

28th Circuit Court 109 W Main St, #144, Marion, VA 24354-2510; phone: 276-782-4044; criminal fax: 276-782-4045; same fax for civil/probate; hours 9AM-5PM (EST). *Felony, Civil Actions Over $15,000, Probate.*
www.courts.state.va.us/courts/circuit.html
Note: Probate is in a separate index at this address.
Civil Records: Access: Mail, fax, online, in person. Both court and visitors may perform in person searches. Search fee: $10.00 per name. Court makes copy: $.50 per page; same fee for self serve. Required to search: name, years to search. Civil cases indexed by defendant, plaintiff; on index cards from 1832, most are computerized since 1/90. Search free at http://208.210.219.132/vacircuit/select.jsp. Also search via LOPAS; call 804-786-5511 to apply. Mail turnaround time 1 week.
Criminal Records: Access: Mail, fax, online, in person. Both court and visitors may perform in person searches. Search fee: $10.00 per name. Court

makes copy: $.50 per page; same fee for self serve. Required to search: name, years to search; also helpful: DOB, SSN. Criminal records on index cards from 1832, most are computerized since 1/90. Online access to criminal records is the same as civil. Mail turnaround time 1 week.
General Information: No juvenile, sealed or adoption records released. Fee to fax documents is $1.00 per page. Certification fee: $2.00. Payee: Clerk of Circuit Court. Personal checks accepted. Prepayment required. SASE requested.

28th General District Court Smythe County Courthouse, Rm 231, 109 W Main St, Marion, VA 24354; phone: 276-782-4047; fax: 276-782-4048; hours 8:30AM-4:30PM (EST). *Misdemeanor, Civil Actions Under $15,000, Eviction, Small Claims.*
Civil Records: Access: Phone, mail, online, in person. Both court and visitors may perform in person searches. No search fee. Court makes copy: $.50 per page. Required to search: name, years to search; also helpful: address. Civil cases indexed by defendant, plaintiff; on computer back to 7/90. Search free at http://208.210.219.132/vadistrict/select.jsp. Also search via LOPAS; call 804-786-5511 to apply. Mail turnaround time 1-2 days.
Criminal Records: Access: Phone, mail, online, in person. Both court and visitors may perform in person searches. No search fee. Court makes copy: $.50 per page. Required to search: name, years to search, DOB; also helpful: SSN. Criminal records on computer back to 7/90. Online access to criminal records is the same as civil. Mail turnaround time 1-2 days.
General Information: Public terminal goes back to 7/1990. No juvenile, sealed records released. No certification fee. Payee: General District Court. Personal checks or Visa, MC accepted. Prepayment required.

South Boston City

Circuit & District Courts
www.courts.state.va.us/courts/circuit.html
Note: See Halifax County.

Southampton County

5th Circuit Court PO Box 190, Courtland, VA 23837; phone: 757-653-2200; hours 8:30AM-5PM (EST). *Felony, Civil Actions Over $15,000, Probate.*
www.courts.state.va.us/courts/circuit.html
Civil Records: Access: Mail, online, in person. Both court and visitors may perform in person searches. Search fee: $5.00 per name. Court makes copy: $.50 per page. Required to search: name, years to search. Civil cases indexed by plaintiff. Civil records on index books from 1749; on computer back to 1990. Search free at http://208.210.219.132/vacircuit/select.jsp. Also search via LOPAS; call 804-786-5511 to apply. Note: Will not certify searches. Mail turnaround time 1-5 days.
Criminal Records: Access: Mail, online, in person. Both court and visitors may perform in person searches. Search fee: $5.00. Court makes copy: $.50 per page. Required to search: name, years to search. Criminal records on index books from 1749; on computer back to 1990. Online access to criminal records is the same as civil. Note: Will not certify searches. Mail turnaround time 1-5 days.
General Information: Public terminal goes back to 1990. No juvenile, sealed, adoption records released. Certification fee: $2.00 per document. Payee: Clerk of Circuit Court. Personal checks accepted. Prepayment required.

5th General District Court PO Box 347, Courtland, VA 23837; phone: 757-653-2673; fax: 757-653-2656; hours 8:30AM-4:30PM (EST). *Misdemeanor, Civil Actions Under $15,000, Eviction, Small Claims.*
Civil Records: Access: Mail, online, in person. Both court and visitors may perform in person searches. No search fee. Court makes copy: $1.00 1st 2 pages; $.50 each add'l. Required to search: name, years to

search. Civil cases indexed by defendant. Civil records on index cards, docket books and computer from 1985, prior records at Circuit Court. Search free at http://208.210.219.132/vadistrict/select.jsp. Also search via LOPAS; call 804-786-5511 to apply. Mail turnaround time 1-5 days.
Criminal Records: Access: Mail, online, in person. Both court and visitors may perform in person searches. No search fee. Court makes copy: $1.00 1st 2 pages; $.50 each add'l. Required to search: name, years to search, DOB; also helpful: SSN. Criminal records on index cards, docket books and computer from 1985, prior records at Circuit Court. Online access to criminal records is the same as civil. Mail turnaround time 1-5 days.
General Information: Public terminal goes back to 1985. No juvenile, sealed, adoption records released. Fee to fax documents is $2.00 per document. No certification fee. Payee: Clerk of General District Court. Personal checks accepted. Credit cards accepted. Prepayment required.

Spotsylvania County

15th Circuit Court PO Box 96, 9113 Courthouse Rd, Spotsylvania, VA 22553; phone: 540-582-7090; fax: 540-582-2169; hours 8AM-4:30PM (EST). *Felony, Civil Actions Over $15,000, Probate.*
www.courts.state.va.us/courts/circuit.html
Civil Records: Access: Online, in person. Visitors must perform in person searches themselves. Court makes copy: $.50 per page. Required to search: name, years to search. Civil cases indexed by defendant, plaintiff; on computer from 1996, on index books from late 1700s. Search free at http://208.210.219.132/vacircuit/select.jsp. Also search via LOPAS; call 804-786-5511 to apply. Note: Mail access limited to specific case only.
Criminal Records: Access: Online, in person. Visitors must perform in person searches themselves. Court makes copy: $.50 per page. Required to search: name, years to search, DOB, SSN. Criminal records on computer from 1996, on index books from late 1700s. Select and search Circuit Courts online at http://208.210.219.132/vacircuit/select.jsp. For information about the statewide online systems, see the state introduction.
General Information: Public use terminal available. No juvenile, sealed, adoption records released. Certification fee: $2.00. Payee: Clerk of Circuit Court. Personal checks accepted. Prepayment required.

15th General District Court Judicial Center, PO Box 339, Spotsylvania, VA 22553; phone: 540-582-7110; fax: 540-582-7288; hours 8AM-4PM (EST). *Misdemeanor, Civil Actions Under $15,000, Eviction, Small Claims.*
Civil Records: Access: Mail, online, in person. Visitors must perform in person searches themselves. No search fee. Court makes copy: $1.00 per page. Required to search: name, years to search. Civil cases indexed by defendant, plaintiff. Civil records go back 10 years; on computer back to 1988. Search free at http://208.210.219.132/vadistrict/select.jsp. Also search via LOPAS; call 804-786-5511 to apply. Mail turnaround time 5 days.
Criminal Records: Access: Mail, online, in person. Visitors must perform in person searches themselves. No search fee. Court makes copy: $1.00 per page. Required to search: name, years to search. Criminal records go back 10 years; on computer back to 1988. Select and search District Courts at http://208.210.219.132/vadistrict/select.jsp. For information about the statewide online systems, see the state introduction. Mail turnaround time 5 days.
General Information: Public terminal goes back to 10 years. No juvenile, sealed records released. Certification fee: $2.00. Payee: Clerk of General District Court. Personal checks accepted. Prepayment required.

Stafford County

15th Circuit Court PO Box 69, Stafford, VA 22554; phone: 540-658-8750; criminal phone: 540-658-8753; civil phone: 540-658-4220; probate phone: 540-658-4176; hours 8AM-4PM (EST). *Felony, Civil Actions Over $15,000, Probate.*
www.co.stafford.va.us/Departments/Courts_&_Legal_Services/Index.shtml

Civil Records: Access: Mail, online, in person. Both court and visitors may perform in person searches. No search fee. Court makes copy: $.50 per page; same fee for self serve. Required to search: name, years to search. Civil cases indexed by defendant, plaintiff. Civil records in index books from 1699, back on computer to 1992. Search free at http://208.210.219.132/vacircuit/select.jsp. Also search via LOPAS; call 804-786-5511 to apply. Mail turnaround time 2-3 weeks.

Criminal Records: Access: Mail, online, in person. Both court and visitors may perform in person searches. No search fee. Court makes copy: $.50 per page; same fee for self serve. Required to search: name, years to search, DOB; also helpful: SSN. Criminal records in index books from 1699, back on computer to 1992. Online access to criminal records is the same as civil. Mail turnaround time 2-3 weeks.

General Information: Public use terminal available. No juvenile, sealed records released. Certification fee: $2.00. Payee: Clerk of Circuit Court. Personal checks accepted. Prepayment required.

15th General District Court 1300 Courthouse Rd, PO Box 940, Stafford, VA 22555; phone: 540-658-8763; criminal phone: 540-658-8935; civil phone: 540-658-4642; fax: 540-658-4834; hours 8:AM-4PM (EST). *Misdemeanor, Civil Actions Under $15,000, Eviction, Small Claims.*

Civil Records: Access: Fax, mail, online, in person. Both court and visitors may perform in person searches. No search fee. Court makes copy: $1.00 per page. Required to search: name, years to search. Civil cases indexed by defendant, plaintiff; on computer since 1986, prior at Circuit Court. Search free at http://208.210.219.132/vadistrict/select.jsp. Also search via LOPAS; call 804-786-5511 to apply. Mail turnaround time 2-7 days.

Criminal Records: Access: Fax, mail, online, in person. Both court and visitors may perform in person searches. No search fee. Court makes copy: $1.00 per page. Required to search: name, years to search. Criminal records on computer since 1986, prior at Circuit Court. Online access to criminal records is the same as civil. Mail turnaround time 2-7 days.

General Information: Public terminal goes back to 1995. No sealed records released. No fee to fax documents. No certification fee. Payee: Clerk of General District Court. Personal checks or Visa, MC accepted. Prepayment required. SASE requested.

Staunton City

25th Circuit Court PO Box 1286, Staunton, VA 24402-1286; phone: 540-332-3874; fax: 540-332-3970; hours 8:30AM-5PM (EST). *Felony, Civil Actions Over $15,000, Probate.*
www.courts.state.va.us/courts/circuit.html

Civil Records: Access: Mail, online, in person. Both court and visitors may perform in person searches. No search fee. Court makes copy: $.50 per page; same fee for self serve. Required to search: name, years to search. Civil cases indexed by defendant, plaintiff; on index books since 1802; on computer back to 1988. Search free at http://208.210.219.132/vacircuit/select.jsp. Also search via LOPAS; call 804-786-5511 to apply.

Criminal Records: Access: Online, in person. Both court and visitors may perform in person searches. Court makes copy: $.50 per page; same fee for self serve. Required to search: name, years to search. Criminal records on index books since 1802; on computer back to 1988. Online access to criminal records is the same as civil.

General Information: Public terminal goes back to 1988. No juvenile, sealed or adoption records released. Fee to fax documents is $.50 per page. Certification fee: $2.00. Payee: Clerk of Circuit Court. Personal checks accepted. Prepayment required.

Staunton General District Court 113 E Beverly St, Staunton, VA 24401-4390; phone: 540-332-3878; fax: 540-332-3985; hours 8:30AM-4:30PM (EST). *Misdemeanor, Civil Actions Under $15,000, Eviction, Small Claims.*

Civil Records: Access: Mail, phone, fax, online, in person. Both court and visitors may perform in person searches. No search fee. Court makes copy: $.50 per page. Required to search: name, years to search; also helpful: address. Civil cases indexed by defendant, plaintiff; on computer back 10 years. Select and search District Courts at http://208.210.219.132/vadistrict/select.jsp. For information about the statewide online systems, see the state introduction. Records are maintained for 10 years. Mail turnaround time 1-5 days.

Criminal Records: Access: Mail, online, in person. Both court and visitors may perform in person searches. No search fee. Court makes copy: $.50 per page. Required to search: name, years to search, DOB. Criminal records indexed on computer since 1991. Online access to criminal records is the same as civil. Records are maintained for 10 years. Mail turnaround time 1-5 days.

General Information: Public terminal has criminal back to 1991 and civil back to 10 years. No certification fee. Payee: Staunton General District Court. Personal checks or Visa, MC accepted. Credit cards accepted for criminal & traffic cases only. Prepayment required.

Suffolk City

Suffolk Circuit Court PO Box 1604, Suffolk, VA 23439-1604; phone: 757-923-2251; fax: 757-934-3490; hours 8:30AM-5PM (EST). *Felony, Civil Actions Over $15,000, Probate.*
www.courts.state.va.us/courts/circuit.html

Civil Records: Access: Online, in person. Visitors must perform in person searches themselves. Court makes copy: $.50 per page. Required to search: name, years to search. Civil cases indexed by defendant, plaintiff; on computer from 1989, on index books from 1866. Search free at http://208.210.219.132/vacircuit/select.jsp. Also search via LOPAS; call 804-786-5511 to apply.

Criminal Records: Access: Online, in person. Visitors must perform in person searches themselves. Court makes copy: $.50 per page. Required to search: name, years to search. Criminal records on computer from 1989, on index books from 1866. Online access to criminal records is the same as civil.

General Information: No juvenile, sealed, adoption records released. Certification fee: $1.50. Payee: Clerk of Circuit Court. Personal checks or Visa, MC accepted. Prepayment required.

5th General District Court 150 N Main St, PO Box 1648, Suffolk, VA 23434; phone: 757-923-2281; fax: 757-925-1790; hours 8AM-4PM (EST). *Misdemeanor, Civil Actions up to $15,000, Eviction, Small Claims.*

Civil Records: Access: Mail, online, in person. Both court and visitors may perform in person searches. Court makes copy: $1.00 1st page, $.50 each add'l. Required to search: name, years to search. Civil cases indexed by defendant, plaintiff; on computer from 1992 prior on index cards. Records destroyed after 10 years. Search free at http://208.210.219.132/vadistrict/select.jsp. Also search via LOPAS; call 804-786-5511 to apply. Mail turnaround time 1 week.

Criminal Records: Access: Online, mail, in person. Visitors must perform in person searches themselves. Court makes copy: $1.00 1st page, $.50 each add'l. Required to search: name, years to search, DOB; also helpful: SSN. Criminal records on computer from 1992, prior on index cards. Online access to criminal records is the same as civil. Mail turnaround time 1 week.

General Information: Public terminal goes back to 1992. No juvenile, sealed, adoptions records released. No certification fee. Payee: Suffolk General District Court. Personal checks or Visa, MC accepted. Prepayment and SASE required.

Surry County

6th Circuit Court 28 Colonial Trail E, PO Box 203, Surry, VA 23883; phone: 757-294-3161; criminal fax: 757-294-0471; same fax for civil/probate; hours 9AM-5PM (EST). *Felony, Civil Actions Over $15,000, Probate.*
www.courts.state.va.us/courts/circuit.html

Civil Records: Access: In person, online. Visitors must perform in person searches themselves. Self serve copy fee: $.50 per page. Required to search: name, years to search. Civil cases indexed by defendant, plaintiff; on cards. Remote online access to court case indexes is via LOPAS; call 804-786-5511 to apply.

Criminal Records: Access: In person, online. Visitors must perform in person searches themselves. Self serve copy fee: $.50 per page. Required to search: name, years to search, DOB; also helpful: SSN. Criminal records on cards. Online access to criminal records is the same as civil.

General Information: Juvenile, sealed records not released. Will not fax documents. Certification fee: $2.00 per document. Payee: Circuit Clerk. Business checks accepted.

6th General District Court Hwy 10 and School St, PO Box 332, Surry, VA 23883; phone: 757-294-5201; fax: 757-294-0312; hours 8:30AM-4:30PM (EST). *Misdemeanor, Civil Actions Under $15,000, Eviction, Small Claims.*

Civil Records: Access: Online, in person. Visitors must perform in person searches themselves. No copy fee. Required to search: name, years to search. Civil cases indexed by defendant, plaintiff; on computer since 11/93, on books from 1985, prior at Circuit Court. Search free at http://208.210.219.132/vadistrict/select.jsp. Also search via LOPAS; call 804-786-5511 to apply.

Criminal Records: Access: Online, in person. Visitors must perform in person searches themselves. No copy fee. Required to search: name, years to search, DOB; also helpful: SSN. Criminal records on computer since 11/93, on books from 1985, prior at Circuit Court. Online access to criminal records is the same as civil.

General Information: Public terminal goes back to 1997. No juvenile, sealed, adoption records released. Certification fee: $2.00 first 2 pages; add copy fee for each add'l page. Payee: General District Court.

Sussex County

6th Circuit Court PO Box 1337, Sussex, VA 23884; phone: 434-246-1017; probate phone: 434-246-1012; fax: 434-246-2203; hours 9AM-5PM (EST). *Felony, Civil Actions Over $15,000, Probate.*
www.courts.state.va.us/courts/circuit.html

Civil Records: Access: Mail, online, in person. Only the court performs in person searches; visitors may not. Search fee: $5.00. Court makes copy: $.50 per page. Required to search: name, years to search. Civil cases indexed by defendant, plaintiff; on index books from 1950. Remote online access to court case indexes is via LOPAS; call 804-786-5511 to apply. Mail turnaround time 1-2 days.

Criminal Records: Access: Mail, online, in person. Only the court performs in person searches; visitors may not. Search fee: $5.00. Court makes copy: $.50 per page. Required to search: name, years to search, DOB, SSN, signed release. Criminal records on index books from 1754; on computer back to 1991. Online access to criminal records is the same as civil. Mail turnaround time 1-2 days.

General Information: No juvenile, sealed, adoption, or confidential records released. Fee to fax documents is $1.00 per page. Certification fee: $2.00. Payee:

[middle column, top] access to criminal records is the same as civil. Mail turnaround time 1 week.

General Information: Public terminal goes back to 1992. No juvenile, sealed, adoptions records released. No certification fee. Payee: Suffolk General District Court. Personal checks or Visa, MC accepted. Prepayment and SASE required.

Clerk of Circuit Court. Personal checks accepted. Prepayment required.

6th Judicial District Court Sussex Cnty Courthouse, 15098 Courthouse Rd, Rte 735, PO Box 1315, Sussex, VA 23884; phone: 434-246-5511; criminal phone: x3273; civil phone: x3240; fax: 434-246-6604; hours 8:30AM-4:30PM (EST). *Misdemeanor, Civil Actions Under $15,000, Eviction, Small Claims.*

Civil Records: Access: Online, in person. Visitors must perform in person searches themselves. Court makes copy: $1.00 minimum for first 2 pages, $.50 each add'l page. Required to search: name, years to search. Civil cases indexed by defendant, plaintiff; on computer from 9/88, on index cards from 1985, prior in Circuit Court. Search free at http://208.210.219.132/vadistrict/select.jsp. Also search via LOPAS; call 804-786-5511 to apply.

Criminal Records: Access: Online, in person. Visitors must perform in person searches themselves. Court makes copy: $1.00 minimum for first 2 pages, thereafter $.50 per page. Required to search: name, years to search, DOB; also helpful: SSN. Criminal records on computer from 9/88, on index cards from 1985, prior in Circuit Court. Online access to criminal records is the same as civil.

General Information: Public terminal goes back to 1988. No juvenile, sealed, adoption records released. No certification fee. Payee: Sussex District Court. Personal checks or Visa, MC accepted. Prepayment required.

Tazewell County

29th Circuit Court PO Box 968, Tazewell, VA 24651-0968; phone: 276-988-1222; criminal fax: 276-988-7501; same fax for civil/probate; hours 8AM-4:30PM (EST). *Felony, Civil Actions Over $15,000, Probate.*
www.courts.state.va.us/courts/circuit.html
Civil Records: Access: Mail, online, in person. Both court and visitors may perform in person searches. No search fee. Court makes copy: $.50 per page; same fee for self serve. Required to search: name, years to search. Civil cases indexed by defendant, plaintiff; on index cards from 1800s. Online access free at http://208.210.219.132/vacircuit/select.jsp. For information about the statewide online systems, see the state introduction. Mail turnaround time 1-3 days.

Criminal Records: Access: Mail, online, in person. Both court and visitors may perform in person searches. No search fee. Court makes copy: $.50 per page; same fee for self serve. Required to search: name, years to search, signed release. Criminal records on computer from 1992. Online access to criminal records is the same as civil. Mail turnaround time 1-3 days.

General Information: Public terminal goes back to 1991. No juvenile, sealed records released. Will fax documents to local or toll free line. Certification fee: $2.00. Payee: Clerk of Circuit Court. Personal checks accepted. Prepayment required.

29th General District Court PO Box 566, Tazewell, VA 24651; phone: 276-988-9057; fax: 276-988-6202; hours 8:30AM-4:30PM (EST). *Misdemeanor, Civil Actions Under $15,000, Eviction, Small Claims.*

Civil Records: Access: Mail, fax, online, in person. Both court and visitors may perform in person searches. No search fee. Court makes copy: $.50 per page. Required to search: name, years to search. Civil cases indexed by defendant, plaintiff; on computer back to 1991, prior records to 1985 at Circuit Court. Search free at http://208.210.219.132/vadistrict/select.jsp. Also search via LOPAS; call 804-786-5511 to apply. Mail turnaround time 1-3 days.

Criminal Records: Access: Mail, fax, online, in person. Both court and visitors may perform in person searches. No search fee. Court makes copy: $.50 per page. Required to search: name, years to search, DOB; also helpful: SSN, signed release.

Criminal records on computer back to 1995, prior records to 1985 at Circuit Court. Online access to criminal records is the same as civil. Mail turnaround time 1-3 days.

General Information: Public use terminal available. No sealed records released. Fee to fax documents is $1.00 per document and $1.00 per page. No certification fee. Payee: Clerk of General District Court. Personal checks or Visa, MC accepted. Prepayment required.

Virginia Beach City

2nd Circuit Court 2425 Nimmo Pky, Virginia Beach, VA 23456-9017; phone: 757-427-4181; criminal phone: 757-427-4186; civil phone: 757-427-4186; probate phone: 757-427-8831; fax: 757-426-5686; hours 8:30AM-5PM (EST). *Felony, Civil Actions Over $15,000, Probate.*
www.vbgov.com/courts/
Note: Probate is a separate index at this same address
Civil Records: Access: Online, in person. Visitors must perform in person searches themselves. Court makes copy: $.50 per page. Required to search: name, years to search. Civil cases indexed by defendant, plaintiff; on computer from 1986, on files from 1960s. Online access free at http://208.210.219.132/vacircuit/select.jsp. For information about the statewide online systems, see the state introduction.

Criminal Records: Access: Online, in person. Visitors must perform in person searches themselves. Court makes copy: $.50 per page. Required to search: name, years to search, DOB; also helpful: SSN. Criminal records on computer from 1986, on files from 1960s. Online access to criminal records is the same as civil.

General Information: Public terminal goes back to late 1986. No juvenile, sealed, presentencing probation report, judges notes or adoption records released. Will not fax documents. Certification fee: $2.00 per document. Payee: Clerk of Circuit Court. Personal checks accepted. Prepayment required.

2nd General District Court 2425 Nimmo Pky, Judicial Center, Virginia Beach, VA 23456-9057; phone: 757-427-8531 Court Info Line; criminal phone: 757-427-4707; civil phone: 757-427-4277; fax: 757-426-5672; hours 8:30AM-4PM (EST). *Misdemeanor, Civil Actions Under $15,000, Eviction, Small Claims.*
www.vbgov.com/courts/
Civil Records: Access: Mail, online, in person. Visitors must perform in person searches themselves. Required to search: name, years to search. Civil cases indexed by defendant, plaintiff; on computer from 1987. Search free at http://208.210.219.132/vadistrict/select.jsp. Also search via LOPAS; call 804-786-5511 to apply. Civil cases decided on or before 01/01/85 retained 10 years, after that date retained 20 years. Mail turnaround time 3-4 weeks.

Criminal Records: Access: Mail, online, in person. Visitors must perform in person searches themselves. Required to search: name, years to search, DOB; also helpful: SSN. Criminal records on computer back ten years, then destroyed. Online access to criminal records is the same as civil. Mail turnaround time 3-4 weeks.

General Information: Public terminal has criminal back to 10 years and civil back to 1987. No juvenile, sealed, adoption or mental records released. No fee to fax documents. No certification fee. Payee: Clerk of General District Court. Personal checks accepted. Prepayment required.

Warren County

Circuit Court 1 E Main St, Front Royal, VA 22630; phone: 540-635-2435; criminal fax: 540-636-3274; same fax for civil/probate; hours 9AM-5PM (EST). *Felony, Civil, Probate.*
www.courts.state.va.us/courts/circuit/warren/home.html

Note: Phone and fax access limited to law enforcement and agencies only. Probate records are in a separate index at this same address.

Civil Records: Access: Mail, online, in person. Both court and visitors may perform in person searches. No search fee. Court makes copy: $.50 per page; same fee for self serve. Required to search: name, years to search. Civil cases indexed by defendant, plaintiff; on archives from 1836; on computer since 1986. Online access free at http://208.210.219.132/vacircuit/select.jsp. For information about the statewide online systems, see the state introduction. Mail turnaround time 1-2 weeks.

Criminal Records: Access: Mail, online, in person. Both court and visitors may perform in person searches. No search fee. Court makes copy: $.50 per page; same fee for self serve. Required to search: name, years to search, DOB; also helpful: SSN. Criminal records on archives from 1836; on computer since 1986. Online access to criminal records is the same as civil. Mail turnaround time 1-2 weeks.

General Information: Public terminal goes back to 1986. No juvenile, sealed, adoption records released. Will fax documents to local or toll-free line. Certification fee: $2.00. Payee: Jennifer R Sims Clerk. Personal checks accepted. Prepayment and SASE required.

26th General District Court 1 E Main St, Front Royal, VA 22630; phone: 540-635-2335; fax: 540-636-8233; hours 8:15AM-4:15PM (EST). *Misdemeanor, Civil Actions Under $15,000, Eviction, Small Claims.*

Civil Records: Access: Mail, fax, online, in person. Both court and visitors may perform in person searches. No search fee. Court makes copy: $.50 per page. Required to search: name, years to search. Civil cases indexed by defendant. Civil records in archives back to 1800s, on computer from 1989. Search free at http://208.210.219.132/vadistrict/select.jsp. Also search via LOPAS; call 804-786-5511 to apply. Mail turnaround time 2-3 days.

Criminal Records: Access: Mail, fax, online, in person. Both court and visitors may perform in person searches. No search fee. Court makes copy: $.50 per page. Required to search: name, years to search. Criminal records in archives, on computer from 1989. Online access to criminal records is the same as civil. Mail turnaround time 2-3 days.

General Information: Public terminal goes back to 1989. No certification fee. Payee: General District Court. Personal checks accepted. Prepayment and SASE required.

Washington County

Circuit Court PO Box 289, Abingdon, VA 24212-0289; phone: 276-676-6224/6226; fax: 276-676-6218; hours 8:30AM-5PM (EST). *Felony, Civil Actions Over $15,000, Probate.*
www.courts.state.va.us/courts/circuit.html
Civil Records: Access: Mail, in person. Both court and visitors may perform in person searches. Search fee: Search fee is determined by time involved. Court makes copy: $.50 per page; same fee for self serve. Required to search: name, years to search within 5 year. Civil cases indexed by defendant, plaintiff; on archives from 1777, on computer from 1991.

Criminal Records: Access: In person only. Visitors must perform in person searches themselves. Court makes copy: $.50 per page; same fee for self serve. Required to search: name, years to search. Criminal records on archives from 1777, on computer from 1991.

General Information: Public terminal goes back to 1990. No juvenile, sealed or adoption records released. Will fax documents to local or toll free line. Certification fee: $2.00. Payee: Clerk, Circuit Court. Personal checks accepted. Prepayment and SASE required.

28th General District Court 191 E Main St, Abingdon, VA 24210; phone: 276-676-6281; fax: 276-676-3136; hours 8:30AM-4:30PM (EST). *Misdemeanor, Civil Actions Under $15,000, Eviction, Small Claims.*
Civil Records: Access: Mail, online, in person. Both court and visitors may perform in person searches. No search fee. Court makes copy: $1.00 for first page, $.50 each add'l. Required to search: name, years to search. Civil cases indexed by defendant, plaintiff; on archives from 1777, on computer from 1994. Search free at http://208.210.219.132/vadistrict/select.jsp. Also search via LOPAS; call 804-786-5511 to apply. Mail turnaround time 1-2 days.
Criminal Records: Access: Mail, online, in person. Both court and visitors may perform in person searches. No search fee. Court makes copy: $1.00 for first page, $.50 each add'l. Required to search: name, years to search. Criminal records on archives from 1777, on computer from 1994. Online access to criminal records is the same as civil. Mail turnaround time 1-2 days.
General Information: Public terminal goes back to 10 years. No sealed records released. Will not fax documents. Certification fee: $2.00. Payee: General District Court. Personal checks or Visa, MC accepted. Prepayment and SASE required.

Waynesboro City

25th Circuit Court 250 S Wayne Ave, PO Box 910, Waynesboro, VA 22980; phone: 540-942-6616; fax: 540-942-6774; hours 8:30AM-5PM (EST). *Felony, Civil Actions Over $15,000, Probate.*
www.courts.state.va.us/courts/circuit.html
Civil Records: Access: Online, in person. Visitors must perform in person searches themselves. Court makes copy: $.50 per page. Required to search: name, years to search. Civil cases indexed by defendant, plaintiff; on computer from 11/88 (some), all on index books from 5/48. Online access free at http://208.210.219.132/vacircuit/select.jsp. For information about the statewide online systems, see the state introduction.
Criminal Records: Access: Online, in person. Visitors must perform in person searches themselves. Court makes copy: $.50 per page. Required to search: name, years to search, DOB; also helpful: SSN. Criminal records on computer from 11/88 (some), all on index books from 5/48. Online access to criminal records is the same as civil.
General Information: Public use terminal available. No juvenile, sealed, adoptions released. Certification fee: $2.00. Payee: Clerk of Circuit Court. Personal checks accepted. Prepayment required.

25th General District Court - Waynesboro 237 Market Ave, PO Box 1028, Waynesboro, VA 22980; phone: 540-942-6636; fax: 540-942-6666; hours 8:30AM-4:30PM (EST). *Misdemeanor, Civil Actions Under $15,000, Eviction, Small Claims.*
www.courts.state.va.us/courts/gd/Waynesboro/home.html
Civil Records: Access: Mail, fax, online, in person. Visitors must perform in person searches themselves. No search fee. No copy fee; same fee for self serve. Required to search: name, years to search. Civil cases indexed by defendant, plaintiff; on computer 10 years. Search court records free at http://208.210.219.132/vadistrict/select.jsp. Mail turnaround time up to 1 week.
Criminal Records: Access: Mail, fax, online, in person. Visitors must perform in person searches themselves. No search fee. No copy fee; same fee for self serve. Required to search: name, years to search. Criminal records on computer for 10 years. Online access to criminal records is the same as civil. Mail turnaround time up to 1 week.
General Information: Public terminal goes back to 10 years. Will fax documents. No certification fee.

Westmoreland County

15th Circuit Court PO Box 307, Montross, VA 22520; phone: 804-493-0108; fax: 804-493-0393; hours 9AM-5PM (EST). *Felony, Civil Actions Over $15,000, Probate.*
www.courts.state.va.us/courts/circuit.html
Note: Probate index is separate.

Civil Records: Access: In person, online. Visitors must perform in person searches themselves. Court makes copy: $.50 per page; same fee for self serve. Required to search: name, years to search. Civil cases indexed by defendant, plaintiff; on index books from 1653. Remote online access to court case indexes is via LOPAS; call 804-786-5511 to apply.
Criminal Records: Access: In person. Visitors must perform in person searches themselves. Court makes copy: $.50 per page; same fee for self serve. Required to search: name, years to search, DOB; also helpful: SSN. Criminal records on index books from 1653.
General Information: No juvenile, sealed, adoption records released. Will not fax documents. Certification fee: $3.00 includes copy fee. Payee: Clerk of Circuit Court. No personal checks accepted. Prepayment required. Will bill copy fees.

15th General District Court PO Box 688, Montross, VA 22520; phone: 804-493-0105; hours 8AM-4:30PM (EST). *Misdemeanor, Civil Actions Under $15,000, Small Claims.*
Civil Records: Access: Mail, online, in person. Both court and visitors may perform in person searches. No search fee. Court makes copy: $1.00 for first page, $.50 each add'l. Required to search: name, years to search. Civil cases indexed by defendant, plaintiff; on computer back 10 years. Search free at http://208.210.219.132/vadistrict/select.jsp. Also search via LOPAS; call 804-786-5511 to apply. Mail turnaround time 1 week.
Criminal Records: Access: Mail, online, in person. Both court and visitors may perform in person searches. No search fee. Court makes copy: $1.00 for first page, $.50 each add'l. Required to search: name, years to search; also helpful: DOB, SSN, date of offense. Criminal records on computer back 10 years. Online access to criminal records is the same as civil. Mail turnaround time 1 week.
General Information: Public terminal goes back to 10 years. All records public. No certification fee. Payee: General District Court. Personal checks accepted. Attorney checks accepted. Visa, MC accepted. Prepayment and SASE required.

Williamsburg City

Circuit & District Courts
www.courts.state.va.us/courts/circuit.html
Note: See James City.

Winchester City

26th Circuit Court 5 N Kent St, Winchester, VA 22601; phone: 540-667-5770; fax: 540-667-6638; hours 9AM-5PM (EST). *Felony, Civil Actions Over $15,000, Probate.*
www.winfredclerk.com
Note: The Winchester Court and the Frederick County Court Clerks are housed in the same judicial center. The offices share microfilming and deed indexing systems.
Civil Records: Access: Online, in person. Visitors must perform in person searches themselves. Court makes copy: $.50 per page; same fee for self serve. Required to search: name, years to search. Civil cases indexed by defendant, plaintiff; on computer from 1985 to present, on index books from 1790. Online access free at http://208.210.219.132/vacircuit/select.jsp. For information about the statewide online systems, see the state introduction.
Criminal Records: Access: Mail, online, in person. Both court and visitors may perform in person searches. No search fee. Court makes copy: $.50 per

page; same fee for self serve. Required to search: name, years to search; also helpful: DOB, SSN. Criminal records on computer from 1985 to present, on index books from 1790. Online access to criminal records is the same as civil. Mail turnaround time same day.
General Information: Public use terminal available. No juvenile, sealed, adoption records released. Will fax documents. Certification fee: $2.00. Payee: Clerk of Circuit Court. Personal checks accepted. Prepayment and SASE required.

26th General District Court 5 N Kent St, PO Box 526, Winchester, VA 22604; phone: 540-722-7208; fax: 540-722-1063; hours 8AM-4PM (EST). *Misdemeanor, Civil Actions Under $15,000, Eviction, Small Claims.*
Civil Records: Access: Online, in person. Visitors must perform in person searches themselves. Court makes copy: $.50 per page. Required to search: name, years to search. Civil cases indexed by defendant, plaintiff; on computer from 1992, on index cards from 1985 to 1987, prior at Circuit Court. Search free at http://208.210.219.132/vadistrict/select.jsp. Also search via LOPAS; call 804-786-5511 to apply.
Criminal Records: Access: Online, in person. Visitors must perform in person searches themselves. Court makes copy: $.50 per page. Required to search: name, years, DOB, SSN, signed release. Criminal records on computer from 1992, on index cards from 1985 to 1987, prior at Circuit Court. Online access to criminal records is the same as civil. Note: Forms for criminal searches available from State Police.
General Information: Public terminal goes back to 10 years. No sealed records released. Certification fee: $2.00. Payee: Clerk of General District Court. Personal checks accepted. Prepayment required.

Wise County

30th Circuit Court PO Box 1248, Wise, VA 24293-1248; phone: 276-328-6111; hours 8:30AM-5PM (EST). *Felony, Civil Actions Over $15,000, Probate.*
www.wisecircuitcourt.com
Civil Records: Access: Phone, fax, mail, online, in person. Both court and visitors may perform in person searches. Search fee: $10.00 per name. Court makes copy: $.50 per page; same fee for self serve. Required to search: name, years, also helpful: address. Civil cases indexed by defendant, plaintiff; on archives from 1856. Online access free at http://208.210.219.132/vacircuit/select.jsp. For information about the statewide online systems, see the state introduction. Also, court indexes and images are at www.courtbar.org. Registration and a fee is required. Records go back to June, 2000. Mail turnaround time 2-3 days.
Criminal Records: Access: Phone, fax, mail, online, in person. Both court and visitors may perform in person searches. Search fee: $10.00 per name. Court makes copy: $.50 per page. Required to search: name, years to search, DOB; also helpful: SSN. Criminal records on archives from 1856. Online access to criminal records is the same as civil. Mail turnaround time 2-3 days.
General Information: Public terminal goes back to 1856. No juvenile, sealed or adoption records released. Will not fax documents. Certification fee: $2.00. Payee: Clerk of Circuit Court. Personal checks accepted. Prepayment required.

30th General District Court Wise County Courthouse, PO Box 829, Wise, VA 24293; phone: 276-328-3426; fax: 276-328-4576; hours 8AM-4PM (EST). *Misdemeanor, Civil Actions Under $15,000, Eviction, Small Claims.*
Civil Records: Access: Phone, mail, online, in person. Both court and visitors may perform in person searches. No search fee. Court makes copy: $.50 per page. Required to search: name, years to search. Civil cases indexed by defendant, plaintiff; on computer back 10 years. Search free at http://208.210.219.132/vadistrict/select.jsp. Also

search via LOPAS; call 804-786-5511 to apply. Mail turnaround time 5 days.

Criminal Records: Access: Phone, mail, online, in person. Both court and visitors may perform in person searches. No search fee. Court makes copy: $.50 per page. Required to search: name, years to search; also helpful: DOB, SSN. Criminal records on computer back 10 years. Online access to criminal records is the same as civil. Mail turnaround time 5 days.

General Information: Public terminal goes back to 10 years. No juvenile, sealed records released. No certification fee. Payee: General District Court. Personal checks accepted. Credit cards accepted. Prepayment required.

Wythe County

27th Circuit Court 225 S 4th St, Rm 105, Wytheville, VA 24382; phone: 276-223-6050; fax: 276-223-6057; hours 8:30AM-5PM (EST). *Felony, Civil Actions Over $15,000, Probate.*
www.courts.state.va.us/courts/circuit.html

Civil Records: Access: In person, online. Both court and visitors may perform in person searches. Court makes copy: $.50 per page; same fee for self serve. Required to search: name, years to search. Civil cases indexed by defendant, plaintiff; on computer from 1989, on index cards/books from 1950s (some back to 1790s). Remote online access to court case indexes is via LOPAS; call 804-786-5511 to apply.

Criminal Records: Access: In person, online. Both court and visitors may perform in person searches. No search fee. Court makes copy: $.50 per page; same fee for self serve. Required to search: name, years to search; also helpful: DOB, SSN. Criminal records on computer from 1989, on index cards/books from 1950s (some back to 1790s). Remote online access to court case indexes is via LOPAS; call 804-786-5511 to apply.

General Information: Public terminal goes back to 1/17/95. No juvenile, sealed, adoption records released. No certification fee. Payee: Clerk of Circuit Court. Personal checks accepted. Prepayment required.

Wythe General District Court 245 S 4th St, #205, Wytheville, VA 24382-2595; phone: 276-223-6075; fax: 276-223-6087; hours 8AM-4:30PM (EST). *Misdemeanor, Civil Actions Under $15,000, Eviction, Small Claims.*

Civil Records: Access: Mail, fax, in person, online. Visitors must perform in person searches themselves. No search fee. Fee is only applied to requests for excessive amounts of information. Court makes copy: $.50 per page; same fee for self serve. Required to search: name, years to search. Civil cases indexed by defendant, plaintiff. Civil records maintained on computer for 10 years, prior at Circuit Court. Search free at http://208.210.219.132/vadistrict/select.jsp. Also search via LOPAS; call 804-786-5511 to apply.

Criminal Records: Access: Online, in person. Visitors must perform in person searches themselves. Court makes copy: $.50 per page; same fee for self serve. Required to search: name, years to search; also helpful: DOB, SSN. Criminal records maintained on computer for 10 years. Online access to criminal records is the same as civil.

General Information: Public terminal goes back to 10 years. Will fax documents. No certification fee. Payee: General District Court. Personal checks or Visa, MC accepted. Prepayment required.

York County

9th Circuit Court PO Box 371, Yorktown, VA 23690; phone: 757-890-3350; criminal phone: 757-890-4104; civil phone: 757-890-4105; probate phone: 757-890-4106; fax: 757-890-3364; hours 9AM-5PM (EST). *Felony, Civil Actions Over $15,000, Probate.*
www.yorkcounty.gov/circuitcourt/
Note: Also includes City of Poquoson. Probate is separate index at this same address.

Civil Records: Access: Online, in person. Visitors must perform in person searches themselves. Court makes copy: $.50 per page; same fee for self serve. Required to search: name, years to search. Civil cases indexed by defendant, plaintiff; on index books from 1950, computerized since 1986. Online access free at http://208.210.219.132/vacircuit/select.jsp. For information about the statewide online systems, see the state introduction.

Criminal Records: Access: Mail, online, in person. Visitors must perform in person searches themselves. Search fee: $5.00 per name. Court makes copy: $.50 per page; same fee for self serve. Required to search: name, years to search, DOB; also helpful: SSN. Criminal records on index books from 1950, computerized since 1986. Online access to criminal records is the same as civil. Mail turnaround time 1 week.

General Information: Public terminal goes back to 1986. No juvenile, sealed, adoption records released. Will not fax documents. Certification fee: $2.00. Payee: Clerk of Circuit Court. Personal checks accepted. Prepayment and SASE required.

9th Judicial District Court York County GDC, PO Box 316, Yorktown, VA 23690-0316; phone: 757-890-3450; fax: 757-890-3459; hours 8:30AM-4:30PM (EST). *Misdemeanor, Civil Actions Under $15,000, Eviction, Small Claims.*
www.yorkcounty.gov/districtcourt

Civil Records: Access: Fax, mail, online, in person. Both court and visitors may perform in person searches. No search fee. Court makes copy: $1.00 for first page, $.50 each add'l. Required to search: name, years to search. Civil cases indexed by defendant, plaintiff; on computer back to 1995; prior to 1985 at Circuit Court. Search free at http://208.210.219.132/vadistrict/select.jsp. Also search via LOPAS; call 804-786-5511 to apply. Mail turnaround time 5 days.

Criminal Records: Access: Fax, mail, online, in person. Both court and visitors may perform in person searches. No search fee. Court makes copy: $1.00 for first page, $.50 each add'l. Required to search: name, years to search, DOB, SSN. Criminal records on computer back to 1995; prior to 1985 at Circuit Court. Online access to criminal records is the same as civil. Mail turnaround time 5 days.

General Information: Public terminal goes back to 1995. No juvenile, sealed, adoption records released. Will fax documents $1.00 1st page, $.50 each add'l. No certification fee. Payee: York County General District Court. Prepayment required.

Virginia Recording Offices

ORGANIZATION: 95 counties and 41 independent cities, 123 recording offices. The recording officer is Clerk of Circuit Court. Fifteen independent cities share the Clerk of Circuit Court with the county - Bedford, Covington (Alleghany County), Emporia (Greenville County), Fairfax, Falls Church (Arlington or Fairfax County), Franklin (Southhampton County), Galax (Carroll County), Harrisonburg (Rockingham County), Lexington (Rockbridge County), Manassas and Manassas Park (Prince William County), Norton (Wise County), Poquoson (York County), South Boston (Halifax County), and Williamsburg (James City County. Charles City and James City are counties, not cities. The City of Franklin is not in Franklin County, the City of Richmond is not in Richmond County, and the City of Roanoke is not in Roanoke County. The entire state is in the Eastern Time Zone (EST).

REAL ESTATE RECORDS: Only a few Clerks of Circuit Court will perform real estate searches. Copy fees and certification fees vary. The independent cities may have separate Assessor Offices.

UCC RECORDS: This was a dual filing state. Until 07/2001, financing statements were filed at the state level and with the Clerk of Circuit Court, except for consumer goods, farm and real estate related collateral, which were filed only with the Clerk of Circuit Court. Now, only real estate related collateral is filed at the county level. Some recording offices will perform UCC searches. Use search request form UCC-11. Searches fees and copy fees vary.

TAX LIEN RECORDS: Federal tax liens on personal property of businesses are filed with the State Corporation Commission. Other federal and all state tax liens are filed with the county Clerk of Circuit Court. They are usually filed in a "Judgment Lien Book." Most counties will not perform tax lien searches.

OTHER LIENS: Judgment, mechanics, hospital, lis pendens.

ONLINE ACCESS: A growing number of Virginia counties and cities provide free access to real estate related information via the Internet. A limited but growing private company network named VamaNet provides free residential, commercial and vacant property and tax records. http://www.vamanet.com/info/home.jsp.

Accomack County

Clerk of Circuit Court, PO Box 126, Accomac, VA 23301-0126. 757-787-5776; fax-757-787-1849; hours: 9AM-5PM.
Index: All land records in one. Only the public may search. Copy fee $.50 per page. Cert fee- $2.00 per page plus copy fee. Payee- Accomack County Clerk of Circuit Court. **Property tax/Assessor-** 757-787-5729.

Albemarle County

Clerk of Circuit Court, 501 E. Jefferson St.; Rm 225, Charlottesville, VA 22902-5176. 434-972-4083; fax-434-293-0298; hours: 8:30AM-4:30PM.
All records in one index. Records indexed on a public use terminal back to 1957. Office will perform a UCC search but public must search other records themselves. UCC search per debtor name- $10.00. Copy fee $.50 per page. Cert fee- $2.00 per doc plus copy fee. Payee- Albemarle County Clerk of Circuit Court. **Other phones:** Treasurer-434-296-5851. **Property tax/Assessor-** 401 McIntire Rd #243, Charlottesville, VA 22902; 434-296-5856.

Alexandria City

Clerk of Circuit Court, 520 King St; Rm 307, Alexandria, VA 22314. 703-838-4044, R/E recording phone-703-838-4066; hours: 9AM-5PM. www.ci.alexandria.va.us
All records in one index. Only the public may search. Copy fee $.50 per page. Cert fee- $2.00 per cert plus copy fee. Payee- Alexandria City Clerk of Circuit Court. **Online access to Assessor, Property records:** Access to city real estate assessments is free at www.ci.alexandria.va.us/city/reasearch/. No name searching. **Other phones:** Treasurer- 703-838-6420; Appraiser/Auditor- 703-838-4646; Elections- 703-838-4050; Vital Records- 703-838-4400. **Property tax/Assessor-** 301 King St, Rm 2600, Alexandria, VA 22314; 703-838-4646.

Alleghany County

Clerk of Circuit Court, PO Box 670, Covington, VA 24426-0670. 540-965-1730; fax-540-965-1732; hours: 8:30AM-5PM. www.alleghanycountyclerk.com
Now has records for the former Clifton Forge City. All records in one index. Records indexed on a public use terminal back to 1968. Only the public may search. Copy fee $.50 per page. Cert fee- $2.00 per doc plus copy fee. Payee- Alleghany County Clerk of Court. **Other phones:** Treasurer- 540-863-6630. **Property tax/Assessor-** 540-863-6640.

Amelia County

Clerk of Circuit Court, PO Box 237, Amelia Court House, VA 23002-0237. 804-561-2128; fax-804-561-6364; hours: 8:30AM-4:30PM.
All records in one index. Only the public may search. Copy fee $.50 per page. Cert fee- $2.00 per cert plus copy fee. Payee- Amelia County Clerk of Circuit Court. **Other phones:** Treasurer- 804-561-2145; Elections- 804-561-3460. **Property tax/Assessor-** 804-561-2158.

Amherst County

Clerk of Circuit Court, PO Box 462, Amherst, VA 24521. 434-946-9321; hours: 8AM-5PM.
All records in one index. Only the public may search. Copy fee $.50 per page. R/E record copy- $1.00 per page, $.50 each add'l after 2 pages. Cert fee- $2.00 per cert plus copy fee. Payee- Amherst County Clerk of Circuit Court. **Other phones:** Treasurer- 434-946-9318. **Property tax/Assessor-** 434-946-9310.

Appomattox County

Clerk of Circuit Court, PO Box 672, Appomattox, VA 24522. 434-352-5275; fax-434-352-2781; hours: 8:30AM-4:30PM.
Separate indices to search include books (liens, UCCs) and computer. Records indexed on a public use terminal back to 1973. Office personnel or visitors may perform searches. Will not search real estate records. UCC search per debtor name- $10.00. Copy fee $.50 per page. Cert fee- None. Payee- Appomattox County Clerk of Circuit Court. **Other phones:** Treasurer- 434-352-5200. **Property tax/Assessor-** same address as above. 434-352-7450.

Arlington County

Clerk of Circuit Court, 1425 N. Courthouse Rd, 6th Fl, Arlington, VA 22201. 703-228-4369; hours: 8AM-4PM. www.co.arlington.va.us
Records indexed on a public use terminal back to 1950. Office will perform a UCC search but public must search other records themselves. Search fee $20.00. Copy fee $.50 per page. Cert fee- $2.00 per doc, plus copy fee. Payee- Arlington County Clerk of Circuit Court. **Online access to Real Estate, Assessor, Trade Name records:** Property records on the County assessor database are free at www.co.arlington.va.us/REAssessments/Scripts/DreaDefault.asp. **Property tax/Assessor-** 703-228-3920.

Augusta County

Clerk of Circuit Court, PO Box 689, Staunton, VA 24402-0689. 540-245-5321, R/E recording phone-540-245-5648, UCC recording phone-540-245-5321; fax-540-245-5318; hours: 8AM-5PM.
All records in one index. Records indexed on a public use terminal back to 1992. Only the public may search. Copy fee $.50 per page. Cert fee- $2.00 per cert plus copy fee. Payee- Augusta County Clerk of Circuit Court. **Online access to Property, Appraisal records:** Click on Augusta County to search property data for free at www.vamanet.com/cgi-bin/LOCS. **Other phones:** Treasurer- 540-245-5660. **Property tax/Assessor-** PO Box 590, Staunton, VA 24401; 540-245-5647.

Bath County

Clerk of Circuit Court, PO Box 180, Warm Springs, VA 24484. 540-839-7226; hours: 8:30AM-4:30PM.
All records in one index. Records indexed on computer back to 2000. Only the public may search. Copy fee $.50 per page. Cert fee- $2.00 per cert plus copy fee. Payee- Bath County Clerk of

Circuit Court. **Online access to Property, Land records:** To access property and land records for free go to www.vamanet.com/cgi-bin/MAPSRCHPGM?LOCAL=BAT. **Other phones:** Treasurer- 540-839-7256. **Property tax/Assessor-** 540-839-7231.

Bedford County

Clerk of Circuit Court, 123 E Main St, Bedford, VA 24523. 540-586-7632; fax-540-586-6197; hours: 8:30AM-5PM.
Only the public may search. Copy fee $.50 per page. Cert fee- $2.50. Payee- Bedford County Clerk of Circuit Court. **Online access to Property Tax records:** Real estate records on the Bedford County GIS site are free at www.co.bedford.va.us/Res/GIS/index.htm; however, no name searching at this time. Records on the City of Bedford are free at www.bedfordva.gov/taxf.shtml. Search by name, address or tax map reference number. Also, access City of Bedford GIS property info free at http://bedfordgis.bedfordva.gov/bedfordcity/search.asp?skipopen=1. **Other phones:** Treasurer- 540-586-7670. **Property tax/Assessor-** 540-586-7626.

Bland County

Clerk of Circuit Court, PO Box 295, Bland, VA 24315-0295. 276-688-4562; fax-276-688-2438; hours: 8AM-6PM.
All records in one index. Records indexed on a public use terminal back to varies. Office will perform a UCC search but public must search other records themselves. Search fee $10.00. Copy fee $1.00 per page. Tax lien copy- $.50. Cert fee- $1.00 per page plus copy fee. Payee- Bland County Clerk of Circuit Court. **Other phones:** Treasurer- 276-688-3741. **Property tax/Assessor-** 276-688-4291.

Botetourt County

Clerk of Circuit Court, PO Box 219, Fincastle, VA 24090. 540-473-8274; hours: 8:30AM-4:30PM.
All records in one index. Office will perform a UCC search but public must search other records themselves. UCC search per debtor name- $10.00. Copy fee $1.00 per page. Cert fee- $2.00 plus copy fee. Payee- Botetourt County Clerk of Circuit Court. **Other phones:** Treasurer- 540-473-8254. **Property tax/Assessor-** 540-473-8254.

Bristol City

Clerk of Circuit Court, 497 Cumberland St; Rm 210, Bristol, VA 24201. 276-645-7321; fax-276-645-7345; hours: 9AM-5PM.
Only the public may search. **Online access to Property, Land records:** To access property and land records free go to www.vamanet.com/cgi-bin/MAPSRCHPGM?LOCAL=BRS. **Other phones:** Treasurer- 276-645-7311. **Property tax/Assessor-** 276-645-7316.

Brunswick County

Clerk of Circuit Court, 216 N. Main St., Lawrenceville, VA 23868. 434-848-2215; fax-434-848-4307; hours: 8:30AM - 5PM.
All records in one index. Only the public may search. Copy fee $.50 per page. Cert fee- $2.00 per doc plus copy fee. Payee- Clerk of Circuit Court. **Other phones:** Treasurer- 434-848-2512; Appraiser/Auditor- 434-848-2313; Elections- 434-848-4414. **Property tax/Assessor-** 228 N Main St, Lawrenceville, VA 23868; 434-848-2313.

Buchanan County

Clerk of Circuit Court, PO Box 929, Grundy, VA 24614. 276-935-6567, R/E recording phone-276-935-6575, UCC recording phone-276-935-6567; fax-276-935-7086; hours: 8:30AM - 5PM.
All records in one index. Records indexed on computer back to 7/1991. Office will perform a UCC and Tax lien search but public must search other records themselves. Search fee $3.00. Copy fee $.50 per page. Cert fee- $2.50 per cert plus

copy fee. Payee- Circuit Court Clerk. **Other phones:** Treasurer- 276-935-6551; Appraiser/Auditor- 276-935-6541; Elections- 276-935-6534; Vital Records- 276-935-6575. **Property tax/Assessor-** 276-935-6542.

Buckingham County

Clerk of Circuit Court, PO Box 107, Buckingham, VA 23921. 434-969-4734; fax-434-959-2043; hours: 8:30AM-4:30PM.
Separate indices to search include deeds, judgments, financing statements. Records indexed on a public use terminal back to 1973. Only the public may search. Copy fee $.50 per page. Cert fee- $2.00 per page plus copy fee. Payee- Clerk of Circuit Court. **Other phones:** Treasurer- 434-969-4744. **Property tax/Assessor-** 434-969-4181.

Buena Vista City

Clerk of Circuit Court, 2039 Sycamore Ave., Buena Vista, VA 24416. 540-261-8627; fax-540-261-8625; hours: 8:30AM-5PM.
All records in one index. Records indexed on computer. Only the public may search. Copy fee $.50 per page. Cert fee- $2.00 per doc plus copy fee. Payee- Clerk of Circuit Court. **Online access to Appraiser, Property records:** Access city appraisal data free at www.vamanet.com/cgi-bin/MAPSRCHPGM?LOCAL=BUE. **Other phones:** Treasurer- 540-261-8621; Elections- 540-261-8627. **Property tax/Assessor-** 540-261-8611.

Campbell County

Clerk of Circuit Court, PO Box 7, Rustburg, VA 24588. 434-592-9517; hours: 8:30AM-4:30PM.
Office will perform a UCC search but public must search other records themselves. UCC search per debtor name- $20.00. Copy fee $.50 per page. Cert fee- $2.00 per cert plus copy fee. Payee- Campbell County Clerk of Circuit Court. **Other phones:** Treasurer- 434-332-9590. **Property tax/Assessor-** 434-322-9518.

Caroline County

Clerk of Circuit Court, PO Box 309, Bowling Green, VA 22427-0309. 804-633-5800; hours: 8:30AM-4PM (Recording Hours 8:30AM-3:45PM).
Separate indices to search include deeds, CIS assignments, PA, ease, etc. Office will perform a UCC search but public must search other records themselves. Search fee $10.00 per name. Copy fee $1.00 per page. R/E record copy- $.50 per page. Cert fee- $2.50 per doc plus copy fee. Payee- Caroline County Clerk of Circuit Court. **Online access to Appraiser, Property records:** Click on Caroline County to search property records for free at www.vamanet.com/cgi-bin/LOCS. **Other phones:** Treasurer- 804-633-5291; Elections- 804-633-9083. **Property tax/Assessor-** 804-633-9834.

Carroll County

Clerk of Circuit Court, PO Box 218, Hillsville, VA 24343-0218. 276-728-3117; fax-276-728-0255; hours: 8AM-5PM. www.chillsnet.org
All records in one index. Records indexed on a public use terminal back to 1985. Only the public may search. Copy fee $.50 per page. Cert fee- $2.00 per doc plus copy fee. Payee- Clerk. **Online access to Real Estate, Judgment, UCC, Plat records:** Access to Carroll county property information is a $25 monthly fee. Username and password required; signup through Clerk of Circuit Court, 276-728-3117. Land index and images go back to 1985; plats to 2002. Access to Town of Hillsville property information is on the gis mapping site at http://arcims2.webgis.net/Hillsville/default.asp. Click on Quick Search to search by name. **Other phones:** Treasurer- 276-728-9421; Appraiser/Auditor- 276-728-3281; Elections- 276-728-2332. **Property tax/Assessor-** 605-17 Pine St, Hillsville, VA 24343; 276-728-3281.

Charles City County

Clerk of Circuit Court, PO Box 86, Charles City, VA 23030-0086. 804-829-9212; fax-804-829-5647;
Only the public may search. Copy fee $.50 per page. Cert fee- $2.50 per doc copy fee. Payee- Clerk, Circuit Court. **Other phones:** Treasurer- 804-829-9205; Elections- 804-829-9210. **Property tax/Assessor-** 804-829-9216.

Charlotte County

Clerk of Circuit Court, PO Box 38, Charlotte Court House, VA 23923. 434-542-5147; fax-434-542-4336; hours: 8:30AM-4:30PM.
Only the public may search. Copy fee $.50 per page. Cert fee- $2.00. Payee- Clerk of Circuit Court. **Other phones:** Treasurer- 434-542-5725. **Property tax/Assessor-** 434-542-5546.

Charlottesville City

Clerk of Circuit Court, 315 E. High St, Charlottesville, VA 22902. 434-970-3766; hours: 8:30AM-4:30PM.
Office will perform a UCC search but public must search other records themselves. UCC search per debtor name- $10.00. Copy fee $.50 per page. Cert fee- $2.00 per cert plus copy fee. Payee- Charlottesville City Clerk of Circuit Court. **Other phones:** Treasurer- 434-296-5851. **Property tax/Assessor-** 434-970-3136.

Chesapeake City

Clerk of Circuit Court, 307 Albemarle Dr, #300, Chesapeake, VA 23322. 757-382-3031, R/E recording phone-757-382-3026, UCC recording phone-757-382-3032; fax-757-382-3034; hours: 8:30-5PM. http://cityofchesapeake.net
All records in one index. Records indexed on computer. Only the public may search. Copy fee $.50 per page. Cert fee- $2.00 per doc plus copy fee. Payee- Clerk of Circuit Court. **Online access to Property Appraiser, Most Wanted records:** Access to property appraiser data is free at http://cityofchesapeake.net/rea/welcome.html. No name searching. Also, search the police most wanted list at http://cityofchesapeake.net/services/depart/police/police/wanted.shtml. **Other phones:** Treasurer- 757-382-6281. **Property tax/Assessor-** 757-382-6235.

Chesterfield County

Clerk of Circuit Court, PO Box 125, Chesterfield, VA 23832-0125. 804-748-1241; fax-804-796-5625; hours: 8:30AM-5PM. www.chesterfield.gov
Separate indices to search include judgments, deeds. Records indexed on a public use terminal back to 1989. Office will perform a UCC search but public must search other records themselves. UCC search per debtor name- $20.00. UCC limited to year 2000. Copy fee $.50 per page. Cert fee- $2.00 per doc. Payee- Circuit Court Clerk. **Online access to Assessor, Property Tax, Property Sale records:** Search real estate assessment data free at www.co.chesterfield.va.us/ManagementServices/RealEstateAssessments/Rea_Search_Home.asp. **Other phones:** Treasurer- 804-748-1201; Elections- 804-748-1471. **Property tax/Assessor-** PO Box 40, Chesterfield, VA 23832-0040; 804-748-1321.

Clarke County

Clerk of Circuit Court, PO Box 189, Berryville, VA 22611. 540-955-5116; fax-540-955-0284; hours: 9AM-4:30PM.
Separate indices to search include judgments, wills, UCC. Only the public may search. Copy fee $.50 per page. Cert fee- $2.50 per cert plus copy fee. Payee- Clarke County Clerk of Circuit Court. **Online access to Property, Appraiser records:** Click on Clarke County to search property data for free at www.vamanet.com/cgi-bin/LOCS. **Other phones:** Treasurer- 540-955-5160. **Property tax/Assessor-** same address as above. 540-955-5108.

Colonial Heights City

Clerk of Circuit Court, PO Box 3401, Colonial Heights, VA 23834. 804-520-9364; fax-804-524-8726; hours: 8:30AM-5PM.

All records in one index. Records indexed on a public use terminal back to 1990 (land records). Office personnel or visitors may perform searches. Search fee $5.00 per name. Copy fee $.50 per page. Cert fee- $2.00 per doc plus copy fee. Payee- Colonial Heights Clerk of Circuit Court. **Other phones:** Treasurer- 804-520-9320; Elections- 804-520-9277. **Property tax/Assessor-** 804-520-9272.

Craig County

Clerk of Circuit Court, PO Box 185, New Castle, VA 24127-0185. 540-864-6141; fax-540-864-7471; hours: 9AM-5PM.

Records indexed on computer back to 9/1999. Only the public may search. Copy fee $.50 per page. Cert fee- $2.00 per cert plus copy fee. Payee- Craig County Clerk of Circuit Court. **Other phones:** Treasurer- 540-864-5641. **Property tax/Assessor-** 540-864-6241.

Culpeper County

Clerk of Circuit Court, 135 W. Cameron St, Rm 103, Culpeper, VA 22701. 540-727-3438; fax-n/a; hours: 8:30AM-4:30PM.

Office will perform a UCC search but public must search other records themselves. UCC search per debtor name- $20.00. Copy fee $.50 per page. Cert fee- $2.00 per cert plus copy fee. Payee- Culpeper County Clerk of Circuit Court. **Other phones:** Treasurer- 540-727-3442; Vital Records- 804-662-6200. **Property tax/Assessor-** 135 W Cameron St, Culpeper, VA 22701; 540-727-3443.

Cumberland County

Clerk of Circuit Court, PO Box 8, Cumberland, VA 23040. 804-492-4442; fax-804-492-4876; hours: 8:30AM-4:30PM.

Separate indices to search include books back to 1749, newer on computer. Records indexed on a public use terminal back to 1993, UCC/judgments back to 2001. Only the public may search. Copy fee $.50 per page. Cert fee- None. Payee- Cumberland County Clerk of Circuit Court. **Other phones:** Treasurer- 804-492-4297. **Property tax/Assessor-** PO Box 77, 1 Courthouse Circle, Cumberland, VA 23040; 804-492-4280, assessor fax- 804-492-3342.

Danville City

Clerk of Circuit Court, PO Box 3300, Danville, VA 24543. 434-799-5168; fax-434-799-6502; hours: 9AM-4:30PM. www.danville-va.gov/home.asp
Office will perform a UCC search but public must search other records themselves. UCC search fee is $20.00. Copy fee $.60 per page. R/E record copy- $.50 per page. Cert fee- $2.00 per doc plus copy fee. Payee- Danville City Clerk of Circuit Court. **Online access to Property, Tax Assessor records:** Access to Danville City assessor online records is free at www.danvillevaassessor.org. **Other phones:** Treasurer- 434-799- 5140; Elections- 434-799-6560. **Property tax/Assessor-** 434-799-5120.

Dickenson County

Clerk of Circuit Court, PO Box 190, Clintwood, VA 24228. 276-926-1616; fax-276-926-6465; hours: 8:30AM-4:30PM. www.dickensonctyva.com
Separate indices to search include Deeds, Wills, Financing Statements. Records indexed on computer. Only the public may search. R/E or tax lien copy- $.50 per page. Cert fee- $2.00 per doc plus copy fee. Payee- Dickenson County Clerk. **Online access to Real Estate, Property Tax records:** Access to the Commissioner of Revenue real estate data is free at http://dcva.tinex.net/html/commissioner.html. **Other phones:** Treasurer- 276-926-1610; Elections- 276-926-1620. **Property tax/Assessor-** 276-926-1646.

Dinwiddie County

Clerk of Circuit Court, PO Box 63, Dinwiddie, VA 23841. 804-469-4540; fax-804-469-5386; hours: 8:30AM-4:30PM.

All records in one index. Only the public may search. Copy fee $.50 per page. Cert fee- $2.00 per cert plus copy fee. Payee- Dinwiddie County Clerk of Circuit Court. **Other phones:** Treasurer- 804-469-4510. **Property tax/Assessor-** 804-469-4507.

Essex County

Clerk of Circuit Court, PO Box 445, Tappahannock, VA 22560. 804-443-3541; fax-804-445-1216; hours: 8:30AM-5PM.

Separate indices to search include deeds, wills, financing statements, judgments. Record index not computerized. Only the public may search. Copy fee $.50 per page. Cert fee- $2.00 per cert plus copy fee. Payee- Essex County Clerk of Circuit Court. **Other phones:** Treasurer- 804-443-4371; Elections- 804-443-4611. **Property tax/Assessor-** 804-443-2661.

Fairfax County

Clerk of the Circuit Court, 4110 Chain Bridge Rd; 3rd Fl, Fairfax, VA 22030. 703-691-7320; 8AM-4PM. www.fairfaxcounty.gov/courts/circuit/land_records_info.htm
As of 1/1/88, Falls Church filings for Zip Codes 22041, 22042, 22043 and 22044 are filed in Fairfax County. Only the public may search. Copy fee $.50 per page. Cert fee- $2.00 per doc plus copy fee. Payee- Fairfax County Clerk of Circuit Court. **Online access to Real Estate, Property Tax, Tax Sale records:** Records on the Dept. of Tax Administration Real Estate Assessment database are free at http://icare.fairfaxcounty.gov/Search/GenericSearch.aspx?mode=ADDRESS. Also, the Automated Information System operates Monday-Saturday 7AM-7PM at 703-222-6740. Hear about property descriptions, assessed values and sales prices. Fax-back service is available. Also, the list of auction properties is free at www.co.fairfax.va.us/dta/auction.htm. Search the City Assessment at for free at www.fairfaxrealestate.org/fairfax208/LandRover.asp. No name searching. **Property tax/Assessor-** 703-222-8234.

Fauquier County

Clerk of Circuit Court, 40 Culpeper St, 1st Fl, Warrenton, VA 20186. 540-347-8608, R/E recording phone-540-347-8748 or 8697, UCC recording phone-540-347-8608; hours: 8AM-4:30PM. www.fauquierrcounty.gov/government/departments/circuitcourt
Separate indices to search. Records indexed on a public use terminal back to 1970. Only the public may search. Copy fee for recordings is $.50 per page. Cert fee- $2.00 per cert plus copy fee. Payee- Fauquier County Clerk of Circuit Court. **Other phones:** Treasurer- 540-347-8691; Elections- 540-347-6972; Land Records Room- 540-347-8748. **Property tax/Assessor-** 10 Hotel St 1st Fl, Warrenton, VA 20186; 540-347-8614.

Floyd County

Clerk of Circuit Court, 100 E. Main St; Rm 200, Floyd, VA 24091. 540-745-9330; hours: 8:30AM-4:30PM; 8:30AM-N Sat.
Only the public may search. Copy fee $.50 per page. Cert fee- $2.00 per cert plus copy fee. Payee- Floyd County Clerk of Circuit Court. **Other phones:** Treasurer- 540-745-9357. **Property tax/Assessor-** 540-745-9345.

Fluvanna County

Clerk of Circuit Court, PO Box 550, Palmyra, VA 22963-0299. 434-591-1970; fax-434-591-1971; hours: 8AM-4:30PM.
Only the public may search. Copy fee $.50 per page. **Online access to Appraiser, Property records:** Click on Fluvanna County to search property data for free at www.vamanet.com/cgi-bin/LOCS.

Other phones: Treasurer- 434-591-1945; Appraiser/Auditor- 434-591-1940; Elections- 434-589-3593. **Property tax/Assessor-** 434-591-1940.

Franklin County

Clerk of Circuit Court, PO Box 567, Rocky Mount, VA 24151. 540-483-3065; fax-540-483-3042; hours: 9AM-4:30PM.

All records in one index. Records indexed on computer back to 1993. Only the public may search. Copy fee $.50 in person; $1.00 per page if mailed. Cert fee- $2.00 per doc plus copy fee. **Online access to Property records:** Access property data free at http://arcims2.webgis.net/va/franklin/. **Other phones:** Treasurer- 757-562-8540. **Property tax/Assessor-** 757-562-8547.

Frederick County

Clerk of Circuit Court, 5 N. Kent St, Winchester, VA 22601. 540-667-5770; fax-540-545-8711; hours: 9AM-5PM. www.winfredclerk.com/standard.htm
Do not confuse this county with Fredericksburg, VA or Frederick, MD. Also, the City of Winchester has a separate filing office. Separate indices to search include land records, marriages, wills, judgments. Records indexed on a public use terminal back to 1983. Only the public may search. Copy fee $.50 per page. Cert fee- $2.50 per cert plus copy fee. Payee- Frederick County Clerk of Circuit Court. **Other phones:** Treasurer- 540-662-6611. **Property tax/Assessor-** 540-662-5303.

Fredericksburg City

Clerk of Circuit Court, PO Box 359, Fredericksburg, VA 22404. 540-372-1066; hours: 8AM-4PM. www.fredericksburgva.gov
Many Fredericksburg addresses are outside the city limits, in Stafford County or Spotsylvania County. Check debtor location carefully. Separate indices to search include computer, books. Office will perform a UCC search but public must search other records themselves. UCC search per debtor name- $20.00. Copy fee $.50 per page. Cert fee- $2.00 per doc plus copy fee. Payee- Fredericksburg City Clerk of Circuit Court. **Online access to Appraiser, Property records:** Click on Fredericksburg City to search for property records for free at www.vamanet.com/cgi-bin/LOCS. **Property tax/Assessor-** 715 Princess Anne St, Fredericksburg, VA 22401; 540-372-1004.

Giles County

Clerk of Circuit Court, PO Box 502, Pearisburg, VA 24134-0501. 540-921-1722; fax-540-921-3825; hours: 9AM-4PM.
Separate indices to search include books, computer. Records indexed on a public use terminal back to 2002. Only the public may search. Copy fee $.50 per page. Cert fee- $3.00 per page includes copy fee. Payee- Giles County Clerk of Circuit Court. **Online access to Appraiser, Property records:** Click on Fluvanna County to search for property records for free at www.vamanet.com/cgi-bin/LOCS. Also, search property info on the county GIS site for free online at http://arcims2.webgis.net/giles/default.asp. To name search click on Quick Search. **Other phones:** Treasurer- 540-921-1240. **Property tax/Assessor-** 130 Main St, Pearisburg, VA 24134-0501; 540-921-3321.

Gloucester County

Clerk of Circuit Court, 7400 Justice Dr Rm 330, Gloucester, VA 23061. 804-693-2502; fax-804-693-2186; hours: 8AM-4:30PM.

All records in one index. Records indexed on a public use terminal back to 1994. Only the public may search. Copy fee $.50 per page. Cert fee- $2.00 per doc plus copy fee. Payee- Clerk of Court. **Online access to Judgment records:** Access to Law and Chancery cases is free at http://208.210.219.132/courtinfo/vacircuit/select.jsp?co

urt=. **Other phones:** Treasurer- 804-693-2141. **Property tax/Assessor-** 804-693-3451.

Goochland County

Clerk of Circuit Court, PO Box 196, Goochland, VA 23063. 804-556-5353; fax-n/a; hours: 8:30AM-5PM. Separate indices to search include computer, older books. Records indexed on a public use terminal back to 1995 (UCC-financing-judgments) and 1994 (land). Office will perform a UCC search but public must search other records themselves. UCC search per debtor name- $20.00. Copy fee $.50 per page. Cert fee- $1.00 per page plus copy fee. Payee- Goochland County Clerk of Circuit Court. **Online access to Property, Assessor records:** Access property records at www.vamanet.com. Choose Goochland as locality to search. **Other phones:** ; Com of Revenue- 804-556-5307. **Property tax/Assessor-** PO Box 10, 1800 Sandy Hook Rd, Goochland, VA 23063; 804-556-5853.

Grayson County

Clerk of Circuit Court, PO Box 130, Independence, VA 24348-0130. 276-773-2231; fax-276-773-3338; hours: 8AM-5PM.
All records in one index. Records indexed on computer back to 1985. Office will perform a UCC search but public must search other records themselves. Search fee $20.00 per name. Copy fee $.50 per page. Cert fee- $2.00 per doc plus copy fee. Payee- Grayson Circuit Court. **Online access to Property records:** Access property data free at http://arcims2.webgis.net/va/grayson/. **Other phones:** Treasurer- 276-773-2571. **Property tax/Assessor-** 276-773-2022.

Greene County

Clerk of Circuit Court, PO Box 386, Stanardsville, VA 22973-0386. 434-985-5208; fax-434-985-6723; hours: 8:15AM-4:30PM.
Record index not computerized. Only the public may search. Copy fee $.50 per page. Cert fee- $2.00 per instrument plus copy fee. Payee- Greene County Circuit Court. **Other phones:** Treasurer- 434-985-5214; Appraiser/Auditor- 434-985-5290; Elections- 434-985-5213; Vital Records- 434-985-5208. **Property tax/Assessor-** 15 Ford Ave, Stanardsville, VA 22973; 434-985-5211.

Greensville County

Clerk of Circuit Court, PO Box 631, Emporia, VA 23847. 434-348-4215; fax-434-348-4020; hours: 9AM-5PM.
Only the public may search. Copy fee $.50 per page. Cert fee- $2.00 per doc plus copy fee. Payee- Deputy Clerk. **Online access to Appraiser, Property records:** Click on Greensville County to search property data for free at www.vamanet.com/cgi-bin/LOCS. **Other phones:** Treasurer- 434-348-4208. **Property tax/Assessor-** 434-348-4229.

Halifax County

Clerk of Circuit Court, PO Box 729, Halifax, VA 24558. 434-476-6211; fax-434-476-2890; hours: 8:30AM-4;30.
Records indexed on a public use terminal back to 1996. Only the public may search. Copy fee $.50 per page. Cert fee- $2.00 per instrument. Payee- Clerk of Circuit Court. **Online access to Property records:** Access property data free at http://arcims2.webgis.net/halifax/. **Other phones:** Treasurer- 434-476-3318; Vital Records- 434-476-6211; 434-476-6688-. **Property tax/Assessor-** 434-476-3314.

Hampton City

Clerk of Circuit Court, PO Box 40, Hampton, VA 23669-0040. 757-727-6105; fax-757-728-3505; hours: 8:30AM-4PM.
All records in one index. Records indexed on computer back to 1991. Only the public may search. Search fee $10.00 for probate, will, or estate. Copy fee $1.00 per page. R/E record copy-

$.50 per page. Cert fee- $2.00 per doc plus copy fee. Payee- Hampton Circuit Court. **Other phones:** Treasurer- 757-727-6374; Elections- 757-727-6218; Vital Records- 757-804-6200. **Property tax/Assessor-** 1 Franklin St, Hampton, VA 23669; 757-727-8311.

Hanover County

Clerk of Circuit Court, PO Box 39, Hanover, VA 23069-0039. 804-365-6150, R/E recording phone-804-365-6120; hours: 8:30AM-4:30PM. www.co.hanover.va.us
Index: Older indices in book; current records computerized. land records indexed on a public use terminal back to 1976. Only the public may search. Copy fee $.50 per page. Cert fee- $2.00 per doc plus copy fee. Payee- Hanover County Clerk of Circuit Court. **Other phones:** Treasurer- 804-365-6050; Registrar 804-365-6080-. **Property tax/Assessor-** PO Box 470, Hanover, VA 23069; 804-365-6029.

Henrico County

Clerk of Circuit Court, PO Box 27032, Richmond, VA 23273. 804-501-4202, R/E recording phone-804-501-4979, UCC recording phone-804-501-5468; hours: 8AM-4PM; (Recording Hours 8AM-3:30PM). www.co.henrico.va.us/clerk/
Separate indices to search. Only the public may search. Copy fee $.50 per page. Cert fee- $2.00 per doc plus copy fee. Payee- Henrico Circuit Court Clerk. **Other phones:** Treasurer- 804-501-7480; Appraiser/Auditor- 804-501-4217; Elections- 804-501-4347; Vital Records- 804-225-5000. **Property tax/Assessor-** 900 East Broad Street, Rm 802, Richmond, Virginia 23219; 804-646-5600.

Henry County

Clerk of Circuit Court, 3160 Kings Mountain Rd. #B, Martinsville, VA 24112. 276-634-4880; hours: 9AM-5PM.
Separate indices to search Deed & land records, UCCs, judgments. Search fee $190.00 unless otherwise indicated. Will not search real estate records. Will search UCC records, but not tax liens. UCC search per debtor name-$.50 per page. Copy fee $.50 per page. Cert fee- $2.00 per doc plus copy fee. Payee- Henry County Clerk of Circuit Court. **Online access to Property records:** Access property data free at http://arcims2.webgis.net/henryco/. City of Martinsville property data also available here online. **Other phones:** Treasurer- 276-624-4675; Appraiser/Auditor- 276-634-4610; Elections- 276-634-4697; Vital Records- 276-634-4880. **Property tax/Assessor-** 276-634-4610.

Highland County

Clerk of Circuit Court, PO Box 190, Monterey, VA 24465-0190. 540-468-2447; fax-540-468-3447; hours: 8:30AM-4:30PM.
Records indexed on a public use terminal back to 2000. Office personnel or visitors may perform searches. Copy fee $.50 per page. Cert fee- $2.00 per instrument; $.50 per page to copy. Payee- Sue Dudley- Clerk. **Other phones:** Treasurer- 540-465-2265; Elections- 540-468-2013. **Property tax/Assessor-** 540-468-2142.

Hopewell City

Clerk of Circuit Court, PO Box 310, Hopewell, VA 23860. 804-541-2239; fax-804-541-2438; hours: 8:30AM-4PM.
All records in one index. Only the public may search. Copy fee $.50 per page. Cert fee- $2.00 per seal, copies not included. Payee- Hopewell City Clerk of Circuit Court. **Online access to Court Appeals Granted, Docket records:** Access to court records is free at www.courts.state.va.us. **Other phones:** Treasurer- 804-541-2240. **Property tax/Assessor-** 804-541-2234.

Isle of Wight County

Clerk of Circuit Court, PO Box 110, Isle of Wight, VA 23397. 757-365-6233; fax-757-357-0884; hours: 9AM-5PM.
Office will perform a UCC search but public must search other records themselves. UCC search per debtor name- $10.00. Copy fee $.50 per page. Cert fee- $2.00 per copy. Payee- Isle of Wight County Clerk of Circuit Court. **Other phones:** Treasurer- 757-357-3191. **Property tax/Assessor-** 757-365-6219.

James City County

Clerk of Circuit Court, 5201 Monticello Ave #6, Williamsburg, VA 23188. 757-564-2242, R/E recording phone-757-564-2349, UCC recording phone-757-564-2242; fax-757-564-2329; 8:30AM-4PM. www.jccegov.com/resources/clerkofcircrt/index.html
This office also handles filings for the City of Williamsburg. Office will perform a UCC search but public must search other records themselves. UCC search per debtor name- $20.00. Copy fee $.50 per page. Cert fee- $2.00 per cert plus copy fee. Payee- Williamsburg-James City County Clerk of Circuit Court. **Online access to Real Estate records:** Records on the James City County Property Information database are free at www.regis.state.va.us/jcc/public/disclaimer.htm. The City of Williamsburg property assessor data is free at www.ci.williamsburg.va.us/dept/realestate/disclaimer.htm. **Other phones:** Treasurer- 757-229-6705. **Property tax/Assessor-** 757-253-6650.

King and Queen County

Clerk of Circuit Court, PO Box 67, King and Queen Court House, VA 23085. 804-785-5984; fax-804-785-5698; hours: 9AM-5PM.
All records in one index. Only the public may search. Copy fee $.50 per page. Cert fee- $1.00 per cert plus copy fee. Payee- King and Queen County Clerk of Circuit Court. **Other phones:** Treasurer- 804-785-5978; Elections- 804-785-5980; Zoning, Planning- 804-785-5975. **Property tax/Assessor-** PO Box 178, King and Queen Court House, VA 23085; 804-785-5976.

King George County

Clerk of Circuit Court, 9483 Kings Highway, #3, King George, VA 22485. 540-775-3322; hours: 8:30AM-4:30PM.
Separate indices to search. Real estate owner, mortgage, and property transfer searches available. Will search UCC records, tax liens not included in UCC search. UCC search per debtor name- $10.00. Copy fee $.50 per page. Cert fee- $2.00 per cert plus copy fee. Payee- King George County Clerk of Circuit Court. **Other phones:** Treasurer- 540-775-2571. **Property tax/Assessor-** 540-775-4664.

King William County

Clerk of Circuit Court, PO Box 216, King William, VA 23086. 804-769-4936; fax-804-769-4991; hours: 8:30AM-4:30PM.
Separate indices to search include computer and book. Records indexed on a public use terminal back to 1999. Only the public may search. Copy fee $.50 per page. Cert fee- $2.00 plus copy fee. Payee- King William County Clerk of Circuit Court. **Other phones:** Treasurer- 804-769-4931; Elections- 804-769-4952. **Property tax/Assessor-** 804-769-4942.

Lancaster County

Clerk of Circuit Court, PO Box 99, Lancaster, VA 22503. 804-462-5611; fax-804-462-9978; hours: 8:30AM-4:30PM. www.lancova.com
Office will perform a UCC search but public must search other records themselves. UCC search fee- $5.00 per UCC. Copy fee $1.00 per page. R/E or tax lien copy- $.50 per page. Cert fee- $2.00 per cert plus copy fee. Payee- Lancaster County Clerk of Circuit Court. **Online access to Chancery, Law**

records: Access to court records is free at www.courts.state.va.us. **Other phones:** Treasurer- 804-462-5630; Elections- 804-462-5277. **Property tax/Assessor-** 804-462-7920.

Lee County

Clerk of Circuit Court, PO Box 326, Jonesville, VA 24263. 276-346-7763; fax-276-346-3440; hours: 8:30AM-5PM.
Office will perform a UCC search but public must search other records themselves. UCC search per debtor name- $10.00. Copy fee $.50 per page. **Other phones:** Treasurer- 276-346-7716. **Property tax/Assessor-** 276-346-7722.

Loudoun County

Clerk of Circuit Court, PO Box 550, Leesburg, VA 20178. 703-777-0270; hours: 8;30AM-4;30PM. www.loudoun.gov/government/
Index: Books. Records indexed on a public use terminal back to 1969. Only the public may search. Copy fee $.50 per page. Cert fee- $2.00 per cert plus copy fee. Payee- Loudoun County Clerk of Circuit Court. **Online access to Property, Assessor records:** Search the property assessor data for free at http://inter1.loudoun.gov/webpdbs/. No name searching; search by address, number, or ID only. **Other phones:** Treasurer- 703-777-0280. **Property tax/Assessor-** 703-777-0260.

Louisa County

Clerk of Circuit Court, PO Box 37, Louisa, VA 23093. 540-967-5312; hours: 8:30AM-5PM (Stop Recording 4:15PM).
All records in one index. Records indexed on a public use terminal back to 1990. Only the public may search. Copy fee $.50 per page. Cert fee- $2.50 per cert plus copy fee. Payee- Louisa County Clerk of Circuit Court. **Property tax/Assessor-** 540-967-3450.

Lunenburg County

Clerk of Circuit Court, 11435 Courthouse Rd., Lunenburg, VA 23952. 434-696-2230; hours: 8:30AM-4:30PM.
Only the public may search. Copy fee $.50 per page. Cert fee- $2.50. Payee- Lunenburg County Clerk of Circuit Court. **Property tax/Assessor-** 434-696-2516.

Lynchburg City

Clerk of Circuit Court, PO Box 4, Lynchburg, VA 24505. 434-455-2620; fax-434-847-1864; hours: 8:15AM-4:45PM.
Office will perform a UCC search but public must search other records themselves. UCC search fee is $20.00 per filing. Copy fee $.50 per page. Cert fee- $2.00 per cert plus copy fee. Payee-Lynchburg City Clerk of Circuit Court. **Other phones:** Treasurer- 434-455-4242. **Property tax/Assessor-** 434-455-3830.

Madison County

Clerk of Circuit Court, PO Box 220, Madison, VA 22727-0220. 540-948-6888; fax-540-948-3759; hours: 8:30AM-4:30PM.
Only the public may search. Copy fee $.50 per page. Cert fee- $2.00. Payee- Clerk of Circuit Court. **Other phones:** Treasurer- 540-948-4409. **Property tax/Assessor-** 540-948-4421.

Martinsville City

Clerk of Circuit Court, PO Box 1206, Martinsville, VA 24114-1206. 276-403-5106; fax-276-403-5232; hours: 9AM-5PM. www.ci.martinsville.va.us/Circuitclerk
Office will perform a UCC search but public must search other records themselves. UCC search per debtor name- $20.00. Copy fee $.50 per page. Cert fee- $2.00 per doc plus copy fee. Payee-Martinsville City Clerk of Circuit Court. **Online access to Property, Deed, Judgment, Will, Marriage, Delinquent Tax records:** Access to Circuit clerk records is at www.ci.martinsville.va.us/Circuitclerk. Fee

is $30.00 per month, or you may search at a rate of $1 per doc. For info, call office of Ashby Pritchett at 276-656-5106 or visit website. **Other phones:** Treasurer-276-403-5240; Other phone- 276-403-5206. **Property tax/Assessor-** 276-403-5131.

Mathews County

Clerk of Circuit Court, PO Box 463, Mathews, VA 23109-0463. 804-725-2550; hours: 8AM-4PM.
All records in one index. Only the public may search. Copy fee $.50 per page. Cert fee- $2.00 per page, plus copy fee. Payee- Mathews County Clerk of Circuit Court. **Other phones:** Treasurer-804-725-2341. **Property tax/Assessor-** PO Box 896, Mathews, VA 23109; 804-725-7168.

Mecklenburg County

Clerk of Circuit Court, PO Box 530, Boydton, VA 23917-0530. 434-738-6191; fax-434-738-6861; hours: 8:30AM-5PM.
Office will perform a UCC search but public must search other records themselves. UCC search fee is $20.00 per name. Copy fee $.50 per page. Cert fee- $2.00 per instrument. Payee- Mecklenburg County Clerk of Circuit Court.

Middlesex County

Clerk of Circuit Court, PO Box 158, Saluda, VA 23149. 804-758-5317; fax-804-758-8637; hours: 8:30AM-4:30PM.
All records in one index. Office will perform a UCC search but public must search other records themselves. Search fee $5.00 per debtor name. Copy fee $.50 per page. Cert fee- $2.00 per page, plus copy fee. Payee- Middlesex County Clerk of Circuit Court. **Other phones:** Treasurer- 804-758-5302; Appraiser/Auditor- 804-758-5331; Elections-804-758-4420. **Property tax/Assessor-** 804-758-5331.

Montgomery County

Clerk of Circuit Court, PO Box 6309, Christiansburg, VA 24068. 540-382-5760; fax-540-382-6937; hours: 8:30AM-4:30PM.
All records in one index. Only the public may search. Copy fee $.50 per page. Cert fee- $2.00 per document plus copy fee. Payee- Clerk of Circuit Court. **Online access to Real Estate, Property Tax records:** Access to the county Tax Parcel Information System database is free online at www.montva.com/departments/plan/igis.php. Records on the Town of Blacksburg GIS site are free at http://arcims2.webgis.net/blacksburg/default.asp?. To name search, click on Quick Search. **Other phones:** Treasurer- 540-382-5723; Appraiser/Auditor- 540-382-5715; Elections- 540-382-5741; Vital Records- 540-382-5760; Public Information Office- 540-381-6887. **Property tax/Assessor-** 540-382-5717.

Nelson County

Clerk of Circuit Court, PO Box 10, Lovingston, VA 22949. 434-263-7020; fax-434-263-7027; hours: 8AM-5PM.
Separate indices to search include manual indices from 1809 to 1993, automated from 1993 to present. Records indexed on a public use terminal back to 1809. Only the public may search. Copy fee $.50 per page. Cert fee- $2.50 per cert plus copy fee. Payee- Nelson County Clerk of Circuit Court. **Other phones:** Treasurer- 434-263-7060. **Property tax/Assessor-** 434-263-7070.

New Kent County

Clerk of Circuit Court, PO Box 98, New Kent, VA 23124-0098. 804-966-9520; fax-804-966-9528; hours: 8:30AM-4:30PM.
Only the public may search. **Online access to Assessor, Property records:** Access to New Kent county assessor records is free at http://data.visionappraisal.com/NewKentCountyVA/. Register free for full data. **Other phones:** Treasurer-804-966-9615. **Property tax/Assessor-** 804-966-9610.

Newport News City

Clerk of Circuit Court, 2500 Washington Ave; Courthouse, Newport News, VA 23607. 757-926-8561, R/E recording phone-757-926-8355, UCC recording phone-757-926-8349; fax-757-926-8531; www.newport-news.va.us
Office will perform a UCC search but public must search other records themselves. UCC search per debtor name- $20.00. Copy fee $.50 per page. **Online access to Assessor, Real Estate records:** Access to the City's "Real Estate on the Web" database is free at http://216.54.20.244/reisweb1. Search by address and parcel number; new "advanced search" may include name searching. **Other phones:** Treasurer-757-247-8731. **Property tax/Assessor-** 757-247-8671.

Norfolk City

Clerk of Circuit Court, 100 St. Paul's Blvd., Norfolk, VA 23510-2773. 757-664-4380; 8:45AM-4:45PM. www.norfolk.gov/Circuit_Court/ccchome.asp
Office personnel or visitors may perform searches. Search fee $10.00 per name. Real estate owner, mortgage, and property transfer searches available. Copy fee $1.00 per page. R/E record copy- $.50 per page. Cert fee- $2.00 per cert plus copy fee. Payee- Clerk, Circuit Court. **Online access to Real Estate, Assessor, Sex Offender Registry, Marriage, Recording, Deed, Judgment, Will records:** Access Clerk of Circuit Court recording data by $50 per month subscription at www.norfolk.gov/Circuit_Court/remote access.asp. Deeds and land records go back to 1988. Judgments, Wills, Marriages, etc, back to 1993. Records on the City of Norfolk Real Estate Property Assessment database are free at www.norfolk.gov/NRealEstate/search.asp. Sex offender registry search for free found at http://sex-offender.vsp.state.va.us/Static/Search.htm. **Other phones:** Treasurer- 757-664-7800; Elections- 757-664-4353. **Property tax/Assessor-** 757-664-4732.

Northampton County

Clerk of Circuit Court, PO Box 36, Eastville, VA 23347-0036. 757-678-0465; fax-757-678-5410;
Only the public may search. Copy fee $2.00 per page. Cert fee- $10.00. Payee- Northampton County Clerk of Circuit Court. **Other phones:** Treasurer- 757-678-0450. **Property tax/Assessor-** 757-678-0446.

Northumberland County

Clerk of Circuit Court, PO Box 217, Heathsville, VA 22473. 804-580-3700; hours: 8:30AM-4:45PM. www.co.northumberland.va.us
Separate index books to search include deed, grantor/grantee, judgments, wills. Office personnel or visitors may perform searches. Office will perform limited searches. No search fee. Copy fee $.50 per page. Cert fee- $.50 per page plus copy fee. Payee- Northumberland County Clerk of Circuit Court. **Online access to Property, Assessor records:** Access Land Book data free at www.co.northumberland.va.us/NH-land-book.htm. **Other phones:** Treasurer- 804-580-5201. **Property tax/Assessor-** PO Box 309, 72 Monument Pl, Heathsville, VA 22473; 804-580-7612.

Nottoway County

Clerk of Circuit Court, PO Box 25, Nottoway, VA 23955. 434-645-9043; fax-434-645-2201; hours: 8:30AM-4PM.
Records indexed on a public use terminal back to 1975. Office will perform a $10.00 UCC search but public must search other records themselves. Copy fee $.50 per page. Cert fee- $2.00 per instrument. Payee- Clerk of Circuit Court. **Online access to Property records:** Access property data free at http://arcims2.webgis.net/va/nottoway/. **Other phones:** Treasurer- 434-645-9318; Appraiser/Auditor-434-645-9317; Elections- 434-645-8148; Vital Records- 434-645-9043 (marriage licenses only). **Property tax/Assessor-** 434-645-9317.

Orange County

Clerk of Circuit Court, PO Box 230, Orange, VA 22960. 540-672-4030; fax-540-672-2939;

Records indexed on a public use terminal back to 1995. Office will perform a UCC search but public must search other records themselves. Search fee $20.00. Copy fee $.50 per page. Cert fee- $2.00 per page plus copy fee. Payee- Clerk of Circuit Court. **Other phones:** Treasurer- 540-672-2656; Appraiser/Auditor- 540-672-4441. **Property tax/Assessor-** 540-672-4441.

Page County

Clerk of Circuit Court, 116 S. Court St, #A, Luray, VA 22835. 540-743-4064; fax-540-743-2338; hours: 9AM-5PM.

Records indexed on computer back to 1981. Will not search real estate records or tax liens. Will search UCC records only if requested in writing on "Information Request" form. UCC search per debtor name- $20.00. Copy fee $.50 per page. Cert fee- $2.00 per doc, plus copy fee. Payee- C. Ron Wilson-Clerk. **Other phones:** Treasurer- 540-743-3975; Elections- 540-743-3986. **Property tax/Assessor-** 101 S Court St, Luray, VA 22835; 540-743-3840.

Patrick County

Clerk of Circuit Court, PO Box 148, Stuart, VA 24171-0148. 276-694-7213; fax-276-694-6943; 9AM-5PM. Records indexed on a public use terminal back to 7/1999. Only the public may search. Copy fee $.50 per page. Cert fee- $2.00 per doc, plus copy fee. Payee- Patrick County. **Online access to Property, Map records:** Access property data free at http://arcims2.webgis.net/patrick/default.asp. Map searching only, no name searching. **Other phones:** Treasurer- 276-694-7257; Elections- 276-694-7206. **Property tax/Assessor-** 276-694-7131x276.

Petersburg City

Clerk of Circuit Court, 7 Courthouse Ave., Petersburg, VA 23803. 804-733-2367, R/E recording phone-804-733-2367 x4122; fax-804-732-5548; 8AM-4PM.

Records indexed on computer from 2001-current; land records prior to year 2001 in deed books. Only the public may search. Copy fee $.50 per page. Cert fee- $2.00 per cert plus copy fee. Payee- Clerk of Court. **Other phones:** Treasurer- 804-733-2321. **Property tax/Assessor-** 804-733-2315.

Pittsylvania County

Clerk of Circuit Court, PO Drawer 31, Chatham, VA 24531. 434-432-7887, R/E recording phone-434-432-7888, UCC recording phone-434-432-7887; fax-434-432-7913; hours: 8:30AM-5PM.

All records in one index. Records indexed on a public use terminal back to 1995. Only the public may search. Copy fee $1.00 per page. Cert fee- $2.00 per cert plus copy fee. Payee- Pittsylvania County Clerk of Circuit Court. **Online access to Real Estate, Assessor records:** Access to county real estate data is free online at www.pittgov.org/real%20search.htm. Most recent assessment data is for the previous year. See Danville City for Real Estate and Lien records online for Danville City. **Other phones:** Treasurer- 434-432-7961; Elections- 434-432-7971. **Property tax/Assessor-** 434-432-7949.

Portsmouth City

Clerk of Circuit Court, PO Box 1217, Portsmouth, VA 23705. 757-393-8671, R/E recording phone-757-393-8530, UCC recording phone-757-393-8671; fax-757-399-4826; hours: 8:30AM-5PM.

Office will perform a UCC search but public must search other records themselves. Copy fee $.50 per page. R/E record copy- $1.00 per page, $.50 each add'l after 2 pages. Cert fee- $2.00 per cert plus copy fee. Payee- Portsmouth Clerk of Circuit Court. **Other phones:** Treasurer- 757-393-8651;

Appraiser/Auditor- 757-393-8771; Elections- 757-393-8644. **Property tax/Assessor-** 757-393-8631.

Powhatan County

Clerk of Circuit Court, PO Box 37, Powhatan, VA 23139-0037. 804-598-5660; fax-804-598-5608; hours: 8:30AM-5PM.

All records in one index. Office will perform a UCC search but public must search other records themselves. UCC search per debtor name- $10.00. Copy fee $.50 per page. UCC or tax lien copy $1.00 per page. Cert fee- $2.00 per cert plus copy fee. Payee- Wm. E. Maxey Jr, Clerk. **Online access to Appraiser, Property records:** Click on Powhatan County to search property data for free at www.vamanet.com/cgi-bin/LOCS. **Other phones:** Treasurer- 804-598-5626; Appraiser/Auditor- 804-598-5617; Elections- 804-598-5604. **Property tax/Assessor-** 5834 Old Buckingham Rd, Powhatan, VA 12139; 804-598-5617.

Prince Edward County

Clerk of Circuit Court, PO Box 304, Farmville, VA 23901. 434-392-5145; hours: 8:30AM-4:30PM.

Only the public may search. Copy fee $.50 per page. Cert fee- $2.50 per cert plus copy fee. Payee- Prince Edward County Clerk of Circuit Court. **Other phones:** Treasurer- 434-392-3404. **Property tax/Assessor-** 434-392-3231.

Prince George County

Clerk of Circuit Court, PO Box 98, Prince George, VA 23875-0098. 804-733-2640; hours: Recording hours 8:30AM-4:30PM.

All records in one index. Records indexed on computer back to 4/1996. Only the public may search. Copy fee $.50 per page. Cert fee- $2.00 per cert plus copy fee. Payee- Prince George County Clerk of Circuit Court. **Other phones:** Treasurer- 804-733-2620. **Property tax/Assessor-** 804-733-2616.

Prince William County

Clerk of Circuit Court, 9311 Lee Ave, Rm 300, Manassas, VA 20110-5598. 703-792-6035; fax-703-792-6083; hours: 8:30AM-4:30PM. www.pwcgov.org/default.aspx?topic=040017

All records in one index. Records indexed on a public use terminal back to 1918 for Deeds. Will not search real estate records. Will search UCC records, but not tax liens. UCC search per debtor name-$10.00. Copy fee $.50 per page. Cert fee- $2.00 per doc plus copy fee. Payee- Clerk of Court. **Online access to Land, Property Assessor records:** Records on the Property Information database are free at http://www4.pwcgov.org/realestate/LandRover.asp. Also, City of Manassas Commissioner of the Revenue's real estate assessment data is online at http://data.visionappraisal.com/ManassasVA/. Free registration is required to access full data. **Other phones:** Vital Records- 703-792-6045 (marriage only). **Property tax/Assessor-** 703-792-6780.

Pulaski County

Clerk of Circuit Court, 45 3rd St. NW, #101, Pulaski, VA 24301. 540-980-7825; fax-540-980-7835; hours: 8:30AM-4:30PM.

All records in one index. Only the public may search. Copy fee $.50 per page. Cert fee- $1.50 per page plus copy fee. Payee- Pulaski County Clerk of Circuit Court. **Online access to Property, GIS records:** Access to the county GIS mapping info is free at http://arcims2.webgis.net/pulaski/default.asp. No name searching. **Other phones:** Treasurer- 540-980-7785; Appraiser/Auditor- 540-980-7753; Elections- 540-980-1222. **Property tax/Assessor-** 540-980-7753.

Radford City

Clerk of Circuit Court, 619 Second St; Courthouse, Radford, VA 24141. 540-731-3610; fax-540-731-3612; hours: 8:30AM-5PM (No machine receipts after 4:30PM).

Will not search real estate records. Will not search UCC records or tax liens. Copy fee $.50 per page. Cert fee- $2.00 per document. Payee- Radford City Clerk of Circuit Court. **Online access to Property records:** Access to City property info on the GIS mapping site is free online at http://arcims2.webgis.net/radfordcity/default.asp. To name search click on Quick Search. **Other phones:** Treasurer- 540-731-3661; Appraiser/Auditor- 540-731-3613; Elections- 540-731-3639; Vital Records- 540-731-3610. **Property tax/Assessor-** 540-731-6248.

Rappahannock County

Clerk of Circuit Court, PO Box 517, Washington, VA 22747-1517. 540-675-5350; fax-540-675-5351; hours: 8:30AM-4:30PM.

All records in one index. Records indexed on a public use terminal back to 1/1995. Only the public may search. Copy fee $.50 per page. Cert fee- $2.00 per doc plus copy fee. Payee- Rappahannock County Clerk of Circuit Court. **Other phones:** Treasurer- 540-675-5360; Appraiser/Auditor- 540-675-5370; Elections- 540-675-5370; Vital Records- 804-662-6200. **Property tax/Assessor-** PO Box 37, Washington, VA 22747; 540-675-5370.

Richmond City

Clerk of Circuit Court, 400 N. 9th St., Richmond, VA 23219. 804-646-6505; hours: 8:45AM-4:45PM.

The City of Richmond is not in Richmond County. It is bordered by Henrico and Chesterfield Counties. Separate indices to search include microfilm, books, computer. Records indexed on a public use terminal back to 1993. Office will perform a UCC search but public must search other records themselves. Copy fee $.50 per page. Cert fee- $2.00 per doc plus copy fee. Payee- Richmond City Clerk of Circuit Court. **Online access to Property, Assessor records:** Search the city's Property & Real Estate Assessment Information free at www.ci.richmond.va.us/departments/gis/webmapper.aspx. If you click on Property Search, you cannot name search, but name searching available through the Webmapper. At the Webmapper page, click on "Advanced Search" then "Assessments" to name search. **Other phones:** Treasurer- 804-646-6474; Appraiser/Auditor- 804-646-5616; Elections- 804-646-5950; Records Rm -804-646-6530.

Richmond County

Clerk of Circuit Court, PO Box 1000, Warsaw, VA 22572-1000. 804-333-3781; fax-804-333-5396; hours: 9AM-5PM. www.co.richmond.va.us

The City of Richmond is a separate filing office and is not located in this county. The following ZIP Codes are the only ones for this county: 22572, 22460, 22472, 22548, and part of 22435. Separate indices to search include land records index, will index. Records indexed on a public use terminal back to 1950 for land records, 1996 for will records. Office will perform a real estate record search but public must search other records themselves. Search fee $10.00 per name. Copy fee $.50 per page. Old records- $1.00 per page. Cert fee- $2.00 per cert plus copy fee. Payee- Richmond County Clerk of Circuit Court. **Other phones:** Treasurer- 804-333-3555; Appraiser/Auditor- 804-333-5062; Elections- 804-333-4772; Vital Records- 804-333-3781. **Property tax/Assessor-** PO Box 366, Warsaw, VA 22572; 804-333-3722.

Roanoke City

Clerk of Circuit Court, Box 2610, Roanoke, VA 24010-2610. 540-853-6702; hours: 8:30AM-4:30PM. www.ci.roanoke.va.us

All records in one index. Records indexed on a public use terminal. Only the public may search. Copy fee $.50 per page. Cert fee- $2.00 per cert plus copy fee. Payee- Roanoke City Clerk of Circuit Court. **Online access to Property, GIS, Tax Appraisal records:** Access to property data is free on the City GIS website online at http://gis.roanokegov.com/text.htm. **Other phones:** Treasurer- 540-853-2561.

Roanoke County

Clerk of Circuit Court, PO Box 1126, Salem, VA 24153-1126. 540-387-6205; fax-540-387-6145; hours: 8:30AM-4:30PM.
Office will perform a UCC search but public must search other records themselves. UCC search per debtor name-$20.00 per name. Copy fee $.50 per page. Cert fee- $2.00 per doc plus copy fee.

Rockbridge County

Clerk of Circuit Court, 2 S. Main St; Court House, Lexington, VA 24450-2599. 540-463-2232; hours: 8:30AM-4:30PM.
Includes City of Lexington. All records in one index. Records indexed on a public use terminal back to 2000. Office will perform a UCC search but public must search other records themselves. Search fee $20.00. Copy fee $.50 per page. Cert fee- $2.50 per doc, plus copy fee. Payee- Clerk's Office. **Online access to Property, Appraiser records:** Access the GIS-property mapping site free at http://quicksearch.webgis.net/search.php?site=va_rockbridge. Access City of Lexington property data free at www.vamanet.com/cgi-bin/MAPSRCHPGM?LOCAL=LEX. **Other phones:** Treasurer- 540-463-2613; Appraiser/Auditor- 540-463-3431; Elections- 540-463-7203. **Property tax/Assessor-** 150 S Main St, Lexington, VA 24450; 540-463-3431.

Rockingham County

Clerk of Circuit Court, Courthouse, Harrisonburg, VA 22801. 540-564-3110; fax-540-564-3127; 9AM-5PM.
Records indexed on a public use terminal back to 1944. Office will perform a UCC search but public must search other records themselves. UCC search fee $20.00 per search, per name. Copy fee $.50 per page. Cert fee- $2.00 per doc. **Online access to Real Estate records:** Access to real estate assessment records at http://rockingham.gisbrowser.com/home.cfm. **Property tax/Assessor-** 540-564-3086.

Russell County

Clerk of Circuit Court, PO Box 435, Lebanon, VA 24266. 276-889-8023; fax-276-889-8003; hours: 8:30AM-5PM.
Office will perform a UCC search but public must search other records themselves. UCC search per debtor name- $20.00. Copy fee $.50 per page. Cert fee- None. Payee- Russell County Clerk. **Other phones:** Treasurer- 276-889-8028. **Property tax/Assessor-** 276-889-8014.

Salem City

Clerk of Circuit Court, PO Box 891, Salem, VA 24153. 540-375-3067, R/E recording phone-540-375-3058, UCC recording phone-540-375-3067; fax-540-375-4039; hours: 8AM-5PM.
Only the public may search. Copy fee $.50 per page. Cert fee- $2.00. Payee- Salem City Clerk of Circuit Court. **Other phones:** Elections- 540-375-3058.

Scott County

Clerk of Circuit Court, 104 E. Jackson St; Courthouse, #2, Gate City, VA 24251-3417. 276-386-3801; fax-276-3862430; hours: 8:30AM-5PM.
All records in one index. Only the public may search. Copy fee $.50 per page. Cert fee- $2.50 per cert. Payee- Scott County Clerk of Circuit Court. **Other phones:** Treasurer- 276-386-7742; Appraiser/Auditor- 276-386-7692; Elections- 276-386-3843; Vital Records- 804-662-6200; Registrar- 276-386-3843. **Property tax/Assessor-** 276-386-7692.

Shenandoah County

Clerk of Circuit Court, PO Box 406, Woodstock, VA 22664-0406. 540-459-6150; fax-540-459-6155; hours: 9AM-5PM.
Office will perform a UCC search but public must search other records themselves. UCC search per debtor name-$20.00. Copy fee $.50 per page. Cert fee- $2.00 per doc plus copy fee. Payee- Shen. Co. Circuit Court. **Other phones:** Treasurer- 540-459-6180. **Property tax/Assessor-** 540-459-6170.

Smyth County

Clerk of Circuit Court, 109 W Main St #144, Marion, VA 24354-2510. 276-782-4044; fax-276-782-4045; hours: 9AM-4:30.
All records in one index. Only the public may search. Copy fee $.50 per page. Cert fee- $2.00 per page includes copy fee. Payee- Smyth County Clerk of Circuit Court. **Online access to Property records:** Access to property records for Smyth County including Marion, Saltville, and Chilhowie Towns are free at http://arcims2.webgis.net/smyth/default.asp. To name search click on Quick Search. **Other phones:** Treasurer- 276-782-4059. **Property tax/Assessor-** 276-782-4040.

Southampton County

Clerk of Circuit Court, PO Box 190, Courtland, VA 23837. 757-653-9245, R/E recording phone-757-653-2200; hours: 8:30AM-5PM.
Includes the City of Franklin. Land records indexed on a public use terminal back to 1970 to current. Only the public may search. They will look up an instrument number or check to see if something has been recorded or if a Deed of Trust has been released. NO extensive searches. UCC search per debtor name-$20.00 per name. Copy fee $.50 per page. Cert fee- $2.00 per cert plus copy fee. Payee- Southampton County Clerk of Circuit Court. **Online access to Appraiser, Property records:** Only the City of Franklin appraisal data is available free at www.vamanet.com/cgi-bin/MAPSRCHPGM?LOCAL=FRA. As far as can be determined, this does not include county appraisal records. **Other phones:** Treasurer- 757-653-3025. **Property tax/Assessor-** 26022 Administration Dr, Courtland, VA 23837; 757-653-3030.

Spotsylvania County

Clerk of Circuit Court, PO Box 96, Spotsylvania, VA 22553-0096. 540-582-7090, R/E recording phone-540-582-7052, UCC recording phone-540-582-7090 X233; fax-540-582-2169; hours: 8AM-3PM.
Separate indices to search include land, wills, judgments, financing statements, marriages, general misc orders, etc. Records indexed on a public use terminal-land records 1980-now; images 9/1993-now, Judgments 1990-now; images 1990-now; Wills/Fiduciary/Financing Statements/Marriage 1996-now, images 7/2002-now; general misc images & indexes from 7/2002-now. Office will perform a UCC search but public must search other records themselves. UCC search fee is $20.00. Copy fee $.50 per page; SASE required for mail return. Cert fee- $2.00 per cert plus copy fee. Payee- Clerk of Circuit Court. **Other phones:** Treasurer- 540-582-7058. **Property tax/Assessor-** 540-582-7132.

Stafford County

Clerk of Circuit Court, PO Box 69, Stafford, VA 22555. 540-659-8752, R/E recording phone-540-658-8752, UCC recording phone-540-658-8758; hours: 8AM-4PM.
Separate indices to search include land records, judgments, financing statements, wills. Only the public may search. Copy fee $.50 per page. Cert fee- $2.00 per cert, does not include copy fee. Payee- Stafford County Clerk of Circuit Court. **Other phones:** Treasurer- 540-658-8700; Appraiser/Auditor- 540-658-4132; Elections- 540-658-4000. **Property tax/Assessor-** PO Box 98, Stafford, VA 22555; 540-658-4132.

Staunton City

Clerk of Circuit Court, PO Box 1286, Staunton, VA 24402-1286. 540-332-3874; fax-540-332-3970; hours: 8;30AM-4;30PM. www.staunton.va.us

All records in one index. Records indexed on a public use terminal back to 1992. Only the public may search. Copy fee $.50 per page. Cert fee- $2.00 per doc plus copy fee. Payee- Circuit Court. **Online access to Property, GIS, Tax Appraisal records:** Access the property mapping system free at http://gis.ci.staunton.va.us:8082/gis/mgdefault.asp. Name searching allowed. **Other phones:** Treasurer- 540-332-3833; Appraiser/Auditor- 540-332-3827; Elections- 540-332-3840. **Property tax/Assessor-** 58 W Beverly St, Staunton, VA 24402; 540-332-3827.

Suffolk City

Clerk of Circuit Court, PO Box 1604, Suffolk, VA 23439-1604. 757-923-2251, R/E recording phone-757-923-2264, UCC recording phone-757-923-2347; hours: 8:30AM-5PM.
Only the public may search. Copy fee $.50 per page. Cert fee- $2.00 per doc, plus copy fee. Payee- Suffolk City Clerk of Circuit Court. **Property tax/Assessor-** 757-923-2400.

Surry County

Clerk of Circuit Court, PO Box 203, Surry, VA 23883-0203. 757-294-3161; fax-757-294-0471; 9AM-5PM.
All records in one index. Only the public may search. Copy fee $.50 per page. $.10 per page from microfilm. Cert fee- $2.00 per cert plus copy fee. Payee- Surry County Clerk of Circuit Court. **Other phones:** Treasurer- 757-294-5206; Elections- 757-294-5213. **Property tax/Assessor-** 757-294-3000.

Sussex County

Clerk of Circuit Court, PO Box 1337, Sussex, VA 23884. 434-246-1012; fax-434-246-2203; 9AM-5PM. www.sussex.k12.va.us/sussex_county/sussex_main.htm
All records in one index. Office will perform a UCC search but public must search other records themselves. UCC search per debtor name- $5.00. Copy fee $.50 per page. Cert fee- $2.00 per cert plus copy fee. Payee- Sussex County Clerk of Circuit Court. **Online access to Land Tax, Marriage records:** A private search company website at http://genealogyresources.org/index.html offers access to records including marriage, census, wills, deeds, land tax, guardian bonds and tithing lists, plus Civil and Revolutionary War. **Other phones:** Treasurer- 434-246-1086. **Property tax/Assessor-** 434-246-1022.

Tazewell County

Clerk of Circuit Court, PO Box 968, Tazewell, VA 24651-0968. 276-988-7541; fax-276-988-7585; hours: 8-AM-4:30PM.
Separate indices to search include deeds, judgments and financing statements. Office will perform a UCC search but public must search other records themselves. UCC search per debtor name- $20.00. Copy fee $.50 per page. Cert fee- $2.00 per doc plus copy fee. Payee- Clerk of Circuit Court. **Online access to Property records:** Access to county Commission of Revenue data is free at www.smartmesh.net/tcva/html/real_estate.html. Information is not always updated in a timely manner. For more details, call 276-988-1235. **Other phones:** Treasurer- 276-988-3000. **Property tax/Assessor-** same address as above. 276-988-1235.

Virginia Beach City

Clerk of Circuit Court, 2425 Nimmo Prky; Judicial Ctr, Virginia Beach, VA 23456-9017. 757-427-8821; fax-757-426-5686; hours: 9AM-5PM. www.vbgov.com/courts/circourt/cclerk/0,1506,8092,00.html
All records in one index. Records indexed on a public use terminal back to 1965. Only the public may search. Copy fee $.50 per page. Cert fee- $2.50 per cert plus copy fee. Payee- Clerk of Circuit Court. **Online access to Real Estate, Property Tax, Assessor, Marriage, Judgment, UCC, Will, Business Name records:** Online access Virginia Beach land records and recordings is free at http://vblandrecords.com/recclkshr/about.asp. But, there is a new fee for images, which is payable by credit card

only. Also, notarized registration for images is required. For credit card account, call 866-793-6505. Direct general questions to Tracey Entwisle at 757-427-8819. Also, you may search the assessor database for free at www.vbgov.com/dept/realestate/. No name searching. **Other phones:** Treasurer- 757-427-4445; Elections-757-427-8683; Public Info Office- 757-427-4111; City Clerk -757-427-4303. **Property tax/Assessor-** 757-427-4601.

Warren County

Clerk of Circuit Court, 1 E. Main St, Front Royal, VA 22630-3382. 540-635-2435; fax-540-636-3274; hours: 9AM-5PM.

Separate indices to search include land records, judgments, UCCs, chancery, law, criminal, marriage, wills. Records indexed on a public use terminal back to 1994. Office will perform a UCC search but public must search other records themselves. UCC search per debtor name- $20.00. Copy fee $.50 per page. Cert fee- $2.00 per doc plus copy fee. Payee- Warren County Circuit Clerk. **Online access to Recording, Deed, Land, Lien, Court, Will, Marriage, UCC records:** Access the Clerk's data on the web; username and password required. For username and password contact Jennifer Sims at 540-635-2435 or at jsims@courts.state.va.us. Images go back to 1994. **Other phones:** Treasurer-540-635-2215; Appraiser/Auditor- 540-635-2651; Elections- 540-635-4327; Vital Records- 540-635-2435. **Property tax/Assessor-** 220 N Commerce Ave, Front Royal, VA 22630; 540-635-2651.

Washington County

Clerk of Circuit Court, PO Box 289, Abingdon, VA 24212. 276-676-6226, R/E recording phone-276-676-6224; fax-276-676-6218; hours: 7:30AM-5PM.

Index: Books, computer. Records indexed on a public use terminal back to 1983. Only the public may search. Copy fee $.50 per page. Cert fee-$2.00 per page plus copy fee. **Online access to Property, Land records:** To access property and land records free go to www.vamanet.com/cgi-bin/mapsrchpgm?local=was. **Other phones:** Treasurer-276-676-6272; Elections- 276-676-6227; Vital Records- 276-676-6265. **Property tax/Assessor-** 276-676-6270.

Waynesboro City

Clerk of Circuit Court, PO Box 910, Waynesboro, VA 22980. 540-942-6616; fax-540-942-6774; hours: 8:30AM-5PM.

Recording do require six digit "PIN" available by calling 540-942-6722, ask for account number. Records indexed on computer back to 1992. Only the public may search. Copy fee $.50 per page. Cert fee- $2.00 per cert plus copy fee. Payee-Waynesboro City Clerk of Circuit Court. **Online access to Property, Appraiser records:** Access to city property appraiser data is free at www.vamanet.com/cgi-bin/LOCS. **Other phones:** Treasurer- 540-942-6606. **Property tax/Assessor-** 540-942-6621/5513.

Westmoreland County

Clerk of Circuit Court, PO Box 307, Montross, VA 22520. 804-493-0108; fax-n/a; hours: 9AM-5PM.

Separate indices to search include deeds, law, chancery, judgments, marriages. Only the public may search. Copy fee $.50 per page. Payee-Westmoreland County Clerk of Circuit Court. **Other phones:** Treasurer- 804-493-0124; Elections-804-493-8898. **Property tax/Assessor-** 804-493-0113.

Winchester City

Clerk of Circuit Court, 5 N. Kent St, Winchester, VA 22601. 540-667-5770; fax-540-667-6638; hours: 9AM-5PM. www.winfredclerk.com

All records in one index. Records indexed on computer. Only the public may search. Copy fee $.50 per page. Cert fee- $2.00 per cert plus copy fee. Payee- Winchester City Clerk of Circuit Court. **Other phones:** Treasurer- 540-667-1815; Appraiser/Auditor- 540-667-1815; Elections- 540-667-1815. **Property tax/Assessor-** 15 N Cameron St, Winchester, VA 22601; 540-667-1815.

Wise County

Clerk of Circuit Court, PO Box 1248, Wise, VA 24293. 276-328-6111; fax-276-328-0039; hours: 8:30AM-5PM. www.courtbar.org

Records indexed on a public use terminal back to 1996. Only the public may search. Copy fee $.50 per page. **Online access to Assessor, Real Estate, Lien, Probate, Marriage, Property Tax, Appraisal records:** Includes City of Norton. For full access fee is $440 annually; see www.courtbar.org website. Free access is at http://arcims2.webgis.net/wise/default.asp; click on Quick Search. The fee service includes index and images, court orders, land documents from 1970 and links to RE tax assessments, 50-year RE, tax maps, plat maps, delinquent taxes, permit images, probate, marriage, judgment liens for 20 years, and more. UCC-1 indices for past 5 years. Also, property data is at http://egov.mixnet.com/wise/search.asp. Egov also offers a $440 per year subscription service. **Other phones:** Treasurer- 276-328-3666; Appraiser/Auditor-276-328-3566. **Property tax/Assessor-** PO Box 1278, Wise, VA 24293; 276-328-3556.

Wythe County

Clerk of Circuit Court, 225 S. Fourth St, Rm 105, Wytheville, VA 24382. 276-223-6050; fax-276-223-6057; hours: 8:30AM-5PM.

All records in one index. Records indexed on a public use terminal back to 1992. Only the public may search. Copy fee $.50 per page. Cert fee-$1.00 per page plus copy fee. Payee- Clerk. **Other phones:** Treasurer- 276-223-6070; Appraiser/Auditor-276-223-6015; Elections- 276-223-6038. **Property tax/Assessor-** 276-223-6015.

York County

Clerk of Circuit Court, PO Box 371, Yorktown, VA 23690. 757-890-3350, R/E recording phone-757-890-4103; fax-757-890-3364; hours: 9AM-4PM. www.yorkcounty.gov/circuitcourt

Separate indices to search include records prior to 1969. Office will perform a UCC search but public must search other records themselves. UCC search per debtor name- $20.00. Copy fee $.50 per page. Cert fee- $2.00 fee plus copy fee. Payee- York County Circuit Court. **Online to Property records:** Property records from the County GIS site are free at www.regis.state.va.us/york/pub/disclaimer.htm. **Other phones:** Treasurer- 757-890-3420 (York Co); City of Poquoson Commissioner- 757-868-3020; City of Poquoson Treasurer -757-868-3015. **Property tax/Assessor-** 757-890-3270.

Virginia County Locator

You will usually be able to find the city name in the City/County Cross Reference below. In that case, it is a simple matter to determine the county from the cross reference. However, only the official US Postal Service city names are included in this index. There are an additional 40,000 place names that people use in their addresses. Therefore, we have also included a ZIP/City Cross Reference immediately following the City/County Cross Reference.

Virginia City/County Cross Reference

ABINGDON Washington
ACCOMAC Accomack
ACHILLES Gloucester
AFTON (22920) Nelson(65), Albemarle(30), Augusta(3)
ALBERTA Brunswick
ALDIE Loudoun
ALEXANDRIA (22311) Alexandria City(93), Fairfax(6)
ALEXANDRIA (22312) Fairfax(76), Alexandria City(23)
ALEXANDRIA Alexandria City
ALEXANDRIA Fairfax
ALFONSO Lancaster
ALTAVISTA Campbell
ALTON Halifax
AMELIA COURT HOUSE Amelia
AMHERST Amherst
AMISSVILLE (20106) Culpeper(62), Rappahannock(33), Fauquier(3)
AMISSVILLE Rappahannock
AMMON Dinwiddie
AMONATE Tazewell
ANDERSONVILLE Buckingham
ANDOVER Wise
ANNANDALE Fairfax
APPALACHIA Wise
APPOMATTOX (24522) Appomattox(98), Buckingham(1)
ARARAT (24053) Patrick(94), Carroll(5)
ARCOLA Loudoun
ARK Gloucester
ARLINGTON (22206) Arlington(97), Alexandria City(2)
ARLINGTON Arlington
ARODA Madison
ARRINGTON (22922) Nelson(96), Amherst(3)
ARVONIA Buckingham
ASHBURN Loudoun
ASHLAND Hanover
ASSAWOMAN Accomack
ATKINS Smyth
ATLANTIC Accomack
AUGUSTA SPRINGS Augusta
AUSTINVILLE (24312) Carroll(60), Wythe(39)
AXTON (24054) Henry(64), Pittsylvania(35)
AYLETT King William
BACOVA Bath
BANCO Madison
BANDY Tazewell
BANK AMERICARD Roanoke City
BARBOURSVILLE (22923) Orange(53), Greene(24), Albemarle(21)
BARHAMSVILLE New Kent
BARREN SPRINGS Wythe
BASKERVILLE Mecklenburg
BASSETT (24055) Henry(94), Franklin(5)
BASTIAN (24314) Bland(71), Tazewell(28)
BASYE Shenandoah
BATESVILLE Albemarle
BATTERY PARK Isle of Wight
BAVON Mathews
BEALETON Fauquier
BEAUMONT Goochland
BEAVERDAM (23015) Hanover(72), Caroline(13), Spotsylvania(12), Louisa(1)
BEAVERLETT Mathews

BEDFORD (24523) Bedford(78), Bedford City(21)
BEE Dickenson
BELLAMY Gloucester
BELLE HAVEN Accomack
BELSPRING Pulaski
BEN HUR Lee
BENA Gloucester
BENT MOUNTAIN (24059) Roanoke(92), Franklin(5), Floyd(2)
BENTONVILLE (22610) Warren(98), Page(1)
BERGTON Rockingham
BERRYVILLE Clarke
BIG ISLAND Bedford
BIG ROCK Buchanan
BIG STONE GAP (24219) Wise(97), Lee(2)
BIRCHLEAF Dickenson
BIRDSNEST Northampton
BISHOP Tazewell
BLACKSBURG Montgomery
BLACKSTONE (23824) Nottoway(91), Brunswick(8)
BLACKWATER (24221) Lee(62), Scott(37)
BLAIRS Pittsylvania
BLAKES Mathews
BLAND Bland
BLOXOM Accomack
BLUE GRASS Highland
BLUE RIDGE (24064) Botetourt(63), Bedford(36)
BLUEFIELD Tazewell
BLUEMONT (20135) Clarke(69), Loudoun(30)
BLUEMONT Loudoun
BOHANNON Mathews
BOISSEVAIN Tazewell
BOONES MILL (24065) Franklin(82), Roanoke(17)
BOSTON (22713) Culpeper(84), Rappahannock(15)
BOWLING GREEN Caroline
BOYCE Clarke
BOYDTON Mecklenburg
BOYKINS Southampton
BRACEY (23919) Mecklenburg(94), Brunswick(5)
BRANCHVILLE Southampton
BRANDY STATION Culpeper
BREAKS Dickenson
BREMO BLUFF Fluvanna
BRIDGEWATER (22812) Rockingham(80), Augusta(19)
BRIGHTWOOD Madison
BRISTOL (24202) Washington(91), Bristol City(5), Scott(2)
BRISTOL Bristol City
BRISTOW Prince William
BROAD RUN (20137) Fauquier(78), Prince William(21)
BROAD RUN Fauquier
BROADFORD (24316) Tazewell(97), Smyth(2)
BROADWAY (22815) Rockingham(98), Shenandoah(1)
BRODNAX (23920) Brunswick(76), Mecklenburg(21), Lunenburg(2)
BROOKE Stafford
BROOKNEAL (24528) Campbell(78), Charlotte(21)

BROWNSBURG Rockbridge
BRUCETOWN Frederick
BRUINGTON King and Queen
BUCHANAN Botetourt
BUCKINGHAM Buckingham
BUENA VISTA (24416) Buena Vista City(77), Rockbridge(22)
BUFFALO JUNCTION (24529) Mecklenburg(98), Halifax(1)
BUMPASS (23024) Louisa(83), Spotsylvania(13), Hanover(3)
BURGESS Northumberland
BURKE Fairfax
BURKES GARDEN Tazewell
BURKEVILLE (23922) Nottoway(91), Prince Edward(8)
BURR HILL Orange
CALLANDS (24530) Pittsylvania(98), Henry(1)
CALLAO (22435) Northumberland(98), Westmoreland(1)
CALLAWAY Franklin
CALVERTON Fauquier
CANA Carroll
CAPE CHARLES Northampton
CAPEVILLE Northampton
CAPRON Southampton
CARDINAL Mathews
CARET (22436) Essex(98), Caroline(1)
CARROLLTON Isle of Wight
CARRSVILLE Isle of Wight
CARSON (23830) Prince George(55), Dinwiddie(30), Sussex(13)
CARTERSVILLE Cumberland
CASANOVA Fauquier
CASCADE Pittsylvania
CASTLETON (22716) Rappahannock(95), Culpeper(4)
CASTLEWOOD Russell
CATAWBA (24070) Roanoke(71), Montgomery(26), Craig(1)
CATHARPIN Prince William
CATLETT Fauquier
CAUTHORNVILLE King and Queen
CEDAR BLUFF (24609) Tazewell(83), Russell(16)
CENTER CROSS (22437) Essex(79), King and Queen(20)
CENTREVILLE Fairfax
CERES (24318) Bland(67), Smyth(32)
CHAMPLAIN (22438) Essex(90), Caroline(9)
CHANCE Essex
CHANTILLY Fairfax
CHANTILLY Loudoun
CHARLES CITY Charles City
CHARLOTTE COURT HOUSE (23923) Charlotte(97), Prince Edward(2)
CHARLOTTESVILLE (22901) Albemarle(82), Charlottesville City(17)
CHARLOTTESVILLE (22903) Charlottesville City(68), Albemarle(31)
CHARLOTTESVILLE Albemarle
CHARLOTTESVILLE Charlottesville City
CHASE CITY (23924) Mecklenburg(93), Lunenburg(4), Charlotte(2)
CHATHAM Pittsylvania
CHECK Floyd
CHERITON Northampton
CHESAPEAKE Chesapeake City

CHESTER Chesterfield
CHESTER GAP Rappahannock
CHILHOWIE (24319) Smyth(76), Washington(23)
CHINCOTEAGUE Accomack
CHINCOTEAGUE ISLAND Accomack
CHRISTCHURCH Middlesex
CHRISTIANSBURG Montgomery
CHURCH ROAD (23833) Dinwiddie(89), Amelia(10)
CHURCH VIEW Middlesex
CHURCHVILLE Augusta
CITY OFFICES Roanoke City
CLAREMONT Surry
CLARKSVILLE Mecklenburg
CLAUDVILLE Patrick
CLEAR BROOK Frederick
CLEVELAND (24225) Russell(97), Dickenson(2)
CLIFFORD Amherst
CLIFTON Fairfax
CLIFTON FORGE (24422) Alleghany(95), Botetourt(3), Clifton Forge City(1)
CLINCHBURG Washington
CLINCHCO Dickenson
CLINTWOOD Dickenson
CLOVER Halifax
CLOVERDALE Botetourt
CLUSTER SPRINGS Halifax
COBBS CREEK Mathews
COBHAM Albemarle
COEBURN (24230) Wise(89), Dickenson(9), Scott(1)
COLEMAN FALLS Bedford
COLES POINT Westmoreland
COLLINSVILLE Henry
COLOGNE King and Queen
COLONIAL BEACH Westmoreland
COLONIAL HEIGHTS (23834) Colonial Heights City(70), Chesterfield(29)
COLUMBIA (23038) Goochland(56), Cumberland(21), Fluvanna(21)
CONCORD (24538) Campbell(77), Appomattox(22)
COPPER HILL Floyd
CORBIN Caroline
COURTLAND (23837) Southampton(96), Sussex(3)
COVESVILLE Albemarle
COVINGTON (24426) Alleghany(49), Covington City(49)
CRADDOCKVILLE Accomack
CRAIGSVILLE Augusta
CREWE Nottoway
CRIDERS Rockingham
CRIMORA Augusta
CRIPPLE CREEK Wythe
CRITZ Patrick
CROCKETT Wythe
CROSS JUNCTION Frederick
CROZET Albemarle
CROZIER Goochland
CRYSTAL HILL Halifax
CULLEN (23934) Charlotte(60), Prince Edward(39)
CULPEPER (22701) Culpeper(89), Orange(7), Madison(3)
CUMBERLAND (23040) Cumberland(91), Buckingham(8)
DABNEYS Louisa

DAHLGREN King George
DALEVILLE Botetourt
DAMASCUS Washington
DANTE (24237) Dickenson(68),
  Russell(31)
DANVILLE (24541) Danville City(77),
  Pittsylvania(22)
DANVILLE Danville City
DARLINGTN HTS Prince Edward
DARLINGTON HEIGHTS Prince Edward
DAVENPORT Buchanan
DAVIS WHARF Accomack
DAYTON Rockingham
DEERFIELD (24432) Augusta(98), Bath(1)
DELAPLANE Fauquier
DELTAVILLE Middlesex
DENDRON Surry
DEWITT Dinwiddie
DIGGS Mathews
DILLWYN (23936) Buckingham(96),
  Cumberland(3)
DINWIDDIE Dinwiddie
DISPUTANTA (23842) Prince George(92),
  Sussex(7)
DOE HILL Highland
DOGUE King George
DOLPHIN Brunswick
DORAN Tazewell
DOSWELL (23047) Hanover(75),
  Caroline(24)
DRAKES BRANCH (23937) Charlotte(94),
  Lunenburg(5)
DRAPER (24324) Pulaski(78), Wythe(21)
DREWRYVILLE Southampton
DRY FORK Pittsylvania
DRYDEN Lee
DUBLIN (24084) Pulaski(94), Bland(5)
DUFFIELD (24244) Scott(83), Lee(16)
DUGSPUR Carroll
DULLES Loudoun
DUMFRIES Prince William
DUNDAS (23938) Brunswick(60),
  Lunenburg(39)
DUNGANNON Scott
DUNN LORING Fairfax
DUNNSVILLE Essex
DUTTON (23050) Mathews(77),
  Gloucester(22)
DYKE (22935) Greene(68), Albemarle(31)
EAGLE ROCK Botetourt
EARLYSVILLE Albemarle
EAST STONE GAP Wise
EASTVILLE Northampton
EBONY Brunswick
EDINBURG Shenandoah
EDWARDSVILLE Northumberland
EGGLESTON Giles
ELBERON Surry
ELK CREEK Grayson
ELKTON (22827) Rockingham(90),
  Page(9)
ELKWOOD Culpeper
ELLISTON (24087) Montgomery(96),
  Roanoke(3)
EMORY Washington
EMPORIA (23847) Greensville(66),
  Emporia City(30), Southampton(2),
  Sussex(1)
ESMONT Albemarle
ETLAN Madison
EVERGREEN Appomattox
EVINGTON (24550) Campbell(89),
  Bedford(10)
EWING Lee
EXETER Wise
EXMORE Northampton
FABER (22938) Nelson(96), Albemarle(3)
FAIRFAX (22032) Fairfax(95), Fairfax
  City(4)
FAIRFAX Fairfax
FAIRFAX Fairfax City
FAIRFAX STATION Fairfax

FAIRFIELD Rockbridge
FALLS CHURCH (22044) Fairfax(93), Falls
  Church City(6)
FALLS CHURCH (22046) Falls Church
  City(69), Fairfax(30)
FALLS CHURCH Fairfax
FALLS CHURCH Falls Church City
FALLS MILLS Tazewell
FANCY GAP Carroll
FARMVILLE (23901) Prince Edward(79),
  Cumberland(18), Buckingham(1)
FARMVILLE Prince Edward
FARNHAM Richmond
FERRUM Franklin
FIELDALE Henry
FIFE Goochland
FINCASTLE Botetourt
FISHERS HILL Shenandoah
FISHERSVILLE Augusta
FLINT HILL Rappahannock
FONESWOOD Richmond
FORD (23850) Dinwiddie(85), Amelia(14)
FOREST (24551) Bedford(87),
  Campbell(11)
FORK UNION Fluvanna
FORT BELVOIR Fairfax
FORT BLACKMORE Scott
FORT DEFIANCE Augusta
FORT EUSTIS Newport News City
FORT LEE (23801) Prince George(98),
  Petersburg City(1)
FORT MITCHELL Lunenburg
FORT MONROE Hampton City
FORT VALLEY Shenandoah
FOSTER Mathews
FRANKLIN (23851) Franklin City(51),
  Southampton(41), Isle of Wight(7)
FRANKTOWN Northampton
FREDERICKSBURG (22401)
  Fredericksburg City(96), Spotsylvania(3)
FREDERICKSBURG (22408)
  Spotsylvania(95), Caroline(3)
FREDERICKSBURG Fredericksburg City
FREDERICKSBURG Spotsylvania
FREDERICKSBURG Stafford
FREE UNION (22940) Albemarle(77),
  Greene(22)
FREEMAN (23856) Brunswick(95),
  Greensville(4)
FRIES Grayson
FRONT ROYAL (22630) Warren(98),
  Clarke(1)
FRONT ROYAL Warren
FT MYER Arlington
FULKS RUN Rockingham
GAINESVILLE Prince William
GALAX (24333) Carroll(35), Grayson(35),
  Galax City(29)
GARRISONVILLE Stafford
GASBURG Brunswick
GATE CITY Scott
GLADE SPRING Washington
GLADEHILL Franklin
GLADSTONE (24553) Nelson(44),
  Amherst(32), Appomattox(12),
  Buckingham(11)
GLADYS Campbell
GLASGOW Rockbridge
GLEN ALLEN (23059) Henrico(78),
  Hanover(21)
GLEN ALLEN Henrico
GLEN LYN Giles
GLEN WILTON Botetourt
GOLDBOND Giles
GOLDVEIN Fauquier
GOOCHLAND Goochland
GOODE Bedford
GOODVIEW Bedford
GORDONSVILLE (22942) Orange(62),
  Louisa(34), Albemarle(2)

GORE Frederick
GOSHEN (24439) Rockbridge(80),
  Augusta(19)
GRAVES MILL Madison
GREAT AMERICAN MAGAZINE Hampton
  City
GREAT FALLS (22066) Fairfax(96),
  Loudoun(3)
GREEN BAY (23942) Prince Edward(67),
  Lunenburg(32)
GREENBACKVILLE Accomack
GREENBUSH Accomack
GREENVILLE Augusta
GREENWAY Fairfax
GREENWOOD Albemarle
GRETNA Pittsylvania
GRIMSTEAD Mathews
GROTTOES (24441) Rockingham(81),
  Augusta(18)
GRUNDY Buchanan
GUM SPRING (23065) Goochland(71),
  Louisa(28)
GWYNN Mathews
HACKSNECK Accomack
HADENSVILLE Goochland
HAGUE Westmoreland
HALLIEFORD Mathews
HALLWOOD Accomack
HAMILTON Loudoun
HAMPDEN SYDNEY Prince Edward
HAMPTON (23665) Hampton City(52),
  York(47)
HAMPTON Hampton City
HANDSOM Southampton
HANOVER (23069) Hanover(41),
  Caroline(33), King William(24)
HARBORTON Accomack
HARDY (24101) Franklin(91), Bedford(8)
HARDYVILLE Middlesex
HARMAN Buchanan
HARRISONBURG (22802) Harrisonburg
  City(50), Rockingham(49)
HARRISONBURG Harrisonburg City
HARTFIELD Middlesex
HARTWOOD Stafford
HAYES Gloucester
HAYMARKET Prince William
HAYNESVILLE Richmond
HAYSI (24256) Dickenson(89),
  Buchanan(10)
HAYWOOD Madison
HEAD WATERS Highland
HEATHSVILLE (22473)
  Northumberland(98), Lancaster(1)
HENRY (24102) Franklin(92), Henry(7)
HERNDON Fairfax
HIGHLAND SPRINGS Henrico
HIGHTOWN Highland
HILLSVILLE Carroll
HILTONS (24258) Scott(85),
  Washington(14)
HINTON Rockingham
HIWASSEE (24347) Pulaski(89),
  Montgomery(10)
HONAKER (24260) Russell(87),
  Buchanan(12)
HOOD Madison
HOPEWELL (23860) Hopewell City(81),
  Prince George(18)
HORNTOWN Accomack
HORSEPEN Tazewell
HOT SPRINGS (24445) Bath(57),
  Alleghany(42)
HOWARDSVILLE (24562) Albemarle(48),
  Buckingham(38), Nelson(12)
HUDDLESTON Bedford
HUDGINS Mathews
HUME Fauquier
HUNTLY Rappahannock
HURLEY Buchanan
HURT Pittsylvania
HUSTLE Essex

HYACINTH Northumberland
INDEPENDENCE Grayson
INDIAN VALLEY Floyd
IRON GATE Alleghany
IRVINGTON Lancaster
ISLE OF WIGHT Isle of Wight
IVANHOE (24350) Wythe(57), Carroll(34),
  Grayson(8)
IVOR (23866) Southampton(59), Isle of
  Wight(40)
IVY Albemarle
JAMAICA Middlesex
JAMES STORE Gloucester
JAMESTOWN James City
JAMESVILLE Northampton
JARRATT (23867) Greensville(91),
  Sussex(8)
JARRATT Greensville
JAVA (24565) Pittsylvania(89), Halifax(10)
JEFFERSONTON Culpeper
JENKINS BRIDGE Accomack
JERSEY King George
JETERSVILLE (23083) Amelia(97),
  Nottoway(2)
JEWELL RIDGE (24622) Tazewell(89),
  Buchanan(10)
JONESVILLE Lee
JORDAN MINES Alleghany
KEELING Pittsylvania
KEEN MOUNTAIN Buchanan
KEENE Albemarle
KEEZLETOWN Rockingham
KELLER Accomack
KENBRIDGE Lunenburg
KENTS STORE (23084) Fluvanna(65),
  Goochland(20), Louisa(14)
KEOKEE Lee
KESWICK (22947) Albemarle(85),
  Fluvanna(11), Louisa(3)
KEYSVILLE (23947) Charlotte(51),
  Lunenburg(39), Prince Edward(9)
KILMARNOCK (22482)
  Northumberland(62), Lancaster(37)
KING AND QUEEN COURT HOUS King
  and Queen
KING GEORGE King George
KING WILLIAM King William
KINSALE Westmoreland
LA CROSSE (23950) Mecklenburg(87),
  Brunswick(12)
LACEY SPRING Rockingham
LACKEY York
LADYSMITH Caroline
LAHORE Orange
LAMBSBURG Carroll
LANEVIEW (22504) Essex(80),
  Middlesex(19)
LANEXA (23089) New Kent(76), James
  City(23)
LAUREL FORK Carroll
LAWRENCEVILLE Brunswick
LEBANON Russell
LEE MONT Accomack
LEESBURG Loudoun
LEON Madison
LEWISETTA Northumberland
LEXINGTON (24450) Rockbridge(71),
  Lexington City(28)
LIGHTFOOT York
LIGNUM Culpeper
LINCOLN Loudoun
LINDEN (22642) Warren(85), Fauquier(14)
LINVILLE Rockingham
LITTLE PLYMOUTH King and Queen
LIVELY Lancaster
LOCUST DALE Madison
LOCUST GROVE (22508) Orange(92),
  Spotsylvania(7)
LOCUST HILL Middlesex
LOCUSTVILLE Accomack
LONG ISLAND (24569) Pittsylvania(86),
  Campbell(7), Halifax(5)

LORETTO Essex
LORTON Fairfax
LOTTSBURG Northumberland
LOUISA (23093) Louisa(92), Goochland(6), Fluvanna(1)
LOVETTSVILLE Loudoun
LOVINGSTON Nelson
LOW MOOR Alleghany
LOWRY Bedford
LUNENBURG Lunenburg
LURAY Page
LYNCH STATION (24571) Campbell(75), Bedford(24)
LYNCHBURG (24502) Lynchburg City(54), Campbell(43), Bedford(2)
LYNCHBURG (24503) Lynchburg City(67), Bedford(32)
LYNCHBURG (24504) Lynchburg City(65), Campbell(33)
LYNCHBURG Lynchburg City
LYNDHURST (22952) Augusta(95), Nelson(2), Waynesboro City(1)
MACHIPONGO Northampton
MACON Powhatan
MADISON HEIGHTS Amherst
MADISON MILLS Madison
MAIDENS (23102) Goochland(79), Louisa(13), Hanover(6)
MANAKIN SABOT Goochland
MANASSAS (20110) Manassas City(84), Prince William(15)
MANASSAS (20109) Prince William(96), Manassas City(3)
MANASSAS (20111) Prince William(63), Manassas Park City(36)
MANASSAS Manassas City
MANASSAS Manassas Park City
MANASSAS Prince William
MANGOHICK King William
MANNBORO Amelia
MANQUIN King William
MAPPSVILLE Accomack
MARION Smyth
MARIONVILLE Northampton
MARKHAM Fauquier
MARSHALL Fauquier
MARTINSVILLE (24112) Henry(65), Martinsville City(34)
MARTINSVILLE Martinsville City
MARYUS Gloucester
MASCOT King and Queen
MASSIES MILL Nelson
MATHEWS Mathews
MATTAPONI King and Queen
MAURERTOWN Shenandoah
MAVISDALE Buchanan
MAX MEADOWS Wythe
MAXIE Buchanan
MC CLURE Dickenson
MC COY Montgomery
MC DOWELL Highland
MC GAHEYSVILLE Rockingham
MC KENNEY Dinwiddie
MC LEAN Fairfax
MEADOWS OF DAN (24120) Patrick(73), Floyd(16), Carroll(10)
MEADOWVIEW Washington
MEARS Accomack
MECHANICSVILLE Hanover
MEHERRIN (23954) Prince Edward(68), Lunenburg(31)
MELFA Accomack
MENDOTA Washington
MEREDITHVILLE Brunswick
MERRIFIELD Fairfax
MERRY POINT Lancaster
MIDDLEBROOK (24459) Augusta(88), Rockbridge(11)
MIDDLEBURG (20117) Loudoun(97), Fauquier(2)
MIDDLEBURG Loudoun

MIDDLETOWN (22645) Frederick(56), Warren(42)
MIDDLETOWN Warren
MIDLAND Fauquier
MIDLOTHIAN Chesterfield
MILES Chesterfield
MILFORD (22514) Caroline(98), King and Queen(1)
MILLBORO Bath
MILLERS TAVERN Essex
MILLWOOD Clarke
MINE RUN Orange
MINERAL (23117) Louisa(86), Spotsylvania(10), Goochland(2)
MINT SPRING Augusta
MITCHELLS Culpeper
MOBJACK Mathews
MODEST TOWN Accomack
MOLLUSK Lancaster
MONETA (24121) Bedford(59), Franklin(40)
MONROE Amherst
MONTEBELLO Nelson
MONTEREY Highland
MONTPELIER (23192) Hanover(92), Louisa(7)
MONTPELIER STATION Orange
MONTROSS Westmoreland
MONTVALE Bedford
MOON Mathews
MORATTICO Lancaster
MOSELEY (23120) Chesterfield(95), Powhatan(4)
MOUNT CRAWFORD (22841) Rockingham(98), Augusta(1)
MOUNT HOLLY Westmoreland
MOUNT JACKSON Shenandoah
MOUNT SIDNEY Augusta
MOUNT SOLON Augusta
MOUNT VERNON Fairfax
MOUTH OF WILSON Grayson
MUSTOE Highland
NARROWS (24124) Giles(97), Bland(2)
NARUNA Campbell
NASSAWADOX Northampton
NATHALIE Halifax
NATURAL BRIDGE Rockbridge
NATURAL BRIDGE STATION Rockbridge
NAXERA Gloucester
NELLYSFORD Nelson
NELSON Mecklenburg
NELSONIA Accomack
NEW CANTON (23123) Buckingham(95), Cumberland(4)
NEW CASTLE Craig
NEW CHURCH Accomack
NEW HOPE Augusta
NEW KENT (23124) New Kent(95), Hanover(4)
NEW MARKET (22844) Shenandoah(91), Rockingham(8)
NEW POINT Mathews
NEW RIVER Pulaski
NEWBERN Pulaski
NEWINGTON Fairfax
NEWPORT (24128) Giles(87), Craig(12)
NEWPORT NEWS (23605) Newport News City(81), Hampton City(18)
NEWPORT NEWS Hampton City
NEWPORT NEWS Newport News City
NEWSOMS Southampton
NEWTOWN King and Queen
NICKELSVILLE (24271) Scott(97), Russell(2)
NINDE King George
NOKESVILLE (20181) Prince William(94), Fauquier(5)
NOKESVILLE Prince William
NORA Dickenson
NORFOLK Norfolk City
NORGE James City

NORTH (23128) Mathews(53), Gloucester(46)
NORTH GARDEN Albemarle
NORTH TAZEWELL Tazewell
NORTON (24273) Norton City(72), Wise(27)
NORWOOD Nelson
NOTTOWAY Nottoway
NUTTSVILLE Lancaster
OAK HALL Accomack
OAKPARK Madison
OAKTON Fairfax
OAKWOOD Buchanan
OCCOQUAN Prince William
OILVILLE (23129) Goochland(96), Hanover(3)
OLDHAMS Westmoreland
ONANCOCK Accomack
ONEMO Mathews
ONLEY Accomack
OPHELIA Northumberland
ORANGE (22960) Orange(90), Madison(9)
ORDINARY Gloucester
ORISKANY Botetourt
ORKNEY SPRINGS Shenandoah
ORLEAN Fauquier
OYSTER Northampton
PAEONIAN SPRINGS Loudoun
PAINT BANK Craig
PAINTER Accomack
PALMYRA Fluvanna
PAMPLIN (23958) Prince Edward(57), Appomattox(29), Charlotte(12)
PARIS (20130) Clarke(73), Fauquier(18), Loudoun(8)
PARIS Fauquier
PARKSLEY Accomack
PARROTT Pulaski
PARTLOW Spotsylvania
PATRICK SPRINGS Patrick
PEARISBURG (24134) Giles(98), Bland(1)
PEMBROKE Giles
PENHOOK (24137) Franklin(79), Pittsylvania(20)
PENN LAIRD Rockingham
PENNINGTON GAP Lee
PETERSBURG (23803) Petersburg City(54), Dinwiddie(25), Chesterfield(20)
PETERSBURG (23805) Petersburg City(60), Prince George(26), Dinwiddie(13)
PETERSBURG Petersburg City
PHENIX Charlotte
PHILOMONT Loudoun
PILGRIMS KNOB Buchanan
PILOT (24138) Floyd(51), Montgomery(48)
PINEY RIVER Nelson
PITTSVILLE Pittsylvania
PLAIN VIEW King and Queen
PLEASANT VALLEY Rockingham
POCAHONTAS Tazewell
POQUOSON Poquoson City
PORT HAYWOOD Mathews
PORT REPUBLIC Rockingham
PORT ROYAL Caroline
PORTSMOUTH Portsmouth City
POUND Wise
POUNDING MILL Tazewell
POWHATAN (23139) Powhatan(97), Cumberland(2)
PRATTS Madison
PRINCE GEORGE Prince George
PROSPECT Prince Edward
PROVIDENCE FORGE (23140) New Kent(59), Charles City(40)
PUNGOTEAGUE Accomack
PURCELLVILLE Loudoun
QUANTICO Prince William
QUANTICO Stafford
QUICKSBURG Shenandoah
QUINBY Accomack
QUINQUE Greene

QUINTON New Kent
RADFORD (24141) Radford City(59), Pulaski(27), Montgomery(11), Floyd(1)
RADFORD Radford City
RADIANT Madison
RANDOLPH (23962) Charlotte(90), Halifax(9)
RAPHINE (24472) Rockbridge(70), Augusta(29)
RAPIDAN (22733) Culpeper(70), Orange(29)
RAPPAHANNOCK ACADEMY Caroline
RAVEN (24639) Tazewell(88), Buchanan(10), Russell(1)
RAWLINGS Brunswick
RECTORTOWN Fauquier
RED ASH Tazewell
RED HOUSE (23963) Charlotte(73), Campbell(21), Appomattox(5)
RED OAK (23964) Charlotte(88), Mecklenburg(11)
REDART Mathews
REDWOOD Franklin
REEDVILLE Northumberland
REGINA Lancaster
REMINGTON (22734) Fauquier(86), Culpeper(13)
REPUBLICAN GROVE Halifax
RESCUE Isle of Wight
RESTON Fairfax
REVA (22735) Culpeper(89), Madison(10)
RHOADESVILLE Orange
RICE (23966) Amelia(53), Prince Edward(46)
RICH CREEK Giles
RICHARDSVILLE Culpeper
RICHLANDS Tazewell
RICHMOND (23235) Chesterfield(72), Richmond City(27)
RICHMOND (23231) Henrico(82), Richmond City(13), Charles City(3)
RICHMOND (23238) Henrico(91), Goochland(8)
RICHMOND (23222) Richmond City(67), Henrico(32)
RICHMOND (23225) Richmond City(83), Chesterfield(16)
RICHMOND (23226) Richmond City(50), Henrico(49)
RICHMOND Chesterfield
RICHMOND Henrico
RICHMOND Richmond City
RIDGEWAY Henry
RILEYVILLE Page
RINER (24149) Montgomery(79), Floyd(20)
RINGGOLD Pittsylvania
RIPPLEMEAD Giles
RIXEYVILLE Culpeper
ROANOKE (24018) Roanoke(85), Roanoke City(14)
ROANOKE (24019) Roanoke(67), Botetourt(21), Roanoke City(11)
ROANOKE (24015) Roanoke City(98), Roanoke(1)
ROANOKE Botetourt
ROANOKE Montgomery
ROANOKE Roanoke
ROANOKE Roanoke City
ROCHELLE Madison
ROCKBRIDGE BATHS Rockbridge
ROCKVILLE (23146) Hanover(73), Goochland(26)
ROCKY GAP Bland
ROCKY MOUNT Franklin
ROLLINS FORK King George
ROSE HILL Lee
ROSEDALE Russell
ROSELAND (22967) Nelson(91), Amherst(8)
ROSELAND Amherst
ROUND HILL Loudoun
ROWE (24646) Buchanan(91), Russell(8)

RUBY Stafford
RUCKERSVILLE (22968) Greene(90), Albemarle(9)
RURAL RETREAT (24368) Wythe(55), Smyth(44)
RUSTBURG Campbell
RUTHER GLEN (22546) Caroline(98), Hanover(1)
RUTHVILLE Charles City
SAINT CHARLES Lee
SAINT PAUL (24283) Wise(95), Russell(3)
SAINT STEPHENS CHURCH (23148) King and Queen(86), Essex(13)
SALEM (24153) Salem City(63), Roanoke(36)
SALEM Salem City
SALTVILLE (24370) Smyth(80), Washington(19)
SALUDA (23149) Middlesex(49), Gloucester(36), King and Queen(13)
SANDSTON Henrico
SANDY HOOK Goochland
SANDY LEVEL Pittsylvania
SANDY POINT Westmoreland
SANFORD Accomack
SAXE Charlotte
SAXIS Accomack
SCHLEY Gloucester
SCHUYLER (22969) Nelson(59), Albemarle(40)
SCOTTSBURG Halifax
SCOTTSVILLE (24590) Fluvanna(47), Albemarle(44), Buckingham(8)
SEAFORD York
SEALSTON King George
SEAVIEW Northampton
SEDLEY (23878) Southampton(97), Sussex(2)
SELMA Alleghany
SEVEN MILE FORD Smyth
SEVERN Gloucester
SHACKLEFORDS King and Queen
SHADOW Mathews
SHARPS Richmond
SHAWSVILLE Montgomery
SHILOH King George
SHIPMAN Nelson
SHORTT GAP Buchanan
SINGERS GLEN Rockingham
SKIPPERS Greensville
SKIPWITH Mecklenburg
SMITHFIELD Isle of Wight
SOMERSET (22972) Orange(95), Madison(4)
SOMERVILLE Fauquier
SOUTH BOSTON Halifax
SOUTH HILL (23970) Mecklenburg(93), Lunenburg(6)
SPARTA Caroline
SPEEDWELL Wythe
SPENCER Henry
SPERRYVILLE (22740) Rappahannock(84), Culpeper(13), Madison(1)

SPOTSYLVANIA Spotsylvania
SPOTTSWOOD (24475) Augusta(96), Rockbridge(3)
SPOUT SPRING Appomattox
SPRING GROVE (23881) Prince George(50), Surry(49)
SPRINGFIELD Fairfax
STAFFORD (22556) Stafford(98), Fauquier(1)
STAFFORDSVILLE Giles
STANARDSVILLE (22973) Greene(98), Madison(1)
STANLEY Page
STANLEYTOWN Henry
STAR TANNERY (22654) Frederick(73), Shenandoah(26)
STATE FARM (23160) Powhatan(66), Goochland(33)
STAUNTON (24401) Staunton City(69), Augusta(30)
STAUNTON Staunton City
STAUNTON Augusta
STEELES TAVERN Augusta
STEPHENS CITY (22655) Frederick(98), Warren(1)
STEPHENSON Frederick
STERLING Loudoun
STERLING PARK Loudoun
STEVENSBURG Culpeper
STEVENSVILLE King and Queen
STONEGA Wise
STONY CREEK (23882) Sussex(71), Dinwiddie(28)
STRASBURG (22657) Shenandoah(84), Warren(15)
STRASBURG Shenandoah
STRATFORD Westmoreland
STUART Patrick
STUARTS DRAFT Augusta
STUDLEY Hanover
SUFFOLK Suffolk City
SUGAR GROVE Smyth
SUMERDUCK Fauquier
SUPPLY Essex
SURRY Surry
SUSAN Mathews
SUTHERLAND Dinwiddie
SUTHERLIN Pittsylvania
SWEET BRIAR Amherst
SWOOPE Augusta
SWORDS CREEK Russell
SYRIA Madison
TANGIER Accomack
TANNERSVILLE Tazewell
TAPPAHANNOCK (22560) Essex(94), King and Queen(5)
TASLEY Accomack
TAZEWELL Tazewell
TEMPERANCEVILLE Accomack
THAXTON Bedford
THE PLAINS Fauquier
THORNBURG Spotsylvania
TIMBERVILLE (22853) Rockingham(95), Shenandoah(4)

TOANO James City
TOMS BROOK Shenandoah
TOPPING Middlesex
TOWNSEND Northampton
TRAMMEL Dickenson
TREVILIANS Louisa
TRIANGLE Prince William
TROUT DALE (24378) Grayson(89), Smyth(10)
TROUTDALE (24378) Grayson(89), Smyth(10)
TROUTVILLE (24175) Botetourt(88), Roanoke(11)
TROY (22974) Fluvanna(77), Louisa(16), Albemarle(5)
TURBEVILLE Halifax
TYRO Nelson
UNION HALL Franklin
UNIVERSITY OF RICHMOND Richmond City
UPPERVILLE (20184) Fauquier(64), Loudoun(35)
UPPERVILLE Fauquier
URBANNA Middlesex
VALENTINES Brunswick
VANSANT Buchanan
VERNON HILL (24597) Halifax(80), Pittsylvania(19)
VERONA Augusta
VESTA Patrick
VESUVIUS (24483) Rockbridge(60), Amherst(20), Nelson(19)
VICTORIA Lunenburg
VIENNA Fairfax
VIEWTOWN (22746) Culpeper(74), Rappahannock(25)
VILLAGE Richmond
VILLAMONT Bedford
VINTON (24179) Bedford(50), Roanoke(49)
VIRGILINA (24598) Halifax(84), Mecklenburg(15)
VIRGINIA BEACH Virginia Beach City
VOLNEY Grayson
WACHAPREAGUE Accomack
WAKE Middlesex
WAKEFIELD (23888) Sussex(54), Southampton(25), Surry(19)
WALKERTON (23177) King and Queen(78), King William(21)
WALLOPS ISLAND Accomack
WARDTOWN Northampton
WARE NECK Gloucester
WARFIELD Brunswick
WARM SPRINGS Bath
WARNER Middlesex
WARRENTON Fauquier
WARSAW (22572) Richmond(93), Westmoreland(6)
WASHINGTON Rappahannock
WATER VIEW Middlesex
WATERFORD Loudoun
WATTSVILLE Accomack
WAVERLY Sussex

WAYNESBORO (22980) Waynesboro City(71), Augusta(28)
WEBER CITY Scott
WEEMS Lancaster
WEIRWOOD Northampton
WEST AUGUSTA Augusta
WEST MCLEAN Fairfax
WEST POINT (23181) King William(85), New Kent(11), King and Queen(3)
WESTMORELAND Westmoreland
WEYERS CAVE (24486) Augusta(85), Rockingham(14)
WHITE HALL Albemarle
WHITE MARSH Gloucester
WHITE PLAINS Brunswick
WHITE POST (22663) Clarke(60), Frederick(34), Warren(4)
WHITE STONE Lancaster
WHITETOP Grayson
WHITEWOOD Buchanan
WICOMICO Gloucester
WICOMICO CHURCH Northumberland
WILLIAMSBURG (23185) James City(46), Williamsburg City(27), York(25)
WILLIAMSBURG (23188) James City(78), York(19), Williamsburg City(1)
WILLIAMSBURG Williamsburg City
WILLIAMSVILLE (24487) Bath(64), Highland(36)
WILLIS (24380) Floyd(93), Carroll(6)
WILLIS WHARF Northampton
WILSONS (23894) Dinwiddie(86), Nottoway(13)
WINCHESTER (22601) Winchester City(93), Frederick(6)
WINCHESTER Frederick
WINCHESTER Winchester City
WINDSOR Isle of Wight
WINGINA (24599) Nelson(85), Buckingham(14)
WIRTZ Franklin
WISE Wise
WITHAMS Accomack
WOLFORD Buchanan
WOLFTOWN Madison
WOODBERRY FOREST Madison
WOODBRIDGE Prince William
WOODFORD (22580) Caroline(90), Spotsylvania(9)
WOODLAWN Carroll
WOODS CROSS ROADS Gloucester
WOODSTOCK Shenandoah
WOODVILLE Rappahannock
WOOLWINE Patrick
WYLLIESBURG Charlotte
WYTHEVILLE Wythe
YALE Sussex
YARDS Tazewell
YORKTOWN York
ZACATA Westmoreland
ZANONI Gloucester
ZUNI (23898) Isle of Wight(69), Southampton(30)

Virginia ZIP/City Cross Reference

20101-20104	DULLES	20132-20134	PURCELLVILLE	20160-20160	LINCOLN
20105-20105	ALDIE	20135-20135	BLUEMONT	20163-20167	STERLING
20106-20106	AMISSVILLE	20136-20136	BRISTOW	20168-20169	HAYMARKET
20107-20107	ARCOLA	20137-20137	BROAD RUN	20170-20172	HERNDON
20108-20113	MANASSAS	20138-20138	CALVERTON	20175-20178	LEESBURG
20115-20116	MARSHALL	20139-20139	CASANOVA	20180-20180	LOVETTSVILLE
20117-20118	MIDDLEBURG	20140-20140	RECTORTOWN	20181-20182	NOKESVILLE
20119-20119	CATLETT	20141-20142	ROUND HILL	20184-20185	UPPERVILLE
20120-20122	CENTREVILLE	20143-20143	CATHARPIN	20186-20188	WARRENTON
20124-20124	CLIFTON	20144-20144	DELAPLANE	20189-20189	DULLES
20128-20128	ORLEAN	20146-20149	ASHBURN	20190-20191	RESTON
20129-20129	PAEONIAN SPRINGS	20151-20153	CHANTILLY	20192-20192	HERNDON
20130-20130	PARIS	20155-20156	GAINESVILLE	20193-20196	RESTON
20131-20131	PHILOMONT	20158-20159	HAMILTON	20197-20197	WATERFORD

20198-20198	THE PLAINS
20199-20199	DULLES
22001-22001	ALDIE
22002-22002	AMISSVILLE
22003-22003	ANNANDALE
22009-22009	BURKE
22010-22010	ARCOLA
22011-22011	ASHBURN
22012-22012	BLUEMONT
22013-22013	BRISTOW
22014-22014	BROAD RUN
22015-22015	BURKE
22016-22016	CALVERTON
22017-22017	CASANOVA

22018-22018	CATHARPIN
22019-22019	CATLETT
22020-22020	CENTREVILLE
22021-22022	FAIRFAX
22024-22024	CLIFTON
22025-22025	DELAPLANE
22026-22026	DUMFRIES
22027-22027	DUNN LORING
22030-22038	FAIRFAX
22039-22039	FAIRFAX STATION
22040-22047	FALLS CHURCH
22060-22060	FORT BELVOIR
22065-22065	GAINESVILLE
22066-22066	GREAT FALLS
22067-22067	GREENWAY
22068-22068	HAMILTON
22069-22069	HAYMARKET
22070-22070	RESTON
22071-22071	HERNDON
22075-22075	LEESBURG
22078-22078	PURCELLVILLE
22079-22079	LORTON
22080-22080	LOVETTSVILLE
22081-22082	MERRIFIELD
22090-22090	HERNDON
22091-22091	RESTON
22092-22092	HERNDON
22093-22093	ASHBURN
22094-22095	HERNDON
22096-22096	RESTON
22101-22102	MC LEAN
22103-22103	WEST MCLEAN
22106-22109	MC LEAN
22110-22111	MANASSAS
22115-22115	MARSHALL
22116-22116	MERRIFIELD
22117-22117	MIDDLEBURG
22118-22120	MERRIFIELD
22121-22121	MOUNT VERNON
22122-22122	NEWINGTON
22123-22123	NOKESVILLE
22124-22124	OAKTON
22125-22125	OCCOQUAN
22128-22128	ORLEAN
22129-22129	PAEONIAN SPRINGS
22130-22130	PARIS
22131-22131	PHILOMONT
22132-22132	PURCELLVILLE
22134-22135	QUANTICO
22140-22140	RECTORTOWN
22141-22141	ROUND HILL
22150-22161	SPRINGFIELD
22170-22170	STERLING PARK
22171-22171	THE PLAINS
22172-22172	TRIANGLE
22176-22176	UPPERVILLE
22180-22185	VIENNA
22186-22186	WARRENTON
22190-22190	WATERFORD
22191-22195	WOODBRIDGE
22199-22199	LORTON
22200-22210	ARLINGTON
22211-22211	FT MYER
22212-22246	ARLINGTON
22300-22336	ALEXANDRIA
22401-22412	FREDERICKSBURG
22421-22421	ALFONSO
22427-22428	BOWLING GREEN
22430-22430	BROOKE
22432-22432	BURGESS
22433-22433	BURR HILL
22435-22435	CALLAO
22436-22436	CARET
22437-22437	CENTER CROSS
22438-22438	CHAMPLAIN
22439-22439	CHANCE
22442-22442	COLES POINT
22443-22443	COLONIAL BEACH
22446-22446	CORBIN
22448-22448	DAHLGREN
22451-22451	DOGUE
22454-22454	DUNNSVILLE
22456-22456	EDWARDSVILLE
22460-22460	FARNHAM
22461-22461	FONESWOOD
22463-22463	GARRISONVILLE
22469-22469	HAGUE
22471-22471	HARTWOOD
22472-22472	HAYNESVILLE
22473-22473	HEATHSVILLE
22476-22476	HUSTLE
22477-22477	HYACINTH
22480-22480	IRVINGTON
22481-22481	JERSEY
22482-22482	KILMARNOCK
22485-22485	KING GEORGE
22488-22488	KINSALE
22501-22501	LADYSMITH
22502-22502	LAHORE
22503-22503	LANCASTER
22504-22504	LANEVIEW
22505-22505	LEWISETTA
22507-22507	LIVELY
22508-22508	LOCUST GROVE
22509-22509	LORETTO
22511-22511	LOTTSBURG
22513-22513	MERRY POINT
22514-22514	MILFORD
22517-22517	MOLLUSK
22520-22520	MONTROSS
22523-22523	MORATTICO
22524-22524	MOUNT HOLLY
22526-22526	NINDE
22528-22528	NUTTSVILLE
22529-22529	OLDHAMS
22530-22530	OPHELIA
22534-22534	PARTLOW
22535-22535	PORT ROYAL
22538-22538	RAPPAHANNOCK ACADEMY
22539-22539	REEDVILLE
22540-22540	REGINA
22542-22542	RHOADESVILLE
22544-22544	ROLLINS FORK
22545-22545	RUBY
22546-22546	RUTHER GLEN
22547-22547	SEALSTON
22548-22548	SHARPS
22549-22549	SHILOH
22552-22552	SPARTA
22553-22553	SPOTSYLVANIA
22554-22556	STAFFORD
22558-22558	STRATFORD
22559-22559	SUPPLY
22560-22560	TAPPAHANNOCK
22565-22565	THORNBURG
22567-22567	UNIONVILLE
22568-22568	MINE RUN
22570-22570	VILLAGE
22572-22572	WARSAW
22576-22576	WEEMS
22577-22577	WESTMORELAND
22577-22577	SANDY POINT
22578-22578	WHITE STONE
22579-22579	WICOMICO CHURCH
22580-22580	WOODFORD
22581-22581	ZACATA
22601-22604	WINCHESTER
22610-22610	BENTONVILLE
22611-22611	BERRYVILLE
22620-22620	BOYCE
22622-22622	BRUCETOWN
22623-22623	CHESTER GAP
22624-22624	CLEAR BROOK
22625-22625	CROSS JUNCTION
22626-22626	FISHERS HILL
22627-22627	FLINT HILL
22630-22630	FRONT ROYAL
22637-22637	GORE
22638-22638	WINCHESTER
22639-22639	HUME
22640-22640	HUNTLY
22641-22641	STRASBURG
22642-22642	LINDEN
22643-22643	MARKHAM
22644-22644	MAURERTOWN
22645-22645	MIDDLETOWN
22646-22646	MILLWOOD
22649-22649	MIDDLETOWN
22650-22650	RILEYVILLE
22651-22651	FRONT ROYAL
22652-22652	FORT VALLEY
22654-22654	STAR TANNERY
22655-22655	STEPHENS CITY
22656-22656	STEPHENSON
22657-22657	STRASBURG
22660-22660	TOMS BROOK
22663-22663	WHITE POST
22664-22664	WOODSTOCK
22701-22701	CULPEPER
22709-22709	ARODA
22711-22711	BANCO
22712-22712	BEALETON
22713-22713	BOSTON
22714-22714	BRANDY STATION
22715-22715	BRIGHTWOOD
22716-22716	CASTLETON
22718-22718	ELKWOOD
22719-22719	ETLAN
22720-22720	GOLDVEIN
22721-22721	GRAVES MILL
22722-22722	HAYWOOD
22723-22723	HOOD
22724-22724	JEFFERSONTON
22725-22725	LEON
22726-22726	LIGNUM
22727-22727	MADISON
22728-22728	MIDLAND
22729-22729	MITCHELLS
22730-22730	OAKPARK
22731-22731	PRATTS
22732-22732	RADIANT
22733-22733	RAPIDAN
22734-22734	REMINGTON
22735-22735	REVA
22736-22736	RICHARDSVILLE
22737-22737	RIXEYVILLE
22738-22738	ROCHELLE
22739-22739	SOMERVILLE
22740-22740	SPERRYVILLE
22741-22741	STEVENSBURG
22742-22742	SUMERDUCK
22743-22743	SYRIA
22746-22746	VIEWTOWN
22747-22747	WASHINGTON
22748-22748	WOLFTOWN
22749-22749	WOODVILLE
22801-22807	HARRISONBURG
22810-22810	BASYE
22811-22811	BERGTON
22812-22812	BRIDGEWATER
22815-22815	BROADWAY
22820-22820	CRIDERS
22821-22821	DAYTON
22824-22824	EDINBURG
22827-22827	ELKTON
22830-22830	FULKS RUN
22831-22831	HINTON
22832-22832	KEEZLETOWN
22833-22833	LACEY SPRING
22834-22834	LINVILLE
22835-22835	LURAY
22840-22840	MC GAHEYSVILLE
22841-22841	MOUNT CRAWFORD
22842-22842	MOUNT JACKSON
22843-22843	MOUNT SOLON
22844-22844	NEW MARKET
22845-22845	ORKNEY SPRINGS
22846-22846	PENN LAIRD
22847-22847	QUICKSBURG
22848-22848	PLEASANT VALLEY
22849-22849	SHENANDOAH
22850-22850	SINGERS GLEN
22851-22851	STANLEY
22853-22853	TIMBERVILLE
22900-22911	CHARLOTTESVILLE
22920-22920	AFTON
22922-22922	ARRINGTON
22923-22923	BARBOURSVILLE
22924-22924	BATESVILLE
22929-22929	COBHAM
22931-22931	COVESVILLE
22932-22932	CROZET
22935-22935	DYKE
22936-22936	EARLYSVILLE
22937-22937	ESMONT
22938-22938	FABER
22939-22939	FISHERSVILLE
22940-22940	FREE UNION
22942-22942	GORDONSVILLE
22943-22943	GREENWOOD
22945-22945	IVY
22946-22946	KEENE
22947-22947	KESWICK
22948-22948	LOCUST DALE
22949-22949	LOVINGSTON
22951-22951	ROSELAND
22952-22952	LYNDHURST
22953-22953	MADISON MILLS
22954-22954	MASSIES MILL
22957-22957	MONTPELIER STATION
22958-22958	NELLYSFORD
22959-22959	NORTH GARDEN
22960-22960	ORANGE
22963-22963	PALMYRA
22964-22964	PINEY RIVER
22965-22965	QUINQUE
22967-22967	ROSELAND
22968-22968	RUCKERSVILLE
22969-22969	SCHUYLER
22971-22971	SHIPMAN
22972-22972	SOMERSET
22973-22973	STANARDSVILLE
22974-22974	TROY
22976-22976	TYRO
22980-22980	WAYNESBORO
22987-22987	WHITE HALL
22989-22989	WOODBERRY FOREST
23001-23001	ACHILLES
23002-23002	AMELIA COURT HOUSE
23003-23003	ARK
23004-23004	ARVONIA
23005-23005	ASHLAND
23009-23009	AYLETT
23011-23011	BARHAMSVILLE
23013-23013	BAVON
23014-23014	BEAUMONT
23015-23015	BEAVERDAM
23016-23016	BEAVERLETT
23017-23017	BELLAMY
23018-23018	BENA
23020-23020	BLAKES
23021-23021	BOHANNON
23022-23022	BREMO BLUFF
23023-23023	BRUINGTON
23024-23024	BUMPASS
23025-23025	CARDINAL
23027-23027	CARTERSVILLE
23029-23029	CAUTHORNVILLE
23030-23030	CHARLES CITY
23031-23031	CHRISTCHURCH
23032-23032	CHURCH VIEW
23035-23035	COBBS CREEK
23037-23037	COLOGNE
23038-23038	COLUMBIA
23039-23039	CROZIER
23040-23040	CUMBERLAND
23042-23042	DABNEYS
23043-23043	DELTAVILLE
23045-23045	DIGGS
23047-23047	DOSWELL
23050-23050	DUTTON
23054-23054	FIFE
23055-23055	FORK UNION
23056-23056	FOSTER
23058-23060	GLEN ALLEN
23061-23061	GLOUCESTER
23062-23062	GLOUCESTER POINT

ZIP Range	Location
23063-23063	GOOCHLAND
23064-23064	GRIMSTEAD
23065-23065	GUM SPRING
23066-23066	GWYNN
23067-23067	HADENSVILLE
23068-23068	HALLIEFORD
23069-23069	HANOVER
23070-23070	HARDYVILLE
23071-23071	HARTFIELD
23072-23072	HAYES
23075-23075	HIGHLAND SPRINGS
23076-23076	HUDGINS
23079-23079	JAMAICA
23080-23080	JAMES STORE
23081-23081	JAMESTOWN
23083-23083	JETERSVILLE
23084-23084	KENTS STORE
23085-23085	KING AND QUEEN COURT HOUS
23086-23086	KING WILLIAM
23089-23089	LANEXA
23090-23090	LIGHTFOOT
23091-23091	LITTLE PLYMOUTH
23092-23092	LOCUST HILL
23093-23093	LOUISA
23101-23101	MACON
23102-23102	MAIDENS
23103-23103	MANAKIN SABOT
23104-23104	MANGOHICK
23105-23105	MANNBORO
23106-23106	MANQUIN
23107-23107	MARYUS
23108-23108	MASCOT
23109-23109	MATHEWS
23110-23110	MATTAPONI
23111-23111	MECHANICSVILLE
23112-23113	MIDLOTHIAN
23114-23114	MILES
23114-23114	MIDLOTHIAN
23115-23115	MILLERS TAVERN
23116-23116	MECHANICSVILLE
23117-23117	MINERAL
23118-23118	MOBJACK
23119-23119	MOON
23120-23120	MOSELEY
23122-23122	NAXERA
23123-23123	NEW CANTON
23124-23124	NEW KENT
23125-23125	NEW POINT
23126-23126	NEWTOWN
23127-23127	NORGE
23128-23128	NORTH
23129-23129	OILVILLE
23130-23130	ONEMO
23131-23131	ORDINARY
23137-23137	PLAIN VIEW
23138-23138	PORT HAYWOOD
23139-23139	POWHATAN
23140-23140	PROVIDENCE FORGE
23141-23141	QUINTON
23142-23142	REDART
23146-23146	ROCKVILLE
23147-23147	RUTHVILLE
23148-23148	SAINT STEPHENS CHURCH
23149-23149	SALUDA
23150-23150	SANDSTON
23153-23153	SANDY HOOK
23154-23154	SCHLEY
23155-23155	SEVERN
23156-23156	SHACKLEFORDS
23157-23157	SHADOW
23160-23160	STATE FARM
23161-23161	STEVENSVILLE
23162-23162	STUDLEY
23163-23163	SUSAN
23168-23168	TOANO
23169-23169	TOPPING
23170-23170	TREVILIANS
23173-23173	UNIVERSITY OF RICHMOND
23175-23175	URBANNA
23176-23176	WAKE
23177-23177	WALKERTON
23178-23178	WARE NECK
23179-23179	WARNER
23180-23180	WATER VIEW
23181-23181	WEST POINT
23183-23183	WHITE MARSH
23184-23184	WICOMICO
23185-23188	WILLIAMSBURG
23190-23190	WOODS CROSS ROADS
23191-23191	ZANONI
23192-23192	MONTPELIER
23200-23298	RICHMOND
23301-23301	ACCOMAC
23302-23302	ASSAWOMAN
23303-23303	ATLANTIC
23304-23304	BATTERY PARK
23306-23306	BELLE HAVEN
23307-23307	BIRDSNEST
23308-23308	BLOXOM
23310-23310	CAPE CHARLES
23313-23313	CAPEVILLE
23314-23314	CARROLLTON
23315-23315	CARRSVILLE
23316-23316	CHERITON
23320-23328	CHESAPEAKE
23336-23336	CHINCOTEAGUE
23336-23336	CHINCOTEAGUE ISLAND
23337-23337	CHINCOTEAGUE
23337-23337	WALLOPS ISLAND
23341-23341	CRADDOCKVILLE
23345-23345	DAVIS WHARF
23347-23347	EASTVILLE
23350-23350	EXMORE
23354-23354	FRANKTOWN
23356-23356	GREENBACKVILLE
23357-23357	GREENBUSH
23358-23358	HACKSNECK
23359-23359	HALLWOOD
23389-23389	HARBORTON
23395-23395	HORNTOWN
23396-23396	OAK HALL
23397-23397	ISLE OF WIGHT
23398-23398	JAMESVILLE
23399-23399	JENKINS BRIDGE
23401-23401	KELLER
23403-23403	LEE MONT
23404-23404	LOCUSTVILLE
23405-23405	MACHIPONGO
23407-23407	MAPPSVILLE
23408-23408	MARIONVILLE
23409-23409	MEARS
23410-23410	MELFA
23412-23412	MODEST TOWN
23413-23413	NASSAWADOX
23414-23414	NELSONIA
23415-23415	NEW CHURCH
23416-23416	OAK HALL
23417-23417	ONANCOCK
23418-23418	ONLEY
23419-23419	OYSTER
23420-23420	PAINTER
23421-23421	PARKSLEY
23422-23422	PUNGOTEAGUE
23423-23423	QUINBY
23424-23424	RESCUE
23426-23426	SANFORD
23427-23427	SAXIS
23429-23429	SEAVIEW
23430-23431	SMITHFIELD
23432-23439	SUFFOLK
23440-23440	TANGIER
23441-23441	TASLEY
23442-23442	TEMPERANCEVILLE
23443-23443	TOWNSEND
23450-23479	VIRGINIA BEACH
23480-23480	WACHAPREAGUE
23481-23481	CARRSVILLE
23482-23482	WARDTOWN
23483-23483	WATTSVILLE
23484-23484	WEIRWOOD
23486-23486	WILLIS WHARF
23487-23487	WINDSOR
23488-23488	WITHAMS
23500-23551	NORFOLK
23600-23603	NEWPORT NEWS
23604-23604	FORT EUSTIS
23605-23628	NEWPORT NEWS
23629-23629	GREAT AMERICAN MAGAZINE
23630-23630	NEWPORT NEWS
23630-23631	HAMPTON
23632-23632	GREAT AMERICAN MAGAZINE
23651-23651	FORT MONROE
23653-23661	HAMPTON
23662-23662	POQUOSON
23663-23681	HAMPTON
23690-23693	YORKTOWN
23694-23694	LACKEY
23696-23696	SEAFORD
23700-23709	PORTSMOUTH
23801-23801	FORT LEE
23803-23806	PETERSBURG
23821-23821	ALBERTA
23822-23822	AMMON
23824-23824	BLACKSTONE
23827-23827	BOYKINS
23828-23828	BRANCHVILLE
23829-23829	CAPRON
23830-23830	CARSON
23831-23831	CHESTER
23832-23832	CHESTERFIELD
23833-23833	CHURCH ROAD
23834-23834	COLONIAL HEIGHTS
23836-23836	CHESTER
23837-23837	COURTLAND
23838-23838	CHESTERFIELD
23839-23839	DENDRON
23840-23840	DEWITT
23841-23841	DINWIDDIE
23842-23842	DISPUTANTA
23843-23843	DOLPHIN
23844-23844	DREWRYVILLE
23845-23845	EBONY
23846-23846	ELBERON
23847-23847	EMPORIA
23850-23850	FORD
23851-23851	FRANKLIN
23856-23856	FREEMAN
23857-23857	GASBURG
23859-23859	HANDSOM
23860-23860	HOPEWELL
23866-23866	IVOR
23867-23867	JARRATT
23868-23868	LAWRENCEVILLE
23870-23870	JARRATT
23872-23872	MC KENNEY
23873-23873	MEREDITHVILLE
23874-23874	NEWSOMS
23875-23875	PRINCE GEORGE
23876-23876	RAWLINGS
23878-23878	SEDLEY
23879-23879	SKIPPERS
23881-23881	SPRING GROVE
23882-23882	STONY CREEK
23883-23883	SURRY
23884-23884	SUSSEX
23885-23885	SUTHERLAND
23887-23887	VALENTINES
23888-23888	WAKEFIELD
23889-23889	WARFIELD
23890-23891	WAVERLY
23893-23893	WHITE PLAINS
23894-23894	WILSONS
23897-23897	YALE
23898-23898	ZUNI
23899-23899	CLAREMONT
23901-23909	FARMVILLE
23911-23911	ANDERSONVILLE
23915-23915	BASKERVILLE
23917-23917	BOYDTON
23919-23919	BRACEY
23920-23920	BRODNAX
23921-23921	BUCKINGHAM
23922-23922	BURKEVILLE
23923-23923	CHARLOTTE COURT HOUSE
23924-23924	CHASE CITY
23927-23927	CLARKSVILLE
23930-23930	CREWE
23934-23934	CULLEN
23935-23935	DARLINGTN HTS
23935-23935	DARLINGTON HEIGHTS
23936-23936	DILLWYN
23937-23937	DRAKES BRANCH
23938-23938	DUNDAS
23939-23939	EVERGREEN
23941-23941	FORT MITCHELL
23942-23942	GREEN BAY
23943-23943	HAMPDEN SYDNEY
23944-23944	KENBRIDGE
23947-23947	KEYSVILLE
23950-23950	LA CROSSE
23952-23952	LUNENBURG
23954-23954	MEHERRIN
23955-23955	NOTTOWAY
23958-23958	PAMPLIN
23959-23959	PHENIX
23960-23960	PROSPECT
23962-23962	RANDOLPH
23963-23963	RED HOUSE
23964-23964	RED OAK
23966-23966	RICE
23967-23967	SAXE
23968-23968	SKIPWITH
23970-23970	SOUTH HILL
23974-23974	VICTORIA
23976-23976	WYLLIESBURG
24000-24040	ROANOKE
24041-24041	BANK AMERICARD
24042-24045	ROANOKE
24046-24046	CITY OFFICES
24048-24050	ROANOKE
24053-24053	ARARAT
24054-24054	AXTON
24055-24055	BASSETT
24058-24058	BELSPRING
24059-24059	BENT MOUNTAIN
24060-24063	BLACKSBURG
24064-24064	BLUE RIDGE
24065-24065	BOONES MILL
24066-24066	BUCHANAN
24067-24067	CALLAWAY
24068-24068	CHRISTIANSBURG
24069-24069	CASCADE
24070-24070	CATAWBA
24072-24072	CHECK
24073-24073	CHRISTIANSBURG
24076-24076	CLAUDVILLE
24077-24077	CLOVERDALE
24078-24078	COLLINSVILLE
24079-24079	COPPER HILL
24082-24082	CRITZ
24083-24083	DALEVILLE
24084-24084	DUBLIN
24085-24085	EAGLE ROCK
24086-24086	EGGLESTON
24087-24087	ELLISTON
24088-24088	FERRUM
24089-24089	FIELDALE
24090-24090	FINCASTLE
24091-24091	FLOYD
24092-24092	GLADEHILL
24093-24093	GLEN LYN
24094-24094	GOLDBOND
24095-24095	GOODVIEW
24101-24101	HARDY
24102-24102	HENRY
24104-24104	HUDDLESTON
24105-24105	INDIAN VALLEY
24111-24111	MC COY
24112-24115	MARTINSVILLE
24120-24120	MEADOWS OF DAN
24121-24121	MONETA
24122-24122	MONTVALE
24124-24124	NARROWS
24126-24126	NEWBERN

24127-24127 NEW CASTLE	24311-24311 ATKINS	24475-24475 SPOTTSWOOD	24624-24624 KEEN MOUNTAIN
24128-24128 NEWPORT	24312-24312 AUSTINVILLE	24476-24476 STEELES TAVERN	24627-24627 MAVISDALE
24129-24129 NEW RIVER	24313-24313 BARREN SPRINGS	24477-24477 STUARTS DRAFT	24628-24628 MAXIE
24130-24130 ORISKANY	24314-24314 BASTIAN	24479-24479 SWOOPE	24630-24630 NORTH TAZEWELL
24131-24131 PAINT BANK	24315-24315 BLAND	24482-24482 VERONA	24631-24631 OAKWOOD
24132-24132 PARROTT	24316-24316 BROADFORD	24483-24483 VESUVIUS	24634-24634 PILGRIMS KNOB
24133-24133 PATRICK SPRINGS	24317-24317 CANA	24484-24484 WARM SPRINGS	24635-24635 POCAHONTAS
24134-24134 PEARISBURG	24318-24318 CERES	24485-24485 WEST AUGUSTA	24637-24637 POUNDING MILL
24136-24136 PEMBROKE	24319-24319 CHILHOWIE	24486-24486 WEYERS CAVE	24639-24639 RAVEN
24137-24137 PENHOOK	24321-24321 CLINCHBURG	24487-24487 WILLIAMSVILLE	24640-24640 RED ASH
24138-24138 PILOT	24322-24322 CRIPPLE CREEK	24501-24515 LYNCHBURG	24641-24641 RICHLANDS
24139-24139 PITTSVILLE	24323-24323 CROCKETT	24517-24517 ALTAVISTA	24646-24646 ROWE
24141-24143 RADFORD	24324-24324 DRAPER	24520-24520 ALTON	24647-24647 SHORTT GAP
24146-24146 REDWOOD	24325-24325 DUGSPUR	24521-24521 AMHERST	24649-24649 SWORDS CREEK
24147-24147 RICH CREEK	24326-24326 ELK CREEK	24522-24522 APPOMATTOX	24651-24651 TAZEWELL
24148-24148 RIDGEWAY	24327-24327 EMORY	24523-24523 BEDFORD	24656-24656 VANSANT
24149-24149 RINER	24328-24328 FANCY GAP	24526-24526 BIG ISLAND	24657-24657 WHITEWOOD
24150-24150 RIPPLEMEAD	24330-24330 FRIES	24527-24527 BLAIRS	24658-24658 WOLFORD
24151-24151 ROCKY MOUNT	24333-24333 GALAX	24528-24528 BROOKNEAL	24659-24659 YARDS
24153-24157 SALEM	24340-24340 GLADE SPRING	24529-24529 BUFFALO JUNCTION	
24161-24161 SANDY LEVEL	24343-24343 HILLSVILLE	24530-24530 CALLANDS	
24162-24162 SHAWSVILLE	24347-24347 HIWASSEE	24531-24531 CHATHAM	
24165-24165 SPENCER	24348-24348 INDEPENDENCE	24533-24533 CLIFFORD	
24167-24167 STAFFORDSVILLE	24350-24350 IVANHOE	24534-24534 CLOVER	
24168-24168 STANLEYTOWN	24351-24351 LAMBSBURG	24535-24535 CLUSTER SPRINGS	
24171-24171 STUART	24352-24352 LAUREL FORK	24536-24536 COLEMAN FALLS	
24174-24174 THAXTON	24354-24354 MARION	24538-24538 CONCORD	
24175-24175 TROUTVILLE	24360-24360 MAX MEADOWS	24539-24539 CRYSTAL HILL	
24176-24176 UNION HALL	24361-24361 MEADOWVIEW	24540-24544 DANVILLE	
24177-24177 VESTA	24363-24363 MOUTH OF WILSON	24549-24549 DRY FORK	
24178-24178 VILLAMONT	24366-24366 ROCKY GAP	24550-24550 EVINGTON	
24179-24179 VINTON	24368-24368 RURAL RETREAT	24551-24551 FOREST	
24184-24184 WIRTZ	24370-24370 SALTVILLE	24553-24553 GLADSTONE	
24185-24185 WOOLWINE	24373-24373 SEVEN MILE FORD	24554-24554 GLADYS	
24201-24209 BRISTOL	24374-24374 SPEEDWELL	24555-24555 GLASGOW	
24210-24212 ABINGDON	24375-24375 SUGAR GROVE	24556-24556 GOODE	
24215-24215 ANDOVER	24377-24377 TANNERSVILLE	24557-24557 GRETNA	
24216-24216 APPALACHIA	24378-24378 TROUT DALE	24558-24558 HALIFAX	
24217-24217 BEE	24378-24378 TROUTDALE	24562-24562 HOWARDSVILLE	
24218-24218 BEN HUR	24379-24379 VOLNEY	24563-24563 HURT	
24219-24219 BIG STONE GAP	24380-24380 WILLIS	24565-24565 JAVA	
24220-24220 BIRCHLEAF	24381-24381 WOODLAWN	24566-24566 KEELING	
24221-24221 BLACKWATER	24382-24382 WYTHEVILLE	24569-24569 LONG ISLAND	
24224-24224 CASTLEWOOD	24401-24407 STAUNTON	24570-24570 LOWRY	
24225-24225 CLEVELAND	24411-24411 AUGUSTA SPRINGS	24571-24571 LYNCH STATION	
24226-24226 CLINCHCO	24412-24412 BACOVA	24572-24572 MADISON HEIGHTS	
24228-24228 CLINTWOOD	24413-24413 BLUE GRASS	24574-24574 MONROE	
24230-24230 COEBURN	24415-24415 BROWNSBURG	24576-24576 NARUNA	
24236-24236 DAMASCUS	24416-24416 BUENA VISTA	24577-24577 NATHALIE	
24237-24237 DANTE	24421-24421 CHURCHVILLE	24578-24578 NATURAL BRIDGE	
24239-24239 DAVENPORT	24422-24422 CLIFTON FORGE	24579-24579 NATURAL BRIDGE STATION	
24243-24243 DRYDEN	24426-24426 COVINGTON	24580-24580 NELSON	
24244-24244 DUFFIELD	24430-24430 CRAIGSVILLE	24581-24581 NORWOOD	
24245-24245 DUNGANNON	24431-24431 CRIMORA	24585-24585 REPUBLICAN GROVE	
24246-24246 EAST STONE GAP	24432-24432 DEERFIELD	24586-24586 RINGGOLD	
24248-24248 EWING	24433-24433 DOE HILL	24588-24588 RUSTBURG	
24249-24249 EXETER	24435-24435 FAIRFIELD	24589-24589 SCOTTSBURG	
24250-24250 FORT BLACKMORE	24437-24437 FORT DEFIANCE	24590-24590 SCOTTSVILLE	
24251-24251 GATE CITY	24438-24438 GLEN WILTON	24592-24592 SOUTH BOSTON	
24256-24256 HAYSI	24439-24439 GOSHEN	24593-24593 SPOUT SPRING	
24258-24258 HILTONS	24440-24440 GREENVILLE	24594-24594 SUTHERLIN	
24260-24260 HONAKER	24441-24441 GROTTOES	24595-24595 SWEET BRIAR	
24263-24263 JONESVILLE	24442-24442 HEAD WATERS	24596-24596 TURBEVILLE	
24265-24265 KEOKEE	24444-24444 HIGHTOWN	24597-24597 VERNON HILL	
24266-24266 LEBANON	24445-24445 HOT SPRINGS	24598-24598 VIRGILINA	
24269-24269 MC CLURE	24448-24448 IRON GATE	24599-24599 WINGINA	
24270-24270 MENDOTA	24449-24449 JORDAN MINES	24601-24601 AMONATE	
24271-24271 NICKELSVILLE	24450-24450 LEXINGTON	24602-24602 BANDY	
24272-24272 NORA	24457-24457 LOW MOOR	24603-24603 BIG ROCK	
24273-24273 NORTON	24458-24458 MC DOWELL	24604-24604 BISHOP	
24277-24277 PENNINGTON GAP	24459-24459 MIDDLEBROOK	24605-24605 BLUEFIELD	
24279-24279 POUND	24460-24460 MILLBORO	24606-24606 BOISSEVAIN	
24280-24280 ROSEDALE	24463-24463 MINT SPRING	24607-24607 BREAKS	
24281-24281 ROSE HILL	24464-24464 MONTEBELLO	24608-24608 BURKES GARDEN	
24282-24282 SAINT CHARLES	24465-24465 MONTEREY	24609-24609 CEDAR BLUFF	
24283-24283 SAINT PAUL	24467-24467 MOUNT SIDNEY	24612-24612 DORAN	
24285-24285 STONEGA	24468-24468 MUSTOE	24613-24613 FALLS MILLS	
24289-24289 TRAMMEL	24469-24469 NEW HOPE	24614-24614 GRUNDY	
24290-24290 WEBER CITY	24471-24471 PORT REPUBLIC	24618-24618 HARMAN	
24292-24292 WHITETOP	24472-24472 RAPHINE	24619-24619 HORSEPEN	
24293-24293 WISE	24473-24473 ROCKBRIDGE BATHS	24620-24620 HURLEY	
24301-24301 PULASKI	24474-24474 SELMA	24622-24622 JEWELL RIDGE	

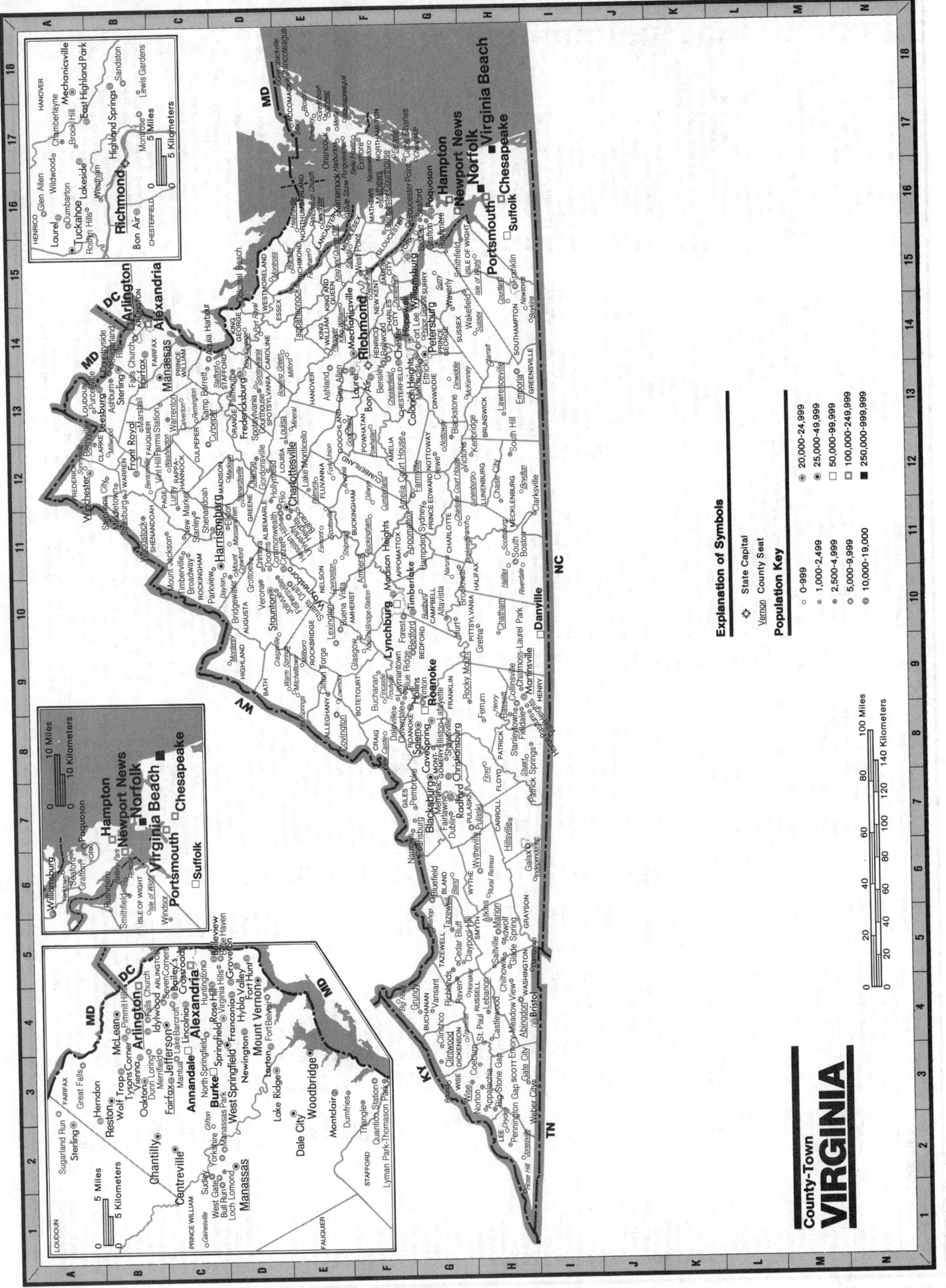

County-Town VIRGINIA

Explanation of Symbols

◇ State Capital

Vernon County Seat

Population Key

○ 0-999
⊙ 1,000-2,499
⊕ 2,500-4,999
◉ 5,000-9,999
◎ 10,000-19,000

⊚ 20,000-24,999
⊛ 25,000-49,999
□ 50,000-99,999
▣ 100,000-249,999
■ 250,000-999,999,999

COUNTIES

(136 Counties and Independent Cities)

Name of County	Population	Location on Map
ACCOMACK	31,703	E-17
ALBEMARLE	68,040	D-11
ALLEGHANY	13,176	E-8
AMELIA	8,787	F-12
AMHERST	28,578	F-10
APPOMATTOX	12,298	F-10
ARLINGTON	170,936	B-14
AUGUSTA	54,677	D-10
BATH	4,799	D-9
BEDFORD	45,656	F-9
BLAND	6,514	G-6
BOTETOURT	24,992	F-8
BRUNSWICK	15,987	H-13
BUCHANAN	31,333	G-4
BUCKINGHAM	12,873	F-11
CAMPBELL	47,572	G-10
CAROLINE	19,217	D-14
CARROLL	26,594	H-7
CHARLES CITY	6,282	F-14
CHARLOTTE	11,688	G-11
CHESTERFIELD	209,274	F-13
CLARKE	12,101	B-12
CRAIG	4,372	F-8
CULPEPER	27,791	C-12
CUMBERLAND	7,825	F-12
DICKENSON	17,620	G-3
DINWIDDIE	20,960	G-13
ESSEX	8,689	E-14
FAIRFAX	818,584	C-14
FAUQUIER	48,741	B-12
FLOYD	12,005	H-7
FLUVANNA	12,429	E-12
FRANKLIN	39,549	G-9
FREDERICK	45,723	A-12
GILES	16,366	F-7
GLOUCESTER	30,131	F-15
GOOCHLAND	14,163	E-12
GRAYSON	16,278	H-5
GREENE	10,297	D-11
GREENESVILLE	8,853	I-13
HALIFAX	29,033	H-10
HANOVER	63,306	E-13
HENRICO	217,881	F-14
HENRY	56,942	I-8
HIGHLAND	2,635	D-9
ISLE OF WIGHT	25,053	H-15
JAMES CITY	34,859	F-15
KING AND QUEEN	6,289	E-14
KING GEORGE	13,527	D-14
KING WILLIAM	10,913	E-14
LANCASTER	10,896	E-15
LEE	24,496	H-2
LOUDOUN	86,129	A-13
LOUISA	20,325	E-12
LUNENBURG	11,419	H-12
MADISON	11,949	D-12
MATHEWS	8,348	F-16
MECKLENBURG	29,241	H-11
MIDDLESEX	8,653	F-15
MONTGOMERY	73,913	G-8
NELSON	12,778	E-10
NEW KENT	10,445	F-14
NORTHAMPTON	13,061	F-17
NORTHUMBERLAND	10,524	E-15
NOTTOWAY	14,993	G-12
ORANGE	21,421	D-13
PAGE	21,690	C-12
PATRICK	17,473	H-8
PITTSYLVANIA	55,655	H-10
POWHATAN	15,328	F-12
PRINCE EDWARD	17,320	G-11
PRINCE GEORGE	27,394	G-14
PRINCE WILLIAM	215,686	C-13
PULASKI	34,496	G-7
RAPPAHANNOCK	6,622	C-12
RICHMOND	7,273	E-15
ROANOKE	79,332	G-8
ROCKBRIDGE	18,350	E-9
ROCKINGHAM	57,482	C-10
RUSSELL	28,667	H-4
SCOTT	23,204	H-3
SHENANDOAH	31,636	B-11
SMYTH	32,370	H-5
SOUTHAMPTON	17,550	H-14
SPOTSYLVANIA	57,403	D-13
STAFFORD	61,236	D-13
SURRY	6,145	G-15
SUSSEX	10,248	G-14
TAZEWELL	45,960	G-5
WARREN	26,142	B-12
WASHINGTON	45,887	H-4
WESTMORELAND	15,480	D-14
WISE	39,573	G-3
WYTHE	25,466	G-6
YORK	42,422	G-15

Name of Independent City	Population	Location on Map
ALEXANDRIA	111,183	B-14
BEDFORD	6,073	G-9
BRISTOL	18,426	H-4
BUENA VISTA	6,406	E-10
CHARLOTTESVILLE	40,341	E-12
CHESAPEAKE	151,976	H-16
CLIFTON FORGE	4,679	E-9
COLONIAL HEIGHTS	16,064	G-14
COVINGTON	6,991	E-8
DANVILLE	53,056	I-10
EMPORIA	5,306	H-13
FAIRFAX	19,622	B-14
FALLS CHURCH	9,578	B-14
FRANKLIN	7,864	H-15
FREDERICKSBURG	19,027	D-13
GALAX	6,670	H-6
HAMPTON	133,793	G-16
HARRISONBURG	30,707	D-11
HOPEWELL	23,101	G-14
LEXINGTON	6,959	E-9
LYNCHBURG	66,049	F-10
MANASSAS	27,957	C-13
MANASSAS PARK	6,734	C-2
MARTINSVILLE	16,162	H-9
NEWPORT NEWS	170,045	G-16
NORFOLK	261,229	H-16
NORTON	4,247	H-3
PETERSBURG	38,386	G-14
POQUOSON	11,005	A-7
PORTSMOUTH	103,907	H-16
RADFORD	15,940	G-7
RICHMOND	203,056	F-14
ROANOKE	96,397	G-8
SALEM	23,756	G-8
SOUTH BOSTON	6,997	H-11
STAUNTON	24,461	D-10
SUFFOLK	52,141	H-15
VIRGINIA BEACH	393,069	H-17
WAYNESBORO	18,549	E-11
WILLIAMSBURG	11,530	G-15
WINCHESTER	21,947	A-12
TOTAL	6,187,358	

CITIES AND TOWNS

Note: The first name is that of the city or town, second, that of the county in which it is located, then the population and location on the map.

Abingdon, Washington, 7,003	H-4
Accomac, Accomack, 466	E-17
•Adwolf, Smyth, 1,292	H-5
Alexandria, Independent City, 111,183	B-14
Altavista, Campbell, 3,686	G-10
Amelia Court House, Amelia	G-13
Amherst, Amherst, 1,060	F-10
•Annandale, Fairfax, 50,975	C-4
Appalachia, Wise, 1,994	H-3
Appomattox, Appomattox, 1,707	G-11
•Aquia Harbour, Stafford, 6,308	C-14
•Arlington, Arlington, 170,936	B-14
•Ashburn, Loudoun, 3,393	B-13
Ashland, Hanover, 5,864	E-14
•Atkins, Smyth, 1,130	H-5
•Bailey's Crossroads, Fairfax, 19,507	C-4
•Barracks, Albemarle, 4,710	D-12
•Bassett, Henry, 1,579	H-8
Bedford, Independent City, 6,073	G-9
Belleview, Fairfax	C-5
•Bellwood, Chesterfield, 6,178	F-14
•Bensley, Chesterfield, 5,093	F-14
Berryville, Clarke, 3,097	B-12
Big Stone Gap, Wise, 4,748	H-3
Blacksburg, Montgomery, 34,590	G-7
Blackstone, Nottoway, 3,497	G-12
Bland, Bland	G-6
•Blue Ridge, Botetourt, 2,840	F-9
Bluefield, Tazewell, 5,363	G-6
•Bon Air, Chesterfield, 16,413	F-13
Bowling Green, Caroline, 727	E-14
Boydton, Mecklenburg, 453	H-12
Bridgewater, Rockingham, 3,918	D-10
Bristol, Independent City, 18,426	H-4
Broadway, Rockingham, 1,209	C-11
Brook Hill, Henrico	A-17
Brookneal, Campbell, 1,344	G-11
Buchanan, Botetourt, 1,222	F-9
Buckingham, Buckingham	F-11
Buena Vista, Independent City, 6,406	E-10
•Bull Run, Prince William, 5,525	C-2
•Burke, Fairfax, 57,734	C-3
Camp Barrett, Stafford	C-14
Cape Charles, Northampton, 1,398	G-17
•Castlewood, Russell, 2,110	H-4
•Cave Spring, Roanoke, 24,053	G-8
Cedar Bluff, Tazewell, 1,290	G-5
•Centreville, Fairfax, 26,585	C-2
•Chamberlayne, Henrico, 4,577	A-17
•Chantilly, Fairfax, 29,337	B-2
Charles City, Charles City	F-14
Charlotte Court House, Charlotte, 531	G-11
Charlottesville, Independent City, 40,341	E-12
Chase City, Mecklenburg, 2,442	H-12
Chatham, Pittsylvania, 1,354	H-10
•Chatmoss-Laurel Park, Henry, 2,194	H-8
Chesapeake, Independent City, 151,976	H-16
•Chester, Chesterfield, 14,986	F-14
Chesterfield, Chesterfield	F-13
Chilhowie, Smyth, 1,971	H-5
Chincoteague, Accomack, 3,572	E-18
Christiansburg, Montgomery, 15,004	G-7
Clarksville, Mecklenburg, 1,243	I-11
•Claypool Hill, Tazewell, 1,468	G-5
Clifton Forge, Independent City, 4,679	E-9
Clinchco, Dickenson	G-4
Clintwood, Dickenson, 1,542	G-3
•Cloverdale, Botetourt, 1,689	F-9
Coeburn, Wise, 2,165	H-3
•Collinsville, Henry, 7,280	H-9
Colonial Beach, Westmoreland, 3,132	D-15
Colonial Heights, Independent City, 16,064	G-14
•Commonwealth, Albemarle, 5,538	D-11
•Countryside, Loudoun, 8,349	B-14
Courtland, Southampton, 819	H-14
Covington, Independent City, 6,991	E-8
Crewe, Nottoway, 2,276	G-12
•Crimora, Augusta, 1,752	D-10
•Crozet, Albemarle, 2,256	E-11
Culpeper, Culpeper, 8,581	C-12
Cumberland, Cumberland	F-12
•Dale City, Prince William, 47,170	E-3
•Daleville, Botetourt, 1,163	F-9
Danville, Independent City, 53,056	I-10
Dinwiddie, Dinwiddie	G-13
•Dooms, Augusta, 1,307	D-11
Dublin, Pulaski, 2,012	G-7
•Dumbarton, Henrico, 8,526	A-16
Dumfries, Prince William, 4,282	E-3
•Dunn Loring, Fairfax, 6,509	B-4
•East Highland Park, Henrico, 11,850	A-17
Eastville, Northampton, 185	F-17
Elkton, Rockingham, 1,935	D-11
•Elliston-Lafayette, Montgomery, 1,243	G-8
•Emory-Meadow View, Washington, 2,248	H-4
Emporia, Independent City, 5,306	H-13
•Ettrick, Chesterfield, 5,290	G-14
Exmore, Northampton, 1,115	F-17
Fairfax, Independent City, 19,622	B-14
•Fairlawn, Pulaski, 2,399	G-7
Falls Church, Independent City, 9,578	B-14
•Falmouth, Stafford, 3,541	D-14
Farmville, Cumberland/Prince Edward, 6,046	G-12
•Ferrum, Franklin, 1,514	G-8
•Fieldale, Henry, 1,018	H-8
Fincastle, Botetourt, 236	F-9
•Fishersville, Augusta, 3,230	D-11
Floyd, Floyd, 396	H-8
•Forest, Bedford, 5,624	G-10
•Fort Belvoir, Fairfax, 8,590	D-4
•Fort Hunt, Fairfax, 12,989	D-5
•Fort Lee, Prince George, 6,895	G-14
•Franconia, Fairfax, 19,882	D-4
Franklin, Independent City, 7,864	H-15
Fredericksburg, Independent City, 19,027	D-13
Front Royal, Warren, 11,880	B-12
Galax, Independent City, 6,670	H-6
Gate City, Scott, 2,214	H-3
Glade Spring, Washington, 1,435	H-5
Glasgow, Rockbridge, 1,140	F-10
•Glen Allen, Henrico, 9,010	A-16
•Gloucester Courthouse, Gloucester, 2,118	F-16
•Gloucester Point, Gloucester, 8,509	G-16
Goochland, Goochland	F-13
Gordonsville, Orange, 1,351	D-12
Grafton, York	G-16
•Great Falls, Fairfax, 6,945	A-3
Gretna, Pittsylvania, 1,339	H-10
Grottoes, Augusta/Rockingham, 1,455	D-11
•Groveton, Fairfax, 19,997	D-5
Grundy, Buchanan, 1,305	G-4
Halifax, Halifax, 688	H-11
•Hampden Sydney, Prince Edward, 1,240	G-12
Hampton, Independent City, 133,793	G-16
Hanover, Hanover	E-14
Harrisonburg, Independent City, 30,707	D-11
Heathsville, Northumberland	E-16
Herndon, Fairfax, 16,139	A-3
•Highland Springs, Henrico, 13,823	B-18
Hillsville, Carroll, 2,008	H-7
•Hollins, Botetourt/Roanoke, 13,305	G-9
•Hollymead, Albemarle, 2,628	D-12
Hopewell, Independent City, 23,101	G-14
•Horse Pasture, Henry, 2,224	H-18
•Huntington, Fairfax, 7,489	C-5
Hurt, Pittsylvania, 1,294	G-10
•Hybla Valley, Fairfax, 15,491	D-5
•Idylwood, Fairfax, 14,710	B-4
Independence, Grayson, 988	I-6
Isle of Wight, Isle of Wight	B-6
•Jefferson, Fairfax, 25,782	C-4
•Jolivue, Augusta, 1,092	D-10
Jonesville, Lee, 927	H-2
Kenbridge, Lunenburg, 1,264	H-12
Kilmarnock, Lancaster/Northumberland, 1,109	E-16
King George, King George	D-14
King William, King William	F-14
King and Queen Court House, King and Queen	F-15
•Lake Barcroft, Fairfax, 8,686	C-4
•Lake Monticello, Fluvanna, 2,331	E-12
•Lake Ridge, Prince William, 23,862	D-3
•Lakeside, Henrico, 12,081	A-17
Lancaster, Lancaster	E-16
•Laurel, Henrico, 13,011	A-16
Lawrenceville, Brunswick, 1,486	H-13
Laymantown, Botetourt, 1,942	F-9
Lebanon, Russell, 3,386	H-4
Leesburg, Loudoun, 16,202	B-13
Lewis Gardens, Henrico	B-18
Lexington, Independent City, 6,959	E-9
•Lincolnia, Fairfax, 13,041	C-4
•Loch Lomond, Prince William, 3,292	C-2
•Lorton, Fairfax, 15,385	D-4
Louisa, Louisa, 1,088	E-12
Lovingston, Nelson	E-11
Lunenburg, Lunenburg	H-12
Luray, Page, 4,587	C-12
Lyman Park-Thomason Park, Prince William	F-3
Lynchburg, Independent City, 66,049	F-10
Madison, Madison, 307	D-12
•Madison Heights, Amherst, 11,700	F-10
Manassas, Independent City, 27,957	C-13
Manassas Park, Independent City, 6,734	C-2
•Mantua, Fairfax, 6,804	C-3
Marion, Smyth, 6,630	H-5
Marshall, Fauquier	B-13
Martinsville, Independent City, 16,162	H-9
Mathews, Mathews	F-16
•McLean, Fairfax, 38,168	B-4
•Mechanicsville, Hanover, 22,027	F-14
•Merrifield, Fairfax, 8,399	B-4
•Merrimac, Montgomery, 1,713	G-7
Middletown, Frederick, 1,061	B-12
•Montclair, Prince William, 11,399	E-3
Monterey, Highland, 222	D-9
•Montrose, Henrico, 6,405	B-17
Montross, Westmoreland, 359	D-15
Mount Jackson, Shenandoah, 1,583	C-11
•Mount Vernon, Fairfax, 27,485	D-5
Narrows, Giles, 2,082	G-7
New Castle, Craig, 152	F-8
New Kent, New Kent	F-15
New Market, Shenandoah, 1,435	C-11
•Newington, Fairfax, 17,965	D-4
Newport News, Independent City, 170,045	G-16
Norfolk, Independent City, 261,229	H-16
•North Springfield, Fairfax, 8,996	C-4
Norton, Independent City, 4,247	H-3
Nottoway, Nottoway	G-12
•Oakton, Fairfax, 24,610	B-3
Onancock, Accomack, 1,434	E-17
Orange, Orange, 2,582	D-12
Palmyra, Fluvanna	E-12
Patrick Springs, Patrick	H-8
Pearisburg, Giles, 2,064	G-7
Pembroke, Giles, 1,064	G-7
Pennington Gap, Lee, 1,922	H-2
Petersburg, Independent City, 38,386	G-14
•Pimmit Hills, Fairfax, 6,019	B-4
Poquoson, Independent City, 11,005	A-7
Portsmouth, Independent City, 103,907	H-16
Powhatan, Powhatan	F-13
Prince George, Prince George	G-14
Pulaski, Pulaski, 9,985	H-7
Purcellville, Loudoun, 1,744	B-13
•Quantico Station, Prince William/Stafford, 7,425	F-3
Radford, Independent City, 15,940	G-7
•Raven, Russell/Tazewell, 2,640	G-5
•Reston, Fairfax, 48,556	B-3
Richlands, Tazewell, 4,456	G-5
Richmond, Independent City, 203,056	F-14
•Rio, Albemarle, 5,133	D-12
Roanoke, Independent City, 96,397	G-8
Rocky Mount, Franklin, 4,098	G-9
•Rose Hill, Fairfax, 12,675	C-4
Roslyn Hills, Henrico	A-16
•Rushmere, Isle of Wight, 1,064	G-15
Rustburg, Campbell	G-10
Saint Paul, Russell/Wise, 1,007	H-4
Salem, Independent City, 23,756	G-8
Saltville, Smyth/Washington, 2,300	H-5
Saluda, Middlesex	F-15
Sandston, Henrico	B-18
Seaford, York	G-16
•Seven Corners, Fairfax, 7,280	C-4
•Shawsville, Montgomery, 1,260	G-8
Shenandoah, Page, 2,213	C-11
Smithfield, Isle of Wight, 4,686	G-15
South Boston, Independent City, 6,997	H-11
South Hill, Mecklenburg, 4,217	H-12
Spotsylvania, Spotsylvania	D-13
•Spotsylvania Courthouse, Spotsylvania, 2,694	D-13
•Springfield, Fairfax, 23,706	C-4
Stafford, Stafford	D-14
Stanardsville, Greene, 257	D-12
Stanley, Page, 1,186	C-11
Stanleytown, Henry, 1,563	H-8
Staunton, Independent City, 24,461	D-10
Stephens City, Frederick, 1,186	B-12
•Sterling, Loudoun, 20,512	B-14
Strasburg, Shenandoah, 3,762	B-12
Stuart, Patrick, 965	H-8
•Stuarts Draft, Augusta, 5,087	E-10
•Sudley, Prince William, 7,321	C-2
Suffolk, Independent City, 52,141	H-15
•Sugarland Run, Loudoun, 9,357	B-14
Surry, Surry, 192	G-15
Sussex, Sussex	H-14
Tappahannock, Essex, 1,550	E-15
Tazewell, Tazewell, 4,176	G-5
•Timberlake, Campbell, 10,314	G-10
Timberville, Rockingham, 1,596	C-11
•Triangle, Prince William, 4,740	F-3
•Tuckahoe, Henrico, 42,629	A-15
•Tysons Corner, Fairfax, 13,124	B-4
•University Heights, Albemarle, 6,900	E-11
•Vansant, Buchanan, 1,187	G-4
•Verona, Augusta, 3,479	D-10
Victoria, Lunenburg, 1,830	H-12
Vienna, Fairfax, 14,852	B-3
•Villa Heights, Henry, 1,021	H-9
•Vint Hill Farms Station, Fauquier, 1,332	C-13
Vinton, Roanoke, 7,665	G-9
Virginia Beach, Independent City, 393,069	H-17
Virginia Hills, Fairfax	C-5
Wakefield, Sussex, 1,070	H-15
Warm Springs, Bath	E-9
Warrenton, Fauquier, 4,830	C-13
Warsaw, Richmond, 961	E-15
Washington, Rappahannock, 198	C-12
Waverly, Sussex, 2,223	G-14
Waynesboro, Independent City, 18,549	E-11
Weber City, Scott, 1,377	H-3
•West Gate, Prince William, 6,565	C-2
West Point, King William, 2,938	F-15
•West Springfield, Fairfax, 28,126	D-4
Westham, Henrico	B-16
Wildwood, Henrico	A-17
Williamsburg, Independent City, 11,530	G-15
Winchester, Independent City, 21,947	A-12
Windsor, Isle of Wight, 1,025	C-5
Wise, Wise, 3,193	G-3
•Wolf Trap, Fairfax, 13,133	B-3
•Woodbridge, Prince William, 26,401	E-3
Woodstock, Shenandoah, 3,182	B-11
Wytheville, Wythe, 8,038	H-6
•Yorkshire, Prince William, 5,699	C-2
Yorktown, York	G-15

Explanation of symbols: •– Census Designated Place (CDP)

General Help Numbers:

Governor's Office
PO Box 40002
Olympia, WA 98504-0002
www.governor.wa.gov

360-902-4111
Fax 360-753-4110
8AM-5PM

Attorney General's Office
PO Box 40100
Olympia, WA 98504-0100
www.atg.wa.gov/

360-753-6200
Fax 360-664-0228
8AM-5PM

Legislative Information Center
PO Box 40600
Olympia, WA 98504-0600
www1.leg.wa.gov/legislature

360-786-7573
Fax 360-786-1293
8AM-5PM

State Archives
State Archives
PO Box 40238
Olympia, WA 98504-0238
www.secstate.wa.gov/archives

360-586-1492
Fax 360-664-8814
8:30AM-4:30PM

State Specifics:

Capital:

Olympia
Thurston County

Time Zone:

PST

Number of Counties:

39

Population:

6,203,788

Web Site:

http://access.wa.gov

State Agencies

Criminal Records

Washington State Patrol, Identification and Criminal History Section, PO Box 42633, Olympia, WA 98504-2633 (Courier address: 3000 Pacific Ave. SE #204, Olympia, WA 98501); 360-705-5100, 360-570-5275-Fax; 8AM-5PM.

www.wsp.wa.gov

Records are available from 1974. Criminal history information is retained at the Identification and Criminal History Section until the offender is age seventy, or ten years from the last date of arrest, whichever is longer. It takes 30 to 45 days if manual; 2 hours if electronic before new records are available for inquiry. Records are indexed on computer. Records are normally destroyed after a court order. 79% of all arrests in database have final dispositions recorded, 70% for those arrests within last 5 years.

Searching: Two types of records available: General Conviction - all convictions and arrests less than one year pending disposition; and Child & Adult Abuse record - only conviction of crimes against persons, certain drug crimes, and financial exploitation crimes. Include the following in your request-date of birth, Social Security Number, sex, race, name and address of subject. Fingerprints are optional. Records are 100% fingerprint-supported. Mail requests are directed to the WSP or e-mail to crimhis@wsp.gov. The following data is not released: non-conviction and arrest information over one year old without disposition. Records without dispositions not released unless the arrest is less than 1 year old.

Access by: mail, in person, online.

Fee & Payment: The fee for a name check is $35.00 per individual (except online). For a fingerprint check, the fee is $30.00 per individual.

Will not conduct FBI fingerprint checks. Fee payee: Washington State Patrol. Prepayment required. Money orders or cashier's checks preferred. Personal checks accepted.

Mail search: Turnaround time: 2 to 3 weeks.

In person search: Requests are returned by mail.

Online search: WSP offers web access through a system called WATCH. The fee per search is $10.00. The exact DOB and exact spelling of the name are required. Credit cards are accepted online. To set up a WATCH account, call 360-705-5100 Ext 5 or email watch.help@wsp.wa.gov.

Other access: See the State Court Administrator's office for information about their criminal records database (JIS-Link).

Statewide Court Records

Administrative Office of Courts, Temple of Justice, PO Box 41174, Olympia, WA 98504-1174 (Courier address: 1206 Quince St SE, Olympia, WA 98504); 360-753-3365, 360-586-8869-Fax; 8AM-5PM.

www.courts.wa.gov

Access by: online.

Online search: The AOC provides facilities that allow one to access information in the Judicial Information System's (JIS) statewide computer. This program of services is called JIS-Link. JIS-Link provides access to all counties and court levels. Fees include a one-time $100.00 per site, a transaction fee of $.065 per record. Case records include criminal, civil, domestic, probate, and judgments. Call 360-357-3365 or visit www.courts.wa.gov/jislink. Supreme Court and Appellate opinions can be found at www.courts.wa.gov/appellate_trial_courts. The webpage offers a notification service also.

Other access: Indexes are available electronically and via microfiche for a fee. Call the JISLink Coordinator for details.

Sexual Offender Registry

Washington State Patrol, SOR, PO Box 42633, Olympia, WA 98504-2633 (Courier address: 3000 Pacific Ave. SE #204, Olympia, WA 98501); 360-705-5100 x3, 360-570-5275-Fax; 8AM-5PM.

www.wsp.wa.gov

It takes only seconds before new records are available for inquiry.

Searching: There is a link to county sex offender sites at www.waspc.org/wa_sex/index.shtml.

Access by: online.

Online search: In cooperation with the Washington Assoc. of Sheriffs and Police Chiefs, online access to Level II and Level III sexual offenders is available at www.waspc.org.

Incarceration Records

Washington Department of Corrections, Office of Correctional Operations, 410 W. 5th, MS-41118, Olympia, WA 98504-1118; 360-753-3317 (Basic info), 360-586-3492 (Public Disclosure), 8AM-5PM M-F.

www.doc.wa.gov

The agency is moving in late 2005 to Tumwater. Phone numbers will change,

Records are available on current and former inmates. It takes 1 to 5 days before new records are available for inquiry.

Searching: Records are not destroyed and eventually archived with Sec. of State office. Include the following in your request-full name, DOB; SSN is helpful. Location, CCO, parole review data, and counselor are released. For anything other than basic information, a written request is required.

Access by: mail, phone, online.

Fee & Payment: A copy fee is $.20 per page; a postage fee applies to all mailed documents.

Mail search: Turnaround time: 1 to 2 weeks.

Phone search: Name searching available by phone; basic information released, no personal information.

Online search: No online searching provided. Email requests can be directed to correspondence@doc1.wa.gov.

Other access: Data is available by subscription for bulk users; for information, contact the Contracts Office at 360-664-0867.

Corporation, Trademarks/Servicemarks, Limited Partnerships, Limited Liability Company

Secretary of State, Corporations Division, PO Box 40234, Olympia, WA 98504-0234 (Courier address: Dolliver Bldg, 801 Capitol Way South, Olympia, WA 98501); 360-753-7115, 360-664-8781-Fax; 8AM-5PM.

www.secstate.wa.gov/corps

Records are available for initial filing documents. Annual reports for the past 5 years are on microfilm, imaged since 2004. It takes less than 1 day before new records are available for inquiry. Records are normally destroyed after 20 years since lapsing, usually.

Searching: All of the information here is public record. Include the following in your request-full name of business, UBI number if available. The copies for a limited partnership are different than corporation documents. Any single document is $1.00 per page plus $.20 per copy for LPs. The Annual Report contains the names of Directors and Officers.

Access by: mail, phone, in person, online.

Fee & Payment: Annual Report is $5.00 per corporate name. Photocopies fee is $10.00 per document, $20.00 if the document needs to be certified. If file exceeds 100 pages, a surcharge of $13.00 per 50 pages is added. Trademark documents are $.50 per page. Fee payee: Secretary of State. Prepayment required. Personal checks accepted. No credit cards accepted.

Mail search: Turnaround time: variable.

Phone search: Information requests are available at this department for limited information.

In person search: Immediate service.

Online search: Search corporation registrations at www.secstate.wa.gov/corps/search.aspx, no fee. Information is updated daily.

Expedited service: Expedited service is available for mail and phone searches. Turnaround time: 48 hours. Add $20.00 per document.

Trade Names

Master License Service, Business & Professions Div, PO Box 9034, Olympia, WA 98507-9034 (Courier address: 405 Black Lake Blvd, Olympia, WA 98507); 360-664-1400, 900-463-6000 (Trade Name Search), 360-570-4959-Fax; 8AM-5PM.

www.dol.wa.gov

Records are available from 1984 (note that everyone re-registered trade names in 1984). It takes 3 weeks before new records are available for inquiry. Records are normally destroyed after 10 years.

Searching: Searching may be done by business name, business address, owner's name, or UBI number. The following data is not released: Social Security Numbers, personal information (height, weight, sex, eye color, etc.), DOB or addresses.

Access by: mail, phone, in person.

Fee & Payment: The search fee is $4.00, which includes 3 business/owner names. Each name variation is considered a separate name. Certification costs an additional $2.00. Fee payee: Washington State Treasurer. Prepayment required. Personal checks accepted, credit cards are not.

Mail search: Turnaround time: 1-2 weeks

Phone search: The 900 number fee is $4.95 for the first minute and $.50 for each additional minute. Average search is 2 minutes.

In person search: Copies cost $.25 per page.

Other access: Records can be purchased on cartridges or 9 track tapes. Information includes date of registration, owner name, state ID numbers, and cancel date if cancelled. Call same number and ask for Jody Miller.

Expedited service: Expedited service is available by fax. Must have an account with a deposit.

Uniform Commercial Code, Federal Tax Liens

Department of Licensing, UCC Records, PO Box 9660, Olympia, WA 98507-9660 (Courier address: 405 Black Lake Blvd, Olympia, WA 98502); 360-664-1530, 360-586-4414-Fax; 8AM-5PM.

www.dol.wa.gov/unfc/uccfront.htm

Records are available from 1967. However, only currently active plus 1 full year are accessible. It takes 2 days before new records are available for inquiry. Records are normally destroyed after one year past lapse date.

Searching: Use search request form UCC-11. The search includes all notices of tax liens filed here. Include the following in your request-debtor name.

Access by: mail, online.

Fee & Payment: A mail or in person request for information is $18.80. A request for information with all copies is $26.57. Fee payee: Department of Licensing. Prepayment required. Credit cards are accepted for online searching only. Personal checks accepted. Credit cards accepted: MasterCard, Visa.

Mail search: Turnaround time: 2 days.

Online search: For online access, go to https://fortress.wa.gov/dol/ucc. There is a $15.00 search fee for a name search. Fee is $26.57 if copies included. Copies are mailed.

Other access: The database may be purchased on microfilm or CD.

State Tax Liens

Records not maintained by a state level agency.

State tax liens are filed at the county level.

Sales Tax Registrations

Department of Revenue, Taxpayer Services, PO Box 47478, Olympia, WA 98504-7478; 360-705-6705, 800-647-7706, 360-705-6655-Fax; hours 8AM-5PM.

www.dor.wa.gov

Records are available from 1992 and are indexed on microfiche and optical imaging. It takes 1-3 days before new records are available for inquiry.

Searching: This agency will provide disclosable information authorized by statute such as tax registration/UBI #, owner's name, business name (DBA), address, open/closing date, account status and SIC/NAICS. For confidential information, submit a signed release. Include the following in your request-business name or owner name, UBI or tax registration number.

Access by: mail, phone, fax, in person, online.

Fee & Payment: There is no search fee, but there is a copy fee of $.15 per page.

Mail search: Turnaround time: 5 business days.

Phone search: Only "public registration" information is available.

Fax search: Turnaround time is 5 business days.

In person search: Appointment required.

Online search: The agency provides a state business records database with free access on the Internet at https://fortress.wa.gov/dor/brd/. Lookups are by owner names, DBAs, and tax reporting numbers. Results show a myriad of data.

Birth Certificates

Department of Health, Center for Health Statistics, PO Box 9709, Olympia, WA 98507-9709 (Courier address: 101 Israel Rd SE, Tumwater WA 98501); 360-236-4300 (Main Number), 360-236-4313 (Credit Card Ordering), 360-352-2586-Fax; 9AM - 4PM.

www.doh.wa.gov

Records are available from July 1, 1907 to present. It takes 2-3 months before new records are available for inquiry. Records are indexed on microfiche, inhouse computer.

Searching: The data on the lower portion of form is confidential. Include the following in your request-full name, names of parents, mother's maiden name, date of birth, place of birth. Please specify if father is not listed on birth certificate.

Access by: mail, phone, fax, in person, online.

Fee & Payment: The search fee is $17.00. Add $5.00 for certification and $6.00 if a credit card is used. Fee payee: Dept of Health. Prepayment required. Personal checks accepted. Major credit cards accepted.

Mail search: Turnaround time: 7 to 8 weeks. Must send your current address and daytime phone number with request. A SASE is requested.

Phone search: You must use a credit card.

Fax search: Same criteria as phone searching.

In person search: Counter service is available for same day requests.

Online search: Records may requested from www.Vitalchek.com, a state-endorsed vendor.

Other access: The Digital archives, launched in 2004, contains various periods for marriages, death, birth, military, naturalization, institution, and various historical records at www.digitalarchives.wa.gov.

Expedited service: Expedited service is available for phone, in person, and fax requests. You must use a credit card. Courier address or Express Mail deliver is an additional costs.

Death Records

Department of Health, Vital Records, PO Box 9709, Olympia, WA 98507-9709 (Courier address: 101 Israel Rd SE, Tumwater, WA 98501); 360-236-4300 (Main Number), 360-236-4313 (Credit Card Ordering), 360-352-2586-Fax; 9AM - 4PM.

www.doh.wa.gov

Records are available from July 1, 1907 to present. It takes 2-6 months before new records are available for inquiry. Records are indexed on microfiche, inhouse computer.

Searching: A written request is required, there is no public viewing. Include the following in your request-full name, date of death, place of death.

Access by: mail, phone, fax, in person, online.

Fee & Payment: The search fee is $17.00. Add $5.00 for certification and $6.00 if a credit card is used. Fee payee: Dept of Health. Prepayment required. Personal checks accepted. Major credit cards accepted.

Mail search: Turnaround time: 7 to 8 weeks. Must send your current address and daytime phone number with request. A SASE is requested.

Phone search: You must use a credit card.

Fax search: Same criteria as phone searching.

In person search: Counter service is available for same day requests.

Online search: Records may requested from www.vitalchek.com, a state-endorsed vendor.

Other access: The Digital archives, launched in 2004, contains various periods for marriages, death, birth, military, naturalization, institution, and various historical records at www.digitalarchives.wa.gov.

Expedited service: Expedited service is available for phone, fax, and in person searches. You must use a credit card. Courier address or Express Mail deliver is an additional cost.

Marriage Certificates

Department of Health, Vital Records, PO Box 9709, Olympia, WA 98507-9709 (Courier address: 101 Israel Rd SE, Tumwater, WA 98501); 360-236-4300 (Main Number), 360-236-4313 (Credit Card Ordering), 360-352-2586-Fax; 9AM - 4PM.

www.doh.wa.gov

Records are available from 1968 to present. It takes 2-4 months before new records are available for inquiry. Records are indexed on microfiche, inhouse computer.

Searching: Written request is required, there is no public viewing. Include the following in your request-names of husband and wife, date of marriage, place or county of marriage.

Access by: mail, phone, fax, in person, online.

Fee & Payment: The search fee is $17.00. Add $5.00 for certification and $6.00 if a credit card is used. Fee payee: Dept of Health. Prepayment required. Personal checks accepted. Major credit cards accepted.

Mail search: Turnaround time: 7 to 8 weeks. Must send your current address and daytime phone number with request. A SASE is requested.

Phone search: You must use a credit card.

Fax search: Same criteria as phone searching.

In person search: Counter service is available for same day requests.

Online search: Records may requested from www.vitalchek.com, a state-endorsed vendor.

Other access: The Digital archives, launched in 2004, contains various periods for marriages, death, birth, military, naturalization, institution, and various historical records at www.digitalarchives.wa.gov.

Expedited service: Expedited service is available for phone, fax, and in person searches. You must use a credit card. Courier address or Express Mail deliver is an additional costs.

Divorce Records

Department of Health, Vital Records, PO Box 9709, Olympia, WA 98507-9709 (Courier address: 101 Israel Rd SE, Tumwater, WA 98501); 360-753-4300 (Main Number), 360-753-4313 (Credit Card Ordering), 360-352-2586-Fax; 9AM - 4PM.

www.doh.wa.gov

Records are available from 1968 to present. It takes 2-4 months before new records are available for inquiry. Records are indexed on microfiche, inhouse computer.

Searching: Include the following in your request-names of husband and wife, date of divorce, place of divorce.

Access by: mail, phone, fax, in person, online.

Fee & Payment: The search fee is $17.00. Add $5.00 for certification and $6.00 if a credit card is used. Fee payee: Dept of Health. Prepayment required. Personal checks accepted. Major credit cards accepted.

Mail search: Turnaround time: 5 weeks. Must send your current address and daytime phone number with request. A SASE is requested.

Phone search: You must use a credit card.

Fax search: Same criteria as phone searching.

In person search: Counter service is available for same day requests.

Online search: Records may requested from www.vitalchek.com, a state-endorsed vendor.

Expedited service: Expedited service is available for phone, fax, and in person searches. You must use a credit card. Courier address or Express Mail deliver is an additional costs.

Workers' Compensation

Labor and Industries, Public Disclosure Unit, PO Box 44632, Olympia, WA 98504-4632; 360-902-5542, 360-902-5529-Fax; 8AM-5PM.

www.lni.wa.gov

There are two forms available on the web - Request for Claim Information and the Request for Public Records.

Records are available for the past 3 years. Prior records are at the State Records Center, but you must go through this office for those records. It takes 1 month before new records are available for inquiry. Records are indexed on computer and microfiche. Records are normally destroyed after 75 years.

Searching: Must have signed release from the claimant on both forms. Written request only. Claims information is not released except as provided under Title 51 of the Revised Code of Washington (RCW). Include the following in your request-claimant name, SSN, claim number, signed release. The DOB is helpful. The following data is not released: chemically-related illness.

Access by: mail, fax, in person.

Fee & Payment: Copy fee is $.15 per page. Certification is additional $.15. Fee payee: L & I

Cashier. Prepayment required if over $100. Personal checks accepted, credit cards are not.

Mail search: Turnaround time: 3 to 5 days. The record information that they send back is taken from microfiche only. No hard file copies released.

Fax search: Fax requests are accepted.

In person search: Must schedule by appointment.

Driver Records

Department of Licensing, Driver Record Section, PO Box 9048, Olympia, WA 98507-9030 (Courier address: 1125 Washington Street SE, Olympia, WA 98504); 360-902-3913, 360-902-3900 (General Information), 360-586-9044-Fax; 8AM-4:30PM.

www.dol.wa.gov

Records available include a 3-year insurance record and the "full" employment record. The 3-year record contains employment or non-employment convictions. The full record contains both. Detailed information on access and forms are found at the web.

It takes 2 to 3 weeks or more before new records are available for inquiry. Records are normally destroyed after 5 years.

Searching: All mail or walk-in requests require a properly signed form, exceptions are for ongoing, pre-approved accounts. Casual requesters must have written consent. In general, records are not provided to third party, even with a signed consent. Include the following in your request-license number, or the name and DOB. The license number is based upon a code of the name and DOB. This code can be confusing (O or 0, *'s) so it is suggested you try name and DOB first. The following data is not released: SSN.

Access by: mail, in person, online.

Fee & Payment: The fee is $5.00 per record. Copies of tickets may be requested by the driver. The fee is $.75 per ticket; the first 5 are free. Fee payee: Department of Licensing Prepayment required. Personal checks accepted. No credit cards accepted.

Mail search: Turnaround time: 2 weeks. There is no charge for a no record found, but do not refund if $5.00 or less specifically requested. A SASE is requested.

In person search: Turnaround time is immediate for up to 5 requests. There is no charge for a no record found.

Online search: You may check the status of a driver license, permit or ID card online for free at https://fortress.wa.gov/dol/ddl/dsd/.

Other access: FTP retrieval is offered for high volume requesters.

Vehicle & Vessel Ownership, Vehicle Identification, Vessel Registration

Department of Licensing, Vehicle Records, PO Box 2957, Olympia, WA 98507-2957 (Courier address: 1125 S Washington MS-48001, Olympia, WA 98504); 360-902-3780, 360-902-3827-Fax; 8AM-5PM.

www.dol.wa.gov

It is recommended that on-going, high volume users enter into a disclosure agreement with this agency; call 360-902-3760.

Records are available for 6 years to present. All motorized boats and sailboats must be titled. All boats must be registered unless under 16 ft with less than a 10 hp motor. It takes 2 to 3 weeks before new records are available for inquiry. Records are indexed on inhouse computer.

Searching: Washington has strict access guidelines that restrict casual requesters. Permitted requesters include attorneys, PI's, insurance companies, and business entities for use in the normal course of business. A special form is required. Include the following in your request-VIN, license plate number. Records cannot be searched by owner or driver name. Requests must be in writing.

Access by: mail, phone, fax, in person, online.

Fee & Payment: The fee for microfilm or microfiche copies are $.75 per page. Fee for photocopy or printouts is $.15 each; no charge under $4.50. There is no charge to "view" a record. Fee payee: Department of Licensing

Mail search: Turnaround time: 2 weeks.

Phone search: Phone ordering is only available for pre-approved, high volume accounts. The system processes by plate number, VIN, WN# & HIN. To set up an account, call 360-902-3760.

Fax search: Approved, ongoing requestors may fax requests.

In person search: Simple requests may be processed while you wait.

Online search: This Internet Vehicle/Vessel Information System is a commercial subscription service and all accounts must be pre-approved. A $25.00 deposit is required and there is a fee per hit. For more information, call 360-902-3760.

Other access: Large bulk lists cannot be released for any commercial purposes. Lists are released to non-profit entities and for statistical purposes. For more information, call 360-902-3760.

Accident Reports

State Patrol, Collision Reports, PO Box 47382, Olympia, WA 98504; 360-570-2355, 360-570-2400-Fax; 8AM-5PM.

www.wsp.wa.gov

Records are available for 6 years plus the present year. It takes 2 to 3 weeks before new records are available for inquiry. Records are normally destroyed after 6 years.

Searching: Include the following in your request-name, date of accident, location of accident. It is strongly suggested to use their request form - Form 300-345-008. The agency will fax a copy of the form, upon request.

Access by: mail, in person.

Fee & Payment: The fee is $5.00 per record. Fee payee: Washington State Patrol. Prepayment required. Personal checks accepted. No credit cards accepted.

Mail search: Turnaround time: 2 weeks. A SASE is requested.

In person search: Walk-in requesters may receive the report with proper credentials, if personnel are available to do the search.

Voter Registration

Access to Records is Restricted.

Secretary of State, Office of Elections Division, PO Box 40229, Olympia, WA 98504-0229; 360-902-4180, 800-448-4881, 360-664-4619-Fax; 8AM-5PM.

www.secstate.wa.gov/elections

All voter information is kept at the local level by the County Auditor (except King County where records are kept by the Dept of Records and Elections). Individual look-ups will not receive SSNs, DOBs, or telephone numbers. However, the Federal Help America Vote Act of 2002 (HAVA) law requires implementation of a central, computerized, statewide voter registration system by 01/01/2006. The state will comply.

GED Certificates

State Board for Community & Technical Colleges, GED Transcripts, PO Box 42495, Olympia, WA 98504-2495 (Courier address: 319 7th Ave, Olympia, WA 98504); 360-704-4410, 360-664-8808-Fax; 8AM-5PM.

www.sbctc.ctc.edu

It takes 2 weeks before new records are available for inquiry.

Searching: Include the following in your request-name, Social Security Number, date of birth, signed release. Also, the city, date of test, and any previous name the record could be under are helpful.

Access by: mail, fax, in person.

Fee & Payment: There is no fee for either verification or a transcript.

Mail search: Turnaround time: 1 week.

Fax search: Same criteria as mail searching.

In person search: Verification is while you wait.

Hunting and Fishing License Information

Department of Fish & Wildlife, Attn: Public Disclosure Officer, 600 Capitol Way, N, Olympia, WA 98501-1091; 360-902-2253, 360-902-2171-Fax; 8AM-5PM.

http://wdfw.wa.gov

Records are available for past 5 years, in this office. It takes up to 3 months before new records are available for inquiry.

Searching: Records cannot be purchased for commercial list purposes. Include the following in your request-name and DOB. All requests must be in writing.

Access by: mail, fax, in person, online.

Fee & Payment: There is no fee for searching individual names. Fees are involved for lists of license holders. Fee payee: WDFW

Mail search: Turnaround time: 1-2 weeks.

Fax search: Fax requests accepted.

In person search: Simple requests may be processed while you wait.

Online search: You may send an email request; check the website for the exact address.

Other access: The database can be purchased for non-commercial purposes only.

Washington State Licensing Agencies

For details about the agency responsible for licensing/certifying/registering an item below or in the Agency Quick Finder section, match an item's number with the number of the agency in the *Licensing Agency Information* section.

Washington Licenses Searchable Online

Acupuncturist #11 .... https://fortress.wa.gov/doh/hpqa1/Application/Credential_Search/profile.asp
Adult Family Home #30 .... www.aasa.dshs.wa.gov/Lookup/AFHRequestv2.asp
Animal Technician #11 .... https://fortress.wa.gov/doh/hpqa1/Application/Credential_Search/profile.asp
Announcer, Athletic Event (Ring) #27 ...... https://fortress.wa.gov/dol/dolprod/profquery/
Applicator, Commercial #5 .... http://agr.wa.gov/PestFert/LicensingEd/ListPrivateApplicators.htm
Architect #26 .... https://fortress.wa.gov/dol/dolprod/profquery/
Architect Corporation #26 .... https://fortress.wa.gov/dol/dolprod/profquery/
Athlete, Professional #27 .... https://fortress.wa.gov/dol/dolprod/profquery/
Athletic Inspector #27 .... https://fortress.wa.gov/dol/dolprod/profquery/
Athletic Judge/Timekeeper/Physian #27 ...https://fortress.wa.gov/dol/dolprod/profquery/
Athletic Mgr/Promoter/Matchmaker #27 ...https://fortress.wa.gov/dol/dolprod/profquery/
Attorney #23 .... http://pro.wsba.org
Auction Company #33 .... www.dol.wa.gov/main/biglist.htm
Auctioneer #33 .... www.dol.wa.gov/main/biglist.htm
Audiologist #11 .... https://fortress.wa.gov/doh/hpqa1/Application/Credential_Search/profile.asp
Bail Bond Agent/Agency #15 .... https://fortress.wa.gov/dol/dolprod/profquery/
Bail Bond Recovery Agent #15 .... https://fortress.wa.gov/dol/dolprod/profquery/
Barber #18 .... https://fortress.wa.gov/dol/dolprod/profquery/
Barber Instructor/School #18 .... https://fortress.wa.gov/dol/dolprod/profquery/
Barber Shop/Mobile/Booth #18 .... https://fortress.wa.gov/dol/dolprod/profquery/
Beauty Shop/Salon/Mobile #18 .... https://fortress.wa.gov/dol/dolprod/profquery/
Boarding Home #30 .... www.aasa.dshs.wa.gov/Lookup/BHRequestv2.asp
Boxer #27 .... https://fortress.wa.gov/dol/dolprod/profquery/
Camping Resort #33 .... www.dol.wa.gov/main/biglist.htm
Cemetery #6 .... https://fortress.wa.gov/dol/dolprod/profquery/
Charitable Gift Annuity #25 .... www.insurance.wa.gov/cgi-bin/PubInfoApps/CharitableGA.exe
Chiropractor #11 .... https://fortress.wa.gov/doh/hpqa1/Application/Credential_Search/profile.asp
Collection Agency #32 .... https://fortress.wa.gov/dol/dolprod/profquery/
Contractor, General, Company #12 .... https://fortress.wa.gov/lni/bbip/
Cosmetologist #18 .... https://fortress.wa.gov/dol/dolprod/profquery/
Cosmetology (Barber) #33 .... www.dol.wa.gov/main/biglist.htm
Cosmetology Instructor/School #18 .... https://fortress.wa.gov/dol/dolprod/profquery/
Counselor #11 .... https://fortress.wa.gov/doh/hpqa1/Application/Credential_Search/profile.asp
Court Reporter #33 .... www.dol.wa.gov/main/biglist.htm
Crematory #6 .... https://fortress.wa.gov/dol/dolprod/profquery/
Dental Hygienist #11 .... https://fortress.wa.gov/doh/hpqa1/Application/Credential_Search/profile.asp
Dentist #11 .... https://fortress.wa.gov/doh/hpqa1/Application/Credential_Search/profile.asp
Dietitian #11 .... https://fortress.wa.gov/doh/hpqa1/Application/Credential_Search/profile.asp
Domestic Insurance Carrier #25 .... https://fortress.wa.gov/oic/laa/LAAMain.aspx
Electrical Contractor/Admin. #12 .... https://fortress.wa.gov/lni/bbip/
Electrician #12 .... https://fortress.wa.gov/lni/bbip/
Embalmer #6 .... https://fortress.wa.gov/dol/dolprod/profquery/
Emergency Medical Technician #11 .... https://fortress.wa.gov/doh/hpqa1/Application/Credential_Search/profile.asp
Employment Agency #32 .... https://fortress.wa.gov/dol/dolprod/profquery/
Employment Directory Service #32 .... https://fortress.wa.gov/dol/dolprod/profquery/
Esthetician Salon/Booth/Mobile #18 .... https://fortress.wa.gov/dol/dolprod/profquery/
Esthetician/Esthetician Instruct. #18 .... https://fortress.wa.gov/dol/dolprod/profquery/
Feedlot #3 .... http://agr.wa.gov/FoodAnimal/Livestock/CertifiedFeedlots.htm
Fishing, Commercial #8 .... www.greatlodge.com/wa-fishhunt/licenses/state_fishgame_front.cgi?st=WA
Funeral Director/Establishment #6 .... https://fortress.wa.gov/dol/dolprod/profquery/
Gaming Operation #24 .... www.wsgc.wa.gov/LicSearch.asp
Gaming-related Occupation #24 .... www.wsgc.wa.gov/LicSearch.asp
Healthcare Service Company #25 .... www.insurance.wa.gov/cgi-bin/PubInfoApps/CGIAuthComp.exe
Hearing Instru. Fitter/Dispenser #11 .... https://fortress.wa.gov/doh/hpqa1/Application/Credential_Search/profile.asp
HMO #25 .... www.insurance.wa.gov/cgi-bin/PubInfoApps/CGIAuthComp.exe
Home Health Care Agency #9 .... www.doh.wa.gov/Licensing.htm
Hospital #9 .... www.doh.wa.gov/Licensing.htm

Hypnotherapist #11 ....https://fortress.wa.gov/doh/hpqa1/Application/Credential_Search/profile.asp
Insurance Agent/Broker #25 ....https://fortress.wa.gov/oic/iaa/LAAMain.aspx
Insurance Company #25.........................www.insurance.wa.gov/cgi-bin/PubInfoApps/CGIAuthComp.exe
Insurance Corp., Resident #25 ....www.insurance.wa.gov/cgi-bin/PubInfoApps/CGIAuthComp.exe
Kickboxer #27 ....https://fortress.wa.gov/dol/dolprod/profquery
Landscape Architect #26 ....https://fortress.wa.gov/dol/dolprod/profquery/
Liquor Store #19......................................www.liq.wa.gov/services/storesearch.asp
Livestock Market #3 ....http://agr.wa.gov/FoodAnimal/Livestock/PublicMarkets.htm
Manicure Shop/Mobile/Booth #18 ....https://fortress.wa.gov/dol/dolprod/profquery/
Manicurist/Esthetician #33 ....www.dol.wa.gov/main/biglist.htm
Manicurist/Manicurist Instruct. #18 ....https://fortress.wa.gov/dol/dolprod/profquery/
Marriage & Family Therapist #11 ....https://fortress.wa.gov/doh/hpqa1/Application/Credential_Search/profile.asp
Massage Therapist #11 ....https://fortress.wa.gov/doh/hpqa1/Application/Credential_Search/profile.asp
Medical Doctor #11 ....https://fortress.wa.gov/doh/hpqa1/Application/Credential_Search/profile.asp
Mental Health Counselor #11 ....https://fortress.wa.gov/doh/hpqa1/Application/Credential_Search/profile.asp
Midwife #11...https://fortress.wa.gov/doh/hpqa1/Application/Credential_Search/profile.asp
Naturopathic Physician #11 ....https://fortress.wa.gov/doh/hpqa1/Application/Credential_Search/profile.asp
Notary Public #17....................................https://fortress.wa.gov/dol/dolprod/profquery/
Nurse/Nursing Assistant #11 ....https://fortress.wa.gov/doh/hpqa1/Application/Credential_Search/profile.asp
Nurse-LPN #11 ....https://fortress.wa.gov/doh/hpqa1/Application/Credential_Search/profile.asp
Nursing Home Administrator #11 ....https://fortress.wa.gov/doh/hpqa1/Application/Credential_Search/profile.asp
Nursing Home #30 ....www.aasa.dshs.wa.gov/Professional/NFDir/directory.asp
Occupational Therapist #11 ....https://fortress.wa.gov/doh/hpqa1/Application/Credential_Search/profile.asp
Ocularist #11...https://fortress.wa.gov/doh/hpqa1/Application/Credential_Search/profile.asp
Optician #11..https://fortress.wa.gov/doh/hpqa1/Application/Credential_Search/profile.asp
Optometrist #11.......................................https://fortress.wa.gov/doh/hpqa1/Application/Credential_Search/profile.asp
Osteopathic Physician #11 ....https://fortress.wa.gov/doh/hpqa1/Application/Credential_Search/profile.asp
Pharmacist #11 ....https://fortress.wa.gov/doh/hpqa1/Application/Credential_Search/profile.asp
Pharmacy Technician #11 ....https://fortress.wa.gov/doh/hpqa1/Application/Credential_Search/profile.asp
Physical Therapist #11............................https://fortress.wa.gov/doh/hpqa1/Application/Credential_Search/profile.asp
Physician Assistant #11 ....https://fortress.wa.gov/doh/hpqa1/Application/Credential_Search/profile.asp
Plumber #12..https://fortress.wa.gov/lni/bbip/
Podiatrist #11 ....https://fortress.wa.gov/doh/hpqa1/Application/Credential_Search/profile.asp
Private Inv. Agency/Trainer #15..............https://fortress.wa.gov/dol/dolprod/profquery/
Private Investigator #15 ....https://fortress.wa.gov/dol/dolprod/profquery/
Professional Athlete #33 ....www.dol.wa.gov/main/biglist.htm
Psychologist #11 ....https://fortress.wa.gov/doh/hpqa1/Application/Credential_Search/profile.asp
Public Accountant-CPA #1 ....www.cpaboard.wa.gov/search/default.htm
Purchasing Group (Insurance) #25..........www.insurance.wa.gov/cgi-bin/PubInfoApps/CGIRiskPG.exe
Radiologic Technologist #11 ....https://fortress.wa.gov/doh/hpqa1/Application/Credential_Search/profile.asp
Recreational Hunting #8 ....www.greatlodge.com/wa-fishhunt/licenses/state_fishgame_front.cgi?st=WA
Referee (Athletic) #27 ....https://fortress.wa.gov/dol/dolprod/profquery/
Respiratory Therapist #11........................https://fortress.wa.gov/doh/hpqa1/Application/Credential_Search/profile.asp
Risk Retention Group #25........................www.insurance.wa.gov/cgi-bin/PubInfoApps/CGIRiskRG.exe
Salon #33..www.dol.wa.gov/main/biglist.htm
Security Guard/Agency #15 ....https://fortress.wa.gov/dol/dolprod/profquery/
Service Contract Provider (Ins) #25.........www.insurance.wa.gov/cgi-bin/PubInfoApps/CGIServiceCP.exe
Sex Offender Treatment Provider #11 ......https://fortress.wa.gov/doh/hpqa1/Application/Credential_Search/profile.asp
Social Worker #11....................................https://fortress.wa.gov/doh/hpqa1/Application/Credential_Search/profile.asp
Speech-Language Pathologist #11 ....https://fortress.wa.gov/doh/hpqa1/Application/Credential_Search/profile.asp
Sport Fishing #8 ....www.greatlodge.com/wa-fishhunt/licenses/state_fishgame_front.cgi?st=WA
Structural Pest Inspector #5.....................http://agr.wa.gov/PestFert/LicensingEd/ListStructuralPestInspectors.htm
Telephone Solicitor #32 ....https://fortress.wa.gov/dol/dolprod/profquery/
Timeshare Seller/Busi./Project #33..........www.dol.wa.gov/main/biglist.htm
Travel Agency #33 ....www.dol.wa.gov/main/biglist.htm
Travel Seller #33.....................................www.dol.wa.gov/main/biglist.htm
Vehicle for Hire #32 ....https://fortress.wa.gov/dol/dolprod/profquery/
Vehicle Sales/Disposal #32 ....https://fortress.wa.gov/dol/dolprod/profquery/
Veterinarian #11......................................https://fortress.wa.gov/doh/hpqa1/Application/Credential_Search/profile.asp
Veterinarian, Livestock #3.......................http://agr.wa.gov/FoodAnimal/Livestock/CertifiedVeterinarians.htm
Veterinary Medical Clerk #11...................https://fortress.wa.gov/doh/hpqa1/Application/Credential_Search/profile.asp
Viatical Settlement Provider #25..............www.insurance.wa.gov/cgi-bin/PubInfoApps/CGIViaticalSP.exe
Whitewater River Outfitter #32.................https://fortress.wa.gov/dol/dolprod/profquery/
Wrestler #27..https://fortress.wa.gov/dol/dolprod/profquery/
X-ray Technician #11 ....https://fortress.wa.gov/doh/hpqa1/Application/Credential_Search/profile.asp

Washington Licensing Quick Finder

Acupuncturist #11	360-236-4700
Adult Family Home #30	360-725-2300
Animal Technician #11	360-236-4700
Announcer, Athletic Event (Ring) #27	360-664-6644
Applicator, Commercial #5	877-301-4555
Applicator, Private Commercial #5	877-301-4555
Architect #26	360-664-1388
Architect Corporation #26	360-664-1388
Athlete, Professional #27	360-664-6644
Athletic Inspector #27	360-664-6644
Athletic Judge/Timekeeper/Physician #27	360-664-6644
Athletic Manager/Promoter/Matchmaker #27	360-664-6644
Attorney #23	206-727-8200
Auction Company #33	360-664-6636
Auctioneer #33	360-664-6636
Audiologist #11	360-236-4700
Bail Bond Agent/Agency #15	360-664-6624
Bail Bond Recovery Agent #15	360-664-6624
Bank #7	360-902-8704
Barber #18	360-664-6626
Barber Instructor/School #18	360-664-6626
Barber Shop/Mobile/Booth #18	360-664-6626
Battery Collector #32	330-664-1400
Beauty Shop/Salon/Mobile #18	360-664-6626
Boarding Home #30	360-725-2300
Boiler Inspector #13	360-902-5270
Boxer #27	360-664-6644
Brand #3	360-902-1855
Bulk Hauler #14	360-664-6466
Business Opportunity Offering #7	360-902-8760
Camping Resort #33	360-664-6646
Cemetery #6	360-664-1555
Charitable Gift Annuity #25	360-725-7144
Check Casher/Seller #7	360-902-8703
Child Care Facility #29	866-482-4325
Child Care Provider #29	866-482-4325
Chiropractor #11	360-236-4700
Cigarette Retailer/Vender/Whlse #32	330-664-1400
Collection Agency #32	360-664-1389
Commodity Registration #7	360-902-8760
Concealed Pistol License #15	360-664-6616
Consumer Loan Company #7	360-902-8703
Contractor, General, Company #12	360-902-5202
Contractor, General, Individual #32	330-664-1400
Cosmetologist #18	360-664-6626
Cosmetology (Barber) #33	360-664-6626
Cosmetology Instructor/School #18	360-664-6626
Counselor #11	360-236-4700
Court Reporter #33	360-664-6633
Credit Union #7	360-902-8701
Crematory #6	360-664-1555
Dental Hygienist #11	360-236-4700
Dentist #11	360-236-4700
Dietitian #11	360-236-4700
Domestic Insurance Carrier #25	360-725-7144
Egg Handler/Dealer #32	330-664-1400
Egg Inspector #4	360-902-1830
Electrical Contractor/Admin. #12	360-902-5269
Electrician #12	360-902-5269
Embalmer #6	360-664-1555
Emergency Medical Technician #11	360-236-2845
Employment Agency #32	360-664-1389
Employment Directory Service #32	330-664-1400
Engineer #10	360-664-1575
Engineering Geologist #21	360-664-1497
Engineering/Land Surveying Company #10	360-664-1575
Escrow Company/Officers #7	360-902-8703
Esthetician Shop/Salon/Booth/Mobile #18	360-664-6626
Esthetician/Esthetician Instructor #18	360-664-6626

Feedlot #3	360-902-1855
Fertilizer Distributor, Bulk #32	330-664-1400
Firearms Dealer #15	360-664-6616
Firearms License, Alien #15	360-664-6616
Fishing, Commercial #8	360-902-2464
Foster Home #31	888-794-1794
Franchise #7	360-902-8760
Fruit/Vegetable Inspector #4	360-902-1832
Funeral Director/Establishment #6	360-664-1555
Gaming Operation #24	360-486-3440
Gaming-related Occupation #24	360-486-3440
Geologist #21	360-664-1497
Grain Inspector/Weigher/Sampler #28	360-902-1921
Healthcare Service Company #25	360-725-7144
Hearing Instrument Fitter/Dispen'r#11	360-236-4700
HMO #25	360-725-7144
Home Health Care Agency #9	360-705-6611
Horse Racing #22	360-459-6462
Horse Racing-related Occupation #22	360-459-6462
Hospital #9	360-705-6611
Hydrogeologist #21	360-664-1497
Hypnotherapist #11	360-236-4700
Insurance Agent/Broker #25	360-725-7144
Insurance Broker, Resident/Non-Resident #25	360-725-7144
Insurance Company #25	360-725-7144
Insurance Corporation, Resident #25	360-725-7144
Investment Advisors #7	360-902-8760
Kickboxer #27	360-664-6644
Land Development Rep #16	306-664-6500/6488
Land Surveyor/SurveyorTrainee #10	360-664-1575
Landscape Architect #26	360-664-1388
Liquor Store #19	360-664-1600
Livestock Brand Record #3	360-902-1855
Livestock Market #3	360-902-1855
Lottery Retailer #32	330-664-1400
Manicure Shop/Mobile/Booth #18	360-664-6626
Manicurist/Esthetician #33	360-664-6626
Manicurist/Manicurist Instructor #18	360-664-6626
Manufactured Home Dealer #14	360-664-6466
Marriage & Family Therapist #11	360-236-4700
Massage Therapist #11	360-236-4700
Medical Doctor #11	360-236-4700
Mental Health Counselor #11	360-236-4700
Midwife #11	360-236-4700
Minor Worker #32	330-664-1400
Mobile Home/Travel Trailer Dealer #14	360-664-6466
Mortgage Broker #7	360-902-8703
Naturopathic Physician #11	360-236-4700
Notary Public #17	360-664-1550
Nurse/Nursing Assistant #11	360-236-4700
Nurse-LPN #11	360-236-4700
Nursery Retailer/Whlse #32	330-664-1400
Nursing Home Administrator #11	360-236-4700
Nursing Homes #30	360-725-2300
Occupational Therapist #11	360-236-4700
Ocularist #11	360-236-4700
Optician #11	360-236-4700
Optometrist #11	360-236-4700
Osteopathic Physician #11	360-236-4700
Pest Control Operator/Consultant, Public #5	877-301-4555
Pesticide Dealer/Manager #5	877-301-4555
Pesticide Demo & Research Applicator #5	877-301-4555
Pesticide Operator/Applicator #5	877-301-4555
Pesticide Private Application #5	877-301-4555
Pharmacist #11	360-236-4700
Pharmacy Technician #11	360-236-4700
Physical Therapist #11	360-236-4700
Physician Assistant #11	360-236-4700
Pilot, Marine, Commercial #2	206-515-3904
Plumber #12	360-902-5207

Podiatrist #11	360-236-4700
Private Investigate/Agency/Trainer #15	360-664-6611
Private Investigator, Armed/Unarmed #15	360-664-6611
Professional Athlete #33	360-664-6644
Psychologist #11	360-236-4700
Public Accountant-CPA #1	360-753-2585
Purchasing Group (Insurance) #25	360-725-7144
Radiologic Technologist #11	360-236-4700
Real Estate Agent/Sales #16	360-664-6500/6488
Real Estate Appraiser, Cert./Licensed #16	306-664-6504/6488
Real Estate Broker #16	360-664-6500/6488
Real Estate LLC, LLP, Corp./Partnership #16	360-664-6500/6488
Recreational Hunting #8	360-902-2464
Referee (Athletic) #27	360-664-6644
Refrigerated Locker #32	330-664-1400
Rental Car #32	330-664-1400
Respiratory Therapist #11	360-236-4700
Risk Retention Group #25	360-725-7144
Salon #33	360-664-6626
Savings & Loan/Savings Bank #7	306-902-8704
School Counselor #20	360-725-6400
School Nurse #20	360-725-6400
School Occ./Physical Therapist #20	360-725-6400
School Principal/Superintendent #20	360-725-6400
School Program Administrator #20	360-725-6400
School Psychologist/Social Worker #20	360-725-6400
Scrap Processor #14	360-664-6466
Securities Broker/Dealer #7	360-902-8760
Securities Salesperson #7	306-902-8760
Security Guard, Private Armed/Unarmed #15	360-664-6611
Security Guard/Agency #15	360-664-6611
Seed Dealer #32	330-664-1400
Service Contract Provider (Ins) #25	360-725-7144
Sex Offender Treatment Provider #11	360-236-4700
Shopkeeper (non-prescription drug)#32	330-664-1400
Snowmobile Dealer #14	360-664-6466
Social Worker #11	360-236-4700
Speech-Language Pathologist #11	360-236-4700
Speed Pathology Audiologist #20	360-725-6400
Sport Fishing #8	360-902-2464
Structural Pest Inspector #5	877-301-4555
Teacher #20	360-725-6400
Telephone Solicitor #32	330-664-1400
Timeshare Seller/Company/Proj'ct #33	360-664-6632
Tow Truck Operator #14	360-664-6466
Travel Agency #33	360-664-6634
Travel Seller #33	360-664-6634
Trust Company #7	360-902-8704
Underground Storage Tank #32	330-664-1400
Vehicle Dealer/Manufacturer #14	360-664-6466
Vehicle for Hire #32	330-664-1400
Vehicle Sales/Disposal #32	330-664-1400
Vehicle Transporter #14	360-664-6466
Vessel Dealer #14	360-664-6466
Veterinarian #11	360-236-4700
Veterinarian, Livestock #3	360-902-1855
Veterinary Medical Clerk #11	360-236-4700
Viatical Settlement Provider #25	360-725-7144
Waste Tire Carrier #32	330-664-1400
Waste Tire Site Owner #32	330-664-1400
Wastewater System Designer/Inspector #10	360-664-1575
Weights & Measures #3	360-902-1857
Whitewater River Outfitter #32	330-664-1400
Wrecker #14	360-664-6466
Wrestler #27	360-664-6644
X-ray Technician #11	360-236-4700

Washington Licensing Agency Information

1 Board of Accountancy, PO Box 9131, Olympia, WA 98507-9131; 360-753-2585, Fax: 360-664-9190. www.cpaboard.wa.gov Email: webmaster@cpaboard.wa.gov Search Database at www.cpaboard.wa.gov/search/default.htm

2 Board of Pilotage Commissioners, 2911 2nd Ave, Seattle, WA 98121-1012; 206-515-3904, Fax: 206-515-3906. Email: larsonp@wsdot.wa.gov

3 Department of Agriculture, Livestock Division, PO Box 42560 (1111 Washington St SE), Olympia, WA 98504-2560; 360-902-1800, Fax: 360-902-2086. http://agr.wa.gov Email: livestockid@agr.wa.gov

4 Department of Agriculture, Food Safety & Animal Health Division, PO Box 42560 (1111 Washington St SE), Olympia, WA 98504-2560; 360-902-1800, Fax: 360-902-2092. http://agr.wa.gov/default.htm

5 Department of Agriculture, Pesticides Management Division, PO Box 42589, Olympia, WA 98504-2589; 877-301-4555, Fax: 360-902-2093. http://agr.wa.gov/PestFert/default.htm Email: mtucker@agr.wa.gov Search Database at http://agr.wa.gov/PestFert/LicensingEd/default.htm Note: Will Provide lists of business names, but not individual names.

6 Department of Licensing, Funeral & Cemetery Licensing Program, PO Box 9012, Olympia, WA 98507-9012; 360-664-1555, Fax: 360-586-4414. www.dol.wa.gov/unfc/funfront.htm Email: funerals@dol.wa.gov Search Database at https://fortress.wa.gov/dol/dolprod/profquery/

7 Department of Financial Institutions, PO Box 41200, (150 Israel Rd SW Tumwater WA 98501), Olympia, WA 98504-1200; 360-902-8700, Fax: 360-586-5068. www.wa.gov/dfi

8 Department of Fish & Wildlife, 600 Capitol Way N, Olympia, WA 98501-1091; 360-902-2954, Fax: 360-902-2171. http://wdfw.wa.gov Email: licensing@dfw.wa.gov

9 Department of Health, Facilities Services Licensing, PO Box 47852, Olympia, WA 98504; 360-236-2900, Fax: 360-236-2901. www.doh.wa.gov/hsqa/fsl/default.htm Email: information@doh.wa.gov Search Database at www.doh.wa.gov/Licensing.htm

10 Department of Licensing, Professional Engineers and Land Surveyors Section, PO Box 9025, Olympia, WA 98507-9025; 360-664-1575, Fax: 360-664-2551. www.dol.wa.gov/engineers/engfront.htm Email: engineers@dol.wa.gov

11 Department of Health, Health Professional Licensing, PO Box 47865 (310 Israel Rd, Tumwater), Olympia, WA 98504; 360-236-4700, Fax: 360-236-4818. www.doh.wa.gov/Licensing.htm Search Database at https://fortress.wa.gov/doh/hpqa1/Application/Credential_Search/profile.asp

12 Department of Labor & Industries, Construction Compliance, PO Box 44000, Olympia, WA 98504-4000; 360-902-5226, Fax: 360-902-5228. www.lni.wa.gov Email: berp235@lni.wa.gov Search Database at www.lni.wa.gov/contractors/contractor.asp

13 Department of Labor & Industries, Boiler Section, PO Box 44410, Olympia, WA 98504-4410; 360-902-5270, Fax: 360-902-5292. www.wa.gov/lni Email: mrod235@lni.wa.gov Search Database at www.lni.wa.gov/TradesLicensing/Boilers/default.asp

14 Department of Licensing, Dealer Services, PO Box 9039, Olympia, WA 98507-9039; 360-664-6466, Fax: 360-586-0479. www.dol.wa.gov/vs/dl-lic.htm Email: dealers@dol.wa.gov

15 Licensing Dept, Public Protection Unit & Firearms Program, Private Investigator, Security Guard, Bail Bond, Recovery Agents, PO Box 9034, Olympia, WA 98507-9034; 360-664-6611, Fax: 360-570-7888. www.dol.wa.gov/ppu/pifront.htm Email: Security@dol.wa.gov Search Database at https://fortress.wa.gov/dol/dolprod/profquery/

16 Department of Licensing, Real Estate & Appraiser Program, PO Box 9015 (2000 4th Ave. W), Olympia, WA 98507-9015; 360-664-6500/664-6488, Fax: 360-586-0998. www.dol.wa.gov/realestate/refront.htm Email: RealEstate@dol.gov

17 Department of Licensing, Notary Section, PO Box 9027 (405 Black Lake Blvd SW), Olympia, WA 98507-9027; 360-664-1550, Fax: 360-586-4414. www.dol.wa.gov/unfc/notfront.htm Email: intnotarie@dol.wa.gov Search Database at https://fortress.wa.gov/dol/dolprod/profquery/

18 Department of Licensing, Cosmetology Division, PO Box 9026, Olympia, WA 98507-9026; 360-664-6626, Fax: 360-664-2550. www.dol.wa.gov/plss/cosfront.htm Email: plssunit@dol.wa.gov Search Database at https://fortress.wa.gov/dol/dolprod/profquery/

19 Liquor Control Board, 3000 Paciic Ave. SE, Olympia, WA 98504-3075; 360-664-1600, Fax: 360-753-2710. www.liq.wa.gov/default.asp Email: wslcb@liq.wa.gov

20 Superintendent of Public Instruction, Professional Education & Certification, PO Box 47200 (Old Capitol Bldg), Olympia, WA 98504-7200; 360-725-6400, Fax: 360-586-0145. www.k12.wa.us/cert Email: cert@ospi.wednet.edu

21 Department of Licensing, Geologist Licensing Program, PO Box 9045, Olympia, WA 98507-9045; 360-664-1497, Fax: 360-664-1495. www.dol.wa.gov/design/geofront.htm Email: geologist@dol.wa.gov

22 Horse Racing Commission, 6326 Martin Way, #209, Olympia, WA 98516-5703; 360-459-6462, Fax: 360-459-6461. Email: whrc@whrc.state.wa.us

23 Bar Association, Washington State Service Center, 2101 4th Ave, 4th Fl, #400, Seattle, WA 98121-2599; 206-443-9722, 800-945-9722, Fax: 206-727-8319. www.wsba.org Email: questions@wsba.org Search Database at http://pro.wsba.org

24 Gambling Commission, PO Box 42400, Olympia, WA 98504-2400; 360-486-3440, Fax: 360-486-3631. www.wsgc.wa.gov Email: cld@wsgc.wa.gov Search Database at www.wsgc.wa.gov/LicSearch.asp

25 Insurance Licensing, P.O. Box 40255, Olympia, WA 98504-0255; 360-725-7144, Fax: 360-664-2782. www.insurance.wa.gov Email: georgiac@oic.wa.gov Search Database at www.insurance.wa.gov

26 Department of Licensing, Business and Professions Division, Architects & Landscape Architects, PO Box 9045, Olympia, WA 98507-9045; 360-664-1388, Fax: 360-664-1495. www.dol.wa.gov/design/arcfront.htm Email: architects@dol.wa.gov Search Database at https://fortress.wa.gov/dol/dolprod/profquery/

27 Department of Licensing, Professional Boxing, Martial Arts & Wrestling Licensing Program, PO Box 9026, Olympia, WA 98507-9026; 360-664-6644, Fax: 360-570-4956. www.dol.wa.gov/plss/pafront.htm Email: plssunit@dol.wa.gov Search Database at https://fortress.wa.gov/dol/dolprod/profquery/

28 Department of Agriculture, Commodity Inspection, 3939 Cleveland Av SE, Olympia, WA 98501; 360-902-1828, Fax: 360-586-5257. http://agr.wa.gov/aboutwsda/divisions/commodityinspection.htm Email: commodity@agr.wa.gov

29 Department of Child Care & Early Learning, PO Box 45480, Olympia, WA 98504; 360-725-4665. http://www1.dshs.wa.gov/esa/dccel/

30 Aging & Adult Services Administration, PO Box 45600, Olympia, WA 98504; 360-725-2300. www.aasa.dshs.wa.gov/default.htm

31 Children's Administration, Dept of Social & Health Services, P.O. Box 45715, Olympia, WA 98504-5715; 360-725-6701, Fax: 360-664-0744. http://www1.dshs.wa.gov/ca/index.asp Email: Children@dshs.wa.gov

32 Department of Licensing, Master License Service, PO Box 9034, Olympia, WA 98507-9034; 360-664-1400, Fax: 360-570-7875. www.dol.wa.gov/mls/reglic.htm Email: MLS@dol.wa.gov

33 Department of Licensing, Professional Licensing Support Services Unit, PO Box 9020 (1125 Washington St. SE), Olympia, WA 98507-9020; 360-664-1400, Fax: 360-664-2550. www.dol.wa.gov/ Email: plssunit@dol.wa.gov Search Database at www.dol.wa.gov/main/biglist.htm

Washington Federal Courts

The following list indicates the district and division name for each county in the state. If the bankruptcy court location is different from the district court, then the location of the bankruptcy court appears in parentheses.

Washington County/Court Cross Reference

County	District	Division
Adams	Eastern	Spokane
Asotin	Eastern	Spokane
Benton	Eastern	Spokane
Chelan	Eastern	Spokane
Clallam	Western	Tacoma (Seattle)
Clark	Western	Tacoma
Columbia	Eastern	Spokane
Cowlitz	Western	Tacoma
Douglas	Eastern	Spokane
Ferry	Eastern	Spokane
Franklin	Eastern	Spokane
Garfield	Eastern	Spokane
Grant	Eastern	Spokane
Grays Harbor	Western	Tacoma
Island	Western	Seattle
Jefferson	Western	Tacoma (Seattle)
King	Western	Seattle
Kitsap	Western	Tacoma (Seattle)
Kittitas	Eastern	Yakima (Spokane)
Klickitat	Eastern	Yakima (Spokane)
Lewis	Western	Tacoma
Lincoln	Eastern	Spokane
Mason	Western	Tacoma
Okanogan	Eastern	Spokane
Pacific	Western	Tacoma
Pend Oreille	Eastern	Spokane
Pierce	Western	Tacoma
San Juan	Western	Seattle
Skagit	Western	Seattle
Skamania	Western	Tacoma
Snohomish	Western	Seattle
Spokane	Eastern	Spokane
Stevens	Eastern	Spokane
Thurston	Western	Tacoma
Wahkiakum	Western	Tacoma
Walla Walla	Eastern	Spokane
Whatcom	Western	Seattle
Whitman	Eastern	Spokane
Yakima	Eastern	Yakima (Spokane)

Standards for Federal Courts: Search fee is $26.00 per item (one party name or case number). Copy fee is $.50 per page. Certification fee is $9.00 per document, double for exemplification, if available. All fees standard unless noted in profile. Mail Search: always enclose a stamped self addressed envelope unless otherwise noted. Most courts accept fax requests or will suggest a copying/search vendor. Before releasing records, all courts require prepayment, unless noted.

Open records are located at the court unless otherwise noted. District courts index by defendant and plaintiff as well as by case number. Bankruptcy courts usually index by debtor and case number. While most courts now have their indexes on computer, many may still maintain index card files as well.

Courts offering internet access via CM-ECF or older RACER, PACER, or Web-PACER systems charge $.08 per page fee unless noted as free. Where PACER is available, the universal sign-up number is 800-676-6856. Find PACER and the US Party/Case Index at http://pacer.psc.uscourts.gov.

US District Court

Eastern District of Washington

Spokane Division Court Clerk, PO Box 1493, Spokane, WA 99210-1493 (courier address: Rm 840, W 920 Riverside, Spokane, WA 99201), 509-353-2150, Fax-509-353-2394. Hours- 8AM-5PM. www.waed.uscourts.gov

Counties: Adams, Asotin, Benton, Chelan, Columbia, Douglas, Ferry, Franklin, Garfield, Grant, Lincoln, Okanogan, Pend Oreille, Spokane, Stevens, Walla Walla, Whitman. Also, some cases from Kittitas, Klickitat and Yakima are heard here.

Searches & Indexing: Results do not include SSN or DOB. Computer and microfiche indexes maintained. New cases in the index 2-3 days after filing date. Records purged every 6 months. Judge McDonald's records maintained in Yakima. All other cases kept in Spokane or Richland Divisions. Search Spokane Division for all cases before 1989.

Fee & Payment: Pay by Visa/MC, money order, cashier's or personal check. Payee: Clerk, US District Court. Prepayment required.

Phone Search: No searching by telephone.

Mail Search: search usually completed- 3 days. SASE not required.

In Person Search: Fee charged if court performs your search. No self-serve copier available.

E-Services: ECF replaces PACER whose records did go back to 7/1989. New records online after 1 day. ECF at https://ecf.waed.uscourts.gov **Other Online Access:** Access weekly calendar at www.waed.uscourts.gov/calendar/default.htm.

Yakima Division Court Clerk, PO Box 1493, Spokane, WA 99201 (courier address: Rm 215, 25 S 3rd St, Yakima, WA 98901), 509-575-5838, Fax-509-454-5752. Hours- 8AM-5PM. www.waed.uscourts.gov

Counties: Kittitas, Klickitat, Yakima. Case hearings are held in Yakima. Direct mail to Spokane. Some cases from Kittitas, Klickitat and Yakima are heard in Spokane or Richland.

Searches & Indexing: Results do not include SSN or DOB. Computer index maintained. For all pre-1989 cases, search at Spokane Division. New cases in the index 1 day after filing date. Records purged every 6 months. Judge McDonald's records maintained in Yakima. All other cases kept in Spokane or Richland Divisions.

Fee & Payment: Pay by Visa/MC, money order, cashier's or personal check. Payee: Clerk, US District Court. Prepayment required.

Phone Search: Some docket information is available by phone.

Mail Search: search usually completed- 1 day. Include SASE for return.

In Person Search: Fee charged if court performs your search. No self-serve copier available.

E-Services: ECF replaces PACER whose records did go back to 7/1989. ECF at https://ecf.waed.uscourts.gov **Other Online Access:** Access weekly calendar at www.waed.uscourts.gov/calendar/default.htm.

US Bankruptcy Court

Eastern District of Washington

Spokane Division Court Clerk, PO Box 2164, Spokane, WA 99210-2164 (courier address: W 904 Riverside, Suite 304, Spokane, WA 99201), 509-353-2404. www.waeb.uscourts.gov

Counties: Adams, Asotin, Benton, Chelan, Columbia, Douglas, Ferry, Franklin, Garfield, Grant, Kittitas, Klickitat, Lincoln, Okanogan, Pend Oreille, Spokane, Stevens, Walla Walla, Whitman, Yakima.

Searches & Indexing: Cases indexed by debtor, creditors, and case number. New cases in the index immediately after filing date.

Fee & Payment: Pay by money order, cashier check, business check. No personal checks. Payee: Clerk, US Bankruptcy Court. Prepayment not required for copy requests; can be billed via mail with results.

Phone Search: Only docket information is available by phone. Press extension 6. Voice Case Information Service available, call 509-353-2404.

Mail Search: search usually completed- 3 days. Include SASE for return.

In Person Search: Fee charged if court performs your search. A copy service is available. No self-serve copier available.

E-Services: ECF replaces PACER whose records did go back to 1997. ECF at https://ecf.waeb.uscourts.gov **Opinions Online:** www.waeb.uscourts.gov/JudicialOpinions/.

US District Court

Western District of Washington

Seattle Division Clerk of Court, US Courthouse, 700 W Stewart St, Seattle, WA 98101 (also use mail address for courier delivery), phone- 206-370-8400, records rm- 206-370-8400, crim dockets- 206-370-8450, civil dockets- 206-370-8450. 9AM-4:30PM. www.wawd.uscourts.gov

Counties: Island, King, San Juan, Skagit, Snohomish, Whatcom.

Searches & Indexing: Computer, microfiche and card indexes maintained. New cases in the index 10 days after filing date. Records purged never.

Fee & Payment: Pay by money order, cashier's or personal check. Payee: Clerk, US District Court. Prepayment required.

Phone Search: Docket information available by phone for civil cases since 1989 and criminal cases since 1992.

Mail Search: search usually completed- 1 week. SASE not required.

In Person Search: permitted. Outside copy service available. Self-serve copier - $.25 per page.

E-Services: ECF replaces PACER. Document images available. PACER records go back to 1988. New records online after 1 day. ECF at https://ecf.wawd.uscourts.gov **Other Online Access:** Calendars and court orders are at www.wawd.uscourts.gov/docs.

Tacoma Division Court Clerk, Clerk's Office, Rm 3100, 1717 Pacific Ave, Tacoma, WA 98402-3200 (also use mail address for courier delivery), 253-593-6313. Hours- 9AM-4:30PM. www.wawd.uscourts.gov

Counties: Clallam, Clark, Cowlitz, Grays Harbor, Jefferson, Kitsap, Lewis, Mason, Pacific, Pierce, Skamania, Thurston, Wahkiakum.

Searches & Indexing: Results do not include SSN or DOB. Computer index maintained, criminal go back to 1990, civil to 1988. Older records on microfiche and card index. New cases in the index immediately after filing date. Records purged never. District-wide searches available back to 1989.

Fee & Payment: Pay by Visa/MC, money order, cashier's or personal check. Payee: Clerk, US District Court. Prepayment required.

Phone Search: No searching by telephone.

Mail Search: search usually completed- 2-5 days. Include SASE for return.

In Person Search: Fee charged if court performs your search. No self-serve copier available.

E-Services: ECF replaces PACER. Document images available. PACER records go back to 1988. New records online after 1 day. ECF at https://ecf.wawd.uscourts.gov **Other Online Access:** Calendars and court orders are at www.wawd.uscourts.gov/docs.

US Bankruptcy Court

Western District of Washington

Seattle Division Clerk of Court, 700 Stewart St #6301, Seattle, WA 98101-1271 (also use mail address for courier delivery), 206-370-5200, Fax- 206-553-0131. Hours- 8:30AM-4:30PM. www.wawb.uscourts.gov

Counties: Clallam, Island, Jefferson, King, Kitsap, San Juan, Skagit, Snohomish, Whatcom.

Searches & Indexing: Cases indexed by debtor, creditors, and case number. Results include last 4 SSN digits. Computer, microfiche, and card indexes maintained. Microfiche goes back to 1984; computer to 2001. Open cases stored by case number. Closed cases stored by year closed, then by case number. New cases in the index 1 day after filing date. Records purged never.

Fee & Payment: Pay by money order, cashier's or personal check. No credit cards. Payee: Clerk, US Bankruptcy Court. Prepayment required.

Phone Search: Voice Case Information Service available, call 888-409-4662 or 206-370-5285.

Mail Search: search usually completed- 2-3 days. Include SASE for return.

In Person Search: Fee charged if court performs your search. Self-serve copier - $.25 per page.

E-Services: PACER online at http://pacer.wawb.uscourts.gov. PACER records go back to 1/1986. New records online after 1 day. ECF at https://ecf.wawb.uscourts.gov **Opinions Online:** www.wawb.uscourts.gov/opinions.htm. **Other Online Access:** Calendars free at www.wawb.uscourts.gov.

Tacoma Division Court Clerk, Suite 2100, 1717 Pacific Ave, Tacoma, WA 98402-3233 (use mail address for courier delivery), 253-593-6310. 8:30AM-4:30PM. www.wawb.uscourts.gov

Counties: Clark, Cowlitz, Grays Harbor, Lewis, Mason, Pacific, Pierce, Skamania, Thurston, Wahkiakum.

Searches & Indexing: Search by debtor's name back to 1987. Results include last 4 SSN digits. Computer index maintained. New cases in the index 1 day after filing. Records purged never.

Fee & Payment: Pay by attorney checks accepted. No debtor business or personal checks accepted. Payee: Clerk, US Bankruptcy Court. Prepayment required.

Phone Search: Voice Case Information Service available, call 888-409-4662 or 206-370-5285.

Mail Search: search usually completed- 1 week. SASE not required.

In Person Search: Fee charged if court performs your search. Self-serve copier - $.15 per page.

E-Services: PACER online at http://pacer.wawb.uscourts.gov. PACER records go back to 1987. New records online after 1 day. ECF at https://ecf.wawb.uscourts.gov **Opinions Online:** www.wawb.uscourts.gov/opinions.htm. **Other Online Access:** Calendars free at www.wawb.uscourts.gov.

Washington County Courts

Court	Jurisdiction	No. of Courts	How Organized
Superior Courts*	General	39	29 Districts
District Courts*	Limited	61	39 Counties
Municipal Courts	Municipal	131	131 Cities

* Profiled in this Sourcebook.

CIVIL									
Court	Tort	Contract	Real Estate	Min. Claim	Max. Claim	Small Claims	Estate	Eviction	Domestic Relations
Superior Courts*	X	X	X	$50,000	No Max		X	X	X
District Courts*	X	X		$0	$50,000	$2500			
Municipal Courts									

CRIMINAL					
Court	Felony	Misdemeanor	DWI/DUI	Preliminary Hearing	Juvenile
Superior Courts*	X				X
District Courts*		X	X	X	
Municipal Courts		X	X		

ADMINISTRATION   Court Administrator, Temple of Justice, PO Box 41174, Olympia, WA, 98504; 360-753-3365, Fax: 360-586-8869. www.courts.wa.gov

COURT STRUCTURE   District Courts retain civil records for 10 years from date of final disposition, then the records are destroyed. District Courts retain criminal records forever.

Washington has a mandatory arbitration requirement for civil disputes for $35,000 or less. However, either party may request a trial in Superior Court if dissatisfied with the arbitrator's decision.

The limit for civil actions in District Court has been increased from $35,000 to $50,000. The small claims maximum limit was raised to $4,000 in 2002.

ONLINE ACCESS   The AOC provides facilities that allow one to access information in the Judicial Information System's (JIS) statewide computer. This program of services is called JIS-Link. JIS-Link provides access to all counties and court levels. Fees include a one-time $100.00 per site, a transaction fee of $.065 per record. Case records include criminal, civil, domestic, probate, and judgments. Call 360-357-3365 or visit www.courts.wa.gov/jislink. Indexes are available electronically and via microfiche for a fee. Call the JISLink Coordinator for details.

At www.courts.wa.gov/appellate_trial_courts you will find Supreme Court and Appellate opinions. The webpage offers a notification service also.

ADD'L INFORMATION   Effective July 25, 2005, a law enacted by the State of Washington mandated a myriad of fee changes for Superior and District courts. Although these changes are related primarily to filing fees, they also pertain to certain copy fees, and certification fees. For example, in the Superior Court the new fee for an uncertified copy is $.50 and $.25 for an electronic computer printout; for a certified copy the fee is $5.00 for the first page and $1.00 for each additional page. Previously the fee per statute was $2.00 for the 1st page and $1.00 each additional per copy, certified or uncertified. At the District Court, the certification fee of $5.00 per document (not page) remains the same.

However, it appears that not all Superior Courts and District Courts are currently complying with the mandated fees changes. Therefore, we suggest that it will take some time before fees reach a true uniform status for copies and certification, if ever.

An SASE is required in most courts that respond to written search requests.

Adams County

Superior Court PO Box 187, 210 W Broadway, Ritzville, WA 99169-0187; phone: 509-659-3257; criminal fax: 509-659-0118; same fax for civil/probate; hours 8:30AM-N, 1-4:30PM (PST). *Felony, Civil, Eviction, Probate.*
Civil Records: Access: Phone, fax, mail, online, in person. Only the court performs in person searches; visitors may not. Search fee: $20.00 per hour. Court makes copy: $.50 per page. Required to search: name, years to search; also helpful: address. Civil cases indexed by defendant, plaintiff. Civil records on computer from 1985, archived from 1900s. Index online from JIS-Link; see www.courts.wa.gov/jislink (also, see state introduction). User ID and password required. Mail turnaround time 1 week.
Criminal Records: Access: Phone, fax, mail, online, in person. Only the court performs in person searches; visitors may not. Search fee: $20.00 per hour. Court makes copy: $.50 per page. Required to search: name, years to search; also helpful: address, DOB, SSN. Criminal records on computer from 1985, archived from 1900s. Index remotely online from JIS-Link; see www.courts.wa.gov/jislink (also, see state introduction). User ID and password required. Mail turnaround time 1 week.
General Information: No sealed, adoption, paternity, mental health, sex offenders (victims) records released. Will fax documents $1.00 per page. Certification fee: $5.00 plus $1.00 each add'l page. Cert fee includes copies. Payee: Adams County Clerk. Business checks accepted. Prepayment and SASE required.

Othello District Court 165 N 1st, Othello, WA 99344; phone: 509-488-3935; fax: 509-488-3480; hours 8:30AM-4:30PM (PST). *Misdemeanor, Civil Actions Under $50,000, Small Claims.*
Civil Records: Access: Phone, fax, mail, online, in person. Only the court performs in person searches; visitors may not. No search fee. Court makes copy: $2.50 for first page, $1.00 each add'l. Required to search: name, years to search; also helpful: address. Civil cases indexed by defendant, plaintiff. Civil records on computer for 10 years, prior on index cards. Index online from JIS-Link; see www.courts.wa.gov/jislink (also, see state introduction). Mail turnaround time 1-3 days.
Criminal Records: Access: Phone, fax, mail, online, in person. Only the court performs in person searches; visitors may not. No search fee. Court makes copy: $2.50 for first page, $1.00 each add'l. Required to search: name, years to search, signed release; also helpful: address, DOB, SSN. Criminal records on computer for 10 years, prior on index cards. Index remotely online from JIS-Link; see www.courts.wa.gov/jislink (also, see state introduction). Mail turnaround time 1-3 days.
General Information: No sealed, juvenile, adoption, paternity, mental health, sex offenders (victims) or (sometimes) DUI records released. No fee to fax documents. Certification fee: $6.00. Payee: Othello District Court. Personal checks accepted. Prepayment and SASE required.

Ritzville District Court 210 W Broadway, Ritzville, WA 99169; phone: 509-659-1002; fax: 509-659-0118; hours 8:30AM-4:30PM (PST). *Misdemeanor, Civil Actions Under $50,000, Small Claims.*
Civil Records: Access: Fax, mail, online, in person. Only the court performs in person searches; visitors may not. No search fee. Court makes copy: $1.00 per page; same fee for self serve. Required to search: name, years to search; also helpful: address. Civil cases indexed by defendant, plaintiff. Civil records on computer from 10/90. Index online from JIS-Link; see www.courts.wa.gov/jislink (also, see state introduction). Mail turnaround time 2 days.
Criminal Records: Access: Fax, mail, online, in person. Only the court performs in person searches; visitors may not. No search fee. Court makes copy: $1.00 per page; same fee for self serve. Required to search: name, years to search, DOB; also helpful: address, SSN. Criminal records on computer from 10/90. Index remotely online from JIS-Link; see www.courts.wa.gov/jislink (also, see state introduction). Mail turnaround time 2 days.
General Information: No sealed, juvenile, adoption, paternity, mental health, sex offenders (victims) or (sometimes) DUI records released. No fee to fax documents. Certification fee: $5.00 1st page, $1.00 ea add'l. Payee: Ritzville District Court. Personal checks accepted. Prepayment and SASE required.

Asotin County

Superior Court PO Box 159, Asotin, WA 99402-0159; phone: 509-243-2081; fax: 509-243-4978; hours 8AM-5PM (PST). *Felony, Civil, Eviction, Probate.*
Civil Records: Access: Phone, fax, mail, online, in person. Only the court performs in person searches; visitors may not. No search fee. Court makes copy: $.50 per page. Required to search: name, years to search; also helpful: address. Civil cases indexed by defendant, plaintiff. Civil records on computer from mid 1985, on microfiche from 1970s, archived from 1895. Index online from JIS-Link; see www.courts.wa.gov/jislink (also, see state introduction). Mail turnaround time 1-5 days.
Criminal Records: Access: Phone, fax, mail, online, in person. Only the court performs in person searches; visitors may not. No search fee. Court makes copy: $.50 per page. Required to search: name, years to search, DOB; also helpful: address, SSN. Criminal records on computer from mid 1985, on microfiche from 1970s, archived from 1895. Index remotely online from JIS-Link; see www.courts.wa.gov/jislink (also, see state introduction). Mail turnaround time 1 day.
General Information: No sealed, juvenile, adoption, paternity, mental health, sex offenders (victims) or (sometimes) DUI records released. Certification fee: $5.00 1st page, $1.00 ea add'l. Cert fee includes copies. Payee: Asotin County Clerk. Personal checks accepted. Prepayment and SASE required.

District Court PO Box 429, Asotin, WA 99402-0429; phone: 509-243-2027; fax: 509-243-2091; hours 8AM-5PM (PST). *Misdemeanor, Civil Actions Under $50,000, Small Claims.*
Civil Records: Access: Fax, mail, online, in person. Only the court performs in person searches; visitors may not. Search fee: $6.00 per name. Court makes copy: $.50 per page; same fee for self serve. Required to search: name, years to search; also helpful: address. Civil cases indexed by defendant, plaintiff. Civil records on computer since 1993; prior records on log books. Index online from JIS-Link; see www.courts.wa.gov/jislink (also, see state introduction). Mail turnaround time up to 2 weeks.
Criminal Records: Access: Fax, mail, online, in person. Only the court performs in person searches; visitors may not. Search fee: $6.00 per name. Court makes copy: $.50 per page; same fee for self serve. Required to search: name, years to search; also helpful: address, DOB, SSN. Criminal records on computer from 1993. Index remotely online from JIS-Link; see www.courts.wa.gov/jislink (also, see state introduction). Mail turnaround time up to 2 weeks.
General Information: No sealed, juvenile, adoption, paternity, mental health, sex offenders (victims) or (sometimes) DUI records released. No fee to fax documents. Certification fee: $12.00 include copies. Payee: Asotin County District Court. Personal checks accepted. Prepayment and SASE required.

Benton County

Superior Court 7320 W Quinault, Kennewick, WA 99336-7690; phone: 509-735-8388; hours 8AM-N, 1-4PM (PST). *Felony, Civil, Probate.*
Civil Records: Access: Mail, in person, online. Only the court performs in person searches; visitors may not. Search fee: $20.00 per hour. Court makes copy: $.50 per page. Required to search: name, years to search; also helpful: address. Civil cases indexed by defendant, plaintiff. Civil records on computer from 1979, pre-1979 on index books. Index online from JIS-Link; see www.courts.wa.gov/jislink (also, see state introduction). Mail turnaround time 10 days.
Criminal Records: Access: Mail, in person, online. Only the court performs in person searches; visitors may not. Search fee: $20.00 per hour. Court makes copy: $.50 per page. Required to search: name, years to search; also helpful: address, DOB, SSN. Criminal records on computer from 1979, pre-1979 on index books. Index remotely online from JIS-Link; see www.courts.wa.gov/jislink (also, see state introduction). Mail turnaround time 10 days.
General Information: No sealed, dependency, adoption, paternity, mental health, sex offenders (victims). Will fax documents $3.00 1st page, $1.00 each add'l. Certification fee: $5.00 plus $1.00 per page after first. Payee: Benton County Clerk. Personal checks accepted. Prepayment and SASE required.

District Court 7122 W Okanogan Pl, Box E, Kennewick, WA 99336; phone: 509-735-8476; 786-5602; fax: 509-736-3069; hours 8AM-N, 1-4PM (PST). *Misdemeanor, Civil Actions Under $50,000, Small Claims.*
Civil Records: Access: Mail, fax, online, in person. Both court and visitors may perform in person searches. Search fee: $10.00 per name. Court makes copy: first 50 copies free, then $.15 each. Required to search: name, years to search; also helpful: address. Civil cases indexed by defendant, plaintiff. Civil records on computer from 7/91. Index online from JIS-Link; see www.courts.wa.gov/jislink (also, see state introduction). Mail turnaround time 10 days.
Criminal Records: Access: Mail, fax, online, in person. Both court and visitors may perform in person searches. Search fee: $10.00 per name. Court makes copy: first 50 copies free, then $.15 each. Required to search: name, years to search, DOB, signed release; also helpful: address, SSN. Criminal records on computer from 7/91, stored from 1988. Index remotely online from JIS-Link; see www.courts.wa.gov/jislink (also, see state introduction). Mail turnaround time 10 days.
General Information: Public terminal goes back to 1992. No sealed, juvenile, adoption, paternity, mental health, sex offenders (victims) or (sometimes) DUI records released. Certification fee: $5.00 per doc. Payee: Benton County District Court. Personal checks accepted. Prepayment required. SASE requested.

Chelan County

Superior Court PO Box 3025, 350 Orondo, Wenatchee, WA 98807-3025; phone: 509-667-6380; fax: 509-667-6611; hours 9AM-5PM (PST). *Felony, Civil, Eviction, Probate, Domestic.*
www.co.chelan.wa.us
Civil Records: Access: Phone, fax, mail, online, in person. Both court and visitors may perform in person searches. Search fee: $20.00 per hour. Court makes copy: $.50 per page; same fee for self serve. Required to search: name, years to search. Civil cases indexed by defendant, plaintiff. Civil docket records on computer back to 1984; prior on microfilm to 1900. Civil records from 1993 forward and probate from 1975 forward by online subscription at web page. Subscribers may also file online. Index online from JIS-Link; see www.courts.wa.gov/jislink (also, see state introduction). Note: Current dockets and schedule are at www.co.chelan.wa.us/scc/scc4.htm. Mail turnaround time 1 day.
Criminal Records: Access: Phone, fax, mail, online, in person. Both court and visitors may perform in person searches. Search fee: $20.00 per hour. Court makes copy: $.50 per page; same fee for self serve. Required to search: full name, years to search; also helpful: address, DOB. Criminal records on computer back to 1984; prior on microfilm to 1900. Records from 1992 forward by online subscription at web page. Subscribers may also file online. Index is

remotely online from JIS-Link; see www.courts.wa.gov/jislink (also, see state introduction). Note: Current dockets and schedule is at www.co.chelan.wa.us/scc/scc4.htm. Mail turnaround time 1 day.

General Information: Public terminal goes back to 1996. No sealed, juvenile, adoption, paternity, mental health, sex offenders (victims) records released. Will fax documents $3.00 1st page, $1.00 each add'l. Certification fee: $5.00 1st page, $1.00 ea add'l. Cert fee includes copies. Payee: Chelan County Clerk. Personal checks and credit cards accepted. Prepayment and SASE required.

Chelan County District Court PO Box 2182, 350 Orondo, Courthouse 4th Fl, Wenatchee, WA 98807; phone: 509-667-6600; fax: 509-667-6456; hours 8:30AM-4:30PM (PST). *Misdemeanor, Civil Actions Under $50,000, Small Claims.*
www.co.chelan.wa.us/dc/dc1.htm

Civil Records: Access: Fax, mail, online, in person. Both court and visitors may perform in person searches. Search fee: $15.00 per name. Court makes copy: $2.00 for first page, $1.00 each add'l. Required to search: name; also helpful: years to search, address. Civil cases indexed by defendant, plaintiff. Civil records on computer from 1984. Records destroyed 3 years from closure. Index online from JIS-Link; see www.courts.wa.gov/jislink (also, see state introduction). Mail turnaround time 1 week.

Criminal Records: Access: Fax, mail, online, in person. Both court and visitors may perform in person searches. Search fee: $15.00 per name. Court makes copy: $2.00 for first page, $1.00 each add'l. Required to search: name, DOB, signed release; also helpful: years to search, address, SSN, aliases. Criminal records on computer. Criminal files may be destroyed 3 years after close of case, infractions destroyed 3 years after close. Index remotely online from JIS-Link; see www.courts.wa.gov/jislink (also, see state introduction). Mail turnaround time 1 week.

General Information: Public terminal has criminal back to 5 years and civil back to 10 years. No sealed, domestic violence victim info, alcohol/probation evaluation records released. Certification fee: $5.00. Payee: Chelan County District Court. Personal checks accepted. Prepayment and SASE required.

Clallam County

Superior Court 223 E 4th St, #9, Port Angeles, WA 98362-3098; phone: 360-417-2508; probate phone: 306-417-2507; hours 8:30AM-4:30PM (PST). *Felony, Civil, Eviction, Probate.*
www.clallam.net/scourt/

Civil Records: Access: Phone, mail, in person. Both court and visitors may perform in person searches. Search fee: $20.00 per hour. Court makes copy: $.10 per page; same fee for self serve. Required to search: name, years to search; also helpful: address. Civil cases indexed by defendant, plaintiff. Civil records on computer from 10/83, on microfiche from 1914, some records on index cards. Mail turnaround time minimum 1 week.

Criminal Records: Access: Phone, mail, online, in person. Both court and visitors may perform in person searches. Search fee: $20.00 per hour. Court makes copy: $.10 per page; same fee for self serve. Required to search: name, years to search; also helpful: address, DOB. Criminal records on computer from 10/83, on microfiche from 1914, some records on index cards. Criminal Index remotely online from JIS-Link; see www.courts.wa.gov/jislink (also, see state introduction). Mail turnaround time minimum 1 week.

General Information: Public terminal goes back to 10/13/83. No sealed, juvenile, adoption, paternity, mental health, sex offenders (victims) records released. Fee to fax documents is $3.00 plus $1.00 per page. Certification fee: $5.00 plus $1.00 per page after first. Payee: Clerk. Business checks accepted. Prepayment and SASE required.

District Court 1 223 E 4th St, Port Angeles, WA 98362; phone: 360-417-2560; fax: 360-417-2403; hours 8:30AM-4:30PM (PST). *Misdemeanor, Civil Actions Under $50,000, Small Claims.*
www.clallam.net/Departments/html/dept_dc1.htm

Note: District 1 Court also has jurisdiction on Civil Anti-Harassment Petitions and Orders.

Civil Records: Access: Mail, fax, online, in person. Visitors must perform in person searches themselves. No search fee. Court makes copy: $.15 per page. Required to search: name, years to search; also helpful: address. Civil cases indexed by defendant, plaintiff. Civil records on computer from 1986. Index online from JIS-Link; see www.courts.wa.gov/jislink (also, see state introduction). Mail turnaround time up to 1 week.

Criminal Records: Access: Mail, fax, online, in person. Visitors must perform in person searches themselves. No search fee. Court makes copy: $.15 per page. Required to search: name, years to search, DOB, signed release; also helpful: address, SSN, nationality. Criminal records on computer from 1986. Index remotely online from JIS-Link; see www.courts.wa.gov/jislink (also, see state introduction). Mail turnaround time up to 1 week.

General Information: Public use terminal available. No sealed, juvenile, adoption, paternity, mental health, sex offenders (victims) or (sometimes) DUI records released. Certification fee: $5.00 per document. Payee: Clallam County District Court 1. Personal checks accepted. Prepayment required.

District Court II 502 E Division St, Forks, WA 98331; phone: 360-374-6383; fax: 360-374-2100; hours 8:30AM-4:30PM (PST). *Misdemeanor, Civil Actions Under $50,000, Small Claims.*
www.clallam.net/Courts/html/court_district_2.htm

Note: Clallam County District Court II serves the West End of Clallam County, including Forks, Neah Bay, Clallam Bay, Sekiu and LaPush.

Civil Records: Access: Mail, online, in person. Both court and visitors may perform in person searches. No search fee. Court makes copy: $.15 per page. Required to search: name, years to search; also helpful: address. Civil cases indexed by defendant, plaintiff. Civil records on computer from 1989, records go back to 1988. Index online from JIS-Link; see www.courts.wa.gov/jislink (also, see state introduction). Mail turnaround time 2 weeks.

Criminal Records: Access: Mail, online, in person. Both court and visitors may perform in person searches. No search fee. Court makes copy: $.15 per page. Required to search: name, years to search DOB; also helpful: address, SSN. Criminal records on computer from 1992 (some back to 1989), on index cards from 1982-1986. Index remotely online from JIS-Link; see www.courts.wa.gov/jislink (also, see state introduction). Mail turnaround time 2 weeks.

General Information: Public terminal has only criminal records. No sealed, juvenile, adoption, paternity, mental health, sex offenders (victims) or (sometimes) DUI records released. Fee to fax documents is $1.00 per page. Certification fee: $5.00 1st page, $1.00 ea add'l. Cert fee includes copies. Payee: Clallam County District II Court. Personal checks accepted. Prepayment and SASE required or provide postage.

Clark County

Superior Court PO Box 5000, Attn: County Clerk, 1200 Franklin St, Vancouver, WA 98666; phone: 360-397-2049 Court Admin.; criminal phone: 360-397-2292; civil phone: 360-397-2292; fax: 360-397-6099; hours 8AM-4:30PM (PST). *Felony, Civil, Eviction, Probate.*
www.clark.wa.gov/courts/superior/index.html

Civil Records: Access: Phone, mail, online, in person, email. Both court and visitors may perform in person searches. Search fee: $20.00 per hour. Court makes copy: $.50 per page; same fee for self serve. Required to search: name, years to search. Civil cases indexed by defendant, plaintiff. Civil records on computer back to 1979 indexed, on microfiche from 1960, and index books prior to 1979. Index online from JIS-Link; see www.courts.wa.gov/jislink (also, see state introduction). Also, daily dockets at www.clark.wa.gov/courts/superior/docket.html. Mail turnaround time 1-3 days.

Criminal Records: Access: Phone, mail, online, in person, email. Both court and visitors may perform in person searches. Search fee: $20.00 per hour. Court makes copy: $.50 per page; same fee for self serve. Required to search: name, years to search, DOB; also helpful: address, signed release (if for employment). Criminal records on computer back to 1979, prior to 1988 on microfilm. Index remotely online from JIS-Link; see www.courts.wa.gov/jislink (also, see state introduction). Also, daily dockets are at www.clark.wa.gov/courts/superior/docket.html. Mail turnaround time 1-3 days.

General Information: Public use terminal available. No sealed, juvenile, adoption, paternity, mental health, sex offenders (victims). Certification fee: $5.00 1st page, $1.00 ea add'l. Payee: County Clerk. Only cashiers checks, money orders and attorney checks accepted. Prepayment required.

District Court PO Box 9806, 1200 Franklin St, Vancouver, WA 98666-8806; criminal phone: 360-397-2424; civil phone: 360-397-2424; fax: 360-397-6044; hours 8AM-5PM (PST). *Misdemeanor, Civil Actions Under $50,000, Small Claims.*
www.clark.wa.gov/courts/district/index.html

Civil Records: Access: Fax, mail, online, in person. Only the court performs in person searches; visitors may not. No search fee. Court makes copy: first 6 free, then $1.00 7-13, $2.00 14-19, etc. Required to search: name, years to search; also helpful: address. Civil cases indexed by defendant, plaintiff. Civil records on computer for approximately ten years. Index online from JIS-Link; see www.courts.wa.gov/jislink (also, see state introduction). Also, daily dockets are at www.clark.wa.gov/courts/district/docket.html. Mail turnaround time 1 week.

Criminal Records: Access: Fax, mail, online, in person. Only the court performs in person searches; visitors may not. No search fee. Court makes copy: first 6 free, then $1.00 7 to 13, $2.00 14-19, etc. Required to search: name, DOB, signed release; also helpful: years to search, address, SSN. Criminal records on computer for approximately five years. Index remotely online from JIS-Link; see www.courts.wa.gov/jislink (also, see state introduction). Also, daily dockets are at www.clark.wa.gov/courts/district/docket.html. Mail turnaround time 1 week.

General Information: No sealed, juvenile, adoption, paternity, mental health, sex offenders (victims) or (sometimes) DUI records released. No fee to fax documents. Certification fee: $5.00 per doc. Payee: Clark County District Court. Personal checks accepted. Prepayment required.

Columbia County

Superior Court 341 E Main St, Dayton, WA 99328; phone: 509-382-4321; criminal fax: 509-382-4830; same fax for civil/probate; hours 8:30AM-N, 1-4:30PM (PST). *Felony, Civil, Eviction, Probate.*

Civil Records: Access: Phone, fax, mail, online, in person. Only the court performs in person searches; visitors may not. Search fee: $20.00 per hour. Court makes copy: $.50 per page; same fee for self serve. Required to search: name, years to search. Civil cases indexed by defendant, plaintiff. Civil records on computer from 1987, some records on index cards and books, archived from 1900s. Index online from JIS-Link; see www.courts.wa.gov/jislink (also, see state introduction). Mail turnaround time 1 week.

Criminal Records: Access: Phone, fax, mail, online, in person. Only the court performs in person searches; visitors may not. Search fee: $20.00 per hour. Court makes copy: $.50 per page; same fee for self serve. Required to search: name, years to search.

Criminal records on computer from 1987, some records on index cards and books, archived from 1900s. Index remotely online from JIS-Link; see www.courts.wa.gov/jislink (also, see state introduction). Mail turnaround time 1 week.

General Information: No sealed, juvenile, adoption, paternity, mental health, sex offenders (victims). Will not fax documents. Certification fee: $5.00 plus $1.00 per page after first. Cert fee includes copies. Payee: Columbia County Clerk. Personal checks accepted. Prepayment and SASE required.

District Court 341 E Main St, Dayton, WA 99328-1361; phone: 509-382-4812; fax: 509-382-4830; hours 8:30AM-4:30PM (PST). *Misdemeanor, Civil Actions Under $50,000, Small Claims.*

Civil Records: Access: Mail, online, in person. Only the court performs in person searches; visitors may not. No search fee. Court makes copy: $.50 per page. Required to search: name, years to search; also helpful: address. Civil cases indexed by plaintiff. Civil records on computer since 5/96; prior on index books. Index online from JIS-Link; see www.courts.wa.gov/jislink (also, see state introduction). Mail turnaround time 7-10 days.

Criminal Records: Access: Mail, online, in person. Only the court performs in person searches; visitors may not. Search fee: Fee may be charged if more than 1 case. Court makes copy: $.50 per page. Required to search: name, years to search, DOB, signed release; also helpful: address. Criminal records on computer from 1996, on books prior. Index remotely online from JIS-Link; see www.courts.wa.gov/jislink (also, see state introduction). Mail turnaround time 7-10 days.

General Information: Will fax documents for $1.00 per page. Certification fee: $5.00 1st page, $1.00 ea add'l. Cert fee includes copies. Payee: District Court. Personal checks accepted. Prepayment and SASE required.

Cowlitz County

Superior Court 312 SW 1st Ave, Attn: County Clerk, Kelso, WA 98626-1724; phone: 360-577-3016; criminal phone: 360-577-3017; hours 8:30-5PM; doors closed at 4:30PM (PST). *Felony, Civil, Eviction, Probate.*
www.co.cowlitz.wa.us/clerk/
Civil Records: Access: Phone, fax, mail, online, in person. Both court and visitors may perform in person searches. Search fee: $10.00 per name. Court makes copy: $.50 per page. Required to search: name, years to search; also helpful: address. Civil cases indexed by defendant, plaintiff. Civil records on computer back to 1982; on microfilm through 1992. Index online from JIS-Link; see www.courts.wa.gov/jislink (also, see state introduction). Mail turnaround time 1-2 days.
Criminal Records: Access: Phone, fax, mail, online, in person. Both court and visitors may perform in person searches. Search fee: $10.00 per name. Court makes copy: $.50 per page. Required to search: name, years to search; also helpful: address, DOB, SSN. Criminal records on computer back to 1982, on microfilm through 1992. Index remotely online from JIS-Link; see www.courts.wa.gov/jislink (also, see state introduction). Mail turnaround time 1-2 days.

General Information: Public terminal goes back to 6/1982. No sealed, juvenile, adoption, paternity, mental health records released. Certain civil and domestic cases are now sealed. Will not fax documents. Certification fee: $5.00 per document. Payee: Cowlitz County Superior Court Clerk. Business checks accepted. No personal checks accepted. Prepayment and SASE required.

District Court 312 SW 1st Ave, Kelso, WA 98626-1724; phone: 360-577-3073; fax: 360-577-3132; hours 8:30AM-5PM (PST). *Misdemeanor, Civil Actions Under $50,000, Small Claims.*
www.co.cowlitz.wa.us
Civil Records: Access: Phone, fax, mail, online, in person. Only the court performs in person searches;

visitors may not. Search fee: $2 mailing fee. Court makes copy: $.15 per page; same fee for self serve. Required to search: name, DOB, years to search; also helpful: address. Civil cases indexed by defendant, plaintiff. Civil records on index cards back to 1992. Index online from JIS-Link; see www.courts.wa.gov/jislink (also, see state introduction). Mail turnaround time 2 weeks.
Criminal Records: Access: Mail, fax, online, in person. Only the court performs in person searches; visitors may not. Search fee: $2.00 for mailing. Court makes copy: $.15 per page; same fee for self serve. Required to search: name, years to search, DOB; also helpful: address, SSN. Criminal records back to 1995. Index remotely online from JIS-Link; see www.courts.wa.gov/jislink (also, see state introduction). Mail turnaround time 2 weeks.
General Information: Will not fax documents. Certification fee: $5.00 per document. Payee: District Court. Personal checks accepted. Prepayment required.

Douglas County

Superior Court PO Box 516, Waterville, WA 98858-0516; phone: 509-745-8529; fax: 509-745-8027; hours 8AM-5PM (PST). *Felony, Civil, Eviction, Probate.*
www.douglascountywa.net/
Note: Clerk is reached at 509-745-8529.
Civil Records: Access: Phone, fax, mail, online, in person. Both court and visitors may perform in person searches. Search fee: $20.00 per hour. Court makes copy: $.50 per page; $.25 if electronic email; same fee for self serve. Required to search: name, years to search; also helpful: address. Civil cases indexed by defendant, plaintiff. Civil records on computer from 1985, archived and on microfiche from 1883, some records on index books. Index online from JIS-Link; see www.courts.wa.gov/jislink (also, see state introduction). Mail turnaround time 1 week.
Criminal Records: Access: Phone, fax, mail, online, in person. Both court and visitors may perform in person searches. Search fee: $20.00 per hour. Court makes copy: $.50 per page; $.25 if electronic email; same fee for self serve. Required to search: name, years to search, DOB; also helpful: address, SSN. Criminal records on computer from 1985, archived and on microfiche from 1883, some records on index books. Index remotely online from JIS-Link; see www.courts.wa.gov/jislink (also, see state introduction). Mail turnaround time 1 week.
General Information: Public terminal goes back to 1985. No sealed, juvenile, adoption, paternity, mental health, sex offenders (victims). Will fax documents $2.00 1st page, $1.00 each add'l. Certification fee: $5.00 1st page, $1.00 ea add'l. Cert fee includes copies. Payee: Douglas County Clerk. Business checks accepted. Prepayment and SASE required.

District Court - Bridgeport PO Box 730, 1206 Columbia Ave, Bridgeport, WA 98813-0730; phone: 509-686-2034; fax: 509-686-4671; hours 8:30AM-4:30PM (PST). *Misdemeanor, Small Claims.*
www.douglascountywa.net/departments/district_court/
Note: This is a rural branch. If record not found in this court, request forwarded to East Wenatchee court (main court).
Civil Records: Access: Fax, mail, in person. Only the court performs in person searches; visitors may not. Search fee: $10.00 per name. Court makes copy: $.15 per page. Required to search: name, years to search; also helpful: address. Civil cases indexed by defendant. Civil records on computer back to 2/95. Index online from JIS-Link; see www.courts.wa.gov/jislink (also, see state introduction). Note: Please use the court's "Request for Information" form. Mail turnaround time 10 days.
Criminal Records: Access: Fax, mail, online, in person. Only the court performs in person searches; visitors may not. Search fee: $10.00 per name. Court

makes copy: $.15 per page. Required to search: name, years to search; also helpful: address, DOB, SSN. Criminal records on computer back to 2/95. Index remotely online from JIS-Link; see www.courts.wa.gov/jislink (also, see state introduction). Note: Please use the court's "Request for Information" form. Mail turnaround time 10 days.
General Information: No sealed, juvenile, adoption, paternity, mental health, sex offenders (victims) or (sometimes) DUI records released. Will fax documents to local or toll free line. Certification fee: $5.00 1st page, $1.00 ea add'l. Cert fee includes copies. Payee: Douglas County District Court Bridgeport. Personal checks accepted. Prepayment and SASE required.

District Court - East Wenatchee 110 3rd St NE, East Wenatchee, WA 98802; phone: 509-884-3536; fax: 509-884-5973; hours 8:30AM-4:30PM (PST). *Misdemeanor, Civil Actions Under $50,000, Small Claims.*
www.douglascountywa.net/departments/district_court/
Note: If record not found in this court, request forwarded to Bridgeport Branch (North) County District Court.
Civil Records: Access: Fax, mail, online, in person. Only the court performs in person searches; visitors may not. Search fee: $10.00. Court makes copy: $.15 per page; same fee for self serve. Required to search: name, years to search; also helpful: address. Civil cases indexed by defendant, plaintiff. Index online from JIS-Link; see www.courts.wa.gov/jislink (also, see state introduction). Record request forms are on the webpage. Mail turnaround time 1 week.
Criminal Records: Access: Fax, mail, online, in person. Only the court performs in person searches; visitors may not. Search fee: $10.00. Court makes copy: $.15 per page; same fee for self serve. Required to search: Full name, address, DOB, SSN. Criminal records on computer back to 1992. Index remotely online from JIS-Link; see www.courts.wa.gov/jislink (also, see state introduction). Mail turnaround time 1 week.
General Information: No sealed, juvenile, adoption, paternity, mental health, sex offenders (victims), Alcohol records, treatment reports released. Will fax documents for $1.00 1st page, $1.00 each add'l. Local faxing only. Certification fee: $5.00. Payee: Douglas District Court. Personal checks accepted. Prepayment and SASE required.

Ferry County

Superior Court 350 E Delaware, #4, Republic, WA 99166; phone: 509-775-5245; hours 8AM-4PM (PST). *Felony, Civil, Probate.*
Civil Records: Access: Phone, mail, online, in person. Both court and visitors may perform in person searches. Search fee: $20.00 per hour. Court makes copy: $2.00 for first page, $1.00 each add'l. Required to search: name, years to search; also helpful: address. Civil cases indexed by defendant, plaintiff. Civil records on computer back to 1987; other records go back to 1900. Index online from JIS-Link; see www.courts.wa.gov/jislink (also, see state introduction). Mail turnaround time 1-4 days.
Criminal Records: Access: Phone, mail, online, in person. Both court and visitors may perform in person searches. Search fee: $20.00 per hour. Court makes copy: $2.00 for first page, $1.00 each add'l. Required to search: name, years to search; also helpful: address, DOB. Criminal records on computer back to 1987; other records go back to 1900. Index remotely online from JIS-Link; see www.courts.wa.gov/jislink (also, see state introduction). Mail turnaround time 1-4 days.
General Information: Public terminal has criminal back to - not known and civil back to 1987. (Public access is very limited.) No sealed, adoption, paternity, mental health or sex offenders (victims). Will fax documents for $2.00 for 1st page and $1.00 each add'l page. Certification fee: $5.00 plus $1.00 each add'l

page. Payee: Ferry County Clerk. Business checks accepted. Prepayment and SASE required.

District Court 350 E Delaware Ave, #6, Republic, WA 99166-9747; phone: 509-775-5244; fax: 509-775-5221; hours 8AM-4PM (PST). *Misdemeanor, Civil Actions Under $50,000, Small Claims.*
www.ferry-county.com
Civil Records: Access: Fax, mail, online, in person. Only the court performs in person searches; visitors may not. No search fee. Court makes copy: $1.00 1st page, $.50 each add'l. Required to search: name, years to search; also helpful: address. Civil cases indexed by case number. Civil records on computer back to 1995; others back to 1995. Index online from JIS-Link; see www.courts.wa.gov/jislink for information (also, see state introduction). Mail turnaround time 1 week.
Criminal Records: Access: Mail, fax, online, in person. Only the court performs in person searches; visitors may not. No search fee. Court makes copy: $1.00 1st page, $.50 each add'l. Required to search: name, years to search, DOB; also helpful: address, SSN, signed release. Criminal records on computer back to 1995; others back to 1995. Index remotely online from JIS-Link; see www.courts.wa.gov/jislink (also, see state introduction). Mail turnaround time 1 week.
General Information: No sealed, juvenile, adoption, paternity, mental health, sex offenders (victims) or (sometimes) DUI records released. No fee to fax documents. Certification fee: $5.00 per cert. Payee: Ferry County District Court. Personal checks accepted. Prepayment and SASE required.

Franklin County

Superior Court 1016 N 4th Ave, Pasco, WA 99301; phone: 509-545-3525; fax: 509-545-2243; hours 8:30AM-5PM (PST). *Felony, Civil, Eviction, Probate.*
www.co.franklin.wa.us
Civil Records: Access: Mail, online, in person, email. Only the court performs in person searches; visitors may not. Search fee: $20.00 per hour. Court makes copy: $.50 per page. Required to search: name, years to search; also helpful: DOB. Civil cases indexed by defendant, plaintiff. Civil records on computer from 7/83, on index books, archived from 1900s. Index online from JIS-Link; see www.courts.wa.gov/jislink (also, see state introduction). Mail turnaround time 1 week.
Criminal Records: Access: Mail, online, in person. Only the court performs in person searches; visitors may not. Search fee: $20.00 per hour. Court makes copy: $.50 per page. Required to search: name, years to search, DOB; also helpful: address, SSN. Criminal records on computer from 7/83, on index books, archived from 1900s. Index remotely online from JIS-Link; see www.courts.wa.gov/jislink (also, see state introduction). Mail turnaround time 1 week.
General Information: No sealed, juvenile, adoption, paternity, mental health, sex offenders (victims). Fee to fax documents is $3.00 1st page, $1.00 each add'l. Certification fee: $5.00 1st page, $1.00 ea add'l. Cert fee includes copies. Payee: Franklin County Superior Court Clerk. Business checks accepted, personal checks are not. Prepayment and SASE required.

District Court 1016 N 4th St, Pasco, WA 99301; phone: 509-545-3593; criminal phone: 509-545-3592; civil phone: 509-545-5810; fax: 509-545-3588; hours 8:30AM-5PM (PST). *Misdemeanor, Civil Actions Under $50,000, Small Claims.*
Civil Records: Access: Mail, online, in person, fax. Only the court performs in person searches; visitors may not. Search fee: $10.00 per name. Court makes copy: $.25 per page. Required to search: name, years to search; also helpful: address. Civil cases indexed by defendant, plaintiff. Civil records on computer from 1993, prior on index cards. Index online from JIS-Link; see

www.courts.wa.gov/jislink (also, see state introduction). Mail turnaround time 7 days.
Criminal Records: Access: Mail, online, in person, fax. Only the court performs in person searches; visitors may not. Search fee: $10.00 per name. Court makes copy: $.25 per page. Required to search: name, years to search, DOB. Criminal records on computer from 1987, prior on index cards. Index remotely online from JIS-Link; see www.courts.wa.gov/jislink (also, see state introduction). Mail turnaround time 7 days.
General Information: No sealed, juvenile, adoption, paternity, mental health, sex offenders (victims) or (sometimes) DUI records released. Will fax documents for no fee. Certification fee: $5.00 per cert. Payee: Franklin District Court. Personal checks accepted. Prepayment and SASE required.

Garfield County

Superior Court PO Box 915, Pomeroy, WA 99347-0915; phone: 509-843-3731; fax: 509-843-1224; hours 8:30AM-N, 1-5PM (PST). *Felony, Civil, Eviction, Probate.*
Civil Records: Access: Phone, fax, mail, online, in person. Only the court performs in person searches; visitors may not. Search fee: $8.00 per hour. Court makes copy: $.50 per page. Self serve copy fee: $.50 per page. Required to search: name, years to search; also helpful: address. Civil cases indexed by defendant, plaintiff. Civil records on docket books, archived from 1882; on computer back to 1993. Index online from JIS-Link; see www.courts.wa.gov/jislink (also, see state introduction). Mail turnaround time 1 week.
Criminal Records: Access: Fax, mail, online, in person, email. Only the court performs in person searches; visitors may not. Search fee: $8.00 per hour. Court makes copy: $.50 per page. Self serve copy fee: $.50 per page. Required to search: name, years to search, DOB; also helpful: address, SSN. Criminal records on docket books, archived from 1882; on computer back to 1993. Index remotely online from JIS-Link; see www.courts.wa.gov/jislink (also, see state introduction). Mail turnaround time 1 week.
General Information: No sealed, juvenile, adoption, paternity, mental health, sex offenders (victims). Will fax documents $.50 per page. Certification fee: $5.00 plus $1.00 per page after first. Cert fee includes copies. Payee: Garfield County Clerk. Personal checks accepted. Prepayment required. SASE requested.

District Court PO Box 817, Pomeroy, WA 99347-0817; phone: 509-843-1002; fax: 509-843-3815; hours 8:30AM-5PM (PST). *Misdemeanor, Civil Actions Under $50,000, Small Claims.*
Civil Records: Access: Mail, online, in person, fax. Only the court performs in person searches; visitors may not. No search fee. Court makes copy: $.25 per page. Required to search: name, years to search; also helpful: address. Civil cases indexed by defendant. Civil records on index cards. Index online from JIS-Link; see www.courts.wa.gov/jislink (also, see state introduction). Mail turnaround time 1 week.
Criminal Records: Access: Mail, online, in person, fax. Only the court performs in person searches; visitors may not. No search fee. Court makes copy: $.25 per page. Required to search: name, years to search, DOB; also helpful: address, SSN. Criminal records on index cards. Index remotely online from JIS-Link; see www.courts.wa.gov/jislink (also, see state introduction). Mail turnaround time 1 week.
General Information: No sealed, juvenile, adoption, mental health, sex offenders (victims) or (sometimes) DUI records released. Certification fee: $5.00. Payee: Garfield County District Court. Personal checks accepted. Prepayment required.

Grant County

Superior Court PO Box 37, Ephrata, WA 98823-0037; phone: 509-754-2011 X430; fax: 509-754-6568; hours 8AM-4:30PM (PST). *Felony, Civil, Eviction, Probate.*
Civil Records: Access: Phone, mail, online, in person. Both court and visitors may perform in person searches. Search fee: $10.00 per name. Court makes copy: $.50 per page; same fee for self serve. Required to search: name, years to search; also helpful: address. Civil cases indexed by defendant, plaintiff. Civil records on computer from 1982, and some on index cards, archived from 1909. Index online from JIS-Link; see www.courts.wa.gov/jislink (also, see state introduction). Mail turnaround time 2 weeks.
Criminal Records: Access: Phone, mail, online, in person. Both court and visitors may perform in person searches. Search fee: $10.00 per name. Court makes copy: $.50 per page; same fee for self serve. Required to search: name, years to search; also helpful: address, DOB, SSN. Criminal records on computer from 1982, and some on index cards, archived from 1909. Index remotely online from JIS-Link; see www.courts.wa.gov/jislink (also, see state introduction). Mail turnaround time 2 weeks.
General Information: Public use terminal available. No sealed, juvenile, adoption, paternity, mental health, sex offenders (victims) records released. Will not fax documents. Certification fee: $5.00 plus $1.00 per page after first. Cert fee includes copies. Payee: Grant County Clerk's Office. Business checks accepted. Prepayment and SASE required.

District Court PO Box 37, Ephrata, WA 98823-0037; phone: 509-754-2011 X628; fax: 509-754-6099; hours 8AM-5PM (PST). *Misdemeanor, Civil Actions Under $50,000, Small Claims.*
www.co.grant.wa.us/
Civil Records: Access: Mail, online, in person. Only the court performs in person searches; visitors may not. Search fee: $20.00 per name. Court makes copy: $2.00 for 1st page, $1.00 each add'l. Required to search: name, years to search; also helpful: address. Civil cases indexed by defendant, plaintiff. Criminal indexed on computer per state retention schedule. Index online from JIS-Link; see www.courts.wa.gov/jislink (also, see state introduction). Mail turnaround time 30 days or more.
Criminal Records: Access: Mail, online, in person. Only the court performs in person searches; visitors may not. Search fee: $20.00 per name. Court makes copy: $2.00 for 1st page, $1.00 each add'l. Required to search: name, years to search, DOB; also helpful: address, SSN. Criminal indexed on computer per state retention schedule. Index remotely online from JIS-Link; see www.courts.wa.gov/jislink (also, see state introduction). Mail turnaround time up to 30 days.
General Information: No sealed, probation, juvenile, adoption, paternity, mental health, sex offenders (victims) or (sometimes) DUI records released. Will fax documents per copy fee rates. Certification fee: $5.00 per page. Payee: Grant County District Court. Personal checks accepted. Prepayment required.

Grays Harbor County

Superior Court 102 W Broadway, Rm 203, Montesano, WA 98563-3606; phone: 360-249-3842; fax: 360-249-6381; hours 8AM-5PM (PST). *Felony, Civil, Eviction, Probate.*
Civil Records: Access: Phone, fax, mail, online, in person. Both court and visitors may perform in person searches. Search fee: $20.00 per name. No fee for records before 1980. Court makes copy: $.50 per page. Required to search: name, years to search; also helpful: address. Civil cases indexed by defendant, plaintiff. Civil records on computer from 12/80, on microfiche from 1856, on index cards. Index online from JIS-Link; see www.courts.wa.gov/jislink (also, see state introduction). Mail turnaround time 5 days.

Criminal Records: Access: Phone, fax, mail, online, in person. Both court and visitors may perform in person searches. Search fee: $20.00 per name. No fee for records before 1980. Court makes copy: $.50 per page. Required to search: name, years to search; also helpful: address, DOB, SSN. Criminal records on computer from 12/80, on microfiche from 1856, on index cards. Index remotely online from JIS-Link; see www.courts.wa.gov/jislink (also, see state introduction). Mail turnaround time 5 days.

General Information: Public terminal goes back to 1980. No sealed, juvenile, adoption, paternity, mental health, sex offenders (victims). No fee to fax documents. Fax available in emergency only. Certification fee: $5.00 1st page, $1.00 ea add'l. Cert fee includes copies. Payee: Grays Harbor County Clerk. Business checks accepted. Prepayment and SASE required.

District Court No 2 PO Box 142, Aberdeen, WA 98520-0035; phone: 360-532-7061; fax: 360-532-7704; hours 8AM-N, 1-5PM (PST). *Civil Actions Under $50,000, Small Claims.*

www.co.grays-harbor.wa.us

Note: This court no longer handles criminal cases.

Civil Records: Access: Fax, mail, online, in person. Only the court performs in person searches; visitors may not. No search fee. Court makes copy: $.50 per page. Required to search: name, years to search; also helpful: address. Civil cases indexed by defendant, plaintiff. Civil records on computer from 4/91, on index cards. Index online from JIS-Link; see www.courts.wa.gov/jislink (also, see state introduction). Mail turnaround time 1 week.

General Information: No sealed, juvenile, adoption, paternity, mental health, sex offenders (victims) or (sometimes) DUI records released. No fee to fax documents. Certification fee: $5.00. Payee: Grays Harbor District Court #2. Personal checks accepted. Prepayment and SASE required.

District Court No 1 102 W Broadway, Rm 202, Montesano, WA 98563; phone: 360-249-3441; fax: 360-249-6382; hours 8AM-N, 1-5PM (PST). *Misdemeanor.*

www.co.grays-harbor.wa.us/info/judicial/

Note: All civil filings and hearings are held in the District Court Dept 2 in Aberdeen.

Criminal Records: Access: Phone, fax, mail, online, in person. Only the court performs in person searches; visitors may not. Search fee: none normally. Court makes copy: $.50 per page; same fee for self serve. Required to search: name, years to search, DOB; also helpful: address, SSN. Criminal records on computer from 4/91, on index cards. Index remotely online from JIS-Link; see www.courts.wa.gov/jislink (also, see state introduction). Mail turnaround time 1 week.

General Information: No sealed, juvenile, adoption, paternity, mental health, sex offenders (victims) records released. Will fax documents for $.25 per page. Certification fee: $5.00. Payee: Grays Harbor District Court #1. Personal checks accepted. Prepayment and SASE required.

Island County

Superior Court PO Box 5000, Coupeville, WA 98239-5000; phone: 360-679-7359; hours 8AM-4:30PM (PST). *Felony, Civil, Eviction, Probate.*

Civil Records: Access: Phone, mail, online, in person. Both court and visitors may perform in person searches. Search fee: $20.00 per hour. Court makes copy: $.25 per page. Self serve copy fee: $.15 per page. Required to search: name, years to search. Civil cases indexed by defendant, plaintiff. Civil records on computer from 7/1984, microfiche from 1889. Archived in Bellingham, WA. Index online from JIS-Link; see www.courts.wa.gov/jislink (also, see state introduction). Mail turnaround time 1 week.

Criminal Records: Access: Phone, mail, online, in person. Both court and visitors may perform in person searches. Search fee: $20.00 per hour. Court makes copy: $.25 per page. Self serve copy fee: $.15

per page. Required to search: name, years to search; also helpful: address, DOB. Criminal records on computer from 7/1984, microfiche from 1889. Archived in Bellingham, WA. Index remotely online from JIS-Link; see www.courts.wa.gov/jislink (also, see state introduction). Mail turnaround time 1 week.

General Information: No sealed, No access to dependency, truancy, adoption, paternity, mental health, sex offenders (victims). Certification fee: $5.00 first page; $1.00 each add'l. Payee: Island county Clerk. Business checks accepted. Prepayment and SASE required.

District Court 800 S 8th Ave, Oak Harbor, WA 98277; phone: 360-675-5988; fax: 360-675-8231; hours 8AM-4:30PM (PST). *Misdemeanor, Civil Actions Under $50,000, Small Claims.*

Note: Records requests are done as time permits. Bottom of priority list.

Civil Records: Access: Fax, mail, online, in person. Both court and visitors may perform in person searches. No search fee. Court makes copy: $.25 per page; $1.00 if electronic docket. Required to search: name, years to search; also helpful: address. Civil cases indexed by defendant. Civil records on computer from 1991, on index by alpha. Index online from JIS-Link; see www.courts.wa.gov/jislink (also, see state introduction). Mail turnaround time 1-7 days.

Criminal Records: Access: Fax, mail, online, in person. Only the court performs in person searches; visitors may not. No search fee. Court makes copy: $.25 per page; $1.00 if electronic docket. Required to search: name, years to search, DOB; also helpful: address, SSN. Criminal records on computer from 1991, on index by alpha. Index remotely online from JIS-Link; see www.courts.wa.gov/jislink (also, see state introduction). Mail turnaround time 1-7 days.

General Information: No sealed, juvenile, adoption, paternity, mental health, sex offenders (victims) or (sometimes) DUI records released. Will fax documents $1.00 per page. Certification fee: $5.00. Payee: Island District Court. Personal checks accepted. Prepayment and SASE required.

Jefferson County

Superior Court PO Box 1220, Port Townsend, WA 98368-0920; phone: 360-385-9125; fax: 360-385-5672; hours 8AM-5PM (PST). *Felony, Civil, Eviction, Probate.*

www.co.jefferson.wa.us/supcourt/

Civil Records: Access: Phone, mail, online, in person. Both court and visitors may perform in person searches. Search fee: $20.00 per hour. Court makes copy: $2.00 per page. Self serve copy fee: $.15 per page. Required to search: name, years to search. Civil cases indexed by defendant, plaintiff. Civil records on computer from 1983, on microfiche from 1890s. Archive in Bellingham, WA. Index online from JIS-Link; see www.courts.wa.gov/jislink (also, see state introduction). Mail turnaround time 2 days.

Criminal Records: Access: Phone, mail, online, in person. Both court and visitors may perform in person searches. Search fee: $20.00 per hour. Court makes copy: $2.00 per page. Self serve copy fee: $.15 per page. Required to search: name, years to search; also helpful: DOB. Criminal records on computer from 1983, on microfiche from 1890s. Archive in Bellingham, WA. Index remotely online from JIS-Link; see www.courts.wa.gov/jislink (also, see state introduction). Mail turnaround time 2 days.

General Information: Public terminal has criminal back to 1983 and civil back to 1988. No sealed, juvenile, adoption, paternity, mental health records released. Certification fee: $5.00 plus $1.00 per page after first. Cert fee includes copies. Payee: County Clerk. Personal checks accepted. Out of state checks not accepted. Prepayment and SASE required.

District Court PO Box 1220, Port Townsend, WA 98368-0920; phone: 360-385-9135; criminal phone: 360-385-9134; civil phone: 360-385-9132; fax: 360-385-9367; hours 8AM-5PM (PST). *Misdemeanor, Civil Actions Under $40,000, Small Claims.*

www.co.jefferson.wa.us

Civil Records: Access: Phone, fax, mail, online, in person. Only the court performs in person searches; visitors may not. No search fee. Court makes copy: $.15 per page. Required to search: name, years to search; also helpful: address. Civil cases indexed by defendant. Civil records on DISCIS computer from 1993, on computer from '90-'93, on log books prior to 1990. Physical files kept 10 years from disposition per retention schedule. Index online from JIS-Link; see www.courts.wa.gov/jislink (also, see state introduction). Mail turnaround time 1 week.

Criminal Records: Access: Phone, fax, mail, online, in person. Only the court performs in person searches; visitors may not. No search fee. Court makes copy: $.15 per page. Required to search: name, DOB; also helpful: years to search, address, SSN. Criminal records on DISCIS computer from 1993, on computer from '90-'93, on log books prior to 1990. Physical files kept 3 years from disposition per retention schedule. Index remotely online from JIS-Link; see www.courts.wa.gov/jislink (also, see state introduction). Mail turnaround time 1 week.

General Information: No sealed, juvenile, adoption, paternity, mental health, sex offenders (victims) records released. Will not fax documents. Certification fee: $6.00 per document. Personal checks accepted. Prepayment and SASE required.

King County

Superior Court 516 3rd Ave, E-609 Courthouse, Seattle, WA 98104-2386; phone: 206-296-9300, 800-325-6165 in state; hours 8:30AM-4:30AM (PST). *Felony, Civil, Eviction, Probate.*

www.metrokc.gov/kcscc

Civil Records: Access: Mail, online, in person. Both court and visitors may perform in person searches. Search fee: $20.00 per hour. Fee $25.00 minimum including copies. Court makes copy: $.50 per page. Self serve copy fee: $.15 to $.25 per page. Required to search: name, years to search. Civil cases indexed by defendant, plaintiff. Civil records on computer since 1979; prior records on microfiche back to 1935. Index online from JIS-Link; see www.courts.wa.gov/jislink (also, see state introduction). Mail turnaround time 2 weeks.

Criminal Records: Access: Mail, online, in person. Both court and visitors may perform in person searches. Search fee: $20.00 per hour. Fee is $25.00 if number of pages unknown. Court makes copy: $.50 per page. Self serve copy fee: $.15 to $.25 per page. Required to search: name, years to search. Criminal records on computer since 1979; prior records on microfiche back to 1938. Index remotely online from JIS-Link; see www.courts.wa.gov/jislink (also, see state introduction). Mail turnaround time 2 weeks.

General Information: Public terminal goes back to 1979. No sealed, juvenile, dependency, adoption, paternity (except for final judgments), mental health, sex offenders (victims) records released. Will not fax documents. Certification fee: $5.00 plus $1.00 per page after first. Payee: King County Superior Court Clerk. Personal checks accepted if in state. Prepayment and SASE required.

District Court East Division - Bellevue 585 112th Ave SE, Bellevue, WA 98004; phone: 206-205-3650 x6; 800-325-6165 +59200; fax: 206-296-0589; hours 8:30AM-4:30PM (PST). *Misdemeanor, Civil Actions Under $50,000, Small Claims.*

www.metrokc.gov/kcdc

Note: Formerly known as the Bellevue Division. Civil Filing Area: Bellevue, Eastgate, Factoria, Mercer Island, Clyde Hill, Beaux Arts, Newcastle.

Civil Records: Access: Phone, mail, online, in person. Both court and visitors may perform in person searches. No search fee. Court makes copy: $.15 per page. Required to search: name, years to search; also helpful: address. Civil cases indexed by defendant, plaintiff. Civil records on computer for past 10 years. Index online from JIS-Link; see www.courts.wa.gov/jislink (also, see state introduction). Mail turnaround time cannot be guaranteed for written requests.

Criminal Records: Access: Phone, mail, online, in person. Both court and visitors may perform in person searches. No search fee. Court makes copy: $.15 per page. Required to search: name, years to search, DOB; also helpful: address, SSN. Criminal records on computer from 1987. Criminal records may be removed after 5 years from disposition. Index remotely online from JIS-Link; see www.courts.wa.gov/jislink (also, see state introduction). Mail turnaround time cannot be guaranteed for written requests.

General Information: Public terminal goes back to 1995. No sealed, juvenile, adoption, paternity, mental health, sex offenders (victims) or (sometimes) DUI records released. Certification fee: $5.00 per doc includes copy fee. Payee: KCDC, Bellevue Division. Personal checks or Visa, MC accepted. Prepayment required.

District Court East Division - Issaquah

5415 220th Ave SW, Issaquah, WA 98029-6839; phone: 206-205-3650 x6; civil phone: 206-205-1747; fax: 206-296-0591; hours 8:30AM-4:30PM (PST). *Misdemeanor, Civil Actions Under $50,000, Small Claims.*

www.metrokc.gov/kcdc

Note: Formerly known as the Issaquah Division. Civil Filing Area: Issaquah, Sammamish, High Point, Preston, Fall City, Snoqualmie, North Bend, Cedar Falls, Tokul, Alpental.

Civil Records: Access: Mail, online, in person. Both court and visitors may perform in person searches. No search fee. Court makes copy: $.15 per page. Required to search: name, years to search; also helpful: address. Civil cases indexed by defendant, plaintiff. Civil records on computer back 10 years. Index online from JIS-Link; see www.courts.wa.gov/jislink (also, see state introduction). Mail turnaround time 1-5 days.

Criminal Records: Access: Mail, online, in person. Both court and visitors may perform in person searches. No search fee. Court makes copy: $.15 per page. Required to search: name, years to search, DOB, signed release; also helpful: address. Criminal records on computer back 5 years. Index remotely online from JIS-Link; see www.courts.wa.gov/jislink (also, see state introduction). Mail turnaround time 1-5 days.

General Information: Public terminal goes back to 1995. No sealed, juvenile, sex offenders (victims) or (sometimes) DUI records released. Certification fee: $5.00 per doc includes copy fee. Payee: Issaquah Division. Personal checks accepted. Prepayment and SASE required.

District Court East Division - Redmond

8601 160th Ave NE, Redmond, WA 98052-3548; phone: 206-296-3667; 206-205-3650 x6; 800-325-6165 x59200; hours 8:30AM-4:30PM (PST). *Misdemeanor, Civil Actions Under $50,000, Small Claims.*

www.metrokc.gov/kcdc

Note: Formerly known as the Northeast Division. Civil Filing Area: Redmond, Kirkland, Woodinville, Bothell, Duvall, Carnation, Juanita.

Civil Records: Access: Mail, online, in person. Both court and visitors may perform in person searches. No search fee. Court makes copy: $.15 per page. Required to search: name, years to search; also helpful: address. Civil cases indexed by defendant, plaintiff. Civil records on computer back 10 years. Index online from JIS-Link; see www.courts.wa.gov/jislink (also, see state introduction). Mail turnaround time 1-2 weeks.

Criminal Records: Access: Mail, online, in person. Both court and visitors may perform in person

searches. No search fee. Court makes copy: $.15 per page. Required to search: name, years to search, DOB; also helpful: address. Criminal records on computer back 5 years. Index remotely online from JIS-Link; see www.courts.wa.gov/jislink (also, see state introduction). Mail turnaround time 1-2 weeks.

General Information: Public terminal goes back to 1995. No sealed, juvenile, adoption, paternity, mental health, sex offenders (victims) or (sometimes) DUI records released. Certification fee: $5.00 per doc includes copy fee. Payee: King County District Court. Personal checks or Visa, MC accepted. Prepayment required.

District Court Shoreline Division

18050 Meridian Ave N, Shoreline, WA 98133-4642; phone: 206-296-3679, 206-205-3650 x6; 800-325-6165 +59200; civil phone: 206-296-3684; fax: 206-296-0594; hours 8:30AM-4:30PM (PST). *Misdemeanor, Civil Actions Under $50,000, Small Claims.*

www.metrokc.gov/kcdc

Note: Civil Filing Area: Shoreline, Kenmore, Lake Forest Park.

Civil Records: Access: Fax, mail, online, in person. Both court and visitors may perform in person searches. No search fee. Court makes copy: $.15 per page. Required to search: name, years to search; also helpful: address. Civil cases indexed by defendant, plaintiff. Civil records on computer from 1985. Index online from JIS-Link; see www.courts.wa.gov/jislink (also, see state introduction). Mail turnaround time 1 week.

Criminal Records: Access: Fax, mail, online, in person. Both court and visitors may perform in person searches. No search fee. Court makes copy: $.15 per page. Required to search: name, years to search; also helpful: address, DOB, SSN. Criminal records on computer from 1987. Index remotely online from JIS-Link; see www.courts.wa.gov/jislink (also, see state introduction). Note: Please limit crim requests to 5 and use their request form. Mail turnaround time 1 week.

General Information: Public terminal goes back to 1995. No sealed, juvenile, adoption, paternity, mental health, sex offenders (victims) or (sometimes) DUI records released. No fee to fax documents. Certification fee: $5.00 per doc includes copy fee. Payee: King County District Court. Personal checks or Visa, MC accepted. Prepayment and SASE required.

District Court South Division - Burien

King County District Court, 601 SW 149th St, Burien, WA 98166-1935; phone: 206-205-3650 x6; 800-325-6165 +59200; fax: 206-296-0124; hours 8:30AM-4:30PM (PST). *Misdemeanor, Civil Actions Under $50,000, Small Claims.*

www.metrokc.gov/kcdc

Note: Formerly located in Vashon. Formerly Southwest Division, name change 12/2002. All civil cases filed at South Division in Kent.

Civil Records: Access: Mail, online, in person. Both court and visitors may perform in person searches. No search fee. Court makes copy: $.15 per page; same fee for self serve. Required to search: name, years to search; also helpful: address. Civil cases indexed by defendant, plaintiff. Civil records on computer back 5 years. Index online from JIS-Link; see www.courts.wa.gov/jislink (also, see state introduction). Mail turnaround time 1 day.

Criminal Records: Access: Mail, online, in person. Both court and visitors may perform in person searches. No search fee. Court makes copy: $.15 per page; same fee for self serve. Required to search: name, years to search; also helpful: address, DOB, SSN. Criminal records on computer from 1987. Index remotely online from JIS-Link; see www.courts.wa.gov/jislink (also, see state introduction). Mail turnaround time 1 day.

General Information: Public terminal goes back to 1995. No sealed, juvenile, adoption, paternity, mental health, sex offenders (victims) or (sometimes) DUI

records released. No fee to fax documents. Certification fee: $5.00 per doc. Payee: Vashon District Court. Personal checks accepted. Prepayment required.

District Court South Division - Kent

1210 S Central, Kent, WA 98032-7426; phone: 206-205-3650 x6; 800-325-6165 +59200; 206-205-9200; hours 8:30AM-4:30PM (PST). *Misdemeanor, Civil Actions Under $50,000, Small Claims.*

www.metrokc.gov/kcdc

Note: Formerly known as Aukeen Division. Civil Filing Area: Enumclaw, Auburn, Black Diamond, Maple Valley, Covington, Algona, Pacific, Ravensdale, Hobart, Federal Way.

Civil Records: Access: Mail, online, in person. Both court and visitors may perform in person searches. No search fee. Court makes copy: $.15 per page. Required to search: name, years to search; also helpful: address. Civil cases indexed by defendant, plaintiff. Civil records on computer 5 years back. Index online from JIS-Link; see www.courts.wa.gov/jislink (also, see state introduction). Mail turnaround time 1 day.

Criminal Records: Access: Mail, online, in person. Both court and visitors may perform in person searches. No search fee. Court makes copy: $.15 per page. Required to search: name, years to search, DOB; also helpful: address, SSN. Criminal records on computer 5 years back. Index remotely online from JIS-Link; see www.courts.wa.gov/jislink (also, see state introduction). Mail turnaround time 1 day.

General Information: Public use terminal available. No sealed, juvenile, adoption, paternity, mental health, sex offenders (victims) or (sometimes) DUI records released. Certification fee: $5.00 per doc includes copy fee. Payee: District Court. Personal checks accepted. Prepayment and SASE required.

District Court West Division - Seattle

516 3rd Ave, #E-327, Courthouse, Seattle, WA 98104-3273; phone: 206-205-3650 x6; 800-325-6165 +59200; criminal phone: 206-296-3565 (crim. traf.); civil phone: 206-296-3550; fax: 206-296-0910; hours 8:30AM-4:30PM (PST). *Misdemeanor, Civil Actions Under $50,000, Small Claims.*

www.metrokc.gov/kcdc

Note: Formerly known as the Seattle Division. Civil Filing Area: Seattle.

Civil Records: Access: Fax, mail, online, in person. Visitors must perform in person searches themselves. No search fee. Court makes copy: $.15 per page. Self serve copy fee: $.25 per page. Required to search: name, years to search; also helpful: address. Civil cases indexed by defendant, plaintiff. Civil records on computer from back 10 years. Index online from JIS-Link; see www.courts.wa.gov/jislink (also, see state introduction). Mail turnaround time 10 days.

Criminal Records: Access: Fax, mail, online, in person. Both court and visitors may perform in person searches. No search fee. Court makes copy: $.15 per page. Self serve copy fee: $.25 per page. Required to search: name, years to search, DOB, signed release; also helpful: address, SSN. Criminal records on computer from back 10 years. Index remotely online from JIS-Link; see www.courts.wa.gov/jislink (also, see state introduction). Mail turnaround time 10 days.

General Information: Public terminal goes back to 1995. (90% of info available to public, other 10% can only be searched by staff.) No sealed, juvenile, adoption, paternity, mental health, sex offenders (victims), treatment plans or (sometimes) DUI records released. Will not fax documents. Certification fee: $5.00 per doc includes copy fee. Payee: King County District Court, Seattle. Personal checks accepted. Prepayment and SASE required.

Kitsap County

Superior Court 614 Division St, MS34, Port Orchard, WA 98366-4699; phone: 360-337-7164; fax: 360-337-4927; hours 8AM-4:30PM (PST). *Felony, Civil, Eviction, Probate.*
www.kitsapgov.com/sc/
Civil Records: Access: Mail, online, in person. Both court and visitors may perform in person searches. Search fee: $20.00 for up to 5 names. Court makes copy: $.50 per page ($.25 if from image media). Self serve copy fee: $.15 per page. Required to search: name, years to search. Civil cases indexed by defendant, plaintiff. Civil records on computer from 1978, on microfiche and archived from 1857. Index online from JIS-Link; see www.courts.wa.gov/jislink (also, see state introduction). Mail turnaround time 2 weeks.
Criminal Records: Access: Mail, online, in person. Both court and visitors may perform in person searches. Search fee: $20.00 for up to 5 names. Court makes copy: $.50 per page ($.25 if from image media). Self serve copy fee: $.15 per page. Required to search: name, years to search; also helpful: address, DOB, SSN. Criminal records on computer from 1978, on microfiche and archived from 1857. Index remotely online from JIS-Link; see www.courts.wa.gov/jislink (also, see state introduction). Mail turnaround time 2 weeks.
General Information: Public use terminal available. No dependencies, adoption or mental illness records released. Will fax documents for $1.00 per page. There is an add'l $5.00 handling fee if copies required. Certification fee: $5.00 1st page, $1.00 ea add'l. Cert fee includes copies. Payee: Kitsap County Clerk. No personal checks accepted. Prepayment required.

District Court 614 Division St, MS 25, Port Orchard, WA 98366-4614; criminal phone: 360-337-7109; civil phone: 360-337-7104; criminal fax: 360-337-4865; civil fax: 360-337-4586; hours 8AM-12:15PM, 1:15-4:30PM (PST). *Misdemeanor, Civil Actions Under $50,000, Small Claims.*
www.kitsapgov.com/dc/
Civil Records: Access: Phone, fax, mail, online, in person. Only the court performs in person searches; visitors may not. No search fee. Court makes copy: $.15 per page. Required to search: name, years to search. Civil cases indexed by defendant, plaintiff. Civil records on computer from 1/95, prior in archives. Index online from JIS-Link; see www.courts.wa.gov/jislink (also, see state introduction). Mail turnaround time 3 days.
Criminal Records: Access: Phone, fax, mail, online, in person. Only the court performs in person searches; visitors may not. No search fee. Court makes copy: $.15 per page. Required to search: name, years to search; also helpful: DOB. Criminal records on computer from 1/95, prior in archives. Index remotely online from JIS-Link; see www.courts.wa.gov/jislink (also, see state introduction). Mail turnaround time 3 days.
General Information: No fee to fax documents. Certification fee: $5.00. Payee: Kitsap County District Court. Personal checks accepted. Prepayment required.

District Court North 614 Division St, MS-25, Port Orchard, WA 98366; phone: 360-337-7109; fax: 360-337-4865; hours 8:30AM-12:15PM; 1:15-4:30PM (PST). *Misdemeanor, Civil Actions Under $50,000, Small Claims.*
Note: The court physical address is 19050 Jensen Way NE, Poulsbo, WA.
Civil Records: Access: Mail, online, in person. Only the court performs in person searches; visitors may not. No search fee. Court makes copy: $.15 per page. Required to search: full name, years to search. Civil cases indexed by defendant, plaintiff. Civil records on computer back 8 years. Index online from JIS-Link; see www.courts.wa.gov/jislink (also, see state introduction). Note: Send all mail requests to Port Orchard District court. Mail turnaround time 2 days.
Criminal Records: Access: Mail, online, in person, phone (1 only). Only the court performs in person searches; visitors may not. No search fee. Court makes copy: $.15 per page. Required to search: name, signed release; also helpful: years to search, DOB. Criminal records on computer back 8 years. Index remotely online from JIS-Link; see www.courts.wa.gov/jislink (also, see state introduction). Note: Send all mail requests to Port Orchard District Court. Mail turnaround time 2 days.
General Information: No dependencies, adoption and mental illness records released. Certification fee: $5.00. Payee: District Court, Kitsap County. Only cashiers checks and money orders accepted. Prepayment and SASE required.

Kittitas County

Superior Court 205 W 5th, Rm 210, Ellensburg, WA 98926; phone: 509-962-7531; fax: 509-962-7667; hours 9AM-N, 1-5PM (PST). *Felony, Misdemeanor, Civil, Eviction, Probate.*
Civil Records: Access: Phone, fax, mail, online, in person. Only the court performs in person searches; visitors may not. Search fee: $10.00 per name. Court makes copy: $.50 per page. Required to search: name, years to search; also helpful: address. Civil cases indexed by defendant, plaintiff. Civil records on computer from 1982, on microfiche and archived from 1890. Some records on index cards. Index online from JIS-Link; see www.courts.wa.gov/jislink (also, see state introduction). Mail turnaround time 2 days.
Criminal Records: Access: Phone, fax, mail, online, in person. Only the court performs in person searches; visitors may not. Search fee: $10.00 per name. Court makes copy: $.50 per page. Required to search: name, years to search; also helpful: address, DOB, SSN. Criminal records on computer from 1982, on microfiche and archived from 1890. Some records on index cards. Index remotely online from JIS-Link; see www.courts.wa.gov/jislink (also, see state introduction). Mail turnaround time 2 days.
General Information: No dependencies, adoption, and mental illness records released. No fee to fax documents. Fax available in emergency only. Certification fee: $5.00 first page; $1.00 each addl. Payee: Kittitas County Clerk. Personal checks accepted. Prepayment required.

District Court Lower Kittitas 205 W 5th, Rm 180, Ellensburg, WA 98926; phone: 509-962-7511; fax: 509-962-7575; hours 9AM-5PM (PST). *Misdemeanor, Civil Actions Under $50,000, Small Claims.*
Civil Records: Access: Mail, online, in person. Only the court performs in person searches; visitors may not. No search fee. No copy fee. Required to search: name, years to search. Civil cases indexed by defendant, plaintiff. Civil records on computer from 8/97, archived back 10 years. Records retained for 20 years. Index online from JIS-Link; see www.courts.wa.gov/jislink (also, see state introduction). Mail turnaround time 7-10 days.
Criminal Records: Access: Fax, mail, online, in person. Only the court performs in person searches; visitors may not. No search fee. No copy fee. Required to search: name, years to search, DOB. Criminal records on computer from 8/97, archived back 10 years. Index remotely online from JIS-Link; see www.courts.wa.gov/jislink (also, see state introduction). Mail turnaround time 7-10 days.
General Information: No dependencies, adoption, and mental illness records released. Will fax documents to local or toll free line. Certification fee: $5.00 includes copy fee. Payee: Lower Kittitas County District Court. Personal checks accepted. Prepayment and SASE required.

District Court Upper Kittitas 700 E 1st, Cle Elum, WA 98922; phone: 509-674-5533; fax: 509-674-4209; hours 7AM-5PM (PST). *Misdemeanor, Civil Actions Under $50,000, Small Claims.*
Civil Records: Access: Mail, online, in person. Only the court performs in person searches; visitors may not. No search fee. Court makes copy: $.25 per page. Required to search: name, years to search. Civil cases indexed by defendant, plaintiff. Civil records on computer since 8/91; prior records archived from 1890, some on index cards. Records retained for 10 years. Index online from JIS-Link; see www.courts.wa.gov/jislink (also, see state introduction). Mail turnaround time 1 week.
Criminal Records: Access: Fax, mail, online, in person. Only the court performs in person searches; visitors may not. No search fee. Court makes copy: $.25 per page. Required to search: name, years to search, DOB, signed release; also helpful: SSN. Criminal records on computer back to 1997; prior records archived from 1890, some on index cards. Records retained for 5 years. Index remotely online from JIS-Link; see www.courts.wa.gov/jislink (also, see state introduction). Mail turnaround time 1 week.
General Information: No dependencies, adoption, and mental illness records released. Fee to fax documents is $1.00 per page. Certification fee: $5.00. Payee: UKCDC. Personal checks or Visa, MC accepted. Prepayment required.

Klickitat County

Superior Court Superior Court Clerk, 205 S Columbus, MS CH-O3, Goldendale, WA 98620; phone: 509-773-5744; hours 9AM-5PM (PST). *Felony, Civil, Eviction, Probate.*
Civil Records: Access: Phone, mail, online, in person. Both court and visitors may perform in person searches. Search fee: $8.00 per hour. Court makes copy: $2.00 for first page, $1.00 each add'l. Required to search: name, years to search; also helpful: address. Civil cases indexed by defendant, plaintiff. Civil records on computer from 9/87. Index online from JIS-Link; see www.courts.wa.gov/jislink (also, see state introduction). Mail turnaround time 1-2 weeks or sooner.
Criminal Records: Access: Phone, mail, online, in person. Both court and visitors may perform in person searches. Search fee: $8.00 per hour. Court makes copy: $2.00 for first page, $1.00 each add'l. Required to search: name, years to search; also helpful: address, DOB, SSN. Criminal records on computer from 9/87; prior on books back to 1886. Index remotely online from JIS-Link; see www.courts.wa.gov/jislink (also, see state introduction). Mail turnaround time 1-2 weeks or sooner.
General Information: Public terminal goes back to 1988. No dependencies, adoption, and mental illness records released. Certification fee: $5.00 plus $1.00 per page after first. Payee: Klickitat County Clerk. No personal checks accepted. Prepayment and SASE required.

East District Court 205 S Columbus, MS-CH11, Goldendale, WA 98620-9290; phone: 509-773-4670; fax: 509-773-4653; hours 8AM-12, 1-5pm (PST). *Misdemeanor, Civil Actions Under $50,000, Small Claims.*
Civil Records: Access: Phone, mail, fax, online, in person. Both court and visitors may perform in person searches. No search fee. Court makes copy: 1st 10 pages free, each add'l page $.15. Required to search: name, years to search. Civil cases indexed by defendant, plaintiff. Civil records on computer from 4/93, on index cards prior. Retained for 10 years. Index online from JIS-Link; see www.courts.wa.gov/jislink (also, see state introduction). Mail turnaround time 1 week.
Criminal Records: Access: Phone, mail, fax, online, in person. Both court and visitors may perform in person searches. No search fee. Court makes copy:

1st 10 pages free, each add'l page $.15. Required to search: name, years to search, DOB. Criminal records on computer from 4/93, on index cards prior. Retained for 10 years. Index remotely online from JIS-Link; see www.courts.wa.gov/jislink (also, see state introduction). Mail turnaround time 1 week.

General Information: No dependencies, adoption, and mental illness records released. Will fax documents to local or toll free line. Certification fee: $5.00. Payee: East District Court. Personal checks accepted. Prepayment and SASE required.

West District Court PO Box 435, White Salmon, WA 98672-0435; phone: 509-493-1190; fax: 509-493-4469; hours 8AM-5PM (PST). *Misdemeanor, Civil Actions Under $50,000, Small Claims.*

Civil Records: Access: Mail, in person, online. Only the court performs in person searches; visitors may not. No search fee. Court makes copy: $1.00 per page. Required to search: name, years to search. Civil cases indexed by defendant, plaintiff. Civil records on computer from 5/93, on docket books. Index online from JIS-Link; see www.courts.wa.gov/jislink (also, see state introduction). Mail turnaround time 3-5 days.

Criminal Records: Access: Mail, in person, online. Only the court performs in person searches; visitors may not. No search fee. Court makes copy: $1.00 per page. Required to search: name, years to search, DOB; also helpful: address. Criminal records on computer from 5/93, on docket books. Index remotely online from JIS-Link; see www.courts.wa.gov/jislink (also, see state introduction). Mail turnaround time 3-5 days.

General Information: No dependencies, adoption, sealed and mental illness records released. Will not fax documents. Certification fee: $6.00 1st page, $1.00 ea add'l. Cert fee includes copies. Payee: West District Court. Personal checks accepted. Prepayment and SASE required.

Lewis County

Superior Court 345 W North St, MS:CLK 01, Chehalis, WA 98532-1900; phone: 360-740-2704; criminal phone: 360-740-1395; civil phone: 360-740-2776; probate phone: 360-740-1177; fax: 360-748-1639; hours 8AM-5PM (PST). *Felony, Misdemeanor, Civil, Eviction, Probate.*

Civil Records: Access: Phone, mail, online, in person. Both court and visitors may perform in person searches. Search fee: $8.00 per hour. Court makes copy: $.50 per page. Required to search: name, years to search; also helpful: address. Civil cases indexed by defendant, plaintiff. Civil records on computer from 1983, archived from 1900s. Index online from JIS-Link; see www.courts.wa.gov/jislink (also, see state introduction). Mail turnaround time up to 7 days.

Criminal Records: Access: Phone, mail, online, in person. Both court and visitors may perform in person searches. Search fee: $8.00 per hour. Court makes copy: $.50 per page. Required to search: name, years to search; also helpful: address, DOB, SSN. Criminal records on computer from 1983, archived from 1900s. Index remotely online from JIS-Link; see www.courts.wa.gov/jislink (also, see state introduction). Mail turnaround time up to 7 days.

General Information: Public terminal goes back to 1983. No dependencies, adoption, paternity, and mental illness records released. Fee to fax documents is $.50 per page. Certification fee: $5.00 1st page, $1.00 ea add'l. Cert fee includes copies. Payee: Lewis County Clerk. Personal checks accepted. Prepayment and SASE required.

District Court PO Box 336, Chehalis, WA 98532-0336; phone: 360-740-1203; fax: 360-740-2779; hours 8AM-5PM (PST). *Misdemeanor, Civil Actions Under $50,000, Small Claims.*

Civil Records: Access: Fax, mail, online, in person. Both court and visitors may perform in person searches. No search fee. Court makes copy: $.25 per page. Required to search: name, years to search. Civil cases indexed by defendant, plaintiff. Civil records on computer from 1983. Records retained 10 years. Index online from JIS-Link; see www.courts.wa.gov/jislink (also, see state introduction). Mail turnaround time 1 week.

Criminal Records: Access: Fax, mail, online, in person. Only the court performs in person searches; visitors may not. No search fee. Court makes copy: $.25 per page. Required to search: name, years to search, DOB, sex, signed release; also helpful: address, SSN. Criminal records on computer since 1981. Records retained for 5 years. Index remotely online from JIS-Link; see www.courts.wa.gov/jislink (also, see state introduction). Mail turnaround time 1 week.

General Information: No dependencies, adoption, and mental illness records released. No fee to fax documents. Certification fee: $5.00 per document. Payee: Lewis County District Court. Personal checks accepted. Prepayment and SASE required.

Lincoln County

Superior Court Box 68, Davenport, WA 99122-0068; phone: 509-725-1401; criminal fax: 509-725-1150; same fax for civil/probate; hours 8AM-5PM (PST). *Felony, Misdemeanor, Civil, Eviction, Probate.*

Note: Probate is in a separate index.

Civil Records: Access: Mail, online, in person. Both court and visitors may perform in person searches. No search fee. Court makes copy: $.50 per page. Required to search: name, years to search; also helpful: address. Civil cases indexed by defendant, plaintiff. Civil records on computer and microfiche from 11/82, archived from 1903. Index online from JIS-Link; see www.courts.wa.gov/jislink (also, see state introduction). Mail turnaround time 4 days.

Criminal Records: Access: Mail, online, in person, phone. Both court and visitors may perform in person searches. No search fee. Court makes copy: $.50 per page. Required to search: name, years to search; also helpful: address, DOB, SSN. Criminal records on computer and microfiche from 11/82, archived from 1903. Index remotely online from JIS-Link; see www.courts.wa.gov/jislink (also, see state introduction). Mail turnaround time 4 days.

General Information: Public terminal goes back to 11/1982. No dependencies, adoption, and mental illness records released. Will not fax documents. Certification fee: $5.00 1st page; $1.00 each add'l page. Payee: Lincoln County Clerk. Business checks accepted. Prepayment and SASE required.

District Court PO Box 329, Davenport, WA 99122-0329; phone: 509-725-2281; fax: 509-725-6481; hours 8AM-5PM (PST). *Misdemeanor, Civil Actions Under $35,000, Small Claims.*

Note: This is a small office with limited time allowable for searches.

Civil Records: Access: Mail, fax, online, in person. Both court and visitors may perform in person searches. Search fee: $25.00 per hour. Court makes copy: $.50. Required to search: name, years to search. Civil cases indexed by defendant. Civil records on computer back to 6/93, in books from 1985. Index online from JIS-Link; see www.courts.wa.gov/jislink (also, see state introduction). Mail turnaround time 1 week.

Criminal Records: Access: Mail, fax, online, in person, phone. Both court and visitors may perform in person searches. Search fee: $25.00 per hour. Court makes copy: $.50. Required to search: name, years to search, DOB. Criminal records on computer back to 6/93; hard copy files back to 1990. Index remotely online from JIS-Link; see www.courts.wa.gov/jislink (also, see state introduction). Mail turnaround time 1 week.

General Information: Public terminal goes back to 1990. No dependencies, adoption, and mental illness records released. Certification fee: $6.00 1st page, $5.00 ea add'l. Cert fee includes copies. Payee: Lincoln County District Court. Business checks accepted. Prepayment and SASE required.

Mason County

Superior Court PO Box 340, Shelton, WA 98584; phone: 360-427-9670 X346; hours 8:30AM-5PM (PST). *Felony, Civil, Eviction, Probate.*

Civil Records: Access: Phone, mail, online, in person. Both court and visitors may perform in person searches. Search fee: $20.00 per hour. Court makes copy: $5.00 for 1st pg. $1.00 each add'l. Required to search: name, years to search; also helpful: address. Civil cases indexed by defendant, plaintiff. Civil records on computer from 1982; on microfiche and archived from 1890; on index or docket books prior to 1982. Index online from JIS-Link; see www.courts.wa.gov/jislink (also, see state introduction). Mail turnaround time 1 week.

Criminal Records: Access: Phone, mail, online, in person. Both court and visitors may perform in person searches. Search fee: $20.00 per hour. Court makes copy: $5.00 for 1st page, $1.00 each add'l. Required to search: name, years to search; also helpful: address, DOB. Criminal records on computer from 1982; on microfiche and archived from 1890; on index or docket books prior to 1982. Index remotely online from JIS-Link; see www.courts.wa.gov/jislink (also, see state introduction). Mail turnaround time 1 week.

General Information: No dependencies, adoption, and mental illness records released. Will not fax documents. Certification fee: $5.00 per document. Payee: Mason County Clerk. Attorney checks accepted. No personal checks accepted. Prepayment and SASE required.

District Court PO Box "O", Shelton, WA 98584-0090; phone: 360-427-9670; criminal phone: X339; civil phone: X343; fax: 360-427-7776; hours 8:30AM-5PM (PST). *Misdemeanor, Civil Actions Under $50,000, Small Claims.*

Civil Records: Access: Mail, in person, online. Only the court performs in person searches; visitors may not. Search fee: $20.00 per name. Fee is for extensive searching. Court makes copy: $.25 per page. Required to search: name, years to search; also helpful: address. Civil cases indexed by defendant, plaintiff. Civil records on computer from 12/92. Index online from JIS-Link; see www.courts.wa.gov/jislink (also, see state introduction). Mail turnaround time 1 week.

Criminal Records: Access: Mail, in person, online. Only the court performs in person searches; visitors may not. Search fee: Will charge $20.00 for extensive search. Court makes copy: $.25 per page. Required to search: name, years to search, DOB, signed release; also helpful: address, SSN. Criminal records on computer from 12/92, prior on index book. Index remotely online from JIS-Link; see www.courts.wa.gov/jislink (also, see state introduction). Mail turnaround time 1 week.

General Information: Certification fee: $5.00 1st page, $.25 ea add'l. Payee: Mason County District Court. Personal checks accepted. Prepayment and SASE required.

Okanogan County

Superior Court PO Box 72, Okanogan, WA 98840; phone: 509-422-7275; probate phone: 509-422-7275; fax: 509-422-7277; probate fax: same; hours 8:30AM-5:00PM (PST). *Felony, Misdemeanor, Civil, Eviction, Probate.*

Civil Records: Access: Phone, fax, mail, online, in person. Only the court performs in person searches; visitors may not. No search fee. Court makes copy: $.50 per page; same fee for self serve. Required to search: name, years to search; also helpful: address. Civil cases indexed by defendant, plaintiff. Civil records on computer from 1994, on hand-written indexes from 1895. Index online from JIS-Link; see www.courts.wa.gov/jislink (also, see state introduction). Mail turnaround time 1-7 days.

Criminal Records: Access: Phone, fax, mail, online, in person. Only the court performs in person searches; visitors may not. No search fee. Court makes copy: $.50 per page; same fee for self serve. Required to search: name, years to search; also helpful: address, DOB, SSN. Criminal records on computer from 1994, on hand-written indexes from 1895. Index remotely online from JIS-Link; see www.courts.wa.gov/jislink (also, see state introduction). Mail turnaround time 1-7 days.

General Information: No dependencies, adoption, and mental illness records released. Certification fee: $5.00 plus $1.00 per page after first. Cert fee includes copies. Payee: Okanogan County Clerk. Personal checks accepted. Prepayment and SASE required.

District Court PO Box 980, Okanogan, WA 98840-0980; phone: 509-422-7170; fax: 509-422-7174; hours 8AM-5PM (PST). *Misdemeanor, Civil Actions Under $50,000, Small Claims.*
www.okanogancounty.org/DC/index.htm
Note: Daily court calendar is at www.okanogancounty.org/DC/calendar.htm.

Civil Records: Access: Phone, fax, mail, in person, online. Both court and visitors may perform in person searches. No search fee. Court makes copy: $1.00 for first page, $.50 each add'l; same fee for self serve. Required to search: name, years to search. Civil cases indexed by defendant, plaintiff. Civil records on computer from 8/91, prior on index cards. Records files maintained 10 years if judgment, otherwise 3 years. Index online from JIS-Link; see www.courts.wa.gov/jislink (also, see state introduction). Mail turnaround time 7 days.

Criminal Records: Access: Phone, fax, mail, in person, online. Both court and visitors may perform in person searches. No search fee. Court makes copy: $1.00 for first page, $.50 each add'l; same fee for self serve. Required to search: name, years to search, DOB. Criminal records on computer from 8/91. Index remotely online from JIS-Link; see www.courts.wa.gov/jislink (also, see state introduction). Mail turnaround time 7 days.

General Information: Public terminal goes back to 8/1991. No alcohol related evaluations, mental illness records released. Will fax documents $1.00 1st page, $.50 each add'l. Certification fee: $5.00 per copy. Cert fee includes copy fee. Payee: Okanogan County District Court. Personal checks accepted. Prepayment required. SASE requested.

Pacific County

Superior Court PO Box 67, South Bend, WA 98586; phone: 360-875-9320; fax: 360-875-9321; hours 8:30AM-4:30PM (PST). *Felony, Civil, Eviction, Probate.*

Civil Records: Access: Phone, mail, online, in person. Both court and visitors may perform in person searches. Search fee: $20.00 per hour. Court makes copy: $.50 per page. Required to search: name, years to search. Civil cases indexed by defendant, plaintiff. Civil records on computer from 2/84, archived from 1887, some on docket books. Index online from JIS-Link; see www.courts.wa.gov/jislink (also, see state introduction). Microfilm copy is an additional $1.00 per page copy fee. Mail turnaround time varies.

Criminal Records: Access: Mail, online, in person. Both court and visitors may perform in person searches. Search fee: $20.00 per hour if searching before 1984. Court makes copy: $.50 per page. Required to search: name, years to search. Criminal records on computer from 2/84, archived from 1887, some on docket books. Index remotely online from JIS-Link; see www.courts.wa.gov/jislink (also, see state introduction). Microfilm copy is an additional $1.00 per page copy fee. Mail turnaround time varies.

General Information: Public terminal goes back to 1887. No dependencies, adoption, and mental illness records released. Certification fee: $5.00 1st page, $1.00 each add'l page. Payee: Pacific County Clerk. Personal checks accepted. Prepayment and SASE required.

District Court North Box 134, South Bend, WA 98586-0134; phone: 360-875-9354; fax: 360-875-9351; hours 9AM-5PM (PST). *Misdemeanor, Civil Actions Under $50,000, Small Claims.*

Civil Records: Access: Phone, fax, mail, online, in person. Only the court performs in person searches; visitors may not. No search fee. Court makes copy: $2.00 for first page, $1.00 each add'l. Required to search: name, years to search; also helpful: address. Civil cases indexed by defendant, plaintiff. Civil records on computer back to 3/93, prior on index cards. Depending on disposition date, civil records retained ten years. Index online from JIS-Link; see www.courts.wa.gov/jislink (also, see state introduction). Mail turnaround time 1-6 weeks.

Criminal Records: Access: Phone, mail, in person, online. Only the court performs in person searches; visitors may not. No search fee. Court makes copy: $2.00 for first page, $1.00 each add'l. Required to search: name, DOB; also helpful: years to search, address, SSN. Criminal Records retained forever, on computer back to 3/93. Index remotely online from JIS-Link; see www.courts.wa.gov/jislink (also, see state introduction). Mail turnaround time 1-6 weeks.

General Information: No dependencies, MVRs, defendant case histories, adoption, and mental illness records released. No fee to fax documents. Certification fee: $5.00. Payee: North District Court. Personal checks accepted. Prepayment and SASE required.

District Court South PO Box 794, Ilwaco, WA 98624; phone: 360-642-9417; fax: 360-642-9416; hours 7:30AM-4:30PM (PST). *Misdemeanor, Civil Actions Under $50,000, Small Claims.*

Civil Records: Access: Phone, fax, mail, online, in person. Only the court performs in person searches; visitors may not. No search fee. Court makes copy: $1.00 for first page, $.10 each add'l. Required to search: name, years to search; also helpful: address. Civil cases indexed by defendant, plaintiff. Civil records on computer for current and open cases. Records retained for 10 years. Index online from JIS-Link; see www.courts.wa.gov/jislink (also, see state introduction). Mail turnaround time 1 week.

Criminal Records: Access: Fax, mail, online, in person. Only the court performs in person searches; visitors may not. No search fee. Court makes copy: $1.00 for first page, $.10 each add'l. Required to search: name; also helpful: years to search, address, DOB, SSN. Criminal records on computer for current and open cases. Records retained for 10 years. Index remotely online from JIS-Link; see www.courts.wa.gov/jislink (also, see state introduction). Mail turnaround time 1 week.

General Information: No dependencies, adoption, and mental illness records released. No fee to fax documents. Certification fee: $6.00 per page includes copy fee. Payee: South District Court. Personal checks accepted. Prepayment and SASE required.

Pend Oreille County

Superior Court PO Box 5020, 229 S Garden Ave, Newport, WA 99156-5020; phone: 509-447-2435; criminal fax: 509-447-2734; same fax for civil/probate; hours 8AM-4:30PM (PST). *Felony, Civil, Eviction, Probate.*

Civil Records: Access: Mail, in person, online. Both court and visitors may perform in person searches. Search fee: $20.00 per hour. Court makes copy: $.50 per page. Required to search: name, years to search; also helpful: address. Civil cases indexed by defendant, plaintiff. Civil records on computer and microfiche from 9/82, archived from 1911, on docket books prior to 9/82. Index online from JIS-Link; see www.courts.wa.gov/jislink (also, see state introduction). Mail turnaround time same day.

Criminal Records: Access: Phone, mail, in person, online. Both court and visitors may perform in person searches. No search fee. Court makes copy: $.50 per page. Required to search: name, years to search; also helpful: address, DOB, SSN. Criminal records on computer and microfiche from 9/82, archived from 1911, on docket books prior to 9/82. Index remotely online from JIS-Link; see www.courts.wa.gov/jislink (also, see state introduction). Mail turnaround time same day.

General Information: No dependencies, adoption, and mental illness records released. Fee to fax documents is $3.00 for the 1st page and $1.00 per page thereafter. Certification fee: $5.00 first page, $1.00 ea add'l. Payee: Pend Oreille County Clerk. Personal checks accepted. Prepayment and SASE required.

District Court PO Box 5030, 229 S Garden Ave, Newport, WA 99156-5030; phone: 509-447-4110; civil phone: 800-359-1506; fax: 509-447-5724; hours 8AM-4:30PM (PST). *Misdemeanor, Civil Actions Under $50,000, Small Claims.*

Civil Records: Access: Phone, fax, mail, online, in person. Both court and visitors may perform in person searches. No search fee. Court makes copy: $.25 per page. Self serve copy fee: none. Required to search: name, years to search; also helpful: address. Civil cases indexed by defendant, plaintiff. Civil records on DISCIS computer from 10/92, on computer from 1989, archived from 1972. Records retained for 10 years. Index online from JIS-Link; see www.courts.wa.gov/jislink (also, see state introduction). Mail turnaround time 10 days.

Criminal Records: Access: Fax, mail, online, in person. Both court and visitors may perform in person searches. No search fee. Court makes copy: $.25 per page. Self serve copy fee: none. Required to search: name, DOB; also helpful: years to search, address, SSN. Criminal records on DISCIS computer from 10/92, on computer from 1989, archived from 1972. Records retained for 10 years. Index remotely online from JIS-Link; see www.courts.wa.gov/jislink (also, see state introduction). Mail turnaround time 10 days.

General Information: No dependencies, adoption, and mental illness records released. No fee to fax documents. Certification fee: $5.00 1st page, $1.00 each add'l, includes copy fee. Payee: Pend Oreille County District Court. Personal checks accepted. Prepayment and SASE required.

Pierce County

Superior Court 930 Tacoma Ave S, Rm 110, Tacoma, WA 98402; phone: 253-798-7455; probate phone: 253-798-7461; fax: 253-798-3428; hours 8:30AM-4:30PM (PST). *Felony, Civil, Eviction, Probate.*
www.co.pierce.wa.us/abtus/ourorg/supct/abtussup.htm

Civil Records: Access: Fax, mail, online, in person. Both court and visitors may perform in person searches. Search fee: $10.00 per hour. Court makes copy: $.50 per page; same fee for self serve. Required to search: name, years to search; also helpful: address. Civil cases indexed by defendant, plaintiff. Civil records on computer from 5/81, archived from 1890. Calendars are online at the website. Also, a statewide index is remotely online (see state introduction). Mail turnaround time 2-5 days.

Criminal Records: Access: Fax, mail, online, in person. Both court and visitors may perform in person searches. Search fee: $10.00 per name. Court makes copy: $.50 per page; same fee for self serve. Required to search: name, years to search, DOB; also helpful: address, SSN. Criminal records on computer from 5/81, archived from 1890. Online access to criminal records is the same as civil. Mail turnaround time 2-5 days.

General Information: Public terminal goes back to 1983. No sealed, juvenile, adoption, paternity, mental health, sex offenders (victims) or (sometimes) DUI records released. Will fax documents; $5.00 minimum. Certification fee: $5.00 plus $1.00 per page after first. Cert fee includes copies. Payee: Pierce County Clerk. Business checks accepted. Prepayment and SASE required.

District Court - Civil Infractions Division

1902 96th St S, Tacoma, WA 98444; phone: 253-798-7474; fax: 253-798-6310; hours 8:30AM-4:30PM M-Th (PST). *Civil Actions Under $50,000, Small Claims, Traffic.*

www.co.pierce.wa.us/abtus/ourorg/distct/abtusd1.htm

Note: District Court #3 in Eatonville, #2 in Gig Harbor, and #4 in Buckley were closed 1/13/03; all civil records were transferred to this court.

Civil Records: Access: Phone, fax, mail, online, in person. Both court and visitors may perform in person searches. Search fee: $20.00 per name. Court makes copy: $5.00 for 1st page, $1.00 each add'l. Required to search: name, years to search, DOB; also helpful: address. Civil cases indexed by defendant, plaintiff. Civil records on computer back to 1990; Records go back 5 years. Index online from JIS-Link; see www.courts.wa.gov/jislink (also, see state introduction) Mail turnaround time 1-2 weeks.

General Information: No sealed, juvenile, adoption, paternity, mental health, sex offenders (victims) or some DUI records released. Will not fax documents. Certification fee: $5.00 plus $1.00 each add'l page. Payee: Pierce County District Court. Personal checks or Visa, MC accepted. Prepayment and SASE required.

District Court - Criminal

930 Tacoma Ave S, Rm 601, Tacoma, WA 98402-2175; phone: 253-798-7457; fax: 253-798-3428; hours 8:30AM-4:30PM (PST). *Misdemeanor.*

www.co.pierce.wa.us/pc/abtus/ourorg/distct/abtusd1.htm

Note: District Court #3 in Eatonville was closed 01/13/03, all misdemeanor were transferred to this court.

Criminal Records: Access: Mail, fax, in person, online. Both court and visitors may perform in person searches. Search fee: $20.00 per name. Court makes copy: $.50 per page. Required to search: name, years to search, DOB; also helpful: address, SSN. Criminal records on computer from 8/1990. Criminal Index remotely online from JIS-Link; see www.courts.wa.gov/jislink (also, see state introduction) Mail turnaround time 1-2 weeks.

General Information: No sealed, juvenile, adoption, paternity, mental health, sex offenders (victims) or some DUI records released. Will not fax documents. Certification fee: $5.00 plus $1.00 each add'l page. Payee: Pierce County District Court. Personal checks or Visa, MC accepted. SASE required.

District Court #2, WA. *Misdemeanor, Civil Actions Under $50,000, Small Claims.*

Note: This court - formerly in Gig Harbor - is closed and records are now houses at the main court in Tacoma.

District Court #3, WA. *Misdemeanor, Civil Actions Under $50,000, Small Claims.*

Note: This court was closed on 01/10/03. All records have been transferred to the Pierce County District Court in Tacoma.

District Court #4, WA. *Misdemeanor, Civil Actions Under $50,000, Small Claims.*

Note: This court was closed on 01/10/03. All records have been transferred to the Pierce County District Court in Tacoma.

San Juan County

Superior Court 350 Court St, #7, Friday Harbor, WA 98250; phone: 360-378-2163; fax: 360-378-3967; hours 8AM-5PM (PST). *Felony, Misdemeanor, Civil, Eviction, Probate.*

www.co.san-juan.wa.us/

Civil Records: Access: Phone, fax, mail, online, in person. Both court and visitors may perform in person searches. Search fee: $20.00 per hour. Court makes copy: $.50 per page. Required to search: name, years to search; also helpful: case number. Civil cases indexed by defendant, plaintiff. Civil records on computer back to 1987, on microfilm and archived from 1890s. Index online from JIS-Link; see

www.courts.wa.gov/jislink (also, see state introduction). Mail turnaround time 3 days.

Criminal Records: Access: Phone, fax, mail, online, in person. Both court and visitors may perform in person searches. Search fee: $20.00 per name. Court makes copy: $.50 per page. Required to search: name, years to search, DOB; also helpful: address, SSN, case number. Criminal records on computer back to 1987, on microfilm and archived from 1890s. Index remotely online from JIS-Link; see www.courts.wa.gov/jislink (also, see state introduction). Note: Only the court may perform in person searches on computer. Mail turnaround time 3 days.

General Information: Public terminal goes back to 1987. No dependencies, adoption, and mental illness records released. Will fax documents $3.00 1st page, $1.00 each add'l. Certification fee: $5.00 plus $1.00 each add'l page. Cert fee includes copies. Payee: San Juan County Clerk. Personal checks accepted. Credit cards accepted. Prepayment and SASE required.

District Court PO Box 127, Friday Harbor, WA 98250-0127; phone: 360-378-4017; fax: 360-378-4099; hours 8:30AM-4:30PM (PST). *Misdemeanor, Civil Actions Under $50,000, Small Claims.*

Civil Records: Access: Mail, in person, online. Only the court performs in person searches; visitors may not. Search fee: none; but $20.00 if an archive search. Court makes copy: $2.00 for first page, $1.00 each add'l. Required to search: name, years to search; also helpful: address. Civil cases indexed by defendant, plaintiff. Civil records on computer from 1993, on index cards prior. Records retained for 10 years. Index online from JIS-Link; see www.courts.wa.gov/jislink (also, see state introduction). Mail turnaround time 1-3 days.

Criminal Records: Access: Mail, in person, fax, online. Only the court performs in person searches; visitors may not. Search fee: none; but $20.00 if an archive search. Court makes copy: $2.00 for first page, $1.00 each add'l. Required to search: name, years to search, signed release; also helpful: address, DOB, SSN. Criminal records on computer from 1993, log book prior. Retained 5 years. Index remotely online from JIS-Link; see www.courts.wa.gov/jislink (also, see state introduction). Mail turnaround time 1-3 days.

General Information: No dependencies, adoption, confidential social files and mental illness records released. Certification fee: $5.00. Payee: San Juan County District Court. Personal checks accepted. Credit cards are accepted through OfficialPayments.Com or 1-877-876-7619. You will need to provide them with your case # or ticket #. Prepayment and SASE required.

Skagit County

Superior Court 205 W Kincaid St, #103, Mount Vernon, WA 98273; phone: 360-336-9440; hours 8:30AM-4:30PM (PST). *Felony, Civil, Eviction, Probate.*

Civil Records: Access: Mail, online, in person. Both court and visitors may perform in person searches. Search fee: $20.00 per hour. Court makes copy: $.25 per page; $1.00 per page is not scanned. Self serve copy fee: $.25 per page. Required to search: name, years to search. Civil cases indexed by defendant, plaintiff. Civil records on computer from 10/81, on microfilm and archived from 1878. Index online from JIS-Link; see www.courts.wa.gov/jislink (also, see state introduction). Mail turnaround time 5 days.

Criminal Records: Access: Mail, online, in person. Both court and visitors may perform in person searches. Search fee: $20.00 per hour. Court makes copy: $.25 per page; $1.00 per page is not scanned. Self serve copy fee: $.25 per page. Required to search: name, years to search. Criminal records on computer from 10/81, on microfilm and archived from 1878. Index remotely online from JIS-Link; see www.courts.wa.gov/jislink (also, see state introduction). Mail turnaround time 5 days.

General Information: Public use terminal available. No dependencies, adoption, and mental illness, juvenile offender prior to 07/01/78 records released. Will not fax documents. Self made copies cannot be certified. Certification fee: $5.00 for first cert page, $1.00 each add'l. Payee: Skagit County Clerk. Only cashiers checks and money orders accepted. Prepayment and SASE required.

District Court PO Box 340, Mount Vernon, WA 98273-0340; phone: 360-336-9319; fax: 360-336-9318; hours 8:30AM-4:30PM (PST). *Misdemeanor, Civil Actions Under $50,000, Small Claims.*

Civil Records: Access: Fax, mail, online, in person. Both court and visitors may perform in person searches. No search fee. Court makes copy: $.50 per page. Required to search: name, years to search; also helpful: address. Civil cases indexed by defendant, plaintiff. Civil records on computer from 1986, archived for 12 years. Open records retained for 10 years. Index online from JIS-Link; see www.courts.wa.gov/jislink (also, see state introduction). Note: Mail search requires a special form. Mail turnaround time 3-4 days.

Criminal Records: Access: Fax, mail, online, in person. Both court and visitors may perform in person searches. No search fee. Court makes copy: $.50 per page. Required to search: name, years to search, DOB; also helpful: SSN. Criminal records prior to 1995 only retained for 5 years. Index remotely online from JIS-Link; see www.courts.wa.gov/jislink (also, see state introduction). Mail turnaround time 3-4 days.

General Information: Public terminal goes back to 1987. No dependencies, alcohol, adoption, and mental illness records released. Certification fee: $5.00 includes copy fee. Payee: District Court, Skagit County. Personal checks accepted. Prepayment and SASE required.

Skamania County

Superior Court PO Box 790, Stevenson, WA 98648; phone: 509-427-9431; fax: 509-427-7386; hours 8:30AM-5PM (PST). *Felony, Civil, Eviction, Probate.*

Civil Records: Access: Phone, mail, online, in person. Only the court performs in person searches; visitors may not. Search fee: $20.00 per hour. Court makes copy: $3.00 first copy, $1.00 ea add'l. Required to search: name, years to search; also helpful: address. Civil cases indexed by defendant, plaintiff. Civil records on computer from 1984, on microfiche and archived from 1900. Index online from JIS-Link; see www.courts.wa.gov/jislink (also, see state introduction). Mail turnaround time 2 days.

Criminal Records: Access: Phone, mail, online, in person. Only the court performs in person searches; visitors may not. Search fee: $20.00 per hour. Court makes copy: $3.00 first copy, $1.00 ea add'l. Required to search: name, years to search; also helpful: address, DOB. Criminal records on computer from 1984, on microfiche and archived from 1900. Index remotely online from JIS-Link; see www.courts.wa.gov/jislink (also, see state introduction). Mail turnaround time 2 days.

General Information: No dependencies, adoption, and mental illness records released. Will fax documents to local or toll free line. Certification fee: $5.00. Payee: Skamania County Clerk. Personal checks accepted. Prepayment and SASE required.

District Court PO Box 790, Stevenson, WA 98648; phone: 509-427-9430; fax: 509-427-7386; hours 8:30AM-5PM (PST). *Misdemeanor, Civil Actions Under $50,000, Small Claims.*

Civil Records: Access: Phone, fax, mail, online, in person. Both court and visitors may perform in person searches. Search fee: $40.00 per hour. Court makes copy: $3.00 for 1st page, $1.00 each add'l. Required to search: name, years to search; also helpful: address. Civil cases indexed by defendant, plaintiff. Civil records on computer go back 10 years. Records retained for 10 years. Index online from

JIS-Link; see www.courts.wa.gov/jislink (also, see state introduction). Mail turnaround time 7 days.

Criminal Records: Access: Phone, fax, mail, online, in person. Both court and visitors may perform in person searches. Search fee: $40.00 per hour. Court makes copy: $3.00 1st page, $1.00 each add'l. Required to search: name, years to search; also helpful: address, DOB, signed release. Criminal records on computer go back 10 years. Records retained for 10 years. Index remotely online from JIS-Link; see www.courts.wa.gov/jislink (also, see state introduction). Mail turnaround time 7 days.

General Information: Public record goes back to 10 years. No dependencies, adoption, and mental illness records released. No fee to fax documents. Certification fee: $5.00. Payee: Skamania County District Court. Personal checks accepted. Prepayment and SASE required.

Snohomish County

Superior Court 3000 Rockefeller, MS 605, Everett, WA 98201; phone: 425-388-3466; hours 8:30AM-5PM (PST). *Felony, Civil Actions, Eviction, Probate.*

www.co.snohomish.wa.us

Civil Records: Access: Phone, mail, online, in person. Both court and visitors may perform in person searches. Search fee: $20.00 per hour, one hr min. Court makes copy: $2.00 first page, $1.00 ea add'l. Self serve copy fee: $.15 per page. Required to search: name, years to search. Civil cases indexed by defendant, plaintiff. Civil records on computer from 1978, prior on database index. Index online from JIS-Link; see www.courts.wa.gov/jislink (also, see state introduction). Mail turnaround time 1 week.

Criminal Records: Access: Phone, mail, online, in person. Both court and visitors may perform in person searches. Search fee: $20.00 per hour, one hr min. Court makes copy: $2.00 first page, $1.00 ea add'l. Self serve copy fee: $.15 per page. Required to search: name, years to search. Criminal records on computer from 1978, prior on database index. Index remotely online from JIS-Link; see www.courts.wa.gov/jislink (also, see state introduction). Mail turnaround time 1 week.

General Information: Public terminal goes back to 1978. No sealed, juvenile, adoption, paternity, mental health, sex offenders (victims). Certification fee: $5.00 plus $1.00 per page after first. Payee: County Clerk or Snohomish County Clerk's Office. Business checks or debit cards accepted; no personal checks. Prepayment and SASE required.

Cascade Division District Court 415 E Burke St, Arlington, WA 98223; phone: 360-435-7700; fax: 360-435-0873; hours 8:30AM-4:30PM (PST). *Misdemeanor, Civil Actions Under $50,000, Small Claims.*

Civil Records: Access: Mail, online, in person. Both court and visitors may perform in person searches. Search fee: $5.00 per name. Court makes copy: $.25 per page. Required to search: name, years to search; also helpful: address. Civil cases indexed by defendant, plaintiff. Civil records on computer from 1985. Index online from JIS-Link; see www.courts.wa.gov/jislink (also, see state introduction). Mail turnaround time 1 week.

Criminal Records: Access: Mail, online, in person. Both court and visitors may perform in person searches. Search fee: $5.00 per name. Court makes copy: $.25 per page. Required to search: name, years to search, DOB; also helpful: address, SSN. Criminal records on computer from 1987. Index remotely online from JIS-Link; see www.courts.wa.gov/jislink (also, see state introduction). Mail turnaround time 1 week.

General Information: Public use terminal available. No sealed, mental health, sex offenders (victims) or some DUI records released. Certification fee: $5.00. Payee: Cascade Division. Personal checks or Visa, MC accepted. Prepayment required.

Everett Division District Court 3000 Rockefeller Ave, MS 508, Everett, WA 98201; phone: 425-388-3331; civil phone: 425-388-3595; fax: 425-388-3565; hours 8:30AM-5PM (PST). *Misdemeanor, Civil Actions Under $50,000, Small Claims.*

Civil Records: Access: Fax, mail, online, in person. Both court and visitors may perform in person searches. No search fee. Court makes copy: $.25 per page. Required to search: complete name, years to search; also helpful: address. Civil cases indexed by defendant, plaintiff. Civil records on computer back to 1986. Index online from JIS-Link; see www.courts.wa.gov/jislink (also, see state introduction). Mail turnaround time 2-3 days.

Criminal Records: Access: Fax, mail, online, in person. Both court and visitors may perform in person searches. No search fee. Court makes copy: $.25 per page. Required to search: complete name, years to search, DOB; also helpful: address, SSN. Criminal records on computer back to 1986. Index remotely online from JIS-Link; see www.courts.wa.gov/jislink (also, see state introduction). Mail turnaround time 1 week.

General Information: Public terminal goes back to 10 years. Limited DUI records released. No fee to fax documents. Certification fee: $5.00. Payee: Everett District Court. Personal checks or Visa, MC, Discover accepted. Prepayment and SASE required.

Evergreen Division District Court 14414 179th Ave SE, Monroe, WA 98272-0625; phone: 360-805-6776; criminal phone: x5792; civil phone: 360-805-6703; fax: 360-805-6755; hours 8:30AM-4:30PM (PST). *Misdemeanor, Civil Actions Under $50,000, Small Claims.*

Civil Records: Access: Mail, in person, online. Only the court performs in person searches; visitors may not. No search fee. Court makes copy: $.25 per page. Required to search: name, years to search; also helpful: address. Civil cases indexed by defendant, plaintiff. Civil records on computer back 10 years; file retained until closure. Index online from JIS-Link; see www.courts.wa.gov/jislink (also, see state introduction). Mail turnaround time 1 week.

Criminal Records: Access: Mail, in person, online. Only the court performs in person searches; visitors may not. No search fee. Court makes copy: $.25 per page. Required to search: name, years to search; also helpful: address, DOB. Criminal records on computer archived 3 years after closure by state. Index remotely online from JIS-Link; see www.courts.wa.gov/jislink (also, see state introduction). Mail turnaround time 1 week.

General Information: No sealed, juvenile, adoption, paternity, mental health, sex offenders (victims) or some DUI records released. Will fax documents for no fee. Certification fee: $5.00 per page. Payee: Evergreen District Court. Personal checks accepted. Prepayment required. SASE requested.

South Division District Court 20520 68th Ave W, Lynnwood, WA 98036-7406; phone: 425-774-8820; fax: 425-744-6820; hours 8:30AM-4:30PM (PST). *Misdemeanor, Civil Actions Under $50,000, Small Claims.*

Civil Records: Access: Mail, online, in person. No search fee. Court makes copy: $.50 per page; same fee for self serve. Required to search: name, years to search. Civil cases indexed by case number. Civil records on computer since 1987. Index online from JIS-Link; see www.courts.wa.gov/jislink (also, see state introduction). Mail turnaround time 2-4 days.

Criminal Records: Access: Mail, online, in person. Only the court performs in person searches; visitors may not. No search fee. Court makes copy: $.50 per page; same fee for self serve. Required to search: name, years to search. Criminal records on computer since 1989. Index remotely online from JIS-Link; see www.courts.wa.gov/jislink (also, see state introduction). Mail turnaround time 2-4 days.

General Information: No sealed, juvenile, adoption, paternity, mental health, sex offenders (victims) or some DUI records released. Certification fee: $5.00

per document. Payee: South District Court. Personal checks accepted. Prepayment required. SASE requested.

Spokane County

Superior Court 1116 W Broadway, Spokane, WA 99260; phone: 509-477-2211; hours 8:30AM-5PM (PST). *Felony, Civil, Eviction, Probate.*

www.spokanecounty.org/clerk/

Civil Records: Access: Phone, mail, online, in person. Both court and visitors may perform in person searches. Search fee: $10.00 per hour. Court makes copy: $.50 per page. Required to search: name, years to search. Civil cases indexed by defendant, plaintiff. Civil records on computer from 1973, archives back to 1800s, docket books prior to computer. Index online from JIS-Link; see www.courts.wa.gov/jislink (also, see state introduction). Mail turnaround time 1-3 days.

Criminal Records: Access: Phone, mail, online, in person. Both court and visitors may perform in person searches. Search fee: $10.00 per hour. Court makes copy: $.50 per page. Required to search: name, years to search; also helpful: DOB. Criminal records on computer from 1973, archives back to 1800s, docket books prior to computer. Index remotely online from JIS-Link; see www.courts.wa.gov/jislink (also, see state introduction). Mail turnaround time 1-3 days.

General Information: Public terminal goes back to 1973. No sealed, juvenile dependency, adoption, paternity, mental health records released. Certification fee: $5.00 plus $1.00 each add'l page. Payee: Spokane County Clerk. Personal checks accepted. Prepayment and SASE required.

District Court 1100 W Mallon, Spokane, WA 99260; phone: 509-477-4770; hours 8:30AM-5PM (PST). *Misdemeanor, Civil Actions Under $50,000, Small Claims.*

www.spokanecounty.org/districtcourt

Civil Records: Access: Phone, mail, online, in person. Only the court performs in person searches; visitors may not. No search fee. Court makes copy: $1.00 per page. Required to search: name, years to search; also helpful: address. Civil cases indexed by defendant, plaintiff. Civil records on computer go back 10 years. Index online from JIS-Link; see www.courts.wa.gov/jislink (also, see state introduction). Mail turnaround time 1 week.

Criminal Records: Access: Phone, mail, online, in person. Only the court performs in person searches; visitors may not. No search fee. Court makes copy: $1.00 per page. Required to search: name, years to search, signed release; also helpful: address, DOB. Criminal records are computer since 1984, but searches are only done for five years time. Index remotely online from JIS-Link; see www.courts.wa.gov/jislink (also, see state introduction). Mail turnaround time 1 week.

General Information: Will not fax documents. Certification fee: $5.00 per cert includes copy fee. Payee: Spokane County District Court. Business checks accepted. Personal checks accepted for civil records only. Prepayment and SASE required.

Stevens County

Superior Court 215 S Oak, Rm 206, Colville, WA 99114; phone: 509-684-7575; hours 8AM-N, 1-4:30PM (PST). *Felony, Civil, Eviction, Probate.*

Civil Records: Access: Phone, mail, online, in person. Only the court performs in person searches; visitors may not. Search fee: $20.00 per hour. Court makes copy: $5.00 for 1st pg, $1.00 each add'l pg. Required to search: name, years to search; also helpful: address. Civil cases indexed by defendant, plaintiff. Civil records on computer from 10-82, microfiche from 1889-1982, archives 1889, index cards prior to 1982. Index online from JIS-Link; see www.courts.wa.gov/jislink (also, see state introduction). Mail turnaround time same day.

Criminal Records: Access: Mail, online, in person. Only the court performs in person searches;

visitors may not. Search fee: $20.00 per hour. Court makes copy: $5.00 for 1st page, $1.00 each add'l. Required to search: name, years to search, DOB; also helpful: address, SSN. Criminal records on computer from 10-82, microfiche from 1889-1982, archives 1889, index cards prior to 1982. Index remotely online from JIS-Link; see www.courts.wa.gov/jislink (also, see state introduction). Mail turnaround time same day.

General Information: No sealed, juvenile, adoption, paternity, mental health, sex offenders (victims). Will not fax documents. Certification fee: Included in copy fee. Payee: Stevens County Clerk. Personal checks accepted. Prepayment and SASE required.

District Court 215 S Oak, Rm 213, Colville, WA 99114; phone: 509-684-5249; fax: 509-684-7571; hours 8AM-N, 1-4:30PM (PST). *Misdemeanor, Civil Actions Under $50,000, Small Claims.*
www.co.stevens.wa.us/distcourt/departments.htm

Civil Records: Access: Mail, online, in person. Only the court performs in person searches; visitors may not. No search fee. Court makes copy: $.15 per page; same fee for self serve. Required to search: name, years to search; also helpful: address. Civil cases indexed by defendant. Civil records on computer from 1/93, prior on docket books to 1988. Index online from JIS-Link; see www.courts.wa.gov/jislink (also, see state introduction). Mail turnaround time 1 week.

Criminal Records: Access: Fax, mail, online, in person. Only the court performs in person searches; visitors may not. No search fee. Court makes copy: $.15 per page; same fee for self serve. Required to search: name, years to search, DOB; also helpful: address, SSN, signed request. Criminal records on computer from 7/93, prior on docket books to 1988. Index remotely online from JIS-Link; see www.courts.wa.gov/jislink (also, see state introduction). Mail turnaround time 1 week.

General Information: No sealed, juvenile, adoption, paternity, mental health, sex offenders (victims) or some DUI records released. Fee to fax documents is $1.00 per page. Certification fee: $5.00 includes copy fee. Payee: Stevens County District Court. Business checks accepted. Prepayment required.

Thurston County

Superior Court Thurston County Clerk, 2000 Lakeridge Dr SW, Bldg 2, Olympia, WA 98502; phone: 360-786-5430; fax: 360-753-4033; hours 8AM-5PM (PST). *Felony, Misdemeanor, Civil, Eviction, Probate.*
www.co.thurston.wa.us/clerk

Civil Records: Access: Phone, mail, in person, email, online. Both court and visitors may perform in person searches. Search fee: $20.00 per hour. Court makes copy: $5.00 for 1st page, $1.00 each add'l. Self serve copy fee: $.25 per page. Required to search: name, years to search; also helpful: address. Civil cases indexed by defendant, plaintiff. Civil records on computer from 7/78, archives back to 1850s. Index online from JIS-Link; see www.courts.wa.gov/jislink (also, see state introduction). Mail turnaround time within 48 hours.

Criminal Records: Access: Phone, mail, in person, email. Both court and visitors may perform in person searches. Search fee: $20.00 per hour. Court makes copy: $5.00 for 1st page, $1.00 each add'l. Self serve copy fee: $.25 per page. Required to search: name, years to search, DOB, signed release; also helpful: address, SSN. Criminal records on computer from 7/78, archives back to 1850s. Index remotely online from JIS-Link; see www.courts.wa.gov/jislink (also, see state introduction). Mail turnaround time 1-7 days.

General Information: Public terminal has criminal back to 1950 and civil back to 1847. No sealed, juvenile, adoption, paternity, mental health, sex offenders (victims). Certification fee: Included in court copy fee. Payee: Thurston County Clerk.

Business checks accepted. Prepayment and SASE required.

District Court 2000 Lakeridge Dr SW, Bldg 3, Olympia, WA 98502; phone: 360-786-5450; fax: 360-754-3359; hours 8:30AM-4PM (PST). *Misdemeanor, Civil Actions Under $50,000, Small Claims.*
www.co.thurston.wa.us/distcrt
Note: Daily court calendars are available at www.co.thurston.wa.us/distcrt/courtcalendars.htm.

Civil Records: Access: Phone, fax, mail, online, in person. Both court and visitors may perform in person searches. No search fee. Court makes copy: $.25 per page. Required to search: name, years to search; also helpful: address. Civil cases indexed by defendant, plaintiff. Civil records on computer from 1983. Index online from JIS-Link; see www.courts.wa.gov/jislink (also, see state introduction). Mail turnaround time 2 weeks.

Criminal Records: Access: Phone, fax, mail, online, in person. Both court and visitors may perform in person searches. No search fee. Court makes copy: $.25 per page. Required to search: name, years to search; also helpful: address, DOB, SSN. Criminal records on computer from 1988. Index remotely online from JIS-Link; see www.courts.wa.gov/jislink (also, see state introduction). Mail turnaround time 2 weeks.

General Information: Public terminal goes back to 1990. No sealed, juvenile, adoption, paternity, mental health, sex offenders (victims) or some DUI records released. Will fax documents. Certification fee: $5.00 includes copy fee. Payee: Thurston County District Court. Personal checks accepted. Prepayment and SASE required.

Wahkiakum County

Superior Court PO Box 116, Cathlamet, WA 98612; phone: 360-795-3558; fax: 360-795-8813; hours 8AM-4PM (PST). *Felony, Misdemeanor, Civil, Eviction, Probate.*

Civil Records: Access: Fax, mail, online, in person. Both court and visitors may perform in person searches. Search fee: $20.00 per hour. Court makes copy: $.50 per page. Required to search: name, years to search. Civil cases indexed by defendant, plaintiff. Civil records on computer from 1988, archives from 1850s. Index online from JIS-Link; see www.courts.wa.gov/jislink (also, see state introduction). Mail turnaround time 1 day.

Criminal Records: Access: Fax, mail, online, in person. Both court and visitors may perform in person searches. Search fee: $20.00 per hour. Court makes copy: $.50 per page. Required to search: name, years to search; also helpful: address, DOB. Criminal records on computer from 1988, archives from 1850s. Index remotely online from JIS-Link; see www.courts.wa.gov/jislink (also, see state introduction). Mail turnaround time 1 day.

General Information: No sealed, juvenile, adoption, paternity, mental health, sex offender victims. Fee to fax documents is $1.00 per page. Certification fee: $5.00 for 1st page, $1.00 ea add'l. Cert fee includes copies. Payee: County Clerk. Personal checks accepted. Prepayment and SASE required.

District Court PO Box 144, Cathlamet, WA 98612; phone: 360-795-3461; fax: 360-795-6506; hours 8AM-4PM (PST). *Misdemeanor, Civil Actions Under $50,000, Small Claims.*

Civil Records: Access: Phone, fax, mail, online, in person. Both court and visitors may perform in person searches. No search fee. Court makes copy: $.25 per page. Required to search: name, years to search; also helpful: address. Civil cases indexed by defendant, plaintiff. Civil records on computer from 1997, index cards back to 1980, archived prior. Index online from JIS-Link; see www.courts.wa.gov/jislink (also, see state introduction). Mail turnaround time 2 days.

Criminal Records: Access: Phone, fax, mail, online, in person. Both court and visitors may perform in

person searches. No search fee. Court makes copy: $.25 per page. Required to search: name, years to search; also helpful: DOB. Criminal records on computer from 1997, index cards back to 1990, archived prior. Index remotely online from JIS-Link; see www.courts.wa.gov/jislink (also, see state introduction). Mail turnaround time 2 days.

General Information: No sealed, juvenile, adoption, paternity, mental health, sex offenders (victims) or some DUI records released. No fee to fax documents. Certification fee: $5.00. Payee: Wahkiakum District Court. Personal checks accepted. Prepayment and SASE required.

Walla Walla County

Superior Court PO Box 836, Walla Walla, WA 99362; phone: 509-527-3221; fax: 509-527-3214; hours 9AM-4PM (PST). *Felony, Civil, Eviction, Probate.*

Civil Records: Access: Phone, mail, in person. Only the court performs in person searches; visitors may not. Search fee: $20.00 per hour. Court makes copy: $.50 per page. Required to search: name, years to search; also helpful: DOB. Civil cases indexed by defendant, plaintiff. Civil records on computer from 7/81, prior in docket books. Mail turnaround time 1 day.

Criminal Records: Access: Phone, mail, in person. Only the court performs in person searches; visitors may not. Search fee: $20.00 per hour. Court makes copy: $.50 per page. Required to search: name, years to search, DOB; also helpful: address, SSN. Criminal records on computer from 7/81, prior in docket books. Mail turnaround time 1 day.

General Information: No sealed, juvenile, adoption, paternity, mental health, sex offenders (victims). Certification fee: $5.00 1st page, $1.00 ea add'l. Cert fee includes copies. Payee: Walla Walla County Clerk. Personal checks not accepted; only cashiers checks and money orders accepted. Prepayment required.

District Court 317 W Rose St, Walla Walla, WA 99362; phone: 509-527-3236; fax: 509-522-3343; hours 9AM-4PM (PST). *Misdemeanor, Civil Actions Under $50,000, Small Claims.*

Civil Records: Access: Mail, online, in person. Only the court performs in person searches; visitors may not. Search fee: $10.00 per name. Court makes copy: $1.00 for first page, $.50 each add'l; same fee for self serve. Required to search: full name, DOB years to search. Civil cases indexed by defendant, plaintiff. Civil records on computer from 7/87, on index books. Records retained for 10 years. Index online from JIS-Link; see www.courts.wa.gov/jislink (also, see state introduction). Mail turnaround time 1-3 days.

Criminal Records: Access: Mail, online, in person. Only the court performs in person searches; visitors may not. Search fee: $5.00 per name. Court makes copy: $1.00 for first page, $.50 each add'l; same fee for self serve. Required to search: full name, DOB years to search, signed release; also helpful: address, SSN. Criminal records on computer from 7/87, on index books. Records retained for 10 years. Index remotely online from JIS-Link; see www.courts.wa.gov/jislink (also, see state introduction). Mail turnaround time 1-3 days.

General Information: No sealed, juvenile, adoption, paternity, mental health, sex offenders (victims) or some DUI records released. Will fax documents for no add'l fee. Certification fee: $5.00 per document; add copy fee for add'l pages. Payee: Walla Walla District Court. Personal checks accepted. Prepayment and SASE required.

Whatcom County

Superior Court PO Box 1144, Bellingham, WA 98227; phone: 360-676-6777; criminal phone: x50014; civil phone: x50018; fax: 360-676-6693; hours 8:30-4:30PM (PST). *Felony, Civil, Eviction, Probate.*

Civil Records: Access: Phone, fax, mail, online, in person. Both court and visitors may perform in person searches. Search fee: No search fee if record is on computer. Court makes copy: $.50 per page. Self serve copy fee: $.15 per page. Required to search: name, years to search; also helpful: address. Civil cases indexed by defendant, plaintiff. Civil records on computer from 1980, archives back to 1800s, index cards. Index online from JIS-Link; see www.courts.wa.gov/jislink (also, see state introduction). Mail turnaround time up to 1 week.

Criminal Records: Access: Phone, fax, mail, online, in person. Both court and visitors may perform in person searches. Search fee: $20.00 per hour. Court makes copy: $.50 per page. Self serve copy fee: $.15 per page. Required to search: name, years to search; also helpful: address, DOB, SSN. Criminal records on computer from 1980, archives back to 1800s, index cards. Index remotely online from JIS-Link; see www.courts.wa.gov/jislink (also, see state introduction). Mail turnaround time up to 1 week.

General Information: Public terminal goes back to 1/2005. No sealed, juvenile, adoption, paternity, mental health, sex offenders (victims). Certification fee: $5.00 1st page, $1.00 ea add'l. Cert fee includes copies. Payee: Whatcom County Clerk. Only cashiers checks and money orders accepted. Prepayment and SASE required.

District Court 311 Grand Ave, #401, Bellingham, WA 98225; phone: 360-676-6770; fax: 360-676-7685; hours 8AM-4:30PM (PST). *Misdemeanor, Civil Actions Under $50,000, Small Claims.*
www.co.whatcom.wa.us
Civil Records: Access: Fax, mail, online, in person. Only the court performs in person searches; visitors may not. No search fee. Court makes copy: $.25 per page. Required to search: name, years to search; also helpful: address. Civil cases indexed by defendant, plaintiff. Civil records on computer since 1984. Index online from JIS-Link; see www.courts.wa.gov/jislink (also, see state introduction). Mail turnaround time 2 days.

Criminal Records: Access: Fax, mail, online, in person. Only the court performs in person searches; visitors may not. No search fee. Court makes copy: $.25 per page. Required to search: name, years to search; also helpful: address, DOB, SSN. Criminal records on computer 10 years back, archived since 1984. Index remotely online from JIS-Link; see www.courts.wa.gov/jislink (also, see state introduction). Mail turnaround time 2 days.

General Information: No sealed, juvenile, adoption, paternity, mental health, sex offenders (victims) or some DUI records released. Certification fee: $5.00 per cert includes copy fee. Payee: Whatcom District Court. Personal checks accepted. Prepayment required.

Whitman County

Superior Court Whitman County Clerk, PO Box 390, Colfax, WA 99111; phone: 509-397-6240; hours 9AM-5PM (PST). *Felony, Civil, Eviction, Probate.*
Civil Records: Access: Phone, fax, mail, online, in person. Only the court performs in person searches; visitors may not. Search fee: $8.00 per hour. Court makes copy: $.15 per page. Required to search: name, years to search; also helpful: address. Civil cases indexed by defendant, plaintiff. Civil records on computer from 1985, archives back to 1887. Index online from JIS-Link; see www.courts.wa.gov/jislink (also, see state introduction). Mail turnaround time 1 week.
Criminal Records: Access: Phone, fax, mail, online, in person. Only the court performs in person

searches; visitors may not. Search fee: $8.00 per hour. Court makes copy: $.15 per page. Required to search: name, years to search, signed release; also helpful: address, DOB, SSN. Criminal records on computer from 1985, archives back to 1887. Index remotely online from JIS-Link; see www.courts.wa.gov/jislink (also, see state introduction). Mail turnaround time 1 week.
General Information: No sealed, juvenile, adoption, paternity, mental health, sex offenders (victims). Will fax documents $4.00 for 1st page, $1.00 each add'l. Certification fee: $5.00 plus $1.00 per page after first. Payee: Whitman County Clerk. Personal checks accepted. Prepayment and SASE required.

District Court 400 N Main St, PO Box 230, Colfax, WA 99111; phone: 509-397-6260; fax: 509-397-5584; hours 8AM-5PM; Public Hours: 8:30AM-4:30PM (PST). *Misdemeanor, Civil Actions Under $50,000, Small Claims.*
Civil Records: Access: Phone, fax, mail, online, in person. Both court and visitors may perform in person searches. Search fee: $8.00. Court makes copy: $.15 per page; same fee for self serve. Required to search: name, years to search; also helpful: address. Civil cases indexed by defendant, plaintiff. Civil records on DISCIS computer system from 7/91, prior on index log. Index online from JIS-Link; see www.courts.wa.gov/jislink (also, see state introduction). Mail turnaround time 2 weeks.
Criminal Records: Access: Phone, fax, mail, online, in person. Both court and visitors may perform in person searches. Search fee: $8.00. Court makes copy: $.15 per page; same fee for self serve. Required to search: name, years to search, DOB; also helpful: address, SSN. Criminal records on DISCIS computer system from 7/91, prior on index log. Index remotely online from JIS-Link; see www.courts.wa.gov/jislink (also, see state introduction). Mail turnaround time 2 weeks.
General Information: Public terminal has criminal back to 7/1991 and civil back to 10 years. No sealed, juvenile, adoption, paternity, mental health, sex offenders (victims) or some DUI records released. Fee to fax documents is $2.00. Certification fee: $5.00. Payee: Whitman County. Personal checks accepted. Prepayment and SASE required.

District Court 325 SE Paradise St, Pullman, WA 99163; phone: 509-332-2065; fax: 509-338-3318; hours 8AM-5PM (PST). *Misdemeanor, Civil Actions Under $50,000, Small Claims.*
Civil Records: Access: Fax, mail, online, in person. Only the court performs in person searches; visitors may not. Search fee: $8.00 per name. Court makes copy: $.15 per page. Required to search: name, years to search; also helpful: address. Civil cases indexed by defendant, plaintiff. Civil records on DISCIS computer system from 7/91; '89-'91 on index. Index online from JIS-Link; see www.courts.wa.gov/jislink (also, see state introduction). Mail turnaround time 1 week.
Criminal Records: Access: Fax, mail, online, in person. Only the court performs in person searches; visitors may not. Search fee: $8.00 per name. Court makes copy: $.15 per page. Required to search: name, years to search; also helpful: address, DOB, SSN. Criminal records on DISCIS computer system from 7/91; '89-'91 on index. Index remotely online from JIS-Link; see www.courts.wa.gov/jislink (also, see state introduction). Mail turnaround time 1 week.
General Information: No sealed, juvenile, adoption, paternity, mental health, sex offenders (victims) or some DUI records released. No fee to fax documents. Certification fee: $6.00. Payee: Whitman District

Court. Personal checks accepted. Prepayment and SASE required.

Yakima County

Superior Court 128 N 2nd St, Rm 314, Yakima, WA 98901; phone: 509-574-1430; probate phone: 509-574-1430; hours 8:30AM-4:30PM (PST). *Felony, Civil, Domestic Relations, Probate.*
www.pan.co.yakima.wa.us/clerk
Civil Records: Access: Phone, mail, in person, online. Only the court performs in person searches; visitors may not. Search fee: $20.00 per hour. Court makes copy: $.50 per page. Microfilm copies $.25 per page. Required to search: name, years to search. Civil cases indexed by defendant, plaintiff. Civil records on computer from 1978, archives back to 1890s. Index online from JIS-Link; see www.courts.wa.gov/jislink (also, see state introduction). Mail turnaround time varies.
Criminal Records: Access: Phone, mail, in person, online. Only the court performs in person searches; visitors may not. Search fee: $20.00 per hour. Court makes copy: $.50 per page. Microfilm copies $.25 per page. Required to search: name, years to search; also helpful: DOB. Criminal records on computer from 1978, archives back to 1890s. Index remotely online from JIS-Link; see www.courts.wa.gov/jislink (also, see state introduction). Mail turnaround time varies.
General Information: No sealed, juvenile, adoption, paternity, mental health, sex offenders (victims). Certification fee: $5.00 plus $1.00 per page after first. Payee: Yakima County Clerk. Business checks accepted, personal checks are not. Prepayment and SASE required.

District Court 128 N 2nd St, Rm 217, Yakima, WA 98901-2631; phone: 509-574-1800; fax: 509-574-1831; hours 8:30AM-4:30PM (PST). *Misdemeanor, Civil Actions Under $50,000, Small Claims.*
www.co.yakima.wa.us/courts
Civil Records: Access: Fax, mail, online, in person. Both court and visitors may perform in person searches. No search fee. Court makes copy: $.15 per page. Required to search: name, years to search; also helpful: address. Civil cases indexed by defendant, plaintiff. Civil records on computer from 1984, generally. Index online from JIS-Link; see www.courts.wa.gov/jislink (also, see state introduction). Note: Search requests to the court must be in writing. Mail turnaround time 2 days.
Criminal Records: Access: Fax, mail, online, in person. Both court and visitors may perform in person searches. No search fee. Court makes copy: $.15 per page. Required to search: name, years to search, DOB; also helpful: address, case number, DRL, SSN. Criminal records on computer from 1984, generally. Index remotely online from JIS-Link; see www.courts.wa.gov/jislink (also, see state introduction). Note: Search requests to the court must be in writing. Mail turnaround time 2 days.
General Information: No sealed or some DUI records released. No fee to fax documents. Certification fee: $5.00 per document. Payee: Yakima County District Court. Personal checks accepted. Credit cards accepted. Prepayment required. SASE requested.

Washington Recording Offices

ORGANIZATION: 39 counties, 39 recording offices. The recording officer is County Auditor. County records are usually combined in a Grantor/Grantee index. The entire state is in the Pacific Time Zone (PST).

REAL ESTATE RECORDS: Many County Auditors will perform real estate searches, including record owner. Search fees and copy fees vary. Copies usually cost $1.00 per page and $2.00 for certification per document. If the Auditor does not provide searches, contact the Assessor for record owner information. Contact the Treasurer (Finance Department in King County) for information about unpaid real estate taxes.

UCC RECORDS: Financing statements are filed at the state level, except for real estate related collateral, which are filed with the County Auditor. Most recording offices will perform UCC searches. Use search request form UCC-11R. Searches fees vary, copy fee is usually $1.00.

TAX LIEN RECORDS: All federal tax liens on personal property are filed with the Department of Licensing. Other federal and all state tax liens are filed with the County Auditor. Most counties will perform tax lien searches. Search fees are usually $8.00 or $10.00 per hour.

ONLINE ACCESS: A number of counties offer access to assessor or real estate records including the larger population counties.

Adams County

County Auditor, 210 W Broadway #200, Ritzville, WA 99169. 509-659-3253; fax-509-659-3254; hours: 8:30AM-4:30PM. www.co.adams.wa.us
All records in one index. Records indexed on a public use terminal back to 3/1998. Office personnel or visitors may perform searches. Search fee $8.00 per hour, 1 hour minimum. Copy fee $1.00 per page. Cert fee- $3.00 per doc includes 1st page copy fee; add copy fee for add'l pages. Payee- County Auditor. **Online access to Property Tax, Sale records:** Access to county property tax and sales records is free at http://adamswa.taxsifter.com/taxsifter/t-parcelsearch.asp. No name searching. **Other phones:** Treasurer- 509-659-3227; Appraiser/Auditor- 509-659-3253; Elections- 509-659-3249; Vital Records- 509-659-3253. **Property tax/Assessor-** 210 W Broadway #105, Ritzville, WA 99169; 509-659-3200.

Asotin County

County Auditor, PO Box 129, Asotin, WA 99402. 509-243-2084, R/E recording phone-509-246-2084; fax-509-243-2087; hours: 7;30AM-5;30PM. www.co.asotin.wa.us
All records in one index. Office personnel may search by written or fax request. General index search fee $10.00 per search. Copy fee $1.00 per page. Cert fee- $3.00 per doc plus copy fee. Payee-Asotin County Auditor. **Online access to Real Estate Recording, Deed records:** Access recording office land data at www.etitlesearch.com; registration required, fee based on usage. **Other phones:** Treasurer- 509-243-2010; Appraiser/Auditor- 509-243-2016; Elections- 509-243-2084; Vital Records- 509-243-2084. **Property tax/Assessor-** same address as above. 509-243-2016.

Benton County

County Auditor, PO Box 470, Prosser, WA 99350. 509-786-5616; fax-509-786-5528; hours: 8AM-5PM. The county also has a second recording office located at 5600 W. Canal, Ste B, Kennewick, WA 99336. Records indexed on a public use terminal back to 1985. Before 1985, on rolls of film. Office personnel or visitors may perform searches. RE search fee for a range of years is $8.00 per hour. Copy fee $1.00 per page. Cert fee- $2.00 per doc plus copy fee. Payee- Benton County Auditor. **Online access to Assessor, Property records:** Assess to Benton County assessor data is free at http://bentonpropertymax.governmaxa.com/propertymax/rover30.asp. Search by parcel ID#, address or map; no name searching. **Other phones:** Treasurer- 509-786-2255; Appraiser/Auditor- 509-736-3085; Elections- 509-786-5618; Vital Records- 509-786-5616. **Property**

tax/Assessor- PO Box 902, Prosser, WA 99350; 509-786-2046.

Chelan County

County Auditor, PO Box 400, Wenatchee, WA 98807. 509-667-6815; fax-509-667-6244; hours: 9AM-5PM. www.co.chelan.wa.us
All records in one index. General index search fee $8.00 per hour. Will search real estate records. Will search UCC records and tax liens. UCC search per debtor name- $8.00 per hour; 1 hour min. Tax lien search fee- $8.00 per hour. Separate federal tax lien search- $8.00 per hour. Separate state tax lien search- $8.00 per hour. Copy fee $1.00 per page. Cert fee- $2.00 per doc plus copy fee. Payee-Chelan County Auditor. **Online access to Grantor/Grantee, Property, Marriage records:** Access to the Auditor's iCRIS database is free at www.co.chelan.wa.us/ad/ad5da.htm. Images go back to 1974; marriage images to 1990. **Other phones:** Treasurer- 509-667-6405; Appraiser/Auditor- 509-667-6368; Elections- 509-667-6808; Vital Records- 360-236-4300. **Property tax/Assessor-** 509-667-6365.

Clallam County

Recording Dept, 223 E. Fourth St #1, Port Angeles, WA 98362. 360-417-2220; fax-360-417-2517; hours: 8:30AM-4:30PM. www.clallam.net
All records in one index. Records indexed on a public use terminal back to 1984. Office will perform a UCC and Tax lien search but public must search other records themselves. Search fee $10.00. Copy fee $1.00 per page. Cert fee- $3.00 1st page, $1.00 each add'l page. Payee- Clallam County Auditor. **Online Property, Assessor records:** Access to assessor property data is free at www.clallam.net/RealEstate/html/land_parcel_search.htm; search by address or property number only. Auditor property maps are also downloadable at www.clallam.net/RealEstate/html/recorded_maps.htm. Auditor records will be online at a later date. **Other phones:** Treasurer- 360-417-2250; Elections- 360-417-2217; Vital Records- 360-417-2303. **Property tax/Assessor-** same address as above. 360-417-2204.

Clark County

County Auditor, PO Box 5000, Vancouver, WA 98666-5000. 360-397-2208; fax-360-397-2137; hours: 8AM-5PM. www.co.clark.wa.us/auditor/
Recording index, 1978 forward. All records in one index granter/grantee index. Search fee $8.00 per hour. Will not search real estate records. Copy fee $1.00 per page. Cert fee- $2.00 per doc, does not include copies. Payee- Clark County Auditor. **Online access to Real Estate, Lien, Vital Statistic, Recording, Most Wanted, Sex Offender records:** Access to County Auditor's database is at

http://auditor.co.clark.wa.us/auditor_new/index.cfm. Court documents are excluded from this index. Also, search maps online for property data at http://gis.clark.wa.gov/ccgis/mol/property.htm. No name searching. **Other phones:** Treasurer- 360-397-2252; Appraiser/Auditor- 360-397-2391; Elections- 360-397-2345; Vital Records- 360-397-2243; Auditor Main Line- 360-397-2241. **Property tax/Assessor-** 1300 Franklin St, 2nd Fl, Vancouver, WA 98660; 360-397-2391.

Columbia County

County Auditor, 341 E. Main St., Dayton, WA 99328-1361. 509-382-4541; fax-509-382-4830; hours: 8:30AM-4:30PM. www.columbiaco.com
Separate indices to search include prior to 1999 in books. Records indexed on a public use terminal back to 1999. Office personnel or visitors may perform searches. Search fee $8.00 per hour. Will not search real estate records. Copy fee $1.00 per page. Cert fee- $2.00 per doc plus copy fee. Payee-Columbia County Auditor. **Other phones:** Treasurer- 509-382-2641; Appraiser/Auditor- 509-382-2131; Elections- 509-382-4541. **Property tax/Assessor-** 509-382-2131.

Cowlitz County

County Auditor, 207 Fourth Ave North, Kelso, WA 98626. 360-577-3006; fax-360-414-5552; hours: 8:30AM-5PM. www.co.cowlitz.wa.us/auditor/
All records in one index. Records indexed on a public use terminal back to 1987. Office will perform a UCC and Tax lien search but public must search other records themselves. General index search fee $8.00 per hour. Copy fee $1.00 per page. Cert fee- $2.00 per doc plus copy fee. Payee- Cowlitz County Auditor. **Online access to Most Wanted, Missing Person records:** Access to sheriff's most wanted, registered sex offender and missing persons lists is free at www.co.cowlitz.wa.us/sheriff/. Also, access to the county building permits list is at http://cowlitz.solidweb.com/permits/permitsearch.asp. **Other phones:** Treasurer- 360-577-3060; Appraiser/Auditor- 360-577-3005; Elections- 360-577-3002; Vital Records- 360-577-5599. **Property tax/Assessor-** same address as above. 360-577-3010.

Douglas County

County Auditor, PO Box 456, Waterville, WA 98858. 509-745-8527, R/E recording phone-509-745-8527 x204; fax-509-745-8812; hours: 8:30AM-4PM. www.douglascountywa.net
Records indexed on a public use terminal back to 1986. Office personnel or visitors may perform searches. Search fee $8.00 per name. Copy fee $1.00 per page. Cert fee- $3.00 1st, $1.00 each

add'l page. Payee- Douglas County Auditor. **Online access to Assessor, Plat, Property records:** Access to the County Parcel Search is free at http://douglaswa.taxsifter.com/taxsifter/T-Parcelsearch.asp. **Other phones:** Treasurer- 509-745-8525; Appraiser/Auditor- 509-884-9403; Elections- 509-745-8527 x203; Vital Records- 509-745-8527 x204. **Property tax/Assessor-** 509-745-8521.

Ferry County

County Auditor, 350 E. Delaware #2, Republic, WA 99166. 509-775-5200; fax-509-775-5208; hours: 8AM-4PM.
Separate indices to search include computer from 2000 to present, prior to 2000 by book index. Records indexed on computer back to 2000. Office personnel or visitors may perform searches. Search fee $8.00 per hour for anything over 15 minutes. Copy fee $1.00 per page. Cert fee- $3.00 1st page, $1.00 add'l page plus copy fee. Payee- Ferry County Auditor. **Other phones:** Treasurer- 509-775-5238; Appraiser/Auditor- 509-775-5209; Elections- 509-775-5208; Vital Records- 509-775-5200. **Property tax/Assessor-** 350 E Delaware #1, Republic, WA 99166.; 509-775-5203.

Franklin County

County Auditor, PO Box 1451, Pasco, WA 99301. 509-545-3536; fax-509-545-3529; hours: 8:30AM-5PM.
Only the public may search. Copy fee $1.00 per page. Cert fee- $3.00 1st page; $1 each add'l. Payee- Franklin County Auditor. **Online access to Assessor, Property, Sex Offender records:** Search for property information by address or parcel number at www.co.franklin.wa.us/assessor. Also, search for residential sales data. Also, search the level 2 sex offenders at www.co.franklin.wa.us/sheriff/?p=14&v=2. Level 3 sex offenders are at www.co.franklin.wa.us/sheriff/?p=14&v=3. **Other phones:** Treasurer- 509-545-3518; Elections- 509-545-3538; Vital Records- 509-586-0207 X229. **Property tax/Assessor-** 509-545-3506.

Garfield County

County Auditor, PO Box 278, Pomeroy, WA 99347-0278. 509-843-1411; fax-509-843-3941; hours: 8:30AM-5PM.
Will look us records if customer knows recording number. Only the public may search. Copy fee $1.00 per page. Cert fee- $2.00 per cert plus copy fee. Payee- Garfield County Auditor. **Other phones:** Treasurer- 509-843-1531; Appraiser/Auditor- 509-843-1411; Elections- 509-843-1411; Vital Records- 509-843-1411. **Property tax/Assessor-** 509-843-3632.

Grant County

County Auditor, PO Box 37, Ephrata, WA 98823. 509-754-2011 x336; hours: 8AM-5PM.
Separate indices to search include grantor/grantee, legal description, parcel number, excise tax aff number. Office will perform a UCC search (must use a UCC 22R search form) but public must search other records themselves. UCC search per debtor name- $8.00 per hour. Copy fee $1.00 per page. Cert fee- $3.00 1st page, $1.00 each add'l plus copy fee. Payee- Grant County Auditor. **Other phones:** Treasurer- 509-754-2011 x353; Appraiser/Auditor- 509-754-2011 x377; Elections- 509-754-2011 x377. **Property tax/Assessor-** same address as above. 509-754-2011 x310.

Grays Harbor County

County Auditor, 101 W. Broadway, #2, Montesano, WA. 98563. 360-249-4232 x2, R/E recording phone-360-249-4232; fax-360-249-3330; hours: 8AM-5PM. www.co.grays-harbor.wa.us
All records in one index. Records indexed on a public use terminal back to 1981. Office will perform a UCC and Tax lien search but public must search other records themselves. Search fee $8.00. Copy fee $1.00 per page. Cert fee- $3.00 for

1st page, $1.00 each add'l pg. **Online access to Assessor, Treasurer, Property Tax, Docket Information, Registered Sex Offenders records:** Access to the county Parcel Database is free at http://bentonpropertymax.governmaxa.com/propertymax/rover30.asp. Search by parcel ID#, address, legal description, but no name searching. Also, Docket information access at www.co.grays-harbor.wa.us/info/clerk/docket/index.htm. Also, Registered Sex Offenders access at www.co.grays-harbor.wa.us/info/sheriff/Offenders/index.html. **Other phones:** Treasurer- 360-249-3751; Appraiser/Auditor- 360-249-4232; Elections- 360-249-4232. **Property tax/Assessor-** 100 W. Broadway, #21, Montesano, WA 98563; 360-249-4121.

Island County

Deputy Auditor, PO Box 5000, Coupeville, WA 98239. 360-679-7366, R/E recording phone-360-240-5549, UCC recording phone-360-679-7366; fax-360-240-5553; hours: 8AM-4:30PM. www.islandcounty.net/auditor
All records in one index. Records indexed back to 1984. Only the public may search. Copy fee $1.00 per page. Cert fee- $2.00 + $1.00 per page plus copy fee. Payee- Island County Auditor. **Online access to Sex Offender records:** Search the sexual offenders and kidnappers list for free at www.islandcounty.net/sheriff/rsolist.htm. **Other phones:** Treasurer- 360-679-7302; Appraiser/Auditor- 360-679-7366; Elections- 360-679-7366; Vital Records- 360-240-5540. **Property tax/Assessor-** 360-679-7303.

Jefferson County

County Auditor, PO Box 563, Port Townsend, WA 98368. 360-385-9116; fax-360-385-9228; hours: 8AM-5PM.
www.co.jefferson.wa.us/auditor/recording/Recording.asp
All records in one index. Office personnel or visitors may perform searches. General index search fee $8.00 per hour. Will search single real estate records but not for a title company. Will search UCC records, search includes tax liens. Copy fee $1.00 per page. Cert fee- $3.00 1st page; $1.00 each add'l page. Payee- Jefferson County Auditor. **Online access to Assessor, Real Estate, Recording, Vital Statistic, Grantor/Grantee, Lien, Deed, UCC, Permit, Restaurant, Inmate, Plat, Permit records:** Access the "Recorded Document Search" database at www.co.jefferson.wa.us/_hidden/disclaimer.htm. Includes grantor/grantee index and records on the County Property (Tax Parcel) Database Tool, also plats and survey images. Also, search for building permits but no name searching. **Other phones:** Treasurer- 360-385-9150; Elections- 360-385-9119. **Property tax/Assessor-** 360-385-9105.

King County

Superintendent of Records, 500 4th Ave; Admin. Bldg, Rm 311, Seattle, WA 98104. 206-296-1570; fax-206-205-8396; hours: 8:30AM-4:30PM. www.metrokc.gov
Records indexed on a public use terminal back to 1991. Office personnel or visitors may perform searches. Search fee $8.00 per 5 year search. Copy fee $1.00 per page. Cert fee- $3.00 per copy. Payee- King County Recorder's Office. **Online access to Real Estate, Lien, Marriage, Recorder, Deed, Judgment, Vital Statistic records:** Access to the recorder's database is free at www.metrokc.gov/recelec/records or at http://146.129.54.93:8193/localization/menu.asp. Also, property records on Dept. of Developmental and Environmental Resources database are free at www.metrokc.gov/ddes/gis/parcel. After the disclaimer page, search by parcel number, address, street intersection, or map. **Other phones:** Treasurer- 206-296-3850; Appraiser/Auditor- 206-296-8683; Elections- 206-296-1565; Vital Records- 206-296-4768; Finance Dept- 206-296-3850. **Property tax/Assessor-** 206-296-7300.

Kitsap County

County Auditor, 614 Division St; Rm 106 /MS 31, Port Orchard, WA 98366. 360-337-4935, R/E recording phone-360-337-7133; fax-360-337-4645; hours: 8AM-4:30PM.
www.kitsapgov.com/aud/default.htm
Records indexed on computer back to 1987. Office personnel or visitors may perform searches. Search fee $8.00. Copy fee $1.00 per page. Cert fee- $3.00 1st page, $1.00 each add'l page. Payee- Kitsap County Auditor. **Online access to Auditor, Property Tax, Grantor/Grantee, Recording, Deed, Lien, Vital Statistic, Judgment records:** Access to the auditor's recording database is free at http://kcwppub4.co.kitsap.wa.us/icris/splash.jsp. Fee to print official documents. Searches can also be performed for property and tax information on the land information system site at http://kcwppub3.co.kitsap.wa.us/website/assessor/search.asp. No name searching. **Other phones:** Treasurer- 360-876-7135; Appraiser/Auditor- 360-227-7129; Elections- 360-337-7128. **Property tax/Assessor-** same address as above. 360-876-7160.

Kittitas County

County Auditor, 205 W. 5th, Ste. #105, Ellensburg, WA 98926-3129. 509-962-7504; fax-509-962-7687; hours: 9AM-5PM. www.co.kittitas.wa.us/
All records in one index. Office personnel or visitors may perform searches. General index search fee $8.00 per name. Will search real estate records. Will search UCC records, tax liens not included in UCC search. Copy fee $1.00 per page. Cert fee- $3.00 1st page, $1.00 each add'l page. **Other phones:** Treasurer- 509-962-7535; Appraiser/Auditor- 509-962-7501; Elections- 509-962-7503; Vital Records- 509-962-7504; Health Department- 509-962-7515. **Property tax/Assessor-** 509-962-7501.

Klickitat County

County Auditor, 205 S. Columbus Ave; MS-CH-2, Goldendale, WA 98620. 509-773-4001; fax-509-773-4244; hours: 9AM-5PM. www.klickitatcounty.org
All records in one index. Records indexed on a public use terminal back to 1981. Office personnel or visitors may perform searches. General index search fee $8.00 per name. Copy fee $1.00 per copy. Cert fee- $3.00 per page plus copy fee. **Other phones:** Treasurer- 509-773-4664; Appraiser/Auditor- 509-773-4001; Elections- 509-773-4001; Vital Records- 509-773-4001; Toll Free Auditor- 800-583-8050. **Property tax/Assessor-** same address as above. 509-773-3715.

Lewis County

County Auditor, PO Box 29, Chehalis, WA 98532-0029. 360-740-1163; fax-360-740-1421; hours: 8AM-5PM.
Separate indices to search include document type or name & date. Records indexed on a public use terminal back to 1988. Office personnel or visitors may perform searches. General index search fee $8.00 per name per 10 years. Copy fee $1.00 per page. Cert fee- $3.00 1st page, $1.00 each page after includes copy fee. **Other phones:** Treasurer- 360-740-1115; Elections- 360-740-1164; Vital Records- 360-236-4313. **Property tax/Assessor-** 360-740-1392.

Lincoln County

County Auditor, PO Box 28, Davenport, WA 99122. 509-725-4971; fax-509-725-0820; hours: 8AM-5PM.
Index: Books and computer. Records indexed on computer back to 1989. Office personnel or visitors may perform searches. General index search fee $8.00 per hour. UCC s $22.00. Copy fee $1.00 per page. Cert fee- $3.00 1st page, $1.00 each add'l. Payee- Lincoln County Auditor. **Other phones:** Treasurer- 509-725-5061; Appraiser/Auditor- 509-725-7011; Elections- 509-725-4971; Vital Records- 509-725-4971. **Property tax/Assessor-** 509-725-7011.

Mason County

County Auditor, PO Box 400, Shelton, WA 98584. 360-427-9670, R/E recording phone-360-427-9670 x467; fax-360-427-8425; hours: 8:30AM - 4:30PM. http://auditor.co.mason.wa.us
Separate indices to search include grantor/grantee, AF number, parcel number, legal description. Records indexed on a public use terminal back to 1985. Office personnel or visitors may perform searches. General index search fee $8.00 per hour. Will search real estate records. Copy fee $1.00 per page. Cert fee- $3.00 for 1st page plus copy fee. Payee- Mason County Auditor. **Online access to Assessor, Property records:** Access to the Assessor data is free at www.co.mason.wa.us/disclaimer.php. Auditor records from 1985 to 2005 are at http://auditor.co.mason.wa.us. **Other phones:** Treasurer- 360-427-9670 x484; Appraiser/Auditor- 360-427-9670 x470; Elections- 360-427-9670 x469; Vital Records- 360-427-9670 x467. **Property tax/Assessor-** PO Box 429, Shelton, WA 98584; 360-427-9670 x491.

Okanogan County

County Auditor, PO Box 1010, Okanogan, WA 98840. 509-422-7240; fax-509-422-7163; hours: 8:30AM-5PM. www.okanogancounty.org
Records indexed on a public use terminal back to 1995. Office personnel or visitors may perform searches. Search fee $8.00 per name. Copy fee $1.00 per page. Cert fee- $2.00 for 1st page. Payee- Okanogan County Auditor. **Online access to Assessor, Property records:** Access to county assessment data is free at www.metrokc.gov/recelec/records/. As of 1/2004, only 50% of the physical real property physical addresses are available. **Other phones:** Treasurer- 509-422-7180; Appraiser/Auditor-   509-422-7240.   **Property tax/Assessor-** 509-422-7190.

Pacific County

County Auditor, PO Box 97, South Bend, WA 98586-9903.   360-875-9318;   fax-360-875-9333;   hours: 8:30AM-4:30PM.
www.co.pacific.wa.us/directory.htm
All records in one index. Office will perform a UCC search but public must search other records themselves. Search fee $8.00. Copy fee $1.00 per page. Cert fee- $3.00 per 1st page, $1.00 each add'l page. Payee- Pacific County Auditor. **Other phones:** Treasurer- 360-875-9421; Appraiser/Auditor- 360-875-9301; Elections- 360-875-9317; Vital Records- 360-875-9318. **Property tax/Assessor-** 360-875-9421.

Pend Oreille County

County Auditor, PO Box 5015, Newport, WA 99156. 509-447-3185; fax-509-447-2475; 8AM-4:30PM.
All records in one index. Records indexed on a public use terminal back to 1996. Office personnel or visitors may perform searches. General index search fee $8.00 per hour. Tax liens with County Treasurer. Copy fee $1.00 per page. Cert fee- $3.00 per doc plus copy fee. Payee- Pend Oreille County Auditor. **Other phones:** Treasurer- 509-447-3612; Appraiser/Auditor- 509-447-4312; Elections- 509-447-3185; Vital Records- 360-236-4300. **Property tax/Assessor-** PO Box 5010, Newport, WA 99156 or, 625 W 4th St, Newport, WA 99156; 509-447-4312.

Pierce County

County Auditor, 2401 S. 35th St; Rm 200, Tacoma, WA 98409. 253-798-7440, R/E recording phone-206-591-7440;   fax-253-798-2761;   hours: 8:30AM-4:30PM. www.piercecountywa.org/auditor
Records indexed on a public use terminal back to 1984. Office will perform a UCC search but public must search other records themselves. General index search fee $8.00 per hour. Cert fee- $3.00 1st page, $1.00 each add'l page. Payee- Pierce County Auditor. **Online access to Assessor, Real Estate, Recording, Deed, Lien, Vital Statistic,**

Judgment, Assumed Name, Inmate records: Search the auditor's recording database for free at http://hartweb.piercecountywa.org/search.asp?cabinet= opr. Also, property records on County Assessor-Treasurer   database   are   free   at www.co.pierce.wa.us/CFApps/atr/epip/search.cfm. Also, the county sexual offender/kidnappers list is at http://pso.co.pierce.wa.us. Marriage records at http://hartweb.piercecountywa.org/search.asp?cabinet= oprmarriage. Also, search inmate info on private company website at www.vinelink.com/index.jsp. **Other phones:** Treasurer- 253-798-6111; Elections- 253-798-7430. **Property tax/Assessor-** 253-798-6111.

San Juan County

County Auditor, PO Box 638, Friday Harbor, WA 98250. 360-378-2161; fax-360-378-6256; hours: 8AM-4:30PM. www.co.san-juan.wa.us
Records indexed on a public use terminal back to 1984. Office personnel or visitors may perform searches. Search fee $8.00 per hour. Copy fee $1.00 per page. Cert fee- $3.00 1st page; $1.00 each add'l page. Payee- San Juan County Auditor. **Online access to Assessor, Property Tax, Auditor, Real Estate, Deed, Lien records:** Online access to assessor property records is free at www.co.san-juan.wa.us/assessor/rpsrch.asp?tp=N.   No   name searching. Also, access to the auditor database of real estate recording records is free at http://sjc-imaging.rockisland.com/SJCdocSearch/?. Images go back to 1997; index goes back to 1/1984. **Other phones:** Treasurer- 360-378-2171; Appraiser/Auditor- 360-378-3357.   **Property tax/Assessor-** 360-378-4729.

Skagit County

County Auditor, PO Box 1306, Mount Vernon, WA 98273-1306. 360-336-9420, R/E recording phone-360-336-9311;   fax-360-336-9429;   hours: 8:30AM-4:30PM. www.skagitcounty.net
All records in one index. Records indexed on a public use terminal back to 3/1979. Office will perform a UCC and Tax lien search but public must search other records themselves. General index search fee $8.00 per hour. Copy fee $1.00 per page. Cert fee- $2.00 per doc plus copy fee. Payee- Skagit County Auditor. **Online access to Recording, Property Tax, Assessor, Treasurer, Deed, Lien, Vital Statistic, Auditor records:** Assessor, Treasurer, Auditor's recorded documents as well as permits are all free at www.skagitcounty.net; click on Records Search. **Other phones:** Treasurer- 360-336-9350; Appraiser/Auditor- 360-336-9310; Elections- 360-336-9305; Vital Records- 360-336-9380. **Property tax/Assessor-** same address as above. 360-336-9370.

Skamania County

County Auditor, PO Box 790, Stevenson, WA 98648-0790.   509-427-9420;   fax-509-427-4165;   hours: 8:30AM-5PM.
http://d30060429.purehost.com/waco/county/skamania.html
Records indexed on a public use terminal back to 1992. Office personnel or visitors may perform searches. Search fee $8.00 per hour. Copy fee $1.00 per page. Cert fee- $3.00 1st page. **Other phones:** Treasurer- 509-427-9410; Appraiser/Auditor- 509-427-9420; Elections- 509-427-9420; Vital Records- 509-427-9420. **Property tax/Assessor-** 509-427-9400.

Snohomish County

County Auditor, 3000 Rockefeller Ave; Dept. R, M/S #204, Everett, WA 98201. 425-388-3483 press 0, R/E recording phone-425-388-3483 x0, UCC recording phone-425-388-3483;   fax-425-259-2777;   hours: 9AM-5PM.
http://www1.co.snohomish.wa.us/Departments/Auditor/
Records indexed on a public use terminal back to 1976. Office personnel or visitors may perform

searches. Search fee $8.00 per name. Copy fee $1.00 per page. Cert fee- $2.00 per doc plus copy fee. Payee- Snohomish County Auditor. **Online access to Real Estate, Assessor, Recording, Marriage, Jail, Offender, Jail Booking records:** Access to the Auditor's office database is free at http://198.238.192.100/localization/menu.asp.   Search on the recorded documents or marriage icons. Also, search the assessor property data for free at http://web5.co.snohomish.wa.us/propsys/asr-tr-propinq/ - no name searching. Search sheriff jail register at http://www1.co.snohomish.wa.us/Departments/Corrections/Services/default.htm.   **Other phones:** Treasurer- 425-388-3366;   Appraiser/Auditor- 425-388-3444; Elections- 425-388-3444. **Property tax/Assessor-** 425-388-3433.

Spokane County

County Auditor, PO Box 2353, Spokane, WA 99210. 509-477-2270; fax-509-477-6451; hours: 8:30AM-5PM. www.spokanecounty.org/auditor
All records in one index. Office personnel or visitors may perform searches. General index search fee $8.00 per hour (1 hour minimum). Will search real estate records. Will search UCC records, tax liens not included in UCC search. Copy fee $1.00 per page. Cert fee- $3.00 1st page; $1.00 each add'l page plus copy fee. Payee- Spokane County Auditor. **Online access to Property Tax, Land records:** Search the County Parcel Locator database for free at www.spokanecounty.org/pubpadal/. No name searching. **Other phones:** Treasurer- 509-456-4713; Appraiser/Auditor- 509-456-3696; Elections- 509-477-2320; Vital Records- 509-324-1522. **Property tax/Assessor-** 1116 W Broadway, 1st Fl, Spokane, WA 99260; 509-477-5793.

Stevens County

County Auditor, 215 S. Oak St., Colville, WA 99114. 509-684-7512;   fax-509-684-8310;   hours: 8AM-4:30PM. www.co.stevens.wa.us
Records indexed on a public use terminal back to 1990. Office personnel or visitors may perform searches. General index search fee $8.00 per hour. Copy fee $1.00 per page. Cert fee- $3.00 1st page; $1.00 each add'l page. Payee- Stevens County Auditor. **Online access to Assessor, Property records:** Access assessor property data free at http://64.85.21.111/screalprop/; no name searching. **Other   phones:**   Treasurer-   509-684-2593; Appraiser/Auditor- 509-684-6161; Elections- 509-684-7514; Vital Records- 509-684-7512; Auditor- 509-684-7511. **Property tax/Assessor-** 509-684-6161.

Thurston County

County Auditor, 2000 Lakeridge Drive SW, Olympia, WA 98502. 360-786-5405; fax-360-786-5223; hours: 8AM-4:30PM. www.co.thurston.wa.us/auditor
All records in one index. Records indexed on a public use terminal back to 1981. Office personnel or visitors may perform searches. General index search fee $8.00 per hour per name. Copy fee $1.00 per page. Cert fee- $3 1st page; $1.00 each add'l. Payee- Thurston County Auditor. **Online access to Assessor, Real Estate, Auditor, Recording records:** Assessor and property data on Thurston GeoData   database   is   free   at www.geodata.org/parcelsrch.asp. No name searching. Also, access the Auditor Recording I-CRIS database, no images, at www.co.thurston.wa.us/auditor. Click on online records. **Other phones:** Treasurer- 360-786-5550; Appraiser/Auditor- 360-786-6410; Elections- 360-786-5408; Vital Records- 360-786-5481. **Property tax/Assessor-** same address as above. 360-786-5410.

Wahkiakum County

County Auditor, PO Box 543, Cathlamet, WA 98612. 360-795-3219; fax-360-795-0824; hours: 8AM-4PM. Only the public may search. Copy fee $1.00 per page. Cert fee- $3.00 1st page; $1.00 each add'l page. Payee- Wahkiakum County Auditor. **Online access to Sheriff Warrant records:** Search the sheriff's warrant list at www.sd.co.wahkiakum.wa.us. **Other phones:** Treasurer- 360-795-8005; Appraiser/Auditor- 360-795-3791; Elections- 360-795-3219; Vital Records- 360-795-6207. **Property tax/Assessor-** 360-795-3791.

Walla Walla County

County Auditor, PO Box 1856, Walla Walla, WA 99362-0356. 509-524-2549; fax-509-526-4806; hours: 9AM-4PM. www.co.walla-walla.wa.us
All records in one index. Office personnel or visitors may perform searches. Search fee $8.00 per hour. Office will not search real estate records. Copy fee $1.00 per page. Cert fee- $3.00 1st page, $1.00 each add'l page. Payee- Walla Walla County Auditor. **Online access to Property Tax, Assessor, Residential Sale, Farm Sale records:** Access to the TaxSifter parcel Search is free at http://wallawallawa.taxsifter.com/taxsifter/T-Parcelsearch.asp. **Other phones:** Treasurer- 509-527-3212; Appraiser/Auditor- 509-527-3216; Elections-509-524-2536. **Property tax/Assessor-** 315 W. Main St, Rm 112, Walla Walla, WA 99362; 509-527-3216, assessor fax- 509-527-3214.

Whatcom County

County Auditor, 311 Grand Ave #103, Bellingham, WA 98225. 360-676-6740, R/E recording phone-360-676-6740 x50013, UCC recording phone-360-676-6740 x50073; fax-360-738-4556; hours: 8:30AM-4:30PA. www.co.whatcom.wa.us/auditor
All records in one index. Records indexed on a public use terminal back to 1988. Only the public may search. General index search fee $8.00 per hour. Copy fee $1.00 per page. Cert fee- $3.00 1st page, $1.00 each add'l page. Payee- Whatcom County Auditor. **Online access to Assessor, Real Estate, Voter Registration records:** Search the assessor parcel database information system free at www.co.whatcom.wa.us/cgibin/db2www/assessor/search/RPSearch.ndt/disclaimer. Also, acquire voter registration lists for political purposes only; information and request information at www.co.whatcom.wa.us/auditor/election_division/labels_lists/index.jsp. **Other phones:** Treasurer- 360-676-6774; Appraiser/Auditor-360-676-6745; Elections- 360-676-6742; Vital Records- 360-676-6740. **Property tax/Assessor-** same address as above. 360-676-6790.

Whitman County

County Auditor, PO Box 350, Colfax, WA 99111-0350. 509-397-6270, UCC recording phone-509-392-6270; fax-509-397-6351; hours: 9AM-5PM (Recording hours are only up until 2:30PM). www.whitmancounty.org
Will search records from 1987 to current. All records in one index. Records indexed on computer. Office personnel or visitors may perform searches. Search fee $8.00 per hour. Will not search real estate records. Will search UCC records. Copy fee $1.00 per page. Cert fee- $3.00 1st page, $1.00 each add'l page plus copy fee. Payee- Whitman County Auditor. **Other phones:** Treasurer- 509-397-6230; Appraiser/Auditor- 509-397-6220; Elections- 509-397-6270; Vital Records- 509-397-6270. **Property tax/Assessor-** N 400 Main, Colfax, WA 99111; 509-397-6220.

Yakima County

County Auditor, 128 N. 2nd St, #117, Yakima, WA 98901. 509-574-1330; fax-509-574-1341; hours: 9AM-4:30PM. www.pan.co.yakima.wa.us
All records in one index. Records indexed on computer back to 1985. Office personnel or visitors may perform searches. Search fee $8.00 per name per hour. Will search real estate records if supplied with specific document titles. Will not do chain of title or tracking of property. Copy fee $1.00 per page. Cert fee- $3.00 1st page, $1.00 each add'l page plus copy fee. Payee- Yakima County Auditor. **Online access to Assessor, Real Estate, Property Tax records:** Assessor and property information on County Assessor database are free at www.co.yakima.wa.us/assessor/propinfo/asr_info.asp. No name searching. Also, treasurer parcel data is free at www.co.yakima.wa.us/treasurer/database/taxes.asp. No name searching. Also, the sheriff's sex offender list at www.pan.co.yakima.wa.us/Sheriff/soffenders.htm.
Other phones: Treasurer- 509-574-2800; Appraiser/Auditor- 509-574-1100; Elections- 509-574-1340; Vital Records- 509-574-1330. **Property tax/Assessor-** 128 N. 2nd St, #112, Yakima, WA 98901; 509-574-1100.

Washington County Locator

You will usually be able to find the city name in the City/County Cross Reference below. In that case, it is a simple matter to determine the county from the cross reference. However, only the official US Postal Service city names are included in this index. There are an additional 40,000 place names that people use in their addresses. Therefore, we have also included a ZIP/City Cross Reference immediately following the City/County Cross Reference.

If you know the ZIP Code but the city name does not appear in the City/County Cross Reference index, look up the ZIP Code in the ZIP/City Cross Reference, find the city name, then look up the city name in the City/County Cross Reference. For example, you want to know the county for an address of Menands, NY 12204. There is no "Menands" in the City/County Cross Reference. The ZIP/City Cross Reference shows that ZIP Codes 12201-12288 are for the city of Albany. Looking back in the City/County Cross Reference, Albany is in Albany County.

Washington - City/County Cross Reference

ABERDEEN Grays Harbor
ACME Whatcom
ADDY Stevens
ADNA Lewis
AIRWAY HEIGHTS Spokane
ALBION Whitman
ALLYN Mason
ALMIRA (99103) Lincoln(88), Grant(11)
AMANDA PARK Grays Harbor
AMBOY (98601) Clark(98), Cowlitz(1)
ANACORTES Skagit
ANATONE Asotin
ANDERSON ISLAND Pierce
APPLETON Klickitat
ARDENVOIR Chelan
ARIEL Cowlitz
ARLINGTON Snohomish
ASHFORD Pierce
ASOTIN Asotin
AUBURN (98092) King(92), Pierce(7)
AUBURN King
BAINBRIDGE ISLAND Kitsap
BARING King
BATTLE GROUND Clark
BAY CENTER Pacific
BEAVER Clallam
BELFAIR Mason
BELLEVUE King
BELLINGHAM (98229) Whatcom(97), Skagit(2)
BELLINGHAM Whatcom
BELMONT Whitman
BENGE Adams
BENTON CITY Benton
BEVERLY Grant
BICKLETON (99322) Klickitat(96), Yakima(3)
BINGEN (98605) Skamania(72), Klickitat(27)
BLACK DIAMOND King
BLAINE Whatcom
BLAKELY ISLAND San Juan
BONNEY LAKE Pierce
BOTHELL King
BOTHELL Snohomish
BOW Skagit
BOYDS Ferry
BREMERTON Kitsap
BREWSTER Okanogan
BRIDGEPORT Douglas
BRINNON Jefferson
BROWNSTOWN Yakima
BRUSH PRAIRIE Clark
BUCKLEY Pierce
BUCODA Thurston
BUENA Yakima
BURBANK Walla Walla
BURLEY Kitsap
BURLINGTON Skagit
BURTON King
CAMANO ISLAND Island
CAMAS Clark
CAMP MURRAY Pierce
CARBONADO Pierce
CARLSBORG Clallam

CARLTON Okanogan
CARNATION King
CARROLLS Cowlitz
CARSON Skamania
CASHMERE Chelan
CASTLE ROCK Cowlitz
CATHLAMET Wahkiakum
CEDARVIEW Pierce
CENTERVILLE Klickitat
CENTRALIA (98531) Lewis(94), Thurston(5)
CHATTAROY Spokane
CHEHALIS Lewis
CHELAN Chelan
CHELAN FALLS Chelan
CHENEY Spokane
CHEWELAH Stevens
CHIMACUM Jefferson
CHINOOK Pacific
CINEBAR Lewis
CLALLAM BAY Clallam
CLARKSTON Asotin
CLAYTON (99110) Stevens(67), Spokane(32)
CLE ELUM Kittitas
CLEARLAKE Skagit
CLINTON Island
COLBERT Spokane
COLFAX Whitman
COLLEGE PLACE Walla Walla
COLTON Whitman
COLVILLE Stevens
CONCONULLY Okanogan
CONCRETE Skagit
CONNELL (99326) Franklin(91), Adams(8)
CONWAY Skagit
COPALIS BEACH Grays Harbor
COPALIS CROSSING Grays Harbor
COSMOPOLIS (98537) Grays Harbor(98), Pacific(1)
COUGAR Cowlitz
COULEE CITY (99115) Grant(88), Douglas(11)
COULEE DAM (99116) Okanogan(82), Douglas(15), Grant(1)
COUPEVILLE Island
COWICHE Yakima
CRESTON Lincoln
CUNNINGHAM Adams
CURLEW Ferry
CURTIS Lewis
CUSICK Pend Oreille
CUSTER Whatcom
DALLESPORT Klickitat
DANVILLE Ferry
DARRINGTON (98241) Snohomish(82), Skagit(17)
DAVENPORT (99122) Lincoln(89), Stevens(10)
DAYTON Columbia
DEER HARBOR San Juan
DEER PARK (99006) Spokane(87), Stevens(10), Pend Oreille(1)
DEMING Whatcom
DIXIE Walla Walla

DOTY Lewis
DRYDEN Chelan
DUPONT Pierce
DUVALL King
EAST OLYMPIA Thurston
EAST WENATCHEE Douglas
EASTON Kittitas
EASTSOUND San Juan
EATONVILLE Pierce
EDMONDS Snohomish
EDWALL (99008) Lincoln(80), Spokane(19)
ELBE (98330) Pierce(82), Lewis(17)
ELECTRIC CITY Grant
ELK (99009) Spokane(78), Pend Oreille(21)
ELLENSBURG Kittitas
ELMA (98541) Grays Harbor(72), Mason(27)
ELMER CITY Okanogan
ELTOPIA Franklin
ENDICOTT Whitman
ENTIAT Chelan
ENUMCLAW (98022) King(95), Pierce(4)
EPHRATA Grant
ETHEL Lewis
EVANS Stevens
EVERETT Snohomish
EVERSON Whatcom
FAIRCHILD AIR FORCE BASE Spokane
FAIRFIELD Spokane
FALL CITY King
FARMINGTON Whitman
FEDERAL WAY King
FERNDALE Whatcom
FORD (99013) Spokane(51), Stevens(46), Lincoln(1)
FORKS Clallam
FOUR LAKES Spokane
FOX ISLAND Pierce
FREELAND Island
FREEMAN Spokane
FRIDAY HARBOR San Juan
FRUITLAND Stevens
GALVIN Lewis
GARFIELD Whitman
GEORGE Grant
GIFFORD Stevens
GIG HARBOR Pierce
GLENOMA Lewis
GLENWOOD Klickitat
GOLD BAR (98251) Snohomish(96), King(3)
GOLDENDALE Klickitat
GOOSE PRAIRIE Yakima
GRAHAM Pierce
GRAND COULEE (99133) Grant(79), Lincoln(11), Douglas(8)
GRANDVIEW Yakima
GRANGER Yakima
GRANITE FALLS Snohomish
GRAPEVIEW Mason
GRAYLAND (98547) Grays Harbor(98), Pacific(1)
GRAYS RIVER Wahkiakum
GREENACRES Spokane

GREENBANK Island
HAMILTON Skagit
HANSVILLE Kitsap
HARRAH Yakima
HARRINGTON Lincoln
HARTLINE Grant
HATTON Adams
HAY Whitman
HEISSON Clark
HOBART King
HOODSPORT Mason
HOOPER Whitman
HOQUIAM Grays Harbor
HUMPTULIPS Grays Harbor
HUNTERS Stevens
HUSUM Klickitat
ILWACO Pacific
INCHELIUM Ferry
INDEX Snohomish
INDIANOLA Kitsap
IONE Pend Oreille
ISSAQUAH King
JOYCE Clallam
KAHLOTUS Franklin
KALAMA Cowlitz
KAPOWSIN Pierce
KELLER (99140) Ferry(98), Stevens(1)
KELSO Cowlitz
KENMORE King
KENNEWICK Benton
KENT King
KETTLE FALLS (99141) Stevens(88), Ferry(11)
KEYPORT Kitsap
KINGSTON Kitsap
KIRKLAND King
KITTITAS Kittitas
KLICKITAT Klickitat
LA CENTER Clark
LA CONNER Skagit
LA GRANDE Pierce
LA PUSH Clallam
LACEY Thurston
LACROSSE Whitman
LAKE STEVENS Snohomish
LAKE TAPPS Pierce
LAKEBAY Pierce
LAKEWOOD Pierce
LAKEWOOD Snohomish
LAMONA Lincoln
LAMONT (99017) Whitman(98), Adams(1)
LANGLEY Island
LATAH Spokane
LAURIER Ferry
LEAVENWORTH Chelan
LEBAM Pacific
LIBERTY LAKE Spokane
LILLIWAUP Mason
LIND Adams
LITTLEROCK Thurston
LONG BEACH Pacific
LONGBRANCH Pierce
LONGMIRE Pierce
LONGVIEW Cowlitz
LOOMIS Okanogan

LOON LAKE Stevens
LOPEZ ISLAND San Juan
LUMMI ISLAND Whatcom
LYLE Klickitat
LYMAN Skagit
LYNDEN Whatcom
LYNNWOOD Snohomish
MABTON Yakima
MALAGA Chelan
MALDEN Whitman
MALO Ferry
MALONE Grays Harbor
MALOTT Okanogan
MANCHESTER Kitsap
MANSFIELD Douglas
MANSON Chelan
MAPLE FALLS Whatcom
MAPLE VALLEY King
MARBLEMOUNT Skagit
MARCUS Stevens
MARLIN (98832) Grant(96), Adams(3)
MARSHALL Spokane
MARYSVILLE Snohomish
MATLOCK Mason
MATTAWA Grant
MAZAMA Okanogan
MCCLEARY Grays Harbor
MCKENNA Pierce
MEAD Spokane
MEDICAL LAKE Spokane
MEDINA King
MENLO Pacific
MERCER ISLAND King
MESA Franklin
METALINE Pend Oreille
METALINE FALLS Pend Oreille
METHOW Okanogan
MICA Spokane
MILTON (98354) Pierce(92), King(7)
MINERAL Lewis
MOCLIPS Grays Harbor
MOHLER Lincoln
MONITOR Chelan
MONROE Snohomish
MONTESANO Grays Harbor
MORTON Lewis
MOSES LAKE Grant
MOSSYROCK Lewis
MOUNT VERNON Skagit
MOUNTLAKE TERRACE Snohomish
MOXEE Yakima
MUKILTEO Snohomish
NACHES Yakima
NAHCOTTA Pacific
NAPAVINE Lewis
NASELLE Pacific
NEAH BAY Clallam
NEILTON Grays Harbor
NESPELEM Okanogan
NEWMAN LAKE Spokane
NEWPORT (99156) Pend Oreille(50),
    Spokane(49)
NINE MILE FALLS (99026) Spokane(54),
    Stevens(45)
NOOKSACK Whatcom
NORDLAND Jefferson
NORTH BEND King
NORTH BONNEVILLE Skamania
NORTH LAKEWOOD Snohomish

NORTHPORT Stevens
OAK HARBOR Island
OAKESDALE Whitman
OAKVILLE (98568) Grays Harbor(97),
    Thurston(2)
OCEAN PARK Pacific
OCEAN SHORES Grays Harbor
ODESSA (99159) Lincoln(86), Adams(13)
OKANOGAN Okanogan
OLALLA Kitsap
OLD NATIONAL BANK Spokane
OLGA San Juan
OLYMPIA Thurston
OMAK Okanogan
ONALASKA Lewis
ORCAS San Juan
ORIENT Ferry
ORONDO Douglas
OROVILLE Okanogan
ORTING Pierce
OTHELLO (99344) Adams(77), Grant(16),
    Franklin(5)
OTIS ORCHARDS Spokane
OUTLOOK Yakima
OYSTERVILLE Pacific
PACIFIC (98047) King(92), Pierce(7)
PACIFIC BEACH Grays Harbor
PACKWOOD Lewis
PALISADES Douglas
PALOUSE Whitman
PARADISE INN Pierce
PARKER Yakima
PASCO Franklin
PATEROS Okanogan
PATERSON Benton
PE ELL Lewis
PESHASTIN Chelan
PLYMOUTH Benton
POINT ROBERTS Whatcom
POMEROY (99347) Garfield(89),
    Columbia(4), Asotin(3), Whitman(1)
PONDEROSA ESTATES Pierce
PORT ANGELES Clallam
PORT GAMBLE Kitsap
PORT HADLOCK Jefferson
PORT LUDLOW Jefferson
PORT ORCHARD Kitsap
PORT TOWNSEND Jefferson
POULSBO Kitsap
PRAIRIE RIDGE Pierce
PRESCOTT Walla Walla
PRESTON King
PROSSER (99350) Benton(96), Klickitat(3)
PULLMAN Whitman
PUYALLUP Pierce
QUILCENE Jefferson
QUINAULT Grays Harbor
QUINCY Grant
RAINIER Thurston
RANDLE Lewis
RAVENSDALE King
RAYMOND Pacific
REARDAN (99029) Lincoln(54),
    Spokane(45)
REDMOND King
REDONDO King
RENTON King
REPUBLIC (99166) Ferry(97),
    Okanogan(2)

RETSIL Kitsap
RICE Stevens
RICHLAND Benton
RIDGEFIELD Clark
RITZVILLE Adams
RIVERSIDE Okanogan
ROCHESTER Thurston
ROCK ISLAND Douglas
ROCKFORD Spokane
ROCKPORT Skagit
ROLLINGBAY Kitsap
RONALD Kittitas
ROOSEVELT Klickitat
ROSALIA (99170) Whitman(55),
    Spokane(44)
ROSBURG Wahkiakum
ROSLYN Kittitas
ROY Pierce
ROYAL CITY Grant
RYDERWOOD Cowlitz
SAINT JOHN Whitman
SALKUM Lewis
SAMMAMISH King
SATSOP Grays Harbor
SEABECK Kitsap
SEAHURST King
SEATTLE King
SEAVIEW Pacific
SEDRO WOOLLEY (98284) Skagit(95),
    Whatcom(4)
SEKIU Clallam
SELAH Yakima
SEQUIM (98382) Clallam(98), Jefferson(1)
SEQUIM Jefferson
SHAW ISLAND San Juan
SHELTON Mason
SILVANA Snohomish
SILVER CREEK Lewis
SILVERDALE Kitsap
SILVERLAKE Cowlitz
SKAMOKAWA Wahkiakum
SKYKOMISH King
SNOHOMISH Snohomish
SNOQUALMIE King
SNOQUALMIE PASS King
SOAP LAKE Grant
SOUTH BEND Pacific
SOUTH CLE ELUM Kittitas
SOUTH COLBY Kitsap
SOUTH PRAIRIE Pierce
SOUTHWORTH Kitsap
SPANAWAY Pierce
SPANGLE Spokane
SPOKANE Spokane
SPRAGUE Lincoln
SPRINGDALE Stevens
STANWOOD Snohomish
STARBUCK Columbia
STARTUP Snohomish
STEHEKIN Chelan
STEILACOOM Pierce
STEPTOE Whitman
STEVENSON Skamania
STRATFORD Grant
SULTAN Snohomish
SUMAS Whatcom
SUMNER Pierce
SUNNYSIDE Yakima
SUQUAMISH Kitsap

TACOMA Pierce
TAHOLAH Grays Harbor
TAHUYA Mason
TEKOA (99033) Whitman(83), Spokane(16)
TENINO Thurston
THE CRESCENT STORE Spokane
THORNTON Whitman
THORP Kittitas
TIETON Yakima
TOKELAND Pacific
TOLEDO Lewis
TONASKET Okanogan
TOPPENISH Yakima
TOUCHET Walla Walla
TOUTLE Cowlitz
TRACYTON Kitsap
TROUT LAKE Klickitat
TUMTUM Stevens
TUMWATER Thurston
TWISP Okanogan
UNDERWOOD Skamania
UNION Mason
UNIONTOWN Whitman
UNIVERSITY PLACE Pierce
USK (99180) Pend Oreille(83),
    Spokane(16)
VADER Lewis
VALLEY Stevens
VALLEYFORD Spokane
VANCOUVER Clark
VANTAGE Kittitas
VASHON King
VAUGHN Pierce
VERADALE Spokane
WAHKIACUS Klickitat
WAITSBURG (99361) Walla Walla(96),
    Columbia(3)
WALDRON San Juan
WALLA WALLA Walla Walla
WALLULA Walla Walla
WAPATO Yakima
WARDEN Grant
WASHOUGAL (98671) Clark(79),
    Skamania(20)
WASHTUCNA Adams
WATERVILLE Douglas
WAUCONDA Okanogan
WAUNA Pierce
WAVERLY Spokane
WELLPINIT Stevens
WENATCHEE Chelan
WEST RICHLAND Benton
WESTPORT Grays Harbor
WHITE SALMON Klickitat
WHITE SWAN Yakima
WILBUR Lincoln
WILKESON Pierce
WILSON CREEK Grant
WINLOCK Lewis
WINTHROP Okanogan
WISHRAM Klickitat
WOODINVILLE (98077) King(92),
    Snohomish(7)
WOODLAND (98674) Cowlitz(66),
    Clark(33)
YACOLT Clark
YAKIMA Yakima
YELM Thurston
ZILLAH Yakima

Washington - Zip/City Cross Reference

Zip Range	City
98001-98002	AUBURN
98003-98003	FEDERAL WAY
98004-98009	BELLEVUE
98010-98010	BLACK DIAMOND
98011-98012	BOTHELL
98013-98013	BURTON
98014-98014	CARNATION
98015-98015	BELLEVUE
98019-98019	DUVALL
98020-98020	EDMONDS
98021-98021	BOTHELL
98022-98022	ENUMCLAW
98023-98023	FEDERAL WAY
98024-98024	FALL CITY
98025-98025	HOBART
98026-98026	EDMONDS
98027-98027	ISSAQUAH
98028-98028	KENMORE
98029-98029	ISSAQUAH
98030-98032	KENT
98033-98034	KIRKLAND
98035-98035	KENT
98036-98037	LYNNWOOD
98038-98038	MAPLE VALLEY
98039-98039	MEDINA
98040-98040	MERCER ISLAND
98041-98041	BOTHELL
98042-98042	KENT
98043-98043	MOUNTLAKE TERRACE
98045-98045	NORTH BEND
98046-98046	LYNNWOOD
98047-98047	PACIFIC
98050-98050	PRESTON
98051-98051	RAVENSDALE
98052-98053	REDMOND
98054-98054	REDONDO
98055-98059	RENTON
98060-98060	SEATTLE
98061-98061	ROLLINGBAY
98062-98062	SEAHURST
98063-98063	FEDERAL WAY
98064-98064	KENT
98065-98065	SNOQUALMIE
98068-98068	SNOQUALMIE PASS
98070-98070	VASHON
98071-98071	AUBURN
98072-98072	WOODINVILLE
98073-98073	REDMOND
98074-98075	SAMMAMISH
98077-98077	WOODINVILLE
98082-98082	BOTHELL
98083-98083	KIRKLAND
98089-98089	KENT
98092-98092	AUBURN
98093-98093	FEDERAL WAY
98100-98109	SEATTLE
98110-98110	BAINBRIDGE ISLAND
98111-98199	SEATTLE
98200-98213	EVERETT
98220-98220	ACME
98221-98221	ANACORTES
98222-98222	BLAKELY ISLAND
98223-98223	ARLINGTON
98224-98224	BARING
98225-98229	BELLINGHAM
98230-98231	BLAINE
98232-98232	BOW
98233-98233	BURLINGTON
98235-98235	CLEARLAKE
98236-98236	CLINTON
98237-98237	CONCRETE
98238-98238	CONWAY
98239-98239	COUPEVILLE
98240-98240	CUSTER
98241-98241	DARRINGTON
98243-98243	DEER HARBOR
98244-98244	DEMING
98245-98245	EASTSOUND
98246-98246	BOW
98247-98247	EVERSON
98248-98248	FERNDALE
98249-98249	FREELAND
98250-98250	FRIDAY HARBOR
98251-98251	GOLD BAR
98252-98252	GRANITE FALLS
98253-98253	GREENBANK
98255-98255	HAMILTON
98256-98256	INDEX
98257-98257	LA CONNER
98258-98258	LAKE STEVENS
98259-98259	LAKEWOOD
98259-98259	NORTH LAKEWOOD
98260-98260	LANGLEY
98261-98261	LOPEZ ISLAND
98262-98262	LUMMI ISLAND
98263-98263	LYMAN
98264-98264	LYNDEN
98266-98266	MAPLE FALLS
98267-98267	MARBLEMOUNT
98270-98271	MARYSVILLE
98272-98272	MONROE
98273-98274	MOUNT VERNON
98275-98275	MUKILTEO
98276-98276	NOOKSACK
98277-98278	OAK HARBOR
98279-98279	OLGA
98280-98280	ORCAS
98281-98281	POINT ROBERTS
98282-98282	CAMANO ISLAND
98283-98283	ROCKPORT
98284-98284	SEDRO WOOLLEY
98286-98286	SHAW ISLAND
98287-98287	SILVANA
98288-98288	SKYKOMISH
98290-98291	SNOHOMISH
98292-98292	STANWOOD
98293-98293	STARTUP
98294-98294	SULTAN
98295-98295	SUMAS
98296-98296	SNOHOMISH
98297-98297	WALDRON
98303-98303	ANDERSON ISLAND
98304-98304	ASHFORD
98305-98305	BEAVER
98310-98314	BREMERTON
98315-98315	SILVERDALE
98320-98320	BRINNON
98321-98321	BUCKLEY
98322-98322	BURLEY
98323-98323	CARBONADO
98324-98324	CARLSBORG
98325-98325	CHIMACUM
98326-98326	CLALLAM BAY
98327-98327	DUPONT
98328-98328	EATONVILLE
98329-98329	GIG HARBOR
98330-98330	ELBE
98331-98331	FORKS
98332-98332	GIG HARBOR
98333-98333	FOX ISLAND
98334-98334	SEQUIM
98335-98335	GIG HARBOR
98336-98336	GLENOMA
98337-98337	BREMERTON
98338-98338	GRAHAM
98339-98339	PORT HADLOCK
98340-98340	HANSVILLE
98342-98342	INDIANOLA
98343-98343	JOYCE
98344-98344	KAPOWSIN
98345-98345	KEYPORT
98346-98346	KINGSTON
98348-98348	LA GRANDE
98349-98349	LAKEBAY
98350-98350	LA PUSH
98351-98351	LONGBRANCH
98352-98352	SUMNER
98353-98353	MANCHESTER
98354-98354	MILTON
98355-98355	MINERAL
98356-98356	MORTON
98357-98357	NEAH BAY
98358-98358	NORDLAND
98359-98359	OLALLA
98360-98360	ORTING
98361-98361	PACKWOOD
98362-98363	PORT ANGELES
98364-98364	PORT GAMBLE
98365-98365	PORT LUDLOW
98366-98367	PORT ORCHARD
98368-98368	PORT TOWNSEND
98370-98370	POULSBO
98371-98375	PUYALLUP
98376-98376	QUILCENE
98377-98377	RANDLE
98378-98378	RETSIL
98380-98380	SEABECK
98381-98381	SEKIU
98382-98382	SEQUIM
98383-98383	SILVERDALE
98384-98384	SOUTH COLBY
98385-98385	SOUTH PRAIRIE
98386-98386	SOUTHWORTH
98387-98387	SPANAWAY
98388-98388	STEILACOOM
98390-98391	SUMNER
98392-98392	SUQUAMISH
98393-98393	TRACYTON
98394-98394	VAUGHN
98395-98395	WAUNA
98396-98396	WILKESON
98397-98397	LONGMIRE
98398-98398	PARADISE INN
98401-98424	TACOMA
98430-98430	CAMP MURRAY
98431-98439	TACOMA
98439-98439	LAKEWOOD
98442-98466	TACOMA
98467-98467	UNIVERSITY PLACE
98471-98492	TACOMA
98492-98492	LAKEWOOD
98493-98497	TACOMA
98497-98497	LAKEWOOD
98498-98499	TACOMA
98499-98499	LAKEWOOD
98501-98508	OLYMPIA
98509-98509	LACEY
98511-98511	TUMWATER
98512-98516	OLYMPIA
98520-98520	ABERDEEN
98522-98522	ADNA
98524-98524	ALLYN
98526-98526	AMANDA PARK
98527-98527	BAY CENTER
98528-98528	BELFAIR
98530-98530	BUCODA
98531-98531	CENTRALIA
98532-98532	CHEHALIS
98533-98533	CINEBAR
98535-98535	COPALIS BEACH
98536-98536	COPALIS CROSSING
98537-98537	COSMOPOLIS
98538-98538	CURTIS
98539-98539	DOTY
98540-98540	EAST OLYMPIA
98541-98541	ELMA
98542-98542	ETHEL
98544-98544	GALVIN
98546-98546	GRAPEVIEW
98547-98547	GRAYLAND
98548-98548	HOODSPORT
98550-98550	HOQUIAM
98552-98552	HUMPTULIPS
98554-98554	LEBAM
98555-98555	LILLIWAUP
98556-98556	LITTLEROCK
98557-98557	MCCLEARY
98558-98558	MCKENNA
98559-98559	MALONE
98560-98560	MATLOCK
98561-98561	MENLO
98562-98562	MOCLIPS
98563-98563	MONTESANO
98564-98564	MOSSYROCK
98565-98565	NAPAVINE
98566-98566	NEILTON
98568-98568	OAKVILLE
98569-98569	OCEAN SHORES
98570-98570	ONALASKA
98571-98571	PACIFIC BEACH
98572-98572	PE ELL
98575-98575	QUINAULT
98576-98576	RAINIER
98577-98577	RAYMOND
98579-98579	ROCHESTER
98580-98580	ROY
98581-98581	RYDERWOOD
98582-98582	SALKUM
98583-98583	SATSOP
98584-98584	SHELTON
98585-98585	SILVER CREEK
98586-98586	SOUTH BEND
98587-98587	TAHOLAH
98588-98588	TAHUYA
98589-98589	TENINO
98590-98590	TOKELAND
98591-98591	TOLEDO
98592-98592	UNION
98593-98593	VADER
98595-98595	WESTPORT
98596-98596	WINLOCK
98597-98597	YELM
98599-98599	OLYMPIA
98601-98601	AMBOY
98602-98602	APPLETON
98603-98603	ARIEL
98604-98604	BATTLE GROUND
98605-98605	BINGEN
98606-98606	BRUSH PRAIRIE
98607-98607	CAMAS
98609-98609	CARROLLS
98610-98610	CARSON
98611-98611	CASTLE ROCK
98612-98612	CATHLAMET
98613-98613	CENTERVILLE
98614-98614	CHINOOK
98616-98616	COUGAR
98617-98617	DALLESPORT
98619-98619	GLENWOOD
98620-98620	GOLDENDALE
98621-98621	GRAYS RIVER
98622-98622	HEISSON
98623-98623	HUSUM
98624-98624	ILWACO
98625-98625	KALAMA
98626-98626	KELSO
98628-98628	KLICKITAT
98629-98629	LA CENTER
98631-98631	LONG BEACH
98632-98632	LONGVIEW
98635-98635	LYLE
98637-98637	NAHCOTTA
98638-98638	NASELLE
98639-98639	NORTH BONNEVILLE
98640-98640	OCEAN PARK
98641-98641	OYSTERVILLE
98642-98642	RIDGEFIELD
98643-98643	ROSBURG
98644-98644	SEAVIEW
98645-98645	SILVERLAKE
98647-98647	SKAMOKAWA
98648-98648	STEVENSON

98649-98649	TOUTLE	
98650-98650	TROUT LAKE	
98651-98651	UNDERWOOD	
98660-98668	VANCOUVER	
98670-98670	WAHKIACUS	
98671-98671	WASHOUGAL	
98672-98672	WHITE SALMON	
98673-98673	WISHRAM	
98674-98674	WOODLAND	
98675-98675	YACOLT	
98682-98687	VANCOUVER	
98801-98801	WENATCHEE	
98802-98802	EAST WENATCHEE	
98807-98807	WENATCHEE	
98811-98811	ARDENVOIR	
98812-98812	BREWSTER	
98813-98813	BRIDGEPORT	
98814-98814	CARLTON	
98815-98815	CASHMERE	
98816-98816	CHELAN	
98817-98817	CHELAN FALLS	
98819-98819	CONCONULLY	
98821-98821	DRYDEN	
98822-98822	ENTIAT	
98823-98823	EPHRATA	
98824-98824	GEORGE	
98826-98826	LEAVENWORTH	
98827-98827	LOOMIS	
98828-98828	MALAGA	
98829-98829	MALOTT	
98830-98830	MANSFIELD	
98831-98831	MANSON	
98832-98832	MARLIN	
98833-98833	MAZAMA	
98834-98834	METHOW	
98836-98836	MONITOR	
98837-98837	MOSES LAKE	
98840-98840	OKANOGAN	
98841-98841	OMAK	
98843-98843	ORONDO	
98844-98844	OROVILLE	
98845-98845	PALISADES	
98846-98846	PATEROS	
98847-98847	PESHASTIN	
98848-98848	QUINCY	
98849-98849	RIVERSIDE	
98850-98850	ROCK ISLAND	
98851-98851	SOAP LAKE	
98852-98852	STEHEKIN	
98853-98853	STRATFORD	
98855-98855	TONASKET	
98856-98856	TWISP	
98857-98857	WARDEN	
98858-98858	WATERVILLE	
98859-98859	WAUCONDA	
98860-98860	WILSON CREEK	
98862-98862	WINTHROP	
98901-98909	YAKIMA	
98920-98920	BROWNSTOWN	
98921-98921	BUENA	
98922-98922	CLE ELUM	
98923-98923	COWICHE	
98925-98925	EASTON	
98926-98926	ELLENSBURG	
98929-98929	GOOSE PRAIRIE	
98930-98930	GRANDVIEW	
98932-98932	GRANGER	
98933-98933	HARRAH	
98934-98934	KITTITAS	
98935-98935	MABTON	
98936-98936	MOXEE	
98937-98937	NACHES	
98938-98938	OUTLOOK	
98939-98939	PARKER	
98940-98940	RONALD	
98941-98941	ROSLYN	
98942-98942	SELAH	
98943-98943	SOUTH CLE ELUM	
98944-98944	SUNNYSIDE	
98946-98946	THORP	
98947-98947	TIETON	
98948-98948	TOPPENISH	
98950-98950	VANTAGE	
98951-98951	WAPATO	
98952-98952	WHITE SWAN	
98953-98953	ZILLAH	
99001-99001	AIRWAY HEIGHTS	
99003-99003	CHATTAROY	
99004-99004	CHENEY	
99005-99005	COLBERT	
99006-99006	DEER PARK	
99008-99008	EDWALL	
99009-99009	ELK	
99011-99011	FAIRCHILD AIR FORCE BASE	
99012-99012	FAIRFIELD	
99013-99013	FORD	
99014-99014	FOUR LAKES	
99015-99015	FREEMAN	
99016-99016	GREENACRES	
99017-99017	LAMONT	
99018-99018	LATAH	
99019-99019	LIBERTY LAKE	
99020-99020	MARSHALL	
99021-99021	MEAD	
99022-99022	MEDICAL LAKE	
99023-99023	MICA	
99025-99025	NEWMAN LAKE	
99026-99026	NINE MILE FALLS	
99027-99027	OTIS ORCHARDS	
99028-99028	SPANGLE	
99029-99029	REARDAN	
99030-99030	ROCKFORD	
99031-99031	SPANGLE	
99032-99032	SPRAGUE	
99033-99033	TEKOA	
99034-99034	TUMTUM	
99036-99036	VALLEYFORD	
99037-99037	VERADALE	
99039-99039	WAVERLY	
99040-99040	WELLPINIT	
99101-99101	ADDY	
99102-99102	ALBION	
99103-99103	ALMIRA	
99104-99104	BELMONT	
99105-99105	BENGE	
99107-99107	BOYDS	
99109-99109	CHEWELAH	
99110-99110	CLAYTON	
99111-99111	COLFAX	
99113-99113	COLTON	
99114-99114	COLVILLE	
99115-99115	COULEE CITY	
99116-99116	COULEE DAM	
99117-99117	CRESTON	
99118-99118	CURLEW	
99119-99119	CUSICK	
99121-99121	DANVILLE	
99122-99122	DAVENPORT	
99123-99123	ELECTRIC CITY	
99124-99124	ELMER CITY	
99125-99125	ENDICOTT	
99126-99126	EVANS	
99127-99127	SAINT JOHN	
99128-99128	FARMINGTON	
99129-99129	FRUITLAND	
99130-99130	GARFIELD	
99131-99131	GIFFORD	
99133-99133	GRAND COULEE	
99134-99134	HARRINGTON	
99135-99135	HARTLINE	
99136-99136	HAY	
99137-99137	HUNTERS	
99138-99138	INCHELIUM	
99139-99139	IONE	
99140-99140	KELLER	
99141-99141	KETTLE FALLS	
99143-99143	LACROSSE	
99144-99144	LAMONA	
99146-99146	LAURIER	
99147-99147	LINCOLN	
99148-99148	LOON LAKE	
99149-99149	MALDEN	
99150-99150	MALO	
99151-99151	MARCUS	
99152-99152	METALINE	
99153-99153	METALINE FALLS	
99154-99154	MOHLER	
99155-99155	NESPELEM	
99156-99156	NEWPORT	
99157-99157	NORTHPORT	
99158-99158	OAKESDALE	
99159-99159	ODESSA	
99160-99160	ORIENT	
99161-99161	PALOUSE	
99163-99165	PULLMAN	
99166-99166	REPUBLIC	
99167-99167	RICE	
99169-99169	RITZVILLE	
99170-99170	ROSALIA	
99171-99171	SAINT JOHN	
99173-99173	SPRINGDALE	
99174-99174	STEPTOE	
99176-99176	THORNTON	
99179-99179	UNIONTOWN	
99180-99180	USK	
99181-99181	VALLEY	
99185-99185	WILBUR	
99200-99256	SPOKANE	
99257-99257	THE CRESCENT STORE	
99258-99258	SPOKANE	
99259-99259	OLD NATIONAL BANK	
99260-99299	SPOKANE	
99301-99302	PASCO	
99320-99320	BENTON CITY	
99321-99321	BEVERLY	
99322-99322	BICKLETON	
99323-99323	BURBANK	
99324-99324	COLLEGE PLACE	
99326-99326	CONNELL	
99327-99327	CUNNINGHAM	
99328-99328	DAYTON	
99329-99329	DIXIE	
99330-99330	ELTOPIA	
99332-99332	HATTON	
99333-99333	HOOPER	
99335-99335	KAHLOTUS	
99336-99338	KENNEWICK	
99341-99341	LIND	
99343-99343	MESA	
99344-99344	OTHELLO	
99345-99345	PATERSON	
99346-99346	PLYMOUTH	
99347-99347	POMEROY	
99348-99348	PRESCOTT	
99349-99349	MATTAWA	
99350-99350	PROSSER	
99352-99352	RICHLAND	
99353-99353	WEST RICHLAND	
99354-99354	RICHLAND	
99356-99356	ROOSEVELT	
99357-99357	ROYAL CITY	
99359-99359	STARBUCK	
99360-99360	TOUCHET	
99361-99361	WAITSBURG	
99362-99362	WALLA WALLA	
99363-99363	WALLULA	
99371-99371	WASHTUCNA	
99401-99401	ANATONE	
99402-99402	ASOTIN	
99403-99403	CLARKSTON	

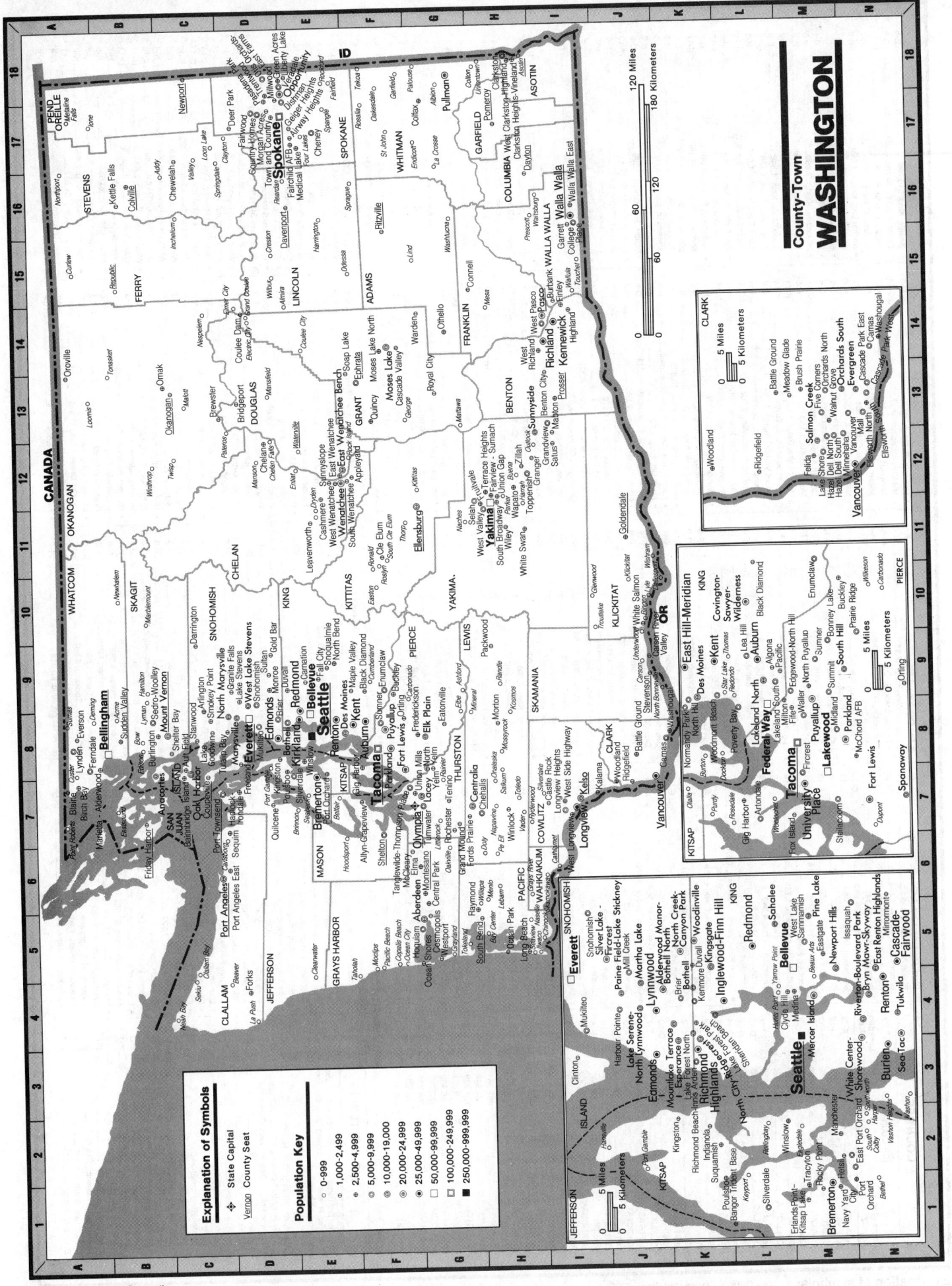

WASHINGTON

County-Town

Explanation of Symbols

✪ State Capital
Vernon County Seat

Population Key
○ 0-999
◉ 1,000-2,499
◉ 2,500-4,999
◉ 5,000-9,999
◉ 10,000-19,000
◉ 25,000-49,999
◉ 50,000-99,999
□ 100,000-249,999
■ 250,000-999,999

Explanation of symbols: ● – Census Designated Place (CDP)

West Virginia

General Help Numbers:

Governor's Office

Office of the Governor
1900 Kanawha Blvd, East
Charleston, WV 25305-0370

304-558-2000
Fax 304-342-7025
8AM-6PM M-TH;
8AM-5PM F

www.state.wv.us/governor

Attorney General's Office

1900 Kanawha Blvd. Rm 26E
Charleston, WV 25305-9924
www.wvs.state.wv.us/wvag/

304-558-2021
Fax 304-558-0140
8:30AM-5PM

Legislative Records

West Virginia State Legislature
State Capitol, Documents
Charleston, WV 25305
www.legis.state.wv.us

304-347-4830
Fax 304-558-1212
8:30AM-4:30PM

State Archives

Archives & History Section
1900 Kanawha Blvd E
Charleston, WV 25305-0300
www.wvculture.org/history/wvsamenu.html

304-558-0230,X168
Fax 304-558-4193
9AM-8PM M-TH, 9-6 F-SA

State Specifics:

Capital:	Charleston Kanawha County
Time Zone:	EST
Number of Counties:	55
Population:	1,815,354
Web Site:	www.wv.gov/

State Agencies

Criminal Records

State Police, Criminal Records Section, 725 Jefferson Rd, South Charleston, WV 25309; 304-746-2277, 304-746-2402-Fax; 8:30AM-4:30PM.

www.wvstatepolice.com

The state will also sell an "incident report" of a specific criminal action for $20.00, call 304-746-2178. FBI checks only available if there is statutory authorization.

Records are available from 1938 on computer. It takes 3 days before new records are available for inquiry. Records are indexed on in house computer (100% of names). Approximately 38% of arrest data is computerized. Records are normally destroyed after the person reaches age 80. 70% of all arrests in database have final dispositions recorded.

Searching: All searches require fingerprints, also FBI fingerprint checks. Include the following in your request-signed release of subject, SSN, DOB, race, sex, and thumbprint. You must use a WV Fingerprint Card and authorization. All records are returned by mail. Search can be initiated in person, results mailed. 100% of the records are fingerprint-supported. All records are released, including those without dispositions.

Access by: mail.

Fee & Payment: The search fee is $20.00 plus $24.00 for an FBI fingerprint check. Certain statutorily-required searches are $10.00, plus the addition FBI fingerprint check fee. Fee payee: West Virginia State Police. Prepayment required. Personal checks not accepted. No credit cards accepted.

Mail search: Turnaround time: 5 to 10 days.

Statewide Court Records

Administrative Office, State Supreme Court of Appeals, 1900 Kanawha Blvd, Bldg 1, Rm E 100, Charleston, WV 25305-0830; 304-558-0145, 304-558-1212-Fax; 9AM-5PM.

www.state.wv.us/wvsca

Except for certain online research capabilities, all court record access must be done at the local level.

Access by: online.

Online search: Supreme Court of Appeals Opinions/Calendar is available at the web page. There are plans for a statewide system to allow access to Circuit, Family and Magistrate records, but it is not yet available. Magistrate Court records are on a private system, see www.swcg-inc.com/products/municipal_courts.html.

Sexual Offender Registry

State Police Headquarters, Sexual Offender Registry, 725 Jefferson Rd, South Charleston, WV 25309; 304-746-2133, 304-746-2403-Fax; 8:30AM-4:30PM.

www.wvstatepolice.com/sexoff

West Virginia currently has over 2026 registered sex offenders.

Records are available from 1994.

Searching: Online access is the only request method. State law does not authorize other access methods.

Access by: online.

Online search: Online searching is available from website, search by county or name.

Incarceration Records

West Virginia Division of Corrections, Records Room, 112 California Ave, Bldg 4, Room 300, Charleston, WV 25305; 304-558-2037, 304-558-5934-Fax; 8AM-5PM.

www.wvf.state.wv.us/wvdoc

Records are available on current and former inmates. It takes up to 4 days before new records are available for inquiry.

Searching: Include the following in your request-full name; DOB and SSN helpful. Location, conviction and sentencing information, and release dates are provided.

Access by: mail, phone, fax, online.

Mail search: Turnaround time: 2 to 4 weeks. SASE is required.

Phone search: Limited name searching permitted

Fax search: Same criteria as mail.

Online search: There is no online searching is available from this agency. However, a private company offers free web access at www.vinelink.com/index.jsp.

Corporation, Limited Liability Company, Limited Partnerships, Trademarks/Servicemarks, Limited Liability Partnerships

Secretary of State, Corporation Division, State Capitol Bldg, Room W151, Charleston, WV 25305-0776; 304-558-8000, 304-558-5758-Fax; 8:30AM-5PM.

www.wvsos.com

Records are available for current active companies. It takes 24 hours before new records are available for inquiry. Records are indexed on inhouse computer.

Searching: Include the following in your request-full name of business. In addition to the initial organizing documents, business records include: Annual Reports, Officers, Directors, Prior (merged) names, Reserved names, mergers and amendments, agents of process and capital stock allocation of corporations.

Access by: mail, phone, fax, in person, online.

Fee & Payment: Copy fee is $1.00 for the first page and $.50 each additional page. Certification is $15.00 plus $5.00 for each amendment. Fee payee: Secretary of State. Prepayment required. Personal checks accepted. Major credit cards accepted.

Mail search: Turnaround time: 24 hours. No SASE is required.

Phone search: They will confirm if a company is active, they will only do three searches per phone call.

Fax search: Fax searching available.

In person search: Simple requests may be processed while you wait.

Online search: Corporation and business types records on the Secretary of State Business Organization Information System are available free online at www.wvsos.com/wvcorporations/. Search by organization name. Certified copies may be ordered online or via email to business@wvsos.com.

Uniform Commercial Code

UCC Division, Secretary of State, Bldg 1, West Wing, Rm 157K, Charleston, WV 25305-0440; 304-558-6000, 304-558-0900-Fax; 8:30AM-5PM.

www.wvsos.com/ucc/main.htm

The agency may place limited information under the website in the future.

Records are available from July 1, 1964. It takes 1 day before new records are available for inquiry. Records are indexed on inhouse computer.

Searching: Use search request form UCC-11. All tax liens are filed at the county level. Terminated filings are researched upon request. Include the following in your request-debtor name.

Access by: mail, phone, fax, in person.

Fee & Payment: The fee is $5.00 per search and $.50 per copy. Fee payee: Secretary of State. Prepayment required. Pre-paid accounts are accepted, but do not send excess amount-search request may be returned. Personal checks accepted. Major credit cards accepted.

Mail search: Turnaround time: 1 day. A SASE is requested.

Phone search: They will bill for telephone searches.

Fax search: Same fees as phone or mail searches. Turnaround time in 24 hours.

In person search: Simple requests may be processed while you wait.

Federal and State Tax Liens

Records not maintained by a state level agency.

All tax liens are filed at the county level.

Sales Tax Registrations

WV State Tax Department, Office of Business Registration, 1001 E Lee St E, Charleston, WV 25301; 304-558-8500, 304-558-8754-Fax; 8:30AM-4:30PM.

www.state.wv.us/taxrev

Records are available for the current year plus four years. It takes 4 to 6 weeks before new records are available for inquiry. Records are normally destroyed after 5 years.

Searching: Will not disclose any information unless you provide a waiver form signed by the taxpayer. Without a waiver, this agency will provide only confirmation if business registered. The waiver form is available at www.state.wv.us/taxrev/uploads/wvari001.pdf. Include the following in your request-business name. This agency will also search by tax business number.

Access by: mail, phone, fax, in person.

Mail search: Turnaround time: 2 weeks or less. A SASE is requested. No fee for mail request.

Phone search: No fee for telephone request.

Fax search: Fax searching available.

In person search: No fee for request. Records are still returned by mail.

Expedited service: Will expedite if requested.

Birth Certificates

Bureau for Public Health, Vital Records, 350 Capitol St, Rm 165, Charleston, WV 25301-3701; 304-558-2931, 304-558-9100, 304-558-1051-Fax; 8:30AM-5PM.

www.wvdhhr.org/bph/oehp/hsc

Records are available from 1917 to present. New records are available for inquiry immediately. Records are indexed on microfiche, inhouse computer.

Searching: This is a closed record state. Records released to immediate family members only. Records forms are available at the webpage. Include the following in your request-full name, names of parents, mother's maiden name, date of birth, place of birth. Online ordering is available from an approved vendor at www.vitalchek.com.

Access by: mail, phone, in person.

Fee & Payment: The fee is $5.00 per name per 3 years searched. Fee payee: Vital Registration. Prepayment required. Personal checks accepted. Major credit cards accepted.

Mail search: Turnaround time: 2 to 3 weeks.

Phone search: See expedited service.

In person search: Turnaround time 15 minutes.

Expedited service: Expedited service is available for fax, phone and online requests. To order by credit card and have 5-7 business days "rush" turnaround time add $15.95. For 3-day processing the total fee is $40.00.

Death Records

Bureau for Public Health, Vital Records, 350 Capitol St, Rm 165, Charleston, WV 25301-3701; 304-558-2931, 304-558-9100, 302-343-2169-Fax; 8AM-4PM.

www.wvdhhr.org/bph/oehp/hsc

Records are available from 1917 on. New records are available for inquiry immediately. Records are indexed on microfiche, inhouse computer.

Searching: This is a closed record state. Records released to immediate family members only. Records forms are available at the webpage. Include the following in your request-full name, date of death, place of death, names of parents, Social Security Number. Online ordering is available from an approved vendor at www.vitalchek.com.

Access by: mail, phone, fax, in person.

Fee & Payment: The fee is $5.00 per name and covers a searching range of three years. Fee payee: Vital Registration. Prepayment required. Personal checks accepted. Major credit cards accepted.

Mail search: Turnaround time: 2 to 3 weeks.

Phone search: See expedited service.

Fax search: Access is provided by VitalChek. Use 866-870-8723 for the fax number. Use of credit card is required.

In person search: Turnaround time 15 minutes.

Expedited service: Expedited service is available for fax, phone and online requests. To order by credit card and have 5-7 business days "rush" turnaround time add $15.95. For 3-day processing the total fee is $40.00.

Marriage Certificates

Bureau for Public Health, Vital Records, 350 Capitol St, Rm 165, Charleston, WV 25301-3701; 304-558-2931, 304-558-9100, 304-343-2169-Fax; 8AM-4PM.

www.wvdhhr.org/bph/oehp/hsc

Records are available from 1964 forward from this agency. Earlier records must be searched at the county level. New records are available for inquiry immediately. Records are indexed on microfiche, inhouse computer.

Searching: This is a closed record state. Records released to immediate family members only. Records forms are available at the webpage. Include the following in your request-names of husband and wife, date of marriage, place or county of marriage. Online ordering is available from an approved vendor at www.vitalchek.com.

Access by: mail, phone, fax, in person.

Fee & Payment: The fee is $5.00 per name and covers a searching range of three years. Fee payee: Vital Registration. Prepayment required. Personal checks accepted. Major credit cards accepted.

Mail search: Turnaround time: 2 to 3 weeks.

Phone search: See expedited service.

Fax search: Available from VitalChek. Use of credit card required.

In person search: Turnaround time 15 minutes.

Expedited service: Expedited service is available for fax, phone and online requests. To order by credit card and have 5-7 business days "rush" turnaround time add $15.95. For 3-day processing the total fee is $40.00.

Divorce Records

Records not maintained by a state level agency.

Records are maintained by the Clerk of Court in the county of divorce.

Workers' Compensation Records

Workers Compensation Commission, Records Management, 4510-D pennsylvania Ave, Charleston, WV 25302; 304-558-5587, 304-926-3400, 304-558-1908-Fax; 8AM-4:30PM.

www.wvwcc.org

Records are available from 1916. New records are available for inquiry immediately. Records are indexed on microfiche.

Searching: Must have a signed release from claimant or be a representative of the employer. They suggest the use of their WC910 Form. You may call for a copy of this form, but they will release no information over the phone. Include the following in your request-claimant name, Social Security Number, date of accident, file number (if known). The following data is not released: psychiatric information.

Access by: mail, in person, online.

Fee & Payment: There are no fees unless extensive copies or searching is needed.

Mail search: Turnaround time: 5 to 10 days. Turnaround time is 1-2 days for microfiche copies and 5-10 days if paper copies are required. A SASE is requested.

In person search: Turnaround time is usually 1 or more days.

Online search: Online access is available via http://ecomp.wvwcc.org/. The site is primarily intended for employers, attorneys, third party administrators, state and federal agencies and the medical community.

Driver License Information, Driver Records

Division of Motor Vehicles, 1800 Kanawha Blvd, Building 3, Rm 124, State Capitol Complex, Charleston, WV 25317; 304-558-4444, 304-558-0465-Fax; 8:30AM-5PM.

www.wvdot.com/6_motorists/dmv/6G_DMV.HTM

Use ZIP Code 25305 for Courier address deliveries.

Records are available for 3 years for all convictions, 10 years for suspensions and revocations. It takes 1 week to 3 months (DUIs immediately) before new records are available for inquiry.

Searching: Casual requesters must have notarized consent of subject to receive records with personal information. The driver's license number and last name are required for a request, DOB and SSN are helpful. The following data is not released:

accidents, speeding 10 mph or less over limit on interstate.

Access by: mail, in person, online.

Fee & Payment: The fee is $5.00 per record including no record founds. Fee payee: Division of Motor Vehicles. Prepayment required. Personal checks accepted. Credit cards accepted.

Mail search: Turnaround time: 3 days.

In person search: Up to seven requests may be received immediately at the counter of this office. Branch offices in at least 15 cities can issue an instant record for the subject-requestor.

Online search: Online access is available 24 hours a day. Batch requesters receive return transmission about 3 AM. Users must access through AAMVAnet. A contract is required and accounts must pre-pay. Fee is $5.00 per record. For more information, call 304-558-3915.

Other access: This agency will sell its DL file to commercial vendors, but records cannot be re-sold.

Vehicle Ownership
Vehicle Identification
Vessel Ownership
Vessel Registration

Division of Motor Vehicles, Information Services, 1606 Washington St East, Charleston, WV 25311; 304-558-0282, 304-558-1012-Fax; 8:30AM-4:30PM.

www.wvdot.com/6_motorists/dmv/6g2_registration.htm

This agency maintains records for unattached mobile homes.

Records are available from 1959 for vehicles, from 1975 for boat registrations, and from 1995 for boat titles. All motorized boats and all sailboats must be registered and titled. It takes 1 to 3 days before new records are available for inquiry.

Searching: High volume requesters must be approved after stating purpose of requests. Casual requesters cannot receive personal information. If doing search by name, it is suggested to also submit address. Boat records can be searched by hull number or WV number. The following data is not released: Social Security Numbers or medical information.

Access by: mail, in person.

Fee & Payment: The fee is $1.00 for registration information, $2.00 per vehicle for lien information, $5.00 per title copy, $15.00 for a complete title history (which includes lien information), and $5.00 for message forwarding. Fee payee: Division of Motor Vehicles. Prepayment required. Do not overpay, they do not have the capacity to refund. Personal checks accepted. No credit cards accepted.

Mail search: Turnaround time: 3 to 5 business days. Return address must appear clearly on the request. A SASE is requested.

In person search: Turnaround time is while you wait if the record is on computer, or 2 days for photocopies.

Other access: The entire state's vehicle file can be purchased. Costs for customized runs depend on programming time. Further resale is prohibited. Call 304-558-0282 for more information.

Accident Reports

Department of Public Safety, Traffic Records Section, 725 Jefferson Rd, South Charleston, WV 25309-1698; 304-746-2128, 304-746-2206-Fax; 8:30AM-5PM.

www.wvstatepolice.com

It is suggested to send a letter explaining purpose of request and state if involved in some manner.

Records are available of incidents investigated by the state police for the past 10 years. It takes 1 to 3 weeks before new records are available for inquiry. Records are normally destroyed after ten years.

Searching: If the State Police did not investigate the incident, the report must be obtained from the local investigating jurisdiction. Include the following in your request-name, date of accident, location of accident. The following data is not released: juvenile records.

Access by: mail, phone, fax, in person.

Fee & Payment: The fee is $20.00 per record. If certified, the cost is $25.00. Fee payee: Superintendent, Division of Public Safety. Prepayment required. Personal checks accepted. No credit cards accepted.

Mail search: Turnaround time: 2 to 3 weeks. A SASE is requested.

Phone search: Records are available by phone.

Fax search: For an extra $5.00 per record, the agency will send data by fax.

In person search: Turnaround time is same day, if record is readily available.

Voter Registration

Sec of State - Election Division, Bldg 1 #157-K, 1900 Kanawha Blvd E, Charleston, WV 25305; 304-558-6000, 304-558-0900-Fax; 8:30AM-4:30PM.

www.wvsos.com/elections/main.htm

Voter information is held by the county clerks, but the state recently implemented a statewide database system.

It takes seconds before new records are available for inquiry.

Searching: Records are open to the public. The following data is not released: phone numbers and SSNs.

Access by: mail, phone, fax, in person.

Fee & Payment: There is no fee for simple requests.

Mail search: Turnaround time: 24 hours. Records are available by mail.

Phone search: Records are available by phone.

Fax search: Records are available by fax.

In person search: Over-the-counter service is available.

Other access: Lists are available, turnaround time is 48 hours. Call for further information.

GED Certificates

WV Dept of Education, GED Office, 1900 Kanawha Blvd E, Bldg 6, Rm 250, Charleston, WV 25305-0330; 304-558-6315, 304-558-4874-Fax; 8AM-4PM.

www.wvabe.org/ged

It takes 8 weeks before new records are available for inquiry. Records are normally destroyed after 8 years, but only if non-passing.

Searching: To search, all of the following is a required: a signed release, name, year of test, date of birth, SSN, city of test, and a copy of or presentation of a current photo ID and daytime phone number.

Access by: mail, fax, in person.

Fee & Payment: There is $10.00 fee for verification. Copies of transcripts are $10.00 each. Fee payee: WV DOE Vocational Division. Prepayment required. Personal checks and money orders accepted. No credit cards accepted.

Mail search: Turnaround time: 7 to 10 days.

Fax search: Only if verification is for job position.

In person search: In person search requests are processed in order received along with mail requests. Depending on workload, one may have to return to pick up results.

Expedited service: The agency will expedite requests if for job verification only.

Hunting and Fishing License Information

Division of Natural Resources, Licensing Division, 1900 Kanawha Blvd E, Bldg 3, Room 624, Charleston, WV 25305; 304-558-2758, 304-558-6208-Fax; 8:30AM-4:30PM.

www.wvweb.com/www/hunting

Records are available for current year only. Records are indexed on inhouse computer. Records are normally destroyed after two years.

Searching: All requests must be in writing. Records are considered public records. Can request through customerservice@dnr.state.wv.us. Include the following in your request-full name, SSN.

Access by: mail, fax, in person.

Fee & Payment: The search fee is $29.00, but only if a record is found. Fee payee: Natural Resources Department. Personal checks accepted. Credit cards accepted: MasterCard, Visa.

Mail search: Turnaround time: 5 to 10 working days. No SASE is required.

Fax search: Fax requests accepted.

In person search: Request must be in writing.

West Virginia State Licensing Agencies

For details about the agency responsible for licensing/certifying/registering an item below or in the Agency Quick Finder section, match an item's number with the number of the agency in the *Licensing Agency Information* section.

West Virginia Licenses Searchable Online

Aesthetician #3	www.wvdhhr.org/bph/wvbc/licensees.cfm
Architect #2	http://wvbrdarch.org/roster/lic/searchdb.asp
Asbestos Clearance Air Monitor #42	www.wvdhhr.org/rtia/allair.cfm
Asbestos Contractor #42	www.wvdhhr.org/rtia/allcon.cfm
Asbestos Inspector #42	www.wvdhhr.org/rtia/allinsp.cfm
Asbestos Laboratory #42	www.wvdhhr.org/rtia/licensing.asp
Asbestos Project Designer #42	www.wvdhhr.org/rtia/alldesign.cfm
Asbestos Supervisor #42	www.wvdhhr.org/rtia/allsup.cfm
Asbestos Worker #42	www.wvdhhr.org/rtia/allwork.cfm
Attorney #14	www.wvbar.org/barinfo/mdirectory/
Barber #3	www.wvdhhr.org/bph/wvbc/licensees.cfm
Barber/Beauty Culture School #3	www.wvdhhr.org/bph/wvbc/licensees.cfm
Contractor, General #24	www.labor.state.wv.us/search/default.asp
Cosmetologist #3	www.wvdhhr.org/bph/wvbc/licensees.cfm
Counselor LPC, Professional #10	www.wvbec.org/alps.htm
Electrician #40	www.wvfiremarshal.org/search.htm
Engineer #33	www.wvpebd.org
Lobbyist #39	www.wvethicscommission.org
Manicurist #3	www.wvdhhr.org/bph/wvbc/licensees.cfm
Medical Corporation #15	www.wvdhhr.org/wvbom/Directory/2003/medcorps2003.pdf
Medical Doctor #15	www.wvdhhr.org/wvbom/Directory/2003/mds2003.pdf
Medical License, Special Volunteer #15	www.wvdhhr.org/wvbom/Directory/2003/specialvolunteer2003.pdf
Medical Professional Company #15	www.wvdhhr.org/wvbom/Directory/2003/pllcs2003.pdf
Nurse-LPN #8	www.lpnboard.state.wv.us/
Occupational Therapist/Assistant #16	www.wvbot.org
Optometrist #41	www.arbo.org/index.php?action=findanoptometrist
Osteopathic Physician/Osteo Assist. #17	www.state.wv.us/bdosteo
Pesticide Applicator #25	www.kellysolutions.com
Physician Assistant #15	www.wvdhhr.org/wvbom/Directory/2003/pas2003.pdf
Podiatrist #15	www.wvdhhr.org/wvbom/Directory/2003/podiatrists2003.pdf
Public Accountant-CPA #1	www.wvboacc.org/Verify_A_Licensee.htm
Radiologic Technologist #9	www.wvrtboard.org/
Real Estate Agent/Broker/Seller #35	www.arello.com/ArelloWeb/ShowPage?command=main
Real Estate Appraiser #34	www.asc.gov/content/category1/appr_by_state.asp
Respiratory Care Practitioner #43	www.wvborc.org/licensees/default.asp
Veterinarian #22	www.wvlicensingboards.com/vetmed/licensed.cfm

West Virginia Licensing Quick Finder

Aesthetician #3	304-558-2924
Animal Technician #22	304.776.8032
Architect #2	304-528-5825
Asbestos Clearance Air Monitor #42	304-558-6720/6768
Asbestos Contractor #42	304-558-6720/6768
Asbestos Inspector #42	304-558-6720/6768
Asbestos Laboratory #42	304-558-6720/6768
Asbestos Project Designer #42	304-558-6720/6768
Asbestos Supervisor #42	304-558-6720/6768
Asbestos Worker #42	304-558-6720/6768
Athlete Agent #36	304-558-6000
Athletic Trainer #26	304-558-7010

Attorney #14	304-558-7815
Barber #3	304-558-2924
Barber/Beauty Culture School #3	304-558-2924
Boat & Canoe Expedition Provider #29	304-558-2784
Boating Business, Whitewater #29	304-558-2784
Charitable Organization #36	304-558-6000
Chiropractor #4	304-746-7839
Contractor, General #24	304-558-7890x122
Cosmetologist #3	304-558-2924
Counselor LPC, Professional #10	304-733-5494
Counselor, Professional #10	304-733-5494
Credit Service Organization #36	304-558-6000
Dental Hygienist #6	304-252-8266

Dentist #6	304-252-8266
Educational Audiologist #26	304-558-7010
Electrician #40	304-558-2191
Embalmer #5	304-558-0302
Emergency Medical Technician-Paramedic #27	304-558-3956
Engineer #33	304-558-3554
First Responder #27	304-558-3956
Fishing Guide #29	304-558-2784
Forester #20	304-324-7557
Forestry Technician #20	304-324-7557
Fund Raiser,For-Profit Profession'l #37	800-982-8297
Funeral Director; Funeral Home #5	304-558-0302

Hearing Aid Specialist #12 304-558-7886
Insurance Adjuster #30 304-558-0610
Insurance Agency / Producer #30 304-558-0610
Insurance Solicitor #30 304-558-0610
Investment Advisor/Represen'tive #38 .. 304-558-2257
Landscape Architect #13 304-727-5501
Lead Abatement Contractor #42 .304-558-6720/6768
Lobbyist #39 304-558-0664
Manicurist #3 304-558-2924
Marriage Registration #36 304-558-6000
Medical Corporation #15 304-558-2921
Medical Doctor #15 304-558-2921
Medical License,Special Volunteer #15 304-558-2921
Medical Professional LLC/Co. #15 304-558-2921
Midwife Nurse #8 304-558-3596
Mine Electrician #32 304-558-1425
Mine Surveyor/Foreman #32 304-558-1425
Miner #32 304-558-1425
Notary Public #36 304-558-6000
Nurse #8 304-558-3596
Nurse Anesthetist #8 304-558-3596

Nurse-LPN #8 304-558-3572
Nursing Home Administrator #31 304-759-0722
Occupational Therapist/Assistant #16 .. 304-285-3150
Optometrist #41 304-558-5901
Osteopathic Physician/Physician Assistant #17
.... 304-723-4638
Pesticide Applicator #25 304-558-2209
Pharmacist #18 304-558-0558
Physical Therapist #19 304-627-2251
Physical Therapist Assistant #19 304-627-2251
Physician Assistant #15 304-558-2921
Podiatrist #15 304-558-2921
Polygraph Examiner #28 .... 304-558-7890 x122
Private Detective #36 304-558-6000
Psychologist #11 304-558-0604
Public Accountant-CPA #1 304-558-3557
Radiologic Technologist #9 304-787-4398
Radon Contractor/Trainer #42 .... 304-558-6720/6768
Rafting Outfitter, Whitewater #29 304-558-2784
Real Estate Agent/Broker/Sales #35 ... 304-558-3555
Real Estate Appraiser #34 304-558-3919

Respiratory Care Practitioner #43 304-558-1382
Sanitarian, Registered/In-Training #23 . 304-558-2981
School Counselor #26 304-558-7010
School Nurse #26 304-558-7010
School Principal #26 304-558-7010
School Psychologist #26 304-558-7010
School Social Services/Attendance Investigator #26
.... 304-558-7010
School Superintendent #26 304-558-7010
Securities Agent #38 304-558-2257
Securities Broker/Dealer #38 304-558-2257
Security Guard #36 304-558-6000
Shooting Reserve #29 304-558-2784
Shot Firer #32 304-558-1425
Social Worker #21 304-558-8816
Speech/Language Pathologist #26 304-558-7010
Supervisor of Instruction #26 304-558-7010
Surveyor, Land #7 304-765-0315
Teacher #26 304-558-7010
Telemarketer #37 304-558-0211
Veterinarian #22 .... 304.776.8032

West Virginia Licensing Agency Information

1 Board of Accountancy, 106 Capitol St, #100, Charleston, WV 25301-2610; 304-558-3557, Fax: 304-558-1325.
www.wvboacc.org/
Email: wvboa@mail.wvnet.edu
Search Database at
www.wvboacc.org/Verify_A_Licensee.htm

2 Board of Architects, PO Box 9125, Huntington, WV 25704-0125;
304-528-5825, Fax: 304-528-5826.
http://wvbrdarch.org
Email: lewilex@wvnvm.wvnet.edu
Search Database at
http://wvbrdarch.org/roster/lic/searchdb.asp

3 Board of Barbers & Cosmetologists, 1716 Pennsylvania Ave, #7, Charleston, WV 25302; 304-558-2924, Fax: 304-558-3450.
www.state.wv.us/wvbc
Email: sholley@state.wv.us
Search Database at
www.wvdhhr.org/bph/wvbc/licensees.cfm

4 Board of Chiropractic Examiners, PO Box 8532 (415 1/2 D St, #6), South Charleston, WV 25303; 304-746-7839, Fax: 304-746-0794.
www.wvboc.com/
Email: wvboc@citynet.net

5 Board of Embalmers & Funeral Directors, 179 Summers St #305, Charleston, WV 25301-2131; 304-558-0302, Fax: 304-558-0660.
www.wvfuneralboard.com/
Email: wvfuneralboard@msn.com   Note: The Funeral Directors Assn. member list is available at www.wvfda.org/members.cfm.

6 Board of Examiners for Dentists/Dental Hygienists, 207 S. Heber St, Beckley, WV 25801; 304-252-8266, Fax: 304-252-2779.
www.wvdentalboard.org
Email: wvbde@charterinternet.com

7 Board of Examiners for Land Surveyors, PO Box 390 (2298 Sutton Lane), Flatwoods, WV 26621; 304-765-0315, Fax: 304-765-0316.

8 Board of Examiners for Reg. Prof. Nurses, 101 Dee Dr, Charleston, WV 25311-1620; 304-558-3596, or 1-877-743-6877, Fax: 304-558-3666.
www.wvrnboard.com/
Email: rnboard@state.wv.us   Note: The LPNs have a separate board at the same address; 304-558-3572; fax: 305-558-4367.

9 Board of Examiners for Radiologic Technology, PO Box 638, Cool Ridge, WV 25825; 304-787-4398, Fax: 304-787-3030.
www.wvrtboard.org/
Email: wvrtboe@charter.net
Search Database at www.wvrtboard.org

10 Board of Examiners in Counseling, PO Box 129, Ona, WV 25545; 800-520-3852.
www.wvbec.org/index.htm
Email: counselingboard@msn.com
Note: Verification requests fee is $20.00 payable to WVBEC; requests are processed in 3 working days. Will fax back results.

11 Board of Examiners of Psychologists, PO Box 3955, Charleston, WV 25339-3955; 304-558-3040, Fax: 304-558-0608.
www.wvpsychbd.org
Email: wvpsychbd@mail.state.wv.us

12 Board of Hearing-Aid Dealers, 701 Jefferson Road, Charleston, WV 25301; 304-558-7886, Fax: 304-558-7886.

13 Board of Landscape Architects, PO Box 1355, St. Albans, WV 25177; 304-727-5501, Fax: 304-727-5580.
www.wvlicensingboards.com/landscape/

14 Board of Law Examiners, 2006 Kanawha Blvd, Charleston, WV 25311; 304-558-2456, Fax: 304-558-2467.   www.state.wv.us/wvsca
Email: suerubenstein@courtswv.org
Search Database at
www.wvbar.org/barinfo/mdirectory/

15 Board of Medicine, 101 Dee Dr #103, Charleston, WV 25311-1620; 304-558-2921 x224, Fax: 304-558-2084.
www.wvdhhr.org/wvbom

16 Board of Occupational Therapy, 3041 University Ave 2nd Fl #6, Kingwood, WV 26537; 304-285-3150.
www.wvbot.org
Email: cathywhalen@wvbot.org

17 Board of Osteopathy, 334 Penco Rd, Weirton, WV 26062-3813; 304-723-4638, Fax: 304-723-6723.
www.wvbdosteo.org/
Email: bdosteo@mail.wvnet.edu

18 Board of Pharmacy, 232 Capitol St, Charleston, WV 25301-2206; 304-558-0558, Fax: 304-558-0572.
www.wvbop.com

19 WV Board of Physical Therapy, 210 Oak Dr #A, Clarksburg, WV 26301; 304-627-2251, Fax: 304-627-2253.   www.wvbopt.com
Email: wvbopt@wvnet.edu   Verifications provided only based on a written request and a $25.00 fee.

20 Board of Registration for Foresters, 625 Parkway, Bluefield, WV 24701; 304-324-7557, Fax: 304-324-7512.
www.wvlicensingboards.com/foresters/index.cfm
Email: tprobert@citlink.net

21 Board of Social Work Examiners, PO Box 5459, (State Capitol Complex, Main Bldg - Rm WB9), Charleston, WV 25361; 304-558-8816, Fax: 304-558-4189.
www.wvsocialworkboard.org/
Email: williju@mail.wvnet.edu

22 Board of Veterinary Medicine, 5509 Big Tyler Road Suite 3, Cross Lanes, WV 25313; 304.776.8032, Fax: 304.776.8256.
www.wvlicensingboards.com/vetmed/
Email: goodww@mail.wvnet.edu

23 Bureau of Public Health, Sanitarian Licensing, 815 Quarrier St, Charleston, WV 25301-2616; 304-558-2981, Fax: 304-558-1071. www.wvdhhr.org/phs/bors/index.asp

24 Contractor Licensing Board, 1900 Kanawha Blvd E, Bldg 6, Rm B-749, Charleston, WV 25305; 304-558-7890 x122, Fax: 304-558-3797. www.labor.state.wv.us/
Search Database at www.labor.state.wv.us/search/default.asp

25 Department of Agriculture, Pesticide Applicator Licensing, 1900 Kanawah Blvd. E., Charleston, WV 25305; 304-558-2209, Fax: 304-558-2228. www.wvagriculture.org/
Search Database at www.kellysolutions.com/

26 Department of Education, 1900 Kanawha Blvd E, Charleston, WV 25305; 304-558-7010, Fax: 304-558-7843. http://wvde.state.wv.us
Email: llkiser@access.k12.wv.us

27 Office of EMS, Bureau of Public Health, 350 Capitol St #515, Charleston, WV 25301-3716; 304-558-3956, Fax: 304-558-1437. www.wvoems.org/

28 Department of Labor, State Capitol Complex, Bldg. 6, Rm 749B, Charleston, WV 25305; 304-558-7890 x122, Fax: 304-558-3797. www.labor.state.wv.us/

29 Division of Natural Resources, 1900 Kanawha Blvd, East Bldg 3, Rm 837, Charleston, WV 25305; 304-558-2784, Fax: 304-558-2873. www.wvdnr.gov/

30 Insurance Commissioner, 1124 Smith St, Charleston, WV 25301; 304-558-0610, Fax: 304-558-4966. www.wvinsurance.gov
Email: agent.licensing@wvinsurance.gov   Note: No longer licenses insurance brokers.

31 Nursing Home Administrators Licensing Board, 5303 Kensington Dr, Cross Lanes, WV 25313; 304-759-0722, Fax: 304-759-0724. www.state.wv.us/wvnha/dspcontactus.cfm

32 Office of Miners Health Safety & Training, 1615 Washington St E, Charleston, WV 25311; 304-558-1425, Fax: 304-558-1282. www.wvminesafety.org/
Email: MINEINFO@mines.state.wv.us

33 Board of Registration for Professional Engineers, 300 Capitol St. Ste 910, Charleston, WV 25301-2703; 304-558-3554, Fax: 304-558-6232.   www.wvpebd.org
Search Database at www.wvpebd.org

34 Real Estate Appraiser Licensing & Certification Board, 2110 Kanawah Blvd E, #101, Charleston, WV 25311; 304-558-3919, Fax: 304-558-3983. www.wvs.state.wv.us/appraise/
Email: wvappbd@wvnvm.wvnet.edu
Search Database at www.asc.gov/content/category1/appr_by_state.asp

35 Real Estate Commission, 1033 Quarrier St, #400, Charleston, WV 25301-2315; 304-558-3555, Fax: 304-558-6442. www.wvrec.org   Email: wvrec@wvrec.state.wv.us
Search Database at www.arello.com/ArelloWeb/ShowPage?command=main

36 Secretary of State, 1900 Kanawha Blvd, Bldg 1, #157-K, Charleston, WV 25305-0770; 304-558-6000, Fax: 304-558-5142. www.wvsos.com
Email: wvsos@wvsos.com

37 Department of Tax & Revenue, Taypayer Services, Telemarketing Registration, Building 1, Room 300W, 1900 Kanawha Boulevard, East, Charleston, WV 25305; 304-558-3356, Fax: 304-558-2324. www.state.wv.us/taxrev/tmkg.htm

38 State Auditor's Office, State Capitol, Rm W110, Charleston, WV 25305; 304-558-2257, Fax: 304-558-4211. www.wvauditor.com
Email: johns@wvauditor.com

39 Ethics Commission, 210 Brooks St #300, Charleston, WV 25301; 304-558-0664, Fax: 304-558-2169. www.wvethicscommission.org/
Email: lsuchy@wvadmin.gov
Search Database at www.wvethicscommission.org

40 State Fire Marshall, 1207 Quarrier, 2nd Fl, Charleston, WV 25301; 304-558-2191, Fax: 304-558-2537. www.wvfiremarshal.org
Email: info@wvfiremarshal.org
Search Database at www.wvfiremarshal.org/search.htm

41 West Virginia Board of Optometry, 723 Kanawha Boulevard #804, Charleston, WV 25301; 304-558-5901, Fax: 304-558-5908. www.wvbo.org
Email: wvbdopt@westvirginia.net
Search Database at www.arbo.org/index.php?action=findanoptometrist

42 Department of Health & Human Resources, Radiation, Toxics and Indoor Air Division, 815 Quarrier St #418, Charleston, WV 25301; 304-558-2981, Fax: 304-558-1289. www.wvdhhr.org/rtia/
Search Database at www.wvdhhr.org/rtia/licensing.asp

43 Board of Respiratory Care, 106 Dee Dr, #1, Charleston, WV 25311; 304-558-1382, Fax: 304-558-1383. www.wvborc.org/topframe.html
Email: info@wvborc.org
Search Database at www.wvborc.org/licensees/default.asp

West Virginia Federal Courts

The following list indicates the district and division name for each county in the state. If the bankruptcy court location is different from the district court, then the location of the bankruptcy court appears in parentheses.

West Virginia County/Court Cross Reference

County	District	Division
Barbour	Northern	Elkins (Wheeling)
Berkeley	Northern	Martinsburg (Wheeling)
Boone	Southern	Charleston
Braxton	Northern	Clarksburg (Wheeling)
Brooke	Northern	Wheeling
Cabell	Southern	Huntington (Charleston)
Calhoun	Northern	Clarksburg (Wheeling)
Clay	Southern	Charleston
Doddridge	Northern	Clarksburg (Wheeling)
Fayette	Southern	Beckley (Charleston)
Gilmer	Northern	Clarksburg (Wheeling)
Grant	Northern	Elkins (Wheeling)
Greenbrier	Southern	Beckley (Charleston)
Hampshire	Northern	Martinsburg (Wheeling)
Hancock	Northern	Wheeling
Hardy	Northern	Elkins (Wheeling)
Harrison	Northern	Clarksburg (Wheeling)
Jackson	Southern	Parkersburg (Charleston)
Jefferson	Northern	Martinsburg (Wheeling)
Kanawha	Southern	Charleston
Lewis	Northern	Clarksburg (Wheeling)
Lincoln	Southern	Huntington (Charleston)
Logan	Southern	Charleston
Marion	Northern	Clarksburg (Wheeling)
Marshall	Northern	Wheeling
Mason	Southern	Huntington (Charleston)
McDowell	Southern	Bluefield (Charleston)
Mercer	Southern	Bluefield (Charleston)
Mineral	Northern	Elkins (Wheeling)
Mingo	Southern	Huntington (Charleston)
Monongalia	Northern	Clarksburg (Wheeling)
Monroe	Southern	Bluefield (Charleston)
Morgan	Northern	Martinsburg (Wheeling)
Nicholas	Southern	Beckley (Charleston)
Ohio	Northern	Wheeling
Pendleton	Northern	Elkins (Wheeling)
Pleasants	Northern	Clarksburg (Wheeling)
Pocahontas	Northern	Elkins (Wheeling)
Preston	Northern	Elkins (Wheeling)
Putnam	Southern	Charleston
Raleigh	Southern	Beckley (Charleston)
Randolph	Northern	Elkins (Wheeling)
Ritchie	Northern	Clarksburg (Wheeling)
Roane	Southern	Charleston
Summers	Southern	Bluefield (Charleston)
Taylor	Northern	Clarksburg (Wheeling)
Tucker	Northern	Elkins (Wheeling)
Tyler	Northern	Clarksburg (Wheeling)
Upshur	Northern	Elkins (Wheeling)
Wayne	Southern	Huntington (Charleston)
Webster	Northern	Elkins (Wheeling)
Wetzel	Northern	Wheeling
Wirt	Southern	Parkersburg (Charleston)
Wood	Southern	Parkersburg (Charleston)
Wyoming	Southern	Beckley (Charleston)

Standards for Federal Courts: See Washington or Wisconsin Federal Courts Section for standards and fees for West Virginia Federal Courts.

US District Court

Northern District of West Virginia

Clarksburg Division Court Clerk, PO Box 2857, Clarksburg, WV 26302-2857 (courier address: 500 W Pike St, Rm 301, Clarksburg, WV 26301), 304-622-8513, Fax-304-623-4551. Hours- 8:30AM-5PM. www.wvnd.uscourts.gov

Counties: Braxton, Calhoun, Doddridge, Gilmer, Harrison, Lewis, Marion, Monongalia, Pleasants, Ritchie, Taylor, Tyler.

Searches & Indexing: Results do not include SSN or DOB. Computer index maintained; civil goes back to 1994, criminal to 1995. Card index also maintained. New cases in the index 1-2 days after filing date. Records purged every 5 years.

Fee & Payment: Pay by Visa/MC/Discover, money order, cashier check. No personal or business checks. Money orders preferred unless it is a known person or business. Payee: Clerk, US District Court. Prepayment required. Will fax back documents.

Phone Search: Only docket information is available by phone. **Mail Search:** search usually completed- 2-3 days. SASE not required.

In Person Search: Fee charged if court performs your search. No self-serve copier available.

E-Services: ECF replaces PACER. Document images available. PACER records go back to 10/1994. New records online after 1 day. ECF at https://ecf.wvnd.uscourts.gov **Opinions Online:** www.wvnd.uscourts.gov/opinions.htm. Opinions go back to 1999.

Elkins Division Court Clerk, PO Box 1518, Elkins, WV 26241 (courier address: 2nd Fl, 300 3rd St, Elkins, WV 26241), phone 304-636-1445, Fax-304-636-5746. Hours- 8AM-5:30PM. www.wvnd.uscourts.gov **Counties:** Barbour, Grant, Hardy, Mineral, Pendleton, Pocahontas, Preston, Randolph, Tucker, Upshur, Webster.

Searches & Indexing: Results do not include SSN or DOB. Computer and card indexes maintained. Civil cases on computer and docket sheets back to 10/1994; criminal back to 10/1995. New cases in the index 1 day after filing date. Records purged every 5 years. District-wide searches available here; case number and cause of action are released.

Fee & Payment: Pay by no business or personal checks accepted. Money orders preferred. Payee: Clerk, US District Court. Prepayment required. Will fax documents $1.00 per page.

Phone Search: Only docket information is available by phone. **Mail Search:** search usually completed- 1-2 days. SASE not required. **In Person Search:** Fee charged if court performs your search. If court personnel assist, search fee is charged. Self-serve copier - $.50 per page.

E-Services: same as Clarksburg Division.

Martinsburg Division Court Clerk, Rm 207, 217 W King St, Martinsburg, WV 25401 (also use mail address for courier delivery), 304-267-8225 x0, Fax-304-264-0434. Hours- 8:30AM-5PM. www.wvnd.uscourts.gov **Counties:** Berkeley, Hampshire, Jefferson, Morgan.

Searches & Indexing: Results do not include SSN or DOB. Both computer and card indexes maintained; computer index goes back to 2001. New cases in the index 2 days after filing date. Records purged every 5 years.

Fee & Payment: Pay by Visa/MC, money order, cashier check. No personal or business checks accepted. Payee: Clerk, US District Court. Prepayment required.

Phone Search: Limited docket information is available by phone. **Mail Search:** search usually completed- 2 weeks. Include SASE for return. **In Person Search:** Fee charged if court performs your search. No self-serve copier available.

E-Services: ECF replaces PACER. Document images available. PACER records go back to 10/1994. New records online after 1 day. ECF at https://ecf.wvnd.uscourts.gov **Opinions Online:** www.wvnd.uscourts.gov/opinions.htm. Opinions go back to 1999.

Wheeling Division Clerk of Court, PO Box 471, Wheeling, WV 26003 (courier address: 12th & Chapline Sts, Wheeling, WV 26003), 304-232-0011, Fax-304-233-2185. Hours- 8:30AM-5PM. www.wvnd.uscourts.gov **Counties:** Brooke, Hancock, Marshall, Ohio, Wetzel.

Searches & Indexing: Results do not include SSN or DOB. Both computer and card indexes maintained. Civil cases on computer back to 10/1994; criminal to 10/1995. New cases in the index immediately after filing date. Records purged every 5 years. **Fee & Payment:** Pay by Visa/MC, money order, cashier check. Payee: Clerk, US District Court. Prepayment required.

Phone Search: Information that is not sealed is available for release via phone. **Mail Search:** search usually completed- soon as work load permits. Include SASE for return. **In Person Search:** Fee charged if court performs your search. Self-serve copier - $.50 per page.

E-Services: same as Clarksburg Division.

US Bankruptcy Court

Northern District of West Virginia

Wheeling Division Court Clerk, PO Box 70, Wheeling, WV 26003 (courier: 12th & Chapline Sts, Wheeling, WV 26003), 304-233-1655. Hours- 8:30AM-5PM. www.wvnb.uscourts.gov

Counties: Barbour, Berkeley, Braxton, Brooke, Calhoun, Doddridge, Gilmer, Grant, Hampshire, Hancock, Hardy, Harrison, Jefferson, Lewis, Marion, Marshall, Mineral, Monongalia, Morgan, Ohio, Pendleton, Pleasants, Pocahontas, Preston, Randolph, Ritchie, Taylor, Tucker, Tyler, Upshur, Webster, Wetzel. Clarksburg location is 324 Main St, Clarksburg, 26302, phone- 304-623-7866.

Searches & Indexing: Results include last 4 SSN digits. A card index is maintained. New cases in the index 24 hours after filing. Records purged never. You may sSearch Clarksburg records.

Fee & Payment: Pay by money order, cashier's or personal check. Payee: Clerk, US Bankruptcy Court. Prepayment required.

Phone Search: Only docket information is available by phone. Voice Case Information Service available, call 800-809-3028 or 304-233-7318. **Mail Search:** search usually completed- 1-2 days. Include SASE for return. **In Person Search:** Fee charged if court performs your search. No self-serve copier available.

E-Services: ECF replaces PACER. Document images available. PACER records go back to early 1990. New records online after 1 day. ECF at https://ecf.wvnb.uscourts.gov **Opinions Online:** www.wvnb.uscourts.gov/courtopinions.htm.

US District Court

Southern District of West Virginia

Beckley Division Court Clerk, PO Drawer 5009, Beckley, WV 25801 (courier address: 110 N. Heber, Beckley, WV 25801), 304-253-7481, Fax-304-253-3252. Hours- 8:30AM-5PM. www.wvsd.uscourts.gov **Counties:** Fayette, Greenbrier, Raleigh, Sumners, Wyoming.

Searches & Indexing: Results do not include SSN or DOB. A card index is maintained. New cases in the index immediately after filing date. Records purged as deemed necessary.

Fee & Payment: Pay by Visa/MC/Discover (in person only), money order, cashier's or personal check. Payee: Clerk, US District Court. Prepayment required. **Phone Search:** Only docket information is available by phone. **Mail Search:**

search usually completed- 2-3 days. Include SASE for return. **In Person Search:** Fee charged if court performs search. Self-serve copier - $.50 per page.

E-Services: ECF replaces PACER. Document images available. PACER records go back to 1991. New records online after 1 day. ECF at https://ecf.wvsd.uscourts.gov **Opinions Online:** www.wvsd.uscourts.gov/district/opinions/. **Other Online Access:** Judges' calendars free at www.wvsd.uscourts.gov/judgetree/index.html.

Bluefield Division Clerk's Office, PO Box 4128, Bluefield, WV 24701 (courier address: 601 Federal St, Bluefield, WV 24701), 304-327-9798, Fax-304-327-6668. Hours- 8:30AM-5PM. www.wvsd.uscourts.gov

Counties: McDowell, Mercer, Monroe.

Searches & Indexing: Results do not include SSN or DOB. A card index is maintained. New cases in the index immediately after filing date.

Fee & Payment: Pay by money order, cashier's or personal check. Payee: Clerk, US District Court. Prepayment required. **Phone Search:** One name may be searched by phone. **Mail Search:** search usually completed- 3 days. Include SASE for return. **In Person:** Fee charged if court performs your search. Self-serve copier - $.50 per page.

E-Services: ECF replaces PACER. Document images available. PACER records go back to 1991. New records online after 1 day. ECF at https://ecf.wvsd.uscourts.gov **Opinions Online:** www.wvsd.uscourts.gov/district/opinions/. **Other Online Access:** Judges' calendars free at www.wvsd.uscourts.gov/judgetree/index.html.

Charleston Division Court Clerk, PO Box 2546, Charleston, WV 25339 (courier address: 300 Virginia St E, #2400, Charleston, WV 25339), 304-347-3000. Hours- 8:30AM-5PM. www.wvsd.uscourts.gov **Counties:** Boone, Clay, Jackson, Kanawha, Lincoln, Logan, Mingo, Nicholas, Putnam, Roane.

Searches & Indexing: All Division records available here on computer. Results do not include SSN or DOB. Both computer and card indexes maintained. New cases in the index immediately after filing date. **Fee & Payment:** Pay by money order, cashier's or personal check. Payee: Clerk, US District Court. Prepayment required.

Phone Search: Only docket information is available by phone. **Mail Search:** search usually completed- 3 days. SASE not required.

In Person Search: Fee charged if court performs your search. Self-serve copier - $.50 per page.

E-Services: ECF replaces PACER. Document images available. PACER records go back to 1991. New records online after 1 day. ECF at https://ecf.wvsd.uscourts.gov **Opinions Online:** www.wvsd.uscourts.gov/district/opinions/. **Other Online Access:** Judges' calendars free at www.wvsd.uscourts.gov/judgetree/index.html.

Huntington Division Clerk of Court, PO Box 1570, Huntington, WV 25716 (courier address: 845 5th Ave, Rm 101, Huntington, WV 25701), 304-529-5588, Fax-304-529-5131. Hours- 8:30AM-5PM. www.wvsd.uscourts.gov

Counties: Cabell, Mason, Wayne.

Searches & Indexing: Results do not include SSN or DOB. Both computer and card indexes maintained. Computer civil index goes back to

1994; criminal to 1994. New cases in the index immediately after filing date.

Fee & Payment: Pay by money order, cashier's or personal check. No credit cards. Payee: Clerk, US District Court. Prepayment required.

Phone Search: Only docket information is available by phone. **Mail Search:** search usually completed- 1-2 days. Include SASE for return. **In Person Search:** Fee charged if court performs your search. Self-serve copier - $.50 per page.

E-Services: same as Charleston Division.

Parkersburg Division Clerk of Court, PO Box 1526, Parkersburg, WV 26102 (courier address: 425 Julianna St, Rm 5102, Parkersburg, WV 26101), 304-420-6490, Fax-304-420-6363. 8:30AM-N, 1-5PM. www.wvsd.uscourts.gov

Counties: Wirt, Wood. **Searches & Indexing:** Results do not include SSN or DOB. Both computer and card indexes maintained. New cases in the index immediately after filing date.

Fee & Payment: Pay by money order, cashier's or personal check. No credit cards. Payee: Clerk, US District Court. Prepayment required.

Phone Search: Only docket information is available by phone. **Mail Search:** search usually completed- 1-2 days. Include SASE for return.**In Person Search:** Fee charged if court performs your search. Self-serve copier - $.50 per page.

E-Services: ECF replaces PACER - records did go back to 1991. New records online after 1 day. ECF at https://ecf.wvsb.uscourts.gov **Opinions Online:** www.wvsd.uscourts.gov/district/opinions/.

US Bankruptcy Court

Southern District of West Virginia

Charleston Division Court Clerk, PO Box 3924, Charleston, WV 25339 (courier address: 300 Virginia St E, Rm 2400, Charleston, WV 25301), 304-347-3000. Hours- 8:30AM-5PM. www.wvsd.uscourts.gov/bankruptcy/index.htm

Counties: Boone, Cabell, Clay, Fayette, Greenbrier, Jackson, Kanawha, Lincoln, Logan, Mason, McDowell, Mercer, Mingo, Monroe, Nicholas, Putnam, Raleigh, Roane, Summers, Wayne, Wirt, Wood, Wyoming.

Searches & Indexing: Results include last 4 SSN digits. Computer index goes back to 12/1/1988. New cases in the index 1 day after filing date.

Fee & Payment: Pay by Visa/MC, money order, cashier's or personal check. Credit cards accepted only from law firms. Payee: Clerk, US Bankruptcy Court. Prepayment required.

Phone Search: Only docket information is available by phone. Voice Case Information Service available, call 304-347-5337. **Mail Search:** search usually completed- 1-2 days. SASE not required. **In Person Search:** Fee charged if court performs your search. No self-serve copier.

E-Services: ECF replaces PACER. Document images available. PACER records go back to 1988. New records online after 1 day. ECF at https://ecf.wvsb.uscourts.gov **Other Access:** limited hearing dockets by day free at www.wvsd.uscourts.gov/bankruptcy/dailydocket.htm

West Virginia County Courts

Court	Jurisdiction	No. of Courts	How Organized
Circuit Courts*	General	55	31 Circuits
Magistrate Courts*	Limited	55	55 Counties
Family Courts	Limited	55	55 Counties
Municipal Courts	Municipal	122	

* Profiled in this Sourcebook.

Court	CIVIL								
	Tort	Contract	Real Estate	Min. Claim	Max. Claim	Small Claims	Estate	Eviction	Domestic Relations
Circuit Courts*	X	X	X	$300	No Max		X		X
Magistrate Courts*	X	X		$0	$5000	$3000		X	X
Family Courts									X
Municipal Courts									

Court	CRIMINAL				
	Felony	Misdemeanor	DWI/DUI	Preliminary Hearing	Juvenile
Circuit Courts*	X				X
Magistrate Courts*		X	X	X	
Municipal Courts			X		

ADMINISTRATION

Administrative Office, Supreme Court of Appeals, 1900 Kanawha Blvd, 1 E 100 State Capitol, Charleston, WV, 25305; 304-558-0145, Fax: 304-558-1212. www.state.wv.us/wvsca

COURT STRUCTURE

The 55 Circuit Courts are the courts of general jurisdiction. Probate is handled by the Circuit Court. Records are held at the County Commissioner's Office.

Family Courts were created by constitutional amendment and were formed as of 01/01/02. Family courts hear cases involving such matters as divorce, annulment, separate maintenance, family support, paternity, child custody, and visitation. Family court judges also conduct final hearings in domestic violence cases.

ONLINE ACCESS

Supreme Court of Appeals Opinions/Calendar is available at the web page. There are plans for a statewide system to allow access to Circuit, Family and Magistrate records, but it is not yet available.

Magistrate Court records are on a private system, see www.swcg-inc.com/products/municipal_courts.html.

ADDITIONAL INFORMATION

There is a statewide requirement that search turnaround times not exceed five business days. However, most courts do far better than that limit. Release of public information is governed by WV Code Sec.29B-1-1 et seq.

📖📖📖📖📖📖

Barbour County

Circuit Court 8 N Main St, Philippi, WV 26416; phone: 304-457-3454; fax: 304-457-2790; hours 8:30AM-4:30PM (EST). *Felony, Civil Actions Over $5,000, Probate.*
Note: Probate is handled by the County Clerk at this address.
Civil Records: Access: Phone, fax, mail, in person. Both court and visitors may perform in person searches. No search fee. Court makes copy: $.50 per page. Required to search: name, years to search. Civil cases indexed by defendant, plaintiff; on microfiche from 1843 to 1980s on index cards back to 1862, on dockets back to 1843. Mail turnaround time 1 day.
Criminal Records: Access: Phone, fax, mail, in person. Both court and visitors may perform in person searches. No search fee. Court makes copy: $.50 per page. Required to search: name, years to search. Criminal records on microfiche from 1843 to 1980s on index cards back to 1862, on dockets back to 1843. Mail turnaround time 1 day.
General Information: Public terminal goes back to 2001. No sealed, juvenile, adoptions, mental health, expunged records released. No fee to fax documents if one or two pages only. Certification fee: $1.00 per cert. Payee: Barbour County Circuit Clerk. Personal checks accepted. Prepayment required. SASE requested.

Magistrate Court PO Box 541, Philippi, WV 26416; phone: 304-457-3676; fax: 304-457-4999; hours 8:30AM-4:30PM (EST). *Misdemeanor, Civil Actions Under $5,000, Eviction, Small Claims.*
Civil Records: Access: Mail, in person. Both court and visitors may perform in person searches. Court makes copy: $.25 per page. Records go back 10 years, computerized since 1997. Phone access limited to one name searched from 8/93 on only. Mail turnaround time varies.

Criminal Records: Access: Mail, in person. Visitors must perform in person searches themselves. Court makes copy: $.25 per page. Required to search: name, years to search. Records go back 10 years, computerized since 1997. Mail turnaround time varies.

General Information: Public terminal has criminal back to 7 years and civil back to 7 years. (Records may be purged, cannot rely on terminal to be true.) Certification fee: $.50 per page. Payee: Barbour County Magistrate Clerk. Prepayment required.

Berkeley County

Circuit Court 110 W King St, Martinsburg, WV 25401-3210; phone: 304-264-1918; probate phone: 304-264-1940; hours 9AM-5PM (EST). *Felony, Civil Actions Over $5,000, Probate.*

Note: Probate is handled by Fiduciary Records Clerk, 100 W King St, Rm 2, Martinsburg, WV 25401.

Civil Records: Access: In person only. Visitors must perform in person searches themselves. Court makes copy: $.50 per page. Required to search: name, years to search. Civil cases indexed by defendant, plaintiff; on computer from 1/1990, on index books from 1863.

Criminal Records: Access: In person only. Visitors must perform in person searches themselves. Court makes copy: $.50 per page. Required to search: name, years to search; also helpful: DOB, SSN. Criminal records on computer from 1/1990, on index books from 1800s.

General Information: Public terminal goes back to 1990. No sealed, juvenile, adoptions, mental health, guardianship records released. Will fax specific case file for $2.00 per page. No certification fee. Payee: Clerk of Circuit Court. Business checks accepted. Prepayment required.

Magistrate Court 120 W John St, Martinsburg, WV 25401; phone: 304-264-1956; fax: 304-263-9154; hours 9AM-4PM (EST). *Misdemeanor, Civil Actions Under $5,000, Eviction, Small Claims.*

Civil Records: Access: Fax, mail, in person. Visitors must perform in person searches themselves. No search fee. Court makes copy: $.25 per page; same fee for self serve. Records stored since 1977. Will fax results for $2.00 per page, pre-paid.

Criminal Records: Access: In person only. Visitors must perform in person searches themselves. No search fee. Court makes copy: $.25 per page; same fee for self serve. Required to search: name, years to search; also helpful: address, DOB, SSN. Records stored since 1977.

General Information: Public terminal goes back to 1993. Certification fee: $.50 per page. Payee: Berkeley County Magistrate Court. Prepayment and SASE required.

Boone County

Circuit Court 200 State St, Madison, WV 25130; phone: 304-369-3925; probate phone: 304-369-7337; fax: 304-369-7326; hours 8AM-4PM (EST). *Felony, Civil Actions Over $5,000, Probate.*

Note: Probate is handled by County Clerk, 200 State St, Madison, WV 25130.

Civil Records: Access: Phone, fax, mail, in person. Both court and visitors may perform in person searches. Court makes copy: $1.00 per page. Required to search: name, years to search. Civil cases indexed by defendant, plaintiff; on computer from 1984 to present, on index books 1956 to present, on dockets back to 1900. Mail turnaround time 1 day.

Criminal Records: Access: Phone, fax, mail, in person. Both court and visitors may perform in person searches. Court makes copy: $1.00 per page. Required to search: name, years to search, signed release. Criminal records on computer from 1984 to present, on index books 1956 to present, on dockets back to 1864. Mail turnaround time 1 day.

General Information: Public terminal goes back to 1984. No sealed, guardianship, juvenile, adoptions, mental health, expunged records released. Fee to fax documents is $5.00 per document. No certification

fee. Payee: Circuit Clerk. Business checks accepted. Prepayment required. SASE requested.

Magistrate Court 200 State St, Madison, WV 25130; phone: 304-369-7364; fax: 304-369-1932; hours 8AM-4PM (EST). *Misdemeanor, Civil Actions Under $5,000, Eviction, Small Claims.*

Civil Records: Access: In person. Both court and visitors may perform in person searches. Court makes copy: $.25 per page; same fee for self serve. Civil records go back to 1977; computerized since 1997.

Criminal Records: Access: In person. Visitors must perform in person searches themselves. Court makes copy: $.25 per page; same fee for self serve. Required to search: name, years to search; also helpful: DOB, SSN. Criminal records go back to 1977; computerized since 1997.

General Information: Public terminal goes back to 1997. No certification fee.

Braxton County

Circuit Court 300 Main St, Sutton, WV 26601; phone: 304-765-2837; probate phone: 304-765-2833; fax: 304-765-2947; hours 8AM-4PM (EST). *Felony, Civil Actions Over $5,000, Probate.*

Note: Email is braxtoncircuit@rtol.net. Probate is located across the hall in the same building.

Civil Records: Access: Phone, fax, mail, in person, email. Both court and visitors may perform in person searches. No search fee. Court makes copy: $.50 per page. Required to search: name, years to search. Civil cases indexed by defendant, plaintiff; on microfiche 1806 to 1910, on dockets back to 1810; on computer back to 1993. Mail turnaround time 2-3 days.

Criminal Records: Access: Phone, fax, mail, in person. Both court and visitors may perform in person searches. No search fee. Court makes copy: $.50 per page. Required to search: name, years to search, signed release. Criminal records on microfiche 1806 to 1910, on dockets back to 1810. Mail turnaround time 2-3 days.

General Information: Public terminal has criminal back to 1987 and civil back to 1993. No adoption, juvenile, mental hygiene records released. Will fax documents $3.00 1st page, $1.00 each add'l. No certification fee. Payee: JW Morris, Clerk. Personal checks accepted. Prepayment and SASE required.

Magistrate Court 307 Main St, Sutton, WV 26601; phone: 304-765-5678; fax: 304-765-3756; hours 8:30AM-4:30PM (EST). *Misdemeanor, Civil Actions Under $5,000, Eviction, Small Claims.*

Civil Records: Access: In person only. Visitors must perform in person searches themselves. Court makes copy: $.50 per page; same fee for self serve. Required to search: name, years to search. Records go back to 1977; on computer back to 1998.

Criminal Records: Access: In person only. Visitors must perform in person searches themselves. Court makes copy: $.50 per page; same fee for self serve. Required to search: name, years to search, DOB; also helpful: address, SSN, signed release. Records go back to 1977; on computer back to 1998. The court will not perform criminal record searches and suggests researchers contact State Police.

General Information: Public terminal goes back to 1998. Fee to fax documents is $2.00 per page. Certification fee: $.50 per page. Payee: Braxton County Magistrate Court. Prepayment required.

Brooke County

Circuit Court Brooke County Courthouse, PO Box 474, Wellsburg, WV 26070; phone: 304-737-3662; probate phone: 304-737-3661; fax: 304-737-0352; hours 9AM-5PM (EST). *Felony, Civil Actions Over $5,000, Probate.*

Note: Probate is handled by County Clerk, 632 Main St, Courthouse, Wellsburg, WV 26070.

Civil Records: Access: Mail, in person. Both court and visitors may perform in person searches. Search fee: $5.00 per name. Court makes copy: $.50

per page; same fee for self serve. Required to search: name; also helpful: years to search. Civil cases indexed by defendant, plaintiff; on dockets and files from prior to 1960 to present, in boxes back to 1800s; computerized records since 1997. Mail turnaround time same day, longer if in archives.

Criminal Records: Access: Mail, in person. Both court and visitors may perform in person searches. Search fee: $5.00 per name. Court makes copy: $.50 per page; same fee for self serve. Required to search: name; also helpful: years to search, DOB, SSN. Criminal records on dockets and files from prior to 1960 to present, in boxes back to 1800s; computerized records since 1997. Mail turnaround time same day, longer if in archives.

General Information: No divorce, juvenile, mental hygiene, adoption records released. Will fax documents for $5.00 per name; Fax charge is $2.00 per page. Certification fee: $.50 per page. Payee: Brooke County Circuit Clerk. Personal checks accepted. Prepayment required.

Magistrate Court 744 Charles St, #4, Wellsburg, WV 26070; phone: 304-737-1321; fax: 304-737-1509; hours 9AM-4PM (EST). *Misdemeanor, Civil Actions Under $5,000, Eviction, Small Claims.*

Civil Records: Access: In person only. Both court and visitors may perform in person searches. Court makes copy: $.25 per page; same fee for self serve. Civil records go back to 1977; computerized back to 1996.

Criminal Records: Access: In person only. Both court and visitors may perform in person searches. Court makes copy: $.25 per page; same fee for self serve. Required to search: name; also helpful: DOB, SSN, signed release. Criminal records go back to 1977; computerized back to 1996.

General Information: Public terminal goes back to 1996. Certification fee: $.50 per page.

Cabell County

Circuit Court PO Box 0545, 750 Fifth Ave, Huntington, WV 25710-0545; phone: 304-526-8622; fax: 304-526-8699; hours 8:30AM-4:30PM (EST). *Felony, Civil Actions Over $5,000, Probate.*

Civil Records: Access: Fax, mail, in person. Both court and visitors may perform in person searches. No search fee. Court makes copy: $.50 per page; same fee for self serve. Required to search: name, years to search. Civil cases indexed by defendant, plaintiff; on computer from 1990 to present. On index books back to 1854. Mail turnaround time 1 day.

Criminal Records: Access: Fax, mail, in person. Both court and visitors may perform in person searches. Search fee: $5.00. Court makes copy: $.50 per page; same fee for self serve. Required to search: name, years to search; also helpful: address, DOB, SSN. Criminal records on computer from 1990 to present. On index books back to 1854. Requests are directed to the state Criminal Investigation Bureau. Mail turnaround time 1 day.

General Information: Public terminal goes back to 1990. No sealed, juvenile, adoptions, mental health, guardianship records released. No certification fee. Payee: Clerk of Circuit Court. Business checks accepted. Prepayment and SASE required.

Magistrate Court 750 5th Ave, Basement, Rm B 113 Courthouse, Huntington, WV 25701; phone: 304-526-8642; fax: 304-526-8646; hours 8:30AM-4:30PM (EST). *Misdemeanor, Civil Actions Under $5,000, Eviction, Small Claims.*

Civil Records: Access: In person only. Visitors must perform in person searches themselves. Court makes copy: $.25 per page. Required to search: name. Records go back to 1977 (1987-1997 storage); on computer back to 1991.

Criminal Records: Access: In person only. Visitors must perform in person searches themselves. Court makes copy: $.25 per page. Required to search: name. Records go back to 1977 (1987-1997 storage); on computer back to 1991.

General Information: Public terminal goes back to 1991. Will fax specific case file for $2.00 per page.

Certification fee: $.50 per page. Cert fee includes copy fee. Payee: Magistrate Court Clerk. Prepayment required.

Calhoun County

Circuit Court PO Box 266, Grantsville, WV 26147; phone: 304-354-6910; probate phone: 304-354-6725; fax: 304-354-6910; probate fax: 304-354-6725; hours 8:30AM-4PM (EST). *Felony, Civil Actions Over $5,000, Probate.*
Note: Probate is located with the County Clerk office.
Civil Records: Access: Phone, fax, mail, in person. Both court and visitors may perform in person searches. No search fee. Court makes copy: $.50 per page; same fee for self serve. Required to search: name, years to search. Civil cases indexed by defendant, plaintiff; on index books from 1800s. Mail turnaround time same day received.
Criminal Records: Access: Phone, fax, mail, in person. Both court and visitors may perform in person searches. No search fee. Court makes copy: $.50 per page; same fee for self serve. Required to search: name, years to search; also helpful: DOB, SSN. Criminal records on dockets from 1900s. Mail turnaround time same day received.
General Information: No adoption, juvenile, divorce, domestic relations, guardianship/conservatorship records released. Will fax documents $3.00 1st page, $.50 each add'l. Certification fee: $.50 per page. Payee: Circuit Clerk. Personal checks accepted. Prepayment required. SASE helpful.

Magistrate Court PO Box 186, Main St, Grantsville, WV 26147; phone: 304-354-6698; civil phone: 304-354-6844; fax: 304-354-6698; hours 8:30AM-12:00; 1-4PM (EST). *Misdemeanor, Civil Actions Under $5,000, Eviction, Small Claims.*
Civil Records: Access: Phone, fax, mail, in person. Both court and visitors may perform in person searches. No search fee. Court makes copy: $.25 per page. Civil records computerized since 1997. Mail turnaround time 1 week.
Criminal Records: Access: In person, fax, mail, phone. Both court and visitors may perform in person searches. No search fee. Court makes copy: $.25 per page. Required to search: name; also helpful: years to search, DOB, SSN. Criminal records computerized since 1997. Mail turnaround time 1 week.
General Information: Public terminal goes back to 1998. Certification fee: $.50 per page. Prepayment and SASE required.

Clay County

Circuit Court PO Box 129, Clay, WV 25043; phone: 304-587-4256; probate phone: 304-587-4269; criminal fax: 304-587-4346; same fax for civil/probate; hours 8AM-4PM (EST). *Felony, Civil Actions Over $5,000, Probate.*
Civil Records: Access: In person only. Both court and visitors may perform in person searches. Court makes copy: $.50 per page. Required to search: name, years to search, address. Civil cases indexed by defendant, plaintiff; on docket books and index books back to 1962, microfilm back to 1858; computerized back to 1998.
Criminal Records: Access: Phone, fax, mail, in person. Both court and visitors may perform in person searches. No search fee. Court makes copy: $.50 per page. Required to search: name, years to search, address, DOB, SSN. Criminal records on docket books and index books back to 1962, microfilm back to 1858; computerized back to 1998.
Note: Court will do name only searches if time allows. Mail turnaround time 3 days.
General Information: Public terminal has criminal back to 1980s and civil back to 1970s. No juvenile, guardianship, conservatorship or mental health records released. Fee to fax documents is $.50 per page. No certification fee. Payee: Clerk of the Circuit Court. Personal checks accepted. Prepayment and SASE required.

Magistrate Court PO Box 393, 200 Main St, Clay, WV 25043; phone: 304-587-2131; fax: 304-587-2727; hours 8:30AM-4:30PM (EST). *Misdemeanor, Civil Actions Under $5,000, Eviction, Small Claims.*
Civil Records: Access: Mail, in person. Both court and visitors may perform in person searches. No search fee. Court makes copy: $.25 per page; same fee for self serve. Civil records go back to 1978; computerized since 2000. Mail turnaround time 5 days.
Criminal Records: Access: Mail, in person. Both court and visitors may perform in person searches. No search fee. Court makes copy: $.25 per page; same fee for self serve. Required to search: name, offense; also helpful: years to search, DOB, SSN. Criminal records go back to 1977; computerized since 2000. Mail turnaround time 5 days.
General Information: Public terminal goes back to 2000. No certification fee.

Doddridge County

Circuit Court 118 E. Court St, West Union, WV 26456; phone: 304-873-2331; fax: 304-873-2260; hours 8:30AM-4PM (EST). *Felony, Civil Actions Over $5,000, Probate.*
Civil Records: Access: Phone, mail, in person. Both court and visitors may perform in person searches. No search fee. Court makes copy: $.50 per page. Required to search: name, years to search. Civil cases indexed by defendant, plaintiff; on index books 1960 to present, archived from 1845 to 1960; computerized records go back to 1999. Mail turnaround time 1-5 days.
Criminal Records: Access: Phone, mail, fax, in person. Both court and visitors may perform in person searches. No search fee. Court makes copy: $.50 per page. Required to search: name, years to search. Criminal records in index books and files from 1948; computerized records go back to 1999. Mail turnaround time 1-5 days.
General Information: No juvenile, adoption, mental, domestic records released. Will fax documents to local or toll free number. No certification fee. Payee: Clerk of Circuit Court. Personal checks accepted. Prepayment and SASE required.

Magistrate Court PO Box 207, West Union, WV 26456; phone: 304-873-2694; fax: 304-873-2643; hours 8AM-4PM (EST). *Misdemeanor, Civil Actions Under $5,000, Eviction, Small Claims.*
Civil Records: Access: In person, mail. Both court and visitors may perform in person searches. No search fee. Court makes copy: $.25 per page; same fee for self serve. Required to search: name, DOB, years to search; also helpful-signed release, SSN. Civil records go back to 1977; on computer back to 1999. Mail turnaround time 5 days.
Criminal Records: Access: In person, mail, fax. Both court and visitors may perform in person searches. No search fee. Court makes copy: $.25 per page; same fee for self serve. Required to search: name, years to search DOB, SSN, signed release; also helpful: offense. Criminal records go back to 1977; on computer back to 1999. Mail turnaround time 5 days.
General Information: Public terminal goes back to 1999. Will fax documents. Certification fee: $.50 per page. Payee: Magistrate Court. Checks accepted. Prepayment required. SASE requested.

Fayette County

Circuit Court 100 Court St, Fayetteville, WV 25840; criminal phone: 304-574-4303/4250; civil phone: 304-574-4249; probate phone: 304-574-4226; hours 8AM-4PM (EST). *Felony, Civil Actions Over $5,000, Probate.*
Note: Probate is handled by County Clerk, PO Box 569, Fayetteville, WV 25840.
Civil Records: Access: Mail, in person, Online. Both court and visitors may perform in person searches. No search fee. Court makes copy: $.50 per page. Required to search: name; also helpful: years to search. Civil cases indexed by defendant, plaintiff; on computer since 1995; prior records on file 1850 to present. Online access to court records via a pay service, see www.swcg-inc.com/products/circuit_express.html or call 800-795-8543. $125 set-up fee plus a $38.00 or $120 monthly fee plan. Mail turnaround time 1 week.
Criminal Records: Access: Mail, in person, online. Both court and visitors may perform in person searches. No search fee. Court makes copy: $.50 per page; same fee for self serve. Required to search: name, years to search; also helpful: DOB, SSN. Criminal records on computer since 1995; prior records on file 1850 to present. Online access same as civil. Mail turnaround time 1 week.
General Information: Public use terminal available. No divorce, adoption, mental, juvenile records released. Certification fee: $5.00 per doc. Payee: Circuit Clerk of Fayette County. No personal checks accepted. Prepayment and SASE required.

Magistrate Court 100 Church St, Fayetteville, WV 25840; phone: 304-574-4279; fax: 304-574-2458; hours 8AM-4PM (EST). *Misdemeanor, Civil Actions Under $5,000, Eviction, Small Claims.*
Civil Records: Access: In person only. Visitors must perform in person searches themselves. Court makes copy: $.25 per page. Required to search: name. Civil records on computer back to 1997, records in-house since 1977.
Criminal Records: Access: In person only. Visitors must perform in person searches themselves. Court makes copy: $.25. Required to search: name, years to search. Criminal records on computer back to 1997, records in-house since 1977.
General Information: Public terminal goes back to 1997. Will fax search specific case file for $2.00 per page. Certification fee: $.50 per page. Payee: Magistrate Court. Prepayment required.

Gilmer County

Circuit Court Gilmer County Courthouse, 10 Howard St, Glenville, WV 26351; phone: 304-462-7241; probate phone: 304-462-7641; criminal fax: 304-462-7038; same fax for civil/probate; hours 8AM-4PM (EST). *Felony, Civil Actions Over $5,000, Probate.*
Note: Probate index is separate and located in the County Clerk's office, downstairs.
Civil Records: Access: Phone, mail, fax, in person. Both court and visitors may perform in person searches. No search fee. Court makes copy: $.50 per page; same fee for self serve. Required to search: name, years to search. Civil cases indexed by defendant, plaintiff; on dockets and files from 1845 to present; computerized back to 1999. Mail turnaround time 1 day.
Criminal Records: Access: Phone, mail, fax, in person. Both court and visitors may perform in person searches. No search fee. Court makes copy: $.50 per page; same fee for self serve. Required to search: name, years to search. Criminal records on dockets and files from 1845 to present; computerized back to 1999. Mail turnaround time 1 day.
General Information: Public terminal goes back to 1999. No juvenile, mental, confidential records released. Fee to fax documents is $1.50 per page with a $3.00 minimum. Certification fee: Copy fee includes certification. Payee: Circuit Clerk. Personal checks accepted.

Magistrate Court Courthouse Annex, Glenville, WV 26351; phone: 304-462-7812; fax: 304-462-8582; hours 8:30AM-4PM (EST). *Misdemeanor, Civil Actions Under $5,000, Eviction, Small Claims.*
Civil Records: Access: Mail, in person. Both court and visitors may perform in person searches. No search fee. Court makes copy: $.25 per page. Required to search: name, DOB, years to search, other names used; also helpful-case number, address, signed release. Civil records on computer back to 2000; other records back to 1977. Mail turnaround time 1-5 days.

Criminal Records: Access: Mail, in person. Both court and visitors may perform in person searches. No search fee. Court makes copy: $.25 per page. Required to search: name, years to search; also helpful: DOB, SSN. Civil records on computer back to 2000; other records back to 1977. Mail turnaround time 1-5 days.

General Information: Public terminal goes back to 2000. Fee to fax documents is $2.00 per document. Certification fee: $.50 per page.

Grant County

Circuit Court 5 Highland Ave, Petersburg, WV 26847; phone: 304-257-4545; fax: 304-257-2593; hours 8:30AM-4:30PM (EST). *Felony, Civil Actions Over $5,000, Probate.*
Note: Send fax to "Attention Circuit Court."
Civil Records: Access: Fax, mail, in person, online. Both court and visitors may perform in person searches. No search fee. Court makes copy: $.50 per page; same fee for self serve. Required to search: name, years to search; also helpful: address. Civil cases indexed by defendant, plaintiff. Computerized records from 1999, on books from 1983, archived back to 1866. Online access to court records via a pay service, see www.swcg-inc.com/products/circuit_express.html or call 800-795-8543. $125 set-up fee plus a $38.00 or $120 monthly fee plan. Mail turnaround time 1-2 days.
Criminal Records: Access: Fax, mail, in person, online. Both court and visitors may perform in person searches. No search fee. Court makes copy: $.50 per page. Required to search: name, years to search, DOB, SSN; also helpful: address. Computerized records from 1999, on books to 1988, archived back to 1866. Online access same as civil. Mail turnaround time 1-2 days.
General Information: Public terminal goes back to 1999. No juvenile, guardianship, adoptions, mental, domestic violence order records released. Fee to fax documents is $1.50 1st page, $.75 each add'l page. Certification fee: $1.50. Payee: Circuit Clerk. Business checks or in state personal checks accepted. Prepayment and SASE required.

Magistrate Court PO Box 216, 5 Highland Ave, Petersburg, WV 26847; phone: 304-257-1289; fax: 304-257-9501; hours 8:30AM-4:30PM (EST). *Misdemeanor, Civil Actions Under $5,000, Eviction, Small Claims.*
Civil Records: Access: Fax, mail, in person. Both court and visitors may perform in person searches. No search fee. Court makes copy: $.50 per page; same fee for self serve. Required to search: Search should include DOB and SSN. Records on computer back to 1994; prior records go back to 1977. Mail turnaround time 2 days.
Criminal Records: Access: Fax, mail, in person. Both court and visitors may perform in person searches. No search fee. Court makes copy: $.50 per page; same fee for self serve. Required to search: name, years to search, DOB, SSN. Records on computer back to 1994; prior back to 1977. Mail turnaround time 1-2 days.
General Information: Public terminal goes back to 1994. Certification fee: $.50 per page. Payee: Grant County Magistrate Court. Prepayment required.

Greenbrier County

Circuit Court PO Drawer 751, Lewisburg, WV 24901; phone: 304-647-6626; fax: 304-647-6666; hours 8:30AM-4:30PM (EST). *Felony, Civil Actions Over $5,000, Probate.*
Civil Records: Access: Mail, in person. Both court and visitors may perform in person searches. Court makes copy: $.50 per page; same fee for self serve. Required to search: name, years to search. Civil cases indexed by defendant, plaintiff. Civil records indexed by general and docket books from 1800s; computerized back to 1994. Mail turnaround time 1-2 days.
Criminal Records: Access: Mail, in person. Both court and visitors may perform in person searches.

Court makes copy: $.50 per page; same fee for self serve. Required to search: name, years to search; also helpful: DOB, SSN, signed release. Criminal records indexed by general and docket books from 1800s; computerized back to1995. No information given over the telephone on criminal matters except to authorized personnel. Mail turnaround time 1-2 days.
General Information: No juvenile, adoptions, mental health records released. Fee to fax documents is $2.50 per page. Certification fee: no cert fee assessed. Payee: Clerk of Circuit Court. Personal checks accepted. Prepayment required.

Magistrate Court 200 N Court St, Lewisburg, WV 24901; phone: 304-647-6632; fax: 304-647-6668; hours 8:30AM-4:30PM (EST). *Misdemeanor, Civil Actions Under $5,000, Eviction, Small Claims.*
Civil Records: Access: Phone, mail, in person. Both court and visitors may perform in person searches. No search fee. Court makes copy: $.25. Civil records on computer back to 1989; other records back to 1977. Mail turnaround time 1-2 days.
Criminal Records: Access: Mail, in person. Both court and visitors may perform in person searches. No search fee. Court makes copy: $.25. Required to search: name, years to search; also helpful: DOB, SSN. Criminal records on computer back to 1989; other records back to 1977. Requests for a background check must be in writing on letterhead. Contact the office for results in three days. If results are to be mailed, include postage or SASE plus the copy fee. Mail turnaround time 1-2 days.
General Information: Public terminal goes back to 1989. Fee to fax documents is $2.00 per page. Certification fee: $.50 plus $.25 per page. Payee: Greenbrier County Magistrate Court. Prepayment required.

Hampshire County

Circuit Court PO Box 343, 66 High St, Romney, WV 26757; phone: 304-822-5022; probate phone: 304-822-5112; fax: 304-822-8257; hours 9AM-4PM M-Th, 9AM-8PM Fri (EST). *Felony, Civil Actions Over $5,000, Probate.*
Note: Probate handled by County Clerk, PO Box 806, Romney, WV 26757.
Civil Records: Access: Fax, mail, in person. Both court and visitors may perform in person searches. No search fee. Court makes copy: $.50 per page. Required to search: name, years to search. Civil cases indexed by defendant, plaintiff; on index files from 1957 to present, on index cards in storage 1885 to 1957. Mail turnaround time 2 days.
Criminal Records: Access: Fax, mail, in person. Both court and visitors may perform in person searches. Search fee: $10.00 per name. Court makes copy: $.50 per page. Required to search: name, years to search. Criminal records on index files from 1957 to present, on index cards in storage 1885 to 1957. Mail turnaround time 2 days.
General Information: Public terminal goes back to 11/2001. No juvenile, divorce or adoption records released. No certification fee. Payee: Clerk of Circuit Court. Personal checks accepted. Prepayment required. Will bill to attorneys. SASE required.

Magistrate Court PO Box 881, 239 W Birch Ln, Romney, WV 26757; phone: 304-822-4311; fax: 304-822-3981; hours 8:00AM-4PM (EST). *Misdemeanor, Civil Actions Under $5,000, Eviction, Small Claims.*
Civil Records: Access: Fax, mail, in person. Both court and visitors may perform in person searches. No search fee. Court makes copy: $.50 per page. Self serve copy fee: $.25 per page. Required to search: name; also helpful-DOB, SSN, years to search, signed release, other names used. Civil records go back to 1977; on computer back to 1993. Mail turnaround time 5 days.
Criminal Records: Access: Fax, mail, in person. Both court and visitors may perform in person searches. No search fee. Court makes copy: $.50 per

page. Self serve copy fee: $.25 per page. Required to search: name, years to search; also helpful: DOB, SSN. Criminal records go back to 1977; on computer back to 1993. Mail turnaround time 5 days.
General Information: Public terminal goes back to 11/2001. Will fax to toll-free numbers no charge. No certification fee. Payee: Magistrate Court Clerk. Only cashiers checks and money orders accepted. Prepayment required.

Hancock County

Circuit Court PO Box 428, New Cumberland, WV 26047; phone: 304-564-3311; probate phone: x279; fax: 304-564-5014; hours 8:30AM-4:30PM (EST). *Felony, Civil Actions Over $5,000, Probate.*
Note: Probate address is PO Box 367.
Civil Records: Access: Fax, mail, in person, online. Both court and visitors may perform in person searches. Search fee: $5.00 per name. Court makes copy: $.50 per page. Required to search: name, years to search; also helpful: address. Civil cases indexed by defendant, plaintiff; on computer since 1972. Online access to court records via a pay service, see www.swcg-inc.com/products/circuit_express.html or call 800-795-8543. $125 set-up fee plus a $38.00 or $120 monthly fee plan. Mail turnaround time same day.
Criminal Records: Access: Fax, mail, in person, online. Both court and visitors may perform in person searches. Search fee: $5.00 per name. Court makes copy: $.50 per page. Required to search: name, years to search, signed release; also helpful: address, DOB, SSN. Criminal records on computer since 1972. Online access to criminal records is the same as civil. Mail turnaround time same day.
General Information: Public terminal goes back to 1972. No adoption, juvenile, mental hygiene released. Fee to fax documents is $2.00 per page. Certification fee: $1.50. Payee: Clerk of Circuit Court. Personal checks accepted. Prepayment and SASE required.

Magistrate Court 106 Court St, New Cumberland, WV 26047; phone: 304-564-3355; fax: 304-564-3852; hours 8:30-4:30pm (EST). *Misdemeanor, Civil Actions Under $5,000, Eviction, Small Claims.*
Civil Records: Access: Mail, in person. Both court and visitors may perform in person searches. Court makes copy: $.25 per page. Civil records on computer since 1996, dockets available since 1977. Phone, fax and mail access limited. Mail turnaround time 1-2 days.
Criminal Records: Access: Mail, in person. Both court and visitors may perform in person searches. No search fee. Court makes copy: $.25 per page. Required to search: name, years to search; also helpful: DOB, SSN. Criminal records on computer since 1996, dockets available since 1977. Phone, fax and mail access limited. Mail turnaround time 1-2 days.
General Information: Public terminal goes back to 1996. Certification fee: $.50 per page.

Hardy County

Circuit Court 204 Washington St, Rm 237, Moorefield, WV 26836; phone: 304-530-0231; hours 9AM-4PM (EST). *Felony, Civil Actions Over $5,000, Probate.*
Civil Records: Access: In person only. Both court and visitors may perform in person searches. No search fee. Court makes copy: $.50 per page; same fee for self serve. Required to search: name, years to search. Civil cases indexed by defendant, plaintiff; on docket books back to 1960 (chrono index in front of book). Computerized records go back to 1995.
Criminal Records: Access: In person only. Both court and visitors may perform in person searches. No search fee. Court makes copy: $.50 per page; same fee for self serve. Required to search: name, years to search, DOB; SSN helpful. Criminal records on docket books back to 1960 (chrono index in front of book). Computerized records go back to 1995.

General Information: No juvenile, mental, domestic records released. Will not fax specific case file. Certification fee: $1.00. Payee: Clerk of Circuit Court. Personal checks accepted. Prepayment required.

Magistrate Court 204 Washington St, Moorefield, WV 26836; phone: 304-538-0212; fax: 304-538-0213; hours 9AM-4PM (EST). *Misdemeanor, Civil Actions Under $5,000, Eviction, Small Claims.*

Civil Records: Access: Fax, mail, in person. Both court and visitors may perform in person searches. No search fee. Court makes copy: $.25 per page; same fee for self serve. Civil records on computer back to 1990; others back to 1977. Mail turnaround time 10 days, 5 days if records on computer.

Criminal Records: Access: Fax, mail, in person. Both court and visitors may perform in person searches. No search fee. Court makes copy: $.25 per page; same fee for self serve. Required to search: name, years to search; also helpful: DOB, SSN. Criminal records on computer back to 1990; others back to 1977. Mail turnaround time 10 days, 5 days if records on computer.

General Information: Public terminal goes back to 1990. Will fax documents for $2.00 per page. Certification fee: $.50 per page. Payee: Hardy County Magistrate Court. Prepayment and SASE required.

Harrison County

Circuit Court 301 W. Main, #301, Clarksburg, WV 26301-2967; phone: 304-624-8640; probate phone: 304-624-8673; fax: 304-624-8710; hours 8:30AM-4:30PM (EST). *Felony, Civil Actions Over $5,000, Probate.*

Note: Probate is handled by County Clerk, 301 W Main St, Courthouse, Clarksburg, WV 26301.

Civil Records: Access: In person only. Visitors must perform in person searches themselves. Court makes copy: $.50 per page. Required to search: name, years to search. Civil cases indexed by defendant, plaintiff; on computer from 1990 to present. On index books back to mid-1800s.

Criminal Records: Access: In person only. Visitors must perform in person searches themselves. Court makes copy: $.50 per page. Required to search: name, years to search; also helpful: DOB, SSN (not available for search). Criminal records on computer from 1990 to present. On index books back to mid-1800s.

General Information: Public terminal goes back to 1990. No adoption, juvenile, guardianship, mental health records released. No certification fee. Payee: Harrison County Circuit Clerk. Only cashiers checks and money orders accepted. Prepayment required.

Magistrate Court 306 Washington Ave, Rm 222, Clarksburg, WV 26301; phone: 304-624-8645; fax: 304-624-8740; hours 8AM-4PM (EST). *Misdemeanor, Civil Actions Under $5,000, Eviction, Small Claims.*

Civil Records: Access: Fax, mail, in person. Both court and visitors may perform in person searches. No search fee. Court makes copy: $.25 per page. Civil records go back to 1980's; computerized since 9/97. Mail turnaround time 5 days.

Criminal Records: Access: Fax, mail, in person. Both court and visitors may perform in person searches. No search fee. Court makes copy: $.25 per page. Required to search: name, years to search; also helpful: DOB, SSN. Criminal records go back to 1980's; computerized since 9/97. Mail turnaround time 5 days.

General Information: Public terminal goes back to 1997. Certification fee: $.50 per page.

Jackson County

Circuit Court PO Box 427, Ripley, WV 25271; phone: 304-373-2214; probate phone: 304-373-2251; fax: 304-372-6237; probate fax: 304-373-0245; hours 9AM-4PM M-F, 9AM-N Sat (EST). *Felony, Civil Actions Over $5,000, Probate.*

Note: Probate is a separate index; probate mailing address is PO Box 800.

Civil Records: Access: Phone, mail, in person. Both court and visitors may perform in person searches. No search fee. Court makes copy: $.50 per page. Required to search: name, years to search. Civil cases indexed by defendant, plaintiff; on index books back to 1800s. Computerized records back to 1999. Mail turnaround time 1-2 days.

Criminal Records: Access: Phone, mail, in person. Both court and visitors may perform in person searches. No search fee. Court makes copy: $.50 per page. Required to search: name, years to search; also helpful: DOB, SSN. Criminal records on index books back to 1800s. Computerized records back to 1999. Mail turnaround time 1-2 days.

General Information: No juvenile, mental, adoption, domestic records released. Will fax documents for $2.00 per page. Certification fee: $2.00 per page includes copies. Payee: Clerk of Circuit Court. Only cashiers checks and money orders accepted. Prepayment and SASE required.

Magistrate Court PO Box 368, Ripley, WV 25271; phone: 304-373-2313; fax: 304-372-7155; hours 9AM-4PM (EST). *Misdemeanor, Civil Actions Under $5,000, Eviction, Small Claims.*

Civil Records: Access: In person only. Visitors must perform in person searches themselves. Court makes copy: $.25 per page; same fee for self serve. Records computerized since 1998, on dockets since 1977.

Criminal Records: Access: In person only. Visitors must perform in person searches themselves. Court makes copy: $.25 per page; same fee for self serve. Required to search: name, years to search; also helpful: DOB, SSN. Records computerized since 1998, on dockets since 1977.

General Information: Public terminal goes back to 1998. Certification fee: $.50 per page. Payee: Jackson County Magistrate Court. Prepayment required.

Jefferson County

Circuit Court PO Box 1234, Charles Town, WV 25414; phone: 304-728-3231; fax: 304-728-3398; hours 8:30AM-5PM (EST). *Felony, Civil Actions Over $5,000.*

Civil Records: Access: In person only. Visitors must perform in person searches themselves. Court makes copy: $.50 per page. Required to search: name, years to search. Civil cases indexed by defendant, plaintiff; on computer back to 1/85; on index books 1960 to 1985. On dockets back 1960 back to 1800s in storage.

Criminal Records: Access: In person only. Visitors must perform in person searches themselves. Court makes copy: $.50 per page. Required to search: name, years to search. Criminal records on computer back to 1/85; on index books 1960 to 1985. On dockets back 1960 back to 1800s in storage.

General Information: Public terminal has criminal back to 1939 and civil back to 1938. No juvenile, guardianship, adoption, or mental health records released. Will fax specific case file to local or toll-free number. Certification fee: $.50 per page; triple seal $3.00. Payee: Circuit Clerk. No personal checks accepted. Prepayment required.

Magistrate Court PO Box 607, 110 N George St, Charles Town, WV 25414; phone: 304-728-3233; fax: 304-728-3235; hours 7:30AM-4:30PM (EST). *Misdemeanor, Civil Actions Under $5,000, Eviction, Small Claims.*

Civil Records: Access: Fax, mail, in person. Both court and visitors may perform in person searches. No search fee. Court makes copy: $.25 per page; same fee for self serve. Civil records on computer back to 1996; others go back to 1977.

Criminal Records: Access: Fax, mail, in person. Both court and visitors may perform in person searches. No search fee. Court makes copy: $.25 per page; same fee for self serve. Required to search: name, years to search, DOB; also helpful: SSN, signed release. Criminal records on computer back to 1996; others go back to 1977.

General Information: Public terminal goes back to 1996. No fee to fax documents. Certification fee: $.50 per page. Payee: Magistrate Clerk. Personal checks accepted. Prepayment required.

Kanawha County

Circuit Court PO Box 2351, 111 Court St, Charleston, WV 25328; phone: 304-357-0440; probate phone: 304-357-0130; fax: 304-357-0473; hours 8AM-5PM (EST). *Felony, Civil Actions Over $5,000, Probate.*

Note: Probate is handled by County Clerk, 409 Virginia St E, Charleston, WV 25301.

Civil Records: Access: In person, online. Visitors must perform in person searches themselves. Court makes copy: $.50 per page. Required to search: name, years to search; also helpful: address. Civil cases indexed by defendant, plaintiff; on computer from 7/1989 to present. On microfiche back to 1800s. Online access to court records via a pay service, see www.swcg-inc.com/products/circuit_express.html or call 800-795-8543. $125 set-up fee plus a $38.00 or $120 monthly fee plan.

Criminal Records: Access: Mail, in person, online. Visitors must perform in person searches themselves. Court makes copy: $.50 per page. Required to search: name, years to search; also helpful: address, DOB, SSN. Criminal records on computer from 7/1989 to present. On microfiche back to 1800s. Online access to criminal records is the same as civil.

General Information: Public terminal goes back to 1989. No juvenile, neglect, adoption, domestic, guardianship, mental health or conservatorship records released. Certification fee: $.50 per page. Payee: Kanawha Circuit Clerk. Business checks accepted. Prepayment required.

Magistrate Court 111 Court St, Charleston, WV 25333; phone: 304-357-0400; fax: 304-357-0205; hours 8:30AM-5PM (EST). *Misdemeanor, Civil Actions Under $5,000, Eviction, Small Claims.*

Civil Records: Access: Mail, in person. Both court and visitors may perform in person searches. No search fee. Court makes copy: $.50 per page. Civil records go back to 1982; computerized records since 1996. Mail turnaround time 14 days.

Criminal Records: Access: Fax, mail, in person. Both court and visitors may perform in person searches. No search fee. Court makes copy: $.50 per page. Required to search: name, years to search; also helpful: DOB, SSN. Criminal records go back to 1982; computerized records since 1991. Mail turnaround time 14 days.

General Information: Public terminal goes back to 1989. Will fax documents to local or toll free line. Certification fee: $.50 per page. Payee: Kanawha Magistrate Court. Personal checks accepted. SASE required.

Lewis County

Circuit Court PO Box 69, Weston, WV 26452; phone: 304-269-8210; probate phone: 304-269-8215; fax: 304-269-8249; probate fax: 304-269-8202; hours 8:30AM-4:30PM (EST). *Felony, Civil Actions Over $5,000, Probate.*

Civil Records: Access: Phone, fax, mail, in person. Only the court performs in person searches; visitors may not. No search fee. Court makes copy: $.50 per page. Required to search: name, years to search. Civil cases indexed by defendant, plaintiff; on index books 1977 to 1992; on computer back to 1984. No index for chancery books back to 1800s. Mail turnaround time 2 days.

Criminal Records: Access: Phone, fax, mail, in person. Only the court performs in person searches; visitors may not. No search fee. Court makes copy: $.50 per page. Required to search: name, years to search; also helpful: SSN. Criminal records on index books 1977 to 1992; on computer back to 1984. No index for chancery books back to 1800s. Mail turnaround time 2 days.

General Information: No adoption, juvenile, domestic records released. Fee to fax documents is $2.00 per page. Certification fee: $1.00 per case. Payee: Clerk of Circuit Court. Business checks accepted. Prepayment required.

Magistrate Court 111 Court St, PO Box 260, Weston, WV 26452; phone: 304-269-8230; fax: 304-269-8239; hours 8:30AM-N, 1-4:30PM (EST). *Misdemeanor, Civil Actions Under $5,000, Eviction, Small Claims.*
Civil Records: Access: In person, mail, fax. Both court and visitors may perform in person searches. No search fee. Court makes copy: $.25 per page; same fee for self serve. Required to search: name, DOB, SSN & years to search. Civil records computerized since 1991, indexed since 1977. Mail turnaround time 5 days.
Criminal Records: Access: In person, mail, fax. Both court and visitors may perform in person searches. No search fee. Court makes copy: $.25 per page; same fee for self serve. Required to search: name, years to search; also helpful: DOB, SSN. Criminal records computerized since 1991. Mail turnaround time 5 days.
General Information: Public terminal has criminal back to 1992 and civil back to 1997. Will fax documents for $2.00 per sheet. Certification fee: $.50 per page. Payee: Lewis County Magistrate Court. Prepayment and SASE required.

Lincoln County

Circuit Court PO Box 338, Hamlin, WV 25523; phone: 304-824-7887 x239; probate phone: x233; hours 9AM-4:30PM (EST). *Felony, Civil Actions Over $5,000, Probate.*
Note: Probate mailing address is PO Box 497; direct records requests to the county clerk at x233.
Civil Records: Access: Phone, mail, in person. Both court and visitors may perform in person searches. No search fee. No copy fee. Required to search: name, years to search. Civil cases indexed by defendant, plaintiff. Civil records computerized since 1991, on index books 1971 to present, on docket books back to 1909. Mail turnaround time immediate to next day.
Criminal Records: Access: Phone, mail, in person. Both court and visitors may perform in person searches. No search fee. No copy fee. Required to search: name, years to search, DOB, SSN; also helpful: address. Criminal records computerized since 1991, on index books 1971 to present, on docket books back to 1909. Mail turnaround time: immediate to next day.
General Information: No juvenile, adoption, divorce or mental hygiene records released. Will fax documents. No certification fee.

Magistrate Court PO Box 573, Hamlin, WV 25523; phone: 304-824-5001 x235; fax: 304-824-5280; hours 9AM-4PM (EST). *Misdemeanor, Civil Actions Under $5,000, Eviction, Small Claims.*
Note: Searches performed by court only on second and fourth Thursday of each month.
Civil Records: Access: Mail, in person. Both court and visitors may perform in person searches. Court makes copy: $.50 per page; same fee for self serve. Required to search: name, DOB, SSN. Mail turnaround time 1-14 days.
Criminal Records: Access: Mail, in person. Both court and visitors may perform in person searches. No search fee. Court makes copy: $.50 per page; same fee for self serve. Required to search: name, years to search; also helpful: DOB, SSN. Mail turnaround time 1-14 days.
General Information: Public terminal goes back to 1998. Will fax documents to local or toll free line.

Logan County

Circuit Court Logan County Courthouse, Rm 311, Logan, WV 25601; phone: 304-792-8550; fax: 304-792-8555; hours 8:30AM-4:30PM (EST). *Felony, Civil Actions Over $5,000, Probate.*
Civil Records: Access: In person only. Visitors must perform in person searches themselves. Court makes copy: $.50 per page. Required to search: name, years to search. Civil cases indexed by defendant, plaintiff; on index books back to 1800s, on computer from 1995.
Criminal Records: Access: Mail, fax, in person. Both court and visitors may perform in person searches. No search fee. Court makes copy: $.50 per page. Required to search: name, years to search, SSN. Criminal records on index books back to 1800s, on computer from 1995. Mail turnaround time 1-2 days.
General Information: No adoptions, juvenile, domestic records released. Fee to fax documents is $1.00 per page. Certification fee: $1.50 plus $.50 per page after first 2. Payee: Clerk of Circuit Court. Only cashiers checks and money orders accepted. Prepayment required. Will bill to attorneys.

Logan Magistrate Court Logan County Courthouse, 300 Stratton St, Logan, WV 25601; phone: 304-792-8651; fax: 304-752-0790; hours 8:30AM-N; 1-4:30PM (EST). *Misdemeanor, Civil Actions Under $5,000, Eviction, Small Claims.*
Civil Records: Access: Fax, mail, in person. Both court and visitors may perform in person searches. Court makes copy: $.25 per page. Records are computerized since 1992. Mail turnaround time 5 days.
Criminal Records: Access: Mail, in person. Both court and visitors may perform in person searches. Search fee: $.50 per name. Court makes copy: $.25 per page. Required to search: name, years to search; also helpful: address, DOB, SSN. Mail turnaround time 5 days.
General Information: Fee to fax documents is $2.00 1st page and $1.50 each addl. Certification fee: $.50 per page. Payee: Logan Magistrate Court. Prepayment required. Prepayment required for copies. SASE requested.

Marion County

Circuit Court PO Box 1269, 217 Adams St, Fairmont, WV 26554; phone: 304-367-5360; fax: 304-367-5374; hours 8:30AM-4:30PM (EST). *Felony, Civil Actions Over $3,000.*
Civil Records: Access: Phone, fax, mail, in person. Both court and visitors may perform in person searches. No search fee. Court makes copy: $.50 per page. Required to search: name, years to search. Civil cases indexed by defendant, plaintiff; on computer from 1/1988 to present. On docket books from 1849 to 1988. Mail turnaround time 2-3 days.
Criminal Records: Access: In person, mail, fax. Visitors must perform in person searches themselves. No search fee. Court makes copy: $.50 per page. Required to search: name, years to search; also helpful: DOB, SSN. Criminal records on computer from 1/1988 to present. On docket books from 1849 to 1988. The court refers all written requests to the Dept of Public Safety. Mail turnaround time 2-3 days.
General Information: Public terminal goes back to 1988. No adoptions, juvenile, mental or guardianship records released. Will fax documents $5.00 1st page, $2.00 each add'l. After 10 pages fee is $1.00 per page. Certification fee: $.50 per page. Payee: Clerk of Circuit Court. Business checks accepted. Prepayment required. SASE requested.

Magistrate Court 200 Jackson St, Fairmont, WV 26554; phone: 304-367-5330; fax: 304-367-5336; hours 8:30AM-4:30PM M-T-W-F; 8:30AM-7PM Th (EST). *Misdemeanor, Civil Actions Under $5,000, Eviction, Small Claims.*
Note: No record checks performed between 11:30AM and 1:30PM.

Civil Records: Access: Mail, in person. Both court and visitors may perform in person searches. No search fee. Court makes copy: $.25 per copy. Civil records go back to 1977; computerized since 1996. Mail turnaround time 5-15 days, ASAP for phone requests, time permitting.
Criminal Records: Access: Mail, in person. Both court and visitors may perform in person searches. No search fee. Court makes copy: $.25 per copy. Required to search: name, years to search; also helpful: DOB, SSN. Criminal records go back to 1977; computerized since 1996. Mail turnaround time 5-15 days, ASAP for phone requests, time permitting.
General Information: Public use terminal available. Will not fax documents. Certification fee: $.50 per page. Payee: Marion County Magistrate Clerk. Personal checks accepted. Prepayment and SASE required.

Marshall County

Circuit Court Marshall County Courthouse, 7th St, Moundsville, WV 26041; phone: 304-845-2130; fax: 304-845-3948; hours 8:30AM-4:30PM M-Th; 8:30AM-5:30PM F (EST). *Felony, Civil Actions Over $5,000.*
Civil Records: Access: Fax, mail, in person. Both court and visitors may perform in person searches. No search fee. Court makes copy: $.50 per page. Self serve copy fee: $.25 per page. Required to search: name, years to search. Civil cases indexed by defendant, plaintiff; on computer since 1/98; prior records on index books and in files from 1836 to present. Mail turnaround time 1-2 days.
Criminal Records: Access: Fax, mail, in person. Both court and visitors may perform in person searches. No search fee. Court makes copy: $.50 per page. Self serve copy fee: $.25 per page. Required to search: name, years to search; also helpful: DOB, SSN. Criminal records on computer since 1/98; prior records on index books and in files from 1836 to present. Mail turnaround time 1-2 days.
General Information: No juvenile, mental, adoption, sealed, conservatorship, guardianship or divorce records released. Fee to fax documents is $2.00 per page. Certification fee: $1.00. Payee: Clerk of Circuit Court. Personal checks accepted. Prepayment required. Will bill to attorneys.

Mason County

Circuit Court Mason County Courthouse, Point Pleasant, WV 25550; phone: 304-675-4400; fax: 304-675-7419; hours 8:30AM-4:30PM (EST). *Felony, Civil Actions Over $5,000, Probate.*
Civil Records: Access: In person only. Visitors must perform in person searches themselves. Court makes copy: $.50 per page; same fee for self serve. Required to search: name, years to search. Civil cases indexed by defendant, plaintiff; on computer from 1994. No time limit on open cases. Index books with data back to 1800s.
Criminal Records: Access: In person only. Visitors must perform in person searches themselves. Court makes copy: $.50 per page; same fee for self serve. Required to search: name, years to search. Criminal records on computer from 1994. No time limit on open cases. Index books with data back to 1800s.
General Information: Public terminal goes back to 1994. No divorce or juvenile records released. No certification fee. Payee: Circuit Court Clerk. Personal checks accepted. Prepayment required.

Magistrate Court 200 6th St, Point Pleasant, WV 25550; phone: 304-675-6840; fax: 304-675-5949; hours 8:30AM-4:30PM (EST). *Misdemeanor, Civil Actions Under $5,000, Eviction, Small Claims.*
Note: Judges offices- 304-675-6400 and 304-675-6636.
Civil Records: Access: Mail, in person. Both court and visitors may perform in person searches. No search fee. Court makes copy: $.10 per page; same fee for self serve. Civil records go back to 1977;

computerized since 1998. Mail turnaround time 3-4 days.

Criminal Records: Access: Mail, in person. Both court and visitors may perform in person searches. No search fee. Court makes copy: $.10 per page; same fee for self serve. Required to search: name, years to search. Criminal records go back to 1977; computerized since 1998. Mail turnaround time 3-4 days.

General Information: Public terminal goes back to 1998. Certification fee: $.50 per page.

McDowell County

Circuit Court PO Box 400, Welch, WV 24801; phone: 304-436-8535; probate phone: 304-436-8544; fax: 304-436-6994; hours 9AM-5PM (EST). *Felony, Civil Actions Over $5,000, Probate.*

Note: Probate is handled by County Clerk, 90 Wyoming St, #109, Welch, WV 24801.

Civil Records: Access: Mail, in person, online. Both court and visitors may perform in person searches. No search fee. Court makes copy: $.50 per page. Required to search: name, years to search. Civil cases indexed by defendant, plaintiff; on index books back to 1800s; on computer back to 1999. Online access to court records via a pay service, see www.swcg-inc.com/products/circuit_express.html or call 800-795-8543. $125 set-up fee plus a $38.00 or $120 monthly fee plan. Mail turnaround time 1 week.

Criminal Records: Access: Mail, in person, online. Both court and visitors may perform in person searches. No search fee. Court makes copy: $.50 per page. Required to search: name, years to search; also helpful: DOB, SSN. Criminal records on index books back to 1800s; on computer back to 1999. Online access same as civil. Mail turnaround time 1 week.

General Information: Public terminal goes back to 1998. No sealed, juvenile, adoption, mental health, guardianship records released. Will fax documents to local or toll free line. Certification fee: $.50 per page. Payee: Clerk of Circuit Court. Business checks accepted. Prepayment and SASE required.

Magistrate Court PO Box 447, Welch, WV 24801; phone: 304-436-8588; fax: 304-436-8575; hours 9AM-5PM (EST). *Misdemeanor, Civil Actions Under $5,000, Eviction, Small Claims.*

Civil Records: Access: Mail, fax, in person. Visitors must perform in person searches themselves. Search fee: none; will search as time permits. Court makes copy: $.25 per page. Records on computer go back to 1999, accessible since 1977. Mail turnaround time 5 days.

Criminal Records: Access: Mail, fax, in person. Both court and visitors may perform in person searches. Search fee: none; will search as time permits. Court makes copy: $.25 per page. Required to search: name, years to search, DOB, SSN. Records on computer go back to 1998, accessible since 1977. Records on criminal now go back to 1997. Mail turnaround time 5 days.

General Information: Public terminal goes back to 1997. Fee to fax documents is $2.00 per page. Certification fee: $.50 per page. Payee: Magistrate Court.

Mercer County

Circuit Court 1501 W Main St, Princeton, WV 24740; phone: 304-487-8323; criminal phone: 304-487-8410 / 304-487-8372; probate phone: 304-487-8336; fax: 304-425-8351; hours 8:30AM-4:30PM (EST). *Felony, Civil Actions Over $5,000.*

Note: Probate court is a separate office at the same address.

Civil Records: Access: Phone, fax, mail, in person. Both court and visitors may perform in person searches. No search fee. Court makes copy: $.50 per page. Required to search: name, years to search. Civil cases indexed by defendant, plaintiff; on computer from 10/1989 to present. On index books from 1930-1989 (Cott System). On index cards back to 1890s. Mail turnaround time 1-2 days.

Criminal Records: Access: Fax, mail, in person. Both court and visitors may perform in person searches. No search fee. Court makes copy: $.50 per page. Required to search: name, years to search; also helpful: DOB, SSN. Criminal records on computer from 10/1989 to present. On index books from 1930-1989 (Cott System). On index cards back to 1890s. Mail turnaround time 1-2 days.

General Information: Public terminal goes back to 10/1989. No juvenile, adoption, mental health, guardianship or conservatorship records released. Will fax documents $2.00 per page. Certification fee: $.50 per page. Payee: Circuit Court Clerk. Business checks accepted. Prepayment required.

Magistrate Court 1519 N Walker St, Princeton, WV 24740; phone: 304-431-7115; hours 8:30AM-4:30PM (EST). *Misdemeanor, Civil Actions Under $5,000, Eviction, Small Claims.*

Civil Records: Access: In person only. Visitors must perform in person searches themselves. Court makes copy: $.25 per page. Required to search: name. Civil records from 1977; computerized back to 1994.

Criminal Records: Access: In person, mail, fax. Visitors must perform in person searches themselves. Court makes copy: $.25 per page. Required to search: name, years to search; also helpful: address, DOB, SSN. Criminal records from 1977; computerized back to 1994. Mail turnaround time 10 days.

General Information: Public terminal goes back to 1994. Will fax documents to local or toll free line. Certification fee: $.50 per page. Payee: Mercer County Magistrate Court. Cashiers checks, money orders, Visa/MC accepted. Prepayment and SASE required.

Mineral County

Circuit Court 150 Armstrong St, Keyser, WV 26726; phone: 304-788-1562; probate phone: 304-788-3924; criminal fax: 304-788-4109; same fax for civil/probate; hours 8:30AM-5PM (EST). *Felony, Civil Actions Over $5,000, Probate.*

Note: Probate court is a separate office at the same address, 2nd Fl, 304-788-3924.

Civil Records: Access: Fax, mail, in person, online. Both court and visitors may perform in person searches. Search fee: $5.00 per name. Court makes copy: $.50 per page; same fee for self serve. Required to search: name, years to search. Civil cases indexed by defendant, plaintiff; on computer 1/1991 to present, on dockets from 1920s. Online access to court records via a pay service, see www.swcg-inc.com/products/circuit_express.html or call 800-795-8543. $125 set-up fee plus a $38.00 or $120 monthly fee plan. Note: Fax access not guaranteed. Mail turnaround time 2-4 days.

Criminal Records: Access: Fax, mail, in person, online. Both court and visitors may perform in person searches. Search fee: $5.00 per name. Court makes copy: $.50 per page; same fee for self serve. Required to search: name, years to search; also helpful: DOB, SSN. Criminal records on computer 1/1991 to present, on dockets from 1920s. Online access to criminal records is the same as civil. Note: Fax access not guaranteed. Mail turnaround time 2-4 days.

General Information: No juvenile, adoption, divorce, mental hygiene, conservatorship or guardianship records released. Will fax documents, no fee. No certification fee. Payee: Clerk of Circuit Court. Personal checks accepted. Prepayment required. SASE requested.

Magistrate Court 105 West St, Keyser, WV 26726; phone: 304-788-2625; fax: 304-788-9835; hours 8:30AM-4:30PM (EST). *Misdemeanor, Civil Actions Under $5,000, Eviction, Small Claims.*

Civil Records: Access: Mail, in person. Both court and visitors may perform in person searches. No search fee. Court makes copy: $.25 per page. Required to search: name, years to search. Civil records on computer back to 1991. Mail turnaround time as time permits.

Criminal Records: Access: Mail, in person. Both court and visitors may perform in person searches. No search fee. Court makes copy: $.25 per page. Required to search: name, years to search; also helpful: DOB, SSN. Records on computer back to 1991. Mail turnaround time: time permitting.

General Information: Public use terminal available. Certification fee: $.50 per page. Payee: Magistrate Court. Prepayment required. SASE requested.

Mingo County

Circuit Court PO Box 435, Williamson, WV 25661; phone: 304-235-0320; probate phone: 304-235-0330; fax: 304-235-0565; hours 8:30AM-4:30PM (EST). *Felony, Civil Actions Over $5,000, Probate.*

Note: Probate is handled by County Clerk, 75 E 2nd Ave, Williamson, WV 25661.

Civil Records: Access: Mail, in person. Both court and visitors may perform in person searches. Search fee: $10.00 per name. Court makes copy: $.50 per page; same fee for self serve. Required to search: name, years to search. Civil cases indexed by defendant, plaintiff; on computer from 1/91 to present, civil on index books back to 1960, chancery books back to 1800s (written or in person only). Mail turnaround time 1-2 weeks.

Criminal Records: Access: Mail, in person. Both court and visitors may perform in person searches. Search fee: $10.00 per name. Court makes copy: $.50 per page; same fee for self serve. Required to search: name, years to search; also helpful: DOB. Criminal records on computer since 1/91, Index books back to 1955. Mail turnaround time 1-2 weeks.

General Information: Public terminal goes back to 1991. No adoption, mental hygiene, juvenile records released. No certification fee. Payee: Mingo County Circuit Clerk. Personal checks accepted. Prepayment and SASE required.

Magistrate Court PO Box 986, Williamson, WV 25661; phone: 304-235-2445; fax: 304-235-3179; hours 8:30AM-4:30PM (EST). *Misdemeanor, Civil Actions Under $5,000, Eviction, Small Claims.*

Civil Records: Access: Phone, mail, fax, in person. Both court and visitors may perform in person searches. No search fee. Court makes copy: $.25 per page. Required to search: name, years to search; also helpful: DOB. Civil records go back to 1977; on computer back to 1998. Mail turnaround time 1 week.

Criminal Records: Access: Phone, mail, fax, in person. Both court and visitors may perform in person searches. No search fee. Court makes copy: $.25 per page. Required to search: name, years to search; also helpful: DOB, SSN. Criminal records go back to 1977; on computer back to 1998. Mail turnaround time 1 week, sooner for phone requests.

General Information: Public terminal goes back to 1998. (Terminal located only in Court Clerk's office.) Fee to fax documents is $2.00 per page or free to toll-free number. Certification fee: $.50 per page. Payee: Magistrate Court. Prepayment required.

Monongalia County

Circuit Court County Courthouse, 243 High St, Rm 110, Morgantown, WV 26505; phone: 304-291-7240; probate phone: 304-291-7236; fax: 304-291-7273; hours 9AM-7PM M; 9AM-5PM T-F (EST). *Felony, Civil Actions Over $5,000, Probate.*

Note: A disclaimer for the Clerk must be included by mail requesters. Estates/Probate is handled by County Clerk, 243 High St, Rm 123, Morgantown, WV 26505.

Civil Records: Access: Mail, in person. Both court and visitors may perform in person searches. Search fee: $5.00 per name. Court makes copy: $.50 per page; same fee for self serve. Required to search: name, years to search. Civil cases indexed by defendant, plaintiff; on computer from 1/90 to present, on index book separated by plaintiff and defendant back to 1865. Mail turnaround time 1 day.

Criminal Records: Access: Mail, in person. Both court and visitors may perform in person searches. Search fee: $5.00 per name. Court makes copy: $.50 per page; same fee for self serve. Required to search: name, years to search; also helpful: DOB, SSN. Criminal records on computer from 1/90 to present, on index book separated by plaintiff and defendant back to 1865. Mail turnaround time 1 day.

General Information: No juvenile, divorce, mental hygiene, divorce, adoption, guardianship, conservatorship or domestic records released. Fee to fax documents is $1.00 per page. No certification fee. Payee: Circuit Clerk. Business checks accepted. Prepayment and SASE required.

Magistrate Court 265 Spruce St, Morgantown, WV 26505; phone: 304-291-7296; fax: 304-284-7313; hours 8AM-7PM (EST). *Misdemeanor, Civil Actions Under $5,000, Eviction, Small Claims.*

Civil Records: Access: Mail, fax, in person. Both court and visitors may perform in person searches. No search fee. Court makes copy: $.25 per page; same fee for self serve. Required to search: name, years to search. Records on computer back to 1999; prior in books back to 1977. Mail turnaround time 10-14 days.

Criminal Records: Access: Mail, fax, in person. Both court and visitors may perform in person searches. No search fee. Court makes copy: $.25 per page; same fee for self serve. Required to search: name, years to search; also helpful: DOB, SSN, signed release. Records on computer go back to 1999; prior in books back to 1977. Mail turnaround time 10-14 days.

General Information: Public terminal goes back to 1999. Certification fee: $.50 per page. Payee: Magistrate Court. Prepayment required.

Monroe County

Circuit Court PO Box 350, Union, WV 24983-0350; phone: 304-772-3017; probate phone: 304-772-3096; fax: 304-772-4497; hours 8AM-4PM (EST). *Felony, Civil Actions Over $5,000, Probate.*
Note: Probate is with the County Clerk, PO Box 350, Union, WV 24983.

Civil Records: Access: Phone, mail, in person. Both court and visitors may perform in person searches. No search fee. Court makes copy: $.50 per page. Include postage with copy fee. Required to search: name, years to search. Civil cases indexed by defendant, plaintiff; on index books 1799 to present; on computer back to 2000. Mail turnaround time 1 week.

Criminal Records: Access: Phone, mail, in person. Both court and visitors may perform in person searches. No search fee. Court makes copy: $.50 per page. Include postage with copy fee. Required to search: name, years to search; also helpful: DOB, SSN. Criminal records on index books 1799 to present; on computer back to 2000. Mail turnaround time 1 week.

General Information: Public terminal has only civil records back to 2000. No juvenile, adoption, divorce records released. Will fax documents to local or toll free line. Certification fee: $1.00 per document. Payee: Clerk of Circuit Court. Personal checks accepted. Prepayment required. SASE requested.

Magistrate Court PO Box 4, Union, WV 24983; phone: 304-772-3321/3176; fax: 304-772-4357; hours 8:30AM-4:30PM (EST). *Misdemeanor, Civil Actions Under $5,000, Eviction, Small Claims.*

Civil Records: Access: Mail, in person. Both court and visitors may perform in person searches. No search fee. Court makes copy: $.25 per page; same fee for self serve. Required to search: name, DOB, SSN. Criminal records go back to 1977; computerized records since 2000. Mail turnaround time 1-2 days.

Criminal Records: Access: Mail, in person, fax. Both court and visitors may perform in person searches. No search fee. Court makes copy: $.25 per page; same fee for self serve. Required to search: name, years to search; also helpful: DOB, SSN.

Criminal records go back to 1977; computerized records since 2000. Mail turnaround time 1-2 days.

General Information: Public terminal goes back to 2001. Will fax documents $2.00. Certification fee: $.50 per page. Payee: Monroe County Magistrate Court. Personal checks accepted. SASE requested.

Morgan County

Circuit Court 77 Fairfax St, #2F, Berkeley Springs, WV 25411-1501; phone: 304-258-8554; probate phone: 304-258-8547; fax: 304-258-7319; hours 9AM-5PM Monday - Friday (EST). *Felony, Civil Actions Over $5,000, Probate.*
Note: Probate is County Clerk's office located at the same address in #1A.

Civil Records: Access: In person only. Visitors must perform in person searches themselves. Court makes copy: $.50 per page; same fee for self serve. Required to search: name, years to search. Civil cases indexed by defendant, plaintiff; on computer back to 1/93, index cards back to 1960; in person searching only on index books back to 1800s.

Criminal Records: Access: In person only. Visitors must perform in person searches themselves. Court makes copy: $.50 per page; same fee for self serve. Required to search: name, years to search; also helpful-DOB, SSN, signed release. Criminal records on computer back to 1/93, index cards back to 1960.

General Information: No juvenile, adoption, mental health, divorce records released. No certification fee. Payee: Kimberly J Jackson, Circuit Clerk. Only cashiers checks and money orders accepted. Prepayment required. Will bill to attorneys.

Magistrate Court 111 Fairfax St, Berkeley Springs, WV 25411; phone: 304-258-8631; fax: 304-258-8639; hours 9AM-4:30PM (EST). *Misdemeanor, Civil Actions Under $5,000, Eviction, Small Claims.*

Civil Records: Access: In person only. Visitors must perform in person searches themselves. Court makes copy: $.25 per page. Civil records go back to 1977; computerized records since 1998.

Criminal Records: Access: In person only. Visitors must perform in person searches themselves. Court makes copy: $.25 per page. Required to search: name, years to search; also helpful: DOB, SSN. Criminal records go back to 1977; computerized records since 1998. Phone, fax and mail access limited.

General Information: Public use terminal available. Certification fee: $.50 per page. Only cashiers checks and money orders accepted.

Nicholas County

Circuit Court 700 Main St #5, Summersville, WV 26651; phone: 304-872-7810; probate phone: 304-872-7820; hours 8:30AM-4:30PM (EST). *Felony, Civil Actions Over $5,000, Probate.*
Note: Probate is handled by County Clerk, 700 Main St, #2, Summersville, WV 26651.

Civil Records: Access: Mail, in person, online. Both court and visitors may perform in person searches. No search fee. Court makes copy: $.50 per page; same fee for self serve. Required to search: name, years to search. Civil cases indexed by defendant, plaintiff; on computer since 1994; prior records on index cards from 1976 to 1994 on dockets back to 1818. Online access to court records via a pay service, see www.swcg-inc.com/products/circuit_express.html or call 800-795-8543. $125 set-up fee plus a $38.00 or $120 monthly fee plan. Mail turnaround time 1 week.

Criminal Records: Access: Mail, in person, online. Both court and visitors may perform in person searches. No search fee. Court makes copy: $.50 per page; same fee for self serve. Required to search: name, years to search; also helpful: DOB, SSN. Criminal records on computer since 1994; prior records on index cards from 1976 to 1994 on dockets back to 1818. Online access same as civil Mail turnaround time 1 week.

General Information: Public use terminal available. No divorce, juvenile, adoption, mental, guardianship

records released. No certification fee. Payee: Circuit Clerk. Personal checks accepted. SASE required.

Magistrate Court 511 Church St, #206, 2nd Fl, Summersville, WV 26651; phone: 304-872-7829; fax: 304-872-7888; hours 8:30AM-4:30PM (EST). *Misdemeanor, Civil Actions Under $5,000, Eviction, Small Claims.*

Civil Records: Access: Mail, in person. Visitors must perform in person searches themselves. Court makes copy: $.25 per page; same fee for self serve. Civil records on computer back to 1990, cases available since 1977. Request must be in writing.

Criminal Records: Access: Mail, in person. Visitors must perform in person searches themselves. Court makes copy: $.25 per page; same fee for self serve. Required to search: name, years to search; also helpful: DOB, SSN. Criminal records on computer back to 1990, cases available since 1977. Request must be in writing.

General Information: Public terminal goes back to 10/90. Certification fee: $.50 per page. Payee: Magistrate Court. Prepayment required.

Ohio County

Circuit Court 1500 Chapline St, City & County Bldg, Rm 403, Wheeling, WV 26003; phone: 304-234-3613; probate phone: 304-234-3656; fax: 304-232-0550; hours 8:30AM-5PM (EST). *Felony, Civil Actions Over $5,000, Probate.*
Note: Probate records are with the county clerk at this address.

Civil Records: Access: Fax, mail, in person, online. Both court and visitors may perform in person searches. Search fee: $5.00 per name. Court makes copy: $.50 per page; same fee for self serve. Required to search: name, years to search. Civil cases indexed by defendant, plaintiff; on computer from 10/1986 to present, on index books back to 1800s. Online access to court records via a pay service, see www.swcg-inc.com/products/circuit_express.html or call 800-795-8543. $125 set-up fee plus a $38.00 or $120 monthly fee plan. Mail turnaround time up to 48 hours.

Criminal Records: Access: Fax, mail, in person, online. Both court and visitors may perform in person searches. Search fee: $5.00 per name. Court makes copy: $.50 per page; same fee for self serve. Required to search: name, years to search; also helpful: DOB, SSN. Criminal records on computer from 10/1986 to present, on index books back to 1800s. Online access to criminal records is the same as civil. Mail turnaround time 1 week for accounts only.

General Information: Public terminal has criminal back to 1986 and civil back to 1986. No domestic, juvenile, mental, adoption records released. Fee to fax documents is $2.00 per page. Certification fee: $1.50 per document for triple seal, includes copies. Payee: Ohio County Circuit Court. Business checks accepted. Prepayment and SASE required.

Magistrate Court Courthouse Annex, 26 15th St, Wheeling, WV 26003; phone: 304-234-3709; fax: 304-234-3898; hours 8:30AM-4:30PM (EST). *Misdemeanor, Civil Actions Under $5,000, Eviction, Small Claims.*

Civil Records: Access: In person, fax, mail. Both court and visitors may perform in person searches. No search fee. Court makes copy: $.25 per page; same fee for self serve. Required to search: name, years to search. Records go back to 1977. Court will only search back to 1997. Mail turnaround time 1 week.

Criminal Records: Access: In person, fax, mail. Both court and visitors may perform in person searches. No search fee. Court makes copy: $.25 per page; same fee for self serve. Required to search: name, years to search; also helpful: DOB, SSN. Records go back to 1977. Court will only search back to 1997. Mail turnaround time 1 week.

General Information: Public use terminal available. Will fax documents. Certification fee: $.50 per page. SASE requested.

Pendleton County

Circuit Court PO Box 846, Franklin, WV 26807; phone: 304-358-7067; fax: 304-358-2152; hours 8:30AM-4PM M-F (EST). *Felony, Civil Actions Over $5,000, Probate.*
Civil Records: Access: Phone, fax, mail, in person. Both court and visitors may perform in person searches. No search fee. Court makes copy: $.50 per page; same fee for self serve. Required to search: name, years to search. Civil cases indexed by defendant, plaintiff; on index books back to 1800s. Mail turnaround time 2-3 days.
Criminal Records: Access: Phone, fax, mail, in person. Both court and visitors may perform in person searches. No search fee. Court makes copy: $.50 per page; same fee for self serve. Required to search: name, years to search; also helpful: DOB, SSN. Criminal records on index books back to 1800s. Mail turnaround time 2-3 days.
General Information: No juvenile, divorce records released. Will fax documents for $2.00 per page. No certification fee. Payee: Pendleton County Circuit Clerk. Local checks accepted. Prepayment and SASE required.

Magistrate Court PO Box 637, Franklin, WV 26807; phone: 304-358-2343; fax: 304-358-3870; hours 8:30AM-4PM (EST). *Misdemeanor, Civil Actions Under $5,000, Eviction, Small Claims.*
Civil Records: Access: Mail, in person. Both court and visitors may perform in person searches. No search fee. Court makes copy: $.25 per page. Required to search: name, years to search. Civil records computerized since 1993. Mail turnaround time 5-10 days.
Criminal Records: Access: Mail, in person. Both court and visitors may perform in person searches. No search fee. Court makes copy: $.25 per page. Required to search: name, years to search. Records computerized since 1993. Mail turnaround time 5-10 days.
General Information: Public terminal goes back to 1993. Will fax documents to local or toll free line. Certification fee: $.50 per page. Payee: Magistrate Court. Prepayment required.

Pleasants County

Circuit Court 301 Court Ln, Rm 201, St. Mary's, WV 26170; phone: 304-684-3513; probate phone: 304-684-3542; hours 8:30AM-4:30PM (EST). *Felony, Civil Actions Over $5,000, Probate.*
Note: Probate is handled by County Clerk, 301 Court Lane, Rm 101, St Mary's, WV 26170.
Civil Records: Access: In person only. Visitors must perform in person searches. Court makes copy: $.50 per page. Required to search: name, years to search. Civil cases indexed by defendant, plaintiff; on computer from 1/1960 to present, on index cards from 1960 to present, on index books back to 1800s.
Criminal Records: Access: In person only. Visitors must perform in person searches. Court makes copy: $.50 per page. Required to search: name, years to search. Criminal records on computer from 1/1960 to present, on index cards from 1960 to present, on index books back to 1800s.
General Information: No domestic, marriage, adoption, juvenile or mental health records released. Certification fee: $.50 per page. Payee: Circuit Clerk. Personal checks accepted. Prepayment required.

Magistrate Court 301 Court Ln, Rm B-6, St Mary's, WV 26170; phone: 304-684-7197; fax: 304-684-3882; hours 8:30AM-4:30PM (EST). *Misdemeanor, Civil Actions Under $5,000, Eviction, Small Claims.*
Civil Records: Access: Phone, in person. Both court and visitors may perform in person searches. Search fee: none, but there is a copy fee. Court makes copy: $.25 per page. Self serve copy fee: $.25 per page. Required to search: name, years to search; also helpful: DOB or SSN. Records go back to 1977, on

computer since mid-2000. Will do some searches over the phone while caller holds.
Criminal Records: Access: Phone, in person. Both court and visitors may perform in person searches. Search fee: none, but there is a copy fee. Court makes copy: $.25 per page. Self serve copy fee: $.25 per page. Required to search: name, years to search; also helpful: DOB, SSN. Records go back to 1977, on computer since mid-2000. Will do some searches over the phone while caller holds.
General Information: Public terminal has criminal back to 2000 and civil back to 2000. Fee to fax results is $2.00 per page. Certification fee: $.50 per page. Payee: Pleasants County Magistrate Court. Prepayment required.

Pocahontas County

Circuit Court 900-D 10th Ave, Marlinton, WV 24954; phone: 304-799-4604; probate phone: 304-799-4549; fax: 304-799-6809; hours 9AM-4:30PM (EST). *Felony, Civil Actions Over $5,000, Probate.*
Civil Records: Access: Phone, mail, in person. Only the court performs in person searches; visitors may not. Court makes copy: $.50 per page; same fee for self serve. Required to search: name, years to search; also helpful: address. Civil cases indexed by defendant, plaintiff; on index books from 1948 to present, order books back to 1800s. Computerized records to 1995. Mail turnaround time same day.
Criminal Records: Access: Phone, mail, in person. Visitors must perform in person searches themselves. Court makes copy: $.50 per page; same fee for self serve. Required to search: name, years to search; also helpful: DOB, SSN. Criminal records on index books from 1948 to present, order books back to 1800s. Computerized records to 1995. Mail turnaround time same day.
General Information: No juvenile, domestic cases involving finances, adoption, guardianship records released. Will fax documents for $1.00 per doc. No certification fee. Payee: Clerk of Circuit Court. Personal checks accepted. Prepayment and SASE required.

Magistrate Court 900 10th Ave, Marlinton, WV 24954; phone: 304-799-6603; fax: 304-799-6331; hours 9AM-4:30PM (EST). *Misdemeanor, Civil Actions Under $5,000, Eviction, Small Claims.*
Civil Records: Access: In person only. Visitors must perform in person searches themselves. Court makes copy: $.25 per page; same fee for self serve. Required to search: name. Records stored since 1977, computerized since 10-14-99.
Criminal Records: Access: In person only. Visitors must perform in person searches themselves. Court makes copy: $.25 per page; same fee for self serve. Required to search: name, years to search; also helpful: DOB, SSN. Records stored since 1977, computerized since 10-14-99.
General Information: Public use terminal available. Certification fee: $.50 per page. Prepayment required.

Preston County

Circuit Court 101 W Main St, Rm 301, Kingwood, WV 26537; phone: 304-329-0047; probate phone: 304-329-0070; fax: 304-329-1417; hours 9AM-5PM M-Th, 9AM-7PM Fri (EST). *Felony, Misdemeanor, Civil Actions Over $5,000, Probate.*
Note: Probate is handled by County Clerk, 101 W Main St, Rm 201, Kingwood, WV 26537.
Civil Records: Access: Phone, fax, mail, in person. Only the court performs in person searches; visitors may not. No search fee. Court makes copy: $.50 per page. Required to search: name, years to search. Civil cases indexed by defendant, plaintiff; on computer from 1/80 to present, on index books 1965 to 1980, chancery file from 1869 to 1965. Mail turnaround time 1 week.
Criminal Records: Access: Phone, fax, mail, in person. Only the court performs in person searches; visitors may not. No search fee. Court makes copy: $.50 per page. Required to search: name, years to

search, DOB, SSN. Criminal records on docket books from 1869 to 1979, records on computer since 1979. Mail turnaround time 1 week.
General Information: No juvenile, adoption, domestic, mental hygiene records released. Fee to fax documents is $2.00 per page. No certification fee. Payee: Betsy Castle, Circuit Clerk. Personal checks accepted. Prepayment and SASE required.

Magistrate Court 328 Tunnelton St, Kingwood, WV 26537; phone: 304-329-2764; fax: 304-329-0855; hours 8:30AM-4:30PM (EST). *Misdemeanor, Civil Actions Under $5,000, Eviction, Small Claims.*
Civil Records: Access: Fax, mail, in person. Both court and visitors may perform in person searches. No search fee. Court makes copy: $.25 per page; same fee for self serve. Civil records go back to 1977; computerized records since 1987. Mail turnaround time 1 week.
Criminal Records: Access: Fax, mail, in person. Both court and visitors may perform in person searches. No search fee. Court makes copy: $.25 per page; same fee for self serve. Required to search: name, years to search; also helpful: DOB, SSN. Criminal records go back to 1977; computerized records since 1987. Mail turnaround time 1 week.
General Information: Public terminal goes back to 1989. Certification fee: $.50 per page. SASE requested.

Putnam County

Circuit Court Putnam County Judicial Bldg, 3389 Winfield Rd, Winfield, WV 25213; phone: 304-586-0203; fax: 304-586-0221; hours 8:30AM-4:30PM M-F (EST). *Felony, Civil Actions Over $5,000, Probate.*
Civil Records: Access: In person, online. Both court and visitors may perform in person searches. Court makes copy: $.50 per page. Required to search: name, years to search. Civil cases indexed by defendant, plaintiff; on computer from 1989 to present, on index books back to 1800s. Online access to court records via a pay service, see www.swcg-inc.com/products/circuit_express.html or call 800-795-8543. $125.00 set-up fee plus a $38.00 or $120.00 monthly fee plan.
Criminal Records: Access: In person, online. Visitors must perform in person searches themselves. No search fee. Court makes copy: $.50 per page. Required to search: name, years to search; also helpful: DOB, SSN. Criminal records on computer from 1982 to present. Online access to criminal records is the same as civil.
General Information: Public use terminal available. No divorce records released. No certification fee. Payee: Circuit Clerk. Business checks accepted. Prepayment required.

Magistrate Court 3389 Winfield Rd, Winfield, WV 25213; phone: 304-586-0234; fax: 304-586-0267; hours 8:30AM-4:30PM (EST). *Misdemeanor, Civil Actions Under $5,000, Eviction, Small Claims.*
Civil Records: Access: Mail, in person. Both court and visitors may perform in person searches. Court makes copy: $.25 per page; same fee for self serve. Records are computerized since 1996, overall records kept since 1977. Mail turnaround time 1 week.
Criminal Records: Access: Mail, in person. Both court and visitors may perform in person searches. No search fee. Court makes copy: $.25 per page; same fee for self serve. Required to search: name, years to search; also helpful: DOB, SSN. Records stored since 1977. Mail turnaround time 1 week.
General Information: Public terminal goes back to 1996. Certification fee: $.50 per page. Payee: Magistrate Court. Prepayment required.

Raleigh County

Circuit Court 215 Main St, Beckley, WV 25801; phone: 304-255-9135; probate phone: 304-255-9123; fax: 304-255-9353; hours 8:30AM-4:30PM (EST). *Felony, Civil Actions Over $5,000, Probate.*
Note: Probate is handled by County Clerk, 215 Main St, Courthouse, Beckley, WV 25801.

Civil Records: Access: In person only. Visitors must perform in person searches themselves. Court makes copy: $.50 per page; same fee for self serve. Required to search: name, years to search. Civil cases indexed by defendant, plaintiff; on master index books from 1977; on computer back to 1997; on dockets back to 1800s.

Criminal Records: Access: Phone, mail, in person. Both court and visitors may perform in person searches. No search fee. Court makes copy: $.50 per page; same fee for self serve. Required to search: name, years to search; also helpful: DOB, SSN. Criminal records on master index books from 1977; on computer back to 1997; on dockets back to 1800s.

General Information: Public terminal has criminal back to 1997 and civil back to 1997. No divorce, juvenile, adoption records released. Fee to fax documents is $2.00 per page. No certification fee. Payee: Clerk of Circuit Court. Business checks accepted. Prepayment required. Will bill to attorneys. SASE required.

Magistrate Court 115 W Prince St, #A, Beckley, WV 25801; phone: 304-255-9197; fax: 304-255-9354; hours 8AM-4PM (EST). *Misdemeanor, Civil Actions Under $5,000, Eviction, Small Claims.*

Civil Records: Access: In person only. Visitors must perform in person searches themselves. Court makes copy: $.25 per page; same fee for self serve. Required to search: name. Civil records go back to 1977, computerized since 1991.

Criminal Records: Access: In person only. Visitors must perform in person searches themselves. Court makes copy: $.25 per page; same fee for self serve. Required to search: name, years to search; also helpful: DOB, SSN, offense, date of offense. Criminal records go back to 1977, on computer back to 1992.

General Information: Public terminal has criminal back to 1992 and civil back to 1991. Will fax specific case file for $2.00 per page. Certification fee: $.50 per page includes copy fee. Prepayment required.

Randolph County

Circuit Court Courthouse, 2 Randolph Ave, Elkins, WV 26241; phone: 304-636-2765; fax: 304-637-3700; hours 8AM-4:30PM (EST). *Felony, Civil Actions Over $5,000, Probate.*

Civil Records: Access: Fax, mail, in person. Visitors must perform in person searches themselves. No search fee. Court makes copy: $.50 per page; same fee for self serve. Required to search: name, years to search. Civil cases indexed by defendant, plaintiff; on computer from 1/91 to present. On index books back to late 1800s.

Criminal Records: Access: Fax, mail, in person. Visitors must perform in person searches themselves. No search fee. Court makes copy: $.50 per page; same fee for self serve. Required to search: name, years to search. Criminal records on computer from 1/91 to present. On index books back to late 1800s.

General Information: Public terminal goes back to 1991. No juvenile, adoption, mental health, or guardianship records released. No certification fee. Payee: Circuit Clerk. Personal checks accepted. Prepayment required.

Magistrate Court #11 Randolph Ave, Elkins, WV 26241; phone: 304-636-5885; fax: 304-636-2510; hours 8AM-4:30PM (EST). *Misdemeanor, Civil Actions Under $5,000, Eviction, Small Claims.*

Civil Records: Access: Mail, in person. Both court and visitors may perform in person searches. No search fee. Court makes copy: $.25 per page; same fee for self serve. Civil records go back to 1977; computerized records since 10/90. Mail turnaround time 3 days.

Criminal Records: Access: Mail, in person. Both court and visitors may perform in person searches. No search fee. Court makes copy: $.25 per page; same fee for self serve. Required to search: name, years to search; also helpful: DOB, SSN. Criminal records go back to 1977; computerized records since 10/90. Mail turnaround time 3 days.

General Information: Public terminal goes back to 1992. Will fax documents for $2.00 per page prepaid. Certification fee: $.50 per page. Prepayment required.

Ritchie County

Circuit Court 115 E. Main St, Harrisville, WV 26362; phone 304-643-2164 x229; civil phone: x1; probate phone: 304-643-2164 x229; fax: 304-643-2534; hours 8AM-4PM (EST). *Felony, Civil Actions Over $5,000, Probate.*
Note: Probate office is located at the same address, but in county clerks office.

Civil Records: Access: Phone, mail, in person. Both court and visitors may perform in person searches. No search fee. Court makes copy: $.50 per page; same fee for self serve. Required to search: name, years to search. Civil cases indexed by defendant, plaintiff; on index cards from 1960 to present. On index books back to mid-1800s; on computer back to 2000. Mail turnaround time 1-2 days.

Criminal Records: Access: Phone, mail, in person. Both court and visitors may perform in person searches. No search fee. Court makes copy: $.50 per page; same fee for self serve. Required to search: name, years to search; also helpful: DOB, SSN. Criminal records on index cards from 1960 to present. On index books back to mid-1800s; on computer back to 2000. Mail turnaround time 1-2 days.

General Information: Public terminal goes back to 2000. No juvenile, mental health, adoption records released. Will not fax documents. No certification fee. Payee: Circuit Clerk. Personal checks accepted. Prepayment required. SASE requested.

Magistrate Court 319 E. Main St, Harrisville, WV 26362; phone: 304-643-4409; fax: 304-643-2098; hours 8AM-4PM (EST). *Misdemeanor, Civil Actions Under $5,000, Eviction, Small Claims.*

Civil Records: Access: Phone, fax, mail, in person. Both court and visitors may perform in person searches. No search fee. Court makes copy: $.25. Civil records go back to 1977; computerized from 1990. Phone, fax or mail access limited. Mail turnaround time 1-2 days, 1-2 hours for phone requests

Criminal Records: Access: Fax, mail, in person. Both court and visitors may perform in person searches. No search fee. Court makes copy: $.25. Required to search: name, years to search; also helpful: DOB, SSN. Criminal records go back to 1977; computerized from 1990. Mail turnaround time 1-2 days, 1-2 hours for phone requests

General Information: Public terminal goes back to 1990. Will fax documents for $2.00 per fax. Certification fee: $.50 per page. Payee: Magistrate Court. Prepayment required.

Roane County

Circuit Court PO Box 122, Spencer, WV 25276; phone: 304-927-2750; fax: 304-927-2164; hours 8:30AM-N, 1-4PM M-F; 9AM-N Sat (EST). *Felony, Civil Actions Over $5,000, Probate.*

Civil Records: Access: Phone, fax, mail, in person. Both court and visitors may perform in person searches. No search fee. Court makes copy: $.50 per page. Required to search: name, years to search. Civil cases indexed by defendant, plaintiff; on index books back to early 1900s; computerized records go back to 1998. Mail turnaround time 1-2 days, less for phone requests.

Criminal Records: Access: Phone, fax, mail, in person. Both court and visitors may perform in person searches. No search fee. Court makes copy: $.50 per page. Required to search: name, years to search; also helpful: DOB, SSN. Criminal records on index books back to early 1900s; computerized records go back to 1998. Mail turnaround time 1-2 days, less for phone requests.

General Information: Public use terminal available. No sealed, juvenile, adoption records released. Will fax documents $1.50 1st page; $1.00 each add'l. Certification fee: $.50 per page. Payee: Beverly

Greathouse. Local checks accepted. Prepayment required.

Magistrate Court 201 Main St, Spencer, WV 25276; phone: 304-927-4750; fax: 304-927-2754; hours 9AM-4PM (EST). *Misdemeanor, Civil Actions Under $5,000, Eviction, Small Claims.*
Note: Record requests can be directed to 304-746-2180.

Civil Records: Access: In person only. Visitors must perform in person searches themselves. Court makes copy: $.25 per page; same fee for self serve. Required to search: name, years to search. Records on computer back to 1997; prior records go back to 1976.

Criminal Records: Access: In person only. Visitors must perform in person searches themselves. Court makes copy: $.25 per page; same fee for self serve. Required to search: name, DOB; also helpful: years to search, SSN. Records on computer back to 1997; prior records go back to 1976.

General Information: Public terminal goes back to 1997. Certification fee: $.50 per page. Payee: Roane County Magistrate Court. Prepayment required. Will bill to attorneys.

Summers County

Circuit Court PO Box 1058, Hinton, WV 25951; phone: 304-466-7103; fax: 304-466-7124; hours 8:30AM-4:30PM (EST). *Felony, Civil Actions Over $5,000, Probate.*

Civil Records: Access: In person only. Visitors must perform in person searches themselves. Self serve copy fee: $.50 per page. Required to search: name, years to search. Civil cases indexed by defendant, plaintiff; on index books back to late 1800s; computerized records since 1998.

Criminal Records: Access: In person only. Both court and visitors may perform in person searches. No search fee. Self serve copy fee: $.50 per page. Required to search: name, years to search; also helpful: DOB, SSN. Criminal records on index books back to 1878, computerized since 1998.

General Information: Public terminal goes back to 1998. No juvenile, adoption, child abuse records released. Will fax specific case file $2.00 per page. Certification fee: $1.00. Payee: Clerk of Circuit Court. Personal checks accepted. Prepayment required.

Magistrate Court PO Box 1059, Hinton, WV 25951; phone: 304-466-7108; criminal fax: 304-466-4912; same fax for civil/probate; hours 9:00AM-4:00PM (EST). *Misdemeanor, Civil Actions Under $5,000, Eviction, Small Claims.*

Civil Records: Access: Phone, fax, mail, in person. Both court and visitors may perform in person searches. No search fee. Court makes copy: $.25. Required to search: name, years to search, other names used; also helpful-address. Civil records on docket back to 1977 and computer back to 1998. Mail turnaround time 1-2 days.

Criminal Records: Access: Phone, fax, mail, in person. Both court and visitors may perform in person searches. No search fee. Court makes copy: $.25. Required to search: name, years to search; also helpful: DOB, SSN. Criminal records on docket books to 1977, and computer back to 1998. Mail turnaround time 1-2 days.

General Information: Public terminal goes back to 1998. Will fax documents for $2.00 per fax. Certification fee: $.50 per page. Payee: Magistrate Court. Prepayment required.

Taylor County

Circuit Court 214 W Main St, Rm 104, Grafton, WV 26354; phone: 304-265-2480; hours 8:30AM-N, 1-4:30PM (EST). *Felony, Civil Actions Over $5,000, Probate.*

Civil Records: Access: Phone, mail, in person. Both court and visitors may perform in person searches. No search fee. Court makes copy: $.50 per page. Required to search: name, years to search. Civil cases indexed by defendant, plaintiff; on index books back to 1844, computerized since 1996. Mail turnaround time 2 days.

Criminal Records: Access: Phone, mail, in person. Both court and visitors may perform in person searches. No search fee. Court makes copy: $.50 per page. Required to search: name, years to search; also helpful: DOB, SSN. Criminal records on index books back to 1929, computerized since 1996. Mail turnaround time 2 days.

General Information: No juvenile, adoptions, mental health records released. Fee to fax documents is $2.00 per page. No certification fee. Payee: Circuit Clerk. Prepayment and SASE required; any add'l fee for postage is 3 times the amount.

Magistrate Court 214 W Main St, Grafton, WV 26354; phone: 304-265-1322; fax: 304-265-5708; hours 8:30AM-4:30PM (EST). *Misdemeanor, Civil Actions Under $5,000, Eviction, Small Claims.*

Civil Records: Access: Mail, in person. Both court and visitors may perform in person searches. Court makes copy: $.25 per page; same fee for self serve. Overall records go back to 1976. Computerized records go back to 1992. Mail turnaround time 1-2 days.

Criminal Records: Access: Mail, in person. Both court and visitors may perform in person searches. No search fee. Court makes copy: $.25 per page; same fee for self serve. Required to search: name, years to search; also helpful: DOB, SSN, signed release. Overall records go back to 1976. Computerized records go back to 1992. Mail turnaround time 1-2 days.

General Information: Public use terminal available. Certification fee: $.50 per page. Payee: Magistrate Court.

Tucker County

Circuit Court 215 1st St, #2, Parsons, WV 26287; phone: 304-478-2606; fax: 304-478-4464; hours 8AM-4PM (EST). *Felony, Civil Actions Over $5,000.*

Civil Records: Access: Mail, in person. Both court and visitors may perform in person searches. Court makes copy: $.50 per page; same fee for self serve. Required to search: name, years to search. Civil cases indexed by defendant, plaintiff; on index books from 1856 to 1996, 1997 to present on computer. Mail turnaround time 2-5 days.

Criminal Records: Access: Mail, in person. Both court and visitors may perform in person searches. No search fee. Court makes copy: $.50 per page; same fee for self serve. Required to search: name, years to search, SSN; also helpful: DOB, case number. Criminal records on index books to 1856 to 1996; 1997 to present on computer. Mail turnaround time 2 days.

General Information: No juvenile, domestic, guardianship, adoption or mental hygiene records released. Fee to fax documents is $2.00 per page, no charge to toll free line. No certification fee. Payee: Circuit Court Clerk. Personal checks accepted; no out of state checks. Prepayment and SASE required.

Magistrate Court 201 Walnut St, Parsons, WV 26287; phone: 304-478-2665; fax: 304-478-4836; hours 8:30AM-4:00PM (EST). *Misdemeanor, Civil Actions Under $5,000, Eviction, Small Claims.*

Civil Records: Access: In person only. Both court and visitors may perform in person searches. Court makes copy: $.25 per page; same fee for self serve. Civil records go back to 1977; computerized since 8/1999.

Criminal Records: Access: In person only. Both court and visitors may perform in person searches. Court makes copy: $.25 per page; same fee for self serve. Required to search: name, years to search; also helpful: DOB, SSN. Criminal records go back to 1977; computerized since 8/1999.

General Information: Public terminal goes back to 8/1999. Will not fax case files. Certification fee: $.50 per page. Prepayment required.

Tyler County

Circuit Court PO Box 8, Middlebourne, WV 26149; phone: 304-758-4811; fax: 304-758-4008; hours 8AM-4PM (EST). *Felony, Civil Actions Over $5,000.*

Civil Records: Access: Phone, mail, fax, in person. Both court and visitors may perform in person searches. No search fee. Court makes copy: $.50 per page; same fee for self serve. Required to search: name, years to search. Civil cases indexed by defendant, plaintiff; on index books back to 1800s; computerized back to 1997. Mail turnaround time 1-2 days.

Criminal Records: Access: Phone, mail, fax, in person. Both court and visitors may perform in person searches. No search fee. Court makes copy: $.50 per page; same fee for self serve. Required to search: name, years to search; also helpful: DOB, SSN. Criminal records on index books back to 1864; computerized back to 1997. Mail turnaround time 1-2 days.

General Information: Public terminal goes back to 1997. No adoption, juvenile, or domestic records released. Fee to fax documents is $5.00 per doc. No certification fee. Payee: Tyler County Circuit Clerk. Personal checks accepted. Prepayment and SASE required.

Magistrate Court PO Box 127, Middlebourne, WV 26149; phone: 304-758-2137; fax: 304-758-2692; hours 9AM-4PM (EST). *Misdemeanor, Civil Actions Under $5,000, Eviction, Small Claims.*

Civil Records: Access: Mail, in person. Both court and visitors may perform in person searches. No search fee. Court makes copy: $.25 per page. Required to search: Name, years to search, other names used, address; also helpful: DOB, SSN. Records go back to 1/1/77; on computer back to 1/1/2000. Mail turnaround time 1 week.

Criminal Records: Access: Mail, in person. Both court and visitors may perform in person searches. No search fee. Court makes copy: $.25 per page. Required to search: name, years to search; also helpful: DOB, SSN. Records go back to 1/1/77; on computer back to 1/1/2000. Mail turnaround time 1 week.

General Information: Public terminal goes back to 1/2000. Will fax documents for $2.00 per page, in advance. Certification fee: $.50 per page includes copy fee. Prepayment required.

Upshur County

Circuit Court 38 W. Main St, Rm 304, Buckhannon, WV 26201; phone: 304-472-2370; probate phone: 304-472-1068; fax: 304-472-2168; probate fax: 304-472-1029; hours 8AM-4:30PM (EST). *Felony, Civil Actions Over $5,000, Probate.* Note: Probate is handled by County Clerk, 40 W Main, Courthouse, Rm 101, Buckhannon, WV 26201.

Civil Records: Access: Fax, mail, in person. Visitors must perform in person searches themselves. No search fee. Court makes copy: $.50 per page. Required to search: name, years to search. Civil cases indexed by defendant, plaintiff; on index books from 1900 to present, on computer from 1/90. Mail turnaround time 1-2 days.

Criminal Records: Access: Fax, mail, in person. Both court and visitors may perform in person searches. Search fee: $5.00 per name. Court makes copy: $.50 per page. Required to search: name, years to search; also helpful: DOB, SSN. Criminal records on computer from 1/90 to present, on index books from 1947 to 1/90, on dockets back to 1800s. Mail turnaround time 1-2 days.

General Information: Public terminal goes back to 1990. No mental health, juvenile, adoption records released. Will fax documents $2.00 per page. Certification fee: $.50 per page. Payee: Circuit Clerk. Business checks accepted. Prepayment required. SASE requested.

Magistrate Court 38 W Main, Rm 204 Courthouse Annex, Buckhannon, WV 26201; phone: 304-472-2053; hours 8AM-4PM (EST). *Misdemeanor, Civil Actions Under $5,000, Eviction, Small Claims.*

Civil Records: Access: Mail, in person. Both court and visitors may perform in person searches. No search fee. Court makes copy: $.25 per page. Civil records from 1977; computerized back to 1996. Mail turnaround time 1-2 days.

Criminal Records: Access: Mail, in person. Both court and visitors may perform in person searches. No search fee. Court makes copy: $.25 per page. Required to search: name; also helpful: DOB, SSN. Criminal records from 1977; computerized back to 1992. Mail turnaround time 1-2 days.

General Information: Public terminal has criminal back to 1992 and civil back to 1995. Will fax documents for $2.00. Certification fee: $.25 per page. Payee: Magistrate Court. Prepayment required.

Wayne County

Circuit Court PO Box 38, Wayne, WV 25570; phone: 304-272-6360; probate phone: 304-272-4372; hours 8AM-4PM M,T,W,F; 8AM-8PM Th (EST). *Felony, Civil Actions Over $5,000, Probate.* Note: Probate is handled by County Clerk, PO Box 248, Wayne, WV 25570.

Civil Records: Access: Phone, mail, in person. Both court and visitors may perform in person searches. No search fee. Court makes copy: $.50 per page; same fee for self serve. Required to search: name, years to search. Civil cases indexed by defendant, plaintiff; on computer back to 1993; prior on index books from 1960 to present. Contact Circuit Clerk for books prior to 1900s. The staff will not conduct genealogical searches. Mail turnaround time 1-2 days.

Criminal Records: Access: In person only. Visitors must perform in person searches themselves. Court makes copy: $.50 per page; same fee for self serve. Required to search: name, years to search, SSN; also helpful: DOB. Criminal records on computer back to 1993; prior on index books from 1960 to present. Contact Circuit Clerk for books prior to 1900s.

General Information: Public terminal goes back to 1993. No juvenile, adoption, mental records released. Will not fax documents. No certification fee. Payee: Clerk of Circuit Court. Business checks accepted. Prepayment and SASE required.

Magistrate Court PO Box 667, Wayne, WV 25570; phone: 304-272-5648/6388; fax: 304-272-5988; hours 8AM-4PM (EST). *Felony, Misdemeanor, Civil Actions Under $5,000, Eviction, Small Claims.*

Civil Records: Access: Phone, fax, mail, in person. Both court and visitors may perform in person searches. No search fee. Court makes copy: $.25 per page; same fee for self serve. Required to search: name; also helpful: years to search, DOB, SSN. Civil records go back to 1977; on computer back to 1996. Mail turnaround time 1-2 days, usually same day for phone requests.

Criminal Records: Access: Fax, mail, in person. Both court and visitors may perform in person searches. No search fee. Court makes copy: $.25 per page; same fee for self serve. Required to search: name; also helpful: years to search, DOB, SSN. Criminal records go back to 1977; on computer back to 1996. Mail turnaround time 1-2 days, usually same day for phone requests.

General Information: Public terminal goes back to 1996. Will fax documents $2.00 per page. Certification fee: $.50 per page. Payee: Wayne County Magistrate Court. Prepayment and SASE required.

Webster County

Circuit Court 2 Court Square, Rm G-4, Webster Springs, WV 26288; phone: 304-847-2421; fax: 304-847-2062; hours 8:30AM-4PM (EST). *Felony, Civil Actions Over $5,000, Probate.*
Civil Records: Access: Phone, fax, mail, in person. Both court and visitors may perform in person searches. No search fee. Court makes copy: $.50 per page. Required to search: name, years to search. Civil cases indexed by defendant, plaintiff; on index cards from 1977 to present, also on computer since 8/99. Mail turnaround time 3-5 days.
Criminal Records: Access: Phone, fax, mail, in person. Both court and visitors may perform in person searches. No search fee. Court makes copy: $.50 per page. Required to search: name, years to search; also helpful: DOB, SSN. Felony dockets back to 1800s. Criminal records also on computer from 8/99. Mail turnaround time 3-5 days.
General Information: No mental health, juvenile, guardianship, adoption, paternity records released. Will fax documents $1.00 per page. Certification fee: $.50 per page. Payee: Clerk of Circuit Court. Personal checks accepted. Prepayment required. SASE requested.

Magistrate Court 2 Court Square, Rm B-1, Webster Springs, WV 26288; phone: 304-847-2613; fax: 304-847-7747; hours 8:30AM-4PM (EST). *Misdemeanor, Civil Actions Under $5,000, Eviction, Small Claims.*
Note: They recommend that criminal searches be directed to the Court Repository in Charleston, 304-746-2180.
Civil Records: Access: Fax, mail, in person. Visitors must perform in person searches themselves. Court makes copy: $.25 per page; same fee for self serve. Civil records go back to 1977; on computer since 2001. Mail turnaround time 7-10 days.
Criminal Records: Access: Fax, mail, in person. Visitors must perform in person searches themselves. Court makes copy: $.25 per page; same fee for self serve. Required to search: name, years to search; also helpful: DOB, SSN. Criminal records go back to 1977; on computer since 2001. Mail turnaround time 7-10 days.
General Information: Public terminal goes back to 2000. Will fax documents to local or toll free line. Certification fee: $.50 per page. Payee: Magistrate Court Clerk. Prepayment required.

Wetzel County

Circuit Court PO Box 263, New Martinsville, WV 26155; phone: 304-455-8219; fax: 304-455-1069; hours 9AM-4:30PM; till 4PM only Thurs; 9AM-N Sat (EST). *Felony, Civil Actions Over $5,000.*
Civil Records: Access: In person only. Visitors must perform in person searches themselves. Court makes copy: $.50 per page. Required to search: name, years to search. Civil cases indexed by defendant, plaintiff; on index books back to mid 1863; computerized back to 1996.
Criminal Records: Access: In person only. Visitors must perform in person searches themselves. Court makes copy: $.50 per page. Required to search: name. Criminal records on index books back to mid 1863; computerized back to 1996.
General Information: Public terminal goes back to 1996. No juvenile, domestic records released. Will fax documents. No certification fee. Payee: Circuit Clerk. Personal checks accepted.

Magistrate Court PO Box 147, New Martinsville, WV 26155; phone: 304-455-5040\5171\2450; fax: 304-455-2859; hours 8:30AM-4:30PM (EST). *Misdemeanor, Civil Actions Under $5,000, Eviction, Small Claims.*
Civil Records: Access: mail, fax, in person. Both court and visitors may perform in person searches.

Required to search: name, DOB, SSN, years to search. Civil records go back to 1995. Mail turnaround time 1-2 days.
Criminal Records: Access: mail, fax, in person. Both court and visitors may perform in person searches. No search fee. Required to search: name, years to search; also helpful: DOB, SSN. Criminal records go back to 1980. Mail turnaround time 1-2 days.
General Information: Public terminal goes back to 11/99. Will fax documents.

Wirt County

Circuit Court PO Box 465, Elizabeth, WV 26143; phone: 304-275-6597; probate phone: 304-275-4271; civil/criminal fax: 304-275-3230; probate fax: 304-275-3418; hours 8:30AM-4PM (EST). *Felony, Civil Actions Over $5,000, Probate.*
Note: Probate records located at the county clerk's office.
Civil Records: Access: Phone, fax, mail, in person. Both court and visitors may perform in person searches. No search fee. Court makes copy: $.10 per page. Required to search: name, years to search. Civil cases indexed by defendant, plaintiff; on index cards from 1848 to present; computerized back to 9/2000.
Criminal Records: Access: Fax, in person. Both court and visitors may perform in person searches. No search fee. Court makes copy: $.10 per page. Required to search: name, years to search, DOB, SSN. Criminal records on index cards from 1848 to present; computerized back to 9/2000. Mail turnaround time same day if possible.
General Information: No juvenile or adoption records released. No fee to fax documents. Certification fee: $.50 per page includes copy fee. Payee: Wirt County Circuit Clerk. Personal checks accepted. Prepayment and SASE required.

Magistrate Court PO Box 249, Elizabeth, WV 26143; phone: 304-275-3641; fax: 304-275-4882; hours 8:30AM-4PM (EST). *Misdemeanor, Civil Actions Under $5,000, Eviction, Small Claims.*
Civil Records: Access: Phone, in person. Both court and visitors may perform in person searches. No search fee. Court makes copy: $.25 per page. Civil records go back 10 years; computerized back to 9/2000.
Criminal Records: Access: Phone, in person. Both court and visitors may perform in person searches. No search fee. Court makes copy: $.25 per page. Required to search: name, years to search; also helpful: address, DOB, SSN. Criminal records go back 10 years; computerized back to 9/2000.
General Information: Public use terminal available. Certification fee: $.50 per page.

Wood County

Circuit Court Wood County Judicial, #2 Government Sq, Parkersburg, WV 26101-5353; phone: 304-424-1700; probate phone: 304-424-1850; fax: 304-424-1804; hours 8:30AM-4:30PM (EST). *Felony, Civil Actions Over $5,000, Probate.*
Note: Probate is handled by County Clerk, PO Box 1474, Parkersburg, WV 26102.
Civil Records: Access: Phone, mail, in person. Both court and visitors may perform in person searches. No search fee. Court makes copy: $.50 per page. Required to search: name, years to search. Civil cases indexed by defendant, plaintiff; on computer from 1978 to present, on index books back to 1885. Mail turnaround time 2-3 days.
Criminal Records: Access: Mail, in person. Both court and visitors may perform in person searches. No search fee. Court makes copy: $.50 per page. Required to search: name, years to search, DOB, SSN. Criminal records on computer since 1979; prior records on index back to 1885. Mail turnaround time 2-3 days.

General Information: Public use terminal available. No juvenile, domestic, adoption, mental hygiene, guardianship records released. No certification fee. Payee: Carole Jones, Clerk. No personal checks accepted. Prepayment required.

Magistrate Court 208 Avery St, Parkersburg, WV 26101; phone: 304-422-3444; hours 8:30AM-4:30PM (EST). *Misdemeanor, Civil Actions Under $5,000, Eviction, Small Claims.*
Civil Records: Access: Mail, in person. Both court and visitors may perform in person searches. No search fee. Court makes copy: $.25 per page. Required to search: name, DOB, SSN, years to search. Civil records go back to 1977; computerized records since 1996. Fax and mail access limited. Mail turnaround time 10 days.
Criminal Records: Access: Mail, in person. Both court and visitors may perform in person searches. No search fee. Court makes copy: $.25 per page. Required to search: name, years to search, address; also helpful: DOB, SSN. Criminal records go back to 1997; computerized since 1996. Fax and mail access limited. Mail turnaround time 10 days.
General Information: Public terminal goes back to 1996. Will fax documents for a fee of $2.00 per rage. Do not fax record search requests, however. Certification fee: $.50 per page includes copy fee. Prepayment and SASE required.

Wyoming County

Circuit Court PO Box 190, Pineville, WV 24874; phone: 304-732-8000 X238; fax: 304-732-7262; hours 9AM-4PM (EST). *Felony, Civil Actions Over $5,000.*
Civil Records: Access: Phone, mail, in person. Both court and visitors may perform in person searches. No search fee. Court makes copy: $.50 per page. Required to search: name, years to search. Civil cases indexed by defendant, plaintiff; on index books back to 1800s. Mail turnaround time 1-2 days, less for phone requests.
Criminal Records: Access: Phone, mail, in person. Both court and visitors may perform in person searches. No search fee. Court makes copy: $.50 per page. Required to search: name, years to search; also helpful: DOB, SSN. Criminal records on index books back to 1800s. Mail turnaround time 1-2 days, less for phone requests.
General Information: Public terminal goes back to 1997. No juvenile, mental hygiene, adoption, or sealed records released. Certification fee: $.50 per page. Payee: David Storer, Circuit Clerk. Business checks accepted. Prepayment required. SASE preferred.

Magistrate Court PO Box 598, Pineville, WV 24874; phone: 304-732-8000 X218; fax: 304-732-7247; hours 9AM-4PM M-Th, 9AM-6PM Fri (EST). *Misdemeanor, Civil Actions Under $5,000, Eviction, Small Claims.*
Civil Records: Access: Mail, in person. Both court and visitors may perform in person searches. Court makes copy: $.25 per copy; same fee for self serve. Civil records from 1977; computerized back to 1995. Mail turnaround time 1-2 days.
Criminal Records: Access: Mail, in person. Both court and visitors may perform in person searches. No search fee. Court makes copy: $.25 per copy; same fee for self serve. Required to search: name, years to search; also helpful: DOB, SSN. Criminal records from 1977; computerized back to 1995. Mail turnaround time 1-2 days.
General Information: Public terminal goes back to 9/1995. Fee to fax results is $2.00 per page. Certification fee: $.75. Payee: Wyoming County Magistrate Court. Prepayment required.

West Virginia Recording Offices

ORGANIZATION: 55 counties, 55 recording offices. The recording officer is County Clerk. The entire state is in the Eastern Time Zone (EST).

REAL ESTATE RECORDS: Most County Clerks will not perform real estate searches. Copy fees are usually $1.50 up to two pages and $1.00 for each additional page. Certification usually costs $1.00 per document.

UCC RECORDS: Financing statements are filed at the state level, except for real estate related collateral, which are filed only with the Register of Deeds. Previous to 07/2001, collateral on consumer goods were are filed in both places, now they are only filed at the state level. Many recording offices will perform UCC searches. Use search request form UCC-11. Searches fees and copy fees vary.

TAX LIEN RECORDS: All federal and state tax liens are filed with the County Clerk. Most counties will not perform tax lien searches.

OTHER LIENS: Judgment, mechanics, lis pendens

ONLINE ACCESS: There is no state-operated system open to public, though a private company offers subscription access to land book assessment information statewide at http://digitalcourthouse.com.

Only one county – Monongalia – offers online access to assessor records.

Barbour County

County Clerk, 8 N. Main St; Courthouse, Philippi, WV 26416. 304-457-2232; fax-304-457-2790; hours: 8:30AM-4:30PM.
Office personnel or visitors may perform searches. Search fee $1.00 per name. Copy fee $1.50 per page. Cert fee- $1.00 per cert. Payee- Barbour County Clerk. **Other phones:** Treasurer- 304-457-2881. **Property tax/Assessor-** 304-457-2336.

Berkeley County

County Clerk, 100 W. King St, Rm 1, Martinsburg, WV 25401. 304-264-1927; fax-304-267-1794; hours: 9AM-5PM.
Only the public may search. Copy fee $1.50 per page. **Other phones:** Treasurer- 304-264-1980; Sheriff- 304-264-1980. **Property tax/Assessor-** 304-264-1901.

Boone County

County Clerk, 200 State St, Madison, WV 25130. 304-369-7337; fax-304-369-7329; hours: 8-4PM.
Only the public may search. Copy fee $1.50 per page plus 1.00 add'l. Cert fee- $1.00. Payee- Boone County Clerk. **Other phones:** Treasurer- 304-369-7391. **Property tax/Assessor-** 304-369-7308.

Braxton County

County Clerk, PO Box 486, Sutton, WV 26601-0728. 304-765-2833; fax-304-765-2093; hours: 8AM-4PM.
All records in one index. Record index not computerized. Only the public may search. Copy fee $1.00 per page. Cert fee- $1.00 per doc plus copy fee. Payee- John D. Jordan-Clerk. **Other phones:** Treasurer- 304-765-2830; Appraiser/Auditor- 304-765-2830; Elections- 304-765-2833; Vital Records- 304-765-2833. **Property tax/Assessor-** same address as above. 304-765-2805.

Brooke County

County Clerk, 632 Main St; Courthouse, Wellsburg, WV 26070. 304-737-3661; fax-304-737-4023; hours: 9AM-5PM, M-F; 9AM-12, SAT.
Separate indices by document type. Only the public may search. Office personal may perform limited search, 1 item. Copy fee $1.50 1st 2 pages; $1.00 each add'l. **Other phones:** Treasurer- 304-737-3663; Elections- 304-737-3668; Vital Records- 304-737-3661. **Property tax/Assessor-** same address as above. 304-737-3667.

Cabell County

County Clerk, 750 Fifth Ave, Rm 108; Cabell County Courthouse, Huntington, WV 25701-2083. 304-526-8625, UCC recording phone-304-526-8631; fax-304-526-8632; hours: 8:30AM-4:30PM. www.cabellcountyclerk.org
Separate indices to search include deeds, liens, wills, financing statements. Records indexed on a public use terminal back to 1/1/1995. Only the public may search. Copy fee $1.50 1st 2 pages; $1.00 each add'l. Cert fee- $1.00 per doc plus copy fee. **Other phones:** Treasurer- 304-526-8672; Elections- 304-526-8633; Vital Records- 304-526-8631. **Property tax/Assessor-** 304-526-8601.

Calhoun County

County Clerk, PO Box 230, Grantsville, WV 26147-0230. 304-354-6725; fax-304-354-6725; hours: 8:30AM-4PM.
Only the public may search. **Other phones:** Treasurer- 304-354-6333; Elections- 304-354-6725; Vital Records- 304-354-6725. **Property tax/Assessor-** 304-354-6958.

Clay County

County Clerk, PO Box 190, Clay, WV 25043. 304-587-4259; fax-304-587-7329; hours: 8AM-4PM.
Only the public may search. Copy fee $1.50 per page. Cert fee- $1.00 plus copy fee. Payee- Clay Count Clerk. **Other phones:** Treasurer- 304-587-4260. **Property tax/Assessor-** 304-587-4258.

Doddridge County

County Clerk, 118 E. Court St, Rm 102, West Union, WV 26456-1297. 304-873-2631; fax-304-873-1840; hours: 8:30AM-4PM.
Office will perform a UCC search but public must search other records themselves. UCC search per debtor name- $10.00. Copy fee $1.50 per page. Cert fee- $1.00 per cert. Payee- Doddridge County Clerk. **Other phones:** Treasurer- 304-873-1000; Elections- 304-873-2631. **Property tax/Assessor-** 304-873-1261.

Fayette County

County Clerk, PO Box 569, Fayetteville, WV 25840. 304-574-4226; fax-304-574-4335; hours: 8AM-4PM.
Separate indices to search include probate, debtor/creditor, grantor/grantee. Office will perform a UCC search but public must search other records themselves. UCC search per debtor name-$1.00 per page. Copy fee $1.00 per page. Cert fee- $.50 per cert plus copy fee. Payee-

Fayette County Clerk. **Other phones:** Treasurer- 304-574-4216; Elections- 304-574-4235. **Property tax/Assessor-** 100 Court St, Fayetteville, WV 25840; 304-574-4244.

Gilmer County

County Clerk, 10 Howard St; Courthouse, Glenville, WV 26351. 304-462-7641; fax-304-462-5134; hours: 8AM-4PM.
Separate indices to search include wills, trust deeds, deeds, liens, assignments, UCC's, appraisements, birth, death, marriage. Record index not computerized. Only the public may search. Copy fee $1.50 1st 2 pages; $1.00 each add'l. Cert fee- $1.00 per doc plus copy fee. Payee- Gilmer County Clerk. **Other phones:** Treasurer- 304-462-7441; Appraiser/Auditor- 304-462-7039; Elections- 304-462-7641; Vital Records- 304-462-7641. **Property tax/Assessor-** same address as above. 304-462-7731.

Grant County

County Clerk, 5 Highland Ave, Petersburg, WV 26847. 304-257-4550; fax-304-257-4207; hours: 8:30AM-4:30PM.
Separate indices to search include general, lien. Records indexed on computer back to 7/1/1979 to current. Office will perform a UCC search but public must search other records themselves. UCC search per debtor name- $2.00. Copy fee $.50 for 1-10 pages, $.25 each add'l. Cert fee- $2.50 per doc, $5.00 for birth, death & marriage plus copy fee. **Other phones:** Treasurer- 304-257-1818; Appraiser/Auditor- 304-257-4550; Elections- 304-257-4550; Vital Records- 304-257-4550; Sheriff- 304-257-1818. **Property tax/Assessor-** same address as above. 304-257-1050.

Greenbrier County

County Clerk, PO Box 506, Lewisburg, WV 24901. 304-647-6602; fax-304-647-6694; hours: 8:30AM-4:30PM.
Separate indices to search include for each category. Record index not computerized. Only the public may search. Copy fee $1.50 1st 2 pages; $1.00 each add'l. Cert fee- $3.00 per cert plus copy fee. Payee- Greenbrier County Clerk. **Other phones:** Treasurer- 304-647-6609; Elections- 304-647-6606; Vital Records- 304-647-6602. **Property tax/Assessor-** 304-647-6615.

Hampshire County

County Clerk, PO Box 806, Romney, WV 26757-0806. 304-822-5112; fax-304-822-4039; hours: 9AM-4PM (Fri open until 8PM).
Separate indices to search include deed, liens, marriages, birth, death, general records. Only the public may search. Copy fee $1.50 1st 2 pages; $1.00 each add'l. Cert fee- $2.50 plus copy fee. Payee- Hampshire County Clerk. **Other phones:** Treasurer- 304-822-4720; Appraiser/Auditor- 304-822-3326; Elections- 304-822-5112; Vital Records- 304-822-5112. **Property tax/Assessor-** 66 N. High St, Romney, WV 26757; 304-822-3326.

Hancock County

County Clerk, PO Box 367, New Cumberland, WV 26047. 304-564-3311 x279, R/E recording phone-304-564-3311 x267, UCC recording phone-304-564-3311 x281; fax-304-564-5941; hours: 8:30AM-4:30PM. http://hancockcountywv.org
Records indexed on computer back to 10/1/1997. Only the public may search. Copy fee $1.50 1st 2 pages, $1.00 each add'l. Cert fee- $3.00 + Copy costs. **Other phones:** Treasurer- 304-564-3311 x262; Appraiser/Auditor- 304-564-3311 x256; Elections- 304-564-3311 x288; Vital Records- 304-564-3311 x280. **Property tax/Assessor-** 304-564-3311 x256.

Hardy County

County Clerk, 204 Washington St; Courthouse - Rm 111, Moorefield, WV 26836. 304-538-2929; fax-304-538-6832; hours: 9AM-4PM.
Only the public may search. Copy fee $1.50 for 1st 2 pages. Cert fee- $1.00. Payee- Hardy County Clerk. **Online access to Deed, Mortgage, Grantor/Grantee records:** Access to Records is free at http://66.101.143.145/. Username Id and Password is hardywv (all small letters). Index goes back to 1/1993. **Other phones:** Treasurer- 304-538-2593. **Property tax/Assessor-** 304-538-6139.

Harrison County

County Clerk, 301 W. Main St; Courthouse, Clarksburg, WV 26301. 304-624-8672; fax-304-624-8575; hours: 8:30AM-4:30PM.
Separate indices to search include grantee/grantor, liens, marriage, death. Only the public may search. Copy fee $1.50 for 1st 2 pages, $1.00 each add'l. Cert fee- $5.00 per cert plus copy fee. Payee- Harrison County Clerk. **Other phones:** Treasurer- 304-624-8550; Elections- 304-624-8615; Vital Records- 304-624-8608. **Property tax/Assessor-** same address as above. 304-624-8510.

Jackson County

County Clerk, PO Box 800, Ripley, WV 25271. 304-373-2250, R/E recording phone-304-373-2259, UCC recording phone-304-373-2258; fax-304-372-5259; hours: 9AM-4PM M-F; 9AM-N Sat.
Separate indices to search include deeds, deed of trust, etc. Records indexed on computer back to 1989. Only the public may search. Copy fee $1.50 for 1st 2 pages; $1.00 each add'l. Cert fee- $1.00 per doc plus copy fee. Payee- Jackson County Clerk. **Other phones:** Treasurer- 304-372-2011 x305; Elections- 304-373-2249; Vital Records- 304-373-2256. **Property tax/Assessor-** 304-372-2241.

Jefferson County

County Clerk, PO Box 208, Charles Town, WV 25414. 304-728-3215, UCC recording phone-304-728-3248; fax-304-728-1957; hours: 9AM-5PM (Fri open until 7PM). www.jeffersoncountyclerk.net
Separate indices to search include judgments, UCC, releases, deeds, deeds of trust, will, plat, and more. Office will perform a UCC search but public must search other records themselves, though the office can assist. UCC search per debtor name- $4.00. Copy fee $1.50 1st 2 pages; $1.00 each add'l. Cert fee- $1.00 per doc plus copy fee. Payee- John Ott, County Clerk. **Other phones:** Treasurer- 304-728-3220; Elections- 304-728-3246;

Vital Records- 304-728-3362. **Property tax/Assessor-** 304-728-3224.

Kanawha County

County Clerk, PO Box 3226, Charleston, WV 25332. 304-357-0130, R/E recording phone-304-357-0244; fax-304-357-0585;
Office will perform a UCC search but public must search other records themselves. UCC search per debtor name- $2.00. Copy fee $1.50 1st 2 pages; $1.00 each add'l. Cert fee- $1.00 per doc plus copy fee. **Other phones:** Treasurer- 304-357-0210; Elections- 304-357-0110; Vital Records- 304-357-0710. **Property tax/Assessor-** 304-357-0250.

Lewis County

County Clerk, PO Box 87, Weston, WV 26452. 304-269-8215; fax-304-269-8202; hours: 8:30AM-4:30PM.
Only the public may search. Copy fee $1.50 1st 2 pages; $1.00 each add'l. Cert fee- $2.00 per doc, plus copy fee. Payee- Lewis County Clerk. **Other phones:** Treasurer- 304-269-8222; Elections- 304-269-8215; Vital Records- 304-269-8215; Second Phone Line- 304-269-8216. **Property tax/Assessor-** 304-269-8205.

Lincoln County

County Clerk, PO Box 497, Hamlin, WV 25523. 304-824-3336; fax-304-824-7972;
Only the public may search. Copy fee $1.50 each 1st 2 pages; $1.00 each add'l. Cert fee- $1.00 per page. **Other phones:** Treasurer- 304-824-3336. **Property tax/Assessor-** 304-824-7878.

Logan County

County Clerk, Stratton & Main St; Courthouse, Rm 101, Logan, WV 25601. 304-792-8600, R/E recording phone-304-792-8697/8603, UCC recording phone-304-792-8606; fax-304-792-8621; 8:30AM-4:30PM.
Separate indices to search include deeds, releases, UCC's, liens, trustee's report of sales, misc, maps, fiduciary. Records indexed on a public use terminal. Only the public may search. Copy fee $2.00 per page. R/E record copy- $1.50 per page. Cert fee- $5.00 per doc plus copy fee. Payee- Glen D. Adkins-County Clerk. **Other phones:** Treasurer- 304-792-8680; Elections- 304-792-8616; Vital Records- 304-792-8615. **Property tax/Assessor-** Rm 212, Logan County Courthouse, Logan, WV 25601; 304-792-8525.

Marion County

County Clerk, PO Box 1267, Fairmont, WV 26555-1267. 304-367-5441, R/E recording phone-304-367-5440; fax-304-367-5448; hours: 8:30AM-4:30PM.
Office will perform a UCC search but public must search other records themselves. UCC search per debtor name- $11.00. General copy fee $1.00 per page. R/E or tax lien copy- $1.50 per page. Cert fee- $2.00 per page. Payee- Marion County Clerk. **Other phones:** Treasurer- 304-367-5303; Appraiser/Auditor- 304-367-5310; Elections- 304-367-5447; Vital Records- 304-367-5453. **Property tax/Assessor-** 304-367-5410.

Marshall County

County Clerk, PO Box 459, Moundsville, WV 26041. 304-845-1220; fax-304-845-5891; 8:30AM-4:30PM.
Separate indices to search include deed, lien, miscellaneous. Records indexed on computer back to 4/2001. Only the public may search. Copy fee $.25 per page. Cert fee- $5.00 per doc plus copy fee. **Other phones:** Treasurer- 304-845-1400; Elections- 304-845-1220; Vital Records- 304-845-1220. **Property tax/Assessor-** 304-845-1490.

Mason County

County Clerk, 200 6th St, Point Pleasant, WV 25550. 304-675-1997; fax-304-675-2521; 8:30AM-4:30PM.
Separate indices to search include grantor, grantee, debtor, estate. Only the public may search. Copy fee $1.50 1st 2 pages; $1.00 each add'l. Cert fee-

$1.00 per cert plus copy fee. Payee- Mason County Clerk. **Other phones:** Treasurer- 304-675-1047; Appraiser/Auditor- 304-675-2918; Elections- 304-675-1997; Vital Records- 304-675-1997. **Property tax/Assessor-** same address as above. 304-675-2840.

McDowell County

County Clerk, 90 Wyoming St; #109, Welch, WV 24801-2487. 304-436-8544, R/E recording phone-304-436-8549, UCC recording phone-304-436-8542; fax-304-436-8576; hours: 9AM-5PM.
Index: More than one index. Record index not computerized. Only the public may search. Copy fee $1.50 per page; $1.00 each add'l. Cert fee- $1.50. Payee- McDowell County Clerk. **Other phones:** Treasurer- 304-436-8527; Appraiser/Auditor- 304-436-8528; Elections- 304-436-8543; Vital Records- 304-436-8542. **Property tax/Assessor-** 304-436-8564.

Mercer County

County Clerk, 1501 Main St., Princeton, WV 24740. 304-487-8312; fax-304-487-8351; hours: 8:30AM-4PM.
Separate indices to search include deed, trust deed, judgment, UCC's, financing, birth, death, marriage, military, misc, etc. Records indexed on computer back to June, 1991. Only the public may search. Copy fee $1.50 1st 2 pages; $1.00 each add'l. Cert fee- $6.00 per 5 pages plus copy fee. Payee- Mercer County Clerk. **Other phones:** Treasurer- 304-425-8366; Elections- 304-487-8339; Vital Records- 304-487-8313; Probate Records- 304-487-8321. **Property tax/Assessor-** PO Box 5429, Princeton, WV 24746; 304-487-8329.

Mineral County

County Clerk, 150 Armstrong St, Keyser, WV 26726. 304-788-3924; fax-304-788-4109; 8:30AM-5PM.
All records in one index. Only the public may search. Copy fee $1.50 1st 2 pages; $1.00 each add'l. Cert fee- $1.50 per 2 pages. Payee- Mineral County Clerk. **Other phones:** Treasurer- 304-788-0341; Appraiser/Auditor- 304-788-3753; Elections- 304-788-3924; Vital Records- 304-788-3924. **Property tax/Assessor-** 304-788-3753.

Mingo County

County Clerk, PO Box 1197, Williamson, WV 25661. 304-235-0330; fax-304-235-0565; 8:30AM-4:30PM.
All records in one index. Records indexed on a public use terminal back to July, 1990. Only the public may search. Copy fee $1.50 1st 2 pages, $.50 each add'l. Cert fee- $5.00 per cert plus copy fee. **Property tax/Assessor-** 304-235-0310.

Monongalia County

County Clerk, 243 High St; Courthouse - Rm 123, Morgantown, WV 26505-5491. 304-291-7230, R/E recording phone-304-291-7235; fax-304-291-7233;
Record index not computerized. Only the public may search. Copy fee $1.50 1st 2 pages; $1.00 each add'l. Cert fee- $1.00 per doc plus copy fee. Payee- Monongalia County Clerk. **Online access to Assessor, Real Estate records:** Access the County Parcel Search database free at www.assessor.org/parcelweb. Search by a wide variety of criteria including owner name and address. **Other phones:** Treasurer- 304-291-7244; Elections- 304-291-7238; Vital Records- 304-291-7234. **Property tax/Assessor-** 243 High St, 2nd Fl, Morgantown, WV 26505; 304-291-7279, assessor fax- 304-291-7220.

Monroe County

County Clerk, PO Box 350, Union, WV 24983. 304-772-3096; fax-304-772-4191; 8:30AM-4:30PM.
Separate indices to search include liens, releases, deeds, leases, fiduciary, PITs. Record index not computerized. Only the public may search. Copy fee $1.50 per page; $1.00 each add'l. Cert fee- $1.00 per doc plus copy fee. Payee- Monroe

County Clerk. **Other phones:** Treasurer- 304-772-3018. **Property tax/Assessor-** same address as above. 304-772-3083.

Morgan County

County Clerk, 77 Fairfax St, #1A; #100, Berkeley Springs, WV 25411. 304-258-8547; fax-304-258-8545; hours: 9AM-5PM M,T,Th; 9AM-1PM W; 9AM-7PM F.

Separate indices to search include. Records indexed on computer from 1997 forward. Also have paper indexes for older documents. Only the public may search. General copy fee $1.00 for 1st 2 pages; $1.00 each add'l. R/E or tax lien copy- $1.50 per page. Cert fee- $1.00 per cert plus copy fee. Payee- Morgan County Clerk. **Other phones:** Treasurer- 304-258-8562; Appraiser/Auditor- 304-258-8570; Elections- 304-258-8547; Vital Records- 304-258-8547. **Property tax/Assessor-** 81 Fairfax St, Berkeley Springs, WV 25411; 304-258-8570.

Nicholas County

County Clerk, 700 Main St; #2, Summersville, WV 26651. 304-872-7820; fax-304-872-9600; hours: 8:30AM-4:30PM.

Separate indices to search include deeds, frauds, lien searches, tax liens, judgment & execution, mechanic liens. Records indexed on a public use terminal. Only the public may search. Copy fee $1.50 1st 2 pages; $1.00 each add'l. Cert fee- $1.00 per cert. **Other phones:** Treasurer- 304-872-3630 x42; Elections- 304-872-7820; Vital Records- 304-872-7820. **Property tax/Assessor-** 304-872-7800.

Ohio County Clerks Office

County Clerk, 1500 Chapline St Rm 205, Wheeling, WV 26003. 304-234-3656; fax-304-234-3829; hours: 8:30AM-5PM.

Separate indices to search include deed, lien, will, birth, death, marriage. Only the public may search. Copy fee $.50 per page. Cert fee- $1.00 per page, copies not included. Payee- Ohio County Clerk. **Other phones:** Treasurer- 304-234-3688. **Property tax/Assessor-** 304-234-3626.

Pendleton County

County Clerk, PO Box 1167, Franklin, WV 26807-0089. 304-358-2505; fax-304-358-2473; hours: 8:30AM-4PM.

Index: Lien and right of ways are in separate indices from regular records. Office will perform a UCC search but public must search other records themselves. UCC search per debtor name- $2.00. Copy fee $1.50 per 2 pages, then $1.00 per page. Cert fee- $1.00 per doc plus copy fee. **Other phones:** Treasurer- 304-358-2214. **Property tax/Assessor-** PO Box 937, Franklin, WV 26807-0937; 304-358-2563.

Pleasants County

County Clerk, 301 Court Lane, Rm 101; Courthouse, St. Marys, WV 26170. 304-684-3542; fax-304-684-7569; hours: 8:30AM-4:30PM.

Separate indices to search include wills, marriages, deaths, deed of trusts, releases, deeds, final settlements of estates. Office will perform a UCC search but public must search other records themselves. UCC search per debtor name- $11.00. Copy fee $1.50 1st 2 pages; $1.00 each add'l. Cert fee- $1.00 per doc plus copy fee. Payee- County Clerk. **Other phones:** Treasurer- 304-684-2285; Appraiser/Auditor- 304-684-3542; Elections- 304-684-3542; Vital Records- 304-684-3542; Sheriff- 304-684-2285. **Property tax/Assessor-** 304-684-3132.

Pocahontas County

County Clerk, 900C 10th Ave, Marlinton, WV 24954. 304-799-4549; fax-304-799-6947; 8:30AM-4:30PM.

All records in one index. Only the public may search, except UCC. Will search UCC records, but not tax liens. UCC search per debtor name- $1.00. Copy fee $1.50 1st 2 pages; $1.00 each add'l. Cert

fee- $1.00 per cert plus copy fee. Payee- Pocahontas County Clerk. **Other phones:** Treasurer- 304-799-4710. **Property tax/Assessor-** 304-799-4750.

Preston County

County Clerk, 101 W. Main St, Rm 201, Kingwood, WV 26537. 304-329-0070; fax-304-329-0198; hours: 9AM-5PM (Fri open until 7PM).

Index: Pre- 2001 indices to search include deeds, liens. Now all in one. Office will perform a UCC search but public must search other records themselves. UCC search per debtor name- $5.00. Copy fee $1.50 for 1st 2 pages; $1.00 each add'l. Cert fee- $1.00 per page plus copy fee. Payee- Preston County Clerk. **Other phones:** Treasurer- 304-329-0105; Appraiser/Auditor- 304-329-0070; Elections- 304-329-0070; Vital Records- 304-329-0070. **Property tax/Assessor-** 101 W. Main St, Rm 203, Kingwood, WV 26537; 304-329-1220.

Putnam County

County Clerk, 3389 Winfield Rd., Winfield, WV 25213-9705. 304-586-0202; fax-304-586-0280; hours: 8AM-4PM.

All records in one index. Records indexed on a public use terminal back to 3/1997. Only the public may search. Copy fee $1.50 1st 2 pages, $1.00 each add'l. Cert fee- $1.00 per cert plus copy fee. Payee- Putnam County Clerk. **Other phones:** Treasurer- 304-586-0204. **Property tax/Assessor-** same address as above. 304-586-0206.

Raleigh County

County Clerk, 215 Main St; Courthouse, Beckley, WV 25801. 304-255-9123, R/E recording phone-304-255-9125, UCC recording phone-304-255-9123; fax-304-255-9352; hours: 8:30AM-4PM.

All records in one index. Records indexed on a public use terminal back to 1990. Only the public may search. Copy fee $1.50 1st 2 pages; $1.00 each add'l. Cert fee- $1.00 per page plus copy fee. Payee- Raleigh County Clerk. **Other phones:** Treasurer- 304-255-9300; Appraiser/Auditor- 304-255-9177; Elections- 304-255-9127; Vital Records- 304-255-9123. **Property tax/Assessor-** same address as above. 304-255-9179.

Randolph County

County Clerk, PO Box 368, Elkins, WV 26241. 304-636-0543; hours: 8AM-4:30PM.

Only the public may search. Copy fee $1.50 1st 2 pages; $1.00 each add'l. Cert fee- $1.00 per cert plus copy fee. Payee- Randolph County Clerk. **Other phones:** Treasurer- 304-636-2100; Sheriff- 304-636-2100. **Property tax/Assessor-** 304-636-2114.

Ritchie County

County Clerk, 115 E. Main St; Courthouse - Rm 201, Harrisville, WV 26362. 304-643-2164, R/E recording phone-304-643-2164 x227, UCC recording phone-304-643-2164 x221; fax-304-643-2906; 8AM-4PM.

Separate indices to search include UCC financing statements, releases prior to July 1, 1985; Estate appraisements prior to 7/1/1985; Appointments & bonds prior to 7/1/1985. Records indexed on a public use terminal back to July, 1985. Only the public may search. Copy fee $1.50 1st 2 pages, $1.00 each add'l. Cert fee- $1.00 per cert plus copy fee. Payee- Ritchie County Clerk. **Other phones:** Treasurer- 304-643-2164 x237; Appraiser/Auditor- 304-643-2164 x242; Elections- 304-643-2164 x225; Vital Records- 304-643-2164 x221; Sheriff- 304-643-2164 x237. **Property tax/Assessor-** 304-643-2164 x242.

Roane County

County Clerk, PO Box 69, Spencer, WV 25276. 304-927-2860; fax-304-927-2489; hours: 8:30AM-4PM M-F; 9AM-N Sat.

Separate indices to search include deeds, liens. Only the public may search. Copy fee $1.50 1st 2

pages, $1.00 each add'l. Cert fee- $1.00 per cert plus copy fee. Payee- Roane County Clerk. **Other phones:** Treasurer- 304-927-2540; Appraiser/Auditor- 304-927-3020; Elections- 304-927-2860; Vital Records- 304-927-2860; Law Enforcement- 304-927-3410; County Commission -304-927-0078. **Property tax/Assessor-** same address as above. 304-927-3020.

Summers County

County Clerk, PO Box 97, Hinton, WV 25951-0097. 304-466-7104; fax-304-466-7146; 8:30AM-4:30PM.

Index: There are separate indices to search. Only the public may search. Copy fee $1.50 1st 2 pages; $1.00 each add'l. Cert fee- None. Payee- Summers County Clerk. **Other phones:** Treasurer- 304-466-7112; Elections- 304-466-7104; Vital Records- 304-466-7104; Sheriff- 304-466-7112. **Property tax/Assessor-** 120 Ballengee St, Hinton, WV 25951; 304-466-7101.

Taylor County

County Clerk, 214 W. Main St, Rm 101; Courthouse, Grafton, WV 26354. 304-265-1401; fax-304-265-3016; hours: 8:30-N; 1-4:30PM.

Separate indices to search include deeds, liens, releases, leases. Some only indexed at front of books. Only the public may search. Copy fee $1.50 1st 2 pages; $1.00 each add'l. Payee- Taylor County Clerk. **Other phones:** Treasurer- 304-265-5766; Elections- 304-265-1401; Vital Records- 304-265-1401. **Property tax/Assessor-** 214 W Main St, Grafton, WV 26354; 304-265-2420.

Tucker County

County Clerk, 215 First St. #3, Parsons, WV 26287. 304-478-2414; fax-304-478-2217; hours: 8AM-4PM.

Separate indices to search include Judgments, Deeds of Trust, and Misc Instruments. Only the public may search. Copy fee $1.50 1st 2 pages; $1.00 each add'l. Cert fee- $1.00 per cert plus copy fee. Payee- Tucker County Clerk. **Other phones:** Treasurer- 304-478-2321; Elections- 304-478-2414; Vital Records- 304-478-2414. **Property tax/Assessor-** 304-478-3727.

Tyler County

County Clerk, PO Box 66, Middlebourne, WV 26149. 304-758-2102; fax-304-758-2126; hours: 8AM-Noon M W F; 8AM-Noon 1PM-4PM T TH.

Separate indices to search. Records indexed on a public use terminal back to 1998. Only the public may search. R/E record copy- $1.50 1st 2 pages; $1.00 each add'l page. Cert fee- $1.00 per cert plus copy fee. **Other phones:** Treasurer- 304-758-4551; Elections- 304-758-2034; Vital Records- 304-758-2102. **Property tax/Assessor-** 304-758-4781.

Upshur County

County Clerk, 40 W. Main St; Courthouse - Rm 101, Buckhannon, WV 26201. 304-472-1068; fax-304-472-1029; hours: 8AM-4:30PM.

All records in one index from 1989 to present, prior to 1989 in individual indexes. Records indexed on computer back to 1984. Only the public may search. Copy fee $1.50 1st 2 pages, $1.00 each add'l. Cert fee- $1.00 per doc includes copy fee. Payee- Upshur County Clerk. **Other phones:** Treasurer- 304-472-1180; Appraiser/Auditor- 304-472-4650; Elections- 304-472-1068; Vital Records- 304-472-1068. **Property tax/Assessor-** 38 W Main St Rm 102, Buckhannon, WV 26201; 304-472-4650.

Wayne County

Clerk of County Commission, PO Box 248, Wayne, WV 25570. 304-272-5974; fax-304-272-5318; hours: 8AM-4PM MTWF; 8AM-8PM TH.

Separate indices to search include Deed (Grantor/Grantee), Debtor (Lien/Release). Only the public may search. R/E or tax lien copy- $1.50 1st 2 pages, $1.00 each add'l page. Cert fee- $1.50 per cert plus copy fee. Payee- Wayne County

Clerk. **Other phones:** Treasurer- 304-272-6721; Elections- 304-272-6370; Vital Records- 304-272-6371. **Property tax/Assessor-** Rm 105 Hendricks St, Wayne, WV 25570; 304-272-6357.

Webster County

County Clerk, 2 Court Sq; Courthouse - Rm G-1, Webster Springs, WV 26288-1054. 304-847-2508; fax-304-847-5780; hours: 8:30AM-4PM.
Index: All are separate before 7/1/1979. Only the public may search. Copy fee $1.50 per page; $1.00 per page after 2nd. Cert fee- $1.00 per page plus copy fee. Payee- Terry J. Payne, Clerk. **Other phones:** Treasurer- 304-847-2006; Elections- 304-847-2508; Vital Records- 304-847-2508. **Property tax/Assessor-** same address as above. 304-847-2110.

Wetzel County

County Clerk, PO Box 156, New Martinsville, WV 26155-0156. 304-455-8224; fax-304-455-5256; hours: 9AM-4:40 M,T,W,F; 9AM-4PM Th; 9AM-N Sat.
Separate indices to search include liens, wills, fiduciary records, marriages, births, deaths, plats, and all deeds including oil/gas, miscellaneous, and releases. Records indexed on a public use terminal back to 1993. Office will perform a UCC search but public must search other records themselves. Will not search real estate records. UCC search per debtor name- $2.00. Copy fee $1.50 per UCC; if

real estate $1.50 1st 2 pages; $1.00 each add'l. Cert fee- $1.00 per doc plus copy fee. **Other phones:** Treasurer- 304-455-8218; Elections- 304-455-8235; Vital Records- 304-455-8224. **Property tax/Assessor-** PO Box 7, New Martinsville, WV 26155; 304-455-8214.

Wirt County

County Clerk, PO Box 53, Elizabeth, WV 26143. 304-275-4271; fax-304-275-3418; hours: 8:30AM-4PM. Record index not computerized. Office will perform a UCC and Tax lien search but public must search other records themselves. No search fee. Copy fee $1.50 1st 2pages, $1.00 add'l per page. Cert fee- $1.00 per cert plus copy fee. Payee- Wirt County Clerk. **Other phones:** Treasurer- 304-275-4222; Elections- 304-275-4271; Vital Records- 304-275-4271. **Property tax/Assessor-** PO Box 548, Elizabeth, WV 26143; 304-275-3192.

Wood County

County Clerk, PO Box 1474, Parkersburg, WV 26102-1474. 304-424-1850, R/E recording phone-304-424-1870, UCC recording phone-304-424-1899; fax-304-424-1864; hours: 8:30AM-4:30PM. www.woodcountywv.com/countyclerk/index.html Separate indices to search include deed, lien. UCC, birth records, death records, wills & appraisement, marriage and military discharge indexes. Office will perform a UCC search but public must search

other records themselves. UCC search per debtor name- $11.00. Copy fee $1.50 1st 2 pages; $1.00 each add'l. Cert fee- $1.00 per cert plus copy fee. Payee- Wood County Clerk. **Online access to Recording, Deed, Will, Death, Birth, Marriage, Lien records:** Access is by dial-up modem; visit www.woodcountywv.com/countyclerk/modem.htm for instructions for free connection. Records go back to July1, 1986. (click on document imaging to download). **Other phones:** Treasurer- 304-424-1910; Appraiser/Auditor- 304-424-1875; Elections- 304-424-1860; Vital Records- 304-424-1844 or 424-1845; Probate- 304-424-1891. **Property tax/Assessor-** 1 Court Sq, #302, Parkersburg, WV 26102; 304-424-1875.

Wyoming County

County Clerk, PO Box 309, Pineville, WV 24874. 304-732-8000; fax-304-732-9659; hours: 8AM-4PM M-TH; 8AM-6PM F.
Separate indices to search include deeds, trust deeds, judgments, UCC's. Only the public may search. Copy fee $1.50 for 1st 2 pages, $1.00 each add'l page. Cert fee- $2.50 per doc plus copy fee. Payee- Wyoming City Clerk. **Other phones:** Treasurer- 304-732-8000; Sheriff- 304-732-8000. **Property tax/Assessor-** PO Box 929, Pineville, WV 24874; 304-732-8000.

West Virginia County Locator

You will usually be able to find the city name in the City/County Cross Reference below. In that case, it is a simple matter to determine the county from the cross reference. However, only the official US Postal Service city names are included in this index. There are an additional 40,000 place names that people use in their addresses. Therefore, we have also included a ZIP/City Cross Reference immediately following the City/County Cross Reference.

If you know the ZIP Code but the city name does not appear in the City/County Cross Reference index, look up the ZIP Code in the ZIP/City Cross Reference, find the city name, then look up the city name in the City/County Cross Reference. For example, you want to know the county for an address of Menands, NY 12204. There is no "Menands" in the City/County Cross Reference. The ZIP/City Cross Reference shows that ZIP Codes 12201-12288 are for the city of Albany. Looking back in the City/County Cross Reference, Albany is in Albany County.

West Virginia City/County Cross Reference

ACCOVILLE Logan
ADRIAN Upshur
ADVENT Jackson
ALBRIGHT Preston
ALDERSON (24910) Greenbrier(73), Summers(20), Monroe(6)
ALKOL Lincoln
ALLEN JUNCTION Wyoming
ALLOY Fayette
ALMA Tyler
ALPOCA Wyoming
ALUM BRIDGE (26321) Lewis(97), Doddridge(1)
ALUM CREEK (25003) Kanawha(54), Lincoln(45)
ALVY Tyler
AMEAGLE Raleigh
AMHERSTDALE Logan
AMIGO Wyoming
AMMA Roane
ANAWALT McDowell
ANMOORE Harrison
ANSTED Fayette
APPLE GROVE Mason
ARBOVALE Pocahontas
ARNETT Raleigh
ARNOLDSBURG Calhoun
ARTHUR Grant
ARTHURDALE Preston
ARTIE Raleigh
ASBURY Greenbrier
ASHFORD Boone
ASHLAND McDowell
ASHTON Mason
ATHENS Mercer
AUBURN Ritchie
AUGUSTA Hampshire
AURORA Preston
AUTO Greenbrier
AVONDALE McDowell
BAISDEN Mingo
BAKER Hardy
BAKERTON Jefferson
BALD KNOB Boone
BALLARD Monroe
BALLENGEE (24919) Summers(54), Monroe(45)
BANCROFT Putnam
BARBOURSVILLE Cabell
BARRACKVILLE Marion
BARRETT Boone
BARTLEY McDowell
BARTOW Pocahontas
BAXTER Marion
BEARDS FORK Fayette
BEAVER Raleigh
BECKLEY Raleigh
BECKWITH Fayette
BEECH BOTTOM Brooke
BEESON Mercer
BELINGTON Barbour
BELLE Kanawha
BELLEVILLE (26133) Wood(98), Jackson(1)
BELMONT Pleasants

BELVA (26656) Nicholas(82), Fayette(14), Clay(2)
BENS RUN Tyler
BENTREE Clay
BENWOOD Marshall
BEREA Ritchie
BERGOO Webster
BERKELEY SPRINGS Morgan
BERWIND McDowell
BETHANY (26032) Brooke(97), Ohio(2)
BEVERLY Randolph
BICKMORE Clay
BIG BEND Calhoun
BIG CREEK Logan
BIG RUN Wetzel
BIG SANDY McDowell
BIG SPRINGS Calhoun
BIM Boone
BIRCH RIVER (26610) Nicholas(96), Webster(3)
BLACKSVILLE Monongalia
BLAIR Logan
BLANDVILLE Doddridge
BLOOMERY Hampshire
BLOOMINGROSE Boone
BLOUNT Kanawha
BLUE CREEK Kanawha
BLUE JAY Raleigh
BLUEFIELD Mercer
BOB WHITE Boone
BOGGS Webster
BOLT Raleigh
BOMONT Clay
BOOMER Fayette
BOOTH Monongalia
BORDERLAND Mingo
BOWDEN (26254) Randolph(96), Tucker(3)
BOZOO Monroe
BRADLEY Raleigh
BRADSHAW McDowell
BRAMWELL Mercer
BRANCHLAND (25506) Lincoln(97), Cabell(2)
BRANDONVILLE Preston
BRANDYWINE Pendleton
BREEDEN Mingo
BRENTON Wyoming
BRETZ Preston
BRIDGEPORT (26330) Harrison(91), Taylor(7), Barbour(1)
BRISTOL (26332) Harrison(97), Doddridge(2)
BROHARD (26138) Wirt(77), Calhoun(22)
BROOKS Summers
BROWNTON Barbour
BRUCETON MILLS Preston
BRUNO Logan
BUCKEYE Pocahontas
BUCKHANNON (26201) Upshur(95), Lewis(3)
BUD Wyoming
BUFFALO Putnam
BUNKER HILL Berkeley
BURLINGTON (26710) Mineral(85), Hampshire(14)

BURNSVILLE (26335) Braxton(55), Gilmer(44)
BURNWELL (25034) Kanawha(50), Putnam(50)
BURTON (26562) Monongalia(56), Wetzel(43)
CABIN CREEK Kanawha
CABINS Grant
CAIRO Ritchie
CALDWELL (24925) Greenbrier(82), Monroe(17)
CALVIN Nicholas
CAMDEN Lewis
CAMDEN ON GAULEY Webster
CAMERON Marshall
CAMP CREEK Mercer
CANABRAKE McDowell
CANEBRAKE McDowell
CANNELTON Fayette
CANVAS Nicholas
CAPELS McDowell
CAPON BRIDGE Hampshire
CAPON SPRINGS Hampshire
CARETTA McDowell
CAROLINA Marion
CASS Pocahontas
CASSVILLE Monongalia
CEDAR GROVE Kanawha
CEDARVILLE (26611) Braxton(56), Gilmer(43)
CENTER POINT Doddridge
CENTRALIA Braxton
CENTURY Barbour
CEREDO Wayne
CHAPMANVILLE (25508) Logan(89), Boone(10)
CHARLES TOWN Jefferson
CHARLESTON Kanawha
CHARLTON HEIGHTS Fayette
CHARMCO Greenbrier
CHATTAROY Mingo
CHAUNCEY Logan
CHESTER Hancock
CHLOE (25235) Calhoun(85), Clay(14)
CIRCLEVILLE Pendleton
CLARKSBURG Harrison
CLAY (25043) Clay(98), Nicholas(1)
CLEAR CREEK Raleigh
CLEAR FORK Wyoming
CLENDENIN (25045) Roane(40), Kanawha(38), Clay(20)
CLEVELAND (26215) Upshur(97), Webster(2)
CLIFTON Mason
CLINTONVILLE Greenbrier
CLIO Roane
CLOTHIER (25047) Boone(58), Logan(41)
COAL CITY Raleigh
COAL MOUNTAIN Wyoming
COALTON Randolph
COALWOOD McDowell
COLCORD Raleigh
COLFAX Marion
COLLIERS Brooke
COMFORT Boone
COOL RIDGE Raleigh

COPEN Braxton
CORA Logan
CORE Monongalia
CORINNE Wyoming
CORINTH Preston
COSTA Boone
COTTAGEVILLE (25239) Jackson(83), Mason(16)
COTTLE Nicholas
COVEL Wyoming
COWEN Webster
COXS MILLS (26342) Gilmer(98), Ritchie(1)
CRAB ORCHARD Raleigh
CRAIGSVILLE Nicholas
CRANBERRY Raleigh
CRAWFORD (26343) Lewis(80), Upshur(19)
CRAWLEY Greenbrier
CRESTON (26141) Wirt(72), Calhoun(27)
CRICHTON Greenbrier
CROWN HILL Kanawha
CRUM Wayne
CRUMPLER McDowell
CUCUMBER McDowell
CULLODEN (25510) Cabell(67), Putnam(21), Lincoln(10)
CUZZART Preston
CYCLONE Wyoming
DAILEY Randolph
DALLAS Marshall
DANESE Fayette
DANIELS Raleigh
DANVILLE Boone
DAVIN (25617) Logan(83), Wyoming(16)
DAVIS Tucker
DAVISVILLE Wood
DAVY (24828) McDowell(98), Wyoming(1)
DAWES Kanawha
DAWMONT Harrison
DEEP WATER Fayette
DELBARTON Mingo
DELLSLOW Monongalia
DELRAY Hampshire
DIANA Webster
DILLE (26617) Clay(98), Nicholas(1)
DINGESS Mingo
DIXIE (25059) Nicholas(85), Fayette(14)
DOROTHY Raleigh
DOTHAN Fayette
DRENNEN Nicholas
DRY CREEK Raleigh
DRYBRANCH Kanawha
DRYFORK (26263) Tucker(66), Randolph(33)
DUCK (25063) Clay(92), Braxton(7)
DUNBAR Kanawha
DUNLOW Wayne
DUNMORE Pocahontas
DURBIN Pocahontas
EAST BANK Kanawha
EAST LYNN Wayne
ECCLES Raleigh
ECKMAN McDowell
EDGARTON Mingo
EDMOND Fayette

EGLON Preston
ELBERT McDowell
ELEANOR Putnam
ELIZABETH (26143) Wirt(85), Ritchie(10), Wood(2), Jackson(1)
ELK GARDEN (26717) Mineral(79), Grant(20)
ELKHORN McDowell
ELKINS Randolph
ELKVIEW (25071) Kanawha(94), Roane(5)
ELLAMORE Randolph
ELLENBORO (26346) Ritchie(50), Pleasants(43), Tyler(6)
ELMIRA Braxton
ELTON Summers
EMMETT Logan
ENGLISH McDowell
ENTERPRISE Harrison
ERBACON Webster
ESKDALE Kanawha
ETHEL Logan
EUREKA Pleasants
EVANS (25241) Jackson(87), Mason(12)
EVERETTVILLE Monongalia
EXCHANGE Braxton
FAIRDALE Raleigh
FAIRLEA Greenbrier
FAIRMONT (26554) Marion(96), Monongalia(3)
FAIRMONT Marion
FAIRVIEW Marion
FALLING ROCK Kanawha
FALLING WATERS Berkeley
FALLS MILL Braxton
FANROCK Wyoming
FARMINGTON Marion
FENWICK Nicholas
FISHER Hardy
FIVE FORKS Calhoun
FLAT TOP Mercer
FLATWOODS Braxton
FLEMINGTON (26347) Taylor(67), Barbour(32)
FOLA Clay
FOLLANSBEE Brooke
FOLSOM Wetzel
FOREST HILL Summers
FORT ASHBY Mineral
FORT GAY Wayne
FORT SEYBERT Pendleton
FORT SPRING Greenbrier
FOSTER Boone
FOUR STATES Marion
FRAMETOWN (26623) Braxton(97), Gilmer(2)
FRANKFORD Greenbrier
FRANKLIN Pendleton
FRAZIERS BOTTOM (25082) Putnam(57), Mason(41)
FREEMAN Mercer
FRENCH CREEK Upshur
FRENCHTON Upshur
FRIARS HILL Greenbrier
FRIENDLY (26146) Tyler(54), Pleasants(45)
GALLAGHER (25083) Kanawha(93), Fayette(6)
GALLIPOLIS FERRY Mason
GALLOWAY Barbour
GANDEEVILLE Roane
GAP MILLS Monroe
GARY McDowell
GASSAWAY Braxton
GAULEY BRIDGE (25085) Fayette(61), Kanawha(38)
GAY (25244) Roane(55), Jackson(44)
GENOA Wayne
GERRARDSTOWN Berkeley
GHENT Raleigh
GILBERT Mingo
GILBOA Nicholas
GILMER Gilmer

GIVEN (25245) Jackson(88), Putnam(11)
GLACE Monroe
GLADY Randolph
GLASGOW Kanawha
GLEN Clay
GLEN DALE Marshall
GLEN DANIEL Raleigh
GLEN EASTON Marshall
GLEN FERRIS Fayette
GLEN FORK Wyoming
GLEN JEAN Fayette
GLEN MORGAN Raleigh
GLEN ROGERS Wyoming
GLEN WHITE Raleigh
GLENDON Braxton
GLENGARY Berkeley
GLENHAYES Wayne
GLENVILLE Gilmer
GLENWOOD (25520) Mason(54), Cabell(45)
GORDON Boone
GORMANIA Grant
GRAFTON Taylor
GRANT TOWN Marion
GRANTSVILLE Calhoun
GRANVILLE Monongalia
GRASSY MEADOWS Greenbrier
GREAT CACAPON Morgan
GREEN BANK Pocahontas
GREEN SPRING Hampshire
GREEN SULPHUR SPRINGS Summers
GREENVILLE Monroe
GREENWOOD (26360) Doddridge(58), Ritchie(31), Tyler(10)
GRIFFITHSVILLE Lincoln
GRIMMS LANDING Mason
GYPSY Harrison
HACKER VALLEY Webster
HALLTOWN Jefferson
HAMBLETON Tucker
HAMLIN (25523) Lincoln(90), Putnam(9)
HAMPDEN Mingo
HANDLEY Kanawha
HANOVER Wyoming
HANSFORD Kanawha
HARMAN (26270) Randolph(97), Pendleton(2)
HARMONY (25246) Roane(94), Jackson(5)
HARPER Raleigh
HARPERS FERRY Jefferson
HARRISON Clay
HARRISVILLE Ritchie
HARTFORD Mason
HARTS (25524) Lincoln(82), Logan(14), Wayne(2)
HAVACO McDowell
HAYWOOD Harrison
HAZELGREEN Ritchie
HAZELTON Preston
HEATERS Braxton
HEDGESVILLE (25427) Berkeley(82), Morgan(17)
HELEN Raleigh
HELVETIA (26224) Randolph(86), Upshur(13)
HEMPHILL McDowell
HENDERSON Mason
HENDRICKS Tucker
HENLAWSON Logan
HENSLEY McDowell
HEPZIBAH Harrison
HERNDON Wyoming
HERNSHAW Kanawha
HEWETT (25108) Boone(89), Logan(10)
HIAWATHA Mercer
HICO Fayette
HIGH VIEW Hampshire
HILLSBORO Pocahontas
HILLTOP Fayette
HINES Greenbrier
HINTON Summers
HOLDEN Logan

HOMETOWN Putnam
HORNER Lewis
HUGHESTON Kanawha
HUNDRED (26575) Wetzel(88), Monongalia(11)
HUNTINGTON (25701) Cabell(97), Wayne(2)
HUNTINGTON (25704) Wayne(58), Cabell(41)
HUNTINGTON Cabell
HUNTINGTON Wayne
HURRICANE Putnam
HUTTONSVILLE Randolph
IAEGER (24844) McDowell(87), Wyoming(12)
IDAMAY Marion
IKES FORK Wyoming
IMPERIAL JUNCTION (25034) Kanawha(50), Putnam(50)
INDEPENDENCE (26374) Preston(67), Monongalia(16), Taylor(15)
INDORE Clay
INDUSTRIAL Harrison
INSTITUTE Kanawha
INWOOD Berkeley
IRELAND (26376) Lewis(87), Braxton(12)
ISABAN McDowell
ITMANN Wyoming
IVYDALE Clay
JACKSONBURG (26377) Wetzel(62), Tyler(37)
JANE LEW (26378) Lewis(89), Harrison(10)
JEFFREY Boone
JENKINJONES McDowell
JESSE Wyoming
JODIE Fayette
JOLO McDowell
JONBEN Raleigh
JOSEPHINE Raleigh
JULIAN Boone
JUMPING BRANCH (25969) Summers(87), Raleigh(12)
JUNCTION Hampshire
JUNIOR Barbour
JUSTICE Mingo
KANAWHA FALLS Fayette
KANAWHA HEAD Upshur
KEARNEYSVILLE (25430) Jefferson(83), Berkeley(16)
KEARNEYSVILLE Jefferson
KEGLEY Mercer
KELLYSVILLE Mercer
KENNA Jackson
KENOVA Wayne
KENTUCK Jackson
KERENS (26276) Randolph(75), Tucker(24)
KERMIT (25674) Mingo(67), Wayne(32)
KESLERS CROSS LANES Nicholas
KEYSER Mineral
KEYSTONE McDowell
KIAHSVILLE Wayne
KIEFFER Greenbrier
KILSYTH Fayette
KIMBALL McDowell
KIMBERLY Fayette
KINCAID Fayette
KINGMONT Marion
KINGSTON Fayette
KINGWOOD Preston
KIRBY (26729) Hampshire(82), Hardy(17)
KISTLER Logan
KOPPERSTON Wyoming
KYLE McDowell
LAHMANSVILLE Grant
LAKE Logan
LAKIN Mason
LANARK Raleigh
LANSING Fayette
LASHMEET Mercer
LAVALETTE Wayne

LAYLAND (25864) Raleigh(78), Fayette(21)
LE ROY (25252) Roane(48), Jackson(44), Wirt(6)
LECKIE McDowell
LEEWOOD Kanawha
LEFT HAND Roane
LEIVASY Nicholas
LENORE Mingo
LEON (25123) Mason(66), Putnam(33)
LERONA Mercer
LESAGE Cabell
LESLIE Greenbrier
LESTER Raleigh
LETART Mason
LETTER GAP Gilmer
LEVELS Hampshire
LEWISBURG Greenbrier
LIBERTY (25124) Putnam(93), Jackson(4), Kanawha(2)
LIMA Tyler
LINDEN Roane
LINDSIDE Monroe
LINN (26384) Gilmer(67), Lewis(31), Braxton(1)
LITTLE BIRCH Braxton
LITTLETON Wetzel
LIZEMORES Clay
LOCHGELLY Fayette
LOCKBRIDGE Summers
LOCKNEY Gilmer
LOGAN Logan
LONDON Kanawha
LONG BRANCH Fayette
LOOKOUT Fayette
LOONEYVILLE Roane
LORADO Logan
LORENTZ Upshur
LOST CITY Hardy
LOST CREEK Harrison
LOST RIVER Hardy
LUMBERPORT Harrison
LUNDALE Logan
LYBURN Logan
LYNCO Wyoming
MABEN Wyoming
MABIE Randolph
MABSCOTT Raleigh
MAC ARTHUR Raleigh
MACFARLAN Ritchie
MADISON Boone
MAHAN Fayette
MAIDSVILLE Monongalia
MALLORY Logan
MAMMOTH Kanawha
MAN Logan
MANNINGTON (26582) Marion(88), Monongalia(10), Harrison(1)
MAPLEWOOD Fayette
MARIANNA Wyoming
MARLINTON Pocahontas
MARTINSBURG Berkeley
MASON Mason
MASONTOWN (26542) Preston(88), Monongalia(11)
MATEWAN Mingo
MATHENY Wyoming
MATHIAS Hardy
MATOAKA (24736) Mercer(85), Wyoming(14)
MAXWELTON Greenbrier
MAYBEURY McDowell
MAYSEL Clay
MAYSVILLE Grant
MC COMAS Mercer
MC GRAWS Wyoming
MC MECHEN Marshall
MC WHORTER Harrison
MCMECHEN Marshall
MEADOR Mingo
MEADOW BLUFF Greenbrier
MEADOW BRIDGE (25976) Fayette(55), Summers(40), Greenbrier(4)

MEADOW CREEK Summers
MEADOWBROOK Harrison
MEDLEY Grant
METZ (26585) Marion(75), Wetzel(25)
MIAMI Kanawha
MIDDLEBOURNE Tyler
MIDKIFF Lincoln
MIDWAY Raleigh
MILAM (26838) Hardy(94), Pendleton(5)
MILL CREEK Randolph
MILLSTONE Calhoun
MILLVILLE Jefferson
MILLWOOD Jackson
MILTON Cabell
MINDEN Fayette
MINERAL WELLS Wood
MINGO Randolph
MOATSVILLE (26405) Barbour(84), Preston(15)
MOHAWK McDowell
MONAVILLE Logan
MONTANA MINES Marion
MONTCALM Mercer
MONTCOAL Raleigh
MONTERVILLE Randolph
MONTGOMERY (25136) Fayette(61), Kanawha(38)
MONTROSE (26283) Randolph(80), Barbour(12), Tucker(6)
MOOREFIELD Hardy
MORGANTOWN Monongalia
MOUNDSVILLE Marshall
MOUNT ALTO (25264) Jackson(65), Mason(34)
MOUNT CARBON Fayette
MOUNT CLARE Harrison
MOUNT GAY Logan
MOUNT HOPE (25880) Raleigh(59), Fayette(40)
MOUNT LOOKOUT Nicholas
MOUNT NEBO Nicholas
MOUNT OLIVE Fayette
MOUNT STORM Grant
MOUNT ZION Calhoun
MOUNTAIN Ritchie
MOYERS Pendleton
MULLENS Wyoming
MUNDAY (26152) Calhoun(92), Wirt(7)
MURRAYSVILLE (26153) Jackson(88), Wood(11)
MYRA Lincoln
MYRTLE Mingo
NALLEN (26680) Fayette(45), Nicholas(43), Greenbrier(10)
NAOMA Raleigh
NAPIER Braxton
NAUGATUCK Mingo
NEBO (25141) Clay(94), Calhoun(5)
NELLIS Boone
NEMOURS Mercer
NEOLA Greenbrier
NETTIE Nicholas
NEW CREEK (26743) Mineral(71), Grant(28)
NEW CUMBERLAND Hancock
NEW HAVEN Mason
NEW MANCHESTER Hancock
NEW MARTINSVILLE Wetzel
NEW MILTON (26411) Doddridge(90), Gilmer(9)
NEW RICHMOND Wyoming
NEWBERNE (26409) Gilmer(55), Ritchie(44)
NEWBURG Preston
NEWELL Hancock
NEWHALL McDowell
NEWTON Roane
NEWTOWN Mingo
NICUT (26633) Calhoun(62), Braxton(34), Gilmer(3)
NIMITZ Summers
NITRO (25143) Kanawha(73), Putnam(26)

NOLAN Mingo
NORMANTOWN (25267) Gilmer(91), Calhoun(4), Braxton(3)
NORTH MATEWAN Mingo
NORTH SPRING Wyoming
NORTHFORK McDowell
NORTON Randolph
OAK HILL Fayette
OAKVALE Mercer
OCEANA Wyoming
ODD (25902) Raleigh(82), Mercer(17)
OHLEY Kanawha
OLD FIELDS (26845) Hardy(97), Hampshire(2)
OMAR Logan
ONA Cabell
ONEGO Pendleton
ORGAS Boone
ORLANDO (26412) Lewis(94), Gilmer(4), Braxton(1)
ORMA Calhoun
OSAGE Monongalia
OTTAWA Boone
OVAPA (25150) Roane(63), Clay(36)
PADEN CITY (26159) Wetzel(64), Tyler(35)
PAGE Fayette
PAGETON McDowell
PALERMO Lincoln
PALESTINE Wirt
PANTHER McDowell
PARKERSBURG Wood
PARSONS (26287) Tucker(98), Preston(1)
PAW PAW (25434) Hampshire(53), Morgan(46)
PAX Fayette
PAYNESVILLE McDowell
PEACH CREEK Logan
PECKS MILL Logan
PEMBERTON Raleigh
PENCE SPRINGS Summers
PENNSBORO (26415) Ritchie(97), Tyler(2)
PENTRESS Monongalia
PERKINS Gilmer
PETERSBURG (26847) Grant(96), Hardy(3)
PETERSTOWN Monroe
PETROLEUM (26161) Ritchie(91), Wood(5), Wirt(3)
PEYTONA Boone
PHILIPPI Barbour
PICKENS (26230) Randolph(92), Webster(7)
PIEDMONT Mineral
PINCH Kanawha
PINE GROVE Wetzel
PINEVILLE Wyoming
PINEY VIEW Raleigh
PIPESTEM (25979) Summers(78), Mercer(21)
PLINY Putnam
POCA Putnam
POE Nicholas
POINT PLEASANT Mason
POINTS Hampshire
POND GAP Kanawha
POOL Nicholas
PORTERS FALLS Wetzel
POWELLTON Fayette
POWHATAN McDowell
PRATT Kanawha
PREMIER McDowell
PRENTER Boone
PRICHARD Wayne
PRINCE Fayette
PRINCEWICK Raleigh
PROCIOUS (25164) Clay(79), Roane(20)
PROCTOR (26055) Marshall(83), Wetzel(16)
PROSPERITY Raleigh
PULLMAN Ritchie
PURGITSVILLE (26852) Hardy(66), Hampshire(27), Mineral(4)

PURSGLOVE Monongalia
QUINNIMONT Fayette
QUINWOOD (25981) Greenbrier(64), Nicholas(35)
RACHEL Marion
RACINE Boone
RAGLAND Mingo
RAINELLE (25962) Fayette(94), Greenbrier(5)
RALEIGH Raleigh
RAMAGE Boone
RAMSEY Fayette
RANGER (25557) Lincoln(97), Wayne(2)
RANSON Jefferson
RAVENCLIFF Wyoming
RAVENSWOOD (26164) Jackson(88), Wood(11)
RAWL Mingo
RAYSAL McDowell
READER Wetzel
RED CREEK Tucker
RED HOUSE (25168) Putnam(68), Kanawha(31)
RED JACKET Mingo
REDSTAR Fayette
REEDSVILLE Preston
REEDY Roane
RENICK Greenbrier
REYNOLDSVILLE Harrison
RHODELL Raleigh
RICHWOOD (26261) Nicholas(98), Greenbrier(1)
RIDGELEY Mineral
RIDGEVIEW Boone
RIDGEWAY Berkeley
RIO (26755) Hampshire(64), Hardy(35)
RIPLEY Jackson
RIPPON Jefferson
RIVERTON Pendleton
RIVESVILLE (26588) Marion(87), Monongalia(12)
ROANOKE Lewis
ROBERTSBURG Putnam
ROBSON Fayette
ROCK Mercer
ROCK CASTLE Jackson
ROCK CAVE (26234) Upshur(95), Webster(4)
ROCK CREEK Raleigh
ROCK VIEW Wyoming
ROCKPORT Wood
RODERFIELD McDowell
ROMNEY Hampshire
RONCEVERTE (24970) Greenbrier(98), Monroe(1)
ROSEDALE (26636) Gilmer(46), Braxton(31), Calhoun(22)
ROSEMONT Taylor
ROSSMORE Logan
ROWLESBURG (26425) Preston(98), Tucker(1)
RUPERT Greenbrier
SABINE Wyoming
SAINT ALBANS Kanawha
SAINT GEORGE (26290) Tucker(95), Preston(4)
SAINT MARYS (26170) Pleasants(93), Ritchie(5)
SALEM (26426) Harrison(92), Doddridge(7)
SALT ROCK Cabell
SAND FORK Gilmer
SAND RIDGE Calhoun
SANDSTONE Summers
SANDYVILLE Jackson
SARAH ANN Logan
SARTON Monroe
SAULSVILLE Wyoming
SAXON Raleigh
SCARBRO Fayette
SCOTT DEPOT Putnam
SECONDCREEK Monroe

SELBYVILLE (26236) Upshur(57), Randolph(42)
SENECA ROCKS Pendleton
SETH Boone
SHADY SPRING Raleigh
SHANKS Hampshire
SHARON Kanawha
SHARPLES Logan
SHENANDOAH JUNCTION Jefferson
SHEPHERDSTOWN (25443) Jefferson(90), Berkeley(9)
SHERMAN Jackson
SHINNSTON (26431) Harrison(96), Taylor(3)
SHIRLEY Tyler
SHOALS Wayne
SHOCK (26638) Gilmer(95), Calhoun(5)
SHORT CREEK Brooke
SIAS Lincoln
SIMON Wyoming
SIMPSON Taylor
SINKS GROVE Monroe
SISTERSVILLE Tyler
SKELTON Raleigh
SKYGUSTY McDowell
SLAB FORK (25920) Raleigh(90), Wyoming(9)
SLANESVILLE Hampshire
SLATYFORK Pocahontas
SMITHBURG Doddridge
SMITHERS Fayette
SMITHFIELD (26437) Wetzel(92), Marion(7)
SMITHVILLE Ritchie
SMOOT Greenbrier
SNOWSHOE Pocahontas
SOD Lincoln
SOPHIA Raleigh
SOUTHSIDE Mason
SPANISHBURG Mercer
SPELTER Harrison
SPENCER Roane
SPRAGUE Raleigh
SPRIGG Mingo
SPRING DALE Fayette
SPRINGFIELD Hampshire
SPURLOCKVILLE (25565) Lincoln(74), Boone(25)
SQUIRE McDowell
STANAFORD Raleigh
STATTS MILLS Jackson
STEPHENSON Wyoming
STIRRAT Logan
STOLLINGS Logan
STOUTS MILLS Gilmer
STRANGE CREEK (26639) Braxton(71), Nicholas(25), Clay(3)
STUMPTOWN (25280) Gilmer(55), Calhoun(44)
SUGAR GROVE Pendleton
SUMERCO Lincoln
SUMMERLEE Fayette
SUMMERSVILLE Nicholas
SUMMIT POINT Jefferson
SUNDIAL Raleigh
SUPERIOR McDowell
SURVEYOR Raleigh
SUTTON Braxton
SWEET SPRINGS Monroe
SWEETLAND Lincoln
SWISS Nicholas
SWITCHBACK McDowell
SWITZER Logan
SYLVESTER Boone
TAD Kanawha
TALCOTT (24981) Summers(86), Monroe(14)
TALLMANSVILLE Upshur
TANNER Gilmer
TAPLIN Logan
TARIFF Roane
TEAYS Putnam

TERRA ALTA Preston
TERRY Raleigh
THACKER Mingo
THOMAS Tucker
THORNTON (26440) Taylor(67), Preston(24), Barbour(7)
THORPE McDowell
THREE CHURCHES Hampshire
THURMOND Fayette
TIOGA (26691) Nicholas(96), Webster(3)
TORNADO (25202) Lincoln(50), Kanawha(49)
TRIADELPHIA Ohio
TROY (26443) Gilmer(85), Doddridge(14)
TRUE Summers
TUNNELTON Preston
TURTLE CREEK Boone
TWILIGHT Boone
TWIN BRANCH McDowell
UNEEDA Boone
UNION Monroe
UPPER TRACT Pendleton
UPPERGLADE Webster
VALLEY BEND Randolph
VALLEY CHAPEL Lewis
VALLEY FORK Clay
VALLEY GROVE (26060) Ohio(98), Brooke(1)

VALLEY HEAD (26294) Randolph(81), Pocahontas(18)
VAN Boone
VARNEY Mingo
VERDUNVILLE Logan
VERNER (25650) Mingo(71), Logan(28)
VICTOR Fayette
VIENNA Wood
VIVIAN McDowell
VOLGA (26238) Barbour(70), Upshur(27), Harrison(1)
VULCAN Mingo
WADESTOWN Monongalia
WAITEVILLE Monroe
WALKER (26180) Wood(92), Wirt(7)
WALKERSVILLE (26447) Lewis(97), Braxton(2)
WALLACE (26448) Harrison(86), Marion(7), Doddridge(5)
WALLBACK (25285) Clay(98), Roane(1)
WALTON Roane
WANA Monongalia
WAR McDowell
WARDENSVILLE Hardy
WARRIORMINE McDowell
WASHINGTON Wood
WAVERLY (26184) Wood(62), Pleasants(37)

WAYSIDE (24985) Monroe(63), Summers(36)
WEBSTER SPRINGS Webster
WEIRTON (26062) Hancock(85), Brooke(14)
WELCH McDowell
WELLSBURG Brooke
WEST COLUMBIA Mason
WEST HAMLIN Lincoln
WEST LIBERTY Ohio
WEST MILFORD Harrison
WEST UNION (26456) Doddridge(94), Tyler(3), Ritchie(1)
WESTON Lewis
WHARNCLIFFE Mingo
WHARTON Boone
WHEELING Ohio
WHITE OAK (25989) Raleigh(98), Summers(1)
WHITE SULPHUR SPRINGS Greenbrier
WHITESVILLE (25209) Raleigh(84), Boone(15)
WHITMAN Logan
WHITMER Randolph
WICK Tyler
WIDEN Clay
WILCOE McDowell
WILEY FORD Mineral

WILEYVILLE Wetzel
WILKINSON Logan
WILLIAMSBURG Greenbrier
WILLIAMSON Mingo
WILLIAMSTOWN Wood
WILSIE Braxton
WILSONBURG Harrison
WILSONDALE (25699) Wayne(74), Mingo(20), Lincoln(5)
WINDSOR HEIGHTS Brooke
WINFIELD Putnam
WINIFREDE Kanawha
WINONA Fayette
WOLF PEN Wyoming
WOLF SUMMIT Harrison
WOLFCREEK Monroe
WOLFE Mercer
WOODVILLE Lincoln
WORTH McDowell
WORTHINGTON (26591) Marion(96), Harrison(3)
WYATT Harrison
WYCO Wyoming
WYOMING Wyoming
YAWKEY Lincoln
YELLOW SPRING Hampshire
YOLYN Logan
YUKON McDowell

West Virginia ZIP/City Cross Reference

ZIP	City
24701-24701	BLUEFIELD
24710-24710	ALPOCA
24712-24712	ATHENS
24714-24714	BEESON
24715-24715	BRAMWELL
24716-24716	BUD
24719-24719	COVEL
24724-24724	FREEMAN
24726-24726	HERNDON
24729-24729	HIAWATHA
24731-24731	KEGLEY
24732-24732	KELLYSVILLE
24733-24733	LASHMEET
24735-24735	MC COMAS
24736-24736	MATOAKA
24737-24737	MONTCALM
24738-24738	NEMOURS
24739-24739	OAKVALE
24740-24740	PRINCETON
24747-24747	ROCK
24751-24751	WOLFE
24801-24801	WELCH
24808-24808	ANAWALT
24810-24810	ASHLAND
24811-24811	AVONDALE
24813-24813	BARTLEY
24815-24815	BERWIND
24816-24816	BIG SANDY
24817-24817	BRADSHAW
24818-24818	BRENTON
24819-24819	CANEBRAKE
24819-24819	CANABRAKE
24820-24820	CAPELS
24821-24821	CARETTA
24822-24822	CLEAR FORK
24823-24823	COAL MOUNTAIN
24824-24824	COALWOOD
24825-24825	CRUMPLER
24826-24826	CUCUMBER
24827-24827	CYCLONE
24828-24828	DAVY
24829-24829	ECKMAN
24830-24830	ELBERT
24831-24831	ELKHORN
24832-24832	ENGLISH
24834-24834	FANROCK
24836-24836	GARY
24839-24839	HANOVER
24841-24841	HAVACO
24842-24842	HEMPHILL
24843-24843	HENSLEY
24844-24844	IAEGER
24845-24845	IKES FORK
24846-24846	ISABAN
24847-24847	ITMANN
24848-24848	JENKINJONES
24849-24849	JESSE
24850-24850	JOLO
24851-24851	JUSTICE
24852-24852	KEYSTONE
24853-24853	KIMBALL
24854-24854	KOPPERSTON
24855-24855	KYLE
24856-24856	LECKIE
24857-24857	LYNCO
24859-24859	MARIANNA
24860-24860	MATHENY
24861-24861	MAYBEURY
24862-24862	MOHAWK
24866-24866	NEWHALL
24867-24867	NEW RICHMOND
24868-24868	NORTHFORK
24869-24869	NORTH SPRING
24870-24870	OCEANA
24871-24871	PAGETON
24872-24872	PANTHER
24873-24873	PAYNESVILLE
24874-24874	PINEVILLE
24877-24877	POWHATAN
24878-24878	PREMIER
24879-24879	RAYSAL
24880-24880	ROCK VIEW
24881-24881	RODERFIELD
24882-24882	SIMON
24883-24883	SKYGUSTY
24884-24884	SQUIRE
24886-24886	SUPERIOR
24887-24887	SWITCHBACK
24888-24888	THORPE
24889-24889	TWIN BRANCH
24891-24891	VIVIAN
24892-24892	WAR
24894-24894	WARRIORMINE
24895-24895	WILCOE
24896-24896	WOLF PEN
24897-24897	WORTH
24898-24898	WYOMING
24899-24899	YUKON
24901-24901	LEWISBURG
24902-24902	FAIRLEA
24910-24910	ALDERSON
24915-24915	ARBOVALE
24916-24916	ASBURY
24917-24917	AUTO
24918-24918	BALLARD
24919-24919	BALLENGEE
24920-24920	BARTOW
24923-24923	BOZOO
24924-24924	BUCKEYE
24925-24925	CALDWELL
24927-24927	CASS
24928-24928	CLINTONVILLE
24931-24931	CRAWLEY
24934-24934	DUNMORE
24935-24935	FOREST HILL
24936-24936	FORT SPRING
24938-24938	FRANKFORD
24939-24939	FRIARS HILL
24941-24941	GAP MILLS
24942-24942	GLACE
24943-24943	GRASSY MEADOWS
24944-24944	GREEN BANK
24945-24945	GREENVILLE
24946-24946	HILLSBORO
24950-24950	KIEFFER
24951-24951	LINDSIDE
24954-24954	MARLINTON
24957-24957	MAXWELTON
24958-24958	MEADOW BLUFF
24961-24961	NEOLA
24962-24962	PENCE SPRINGS
24963-24963	PETERSTOWN
24966-24966	RENICK
24970-24970	RONCEVERTE
24973-24973	SARTON
24974-24974	SECONDCREEK
24976-24976	SINKS GROVE
24977-24977	SMOOT
24980-24980	SWEET SPRINGS
24981-24981	TALCOTT
24983-24983	UNION
24984-24984	WAITEVILLE
24985-24985	WAYSIDE
24986-24986	WHITE SULPHUR SPRINGS
24991-24991	WILLIAMSBURG
24993-24993	WOLFCREEK
25002-25002	ALLOY
25003-25003	ALUM CREEK
25004-25004	AMEAGLE
25005-25005	AMMA
25007-25007	ARNETT
25008-25008	ARTIE
25009-25009	ASHFORD
25010-25010	BALD KNOB
25011-25011	BANCROFT
25013-25013	BARRETT
25014-25014	BEARDS FORK
25015-25015	BELLE
25018-25018	BENTREE
25019-25019	BICKMORE
25021-25021	BIM
25022-25022	BLAIR
25024-25024	BLOOMINGROSE
25025-25025	BLOUNT
25026-25026	BLUE CREEK
25028-25028	BOB WHITE
25030-25030	BOMONT
25031-25031	BOOMER
25033-25033	BUFFALO
25034-25034	BURNWELL
25034-25034	IMPERIAL JUNCTION
25034-25034	BURNWELL
25035-25035	CABIN CREEK
25036-25036	CANNELTON
25039-25039	CEDAR GROVE
25040-25040	CHARLTON HEIGHTS
25043-25043	CLAY
25044-25044	CLEAR CREEK
25045-25045	CLENDENIN
25046-25046	CLIO
25047-25047	CLOTHIER
25048-25048	COLCORD
25049-25049	COMFORT
25051-25051	COSTA
25052-25052	CROWN HILL
25053-25053	DANVILLE
25054-25054	DAWES
25057-25057	DEEP WATER
25059-25059	DIXIE
25060-25060	DOROTHY
25061-25061	DRYBRANCH
25062-25062	DRY CREEK
25063-25063	DUCK
25064-25064	DUNBAR
25067-25067	EAST BANK
25070-25070	ELEANOR
25071-25071	ELKVIEW
25075-25075	ESKDALE
25076-25076	ETHEL
25079-25079	FALLING ROCK
25080-25080	FOLA
25081-25081	FOSTER
25082-25082	FRAZIERS BOTTOM
25083-25083	GALLAGHER
25085-25085	GAULEY BRIDGE
25086-25086	GLASGOW
25088-25088	GLEN
25090-25090	GLEN FERRIS
25093-25093	GORDON
25095-25095	GRIMMS LANDING
25102-25102	HANDLEY
25103-25103	HANSFORD
25105-25105	HARRISON
25106-25106	HENDERSON
25107-25107	HERNSHAW
25108-25108	HEWETT

25109-25109 HOMETOWN	25258-25258 LOCKNEY	25567-25567 SUMERCO	25840-25840 FAYETTEVILLE
25110-25110 HUGHESTON	25259-25259 LOONEYVILLE	25568-25568 SWEETLAND	25841-25841 FLAT TOP
25111-25111 INDORE	25260-25260 MASON	25569-25569 TEAYS	25843-25843 GHENT
25112-25112 INSTITUTE	25261-25261 MILLSTONE	25570-25570 WAYNE	25844-25844 GLEN DANIEL
25113-25113 IVYDALE	25262-25262 MILLWOOD	25571-25571 WEST HAMLIN	25845-25845 GLEN FORK
25114-25114 JEFFREY	25264-25264 MOUNT ALTO	25572-25572 WOODVILLE	25846-25846 GLEN JEAN
25115-25115 KANAWHA FALLS	25265-25265 NEW HAVEN	25573-25573 YAWKEY	25847-25847 GLEN MORGAN
25118-25118 KIMBERLY	25266-25266 NEWTON	25601-25601 LOGAN	25848-25848 GLEN ROGERS
25119-25119 KINCAID	25267-25267 NORMANTOWN	25606-25606 ACCOVILLE	25849-25849 GLEN WHITE
25120-25120 KINGSTON	25268-25268 ORMA	25607-25607 AMHERSTDALE	25851-25851 HARPER
25121-25121 LAKE	25270-25270 REEDY	25608-25608 BAISDEN	25853-25853 HELEN
25122-25122 LEEWOOD	25271-25271 RIPLEY	25611-25611 BRUNO	25854-25854 HICO
25123-25123 LEON	25272-25272 ROCK CASTLE	25612-25612 CHAUNCEY	25855-25855 HILLTOP
25124-25124 LIBERTY	25274-25274 SAND RIDGE	25614-25614 CORA	25856-25856 JONBEN
25125-25125 LIZEMORES	25275-25275 SANDYVILLE	25617-25617 DAVIN	25857-25857 JOSEPHINE
25126-25126 LONDON	25276-25276 SPENCER	25620-25620 EMMETT	25859-25859 KILSYTH
25130-25130 MADISON	25279-25279 STATTS MILLS	25621-25621 GILBERT	25860-25860 LANARK
25131-25131 MAHAN	25280-25280 STUMPTOWN	25623-25623 HAMPDEN	25862-25862 LANSING
25132-25132 MAMMOTH	25281-25281 TARIFF	25624-25624 HENLAWSON	25864-25864 LAYLAND
25133-25133 MAYSEL	25283-25283 VALLEY FORK	25625-25625 HOLDEN	25865-25865 LESTER
25134-25134 MIAMI	25285-25285 WALLBACK	25628-25628 KISTLER	25866-25866 LOCHGELLY
25135-25135 MONTCOAL	25286-25286 WALTON	25630-25630 LORADO	25867-25867 LONG BRANCH
25136-25136 MONTGOMERY	25287-25287 WEST COLUMBIA	25631-25631 LUNDALE	25868-25868 LOOKOUT
25139-25139 MOUNT CARBON	25300-25396 CHARLESTON	25632-25632 LYBURN	25870-25870 MABEN
25140-25140 NAOMA	25401-25402 MARTINSBURG	25634-25634 MALLORY	25871-25871 MABSCOTT
25141-25141 NEBO	25410-25410 BAKERTON	25635-25635 MAN	25873-25873 MAC ARTHUR
25142-25142 NELLIS	25411-25411 BERKELEY SPRINGS	25636-25636 MONAVILLE	25874-25874 MAPLEWOOD
25143-25143 NITRO	25413-25413 BUNKER HILL	25637-25637 MOUNT GAY	25875-25875 MC GRAWS
25147-25147 OHLEY	25414-25414 CHARLES TOWN	25638-25638 OMAR	25876-25876 SAULSVILLE
25148-25148 ORGAS	25419-25419 FALLING WATERS	25639-25639 PEACH CREEK	25878-25878 MIDWAY
25149-25149 OTTAWA	25420-25420 GERRARDSTOWN	25643-25643 ROSSMORE	25879-25879 MINDEN
25150-25150 OVAPA	25421-25421 GLENGARY	25644-25644 SARAH ANN	25880-25880 MOUNT HOPE
25152-25152 PAGE	25422-25422 GREAT CACAPON	25645-25645 STIRRAT	25882-25882 MULLENS
25154-25154 PEYTONA	25423-25423 HALLTOWN	25646-25646 STOLLINGS	25901-25901 OAK HILL
25156-25156 PINCH	25425-25425 HARPERS FERRY	25647-25647 SWITZER	25902-25902 ODD
25158-25158 PLINY	25427-25427 HEDGESVILLE	25648-25648 TAPLIN	25904-25904 PAX
25159-25159 POCA	25428-25428 INWOOD	25649-25649 VERDUNVILLE	25905-25905 PEMBERTON
25160-25160 POND GAP	25429-25430 KEARNEYSVILLE	25650-25650 VERNER	25906-25906 PINEY VIEW
25161-25161 POWELLTON	25431-25431 LEVELS	25651-25651 WHARNCLIFFE	25907-25907 PRINCE
25162-25162 PRATT	25432-25432 MILLVILLE	25652-25652 WHITMAN	25908-25908 PRINCEWICK
25163-25163 PRENTER	25434-25434 PAW PAW	25653-25653 WILKINSON	25909-25909 PROSPERITY
25164-25164 PROCIOUS	25437-25437 POINTS	25654-25654 YOLYN	25910-25910 QUINNIMONT
25165-25165 RACINE	25438-25438 RANSON	25661-25661 WILLIAMSON	25911-25911 RALEIGH
25166-25166 RAMAGE	25440-25440 RIDGEWAY	25665-25665 BORDERLAND	25912-25912 RAMSEY
25168-25168 RED HOUSE	25441-25441 RIPPON	25666-25666 BREEDEN	25913-25913 RAVENCLIFF
25169-25169 RIDGEVIEW	25442-25442 SHENANDOAH JUNCTION	25667-25667 CHATTAROY	25914-25914 REDSTAR
25172-25172 ROBERTSBURG	25443-25443 SHEPHERDSTOWN	25669-25669 CRUM	25915-25915 RHODELL
25173-25173 ROBSON	25444-25444 SLANESVILLE	25670-25670 DELBARTON	25916-25916 SABINE
25174-25174 ROCK CREEK	25446-25446 SUMMIT POINT	25671-25671 DINGESS	25917-25917 SCARBRO
25177-25177 SAINT ALBANS	25501-25501 ALKOL	25672-25672 EDGARTON	25918-25918 SHADY SPRING
25180-25180 SAXON	25502-25502 APPLE GROVE	25674-25674 KERMIT	25919-25919 SKELTON
25181-25181 SETH	25503-25503 ASHTON	25676-25676 LENORE	25920-25920 SLAB FORK
25182-25182 SHARON	25504-25504 BARBOURSVILLE	25678-25678 MATEWAN	25921-25921 SOPHIA
25183-25183 SHARPLES	25505-25505 BIG CREEK	25682-25682 MEADOR	25922-25922 SPANISHBURG
25185-25185 MOUNT OLIVE	25506-25506 BRANCHLAND	25684-25684 MYRTLE	25926-25926 SPRAGUE
25186-25186 SMITHERS	25507-25507 CEREDO	25685-25685 NAUGATUCK	25927-25927 STANAFORD
25187-25187 SOUTHSIDE	25508-25508 CHAPMANVILLE	25686-25686 NEWTOWN	25928-25928 STEPHENSON
25189-25189 SUNDIAL	25510-25510 CULLODEN	25687-25687 NOLAN	25931-25931 SUMMERLEE
25193-25193 SYLVESTER	25511-25511 DUNLOW	25688-25688 NORTH MATEWAN	25932-25932 SURVEYOR
25201-25201 TAD	25512-25512 EAST LYNN	25690-25690 RAGLAND	25934-25934 TERRY
25202-25202 TORNADO	25514-25514 FORT GAY	25691-25691 RAWL	25936-25936 THURMOND
25203-25203 TURTLE CREEK	25515-25515 GALLIPOLIS FERRY	25692-25692 RED JACKET	25938-25938 VICTOR
25204-25204 TWILIGHT	25517-25517 GENOA	25693-25693 SPRIGG	25942-25942 WINONA
25205-25205 UNEEDA	25519-25519 GLENHAYES	25694-25694 THACKER	25943-25943 WYCO
25206-25206 VAN	25520-25520 GLENWOOD	25696-25696 VARNEY	25951-25951 HINTON
25208-25208 WHARTON	25521-25521 GRIFFITHSVILLE	25697-25697 VULCAN	25957-25957 BROOKS
25209-25209 WHITESVILLE	25523-25523 HAMLIN	25699-25699 WILSONDALE	25958-25958 CHARMCO
25211-25211 WIDEN	25524-25524 HARTS	25700-25779 HUNTINGTON	25961-25961 CRICHTON
25213-25213 WINFIELD	25526-25526 HURRICANE	25801-25802 BECKLEY	25962-25962 RAINELLE
25214-25214 WINIFREDE	25529-25529 JULIAN	25810-25810 ALLEN JUNCTION	25965-25965 ELTON
25231-25231 ADVENT	25530-25530 KENOVA	25811-25811 AMIGO	25966-25966 GREEN SULPHUR SPRINGS
25234-25234 ARNOLDSBURG	25534-25534 KIAHSVILLE	25812-25812 ANSTED	25967-25967 HINES
25235-25235 CHLOE	25535-25535 LAVALETTE	25813-25813 BEAVER	25969-25969 JUMPING BRANCH
25237-25237 CLIFTON	25537-25537 LESAGE	25814-25814 BECKWITH	25971-25971 LERONA
25239-25239 COTTAGEVILLE	25540-25540 MIDKIFF	25816-25816 BLUE JAY	25972-25972 LESLIE
25241-25241 EVANS	25541-25541 MILTON	25817-25817 BOLT	25973-25973 LOCKBRIDGE
25243-25243 GANDEEVILLE	25544-25544 MYRA	25818-25818 BRADLEY	25976-25976 MEADOW BRIDGE
25244-25244 GAY	25545-25545 ONA	25820-25820 CAMP CREEK	25977-25977 MEADOW CREEK
25245-25245 GIVEN	25546-25546 PALERMO	25823-25823 COAL CITY	25978-25978 NIMITZ
25246-25246 HARMONY	25547-25547 PECKS MILL	25825-25825 COOL RIDGE	25979-25979 PIPESTEM
25247-25247 HARTFORD	25550-25550 POINT PLEASANT	25826-25826 CORINNE	25981-25981 QUINWOOD
25248-25248 KENNA	25555-25555 PRICHARD	25827-25827 CRAB ORCHARD	25984-25984 RUPERT
25249-25249 KENTUCK	25557-25557 RANGER	25828-25828 CRANBERRY	25985-25985 SANDSTONE
25250-25250 LAKIN	25559-25559 SALT ROCK	25831-25831 DANESE	25986-25986 SPRING DALE
25251-25251 LEFT HAND	25560-25560 SCOTT DEPOT	25832-25832 DANIELS	25988-25988 TRUE
25252-25252 LE ROY	25562-25562 SHOALS	25833-25833 DOTHAN	25989-25989 WHITE OAK
25253-25253 LETART	25563-25563 SIAS	25836-25836 ECCLES	26003-26003 WHEELING
25255-25255 LETTER GAP	25564-25564 SOD	25837-25837 EDMOND	26030-26030 BEECH BOTTOM
25256-25256 LINDEN	25565-25565 SPURLOCKVILLE	25839-25839 FAIRDALE	26031-26031 BENWOOD

26032-26032	BETHANY
26033-26033	CAMERON
26034-26034	CHESTER
26035-26035	COLLIERS
26036-26036	DALLAS
26037-26037	FOLLANSBEE
26038-26038	GLEN DALE
26039-26039	GLEN EASTON
26040-26040	MC MECHEN
26040-26040	MCMECHEN
26041-26041	MOUNDSVILLE
26047-26047	NEW CUMBERLAND
26050-26050	NEWELL
26055-26055	PROCTOR
26056-26056	NEW MANCHESTER
26058-26058	SHORT CREEK
26059-26059	TRIADELPHIA
26060-26060	VALLEY GROVE
26062-26062	WEIRTON
26070-26070	WELLSBURG
26074-26074	WEST LIBERTY
26075-26075	WINDSOR HEIGHTS
26101-26104	PARKERSBURG
26105-26105	VIENNA
26106-26106	PARKERSBURG
26120-26121	MINERAL WELLS
26133-26133	BELLEVILLE
26134-26134	BELMONT
26135-26135	BENS RUN
26136-26136	BIG BEND
26137-26137	BIG SPRINGS
26138-26138	BROHARD
26141-26141	CRESTON
26142-26142	DAVISVILLE
26143-26143	ELIZABETH
26144-26144	EUREKA
26145-26145	FIVE FORKS
26146-26146	FRIENDLY
26147-26147	GRANTSVILLE
26148-26148	MACFARLAN
26149-26149	MIDDLEBOURNE
26150-26150	MINERAL WELLS
26151-26151	MOUNT ZION
26152-26152	MUNDAY
26153-26153	MURRAYSVILLE
26155-26155	NEW MARTINSVILLE
26159-26159	PADEN CITY
26160-26160	PALESTINE
26161-26161	PETROLEUM
26162-26162	PORTERS FALLS
26164-26164	RAVENSWOOD
26167-26167	READER
26169-26169	ROCKPORT
26170-26170	SAINT MARYS
26173-26173	SHERMAN
26175-26175	SISTERSVILLE
26178-26178	SMITHVILLE
26179-26179	TANNER
26180-26180	WALKER
26181-26181	WASHINGTON
26184-26184	WAVERLY
26185-26185	WICK
26186-26186	WILEYVILLE
26187-26187	WILLIAMSTOWN
26201-26201	BUCKHANNON
26202-26202	FENWICK
26203-26203	ERBACON
26205-26205	CRAIGSVILLE
26206-26206	COWEN
26207-26207	COTTLE
26208-26208	CAMDEN ON GAULEY
26209-26209	SNOWSHOE
26210-26210	ADRIAN
26214-26214	CENTURY
26215-26215	CLEVELAND
26217-26217	DIANA
26218-26218	FRENCH CREEK
26219-26219	FRENCHTON
26222-26222	HACKER VALLEY
26224-26224	HELVETIA
26228-26228	KANAWHA HEAD
26229-26229	LORENTZ
26230-26230	PICKENS
26234-26234	ROCK CAVE
26236-26236	SELBYVILLE
26237-26237	TALLMANSVILLE
26238-26238	VOLGA
26241-26241	ELKINS
26250-26250	BELINGTON

26253-26253	BEVERLY
26254-26254	BOWDEN
26257-26257	COALTON
26259-26259	DAILEY
26260-26260	DAVIS
26261-26261	RICHWOOD
26263-26263	DRYFORK
26264-26264	DURBIN
26266-26266	UPPERGLADE
26267-26267	ELLAMORE
26268-26268	GLADY
26269-26269	HAMBLETON
26270-26270	HARMAN
26271-26271	HENDRICKS
26273-26273	HUTTONSVILLE
26275-26275	JUNIOR
26276-26276	KERENS
26278-26278	MABIE
26280-26280	MILL CREEK
26281-26281	MINGO
26282-26282	MONTERVILLE
26283-26283	MONTROSE
26285-26285	NORTON
26287-26287	PARSONS
26288-26288	WEBSTER SPRINGS
26289-26289	RED CREEK
26290-26290	SAINT GEORGE
26291-26291	SLATYFORK
26292-26292	THOMAS
26293-26293	VALLEY BEND
26294-26294	VALLEY HEAD
26296-26296	WHITMER
26298-26298	BERGOO
26299-26299	BOGGS
26301-26306	CLARKSBURG
26320-26320	ALMA
26321-26321	ALUM BRIDGE
26322-26322	ALVY
26323-26323	ANMOORE
26325-26325	AUBURN
26327-26327	BEREA
26328-26328	BLANDVILLE
26330-26330	BRIDGEPORT
26332-26332	BRISTOL
26334-26334	BROWNTON
26335-26335	BURNSVILLE
26337-26337	CAIRO
26338-26338	CAMDEN
26339-26339	CENTER POINT
26342-26342	COXS MILLS
26343-26343	CRAWFORD
26344-26344	DAWMONT
26346-26346	ELLENBORO
26347-26347	FLEMINGTON
26348-26348	FOLSOM
26349-26349	GALLOWAY
26350-26350	GILMER
26351-26351	GLENVILLE
26354-26354	GRAFTON
26360-26360	GREENWOOD
26361-26361	GYPSY
26362-26362	HARRISVILLE
26366-26366	HAYWOOD
26367-26367	HAZELGREEN
26369-26369	HEPZIBAH
26372-26372	HORNER
26374-26374	INDEPENDENCE
26375-26375	INDUSTRIAL
26376-26376	IRELAND
26377-26377	JACKSONBURG
26378-26378	JANE LEW
26383-26383	LIMA
26384-26384	LINN
26385-26385	LOST CREEK
26386-26386	LUMBERPORT
26401-26401	MC WHORTER
26404-26404	MEADOWBROOK
26405-26405	MOATSVILLE
26407-26407	MOUNTAIN
26408-26408	MOUNT CLARE
26409-26409	NEWBERNE
26410-26410	NEWBURG
26411-26411	NEW MILTON
26412-26412	ORLANDO
26415-26415	PENNSBORO
26416-26416	PHILIPPI
26419-26419	PINE GROVE
26421-26421	PULLMAN
26422-26422	REYNOLDSVILLE

26423-26423	ROANOKE
26424-26424	ROSEMONT
26425-26425	ROWLESBURG
26426-26426	SALEM
26430-26430	SAND FORK
26431-26431	SHINNSTON
26434-26434	SHIRLEY
26435-26435	SIMPSON
26436-26436	SMITHBURG
26437-26437	SMITHFIELD
26438-26438	SPELTER
26439-26439	STOUTS MILLS
26440-26440	THORNTON
26443-26443	TROY
26444-26444	TUNNELTON
26446-26446	VALLEY CHAPEL
26447-26447	WALKERSVILLE
26448-26448	WALLACE
26451-26451	WEST MILFORD
26452-26452	WESTON
26456-26456	WEST UNION
26461-26461	WILSONBURG
26462-26462	WOLF SUMMIT
26463-26463	WYATT
26501-26508	MORGANTOWN
26519-26519	ALBRIGHT
26520-26520	ARTHURDALE
26521-26521	BLACKSVILLE
26522-26522	BOOTH
26523-26523	BRANDONVILLE
26524-26524	BRETZ
26525-26525	BRUCETON MILLS
26527-26527	CASSVILLE
26529-26529	CORE
26530-26530	CUZZART
26531-26531	DELLSLOW
26533-26533	EVERETTVILLE
26534-26534	GRANVILLE
26535-26535	HAZELTON
26537-26537	KINGWOOD
26541-26541	MAIDSVILLE
26542-26542	MASONTOWN
26543-26543	OSAGE
26544-26544	PENTRESS
26546-26546	PURSGLOVE
26547-26547	REEDSVILLE
26554-26555	FAIRMONT
26559-26559	BARRACKVILLE
26560-26560	BAXTER
26561-26561	BIG RUN
26562-26562	BURTON
26563-26563	CAROLINA
26566-26566	COLFAX
26568-26568	ENTERPRISE
26570-26570	FAIRVIEW
26571-26571	FARMINGTON
26572-26572	FOUR STATES
26574-26574	GRANT TOWN
26575-26575	HUNDRED
26576-26576	IDAMAY
26578-26578	KINGMONT
26581-26581	LITTLETON
26582-26582	MANNINGTON
26585-26585	METZ
26586-26586	MONTANA MINES
26587-26587	RACHEL
26588-26588	RIVESVILLE
26589-26589	WADESTOWN
26590-26590	WANA
26591-26591	WORTHINGTON
26601-26601	SUTTON
26610-26610	BIRCH RIVER
26611-26611	CEDARVILLE
26612-26612	CENTRALIA
26615-26615	COPEN
26617-26617	DILLE
26618-26618	ELMIRA
26619-26619	EXCHANGE
26620-26620	FALLS MILL
26621-26621	FLATWOODS
26623-26623	FRAMETOWN
26624-26624	GASSAWAY
26626-26626	GLENDON
26627-26627	HEATERS
26629-26629	LITTLE BIRCH
26631-26631	NAPIER
26633-26633	NICUT
26634-26634	PERKINS
26636-26636	ROSEDALE

26638-26638	SHOCK
26639-26639	STRANGE CREEK
26641-26641	WILSIE
26651-26651	SUMMERSVILLE
26656-26656	BELVA
26660-26660	CALVIN
26662-26662	CANVAS
26667-26667	DRENNEN
26671-26671	GILBOA
26674-26674	JODIE
26675-26675	KESLERS CROSS LANES
26676-26676	LEIVASY
26678-26678	MOUNT LOOKOUT
26679-26679	MOUNT NEBO
26680-26680	NALLEN
26681-26681	NETTIE
26683-26683	POE
26684-26684	POOL
26690-26690	SWISS
26691-26691	TIOGA
26704-26704	AUGUSTA
26705-26705	AURORA
26707-26707	BAYARD
26710-26710	BURLINGTON
26711-26711	CAPON BRIDGE
26713-26713	CORINTH
26714-26714	DELRAY
26716-26716	EGLON
26717-26717	ELK GARDEN
26719-26719	FORT ASHBY
26720-26720	GORMANIA
26722-26722	GREEN SPRING
26726-26726	KEYSER
26729-26729	KIRBY
26731-26731	LAHMANSVILLE
26734-26734	MEDLEY
26739-26739	MOUNT STORM
26743-26743	NEW CREEK
26750-26750	PIEDMONT
26753-26753	RIDGELEY
26755-26755	RIO
26757-26757	ROMNEY
26761-26761	SHANKS
26763-26763	SPRINGFIELD
26764-26764	TERRA ALTA
26765-26765	THREE CHURCHES
26767-26767	WILEY FORD
26769-26769	EGLON
26801-26801	BAKER
26802-26802	BRANDYWINE
26804-26804	CIRCLEVILLE
26806-26806	FORT SEYBERT
26807-26807	FRANKLIN
26808-26808	HIGH VIEW
26810-26810	LOST CITY
26811-26811	LOST RIVER
26812-26812	MATHIAS
26813-26813	MOYERS
26814-26814	RIVERTON
26815-26815	SUGAR GROVE
26816-26816	ARTHUR
26817-26817	BLOOMERY
26818-26818	FISHER
26823-26823	CAPON SPRINGS
26824-26824	JUNCTION
26833-26833	MAYSVILLE
26836-26836	MOOREFIELD
26838-26838	MILAM
26845-26845	OLD FIELDS
26847-26847	PETERSBURG
26851-26851	WARDENSVILLE
26852-26852	PURGITSVILLE
26855-26855	CABINS
26865-26865	YELLOW SPRING
26866-26866	UPPER TRACT
26884-26884	SENECA ROCKS
26886-26886	ONEGO

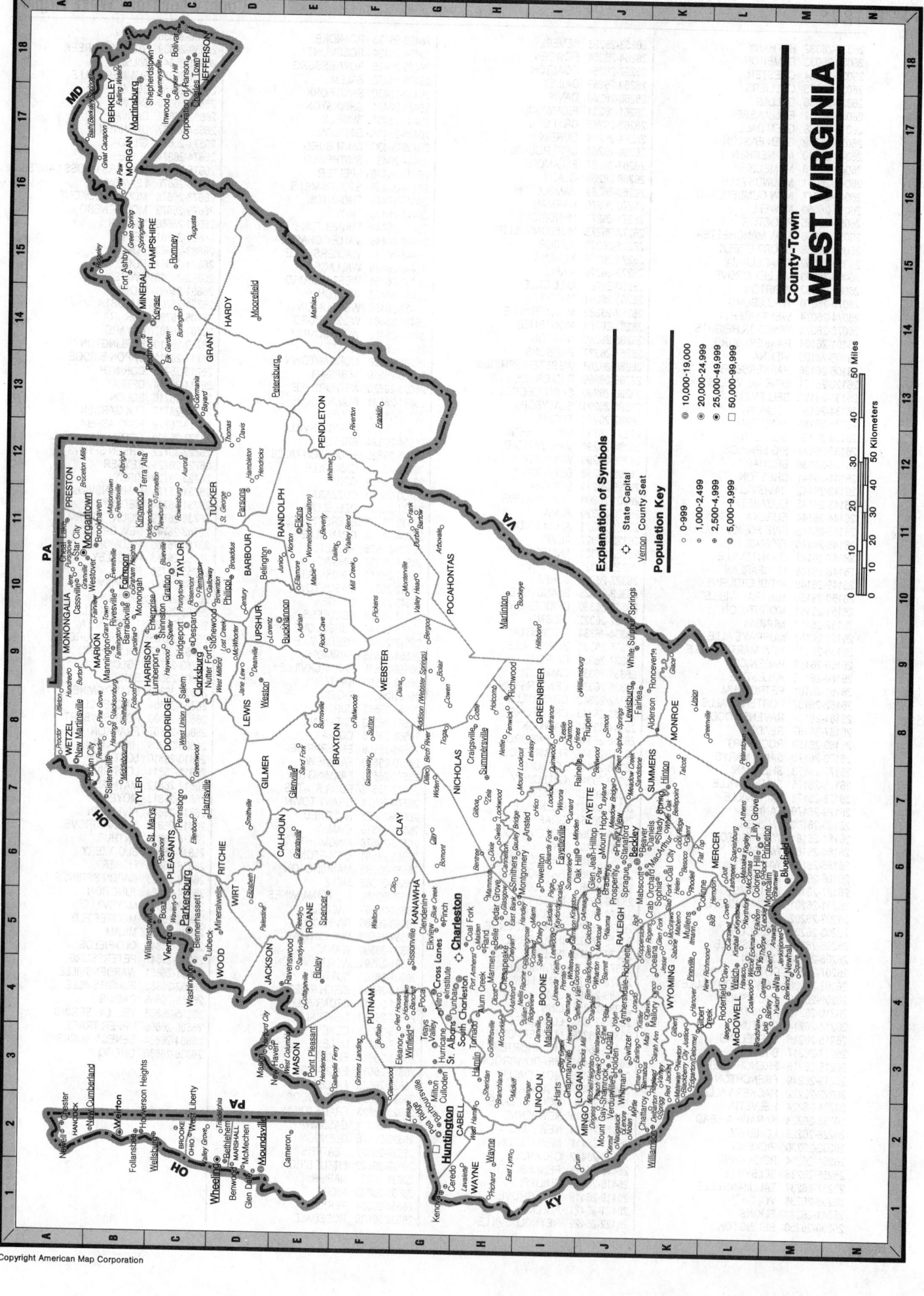

County-Town
WEST VIRGINIA

Explanation of Symbols

✪ State Capital

⌖ Vernon ○ County Seat

Population Key

○ 0-999
● 1,000-2,499
◉ 2,500-4,999
◉ 5,000-9,999
◎ 10,000-19,000
◉ 20,000-24,999
◉ 25,000-49,999
□ 50,000-99,999

50 Miles

50 Kilometers

Explanation of symbols: ●– Census Designated Place (CDP)

Wisconsin

General Help Numbers:

Governor's Office
PO Box 7863
Madison, WI 53707-7863
www.wisgov.state.wi.us

608-266-1212
Fax 608-267-8983
8AM-5PM

Attorney General's Office
Justice Department
PO Box 7857
Madison, WI 53707-7857
www.doj.state.wi.us

608-266-1221
Fax 608-267-2779
8AM-5PM

Legislative Records
Legislative Reference Bureau
PO Box 2037
Madison, WI 53701-2037
www.legis.state.wi.us

608-266-0341
Fax 608-266-5648
7:45AM-5PM

State Archives
Archives Division
816 State St
Madison, WI 53706
www.wisconsinhistory.org/libraryarchives/

608-264-6460
Fax 608-264-6486
8AM-5PM M-F, 9-4 SA

State Specifics:

Capital:

Madison
Dane County

Time Zone:

CST

Number of Counties:

72

Population:

5,509,026

Web Site:

www.wisconsin.gov

State Agencies

Criminal Records

Wisconsin Department of Justice, Crime Information Bureau, Record Check Unit, PO Box 2688, Madison, WI 53701-2688 (Courier address: 17 W Main St, Madison, WI 53703); 608-266-5764, 608-266-7780 (Online Questions), 608-267-4558-Fax; 8AM-4:30PM.

www.doj.state.wi.us

Records are available from July 1971 (when the agencies were required to save records) and are computerized. It takes 4 days before new records are available for inquiry. Records are indexed on inhouse computer. Records are maintained indefinitely. 100% of arrest records are fingerprint supported. 76% of all arrests in database have final dispositions recorded, 67% for those arrests within last 5 years.

Searching: Criminal record information is open to the public per statute 3-21-91. Certain statutorily-required searches require fingerprints. Include the following in your request-sex, race, full name, date of birth. Fingerprints are optional. All requests must be in writing. You must have an account with CIB in order to submit fingerprint cards. The account application can be downloaded from the web. The following data is not released: juvenile records. All records are released, including those without dispositions.

Access by: mail, fax, in person, online.

Fee & Payment: The fee is $18.00 per individual for a name search, and only $15.00 if a fingerprint search. Non-profits made submit name searches for $7.00 per record. If a statutorily-required search also requires an FBI fingerprint check, add $24.00. Fee payee: Wisconsin Department of Justice. Prepayment required. Personal checks accepted. VISA and MC accepted at web site only.

Mail search: Turnaround time: 7 to 10 days. A SASE is requested.

Fax search: Incoming fax permitted only for customers with accounts. Customers wishing to fax requests must provide CIB with a supply of self-addressed, stamped return envelopes.

In person search: Records are returned by mail.

Online search: The agency offers Internet access at http://wi-recordcheck.org. An account with PIN is required or a credit card can be used. Records must be "picked up" at the website within 10 days. They are not returned by mail. Fee is $13 per request, $7.00 if a non-profit, and $10.00 if a government agency. Only daycare centers and other caregivers can receive immediate online response but pay an additional $2.50 per record.

Other access: There is a free Internet service for access to the state's Circuit Courts' records, except for and Portage county. Visit http://wcca.wicourts.gov/index.xsl.

Statewide Court Records

Director of State Courts, Supreme Court, PO Box 1688, Madison, WI 53701-1688; 608-266-6828, 608-267-0980-Fax; 8AM-5PM.

http://wicourts.gov

It takes up to 4 hours before new records are available for inquiry.

Access by: online.

Online search: Wisconsin Circuit Court Access (WCCA) allows users to view circuit court case information at http://wcca.wicourts.gov. Data is available from all counties except Portage County offers only probate records online. WCCA provides detailed information about circuit cases and for civil cases on either a statewide or county basis. The system displays judgment and judgment party information and offers the ability to generate reports. Appellate and Supreme Courts opinions are available from the main web page.

Other access: Bulk access to data may be arranged on contract, fees are involved. Contact the Office of Court Operations at 608-266-3121 for details.

Sexual Offender Registry

Department of Corrections, Sex Offender Registry Program, PO Box 7925, Madison, WI 53707-7925 (Courier address: 3099 E Washington Avenue, Madison, WI 53704); 608-240-5830, 608-240-3355-Fax; 7:45AM-4:30PM.

http://offender.doc.state.wi.us/public

Information stored in the database is accessible on a limited basis to victims, neighborhood watch programs, and the general public. One may also search at the local law enforcement level.

Records are available from 1998 to present. Records are normally destroyed after the registration discharge date.

Searching: The following data is not released: victim profile and data, juvenile adjudication, exact residence address.

Access by: mail, online.

Mail search: Turnaround time: 1-2 weeks.

Online search: Search for offenders by name or location at the website. Second website address is http://widocoffenders.org.

Incarceration Records

Wisconsin Department of Corrections, Bureau of Technology Management, PO Box 8980, Madison, WI 53708-8980 (Courier address: 3099 E Washington Ave, Madison, WI 53708); 608-240-5741, 608-240-3385-Fax; 7:30AM-4PM.

www.wi-doc.com

Records are available on current and former inmates. It takes 10 days before new records are available for inquiry. Records are indexed on inhouse computer. Records are normally destroyed after 5 years beyond termination.

Searching: Computerized records go back to 1961. Include the following in your request-first and last name and the DOB. Location, conviction and sentencing information, and release dates are provided.

Access by: mail, phone, fax, online.

Fee & Payment: Copies are $.15 per page, there is no search fee. Fee payee: Department of Corrections Personal checks accepted.

Mail search: Turnaround time: 5 to 10 working days.

Phone search: For phone search, call number above.

Fax search: Requests are accepted by fax.

Online search: No online searching is available for the public from this agency, however a private company provides free web access at www.vinelink.com/index.jsp.

Corporation, Limited Partnership, Limited Liability Company, Limited Liability Partnerships

Division of Corporate & Consumer Services, Corporation Record Requests, PO Box 7846, Madison, WI 53707-7846 (Courier address: 345 W Washington Ave, 3rd Floor, Madison, WI 53703); 608-261-7577, 608-267-6813-Fax; 7:45AM-4:30PM.

www.wdfi.org

Records are available from 1873. Any records that are not at this office are kept at the State Records Center or the State Archives, but you must go through this office for access. New records are available for inquiry immediately. Records are indexed on inhouse computer, microfilm.

Searching: Include the following in your request-full name of business. In addition to the articles of incorporation, corporation records include the following information: Annual Reports of Officers/Directors, merger information and Name Changes.

Access by: mail, phone, fax, in person, online.

Fee & Payment: ID reports are $10.00, simple copy work is $5.00 per document. Short form certificates of status are $10.00. Certified copies are $10.00 plus. In-person copies are $.25 do it yourself. Fee payee: Department of Financial Institutions. Prepayment required. Personal checks accepted. Credit cards accepted; Visa or MasterCard

Mail search: Turnaround time: 7 to 10 days. A SASE is requested.

Phone search: No fee for telephone request. They will only give a verbal response from the on-screen information.

Fax search: Requires use of a credit card.

In person search: Turnaround time is while you wait.

Online search: Selected elements of the database ("CRIS" Corporate Registration System) are available online on the department's website at www.wdfi.org/corporations/crispix.

Other access: Some data is released in database format and is available electronically via email or on CD.

Expedited service: Expedited service is available for mail searches. Turnaround time: 2 days. Add $25.00 per item.

Trademarks/Servicemarks, Trade Names

Secretary of State, Tradenames/Trademarks Division, PO Box 7848, Madison, WI 53707-7848 (Courier address: 30 W Mifflin St, 10th Floor, Madison, WI 53702); 608-266-5653, 608-266-3159-Fax; 7:45AM-4:30PM.

www.sos.state.wi.us

Records are available for the past 20 years. It takes 7-14 working days before new records are available for inquiry. Records are indexed on computer. Records are normally destroyed after 2 years after expiration.

Searching: All information is considered public record and they will release any information they have. Note that the data is not computerized. Include the following in your request-trademark/servicemark name, name of owner, date of application.

Access by: mail, phone, fax, in person.

Fee & Payment: There is no fee to see if a mark is listed. Plain copies of one record costs $2.00. For certified copies, the cost is $6.00 minimum, depending on the number of pages in the file. Fee payee: Secretary of State. Prepayment required. Personal checks accepted. No credit cards accepted.

Mail search: Turnaround time: 7 to 10 days. SASE not required but does insure quicker response.

Phone search: They will pull the file and give all available information over the phone.

Fax search: Same fees apply, $2.00 per copy if returned by fax. Turnaround time in 7 to 10 days.

In person search: There is no public access to copier. Staff will pull cards and forms for free inspection; staff will make copies for fees listed.

Uniform Commercial Code, Federal and State Tax Liens

Department of Financial Institutions, CCS/UCC, PO Box 7847, Madison, WI 53707-7847 (Courier address: 345 W Washington Ave 3rd Fl, Madison, WI 53703); 608-261-9548, 608-264-7965-Fax; 7:45AM-4:30PM.

www.wdfi.org

Records are available from 1965, if still in effect. It takes 48 hours before new records are available for inquiry. Records are indexed on inhouse computer. Records are normally destroyed after 10 years past effectiveness.

Searching: Use search request form UCC-11. Generally, the search includes federal tax liens filed on businesses. Federal tax liens filed on people, and all state tax liens are filed at the county level. Include the following in your request-debtor name.

Access by: mail, phone, fax, in person, online.

Fee & Payment: There is no search fee. Copies are $4.00 per original file number. Certified copies are $15.00 per file number. Fee payee: Department of Financial Institutions. Prepayment required. Personal checks accepted. No credit cards accepted.

Mail search: Turnaround time: up to 5 days.

Phone search: Call for uncertified information, some data is given over the phone.

Fax search: Turnaround time is 2-7 days.

In person search: Simple requests may be processed while you wait.

Online search: There is free Internet access for most records. Some records may require a $1.00 fee. You may do a free debtor name search at www.wdfi.org/ucc/search/. Instant filings are available immediately.

Other access: Bulk Index data is available on CD. The initial subscription is $3,000, monthly updates are $250.00. Images are available on CD for $200 per month.

Sales Tax Registrations

Revenue Department, Sales & Use Tax Division, PO Box 93389, Madison, WI 53293 (Courier address: 3125 Rimrock Rd, Madison, WI 53713); 608-266-2776, 608-267-1030-Fax; 7:45AM-4:30PM.

www.dor.state.wi.us

The information contained on the seller's permit is not confidential, so it may be provided to requester who inquires if a particular seller has a seller's permit.

Records are available from 1963. Records are indexed on inhouse computer.

Searching: The department can disclose the real name, business name, address, and seller's permit number. Include the following in your request-business name, tax permit number. The more information provided, the easier the search can be conducted. Specific account numbers (i.e., FEIN, SP, etc.) can be more easily used than can names (i.e., real or business).

Access by: mail, phone, fax, in person.

Fee & Payment: There is no search fee, no copy fee.

Mail search: Turnaround time: 2 to 3 weeks. A SASE is requested.

Phone search: Records are available by phone.

Fax search: Records may be requested via fax.

In person search:

Birth Certificates

Bureau of Health Information and Policy, Vital Records, PO Box 309, Madison, WI 53701-0309 (Courier address: One W Wilson St, Room 158, Madison, WI 53702); 608-266-1373, 608-266-1371 (Recording), 608-267-7820 (Genealogy), 608-255-2035-Fax; 8AM-4:15PM.

www.dhfs.wisconsin.gov/vitalrecords

Records are available from 1907 on. This office has the original records. The county of issue has a copy. New records are available for inquiry immediately.

Searching: Must have a signed release from person of record or immediate family member and include the reason for the inquiry for certified copies. Uncertified copy requests do not require a release or a reason, but cannot be expedited. Include the following in your request-full name, names of parents, mother's maiden name, date of birth, place of birth, relationship to person of record, reason for information request.

Access by: mail, fax, in person, online.

Fee & Payment: The fee is $12.00 per name. Add $3.00 per name per copy for additional copies. Uncertified copies are the same price. Fee payee: State of WI Vital Records. Prepayment required. Credit cards fax and online service only. Personal checks accepted. Major credit cards accepted.

Mail search: Turnaround time: 4 weeks. A SASE is requested.

Fax search: See expedited service through Vitalchek.

In person search: Turnaround time 2 to 4 hours.

Online search: Records may be ordered online via www.vitalchek.com, a state approved vendor.

Expedited service: Expedited service is available in person from this agency for an additional $10.00. If www.vitalchek.com used (fax, online), add $6.00 for use of credit card and shipping costs.

Death Records

Bureau of Health Information and Policy, Vital Records, PO Box 309, Madison, WI 53701-0309 (Courier address: One W Wilson St, Room 158, Madison, WI 53702); 608-266-1373, 608-266-1371 (Recording), 608-267-7820 (Genealogy), 608-255-2035-Fax; 8AM-4:15PM.

www.dhfs.wisconsin.gov/vitalrecords

Records are available from 1907 on. This office has the original records. The county of issue has a copy. New records are available for inquiry immediately.

Searching: Must have a signed release from immediate family member for certified copies. Uncertified copy requests do not require a release. Include the following in your request-full name, date of death, place of death, relationship to person of record, reason for information request.

Access by: mail, fax, in person, online.

Fee & Payment: The fee is $7.00 per name search. Add $3.00 per name per copy for additional copies. Uncertified copies are the same fee, but cannot be expedited. Fee payee: State of WI Vital Records. Prepayment required. Credit cards fax and online service only. Personal checks accepted. Major credit cards accepted.

Mail search: Turnaround time: 4 weeks. A SASE is requested.

Fax search: See expedited service through Vitalchek.

In person search: Turnaround time 2 to 4 hours.

Online search: Records may be ordered online via www.vitalchek.com, a state approved vendor.

Expedited service: Expedited service is available in person from this agency for an additional $10.00. If www.vitalchek.com used (fax, online), add $6.00 for use of credit card and shipping costs.

Marriage Certificates

Bureau of Health Information and Policy, Vital Records, PO Box 309, Madison, WI 53701-0309 (Courier address: One W Wilson St, Room 158, Madison, WI 53702); 608-266-1373, 608-266-1371 (Recording), 608-267-7820 (Genealogy), 608-255-2035-Fax; 8AM-4:15PM.

www.dhfs.wisconsin.gov/vitalrecords

Records are available from 1907 on. This office has the original records. The county of issue has a copy. New records are available for inquiry immediately.

Searching: Must have a signed release from the named parties for certified copies. Requests for uncertified copies do not require a release. Include the following in your request-names of husband and wife, date of marriage, place or county of marriage, reason for information request.

Access by: mail, fax, in person, online.

Fee & Payment: The fee is $7.00 per name search. Add $3.00 per name per copy for additional copies. The fee is the same for uncertified copies, but cannot be expedited. Fee payee: State of WI Vital Records. Prepayment required. Credit cards fax and online service only. Personal checks accepted. Major credit cards accepted.

Mail search: Turnaround time: 4 weeks. A SASE is requested.

Fax search: See expedited service through Vitalchek.

In person search: Turnaround time 2 to 4 hours.

Online search: Records may be ordered online via www.vitalchek.com, a state approved vendor.

Expedited service: Expedited service is available in person from this agency for an additional $10.00. If www.vitalchek.com used (fax, online), add $6.00 for use of credit card and shipping costs.

Divorce Records

Bureau of Health Information and Policy, Vital Records, PO Box 309, Madison, WI 53701-0309 (Courier address: One W Wilson St, Room 158, Madison, WI 53702); 608-266-1373, 608-266-1371 (Recording), 608-267-7820 (Genealogy), 608-255-2035-Fax; 8AM-4:15PM.

www.dhfs.wisconsin.gov/vitalrecords

Records are available from 1907. New records are available for inquiry immediately.

Searching: Must have a signed release from the persons of record for a certified copy. Requests for uncertified copies do not require a release. Include the following in your request-names of husband and wife, date of divorce, place of divorce, case number (if known), reason for information request.

Access by: mail, fax, in person, online.

Fee & Payment: The fee is $7.00 per name search. Add $3.00 per name per copy for additional copies. Uncertified copies are the same fee, but cannot be expedited. Fee payee: State of WI Vital Records. Prepayment required. Credit cards fax and online service only. Personal checks accepted. Major credit cards accepted.

Mail search: Turnaround time: 4 weeks. Uncertified requests can take up to 4 months to process. A SASE is requested.

Fax search: See expedited service through Vitalchek.

In person search: Turnaround time 2 to 4 hours if expedite fee paid.

Online search: Records may be ordered online via www.vitalchek.com, a state approved vendor.

Expedited service: Expedited service is available in person from this agency for an additional $10.00. If www.vitalchek.com used (fax, online), add $6.00 for use of credit card and shipping costs.

Workers' Compensation Records

Dept of Workforce Development, Worker's Compensation Division, PO Box 7901, Madison, WI 53707-7901 (Courier address: 201 E Washington Ave, Madison, WI 53707); 608-266-3280, 608-260-2503-Fax; 7:45AM-4:30PM.

www.dwd.state.wi.us/wc

Records are available for 12 years from last benefit payment. New records are available for inquiry immediately. Records are indexed on microfilm, inhouse computer. Records are normally destroyed after 12 years if they are inactive. May be on microfilm if there was activity in the last couple of years.

Searching: Must have release from claimant or be a party to the claim. Must also specify what records you request. Include the following in your request-claimant name, date of accident, employer, and either claim number or SSN. It is suggested to call first so that they can locate records.

Access by: mail, fax, in person.

Fee & Payment: There is a $3.00 service fee plus $.20 per copy fee, $2.00 if certified. Fee payee: Workforce Department. Prepayment required. Personal checks accepted. No credit cards accepted.

Mail search: Turnaround time: 1 to 2 weeks. A SASE is requested.

Fax search: Fax requests accepted.

In person search: Requester must show how connected to party. If you make the copies, the fee is $.10 per page, exact change required.

Driver Records

Division of Motor Vehicles, Records & Licensing Info. Section, PO Box 7995, Madison, WI 53707-7995 (Courier address: 4802 Sheboygan Ave, Room 350, Madison, WI 53707); 608-266-2353, 608-267-3636-Fax; 7:30AM-5:15PM.

www.dot.wisconsin.gov

Copies of tickets may be obtained from this address for $5.50 per citation.

Records are available for 5 years from date of conviction for moving violations and suspensions/revocations, 55 years from date of convictions for alcohol-related violations, and 20 years withdrawal based on damage judgment. It takes no more than 15 days before new records are available for inquiry.

Searching: Driver record information can be obtained per DPPA guidelines. Casual requesters must submit Form MV2896 which requires signature of the subject. This form may be downloaded from the web. The driver license number, or full name, DOB and sex are required when ordering a record. The driver's address is included as part of the search for approved requesters. There is no public counter for walk-in requests. The following data is not released: ID

card information, SSN, juvenile record entries, arrests and medical information.

Access by: mail, phone, online.

Fee & Payment: The fee is $5.00 per driving record. Fee payee: Registration Fee Trust Prepayment required. Personal checks accepted. No credit cards accepted.

Mail search: Turnaround time: 5 business days.

Phone search: Pre-approved accounts may order driving records by phone or fax. The fee is $6.00 if a human operator reads back the record or $5.00 for a digitized computer readback of record.

Online search: Commercial online access is available for high volume users only, fee is $5.00 per record. Call 608-266-2353 for more information. Approved accounts may email requests to driverrecords.dmv@dot.state.wi.us. The Employer Notification program provides a an employee's MVR when an accident, suspension, revocation or out of service order occurs. Cost is $20.00 to sign up and $2.00 per employee. Call 608-266-5769 to set up the program.

Other access: The agency offers a magnetic tape retrieval system for high volume users. The agency will, also, sell its license file without histories to qualified entities. For more information, call 608-266-2353.

Vehicle Ownership
Vehicle Identification

Department of Transportation, Vehicle Records Section, PO Box 7911, Madison, WI 53707-7911 (Courier address: 4802 Sheboygan Ave, Room 102, Madison, WI 53707); 608-266-3666, 608-266-1466 (Registration Laws), 608-267-6966-Fax; 8AM-4:30PM.

www.dot.wisconsin.gov

Records are available for 7 years to present. It takes 2-3 days before new records are available for inquiry. Records are normally destroyed after 7 years after expiration.

Searching: All DPPA restrictions apply. All casual or occasional requestors must submit a request form MV2896. If the request is not for a permissible use, the subject's signature is necessary. The state no longer offers in-person access to records. Depending on what record is required, records can be looked up by name, VIN, plate or by name & city or county.

Access by: mail, phone.

Fee & Payment: The fee is $5.00 per record, including lien searches. An additional $5.00 is charged for certification. The photocopy fee is $.25 per page. Fee payee: Registration Fee Trust. Prepayment required. Personal checks accepted. No credit cards accepted.

Mail search: Turnaround time: 5 business days. A SASE is requested.

Phone search: Only approved requesters may order records by phone.

Other access: This agency offers a variety of methods of obtaining bulk registration lists on cartridge and microfiche. FTP output by a specific request list is available only to law enforcement. Call 608-266-0898 for more information. All DPPA restrictions apply.

Accident Reports

Division of Motor Vehicles, Traffic Accident Section, PO Box 7919, Madison, WI 53707-7919 (Courier address: 4802 Sheboygan Ave, Room 804, Madison, WI 53707); 608-266-8753, 608-267-0606-Fax; 7:30AM-4:30PM.

www.dot.wisconsin.gov

Records are available for 4 years to present. It takes 30 days, on average, from receipt of report before new records are available for inquiry. Records are normally destroyed after 4 years.

Searching: The information is public record. Records can be accessed by driver license number, by plate number, or by accident report number. If none of these items are available, the full name, DOB, and date of accident will be used. The following data is not released: juvenile records.

Access by: mail, phone.

Fee & Payment: The fees are $6.00 for operator reports and $6.00 for police reports. Fee payee: Registration Fee Trust. Prepayment is required if charges are above $6.00. Personal checks accepted. No credit cards accepted.

Mail search: Turnaround time: 72 hours. No SASE is required.

Phone search: 24 hour automated messaging system available to request copies.

Vessel Ownership
Vessel Registration

Department of Natural Resources, Boat Registration, PO Box 7921, Madison, WI 53707 (Courier address: 101 S Webster, Madison, WI 53703); 608-266-2621, 608-264-6130-Fax; 7:45AM-4:30PM.

www.dnr.wi.gov

Records are available from 1978 to present. Records are indexed on computer. All motorized boats and all sailboats must be registered. All motorized boats and all sailboats, if 16 ft or over, must be titled. Lien information shows on title records. It takes up to 3 months before new records are available for inquiry. Records are normally destroyed after 10 years.

Searching: To search one of the following is required: name, hull ID #, or boat registration #.

Access by: mail, phone, fax, in person.

Fee & Payment: There is no search fee for 10 names or less. If over 10 names, then the fees for purchasing lists ($100) are imposed. Fee payee: DNR. Prepayment required. Personal checks accepted. No credit cards accepted.

Mail search: Turnaround time: 1 to 2 days. No SASE is required.

Phone search: Records are available by phone, if under 10 records.

Fax search: Same criteria as mail searching.

In person search: Unless the search is a simple record check, records are returned by mail the next day.

Other access: Bulk lists may be purchased. Call the number above or visit the web page.

Voter Registration

Access to Records is Restricted.

State Elections Board, PO Box 2973,, Madison, WI 53701 (Courier address: 17 W Main #310, Madison, WI 53703); 608-266-8005, 608-267-0500-Fax; 7:45AM-4:30PM.

http://elections.state.wi.us

All records are maintained at the municipal level. However, per the Federal Help America Vote Act of 2002 (HAVA) the implementation of a central, computerized, statewide voter registration system will be in place 01/01/2006. Records will be available for political purposes. Records are open to the public, but personal identifiers are cloaked.

GED Certificates

Department of Public Instruction, GED Program, PO Box 7841, Madison, WI 53707-7841 (Courier address: 125 S Webster, Madison, WI 53707); 608-267-2275, 800-441-4563, 608-267-9275-Fax; 8AM-4:30PM.

www.dpi.state.wi.us

It takes minutes before new records are available for inquiry. Records are normally destroyed after 7 years.

Searching: Include the following in your request-name, SSN, DOB, and year test was taken. For a transcript, include a signed release.

Access by: mail, phone, fax, in person.

Fee & Payment: there is no fee for a verification, the fee is $15.00 for a copy of a transcript or diploma. Fee payee: WI Department of Public Instruction   Credit cards are accepted for transcripts.

Mail search: Turnaround time: 1 week. No SASE is required.

Phone search: A requester must leave a message, with all required data. The agency will then call back with verification.

Fax search: Same criteria as mail or phone searching.

In person search: An appointment is required. Simple requests may be processed while you wait.

Expedited service: Expedited service is available for mail requests. Fee is $25.00. Turnaround time: 48 hours.

Hunting and Fishing License Information

Access to Records is Restricted.

Fish & Game Licensing Division, Records Manager - CS/G3, PO Box 7924, Madison, WI 53707 (Courier address: 101 S Webster St, Madison, WI 53703); 608-266-2621, 608-261-0770 (List Sales), 608-261-4380-Fax; 8AM-4:30PM.

www.dnr.state.wi.us

They do not provide name searching, but will sell lists by license type. There is an opt out provision in place, and 50% of the licensees have opted out.

Wisconsin State Licensing Agencies

For details about the agency responsible for licensing/certifying/registering an item below or in the Agency Quick Finder section, match an item's number with the number of the agency in the *Licensing Agency Information* section.

Wisconsin Licenses Searchable Online

Accounting Firm #2	http://drl.wi.gov/lookupjump.htm
Acupuncturist #4	http://drl.wi.gov/drl/drllookup/LicenseLookupServlet?page=lookup_health
Adjustment Service Company #6	www.wdfi.org/fi/lfs/licensee_lists
Aesthetics Establ./Specialty School #2	http://drl.wi.gov/lookupjump.htm
Aesthetics Instructor #1	http://drl.wi.gov/lookupjump.htm
Ambulance Service Provider #7	http://dhfs.wisconsin.gov/ems/Provider/WICounties.htm
Appraiser, General/Residential #1	http://drl.wi.gov/lookupjump.htm
Architect #1	http://drl.wi.gov/lookupjump.htm
Architectural Corporation #2	http://drl.wi.gov/lookupjump.htm
Art Therapist #4	http://drl.wi.gov/drl/drllookup/LicenseLookupServlet?page=lookup_health
Attorney #16	www.wisbar.org/lawyersearch/mainform.cfm
Auction Company #2	http://drl.wi.gov/lookupjump.htm
Auctioneer #1	http://drl.wi.gov/lookupjump.htm
Audiologist #4	http://drl.wi.gov/drl/drllookup/LicenseLookupServlet?page=lookup_health
Bank #5	www.wdfi.org/fi/savings_institutions/licensee_lists/
Barber #1	http://drl.wi.gov/lookupjump.htm
Barber School #2	http://drl.wi.gov/lookupjump.htm
Barber/Apprentice/Instrct./Mgr. #1	http://drl.wi.gov/lookupjump.htm
Boiler Repairer #3	http://apps.commerce.state.wi.us/SB_Credential/SB_CredentialApp
Boxer #1	http://drl.wi.gov/lookupjump.htm
Boxing Club, Amateur or Professional #2	http://drl.wi.gov/lookupjump.htm
Boxing Show #2	http://drl.wi.gov/lookupjump.htm
Building Inspector #3	http://apps.commerce.state.wi.us/SB_Credential/SB_CredentialApp
Cemetery Authority/Warehouse #2	http://drl.wi.gov/lookupjump.htm
Cemetery Salespers'n/Preneed Seller #1	http://drl.wi.gov/lookupjump.htm
Charitable Organization #2	http://drl.wi.gov/lookupjump.htm
Check Seller #6	www.wdfi.org/fi/lfs/licensee_lists
Chiropractor #4	http://drl.wi.gov/drl/drllookup/LicenseLookupServlet?page=lookup_health
Collection Agency #6	www.wdfi.org/fi/lfs/licensee_lists
Cosmetologist #1	http://drl.wi.gov/lookupjump.htm
Cosmetology Instr./Mgr./Apprentice #1	http://drl.wi.gov/lookupjump.htm
Cosmetology School #2	http://drl.wi.gov/lookupjump.htm
Counselor, Professional #4	http://drl.wi.gov/drl/drllookup/LicenseLookupServlet?page=lookup_health
Credit Service Organization #5	www.wdfi.org/fi/cu/chartered_lists/default.asp
Credit Union #5	www.wdfi.org/fi/cu/chartered_lists/default.asp
Currency Exchange #6	www.wdfi.org/fi/lfs/licensee_lists
Dance Therapist #4	http://drl.wi.gov/drl/drllookup/LicenseLookupServlet?page=lookup_health
Debt Collector #6	www.wdfi.org/fi/lfs/licensee_lists
Dental Hygienist #4	http://drl.wi.gov/drl/drllookup/LicenseLookupServlet?page=lookup_health
Dentist #4	http://drl.wi.gov/drl/drllookup/LicenseLookupServlet?page=lookup_health
Designer of Engineering Systems #1	http://drl.wi.gov/lookupjump.htm
Dietitian #4	http://drl.wi.gov/drl/drllookup/LicenseLookupServlet?page=lookup_health
Drug Distributor/Mfg #2	http://drl.wi.gov/lookupjump.htm
Electrical Inspector #3	http://apps.commerce.state.wi.us/SB_Credential/SB_CredentialApp
Electrician #3	http://apps.commerce.state.wi.us/SB_Credential/SB_CredentialApp
Electrologist/Electrology Instructor #1	http://drl.wi.gov/lookupjump.htm
Electrology Establ./School #2	http://drl.wi.gov/lookupjump.htm
Engineer/Engineer in Training #1	http://drl.wi.gov/lookupjump.htm
Engineering Corporation #2	http://drl.wi.gov/lookupjump.htm
Firearms Permit #2	http://drl.wi.gov/lookupjump.htm
Fireworks Manufacturer #3	http://apps.commerce.state.wi.us/SB_Credential/SB_CredentialApp
Fund Raiser, Professional #1	http://drl.wi.gov/lookupjump.htm
Fund Raising Counsel #2	http://drl.wi.gov/lookupjump.htm
Funeral Director/Director Apprentice #1	http://drl.wi.gov/lookupjump.htm
Funeral Establism't/Preneed Seller #2	http://drl.wi.gov/lookupjump.htm
Geologist #1	http://drl.wi.gov/lookupjump.htm

Geology Firm #2	http://drl.wi.gov/lookupjump.htm
Hearing Instrument Specialist #4	http://drl.wi.gov/drl/drllookup/LicenseLookupServlet?page=lookup_health
Home Inspector #1	http://drl.wi.gov/lookupjump.htm
HVAC Contractor #3	http://apps.commerce.state.wi.us/SB_Credential/SB_CredentialApp
Hydrologist #1	http://drl.wi.gov/lookupjump.htm
Hydrology Firm #2	http://drl.wi.gov/lookupjump.htm
Insurance Company #6	http://badger.state.wi.us/agencies/oci/dir_ins.htm
Insurance Premium Financier #6	www.wdfi.org/fi/lfs/licensee_lists
Interior Designer #1	http://drl.wi.gov/lookupjump.htm
Investment Advisor/Advisor Rep #10	www.wdfi.org/fi/securities/licensing/licensee_lists/default.asp
Land Surveyor #1	http://drl.wi.gov/lookupjump.htm
Landscape Architect #1	http://drl.wi.gov/lookupjump.htm
Loan Company #6	www.wdfi.org/fi/lfs/licensee_lists
Loan Solicitor/Originator #5	www.wdfi.org/fi/
Lobbying Organization, Principal #11	http://ethics.state.wi.us/Scripts/2003Session/OELMenu.asp
Lobbyist #11	http://ethics.state.wi.us/Scripts/2003Session/LobbyistsMenu.asp
Manicurist Establ./Specialty School #2	http://drl.wi.gov/lookupjump.htm
Manicurist/Manicurist Instructor #1	http://drl.wi.gov/lookupjump.htm
Marriage & Family Therapist #4	http://drl.wi.gov/drl/drllookup/LicenseLookupServlet?page=lookup_health
Massage Therapist/Bodyworker #4	http://drl.wi.gov/drl/drllookup/LicenseLookupServlet?page=lookup_health
Medical Doctor/Surgeon #4	http://drl.wi.gov/drl/drllookup/LicenseLookupServlet?page=lookup_health
Midwife Nurse #4	http://drl.wi.gov/drl/drllookup/LicenseLookupServlet?page=lookup_health
Mobile Home & RV Dealer #6	www.wdfi.org/fi/lfs/licensee_lists
Mortgage Banker/Broker #5	www.wdfi.org/fi/
Motorcycle Dealer #6	www.wdfi.org/fi/lfs/licensee_lists
Music Therapist #4	http://drl.wi.gov/drl/drllookup/LicenseLookupServlet?page=lookup_health
Nurse-RN/LPN #4	http://drl.wi.gov/drl/drllookup/LicenseLookupServlet?page=lookup_health
Nursing Home Administrator #1	http://drl.wi.gov/lookupjump.htm
Occupational Therapist/Assistant #4	http://drl.wi.gov/drl/drllookup/LicenseLookupServlet?page=lookup_health
Optometrist #4	http://drl.wi.gov/drl/drllookup/LicenseLookupServlet?page=lookup_health
Osteopathic Physician #4	http://drl.wi.gov/drl/drllookup/LicenseLookupServlet?page=lookup_health
Payday Lender #6	www.wdfi.org/fi/lfs/licensee_lists
Pesticide Applicator #9	www.kellysolutions.com/WI/Applicators/index.asp
Pesticide Applicator Business #9	www.kellysolutions.com/WI/Business/searchbyCity.asp
Pesticide Dealer #9	www.kellysolutions.com/WI/Dealers/searchbyCity.asp
Pharmacist #4	http://drl.wi.gov/drl/drllookup/LicenseLookupServlet?page=lookup_health
Pharmacy #4	http://drl.wi.gov/drl/drllookup/LicenseLookupServlet?page=lookup_health
Physical Therapist #4	http://drl.wi.gov/drl/drllookup/LicenseLookupServlet?page=lookup_health
Physician Assistant #4	http://drl.wi.gov/drl/drllookup/LicenseLookupServlet?page=lookup_health
Plumber #3	http://apps.commerce.state.wi.us/SB_Credential/SB_CredentialApp
Podiatrist #4	http://drl.wi.gov/drl/drllookup/LicenseLookupServlet?page=lookup_health
Private Detective / Detective Agency #2	http://drl.wi.gov/lookupjump.htm
Psychologist #4	http://drl.wi.gov/drl/drllookup/LicenseLookupServlet?page=lookup_health
Public Accountant #1	http://drl.wi.gov/lookupjump.htm
Real Estate Agent/Broker/Sales #1	http://drl.wi.gov/lookupjump.htm
Real Estate Appraiser #1	http://drl.wi.gov/lookupjump.htm
Real Estate Business Entity #2	http://drl.wi.gov/lookupjump.htm
Respiratory Care Practitioner #4	http://drl.wi.gov/drl/drllookup/LicenseLookupServlet?page=lookup_health
Sales Finance/Loan Company #6	www.wdfi.org/fi/lfs/licensee_lists
Savings & Loan Financier #6	www.wdfi.org/fi/lfs/licensee_lists
Savings Institution #5	www.wdfi.org/fi/savings_institutions/licensee_lists/
School Librarian/Media Specialist #15	www.dpi.state.wi.us/dpi/dlsis/tel/lisearch.html
School Psychology Private Practice #4	http://drl.wi.gov/drl/drllookup/LicenseLookupServlet?page=lookup_health
Securities Broker/Dealer/Agent #10	www.wdfi.org/fi/securities/licensing/licensee_lists/default.asp
Security Guard #1	http://drl.wi.gov/lookupjump.htm
Social Worker #4	http://drl.wi.gov/drl/drllookup/LicenseLookupServlet?page=lookup_health
Soil Science Firm #2	http://drl.wi.gov/lookupjump.htm
Soil Scientist #1	http://drl.wi.gov/lookupjump.htm
Soil Tester #3	http://apps.commerce.state.wi.us/SB_Credential/SB_CredentialApp
Speech Pathologist/Audiologist #4	http://drl.wi.gov/drl/drllookup/LicenseLookupServlet?page=lookup_health
Teacher #15	www.dpi.state.wi.us/dpi/dlsis/tel/lisearch.html
Timeshare Salesperson #1	http://drl.wi.gov/lookupjump.htm
Veterinarian/Veterinary Technician #4	http://drl.wi.gov/drl/drllookup/LicenseLookupServlet?page=lookup_health
Welder #3	http://apps.commerce.state.wi.us/SB_Credential/SB_CredentialApp

Wisconsin Licensing Quick Finder

Accounting Firm #2 608-261-7096
Acupuncturist #4 608-266-8794
Adjustment Counselor #6 608-261-7578
Adjustment Service Company #6 608-261-7578
Aesthetics Establ./Specialty School #2 . 608-261-2390
Aesthetics Instructor #1 608-266-2112
Ambulance Service Provider #7 608-266-1568
Appraiser, General/Residential #1 608-266-2112
Architect #1 608-266-5511
Architectural Corporation #2 608-261-7096
Art Therapist #4 608-266-8794
Asbestos Worker #17 608-261-6876
Attorney #16 608-250-6125
Auction Company #2 608-261-7096
Auctioneer #1 608-266-5511
Audiologist #4 608-266-8794
Bank #5 608-261-7578
Barber #1 608-266-2112
Barber School #2 608-261-2390
Barber/Apprentice/Instrct./Mgr. #1 608-266-2112
Beer Wholesaler #8 608-266-2776
Boiler Repairer #3 608-261-8500
Boxer #1 608-266-5511
Boxing Club, Amateur or Prof. #2 608-261-7096
Boxing Show #2 608-261-2390
Building Inspector #3 608-261-8500
Business Tax Registration #8 608-266-2776
Cemetery Authority/Warehouse #2 608-261-2390
Cemetery Pre-Need Seller #1 608-266-5511
Cemetery Salesperson #1 608-266-5511
Charitable Gaming #14 608-270-2555
Charitable Organization #2 608-261-7096
Check Seller #6 608-261-7578
Chiropractor #4 608-266-8794
Cigarette & Tobacco Distributor/Vendor/Multiple
    Retailer #8 608-266-2776
Cigarette & Tobacco Warehouser/Wholesaler/
    Jobber #8 608-266-2776
Collection Agency #6 608-261-7578
Cosmetologist #1 608-266-2112
Cosmetology Instr./Mgr./Apprentice #1 . 608-266-2112
Cosmetology School #2 608-261-7096
Counselor, Professional #4 608-266-8794
Credit Service Organization #5 608-266-9543
Credit Union #5 608-266-9543
Currency Exchange #6 608-261-7578
Dance Therapist #4 608-266-8794
Debt Collector #6 608-261-7578
Dental Hygienist #4 608-266-8794
Dentist #4 608-266-8794
Designer of Engineering Systems #1 ... 608-266-5511
Dietitian #4 608-266-8794
Director of Instruction #15 608-266-1027

Dog Racing Professional #14 608-270-2555
Drug Distributor/Mfg #2 608-261-7096
Electrical Inspector #3 608-261-8500
Electrician #3 608-261-8500
Electrologist/Electrology Instructor #1 .. 608-266-2112
Electrology Establ./School #2 608-261-7096
Employee Benefits Plan Administrator #12
    608-267-1238
EMT/Paramedic #7 608-266-1568
Engineer/Engineer in Training #1 608-266-5511
Engineering Corporation #2 608-261-7096
Excise Tax Permit #8 608-266-2776
Fertilizer #9 608-224-4541
Firearms Permit #2 608-261-7096
Fireworks Manufacturer #3 608-261-8500
Fuel Tax Permit #8 608-266-2776
Fund Raiser, Professional #1 608-266-5511
Fund Raising Counsel #2 608-261-7096
Funeral Director/Director Apprentice #1 608-266-2112
Funeral Establishment #2 608-261-2390
Funeral Pre-Need Seller #1 608-266-5511
Geologist #1 608-266-2112
Geology Firm #2 608-261-2390
Hearing Instrument Specialist #4 608-266-8794
Home Inspector #1 608-266-5511
HVAC Contractor #3 608-261-8500
Hydrologist #1 608-266-2112
Hydrology Firm #2 608-261-2390
Indian Gaming Vendor #14 608-270-2555
Insurance Company #6 608-261-7578
Insurance Intermediary #12 608-266-8699
Insurance Premium Finance Company #6
    608-261-7578
Interior Designer #1 608-266-5511
Investment Advisor/Advisor Rep #10 ... 608-266-3693
Land Surveyor #1 608-266-5511
Landscape Architect #1 608-266-5511
Liquor, Wholesale #8 608-266-2776
Loan Company #6 608-261-7578
Loan Solicitor/Originator #5 608-261-7578
Lobbying Organization, Principal #11 .. 608-266-8123
Lobbyist #11 608-266-8123
Manicurist Establ./Specialty School #2 608-261-2390
Manicurist/Manicurist Instructor #1 608-266-2112
Marriage & Family Therapist #4 608-266-8794
Massage Therapist/Bodyworker #4 608-266-8794
Medical Doctor/Surgeon #4 608-266-8794
Midwife Nurse #4 608-266-8794
Mobile Home & RV Dealer #6 608-261-7578
Mortgage Banker/Broker #5 608-261-7578
Motorcycle Dealer #6 608-261-7578
Music Therapist #4 608-266-8794
Notary Public #13 608-266-5594

Nurse-RN/LPN #4 608-266-8794
Nursing Home Administrator #1 608-266-2112
Occupational Therapist/Assistant #4 ... 608-266-8794
Optometrist #4 608-266-8794
Osteopathic Physician #4 608-266-8794
Payday Lender #6 608-261-7578
Pesticide Applicator/Application Business #9
    608-224-4548
Pesticide Dealer #9 608-224-4548
Pesticide Vet Clinic #9 608-224-4548
Pharmacist #4 608-266-8794
Pharmacy #4 608-266-8794
Physical Therapist #4 608-266-8794
Physician Assistant #4 608-266-8794
Plumber #3 608-261-8500
Podiatrist #4 608-266-8794
Private Detective #1 608-266-5511
Private Detective Agency #2 608-261-7096
Psychologist #4 608-266-8794
Public Accountant #1 608-266-5511
Racing/Racing Vendor #14 608-270-2555
Real Estate Agent/Broker/Sales #1 608-266-5511
Real Estate Appraiser #1 608-266-2112
Real Estate Business Entity #2 608-261-2390
Respiratory Care Practitioner #4 608-266-8794
Sales Finance/Loan Company #6 608-261-7578
Sales Withholding Tax Registration #8 . 608-266-2776
Sanitarian #17 608-267-4784
Savings & Loan Sales Finance Company #6
    608-261-7578
Savings Institution #5 608-261-4335
School Counselor #15 608-266-1027
School Librarian/Media Specialist #15 . 608-266-1027
School Nurse #15 608-266-1027
School Principal/Superintendent/Bus. Mgr #15
    608-266-1027
School Psycholog't/Social Worker #15 . 608-266-1027
School Psychology Private Practice #4 608-266-8794
Securities Broker/Dealer/Agent #10 608-266-3693
Security Guard #1 608-266-5511
Social Worker #4 608-266-8794
Soil Science Firm #2 608-261-7096
Soil Scientist #1 608-266-2112
Soil Tester #3 608-261-8500
Speech Pathologist/Audiologist #4 608-266-8794
Teacher #15 608-266-1027
Timeshare Salesperson #1 608-266-5511
Veterinarian/Veterinary Technician #4 . 608-266-8794
Viatical Settlement Broker #12 608-266-8699
Vocational Education Coordinator, Local #15
    608-266-1027
Welder #3 608-261-8500
Wine Distributor, Public #8 608-266-2776

Wisconsin Licensing Agency Information

1 Department of Regulation and Licensing, Division of Business Professional Licensure & Reg - Individuals, PO Box 8935 (1400 E Washington), Madison, WI 53708-8935; 608-266-5511, Fax: 608-267-3816. http://drl.wi.gov/index.htm
Email: dorl@drl.state.wi.us
Search Database at http://drl.wi.gov/lookupjump.htm Note: Lists may be obtained.

2 Dept of Regulation & Licensing, Division of Business Licensure & Regulation - Entities, PO Box 8935 (1400 E Washington), Madison, WI 53708-8935; 608-266-5511, Fax: 608-267-3816. http://drl.wi.gov/index.htm
Email: dorl@drl.state.wi.us
Search Database at http://drl.wi.gov/lookupjump.htm Note: Lists may be obtained.

3 Department of Commerce, Safety & Buildings, PO Box 7082, 201 W Washington Ave, Madison, WI 53707-2689; 608-261-8500, Fax: 608-267-0592. www.commerce.wi.gov/
Search Database at http://apps.commerce.state.wi.us/SB_Credential/SB_CredentialApp

4 Bureau of Health Services Professions, PO Box 8935 (1400 E Washington Ave), Madison, WI 53708-8935; 608-266-0145, Fax: 608-261-7083. http://drl.wi.gov/prof/burhsvc.htm
Email: dorl@drl.state.wi.us
Search Database at http://drl.wi.gov/drl/drllookup/LicenseLookupServlet?page=lookup_health Note: This department recommends an internet search; if not, inquire by mail. Phone verifications may not be accepted.

5 Department of Financial Institutions, Division of Banking, PO Box 7876 (345 W Washington Av, 4th Fl), Madison, WI 53707-7876; 608-261-7578, Fax: 608-261-6889. www.wdfi.org
Email: info@dfi.state.wi.us
Search Database at www.wdfi.org/fi/savings_institutions/licensee_lists/ Note: Division of Financial Inst. - dfi - offers both an online list system and telephone system for verifications.

6 Department of Financial Institutions, Licensed Financial Services, 345 W Washington Ave, Madison, WI 53707-7876; 608-261-7578, Fax: 608-261-7200.
www.wdfi.org/fi/lfs/
Search Database at www.wdfi.org/fi/lfs/licensee_lists/ Note: Also offers an online list system for verifications.

7 Division of Public Health, Bureau of EMS and IP, 1 W Wilson St, Rm 118, Madison, WI 53703; 608-267-9777, 266-1568, Fax: 608-261-6392. http://dhfs.wisconsin.gov/ems/
Email: webmaildph@dhfs.state.wi.us

8 Department of Revenue, 2135 Rimrock Rd, Madison, WI 53713; 608-266-2772, Fax: 608-267-1030. www.dor.state.wi.us
Email: sales10@dor.state.wi.us

9 Department of Agriculture, Trade & Consumer Protection, Applicator Certification & Licensing, 2811 Agriculture Dr, Madison, WI 53718; 608-224-4548, Fax: 608-224-4656.
www.datcp.state.wi.us/index.jsp
Email: bonnie.bruns@datcp.state.wi.us
Search Database at www.datcp.state.wi.us/arm/agriculture/pest-fert/pesticides/data/index.jsp

10 Department of Financial Institutions, Division of Securities, PO Box 1768, Madison, WI 53701; 608-266-1064, Fax: 608-264-7979.
www.wdfi.org/fi/securities/
Email: info@dfi.state.wi.us
Search Datab ase at www.wdfi.org/fi/securities/licensing/licensee_lists/default.asp Note: These lists only contain firm info. No agents or investment adviser reps are searchable from the DFI website.

11 Ethics Board, 44 E Mifflin St, #601, Madison, WI 53703-2800; 608-266-8123, Fax: 608-264-9319. http://ethics.state.wi.us
Email: ethics@ethics.state.wi.gov
Search Database at http://ethics.state.wi.us/LobbyingRegistrationReports/LobbyingOverview.htm

12 Office of the Commissioner of Insurance, 125 S Webster St, Madison, WI 53702; 608-266-3585, Fax: 608-266-9935.
http://badger.state.wi.us/agencies/oci/oci_home.htm
Email: agentlicensing@oci.state.wi.us Note: For list of licence types go to www.oci.wi.gov.

13 Office of Secretary of State, PO Box 7848, Madison, WI 53707-7848; 608-266-5594, Fax: 608-266-3159.
www.state.wi.us/agencies/sos

14 Department of Administration, Division of Gaming/Racing, 2005 W Beltline Hwy, #201 [PO Box 8979 (53708)], Madison, WI 53713; 608-270-2555, Fax: 608-270-2564.
www.doa.state.wi.us/gaming/index.asp
Email: racingweb@doa.state.wi.us

15 Teacher Education, Department of Public Instruction, PO Box 7841, Madison, WI 53707-7841; 608-266-1027, Fax: 608-264-9558.
www.dpi.state.wi.us/dpi/dlsis/tel/
Email: tcert@dpi.state.wi.us
Search Database at www.dpi.state.wi.us/dpi/dlsis/tel/lisearch.html Note: At the search page, enter the User Name "view" and the Password, "1234567" then click "ok".

16 State Bar Association, PO Box 7158 (5302 Eastpark Blvd.), Madison, WI 53707; 608-257-3838, Fax: 608-257-5502.
www.wisbar.org
Email: service@wisbar.org
Search Database at www.wisbar.org/lawyersearch/mainform.cfm

17 Department of Health & Family Svcs, Occupational Health, 1 W Wilson St, Perry Manor, Madison, WI 53703; 608-267-2297, Fax: 608-266-9711. www.dhfs.wisconsin.gov

Wisconsin Federal Courts

The following list indicates the district and division name for each county in the state. If the bankruptcy court location is different from the district court, then the location of the bankruptcy court appears in parentheses.

Wisconsin County/Court Cross Reference

County	District	Division
Adams	Western	Madison
Ashland	Western	Madison (Eau Claire)
Barron	Western	Madison (Eau Claire)
Bayfield	Western	Madison (Eau Claire)
Brown	Eastern	Milwaukee
Buffalo	Western	Madison (Eau Claire)
Burnett	Western	Madison (Eau Claire)
Calumet	Eastern	Milwaukee
Chippewa	Western	Madison (Eau Claire)
Clark	Western	Madison (Eau Claire)
Columbia	Western	Madison
Crawford	Western	Madison
Dane	Western	Madison
Dodge	Eastern	Milwaukee
Door	Eastern	Milwaukee
Douglas	Western	Madison (Eau Claire)
Dunn	Western	Madison (Eau Claire)
Eau Claire	Western	Madison (Eau Claire)
Florence	Eastern	Milwaukee
Fond du Lac	Eastern	Milwaukee
Forest	Eastern	Milwaukee
Grant	Western	Madison
Green	Western	Madison
Green Lake	Eastern	Milwaukee
Iowa	Western	Madison
Iron	Western	Madison (Eau Claire)
Jackson	Western	Madison (Eau Claire)
Jefferson	Western	Madison
Juneau	Western	Madison (Eau Claire)
Kenosha	Eastern	Milwaukee
Kewaunee	Eastern	Milwaukee
La Crosse	Western	Madison (Eau Claire)
Lafayette	Western	Madison
Langlade	Eastern	Milwaukee
Lincoln	Western	Madison (Eau Claire)
Manitowoc	Eastern	Milwaukee
Marathon	Western	Madison (Eau Claire)
Marinette	Eastern	Milwaukee
Marquette	Eastern	Milwaukee
Menominee	Eastern	Milwaukee
Milwaukee	Eastern	Milwaukee
Monroe	Western	Madison (Eau Claire)
Oconto	Eastern	Milwaukee
Oneida	Western	Madison (Eau Claire)
Outagamie	Eastern	Milwaukee
Ozaukee	Eastern	Milwaukee
Pepin	Western	Madison (Eau Claire)
Pierce	Western	Madison (Eau Claire)
Polk	Western	Madison (Eau Claire)
Portage	Western	Madison (Eau Claire)
Price	Western	Madison (Eau Claire)
Racine	Eastern	Milwaukee
Richland	Western	Madison
Rock	Western	Madison
Rusk	Western	Madison (Eau Claire)
Sauk	Western	Madison
Sawyer	Western	Madison (Eau Claire)
Shawano	Eastern	Milwaukee
Sheboygan	Eastern	Milwaukee
St. Croix	Western	Madison (Eau Claire)
Taylor	Western	Madison (Eau Claire)
Trempealeau	Western	Madison (Eau Claire)
Vernon	Western	Madison (Eau Claire)
Vilas	Western	Madison (Eau Claire)
Walworth	Eastern	Milwaukee
Washburn	Western	Madison (Eau Claire)
Washington	Eastern	Milwaukee
Waukesha	Eastern	Milwaukee
Waupaca	Eastern	Milwaukee
Waushara	Eastern	Milwaukee
Winnebago	Eastern	Milwaukee
Wood	Western	Madison (Eau Claire)

Standards for Federal Courts: Search fee is $26.00 per item (one party name or case number). Copy fee is $.50 per page. Certification fee is $9.00 per document, double for exemplification, if available. All fees standard unless noted in profile. Mail Search: always enclose a stamped self addressed envelope unless otherwise noted. Most courts accept fax requests or will suggest a copying/search vendor. Before releasing records, all courts require prepayment, unless noted.

Open records are located at the court unless otherwise noted. District courts index by defendant and plaintiff as well as by case number. Bankruptcy courts usually index by debtor and case number. While most courts now have their indexes on computer, many may still maintain index card files as well.

Courts offering internet access via CM-ECF or older RACER, PACER, or Web-PACER systems charge $.08 per page fee unless noted as free. Where PACER is available, the universal sign-up number is 800-676-6856. Find PACER and the US Party/Case Index at http://pacer.psc.uscourts.gov.

US District Court

Eastern District of Wisconsin

Milwaukee Division Clerk's Office, Rm 362, 517 E Wisconsin Ave, Milwaukee, WI 53202 (also use mail address for courier delivery), 414-297-3372, Fax-414-297-3203. Hours- 8:30AM-4:30PM. www.wied.uscourts.gov

Counties: Brown, Calumet, Dodge, Door, Florence, Fond du Lac, Forest, Green Lake, Kenosha, Kewaunee, Langlade, Manitowoc, Marinette, Marquette, Menominee, Milwaukee, Oconto, Outagamie, Ozaukee, Racine, Shawano, Sheboygan, Walworth, Washington, Waukesha, Waupaca, Waushara, Winnebago.

Searches & Indexing: Results include last 4 SSN digits, also birth year. Computer index maintained; civil back to 1991, criminal to 1993. New cases in the index immediately after filing date. Records purged never.

Fee & Payment: Pay by money order, cashier's or personal check. Payee: Clerk, US District Court. Prepayment required.

Phone Search: Docket information available via phone if you provide case number or party names.

Mail Search: search usually completed- 3 days. Include SASE for return.

In Person Search: Fee charged if court performs your search. Self-serve copier - $.25 per page.

E-Services: ECF replaces PACER whose records did go back to 1991. New records online after 1 day. ECF at https://ecf.wied.uscourts.gov

US Bankruptcy Court

Eastern District of Wisconsin

Milwaukee Division Court Clerk, Rm 126, 517 E Wisconsin Ave, Milwaukee, WI 53202 (also use mail address for courier delivery), 414-297-3291, records rm- 414-297-4111. Hours- 8:30AM-4:30PM. www.wieb.uscourts.gov

Counties: Brown, Calumet, Dodge, Door, Florence, Fond du Lac, Forest, Green Lake, Kenosha, Kewaunee, Langlade, Manitowoc, Marinette, Marquette, Menominee, Milwaukee, Oconto, Outagamie, Ozaukee, Racine, Shawano, Sheboygan, Walworth, Washington, Waukesha, Waupaca, Waushara, Winnebago.

Searches & Indexing: Computer index goes back to 1986. Computer index maintained. New cases in the index 1-2 days after filing date. Records purged after case is closed.

Fee & Payment: Pay by money order, cashier's or personal check. Payee: Clerk, US Bankruptcy Court. Prepayment required.

Phone Search: Voice Case Information Service available, call 877-781-7277 or 414-297-3582.

Mail Search: search usually completed- 3 days. Include SASE for return.

In Person Search: Fee charged if court performs your search. Self-serve copier - $.25 per page.

E-Services: PACER online at http://pacer.wieb.uscourts.gov. PACER records go back to 1991. New records online after 1 day. ECF

at https://ecf.wieb.uscourts.gov **Opinions Online:** www.wieb.uscourts.gov/JUDCAL4i/judpol4i_index.htm. Limited opinions. **Other Online Access:** Calendars at www.wieb.uscourts.gov/judcal4i/judcal4i_calendars.htm.

US District Court

Western District of Wisconsin

Madison Division Court Clerk, PO Box 432, Madison, WI 53701 (courier address: 120 N Henry St, Madison, WI 53703), 608-264-5156. Hours-8AM-4:30PM. www.wiwd.uscourts.gov

Counties: Adams, Ashland, Barron, Bayfield, Buffalo, Burnett, Chippewa, Clark, Columbia, Crawford, Dane, Douglas, Dunn, Eau Claire, Grant, Green, Iowa, Iron, Jackson, Jefferson, Juneau, La Crosse, Lafayette, Lincoln, Marathon, Monroe, Oneida, Pepin, Pierce, Polk, Portage, Price, Richland, Rock, Rusk, Sauk, Sawyer, St. Croix, Taylor, Trempealeau, Vernon, Vilas, Washburn, Wood.

Searches & Indexing: Results do not include SSN or DOB. Computer index maintained back to 1990; on microfiche to 1980; also on card file. New cases in the index 24 hours after filing date. Records purged never. District-wide searches available here.

Fee & Payment: Pay by money order, cashier's or personal check. No credit cards. Payee: Clerk, US District Court. Prepayment required.

Phone Search: Only docket information is available by phone.

Mail Search: search usually completed- 24 hours. Include SASE for return.

In Person Search: Fee charged if court performs your search. No self-serve copier available.

E-Services: PACER online at http://pacer.wiwd.uscourts.gov. Document images available. PACER records go back to 1990. New records online after 1 day. ECF at (Currently in the process of implementing CM-ECF.) **Opinions:** www.wiwd.uscourts.gov/opinsearch/index.html. **Other Online Access:** Weekly court calendars free at www.wiwd.uscourts.gov/calendar/calfrm.html

US Bankruptcy Court

Western District of Wisconsin

Eau Claire Division Court Clerk, PO Box 5009, Eau Claire, WI 54702-5009 (courier address: 500 S Barstow St, Eau Claire, WI 54702), 715-839-2980, Fax-715-839-2996. Hours- 8AM-4:30PM. www.wiw.uscourts.gov/bankruptcy

Counties: Ashland, Barron, Bayfield, Buffalo, Burnett, Chippewa, Clark, Douglas, Dunn, Eau Claire, Iron, Jackson, Juneau, La Crosse, Lincoln, Marathon, Monroe, Oneida, Pepin, Pierce, Polk, Portage, Price, Rusk, Sawyer, St. Croix, Taylor, Trempealeau, Vernon, Vilas, Washburn, Wood. This Division has satellite offices in LaCrosse and Wausau.

Searches & Indexing: Results include last 4 SSN digits. Computer index maintained. New cases in the index 1 day after filing date.

Fee & Payment: Pay by money order, cashier's, business or attorney checks. No personal checks. Payee: Clerk, US Bankruptcy Court. Prepayment required.

Phone Search: Limited docket information available by phone. Voice Case Information Service available, call VCIS at 800-743-8247 or 608-264-5035.

Mail Search: search usually completed- 2 days. SASE not required.

In Person Search: Fee charged if court performs your search. No self-serve copier available.

E-Services: ECF replaces PACER whose records did go back to 4/1991. New records online after 1 day. ECF at https://ecf.wiwb.uscourts.gov. Document images available. **Opinions Online:** www.wiw.uscourts.gov/bankruptcy/decision_home.htm.

Madison Division Court Clerk, PO Box 548, Madison, WI 53701 (courier address: Rm 340, 120 N Henry St, Madison, WI 53703), 608-264-5178, Fax-608-264-5105. Hours- 8AM-4:30PM. www.wiw.uscourts.gov/bankruptcy

Counties: Adams, Columbia, Crawford, Dane, Grant, Green, Iowa, Jefferson, Lafayette, Richland, Rock, Sauk.

Searches & Indexing: Results include last 4 SSN digits. Computer index maintained. New cases in the index 24 hours after filing date.

Fee & Payment: Pay by money order, cashier check, business check. No personal checks. Payee: Clerk, Bankruptcy Court. Prepayment required.

Phone Search: Limited docket information available by phone. Voice Case Information Service available, call VCIS at 800-743-8247 or 608-264-5035.

Mail Search: search usually completed- 5 days. SASE not required.

In Person Search: Fee charged if court performs your search. No self-serve copier available.

E-Services: ECF replaces PACER whose records did go back to 4/1991. New records online after 1 day. ECF at https://ecf.wiwb.uscourts.gov. Document images available. **Opinions Online:** www.wiw.uscourts.gov/bankruptcy/decision_home.htm

Wisconsin County Courts

Court	Jurisdiction	No. of Courts	How Organized
Circuit Courts*	General	74	69 Circuits
Municipal Courts	Municipal	226	
Probate Courts*	Probate	72	

* Profiled in this Sourcebook.

CIVIL									
Court	Tort	Contract	Real Estate	Min. Claim	Max. Claim	Small Claims	Estate	Eviction	Domestic Relations
Circuit Courts*	X	X	X	$0	No Max	$5000	X	X	X
Municipal Courts									
Probate Courts*							X		

CRIMINAL					
Court	Felony	Misdemeanor	DWI/DUI	Preliminary Hearing	Juvenile
Circuit Courts*	X	X	X	X	X
Municipal Courts			X		X
Probate Courts*					

ADMINISTRATION

Director of State Courts, Supreme Court, PO Box 1688, Madison, WI, 53701; 608-266-6828, Fax: 608-267-0980. http://wicourts.gov

COURT STRUCTURE

The Circuit Court is the court of general jurisdiction. The Register in Probate maintains guardianship and mental health records, most of which are sealed but may be opened for cause with a court order. In some counties, the Register also maintains termination and adoption records, but practices vary widely across the state.

Most Registers in Probate are putting pre-1950 records on microfilm and destroying the hard copies. This is done as "time and workloads permit," so microfilm archiving is not uniform across the state.

The small claims limit was raised to $5000 in mid-1995.

ONLINE ACCESS

Wisconsin Circuit Court Access (WCCA) allows users to view circuit court case information at http://wcca.wicourts.gov/ which is the Wisconsin court system web site. Data is available from all counties except only probate records are available from Portage. Searches can be conducted statewide or county by county. WCCA provides detailed information about circuit cases and for civil cases, the program displays judgment and judgment party information. WCCA also offers the ability to generate reports. In addition, public access terminals are available at each court. Due to statutory requirements, WCCA users will not be able to view restricted cases. There are probate records for all counties. Appellate and Supreme Courts opinions are available from the main web page.

ADDITIONAL INFORMATION

The statutory fee schedule for the Circuit Courts is as follows: Search Fee - $5.00 per name; Copy Fee - $1.25 per page; Certification Fee - $5.00. In about half the Circuit Courts, no search fee is charged if the case number is provided.

The fee schedule for probate is as follows: Search Fee - $4.00 per name; Certification Fee - $3.00 per document plus copy fee; Copy Fee - $1.00 per page.

PROBATE COURTS

Probate filing is a function of the Circuit Court; however, each county has a Register in Probate who maintains and manages the probate records. Probate records are available online at the web page.

Adams County

Circuit Court PO Box 220, Friendship, WI 53934; phone: 608-339-4208; fax: 608-339-4503; hours 8AM-4:30PM (CST). *Felony, Misdemeanor, Civil, Eviction, Small Claims.*
Civil Records: Access: Phone, mail, online, in person. Both court and visitors may perform in person searches. Search fee: $5.00 per name. Court makes copy: $1.25 per page. Required to search: name, years to search. Civil records on computer from 1993, on index cards and books from 1950. Historical societies have previous records and indexes. Organized 1848. Civil court records free online at http://wcca.wicourts.gov/index.xsl. Mail turnaround time 1-2 days.
Criminal Records: Access: Phone, mail, online, in person. Both court and visitors may perform in person searches. Search fee: $5.00 per name. Court makes copy: $1.25 per page. Required to search: name, years to search, DOB. Criminal records on computer from 1993, on index cards and books from 1950. Historical societies have previous records and indexes. Organized 1848. Access criminal index free at http://wcca.wicourts.gov/index.xsl. Mail turnaround time 1-2 days.
General Information: Public terminal goes back to 1993. No juvenile, paternity, financial, PSI reports released. Fee to fax documents is $1.25 per page. Certification fee: $5.00 includes copies. Payee: Clerk of Court. Personal checks accepted. Prepayment and SASE required.

Register in Probate PO Box 200, Friendship, WI 53934; phone: 608-339-4213; fax: 608-339-4503; hours 8AM-4:30PM (CST). *Probate.*
Note: Probate records free online at http://wcca.wicourts.gov/index.xsl.

Ashland County

Circuit Court Courthouse, 201 W Main St, Rm 307, Ashland, WI 54806; phone: 715-682-7016; fax: 715-682-7919; hours 8AM-N, 1-4PM (CST). *Felony, Misdemeanor, Civil, Eviction, Small Claims.* www.co.ashland.wi.us
Civil Records: Access: Phone, fax, mail, online, in person. Both court and visitors may perform in person searches. Search fee: $5.00 per name. Court makes copy: $1.25 per page. Required to search: name, years to search. Civil cases indexed by defendant, plaintiff; on index cards and index books concurrently from 1960. Organized 1860. Civil court records free online at http://wcca.wicourts.gov/index.xsl. Mail turnaround time 1-2 days.
Criminal Records: Access: Fax, mail, online, in person. Both court and visitors may perform in person searches. Search fee: $5.00 per name. Court makes copy: $1.25 per page. Required to search: name, years to search, DOB. Criminal records on computer back to 1994. Access criminal index free at http://wcca.wicourts.gov/index.xsl. Mail turnaround time 1-2 days.
General Information: Public terminal goes back to 1994. No juvenile or paternity records released. Will fax documents for $1.25 per page. Certification fee: $5.00 per cert. Payee: Clerk of Court. Local or pre-approved checks accepted. Prepayment and SASE required.

Register in Probate Courthouse, Rm 203, 201 W Main, Ashland, WI 54806; phone: 715-682-7009; fax: 715-682-7919; hours 8AM-N, 1-4PM (CST). *Probate.*
Free search at http://wcca.wicourts.gov/index.xsl.

Barron County

Circuit Court Barron County Justice Center, 1420 State Hwy 25 N, Barron, WI 54812; phone: 715-537-6265; criminal phone: 715-537-6268; civil phone: 715-537-6271; probate phone: 715-537-6261; fax: 715-537-6269; hours 8AM-4:30PM (CST). *Felony, Misdemeanor, Civil, Eviction, Small Claims.*

Civil Records: Access: Online, in person. Visitors must perform in person searches themselves. Court makes copy: $1.25 per page. Required to search: name, years to search. Civil cases indexed by defendant, plaintiff; on computer, index cards from 1983. Organized 1859. Civil court records free online at http://wcca.wicourts.gov/index.xsl.
Criminal Records: Access: Online, in person. Visitors must perform in person searches themselves. Court makes copy: $1.25 per page. Required to search: name, years to search. Criminal records on computer, index cards from 1983. Organized 1859. Access criminal index free at http://wcca.wicourts.gov/index.xsl.
General Information: Public terminal goes back to mid-1993. No expunged, paternity or sealed records released. Will fax documents for $2.00 per page. Certification fee: $5.00 per document. Payee: Clerk of Court. Personal checks accepted. Prepayment required.

Register in Probate Barron Justice Ctr, 1420 State Hwy 25 N, Rm 2700, Barron, WI 54812; phone: 715-537-6261; fax: 715-537-6769; hours 8AM-4:30PM (CST). *Probate.*
Free search at http://wcca.wicourts.gov/index.xsl.

Bayfield County

Circuit Court 117 E 5th, Washburn, WI 54891; phone: 715-373-6108; fax: 715-373-6153; hours 8AM-4PM (CST). *Felony, Misdemeanor, Civil, Eviction, Small Claims.*
Civil Records: Access: Mail, online, in person. Both court and visitors may perform in person searches. Search fee: $5.00 per name. Court makes copy: $1.25 per page; same fee for self serve. Required to search: name, years to search. Civil cases indexed by defendant, plaintiff; on computer for all open cases since 1982, on index cards from 1979, index books in archives from 1845 to 1979. Civil court records free online at http://wcca.wicourts.gov/index.xsl. Mail turnaround time 1-2 days.
Criminal Records: Access: Mail, online, in person. Both court and visitors may perform in person searches. Search fee: $5.00 per name. Court makes copy: $1.25 per page; same fee for self serve. Required to search: name, years to search, DOB. Criminal records on computer since 3/93. Criminal index free at http://wcca.wicourts.gov/index.xsl. Mail turnaround time 1-2 days.
General Information: Public terminal goes back to 1993. No sealed records released. Fee to fax documents is $2.50 per page. Certification fee: $5.00. Payee: Clerk of Court. Personal checks accepted. Prepayment and SASE required.

Register in Probate PO Box 536, 117 E 5th St, Washburn, WI 54891; phone: 715-373-6108; fax: 715-373-6153; hours 8AM-4PM (CST). *Probate.*
Free search at http://wcca.wicourts.gov/index.xsl.

Brown County

Circuit Court PO Box 23600, Green Bay, WI 54305-3600; phone: 920-448-4161; probate phone: 920-448-4275; fax: 920-448-4156; hours 8AM-4:30PM (CST). *Felony, Misdemeanor, Civil, Eviction, Small Claims.*
Civil Records: Access: Mail, online, in person. Both court and visitors may perform in person searches. Search fee: $5.00 per name. Court makes copy: $1.25 per page. Required to search: name, years to search. Civil cases indexed by defendant, plaintiff; on computer since 1990, on microfiche from 1987-1990, archives from 1962-1990. Crossed on index cards from 1972, index books from 1982. Records free online at http://wcca.wicourts.gov/index.xsl. Mail turnaround time 10 days.
Criminal Records: Access: Mail, online, in person. Both court and visitors may perform in person searches. Search fee: $5.00 per name. Court makes copy: $1.25 per page. Required to search: name, years to search, DOB. Criminal records on computer since 1990, on microfiche from 1987-1990, archives from 1962-1990. Crossed on index cards from 1972, index books from 1982. Access criminal index free at http://wcca.wicourts.gov/index.xsl. Mail turnaround time 10 days.
General Information: Public terminal has criminal back to 1991 and civil back to 1990. No juvenile or preadjudicated paternity records released. Certification fee: $5.00. Payee: Brown County Clerk of Court. Personal checks accepted. Prepayment and SASE required.

Register in Probate PO Box 23600, Green Bay, WI 54305-3600; phone: 920-448-4275; fax: 920-448-6208; hours 8AM-4:30PM (CST). *Probate.*
Free search at http://wcca.wicourts.gov/index.xsl.

Buffalo County

Circuit Court 407 S 2nd, PO Box 68, Alma, WI 54610; phone: 608-685-6212; fax: 608-685-6211; hours 8AM-4:30PM (CST). *Felony, Misdemeanor, Civil, Eviction, Small Claims.*
Civil Records: Access: Phone, fax, mail, online, in person. Both court and visitors may perform in person searches. Search fee: $5.00 per name. Court makes copy: $1.25 per page. Required to search: name, years to search. Civil cases indexed by defendant, plaintiff; on computer from 1994, on index cards from 1979. No civil records available before 1962. Civil court records free online at http://wcca.wicourts.gov/index.xsl. Mail turnaround time 1 week.
Criminal Records: Access: Phone, fax, mail, online, in person. Both court and visitors may perform in person searches. Search fee: $5.00 per name. Court makes copy: $1.25 per page. Required to search: name, years to search. Criminal records on computer from 1994. Felonies retained 50 years; misdemeanors 20 years. Access criminal index free at http://wcca.wicourts.gov/index.xsl. Mail turnaround time 1 week.
General Information: Public terminal goes back to 1994. No closed records released. Fee to fax documents is $1.25 per page. Certification fee: $5.00 per document. Payee: Buffalo County Clerk of Court. Personal checks accepted. Prepayment and SASE required.

Register in Probate 407 S 2nd, PO Box 68, Alma, WI 54610; phone: 608-685-6202; fax: 608-685-6211; hours 8AM-4:30PM (CST). *Probate.*
Free search at http://wcca.wicourts.gov/index.xsl.

Burnett County

Circuit Court 7410 County Road K, #115, Siren, WI 54872; phone: 715-349-2147; probate phone: 715-349-2177; fax: 715-349-7659; hours 8:30AM-4:30PM (CST). *Felony, Misdemeanor, Civil, Eviction, Small Claims.*
Civil Records: Access: Mail, online, in person. Both court and visitors may perform in person searches. Search fee: $5.00 per name. Court makes copy: $1.25 per page. Required to search: name, years to search. Civil cases indexed by defendant, plaintiff; on computer from 10/92, on index books from 1800s. Organized 1856. Civil court records free online at http://wcca.wicourts.gov/index.xsl. Mail turnaround time 1-2 days.
Criminal Records: Access: Mail, online, in person. Both court and visitors may perform in person searches. Search fee: $5.00 per name. Court makes copy: $1.25 per page. Required to search: name, years to search. Criminal records on computer from 10/92, on index books from 1800s. Organized 1856. Access criminal index free at http://wcca.wicourts.gov/index.xsl. Mail turnaround time 1-2 days.
General Information: Public terminal goes back to 1992. No paternity, juvenile, sealed or confidential records released. Will fax documents to local or toll free line. Fees must be paid in advance. Certification fee: $5.00 per document. Payee: Clerk of Courts. Personal checks accepted. Prepayment and SASE required.

Register in Probate 7410 County Road K #110, Siren, WI 54872; phone: 715-349-2177 x0301; fax: 715-349-7659; hours 8:30AM-4:30PM (CST). *Probate.*

Free search at http://wcca.wicourts.gov/index.xsl. This court also holds Juvenile, Guardianship, Mental Commitments, Adoptions, and Term. of Parental Right.

Calumet County

Circuit Court 206 Court St, Chilton, WI 53014; phone: 920-849-1414; fax: 920-849-1483; hours 8AM-4:30PM (CST). *Felony, Misdemeanor, Civil, Eviction, Small Claims.*
Civil Records: Access: Mail, online, in person. Both court and visitors may perform in person searches. Search fee: $5.00 per name. Court makes copy: $1.25 per page. Required to search: name, years to search. Civil cases indexed by defendant, plaintiff; on computer from 1992, index cards from 1978, index books from 1800s. Civil court records free online at http://wcca.wicourts.gov/index.xsl. Mail turnaround time 2 days.
Criminal Records: Access: Mail, online, in person. Both court and visitors may perform in person searches. Search fee: $5.00 per name. Court makes copy: $1.25 per page. Required to search: name, years to search, DOB. Criminal records on computer from 1992, index cards from 1978, index books from 1800s. Access criminal index free at http://wcca.wicourts.gov/index.xsl. Mail turnaround time 2 days.
General Information: Public use terminal available. No juvenile or paternity records released. Certification fee: $5.00. Payee: Clerk of Court. Personal checks accepted. Prepayment and SASE required.

Register in Probate 206 Court St, Chilton, WI 53014-1198; phone: 920-849-1455; fax: 920-849-1483; hours 8AM-N, 1-4:30PM (CST). *Probate.*
Free search at http://wcca.wicourts.gov/index.xsl.

Chippewa County

Circuit Court 711 N Bridge St, Chippewa Falls, WI 54729-1879; phone: 715-726-7758; probate phone: 715-726-7737; fax: 715-726-7786; hours 8AM-4:30PM (CST). *Felony, Misdemeanor, Civil, Eviction, Small Claims.*
Civil Records: Access: Mail, fax, online, in person. Both court and visitors may perform in person searches. Search fee: $5.00 per name. Court makes copy: $1.25 per page. Required to search: name, years to search; also helpful: address, records sought. Civil cases indexed by defendant, plaintiff; on computer from 1990, index cards from 1979, index books from 1900s. Civil court records free online at http://wcca.wicourts.gov/index.xsl. Mail turnaround time same as criminal.
Criminal Records: Access: Mail, fax, online, in person. Both court and visitors may perform in person searches. Search fee: $5.00 per name. Court makes copy: $1.25 per page. Required to search: name, years to search, DOB; also helpful: SSN. Criminal records on computer from 1990, index cards from 1979, index books from 1900s. Access criminal index free at http://wcca.wicourts.gov/index.xsl. Mail turnaround time 10 days or less; up to 30 days if pre-1990.
General Information: Public use terminal available. Paternity records released only to party or attorney of record, or with written court authorization. Fee to fax documents is $2.00 for 1st page and $1.00 per page thereafter. Certification fee: $5.00. Payee: Chippewa County Clerk of Courts. Personal checks accepted. Prepayment and SASE required.

Register in Probate 711 N Bridge St, Chippewa Falls, WI 54729; phone: 715-726-7737; fax: 715-738-2626; hours 8AM-4:30PM (CST). *Probate.*
Free search at http://wcca.wicourts.gov/index.xsl.

Clark County

Circuit Court 517 Court St, Neillsville, WI 54456-1971; phone: 715-743-5181; fax: 715-743-5120; hours 8AM-4:30PM (CST). *Felony, Misdemeanor, Civil, Eviction, Small Claims.*
Civil Records: Access: Mail, online, in person. Both court and visitors may perform in person searches. Search fee: $5.00 per name. Court makes copy: $.30 per page. Required to search: name, years to search. Civil cases indexed by defendant, plaintiff; on computer from 1994, on index cards from 1981, index books from 1900s. Civil court records free online at http://wcca.wicourts.gov/index.xsl. Mail turnaround time 1-2 weeks.
Criminal Records: Access: Mail, online, in person. Both court and visitors may perform in person searches. Search fee: $5.00 per name. Court makes copy: $.30 per page. Required to search: name, years to search. Criminal records on computer from 1994, on index cards from 1981, index books from 1900s. Access criminal index free at http://wcca.wicourts.gov/index.xsl. Mail turnaround time 1-2 weeks.
General Information: Public terminal goes back to 1993. No sealed or paternity records released. Will fax documents. Certification fee: $5.00 per doc. Payee: Clerk of Court. Personal checks accepted. Prepayment and SASE required.

Register in Probate 517 Court St, Rm 403, Neillsville, WI 54456; phone: 715-743-5172; fax: 715-743-5120; hours 8AM-4:30PM (CST). *Probate.*
Note: There is a $4.00 search fee. Also, probate records free online at http://wcca.wicourts.gov/index.xsl.

Columbia County

Circuit Court PO Box 587, Portage, WI 53901; phone: 608-742-9642; criminal phone: 608-742-9643; civil phone: 608-742-9624; probate phone: 608-742-9636; criminal fax: 608-742-9601; same fax for civil/probate; hours 8AM-4:30PM (CST). *Felony, Misdemeanor, Civil, Eviction, Small Claims, Probate.*
Civil Records: Access: Mail, online, in person. Both court and visitors may perform in person searches. Search fee: $5.00 per name. Court makes copy: $1.25 per page. Required to search: name, years to search. Civil cases indexed by defendant, plaintiff; on computer from 1994, on microfiche to 1960s, concurrent index cards/books from 1940s. Civil and probate court records free online at http://wcca.wicourts.gov/index.xsl. Mail turnaround time 1-2 weeks.
Criminal Records: Access: Mail, online, in person. Both court and visitors may perform in person searches. Search fee: $5.00 per name. Court makes copy: $1.25 per page. Required to search: name, years to search, DOB. Criminal records on computer from 1994, on microfiche to 1960s, concurrent index cards/books from 1940s. Access criminal index free at http://wcca.wicourts.gov/index.xsl. Mail turnaround time 1-2 weeks.
General Information: Public terminal goes back to 1994. No juvenile or paternity records released. Fee to fax documents is $1.25 per page. Certification fee: $5.00. Payee: Clerk of Court. Personal checks accepted. Prepayment and SASE required.

Crawford County

Circuit Court 220 N Beaumont Rd, Prairie Du Chien, WI 53821; phone: 608-326-0211; criminal phone: 608-326-010; civil phone: 608-326-0208; probate phone: 608-326-0206; hours 8AM-4:30PM (CST). *Felony, Misdemeanor, Civil, Eviction, Small Claims.*
Civil Records: Access: Mail, online, in person. Both court and visitors may perform in person searches. Search fee: $5.00 per name. Court makes copy: $1.25 per page. Required to search: name, years to search. Civil cases indexed by defendant, plaintiff; on computer from 1993, on index cards from 1984, index

books from 1900. Historical Society has archives. Civil court records free online at http://wcca.wicourts.gov/index.xsl. Mail turnaround time 10 working days.
Criminal Records: Access: Mail, online, in person. Both court and visitors may perform in person searches. Search fee: $5.00 per name. Court makes copy: $1.25 per page. Required to search: name, years to search. Criminal records on computer from 1993, on index cards from 1984, index books from 1900. Historical Society has archives. Access criminal index free at http://wcca.wicourts.gov/index.xsl. Mail turnaround time 10 working days.
General Information: Public terminal goes back to mid-1993. No juvenile, paternity, mental records released. Will not fax documents. Certification fee: $5.00. Payee: Clerk of Court. Personal checks accepted. Prepayment and SASE required.

Register in Probate 220 N Beaumont Rd, Prairie Du Chien, WI 53821; phone: 608-326-0206; fax: 608-326-0288; hours 8AM-4:30PM (CST). *Probate.*
Free search at http://wcca.wicourts.gov/index.xsl.

Dane County

Circuit Court 210 Martin Luther King Jr Blvd, Rm GR10, Madison, WI 53703; phone: 608-266-4311; probate phone: 608-266-4331; fax: 608-267-8859; hours 7:45AM-4:30PM (CST). *Felony, Misdemeanor, Civil, Eviction, Small Claims.*
www.co.dane.wi.us/clrkcort/clrhome.htm
Civil Records: Access: Fax, mail, online, in person. Both court and visitors may perform in person searches. Search fee: $5.00 per name. Court makes copy: $1.25 per page. Required to search: name, years to search. Civil cases indexed by defendant, plaintiff; on computer from 1981, on microfiche from 1976, plaintiff index books 1848. Civil court records free online at http://wcca.wicourts.gov/index.xsl. Mail turnaround time 2-3 days.
Criminal Records: Access: Fax, mail, online, in person. Both court and visitors may perform in person searches. Search fee: $5.00 per name. Court makes copy: $1.25 per page. Required to search: name, years to search, DOB. Criminal records on computer from 1983, index back to 1848. Access criminal index free at http://wcca.wicourts.gov/index.xsl. Mail turnaround time 2-3 days.
General Information: Public terminal has criminal back to 1983 approx and civil back to 1990s. (Small claims available back to 1984.) No "confidential records" released. Will fax documents $.50 for 1st 5 pages, $.23 for each add'l 5 pages or fraction thereof. Certification fee: $5.00 per document. Payee: Dane County Clerk of Courts. Personal checks accepted. Prepayment and SASE required.

Register in Probate 210 Martin Luther King Jr Blvd, Rm 305, Madison, WI 53703-3344; phone: 608-266-4331; fax: 608-267-4152; hours 7:45AM-4:30PM (CST). *Probate.*
Free search at http://wcca.wicourts.gov/index.xsl.

Dodge County

Circuit Court 210 W Center St, Juneau, WI 53039; phone: 920-386-3820; fax: 920-386-3587; hours 8AM-4:30PM (CST). *Felony, Misdemeanor, Civil, Eviction, Small Claims.*
Civil Records: Access: Mail, online, in person. Both court and visitors may perform in person searches. Search fee: $5.00 per name. Court makes copy: $1.25 per page. Required to search: name, years to search. Civil cases indexed by defendant, plaintiff; on computer from 1993, on index cards from 1986, microfiche from 1972, index books from 1950s. Civil court records free online at http://wcca.wicourts.gov/index.xsl. Mail turnaround time 1-2 days.
Criminal Records: Access: Mail, online, in person. Both court and visitors may perform in person

searches. Search fee: $5.00 per name. Court makes copy: $1.25 per page. Required to search: name, years to search, DOB. Criminal records on computer from 1993, on index cards from 1986, microfiche from 1972, index books from 1950s. Access criminal index free at http://wcca.wicourts.gov/index.xsl. Mail turnaround time 1-2 days.

General Information: Public terminal goes back to 1990. No juvenile or John Doe records released. Fee to fax documents is $1.50 per page. Certification fee: $5.00 per doc. Payee: Clerk of Courts. Personal checks accepted. Prepayment and SASE required.

Register in Probate 210 W Center St, Juneau, WI 53039-1091; phone: 920-386-3550; hours 8AM-4:30PM (CST). *Probate.*

Note: $4.00 search fee; records computerized since 1992. Also, probate records free at http://wcca.wicourts.gov/index.xsl.

Door County

Circuit Court PO Box 670, Sturgeon Bay, WI 54235; phone: 920-746-2205; fax: 920-746-2520; hours 8AM-4:30PM (CST). *Felony, Misdemeanor, Civil, Eviction, Small Claims.*

Civil Records: Access: Mail, online, in person. Both court and visitors may perform in person searches. Search fee: $5.00 per file. Court makes copy: $1.25 per page; same fee for self serve. Required to search: name, years to search. Civil cases indexed by defendant, plaintiff; on computer from 4/93, on index cards from 1984. Civil court records free online at http://wcca.wicourts.gov/index.xsl. Mail turnaround time 2-3 days.

Criminal Records: Access: Mail, online, in person. Both court and visitors may perform in person searches. Search fee: $5.00 per file. Court makes copy: $1.25 per page; same fee for self serve. Required to search: name, years to search, DOB. Criminal records on computer from 4/93, on index cards from 1984, index books from 1900s. Access criminal index free at http://wcca.wicourts.gov/index.xsl. Mail turnaround time 2-3 days.

General Information: Public terminal has only civil records back to 4/1993. No financial or paternity records released. Fee to fax documents is $3.00 per document. Certification fee: $5.00 per document. Payee: Clerk of Court. Personal checks accepted. Prepayment and SASE required.

Register in Probate PO Box 670, 421 Nebraska St, Rm C375, Sturgeon Bay, WI 54235-2470; phone: 920-746-2482; hours 8AM-4:30PM (CST). *Probate.* Free search at http://wcca.wicourts.gov/index.xsl.

Douglas County

Circuit Court 1313 Belknap, Superior, WI 54880; criminal phone: 715-395-1240; civil phone: 715-395-1233; fax: 715-395-1421; hours 8AM-4:30PM (CST). *Felony, Misdemeanor, Civil, Eviction, Small Claims.*

Civil Records: Access: Mail, online, in person. Both court and visitors may perform in person searches. Search fee: $5.00 per name. Court makes copy: $1.25 per page. Required to search: name, years to search. Civil cases indexed by defendant, plaintiff; on computer since 1994; prior records on index cards from 1976, index books from 1900s. Civil court records free online at http://wcca.wicourts.gov/index.xsl. Mail turnaround time 1-2 weeks.

Criminal Records: Access: Mail, online, in person. Both court and visitors may perform in person searches. Search fee: $5.00 per name. Court makes copy: $1.25 per page. Required to search: name, years to search; also helpful: DOB. Criminal records on computer since 1994; prior records on index cards from 1976, index books from 1900s. Access criminal index free at http://wcca.wicourts.gov/index.xsl. Mail turnaround time 1-2 weeks.

General Information: Public terminal goes back to 1994. No juvenile or paternity records released. Will

fax documents for $1.00 per page. Certification fee: $5.00 per document. Payee: Clerk of Courts. Only cashiers checks and money orders accepted. Douglas County personal checks accepted. Prepayment and SASE required.

Register in Probate 1313 Belknap, Superior, WI 54880; phone: 715-395-1220; fax: 715-395-1550; hours 8AM-4:30PM (CST). *Probate.* Free search at http://wcca.wicourts.gov/index.xsl. This court also takes care of Guardianship, Mental Commitment, Adoptions

Dunn County

Circuit Court 615 Stokke Parkway, #1500, Menomonie, WI 54751; phone: 715-232-2611; fax: 715-232-6888; hours 8AM-4:30PM (CST). *Felony, Misdemeanor, Civil, Eviction, Small Claims.*

Civil Records: Access: Mail, online, in person. Both court and visitors may perform in person searches. Search fee: $5.00 per name. Court makes copy: $1.25 per page. Required to search: name, years to search. Civil cases indexed by defendant, plaintiff; on computer from 1987, index cards from 1977, index books from 1900s, archives from 1970. Civil court records free online at http://wcca.wicourts.gov/index.xsl. Mail turnaround time 2-3 days.

Criminal Records: Access: Mail, online, in person. Both court and visitors may perform in person searches. Search fee: $5.00 per name. Court makes copy: $1.25 per page. Required to search: name, years to search, DOB. Criminal records on computer from 1987, index cards from 1977, index books from 1900s, archives from 1970. Access criminal index free at http://wcca.wicourts.gov/index.xsl. Mail turnaround time 2-3 days.

General Information: Public terminal goes back to 1987. No juvenile, family financial, sealed records released. Certification fee: $5.00 per document. Payee: Clerk of Court. Personal checks accepted. Prepayment required.

Register in Probate 615 Stokke Pky, #1300, Menomonie, WI 54751; phone: 715-232-6782; fax: 715-232-6782; hours 8AM-4:30PM (CST). *Probate.* Free search at http://wcca.wicourts.gov/index.xsl.

Eau Claire County

Circuit Court 721 Oxford Ave, Eau Claire, WI 54703; phone: 715-839-4816; fax: 715-839-4817; hours 8AM-5PM (CST). *Felony, Misdemeanor, Civil, Eviction, Small Claims.*

Civil Records: Access: Mail, online, in person. Both court and visitors may perform in person searches. Search fee: $5.00 per name. Court makes copy: $1.25 per page. Self serve copy fee: $.25 per page. Required to search: name, years to search. Civil cases indexed by defendant, plaintiff; on computer from 7/92, on index cards from 1970, index books from 1968. Civil court records free online at http://wcca.wicourts.gov/index.xsl. Mail turnaround time 1-10 days.

Criminal Records: Access: Mail, online, in person. Both court and visitors may perform in person searches. Search fee: $5.00 per name. Court makes copy: $1.25 per page. Self serve copy fee: $.25 per page. Required to search: name, years to search, DOB. Criminal records on computer from 7/92, on index cards from 1970, index books from 1968. Access criminal index free at http://wcca.wicourts.gov/index.xsl. Mail turnaround time 1-10 days.

General Information: Public terminal goes back to 7/1992. No paternity, financial disclosure, expungment or sealed records released. Will fax documents. Certification fee: $5.00 per document. Payee: Clerk of Court-Eau Claire County. Personal checks accepted. Prepayment and SASE required.

Register in Probate 721 Oxford Ave, Rm 2201, Eau Claire, WI 54703; phone: 715-839-4823; fax: 715-831-5835; hours 8AM-N, 1-5PM (CST). *Probate.*

Free search at http://wcca.wicourts.gov/index.xsl.

Florence County

Circuit Court PO Box 410, Florence, WI 54121; phone: 715-528-3205; fax: 715-528-5470; hours 8:30AM-4PM (CST). *Felony, Misdemeanor, Civil, Eviction, Small Claims.*

Civil Records: Access: Mail, online, in person. Both court and visitors may perform in person searches. Search fee: $5.00 per name. Court makes copy: $1.25 per page. Required to search: name, years to search. Civil cases indexed by defendant, plaintiff; on computer from 1991; prior records on index books from 1900s. Civil court records free online at http://wcca.wicourts.gov/index.xsl. Mail turnaround time 2 weeks.

Criminal Records: Access: Mail, online, in person. Both court and visitors may perform in person searches. Search fee: $5.00 per name. Court makes copy: $1.25 per page. Required to search: name, years to search. Criminal records on computer from 1991; prior records on index books from 1900s. Access criminal index free at http://wcca.wicourts.gov/index.xsl. Mail turnaround time 2 weeks.

General Information: Public use terminal available. No juvenile, mental health, adoption or guardianship records released. Certification fee: $4.00. Payee: Clerk of Courts. Personal checks accepted. Prepayment and SASE required.

Register in Probate PO Box 410, 501 Lake Ave, Florence, WI 54121; phone: 715-528-3205; fax: 715-528-5470; hours 8:30AM-12;30, 1-4PM (CST). *Probate.*

Free search at http://wcca.wicourts.gov/index.xsl.

Fond du Lac County

Circuit Court 160 S Macy, Fond du Lac, WI 54936-1355; phone: 920-929-3040; fax: 920-929-3933; hours 8AM-4:30PM (CST). *Felony, Misdemeanor, Civil, Eviction, Small Claims.*

Civil Records: Access: Mail, online, in person. Both court and visitors may perform in person searches. Search fee: $5.00 per name. Court makes copy: $1.25 per page. Required to search: name, years to search. Civil cases indexed by defendant, plaintiff; on computer from 1990, index cards from 1978, microfiche 1836 to 1978, archives prior to 1900s. Old files destroyed, on microfiche or in Historical Society. Civil court records free online at http://wcca.wicourts.gov/index.xsl. Mail turnaround time 1-2 days.

Criminal Records: Access: Mail, online, in person. Both court and visitors may perform in person searches. Search fee: $5.00 per name. Court makes copy: $1.25 per page. Required to search: name, years to search, DOB. Criminal records on computer from 1990, index cards from 1978, microfiche 1836 to 1978, archives prior to 1900s. Old files destroyed, on microfiche or in Historical Society. Access criminal index free at http://wcca.wicourts.gov/index.xsl. Mail turnaround time 1-2 days.

General Information: No juvenile or paternity records released. Fee to fax documents is $2.00 per document. Certification fee: $5.00 per doc. Payee: Clerk of Circuit Court. Personal checks accepted. Prepayment and SASE required.

Register in Probate PO Box 1576, 160 S Macy St, Fond du Lac, WI 54936-1576; phone: 920-929-3084; fax: 920-906-5540; hours 8AM-4:30PM (CST). *Probate.*

Free search at http://wcca.wicourts.gov/index.xsl.

Forest County

Circuit Court 200 E Madison St, Crandon, WI 54520; phone: 715-478-3323; fax: 715-478-3211; hours 8:30AM-4:30PM (CST). *Felony, Misdemeanor, Civil, Eviction, Small Claims.*
Civil Records: Access: Mail, online, in person. Both court and visitors may perform in person searches. Search fee: $5.00 per name. Court makes copy: $1.25 per page. Self serve copy fee: $.10 per page plus tax. Required to search: name, years to search. Civil cases indexed by defendant, plaintiff; on computer from 1994, on index cards from 1979, index books from 1920s. Civil court records free online at http://wcca.wicourts.gov/index.xsl. Mail turnaround time 1-2 days.
Criminal Records: Access: Mail, online, in person. Both court and visitors may perform in person searches. Search fee: $5.00 per name. Court makes copy: $1.25 per page. Self serve copy fee: $.10 per page plus tax. Required to search: name, years to search, DOB. Criminal records on computer from 1994, on index cards from 1979, index books from 1920s. Access criminal index free at http://wcca.wicourts.gov/index.xsl. Mail turnaround time 1-2 days.
General Information: Public terminal goes back to 1994. No juvenile, paternity records released. Fee to fax documents is $1.25 per page. Certification fee: $5.00 per document. Payee: Clerk of Court. Personal checks accepted. Prepayment and SASE required.

Register in Probate 200 E Madison St, Crandon, WI 54520; phone: 715-478-2418; fax: 715-478-2430; hours 8:30AM-12;00,1-4:30PM (CST). *Probate.*
Free search at http://wcca.wicourts.gov/index.xsl.

Grant County

Circuit Court PO Box 110, Lancaster, WI 53813; phone: 608-723-2752; fax: 608-723-7370; hours 8AM-4:30PM (CST). *Felony, Misdemeanor, Civil, Eviction, Small Claims.*
Civil Records: Access: Phone, mail, fax, online, in person. Both court and visitors may perform in person searches. No search fee. Court makes copy: $1.25 per page. Required to search: name, years to search. Civil cases indexed by defendant, plaintiff; on computer from 10/93, on index books from 1900s. Civil court records free online at http://wcca.wicourts.gov/index.xsl. Mail turnaround time 2 weeks.
Criminal Records: Access: Phone, mail, fax, online, in person. Both court and visitors may perform in person searches. No search fee. Court makes copy: $1.25 per page. Required to search: name, years to search. Criminal records on computer from 10/93, on index books from 1900s. Access criminal index free at http://wcca.wicourts.gov/index.xsl. Mail turnaround time 2 weeks.
General Information: Public use terminal available. No juvenile, paternity records released. Will fax documents to local or toll free line. Certification fee: $5.00 per document. Payee: Clerk of Court. Personal checks accepted. Prepayment and SASE required.

Register in Probate 130 W Maple St, Rm A360, Lancaster, WI 53813; phone: 608-723-2697; fax: 608-723-7370; hours 8AM-4:30PM (CST). *Probate.*
Note: $4.00 search fee, records computerized since 1993. Probate records free at http://wcca.wicourts.gov/index.xsl.

Green County

Circuit Court 1016 16th Ave, Monroe, WI 53566; phone: 608-328-9433; fax: 608-328-9459; hours 8AM-4:30PM (CST). *Felony, Misdemeanor, Civil, Eviction, Small Claims.*
www.co.green.wi.gov/
Civil Records: Access: Mail, online, in person. Both court and visitors may perform in person searches. Search fee: $5.00 per name. Court makes copy: $1.25 per page. Required to search: name, years to search;

also helpful: address. Civil cases indexed by defendant, plaintiff; on index cards from 1984, index books from 1900s; computerized back to 1994. Civil court records free online at http://wcca.wicourts.gov/index.xsl. Mail turnaround time 1-2 days.
Criminal Records: Access: Mail, online, in person. Both court and visitors may perform in person searches. Search fee: $5.00 per name. Court makes copy: $1.25 per page. Required to search: name, years to search; also helpful: DOB. Criminal records on index cards from 1984, index books from 1900s; computerized back to 1994. Access criminal index free at http://wcca.wicourts.gov/index.xsl. Mail turnaround time 1-2 days.
General Information: Public terminal goes back to 1994. No juvenile, paternity or sealed records released. Will fax documents for $1.00 per page. Certification fee: $5.00 per doc. Payee: Clerk of Court. Personal checks accepted. Prepayment and SASE required.

Register in Probate 1016 16th Ave, Monroe, WI 53566; phone: 608-328-9567; fax: 608-328-9459; hours 8AM-12, 1PM-4:30PM (CST). *Probate.*
Free search at http://wcca.wicourts.gov/index.xsl.

Green Lake County

Circuit Court 492 Hill St, PO Box 3188, Green Lake, WI 54941; phone: 920-294-4142; hours 8AM-4:30PM (CST). *Felony, Misdemeanor, Civil, Eviction, Small Claims.*
www.co.green-lake.wi.us
Civil Records: Access: Mail, online, in person. Both court and visitors may perform in person searches. Search fee: $5.00 per name. Court makes copy: $1.25 per page. Required to search: name, years to search. Civil cases indexed by defendant, plaintiff; on computer from 4/93, on index cards since 1900s. Civil court records free online at http://wcca.wicourts.gov/index.xsl. Mail turnaround time 1-3 days.
Criminal Records: Access: Mail, online, in person. Both court and visitors may perform in person searches. Search fee: $5.00 per name. Court makes copy: $1.25 per page. Required to search: name, years to search. Criminal records on computer from 4/93, on index cards since 1900s. Access criminal index free at http://wcca.wicourts.gov/index.xsl. Mail turnaround time 1-3 days.
General Information: Public terminal goes back to 1993. No paternity or juvenile ordinance records released. Certification fee: $5.00 per doc. Payee: Clerk of Circuit Clerk. Personal checks accepted. Prepayment and SASE required.

Register in Probate 492 Hill St, PO Box 3188, Green Lake, WI 54941; phone: 920-294-4044; hours 8AM-4:30PM (CST). *Probate.*
Free search at http://wcca.wicourts.gov/index.xsl.

Iowa County

Circuit Court 222 N Iowa St, Dodgeville, WI 53533; phone: 608-935-0395; probate phone: 608-935-0347; fax: 608-935-0386; hours 8:30AM-4:30PM (CST). *Felony, Misdemeanor, Civil, Eviction, Small Claims.*
Civil Records: Access: Mail, online, in person. Both court and visitors may perform in person searches. Search fee: $5.00 per name. Court makes copy: $1.25 per page. Required to search: name, years to search. Civil cases indexed by defendant, plaintiff; on computer from 1992, index cards from 1987, archives from 1917, index books from 1829. Civil court records free online at http://wcca.wicourts.gov/index.xsl. Mail turnaround time same day.
Criminal Records: Access: Mail, online, in person. Both court and visitors may perform in person searches. Search fee: $5.00 per name. Court makes copy: $1.25 per page. Required to search: name, years to search, DOB. Criminal records on computer from 1992, index cards from 1987, archives from 1917,

index books from 1829. Access criminal index free at http://wcca.wicourts.gov/index.xsl. Mail turnaround time same day.
General Information: Public terminal goes back to 1992. No adoption, paternity or mental records released. Fee to fax back- $5.00 plus $1.25 per page. Certification fee: $5.00 per doc. Payee: Clerk of Court. Personal checks accepted. Prepayment and SASE required.

Register in Probate 222 N Iowa St, Rm 206, Dodgeville, WI 53533; phone: 608-935-0347; fax: 608-935-0386; hours 8:30AM-N, 12;30-4:30PM (CST). *Probate.*
Free search at http://wcca.wicourts.gov/index.xsl.

Iron County

Circuit Court 300 Taconite St, #207, Hurley, WI 54534; phone: 715-561-4084; fax: 715-561-4054; hours 8AM-4PM (CST). *Felony, Misdemeanor, Civil, Eviction, Small Claims.*
Civil Records: Access: Phone, mail, online, in person. Both court and visitors may perform in person searches. Search fee: $5.00 per name. Court makes copy: $1.25 per page. Required to search: name, years to search. Civil cases indexed by defendant, plaintiff; on index cards from 1989, index books from 1920. Civil court records free online at http://wcca.wicourts.gov/index.xsl. Note: Phone access for title companies only. Mail turnaround time 2-3 days.
Criminal Records: Access: Mail, online, in person. Both court and visitors may perform in person searches. Search fee: $5.00 per name. Court makes copy: $1.25 per page. Required to search: name, years to search, DOB. Criminal records on index cards from 1989, index books from 1920. Access criminal index free at http://wcca.wicourts.gov/index.xsl. Mail turnaround time 2-3 days.
General Information: Public terminal goes back to 1993. No juvenile or paternity records released. Will fax documents to local or toll free line. Certification fee: $5.00 per doc. Payee: Clerk of Court. Personal checks accepted. Prepayment and SASE required.

Register in Probate 300 Taconite St, #209, Hurley, WI 54534; phone: 715-561-3434; fax: 715-561-4054; hours 8AM-4PM (CST). *Probate.*
Free search at http://wcca.wicourts.gov/index.xsl.

Jackson County

Circuit Court 307 Main St, Black River Falls, WI 54615; phone: 715-284-0208; probate phone: 715-284-0213; fax: 715-284-0270; hours 8AM-4:30PM (CST). *Felony, Misdemeanor, Civil, Eviction, Small Claims.*
www.co.jackson.wi.us
Civil Records: Access: Mail, online, in person. Both court and visitors may perform in person searches. Search fee: $5.00 per name. Court makes copy: $1.25 per page. Required to search: name, years to search. Civil cases indexed by defendant, plaintiff; on computer from 6/92, on index cards from 1979, index books to 1980, files and indexes prior to 1980 destroyed. Civil court records free online at http://wcca.wicourts.gov/index.xsl. Mail turnaround time 1-4 days.
Criminal Records: Access: Mail, online, in person. Both court and visitors may perform in person searches. Search fee: $5.00 per name. Court makes copy: $1.25 per page. Required to search: name, years to search, DOB. Criminal records on computer from 6/92. Felonies 1879 to 1927 at State Historical Society. Access criminal index free at http://wcca.wicourts.gov/index.xsl. Mail turnaround time 1-4 days.
General Information: Public terminal goes back to 1992. No juvenile or pre-judgment paternity records released. Will fax documents $3.00; must be pre-paid. Certification fee: $5.00. Payee: Clerk of Court. Personal checks accepted. I. Prepayment required. Prepayment required if over $5.00. SASE required.

Register in Probate 307 Main St, Black River Falls, WI 54615; phone: 715-284-0213; fax: 715-284-0277; hours 8AM-4:30PM (CST). *Probate.* Free search at http://wcca.wicourts.gov/index.xsl.

Jefferson County

Circuit Court 320 S Main St, Jefferson, WI 53549; phone: 920-674-7150; fax: 920-674-7425; hours 8AM-4:30PM (CST). *Felony, Misdemeanor, Civil, Eviction, Small Claims.*
Civil Records: Access: Mail, online, in person. Both court and visitors may perform in person searches. Search fee: $5.00 per name. Court makes copy: $1.25 per page. Required to search: name, years to search. Civil cases indexed by defendant, plaintiff; on computer from 1992, on index cards from 1979, index books from late 1800s. Civil court records free online at http://wcca.wicourts.gov/index.xsl. Mail turnaround time 2-3 days.
Criminal Records: Access: Mail, online, in person. Both court and visitors may perform in person searches. Search fee: $5.00 per name. Court makes copy: $1.25 per page. Self serve copy fee: $1.00 per page. Required to search: name, years to search, DOB. Criminal records on computer from 1992, on index cards from 1979, index books from late 1800s. Access criminal index free at http://wcca.wicourts.gov/index.xsl. Mail turnaround time 2-3 days.
General Information: Public terminal goes back to 1992. No juvenile or mental health records released. Certification fee: $5.00. Payee: Clerk of Courts. Personal checks accepted. Prepayment and SASE required.

Register in Probate 320 S Main St, Jefferson, WI 53549; phone: 920-674-7245; fax: 920-675-0134; hours 8AM-4:30PM (CST). *Probate.* Free search at http://wcca.wicourts.gov/index.xsl.

Juneau County

Circuit Court 200 Oak St, Juneau County Justice Ctr, Mauston, WI 53948; phone: 608-847-9356; fax: 608-847-9360; hours 8AM-4:30PM (CST). *Felony, Misdemeanor, Civil, Eviction, Small Claims.* http://wicourts.gov/casesearch.htm
Civil Records: Access: Mail, online, in person. Both court and visitors may perform in person searches. Search fee: $5.00 per name. Fee is per case. Court makes copy: $1.25 per page. Required to search: name, years to search, DOB. Civil cases indexed by defendant, plaintiff; on computer from 1988, index cards from 1977, index books from 1900, microfiche from 1856-1900. Civil court records free online at http://wcca.wicourts.gov/index.xsl. Mail turnaround time 1 week.
Criminal Records: Access: Mail, online, in person. Both court and visitors may perform in person searches. Search fee: $5.00 per name. Court makes copy: $1.25 per page. Required to search: name, years to search, DOB. Criminal records on computer from 1988, index cards from 1977, index books from 1900, microfiche from 1856-1900. Access criminal index free at http://wcca.wicourts.gov/index.xsl. Mail turnaround time 1 week.
General Information: Public terminal goes back to 1996. No juvenile, confidential family or paternity records released. Certification fee: $5.00 per doc. Payee: Juneau County Clerk of Court. Personal checks accepted. Prepayment and SASE required.

Register in Probate 200 Oak St, Rm 2300, Mauston, WI 53948; phone: 608-847-9346; fax: 608-847-9349; hours 8AM-4:30PM (CST). *Probate.* Free search at http://wcca.wicourts.gov/index.xsl.

Kenosha County

Circuit Court 912 56th St, Kenosha, WI 53140; phone: 262-653-2664; fax: 262-653-2435; hours 8AM-5PM (CST). *Felony, Misdemeanor, Civil, Eviction, Small Claims.*
Civil Records: Access: Mail, online, in person. Both court and visitors may perform in person searches.

Search fee: $5.00 per name. Court makes copy: $1.25 per page. Required to search: name, years to search. Civil cases indexed by defendant, plaintiff; on computer from 1989, index cards from 1960, microfiche from 1850. Civil court records free online at http://wcca.wicourts.gov/index.xsl. Mail turnaround time 1-2 days.
Criminal Records: Access: Mail, online, in person, fax. Both court and visitors may perform in person searches. Search fee: $5.00 per name. Court makes copy: $1.25 per page. Required to search: name, years to search; also helpful: DOB, SSN. Criminal records on computer from 1989, index cards from 1960, microfiche from 1850. Access criminal index free at http://wcca.wicourts.gov/index.xsl. Mail turnaround time 1-2 days.
General Information: Public terminal goes back to 1995. No juvenile or paternity records released. Will fax documents to local or toll free line. Certification fee: $5.00. Payee: Clerk of Court. Personal checks accepted. Prepayment and SASE required.

Register in Probate Courthouse, Rm 304, 912 56th St, Kenosha, WI 53140; phone: 262-653-2675; fax: 262-653-2673; hours 8AM-5PM (CST). *Probate.*
Note: $4.00 per search, records indexed on computer back to 1992; cards prior. Probate records free at http://wcca.wicourts.gov/index.xsl.

Kewaunee County

Circuit Court 613 Dodge St, Kewaunee, WI 54216; phone: 920-388-7144; criminal phone: 920-388-7153; civil phone: 920-388-7146; fax: 920-388-3139; hours 8AM-4:30PM (CST). *Felony, Misdemeanor, Civil, Eviction, Small Claims.* http://wicourts.gov/casesearch.htm
Civil Records: Access: Phone, mail, online, in person. Both court and visitors may perform in person searches. Search fee: $5.00 per name. Court makes copy: $1.25 per page; same fee for self serve. Required to search: name, years to search. Civil cases indexed by defendant, plaintiff. Computerized records from 1993, civil records on index cards from 1950, index books from 1852. Civil court records free online at http://wcca.wicourts.gov/index.xsl. Mail turnaround time 1-2 days.
Criminal Records: Access: Phone, mail, online, in person. Both court and visitors may perform in person searches. Search fee: $5.00 per name. Court makes copy: $1.25 per page; same fee for self serve. Required to search: name, years to search, DOB. Computerized records from 1993, criminal records on index cards from 1950, index books from 1852. Access criminal index free at http://wcca.wicourts.gov/index.xsl. Mail turnaround time 1-2 days.
General Information: Public terminal goes back to 1993. No paternity records released. Will fax documents for $1.00 1st page, $.50 each add'l page. Certification fee: $5.00 per document. Payee: Clerk of Circuit Court. Personal checks accepted. Prepayment and SASE required.

Register in Probate 613 Dodge St, Kewaunee, WI 54216; phone: 920-388-7143; fax: 920-388-3139; hours 8AM-4:30PM (CST). *Probate.* Free search at http://wcca.wicourts.gov/index.xsl.

La Crosse County

Circuit Court 333 Vine St, La Crosse, WI 54601; phone: 608-785-9590/9573; fax: 608-789-7821; hours 8:30AM-5PM (CST). *Felony, Misdemeanor, Civil, Eviction, Small Claims.*
Civil Records: Access: Fax, mail, online, in person. Both court and visitors may perform in person searches. Search fee: $5.00 per name. Court makes copy: $1.25 per page. Required to search: name, years to search. Civil cases indexed by defendant, plaintiff; on computer from 1993, on index cards from 1983, index books from 1917. Civil court records free online at http://wcca.wicourts.gov/index.xsl. Mail turnaround time 1-2 days.

Criminal Records: Access: Fax, mail, online, in person. Both court and visitors may perform in person searches. Search fee: $5.00 per name. Court makes copy: $1.25 per page. Required to search: name, years to search; also helpful: DOB. Criminal records on computer from 1993, on index cards from 1983, index books from 1917. Access criminal index free at http://wcca.wicourts.gov/index.xsl. Mail turnaround time 1-2 days.
General Information: Public terminal has criminal back to 1983 and civil back to 1993. No juvenile, paternity or finances in family records released. Fee to fax documents is $1.25 per page. Certification fee: $5.00 per doc. Payee: Clerk of Courts. Personal checks accepted. Prepayment and SASE required.

Register in Probate 333 Vine St, Rm 1201, La Crosse, WI 54601; phone: 608-785-9882; hours 8:30AM-5PM (CST). *Probate.* Free search at http://wcca.wicourts.gov/index.xsl.

Lafayette County

Circuit Court 626 Main St, Darlington, WI 53530; phone: 608-776-4832; probate phone: 608-776-4811; hours 8AM-4:30PM (CST). *Felony, Misdemeanor, Civil, Eviction, Small Claims.*
Civil Records: Access: Mail, online, in person. Both court and visitors may perform in person searches. Search fee: $5.00 per name. Court makes copy: $1.25 per page. Required to search: name, years to search. Civil cases indexed by defendant. Civil records on index cards from 1973, index books from 1900; computerized back to 1993. Civil court records free online at http://wcca.wicourts.gov/index.xsl. Mail turnaround time 2-3 days.
Criminal Records: Access: Mail, online, in person. Both court and visitors may perform in person searches. Search fee: $5.00 per name. Court makes copy: $1.25 per page. Required to search: name, years to search. Criminal records on index cards from 1973, index books from 1900; computerized back to 1993. Access criminal index free at http://wcca.wicourts.gov/index.xsl. Mail turnaround time 2-3 days.
General Information: Public terminal goes back to 1993. No juvenile records released. Will not fax documents. Certification fee: $5.00 per document. Payee: Clerk of Circuit Court. Personal checks accepted. Prepayment and SASE required.

Register in Probate 626 Main St, Rm 302, Darlington, WI 53530; phone: 608-776-4811; hours 8AM-N, 1-4:30PM (CST). *Probate.* Free search at http://wcca.wicourts.gov/index.xsl.

Langlade County

Circuit Court 800 Clermont St, Antigo, WI 54409; phone: 715-627-6215; hours 8:30AM-4:30PM (CST). *Felony, Misdemeanor, Civil, Eviction, Small Claims.*
Civil Records: Access: Mail, online, in person. Both court and visitors may perform in person searches. Search fee: $5.00 per name. Court makes copy: $1.25 per page; same fee for self serve. Required to search: name, years to search. Civil cases indexed by defendant, plaintiff;. on index books from 1905, computerized since 1993. Civil court records free online at http://wcca.wicourts.gov/index.xsl. Mail turnaround time 2-3 days.
Criminal Records: Access: Mail, online, in person. Both court and visitors may perform in person searches. Search fee: $5.00 per name. Court makes copy: $1.25 per page; same fee for self serve. Required to search: name, years to search. Criminal records on index books from 1905, computerized since 1993. Access criminal index free at http://wcca.wicourts.gov/index.xsl. Mail turnaround time 2-3 days.
General Information: Public terminal goes back to 1993. No confidential records released. Will not fax documents. Certification fee: $5.00 per cert. Payee: Clerk of Court. Personal checks accepted. Prepayment and SASE required.

Register in Probate 800 Clermont St, Antigo, WI 54409; phone: 715-627-6213; fax: 715-627-6329; hours 8:30AM-4:30PM (CST). *Probate.* Note: There is a $4.00 search fee. Probate records free at http://wcca.wicourts.gov/index.xsl.

Lincoln County

Circuit Court 1110 E Main St, Merrill, WI 54452; phone: 715-536-0319; fax: 715-536-0361; hours 8AM-4:30PM (CST). *Felony, Misdemeanor, Civil, Eviction, Small Claims.*

Civil Records: Access: Mail, online, in person. Both court and visitors may perform in person searches. Search fee: $5.00 per name. Court makes copy: $1.25 per page. Required to search: name, years to search. Civil cases indexed by defendant. Civil records on computer from 1990, index cards from 1982, index books from 1900s. Civil court records free online at http://wcca.wicourts.gov/index.xsl. Mail turnaround time 1-2 days.

Criminal Records: Access: Mail, online, in person. Both court and visitors may perform in person searches. Search fee: $5.00 per name. Court makes copy: $1.25 per page. Required to search: name, years to search; also helpful: DOB, SSN. Criminal records on computer from 1990, index cards from 1982, index books from 1900s. Access criminal index free at http://wcca.wicourts.gov/index.xsl. Mail turnaround time 1-2 days.

General Information: Public terminal goes back to 1990. No paternity or sealed records released. Will fax documents for $1.00 per fax. Cannot fax Certified copies. Certification fee: $5.00 per document. Payee: Clerk of Court. Local personal checks accepted. Prepayment and SASE required.

Register in Probate 1110 E Main St, Merrill, WI 54452; phone: 715-536-0342; 536-0378; fax: 715-539-2762; hours 8:15AM-N, 1-4:30PM (CST). *Probate.*

Free search at http://wcca.wicourts.gov/index.xsl.

Manitowoc County

Circuit Court PO Box 2000, Manitowoc, WI 54221-2000; phone: 920-683-4030; fax: 920-683-2733; hours 8:30AM-5PM M; 8:30AM-4:30PM T-F (CST). *Felony, Misdemeanor, Civil, Eviction, Small Claims.*

Civil Records: Access: Phone, mail, online, in person. Both court and visitors may perform in person searches. Search fee: $5.00 per name. Court makes copy: $1.25 per page. Required to search: name, years to search. Civil cases indexed by defendant, plaintiff; on computer from 1993, on index cards from 1962, index books from 1906, Historical Society has prior records. Civil court records free online at http://wcca.wicourts.gov/index.xsl. Note: Prior written agreement with court required for phone access. Mail turnaround time 5-7 days.

Criminal Records: Access: Phone, mail, online, in person. Both court and visitors may perform in person searches. Search fee: $5.00 per name. Court makes copy: $1.25 per page. Required to search: name, years to search, DOB. Criminal records on computer from 1993, on index cards from 1962, index books from 1906, Historical Society has prior records. Access criminal index free at http://wcca.wicourts.gov/index.xsl. Note: Prior written agreement with court required for phone access. Mail turnaround time 5-7 days.

General Information: Public terminal goes back to 1993. No confidential records released. Will fax documents for $3.00 plus $1.25 per page, either prepaid or within 48 hours. Certification fee: $5.00 per document. Payee: Clerk of Circuit Court. Personal checks accepted. Prepayment required. SASE requested.

Register in Probate 1010 S 8th St, Rm 116, Manitowoc, WI 54220; phone: 920-683-4016; fax: 920-683-5182; hours 8:30AM-4:30PM T-F; 8:30AM-5PM M (CST). *Probate.*

Free search at http://wcca.wicourts.gov/index.xsl.

Marathon County

Circuit Court 500 Forest St, Wausau, WI 54403; phone: 715-261-1300; criminal phone: 715-261-1280; civil phone: 715-261-1300; criminal fax: 715-261-1279; civil fax: 715-261-1319; hours 8AM-5PM (Summer hours 8AM-4:30PM Memorial-Labor Day) (CST). *Felony, Misdemeanor, Civil, Eviction, Small Claims.*

Note: Small claims phone is 261-1310; Traffic, 261-1270. Fax for criminal is 715-261-1279.

Civil Records: Access: Mail, online, in person. Both court and visitors may perform in person searches. Search fee: $5.00 per name. Court makes copy: $1.25 per page. Required to search: name, years to search. Civil cases indexed by defendant, plaintiff; on computer from 1992, on index cards from 1979. Civil court records free online at http://wcca.wicourts.gov/index.xsl. Note: All requests must be in writing, using their form if possible. Mail turnaround time 1-3 days.

Criminal Records: Access: Mail, online, in person. Both court and visitors may perform in person searches. Search fee: $5.00 per name. Court makes copy: $1.25 per page. Required to search: name, years to search, DOB. Criminal records on computer from 1992, on index cards from 1979, index books from 1900s. Access criminal index free at http://wcca.wicourts.gov/index.xsl. Note: All requests must be in writing, using their form if possible. Mail turnaround time 1-3 days.

General Information: Public terminal goes back to 1991. No mental health or juvenile records released. Will fax documents to local or toll free line. Certification fee: $5.00 per Cert. Payee: Clerk of Court. Personal checks accepted. Prepayment required. SASE helpful.

Register in Probate 500 Forest St, Wausau, WI 54403; phone: 715-261-1260; fax: 715-261-1269; hours 8AM-5PM (CST). *Probate.*

Free search at http://wcca.wicourts.gov/index.xsl.

Marinette County

Circuit Court 1926 Hall Ave, Marinette, WI 54143-1717; phone: 715-732-7450; probate phone: 715-732-7475; hours 8:30AM-4:30PM (CST). *Felony, Misdemeanor, Civil, Eviction, Small Claims.* **Civil Records:** Access: Mail, online, in person. Both court and visitors may perform in person searches. Search fee: $5.00 per name. Court makes copy: $1.25 per page. Required to search: name, years to search. Civil cases indexed by defendant, plaintiff; on computer from 1989, index cards from 1980, index books from 1906, prior records at Historical Society. Civil court records 1994 to present are free online at http://wcca.wicourts.gov/index.xsl. Mail turnaround time 2-3 days.

Criminal Records: Access: Mail, online, in person. Both court and visitors may perform in person searches. Search fee: $5.00 per name. Court makes copy: $1.25 per page. Required to search: name, years to search, DOB. Criminal records on computer from 1989, index cards from 1980, index books from 1906, prior records at Historical Society. Access criminal index free at http://wcca.wicourts.gov/index.xsl. Mail turnaround time 2-3 days.

General Information: Public terminal goes back to 1994. No paternity records released. Will fax documents to local or toll free line. Certification fee: $5.00. Payee: Clerk of Courts. Personal checks accepted. Prepayment and SASE required.

Register in Probate 1926 Hall Ave, Marinette, WI 54143-1717; phone: 715-732-7475; fax: 715-732-7561; hours 8:30AM-4:30PM (CST). *Probate.*

Free search at http://wcca.wicourts.gov/index.xsl.

Marquette County

Circuit Court PO Box 187, 77 W Park St, Montello, WI 53949; phone: 608-297-9136 x202; fax: 608-297-9188; hours 8AM-N, 12:30-4:30PM (CST). *Felony, Misdemeanor, Civil, Eviction, Small Claims.*

Civil Records: Access: Phone, mail, online, in person. Both court and visitors may perform in person searches. Search fee: $5.00 per name. Court makes copy: $1.25 per page. Required to search: name, years to search. Civil cases indexed by defendant, plaintiff; on index books from 1983, prior records at Historical Society; computerized back to 1996. Civil court records free online at http://wcca.wicourts.gov/index.xsl. Mail turnaround time 7-10 days.

Criminal Records: Access: Mail, online, in person. Both court and visitors may perform in person searches. Search fee: $5.00 per name. Court makes copy: $1.25 per page. Required to search: name, years to search, DOB, full name. Criminal records on index books from 1900s, prior records at Historical Society; computerized back to 1996. Access criminal index free at http://wcca.wicourts.gov/index.xsl. Mail turnaround time 7-10 days.

General Information: Public terminal goes back to 1996. No adoption, juvenile, paternity, guardianship, mental or termination of parental right records released. Fee to fax documents is $2.00 per page. Certification fee: $5.00 per doc. Payee: Clerk of Circuit Court. Personal checks accepted. Prepayment required. SASE requested.

Register in Probate 77 W Park St, PO Box 749, Montello, WI 53949; phone: 608-297-9105; fax: 608-297-9188; hours 8AM-4:30PM (CST). *Probate.* Free search at http://wcca.wicourts.gov/index.xsl.

Menominee County

Circuit Court PO Box 279, Keshena, WI 54135; phone: 715-799-3313; fax: 715-799-1322; hours 8AM-4:30PM (CST). *Felony, Misdemeanor, Civil, Eviction, Small Claims.*

Civil Records: Access: Mail, online, in person. Both court and visitors may perform in person searches. Search fee: $5.00 per name. Court makes copy: $1.25 per page. Required to search: name, years to search. Civil cases indexed by defendant, plaintiff. Civil records are indexed by cards, kept in files since 1979, computerized since 1992. Older records are at the Historical Society. Civil court records free online at http://wcca.wicourts.gov/index.xsl. Mail turnaround time 3-4 days.

Criminal Records: Access: Mail, online, in person, fax. Both court and visitors may perform in person searches. Search fee: $5.00 per name. Court makes copy: $1.25 per page. Required to search: name, years to search, DOB. Criminal records are indexed by cards, kept in files since 1979, computerized since 1992. Older records are at the Historical Society. Access criminal index free at http://wcca.wicourts.gov/index.xsl. Mail turnaround time 3-4 days.

General Information: No juvenile, mental, adoption. Will fax documents to local or toll free line. Certification fee: $5.00. Payee: Clerk of Court. Personal checks accepted. SASE helpful.

Register in Probate 311 N Main St, Rm 203, Shawano, WI 54166; phone: 715-526-8631; fax: 715-526-8622; hours 8AM-4:30PM (CST). *Probate.* Note: Tribal probate records only in Keshena (Menominee Tribal Court); Non-tribal records are in Shawano County; Shawano County info given here. Probate records free at http://wcca.wicourts.gov/index.xsl.

Milwaukee County

Circuit Court - Civil 901 N 9th St, Rm G-9, Milwaukee, WI 53233; phone: 414-278-4120; fax: 414-223-1256; hours 8AM-5PM (CST). *Civil, Eviction, Small Claims.*

Civil Records: Access: Mail, online, in person. Both court and visitors may perform in person searches. Search fee: $5.00 per name. Court makes copy: $1.25 per page. Self serve copy fee: $.25 per page. Required to search: name, years to search; also helpful-DOB or SSN. Civil cases indexed by defendant, plaintiff; on computer from 1985, on microfiche from 1949, prior with County Historical Society. Civil court records free online at http://wcca.wicourts.gov/index.xsl. Mail turnaround time 1-2 weeks.

General Information: Public terminal has only civil records back to 1985. (Terminal in Rm 117 of Safety Bldg.) No paternity records released. Certification fee: $5.00. Payee: Milwaukee County Clerk of Circuit Court. Personal checks accepted. Prepayment and SASE required.

Circuit Court - Criminal Division 821 W State St, Milwaukee, WI 53233; phone: 414-278-4121, 2784599; fax: 414-223-1262; hours 8AM-5PM (CST). *Felony, Misdemeanor.*
http://204.194.250.11

Criminal Records: Access: Fax, mail, online, in person. Both court and visitors may perform in person searches. Search fee: $5.00 per name (no fee if case number provided). Court makes copy: $1.25 per page. Required to search: name, years to search, DOB. Criminal records on computer from 10/86, index books and cards prior. Access criminal index free at http://wcca.wicourts.gov/index.xsl. Also, criminal case records on Milwaukee Municipal Court Case Information System database are free at www.court.ci.mil.wi.us/. Search by Case Number, by Citation Number, or by Name. Note: Additional search time needed for older records in storage off-site. Mail turnaround time 4 days.

General Information: Public terminal has only criminal records. No sealed records released. No fee to fax documents, but search fees still apply. Certification fee: $5.00. Payee: Clerk of Circuit Court. Personal checks accepted. Prepayment and SASE required.

Register in Probate 901 N 9th St, Rm 207, Milwaukee, WI 53233; phone: 414-278-4444; fax: 414-223-1814; hours 8AM-4:30PM (CST). *Probate.*
Free search at http://wcca.wicourts.gov/index.xsl.

Monroe County

Circuit Court 112 S Court St, #203, Sparta, WI 54656-1764; phone: 608-269-8745; criminal phone: 608-269-8962; civil phone: 608-269-8748; probate phone: 608-269-8701; fax: 608-269-8781; hours 8AM-4:30PM (CST). *Felony, Misdemeanor, Civil, Eviction, Small Claims.*

Civil Records: Access: Fax, mail, online, in person. Both court and visitors may perform in person searches. Search fee: $5.00 per name. Court makes copy: $1.25 per page. Required to search: name, years to search. Civil cases indexed by defendant, plaintiff; on computer and cards. Civil court records free online at http://wcca.wicourts.gov/index.xsl. Mail turnaround time 1 week.

Criminal Records: Access: Fax, mail, online, in person. Both court and visitors may perform in person searches. Search fee: $5.00 per name. Court makes copy: $1.25 per page. Required to search: name, years to search. Criminal records on computer and cards. Access criminal index free at http://wcca.wicourts.gov/index.xsl. Mail turnaround time 1 week.

General Information: Public terminal goes back to 1993. (Traffic records on terminal go back to 1996.) No paternity, medical or financial records released. Will fax documents $1.25 per page; no charge to toll free line. Certification fee: $5.00 per document. Payee: Clerk of Court. Local checks accepted. Prepayment and SASE required.

Register in Probate 112 S Court, Rm 301, Sparta, WI 54656-1765; phone: 608-269-8701; fax: 608-269-8950; hours 8AM-N, 12;30-4;30PM (CST). *Probate.*
Free search at http://wcca.wicourts.gov/index.xsl.

Oconto County

Circuit Court 301 Washington St, Oconto, WI 54153; phone: 920-834-6855; fax: 920-834-6867; hours 8AM-4PM (CST). *Felony, Misdemeanor, Civil, Small Claims.*

Civil Records: Access: Mail, online, in person. Both court and visitors may perform in person searches.

Search fee: $5.00 per name. Court makes copy: $1.25 per page. Required to search: name, years to search. Civil cases indexed by defendant, plaintiff; on computer since 1994; prior records on index books from 1930s. Historical Society has earlier records. Civil court records free online at http://wcca.wicourts.gov/index.xsl. Mail turnaround time 1-2 days.

Criminal Records: Access: Mail, online, in person. Both court and visitors may perform in person searches. Search fee: $5.00 per name. Court makes copy: $1.25 per page. Required to search: name, years to search, DOB. Criminal records on computer since 1994; prior records on index books from 1930s; Historical Society has earlier records. Access criminal index free at http://wcca.wicourts.gov/index.xsl. Mail turnaround time 1-2 days.

General Information: Public terminal goes back to 1994. No juvenile or paternity records released. Certification fee: $5.00 per doc. Payee: Oconto County Clerk of Court. Personal checks accepted. Prepayment and SASE required.

Register in Probate 301 Washington St, Oconto, WI 54153; phone: 920-834-6839; fax: 920-834-6867; hours 8AM-4PM (CST). *Probate.*
Free search at http://wcca.wicourts.gov/index.xsl.

Oneida County

Circuit Court PO Box 400, Rhinelander, WI 54501; phone: 715-369-6120; criminal phone: 715-369-6123; civil phone: 715-369-6124; probate phone: 715-369-6159; fax: 715-369-6160; hours 8AM-4:30PM (CST). *Felony, Misdemeanor, Civil, Eviction, Small Claims.*

Civil Records: Access: Mail, online, in person. Both court and visitors may perform in person searches. Search fee: $5.00 per name. Court makes copy: $1.25 per page. Self serve copy fee: $.25 per page. Required to search: name, years to search. Civil cases indexed by defendant, plaintiff; on computer from 1992, index cards from 1980, index books from 1900s. Civil court records free online at http://wcca.wicourts.gov/index.xsl. Mail turnaround time 1 week.

Criminal Records: Access: Mail, online, in person. Both court and visitors may perform in person searches. Search fee: $5.00 per name. Court makes copy: $1.25 per page. Self serve copy fee: $.25 per page. Required to search: name, years to search, DOB. Criminal records on computer from 1992, index cards from 1980, index books from 1900s. Access criminal index free at http://wcca.wicourts.gov/index.xsl. Mail turnaround time 1 week.

General Information: Public terminal goes back to 1992. No paternity records released. Will fax documents $1.25 per page. Certification fee: $5.00 per document. Payee: Clerk of Court. Personal checks accepted. Prepayment required.

Register in Probate PO Box 400, 1 Oneida St, Rhinelander, WI 54501; phone: 715-369-6159; hours 8AM-12, 1-4:30PM (CST). *Probate.*
Free search at http://wcca.wicourts.gov/index.xsl.

Outagamie County

Circuit Court 320 S Walnut St, Appleton, WI 54911; phone: 920-832-5130; civil phone: 920-832-5136; fax: 920-832-5115; hours 8:00AM-4:30PM (CST). *Felony, Misdemeanor, Civil, Eviction, Small Claims.*
Note: Small claims and eviction records at 920-832-5135.

Civil Records: Access: In person, online, mail. Visitors must perform in person searches themselves. Search fee: $5.00. Court makes copy: $1.25 per page; same fee for self serve. Required to search: name, years to search. Civil cases indexed by defendant, plaintiff; on computer from 10/87, index cards from 1983, index books from 1901, some records on microfiche. Civil court records free

online at http://wcca.wicourts.gov/index.xsl. Mail turnaround time 2-3 days.

Criminal Records: Access: Mail, in person, online. Both court and visitors may perform in person searches. Search fee: $5.00 per name. Court makes copy: $1.25 per page; same fee for self serve. Required to search: name, years to search, DOB. Criminal records on computer from 10/87, index cards from 1983, index books from 1901, some records on microfiche. Criminal court records free online at http://wcca.wicourts.gov/index.xsl. Mail turnaround time 2-3 days.

General Information: Public terminal has criminal back to 13 years and civil back to 10/1987. No adoption or juvenile records released. Will fax documents for $1.25 per page. Certification fee: $5.00 per document. Payee: Clerk of Court. Personal checks accepted. Prepayment and SASE required.

Register in Probate 320 S Walnut St, Appleton, WI 54911; phone: 920-832-5601; fax: 920-832-5115; hours 8:30AM-N, 1-5PM (CST). *Probate.*
Free search at http://wcca.wicourts.gov/index.xsl.

Ozaukee County

Circuit Court 1201 S Spring St, Port Washington, WI 53074; phone: 262-284-8409; fax: 262-284-8491; hours 8:30AM-5PM (CST). *Felony, Misdemeanor, Civil, Eviction, Small Claims.*
www.co.ozaukee.wi.us/ClerkCourts/default.htm

Civil Records: Access: Mail, online, in person. Both court and visitors may perform in person searches. Search fee: $5.00 per name. Court makes copy: $1.25 per page ($1.00 if probate); same fee for self serve. Required to search: name, years to search. Civil cases indexed by defendant, plaintiff; on computer from 1991, index cards from late 1950s. Civil court records free online at http://wcca.wicourts.gov/index.xsl. Access is also with the use of county "Remote Access". This data is for inquiries only and includes civil, family, and traffic courts. For info, contact the Technology Resources Dept. at 262-284-8309. Mail turnaround time 1 week.

Criminal Records: Access: Mail, online, in person. Both court and visitors may perform in person searches. Search fee: $5.00 per name. Court makes copy: $1.25 per page; same fee for self serve. Required to search: name, years to search, DOB. Criminal records on computer from 1989. Access criminal index free at http://wcca.wicourts.gov/index.xsl. Mail turnaround time 1 week.

General Information: Public terminal has criminal back to 1987 and civil back to 1991. No paternity records released. Certification fee: $5.00. Payee: Clerk of Court. Business checks or in state personal checks accepted. Prepayment and SASE required.

Register in Probate PO Box 994, 1201 S Spring St, Port Washington, WI 53074; phone: 262-284-8370/8409; fax: 262-284-8491; hours 8:30AM-5PM (CST). *Probate.*
Free search at http://wcca.wicourts.gov/index.xsl.

Pepin County

Circuit Court PO Box 39, Durand, WI 54736; phone: 715-672-8861; fax: 715-672-8894; hours 8:30AM-N, 12:30-4:30PM (CST). *Felony, Misdemeanor, Civil, Eviction, Small Claims.*

Civil Records: Access: Mail, online, in person. Both court and visitors may perform in person searches. Search fee: $5.00 per name. Court makes copy: $1.25 per page. Required to search: name, years to search. Civil cases indexed by plaintiff. Civil records on computer from 1995, index books from 1900s. Civil court records free online at http://wcca.wicourts.gov/index.xsl. Mail turnaround time 1 week.

Criminal Records: Access: Mail, online, in person. Both court and visitors may perform in person searches. Search fee: $5.00 per name. Court makes copy: $1.25 per page. Required to search: name, years to search, DOB. Criminal records on computer from 1995, index books from 1900s. Access criminal index free at http://wcca.wicourts.gov/index.xsl. Mail turnaround time 1 week.

General Information: Public terminal goes back to 1995. No minor or financial divorce records released. Will fax documents to local or toll free line. Certification fee: $5.00 per document. Payee: Clerk of Court. Personal checks accepted. Prepayment and SASE required.

Register in Probate PO Box 39, 740 7th Ave W, Durand, WI 54736; phone: 715-672-8859/715-672-8868; fax: 715-672-8521; hours 8:30AM-N, 1-4:30PM (CST). *Probate.*

Free search at http://wcca.wicourts.gov/index.xsl.

Pierce County

Circuit Court PO Box 129, Ellsworth, WI 54011; phone: 715-273-3531; fax: 715-273-6855; hours 8AM-5PM (CST). *Felony, Misdemeanor, Civil, Eviction, Small Claims.*

Civil Records: Access: Mail, online, in person. Both court and visitors may perform in person searches. Search fee: $5.00 per name. Fee is by type of case. Court makes copy: $1.25 per page. Required to search: name, years to search. Civil cases indexed by defendant, plaintiff. Civil records are retained 20 years; on computer back to 1994. Archives in River Falls. Civil court records free online at http://wcca.wicourts.gov/index.xsl. Mail turnaround time 2-3 days.

Criminal Records: Access: Mail, online, in person. Both court and visitors may perform in person searches. Search fee: $5.00 per name. Court makes copy: $1.25 per page. Required to search: name, years to search, DOB. Felony records are retained 50-75 years; misdemeanors for 20. Criminal records on computer back to 1994. Archives in River Falls. Access criminal index free at http://wcca.wicourts.gov/index.xsl. Mail turnaround time 2-3 days.

General Information: Public terminal goes back to 1994. No sealed records released. Will fax documents for $1.25 per page. Certification fee: $5.00. Payee: Clerk of Court. Personal checks accepted. Prepayment and SASE required.

Register in Probate PO Box 97, 414 W Main, Ellsworth, WI 54011; phone: 715-273-3531 x6460; fax: 715-273-6794; hours 8AM-5PM (CST). *Probate.*

Free search at http://wcca.wicourts.gov/index.xsl.

Polk County

Circuit Court PO Box 549, 1005 W Main St, Balsam Lake, WI 54810; phone: 715-485-9299; fax: 715-485-9262; hours 8:30AM-4:30PM (CST). *Felony, Misdemeanor, Civil, Eviction, Small Claims.*

Civil Records: Access: Mail, online, in person. Both court and visitors may perform in person searches. Search fee: $5.00 per name per record/file. Court makes copy: $1.25 per page. Required to search: name, years to search. Civil cases indexed by defendant, plaintiff. Civil records go back to 1970s; on computer back to 1992. Civil court records free online at http://wcca.wicourts.gov/index.xsl. Mail turnaround time 2 days.

Criminal Records: Access: Mail, online, in person. Both court and visitors may perform in person searches. Search fee: $5.00 per name. Fee is per record/file. Court makes copy: $1.25 per page. Required to search: name, years to search, DOB. Criminal records go back to 1970s; on computer back to 1992. Access criminal index free at http://wcca.wicourts.gov/index.xsl. Mail turnaround time 2 days.

General Information: Public terminal goes back to 9/1992. No juvenile, paternity or confidential records released. Will fax documents to local or toll free line. Certification fee: $5.00 per doc. Payee: Clerk of Court. Personal checks accepted. Prepayment and SASE required.

Register in Probate 1005 W Main, #500, Balsam Lake, WI 54810; phone: 715-485-9238; fax: 715-485-9275; hours 8:30AM-4:30PM (CST). *Probate.*

www.co.polk.wi.us

Free search at http://wcca.wicourts.gov/index.xsl.

Portage County

Circuit Court (Branches 1, 2 & 3) 1516 Church St, Stevens Point, WI 54481; phone: 715-346-1364; fax: 715-346-1236; hours 7:30AM-4:30PM (CST). *Felony, Misdemeanor, Civil, Eviction, Small Claims.*

Civil Records: Access: Mail, in person, online. Both court and visitors may perform in person searches. Search fee: $5.00 per name. Court makes copy: $1.25 per page. Required to search: name, years to search. Civil cases indexed by defendant, plaintiff; on computer from 6/91, index cards from 1980, index books from 1900s. Internet access is upon approval. Request in writing to Data Processing Dept, 1462 Strong Ave, Stevens Point 54481. Explain purpose of record requests. Mail turnaround time 10 working days.

Criminal Records: Access: Mail, in person, online. Both court and visitors may perform in person searches. Search fee: $5.00 per name. Court makes copy: $1.25 per page. Required to search: name, years to search, address, DOB, SSN, signed release. Criminal records on computer from 6/91, index cards from 1980, index books from 1900s. Internet access is upon approval. Request in writing to Data Processing Dept, 1462 Strong Ave, Stevens Point 54481. Explain purpose of record requests. Mail turnaround time 10 working days.

General Information: Public terminal goes back to 1990. No expunged records released. Will fax documents to local or toll free line. Certification fee: $5.00 per doc. Payee: Clerk of Court. Business checks accepted. Prepayment and SASE required.

Register in Probate 1516 Church St, Stevens Point, WI 54481; phone: 715-346-1362; fax: 715-346-1486; hours 7:30AM-4:30PM (CST). *Probate.*

Free search at http://wcca.wicourts.gov/index.xsl.

Price County

Circuit Court Courthouse, 126 Cherry St, Phillips, WI 54555; phone: 715-339-2353; fax: 715-339-5114; hours 8AM-N, 1-4:30PM (CST). *Felony, Misdemeanor, Civil, Eviction, Small Claims.*

Civil Records: Access: Mail, online, in person. Both court and visitors may perform in person searches. Search fee: $5.00 per name. Court makes copy: $1.25 per page. Required to search: name, years to search. Civil cases indexed by defendant, plaintiff; on computer from 1997, prior on index books. Civil court records free online at http://wcca.wicourts.gov/index.xsl. Mail turnaround time 1-2 days.

Criminal Records: Access: Mail, online, in person. Both court and visitors may perform in person searches. Search fee: $5.00 per name. Court makes copy: $1.25 per page. Required to search: name, years to search, DOB; also helpful: SSN. Criminal records on computer from 1997, prior on index books. Access criminal index free at http://wcca.wicourts.gov/index.xsl. Mail turnaround time 1-2 days.

General Information: Public terminal goes back to 1993. No confidential records per statute or order released. Will fax documents to local or toll free line. Certification fee: $5.00 per document. Payee: Clerk of Circuit Court. Personal checks accepted. Prepayment and SASE required.

Register in Probate Courthouse, 126 Cherry St, Rm209, Phillips, WI 54555; phone: 715-339-3078; fax: 715-339-3079; hours 8AM-4:30PM (CST). *Probate.*

Free search at http://wcca.wicourts.gov/index.xsl.

Racine County

Circuit Court 730 Wisconsin Ave, Racine, WI 53403; phone: 262-636-3333; probate phone: 262-636-3137; civil/criminal fax: 262-636-3341; probate fax: 262-636-3870; hours 8AM-5PM (CST). *Felony, Misdemeanor, Civil, Eviction, Small Claims, Probate.*

Civil Records: Access: Mail, online, in person. Both court and visitors may perform in person searches. Search fee: $5.00 per name. Court makes copy: $1.25 per page; same fee for self serve. Required to search: name, years to search. Civil cases indexed by defendant, plaintiff; on computer from 1990, index cards from 1970, archives prior to 1970. Civil court records free online at http://wcca.wicourts.gov/index.xsl. Mail turnaround time 1-2 weeks.

Criminal Records: Access: Mail, online, in person. Both court and visitors may perform in person searches. Search fee: $5.00 per name. Court makes copy: $1.25 per page; same fee for self serve. Required to search: name, years to search, DOB. Criminal records on computer from 1990, index cards from 1970, archives prior to 1970. Access criminal index free at http://wcca.wicourts.gov/index.xsl. Mail turnaround time 1-2 weeks.

General Information: Public terminal goes back to 1994. No adoption, juvenile, paternity or mental commitment records released. Will fax documents to local or toll free line. Certification fee: $5.00 per document includes copy fee. Payee: Clerk of Court. Personal checks accepted. Prepayment and SASE required.

Register in Probate 730 Wisconsin Ave, Racine, WI 53403; phone: 262-636-3137; fax: 262-636-3870; hours 8AM-5PM (CST). *Probate.*

Free search at http://wcca.wicourts.gov/index.xsl.

Richland County

Circuit Court PO Box 655, Richland Center, WI 53581; phone: 608-647-3956; hours 8:30AM-4:30PM (CST). *Felony, Misdemeanor, Civil, Eviction, Small Claims.*

Civil Records: Access: Mail, online, in person. Both court and visitors may perform in person searches. Search fee: $5.00 per name. Court makes copy: $1.25 per page. Required to search: name, years to search. Civil cases indexed by defendant, plaintiff; on index cards from 1982, index books from 1972, archives prior to 1972, on computer back to 1993. Civil court records free online at http://wcca.wicourts.gov/index.xsl. Mail turnaround time within 2 days.

Criminal Records: Access: Mail, online, in person. Both court and visitors may perform in person searches. Search fee: $5.00 per name. Court makes copy: $1.25 per page. Required to search: name, years to search, DOB. Criminal records on index cards from 1982, index books from 1972, archives prior to 1972, on computer back t0 1993. Access criminal index free at http://wcca.wicourts.gov/index.xsl. Mail turnaround time 1 week.

General Information: Public use terminal available. No juvenile or paternity records released. Certification fee: $5.00 per certificate. Payee: Clerk of Circuit Court. Personal out-of-state checks not accepted. Prepayment and SASE required.

Register in Probate PO Box 427, Richland Center, WI 53581; phone: 608-647-2626; fax: 608-647-6134; hours 8:30AM-N, 1-4:30PM (CST). *Probate.*

Free search at http://wcca.wicourts.gov/index.xsl.

Rock County

Circuit Court 51 S Main, Janesville, WI 53545; phone: 608-743-2200; fax: 608-743-2223; hours 8AM-5PM (CST). *Felony, Misdemeanor, Civil, Eviction, Small Claims.*

Civil Records: Access: Mail, online, in person. Both court and visitors may perform in person searches. Search fee: $5.00 per name. Court makes copy: $1.25

per page. Required to search: name, years to search. Civil cases indexed by defendant, plaintiff; on computer from 6/93, on index cards from 6/91, index books from 1940, archives prior to 1940. Civil court records free online at http://wcca.wicourts.gov/index.xsl. Mail turnaround time 2-3 days.

Criminal Records: Access: Mail, online, in person. Both court and visitors may perform in person searches. Search fee: $5.00 per name. Court makes copy: $1.25 per page. Required to search: name, years to search, DOB. Criminal records on computer from 6/93, on index cards from 6/91, index books from 1940, archives prior to 1940. Access criminal index free at http://wcca.wicourts.gov/index.xsl. Mail turnaround time 2-3 days.

General Information: Public use terminal available. No juvenile, paternity or sealed records released. Certification fee: $5.00. Payee: Clerk of Court. Personal checks accepted. Prepayment and SASE required.

Circuit Court - South Janesville Courthouse, 51 S Main St, Janesville, WI 53545; phone: 608-743-2200; criminal phone: 608-743-2211; civil phone: 608-743-2210; fax: 608-743-2223; hours 8AM-5PM (CST). *Felony, Misdemeanor, Civil, Eviction, Small Claims.*

Civil Records: Access: Mail, online, in person. Both court and visitors may perform in person searches. Search fee: $5.00 per name. Court makes copy: $1.25 per page. Required to search: name, years to search. Civil cases indexed by defendant, plaintiff; on computer from mid-1993, on index cards from 1970s, index books from 1900s in vault. Civil court records free online at http://wcca.wicourts.gov/index.xsl. Mail turnaround time 1 week.

Criminal Records: Access: Mail, online, in person. Both court and visitors may perform in person searches. Search fee: $5.00 per name. Court makes copy: $1.25 per page. Required to search: name, years to search, DOB. Criminal records on computer from mid-1993, on index cards from 1970s, index books from 1900s in vault. Access criminal index free at http://wcca.wicourts.gov/index.xsl. Mail turnaround time 1 week.

General Information: Public terminal goes back to 1993. No paternity records released. Certification fee: $5.00. Payee: Clerk of Court. Personal checks accepted. Prepayment and SASE required.

Register in Probate 51 S Main, Janesville, WI 53545; phone: 608-757-5635; fax: 608-757-5769; hours 8AM-5PM (CST). *Probate.*
Free search at http://wcca.wicourts.gov/index.xsl.

Rusk County

Circuit Court 311 Miner Ave E, #L350, Attn: Clerk of Circuit Court, Ladysmith, WI 54848; phone: 715-532-2108; probate phone: 715-532-2147; fax: 715-632-2110; probate fax: 715-532-2266; hours 8AM-4:30PM (CST). *Felony, Misdemeanor, Civil, Small Claims.*

Civil Records: Access: Mail, online, in person, phone, fax. Both court and visitors may perform in person searches. Search fee: $5.00 per name, no charge for persons performing their own search. Court makes copy: $1.25 per page. Required to search: name, years to search. Civil cases indexed by defendant, plaintiff; on computer from 1992, on index cards from 1978, index books from 1901. Civil court records free online at http://wcca.wicourts.gov/index.xsl. Note: Phone requests are accepted if the case number is known. Mail turnaround time 5 days.

Criminal Records: Access: Mail, online, in person, online. Both court and visitors may perform in person searches. Search fee: $5.00 per name, no charge for persons performing their own search. Court makes copy: $1.25 per page. Required to search: name, years to search, DOB. Criminal records on computer from 1992, on index cards from 1978, index books from 1901. Access criminal index free at http://wcca.wicourts.gov/index.xsl. Note: Phone

requests are accepted if the case number is known. Mail turnaround time 5 days.

General Information: Public terminal goes back to 1992. No juvenile or paternity records released. Will fax documents for $1.25 per page plus $5.00 search fee per name. Certification fee: $5.00 per document. Payee: Clerk of Court. Personal checks accepted. Prepayment and SASE required.

Register in Probate 311 E Miner Ave, #C-330, Ladysmith, WI 54848; phone: 715-532-2147; fax: 715-532-2266; hours 8AM-4:30PM (CST). *Probate.*
Free search at http://wcca.wicourts.gov/index.xsl.

Sauk County

Circuit Court 515 Oak St, Baraboo, WI 53913; phone: 608-355-3287; fax: 608-355-3514; hours 8AM-4:30PM (CST). *Felony, Misdemeanor, Civil, Eviction, Small Claims.*

Civil Records: Access: Mail, online, in person. Both court and visitors may perform in person searches. Search fee: $5.00 per name per index. Court makes copy: $1.25 per page. Required to search: name, years to search. Civil cases indexed by defendant, plaintiff; on computer from 1990, index cards from 1980, index books from 1967. Civil court records free online at http://wcca.wicourts.gov/index.xsl. Mail turnaround time 2-3 days.

Criminal Records: Access: Mail, online, in person. Both court and visitors may perform in person searches. Search fee: $5.00 per name per index. Court makes copy: $1.25 per page. Required to search: name, years to search. Criminal records on computer from 1990, index cards from 1980, index books from 1967. Access criminal index free at http://wcca.wicourts.gov/index.xsl. Mail turnaround time 2-3 days.

General Information: Public terminal goes back to 1993. No paternity, juvenile records released. Fee to fax documents is $5.00 1st page, $1.00 each add'l plus tax. Certification fee: $5.00 per doc. Payee: Clerk of Court. Personal checks accepted. Prepayment and SASE required.

Register in Probate 515 Oak St, Baraboo, WI 53913; phone: 608-355-3226; fax: 608-355-3498; hours 8AM-4:30PM (CST). *Probate.*
www.co.sauk.wi.us/dept/reginprobate/index.html
Free search at http://wcca.wicourts.gov/index.xsl.

Sawyer County

Circuit Court PO Box 508, Hayward, WI 54843; phone: 715-634-4887; fax: 715-638-3297; hours 8AM-4PM (CST). *Felony, Misdemeanor, Civil, Eviction, Small Claims.*

Civil Records: Access: Mail, online, in person. Both court and visitors may perform in person searches. Search fee: $5.00 per name. Court makes copy: $1.25 per page. Required to search: name, years to search. Civil cases indexed by defendant, plaintiff; on index cards from 7/85, prior on books. Civil court records free online at http://wcca.wicourts.gov/index.xsl. Mail turnaround time 3 days.

Criminal Records: Access: Mail, online, in person. Both court and visitors may perform in person searches. Search fee: $5.00 per name. Court makes copy: $1.25 per page. Required to search: name, years to search. Criminal records on index cards from 7/85, prior on books. Access criminal index free at http://wcca.wicourts.gov/index.xsl. Mail turnaround time 3 days.

General Information: Public terminal goes back to 4/1993. No juvenile or paternity records released. Certification fee: $5.00 per document. Payee: Clerk of Court. Personal checks accepted. Prepayment and SASE required.

Register in Probate PO Box 447, Hayward, WI 54843; phone: 715-634-7519; fax: 715-638-3297; hours 8AM-4PM (CST). *Probate.*
Free search at http://wcca.wicourts.gov/index.xsl.

Shawano County

Circuit Court 311 N Main, Rm 206, Shawano, WI 54166; phone: 715-526-9347; probate phone: 715-526-8631; fax: 715-526-4915; hours 8AM-4:30PM (CST). *Felony, Misdemeanor, Civil, Eviction, Small Claims.*
www.co.shawano.wi.us/

Civil Records: Access: Fax, mail, online, in person. Both court and visitors may perform in person searches. Search fee: $5.00 per name. Court makes copy: $1.25 per page. Required to search: name, years to search. Civil cases indexed by defendant, plaintiff; on computer from 1993, on index books from 1930s, prior in archives. Civil court records free online at http://wcca.wicourts.gov/index.xsl. Mail turnaround time 10-20 days.

Criminal Records: Access: Fax, mail, online, in person. Both court and visitors may perform in person searches. Search fee: $5.00 per name. Court makes copy: $1.25 per page. Required to search: name, years to search, DOB. Criminal records on computer from 1993, on index books from 1930s, prior in archives. Access criminal index free at http://wcca.wicourts.gov/index.xsl. Mail turnaround time 10-20 days.

General Information: Public terminal goes back to 3/1993. No juvenile, closed files or mental records released. Will fax documents $1.25 per page, add $2.50 for long distance. Certification fee: $5.00. Payee: Clerk of Court. Personal checks accepted. Prepayment and SASE required.

Register in Probate 311 N Main, Rm 203, Shawano, WI 54166; phone: 715-526-8631; fax: 715-526-8622; hours 8AM-4:30PM (CST). *Probate.* Note: This is also the location of Menominee County Probate. Tribal probate records are not housed here; tribal records are at Keshena (Menominee Tribal Court). Also, probate records free at http://wcca.wicourts.gov/index.xsl.

Sheboygan County

Circuit Court 615 N 6th St, Sheboygan, WI 53081; phone: 920-459-3068; fax: 920-459-3921; hours 8AM-5PM (CST). *Felony, Misdemeanor, Civil, Eviction, Small Claims.*
www.co.sheboygan.wi.us/html/d_crtclrk.html

Civil Records: Access: Mail, online, in person. Both court and visitors may perform in person searches. Search fee: $5.00 per case. Court makes copy: $1.25 per page. Required to search: name, years to search; also helpful: address. Civil cases indexed by defendant, plaintiff; on computer since 1992; prior records on index cards from 1960, index books from 1860s, archives prior to 1971. Civil court records free at http://wcca.wicourts.gov/index.xsl. Mail turnaround time 2-3 days.

Criminal Records: Access: Mail, online, in person. Both court and visitors may perform in person searches. Search fee: $5.00 per case. Court makes copy: $1.25 per page. Required to search: name, years to search, DOB; also helpful: address. Criminal records on computer since 1992; prior records on index cards from 1960, index books from 1860s, archives prior to 1971. Access criminal index free at http://wcca.wicourts.gov/index.xsl. Mail turnaround time 2-3 days.

General Information: Public terminal goes back to 1992. (Public access is same info as on internet.) No juvenile or paternity records released. Will fax documents for pre-paid $3.00. Certification fee: $5.00 per document. Payee: Clerk of Circuit Court. Personal checks accepted. Prepayment and SASE required.

Register in Probate 615 N 6th St, Sheboygan, WI 53081; phone: 920-459-3050, 459-3202, 459-3051; fax: 920-459-0541; hours 8AM-5PM (CST). *Probate.*
Note: There is a $4.00 search fee. Probate records free at http://wcca.wicourts.gov/index.xsl.

St. Croix County

Circuit Court 1101 Carmichael Rd, Hudson, WI 54016; phone: 715-386-4630; criminal phone: 715-386-4631; civil phone: 715-386-4633; probate phone: 715-386-4619; hours 8AM-5PM (CST). *Felony, Misdemeanor, Civil, Eviction, Small Claims.*
Civil Records: Access: Mail, online, in person. Both court and visitors may perform in person searches. Search fee: $5.00 per name. Court makes copy: $1.25 per page. Required to search: name, years to search. Civil cases indexed by defendant, plaintiff; on computer from 10/92, on index cards from 1982, index books from 1965. Civil court records free online at http://wcca.wicourts.gov/index.xsl. Mail turnaround time within 10 days.
Criminal Records: Access: Mail, online, in person. Both court and visitors may perform in person searches. Search fee: $5.00 per name. Court makes copy: $1.25 per page. Required to search: name, years to search, DOB. Criminal records on computer from 10/92, on index cards from 1982, index books from 1900s. Access criminal index free at http://wcca.wicourts.gov/index.xsl. Mail turnaround time 5-10 days.
General Information: Public terminal goes back to 1992. No juvenile forfeitures, paternity, some case specific documents or sealed records released. Will fax documents for $1.25 per page. Certification fee: $5.00. Payee: Clerk of Court. Personal checks accepted. Prepayment and SASE required.

Register in Probate 1101 Carmichael Rd, Rm 2242, Hudson, WI 54016; phone: 715-386-4618; fax: 715-381-4318; hours 8AM-5PM (CST). *Probate.*
Free search at http://wcca.wicourts.gov/index.xsl.

Taylor County

Circuit Court 224 S 2nd St, Medford, WI 54451-1811; phone: 715-748-1425; probate phone: 715-748-1435; fax: 715-748-2465; hours 8:30AM-4:30PM (CST). *Felony, Misdemeanor, Civil, Eviction, Small Claims.*
Civil Records: Access: Mail, online, in person. Both court and visitors may perform in person searches. Search fee: $5.00 per name. Court makes copy: $1.25 per page. Required to search: name, years to search. Civil cases indexed by defendant, plaintiff; on computer from 1989; prior records index books from 1917. Civil court records free online at http://wcca.wicourts.gov/index.xsl. Mail turnaround time 1-2 days.
Criminal Records: Access: Mail, online, in person. Both court and visitors may perform in person searches. Search fee: $5.00 per name. Court makes copy: $1.25 per page. Required to search: name, years to search, DOB. Criminal records on computer from 1989; prior records index books from 1917. Access criminal index free at http://wcca.wicourts.gov/index.xsl. Mail turnaround time 1-2 days.
General Information: Public terminal goes back to 1989. No sealed records released. Will fax documents to a local or toll free line. Certification fee: $5.00 per doc. Payee: Clerk of Circuit Court. Personal checks accepted. Prepayment and SASE required.

Register in Probate 224 S 2nd, Medford, WI 54451; phone: 715-748-1435; fax: 715-748-1524; hours 8:30AM-4:30PM (CST). *Probate.*
Free search at http://wcca.wicourts.gov/index.xsl.

Trempealeau County

Circuit Court PO Box 67, 36245 Main St, Whitehall, WI 54773; phone: 715-538-2311; hours 8AM-4:30PM (CST). *Felony, Misdemeanor, Civil, Eviction, Small Claims.*
Civil Records: Access: Mail, online, in person. Both court and visitors may perform in person searches. Search fee: $5.00 per name. Court makes copy: $1.25 per page. Required to search: name, years to search. Civil cases indexed by defendant, plaintiff; on computer from 1993, on index cards from 1987, index

books from 1940, archives prior to 1940. Civil court records free online at http://wcca.wicourts.gov/index.xsl. All mail requests must be in writing. Mail turnaround time 2-3 days.
Criminal Records: Access: Mail, online, in person. Both court and visitors may perform in person searches. Search fee: $5.00 per name. Court makes copy: $1.25 per page. Required to search: name, years to search, DOB. Criminal records on computer from 1993, on index cards from 1987, index books from 1940, archives prior to 1940. Access criminal index free at http://wcca.wicourts.gov/index.xsl. All mail requests must be in writing. Mail turnaround time 2-3 days.
General Information: Public terminal goes back to 1994. No juvenile, paternity or child support records released. Will fax documents $2.00 per page. Certification fee: $5.00 per doc. Payee: Clerk of Circuit Court. Personal checks accepted. Prepayment and SASE required.

Register in Probate 36245 Main St, PO Box 67, Whitehall, WI 54773; phone: 715-538-2311 X238; fax: 715-538-4123; hours 8AM-4:30PM (CST). *Probate.*
Free search at http://wcca.wicourts.gov/index.xsl.

Vernon County

Circuit Court PO Box 426, Viroqua, WI 54665; phone: 608-637-5340; criminal phone: 608-637-5338; civil phone: 608-637-5338; fax: 608-637-5554; hours 8:30AM-4:30PM (CST). *Felony, Misdemeanor, Civil, Eviction, Small Claims.*
Civil Records: Access: Phone, fax, mail, online, in person. Both court and visitors may perform in person searches. Search fee: $5.00 per name. Court makes copy: $1.25 per page; same fee for self serve. Required to search: name, years to search, DOB. Civil cases indexed by defendant, plaintiff; on computer back to 1993; on index books & cards 1950 to 1992. Civil court records free online at http://wcca.wicourts.gov/index.xsl. Mail turnaround time 2-3 days.
Criminal Records: Access: Phone, fax, mail, online, in person. Both court and visitors may perform in person searches. Search fee: $5.00 per name. Court makes copy: $1.25 per page; same fee for self serve. Required to search: name, years to search; also helpful: DOB. Criminal records on computer back to 1993; on index books & cards 1950 to 1992. Access criminal index free at http://wcca.wicourts.gov/index.xsl. Mail turnaround time 2-3 days.
General Information: Public terminal goes back to 1993. No paternity or juvenile records released. Will fax documents. Certification fee: $5.00 per document. Payee: Clerk of Court. Personal checks accepted. Prepayment required. Will bill to attorneys credit agencies. SASE required.

Register in Probate PO Box 448, 400 Courthouse Sq, Viroqua, WI 54665; phone: 608-637-5347; fax: 608-637-5554; hours 8:30AM-4:30PM (CST). *Probate.*
Free search at http://wcca.wicourts.gov/index.xsl.

Vilas County

Circuit Court 330 Court St, Eagle River, WI 54521; criminal phone: 715-479-3633; civil phone: 715-479-3632; fax: 715-479-3740; hours 8AM-4PM (CST). *Felony, Misdemeanor, Civil, Eviction, Small Claims.*
Civil Records: Access: Mail, online, in person. Both court and visitors may perform in person searches. Search fee: $5.00 per name. Court makes copy: $1.25 per page. Self serve copy fee: $.25 per page. Required to search: name, years to search. Civil records on computer back to 1992, index cards from 1978, index books from 1900s. Civil court records free online at http://wcca.wicourts.gov/index.xsl. Mail turnaround time 2 weeks.

Criminal Records: Access: Mail, online, in person. Both court and visitors may perform in person searches. Search fee: $5.00 per name. Court makes copy: $1.25 per page. Self serve copy fee: $.25 per page. Required to search: name, years to search, DOB. Criminal records on computer back to 1992; index cards from 1978, index books from 1900s. Access criminal index free at http://wcca.wicourts.gov/index.xsl. Mail turnaround time 2 weeks.
General Information: Public terminal goes back to 1992. No paternity records released. Fee to fax documents is $1.25 per page. Certification fee: $5.00. Payee: Clerk of Circuit Court. Personal checks accepted. Prepayment and SASE required.

Register in Probate 330 Court St, Eagle River, WI 54521; phone: 715-479-3642; fax: 715-479-3740; hours 8AM-4PM (CST). *Probate.*
Free search at http://wcca.wicourts.gov/index.xsl.

Walworth County

Circuit Court PO Box 1001, 1800 County Rd NN, Elkhorn, WI 53121-1001; phone: 262-741-7012; criminal phone: 262-741-7024-felony; 62-741-7052-Misd.; civil phone: 262-741-7023; fax: 262-741-7050; hours 8AM-5PM (CST). *Felony, Misdemeanor, Civil, Eviction, Small Claims.*
www.co.walworth.wi.us
Note: Misdemeanor phone number is 262-741-7052.

Civil Records: Access: Mail, in person, online. Both court and visitors may perform in person searches. Search fee: $5.00 per name. Court makes copy: $1.25 per page. Required to search: name, years to search. Civil cases indexed by defendant, plaintiff; on computer from 1989, index cards/books from 1836. Civil court records are free online at http://wcca.wicourts.gov/index.xsl. Mail turnaround time 1-2 days.
Criminal Records: Access: Mail, in person, online. Both court and visitors may perform in person searches. Search fee: $5.00 per name. Court makes copy: $1.25 per page. Required to search: name, years to search, DOB. Criminal records on computer from 1989, index cards/books from 1836 (organized). Access criminal index free at http://wcca.wicourts.gov/index.xsl. Mail turnaround time 1-2 days.
General Information: Public use terminal available. No sealed records released. Will fax documents for $1.25 per page. Certification fee: $5.00 per document. Payee: County Clerk of Courts. Business checks or Visa, MC accepted. Credit cards accepted in person only. Prepayment and SASE required.

Register in Probate PO Box 1001, 1800 County Rd NN, Elkhorn, WI 53121; phone: 262-741-7014; fax: 262-741-7002; hours 8AM-5PM (CST). *Probate.*
Free search at http://wcca.wicourts.gov/index.xsl.

Washburn County

Circuit Court PO Box 339, Shell Lake, WI 54871; phone: 715-468-4677; fax: 715-468-4678; hours 8AM-4:30PM (CST). *Felony, Misdemeanor, Civil, Eviction, Small Claims.*
Civil Records: Access: Mail, online, in person. Both court and visitors may perform in person searches. Search fee: $5.00 per name. Court makes copy: $1.25 per page. Required to search: name, years to search. Civil cases indexed by defendant, plaintiff; on computer since 1993 (civil money judgments back to 1/1/90); on index books from 1883. Civil court records free online at http://wcca.wicourts.gov/index.xsl. Mail turnaround time 2-3 days.
Criminal Records: Access: Mail, online, in person. Both court and visitors may perform in person searches. Search fee: $5.00 per name. Court makes copy: $1.25 per page. Required to search: name, years to search; also helpful: DOB. Criminal records on computer since 1993; on index books from 1883.

Access criminal index free at http://wcca.wicourts.gov/index.xsl. Mail turnaround time 2-3 days.

General Information: Public terminal goes back to 1993. No sealed records released. Will fax documents to local or toll free line. Certification fee: $5.00 per document. Payee: Clerk of Court. Personal checks accepted. Prepayment and SASE required.

Register in Probate PO Box 316, 10 Fifth St, Shell Lake, WI 54871; phone: 715-468-4688; fax: 715-468-4678; hours 8AM-N, 1-4:30PM (CST). *Probate.*

Free search at http://wcca.wicourts.gov/index.xsl.

Washington County

Circuit Court PO Box 1986, West Bend, WI 53095-7986; phone: 262-335-4341; fax: 262-335-4776; hours 8AM-4:30PM (CST). *Felony, Misdemeanor, Civil, Eviction, Small Claims.*
www.co.washington.wi.us/washington/department.jsp?dept=COC
Civil Records: Access: Mail, fax, online, in person. Both court and visitors may perform in person searches. Search fee: $5.00 per name. Court makes copy: $1.25 per page. Required to search: name, years to search; also helpful: address. Civil cases indexed by defendant, plaintiff; on computer from 1986, index cards from 1976, index books from 1836. Civil court records free online at http://wicourts.gov/. Mail turnaround time 1 week.
Criminal Records: Access: Mail, fax, online, in person. Both court and visitors may perform in person searches. Search fee: $5.00 per name. Court makes copy: $1.25 per page. Required to search: name, years to search, DOB; also helpful: address. Criminal records on computer from 1986, index cards from 1976, index books from 1836. Access criminal index free at http://wcca.wicourts.gov/index.xsl. Mail turnaround time 1 week.
General Information: Public terminal goes back to 1986. No paternity records released prior to adjudication. Will fax documents to local or toll free line. Certification fee: $5.00. Payee: Clerk of Court. Personal checks accepted. Prepayment and SASE required.

Register in Probate PO Box 82, 432 E Washington St, West Bend, WI 53095-0082; phone: 262-335-4334; fax: 262-306-2224; hours 8AM-4:30PM (CST). *Probate.*
www.co.washington.wi.us/pjc
Free search at http://wcca.wicourts.gov/index.xsl.

Waukesha County

Circuit Court Clerk 515 W Moreland Blvd, Waukesha, WI 53188; criminal phone: 262-548-7484; civil phone: 262-548-7525; hours 8AM-4:30PM (CST). *Felony, Misdemeanor, Civil, Eviction, Small Claims.*
http://circuitcourts.waukeshacounty.gov
Civil Records: Access: Mail, online, in person. Both court and visitors may perform in person searches. Search fee: $5.00 per name. Court makes copy: $1.25 per page. Required to search: name, years to search. Civil cases indexed by defendant, plaintiff; on computer back to 1994. Civil court records free online at http://wcca.wicourts.gov/index.xsl. Mail turnaround time 2-3 days.
Criminal Records: Access: Mail, online, in person. Both court and visitors may perform in person searches. Search fee: $5.00 per name. Court makes copy: $1.25 per page. Required to search: name, years to search, DOB. Criminal records indexed on computer back to 1994; on microfilm back to 1980; index cards to 1940. Access criminal index free at http://wcca.wicourts.gov/index.xsl. Mail turnaround time 2-3 days.
General Information: Public terminal has criminal back to 1996 and civil back to 1994. No paternity, mental commitment records released. Fee to fax documents is $3.00 per document plus $1.25 per page.

Certification fee: $5.00 per document. Payee: Clerk of Circuit Court. Personal checks accepted. Credit cards accepted. Accepted in person only. Prepayment and SASE required.

Register in Probate 515 W Moreland, Rm 380, Waukesha, WI 53188; phone: 262-548-7468; fax: 262-896-8397; hours 8AM-4:30PM M-F (CST). *Probate.*
Free search at http://wcca.wicourts.gov/index.xsl.

Waupaca County

Circuit Court 811 Harding St, Waupaca, WI 54981; phone: 715-258-6460; fax: 715-258-6497; hours 8AM-4PM (CST). *Felony, Misdemeanor, Civil, Eviction, Small Claims.*
Civil Records: Access: Mail, in person, online. Both court and visitors may perform in person searches. Search fee: $5.00 per name. Court makes copy: $1.25 per page. Computer document copy fee $.50 per page. Required to search: name, years to search. Civil cases indexed by defendant, plaintiff; on computer from 1992. Civil court records free online at http://wcca.wicourts.gov/index.xsl. Mail turnaround time 3-4 days.
Criminal Records: Access: Mail, online, in person. Both court and visitors may perform in person searches. Search fee: $5.00 per name. Court makes copy: $1.25 per page. Computer document copy fee $.50 per page. Required to search: name, years to search. Criminal records on computer from 1992. Access criminal index free at http://wcca.wicourts.gov/index.xsl. Mail turnaround time 3-4 days.
General Information: Public use terminal available. No juvenile, JO, paternity excluding past judgments released. Certification fee: $5.00 per document. Payee: Clerk of Court. Business check and personal in-state check accepted. Prepayment and SASE required.

Register in Probate 811 Harding St, Waupaca, WI 54981; phone: 715-258-6429; probate phone: 715-258-6431 Dep Reg.; fax: 715-258-6440; hours 8AM-4PM (CST). *Probate.*
Free search at http://wcca.wicourts.gov/index.xsl.

Waushara County

Circuit Court PO Box 507, Wautoma, WI 54982; phone: 920-787-0441; fax: 920-787-0481; hours 8AM-4:30PM (CST). *Felony, Misdemeanor, Civil, Eviction, Small Claims.*
Civil Records: Access: Mail, fax, online, in person. Both court and visitors may perform in person searches. Search fee: $5.00 per name. fee only if court does search. Court makes copy: $1.25 per page. Required to search: name, years to search. Civil cases indexed by defendant. Civil records on computer from 1992, index cards to 1978, index books prior. Civil court records free online at http://wcca.wicourts.gov/index.xsl. Mail turnaround time 1 day.
Criminal Records: Access: Mail, fax, online, in person. Both court and visitors may perform in person searches. Search fee: $5.00 per name. Fee applies if court does search. Court makes copy: $1.25 per page. Required to search: name, years to search, DOB. Criminal records on computer from 1993, prior on cards and books. Access criminal index free at http://wcca.wicourts.gov/index.xsl. Mail turnaround time 1 week.
General Information: Public terminal goes back to 1993. Will fax documents if prepaid. Certification fee: $5.00. Payee: Clerk of Court. Personal in-state checks accepted; money orders for out of state requests. Prepayment and SASE required.

Register in Probate PO Box 508, Wautoma, WI 54982; phone: 920-787-0448; fax: 920-787-0481; hours 8AM-4:30PM (CST). *Probate.*
www.co.waushara.wi.us/
Free search at http://wcca.wicourts.gov/index.xsl.

Winnebago County

Circuit Court PO Box 2808, Oshkosh, WI 54903-2808; phone: 920-236-4848; criminal phone: 920-236-4855; civil phone: 920-236-4848; probate phone: 920-236-4833; fax: 920-424-7780; hours 8AM-4:30PM (CST). *Felony, Misdemeanor, Civil, Eviction, Small Claims.*
Civil Records: Access: Mail, fax, online, in person. Both court and visitors may perform in person searches. Search fee: $5.00 per name. Court makes copy: $1.25 per page. Required to search: name, years to search. Civil cases indexed by defendant, plaintiff. Civil records are on computer since 1990, prior on books and cards to 1970. Historical Society has records to 1938. Civil court records free online at http://wcca.wicourts.gov/index.xsl. Mail turnaround time 1 week.
Criminal Records: Access: Mail, fax, online, in person. Both court and visitors may perform in person searches. Search fee: $5.00 per name. Court makes copy: $1.25 per page. Required to search: full name, years to search, DOB. Criminal records are on computer since 1990, prior on books and cards. organized since 1938. Access criminal index free at http://wcca.wicourts.gov/index.xsl. Mail turnaround time 1 week.
General Information: Public terminal has criminal back to 1990 and civil back to 1992. No juvenile, paternity, financial records released. Fee to fax documents is $1.25 per page. Certification fee: $5.00. Payee: Clerk of Courts. Personal checks accepted. Prepayment and SASE required.

Register in Probate PO Box 2808, 415 Jackson St, Oshkosh, WI 54903-2808; phone: 920-236-4833; fax: 920-424-7536; hours 8AM-N, 1-4:30PM (CST). *Probate.*
Note: There is a $4.00 search fee. Probate records free at http://wcca.wicourts.gov/index.xsl.

Wood County

Circuit Court 400 Market St, PO Box 8095, Wisconsin Rapids, WI 54494-958095; phone: 715-421-8490; civil phone: 715-421-8807; fax: 715-421-8691; hours 8AM-4:30PM (CST). *Felony, Misdemeanor, Civil, Eviction, Small Claims.*
Civil Records: Access: Mail, online, in person. Both court and visitors may perform in person searches. Search fee: $5.00 per name. Court makes copy: $1.25 per page. Required to search: name, years to search. Civil cases indexed by defendant, plaintiff; on computer from 1983, microfiche from 1856-1980s. Civil court records free online at http://wcca.wicourts.gov/index.xsl. Mail turnaround time within 10 days.
Criminal Records: Access: Mail, online, in person. Both court and visitors may perform in person searches. Search fee: $5.00 per name. Court makes copy: $1.25 per page. Required to search: name, years to search, DOB. Criminal records on computer from 1980; manual search required for pre-1980 records. Access criminal index free at http://wcca.wicourts.gov/index.xsl. Mail turnaround time within 10 days.
General Information: Public use terminal available. No paternity or sealed records released. Will fax documents to local or toll free line. Certification fee: $5.00. Payee: Clerk of Court. Personal checks accepted. Prepayment and SASE required.

Register in Probate PO Box 8095, 400 Market St, County Courthouse, Wisconsin Rapids, WI 54495-8095; phone: 715-421-8523; fax: 715-421-8896; hours 8AM-4:30PM (CST). *Probate.*
Note: Court also holds guardianships, juveniles, mental and adoption records. Probate records free at http://wcca.wicourts.gov/index.xsl.

Wisconsin Recording Offices

ORGANIZATION: 72 counties, 72 recording offices. The recording officers are Register of Deeds and Clerk of Court (state tax liens). The entire state is in the Central Time Zone (CST).

REAL ESTATE RECORDS: Registers will not perform real estate searches. Copy fees and certification fees vary. Assessor telephone numbers are for local municipalities or for property listing agencies. Counties do not have assessors. Copies usually cost $2.00 for the first page and $1.00 for each additional page. Certification usually costs $.25 per document. The Treasurer maintains property tax records.

UCC RECORDS: Financing statements are filed at the state level, except for real estate related collateral, which are filed with the Register of Deeds. However, prior to 07/2001, consumer goods and farm collateral were also filed at the Register of Deeds and these older records can be searched there. Many recording offices will no longer perform UCC searches. Use search request form UCC-11 for mail-in searches. Searches fees are usually $10.00 to $15.00 per debtor name. Copy fees are usually $2.00 1st page and $1.00 each add'l page.

TAX LIEN RECORDS: Federal tax liens on personal property of businesses are filed with the Secretary of State. Only federal tax liens on real estate are filed with the county Register of Deeds. State tax liens are filed with the Clerk of Court, and at the State Treasurer at the Dept. of Revenue. Refer to the County Court Records section for information about Wisconsin courts. Most but not all Registers will perform federal tax lien searches. Search fees vary, but copy fees are $2.00 1st page and $1.00 each add'l page.

OTHER LIENS: Judgment, mechanics, breeders.

ONLINE ACCESS: A number of cities and a few counties offer online access to assessor and property records.

Adams County

Register of Deeds, PO Box 219, Friendship, WI 53934-0219. 608-339-4206; hours: 8AM-4:30PM.
Only the public may search. For state tax liens, see clerk of court. Copy fee $2.00 1st page, $1.00 each add'l page. Payee- Adams County Register of Deeds.

Ashland County

Register of Deeds, 201 W. Main St, Rm 206, Ashland, WI 54806. 715-682-7008; fax-715-682-7035; hours: 8AM-4PM. www.co.ashland.wi.us
All records in one index. Only the public may search. For state tax liens, see clerk of court. Copy fee $2.00 1st page, $1.00 each add'l page. Cert fee- $1.00 per doc plus copy fee. Payee- Register of deeds. **Online access to Property, Assessor records:** Search property records free at www.ashlandcogiws.com/textsearch/index.htm. **Other phones:** Treasurer- 715-682-7012; Elections- 715-682-7000; Vital Records- 715-682-7008.

Barron County

Register of Deeds, 330 E. LaSalle, Rm 201, Barron, WI 54812. 715-537-6210; fax-715-537-6277; hours: 8AM-4PM. www.co.barron.wi.us
Index: Book, computer. Records indexed on a public use terminal back to 1999. Office will perform a UCC and Tax lien search but public must search other records themselves. Search fee $15.00 per debtor. Copy fee $2.00 1st page, $1.00 each add'l page. Cert fee- $1.00 per doc plus copy fee. Payee- Barron County Register of Deeds. **Online access to Land, Assessor, Recorder, Real Estate, Deed, Lien records:** Access land records at www.gcssoftware.com/product/web_search.asp.
Registration, $300.00 annual fee, username, password required; call Yvonne at the county treasurer's office, 715-537-6280. Also, recorder office data by subscription on either the Laredo system using subscription and fees or the Tapestry System using credit card, https://tapestry.fidlar.com/tapsearch.aspx; $3.99 search; $.50 per image. **Other phones:** Treasurer- 715-537-6280; Vital Records- 715-537-6210. **Property tax/Assessor-** 715-537-6313.

Bayfield County

Register of Deeds, PO Box 813, Washburn, WI 54891. 715-373-6119; hours: 8AM-4PM.
Only the public may search. For state tax liens, see clerk of court. Copy fee $2.00 1st page, $1.00 each add'l page. Cert fee- $.25 per page. Payee- Bayfield County Register of Deeds. **Other phones:** Treasurer- 715-373-6131. **Property tax/Assessor-** 715-373-6131.

Brown County

Register of Deeds, PO Box 23600, Green Bay, WI 54305-3600. 920-448-4470, R/E recording phone-920-448-4439, UCC recording phone-920-448-4468; fax-920-448-4449; hours 8AM-4:30PM.
www.co.brown.wi.us/rod
All records in one index. Only the public may search. Copy fee $2.00 1st page, $1.00 each add'l page. Cert fee- $1.00 per doc plus copy fee. Payee- Register of Deeds. **Online access to Real Estate, Recording, Deed, Lien records:** Recorder office data by subscription on either the Laredo system using subscription and fees or the Tapestry System using credit card, https://tapestry.fidlar.com/tapsearch.aspx; $3.99 search; $.50 per image. Also, land records without name searching is at www.co.brown.wi.us/treasurer/landrecordssearch/entryform.asp. And land records can be downloaded from an ftp site; contact the Land Information office at 920-448-6295 to register and user information. **Other phones:** Treasurer- 920-448-4074; Elections- 920-448-4016; Vital Records- 920-448-4474. **Property tax/Assessor-** same address as above. not known.

Buffalo County

Register of Deeds, PO Box 28, Alma, WI 54610-0028. 608-685-6230; fax-608-685-6213;
Only the public may search. For state tax liens, see clerk of court. Copy fee $2.00 1st page, $1.00 each add'l page. **Online access to Land, Property Tax records:** Access to county land records is free at www.gcssoftware.com/applications/search/index.asp?County=Buffalo. **Other phones:** Treasurer- 608-685-6214.

Burnett County

Register of Deeds, 7410 County Rd K #103, Siren, WI 54872. 715-349-2183; fax-715-349-2037; hours: 8:30AM-4:30PM. www.burnettcounty.com
All records in one index. Only the public may search. For state tax liens, see clerk of court. Copy fee $2.00 1st page, $1.00 each add'l page. Cert fee- $1.00 per page plus copy fee. Payee- Burnett County Register of Deeds. **Online access to Property, Tax Assessor records:** Access to limited county property and assessment records is free at http://burnettims.homeip.net/. No name searching. For full data, an online subscription service is $100 per year. **Other phones:** Treasurer- 715-349-2187; Elections- 715-349-2173; Vital Records- 715-349-2183.

Calumet County

Register of Deeds, 206 Court St, Chilton, WI 53014. 920-849-1441; fax-920-849-1616; hours: 8AM-4:30PM. www.co.calumet.wi.us
All records in one index. Records indexed on a public use terminal back to 1991. Only the public may search. Copy fee $2.00 1st page, $1.00 each add'l page. Cert fee- $1.00 per doc + copy fees. Payee- Register of Deeds. **Online access to Assessor, Property Tax records:** Access to assessor property tax data is free at http://calum400.co.calumet.wi.us/nsccalo/nsclndrec. **Property tax/Assessor-** same address as above. 920-849-1457.

Chippewa County

Register of Deeds, 711 N Bridge St, Chippewa Falls, WI 54729-1876. 715-726-7994; fax-715-726-4582; hours: 8AM-4:30 PM
www.co.chippewa.wi.us/Departments/RegisterDeeds
All records in one index. Office will perform a UCC search but public must search other records themselves. Will search for one or two real estate records. UCC search per debtor name- $15.00. Copy fee $2.00 1st page, $1.00 each add'l page. Cert fee- $1.00 per page plus copy fee. Payee- Register of Deeds. **Online access to Recording, Deed, Judgment, Real Estate records:** Search Register of Deeds data at www.landshark.co.chippewa.wi.us, index search is free, but fees apply for images and copies, $2.00 1st page, $1.00 2nd page. Credit cards accepted. **Other phones:**

Treasurer- 715-726-7965; Elections- 715-726-7980; Vital Records- 715-726-7994.

Clark County

Registrar, PO Box 384, Neillsville, WI 54456-0384. 715-743-5162, R/E recording phone-715-743-5163; fax-715-743-5154; 8-4:30PM. www.co.clark.wi.us Separate indices to search include Computer and Books-Fed Tax Liens, Grantee/Grantor, Tract, Misc, Corp. Only the public may search. Copy fee $2.00 1st page, $1.00 each add'l page. Cert fee- $1.00 per doc, plus copy fee. Payee- Clark County Register of Deeds. **Online access to Assessor, Property records:** Search for assessor/property tax information on the county GIS-mapping site at www.co.clark.wi.us/Website/ClarkIMS/viewer.htm. Search by PIN or address. **Other phones:** Treasurer- 715-743-5155; Elections- 715-743-5148; Vital Records- 715-743-5163.

Columbia County

Register of Deeds, PO Box 133, Portage, WI 53901. 608-742-9677; fax-608-742-9875; hours: 8AM-4:30PM. www.co.columbia.wi.us All records in one index. Records indexed on computer back to 11/1/1987. Only the public may search. Copy fee $2.00 1st page, $1.00 each add'l page. Cert fee- $1.00 per record plus copy fee. Payee- Register of Deeds. **Online access to Property Tax, Land records:** Search the land records system for free at www.co.columbia.wi.us/landrecords. **Other phones:** Treasurer- 608-742-9613. **Property tax/Assessor-** 608-742-9677.

Crawford County

Register of Deeds, 220 N. Beaumont Rd, Prairie du Chien, WI 53821. 608-326-0219; fax-608-326-0220; 8AM-4;30PM. http://crawfordcounty-wi-us.org All records in one index. Records indexed on computer back to 6/28/2001. Office personnel or visitors may perform searches. For state tax liens, see clerk of court. Copy fee $2.00 1st page, $1.00 each add'l page. Cert fee- $3.00 1st page, $1.00 each add'l. Payee- Register of Deeds. **Other phones:** Treasurer- 608-326-0203; Vital Records- 608-326-0219.

Dane County

Register of Deeds, PO Box 1438, Madison, WI 53701. 608-266-4141, R/E recording phone-608-266-4144 (2-4 PM only); fax-608-267-3110; hours: 7:45AM-4PM. www.co.dane.wi.us/regdeeds/rdhome.htm The Register of Deeds will only release information over the phone between the hours of 2-4PM. You can email the agency if you have questions. All records in one index. Records indexed on a public use terminal back to 1978. Only the public may search. Will search limited real estate records from 2PM-4PM only. Copy fee $2.00 1st page, $1.00 each add'l page. Cert fee- $1.00 per doc plus copy fee. Payee- Register of Deeds. **Online access to Assessor, Property Tax, Recording, Real Estate, Deed, Lien records:** A fee-based system is at www.co.dane.wi.us/regdeeds/laredotapestry/accesstorealestate.htm. $3.99 search; $.50 per image. Also, access recording office land data at www.etitlesearch.com; registration required, fee based on usage. Also, the City of Madison tax assessor database is accessible at www.ci.madison.wi.us/assessor/property.html. Also, search property info for Towns of Cross Plains, Mazomanie, Berry, Medina at www.wendorffassessing.com/municipalities.htm. Also, Professional companies may register to use assessor/land record services at www.co.dane.wi.us and select "AccessDane" from the bottom of this home page. **Other phones:** Treasurer- 608-266-4151; Elections- 608-266-4121; Vital Records- 608-266-4142; General Number- 608-266-4141.

Dodge County

Register of Deeds, 127 E. Oak St; Admin. Bldg., Juneau, WI 53039-1391. 920-386-3720, UCC recording phone-920-386-3723; fax-920-386-3902; hours: 8AM-4:30PM. www.co.dodge.wi.us Separate indices to search include computer to 4/1987, paper before that. Records indexed on a public use terminal back to 4/1987. Office will perform a UCC search but public must search other records themselves. Copy fee $2.00 1st page, $1.00 each add'l page. Cert fee- $1.00 per page plus copy fee. Payee- Dodge County Register of Deeds. **Other phones:** Treasurer- 920-386-3782; Vital Records- 920-386-3720. **Property tax/Assessor-** 920-386-3770.

Door County

Register of Deeds, PO Box 670, Sturgeon Bay, WI 54235-0670. 920-746-2270, UCC recording phone-608-261-9548 (Madison); fax-920-746-2525; hours: 8AM-4:30PM. Separate indices to search include grantor/Grantee, Tracts. Grantor/Grantee indexed on computer back to 1982. Office will perform a UCC search but public must search other records themselves. Separate federal tax lien search- $15.00 per debtor. For state tax liens, see clerk of court. Copy fee $2.00 1st page, $1.00 each add'l page. Cert fee- $2.00 1st page, $1.00 add'l page, plus copy fee. Payee- Register of Deeds. **Other phones:** Treasurer- 920-746-2286; Vital Records- 920-746-2270. **Property tax/Assessor-** same address as above. 920-746-2905.

Douglas County

Register of Deeds, PO Box 847, Superior, WI 54880. 715-395-1463, R/E recording phone-715-395-1350, UCC recording phone-715-395-1463; fax-715-395-1553; 8AM-4:30PM. www.douglascountywi.org All records in one index. Only the public may search. For state tax liens, see clerk of court. Copy fee $2.00 1st page, $1.00 each add'l page. Cert fee- $3.00 1st page plus copy fee. Payee- Register of Deeds. **Online access to Land records:** For access to county land records, use Landshark to go to http://rdlandshark.douglascountywi.org. **Other phones:** Treasurer- 715-395-1348; Elections- 715-395-1397; Vital Records- 715-395-1463; City of Superior- 715-395-7222; County Tax Lister -715-395-1386.

Dunn County

Register of Deeds, 800 Wilson Ave, Menomonie, WI 54751. 715-232-1228; fax-715-232-1229; hours: 8AM-4:30PM. Only the public may search. For state tax liens, see clerk of court. Copy fee $2.00 1st page, $1.00 each add'l page. Cert fee- $1.00. Payee- Dunn County Register of Deeds. **Online access to Recording, Real Estate, Deed, Lien records:** Recorder office data by subscription on either the Laredo system using subscription and fees or the Tapestry System using credit card, https://tapestry.fidlar.com/tapsearch.aspx; $3.99 search; $.50 per image. **Other phones:** Treasurer- 715-232-3789. **Property tax/Assessor-** 715-232-1401.

Eau Claire County

Register of Deeds, PO Box 718, Eau Claire, WI 54702. 715-839-4745; hours: 8AM-5PM. www.co.eau-claire.wi.us/ Only the public may search. Copy fee $2.00 1st page, $1.00 each add'l page. Cert fee- $1.00 per cert plus copy fee. Payee- Eau Claire County Register of Deeds. **Online access to Recording, Real Estate, Deed, Lien, Warrant, Most Wanted records:** Recorder office data by subscription on either the Laredo system using subscription and fees or the Tapestry System using credit card, https://tapestry.fidlar.com/tapsearch.aspx; $3.99 search; $.50 per image. Search the sheriff's most wanted list and warrants list at www.co.eau-claire.wi.us/sheriff/sheriff.asp. **Other phones:** Treasurer- 715-839-4805; Elections- 715-839-4801;

Vital Records- 715-839-4745. **Property tax/Assessor-** 715-839-4741.

Florence County

Register of Deeds, PO Box 410, Florence, WI 54121-0410. 715-528-4252; fax-715-528-5470; 8:30-4PM. All records in one index. Records indexed on computer. Only the public may search. Will do limited real estate search. For state tax liens, see clerk of court. Copy fee $2.00 1st page, $1.00 each add'l page. Cert fee- $1.00. Payee- Register of Deeds. **Other phones:** Treasurer- 715-528-3204.

Fond du Lac County

Register of Deeds, PO Box 509, Fond du Lac, WI 54935-0509. 920-929-3018, R/E recording phone-920-929-3021, UCC recording phone-920-929-3022; fax-920-929-3293; hours: 8AM-4:30PM. www.co.fond-du-lac.wi.us All records in one index. Records indexed on a public use terminal back to 1989. Only the public may search. For state tax liens, see clerk of court. Copy fee $2.00 1st page, $1.00 each add'l page. Cert fee- $1.00 per doc plus copy fee. Payee- Fond du Lac County Register of Deeds. **Online access to Property, Assessor, GIS Mapping records:** Access to the GIS-mapping site at www.co.fond-du-lac.wi.us/Website/FondduLacIMS/viewer.htm. Click on search to search by address or parcel number. No name searching. **Other phones:** Treasurer- 920-929-3010; Elections- 920-929-3000; Vital Records- 920-929-3019. **Property tax/Assessor-** same address as above. 920-929-3010.

Forest County

Register of Deeds, 200 E. Madison St, Crandon, WI 54520. 715-478-3823; fax-715-478-3837; hours: 8:30AM-N, 1-4:30PM. Office will perform a UCC search but public must search other records themselves. UCC search per debtor name- $10.00. For state tax liens, see clerk of court. Copy fee $2.00 1st page, $1.00 each add'l page. Cert fee- $1.00 per cert plus copy fee. Payee- Forest County Register of Deeds. **Online access to Land, Assessor records:** Access to county property and assessor data free is at www.gcssoftware.com/applications/search/index.asp?County=Forest. **Other phones:** Treasurer- 715-478-2412; Elections- 715-478-2422; Vital Records- 715-478-3823.

Grant County

Register of Deeds, PO Box 391, Lancaster, WI 53813-608-723-2727; fax-608-723-4048; 8AM-4:30PM. All records in one index. Records indexed on a public use terminal back to 1989. Only the public may search. For state tax liens, see clerk of court. Copy fee $2.00 1st page, $1.00 each add'l page. Cert fee- $1.00 per doc, plus copy fee. Payee- Register of Deeds. **Online access to Land, Assessor records:** Access to county property and assessor data is at www.gcssoftware.com/product/web_search.asp. Registration, $200.00 annual fee, username, and password required; call John at the Tax Lister office, 608-723-2666. **Other phones:** Treasurer- 608-723-2604; Elections- 608-723-2675; Vital Records- 608-723-2727. **Property tax/Assessor-** same address as above. 608-723-2666.

Green County

Register of Deeds, 1016 16th Ave; Courthouse, Monroe, WI 53566. 608-328-9439; fax-608-328-2835; hours: 8AM-5PM. Only the public may search. For state tax liens, see clerk of court. Copy fee $2.00 1st page, $1.00 each add'l page. Payee- Green County Register of Deeds.

Green Lake County

Register of Deeds, PO Box 3188, Green Lake, WI 54941-3188. 920-294-4021; fax-920-294-4165; hours: 8AM-4:30PM. www.co.green-lake.wi.us All records in one index. They will do a quick search for 1 item or Property. Copy fee $2.00 1st page, $1.00 each add'l page. Cert fee- $2.00 per doc plus copy fee. **Other phones:** Treasurer- 920-294-4018; Vital Records- 920-294-4021.

Iowa County

Register of Deeds, 222 N. Iowa St, Dodgeville, WI 53533. 608-935-0396; fax-608-935-3024; hours: 8:30AM-4:30PM.
Only the public may search. For state tax liens, see clerk of court. Copy fee $2.00 1st page, $1.00 each add'l page. Cert fee- $1.00 plus copy fee. Payee- Iowa County Register of Deeds. **Other phones:** Treasurer- 608-935-0397; Elections- 608-935-0399; Vital Records- 608-935-0396.

Iron County

Register of Deeds, 300 Taconite St #102, Hurley, WI 54534. 715-561-2945; fax-715-561-2928; hours: 8AM-4PM.
All records in one index. Only the public may search. Copy fee $2.00 1st page, $1.00 each add'l page. Cert fee- $2.00 per page. **Other phones:** Treasurer- 715-561-2883; Appraiser/Auditor- 715-561-2883; Vital Records- 715-561-2945. **Property tax/Assessor-** 715-561-2883.

Jackson County

Register of Deeds, 307 Main, Black River Falls, WI 54615. 715-284-0205; fax-715-284-0204; hours: 8AM-4PM. www.co.jackson.wi.us
All records in one index. Records indexed on a public use terminal back to 1986. Office will perform a Tax lien search but public must search other records themselves. For state tax liens, see clerk of court. General copy fee $2.00 1st page, $1.00 each add'l page. Tax lien copy- $1.00 per page. Cert fee- $1.00 per doc plus copy fee. Payee- Register of Deeds. **Other phones:** Treasurer- 715-284-0226. **Property tax/Assessor-** 715-284-0203.

Jefferson County

Register of Deeds, PO Box 356, Jefferson, WI 53549. 920-674-7235; hours: 8AM-4:30PM. www.co.jefferson.wi.us
Office will perform a tax lien search but public must search other records themselves. Search fee $10.00 per debtor. Copy fee $2.00 1st page, $1.00 each add'l page. Cert fee- $1.00 per doc plus copy fee. Payee- Jefferson County Register of Deeds. **Online access to Grantor/Grantee, Treasurer, GIS-Mapping, Assessor Property Tax records:** Call 920-674-7254 for info and fee. **Other phones:** Treasurer- 920-674-7250; Elections- 920-674-7140; Vital Records- 920-674-7235.

Juneau County

Register of Deeds, 220 E. State St. #212, Mauston, WI 53948-1379. 608-847-9325; fax-608-847-9402; hours: 8AM-N, 12:30-4:30PM. www.juneaucounty.com/
All records in one index. Records indexed on a public use terminal back to 9/1/89 for grantor/grantee - back to Mid-May 99 for track index. Only the public may search. For state tax liens, see clerk of court. Copy fee $2.00 1st page, $1.00 each add'l page. Cert fee- $3.00 1st page, $1.00 each add'l pages per real estate doc plus copy fee. Payee- Register of Deeds. **Other phones:** Treasurer- 608-847-9308; Elections- 608-847-9302; Vital Records- 608-847-9325.

Kenosha County

Register of Deeds, 1010 56 St., Kenosha, WI 53140. 262-653-2444, R/E recording phone-414-653-2441; fax-262-653-2564; hours: 8AM-5PM. www.kenosha.org
Records indexed on computer. Only the public may search. Copy fee $2.00 1st page, $1.00 each add'l page. Cert fee- $1.00 per page plus copy fee. Payee- Kenosha Register of Deeds. **Online access to Real Estate, Lien, Vital Statistic, Assessor records:** Access to recorder records requires a set-up fee is $500, plus $6.00 per hour usage fee. The system operates 24 hours daily; records date back to 5/1986.

Federal tax liens and lending agency information is available. For further information, contact Joellyn Storz at 262-653-2511. Also, search the Kenosha City Assessor's property database for free at www.kenosha.org/departments/assessor/search.html. No name searching. **Other phones:** Treasurer- 414-653-2542; Vital Records- 262-653-2444. **Property tax/Assessor-** 414-653-2545.

Kewaunee County

Register of Deeds, 613 Dodge St, Kewaunee, WI 54216-1398. 920-388-7126, R/E recording phone-920-388-7126/7127/7128; fax-920-388-7129; hours: 8AM-4:30PM. www.kewauneeco.org
All records in one index. Records indexed on a public use terminal back to 2/1992. Office will perform a UCC search but public must search other records themselves. Search fee $15.00. Copy fee $2.00 1st page, $1.00 each add'l page. Cert fee- $1.00 per doc plus copy fee. Payee- Register of Deeds. **Online access to Grantor/Grantee, Deed, Tract & Image, GIS Mapping, Property Tax, Real Estate records:** Access to Register of Deeds data should be at www.kewauneeco.org/subpages/Dep artments/ROD/Register%20of%20Deeds.htm. Click on Documents and Images. Also, search land and tax records free at www.gcssoftware.com/applic ations/search/index.asp?County=Kewaunee. **Other phones:** Treasurer- 920-388-7152; Elections- 920-388-7133; Vital Records- 920-388-7127.

La Crosse County

Register of Deeds, 400 N. 4th St, Rm 1220; Admin. Ctr, La Crosse, WI 54601-3200. 608-785-9644, R/E recording phone-608-785-9652, UCC recording phone-608-785-9651; fax-608-785-9643; 8:30AM-5PM. www.co.la-crosse.wi.us/Departments/departments.htm
The county participates on the www.landrecords.net site. Fees are involved. Office will perform a tax lien search but public must search other records themselves. Federal tax lien search- $15.00 per debtor. For state tax liens, see clerk of court. Copy fee $2.00 1st page, $1.00 each add'l. Cert fee- $1.00 per doc + copy fees. Payee- Register of Deeds. **Online access to Land, Deed, Property Owner, Recording, Lien records:** Recorder office data by subscription on either the Laredo system using subscription and fees or the Tapestry System using credit card, https://tapestry.fidlar.com/tapsearch.aspx; $3.99 search; $.50 per image. Index back to 1992; images to 6/1992. Also, search for property owner and land information for free at www.co.la-crosse.wi.us/Departments/LIO/main_search_page.htm. **Other phones:** Treasurer- 608-785-9711; Vital Records- 608-785-9652. **Property tax/Assessor-** 608-785-7525.

Lafayette County

Register of Deeds, PO Box 170, Darlington, WI 53530. 608-776-4838; fax-608-776-4991; 8AM-4:30PM.
Index: Books and computer back to 1/1/1995. Only the public may search. For state tax liens, see clerk of court. Copy fee $2.00 1st page, $1.00 each add'l page. Cert fee- $1.00 per page plus copy fee. Payee- Register of Deeds. **Online access to Recording, Real Estate, Deed, Lien records:** Recorder office data by subscription on either the Laredo system using subscription and fees or the Tapestry System using credit card, https://tapestry.fidlar.com/tapsearch.aspx; $3.99 search; $.50 per image. **Other phones:** Treasurer- 608-776-4862; Elections- 608-776-4850; Vital Records- 608-776-4838.

Langlade County

Register of Deeds, 800 Clermont St, Antigo, WI 54409. 715-627-6209; fax-715-627-6303; hours: 8:30AM-4:30PM. http://co.langlade.wi.us
Separate indices to search include tract, grantor/grantee. Records indexed on computer back to 1994. Office personnel or visitors may perform searches. For state tax liens, see clerk of court. Copy fee $2.00 1st page, $1.00 each add'l

page. Cert fee- $1.00 per cert plus copy fee. Payee-Register of Deeds. **Other phones:** Treasurer- 715-627-6204; Elections- 715-627-6200; Vital Records-715-627-6209. **Property tax/Assessor-** 715-627-6207.

Lincoln County

Register of Deeds, 1110 E. Main; Courthouse, Merrill, WI 54452. 715-536-0318; fax-715-536-0360; www.co.lincoln.wi.us
Office will perform a UCC search but public must search other records themselves. UCC search per debtor name- $10.00. For state tax liens, see clerk of court. Copy fee $2.00 1st page, $1.00 each add'l page. **Online access to Land records:** Access to county land records is free at www.lrs.co.lincoln.wi.us/apps/lrs/. No name searching. **Other phones:** Treasurer- 715-536-0315; Elections- 715-536-0359; Vital Records- 715-536-0318. **Property tax/Assessor-** 715-536-0479.

Manitowoc County

Register of Deeds, PO Box 421, Manitowoc, WI 54221-0421. 920-683-4010, R/E recording phone-920-683-4011, UCC recording phone-920-683-4010; fax-920-683-2702; hours: 8:30AM-4:30PM. www.manitowoc-county.com
Office personnel or visitors may perform searches. Search fee $10.00 per name. Will not search real estate records. For state tax liens, see clerk of court. Copy fee $2.00 1st page, $1.00 each add'l page. Cert fee- $1.00 per page. Payee- Register of Deeds. **Online access to Assessor, Real Estate records:** Access to the City of Manitowoc Assessor database at http://assessor.manitowoc.org/default.htm. No name searching. Access Two Rivers assessor data free at http://tworivers.patriotproperties.com/default.asp. **Other phones:** Treasurer- 920-683-4020; Vital Records- 920-683-4509. **Property tax/Assessor-** 920-683-4425.

Marathon County

Register of Deeds, 500 Forest St; Courthouse, Wausau, WI 54403-5568. 715-261-1470; fax-715-261-1488; hours: 8AM-4:30PM. www.co.marathon.wi.us
All records in one index. Records indexed on computer back to 1986. Only the public may search. For state tax liens, see clerk of court. Copy fee $2.00 1st page, $1.00 each add'l page. Cert fee- $1.00 per doc plus copy fee. Payee- Register of Deeds. **Online access to Land records:** Access to county property records is free at www.co.marathon.wi.us/online/apps/lrs/index.asp. No name searching. **Other phones:** Treasurer- 715-261-1150; Elections- 715-261-1500; Vital Records- 715-261-1470. **Property tax/Assessor-** 715-843-1300.

Marinette County

Register of Deeds, 1926 Hall Ave; Courthouse, Marinette, WI 54143. 715-732-7550; fax-715-732-7532; hours: 8:30AM-4:30PM. www.marinettecounty.com
Separate indices to search include computer, tract, grantor/grantee. Records indexed on a public use terminal back to 2000. Only the public may search. For state tax liens, see clerk of court. Copy fee $2.00 1st page, $1.00 each add'l page. Cert fee- $1.00 per cert plus copy fee. Payee- Marinette County Register of Deeds. **Other phones:** Treasurer- 715-732-7430.

Marquette County

Register of Deeds, PO Box 236, Montello, WI 53949-0236. 608-297-9132, R/E recording phone-608-297-9136 x232; fax-608-297-7606; hours: 8AM-N, 12:30-4:30PM.
Office will perform a tax lien search but public must search other records themselves. Will do federal tax lien search for the cost of copies. For state tax liens, see clerk of court. Copy fee $2.00 1st page, $1.00 each add'l page. Cert fee- $1.00 per doc plus copy fee. Payee- Marquette County Register of Deeds. **Other phones:** Treasurer- 608-

297-9148; Vital Records- 608-297-9136 x232. **Property tax/Assessor**- 608-297-9148.

Menominee County

Register of Deeds, PO Box 279, Keshena, WI 54135-0279. 715-799-3312; fax-715-799-1322; hours: 8AM-4:30PM.
All records in one index. Records indexed on computer. Office personnel or visitors may perform searches. Search fee $10.00. Real estate records are found at D.F.I. Copy fee $2.00 1st page, $1.00 each add'l page. **Other phones:** Treasurer- 715-799-3315; Appraiser/Auditor- 715-799-3001; Elections- 715-799-3311; Vital Records- 715-799-3312. **Property tax/Assessor**- 715-799-3315.

Milwaukee County

Register of Deeds, 901 N. 9th St, Rm 103, Milwaukee, WI 53233. 414-278-4011, R/E recording phone-414-278-4005, UCC recording phone-414-278-4006; fax-414-223-1257; hours: 8AM-4:30PM. www.milwaukee.gov
Recorder office data by subscription on either the Laredo system using subscription and fees or the Tapestry System using credit card, https://tapestry.fidlar.com/tapsearch.aspx; $3.99 search; $.50 per image at landrecords.net. All records in one index. Records indexed on a public use terminal back to 1988. Office personnel or visitors may perform searches. Search fee $10.00 per name. Copy fee $2.00 1st page, $1.00 each add'l page. Cert fee- 1.00 per doc plus copy fee. **Online access to Real Estate, Property Sale, Recorder, Deed, Lien records:** Property, assessment data & sales data on Milwaukee City (not county) Assessor database is free at www.milwaukee.gov/display/router.asp?docid=720. No name searching. Search Greendale, Brown Deer, Oak Creek at www.gcssoftware.com/product/web_search.asp. Search the City of Cudahy assessor property data for free online at http://exch02.ci.cudahy.wi.us/Scripts/GVSWeb.dll/Search, and Wauwatosa property at www.wauwatosa.net/display/router.asp?DocID=961. No name searching. Also, search Franklin assessor at www.ci.franklin.wi.us/dynamic/pagetemplate.cfm?template=assessmentSearch.cfm. Glendale assessor is at http://ts.glendale-wi.org; West Allis at www.ci.westallis.wi.us/asp/search_form.asp. No name searching. **Other phones:** Treasurer- 414-278-4033; Elections- 414-278-4060; Vital Records- 414-278-4003. **Property tax/Assessor**- 414-286-3651.

Monroe County

Register of Deeds, 202 S. "K" St, Rm 2, Sparta, WI 54656. 608-269-8716; fax-608-269-8715; hours: 8AM-4:30PM. www.co.monroe.wi.us
All records in one index. Records indexed on a public use terminal back to 1996. Only the public may search. Copy fee $2.00 1st page, $1.00 each add'l page. Cert fee- $1.00 per cert plus copy fee. Payee- Monroe County Register of Deeds. **Other phones:** Treasurer- 608-269-8710; Vital Records- 608-269-8716.

Oconto County

Register of Deeds, 301 Washington St, Rm 2035, Oconto, WI 54153-1699. 920-834-6807; hours: 8AM-4PM. www.co.oconto.wi.us
One index since 1/1/2000. Federal tax liens may be searched separately. All records in one index. Will not search real estate records. Will search UCC records through to 6/30/2001 only. UCC search does not include federal tax liens. UCC search per debtor name- $15.00. Separate federal tax lien search-$15.00 per debtor. For state tax liens, see clerk of court. Copy fee $2.00 1st page, $1.00 each add'l page. Cert fee- $1.00 per cert plus copy fee. Payee-Oconto County Register of Deeds. **Online access to Property, Assessor records:** Access to the county SOLO tax parcel search is free or by subscription at http://solo.co.oconto.wi.us/ocontoco/. Subscription fee is $300 per calendar year. Phone 920-834-6800 for information. Access to Registrar of Deeds by

subscription or escrow account at https://landshark.co.oconto.wi.us. The free service does not include name searching. **Other phones:** Treasurer- 920-834-6813; Vital Records- 920-834-6807; Real Property Lister- 920-834-6827.

Oneida County

Register of Deeds, PO Box 400, Rhinelander, WI 54501. 715-369-6150; fax-715-369-6222; hours: 8AM-4:30PM.
All records in one index. Office will perform a UCC search but public must search other records themselves. UCC search per debtor name- $15.00. Separate federal tax lien search- $2.00 per debtor. For state tax liens, see clerk of court. Copy fee $2.00 1st page, $1.00 each add'l. Cert fee- $1.00 per page. Payee- Oneida County Register of Deeds. **Other phones:** Treasurer- 715-369-6137. **Property tax/Assessor**- 715-369-6137.

Outagamie County

Register of Deeds, 410 S. Walnut St, CAB 205, Appleton, WI 54911-5999. 920-832-5095; fax-920-832-2177; hours: 8AM-4:30PM; Summer hours: 7AM-3:30PM. www.co.outagamie.wi.us
All records in one index. Only the public may search. For state tax liens, see clerk of court. Copy fee $2.00 1st page, $1.00 each add'l page. Cert fee- $1.00 per page plus copy fee. **Online access to Real Estate, Recorder, Deed, Judgment, Treasurer, Property Tax, GIS-Mapping Inmate, Offender records:** Access recorder and treasurer records via subscription on PRISM System, see www.co.outagamie.wi.us/planning/prismnew.pdf or call 920-832-4357. Basic plan- $50.00 per month plus $.06 per minute. Advanced plan with images- $100 per month and $.12 per minute. Search inmate information free on private company website at www.vinelink.com/offender/searchNew.jsp?siteID=50002. **Other phones:** Treasurer- 414-832-5065; Elections- 920-832-5077; Vital Records- 920-832-5095; Abstracting Phone- 920-832-5114; Tax Lister - 920-832-5665. **Property tax/Assessor**- 410 Walnut St, Appleton, WI 54911; not known.

Ozaukee County

Register of Deeds, PO Box 994, Port Washington, WI 53074-0994. 262-284-8260; fax-262-284-8268; hours: 8:30AM-5PM. www.co.ozaukee.wi.us
Records indexed on computer. Only the public may search. For state tax liens, see clerk of court. Copy fee $2.00 1st page, $1.00 each add'l page. Cert fee- $1.00 per doc plus copy fee. Payee-Register of Deeds. **Online access to Recording, Real Estate, Grantor/Grantee, Vital Statistic, Property Tax, Tracts, Civil Court records:** Access is by "Remote Access" requiring dial-up modem. This data is for inquiries only and includes civil, family, and traffic courts with Register of Deeds (back to 1960's) and Treasurer (back 11 years) property data. Software is supplied by the county. First month is free, then $50.00 per month subscription. For info, contact the Technology Resources Dept. at 262-284-8309. Also, recorder office data by subscription on either the Laredo system using subscription and fees or the Tapestry System using credit card, online at https://tapestry.fidlar.com/tapsearch.aspx; $3.99 search; $.50 per image. **Other phones:** Treasurer- 262-284-8280; Vital Records- 262-284-8260.

Pepin County

Register of Deeds, PO Box 39, Durand, WI 54736. 715-672-8856; fax-715-672-8677; hours: 8:30AM-N, 12:30-4:30. www.co.pepin.wi.us
Index: books. Records indexed on a public use terminal back to 1994. Office will perform a Tax lien search but public must search other records themselves. Search fee $15.00. Copy fee $2.00 1st page, $1.00 each add'l page. Cert fee- $1.00 per doc plus copy fee. Payee- Register of Deeds. **Online access to Land, Property Tax, Map records:** Access maps, land record/tax data at

www.co.pepin.wi.us. **Other phones:** Treasurer- 715-672-8850; Vital Records- 715-672-8856.

Pierce County

Register of Deeds, PO Box 267, Ellsworth, WI 54011-0267. 715-273-3531 x418; fax-715-273-6861; hours: 8AM-5PM. www.co.pierce.wi.us
Separate indices to search include tract index books and grantor/grantee books up to 1998, then computer. Records indexed on computer from 1998 to present. Only the public may search. For state tax liens, see clerk of court. Copy fee $2.00 1st page, $1.00 each add'l page. Cert fee- $1.00 per doc plus copy fee. Payee- Register of Deeds. **Online access to Real Estate, Assessor, Property Tax, Recording, Deed, Lien records:** Access to county property data is free at www.co.pierce.wi.us/Disclaimer.htm. Click on Property Data Search. Also, recorder office data by subscription on either the Laredo system using subscription and fees or the Tapestry System using credit card, https://tapestry.fidlar.com/tapsearch.aspx; $3.99 search; $.50 per image. Visit www.co.pierce.wi.us/reg_of_deeds/Records.access.page.htm for more Tapestry info. Records go back to 1998. **Other phones:** Treasurer- 715-273-3531 x307-8; Vital Records- 715-273-3531 x418. **Property tax/Assessor**- 715-273-3531.

Polk County

Register of Deeds, PO Box 335, Balsam Lake, WI 54810-0335. 715-485-9240; fax-715-485-9202; hours: 8:30AM-4:30PM. www.co.polk.wi.us
All records in one index. Records indexed on a public use terminal back to 9/1995. Only the public may search. For state tax liens, see clerk of court. Copy fee $2.00 1st page, $1.00 each add'l page. Cert fee- $1.00 per doc plus copy fee. Payee-Register of Deeds. **Online access to Assessor, Land records:** For assessor and land records free go to www.gcssoftware.com/applications/search/index.asp?County=Polk. **Other phones:** Treasurer- 715-485-9254; Elections- 715-485-9223; Vital Records- 715-485-9240.

Portage County

Register of Deeds, 1516 Church St; County-City Bldg., Stevens Point, WI 54481. 715-346-1428; fax-715-345-5361; hours: 7:30-4:30. www.co.portage.wi.us
Office personnel or visitors may perform searches. Search fee $10.00 per name. For state tax liens, see clerk of court. Copy fee $2.00 1st page, $1.00 each add'l page. Cert fee- $1.00 per cert. Payee-Register of Deeds. **Online access to Property Tax, Assessor, Recording, Land, Deed, Criminal Complaint records:** Access to county records is free at www.co.portage.wi.us. Registration required; searching is free; fee for copies of images. Property tax data does not include Steven Point City. **Other phones:** Treasurer- 715-346-1428. **Property tax/Assessor**- 715-346-1553.

Price County

Register of Deeds, 126 Cherry, Phillips, WI 54555. 715-339-2515; hours: 8AM-N, 1-4:30PM.
Office personnel or visitors may perform searches. No search fee. Will not search UCC records. For state tax liens, see clerk of court. Copy fee $2.00 1st page, $1.00 each add'l page. Cert fee- $1.00 per cert. Payee- Price County Register of Deeds.

Racine County

Register of Deeds, 730 Wisconsin Ave, Racine, WI 53403. 262-636-3208, UCC recording phone-262-636-3849; fax-262-636-3851; hours: 8AM-5PM. www.goracine.org
Separate indices to search include grantor/grantee, address, tax key number, legal description. Records indexed on computer back to mid-1993. Office personnel or visitors may perform searches. Search fee $5.00-$10.00 depending on dates. For state tax liens, see clerk of court. Copy fee $2.00 1st page, $1.00 each add'l page. Cert fee- $1.00

per doc plus copy fee. Payee- Racine County Register of Deeds. **Other phones:** Treasurer- 262-636-3238; Elections- 262-636-3122; Vital Records- 262-636-3477.

Richland County

Register of Deeds, PO Box 337, Richland Center, WI 53581. 608-647-3011; hours: 8:30AM-4:30PM. All records in one index. Will search real estate records. Will search UCC records, search includes federal tax liens if requested. UCC search per debtor name- $10.00. Separate federal tax lien search- $10.00 per debtor. For state tax liens, see clerk of court. Copy fee $2.00 1st page, $1.00 each add'l page. Cert fee- $1.00 per cert plus copy fee. Payee- Richland County Register of Deeds. **Online access to Property, Assessor, GIS records:** Access property data free at www.rclrs.net. **Other phones:** Treasurer- 608-647-3658; Vital Records- 608-647-3011. **Property tax/Assessor-** 181 W Seminary St, Richland Center, WI 53581; 608-647-3658.

Rock County

Register of Deeds, 51 S. Main St, Janesville, WI 53545. 608-757-5650, UCC recording phone-608-757-5657; fax-608-757-5563; hours: 8AM-5PM. www.co.rock.wi.us/departments/reg_deeds.htm Only the public may search. Copy fee $2.00 1st page, $1.00 each add'l page. Cert fee- $1.00 per cert plus copy fee. Payee- Rock County Register of Deeds. **Online access to Assessor, Real Estate records:** City of Janesville Assessor database are free at www.ci.janesville.wi.us/Scripts2/gvsweb.dll/search. No name searching. Also, search Evansville property assessor records for free at www.wendorffas sessing.com/Evansville%20options.htm. No name searching. **Other phones:** Vital Records- 608-757-5656.

Rusk County

Register of Deeds, 311 Miner Ave. Rm#N132, Ladysmith, WI 54848-0311. 715-532-2139; fax-715-532-2194; hours: 8AM-4:30PM. www.ruskcounty.org/services/deeds.asp Add'l register of deeds info at www.ruskcounty.org/docs/brochure4.doc. All records in one index. Records indexed on a public use terminal back to 1999. Only the public may search. For state tax liens, see clerk of court. Copy fee $2.00 1st page, $1.00 each add'l page. Cert fee- $1.00 per page plus copy fee. Payee- Rusk County Register of Deeds. **Online access to Property, Assessor records:** Access assessor land data free at www.ruskcogiws.com/textsearch/index.htm.

Sauk County

Register of Deeds, 505 Broadway St., Baraboo, WI 53913. 608-355-3288; fax-608-355-3292; hours: 8AM-4:30PM. www.co.sauk.wi.us/dept/regodeed/index.html All records in one index. Records indexed on a public use terminal back to 1987. Only the public may search. Copy fee $2.00 1st page, $1.00 each add'l page. Cert fee- $1.00 per doc plus copy fee. Payee- Register of Deeds. **Online access to Property, Assessor records:** Search Village of Spring Green property data for free at www.wendorffassessing.com/Spring%20Green%20opt ions.htm. No name searching. Also, search Village of Plain property data at www.wendorffassessi ng.com/Plain%20options.htm. **Other phones:** Treasurer- 608-355-3276. **Property tax/Assessor-** 608-355-5581.

Sawyer County

Register of Deeds, PO Box 686; 10610 Main St, Hayward, WI 54843-0686. 715-634-4867; fax-715-634-6839; 8AM-4PM. http://sawyercountygov.org Will not search real estate records. Will not search UCC records or tax liens. Copy fee $2.00 1st page, $1.00 each add'l page. Cert fee- $1.00 per page plus $2.00 per page to copy. **Online access to Recording, Real Estate, Deed, Lien records:** Recorder office

data by subscription on either the Laredo system using subscription and fees or the Tapestry System using credit card, https://tapestry.fidlar.com/tapsearch.aspx; $3.99 search; $.50 per image. **Other phones:** Treasurer- 715-634-4868; Elections- 715-634-4866; Vital Records- 715-634-4867. **Property tax/Assessor-** 715-634-4868.

Shawano County

Register of Deeds, 311 N. Main, Shawano, WI 54166. 715-524-2129, R/E recording phone-715-526-4619; fax-715-524-5157; hours: 8AM-4:30PM. www.co.shawano.wi.us All records in one index. Records indexed on a public use terminal back to 1986. Only the public may search. For state tax liens, see clerk of court. Copy fee $2.00 per page. Cert fee- $1.00 per doc plus copy fee. **Other phones:** Treasurer- 715-524-9130; Elections- 715-526-4841; Vital Records- 715-524-2129. **Property tax/Assessor-** 715-524-9130.

Sheboygan County

Register of Deeds, 508 New York Ave, 2nd Fl, Sheboygan, WI 53081. 920-459-3023; 8AM-5PM. Only the public may search. Copy fee $2.00 1st page; $1.00 each add'l. Cert fee- $1.00 per cert plus copy fee. Payee- Register of Deeds. **Online access to Recording, Deed, Real Estate, Tax Lien records:** Recorder office data by subscription on either the Laredo system using subscription and fees or the Tapestry System using credit card, https://tapestry.fidlar.com/tapsearch.aspx; $3.99 search; $.50 per image. Index back to 1/1992; images to 5/1994. **Other phones:** Treasurer- 920-459-3015.

St. Croix County

Register of Deeds, 1101 Carmichael Rd., Hudson, WI 54016. 715-386-4652; fax-715-386-4687; hours: 8AM-5PM. www.co.saint-croix.wi.us Only the public may search. Copy fee $2.00 1st page, $1.00 each add'l page. Cert fee- $1.00 per page plus copy fee. Payee- Register of Deeds. **Online access to Recording, Real Estate, Deed, Lien records:** Recorder office data by subscription on either the Laredo system using subscription and fees or the Tapestry System using credit card, https://tapestry.fidlar.com/tapsearch.aspx; $3.99 search; $.50 per image. **Other phones:** Treasurer- 715-386-4645; Vital Records- 715-386-4653. **Property tax/Assessor-** same address as above. 715-386-4677.

Taylor County

Register of Deeds, 224 S 2nd St, Medford, WI 54451-1811. 715-748-1483; fax-715-748-1446; hours: 8:30AM-4:30PM. www.co.taylor.wi.us/departments/registerofdeeds/r odmain.htm Office personnel or visitors may perform searches. Search fee $15.00 per name. UCC search per debtor name- $10.00. For state tax liens, see clerk of court. Copy fee $2.00 1st page, $1.00 each add'l page. Cert fee- $1.00 per cert plus copy fee. Payee- Taylor County Register of Deeds. **Online access to Real Estate - 1995 forward records:** Found at https://landshark.co.taylor.wi.us/eddie/login.jsp; username and password required. Records go back to 1998. Index search is free; images are $2.00 1st page, $1.00 each add'l. **Other phones:** Treasurer- 715-748-1466; Vital Records- 715-748-1483. **Property tax/Assessor-** 715-748-1465.

Trempealeau County

Register of Deeds, PO Box 67, Whitehall, WI 54773. 715-538-2311, R/E recording phone-715-538-2311 x244; 8AM-4:30PM. www.tremplocounty.com All records in one index. Only the public may search. For state tax liens, see clerk of court. Copy fee $2.00 1st page, $1.00 each add'l page. Cert fee- $1.00 per cert plus copy fee. Payee- Trempealeau County Register of Deeds. **Online access to Real Estate, Assessor records:** Access to the county assessor's database is free at

www.tremplocounty.com/Search. **Other phones:** Treasurer- 715-538-2311 x219; Vital Records- 715-538-2311 x244. **Property tax/Assessor-** 715-538-2311 x248.

Vernon County

Register of Deeds, PO Box 46, Viroqua, WI 54665. 608-637-5371; fax-608-637-5304; hours: 8:30AM-4:30PM. All records in one index. Records indexed on a public use terminal back to approx., July, 2000. Office will perform a UCC search but public must search other records themselves. UCC search per debtor name- $15.00. Copy fee $2.00 1st page, $1.00 each add'l page. Cert fee- $1.00 per cert plus copy fee. Payee- Vernon County Register of Deeds. **Other phones:** Treasurer- 608-637-5365; Elections- 608-637-5304; Vital Records- 608-637-5371. **Property tax/Assessor-** 608-637-5365.

Vilas County

Register of Deeds, 330 Court St., Eagle River, WI 54521. 715-479-3660; fax-715-479-3695; hours: 8AM-4PM. http://co.vilas.wi.us All records in one index. Records indexed on a public use terminal. Only the public may search. Copy fee $2.00 1st page, $1.00 each add'l page. Cert fee- $1.00 per doc plus copy fee. Payee- Register of Deeds. **Other phones:** Treasurer- 715-479-3610; Vital Records- 715-479-3660. **Property tax/Assessor-** same address as above. contact treasurer for info.

Walworth County

Register of Deeds, PO Box 995, Elkhorn, WI 53121-0995. 262-741-4233; fax-262-741-4947; hours: 8AM-5PM. www.co.walworth.wi.us All records in one index. Only the public may search. Copy fee $2.00 1st page, $1.00 each add'l page. Cert fee- $1.00 per doc plus copy fee. Payee- Refgister of Deeds. **Online access to Property Tax, Recording, Grantor/Grantee, Deed records:** Search the Register of Deeds index for free on the county e-government web page at www.co.walworth.wi.us. Click on "Public Records." Online records go as far back as 1976. Also, search the treasurer's tax roll list under "Tax Roll Documents" on the county e-government web page. Also search the Village of Walworth property data for free at www.wendorffassessing.com/Walworth%20options.ht m. **Other phones:** Treasurer- 262-741-4251; Elections- 262-741-4241; Vital Records- 262-741-4235. **Property tax/Assessor-** 100 W. Walworth St, Elkhorn, WI 53121; 262-741-4255.

Washburn County

Register of Deeds, PO Box 607, Shell Lake, WI 54871. 715-468-4616; fax-715-468-4658; 8AM-4:30PM. All records in one index. Office personnel (except for real estate records) or visitors may perform searches. Search fee $10.00 per name. For state tax liens, see clerk of court. Copy fee $2.00 1st page, $1.00 each add'l. Cert fee- $1.00 per doc plus copy fee. Payee- Register of deeds. **Other phones:** Treasurer- 715-468-4650; Elections- 715-468-4605; Vital Records- 715-468-4616. **Property tax/Assessor-** 715-468-4696.

Washington County

Register of Deeds, PO Box 1986, West Bend, WI 53095-7986. 262-335-4318, R/E recording phone-262-335-4320; fax-262-335-6866; hours: 8AM-4:30PM. www.co.washington.wi.us/washington/contacts.jsp Only the public may search. For state tax liens, see clerk of court. Copy fee $2.00 per page. Cert fee- $3.00 1st page; $1.00 each add'l. Payee- Register of Deeds. **Other phones:** Treasurer- 262-335-4325; Elections- 262-335-4468; Vital Records- 262-335-4321. **Property tax/Assessor-** 262-335-4370.

Waukesha County

Register of Deeds, 1320 Pewaukee Rd, Rm 110, Waukesha, WI 53188. 262-548-7863, R/E recording phone-262-548-7590, UCC recording phone- 262-548-7585;   hours: 8AM-4:30PM. www.waukeshacounty.gov/departments/register All records in one index. Only the public may search. Copy fee $2.00 1st page; $1.00 each add'l. Cert fee- $1.00 per page plus copy fee. Payee-Waukesha County Register of Deeds. **Online access to Property, Assessor, Recording, Deed, Lien, Marriage, UCC, Personal Property records:** Access the recorder database free at http://dwprd.waukeshacounty.gov/applications/production/ROD_TRACT_DOCUMENTS/. Also, for access to county property assessment go to www.wauwatosa.net/display/router.asp?DocID=961. Also, search county tax listing at http://dwprd.waukeshacounty.gov/applications/production/ROD_TAX_LISTING/. No name searching at either of these sites. Also search assessor property data at www.ci.waukesha.wi.us/Parcel/DataInquiry1.jsp. No name search. Also, search City of Waukesha assessor property database or sales lists for free at www.ci.waukesha.wi.us/Assessor/propertySalesInformation.html. Search City personal property at www.ci.waukesha.wi.us/Assessor/Documents/ppAssessmentRoll.txt. **Other phones:** Treasurer- 262-548-7576. **Property tax/Assessor-** 262-542-0455.

Waupaca County

Register of Deeds, PO Box 307, Waupaca, WI 54981. 715-258-6250; fax-715-258-6212; hours: 8AM-4PM. http://public1.co.waupaca.wi.us/eddie/login.jsp All records in one index. Records indexed on computer back to 1982. Only the public may search. Copy fee $2.00 1st page, $1.00 each add'l page. Cert fee- $3.00 1st page, $1.00 each add'l page. Payee- Register of Deeds. **Online access to Register of Deed, Land, Property records:** Access to the Register of Deeds data requires subscription, username and password. Annual fee is $125.00. For info, call 715-258-6235 or visit http://216.56.10.105/access/default.asp?access=2. Register of Deeds also has a second subscription access website for land records; visit https://public1.co.waupaca.wi.us/eddie/registration.jsp. Records go back to 1982; monthly or daily subscriptions are available. Also, access land information office data free at http://public1.co.waupaca.wi.us/gisaccess/access.asp?access=1. A fee and registration is required for name searching. **Other phones:** Treasurer- 715-258-6220; Elections- 715-258-6200; Vital Records- 715-258-6250. **Property tax/Assessor-** 715-258-6215.

Waushara County

Register of Deeds, PO Box 338, Wautoma, WI 54982. 920-787-0444; fax-920-787-0425; hours: 8AM-4:30PM. www.co.waushara.wi.us All records in one index. Records indexed on a public use terminal back to 1993. Only the public may search. Copy fee $2.00 1st page, $1.00 each add'l. Cert fee- $1.00 per doc, plus copy fee. Payee- Register of Deeds. **Online access to Property, Assessor records:** Search property data free on the county land information system at www.co.waushara.wi.us/Website/WausharaPA/viewer.htm. **Other phones:** Treasurer- 920-787-0445; Elections- 920-787-0442; Vital Records- 920-787-0444.

Winnebago County

Register of Deeds, PO Box 2808, Oshkosh, WI 54903-2808. 920-236-4883, R/E recording phone-920-236-4881, UCC recording phone-920-236-4883; fax-920-303-3025;   hours   8AM-4:30PM. www.co.winnebago.wi.us All records in one index. Records indexed on a public use terminal back to 1997. Only the public may search. For state tax liens, see clerk of court. Copy fee $2.00 1st page, $1.00 each add'l page. Cert fee- $1.00 per cert plus copy fee. Payee-Winnebago County Register of Deeds. **Online access to Assessor, Real Estate, Recording, Deed, Lien records:** Recorder office data by subscription on either the Laredo system using subscription and fees or the Tapestry System using credit card, https://tapestry.fidlar.com/tapsearch.aspx; $3.99 search; $.50 per image. Also, property records on the City of Oshkosh assessor database are free at www.ci.oshkosh.wi.us/assessor/ProcessSearch.asp?cmd=NewSearch. Also, City of Neenah property data is at www.ci.neenah.wi.us/PropInfo/PropertyAssessmentSearch.asp but no name searching. Also, records on the City of Menasha Tax Roll Information database are free at www.cityofmenasha-wi.gov. **Other phones:** Treasurer- 920-236-4777; Elections- 920-236-4888; Vital Records- 920-236-4882. **Property tax/Assessor-** 920-236-4775.

Wood County

Register of Deeds, PO Box 8095, Wisconsin Rapids, WI 54495. 715-421-8450; hours: 8AM-4:30PM. www.co.wood.wi.us All records in one index. Records indexed on a public use terminal back to 1980. Only the public may search. Copy fee $2.00 1st page, $1.00 each add'l page. Cert fee- $1.00 per cert plus copy fee. Payee- Wood County Register of Deeds. **Online access to Recording, Real Estate, Deed, Lien records:** Recorder office data by subscription on either the Laredo system using subscription and fees or the Tapestry System using credit card, https://tapestry.fidlar.com/tapsearch.aspx; $3.99 search; $.50 per image. **Other phones:** Treasurer- 715-421-8484. **Property tax/Assessor-** 715-421-8484.

Wisconsin County Locator

You will usually be able to find the city name in the City/County Cross Reference below. In that case, it is a simple matter to determine the county from the cross reference. However, only the official US Postal Service city names are included in this index. There are an additional 40,000 place names that people use in their addresses. Therefore, we have also included a ZIP/City Cross Reference immediately following the City/County Cross Reference.

If you know the ZIP Code but the city name does not appear in the City/County Cross Reference index, look up the ZIP Code in the ZIP/City Cross Reference, find the city name, then look up the city name in the City/County Cross Reference. For example, you want to know the county for an address of Menands, NY 12204. There is no "Menands" in the City/County Cross Reference. The ZIP/City Cross Reference shows that ZIP Codes 12201-12288 are for the city of Albany. Looking back in the City/County Cross Reference, Albany is in Albany County.

Wisconsin City/County Cross Reference

ABBOTSFORD (54405) Clark(71), Marathon(28)
ABRAMS Oconto
ADAMS Adams
ADELL Sheboygan
AFTON Rock
ALBANY Green
ALGOMA (54201) Kewaunee(96), Door(3)
ALGOMA Kewaunee
ALLENTON (53002) Washington(97), Dodge(2)
ALMA Buffalo
ALMA CENTER Jackson
ALMENA Barron
ALMOND (54909) Portage(88), Waushara(11)
ALTOONA Eau Claire
AMBERG Marinette
AMERY Polk
AMHERST Portage
AMHERST JUNCTION Portage
ANIWA (54408) Marathon(56), Shawano(39), Langlade(4)
ANTIGO (54409) Langlade(97), Marathon(1), Shawano(1)
APPLETON (54914) Outagamie(97), Winnebago(2)
APPLETON (54915) Outagamie(53), Calumet(32), Winnebago(13)
APPLETON Outagamie
ARCADIA (54612) Trempealeau(89), Buffalo(10)
ARENA Iowa
ARGONNE Forest
ARGYLE (53504) Lafayette(75), Green(25)
ARKANSAW (54721) Pepin(88), Pierce(6), Dunn(5)
ARKDALE Adams
ARLINGTON (53911) Columbia(93), Dane(6)
ARMSTRONG CREEK (54103) Forest(82), Marinette(16), Florence(1)
ARPIN Wood
ASHIPPUN Dodge
ASHLAND (54806) Ashland(86), Bayfield(13)
ATHELSTANE (54104) Marinette(97), Oconto(1), Forest(1)
ATHENS (54411) Marathon(97), Taylor(2)
AUBURNDALE (54412) Wood(75), Marathon(24)
AUGUSTA Eau Claire
AVALON (53505) Rock(98), Walworth(1)
AVOCA Iowa
BABCOCK Wood
BAGLEY Grant
BAILEYS HARBOR Door
BALDWIN St. Croix
BALSAM LAKE Polk
BANCROFT (54921) Portage(89), Adams(8), Waushara(1)
BANGOR La Crosse
BARABOO Sauk
BARNEVELD Iowa
BARRON Barron

BARRONETT (54813) Barron(51), Burnett(31), Washburn(16)
BASSETT Kenosha
BAY CITY Pierce
BAYFIELD Bayfield
BEAR CREEK (54922) Outagamie(54), Waupaca(45)
BEAVER DAM Dodge
BEETOWN Grant
BELDENVILLE Pierce
BELGIUM (53004) Ozaukee(98), Sheboygan(1)
BELLEVILLE (53508) Dane(72), Green(27)
BELMONT Lafayette
BELOIT Rock
BENET LAKE Kenosha
BENOIT Bayfield
BENTON Lafayette
BERLIN (54923) Green Lake(71), Waushara(25), Winnebago(3)
BIG BEND Waukesha
BIG FALLS Waupaca
BIRCHWOOD (54817) Washburn(40), Sawyer(31), Barron(24), Rusk(2)
BIRNAMWOOD (54414) Shawano(77), Marathon(21)
BLACK CREEK (54106) Outagamie(98), Shawano(1)
BLACK EARTH Dane
BLACK RIVER FALLS (54615) Jackson(98), Monroe(1)
BLAIR (54616) Trempealeau(96), Jackson(3)
BLANCHARDVILLE (53516) Lafayette(57), Green(21), Iowa(18), Dane(2)
BLENKER Wood
BLOOM CITY Richland
BLOOMER Chippewa
BLOOMINGTON Grant
BLUE MOUNDS (53517) Dane(62), Iowa(37)
BLUE RIVER (53518) Richland(70), Grant(24), Crawford(5)
BONDUEL (54107) Shawano(96), Outagamie(3)
BOSCOBEL (53805) Grant(68), Crawford(31)
BOULDER JUNCTION Vilas
BOWLER Shawano
BOYCEVILLE Dunn
BOYD (54726) Chippewa(62), Eau Claire(37)
BRANCH Manitowoc
BRANDON (53919) Fond du Lac(98), Green Lake(1)
BRANTWOOD Price
BRIGGSVILLE (53920) Marquette(67), Adams(32)
BRILL Barron
BRILLION (54110) Calumet(79), Manitowoc(18), Brown(2)
BRISTOL Kenosha
BRODHEAD (53520) Green(74), Rock(25)
BROKAW Marathon
BROOKFIELD Waukesha

BROOKLYN (53521) Green(45), Dane(31), Rock(23)
BROOKS Adams
BROWNSVILLE (53006) Dodge(70), Fond du Lac(29)
BROWNTOWN (53522) Green(92), Lafayette(7)
BRUCE Rusk
BRULE (54820) Douglas(69), Bayfield(30)
BRUSSELS Door
BRYANT Langlade
BURLINGTON (53105) Racine(67), Walworth(19), Kenosha(13)
BURNETT Dodge
BUTLER Waukesha
BUTTE DES MORTS Winnebago
BUTTERNUT (54514) Ashland(53), Price(39), Iron(7)
BYRON Fond du Lac
CABLE (54821) Bayfield(98), Sawyer(1)
CADOTT (54727) Chippewa(91), Eau Claire(8)
CALEDONIA Racine
CAMBRIA (53923) Columbia(88), Green Lake(11)
CAMBRIDGE (53523) Dane(50), Jefferson(49)
CAMERON Barron
CAMP DOUGLAS (54618) Juneau(63), Monroe(36)
CAMP LAKE Kenosha
CAMPBELLSPORT (53010) Fond du Lac(94), Washington(4)
CAROLINE Shawano
CASCADE (53011) Sheboygan(91), Fond du Lac(8)
CASCO (54205) Kewaunee(97), Door(2)
CASHTON (54619) Monroe(77), Vernon(21), La Crosse(1)
CASSVILLE Grant
CATARACT Monroe
CATAWBA Price
CATO Manitowoc
CAZENOVIA (53924) Richland(96), Sauk(3)
CECIL (54111) Shawano(90), Oconto(9)
CEDAR GROVE (53013) Sheboygan(84), Ozaukee(15)
CEDARBURG (53012) Ozaukee(95), Washington(4)
CENTURIA Polk
CHASEBURG Vernon
CHELSEA Taylor
CHETEK (54728) Barron(87), Rusk(11), Dunn(1)
CHILI (54420) Clark(96), Wood(3)
CHILTON (53014) Calumet(97), Manitowoc(2)
CHIPPEWA FALLS (54729) Chippewa(97), Eau Claire(2)
CHIPPEWA FALLS Chippewa
CLAM LAKE (54517) Ashland(93), Sawyer(6)
CLAYTON (54004) Polk(59), Barron(40)

CLEAR LAKE (54005) Polk(79), St. Croix(11), Dunn(5), Barron(3)
CLEVELAND (53015) Manitowoc(86), Sheboygan(14)
CLINTON (53525) Rock(97), Walworth(2)
CLINTONVILLE (54929) Waupaca(69), Shawano(29), Outagamie(1)
CLYMAN Dodge
COBB Iowa
COCHRANE Buffalo
COLBY (54421) Clark(74), Marathon(25)
COLEMAN (54112) Marinette(76), Oconto(23)
COLFAX (54730) Dunn(77), Chippewa(22)
COLGATE (53017) Washington(72), Waukesha(27)
COLLINS Manitowoc
COLOMA (54930) Waushara(83), Adams(14), Marquette(2)
COLUMBUS (53925) Columbia(82), Dodge(13), Dane(4)
COMBINED LOCKS Outagamie
COMSTOCK (54826) Barron(62), Polk(37)
CONOVER Vilas
CONRATH Rusk
COON VALLEY (54623) Vernon(52), La Crosse(47)
CORNELL Chippewa
CORNUCOPIA Bayfield
COTTAGE GROVE Dane
COUDERAY Sawyer
CRANDON Forest
CRIVITZ (54114) Marinette(91), Oconto(8)
CROSS PLAINS Dane
CUBA CITY (53807) Grant(86), Lafayette(13)
CUDAHY Milwaukee
CUMBERLAND (54829) Barron(91), Polk(8)
CURTISS (54422) Clark(94), Taylor(5)
CUSHING Polk
CUSTER (54423) Portage(98), Marathon(1)
DALE Outagamie
DALLAS Barron
DALTON (53926) Green Lake(72), Marquette(15), Columbia(12)
DANBURY (54830) Burnett(93), Douglas(6)
DANE Dane
DARIEN (53114) Walworth(84), Rock(15)
DARLINGTON Lafayette
DE FOREST (53532) Dane(97), Columbia(2)
DE PERE (54115) Brown(92), Outagamie(7)
DE SOTO (54624) Vernon(89), Crawford(10)
DEER PARK (54007) St. Croix(67), Polk(32)
DEERBROOK Langlade
DEERFIELD Dane
DELAFIELD Waukesha
DELAVAN Walworth
DELLWOOD Adams
DENMARK (54208) Brown(53), Kewaunee(38), Manitowoc(7)

DICKEYVILLE Grant
DODGE Trempealeau
DODGEVILLE Iowa
DORCHESTER (54425) Clark(83),
  Marathon(9), Taylor(6)
DOUSMAN (53118) Waukesha(96),
  Jefferson(3)
DOWNING (54734) Dunn(94), St. Croix(5)
DOWNSVILLE Dunn
DOYLESTOWN Columbia
DRESSER Polk
DRUMMOND Bayfield
DUNBAR Marinette
DURAND (54736) Pepin(82), Buffalo(17)
EAGLE (53119) Waukesha(93),
  Walworth(4), Jefferson(2)
EAGLE RIVER (54521) Vilas(78),
  Oneida(19), Forest(1)
EAST ELLSWORTH Pierce
EAST TROY (53120) Walworth(97),
  Racine(2)
EASTMAN Crawford
EAU CLAIRE (54703) Eau Claire(89),
  Chippewa(10)
EAU CLAIRE Eau Claire
EAU GALLE (54737) Dunn(96), Pepin(3)
EDEN Fond du Lac
EDGAR Marathon
EDGERTON (53534) Rock(84), Dane(13),
  Jefferson(2)
EDGEWATER Sawyer
EDMUND Iowa
EGG HARBOR Door
ELAND (54427) Marathon(66),
  Shawano(33)
ELCHO (54428) Langlade(96), Oneida(3)
ELDERON Marathon
ELDORADO Fond du Lac
ELEVA (54738) Eau Claire(58),
  Trempealeau(40), Buffalo(1)
ELK MOUND (54739) Dunn(62),
  Chippewa(37)
ELKHART LAKE (53020) Sheboygan(93),
  Manitowoc(3), Calumet(2)
ELKHORN Walworth
ELLISON BAY Door
ELLSWORTH Pierce
ELM GROVE Waukesha
ELMWOOD (54740) Pierce(79), Dunn(20)
ELROY (53929) Juneau(82), Monroe(11),
  Vernon(5)
ELTON Langlade
EMBARRASS Waupaca
EMERALD St. Croix
EMERALDX St. Croix
ENDEAVOR Marquette
EPHRAIM Door
ETTRICK (54627) Trempealeau(91),
  Jackson(8)
EUREKA Winnebago
EVANSVILLE (53536) Rock(96), Green(3)
EXELAND (54835) Sawyer(89), Rusk(10)
FAIRCHILD (54741) Jackson(51), Eau
  Claire(48)
FAIRWATER Fond du Lac
FALL CREEK Eau Claire
FALL RIVER (53932) Columbia(95),
  Dodge(4)
FENCE (54120) Florence(78),
  Marinette(21)
FENNIMORE Grant
FERRYVILLE (54628) Crawford(93),
  Vernon(6)
FIFIELD Price
FISH CREEK Door
FOND DU LAC Fond du Lac
FONTANA Walworth
FOOTVILLE Rock
FOREST JUNCTION Calumet
FORESTVILLE (54213) Door(85),
  Kewaunee(14)

FORT ATKINSON (53538) Jefferson(97),
  Rock(2)
FOUNTAIN CITY Buffalo
FOX LAKE Dodge
FOXBORO Douglas
FRANCIS CREEK Manitowoc
FRANKLIN Milwaukee
FRANKSVILLE Racine
FREDERIC (54837) Polk(81), Burnett(18)
FREDONIA (53021) Ozaukee(88),
  Washington(11)
FREEDOM Outagamie
FREMONT (54940) Waupaca(51),
  Waushara(29), Winnebago(14),
  Outagamie(4)
FRIENDSHIP Adams
FRIESLAND Columbia
GALESVILLE Trempealeau
GALLOWAY Marathon
GAYS MILLS Crawford
GENESEE DEPOT Waukesha
GENOA Vernon
GENOA CITY (53128) Walworth(80),
  Kenosha(19)
GERMANTOWN Washington
GILE Iron
GILLETT (54124) Oconto(87),
  Menominee(9), Shawano(2)
GILLETT Oconto
GILLETT Shawano
GILMAN (54433) Taylor(80), Chippewa(19)
GILMANTON Buffalo
GLEASON (54435) Lincoln(69),
  Langlade(30)
GLEN FLORA Rusk
GLEN HAVEN Grant
GLENBEULAH Sheboygan
GLENWOOD CITY St. Croix
GLIDDEN Ashland
GOODMAN (54125) Marinette(98),
  Forest(1)
GORDON Douglas
GOTHAM Richland
GRAFTON Ozaukee
GRAND MARSH Adams
GRAND VIEW Bayfield
GRANTON Clark
GRANTSBURG (54840) Burnett(98),
  Polk(1)
GRATIOT Lafayette
GREEN BAY Brown
GREEN LAKE Green Lake
GREEN VALLEY Shawano
GREENBUSH Sheboygan
GREENDALE Milwaukee
GREENLEAF (54126) Brown(96),
  Manitowoc(3)
GREENVILLE Outagamie
GREENWOOD Clark
GRESHAM Shawano
GURNEY Iron
HAGER CITY Pierce
HALES CORNERS Milwaukee
HAMMOND St. Croix
HANCOCK (54943) Waushara(81),
  Adams(18)
HANNIBAL Taylor
HANOVER Rock
HARSHAW Oneida
HARTFORD (53027) Washington(96),
  Dodge(3)
HARTLAND Waukesha
HATLEY Marathon
HAUGEN Barron
HAWKINS (54530) Rusk(71), Price(27)
HAWTHORNE Douglas
HAYWARD (54843) Sawyer(96),
  Washburn(3)
HAZEL GREEN (53811) Grant(94),
  Lafayette(5)
HAZELHURST Oneida
HEAFFORD JUNCTION Lincoln

HELENVILLE Jefferson
HERBSTER Bayfield
HERTEL Burnett
HEWITT Wood
HIGH BRIDGE Ashland
HIGHLAND (53543) Iowa(91), Grant(8)
HILBERT Calumet
HILLPOINT (53937) Sauk(63),
  Richland(36)
HILLSBORO (54634) Vernon(79),
  Richland(19), Juneau(1)
HILLSDALE Barron
HINGHAM Sheboygan
HIXTON Jackson
HOLCOMBE (54745) Chippewa(87),
  Rusk(12)
HOLLANDALE (53544) Iowa(97), Dane(1)
HOLMEN La Crosse
HONEY CREEK Walworth
HORICON Dodge
HORTONVILLE Outagamie
HOULTON St. Croix
HUBERTUS Washington
HUDSON St. Croix
HUMBIRD (54746) Clark(77), Jackson(22)
HURLEY Iron
HUSTISFORD Dodge
HUSTLER Juneau
INDEPENDENCE (54747)
  Trempealeau(82), Buffalo(17)
IOLA (54945) Waupaca(96), Portage(3)
IOLA Waupaca
IRMA Lincoln
IRON BELT Iron
IRON RIDGE Dodge
IRON RIVER Bayfield
IXONIA (53036) Jefferson(73), Dodge(19),
  Waukesha(6)
JACKSON Washington
JANESVILLE Rock
JEFFERSON Jefferson
JIM FALLS Chippewa
JOHNSON CREEK Jefferson
JUDA Green
JUMP RIVER Taylor
JUNCTION CITY (54443) Portage(95),
  Marathon(2), Wood(2)
JUNEAU Dodge
KANSASVILLE (53139) Racine(85),
  Kenosha(14)
KAUKAUNA (54130) Outagamie(95),
  Brown(2), Calumet(1)
KELLNERSVILLE Manitowoc
KEMPSTER Langlade
KENDALL (54638) Monroe(88), Vernon(9),
  Juneau(2)
KENNAN Price
KENOSHA Kenosha
KESHENA Menominee
KEWASKUM (53040) Washington(76),
  Sheboygan(13), Fond du Lac(9)
KEWAUNEE Kewaunee
KIEL (53042) Manitowoc(95), Calumet(4)
KIELER Grant
KIMBERLY Outagamie
KING Waupaca
KINGSTON Green Lake
KNAPP (54749) Dunn(88), St. Croix(11)
KOHLER Sheboygan
KRAKOW (54137) Shawano(76),
  Oconto(23)
LA CROSSE La Crosse
LA FARGE (54639) Vernon(93),
  Richland(6)
LA POINTE Ashland
LA VALLE (53941) Sauk(97), Juneau(1)
LAC DU FLAMBEAU (54538) Vilas(90),
  Oneida(5), Price(4)
LADYSMITH Rusk
LAKE DELTON Sauk
LAKE GENEVA Walworth
LAKE MILLS Jefferson

LAKE NEBAGAMON Douglas
LAKE TOMAHAWK Oneida
LAKEWOOD Oconto
LANCASTER Grant
LAND O LAKES Vilas
LANNON Waukesha
LAONA Forest
LARSEN Winnebago
LEBANON Dodge
LENA (54139) Oconto(98), Marinette(1)
LEOPOLIS Shawano
LEWIS Polk
LILY Langlade
LIME RIDGE Sauk
LINDEN Iowa
LITTLE CHUTE Outagamie
LITTLE SUAMICO Oconto
LIVINGSTON (53554) Grant(70), Iowa(29)
LODI (53555) Columbia(92), Dane(7)
LOGANVILLE Sauk
LOMIRA (53048) Dodge(97), Fond du
  Lac(2)
LONE ROCK (53556) Richland(83),
  Sauk(16)
LONG LAKE (54542) Forest(65),
  Florence(34)
LOWELL Dodge
LOYAL Clark
LUBLIN (54447) Taylor(97), Clark(2)
LUCK (54853) Polk(94), Burnett(5)
LUXEMBURG (54217) Kewaunee(88),
  Door(5), Brown(5)
LYNDON STATION (53944) Juneau(88),
  Sauk(11)
LYNXVILLE Crawford
LYONS Walworth
MADISON Dane
MAIDEN ROCK Pierce
MALONE (53049) Fond du Lac(92),
  Calumet(7)
MANAWA Waupaca
MANCHESTER Green Lake
MANITOWISH WATERS (54545) Vilas(98),
  Iron(1)
MANITOWOC Manitowoc
MAPLE Douglas
MAPLEWOOD Door
MARATHON Marathon
MARENGO Ashland
MARIBEL (54227) Manitowoc(98),
  Brown(1)
MARINETTE Marinette
MARION (54950) Shawano(50),
  Waupaca(49)
MARKESAN (53946) Green Lake(97),
  Fond du Lac(2)
MARQUETTE Green Lake
MARSHALL (53559) Dane(98),
  Jefferson(1)
MARSHALL FIELDS Milwaukee
MARSHFIELD (54449) Wood(93),
  Marathon(6)
MARSHFIELD Wood
MASON (54856) Bayfield(97), Ashland(2)
MATHER Juneau
MATTOON Shawano
MAUSTON Juneau
MAYVILLE Dodge
MAZOMANIE (53560) Dane(96), Iowa(3)
MC FARLAND Dane
MC NAUGHTON Oneida
MEDFORD Taylor
MEDINA Outagamie
MELLEN Ashland
MELROSE Jackson
MENASHA (54952) Winnebago(89),
  Calumet(10)
MENOMONEE FALLS Waukesha
MENOMONIE Dunn
MEQUON Ozaukee
MERCER Iron

MERRILL (54452) Lincoln(88), Marathon(11)
MERRILLAN (54754) Jackson(85), Clark(14)
MERRIMAC (53561) Sauk(86), Columbia(13)
MERTON Waukesha
MIDDLETON Dane
MIKANA Barron
MILAN Marathon
MILLADORE (54454) Wood(87), Portage(12)
MILLSTON Jackson
MILLTOWN Polk
MILTON Rock
MILWAUKEE Milwaukee
MINDORO (54644) La Crosse(96), Jackson(3)
MINERAL POINT (53565) Iowa(87), Lafayette(12)
MINOCQUA (54548) Oneida(78), Vilas(21)
MINONG (54859) Washburn(88), Douglas(11)
MISHICOT Manitowoc
MONDOVI (54755) Buffalo(63), Eau Claire(12), Dunn(11), Pepin(11)
MONROE Green
MONTELLO (53949) Marquette(98), Green Lake(1)
MONTFORT (53569) Grant(66), Iowa(33)
MONTICELLO Green
MONTREAL Iron
MORRISONVILLE Dane
MOSINEE (54455) Marathon(97), Portage(2)
MOUNT CALVARY Fond du Lac
MOUNT HOPE Grant
MOUNT HOREB Dane
MOUNT STERLING Crawford
MOUNTAIN Oconto
MUKWONAGO (53149) Waukesha(90), Walworth(7), Racine(1)
MUSCODA (53573) Grant(52), Richland(40), Iowa(7)
MUSKEGO (53150) Waukesha(98), Racine(1)
NASHOTAH Waukesha
NECEDAH Juneau
NEENAH Winnebago
NEILLSVILLE Clark
NEKOOSA (54457) Wood(57), Adams(39), Juneau(3)
NELSON Buffalo
NELSONVILLE Portage
NEOPIT Menominee
NEOSHO Dodge
NESHKORO (54960) Marquette(59), Waushara(35), Green Lake(5)
NEW AUBURN (54757) Chippewa(66), Barron(17), Dunn(9), Rusk(6)
NEW BERLIN Waukesha
NEW FRANKEN Brown
NEW GLARUS (53574) Green(98), Dane(1)
NEW HOLSTEIN (53061) Calumet(95), Fond du Lac(4)
NEW HOLSTEIN Calumet
NEW LISBON Juneau
NEW LONDON (54961) Waupaca(81), Outagamie(18)
NEW MUNSTER Kenosha
NEW RICHMOND (54017) St. Croix(98), Polk(1)
NEWBURG Washington
NEWTON Manitowoc
NIAGARA (54151) Marinette(66), Florence(33)
NICHOLS Outagamie
NORTH FREEDOM Sauk
NORTH LAKE Waukesha
NORTH PRAIRIE Waukesha
NORWALK Monroe

OAK CREEK Milwaukee
OAKDALE Monroe
OAKFIELD (53065) Fond du Lac(91), Dodge(8)
OCONOMOWOC (53066) Waukesha(94), Jefferson(3), Dodge(1)
OCONTO Oconto
OCONTO FALLS (54154) Oconto(96), Shawano(3)
ODANAH Ashland
OGDENSBURG Waupaca
OGEMA Price
OJIBWA Sawyer
OKAUCHEE Waukesha
OMRO Winnebago
ONALASKA La Crosse
ONEIDA (54155) Brown(59), Outagamie(40)
ONTARIO (54651) Vernon(61), Monroe(38)
OOSTBURG Sheboygan
OREGON Dane
ORFORDVILLE Rock
OSHKOSH Winnebago
OSSEO (54758) Trempealeau(71), Eau Claire(17), Jackson(11)
OWEN (54460) Clark(96), Taylor(3)
OXFORD (53952) Marquette(51), Adams(48)
PACKWAUKEE Marquette
PALMYRA Jefferson
PARDEEVILLE (53954) Columbia(96), Marquette(3)
PARK FALLS (54552) Price(92), Iron(7)
PATCH GROVE Grant
PEARSON Langlade
PELICAN LAKE (54463) Oneida(95), Langlade(4)
PELL LAKE Walworth
PEMBINE Marinette
PEPIN Pepin
PESHTIGO (54157) Marinette(98), Oconto(1)
PEWAUKEE Waukesha
PHELPS Vilas
PHILLIPS Price
PHLOX Langlade
PICKEREL (54465) Langlade(59), Forest(40)
PICKETT (54964) Winnebago(80), Fond du Lac(19)
PIGEON FALLS Trempealeau
PINE RIVER (54965) Waushara(98), Waupaca(1)
PITTSVILLE (54466) Wood(79), Clark(10), Jackson(9)
PLAIN Sauk
PLAINFIELD (54966) Waushara(85), Portage(13), Adams(1)
PLATTEVILLE (53818) Grant(95), Lafayette(3)
PLEASANT PRAIRIE Kenosha
PLOVER Portage
PLUM CITY Pierce
PLYMOUTH Sheboygan
POPLAR Douglas
PORT EDWARDS Wood
PORT WASHINGTON Ozaukee
PORT WING Bayfield
PORTAGE Columbia
PORTERFIELD Marinette
POSKIN Barron
POTOSI Grant
POTTER Calumet
POUND (54161) Marinette(53), Oconto(46)
POWERS LAKE Kenosha
POY SIPPI Waushara
POYNETTE Columbia
PRAIRIE DU CHIEN (53821) Crawford(98), Grant(1)
PRAIRIE DU SAC (53578) Sauk(90), Columbia(9)

PRAIRIE FARM (54762) Barron(94), Dunn(5)
PRENTICE Price
PRESCOTT Pierce
PRESQUE ISLE Vilas
PRINCETON (54968) Green Lake(93), Marquette(6)
PULASKI (54162) Shawano(62), Brown(28), Oconto(8)
RACINE (53403) Racine(98), Kenosha(1)
RACINE Racine
RADISSON Sawyer
RANDOLPH (53956) Dodge(57), Columbia(39), Green Lake(3)
RANDOLPH Columbia
RANDOM LAKE (53075) Sheboygan(93), Ozaukee(5)
READFIELD Waupaca
READSTOWN (54652) Vernon(96), Crawford(3)
REDGRANITE Waushara
REEDSBURG Sauk
REEDSVILLE Manitowoc
REESEVILLE Dodge
REWEY Iowa
RHINELANDER Oneida
RIB LAKE (54470) Taylor(96), Price(2)
RICE LAKE Barron
RICHFIELD Washington
RICHLAND CENTER Richland
RIDGELAND (54763) Dunn(84), Barron(15)
RIDGEWAY Iowa
RINGLE Marathon
RIO Columbia
RIPON (54971) Fond du Lac(82), Green Lake(13), Winnebago(4)
RIVER FALLS (54022) Pierce(74), St. Croix(25)
ROBERTS St. Croix
ROCHESTER Racine
ROCK FALLS Dunn
ROCK SPRINGS Sauk
ROCKFIELD Washington
ROCKLAND (54653) La Crosse(90), Monroe(9)
ROSENDALE Fond du Lac
ROSHOLT (54473) Portage(79), Marathon(20)
ROTHSCHILD Marathon
ROYALTON Waupaca
RUBICON Dodge
RUDOLPH (54475) Wood(86), Portage(13)
SAINT CLOUD (53079) Fond du Lac(92), Sheboygan(7)
SAINT CROIX FALLS Polk
SAINT FRANCIS Milwaukee
SAINT GERMAIN (54558) Vilas(89), Oneida(10)
SAINT JOSEPH St. Croix
SAINT NAZIANZ Manitowoc
SALEM Kenosha
SAND CREEK Dunn
SARONA (54870) Washburn(96), Barron(3)
SAUK CITY (53583) Sauk(85), Dane(13)
SAUKVILLE Ozaukee
SAXEVILLE Waushara
SAXON (54559) Iron(94), Ashland(5)
SAYNER Vilas
SCANDINAVIA (54977) Waupaca(94), Portage(5)
SCHOFIELD Marathon
SENECA Crawford
SEXTONVILLE Richland
SEYMOUR (54165) Outagamie(95), Shawano(3), Brown(1)
SHARON (53585) Walworth(96), Rock(3)
SHAWANO Shawano
SHEBOYGAN Sheboygan
SHEBOYGAN FALLS Sheboygan
SHELDON (54766) Rusk(59), Taylor(39)
SHELL LAKE (54871) Washburn(65), Burnett(34)

SHERWOOD Calumet
SHIOCTON (54170) Outagamie(93), Shawano(5)
SHULLSBURG Lafayette
SILVER LAKE Kenosha
SINSINAWA Grant
SIREN (54872) Burnett(97), Polk(2)
SISTER BAY Door
SLINGER Washington
SOBIESKI Oconto
SOLDIERS GROVE (54655) Crawford(83), Richland(12), Vernon(3)
SOLON SPRINGS (54873) Bayfield(50), Douglas(49)
SOMERS Kenosha
SOMERSET St. Croix
SOUTH MILWAUKEE Milwaukee
SOUTH RANGE Douglas
SOUTH WAYNE Lafayette
SPARTA Monroe
SPENCER (54479) Marathon(56), Clark(42)
SPOONER (54801) Washburn(83), Burnett(16)
SPRING GREEN (53588) Sauk(77), Iowa(21)
SPRING VALLEY (54767) Pierce(95), St. Croix(3), Dunn(1)
SPRINGBROOK Washburn
SPRINGFIELD Walworth
STANLEY (54768) Chippewa(73), Clark(16), Eau Claire(6), Taylor(2)
STAR LAKE Vilas
STAR PRAIRIE (54026) Polk(61), St. Croix(38)
STETSONVILLE (54480) Taylor(95), Marathon(4)
STEUBEN Crawford
STEVENS POINT Portage
STITZER Grant
STOCKBRIDGE Calumet
STOCKHOLM (54769) Pepin(81), Pierce(18)
STODDARD (54658) Vernon(89), La Crosse(10)
STONE LAKE (54876) Sawyer(68), Washburn(31)
STOUGHTON (53589) Dane(98), Rock(1)
STRATFORD Marathon
STRUM (54770) Trempealeau(76), Eau Claire(23)
STURGEON BAY Door
STURTEVANT (53177) Racine(91), Kenosha(8)
SUAMICO Brown
SULLIVAN Jefferson
SUMMIT LAKE Langlade
SUN PRAIRIE Dane
SUPERIOR Douglas
SURING (54174) Oconto(91), Menominee(8)
SUSSEX Waukesha
TAYLOR (54659) Jackson(91), Trempealeau(8)
THERESA (53091) Dodge(94), Washington(5)
THIENSVILLE Ozaukee
THORP (54771) Clark(92), Taylor(7)
THREE LAKES (54562) Oneida(95), Forest(4)
TIGERTON (54486) Shawano(92), Waupaca(7)
TILLEDA Shawano
TISCH MILLS Manitowoc
TOMAH Monroe
TOMAHAWK (54487) Lincoln(88), Oneida(11)
TONY Rusk
TOWNSEND Oconto
TREGO Washburn
TREMPEALEAU Trempealeau
TREVOR Kenosha

TRIPOLI (54564) Oneida(47), Lincoln(36), Price(16)
TUNNEL CITY Monroe
TURTLE LAKE (54889) Barron(76), Polk(23)
TWIN LAKES Kenosha
TWO RIVERS Manitowoc
UNION CENTER Juneau
UNION GROVE (53182) Racine(90), Kenosha(9)
UNITY (54488) Clark(68), Marathon(31)
UPSON Iron
VALDERS Manitowoc
VAN DYNE (54979) Fond du Lac(87), Winnebago(12)
VERONA Dane
VESPER Wood
VIOLA (54664) Richland(66), Vernon(33)
VIROQUA (54665) Vernon(98), Crawford(1)
WABENO Forest
WALDO Sheboygan
WALES Waukesha
WALWORTH Walworth

WARRENS (54666) Monroe(82), Jackson(17)
WASCOTT Douglas
WASHBURN Bayfield
WASHINGTON ISLAND Door
WATERFORD Racine
WATERLOO (53594) Jefferson(81), Dodge(14), Dane(3)
WATERTOWN Dodge
WAUKAU Winnebago
WAUKESHA Waukesha
WAUNAKEE Dane
WAUPACA (54981) Waupaca(91), Waushara(4), Portage(3)
WAUPUN (53963) Dodge(51), Fond du Lac(48)
WAUSAU Marathon
WAUSAUKEE Marinette
WAUTOMA (54982) Waushara(97), Marquette(2)
WAUZEKA Crawford
WEBSTER Burnett
WEST BEND Washington
WEST SALEM La Crosse

WESTBORO (54490) Taylor(95), Price(4)
WESTBY (54667) Vernon(98), La Crosse(1)
WESTFIELD (53964) Marquette(96), Adams(2), Waushara(1)
WEYAUWEGA (54983) Waupaca(90), Waushara(9)
WEYERHAEUSER Rusk
WHEELER Dunn
WHITE LAKE (54491) Langlade(91), Oconto(8)
WHITEHALL Trempealeau
WHITELAW Manitowoc
WHITEWATER (53190) Walworth(76), Rock(13), Jefferson(9)
WILD ROSE Waushara
WILLARD Clark
WILLIAMS BAY Walworth
WILMOT Kenosha
WILSON St. Croix
WILTON Monroe
WINDSOR Dane
WINNECONNE (54986) Winnebago(98), Waushara(1)

WINTER Sawyer
WISCONSIN DELLS (53965) Columbia(38), Sauk(31), Adams(23), Juneau(6)
WISCONSIN RAPIDS (54494) Wood(92), Portage(6)
WISCONSIN RAPIDS Wood
WITHEE (54498) Clark(90), Taylor(9)
WITTENBERG (54499) Shawano(71), Marathon(27), Portage(1)
WONEWOC (53968) Juneau(67), Sauk(24), Vernon(6), Richland(1)
WOODFORD Lafayette
WOODLAND Dodge
WOODMAN Grant
WOODRUFF (54568) Vilas(67), Oneida(32)
WOODVILLE St. Croix
WOODWORTH Kenosha
WRIGHTSTOWN (54180) Brown(95), Outagamie(4)
WYEVILLE Monroe
WYOCENA Columbia
ZACHOW Shawano
ZENDA Walworth

Wisconsin ZIP/City Cross Reference

53001-53001 ADELL
53002-53002 ALLENTON
53003-53003 ASHIPPUN
53004-53004 BELGIUM
53005-53005 BROOKFIELD
53006-53006 BROWNSVILLE
53007-53007 BUTLER
53008-53008 BROOKFIELD
53009-53009 BYRON
53010-53010 CAMPBELLSPORT
53011-53011 CASCADE
53012-53012 CEDARBURG
53013-53013 CEDAR GROVE
53014-53014 CHILTON
53015-53015 CLEVELAND
53016-53016 CLYMAN
53017-53017 COLGATE
53018-53018 DELAFIELD
53019-53019 EDEN
53020-53020 ELKHART LAKE
53021-53021 FREDONIA
53022-53022 GERMANTOWN
53023-53023 GLENBEULAH
53024-53024 GRAFTON
53026-53026 GREENBUSH
53027-53027 HARTFORD
53029-53029 HARTLAND
53031-53031 HINGHAM
53032-53032 HORICON
53033-53033 HUBERTUS
53034-53034 HUSTISFORD
53035-53035 IRON RIDGE
53036-53036 IXONIA
53037-53037 JACKSON
53038-53038 JOHNSON CREEK
53039-53039 JUNEAU
53040-53040 KEWASKUM
53042-53042 KIEL
53044-53044 KOHLER
53045-53045 BROOKFIELD
53046-53046 LANNON
53047-53047 LEBANON
53048-53048 LOMIRA
53049-53049 MALONE
53050-53050 MAYVILLE
53051-53052 MENOMONEE FALLS
53056-53056 MERTON
53057-53057 MOUNT CALVARY
53058-53058 NASHOTAH
53059-53059 NEOSHO
53060-53060 NEWBURG
53061-53062 NEW HOLSTEIN
53063-53063 NEWTON

53064-53064 NORTH LAKE
53065-53065 OAKFIELD
53066-53066 OCONOMOWOC
53069-53069 OKAUCHEE
53070-53070 OOSTBURG
53072-53072 PEWAUKEE
53073-53073 PLYMOUTH
53074-53074 PORT WASHINGTON
53075-53075 RANDOM LAKE
53076-53076 RICHFIELD
53077-53077 ROCKFIELD
53078-53078 RUBICON
53079-53079 SAINT CLOUD
53080-53080 SAUKVILLE
53081-53083 SHEBOYGAN
53085-53085 SHEBOYGAN FALLS
53086-53086 SLINGER
53088-53088 STOCKBRIDGE
53089-53089 SUSSEX
53090-53090 WEST BEND
53091-53091 THERESA
53092-53092 THIENSVILLE
53093-53093 WALDO
53094-53094 WATERTOWN
53095-53096 WEST BEND
53097-53097 MEQUON
53098-53098 WATERTOWN
53099-53099 WOODLAND
53101-53101 BASSETT
53102-53102 BENET LAKE
53103-53103 BIG BEND
53104-53104 BRISTOL
53105-53105 BURLINGTON
53108-53108 CALEDONIA
53109-53109 CAMP LAKE
53110-53110 CUDAHY
53114-53114 DARIEN
53115-53115 DELAVAN
53118-53118 DOUSMAN
53119-53119 EAGLE
53120-53120 EAST TROY
53121-53121 ELKHORN
53122-53122 ELM GROVE
53125-53125 FONTANA
53126-53126 FRANKSVILLE
53127-53127 GENESEE DEPOT
53128-53128 GENOA CITY
53129-53129 GREENDALE
53130-53130 HALES CORNERS
53132-53132 FRANKLIN
53137-53137 HELENVILLE
53138-53138 HONEY CREEK
53139-53139 KANSASVILLE

53140-53144 KENOSHA
53146-53146 NEW BERLIN
53147-53147 LAKE GENEVA
53148-53148 LYONS
53149-53149 MUKWONAGO
53150-53150 MUSKEGO
53151-53151 NEW BERLIN
53152-53152 NEW MUNSTER
53153-53153 NORTH PRAIRIE
53154-53154 OAK CREEK
53156-53156 PALMYRA
53157-53157 PELL LAKE
53158-53158 PLEASANT PRAIRIE
53159-53159 POWERS LAKE
53167-53167 ROCHESTER
53168-53168 SALEM
53170-53170 SILVER LAKE
53171-53171 SOMERS
53172-53172 SOUTH MILWAUKEE
53176-53176 SPRINGFIELD
53177-53177 STURTEVANT
53178-53178 SULLIVAN
53179-53179 TREVOR
53181-53181 TWIN LAKES
53182-53182 UNION GROVE
53183-53183 WALES
53184-53184 WALWORTH
53185-53185 WATERFORD
53186-53189 WAUKESHA
53190-53190 WHITEWATER
53191-53191 WILLIAMS BAY
53192-53192 WILMOT
53194-53194 WOODWORTH
53195-53195 ZENDA
53200-53234 MILWAUKEE
53235-53235 SAINT FRANCIS
53237-53259 MILWAUKEE
53260-53260 MARSHALL FIELDS
53263-53295 MILWAUKEE
53400-53490 RACINE
53501-53501 AFTON
53502-53502 ALBANY
53503-53503 ARENA
53504-53504 ARGYLE
53505-53505 AVALON
53506-53506 AVOCA
53507-53507 BARNEVELD
53508-53508 BELLEVILLE
53510-53510 BELMONT
53511-53512 BELOIT
53515-53515 BLACK EARTH
53516-53516 BLANCHARDVILLE
53517-53517 BLUE MOUNDS

53518-53518 BLUE RIVER
53520-53520 BRODHEAD
53521-53521 BROOKLYN
53522-53522 BROWNTOWN
53523-53523 CAMBRIDGE
53525-53525 CLINTON
53526-53526 COBB
53527-53527 COTTAGE GROVE
53528-53528 CROSS PLAINS
53529-53529 DANE
53530-53530 DARLINGTON
53531-53531 DEERFIELD
53532-53532 DE FOREST
53533-53533 DODGEVILLE
53534-53534 EDGERTON
53535-53535 EDMUND
53536-53536 EVANSVILLE
53537-53537 FOOTVILLE
53538-53538 FORT ATKINSON
53540-53540 GOTHAM
53541-53541 GRATIOT
53542-53542 HANOVER
53543-53543 HIGHLAND
53544-53544 HOLLANDALE
53545-53548 JANESVILLE
53549-53549 JEFFERSON
53550-53550 JUDA
53551-53551 LAKE MILLS
53553-53553 LINDEN
53554-53554 LIVINGSTON
53555-53555 LODI
53556-53556 LONE ROCK
53557-53557 LOWELL
53558-53558 MC FARLAND
53559-53559 MARSHALL
53560-53560 MAZOMANIE
53561-53561 MERRIMAC
53562-53562 MIDDLETON
53563-53563 MILTON
53565-53565 MINERAL POINT
53566-53566 MONROE
53569-53569 MONTFORT
53570-53570 MONTICELLO
53571-53571 MORRISONVILLE
53572-53572 MOUNT HOREB
53573-53573 MUSCODA
53574-53574 NEW GLARUS
53575-53575 OREGON
53576-53576 ORFORDVILLE
53577-53577 PLAIN
53578-53578 PRAIRIE DU SAC
53579-53579 REESEVILLE
53580-53580 REWEY

53581-53581	RICHLAND CENTER	53958-53959	REEDSBURG	54164-54164	GILLETT
53582-53582	RIDGEWAY	53960-53960	RIO	54165-54165	SEYMOUR
53583-53583	SAUK CITY	53961-53961	ROCK SPRINGS	54166-54166	SHAWANO
53584-53584	SEXTONVILLE	53962-53962	UNION CENTER	54169-54169	SHERWOOD
53585-53585	SHARON	53963-53963	WAUPUN	54170-54170	SHIOCTON
53586-53586	SHULLSBURG	53964-53964	WESTFIELD	54171-54171	SOBIESKI
53587-53587	SOUTH WAYNE	53965-53965	WISCONSIN DELLS	54173-54173	SUAMICO
53588-53588	SPRING GREEN	53968-53968	WONEWOC	54174-54174	SURING
53589-53589	STOUGHTON	53969-53969	WYOCENA	54175-54175	TOWNSEND
53590-53591	SUN PRAIRIE	54001-54001	AMERY	54176-54176	GILLETT
53593-53593	VERONA	54002-54002	BALDWIN	54177-54177	WAUSAUKEE
53594-53594	WATERLOO	54003-54003	BELDENVILLE	54180-54180	WRIGHTSTOWN
53595-53595	DODGEVILLE	54004-54004	CLAYTON	54182-54182	ZACHOW
53596-53596	SUN PRAIRIE	54005-54005	CLEAR LAKE	54201-54201	ALGOMA
53597-53597	WAUNAKEE	54006-54006	CUSHING	54202-54202	BAILEYS HARBOR
53598-53598	WINDSOR	54007-54007	DEER PARK	54203-54203	BRANCH
53599-53599	WOODFORD	54009-54009	DRESSER	54204-54204	BRUSSELS
53700-53794	MADISON	54010-54010	EAST ELLSWORTH	54205-54205	CASCO
53801-53801	BAGLEY	54011-54011	ELLSWORTH	54206-54206	CATO
53802-53802	BEETOWN	54012-54012	EMERALD	54207-54207	COLLINS
53803-53803	BENTON	54012-54012	EMERALDX	54208-54208	DENMARK
53804-53804	BLOOMINGTON	54013-54013	GLENWOOD CITY	54209-54209	EGG HARBOR
53805-53805	BOSCOBEL	54014-54014	HAGER CITY	54210-54210	ELLISON BAY
53806-53806	CASSVILLE	54015-54015	HAMMOND	54211-54211	EPHRAIM
53807-53807	CUBA CITY	54016-54016	HUDSON	54212-54212	FISH CREEK
53808-53808	DICKEYVILLE	54017-54017	NEW RICHMOND	54213-54213	FORESTVILLE
53809-53809	FENNIMORE	54020-54020	OSCEOLA	54214-54214	FRANCIS CREEK
53810-53810	GLEN HAVEN	54021-54021	PRESCOTT	54215-54215	KELLNERSVILLE
53811-53811	HAZEL GREEN	54022-54022	RIVER FALLS	54216-54216	KEWAUNEE
53812-53812	KIELER	54023-54023	ROBERTS	54217-54217	LUXEMBURG
53813-53813	LANCASTER	54024-54024	SAINT CROIX FALLS	54220-54221	MANITOWOC
53816-53816	MOUNT HOPE	54025-54025	SOMERSET	54226-54226	MAPLEWOOD
53817-53817	PATCH GROVE	54026-54026	STAR PRAIRIE	54227-54227	MARIBEL
53818-53818	PLATTEVILLE	54027-54027	WILSON	54228-54228	MISHICOT
53820-53820	POTOSI	54028-54028	WOODVILLE	54229-54229	NEW FRANKEN
53821-53821	PRAIRIE DU CHIEN	54082-54082	SAINT JOSEPH	54230-54230	REEDSVILLE
53824-53824	SINSINAWA	54082-54082	HOULTON	54231-54231	ALGOMA
53825-53825	STITZER	54101-54101	ABRAMS	54232-54232	SAINT NAZIANZ
53826-53826	WAUZEKA	54102-54102	AMBERG	54234-54234	SISTER BAY
53827-53827	WOODMAN	54103-54103	ARMSTRONG CREEK	54235-54235	STURGEON BAY
53901-53901	PORTAGE	54104-54104	ATHELSTANE	54240-54240	TISCH MILLS
53910-53910	ADAMS	54106-54106	BLACK CREEK	54241-54241	TWO RIVERS
53911-53911	ARLINGTON	54107-54107	BONDUEL	54245-54245	VALDERS
53913-53913	BARABOO	54110-54110	BRILLION	54246-54246	WASHINGTON ISLAND
53916-53917	BEAVER DAM	54111-54111	CECIL	54247-54247	WHITELAW
53919-53919	BRANDON	54112-54112	COLEMAN	54300-54344	GREEN BAY
53920-53920	BRIGGSVILLE	54113-54113	COMBINED LOCKS	54401-54403	WAUSAU
53921-53921	BROOKS	54114-54114	CRIVITZ	54404-54404	MARSHFIELD
53922-53922	BURNETT	54115-54115	DE PERE	54405-54405	ABBOTSFORD
53923-53923	CAMBRIA	54119-54119	DUNBAR	54406-54406	AMHERST
53924-53924	CAZENOVIA	54120-54120	FENCE	54407-54407	AMHERST JUNCTION
53925-53925	COLUMBUS	54121-54121	FLORENCE	54408-54408	ANIWA
53926-53926	DALTON	54123-54123	FOREST JUNCTION	54409-54409	ANTIGO
53927-53927	DELLWOOD	54124-54124	GILLETT	54410-54410	ARPIN
53928-53928	DOYLESTOWN	54125-54125	GOODMAN	54411-54411	ATHENS
53929-53929	ELROY	54126-54126	GREENLEAF	54412-54412	AUBURNDALE
53930-53930	ENDEAVOR	54127-54127	GREEN VALLEY	54413-54413	BABCOCK
53931-53931	FAIRWATER	54128-54128	GRESHAM	54414-54414	BIRNAMWOOD
53932-53932	FALL RIVER	54129-54129	HILBERT	54415-54415	BLENKER
53933-53933	FOX LAKE	54130-54130	KAUKAUNA	54416-54416	BOWLER
53934-53934	FRIENDSHIP	54131-54131	FREEDOM	54417-54417	BROKAW
53935-53935	FRIESLAND	54135-54135	KESHENA	54418-54418	BRYANT
53936-53936	GRAND MARSH	54136-54136	KIMBERLY	54419-54419	CHELSEA
53937-53937	HILLPOINT	54137-54137	KRAKOW	54420-54420	CHILI
53939-53939	KINGSTON	54138-54138	LAKEWOOD	54421-54421	COLBY
53940-53940	LAKE DELTON	54139-54139	LENA	54422-54422	CURTISS
53941-53941	LA VALLE	54140-54140	LITTLE CHUTE	54423-54423	CUSTER
53942-53942	LIME RIDGE	54141-54141	LITTLE SUAMICO	54424-54424	DEERBROOK
53943-53943	LOGANVILLE	54143-54143	MARINETTE	54425-54425	DORCHESTER
53944-53944	LYNDON STATION	54149-54149	MOUNTAIN	54426-54426	EDGAR
53945-53945	MANCHESTER	54150-54150	NEOPIT	54427-54427	ELAND
53946-53946	MARKESAN	54151-54151	NIAGARA	54428-54428	ELCHO
53947-53947	MARQUETTE	54152-54152	NICHOLS	54429-54429	ELDERON
53948-53948	MAUSTON	54153-54153	OCONTO	54430-54430	ELTON
53949-53949	MONTELLO	54154-54154	OCONTO FALLS	54432-54432	GALLOWAY
53950-53950	NEW LISBON	54155-54155	ONEIDA	54433-54433	GILMAN
53951-53951	NORTH FREEDOM	54156-54156	PEMBINE	54434-54434	JUMP RIVER
53952-53952	OXFORD	54157-54157	PESHTIGO	54435-54435	GLEASON
53953-53953	PACKWAUKEE	54159-54159	PORTERFIELD	54436-54436	GRANTON
53954-53954	PARDEEVILLE	54160-54160	POTTER	54437-54437	GREENWOOD
53955-53955	POYNETTE	54161-54161	POUND	54439-54439	HANNIBAL
53956-53957	RANDOLPH	54162-54162	PULASKI	54440-54440	HATLEY

54441-54441	HEWITT
54442-54442	IRMA
54443-54443	JUNCTION CITY
54444-54444	KEMPSTER
54445-54445	LILY
54446-54446	LOYAL
54447-54447	LUBLIN
54448-54448	MARATHON
54449-54449	MARSHFIELD
54450-54450	MATTOON
54451-54451	MEDFORD
54452-54452	MERRILL
54453-54453	MILAN
54454-54454	MILLADORE
54455-54455	MOSINEE
54456-54456	NEILLSVILLE
54457-54457	NEKOOSA
54458-54458	NELSONVILLE
54459-54459	OGEMA
54460-54460	OWEN
54462-54462	PEARSON
54463-54463	PELICAN LAKE
54464-54464	PHLOX
54465-54465	PICKEREL
54466-54466	PITTSVILLE
54467-54467	PLOVER
54469-54469	PORT EDWARDS
54470-54470	RIB LAKE
54471-54471	RINGLE
54472-54472	MARSHFIELD
54473-54473	ROSHOLT
54474-54474	ROTHSCHILD
54475-54475	RUDOLPH
54476-54476	SCHOFIELD
54479-54479	SPENCER
54480-54480	STETSONVILLE
54481-54482	STEVENS POINT
54484-54484	STRATFORD
54485-54485	SUMMIT LAKE
54486-54486	TIGERTON
54487-54487	TOMAHAWK
54488-54488	UNITY
54489-54489	VESPER
54490-54490	WESTBORO
54491-54491	WHITE LAKE
54492-54492	STEVENS POINT
54493-54493	WILLARD
54494-54495	WISCONSIN RAPIDS
54498-54498	WITHEE
54499-54499	WITTENBERG
54501-54501	RHINELANDER
54511-54511	ARGONNE
54512-54512	BOULDER JUNCTION
54513-54513	BRANTWOOD
54514-54514	BUTTERNUT
54515-54515	CATAWBA
54517-54517	CLAM LAKE
54519-54519	CONOVER
54520-54520	CRANDON
54521-54521	EAGLE RIVER
54524-54524	FIFIELD
54525-54525	GILE
54526-54526	GLEN FLORA
54527-54527	GLIDDEN
54528-54528	GURNEY
54529-54529	HARSHAW
54530-54530	HAWKINS
54531-54531	HAZELHURST
54532-54532	HEAFFORD JUNCTION
54534-54534	HURLEY
54536-54536	IRON BELT
54537-54537	KENNAN
54538-54538	LAC DU FLAMBEAU
54539-54539	LAKE TOMAHAWK
54540-54540	LAND O LAKES
54541-54541	LAONA
54542-54542	LONG LAKE
54543-54543	MC NAUGHTON
54545-54545	MANITOWISH WATERS
54546-54546	MELLEN
54547-54547	MERCER
54548-54548	MINOCQUA

54550-54550 MONTREAL	54659-54659 TAYLOR	54774-54774 CHIPPEWA FALLS	54890-54890 WASCOTT
54552-54552 PARK FALLS	54660-54660 TOMAH	54801-54801 SPOONER	54891-54891 WASHBURN
54554-54554 PHELPS	54661-54661 TREMPEALEAU	54805-54805 ALMENA	54893-54893 WEBSTER
54555-54555 PHILLIPS	54662-54662 TUNNEL CITY	54806-54806 ASHLAND	54895-54895 WEYERHAEUSER
54556-54556 PRENTICE	54664-54664 VIOLA	54810-54810 BALSAM LAKE	54896-54896 WINTER
54557-54557 PRESQUE ISLE	54665-54665 VIROQUA	54812-54812 BARRON	54901-54906 OSHKOSH
54558-54558 SAINT GERMAIN	54666-54666 WARRENS	54813-54813 BARRONETT	54909-54909 ALMOND
54559-54559 SAXON	54667-54667 WESTBY	54814-54814 BAYFIELD	54911-54919 APPLETON
54560-54560 SAYNER	54669-54669 WEST SALEM	54816-54816 BENOIT	54921-54921 BANCROFT
54561-54561 STAR LAKE	54670-54670 WILTON	54817-54817 BIRCHWOOD	54922-54922 BEAR CREEK
54562-54562 THREE LAKES	54671-54671 WYEVILLE	54818-54818 BRILL	54923-54923 BERLIN
54563-54563 TONY	54701-54703 EAU CLAIRE	54819-54819 BRUCE	54926-54926 BIG FALLS
54564-54564 TRIPOLI	54720-54720 ALTOONA	54820-54820 BRULE	54927-54927 BUTTE DES MORTS
54565-54565 UPSON	54721-54721 ARKANSAW	54821-54821 CABLE	54928-54928 CAROLINE
54566-54566 WABENO	54722-54722 AUGUSTA	54822-54822 CAMERON	54929-54929 CLINTONVILLE
54568-54568 WOODRUFF	54723-54723 BAY CITY	54824-54824 CENTURIA	54930-54930 COLOMA
54601-54603 LA CROSSE	54724-54724 BLOOMER	54826-54826 COMSTOCK	54931-54931 DALE
54610-54610 ALMA	54725-54725 BOYCEVILLE	54827-54827 CORNUCOPIA	54932-54932 ELDORADO
54611-54611 ALMA CENTER	54726-54726 BOYD	54828-54828 COUDERAY	54933-54933 EMBARRASS
54612-54612 ARCADIA	54727-54727 CADOTT	54829-54829 CUMBERLAND	54934-54934 EUREKA
54613-54613 ARKDALE	54728-54728 CHETEK	54830-54830 DANBURY	54935-54937 FOND DU LAC
54614-54614 BANGOR	54729-54729 CHIPPEWA FALLS	54832-54832 DRUMMOND	54940-54940 FREMONT
54615-54615 BLACK RIVER FALLS	54730-54730 COLFAX	54834-54834 EDGEWATER	54941-54941 GREEN LAKE
54616-54616 BLAIR	54731-54731 CONRATH	54835-54835 EXELAND	54942-54942 GREENVILLE
54617-54617 BLOOM CITY	54732-54732 CORNELL	54836-54836 FOXBORO	54943-54943 HANCOCK
54618-54618 CAMP DOUGLAS	54733-54733 DALLAS	54837-54837 FREDERIC	54944-54944 HORTONVILLE
54619-54619 CASHTON	54734-54734 DOWNING	54838-54838 GORDON	54945-54945 IOLA
54620-54620 CATARACT	54735-54735 DOWNSVILLE	54839-54839 GRAND VIEW	54946-54946 KING
54621-54621 CHASEBURG	54736-54736 DURAND	54840-54840 GRANTSBURG	54947-54947 LARSEN
54622-54622 COCHRANE	54737-54737 EAU GALLE	54841-54841 HAUGEN	54948-54948 LEOPOLIS
54623-54623 COON VALLEY	54738-54738 ELEVA	54842-54842 HAWTHORNE	54949-54949 MANAWA
54624-54624 DE SOTO	54739-54739 ELK MOUND	54843-54843 HAYWARD	54950-54950 MARION
54625-54625 DODGE	54740-54740 ELMWOOD	54844-54844 HERBSTER	54951-54951 MEDINA
54626-54626 EASTMAN	54741-54741 FAIRCHILD	54845-54845 HERTEL	54952-54952 MENASHA
54627-54627 ETTRICK	54742-54742 FALL CREEK	54846-54846 HIGH BRIDGE	54956-54957 NEENAH
54628-54628 FERRYVILLE	54743-54743 GILMANTON	54847-54847 IRON RIVER	54960-54960 NESHKORO
54629-54629 FOUNTAIN CITY	54744-54744 HILLSDALE	54848-54848 LADYSMITH	54961-54961 NEW LONDON
54630-54630 GALESVILLE	54745-54745 HOLCOMBE	54849-54849 LAKE NEBAGAMON	54962-54962 OGDENSBURG
54631-54631 GAYS MILLS	54746-54746 HUMBIRD	54850-54850 LA POINTE	54963-54963 OMRO
54632-54632 GENOA	54747-54747 INDEPENDENCE	54851-54851 LEWIS	54964-54964 PICKETT
54634-54634 HILLSBORO	54748-54748 JIM FALLS	54853-54853 LUCK	54965-54965 PINE RIVER
54635-54635 HIXTON	54749-54749 KNAPP	54854-54854 MAPLE	54966-54966 PLAINFIELD
54636-54636 HOLMEN	54750-54750 MAIDEN ROCK	54855-54855 MARENGO	54967-54967 POY SIPPI
54637-54637 HUSTLER	54751-54751 MENOMONIE	54856-54856 MASON	54968-54968 PRINCETON
54638-54638 KENDALL	54754-54754 MERRILLAN	54857-54857 MIKANA	54969-54969 READFIELD
54639-54639 LA FARGE	54755-54755 MONDOVI	54858-54858 MILLTOWN	54970-54970 REDGRANITE
54640-54640 LYNXVILLE	54756-54756 NELSON	54859-54859 MINONG	54971-54971 RIPON
54641-54641 MATHER	54757-54757 NEW AUBURN	54861-54861 ODANAH	54974-54974 ROSENDALE
54642-54642 MELROSE	54758-54758 OSSEO	54862-54862 OJIBWA	54975-54975 ROYALTON
54643-54643 MILLSTON	54759-54759 PEPIN	54864-54864 POPLAR	54976-54976 SAXEVILLE
54644-54644 MINDORO	54760-54760 PIGEON FALLS	54865-54865 PORT WING	54977-54977 SCANDINAVIA
54645-54645 MOUNT STERLING	54761-54761 PLUM CITY	54866-54866 POSKIN	54978-54978 TILLEDA
54646-54646 NECEDAH	54762-54762 PRAIRIE FARM	54867-54867 RADISSON	54979-54979 VAN DYNE
54648-54648 NORWALK	54763-54763 RIDGELAND	54868-54868 RICE LAKE	54980-54980 WAUKAU
54649-54649 OAKDALE	54764-54764 ROCK FALLS	54870-54870 SARONA	54981-54981 WAUPACA
54650-54650 ONALASKA	54765-54765 SAND CREEK	54871-54871 SHELL LAKE	54982-54982 WAUTOMA
54651-54651 ONTARIO	54766-54766 SHELDON	54872-54872 SIREN	54983-54983 WEYAUWEGA
54652-54652 READSTOWN	54767-54767 SPRING VALLEY	54873-54873 SOLON SPRINGS	54984-54984 WILD ROSE
54653-54653 ROCKLAND	54768-54768 STANLEY	54874-54874 SOUTH RANGE	54985-54985 WINNEBAGO
54654-54654 SENECA	54769-54769 STOCKHOLM	54875-54875 SPRINGBROOK	54986-54986 WINNECONNE
54655-54655 SOLDIERS GROVE	54770-54770 STRUM	54876-54876 STONE LAKE	54990-54990 IOLA
54656-54656 SPARTA	54771-54771 THORP	54880-54880 SUPERIOR	
54657-54657 STEUBEN	54772-54772 WHEELER	54888-54888 TREGO	
54658-54658 STODDARD	54773-54773 WHITEHALL	54889-54889 TURTLE LAKE	

County-Town
WISCONSIN

Explanation of Symbols

✧ State Capital

Vernon County Seat

Population Key

○ 0-999
⊕ 1,000-2,499
⊕ 2,500-4,999
⊙ 5,000-9,999
⊙ 10,000-19,000
⊙ 20,000-24,999
⊙ 25,000-49,999
□ 50,000-99,999
□ 100,000-249,999
■ 250,000-999,999

Explanation of symbols: ● – Census Designated Place (CDP)

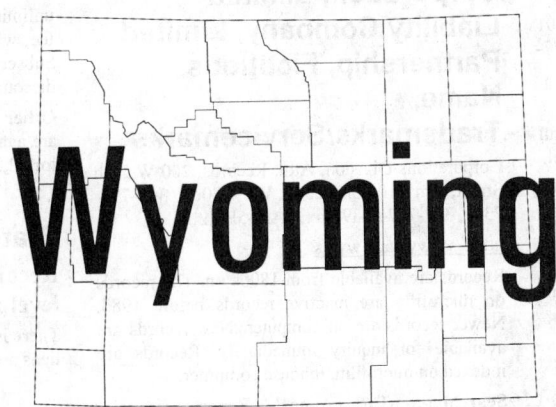

Wyoming

General Help Numbers:

Governor's Office

State Capitol Building, Rm 124
Cheyenne, WY 82002-0010

307-777-7434
Fax 307-632-3909
8AM-5PM

www.wyoming.gov/governor/governor_home.asp

Attorney General's Office

200 W 24thth Street
Cheyenne, WY 82002

307-777-7841
Fax 307-777-6869
8AM-5PM

http://attorneygeneral.state.wy.us

Legislative Records

Wyoming Legislature
State Capitol, Room 213
Cheyenne, WY 82002

307-777-7881
Fax 307-777-5466
8AM-5PM

http://legisweb.state.wy.us

State Archives

Archives Division
2301 Central Ave, Barrett Bldg
Cheyenne, WY 82002

307-777-7826
Fax 307-777-7044
8AM-5PM M-F
(Research Area 8AM-4:45PM)

http://wyoarchives.state.wy.us/index.htm

State Specifics:

Capital:	Cheyenne Laramie County
Time Zone:	MST
Number of Counties:	23
Population:	506,529
Web Site:	www.wyoming.gov

State Agencies

Criminal Records

Division of Criminal Investigation, Criminal Record Unit, 316 W 22nd St, Cheyenne, WY 82002; 307-777-7523, 307-777-7252-Fax; 8AM to 5PM.

http://attorneygeneral.state.wy.us/dci/index.html

A record inquiry includes all reported felonies, high misdemeanors and other specified misdemeanors, but not municipal ordinance violations. authorized by state law, the check may include federal records held by FBI.

Records are available from 1941 on. It takes up to 10 days before new records are available for inquiry. Records are indexed on inhouse computer.

100% of arrest records are fingerprint supported. 79% of all arrests in database have final dispositions recorded, 65% for those arrests within last 5 years.

Searching: First, obtain a Request for Criminal Record Packet from the address above or by telephoning this agency. Include the following in your request-notarized waiver from subject, name, set of fingerprints, date of birth, Social Security Number, number of years to search. Use the WY standard 8" x 8" orange fingerprint card. Must also complete all information and waiver is on the back of this office's fingerprint card. The following data is not released: juvenile records. Records include all felony and major misdemeanor arrests and convictions.

Access by: mail, in person.

Fee & Payment: The search fee is $15.00 plus an additional $5.00 if this office must perform the fingerprinting. The fee is $10.00 if the applicant is providing volunteer services, plus the fingerprinting fee if applicable. The FBI fingerprint check is an add'l $24.00. Fee payee: Office of the Attorney General. Prepayment required. Money order, cash or certified checks only. No credit cards accepted.

Mail search: Turnaround time: 2 to 4 weeks. A SASE is requested. **In person search:** Proper forms are required to be filled out.

Statewide Court Records

Court Administrator, Supreme Court Bldg, 2301 Capitol Ave, Cheyenne, WY 82002; 307-777-7583, 307-777-3447-Fax; 8AM-5PM.

www.courts.state.wy.us

Except for certain online research capabilities, all court record access must be done at the local level.

Access by: online.

Online search: Supreme Court opinions available at web, listed by date. Wyoming's statewide case management system is for internal use only. Planning is underway for a new case management system that will ultimately allow public access.

Sexual Offender Registry

Division of Criminal Investigation, ATTN: WSOR, 316 W 22nd St, Cheyenne, WY 82002-0001; 307-777-7809, 307-777-7252-Fax; 8AM to 5PM.

http://attorneygeneral.state.wy.us/dci/index.html

Wyoming law defines a sex offender subject to registration as a person convicted of a sex offense in which the victim was a minor and the offender was at least eighteen (18) years of age or an aggravated sex offense.

Searching: The County Sheriff's Office or other law enforcement agency maintains a file and forwards the information to the Wyoming Division of Criminal Investigation (DCI).

Access by: online.

Online search: The Internet is the search method offered by this agency to the public. Search is by county. The website contains offenders found to have a high risk of re-offense. Data includes name, address, date and place of birth, date and place of conviction, crime for which convicted, photograph and physical description.

Incarceration Records

Wyoming Department of Corrections, 700 W. 21st Street,, Cheyenne, WY 82002; 307-777-7405, 307-777-7479-Fax; 8AM-5PM.

http://doc.state.wy.us/corrections.asp

Records are available on current and former inmates. It takes a minimum of 30 days before new records are available for inquiry.

Searching: Include the following in your request-full name. DOB and SSN are helpful. Location, conviction and sentencing information, and release dates are provided. Limited search requests honor via email at mbrazz@wdoc.state.wy.us. The following data is not released: probation and parole data, medical, and mental health problems

Access by: mail, phone, fax, online.

Fee & Payment: The fee is $.50 per page. Fee payee: Wyoming Dept of Corrections Prepayment required. Personal checks accepted.

Mail search: Turnaround time: 1 to 2 weeks. A SASE is requested.

Phone search: Name searching available by phone.

Fax search: Can request via fax.

Online search: No searching online direct from this agency; a private company provides access to DOC records at www.vinelink.com/index.jsp. However, one may send requests to this agency via email, from the webpage.

Corporation, Limited Liability Company, Limited Partnership, Fictitious Name, Trademarks/Servicemarks

Corporations Division, Attn: Records, 200 W 24th Street, Rm 110, Cheyenne, WY 82002; 307-777-7311, 307-777-5339-Fax; 8AM-5PM.

http://soswy.state.wy.us

Records are available from 1800s on. The records on microfilm are inactive records before 1983. Newer records are on computer. New records are available for inquiry immediately. Records are indexed on microfilm, inhouse computer.

Searching: The Annual Report financial information (Appendix I Worksheet filed with Annual Report) is not released. Include the following in your request-full name of business. In addition to the articles of incorporation, corporation records include the following information: Annual Reports, Officers, Directors, DBAs, Prior (merged) names, Inactive and Reserved names.

Access by: mail, fax, in person, online.

Fee & Payment: Copy fees are $.50 per page for the first 10 pages and $.15 for each additional page. Certification is $3.00. If you only need a couple pages and are not certifying the document (and are nice), usually there is no charge. Fee payee: Secretary of State. They will invoice for copies and certificates. Prepaid accounts are available. Personal checks accepted. No credit cards accepted.

Mail search: Turnaround time: 1 to 2 days. A SASE is requested.

Fax search: Turnaround time is 24-48 hours.

In person search: You may request information in person.

Online search: Information is available through the Internet site listed above. You can search by corporate name or even download the whole file. Also, they have 2 pages of excellent searching tips.

Uniform Commercial Code, Federal Tax Liens

Secretary of State, UCC Division - Records, 200 W 24th Street, Room 110, Cheyenne, WY 82002-0020; 307-777-5372, 307-777-5988-Fax; 8AM-5PM.

http://soswy.state.wy.us/uniform/uniform.htm

Records are available for five years on computer, since the "beginning" on microfiche. Records are indexed on inhouse computer and microfiche.

Searching: The search includes federal tax liens on businesses and state tax liens filed by state agencies. Include the following in your request-debtor name.

Access by: mail, fax, in person, online.

Fee & Payment: The search fee is $10.00. Copies cost $.50 each. Fee payee: Secretary of State. Prepayment required. Personal checks accepted. No credit cards accepted.

Mail search: Turnaround time: 3 days. Please include your phone number with all requests.

Fax search: Requests may be faxed in.

In person search: Simple requests may be processed while you wait.

Online search: The online filing system permits unlimited record searching. There is a $150 annual fee, with no additional fees charged for searches. Subscribers are entitled to do filings at a 50% discount. Visit the webpage.

Other access: Lists of filings on CD or diskette are available for purchase. Download the database for $2,000 per year.

State Tax Liens

Records not maintained by a state level agency.

There is no state income tax. All other state tax liens are filed at the county level.

Sales Tax Registrations

Department of Revenue, Excise Tax Division, Herschler Bldg, 122 W 25th St, Cheyenne, WY 82002-0110; 307-777-5200, 307-777-3632-Fax; 8AM-5PM.

http://revenue.state.wy.us

Records are available for at least three years: cancelled licenses are purged every two years. It takes 10 to 14 days before new records are available for inquiry. Records are normally destroyed after 6 to 10 years after case closure.

Searching: This agency will only confirm that the business is registered. They will provide no other information except to an owner or officer of the business. Requests may be e-mailed, visit the website for the proper e-mail address. Include the following in your request-business name, and ID of the requester. They will also search by tax permit number. Annual reports may be retrieved from the webpage.

Access by: mail, phone, in person.

Fee & Payment: For paper copies or from microfilm, copy fee is $.50 each first 10 pages, $.15 each add'l with a $10.00 minimum. For computer images, copy fee is $1.00 per page first 10 pages, then $.30 each additional with a $35.00 minimum. Fee payee: WY Dept of Revenue

Mail search: Turnaround time: 7 to 10 days. A SASE is requested. No search fee for mail request.

Phone search: No search fee for telephone request.

In person search: No search fee for request.

Birth Certificates

Wyoming Department of Health, Vital Records Services, Hathaway Bldg, Rm 172, Cheyenne, WY 82002; 307-777-7591, 307-635-4103-Fax; 8AM-5PM.

http://wdhfs.state.wy.us/vital_records

Records are available from July 1909 to present. New records are available for inquiry immediately. Records are indexed on microfilm, inhouse computer.

Searching: Must have a signed release from person of record or parent or guardian. Include the following in your request-full name, names of parents, mother's maiden name, date of birth, place of birth, relationship to person of record. Must include signature of requester and copy of photo ID.

Access by: mail, fax, in person.

Fee & Payment: Search fee is $12.00 per name per 5 years searched. Fee includes certification.

Use of credit card is an additional $5.00 for expedited service. Fee payee: Vital Records Services. Prepayment required. Personal checks accepted. Major credit cards accepted.

Mail search: Turnaround time: 3 to 4 working days. No SASE is required.

Fax search: See expedited services.

In person search: Turnaround time is 15 minutes.

Expedited service: Expedited service is available for fax searches. Turnaround time: next day. Include $18.25 for credit card fee and for overnight delivery.

Death Records

Wyoming Department of Health, Vital Records Services, Hathaway Bldg, Cheyenne, WY 82002; 307-777-7591, 307-635-4103-Fax; 8AM-5PM.

http://wdhfs.state.wy.us/vital_records

Records are available from May 1945 to present. If record is more than 50 years old, it must be obtained from the Wyoming State Archives (307-777-7826). New records are available for inquiry immediately. Records are indexed on microfilm, inhouse computer.

Searching: Must have a signed release from immediate family member. The agency will verify information to family member, such as aunts and uncles, but will not release copies. Include the following in your request-full name, date of death, place of death, relationship to person of record, reason for information request. Must include signature and copy of photo ID with request.

Access by: mail, fax, in person.

Fee & Payment: Search fee is $9.00 per name if year is known; fee is $12.00 per name per 5 years if date is unknown. All copies are certified. Use of credit card for expedited service an extra $5.00. Fee payee: Vital Records Services. Prepayment required. Personal checks accepted. Major credit cards accepted.

Mail search: Turnaround time: 3 to 4 working days. No SASE is required.

Fax search: See expedited services.

In person search: Turnaround time is 15 minutes.

Expedited service: Expedited service is available for fax searches. Turnaround time: next day. Include $18.25 for credit card fee and for overnight delivery.

Marriage Certificates

Wyoming Department of Health, Vital Records Services, Hathaway Bldg, Cheyenne, WY 82002; 307-777-7591, 307-635-4103-Fax; 8AM-5PM.

http://wdhfs.state.wy.us/vital_records

Records are available from May 1941 to present. If record is more than 50 years old, it must be obtained from the Wyoming State Archives (307-777-7826). New records are available for inquiry immediately. Records are indexed on microfilm, inhouse computer.

Searching: Must have a signed release from persons of record. Include the following in your request-names of husband and wife, date of marriage, place or county of marriage, relationship to person of record, reason for information request, wife's maiden name. Signature and copy of photo ID must be included in request.

Access by: mail, fax, in person.

Fee & Payment: The fee is $12.00 per record and an additional $5.00 if a credit card is used for expedited service. Fee payee: Vital Records Services. Prepayment required. Personal checks accepted. Major credit cards accepted.

Mail search: Turnaround time: 3 to 4 working days. No SASE is required.

Fax search: See expedited services.

In person search: Turnaround time is 15 minutes.

Expedited service: Expedited service is available for fax searches. Turnaround time: next day. Include $18.25 for credit card fee and for overnight delivery.

Divorce Records

Wyoming Department of Health, Vital Records Services, Hathaway Bldg, Cheyenne, WY 82002; 307-777-7591, 307-635-4103-Fax; 8AM-5PM.

http://wdhfs.state.wy.us/vital_records

Records are available from May 1941 to present. If record is more than 50 years old, it must be obtained from the Wyoming State Archives (307-777-7826). New records are available for inquiry immediately. Records are indexed on microfilm, inhouse computer.

Searching: Must have a signed release from person of record. Include the following in your request-names of husband and wife, date of divorce, place of divorce, relationship to person of record. Include copy of photo ID with request.

Access by: mail, fax, in person.

Fee & Payment: Fee is $12.00 per record. Fee payee: Vital Records Services. Prepayment required. Personal checks accepted. Major credit cards accepted.

Mail search: Turnaround time: 3 to 4 working days.

Fax search: See expedited services.

In person search: Turnaround time is 30 minutes.

Expedited service: Expedited service is available for fax searches. Turnaround time: next day. Include $18.25 for credit card fee and for overnight delivery.

Workers' Compensation Records

Employment Department, Workers Compensation Division, 1510 E Pershing Blvd, Cheyenne, WY 82002; 307-777-7159, 307-777-5946-Fax; 8AM-4:30PM.

http://wydoe.state.wy.us/doe.asp?ID=9

Records are available from 1987 on computer. Records are on microfiche from 1919 to 1987. Searches on microfiche must include the date of injury, county of injury, employer and body part affected. It takes 3 days before new records are available for inquiry. Records are normally destroyed after document image saved on computer, usually 45 days from closure.

Searching: Only the injured party, employer or legal counsel for either party can obtain records from this agency. Include the following in your request-claimant name, Social Security Number. The only information released is case #, date of injury, body part, employer at time of injury, or other information specifically authorized by claimant.

Access by: mail, fax.

Fee & Payment: No search fee. The copy fee is $.25 per copy. Fee payee: Wyoming Workers' Compensation

Mail search: Turnaround time: variable. Send release form with request to Gary Lord at address above. No SASE is required.

Fax search: They will fax results with appropriate request.

Driver License Information, Driver Records

Wyoming Department of Transportation, Driver Services, 5300 Bishop Blvd, Cheyenne, WY 82009-3340; 307-777-4800, 307-777-4773-Fax; 8AM-5PM.

www.dot.state.wy.us

Authorized requesters may obtain ticket information from the address above for a fee of $5.00 per citation.

Records are available for 3 years from offense date for moving violations, 5 years from conviction date for DWUIs, and 3 to 5 years based on original charge for suspensions. Accidents are shown only if driver has no insurance. Records are normally destroyed after 10 years.

Searching: Companies requesting records must complete and file the DPPA form found on the website. Casual requesters cannot obtain records with personal information without signed release from subject. Include the following in your request-name and DOB and DL or SSN. The following data is not released: medical information.

Access by: mail, fax, in person, online.

Fee & Payment: The fee is $5.00 per record, $3.00 by FTP. Add $6.00 if credit card used. Fee payee: Department of Transportation. Prepayment required. Personal checks accepted. No credit cards accepted.

Mail search: Turnaround time: 3 business days.

Fax search: Approved, ongoing requesters may send fax requests.

In person search: Normal turnaround time is while you wait. Individual licensees may request a copy of their own record at any field office.

Online search: This method is available using FTP technology. Only approved vendors and permissible users are supported. Write Deb Ornelas at the above address for details.

Other access: Magnetic tape retrieval is available at $3.00 per record. The entire driver license file may be purchased for $2,500. Write or call 307-777-4842 for details.

Vehicle Ownership Vehicle Identification

Wyoming Dept. of Transportation, Motor Vehicle Services, 5300 Bishop Blvd, Cheyenne, WY 82009-3340 (Courier address: 5300 Bishop Blvd, Cheyenne, WY 82002); 307-777-4851, 307-777-4714, 307-777-4772-Fax; 8AM-5PM.

http://wydotweb.state.wy.us/web/vehicle_services/index.html

At the website, click on "Vehicle Services" for detailed WY DOT vehicle information. Also, the web site provides access to the request forms needed.

Records are available for 40 years on titles and 80 years on registrations. It takes 3 to 15 days before new records are available for inquiry.

Searching: Requests must be for a permissible use per DPPA. A "Privacy Disclosure Agreement" will need to be signed. Casual requesters cannot obtain records unless written consent of subject is provided and reason for request is approved by MVS. Lien records are not available from the state and must be obtained from the one of the 23 Wyoming county clerk offices.

Access by: mail, fax, in person.

Fee & Payment: The fee is $5.00 per record. Credit cards accepted for an additional $4.95 fee. Fee payee: WY Department of Transportation. Prepayment required. Personal checks accepted. Credit cards accepted.

Mail search: Turnaround time: 1 week. No SASE is required.

Fax search: Approved requester may search by fax using a credit card.

In person search: Turnaround time is normally in a few minutes.

Other access: Bulk information is available, customized lists can be obtained, per DPPA. For more information, call the Motor Vehicle Services at 307-777-4714.

Accident Reports

Highway Safety Program, Accident Records Section, 5300 Bishop Blvd, Cheyenne, WY 82009; 307-777-4450, 307-777-4250-Fax; 8AM-5PM.

The agency refers to these reports as "Crash Reports."

Records are available for It takes 10 to 30 days before new records are available for inquiry.

Searching: Accident reports (done by the officer) are considered open public record reports. Reports compiled by individuals involved are closed. Include the following in your request-date of accident, location of accident, full name, date of birth.

Access by: mail, phone, in person.

Fee & Payment: The fee is $3.00 per record uncertified and $5.00 certified. Fee payee: Department of Transportation. Prepayment required. Personal checks accepted. No credit cards accepted.

Mail search: Turnaround time: 1 week to 10 days.

Phone search: Searches may be done by phone, but no copies are sent until payment is received.

In person search: In-person requests are normally processed in a few of minutes.

Vessel Ownership, Vessel Registration

Wyoming Game & Fish Dept, Watercraft Section, 5400 Bishop Blvd, Cheyenne, WY 82006; 307-777-4575, 307-777-4610-Fax; 8AM-5PM M-F.

http://gf.state.wy.us

Records are available for the last 3 years. The state does not issue titles. All motorized boats must be registered. It takes 10 days before new records are available for inquiry. Records are indexed on computer. Records are normally destroyed after 3 years.

Searching: To search you must provide one of the following: name, Wyoming number, or hull ID number.

Access by: mail, phone, fax, in person.

Fee & Payment: There is no search fee.

Mail search: Turnaround time: 2 to 3 days. Turnaround time is 1 week if archived info is needed.

Phone search: Records are available by phone.

Fax search: Information can be faxed back.

In person search: No fee for request. Turnaround time is immediate if the file is not archived.

Other access: Printed lists are available, call for further details.

Voter Registration

Access to Records is Restricted.

Secretary of State - Election Division, 200 W 24th Street, Wyoming State Capitol, Cheyenne, WY 82002-0020; 307-777-7186, 307-777-7640-Fax; 8AM-5PM.

http://soswy.state.wy.us/election/election.htm

Individual look-ups can also be done at the county level. The SSN and DOB are not released. The state will sell all or part of its database, but only for political reasons. Commercial use is not permitted.

GED Certificates

Department of Workforce Services, GED Program, 122 W 25th Street, Cheyenne, WY 82002; 307-777-6911, 307-777-5857-Fax; 8AM-5PM M-F.

www.wyomingworkforce.org

Records are available from 1950's forward. It takes seconds before new records are available for inquiry.

Searching: To request a transcript or have one sent to employer or college, the following is required: signed release from subject, full name, SSN, and date of birth. Test date is helpful. Request form can be downloaded from webpage.

Access by: mail, fax, in person.

Fee & Payment: There is no fee for verifications or transcripts.

Mail search: Turnaround time: 48 hours. No SASE is required.

Fax search: Same criteria as mail searching.

In person search: Turnaround time is typically 10 minutes for verifications or transcripts if Chief Examiner is available. Otherwise mailed.

Hunting and Fishing License Information

Game & Fish Department, License Section, 5400 Bishop Blvd, Cheyenne, WY 82006; 307-777-4600 (Licensing Section), 307-777-4655 (License Draw), 307-777-4679-Fax; 8AM-5PM.

http://gf.state.wy.us

They maintain a central database for lottery (big game, moose, big horn sheep, elk, deer & antelope) permits and periodically add license permits sold by agents throughout the state.

Records are available from 3 years present on computer, 10 years on microfiche.

Searching: Include the following in your request-full name, date of birth, Social Security Number. The following data is not released: Social Security Numbers.

Access by: mail, phone, fax, in person.

Fee & Payment: Fees are incurred if there is extensive searching or lists are involved. Call first. Fee payee: Wyoming Game and Fish. Prepayment required. Money orders and cashier's checks are preferred. No credit cards accepted.

Mail search: Turnaround time: 1 to 3 days. No SASE is required.

Phone search: Records are available by phone.

Fax search: Fax searching available.

In person search: Simple requests may be processed while you wait.

Other access: They have mailing and label lists available. Call 800-548-9453 for more information.

Wyoming State Licensing Agencies

For details about the agency responsible for licensing/certifying/registering an item below or in the Agency Quick Finder section, match an item's number with the number of the agency in the *Licensing Agency Information* section.

Wyoming Licenses Searchable Online

Attorney #9 .... www.wyomingbar.org/directory/index.html
Bank #23 .... http://audit.state.wy.us/banking/banking/bankingregulatedentities.htm
Check Casher #23 .... http://audit.state.wy.us/banking/uccc/uccclicensees.htm
Chiropractor #32 .... http://plboards.state.wy.us/chiropractic
Collection Agency #24 .... http://audit.state.wy.us/banking/cab/cablicensees.htm
Engineer #27 .... www.wrds.uwyo.edu/wrds/borpe/roster/roster.html
Feed/Fertilizer #1 .... www.kellysolutions.com/wy/
Funeral Pre-Need Agent #8 .... http://insurance.state.wy.us/search/search.asp
Geologist #18 .... http://wbpgweb.uwyo.edu/roster_search.asp
Guide, Outdoor #13 .... http://outfitte.state.wy.us/directory.html
Insurance Claims Adjuster #8 .... http://insurance.state.wy.us/search/search.asp
Insurance Consul't/ Producer/ Serv Rep #8 .... http://insurance.state.wy.us/search/search.asp
Lender, Supervised #23 .... http://audit.state.wy.us/banking/uccc/uccclicensees.htm
Lobbyist #36 .... http://soswy.state.wy.us/election/lob-list.htm
Medical Doctor #10 .... http://wyomedboard.state.wy.us/roster.asp
Motor Club Agent #8 .... http://insurance.state.wy.us/search/search.asp
Optometrist #6 .... www.arbo.org/index.php?action=findanoptometrist
Outfitter #13 .... http://outfitte.state.wy.us/directory.html
Pawnbroker #23 .... http://audit.state.wy.us/banking/uccc/uccclicensees.htm
Pharmacist / Pharmacy Tech #14 .... http://pharmacyboard.state.wy.us/search.asp
Physician Assistant #10 .... http://wyomedboard.state.wy.us/PARoster.asp
Psychologist #16 .... http://plboards.state.wy.us/psychology
Public Accountant-CPA, Individ'l/Firm #29 .... http://cpaboard.state.wy.us/database.aspx
Real Estate Appraiser #21 .... www.asc.gov/content/category1/appr_by_state.asp
Rent-to-own Company #23 .... http://audit.state.wy.us/banking/uccc/uccclicensees.htm
Sales Finance Company #23 .... http://audit.state.wy.us/banking/uccc/uccclicensees.htm
Savings & Loan Association #23 .... http://audit.state.wy.us/banking/banking/bankingregulatedentities.htm
Surplus Line Broker, Resident #8 .... http://insurance.state.wy.us/search/search.asp
Surveyor, Land #27 .... www.wrds.uwyo.edu/wrds/borpe/roster/roster.html
Trust Company #23 .... http://audit.state.wy.us/banking/banking/bankingregulatedentities.htm

Wyoming Licensing Quick Finder

Architect #30 307-777-5403
Attorney #9 307-632-9061
Bank #23 307-777-6605
Barber/Barber Shop #2 307-777-8572
Bus Driver #31 307-777-3340
Check Casher #23 307-777-6605
Child Care Licensee/Subsidy #22 307-777-6848
Chiropractor #32 307-777-6529
Coach, Athletic #35 307-777-7291
Collection Agency #24 307-777-3497
Coroner/Deputy Coroner #39 307-777-7718
Cosmetologist / Cosmo. Instructor #3 . 307-777-3534
Counselor, Professional #30 307-777-7387
Dentist / Dental Assistant #4 307-777-6529
Dental Hygienist #4 307-777-6529
Detention Officer #39 307-777-7718
Dispatcher law enforcement-related#39 307-777-7718
Educational Diagnostician #35 307-777-7291
Electrician, Master/Journey'n/Apr. #26 . 307-777-7991
Embalmer #5 307-777-5403
Emergency Medical Technician #40 307-777-7955
Engineer #27 307-777-6155
Esthetician #3 307-777-3534
Feed/Fertilizer #1 307-777-7324
Funeral Director #5 307-777-5403
Funeral Pre-Need Agent #8 307-777-7344
Geologist #18 307-742-1118
Guide, Outdoor #13 307-635-1589
Hearing Aid Specialist #7 307-777-6529
Insurance Claims Adjuster #8 307-777-7344
Insurance Consultant / Producer #8 307-777-7344

Insurance Service Rep #8 307-777-7344
Jockey/Jockey Apprentice #38 307-777-5887
Landscape Architect #30 307-777-5403
Law Enforcement Officer #39 307-777-7718
Lender, Supervised #23 307-777-6605
Lobbyist #36 307-777-7186
Manicurist/Nail Technician #3 307-777-3534
Marriage & Family Therapist #30 307-777-7387
Medical Doctor #10 307-778-7053
Mine Foreman #33 307-362-5222
Mine Inspector/Examiner #33 307-362-5222
Motor Club Agent #8 307-777-7344
Notary Public #36 307-777-5407
Nurse -LPN #37 877-626-2681
Nursing Assistant #37 877-626-2681
Nursing Home Administrator #12 307-432-0465
Occupational Therapist / Assist't #12 .. 307-432-0488
Optometrist #6 307-777-3507
Outfitter #13 307-635-1589
Pari-Mutuel Employee/Official #38 307-777-5887
Pawnbroker #23 307-777-6605
Peace Officer #39 307-777-7718
Pesticide Aircraft #1 307-777-7324
Pesticide Applicator, Commercial #1 .. 307-777-7324
Pharmacist / Pharmacy Tech. #14 307-234-0294
Physical Therapist #15 307-777-3507
Physician Assistant #10 307-778-7053
Podiatrist #19 307-777-3507
Property Appraiser #25 307-777-7141
Psychiatrist #10 307-778-7053
Psychological Practitioner #16 307-333-6529

Psychologist #16 307-777-6529
Public Accoun't-CPA, person/firm #29 .. 307-777-7551
Racetrack Security Employee #38 307-777-5887
Racing Event #38 307-777-5887
Racing Permittee/Employee/Offic'l #38 307-777-5887
Radiation (Ionizing) Agent #17 307-777-3507
Radiologic Technologist/Technic'n #17 307-777-3507
Radiopharmaceutical Agent #17 307-778-2068
Real Estate Agent #21 307-777-7141
Real Estate Appraiser #21 307-777-7141
Rent-to-own Company #23 307-777-6605
Sales Finance Company #23 307-777-6605
Savings & Loan Association #23 307-777-6605
School Counselor / Librarian #35 307-777-7291
School Principal / Superintendent #35 . 307-777-7291
School Psychologist #16 307-777-6529
Securities Agent #34 307-777-7370
Securities Broker/Dealer #34 307-777-7370
Social Worker #30 307-777-7387
Speech Pathologist/Audiologist #28 307-777-6529
Substitute Teacher #35 307-777-7291
Surplus Line Broker, Resident #8 307-777-7344
Surveyor, Land #27 307-777-6155
Teacher #35 307-777-7291
Travel & Baggage Agent #8 307-777-7344
Truck Driver #31 307-777-3340
Trust Company #23 307-777-6605
Veterinarian #20 307-777-3507
Water Dist/Collection Operator #42 307-777-7781
Water/Waste Water Treatment Plant
   Operator #42 307-777-7781

Wyoming Licensing Agency Information

1 Technical Services Department, Board of Agriculture, 2219 Carey Ave, Cheyenne, WY 82002-0100; 307-777-7324, Fax: 307-777-6593. http://wyagric.state.wy.us/techserv/tsindex.html Email: huhden@state.wy.us   Note: Will sell lists.

2 Board of Barber Examiners, 2515 Warren Ave. #302, Cheyenne, WY 82002; 307-777-8572.

3 Board of Cosmetology, 2515 Warren Ave, #302, Cheyenne, WY 82002; 307-777-3534, Fax: 307-777-3681. Email: babern@state.wy.us

4 Board of Dental Examiners, 2020 Carey Ave #201, Cheyenne, WY 82002; 307-777-6529, Fax: 307-777-3508. http://plboards.state.wy.us/dental

5 Board of Embalming, 2020 Carey Ave, #201, Cheyenne, WY 82002; 307-777-5403, Fax: 307-777-3508.

6 Board of Examiners in Optometry, 2020 Carey Ave, #201, Cheyenne, WY 82002; 307-777-3507, Fax: 307-777-3508. Email: nbrown1@missc.wy.state.us Search Database at www.arbo.org/index.php?action=findanoptometrist

7 Board of Hearing Aid Specialists, 2020 Carey Ave, #201, Cheyenne, WY 82002; 307-777-6529, Fax: 307-777-3508. http://plboards.state.wy.us/hearingaid/index.asp

8 Board of Insurance Agents Examiners, 122 W 25th St, Cheyenne, WY 82002-0040; 307-777-7344, Fax: 307-777-5895. http://insurance.state.wy.us/ Email: gnalde@state.wy.us   Search Database at http://insurance.state.wy.us/search/search.asp

9 Board of Law Examiners, PO Box 109 (500 Randall Ave.), Cheyenne, WY 82003; 307-632-9061, Fax: 307-630-3737. http://www.wyomingbar.org

10 Board of Medicine, 211 W 19th St, 2nd Fl, Cheyenne, WY 82002; 307-778-7053, 800-438-5784, Fax: 307-778-2069. http://wyomedboard.state.wy.us Email: wyomedical@wyomedicalboard.org

11 Department of Environmental Quality, Water Quality Division, 122 W 25th St, Herschler Bldg 4th Fl-W, Cheyenne, WY 82002; 307-777-7781, Fax: 307-777-5973. http://deq.state.wy.us/wqd/index.asp?pageid=5

12 Board of Occupational Therapy, 1114 Logan Ave, Cheyenne, WY 82002; 307-432-0488, Fax: 307-432-0492. http://plboards.state.wy.us/ Email: kspire@state.wy.us

13 Board of Outfitters & Professional Guides, 1950 Bluegrass Circle #280, Cheyenne, WY 82002; 307-635-1589, Fax: 307-777-6715. http://outfitters.state.wy.us Email: jflagg@state.wy.us   Search Database at http://outfitte.state.wy.us/directory.html

14 Board of Pharmacy, 632 S David S, Casper, WY 82601-3189; 307-234-0294, Fax: 307-234-7226. http://pharmacyboard.state.wy.us Email: wybop@state.wy.us   Search Database at http://pharmacyboard.state.wy.us/search.asp

15 Board of Physical Therapy, 2020 Carey Ave, #201, Cheyenne, WY 82002; 307-777-3507, Fax: 307-777-3508. Email: nbrown@missc.wy.state.us

16 Board of Psychology, 2020 Carey Ave, #201, Cheyenne, WY 82002; 307-777-6529, Fax: 307-777-3508. http://plboards.state.wy.us/psychology

17 Board of Radiologic Technologists, 2020 Carey Ave, #201, Cheyenne, WY 82002; 307-777-3507, Fax: 307-777-3508. http://plboards.state.wy.us/radiology/index.asp Email: nbrown@missc.wy.state.us

18 Board of Registration for Professional Geologists, 1465 N. 4th Street # 109, Laramie, WY 82072-2066; 307-742-1118, Fax: 307-742-1120. http://wbpgweb.uwyo.edu Email: wbpg@state.wy.us   Search Database at http://wbpgweb.uwyo.edu/roster_search.asp

19 Board of Registration in Podiatry, 2020 Carey Ave, #201, Cheyenne, WY 82002; 307-777-3507, Fax: 307-777-3508. Email: nbrown@missc.wy.state.us

20 Board of Veterinary Medicine, 2020 Carey Ave, #201, Cheyenne, WY 82002; 307-777-3507, Fax: 307-777-3508. Email: nbrown@missc.wy.state.us

21 Real Estate Appraiser Board, 2020 Carey Ave, #100, Cheyenne, WY 82002; 307-777-7141, Fax: 307-777-3796. http://realestate.state.wy.us

22 Child Care Certification Board, 2300 Capitol Ave, Hathaway Bldg., Room 337, Cheyenne, WY 82002-0490; 307-777-6350, Fax: 307-777-3659. http://dfsweb.state.wy.us

23 Department of Audit, Division of Banking, 122 W 25th St, Herschler Bldg 3 E, Cheyenne, WY 82002; 307-777-7797, Fax: 307-777-3555. http://audit.state.wy.us/banking/default.htm Search Database at http://audit.state.wy.us/banking/banking/bankingregulatedentities.htm

24 Department of Audit, Collecting Agency Board, Herschler Bldg, 3rd Fl, 122 W 25th St, Cheyenne, WY 82002; 307-777-3497, Fax: 307-777-3555. http://audit.state.wy.us/banking/default.htm Email: ssmith@audit.state.wy.us Search Database at http://audit.state.wy.us/banking/cab/cablicensees.htm

25 Real Estate Commission, Appraiser Board, 2020 Carey Avenue, Suite 100, Cheyenne, WY 82002-0180; 307-777-7141. http://realestate.state.wy.us/ Email: jburtol@missc.state.wy.us

26 Electrical Board, Herschler Bldg, 1st Fl W, Cheyenne, WY 82002; 307-777-7288, Fax: 307-777-7119.   Email: jnoel@state.wy.us

27 Engineers & Professional Land Surveyors, 2424 Pioneer Ave, #400, Cheyenne, WY 82001; 307-777-6155, Fax: 307-777-3403. www.wrds.uwyo.edu/wrds/borpe/borpe.html Email: wyopepls@qwest.net   Search Database at www.wrds.uwyo.edu/wrds/borpe/roster/roster.html

28 Examiners for Speech Pathology & Audiology, 2020 Carey Ave, #201, Cheyenne, WY 82002; 307-777-6529, Fax: 307-777-3508. http://plboards.state.wy.us/speech/index.asp Note: Roster of Licensees available.

29 Board of Certified Public Accountants, 2020 Carey Ave, #100, Cheyenne, WY 82002; 307-777-7551, Fax: 307-777-3796. http://cpaboard.state.wy.us Email: pmorga@state.wy.us Search Database at http://cpaboard.state.wy.us/database.aspx

30 Professional Licensing Boards, 2020 Carey Ave, #201, Cheyenne, WY 82002; 307-777-3628, Fax: 307-777-3508.

31 Driver Svcs, Department of Transportation, 5300 Bishop Blvd, Cheyenne, WY 82009-3340; 307-777-3340, Fax: 307-777-4289. http://dot.state.wy.us

32 Board of Chiropractic Examiners, 2020 Carey Ave, #201, Cheyenne, WY 82002; 307-777-6529, Fax: 307-777-3508. http://plboards.state.wy.us/chiropractic

33 Mining Council, PO Box 1094, Rock Springs, WY 82901; 307-362-5222, Fax: 307-362-5233.

34 Securities Division, Office of Secretary of State, 200 West 24th Street, The Capitol Building, Rm 109, Cheyenne, WY 82002; 307-777-7370, Fax: 307-777-5339. http://soswy.state.wy.us/securiti/securiti.htm Email: securities@state.wy.us

35 Professional Teaching Standards Board, 1920 Thomes Ave. #400, Cheyenne, WY 82002; 307-777-7291, Fax: 307-777-8718. Email: lstowe@state.wy.us

36 Secretary of State, Elections/Notary Division, Joseph B Meyer, State Capitol Bldg, Cheyenne, WY 82002; 307-777-7378, Fax: 307-777-6217. http://soswy.state.wy.us Email: secofstate@missc.state.wy.us

37 Board of Nursing, 2020 Carey Ave, #110, Cheyenne, WY 82002; 307-777-7601; voice verification 877-626-2681, Fax: 307-777-3519. http://nursing.state.wy.us Email: rpoupp@state.wy.us   Note: Call for prices.

38 Pari-Mutuel Commission, 2515 Warren Ave, #301, Cheyenne, WY 82002; 307-777-5887, Fax: 307-777-5700. http://parimutuel.state.wy.us/

39 P.O.S.T. Commission, 1710 Pacific Ave, Cheyenne, WY 82002; 307-777-7718, Fax: 307-638-9706.

40 Office of Emergency Medical Svcs, 2300 Capital Ave, Hathaway Bldg 4th Fl, Cheyenne, WY 82002; 307-777-7955, Fax: 307-777-5639. http://wdhfs.state.wy.us/ems/

Wyoming Federal Courts

The following list indicates the district and division name for each county in the state.

Wyoming County/Court Cross Reference

County	Division		County	Division
Albany	Cheyenne		Natrona	Cheyenne
Big Horn	Cheyenne		Niobrara	Cheyenne
Campbell	Cheyenne		Park	Cheyenne
Carbon	Cheyenne		Platte	Cheyenne
Converse	Cheyenne		Sheridan	Cheyenne
Crook	Cheyenne		Sublette	Cheyenne
Fremont	Cheyenne		Sweetwater	Cheyenne
Goshen	Cheyenne		Teton	Cheyenne
Hot Springs	Cheyenne		Uinta	Cheyenne
Johnson	Cheyenne		Washakie	Cheyenne
Laramie	Cheyenne		Weston	Cheyenne
Lincoln	Cheyenne			

US District Court

District of Wyoming

Cheyenne Division Court Clerk, 2120 Capitol Ave, Rm 2141, Cheyenne, WY 82001 (also use mail address for courier delivery), 307-433-2120, Fax-307-433-2152. Hours- 8AM-5PM. www.ck10.uscourts.gov/wyoming/district/index.html

Counties: All counties in Wyoming. Some criminal records are held in Casper but all are available electronically here.

Searches & Indexing: Results do not include SSN or DOB. Computer index back to 1992 maintained. Records older than 1992 on microfiche. New cases in the index 1-2 days after filing date. Records purged once yearly.

Fee & Payment: Pay by money order, cashier's or personal check. Payee: Clerk, US District Court. Prepayment required.

Mail Search: search usually completed- 1-2 days. SASE not required.

In Person Search: Fee charged if court performs your search. No self-serve copier available.

E-Services: ECF replaces PACER whose records did go back to 1988. New records online after 1 day. ECF at https://ecf.wyd.uscourts.gov

US Bankruptcy Court

District of Wyoming

Cheyenne Division Court Clerk, 2120 Capitol Ave, #6004, Cheyenne, WY 82001 (also use mail address for courier delivery), 307-433-2200. Hours- 8:30AM-N, 1-4PM. www.wyb.uscourts.gov

Counties: All counties in Wyoming.

Searches & Indexing: Both computer and card indexes maintained. New cases in the index 24 hours after filing date. Records purged yearly.

Fee & Payment: Pay by money order, cashier's or personal check. No debtor's checks accepted. Payee: Clerk, US Bankruptcy Court. Prepayment required.

Phone Search: Voice Case Information Service available, call VCIS at 888-804-5537 or 307-433-2238.

Mail Search: search usually completed- 1-2 days. Include SASE for return.

In Person Search: Fee charged if court performs your search. Self-serve copier available from the computer terminal - $.10 per page.

E-Services: ECF replaces PACER whose records did go back 1 year. ECF at https://ecf.wyb.uscourts.gov. Document images available. Opinions may be available at the main website.

Standards for Federal Courts: Search fee is $26.00 per item (one party name or case number). Copy fee is $.50 per page. Certification fee is $9.00 per document, double for exemplification, if available. All fees standard unless noted in profile. Mail Search: always enclose a stamped self addressed envelope unless otherwise noted. Most courts accept fax requests or will suggest a copying/search vendor. Before releasing records, all courts require prepayment, unless noted.

Open records are located at the court unless otherwise noted. District courts index by defendant and plaintiff as well as by case number. Bankruptcy courts usually index by debtor and case number. While most courts now have their indexes on computer, many may still maintain index card files as well.

Courts offering internet access via CM-ECF or older RACER, PACER, or Web-PACER systems charge $.08 per page fee unless noted as free. Where PACER is available, the universal sign-up number is 800-676-6856. Find PACER and the US Party/Case Index at http://pacer.psc.uscourts.gov.

Wyoming County Courts

Court	Jurisdiction	No. of Courts	How Organized
District Courts*	General	23	9 Districts
Circuit Courts*	Limited	27	23 Counties
Municipal Courts	Municipal	80	

* Profiled in this Sourcebook.

Court	CIVIL								
	Tort	Contract	Real Estate	Min. Claim	Max. Claim	Small Claims	Estate	Eviction	Domestic Relations
District Courts*	X	X	X	$3000/$7000	No Max		X		X
Circuit Courts*	X	X	X	$0	$7000	$3000		X	X
Municipal Courts									

Court	CRIMINAL				
	Felony	Misdemeanor	DWI/DUI	Preliminary Hearing	Juvenile
District Courts*	X				X
Circuit Courts*		X	X	X	
Municipal Courts		X	X		

ADMINISTRATION

Court Administrator, 2301 Capitol Av, Supreme Court Bldg, Cheyenne, WY, 82002; 307-777-7583, Fax: 307-777-3447. www.courts.state.wy.us

COURT STRUCTURE

Each county has a District Court ("higher" jurisdiction) and a Circuit. Prior to 2003, for their "lower" jurisdiction court some counties had Circuit Courts and others had Justice Courts. Effective January 1, 2003 all Justice Courts became Circuit Courts and follow Circuit Court rules.

Circuit Courts handle civil claims up to $7,000 while Justice Courts handle civil claims up to $3,000. The District Courts take cases over the applicable limit in each county. Three counties have two Circuit Courts each: Fremont, Park, and Sweetwater. Cases may be filed in either of the two court offices in those counties, and records requests are referred between the two courts. Municipal courts operate in all incorporated cities and towns. Their jurisdiction covers all ordinance violations, and it has no civil jurisdiction. The municipal court judge may assess penalties of up to $750 and/or six months in jail.

Probate is handled by the District Court.

ONLINE ACCESS

Wyoming's statewide case management system is for internal use only. Planning is underway for a new case management system that will ultimately allow public access. Appellate and Supreme Court opinions available at web, listed by date.

Albany County

2nd Judicial District Court County Courthouse, 525 Grand, Rm 305, Laramie, WY 82070; phone: 307-721-2508; hours 9AM-5PM (MST). *Felony, Civil Actions Over $7,000, Probate.*
Civil Records: Access: Phone, mail, in person. Both court and visitors may perform in person searches. Search fee: $10.00 per name. Court makes copy: $1.00 for first page, $.50 each add'l. Required to search: name; also helpful: years to search. Civil cases indexed by defendant, plaintiff. Civil records on computer go back to 1988, prior records on card index to 1890. Limit calls to three names. Mail turnaround time same day.
Criminal Records: Access: Mail, in person. Both court and visitors may perform in person searches. Search fee: $10.00 per name. Search results can be phoned back to a toll-free number only. Court makes copy: $1.00 for first page, $.50 each add'l. Required to search: name, years to search, DOB. Criminal records on computer go back to 1988, prior records on card index to 1890. Mail turnaround time same day.
General Information: No sex offenses records released, signed release required for child support cases. Will fax results to toll-free number only. No certification fee. Payee: Clerk of District Court. Personal checks accepted. Prepayment and SASE required.

Albany Circuit Court County Courthouse, 525 Grand, Rm 105, Laramie, WY 82070; phone: 307-742-5747; fax: 307-742-5610; hours 8AM-5PM (MST). *Misdemeanor, Civil Actions Under $7,000, Eviction, Small Claims.*
Civil Records: Access: Mail, in person. Both court and visitors may perform in person searches. Search fee: $10.00 per name. Court makes copy: $1.00 for 1st page, $.50 each add'l. Required to search: name, years to search. Civil cases indexed by defendant, plaintiff. Civil records on computer from 1993, prior on docket books to 1984. Mail turnaround time same day if possible.
Criminal Records: Access: Mail, in person, fax. Both court and visitors may perform in person searches. Search fee: $10.00 per name. Court makes copy: $1.00 for 1st page, $.50 each add'l. Required to search: name, years to search, DOB. Criminal records on computer from 1990, prior on docket books to 1984. Mail turnaround time same day if possible.
General Information: No SSN or family violence records released. Fee to fax results is $2.00 per document. Certification fee: $5.00 per document. Payee: Albany Circuit Court. In state personal checks accepted. Prepayment and SASE required.

Big Horn County

5th Judicial District Court PO Box 670, Basin, WY 82410; phone: 307-568-2381; criminal fax: 307-568-2791; same fax for civil/probate; hours 8AM-N, 1-5PM (MST). *Felony, Civil Actions Over $7,000, Probate.*

Civil Records: Access: Fax, mail, in person. Both court and visitors may perform in person searches. Search fee: $10.00 per name. Court makes copy: $1.00 for first page, $.50 each add'l. Required to search: name, years to search. Civil cases indexed by defendant, plaintiff. Civil records on computer 1988, on microfiche 1982, 1970 to present on cards. Mail turnaround time 24 hours.

Criminal Records: Access: Fax, mail, in person. Both court and visitors may perform in person searches. Search fee: $10.00 per name. Court makes copy: $1.00 for first page, $.50 each add'l. Required to search: name, years to search. Criminal records on computer 1989, on microfiche 1982, 1970 to present on cards. Mail turnaround time 24 hours.

General Information: Some confidential records not released. Will fax results for $2.00. Certification fee: $.50 per page. Payee: Clerk of Court. Business checks accepted. Prepayment and SASE required.

Basin Circuit Court PO Box 749, Basin, WY 82410; phone: 307-568-2367; fax: 307-568-2554; hours 8AM-5PM (MST). *Misdemeanor, Civil Actions Under $7,000, Small Claims.*

Note: Note that misdemeanor records from this Basin Court and the Lovell Court are not combined.

Civil Records: Access: Fax, mail, in person. Only the court performs in person searches; visitors may not. Search fee: $10.00 per name. Court makes copy: $1.00 for 1st page, $.50 each add'l. Required to search: name, years to search; also helpful: address. Civil cases indexed by defendant. Civil records on microfiche 1985. Mail turnaround time 1 day.

Criminal Records: Access: Fax, mail, in person. Only the court performs in person searches; visitors may not. Search fee: $10.00 per name. Court makes copy: $1.00 for 1st page, $.50 each add'l. Required to search: name, DOB; also helpful: SSN. Criminal records on computer since 1990, microfiche 1985. Mail turnaround time 1 day.

General Information: No sex or juvenile offenses released. Fee to fax results is $2 per document. Certification fee: $5.00 per document. Payee: Basin Circuit Court. Personal checks accepted. Prepayment required.

Lovell Circuit Court PO Box 595, Lovell, WY 82431; phone: 307-548-7601; fax: 307-548-9691; hours 8AM-5PM (MST). *Misdemeanor, Civil Actions Under $7,000, Small Claims.*

Note: Note that misdemeanor records from the Basin Circuit Court and this Lovell Court are not combined.

Civil Records: Access: Fax, mail, in person. Only the court performs in person searches; visitors may not. Search fee: $10.00 per name. Court makes copy: $1.00 for 1st page, $.50 each add'l. Required to search: name, years to search; also helpful: address. Civil cases indexed by defendant. Civil records computerized since 01/99. Mail turnaround time 1 day.

Criminal Records: Access: Fax, mail, in person. Only the court performs in person searches; visitors may not. Search fee: $10.00 per name. Court makes copy: $1.00 for 1st page, $.50 each add'l. Required to search: name, DOB; also helpful: SSN. Criminal records on computer since 1990. Mail turnaround time 1 day.

General Information: No sex or juvenile offenses released. Fee to fax results is $2.00 per document. Certification fee: $5.00 per document. Payee: Lovell Circuit Court. Personal checks accepted. Prepayment required.

Campbell County

6th Judicial District Court PO Box 817, 500 S Gillette, Gillette, WY 82717; phone: 307-682-3424; criminal fax: 307-687-6209; same fax for civil/probate; hours 8AM-5PM (MST). *Felony, Civil Actions Over $7,000, Probate.*

Civil Records: Access: Fax, mail, in person. Visitors must perform in person searches themselves. Search fee: $10.00 per name. Court makes copy: $1.00 for first page, $.50 each add'l. Self serve copy fee: $.25 per page. Required to search: name, years to search. Civil cases indexed by defendant. Civil records archived from 1913; on computer back to 1983. Mail turnaround time 1-2 days.

Criminal Records: Access: Fax, mail, in person. Visitors must perform in person searches themselves. Search fee: $10.00 per name. Court makes copy: $1.00 for first page, $.50 each add'l. Self serve copy fee: $.25 per page. Required to search: name, years to search. Criminal records archived from 1913; on computer back to 1983. Mail turnaround time 1-2 days.

General Information: Public terminal goes back to 1986. Names of victims in sex cases, confidential records not released. Will fax results $1.00 per page. Certification fee: $1.00 per certification. Payee: Clerk of District Court. Personal checks accepted. Out of state checks not accepted. Prepayment required.

Campbell Circuit Court 500 S Gillette Ave, #301, Gillette, WY 82716; phone: 307-682-2190; fax: 307-687-6214; hours 8AM-5PM (MST). *Misdemeanor, Civil Actions Under $7,000, Eviction, Small Claims.*

Civil Records: Access: Mail, in person. Only the court performs in person searches; visitors may not. Search fee: $10.00 per name. Court makes copy: $1.00 for 1st page, $.50 each add'l; same fee for self serve. Required to search: name, years to search; also helpful: address. Civil cases indexed by defendant, plaintiff. Civil records on computer since 1983, archives from 1979. Mail turnaround time 2 days.

Criminal Records: Access: Mail, in person. Only the court performs in person searches; visitors may not. Search fee: $10.00 per name. Court makes copy: $1.00 for 1st page, $.50 each add'l; same fee for self serve. Required to search: name, years to search, DOB; also helpful: address. Criminal records on computer since 1983, archives from 1979. Mail turnaround time 1-2 days; longer for cases prior to 2001.

General Information: No sex related cases released. Fee to fax results is $2 per document. Certification fee: $5.00 per document. Payee: Campbell County Circuit Court. Personal checks accepted. Prepayment required. SASE requested.

Carbon County

Carbon County District Court Clerk of District Court, PO Box 67, Rawlins, WY 82301; phone: 307-328-2628; fax: 307-328-2629; hours 8AM-5PM (MST). *Felony, Civil Actions Over $7,000, Probate.*

Civil Records: Access: Phone, fax, mail, in person. Both court and visitors may perform in person searches. Search fee: $10.00 per name. Court makes copy: $1.00 for first page, $.50 each add'l; same fee for self serve. Required to search: name, years to search; also helpful: address. Civil cases indexed by defendant, plaintiff. Civil records on file from late 1800s, index cards, docket books, then computer 1997. Public can search on the manual index. Mail turnaround time 4-5 days.

Criminal Records: Access: Phone, fax, mail, in person. Both court and visitors may perform in person searches. Search fee: $10.00 per name. Court makes copy: $1.00 for first page, $.50 each add'l; same fee for self serve. Required to search: name, years to search; also helpful: address, DOB, SSN. Criminal records on index cards and docket books; on computer since 1997. Public can search on the manual index. Mail turnaround time 4-5 days.

General Information: No juvenile or adoption records released. Fee to fax results depends on number of pages. No certification fee. Payee: Clerk of District Court, Carbon County. Personal checks accepted. Prepayment and SASE required.

Carbon Circuit Court Attn: Chief Clerk, Courthouse Bldg, 415 W Pine St, Rawlins, WY 82301; phone: 307-324-6655; fax: 307-324-9465; hours 8AM-5PM (MST). *Misdemeanor, Civil Actions Under $7,000, Eviction, Small Claims.*

Civil Records: Access: Mail, fax, in person. Only the court performs in person searches; visitors may not. Search fee: $10.00 per name. Court makes copy: $1.00 for 1st page, $.50 each add'l. Required to search: name, years to search; also helpful: address. Civil cases indexed by defendant, plaintiff. Civil records on computer back to 3/95. Mail turnaround time 1 week.

Criminal Records: Access: Mail, fax, in person. Only the court performs in person searches; visitors may not. Search fee: $10.00 per name. Court makes copy: $1.00 for 1st page, $.50 each add'l. Required to search: name, years to search, DOB. Criminal records on computer back to 8/87. Mail turnaround time 1 week.

General Information: Names of victims not released in sex related cases. Will fax results to a toll-free line. Certification fee: $5.00 per document. Payee: Circuit Court of Carbon County. Personal checks accepted. Prepayment and SASE required.

Converse County

8th Judicial District Court Box 189, Douglas, WY 82633; phone: 307-358-3165; criminal fax: 307-358-9783; same fax for civil/probate; hours 8AM-5PM (MST). *Felony, Civil Actions Over $7,000, Probate.*

Civil Records: Access: Phone, fax, mail, in person. Both court and visitors may perform in person searches. Search fee: $10.00 per name or case. Court makes copy: $.25 per page. Self serve copy fee: $.10 per page. Required to search: name, years to search; also helpful: address. Civil cases indexed by defendant, plaintiff. Civil records on card file from 1888. Mail turnaround time usually same day.

Criminal Records: Access: Phone, fax, mail, in person. Both court and visitors may perform in person searches. Search fee: $10.00 per name or case. Court makes copy: $.25 per page. Self serve copy fee: $.10 per page. Required to search: name, years to search; also helpful: address, DOB, SSN. Criminal records on card file from 1800. Mail turnaround time usually same day.

General Information: No juvenile, adoptions or mental cases released. Will fax results $2.00 per page. Certification fee: $1.00 plus $.50 each add'l page. Payee: Clerk of District Court. Only cashiers checks and money orders accepted. Prepayment required.

Converse Circuit Court 107 N 5th St, #231, PO Box 45, Douglas, WY 82633; phone: 307-358-2196; fax: 307-358-2501; hours 8AM-5PM (MST). *Misdemeanor, Civil Actions Under $7,000, Eviction, Small Claims.*

Civil Records: Access: Mail, in person. Both court and visitors may perform in person searches. Search fee: $10.00 per name. Court makes copy: $1.00 for 1st page, $.50 each add'l. Required to search: name, years to search. Civil cases indexed by defendant, plaintiff. Civil records on computer from 1994, card file prior. Mail turnaround time 1-2 days.

Criminal Records: Access: Mail, in person. Both court and visitors may perform in person searches. Search fee: $10.00 per name. Court makes copy: $1.00 for 1st page, $.50 each add'l. Required to search: name, years to search, DOB also helpful: address, SSN. Criminal records on computer from 1990, card file prior. Mail turnaround time 1-2 days.

General Information: No sealed records released. Fee to fax results is $2.00 per document. Certification fee: $2.00 per document. Payee: Circuit Court of Converse County. Only cashiers checks and money orders accepted. Prepayment required.

Crook County

6th Judicial District Court Box 904, Sundance, WY 82729; phone: 307-283-2523; criminal fax: 307-283-2996; same fax for civil/probate; hours 8AM-5PM (MST). *Felony, Civil Actions Over $7,000, Probate, High Misdemeanor pre-7/1/02.*
Note: High misdemeanor cases no longer heard by this court, effective 7/1/02; High misdemeanor records prior to that date can be found here.
Civil Records: Access: Mail, in person. Both court and visitors may perform in person searches. Search fee: $10.00 per name. Court makes copy: $.50 per page; same fee for self serve. Required to search: name, years to search; also helpful: address. Civil cases indexed by defendant, plaintiff. Civil records on card file from late 1800s; on computer back to 1999. The civil limit was raised from $3,000 to $7,000 on 7/1/2002. Cases prior to that date remain with this court. Mail turnaround time usually same day.
Criminal Records: Access: Mail, in person. Both court and visitors may perform in person searches. Search fee: $10.00 per name. Court makes copy: $.50 per page; same fee for self serve. Required to search: name, years to search; also helpful: address, DOB, SSN. Criminal records on card file from late 1800s; on computer back to 1999. As of 7/1/02, high misdemeanor cases are no longer heard by this court, however, cases prior to that date will remain here. Mail turnaround time usually same day.
General Information: No sealed records released. Will fax results for $2.00 per page. Certification fee: $1.00 per certification. Payee: Clerk of District Court. Business checks accepted. Prepayment and SASE required.

Circuit Court PO Box 650, Sundance, WY 82729; phone: 307-283-2929; fax: 307-283-2931; hours 8AM-5PM (MST). *Misdemeanor, Civil Actions Under $7,000, Small Claims.*
Note: This former Justice Court became a Circuit Court on 7/1/2002.
Civil Records: Access: Mail, fax, in person. Only the court performs in person searches; visitors may not. Search fee: $10.00 per name. Court makes copy: $1.00 for 1st page, $.50 each add'l. Required to search: name, years to search; also helpful: address. Civil cases indexed by defendant, plaintiff. Civil records on cards, archives back to 1977; on computer back to 1998. Mail turnaround time 3-5 days.
Criminal Records: Access: Mail, fax, in person. Only the court performs in person searches; visitors may not. Search fee: $10.00 per name. Court makes copy: $1.00 for 1st page, $.50 each add'l. Required to search: name, years to search, DOB, SSN. Criminal records go back to 1983; on computer back to 1992. Mail turnaround time 3-5 days.
General Information: No sex related cases released. Fee to fax results is $2.00 per document; no charge if $20.00 search fee is paid. Certification fee: $5.00 per document. Payee: Crook County Circuit Court. Personal checks accepted. Prepayment and SASE required.

Fremont County

9th Judicial District Court PO Box 370, Lander, WY 82520; phone: 307-332-1134; fax: 307-332-1143; hours 8AM-N, 1-5PM (MST). *Felony, Civil Actions Over $7,000, Probate.*
Civil Records: Access: Phone, fax, mail, in person. Both court and visitors may perform in person searches. Search fee: $10.00 per name. Court makes copy: $.25 per page; same fee for self serve. Required to search: name, years to search; also helpful: address. Civil cases indexed by defendant, plaintiff. Civil records on computer since 1992, in books since 1991, on microfiche since 1939 and on card file from 1898. Mail turnaround time same day.
Criminal Records: Access: Phone, fax, mail, in person. Both court and visitors may perform in person searches. Search fee: $10.00 per name. Court makes copy: $.25 per page; same fee for self serve. Required to search: name, years to search; also

helpful: address, DOB, SSN. Criminal records on computer since 1992, in books since 1991, on microfiche since 1939 and on card file from 1898. Mail turnaround time same day.
General Information: Public terminal goes back to 1993. No juvenile, involuntary hospitalization or adoption records released. No fee to fax results. No certification fee. Payee: Clerk of District Court. Personal checks accepted. SASE required.

Dubois Circuit Court Box 952, Dubois, WY 82513; phone: 307-455-2920; fax: 307-455-2132; hours 8AM-2:00PM (MST). *Misdemeanor, Civil Actions Under $7,000, Eviction, Small Claims.*
Note: This is a satellite of the Lander Court.
Civil Records: Access: Mail, in person. Both court and visitors may perform in person searches. Search fee: $10.00 per name. Court makes copy: $1.00 for 1st page, $.50 each add'l. Required to search: name, years to search. Civil cases indexed by defendant, plaintiff. Civil records on index. Mail turnaround time 2 days.
Criminal Records: Access: Mail, in person. Both court and visitors may perform in person searches. Search fee: $10.00 per name. Court makes copy: $1.00 for 1st page, $.50 each add'l. Required to search: name, years to search; also helpful: DOB. Criminal records on computer since 12/98; prior records on indexes. Mail turnaround time 2 days.
General Information: No juvenile, sexual data released. Fee to fax results is $2.00 per document. Certification fee: $5.00 per document. Payee: Fremont County Court. Personal checks accepted. Prepayment and SASE required.

Lander Circuit Court 450 N 2nd, Rm 230, Lander, WY 82520; phone: 307-332-3239; fax: 307-332-1152; hours 8AM-5PM (MST). *Misdemeanor, Civil Actions Under $7,000, Eviction, Small Claims.*
Note: This is the main Circuit Court for Fremont County.
Civil Records: Access: Phone, fax, mail, in person. Both court and visitors may perform in person searches. Search fee: $10.00 per name. Court makes copy: $1.00 for 1st page, $.50 each add'l. Required to search: name, years to search; also helpful: address. Civil cases indexed by defendant, plaintiff. Civil records on computer from 1988, archive back to 1979. Mail turnaround time 2 days.
Criminal Records: Access: Phone, fax, mail, in person. Both court and visitors may perform in person searches. Search fee: $10.00 per name. Court makes copy: $1.00 for 1st page, $.50 each add'l. Required to search: name, years to search; also helpful: address, DOB, SSN. Criminal records on computer from 1988, archive back to 1979. Mail turnaround time 2 days.
General Information: No juvenile or sexual data released. Fee to fax results is $2.00 per document. Certification fee: $5.00 per document. Payee: Circuit Court. In state personal checks accepted. Prepayment and SASE required.

Riverton Circuit Court 818 S Federal Blvd, Riverton, WY 82501; phone: 307-856-7259; fax: 307-857-3635; hours 8AM-5PM (MST). *Misdemeanor, Civil Actions Under $7,000, Eviction, Small Claims.*
www.courts.state.wy.us/Brochure_files/ccriv.htm
Civil Records: Access: Mail, in person. Only the court performs in person searches; visitors may not. Search fee: $10.00 per name. Court makes copy: $1.00 for 1st page, $.50 each add'l. Required to search: name, years to search. Civil cases indexed by defendant, plaintiff. Civil records are computerized since 1997; prior in books to 1981. Mail turnaround time 2 days.
Criminal Records: Access: Mail, in person. Only the court performs in person searches; visitors may not. Search fee: $10.00 per name. Court makes copy: $1.00 for 1st page, $.50 each add'l. Required to search: name, years to search, DOB; also helpful: SSN. Criminal records on computer since 1989; prior in books to 1981. Mail turnaround time 2 days.

General Information: No sex released cases released. Fee to fax results is $2.00 per document. Certification fee: $5.00 per document. Payee: Fremont County Circuit Court. In state personal checks accepted. Prepayment and SASE required.

Goshen County

8th Judicial District Court PO Box 818, Clerk of District Court, 2125 E "A" St #236, Torrington, WY 82240; phone: 307-532-2155; fax: 307-532-8608; hours 7:30AM-4PM (MST). *Felony, Civil Actions Over $7,000, Probate.*
Civil Records: Access: Mail, in person. Both court and visitors may perform in person searches. Search fee: $10.00 per name. Court makes copy: $1.00 for first page, $.50 each add'l. Required to search: name, years to search; also helpful: address. Civil cases indexed by defendant, plaintiff. Civil records on index file only since 1913. Mail turnaround time 3-4 days.
Criminal Records: Access: Mail, in person. Both court and visitors may perform in person searches. Search fee: $10.00 per name. Court makes copy: $1.00 for first page, $.50 each add'l. Required to search: name, years to search; also helpful: address, DOB, SSN. Criminal records on index file only since 1913, on computer back to 2004. Mail turnaround time 3-4 days.
General Information: No juvenile records released. Will fax results, prefer toll free line. Certification fee: $.50 per page. Payee: Clerk of District Court. In state personal checks accepted. Prepayment and SASE required.

Goshen Circuit Court Drawer BB, Torrington, WY 82240; phone: 307-532-2938; criminal phone: X250; civil phone: X251; fax: 307-532-5101; hours 7AM-4PM (MST). *Misdemeanor, Civil Actions Under $7,000, Eviction, Small Claims.*
Civil Records: Access: Mail, in person. Only the court performs in person searches; visitors may not. Search fee: $10.00 per name. Court makes copy: $1.00 for 1st page, $.50 each add'l. Required to search: name, years to search; also helpful: address. Civil cases indexed by case number, defendant. Civil records go back to 1988; on computer back to 3/97, prior archived. Mail turnaround time 3-4 days.
Criminal Records: Access: Mail, in person. Only the court performs in person searches; visitors may not. Search fee: $10.00 per name. Court makes copy: $1.00 for 1st page, $.50 each add'l. Required to search: name, years to search, DOB; also helpful: address, SSN. Criminal records go back to 10/92; on computer back to 4/89 for disposition data, to 1984 for felonies or high misdemeanors, prior archived. Mail turnaround time 3-4 days.
General Information: No juvenile records released. Fee to fax results is $2.00 per document. Certification fee: $5.00 per document. Payee: Circuit Court 8th Judicial District. Personal checks accepted. Prepayment and SASE required.

Hot Springs County

5th Judicial District Court 415 Arapahoe St, Thermopolis, WY 82443; phone: 307-864-3323; fax: 307-864-3210; hours 8AM-5PM (MST). *Felony, Civil Actions Over $7,000, Probate.*
Civil Records: Access: Mail, in person. Both court and visitors may perform in person searches. Search fee: $10.00 per name. Court makes copy: $1.00 for 1st page, $.50 each add'l. Self serve copy fee: $.50 per page. Required to search: name, years to search; also helpful: address. Civil cases indexed by defendant, plaintiff. Civil records on card index back to 1900s. Mail turnaround time 1 day.
Criminal Records: Access: Mail, in person. Both court and visitors may perform in person searches. Search fee: $10.00 per name. Court makes copy: $1.00 for 1st page, $.50 each add'l. Self serve copy fee: $.50 per page. Required to search: name, years to search, DOB, SSN; also helpful: address. Criminal records on card index back to 1900s. Mail turnaround time 1 day.

General Information: No juvenile, adoption or sexual data released. Will fax results to a local or toll free line. Certification fee: $.50 per page. Payee: Clerk of District Court. Personal checks accepted. Prepayment and SASE required.

Hot Springs Circuit Court 417 Arapahoe St, Thermopolis, WY 82443; phone: 307-864-5161; fax: 307-864-2067; hours 8AM-5PM (MST). *Misdemeanor, Civil Actions Under $7,000, Small Claims.*

Civil Records: Access: Mail, in person. Only the court performs in person searches; visitors may not. Search fee: $10.00 per name. Court makes copy: $1.00 for 1st page, $.50 each add'l. Required to search: name, years to search. Civil cases indexed by defendant, plaintiff. Civil records on computer from 1990, prior in card file. Mail turnaround time 2-3 days.

Criminal Records: Access: Mail, in person. Only the court performs in person searches; visitors may not. Search fee: $10.00 per name. Court makes copy: $1.00 for 1st page, $.50 each add'l. Required to search: name, years to search. Criminal records on computer from 1990, prior in card file to 1980. Mail turnaround time 2-3 days.

General Information: No closed case records released. Fee to fax results is $2 per document. Certification fee: $5.00 per document. Payee: Circuit Court. Business checks accepted. Prepayment and SASE required.

Johnson County

4th Judicial District Court 76 N Main, Buffalo, WY 82834; phone: 307-684-7271; fax: 307-684-5146; hours 8AM-5PM (MST). *Felony, Civil Actions Over $7,000, Probate.*

Civil Records: Access: Fax, mail, in person. Both court and visitors may perform in person searches. Search fee: $10.00 per name. Court makes copy: $1.00 first page; $.50 each add'l page; same fee for self serve. Required to search: name, years to search; also helpful: address. Civil cases indexed by defendant, plaintiff. Civil records on computer from 1989, card index since 1892. Mail turnaround time 1 week.

Criminal Records: Access: Fax, mail, in person. Both court and visitors may perform in person searches. Search fee: $10.00 per name. Court makes copy: $1.00 first page; $.50 each add'l page; same fee for self serve. Required to search: name, years to search; also helpful: address, DOB, SSN. Criminal records on computer from 1989, card index since 1892. Mail turnaround time 1 week.

General Information: No adoption or juvenile records released. Will fax results for $1.00 per page. Certification fee: $.50 per page. Payee: Clerk of District Court. In state personal checks accepted. Prepayment and SASE required.

Circuit Court 76 N Main St, Buffalo, WY 82834-1847; phone: 307-684-5720; fax: 307-684-7308; hours 8AM-5PM (MST). *Misdemeanor, Civil Actions Under $7,000, Small Claims.*
www.courts.state.wy.us/Brochure_files/jpbuf.htm
Note: Formally a Justice Court; became a Circuit Court on 1/03.

Civil Records: Access: Mail, fax, in person. Both court and visitors may perform in person searches. Search fee: $10.00. Court makes copy: $1.00 for 1st page; $.50 each add'l. Required to search: name, years to search; also helpful: address. Civil cases indexed by defendant, plaintiff. Civil records on computer since 1995; prior records on index cards. Mail turnaround time 2 days.

Criminal Records: Access: Mail, fax, in person. Both court and visitors may perform in person searches. Search fee: $10.00 per name. Court makes copy: $1.00 1st page; $.50 each add'l. Required to search: name, years to search, DOB; also helpful: SSN. Criminal records on computer since 5/90, card index back to 1979. Mail turnaround time 2 days.

General Information: Public terminal has criminal back to 1990 and civil back to 1995. No sex cases released. Will fax results for $2.00. Certification fee: $5 per document. Payee: Circuit Court. Personal checks accepted. Prepayment and SASE required.

Laramie County

1st Judicial District Court 309 W 20th St, #3205, PO Box 787, Cheyenne, WY 82003; phone: 307-633-4270; fax: 307-633-4277; hours 8AM-5PM (MST). *Felony, Misdemeanor, Civil Actions Over $7,000, Probate.*
www.laramiecounty.com/departments/district_court/index.asp

Civil Records: Access: Fax, mail, in person. Both court and visitors may perform in person searches. Search fee: $10.00 per name. Court makes copy: $1.00 for first page, $.50 each add'l; same fee for self serve. Required to search: name. Civil cases indexed by defendant, plaintiff. Civil records on card index to 1890; on computer back to 1992. Mail turnaround time 2 days.

Criminal Records: Access: Fax, mail, in person. Both court and visitors may perform in person searches. Search fee: $10.00 per name. Court makes copy: $1.00 for first page, $.50 each add'l; same fee for self serve. Required to search: name, years to search, DOB, SSN. Criminal records on card index to 1890; on computer back to 1992. Mail turnaround time 2 days.

General Information: Public terminal goes back to 1992. No juvenile or paternity records released. No fee to fax results. Will fax to 800 numbers only. Certification fee: $.50 per page. Payee: Laramie County Clerk of District Court. Business checks accepted. Prepayment and SASE required.

Laramie County Circuit Court 309 W 20th St, Rm 2300, Cheyenne, WY 82001; criminal phone: 307-633-4298; civil phone: 307-633-4326; fax: 307-633-4392; hours 8AM-5PM (MST). *Misdemeanor, Civil Actions Under $7,000, Eviction, Small Claims.*

Civil Records: Access: Fax, mail, in person. Both court and visitors may perform in person searches. Search fee: $10.00 per name. Court makes copy: $1.00 for 1st page, $.50 each add'l. Required to search: name, years to search; also helpful: address. Civil cases indexed by defendant, plaintiff. Civil records on computer from 1992, card index from late 1977. Mail turnaround time 48 hours.

Criminal Records: Access: Fax, mail, in person. Both court and visitors may perform in person searches. Search fee: $10.00 per name. Court makes copy: $1.00 for 1st page, $.50 each add'l. Required to search: name, years to search; also helpful: address. Criminal records on computer from 1988, card index from late 1977. Mail turnaround time 48 hours.

General Information: Public terminal has criminal back to 1988 and civil back to 1992. Fee to fax results is $2.00 per document. Certification fee: $5.00 per document. Payee: Laramie County Circuit Court. Business checks or in state checks only. Prepayment and SASE required.

Lincoln County

3rd Judicial District Court PO Drawer 510, Kemmerer, WY 83101; phone: 307-877-9056; fax: 307-877-6263; hours 8AM-5PM (MST). *Felony, Civil Actions Over $7,000, Probate.*

Civil Records: Access: Fax, mail, in person. Both court and visitors may perform in person searches. Search fee: $10.00 per name. Court makes copy: $1.00 for first page, $.50 each add'l; same fee for self serve. Required to search: name; also helpful: years to search, address. Civil cases indexed by defendant. Civil records on card index and computer back to 1916. Mail turnaround time same day.

Criminal Records: Access: Fax, mail, in person. Both court and visitors may perform in person searches. Search fee: $10.00 per name. Court makes copy: $1.00 for first page, $.50 each add'l; same fee for self serve. Required to search: name; also helpful: years to search, address, DOB, SSN. Criminal records on card index and computer back to 1916. Mail turnaround time same day.

General Information: No juvenile, sexual or PD records released. Will fax results $5.00 per doc. Certification fee: $2.50. Payee: 3rd Judicial District Court. Personal checks accepted. Prepayment and SASE required.

Lincoln Circuit Court PO Box 949, Kemmerer, WY 83101; phone: 307-877-4431; fax: 307-877-4936; hours 8AM-5PM (MST). *Misdemeanor, Civil Actions Under $7,000, Eviction, Small Claims.*

Civil Records: Access: Mail, in person. Only the court performs in person searches; visitors may not. Search fee: $10.00 per name. Court makes copy: $1.00 for 1st page, $.50 each add'l. Required to search: name, years to search. Civil cases indexed by defendant, plaintiff. Civil records on computer from 1/90, card index from 1984, prior data in archives. All search requests must be in writing. Mail turnaround time same day.

Criminal Records: Access: Mail, in person. Only the court performs in person searches; visitors may not. Search fee: $10.00 per name. Court makes copy: $1.00 for 1st page, $.50 each add'l. Required to search: name, years to search, DOB; also helpful: SSN. Criminal records on computer from 10/90, card index from 1984, prior in archives. All search requests must be in writing. Mail turnaround time same day.

General Information: No sexual or PD records released. Will fax results to local or toll free line. Certification fee: $5.00 per document. Payee: Lincoln Circuit Court. Business checks accepted. Out of state checks not accepted. Prepayment required. SASE requested.

Natrona County

7th Judicial District Court PO Box 2510, Clerk of District Court, 200 N Center, Casper, WY 82602; phone: 307-235-9243; fax: 307-235-9496; hours 8AM-5PM (MST). *Felony, Civil Actions Over $7,000, Probate.*
Note: The 9496 fax number is for record room. The non-record request fax number to clerk is 307-235-9493. No misdemeanor records, unless they were originally felony charges.

Civil Records: Access: Phone, fax, mail, in person. Both court and visitors may perform in person searches. Search fee: $10.00 per name. Court makes copy: $1.00 for first page, $.50 each add'l. Self serve copy fee: $.15 per page if non-court doc. Required to search: name, years to search; also helpful: address. Civil cases indexed by defendant, plaintiff. Civil records on computer, microfiche from 1891. Mail turnaround time 5 days.

Criminal Records: Access: Phone, fax, mail, in person. Both court and visitors may perform in person searches. Search fee: $10.00 per name. Court makes copy: $1.00 for first page, $.50 each add'l. Self serve copy fee: $.15 per page if non-court doc. Required to search: name, years to search; also helpful: address, DOB, SSN. Criminal records on computer, microfiche from 1891. Mail turnaround time 5 days.

General Information: Public terminal goes back to 1891. (Public terminal in Rm 202.) No adoption, juvenile, paternity, mental health records released. Will fax results $.30 per page plus $2.00 fee. Certification fee: $1.00 certify, $5.00 to authenticate. Payee: Clerk of District Court. Business checks accepted. Prepayment and SASE required.

Natrona Circuit Court 201 N David, Floor 5, Casper, WY 82601; phone: 307-235-9266; fax: 307-235-9331; hours 8AM-5PM (MST). *Misdemeanor, Civil Actions Under $7,000, Eviction, Small Claims.*

Civil Records: Access: Mail, in person. Only the court performs in person searches; visitors may not. Search fee: $10.00. Court makes copy: $1.00 for 1st page, $.50 each add'l. Required to search: name, years to search; also helpful: address. Civil cases indexed by defendant, plaintiff. Civil records on computer from 1994, on microfiche from 1891. All search requests must be in writing. Mail turnaround time 2-5 days.

Criminal Records: Access: Mail, in person. Only the court performs in person searches; visitors may not. Search fee: $10.00 per name. Court makes copy: $1.00 for 1st page, $.50 each add'l. Required to search: name, years to search; also helpful: address, DOB, SSN. Criminal records on computer from 1989, microfiche from 1891. All search requests must be in writing. Mail turnaround time 2-5 days.

General Information: No sexual, abuse records released. Fee to fax documents is $2.00 per doc; fax available for 800 numbers only. Certification fee: $5.00 per document. Payee: Natrona Circuit Court. Personal checks accepted. Prepayment and SASE required.

Niobrara County

8th Judicial District Court Clerk of District Court, PO Box 1318, Lusk, WY 82225; phone: 307-334-2736; criminal fax: 307-334-2703; same fax for civil/probate; hours 8AM-N, 1-4PM (MST). *Felony, Civil Actions Over $7,000, Probate.*

Civil Records: Access: Mail, in person. Visitors must perform in person searches themselves. Search fee: $10.00 per name. Court makes copy: $1.00 for first page, $.50 each add'l. Required to search: name, years to search. Civil cases indexed by defendant, plaintiff. Civil records on card index from early 1900s. Mail turnaround time 2 days.

Criminal Records: Access: Mail, in person. Both court and visitors may perform in person searches. Search fee: $10.00 per name. Court makes copy: $1.00 for 1st page, $.50 each add'l. Required to search: name, years to search, DOB, SSN. Criminal records on card index from 1913. Mail turnaround time 2 days.

General Information: No juvenile or adoption related released, no PD released. Fee to fax results is $1.00 per page. Certification fee: $.50 per page. Payee: Niobrara Clerk of District Court. No personal checks accepted. Prepayment and SASE required.

Circuit Court PO Box 209, 223 S Main St, Lusk, WY 82225; phone: 307-334-3845; fax: 307-334-3846; hours 9AM-N, 1-5PM (MST). *Misdemeanor, Civil Actions Under $7,000, Small Claims.*

Note: This was a Justice Court until 01/03.

Civil Records: Access: Mail, in person. Both court and visitors may perform in person searches. Search fee: $10.00 per name. Court makes copy: $1.00 for 1st page; $.50 each add'l. Required to search: name, years to search; also helpful: address. Civil cases indexed by plaintiff. Civil records on computer back to 2003, also index cards. Mail turnaround time 2 days.

Criminal Records: Access: Mail, in person. Both court and visitors may perform in person searches. Search fee: $10.00 per name. Court makes copy: $1.00 for 1st page, $.50 each add'l. Required to search: name, years to search, DOB, SSN, signed release; also helpful: address. Criminal records on computer from 1988, prior archived. Mail turnaround time 2 days.

General Information: No juvenile data released. Fee to fax results is $2 per doc. Certification fee: $5 per document. Payee: Niobrara Circuit Court. Personal checks accepted. Prepayment required. SASE requested.

Park County

5th Judicial District Court Clerk of District Court, PO Box 1960, Cody, WY 82414; phone: 307-527-8690; criminal fax: 307-527-8687; same fax for civil/probate; hours 8AM-5PM (MST). *Felony, Civil Actions Over $7,000, Probate.*
www.wtp.net/parkco/districtcourt.htm
Civil Records: Access: Phone, fax, mail, in person. Both court and visitors may perform in person searches. Search fee: $10.00 per name. Court makes copy: $1.00 for first page, $.50 each add'l. Required to search: name, years to search; also helpful: address.

Civil cases indexed by defendant, plaintiff. Civil records on computer from 1989, card index back to 1911. Mail turnaround time 6 hours.

Criminal Records: Access: Phone, fax, mail, in person. Both court and visitors may perform in person searches. Search fee: $10.00 per name. Court makes copy: $1.00 for first page, $.50 each add'l. Required to search: name, years to search; also helpful: DOB, SSN. Criminal records on computer from 1989, card index back to 1911. Mail turnaround time same day.

General Information: Public use terminal available. No juvenile, adoptions or PD released. Fee to fax results is $2.00 per page. Certification fee: $.50 per page. Payee: Clerk of District Court. Personal checks not accepted. Prepayment required. SASE preferred.

Cody Circuit Court 1002 Sheridan Ave, Cody, WY 82414; phone: 307-527-8590; fax: 307-527-8596; hours 8AM-5PM (MST). *Misdemeanor, Civil Actions Under $7,000, Eviction, Small Claims.*

Note: On January 2, 1995 this court changed status from a Justice Court to a Circuit Court. They also have records for the Powell Circuit Court Branch.

Civil Records: Access: Mail, in person. Only the court performs in person searches; visitors may not. Search fee: $10.00 per name. Court makes copy: $1.00 for 1st page, $.50 each add'l. Required to search: name, years to search; also helpful: address. Civil cases indexed by defendant, plaintiff. Civil records on computer since 8/95; limited records available prior to 8/95. Mail turnaround time 5 days.

Criminal Records: Access: Mail, in person. Only the court performs in person searches; visitors may not. Search fee: $10.00 per name. Court makes copy: $1.00 for 1st page, $.50 each add'l. Required to search: name, years to search, DOB, SSN (one or other is required) also helpful: address. Criminal records on computer since 1990; limited records available prior to 1990. Mail turnaround time 5 days.

General Information: No sexual or confidential data released. Will fax results to local or toll free line. Certification fee: $5.00 per document. Payee: Park County Circuit Court. Business checks accepted. Prepayment and SASE required.

Powell Circuit Court 109 W 14th, Powell, WY 82435; phone: 307-754-8890; fax: 307-754-8896; hours 8AM-N, 1-5PM (MST). *Misdemeanor, Civil Actions Under $7,000, Eviction, Small Claims.*

Note: Powell court misdemeanor records are also available at the main Circuit Court in Cody.

Civil Records: Access: Mail, in person. Only the court performs in person searches; visitors may not. Search fee: $10.00 per name. Court makes copy: $1.00 for 1st page, $.50 each add'l. Required to search: name, years to search. Civil cases indexed by defendant, plaintiff. Civil records on computer from 1995; prior records very poor. Mail turnaround time 1 week.

Criminal Records: Access: Mail, in person. Only the court performs in person searches; visitors may not. Search fee: $10.00 per name. Court makes copy: $1.00 for 1st page, $.50 each add'l. Required to search: name, years to search, DOB or SSN. Criminal records on computer from 1991; prior records very poor. Mail turnaround time 1 week.

General Information: No sexual, confidential records released. Fee to fax results is $2.00 per document. No certification fee. Payee: Park County Circuit Court. Personal checks accepted. Prepayment and SASE required.

Platte County

8th Judicial District Court PO Box 158, Wheatland, WY 82201; phone: 307-322-3857; fax: 307-322-5402; hours 8AM-5PM (MST). *Felony, Civil Actions Over $7,000, Probate.*

Civil Records: Access: Mail, fax, in person. Both court and visitors may perform in person searches. Search fee: $10.00 per name. Court makes copy: $1.00 for first page, $.50 each add'l. Required to search: name, years to search; also helpful: address.

Civil cases indexed by defendant. Civil records on card file index last 15 yrs, then to archives. Mail turnaround time same day.

Criminal Records: Access: Mail, fax, in person. Both court and visitors may perform in person searches. Search fee: $10.00 per name. Court makes copy: $1.00 for first page, $.50 each add'l. Required to search: name, years to search; also helpful: address, DOB, SSN. Criminal records on card file index last 15 yrs, then to archives. Mail turnaround time same day.

General Information: No juvenile data released. Will fax results to local or toll free line. Certification fee: $.50 per page. Payee: Clerk of the Court. Personal checks accepted. Prepayment and SASE required.

Circuit Court PO Box 306, Wheatland, WY 82201; phone: 307-322-3441; fax: 307-322-1371; hours 8AM-5PM (MST). *Misdemeanor, Civil Actions Under $3,000, Small Claims.*

Note: This former Justice Court became a Circuit Court as of 01/03.

Civil Records: Access: Phone, mail, fax, in person. Only the court performs in person searches; visitors may not. Search fee: $10.00 per name. Court makes copy: included in search fee. Required to search: name, years to search; also helpful: address. Civil cases indexed by defendant. Civil records on computer since 11/95; on card index since 1976. Fax copy of check, when faxing. Mail turnaround time 2 days.

Criminal Records: Access: Phone, mail, fax, in person. Only the court performs in person searches; visitors may not. Search fee: $10.00 per name. Court makes copy: included in search fee. Required to search: name, years to search, signed release, DOB; also helpful: address, SSN. Criminal records on computer from 11/92, card index from 1976. Fax copy of check, when faxing. Mail turnaround time 2 days.

General Information: No juvenile data released. Fee to fax results is included in search fee. Certification fee: $5.00 per document. Payee: Platte County Circuit Court. Business checks accepted. Prepayment and SASE required.

Sheridan County

4th Judicial District Court 224 S. Main, #B-11, Sheridan, WY 82801; phone: 307-674-2960; fax: 307-674-2589; hours 8AM-5PM (MST). *Felony, Civil Actions Over $7,000, Probate.*

Civil Records: Access: Phone, mail, fax, in person. Both court and visitors may perform in person searches. Search fee: Circuit Court. Court makes copy: $1.00 for first page, $.50 each add'l. Required to search: name, years to search. Civil cases indexed by defendant, plaintiff. Civil records archived from 1800s. Mail turnaround time 1 week.

Criminal Records: Access: Phone, mail, fax, in person. Both court and visitors may perform in person searches. Search fee: $10.00 per name. Court makes copy: $1.00 for first page, $.50 each add'l. Required to search: name, years to search, DOB, SSN. Criminal records archived from late 1800s. Mail turnaround time 1 week.

General Information: No sex related, juvenile or adoption cases released except by judges permission. Fee to fax results is $5.00 per doc. Certification fee: $.50 per page. Payee: Clerk of District Court. Personal checks accepted. Prepayment and SASE required.

Circuit Court 224 S Main, #B-7, Sheridan, WY 82801; phone: 307-674-2940; fax: 307-674-2944; hours 8AM-5PM (MST). *Misdemeanor, Civil Actions Under $7,000, Eviction, Small Claims.*

Civil Records: Access: Mail, in person. Only the court performs in person searches; visitors may not. Search fee: $10.00 per name. Court makes copy: $1.00 for 1st page, $.50 each add'l. Required to search: name, years to search; also helpful: DOB, SSN, address. Civil cases indexed by defendant, plaintiff. Civil records on cards from 1983; computerized records go back to 1983. Mail turnaround time 48 hours.

Criminal Records: Access: Mail, in person. Only the court performs in person searches; visitors may not. Search fee: $10.00 per name. Court makes copy: $1.00 for 1st page, $.50 each add'l. Required to search: name, years to search; also helpful: address, DOB, SSN. Criminal records on computer from 1983, on cards from 1983. Mail turnaround time 48 hours.
General Information: Identity of victims not released in sexual assault cases. Certification fee: $5.00 per document. Payee: Sheridan Circuit Court. Personal checks accepted. Prepayment and SASE required.

Sublette County

9th Judicial District Court PO Box 764, Pinedale, WY 82941-0764; phone: 307-367-4376; criminal fax: 307-367-6474; same fax for civil/probate; hours 8AM-5PM (MST). *Felony, Civil Actions Over $7,000, Probate.*
Civil Records: Access: Mail, in person. Both court and visitors may perform in person searches. Search fee: $10.00 per name. Court makes copy: $1.00 for first page, $.50 each add'l; same fee for self serve. Required to search: name; also helpful: years to search, address. Civil cases indexed by defendant, plaintiff. Civil records on card file from 1923. Mail turnaround time same day.
Criminal Records: Access: Mail, in person. Both court and visitors may perform in person searches. Search fee: $10.00 per name. Court makes copy: $1.00 for first page, $.50 each add'l; same fee for self serve. Required to search: name, years to search; also helpful: address, DOB, SSN. Criminal records go back to 1923. Mail turnaround time same day.
General Information: No PD or juvenile records released. Will fax results for $3.00 1st page, $1.00 each add'l. No certification fee. Payee: Clerk of District Court. Personal checks accepted. Prepayment and SASE required.

Sublette Circuit Court PO Box 1796, 40 S Fremont Ave, Pinedale, WY 82941; phone: 307-367-2556; fax: 307-367-2658; hours 8AM-5PM (MST). *Misdemeanor, Civil Actions Under $7,000, Eviction, Small Claims.*
Civil Records: Access: Mail, in person. Only the court performs in person searches; visitors may not. Search fee: $10.00 per name. Court makes copy: $1.00 for 1st page, $.50 each add'l. Required to search: name, years to search; also helpful: address. Civil cases indexed by defendant & plaintiff. Civil records go back 21 years, computerized from 1998. Mail turnaround time 2 business days.
Criminal Records: Access: Mail, in person. Only the court performs in person searches; visitors may not. Search fee: $10.00 per name. Court makes copy: $1.00 for 1st page, $.50 each add'l. Required to search: name, years to search; also helpful: address, SSN. Criminal records on computer back to 1993. Mail turnaround time 2 business days.
General Information: Will fax back documents no charge. No certification fee. Payee: Circuit Court of Sublette County. Will accept in state checks only. Prepayment required.

Sweetwater County

3rd Judicial District Court PO Box 430, Green River, WY 82935; phone: 307-872-6440; fax: 307-872-6439; hours 9AM-5PM (MST). *Felony, Civil Actions Over $7,000, Probate.*
Civil Records: Access: Phone, fax, mail, in person. Both court and visitors may perform in person searches. Search fee: $10.00 per name. Court makes copy: $1.00 for first page, $.50 each add'l. Required to search: name, years to search. Civil cases indexed by defendant, plaintiff. Civil records on computer from 1985, on microfiche from 1960, archived from late 1800. Mail turnaround time same day.
Criminal Records: Access: Phone, fax, mail, in person. Both court and visitors may perform in person searches. Search fee: $10.00 per name. Court makes copy: $1.00 for first page, $.50 each add'l. Required to search: name, years to search. Criminal

records on computer from 1985, on microfiche from 1960, archived from late 1800. Mail turnaround time same day.
General Information: Public terminal goes back to 1985. No juvenile, paternity, or adoption records released. Will fax results $2.00 plus $.50 per page. Certification fee: 1st page free, $.50 each add'l. Payee: Clerk of District Court. Business checks accepted. Prepayment and SASE required.

Green River Circuit Court PO Drawer 1720, Green River, WY 82935; phone: 307-872-6460; fax: 307-872-6375; hours 8AM-5PM (MST). *Misdemeanor, Civil Actions Under $7,000, Eviction, Small Claims.*
Civil Records: Access: Mail, in person. Only the court performs in person searches; visitors may not. Search fee: $10.00. Court makes copy: $1.00 for 1st page, $.50 each add'l. Required to search: name, years to search. Civil cases indexed by defendant, plaintiff. Civil records on computer from 1994, in card file from 1978-1994, archived prior to 1978. Requests must be in writing. Mail turnaround time same day.
Criminal Records: Access: Mail, in person. Only the court performs in person searches; visitors may not. Search fee: $10.00 per name. Court makes copy: $1.00 for 1st page, $.50 each add'l. Required to search: name, years to search, DOB; also helpful: SSN. Criminal Records computerized since 1990, on card file from 1978 to 1990. Requests must be in writing. Mail turnaround time same day.
General Information: No sealed, sexual assault records released. Fee to fax results is $2.00 per fax. Certification fee: $5.00 per document. Payee: Sweetwater County Circuit Court. Business checks accepted. In-state checks only. Prepayment required.

Sweetwater Circuit Court PO Box 2028, 731 "C" St, Rock Springs, WY 82902; phone: 307-352-6817; fax: 307-352-6758; hours 8AM-5PM (MST). *Misdemeanor, Civil Actions Under $7,000, Eviction, Small Claims.*
Civil Records: Access: Fax, mail, in person. Only the court performs in person searches; visitors may not. Search fee: $10.00 per name. Court makes copy: $1.00 for 1st page, $.50 each add'l. Required to search: name, years to search; also helpful: address. Civil cases indexed by defendant, plaintiff. Civil records on computer from 1995, archived to 1981. Mail turnaround time 2 days.
Criminal Records: Access: Fax, mail, in person. Only the court performs in person searches; visitors may not. Search fee: $10.00 per name. Court makes copy: $1.00 for 1st page, $.50 each add'l. Required to search: name, years to search; also helpful: address, DOB, SSN. Criminal records on computer from 1989, archived to 1981. Mail turnaround time 2 days.
General Information: No sexual assault, sealed records released. Fee to fax results is $2.00 per doc. Certification fee: $5.00 per doc. Payee: Sweetwater Circuit Court. Business checks accepted. Prepayment and SASE required.

Teton County

9th Judicial District Court PO Box 4460, Jackson, WY 83001; phone: 307-733-2533; fax: 307-734-1562; hours 8AM-5PM (MST). *Felony, Civil Actions Over $7,000, Probate.*
Civil Records: Access: Phone, fax, mail, in person. Both court and visitors may perform in person searches. Search fee: $10.00 per name. Court makes copy: $1.00 for first page, $.50 each add'l. Required to search: name, years to search; also helpful: address. Civil cases indexed by defendant, plaintiff. Civil records on computer since 1990, card index back to 1920s. Mail turnaround time 2 days.
Criminal Records: Access: Phone, fax, mail, in person. Both court and visitors may perform in person searches. Search fee: $10.00 per name. Court makes copy: $1.00 for first page, $.50 each add'l. Required to search: name, years to search; also helpful: address, DOB, SSN. Criminal records on

computer since 1990, card index back to 1920s. Mail turnaround time 2 days.
General Information: Public use terminal available. No juvenile or adoption records released. Will fax results to local or toll free line. Certification fee: $.50 per page. Payee: Clerk of District Court. Personal checks accepted. Prepayment and SASE required.

Circuit Court PO Box 2906 (180 S King St), Jackson, WY 83001; phone: 307-733-7713; fax: 307-733-8694; hours 8AM-5PM (MST). *Misdemeanor, Civil Actions Under $7,000, Small Claims under $3,000.*
Note: This was a Justice Court until 01/03.
Civil Records: Access: Mail, in person. Only the court performs in person searches; visitors may not. Search fee: $10.00 per name. Court makes copy: $1.00 for 1st page, $.50 each add'l. Required to search: name, years to search; also helpful-DOB, SSN. Civil cases indexed by defendant, plaintiff. Civil records on docket books back to 1979. Actual files 5 years. Mail turnaround time 3-4 days; may be longer for pre-1992 criminal records.
Criminal Records: Access: Mail, in person. Only the court performs in person searches; visitors may not. Search fee: $10.00 per name. Court makes copy: $1.00 for 1st page, $.50 each add'l. Required to search: name, years to search, DOB, SSN. Criminal records citations on computer from 1991. No citation record older than 5 years. On docket books and files back to 1979. Mail turnaround time 3-4 days; may be longer for pre-1992 criminal records.
General Information: No juvenile, sexual or PD released. Fee to fax results is $2.00 per document. Certification fee: $5.00 per document. Payee: Teton County Circuit Court. Personal checks accepted. Prepayment required. SASE requested.

Uinta County

3rd Judicial District Court PO Drawer 1906, Attn: Clerk of District Court, Evanston, WY 82931; phone: 307-783-0456; fax: 307-783-0400; hours 8AM-5PM (MST). *Felony, Civil Actions Over $7,000, Probate.*
www.uintacounty.com
Civil Records: Access: Mail, in person. Visitors must perform in person searches themselves. Search fee: $10.00 per name. Court makes copy: $1.00 first page; $.50 each add'l. Required to search: name, years to search; also helpful: address. Civil cases indexed by defendant, plaintiff. Civil records on microfiche from the late 1800s. Mail turnaround time 1 day.
Criminal Records: Access: Phone, fax, mail, in person. Visitors must perform in person searches themselves. Search fee: $10.00 per name. Court makes copy: $1.00 first page; $.50 each add'l. Required to search: name, years to search, DOB, SSN; also helpful: address. Criminal records on microfiche since 1938. Mail turnaround time 1 day.
General Information: Signed notarized release necessary on confidential cases. Fee to fax results is $1.00 per page, if not related to an already paid search. Certification fee: $.50 per seal. Payee: Clerk of District Court. Personal checks accepted. Prepayment and SASE required.

Uinta Circuit Court 225 9th St, 2nd Fl, Evanston, WY 82931; phone: 307-789-2471; fax: 307-789-5062; hours 8AM-5PM (MST). *Misdemeanor, Civil Actions Under $7,000, Eviction, Small Claims.*
Civil Records: Access: Mail, in person. Only the court performs in person searches; visitors may not. Search fee: $10.00 per name. Court makes copy: $1.00 for 1st page, $.50 each add'l. Required to search: name, years to search; also helpful: address. Civil cases indexed by defendant. Civil records on computer from 1994, prior on card index. All requests must be in writing. Mail turnaround time 1 week.
Criminal Records: Access: Mail, in person. Only the court performs in person searches; visitors may not. Search fee: $10.00 per name. Court makes copy:

$1.00 for 1st page, $.50 each add'l. Required to search: name, years to search; also helpful: address, DOB, SSN. Criminal records on computer since 1989, prior on index cards. All requests must be in writing. Mail turnaround time 1 week.

General Information: No juvenile records released. Fee to fax results is $2.00 per document. Certification fee: $5.00 per doc. Payee: Uinta County Court. Out of state checks not accepted. Prepayment required. SASE requested.

Washakie County

5th Judicial District Court PO Box 862, Worland, WY 82401; phone: 307-347-4821; fax: 307-347-4325; hours 8AM-5PM (MST). *Felony, Civil Actions Over $7,000, Probate.*

Civil Records: Access: Fax, mail, in person. Both court and visitors may perform in person searches. Search fee: $10.00 per name. Court makes copy: $1.00 for first page, $.50 each add'l; same fee for self serve. Required to search: name; also helpful: years to search, address. Civil cases indexed by defendant. Civil records on computer back to 1985, prior on file index. Mail turnaround time same day when possible.

Criminal Records: Access: Phone, fax, mail, in person. Both court and visitors may perform in person searches. Search fee: $10.00 per name. Court makes copy: $1.00 for first page, $.50 each add'l; same fee for self serve. Required to search: name, years to search; also helpful: address, DOB, SSN. Criminal records on computer back to 1985, prior on file index. Mail turnaround time same day when possible.

General Information: No juvenile, sexual or PD released. Will fax results $1.00 per page. Certification fee: $.50 per document. Payee: Clerk of Court. Personal checks accepted. Prepayment and SASE required.

Circuit Court PO Box 927, Worland, WY 82401; phone: 307-347-2702; fax: 307-347-8459; hours 8AM-5PM (MST). *Misdemeanor, Civil Actions Under $7,000, Small Claims.*

Note: This was a Justice Court until 01/03.

Civil Records: Access: Mail, fax. Only the court performs in person searches; visitors may not. Search fee: $10.00 per name. Court makes copy: $1.00 for 1st page; $.50 each add'l. Required to search: name, years to search. Civil cases indexed by defendant. Civil records on computer since 1998, on card index from late 1970, prior archived. Mail turnaround time same day.

Criminal Records: Access: Mail, fax, in person. Only the court performs in person searches; visitors may not. Search fee: $10.00 per name. Court makes copy: $1.00 for 1st page; $.50 each add'l. Required to search: name, years to search, DOB; also helpful: SSN. Criminal records on computer since 1995, on card index from late 1970, prior archived. Mail turnaround time same day.

General Information: No juvenile or PD released; criminal only. Fee to fax results is $2.00 per document. Certification fee: $5.00 per document. Payee: Circuit Court. Personal checks accepted. Prepayment required.

Weston County

6th Judicial District Court 1 W Main, Newcastle, WY 82701; phone: 307-746-4778; criminal fax: 307-746-4778; same fax for civil/probate; hours 8AM-5PM (MST). *Felony, Civil Actions Over $7,000, Probate.*

Civil Records: Access: Mail, fax, in person. Both court and visitors may perform in person searches. Search fee: $10.00 per name. Court makes copy: $1.00 for 1st page, $.50 each add'l. Required to search: name; also helpful: years to search, address. Civil cases indexed by defendant, plaintiff. Civil records on card index from 1913; computerized back to 1999. Mail turnaround time same day.

Criminal Records: Access: Phone, fax, mail, in person. Both court and visitors may perform in person searches. Search fee: $10.00 per name. Court makes copy: $1.00 for 1st page, $.50 each add'l. Required to search: name; also helpful: years to search, address, DOB, SSN. Criminal records on card index from 1913; computerized back to 1999. Mail turnaround time same day.

General Information: No juvenile, sexual or PD released. Fee to fax results is $2.00 per page. Certification fee: $.50 per certification. Payee: Clerk of District Court. Personal checks accepted. Prepayment and SASE required.

Circuit Court 6 W Warwick, Newcastle, WY 82701; phone: 307-746-3547; fax: 307-746-3558; hours 8AM-5PM (MST). *Misdemeanor, Civil Actions Under $7,000, Small Claims.*

Note: This was a Justice Court until 01/03.

Civil Records: Access: Mail, fax, in person. Only the court performs in person searches; visitors may not. Search fee: $10.00 (no charge if in person). Court makes copy: $1.00 first page; $.50 each add'l; same fee for self serve. Required to search: name, DOB, years to search; also helpful: address. Civil cases indexed by defendant. Civil records in files back to 1970s; on computer back to 1998. Mail turnaround time minimum 1 day.

Criminal Records: Access: Fax, mail, in person. Only the court performs in person searches; visitors may not. Search fee: $10.00 (no charge if in person). Court makes copy: $1.00 first page; $.50 each add'l; same fee for self serve. Required to search: name, years to search, DOB; also helpful: address, offense, date of offense, SSN. Criminal records in files back to 1970s; on computer back to 1996. Mail turnaround time minimum 1 day.

General Information: Fee to fax results is $2.00 per document or no charge if search fee paid. Certification fee: $5.00 per document. Payee: Circuit Court. Business checks accepted. Prepayment required.

Wyoming Recording Offices

ORGANIZATION: 23 counties, 23 recording offices. The recording officer is County Clerk. The entire state is in the Mountain Time Zone (MST).

REAL ESTATE RECORDS: County Clerks will not perform real estate searches. Copy fees are usually $1.00 per page, and certification fees are usually $2.00 per document. The Assessor maintains property tax records.

UCC RECORDS: Since 07/1/2001, all filings have been centralized at the state. Prior, financing statements were usually filed with the County Clerk and accounts receivable and farm products require dula filing at the state level as well. All recording offices will perform UCC searches. Use search request form UCC-11. Searches fees are usually $10.00 per debtor name. Copy fees vary.

TAX LIEN RECORDS: Federal tax liens on personal property of businesses are filed with the Secretary of State. Other federal and all state tax liens are filed with the County Clerk. Most counties will perform tax lien searches. Search fees are usually $10.00 per name.

ONLINE ACCESS: Teton county offers online access to the County Clerk's database of recorded documents.

Albany County

County Clerk, 525 Grand Ave. Rm202, Laramie, WY 82070. 307-721-5516, R/E recording phone-307-721-2547, UCC recording phone-307-721-2541; fax-307-721-2544; hours: 9AM-5PM.
Records indexed on computer back to 1997. Only the public may search. Copy fee $.25 per page. Cert fee- $3.00 per copy. Payee- Albany County Clerk. **Other phones:** Treasurer- 307-721-2502; Appraiser/Auditor- 307-721-2511; Elections- 307-721-2546; Vital Records- 307-777-7591. **Property tax/Assessor-** 307-721-2511.

Big Horn County

County Clerk, PO Box 31, Basin, WY 82410. 307-568-2357; fax-307-568-9375; hours: 8AM-5PM. www.bighorncountywy.gov
Separate indices to search include receiving books, bound books. Office will perform a UCC search but public must search other records themselves. Will search computerized UCC records only, search includes tax liens. UCC search per debtor name-$10.00. Separate federal/state tax lien search-$10.00 per debtor. Copy fee $1.00 per page. Tax lien copy- $10.00 per name. Cert fee- $2.00 per doc plus copy fee. Payee- Big Horn County Clerk. **Other phones:** Treasurer- 307-568-2578; Elections-307-568-2357; Vital Records- 307-568-2357. **Property tax/Assessor-** PO Box 547, Basin, Wy 82410; 307-568-2547, assessor fax- 307-568-2013.

Campbell County

County Clerk, PO Box 3010, Gillette, WY 82717-3010. 307-682-7285; fax-307-687-6455; hours: 8AM-5PM.
Record index not computerized. Office personnel or visitors may perform searches. Search fee $10.00 per name. Will not search real estate records. Copy fee $.50 each then $.15 each after 1st 10 pages. Cert fee- $5.00 per doc plus copy fee. Payee- Campbell County Clerk. **Property tax/Assessor-** 307-682-7266.

Carbon County

County Clerk, PO Box 6; Courthouse, Rawlins, WY 82301. 307-328-2664, R/E recording phone-307-328-2677, UCC recording phone-307-328-2667; fax-307-328-2669; hours: 8AM-5PM.
Records indexed on a public use terminal back to 1992. Office personnel or visitors may perform searches. Search fee $10.00 per name. Copy fee $.25 per page. Cert fee- $3.00 per doc plus copy fee. Payee- Carbon County Clerk. **Other phones:** Treasurer- 307-328-2662; Elections- 307-328-2650; Vital Records- 307-328-2670. **Property tax/Assessor-** 307-328-2637.

Converse County

County Clerk, 107 North 5th St; #114, Douglas, WY 82633-0990. 307-358-2244; fax-307-358-5998; hours: 8AM-5PM.
All records in one index. Office will perform a UCC search but public must search other records themselves. Copy fee $.50 per page. Cert fee- $2.00 per doc plus copy fee. **Other phones:** Treasurer- 307-358-3120; Elections- 307-358-2244. **Property tax/Assessor-** PO Box 57, Douglas, WY 82633; 307-358-2741.

Crook County

County Clerk, PO Box 37, Sundance, WY 82729. 307-283-1323; fax-307-283-3038; hours: 8AM-5PM.
All records in one index. Office will perform a UCC search but public must search other records themselves. Tax liens included in UCC search. UCC search per debtor name- $10.00. Separate federal tax lien search- $10.00 per debtor. Copy fee $.50 per page. Cert fee- $3.00 per doc plus copy fee. Payee- Crook County Clerk. **Other phones:** Treasurer- 307-283-1244. **Property tax/Assessor-** PO Box 365, Sundance, WY 82729; 307-283-2054.

Fremont County

County Clerk, 450 N. 2nd St; Rm 220, Lander, WY 82520. 307-332-2405, R/E recording phone-307-332-1127, UCC recording phone-307-332-1125; fax-307-332-1132; hours: 8AM-5PM. www.fremontcounty.org
All records in one index. Records indexed on computer. Office will perform a UCC and Tax lien search but public must search other records themselves. General index search fee $10.00 per name. Copy fee $.75 per page. Cert fee- $3.00 per page plus copy fee. Payee- Fremont County Clerk. **Other phones:** Treasurer- 307-322-1105; Elections- 307-332-1089; Vital Records- 307-332-1127. **Property tax/Assessor-** 307-332-1188.

Goshen County

County Clerk, PO Box 160, Torrington, WY 82240. 307-532-4051; fax-307-532-7375; hours: 7:30AM-4PM.
Only the public may search. Copy fee $1.00 per page. Cert fee- $5.00. Payee- Goshen County Clerk. **Other phones:** Treasurer- 307-532-5151; Elections- 307-532-4051. **Property tax/Assessor-** 307-532-2349.

Hot Springs County

County Clerk, 415 Arapahoe St; Courthouse, Thermopolis, WY 82443-2783. 307-864-3515; fax-307-864-3333; hours: 8AM-5PM.
Record index not computerized. Office will perform a UCC search but public must search other records themselves. UCC search per debtor name- $10.00. Copy fee $.25 per page. Cert fee- $3.00 per doc plus copy fee. Payee- Hot Springs County Clerk. **Other phones:** Treasurer- 307-864-3616. **Property tax/Assessor-** 307-864-3414.

Johnson County

County Clerk, 76 N. Main St, Buffalo, WY 82834. 307-684-7272; fax-307-684-2708; hours: 8AM-5PM. www.johnsoncountywyoming.org
Separate indices to search include surface ownership index and mineral ownership index. Record index not computerized. Office will perform a UCC search but public must search other records themselves. Search fee $10.00 per name. Copy fee $.50 per page. Cert fee- $3.00 per doc plus copy fee. Payee- Johnson County Clerk. **Other phones:** Treasurer- 307-684-7302. **Property tax/Assessor-** same address as above. 307-684-7392.

Laramie County

County Clerk, PO Box 608, Cheyenne, WY 82003. 307-633-4351, R/E recording phone-307-633-4350; fax-307-633-4240; hours: 8AM-5PM. www.laramiecountyclerk.com
Records indexed on a public use terminal back to 1985. Office personnel or visitors may perform searches. Search fee $10.00 per name. Copy fee $.25 per page. Cert fee- $3.00 per doc plus copy fee. **Other phones:** Treasurer- 307-633-4225; Elections- 307-633-4242; Vital Records- 307-777-7591. **Property tax/Assessor-** 307-633-4307.

Lincoln County

County Clerk, PO Box 670, Kemmerer, WY 83101-0670. 307-877-9056, R/E recording phone-307-877-9056 x305, UCC recording phone-307-877-9056 x304; fax-307-877-3101; hours: 8AM-5PM. www.lincolncountywy.org
Record index not computerized. Office will perform a UCC search but public must search other records themselves. UCC search per debtor name- $10.00 per name. Copy fee $.50 per page. Cert fee- $3.00 per doc plus copy fee. Payee- Lincoln County Clerk. **Other phones:** Treasurer- 307-877-9056 x345; Elections- 307-877-9056 x303. **Property tax/Assessor-** 307-877-9056 x330.

Natrona County

County Clerk, PO Box 863, Casper, WY 82602. 307-235-9270, R/E recording phone-307-235-9206, UCC recording phone-307-235-9207; fax-307-235-9367; hours: 8AM-5PM. www.natronacounty-wy.gov
Search fee $10.00 per debtor. Will not search real estate records. Will search UCC records. Copy fee $.25 per page. Cert fee- $3.00 per doc plus copy fee. Payee- Natrona County Clerk. **Other phones:** Treasurer- 307-235-9370; Elections- 307-235-9217; Vital Records- 307-777-7591. **Property tax/Assessor-** 200 N Center #140, Casper, WY 82601; 307-235-9444.

Niobrara County

County Clerk, PO Box 420, Lusk, WY 82225. 307-334-2211; fax-307-334-3013; hours: 8AM-4PM.
Separate indices to search include Deeds, Mtgs, Misc. Record index not computerized. Office will perform a UCC search but public must search other records themselves. Copy fee $.25 per page. Cert fee- $3.00. **Other phones:** Treasurer- 307-334-2432; Elections- 307-334-2211; Vital Records- 307-777-7591. **Property tax/Assessor-** PO Box 120, Lusk, WY 82225; 307-334-3201.

Park County

County Clerk, 1002 Sheridan Ave.; Courthouse, Cody, WY 82414. 307-527-8600; fax-307-527-8626; hours: 8AM-N, 1-5PM.

www.parkcounty.us/countyclerk.htm
All records in one index. Records indexed on a public use terminal. Office will perform a UCC search but public must search other records themselves. UCC search or tax lien search per debtor name- $10.00. Copy fee $.50 per page; $.25 self serve. Cert fee- $5.00 per cert plus copy fee. Payee- park County Clerk. **Online access to Warrants, Most Wanted, Sex Offender records:** Search the sheriff's lists free at www.cityofcody.com/cpd/. **Other phones:** Treasurer- 307-527-8630; Elections- 307-527-8620. **Property tax/Assessor-** 307-527-8650.

Platte County

County Clerk, PO Drawer 728, Wheatland, WY 82201. 307-322-2315; fax-307-322-2245; hours: 7AM-4PM.
All records in one index. Records indexed on computer back to 2/2002. Search fee $10.00 per name. Will not search real estate records. Copy fee $.50 per page. Cert fee- $3.00 plus copy fee. Payee- Platte County Clerk. **Other phones:** Treasurer- 307-322-2092; Elections- 307-322-2315.

Property tax/Assessor- PO Box 895, Wheatland, WY 82201; 307-322-2858.

Sheridan County

County Clerk, 224 S. Main St; #B-2, Sheridan, WY 82801-9998. 307-674-2500; fax-307-674-2529; hours: 8AM-5PM.
Record index not computerized. Office personnel or visitors may perform searches. Search fee $10.00 per name. Copy fee $1.00 per page. Cert fee- $5.00 per doc plus copy fee. Payee- Sheridan County Clerk. **Other phones:** Treasurer- 307-674-6522; Elections- 307-674-2515. **Property tax/Assessor-** 307-674-2535.

Sublette County

County Clerk, PO Box 250, Pinedale, WY 82941-0250. 307-367-4372; fax-307-367-6396; hours: 8AM-5PM.
All records in one index. Records indexed on a public use terminal back to 1993. Office will perform a UCC and Tax lien search but public must search other records themselves. Search fee $10.00. Copy fee $.25 per page. Cert fee- $3.00 per page plus copy fee. Payee- County Clerk. **Other phones:** Treasurer- 307-367-4373; Elections- 307-367-4372. **Property tax/Assessor-** PO Box 2057, Pinedale, WY 82941; 307-367-4374.

Sweetwater County

County Clerk, PO Box 730, Green River, WY 82935. 307-872-6400, R/E recording phone-307-872-6409, UCC recording phone-307-872-6406 or 6407; fax-307-872-6337; hours: 9AM-5PM.

www.co.sweet.wy.us/clerk
Separate indices to search include grantor/grantee, legal description. Records indexed on a public use terminal back to 1985. Only the public may search. Copy fee $.25 per copy. Cert fee- $3.00 per doc plus copy fee. Payee- Sweetwater County Clerk. **Other phones:** Treasurer- 307-872-6389; Appraiser/Auditor- 307-872-6400; Elections- 307-872-6400; Vital Records- 307-872-6407 (marriage only). **Property tax/Assessor-** 80 W Flaming Gorge Way #122, Green River, WY 82935; 307-872-6416.

Teton County

County Clerk, PO Box 1727, Jackson, WY 83001. 307-733-4430, UCC recording phone-307-733-4433; fax-307-739-8681; hours: 8AM-5PM.
http://www2.tetonwyo.org/clerk/
All records in one index. Records indexed on a public use terminal back to 3/1991. Only the public may search. Copy fee $1.00 per page. Cert

fee- $5.00 per page plus copy fee. **Online access to Real Estate, Lien, Recording records:** Access to the Clerk's database of scanned images is free at http://www2.tetonwyo.org/clerk/query/. Search for complete documents back to 7/1996; partial documents back to 4/1991. **Other phones:** Treasurer- 307-733-4770; Elections- 307-733-7733; Vital Records- 307-777-7591. **Property tax/Assessor-** 307-733-4960.

Uinta County

County Clerk, PO Box 810, Evanston, WY 82931-0810. 307-783-0308, R/E recording phone-307-783-0304, UCC recording phone-307-783-0308; fax-307-783-0376; hours: 8AM-5PM.
www.uintacounty.com
All records in one index. Records indexed on a public use terminal. Office will perform a UCC and Tax lien search but public must search other records themselves. Search fee $10.00 per name. Will not search real estate records. Will search UCC records, search includes tax liens. UCC search per debtor name- $10.00. Copy fee $.25 per page. Cert fee- $3.00 per doc plus copy fee. Payee- Uinta County Clerk. **Other phones:** Treasurer- 307-783-0332; Elections- 307-783-0423; Vital Records- 307-783-0304. **Property tax/Assessor-** same address as above. 307-783-0336.

Washakie County

County Clerk, Box 260, Worland, WY 82401-0260. 307-347-3131; fax-307-347-9366; hours: 8AM-5PM.
www.washakiecounty.net
Records indexed on computer back to 1985. Office personnel or visitors may perform searches. Search fee $10.00 per name. Will not search real estate records. Copy fee $.25; real estate $1.00 per page. Cert fee- $3.00 per doc plus copy fee. Payee- Washakie County Clerk. **Other phones:** Treasurer- 307-347-2031; Elections- 307-347-3131; Vital Records- 307-347-3131. **Property tax/Assessor-** 307-347-2831.

Weston County

County Clerk, 1 W. Main, Newcastle, WY 82701. 307-746-4744; fax-307-746-9505; hours: 8AM-5PM.
Record index not computerized. Office will perform a UCC search but public must search other records themselves. UCC search per debtor name- $10.00. Copy fee $.50 per page. Cert fee- $3.00 per cert. Payee- Weston County Clerk. **Other phones:** Treasurer- 307-746-2852. **Property tax/Assessor-** 307-746-4633.

Wyoming County Locator

You will usually be able to find the city name in the City/County Cross Reference below. In that case, it is a simple matter to determine the county from the cross reference. However, only the official US Postal Service city names are included in this index. There are an additional 40,000 place names that people use in their addresses. Therefore, we have also included a ZIP/City Cross Reference immediately following the City/County Cross Reference.

If you know the ZIP Code but the city name does not appear in the City/County Cross Reference index, look up the ZIP Code in the ZIP/City Cross Reference, find the city name, then look up the city name in the City/County Cross Reference. For example, you want to know the county for an address of Menands, NY 12204. There is no "Menands" in the City/County Cross Reference. The ZIP/City Cross Reference shows that ZIP Codes 12201-12288 are for the city of Albany. Looking back in the City/County Cross Reference, Albany is in Albany County.

Wyoming City/County Cross Reference

AFTON Lincoln
ALADDIN Crook
ALBIN Laramie
ALCOVA Natrona
ALPINE Lincoln
ALTA Teton
ALVA Crook
ARAPAHOE Fremont
ARMINTO Natrona
ARVADA (82831) Campbell(37), Sheridan(32), Johnson(29)
AUBURN Lincoln
BAGGS Carbon
BAIROIL Sweetwater
BANNER (82832) Sheridan(80), Johnson(19)
BASIN Big Horn
BEDFORD Lincoln
BEULAH Crook
BIG HORN Sheridan
BIG PINEY Sublette
BILL Converse
BONDURANT Sublette
BOSLER Albany
BOULDER Sublette
BUFFALO Johnson
BUFORD (82052) Albany(68), Laramie(31)
BURLINGTON (82411) Big Horn(97), Park(2)
BURNS Laramie
BYRON Big Horn
CARLILE Crook
CARPENTER Laramie
CASPER Carbon
CASPER Natrona
CENTENNIAL Albany
CHEYENNE Laramie
CHUGWATER (82210) Platte(80), Goshen(20)
CLEARMONT Sheridan
CODY Park
COKEVILLE Lincoln
CORA Sublette
COWLEY Big Horn
CROWHEART Fremont
DANIEL Sublette
DAYTON Sheridan
DEAVER (82421) Big Horn(85), Park(14)
DEVILS TOWER Crook

DIAMONDVILLE Lincoln
DIXON Carbon
DOUGLAS Converse
DUBOIS Fremont
EDGERTON Natrona
ELK MOUNTAIN Carbon
EMBLEM Big Horn
ENCAMPMENT Carbon
ETNA Lincoln
EVANSTON Uinta
EVANSVILLE (82636) Natrona(97), Converse(2)
FARSON Sweetwater
FE WARREN AFB Laramie
FORT BRIDGER Uinta
FORT LARAMIE Goshen
FORT WASHAKIE Fremont
FOUR CORNERS Weston
FRANNIE Park
FREEDOM Lincoln
FRONTIER Lincoln
GARRETT Albany
GILLETTE Campbell
GLENDO (82213) Platte(98), Converse(1)
GLENROCK Converse
GRANGER Sweetwater
GRANITE CANON Laramie
GREEN RIVER Sweetwater
GREYBULL Big Horn
GROVER Lincoln
GUERNSEY Platte
HAMILTON DOME Hot Springs
HANNA Carbon
HARTVILLE Platte
HAWK SPRINGS Goshen
HILAND (82638) Natrona(87), Fremont(12)
HILLSDALE Laramie
HORSE CREEK Laramie
HUDSON Fremont
HULETT Crook
HUNTLEY Goshen
HYATTVILLE Big Horn
IRON MOUNTAIN Laramie
JACKSON Teton
JAY EM Goshen
JEFFREY CITY Fremont
JELM Albany
KAYCEE (82639) Johnson(92), Natrona(7)
KEELINE Niobrara

KELLY Teton
KEMMERER Lincoln
KINNEAR Fremont
KIRBY Hot Springs
LA BARGE Lincoln
LAGRANGE (82221) Goshen(97), Laramie(2)
LANCE CREEK Niobrara
LANDER Fremont
LARAMIE Albany
LEITER Sheridan
LINCH Johnson
LINGLE Goshen
LITTLE AMERICA Sweetwater
LONETREE Uinta
LONETREE Uinta
LOST SPRINGS (82224) Converse(85), Niobrara(14)
LOVELL Big Horn
LUSK Niobrara
LYMAN Uinta
LYSITE Fremont
MANDERSON (82432) Park(75), Big Horn(24)
MANVILLE Niobrara
MC FADDEN Carbon
MC KINNON Sweetwater
MEDICINE BOW (82329) Carbon(77), Albany(22)
MEETEETSE Park
MERIDEN Laramie
MIDWEST Natrona
MILLS Natrona
MOORCROFT (82721) Crook(60), Campbell(39)
MOOSE Teton
MORAN Teton
MOUNTAIN VIEW Uinta
NATRONA Natrona
NEWCASTLE Weston
NODE Niobrara
OPAL Lincoln
OSAGE Weston
OSHOTO (82724) Crook(77), Campbell(22)
OTTO Big Horn
PARKMAN Sheridan
PAVILLION Fremont
PINE BLUFFS Laramie
PINEDALE Sublette

POINT OF ROCKS Sweetwater
POWDER RIVER Natrona
POWELL Park
RALSTON Park
RANCHESTER Sheridan
RAWLINS Carbon
RECLUSE Campbell
RELIANCE Sweetwater
ROBERTSON Uinta
ROCK RIVER (82083) Carbon(55), Albany(44)
ROCK SPRINGS Sweetwater
ROZET Campbell
SADDLESTRING Johnson
SAINT STEPHENS Fremont
SARATOGA Carbon
SAVERY Carbon
SHAWNEE Converse
SHELL Big Horn
SHERIDAN Sheridan
SHOSHONI Fremont
SINCLAIR Carbon
SMOOT Lincoln
STORY (82842) Sheridan(91), Johnson(8)
SUNDANCE (82729) Crook(95), Weston(4)
SUPERIOR Sweetwater
TEN SLEEP Washakie
TETON VILLAGE Teton
THAYNE Lincoln
THERMOPOLIS Hot Springs
TIE SIDING Albany
TORRINGTON Goshen
UPTON (82730) Weston(85), Crook(14)
VAN TASSELL (82242) Niobrara(59), Goshen(40)
VETERAN Goshen
WALCOTT Carbon
WAMSUTTER Sweetwater
WAPITI Park
WESTON (82731) Campbell(96), Crook(4)
WHEATLAND (82201) Platte(98), Albany(1)
WILSON Teton
WOLF Sheridan
WORLAND Washakie
WRIGHT Campbell
WYARNO Sheridan
YELLOWSTONE NATIONAL PARK Park
YODER Goshen

Wyoming ZIP/City Cross Reference

82001-82003	CHEYENNE	82321-82321	BAGGS	82631-82631	BILL	82923-82923	BOULDER
82005-82005	FE WARREN AFB	82322-82322	BAIROIL	82633-82633	DOUGLAS	82925-82925	CORA
82006-82010	CHEYENNE	82323-82323	DIXON	82635-82635	EDGERTON	82926-82926	ROCK SPRINGS
82050-82050	ALBIN	82324-82324	ELK MOUNTAIN	82636-82636	EVANSVILLE	82929-82929	LITTLE AMERICA
82051-82051	BOSLER	82325-82325	ENCAMPMENT	82637-82637	GLENROCK	82930-82931	EVANSTON
82052-82052	BUFORD	82327-82327	HANNA	82638-82638	HILAND	82932-82932	FARSON
82053-82053	BURNS	82329-82329	MEDICINE BOW	82639-82639	KAYCEE	82933-82933	FORT BRIDGER
82054-82054	CARPENTER	82331-82331	SARATOGA	82640-82640	LINCH	82934-82934	GRANGER
82055-82055	CENTENNIAL	82332-82332	SAVERY	82642-82642	LYSITE	82935-82935	GREEN RIVER
82057-82057	LARAMIE	82334-82334	SINCLAIR	82643-82643	MIDWEST	82936-82936	LONETREE
82058-82058	GARRETT	82335-82335	WALCOTT	82644-82644	MILLS	82936-82936	LONTETREE
82059-82059	GRANITE CANON	82336-82336	WAMSUTTER	82646-82646	NATRONA	82937-82937	LYMAN
82060-82060	HILLSDALE	82401-82401	WORLAND	82648-82648	POWDER RIVER	82938-82938	MC KINNON
82061-82061	HORSE CREEK	82410-82410	BASIN	82649-82649	SHOSHONI	82939-82939	MOUNTAIN VIEW
82062-82062	IRON MOUNTAIN	82411-82411	BURLINGTON	82701-82701	NEWCASTLE	82941-82941	PINEDALE
82063-82063	JELM	82412-82412	BYRON	82710-82710	ALADDIN	82942-82942	POINT OF ROCKS
82070-82073	LARAMIE	82414-82414	CODY	82711-82711	ALVA	82943-82943	RELIANCE
82080-82080	MC FADDEN	82420-82420	COWLEY	82712-82712	BEULAH	82944-82944	ROBERTSON
82081-82081	MERIDEN	82421-82421	DEAVER	82713-82713	CARLILE	82945-82945	SUPERIOR
82082-82082	PINE BLUFFS	82422-82422	EMBLEM	82714-82714	DEVILS TOWER	83001-83002	JACKSON
82083-82083	ROCK RIVER	82423-82423	FRANNIE	82715-82715	FOUR CORNERS	83011-83011	KELLY
82084-82084	TIE SIDING	82426-82426	GREYBULL	82716-82718	GILLETTE	83012-83012	MOOSE
82190-82190	YELLOWSTONE NATIONAL PARK	82427-82427	HAMILTON DOME	82720-82720	HULETT	83013-83013	MORAN
82201-82201	WHEATLAND	82428-82428	HYATTVILLE	82721-82721	MOORCROFT	83014-83014	WILSON
82210-82210	CHUGWATER	82430-82430	KIRBY	82723-82723	OSAGE	83025-83025	TETON VILLAGE
82212-82212	FORT LARAMIE	82431-82431	LOVELL	82724-82724	OSHOTO	83101-83101	KEMMERER
82213-82213	GLENDO	82432-82432	MANDERSON	82725-82725	RECLUSE	83110-83110	AFTON
82214-82214	GUERNSEY	82433-82433	MEETEETSE	82727-82727	ROZET	83111-83111	AUBURN
82215-82215	HARTVILLE	82434-82434	OTTO	82729-82729	SUNDANCE	83112-83112	BEDFORD
82217-82217	HAWK SPRINGS	82435-82435	POWELL	82730-82730	UPTON	83113-83113	BIG PINEY
82218-82218	HUNTLEY	82440-82440	RALSTON	82731-82731	WESTON	83114-83114	COKEVILLE
82219-82219	JAY EM	82441-82441	SHELL	82732-82732	WRIGHT	83115-83115	DANIEL
82220-82220	KEELINE	82442-82442	TEN SLEEP	82801-82801	SHERIDAN	83116-83116	DIAMONDVILLE
82221-82221	LAGRANGE	82443-82443	THERMOPOLIS	82831-82831	ARVADA	83118-83118	ETNA
82222-82222	LANCE CREEK	82450-82450	WAPITI	82832-82832	BANNER	83119-83119	FAIRVIEW
82223-82223	LINGLE	82501-82501	RIVERTON	82833-82833	BIG HORN	83120-83120	FREEDOM
82224-82224	LOST SPRINGS	82510-82510	ARAPAHOE	82834-82834	BUFFALO	83121-83121	FRONTIER
82225-82225	LUSK	82512-82512	CROWHEART	82835-82835	CLEARMONT	83122-83122	GROVER
82227-82227	MANVILLE	82513-82513	DUBOIS	82836-82836	DAYTON	83123-83123	LA BARGE
82228-82228	NODE	82514-82514	FORT WASHAKIE	82837-82837	LEITER	83124-83124	OPAL
82229-82229	SHAWNEE	82515-82515	HUDSON	82838-82838	PARKMAN	83126-83126	SMOOT
82240-82240	TORRINGTON	82516-82516	KINNEAR	82839-82839	RANCHESTER	83127-83127	THAYNE
82242-82242	VAN TASSELL	82520-82520	LANDER	82840-82840	SADDLESTRING	83128-83128	ALPINE
82243-82243	VETERAN	82523-82523	PAVILLION	82842-82842	STORY	83414-83414	ALTA
82244-82244	YODER	82524-82524	SAINT STEPHENS	82844-82844	WOLF		
82301-82301	RAWLINS	82601-82615	CASPER	82845-82845	WYARNO		
82310-82310	JEFFREY CITY	82620-82620	ALCOVA	82901-82902	ROCK SPRINGS		
		82630-82630	ARMINTO	82922-82922	BONDURANT		

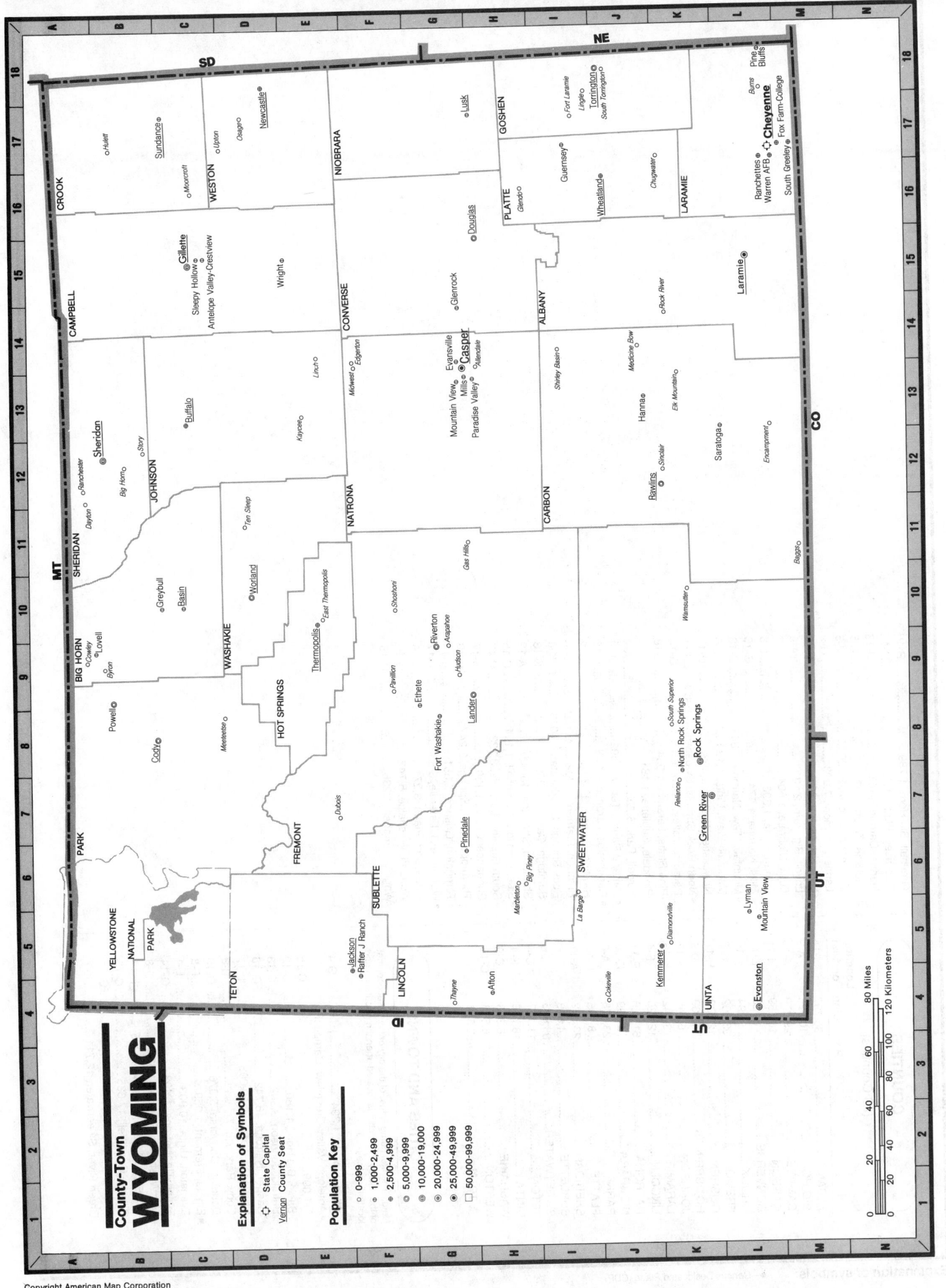

County-Town
WYOMING

Explanation of Symbols

◇ State Capital
Vernon County Seat

Population Key

- ○ 0-999
- ◉ 1,000-2,499
- ⊕ 2,500-4,999
- ◉ 5,000-9,999
- ◉ 10,000-19,000
- ◉ 20,000-24,999
- ◉ 25,000-49,999
- ☐ 50,000-99,999

80 Miles
120 Kilometers

COUNTIES

(23 Counties)

Name of County	Population	Location on Map
ALBANY	30,797	I-14
BIG HORN	10,525	A-9
CAMPBELL	29,370	A-14
CARBON	16,659	I-11
CONVERSE	11,128	E-14
CROOK	5,294	A-16
FREMONT	33,662	D-6
GOSHEN	12,373	H-17
HOT SPRINGS	4,809	D-8
JOHNSON	6,145	B-12
LARAMIE	73,142	K-16
LINCOLN	12,625	F-4
NATRONA	61,226	E-11
NIOBRARA	2,499	E-16
PARK	23,178	A-6
PLATTE	8,145	H-16
SHERIDAN	23,562	A-11
SUBLETTE	4,843	F-6
SWEETWATER	38,823	I-6
TETON	11,172	C-4
UINTA	18,705	K-4
WASHAKIE	8,388	C-9
WESTON	6,518	C-16
TOTAL	**453,588**	

CITIES AND TOWNS

Note: The first name is that of the city or town, second, that of the county in which it is located, then the population and location on the map.

Afton, Lincoln, 1,394	G-4
• Antelope Valley-Crestview, Campbell, 1,099	C-15
Basin, Big Horn, 1,180	C-10
Buffalo, Johnson, 3,302	C-13
Casper, Natrona, 46,742	G-13
Cheyenne, Laramie, 50,008	L-17
Cody, Park, 7,897	B-8
Douglas, Converse, 5,076	G-15
• Ethete, Fremont, 1,059	F-8
Evanston, Uinta, 10,903	L-4
Evansville, Natrona, 1,403	G-14
• Fort Washakie, Fremont, 1,334	G-8
Fox Farm-College, Laramie, 2,965	L-17
Gillette, Campbell, 17,635	C-15
Glenrock, Converse, 2,153	G-14
Green River, Sweetwater, 12,711	K-7
Greybull, Big Horn, 1,789	B-10
Guernsey, Platte, 1,155	I-17
Hanna, Carbon, 1,076	J-13
Jackson, Teton, 4,472	E-5
Kemmerer, Lincoln, 3,020	J-5
Lander, Fremont, 7,023	G-9
Laramie, Albany, 26,687	L-15
Lovell, Big Horn, 2,131	A-9
Lusk, Niobrara, 1,504	G-17
Lyman, Uinta, 1,896	L-5
Mills, Natrona, 1,574	G-13
• Mountain View, Natrona, 1,345	G-13
Mountain View, Uinta, 1,189	L-5
Newcastle, Weston, 3,003	D-18
• North Rock Springs, Sweetwater, 2,471	K-7
Paradise Valley, Natrona	G-13
Pine Bluffs, Laramie, 1,054	L-18
Pinedale, Sublette, 1,181	G-6
Powell, Park, 5,292	A-9
• Rafter J Ranch, Teton, 1,092	F-4
• Ranchettes, Laramie, 4,038	L-16
Rawlins, Carbon, 9,380	J-12
Riverton, Fremont, 9,202	G-9
Rock Springs, Sweetwater, 19,050	K-8
Saratoga, Carbon, 1,969	K-13
Sheridan, Sheridan, 13,900	A-12
• Sleepy Hollow, Campbell, 1,194	C-15
• South Greeley, Laramie, 3,723	M-17
Sundance, Crook, 1,139	B-17
Thermopolis, Hot Springs, 3,247	E-10
Torrington, Goshen, 5,651	I-18
• Warren AFB, Laramie, 3,832	L-17
Wheatland, Platte, 3,271	I-16
Worland, Washakie, 5,742	D-10
Wright, Campbell, 1,236	D-15

Explanation of symbols: • – Census Designated Place (CDP)

U.S. Territories

Guam - Puerto Rico - Virgin Islands

Guam Records

Guam Driving Records

Superior Court
Traffic Violations Bureau
120 W. O'Brien
Hagatna, Guam 96910

(671) 475-3274
(671) 472-2856 fax
http://ns.gov.gu/revtax/dmv.html

Records are public. To request by mail, submit name, DOB and SSN. Include a self-addressed, stamped envelope. In person requests are permitted. The fee is $1.50 for clearance and then $1.00 per citation on the record. Make checks payable to Superior Court of Guam. They will not fax back requests.

Guam Vehicle Records

Department of Revenue & Taxation
Vehicle Records
PO Box 23607, GMF
Barrigada, Guam 96921

(671) 475-1816

Vehicle records are not considered public records.
You must have a court order and then submit request on their form

Guam Recording Office

Guam Department of Revenue & Taxation
Clerk, PO Box 23605
GMF, GU 96921

671-475-5000 x815; Fax 671-472-2643.
Will not search real estate records. Will search UCC records, but not tax liens.
UCC search per debtor name- $5.00. Payee- Treasurer of Guam.

Guam Federal Courts

Office of the Clerk of Court
520 W Soledad Ave, 4th Fl
US Courthouse, RM 460
Hagatna, Guam 96910

671-473-9100, Fax: 671-473-9152
www.gud.uscourts.gov   Hours 8AM-3PM

Counties: Guam. Address Bankruptcy requests to the Guam Bankruptcy Division.

Searches & Indexing: Results include last 4 SSN digits only. Pre-2000 index is manual index cards. New cases in the index 1 day after filing date. Records purged never. All records including archives are located here. All closed case records maintained here.

Fee & Payment: Pay by personal checks accepted. No credit cards. Payee: Clerk, Guam District Court.

Phone Search: No searching by telephone.

Mail Search: search usually completed- same day. Expect a longer return time of mail. Include SASE for return.

In Person Search: Fee charged if court performs your search.

E-Services: PACER online at https://pacer.login.uscourts.gov/cgi-bin/login.pl?court_id=gudc. PACER records go back to 2002. ECF at https://ecf.gub.uscourts.gov

Opinions Online: www.gud.uscourts.gov/opinions.htm.

Other Online Access: Now participates in the US Party case index. Court calendars at www.gud.uscourts.gov/calendar/calnotsealed30.htm.

Guam City/County Cross Reference

AGANA HEIGHTS Guam	DEDEDO Guam	MONGMONG Guam	TAMUNING Guam
AGAT Guam	HAGATNA Guam	PITI Guam	UMATAC Guam
ASAN Guam	INARAJAN Guam	SANTA RITA Guam	YIGO Guam
BARRIGADA Guam	MANGILAO Guam	SINAJANA Guam	YONA Guam
CHALAN PAGO Guam	MERIZO Guam	TALOFOFO Guam	

Guam ZIP/City Cross Reference

96910-96910 AGANA	96915-96915 SANTA RITA	96922-96922 ASAN	96928-96928 AGAT
96910-96910 HAGATNA	96916-96916 MERIZO	96923-96923 MANGILAO	96929-96929 YIGO
96911-96911 TAMUNING	96917-96917 INARAJAN	96924-96924 CHALAN PAGO	96930-96930 TALOFOFO
96912-96912 DEDEDO	96918-96918 UMATAC	96925-96925 PITI	96931-96931 TAMUNING
96913-96913 BARRIGADA	96919-96919 AGANA HEIGHTS	96926-96926 SINAJANA	96932-96932 AGANA
96914-96914 YONA	96921-96921 BARRIGADA	96927-96927 MONGMONG	96932-96932 HAGATNA

Puerto Rico Records

Puerto Rico Driving Records

Department of Transportation
Services Division
PO Box 41243 - Minillas Station
San Juan, PR 00940-1243

(787) 767-4425

www.gobierno.pr/GPRPortal/Inicio

The request must include full name and SSN, signed release from subject is suggested. The fee is $1.50 per record made payable to the Secretary of the Treasury.

Puerto Rico Federal Courts

US District Court

Court Clerk, Clemente-Ruiz-Nazario US Courthouse, 150 Carlos Chardon St, Hato Rey, Puerto Rico 00918 (also use mail address for courier delivery), 787-772-3000, records rm- 787-772-3025, Fax-787-766-5693. Hours- 8:30AM-4:45PM. www.prd.uscourts.gov

Searches & Indexing: Cases indexed by and case number. Results do not include SSN or DOB. New cases in the index 1-2 days after filing date. Records purged never.

Fee & Payment: Pay by money order or cashier's check. Payee: Clerk, U.S. District Court. Prepayment required.

Phone Search: No searching by telephone.

Mail Search: An SASE required.

In Person Search: Fee charged if court performs your search.

E-Services: ECF replaces PACER. ECF at https://ecf.prd.uscourts.gov **Other Online Access:** Participates in the US Party Case Index.

US Bankruptcy Court

Court Clerk, US Post Office & Courthouse Building, 300 Recinto Sur #109, San Juan, Puerto Rico 00901 (also use mail address for courier delivery), 787-977-6000, Fax-787-977-6008. Hours- 8AM-4PM. www.prb.uscourts.gov

Searches & Indexing: Cases indexed by debtor name and case number. Results include SSN. Computer index maintained. New cases in the index immediately after filing date. Closed cases shipped to Missouri Records Center 3 months after case closed.

Fee & Payment: Pay by money order or cashier's check. No personal checks. Payee: Clerk, U.S. Bankruptcy Court. Prepayment required. **Phone Search:** No searching by telephone. **Mail Search:** An SASE required. **In Person Search:** Fee charged if court performs your search.

E-Services: Access PACER at https://pacer.login.uscourts.gov/cgi-bin/login.pl?court_id=prbk. PACER toll-free: 800-792-8338. PACER local phone: 787-977-6140. ECF at https://ecf.prb.uscourts.gov **Opinions Online:** www.prb.uscourts.gov/Isys/isyswebext.dll?op=get&uri=/isysmenu.html. **Other Online Access:** Access judges' calendars by name at www.prb.uscourts.gov/Judge.htm.

Puerto Rico County Locator

Puerto Rico ZIP/City Cross Reference

ADJUNTAS Adjuntas
AGUADA Aguada
AGUADILLA Aguadilla
AGUAS BUENAS Aguas Buenas
AGUIRRE Guayama
AIBONITO Aibonito
ANASCO Anasco
ANGELES Utuado
ARECIBO Arecibo
ARROYO Arroyo
BAJADERO Arecibo
BARCELONETA Barceloneta
BARRANQUITAS Barranquitas
BAYAMON Bayamon
BOQUERON Cabo Rojo
CABO ROJO Cabo Rojo
CAGUAS Caguas
CAMUY Camuy
CANOVANAS Canovanas
CAROLINA (00979) San Juan(59), Carolina(40)
CAROLINA Carolina
CAROLINA San Juan
CASTANER Lares
CATANO Catano
CAYEY Cayey
CEIBA Ceiba
CIALES Ciales
CIDRA Cidra

COAMO Coamo
COMERIO Comerio
COROZAL Corozal
COTO LAUREL Ponce
CULEBRA Culebra
DORADO Dorado
ENSENADA Guanica
FAJARDO Fajardo
FLORIDA Florida
FORT BUCHANAN Bayamon
GARROCHALES Arecibo
GUANICA Guanica
GUAYAMA Guayama
GUAYAMA Guayanilla
GUAYANILLA Guayanilla
GUAYNABO Catano
GUAYNABO Guaynabo
GUAYNABO San Juan
GURABO Gurabo
HATILLO Hatillo
HORMIGUEROS Hormigueros
HUMACAO Humacao
ISABELA Isabela
JAYUYA Jayuya
JUANA DIAZ Juana Diaz
JUNCOS Juncos
LA PLATA Aibonito
LAJAS Lajas
LARES Lares

LAS MARIAS (00670) Camuy(55), Anasco(44)
LAS PIEDRAS Las Piedras
LOIZA Loiza
LUQUILLO Luquillo
MANATI Manati
MARICAO Maricao
MAUNABO Maunabo
MAYAGUEZ Mayaguez
MERCEDITA Ponce
MOCA Moca
MOROVIS Morovis
NAGUABO Naguabo
NARANJITO Naranjito
OROCOVIS Orocovis
PALMER Rio Grande
PATILLAS Patillas
PENUELAS Penuelas
PONCE Ponce
PUERTO REAL Fajardo
PUNTA SANTIAGO Humacao
QUEBRADILLAS Quebradillas
RINCON Rincon
RIO BLANCO Naguabo
RIO GRANDE (00745) Humacao(84), Rio Grande(12), Canovanas(3)
ROOSEVELT ROADS Ceiba
ROSARIO San German
SABANA GRANDE Sabana Grande

SABANA HOYOS Arecibo
SABANA SECA Toa Baja
SAINT JUST Trujillo Alto
SAINT JUST CONTRACT Trujillo Alto
SALINAS Salinas
SAN ANTONIO Aguadilla
SAN GERMAN San German
SAN JUAN San Juan
SAN LORENZO San Lorenzo
SAN SEBASTIAN San Sebastian
SANTA ISABEL Santa Isabel
ST JUST Trujillo Alto
TOA ALTA Toa Alta
TOA BAJA Toa Baja
TRUJILLO ALTO (00976) Trujillo Alto(98), San Juan(1)
TRUJILLO ALTO Trujillo Alto
UTUADO Utuado
VEGA ALTA Vega Alta
VEGA BAJA (00694) Vega Alta(59), Vega Baja(40)
VEGA BAJA Vega Baja
VIEQUES Vieques
VILLALBA Villalba
YABUCOA Yabucoa
YAUCO Yauco

Puerto Rico ZIP/City Cross Reference

00601-00601 ADJUNTAS	00664-00664 JAYUYA	00721-00721 PALMER	00778-00778 GURABO
00602-00602 AGUADA	00667-00667 LAJAS	00723-00723 PATILLAS	00780-00780 COTO LAUREL
00603-00605 AGUADILLA	00669-00669 LARES	00725-00727 CAGUAS	00782-00782 COMERIO
00606-00606 MARICAO	00670-00670 LAS MARIAS	00728-00728 PONCE	00783-00783 COROZAL
00610-00610 ANASCO	00674-00674 MANATI	00729-00729 CANOVANAS	00784-00785 GUAYAMA
00611-00611 ANGELES	00676-00676 MOCA	00730-00734 PONCE	00786-00786 LA PLATA
00612-00614 ARECIBO	00677-00677 RINCON	00735-00735 CEIBA	00791-00792 HUMACAO
00616-00616 BAJADERO	00678-00678 QUEBRADILLAS	00736-00737 CAYEY	00794-00794 BARRANQUITAS
00617-00617 BARCELONETA	00680-00682 MAYAGUEZ	00738-00738 FAJARDO	00795-00795 JUANA DIAZ
00622-00622 BOQUERON	00683-00683 SAN GERMAN	00739-00739 CIDRA	00901-00933 SAN JUAN
00623-00623 CABO ROJO	00685-00685 SAN SEBASTIAN	00740-00740 PUERTO REAL	00934-00934 FORT BUCHANAN
00624-00624 PENUELAS	00687-00687 MOROVIS	00741-00741 PUNTA SANTIAGO	00935-00940 SAN JUAN
00627-00627 CAMUY	00688-00688 SABANA HOYOS	00742-00742 ROOSEVELT ROADS	00949-00951 TOA BAJA
00631-00631 CASTANER	00690-00690 SAN ANTONIO	00744-00744 RIO BLANCO	00952-00952 SABANA SECA
00636-00636 ROSARIO	00692-00692 VEGA ALTA	00745-00745 RIO GRANDE	00953-00954 TOA ALTA
00637-00637 SABANA GRANDE	00693-00694 VEGA BAJA	00751-00751 SALINAS	00955-00955 SAN JUAN
00638-00638 CIALES	00698-00698 YAUCO	00754-00754 SAN LORENZO	00956-00961 BAYAMON
00641-00641 UTUADO	00703-00703 AGUAS BUENAS	00757-00757 SANTA ISABEL	00962-00963 CATANO
00646-00646 DORADO	00704-00704 AGUIRRE	00765-00765 VIEQUES	00964-00964 SAN JUAN
00647-00647 ENSENADA	00705-00705 AIBONITO	00766-00766 VILLALBA	00965-00971 GUAYNABO
00650-00650 FLORIDA	00707-00707 MAUNABO	00767-00767 YABUCOA	00975-00975 SAN JUAN
00652-00652 GARROCHALES	00714-00714 ARROYO	00769-00769 COAMO	00976-00977 TRUJILLO ALTO
00653-00653 GUANICA	00715-00715 MERCEDITA	00771-00771 LAS PIEDRAS	00978-00978 SAINT JUST
00656-00656 GUAYANILLA	00716-00717 PONCE	00772-00772 LOIZA	00978-00978 ST JUST
00659-00659 HATILLO	00718-00718 NAGUABO	00773-00773 LUQUILLO	00978-00978 SAINT JUST CONTRACT
00660-00660 HORMIGUEROS	00719-00719 NARANJITO	00775-00775 CULEBRA	00979-00999 CAROLINA
00662-00662 ISABELA	00720-00720 OROCOVIS	00777-00777 JUNCOS	

Virgin Islands Records

Virgin Islands Driving Records

Criminal Justice Complex
Records Bureau
St. Thomas, Virgin Islands 00802

340-774-2211 x5523

www.bvi.gov.vg

The request must include a signed release from the subject. Submit photocopy of the driver's license, a self-addressed, stamped envelope. The fee is $5.00 in certified funds, made payable to the Government of the Virgin Islands. Turnaround time is 1-2 days.

Virgin Islands Vehicle Records

Virgin Island Police Department
C/O Motor Vehicle Bureau
Sub Base
St. Thomas, Virgin Islands 00801

(340) 774-5765

They will verify information over the phone, including lien information. To do a record request, submit a license plate number of VIN, $20.00 in certified funds, and a self-addresses, stamped envelope. Make check payable to Government of the Virgin Islands.

Virgin Islands Recording Offices

St. Croix

Recorder of Deeds, 1131 King St; #101, Christiansted, VI 00820-4970. 340-773-6449; fax-340-773-0330; hours: 8AM-5PM.
Also has offices in St. Thomas (340-776-8505 - see separate listing), St. John (340-776-6737), and Fredericksted (340-772-3115). Separate indices to search include books, computer. public use terminal available. Office personnel or visitors may perform searches. Will not search R/E or tax lien records. Copy fee $5.00 per page. Cert fee- $10.00 for 1st page; $1.00 each add'l pg. **Online access to Property, Assessor, Real Estate, Recording, Deed, Judgment records:** Access to computerized records is to be available at www.ltg.gov.vi late 2005. Also, property valuation data to be available at www.vipropertyrevaluation.com/index.htm. **Other phones:** Treasurer- 340-773-1105; Appraiser/Auditor- 340-773-6459; Elections- 340-773-1021; Vital Records- 340-773-1311 or 773-9376. **Property tax/Assessor-** same address as above. 340-773-6459, assessor fax- 340-773-0330.

St. Thomas

Recorder of Deeds, Div. of Corporations & Trademarks; Kongens Gade #18, St. Thomas, VI 00802. 340-774-9906, UCC recording phone-340-776-8515; fax-340-774-1270; hours: 8AM-5PM. www.ltg.gov.vi/departments/recorder.html
All records in one index. Records indexed on a public use terminal back to 9/1999; earlier records being added. Office is limited to preparation of $20.00 title and encumbrance statements only; other searches done by visitors. Copy fee $1.00 per page. Cert fee- $10.00 per doc plus copy fee. Payee- Government of VI. **Online access to Property, Assessor, Real Estate, Recording, Deed, Judgment records:** Access to computerized records is to be available at www.ltg.gov.vi late 2005. Also, property valuation data to be available at www.vipropertyrevaluation.com/index.htm. **Property tax/Assessor-** same address as above. 340-776-8505, assessor fax- 340-776-4612.

Virgin Islands County Locator

V. I. City/County Cross Reference

CHRISTIANSTED St. Croix
CHRISTIANSTED (00820) St. Croix(78), St. Thomas(21)
FREDERIKSTED St. Croix
KINGSHILL St. Croix
SAINT JOHN St. John
SAINT THOMAS St. Thomas

V. I. ZIP/City Cross Reference

00801-00805	SAINT THOMAS
00820-00824	CHRISTIANSTED
00830-00831	SAINT JOHN
00840-00841	FREDERIKSTED
00850-00851	KINGSHILL

Canada

Canadian Criminal Records
Canadian Parole/Pardon Information
Canadian Driving Records

Canadian Criminal Records

Information and Identification Services
Directorate of the Royal Canadian Mounted Police (RCMP)

Searches requests may be directed to the Royal Canadian Mounted Police's Information and Identification Services:

Mailing address:

RCMP
Civil Fingerprint Screening Services
PO Box 8885
Ottawa, Ontario K1G 3M8   Canada

Courier address:

RCMP
National Police Services Building, Loading Dock #1
Information and Identification Services,
Civil Fingerprint Screening Services,
1200 Vanier Parkway
Ottawa, Ontario K1A 0R2   Canada

Telephone Information:

613-998-6362

You may follow the prompts, but in most call scenarios, you are prompted to leave a message. Please allow up to three business days for a response.

General Web Site:

www.rcmp.gc.ca/crimrec/crimrec_e.htm

Criminal Record Checks Information Web Site:

www.rcmp.gc.ca/crimrec/finger2_e.htm#Obtain

Email Information requests:

civilnps@rcmp-grc.gc.ca

...continued

Searches may be performed by mail and in person. A messenger and courier service may be used. Also, to speed return, include a postal paid overnight or expedited envelope; in fact, a postage paid envelope of some form is required for all mail requests.

Certified criminal records will be provided to subjects seeking employment, adoptions, Canadian citizenship, foreign travel, border crossing permits, landed immigrant status or immigration to Canada, refugee status, visa/waiver applications, work permits, or volunteer positions. Criminal records are kept on file until the subject is eighty years old if no criminal activity has been reported within the last 10 years. In the case of a subject serving term of life imprisonment, of a "dangerous offender", or a subject of the age of 80 who is still incarcerated, the criminal record is retained until the sentence is completed and no additional crimes have been committed for 10 years, the subject reaches the age of 100, or the subject dies and the death is supported by fingerprints.

Search requirements: full name, DOB, sex, and SASE. A release and a fingerprint form is required. The Canadian fingerprint release form C-216C should be used when possible. If the form is not available, an official fingerprint from the police department may be substituted. The form used should be completed and signed by the officer taking the fingerprints. The form should include the reason for the application (i.e. employment, etc.) Requests of records for purposes of employment or volunteer work must indicate the job title or position sought on the fingerprint form.

Records will only be released to the subject, unless a release is included with the request. The release must authorize the RCMP to provide criminal record information to a specific individual or agency. The release must also include a statement that the subject is aware that refusal to give consent to release will not negatively affect the request. The consent must be an original document. A photocopied or faxed release will not be accepted.

The search fee is $25.00 (Canadian), or $18.00 (U.S.), payable to the Receiver General of Canada by certified check or money order. The fee is waived on searches done for Canadian citizenship, employment with the Canadian federal government or police forces, immigration to Canada, refugee status or volunteer work (requires written confirmation from a registered non-profit organization).

Turnaround time is 4-6 weeks. Inquiry calls regarding record requests should be directed to 613-998-6362. To receive results by courier, include prepaid return packaging. Additional funds will not be accepted for express delivery of results.

Canadian Pardons & Paroles

National Parole Board of Canada

Website:

www.npb-cnlc.gc.ca

The website provides a wealth of information on parole rules and parolee records.

Canadian Pardons

For questions relating to the status of pardon applications, call this toll-free number:

1-800-874-2652

Mailing address for the Pardons Sections is:

Pardon Section
Clemency and Investigations Division
National Parole Board
410 Laurier Avenue West
Ottawa, Ontario K1A 0R1

Note: Requests must be made by the subject. Notice must include full name, date of birth, personal reference number, if available, and subject's signature.

Canadian Driving Records

Note: All record search fees are quoted in Canadian Dollars.

Alberta

Motor Vehicle Division
Alberta Service Bureau
Scotia Place, Main Floor, M23
10060 Jasper Ave
Edmonton, Alberta T5J 3R8
(780) 944-1204
(780) 423-0285 fax

www3.gov.ab.ca/gs/services/mv/

Driving Records   Records are privatized and require the signed, notarized release of the subject. The cost of a record search is $30.17. Processing time is same day. The name, DOB, license number, reason for request, and a signed release from subject are required for a search. Records may be searched by mail or in person.

Vehicle Records   With the exception of lien information ($20.70 fee) records are generally not released to the public. If permitted, records can be searched by owner's name, VIN number and/or by plate number.

British Columbia

Driver Services
ICBI Licensing Department
910 Government Street
PO Box 3750
Victoria, British Columbia V8W 3Y5
(250) 978-8300 or (800) 950-1498
(250) 978-8001 fax
www.icbc.com

Driving Records   The cost of a record search is $5.00 (no fee if your own record). Processing time is 2 to 3 days. The name, DOB, license number and a signed release from subject are required for a search. Records may be searched by mail or in person. Will fax back. Will accept MasterCard and Visa. Information is not available online at this time.

Vehicle Records   Records are not available. However, by calling (800) 464-5050, one can get a verbal verification if a vehicle was involved in an accident.

Manitoba

Division of Driver & Vehicle License
Suspension & Records
1075 Portage Ave
Winnipeg, Manitoba R3G 0S1
(204) 945-6945 (Driver)
(204) 945-5357 (Driver-fax)
(204) 945-7366 (Vehicle)

www.gov.mb.ca/tgs/ddvl/index.html

Driving Records The cost of a record search is $10.00, there is also a search on CDL drivers which is $10.00. Accident reports at $10.70. Prepayment is required, checks or money orders to be made out to Minister of Finance. The processing time is 1 to 2 days. The name, DOB, license number and a signed release from subject are required for a search. Records may be searched by mail, fax or in person and they will return by fax. MasterCard and Visa accepted.

Vehicle Records   Information is not available to the general public, but they will confirm the number of vehicle owners and accident history information. To permissible users, vehicle records can be searched by owner's name, VIN number and/or by plate number. For Lien information call (204) 945-3123.

New Brunswick

Department of Public Safety
Licensing & Records Branch
Driver (or Vehicle) Records
PO Box 6000
Fredericton, New Brunswick E3B 5H1
(506) 684-7901
(506) 453-7455

www.gnb.ca/0276/index-e.asp

Driving Records   The cost of a driving record search is $10.00 and **Accident Reports** are $8.00. The processing time is same day. The name, DOB and License number are required for a search. Records may be searched by mail, in person or online. Records can be returned by fax.

An online, interactive system is available from a designated vendor. Fee is $10.00 per record. For more information about setting up an account call (888) 624-2265 or fax 902-422-1675.

Vehicle Records   Vehicle records searches are done through Data Entry at (506) 453-2084, fee is $8.00 per record. Vehicle records can be searched by owner's name, VIN number and/or by plate number. Signed release required. Credit cards are not accepted. Lien information is released only to parties involved; call the Registry Office at (506) 453-2817.

Newfoundland

Motor Vehicle Registration
Driver Records Division
PO Box 8710
St Johns, Newfoundland A1B 4J5
(709) 729-2519
(709) 729-2515 (Driver fax)
(709) 729-3399 (Vehicle fax)

www.gov.nf.ca/gsl/gs/mr

Driving Records   The cost of a driving record search is $10.00. The processing time is in less than a week. The name and either DOB or license number, and the signature of the requester are required for a search. Records may be searched by mail or in person. Visa, MasterCard and Debit Cards are accepted. Records returned by fax incur an additional $5.00 fee.

Vehicle Records   With the exception of lien information records are generally not released to the public. If permitted, records can be searched by owner's name, VIN number and/or by plate number.

Lien Records   Lien searches have been privatized. Search companies are listed on the web under personal Property Registry at:

www.gov.nl.ca/gs/cca/cr/prop-about.stm

Northwest Territories

Department of Transportation
Motor Vehicle Division
Yellow Knife Registries
Box 1320
Yellow Knife, Northwest Territories
X1A 2L9
(867) 873-7487
(867) 669-9094 fax
www.gov.nt.ca

Driving Records   The cost of a driving record is $12.14. Visa, MasterCard and Debit Cards are accepted. The name, DOB, license number, and a signed release from subject are required for a search. Records may be searched by mail or in person, or by fax. Processing time is 1 to 2 days. Information is not available online at this time.

Vehicle Records   Vehicle records are closed and unavailable. Lien information is available from a different office, call (876) 873-7493 for more information.

Nova Scotia

Department of Transportation
PO Box 1652
Halifax, Nova Scotia B3J 2Z3
(902) 424-5851
(902) 424 0720 fax

www.gov.ns.ca/snsmr/rmv

Driving Records   The cost of a record search is $15.00. Make checks payable to Registry of Motor Vehicles. Visa, MasterCard and Debit Cards are accepted. The processing time is 1 to 2 weeks by mail, immediate in person, and same day for fax. The name, DOB and a signed release from subject are required for a search. The license number is helpful. Records may be searched by mail or fax (credit card required).

An online, interactive system is available from a designated vendor. Fee is $15.00 per record. For more information about setting up an account call (888) 624-2265 or fax 902-422-1675.

Vehicle Records Vehicle record information is not available to the general public.

Lien Records   Lien information is held at the Registry of Deeds at (902) 424-8571. However, you can only search in person. They recommend a vendor, Info Fax Research, at (888) 356-4636.

Ontario

Ministry of Transportation
2680 Keele
Downsview, Ontario M3M 3E6
(416) 235-2999
(416) 235-4009 fax

www.mto.gov.on.ca

Driving Records   Both driving and vehicle records may be obtained from kiosks and mall kiosks. Driver's address is not released. The cost of a driving record or accident report is $12.00, add $6.00 for certification. Reports on commercial driving only is $5.00. Credit cards and debit cards are accepted with fax service. They would prefer fax requests instead of mail requests. The name, DOB and license number required for a search. Records may be ordered online, also a license check can be ordered online for $2.00. Records are turned by mail.

Vehicle Records   Permitted requesters may search vehicle records by owner's name, VIN number and/or by plate number for $12.00. Addresses are not released. Lien information is shown only when a Used Vehicle Information Package is purchased for $20.00.

Prince Edward Island

Highway Safety Division
Records Division
33 Riverside Dr
PO Box 2000
Charlottetown, Prince Edward Island
C1A 7N8
(902) 368-5210
(902) 368-5236 (Driver fax)
www.gov.pe.ca/infopei/transportation/land

Driving Records   The cost of a record search is $15.00. Records may be searched by mail or in person. Processing time is 1 to 2 days for mail requests. The name, DOB, license number and a signed release from subject are required for a search. Credit cards are accepted for payment. Information is not available online at this time.

Vehicle Records   Records are closed to private individuals and the insurance industry. Lien information is released only upon request at courthouses.

Quebec

Driving Records Division
SAAQ
333 Jean LeSage
PO Box 19600
Quebec, Quebec G1K 8J6
(418) 643-7620
www.saaq.gouv.qc.ca

Driving Records   Records may be ordered by mail or at Service Centers throughout the province. The cost of a record search is $8.00. Processing time is 2 to 3 days. The full name, DOB, license number, requester's phone number, and a signed release from subject are required for a search. Records may be searched by mail or in person.

Vehicle Records   Release of information is extremely restrictive. The agency will confirm, but will not do searches.

Saskatchewan

Driver Abstracts
Saskatchewan Government Insurance
2260 11th Ave
Regina, Saskatchewan S4P 2N7
(306) 775-6198
(306) 775-6681 fax

www.sgi.sk.ca

Driving Records   The cost of a record search is $10.00. MasterCard and Visa are accepted. Processing time is 1 week by mail and 1 hour if credit card signature available. The name, DOB, license number and a signed release from subject are required for a search. Records may be searched by mail or fax. Information is not available online at this time.

Vehicle Records   Vehicle records are not released to the general public. Permissible requesters can be search by owner's name, VIN number and/or by plate number. Lien information is shown.

Yukon

Motor Vehicle Department
Yukon Territory
Government of Yukon
PO Box 2703
Whitehorse, Yukon Y1A 2C6
(867) 667-5315
(867) 393-6220 fax
www.gov.yk.ca

Driving Records   The cost of a driving record is $10.00, Mastercard and Visa are accepted. Processing time is same day. The name, DOB, license number and a signed release from subject are required for a search. Records may be searched by mail or fax. Information is not available online at this time.

Vehicle Records   Vehicle records can be searched by owner's name, VIN number and/or by plate number. Records are not available unless a signed, notarized release is presented. The fee is $10.00 per record. Lien information is available from Corporate Affairs at (867) 667-5442.

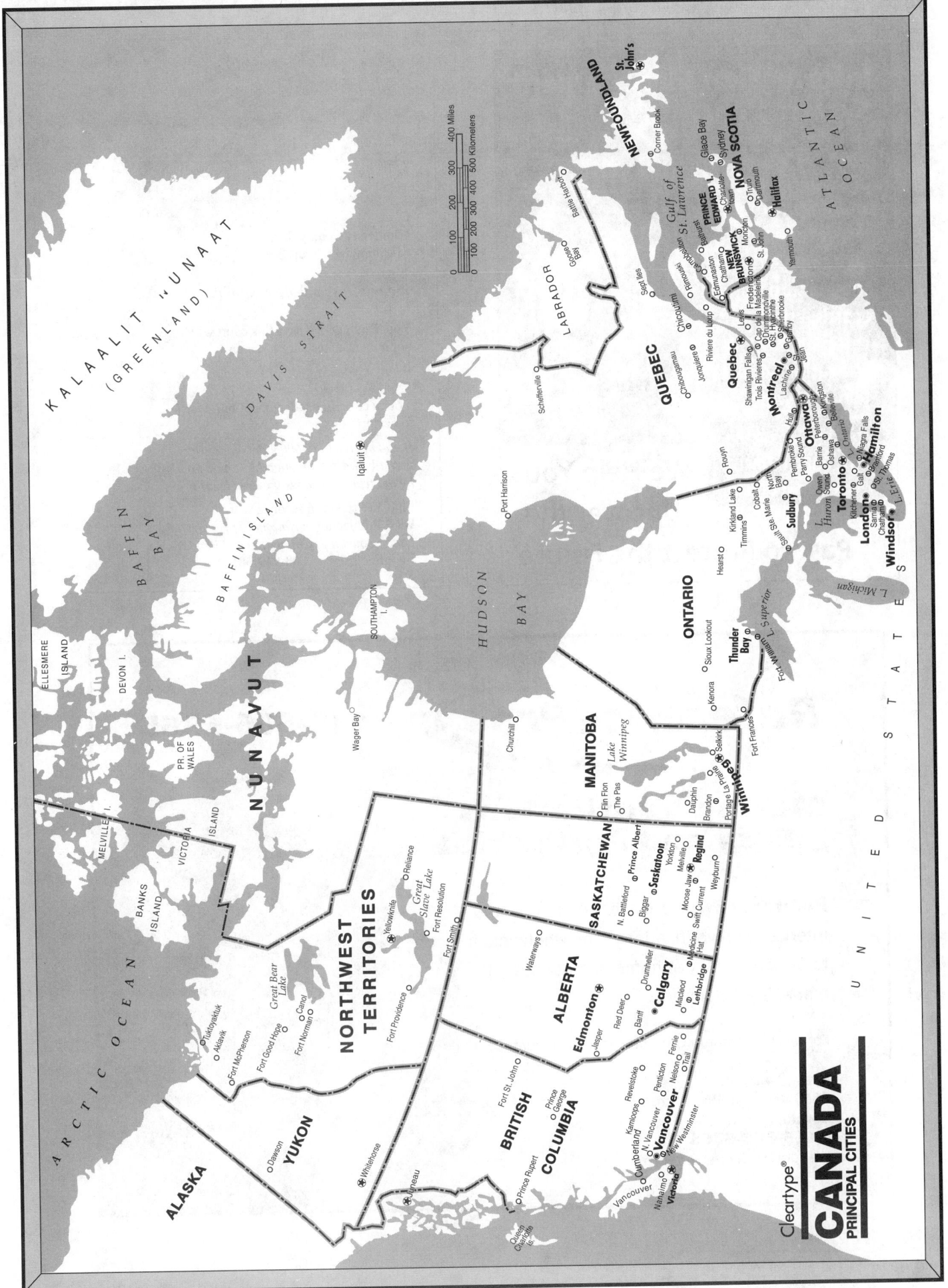

Cleartype®
CANADA
PRINCIPAL CITIES

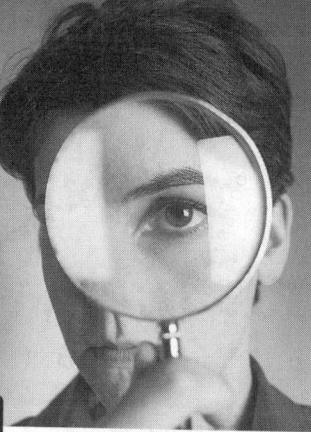

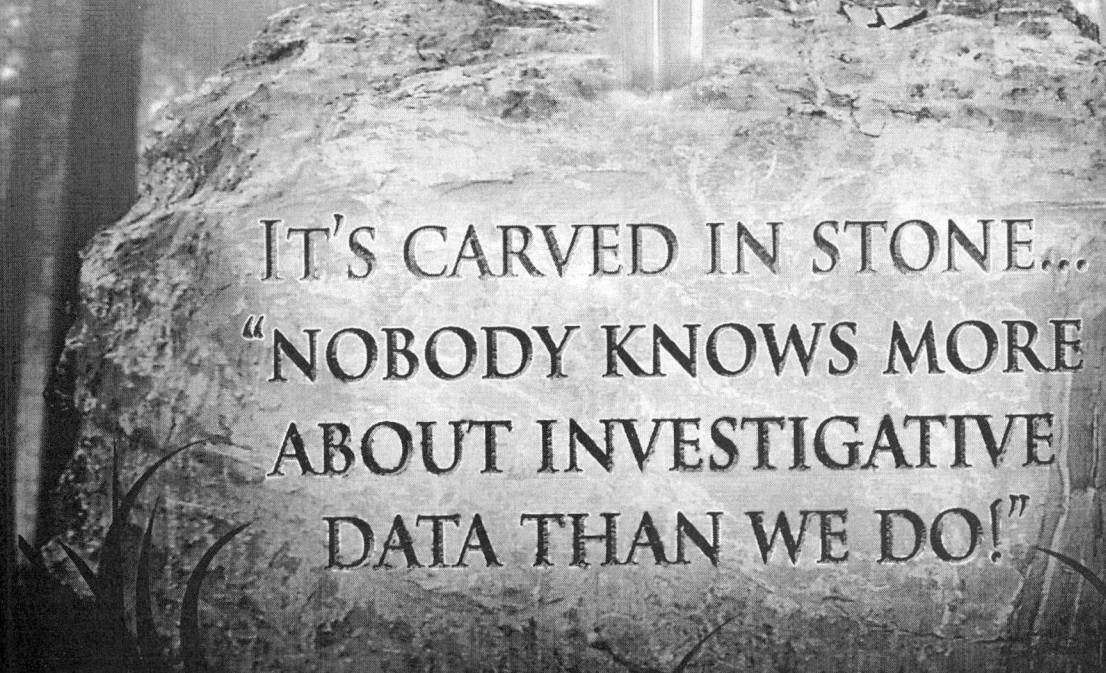

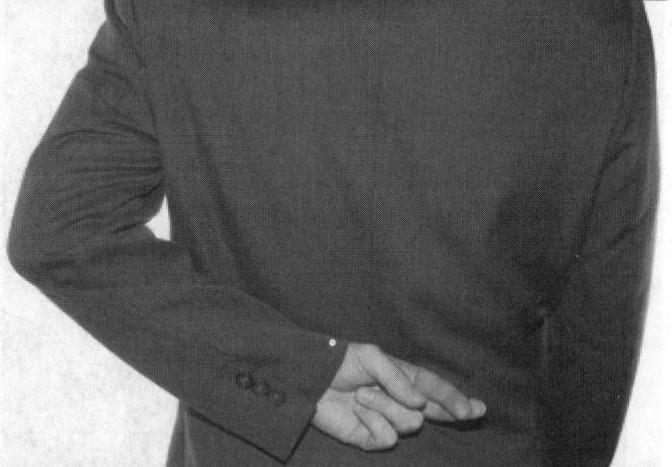